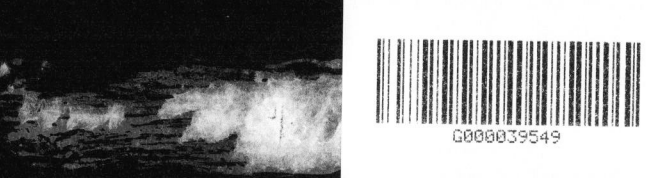

International
WHO'S WHO in

2005

Classical
MUSIC

International WHO'S WHO in

2005

Classical MUSIC

21st Edition

Routledge
Taylor & Francis Group

LONDON AND NEW YORK

First published 1935

ISBN: 1 85743 2959
ISSN: 1740-0155

Series Editor: Robert J. Elster
Associate Editor: Alison Neale
Technology Editor: Ian Preston
Assistant Editor: Meena Khan
Freelance Editorial Team: Annabella Gabb, Justin Lewis
Administrative Assistant: Charley McCartney

Typeset by Data Standards Limited, Frome
Printed and bound by Polestar Wheatons, Exeter

FOREWORD

The 21st edition of the INTERNATIONAL WHO'S WHO IN CLASSICAL MUSIC provides biographical information on over 8,000 prominent people in the fields of classical and light classical music, including composers, instrumentalists, conductors, singers, arrangers, writers and managers. The biographies include information on career, education, repertoire, compositions, recordings, publications and, where available, personal and contact details.

For each edition, entrants are given the opportunity to make necessary amendments and additions to their biographies. Supplementary research is done by the editorial department in order to ensure that the book is as up to date as possible on publication.

In addition to the biographical information, the directory section provides appendices of orchestras, opera companies, festivals, music organizations, major competitions and awards, music libraries and music conservatoires. The introduction contains a list of abbreviations and international telephone codes. The names of entrants whose death has been reported over the past year are included in the obituary.

Readers are referred to the book's companion title in The Europa Biographical Reference Series, the INTERNATIONAL WHO'S WHO IN POPULAR MUSIC, for a comprehensive collection of information on the most famous and influential people in the popular music industry.

The assistance of the individuals and organizations included in this publication in providing up-to-date material is invaluable, and the editors would like to take this opportunity to express their appreciation.

March 2005

ALPHABETIZATION KEY

The list of names is alphabetical, with the entrants listed under surnames. If part of an entrant's surname is in parentheses, indicating that this name is not usually used, this will be ignored for the purposes of the alphabetical listing.

If an entrant's name is spelt in a variety of ways, a cross reference is provided. An entrant who is known by a pseudonym or by an abbreviation of their name is either listed under this name or a cross reference is provided. Multiple pseudonyms are cross referenced where considered necessary.

Pseudonyms that include numbers as part of the name are listed alphabetically under the spelling of that number, e.g. 3-D is alphabetized as three-d.

All names beginning Mc or Mac are treated as Mac, e.g. McDevitt before MacDonald.

Names with Arabic prefixes are normally listed after the prefix, except when requested otherwise by the entrant.

In the case of surnames beginning with De, Des, Du, van or von the entries are normally found under the prefix.

Names beginning St are listed as if they began Saint, e.g. St Germain before Salamun.

CONTENTS

ABBREVIATIONS

AA	Associate in Arts	bros	brothers
AB	Alberta; Bachelor of Arts	BS	Bachelor of Science; Bachelor of Surgery
ABC	Australian Broadcasting Corporation; Australian Broadcasting Commission	BSc	Bachelor of Science
		BSE	Bachelor of Science in Engineering (USA)
AC	Companion of the Order of Australia	BSFA	British Science Fiction Association
ACA	American Composers' Alliance	BTh	Bachelor of Theology
Acad.	Academy	BTI	British Theatre Institute
ACLS	American Council of Learned Societies		
ACT	Australian Capital Territory	c.	circa; child, children
Admin.	Administrator, Administrative	CA	California
AFofM	American Federation of Musicians	CAMI	Columbia Artists Management International
AFTRA	American Federation of Television and Radio Artists	CBC	Canadian Broadcasting Corporation
AG	Aktiengesellschaft (Joint Stock Company)	CBE	Commander of (the Order of) the British Empire
AGMA	American Guild of Musical Artists	CBS	Columbia Broadcasting System
AIDS	acquired immunodeficiency syndrome	CBSO	City of Birmingham Symphony Orchestra
AK	Alaska	CCMA	Canadian Country Music Association
aka	also known as	CD	compact disc
AL	Alabama	CD-ROM	compact disc read-only memory
ALCS	Authors' Lending and Copyright Society	CEO	Chief Executive Officer
AM	Member of the Order of Australia; Master of Arts; amplitude modulation	Chair.	Chairman, Chairwoman, Chairperson
		Cia	Companhia
AO	Officer of the Order of Australia	Cía	Compañía
Apdo	Apartado (Post Box)	Cie	Compagnie
approx.	approximately	circ.	circulation
APRA	Australian Performing Rights Society	CMA	Country Music Association
Apt	Apartment	CMG	Companion of (the Order of) St Michael and St George
apto	apartamento	CNRS	Centre National de la Recherche Scientifique
A & R	Artists and Repertoire	c/o	care of
AR	Arkansas	Co.	Company; County
ARCA	Associate of the Royal College of Art	CO	Colorado; Chamber Orchestra
ARCM	Associate of the Royal College of Music	Col.	Colonia, Colima (hill)
ARCO	Associate of the Royal College of Organists	Coll.	College
ARCS	Associate of the Royal College of Science	Comm.	Commission
ASCAP	American Society of Composers, Authors and Publishers	Commdr	Commandeur
Asscn	Association	COO	Chief Operating Officer
Assoc.	Associate	Corpn	Corporation
Asst	Assistant	CP	Case Postale; Caixa Postal; Casella Postale (Post Box)
ATD	Art Teacher's Diploma	Cres.	Crescent
Aug.	August	CRNCM	Companion, Royal Northern College of Music
autobiog.	autobiography	Ct	Court
Avda	Avenida (Avenue)	CT	Connecticut
AZ	Arizona	Cttee	Committee
		CUNY	City University of New York
b.	born	CVO	Commander of the Royal Victorian Order
BA	Bachelor of Arts	CWA	(British) Crime Writers' Association
BAC&S	British Academy of Composers and Songwriters		
BAFTA	British Academy of Film and Television Arts	d.	daughter(s)
BArch	Bachelor of Architecture	DBE	Dame Commander of (the Order of) the British Empire
BASCA	British Association of Songwriters, Composers and Authors (now BAC&S)	DC	District of Columbia; Distrito Central
		DD	Doctor of Divinity
BBC	British Broadcasting Corporation	Dd'ES	Diplôme d'études supérieures
BC	British Columbia	DE	Delaware
BCL	Bachelor of Civil Law	Dec.	December
BD	Bachelor of Divinity	DEd	Doctor of Education
Bd	Board	Dept	Department
Bdwy	Broadway	D. ès L.	Docteur ès Lettres
BE	Bachelor of Engineering; Bachelor of Education	D. ès Sc.	Docteur ès Sciences
BEd	Bachelor of Education	devt	development
BEng	Bachelor of Engineering	DF	Distrito Federal
BFA	Bachelor in Fine Arts	DFA	Doctor of Fine Arts; Diploma of Fine Arts
BFI	British Film Institute	DHL	Doctor of Hebrew Literature
biog.	biography	DipEd	Diploma in Education
BJ	Bachelor of Journalism	DipTh	Diploma in Theology
Bldg	Building	Dir	Director
BLitt	Bachelor of Letters	DJ	disc jockey
BLS	Bachelor in Library Science	DJur	Doctor of Law
Blvd	Boulevard	DLitt	Doctor of Letters
BM	Bachelor of Music; Bachelor of Medicine	DM	Doctor of Music
BME	Bachelor of Music Education	DMA	Doctor of Musical Arts
BMEd	Bachelor of Music Education	DME	Doctor of Musical Education
BMI	Broadcast Music Inc	DMEd	Doctor of Musical Education
BMus	Bachelor of Music	DMus	Doctor of Music
BP	Boîte postale (Post Box)	DMusEd	Doctor of Music Education
BPhil	Bachelor of Philosophy	DN	Distrito Nacional

ABBREVIATIONS

DPhil	Doctor of Philosophy	Jan.	January
dpto	departamento	JD	Doctor of Jurisprudence
Dr(a)	Doctor(a)	JP	Justice of the Peace
DSc	Doctor of Science	Jr	Junior
DSocSci	Doctor of Social Science	jt	joint
DTh	Doctor of Theology		
DVD	digital versatile disc	KBE	Knight Commander, Order of the British Empire
		KCVO	Knight Commander of the Royal Victorian Order
E	East(ern)	km	kilometre(s)
EC	European Community	KS	Kansas
Ed.	Editor	KY	Kentucky
Edif.	Edificio (Building)		
edn	edition	LA	Louisiana
e.g.	exempli gratia (for example)	LAMDA	London Academy of Music and Dramatic Art
EMI	Electrical and Musical Industries	LEA	Local Education Authority
ENO	English National Opera	L. ès L.	Licencié ès Lettres
EP	extended-play (record)	L. ès Sc.	Licencié ès Sciences
esq.	esquina (corner)	LHD	Doctor of Humane Letters
etc.	et cetera	Lic. en Let.	Licenciado en Letras
EU	European Union	LLB	Bachelor of Laws
eV	eingetragener Verein	LLD	Doctor of Laws
Exec.	Executive	LL.L	Licentiate of Laws
		LLM	Master of Laws
f.	founded	LP	long-playing (record)
Feb.	February	LPO	London Philharmonic Orchestra
FL	Florida	LRCP	Licenciate, Royal College of Physicians, London
FLS	Fellow of the Linnaean Society	LRSM	Licenciate, Royal Schools of Music
FM	frequency modulation	LSE	London School of Economics and Political Science
FMA	Florida Music Association	LSO	London Symphony Orchestra
fmr(ly)	former(ly)	Lt	Lieutenant
FRAM	Fellow of the Royal Academy of Music	LTCL	Licenciate of Trinity College of Music, London
FRCM	Fellow of the Royal College of Music	Ltd	Limited
FRCO	Fellow of the Royal College of Organists	LW	long wave
FRGS	Fellow of the Royal Geographical Society	LWT	London Weekend Television
FRHistS	Fellow of the Royal Historical Society		
FRS	Fellow of the Royal Society	m.	married
FRSA	Fellow of the Royal Society of Arts	MA	Massachusetts; Master of Arts
FRSL	Fellow of the Royal Society of Literature	Man.	Manager; Managing
		MAT	Master of Arts and Teaching
GA	Georgia	MB	Manitoba
Gen.	General	MBA	Master of Business Administration
GmbH	Gesellschaft mit beschränkter Haftung (Limited Liability Company)	MBE	Member of (the Order of) the British Empire
		MC	master of ceremonies
GMT	Greenwich Mean Time	MD	Maryland; Music Director
Gov.	Governor	MDiv	Master in Divinity
GP	General Practitioner	ME	Maine
GPO	General Post Office	MEd	Master in Education
GRSM	Graduate of the Royal School of Music	mem.	member
GSMD	Guildhall School of Music and Drama, London (formerly GSM)	MEngSc	Master of Engineering
		Met	Metropolitan Opera House, New York
		MFA	Master of Fine Arts
hc	honoris causa	MHRA	Modern Humanities Research Association
HHD	Doctor of Humanities	MHz	megahertz (megacycles)
HI	Hawaii	MI	Michigan
HIV	human immunodeficiency virus	MIDI	Musical Instrument Digital Interface
HM	His (or Her) Majesty	mil.	military
HMV	His Master's Voice	MIT	Massachusetts Institute of Technology
Hon.	Honorary; Honourable	MLA	Modern Language Association
Hons	Honours	MLitt	Master of Letters; Master of Literature
HRH	His (or Her) Royal Highness	MLS	Master in Library Science
HS	Heraldry Society	MM	Master of Music
		MME	Master of Music Education
IA	Iowa	MMEd	Master of Music Education
IBA	Independent Broadcasting Authority	MMus	Master of Music
ID	Idaho	MN	Minnesota
i.e.	id est (that is to say)	MO	Missouri
IL	Illinois	MOBO	Music of Black Origin
IMC	International Music Council	MP	Member of Parliament
IMMIE	Indian Music Excellence (award)	MPh	Master of Philosophy (USA)
IN	Indiana	MPhil	Master of Philosophy
Inc.	Incorporated	MRCS	Member, Royal College of Surgeons of England
incl.	including	MS	Mississippi; Master of Science; manuscript
Inst.	Institute	MSA	Memphis Songwriters' Association
int.	international	MSc	Master of Science
IPC	Institute of Professional Critics	MSO	Melbourne Symphony Orchestra
ISM	Incorporated Society of Musicians	MT	Montana
IRCAM	Institut de Recherche et Coordination Acoustique/Musique	Mt	Mount
		MTh	Master of Theology
ISCM	International Society for Contemporary Music	MTV	Music Television
ISM	Incorporated Society of Musicians	MusB	Bachelor of Music
ITA	Independent Television Authority	MusD	Doctor of Music
ITN	Independent Television News	MusDoc	Doctor of Music
ITV	Independent Television	MusM	Master of Music

ix

ABBREVIATIONS

MVO	Member of the Royal Victorian Order
MW	medium wave
MWA	Mystery Writers of America
N	North(ern)
NABOB	National Association of Black Owned Broadcasters
NARAS	National Academy of Recording Arts & Sciences
NAS	National Academy of Songwriters
nat.	national
NB	New Brunswick
NBC	National Broadcasting Company
NC	North Carolina
ND	North Dakota
NDD	National Diploma in Design
NE	Nebraska; North-east(ern)
NEA	National Endowment for the Arts
NEH	National Endowment for the Humanities
NF	Newfoundland
NFSPS	National Federation of State Poetry Societies
NH	New Hampshire
NHK	Nippon Hoso Kyokai (Japanese broadcasting system)
NJ	New Jersey
NM	New Mexico
NME	New Musical Express
no.	number
Nov.	November
nr	near
NRK	Norsk Rikskringkasting (Norwegian broadcasting system)
NS	Nova Scotia
NSAI	Nashville Songwriters' Association International
NSW	New South Wales
NT	Northwest Territories; Northern Territory
NU	Nunavut Territory
NUJ	National Union of Journalists
NV	Nevada
NW	North-west(ern)
NY	New York (State)
NYPO	New York Philharmonic Orchestra
NYSO	New York Symphony Orchestra
NZSA	New Zealand Society of Authors
OBE	Officer of (the Order of) the British Empire
Oct.	October
Of.	Oficina (Office)
OH	Ohio
OK	Oklahoma
ON	Ontario
ONZ	Order of New Zealand
ONZM	Officer, New Zealand Order of Merit
OR	Oregon
org.	organization
ORTF	Office de Radiodiffusion-Télévision Française
OST	original soundtrack
OUP	Oxford University Press
p.	page
PA	Pennsylvania
PBS	Public Broadcasting Service
PE	Prince Edward Island
PEN	Poets, Playwrights, Essayists, Editors and Novelists (Club)
PETA	People for the Ethical Treatment of Animals
PF	Postfach (Post Box)
PGCE	Post Graduate Certificate of Education
PhB	Bachelor of Philosophy
PhD	Doctor of Philosophy
PhL	Licenciate of Philosophy
Pl.	Place
PLC	Public Limited Company
PMB	Private Mail Bag
pnr	partner
PO	Philharmonic Orchestra
PO Box	Post Office Box
Pres.	President
PR(O)	Public Relations (Officer)
Prod.	Producer
Prof.	Professor
promo	promotional
PRS	Performing Right Society
pt.	part
Pty	Proprietary
Publ.(s)	Publication(s)

QC	Québec
QEH	Queen Elizabeth Hall, London
Qld	Queensland
QSO	Queen's Service Order; Queensland Symphony Orchestra
q.v.	quod vide (to which refer)
RADA	Royal Academy of Dramatic Art
RAH	Royal Albert Hall, London
RAI	Radio Audizioni Italiane
RAM	Royal Academy of Music
R&B	Rhythm and Blues
RCM	Royal College of Music
RCO	Royal College of Organists
Rep.	Republic
retd	retired
rev. edn	revised edition
RFH	Royal Festival Hall, London
RGS	Royal Geographical Society
RI	Rhode Island
RIAS	Radio im Amerikanischen Sektor
RLPO	Royal Liverpool Philharmonic Orchestra
RMA	Royal Musical Association
RMCM	Royal Manchester College of Music
RNCM	Royal Northern College of Music, Manchester
RNLI	Royal National Life-boat Institution
RO	Radio Orchestra
ROC	Rock Out Censorship
ROH	Royal Opera House, Covent Garden
rpm	revolutions per minute
RPO	Royal Philharmonic Orchestra
RSA	Royal Society of Arts
RSAMD	Royal Scottish Academy of Music and Drama
RSC	Royal Shakespeare Company
RSL	Royal Society of Literature
RSNO	Royal Scottish National Orchestra (formerly SNO)
RSO	Radio Symphony Orchestra
RSPB	Royal Society for Protection of Birds
RTÉ	Radio Telefís Éireann
RTF	Radiodiffusion-Télévision Française
RTS	Royal Television Society
S	South(ern); San
s.	son(s)
SA	Société Anonyme, Sociedad Anónima (Limited Company); South Australia
SACEM	Société d'Auteurs, Compositeurs et Editeurs de Musique
SAG	Screen Actors' Guild
SC	South Carolina
SD	South Dakota
SE	South-east(ern)
Sec.	Secretary
Sept.	September
SFWA	Science Fiction and Fantasy Writers of America
SGA	Songwriters' Guild of America
SK	Saskatchewan
SL	Sociedad Limitada
SO	Symphony Orchestra
SOAS	School of Oriental and African Studies
SOCAN	Society of Composers, Authors and Music Publishers of Canada
SOSA	State Opera of South Australia
SPNM	Society for the Promotion of New Music
Sr	Senior
St	Saint
Sta	Santa
STB	Bachelor of Sacred Theology
STD	Doctor of Sacred Theology
Ste	Sainte
STL	Reader or Professor of Sacred Theology
STM	Master of Sacred Theology
str	strasse
SUNY	State University of New York
SVSA	South West Virginia Songwriters' Association
SW	South-west(ern); short wave
TCL	Trinity College of Music, London
TLS	Times Literary Supplement
TN	Tennessee
trans.	translated; translation; translator
Treas.	Treasurer
TV	television
TX	Texas

u.	utca (street)	VC	Victoria Cross
UCLA	University of California at Los Angeles	VHF	very high frequency
UHF	ultra-high frequency	VI	(US) Virgin Islands
UK	United Kingdom (of Great Britain and Northern Ireland)	Vic.	Victoria
ul.	ulitsa (street)	Vol.(s)	Volume(s)
UN	United Nations	VSO	Victoria State Opera
UNESCO	United Nations Educational, Scientific and Cultural Organization	VT	Vermont
UNICEF	United Nations Children's Fund	W	West(ern)
Univ.	University	WA	Western Australia; Washington (State)
Urb.	Urbanización (urban district)	WI	Wisconsin
US(A)	United States (of America)	WNO	Welsh National Opera
USSR	Union of Soviet Socialist Republics	WV	West Virginia
UT	Utah	WY	Wyoming
VA	Virginia	YT	Yukon Territory

INTERNATIONAL TELEPHONE CODES

To make international calls to telephone and fax numbers listed in the book, dial the international code of the country from which you are calling, followed by the appropriate code for the country you wish to call (listed below), followed by the area code (if applicable) and telephone or fax number listed in the entry.

	Country code	+ or – GMT*		Country code	+ or – GMT*
Afghanistan	93	+4½	Dominica	1 767	−4
Albania	355	+1	Dominican Republic	1 809	−4
Algeria	213	+1	Ecuador	593	−5
Andorra	376	+1	Egypt	20	+2
Angola	244	+1	El Salvador	503	−6
Antigua and Barbuda	1 268	−4	Equatorial Guinea	240	+1
Argentina	54	−3	Eritrea	291	+3
Armenia	374	+4	Estonia	372	+2
Australia	61	+8 to +10	Ethiopia	251	+3
Australian External Territories:			Fiji	679	+12
Australian Antarctic Territory	672	+3 to +10	Finland	358	+2
Christmas Island	61	+7	Finnish External Territory:		
Cocos (Keeling) Islands	61	+6½	Åland Islands	358	+2
Norfolk Island	672	+11½	France	33	+1
Austria	43	+1	French Overseas Departments:		
Azerbaijan	994	+5	French Guiana	594	−3
The Bahamas	1 242	−5	Guadeloupe	590	−4
Bahrain	973	+3	Martinique	596	−4
Bangladesh	880	+6	Réunion	262	+4
Barbados	1 246	−4	French Overseas Collectivité		
Belarus	375	+2	Départementale:		
Belgium	32	+1	Mayotte	269	+3
Belize	501	−6	Overseas Collectivité Territoriale:		
Benin	229	+1	Saint Pierre and Miquelon	508	−3
Bhutan	975	+6	French Overseas Territories:		
Bolivia	591	−4	French Polynesia	689	−9 to −10
Bosnia and Herzegovina	387	+1	Wallis and Futuna Islands	681	+12
Botswana	267	+2	French Overseas Country:		
Brazil	55	−3 to −4	New Caledonia	687	+11
Brunei	673	+8	Gabon	241	+1
Bulgaria	359	+2	Gambia	220	0
Burkina Faso	226	0	Georgia	995	+4
Burundi	257	+2	Germany	49	+1
Cambodia	855	+7	Ghana	233	0
Cameroon	237	+1	Greece	30	+2
Canada	1	−3 to −8	Grenada	1 473	−4
Cape Verde	238	−1	Guatemala	502	−6
The Central African Republic	236	+1	Guinea	224	0
Chad	235	+1	Guinea-Bissau	245	0
Chile	56	−4	Guyana	592	−4
China, People's Republic	86	+8	Haiti	509	−5
Special Administrative Regions:			Honduras	504	−6
Hong Kong	852	+8	Hungary	36	+1
Macao	853	+8	Iceland	354	0
China (Taiwan)	886	+8	India	91	+5½
Colombia	57	−5	Indonesia	62	+7 to +9
The Comoros	269	+3	Iran	98	+3½
Congo, Democratic Republic	243	+1	Iraq	964	+3
Congo, Republic	242	+1	Ireland	353	0
Costa Rica	506	−6	Israel	972	+2
Côte d'Ivoire	225	0	Italy	39	+1
Croatia	385	+1	Jamaica	1 876	−5
Cuba	53	−5	Japan	81	+9
Cyprus	357	+2	Jordan	962	+2
'Turkish Republic of Northern Cyprus'	90 392	+2	Kazakhstan	7	+6
Czech Republic	420	+1	Kenya	254	+3
Denmark	45	+1	Kiribati	686	+12 to +13
Danish External Territories:			Korea, Democratic People's Republic		
Faroe Islands	298	0	(North Korea)	850	+9
Greenland	299	−1 to −4	Korea, Republic (South Korea)	82	+9
Djibouti	253	+3	Kuwait	965	+3

xii

	Country code	+ or – GMT*		Country code	+ or – GMT*
Kyrgyzstan	996	+5	Serbia and Montenegro	381	+1
Laos	856	+7	Seychelles	248	+4
Latvia	371	+2	Sierra Leone	232	0
Lebanon	961	+2	Singapore	65	+8
Lesotho	266	+2	Slovakia	421	+1
Liberia	231	0	Slovenia	386	+1
Libya	218	+1	Solomon Islands	677	+11
Liechtenstein	423	+1	Somalia	252	+3
Lithuania	370	+2	South Africa	27	+2
Luxembourg	352	+1	Spain	34	+1
Macedonia, former Yugoslav republic	389	+1	Sri Lanka	94	+6
Madagascar	261	+3	Sudan	249	+2
Malawi	265	+2	Suriname	597	–3
Malaysia	60	+8	Swaziland	268	+2
Maldives	960	+5	Sweden	46	+1
Mali	223	0	Switzerland	41	+1
Malta	356	+1	Syria	963	+2
Marshall Islands	692	+12	Tajikistan	992	+5
Mauritania	222	0	Tanzania	255	+3
Mauritius	230	+4	Thailand	66	+7
Mexico	52	–6 to –7	Timor-Leste	670	+9
Micronesia, Federated States	691	+10 to +11	Togo	228	0
Moldova	373	+2	Tonga	676	+13
Monaco	377	+1	Trinidad and Tobago	1 868	–4
Mongolia	976	+7 to +9	Tunisia	216	+1
Morocco	212	0	Turkey	90	+2
Mozambique	258	+2	Turkmenistan	993	+5
Myanmar	95	+6½	Tuvalu	688	+12
Namibia	264	+2	Uganda	256	+3
Nauru	674	+12	Ukraine	380	+2
Nepal	977	+5¾	United Arab Emirates	971	+4
Netherlands	31	+1	United Kingdom	44	0
Netherlands Dependencies:			United Kingdom Crown Dependencies	44	0
Aruba	297	–4	United Kingdom Overseas Territories:		
Netherlands Antilles	599	–4	Anguilla	1 264	–4
New Zealand	64	+12	Ascension Island	247	0
New Zealand's Dependent and Associated			Bermuda	1 441	–4
Territories:			British Virgin Islands	1 284	–4
Tokelan	690	–10	Cayman Islands	1 345	–5
Cook Islands	682	–10	Diego Garcia (British Indian Ocean		
Niue	683	–11	Territory)	246	+5
Nicaragua	505	–6	Falkland Islands	500	–4
Niger	227	+1	Gibraltar	350	+1
Nigeria	234	+1	Montserrat	1 664	–4
Norway	47	+1	Pitcairn Islands	872	–8
Norwegian External Territory:			Saint Helena	290	0
Svalbard	47	+1	Tristan da Cunha	2 897	0
Oman	968	+4	Turks and Caicos Islands	1 649	–5
Pakistan	92	+5	United States of America	1	–5 to –10
Palau	680	+9	United States Commonwealth Territories:		
Palestinian Autonomous Areas	970	+2	Northern Mariana Islands	1 670	+10
Panama	507	–5	Puerto Rico	1 787	–4
Papua New Guinea	675	+10	United States External Territories:		
Paraguay	595	–4	American Samoa	1 684	–11
Peru	51	–5	Guam	1 671	+10
The Philippines	63	+8	United States Virgin Islands	1 340	–4
Poland	48	+1	Uruguay	598	–3
Portugal	351	0	Uzbekistan	998	+5
Qatar	974	+3	Vanuatu	678	+11
Romania	40	+2	Vatican City	39	+1
Russian Federation	7	+2 to +12	Venezuela	58	–4
Rwanda	250	+2	Viet Nam	84	+7
Saint Christopher and Nevis	1 869	–4	Yemen	967	+3
Saint Lucia	1 758	–4	Zambia	260	+2
Saint Vincent and the Grenadines	1 784	–4	Zimbabwe	263	+2
Samoa	685	–11			
San Marino	378	+1			
São Tomé and Príncipe	239	0			
Saudi Arabia	966	+3			
Senegal	221	0			

* The times listed compare the standard (winter) times in the various countries. Some countries adopt Summer (Daylight Saving) Time—i.e. +1 hour—for part of the year.

OBITUARY

ALLANBROOK, Douglas Phillips	29 January 2003
AM BACH, Rudolf	6 March 2004
APIVOR, Denis	27 May 2004
BALLIF, Claude	24 July 2004
BENEŠ, Juraj	10 September 2004
BERNSTEIN, Elmer	18 August 2004
BRONHILL, June	25 January 2005
BROWN, Iona	5 June 2004
BULLER, John	9 September 2004
CAROSIO, Margherita	10 January 2005
CONE, Edward T(oner)	23 October 2004
DAVIES, Hugh Seymour	1 January 2005
DE LOS ANGELES, Victoria	15 January 2005
DOLIN, Samuel	13 January 2002
FENNELL, Frederick	7 December 2004
FRECCIA, Massimo	December 2004
FRIEDMAN, Erick	30 March 2004
GHIAUROV, Nicolai	2 June 2004
GOOSSENS, Sidonie	15 December 2004
HAMBURGER, Paul Philip	11 April 2004
HANUS, Jan	30 July 2004
HEENAN, Ashley (David Joseph)	6 September 2004
HELFFER, Claude	27 October 2004
KALLIR, Lilian	25 October 2004
KLEIBER, Carlos	13 July 2004
KOVARICEK, František	7 January 2003
LEIGH, Adèle	23 May 2004
MERRILL, Robert	23 October 2004
NAPIER, Marita	16 February 2004
PERGAMENSHIKOV, Boris	30 April 2004
PRAUSNITZ, Frederik William	12 November 2004
RANKIN, Nell	13 January 2005
SAMS, Eric	13 September 2004
SCHMIDT, Trudliese	24 June 2004
SHARPE, Terence	26 June 2004
SMITH, Ronald	27 May 2004
SOULIOTIS, Elena	4 December 2004
SOUZAY, Gérard	17 August 2004
STEIN, Leonard	24 June 2004
STEVENS, Denis William	1 April 2004
TAILLON, Jocelyne	10 June 2004
TEBALDI, Renata	19 December 2004
VAZSONYI, Balint	18 January 2003
VONK, Hans	29 August 2004
WATANABE, Yoko	15 July 2004
WALLBERG, Heinz	27 September 2004
WERLE, Lars Johan	3 August 2001
YOUNG, Percy Marshall	9 May 2004

Biographies

Biographies

A

AADLAND, Eivind; Norwegian violinist; b. 19 Sept. 1956, Bergen. *Education:* Norwegian State Music Acad., Oslo with Camilla Wicks, Int. Menuhin Music Acad., Switzerland with Alberto Lysy and Yehudi Menuhin, masterclasses with Sándor Végh. *Career:* fmrly concertmaster, Bergen Philharmonic Orchestra; Music Dir, European Community Chamber Orchestra 1988–; has appeared in major halls and festivals world-wide, including Musikverein, Vienna, Concertgebouw, Amsterdam, Salle Pleyel, Paris and Gewandhaus, Leipzig. *Recordings:* 12 albums. *Address:* Arupsgate 10, 0192 Oslo, Norway.

AAQUIST, Svend; Danish composer, conductor and computer programmer; b. 1948. *Education:* Univ. of Copenhagen, Royal Danish Acad. of Music, Copenhagen; int. courses with teachers, including Elisabeth Klein, Arne Hammelboe, Michel Tabachnik. *Career:* debut 1969; conductor for numerous choirs, chamber ensembles and orchestras 1969–; High School teacher 1969–75; Teacher of Conducting, Royal Danish Acad. of Music and State Acad. of Music at Esbjerg; numerous workshops and seminars for musical and conducting courses; Chief Conductor and Artistic Dir, Esbjerg Symphony Orchestra; Artistic Adviser, Esbjerg Ensemble 1984–; appeared in many concerts, festivals, radio and television recordings, in Denmark and abroad; concerts given with many orchestras, including Odense Symphony Orchestra; concert tours with West German Chamber Orchestra, Ensemble Modern 1981, 1982, 1984; mem., LUT and LYT (co-founder), Danish State Music Council, Nordic Composers' Council (pres. 1973–74), Soc. for Publication of Danish Music (bd mem. 1974–84), Danish Composers' Soc. (chair. 1973–74), DUT Danish ISCM (chair. 1980–84). *Compositions include:* Pentagram 1969, Salut-Salut 1970, Ke-Tjak 1973, Unite 1974, Sinfonia Sisyphus 1976, Malinche 1979, Sun 1983, Hymn With Dances 1985, cello solo The Lilac Shall Bloom 1976, Tai Yang 1986, High Voltage Rag 1991, Le Malade Imaginaire 1994, Babylon 1996. *Address:* Bruserup Strand 9, 4873 Væggerløse, Denmark. *Telephone:* 54-16-70-00 (office); 54-17-82-20 (home). *E-mail:* aa@ajourdata.dk (office); svend@aaquist .com (home).

ABAJAN, Maria; Singer (Soprano); b. 1950, Eriwan, Armenia. *Education:* Studied at Eriwan and Tchaikovsky Conservatory in Moscow; Further studies at Los Angeles. *Career:* Moved to USA in 1977; Successful at singing competitions in New York, San Francisco, Italy and Mexico; Appeared in Europe, 1985–, notably as Turandot in Liège, Abigaille in Nabucco, (Brussels, 1987) and Aida in Zürich; Has sung Leonora in Trovatore and Elisabeth de Valois at Hamburg, Tosca and Amelia in Ballo in Maschera in Essen; Appeared as Tosca with Scottish Opera, Glasgow, in 1990; Vienna Staatsoper, 1991–92, as Tosca and the Forza Leonora; Season 1993 as Abigaille at Bregenz, and Giorgetta at Madrid; Sang Santuzza in Cavalleria Rusticana at the Berlin Staatsoper and Nice, 1997, 1999. *Address:* c/o Scottish Opera, 39 Elmbank Crescent, Glasgow G2 4PT, Scotland.

ABBADO, Claudio; Italian conductor; b. 26 June 1933, Milan; one c. *Education:* Giuseppe Verdi Conservatory, Milan and Acad. of Music, Vienna with Hans Swarowsky. *Career:* debut La Scala, Milan in concert celebrating tercentenary of A. Scarlatti 1960 conducted opening of La Scala season 1967; Music Dir Teatro alla Scala, Milan 1968–86, Vienna Philharmonic Orchestra 1972–, London Symphony Orchestra 1979–88, Vienna State Opera 1986–91; Principal Conductor Chamber Orchestra of Europe 1981; Principal Guest Conductor Chicago Symphony Orchestra 1982–85; Gen. Music Dir City of Vienna 1987–; Music Dir and Principal Conductor Berlin Philharmonic Orchestra 1989–2002; Artistic Dir Salzburg Easter Festival 1994; f. European Community Youth Orchestra 1978, La Filharmonica della Scala 1982, Gustav Mahler Jugendorchester, Vienna 1986, Wien Modern (Modern Vienna) Contemporary Art Festival 1988, Vienna Int. Competition for Composers 1991, Encounters in Berlin (Chamber Music Festival) 1992, Lucerne Festival Orchestra 2001; has conducted on tours world-wide, with numerous orchestras. *Publications:* Musica sopra Berlino (Nonino Award 1999) 1998, Suite Concertante from the Ballet Hawaii 2000, La Casa del Suoni (juvenile). *Honours:* Dr hc (Aberdeen) 1986, (Ferrara) 1990, (Cambridge) 1994; Mozart Medal (Vienna) 1973, Gold Medal, Int. Gustav Mahler Gesellschaft (Vienna) 1985, Amadeus (Ferrara) 1996, award from the Presidency of the Council of Ministers 1997, Athena-Giovani e Cultura Award (Univ. of Milan) 1999, Conductor of the Year, Opernwelt Review 2000, Oscar della Lirica 2001, Praemium Imperiale 2003; Grand Cross, Order of Merit (Italy) 1984, Officier, Légion d'Honneur, Bundesverdienstkreuz (Germany) 1992, Ehrenring, City of Vienna 1994. *Current Management:* Askonas Holt Ltd, Lonsdale Chambers, 27 Chancery Lane, London, WC2A 1PF, England. *Telephone:* (20) 7400-1700. *Fax:* (20) 7400-1799. *E-mail:* info@askonasholt.co .uk. *Website:* www.askonasholt.co.uk.

ABBADO, Marcello, DipMus; Italian composer; b. 7 Oct. 1926, Milan. *Education:* Milan Conservatory. *Career:* soloist and conductor in Europe, America, Africa, Asia 1944–; performed all Debussy and all piano concertos of Mozart; Prof. of Piano at Conservatories of Cagliari, Venice and Milan, and of Composition at Parma and Bologna 1950; Dir, Liceo Musicale, Piacenza 1958, Rossini Conservatory, Pesaro 1966, Verdi Conservatory, Milan 1972–96; founder, Symphony Orchestra Verdi, Milan 1993; jury mem., int. competitions of chamber music, composition, conducting, piano, violin, voice and others world-wide; mem. Admin. Council, Teatro alla Scala 1973–96; mem. Fondazione Curci (Naples), Fondazione Puccini (Lucca). *Compositions include:* ballet: Scena Senza Storia, Hawaii 2000, Suite Concertante from the Ballet Hawaii 2000; orchestral: Concerto for Orchestra, Hommage à Debussy, Costruzioni for five Small Orchestras, Variazioni sopra un tema di Mozart, Risonanze for two pianos and chamber orchestra, La strage degli innocenti for vocal soloists, choir and orchestra, seven Ricercari and six Intermezzi for violin and orchestra, Quadruplo Concerto for piano, violin, viola, cello and orchestra 1970, Double Concerto for violin, piano and double chamber orchestra, L'Idea fissa for violin 'scordato' and percussion orchestra 1994, Ottavo Ricercare for violin and orchestra 1997, Concerto for flute and orchestra 2002, Ten Songs of Sicily for voice, violin and orchestra, Velicianie Aleksandr Nevsky for violin and choir, The Bells of Moscow for violin and percussion 1998, Lento e Rondo for violin and percussions, Musica Celeste for violin and orchestra, 15 Poesie T'ang for voice and four instruments, Ciapo for voice and nine instruments, Three Quatuor, Duo for violin and cello, Fantasia No. 1 for 12 instruments, Fantasia No. 2 for four instruments and 31 percussion, Capriccio su un tema di Paganini for violin and piano, Chaconne for solo violin, Riverberazioni for wind instruments and piano, Divertimento for 4 winds and piano, Concertante for piano and instrument, Sonata for flute, Incastri No. 1 and No. 2 for winds, Lamento for the Mother's Death for clavichord, Variazioni sopra un minuetto di Bach for piano, Aus dem Klavier for piano, Responsorio for choir and organ, Sarà Sara for guitar, Ostinato on a Rhythmic Motif from the Overture to Il Signor Bruschino by Rossini, for piano, string orchestra and percussions 1994, Nuova Costruzione for Wind Octet 2002, Australia, for violin, didgeridoo and percussions 2002, Asif Saleem Nasreen No. 1 and No. 2 for violin, alto, cello and string orchestra 2002, Six Ninne Nanne for solo voice, Vocalizzo on Ma se mi toccano, from Rossini's Il Barbiere di Siviglia, for voice and piano, Desprez; Entre Paris et la France, Fijetto dei corni, for choir 1999, Harmonic Variations for orchestra on Mozart's Marche Funèbre del Signor Maestro Contrapunto, DV 453a 2000, Costruzione for 12 cellos 2001, Risonanza magnetica for piano and percussion orchestra 2003, Music for Jean Cocteau's La voix humaine 2003, Concerto for harp and strings orchestra 2003, Il buio negli occhi (scenic action) 2003. *Address:* Viale Monza 9, 20125 Milan, Italy.

ABBADO, Roberto; conductor; b. 1954, Milan, Italy. *Education:* Pesaro and Milan Conservatories, studied with Franco Ferrara in Rome and at Teatro La Fenice, Venice. *Career:* debut with Orchestra of Accademia Santa Cecilia 1977; operatic debut with a new production of Simon Boccanegra at Macerata 1978; festival appearances at Edinburgh 1982, Israel 1984, Lille and Munich 1989; Chief Conductor, Munich Radio Orchestra 1991; engagements with Staatskapelle Dresden, Bamberg Symphony, Orchestre National de France, RAI Turin, The Orchestra of St Luke's in New York, Maggio Musicale Fiorentino Orchestra; opera engagements at La Scala with world premieres of Flavio Testi's Il Sosia and Riccardo III and a new production of Don Pasquale; Vienna State Opera with a new production of La Cenerentola; Bayerische Staatsoper, Munich, with a new production of La Traviata 1993, and Adriana Lecouvreur, Manon Lescaut, Don Pasquale; conducted La Forza del Destino at San Francisco 1993; appeared at Rome, Florence, Bologna, Venice, Berlin Deutsche Oper, Zürich, Barcelona and Tokyo with Teatro Comunale Bologna 1993; conducted Adriana Lecouvreur at the Metropolitan, New York 1994; Opéra Bastille debut in Lucia di Lammermoor 1995; Houston Grand Opera debut in Norma 1996; Aida at the 1997 Munich Festival; Le Comte Ory at Florence 1998. *Recordings include:* Bellini's I Capuleti e i Montecchi 1998. *Honours:* Deutsche Phono Akademi Echo Klassic Deutscher Schallplattenpreis (for recording of Rossini's Tancredi) 1997. *Current Management:* M. L. Falcone Public Relations, 155 W 68th Street, New York, NY 10023, USA. *Fax:* (212) 787-9638 (office).

ABBOTT, Jocelyn, ARCT, BMus, LRAM, DipRAM, ARAM; Concert Pianist; b. 15 Sept. 1954, Toronto, Canada. *Education:* Victoria Conservatory of Music, Victoria BC; Royal Conservatory of Music, Toronto; Univ. of Victoria; Royal Academy of Music, London. *Career:* concerts and recordings as soloist and accompanist, and since 1992 as part of ensemble The Abbott O'Gorman Piano Duo with Laura O'Gorman, including commissioning transcriptions and arranging orchestral repertoire; mem. Incorporated Society of Musicians. *Recordings:* Ravel à quatre mains, 1994; Classical Jazz à quatre mains, 1999. *Publications:* contrib. to Pianist Magazine. *Honours:* Associate of the Royal Academy of Music, 1987; 'Steinway Artist' Status, 1996. *Address:* Cubitt Music Management, 40 Cubitt Terrace, London, SW4 6AR, England (office). *Telephone:* (777) 1725002 (office). *Fax:* (20) 7720–8660 (office). *E-mail:* rjordan@cubittmusic.co.uk (office). *Website:* www.cubittmusic.co.uk (office).

ABDRASAKOV, Askar; Singer (bass); b. 1960, Ufa, Urals, Russia. *Education:* Ufa Conservatoire and with Irina Arkipova in Moscow. *Career:* soloist with the Bashkirian Opera from 1990, as Sobakin (The Tsar's Bride), Konchak in Prince Igor, Gremin, Zuniga, Sparafucile and Rossini's Don Basilio; recital with Arkhipova at the Wigmore Hall, 1994 and Rimsky's Invisible City of Kitezh at the Bregenz Festival, 1995; in recital at the Châtelet, Paris, the Bonze in Stravinsky's Nightingale under Pierre Boulez in Paris and London, Rimsky's Tsar Saltan at Florence and the Grand Inquisitor in Don Carlos at Bologna, 1996–98; concerts include the Verdi Requiem, Puccini Messa di Gloria; Russian and French songs and Lieder. *Honours:* prizewinner at the 1991 Glinka Competition; winner, Chaliapin Bass Competition at Kazan, 1994; Grand Prix, Maria Callas Competition in Athens, 1995. *Current Management:* Askonas Holt Ltd, Lonsdale Chambers, 27 Chancery Lane, London, WC2A 1PF, England. *Telephone:* (20) 7400-1700. *Fax:* (20) 7400-1799. *E-mail:* info@askonasholt.co.uk. *Website:* www .askonasholt.co.uk.

ABE, Keiko Kimura; Japanese marimba player and composer; b. 18 April 1937, Tokyo. *Education:* studied xylophone with Eiichi Asabuki, Tokyo Gakugei Univ. composition with Shosuke Ariga and Toshio Kashiwagi, percussion with Masao Imamura and Yusuke Oyake. *Career:* joined Tokyo Marimba Group 1962; Lecturer, Tôhô Gakuen Coll. of Music, Tokyo 1969–88; annual recital tours of Europe, N America and Asia from 1981; Yamaha released standard five-octave marimba based on her ideas 1984; Prof., Tôhô Gakuen Coll. of Music, Tokyo 1988–; Visiting Prof., Utrecht Conservatoire. *Compositions:* Variations on Japanese Children's Songs, Mi-Chi, Ancient Vase, Wind in the Bamboo Grove, Memories of the Seashore, Prism, Little Windows, Frogs, Wind Sketch, Tambourin Paraphrase, Voice of Matsuri Drums, Itsuki Fantasy for Six Mallets, Ban-ka, Piacer d'amor, Alone, Kazak Lullaby, Marimba d'amore, Dream of the Cherry Blossoms, Prism Rhapsody II. *Recordings include:* Keiko Abe: Art of Marimba. *Address:* c/o Tôhô Gakuen Coll. of Music, 1-41-1 Wakaba-chô, Chôfu-shi, 182–0003 Tokyo, Japan (office).

ABEL, Yves; Conductor; b. 1963, Canada. *Education:* Univ. of Toronto; Royal Conservatory; Mannes Coll. of Music; Tanglewood Music Center, with Leonard Bernstein, Seiji Ozawa, Gunther Herbig and Roger Norrington. *Career:* conducted La Traviata at New York City Opera, televised on Live From Lincoln Center series; La Cenerentola with Seattle Opera; La Belle Hélène, with Opera Theatre of St Louis; Roméo et Juliette with Florida Grand Opera; Herold's Zampa at 1993 Wexford Festival and Wagner's Das Liebesverbot at 1994 Festival, also conducting Brahms' Ein Deutsches Requiem; Rigoletto with Opera Lyra Ottawa; Massenet's Werther at Skylight Opera; Dido and Aeneas at Canada's Elora Festival, broadcast nationwide on CBC Radio; Madama Butterfly with Opera Theater of Connecticut; Music Dir, L'Opéra Français de New York, with performances at Lincoln Center and Alice Tully Hall, conducting Offenbach's Barbe-Bleue, Médée by Cherubini and Le Comte Ory by Rossini; recently acclaimed debuts include Don Carlos with Opera North, Le Comte Ory with Glynde-bourne Festival Opera, Hamlet with San Francisco Opera, L'Elisir d'amore with Royal Danish Opera, Rossini Opera Festival and performances of Faust with Paris Opéra; debut at Lyric Opera of Chicago with L'Elisir d'amore, Seattle Opera for Forza del Destino, Netherlands Opera for Barbiere and a revival of Les Dialogues des Carmélites, the Royal Danish Opera for Verdi, the WNO for Leonore, 2000, and Bilbao Opera for Barbiere di Siviglia; third season at Metropolitan Opera with Carmen, with Domingo and Denyce Graves; engaged at the Lyric Opera in Chicago for Barbiere, 2001; recent concert engagements with Toronto Symphony, Orquestra Ciudad de Granada and National Arts Center in Ottawa; Season 2002–03 with the Metropolitan Opera (Carmen) and the Netherlands Opera, as well as new productions with the Santa Fe Opera (Così fan tutte), the Dallas Opera (Ermione), the Deutsche Oper Berlin (Don Pasquale) and the Teatro Comunale di Bologna (Iphigénie en Tauride). *Current Management:* Askonas Holt Ltd, Lonsdale Chambers, 27 Chancery Lane, London, WC2A 1PF, England. *Telephone:* (20) 7400-1700. *Fax:* (20) 7400-1799. *E-mail:* info@askonasholt.co.uk. *Website:* www.askonasholt .co.uk.

ABELL, David; Conductor; b. 1965, USA. *Education:* Yale University and Juilliard School, New York; Further study with Leonard Bernstein and Nadia Boulanger. *Career:* Many appearances in USA and Europe

with leading orchestras; London resident from 1996; Concerts with City of Birmingham Symphony Orchestra, Royal Philharmonic, Royal Scottish National Orchestra, and BBC Concert Orchestra; Rossini's La Gazza Ladra with Opera North, Madama Butterfly and Carmen at the Royal Albert Hall; US engagements with New York City Opera, Washington and Michigan Operas, Seattle and Alabama Symphonies; Italian debut 1999, with Rigoletto at the Lugio Musicale Trapanese; Season 2001 with the Brighton Philharmonic, BBC Concert Orchestra at the Covent Garden Festival, Sinfonia Viva, Ulster Orchestra, and Hong Kong Philharmonic; Conducted Rodgers & Hammerstein's Oklahoma! at the London Proms, 2002. *Current Management:* IMG Artists, Lovell House, 616 Chiswick High Road, London W4 5RV, England.

ABENIUS, Folke; Producer and Professor; b. 8 Oct. 1933, Stockholm, Sweden; m., 1 s., 1 d. *Education:* Royal University College of Music, Stockholm; Opera Producing, Germany. *Career:* Debut: Royal Court Theatre, Drottwingholm; Producer, Malmo City Theatre, 1960–67; Producer, Royal Opera House, Stockholm, 1967–71 and 1984–91; Artistic leader, Opera House, Goteborg, 1971–77; General Manager, Royal Opera House, Stockholm, 1978–84; Professor, University College of Opera, Stockholm, 1991–, among others; Ring des Nibelungen, Rosenkavalier, Ariadne, Lohengrin, Traviata, Otello, I Vespri Siciliani, Elektra, Fidelio, Zauberflöte and Figaro; Guest producer, Copenhagen, Oslo, Helsinki, Hamburg, Kiel, Braunschweig; mem, Royal Academy of Music, Stockholm. *Honours:* Litteris et Artibus. *Address:* Karlavagen 83, 114 59 Stockholm, Sweden.

ABESHOUSE, Warren; Australian composer; b. 8 May 1952, Sydney, NSW. *Education:* State Conservatoire, NSW. *Career:* ABC Radio and Television 1975–87; Office Man. 1994–. *Compositions include:* Five Bagatelles for Piano, 1972; Two Piano Sonatas, 1975, 1986; Psalm 70 for Chorus and Organ, 1975; Four Characteristic Pieces for Clarinet, 1976; Two Bagatelles for Cello, 1976; Lemmata, Essay for Orchestra, 1977; On Love for Tenor and Piano, 1980; Shadow Darkly for Oboe and Strings, 1990; The Christopher Sonatina for Piano, 1991; Womblemov for Horn, Cello and Timpani, 1993; Lament for Piano, 1993. *Honours:* First Prize, Original work for solo instrument, City of Sydney Eisteddfod, 1990. *Address:* c/o APRA, 1A Eden Street, Crows Nest, NSW 2065, Australia.

ABLINGER-SPERRHACKE, Wolfgang; Austrian singer (tenor); b. 1967, Zell am See. *Education:* studied in Vienna with Gerhard Kahry. *Career:* first became mem. of Landestheater, Linz, then joined Basel Opera and Gärtnerplatz, Munich; debut at Opéra Nat. de Paris 1997, subsequently sang there Goro/Madama Butterfly (also Theatre Olympics, Japan), Monostatos, Dr Blind/Die Fledermaus, 1st Jew/Salome, premiere of Phillippe Manoury's K; other engagements have included Vašek, Reverend Horace Adams/Peter Grimes and Monostatos at Glyndebourne Festival, Spoletta/Tosca and Valzacchi/Der Rosenkava-lier (La Monnaie), Dr Cajus/Falstaff (Aix, Madrid, Champs-Elysées), Mime/Das Rheingold (Dresden), Mime/Siegfried (Toulouse, Madrid), Regista/Un re in ascolto (Frankfurt), Pedrillo/Die Entführung aus dem Serail (La Conma), Trimalchio/Madema's Satyricon (Nancy); has worked with many conductors including Jordan, Conlon, Bychkov, Steinberg, Pappano and López Cobos; has appeared widely in concert, including recently Concertgebouw, Sao Paulo (Mahler's Lied von der Erde), Melbourne (Gurrelieder/Schönberg.); future engagements include Strasbourg (Aegisth/Elektra, Loge/Rheingold), Nancy (Haupt-maxm/Wozzeck), Madrid (Pedrillo). *Recordings:* DVD: Falstaff, Die Fledermaus. *Current Management:* IMG Artists, Lovell House, 616 Chiswick High Road, London, W4 5RX, England.

ABRAHAMSEN, Hans; Composer; b. 23 Dec. 1952, Copenhagen, Denmark. *Education:* Studied horn, theory, and music history at Royal Danish Conservatory, Copenhagen, 1969–71; Composition with Pelle Gudmundsen-Holmgreen and Per Norgard at Jutland Academy of Music, Ârhus. *Compositions:* Orchestral: Foam, 1970; Symphony in C, 1972; Symphony No. 1, 1974; Stratifications, 1973–75; Nach und Trompeten, 1981; Marchenbilder for 14 players, 1984; Cello Concerto, 1987; Chamber: Fantasy Pieces After Hans Jorgen Nielsen for Flute, Horn, Cello and Piano, 1969, revised, 1976; October for Piano Left Hand, 1969, revised 1976; Round And In Between for Brass Quintet, 1972; 2 Woodwind Quintets: No. 1, Landscapes, 1972, No. 2, Walden, 1978; Nocturnes for Flute and Piano, 1972; Flowersongs for 3 Flutes, 1973; Scraps for Cello and Piano, 1973; 2 String Quartets: No. 1, 1973, No. 2, 1991, 10 Preludes, 1973, No. 2, 1981; Flush for Saxophone, 1974, revised, 1979; Double for Flute and Guitar, 1975; Winternacht for 7 instruments, 1976–79; Canzone for Accordion, 1978; Geduldspiel for 10 instruments, 1980; 6 Pieces for Violin, Horn and Piano, 1984; 10 Studies for Piano, 1983–87; Herbst for Tenor, Flute, Guitar and Cello, 1970–72, revised, 1977; Universe Birds for 10 Sopranos, 1973; Songs of Denmark for Soprano and 5 Instruments, 1974, revised 1976; Aria for Soprano and 4 Instruments, 1979; Autumn Song for Soprano and Ensemble, 1992. *Address:* c/o CODA, PO Box 2154, 1016, Copenhagen K, Denmark.

ACEL, Ervin; Music Director and Conductor; b. 3 June 1935, Timisoara, Romania; 1 s. *Education:* Choral conducting, C Porumbescu Conservatory, Bucharest, 1953–58; Orchestral conducting, Cluj-Napoca Conservatory, Romania, 1958–60; Orchestral conducting; Masterclass. *Career:* Debut: Botosani Symphonic Orchestra, 1963; Conductor, Botosani State Philharmonic Orchestra, Romania, 1960–63; Principal Conductor, 1963–91, Director, 1984–91, Oradea Philharmonic Orchestra, Romania; Music Director, Szeged Symphony Orchestra, Hungary, 1991–99; Toured throughout Europe, USA, Japan, Mexico, Brazil, Taiwan, Singapore; Worked with numerous operas including Dresden Staatsoper, Grand Opera Dublin, various Romanian operas, Szeged Opera and Szeged Festival Opera; Professor in Conducting of Internationale Musik Seminar in Vienna, Austria, 1996; Guest Professor, Conducting Class, Universität für Musik und darstellende Kunst, Vienna, 1997. *Recordings:* Over 35 albums including J. Haydn Harpsichord concertos, Bach Harpsichord concertos, Mozart flute concertos, Mozart violin concertos, Schubert symphonies, Tchaikovsky string serenade, Mahler Kindertotenlieder, Kabalevsky symphonies, Flute concertos by Ibert and Nielsen. *Honours:* Cultural Order, Romania, 1978; Sebetia Ter, Italy, 1998. *Address:* 9725 Köszegszerdahely, Hegyi u. 15, Hungary.

ACHIM, Erzsébet; Organist; b. 6 Nov. 1954, Gyula, Hungary; m. Miklós Thaisz, 21 Oct 1978, 2 s. *Education:* Bartók Béla Konzervatórium; Faculty of Choir-Leading, Faculty of Organ, Ferenc Liszt Academy of Music, Budapest. *Career:* Played piece by Bartók for Hungarian Radio, age 5; Performs at organ concerts and concerts with orchestra, also as soloist and with choirs; Teaches church music; Several interviews and concerts broadcast by Hungarian radio and television; mem, Hungarian Church Music Society. *Recordings:* Several of chamber music, 1990–96; Handel, 6 Organ Concertos op 4, 1994; Glocken und Orgeln in Selm, 1999. *Contributions:* Articles in Magyar Nemzet, other Hungarian dailies, Uj Magyarország, Der Landbote, Switzerland, Südwest Presse, Germany, BBC Music Magazine. *Honours:* Extra Prize for Interpretation of Hungarian Composers, Ferenc Liszt International Musical Competition, 1978. *Address:* Apor Vilmos tér 3, 1124 Budapest, Hungary.

ACHUCCARO, Joaquin; Concert Pianist; b. 1 Nov. 1936, Bilbao, Spain. *Education:* Accademia Chigiana and with Walter Gieseking. *Career:* Many solo and concert performances world-wide from 1959, including appearances with the Berlin and New York Philharmonic, London Symphony and Philharmonia Orchestras, Orchestre National de France and Warsaw National Orchestra; Has also featured as soloist-conductor with chamber orchestras in the United Kingdom, Italy, Germany and Spain; from 1989 teacher at Southern Methodist University, Dallas; BBC recitals on tour, 1997. *Recordings include:* albums of Granados, Falla, Schubert, Ravel, Debussy and Brahms. *Honours:* Winner, 1959 Liverpool International Competition. *Current Management:* Olivia Ma Artists' Management, 65 Campden Street, London W8 7EL, England.

ACKER, Dieter; Composer and Teacher; b. 3 Nov. 1940, Sibiu-Hermannstadt, Romania. *Education:* Studied piano, organ, theory with Fr Xav Dressler, Sibiu, 1950–58; Composition with Sigismund Todutá, Cluj Conservatory, 1959–64. *Career:* Teacher of Theory and Composition, Cluj Conservatory, 1964–69; Teacher, Robert Schumann Conservatory, Düsseldorf, 1969–72; Teacher of Theory and Composition, 1972–76, Professor of Composition, 1976–, Munich Hochschule für Musik. *Compositions include:* Symphony No. 1, 1977–78; Eichendorff-Sonata for clarinet and piano, 1983; Mörike-Sonata for cello and piano, 1978; Bassoon Concerto, 1979–80; Violin Concerto No. 1, 1981; Piano Concerto, 1984; Piano Trio No. 2, 1984; String Trio No. 3, 1987; String Quartet No. 5, 1990–95; Music for Two Horns and Strings, 1991; Piano Trio No. 3, 1992; Symphony No. 3, 1992; Sinfonia Breve for brass, 1993; Notturno, for string orchestra, 1994; Violin Concerto No. 2, 1994–95; Sonata for two pianos, 1993; Sonata for Piano No. 2, 1993; Trinklieder for vocal quartet and piano, 1994; Sonata for Bassoon and Piano, 1996; Vocal music; Organ Music. *Recordings include:* Nachtstücke for two flutes; Piano Trio Stigmen; Rilke Sonate for violin and piano. *Honours:* Prag 1996 Prize for String Quartet No. 1; Johann-Wenzel-Stamitz-Prize, Stuttgart, 1970; Lions Club International Prize for String Quartet No. 4, Düsseldorf, 1973; Prix Henriette Renié for Music for Strings and Harp, Paris, 1988; Johann-Wenzel-Stamitz-Prize, Mannheim, 1990. *Address:* Kleiststrasse 12, 85521 Munich-Ottobrunn, Germany.

ACKERT, Stephen, DMus; American musician; b. 13 May 1944. *Education:* Univ. of Wisconsin, Madison Northwestern Univ., Evanston, IL. *Career:* resident keyboard artist and Music Dir of resident orchestra, Nat. Iranian Radio and Television Network, Tehran 1974–78; Dir of Music St Margaret's Episcopal Church, Washington, DC 1979–86; music program specialist, Nat. Gallery of Art, Washington, DC 1986–2004; Head of Music Dept, Nat. Gallery of Art 2004–; concert organist; teacher of applied organ; host of weekly classical music broadcasts on WOBC, Oberlin, OH and the Nat. Iranian Radio and Television Network, Tehran. *Publications:* articles in The American Organist. *Honours:* Fulbright Scholarship, Robert F. Smith Research Fellowship, Nat. Federation of Music Clubs Award, Alumnus of the Year Award, Oberlin Coll. 2002. *Address:* National Gallery of Art, Washington, DC 20565, USA (office). *Telephone:* (202) 842 6075 (office). *Fax:* (202) 842 2407 (office). *E-mail:* S-Ackert@nga.gov (office). *Website:* www.nga.gov (office).

ACOSTA, Adolovna P.; Concert Pianist, Music Teacher and Music Director; b. 3 Feb. 1946, Manila, Philippines. *Education:* Graduate Studies, Ethnomusicology, Wesleyan University, Connecticut, 1968–69; Teacher's Diploma, 1965, BM, Piano, 1966, MM, 1968, University of the Philippines; MS, Piano, The Juilliard School, 1971. *Career:* Solo recitals in New York including Carnegie Recital Hall, Alice Tully Hall, Merkin Concert Hall; Solo recitals in Wigmore Hall and Purcell Hall, London; Sunderland Art Gallery, Wolverhampton Art Gallery, England; Salle Cortot, Paris; Copenhagen and Stockholm; Solo recitals in Cultural Centre of the Philippines and Abelardo Hall, University of the Philippines; Soloist, four times, with the University of the Philippines Symphony Orchestra; Radio performances in Sweden, Philippines and the USA; Recitals in Philippine Consulates and Embassies; Jury Member, East and West Artists International Auditions, 1971, New York Chopin Competition, 1984; Former faculty mem., The Juilliard School Pre-College Division and New York University. *Recordings:* Andalucia and Danzas Afro Cubanas of Ernesto Lecuona; Piano Music of Carl Nielsen for Musical Heritage Society. *Address:* 310 Riverside Drive, Apt 313, New York, NY 10025, USA.

ACS, Janos; Conductor; b. 23 March 1952, Hungary; Divorced, 1 s., 2 d. *Education:* Diplomas in Flute, Pianoforte and Composition from Bela Bartók Institute, F. Liszt Academy, Budapest; Organ Diploma from Verdi Conservatorio, Milan. *Career:* debut, Fidelio at Teatro Carlo Felice, Genoa in 1979; Idomeneo at Opera di Roma, Tancredi at La Fenice, Falstaff, I Capuleti, Amico Fritz at Arena di Verona, Offenbach at Comunale di Firenze, La Bohème at Frankfurt, Symphonic Programmes in Tokyo, Manon, Pagliacci, La Traviata, and Otello in Denver, Carmen, Il Trovatore, and Tristan und Isolde in Pretoria, Faust in Hong Kong, and Luciano Pavarotti recital in Budapest; One of Pavarotti's conductors; Principal Conductor, Pact Theater, Pretoria, 1983–88; Principal Conductor at Opera Colorado in Denver, USA, 1985–91; mem, Co-Director, Franz Liszt Society of Germany. *Recordings:* Bellini Overtures; Donizetti Overtures; I Puritani; Carmen, video of Pact Theater in Pretoria; Respighi's Gli Uccelli, Trittico Botticelliano. *Honours:* Respighi Memorial Concert and Prize, 1985. *Address:* Via Carducci, 38, 2100 Milan, Italy.

ADAM, Theo; Singer (Bass Baritone) and Producer; b. 1 Aug. 1926, Dresden, Germany. *Education:* Sang in Dresden Kreuzchor and studied with Rudolf Dietrich in Dresden and in Weimar. *Career:* Debut: Dresden in 1949 as the Hermit in Der Freischütz; Berlin State Opera from 1952; Bayreuth debut in 1952 as Ortel in Meistersinger, later sang Wotan, Gurnemanz, King Henry, Pogner, Sachs and Amfortas; Covent Garden debut in 1967 as Wotan, Metropolitan Opera debut in 1969 as Sachs; Guest appearances include Hamburg, Vienna, Budapest and Chicago with roles including Berg's Wozzeck and Verdi's King Philip; Sang in and produced the premiere production of Dessau's Einstein at Berlin State Opera in 1974; Sang at Salzburg Festival, 1981, 1984 in premieres of Cerha's Baal and Berio's Un Re in Ascolto; In 1985 sang at reopened Semper Opera House, Dresden, in Der Freischütz and as Ochs in Der Rosenkavalier; Sang Don Alfonso at Tokyo in 1988 and La Roche in Capriccio at Munich Festival, 1990; Staged Graun's Cesare e Cleopatra for the 250th Anniversary of the Berlin State Opera, 1992; Sang Schigolch in Lulu at the Festival Hall in London, 1994 and at the Berlin Staatsoper, 1997; Sang in Henze's Bassarids at Dresden, 1997; Sang in the premiere of Weill's The Eternal Road, Chemnitz 1999; Season 2001 as Schigolch in Lulu at Palermo and Pimen in Boris Godunov at the Komische Oper, Berlin. *Recordings:* Bach Cantatas; Freischütz; Parsifal; Meistersinger; Die Zauberflöte; Così fan tutte; Der Ring des Nibelungen; St Matthew Passion; Fidelio; Krenek's Karl V; Baal; Dantons Tod; Rosenkavalier; Die schweigsame Frau. *Publications:* Seht, hier ist Tinte, Feder, Papier…, autobiography, 1983. *Address:* Schillerstrasse, 8054 Dresden, Germany.

ADAMIS, Mihalis; Composer and Choral Director; b. 19 May 1929, Piraeus, Greece; m. Pany Carella, 30 July 1973, 2 s. *Education:* Theology Degree, Athens University, 1954; Byzantine Music Degree, Piraeus Conservatory, 1955; Composition Degree, Hellenicon Conservatory, 1959; Graduate studies in composition, electronic music, Byzantine Paleography, Brandeis University, Boston, USA, 1962–65. *Career:* Founder and Director of Hellenic Royal Palace Boys Choir, 1950–67 and Athens Chamber Chorus, 1958–61; Taught Byzantine Music, directed choir, Greek Orthodox College of Theology, Boston, USA, 1961–63; Founder of first electronic music studio in Athens, Greece in 1968; Head of Music Department, Choir Director, Pierce College, Athens, 1968–; Many festival commissions including: Hellenic

Weeks of Contemporary Music, 1967–72, English Bach Festival, 1971, 1973; World-wide performances of works include: ONCE Festival, USA, 1962, Barcelona, 1973, Leicester, 1976, Greek Month in London, 1975, 1989, Art Weeks throughout Europe, Middle and Far East; Many international radio and television broadcasts; Toured Europe and the Americas with ballet piece, Genesis, 1973; President, Supreme Council for Music, Ministry of Culture, 1993. *Compositions include:* Epallelon for Orchestra; Anakyklesis; Hirmos for voices; Kratema; Vision of God for mixed chorus and orchestra, 1997; Who is as Great as God? for women's chorus, 1999; Melos for alto saxophone, 2000. *Recordings:* Genesis; Apocalypsis; Minyrismos; Metallic Sculptures; Byzantine Passion; Psalmic Ode. *Address:* Gravias 43, 15342 Ayia Paraskevi, Athens, Greece.

ADAMS, Byron; Composer, Conductor, Author and Teacher; b. 9 March 1955, Atlanta, Georgia, USA. *Education:* BM, Jacksonville University, 1977; MM, University of Southern California, 1979; DMA, Cornell University, 1984. *Career:* Composer-in-Residence, Music Center, University of the South, 1979–84; Guest Composer, 26th Warsaw Autumn Festival, 1983, and San Francisco Conservatory, 1986; Lecturer, Cornell University, New York City, 1985–87; Assistant Professor, Associate Professor, University of California at Riverside. *Compositions:* Quintet for piano and strings, 1979; Concerto for trumpet and string orchestra, 1983; Sonata for trumpet and piano, 1983; Concerto for violin and orchestra, 1984; Go Lovely Rose for male chorus, 1984; Missa brevis, 1988; Three Epitaphs, 1988. *Recordings:* Nightingales, 1979; Serenata aestiva, 1986. *Contributions:* The Instrumentalist; Musical Quarterly; Notes. *Address:* Department of Music, University of California at Riverside, Riverside, CA 92521, USA.

ADAMS, David; Composer, Conductor and Librettist; b. 19 April 1949, Box Hill, Victoria, Australia. *Education:* BA, Canberra School of Music, 1976. *Career:* Lowther Hall Anglican Girls Grammar School, 1977–81; Scotch College, 1978–83; Melbourne College of Advanced Education, 1985–87; Commissions from Sydney Dance Company, Australian Musicians Guild and the British Musical Society, 1987. *Compositions include:* Memories of the Future for guitar and harpsichord, 1979; Strangers, ballet, for string quartet, oboe, horn and percussion, 1981; being divinely for soprano, percussion and strings, 1983; Variations for oboe and guitar, 1983; In Memoriam, for soprano and ensemble, 1984; Fan Fare for chorus, orchestra, soprano and viola, 1985; Time Locked in his Tower, music theatre for flutes, guitar and percussion, 1987; In My Craft of Sullen Art for soprano and viola, 1994; Lunar aspects, song cycle for soprano and guitar, 1996. *Honours:* Winner, Australian Composition Sections at Geelong Eisteddfod, also Bandigo Eisteddfod, 1981–83. *Address:* c/o APRA, 1A Eden Street, Crows Nest, NSW 2065, Australia.

ADAMS, John Coolidge; Composer and Conductor; b. 15 Feb. 1947, Worcester, MA, USA. *Education:* studied clarinet with father and Felix Viscuglia; BA, 1969, MA, 1971, Harvard College; studied composition with Leon Kirchner, David Del Tredici and Roger Sessions. *Career:* appearances as clarinettist and conductor; Head, Composition Department, San Francisco Conservatory, 1971–81; Adviser on New Music, 1978, Composer-in-Residence, 1982–85, San Francisco Symphony Orchestra; conducted Nixon in China at 1988 Edinburgh Festival; Creative Adviser, St Paul Chamber Orchestra, MN, 1988–89; The Death of Klinghoffer premiered at Brussels, Lyon and Vienna, 1991 (London premiere at Barbican Hall, 2002); I Was Looking at the Ceiling, performed at Berkeley, New York, Paris, Edinburgh and Hamburg, 1995. *Compositions:* Operas: Nixon in China, 1987; The Death of Klinghoffer, 1991; Musical: I Was Looking at the Ceiling and then I Saw the Sky, 1995; Orchestral: Common Tones In Simple Time, 1979; Harmonium for Chorus and Orchestra, 1980; Grand Pianola Music for 2 Sopranos, 2 Pianos and Small Orchestra, 1981–82; Shaker Loops for String Orchestra, 1983; Harmonielehre, 1984–85; Fearful Symmetries, 1988; The Wound-Dresser for Baritone and Orchestra, 1989; Eros Piano for Piano and Orchestra, 1989; Liszt's La Lugubre Gondola, and Wiegenlied arranged for orchestra, 1989; Violin Concerto, 1993; Gnarly Buttons, 1996; Slonimsky's Earbox, 1996; Naive and Sentimental Music, 1998; Nativity, El Niño, oratorio, 2000; Chamber: Piano Quintet, 1970; American Standard for Unspecified Ensemble, 1973; Grounding for 3 Solo Voices, Instruments and Electronics, 1975; Onyx for Tape, 1976; Piano: Ragamarole, 1973; China Gates, 1977; Phrygian Gates, 1977; On the Transmigration of Souls, 2002. *Honours:* Guggenheim Fellowship, 1982. *Current Management:* Boosey & Hawkes Ltd, 295 Regent Street, London W1R 8JH, England.

ADAMS, (Harrison) Leslie, PhD; American composer and teacher; b. 30 Dec. 1932, Cleveland, OH. *Education:* Glenville High School, Oberlin Coll. Conservatory of Music, OH, Calif. State Univ. at Long Beach, Ohio State Univ. *Career:* piano accompanist for ballet and dance companies in New York, numerous performances of his compositions 1957–62; Assoc. Musical Dir, Karamu House, Cleveland, OH 1964–65; composer-in-residence 1979–80; Musical Dir, Kaleidoscope Players, Raton, NM 1967–68; composer-in-residence, Cuyahoga Community Coll., Cleve-

land 1980, Cleveland Music School Settlement 1981–82; founder and Pres., Accord Assocs. Inc. 1980–86, Exec. Vice-Pres. and composer-in-residence 1986–92; Exec. Vice-Pres. and composer-in-residence, Creative Arts Inc. 1997–; teacher, Soehl Jr High School, Linden, NJ 1962–63, secondary schools in Raton, NM 1966–67; Asst Prof. of Music, Fla A&M Univ., Tallahassee 1968; Assoc. Prof. of Music, Dir of the Univ. Choir, Dir of Choral Clinics, Univ. of Kan., Lawrence 1970–78; mem. advisory council, Musical Arts Asscn (Cleveland Orchestra) 1982; mem. American Choral Dirs' Asscn, American Guild of Organists. *Compositions:* Hark, to the Shouting Wind! 1951, I Hear A Voice 1951, Night 1951, The Constant Lover 1951, Break, Break, Break 1951, Teach Me, O Lord (from Psalm 119) 1951, Turn Away Mine Eyes 1951, Four Pieces for piano 1951, Pastorale for violin and piano 1952, Asperges Me for chorus 1952, Two Vachel Lindsay Songs 1952–53, Of Man's First Disobedience (from Paradise Lost) 1953, On the Sea 1953, Seven Amen Chorale Responses 1953, Intermezzo for violin and piano 1953, Theme and Variations in A-flat Major (or Variations on a Serious Theme) 1953, A Kiss in Xanadu (ballet) 1954, The Congo 1955, Romance for orchestra 1960, Five Songs on Texts by Edna St Vincent Millay (or Five Millay Songs) 1960, Six Songs (on Texts by African-American Poets) 1961, A White Road 1961, Sonata for violin and piano 1961, Three Preludes for piano 1961, Sonata for horn and piano 1961, Contrasts for piano 1961, Concerto for piano and orchestra (or CitiScape) 1964, All the Way Home 1965, Madrigal for chorus 1969, Love Song for chorus 1969, Hosanna to the Son of David for chorus 1969, Psalm 121 for chorus 1969, Under the Greenwood Tree for chorus 1969, Psalm 23 for chorus 1970, There Was an Old Man for chorus 1970, Vocalise for chorus 1973, Man's Presence: A Song of Ecology for chorus 1975, Trombone Quartet 1975, Sonata for cello and piano 1975, Etude in G Minor 1977, Prelude and Fugue for organ 1979, Ode to Life for orchestra 1979, Dunbar Songs (or Three Songs on Texts of Paul Laurence Dunbar) 1981, Christmas Lullaby 1983, Night Song for flute and harp 1983, Symphony No. 1 1983, The Righteous Man: A Cantata to the Memory of Dr Martin Luther King Jr (or Cantata No. 1) 1985, Blake (opera) 1986, The Wider View 1988, Hymn to Freedom 1989, Love Expressions 1990, Love Memory 1990, What Love Brings 1991, A Christmas Wish for chorus 1991, Offering of Love for organ 1991, Amazing Grace 1992, Song of the Innkeeper's Children 1992, Song to Baby Jesus 1992, Christmas Lullaby for orchestra with chorus 1993, Song of Thanks 1993, Love Request 1993, Lullaby Eternal 1993, Anniversary Song 1993, Flying 1993, Midas, Poor Midas 1994, From a Hotel Room 1994, Daybirth 1994, Western Adventure for orchestra 1994, Hymn to All Nations for chorus 1997. *Publications:* contrib. articles The Mahlerian Mystique 1969, The Problems of Composing Choral Music for High School Use 1973. *Honours:* Nat. Asscn of Negro Women Inc. Composition Competition, New York 1963, Nat. Educ. Defense Act Fellowship 1969–70, Christian Arts Inc. Nat. Award for Original Composition for Choral Ensemble, New York 1974, Nat. Endowment for the Arts Award 1979, Rockefeller Foundation Study and Conference Center, Bellagio Italy 1979, Yaddo Artists Colony, Saratoga Springs NY 1980, 1984, Cleveland Foundation Fellow 1980, Jennings Foundation Fellow 1981, 'Meet The Artist' Cleveland Ohio Public Schools. *Current Management:* Creative Arts Inc., 9409 Kempton Avenue, Cleveland, OH 44108, USA. *Fax:* (216) 451-5159 (office). *E-mail:* CreativeArtsInc@webtv.net (office).

ADAMS-BARBARO, Jennifer; Singer (Soprano); b. 22 March 1953, London, England. *Education:* Guildhall School of Music and Drama. *Career:* Opera debut aged 15, Juliet in Gounod's Romeo and Juliet; Operatic roles, Gretel, Galatea, Euridice, Dido, Micaela, Naiad and Turandot; Star singer on Friday Night is Music Night, 1985; Glyndebourne Festival Opera; Mozart Requiem, Swansea Festival, Jane Glover, 1991. *Recordings:* Numerous BBC solo recordings including Rossini Petite Messe, Verdi Four Sacred Pieces with BBC Symphony Orchestra; Promenade concert; Video, Bartók Five Village Scenes with Pierre Boulez, Concertgebouw, Amsterdam. *Honours:* World Finalist in Luciano Pavarotti Prize, 1985; AGSM. *Address:* 68 Bellingham Road, Catford, London SE6 2PT, England.

ADÈS, Thomas Joseph Edmund, MA, MPhil; British composer, pianist and conductor; *Artistic Director, Aldeburgh Festival;* b. 1 March 1971, London; s. of Timothy Adès and Dawn Adès. *Education:* Univ. Coll. School, Guildhall School of Music, King's Coll., Cambridge, St John's Coll., Cambridge. *Career:* solo recitalist with the Composers' Ensemble 1992; PLG Young Concert Artists Platform concert at the Purcell Room 1993; Composer in Assoc., Hallé Orchestra 1993–95; Lecturer, Univ. of Manchester 1993–94; Fellow Commoner in Creative Arts, Trinity Coll., Cambridge 1995–97; Benjamin Britten Prof. of Music, RAM 1997–99; Musical Dir Birmingham Contemporary Music Group 1998–2000; Artistic Dir Aldeburgh Festival 1999–; conducted the BBC Symphony Orchestra at the BBC Proms, London 2002. *Compositions:* Five Eliot Landscapes 1990, Chamber Symphony 1990, Catch 1991, Darkness Visible 1992, Under Hamelin Hill 1992, Fool's Rhymes 1992, Still Sorrowing 1993, Life Story 1993, Living Toys 1993, . . . but all shall be well 1993, Sonata da Caccia 1994, The Origin of the Harp 1994,

Arcadiana 1994, Powder Her Face 1995, Traced Overhead 1995–96, These Premises are Alarmed 1996, Asyla 1997, Concerto Conciso 1997–98, America (A Prophecy) 1999, January Writ 1999, Piano Quintet 2000, Brahms 2001, The Tempest 2004. *Television includes:* Music for the 21st Century: Thomas Adès (Channel 4), Powder Her Face (Channel 4). *Honours:* Lutine Prize, GSM 1986, winner Paris Rostrum, for best piece by composer under 30 1994, Royal Philharmonic Prize 1997, Elise L. Stoeger Prize 1996, Royal Philharmonic Society Award for Large-scale Composition 1997, Salzburg Easter Festival Prize 1999, Ernst von Siemens Prize 1999, Grawemeyer Prize 2000, Hindemith Prize 2001, ISCM Young Composers Award 2002. *Address:* c/o Faber Music Ltd, 3 Queen Square, London, WC1N 3AU, England (office). *Telephone:* (20) 7833-7911 (office). *Fax:* (20) 7833-7939 (office). *E-mail:* sally.cavender@fabermusic.com (office). *Website:* www.fabermusic.com (office).

ADEY, Christopher, ARAM, FRAM, FRCM, FRWCMD; conductor; b. 1943, Essex, England. *Education:* Royal Acad. of Music, London, principally as violinist with Manoug Parikian. *Career:* violinist –1973 mainly with Halle and London Philharmonic Orchestras; debut as conductor in 1973; Assoc. Conductor, BBC Scottish Symphony Orchestra 1973–76; cycle of the complete Martinů symphonies for BBC 1975; frequent guest appearances throughout the UK and with the leading London orchestras; Assoc. Conductor, Ulster Orchestra 1981–84; has worked in most European countries, Middle and Far East, Canada and USA; frequent broadcasts for BBC and abroad; extensive repertoire covering symphonic and chamber orchestra works of all periods and including choral works and opera; Prof. of Conducting, Royal Coll. of Music 1979–92; orchestral trainer at conservatoires throughout the UK and maintains a large commitment to guest conducting with county, nat. and int. youth orchestras; Principal Conductor, Nat. Youth Orchestra of Wales 1996–2002; Chief Conductor and Artistic Dir, Royal Oman Symphony Orchestra 2001–. *Publications:* Orchestral Performance: A Guide for Conductors and Players 1998. *Honours:* Commemorative Medal of Czech Government 1986. *Address:* c/o Richard Haigh, Performing Arts, 6 Windmill Street, London, W1P 1HF, England.

ADKINS, Cecil Dale; Musicologist; b. 30 Jan. 1932, Red Oak, Iowa, USA. *Education:* BFA, University of Omaha, 1953; MM, University of South Dakota, 1959; PhD, University of Iowa, 1963. *Career:* Assistant Conductor and Arranger, Fourth Armoured Division Band, Fort Hood, Texas, 1954–55; Director of Instrumental Music, Paullina, IA, 1955–60; Graduate Assistant, University of Iowa, 1960–63; Instructor, Music department, Mount Mercy College, Cedar Rapids, IA, 1960–63; Professor of Music, University of North Texas, Denton, 1963–, Regents Professor, 1988–, Chairman, International Musicological Society's Center for Musicological Works in Progress, 1969–; President, American Musical Instrument Society, 1987–91; mem, American Musicological Society; International Musicological Society; American Musical Instrument Society; Dansk Selskab for Musikforskning. *Publications:* Editor, Doctoral Dissertations in Musicology, 5th edition, 1971, 7th edition, 1984, with A Dickinson, 8th edition, 1989; The A flat y'Berg Positive Organ: Basle, Historical Museum 1927–28, Description and Technical Drawing, 1979; A Trumpet by Any Other Name: A History of the Trumpet Marine, with A Dickinson, 1987; Four Historical Trumpet Marines, Description and Technical Drawings, 1987; Doctoral Dissertations in Musicology, Second Series No. 1, 1990, No. 2, 1996. *Contributions:* articles in many journals and reference works. *Honours:* Francis Densmore Prize for best Journal Article on Instruments, American Musical Instrument Society, 1992; Curt Sachs Award, American Musical Instrument Society, 1999. *Address:* c/o College of Music, University of North Texas, Denton, TX 76203, USA.

ADLER, Samuel Hans, BM, MA; composer, conductor and music teacher; *Composition Faculty Member, Juilliard School of Music;* b. 4 March 1928, Mannheim, Germany; m. 1st Carol Ellen Stalker (divorced 1988); two d.; m. 2nd Emily Freeman Brown 1992. *Education:* Boston Univ., Harvard Univ., studied composition with Herbert Fromm, Hugo Norden, Walter Piston, Randall Thompson, Paul Hindemith and Aaron Copland, musicology with Karl Geiringer, conducting with Serge Koussevitzky at Berkshire Music Centre, Tanglewood. *Career:* founder and first conductor, 7th Army Symphony Orchestra 1952; Dir of Music, Temple Emanu-El, Dallas 1953–66; conductor, Dallas Lyric Theatre 1955–57; Prof. of Composition, North Texas State Univ., Denton 1957–66; Prof. of Composition 1966–95, Prof. Emeritus 1966–95, Chair Composition Dept 1973–95, Eastman School of Music, Rochester, NY; guest conductor, symphony orchestras and opera cos. worldwide; guest lecturer in USA and other countries; teacher of composition, Juilliard School of Music, New York, Composition Faculty mem. 1997–; mem. professional organizations. *Compositions include:* operas: The Outcasts of Poker Flat 1959, The Wrester 1970, The Lodge of Shadows 1973; orchestral works include: six symphonies 1953–85, Rhapsody for violin and orchestra 1961, Elegy for string orchestra 1962, Requiescat in Pace in memory of President John F. Kennedy 1963, Concerto for orchestra 1971, Sinfonietta 1971, Flute Concerto 1977, Piano Concerto No. 1 1983,

Time in Tempest Everywhere for orchestra 1993, Guitar Concerto 1994, Cello Concerto 1995, Piano Concerto No. 2 1996; chamber music includes: eight string quartets 1945, 1950, 1953, revised 1964, 1963, 1969, 1975, 1981, 1990, organ pieces. *Publications include:* Anthology for the Teaching of Choral Conducting 1971, Sight Singing 1979, The Study of Orchestration 1982; contrib. to numerous journals. *Honours:* several hon. degrees; American Acad. and Inst. of Arts and Letters Music Award, ASCAP Aaron Copland Award for Lifetime Achievement 2003. *Address:* 9412 Sheffield Road, Perrysburg OH 43551, USA. *Telephone:* (419) 666-9519 (home). *Fax:* (419) 666-6417 (home).

ADNI, Daniel; Concert Pianist; b. 6 Dec. 1951, Haifa, Israel. *Education:* Paris Conservatoire, 1968–69. *Career:* Debut: London, 1970; Since debut played as soloist with most orchestras in the United Kingdom, Israel, Netherlands, Germany, USA, Far East and Japan; Solo recitals in many major cities and festivals; Also played chamber music at such festivals as Kuhmo, Finland; Numerous broadcasts on various radio stations including BBC; Joined The Solomon Trio in 1994. *Recordings:* Over 21 records including: works by Chopin and Debussy, Complete Songs Without Words by Mendelssohn, Complete Grieg Lyric Pieces, Piano Music by John Ireland and Percy Grainger, Mendelssohn Preludes and Fugues op 35, Schubert Sonatas, Concertos by Saint-Saëns and Mendelssohn, and Rhapsody in Blue by Gershwin. *Honours:* Winner of many prizes for piano, Solfège and sight-reading, Paris Conservatoire, 1969; Winner, Young Concert Artists, New York, 1976; Winner, Phillip M Fanuett Prize, New York, 1981. *Address:* 64A Menelik Road, London NW2 3RH, England.

ADOLPHE, Bruce; American composer; *Artistic Advisor and Education Advisor, Chamber Music Society of Lincoln Center;* b. 31 May 1955, New York City. *Education:* Juilliard School, New York. *Career:* taught at New York Univ. Tisch School 1983, Yale Univ. 1984–85; Composer-in-Residence, 92nd Street Y School Concert Series 1988–90, Santa Fe Chamber Music Festival 1989, La Jolla SummerFest 1998–2001, 2003, 2005, Music from Angel Fire 1984, 1995 and many other festivals; Artistic Advisor and Educ. Advisor, Chamber Music Soc. of Lincoln Center, New York 1992–; Creative Dir PollyRhythm Productions; his operas have been performed in Boston and New York; comms from Orpheus Chamber Orchestra, Chamber Music Soc. of Lincoln Center, Itzhak Perlman, Beaux Arts Trio, Chamber Orchestra of Philadelphia, Brentano String Quartet, Metropolitan Opera Guild, Chicago Chamber Musicians, Chicago Humanities Festival, and many others. *Compositions include:* The Tell-Tale Heart (one-act opera after Edgar Allan Poe) 1982, Mikhoels The Wise (opera in two acts) 1982, The False Messiah (opera in two acts) 1983, The Amazing Adventure of Alvin Allegretto (one-act comic children's opera) 1994, Oceanophony (for chamber ensemble and actors, poems by Kate Light) 2004, Red Dogs and Pink Skies: A Musical Celebration of Paul Gauguin 2003, Time Flies (for chamber orchestra) 2004, What Dreams May Come? (for chamber orchestra) 2005, Violin Concerto 2005, Songs of Life and Love: to Poems by Persian, Arab, Israeli, and American Women (for mezzo-soprano and piano) 2005. *Recordings:* many recordings with PollyRhythm Productions, Telarc, Naxos, Delos, Koch, CRI and Summit. *Publications:* The Mind's Ear 1990, What To Listen For In The World 1996, Of Mozart, Parrots, and Cherry Blossoms in the Wind: A Composer Explores Mysteries of the Musical Mind 1999. *Address:* Chamber Music Society of Lincoln Center, 70 Lincoln Center Plaza, 10th Floor, New York, NY 10024, USA (office). *Telephone:* (212) 875-5775 (office). *Website:* www.chambermusicsociety.org (office); www.pollyrhythm.com (office).

ADORJÁN, András; Flautist; b. 26 Sept. 1944, Budapest, Hungary. *Education:* Dentist Diploma, Copenhagen, 1968; Musical Studies with Jean-Pierre Rampal and Aurèle Nicolet. *Career:* Principal with the orchestra of the Royal Opera, Stockholm, 1970–72; Gurzenich Orchestra, Cologne, 1972–73; Sudwestfunk Baden-Baden, 1973–74 and Bavarian Radio Symphony Orchestra, 1974–88; Teacher at the Nice Summer Academy from 1971–1985; Professor at the Musikhochschule at Cologne, Germany from 1987 and the Musikhochschule München from 1996; Gave the 1981 premiere of Ground, concerto for Flute and Orchestra by Sven-Erik Werner; Dedication of Moz-Art à la Mozart by Alfred Schnittke, 1990; Concerto for Flute and Harp by Edison Denisov, 1995. *Recordings:* Over 90 including the first complete recording of all 14 flute concertos by François Devienne. *Address:* Musikhochschule München, Arcisstr 12, 80333 Munich, Germany.

AFANASSIEV, Valery; Pianist; b. 1947, Moscow, Russia. *Education:* Studied at the Moscow Conservatory with Emil Gilels. *Career:* Debut: Moscow, 1962; Performances throughout Eastern Europe after winning 1969 Bach Competition at Leipzig; Settled in Brussels, 1974, Versailles thereafter; Chamber musician with violinist Gidon Kremer; Concerts throughout Europe, Japan and USA; Performs in own plays as actor and pianist, has done these one-man shows in several countries and in 4 languages. *Recordings:* Bach, Beethoven, Brahms, Mozart and Schubert with major recording companies including most recently Das Wohltemperierte Klavier Complete Vols I and II, by J. S. Bach, 1997; Sonatas D

958, D 959, D960 by Schubert, 1997; Diabelli Variations and Chopin's Nocturnes. *Publications:* 4 novels (in French); 2 Theatrical Plays inspired by Mussorgsky's Pictures at an Exhibition and Schumann's Kreisleriana. *Honours:* Winner, Queen Elisabeth of the Belgians Competition, Brussels, 1972. *Address:* 1 square de Furstenberg, 78150 Le Chesnay, France.

AFANASYEVA, Veronika; Violinist; b. 1960, Moscow, Russia. *Education:* Studied at Central Music School, Moscow. *Career:* Co-Founder of Quartet Veronique in 1989; Many concerts in Russia notably in the Russian Chamber Music Series and 150th birthday celebrations for Tchaikovsky in 1990; Masterclasses at Aldeburgh Festival in 1991; Concert tour of the United Kingdom in season 1992–93; Repertoire includes works by Beethoven, Brahms, Tchaikovsky, Bartók, Shostakovich and Schnittke. *Recordings include:* Schnittke's 3rd Quartet. *Honours:* With Quartet Veronique: Winner, All-Union String Quartet Competition at St Petersburg, 1990–91, 3rd Place, International Shostakovich Competition at St Petersburg, 1991. *Address:* c/o Sonata (Quartet Veronique), 11 Northgate Street, Glasgow G20 7AA, Scotland.

AGACHE, Alexandru; Singer (Baritone); b. 16 Aug. 1955, Cluj, Romania. *Education:* Studied in Cluj. *Career:* Debut: As Silvano in Ballo in Maschera, Cluj, 1979; Has sung Sharpless, Don Giovanni, Malatesta and Verdi's Posa, Luna, Nabucco and Germont at Cluj; Further appearances in Dresden, Budapest and Ankara; Sang Don Giovanni at Livorno and Toulon, 1987, Renato at Covent Garden followed by Enrico Ashton in Lucia di Lammermoor and Simon Boccanegra in a new production of Verdi's opera in 1991; La Scala debut as Belcore in L'Elisir d'amore, 1988; Marquis di Posa in Hamburg, 1988 and La Fenice, Venice, in 1992; Sang Renato in Ballo in Maschera in Zürich and Düsseldorf, 1989, Marcello in La Bohème at Lyon Opéra in 1991 and Renato at Opéra Bastille in Paris in 1992; Sang Amonasro at Covent Garden, 1994, returning 1997 and 2002 for Simon Boccanegra; Met debut as Boccanegra, 1999. *Recordings include:* Golem The Rebel by Nicolas Bretan; Video of Covent Garden performance of Simon Boccanegra under Solti. *Address:* c/o Stafford Law Associates, 6 Barham Close, Weybridge, Surrey KT 13 9 PR, England.

AGAZHANOV, Artyomovich; Composer and Pianist; b. 3 Feb. 1958, Moscow, Russia. *Education:* piano and composition at Moscow Central Music School, 1965–76; further study at Moscow State Tchaikovsky Conservatoire. *Career:* teacher at Moscow Central Music School 1983–; concert appearances as composer and pianist in Russia, Bulgaria, Italy, Germany, including festivals: Moscow autumne 1986, 1987, 1989 and 1994, Moscow Stars 1989, and International Music Festival 1988; mem. Union of Russian Composers. *Compositions include:* Pax in terra for orchestra, 1983; On Beauty, Sorrow, Laughter and Grieving (cantata no. 2), for high soprano and large orchestra, texts by Issa Kobayashi, Matsuo Basho, Ihara Saikaku, 1983; Gloria (cantata no. 3) for soprano, mezzo-soprano, tenor, baritone, mixed chorus, large orchestra, tape ad libitum, 1984; Way of the Poet (cantata no. 4), for tenor, mixed chorus, large orchestra, text by Mikhail Lermontov, 1989; Kolobrod, music for film, 1990; Incite the City to Rebellion, music for film, 1992; Confessing Sinner (cantata no. 5), for mezzo-soprano, tenor, tenor/baritone, bass, large orchestra, tape ad libitum, 2000; Farewell in June, music for film, 2003. *Recordings:* Vision for Violin and Piano, 1988; Sonata for Violoncello and Piano, 1989; Gust, overture for Orchestra, 1989; From 3 till 6 for Piano, 1989; Variations on Theme by Chopin for Piano, 1992; 6 Japanese Hokku for Soprano and Piano, 1993; Way of the Poet (cantata no. 4), vocal symphony poem for Tenor, Mixed Choir and Full Orchestra, 1994; Without trace, vocal cycle for contralto and piano, 1999. *Publications:* Without Colouring The Truth 1993. *Honours:* All Union Competition of Young Composers 1981. *Address:* Brusov 8–10 Apt 55, Moscow 103009, Russia. *E-mail:* aaartem_@mtu-net.ru.

AGHOVA, Livia; Singer (Soprano); b. 1961, Slovakia, Czechoslovakia. *Education:* Studied in Bratislava. *Career:* Sang in opera at Bratislava, 1983–88; Mozart's Susanna, Donna Elvira and Pamina, Mimi, Micaela and Marguerite in Faust; National Theatre, Prague, 1988–; Marenka Marzellina and Martinů's Julietta; Berlin Staatsoper as Antonia in Hoffmann; Munich Staatsoper as Xenia in Dvořák's Dimitri; As Donna Elvira, Savonlinna Festival, 1991; Liu in Turandot, Houston, 1994; Puccini's Lauretta, Prague, 1996; Other roles include Jenůfa, Strauss's Sophie, Gounod's Juliette and Nedda in Pagliacci; Concerts include Beethoven's Ninth and Dvořák's St Ludmilla and The Spectre's Bride; Sang Janáček's Vixen at Venice, 1999. *Recordings:* Dimitri, Supraphon; Janáček's Osud, Orfeo; Glagolitic Mass. *Address:* c/o Music International, 13 Ardilaun Road, London N5 2QR, England.

AGNEW, Paul; Singer (tenor); b. 1964, Glasgow, Scotland. *Education:* Chorister at St Chad's Cathedral, Birmingham; Lay-Clerkships at Birmingham and Lichfield Cathedrals; Choral Scholar at Magdalen College, Oxford. *Career:* Tours with the Consort of Musicke to Germany, Switzerland, Netherlands, Italy, Spain, Austria, Sweden and Australia; Handel songs in the National Gallery, London with the Parley of

Instruments; Promenade Concerts debut in 1989 in The Judgement of Paris; Has sung the Evangelist in the St Matthew Passion for the London Handel Orchestra; South Bank debut at the Purcell Room celebrating the centenary of Ivor Gurney's birth; Engaged for the St John Passion with the Schola Cantorum of Basle and for Les Noces in Zürich; Tour of the USA with the Festival of Voices directed by Paul Hillier; Sang in Monteverdi Madrigals with the Consort of Musicke at Promenade Concerts in 1993; Palais Garnier, Paris, 1996, as Rameau's Hippolyte; Sang with New London Consort at the Purcell Room, London, 1997; Season 1999 with Charpentier's Extremum Dei Judicum and Lalande's Dies Irae at the London Prom concerts; Sang in Rameau's Platée at the Palais Garnier; Season 2000 in Rameau's La Guirlande at Cologne and Acis and Galatea at the Salzburg Easter Festival. *Recordings include:* Monteverdi Madrigals. *Current Management:* Hazard Chase Ltd, Norman House, Cambridge Place, Cambridge, CB2 1NS, England. *Telephone:* (1223) 312400. *Fax:* (1223) 460827. *Website:* www.hazardchase.co.uk.

AGOPOV, Vladimir; Composer; b. 23 Nov. 1953, Voroshilovgrad, USSR; m. 16 June 1977, 2 s., 1 d. *Education:* Graduated, Composition major, Moscow Conservatoire, 1977. *Career:* Debut: Diploma Concert, Moscow, 1977; mem, Society of Finnish Composers. *Compositions:* Music for Chamber Orchestra, 1982; Ergo for violin and piano, 1985; Tres viae, Concerto for Cello and Orchestra, op 10, 1987; Decimetto, 1997. *Recordings:* Sonata for clarinet and piano, 1991; Concerto for cello and orchestra, 1992; Siciliana, 1992. *Honours:* Competition in Kouvola, Finland, 1982; Sibelius Violin Competition for Composers, 1985. *Address:* Limingantie 24, 00520 Helsinki, Finland.

AGUERA, Luc-Marie; Violinist; b. 1960, France. *Education:* Paris Conservatoire with Jean-Claude Pennetier and with members of the Amadeus and Alban Berg Quartets. *Career:* Member of the Ysaÿe String Quartet from 1985; Many concert performances in France, Europe, America and the Far East; Festival engagements at Salzburg, Tivoli, Bergen, Lockenhaus, Barcelona and Stresa; Many appearances in Italy notably playing the Haydn Quartets of Mozart; Tours of Japan and USA in 1990 and 1992. *Recordings:* Mozart Quartet K421 and Quintet K516; Ravel, Debussy and Mendelssohn Quartets. *Honours:* Grand Prix Evian International String Quartet Competition, 1988; Special Prizes for Best Performances of a Mozart Quartet, the Debussy Quartet and a contemporary work; 2nd Prize, Portsmouth International String Quartet Competition, 1988. *Current Management:* Artist Management International Ltd, 12–13 Richmond Buildings, Dean Street, London W1V 5AF, England.

AHLIN, Sven Åke; Swedish composer; b. 6 April 1951, Sundsvall; m. Emma Rosendal 1989; two s. one d. *Education:* Royal Coll. of Music, Stockholm, Indiana Univ., USA. *Career:* debut, Stockholm 1977; numerous performances of his choir music and chamber music in Sweden, including trombone concerto with Christian Lindberg as soloist in Jönköping; broadcasts include four first performances by the Swedish Radio Choir, and piano concerto with Mats Widlund as soloist; performances abroad in Norway, Iceland, Russia, France, Spain, Hungary and the Netherlands; mem. Soc. of Swedish Composers. *Compositions:* Al Fresco, piano concerto; Narratives, trombone concerto; Across for orchestra; Ritual for Huitzilopochtli; Choral music including Dream of Elysium; Clashing Worlds; I have a dream; Concertos: Al fresco (piano); Narratives (trombone); Turning Points (String Quartet No. 2), 1997; Concerto for vihuela and string orchestra, 1998; Skuggan av ett regn (The shadow of a rain) for mezzo-soprano and chamber ensemble; numerous pieces of chamber music. *Address:* Ålstorp, Mossehus, 312 94 Laholm, Sweden. *Telephone:* (430) 61027. *Fax:* (430) 63018. *E-mail:* stringendo@rixtele.com.

AHLSTEDT, Douglas; Singer (Tenor); b. 16 March 1945, Jamestown, NY, USA. *Education:* Studied at State University, New York and Eastman School, Rochester. *Career:* Debut: As Ramiro in La Cenerentola, Western Opera Theater, San Francisco, 1971; Sang at Metropolitan Opera from season 1974–75, with debut as Italian Singer in Rosenkavalier, then as Fenton in Falstaff; Member of Deutsche Oper Düsseldorf, 1975–84, and guest appearances in Vienna, Hamburg, Zürich and Karlsruhe; Returned to New York in 1983 and sang Iopas in Les Troyens, Almaviva in Barbiere di Siviglia and Debussy's Pelléas, 1988; Salzburg Festival as Alfinoma in the Henze-Monteverdi Il Ritorno d'Ulisse, 1985; Teatro San Carlo in Naples as Orestes in Ermione by Rossini, 1988; Other engagements in Dallas, Philadelphia and Santiago as Don Ottavio, Genoa, Avignon and Rome as Idreno in Semiramide, 1982; Other roles include Tamino, Jacquino in Fidelio, Narcisio in Turco in Italia, the Fox in Cunning Little Vixen and Peter Quint in The Turn of the Screw; Sang Dorvil in La Scala di Seta in Stuttgart, 1991; Zürich Opera as Flamand in Capriccio, 1992. *Recordings include:* Video of Il Ritorno d'Ulisse, Salzburg, 1985. *Address:* c/o Staatstheater Stuttgart, Oberer Schlossgarten 6, 7000 Stuttgart, Germany.

AHNSJO, Claes Haakon; Singer (Tenor); b. 1 Aug. 1942, Stockholm, Sweden; m. Helena Jungwirth. *Education:* Studied in Stockholm with Erik Saeden, Aksel Schiotz and Max Lorenz. *Career:* Debut: Royal Opera Stockholm in 1969 as Tamino; Sang in Stockholm until 1973, then with the Munich Opera notably in operas by Mozart and Rossini; Drottningholm Opera from 1969; Bayreuth Festival, 1973; Kennedy Music Center, NY, 1974 in Die Jahreszeiten by Haydn; Guest appearances in Frankfurt, Cologne, Tokyo, Hamburg, Stuttgart and Nancy; Concert tours of Italy and Spain; Sang at Munich in 1985 as the Painter in Lulu, and in the premiere of Le Roi Bérenger by Sutermeister; Sang at Berlin in 1987 as Ramiro in La Cenerentola by Rossini; Sang Wolfgang Capito in Mathis der Maler and the Abbé in Adriana Lecouvreur, 1989; Munich Festival in premiere of Penderecki's Ubu Rex in 1991; Season 1997–98 in Monteverdi's Poppea and as Melot in Tristan und Isolde; Director of the Stockholm Royal Opera, from 1999/2000. *Recordings:* Bastien und Bastienne; Orlando Paladino, La Vera Costanza and L'Infedeltà Delusa by Haydn; Betulia Liberata by Mozart; Die Lustigen Weiber von Windsor; Bruckner's Te Deum. *Address:* c/o Bayerische Staatsoper, Pf 745, 8000 Munich 1, Germany.

AHO, Kalevi; Composer, Teacher and Writer on Music; b. 9 March 1949, Forssa, Finland. *Education:* Diploma, Sibelius Academy, Helsinki, 1971; Studied composition with Einojuhani Rautavaara, Boris Blacher at Staatliche Hochschule für Musik und Darstellende Kunst, Berlin, 1971–72. *Career:* Lecturer on Music, University of Helsinki, 1974–88; Professor of Composition, Sibelius Academy, Helsinki, 1988–93; Composer-in-Residence, Sinfonia Lahti, Finland, 1992–; Free artist in Helsinki, 1993–. *Compositions include:* Works for the stage: Avain (The Key), dramatic monologue for baritone and chamber orchestra, 1977–78; Hyönteisedämää (Insect Life), comic opera, 1985–87; Ennen kuin me kaikki olemme hukkuneet (Before We Are All Drowned), opera, 1995–99; Salaisuuksien kirja (The Book of Secrets), opera for soloists, choir and orchestra, 1998; Orchestral works: Symphonies Nos 1–11, 1969–1998, Concertos and chamber symphonies; Pergamon, for four instrumental groups, voices and organ, 1990; Hiljaisuus, for orchestra, 1982; Tristia, fantasy for wind orchestra, 1999; Chamber Music: Quintets and Quartets include: Quintet for flute, oboe, violin, viola and cello, 1977; Quintet for alto saxophone, bassoon, viola, cello and double bass; Sonata for oboe and piano, 1985; Sonatine for two pianos, 1997; Ballade, for flute, bassoon, cello and piano, 1999; Solo instruments: Sonata for violin, 1973; In memoriam for organ, 1980; Piano Sonata, 1980; Sonata No. 2 for accordion, mustat linnet (Black Birds), 1990; Solo III for flute, 1991–92; Solo IV for Cello, 1997; Solo V for bassoon, 1999; Solo VI for double bass, 1999; Clarinet Quintet, 1999; Vocal works: Lasimaalaus (Stained Glass), for female choir, 1975; Kiinalaisia lauluja (Chinese Songs) soprano and orchestra, 1997; Kolme Bertrandin monologia (Three Monologues of Bertrand), baritone and orchestra, 1999; Orchestrations and arrangements: Modest Mussorgsky: Songs and Dances of Death, 1984; Uuno Klami, Whirls (illustrations of the ballet act, 1988) Erik Tulindberg, string quartets; Sibelius, Karelia, reconstruction, 1997. *Recordings:* Complete works recorded. *Publications include:* Finnish Music and the Kalevala, 1985; Finnish Music, co-author, 1996; Art and Reality, 1997. *Honours:* Leonie Sonning Prize, Copenhagen, 1974; Award of City of Hamburg, 1982; Henrik Steffens Prize, 1990; Flisaka '96 Prize, Toruń, Poland, 1996; Award, Stiftung Kulturfonds, Berlin, 1998; Pro Finlandia, 1999. *Address:* Taivaiskalliontie 15, 00600 Helsinki, Finland.

AHRENS, Hans-Georg; Singer (bass baritone); b. 1947, Hitzacker an der Elbe, Germany. *Education:* Berlin Musikhochschule. *Career:* Sang at Mainz Opera, 1973–75; Augsburg, Kassel and Kiel; Ludwigsburg Festival, 1978 as Leporello and Figaro, 1989; As Gauguin in Rautavaara's Vincent, Kiel Opera, 1991; Sang Don Alfonso, Wiesbaden Festival, 1992 and the Doctor in Wozzeck, Brunswick, 1996; Season 1997 at Kiel in the stage premiere of The Magic Fountain by Delius, Hagen in Götterdämmerung, 2000. Other roles include Wagner's King Henry, Marke and Gurnemanz, Gianni Schicchi, Dulcamara and Schigolch in Lulu; Concerts in music by Bach. *Recordings:* Don Giovanni, Electrola; Così fan tutte, Harmonia Mundi. *Address:* Bühnen der Landeshaupstadt Kiel, Rathausplatz 4, 24103 Kiel, Germany.

AIKIN, Laura; Singer (soprano); b. 1965, Buffalo, USA. *Education:* Studied at Buffalo, New York and Indiana University; Vocal studies with Reri Grist in Munich. *Career:* Appearances at the Staatsoper Berlin and elsewhere in Europe as Amenaide in Tancredi (Zürich), 1996, the Queen of Night, Adele and Gretel; Deutsche Oper Berlin debut as Madame Herz in Mozart's Schauspieldirektor; Schwetzingen Festival in L'Opera Seria by Florian Gassmann, under René Jacobs; Salzburg Festival recital with Maurizio Pollini, in Schubert's Hirt auf den Felsen, 1995; Strauss's Zerbinetta at the Vienna Staatsoper and a Jonathan Miller production of Ariadne auf Naxos at Florence, 1997; Il trionfo del Tempo by Handel at the Styriate Festival with Nicolas Harnoncourt and Concentus Musicus, 1997; Appearances in Berlin as Lulu and Silvia in Haydn's L'Isola disabitata; Further concerts include Schoenberg's

oratorio Die Jakobsleiter under Michael Gielen, Beethoven's Christus am Ölberg with Daniel Barenboim in Jerusalem and Chicago, and Pierre Boulez 70th birthday celebrations at Carnegie Hall; Met debut as the Queen of Night; Madeleine in Le Postillon de Lonjumeau at the Berlin Staatsoper, 1998; Numerous appearances with The Ensemble Intercontemporain including: Salzburg, Edinburgh and Schleswig Holstein Festivals; Handel's Alcina at the Beaune Festival with Les Arts Florissants and William Christie; Ariadne at the Chicago Lyric; Suite from Prometeo by Luigi Nono with Claudio Abbado and the Berlin Philharmonic at Carnegie Hall, 1999; Season 1999–2000 engaged for Fidelio and Ariadne at La Scala, for Lulu at Zürich, Ariadne at Munich and Die schweigsame Frau at Vienna; Sang Lulu for Netherlands Opera, 2001. *Honours:* Winner, Lake Constance International Competition; Deutsche Akademische Austauschdienst Scholar, Munich, 1990–92. *Current Management:* Ingpen & Williams Ltd, 7 St George's Court, 131 Putney Bridge Road, London, SW15 2PA, England.

AINSLEY, John Mark; Singer (tenor); b. 9 July 1963, Crewe, England. *Education:* Oxford University. *Career:* Many concert performances from 1985 with the Taverner Consort, the New London Consort and London Baroque; Appearances in Mozart Masses at The Vienna Konzerthaus with Heinz Holliger, Handel's Saul at Göttingen with John Eliot Gardiner and the Mozart Requiem under Yehudi Menuhin at Gstaad and Pulcinella at the Barbican under Jeffrey Tate; Other concerts with the Ulster Orchestra and the Bournemouth Sinfonietta; US Debut at Lincoln Center in the B minor Mass with Christopher Hogwood; Opera debut at the Innsbruck Festival in Scarlatti's Gli Equivoci nel Sembiante; English National Opera in 1989 in The Return of Ulysses; Title role in Méhul's Joseph for Dutch Radio, Handel's Acis in Stuttgart and Solomon for Radio France, under Leopold Hager; Has sung Mozart's Tamino for Opera Northern Ireland and Ferrando for Glyndebourne Touring Opera; Engaged in Falstaff for Scottish Opera and Idomeneo for Welsh National Opera; Sang Ferrando at Glyndebourne Festival in 1992, and Don Ottavio in 1994; Haydn's The Seasons with the London Classical Players; Promenade Concerts in London, 1993; Stravinsky concert under Andrew Davis at the Festival Hall, 1997; Engaged in Monteverdi's Orfeo for the 1999 Munich Festival; Jupiter in Semele for ENO, 1999; Season 2000 as Idomeneo at Sydney, Lensky for ENO, and Jupiter at San Francisco; Bach's St Matthew Passion at the London Proms, 2002. *Recordings include:* Handel's Nisi Dominus, under Simon Preston, and Purcell's Odes with Trevor Pinnock; Mozart's C minor Mass with Hogwood and Great Baroque Arias with the King's Consort; Acis and Galatea; Saul. *Current Management:* Askonas Holt Ltd, Lonsdale Chambers, 27 Chancery Lane, London, WC2A 1PF, England. *Telephone:* (20) 7400-1700. *Fax:* (20) 7400-1799. *E-mail:* info@askonasholt.co.uk. *Website:* www.askonasholt.co.uk.

AITKEN, Hugh; Composer and Teacher; b. 7 Sept. 1924, NY, USA. *Education:* Studied composition with Wagenaar, Persichetti and Ward at the Juilliard School; MS, 1950. *Career:* Taught privately and at the Juilliard Preparatory Division, 1950–65; Faculty, Juilliard School, 1960–70; Professor, William Paterson College, 1970–. *Compositions:* Stage: Felipe, opera, Fables, chamber opera, and dance scores; Other: 3 Violin Concertos, 1984, 1988, Oratorio, The Revelation of St John The Divine, 1953–90, 10 Solo Cantatas, In Praise Of Ockeghem for Strings, Rameau Remembered for Flute and Chamber Orchestra, Happy Birthday, overture; Opus 95 Revisited for String Quartet, unaccompanied works for various instruments, Duo for Cello and Piano, Trios for 11 Players, Quintet for Oboe and String Quartet. *Recordings include:* Piano Fantasy and 2 Cantatas. *Publications:* Various. *Honours:* National Academy of Arts and Letters, 1988; Several grants, National Endowment for the Arts. *Address:* Music Department, William Paterson College of New Jersey, Wayne, NJ 07470, USA.

AITKEN, Robert Morris; Flautist, Teacher and Composer; b. 28 Aug. 1939, Kentville, Nova Scotia, Canada; m. Marion I Ross. *Education:* Studied flute as child in Pennsylvania, later with Nicholas Fiore, Royal Conservatory of Music, Toronto, 1955–59; Composition with Barbara Pentland, University of British Columbia, and with John Weinzweig; Electronic music with Myron Schaeffer; Flute with various teachers, 1964–65; MMus, University of Toronto, 1964. *Career:* Principal Flautist with Vancouver Symphony Orchestra, 1958–59, Stratford Festival Orchestra, Ontario, 1962–64; Soloist with orchestras and chamber music player with many tours abroad; Artistic Director of Music Today, Shaw Festival, Niagara-on-the-Lake, 1970–72, and New Music Concerts, Toronto, 1971–; Advanced studies in music programme, 1985–89; Professor of Flute, Staatliche Hochschule für Musik, Freiburg im Breisgau, 1988–. *Compositions include:* Rhapsody for Orchestra, 1961; Music for Flute and Electronic Tape, 1963; Concerto for 12 Solo Instruments, 1964; Kebyar for Flute, Clarinet, 2 Double Basses, Percussion and Tape, 1971; Shadows III, Nira for Solo Violin, Flute, Oboe, Viola, Double Bass, Piano and Harpsichord, 1974–88; Icicle for Flute, 1977; Folia for Woodwind Quintet, 1980; Berceuse for Flute and Orchestra, 1992; My Song, for 2 flutes, 1994. *Recordings:* Various compositions recorded; Many albums as soloist and chamber music artist. *Address:* 14 Maxwell Avenue, Toronto, ON, M5P 2B5, Canada.

AJMONE-MARSAN, Guido; Orchestral Conductor; b. 24 March 1947, Turin, Italy; m. Helle Winkelhorn 1971. *Education:* BMus, Conducting and Clarinet, Eastman School of Music, New York, USA, 1968; studied with F. Ferrara at Conservatory of St Cecilia, Rome, Italy, 1968–71. *Career:* Chief Conductor of the Gelders Orchestra, Arnhem, Netherlands, 1982–86; Music Adviser and Principal Conductor of the Orchestra of Illinois at Chicago, USA, 1982–87; Music Director of Opera House, Essen, Germany, 1986–90; Guest Conductor for many international orchestras and opera houses including: Jerusalem Symphony, Philharmonia, London Symphony, Covent Garden Opera, NHK Japan, Welsh National Opera, Spoleto Festival, La Scala Orchestra, Metropolitan Opera and English National Opera, New York City Opera, Teatro Colón, Buenos Aires, Opera of Santiago, Chile; Scottish Opera; mem, Royal Philharmonic Society. *Recordings:* Many for Radio broadcast with radio orchestras in Czechoslovakia, the United Kingdom, Germany, Japan, Australia, Netherlands, Denmark, Italy and France. *Honours:* Many Prizes, Cantelli Competition, Milan, 1969, Mitropoulos, NY, 1970, Winner, Rupert Foundation Conducting Competition, with one year assistantship to London Symphony, 1973, Winner, G Solti Competition, Chicago, 1973; The Deane Sherman Performing Arts Award, MD, USA, 1992. *Current Management:* Athole Still International Management, Forresters Hall, 25–27 Westow Street, London, SE19 3RY, England. *Telephone:* (20) 8771-5271. *Fax:* (20) 8768-6600. *Website:* www .atholestill.com. *Address:* 57 Wood Vale, London, N10 3DL, England. *E-mail:* marsan@vale57.fsnet.co.uk.

AKIMOV, Yevgeny; Singer (Tenor); b. 1970, St Petersburg, Russia. *Education:* St Petersburg Conservatoire. *Career:* Kirov Opera at the Mariinsky Theatre from 1996; roles have included Rossini's Almaviva, Froh in Das Rheingold, the Fisherman in Stravinsky's Nightingale and the Indian Merchant in Rimsky-Korsakov's Sadko; Sang the Simpleton in Boris Godunov with the Kirov at Covent Garden, 1997 and appeared in Parsifal at the Royal Albert Hall, 1999; Other roles include Cassio in Otello and Antonio in Prokofiev's Betrothal in a Monastery; Appearances with the Kirov Opera at the Royal Opera House, London, 2000; Mussorgsky's Boris Godunov at the London Proms, 2002. *Honours:* Prizewinner, 1st International Pechkovsky Singing Competition, 1994. *Address:* c/o Kirov Opera, Mariinsky Theatre, Mariinsky Square, St Petersburg, Russia.

AKIYAMA, Kazuyoshi; Conductor; b. 2 Jan. 1941, Tokyo, Japan. *Education:* Studied conducting with Hideo Saito, Toho School of Music, Tokyo. *Career:* Debut: Tokyo Symphony Orchestra, 1964; Music Director of the Tokyo Symphony Orchestra, 1964; Conductor, Japanese Orchestras; Music Director, American Symphony Orchestra, New York, 1973–78; Resident Conductor and Music Director, Vancouver Symphony Orchestra, BC, 1972–85; Music Director, Syracuse Symphony Orchestra, NY, 1985–. *Address:* c/o Syracuse Symphony Orchestra, 411 Montgomery Street, Syracuse, NY 13202, USA.

AKOKA, Gérard; Conductor; b. 2 Nov. 1949, Paris, France. *Education:* Studied at the Paris Conservatoire, at the Accademia di Santa Cecilia and with Jean Martinon, Igor Markevitch, Sergiu Celibidache and Franco Ferrara. *Career:* Former assistant to Daniel Barenboim and Leonard Bernstein; Assistant to Boulez at Orchestre de Paris (1977) and musical director of the Lorraine Philharmonic, 1983–84; Recent engagements in Taiwan and elsewhere in the Far East. *Address:* c/o Taipei City Symphony Orchestra, 25 Pa Teh Road, Sec 3, Taipei 10560, Taiwan.

AKOS, Francis (Ferenc), DipMusEd; violinist and conductor; b. 30 March 1922, Budapest, Hungary; m. Phyllis Malvin Sommers 1981; two d. by previous marriage. *Education:* Franz Liszt Acad. of Music, Budapest. *Career:* debut, Mozart Concerto in D No. 4 for violin and orchestra, Budapest 1938; Concertmaster, Budapest Concert Orchestra 1945–46, Royal Opera and Philharmonic Soc. of Budapest 1947–48, Gothenburg (Sweden) Symphony Orchestra 1948–50, Municipal Opera (now Deutsche Oper), Berlin 1950–54, Minneapolis Symphony Orchestra 1954–55; Asst Concertmaster, Chicago Symphony Orchestra 1955–2004, Concertmaster Emeritus 1997–; also performed at Salzburg Festival, Scandinavian Festival in Helsinki, Prades Festival, and Berlin, Bergen and Vienna Festivals; founder and Conductor, The Chicago Strings chamber orchestra 1961–; founder and Conductor, The Highland Park strings 1979–. *Honours:* first prize Reményi Competition, Budapest 1939, first prize Hubay Competition, Budapest 1939. *Address:* 1310 Maple Avenue # 3B, Evanston, IL 60201, USA (home). *Telephone:* (847) 866-8832 (home). *E-mail:* violaki310@yahoo.com (home).

ALAGNA, Roberto; Singer (tenor); b. 7 June 1963, Clichy-sur-Bois, France; m. Angela Gheorghiu 1996. *Education:* studied in France and Italy. *Career:* debut, Plymouth 1988, as Alfredo in La Traviata for Glyndebourne Touring Opera; Sang Rodolfo at Covent Garden (1990)

and has returned for Gounod's Roméo and Don Carlos, 1994–96; Sang Donizetti's Roberto Devereux at Monte Carlo (1992) and the Duke of Mantua at the Vienna Staatsoper (1995); Sang Don Carlos at the Théâtre du Châtelet, Paris, 1996; American appearances at Chicago and New York (debut at Met 1996, as Rodolfo); Alfredo at La Scala, Milan; Season 1999–2000 with Mascagni's L'Amico Fritz at Monte Carlo and Gounod's Romeo at Covent Garden (returned 2002, in new production of La Rondine, by Puccini; Engaged as Gounod's Faust at Covent Garden, 2005. *Recordings include:* Gounod's Roméo et Juliette (video), La Traviata, from La Scala, Don Carlos, Tosca 2002, Il Trovatore. *Honours:* winner, Pavarotti Competition 1988. *Address:* c/o Royal Opera House (Contracts), Covent Garden, London WC2E 9DD, England.

ALAIMO, Simone; Singer (Bass Baritone); b. 3 Feb. 1950, Villabate, Palermo, Italy; m. Vittorio Mazzoni, 30 April 1988, 1 s., 1 d. *Education:* Literary studies at University of Palermo; Scuola di Perfezionamento Teatro alla Scala di Milano per Giovani Lirici. *Career:* Debut: In Don Pasquale at Pavia, 1977; Appearances at La Scala, Teatro dell Opera, Rome, Teatro Comunale, Florence, Teatro San Carlo, Naples, Chicago, San Francisco, Dallas, Vienna, Monaco, Paris, Madrid, Barcelona, Lisbon and Marseilles; Radio and television appearances in Luisa Miller, Cavalleria Rusticana and Zaira; Sang Mustafà in L'Italiana in Algeri at San Francisco in 1992 followed by Dulcamara, Rossini's Don Basilio at Genoa in 1992; New York Met from 1995, as Mozart's Figaro and Rossini's Basilio; Faraone in Mosè in Egitto at Covent Garden, 1994; Rossini's Basilio at Genoa, 1998; First modern production of Donizetti's Alahor in Granata, Seville, 1998; Appeared in film of Il Barbiere di Siviglia; Mustafà for New Israeli Opera, 2000; Season 2003 as Rossini's Don Magnifico at Covent Garden. *Recordings:* La Cenerentola; Don Giovanni; Il Turco in Italia; Maria Stuarda; I Masnadieri; L'Ebreo; Torquato Tasso; L'Esule di Roma; Convenienze Teatrali; Barbiere di Siviglia; (Bongiovanni). *Honours:* Lions Prize, 1977; Voce Verdiane di Busseto International Competition, 1978; Beniamino Gigli di Macerata International Competition, 1978; Maria Callas International Competition, 1980. *Address:* Via Pacevecchia, Parc Conim, 82100 Benevento, Italy.

ALAIN, Marie-Claire; French organist; b. 10 Aug. 1926, Saint-Germain-en-Laye; d. of Albert Alain and Magdeleine Alain (née Alberty); m. Jacques Gommier 1950; one s. one d. *Education:* Institut Notre Dame, Saint-Germain-en-Laye, Conservatoire Nat. Supérieur de Musique, Paris. *Career:* organ teacher, Conservatoire de Musique de Paris; Lecturer, Summer Acad. for organists, Haarlem, Netherlands 1956–72; organ teacher, Conservatoire de Musique de Rueil-Malmaison 1978–94; numerous concerts throughout world 1955–; lecturer at numerous univs throughout world; expert on organology to Minister of Culture, Commission des Orgues des Monuments Historiques 1965–2002. *Recordings:* over 250 records, including complete works of J. Alain, C.P.E. Bach, J.S. Bach, C. Balbastre, G. Böhm, N. Bruhns, D. Buxtehude, L. N. Clérambault, F. Couperin, L. C. Daquin, C. Franck, N. de Grigny, J. A. Guilain, G. F. Handel, J. Haydn, F. Mendelssohn, A. Vivaldi. *Publication:* Notes critiques sur l'œuvre d'orgue de Jehan Alain 2001. *Honours:* Commdr, Légion d'honneur; Commdr, Ordre du Mérite; Commdr des Arts et Lettres; Hon. DHumLitt (Colorado State Univ.); Hon. DMus (Southern Methodist Univ., Dallas, Boston Conservatory); Dr hc (Acad. Sibelius, Helsinki); numerous prizes for recordings and performances, including Buxtehudepreis (Lübeck, Germany), Prix Léonie Sonning (Copenhagen, Denmark), Prix Franz Liszt (Budapest) 1987. *Address:* 4 rue Victor Hugo, 78230 Le Pecq, France. *Telephone:* 1-30-87-08-65. *Fax:* 1-30-61-43-61.

ALARIE, Pierrette Marguerite; Singer (soprano) and Teacher; b. 9 Nov. 1921, Montreal, Canada; m. Leopold Simoneau, 1946. *Education:* Studied voice and acting with Jeanne Maubourg and Albert Roberval; Voice with Salvator Issaurel, 1938–43, with Elisabeth Schumann, Curtis Institute of Music, Philadelphia, 1943–46. *Career:* Debut: Operatic debut at Montreal in 1943; Metropolitan Opera debut as Oscar in Un Ballo in Maschera, 1945; European debut in Paris, 1949; Sang in opera, concert and recital in leading North American and European music centres; Retired from operatic stage in 1966, with farewell appearance as soloist in Handel's Messiah with Montreal Symphony Orchestra, 1970; Taught voice. *Recordings:* numerous including album of Mozart arias with husband. *Honours:* Winner, Metropolitan Opera Auditions of the Air, 1945; Officier of the Order of Canada, 1967; Winner, Grand Prix du Disque, 1961; Honorary Doctorate, McGill University, 1994.

ALBANESE, Licia; Italian fmr singer (soprano); b. 22 July 1913, Bari; m. Joseph Gimma, 7 April 1945. *Education:* Studied voice with Emanuel De Rosa, Bari and Giuseppina Baldassare-Tedeschi, Milan. *Career:* operatic debut as Butterfly, Teatro Lirico, Milan, 1934; formal operatic debut, New York as Cio-Cio San, 1940 and sang there until 1966 (286 performances in 17 roles); appeared in concerts; taught singing; roles included Butterfly, Violetta, Zerlina, Desdemona, Susanna, Manon, Tosca, Gounod's Marguerite, Mimi. *Recordings:* NBC radio broadcasts under Toscanini. *Honours:* Order of Merit of Italy; Lady Grand Cross of the Equestrian Order of the Holy Sepulchre. *Address:* Nathan Hale Drive, Wilson Point South, Norwalk, CT 06854, USA.

ALBERGA, Eleanor; Composer; b. 30 Sept. 1949, Kingston, Jamaica. *Education:* Studied at the Royal Academy of Music, London, from 1970. *Career:* Has performed with an African dance company and played piano for the London Contemporary Dance Theatre. *Compositions:* Mobile I for orchestra, 1983; Jamaican Medley for piano, 1983; Clouds for piano quintet, 1984; Ice Flow for piano, 1985; Stone Dream for prepared piano and tape, 1986; Suite for piano 4 hands, 1986; Mobile II for ensemble, 1988; Whose Own for prepared piano and sound processor, 1988; Sun Warrior for orchestra, 1990; Dancing with the Shadows for ensemble, 1991; Jupiter's Fairground for orchestra, 1991; Snow White and the Seven Dwarfs, for narrators and orchestra, 1994; 2 String Quartets, 1993, 1994; The Wild Blue Yonder for piano and violin, 1995; Under Light Manners, for saxophones and ensemble, 1997; Only a Wish Away, for piano, 1997. *Address:* 166 Bethnal Green Road, London E2 6 DL, England.

ALBERMAN, David; Violinist; b. 1959, London, England. *Education:* Private tuition with Mary Long, Emanuel Hurwitz, Sheila Nelson, Vera Kantrovich, Igor Ozim in Cologne; LRAM, 1975; MA in Greats, Classical Languages and Literature, Merton College, Oxford, 1981. *Career:* Leader of the National Youth Orchestra of Great Britain, 1977; Has performed with the London Mozart Players, Royal Philharmonic Orchestra, London Symphony, Associate Member, 1983–85, and the Academy of St Martin-in-the-Fields; Former leader of the Chamber Orchestra of Europe; Has performed music by Lutoslawski, Penderecki, Osborne and Bainbridge with such groups as the Ballet Rambert and Divertimenti; Member, Arditti Quartet, 1986–94; Many performances at festivals across Europe and North America; Resident string tutor at the Darmstadt Fereinkurse for New Music from 1986; Music in camera programme for BBC television, 1987; Cycle of Schoenberg's Quartets at the Purcell Room, London, November 1988; recital in the Russian Spring Series at South Bank, May 1991; Performed in all the quartets of Berg, Webern and Schoenberg at Antwerp, Cologne, Frankfurt, London and Paris, 1991–93; Took part in the premieres of quartets by Bose, No. 3, 1989; Bussotti, 1988; John Cage, Music for 4, 1988, 4, 1989; Ferneyhough, Nos 3 and 4; Gubaidulina, No. 3, 1987; Harvey, No. 2; Kagel, No. 3, 1987; Nancarrow, No. 3, 1988; Pousseur, No. 2, 1989; Rihm, Nos 6 and 8; Xenakis, Akea, Piano Quintet, 1986, Tetora, 1991, Isang Yun, Flute Quintet, 1987; Premiere of Nono's Hay que caminar sonando for violin duo, with Irvine Arditti, Violin, 1989. *Recordings include:* Elliott Carter's Quartets; Quartets by Ferneyhough. *Address:* 14 Fairmead Road, London N19 4 DF, England.

ALBERT, Donnie Ray; Singer (Bass-baritone); b. 1950, Louisiana, USA. *Career:* Sang Gershwin's Porgy at Houston (1976) and sang there regularly until 1990; Guest appearances at the New York City Opera (Scarpia, 1978), Washington Opera (Amonasro, 1990), Boston, San Francisco and elsewhere in the USA; Appearances in Berlin and Florence as Porgy; Other roles include Carlos in Ernani, Monterone, Nabucco, Iago, Jack Rance, Jochanaan, Escamillo, Varlaam, and the title role in Gruenberg's Emperor Jones; Season 1996 as Wagner's Dutchman at Cologne and Hidraot in Gluck's Armide at La Scala; Villains in Hoffmann at Cologne, 1998; Season 1999–2000 as Macbeth at Cologne, Amonasro at Cincinnati and Gershwin's Porgy at Munich; Concert engagements in New York, Los Angeles and Chicago. *Address:* c/o Houston Grand Opera, 510 Preston Avenue, Houston, TX 77002, USA.

ALBERT, Marian; Singer (Tenor); b. 1961, Poznań, Poland. *Education:* Studied at Lubin, Poznan and the Salzburg Mozarteum. *Career:* Choir and orchestra director in Poland, 1982–87; Sang Fenton, Vladimir in Price Igor, Lensky, Tamino, Narciso in Il Turco in Italia and Amenofi in Rossini's Mosè, Poznan Opera, 1988–; Guest at Brussels as Tamino and Wagner's Froh; Antwerp as Cavaradossi and Berne as Belmonte; Belmonte, Strauss's Brighella and Giannetto in La Gazza Ladra, Theater am Gärtnerplatz, Munich, 1992; Cadi in Der Barbier von Bagdad by Cornelius, Frankfurt, 1994; Appearances at Salzburg Mozartwochen and Prague Spring Festivals. *Address:* Theater am Gärtnerplatz 3, 8000 Munich 5, Germany.

ALBERT, Thomas; Conductor and Director; b. 1950, Germany. *Career:* Violinist with La Petite Bande and the Musikalische Compagney; Founded Fiori Musicale, 1978, for the performances of Baroque music; Founded, Forum Alte Musik, 1982; Bremen Academy of Early Music, 1986; Teacher, Hamburg Academy of Music and Strasbourg Conservatoire; Professor, Bremen Academy of Music, 1989; Artistic Director, Bremen Music Festival, 1989. *Recordings:* Bach Cantatas 56 and 82; Keiser's Masagniello Furioso; Lubeck Cantatas. *Address:* c/o Bremen Academy of Music, Bremen, Germany.

ALBERT, Werner Andreas; Conductor; b. 1935, Weinheim, Germany. *Education:* Studied at the Mannheim Hochschule für Musik and at Heidelberg University; Conducting studies with Herbert von Karajan and Hans Rosbaud. *Career:* Chief Conductor of the North West German Philharmonic, Gulbenkian Orchestra, Lisbon, Nuremberg Symphony Orchestra, Queensland Symphony Orchestra, Queensland Philharmonic Orchestra, Australian and the Bavarian Youth Orchestra; Senior Lecturer at Nuremberg Conservatorium; Professor of Queensland University; President, Siegfried Wagner Society. *Recordings include:* Oboe Concertos by Leclair, Haydn and Dittersdorf; Beethoven's 9th Symphony; Rossini's Petite Messe Solennelle; Cello Concertos by Sutermeister; Mozart's Clarinet Concerto and Horn Concerto K447; Puccini's Messa di Gloria. *Honours:* First Prize, German Recording Industry, 1994; American Menza Award, 1994; Music Prize, Bavarian Academy of Fine Arts, 1998. *Current Management:* Arts Management, 790 George Street, Sydney 2000, Australia. *Address:* Rankestrasse 19, 90461 Nürnberg, Germany.

ALBERY, Tim; British stage director; b. 5 May 1952, Harpenden, England. *Career:* has produced plays for Liverpool Playhouse, Liverpool Everyman, Contact Theatre, Manchester, The Half Moon, ICA, Almeida and Royal Court Theatres, London; has directed plays in Germany and Netherlands; Dir, ICA Theatre, London 1981–82; directed Schiller at Greenwich Theatre and at Royal Shakespeare Co.; Shakespeare for the Old Vic and Racine at the Nat. Theatre; debut as Opera Dir, The Turn of the Screw at Batignano, Italy 1983; other work includes The Midsummer Marriage, Don Giovanni, La Finta Giardiniera, Così fan Tutte, One Touch of Venus, The Trojans and Katya Kabanova for Opera North; The Rape of Lucretia at Gothenburg 1987; La Wally at Bregenz 1990; Billy Budd, Beatrice and Benedict, Peter Grimes and Lohengrin for ENO 1988, 1990, 1991 and 1993, also From the House of the Dead 1997, War and Peace 2000; Berlioz's Benvenuto Cellini in Amsterdam 1991; Don Carlos for Opera North 1993; Chérubin for Royal Opera House and Fidelio 1994, The Ring Cycle for Scottish Opera 2000; Beatrice and Benedict at Santa Fe 1998; The Ring Cycle for Scottish Opera 2000–03; Passion for Minn. Opera. *Address:* c/o Harriet Cruikshank, 97 Old Lambeth Road, London, SW8 1XU, England.

ALBIN, Roger; Conductor and Cellist; b. 30 Sept. 1920, Beausoleil, France. *Education:* Studied with Umberto Benedetti at Monte Carlo from 1926; Paris Conservatoire with Henri Busser, Milhaud and Olivier Messiaen. *Career:* Played cello at Monte Carlo, The Paris Opéra and at the Société des Concerts du Conservatoire; Duo partnership with pianist Claude Helffer, 1949–57; Studied further with Roger Desormière, Carl Schuricht and Hans Rosbaud, and conducted from 1957 with chorus at the Opéra Comique, Paris; Musical Director at Nancy, 1960–61, Toulouse, 1961–66 and French Radio Orchestra at Strasbourg, 1966–75; Cellist with the French National Orchestra, 1978–81, also a member of the orchestra's String Sextet; Professor of Chamber Music at the Strasbourg Conservatory, 1981–87. *Recordings:* As cellist: Prokofiev's Concerto and Ravel's Trio; Fauré's Fantasie and the Fantasie for Piano and Orchestra by Debussy; Ibert's Diane Poitiers. *Honours:* Premier Prix in cello class at the Paris Conservatoire, 1936.

ALBRECHT, Georg-Alexander; Conductor; b. 15 Feb. 1935, Bremen, Germany. *Education:* Studied violin, piano and composition, 1942–54. *Career:* Debut: As conductor, 1949; Chief Conductor at the Bremen Opera, 1958–61, Hannover Opera from 1961; Guest Conductor with the Dresden Staatskapelle, the Berlin Philharmonic and other German orchestras; Professor at the Hannover Conservatory. Repertory includes the 1st Symphony of Wolfgang Rihm (premiere, 1984). *Address:* c/o Hochschule für Musik Hannover, Emmichplatz 1, 3000 Hannover 1, Germany.

ALBRECHT, Gerd; Conductor; b. 19 July 1935, Essen, Germany. *Education:* Studied conducting with Wilhelm Bruckner-Ruggenerg, Hamburg Hochschule für Musik and musicology at the Universities of Kiel and Hamburg. *Career:* Repetiteur and Conductor, Wurttemberg State Theater, Stuttgart, 1958–61; First Conductor, Mainz, 1961–63; Generalmusikdirektor, Lubeck, 1963–66 and Kassel, 1966–72; Chief Conductor, Deutsche Oper, West Berlin, 1972–79 and Tonhalle Orchestra, Zürich, 1975–80; Guest Conductor with Vienna State Opera, 1976–; Conducted the premieres of Henze's Telemanniana in Berlin in 1967, Fortner's Elisabeth Tudor in Berlin in 1972, Henze's Barcarola in Zürich in 1980 and Reimann's Troades at Munich in 1986; Guest appearances with various European and North American opera companies and orchestras; Chief Conductor, Der fliegende Holländer at Covent Garden in 1986; Chief Conductor, Hamburg State Opera and Philharmonic State Orchestra, 1988–; Conducted Schreker's Der Schatzgräber at Hamburg, 1989–90 followed by Idomeneo and Tannhäuser; Conducted Tchaikovsky's Maid of Orleans at the 1990 Munich Festival, with Waltraud Meier; Chief Conductor of the Czech Philharmonic Orchestra, 1992–94; Hamburg State Opera from 1995; Season 1992 with Dvořák's Dimitri at Munich, Reimann's Troades at Frankfurt and Tannhäuser at Barcelona; Premiere of Schnittke's Historia von D Johann Fausten at Hamburg, 1995; Gurlitt's Wozzeck at Florence, 1998. *Recordings include:* album of Der Schatzgräber. *Honours:* Winner,

Besançon, 1957; Conducting Conpetitions, Hilversum, 1958. *Address:* c/o Hamburg State Opera, Postfach 302448, 2000 Hamburg 36, Germany.

ALBRECHT, Theodore John; Orchestra Conductor and Musicologist; b. 24 Sept. 1945, Jamestown, NY, USA; m. Carol Padgham 1976. *Education:* BME, St Mary's Univ. 1967, MM 1969, PhD 1975, North Texas State Univ. *Career:* Asst Prof., Appalachian State Univ. 1975–76; Conductor, German Orchestra of Cleveland 1977–80; Music Dir, Northland Symphony Orchestra, Kansas City, MO 1980–87; Prof., Park Coll. 1980–92; Music Dir, Philharmonia of Greater Kansas City 1987–92; Prof., Kent State Univ., Kent, OH 1992–; notable performances include US premieres of Bruckner Dialog by Gottfried von Einem 1982, Symphony in C, op 46 by Hans Pfitzner 1983, Ludi Leopoldini by Gottfried von Einem 1984; first American conductor to conduct all nine Dvořák symphonies; world premiere of Song of the Prairie by Timothy Corrao 1987. *Publications:* Dika Newlin, Friend and Mentor: A Birthday Anthology (ed.) 1973; translation of Felix Weingartner's On the Performance of the Symphonies of Mozart 1985, translations of Felix Weingartner's Schubert and Schumann 1986, Thayer, Salieri, Rival of Mozart (ed.) 1989, Letters to Beethoven and Other Correspondence, three vols 1996, Beethoven im Gespräch 2002. *Honours:* Deems Taylor Award, ASCAP 1997. *Address:* 1635 Chadwick Drive, Kent, OH 44240, USA. *E-mail:* talbrecht@kent.edu.

ALCANTARA, Theo; Conductor; b. 16 April 1941, Cuenca, Spain; m. Susan Alcantara. *Education:* Madrid Conservatory and Salzburg Mozarteum. *Career:* Conductor, Frankfurt am Main, 1964–66; Director of orchestras, University of Michigan, Ann Arbor, 1968–73; Music Director, Grand Rapids Symphony Orchestra, MI, 1973–78; Music Director, Phoenix Symphony Orchestra, 1978–89; Artistic Director, Music Academy of the West, Santa Barbara, CA, 1981–84; Principal Conductor, Pittsburgh Opera, 1987–; Conducted Elektra at Pittsburgh, 1989. *Honours:* Silver Medal, Mitropoulos Competition, 1966. *Current Management:* ICM Artists Ltd, 40 West 57th Street, New York, NY 10019, USA.

ALDEN, David; Stage Director; b. 16 Sept. 1949, New York City, USA. *Career:* Has directed the premieres of Stephen Burton's The Duchess of Malfi, Wolf Trap, 1978, Pasatieri's Washington Square and Conrad Susa's Don Perlimpin at San Francisco, Fidelio and Wozzeck at the Metropolitan Opera, and Rigoletto, Wozzeck and Mahagonny for Scottish Opera; Productions of The Rake's Progress for Netherlands Opera and at the Israel Festival, Werther at Nancy and the US premiere of Judith by Siegfried Matthus at Sante Fe in 1990; English National Opera with Mazeppa, Simon Boccanegra, A Masked Ball and double bill of Oedipus Rex and Duke Bluebeard's Castle in 1991; Staged Tristan and Isolde for ENO, 1996; Affiliations with opera at the Academy, New York, with La Calisto and New Israel Opera with Les Contes d'Hoffmann, La Bohème and the world premiere of Noam Sheriff's The Sorrows of Job; Monteverdi's Poppea for the Bavarian State Opera, 1997; Engaged for Handel's Ariodante at Houston, 2001. *Address:* c/o English National Opera, St Martin's Lane, London WC2 4ES, England.

ALDULESCU, Radu; Italian concert cellist; b. 17 Sept. 1922, Piteasca-Pasarea, Romania. *Education:* began to study cello aged 6; Bucharest Conservatory. *Career:* debut, soloist with Bucharest Radio Symphony Orchestra, 1941; soloist with the Georges Enescu Philharmonic, Bucharest, 1945–46 and with all the important Philharmonic Orchestras in Europe, South America and South Africa; Asst to Gaspar Cassado, 1964–, and formed string trio, Trio d'Archi di Roma, with Salvatore Accardo and A. Luigi Bianchi, 1972; chamber recitals with Carlo Zecchi; performed at many international festivals including Berlin, Rome, Barcelona, Prague, Salzburg, Granada, Copenhagen, Hannover, Gstaad, San Salvador; regularly participated in chamber music concerts with Yehudi Menuhin, Sándor Végh, Wolfgang Schneiderhan, Alberto Lysy, Salvatore Accardo, Rostropovich, Yo-Yo Ma and many others; teacher at many conservatories including Basle, Maastricht, Conservatoire Européen de Musique, Paris, International Menuhin Acad., Gstaad; Centre d'estudis musicals, Barcelona; masterclasses in Rome, Berlin, Paris, Geneva, Buenos Aires, Nantes, Weimar, Freiburg, Prussia Cove (Cornwall), Assisi, Taormina, Santiago de Compostela and Granada; mem., Philharmonic Acad. of Bologna, Acad. Tiberina, Rome. *Recordings include:* Beethoven Sonatas (two vols); Concertos and Recitals (six vols); historical recordings series. *Honours:* Harriet Cohen International Music Award, Best Cellist of the Year, London, 1967; Cavaliere Ufficiale dell'Ordine al Merito della Republica Italiana awarded by the President and Government of Italy, 1972; Saggitario d'Oro and Gonfalone d'Oro, Italy. *Address:* 30 avenue Malausséna 2è dr, 06000 Nice, France.

ALEKSASHKIN, Sergei; Singer (Bass-baritone); b. 1954, Saratov, Russia. *Education:* Studied at the Saratov Conservatory, graduated 1982; La Scala. *Career:* Appearances as Don Giovanni, Mephistopheles, Sarastro, Gremin in Eugene Onegin and Philip II in Don Carlos, Kirov

Opera, 1989; Kutuzov in War and Peace, Rossini's Basilio, King Henry in Lohengrin and Rimsky's Ivan the Terrible; Tours of Japan and USA, with the Kirov; Sang Rachmaninov's Miserly Knight at Venice, 1998; Balducci in Benvenuto Cellini at the Festival Hall, London, 1999; Boris Godunov under Abbado at Salzburg; Season 2000–01 as the Grand Inquisitor and Leporello at St Petersburg and the General in The Gambler by Prokofiev at the New York Met; Concerts include Shostakovich's 13th Symphony with Solti, Bach's B Minor Mass, Mozart's Requiem; Beethoven's Choral Symphony and the Verdi Requiem. *Address:* c/o Kirov Opera, 1 Theatre Square, St Petersburg, Russia.

ALER, David; Singer (Baritone); b. 26 April 1959, Stockholm, Sweden. *Education:* Studied in Gothenburg with Jacqueline Delman until 1987; Further studies with Geoffrey Parsons, Janet Baker, Kim Borg and Galina Vishnevskaya. *Career:* Sang at Landestheater Coburg and in Sweden, 1988–, as Don Giovanni, Guglielmo and Tarquinius in The Rape of Lucretia; Appeared in Vadstena and Reykjavík, 1988–89 in the premiere production of Someone I Have Seen by Karolina Eriksdottir; Stora Theater in Gothenburg as Schaunard in La Bohème, 1989; Drottningholm Festival 1996, as Allworthy in Tom Jones by Philidor; Salzburg Festival 1998, as Frère Mass ée in St François d'Assise; Concert engagements in Stockholm with Drottningholm Baroque Ensemble and Chapelle Royale of Versailles. *Address:* c/o M & M Lyric Artists, 140 Battersea Park Road, London SW11 5 NY, England.

ALER, John; Singer (Tenor); b. 4 Oct. 1949, Baltimore, MD, USA. *Education:* Bachelor and Master degrees in Voice Performance, School of Music, Catholic University of America, 1972; Juilliard School of Music, American Opera Center and Opera Training Department, 1972–75; Studied with Oren Brown and Martin Isepp. *Career:* Has sung in opera, oratorio and recitals in USA, Canada, the United Kingdom and most of Europe; Many appearances including Tanglewood, Glyndebourne and Aix-en-Provence Festivals, Salzburg Festival, La Scala and London Proms; Has sung with major national and international orchestras; Vienna Staatsoper debut 1982; Toured Japan with Royal Opera, Covent Garden, 1986; Toured Taiwan with Ludwigsburg Festival Chorus and Orchestra, 1987; Sang Eumolpus in Stravinsky's Persephone at Promenade Concerts, London, 1993. *Recordings include:* Handel's Messiah, 1986; Bizet's Les Pêcheurs des Perles, 1989; Songs and Duos of Saint-Saëns, with John Ostendorf and John van Buskirk, 1989; Enesco's Oedipe; Semele, with Kathleen Battle, 1990; Title role in Gazzaniga's Don Giovanni; Orfeo, 1990; Stravinsky works with London Sinfonietta, 1990; Rossini's Songs of My Old Age, 1991; Handel's Joshua, 1991; Gounod's Mors et Vita with Orchestre du Capitole de Toulouse under Michel Plasson, 1992; Dvořák's Stabat Mater with New Jersey Symphony, 1994; Merry Widow, Glyndebourne company in concert, 1994; Songs We Forgot to Remember, 1996. *Honours:* Grammy Award for Best Classical Vocal Soloist for Berlioz Requiem, 1985; Featured on 2 Grammy winning albums, Best Classical Album for Bartók–Cantata Profana and Best Opera Recording for Handel–Semele, 1994. *Current Management:* Herbert Barrett Management. *Address:* c/o Mary Lynn Fixler, Herbert Barrett Management, 266 W 37th Street, New York, NY 10018, USA.

ALEXANDER, Haim; Composer; b. 9 Aug. 1915, Berlin, Germany; m. 6 Jan 1941, 2 s. *Education:* Sternsches Conservatory, Berlin; Graduated, Palestine Conservatory and Academy of Music, 1945; Higher Studies, Freiburg, Germany. *Career:* Teacher of Piano and Theory, 1945–; Associate Professor, Composition and Theory, Head, Department of Theoretical Subjects, Rubin Academy of Music, Jerusalem, 1971–82; Associate Professor, 1972–76, Full Professorship, 1976–, Theoretical Subjects, Department of Musicology, University of Tel-Aviv; Retired 1982, but continuing part-time work. *Compositions include:* Miscellaneous works for piano, 2 pianos, chamber music, pieces based on Oriental Folklore, choral music, songs for voice and piano, works for orchestra; My Blue Piano, Lyrics by Else Lasker-Schüler, for 8 women's voices and percussion, 1990; Piano Sonata, 1994; Late Love for chamber orchestra, 1997; The West-Eastern Bridge, for organ solo, 1998; Two Ballads Recollected, for string quartet, 1998. *Publications:* Improvisation am Klavier, in German, 1986. *Contributions:* Encyclopaedia Hebraica. *Honours:* Golden Feather Prize for Lifetime Achievement from ACUM, 1996; The Israel Prime Minister's Prize for his life achievements, 2001. *Address:* 55 Tschernichowsky Street, 92587 Jerusalem, Israel.

ALEXANDER, Leni; Composer; b. 8 June 1924, Breslau, Germany; m. Ernst Bodenhöfer, 24 Dec 1941, divorced, 2 s., 1 d. Emigrated to Chile from Hamburg in 1939. *Education:* Real-Gymnasium Hamburg, 1939; Diploma Montessori, University of Chile, 1945; Piano, cello, Composition with Fre Focke; Conservatoire de Paris with Olivier Messiaen and composition studies with René Leibowitz, 1954. *Career:* Public concerts of symphonique works in: Santiago de Chile, Buenos Aires, Paris, Rome, New York, Cologne (Chamber Music), Venice, Toulouse, Tokyo and Stuttgart; Film Music, ballet music in Santiago; Special broadcast commission, San Francisco. *Compositions include:* Cuarteto para Cuerdas, 1957; Cantata From Death to Morning; Equinoccio; ... ils se sont perdus dans l'espace etoile..., 1975; Aulicio II, 1985; Time and Consummation; Tessimenti; Adras; Par Quoi? A Quoi? Pour Quoi?; Maramoh; Los Disparates; Sous le quotidien, decelez l'inexplicable;... Est-ce donc si doux cette vie?... Ballet Music: Soon we shall be one, 1959, Les trois visages de la lune, 1966, Un medecin de campagne, Schigan for Organ, 1989, Dishona for Voice, Saxophone and 3 Percussions, 1988. *Contributions:* Music and Psychoanalysis; Alban Berg; The Music Which Freud Never Heard; Psychoanalytic Variations about a theme by Gustav Mahler. *Address:* c/o Beatrice Bodenhofer, Arzobispo Casanova, 24 Bellavista, Santiago de Chile.

ALEXANDER, Roberta; Singer (Soprano); b. 3 March 1949, Lynchburg, VA, USA. *Education:* Studied at the University of Michigan and with Herman Woltman at the Royal Conservatory, The Hague. *Career:* European debut as Rossini's Fanny, La Cambiale di Matrimonio, Netherlands Opera in 1975; Sang Pamina at Houston in 1980 and Strauss's Daphne at Santa Fe in 1981; Covent Garden debut as Mimi in La Bohème; Metropolitan debut in 1983 as Zerlina and returned to New York as Jenůfa, Mimi, Vitellia, Countess and Gershwin's Bess; Sang at Netherlands Opera as Vitellia, Fiordigili and Violetta, Vienna State Opera as Donna Elvira, Jenůfa, and Hamburg State Opera as Elettra in Idomeneo, Donna Elvira and Countess; Glyndebourne debut in 1989 as Jenůfa; Sang Mozart's Vitellia at Zürich in 1989 and Elettra, Idomeneo, at the Hamburg Staatsoper in 1990; Sang Vitellia at Glyndebourne 1995; Donna Elvira at Fort Lauderdale, 1997; Concert appearances include Strauss Four Last Songs with Los Angeles Philharmonic under Previn, and San Francisco Symphony, Mahler No. 4 with Boston Symphony under Ozawa, Concertgebouw under Haitink, Cleveland under Ashkenazy, and Mahler No. 8 at the Salzburg Festival under Maazel; Concerts with Concentus Musicus Wien under Harnoncourt; Engaged for premiere of Angels in America, by Peter Eötvös, Paris Châtelet, 2004. *Recordings:* Mahler No. 4; Porgy and Bess excerpts; St John Passion; Giulio Cesare excerpts; Don Giovanni; Telemann Cantatas; Songs by Ives, Strauss, Mozart, Bernstein, Barber and Puccini; Goldschmidt's Beatrice Cenci and Der gewaltige Hahnrei. *Address:* c/o IMG Artists Europe, Lovell House, 616 Chiswick High Road, London W4 5RX, England.

ALEXANDRA, Liana; Romanian composer; *Professor, National University of Music;* b. 27 May 1947, Bucharest; m. Serban Nichifor. *Education:* studied at Bucharest Univ. of Music, at Weimar and Darmstadt, Germany and in USA. *Career:* Prof., Doctor in Musicology teaching Orchestration, Musical Analysis and Composition, Univ. of Music, Bucharest 1971–. *Compositions:* over 100 works include seven symphonies, six concertos for different instruments and orchestra, three operas, one ballet, biblical cantata (Voice-Decalog) Jerusalem, 60 chamber works, choral music. *Recordings:* radio broadcasts and album recordings in Romania, Israel, USA, Netherlands, Belgium, Denmark, Germany, Italy, Spain, Australia, Austria. *Publications:* books and articles published in Romania, Germany and Israel. *Honours:* Order of Cultural Merit (Second Class), Romania 2004; Gaudeamus Prize (Netherlands) 1979, 1980, Magadine Prize 1982, Bee-Sheva (Israel) 1986, Mannheim-Bedock Prize 1989, UNNA Prize (Dortmund) 1991, Int. Commendation of Success (USA) 2000, The 20th Century (USA) 2000, Int. Personality of the Year (UK) 2001, Researcher of the Year, American Biographical Inst. 2001, Woman of the Year, American Biographical Inst. 2002, Prize for Electroacoustic Composition (France) 2003, 2004, Int. Peace Prize, United Cultural Convention 2003. *Address:* Str. Rosia Montana Nr 4, Bloc 05, Scara 4, Apt 165, 060955 Bucharest, Romania (home). *Telephone:* (21) 772-30-29 (home). *E-mail:* lianaalexandra@pcnet.ro (home). *Website:* romania-on-line.net/whoswho/AlexandraLiana.htm (home).

ALEXASHKIN, Sergei; Singer (bass); b. 1960, Saratov, Russia. *Education:* Studied at the Saratov Conservatoire and at La Scala. *Career:* Member of the Kirov Opera from 1984, including tours to the Edinburgh Festival, 1991, and New York Metropolitan, 1992; Roles have included Mussorgsky's Boris, Rangoni and Dosifei, Sobakin in The Tsar's Bride, Ivan Susanin, Glinka's Ruslan and Farlaf, Kutuzov in War and Peace and Rimsky's Ivan the Terrible; Engagements at Frankfurt and Salzburg in Boris Godunov, at Vienna in Prince Igor, and The Damnation of Faust at Rome; Other roles include Verdi's Philip II, Fiesco, Ramfis and Procida, Gounod's Mephistopheles, Sarastro, and Don Giovanni; Concerts include Shostakovich's 13th Symphony with the Chicago Symphony Orchestra, 1995, Mussorgsky's Songs and Dances of Death (the United Kingdom debut with the BBC Philharmonic Orchestra under Solti, 1996), and Shostakovich's 14th Symphony, at the Vienna Konzerthaus and Ferrara Musica. *Recordings include:* The Fiery Angel and Sadko. *Current Management:* Askonas Holt Ltd, Lonsdale Chambers, 27 Chancery Lane, London, WC2A 1PF, England. *Telephone:* (20) 7400-1700. *Fax:* (20) 7400-1799. *E-mail:* info@askonasholt.co.uk. *Website:* www.askonasholt.co.uk.

ALEXEEV, Dmitri; Pianist; b. 10 Aug. 1947, Moscow, Russia; m. Tatiana Sarkissova, 1 d. *Education:* Piano Studies from age of 5; Entered Central Music School, Moscow Conservatory, aged 6; Postgraduate Studies, Dmitri Bashkirov, Moscow. *Career:* Debut: London, 1975, Vienna, 1975, Chicago 1976, New York, 1978, Paris; Numerous appearances, great orchestras world-wide; English recitals include: Major music societies and festivals (Aldeburgh, Edinburgh); Regular performances throughout Russia, Europe, USA, Japan, Australia; Solo appearances; Concerts with soprano Barbara Hendricks (London, Stockholm, Frankfurt, Munich, Milan, Florence, Russia, France); Season 2000–01 with the premiere of Penderecki's Sextet in Vienna, concerts with the Concertgebouw, St Petersburg Philharmonic and Brabants Orchestras; Benelux tour with Moscow Radio Symphony Orchestra; Festivals include: Edinburgh, Aldeburgh, Prague Spring, Maggio Musicale in Florence, Ravinia, Nantaali, Berlin,Bordeaux and the Lille Piano Festival as part of the celebrations for the European Capital of Culture; As a chamber musician he has collaborated with artists such as Mstislav Rostropovich, Lynn Harrell, Truls Mørk, Yuri Bashmet and Joshua Bell. Recent recitals include: the Medtner Piano Concerto No 1 with the Natherlands Radio Philharmonic at the Concertgebouw, the Schumann Concerto with the Royal Philharmonic Orchestra and Daniele Gatti in Frankfurt and London, three concerts at the Bridgewater Hall in Manchester with the Halle Orchestra and three performances on tour with the Royal Flanders Philharmonic. *Recordings include:* Piano concertos by Schumann, Grieg, Rachmaninov, Prokofiev, Shostakovich, Scriabin, Medtner and solo works by Brahms, Rachmaninov, Schumann, Chopin and Liszt; Spirituals with Barbara Hendricks; Chopin Waltzes; Chopin Preludes; Grieg and Schumann Concertos with Yuri Temirkanov and Royal Philharmonic Orchestra; Scriabin–Prometheus/Philadelphia Orchestra (R Muti); Schumann's Kreisleriana and Etudes Symphoniques; Shostakovich Concertos with the English Chamber Orchestra, Classics for Pleasure; Hyperion, Medtner, Piano Concerto and Piano Quintet, BBC Symphony; BMG Rachmaninov, Paganini Rhapsody, St Petersburg Philharmonic; Rachmaninov Complete Preludes and Moments Musicaux. *Honours:* Top Honours at the Marguérite Long Competition, Paris, 1969, the George Enescu Competition, Bucharest, 1970 and at the Tchaikovsky Competition in Moscow in 1974; First Prize, Leeds International Piano Competition, 1975; Edison Award, 1994. *Current Management:* IMG Artists. *Address:* c/o IMG Artists Europe, Lovell House, 616 Chiswick High Road, London W4 5RX, England.

ALEXEYEV, Anya; Concert Pianist; b. 1970, Moscow, Russia. *Education:* Studied with Dmitri Bashkirov at the Moscow Conservatoire and at the Royal College of Music, with Irina Zaritskaya, 1990–. *Career:* Frequent appearances in Russia and at the major London venues: Barbican Centre, South Bank and St John's Smith Square; Wigmore Hall recital, 1994; Tour of South America 1993 and with the Lithuanian Symphony Orchestra on tour to the United Kingdom, in Concerto No. 2 by Shostakovich; Rachmaninov 2 and Beethoven 4 with the Philharmonia in South Africa; Season 1994–95 with recitals in Ireland and at Festivals in Belgium, Spain, France and Finland; Schumann's Concerto with the Bournemouth Symphony Orchestra, the Grieg Concerto with the Royal Scottish National Orchestra, the United Kingdom tour with the Moscow State Orchestra and recitals at the Bath and Brighton Festivals; the United Kingdom tour with the Russian Symphony Orchestra, 2001; Past engagements have included performances with orchestras including the Philharmonia, BBC Philharmonic, London Mozart Players, Deutschland Radio, Vienna Chamber, National Symphony, Quebec Symphony and St Petersburg Philharmonic with Yuri Temirkanov; also solo recitals at major venues and festivals throughout Europe, regular appearances at the Wigmore Hall in London and appearances with various groups in the United Kingdom, Austria, Sweden and Finland. *Honours:* Winner, Newport International Piano Competition, 1991. *Current Management:* Harrison/Parrott Ltd, 12 Penzance Place, London, W11 4PA, England. *Telephone:* (20) 7229 9166. *Fax:* (20) 7221 5042. *Website:* www.harrisonparrott.com.

ALEXEYEV, Valery; Singer (Baritone); b. 1954, Novosibirsk, Siberia. *Education:* Studied in Novosibirsk and Milan. *Career:* Sang with the Kirov Opera, St Petersburg, 1984 in Prokofiev's War and Peace, The Enchantress by Tchaikovsky and the baritone leads in Prince Igor, Eugene Onegin and Boris Godunov; As Tomsky in The Queen of Spades, Vienna Staatsoper, 1996; As Ruprecht in Prokofiev's Fiery Angel, Covent Garden, 1992; Iago in Otello, Barcelona, 1992; Boris in Lady Macbeth, Frankfurt, 1993; Sang Nabucco, Bregenz Festival, 1993 and Rangoni in Boris Godunov, Salzburg, 1994; Sang Escamillo at Verona, 1995; Eugene Onegin, Zürich, 1996; Season 2000–01 as Giancotto in Francesca da Rimini at Buenos Aires, Iago for the Berlin Staatsoper and Count Luna at the New York Met; Other roles include Scarpia, Verdi's Miller, Santiago; Don Giovanni, Rigoletto, Mazeppa, Posa in Don Carlos and Valentin in Faust. *Recordings:* Otello. *Address:* c/o Kirov Opera, 1 Theatre Square, St Petersburg, Russia.

ALGIERI, Stefano; Singer (Tenor); b. 1959, USA. *Career:* Sang at Bielefeld Opera, 1984–86; Verdi's Riccardo, Essen, 1986–87; As Turiddu, New York City Opera, 1986 and Radames at Costa Mesa Opera, 1988; Boris in Katya Kabanova, Amsterdam, Paris and Berlin; 1998–99 season as Don Carlos, Toronto; Don José, New Orleans; Andrea Chénier, Strasbourg; Sang Verdi's Alvaro and Pollione in Norma, Scottish Opera, 1990 and 1993 and Laca in Jenůfa, Bonn, 1994; Other roles include Puccini's Des Grieux, Dublin, 1991; Manrico, Lisbon. *Address:* c/o Scottish Opera, 39 Elmbank Crescent, Glasgow G2 4PT, Scotland.

ALI-ZADEH, Franghiz; Composer and Pianist; b. 29 May 1947, Baku, Azerbaijan, Russia. *Education:* Studied at the Baku Conservatory, 1970–76. *Career:* Teacher at the Baku Conservatory from 1977. *Compositions include:* The Legend about White Horseman, rock opera, 1985; Piano concerto, 1972; Symphony, 1976; Concerto for chamber orchestra, 1986; Songs about the Motherland, oratorio, 1978; Ode for chorus and orchestra, 1980; 2 piano sonatas, 1970, 1990; String Quartet, 1974, and other chamber music; Crossings for chamber ensemble, 1992; Songs; Empty Cradle, ballet, 1993; String Quartets Nos 3 and 4, 1995, 1998; Journey to the Immortal for baritone, chorus and ensemble, 1995–99. *Address:* c/o RAO, Bolchaia Bronnai 6a, Moscow 103670, Russia.

ALIBERTI, Lucia; Singer (Soprano); b. 1957, Messina, Sicily, Italy. *Education:* Studied at the Messina Conservatory. *Career:* Debut: Teatro Sperimentale, Spoleto in 1978 as Amina in La Sonnambula; Spoleto Festival in 1979 as Amina, Wexford Festival in 1979 in Crispino e la Comare by the brothers Ricci; Returned in 1980 in Un Giorno di Regno and in 1983 as Linda di Chamounix; Sang at Piccola Scala Milan in 1980 as Elisa in Il Re Pastore by Mozart, then in Handel's Ariodante; Glyndebourne Festival in 1980 as Nannetta and also at La Scala Milan in 1981; Sang at the Teatro Bellini Catania in 1982 as Elvira in I Puritani and Olympia in Les Contes d'Hoffmann; Deutsche Oper Berlin and Munich Opera in 1983 as Lucia and Gilda; Cologne and Zürich in 1985 and 1986 as Violetta; Sang title role in Rossini's La Donna del Lago followed by Norma at Catania in 1990; Sang Violetta at Hamburg, 1993; Norma at Buenos Aires, 1995; Lucia di Lammermoor at La Scala, 1997; Season 2001 as Imogene in Bellini's Il Pirata at Catania and as Donizetti's Anna Bolena at the Deutsche Oper, Berlin. *Recordings include:* La Buona Figliuola by Piccinni; L'Arte del Bel Canto. *Address:* Oper der Stadt Bonn, Am Boselagerhof 1, 5300 Bonn, Germany.

ALIEV, Eldar; Singer (Bass); b. 1968, Baku, Russia. *Education:* Baku Conservatory, and with Anatoly Eusev. *Career:* Debut: Sarastro in Die Zauberflöte, conducted by Peter Maag, Treviso, 1994; Appearances at the Wexford Festival, in Giordano's Siberia, in Verdi's Attila at Genoa, as Sparafucile in Rigoletto at Lausanne, and Debussy's Arkel at Bologna; Commendatore in Don Giovanni at the Berlin State Opera, and Opéra Bastille, Paris, 2001; Further roles include Puccini's Colline, Ferrando in Il trovatore, Philip II (Don Carlo), Baldassare in La Favorita and Oroveso in Norma; Sang Capiello in I Capuleti e i Montecchi at Covent Garden, 2001; Concert repertoire includes Beethoven's 9th and Shostakovich's 13th Symphonies, and the Verdi and Mozart Requiems; Engaged as Banquo in Macbeth at the Opéra Bastille and as Timur in Turandot for Netherlands Opera. *Address:* Opéra Bastille, 120 rue de Lyon, 75012 Paris, France.

ALLDIS, John; Conductor; b. 10 Aug. 1929, London, England; m. Ursula Mason, 23 July 1960, 2 s. *Education:* Felsted School, 1943–47; Choral Scholar, King's College, Cambridge, 1949–52; ARCO, 1954; MA, 1957. *Career:* Founder and Conductor, John Alldis Choir, 1962–; Professor, Guildhall School of Music, 1966–77; Founder and Conductor, London Symphony Chorus, 1966–69; Conductor of London Philharmonic Choir, 1969–82; Conductor of Danish Radio Choir, 1972–77; Musical Director, Groupe Vocal de France, 1978–83. *Recordings:* Over 50 various recordings with John Alldis Choir, of contemporary music and opera; Beethoven's Missa Solemnis (Klemperer), Elgar's The Dream of Gerontius (Boult), Berlioz's Grande Messe des Morts, (Colin Davis) and L'Enfance du Christ, Ives Symphony No. 4, (Serebrier), Mozart's Die Entführung, (Davis), Puccini's Turandot, (Mehta), Tchaikovsky's Eugene Onegin, (Solti) and Vivaldi's Sacred Choral Works, Negri. *Honours:* Various awards and Grammy nominations; Gold Disc with London Philharmonic Choir, 1977; FGSM, 1976; Fellow, Westminster Choir College, Princeton, NJ, USA, 1978; Chevalier des Arts et des Lettres, 1984. *Current Management:* Allied Artists. *Address:* 3 Wool Road, Wimbledon, London SW20 0HN, England.

ALLEN, Betty; Singer (Mezzo-Soprano), Teacher and Administrator; b. 17 March 1930, Campbell, OH, USA; m. Ritten Edward Lee III, 17 Oct 1953, 1 s., 1 d. *Education:* Wilberforce University, 1944–46; Certificate, Hartford School of Music, 1953; Private vocal studies with Zinka Milanov; Berkshire Music Center, Tanglewood. *Career:* Soloist, Bernstein's Jeremiah Symphony, Tanglewood, 1951; Appeared in Thomson's Four Saints in Three Acts, New York 1952; Debut at New York City Opera in Kern's Queenie, 1954; Toured Europe under auspices of the US State Department, 1955; New York recital debut at Town Hall in 1958; Formal operatic debut at Teatro Col ón, Buenos Aires as Jocasta in Oedipus Rex, 1964; USA operatic debut at San Francisco, 1966 and Metropolitan Opera debut in 1973; Appearances with other USA opera companies; Many concert engagements; Teacher at Manhattan School of Music in New York, 1969, North Carolina School of the Arts at Winston-Salem, 1978–87 and Philadelphia Musical Academy, 1979; Executive Director, Harlem School of the Arts, 1979–; Teacher of masterclasses in voice at Teatro Col ón, Buenos Aires, 1985–86 and Curtis Institute of Music, Philadelphia, 1987–. *Recordings:* Various. *Address:* c/o Harlem School of the Arts, 645 St Nicholas Avenue, New York, NY 10030, USA.

ALLEN, Giselle; Singer (soprano); b. 1970, Belfast, N Ireland. *Education:* University of Wales; Guildhall School. *Career:* Roles included Janáček's Fox, Britten's Helena and Suor Angelica, GSMD, London; Walton's Cressida, Ischia; Musetta and Tatiana for Clonter Opera; Svatava in Sarka by Fibich, Wexford; Massenet's Iris, Holland Park; Helena at Singapore; Massenet's Salomé at Dublin, 2000; Concerts include Messiah, Albert Hall with David Willcocks; The Vaughan Williams Serenade with Simon Rattle and recitals in Northern Ireland, 1998–99 season. *Honours:* Guildhall and Ricordi Singing Prizes, GSMD. *Current Management:* Hazard Chase, Norman House, Cambridge Place, Cambridge CB2 1NS, England. *Telephone:* (1223) 312400. *Fax:* (1223) 460827. *Website:* www.hazardchase.co.uk. *Address:* Music International, 13 Ardilaun Road, London N5 2AR, England.

ALLEN, Paschal; Singer (Baritone); b. 1960, Armagh, Northern Ireland. *Education:* Studied in Belfast and at Guildhall School, London, with Norman Walker. *Career:* Appearances at the Wexford and Glyndebourne Festivals, with English National Opera and for Dublin Grand Opera; Repertoire includes Leporello, Bartolo, Colline in La Bohème, Kecal (The Bartered Bride), Figaro and Sarastro; Frequent tours with the English Opera Group; Concerts at the Edinburgh and Aldeburgh Festivals; Broadcasts for BBC and Radio Telefis Eireann; Engagements for the Royal Opera, Covent Garden, include English stage premiere of Hindemith's Mathis der Maler, directed by Peter Sellars, 1995. *Address:* c/o Royal Opera House (Contracts), Covent Garden, London WC2E 9 DD, England.

ALLEN, Sir Thomas Boaz, Kt, FRCM; British opera singer (baritone); b. 10 Sept. 1944, Seaham Harbour, Co. Durham; s. of Thomas Boaz Allen and Florence Allen; m. 1st Margaret Holley 1968 (divorced 1986); one s.; m. 2nd Jeannie Gordon Lascelles 1988; one step-s. one step-d. *Education:* Robert Richardson Grammar School, Ryhope, Royal Coll. of Music, London. *Career:* prin. baritone, Welsh Nat. Opera 1969–72, Royal Opera House, Covent Garden 1972–78; freelance opera singer 1978–, singing at Glyndebourne Opera 1973, ENO, London Coliseum 1986, La Scala 1987, Chicago Lyric Opera 1990, Royal Albert Hall 2000, London Proms 2002, Royal Opera House, Covent Garden 2003; Prince Consort Prof. Royal Coll. of Music 1994; Hambro Visiting Prof. of Opera Univ. of Oxford 2000–01, currently Fellow Jesus Coll.; Pres. British Youth Opera 2000–. *Art Exhibitions:* Chelsea Festival 2001, Salisbury Playhouse 2001. *Performances include:* Die Zauberflöte 1973, Le Nozze di Figaro 1974, Così fan Tutte 1975, Don Giovanni 1977, The Cunning Little Vixen 1977 and Simon Boccanegra, Billy Budd, La Bohème, L'Elisir d'Amore, Faust, Albert Herring, Die Fledermaus, La Traviata, A Midsummer Night's Dream, Die Meistersinger von Nürnberg; as producer Albert Herring 2002. *Film:* Mrs Henderson Presents 2005. *Publication:* Foreign Parts: A Singer's Journal 1993. *Honours:* Hon. Fellow RAM, Univ. of Sunderland; Hon. MA (Newcastle) 1984, Hon. DMus (Durham) 1988, Hon. DMus (Birmingham) 2004; Queen's Prize 1967, Gulbenkian Fellow 1968, Royal Philharmonic Soc. BBC Radio 3 Listeners' Award 2004. *Current Management:* Askonas Holt Ltd, Lonsdale Chambers, 27 Chancery Lane, London, WC2A 1PF, England. *Telephone:* (20) 7400-1700. *Fax:* (20) 7400-1799. *E-mail:* info@askonasholt.co.uk. *Website:* www.askonasholt.co.uk.

ALLIK, Kristi; Composer and Teacher; b. 6 Feb. 1952, Toronto, Ontario, Canada. *Education:* Studied at Toronto University, at Princeton, and at the University of Southern California. *Career:* Teacher at Queen's University, Kingston, Ontario, from 1988; Co-founder of electronic music studio at Queen's. *Compositions include:* Loom Sword River, opera, 1982; Of all the People for voices and ensemble, 1983, Skyharp, sound sculpture, 1991; Multi-media works with electronics Electronic Zen Garden (1983), Rondeau (1985), Comatose (1986), Rhythm and Culture (1986), Till Rust do us Part (1988), Vitamin B-52 (1989); Piano trio, 1979; Lend me your Harp for chorus and chamber orchestra, 1981; Zone Two for ensemble, 1984; Rohan for cello and chamber orchestra, 1988; Trio for clarinet, piano and low voice, 1989; Three Textures for strings, 1992; Illustrated Earth for orchestra, 1995; Nel mezzo del camina for soprano, guitar and tape, 1995. *Address:* c/o Queen's University, School of Music, Kingston, Ontario K7L 3N6, Canada.

ALLIOT-LUGAZ, Colette; Singer (Soprano); b. 20 July 1947, Notre-Dame-de-Bellecombe, France. *Education:* Studied at Bonneville with Magda Fonay-Besson in Geneva and at the Opera Studio Paris with Rene Koster and Vera Rozsa; Further study at the Lyon Conservatoire. *Career:* Has sung widely in France and elsewhere as Mozart's Pamina, Cherubino and Zerlina; Engagements as Messager's Véronique, Rosina and Weber's Aennchen and in operas by Monteverdi, Haydn and Rameau; Has often appeared as Debussy's Mélisande notably at the Lyon Opéra in 1980; Festival performances at Aix and Glyndebourne and at the Paris Opéra and the Théâtre de la Monnaie, Brussels; Modern repertory includes La Passion de Gilles by Boesmans, creation 1983, and Berio's Opera; Sang Ascanius in Les Troyens at the opening of the Opéra Bastille, Paris in 1990; Appeared as Lully's Alceste at the Théâtre des Champs-Elysées, 1992; Season 1992–93 as Gluck's Alceste at Montpellier and Siebel in Faust at the Paris Opéra; Sang in Les Troyens by Berlioz with the Toulouse Orchestra under the direction of Michel Plasson at Toulouse and Athens, 1994; During 1995 gave many concerts with the Orchestra des Pays de Savoie; Sang a concert version of Pulcinella by Stravinsky at the Salle Pleyel, 1996, and the Brahms Requiem at Lyon, 1997; Season 1997–98 sang with the Cantate des Alpes in many concerts of traditional alpine songs throughout the Rhône-Alpes region. *Recordings include:* Pelléas et Mélisande, conducted by Charles Dutoit; Fragoletto in Les Brigands by Offenbach; Campra's Tancrède; Video of Pelléas et Mélisande, from Lyon (Arthaus). *Honours:* The Nadia and Lili Boulanger Prize, Académie des Beaux-Arts, Paris, 1993. *Address:* Les Frasses, 73590 Notre Dame de Bellecombe, France.

ALLISON, John, BMus, PhD, ARCO; British editor and critic; *Editor, Opera;* b. 20 May 1965, Cape Town, S Africa; s. of David Allison and Adele Allison; m. Nicole Galgut. *Education:* Univ. of Cape Town. *Career:* fmr organist at Cape Town Cathedral; music critic for The Times; Ed. Opera magazine 2000–. *Publications:* Edward Elgar: Sacred Music 1994, Mitchell Beazley Pocket Guide to Opera 1998; contrib. to Opera News, BBC Music Magazine, Classic FM Magazine, Financial Times, London Evening Standard, The Observer, The Australian, New Grove Dictionary of Music and Musicians, The New Penguin Opera Guide, Music and Words—Essays in Honour of Andrew Porter. *Address:* Opera Magazine, 36 Black Lion Lane, London, W6 9BE, England (office). *E-mail:* editor@operamag.clara.co.uk (office). *Website:* www.opera.co.uk (office).

ALLISTER, Jean Maria, LRAM, FRAM, FGSM; singer; b. 26 Feb. 1932, Northern Ireland; m. 1st Edgar Fleet 1955; one s.; m. 2nd René Atkinson 1974. *Education:* Royal Acad. of Music, London. *Career:* debut, Royal Albert Hall, London 1954; many oratorio and recital performances, England and abroad 1954–80; Henry Wood Promenade Concerts 1959–70; premiere, In Terra Pax 1960; Three Choirs Festivals 1961–77; appeared in L'Italiana in Algeri, Camden Festival 1961; Sadler's Wells Opera debut 1962; sang at Glyndebourne 1962–68; British premiere, Henze's Novae de Infinito Laudes, Leeds 1965; Alexander Nevsky, Festival Hall 1968; L'Ormindo, Munich 1969; Covent Garden debut as Page in Salome 1970; Scipio, Handel Opera Soc., Herrenhausen and Drottningholm 1970; premiere, John Gardner's The Visitors 1972; Delius's Koanga, Sadler's Wells Opera 1972; British premiere, F. Martin's Requiem 1975; final appearances before retiring from public performance, Jenůfa, Opera North 1980. *Recordings:* Stravinsky Mass (L'Oiseau Lyre) conducted by C. Davis, Pirates of Penzance, Ruddigore (D'Oyly Carte), Gilbert and Sullivan Selection, Koanga, Cavalli L'Ormindo, The Mikado (Sadler's Wells Orchestra), Gilbert and Sullivan Spectacular (various, London Concert Orchestra), Malcolm Arnold The Composer/The Conductor: A 75th Birthday Tribute (Song of Simeon), Dido and Aeneas (Purcell conducted by Britten with the English Opera Group Orchestra, reissue) 1999. *Publications:* Sing Solo Soprano (ed.) 1985. *Honours:* Minnie Hauk Prize 1953, Fellow Emeritus GSM. *Address:* Little Paddock, Elm Crescent, Charlbury, Oxfordshire OX7 3PZ, England.

ALLMAN, Robert; Singer (Baritone); b. 8 June 1927, Melbourne, Australia. *Education:* Studied with Horace Stevens, at the Melbourne Conservatory, with Marjorie Smith in Sydney and with Dominique Modesti in Paris, 1955–57. *Career:* Sang with the Victoria National Opera Company, 1952, and Royal Opera House, Covent Garden in 1956 as Escamillo; Guest appearances at Sadler's Wells and at Berlin Staatsoper, Hamburg as Iago, Frankfurt, Munich and Cologne until 1967; Appearances in Australia from 1960 as Rigoletto, Jochanaan in Salome, Macbeth, Escamillo, Scarpia, Belcore and Valentine; Sang Don Giovanni, Iago and Nabucco, 1970–71, with the Elizabethan Opera Company; Further guest engagements at Stuttgart, Düsseldorf, Kassel, Zürich and Strasbourg as Macbeth and Simon Boccanegra; Glyndebourne Festival in 1979 as Pizarro; Member of the Australian Opera at Sydney from 1971; Sang Amonasro in Aida at Brisbane in 1988; Many concert performances notably in Messiah. *Address:* c/o Lyric Opera of Queensland, PO Box 677, South Brisbane, Queensland 4101, Australia.

ALLWOOD, Ralph, BA; teacher; b. 30 April 1950, Walton-on-Thames, England. *Education:* Tiffin School, Durham Univ., Univ. of Cambridge. *Career:* Precentor and Dir of Music, Eton Coll. 1985–; founded and directs the five annual Eton Choral Courses; Dir Rodolfus Choir; Dir Windsor and Eton Choral Society; adjudicator for Sainsbury's Choir of the Year and the Llangollen International Eisteddfod; choral advisor for Novello and Co. Ltd. *Recordings:* Music from Eton, 1986; I will lift up mine eyes, 1986; A Sequence for the Ascension, 1992; Mater Ora Filium, 1993; Music from Eton Choirbook, 1994; Grier: Twelve Anthems, 1995; Among the leaves so Green, 1996; Choral evensong from Eton College, 1997; Welsh Songs, Hymns and Anthems, 1997; Parry: Songs of Farwell, 1998; Eberlin: Sacred Choral Music, 1999; Christmas Music from Eton College, 2000; By Special Arrangement, 2002; A Christmas Collection, 2003. *Honours:* Hon. FRSCM 2002, Hon. ARAM 2003. *Address:* Eton College, Eton, Berkshire SL4 6EW, England (office). *Telephone:* (1753) 671169 (office). *Fax:* (1753) 671170 (office). *E-mail:* r.allwood@ etoncollege.org.uk (office). *Website:* www.etoncollege.com (office).

ALMERARES, Paula; Singer (Soprano); b. 1970, Argentina. *Education:* Studied in Buenos Aires. *Career:* Debut: Soloist in Mahler's 4th Symphony, La Plata, 1990; Stage debut as Mimi, La Plata, 1990; Early roles were Musetta, Micaela and Donizetti's Norina; Sang in Roméo et Juliette, Don Pasquale, La Bohème and Falstaff, Teatro Col ón Buenos Aires, 1992; Offenbach's Antonia with Alfredo Kraus, 1993; Gounod's Juliette, 1996; Premiere of Mario Peruso's Guayaquil, 1993; Zarzuelas with Placido Domingo, Teatro Avenida, Buenos Aires, 1994; Gluck's Euridice, Venice, 1995; Sang at Trieste, 1996 as Adina in L'Elisir d'amore; Adina at Washington and Euridice at Naples, 1998 season; La Traviata, Il Barbiere, L'Elisir d'amore, Pittsburgh Opera; In Italy, La Sonnambula, I Puritani, Il Corsaro, La Traviata, L'Elisir d'amore and Massenet's Manon; Sang Massenet's Manon at Genoa, 1999. *Recordings:* Giulietta e Romeo (N Vaccai) first recording. *Honours:* Best Soprano, Belvedere Competition, Vienna, 1993; Winner of Traviata 2000 Competition, Pittsburgh, 1994. *Current Management:* CAMI. *Address:* c/o CAMI Z/G, 165 West 57th Street, New York, NY 10019, USA.

ALONSO, Odon; Conductor; b. 28 Feb. 1925, La Baneza, Leon, Spain. *Education:* Studied at the Madrid Conservatoire and in Siena and Vienna. *Career:* Choral Director of the Madrid Soloists, 1952, specializing in Music of the Spanish Renaissance and Baroque; Conducted the Spanish National Orchestra, 1952–56, Madrid Philharmonic, 1956–58; Directed the Zarzuela Theatre at Madrid, 1956–57; Conducted the Spanish Radio and Television Orchestra from 1968; Guest engagements at the Vienna Volksoper, New York City Opera, Teatro Liceo Barcelona and the Madrid Opera. *Recordings include:* Guitar Concertos by Vivaldi and Rodrigo, with Narciso Ypes; Turina's Rapsodia Sinfonica.

ALONSO-CRESPO, Eduardo; Composer and Conductor; b. 18 March 1956, Tucuman, Argentina. *Education:* Civil Engineering, National University of Tucuman; Professor of Piano, School of Musical Arts, National University of Tucuman; MFA, Conducting, Carnegie Mellon University, Pittsburgh. *Career:* Debut: Conducting: Carnegie Mellon Philharmonic in Ginastera, USA, 1987; Tucuman Symphony in Alonso-Crespo, Mozart, Brahms, Argentina, 1988; Assistant Conductor, Pittsburgh Civic Orchestra, 1988–90; Associate Conductor, Carnegie Mellon Philharmonic, 1989–91; Music Director, Tucuman Symphony Orchestra and Carnegie Mellon Contemporary Ensemble, 1989–; Orquesta de Tucuman, seasons 1991, 1992; Carnegie Mellon Wind Ensemble, 1991–92; Conductor-in-Residence, Carnegie Mellon University, 1991–92; Guest conducting, Argentina, USA. *Compositions include:* Gorbachev, Two-Act Opera; Juana, La Loca, One-Act Opera; Putzi, One-Act Opera; Medea, Ballet, for Chorus and Orchestra; Piano Concerto No. 1, Commentaries on Three Waltzes by Alberdi; Two Stories of Birds for Orchestra; Sinfonietta for String Orchestra. *Address:* Marcos Paz 250, Tucuman 4000, Argentina.

ALPENHEIM, Ilse Von; Pianist; b. 11 Feb. 1927, Innsbruck, Austria; m. Antal Dorati, 16 Dec 1969, deceased 1988. *Education:* Studied with Franz Ledwinka and Winfried Wolf, Salzburg Mozarteum. *Career:* Soloist with major European and USA Orchestras; Many engagements as Recitalist and Chamber-Music Player. *Recordings:* For Desto; Turnabout; Vox, Philips and Pantheon; Haydn Piano Music Complete, Schubert Chamber Music with Piano Complete.

ALPERIN, Yoram; Cellist; b. 1945, Romania. *Education:* Studied with Uzi Wiezel, Rubin Academy of Music, Tel-Aviv. *Career:* Member and solo appearances with Israel Philharmonic, 1971–; Co-founded Jerusalem String Trio, 1977, giving many concerts, Israel and Europe, 1981–; Repertoire includes String Trios by Beethoven, Dohnányi, Mozart, Reger, Schubert and Taneyev, Piano Quartets by Beethoven, Brahms, Dvořák, Mozart and Schumann; Concerts with Radu Lupu and Daniel Adni. *Recordings:* Several albums. *Address:* c/o Ariën Arts & Music, de Boeystraat 6, B-2018 Antwerp, Belgium.

ALSOP, Marin, MusM; American violinist and conductor; *Principal Conductor, Bournemouth Symphony Orchestra*; b. 16 Oct. 1956, Manhattan, NY; d. of LaMar Alsop and Ruth Alsop. *Education:* Yale Univ., Juilliard School of Music. *Career:* began piano studies aged two, violin studies aged five; entered Juilliard Pre-Coll. 1963; freelance violinist with New York Symphony Orchestra, Mostly Mozart, New York Chamber Symphony, American Composers Orchestra, several Broadway shows 1976–79; began conducting studies with Carl Bamberger 1979, Harold Farberman 1985; f. String Fever (14-piece swing band) 1981; Founder and Dir Concordia Orchestra 1984–; debut with London Symphony Orchestra 1988; Assoc. Conductor Richmond Symphony 1988; studied with Leonard Bernstein, Seiji Ozawa and Gustav Meier, Tanglewood Music Center 1989; Music Dir Eugene Symphony, OR 1989–96, Conductor Laureate 1996–; Music Dir Long Island Philharmonic 1990–96; debut with Philadelphia Orchestra and Los Angeles Philharmonic 1990; Music Dir Cabrillo Music Festival 1992–; Music Dir Colorado Symphony, Denver 1993–; debut Schleswig Holstein Music Festival 1993; Creative Conductor Chair. St Louis Symphony Orchestra 1996–98; Prin. Guest Conductor, Royal Scottish Nat. Symphony 1999–; Prin. Guest Conductor, City of London Sinfonia 1999–; Prin. Conductor Bournemouth Symphony Orchestra (first woman to lead UK symphony orchestra) 2001–; debut with ENO 2003; teacher Nat. Orchestral Inst. 1991–, Oberlin Coll. 1998, Interlochen Center for the Arts 1998, Curtis Inst. 1998. *Recordings include:* Fever Pitch, Fanfares for the Uncommon Woman, Saint-Saens, Blue Monday, Victory Stride, Fiddle Concerto for Violin and Orchestra, Gorgon, Music of Edward Collins, Too Hot to Handel, Barber Vols I–IV, Passion Wheels, Tchaikovsky Symphony No. 4, Bernstein Chichester Psalms. *Honours:* Leonard Bernstein Conducting Fellow, Tanglewood Music Festival 1988, 1989; Hon. DLitt (Gonzaga Univ.) 1995; Stokowski Conducting Competition 1988, Koussevitszky Conducting Prize 1989, American Soc. of Composers, Authors and Publishers (ASCAP) Award for Adventuresome Programming of Contemporary Music 1991, Univ. of Colorado Distinguished Service Award 1997, State of Colorado Gov.'s Award for Excellence in the Arts 1998, Royal Philharmonic Soc. Conducting Award 2003, Gramophone Artist of the Year 2003. *Current Management:* 21C Media Group Inc., 30 W 63rd Street, Suite 15S, New York, NY 10023, USA. *Telephone:* (212) 842-0080. *Fax:* (212) 842-0034. *E-mail:* MarinAlsop@aol.com (office); info@21cmediagroup.com (office). *Website:* www.marinalsop.com (office).

ALSTED, Birgitte; Composer and Violinist; b. 15 June 1942, Odense, Denmark. *Education:* Violin Studies, Royal Danish Academy of Music; Music Academy, Warsaw, Poland; Composition Seminars with Per Norgard, Copenhagen. *Career:* Performer of new music in, Det unge Tonekunstnerselskab; Kvinder i Musik; Danmarks Radio, Television Acting Musician, Experimental Theatre; Teacher, Compositions performed in DUT, Radio, Television, KIM, Paris, Rome, New York, Mexico City, Berlin, Stockholm, London; Commissions, Contemporary Dance Theatre, London, Nordiske Forum 88, Danmarks Radio; mem, Dansk Komponistforening; Kvinder i Musik; Det Unge Tonekunstnerselskab. *Compositions include:* Klumpe, 1972; Stykke 2, 1973; 12 toner i Zoo, 1973; Smedierne i Granada, 1976; Strygekvartet i CD, 1977; Konkurrence, 1979; Haiku-Sange, 1979; Solen og jeg, 1981; Gentagne Gange, 1980; Solen på Moddingen, 1982; Phasing Moon Facing Changing, 1983; Antigone, 1983; Kaere Allesammen, 1984; På Afstand af Bolgen, 1984–85; Om Natten, 1985; Skiftetid, 1985; Kindleins Schlaflied, 1986; Frokost i det Gronne, 1985; Nostalgisk Extranummer, 1985; Extra Nostalgisk no. 2, 1986; Espressione Emotionale, 1987; Fatsy, 1987; Dromme-spil, 1988; Opbrud, 1988; Vakst, 1989; Lyst, 1990; 2 sange til Doden, 1990; Episoder til Thomas, 1991; Havet ved Forår, 1991; Karen's Å, 1992; Unoder, 1992; Natterdag, 1992; Berceuse Neptunoise, 1993; Spring I, 1994; Stelle, 1995; Sorgsang, 1995; Hojsang, 1995; She Cinderella, opera, 1996; Church Bells for orchestra, 1996; Lament for baritone and piano, 1996; Very Sure, electro-acoustic, 1997. *Recordings:* Antigone; Frokost i det Gronne; Vakst; Natterdag; To Sange til Doden; Sorgsang. *Honours:* Komponistforemingens Jubilaeumslegat, 1985; Gustav Enna's Mindelegat, 1988; Several grants, Art Foundation of Danish State, including 3 years, 1980–83. *Address:* Dansk Komponistforening, Grabrodretorv 16, 1154 Copenhagen K, Denmark.

ALTENA, Marius van; Singer (Counter-Tenor); b. 10 Oct. 1938, Amsterdam, Netherlands; m. Marianne Syses, 2 s. *Education:* Piano Diploma A and B, Singing Diploma A and B, Conservatory of Music, Amsterdam. *Career:* Debut: Germany, 1970; Concerts throughout Europe and the US with early music groups; Further tours to Japan and Australia; Holland Festival, 1974, in Eumelio by Agazzari and in Seelewig by Staden; Returned 1980, for Gluck's L'Isle de Merlin; Performed with Vienna-based group Spectaculum, 1980–84, in stage works by Fux, Leopold I and Conti; Later turned to conducting. *Recordings include:* Leopold I's Il figliuol prodigo; Madrigals by Monteverdi (RCA); Bach Concertos with Harnoncourt and Gustav Leonhardt, 1985; Hodges Ensemble with Paul V Nevel, 1990–97;

Camerata Trajectina, 1988–97. *Address:* Bloemberg 8, 7924 PW Veeningen, Netherlands.

ALTENBURGER, Christian; Violinist; b. 5 Sept. 1957, Heidelberg, Germany. *Education:* Graduated Vienna Academy of Music, 1973; Graduated, Juilliard School, New York, 1978; Studied Violin with father and Dorothy DeLay. *Career:* Debut: First appearance in 1964; Formal debut, Recital, Musikverein, Vienna, 1976; Soloist with various major orchestras in Europe and the USA; With Bruno Canino played the Sonata by Strauss, Schoenberg's Fantasy and Bartók's 2nd Sonata, Salzburg Festival, 1990. *Recordings:* For Arabesque; ProArte.

ALTMEYER, Jeannine; Singer (Soprano) b. 2 May 1948, La Habra, California, USA. *Education:* Studied with Martial Singher and Lotte Lehmann in Santa Barbara, California; Attended the Salzburg Mozarteum. *Career:* Operatic debut as the Heavenly Voice in Don Carlos, Metropolitan Opera, New York, 25 September 1971; Appeared with the Chicago Lyric Opera, 1972, in Salzburg, 1973 and at Bayreuth, 1979; Member of the Wurttemberg State Theatre, Stuttgart, 1975–79; Then sang throughout Europe, achieving success as a Wagnerian; Roles: Elsa, Eva, Sieglinde, Isolde, Elisabeth, Gutrune and Brünnhilde; Sang Isolde at Bayreuth, 1986; Paris Opéra and Los Angeles, 1987 as Chrysothemis, Isolde; Brünnhilde in Götterdämmerung at the Zürich Opera, 1989; Sang Leonore at La Scala, 1990; Turin 1991, as Goldmark's Queen of Sheba; Sang Brünnhilde in Götterdämmerung for Netherlands Opera, 1998; Elektra at Aachen, 1999. *Recordings:* Sang Brünnhilde in The Ring under Janowski; Video and DVD of Die Walküre, in production from Bayreuth. *Address:* c/o Theateragentur Dr Germinal Hilbert, Maximilianstrasse 22, 8000 Munich 22, Germany.

ALTMEYER, Theodor Daniel; Singer (tenor); b. 16 March 1931, Eschweiler, Aachen, Germany. *Education:* Studied in Cologne with Clemens Glettenberg, 1953–56. *Career:* Sang at the Städtische Oper Berlin, 1955–60, notably in the 1958 premiere of Diary of a Madman by Searle; Sang at Hannover from 1960, in operas by Rossini, Lortzing and Mozart, and as Pfitzner's Palestrina; Sang in Stuttgart from 1958; Vienna from 1969; Many concert appearances, often as the Evangelist in the Passions of Bach; Guest engagements in France, Austria, Italy, Belgium, England, Switzerland and Netherlands; Festivals of Venice, Lucerne, Montreux, Ansbach, Vienna, Florence and Naples; Professor at the Hannover Musikhochschule from 1974. *Recordings:* St Matthew and St John Passions of Bach, Dettinger Te Deum by Handel, Beethoven and Haydn Masses, Bach Cantatas; Evangelist in the St Luke Passion by Telemann and the St John Passion by Schütz; Schütz St Matthew Passion. *Address:* Hochschule für Musik und Theater Hannover, Emmichplatz 1, 3 Hannover, Germany.

ALVA, Luigi; Singer (Tenor); b. 10 April 1927, Lima, Peru. *Education:* Studied with Rosa Morales in Lima and with Emilio Ghiradini and Ettore Campogalliani in Milan. *Career:* Debut: Sang at Lima in the Zarzuela Luisa Fernanda, 1949; Beppe in Pagliacci, 1950; Sang Paolino in Cimarosa's Il matrimonio segreto at La Scala, 1955; Salzburg Festival, 1957–58, as Fenton in Falstaff and Ferrando in Così fan tutte; Sang Rossini's Almaviva more than 300 times, starting with La Scala, 1956; Returned to Milan in 1958 for the local premiere of Janáček's The Cunning Little Vixen and world premieres of Una domanda di matrimonio by Luciano Chailly and Malipiero's La donna e mobile; appeared in Holland Festival in 1959 in Il mondo della luna by Haydn and made his Covent Garden debut in 1960; Glyndebourne Festival, 1961–62, as Nemorino in L'Elisir d'amore; Aix-en-Provence from 1960, Vienna Staatsoper from 1961; Metropolitan Opera, 1964–76 as Ernesto in Don Pasquale, Almaviva, Lindoro in L'Italiana in algeri and Mozart's Tamino; Other appearances in Hamburg, Berlin, Moscow, Edinburgh, Stockholm, Lisbon, Venice, Florence and Mexico City; Artistic Director of Prolirica in Lima from 1982; Retired as singer, 1989. *Recordings include:* Il Barbiere di Siviglia, Il matrimonio segreto and Falstaff (Columbia); La Cenerentola (Deutsche Grammophon); Handel's Alcina, L'Italiana in Algeri and Mozart's Il re pastore (Decca); Haydn's L'Isola disabitata (Philips); Alfonso und Estrella by Schubert (Melodram). *Address:* La Scala Opera, Via Drammatici 21, 20121 Milan, Italy.

ALVARES, Eduardo; Singer (Tenor); b. 10 June 1947, Rio de Janeiro, Brazil. *Career:* Stated career in Europe, (debut as Don José) Linz, Frankfurt, Vienna and Stuttgart, returned to Brazil and then sang Des Grieux (Manon Lescaut) at Metropolitan, and Netherlands Opera (also Dick Johnson in Fanciulla del West), Manrico in Il Trovatore for Opera North and Calaf in Turandot for Scottish Opera; English National Opera as Radames in Aida, 1985 and Cavaradossi, 1987; Teatro Municipal Rio de Janeiro, 1987–88, as Don José and Bacchus; Other roles include Alfredo, Gabriele Adorno, Don Carlos, Faust, Werther and Alva in Lulu; Wexford Festival, 1983–84, in Hans Heiling and The Kiss. *Address:* c/o English National Opera, London Coliseum, St Martin's Lane, London WC2N 4ES, England.

ALVAREZ, Carlos; Singer (Baritone); b. 1963, Malaga, Spain. *Education:* Studied at the Malaga Conservatory. *Career:* Sang Morales in Carmen with Luis Lima and gave concert with him at the Teatro Arriaga in Bilbao; Further appearances at the Teatro La Zarzuela, Madrid, Teatro Colón Buenos Aires, Vienna Staatsoper, La Scala Milan and Royal Opera, Covent Garden; Operas have included Eugene Onegin (at Madrid), La Bohème, Il Barbiere di Siviglia (Zürich), La Traviata works Fedora (London), Don Carlos (Mannheim) and Madama Butterfly (Milan); Frequent appearances with Placido Domingo, including Il Guarany by Gomes at Bonn and concerts in Tokyo, Berlin, Madrid and Seville; Les Troyens with the London Symphony at the Barbican Hall, under Colin Davis, 1993; Guest engagements in New York, Geneva and Washington; Posa in Don Carlos at Salzburg, 1998; Don Giovanni at the Vienna Theater an der Wien, 1999; Season 2000–01 as Germont at Zürich, Don Carlo in Ernani at Madrid and Posa in Don Carlos at the Vienna Staatsoper; Rigoletto at Covent Garden, 2002. *Address:* c/o Opernhaus Zürich, Falkenstrasse 1, 8008 Zürich, Switzerland.

ALVES DA SILVA, Luiz; singer (countertenor); b. 1961, Brazil. *Career:* sang with various European vocal groups, including the Clemencic Consort, Vienna, Hesperion XX, Instituzioni Harmoniche of Bologne, Capella Real of Barcelona and Ensemble Turicum; Zürich Opera Studio 1990; Achilles in Handel's Deidamia; Vienna Konzerthaus, 1990 as Mozart's Ascanio; Sang at Ulm and Zürich in Ligeti's Le Grand Macabre and Britten's Oberon at Biel; Baroque and contemporary works on stage and the concert platform. *Recordings:* GG Brunetti's Stabat Mater. *Address:* c/o Opernhaus Zürich, Falkenstrasse 1, 8008 Zürich, Switzerland.

ALWYN, Kenneth, ARAM, FRAM; conductor; b. 28 July 1928, Croydon, England; m. Mary Law; two d. *Education:* Royal Schools of Music, London. *Career:* debut, London; Conductor, Royal Choral Union, New Zealand; Sadler's Wells Theatre Ballet; Royal Ballet, Royal Opera House, Covent Garden; BBC Staff Conductor; Principal Conductor, Yomiuri Nippon Symphony Orchestra, Tokyo; Musical Dir, Philomusica; radio and television presenter; mem. Incorporated Soc. of Musicians, BBC Central Music Advisory Cttee. *Compositions:* various concert, radio and television commissions. *Recordings:* major recordings with leading orchestras; conductor of first stereophonic recordings by Decca with London Symphony Orchestra 1958, Tchaikovsky's 1812 Overture; complete recording, Hiawatha, with Bryn Terfel and Welsh National Opera 1991. *Honours:* Mann's Prize for Conducting 1951, Gramophone Award for Best Film Music 1998. *Address:* Horelands, West Chiltington Lane, West Sussex RH14 9EA, England.

ÅM, Magnar; composer; b. 9 April 1952, Trondheim, Norway. *Education:* Bergen Conservatory, studied in Lidholm, Stockholm. *Compositions include:* Prayer for soprano, chorus and string orchestra, 1972; Song for brass and percussion, 1974; Dance for harp, guitar and harpsichord, 1977; Octet, 1977; Point Zero for soprano, alto, chorus, children's chorus and amateur orchestra, 1979; 2 alternative versions; Ajar, double-bass concerto, 1981; A Cage-bird's Dream, multimedia piece, 1981; Inconceivable Father for Child Soprano, children's chorus, bass clarinet, timpani, double bass and organ, 1982; My Planet, My Soul, symphony, 1982; Piano pieces; Like a Leaf on the River, for guitar, 1983; Omen, for violin, horn, piano, 1983; Conqilia for violin, horn, piano, recitor, 1984; Right Through All This, for orchestra, 1985; Freetonal Conversations, for violin, cello and piano, 1986; Hovering depths for double bass, 1986; A Miracle and a Tear, for mixed chorus, 1987; If We Lift As One, for orchestra, 1988; Tonebath, experience room, 1989; And Let the Boat Slip Quietly Out, for orchestra, 1989; ... And Life, an oratorio, 1990; Quiet Ruby, for choir, 1992; Glimpses of an Embrace, for trumpet, horn and mountain echoes, 1994; Among Mirrors, for violin, cello and piano, 1995; Be Quiet, My Heart, for orchestra, 1995; The Silver Cord for string quartet, 1996; On the Wings of the Ka-bird, for choir, 1996; The Wondering and the Wonder, for orchestra and dolphins, 1996; You Are Loved, for soprano, choir (SSA), two horns and harp, 1997; But in the Middle of the Whirl, for Hardanger-fiddle, cello and piano, 1998; Wandering Heaven, for alto voice and string sextet, 1998; 5 Paradoxes, for organ, 1999; Tree of Tenderness (an oratorio), 1999; Aching Hard, Aching Soft for solo violin, 2000; Here In the Resurrection for string quartet and recitor, 2001; Lonely/Embraced for bassoon and orchestra, 2003. *Recordings:* Hovering Depths; Study on a Norwegian Hymn; Point Zero; Like a Leaf on the River; The Silver Cord; Gratia; The Light in your Chest; You Are Loved; Wandering Heaven; Va Bene; Octet–in nude. *Address:* Vevendelvegen 46, 6100 Volda, Norway. *E-mail:* magnar.am@online.no. *Website:* www.magnaram.com.

AMACHER, Maryanne, BFA; American composer and multi-media artist; b. 25 Feb. 1942, Kates, PA. *Education:* University of Pennsylvania with George Rochberg, Univs of Pennsylvania and Illinois, studied with Karlheinz Stockhausen. *Career:* taught in the Experimental Music Studio at the School of Engineering, University of Illinois, 1964–66; Creative Associate at the Center of Creative and Performing Arts, State University, New York, 1966–67; Fellow at the Massachusetts Institute of Technology, 1972–76; Fellow at Radcliffe College, Harvard, 1978–79; Sound experiments with John Cage and Merce Cunningham; Has

initiated various projects with natural sound experiments in the local environemnt. *Compositions include:* City Links, performed in New York, Buffalo, Paris and Chicago, 1967–79; Lecture on the Weather, collaboration with Cage, 1975; Remainder, dance music for Merce Cunningham, for Tape and Electronics, 1976; Mixed Media works include Sound-Joined Rooms, 1980–82; Close Up; Intelligent Life, 1982; Music for the Webern Car; Mini-Sound Series, 1985–; Petra for 2 pianos, 1991. *Honours:* Multi-Media Award from New York State Council of Arts, 1978–79; Composition Award from the National Endowment of the Arts, 1978–79; Beard Arts Fund, 1980. *Address:* ASCAP, ASCAP Building, 1 Lincoln Plaza, New York, NY 10023, USA.

AMADUCCI, Bruno; Conductor; b. 5 Jan. 1935, Viganello-Lugano, Switzerland. *Education:* Conservatorio Giuseppe Verdi, Milan, Italy; Ecole normale de Musique, Paris, France. *Career:* 1st Concert, Mozart Requiem, Swiss Radio Monteceneri, 1951; 1st Public Concert with Alfred Cortot and Orchestra, Pomeriggi Musicali, Milan, 1951; Former Conductor, Metropolitan Opera, Vienna State Opera, Vienna Symphony Orchestra, Paris Opéra, Deutsche Oper, Berlin; Member of Jury, Concorso Voci Verdiane, Busseto, Italy and Concours Internationale, Geneva. *Publications:* L'Amfiparnaso de Orazio Vecchi par rapport au développement de l'expression du langage musicale, 1951; La Musica nella Svizzera Italiana e La Presenzadella Radio-Orchestra, 1973; The Puccini Dynasty, 1973. *Address:* Casella Postale, Lugano, 6901, Switzerland.

AMARA, Lucine; Singer (Soprano); b. 1 March 1925, Hartford, Connecticut, USA. *Education:* Studied voice with Stella Eisner-Eyn in San Francisco; Attended the Music Academy of West Santa Barbara, 1947 and the University of Southern California, Los Angeles, 1949–50. *Career:* Member, San Francisco Opera Chorus, 1945–46; Concert debut, San Francisco Opera, sang at the Hollywood Bowl, 1948; Metropolitan Opera debut, 1950; Regular Appearances there in subsequent seasons; Sang at the Glyndebourne Festival, 1954–58, as Strauss's Ariadne and Mozart's Donna Elvira; Edinburgh Festival 1954, Vienna State Opera 1960, Russia 1965, China 1983; Major Roles, Gluck's Euridice, Verdi's Aida and Leonora (Il Trovatore), Puccini's Mimi and Leoncavallo's Nedda; Sang Mère Marie in Dialogues des Carmélites at the Met, 1987; Sang with the Metropolitan Opera for 41 years. *Recordings:* Bohème as Musetta, Beecham conducting; Lohengrin as Elsa, Leinsdorf conducting; Verdi Requiem, Ormandy conducting. *Honours:* 1st Prize, Atwater Kent Auditions, 1948. *Address:* 260 West End Avenue, Suite 7A, New York, NY 10023, USA.

AMBACHE, Diana Bella, BA, ARAM, LRAM; British pianist, orchestra director, musicologist, academic and broadcaster; *Musical Director, Ambache Chamber Orchestra;* b. 18 June 1948, Kent, England; m. Jeremy Polmear 1982. *Education:* Royal Acad. of Music, Univ. of Sheffield. *Career:* debut, Purcell Room 1979; founder and Musical Dir, Mozart Chamber Orchestra 1977–83; founder and Musical Dir, Ambache Chamber Orchestra 1984–; int. touring to 33 countries on five continents 1977–; first performances of Complete Version in Modern Times of Mozart, Rondo in D, K386 1980; Dussek Piano Concerto in G Minor Opus 49 1981; Fantasy for Piano by Francis Shaw 1982; many British premieres of piano concertos and chamber music by G. Tailleferre, Clara Schumann, Fanny Mendelssohn, Kozeluch, Benda, Michael Haydn, Amy Beach, Helen Hopekirk, Luise Le Beau and others; Lecturer for Martin Randall Travel; broadcasts for BBC World Service, BBC Radio 4, BBC Radio 3, Classic FM; Artistic Dir, Women of Note 1995–97. *Recordings include:* four of Mozart's piano concertos and chamber music by Mozart, Beethoven, Louise Farrenc, Amy Beach and Ottorino Respighi, Sweet Melancholy: 20th Century oboe and piano English collection, Old Masters, New Mistresses (concert series) 2002–04. *Honours:* Gold Medal Associated Bd 1966, scholarship to Royal Acad. of Music 1967; exhibition from Univ. of Sheffield 1970. *Address:* 9 Beversbrook Road, London N19 4QG, England (office). *Telephone:* (20) 7263-4027 (office). *E-mail:* polmear.ambache@telinco.co.uk (office). *Website:* www.ambache.co.uk; www.womenofnote.co.uk.

AMIRKHANIAN, Charles Benjamin; Composer; b. 19 Jan. 1945, Fresno, California, USA. *Education:* BA, English Literature, California State University, Fresno, 1967; MA, Interdisciplinary Creative Arts, San Francisco State University, 1969; MFA, Mills College, Oakland, California, 1980; Studied electronic music and sound recording techniques with David Behrman, Robert Ashley and Paul de Marinis. *Career:* Composer-in-Residence, Ann Halprin's Dancers Workshop Company, 1968–69; Music Director, KPFA Radio, Berkeley, California, 1969–; Lecturer, San Francisco State University, 1977–80. *Compositions:* Live-Performance: Canticle No. 1 for Percussion Quartet, 1963; Canticle No. 2 for Flute and Timpani, 1963; Canticle No. 3 for Percussion Trio, 1966; Canticle No. 4 for Percussion Quartet, 1966; Ode to Gravity, Theatre Piece, 1967; Spurlo Music, Theatre Piece, 1979; Text-Sound (Tape): Oratora Konkurso Rezulto: Autoro de la Jara (Portrait of Lou Harrison), 1970; Each'll, 1971; If In Is, 1971; Sound Nutrition, 1972; Heavy Aspirations (Portrait of Nicolas Slonimsky),

1973; Seatbelt Seatbelt, 1973; She She and She, 1974; Mahogany Ballpark, 1976; Dutiful Ducks, 1977; Audience, 1978; Dreams Freud Dreamed, 1979; Hypothetical Moments (in the Intellectual Life of Southern California), 1981; Dog of Stravinsky, 1982; The Real Perpetuum Mobile, 1984. *Address:* c/o ASCAP, ASCAP Building, 1 Lincoln Plaza, New York, NY 10023, USA.

AMORETTI, Ruben; Singer (Tenor); b. 1968, Burgos, Spain. *Education:* Studied in Berne; Bloomington, Indiana. *Career:* Sang Rossini's Almaviva at Bilbao, Zürich, Stuttgart and Porto, 1995; Scarlatti's Il Trionfo del onore and Massenet's Le Portrait de Manon, Geneva Opera; Sang Flamino in L'amore dei tre re by Montemezzi, Vienna, 1996; Concert repertory includes Bach, Magnificat, Mendelssohn's Elijah, Rossini's Petite Messe, Berlioz Te Deum and Puccini's Messa di Gloria. *Recordings:* Songs by Falla, Verdi, Bellini and Respighi, Gallo. *Address:* c/o Opernhaus Zürich, Falkenstrasse 1, 8008 Zürich, Switzerland.

AMOYAL, Pierre; Violinist; b. 22 June 1949, Paris, France. *Education:* Studied at the Paris Conservatoire and with Jascha Heifetz between 1966 and 1971. *Career:* Debut: Paris 1971, in the Berg Concerto, with the Orchestre de Paris; Appearances with the BBC Symphony Orchestra, Hallé Orchestra, London Philharmonic, Philharmonia, Berlin Philharmonic, Boston Symphony, Cleveland Orchestra, Philadelphia Orchestra and Orchestras in Canada and France; Conductors include Karajan, Ozawa, Boulez, Dutoit, Sanderling, Maazel, Solti, Prêtre, Masur and Rozhdestvensky; Plays Concertos by Berg, Schoenberg and Dutilleux, in addition to the standard repertory; Played Brahms Concerto with the Royal Philharmonic Orchestra, 1995; Artist in Residence at Beaumaris Festival in Wales, 1995; Recitals at St John's Smith Square for the BBC; New York Carnegie Hall debut 1985; Professor at the Paris Conservatoire from 1977; Professor at the Lausanne Conservatoire; Dvořák Concerto at Lisbon, 2003. *Recordings:* Concertos by Dutilleux, Respighi and Saint-Saëns with the Orchestre National conducted by Charles Dutoit; Chamber music (sonatas by Brahms, Fauré and Franck) with Pascal Rogé; Schoenberg Concerto with the London Symphony Orchestra conducted by Boulez. *Honours:* Ginette Neveu Prize, 1963; Paganini Prize, 1964; Enescu Prize, 1970. *Address:* c/o Patrick Voullaire, Park Offices, 121 Dora Road, London SW19 7JT, England.

AMRAM, David, BA; American composer, conductor and multi-instrumentalist; b. 17 Nov. 1930, Philadelphia, PA; m. Lora Lee 1979; one s. two d. *Education:* George Washington University. *Career:* pioneer of the French horn in jazz and Latin music during the late 1940s; World tours as a jazz player, multi-instrumentalist, folklorist, composer and conductor; Director of Music, New York Shakespeare Festival, 1956–67; Director of Music, Lincoln Center Theater, 1963–65; Director of Music, Young People's Concerts and Parks Concerts, Brooklyn Philharmonic, 1971–98; Guest conducts annually with 14 orchestras including Montreal, Toronto, Grant Park and Milwaukee Orchestras; mem. BMI. *Compositions:* Over 100 orchestral, choral, operatic and chamber works including American Dance Suite (all published by C F Peters); Kokopelli: A Symphony in Three Movements premiered by the Nashville Symphony Orchestra, 1997; Trombone Alone, 1996. Commissioned work to celebrate the opening of the Jefferson Wing of the Library of Congress, 1995; A Little Rebellion: Thomas Jefferson, for narrator and orchestra; Composed music for films, The Manchurian Candidate and Splendour in the Grass; Flute Concerto, Giants of the Night commissioned by James Galway for the year 2000. *Recordings:* over 40 recordings of his own compositions; 15 albums as soloist. *Publications:* Vibrations: The Musical Times of David Amram, 1968. Symphonic Works performed by New York Philharmonic, Boston Symphony, Philadelphia Orchestras, one of US 20 most performed composers of concert music, since 1974. *Address:* c/o Ed Keane Associates, 32 St Edward Road, Boston, MA 02128, USA.

AMSELLEM, Norah; Singer (Soprano); b. 1970, Paris, France. *Education:* Studied in New York; Participant in Met's Young Artist Development Program. *Career:* Debut: Micaela at the Metropolitan Opera, 1995; Concert debut at Alice Tully Hall, New York; Opera appearances as Micaela at the Opéra Bastille, Paris, and Lyon; Liu at the Met and Mozart's Countess at the 1997 Glyndebourne Festival; Season 1997–98 as Micaela at the Met, under James Levine and with Placido Domingo, Liu in debut at the San Francisco Opera; Norina (Don Pasquale) and Gounod's Juliette at the Grand Théâtre, Bordeaux; Manon of Massenet at La Scala, Milan, and in Toulouse and Bordeaux; Micaela in Monte Carlo and Japan. *Address:* c/o Metropolitan Opera, Lincoln Center, New York, NY 10023, USA.

AMY, Gilbert; Conductor, Music Educator and Composer; b. 29 Aug. 1936, Paris, France. *Education:* Studied piano with Loriod and composition with Milhaud and Messiaen at the Paris Conservatory, attended Boulez's courses in new music at Darmstadt. *Career:* Commenced conducting 1962; Director, Domaine Musical, Paris, 1967–73; Founder-Conductor, Nouvel Orchestre Philharmonique de

Radio France, Paris, 1976–81; Taught analysis and composition, Yale University, 1982; Director, Lyon Conservatory, 1984–. *Compositions:* Orchestral: Mouvements, 1958; Diaphonies, 1962; Antiphonies for 2 orchestras, 1964; Triade, 1965; Chant, 1968–69, revised 1980; Refrains, 1972; Orchestrale, 1985; Chamber: Piano Sonata, 1967–68; Epigrammes for piano, 1961; Inventions for ensemble, 1959–61; Alpha-Beth for wind sextet, 1963–64; Cycle for percussion sextet; 7 Bagatelles for organ, 1975; Quasi scherzando for cello, 1981; 2 String Quartets, 1992, 1995; Cantata breve for soprano and 3 instruments, 1957; D'un Espace deploye for soprano, 2 pianos and 2 orchestral groups, 1973; Strophe for soprano and orchestra, 1965–77; Une saison en enfer for soprano, piano, percussion and tape; Messe for soloists, chorus and orchestra, 1982–3; Ecrits sur toiles for reciter and small ensemble, 1983; Posaunen for four trombones, 1986; Choros for soloists, chorus and orchestra, 1989; Trois Scènes, for orchestra, 1995; Le Premier Cercle, opera in 4 acts premiered Lyon, 1999. *Address:* c/o Conservatoire National superieur de Musique de Lyon, 3 Quai Chauveau, 69009 Lyon, France.

AN, Chengbi-Seungpil, BA; Composer; b. 25 July 1967, China. *Education:* CNSM Paris, Shanghai Conservatory of Music. *Career:* debut as pianist, aged 7; Lecturer, Department of Composition, Shanghai Conservatory of Music 1993–94; teaching asst, Department of Composition, Shanghai Conservatory of Music 1991–93; Yanbian Korean Arts Troupe of Jilin, Beijing Chinese Arts Troupe 1984–86. *Compositions:* Hyun-Oh, 1998; Ressac, 1997; Electronic Music, 1996; Scintillations, 1996; Nong-mou, 1995; Symphony Movements, 1994; Ru, 1993; A Work, 1993; Lu, 1992; The Light of the Universe, 1992; Symphony Fantasy, 1991; Lou Shi Ming, 1990; Symphony Overture, 1990; Works, 1989; Mingwu, 1988; Ten Variations in Eight Notes, 1988; Sanjo, 1987; A Work, 1987; Arirang Suite, 1986; Unaccompanied Pieces, 1986; Parting, 1985; Piano Suite, 1985; Piano Piece, 1985. *Address:* 7 etg app 75, 2 rue des Cites, 93300 Aurervilliers, France.

ANASTASSOV, Orlin; Bulgarian singer (bass); b. 1976, Rousse, Bulgaria. *Education:* studied in Sofia with Nicola Ghiuselev. *Career:* debut singing Ramfis in Aida on tour to Germany with Ruse Opera; sang Rossini's Don Basilio at La Scala, Milan 1999; appearances in Faust, Aida, and La Sonnambula at Madrid, Berlin, Washington, and Munich; concerts with Colin Davis and the London Symphony Orchestra; season 2000–01 as Bellini's Oroveso at Rome, Sparafucile in Rigoletto at Hamburg and Verdi Requiem in Paris, Monte Carlo and Amsterdam; Ramfis in Vienna, Verona and Berlin; sang Federico Barbarossa in Verdi's La Battaglia in concert, with the Royal Opera at the Festival Hall, London 2000. *Current Management:* Ernesto Palacio Artists Management, Via Donizetti 11, 24050 Lurano (BG), Italy. *Address:* c/o London Symphony Orchestra (contracts), Barbican Centre, Silk Street, London EC2Y 8DS, England.

ANDERSEN, Bo; Composer, Organist and Musicologist; b. 10 Nov. 1963, Denmark. *Education:* Department of Musicology and Nordic Philology, University of Copenhagen; Composition with Ib Nørholm, music theory with Yngve Trede and orchestration with Erik Norby, Royal Danish Academy of Music, Copenhagen, 1988–95; Examination as Organist at the Royal Academy, Copenhagen, 1990, after private studies. *Career:* Numerous performances of most of his works, many commissions from ensembles and soloists; mem, Danish Composer's Association; Society for Publication of Danish Music. *Compositions:* Main Works: Vier Stücke im alten Stil, (String Quartet, No. 1), 1989 (revised 2001); Pezzo Concertante, 4 accordions and 2 percussionists, 1991, Pensieri notturni No. 1 for 3 woodwinds (former Serenade), flute, clarinet and bassoon, 1991 (revised, 1998); Moments Musicaux for 2 accordions, 1999 (revised 2001); Three Flowersongs for soprano and piano, 2000–01, texts by Kirsten Ahlemann; A Fantasia for the Viol for solo cello, 1999; Invocation for solo flute, 1993 (revised 2001); Dream Calls for trumpet, percussion and orchestra; Concerto for trombone and orchestra. *Honours:* Astrid and Aksel Agerby Memorial Grant, 1993; Several grants from the Danish State Arts Foundation. *Address:* c/o S E Mielche, Frederiksberg Allé 78 1.mf, 1820 Frederiksberg C, Denmark.

ANDERSEN, Karsten; Conductor and Violinist; b. 16 Feb. 1920, Kristiania (now Oslo), Norway. *Education:* Studied in Norway and Italy. *Career:* Violinist and Conductor; Music Director, Stavanger Symphony Orchestra, 1945–65; Bergen Symphony Orchestra, 1965–85; Iceland Symphony Orchestra, 1973–80; Guest Conductor of Orchestras in Europe and the USA. *Recordings:* For Composers Recording Inc: Norskkultturrads Klassikerserie; Philips, including Svendsen's Concertos for Violin and Cello and Egge's Symphony No. 1.

ANDERSEN, Stig Fogh; Singer (Tenor); b. 24 Feb. 1950, Horsholm, Denmark; m. Tina Kiberg. *Education:* Studied at the Århus and Copenhagen Conservatories. *Career:* Sang at Århus from 1978 and made debut at Royal Opera Copenhagen, 1980, as Macduff in Macbeth; Many appearances in Copenhagen and elsewhere as guest, singing Tamino (1985), Sergei in Shostakovich's Lady Macbeth (1990), Don José

(1992), Leander in Maskarade, Don Carlos, Lensky, Otello and Florestan; sang Siegfried at Århus, 1994; Cardinal Albrecht in Mathis der Maler at Covent Garden, 1995; Siegfried in The Ring at the Albert Hall and in Birmingham for the Royal Opera, 1998; Meistersinger and Tannhäuser, Munich, 1999; Siegfried in The Ring, Metropolitan Opera House, New York, 2000; Tristan in Houston, 2000; Parsifal, at Covent Garden, 2001; Season 2000–01 as Herman in The Queen of Spades at Copenhagen, Siegfried at Mannheim and Geneva, and Tannhäuser at the Deutsche Oper Berlin; Title role in new production of Siegfried at Munich, 2002. *Recordings:* Das Buch mit 7 Siegeln by Franz Schmidt (EMI). *Honours:* Ridder Af Danebrog, 1 Grad, 2000. *Address:* c/o Det Kongelige Teater, Box 2185, 1017 Copenhagen, Denmark.

ANDERSEN, Terje; Singer (tenor); b. 1970, Oslo, Norway. *Education:* Guildhall School and National Opera Studio, London; Milan with Franco Corelli. *Career:* Early roles in The Rape of Lucretia, The Carmelites and L'Enfant et les Sortilèges; Engagements at Oslo, as Tamino, and Macduff at Stuttgart; English National Opera as Nemorino, and Glyndebourne Festival as Gabriele Adorno; Alfredo in La Traviata on tour with Welsh National Opera; Froh in Das Rheingold and Mozart's Tamino for Münster Opera; Season 2001–2002 as Rodolfo and Pinkerton for the Royal Opera Stockholm, Cavaradossi in Tosca at Koblenz and Macduff for Singapore Lyric Opera; Concerts include the Verdi, Dvořák and Mozart Requiems, Elijah, Mors et Vita by Gounod and Bach's Christmas Oratorio. *Current Management:* Athole Still International Management, Forresters Hall, 25–27 Westow Street, London, SE19 3RY, England. *Telephone:* (20) 8771-5271. *Fax:* (20) 8768-6600. *Website:* www.atholestill.com.

ANDERSON, Avril; Composer; b. 10 June 1953, Southsea, Hampshire, England. *Education:* Studied at the Royal College of Music with Humphrey Searle and John Lambert, 1972–76, at the New England Conservatory, with David del Tredici at New York and with Jonathan Harvey at Sussex University. *Career:* Co-artistic Director of the contemporary music group Sounds Positive, 1987; Composer-in-Residence, The Young Place, London Contemporary Dance School; PRS Composer in Education 1996–97; Adjunct Professor, University of Notre Dame, London Programme. *Compositions:* Mono-staus for 3 clarinets, 1975; Où allons nous? for soprano and orchestra, 1976; Edward II, opera in 1 act, 1978; Black Eyes in an Orange Sky for soprano and piano, 1979; Private Energy for soprano and ensemble, 1983; Dynamics of Matter for piano, 1989; Winds of Change, 1989; Beating the System, 1993; Repetitive Strain for organ, 1995; Deadwood, 1996; Sephardic Songs, 1996; Dead on Time for ensemble, 1998; Nature's Voice, dance score, 1998; Rest Assured, 1999. *Recordings:* Deadwood; Sephardic Songs; Rest Assured. *Honours:* Cobbett Prize; Sullivan and Farrar Prize. *Address:* 28 Cavendish Avenue, London N3 3QN, England.

ANDERSON, Barry; Singer (Baritone); b. 1959, Australia. *Education:* Studied in Vienna and Milan. *Career:* Appearances at Naples as Verdi's Renato; At Catania as Rigoletto; At Cagliari as Count Luna; As Puccini's Sharpless and as Michonnet in Adriana Lecouvreur, Trieste, 1989; Bergamo Opera as Warney in Donizetti's Elisabetta al Castello di Kenilworth; Dresden Staatsoper as Macbeth and Munich Opera as Sharpless; As Macbeth, Simon Boccanegra and Rigoletto, Cologne Opera, 1991–94; Season 1993: As Mozart's Bartolo at the Deutsche Oper, Berlin; Ezio in Verdi's Attila at Buenos Aires; Other repertory includes Verdi's Il Corsaro, at Nîmes; Sang Mascagni's Gianni Rantzau, Livorno, 1991; Sang Germont at Jesi, 2000; Valentin in Gounod's Faust at Cachiari, 1996; Don Carlo in Verdi's Ernani at Montpellier, 1999; Michele in Il Tabarro by Puccini at Sydney Opera House, 2001; Gianni Schicchi by Puccini at Nantes, 2002. *Recordings:* Elisabetta Al Castello Di Kenilworth, Donizetti; I Rantzau, Mascagni; L'Arlesiana, Cilea; Zanà, Leoncavallo. *Address:* c/o Jennifer Eddy Artists, Suite 11, The Clivedon, 596 St Kilda Road, Melbourne, Victoria 3004, Australia. *Telephone:* (39) 0438415869. *Fax:* (39) 0438427866. *E-mail:* barry.tone .anderson@sii.it.

ANDERSON, Beth, BA, MA, MFA; American composer and musician (piano); b. 3 Jan. 1950, Lexington, KY; m. Elliotte Rusty Harold. *Education:* Univ. of California at Davis with Larry Austin and John Cage, Mills Coll., Oakland with Terry Riley and Robert Ashley. *Career:* founder Ear Magazine, New York 1975; solo performer as vocalist and piano accompanist at dance studios; Nat. Endowment for the Arts grant, Nat. Public Radio Satellite Program Development Fund grant; mem. New York Women Composers, Int. Alliance of Women in Music, Poets and Writers. *Compositions include:* April Swale for viola and harpsi-chord, August Swale for woodwind quintet, Belgian Tango, Brass Swale for brass quintet, Elizabeth Rex: Or The Well Bred Mother Goes To Camp (musical), Flute Swale for harpsichord, German Swale for tape, Guitar Swale for guitar duet, January Swale for string quartet, Joan (oratorio), March Swale for string quartet, May Swale for viola solo, Minnesota Swale for orchestra, Mourning Dove Swale for string orchestra, Net Work, New Mexico Swale for chamber ensemble, Nirvana Manor (musical), Pennyroyal Swale for string quartet, Queen Christina

(opera), Revel for orchestra, Rhode Island Swale for harpsichord, Riot Rot (text-sound piece), Rosemary Swale for string quartet, Saturday/Sunday Swale for brass quintet, September Swale for mandolin and guitar, Soap Tuning (musical), The Fat Opera (musical), Three Swales for string orchestra, Trio: Dream In 'D'. *Publications:* Beauty is Revolution, The Internet for Women in Music. *Current Management:* Jeffrey James Arts Consulting, 316 Pacific Street, Massapequa Park, NY 11762, USA.

ANDERSON, David Maxwell; Singer (Tenor); b. 1964, Scotland. *Education:* Studied at the Glasgow Academy and Queen's College, Cambridge; Royal College of Music from 1986, National Opera Studio, 1989. *Career:* Debut: Rinuccio in Gianni Schicchi for Opera North, 1990; Has sung Rinuccio for English National Opera; Rodolfo in La Bohème for Scottish Opera and Glyndebourne Touring Opera, Pinkerton in Madama Butterfly for Opera North, the Duke of Mantua in Rigoletto for Opera North and the Teatro di Pisa, Alfredo in La Traviata for the Teatro di Pisa and Opera North; Other roles include Števa in Jenůfa (English National Opera) and Oronte in I Lombardi (Opera North); Engaged as Anatole in Samuel Barber's Vanessa at Monte Carlo, 2001; Concert engagements include the Verdi Requiem (David Willcocks), Vaughan Williams Serenade to Music (Vernon Handley), Bruckner Te Deum (Alexander Gibson and John Eliot Gardiner), and the Rossini Stabat Mater (Rafael Frühbeck de Burgos). *Address:* 26 Aberdare Gardens, London NW6 3QA, England.

ANDERSON, Julian; Composer; b. 1967, London, England. *Education:* BMus, Royal College of Music, London; Further study with Tristan Murail in Paris, Alexander Goehr at Cambridge and with Oliver Knussen; Attendance at the Dartington International Summer School, the Britten-Pears School (1992) and Tanglewood (1993). *Career:* Free-lance Composer, with performances at the 1996 International Rostrum of Composers (Paris), at the Brighton, Huddersfield Contemporary Music and Cambridge Elgar Festivals; Further performances at the 1995 Ars Musica Festival, Brussels, London Proms, Tanglewood and 1996 Warsaw Festival; Professor of Composition RCM; Composer in Focus to the London PO, 2002–03. *Compositions include:* Diptych, 2 movements for orchestra, 1991–95; Khorovod for 15 players, 1994; The Bearded Lady, for oboe, clarinet and piano, 1994; The Colour of Pomegranates for alto flute and piano, 1994; Scherzo with Trains for four clarinets, 1989–93; Tiramisu for ten players, 1994–95; I'm Nobody who Are You for tenor, violin and piano, 1995; Three Parts off the Ground for 13 players, 1995; Piano Etudes Nos 1 and 2, 1995–96; The Crazed Moon for orchestra, 1995–96; Past Hymns for 15 solo strings, 1996; Poetry Nearing Silence, Divertimento for 7 instruments, 1997; BBC Commission for the 1998 Promenade Concerts; The Stations of the Sun, 1998; Towards Poetry, extended ballet version of Poetry Nearing Silence, 1998; Alhambra Fantasy, for 16 players, 2000; The Bird Sings with its Feathers, ballet for chamber orchestra, 2001; Shir Hashirim, for soprano and chamber orchestra, 2001; Imagin'd Corners, for orchestra, 2002. *Address:* c/o Faber Music, 3 Queen Square, London WC1N 3AU, England.

ANDERSON, June; Singer (Soprano); b. 30 Dec. 1952, Boston, USA. *Education:* Won Rockefeller Foundation Scholarship to the Metropoli-tan Opera, New York in 1970. *Career:* New York City Opera, 1978–84; Appearances in Italy, Palermo, Florence, La Scala, Milan, Venice, Rome, Bologna; Debut Vienna State Opera, 1987, Naples, 1988; Other European appearances, Hamburg, Geneva, Bordeaux, Paris, Madrid, Nice, Prague Festival, Pesaro, Aix-en-Provence Festival, 1988; Metro-politan Opera, 1989 (debut as Gilda); Royal Opera House, London (debut 1986) as Semiramide in a concert performance of Rossini's opera; Other roles include Gilda and Giulietta in Bellini's I Capuleti at La Scala; Lucia di Lammermoor and Isabelle in Robert le Diable, Paris Opéra; Rossini's Armida at Pesaro and Desdemona at San Francisco; Sang in concert at opening of the Bastille Opéra Paris, 1989; Luciano Pavarotti 30th Anniversary Gala at Reggio Emilia, 1991; Television appearances in Beethoven's Ninth Symphony, Berlin, Bernstein, and title role in Lusia Miller, Lyon Opera; Bellini's Elvira in a new production of I Puritani at Covent Garden, May 1992; Sang Zoraide in Rossini's Ricciardo e Zoraide at Pesaro, 1990; Giovanna d'Arco at Covent Garden, 1996; Engaged as Norma at Geneva, 1999; Sang Violetta at the Met 2001. *Recordings include:* Mosè in Egitto, La Jolie Fille de Perth, Le Postillon de Longjumeau, La Fille du Régiment, Maometto II, La Muette de Portici. *Address:* c/o Metropolitan Opera, Lincoln Center, New York, NY 10023, USA.

ANDERSON, Laurie P., MFA; American performance artist and musician (keyboards, violin) and writer; b. 5 June 1947, Wayne, IL; d. of Arthur T. Anderson and Mary Louise (née Rowland) Anderson. *Education:* Columbia Univ., Barnard Coll. *Career:* instructor in Art History, City Coll., CUNY 1973–75; freelance critic Art News, Art Forum; composer and performer multi-media exhbns; Artist-in-Resi-dence, ZBS Media 1974. *Exhibitions include:* solo shows: Barnard Coll. 1970, Harold Rivkin Gallery, Washington 1973, Artists' Space, New

York 1974, Holly Solomon Gallery, New York 1977, 1980–81, Museum of Modern Art 1978, Queen's Museum, New York 1984, Barbican, London 2002; numerous group exhbns 1972–. *Other projects:* New York Social Life, Voices From The Beyond, Talk Normal, Natural History, Happiness 2002. *Film performances:* Carmen, Personal Service Announcements, Beautiful Red Dress, Talk Normal, Alive From Off Center, What You Mean We?, Language Is A Virus, This Is The Picture, Sharkey's Day, Dear Reader, Home of the Brave (writer, dir, performer) 1986, Puppet Motel (CD-ROM) 1995. *Recordings include:* O Superman 1981, Big Science 1982, United States 1983, Mister Heartbreak 1984, Strange Angels 1989, Bright Red 1994, The Ugly One With The Jewels And Other Stories 1995, Live At Town Hall, New York City 2002; film scores: Home Of The Brave 1986, Swimming To Cambodia, Monster In A Box. *Publications:* The Package 1971, October 1972, Transportation, Transportation 1973, The Rose and the Stone 1974, Notebook 1976, Artifacts at the End of a Decade 1981, Typisch Frac 1981, United States 1984, Empty Places: A Performance 1989, Laurie Anderson's Postcard Book 1990, Stories from the Nerve Bible 1993. *Honours:* Guggenheim Fellow 1983, Dr hc (Art Inst. of Chicago), (Philadelphia Coll. of the Arts). *Current Management:* Primary Talent International, Fifth Floor, 2–12 Pentonville Road, London, N1 9PL, England. *Telephone:* (20) 7833-8998. *Fax:* (20) 7833-5992.

ANDERSON, Lorna; British singer (soprano); b. 1962, Glasgow, Scotland. *Education:* Royal Scottish Acad. of Music (with Patricia MacMahon); Royal Coll. of Music, London. *Career:* concerts with Bach Choir, English Concert under Trevor Pinnock, and Scottish Chamber Orchestra; tour of Spain and Poland and appearances at Kings Lynn, City of London, Brighton, Edinburgh and Aldeburgh Festivals; sang with London Baroque under Charles Medlam, with the London Mozart Players under Andrew Parrott and the Bournemouth Sinfonietta under Roger Norrington 1988; Promenade Concert debut 1988; further concerts with London Classical Players, Orchestra of the Age of Enlightenment, Scottish Nat. Orchestra, Florilegium, The King's Consort, BBC Scottish Symphony Orchestra; sang Innocenza in first modern revival of Marazzoli's La Vita Humana, Scottish Early Music Consort, Glasgow 1990; The Fairy Queen with the Sixteen, Queen Elizabeth Hall 1990; Les Noces with Pierre Boulez and Ensemble Intercontemporain 1990, 1992; Morgana in Alcina, Halle Handel Festival and Innsbruck Festival 1992; Mozart Mass in C minor with Scottish Chamber Orchestra under Charles Mackerras 1992; sang in Bach's St John Passion, Royal Festival Hall, London 1997; opera: Clorinda in Il Combattimento di Tancredi e Clorinda, Netherlands Opera 1991, 1993, Pulcheria in Handel's Riccardo Primo, Göttingen 1996; title role in Theodora, Glyndebourne Touring Opera 1997. *Recordings include:* The Fairy Queen with Harry Christophers/The Sixteen, Linley Shakespeare Ode with The Parley of Instruments; Hyperion Complete Schubert; Hyperion Complete Britten Folksongs; Complete Scottish Folksong arrangements by Joseph Haydn with Haydn Trio Eisenstadt for Joan Records; Hyperion: L'Allegro (Handel), The King's Consort; Semper Amor with Apollo Chamber Players for London Independent Records; Messiah with David Willcocks and Mormon Tabernacle Choir. *Honours:* First Prize in Peter Pears and Royal Overseas League Competition 1984, Purcell-Britten Prize for Concert Singers, Aldeburgh 1986. *Current Management:* Andrew Rosner, Allied Artists, 42 Montpelier Square, London, SW7 1JZ, England. *Telephone:* (20) 7589-6243. *Fax:* (20) 7581-5269. *E-mail:* info@alliedartists.co.uk. *Website:* www.alliedartists.co.uk.

ANDERSON, (Leonard) Mark, BMus, LRAM, PPRNCM; pianist; b. 8 Oct. 1963, Eureka, CA, USA. *Education:* San Jose State University, Royal Northern College of Music, Manchester. *Career:* debut New York, 1988; San Francisco, 1988; Tokyo, 1992; Toronto, 1993; London, 1994; Zürich, 1994; Alice Tully Hall, New York, 1994; Performances at major venues world-wide with leading orchestras and conductors. *Recordings:* Various solo piano works of Liszt, Brahms and Schumann; Brahms First Piano Concerto with the Hungarian State Symphony Orchestra, Adam Fischer conducting; Liszt Recital, 1996; Brahms Variations, op 118 and 119, 1997; Live solo concert of works by Copland and Gershwin, 1999. *Contributions:* Piano Quarterly; Keyboard Stylist. *Honours:* Winner, Leeds Pianoforte Competition, 1993; 1st Prize, William Kapell International Piano Competition, Washington DC, 1994. *Address:* 253 Tomas Way, Pleasanton, CA 94566, USA.

ANDERSON, Nicholas Maurice William, MA; Musician, Writer and Producer; b. 29 March 1941, Exeter, Devon; m.; one d. *Education:* Westminster School, London, New Coll., Oxford, Univ. Coll., Durham. *Career:* Editorial Man., Decca Record Co Ltd 1968–71; music producer, BBC Radio 3 1971–91; music consultant to Warner Music 1991–97, 2002–; freelance record producer to Harmonia Mundi, Virgin Classics, Chandos Record Co; Dir, Collegium Musicum 90. *Recordings as producer:* over 50 albums for Collegium Musicum 90. *Publications:* Baroque Music from Monteverdi to Handel 1994; contributions to A Companion to the Concerto 1988, Cambridge Guide to the Arts in

Britain 1991, Oxford Composer Companions: J. S. Bach 2000, New Grove Dictionary of Music and Musicians. *Address:* The Old Bank House, Nether Stowey, TA5 1NG, England. *Telephone:* (1278) 733747 (home). *Fax:* (1278) 732840 (home). *E-mail:* nicholas.anderson@btinternet.com (home).

ANDERSON, Robert David, MA, FSA; conductor, writer and editor; b. 20 Aug. 1927, Shillong, Assam, India. *Education:* Gonville and Caius Coll., Cambridge. *Career:* Asst Ed., Record News 1954–56; Asst Master and Dir of Music, Gordonstoun School, Scotland 1956–62; Conductor, Moray Choral Union; Asst Conductor, Spoleto Festival 1962; Conductor, St Bartholomew's Hospital Choral Soc. 1965–90; Assoc. Ed., The Musical Times 1967–85; critic, The Times 1967–72; contrib. to BBC Music Weekly and other programmes; co-ordinating Ed., Elgar Complete Edition 1983–2003; television programme on Paganini (BBC 2) 1971; Prof. of History, State Univ. of Rostov-on-Don 2002; mem. Egypt Exploration Soc., Royal Musical Asscn. *Recordings:* Mozart Sacred Music, Elgar Church Music. *Publications:* Catalogue of Egyptian Antiquities in the British Museum III, Musical Instruments 1976, Wagner 1980, Wagner, in Heritage of Music III 1989, Elgar in Manuscript 1990, Elgar 1993, Music and Dance in Pharaonic Egypt in Civilisations of the Ancient Near East IV 1995, Elgar and Chivalry 2002. *Honours:* Hon. DMus (City Univ.) 1985, Hon. DHist (Russian State Univ. for Humanities, Moscow) 2000; Liveryman, Worshipful Co. of Musicians 1977. *Address:* 54 Hornton Street, London W8 4NT, England.

ANDERSON, (Evelyn) Ruth; composer and flautist; b. 21 May 1928, Kalispell, Montana, USA. *Education:* University of Washington, Columbia and Princeton Univs with Earl Kim and Ussachevsky; further studies with Nadia Boulanger, Darius Milhaud and Jean-Pierre Rampal. *Career:* Flautist with the Totenberg Instrumental Ensemble, the Portland and Seattle Symphony Orchestras and the Boston Pops Orchestra during the 1950s; Orchestrator for NBC Television and Broadway shows; Teacher of Composition and Electronic Music at Hunter College, New York, from 1966. *Compositions include:* The Pregnant Dream, 1968; DUMP, Collage, 1970; 3 Studies, 1970; State of the Union Message, Collage, 1973; Conversations, 1974; Dress Rehearsal, 1976; I Come Out of your Sleep, 1979; Mixed Media: Centering, Dance, for 4 performers and live electronics, 1979; Sound Sculptures: Sound Environment, 1975; Time and Tempo, 1984. *Recordings include:* 1750 Arch, 1977; Opus One, 1981; CRI, 1997, 1998; XI, 1998. *Honours:* Five MacDowell Colony Fellowships, 1957–73; Fulbright Scholarships, 1958, 1959; Martha Baird Rockefeller Fund; Alice M Ditson Fund. *Address:* c/o ASCAP, ASCAP Building, 1 Lincoln Plaza, New York, NY 10023, USA.

ANDERSON, Sylvia; Singer (Mezzo-Soprano); b. 1938, Denver, Colorado, USA; m. Matthias Kuntzsch. *Education:* Studied at the Eastman School with Anna Kaskas and at the Cologne Musikhochschule with Ellen Bosenius. *Career:* Debut: Cologne 1962, as Fyodor in Boris Godunov; Sang at the Hamburg Staatsoper, 1965–69, notably as Ophelia in the 1968 premiere of Searle's Hamlet; Bayreuth Festival, 1970–71; Salzburg Festival, 1973, in the premiere of De Temporum fine Comoedia by Orff; Guest appearances in Zürich, Stuttgart, Frankfurt, Düsseldorf, Brussels, Barcelona, Trieste and Amsterdam; Bayreuth 1970–71, as Schwertleite, Magdalena and Flosshilde; US engagements at the Metropolitan and New York City Operas, and in San Francisco, Washington and Santa Fe; Repertoire included Operas by Gluck, Purcell, Rossini, Verdi, Wagner and modern composers; Many concert appearances. *Recordings:* Schubert Masses; De Temporum fine Comoedia.

ANDERSON, Thomas Jefferson, Jr; Composer and Music Educator; b. 17 Aug. 1928, Coatesville, Pennsylvania, USA; m., 3 c. *Education:* BMus, West Virginia State College, 1950; MEd, Pennsylvania State University, 1951; Studied Composition with Scott Huston, Cincinnati Conservatory of Music, 1954; PhD, University of Iowa, 1958; With Philip Bezanson and Richard Hervig; With Darius Milhaud, Aspen School of Music, 1964. *Career:* Teacher, Instrumental Music, High Point, North Carolina Public Schools, 1951–54; Instructor, West Virginia State College, Institute, West Virginia, 1955–56; Professor of Music, Chairman of Music Department, Langston (Oklahoma) University, 1958–63; Professor of Music, Tennessee State University, Nashville, 1963–69; Orchestrated first complete performance of Treemonisha by Scott Joplin, 1972; Composer-in-Residence, Atlanta, Georgia, 1971–72; Professor of Music, Chairman, Music Department 1972–80, Chair, Austin Fletcher Professor of Music 1976–90, Emeritus 1990, Tufts University, Medford, Massachusetts; Doctor of Music, Honoris Causa, Bridgewater State College, 1991; Scholar-in-Residence, The Rockefeller Foundation, Study and Conference Centre, Bellagio, Italy, 1984, 1994; fellowship, John Simon Guggenheim Foundation, 1988; Fellow, National Humanities Centre, Research Triangle Park, North Carolina, 1996–97. *Compositions include:* Stage, The Shell Fairy, operetta, 1976–77; Re-Creation for 3 Speakers, Dancer and 6 Instruments, 1978; Spirtuals, for orchestra, jazz quartet, chorus, children's choir, tenor and narrator, 1979; Soldier Boy, Soldier, opera, 1982; Walker, chamber opera with words by Derek Walcott, 1992; Orchestral, Introduction and Allegro, 1959; Classical Symphony, 1961; 6 Pieces for Clarinet and Chamber Orchestra, 1962; Symphony in 3 Movements, 1964; Songs of Illumination, song cycle, 1990; Whatever Happened to the Big Bands, 1991; Bahia, Bahia, for chamber orchestra, 1991; Spirit Songs commissioned by Yo-Yo Ma, for cello and piano, 1993; Here in the Flesh, hymn, 1993; 7 Cabaret Songs, for jazz singer, 1994; Flute, viola, cello and piano, Broke Baroque for violin and piano, 1996; Shouts, 1997; Huh? What did you say? for solo clarinet, string trio and solo violin, 1998; Boogie Woogie Fantasy for solo piano, 1999; Game Play for flute, viola, cello, harp, 2002; Slavery Documents for chorus, orchestra, soloists, 2002. *Recordings:* Chamber Symphony: London Philharmonic Orchestra, James Dixon conductor; Variations on a Theme by M B Tolson; Contemporary Chamber Ensemble, Arthur Weisberg conductor; Squares: Baltimore Symphony Orchestra, Paul Freeman conductor; Intermezzi, Videmus, Vivian Taylor, Artistic Director. *Honours:* Honorary DMA, College of the Holy Cross, 1983 and St Augustine's College, 1996; Honorary DM, West Virginia State College, 1984 and Bridgewater State College, 1991; Honorary DFA Northwestern University, 2002. *Address:* 111 Cameron Glen Drive, Chapel Hill, NC 27516, USA.

ANDERSON, Valdine; Singer (soprano); b. 1965, Canada. *Career:* Appearances with Edmonton Opera as Mozart's Blonde and Pamina, and with Vancouver Opera as Micaela; Contemporary repertory includes Lutoslawski's Chatefleurs et Chantefables (composer conducting), Michael Torke's Book of Proverbs, Gorecki's Symphony of Sorrowful Songs (Vancouver Symphony Orchestra) and the Maid in Powder Her Face by Thomas Adés (premiere, at the Cheltenham Festival); Varèse Offrandes with the BBC Scottish Symphony Orchestra, Berg's Altenberhlieder, Benjamin's A Mind of Winter, Kurtag's The Sayings of Peter Bornemisza; Season 1997 with Carmina Burana (Edmonton Symphony Orchestra), Messiah in Winnipeg and a Maxwell Davies premiere with Vancouver New Music; Other repertory includes Britten's Spring Symphony (Aldeburgh, 1995); Beethoven's Ninth (Toronto Symphony Orchestra) and Ein Deutsches Requiem; Sang Suzel in the premiere of Dr Ox's Experiment by Bryars, ENO, 1998; Oliver Knussen's Where the Wild Things Are and Higglety, Pigglety, Pop! at the London Proms, 2002. *Current Management:* Ingpen & Williams Ltd, 7 St George's Court, 131 Putney Bridge Road, London, SW15 2PA, England.

ANDERSON-JAQUEST, Tommie Crowell, BMus, MA, MMus, DMus, PhD; American singer (soprano), academic and musician (piano); *Principal Lecturer, Regents Business School*; b. 22 Feb. 1941; m. Gordon N. Jaquest 1993. *Career:* various professional solo recitals, concerts and operatic appearances, USA; has sung with the Chicago Lyric Opera and San Francisco Opera; major roles include Lady Billows (Albert Herring), Countess (Marriage of Figaro), title role in Suor Angelica, Nedda (Pagliacci), Magda (The Consul), Pamina (The Magic Flute), title role in Medea, Antonia (Tales of Hoffmann), Marschallin (Der Rosenkavalier); econ. analyst, Int. Coffee Org., London; Principal Lecturer and Academic Leader, Regent's Business School, London; writing and lecturing in the fields of music, int. relations; mem. American Guild of Musical Artists, Incorporated Soc. of Musicians (UK), Royal Inst. of Int. Affairs (UK), Higher Educ. Acad. (UK). *Address:* Regents Business School, Regents' College, Regents' Park, London, NW1 4NS, England (office); 29 Little Meadow, Loughton, Milton Keynes, Bucks. MK5 8EH, England (home). *Telephone:* (20) 7487-7676 (office); (1908) 240988 (home). *Fax:* (20) 7487-7602 (office); (1908) 240988 (home). *E-mail:* Andersot@regents.ac.uk (office); tscanderson@msn.com (home). *Website:* www.regents.ac.uk (office).

ANDERSSON, Anders; Singer (Tenor); b. 1954, Sweden. *Education:* Studied at the Stockholm Music High School and Ave Opera Studio of the Royal Opera. *Career:* Debut: As Erland in Singoalla by de Frumerie, also at Savonlinna, Stockholm, 1989; Sang Gunnar in Den Fredlose by Inger Wikstrom at Ulriksdal, 1989; As Gudmund in Stenhammar's Gildet pa Solhaug at Norrlands operan, 1990; Title role in a revival of J G Naumann's Gustaf Wasa, Stockholm, 1992; Sang Samson, and the Emperor in Turandot, Folkoperan, Stockholm, 1993; Concert appearances and teaching engagements. *Recordings:* Gustaf Wasa. *Address:* c/o Kungliga Teatern, PO Box 16094, 10322 Stockholm, Sweden.

ANDERSSON, B. Tommy; Conductor and Composer; b. 26 July 1964, Borås, Sweden. *Education:* Royal College of Music, Stockholm. *Career:* Debut: Le nozze di Figaro, Södra Teatern, Stockholm, 1992; Recurrent engagements with opera houses in Stockholm, Göteborg, Malmö, Umeå, Vadstena and Karlstad, including Die Geisterinsel (Reichardt), 1992; Fidelio (Beethoven), 1997; Il Prigioniero (Dallapiccola), 1997; Un ballo in maschera (Verdi), 1998; Wozzeck (Berg), 1999; Orlando (Handel), 2000; The Cunning Little Vixen (Janáček), 2000; Macbeth (Sandström), 2001; Lulu (Berg), 2002; Recurrent concert engagements with all big

orchestras and most chamber orchestras in Sweden; Guest conducting in Germany, the United Kingdom, Switzerland, Netherlands, Finland, Denmark, Norway, Iceland, Uruguay, Czechoslovakia, Romania and Hungary; First performance of more than 120 works, including 11 operas; Artistic Director for KammarensembleN, an ensemble for contemporary music, 1994–99; Principal Conductor of Stockholm Symphonic Wind Ensemble, 1998–, Prof. of Orchestral Studies at Gothenburg Univ. School of Music, 2003–; mem. Fellow of the Royal Swedish Academy of Music; Swedish Composers Association; Swedish Section of ISCM; Swedish Conductors Association. *Compositions:* Concerto for Piano, Winds and Percussion, 1984; Stabat Mater, 1985; Te Deum, 1987; Impromptu for Clarinet and Vibraphone, 1987; Sonata for Percussion and Piano, 1987 Conflicts for Percussion Ensemble, 1988; Intrada for Winds and Percussion, 1989; A Bed of Roses for Percussion Ensemble, 1989; Concerto for Horn and Orchestra, 1993; Dark Shadows for Recorder and Marimba, 1990; Apollo, Concerto for Percussion Solo and Orchestra, 1995; Antique for Male Voice and Piano, 19999; Satyricon for Large Orchestra, 2000; Sonnet XVIII for mixed choir a cappella, 2002; Games for Gito for Wind Quintet, 2002; Reflections, Concerto for Soprano Saxophone and Orchestra, 2003.. *Recordings:* Including music by Atterberg, Hallén, Hallström, Nysteom and Auber; Several recordings of Swedish contemporary music with a.o. Swedish Radio Symphony Orchestra, Royal Stockholm Philharmonic Orchestra and KammarensembleN.. *Honours:* Swedish Royal Academy Scholarships 1990, 1993; Crusell Award for Young Conductors, 1993; Sten Frykberg Award, 1994; Crystal Prize for Interpretation of Contemporary Music, 1995; Swedish Composers Association Interpreters Prize, 1998. *Current Management:* Svenska Konsertbyrån AB. *Address:* Jungfrugatan 45, 114 44 Stockholm, Sweden. *E-mail:* bta@chello.se.

ANDERSSON, Laila; Singer (Soprano); b. 30 March 1941, Losen, Blekinge, Sweden; m. Ulf Palme, 1984. *Education:* Studied with Sylvia Mang-Borenberg, Ragnar Hulten, and Hjordis Schymberg in Stockholm. *Career:* Royal Opera Stockholm from 1964, as Susanna, Leonore (Il Trovatore), Mathilde (Guillaume Tell), Madama Butterfly, Jenůfa and Sophie; Sang in the premieres of Herr von Hancken by Blomdahl 1965 and Granskibbutzen by Karkoff, 1975; Sang the title role in Berg's Lulu, 1977; Frequent visits to the Drottningholm Festival from 1967 (Gustaf Adolf och Ebba Brahe by the Abbé Vogler, 1973); Guest engagements at the Edinburgh Festival 1974, Copenhagen, Wiesbaden, Helsinki and Oslo; Sang Tosca at Stockholm, Grenoble and Bonn, 1977, Salome at the Metropolitan (debut, 1981), Gelsenkirchen, Vienna, Rio de Janeiro, Berlin and Montreal, 1985; Sang Brünnhilde at Århus, Denmark, 1987; Fidelio at Washington and Montreal, 1988; Sang Tiresias in the premiere of Backanterna by Daniel Börtz, 1992; as Elektra, Stockholm Opera, 1993; Stockholm 1994, in the premiere of Schederin's Lolita; Member of the Nya Bjorling Vocal Quartet; Chairman, Theatre Order, 750 Sisters; Member of Royal Swedish Academy of Music. *Honours:* Singer of the Royal Court, 1985; Litteris et Artibus, 1992. *Address:* Köpmantorget 10, 111 31 Stockholm, Sweden.

ANDERSZEWSKI, Piotr; Concert Pianist; b. 4 April 1969, Warsaw, Poland. *Education:* Studied at the Conservatories of Lyon and Strasbourg, University of Southern California in Los Angeles; Chopin Academy, Warsaw. *Career:* recitals in Poland, USA and France; Wigmore Hall, London debut, Feb 1991; Further British engagements include the Harrogate Festival, 1991 and concerts with the Royal Liverpool Philharmonic and Hallé Orchestras; Festival Hall debut with the London Philharmonic conducted by Franz Welser-Möst; Recordings for Polish radio and television; European recital tour, Autumn 1992; Regular duo partner with violinist Viktoria Mullova, 1992–93 season; Edinburgh Festival debut in recital, 1994; Concert performances with City of Birmingham Symphony Orchestra, Sept 1994, Ulster Orchestra, Feb 1995, Lahti Symphony, Oct 1994 and National Symphony Orchestra of Ireland, May 1995. *Recordings:* Recital with Viktoria Mullova: Prokofiev, Sonata for Violin and Piano No. 1 Op 80; Debussy, Sonata for Violin and Piano; Janáček, Sonata for Violin and Piano; Brahms Sonatas for Piano and Violin; Bach, Beethoven and Webern, solo; Bach, keyboard works. *Honours:* Chosen as one of five internationally known young pianists to receive International Piano Foundation Scholarship at IPF on Lake Como, Italy, 1994–95. *Current Management:* Askonas Holt Ltd, Lonsdale Chambers, 27 Chancery Lane, London, WC2A 1PF, England. *Telephone:* (20) 7400-1700. *Fax:* (20) 7400-1799. *E-mail:* info@askonasholt.co.uk. *Website:* www .askonasholt.co.uk.

ANDONIAN, Andrea; Singer (Mezzo-Soprano); b. 1950, Colorado, USA. *Education:* Studied at Florida and Ohio Universities and Operastudio in Cologne. *Career:* Sang at Cologne Offenbach Theatre, 1977–78; Engaged at Krefeld-Monchengladbach, 1978–85; Has sung with Deutsche Oper Berlin, 1986–; Guest appearances, Germany and elsewhere, in repertory including Cherubino, Dorabella, Ramiro in Mozart's Finta Giardiniera, Idamante in Idomeneo and Annio in La Clemenza di Tito; Humperdinck's Hansel, Siebel in Faust, the Prince in Massenet's

Cendrillon, and Britten's Lucretia and Hermia; Sang Urbain in Les Huguenots with Deutsche Oper, 1987, and at Covent Garden, 1991; Paris Opéra-Comique, 1992, in Rossini's L'Occasione fa il Ladro, La Scala di Seta, La Cambiale di Matrimonio and Il Signor Bruschino; Mrs Sedley in Peter Grimes at Cologne, 1994; Season 1999–2000 at Cologne, as Annina in La Traviata, Wellgunde in Götterdämmerung, Larina in Eugene Onegin and Sycorax in Spohr's Faust. *Recordings include:* Schumann's Requiem. *Address:* Deutsche Oper Berlin, Richard Wagnerstrasse 10, 1000 Berlin 10, Germany.

ANDRADE, Levine; Violist; b. 1954, Bombay, India. *Education:* Studied Violin at the Yehudi Menuhin School with Robert Mastres; Studied with Menuhin and Nadia Boulanger; Viola studies with Patrick Ireland; Royal Academy of Music from 1969 with Frederick Grinke, Max Gilbert, Sidney Griller and Colin Hampton. *Career:* Co-founded the Arditti String Quartet, 1974 and member until 1989; Frequent concerts with the London Symphony Orchestra, Royal Philharmonic, Academy of St Martin-in-the-Fields, the London Sinfonietta and the London Mozart Players; Guest Professor at the Royal Academy of Music; Many concerts with the Arditti Quartet in Europe and North America; Festival engagements at Aldeburgh, Bath, BBC Proms, Berlin, Budapest, Paris, Venice Biennale, Vienna and Warsaw; Music in Camera programme, BBC television, 1987; Series of seven recitals for Radio 3, 1987; Played in all Schoenberg's quartets in a single recital, Queen Elizabeth Hall, London, November, 1988; Took part in the premieres of quartets by Georges Aperghis, 1985; Berio, Divertimento for Trio, 1987; Bose, No. 3, 1989; Britten, Quartettino, 1983; Gavin Bryars, 1985; Bussotti, 1988; John Cage, Music for 4, 1988; Davies, 1983; Ferneyhough, Numbers 2 and 3; Gubaidulina No. 3, 1987; Harvey, Numbers 1 and 2; Hindemith Quartet 1915, 1986; Kagel, 1987; Nancarrow, No. 3, 1988; Ohana, No. 2, 1982; Pousseur, No. 2, 1989; Premiered quartets by Michael Finnissy, Michael Nyman and Tim Souster. *Recordings include:* Henze's Five String Quartets. *Honours:* Deutsche Schallplattenpreis for Henze Quartets, 1987. *Address:* 80 Whellock Road, London W4 1DJ, England.

ANDRADE, Rosario; Singer (Soprano); b. 6 April 1951, Veracruz, Mexico. *Education:* Studied in Veracruz and Accademia di Santa Cecilia, Rome. *Career:* Debut: As Madama Butterfly, Mexico City, 1974; Sang at Glyndebourne Festival as Donna Elvíra in Don Giovanni, 1977–78; Many guest appearances in Europe and North America, Brussels, 1978, Lyon (in Cavalli's La Calisto), 1979, Warsaw, 1981–82, Connecticut, 1987, Pittsburgh and Mississippi Opera Company, 1988; Metropolitan Opera debut, 1982, as Antonia in Les Contes d'Hoffmann, returning as Manon, 1986; Other roles include Mimi, Micaela, Marguerite, Donna Anna, Aida and Maddalena in Andrea Chénier; Concert repertory includes Marguerite in La Damnation de Faust. *Address:* c/o Metropolitan Opera, Lincoln Center, New York, NY 10023, USA.

ANDRASOVAN, Tibor; Conductor and Composer; b. 3 April 1917, Slovenska, Lupca, Czechoslovakia; m. (1) Ivanka Dimitrová, 16 July 1948, 1 s., 2 d., (2) Mária Kutejová, 21 Oct 1973. *Education:* Pedagogic University; Pupil of E Suchon and A Moyses at the Bratislava Conservatory; The Master School of Music, Prague. *Career:* Professor, 1941; Conductor since 1945; Repetiteur, Slovak National Theatre, 1946–57; Artistic Director, Slovak Folk Artistic Ensemble, 1955–58, 1969–74. *Compositions:* Stage: Gelo the Joker, 1957; The Quadrille, Operetta, 1960; The White Disease, Music Drama, 1967; The Gamekeeper's Wife, Opera, 1973–74; The King of Fools, Musical, 1982; Ballets: Orpheus and Euridice, 1948; The Song of Peace, 1949; The Festival of Solstice, 1985; Orchestral: Little Goral, Overture, 1961; Concerto for Cembalo and Strings, 1977; Chamber: String Quartet, Folklorica, 1976; Partita Romantica for Piano, 1983; Tokajik, Cantata for Soprano, Chorus and Orchestra, 1975; The Echoes of the Uprising Mountains, Song Cycle for Narrator, Soprano, Tenor and Piano, 1979; The Recruit Songs, Song Cycle, 1973; The Pines Whispered, Song Cycle for Soprano and Piano, 1976; The Woman and Muse, Song Cycle for Bass-Baritone and Piano, 1978; Also Incidental Music, Film Scores and Music for Folk Ensembles. *Publications:* Tonal System of Slovak Music, 1996. *Address:* c/o SOZA, Bratislava 3, 821 08 Bratislava, Slovakia.

ANDRASSY, Gabor; Singer (Bass); b. 1951, Transylvania, Romania. *Career:* Sang at the Berne Opera, 1979–81, then at Krefeld, 1981–87; Karlsruhe, 1988–90, with guest appearances at Geneva, Théâtre des Champs-Elysées Paris, as Fafner in The Ring and at Seattle (1989) as Wagner's Daland; Has performed widely in France as King Marke at Nantes, Hunding and Hagen at Nice, and Fafner, Boris Godunov and Ivan Khovansky at Strasbourg, 1991–92; Seattle Opera in The Ring and as Rocco in Fidelio; Other roles include the Commendatore in Don Giovanni, Boris Godunov and King Philip, King Henry and Grand Inquisitor; Season 1995–96, as Walter in Luisa Miller at Strasbourg and Capitan in the premiere of Florencia en las Amazonas by Daniel Cátan at Houston; Sang in Der Freischütz at Seattle, 1999, and Sarastro in Die Zauberflöte; Season 2000–01 as Dansker in Billy Budd, at Seattle and

Los Angeles. *Address:* c/o Merle Hubbard Management, 133 West 71st Street, Apt 8a, New York, NY 10023, USA.

ANDRÉ, Martin; Conductor; b. 10 Dec. 1960, West Wickham, England. *Education:* Studied at the Yehudi Menuhin School, the Royal College of Music and Cambridge University. *Career:* Played with the National Youth Orchestra as Percussionist from 1970; Founded the Mozart Chamber Ensemble at Cambridge and was appointed conductor of the University Orchestra and Chorus, and the University Chamber Orchestra; Conducted his edition of Purcell's King Arthur at Cambridge and the Minack Theatre, Cornwall, 1982; Has worked with the Welsh National Orchestra from 1982, leading Aida, Jenůfa, Ernani, Rigoletto, Madama Butterfly, Un Ballo in Maschera, Eugene Onegin and Il Barbiere di Siviglia; Vancouver Opera from season 1986–87 with Janáček's From the House of the Dead and Cunning Little Vixen, Ariadne auf Naxos, La Traviata and La Bohème; Seattle Opera 1987, Carmen; London concert debut January 1987, with the English Chamber Orchestra at the Barbican; Further concerts with the Scottish Chamber Orchestra and the Northern Sinfonia; Scottish Opera from 1989, The Merry Widow and La Clemenza di Tito; Conducted The Love of Three Oranges at the English National Opera, 1990, and at Teatro São-Carlos, Lisbon, 1991; Madama Butterfly for Opera North; World premiere, The Bacchae by John Buller for ENO, 1992; Music Director, English Touring Opera, 1993; Recent notable debuts include Verdi's Un Ballo in Maschera at the Royal Opera House Covent Garden; Conducted the United Kingdom premiere of Matthus' Cornet Christoph Rilke's Song of Love and Death for Glyndebourne Touring Opera; The Makropulos Case for GTO in 1997; Engagements with the New Israeli Opera include conducting Don Pasquale and Love for Three Oranges; The Magic Flute for Opera Northern Ireland, 1998. *Current Management:* Ingpen & Williams Ltd, 7 St George's Court, 131 Putney Bridge Road, London, SW15 2PA, England.

ANDRÉ, Maurice; Trumpeter; b. 21 May 1933, Ales, France. *Education:* Studied with his father and with Sabarich at the Paris Conservatoire. *Career:* Soloist with the Concerts Lamoureux, 1953–60, L'Orchestre Philharmonique of ORTF (French Radio), 1953–62, and the orchestra of the Opéra-Comique, Paris, 1962–67; Many concert performances in Europe; North American Professor at the Paris Conservatoire, 1967–78; Composers who have written for him include Boris Blacher (Concerto 1971), Charles Chaynes, Marcel Landowski, Jean-Claude Eloy, Harold Genzmer, Bernhard Krol, Jean Langlais (Chorals for trumpet and organ), Henri Tomasi and André Jolivet (Arioso barocco, 1968). *Honours:* First prizes at International Competitions in Geneva, 1955 and Munich, 1963.

ANDREAE, Marc Edouard; Conductor; b. 8 Nov. 1939, Zürich, Switzerland. *Education:* Zürich Conservatory; University of Zürich; Study with Nadia Boulanger in Paris, with Franco Ferrara in Rome. *Career:* Chief Conductor, Broadcasting Orchestra of Italian Switzerland, Lugano, 1991; Regular Guest, numerous European, US and Japanese symphony orchestras and at festivals, Paris, Berlin, Lucerne, Vienna, Salzburg, Ascona, Brescia; Numerous concerts and operas for television including Eurovision; Music and Artistic Director of the Angelicum in Milan, Italy, 1990–93; mem, Swiss Music Edition (past president). *Recordings:* With NDR Hamburg, Hamburg Philharmonic Orchestra, Munich Philharmonic, Cologne Radio Symphony Orchestra, Bamberg Symphony, National Orchestra of France, NHK Symphony Orchestra, Tokyo. *Publications:* Music of Weber, Rossini, Donizetti, Schumann, Lortzing, Tchaikovsky and Liszt. *Honours:* 1st Prize, Swiss National Competition, 1966; 2 Grand Prix, Italian Record Critics, 1974; LP Techno Distinction, Tokyo, 1975. *Address:* Via Moretto 6, 6924 Sorengo, Switzerland. *E-mail:* marc.andreae@bluewin.ch.

ANDREESCU, Horia; Conductor; b. 18 Oct. 1946, Brasov, Romania. *Education:* Studied at the Brasov School of Music and the Bucharest Conservatoire; Further study with Hans Swarowsky in Vienna and Sergiu Celibidache in Munich. *Career:* Chief Conductor of Ploiesti Philharmonic, 1974–87; Permanent Guest Conductor, Mecklenburgische Staatskapelle Schwerin, 1979–90; Permanent Guest Conductor, Radio Symphony Orchestra, Berlin, 1981–91; Permanent Guest Conductor, Dresden Philharmonia, 1983–91; Joint Artistic Director of the George Enescu Philharmonic at Bucharest, 1987–; Professor, Academy of Music, 1988–90; Conductor, Virtuosi of Bucharest Chamber Orchestra; Conductor, Bucharest George Enescu Philharmonic Orchestra; Chief Conductor and General Music Director, Bucharest National Radio Orchestra, 1992–. *Recordings include:* The first complete orchestral work of George Enescu; Recorded for Radio Bucharest, Radio East Berlin (Haydn, Brahms, Wagner, Stravinsky, Hindemith, Prokofiev), Radio Leipzig (Bartók), BBC (Haydn, Mozart, Beethoven, Tchaikovsky), Radio Madrid, Radio Copenhagen and Radio Suisse Romande. *Honours:* Prizewinner at Geneva and Copenhagen Competitions. *Address:* c/o Radio Romania, Directia Formatilor Muzicale, Str General Berthelot 62–68, Bucharest, Romania.

ANDREEV, Andrei; Violinist; b. 1950, Crimea, USSR. *Career:* Co-founded Rachmaninov Quartet under auspices of Sochi State Philharmonic Society, Crimea, 1974; Many concerts in former Soviet Union; From season 1975–76 tours to Switzerland, Austria, Bulgaria, Norway and Germany; Participation in Shostakovich Chamber Music Festival, Vilnius, 1976 and festivals in Moscow and St Petersburg; Repertoire includes works by Haydn, Mozart, Beethoven, Bartók, Brahms, Schnittke, Shostakovich, Boris Tchaikovsky, Chalayev and Meyerovich. *Honours:* With Rachmaninov Quartet: Prizewinner at First All-Union Borodin String Quartet Competition, 1987. *Current Management:* Sonata, Glasgow, Scotland. *Address:* 11 North Park Street, Glasgow, G20 7AA, Scotland.

ANDREW, Jon; Singer (Tenor); b. 1936, New Zealand. *Education:* Studied in Auckland. *Career:* Debut: As Don José in Carmen, Auckland, 1982; Sang with Sadler's Wells Opera, 1963–68, as Ricardo, Radames, Don José, and Agrippa in the British premiere of The Fiery Angel (New Opera Company); Sang in Germany, 1969–, notably in Karlsruhe, Mannheim and Düsseldorf in Wagner roles including Siegmund in Die Walküre; Glyndebourne Festival as the Italian Singer in Rosenkavalier, 1965; Covent Garden, 1967 and 1974, as Froh in Das Rheingold and Dimitri in Boris Godunov; Further appearances with Welsh National Opera, Handel Opera Society, 1967, and at San Diego as Siegmund and Otello, 1975–76; Also sang Siegmund at Madrid, Berlin Staatsoper, and with English National Opera, 1975; Wexford Festival as Pedro in Tiefland, 1978; Further engagements at La Scala, Milan, and Nice and Santiago, 1981; Other roles have included Turiddu, Erik in Fliegende Holländer, Max in Der Freischütz, Laca in Jenůfa, and Bob Boles in Peter Grimes. *Address:* c/o English National Opera, St Martin's Lane, London WC2 4ES, England.

ANDREW, Sarah; Bassoonist; b. 1975, England. *Education:* Royal College of Music, with Martin Gatt, and in Vienna. *Career:* Co-founded Aurora Ensemble 1997, with wide range of wind quintet repertory, including commissioned works performed throughout Britain; Venues include ORF studios, Vienna, Purcell Room (London), Cheltenham and English Music Festivals, South Bank Centre Rimsky-Korsakov Festival and International Akademia Prag-Wien-Budapest; BBC Radio 3 Young Artists' Forum Series; Education project Sounds Exciting (2000) and performance visits to educational establishments; Schubert's Octet at the National Gallery London 2001 with Piros Ensemble (founded 2000). *Honours:* Prizewinner, Music d'Ensemble Competition, Paris 2001. *Address:* c/o Royal College of Music, Prince Consort Road, London, SW7 2 BS, England.

ANDRIESSEN, Louis; Composer; b. 6 June 1939, Utrecht, Netherlands. *Education:* studied with his father, Hendrik Andriessen, with Kees van Baaren, Royal Conservatory of Music, The Hague 1957–62, with Luciano Berio, Milan 1962–63. *Career:* Trilogy of the Last Day received the United Kingdom premiere at the 1999 London Prom concerts; Passion—The Music of Louis Andriessen, concert series at South Bank Centre, London 2002. *Compositions:* Stage: Reconstructie, Opera, 1968–69, in collaboration with 4 colleagues; Matthew Passion, 1976; Orpheus, 1977; George Sand, 1980; Orchestral: What it's Like for live Electronic Improvisers and 52 Strings, 1970; Uproar for 16 Winds, 6 Percussionists and Electronic Instruments, 1970; The 9 Symphonies of Beethoven for Promenade Orchestra and Ice Cream Bell, 1970; Symphony for Open Strings, 1978; Velocity, 1983; De Stijl, 1985; Chamber: Flute Sonata, 1956; Percosse for Flute, Trumpet, Bassoon and Percussion, 1958; A Flower Song I for Violin, 1963, II for Oboe, 1963; and III for Cello, 1964; Double for Clarinet and Piano, 1965; Souvenirs d'enfance for Piano and Tape, 1966; The Persistence for Piano and Winds, 1972; Felicitatie for 3 Trumpets, 1979; Disco for Violin and Piano, 1982; Overture to Orpheus for Harpsichord, 1982; Piano Pieces; Nocturne for Soprano and Chamber Orchestra, 1959; Il Principe for 2 Choirs, Winds, Piano and Bass Guitar, 1974; The State for 4 Women's Voices and 27 Instruments, 1972–76; Mausoleum for 2 Baritones and Chamber Ensemble, 1979, revised 1981; Time for Choir and Orchestra, 1981; Madrigal Concerto for Choir, 1984; 3 Dancing on the Bones for children's voices and ensemble, 1997; Collaboration with Peter Greenaway in 1991 television series Not Mozart: M is for Man, Music, Mozart; Rosa, a horse opera, 1994; Trilogy of the Last Day for orchestra, 1998; Writing to Vermeer, music theatre, 1999. *Address:* Boosey & Hawkes Music Publishers, 295 Regent Street, London, W1, England.

ANDSNES, Leif Ove; Norwegian pianist; b. 7 April 1970, Stavanger. *Education:* Music Conservatory of Bergen with Jiri Hlinka. *Career:* debut, Oslo 1987; British debut, Edinburgh Festival with the Oslo Philharmonic and Mariss Jansons 1989; US debut, with Cleveland Symphony and Neeme Järvi; concerts include performances with the London Symphony Orchestra, Berlin Philharmonic, Orchestre de Paris, Tonhalle Orchester, New York Philharmonic, Cleveland Orchestra, San Francisco Symphony and others; performed Grieg's Piano Concerto in A minor at The Last Night of the Proms 2002; recitals include appearances at the Wigmore Hall and Barbican Hall, London, Herkulessaal, Munich,

Konzerthaus, Vienna, Concertgebouw, Amsterdam, Carnegie Hall, New York. *Recordings include:* Grieg A Minor and Liszt A Major concerti; Janáček, Solo Piano Music; Chopin, Sonatas and Grieg, Solo Piano Music; Brahms and Schumann works for piano and viola with Lars Anders Tomter; Haydn Piano Concerti (Gramophone Award, 1999); Liszt piano works, Britten and Shostakovich piano concertos. *Honours:* Commdr, Royal Norwegian Order of St Olav 2002, First Prize at the Hindemith Competition, Frankfurt, Gilmore Artist Award 1980, Gramophone Award for Best Concerto Recording 2000, for Best Instrumental Recording 2002. *Current Management:* Kathryn Enticott, IMG Artists, Lovell House, 616 Chiswick High Road, London, W4 5RX, England. *Telephone:* (20) 8233-5800 (office). *Fax:* (20) 8233-5800 (office). *E-mail:* artistseurope@imgworld.com. *Website:* www.imgartists.com; www.andsnes.com (home).

ANGAS, Richard; Singer (Bass); b. 1942, Surrey, England. *Education:* Studied in Vienna and London. *Career:* Debut: With Scottish Opera as Fafner in The Ring; Appearances with the Welsh National Opera and at Covent Garden; Performances in Germany as King Mark and King Henry, Baron Ochs, Osmin, Rocco and Mephistopheles; Engagements throughout Europe, Israel, Australia and South America in Oratorio and Recital; English National Opera as Monteverdi's Seneca and Pluto, Basilio in Il Barbiere di Siviglia, Pimen (Boris Godunov), Daland (The Flying Dutchman) and Jupiter (Orpheus in the Underworld); The Mikado, 1990, and Bartolo in Figaro; The Doctor in a new production of Wozzeck, 1990; Has sung in the world premiere of Birtwistle's The Mask of Orpheus, 1986, and the British premiere of The Making of the Representative for Planet 8 by Philip Glass, 1988; Sang in The Love for Three Oranges with Opera North, Leeds; Debut in Paris, Opéra Garnier, as Pontius Pilate in Höller's Master and Margarita, 1991; Debut in USA as Rocco in Fidelio, 1994; Tosca and The Mikado for ENO, 1994; Mulhouse, 1996, as the Commandant in From the House of the Dead; Season 1998 with Pistol in Falstaff at Garsington and Sarastro at Belfast; Season 1999–2000 as Waldner in Arabella for Opera North, Aga in Martinu's Greek Passion at Bregenz (repeated at Covent Garden) and the High Priest in Nabucco for ENO. *Address:* c/o Musichall Ltd, Vicarage Way, Ringmer, East Sussex, BN8 5 LA, England.

ANGEL, Marie; Singer (Soprano); b. 30 July 1953, Pinnaroo, South Australia; m. David Freeman. *Career:* Has sung with Opera Factory London and Opera Factory Zürich in Così fan tutte (Fiordiligi, also televised); The Knot Garden (Denise); Birtwistle's Punch and Judy (Pretty Polly); Aventures by Ligeti; Mahagonny Songspiel; Gluck's Iphigenia operas (title role); Donna Anna and Mozart's Countess Fiordiligi, 1991, all 3 televised; Other roles include Euridice in Monteverdi's Orfeo and Hecate and the Oracle of the Dead in the premiere of The Mask of Orpheus, 1986 for the English National Opera; Mozart's Queen of Night for Welsh National Opera; Musetta for Opera North; Sang Berio's Recital at South Bank and Jo-Ann for Glyndebourne Touring Opera in Tippett's New Year; Created the role of Morgana Le Fay in the premiere of Birtwistle's Gawain at Covent Garden, May 1991; Sang Monteverdi's Poppea in a new production by Opera Factory, 1992; Has also sung Donna Anna for Victoria State Opera and appeared with Houston Grand Opera and at the New York City Opera; Created the role of Esmerelda in Rosa, the opera by Peter Greenaway and Louis Andriessen at the Music Theatre, Amsterdam, 1994; Sang Hecate in The Mask of Orpheus at the Festival Hall, London, 1996 (recorded) English National Opera 1996, as Countess de la Roche in Zimmermann's Die Soldaten, and at Basle, 1998–99; Kagel's Aus Deutschland, Dichterin and Kammersängerin, Basle and Holland Festivals, 1997; In Satyricon by Maderna, sang Fortunata for Basle and toured to Venice, 1998; Sang title role in Die Lustige Witwe at Basle Theatre, 1999. *Recordings:* Gawain, 1994; Andriessen's Rosa, recorded and filmed, 1998; Prospero's Books, P. Greenaway, recorded and filmed (Nyman), 1989; Hannover, Europera 5, John Cage, 2001/2002; Nyman's Facing Goya, Spanish Tour, recorded 2002. *Current Management:* Allied Artists Agency, London. *Address:* 42 Montpelier Square, London SW7 1JZ, England.

ANGEL, Ryland; Singer (Countertenor); b. 22 Nov. 1966, England. *Education:* Vocal studies with David Mason in London and Gerald Lesne. *Career:* Appearances in Handel's Amadigi at the Karlsruhe Festival, 1996–97, Purcell's Dido and Aeneas, Blow's Venus and Adonis with René Jacobs at De Vlaamse Opera; Peri's Euridice with Opera Normandie, the medieval Play of Daniel in New York and a staged production of Caldara's oratorio La Santissima Annunziata with Le Parlement de Musique at the Louvre, Paris; Settings of Orfeo by Monteverdi and Gluck with English National Opera and English Touring Opera, Purcell Fairy Queen with the English Bach Festival and for ENO, 1998; Further concerts with La Chapelle Royale, Le Concert Spirituel and Les Jeunes Solistes; Festival appearances at Lucerne, BBC Proms, Athens, Lufthansa Baroque Festival (London) and Venice International Contemporary Music Festival; Solo recitals in Paris; Sang Zephyrus in Mozart's Apollo et Hyacinthus, Britten

Theatre, London, 1998; Further engagements include: Bertarido in Handel's Rodelinda with Il Combattimento in Amsterdam, and a concert tour with La Fenice; Season 1999–2000 with the title role in Handel's Radamisto at St Louis Festival and Non Erat Bonus by Brixi with Musiktheater Transparant. *Address:* 39 Rue de Rivoli, 75004, Paris, France.

ANGELICH, Nicholas; American pianist; b. 1970, Cincinnati, OH. *Education:* Conservatoire Nat. Superieur de Musique, Paris, France with Aldo Ciccolini, Yvonne Loriod and Michel Beroff, numerous masterclasses. *Career:* resident pianist of the Fondation Internationale per il Pianoforte, Cadennabia, Italy 1996; performed at the Fourth Annual Miami Int. Piano Festival of Discovery 2001. *Recordings:* Rachmaninov: Etudes–Tableaux, Brahms: Sonates pour alto et piano (with Laurent Verney), Ravel: Miroirs, Gaspard de la nuit, La Valse, Liszt: Les Années de pèlerinage, Brahms: Piano Trios (with Renaud and Gautier Capuçon). *Honours:* Second Prize R. Casadesus Int. Competition, Cleveland 1989, Fifth Prize Tokyo Int. Competition, First Prize Gina Bachauer Int. Competition 1994, Second Prize Umberto Micheli Competition 1997. *Address:* c/o Virgin Classics, EMI Group plc, 27 Wrights Lane, London, W8 5SW, England.

ANGELO, Mariana; Singer (Soprano); b. 1954, Sofia, Bulgaria. *Education:* Studied at Conservatoire of Sofia. *Career:* Sang at the Komische Oper Berlin, 1978–84; Berne Opera, 1984–86; Has appeared at the Nationaltheater Mannheim, 1987–, and has sung as guest at Dresden, Karlsruhe, Sofia, Graz, Nancy, Paris, Ghent and Antwerp; Lausanne Opera, 1989, as Liu in Turandot; Other roles include Verdi's Leonora (Il Trovatore and La Forza del Destino), Amelia Grimaldi, Aida, Violetta and Desdemona; Puccini's Mimi, Manon Lescaut and Madama Butterfly; Nedda, Tatiana and Mathilde in Guillaume Tell; Sang Aida at the Berlin Staatsoper, 1991. *Address:* c/o Music International, 13 Ardilaun Road, London N5 2QR, England.

ANGERER, Paul; Conductor, Violist and Composer; b. 16 May 1927, Vienna, Austria; m. Anita Rosser, 18 June 1952, 2 s., 2 d. *Education:* Studies in Theory, Piano, Violin and Organ, Hochschule für Musik, Vienna and at Vienna Conservatory, 1941–46. *Career:* Violist, 1947, Principal Violist, 1953–56, Vienna Symphony Orchestra; Violist, Zürich Tonhalle Orchestra, 1948, Orchestre de la Suisse Romande, Geneva, 1949–52; Director, Chief Conductor, Vienna Chamber Orchestra, 1956–63; Composer, Conductor, Burgtheater, Vienna, 1960–64; Principal Conductor, Bonn City Theatre, 1964–66; Permanent Guest Conductor, Haydn Symphonic Orchestra of Bolzano and Trento, 1960–90; Musical Opera Director, Ulm Theatre, 1966–68, Salzburg Landestheater, 1968–72; Artistic Director, Hellbrunn Festival, 1970–71; Director, SW German Chamber Orchestra, 1972–82; Professor, Hochschule für Musik, Vienna, 1983–92; Numerous tours as Guest Conductor; Leader, Concilium Musicum; Editor, Baroque and Pre-Classical Music and works by Joseph Lanner; 1984–2001 Moderator ORF, on 2001 Radio Stephansdom. *Compositions include:* Orchestral pieces; Chamber works; Viola and Piano Concertos; A Dramatic Cantata; Television Opera; Works for Organ, Harp, Viola, Harpsichord. *Recordings:* Numerous recordings as soloist, conductor and instrumentalist. *Honours:* Nestroy-Ring der Stadt Wien, 1999. *Address:* Esteplatz 3, 1030 Vienna, Austria.

ANGERMÜLLER, Rudolph Kurt; German/Austrian Music Editor and Music Librarian; *General Secretary, International Mozarteum Foundation;* b. 2 Sept. 1940, Bielefeld, Germany; m. Hannelore Johannböke, one s., one d. *Education:* MA; PhD 1970; Graduate, Försterling Conservatory of Music, Bielefeld. *Career:* Assistant, Musicology Institute, University of Salzburg; Chief Editor, New Mozart Edition, and Librarian, International Mozarteum Foundation, 1972–; Chief of Research Department International Mozarteum Foundation, 1981–; General Secretary, International Mozarteum Foundation, 1988–; Professor, 1993; mem, International Musicological Society; Society for Music Research; Austrian Musicological Society. *Publications:* Untersuchungen zur Geschichte des Carmen-Stoffes, 1967; Antonio Salieri, Sein Leben und seine weltlichen Werke unter besonderer Berücksichtigung seiner grossen Opern, 3 Vols, 1971, 1972, 1974; W A Mozarts Musikalische Umwelt in Paris, 1778, Eine Dokumentation, 1982; Mozart's Operas, 1988; Ich johannes chrisostomus Amadeus Wolfgangus Sigismundus Mozart, 1991; Mozarts Reisen in Italien, 1994; Franz Xaver Wolfgang Mozart, Reisetagebuch 1819–1821, 1994; Mozart auf der Reise nach Prag, Dresden, Leipzig und Berlin, 1995; Geistliche Werke von Antonio Salieri in der Hofkapelle in Wien, 1996; Francesco Benucci: Mozarts erster Figaro und Guglielmo, 1998; Pariser Don Juan: Rezensionen 1805–1806, 1998; Antonio Salieri: Dokumente seines Lebens, 2000. *Contributions:* Bulletin of the International Mozarteum Foundation; Mozart-Jahrbuch; Haydn-Jahrbuch; Die Musikforschung; Österreichische Musikzeitschrift; Wiener Figaro; Musical Times; Deutsches Jahrbuch für Musikwissenschaft; Numerous other professional journals and books. *Honours:* Socio Accademia degli Agiati Rovereto, 1995; Socio d'onore R Accademia Filarmonica di Bologna,

1997; Stella d'oro al valor mozartiano, 2001. *Address:* 92A Moosstrasse, 5020 Salzburg, Austria. *Telephone:* 826735 (office).

ANGUS, David Anthony; Conductor; b. 2 Feb. 1955, Reading, England; m., 1 d. *Education:* Surrey University; Leeds University; Royal Northern College of Music. *Career:* Debut: Chorister at King's College, Cambridge; Chorus Master and Staff Conductor, Glyndebourne, 1989–95; Freelance; Conducted most major orchestras in the United Kingdom including London Philharmonic Orchestra; Many performances at Glyndebourne; Appears regularly in Italy; Principal conductor of the Symphony Orchestra of Flanders; Broadcasts with BBC Orchestra and BBC Singers; Conductor, British Opera premieres, Brighton Festival; Appeared in Denmark, Norway, Finland, Austria, Belgium and France; Specialises in Mozart, romantic and 20th Century opera. *Recordings:* Britten's Curlew River; Modern British choral and orchestral works with London Philharmonic Orchestra. *Honours:* 3 Ricordi prizes for opera conducting, 1985–87; Finalist, Leeds conductors Competition, 1988. *Current Management:* Patrick Garvey Management, Top Floor, 59 Lansdowne Place, Hove, East Sussex BN3 1FL, England.

ANHALT, Istvan, OC; Canadian composer, writer and educator; *Professor Emeritus, Queen's University;* b. 12 April 1919, Budapest, Hungary. *Education:* Royal Hungarian Acad. of Music, Conservatoire National de Musique de Paris, France, composition with Zoltán Kodály and Nadia Boulanger, conducting with Louis Fourestier, piano with Soulima Stravinsky. *Career:* appointed as a Lady Davis Fellow and Asst Prof. to Faculty of Music, McGill Univ., Montréal, Canada 1949, later Assoc. and full Prof.; carried out experimentation and compositional work at electronic music laboratory of National Research Council of Canada, Ottawa, Columbia-Princeton Electronic Music Centre and Bell Telephone Laboratories; installed electronic music studio and appointed dir; mem. of the senate, McGill Univ. 1968; appointed Visiting Slee Prof., New York State Univ. at Buffalo 1969; Head of Music, Queen's Univ., Kingston, ON 1971–81, Emeritus Prof. 1984–. *Compositions include:* dramatic works: Arc en Ciel 1951, Cycle of 4 musico-dramatic (operatic) works: La Tourangelle: A Musical Tableau 1975, Winthrop: A Musical Pageant 1983, Traces (Tikkun): A Pluri-drama for solo lyric baritone and orchestra 1995, Millennial Mall (Lady Diotima's Walk): A Voice-Drama for the Imagination for solo lyric soprano, choir and orchestra 1998; orchestral: Interludium 1950, Symphony No. 1 1958, Symphony of Modules, Symphony No. 2 1967, Simulacrum 1987, Sparkskraps 1988, Sonance Resonance (Welche Töne?) 1989, Twilight Fire (Baucis' and Philemon's Feast) 2001, The Tents of Abraham (A Mirage-Midrash) 2003; chorus: The Bell-Man 1954, revised 1980, Three Songs of Love 1951, revised 1998, Three Songs of Death 1954, Journey of the Magi 1951, Thisness a duo-drama for mezzo-soprano and pianist 1986, Cento for choir with tape; chamber music: Funeral Music, for chamber ensemble 1951, Trio for violin, cello and piano 1953, Sonata for violin and piano 1954, Sonata for piano 1951, Fantasia for piano 1954, Electronic Tape: Electronic Composition Nos 1–4 1959–62, Foci for soprano and chamber orchestra with tape, Doors... Shadows (Glenn Gould in Memory) String Quartet 1992. *Recordings include:* Cento, Fantasia for Piano, Foci, Sonata for Violin and Piano, Trio for violin, cello and piano. *Publications:* Alternative Voices, Essays on Contemporary Vocal and Choral Composition 1984, Istvan Anhalt Pathways and Memory (eds Robin Elliott and Gordon E. Smith) 2001, numerous other publications and papers. *Honours:* DMus hc (McGill Univ.) 1982, Hon. LLD (Queen's Univ.) 1992, personal papers and manuscripts held in the Music Division, National Library of Canada, Ottawa, ON. *Address:* 274 Johnson Street, Kingston, ON K7L 1Y4, Canada (home).

ANIEVAS, Agustin; Pianist and Teacher; b. 11 June 1934, New York, USA. *Education:* Commenced piano lessons at age 4 with his mother; was a pupil of Steuermann, Samaroff and Marcus at the Juilliard School of Music, New York. *Career:* Formal debut as soloist with the Little Orchestra Society, New York, 1952; Later toured North and South America, Australia and the Far East; Professor of Piano, Brooklyn College of the City University of New York, 1974–. *Recordings:* For Angel-EMI and Seraphim, notably of music by Bartók, Prokofiev, Rachmaninov, Chopin and Liszt. *Honours:* Concert Artists Guild Award, 1959; First Prize, Dimitri Mitropoulos Competition, 1961. *Address:* c/o Music Department, Brooklyn College of the City University of New York, Brooklyn, NY 11210, USA.

ANISIMOV, Alexander; Singer (bass); b. 1960, Krasnoyarsk, Russia. *Education:* Studied with Ekaterina Yofel in Krasnoyarsk. *Career:* Joined the Bolshoi Theatre Moscow and sang major roles in Glinka's Ivan Susanin and Tchaikovsky's Iolanta; Season 1992 as the Grand Inquisitor in Don Carlos at La Scala and the Old Prisoner in Lady Macbeth of the Mtsensk District at the Opéra Bastille, Paris; Prince Gremin in Eugene Onegin, at the Théâtre du Châtelet; Season 1993–94 as the Commendatore at La Scala, Sparafucile, in Rigoletto at the Berlin Staatsoper and the Glagolitic Mass with the London Philharmonic; US debut at the New York Met in Lady Macbeth and also at the Bastille; Season 1994–95 as Il Bonzo in Madama Butterfly at the Bastille; Season

1995–96 as Lodovico in Otello, Sparafucile and Commendatore in Don Giovanni at the Met, King Dodon in The Golden Cockerel at Nice, the Verdi Requiem in Tel-Aviv and Oroveso in Norma at the Carnegie Hall; Season 1996–97 as Timur in Turandot at Chicago and the Metropolitan Opera House, New York and Pimen in Boris Godunov at Frankfurt; Season 1997–98 Boris in Boris Godunov with Milwaukee Symphony Orchestra, Ramphis in Aida at Dallas, Pimen in Boris Godunov at Frankfurt and concerts at the Colmar International Festival; Season 1998–99 as Oroveso in Norma with the Canadian Opera Company, King Rene in Iolanthe in Toronto, Verdi's Requiem with Madrid Philharmonic Orchestra and Antwerp Opera, Tom in Un Ballo in Maschera at San Diego; Inquisitor in Don Carlo at Palm Beach; Season 1999–2000 with Basilio in Il Barbiere at Las Palmas and in Don Carlo at Barcelona; Further engagements include: Lady Macbeth of Mtsensk at the Dresden Staatsoper, Boris Godunov at Seattle, Fiesco in Simon Boccanegra in Nancy. Recordings include: Russian Church Music; Don Carlos; Eugene Onegin. Honours: Prizewinner, Glinka Competition, 1987; Prizewinner Tchaikovsky Competition, 1990. Current Management: Askonas Holt Ltd, Lonsdale Chambers, 27 Chancery Lane, London, WC2A 1PF, England. Telephone: (20) 7400-1700. Fax: (20) 7400-1799. E-mail: info@askonasholt.co.uk. Website: www.askonasholt.co.uk.

ANISIMOVA, Tanya; cellist; b. 15 Feb. 1966, Grozny, Russia; m. Victor Taratuta 1989. Education: Central Music School, Moscow, 1975–84; Studied Cello with Natalia Shakhovskaya, Igor Gavrysh, Galina Kozolupov, graduated with honours, 1984–89; Assistantship, Cello, String Quartet, Graduate School, Moscow Conservatory, 1989–90; Studied with George Neikrug, Artist's Diploma, Boston University, 1990–92; Graduate Studies with Aldo Parisot, Yale University School of Music, 1992–. Career: Solo Recitals, Russia, Massachusetts, Virginia, Washington DC, and Soloist with Orchestras, Young Performers Series, Moscow, Minsk, Gorky, Ulianovsk, Lugansk and local Philharmonic Orchestras, Russia, and Central Massachusetts Symphony, USA, 1985–91; With Glazunov String Quartet, Russia, Poland, Greece, Japan, Germany; Artist-in-Residence, Banff Music Festival, 1993. Recordings: Moscow State Radio, 1987; With Glazunov String Quartet, Athens Radio, Greece, 1989; WBGH Public Radio, Boston, Massachusetts, 1991; WCUW Radio, Worcester, Massachusetts, 1992. Publications: contrib. to magazines, reviews, journals. Honours: 1st Prize, Concertino Praha International Competition, Prague, 1981; 1st Prize, All-Union String Quartet Competition, Voronezh, Russia, 1987. Address: c/o Aldo Parisot, Yale University, School of Music, PO Box 2104A, Yale Station, New Haven, CT 06520, USA.

ANISSIMOV, Alexander; Russian conductor; b. 1947. Education: St Petersburg Conservatory and Moscow Conservatory. Career: Principal Conductor, Bolshoi Theatre, Belarus 1980; f. and conductor, Nat. Youth Orchestra of Belarus; Principal Guest Conductor, Radio Telefís Éireann (RTÉ) Nat. Symphony Orchestra, Dublin 1995–98, Principal Conductor 1998–2001, Conductor Emeritus 2001–; regular guest conductor with Nat. Youth Orchestra of Ireland; Principal Conductor, Belorussian State Philharmonic 1996, Nat. Philharmonic Orchestra of Belarus 2001, Opera Rostov-on-the-Don, Russia 2003; he has conducted world-wide, including the Bolshoi Theatre (Moscow), Kirov Opera (St Petersburg), Opéra Bastille (Paris), Staatsoper Hamburg, Komische Oper Berlin, State Opera of South Australia, Norske Opera (Oslo), North Holland Sinfonia, Concertgebouw (Amsterdam), Opera Ireland, Teatro del Liceo (Barcelona), Teatro Colón (Buenos Aires), San Francisco Opera, Houston Grand Opera, La Fenice (Venice), Florence Opera; Hon. Pres. Wagner Soc. of Ireland 2002–. Recordings: Beethoven Symphony No. 9 in D minor, Alexander Konstantinovich Glazunov Orchestral Works Vol. 1 (Raymonda, Op. 57), Vol. 5 (Symphonies Nos 2 & 7 "Pastoral"), Vol. 7 (Symphonies Nos 1 "Slavyanskaya" & 4), Vol. 8 (The Seasons, Op. 67, Op. 52, Op. 81), Vol. 12 (Symphonies Nos 3 & 9), Vol. 13 (Symphony No. 6, Op. 58 Symphonic Poem "The Forest", Op. 19), Vol. 15 (Symphonies Nos 5 & 8), Rachmaninov Symphony No. 1 and Op. 13 Caprice Bohémien and Op. 12, Rachmaninov Symphony No. 2, Rachmaninov Symphony No. 3 and Op. 44 Mélodie in E Polichinelle, Rachmaninov The Bells Op. 35, Mahler Symphony No. 2 "The Resurrection", Anton Rubinstein The Demon, Tchaikovsky Symphony No. 5 and Concerto No. 1, Classical Favourites Vols 1 and 2, Vivat Opera Live 1999. Honours: Hon. DMus (Nat. Univ. of Ireland) 2001. Current Management: Askonas Holt Ltd, Lonsdale Chambers, 27 Chancery Lane, London, WC2A 1PF, England. Telephone: (20) 7400-1700. Fax: (20) 7400-1799. E-mail: info@askonasholt.co.uk. Website: www.askonasholt.co.uk. Address: c/o RTE National Symphony Orchestra, Radio Telefís Eireann, Donnybrook, Dublin 4, Ireland. Website: www.alexanderanissimov.com.

ANNEAR, Gwynneth; singer (soprano, mezzo-soprano); b. 1939, Tailenbend, South Australia. Education: University of Adelaide, Royal College of Music, London. Career: debut, sang in Amahl and the Night Visitors while at the Royal College of Music, 1964; Sang the title role in Anna Bolena by Donizetti at the 1965 Glyndebourne Festival; Tour of Italy with Italian Company, 1968, in Fidelio and Così fan tutte; Has sung at the Camden Festival and with opera companies in Australia; Frequent broadcasts and concert engagements; Glyndebourne Festival 1970 and 1973, First Lady in Die Zauberflöte. Address: c/o Australian Opera, Sydney Opera House, Sydney, NSW, Australia.

ANRAKU, Mariko; Harpist; b. 7 March 1970, Japan. Education: BM, MM, Juilliard School, New York; Royal Conservatory of Music, Toronto, Canada. Career: Debut: Soloist, Toronto Symphony; Recitals, Weill Recital Hall, Carnegie Hall, New York; Jordan Hall, Boston; LA County Museum; Opéra-Comique, Paris; Casals and Kioi Halls, Tokyo; Soloist, Many orchestras; Spoleto Festival, Italy; Newport Festival; Festival of the Sound; Takefu Festival, Tanglewood; Banff Festival; Harpist, Metropolitan Opera Orchestra. Recordings: Mariko Anraku harp recital I and II, 1997 and 1998. Honours: 3rd prize and the Pearl Chertok prize, The International Harp Contest, Israel, 1992; 1st prize, The 1st Harp contest, Japan, 1989; Pro Musicis International Award, 1993. Address: c/o The Metropolitan Opera Orchestra, Lincoln Center, NY, NY 10023, USA.

ANSELL, Gillian; Violist; b. 1968, Auckland, New Zealand. Education: Studied at Royal College of Music, London, and with Igor Ozim and the Amadeus Quartet in Cologne. Career: Played with Kent Opera Orchestra, Chamber Orchestra of Europe and Philharmonia, 1984–; Co-Founded New Zealand String Quartet, under auspices of Music Federation of New Zealand, 1987; Debut Concert, Wellington, May 1988; Concerts at Tanglewood School, USA, Banff International Competition, Canada; Performances with Lindsay Quartet at International Festival of the Arts, Wellington, 1990; Soloist with New Zealand Symphony Orchestra; Artist-in-Residence, Victoria University, Wellington; Tour to Australia for Musica Viva Australia, 1990; New Zealand tours, 1992; Concerts in New York, 1993. Current Management: Ingpen & Williams Ltd, 7 St George's Court, 131 Putney Bridge Road, London, SW15 2PA, England.

ANTHONY, Charles; Singer (Tenor); b. 15 July 1929, New Orleans, Louisiana, USA. Education: Studied voice with Dorothy Hulse at Loyola University; Continued training with Riccardo Picozzi and Giuseppe Ruisi in Italy. Career: Won Metropolitan Opera Auditions of the Air, 1952; Metropolitan debut 1954, as Missail in Boris Godunov; Later sang Ernesto in Don Pasquale, Almaviva in Il Barbiere di Siviglia, David in Die Meistersinger and Nemorino in L'Elisir d'amore; Has sung nearly 2000 performances with Metropolitan company; Also sang as guest in Dallas, Santa Fe and Boston; Sang Eisslinger in a new production of Die Meistersinger at the Metropolitan, 1993. Address: c/o Metropolitan Opera House, Lincoln Center, New York, NY 10023, USA.

ANTHONY, Susan; Singer (Soprano); b. 1959, Michigan, USA. Education: Zürich Opera Studio. Career: Appearances in opera throughout Europe from 1985; Berlin Staatsoper from 1991 as the Trovatore Leonora, Ines in L'Africaine; Elena in Vespri Siciliani and Eva in Die Meistersinger, 1994; Sang Strauss's Daphne, 1991, and Leonore in Fidelio, 1996, Rome Opera; Bregenz, 1995; Season 1995–96 as Tatiana at Cologne and Elsa in Lohengrin at the Vienna Staatsoper; Geneviève in Chausson's Roi Arthus at Bregenz and Cologne and Freia in Das Rheingold at La Scala and Hamburg; Season 1997 in Fidelio at Buenos Aires; Season 1998: as Leonore in Paris; Marie in Wozzeck at Montpellier; Sang Maria in Strauss's Friedenstag at Dresden; Senta in Tokyo and Fidelio in Vienna; Season 1999 as Elsa in Paris and Vienna; Ariadne and Empress in Frau ohne Schatten in Dresden; Liebe der Danaë in Munich and Marie in Wozzeck in Cologne; Season 2000 with Salome in Bologna, Ariadne at La Scala and Frau ohne Schatten in Dresden; Die Frau ohne Schatten at Vienna Staatsoper, Barcelona; World premiere of 'K' by Phillipe Manouri, Bastille Opéra; Brünnhilde (Siegfried) at Grand Théâtre, Geneva; Elektra at Santa Fe Opera; Season 2002–04 in Paris as the Empress in Strauss's Frau and also in Vienna and Dresden and new productions in the Deutsche Oper, Berlin, Washington, Rome, Barcelona and two in Tokyo; Senta in Mardrid, 2003, with Barenboim. Recordings: Traumgörge (Zemlinsky); Roi Arthus (Chausson). Honours: Openwelt Singer of the Year, 1995–96, 1997–98. Current Management: Laifer Artists Management (NY); IMG Artists (Paris). Address: c/o Laifer Artists Management, 410 West 24th Street, Suite 2i, New York, NY 10011-1369, USA.

ANTINORI, Nazzareno; Singer (Tenor); b. 1950, Anzio, Italy. Education: Accademia di Santa Cecilia, Rome. Career: Sang Pinkerton, Rome Opera, 1979, repeated at Verona Arena, 1983; Appearances at Naples, Trieste, Macerata and Palermo; Sang Forresto in Atilla by Verdi, La Scala, Milan, 1991; Other roles have included Verdi's Ismaele, Alfredo, Malcolm and Don Carlos, Cavaradossi, Maurizio in Adriana Lecouvreur and Števa in Jenůfa; Cavaradossi at Macerata, 1995; Season 1998 as Ismaele at Rome and Verona. Recordings: Tosca and Madama Butterfly. Honours: Winner, Maria Callas Competition, 1980. Address: c/o Rome Opera, Piazza B Gigli 8, 00184 Rome, Italy.

ANTOINE, Bernadetta; Singer (Soprano); b. 8 March 1940, Nancy, France. *Education:* Studied at the Conservatories of Nancy and Paris. *Career:* Debut: Theatre Region Parisienne 1967, as Musetta; Has sung at the Grand Opéra and the Opéra-Comique, Paris and in Lyon, Marseille, Toulouse, Rouen, Hamburg, Brussels, Lisbon and Geneva; ORTF, Radio France, in the 1972 premiere of Don Juan ou l'amour de la geometrie by Semenov; Strasbourg 1974, in the premiere of Les Liaisons Dangereuses by Prey; Repertoire includes works by Gluck, Mozart, Puccini, Berlioz, Debussy, Poulenc, Britten and Prokofiev; Many concert appearances; Member of the Saarbrücken Opera, 1985–86.

ANTOKOLETZ, Elliott Maxim, BA, MA, PhD; American musicologist and writer; *Professor of Musicology, University of Texas at Austin;* b. 3 Aug. 1942, Jersey City, NJ; m. Juana Canabal 1972; one s. *Education:* Juilliard School of Music, Hunter Coll., Graduate School and Univ. Center CUNY. *Career:* Lecturer and mem. of faculty string quartet, Queens Coll., CUNY 1973–76; Prof. of Musicology 1976–, Head Musicology Division 1992–94, Univ. of Texas at Austin; co-ed., Int. Journal of Musicology 1992–; mem. American Musicological Soc. *Publications:* The Music of Béla Bartók: A Study of Tonality and Progression in Twentieth-Century Music 1984, Béla Bartók: A Guide to Research 1988, Twentieth Century Music 1992, Bartók Perspectives (ed. with V. Fischer and B. Suchoff) 2000, Musical Symbolism in the Operas of Debussy and Bartók 2004; contrib. three chapters to The Bartók Companion, one chapter to Sibelius Studies; contrib. to scholarly books and professional journals. *Address:* c/o School of Music, University of Texas at Austin, Austin, TX 78712, USA.

ANTONACCI, Anna-Caterina; Italian singer (soprano); b. 5 April 1961, Ferrara. *Education:* Bologna Conservatory. *Career:* initial experience in Bologna Comunale Theatre Chorus; debut as Rosina, Arezzo 1986; subsequent roles include Flora in La traviata, Bologna, Dorliska in Torvaldo and Dorliska, Savona 1988, Elcia in Mosè in Egitto, Rome 1988 and London 1994, Horatia in Gli Orazi ed i Curiazi, Cimarosa, Rome 1989 and Lisbon, Elizabeth in Maria Stuarda, Bari 1989, Ninetta in La gazza ladra, Philadelphia 1989, and Zelmira, Rome 1989; sang Fiordiligi at Venice and Macerata, Adalgisa at Catania, Polyxena in Manfroce's Ecuba and the title role of Paisiello's Elfrida at Savona 1990; Anaide in Mosè, Bologna 1991, Semiramide Catania 1991, Elisabetta, regina d'Inghilterra, Naples 1991, title role of Ermione, Rome 1991, London 1992 (also Buenos Aires, San Francisco concert performance and Glyndebourne for two seasons), Elena in La donna del lago, Amsterdam 1992; other roles at this time include Mayr's La rosa bianca e la rosa rossa at Bergamo, Polissena in Manfroce's Ecuba; sang Donna Elvira in Ferrara, Gluck's Alceste in Vienna and Berlin and Gluck's Armide at La Scala; an Adalgisa in Catania 1990, which she later sang at San Francisco and in Naples 1995; sang Monteverdi's Poppea in Bologna, Milan and Buenos Aires, the title role in Gluck's Armide at La Scala 1996, and Angelina in La Cenerentola, Toronto 1996; season 1999 included Fiordiligi at Naples, Rodelinda at Glyndebourne, Donna Elvira at Vienna and Ravenna, and Gluck's Armide and Paisiello's Nina at La Scala; season 2001–02, sang Dido at Florence, Marchesa del Poggia in Un giorno di regno at Bologna, and Elisabetta in a concert performance of Maria Stuarda in Edinburgh; recent roles include Agrippina at the Barbican 2003, Cassandra in Les Troyens at the Chatelet Theatre 2003, Carmen for Glyndebourne 2004, Cherubini's Medea at the Chatelet in 2005. *Recordings include:* Paisiello's Elfrida, Mayr's La Rosa Bianca e La Rosa Rossa, Polissena in Manfroce's Ecuba, Fiordiligi in Così fan tutte, Ermione, Puccini's Messa di Gloria, Stravinsky's Pulcinella, Pergolesi's Stabat Mater. *Honours:* won Verdi Competition, Busseto 1987, Pavarotti Competition, Philadelphia 1988, Maria Callas Competition 1988. *Current Management:* Askonas Holt Ltd, Lonsdale Chambers, 27 Chancery Lane, London, WC2A 1PF, England. *E-mail:* info@askonasholt.co.uk (office).

ANTONIOU, Theodore; Composer, Conductor and Teacher; b. 10 Feb. 1935, Athens, Greece. *Education:* Studied violin, voice and theory, National Conservatory, Athens, 1947–58; Composition with Yannis Papaioannou, Hellenic Conservatory, 1956–61; Composition and Conducting with Gunter Bialas, Munich Hochschule für Musik, 1961–65; Attended the Darmstadt Summer Courses, 1963–65. *Career:* Active as a Conductor with various contemporary music groups; Teacher of Composition and Orchestration, Stanford University, 1969–70, University of Utah, 1970, Philadelphia Music Academy 1970–75, Berkshire Music Center, Tanglewood, 1975, University of Pennsylvania, 1978, Boston University, 1979–. *Compositions:* Stage Periander, opera, 1977–79; Ballets, Bacchae, 1980, and The Magic World, 1984; Music Theatre pieces, including The Imaginary Cosmos, ballet, 1984; Bacchae, opera, 1992; Monodrama for actor and ensemble, 1992; Oedipus at Colonus, opera, 1998; Mixed media scores; Incidental music to various dramas; Film Scores; Orchestral, Concerto for clarinet, trumpet, violin and orchestra, 1959; Antithese, 1962; Piano Concertino, 1962; Jeux for cello and strings, 1963; Micrographies, 1964; Violin Concerto, 1965; Kinesis ABCD for 2 string orchestras, 1966; Threnos for wind ensemble,

piano, percussion and double bass, 1972; Double Concerto for percussion and orchestra, 1977; The GBYSO Music, 1982; Various Choral Works, Solo Vocal Pieces and Chamber Music with Tape including Ode for soprano and ensemble, 1992. *Recordings:* As Conductor of his own works and of works by other contemporary composers. *Honours:* Many commissions and awards. *Address:* c/o Music Department, Boston University, Boston, MA 02215, USA.

ANTONIOZZO, Alfonso; Singer (Bass-Baritone); b. 1963, Italy. *Education:* Studied with Sesto Bruscantini. *Career:* Sang at the Montepulciano Festival from 1986, Florence and Torre del Festival, 1987, Bologna, 1988; Has appeared widely in Italy in Turandot (as Ping), Rossini's L'occasione fa il ladro, Adina and Il Barbiere di Siviglia; San Francisco, 1992, as Taddeo in L'Italiana in Algeri; Other roles include Pistol in Falstaff, Bizet's Don Procopio, Schaunard in La Bohème and Patroclus in Paer's Achille; Season 1995–96 as Mustafà in Rossini's Adina at Rome and Don Magnifico at Monte Carlo, San Francisco and Dallas 1996, as Leporello. *Recordings include:* Don Procopio and Cimarosa's I traci amanti (Bongiovanni). *Address:* c/o PG & PM, 7 Whitehorse Close, Royal Mile, Edinburgh, EH8 8BU, Scotland.

ANTONSEN, Ole Edvard; Trumpeter; b. 25 April 1962, Ringsaker, Norway. *Education:* Studied with Harry Kvaebek at the Norwegian State Academy of Music, Diploma 1982. *Career:* Played with the Oslo Philharmonic 1982–90; Solo career from 1990; Concerto appearances with Atlanta Symphony, Dresdner Philharmonie, Stuttgart Chamber Orchestra. I Fiamminghi Chamber Orchestra, Wurtembergisches Kammerorchester, Swedish Radio Symphony Orchestra, Oslo and Bergen Philharmonic Orchestras in Sweden, Kioi Sinfonietta, Tokyo, Israel Chamber Orchestra, Orchestre de la Suisse Romande, Leipzig Radio Orchestra, Prague Symphony, London Festival Orchestra, Royal Swedish Chamber Orchestra and Cantilena (Scotland); Tour of 15 different countries 1989, including Russia and Brazil; Season 1990 with Paris debut (Oslo Philharmonic) and engagements in Spain, USA (New York and Washington recitals), West Germany and Switzerland; Plays jazz and contemporary music as well as the standard classics; 1995–96 included a recital debut with Wayne Marshall at the Royal Festival Hall, London; Appearances for the Istanbul International, City of London and Bermuda Festivals, concerts in Germany, Switzerland, Scandinavia and Austria and a 6th tour of Japan; 1997 included a return to the Schleswig-Holstein Festival, a tour with Dmitri Sitkovetsky and the New European String Orchestra and engagements in Europe, North America and the Far East; Recital with the Norwegian Chamber Orchestra, conducted by Iona Brown; with Wayne Marshall and the ECO, 1992; Berlin Philharmonic Orchestra with M Jansons and M Rudy for EMI. *Recordings include:* Tour de Force, 1993; Trumpet and piano recital with Wolfgang Sawallisch in 1996. *Honours:* First prize at the 1987 CIEM-Competition in Geneva; Laureat of the 1989 UNESCO Competition in Bratislava; Norwegian Grammy; Arets, Spillemann, for his Norwegian recording, Tour de Force, 1992.

ANTUNES, Jorge, PhD; university professor, composer, conductor and violinist; b. 23 April 1942, Rio de Janeiro, Brazil; m. Mariuga Lisboa Antunes 1969; three s. *Education:* University of Brazil, Instituto Torcuato di Tella, Buenos Aires, Sorbonne, Univ. of Paris, France. *Career:* Prof. of Composition, Dir of Electronic Music Laboratory, Co-ordinator of Composition and Conducting, General Co-ordinator of Nucleus for Studies and Research in Sonology, Univ. of Brasília; television and radio appearances; mem. Academia Brasileira de Música, Brazilian Society for Electroacoustic Music (pres. 2004). *Compositions:* Cromorfonetica, 1969; Tartinia MCMLXX, 1970; Para Nascer Aqui, 1970–71; Macroformobiles 1, 1972–73; Catastrophe Ultra-Violette, 1974; Plumbea Spes, 1976; Congadasein, 1978; Elégie Violette pour Monseigneur Romero, 1980; Qorpo-Santo, opera, 1983; Sinfonia das Diretas, 1984; Dramatic Polimaniquexixe, 1985; Modinha para Mindinha, 1986; Serie Meninos, for young violinist and tape, 1986–87; Amerika 500, 1992; Olga, opera, 1993; Rimbaudiannisia MCMXCV, for children's choir, lights, masks and orchestra, 1994; Ballade Dure, electro-acoustic music, 1995; La beauté indiscrète d'une note violette, 1995; Cantata dos Dez Povos, 1999; Sinfonia em cinco movimentos, 2000; Eloquens, 2003; Toccata Irisée, 2004. *Recordings include:* Jorge Antunes–Musica Eletronica, 1975; Jorge Antunes Com A Orquestra Sinfonica Brasileira, 1978; No Se Mata La Justicia–Jorge Antunes, 1982; Musica Eletronica 70s, Vol. I, 1994; Musica Eletronica 70s, Vol. II, 1995; Musica Eletronica 90s Vol.III, 1997; Savage Songs, early Brazilian electronic music by Jorge Antunes, Pogus, NY, 2001. *Publications:* Sobre a correspondência entre os s. e as cores 1982, Notaçao na música contemporânea 1989, Uma Poética Musical brasileira e revolucionária 2002, Sons Novos para o piano, a harpa eo violão 2004. *Honours:* first prize Premio Angelicum di Milano 1971, Premio Vitae, Brazil 1991, Premio APAC 1992, Prix Musica Criativa 1994, Cidadão Honorário de Brasília 2002; Chevalier, Ordre des Arts et des Lettres 2002. *Address:* Universidade de Brasilia, Departmento de Música, 70910-970 Brasilia,

DF, Brazil. *Fax:* (55) 61-368-1797. *E-mail:* antunes@unb.br. *Website:* www.americasnet.com.br/antunes.

ANTUNES DE OLIVEIRA, Glacy; Concert Pianist; b. 15 Oct. 1943, Goiania, Goias, Brazil. *Education:* Graduated, Conservatory of Music, Federal University of Goias; Master's Degree, National School of Music, Federal University of Rio de Janeiro; PhD, Institute of Arts, Federal University of Goias; Postgraduate work, Rio de Janeiro and USA; Has worked under Professor José Kliass, São Paulo, and at Brigham Young University, Utah. *Career:* Recitals, Solo and Chamber Music, all over Brazil, North and South America, Germany, Switzerland, Austria; Founder, Director, Musika Centro de Estudos, Goiania; President, National Piano Competition, Co-ordinator, Postgraduate Diploma Course in Music, Institute of Arts, Federal University. *Recordings:* 3 as Soloist with Orquestra de Camara de Blumenau. *Address:* Rua 19 No. 32 S Oeste, Goiania, Goias 740001-970, Brazil.

ANZAGHI, Davide; Composer and Teacher; b. 29 Nov. 1936, Milan, Italy. *Education:* Graduated, Milan Conservatory, 1957; Studied Composition with E Pozzoli, A Maggioni, G Ghedini and F Donatoni. *Career:* Teacher of Composition, Milan Conservatory; mem, President of Novurgia (Associazione Italiana per l'Arte, lo Spettacolo, la Cultura, Oggi). *Compositions:* Orchestral: Limbale, 1973; Ausa, 1973; Egophonie, 1974; Aur'ore for chorus and orchestra, 1975–76; Ermosonio, 1978; Anco, 1987; First Piano Concerto, 1987–88; Second Piano Concerto, 1990–91; Concerto Breve for clarinet and strings, 1990–91; Concerto for violin and orchestra, 1992; Third Piano Concerto 1993; Archindò for violin and strings, 1998; Chamber: Limine for string trio, 1971; In-Chiostro for 2 violins and viola, 1975, revised 1982; Alena for 10 wind instruments, 1976; Remota for 7 players, 1977; Alia for bass clarinet and piano, 1980; Oiseau Triste for piccolo and piano, 1980; Soavodia for clarinet and piano, 1980; Eco for cello and piano, 1980; Oniram for soprano and piano, 1980; Tornelli for oboe and piano, 1981; Labia for string quartet, 1982; Ricrio for brass octet, 1982; Soliludio for flute, clarinet, violin, cello and piano, 1982; Mitofania for flute, clarinet, violin, cello, piano and percussion, 1982; For Four for string quartet, 1983; Airy for clarinet, 1983; Halpith for flute, 1984; Elan for 9 instruments, 1984; Pri-ter for string quartet, 1985; Queen That for wind quintet, 1985; Apogeo for 5 instruments, 1987; Tremes for viola and piano, 1988; Viol-Once-All, 3 Pieces for cello, 1988; Settimino for clarinet, horn, bassoon, piano, violin, viola and cello, 1992; Invenzione, Schizzo, Variazioni for guitar, 1994; Elea for violin and piano, 1994; Riturgia for two recitant voices, chorus and orchestra, 1994; Chitattro and Repetita for 4 guitars, 1995; Phantasus for cello and piano, 1995; Ludus for ensemble, 1995; Musica per 3 for violin, cello and piano, 1996; Declinava un'estate inquieta, for recitant, piano and percussion, 1996; D'Ance for accordion; In nomine Filii, Oratorio for recitant, chorus, soprano and ensemble, 1997; Chifla, for flute and guitar, 1997; Il Labirinto di Sangue for recitant, 2 pianos and 2 percussion, 1998; Rondò per Pia for sax soprano, 1999; Piano Pieces: Segni, 1968–70; Ritografia, 1971; Revenants, 1981; Segni e Suoni, 1983; Due Intermezzi, 1983; Due Improvvisi, 1985; Variazioni, 1991; Sèpalo for 4 hands; Marcia Funebre con Variazioni, 1997; Notturni d'Averno, 1999. *Address:* Via Previati 37, 20149 Milan, Italy.

APONTE-LEDÉE, Rafael; Composer and Teacher; b. 15 Oct. 1938, Guayama, Puerto Rico. *Education:* Studies in piano, harmony, counterpoint and composition at Madrid Conservatory, 1957–64 with Cristobal Halffter; Further study with Alberto Ginastera at the Latin American Institute of Higher Musical Studies, Di Tella Institute, Buenos Aires, diploma in 1966. *Career:* Teacher of theory and composition, University of Puerto Rico, 1968–73, and the Puerto Rico Conservatory of Music, 1968–; Promoter of avant-garde music festivals; mem, Musical Director of Latin American Foundation for Contemporary Music. *Compositions include:* Orchestral: Elejia, 1965, revised, 1967, Impulsos, in memoriam Julia de Burgos, 1967, Dos Cuentos Para Orquesta, 1987, Canción De Albada Y Epitafio, 1991; Orchestra and Soloist: Cantata, 1988; Chamber Orchestra: A Flor De Piel with 2 singers; Chamber Opera: El Paseo de Buster Keaton; Solo Instruments: Tres Bagatelas for Guitar, Tema Y Seis Diferencias for Piano; Chamber: Dialogantes for Flute and Viola, 1965; Piano pieces, many other works for various instruments, guitar; Canción de Albada for orchestra, 1991. *Recordings:* Musica de Cámara, 1976; La Canción De Arte Puertorriquena with Margarita Castro, 1989; La Musica De Rafael Aponte Ledée. *Publications:* Tema y seis diferencias; SOMBRAS, Zona de Carga y Descarga; La Ventana Abierta. *Honours:* ASCAP, 1989, 1990, 1991. *Address:* c/o Conservatorio de Musica de Puerto Rico, Apdo 41227, Minillas Station, Santurce, Puerto Rico 00940.

APPEL, Andrew; Harpsichordist; b. 8 June 1951, New York City, USA. *Education:* Duke University, 1969–71; Doctorate, Juilliard School, 1983. *Career:* Debut: Carnegie Recital Hall, 1977; Solo recitals in Europe and USA; Director of Four Nations Ensemble; Festival participation at Spoleto, Aston Magna; Teacher at Temple University, Juilliard, Princeton; Mostly Mozart; mem, American Musical Society;

Early Music America; South Eastern Historical Keyboard Society. *Recordings:* Bach, Works for Harpsichord, 1983; Couperin, Works for Harpsichord, 1989; JB Bach-Bridge, 1987; Couperin, 1991. *Publications:* Gaspard Le Roux–Complete Works, 1989. *Honours:* 1st Prize, Erwin Bodkey Competition, 1977. *Address:* 39 Plaza Street, Brooklyn, NY 11217, USA.

APPELGREN, Curt; Singer (bass baritone); b. 1945, Sweden. *Career:* Began as a violinist and later made his debut as a singer at the Drottningholm Court Theatre as Dulcamara in L'Elisir d'amore; Sang Pogner in Götz Friedrich's production of Die Meistersinger at the Royal Opera in Stockholm; Other Swedish roles include Cimarosa's Maestro di Capella, Jokanaan in Salome and Leporello in Don Giovanni; Sang Oxenstierna in the premiere of Christina by Hans Gefors, 1986; Perugia Festival in Spontini's La Vestale; Sung at Glyndebourne as Rocco and Bottom, and in Peter Hall's productions of Fidelio and A Midsummer Night's Dream; Sang Bottom at the Hong Kong Festival and Rossini's Basilio at Glyndebourne; Appearances with the London Choral Society and the London Philharmonic Orchestra at the Festival Hall; Sang Johann in a revival of Vogler's Gustaf Adolf och Ebba Braha at Drottningholm, 1990; King Mark in Tristan und Isolde at the Festival Hall, London, 1993; Glyndebourne 1995, as Publio in La Clemenza di Tito; Oroveso in Norma at Stockholm, 1997. *Current Management:* Askonas Holt Ltd, Lonsdale Chambers, 27 Chancery Lane, London, WC2A 1PF, England. *Telephone:* (20) 7400-1700. *Fax:* (20) 7400-1799. *E-mail:* info@askonasholt.co.uk. *Website:* www.askonasholt.co.uk.

ARAD, Atar; Violist; b. 1943, Israel. *Career:* Member of the Cleveland Quartet, 1980–87; Regular tours of USA, Canada, Europe, Japan, South America and the Middle East; Faculty of Indiana University, Bloomington; Concerts in Paris, Lyon, London, Bonn, Prague, Brussels and Houston; Appeared at Salzburg, Edinburgh, Aspen, Mostly Mozart and Lucerne festivals; In addition to standard repertory performs works by John Harbison, Samuel Adler, Christopher Rouse, Toru Takemitsu and Solo Sonata for Viola by Atar Arad. *Recordings:* Repertoire from Mozart to Ravel; Recordings in collaboration with Cleveland Quartet, Emanuel Ax and Yo-Yo Ma. *Address:* 1657 Bellemeade Avenue, Bloomington, IN 47401, USA.

ARAGALL, Giacomo; Singer (Tenor); b. 6 June 1939, Barcelona, Spain. *Education:* Studied with Francesco Puig in Barcelona and with Vladimir Badiali in Milan. *Career:* Debut: La Fenice, Venice, 1963 in the first modern performance of Verdi's Jerusalem; La Scala, Milan, in 1963 as Mascagni's Fritz; In 1965 sang in Haydn's Le Pescatrici with Netherlands Opera and at the Edinburgh Festival; Vienna Staatsoper debut in 1966 as Rodolfo in La Bohème; Covent Garden debut in 1966 as the Duke of Mantua; Metropolitan Opera debut in 1968; Guest appearances in Berlin, Italy, San Francisco and at the Lyric Opera Chicago; Sang at San Carlo Opera Naples in 1972 in a revival of Donizetti's Caterina Cornaro; Festival appearances at Bregenz and Orange in 1984 as Cavaradossi and Don Carlos; Sang Gabriele Adorno at Barcelona in 1990 and Don Carlos at the Orange Festival in 1990; Sang Rodolfo at Barcelona in 1991 and Don Carlos at the Deutsche Oper Berlin, 1992; Sang Cavaradossi at the Opéra Bastille, 1994. Other roles include Pinkerton, Romeo in I Capuleti e i Montecchi, Werther, and Gennaro in Lucrezia Borgia. *Recordings:* La Traviata; Lucrezia Borgia; Faust; Rigoletto; Simon Boccanegra; Madama Butterfly. *Address:* c/o Stafford Law Associates, 6 Barham Close, Weybridge, Surrey KT 13 9 PR, England.

ARAIZA, (José) Francisco; singer (tenor); b. 4 Oct. 1950, Mexico City, Mexico; m. (divorced); two s. two d. *Education:* Univ. of Mexico City; vocal studies with Irma Gonzalez and Erika Kubacsek (repertory). *Career:* debut as First Prisoner in Beethoven's Fidelio, Mexico City 1970; with Karlsruhe Opera 1974–78; permanent member of Zürich Opera House 1978–; guest appearances in Vienna, Munich, Hamburg, Berlin, Covent Garden London, Opéra Bastille Paris, La Scala Milan, Rome, Parma, Barcelona, Madrid, San Francisco, Chicago, Buenos Aires and Japan; also at the international festivals of Aix-en-Provence, Orange, Bayreuth, Salzburg (debut in 1980 under Karajan), Edinburgh, Rossini Festival, Pesaro, Schubert Festival, Hohenems, Richard Strauss Festival, Garmisch; operatic repertoire ranges from Mozart and Rossini in 1983 to dramatic Italian and French repertory to Wagner roles such as Lohengrin in Venice 1990 and Walther in Die Meistersinger von Nürnberg with Metropolitan Opera in New York 1993; Season 1999–2000 at the Berlin Staatsoper as Pollione in Norma and Wagner's Walther; Gounod's Roméo at Karlsruhe and Loge in Das Rheingold at Zürich 2000–01; renowned Lieder and concert singer; masterclasses in Munich, Vienna; Prof., Staatliche Hochschule für Musik, Stuttgart, Germany (appointed by Ministry of Baden-Würtenberg) 2003. *Recordings include:* Die schöne Müllerin; All major Mozart roles including Tamino, Belmonte, Ferrando, Don Ottavio and Idomeneo; Il Barbiere di Siviglia, Faust, Les Contes d'Hoffmann, La Bohème, Hagenbach in La Wally, Der Freischütz; Das Lied von der Erde, Beethoven's 9th Symphony, Die Schöpfung and Mozart's Requiem; Arias and Lieder;

Several videos including: La Cenerentola; The Abduction from the Seraglio. *Honours:* Deutscher Schallplattenpreis; Orphee d'Or; Mozart Medal, Univ. of Mexico City; Otello d'Oro: Goldener Merkur, Best Performer's Award, Munich 1996. *Current Management:* Kunstlermanagement, M Kursidem, Tal 15, 80331 Munich, Germany.

ARASON, Jon Runar; Singer (Tenor); b. 29 March 1962, Iceland. *Education:* Studied in Iceland with Magnus Johnnson; Sweden with Harald Ek. *Career:* Debut: Rodolfo, La Bohème, at Århus, Denmark, 1995; Sang roles of Pinkerton in Madama Butterfly and First Jew in Salome, Gothenburg Opera, 1996–97; Duke in Rigoletto, Oslo Opera, 1996–97; Pinkerton, 1997–98; Rodolfo, La Bohème; Worked at operas in both Reykjavík and Gothenburg as chorus member; Mozart's Magic Flute; Roderigo in Otello; Borsa, Rigoletto; Bardolfo, Falstaff; Beppe, Donizetti's Rita; Swan, Orff's Carmina Burana; Tenor, Rossini's Stabat Mater. *Address:* c/o Oslo Arts Management AS, Den Gamle Logen, Grev Wedels Plass 2, 0151 Oslo 1, Norway.

ARAYA, Graciela; singer (mezzo-soprano); b. 16 May 1958, Santiago, Chile. *Education:* studied in Santiago and São Paulo. *Career:* debut, as Maddalena in Rigoletto, Santiago, 1981; Sang in South America until 1985; Sang in Germany in Weise von Liebe und Tod by Matthus, Deutsche Oper Berlin, 1985; and as Cherubino, Hansel, Cenerentola, Britten's Lucretia and Sesto in Handel's Giulio Cesare, 1989, Deutsche Oper am Rhein from 1986; Guest appearances as Massenet's Charlotte, Stuttgart; As Octavian and Rosina, Aachen; and as Carmen, Bremen; Season 1994–95: as Enriquetta in I Puritani, Vienna Staatsoper in premiere of Schnittke's Gesualdo; US debut as Carmen, Costa Mesa, 1995; Mignon by Thomas at the Vienna Volksoper, 1996; Season 1998 as Maddalena at Antwerp and Amastre in Serse, Geneva; Charlotte, Venice; Season 2000–01 as Countess Geschwitz in Lulu at Vienna, Clairon in Capriccio at Amsterdam, and Maddalena in Rigoletto at Antwerp. *Current Management:* Robert Gilder & Co., Enterprise House, 59–65 Upper Ground, London, SE1 9PQ, England. *Telephone:* (20) 7928-9008. *Fax:* (20) 7928-9755. *E-mail:* rgilder@robert-gilder.com.

ARCHER, Neill; Singer (tenor); b. 31 Aug. 1961, Northampton, England. *Education:* Studied at the University of East Anglia and the Brevard Music Centre in North Carolina. *Career:* Concert engagements with the London Philharmonic, BBC Symphony, English Baroque Soloists and the Junge Deutsche Philharmonie; Promenade Concerts debut in 1983 with Babylon The Great is Fallen, by Alexander Goehr; Festival Hall debut in Mozart's Requiem followed by Schoenberg's Moses und Aron under John Pritchard; Sang in Bach's St John Passion at the Accademia di Santa Cecilia in Rome, the St Matthew Passion in Stavanger and Schumann's Das Paradies und die Peri at Paris Opéra; Season 1987–88 with Tamino for Kent Opera, Ferrando for Scottish Opera and Don Ottavio with Welsh National Opera; Teatro Regio Turin in 1988 in Testi's Riccardo III; Returned to Italy as Andres in Wozzeck at Parma; Buxton Festival in 1988 as Ubaldo in Haydn's Armida followed by Carmina Burana at the Edinburgh Festival; Sang Ferrando in Così fan tutte for Opera Factory, also televised; Season 1989–90 included Almaviva in Oslo and for Opera North; Sang at English National Opera and Covent Garden in 1991 as Tamino and Jacquino; Sang Pylade in Iphigénie en Tauride at Basle in 1991; Season 1991–92 included Don Ottavio in New Zealand and Pelléas with WNO in a Pierre Boulez/Peter Stein presentation of Debussy's opera; Sang the Steersman in a new production of Der fliegende Holländer at Covent Garden in 1992; Season 1994 as Tamino for ENO and Almaviva at Garsington; Opera North 1996, as Achille in Gluck's Iphigenie en Aulide and 1998 as Jenik; Retired from stage 1999 and became Anglican priest. *Current Management:* Athole Still International Management, Forresters Hall, 25–27 Westow Street, London, SE19 3RY, England. *Telephone:* (20) 8771-5271. *Fax:* (20) 8768-6600. *Website:* www.atholestill.com.

ARCHIBALD, Ann; Singer (Soprano); b. 1967, Scotland. *Education:* Studied at the Royal Scottish Academy of Music and Drama with Elizabeth Izatt. *Career:* Concert debut with the City of Glasgow Philharmonic at Glasgow Royal Concert Hall; Concert repertory includes Carmina Burana, Handel and Bach Cantatas (Göttingen Festival), Beethoven's Ninth (with the Royal Scottish National Orchestra) and Mahler's 4th Symphony; Opera debut 1992, as Papagena with Scottish Opera; Further appearances as Second Niece in Peter Grimes, Mozart's Barbarina and Mrs Honor in Tom Jones by Philidor (Drottningholm Festival, 1995); Season 1995–96 as Musetta and the Sandman in Hansel and Gretel for Scottish Opera, and in Monteverdi's Orfeo for English National Opera; Sang the role of Fish in Broken Strings in a Param Vir double bill for Scottish Opera, 1998 and Exultate Jubilate with the Scottish Chamber Orchestra. *Recordings:* Carmina Burana with the Royal Philharmonic Orchestra. *Honours:* Numerous prizes with the Royal Scottish Academy. *Current Management:* Askonas Holt Ltd, Lonsdale Chambers, 27 Chancery Lane, London, WC2A 1PF, England. *Telephone:* (20) 7400-1700. *Fax:* (20) 7400-1799. *E-mail:* info@askonasholt.co.uk. *Website:* www.askonasholt .co.uk.

ARDAM, Elzbieta; Singer (Mezzo-Soprano); b. 22 Sept. 1959, Kielczewo, Poland; m. Udo Gefe, 24 May 1991, 1 s. *Education:* Conservatory of Poznan, 1985. *Career:* Debut: Santuzza, 1983; Reigen, World Premier at Brussels, 1983, Orfeo, La Scala di Milan, Emelia in Otello, Chicago Symphony and New York Carnegie Hall; Brussels from 1987, as Gluck's Orpheus, Ottone in Poppea, Anna in Les Troyens and Donna Elvira; Frankfurt 1995 as Waltraute and Third Norn; Season 2000–01 as Gaea in Strauss's Daphne at Karlsruhe, Monteverdi's Ottone and Federica in Luisa Miller for Frankfurt Opera; mem, Teatr Wieki, Poznan, 1982–87. *Recordings:* Janáček Diary; Boesmans Reigen. *Honours:* Silver Medal, Geneva, 1981; Tchaikovsky Bronze Medal, Moscow, 1982; R Vinas Bronze Medal, Barcelona, 1984. *Address:* Gartenstrasse 38, 60596 Frankfurt, Germany.

ARDEN-GRIFFITH, Paul, GRSM, ARMCM; British singer (tenor); b. 18 Jan. 1952, Stockport, England. *Education:* Royal Manchester Coll. of Music, Cantica Voice Studio, London. *Career:* debut as Puck in Benjamin Britten's Midsummer Night's Dream, Sadler's Wells Theatre, London 1973; other performances include Franz Lehar's The Merry Widow, Henze's We Come to the River, Britten's Paul Bunyan, Carlisle Floyd's Of Mice and Men, Carl Orff's Carmina Burana, Prokofiev's The Duenna, Count Almaviva in Barber of Seville, Puccini's Il Tabarro, Rossini's Count Ory, La Traviata, Mozart's Die Zauberflöte, Phantom of the Opera, The Legendary Lanza, Babes in the Wood, Sunset Boulevard, That Old Minstrel Magic; concerts and cabarets include London Dorchester Hotel, Hyde Park Intercontinental, Picadilly Theatre, The Belfry Club, Savoy Hotel, Tramshed, Theatre Royal Drury Lane, The Limelight Club, Royal Artillery House; world-wide concert tours, festival appearances, masterclasses and lecture tours of UK music colls and arts faculties; founder mem. Arts Council Opera 80, the United Kingdom Touring Co.; Pres. Barezzi Theatre School; recent performances include Strauss' Die Fledermaus with WNO 2001, Puccini's La Bohème with Somerset Opera 2003, Sondheim's Sweeney Todd at Covent Garden 2003–04; Strauss' Die Fledermaus with Opera Holland Park, London 2004. *Recordings:* The Song Is You 1986, Phantom Of The Opera (original cast recording) 1987, An Evening With Alan Jay Lerner 1987, Minstrel Magic (cast soundtrack) 1993, A Minstrel On Broadway 1994, Encore! 1995, The Classic Collection 1995, Accolade! 1996. *Honours:* Gwilym Gwalchmai Jones Scholarship for Singing 1974. *Current Management:* Ken Spencer Personal Management, 138 Sandy Hill Road, London, SE18 7BA, England. *Telephone:* (20) 8854-2558. *Fax:* (20) 8854-2558.

ARDITTI, Irvine; Violinist; b. 8 Feb. 1953, London, England; m. Jenny Whitelegg, 3 s. *Education:* Royal Academy of Music with Clarence Myerscough and Manoug Parikian, 1969–74. *Career:* Concert Violinist; Co-Founder, Leader, Arditti String Quartet with many 20th Century performances world-wide, 1974–; Co-leader, London Symphony Orchestra, 1976–80; Engagements, major festivals in cities throughout Europe including Aldeburgh, Bath, BBC Proms, Berlin, Budapest, Paris, Venice Biennale, Vienna, Warsaw and USA; Resident String Tutor, Darmstadt Ferienkurse for New Music, 1982–; BBC television Music in Camera, Radio 3 series of 7 recitals, 1987; All Schoenberg's quartets in single recital, Queen Elizabeth Hall, London, November, 1988; Solo appearances in Turin, Brussels, Berlin, Belgian and Turin Radio Symphony Orchestras, London Sinfonietta, Spectrum and Ensemble Cologne; World Premiere, solo works by various composers including J Dillon, J Harvey and Xenakis; With Arditti Quartet has given complete quartets of Berg, Webern and Schoenberg and numerous other composers; Promenade concert debut with United Kingdom premiere of L Francesconi's Rita Neurali in 1993. *Recordings:* Complete Kurtag Quartets, Lachenmann, Dutilleux, and Nono; Rihm, Harvey Quartets; La Lontanza for violin and tape. *Publications:* Premiere of New Work for Violin and Orchestra by Liebermann, 1994. *Honours:* Gold Medal. Worshipful Society of Musicians, 1994; Chamber Music Award, Royal Philharmonic Society. *Address:* c/o Lorraine Lyons, 12 Chatteris Avenue, Harold Hill, Romford, Essex RM3 8JX, England.

ARDOVA, Asya; Pianist, Publisher, Musicologist, Book Translator and Music Teacher; b. 11 Oct. 1972, St Petersburg, Russia. *Education:* Music College at St Petersburg Conservatoire, 1993; St Petersburg Pedagogical University, 1999. *Career:* Debut: Shostakovich Preludes and Fugues, St Petersburg, 1996; Concerts in St Petersburg and elsewhere in Russia; Festivals include Musical Spring, St Petersburg, 1998–2000; Congress of Composers, 2000; International Children's Festival, St Petersburg, 2001. *Publications include:* Monographs on Arkhidimandritov, Firtich; Translation from Russian into English and publication of: Vivaldi 'The Seasons' (poems), J. S. Bach Six Flute Sonatas (preface and commentaries); S. Slonimsky 'The Visions of Ioann Grozny' (libretto and commentaries; B. Tischenko 'Letters of D. D. Shostakovich to B. Tischenko', 2000. *Honours:* Diploma of the St Petersburg Pedagogical University, 1999; Secretary of the Association of Modern Music (AMM). *Address:* Belgradskaya St 44-1-44, St Petersburg, Russia.

ARENS, Rolf-Dieter; Pianist; b. 16 Feb. 1945, Zinnwald, Germany. *Education:* Studied at the Leipzig Musikhochschule, 1963–68. *Career:* Many appearances in Germany and elsewhere in Europe as soloist and chamber musician; Soloist with the Berlin Symphony Orchestra, from 1986; Teacher at the Leipzig Hochschule from 1970, Franz Liszt Hochschule, Weimar, 1976. *Honours:* Prizewinner at the Budapest International Competition, 1966, Bach International at Leipzig, 1968, Long-Thibaud Competition at Paris, 1971. *Address:* c/o Hochschule für Musik Franz Liszt, Platz der Demokratie 2–3, 5300 Weimar, Germany.

AREVALO, Octavio; Singer (tenor); b. 1963, Mexico City, Mexico. *Education:* Studied at the Verdi Conservatoire, Milan, 1984–85; Further study with Ernst Haefliger and James King in Munich. *Career:* Concert appearances in Switzerland, in Bach's Christmas Oratorio and Mozart's C Minor Mass; Stage debut as Paolino in Il Matrimonio Segreto at the Gärtnerplatz Theatre, Munich, 1989; Sang Tamino at Mexico City, 1990; Stadttheater Lucerne, as Mozart's Belmonte, Tamino and Don Ottavio, Nemorino, Rodolfo and Pinkerton, 1991–; Vienna Staatsoper debut as Nemorino, 1992; Season 1994–95 as Rinuccio in Gianni Schicchi at the Komische Oper Berlin, Ferrando (Così fan tutte) at Mexico City, Verdi's Fenton in Madrid and Polyceute in Donizetti's Les Martyrs at Nancy; Season 1996–97 in Le Roi Arthus by Chausson at the Bregenz Festival, Orombello in Beatrice di Tenda at the Deutsche Oper Berlin and Leicester in Maria Stuarda at the Herkulessahl, Munich; Further concert repertory includes Dvořák's Stabat Mater (in Zürich), the Verdi Requiem (Moscow) and Bruckner's Te Deum (Madrid, 1997). *Recordings include:* Rossini's Il Signor Bruschino and Semiramide. *Current Management:* Askonas Holt Ltd, Lonsdale Chambers, 27 Chancery Lane, London, WC2A 1PF, England. *Telephone:* (20) 7400-1700. *Fax:* (20) 7400-1799. *E-mail:* info@askonasholt.co.uk. *Website:* www.askonasholt.co.uk.

ARGENTA, Nancy; singer (soprano); b. 17 Jan. 1957, Nelson, BC, Canada. *Education:* Univ. of Western Ont., studied singing in Germany and with Peter Pears, Gerard Souzay, Vera Rozsa. *Career:* appearances at the Vienna and Schwetzingen Festivals with London Baroque; sang in Scarlatti's La Giuditta in Italy, Mozart Mass in C minor with the English Chamber Orchestra, Handel's Messiah and Giulio Cesare in Canada; concerts with the Songmakers' Almanac; opera engagements as Susanna with WNO, Haydn's L'Infedeltà Delusa in Paris, Brussels and Cologne, Astreia in Handel's Tamerlano at the Opéra de Lyon, La Chasseuresse in Rameau's Hippolyte et Aricie and Purcell's King Arthur at Aix-en-Provence; sang the title role in L'Incoronazione di Poppea, on South Bank, London; Purcell's Dido in Utrecht, Paris, Beaune and Saintes; further concerts in the Schoenberg Reluctant Revolutionary series on South Bank and Cupid in Venus and Adonis by Blow at the 1989 Promenade Concerts; sang Vespina in Haydn's L'Infedeltà Delusa, Antwerp 1990; Rossanne in the N American premiere of Floridante, Toronto 1990; sang Clärchen's songs in Beethoven's Egmont at the Festival Hall 1991; Mozart's Requiem at the 1991 Proms, conducted by Roger Norrington; debut in 1996 at the Salzburg, Flanders and Budapest Festivals, singing Euridice in Gluck's Orfeo ed Euridice with Ivan Fischer and the Budapest Festival Orchestra; also performed with Tafelmusik in Toronto, the Nat. Arts Centre Ottawa, the Scottish Chamber Orchestra, Ensemble Baroque de Limoges, the Orchestra of the Age of Enlightenment, Acad. of Ancient Music and at the Ansbach, Halle and Spitalfields Festivals; Mahler's 2nd Symphony at the Festival Hall 1997; Mozart's Exultate Jubilate and Haydn's Nelson Mass at the 1999 London Proms. *Recordings include:* Handel's Solomon and the Magnificat by Bach, Bach B Minor Mass, St John Passion and Christmas Oratorio, Monteverdi's Orfeo, Handel's Tamerlano, Barbarina in Le nozze di Figaro, Mozart's Requiem and Don Giovanni, Bach Solo Cantatas, Handel's Saul. *Current Management:* Askonas Holt Ltd, Lonsdale Chambers, 27 Chancery Lane, London, WC2A 1PF, England. *Telephone:* (20) 7400-1700 (office). *Fax:* (20) 7400-1799 (office). *E-mail:* info@askonasholt.co .uk (office). *Website:* www.askonasholt.co.uk (office).

ARGENTO, Dominick; Composer and Teacher; b. 27 Oct. 1927, York, PA, USA. *Education:* Studied with Nicolas Nabokov and Hugo Weisgall at the Peabody Conservatory of Music, Baltimore, BA, 1951; Piano with Pietro Scarpini and composition with Luigi Dallapiccola at the Florence Conservatory, 1951–52; Studied composition with Bernard Rogers, Howard Hanson and Alan Hovhaness at the Eastman School of Music, PhD, 1957. *Career:* Teacher of theory and composition, 1958–, Regents Professor, 1979–, University of Minnesota; European premiere of the Dream of Valentino at Kassel, 1999; Compositions include: Operas: The Boor, 1957, Christopher Sly, 1962–63, The Shoemaker's Holiday, 1967, The Voyage of Edgar Allan Poe, 1975–76, Casanova's Homecoming, 1980–84; The Aspern Papers, 1988; The Dream of Valentino, 1993; Monodramas: A Water Bird Talk, 1974; Ballets: The Resurrection Of Don Juan, 1955, Incidental music to plays; Orchestral: Ode To The West Wind, concerto for Soprano and Orchestra, 1956, Bravo Mozart!, 1969, In Praise Of Music, 1977, Le Tombeau d'Edgar Poe, 1985; Chamber:

Divertimento for Piano and Strings, 1954; Songs About Spring for Soprano and Piano or Chamber Orchestra, 1954, The Revelation Of St John The Divine for Tenor, Men's Voices, Brass and Percussion, 1966, Letters From Composers for Tenor and Guitar, 1968, To Be Sung Upon The Water, song cycle for High Voice, Clarinet and Piano, 1972, From The Diary Of Virginia Woolf, song cycle for Mezzo-Soprano and Piano, 1974, I Hate And I Love, song cycle for Chorus and Percussion, 1981, Te Deum for Chorus and Orchestra, 1987; Spirituals and Swedish Chorales, 1994; Walden Pond for chorus, 3 cellos and harp, 1996; A Few Words About Chekhov for mezzo-soprano, baritone and piano, 1996; mem, Institute of Arts and Letters, 1980. *Honours:* Fulbright Fellowship, 1951–52; Guggenheim Fellowships, 1957, 1964; Pulitzer Prize in Music, 1975; Numerous commissions; Honorary Doctorates. *Address:* c/o Boosey & Hawkes Ltd, 295 Regent Street, London W1R 8JH, England.

ARGERICH, Martha; Pianist; b. 5 June 1941, Buenos Aires, Argentina. *Education:* Studied with V Scaramuzza in Argentina and with Friedrich Gulda, Madeleine Lipatti, Nikita Magaloff and Michelangeli in Europe. *Career:* Debut: 1946; Gave recitals in Buenos Aires, 1949, 1952; Moved to Europe in 1955; London debut in 1964; Soloist with the world's leading orchestras; Often heard in Chopin, Liszt, Schumann, Prokofiev and Bartók; Duo partnership with the violinist Gidon Kremer; London recital in 1988 with sonatas by Schumann, Franck and Bartók; Played Beethoven's 3rd Concerto with Chamber Orchestra of Europe at the Barbican Hall, London, 1991; Schumann Concerto at the BBC London Proms, 2000; Ravel's Concerto in G major at the London Proms, 2002. *Honours:* Winner, International Music Competition, Geneva, 1957; Winner, Busoni Competition, Bolzano, 1957; 1st Prize, Seventh Warsaw International Chopin Competition, 1965; Polish Radio Prize, 1965.

ARGIRIS, Spiros; Conductor; b. 24 Aug. 1948, Athens, Greece. *Education:* Studied piano with Alfons Kontarsky, conducting with Hans Swarowsky; With Nadia Boulanger in Paris. *Career:* Conducted at opera houses in Berlin, Hamburg, Cologne and elsewhere in Germany; Has led concerts at the Venice Biennale and at the Maggio Musicale, Florence; Musical Director of the Festival of Two Worlds, Spoleto-Charleston, 1986; Conducted Salome in 1989; Musical Director of the Trieste Opera, 1987, leading The Queen of Spades in 1988 and Il Barbiere di Siviglia and Parsifal in 1989; Conducted Elektra at the Teatro Nuovo, Spoleto, 1990; Parsifal and Le nozze di Figaro at Charleston; Modern repertoire includes Henze's El Rey de Harlem, premiere 1980, and Hans Jurgen von Bose's Die Nacht aus Blei, premiere 1981; Appointed Musical Director of the Opera and Orchestre Philharmonique at Nice, 1988. *Address:* Orchestre Philharmonique de Nice, Opera de Nice, Rue Saint Francois de Paule, 06300 Nice, France.

ARHO, Anneli; Composer; b. 12 April 1951, Helsinki, Finland. *Education:* Studied at the Sibelius Academy, Helsinki, and with Klaus Huber and Brian Ferneyhough at Freiburg. *Career:* Teacher at the Sibelius Academy from 1979. *Compositions:* Minos for harpsichord, 1978; Answer for mezzo, horn and string quartet, 1978; Once upon a Time for wind quintet, 1979; Par comparison for 3 cellos, 1981; Les temps emboîtés for 3 cellos, 1987. *Address:* c/o Sibelius Academy of Music, Töölönkatu 28, 00260 Helsinki, Finland.

ARISTO, Giorgio; Singer (Tenor); b. 28 Dec. 1950, New York City, USA. *Education:* Studied at Manhattan School of Music and in Milan and Zürich. *Career:* Sang at Passau, 1979–81, as the Duke in Rigoletto, Rodolfo in La Bohème and Rossini's Count Almaviva; Engaged in Essen, 1981–83; Hannover, 1983–; Guest appearances in Düsseldorf as Don José, Vienna as Massenet's Werther, Munich in The Bartered Bride and Copenhagen as Cavaradossi; Season 1988–89 as Calaf in Nantes and Andrea Chénier in Toulon and Liège; Other roles include Alfredo and Turiddu; Munich Opera from 1992, as Cavaradossi and Manrico; Many concert appearances. *Address:* c/o Bayerische Staatsoper, Max-Joseph-Platz, D–80539 Munich, Germany.

ARKADIEV, Mikhail; Pianist and Composer; b. 1958, Moscow, Russia. *Education:* Graduated from the Tchaikovsky Conservatoire, Moscow, 1978; Gnessin Institute, 1988. *Career:* Solo performances throughout Russia and recital accompanist to baritone Dmitri Hvorostovsky, 1990–; Tours to Europe, America, East Asia and the Pacific Music Festival; Solo debut in Berlin, 1990; Chair of the Piano Department at the Academy of Choral Art in Moscow. *Compositions include:* Mass for Choir And Organ; Vocal and chamber works. *Publications include:* The Temporal Structures of New European Music; An Essay in Phenomenological Study, 1992.

ARKHIPOVA, Irina Konstantinova; Singer (mezzo-soprano); b. 2 Dec. 1925, Moscow, USSR. *Education:* Studied with Leonid Savranski at the Moscow Conservatory. *Career:* Sang at Sverdlovsk 1954–56; Member of the Bolshoi Opera, Moscow from 1956; Has sung Azucena, Marina, Marfa (Khovanshchina), Amneris, Eboli and Charlotte; Further Russian repertoire includes Lyubasha (The Tsar's Bride), Polina and Lyubov (The Queen of Spades), and parts in the Bolshoi premieres of

War and Peace and The Story of a Real Man by Prokofiev, Khrennikov's The Mother and Shchedrin's Not Love Alone; Teatro San Carlo Naples 1960, as Carmen; La Scala Milan, 1964, as Helen in War and Peace (with the Bolshoi Company); 1967–71, as Marfa and Marina; Orange and Covent Garden, 1972 and 1975, as Azucena; San Francisco, 1972, as Amneris; Savonlinna Festival, Finland, 1989 as Marfa in Khovanshchina; Sang Ulrica at Covent Garden, 1988; Appeared with the Kirov Opera at the Metropolitan, (the Countess in The Queen of Spades), 1992; and as the Nurse in Eugene Onegin at the Théâtre du Châtelet, 1992. *Recordings:* War and Peace, Khovanshchina, Boris Godunov, The Snow Maiden, The Queen of Spades, Mazeppa, Alexander Nevsky by Prokofiev. *Honours:* People's Artist of the USSR, 1966. *Current Management:* Askonas Holt Ltd, Lonsdale Chambers, 27 Chancery Lane, London, WC2A 1PF, England. *Telephone:* (20) 7400-1700. *Fax:* (20) 7400-1799. *E-mail:* info@askonasholt.co.uk. *Website:* www .askonasholt.co.uk.

ARMENGUARD, Jean-Pierre; Pianist; b. 17 June 1943, Clermont-Ferrand, France. *Education:* Studied at the Ecole Normale and the Sorbonne, Paris, and with Jacques Février. *Career:* Has performed throughout France and elsewhere in Europe in a wide repertory, including 20th century music; Founded the Sainte-Baume music festival and co-founded (1970) a trio with clarinet and piano; French cultural ambassador to Sweden (1982–85) and to Greece (1985–88). *Publications include:* History of Music from the time of Beethoven.

ARMILATO, Fabio; Singer (Tenor); b. 1963, Genoa, Italy. *Education:* Paganini Conservatoire and the Academia Virgiliana, Mantua. *Career:* Debut: Teatro Pergolesi di Jesi, 1986, as Licinio in La Vestale; Appearances at La Scala and throughout Italy as Faust in Mefistofele, Alfredo, Edgardo, Turiddu, Pinkerton and Gabriele Adorno; Vlaamse Opera Antwerp as Don Carlos, Rodolfo, Des Grieux and Cavaradossi; North American debut at the New York City Opera as Don José; Metropolitan Opera as Radames, Gabriele, Turiddu, Manrico and Loris in Fedora; San Francisco Opera from 1994, as Manrico and Radames, (1997); Further engagements with the Houston Opera as Pinkerton, at Pittsburgh as Don José, Buenos Aires as Andrea Chénier and in Paris as Cavaradossi (also at Antwerp, 1996); Sang Radames at Verona and the New York Met, Faust at Buenos Aires, 1999; Season 2000–01 as Puccini's Ramirez at Nice, Andrea Chénier for the Vienna Staatsoper (returned as Don Carlos), and as Manrico for Washington Opera. *Honours:* Winner, 1986 Tito Schipa Competition. *Address:* c/o Music International, 13 Ardilaun Road, London N5 2QR, England.

ARMITSTEAD, Melanie; Singer (Soprano); b. 1957, England. *Education:* Studied at Guildhall School of Music. *Career:* Debut: Frasquita and Micaela in Carmen for Scottish Opera; Appearances with Kent Opera, 1987–, as Venus in Rameau's Pygmalion, First Lady in The Magic Flute, and Minerva in The Return of Ulysses; Scottish Opera debut as Titania in Eugene Onegin in 1988 returning as Fiordiligi; English National Opera and Opera North debuts in 1990 as Nicoletta in The Love for Three Oranges and Mélisande in Ariane et Barbe-Bleue; Returned to Leeds as Xenia in Boris Godunov in 1992; Created the Niece in Fenelon's Le Chevalier Imaginaire, Théâtre du Châtelet, Paris, 1992; Concert performances with Liverpool Philharmonic, the Halle and Royal Philharmonic; Season 1989–90 included Vivaldi's Gloria with English Chamber Orchestra, Messiah with Tokyo Philharmonic, St John Passion in Netherlands, and Bach's Magnificat at the Barbican Hall; Recitalist at the Wigmore Hall (Debut 1987), Purcell Room and Queen Elizabeth Hall; Appearances with the pianist Julian Drake and oboist Nicholas Daniel. *Address:* c/o Opera North, The Grand Theatre, 46 New Briggate, Leeds, Yorkshire LS1 6NU, England.

ARMSTRONG, Karan; Singer (soprano); b. 14 Dec. 1941, Horne, Montana, USA; m. Götz Friedrich (died 2000). *Education:* Studied in Minnesota with Thelma Halverson, California with Lotte Lehmann and Fritz Zweig. *Career:* Debut: Metropolitan Opera in 1969 in Hansel and Gretel; Appearances with opera companies in Houston, Seattle, Cincinnati and Portland; Roles include Donizetti's Norina, Puccini's Butterfly, Verdi's Alice Ford and Wagner's Eva; Sang at New York City Opera, 1975–78 as Minnie, Tosca, Concepcion and the Queen of Shemakha; European debut at Strasbourg in 1976 as Salomé; Guest appearances in Munich, Frankfurt, Geneva, Oslo and Vienna; Bayreuth debut in 1979 as Elsa; World premiere performances in Von Einem's Jesu Hochzeit, Vienna in 1980, Sinopoli's Lou Salomé at Munich in 1981 and Berio's Un Re in Ascolto at Salzburg in 1984; Covent Garden in 1981 as Lulu in the first British performance of the 3 act version of Berg's opera; Other roles include Berg's Marie and the Woman in Schoenberg's Erwartung; Sang Katerina Izmailova at Berlin in 1988 and Emilia Marty and Regina in Mathis der Maler, 1990; Wiesbaden Festival in 1989 as Katya Kabanova, Alice Ford at Los Angeles in 1990 followed by Leonore; Sang Wagner's Sieglinde and Gutrune at Covent Garden in 1991, Janáček's Emilia Marty at Los Angeles in 1992, and Megara in the premiere of Desdemona und Ihre Schwestern by Siegfried Matthus at Schwetzingen Festival in 1992; Concert appearances in the Four Last

Songs of Strauss, Zemlinsky's Lyric Symphony and the Bruchstücke from Wozzeck; Sang Schoenberg's Woman at the Deutsche Oper Berlin, 1994; Jocasta in Enescu's Oedipe at Berlin, 1996; Floyd's Susannah in 1997; Sang Brünnhilde in Götterdämmerung at Helsinki, 1998; Season 2000-01 as the Marschallin and Wagner's Venus at the Deutsche Oper Berlin, Weill's Begbick at Genoa. *Recordings include:* Elsa in Lohengrin from Bayreuth. *Current Management:* Harrison/Parrott Ltd, 12 Penzance Place, London, W11 4PA, England. *Telephone:* (20) 7229 9166. *Fax:* (20) 7221 5042. *Website:* www.harrisonparrott.com.

ARMSTRONG, Sir Richard, Kt, CBE; British conductor; b. 1 July 1943, Leicester, England. *Education:* Univ. of Cambridge. *Career:* mem. of music staff, Royal Opera, Covent Garden 1966–68; Music Dir, WNO 1973–86; Covent Garden debut in 1982 with Billy Budd, returning for Andrea Chénier, Un Ballo in Maschera and Don Carlos 1989; conducted Elektra, Die Frau ohne Schatten, Wozzeck, operas by Janácek, The Midsummer Marriage and Peter Grimes; led the WNO in The Ring at Covent Garden 1986; guest engagements with Netherlands Opera in Elektra, Komische Oper Berlin in Peter Grimes, Frankfurt in Der fliegende Holländer, with new productions of Elektra and Ariadne auf Naxos and at Geneva in Don Carlos; conducted the premiere of John Metcalf's Tornrak for WNO 1990, followed by Otello and House of the Dead; Music Dir, Scottish Opera 1993–; conducted Moses und Aron and La Voix Humaine at the 1992 Edinburgh Festival, Werther at Toulouse 1997; British stage premiere of Magic Fountain by Delius, Scottish Opera 1999; new production of Parsifal 2000; Wagner's Ring Cycle 2003. *Honours:* Royal Philharmonic Soc. opera award 2004. *Current Management:* Ingpen & Williams Ltd, 7 St George's Court, 131 Putney Bridge Road, London, SW15 2PA, England.

ARMSTRONG, Sheila Ann, FRAM; British opera and concert singer (soprano); b. 13 Aug. 1942, Ashington, England; d. of William R. Armstrong and Janet Armstrong; m. David E. Cooper 1980 (divorced 1999). *Education:* Hirst Park Girls' School, Ashington, Northumberland and Royal Acad. of Music. *Career:* sang Despina in Così fan tutte at Sadler's Wells 1965, Belinda in Dido and Aeneas, Glyndebourne 1966, Mozart's Pamina and Zerlina and Fiorila in Rossini's Il Turco in Italia, Glyndebourne; sang in the premiere of John McCabe's Notturni ed Alba at Three Choirs Festival 1970; New York debut with New York Philharmonic 1971; sang with Los Angeles Philharmonic under Mehta; Covent Garden debut as Marzelline in Fidelio 1973; sang Donizetti's Norina and Mozart's Donna Elvira for Scottish Nat. Opera; concert engagements included Messiah at the Concertgebouw, tour of the Far East with the Bach Choir, Britten's Spring Symphony, Strauss' Four Last Songs with Royal Philharmonic, Elgar's Oratorios and the Sea Symphony by Vaughan Williams; Pres. Kathleen Ferrier Soc., trustee Kathleen Ferrier Award; Fellow Hatfield Coll., Univ. of Durham 1992; mem. Royal Philharmonic Soc.. *Recordings include:* Samson, Dido and Aeneas, Mozart's Requiem, Carmina Burana, Elgar's Apostles, The Pilgrim's Progress, Cantatas by Bach, Haydn's Stabat Mater, Beethoven's Ninth Symphony, Mahler's 2nd and 4th. *Honours:* Hon. MA (Newcastle); Hon. DMus (Durham) 1991; Mozart Prize 1965, Kathleen Ferrier Memorial Award 1965. *Address:* Harvesters, Tilford Road, Hindhead, Surrey, GU26 6SQ, England.

ARNAULD, Serge; Composer and Scholar; b. 16 Nov. 1944, Geneva, Switzerland; m. Christiane Wirz, 16 Jan 1965, 3 s., 1 d. *Education:* Maîtrise, Philosophy with Professor Vladimir Jankelevitch, Sorbonne, Paris, 1973; Studied composition with Darius Milhaud, Marcel Landowski, Adrienne Clostre and Louis Saguer. *Career:* Radio: Swiss selection for Paul Gilson Prize and Prix Italia with Pugilat, 1979, and mini-operas, Masculin-Singulier, 1987; Films: Jean-Luc Godard's Sauve qui Peut (La Vie) et Passion, participated as actor; Musicology: Les Manuscrits de Carpentras, 1979, Scènes de la Vie Judéo-Comtadine, 1980; Founder and Artistic Director for International Music Festival from the Academies of Rome, 1984–88; Collaborateur à la dramaturgie au Grand Théâtre de Genève, 1989–2001. *Compositions:* Le Jeu De La Tarasque, ballet-pantomime, 1985; L'Esprit De Genève, directed by Jean-Louis Martinoty, 1986, to commemorate the 450th anniversary of the Reformation in Geneva; Le Double et sa doublure, cabaret songs (with Louis Saguer, 1990); Guillaume Tell en Jacobin, to commemorate the bicentenary of the French Revolution and for the 700th anniversary of the Swiss Confederation, 1991; 3 Lettres, ballet dissocié, 1993; Signes des Temps, 1997; Opéra Imaginaire (La Vie à deux), 1999; Dramaturge du spectacle musical, Le Petit Prince, music by Richard Cocciante, performed at Casino de Paris, Oct 2002. *Recordings:* Cantates Ambivalentes; Requiem de Pâques; L'Amour. *Publications:* La Cotonalité and Le Système Hexacordal, Paris, 1968–69; Le Chalet dans tous ses états (la construction de l'imaginaire helvétique), 1999–2000; De Genève, et du Théâtre: culte sans image—culture de son image, 2001–03. *Honours:* Member, Institut Suisse, Rome, 1983. *Address:* 6 rue de la Mairie, 1207 Geneva, Switzerland.

ARNELL, Richard Anthony Sayer; Composer; b. 15 Sept. 1917, Hampstead, London, England; m. Joan Heycock 1992. *Education:* Hall

School, University College School, London; Royal College of Music. *Career:* Music Consultant, BBC North American Service, 1943–46; Lecturer, Royal Ballet School, 1958–59; Editor, The Composer, 1961–64; Chairman, Composers Guild of Great Britain, 1964, 1974–75, Vice-President, 1992–; Visiting Fulbright Professor, Bowdoin College, Maine, 1967–68. Hofstra University, New York, 1968–70; Music Director, Board Member, London International Film School, 1975–88; Music Director, Ram Filming Ltd, 1980–85; Vice-President, Friends of Trinity College of Music Junior Department, 1987–; Founder Chairman, Tadcaster Civic Society Arts Committee, 1988–91; Founder Chairman, Saxmundham Music and Arts, 1992–95, Resident, 1995–; mem, Composers Guild of Great Britain; BETC Union; Savage Club. *Compositions:* Operas: Love in Transit; Moonflowers; Ballets: Punch and the Child; Harlequin in April; The Great Detective; The Angels; Orchestral: 6 Symphonies; 2 Concertos for Violin; Concerto for Harpsichord; 2 Concertos for Piano; Symphonic Portrait Lord Byron; Landscapes and Figures; Robert Faherty; Impression; Ode to Beecham, 1986; Xanadu, 1992; Chamber: 6 String Quartets; 2 Quintets; Piano Trio; Piano Works; Music for Wind Instruments; Brass Instruments; Electronic Music; Song Cycles; Numerous film scores. *Publications:* Technique of Film Music (co-editor). *Honours:* Tadcaster Town Council Merit Award, 1990. *Address:* c/o British Music Information Centre, 11 Stratford Place, London, W1, England.

ARNESTAD, Finn Oluf Bjerke; Composer and Music Critic; b. 23 Sept. 1915, Oslo, Norway. *Education:* Studied violin and piano at Oslo, composition with Bjarne Brustad, African and Oriental Folk Music in Paris, 1952. *Career:* Music Critic in Oslo. *Compositions:* Orchestral: Constellation, 1948, Conversation for Piano and Orchestra, 1950, Meditation, 1952, INRI, 2 suites from a symphonic mystery play, 1952–55, Violin Concerto, 1957, Aria Appassionata, 1962, Cavatina Cambiata, 1965, Overture, 1970, Toccata, 1972, Arabesque, 1975, Piano Concerto, 1976, Mouvement Concertant for Double Bass and Orchestra, 1978; Chamber: String Quartet, 1947, Sextet for Flute, Clarinet, Bassoon, Violin, Cello and Piano, 1959, Quintet for Flute and Strings, 1962, Suite In Old Dance Rhythms for Flute, Oboe, Harpsichord and Strings, 1966, Trombone Sonata, 1971, Solo Violin Sonata, 1980, Solo Double Bass Sonata, 1980, Piano Music; Several vocal works.

ARNET, Marie; Singer (soprano); b. 1970, Solna, Sweden. *Education:* Royal Academies, Stockholm and London; London Opera Studio. *Career:* Anne Trulove, in The Rake's Progress and Mozart's Sandrina and Barbarina for RAM; Adelaide in Handel's Lotario for the London Handel Society; Susanna for Clonter Opera, Rossini's Berta for British Youth Opera, and in Burning Mirrors, for ENO Studio; Recitals and Oratorios in Sweden, Qatar, Brussels, Aix-en-Provence and Sicily; Barbarina in Le nozze di Figaro at the Glyndebourne Festival 2001; Studies with Alison Pearce at the National Opera Studio; Concert repertoire includes Bach's St John Passion, Mahler's Symphony no. 2 and 4, Brahms, Fauré and Mozart Requiems, Rossini's Petite Messe Solonelle, Pergolesi's Stabat Mater, Haydn's Nelson Mass and The Creation, Bruckner's Te Deum and television appearances in Madrid in performances of Child of Our Time, Berlioz's L'enfance du Christ at the Three Choirs Festival and Mozart's Requiem with Paul McCreesh and the Gabrieli Consort; Engagements include Barbarina in Le Nozze di Figaro at Glyndebourne, Diana in Iphigénie en Aulide at Glyndebourne, Sophie in Der Rosenkavalier at Opera North (debut) and Pamina in Die Zauberflöte for Scottish Opera; Debut as Ilia in Idomeneo at the Glyndebourne Festival under Sir Simon Rattle. *Current Management:* Hazard Chase, Norman House, Cambridge Place, Cambridge CB2 1NS, England. *Telephone:* (1223) 312400. *Fax:* (1223) 460827. *Website:* www .hazardchase.co.uk. *Address:* c/o National Opera Studio, Morley College, 61 Westminster Bridge Road, London, SE1 7XT, England.

ARNOLD, David Charles; American opera and concert singer (baritone); b. 1949, Atlanta, GA. *Career:* debut, Metropolitan Opera as Enrico in Lucia; ENO as Escamillo in Carmen; New York City Opera as Zurga in Les Pêcheurs de Perles; Escamillo in Carmen, Komische Oper Berlin; performances of many world premieres, including John Harbison's Full Moon in March and his Winter's Tale, David Diamond's Ninth Symphony for Baritone and Orchestra, Leonard Bernstein conducting at Carnegie Hall, Charles Fussell's Specimen Days, James Ynaut's Such Was the War; two guest appearances at the White House singing Berlioz's L'Enfance du Christ and performance of American song repertoire; performances of Amonasro in Aida with Opera Company of Boston, L'Opéra de Montréal and Opera Omaha and Le nozze di Figaro with L'Opéra de Québec; performances with most leading orchestras, including The Boston Symphony for six seasons, St Louis Symphony, Atlanta Symphony, American Symphony Orchestra, San Francisco Symphony, Chicago Symphony, Buffalo Philharmonic, Singapore Symphony Orchestra, The Spoleto Festivals, Philadelphia Orchestra and the Israel Philharmonic. *Recordings:* Schoenberg's Gurrelieder, Boston Symphony; Harbison's Full Moon in March; Judith Lang's Zaimont's Magic World; Mendelssohn's Walpurgisnacht; Beetho-

ven's 9th Symphony; Mozart's Requiem; Haydn's Lord Nelson Mass; Cherubini's Médée; Elijah; Bach's St Matthew Passion; Scott McLean's Scripture Songs; Moravec's Songs of Love and War. *Current Management:* William Knight, Grant House, 309 Wood Street, Burlington, NJ 08016, USA.

ARNOLD, Sir Malcolm Henry, CBE, FTCL, FRNCM; British composer; b. 21 Oct. 1921, Northampton, England; s. of William Arnold and Annie Arnold (née Hawes); two s. one d. *Education:* Royal Coll. of Music, London, trumpet with Ernest Hall, piano with Hurst Bannister, composition with Gordon Jacob. *Career:* first trumpet, London Philharmonic Orchestra 1942–49 (excluding break for military service and short time with BBC Symphony Orchestra); numerous appearances on concert platform as soloist in Haydn, Goedicke, Riisager and other concertos; Mendelssohn Scholarship for study in Italy 1948; composer of wide range of concert music and nearly 120 film scores; Omnibus 70th Birthday 1991. *Compositions include:* Two operas, The Dancing Master, 1951 and The Open Window, 1956; Ballets, Homage to the Queen, for the 1953 Coronation, Rinaldo and Armida, 1955 and Electra, 1963; Orchestral, 9 Symphonies, 1951, 1953, 1954, 1960, 1961, 1967, 1973, 1979, 1987; 10 Overtures, including Beckus the Dandipratt, 1948 and Tam O'Shanter, 1955; Toy Symphony, 1957; Concertos: for clarinet, 1951 and 1974, oboe 1952, flute 1954 and 1972, harmonica 1954, guitar 1961, horn 1947 and 1956, viola 1971, two violins 1962; Trumpet Concerto commissioned by the Royal Coll. of Music in celebration of its foundation in 1988; Recorder Concerto for Michala Petri, 1988; Cello Concerto commissioned by the Royal Philharmonic Soc. for Julian Lloyd Webber, first performance Royal Festival Hall, London, 1989; Two Brass Quintets 1961 and 1988 and Two String Quartets, 1951 and 1975; Children's pieces include music for The Turtle Drum for BBC television; Film music includes The Bridge on the River Kwai (awarded Hollywood Oscar, 1958); The Inn of the Sixth Happiness; Whistle Down the Wind; Wind Octet, 1989; Four Welsh Dances, 1989; Flourish for a Battle for RAF Battle of Britain, 1990; Robert Kett Overture, 1990; Manx Suite, 1990; Fantasy for Recorder and String Quartet, 1991. *Recordings:* Chandos, string quartets; Film Suites; Conifer Symphonies 6, 7, 8; Koch: Piano and Chamber Music; Wind Band and Orchestra Overtures. *Honours:* Hon. DMus (Exeter) 1969, (Durham) 1982, (Leicester) 1983, Hon. DHumLitt (Miami), (Oxford, USA) 1990; Bard of the Cornish Gorsedd 1969, W. W. Cobbett Prize 1941, hon. mem. Royal Acad. of Music, London, Ivor Novello Award for Outstanding Services to British Music 1985, Wavendon All Music Composer of the Year 1987, ISM Distinguished Musician Award 2004. *Address:* c/o Anthony Day, 26 Springfields, Attleborough, Norfolk NR17 2PA, England. *Telephone:* (1953) 455420. *Fax:* (1953) 455420. *E-mail:* musicunited@btopenworld .com. *Website:* www.malcolmarnold.co.uk.

ARONICA, Roberto; Singer (Tenor); b. 1968, Italy. *Education:* Studied with Carlo Bergonzi. *Career:* Appearances as Rodolfo, Turin, 1992; As Donizetti's Edgardo at Macerata as Alfredo, at Treviso, 1995; Guest engagements as the Duke of Mantua, Santiago, 1992; As Alfredo, Welsh National Opera; As Rodolfo and Alfredo, San Francisco, 1993 and 1995; Further appearances as Rodolfo at La Scala, 1996; As Rodolfo, Opéra Bastille, Paris and Tel-Aviv, 1998; Season 2000–01 as Alfredo at the New York Met and the Duke of Mantua at Chicago. *Address:* c/o San Francisco Opera, Van Ness Avenue, San Francisco, CA 94102 USA.

ARONOFF, Josef; Violinist, Violist and Conductor; b. 13 June 1932, Budapest, Hungary; m. Astrid Gray, 3 s., 1 d. *Education:* Franz Liszt Academy of Music, Budapest; Guildhall School of Music, London; MBC (United Kingdom); AGSM; LRAM. *Career:* Radio and television appearances, Hungary, Austria, the United Kingdom, Portugal, France, Germany, USA, Hong Kong, Australia; Professor, Royal Manchester College of Music, England, 1965–70; Head of String Department, Queensland Conservatorium of Music, Australia, 1970–75; Musical Director, Conservatorium Chamber Orchestra, 1970–75; Musical Director, Artemon Ensemble and Orchestra, 1971–; Concertmaster, Director of Instrumental Studies, Darling Downs Institute of Advanced Education, 1975–77; Conductor, Allegri Players, 1975–77; Senior Lecturer, Adelaide College of Arts, 1977–79; Musical Director, South-Western Symphony Orchestra, 1977–79; Professor, Guildhall School of Music and Drama, England, 1979–88; Professor, Birmingham School of Music, 1979–88; Senior Examiner, Australian Music Examination Board, 1988–. *Recordings:* Viola Concerto 1989 by C Reichard-Gross; Memories of Sunny Days for Violin and Orchestra by C Reichard-Gross, with Hungarian Northern Symphony Orchestra, soloist Josef Aronoff (viola/violin), conductor Laszlo Kovacs. *Current Management:* Camerata Artists, United Kingdom; Austral Artists, Australia. *Address:* 40 Isabella Street, Tarragindi, Brisbane, Queensland 4121, Australia.

ARP, Klaus; Conductor and Composer; b. 2 April 1950, Soltau, Germany. *Education:* Piano, Conducting, Composition, Staatliche Hochschule für Musik, Hamburg. *Career:* Debut: Hamburgische Staatsoper, 1979; Pianist, Hamburgische Staatsoper, 1975; Conductor, Hamburg Youth Orchestra, 1979; First Kapellmeister Opera Theater, Koblenz, 1981;

Chief Conductor, Radio Orchestra, Sudwestfunk, Baden-Baden 1987–95; Artistic Director, Villa Musica, Mainz, 1992–; Professor of Conducting, Staatliche Hochschule für Musik, Heidelberg-Mannheim, 1993–. *Compositions:* Odysseus auf Ogygia, opera, world premiere, Koblenz, 1979. *Recordings include:* Faust, opera by Louis Spohr, 1989; Adolphe Adam, Le Postillion de Lonjumeau; Stravinsky, Le Chant du Rossignol. *Current Management:* Herwald Artists Management. *Address:* Schillerstr 60, 67071 Ludwigshafen, Germany.

ARROYO, Martina; Singer (Soprano); b. 2 Feb. 1936, Harlem, NY, USA. *Education:* BA, Hunter College of the City University of New York, 1956. *Career:* Sang in the US premiere of Pizzetti's Assassinio nella Cattedrale, NY, 1958; Metropolitan Opera debut as the Heavenly Voice in Don Carlos, 1959; Appeared in Europe from 1963 singing at the Vienna State Opera, Berlin State Opera, Zürich Opera, Covent Garden London and Paris Opéra; Sang major roles at the Metropolitan Opera from 1965 with debut as Aida; Sang several Verdi roles as well as Wagner's Elsa and Mozart's Donna Anna; Concert performances in music by Varèse, Dallapiccola and Stockhausen; Metropolitan Opera in Aida, (Santuzza, 1986–87) and Seattle Opera in 1988 in Turandot. *Recordings:* Various including Verdi's Sicilian Vespers, Un Ballo in Maschera and La Forza del Destino. *Honours:* Winner, Metropolitan Opera Auditions of the Air, 1958; Honorary DHL, Hunter College, CUNY, 1987. *Address:* c/o Thea Dispeker Inc, 59 East 54th Street, New York, NY 10022, USA.

ARTAUD, Pierre-Yves; Flautist; b. 13 July 1946, Paris, France. *Education:* Studied at the Paris Conservatoire, graduated 1970. Played the piccolo in the Orchestre Philharmonique, Ile-de-France, 1964–68, and flute with the Orchestra Laetitia Musica, 1971; Directed contemporary flute studies at Sainte-Baume, 1973–80; Visiting Professor at Pecs and Csingrad in Hungary from 1978; Responsible for instrumental research at IRCAM, Paris, Electronic Music Studio, 1981; Professor at Darmstadt, 1982; Performer in recital groups including Arcadie, quartet of flutes, 1964, Da Camera, wind quintet, 1970–72, and the Albert Roussel Quintet, 1973–74; Collaboration with harpist Sylvie Beltrando and harpsichordist Pierre Bouyer; Has premiered works by Brian Ferneyhough, Betsy Jolas, Tristan Murail, Franco Donatoni, Maurice Ohana and André Boucourechliev; Professor of Chamber Music at Paris Conservatoire from 1985 and of Flute from 1987. *Publications:* La Flute, 1987. *Honours:* 1st Prize at the Conservatoire, 1969 and 1970; Medal Of Arts, Sciences and Letters, 1978; Grand Prix of French Contemporary Music Interpretation, 1982; Prix de l'Academie du Disque Français, 1984; Prix Charles Inos, 1985. *Address:* 209 Avenue Jean Jaurès, 75079 Paris, France.

ARTETA, Ainhoa; Singer (Soprano); b. 1966, Spain. *Career:* Appearances at North American opera houses from 1990, including Tarrytown, NY as Ah-Joe in Leoni's L'Oracolo; Other roles have included Violetta, Gilda and Liu in Turandot; Sang Micaela in Carmen for Scottish Opera, 1992; As Olga in Fedora, and Mimi; Leila in Les Pêcheurs de perles, Seattle, 1994; Magda in La Rondine, Bonn; Mimi for Netherlands Opera; Zarzuela performances with Placido Domingo, Hamburg, 1996; Season 1998: As Magda at Washington; Violetta at Cincinnati. *Recordings:* Dona Francesquita by Vives. *Honours:* Metropolitan Auditions and Placido Domingo Competition, 1993; Sang Musetta in La Bohème at the New York Met, 2000. *Address:* c/o Washington Opera, John F Kennedy Center, Washington DC 20566, USA.

ARTYOMOV, Vyacheslav; Composer; b. 29 June 1940, Moscow, Russia. *Education:* Studied composition with Pirumov and Sidelnikov; Graduated, Moscow Conservatory, 1968. *Compositions:* Piano Concerto, 1961; 2 Clarinet Sonatas, 1966, 1971; Variations, Nestling Antsali for Flute and Piano, 1974; Capriccio For New Year's Eve for Soprano, Saxophone, Baritone Saxophone and Vibraphone, 1975; Totem for Percussion Group, 1976; A Symphony Of Elegies, 1977; Way To Olympus for Orchestra, 1984; In Memoriam, symphony for Violin Solo and Orchestra, 1968–84; Tristia for Orchestra, 1983; Invocations for Soprano and Percussion Group, 1981; Moonlight Dreams, cantata, for Soprano (mezzo-soprano), Alto Flute, Cello and Piano, 1982; Hymns Of Sudden Wafts for Ensemble, 1985; Gurian Hymns for 3 Violins and Orchestra, 1986; Requiem for Soloists, 2 Choirs and Orchestra, 1988; Sola Fide (By Faith Alone), ballet, 1987; Ave Maria for soprano and chorus, 1989; Hymns of Fiery Torches for ensemble, 1994; Various works for different instruments. *Address:* c/o RAO, Bolchaia Bronnai 6-1, Moscow 103670, Russia.

ARTZT, Alice Josephine, BA; American classical guitarist and writer and teacher; b. 16 March 1943, Philadelphia, PA; d. of Harriett Green Artzt and Maurice G. Artzt; m. Bruce B. Lawton, Jr. *Education:* Columbia Univ. and studied composition with Darius Milhaud and guitar with Julian Bream, Ida Presti and Alexandre Lagoya. *Career:* taught guitar at Mannes Coll. of Music, New York 1966–69, Trenton State Univ. 1977–80; world-wide tours as soloist 1969–; f. Alice Artzt Guitar Trio (with M. Rutscho and R. Burley) 1989; toured in duo with R.

Burley; fmr mem. Bd of Dirs Guitar Foundation of America (Chair. 1986–89). *Recordings include:* Bach and His Friends, Guitar Music by Fernando Sor, Guitar Music by Francisco Tarrega, 20th Century Guitar Music, English Guitar Music, The Music of Manuel Ponce, The Glory of the Guitar, Virtuoso Romantic Guitar, Musical Tributes, Variations, Passacaglias and Chaconnes, American Music of the Stage and Screen, Alice Artzt Classic Guitar, Alice Artzt Plays Original Works. *Publications:* The Art of Practicing, The International GFA Guitarists' Cookbook (ed.), Rythmic Mastery 1997; numerous articles in guitar and music periodicals. *Honours:* several Critics' Choice Awards. *Address:* 51 Hawthorne Avenue, Princeton, NJ 08540, USA. *Telephone:* (609) 921-6629. *Fax:* (609) 924-0091. *E-mail:* guitartzt@aol.com (home).

ARUHN, Britt Marie; Singer (soprano); b. 11 Nov. 1943, Motala, Sweden. *Education:* Stockholm Acad. of Music. *Career:* debut, Stockholm in Les Contes d'Hoffmann, 1974; has sung at Stockholm and the Drottningholm Festival as Norina, Zerbinetta, Gilda, Violetta, Mélisande, Susanna, Rosina, Musetta, Mimi, Marguerite, Nedda, Sophie, Gepopo and Adina; Staatsoper Dresden as Gilda and Sophie, 1976; Covent Garden as Zerbinetta, 1978; Wiener Staatsoper as Gilda, 1978, Sophie, 1980; Paris as Gepopo in Der Grosse Makaber and Zdenka, 1981; Hamburg Staatsoper as Olympia, 1981, Musetta, 1982; Brussels as La Fée in Cendrillon, La Comtesse in Le Conte d'Ory and Musetta, 1983, Mélisande and Susanna, 1984, Adèle, 1985, Sandrina in La Finta Giardiniera (and at Drottningholm), 1987; La Scala as Lucio Cinna in Lucio Silla, 1984; Drottningholm as Sandrina, 1987 and in Luigi Rossi's Orfeo, 1997; Helsinki as Violetta, 1988; Oslo as Violetta, 1991. *Recordings include:* Brahms' Ein Deutsches Requiem; Strauss' Vier Letzte Lieder. *Film:* First Lady in The Magic Flute, 1974. *Honours:* Royal Court Singer, 1998. *Address:* Kungliga Operan, PO Box 16094, 10322 Stockholm (office); Fornborgsgrand 12A, 16858 Bromma, Sweden (home). *Fax:* (8) 374320 (home). *E-mail:* bmaruhn@hem.utfors.se (home).

ARVIDSSON, Bjorn; Singer (Tenor); b. 1965, Stockholm. *Education:* Studied singing, Sundsgarden, Malmo; Guildhall School of Music and Drama with Laura Sarti, 1992. *Career:* Sang Bernini Opera: Nemorino, Wexford Festival; Title role, Robinson Crusoe, British Youth Opera; Travelling Opera; Appearances in Holland Park, Don Ottavio and Beppe; Rodolfo for Kentish Opera; Liverpool Playhouse; Toured with Pavilion Opera as Tamino; The Count of Luxembourg, D'Oyly Carte; Liberto in Poppea for Welsh National Opera; Appeared in Antwerp; Opera Project; Tour of Ireland with Co-opera; Alfredo at the Théâtre de Caen; Regular appearances in concert and oratorio; 1999 International Festival, Aix en Provence, Academie Européene de Musique; Toured France, Italy and Switzerland. *Recordings:* Several roles in The Coronation of Poppea, Welsh National Opera for BBC. *Address:* 58 Alexandra Park Road, London N10 2AD, England.

ASAWA, Brian; Singer (Countertenor); b. 1966, USA. *Education:* Studied in New York. *Career:* Season 1995 as Britten's Oberon with the London Symphony Orchestra, Endimione in La Calisto at Brussels, Arsamenes in Handel's Xerxes at the Cologne Opera and a Wigmore Hall recital with Melvyn Tan; Season 1996–97 in Handel's Semele at the Berlin Staatsoper, Monteverdi's Orfeo in Amsterdam and Lyon and Orlofsky in Die Fledermaus for San Francisco Opera; Seattle and Göttingen debuts as Arsamenes, Opéra Bastille and Covent Garden debuts as Tolomeo in Giulio Cesare; Season 1997–98 in Mozart's Mitridate for Lyon Opéra and Monteverdi's Nero for Australian Opera, and Dallas Opera debut in Handel's Ariodante; Handel's Admeto in Australia and at Montpellier, 1998; Recitals at Lincoln Center, the Geneva Opera, Sydney Festival and on tour to Japan; Season 2000–01 as Farnace in Mozart's Mitridate at the Paris Châtelet, Handel's Tolomeo in Sydney, Baba the Turk in The Rake's Progress for San Francisco Opera and Britten's Oberon at Naples. *Recordings include:* A Midsummer Night's Dream; Arsamenes in Handel's Serse and Farnace in Mozart's Mitridate; Solo recitals; The Dark is My Delight; A Midsummer Night's Dream; Vocalise. *Honours:* Winner, Metropolitan Opera Auditions, 1991; Richard Tucker Foundation grant, 1993; Prizewinner, Placido Domingo Operalia Competition, 1994. *Current Management:* Askonas Holt Ltd, Lonsdale Chambers, 27 Chancery Lane, London, WC2A 1PF, England. *Telephone:* (20) 7400-1700. *Fax:* (20) 7400-1799. *E-mail:* info@askonasholt.co.uk. *Website:* www.askonasholt.co.uk.

ASAZUMA, Fumiki, BMus; Japanese professor of viola, conductor and viola d'amore player; b. 23 Aug. 1931, Tokyo; m. Michiko Nagamatsu 1957; one s. two d. *Education:* Tokyo National University of Fine Arts and Music, Vienna Academy. *Career:* violist, NHK Symphony Orchestra, Tokyo, 1956–62; Professor of Viola, Tokyo National University of Fine Arts and Music, 1962–; Director and Conductor, Tokio Akademiker Ensemble (Kammerorchester) Tokyo, 1968–; Many television and radio appearances, NHK and especially on FM-Tokyo, 1968–85; President, Japan Viola Research Society; The Dolmetsch Foundation; Japan Musicology Society; Nippon Conductors Association; Rotary Club. *Recordings:* with Tokio Akademiker Ensemble: 3 Divertimentos by

Mozart, 1972, Stamitz, Bach, Mozart, 1975, Flute Concertos by Vivaldi with Christian Larde, 1975, Mozart with Christian Larde and Marie Claire Jamet, 1977, Doppler, Fauré, Gluck, Kreisler, Genin, with Paula Robison, 1984. *Publications:* Translator, The Interpretation of the Music of the XVII and XVIII Centuries by Arnold Dolmetsch, 1966. *Address:* 13-17 Hachiyama, Shibuya-ku, Tokyo 150, Japan.

ASBURY, Stefan; Conductor; b. 2 July 1965, Dudley, West Midlands, England. *Education:* Univ. of Oxford, Royal Coll. of Music with Oliver Knussen, Tanglewood Music Centre. *Career:* engagements with SWR Stuttgart, SWR Sinfonieorchester Baden-Baden & Freiburg, WDR Cologne, NDR Hamburg, NDR Hannover, Deutschland Radio, RIAS Kammerchor, Århus Symphony, Norwegian Radio Orchestra, Royal Scottish Nat. Orchestra and contemporary ensembles, including Ensemble Modern, musikFabrik, Asko Ensemble, London Sinfonietta, Klangforum Wien, Ensemble Intercontemporain; festival appearances include Berlin Festival, Wien Modern, Ultima Festival, Venice Biennale; opera includes premiere of Rob Zuidam's Freeze at Munich Biennale, Birtwistle's Punch & Judy and Chagas Rosa's Melodias Estranhas with Remix Ensemble, Weir's The Blond Eckbert with NDR Hannover, premieres of Staud's Berenice at Munich Biennale and Berlin Festival 2004, and van Vlijmen's Thyeste at La Monnaie. *Recordings:* Harvey, One Evening with Ensemble Intercontemporain. *Honours:* Leonard Bernstein Fellowship, Tanglewood, 1990; Conducting Prize, Munich Biennale, 1994. *Current Management:* Harrison Parrott Ltd, 12 Penzance Place, London, W11 4PA, England. *Telephone:* (20) 7229 9166. *Fax:* (20) 7221 5042. *E-mail:* nicole.rochman@harrisonparrott.co.uk. *Website:* www.harrisonparrott.com.

ASCHENBACH, Hans; Singer (Tenor); b. 1965, Idaho, USA (Swedish and German parents). *Education:* Studied in Idaho and with Neville Marriner. *Career:* Engagements at the New Orleans Opera, Lyric Opera of Queensland, New York Metropolitan, English National Opera and Connecticut Opera; Sang Schoenberg's Aron with the Leipzig Opera and in concert with the Philharmonic Orchestra at the Festival Hall, London, 1996; Other roles include Alwa in Lulu, Nuremberg Opera, 1996; Season 2000–01 as Lohengrin at Weimar and Tannhäuser at Schwerin; Concerts at Carnegie Hall and throughout Europe. *Address:* c/o Stadtische Buhnen Nurnberg, Richard Wagner Platz 2-10, 8500 Nurnberg 70, Germany.

ASGEIRSSON, Jón Gunnar; Icelandic music educator; b. 11 Oct. 1928, Isafjördur; m. Elisabet Thorgeirsdottir 1955; two s. one d. *Education:* Reykjavík Music School, Royal Scottish Academy of Music, Glasgow. *Career:* music teacher at elementary school, Hafnarfjördur 1958–62; music teacher 1962–81, Lecturer 1981–94, Prof. 1994–98, College of Education; music critic for Morgunbladid 1970–; mem. Société de Compositeurs d'Islande, Tónskáldafélag Islands. *Compositions:* Orchestral: Folklore Rhapsody; Lilja, symphonic poem; A Poem of Seven Strings; Blindisleikur, ballet suite; Three Concertos, for Cello and Orchestra, for Horn and Orchestra, for Clarinet and Orchestra; Ancient Dances Suite; Chamber music: Woodwinds Octet; 2 Woodwind Quintets; Folkloric Quintet for Piano and String Quartet; Four Movements for Solo Guitar; String Quartet, 2000; Ten Icelandic Folk Songs for solo guitar, 2000; Choral works and songs; Numerous arrangements of Icelandic folksongs and dances; Operas: Thrymskvida, based on mythological poem; Galdra-Loftur, based on a play by Johann Sigurjónsson. *Recordings:* For Icelandic Broadcasting Service; Ten Icelandic Folk Songs, 1999; Galdia Loftw (opera); Svarfálfa dans (Dance of the Black Elves). *Honours:* 1st Prize in Opera Competition, Icelandic National Theatre, 1974. *Address:* Flókagata 56, 105 Reykjavík, Iceland.

ASHE, Rosemary Elizabeth, LRAM, ARAM; British singer (soprano); b. 1953, England; m. Roderick Jones. *Education:* Royal Acad., London Opera Centre. *Career:* sang in the premiere of Tavener's Thérèse at Covent Garden 1979, for ENO has sung Papagena, Esmeralda (Bartered Bride), Fiakermilli (Arabella), Venus (Orpheus in the Underworld) and ZouZou (La Belle Vivette); other roles include the Queen of Night and Julie Laverne (Showboat) for Opera North, Despina (Così fan tutte) and Lucy Lockitt (The Beggar's Opera) on BBC television), Frasquita (Earl's Court and Japan), Josephine (HMS Pinafore) at City Center New York, Musetta, for Opera Northern Ireland, Offenbach's Hélène at Sadler's Wells and Clorinda in La Cenerentola at the Garsington Festival, Dinah in Trouble in Tahiti for Musiktheater Transparent in Antwerp; season 1994–95 as Shakespeare's Hermia at Barbados and in Brand's Maschinist Hopkins in Amsterdam; performed in Coward's After the Ball at the Covent Garden Festival 1999; many appearances in musicals; created role of Carlotta in Andrew Lloyd Webber's The Phantom of the Opera; created role of Felicia Gabriel in The Witches of Eastwick at the Theatre Royal, Drury Lane, London 2000–01 and also at the Princess Theatre, Melbourne 2002; Madame Thenardier in Les Miserables 2002–03; Miss Andrew in Mary Poppins, Prince Edward Theatre, London 2004–. *Recordings:* original cast recordings of The Phantom of the Opera, The Boyfriend, Bitter Sweet, Kismet, Oliver!, The Student Prince, The Killer Soprano. *Current Management:* Hilary Gagan Associates, 187 Drury Lane, London, WC2B 5QD, England. *Telephone:* (20) 7404-8794 (office). *Fax:* (20) 7430-1869 (office). *Website:* hilary@hgassoc.freeserve.co.uk (office). *E-mail:* rosie@rosemaryashe.com. *Website:* www.rosemaryashe.com.

ASHER, Nadine; Singer (Contralto); b. 1957, Chicago, Illinois, USA. *Education:* Studied at Indiana University and Juilliard, New York. *Career:* Sang at first in concert, then opera engagement at Kiel from 1984; Guest appearances at Heidelberg, Munster and Lucerne, as Bostania in Cornelius's Barbier von Bagdad; Zürich Opera from 1987, as Wagner's Flosshilde and Grimgerde, Edwige in Guillaume Tell and Ulrica (Ballo in maschera); Zürich 1996 in the premiere of Schlafes Bruder by H Willi. *Address:* c/o Opernhaus Zürich, Falkenstrasse 1, 8008 Zürich, Switzerland.

ASHKENASI, Shmuel; Violinist; b. 1940, Israel. *Education:* Studied with Ilona Feher in Israel and with Efrem Zimbalist at the Curtis Institute in Philadelphia. *Career:* Concert tours of the US, Europe, Russia and Japan; Co-founded the Vermeer String Quartet at the Marlboro Festival in 1970; Performances in all major US centres and in Europe, Israel and Australia; Festival engagements at Tanglewood, Aspen, Spoleto, Edinburgh, Mostly Mozart in New York, Aldeburgh, South Bank, Sante Fe, Chamber Music West and the Casals Festival; Resident Quartet for Chamber Music Chicago; Masterclasses at the Royal Northern College of Music, Manchester; Member of the Resident Artists Faculty of Northern Illinois University. *Recordings:* Paganini Concertos with the Vienna Symphony Orchestra; Mozart Concerto K219 and Beethoven Romances; Quartets by Beethoven, Dvořák, Verdi and Schubert; Brahms Clarinet Quintet with Carl Leister. *Honours:* Winner, Merriweather Post Contest, Washington DC; Finalist of Queen Elisabeth Competition, Brussels; 2nd Prize, Tchaikovsky International Competition, Moscow. *Address:* c/o Allied Artists, Vermeer Quartet, 42 Montpelier Sq., London, SW7 1JZ, England.

ASHKENAZY, Dimitri; clarinettist; b. 1969, New York, USA. *Education:* Lucerne Conservatory with Giambattista Sisini. *Career:* concerts 1992–93 at the Hollywood Bowl and with the Royal Philharmonic in London (Mozart's Concerto); first tour of Japan 1993, followed by Maxwell Davies's Strathclyde Concerto No. 4 with the composer conducting; 1994 premiere of Marco Tutino's concerto at La Scala; collaborations with Barbara Bonney 1995, 1997, 1998, 2003 and Krzysztof Penderecki 1997, 1998, 1999; season 1996–97 with the premiere of Filippo del Corno's Concerto and concerts in Japan with the European Soloists Ensemble; tours with Sinfonia Varsovia in Spain and Poland playing Penderecki's concerto with the composer conducting 1998–99, and collaboration with Edita Gruberova 1999; appearance at Casals Festival, Puerto Rico 2000; tours of Japan 2000, 2002, including duo recitals with Vovka Ashkenazy and appearance with Gary Bertini at Suntory Hall, Tokyo; appearances in S Africa with KwaZulu-Natal Philharmonic 2002–03, with Brodsky Quartet 1999–2004; duo recitals with Vladimir Ashkenazy in Germany and Austria 2003; world premiere of Maxwell Davies's Clarinet Quintet, Hymn to Artemis Locheia with The Brodsky Quartet at the Lucerne Festival 2004; Berlin debut with the Rundfunk-Sinfonie-Orch. Berlin, Konzerthaus 2004. *Recordings include:* Rossini Variations in C; Richard Strauss Duet-Concertino; Stravinsky Ebony Concerto; Stravinsky Chamber Music; Françaix Clarinet Concerto; Finzi, Copland, Bozza Clarinet Concertos; Blacher Clarinet Concerto. *Current Management:* Harrison/Parrott Ltd, 12 Penzance Place, London, W11 4PA, England. *Telephone:* (20) 7229 9166. *Fax:* (20) 7221 5042. *Website:* www.harrisonparrott.com. *E-mail:* dasliedvondererde@bluemail.ch (home).

ASHKENAZY, Vladimir; Pianist and Conductor; b. 6 July 1937, Gorky, USSR; m. Thorunn Sofia Johannsdottir 1961, 2 s., 3 d. *Education:* Moscow Central Music School, 1945–55; Moscow Conservatory, 1955–63. *Career:* Concert appearances throughout the world, solo recitals and with major orchestras; Conductor of major orchestras especially the Philharmonia, the Concertgebouw (Amsterdam) and the Cleveland Orchestras; Music Director, the Royal Philharmonic Orchestra, 1987–94; Music Director, the Berlin Radio Symphony Orchestra (now called Deutsches Symphonie Orchester Berlin), 1989–99; Conducted at the Prokofiev Centenary Celebrations at the Festival Hall, London, 1991; Promenade Concerts, London, 1991, with the European Community Youth Orchestra; La Mer, 8th Symphony by Shostakovich, and the Royal Philharmonic, Tippett's Concerto for Double String Orchestra and Walton's 1st Symphony, conducted works by Walton (Henry V, Cello Concerto and Belshazzar's Feast) at the Festival Hall, London, 1993; Conducted the Deutsches Symphony Orchestra in Mahler's 8th Symphony, 1996 (tour of South America 1997 and engaged for the 1998 Salzburg Festival); Music Director of the Czech Philharmonic, 1998–. *Recordings:* Over 100 including works by Mozart, Prokofiev, Beethoven, Liszt, Chopin, Schumann and Brahms. *Honours:* 2nd Prize, Chopin International Competition, 1955; 1st Prize, Queen Elisabeth of Belgium Competition, Brussels, 1965; 1st Prize, Tchaikovsky Competition, 1962. *Current Management:* Harrison/Parrott Ltd,

12 Penzance Place, London, W11 4PA, England. *Telephone:* (20) 7229 9166. *Fax:* (20) 7221 5042. *Website:* www.harrisonparrott.com. *Address:* Käppelistrasse 15, 6045 Meggen, Switzerland.

ASHKENAZY, Vovka; Pianist; b. 1961, Moscow, Russia; (Son of preceding). m. Ariane Haering. *Education:* Early piano studies in Iceland with Rögnvaldur Sigurjonsson; Moved to England 1977 and completed studies at Royal Northern College of Music, 1983. *Career:* Debut: Barbican Hall, London, 1983 in Tchaikovsky 1st Piano Concerto with London Symphony Orchestra; Concerts in Germany, Italy, Netherlands, France and Canada; Appearances with most London orchestras in concertos by Brahms, Schumann, Grieg, Tchaikovsky and Rachmaninov; US debut with Los Angeles Philharmonic, at Hollywood Bowl; Recital tour of Israel and tours of Australia and Japan; Appearances in many countries including: Austria, Australia, Belgium, Canada, Denmark, France, Greece, Guatemala, Germany, Netherlands, Iceland, Italy, Ireland, Japan, Malta, Norway, New Zealand, Finland, Russia, Israel, Switzerland and Spain. *Recordings:* Arensky and Tchaikovsky Piano Trios; Bartók Sonata for Two Pianos and Percussion. *Current Management:* c/o Jens Gunnar Becker, Grünstrasse 13, 58313 Herdecke, Germany.

ASHLEY, Robert Reynolds; Composer; b. 28 March 1930, Ann Arbor, MI, USA. *Education:* Studied theory at University of Michigan, Ann Arbor, BMus in 1952, Piano and composition at Manhattan School of Music, NY, MMus in 1952; Postgraduate studies in acoustics and composition at University of Michigan, 1957–60. *Career:* Active with Milton Cohen's Space Theater, 1957–64, the ONCE Festivals and ONCE Group, 1959–69, and the Sonic Arts Union, 1966–76; Toured with these groups in the US and Europe; Director, Center for Contemporary Music, Mills College, Oakland, CA, 1969–81. *Compositions include:* Operas: That Morning Thing, 1967, Atlanta (Acts of God), 1982; Television operas Now Eleanor's Idea (1993), Foreign Experiences (1994), The Immortality Songs (1994–98), Balseros (1997); Various electronic music theatre pieces including Heat, 1961, Public Opinion Descends Upon The Demonstrators, 1961, Kittyhawk: An Antigravity Piece, 1964, Night Train, 1965, The Trial Of Anne Opie Wehrer And Unknown Accomplices For Crimes Against Humanity, 1968, Fancy Free, 1970, It's There, 1970; Films; Video Operas: Music With Roots In The Aether, 1976, Title Withdrawn, 1976, The Lessons, 1981, Atlanta Strategy, 1984; Commission from Florida Grand Opera for opera on the Cuban 'Rafters', 1997; Instrumental pieces including Fives for 2 Pianos, 2 Percussion and String Quintet, 1962, In Memoriam… Kit Carson, opera, 1963, Odalisque, 1985, Superior Seven, 1988; Piano pieces. *Address:* 10 Beach Street, New York, NY 10013, USA.

ASHMAN, David; Singer (baritone); b. 1965, England. *Education:* Royal Academy of Music, London. *Career:* Debut: Sang Belcore in L'Elisir d'amore for Gemini Opera; Appearances as Falke in Die Fledermaus for London City Opera, Ajax in La Belle Hélène for New Sadler's Wells Opera and title role in the premiere of The Plumber's Gift by David Blake for English National Opera, 1989; The Speaker in Die Zauber- flöte, Rossini's Bartolo, Mozart's Figaro and Malatesta in Don Pasquale for the London Opera Players; Season 1994 with Glydebourne Touring Opera, including appearances in Il Barbiere di Siviglia. *Honours:* Andrew Sykes Award, Van Smit Prize and Peter Moores Foundation Scholarship, RAM.

ASHMAN, Mike; British opera director and administrator; *Artistic Director, Opera Zuid;* b. 16 April 1950, Hertford, Herts.. *Career:* Assoc. Producer for Royal Coll. of Music Opera School, London 1989–98; Artistic Dir Opera Zuid, Maastrict, Netherlands 2000–04; has directed for Royal Opera House, Covent Garden, Welsh Nat. Opera, Scottish Opera Go-Round, Opera Holland Park, Opera Ireland and Banff Centre, Alberta; has made performing translations of The Bartered Bride and Weill's Der Jasager. *Recent productions:* for Opera Zuid: Dutch premiere of Death in Venice 2001, Jenufa 2003, Un Ballo in Maschera 2003, Der fliegende Hollander 2004; for Cincinnati Opera: Le Nozze di Figaro 2002; for Royal Danish Opera: L'Elisir d'Amore 1999; for Den Norske Opera: Der fliegende Hollander 1999, Der Ring des Nibelungen 1993–97; French premieres of Cox and Box and Trial by Jury, Musee d'Orsay, Paris 1999. *Publications:* contributes regular articles on operatic subjects (especially Wagner) to books, journals, newspapers and record booklets. *Address:* 22 Little Brook Road, Roydon, Essex, CM19 5LR, England.

ASHWORTH, Valerie Grace; Pianist; b. 12 Sept. 1956, Sale, Cheshire, England; m. Vincent Pirillo, 2 d. *Education:* Chetham's School of Music, Manchester, 1969–75; Studied with Kendall Taylor at Royal College of Music, London, 1975–79; Masterclasses in solo repertoire with William Glock, Albert Ferber, Rudolf Firkusny, Hochschule für Musik, Vienna, 1979–81; ARCM, Piano Performer, 1971; LLRAM, Piano Performer, 1974; ARCM, Teacher's Diploma, 1977. *Career:* Debut: Radio debut, Young Artists, 1969; Soloist, chamber musician and accompanist in England, France, Switzerland, Italy, Denmark, Germany, Japan,

Hungary and Austria; Television debut on John Amis Music On Two, 1972 and Austrian television debut in 1982; American debut at Carnegie Hall in 1989; Official accompanist including Jacqueline du Pré masterclasses, England, 1979, Summer Academy, Nice, France, 1980, Irwin Gage in Zürich, 1984–86, Carinthia Summer 1984 and Summer Academy at Salzburg in 1991; Teaching Contract: Coach, String Department, 1982–87, Vocal Department, 1987–89, Hochschule für Musik at Vienna; Taught piano at University of Osnabruck, 1989–93. *Current Management:* Wilhelm Hansen, Denmark.

ASIKAINEN, Matti Tapio; Pianist and Composer; b. 25 June 1957, Hankasalmi, Finland. *Education:* MA, Musicology, University of Jyväskylä, Finland, 1996; Pianist Diploma, Sibelius Academy, Helsinki, 1985; MA, Piano Department, Moniuszko Academy of Music, Gdańsk, Poland, 1991. *Career:* debut, Concert Hall of Sibelius Academy, Helsinki, 1974; recordings for Finnish Broadcasting Company, 1971–; appearances on Finnish, Lithuanian and Polish television; solo recitals also in Russia and Italy, including Incontri di Serra Maiori Festival; participant, Probaltica Festival of Chamber Music, Poland; soloist, Symphony Orchestras of Polish Philharmonia; mem. Int. Rachmaninoff Soc., England, Chopin Soc. of Finland, Asscn of Finnish Piano Teachers. *Publications:* contributions to music magazines and reviews. *Honours:* Vienna Musikseminar Int. Piano Competition, 1985; Knight Cross of Merit, Order of Merit (Polish President's award), 2002. *Address:* Pyynpolku 5, 40900 Säynätsalo, Finland. *Telephone:* (14) 378-2827. *Fax:* (14) 260-1331.

ASKER, Bjorn; Singer (Baritone); b. 23 Sept. 1941, Stockholm, Sweden. *Education:* Royal Music Academy, Stockholm; With Tito Gobbi in Rome. *Career:* Many appearances at Royal Opera, Stockholm, from 1969, including the premiere of Werle's Tintomara, 1973 and as Don Giovanni, Macbeth, Rossini's Figaro, Telramund, Wotan, Kurwenal, Alberich and Simon Boccanegra; Guest appearances at Helsinki, Tel-Aviv and the Drottningholm Festival; Sang Renato in Un Ballo in Maschera at Stockholm, 1986; Lionel in Tchaikovsky's Maid of Orleans, Rigoletto and Wagner's Dutchman; Amfortas in Mexico and USA; Many concert and recital dates. *Honours:* Swedish Court Singer, 1983. *Address:* Stockholm Royal Opera, PO Box 15094, 10322 Stockholm, USA.

AST, Jochen Van; Singer (Baritone); b. 1970, Amsterdam. *Education:* Studied in Jerusalem; Guildhall School. *Career:* Appearances with The Opera Company, Kent Opera; British Youth Opera and in Hong Kong; Roles have included Mozart's Count and Guglielmo, Dandini in Cenerentola, Clonter Opera; Purcell's Aeneas and Marullo in Rigoletto, Stowe Opera; Purcell's Fairy Queen at Athens and Granada; Le Bourgeois Gentilhomme, Covent Garden; Fledermaus on tour to the USA, 1999; Gershwin's Of Thee I Sing, debut with Opera North, 1998; Concerts include Bach's Passions and Magnificat; Messiah; Judas Maccabaeus; Haydn's Creation and Seasons; Mozart's Requiem. *Address:* Music International, 13 Ardilaun Road, London N5 2QR, England.

ASTI, Eugene; Pianist; b. 1962, USA. *Education:* Mannes College of Music, Fontainebleau, France; Guildhall School, London. *Career:* appearances at the Aldeburgh, Arundel and Cheltenham Festivals; accompanist for Margaret Price throughout Europe and recitals with Felicity Lott; Wigmore Hall debut with Elizabeth Connell; further recitals with Alison Buchanan, Susan Gritton, Nancy Argenta and Rebecca Evans; Schubert's Winterreise with Stephen Varcoe; Brahms and Mendelssohn recital series in London and Bristol 1997; Strauss/ Poulenc recital series, London 1999; Schumann series, London 2003; recitals at Lincoln Center and Weill Recital Hall, New York; Musikverein, Vienna; regular appearances with Sophie Daneman and Stephan Loges; broadcasts on BBC Radio 3. *Recordings:* Songs by Felix and Fanny Mendelssohn; Clara Schumann; Eric Coates. *Honours:* Ferdinand Rauter Award (Richard Tauber Competition) for piano accompaniment; Megan Foster Award (Maggie Teyte Competition) for piano accompaniment. *Current Management:* Harlequin Artist Agency, 203 Fidlas Road, Cardiff CF4 5NA, Wales.

ASTON, Peter George, DPhil, GBSM, FTCL, FCI, ARCM, FRSCM, FRSA; British composer, conductor and academic; b. 5 Oct. 1938, Birmingham, England; m. Elaine Veronica Neale 1960; one s. *Education:* Birmingham School of Music, Univ. of York. *Career:* Lecturer in Music, Univ. of York 1964–72, Sr Lecturer 1972–74; Prof. and Head of Music, School of Fine Arts and Music, Univ. of East Anglia, Norwich 1974–98, Professorial Fellow 1998–2001, Prof. of Music Emeritus 2001–, Dean 1981–84; Dir, The Tudor Consort 1959–65; Conductor, English Baroque Ensemble 1967–70, Aldeburgh Festival Singers 1974–88; Principal Guest Conductor, Sacramento Bach Festival, USA 1993–99, Incontri Corali, Italy 1996, Schola Cantorum Gedanensis, Poland 1999; Series Ed., UEA Recordings 1979–98; jt and founder Artistic Dir, Norwich Festival of Contemporary Church Music 1981–; Lay Canon, Norwich Cathedral 2002–; Chair., Eastern Arts Asscn Music Panel 1976–81; Chair., Norfolk

Asscn for the Advancement of Music 1990–93, Pres. 1993–98; Guild of Church Musicians Academic Bd 1996–; Royal School of Church Music Norfolk and Norwich Area Cttee 1998–. *Compositions:* chamber music, opera, Church music, numerous choral and orchestral works, including I Am the True Vine for chorus and organ 1999, editions of Baroque music, including complete works of George Jeffreys. *Recordings:* Mellers' Life Cycle; Jeffreys' Anthems and Devotional Songs; Choral music by Holst and Britten; Numerous choral and orchestral works. *Publications:* The Music of York Minster 1972, Sound and Silence (co-author) 1970, Music Theory in Practice (three vols) 1992–93. *Honours:* Hon. RCM 1991, FGCM 1995. *Address:* 9 Bourne Close, Long Stratton, Norwich NR15 2RW, England.

ATANASIU, George; Cellist, Conductor; b. 15 Nov. 1958, Galati, Romania; 2 s. *Education:* Studied at Bucharest Academy of Music with Serafim Antropov, Petre Lefterescu, Uzi Wiesel and Laszlo Meszo; Bayreuth Youth Festival; Weimar International Music Seminar; Hitzaker Chamber Music Academy. *Career:* Debut: Soloist with Galati Youth Orchestra, Golterman cello concerto, aged 13; Cello Professor, Rowan University of New Jersey and Conductor of PYPO Orchestra and Enescu Piano Trio, 1988–; Appeared as soloist or in recitals on radio and television in Romania, USA, Germany, Italy, Spain, Switzerland, Hungary, Austria, the United Kingdom and Venezuela; Performed at Bayreuth Youth Festival, Weimar International Music Seminar, Hitzacker Chamber Music Academy, Carmel Bach Festival, California and George Enescu International Festival, Bucharest; Principal cellist of the Garden State Philharmonic, 1988–90; South Jersey Symphony Orchestra, 1990–94; mem, American String Teacher Association. *Recordings:* George Enescu Trio in A minor no. 2. *Honours:* Winner of Romania National Competition, cello, 1975, 1983; Chamber music, 1979; Bronze medal at International Chamber Music Competition, Florence, 1983. *Current Management:* GAIAM-ARTS. *Address:* 505 Bloomfield Avenue, Drexel Hill, PA 19026, USA.

ATHERTON, David, OBE, MA, LRAM, LTCL, LGSM; British conductor; *Conductor Laureate, Hong Kong Philharmonic Orchestra;* b. 3 Jan. 1944, Blackpool; s. of Robert Atherton and Lavinia Atherton; m. Ann Gianetta Drake 1970; one s. two d. *Education:* Univ. of Cambridge. *Career:* Répétiteur, Royal Opera House, Covent Garden 1967–68; Resident Conductor, Royal Opera House 1968–79; Artistic Dir and Conductor, London Stravinsky Festival 1979–82, Ravel/Varèse Festival 1983–84; debut La Scala, Milan 1976, San Francisco Opera 1978, Metropolitan Opera, New York 1984; youngest-ever conductor at Henry Wood Promenade Concerts, London 1968; debut Royal Festival Hall, London 1969; has conducted performances in Europe, Middle East, Far East, Australasia, N America 1970–; Music Dir and Prin. Conductor San Diego Symphony Orchestra 1980–87; Prin. Conductor and Artistic Adviser Royal Liverpool Philharmonic Orchestra 1980–83, Prin. Guest Conductor 1983–86; Prin. Guest Conductor BBC Symphony Orchestra 1985–89; Music Dir and Prin. Conductor Hong Kong Philharmonic Orchestra 1989–2000, Conductor Laureate 2000–; Artistic Dir Mainly Mozart Festival, Southern Calif. 1989–, London Sinfonietta 1967–73, 1989–91 (Founder 1967); Prin. Guest Conductor BBC Nat. Orchestra of Wales 1994–97; Co-Founder, Pres. and Artistic Dir Global Music Network 1998–; Licentiate, Trinity Coll. of Music, Guildhall School of Music and Drama. *Publications:* The Complete Instrumental and Chamber Music of Arnold Schoenberg and Roberto Gerhard (ed.) 1973, Pandora and Don Quixote Suites by Roberto Gerhard (ed.) 1973; contrib. to The Musical Companion 1978, The New Grove Dictionary 1981. *Honours:* Conductor of the Year Award, Composers' Guild of GB 1971, Edison Award 1973, Grand Prix du Disque Award 1977, Koussevitzky Award 1981, Int. Record Critics' Award 1982, Prix Caecilia 1982. *Current Management:* Askonas Holt Ltd, Lonsdale Chambers, 27 Chancery Lane, London, WC2A 1PF, England. *Telephone:* (20) 7400-1700. *Fax:* (20) 7400-1799. *E-mail:* info@askonasholt.co.uk. *Website:* www.askonasholt.co.uk.

ATHERTON, Diane; Singer (Soprano); b. 1970, Yorkshire, England. *Education:* Guildhall School, London. *Career:* Appearances in Mendelssohn's Midsummer Night's Dream, as Eva in Joseph Tal's The Garden and Carmina Burana by Orff, all at the Queen Elizabeth Hall, London; Britten's Aminta in Mozart's Il re Pastore at Aldeburgh; Opera Holland Park as Musetta, and as Mozart's Zerlina, Pamina and Susanna; British tour in Strauss Gala, conducted by Christopher Warren-Green; Handel's Messiah for HTV, Wales; Sang Pythia in the British premiere of Oresteia by Xenakis, for the English Bach Festival, Linbury Studio, Covent Garden, 2000. *Recordings include:* Purcell's Fairy Queen (Naxos). *Address:* c/o English Bach Festival, Linbury Theatre, Royal Opera, Covent Garden, London WC2, England.

ATHERTON, Joan, GRSM, ARCM; British violinist; b. 6 April 1948, Blackpool, England; two d. *Education:* Royal Coll. of Music, London. *Career:* freelance violinist, solo, chamber and orchestral player; principal with London Sinfonietta 1970–; mem. Inc. Soc. of Musicians, Musicians' Union. *Honours:* Tagore Gold Medal 1970. *Address:* 12 Addison Way, London, NW11 6AJ, England (office). *Telephone:* (20) 8455-0658 (office). *Fax:* (20) 8201-9704 (office). *E-mail:* joan@atherton80.freeserve.co.uk (office).

ATHERTON, Michael, MA; Australian composer and musician and writer; *Director of Research, College of Arts, University of Western Sydney;* b. 17 Feb. 1950, Liverpool, England. *Education:* Univ. of New South Wales, Univ. of Sydney, Univ. of New England, USA. *Career:* Artist-in-Residence, Australian Museum 1993; Foundation Prof. of Music, Univ. of Western Sydney 1993–, Chair of Contemporary Arts 1999–, currently Dir of Research, Coll. of Arts; performer of classical, early music, folk and Asia Pacific instruments in various groups internationally; serves on State and Commonwealth Ministerial Cttees for the Arts. *Compositions include:* The Mahogany Ship for choir, strings and percussion 1993; Exhortation for double choir and percussion 1996; Namatjira for choir 1995; Songs for Imberombera for choir, strings and percussion 1997; Theme for Children's Hospital, Australian Broadcasting Corporation Television 1997; I Saw Eternity for double SATB 1999; Score for the feature film Dogwatch 1999, Kamawarah for orchestra 2001. *Recordings:* Ankh (CD of ancient Egyptian music) 1998, Abundance 2003, Melismos (CD of ancient Greek music) 2004. *Honours:* Centenary Medal for Services to Society (Music). *Address:* Locked Bag 1797, University of Western Sydney, Penrith, 5th DC, NSW 1797 (office); 10/1 Kiara Close, North Sydney, NSW 2060, Australia (home). *Telephone:* (2) 9772-6306 (office). *Fax:* (2) 9772-6737 (office). *E-mail:* m.atherton@uws.edu.au (office).

ATKINSON, Ann, BEd, LRAM; Welsh singer (mezzo-soprano); b. 24 Aug. 1965, Corwen, Clwyd; m. Kevin John Sharp. *Education:* Univ. of Wales; Royal Acad. of Music, with Kenneth Bowen; and with Ryland Davies. *Career:* performed with Britain's leading opera companies, including Scottish Opera, Glyndebourne Festival and Touring Opera, Wexford Festival Opera; operatic roles include Carmen for Garden Opera, Azucena and Ines (Il Trovatore) for Scottish Opera, Niklausse (Tales of Hoffmann), Larina and Filipyevna (Eugene Onegin), Annina (La Traviata) for Glyndebourne, Maddalena (Rigoletto), Marcellina (Le Nozze di Figaro); also sang Mamma Lucia (Cavalleria Rusticana) in Ho Chi Minh City; created roles of Mrs Baines in Andrew Gant's The Basement Room and Ann Clwyd, MP in world premiere of Alun Hoddinott's opera Tower for Opera Box; many concert performances include Verdi's Requiem, Beethoven's 9th Symphony; Brahms' Alto Rhapsody, Mozart's Requiem, Mendelssohn's Elijah (QEH), Handel's Messiah; conductor of two male voice choirs, Cor Meibion Bro Glyndwr and Cor Meibion Froncysyllte. *Honours:* Winner, Nat. Eisteddfod of Wales; Llangollen Int. Eisteddfod. *Current Management:* Helen Sykes Artists Management, 100 Felsham Road, Putney, London, SW15 1DQ, England. *Address:* Glaslwyn, Mill Street, Corwen, Denbighshire, LL21 0AU, England (home). *Telephone:* (1490) 412735 (home). *E-mail:* annatkinson@ntlworld.com (home).

ATKINSON, Lynton; British singer (tenor); b. 11 Oct. 1962, London, England. *Education:* studied in Cambridge with George Guest, London with David Mason and Gita Denise. *Career:* concert appearances in festivals at Innsbruck, Utrecht, Malta, Brighton and Edinburgh; Sang at cathedrals of Canterbury, Wells, Durham and Birmingham, at King's College Cambridge and the Sheldonian Theatre in Oxford; Has sung in Bach's St John Passion on tour to Spain, the St Matthew Passion in Bad Homburg and L'Incoronazione di Poppea at the Spitalfields Festival; Vienna in 1989 with Handel's Susanna under Martin Haselbrock; Sang Alfredo in a production of La Traviata in Mauritius; Handel's Belshazzar with Concerto Köln in Germany and Italy; Sang at Edinburgh Festival and in Poland with the City of London Sinfonia under Richard Hickox; Covent Garden, 1990–91 as First Prisoner in Fidelio and Ywain in the world premiere of Birtwistle's Gawain; Sang at Buxton Festival and Spitalfields in 1991 in Il Sogno di Scipione by Mozart and Acis and Galatea; Season 1992 as Nathaniel in Hoffmann and Zefirino in Il Viaggio a Reims at Covent Garden. *Recordings include:* L'Incoronazione di Poppea; Video of Covent Garden Fidelio as First Prisoner. *Honours:* Prizewinner, Alfredo Kraus International Singing Competition, Las Palmas, 1990. *Address:* c/o The City of Birmingham Choir, 47 Lonsdale Road, Walsall, WS5 3HJ, England.

ATLANTOV, Vladimir; Singer (Tenor); b. 19 Feb. 1939, Leningrad, USSR. *Education:* Studied with N Bolotina at the Leningrad Conservatory and at La Scala opera school, Milan. *Career:* Sang at the Kirov Theatre, Moscow from 1963, Bolshoi Theatre from 1967, roles include Lenski, Hermann, Don Carlos, Radames, Don José, Alfredo, Cavaradossi and Canio; Vienna Staatsoper 1971; Vladimir in Prince Igor with the Bolshoi company at La Scala, 1973; Deutsche Oper Berlin 1974, as Cavaradossi; Has also sung baritone roles from 1977, notably Posa in Don Carlos; Munich 1980, as Otello; Covent Garden 1989 as Canio in Pagliacci (also at Kenwood, Lakeside); Sang Samson at Berlin, Deutsche Oper, 1989; Otello at Covent Garden, 1990 followed by Hermann at La Scala and Canio at the Caracalla Festival, Rome; Sang Samson for Opera Pacific at Costa Mesa, 1992 and Otello there in 1997; Concert tours of Canada, Europe and Japan. *Recordings:* Prince Igor, Eugene Onegin, Francesca da Rimini by Rachmaninov, Iolanta by Tchaikovsky, Ruslan and Ludmila, The Stone Guest by Dargomyzhsky. *Honours:* People's Artist of the RSFSR, 1972. *Address:* c/o Allied Artists Agency, 42 Montpelier Square, London SW7 1JZ, England.

ATLAS, Allan Warren; Musicologist; b. 19 Feb. 1943, New York, USA. *Education:* BA, Hunter College of the City University of New York, 1964; MA, 1966, PhD, 1971, New York University. *Career:* Faculty, Brooklyn College, 1971–; Visiting Professor, New York University, 1971, 1984, 1986; Executive Officer, PhD and DMA Programs in Music, Director, Center for the Study of Free-Reed Instruments, Graduate School, City University of New York. *Publications:* The Cappella Giulia Chansonnier: Rome, Biblioteca Apostolica Vaticana, CG XIII. 27, 2 vols, 1975–76; Music at the Aragonese Court of Naples, 1985; The Wheatstone English Concertina in Victorian England, 1996; Renaissance Music, 1998; Anthology of Renaissance Music, 1998. *Contributions:* Articles in the New Grove Dictionary of Music and Musicians and in various journals. *Address:* 945 Cedar Lane, Woodmere, NY 11598, USA.

ATTROT, Ingrid; Singer (Soprano); b. 1961, Canada. *Education:* Graduated, University of Toronto's Opera School, 1985; Britten-Pears School at Aldeburgh; National Opera Studio, 1986–87. *Career:* Has appeared as Mozart's Countess and Donna Anna and Meg Page in Sir John In Love by Vaughan Williams, Ibert's Angélique and Respighi's Maria Egiziaca; Sang Madeline in Debussy's Fall of the House of Usher at Elizabeth Hall, 1989; Wigmore Hall and Purcell Room recitals in 1989; Handel's Ode to St Cecilia with Charles Dutoit and the Montreal Symphony; Bach's B minor Mass in Montreal; Vivaldi's Gloria in Ottawa and New York under Trevor Pinnock; Mendelssohn's Midsummer Night's Dream under Neville Marriner at the Festival Hall; Season 1989–90 with Carmina Burana and the Petite Messe Solennelle; Szymanowski recital at the Purcell Room; Handel's Floridante in Canada and California; Stravinsky's Les Noces in Antwerp and Elgar's The Kingdom; Tour of Russia with English National Opera productions of Macbeth and The Turn of The Screw; Season 1992 as Mathilde in Guillaume Tell for Haddo House Opera and the Governess in The Turn of the Screw for Pimlico Opera; Sang Donna Anna at Belfast, 1994. *Honours:* Winner, Eckhardt-Gramatte Competition for Contemporary Music, Canada; Awards from Canada Council, University of Toronto, the Canadian Aldeburgh Foundation and the Friends of Covent Garden. *Address:* Juggs Cottage, Forebridge, Little Bedwyn, Marlborough, Wiltshire SN8 3JS, England.

ATZMON, Moshe; Conductor; b. 30 July 1931, Budapest, Hungary. *Education:* Studied cello in Hungary and continued musical training in Israel where he studied horn and piano; Further studies at the Tel-Aviv Academy of Music, 1958–62; Composition studies at the Guildhall School of Music, London. *Career:* Played horn in Israel Symphony and opera orchestras; Chief Conductor, Sydney Symphony Orchestra, 1969–71, Basle Symphony Orchestra, 1972–77, North German Radio Symphony Orchestra, Hamburg, 1972–76 and Tokyo Metropolitan Symphony Orchestra, 1978–82; Co-Principal Conductor of American Symphony Orchestra, NY, 1982–84; Chief Conductor of Nagoya Philharmonic Orchestra, 1986–92; Director of the Dortmund Orchestra in 1991; Conducted Siegfried, Buenos Aires Filarmónica concert, 1996. *Recordings include:* Mendelssohn Overtures; Liszt's Piano Concertos with Garrick Ohlsson; Brahms' Double Concerto and Serenade Op 11; Bach's E major and A minor Violin Concertos with Schneiderhan; Works for piano and orchestra by Addinsell, Litolff, Gottschalk and Rachmaninov. *Honours:* 1st Prize, Conducting, Guildhall School of Music, 1963; 1st Prize, Liverpool International Conductors' Competition, 1964. *Address:* PGM, Top floor, 59 Lansdowne Place, Hove, East Sussex BN3 1 FL, England.

AUBERSON, Jean Marie; Conductor; b. 2 May 1920, Chavorney, Vaud, Switzerland. *Education:* Studied at the Lausanne Conservatory; Studied conducting with Van Kampen at Siena and with Gunther Wand in Cologne, 1950–51. *Career:* Played violin with the Lausanne Chamber Orchestra, 1943–46, and Suisse Romande Orchestra, 1946–49; Conducted the Lausanne Chamber Orchestra, then the Radio Beromunster Orchestra at Zürich, the Suisse Romande Orchestra and the Zürich Tonhalle; Ballet evenings at the Geneva Opera and the Hamburg Staatsoper; Further career with Orchestra of Radio Basle and of Ville de Saint-Gall; Conducted the premieres of the ballet Paris by Henri Sauguet in 1964, Ginastera's Piano Concerto in 1977 and La Folie de Tristan by Schibler in 1980. *Recordings include:* Mozart C minor Mass with the Vienna Philharmonic; Handel's Organ Concertos with Lionel Rogg and the Geneva Baroque Orchestra; Tchaikovsky's Violin Concerto with Tibor Varga; Oboe Concertos by CPE Bach, Marcello and Bellini, with Heinz Holliger. *Address:* c/o Grand Théâtre de Genève, 11 Boulevard du Théâtre, 1211 Geneva 11, Switzerland.

AUDI, Pierre; Stage Director; b. 1957, Beirut, Lebanon. *Education:* Exeter College, Oxford, 1975–78. *Career:* Founded the Almeida Theatre, Islington, London, 1979; Director of theatre and annual contemporary music festival until 1989; Artistic Director of Netherlands Opera from 1988, productions include Schoenberg's Die Glückliche Hand, Feldman's Neither and Monteverdi's Il Ritorno d'Ulisse, part of a complete cycle and Wagner's Ring, concluding in 1998; Directed stage works by Wolfgang Rihm, Michael Finnissy (The Undivine Comedy) and John Casken (Golem) for the Almeida Theatre; Opera North 1990 with the British stage premiere of Verdi's Jerusalem; Produced Birtwistle's Punch and Judy for Netherlands Opera in 1993; Staged premiere of Henze's Venus and Adonis at Munich, 1997. *Honours:* Lesley Boosey Award, 1990. *Current Management:* Ingpen & Williams Ltd, 7 St George's Court, 131 Putney Bridge Road, London, SW15 2PA, England.

AUGUIN, Philippe; Conductor; b. 1962, France. *Education:* Studied in Vienna and Florence. *Career:* Musical assistant to Herbert von Karajan, 1986–; Associated with Georg Solti at the Salzburg Festival; La Scala Milan, with Don Giovanni, La Damnation de Faust, Die Zauberflöte and Figaro, 1993–; Covent Garden with La Traviata and Un Ballo in Maschera, 1994; Music Director of the Braunschweig Opera leading Tristan und Isolde, Parsifal, Salome, Pelléas et Mélisande and Wozzeck, 1994–; Mahler and Schoenberg cycles with Czech and Royal Philharmonics, Dresden State Orchestra and Orchestre National de France; Principal Conductor of the Staatsheater Stuttgart, with Tannhäuser, Elektra, Lohengrin, Rosenkavalier and Ariadne; Otello at the Hamburg Staatsoper, Der fliegende Holländer at Leipzig and La Sonnambula at Cologne; Salzburg Festival, 1991–; with Fidelio, 1996; Season 1996–97 with Figaro at La Scala, Tannhäuser for Australian Opera, Le Roi Arthus in Cologne and concerts with the Royal Scottish National; Music Director, Nuremberg Opera/State Theatre, 1998–; La Forza del Destino at La Scala, 1999. *Current Management:* Askonas Holt Ltd, Lonsdale Chambers, 27 Chancery Lane, London, WC2A 1PF, England. *Telephone:* (20) 7400-1700. *Fax:* (20) 7400-1799. *E-mail:* info@askonasholt.co .uk. *Website:* www.askonasholt.co.uk.

AUSTBÖ, Hakon; Pianist; b. 22 Oct. 1948, Kongsberg, Norway. *Education:* Studied in Norway and at the Paris Conservatoire and Ecole Normale de Musique, 1966–71; Juilliard School, New York, USA, 1971–72; Staatliche Hochschule für Musik, Munich, Germany, 1972–74; Private studies in London. *Career:* Played with Bergen Philharmonic Orchestra, 1963; First Oslo recital, 1964; Concert and solo engagements throughout Scandinavia and Europe; Piano duo with Marina Horak, and chamber concerts with Trio du Nord until 1985; Numerous radio and television performances. *Honours:* Winner of the 1971 Messiaen Competition at Royan and prizewinner at the Scriabin Competition, Oslo (1972) and the Ravel Competition at Paris (1975); Professor at the University of Utrecht from 1979. *Address:* c/o Utrechts Conservatorium, Mariaplaats 28, 3511 LL Utrecht, Netherlands.

AUSTIN, Larry Don; Composer and Music Educator; b. 12 Sept. 1930, Duncan, Oklahoma, USA; m. Edna Navarro 1953, 2 s., 3 d. *Education:* BME, 1951, MM, 1952, University of North Texas, Denton; Studied with Darius Milhaud, Mills College, Oakland, CA, 1955; Seymour Shifrin and Andrew Imbrie, University of California, Berkeley, 1955–58; Computer music workshops, Stanford University, 1969; Massachusetts Institute of Technology, 1978. *Career:* Professor, 1958–72, Director of University's bands, 1958–72, Co-director, New Music Ensemble, 1963–68, University of California, Davis; Publisher and Owner, Source and Composer/ Performer Edition, 1966–; University of South Florida, Tampa, 1972–78, University of North Texas, 1978–. *Compositions include:* Woodwind Quintet, 1949; Mass for Chorus and Orchestra, 1955–58; Quartet Three, electronic music on tape, 1971; Quadrants, 1–11; Catalogo Sonoro-Narcisso for Viola and Tape, 1978; Protoforms, hybrid musics for 3 Sopranos and Computer, 1980; Euphonia: A Tale Of The Future, opera, 1982; Sonata Concertante for Pianist and Computer, 1983–84; Violet's Invention for Piano, 1988; A Universe Of Symphony: The Earth, Life Pulse And Heavens, 1974–93; Accidents Two: Sound Projections for Piano with Computer Music, 1992; Electro-acoustic music, including Variations... Beyond Pierrot, 1995; Shin-Edo: CityscapeSet, 1996; BluesAx, 1996; Djuro's Tree, 1997; Taragato, 1998; Singing! For baritone and tape, 1998. *Publications:* Learning to Compose: Modes, Materials and Models of Musical Invention, with Thomas Clark, 1988. *Contributions:* Articles in various publications. *Honours:* numerous grants, commissions and awards. *Address:* 2109 Woodbrook, Denton, TX 76205, USA.

AUSTIN-PHILIPS, Eric; Composer and Conductor; b. 12 Oct. 1947, Melbourne, Victoria, Australia. *Education:* BMus, University of Melbourne; Composition with John McCabe and conducting with Roger Norrington, 1975. *Career:* Faculty Member, The University High School, 1972–; Conductor, Music Critic. *Compositions include:* Portraits of my Friends and Others, for flute, oboe, clarinet, bassoon and piano, 1973; Nirthanjali for mandolin and orchestra, 1973; Into the Air for piano, 1976; Macavity: The Mystery Cat, for choir, 1981; Comfits and

Joys for soprano, choir and strings, 1982; The Black Swan, for choir, 1984; Sinfonietta No. 2 for plectra ensemble, 1986; Commissions from the British Music Society (1972), Melbourne Mandolin Orchestra and The Melbourne Chronicle (1982). *Honours:* Dorian Le Gallienne Prize, 1972. *Address:* c/o APRA, 1A Eden Street, Crows Nest, NSW 2065, Australia.

AUVINEN, Ritva; singer (soprano); b. 1945, Finland. *Education:* Sibelius Academy, Helsinki, studied with Gina Cigna in Rome and Peter Klein in Vienna. *Career:* Debut: Helsinki concert, 1965; Many appearances with the Finnish National Opera from 1965, notably as Riita in the premiere of Kokkonen's The Last Temptations, 1975, also at the New York Met, 1983; Other roles include Renata in Prokofiev's The Fiery Angel, 1985; Strauss's Ariadne, 1986; Janáček's Emilia Marty, 1988; Lady Macbeth at the Savonlinna Festival, 1993; Guest engagements at St Petersburg, Zürich and Stockholm, with concerts and recitals in New York, London, Vienna and Salzburg; Sang Ms Lovett in Sondheim's Sweeney Todd at Helsinki 1997–98; Premiere of Tapio Tuomela's Mother and Daughter at Helsinki (concert) 1999. *Address:* Finnish National Opera, PO Box 176, Helsingkatu 58, 00251 Helsinki, Finland.

AVDEYEVA, Larisa Ivanova; Singer (mezzo-soprano); b. 21 June 1925, Moscow, Russia; m. Evgeny Svetlanov. *Education:* Stanislavsky Opera Studio. *Career:* Sang at the Stanislavsky Music Theatre, Moscow from 1947 as Offenbach's La Périchole, Susuki in Madama Butterfly and in Khrennikov's Into The Storm and Molchanov's The Stone Flower; Bolshoi Theatre in Moscow from 1952 as Olga in Eugene Onegin, Marina in Boris Godunov, Lehl in The Snow Maiden by Rimsky-Korsakov, Konchakovna in Prince Igor, Akhrosimova in Prokofiev's War and Peace, Carmen, and the Sorceress in the opera by Tchaikovsky; Has toured as opera and concert singer in Canada, Europe, USA and the Far East. *Honours:* People's Artist of RSFSR, 1964. *Address:* c/o Bolshoi Theatre, Pr Marxa 8-2, 103009 Moscow, Russia.

AVELING, Valda; Harpsichordist; b. 16 May 1920, Sydney, Australia. *Education:* Performers and Teachers Diplomas, New South Wales Conservatorium of Music, 1936. *Career:* Debut: Town Hall, Sydney, with Malcolm Sargent, 1938; Appearances with all leading orchestras and at all Music Festivals in the United Kingdom; Frequent concert and record collaboration with Richard Bonynge and Joan Sutherland; Numerous recitals as Duo with Evelyn Barbirolli (oboe); Numerous tours of Europe, Canada and Far East including tour of Germany as joint soloist with Yehudi Menuhin; Performances at Rome Harpsichord Festival, Italy, 1971, 1972; Four visits to Australia for Australian Broadcasting Commission, latest 1976; Recital, University of Indiana, USA, 1976. *Recordings include:* Scarlatti Sonatas for harpsichord, for EMI, 1976; Chio Mi Scordi di Te, Mozart; Harpsichord Pieces, Thomas Morley; The Collection of Historic Instruments at the Victoria and Albert Museum, London; Music for Four Harpsichords; Harpsichord Continuo. *Contributions:* Music and Musicians. *Honours:* Honorary FTCL; Awarded O.B.E., 1982. *Address:* 15 Priory Road, London NW6 4NN, England.

AVNI, Tzvi Jacob; Composer and Music Educator; b. 7 Sept. 1927, Saarbrucken, Germany (living in Israel since 1935); m. Hanna Avni, 26 Aug 1979, 1 s., 1 d. *Education:* Diploma in Theory and Composition, Israel Music Academy, Tel-Aviv, 1958; Further studies in USA, 1962–64. *Career:* Director, AMLI Central Music Library, Tel-Aviv, 1961–75; Director, Electronic Music Studio, 1977–1995, Professor of Music Theory and Composition, Rubin Academy, Jerusalem, 1971–; North Eastern University, Boston, 1993–94; Queens College, New York, 1994–95; mem, Israel Composers League, Chairman 1978–80; Chairman of Israel Jeunesses Musicales. *Compositions include:* Two String Quartets, Wind Quintet, Five Pantomimes for 8 Players; Works for choir, various electronic pieces, works for ballet, art films and radio plays; Vitrage for Harp Solo, 1990; Desert Scenes, symphony in 3 movements, 1990; Three Lyric Songs on P Celan Poems for Mezzo Soprano, English Horn and Harp, 1990; Fagotti Fugati for 2 Bassoons, 1991; Variations on a Sephardic Tune for Recorder Ensemble, 1992; Haleluyah for Mixed Choir, 1993; Triptych for Piano, 1994; The Three Legged Monster, musical legend, for Narrator, Piano and Small Orchestra with text by Hanna Avni, 1994; Anthropomorphic Landscapes, No. 1 Flute Solo, No. 2 Oboe Solo, No. 3 Clarinet Solo; Songs and Melodies, for mixed choir, in memory of Itzhak Rabin, 1996–97; Pray for the Peace of Jerusalem for symphony orchestra, 1997; Se Questo é un Uomo, five songs for soprano and orchestra on poems by Primo Levi, 1998; The Ship of Hours, four orchestral sketches on paintings by M Ardon, 1999; Apropos Klee, four pieces for choir and instruments on Paul Klee Paintings, 2000; Bassoon Concerto, 2001. *Recordings include:* Love Under a Different Sun, Chamber-Vocal Works; Program Music 1980 with Israel Philharmonic and Mehta; Piano Sonata No. 1; String Quartet No. 1 (Summer Strings), Israeli String Quartet; 5 Variations for Mr 'K', for percussion; Epitaph (sonata No. 2) for Piano, 1998. *Publications include:* An Orchestra is Born; Editor of Gittit, Israel, 1966–80. *Contributions:* Dictionary of 20th Century Music; Music in Israel. *Honours:* The Israel Prime-Minister's Prize for life achieve-

ments, 1998; The Saarland (Germany) State Prize for life achievement, 1998; The Israel State Prize in Music, 2001. *Address:* 54 Bourla Street, Tel-Aviv 69364, Israel.

AVSHALOMOV, Jacob David; Conductor and Composer; b. 28 March 1919, Tsintao, China. *Education:* Studied with his father, Aaron Avshalomov in Shanghai, with Ernst Toch in Los Angeles, 1938, at Reed College in Portland, Oregon, 1939–41 and with Bernard Rogers at Eastman School of Music, Rochester, New York, 1941–43. *Career:* Teacher, 1947–54, Conductor of Chorus and Orchestra, Columbia University; US premieres, Bruckner Mass in D, Handel's Triumph of Time and Truth, Tippett's A Child of Our Time; Conductor of Portland Junior Symphony Orchestra, 1954–78 and Portland Youth Philharmonic, 1978–94. *Compositions include:* The Taking of T'Ung Kuan for Orchestra, 1943, revised, 1953; Sinfonietta, 1946; Evocations for Clarinet and Chamber Orchestra, 1947; Sonatine for Viola and Piano, 1947; Prophecy for Cantor, Chorus and Organ, 1948; How Long, O Lord, cantata, 1948–49; Tom O'Bedlam for Chorus, 1953; Psalm 100 for Chorus and Wind Instruments, 1956; Inscriptions At The City Of Brass for Female Narrator, Chorus and Orchestra, 1956; Phases Of The Great Land for Orchestra, 1959; Symphony: The Oregon, 1959–61, Revised Jubilee version 1999; City Upon The Hill for Narrator, Chorus, Orchestra and Liberty Bell, 1965; The Thirteen Clocks for 2 Storytellers and Orchestra, 1973; Raptures for Orchestra, 1975; Quodlibet Montagna for Brass Sextet, 1975; Praises From The Corners Of The Earth for Chorus and Orchestra, 1976; Songs for Alyce, 1976; The Most Triumphant Bird, chorus, piano and viola concertante, text Emily Dickinson, 1986; Glorious The Assembled Fires for Chorus and Orchestra, 1990; Songs in Season for chorus, C, B and piano, 1993; Songs from the Goliards, chorus and cello, 1994; His Fluid Aria for chorus and bass clarinet, 1995; Doris Songs for mezzo and guitar, 1997; Seasons' Greetings for full orchestra, 1997. *Recordings:* Collections of contemporary American music; Phases of the great Land Cantata: How Long O Lord; Taking of Tung Kuan Prophecy; Open Sesame; Praises from the Corners of the Earth, Raptures for Orchestra, Symphony of Songs; Three Generations Avshalomov; 24 songs; Fabled Cities; Music for Virtuoso Chorus and Virtuosolo Instruments; Conducted Aaron Avshalomov's orchestral works, 1999. *Publications:* The Concerts Reviewed, 65 Years of the Portland Youth Philharmonic, 1989; Avshalomows' Winding Way (biography of father, Aaron, and Jacob), 2001. *Address:* 2741 SW Fairview Blvd, Portland, OR 97201, USA. *Website:* www.composers.com/avshalomov.

AWAD, Emil; Composer, Conductor and Educator; b. 2 Aug. 1963, Mexico. *Education:* BM, Manhattan School of Music; PhD, Composition, Harvard University, 1995. *Career:* Artistic Director, Dudley Orchestra, Harvard, 1989–93, Ensemble de las Rosas, 1994–96, Fin de Siglo en Xalapa, 1998–; Guest Conductor, Manhattan Contemporary Ensemble, Harvard Contemporary Ensemble, Orquesta de Cámara de Bellas Artes; Artistic Director for over 100 premieres in Mexico, 1994–, including works by Babbitt, Carter, Davidovsky, Kim, and Martino; Chair, Composition Department, Conservatorio de las Rosas, 1994–98; Director of Graduate Studies, Professor, Music Department, Universidad Veracruzana, 1999–. *Compositions include:* Duo for violin and Piano, Guitar Quartet, Woodwind Trio, Pashkat, women's chorus, harp and string orchestra; Zazil for orchestra; Piedras Sueltas, text by Octavio Paz, for flute, violin, viola, cello, piano, soprano.. *Recordings:* Artificios, Cuarteto Manuel M. Ponce. Quindecim Recordings 2002.. *Publications:* La Parte del Oyente, Ciencia con Arte.. *Honours:* Harvard Grant; Manhattan School of Music Merit Scholarship; Juilliard School of Music Composition Prize; Fellow, Composer-in-Residence, Universidad Veracruzana, 1998–99. *Address:* Facultad de Música, Universidad Veracruzana, Barragán No. 32, Xaiapa, Veracruz CP 91000, Mexico.

AX, Emanuel, BA; pianist; b. 8 June 1949, Lvov, Poland; m. Yoko Nozaki 1974; one s. one d. *Education:* Columbia University, NY, USA, Juilliard School of Music. *Career:* concert pianist, 1974–; appearances in USA and abroad; Performances with major orchestras including the New York Philharmonic, Philadelphia Orchestra, Chicago Symphony Orchestra, Los Angeles Philharmonic Orchestra, Cleveland Orchestra, Concertgebouw Orchestra, NHK Symphony and London Philharmonic; Played Beethoven's 2nd Concerto with London Philharmonic at the Festival Hall in 1991, and Brahms 1st Concerto at Promenade Concerts in 1991; Mozart's D minor Concerto at the 1994 Proms; World premieres of concertos by John Adams with the Cleveland Orchestra, 1997, Christopher Rouse (New York Philharmonic, 1999), Bright Sheng (Boston Symphony, 2000); All-Beethoven concerto cycles with New York Philharmonic at Lincoln Center Festival, 1999, and Cleveland Orchestra, 2001; Mozart K482 at London Proms 2000; Schoenberg concerto at Salzburg Festival, 2000; Beethoven's Concerto No. 4 in G Major at the London Proms, 2002; mem, Advisory Board, Palm Beach Festival; Chopin Society. *Recordings:* With Philadelphia Orchestra, Chicago Symphony, Cleveland Quartet and Guarneri Quartet; Brahms Concerto (Boston Symphony/Haitink); Adams Concerto (Cleveland

Orchestra); Chamber music with Yo-Yo Ma, Isaac Stern, Jaime Laredo; Duos with Yo-Yo Ma. *Honours:* 1st Prize, Arthur Rubenstein International Piano Master Competition, 1974; Record of the Year Award, Stereo Review, 1977; 1 of 5 Best Records of the Year Award, Time Magazine, 1977; Avery Fisher Award, 1979. *Current Management:* ICM Artists Ltd, 40 W 57th Street, New York, NY 10019, USA. .

AXERLIS, Stella; Singer (Soprano); b. 5 March 1944, Alexandria, Greece. *Education:* Studied at the University of Melbourne, Australia. *Career:* Debut: Hagen, Germany, in 1968 as Aida; Sang at the Deutsche Oper am Rhein, Düsseldorf, 1970–85 as Leonore, Elisabeth de Valois, Lady Macbeth, Senta, Venus, Sieglinde, Gutrune, Tatiana, Marina, the Marschallin, Jenůfa, Santuzza and Madama Butterfly; Guest appearances in Hamburg, Cologne, Kassel, Amsterdam, Paris, Sydney and Covent Garden in London; Zürich Opera in 1986 as the Kostelnicka in Jenůfa; Sang Ortrud in Lohengrin at Sydney, 1987. *Address:* Deutsche Oper am Rhein, Heinrich Heine Allee, Düsseldorf, Germany.

AYDIN, Özgür; Pianist; b. 4 June 1972, Boulder, Colorado, USA. *Education:* Studied at the Ankara Conservatory and the Royal College of Music, London; Studying at the Hannover Musikhochschule. *Career:* Appeared at the 1994 Salzburg Festival and the 1995 Schleswig-Holstein Music Festival; Concerts broadcast by Classic FM, London, 1993, ABC Sydney, 1996, North German Radio, 1997; Played Brahms' first piano concerto with the Bavarian Radio Symphony Orchestra, Herkules-Saal München, live broadcast by Bavarian Radio and television, 1997; Appeared at the International Istanbul Music Festival and the Rheingau Music Festival in 1998; Concerts broadcast by Deutschland Radio Berlin and North German Radio, 1998. *Honours:* Winner of the 46th International Music Competition of the ARD, Munich, 1997; Nippon Music Award, Tokyo, 1997. *Address:* Roscherstrasse 3, 30161 Hannover, Germany.

AYKAL, Gurer; music director and conductor; b. 1942, Turkey; m. (deceased); three s. *Education:* Ankara State Conservatory, Guildhall School of Music, London, Accademia Santa Cecilia, Pontifical Inst. of Sacred Music with Dominico Bartolucci, studied with Andre Previn and George Hurst in London. *Career:* resident conductor under direction of Franco Ferrera, Accademia Santa Cecilia 1973; apptd permanent conductor of Presidential Symphony Orchestra, Turkey; founder, Ankara Chamber Orchestra; toured Russia as conductor of Moscow State Symphony Orchestra 1984; toured South America and Caribbean Islands as conductor of English Chamber Orchestra; Music Dir and conductor, Lubbock Symphony Orchestra, TX 1987–93; conducted Istanbul Symphony Orchestra 1989; principal guest conductor of Amsterdam Concertgebouw Chamber Orchestra 1989; Music Dir and conductor, El Paso Symphony Orchestra, TX 1992–. *Recordings:* works with London Philharmonic Orchestra. *Honours:* Turkish Government State Artist 1981. *Address:* El Paso Symphony Orchestra, 10 Civic Center Plaza, El Paso, TX 79901, USA.

AYLDON, John; Singer (Bass baritone); b. 1950, London. *Career:* Appearances with D'Oyly Carte Opera, until 1982, with tours to North America, Austrialia and New Zealand; Engagements from 1982 with Canadian Opera; New Sadler's Wells, Welsh National, Dublin Grand Opera and at the Wexford Festival; Roles include Geronimo in Il Matrimonio Segreto, Don Pasquale, Sacristan in Tosca, Frank in Die Fledermaus and Schaunard in La Bohème, Concian in Wolf-Ferrari's I Quattro Rusteghi, Otec in Smetana's The Kiss and Pooh-Bah in The Mikado. *Address:* Music International, 13 Ardilaun Road, London N5 2QR, England.

AYRTON, Norman Walter; British theatre and opera director; b. 25 Sept. 1924, London, England. *Education:* Old Vic Theatre School, London with Michael Saint Denis. *Career:* war service, RNVR 1939–45;

mem., Old Vic Co. 1949, Festival Season 1951; repertory at Farnham and Oxford 1949–50; staff mem., Old Vic Theatre School 1949–52; opened own teaching studio 1952; began dramatic coaching for Royal Opera House, Covent Garden 1953; Asst Prin. 1954–66, Prin. 1966–72, London Acad. of Music and Dramatic Art; taught at Shakespeare Festival, Stratford, Ont., Canada and Royal Shakespeare Theatre, England 1959–62; Dir, Artaxerxes for Handel Opera Soc., Camden Festival 1963, La Traviata at Covent Garden 1963, Manon at Covent Garden 1964, Sutherland-Williamson Grand Opera Season, Australia 1965, Britten's Midsummer Night's Dream, Sydney 1973, Lakmé for Australian Opera 1976, Der Rosenkavalier for Australian Opera Centre 1983; guest dir for many int. productions 1973–84; Faculty, Juilliard School of Music, New York 1974–85; Stage Dir, American Opera Center 1979–85, Vancouver Opera 1975–83, Melbourne Theatre Co. 1974–, Hartford Stage Co. and American Stage Festival 1978–, Spoleto Festival, USA 1984, Vassar Coll., New York 1990–, Utah Shakespeare Festival 1994, Cornell Univ., New York 1995, 1998 and Sarah Lawrence Coll., New York 1994, 1997, 2001; Dir of Opera, Royal Acad. of Music 1986–90; Dean, British American Drama Acad. 1986–98, Fla State Univ. 1997–. *Honours:* Hon. RAM 1989. *Address:* c/o British American Drama Academy, 14 Gloucester Gate, London, NW1 4HG, England (office); 40a Birchington Road, London, NW6 4LJ, England (home). *Telephone:* (20) 7487-0730 (office); (20) 7328-6056 (home). *Fax:* (20) 7487-0731 (office).

AZARMI, Nassrin; Singer (Soprano); b. 5 Jan. 1949, Brujderd, Iran. *Education:* Studied in Tehran and Cologne. *Career:* Debut: As Mozart's Despina, Tehran, 1967; Sang at the Vienna Volksoper, 1968–69; Linz, 1969–71; Deutsche Oper am Rhein, Düsseldorf from 1971 as Mozart's Queen of Night, Pamina, Susanna and Constanze, Adina in L'Elisir d'amore, Offenbach's Olympia, Rossini's Elvira; Guest appearances include Berg's Lulu at Antwerp, 1982; In Die Zauberflöte at Salzburg, 1990; Sang Musetta at Düsseldorf, 1993; Further roles have included Nicolai's Frau Fluth, Gilda, Micaela, Strauss's Aminta and Nannetta in Falstaff; Concert and oratorio engagements. *Address:* c/o Deutsche Oper am Rhein, Heinrich Heine Allee 16a, 40213 Düsseldorf, Germany.

AZEVEDO, (António) Sérgio Arede Torrado Marques; Portuguese composer; b. 23 Aug. 1968, Coimbra. *Education:* Academia de Amadores de Música, Escola Superior de Música, Lisbon. *Career:* teacher at Escola Superior de Música; ed. for Portuguese Nat. Radio. *Compositions include:* Coral I 1991, Tranquilo 1997, Retábulo de Brecht (music theatre) 1998, Festa 1998, Concerto for two pianos and chamber orchestra 1999–2000. *Publications:* 1958–1998: Forty Years of Contemporary Music in Portugal, World New Music Magazine 1998, A invenção dos sons 1998. *Address:* R. João de Barros, lote 21, 1 Esq. Alapraia, São João do Estoril, 2765 Estoril, Portugal. *Telephone:* 9 6339 7727. *Fax:* 2 1466 5042. *E-mail:* sergio.aze@sapo.pt.

AZZOLINI, Sergio; Italian bassoonist; b. 15 Jan. 1967, Bolzano. *Education:* Claudio Monteverdi Conservatory of Music with Romano Santi, Bolzano, and Hanover Musikhochschule with Klaus Thunemann. *Career:* principal solo bassoon, European Community Youth Orchestra; Prof., Stuttgart Musikhochschule 1989–98; Prof., Basle State Acad. of Music 1998–; directs his own ensemble, Il Proteo; mem., Ma'alot Quintetts, Sabine Meyer Bläserensemble, Maurice Bourgue Trio, and several early music groups; under contract to EMI for future chamber music recordings. *Honours:* first prizes in int. competitions at Ancona, Prague, Belgrade, Martigny, Bonn, first prize C.M. von Weber competition, Munich. *Address:* Caroline Martin Musique, 126 rue Vieille du Temple, 75003 Paris, France (office). *Website:* www.caroline-martin-musique.com (office).

B

BABBITT, Milton (Byron); Composer, Music Educator and Music Theorist; b. 10 May 1916, Philadelphia, PA, USA; m. Sylvia Miller, 27 Dec 1939, 1 d. *Education:* Studied violin, clarinet and saxophone in childhood; Mathematics, University of PA; BA, New York University, 1935; MFA, Princeton University, 1942; Studied music with Marion Bauer and Philip James and privately with Roger Sessions. *Career:* Teacher, Music Faculty, 1938–42, 1948–84, Mathematics Faculty, 1942–45, William Shubael Conant Professor, 1966–84, Professor Emeritus, Princeton University; Director, Columbia-Princeton Electronic Music Center, 1959–84; Member, Composition Faculty, Juilliard School, NY, 1972–; Guest Lecturer, many USA and European colleges and universities; PhD, Princeton University, 1992; President, 1951–52, International Society of Contemporary Music. *Compositions include:* Orchestral: Fabulous Voyage, 1946, Ars Combinatoria, 1981, Piano Concerto, 1985; Transfigured Notes for strings, 1986; Piano concerto No. 2, 1998; Chamber: 5 String Quartets, 1948–82, Woodwind Quartet, 1953, Sextets for Violin and Piano, 1966, My Ends Are My Beginnings for Clarinet, 1978, Dual for Cello and Piano, 1980, Groupwise for 7 Instruments, 1983, Sheer Pluck for Guitar, 1984, Fanfare for Double Brass Sextet, 1987, Whirled Series for Saxophone and Piano, 1987, The Crowded Air for 11 Instruments, 1988; None but the Lonely Flute, 1991; Septet, But Equal, 1992; Around the Horn, 1993; No Longer Very Clear, for soprano and four instruments, 1994; Triad, clarinet, viola and piano, 1994; Piano Quintet, 1995; When Shall We Three Meet Again? For flute, clarinet and vibraphone, 1996; Manifold Music for organ, 1996; Solo piano pieces, choruses, songs and tape pieces including No Longer Very Clear for soprano and ensemble, 1994. *Publications:* Milton Babbitt: Words about Music, the Madison lectures, 1987. *Contributions:* Articles in various journals. *Honours:* American Academy and Institute of Arts and Letters Gold Medal in Music, 1988. *Address:* 222 Western Way, Princeton, NJ 08540, USA.

BABINGTON, Amanda-Louise, BMus, MusM; British musician and musicologist; b. 12 Oct. 1979, Oxford. *Education:* Univ. of Manchester. *Career:* Academie D'Ambronay, Handel's Athalia, Paul McCreesh 2003; Britten Pears Orchestra, Handel, Richard Egarr 2002, Charpentier, Emmanuelle Haim 2003, Bach, Richard Egarr 2003, Mozart and Handel, Paul McCreesh and Richard Egarr 2004; Les Talens Lyrique, Handel, 2004; Leeds Baroque Orchestra 2000–; Contemporary Baroque (ensemble) 2001–; mem. Musicians' Union. *Recordings:* Wagner Prelude to Die MeisterSinger, Ravel Daphnis and Chloé, National Youth Orchestra of Scotland, Takho Yuasa 1999. *Publications:* Handel's Solo Sonatas, Early Music Performer Issue II March 2003. *Honours:* Scottish Arts Trust 2003, 2002, 2001, SRP Walter Bergmann Memorial Fund 2001, The Robert Nicol Trust 2001, Proctor Gregg Travel Award 2001, 2000, 1999. *Address:* 9 Patterson Avenue, Chorlton, Manchester, M21 9NB, England (home). *Telephone:* (161) 881-1672 (home). *E-mail:* ababington@hotmail.com (home).

BABYKIN, Anatol; Singer (Bass); b. 29 Sept. 1944, Tscheljabinsk, Russia. *Education:* Studied at the Astrakhan Conservatory until 1976. *Career:* Member of the Bolshoi Opera at Moscow from 1976; Roles have included King René (Iolanthe), Gremin (Eugene Onegin), Leporello in The Stone Guest by Dargomyzhsky and Don Alfonso (Così fan tutte); Sang with the Bolshoi at the Edinburgh Festival in 1991, operas by Tchaikovsky and Rimsky-Korsakov. *Address:* c/o Bolshoi Opera, 103009 Moscow, Russia.

BACELLI, Monica; Singer (Mezzo-Soprano); b. 1960, Italy. *Career:* Debut: As Mozart's Dorabella, Spoleto Festival, 1987; Sang Zerlina at Rome, 1990; Cecilio in Mozart's Lucio Silla, San Francisco, 1991; Appearances as Cherubino, Salzburg Festival, 1992; Covent Garden Vienna State Opera and Rossini Festival, Pesaro; Roles include Rosina, Nicklausse, Ravel's Child and Mozart's Idamante, Idomeneo; Season 1998 with Cherubino, Rome; Sang Ascanio in Benvenuto Cellini in concert, at the Barbican, London, 1999; Season 1999–2000: Premiere of Berio's Cronaca del Luogo, Salzburg; Rossini's Isabella for Netherlands Opera; Ottavia in Poppea at Florence and Bellini's Romeo at Catania; Berio's Outis at La Scala and the Châtelet, Paris; Season 2001 in Handel's Tamerlano at Halle. *Recordings:* La Finta giardiniera, Teldec; Le nozze di Figaro. *Address:* c/o Netherlands Opera, Waterlooplein 22, 1011 Amsterdam, Netherlands.

BACH, Andreas; Pianist; b. 29 July 1968, Dennbach, Germany. *Education:* First music lessons, 1973–80; Studied with Professor Karl-Heinz Kammerlung, Hannover. *Career:* Debut: Alte Opera, Frankfurt in 1984; Appearance in Eurovision Competition, 1984; 1st tour to USA with debuts at New York, San Francisco and Washington DC, 1987 and to Japan, 1988; Several further tours to USA and appearances in France, England, Switzerland, Italy and Portugal. *Recordings:* Schumann Op 6, Op 7, 1989; Beethoven Op 7, Op 31 No. 2, Op 126, Novalis,

1990. *Honours:* Winner, several Youth Competitions, 1975–84; Bernhard Sprengel Prize for Music, 1985; Kulturpreis von Rheinland-Pfalz, 1990. *Address:* c/o Concerto Winderstein, Leopoldstrasse 25, D–80802, Munich, Germany.

BACH, Jan Morris, BMus, MMus, DMA; American composer and fmr educator; b. 11 Dec. 1937, Forrest, IL; m. Dalia Zakaras 1971; two d. *Education:* Univ. of Illinois, Urbana-Champaign. *Career:* asst first horn, US Army Band 1962–65; instructor in music, Univ. of Tampa, FL 1965–66; Prof. of Music, Northern Illinois Univ., Dekalb 1966–98, Distinguished Research Prof. Emer. 1998–; Presidential Research Prof., Northern Illinois Univ. 1982–86; mem. American Soc. of Composers, Authors and Publishers, BMI. *Compositions include:* Four Two-Bit Contraptions, 1967; Skizzen, 1967; Burgundy Variations, 1968; Woodwork, 1970; Eisteddfod, 1972; The System, 1973; Piano Concerto, 1975; The Eve of St Agnes, for antiphonal wind ensemble, 1976; Praetorius Suite, 1977; Canon and Caccia, for five French horns, 1977; Happy Prince, 1978; Quintet for Tuba and Strings, 1978; Gala Fanfare, 1979; The Student from Salamanca, 1979; Rounds and Dances, 1980; Sprint, 1982; French Suite, for unaccompanied horn, 1982; Horn Concerto, 1983; Dompes and Jompes, 1986; Harp Concerto, 1986; Concerto for Trumpet and Wind Ensemble, 1987; Concerto, for Euphonium and Orchestra, 1990; Anachronisms, for string quartet. 1991; People of Note, 1993; Concerto for Steel Pan and Orchestra, 1994; The Last Flower, 1995; Foliations, 1995; Concertino for Bassoon and Strings, 1996; Pilgrimage, 1997; Variations on a theme of Brahms, 1997; Choral: Hair Today, 1977; Dear God, 1998; In the Hands of the Tongue, 1999; The Duel, 2000; Songs of the Streetwise, 2000. *Recordings include:* Laudes for Brass Quintet; Skizzen for Woodwind Quintet; Four Two-Bit Contraptions; Eisteddfod, 1972; My Very First Solo, 1973; Praetorius Suite, 1976; Concert Variations, for Euphonium and Piano, 1977; Fanfare and Fugue for Five Trumpets, 1979; Rounds and Dances, 1980; Triptych, for Brass Quintet, 1989; Steel Pan Concerto, 1994; The Duel, 2000; Horn Concerto 2005, Gala Fanfare 2005, French Suite 2005, Helix 2005. *Honours:* Award for Excellence in Undergraduate Education, Northern Illinois Univ. 1978. *Address:* PO Box 403, Wasco, IL 60183, USA. *E-mail:* janbach@janbach.com. *Website:* www.janbach.com.

BACH, Mecthild; Singer (Soprano); b. 1970, Limburg an der Lehn, Germany. *Education:* Frankfurt Musikhochschule with Elsa Calveti; Hartmut Holl and Michael Schneider, Studio for Early Music; Vera Rozsa and Laura Sarti in London. *Career:* Darmstadt Staatstheater and the opera studio of the Deutsche Oper am Rhein, Düsseldorf, Heidelberg Opera, 1991–96; Stage and concert appearances with conductors Frieder Bernius, Reinhard Goebel, Michael Schneider and Sigiswald Kuijken. *Recordings:* Flavio in Jommelli's Il Vologeso, Orfeo; Jommelli's Didone Abbandonata as Selene, Orfeo; Gristostomo in Telemann's Don Quichotte; Durante's Lamentations; Monteverdi's Vespers; Mendelssohn's Lobesgesang; Handel's Acis and Galatea and Ode for St Cecilia's Day; Mozart Masses. *Address:* c/o Heidelberg Opera, Friedrickstrasse 5, 69117 Heidelberg, Germany.

BACHLUND, Gary; Singer (Tenor); b. 1958, New York, NY, USA. *Education:* Studied in New York. *Career:* Sang Parsifal at Carnegie Hall and appeared in operas by Mussorgsky, Wagner (Das Rheingold) and Gounod (Roméo et Juliette) at the Metropolitan Opera; Sang Strauss's Bacchus with Minnesota Opera; Florestan for Boston Opera and Don José for Scottish Opera at Glasgow (European debut, 1986); Other roles include Agrippa in The Fiery Angel, Jimmy in Mahagonny and Aegisthus in Elektra (all at Los Angeles); Ennée in Les Troyens at the Opéra Bastille, Paris, 1990 and Wagner's Erik at Cologne (1992); Sang Tristan at Milwaukee, 1993 (also at Brunswick, 1996); Santiago 1993, as Don José; Kaiserslautern, 1995, Tannhäuser; Season 2000 as Tristan at Honolulu and Dmitri in Boris Godunov at Kassel. *Address:* c/o Musicaglotz, 11 rue le Verrier, F–75006, Paris, France.

BACHMANN, Rhonda; Singer (Soprano); b. 24 Oct. 1952, Chicago, Illinois, USA; m. Arthur Hammond, 24 Aug 1986, deceased 1991. *Education:* Conservatoire National Superieur de Musique de Paris, 1972–76. *Career:* Chicago Opera Theatre, 1979–80; Opéra de Lyon, 1981; Opéra de Wallonie, Belgium, 1982; Opéra du Rhin, Strasbourg, 1981–84; Théâtre du Palais Royal, Paris, 1981; Concerts include, Radio France 1980; 1989–1993 Marie Antoinette Bicentennial, Naantali Festival, Finland, 1981; Salle Gaveau, Paris, 1981; Royal Opera House, Friends of Covent Garden Christmas Gala, 1985; Institut Français London, 1986; Pavillon Dauphine, Paris, 1986; Many recitals and chamber music concerts in Paris, Germany, Italy, including the music of Vivaldi, Bach, Handel, Mozart, Schubert, Spohr, Brahms, Schoenberg, Ravel and Dowland; Appearances on television, New York, Paris, Marseilles; Acted in 3 films, 1974–76; Leading role, Harriet Smithson, The Life of Berlioz, 1981; Toured extensively with recital in 18th

Century Costume as Queen Marie Antoinette, Songs for the Queen, Songs for the Revolution, 7 programmes, 175 performances of which 73 in the Grand Trianon, Versailles, 1988–2000; Tours to America, England, Scotland, Ireland, Bulgaria, Austria with Peter Gellhorn, piano; 13 recital programmes, Malibran and Viardot (bel canto repertoire), The Romantic Nightingale (Lieder) and From Times of War (20th century up to 1948), tours to Italy, France, Austria and the United Kingdom, Covent Garden Festival, 55 performances, with Peter Gellhorn, piano, 1992–2001. *Recordings:* Cassettine: Quand tu étais petit, Lieder in French translation by Mozart, Schubert and Brahms with Noel Lee, piano; Video: Queen Marie Antoinette and the Kindling Fire, with Peter Gellhorn, piano, 2000. *Address:* 7 Norfolk House, Courtlands, Sheen Road, Richmond, Surrey TW10 5AT, England.

BACK, Andrée; Singer (Soprano); b. 1950, England. *Education:* Studied at the Royal College of Music. *Career:* Has sung in oratorios, recitals and symphony concerts with appearances in most major European and American cities; Frequent engagements in Switzerland, Norway, Austria, Belgium and the Netherlands (Radio Symphony Orchestra, Rotterdam); Has sung in Carmina Burana at Liège, Siegen and Edinburgh, Berlioz's La Mort de Cléopâtre with Berlin Symphony Orchestra, Mozart's Requiem and Coronation Mass in Marienstatt with the Bonn Bach Choir, and Mozart Concert Arias with the Schwabische Symphony Orchestra; Sang in Mahler's 4th Symphony at Cheltenham Festival and in A Child of Our Time at Bury St Edmunds, Telemann Cantatas in Hamburg and Haydn's Berenice and Strauss's Four Last Songs with the Billings Symphony Orchestra, 1989; Other concert repertoire includes Bach's Mass in B minor, Magnificat, Passions and Christmas Oratorio, Beethoven's Missa Solemnis, Mass in C and Choral Symphony, Requiems by Brahms, Fauré, Britten and Verdi, Handel's Messiah, Judas Maccabaeus, Jephtha, Joshua, Acis and Galatea, Hercules, Israel in Egypt, Samson, Saul and Chandos Anthems, Janáček's Glagolitic Mass, Mahler's 2nd and 8th Symphonies, Rückert Lieder, Schubert's Salve Regina, Masses, Vivaldi's Gloria and Magnificat, Wagner's Wesendonck Lieder. *Address:* Mancroft Towers, Oulton Broad, Lowestoft, Suffolk NR32 3PS, England.

BACQUIER, Gabriel; Singer (Baritone); b. 17 May 1924, Beziers, France. *Education:* Studied at the Paris Conservatoire. *Career:* Debut: Sang in Landowski's Le Fou at Nice in 1950; Sang in Brussels, 1953–56 and at the Opéra Comique, Paris, 1956–58; Appeared at the Paris Opéra from 1958 as Escamillo, Valentin, Rigoletto, Simon Boccanegra and Boris Godunov; Aix-en-Provence in 1960 as Don Giovanni, Glyndebourne Festival in 1962 as Mozart's Count, and Covent Garden in 1964 as Riccardo in I Puritani and Scarpia; US debut in 1962 at Chicago as the High Priest in Samson et Dalila; Metropolitan Opera, 1964–79 as Don Pasquale, the Villains in Les Contes d'Hoffmann, Iago, Leporello, Golaud and Rossini's Bartolo; Holland Festival in 1972 as Falstaff; Teatro Fenice, Venice, 1973–74; Teacher at the Paris Conservatoire until 1987; Sang Sancho Panza in Massenet's Don Quichotte at Florence and Monte Carlo, 1992; Debussy's Arkel at Lille, 1996. *Recordings include:* Guillaume Tell; Gounod's Mireille and Roméo et Juliette; La Belle Hélène; Lakmé; Les Huguenots; Don Giovanni; Les Contes d'Hoffmann; Così fan tutte; Le nozze di Figaro; Don Quichotte; La Favorite by Donizetti; Thais by Massenet; Ariane et Barbe-Bleue by Dukas. *Address:* c/o M. Jean-Marie, Poilvé, 16 Avenue Franklin D. Roosevelt, F–75008, Paris, France.

BACRI, Nicolas; French composer; b. 23 Nov. 1961, Paris. *Education:* Paris Conservatoire, Acad. de France in Rome. *Career:* Head of Chamber Music Dept, Radio France 1987–91; composer-in-residence, Casa de Velasquez, Spain 1991–93, Orchestre de Picardie 1996–98, CNR de Bayonne 2001. *Compositions include:* Quatuor à cordes 1980, Concerto pour violon 1982–83, Symphonie No. 1 1983–84, Concerto pour violoncelle 1985–87, Fleur et le miroir magique (conte lyrique for children) 1996–97, Symphonie No. 6 1998, Concerto da camera pour clarinette 1999, Concerto pour trompette No. 2 2000. *Recordings include:* Concerto pour violoncelle Folia, Requiem, Tre canti e finale, Etcetera, Concerto pour trompette, Verany Arion. *Honours:* first prize for composition, Paris Conservatoire 1983, Grand Prix Académie du Disque 1993, Lauréat de la Fondation d'entreprise Natexis 1993–96. *Address:* c/o Peer Musikverlag, Muhlenkamp 45, 22303 Hamburg, Germany (office). *Website:* www.peermusic-classical.de.

BACULEWSKI, Krzysztof Jan; Composer; b. 26 Dec. 1950, Warsaw, Poland; m. Agnieszka Dmowska, 20 Dec 1979. *Education:* MA, Academy of Music, Warsaw, 1974; Postgraduate Studies, Conservatoire National Supérieur de Musique, Paris, 1976–77; PhD, Warsaw University, 1982. *Career:* Debut: Warsaw, 1975; Many Compositions Performed at Warsaw Autumn International Festival of Contemporary Music and Abroad, including USA, France, Germany, Finland, Hungary, South America; Professor, Music Academy, Warsaw, 1998–; mem, Polish Composers Union; ISCM; Society of Authors ZAiKS. *Compositions:* Vivace e Cantilena for Chamber Ensemble, 1975; Epitaphium for Orchestra, 1973; Ground for Orchestra, 1981; Concerto for Orchestra,

1983; A Walking Shadow for Orchestra, 1990; Antitheton I, for Piano Trio, 1989; Antitheton II, for Baroque instruments, 1996. *Recordings:* Sonata for Percussion, Rilke-Lieder for Choir a Cappella, Nox Ultima, Motet for Choir a Cappella, The Profane Anthem to Anne, text by John Donne, a Cantata; Chansons Romanesques et Frivoles for voice and baroque instruments, 1998; Sonata Canonica for two violins, 1998. *Contributions:* Ruch Muzyczny; Studio. *Publications:* Polish Musical Output, 1945–1984, 1987; Vol. X (Contemporary Music), The History of Polish Music, 1996. *Honours:* Many Prizes at Polish Competitions. *Address:* ul Ludwika Hirszfelda 8 m 42, 02-776 Warsaw, Poland.

BADER, Hans-Dieter; Singer (Tenor); b. 16 Feb. 1938, Stuttgart, Germany. *Education:* Studied with Rudolf Gehrung and in Stuttgart. *Career:* Debut: Stuttgart Staatsoper in 1960 as Arturo in Lucia di Lammermoor; Sang at Brunswick, Karlsruhe, Essen, Kassel and Mannheim; Appeared in Hannover, 1965–84 as Rodolfo in La Bohème, Faust at Nuremberg, Hamburg, Düsseldorf, Strasbourg and Vienna Volksoper; Other roles include Ferrando in Così fan tutte and the Duke of Mantua; Season 1995–96, as Herod in Salome and Tiresias in Orff's Antigonae at Hannover; Strauss's Emperor at Kiel; Season 2000–01 as Shuisky in Boris Godunov and Aegisthus in Elektra, at Hannover. *Recordings include:* Reger's Requiem; Sly by Wolf-Ferrari; Strauss's Feuersnot. *Address:* Staatstheater Hannover, Opernhaus, Opernplatz 1, 30159 Hannover, Germany.

BADIAN, Maya; Composer and Musicologist; b. 18 April 1945, Bucharest, Romania; m. Lucian Munteanu, 1 s. (died 1989). *Education:* MMus, Composition, Music Academy of Bucharest, Bucharest; DMus, Composition, Montreal University, Montreal, Canada. *Career:* Debut: Symphonic Movement, Romania in 1968; Musical Director for RTV, Bucharest, 1968–72; Professor of Composition and Keyboard, Bucharest, 1972–87; Settled in Montreal, Canada since 1987; Teacher at the Montreal University since 1990; Musicology writings; Lecturer at international contemporary music festivals and congress in Europe and Canada; Concerts in Europe, USA and Canada; Member of various international juries. *Compositions:* Over 50 works including: Symphonic: Holocaust–In Memoriam, symphony; Concertante music: Concertos for Piano, for Violin, for Guitar, for Cello, for Marimba and Vibraphone for Clarinet and Saxophone for 4 Timpani (To Mircea Badian); Children's World for orchestra, 1997; Vocal-Orchestral works: Canada 125–Cantata Profana, Towards The Pinnacle, poem for Soprano; Chamber: Concerto for Horn and Percussion, Solos, duos, trios and other chamber ensembles. *Recordings:* Maya Badian, Romania, 1977; Towards The Pinnacle, Canada, 1994. *Publications:* All compositions published in Lucian Badian Editions, Canada. *Contributions:* Various musical periodicals; RTV interviews. *Honours:* All her archival documents and manuscripts are deposited at the Manuscript Collection, Music Division, National Library of Canada, Ottawa. *Address:* No. 2001, 1140 Fisher Avenue, Ottawa, Ontario K1Z 8M5, Canada.

BADINSKI, Nikolai; Composer, Violinist and Pedagogue; b. 19 Dec. 1937, Sofia, Bulgaria. *Education:* Diploma, Academy of Music, Sofia, 1956–61; Masterclass, Composition, Academy of Arts, East Berlin, 1967–70; Scholarships for Masterclasses, Accademia Musicale, Siena, Italy, 1975, 1976. *Career:* Active as Composer, University Teacher in Berlin, Sofia, Halle; Concert Violinist; Concertmaster; Special Adviser for Music Education, String Quartet; Active in the Darmstadt International Courses for New Music, 1974–78; Guest Professor, Universities of Stockholm and Copenhagen; Assistant to Max Deutsch, Sorbonne and Ecole Normale de Musique, Paris, 1982; Living in Paris (Scholar of the French Government), 1985–86; Composer-in-Residence (California); Appearances at various Festivals; Numerous performances, radio and television broadcaster; mem, European Academy of Arts, Sciences and Humanities (Paris). *Compositions:* Numerous compositions including 3 Symphonies, Several Concertos for instruments and orchestra; Widerspiegelungen der Weisheit for S, B, choir and orchestra, Ballets, Music for Orchestra, Chamber Music; 3 Espressioni for soprano and tape, 1981; Cantico di S Francesco for baritone and tape, 1981–82; Vocal, Organ Music; Electro-acoustic Music; Schwendes Bei Märchen, Traumvisionen, Dostoevsky Reflections, Homage to Kafka, Rotation (in Memory of a Cosmonaut), Phoenixe, Sevtopolis; Water Music, 1980; Musik mit Papier; Luftmusik, 1980–81; Musicvisual Correspondence P, 1980–82; Six Capricci for baritone and piano, 1991; Seven Memorial Stones, In memorium of the Holocaust Victims–A Requiem; Die trunkene Fledermaus for orchestra. *Contributions:* Freelance Contributor to the BBC, London. *Address:* Fröaufstr 3, 12161 Berlin, Germany.

BADURA-SKODA, Eva; Musicologist; b. 15 Jan. 1929, Munich, Germany; m. Paul Badura-Skoda, 4 c. *Education:* Universities of Heidelberg, Vienna and Innsbruck; PhD, 1953; Hochschule für Musik, Vienna. *Career:* Freelance Lecturer and Writer, until 1962; Summer School Lecturer, Mozarteum Salzburg; Professor, University of Wisconsin, 1964–74; Guest Professor, University of Boston, 1976; Queen's University, Kingston, Canada, 1979; McGill University, Montreal, Canada,

1981–82, Winter-term; Universitat Goettingen, 1982–83; mem, International Musicological Society; Haydn Institute, Cologne; Zentralinstitut für Mozart-Forschung des Mozarteums, Salzburg. *Publications:* Mozart Interpretation, 1957; Interpreting Mozart on the Keyboard, 1961; Mozart's C Minor Piano Concerto, 1971; An Unknown Singspiel by Joseph Haydn, 1972; Schubert Studies, 1982; Internationaler Joseph Haydn Kongress Wien 1982 Congress Report, Henle Verlag Munich, 1985; Aspects of Performance Practice, 1994. *Contributions:* Musical Journals; New Grove Dictionary of Music and Musicians, 1980; More than 100 scholarly articles on History of Viennese Classical Music and History of the Fortepiano. *Honours:* Austrian Decoration: Honorary Cross Litteris et Artibus; 3 University Grants. *Address:* Zuckerkandlgasse 14, 1190 Vienna, Austria.

BADURA-SKODA, Paul; Pianist; b. 6 Oct. 1927, Vienna, Austria; m. Eva Badura-Skoda, 4 c. *Education:* Studied Conducting and Piano at State Conservatory, Vienna; Masterclass of Edwin Fischer, Lucerne. *Career:* Concert Pianist from 1948, notably in works by Mozart, Beethoven and Schubert; New York debut 1953; Tokyo, 1959; Moscow debut, 1964; Duets with violinist D Oistrakh; Held annual master classes, formerly in Edinburgh and Salzburg, latterly at Siena Festival; Artist-in-Residence, University of Wisconsin, 1966–71; Premieres of Martin's 2nd Piano Concerto, 1970 and Fantasie sur des rhythmes flamencos, 1973; Numerous recordings. *Compositions:* Mass in D; Sonata romantique for flute and piano, 1994; Cadenzas to piano and violin concertos by Mozart and Haydn. *Publications:* Mozart Interpretation 1957 (with wife); The Piano Sonatas of Beethoven (with Jörg Demus) 1970; Interpreting Bach at the Keyboard, 1993; Editions of works by Schubert, Mozart and Chopin. *Honours:* Chevalier de la Légion d'Honneur, France, 1992; Cross of Honour, Austria, 1977. *Address:* c/o 3116 Live Oak Street, Dallas, TX 75204, USA.

BAEK, Kwang-Hoon; Singer (baritone) and Choir Conductor; b. 29 April 1954, Soon-Chun City, Korea; m. Kyung-Nyum Park, 7 June 1987, 1 s. *Education:* Kyung-Hee University, Seoul; postgraduate studies of singing and choir conducting, Music University, Wuppertal, Germany. *Career:* Debut: As Scarpia in Tosca at National Theatre, Seoul; Freelance Singer and Choir Conductor; Schubert's Winterreise, KBS Broadcasting Station, 1989; Has sung main parts in Tosca, La Traviata, Pagliacci, Le nozze di Figaro, Cavalleria Rusticana, Noye's Fludde, Madama Butterfly, Un Ballo in Maschera in Korea and Slovakia; mem, Schubert Association, Seoul; Opera Association, Seoul; Deutscher Liederverein, Germany. *Recordings:* Winterreise; Hymns Solo; Conductor, The Creation by Haydn. *Address:* 101 Ho, 1428-7, Seocho-Dong, Seocho-Ku, Seoul, Republic of Korea.

BAERG, Theodore; Singer (Baritone); b. 19 Dec. 1952, Toronto, Canada. *Career:* Debut: Canadian Opera Company, 1978, as Monterone in Rigoletto; Sang in the Canadian premiere of Tchaikovsky's The Maid of Orleans (1980) and in Lulu, The Merry Widow and Die Zauberflöte (Papageno); Other roles include Mozart's Count (Hamilton Opera, 1984), Rossini's Figaro (Vancouver) and Ramiro in L'Heure Espagnole (Glyndebourne, 1988); Guested as Marcello in La Bohème at San Diego (1990) and Papageno at Washington (1991); Toronto, 1992, in the premiere of Mario and the Magician by Harry Somers. *Address:* c/o Canadian Opera Company, 227 Front Street East, Toronto, Ontario M5A 1E8, Canada.

BAEVA, Vera; Composer and Pianist; b. 18 March 1930, Burgas, Bulgaria. *Education:* Graduated Sofia State Academy, 1953. *Career:* Conducted the chorus of Radio Sofia, from 1954; Lecturer at the Sofia State Academy from 1986; Teacher of chamber music at the Open Society Foundation, 1993. *Compositions:* Five Impressions for piano, 1973; Four Songs, 1975; 2 Preludes for cello, 1984; Nostalgichno for chamber ensemble, 1986; Sonata for piano 4 hands, 1988; Butterfly for female voices and ensemble, 1989; Tristezza for violin, 1990; Dance around the Fire of the God Tangra for male voices and ensemble, 1991. *Address:* c/o Union of Bulgarian Composers, Rue IV Vazov, BG-1000 Sofia, Bulgaria.

BAGINSKI, Zbigniew; Composer and Teacher; b. 19 Jan. 1949, Stettin, Poland; m. Alicja, 23 Aug 1988, 2 d. *Education:* MA, High School of Music, Warsaw, 1972. *Career:* Many performances of compositions in Germany, the United Kingdom, Denmark, Sweden, USA, USSR, Netherlands, Hungary, Cuba; Assistant Professor, 1978–88, Associate Professor 1988–; Vice-Dean, Faculty of Composition, Conducting and Music Theory, 1987–90, Academy of Music Frederic Chopin, Warsaw; mem, Polish Composers Union, Vice-President of Warsaw Branch, 1985–89, General Secreatry, 1989. *Compositions:* Sinfonia Notturna, 1984; Concerto for Harpsichord and Orchestra, 1985; Oh, Sweet Baroque Suite for String Orchestra, 1985; Symphony in Seven Scenes, 1988; String Quartet No. 3, 1992; Mass for chorus, 1995; Little Elegiac Symphony, 1995; Piano Concerto, 1995; Violin Concerto, 1996; Canons, Scherzos and Epigrams, 1987; Nocturne-Berceusee, 1989; Trio with Coda, 1983; Piano Quartet, 1990; Refrain for 2 Pianos, 1975; Acho for

Organ, 1974; Expeditions on the Other Side, 1973. *Address:* ul Schillera 8 m 5, 00-248 Warsaw, Poland.

BAGLIONI, Bruna; Singer (mezzo-soprano); b. 8 April 1947, Frascati, Italy. *Education:* studied with Gina Maria Rebori and Walter Cataldi-Tassoni in Rome. *Career:* debut, Festival Dei Due Mondi, Spoleto in Boris Godunov 1970, soon afterwards sang La Favorita in Bologna with Luciano Pararotti; has sung at major theatres including La Favorita, Norma, Un Ballo In Maschera, Cavalleria Rusticana at La Scala, Milan; La Fenice, Venice; San Carlo, Naples; Trieste; Rome; Bologna; Palermo; Torino; Arena of Verona for 21 years; Eboli in Don Carlos at Covent Garden, London; Metropolitan, New York; Tokyo; Berlin; Munich; Hamburg; Paris; Vienna; Particularly identified with the role of Verdi's Amneris; Major tours include: Norma in Moscow with La Scala Milan; Dalila in Samson and Dalila with the Met of New York and with Covent Garden in Korea and Japan; Repertoire includes Verdi: Amneris in Aida, Azucena in Il Trovatore, Ulrica in Un Ballo in Maschera, Eboli in Don Carlos, Preziosilla in La Forza del Destino, Fenena in Nabucco and Messa da Requiem; Laura in La Gioconda of Ponchielli, Charlotte in Werther by Massenet; Leonore in Donizetti's la Favorite; Fedora; Dalila in Samson et Dalila; Santuzza in Cavalleria Rusticana; Giovanna Seymour in Anna Bolena; Carmen; Principessa of Bouillon in Adrian Lecouvreur; Adalgisa in Norma. *Recordings include:* videos: Don Carlos at Covent Garden; Nabucco at Arena of Verona; Aida in Luxor; albums: Norma with La Scala in Moscow; Luisa Muiller at La Scala, Milan; La Favorita in Bern. *Address:* Vicolo Manara 9, 00044 Frascati, Rome, Italy.

BAGRATUNI, Suren; Cellist; b. 17 March 1963, Yerevan, Armenia. *Education:* Yerevan State Komitas Conservatory; Moscow State Tchaikovsky Conservatory; New England Conservatory, Boston; Central Music School (Yerevan). *Career:* Debut: Solo in Yerevan, 1976; With an orchestra in Yerevan, 1978; Solo recitals in Grand Hall, Moscow Conservatory; Carnegie (Weill), New York; Jordan and Symphony Halls, Boston; Gasteig-Munchen; Gaveau-Paris; Alice Tully; Merkin, New York; Tonhalle, St Gallen, Switzerland; Professor, Michigan State University; Concertos and recitals throughout the world; mem, Nobilis Trio. *Recordings:* Solo Cello and Two Cellos, 1995; Shostakovich, Prokoviev–Sonatas, 1997; Trios by Beethoven (Op 1, No. 3) Brahms (Op 8), Tchaikovsky, Rachmaninov, 1997; Babajanian, Trio, 1997; Short Pieces for cello and piano, 1997; Shostakovich and Prokofiev Cello Sonatas (Great Russian Cello Sonatas, Ongaku), 1998; Rachmaninov, Debussy-Sonatas; Stravinsky Suite Italienne, 2001. *Honours:* First Prize, Armenia National, 1980; First Prize, Trancaucasus, 1981; Winner, USSR National, 1981; Silver Medal, Tchaikovsky, 1986; First Prize, Vittorio Gui, 1988. *Current Management:* Boston Classical Artists. *Address:* 1291 Sebewaing Road, Okemos, MI 48864-3450, USA. *E-mail:* bagratuni@yahoo.com.

BAHK, Jehi; Austrian violinist; b. 26 June 1971, Vienna. *Education:* Vienna Acad. for Music and Performing Arts. *Career:* debut, Konzerthaus, Vienna 1995; founding mem. and leader, Hugo Wolf Quartet 1993–; Salzburg Mozarteum, Schubertiade Feldkirch, Carinthian Summer 1996; Munich Herkules-Saal, Nurnberg Kaiserburg, Prague, Rudolfinum 1997; Edinburgh Festival, Carnegie Hall, New York 1998; Musikverein Vienna, Cité de la musique Paris, Palais des Beaux-Arts Brussels, Philharmonie Cologne 1999; Wigmore Hall London, Philharmonie Berlin 2000; Tonhalle Zürich 2003; Amsterdam Concertgebouw, Birmingham Symphony Hall, Megaron Athens; Prof. of Violin, German School of Music, Weimar 2005–; Kangnam Univ., Republic of Korea 2005–. *Publications:* Hugo Wolf, Italian Songbook (vol. two, arrangement for string quartet and voice) 2003. *Honours:* first prize Int. Competition for String Quartets, Cremona, Italy 1995. *Current Management:* Till Dönch Künstlermanagement, Rögergasse 24–26/G2, 1090 Vienna, Austria. *Telephone:* (1) 470-80-83. *Fax:* (1) 479-69-71. *E-mail:* cora@doench.at. *Website:* www.doench.at. *Address:* Schützengasse 13/12, 1030 Vienna, Austria (office). *Website:* www.jehibahk.com.

BAILES, Anthony James; lutenist; b. 18 June 1947, Bristol, England; m. Anne Van Royen. *Education:* Bulmershe Coll. of Further Education, studied with Michael Watson in Bristol, Diana Poulton in London, Gusta Goldschmidt in Amsterdam, Eugen M. Dombois (Schola Cantorum Basiliensis). *Career:* debut, Purcell Room 1971; solo concerts and tours throughout Europe and Scandinavia; many recordings both solo and in ensemble; Prof. of Lute; hon. mem. Lute Soc., Svenska Gitarr Och Luta Sallskapet; mem. Schweizerische Clavichord Gesellschaft. *Recordings include:* Pieces de Luth, Lauten Galanterie, A Musical Banquet, Airs de Cour, Lautenmusik der Habsbergische Lande. *Publications:* An Introduction to 17th-Century Lute Music 1983, Lessons for the Lute (with A. Van Royen) 1983, 32 Easy Pieces for Baroque Lute 1984; contrib. articles to various journals and magazines. *Honours:* Edison Klassiek 1977. *Address:* Hollenweg 3A, 4144 Arlesheim, Switzerland.

BAILEY, Judith (Margaret); Composer and Conductor; b. 18 July 1941, Camborne, Cornwall, England. *Education:* Studied at the Royal

Academy of Music, 1959–63. *Career:* Conductor and composer from 1971; mem, BASCA; BASBWE; COMA; Cornish Music Guild; Portsmouth District Composers Alliance. *Compositions:* Trencrom, symphonic poem, 1978; 2 symphonies, 1981, 1982; Seascape for women's chorus, woodwind trio and orchestra, 1985; Penwith, overture, 1986; Fiesta for orchestra, 1988; Concerto for clarinet and strings, 1988; Havas for orchestra, 1991; Joplinesque for wind band; Festive Concert Piece for wind band; Chamber music. *Publications:* Most compositions are published. *Address:* c/o British Music Information Centre, 10 Stratford Place, London W1N 9 AE, England.

BAILEY, Norman Stanley, CBE, BMus; British opera and concert singer (baritone); b. 23 March 1933, Birmingham, England; m. 1st Doreen Simpson 1957 (divorced 1983); two s. one d.; m. 2nd Kristine Ciesinki 1985. *Education:* Rhodes University, South Africa, Vienna State Academy, Austria; performers' and teachers' licenciate in singing, diplomas in opera, lieder and oratori. *Career:* debut, Linz, 1960; Principal Baritone, Sadler's Wells Opera, London, 1967–71; Regular engagements at world's major opera houses and festivals including: La Scala, Milan, Royal Opera House, Covent Garden; 1st British Hans Sachs in Meistersinger, 1969 at Bayreuth Wagner Festival, also sang Amfortas there; Sang at: Vienna State Opera, Metropolitan Opera, NY, Paris Opéra, Edinburgh Festival, Hamburg State Opera, Munich State Opera, English National Opera, Scottish Opera; In 1985 sang in the world premiere of Goehr's Behold The Sun, at Duisburg; Performances for BBC include: Falstaff, Germont in La Traviata, The Flying Dutchman, Macbeth; Has also sung: Sharpless with Scottish Opera, Britten's Theseus for Opera London, Sadler's Wells and Stromminger in La Wally for Bregenz Festival, 1990; Sang in Reginald Goodall's Memorial Concert, Wahnmonolog, Festival Hall, 1991; Season 1992 as Sharpless in Madama Butterfly for ENO and King René in Tchaikovsky's Yolanta for Opera North; Sang Oroveso in Bellini's Norma for Opera North, 1993; Glyndebourne debut, as Schigolch in Lulu, 1996 (also televised); Sang Landgrave in Tannhäuser for Opera North, 1997 and Gremin in Eugene Onegin, 1998; mem, Baha'i World Community. *Recordings include:* The Ring, Goodall; Meistersinger; Der fliegende Holländer, Solti; Walküre, Klemperer. *Honours:* Honorary RAM, 1981; Honorary Doctor of Music, 1986. *Address:* 84 Warham Road, South Croydon, Surrey CR2 6LB, England.

BAILEY, Simon; Singer (baritone); b. 1970, England. *Education:* Royal Northern College of Music and Clare College, Cambridge; Academy of Teatra alla Scala, Milan. *Career:* Appearances at La Scala in supporting roles in La Bohème, Carmélites, Wozzeck, Peter Grimes and Ariadne auf Naxos; Season 2001–02 with Jeffrey Tate, James Conlon and Riccardo Muti; Roles in Turandot and Verdi's Un giorno de regno; Premieres of Tatiana by Corghi, and in Figaro at Rouen; Season 2002–03 at Frankfurt Opera in Salome, Hercules by Handel, Der Schatzgräber by Schreker, Berio's Un re in ascolto, Manon and Verdi's Jérusalem; Papageno in Die Zauberflöte and Dulcamara in L'elisir d'amore. *Current Management:* Hazard Chase, Norman House, Cambridge Place, Cambridge CB2 1NS, England. *Telephone:* (1223) 312400. *Fax:* (1223) 460827. *Website:* www.hazardchase.co.uk.

BAILLIE, Alexander; Concert Cellist; b. 6 Jan. 1956, Stockport, Lancashire, England. *Education:* Studied with Jacqueline du Pré, at the Royal College of Music and with André Navarra in Vienna. *Career:* Many performances with leading British Orchestras; Concerts in Europe and North America include the first Canadian performance of Penderecki's 2nd Concerto; Tour of the United Kingdom with the Budapest String Orchestra, 1991, followed by tour of the Far East; Promenade Concert appearances include the Concerto by Colin Matthews, 1984, Henze's Sieben Liebeslieder, Takemitsu's Orion and Pleiades 1989, Schumann Concerto, 1990 and the Delius Concerto, 1993; Has premiered works by Lutoslawski (Grave), Schnittke (Sonata for Cello and Piano), Gordon Crosse (Wave-Songs) and Takemitsu (Orion and Pleiades); Principal Guest Artist with the East of England Orchestra; Concerts with the Villiers Piano Quartet; Recital debut at the Kennedy Center in Washington, 1992; Season 1993 with US Concerto debut, Boston Philharmonic, and visits to the Edinburgh and Harrogate Festivals; Recital of unaccompanied works at the Wigmore Hall, London, 1997; Professor at the Royal Academy of Music. *Recordings include:* Tippett Triple Concerto with Ernst Kovacic and Gerard Causse; Concertos by Elgar, Colin Matthews and Bernard Stevens; Frank Bridge's Oration, the Britten Cello Suites and Sonata; Sonatas by Rachmaninov, Shostakovich, Prokofiev and Schnittke. *Honours:* Prizewinner in competitions at Budapest (Casals) and Munich (ARD). *Current Management:* TransArt (UK) Ltd, Cedar House, 10 Rutland Street, Filey, YO14 9JB, North Yorkshire, England. *Telephone:* (1723) 515819. *Fax:* (1723) 514678. *E-mail:* transartuk@transartuk .com. *Website:* www.transartuk.com.

BAILLIE, Peter; Singer (Tenor); b. 29 Nov. 1933, Hastings, New Zealand. *Education:* Studied in Australia and New Zealand. *Career:* Sang with New Zealand Opera and the Elizabethan Opera Trust at Sydney, from 1963; Roles included Tamino, Ferrando, Jacquino (Fidelio) and Gounod's Faust; Member of the Vienna Volksoper, 1967–88, in such character roles as Mozart's Bartolo and Monostatos, Albert Herring and Nando in Tiefland; Also appeared in The Bartered Bride, From the House of the Dead and Zemlinsky's Kleider machen Leute; Glyndebourne debut, 1968, as Hervey in Anna Bolena, Wexford, 1968 (Mozart's Titus) and Salzburg, 1971 (first modern revival of Mozart's Mitridate); Other roles include Ernesto in Don Pasquale, Malcolm in Macbeth and Svatopluk Cech in The Excursions of Mr Brouček; Sang Mozart's Basilio for Wellington City Opera, 1995. *Address:* c/o Volksoper, Währingerstrasse 78, 1090 Vienna, Austria.

BAINBRIDGE, Elizabeth; British singer (mezzo-soprano); b. 28 March 1936, Lancashire, England. *Education:* Guildhall School with Norman Walker. *Career:* debut, Glyndebourne 1963 in Die Zauberflöte; sang in British premiere of Rossini's La Pietra del Paragone, London 1963; mem., Covent Garden Opera from 1965, in Butterfly (Suzuki), The Midsummer Marriage, Götterdämmeruug (Norn); Falstaff (Mistress Quickly), Les Troyens, Un Ballo in Maschera (Arvidson), Troilus and Cressida and Lulu, Erda, (Rheingold, Siegfried), Amelia, Otello, Jenůfa (Grandmother), Onegin (Nurse), Aida (Amneris); tours to La Scala, Milan 1976; Far East, 1979; Los Angeles; Athens Festival; guest appearances with ENO, Scottish Opera, WNO; US debut, Chicago, 1977 in Peter Grimes; Buenos Aires debut, 1979; Israel, Jenůfa, 1993, 1995; Covent Garden, First Maid in Elektra, Innkeeper's Wife in The Cunning Little Vixen, 1990; Peter Grimes, Dublin Grand Opera Society; Widow Sweeney in The Rising of the Moon, Wexford Festival; sang the Hostess in the Covent Garden premiere of Prokofiev's The Fiery Angel, 1992; Grandmother Burjya in Jenůfa at Geneva, 2001. *Recordings include:* Dido and Aeneas, Sorceress; Sir John in Love, Mistress Ford; The Rape of Lucretia, Bianca; Peter Grimes, Auntie; Cendrillon, Dorothée; Filipyevna in Eugene Onegin for EMI; Troilus and Cressida; Midsummer Marriage. *Address:* Buckleys, Forestside, Rowlands Castle, Hants PO9 6ED, England.

BAINBRIDGE, Simon (Jeremy); Composer and Conductor; b. 30 Aug. 1952, London, England; m. Lynda Richardson, 17 July 1980, 1 d. *Education:* Central Tutorial School for Young Musicians (now Purcell School), 1965–66; Highgate School, 1966–69; Royal College of Music, 1969–72; Studied Composition with John Lambert at the Berkshire Music Center, Tanglewood, Massachusetts, USA, 1973–74, with Gunther Schuller. *Career:* Freelance Composer, 1972–; His music performed extensively in the United Kingdom, USA, Europe, Australia; Has worked as Conductor with BBC Symphony Orchestra, BBC Scottish Symphony Orchestra, Bournemouth Symphony Orchestra, London Sinfonietta, Northern Sinfonia, Nash Ensemble, Composers' Ensemble, Capricorn and Divertimenti; Teaches composition at Royal College of Music and Guildhall School of Music and Drama; mem, Executive Committees: Society for the Promotion of New Music; International Society for Contemporary Music; Association of Professional Composers. *Compositions include:* Wind Quintet; String Quartet; String Sextet; Clarinet Quintet; Works for small and large Chamber Ensembles, with and without voice; Choral Music; Works for large orchestra; Dance Score for Rambert Dance Company; Music for 2 Madame Tussaud Exhibitions, London and Amsterdam; Double Concerto for oboe, clarinet and chamber orchestra, 1990; Clarinet Quintet, 1993; Henry's Mobile for viol consort, 1995; Landscape and Memory for horn and ensemble, 1995; 4 Primo Levi Settings for mezzo-soprano, clarinet, viola and piano, 1996; 'Tis Time I Think for soprano and string quartet, 1996; Eicha for mezzo-soprano, chorus and wind ensemble, 1997; Chant for 12 amplified voices and ensemble, 1998; Three Pieces for orchestra, 1998; Guitar Concerto, 1998; Towards the Bridge for large ensemble, 1999; Dances for Moon Animals for guitar, 1999; Scherzi for orchestra, 2000; Voices, for bassoon and 12 strings, 2001. *Recordings:* Music of Simon Bainbridge: Fantasia for Double Orchestra–BBC Symphony Orchestra/Composer, Viola Concerto–London Sinfonietta/ Michael Tilson Thomas-Walter Trampler Viola, Concertante in moto perpetuo-Composers' Ensemble/composer-Nicholas Daniel oboe. *Honours:* Margaret Lee Crofts Fellowship, USA, 1973; Leonard Bernstein Fellowship, USA, 1974; Forman Fellowship, 1976; USA-UK Bicentennial Fellowship, 1978; Published by United Music Publishers, Novello-Music Sales. *Address:* 38 Constantine Road, London NW3 2NG, England.

BAIOCCHI, Regina Harris, BA; American composer and musician; b. 16 July 1956, Chicago, IL. *Education:* Richards Vocational High School, Chicago, Paul Laurence Dunbar Vocational High School, Roosevelt Univ., Ill. Inst. of Tech., Inst. of Design, Chicago, New York Univ., DePaul Univ. *Career:* began composing aged ten; Orchestral Suite performed at Detroit Symphony Orchestra/Unisys Corpn Symposium 1992; composer-in-residence, Mostly Music Inc. 1992; guest composer, Wayne State Univ., Detroit 1993–94; guest composer/public relations lecturer, Northeastern Ill. Univ., Chicago 1993–94; guest composer, Columbia Coll., Chicago 1995, Northwestern Univ., Evanston 1996;

composer, Musical Dir, Steppenwolf Theatre, Chicago 1997. *Compositions:* Equipoise by Intersection for piano 1978, Realizations for strings 1978, Chasé 1979, Who Will Claim The Baby? for chorus 1984, Send Your Gifts for chorus 1984, Father We Thank You for chorus 1986, Zora Neale Hurston Songs 1989, Psalm 138 for chorus 1990, We Real Cool for jazz ensemble 1990, Miles Per Hour (Jazz Sonatina) for trumpet 1990, Autumn Night for flute 1991, Crystal Stair for vocal ensemble 1991, Foster Pet 1991, Langston Hughes Songs 1991, Orchestral Suite 1991–92, Sketches for piano trio 1992, Shadows 1992, A Few Black Voices 1992, Teddy Bear Suite for orchestra 1992, Legacy 1992, Bwana's Libation 1992, QFX 1993, Much in Common for vocal ensemble 1993, Nobody's Child for chorus 1993, Mason Room 1993, Three Pieces for Greg 1994, Deborah for percussion 1994, Liszten, My Husband is Not a Hat for piano 1994, After the Rain 1994, Friday Night 1995, Darryl's Rose 1995, Gbeldahoven: No One's Child (opera) 1996, African Hands for orchestra with soloists 1997, Skins for percussion 1997, Dreamhoppers 1997, Nikki Giovanni 1997, Muse for orchestra 1997, Message to My Muse 1997, Dream Weaver 1997. *Honours:* City of Chicago Dept of Cultural Affairs CAAP grant 1992–94, 1996, AT&T grant 1994, Nat. Endowment for the Arts/Randolph Street Gallery Regional Artist Program grant 1995, Chicago Music Asscn Award 1995, ASCAP Special Awards grants 1996, 1997, Art Inst. of Chicago and the Lila Wallace/Reader's Digest Fund Award 1997. *Address:* PO Box 450, Chicago, IL 60690-0450, USA (office).

BAIRD, Janice; Singer (soprano); b. 1960, New York, USA. *Education:* Studied with Astrid Varnay and Birgit Nilsson; City University of New York. *Career:* Sang as mezzo-soprano throughout the USA; Dramatic soprano roles in opera throughout Germany from 1991; Season 1998 at Chemnitz as Elektra, Leonore, and Brünnhilde; Leonore at the Deutsche Oper Berlin, 1999, and Brünnhilde in Der Ring an einem Abend; Salome at the Vienna Staatsoper and the Berlin Staatsoper; Season 1999–2000 as Brünnhilde at Gothenburg and Geneva; Season 2000–2001 in The Ring at Catania, Salome in Berlin and Turandot at the Opéra du Rhin, Strasbourg. *Current Management:* Athole Still International Management, Forresters Hall, 25–27 Westow Street, London, SE19 3RY, England. *Telephone:* (20) 8771-5271. *Fax:* (20) 8768-6600. *Website:* www.atholestill.com.

BAIRD, Julianne; Singer (Soprano); b. 10 Dec. 1952, Stateville, North Carolina, USA. *Education:* Studied at Eastman School with Masako Ono Toribara and at Stanford University; Further study with Walter Berry and Harnoncourt, and at Salzburg Mozarteum. *Career:* Sang in New York with Waverly Consort and Concert Royal; Stage debut in Handel's Il Pastor Fido; Later appearances at Santa Fe, Washington DC, Philadelphia and Los Angeles in operas by Gluck, Mozart, Purcell, Charpentier and Gagliano; Concert engagements in sacred music by Bach and French Baroque music; Sang in Dido and Aeneas with Academy of Ancient Music at the Barbican Hall, London, 1992; Teacher at Rutgers University. *Recordings include:* Handel's Imeneo, Acis and Galatea, Joshua and Siroe; Cantatas by Bach, Telemann and Clerambault; Bach's Magnificat and B Minor Mass; J C Bach's Amadis de Gaule; La Serva Padrona by Pergolesi and Monteverdi's Orfeo; Handel's Faramondo (Vox, 1996). *Contributions:* Journals such as Continuo and Early Music. *Address:* c/o Washington Opera, John F Kennedy Center for the Performing Arts, Washington DC 20566, USA.

BAKELS, Kees; Conductor; b. 14 Jan. 1945, Amsterdam, Netherlands. *Education:* Studied at the Amsterdam Conservatory and at the Accademia Chigiana in Siena with Franco Ferrara and Bruno Rigacci; Further study with Kiril Kondrashin. *Career:* Associate Conductor of the Amsterdam Philharmonic and Principal Guest Conductor of the Netherlands Chamber Orchestra; Tours to England, Belgium, Spain and the USA; Has led all the major Dutch Orchestras and has guested with the Warsaw Philharmonic, BBC Philharmonic, BBC National Orchestra of Wales, San Diego, Quebec and Oregon Symphony Orchestras; New Belgian Chamber Orchestra; Ulster Orchestra; Scottish Chamber; Bournemouth Sinfonietta; Royal Liverpool Philharmonic; Appeared with the National Youth Orchestra at the 1985 Promenade Concerts; Chief Guest Conductor with the Bournemouth Symphony and Principal Conductor of Netherlands Radio Symphony Orchestra, 1993–; Has worked with the soloists Yehudi Menuhin, Claudio Arrau, Pierre Fournier, Paul Tortelier, David Oistrakh and Ruggiero Ricci; Appearances with Netherlands Opera in Nabucco, Ariadne auf Naxos, Carmen, Lucia di Lammermoor, Idomeneo and I Puritani; San Diego Opera, Oberto and Madama Butterfly; Vancouver Opera, Carmen, Così fan tutte, Le nozze di Figaro and Die Zauberflöte; Conducted the Lyon Opéra in Cinderella (also on tour to Poland); Welsh National Opera with Die Zauberflöte, La Bohème and Carmen; At English National Opera has led Aida and Fidelio; Conducted Carmen at San Diego, 1992; Season 1992/93 with engagements in the United Kingdom, the Netherlands and Denmark; US appearances with the Florida Symphony, Oregon Symphony and Calgary Philharmonic; Concert performance of Roberto Devereux with Netherlands Radio

Symphony at the Concertgebouw; Four concerts with Tokyo Metropolitan Symphony Orchestra; Further engagements (2000–2001) include concerts with L'Orchestre Philharmonique de Monte-Carlo, Saarbrucken Radio and the BBC Symphony Orchestra. *Recordings:* Vaughan Williams Symphonies with the Bournemouth Symphony; Complete Nielsen Concerti with the Bournemouth Symphony Orchestra. *Address:* IMG Artists, Lovell House, 616 Chiswick High Road, London W4 5RX, England.

BAKER, Alice; Singer (Mezzo Soprano); b. 27 March 1961, Detroit, Michigan, USA. *Education:* Bachelor of Arts, Oakland University, USA; Master of Arts, California State University, Los Angeles, USA; Apprenticeships with Lyric Opera of Chicago and San Diego Opera; Private study and both degrees with specialisation in music performance. *Career:* Debut: In USA, Opera, in alternating productions of Otello with Plácido Domingo and Madama Butterfly with Leona Mitchell, Los Angeles, 1986; European debut as Carmen opposite José Carreras at Teatro dell'Opera di Roma, 1987; In Europe has appeared in Rome as Giulio Cesare, 1998; Carmen, 1987; Isabella, 1987; L'Italiana in Algeri, 1987; Siebel, Faust, 1988; Suzuki, Madama Butterfly, 1990; Stabat Mater, 1989; In Turin as Elisabeth I in Maria Stuarda, 1999; As the Old Lady, Candide, 1997; In Venice, Leonora, La Favorita, 1988; Concert in Debussy's La Damoiselle Elue, 1989; In concert in smaller cities, Santa Margherita, Verdi Requiem, 1998 and Beethoven's 9th Symphony, 1997; Verona, in recital, 1989; Rome, in recital, 1996; Mantua, La Forza del Destino, 1999; United Kingdom debut with Wexford Festival Opera, 1988, as Carlotta in Elisa e Claudio; On tour to London at Queen Elizabeth Hall; In Germany as Rosina in Il Barbiere di Siviglia at Frankfurt Opera, 1988, 1989, 1990; Brahms Alto Rhapsody, 1992; In Spain in title role of La Cenerentola, Teatro Liceu, Barcelona, 1992; In Norway in concert with Stavanger Symphony, Mozart Grand Mass in C Minor, 1989; In Slovenia at International Festival Ljubjana, Verdi Requiem, 1998; Carmen, 2000; In USA and Canada: return engagements in Los Angeles to sing the title role in Cenerentola, 1988; Revivals of Otello, 1989; Hermia in A Midsummer Night's Dream, 1988; The Mother Superior in The Fiery Angel, 1989; Vancouver Opera debut, Suzuki in Madama Butterfly, 1995; Edmonton Opera as Cornelia in Giulio Cesare, 1994; Amneris in Aida for Greenville Opera, 1988; Preziosilla in La Forza del Destino, Washington Opera, Kennedy Center, Washington DC, 1989; Ruggero in Alcina, Opera Theatre of St Louis, 1987; Concert debuts in USA, Parsifal, Los Angeles Philharmonic, Hollywood Bowl, 1985; Parsifal, Carnegie Hall, New York, 1986; Lyric Opera of Chicago debut as Peep-Bo in Peter Sellers' The Mikado, 1983; St Louis Symphony, Mahler Third, 1988, return appearances for Otello, 1989; Pittsburgh Symphony debut in Rossini's Stabat Mater, 1989; Festival Internazionale Valentiniano, Rieti, Italy, Rossini's Stabat Mater with Moscow State Orchestra, 2000; Manzoni Requiem of Verdi, 2001; Recital tour in USA of songs by American and British composers and by Bizet, 2001. *Current Management:* MIA Management (Italy only); CMI Arts (rest of world). *E-mail:* info@cmi-arts.com. *Website:* digilander.iol.it/cmi.

BAKER, Claude; Composer; b. 12 April 1948, Lenoir, North Carolina, USA. *Education:* Eastman School, Rochester. *Career:* Professor, University of Louisville, 1976–88; Indiana University School of Music, Bloomington, from 1988; Composer in Residence, St Louis Symphony Orchestra, 1991–99. *Compositions:* Canzonet for solo tuba, 1972; Elegy for Solo Violin, 1979; Divertissement for clarinet, violin, cello and piano, 1980; Omaggi e Fantasie for tuba and piano, 1981, revised 1987; The Glass Bead Game for orchestra, 1982; Omaggi e Fantasie for double bass and piano, 1984; 4 Nachtszenen for harp, 1985, revised 1990; Fantasy Variations for string quartet, 1986; Tableaux Funèbres for piano and string quartet, 1988, revised 2003; Three Pieces for 5 timpani, 5 rototoms and wind ensemble, 1990; Shadows for orchestra 1990; Awaking the Winds for orchestra, 1993, for chamber orchestra, 1994; Whispers and Echoes for orchestra, 1995; Into the Sun, for mezzo-soprano and orchestra, 1996; Flights of Passage for piano, 1998; Sleepers Awake for mezzo-soprano, percussion and strings, 1998; The Mystic Trumpeter for orchestra, 1999; Symphony No.1, 2000; Aus Schwanengesang for orchestra, 2001; Three Fantasy Pieces for viola and percussion, 2002. *Honours:* ASCAP Serious Music Awards, annually 1976–; George Eastman Prize, 1985; Eastman-Leonard Prize, 1988; Acad. Award in Music, American Acad. of Arts and Letters, 2002Fellowships: John Simon Guggenheim Memorial Foundation, 2001; Koussevitzky Music Foundation, 2002; Bogliasco Foundation, 2002. *Address:* School of Music, Indiana University, Bloomington, IN 47405, USA. *Telephone:* (812) 855-7423. *E-mail:* bakerwc@indiana.edu.

BAKER, Gregg; singer (baritone); b. 7 Dec. 1955, Chicago, Illinois, USA. *Education:* Northwestern University, studied with Andrew Smith. *Career:* Sang on Broadway in musicals; Metropolitan Opera debut, as Crown in Porgy and Bess, 1985, appearing later as Escamillo and the High Priest in Samson and Delilah; Has also sung Crown at Glyndebourne, 1985, and in Helsinki and Tulsa; Concert performance of Porgy and Bess at the Queen Elizabeth Hall, London, 1989; Other roles include Ford in Falstaff, Count Almaviva and Marcello in La Bohème; Old Vic Theatre, London in Carmen Jones, 1991; Sang Crown in Porgy and Bess at Covent Garden, London and Savonlinna Festival, Finland, 1992; Caesaerea 1993 as Amonasro; Jokanaan at Philadelphia and Detroit, 1995–96; Jokanaan in Salome at Vancouver 1997; Italian debut as Escamillo, at the 1996 Verona Festival; Season 2000 as Amonasro at Houston, Scarpia at Philadelphia, and Escamillo at Naples. *Recordings include:* Porgy and Bess. *Current Management:* Pinnacle Arts Management Inc., 889 Ninth Avenue, Second Floor, New York, NY 10019, USA. *Telephone:* (212) 397-7915. *Fax:* (212) 397-7920. *Website:* pinnaclearts.com.

BAKER, Israel; Violinist; b. 11 Feb. 1921, Chicago, IL, USA. *Education:* Studied with Adolf Pick, Chicago Conservatory, Louis Persinger at Juilliard School of Music in New York, Jacques Gordon and Bronislaw Huberman. *Career:* Soloist with various orchestras; Concertmaster; Many chamber music appearances including 2nd violinist, Heifetz-Piatigorsky Chamber Concerts; Often heard in Schoenberg's Concerto and Berg's Chamber Concerto; Member of Pacific Art Trio; Professor of Music at Scripps College, Claremont, CA. *Recordings:* Various as soloist and chamber music player, including works by Ives, Antheil, Kubik and Stravinsky. *Address:* c/o Scripps College, Claremont, California, USA.

BAKER, Dame Janet (Abbott); Singer (mezzo-soprano); b. 21 Aug. 1933, Hatfield, Yorkshire, England; m. James Keith Shelley, 1957. *Education:* The College for Girls, York; Vocal Studies with Helene Isepp and Meriel St Clair in London. *Career:* Debut: Oxford University Opera Club, 1956, as Roza in The Secret by Smetana; Sang in concert, and in opera as Gluck's Orpheus, London 1958, and Pippo in La Gazza Ladra at the 1959 Wexford Festival; Sang Eduige in Handel's Rodelinda, London 1959, and the title roles in Tamerlano, Ariodante, Orlando and Admeto, Birmingham, 1962–68; Rameau's Hippolyte et Aricie, 1965; Sang in Mahler's Resurrection Symphony at the 1961 Edinburgh Festival; English Opera Group from 1962, as Dido, Polly in The Beggar's Opera and Lucretia; Sang in the premieres of Britten's Owen Wingrave, 1971 and Phaedra, 1976; New York concert debut, 1966; Scottish Opera debut 1967, as Dorabella, followed by Dido in The Trojans, Octavian, and the Composer in Ariadne auf Naxos; Glyndebourne Festival, 1965–72, as Dido, Diana-Jupiter in La Calisto and Penelope in Il Ritorno d'Ulisse; Covent Garden, 1966–74, as Hermia in A Midsummer Night's Dream, Dido, Kate in Owen Wingrave and Vitellia in La Clemenza di Tito; With English National Opera appeared as Poppea, 1971, Mary Stuart, 1973, Charlotte, 1976 and Julius Caesar; Concert repertory included works by Mahler, Elgar, Britten, Brahms and Bach; Lieder by Schubert and French and English Songs; Retired from opera 1982, singing Gluck's Orpheus at Glyndebourne and Alceste at Covent Garden; Sang Orpheus in a concert performance at Carnegie Hall and retired 1989; Appointed Chancellor of York University, 1991; Trustee, Foundation for Sport and the Arts, 1991; mem, Fellow of the Royal Society of Arts, 1979. *Recordings include:* The Angel in The Dream of Gerontius; Dido and Aeneas; La Calisto; Mozart's Requiem; I Capuleti e i Montecchi; Maria Stuarda; The Rape of Lucretia and Owen Wingrave; Duets with Dietrich Fischer-Dieskau; Handel's Messiah, Judas Maccabaeus and Ariodante; La Clemenza di Tito; Verdi Requiem; Orfeo ed Euridice; Labels include Erato, Deutsche Grammophon, EMI and Philips. *Publications:* Full Circle, Autobiography, 1982. *Honours:* C.B.E., 1970; D.B.E., 1976; Shakespeare Prize, Hamburg, 1971; Honorary Fellow, St Anne's College, Oxford, 1975; Copenhagen Sonning Prize, 1979; Honorary DMus from Birmingham, Leicester, London, Hull, Oxford, Leeds, Lancaster and York Universities; Honorary DMus, Cambridge, 1984; Honorary Fellow, Downing College, Cambridge, 1985; Gold Medal, Royal Philharmonic Society, 1990; Companion of Honour, 1994; Commander of the French Order of Arts and Letters, 1995. *Current Management:* TransArt (UK) Ltd, Cedar House, 10 Rutland Street, Filey, YO14 9JB, North Yorkshire, England. *Telephone:* (1723) 515819. *Fax:* (1723) 514678. *E-mail:* transartuk@transartuk.com. *Website:* www .transartuk.com.

BAKER, Mark; Singer (Tenor); b. 1953, Tulsa, Oklahoma, USA. *Education:* Bachelor of Music, 1984, Masters Degree in Counselling, 1986, Indiana University. *Career:* Metropolitan Opera from 1986, as Paris in Roméo et Juliette (debut role), Narraboth in Salome, Froh in Das Rheingold and Melot in Tristan und Isolde; Glimmerglass Opera, 1987, as Lensky in Eugene Onegin, Santa Fe, 1988 (Erik in Fliegende Holländer), Glyndebourne Touring Opera, 1990, as Florestan; Sang Števa in Jenůfa and Ferrando in Così fan tutte at 1989 Glyndebourne Festival; Nantes, 1991, as Monteverdi's Ulisse, Théâtre du Châtelet, Paris, 1992 and Met, 1997, as the Drum Major in Wozzeck; Season 1995–96 as Siegmund at Santiago and Vladimir in Prince Igor at San Francisco; Laca in Jenůfa at Santiago, 1998; Engaged as Samson in Samson et Dalila and Tom in The Great Gatsby at the Met (world premiere, 1999–2000) and Siegmund in Die Walküre at San Francisco Opera; Season 2000–01 as the Drum Major in Wozzeck at Dallas and

Samson for Cleveland Opera. *Recordings include:* Jenůfa, from Glyndebourne (Virgin Classics). *Honours:* Winner in the Metropolitan Opera National, 1986. *Current Management:* Munro Artist's Management. *Address:* c/o Metropolitan Opera, Lincoln Plaza, New York, NY 10023, USA.

BAKER, Michael Conway; Canadian composer and lecturer; b. 13 March 1937, West Palm Beach, FL, USA; m. Penny Anne Baker. *Education:* BMus, Univ. of British Columbia, 1966; MA, Western Washington State Coll., 1972. *Career:* film and concert composer; over almost 25 years has taught and developed music programmes for children of all ages, adult education and univ. students; taught two courses at Univ. of British Columbia as well as one extension course at Simon Fraser Univ.; Composer-in-Residence for Vancouver School Board; now retired; mem., ALCM. *Compositions include:* Counterplay for viola and strings, 1971; Concerto for flute and strings, 1974; Sonata for piano, 1974; Concerto for piano and orchestra, 1976; Symphony No. 1, Highland, 1977; Washington Square, 60-minute ballet for orchestra, 1978; Evocations for flute, quartet and orchestra, 1982; Seven Wonders: A Song Cycle for soprano and piano, 1983; Chanson Joyeuse for orchestra, 1987; Intermezzo for flute and harp, 1988; Through the Lions' Gate: Tone Poems for orchestra, 1989; Capriccio for clarinet and orchestra, 1991; Cinderella—Frozen in Time, 90-minute ice ballet, 1993; Century Symphony (no. 2), 1994; Summit Concerto for trumpet and orchestra, 1995; Vancouver Variations, 1996; His Fanfare to Expo '86 opened the proceedings in Vancouver. *Recordings:* 116 concert works and 180 film projects. *Honours:* Juno, Best Classical Composition, 1991; Order of British Columbia, 1997. *Address:* 2440 Treetop Lane, North Vancouver, BC V7H 2K5, Canada.

BAKER, Richard Douglas James, MA; British broadcaster and writer; b. 15 June 1925, Willesden, London, England; m. Margaret Celia Baker; two s. *Education:* Peterhouse, Cambridge. *Career:* debut as actor 1948, as BBC announcer 1950; actor 1948–49; teacher 1949–50; BBC television news reader 1954–82; panellist on Face the Music (BBC TV) 1964–79; presenter of television concerts 1960–85; presenter of numerous radio programmes, including These You Have Loved (Radio 4) 1972–77, Baker's Dozen (Radio 4) 1977–88, Melodies For You (Radio 2) 1988–94, 1999–, Richard Baker Compares Notes (Radio 4) 1989–95, Music for a While (World Service) 1990–91, In Tune (Radio 3) 1992, (Classic FM) 1995–97, Sound Stories (Radio 3) 1998–99; numerous concert appearances as narrator and compere. *Recordings as narrator:* Peter and the Wolf, Young Person's Guide to the Orchestra, Façade (with Susana Walton). *Publications:* The Magic of Music, 1975; Richard Baker's Music Guide, 1979; Mozart, 1982, new illustrated edition, 1991; Schubert, an illustrated biography, 1997. *Current Management:* Stephanie Williams Artists, 9 Central Chambers, Wood Street, Stratford Upon Avon CV37 6JQ, England.

BAKER, Simon; Singer (Countertenor); b. 1973, Edinburgh, Scotland. *Education:* Edinburgh Academy and Christ's Hospital; Royal College of Music, with Ashley Stafford. *Career:* Sang Handel's Ottone, and Claudio in the modern premiere of Silla at the 23rd London Handel Festival, 2000; Arsamenes in Xerxes for British Youth Opera at the Queen Elizabeth Hall, Messiah in Dublin and London and Canticles by Britten for the Spitalfields Winter Festival; Season 2001 with Flavio for the London Handel Festival, St Matthew Passion at Wells Cathedral, St John Passion at Christ's Hospital and Fileno in Handel's Clori, Tirsi e Fileno for the Covent Garden Festival; other roles include Nero in Monteverdi's Poppea. *Recordings:* Silla, by Handel conducted by Denys Darlow. *Honours:* Featured Artist, Great British Hopes, London Times 2000. *Address:* c/o Royal College of Music, Prince Consort Road, London SW7 2 BS, England.

BAKHCHIEV, Alexander; Pianist; b. 27 July 1930, Moscow, USSR; m. Elena Sorokina, 28 Nov 1962, 1 d. *Education:* MA, Performance, 1953, completed postgraduate courses, 1956, Moscow Conservatory. *Career:* Debut: Solo programme, Liszt, Beethoven Hall, Bolshoi Theatre, Moscow, 1954; State television and radio, over 35 years; Solo, with orchestra, in chamber music ensembles, with singers; Regular duo with wife; Played with orchestras conducted by Rozhdestvensky, Svetlanov, Kondrashin, Chaikin, with V Popov (bassoon), A Korneyev (flute), others; Performed, France, 1954; Chamber music concerts, 1970s; Many educational television and radio series; Concerts all over USSR, including Moscow State Conservatory and with St Petersburg Philharmonic; Duets, Soviet and British modern music, England, 1989; International festivals including Mozart Festival, Tokyo, 1991; Teaching Chamber Ensemble, Moscow State Conservatory, 1990–; 8 programmes, all Schubert piano duets (with wife); Piano duo festivals, Novosibirsk, Ekaterinburg, 1993–95; Piano Duet lecture series for teachers and students, Russia; Music dedicated to him and wife by Boyarsky, Lubovksy, Fried, Moore; Gubaidulina's concerto Introitus written for him. *Recordings:* About 70; Solo recordings include Haydn, Liszt, Bach, Handel, Rubinstein, Arensky, Liadov, Lyapunov, Mussorgsky, Borodin; Ensembles: All sonatas, flute, harpsichord, Bach,

Handel; Vivaldi (with A Korneyev); With Valery Popov: Masterpieces of Baroque; Czechoslovakian music, bassoon, piano; Series: Early Mozart, solo, ensembles; Duets with wife: Schubert, all Mozart, Rachmaninov, Russian Salon Piano Music; Music of France; Albums: Music of Old Vienna; J. S. Bach, his family and pupils. *Current Management:* Vadim Dubrovitsky Producer Firm, Ramenki Gallery, Ramenki Str 6-2, 117607 Moscow, Russia. *Address:* 4-32 Koshkin str, Moscow 115409, Russia.

BAKKE, Ruth; Composer and Organist; b. 2 Aug. 1947, Bergen, Norway. *Education:* Studied at the Bergen Conservatory and Oslo University and in the USA. *Career:* Organist at the Storetveit Church, Bergen, from 1973. *Compositions:* Organ sonata, 1970; Colour Clouds for orchestra, 1972; Rumus for chamber orchestra, 1976; Bonn for organ, soprano and guitar, 1976; Trollsuite for string quartet, 1981; Into the Light for violin and organ, 1982; Meditation for horn and organ, 1986; Nonsense for solo voice, 1990; Sphaerae for organ, 1992; Suite ACD for Renaissance instruments, 1992; Psalm 2000 for organ and tuba, 1993. *Address:* c/o TONO, 4 Galleri Oslo, Toyenbekken 21, Postboks 9171, Gronland, 0134 Oslo 1, Norway.

BAKST, Lawrence; Singer (Tenor); b. 1955, Washington, District of Columbia, USA. *Education:* Studied in America and Europe. *Career:* Sang Radames with Opera Delaware and Kentucky Operas; Verdi's Don Carlos at several Italian centres; Macduff in New Jersey, Barcelona and Marseilles; Gabriele Adorno, Riccardo, Manrico, Canio, Calaf and Faust in Mefistofeles; Appearances at the New York City Opera, Zagreb, Wexford, Detmold, Wuppertal and the Opera Forum in Holland; Season 1990–91 as Faust, Cavaradossi and Edgar (Lucia di Lammermoor) in Wuppertal; Bob Boles in Peter Grimes at Marseilles and Pylade in Iphigénie en Tauride at the Opéra de Bastille, Paris; Sang Pylade with the Tanztheater of Wuppertal at Rome, 1992; Sang Puccini's Calaf at Kiel, 1995; Pylade in Iphigénie en Tauride at Rio de Janeiro, 1997. *Honours:* Winner, Metropolitan Opera National Council Auditions Competition; Premier Grand Prix and Best Tenor Award in the Vinas Competition, Barcelona; Concours International de Chant, Toulouse; 1st Prize, G B Viotti Competition, Vercelli. *Address:* c/o Music International, 13 Ardilaun Road, London N5 2QR, England.

BALADA, Leonardo; composer and professor; b. 22 Sept. 1933, Barcelona, Spain; m. 1st; one s.; m. 2nd Joan Winer 1979. *Education:* Barcelona Conservatory, New York Coll. of Music, Juilliard School of Music, Mannes Coll. of Music, studied with Copland, Tansman, Persichetti, Markevitch. *Career:* teacher, United Nations International School 1963–70; Faculty 1970–75, Prof. 1975–90, Univ. Prof. 1990–, Carnegie-Mellon Univ.. *Compositions include:* Opera: Christopher Columbus, 1987, premiered in 1989, Barcelona Opera, with José Carreras and Monserrat Caballé singing leading roles; Orchestral: Piano Concerto, 1964, Guitar Concerto, 1965, Guernica, 1966, Bandoneon Concerto, 1970, Steel Symphony, 1972, Ponce de Leon for narrator and orchestra, 1973, Homage to Casals and Sarasate, 1975, Sardana, 1979, Quasi un Pasodoble, premiered with New York Philharmonic, 1981, Alegrias for flute and string orchestra, 1988, Symphony No. 4, premiered by the Lausanne Chamber Orchestra, 1992, Music for oboe and orchestra, Lorin Maazel and the Pittsburgh Symphony Orchestra, 1993, Shadows, Cincinnati Symphony Orchestra, 1995, Morning Music, premiered by Julius Baker flute, and Carnegie Mellon Philharmonic, 1995; Concierto Magico, for guitar and orchestra, 1997, premiered by guitarist Angel Romero and the Cincinnati Symphony Orchestra, 1998; No-Res, revised, 1997; Cantata, with Barcelona Symphony Orchestra and National Chorus of Spain, 1997; Folk Dreams for orchestra, 1998, premiere National Orchestra of Ireland; Concerto for Piano and Orchestra No. 3, 1999, premiere Berlin Radio Symphony Orchestra; Passacaglia for orchestra, 2000; Music for Flute and Orchestra, 2000. *Recordings include:* Steel Symphony with Pittsburgh Symphony Orchestra under Lorin Maazel; Torquemada, cantata; Concerto for Piano, Winds and Percussion; Music for Oboe and Orchestra; Maria Sabina, Cantata with Louisville Orchestra; Divertimentos for string orchestra. *Honours:* Nat. Composition Prize of Catalonia, Barcelona 1993. *Address:* c/o Music Associates of America, 224 King Street, Engelwood, NJ 07631, USA.

BALASHOV, Oleg; Singer (Tenor); b. 1968, Moscow, Russia. *Education:* Graduated Moscow Conservatoire 1999. *Career:* Sang with Moscow Municipal Theatre New Opera from 1998; Young Singers' Academy of the Mariinsky Theatre, St Petersburg, 1999–; Roles with the Kirov Opera and elsewhere have included Andrei in Mazeppa, Vaudémont in Tchaikovsky's Iolanta, Kuragin in War and Peace by Prokofiev, and Verdi's Alfredo; Further engagements as Mozart in Rimsky-Korsakov's Mozart and Salieri, Lukov in Rimsky's The Tsar's Bride, Sinodal in The Demon by Rubinstein and Grigory in Boris Godunov; Appearances with the Kirov Opera in summer season at Covent Garden 2000 as Prince Anatol Kuragin in War and Peace. *Address:* c/o Kirov Opera, Mariinsky Theatre, Mariinsky Square, St Petersburg, Russia.

BALASSA, Sándor; Composer and Teacher of Orchestration; b. 20 Jan. 1935, Budapest, Hungary; m. 1st Irene Balogh 1957; one s. one d.; m. 2nd Marianne Orosz 1994. *Education:* choral leadership, Bela Bartók Conservatory, Budapest; composition diploma, Liszt Academy, Budapest. *Career:* debut, 1965; radio broadcasts, including Legend (21 stations) 1971, Requiem for Lajor Kassak (30 stations) 1972–73, Xenia (BBC) 1974; works performed abroad; commissions, including from Koussevitzky Music Foundation; Teacher of Orchestration, Academy of Music, Budapest; retired in 1996; mem. Hungarian Art Academy (vicepres.). *Compositions include:* The Man Outside, opera, 1973–76; The Third Planet, opera, 1986–87; Karl and Anna, opera in 3 acts, 1987–92; Damjanich's Prayer, mixed choir, 1992; Tündér Ilona, orchestra, 1992; Prince Csaba, string orchestra, 1993; Bölcskei Concerto, string orchestra, 1993; Szonatina, harp, 1993; Divertimento, 2 cimbaloms, 1993; John's Day Music, violin solo, 1993; Little Garland, trio for flute, viola, harp, 1993; Dances of Mucsa, orchestra, 1994; String Quartet, 1995; A nap fiai, for orchestra, 1995; Nyirbatori harangok, for brass, 1996; Preludiums and Fantasia, for organ, 1997; Four Portraits, for orchestra, 1996; 301-s parcella, for orchestra, 1997; Pécs Concerto, 1998; Hungarian Coronation Music, 1998; Hun's Valley, 1999; Woodcutter for male choir, 1998; Winter Cantata for children's choir, 1998; Chant of the Moon and Anthem of the Sun for male choir, 1999; Duets for flute and harp, 1998; Pastoral and Rondo for violin and horn, 1999; Földindulás, opera in 3 acts, 1999–2001; Double concerto for oboe and horn, 2002; Fantasy for harp and string orchestra, 2002; Commissions include Calls and Cries (Boston Symphonic Orchestra Centennial); The Day Dreamer's Diary, orchestra (Elizabeth Sprague Coolidge Foundation, Washington); Three Fantasies (BBC Philharmonic Orchestra); Summer interlude for oboe and piano; Eight movements for two clarinets; The Secret of the Heart, cantata; Fantasy for Harp and String Orchestra; Flowers of October for orchestra; Songs from street Sümegvár; Six duets for two violins; Gödöllö concertino for guitar orchestra; Sun-Mountains excursion for youth string orchestra; Il Szonetina for piano; Zenia II – nonet. *Recordings:* Antinomia, trio for soprano, clarinet, cello; Xenia, nonet; Requiem for Lajos Kassak; Iris, orchestra; Cantata Y; Lupercalia, orchestra; Tabulae, chamber orchestra; The Island of Everlasting Youth, orchestra; Pécs Concerto, Four POrtraits, Parcel No. 301; Karl and Anna, opera. *Honours:* Bartók-Pásztory Prize, 1999. *Address:* Sumegvar u.18, 1118 Budapest, Hungary.

BALATSCH, Norbert; Chorus Master; b. 10 March 1928, Vienna, Austria. *Education:* Studied at the Vienna Music Academy; Private studies in cello and piano. *Career:* Sang with the Vienna Boys' Choir as a child, then directed after graduation; Directed the Vienna Mens' Chorus, then from 1952 the chorus of the Vienna Staatsoper (Chorus Master 1978–84); Director of the Bayreuth Festival Chorus from 1972 together with the Philharmonic Chorus, London (1974–79); Chorus of Accademia di Santa Cecilia, Rome from 1984; Has directed sacred works by Mozart, Haydn and others at the chapel of the Viennese Court; Led the chorus in Der fliegende Holländer at Bayreuth, 1990; Nikikai Chorus Group of Tokyo in Lohengrin, 1997. *Address:* Festspielhaus, 8580 Bayreuth, Germany.

BALDWIN, Dalton; Pianist; b. 19 Dec. 1931, Summit, New Jersey, USA. *Education:* Juilliard School of Music, New York; BM, Oberlin College Conservatory of Music; Studies with Nadia Boulanger, Madeleine Lipatti, Paris; Special coaching from Sibelius, Barber, Poulenc, et al. *Career:* Toured extensively as Accompanist including: Gerard Souzay, Elly Ameling, Marilyn Horne and Jessye Norman; Took part with Souzay in the premiere of Rorem's War Scenes, 1969. *Recordings:* Numerous recordings including the complete songs of Fauré, Debussy, Ravel and Poulenc. *Address:* c/o Columbia Artists Management, 165 West 57th Street, NY 10019, USA.

BALKIND, Jonathan (Paul Brenner); Impresario; b. 6 July 1946, Los Angeles, California, USA. *Education:* Cambridge University; Architectural Association, London. *Career:* Historic Buildings Inspector for GLC/English Heritage with special responsibility for Spitalfields, 1974–88; Board Member, Adviser, Endymion Ensemble, 1980–; General and Artistic Director, Opera London, 1988–; Director, Songbird Films (Music and Arts); Artistic Adviser, City of London Sinfonia, 1988–91; Chairman, Collegium Music '90; Founder, Spitalfields Festival and Director, 1976–82; Festivals of Handel, 1977, Early Music, 1978, English Music, 1979, Young Mozart, 1980; Produced Mozart Lucio Silla, last performances by Janet Baker of Dido and Aeneas and many other concerts and first performances; Produced operas for stage in Spitalfields and other festivals, Barbican, South Bank and Sadler's Wells, including Gluck's Armide, 1982, (Spitalfields), broadcast BBC, Handel's Alcina, restaged in Los Angeles, Monteverdi's L'Incoronazione di Poppea, and Britten's A Midsummer Night's Dream (all 4 recorded); Produced extensive music theatre with Endymion Ensemble, including Birtwistle's Punch and Judy with Opera Factory; Directed operas by Gluck, Mozart and Mussorgsky; Music Adviser: BBC television films Janet Baker–Full Circle, 1982, Jessye Norman–Singer, 1986, and dance documentaries for Channel 4; Beethoven in Love for BBC. *Contributions:* Frequently to various publications; Notes for concerts by Endymion Ensemble and City of London Sinfonia; Editor, festival and opera programmes. *Honours:* Nominee, ABSA/Daily Telegraph Orb Award, 1991. *Address:* 45 Chalcot Road, London NW1 8LS, England.

BALKWILL, Bryan Havell, FRAM; British conductor; b. 2 July 1922, London, England; m. Susan Elizabeth Roberts 1949; one s. one d. *Education:* Royal Academy of Music. *Career:* debut, New London Opera Co. 1947; Conductor, New London Opera 1947–49; Glyndebourne, Wexford Festivals, 1950–64; Sadler's Wells, English National Opera, Royal Opera House, Covent Garden, 1959–65; toured USSR with the English Opera Group, conducting Albert Herring and A Midsummer Night's Dream with Covent Garden in London; gave premiere of Bennett's A Penny for a Song at Sadler's Wells, London 1967; Musical Dir, Welsh National Opera 1963–67; freelance, opera and concerts in the UK, Europe, USA and Canada; Prof. of Conducting, Indiana Univ., USA 1977–92; life mem. Royal Philharmonic Society. *Recordings:* Madama Butterfly Highlights, Sadler's Wells Opera; Recital with Geraint Evans and Suisse Romande Orchestra. *Address:* 8 The Green, Wimbledon Common, London SW19 5AZ, England.

BALL, Christopher, ARAM, LRAM, ARNCM; British composer, conductor and professor; b. 7 July 1936, Leeds. *Education:* Royal Academy of Music, Royal Northern College of Music, Guildhall School of Music. *Career:* debut as Dir, Praetorius Consort, Wigmore Hall 1971; conductor, BBC Philharmonic, BBC Scottish Symphony Orchestra, Ulster Orchestra, City of Birmingham Symphony Orchestra, Vancouver Symphony Orchestra, Royal Opera House Covent Garden Orchestra, Bavarian Opera Orchestra, Maggio Musicale Orchestra of Florence; mem Performing Right Soc., RAM Club, Composers' Guild. *Compositions:* Recorder Concerto, The Piper of Dreams; Oboe concerto; Flute concerto; Orchestral dances; Dance contrasts for full orchestra; wind quintet, Scenes from a comedy; Pagan Piper; Pan Overheard; On a Summer Day; Celtic Moods; Adderbury in Spring; The Coming of Summer; Autumn Landscape; Christmas at the Rookery. *Recordings:* Dances From Terpsichore; German And Polish Dances; The Dancing School Of Lambrangi; Orchésographie; Music By Holborne; Recordings by London Baroque Trio; The Praetorius Consort; Joyful Noyse. *Honours:* Gold medal for orchestral playing; John Solomon wind prize; Ricordi conducting prize. *Address:* 122 Wigmore Street, London W1U 3RX, England.

BALL, Michael, DMus, ARCM; Composer; b. 10 Nov. 1946, Manchester, England. *Education:* Royal Coll. of Music. *Career:* compositions covering most areas, including five commissions from the BBC and many brass band works; mem. British Acad. of Composers and Songwriters, Incorporated Soc. of Musicians, Soc. for the Promotion of New Music. *Compositions include:* Sainte Marye Virgine, 1979; Resurrection Symphonies, 1982; Frontier!, 1984; A Hymne to God my God, 1984; Omaggio, 1986; Danses vitales: Danses macabres, 1987; Nocturns, 1990; Midsummer Music, 1991; The Belly Bag (opera), 1992; Chaucer's Tunes, 1993; Whitsun Wakes, 1997. *Honours:* Octavia Travelling Scholarship. *Address:* 31 Sefton, Rochestown Avenue, Dun Laoghaire, Co. Dublin, Ireland (home). *E-mail:* michaelball@iol.ie. .

BALLARD, Louis; Composer; b. 6 July 1931, Devil's Promenade, Oklahoma, USA. *Education:* Studied at Oklahoma and Tulsa Universities; MM, 1962; Further study with Milhaud, Bela Rozsa, Castelnuovo-Tedesco and Carlos Surinach. *Career:* Programme Director, Bureau of Indian Affairs, Washington, District of Columbia, 1979–. *Compositions include:* Koshare, ballet on Indian themes, 1966; The God will Hear, cantata, 1966; Four Moons, ballet, 1967; Ritmo Indio for wind instruments, 1968; Dialogue Differgutia, oratorio with orchestra and soloists; Katcin Dances for cello and piano, 1970; Desert Trilog for winds, strings and percussion, 1971; Cacega Ayuwipi for percussion ensemble, 1973; Devil's Promenade for orchestra, 1973; Incident at Wounded Knee for orchestra, 1974; Thus Spake Abraham, cantata, 1976; City of Fire for piano; City of Silver, piano; City of Light, piano; Companion of Talking God for orchestra, 1982; Fantasy Aborigine III for orchestra, 1984; Fantasy Aborigine No. 5, 1986, No. 6 'Niagara', 1991; The Maid of the Mist and the Thunderbeings, dance, 1991; The Lonely Sentinel for ensemble, 1993; Feast Day, sketch for orchestra, 1994; The Fire Moon, string quartet, 1997. *Publications include:* My Music Reaches to the Sky, 1973; Music of North American Indians, 1974. *Address:* c/o ASCAP, ASCAP Building, 1 Lincoln Plaza, New York, NY 10023, USA.

BALLEYS, Brigitte; singer (mezzo-soprano); b. 18 June 1959, Martigny, Wallis, Switzerland. *Education:* Bern Conservatory with Jakob Stämpfli, studied with Elisabeth Schwarzkopf. *Career:* sang in concert from 1982, notably in sacred music by Bach, the Brahms Alto Rhapsody, Masses by Mozart, Haydn, Schubert, Bruckner, Dvořák and Rossini; Schumann and Mahler Lieder; appearances in Switzerland, Germany, Austria, Italy, France, Portugal, Spain, South America, USA, Czecho-

slovakia; festival engagements at Zürich, Lucerne, Florence and Siena; recitalist in songs by de Falla, Shostakovich, Schoeck and Wolf-Ferrari, as well as French chansons and German songs; sang in opera at Freiburg 1985, with guest appearances at Zürich, Geneva, Avignon, Schwetzingen, Lausanne, and Montpellier; Vienna Staatsoper 1987, as Cherubino conducted by Leinsdorf; sang Octavian in Bern, Montpellier, Toulouse 1990; season 1992 as Fragoletto in Offenbach's Les Brigands at Amsterdam and Ramiro in Jean-Claude Malgoire's Vivaldi pastiche Montezuma at Monte Carlo; sang Nerone in Monteverdi's Poppea at Amsterdam 1996; other roles include Jocasta in Oedipus Rex (at Palermo), Gluck's Orpheus, Ottavia in Coronation of Poppea, Charlotte in Werther by Massenet, Meg Page and Orlofsky, Mrs Montgomery in L'Héritière by Damasé (at Marseilles); Geneviève in Debussy's Pelléas at the Paris Opéra-Comique 1998 and at La Scala, Milan 2004; season 1999 sang Sesto in Giulio Cesare by Handel at Montpellier and the title role in Didon by Henri Desmarest at Beaune, Versailles and Metz; sang Isadora in Le Foy by Marcel Landowski at Montpellier 2000; sang in Nerone at BAM Festival, Brooklyn, NY 2002; teacher at Lausanne Conservatoire 2001–. *Recordings include:* La Demoiselle Elue by Debussy and Janáček's Diary of One who Disappeared; Mendelssohn's St Paul and Die Zauberflöte, as Second Lady; Zelenka's Requiem; Leguerney, Melodies; Martucci, Canzone de Ricordi; Respighi, Il Tramonto; Les Nuits d'Été by Berlioz; Schumann, Lieder; Honegger, Judith; Frank Martin, In Terra Pax; Ernest Bloch's 4 chants d'automne; Frank Martin's Der Cornet; Löffler's Melodies; Chants du Japon. *Honours:* first prize Benson and Hedges in London 1983, Special Prize for Lied. *Address:* Bächtoldstrasse 1, 8044 Zürich; Chemin des Planches 19, 1008 Prilly, Switzerland. *Telephone:* (21) 634-4877.

BALLISTA, Antonio; Pianist; b. 30 March 1936, Milan, Italy. *Education:* Studied piano and composition Milan Conservatory, graduated 1955. *Career:* Toured widely as a soloist, also many duo recitals with the pianist Bruno Canino; Took part in the premieres of Rapsodia (1984), by Davidee Anzaghi, Concerto for two pieces by Berio (1973), Tableaux Vivants (1964), by Berio, Fogliod'album (1969), by Bussotti, Couplets (1979), by Castiglioni, B.A.C.H. (1970) and Piano Concerto (1976), by Aldo Clementi, Estratto (1969), by Donatoni and De La Nuit, 1971, by Sciarrino; Professor at Giuseppe Verdi Conservatory from 1964. *Recordings:* Several recordings of contemporary works. *Address:* c/o Ingrassia, Via San Zanobi 7, 1–50018 Scandicci (Fi), Italy.

BALOGH, Endre; Violinist; b. 1954, Los Angeles, California, USA. *Education:* Attended Yehudi Menuhin's School, England, at age 9; Violin studies with Joseph Piastro, Manuel Compinsky and Mehli Mehta. *Career:* Debut: New York Town Hall, 1971; Played 1st concerto with orchestra at age 6; Recital, Los Angeles, at age 15; 1st European tour including concerts in Berlin and London, 1973; Performed in Austria, Netherlands and Italy; Recital for BBC, London, and on-the-air, Amsterdam; Appearances with various orchestras including Los Angeles Philharmonic and Washington, Seattle, Honolulu and other Symphony Orchestras; Numerous recitals in key US cities; Performed with Berlin Philharmonic, Rotterdam Philharmonic, Frankfurt Symphony, Tonhalle Orchestra of Zürich, Basel Symphony; As soloist with orchestra under conductors Zubin Mehta, Lawrence Foster, Henry Lewis, Vladimir Golschmann, Milton Katims, Hirouko Iwaki, Edo de Waart; Numerous appearances with American Youth Symphony, under Mehli Mehta; Played many benefits for State of Israel, United Nations, Philosophical Research Society and others; Violinist, Pacific Trio, throughout USA and Canada. *Recordings:* Pacific Trio, 1990; Brahms C major and Shostakovich E major trios. *Address:* c/o UCLA, Music Faculty, 405 Hilgard Ave, Los Angeles, CA 90024, USA.

BALSACH, Llorenç; composer and music theorist; b. 16 April 1953, Sabadell, Barcelona, Spain; m. Sedes Garcia-Cascon 1991. *Education:* University of Barcelona, Sabadell and Barcelona Conservatories of Music, composition with Josep Soler. *Career:* freelance composer, 1976–; commissions, Baden-Baden Südwestfunk Orchestra, 1979, Associació Catalana de Compositors, 1983, 1991, CDMC, Barcelona City Council, 1991, Vallès Symphony Orchestra, 1991, Spanish Ministry of Culture, 1992, Radio Nacional de España, 1993, 1994, film Entreacte, 1985, and stage works; Creator, pioneer music software in GADIN Company, 1983–87; Editor, LA MA DE GUIDO Music Publishing House editions, 1986–; Consultant, Phonos, Pompeu Fabra University, 1994–. *Compositions include:* Orchestral: Gran Copa especial, 1979; Poema Promiscu, 1981; Visions grotesques, 1992; Quatre dibuìxos per a guitarra i cordes, 1994; Chamber: De Caldetes a Moià, 1979; Suite Gàstrica, 1979; Rondó, 1983; Musica-Màgica, 1992; Trìo per a cordes, 1992; Tres converses for 10 instruments, 1997; Música groga, 1980; Sis cançons breus, 1982; Olis d'olimpia, 1991. *Address:* Les Planes 37, 08201 Sabadell, Barcelona, Spain.

BALSADONNA, Renato; Italian conductor and repetiteur; b. 1966, Venice; one s. *Education:* Milan Conservatoire. *Career:* chorus repetiteur and Asst Chorus Master, Opéra de Basle 1993; Asst Chorus Master, La Monnaie, Brussels 1995; Dir of Chorus 1997; Asst Dir, Bayreuth

Festival Chorus 1999; Chorus Dir, Royal Opera House, Covent Garden 2004. *Address:* c/o Royal Opera House, Covent Garden, London, WC2E 9DD, England (office).

BALSLEV, Lisbeth; Singer (soprano); b. 21 Feb. 1945, Abenraa, Denmark. *Education:* Vestjysk Conservatory in Esbjerg, Denmark; Royal Opera School, Copenhagen. *Career:* Debut: Copenhagen, 1976, as Jaroslavna in Prince Igor; Sang Mozart's Fiordiligi, Leonora in Il Trovatore and Wagner's Senta in Copenhagen; Bern Opera, 1977, as Electra in Idomeneo; Bayreuth from 1978, as Senta in Der fliegende Holländer; Hamburg Opera debut, 1979, as Elsa in Lohengrin; Munich Staatsoper, 1979, in the title role of Iphigénie en Tauride by Gluck; Guest appearances in Dresden, Amsterdam, Berlin, Stuttgart, Cologne and Frankfurt; La Scala, Milan, 1987, as Salome; Lisbon and Berne, 1987, Senta and Elisabeth; Turin and Florence, 1988, as Wagner's Isolde; Leonore in Fidelio with Cologne Opera, Hong Kong, 1989; Isolde in a concert performance of Tristan und Isolde with Jutland Opera, Edinburgh Festival, 1990; Agave in The Bassarids at Düsseldorf, 1991; Nice, 1993 and Montpellier, 1996, as Isolde; Debut as Elektra at Århus, 1998. *Recordings include:* Senta in Der fliegende Holländer from Bayreuth. *Current Management:* Ingpen & Williams Ltd, 7 St George's Court, 131 Putney Bridge Road, London, SW15 2PA, England.

BALTHROP, Carmen (Arlen); Singer (Soprano); b. 14 May 1948, Washington DC, USA. *Education:* Studied at the University of Maryland, College Park and the Catholic University of America. *Career:* Debut: Washington DC in 1973 as Virtue in L'Incoronazione di Poppea, and as Minerva in the US premiere of Il Ritorno d'Ulisse, 1974; Sang the title role in Scott Joplin's Treemonisha at Houston Opera in 1975; In 1977 sang in Cavalli's L'Egisto at Wolf Trap and made her Metropolitan debut as Pamina; Sang at New York City Opera in 1978 as Roggiero in Rossini's Tancredi; Innsbruck Early Music Festival in 1980 as Monteverdi's Poppea, in the edition by Alan Curtis; Sang Poppea at Spoleto in 1979 and Santa Fe in 1986; Sang in Venice as Gluck's Euridice and Poppea in Handel's Agrippina, 1982–83; Michigan Opera Theater as Treemonisha and Pamina, 1982–84; Sang Gretel at Milwaukee, 1995; Created the title role in Vanqui by Leslie Burrs for Opera Columbus 1999. *Recordings include:* Treemonisha. *Honours:* Winner, Metropolitan Opera Auditions, 1975. *Address:* c/o Santa Fe Opera, PO Box 2408, Santa Fe, NM 878504, USA.

BALTSA, Agnes; Singer (Mezzo-Soprano); b. 19 Nov. 1944, Lefkas, Greece; m. Gunter Missenhardt, 1974. *Education:* Study in Athens with Nunuka Fragia-Spilopoulos; Frankfurt with Herbert Champian. *Career:* Debut: Frankfurt Opera, 1968, as Cherubino in Figaro; Octavian in Der Rosenkavalier at the Vienna Staatsoper, 1969; Guest appearances in Hamburg, Athens, Berlin, Munich, Barcelona and Belgrade; US debut, 1971, with Houston Opera, as Carmen; Concert tour of USA, 1976, with Karajan; Salzburg Festival from 1970, in Bastien et Bastienne and as Herodias in Salome, Eboli in Don Carlos and as Octavian; Covent Garden debut, 1976; Returned to London as Giulietta in Les Contes d'Hoffmann, Adalgisa in Norma, as Romeo in I Capuleti e i Montecchi, 1984, as Isabella in L'Italiana in Algeri, 1987, and as Eboli in Don Carlos, 1989; Metropolitan Opera debut, 1979, as Octavian; Returned to New York, 1987, as Carmen; Sang Santuzza, Vienna Staatsoper, 1989; Cenerentola and Dalila, Covent Garden, 1990–91; Season 1992–93 as Elisabeth in Maria Stuarda at Barcelona and Azucena at the Vienna Staatsoper; Sang Dalila at Zürich, 1996; Carmen at Madrid, 1999; Orlofsky in Die Fledermaus at Vienna, 2000; Other roles include Berlioz's Dido, Gluck's Orfeo, Mozart's Dorabella and Fides in Le Prophète (Vienna Staatsoper, 1998); Season 2000–01 as Santuzza at the Vienna Staatsoper and Despina for Zürich Opera. *Recordings:* Roles in Salome, Don Carlos, Aida, Orfeo ed Euridice, Così fan tutte, Les Contes d'Hoffmann, I Capuleti e i Montecchi, Mitridate, Die Zauberflöte, Rosenkavalier, Don Giovanni, Ascanio in Alba, Le nozze di Figaro. *Address:* c/o Royal Opera House (Contracts), Covent Garden, London WC2E 9 DD, England.

BALUN, Frantisek; Singer (Baritone); b. 13 Sept. 1948, Chminianska Nová Ves, Czechoslovakia; m. Melánia Balúnová, 3 s., 1 d. *Education:* The State Conservatory in Brno, Czech Republic (with Professor Richard Novák). *Career:* Debut: Theater of the Jonás Záborsky, Presov, 1968; Slovak National Theatre, Bratislava 1972–77; The State Theatre, Kosice, 1977–; Tchaikovsky's Iolanta; Ravel, The Spanish Hour; Sang Nabucco in Paris, 1994; Sang in Germany: Bettelstudent, 1996, Carmen, 1997; Sang in Austria: Nabucco, and Carmen, 1997; In Czech Republic: Il Trovatore, Madama Butterfly; Opera and operetta arias; Folk songs for Slovak Radio; mem, Ján Cikker Foundation. *Honours:* Prize of the Musical Fund for Tosca (Scarpia), Il Trovatore (Luna); Annual Prize of the Musical Fund and the Ministry of Culture for the performance of Mr Scrooge by Ján Cikker. *Current Management:* Opera Director, East Slovak State Theatre, Kosice. *Address:* Dvorkinova 6, 040 22 Kosice, Slovakia.

BALZANI, Vincenzo; Concert Pianist; b. 1965, Milan, Italy. *Education:* Studied at the Giuseppe Verdi Conservatory in Milan with Alberto Mozzati. *Career:* Debut: Has performed in public from age 14; Italian engagements at La Fenice Venice, the Comunale of Bologna, the Verdi Theatre in Trieste and the Academia Filarmonica Romana; Further appearances in France, Germany and Spain; London recital debut at the Purcell Room in 1989 playing Scarlatti Sonatas, Brahms Paganini Variations, Gaspard de la Nuit, Chopin Etudes Op 10 and Liszt Rigoletto Paraphrase. *Recordings include:* Music by Liszt, Mozart and Hummel; Chopin Etudes Op 10. *Honours:* Liszt Prize at the Maria Canals Competition in Barcelona.

BAMBERGER, David, BA; American opera director and producer; b. 14 Oct. 1940, Albany, NY; m. Carola Beral; one s. *Education:* Yale University School of Drama, Université de Paris, France, Swarthmore College. *Career:* Stage Director/Producer: The Barber of Seville, The Magic Flute, Der Rosenkavalier, New York City Opera; Rigoletto, Lucia di Lammermoor, National Opera, Santiago, Chile; Madama Butterfly, Don Pasquale, Cincinnati Opera; Don Pasquale, Pittsburgh Opera; The Flying Dutchman, Harford Opera Company; Producer/Director, Don Giovanni, Four Saints in Three Acts, Madama Butterfly, Così fan tutte; The Gondoliers, Die Fledermaus, Menotti's Tamu-Tamu (1st production after world premiere), Oberlin Music Theatre, Ohio; General Director, Cleveland Opera, 1976–, 50 productions including La Traviata, La Bohème, Daughter of the Regiment, Tosca, Aida, Faust, Falstaff, The Medium, The Secret Marriage, The Merry Widow, Holy Blood and Crescent Moon (world premiere); Artistic Director, Toledo (Ohio) Opera, 1983–85, staged Faust, Don Pasquale, Aida, Barber of Seville. *Address:* 1422 Euclid Avenue, Cleveland, OH 44115, USA.

BAMERT, Matthias; Conductor and Composer; b. 5 July 1942, Ersigen, Switzerland; m. Susan Bamert, 2 c. *Education:* Studied in Bern and Paris; Principal composition teachers: Jean Rivier and Pierre Boulez. *Career:* First oboist, Mozarteum Orchestra, Salzburg, 1965–69; Assistant conductor, American Symphony Orchestra, New York, 1970–71; Joined the conducting staff of the Cleveland Orchestra, 1971; Music director, Basle Radio Symphony Orchestra, 1977–83; Principal guest conductor, Scottish National Orchestra, Glasgow, and Director, Musica Nova, Glasgow, 1985–90; Conducted Schoenberg's Violin Concerto, 1988; Conducted Ulster Orchestra, Belfast, 1991 in Nielsen's Helios Overture, Sibelius's 2nd Symphony and works by Sandström m and Saariaho; Promenade concerts, London, 1991, with BBC Symphony in Liszt's Hunnenschlacht, Alexander Nevsky, premiere of Martin Butler's O Rio; Conducted the National Youth Orchestra in music by Mussorgsky and Birtwistle (Gawain's Journey) at the 1993 Proms; Led the BBC Philharmonic in the premiere of Roberto Gerhard's 1930s ballet, Soirées de Barcelone, 1996; Principal conductor of the London Mozart Players from 1993; Toured Switzerland with the Royal Philharmonic, and Japan with the London Mozart Players; Engagements for the 1997–98 season included: Luzern Festival, Orchestre de Paris, tours to Netherlands, Spain and Switzerland with the LMP; North American concerts with the Cleveland Orchestra, Houston and Pittsburgh symphonies; Conducted world premieres of Takemitsu, Denisov, Holliger, Erb, Huber, Casken, Dillon and Rihm; Conducted Weill's Propheten at the 1998 London Proms; Season 1999 with Mozart Flute Concerto and 40th Symphony at the Proms. *Compositions:* Concertino for English horn, string orchestra and piano, 1966; Septuria Lunaris for orchestra, 1970; Rheology for string orchestra, 1970; Mantrajana for orchestra, 1971; Once upon an Orchestra for narrator, 12 dancers and orchestra, 1975; Ol-Okun for string orchestra, 1976; Keepsake for orchestra, 1979; Circus Parade for narrator and orchestra, 1979. *Recordings:* Pelléas et Mélisande with Scottish National Orchestra; Complete symphonies of Hubert Parry with the London Philharmonic; Frank Martin; Contributed to Contemporaries of Mozart with London Mozart Players; Recordings with BBC Philharmonic of Stokowski's transcriptions and Korngold. *Honours:* Received the first George Szell Memorial Award, 1971. *Address:* c/o Scottish National Orchestra, 3 La Belle Place, Glasgow G3 7LH, Scotland.

BAMPTON, Rose E., BMus, LHD; American concert and opera singer (soprano); b. 28 Nov. 1909, Cleveland, OH; m. Wilfred Pelletier. *Education:* Curtis Institute of Music, Philadelphia, Drake University, Iowa. *Career:* debut, Metropolitan Opera, New York City, 1932, as Laura in La Gioconda; Metropolitan Opera, New York, 1932–50, notably as Leonora (Il Trovatore), Sieglinde, Kundry and Donna Anna; Covent Garden, London, England, 1937; As Amneris, Teatro Colón, Buenos Aires, Argentina, 1945–50; Sang Daphne in the first South American performance of the Opera by Strauss, 1948; Chicago Opera, San Francisco Opera; Voice faculty, Manhattan School of Music, 1962–82; Juilliard School of Music, 1974–. *Recordings:* Gurrelieder, Stokowski; Fidelio, Toscanini; Operatic Arias, Wilfred Pelletier. *Honours:* Hon. LHD (Holart and William Smith Colls, Geneva and New York) 1978. *Address:* 322 E 57th Street, New York, NY 10022, USA.

BANDITELLI, Gloria; Singer (Mezzo-Soprano); b. 1954, Italy. *Career:* Sang first in Sacchini's Fra Donato, for RAI, Naples; Siena, 1980, in Cavalieri's La Rappresentazione; Teatro Vale Rome, 1982, in Gagliano's Dafne, Innsbruck Festival, 1983, as Cesti's Tito, followed by Handel's Rodrigo, Medea in Cavalli's Giasone, Teodota in Handel's Flavio and Amastris in Serse; Bologna, 1984 and 1991, in Gluck's Armide and as Maria in Mosè in Egitto; La Scala, Milan, 1988, in Jommelli's Fetonte, Utrecht Festival, 1988, in Giasone and Montpellier, 1989, as Gluck's Orpheus; Concerts include Mozart's Requiem in Vienna, on 200th anniversary of his death; Sang the Messenger in Monteverdi's Orfeo at Palermo, 1996; Monteverdi's Penelope at Palermo 1998; Season 2000–01 in Monteverdi's Orfeo and Poppea at Beaune, and in Dido and Aeneas at Florence. *Recordings include:* Le Cinesi by Gluck (Harmonia Mundi), Pergolesi's Adriano in Siria (Bongiovanni) and Penelope in Monteverdi's Ulisse (Nuova Era). *Address:* c/o Teatro Massimo di Palermo, Via R. Wagner 2, 90139 Palermo, Italy.

BANKS, Barry; British singer (tenor); b. 1960, Stoke-on-Trent, England. *Education:* Royal Northern Coll. of Music with Josef Ward. *Career:* sang Tamino and Don Ottavio at Royal Northern Coll. of Music; Covent Garden debut as Beppe in Pagliacci 1989; ENO Tom Rakewell, Don Ottavio, Nemorino; at Covent Garden Brighella (Ariadne). *Honours:* Peter Moores Foundation Scholarship 1983. *Current Management:* Harrison/Parrott Ltd, 12 Penzance Place, London, W11 4PA, England. *Telephone:* (20) 7229 9166. *Fax:* (20) 7221 5042. *Website:* www .harrisonparrott.com.

BANNATYNE-SCOTT, Brian; Singer (bass); b. 4 Nov. 1955, Edinburgh, Scotland; m. Frances Stewart Leaf 1979, 1 s., 1 d. *Education:* St Andrew's University; Guildhall School of Music; Further study with Norman Bailey. *Career:* Debuts at La Fenice Venice, 1981, and the Rome Opera, 1982; Scottish Opera from 1982, as Colline, Don Fernando (Fidelio), Nourabad (The Pearl Fishers) and the Speaker in The Magic Flute; English National Opera from 1987 as Monterone (Rigoletto), Pogner and the Commendatore (1991); Varlaam (Boris Godunov), Opera North and BBC Prom, 1992; Banquo, ENO, 1993; Sang Fafner and Hagen in the City of Birmingham Touring Opera version of The Ring; Tour of Europe as Cold Genius in Purcell's King Arthur; Salzburg Festival debut, 1991, as Polyphemus in Acis and Galatea; Bermuda Festival, 1991, as Don Alfonso in Così fan tutte; Concert engagements with leading British orchestras; Has sung Christus in the St John Passion settings of Bach and Arvo Pärt (in Italy, Germany and Japan); Stravinsky's Les Noces with London Sinfonietta and Simon Rattle, 1993; Aldeburgh masterclasses with Galina Vishnevskaya (also televised) and recital at 1990 Prom Concert; *Appearances:* The Trojans, London Symphony Orchestra, 1993, 1994; Swallow in Peter Grimes, Nantes; Bastille Opéra, Tosca; Gurrelieder, City of Birmingham Symphony Orchestra; Flanders Festival, Handel's Chandos Anthems; Liège, Der Kaiser von Atlantis; 1995: Bartolo in Figaro, Bermuda Festival; Sarastro in Magic Flute, Nantes; Purcell's King Arthur in Europe and Buenos Aires; Sang Araspe in Handel's Tolomeo at Halle, 1996. *Recordings include:* King Arthur; Poppea; Dioclesian and Timon of Athens; The Wreckers; A Midsummer Night's Dream; Tolomeo. *Current Management:* Musicmakers International Artists Representation, Tailor House, 63–65 High Street, Whitwell, Hertfordshire SG4 8AH, England. *Telephone:* (1438) 871708. *Fax:* (1438) 871777. *E-mail:* musicmakers@compuserve.com. *Website:* www.operauk.com.

BANSE, Juliane; Singer (Soprano); b. 10 July 1969, Tettnang, Wurttemberg, Germany. *Education:* Trained as ballet dancer in Zürich; Vocal Studies in Zürich and with Brigitte Fassbaender and Daphne Evangelatos in Munich. *Career:* Debut: Sang Pamina in Harry Kupfer's production of Die Zauberflöte at Komische Oper Berlin, 1989; Engagements at Komische Oper as Ilia and Susanna, 1991–92; Pamina in Stuttgart and Brussels; Sophie in Rosenkavalier at Landestheater Salzburg and Zerlina at Glyndebourne, 1994, 1995; Sophie, Susanna, Pamina and Zdenka; Contract with Vienna State Opera, 1993–; Concert repertoire includes all major oratorio repertoire; European concert performances with Orchestre de Bastille, Paris, Mahler's 4th Symphony with Vienna Philharmonic Orchestra under Claudio Abbado; Many Lieder recitals throughout Europe; US debut in 1995 in St Louis and Indianapolis; Sang in Henze's Raft of the Medusa at the Festival Hall, London, 1997; Season 1998 as Musetta at Cologne and Manon at the Deutsche Oper, Berlin; Mahler's 4th Symphony with Cleveland and Philadelphia Orchestra; Mahler's 2nd Symphony with the Vienna Philharmonic and Simon Rattle at the 1999 London Prom Concerts; Created the title role in Holliger's Schneewittchen, Zürich, 1998; Season 2000 as Pamina at the Vienna Staatsoper, and soloist in the premiere of Lukas Passion by Wolfgang Rihm (Stuttgart). *Recordings include:* Lieder by Schoeck; Bach's Christmas Oratorio with the Windsbacher Knabenchor; Berg's Lulu Suite and Altenberg Lieder with Vienna Philharmonic Orchestra, Claudio Abbado; Mendelssohn's Paulus with H Rilling; Video of Don Giovanni, Glyndebourne 1995 (Warner). *Honours:* Winner, Kulturforum Competition, Munich, 1989; Schubert

Award, Vienna, 1993. *Current Management:* Künstlersekretariat am Gasteig, Rosenleimerstr, 52, 81669 Munich, Germany. *Address:* c/o IMG Artists, Lovell House, 616 Chiswick High Road, London W4 5RX, England.

BAPTISTE, Eric; French radio executive; *Director-General, International Confederation of Societies of Authors and Composers. Education:* École nationale d'administration. *Career:* Gen. Man., Radio France Int. 1990–95; Vice-Pres., Radio Néo; Dir-Gen., Int. Confed. of Socs of Authors and Composers (CISAC) 1998–; chair. of govt think tank on digital convergence. *Publications:* Rapport sur les relations entre les diffuseurs télévisuels et les producteurs cinématographiques et audio-visuals 1999, L'infosphère: stratégies des medias et role de l'État 2000. *Address:* c/o CISAC, 20–26 blvd du Parc, 92200 Neuilly-sur-Seine, France. *Telephone:* 1-55-62-08-50. *Fax:* 1-55-62-08-60. *E-mail:* cisac@ cisac.org. *Website:* www.cisac.org.

BÄR, Olaf; Singer (Baritone); b. 19 Dec. 1957, Dresden, Germany. *Career:* Studied in Dresden, sang in Dresden Kreuzchor, 1966–75, and was a principal member of Dresden State Opera until 1991; British debut, Nov 1983, at Wigmore Hall; Returned summer 1985; Covent Garden debut, 1985, as Harlekin in Ariadne auf Naxos; Aix-en-Provence Festival, 1986, in Ariadne; Die Zauberflöte at La Scala; Glyndebourne Festival, 1987, as the Count in Capriccio; Aix, 1988, as Guglielmo in Così fan tutte, conducted by Jeffrey Tate; Concert performances, Europe and USA; US debut, 1987, as Christus in the St Matthew Passion with the Chicago Symphony Orchestra conducted by Solti; Tours of Australia, 1989, 1993, Japan, 1989, 1992; Created roles in premieres of operas by Matthus, 1985, and Mayer, 1989; At Covent Garden Opera sang Papageno, 1991; Glyndebourne as Don Giovanni, 1991; Sang in Britten's War Requiem; Oliver in Capriccio, Opernhaus Zürich, 1992; Marcello in La Bohème, Staatsoper Dresden, 1992; Count in Le nozze di Figaro, Netherlands Opera Amsterdam, 1993; Operatic debut, USA as Papageno, Chicago, 1996; Sang in Schubert's Alfonso und Estrella at the 1997 Vienna Festival; Mozart's Count at Rome and Wolfram in Tannhäuser by Wagner at Dresden, 1998; New production of Ariadne auf Naxos at Dresden, 1999 and Die Fledermaus at the 1999 Vienna Festival; Sang Froila in Schubert's Alfonso und Estrella at Zürich, 2001. *Recordings:* Schumann Dichterliebe Op 48 and Liederkreis Op 39, Kerner-Lieder Op 35 and Liederkreis Op 24; Schubert Die schöne Müllerin, Winterreise and Schwanengesang; Wolf Mörike Lieder; Brahms Lieder; Beethoven Lieder; Mozart Arien; Bach Christmas Oratorio with John Eliot Gardiner and the Monteverdi Choir; Christus in the St Matthew-Passion (Arias), conductor J E Gardiner; St Matthew-Passion (Christus), conductor Georg Solti; St John-Passion (Arias), conductor Peter Schreier; Fauré and Duruflé Requiems; Further recordings include Papageno in Mozart's Die Zauberflöte; Adam in Haydn's Creation and Harlekin in Strauss's Ariadne auf Naxos; Hugo Wolf: Italienisches Liederbuch (with Dawn Upshaw); Spanisches Liederbuch (with Ann-Sophie von Otter). *Honours:* Robert-Schumann Preis der Stadt Zwickau, 1998. *Current Management:* IMG Artists Vocal Division, Lovell House, 616 Chiswick High Road, London W4 5RX, England. *Address:* Steglichstr 6, 01324 Dresden, Germany.

BARAB, Seymour; Composer and Cellist; b. 9 Jan. 1921, Chicago, Illinois, USA. *Education:* Studied the cello with Gregor Piatigorsky and Edmund Kurtz. *Career:* Performed first as church organist in Chicago; Played the cello in symphony orchestras of Indianapolis, Cleveland, Portland and San Francisco, 1940–60; Assisted in the organisation of the Composers Quartet and the New York Pro Musica; Has taught at Rutgers, the State University of New Jersey and the New England Conservatory. *Compositions include:* Operas: Chanticleer, after Chaucer, Aspen, 1956; A Game of Chance, Illinois, 1957; Little Red Riding Hood, New York, 1962; The Toy Shop, New York, 1978; A Piece of String, Colorado, 1985; The Maker of Illusion, New York, 1985; Song settings of A Child's Garden of Verses and Songs of Perfect Propriety. *Address:* c/o ASCAP, ASCAP Building, 1 Lincoln Plaza, New York, NY 10023, USA.

BARABAS, Sari; Singer (Soprano); b. 14 March 1914, Budapest, Hungary; m. Franz Klarwein (1914–91). *Education:* Studied in Budapest. *Career:* Debut: Budapest in 1939 as Gilda in Rigoletto; Member of the Hamburg Staatsoper from 1949; Sang in San Francisco in 1950 as the Queen of Night and Glyndebourne, 1953–57 as Constanze in Die Entführung, Adèle in Le Comte Ory and Zerbinetta in Ariadne auf Naxos; Florence Maggio Musicale in 1955; Guest appearances in Germany and Austria in operettas; Sang in London in 1969 in The Great Waltz. *Recordings include:* Le Comte Ory from the Glyndebourne Festival, 1956; Excerpts from works by Johann Strauss, Gasparone, Telefunken.

BARAN, Peter; Cellist; b. 16 March 1950, Bratislava, Czechoslovakia; m. Beata Baranova, 15 Aug 1975, 2 s. *Education:* Music School, Bratislava, 1956–65; Conservatory, Bratislava, 1965–72; Hochschule für Musik und Darstellende Kunst, Vienna, 1979–83. *Career:* Debut: Haydn's Cello

Concerto in D major, 1972; Slovak Philharmonic Orchestra, 1972–; Suchon Quartet, 1973–77; Bratislava Chamber Harmony, 1973–80; Capella Istropolitana Chamber Orchestra, 1982–89; Bratislava String Trio, 1985–; Kontrapunkte, ensemble of 20th century music, Vienna, 1988–; Concertmaster, Slovak Philharmonic Orchestra, 1989–; Soloist and Member, Orchestra Ensemble Kanazawa, Japan, 1992–; Major performances, solo: Concerto for 2 Celli (Handel) with Slovak Philharmonic Orchestra, 1984; Symphonia Concertante (Haydn) with Slovak Chamber Orchestra, 1985; Cello Concerto op 33 (Saint-Saëns) with Slovak Philharmonic Orchestra, 1985; Concerto for String Trio and Orchestra (C Stamitz), 1987; Quatuor pour la fin du temps (Messiaen) at BHS Festival, 1987; Brahms Double Concerto and Sonata da Camera and Orchestra (Martinů), both with Slovak Philharmonic Orchestra, 1993; Don Quixote with Slovak Philharmonic, 1997; Cellist, Kyoto Symphony Orchestra; Slovak and Austrian Radio performances: 'Hunt' Quartet (Mozart); Cello Concerto in C major (Haydn); For television: Sonata in F major, op 99 (Brahms); String Trio Serenade (Dohnányi); Divertimento (Mozart); Trio in G major (Hummel); Little Trio (A Moyzes); Ernest Bloch, Schelomo, Hebraic Rhapsody for Violoncello and orchestra; mem, Slovak Music Union; Musicians' Union, Japan. *Recordings:* Vivaldi: Cello Concerto in A minor, Concerto in G minor for 2 celli; Beethoven: Septet, op 20; String Trio in G major by Hummel; Clarinet Quartet E flat, J N Hummel and Concerto for string trio and orchestra, C Stamitz; Concerto No. 1 G Major by C Stamitz. *Address:* Medena 35, 81102 Bratislava, Slovakia.

BARANOWSKI, Marcin; Violinist and Professor; b. 30 Nov. 1961, Poznań, Poland; m. Monika Rosenkiewicz 2000. *Education:* Academy of Music, Poznań, Poland 1985. *Career:* debut, State Philharmonic Orchestra, Poznan 1984; Karol Szymanowski Violin Concerto; mem. of Amadeus Chamber Orchestra 1981–; concerts all over the world; over 20 recordings; television and radio appearances; Polish String Quartet, 1994; Leader of the second violin, Amadeus Chamber Orchestra, 1995; Prof., Paderewski Academy of Music. *Recordings:* Amadeus Chamber Orchestra, 1989 and 1993. *Honours:* Third Prize, International Chamber Music Competition, Łódź, Poland, 1983; Award of Ministry of Culture, 1992. *Current Management:* Warsaw Artistic Management. *Address:* ul Rozana, 5A/2, 61577 Poznań, Poland. *E-mail:* marcin.b@inetia.pl.

BARANTSCHIK, Alexander; Violinist; b. 1953, Leningrad, USSR. *Education:* Studied at the Leningrad Conservatory, 1960–72, with Professor Waiman, 1972–77. *Career:* Gave concerts in Russia, then emigrated, 1979, becoming leader of the Bamberg Symphony Orchestra; Leader of the Radio Philharmonic Orchestra of the Netherlands, 1982; Solo engagements with leading orchestras in Germany, Netherlands, the United Kingdom and Hungary; Appearances in Russia with the Kazan Symphony and the Leningrad Philharmonic; Performed the Sibelius Concerto with the London Symphony in Spain, 1987, Prokofiev's 1st in the USA and London, 1989–90; Leader of the London Symphony Orchestra from 1989, played the Tchaikovsky Concerto with the orchestra, Mar 1991, Bach on tour to the USA, Aug 1991; Brahms Double Concerto at the Barbican, 1997. *Honours:* Winner, International Violin Competition at Sion, 1980. *Address:* c/o London Symphony Orchestra, Barbican Centre, London EC 2Y 8 DS, England.

BARBACINI, Paolo; Singer (tenor); b. 20 Nov. 1946, Reggio Emilia, Italy. *Career:* Has sung throughout Italy in operas by Mozart and Rossini, notably Don Giovanni, Il Re Pastore, Cenerentola, Il Turco in Italia, Adina and Aureliano in Palmira; La Scala Milan from 1980, in Falstaff and Figaro and on tour to Tokyo and Sofia; Has sung in La Pietra del Paragone for the Israel Festival, Il Turco in Italia in Aix and Rossini's Elisabetta in Turin and on tour to the USA; Modern repertoire includes Manzoni's Doctor Faustus (premiere, at La Scala, 1985), Wozzeck, Orff's Catulli Carmina and the premiere of Bussotti's L'Ispirazione (Florence, 1988); Sang Pang in Turandot at Macerata, 1996 and Bologna, 1997; Season 2000–01 as the Doctor in Penderecki's Devils of Loudun at Turin and as Bardolph in Falstaff at La Scala. *Current Management:* Athole Still International Management, Forresters Hall, 25–27 Westow Street, London, SE19 3RY, England. *Telephone:* (20) 8771-5271. *Fax:* (20) 8768-6600. *Website:* www.atholestill.com.

BARBAUX, Christine; Singer (Soprano); b. 1955, Saint-Mande, France. *Education:* Studied at Paris Conservatory. *Career:* Debut: Strasbourg, as Despina, 1977; Sang Barbarina in Le nozze di Figaro in Paris, 1978, Vienna and Salzburg under Karajan; Further engagements in Geneva in The Love of Three Oranges, 1984; Théâtre de la Monnaie, Brussels, as Servilia in La Clemenza di Tito and Sophie in Rosenkavalier, 1982, 1986, Aix-en-Provence as Sophie, Amsterdam and Norina, 1988; Salzburg Festival as Servilia, 1988; Other roles include Ophelia in Hamlet by Thomas, Gilda, and Blanche Force in Les Dialogues des Carmélites; Sang Alice Ford in Falstaff at Bonn, 1991; Sang Contesse Fedora in Donizetti's Gli Esiliati di Siberia at Montpellier, 1999. *Recordings include:* Werther and Pelléas et Mélisande; Fauré's

Pénélope; Le nozze di Figaro. *Address:* c/o Opéra de Montpellier, 11 Blvd. Victor Hugo, 34967 Montpellier, Cédex, France.

BARBER, Graham (David); British organist; b. 30 Dec. 1948, London, England; m. Dianne Mackay, 20 July 1990; one d. *Education:* BA 1970, MMus, 1971, University of East Anglia; Royal Northern College of Music; ARNCM Piano, 1974; Piano Accompaniment. distinction, 1975. *Career:* Debut: Royal Festival Hall, London, 1978; International Concert Organist; Musical Director, Chorus Master, Harpsichordist, Piano Accompanist, Coach; Frequent BBC radio appearances as Organist, mainly featuring German Baroque music and Max Reger; Lecturer in Music, University of Leeds, 1981–; Chorus Master, Leeds Philharmonic Society. 1983–92; Curator, Historic Schulze Organ, St Bartholomew's Church, Armley, 1986–; Chorus Master, Sheffield Philharmonic Chorus, 1987–97; Tutor in Organ Studies, The Royal Northern College of Music, 1995–; Professor of Performance Studies, University of Leeds, 1998–; Fellow, Royal College of Organists; Adviser, Board Member, Percy Whitlock Trust; Incorporated Society of Musicians; BIOS; ABC; Karg Elert Society, President, 1998; Incorporated Association of Organists. *Recordings:* Numerous including: Johann Gottfried Walther Organ Works, Reid Concert Hall, Edinburgh; Franz Schmidt: Organ Works; English Romantic at Truro Cathedral; Bach Neumeister Chorales and Early Organ Works, Vol. 1 and 2; Organ Music from Salisbury Cathedral; The Sandtner Organ at Villingen Münster; The Klais Organ at Altenberg Dom; Complete Organ Works of Percy Whitlock (3 vols). *Contributions:* Musical Times, 1984; Cambridge Companion to the Organ, 1998. *Honours:* Limpus and F J Reed Prizes, FRCO Exams, 1969. *Address:* 16, Vernon Road, Harrogate, HG2 8 DE, England. *E-mail:* g.d.barber@leeds.ac.uk.

BARBER, Kimberley; Singer (mezzo-soprano); b. 1961, Canada. *Career:* Debut: Sang Hansel in Hansel and Gretel for Calgary Opera, 1985; Has sung widely in Canada and in Europe in travesti roles by Mozart, Rossini and Strauss; Also sings Massenet's Cendrillon, Nicklausse in Les Contes d'Hoffmann and Lazuli in L'Etoile; Frankfurt Opera from 1989, as the Composer, Hermia, Ramiro (La finta giardiniera), Dorabella, Cherubino and Rosina; Sang Pauline in The Gambler for English National Opera and has appeared in concert with the Chicago, Toronto and Cincinnati Symphonies; New York and Wigmore Hall concert debuts, 1994. *Current Management:* Athole Still International Management, Forresters Hall, 25–27 Westow Street, London, SE19 3RY, England. *Telephone:* (20) 8771-5271. *Fax:* (20) 8768-6600. *Website:* www.atholestill.com.

BARBIROLLI, Evelyn; Musician, Adjudicator, Lecturer and Oboist; b. 24 Jan. 1911, Wallingford, England; m. Sir John Barbirolli CH, 5 July 1939. *Education:* Royal College of Music, London. *Career:* Scottish, London Symphony, Glyndebourne Festival Opera Orchestras, 1932–39; Soloist and Chamber Music Player later; mem, Incorporated Society of Musicians, Ex-President. *Compositions:* Oboe Technique; The Oboist's Companion; Many arrangements and editions for oboe. *Recordings:* Concertos by Haydn, Mozart, Corelli, Handel, Pergolesi, Cimarosa, Albinoni, Marcello. *Publications:* Oboe Technique, 1953, 3rd edition, 1987, translated into Japanese and Norwegian; The Oboist's Companion, 3 vols; A Tune for Oboe; A Book of Scales for The Oboe. *Contributions:* Many articles for various magazines. *Honours:* O.B.E., 1984; DMus; MA; FRCM; RAM; FRNCM; RTCL. *Address:* 15a Buckland Crescent, London NW3 5 DH, England.

BARBIZET, Pierre; French pianist; b. 20 Sept. 1922, Arica, Chile. *Education:* Paris Conservatoire. *Career:* many performances as soloist and chamber musician, notably with violinist Christian Ferras; frequent performances of Chabrier, and Dir of Marseilles Conservatory, 1963–. *Recordings include:* complete Beethoven violin sonatas, with Christian Ferras. *Honours:* prizewinner, Long-Thibaud Competition. *Address:* Conservatoire National de Marseille, 2 Place Carli, 13001 Marseille, France.

BARBONI YANS, Geneviève, PhD; stage designer and costume designer; b. 26 Dec. 1947, Montegnée, Belgium. *Education:* Univ. of Liège, Belgium, Univ. of Reims, France. *Career:* debut as opera producer, at Opera House, Liège, Belgium; broadcast: introductions to concerts, RTB, Liège, 1969; staging (set, costumes): Walloon Gala, Li Voyèdje di Tchaudfontaine, opera by J.-N. Hamal, Liège, 1970; Ravel, ballet gala, Grand Théâtre, Nancy, 1975; staging for television and radio: Evolution of the Opera in Emilia-Romagna, RAI Bologna, 1982; Man., Centro Canto Cesenatico, specialised services for the education, re-education and improvement of the speaking and singing voice, 1991–; transcriptions of operas: Cavalli's L'Hipermestra, Stradella's La Circe; mem., Voice Foundation, Philadelphia, Italian Society of Phonatricians and Logopedists. *Recordings:* Li Voyèdje di Tchaudfontaine (video), 1970. *Publications:* Un opéra de Francesco Cavalli, pour la cour de Florence: L'Hipermestra, 1979; Contributo alla storia della gestione degli spettacoli nel Ducato Estense dal 1650 al 1790, 1994; contrib. to magazines and journals in Italy. *Address:* Via Viola 13, 47042 Cesenatico, Italy.

BARCE, Ramon; Composer; b. 16 March 1928, Madrid, Spain; m. Elena Martin, 22 June 1984. *Education:* Conservatory of Madrid, 1950–54; PhD, 1956. *Career:* Foundation Member, Group Nueva Musica, 1958; Foundation Member, Group Zaj, 1964; Foundation Member, Group Sonda, 1967; Editor, contemporary music magazine 'Sonda', 1967–74; Musical Critic, newspaper 'Ya', 1971–78; Foundation Member Asociacion de Compositores Sinfonicos Espanoles and First President, 1976–88; mem, Asociacion de Compositores Sinfonicos Espanoles;Sociedad Espanola de Musicologia; Sociedad General de Autores y Editores. *Compositions:* six Symphonies 1975, 1982, 1983, 1984, 1995, 1998; Concert for Piano, 1974; Nine Conciertos de Lizara, 1973–88; Forty Eight Preludios for Piano, 1973–83; Ten String Quartets, 1958–94; Coral hablado, 1966; Melodramas Oleada and Hacia manana hacia hoy, 1982, 1987; Nuevas polifonias I–II, 1971, 1985; Parabola, 1963 and Travesia 1979 for brass quintet. *Recordings:* Canada-Trio 1970 and 1993; Twenty Four Preludios, 1987; Obertura fonética, 1977, 1979 and 1994; Siala, 1973; Estudio de valores for piano, 1992; Sonata No. 3 for violin and piano, 1990; Sintesis de Siala, 1993; Musica funebre, 1979, 1994; Tango para Yvar, 1995. *Publications:* Fronteras de la musica, 1985; Tiempo de tinieblas y algunas sonrisas, 1992; Boccherini en Madrid, 1992; Translations of Harmonielehre of Schoenberg 1974, Alois Haba 1984 and Schenker 1990. *Contributions:* 12 advertencias para una sociologia de la musica in Coloquio Artes 72, Lisbon 1987; La vanguardia y yo in Revista Musical Catalana 59, Barcelona, 1989. *Honours:* National Prize of Music, 1973; Prize of Comunidad de Madrid, 1991; Medalla de Oro al m érito en las Bellas Artes, 1996. *Address:* Valdevarnes 35, 28039 Madrid, Spain.

BARCELLONA, Daniela; Singer (Mezzo-Soprano); b. 1973, Trieste, Italy. *Education:* Studied in Trieste. *Career:* Early appearances at Spoleto, Florence, Bordeaux, Rome, Wexford Festival and Geneva. Season 1998–99 as Orsini in Lucrezia Borgia at La Scala, Arsace in Semiramide at Genoa and Isabella (L' Italiana in Algeri) at Verona; Rome Opera as Rossini's Rosina and in La Fiamma by Respighi; Further engagements as Vivaldi's Bajazet at Istanbul, as Rossini's Tancredi Pesaro and Jane Seymour in Anna Bolena at Naples; Concerts include the Verdi Requiem (in Dresden, Rome, Berlin and elsewhere), Roméo et Juliette by Berlioz (Barbican Hall, London, 2000), Beethoven's Missa Solemnis at the Concertgebouw and Rossini's Stabat Mater; New York Met debut 2001, in a Verdi Gala, returning for Bellini's Norma; Ginevra di Scozia by Mayr at Trieste, Malcolm in La Donna del Lago at Pesaro; Season 2002 as Romeo in Bellini's Capuleti et i Montecchi in Paris and Isabella in Rome. *Recordings include:* La Fedeltà Premiata by Haydn (Arabesque); Verdi Requiem. *Address:* c/o Theateragentur Dr Germinal Hilbert, Maximilianstr. 22, 80539 Munich, Germany.

BARCLAY, Yvonne; Singer (Soprano); b. 1965, Ayrshire, Scotland. *Education:* Royal Scottish Academy, Glasgow; National Opera Studio, London. *Career:* Appearances with the Royal Opera, Covent Garden, as Frasquita in Carmen, Mozart's Barbarina and Papagena, Priestess in Aida and Javotte in Manon; English Bach Festival as Belinda in Dido and Aeneas, Gluck's Euridice and in The Fairy Queen (2001); English National Opera as Lucia in The Rape of Lucretia, Echo in Ariadne auf Naxos, Sandman in Hansel and Gretel and Euridice in Monteverdi's Orfeo; Opera North as Eurydice in Orpheus in the Underworld; Glyndebourne Touring Opera as Blondchen in Die Entführung and Mélisande in Pelléas et Mélisande; for Scottish Opera roles in Die Zauberflöte, Hansel and Gretel, L'Egisto by Cavalli and Death in Venice; Emmie in Albert Herring for Glyndebourne and Far East tour as Norina in Don Pasquale; Further engagements include Blondchen and Gretel at the Leipzig Opera and First Niece in Peter Grimes at the Paris Châtelet, and in Lisbon and Bremen. Frequent concert appearances and broadcasts. *Recordings:* Josephine in HMS Pinafore for D'Oyly Carte Opera, First Niece Peter Grimes (Grammy Award). *Address:* Music International, 13 Ardilaun Road, London, N5 2QR, England.

BARCZA, Peter; Singer (Baritone); b. 23 June 1949, Stockholm, Sweden. *Education:* Graduated Toronto University, 1971. *Career:* Sang with Canadian Touring Opera, 1972–73, notably as Guglielmo (Così fan tutte), Papageno, Enrico (Lucia di Lammermoor), Marcello and Germont; Guest appearances at Memphis (1981), New Orleans (from 1985), Seattle and the New York City Opera (from 1990); European appearances include Monteverdi's Ulisse at Bad Hersfeld; Other roles include Rossini's Figaro, Malatesta (Don Pasquale), Luna, Ping (Turandot), Valentin (Faust), and Rangoni in Boris Godunov. *Address:* c/o New York City Opera, Lincoln Center, New York, NY 10023, USA.

BARDON, Patricia; Singer (mezzo-soprano); b. 1964, Ireland. *Career:* Operatic engagements include Arsace in Semiramide at La Fenice, Venice; Carmen, Hamburg Staatsoper and Welsh National Opera; Penelope in Il Ritorno d'Ulisse at the Maggio Musicale Florence; Orlando in New York, Paris and Lyon; Smeaton in Anna Bolena at San

Francisco; Amastris in Xerxes at the Munich Staatsoper; Juno in Sémele at Innsbruck; 3rd Lady in Die Zauberflöte at Verona and roles in Rigoletto, Mosè in Egitto, Guillaume Tell and Mefistofele for Royal Opera at Barbican Hall; Concert engagements have taken her to USA, Canada, Japan and all major European Centres including La Scala, La Monnaie, (Brussels), BBC Proms London, Edinburgh, Aix en Provence and Montreux Festivals, Concertgebouw, Amsterdam and Schauspielhaus, Berlin; Season 2000–01 as Erda in The Rhinegold, for ENO, and Ursule in Béatrice et Bénédict for Netherlands Opera. *Recordings include:* Orlando, Elijah, Olga in Eugene Onegin and Giovanna in Rigoletto. *Honours:* Prizewinner, Cardiff Singer of the World Competition. *Current Management:* Ingpen & Williams Ltd, 7 St George's Court, 131 Putney Bridge Road, London, SW15 2PA, England.

BARENBOIM, Daniel; Pianist and Conductor; b. 15 Nov. 1942, Buenos Aires, Argentina; m. (1) Jacqueline Du Pré, 1967 (deceased 1987), (2) Elena Bashkirova, 1988, 2 s. *Education:* Studied with father; Accademia di Santa Cecilia, Rome; Conducting, Salzburg, 1954. *Career:* Debut: Buenos Aires, 1949; Played at Salzburg Mozarteum, 1951; Israel Philharmonic, 1953–; British debut, 1955; Played a Mozart concerto, Festival Hall, 1956, with Royal Philharmonic; New York debut, conducted by Stokowski, 1957; Berlin Philharmonic, 1963–; New York Philharmonic, 1964–; Many appearances with London Philharmonic and Chicago Symphony; Conducting debut, Israel, 1962, then tour of Australia; Conductor, Pianist, English Chamber Orchestra, 1964–; Tours, Latin America, Far East; Directed South Bank Summer Music Festival, London, 1968–70; Premiere of Goehr's Piano Concerto, Brighton, 1972; Conducted Don Giovanni and Figaro, Edinburgh Festival, 1973, 1975; Music Director, Orchestre de Paris, 1975–89; Conducted Tristan und Isolde, Bayreuth, 1981, Der Ring des Nibelungen, 1988–90; Concert, Bayreuth Festspielhaus, 1986, for centenary of Liszt's death; Tristan at the 1995 Bayreuth Festival; Artistic Director, Mozart Festival, Paris, 1983–, Don Giovanni, Così fan tutte, Figaro, 1986; Accompanied Janet Baker and Dietrich Fischer-Dieskau in Lieder; Chamber music with Pinchas Zukerman and Itzhak Perlman; Many complete cycles of Beethoven Piano Sonatas, notably television series from historic houses in Vienna; Music Director, Chicago Symphony, Berlin Staatsoper, 1991–; Concerts with Berlin Philharmonic in London, 1990 (Bruckner 7th, Beethoven 3rd, Schubert 8th); Conducted Parsifal excerpts, Chicago, 1990; Played Brahms D minor Concerto, Festival Hall, Philharmonia, 1991; Mozart 200 Festival, English Chamber Orchestra, Barbican (K183, K543, K271) Conducted the Vienna Philharmonic in Mozart and Bruckner, Festival Hall, 1997; Busoni's Doktor Faust at the Berlin Staatsoper, 1998; Season 1999 with Wagner Festival in Berlin; Premiere of Elliott Carter's What Next? at the Staatsoper, 1999; Birtwistle's The Last Supper, 2000; Two complete Wagner cycles, Berlin, 2002; Concert for Peace, numerous locations world-wide 2003. *Recordings include:* Berlioz cycle; Beethoven Concertos as soloist and conductor; Mozart Concertos, English Chamber Orchestra; Don Giovanni; Le nozze di Figaro; Complete Mozart Piano Sonatas; Liszt Cycle, sound and video; Tristan und Isolde (Teldec), 1995; Lohengrin, 1999. *Publication:* A Life in Music (jtly) 1991, Parallels and Paradoxes (with Edward W. Said) 2003. *Honours:* Beethoven Medal, 1958; Paderewski Medal, 1963; Beethoven Society Medal, 1982, Wolf Prize. *Current Management:* Askonas Holt Ltd, Lonsdale Chambers, 27 Chancery Lane, London, WC2A 1PF, England. *Telephone:* (20) 7400-1700. *Fax:* (20) 7400-1799. *E-mail:* info@askonasholt.co.uk. *Website:* www.askonasholt.co.uk.

BARGIELSKI, Zbigniew, PhD; Austrian (b. Polish) composer; *Professor and Head of Department of Composition and Theory of Music, Bydgoszcz Academy of Music;* b. 21 Jan. 1937, Lomza, Poland. *Education:* studies in piano at Lublin Conservatory, Warsaw Conservatory with Szeligowski, Music Acad., Katowice with Boleslaw Szabelski; composition studies with Nadia Boulanger in Paris and at Graz. *Career:* music critic and journalist; Pres. Young Polish Composers 1967–70; Sec. Polish Composers Asscn, Warsaw 1967–70; premiere of opera In a Small Country House (The Little Haunted Manor) at Warsaw Grand Theatre 1984; mem. Polish Composer's Asscn, Österreichischer Komponistenbund; Prof. and Head of Dept of Composition and Theory of Music, Bydgoszcz Acad. of Music, Poland 2002–; compositions have been performed throughout Europe, in USA, Australia and South America and at int. festivals for contemporary music including Warsaw-Autumn, Muzicki Biennale Zagreb, Festival de Paris, Steirischer Herbst, Graz, Austria, Leningrad Spring, Encontros Gulbenkian, Lisbon, Helsinki Festival, Tsumari Triennale, Festival de Strasbourg, World Music Festival, and others. *Compositions include:* Danton, or Some Scenes from the History of the Great French Revolution (opera) 1968–69, The Little Prince (musical tale) 1970, Alice in Wonderland (youth opera) 1972, Phantoms do not Lie (comic opera) 1981, Parades for orchestra 1965, Percussion Concerto 1975, Espace étrapé for orchestra 1973, Violin Concerto 1975, Ballads for wind and percussion 1976, String Quartet No. 1 1976, String Quarter No. 2 ('Primaverile') 1980, String Quartet No. 3 ('Still Life with a Scream') 1985, In Nobody's Land (oratorio) 1989, Requiem for orchestra 1991–92, Trigonalia for guitar, accordion, percussion and chamber orchestra 1994, String Quarter No. 4 ('Le temps ardent') 1994, Fountain of hope for alto saxophone and marimba 1995, Dance on the Verge of Light for chamber ensemble 1995, A la recherche du son perdu for flute 1996, Landscape of remembrance for violin, cello and piano 1996, A la espagnola for guitar 1996, Hierofania for five percussionists 1996, Forgotten – Regained for violin 1996, Slapstick for chamber orchestra 1997, Tango for chamber ensemble 1997, Shrine for an Anonymous Victim, (computer musiic) 1999, Light Cross (computer music) 2000, Towards Organic Geometry (computer music) 2001, String Quartet No. 5 ('Le temps qui n'est plus) 2001, Music for Children for piano 2001–02, Le cristal flamboyant for harpsichord and tape 2002, Jeux à trois for three accordions 2003. *Recordings:* works by Zbigniew Bargielski 1996. *Publications:* Sacrum in der Musik 1996. *Honours:* Order 'Merit for Polish Culture' 1990; Officer's Cross, Order of Polonia Restituta 1995; First Prize, Young Polish Composers Competition (Warsaw) 1965, Arthur Malawski Composer's Competition Award, Kraków 1976, UNESCO Int. Composer's Rostrum Award, Paris 1981, 1995, Austrian Govt Grant of the German Academic Exchange Service 1985, First Prize, Int Composers Competition 1986, Anton Benya Prize (Vienna) 2000, Polish Composers' Union Prize (Warsaw) 2001. *Address:* c/o Society of Authors ZAiKS, 2 Hipoteczna Street, 00 092 Warsaw, Poland (office). *Telephone:* (52) 321-11-42 (office). *E-mail:* sekr@amuz.bydgoszcz.pl (office). *Website:* www.amuz.bydgoszcz.pl (office); www.bargielski.com (home).

BARHAM, Edmund; Singer (Tenor); b. 22 March 1950, Beckenham, England. *Education:* Studied at the Trinity College of Music, London, and the London Opera Centre. *Career:* Sang leading lyric roles in Wuppertal, then became a member of the company of the Theater am Gärtnerplatz, Munich; Many appearances at leading German opera houses; English National Opera from 1985, as Jenik in The Bartered Bride, Turiddu, Narroboth in Salome, Pinkerton, Cavaradossi, Gabriele Adorno, and Vakula in the first British production of Rimsky-Korsakov's Christmas Eve, 1988; Engagements with Opera North as Don José, Boris in Katya Kabanova and Dimitri in Boris Godunov; Sang in the Gounod Grande Messe Solennelle for BBC television; Sang Alfredo, English National Opera, 1990, and Macduff in a new production of Macbeth (also on tour to USSR); Sang Manrico at St Gallen, 1991; Don Carlos, English National Opera, 1992; Overseas appearances include The Rise and Fall of Mahagonny and Adriana Lecouvreur in Switzerland, Howard Blake's Benedictus in Norway, and Don José at the Bregenz Festival; Engaged as Otello for the Victoria State Opera, 1993; Manrico in Il Trovatore for Opera North, 1994; Don José for Welsh National Opera, 1997; Sang Otello at Halle, 2000. *Recordings:* First Armed Man in Die Zauberflöte; 18th Century English Songs for orchestra and chorus; Rossini's Petite Messe Solennelle. *Address:* c/o Stafford Law Associates, 6 Barham Close, Weybridge, Surrey KT 13 9 PR, England.

BARK, Jan; Composer; b. 19 April 1934, Harnosand, Sweden. *Education:* Studied in Stockholm with Larsson, Blomdahl and Ligeti; Further study in Far East. *Career:* Worked at Tape Music Center, San Francisco, and with Swedish Broadcasting Service; Co-Founder, Culture Quartet (4 trombones) with Folk Rabe. *Compositions include:* Piano Sonata, 1957; 2 string quartets, 1959, 1962; Metakronismer for orchestra, 1960; Lamento for ensemble, 1962; Boca Chica for chamber ensemble, 1962; Pyknos for orchestra, 1962; Missa Bassa for small orchestra with 7 conductors, 1964; Nota for mixed chorus, 1964; Bar, electronic music; Light Music for chorus a cappella, 1968; Lyndon Bunk Johnson, 1968; Irk-Ork for chamber ensemble, 1970; Memoria in memoria for chamber ensemble, 1974; Utspel for band, 1978; Malumma for tuba and band, 1984; Concerto for orchestra, 1985; Beacon for 4 trombones, 1996; Theatre and film music. *Address:* c/o STIM, Sandhamnsgatan 79, PO Box 27372, 102 54 Stockholm, Sweden.

BARKAUSKAS, Vytautas (Pranas Marius); Composer and Professor; b. 25 March 1931, Kaunas, Lithuania; m. (1) Elena Tverijonaite, 27 July 1954, (2) Tiina Vabrit, 20 Dec 1984, (3) Svetlana Cherniavska, 15 Feb 1991, 1 s., 1 d. *Education:* Lithuanian State Conservatory, Vilnius, 1953–59. *Career:* Accompanist, Vilnius College of Music, 1954–58; Instructor, House of the People's Creative Work of the Republic, 1958–61; Professor, Theory, Composition, Lithuanian State Academy of Music, Vilnius, 1961–; mem, Union of Composers, Lithuania. *Compositions include:* 5 symphonies, 1962, 1971, 1979, 1984, 1986; Intimate Composition for oboe and 12 string, 1968; Three Aspects for symphony orchestra, 1969; Contrast Music for flute, cello and percussion, 1969; Gloria Urbi, organ, 1972; Prelude and Fugue, chorus, 1974; Legend About Love, opera, 1975; Salute Your Land, oratorio-mystery, 1976; Sonatas for violin and piano, No. 1 Sonata subita, 1976, No. 2 Dialogue, 1978, No. 3, 1984; Open Window, mezzo-soprano, 5 instruments, 1978; Rondo capriccioso, 1981; Concerto for viola and chamber orchestra, 1981; The Sun, symphonic picture, 1983; Duo Sonata, violin, viola, 1984; Sonata for 2 pianos and 3 performers, 1984; Sextet, 1985;

Cantus Amores, cantata, 1986; Sonata for double bass and piano, 1987; Hope, oratorio, 1988; The Second Legend of Ciurlionis, piano, 1988; Credo, organ, 1989; Concerto for Piano and Orchestra, 1992; Konzertstück für Orchester No. 1, 1992; Concert Suite, cello, piano, 1993; Reminiscence, harpsichord, 1993; Intimate Music, op 100, flute, percussion, 1993; Divertimento, piano 6 hands, 1993; The Third Legend of Ciurtionis, piano, 1993; Inspiration, organ, 1994; Konzertstück No. 2 für Orchester, 1994; Trio a deux, violin, viola, cello, 1995; Allegro Brillante for two pianos, 1996; Modus vivendi for violin, cello and piano, 1996; Scherzo for violin and chamber orchestra, 1996; Duo for guitar and piano, 1997; Toccamento No. 2 for viola solo, violin, cello and piano, 1998; Here and Now music for symphonic orchestra, 1998; Symphony No. 6, 2001. *Recordings:* Ars vivendi, 1992; Cavalli, 1993; Proud Sound, 1995; Lithuanian New Music series, 1997. *Address:* Saltiniu Street 11/15 b. 44, Vilnius 2006, Lithuania.

BARKER, Cheryl; Singer (Soprano); b. 22 April 1960, Sydney, Australia; m. Peter Coleman-Wright. *Education:* Studied with Joan Hammond. *Career:* Debut: Sang Mozart's Blondchen at Adelaide, 1984; Appearances as the Governess in The Turn of the Screw, Princess in Rusalka, Oksana in Rimsky's Christmas Eve, with English National Opera from 1989; Sang Cherubino and Marzelline, Glyndebourne Touring Opera, 1989; Sang Mozart's Annio, Tatiana in Eugene Onegin and Adina, L'Elisir d'amore, Scottish Opera, 1991–94; Sang Tatiana at Sydney, 1994; Violetta at Auckland, 1995; Season 1996 in The Midsummer Marriage at Covent Garden and as Suor Angelica at Antwerp; Season 1997–98 as Butterfly for Opera Australia, Falla's Salud at Brussels, Liu in Turandot and Butterfly for English National Opera; Season 2000–01 as Butterfly and Suor Angelica at ENO and Donna Elvira for Australian Opera; Title role in new production of Tosca for ENO, 2002. *Recordings:* La Bohème. *Address:* c/o English National Opera, St Martin's Lane, London WC2N 4ES, England.

BARKER, Noelle, OBE, MA, FGSM; singing teacher; b. 28 Dec. 1928, Aberdeen, Scotland; m. Christopher Peake; three c. *Education:* Aberdeen University, Dartington Hall; Amsterdam Conservatory, Munich Academy, studied with Hans Hotter. *Career:* debut, Royal Festival Hall, London; oratorio, Lieder and contemporary music with leading choral societies and ensembles; appearances with Three Choirs and at various festivals; sang with the English Opera Group, London Sinfonietta and Dreamtiger Ensemble; broadcasts on BBC and European stations; Prof., Guildhall School of Music and Drama, Royal Acad., London and Conservatoire National, Paris; private teaching in London and Paris; masterclasses world-wide and jury mem. of various int. competitions; Dir, British Youth Opera; co-ed., Pathodia Sacra e Profana; ed., The Junior Recitalist. *Recordings:* complete solo vocal works of Messiaen, Jazz Songs. *Honours:* Hon. RAM 1999. *E-mail:* noellebarker@onetel.com. *Address:* Brontë Cottage, 89 South End Road, London NW3 2RJ, England (home). *Telephone:* (20) 7794-3615 (home).

BARKER, Paul (Alan); Composer; b. 1 July 1956, Cambridge, England; m. (1) Christine Susan Barker, 3 Sept 1977, divorced 1991, (2) Maria Huesca, 23 May 1992. *Education:* Guildhall School of Music, 1974–78; GGSM 1st Class; MMus, Durham University, 1983–85. *Career:* Visiting Lecturer, City University, 1978–83; Musical Director of Dancers Anonymous, 1979–86; Associate Lecturer, Kingsway-Princeton College, 1984–90; Artistic Director of Modern Music Theatre Troupe, 1985–94; Composer in Residence, West Sussex, 1991–93; Composer in Association, London Mozart Players 1993–; Lecturer, Hertfordshire University, 1997–; mem, Executive Committee, APC; Honorary Associate Member, OMTF; PCS Committee of ISM. *Compositions include:* Operas: The Marriages Between Zones 3, 4 and 5, The Place, 1985, Phantastes, Camden Festival 1986, The Pillow Song, 1988, La Malinche, 1989, Albergo Empedocle, 1990, Dirty Tricks, 1997, at London International Opera Festival and Prologue at Festival del Centro Historico, Mexico City, 1992; 10 Contemporary dance scores for European companies; Orchestral works include Fantasy on Four Notes, 1978; Instrumental ensemble, vocal, choral and chamber works; Music for Theatre; Children's Operas and educational music; Three Songs for Sylvia, commissioned by London Festival Orchestra, Bristol Cathedral, 1994; Concerto for 8, for London Mozart Players, Henley Festival, 1995; Concerto for Violin and Orchestra for Tasmin Little and London Mozart Players 1996. *Recordings:* Barbican Fanfare, 1979; The Pied Piper of Hamelin, 1980. *Honours:* Royal Philharmonia Society Prize for Composition, 1978. *Current Management:* Modern Music Theatre Troupe. *Address:* Flat 3, 33 Hopton Road, London SW16 2EH, England.

BARKIN, Elaine R(adoff); Composer, Music Educator and Writer on Music; b. 15 Dec. 1932, New York, NY, USA; m. George J Barkin, 28 Nov 1957, 3 s. *Education:* BA, Music, Queens College, 1954; MFA, Composition 1956, PhD, Composition and Theory 1971, Brandeis University; Certificate in Composition and Piano, Berlin Hochschule für Musik, 1957; Studied with Karol Rathaus, Irving Fine, Boris Blacher, Arthur Berger and Harold Shapero. *Career:* Assistant to Co-Editor, Perspectives of New Music, 1963–85; Lecturer in Music, Queens

College, 1964–70; Sarah Lawrence College, 1969–70; Assistant, Associate Professor of Music Theory, University of Michigan, 1970–74; Visiting Assistant Professor, Princeton University, 1974; Associate Professor 1974–77, Professor 1977–97, Composition and Theory, University of California, Los Angeles; Guest Lecturer at various colleges and universities. *Compositions:* String Quartet, 1969; Sound Play for violin, 1974; String Trio, 1976; Plein Chant, alto flute, 1977; Ebb Tide, 2 vibraphones 1977;... the Supple Suitor... for soprano and 5 players, 1978; De Amore, chamber mini-opera, 1980; Impromptu for violin, cello and piano, 1981; Media Speak, theatre piece, 1981; At the Piano, piano, 1982; For String Quartet, 1982; Quilt Piece, graphic score for 7 instruments, 1984; On the Way to Becoming, for 4-track Tape Collage, 1985; Demeter and Persephone for violin, tape, chamber ensemble and dancers, 1986; 3 Rhapsodies, flutes and clarinet, 1986; Encore for Javanese Gamelan Ensemble, 1988; Out of the Air for Basset Horn and Tape, 1988; To Whom It May Concern, 4-track Tape Collage, Reader, 1989; Legong Dreams, Oboe, 1990 (and since 1980 many improvised group and duo sessions on tape); Gamélange, harp and mixed gamelan band, 1992; Five Tape Collages, Open Space CD #3, 1993; For My Friends' Pleasure, for soprano and harp, 1993; Touching All Bases, electric bass, percussion, Balinese gamelan, 1996; Music for Soloists and Small Ensembles (1974–1993), Open Space CD #12, 1999; Poem for winds and percussion, 1999; Song for Sarah, violin, 2001. *Publications:* An Anthology, music, text and graphics, 1997. *Honours:* Fulbright Award, 1957; NEA Awards, 1975, 1979; Rockefeller Foundation, 1980; Meet the Composer, 1994. *Address:* Department of Music, 405 Hilgard Avenue, University of California, Los Angeles, CA 90095, USA.

BARKL, Michael Laurence Gordon; Composer; *Head Teacher of Music, Illawarra Institute of Technology;* b. 9 Aug. 1958, Sydney, NSW, Australia; m. Sharyn Lee 1986, 1 d. *Education:* BMus, New South Wales State Conservatorium of Music, 1981; FTCL, Trinity College of Music, London, 1982; MMus, University of New England, 1986; DipEd, Sydney College of Advanced Education, 1986; PhD, Deakin University, 1995. *Career:* Tutor, University of New England, 1982; Head Teacher of Music, Illawarra Institute of Technology 1987–; commissions from Seymour Group, Synergy, Elision, Duo Contemporain, Manly Art Gallery and Orange City Council. *Compositions include:* The Time, The Time, for choir, 1981; Voce di Testa and Voce di Petto, for orchestra, 1981–82; Chroma for harpsichord, 1981; Drumming for piano, 1983; Psychonaut for chorus, 1983; Iambus for wind quintet and strings, 1983; Cabaret for orchestra, 1985; Expressive and Ferocious, for string quartet, 1985; Backyard Swing for concert band, 1986; Blues for clarinet and marimba, 1986; Rondo for chamber orchestra, 1988; Disco for percussion quartet, 1989; Smoky for harpsichord, 1997. *Honours:* Segnalata, Valentino Bucchi competition for Composition, Italy, 1981. *Address:* 119 Combermere Street, Goulburn, NSW 2580, Australia.

BARLEY, Matthew; Concert Cellist; b. 1965, England. *Education:* Guildhall School, London; Moscow Conservatoire. *Career:* debut, Shostakovich First Concerto with London SO at Barbican Hall; guest principal with the LSO, London Philharmonic Orchestra, Philharmonia, RPO, London Sinfonietta; solo and chamber music engagements in North America, Asia, Australasia and throughout Europe; concertos with London Sinfonietta, Orchestra Internazionale d'Italia, Royal Scottish National Orchestra, Brno Symphony Orchestra, Athens Camerata, Hong Kong Sinfonietta, New Zealand Symphony Orchestra; festival appearances at Taranaki, New Zealand, WOMAD, Lucerne, Prague Autumn, Dijon, Koshigaya, Harrogate, Norwich, Dartington, Chester, Salisbury, City of London, Cheltenham; premieres of works by John Woolrich, Carl Vine, Peter Wiegold, Fraser Trainer, Detlev Glanert, Dave Maric, Deirdre Gribben; non-classical collaboration with Viktoria Mullova, Amjad Ali Khan, Julian Joseph, Django Bates and others; founder of performance and education group, Between the Notes, 1997. *Recordings include:* Through the Looking Glass, The Silver Swan, Strings Attached. *Current Management:* Askonas Holt Ltd, Lonsdale Chambers, 27 Chancery Lane, London, WC2A 1PF, England. *Telephone:* (20) 7400-1700. *Fax:* (20) 7400-1799. *E-mail:* info@askonasholt.co.uk. *Website:* www.askonasholt.co.uk; www.matthewbarley.com; www.betweenthenotes.co.uk.

BARLOW, Clara; Singer (Soprano); b. 28 July 1928, Brooklyn, New York, USA. *Education:* Studied with Cecile Jacobson in New York. *Career:* Debut: Berne Opera 1962, as Venus in Tannhäuser; Sang at Oberhausen, 1963–65, Kiel 1965–66; Komische Oper Berlin 1967, as Donna Anna; Engaged at Wiesbaden 1967–69, Zürich 1969–70; Guest appearances at the Spoleto Festival (as Isolde, 1968), San Diego (1969) and the Metropolitan Opera (as Leonore, 1970); Returned to New York 1974, as Isolde; Deutsche Oper Berlin 1970, Vienna Staatsoper 1973; Sang Fata Morgana in The Love of Three Oranges at La Scala 1974; Appearances as Brünnhilde at Seattle (1970–72 and 1976) and Dallas (1981); Scottish Opera 1973, as Isolde; Further appearances at Dresden, Stuttgart, Hamburg, Munich, Chicago (1976–77), Houston, Copenhagen, Toronto, Budapest and Mexico City; Stadttheater Bremen 1985–86, as Elektra

and Leonore; Other roles have included the Dyer's Wife (Die Frau ohne Schatten), Agathe, Senta, Elsa, Elisabeth, Ariadne, Salome, Aida, Elisabeth de Valois, Jenůfa, Marina (Boris Godunov) and Giulietta in Les Contes d'Hoffmann. *Address:* c/o Bremer Theater, Postfach 101046, 2800 Bremen, Germany.

BARLOW, Stephen; Conductor; b. 30 June 1954, Seven Kings, Essex; m. Joanna Lumley. *Education:* Studied in Canterbury, at Trinity College, Cambridge, and Guildhall School of Music. *Career:* Founded New London Chamber Group, based at the Riverside Studios, Hammersmith; Guest conductor of opera at the Guildhall School, notably Falstaff and Maw's The Rising of the Moon; Glyndebourne Festival and Tour, 1979–85, leading Die schweigsame Frau, Der Rosenkavalier, Arabella, Oliver Knussen double bill, Così fan tutte, Gluck's Orfeo, The Rake's Progress and Love of Three Oranges; For English National Opera has conducted The Flying Dutchman, Carmen, Abduction from the Seraglio, The Damnation of Faust, La Cenerentola, L'italiana in Algeri, Barber of Seville; Scottish Opera from 1983, with Hansel and Gretel, The Bartered Bride, Intermezzo; Conducted Opera 80 from its inception, Musical Director from 1987, leading Marriage of Figaro, A Masked Ball, The Rake's Progress, The Merry Widow, 1989–90; Covent Garden debut, 1989, with Turandot, returning for Die Zauberflöte in 1991; San Francisco Opera, 1990, Capriccio; Has also worked for Opera North and Vancouver Opera; Australian debut, Melbourne, in Die Zauberflöte, 1991; Conducted Faust for Opera Northern Ireland, 1992; Conducted Capriccio in Catania, Marriage of Figaro at Garsington, Carmen in Adelaide; Madama Butterfly at Auckland, 1994 and in Belfast, 1997; Season 1998 with Falstaff at Garsington; Concert engagements with the English Chamber Orchestra, City of London Sinfonia, London Sinfonietta, City of Birmingham Symphony, Royal Liverpool Philharmonic, Scottish Chamber Orchestra, BBC Scottish and Bournemouth Sinfonietta; Concerts in Spain, Netherlands, Germany; BBC National Orchestra of Wales, Radio Philharmonic Orchestra, Hilversum; New Zealand, Vancouver, Melbourne and Detroit Symphony Orchestras, BBC Philharmonic; Artistic Director, Opera Northern Ireland, 1996–98; Music Director Queensland Philharmonic Orchestra, 1996–98. *Honours:* Fellow, Royal College of Organists, 1972; Fellow, Guildhall School of Music and Drama, 1985. *Current Management:* Musichall. *Address:* c/o Musichall, Vicarage Way, Ringmer, East Sussex BN8 5 LA, England.

BARNARD, Keith, AMus; British composer, poet and teacher; b. 26 Oct. 1950, London, England. *Education:* Trinity Coll. of Music, London; studied composition with Arnold Cooke; Int. Writers' Asscn, Int. Poets' Acad., Madras, India. *Career:* teacher of piano, music theory and composition 1972–; numerous concerts and recitals of his own compositions; conductor, multicultural concert; mem. Performing Right Asscn, Musicians' Union, New Age Music Asscn. *Compositions include:* Healing 1–4 for Piano, Colour Harmonies for Keyboard Synthesizer, Healing Rays of Emerald-Blue for 5 Flutes, The Golden Temple of Wisdom for 4 Flutes, Angelic Nocturne for Piano. *Publications:* Outer World Poems 1982, The Sacred Cup 1982, The Legend of Bran 1982, The Legend of Fonn 1983, The Adventures of Fionn Mac Chumail 1984, Heroes and Rituals 1984, Dreams of Wisdom 1986, Visions 1988, Perspectives 1989, Dream Soul 1990, Kingdoms 1991; contrib. to East-West Voices, Rising Stars, Samvedana-Creative Bulletin, Poet International, Souvenir Tribute to Professor Saidhana, Canopy, Indian Literary Journal. *Address:* 115 San Jose Avenue, Santa Cruz, CA 96060, USA.

BARNARD, Trevor John, ARAM, ARCM, GradMIMIT, LPIBA; pianist and academic; b. 3 Jan. 1938, London, England; m. Helen Richmond 1974. *Education:* Royal Academy of Music, Royal College of Music, Inst. of Musical Instrument Technology, studied with Herbert Fryer, Harold Craxton. *Career:* pianist-in-residence, Boston Univ. Radio 1967–71; Faculty, New England Conservatory, Boston, MA 1968–72; piano tutor, Monash Univ., Australia 1972–74; Lecturer in Music, Melbourne Coll. of Advanced Education 1974–88; Lecturer in Music, Univ. of Melbourne and examiner, Australian Music Examinations Board 1989–2003; many appearances as pianist, BBC and ABC television; Music-in-the-Round Chamber Music Festivals; many orchestras, music socs; mem. Australian Musicians' Guild (hon. sec. 1982–93), Camberwell Music Soc. (pres. 1990–2000, hon. life mem. 2000–). *Recordings:* An Introduction to Piano Music; Bliss Piano Concerto; J. S. Bach transcriptions and piano music from Australia; Busoni 24 preludes; Bliss Sonata; Blue Wrens, piano music from Australia. *Recordings for television and film:* Schumann and Bliss concerti, Mozart, Concerto Rondo (K382). *Publications:* Pedalling and Other Reflections on Piano Teaching, 1991; A Guide to the Study of Solo Piano Repertoire at Tertiary Level, 1996; contrib. to Clavier (journal), 1998–2002; Australia Music Teacher (magazine) 1992–. *Honours:* Full Scholarship Royal Coll. of Music 1955. *Address:* 10 Grosvenor Road, Glen Iris, Vic. 3146, Australia.

BARNEA, Sever (Aurelian); Romanian singer (baritone); *First Soloist, Baritone, National Opera, Bucharest;* b. 1 July 1960, Bucharest; one s. *Education:* piano principal study, Lyceum of Art, singing principal study, Universitatea de Muzica, int. music classes, Weimar. *Career:*

First Perm. Baritone, Romanian Nat. Opera Bucharest, 1989; Mozart, Papageno in The Magic Flute; Figaro in Le nozze di Figaro; title role in Don Giovanni; Donizetti, Dr Malatesta in Don Pasquale and Dulcamara in L'Elisir d'amore; Verdi, Amonasro in Aida; Iago in Otello; title role in Falstaff; Gounod, Mephisto in Faust; Rossini, Mustafa in Italiana in Algeri; Bartolo in Il Barbiere di Siviglia; Basilio in La Cenerentola, Saint-Saëns, The Grand Priest of Dagon in Samson and Delilah; Ponchielli, Barnaba in Gioconda; Gomes in C Gomes, Don Gil de Tarragona in Maria Tudor; Puccini, Marcello in La Bohème; Madama Butterfly; Scarpia in Tosca; Ping in Turandot; Bizet, Escamillo in Carmen; Tchaikovsky, title role in Eugene Onegin; Wagner, Holländer in Der fliegende Holländer; Georges Enescu, title role in Oedipe; Pascal Bentoiu, Laertes in Hamlet; Nicolae Bretan, title role in Golem; Bach; Haydn; Fauré; Carl Orff. *Recordings:* Romanian national radio and television, Bulgaria; BBC; Participated in several festivals at Georges Enescu International Festival, Romania; Temps Musicaux, Ramatuelle Festival Anvers sur Oise, France; Medway Arts Festival, 1995; Athens Festival; Toured Austria, Belgium, France, Spain, Bulgaria, Germany, Greece, Switzerland, Netherlands, United Kingdom, Italy, Hungary, Poland, Japan, Albania, Moldova, Macedonia. *Honours:* Performanta in Spectacolul de Opera Award, Actualitatie Musicale 2000, Meritul Cultural in Grad Cavaler Presidential Award 2004. *Address:* Str. Compozitorilor 1 Mai, 32 B1 F8, Sc B apt 24 Sector VI, Cod 61634 Bucharest, Romania. *Telephone:* (21) 7252429; (745) 074023. *Fax:* (21) 3120505. *E-mail:* severbarnea@pcnet.ro. *Website:* www.geocities.com/severbarnea.

BARNES, Gerald Linton, FRCO, GRSM, ARAM, ARCM; Musician; b. 6 June 1935, Hampstead, England; m. Rachel Mary Townsend. *Education:* Kilburn Grammar School, Hertford Coll., Oxford, Royal Acad. of Music. *Career:* Organist, Bloomsbury Central Church 1956–81; St Columba's Pont Street 1988–; Prof., examiner London Coll. of Music 1965–; Lecturer City Literary Inst. 1971–; conductor, Elysian Choir 1975–, Wembley Philharmonic Soc. 1981, Thiman Orchestra of London 1985–; appeared as organist on television, radio and at cathedrals, univs and major concert halls in England, Europe and USA; mem. Savage Club, Royal Soc. of Musicians. *Compositions:* hymn tunes and anthems. *Recordings:* various organ recordings. *Publications:* contrib. to Musical Times, Musical Opinion and choral and musical journals. *Honours:* Hon. FLCM 1985. *Address:* 35 Dollis Avenue, London, N3 1BY, England (home). *Telephone:* (20) 8346-6637 (home).

BAROVÁ, Anna; Singer (mezzo-soprano); b. 1932, Plzeň, Czechoslovakia. *Education:* Prague Acad. *Career:* sang at the Leipzig Opera, 1959–69, notably in the 1961 German premiere of Prokofiev's War and Peace, as Sonia; guested widely in former E Germany; sang at the Janáček Opera, Brno, 1969–92; roles included Dorabella, Rosina, Carmen, Ulrica, Suzuki, Olga; concert repertory includes Beethoven's Ninth, the Verdi, Mozart and Dvořák Requiems, Dvořák's Stabat, and vocal recitals; Prof., Janáček Acad. of Performing Arts, Brno, 1990–. *Recordings include:* The Devil and Kate by Dvořák, Eva by Foerster, Jenůfa by Janáček. *Address:* Kotlanova 1c, 628 00 Brno, Czech Republic.

BARRELL, David; Singer (Baritone); b. 1962, England. *Education:* London University and the Royal Academy of Music; Opera Center at the Juilliard School, New York. *Career:* Sang Gounod's Ourrais (Mireille) and Don Giovanni at Juilliard; Appearances at the Spoleto Festivals (Italy and USA) 1986; Wexford Festival 1987 and Britten's Demetrius at the Bloomsbury Festival; Welsh National Opera as Ottokar in Der Freischütz, The Speaker in Die Zauberflöte, Don Carlos (Ernani) and Germont; Season 1992–93 as Rossini's Figaro and Alfonso in La Favorita, with WNO at Covent Garden; Sang 'I' in the British premiere production of Schnittke's Life with an Idiot (English National Opera, 1994); Šiškov in House of the Dead in Nice; Wolfram in Tannhäuser for Chelsea Opera Group and Thaos in Iphigénie en Tauride at the 1996 Edinburgh Festival; Season 1996–97 with Germont for Opera Northern Ireland, Major Haudy in Zimmermann's Die Soldaten for ENO, Puccini's Marcello, The Forester in The Cunning Little Vixen and Balstrode in Peter Grimes, for Scottish Opera; Mandryka in Arabella at Glyndebourne Festival; Concerts include: The Brahms Requiem, Carmina Burana, Elijah and Elgar's The Kingdom; Premiere of Tippett's Tempest Suite, season 1995–96; Season 1997–98 as Josquin Desprez in Pfitzner's Palestrina at the Metropolitan, New York, Thaos in Iphigénie en Tauride at Rio de Janeiro, Tokyo and Madrid, and Redburn in Billy Budd for ENO. *Honours:* Winner, New York Oratorio Society International Soloist Competition, Carnegie Hall; Associate of Royal Academy of Music. *Address:* Allied Artists, 42 Montpelier Square, London SW7 1JZ, England.

BARRERA, Giulia; Singer (Soprano); b. 28 April 1942, Brooklyn, New York, USA. *Education:* Studied in New York with Dick Marzollo. *Career:* Debut: New York City Opera, 1963, as Aida; Sang in Baltimore, New Orleans, Pittsburgh, Washington and Seattle; Member of New York City Opera: Roles included Verdi's Amelia and Leonora (Il Trovatore), Santuzza, Don Giovanni, Sieglinde in Die Walküre, Tosca,

Manon Lescaut, Venus in Tannhäuser and Monteverdi's Euridice; Guest appearances in Copenhagen, Rome, Parma, Cardiff, Montreal and Nuremberg. *Recordings include:* The Mother in Dallapiccola's Il Prigioniero.

BARRETT, Richard; British composer and classical guitarist; b. 7 Nov. 1959, Swansea, Wales. *Education:* studied with Peter Wiegold and in Darmstadt. *Career:* teacher, Darmstadt, 1986 and 1988; Co-director, Ensemble Expose. *Compositions:* Essay in Radiance for ensemble, 1983; Principia for baritone and piano, 1984; Cogitum for mezzo and ensemble, 1985; Illuminer le temps for ensemble, 1986; Ne Songe plus a fuir for amplified cello, 1986; Temptation for ensemble, 1986; Alba for bassoon and electronics, 1987; Recticule for violin, 1988; The Unthinkable for electronics and tape, 1989; Dark Ages for cello, 1990; Another Heavenly Day for ensemble, 1990; Lieder vom wasser for soprano and ensemble; Basalt for trombone, 1991; Praha for cello, 1991; Negatives for guitar and ensemble, 1992; Knospend–gespaltener for clarinet, 1993; Vanity for orchestra, 1994; Trawl for 5 players, 1994–97; Von Hinter dem Schmerz for amplified cello, 1992–97; Opening of the Mouth for 2 female voices, instruments, tapes and live electronics, 1992–97; Stress for string quartet, 1995–97; Unter Wasser, opera for mezzo-soprano and 13 instruments, 1995–98. *Address:* c/o British Music Information Centre, 19 Stratford Place, London W1N 9AE, England.

BARRIÈRE, Jean-Baptiste (Marie); Composer and Director of Musical Research; b. 2 Jan. 1958, Paris, France; m. Kaija Saariaho, 26 May 1984. *Education:* Licence, Mathematical Logic, 1980, DEA Philosophy, 1981, Doctorate in Philosophy, 1987, University of Paris I, Panthéon Sorbonne. *Career:* Member of the Synthesizer Ensemble of the Centre Européen pour la Recherche Musicale, Metz, 1976–77; Researcher, Composer, 1981–84, Director of Musical Research, 1984–97, Institut de Recherche et de Co-ordination Acoustique Musique, Paris; mem, Collectif pour la Recherche en Information Musicale. *Compositions:* Pandémonium: Ville Ouverte, 1975; Pandémonium: Non, Jamais l'Esperance, 1976; Sophistic Variations, 1980; Chreode I, 1983; Collisions, 1984; Epigénèse, 1986; Hybris, 1987; World Skin, 1997; Cellitude, 1998; Time Dusts, 1998. *Recordings:* Pandémonium: Ville Ouverte, 1977; Pandémonium: Non, Jamais l'Esperance, 1978. *Publications:* Le Timbre: Métaphores pour la Composition, 1987–88; Actes du Symposium Systèmes Personnels et Informatique Musicale, 1987. *Contributions:* Chreode I: A Path to a New Music with the Computer, for Contemporary Music Review No. 1, 984; Mutations de l'Escriture, Mutations du Matériau, for Inharmoniques No. 1, 1987. *Honours:* Digital Music Prize in the Electro-Acoustic Music Competition, Bourges, France, 1983; Prix Ars Electronica, Linz, 1998. *Address:* c/o Centre de la Musique Contemporain, Cité de la Musique, 16 Place de la Fontaine, F–75019 Paris, France.

BARRON, Bebe; Composer; b. 16 June 1927, Minneapolis, Minnesota, USA. *Education:* Studied at the Universities of Minnesota and Mexico and in New York with Riegger and Cowell. *Career:* With husband Louis Barron (1920–89) co-founded electro-acoustic music studio in New York, 1949; Secretary of the Society for Electro-Acoustic Music from 1985. *Compositions:* With Louis Barron, Dramatic Legend, 1955; Ballet, 1956; Heavenly Menagerie, 1952; For an Electronic Nervous System, 1954; Music of Tomorrow, 1960; Spaceboy, 1971; The Circe Circuit, 1982; Elegy for a Dying Planet, 1982; Film scores, including Forbidden Planet, 1956, and Cannabis, 1975. *Address:* c/o ASCAP, ASCAP House, 1 Lincoln Plaza, New York, NY 10023, USA.

BARROSO, Sergio; Composer and Synthesist; b. 4 March 1946, Havana, Cuba. *Education:* Composition; Piano; Organ; Theory; National Conservatory, Havana, 1950–66; Postgraduate, Prague Superior Academy of Music; Orchestral Conducting, University of Havana; Computer Music, CCRMA, Stanford University, USA. *Career:* Professor; Composition; Institute of Arts, Havana; Performances include: Monte Carlo Theatre, 1972; Warsaw Autumn Festivals, 1972, 1985; Budapest Opera, 1976; Teatro de la Zarzuela, Madrid, 1976; MET-Lincoln Center, New York, 1977–78; San Francisco Opera, 1977; Bratislava Philharmonic Hall, 1979; ISCM Festival, Belgium, 1980, Oslo, 1990; IRCMA, Paris, 1980; Array, Toronto, 1981; Utrecht Conservatorium, Netherlands, 1982; Manuel de Falla Festival, Granada, 1985; Wired Society, Toronto, 1986; ACREQ, Montreal, 1987; Museo Tamayo, Mexico City, 1988; National Arts Centre, Ottawa, 1988; South Bank Centre, London, 1989; Toronto New Music Concerts, 1990; Sub-Tropics Festival, Miami, 1991; LIEM, Centro Reina Sofia, Madrid, 1991; ICMC, Montreal, 1991; New Music Across America, Seattle, 1992; Others. *Compositions:* 2 ballets; Plásmasis, 1970; La Casa de Bernarda Alba, 1975; Oboe Concerto, 1968; Yantra IV flute, tape, 1982; Ireme, voice, percussion, tape, 1985; En Febrero Mueren las Flores, violin, tape, 1987; Tablao, guitar, tape, 1991; Concerto for violin and orchestra, 1992; Synthesizers: Soledad, 1987; Canzone, 1988; La Fiesta, synthesizers, tape, 1989; La Fiesta Grande, synthesizers, orchestra, 1990; Cronicas de Ultrasueño, oboe, synthesizers, 1992; Sonatada, 1992; Concerto for viola and orchestra, 1996; Viola Desnuda, viola solo, 1997; La Noche, viola, bass clarinet and tape, 1997;

Sandunga, viola or clarinet and tape, 1998; Cuartetas, viola, bass clarinet, piano and tape, 1999; Callejero, bass clarinet and tape, 1999; Pregones, cello and tape, 2000. *Recordings:* Digital Keyboard Music, 1988; Cronicas, 1995; Concerto for viola and Concerto for violin, 1998; Charangas Delirantes, solo and electronic works, 1998; Viola Desnuda, 2000. *Address:* IREME EMS, 7938, 122 A Street, Surrey, British Columbia, V3W 3T3, Canada.

BARRUECO, Manuel; American classical guitarist; b. 16 Dec. 1952, Santiago de Cuba, Cuba. *Education:* Eŝteban Salas Conservatory, Santiago de Cuba and the Peabody Conservatory, Maryland. *Career:* debut, New York, 1974; many concert appearances as soloist; faculty mem. at the Peabody Conservatory and assisted in the creation of a faculty for guitar at the Manhattan School of Music; gave the US premiere of Takemitsu's guitar concerto, 1985. *Recordings include:* Rodrigo, with Placido Domingo; Bach Sonatas; Albeniz, Turina, solo. *Honours:* Concert Artists' Guild Award, 1974. *Current Management:* M. B. General Management, PO Box 4466, Timonium, MD 21094-4466, USA.

BARRY, Gerald; Composer; b. 28 April 1952, Clarecastle, Ireland. *Education:* Studied in Cologne with Stockhausen and Kagel; Studied organ with Piet Kee in Amsterdam. *Compositions:* Principal works include: Chevaux de frise for orchestra (performed at the 1988 Proms); The Intelligence Park, opera (ICA commission, first performed at the 1990 Almeida Festival); The Triumph of Beauty and Deceit (Channel 4 television commission, 1992, 1993); The Conquest of Ireland, vocal and orchestral work (BBC Symphony Orchestra commission); String Quartet, 1994; The Ring for chorus and orchestra, 1995; Quintet, 1995; Octet, 1995; Piano Quintet No. 2, 1996; The Road for orchestra, 1997. *Recordings:* Piano and Chamber music–Noriko Kawai, piano, with the Nua Nos ensemble. *Contributions:* The Intelligence Park, to Contemporary Music Review, Vol. 5; Irish Wit, to The Musical Times, Sept 1993; Bob's Your Uncle, to The Musical Times, April 1995. *Current Management:* Oxford University Press. *Address:* Oxford University Press, 70 Baker St, London W1M 1DJ, England.

BARSHAI, Rudolf; Conductor; b. 28 Sept. 1924, Labinskaya, USSR; m. (1) 3 s., (2) Elena Raskova. *Education:* Conducting course under Ilya Musin, Leningrad; Violin and Viola studies with Lev Zeitlin, Moscow Conservatory. *Career:* Solo Violinist, Moscow Philharmonic Quartet, Member, Borodin and Tchaikovsky Quartets, Founder and Conductor, Moscow Chamber Orchestra, Guest Conductor, Moscow Philharmonic, State Orchestra of USSR, USSR Radio Orchestra, 1955–77; Guest Conductor, New Israel Orchestra, 1977–, also London Symphony, London Philharmonic and Royal Philharmonic Orchestras, BBC London, Philharmonia, English Chamber Orchestra, Scottish National Orchestra, City of Birmingham Symphony Orchestra, BBC Philharmonic, Vienna Symphony, Orchestre National de France, Orchestre de Paris, Mozarteum Salzburg, Tokyo Philharmonic, Yomiuri and NHK Orchestras, RAI Turin, Pittsburgh Symphony, Swiss Radio Orchestra, Bavarian Radio Symphony Orchestra, Munich, Radio Symphony Orchestra, Hamburg, Radio Symphony Orchestra, Cologne, Tonhalle Orchestra Zürich; Principal Conductor, Bournemouth Symphony, 1982–88; Music Director, Vancouver Symphony, 1985–88; Principal Guest Conductor, Orchestral National de France, 1987–88; President, International Toscanini Conductors' Competition, 1986–93. *Compositions:* Arrangements of Bach; Art of the Fugue; Musical Offering; Shostakovich: Chamber Symphony op 49a, op 110a, op 83a, Symphony for Strings op 118a, Symphony for Woodwinds and Strings, op 73a; Prokofiev: Visions Fugitives, others. *Recordings:* Many including works by Bach, Vivaldi, Corelli, Mozart, Haydn, Beethoven, Schubert, Brahms, Mahler, Stravinsky, Bartók, Shostakovich, Tchaikovsky, Tippett, Prokofiev, for various labels. *Honours:* Grand Prix du Disque; Honorary Doctorate, University of Southampton, 1985. *Current Management:* Askonas Holt Ltd, Lonsdale Chambers, 27 Chancery Lane, London, WC2A 1PF, England. *Telephone:* (20) 7400-1700. *Fax:* (20) 7400-1799. *E-mail:* info@askonasholt.co.uk. *Website:* www.askonasholt.co.uk. *Address:* Concerto Winderstein, Leopoldstrasse 25, Munich 80802, Germany.

BARSTOW, Dame Josephine Clare; Opera Singer; b. 27 Sept. 1940, Sheffield, Yorkshire, England; m. (1) Terry Hands, (2) Ande Anderson, 25 Oct 1969. *Education:* BA, English, Birmingham University; London Opera Centre, one year. *Career:* Debut: 1964, Opera for All; Has appeared with all major British Opera Companies; In world premieres of The Knot Garden and The Ice Break by Tippett and We Come to the River by Henze at Covent Garden; The Story of Vasco, by Gordon Crosse, at ENO; Summer, 1986, at Salzburg Festival in leading role in Penderecki's Die schwarze Maske; Has sung in all major houses in USA, Germany, including Bayreuth, France, Switzerland, Italy, Buenos Aires, Africa and Russia, at the Bolshoi; Main Roles in Verdi and Strauss, frequently Salome and Janáček, Mozart, Puccini, Beethoven and Wagner; Role of Kate in Kiss Me Kate; Sang Odabella in a new production of Attila at Covent Garden; Amelia in Un Ballo in Maschera

at Salzburg, 1990; Ellen Orford in a new production of Peter Grimes, ENO, 1991; Sang Leonora in a new production of La Forza del Destino for ENO, 1992; Chrysothemis in Elektra at Houston, 1993; Elizabeth I in Gloriana for Opera North at Covent Garden, 1994; The Kostelnicka for Opera North, 1995, returned 1997, as Elizabeth I; Mère Marie in Carmelites for ENO, 1999; Covent Garden, 2001, as the Kabanicha in Katya Kabanova; Sang the Kostleniĉka in Jenûfa for Opera North, 2002. *Recordings:* The Knot Garden by Michael Tippett; Recital of Verdi Arias and Ballo in Maschera under Karajan; Four Opera Finales; Gloriana, title role; Kiss Me Kate; Albert Herring. *Honours:* Critics Prize, Berliner Zeitung; Best Debut, Buenos Aires; Honorary Doctorate of Music, Birmingham University, C.B.E., 1985; Fidelio Medal; D.B.E., 1995; Honorary Doctorate of Music, Kingston University, 1999. *Current Management:* Askonas Holt Ltd, Lonsdale Chambers, 27 Chancery Lane, London, WC2A 1PF, England. *Telephone:* (20) 7400-1700. *Fax:* (20) 7400-1799. *E-mail:* info@askonasholt.co.uk. *Website:* www.askonasholt.co.uk.

BARTA, Ales; Organist; b. 30 Aug. 1960, Rychnov, Czechoslovakia; m. 25 Feb 1984. *Education:* Conservatoire in Brno; Academy of Music, Prague. *Career:* Debut: With Prague Symphony Orchestra, Prague Spring Festival, 1984; Foreign tours of Denmark, 1979, Austria, 1983, Hungary, 1984, 1985, Turkey, 1985, Germany, 1986, 1990, France, 1987, Russia, 1988; USA debut at concert of Czech music, New York, 1990; Festival appearances: Recitals at Prague Spring Festival, 1984, 1988 and 1991, Avignon Festival, 1987, Istanbul Festival, 1985, Leipzig Festival, 1986; Debut with Prague Radio Symphony Orchestra, Berlin Festival, 1987. *Recordings:* Organ recital, Bach, Reger and Flosman, 1986; Organ recital, Bach, 1991; Organ recital, Live recording, Bach, Reger, Sokola, 1992. *Honours:* 1st Prize, Anton Bruckner International Organ Competition, Linz, 1982; 1st Prize, Czech Organists Competition, 1984; 1st Prize, Prague Spring International Organ Competition, 1984. *Address:* Nuselska 6, 14000 Prague 4, Czech Republic.

BÁRTA, Jiri; Czech composer; b. 19 June 1935, Sumice; m. Jindra Bartova 1964; one d. *Education:* conservatoire; Janáček Acad. of Music and Dramatic Arts, Brno, Czechoslovakia. *Career:* debut, Concerto for Orchestra 1962; music theory teacher, Conservatory, Brno 1968–; mem. Asscn of Composers and Music Publicists, Camerata Brno. *Compositions:* Lyric Variations for Violin and Piano, Melancholy and Defiance for Violin, Cello and Piano, Concerto da Camera per Pianoforte ed Archi, Reliefs for Orchestra, Music for Strings: In Memoriam Miloslav Istvan, Chitra Chamber Opera, Concerto for Viola and Orchestra, Concertino for Piano, Harpsichord and Chamber Orchestra. *Recordings:* Camerata Brno Live I (two Impromptus for Piano), Camerata Brno Live II (Drink from the Vine), Czech Radio. *Honours:* Prizes, Union of Czech Composers 1986, Czech Musical Fund 1990, 1991. *Address:* Solnicni 5-9, 602 00 Brno, Czech Republic.

BARTA, Michael (Mihaly); Violinist and University Professor; b. 6 Feb. 1954, Budapest, Hungary; m. Irene Barta, 3 May 1980, 1 s. *Education:* Béla Bartók Conservatory, 1964–69; F Liszt Academy, Budapest, 1969–75; Postgraduate study with Arthur Grumiaux, –1975. *Career:* Concerts, Wigmore Hall, London, Tokyo, Frankfurt, Carnegie Recital Hall, New York, Detroit Arts Institute, Austria; Radio: Radio France, Scottish BBC, Radio Bremen, Berlin, Hungarian Radio, WDR Köln, PBS USA; Concerts in Sofia Conservatory, La Valetta (Malta), Budapest (Franz Liszt Academy); Hungarian Television, PBS-USA; Malta, Bulgaria, Latvia, Spain. *Recordings:* Goldmark Suite for Violin and Piano; Prokofiev: Sonata for Two Violins; Numerous recordings for major labels and national and international radio stations. *Honours:* 2nd Prize, Joseph Szigeti International Competition, Budapest, 1973; Gold Medal, Belgian Eugene Ysaÿe Society, 1973; Special Prize, finals, Tchaikovsky International Competition, Moscow, 1974. *Address:* 45 Twin Creeks Lane, Murphysboro, IL 62966, USA.

BARTELINK, Bernard G. M.; Organist and Composer; b. 24 Nov. 1929, Enschede, Netherlands; m. Rina Stolwyk 1955, 2 s. *Education:* Diploma, Composition, 1955, Prix d'excellence, organ, 1954, Amsterdam Conservatory. *Career:* Recitals in major concert halls and cathedrals in the United Kingdom, Europe and USA; Radio appearances in many countries; Professor of organ at Sweelinck Conservatory, Amsterdam until 1989; Organist at St Bavo Cathedral, Haarlem, –1999. *Compositions:* The Beatitudes for voice and organ; Works for organ, choir and chamber music, commissioned by Dutch Government, City of Amsterdam. *Recordings:* Several solo albums. *Honours:* First prize, International Organ Improvisation Contest, Haarlem, 1961; Knight in the Papal Order of St Sylvester; Silver Medal of the Academic Society, Arts, Sciences and Letters, Paris; Officer in the Order of Oranje-Nassau. *Address:* Leeghwaterstraat 14, 2012 GD Haarlem, Netherlands.

BARTH, Ned; Singer (Baritone); b. 1963, Syracuse, New York. *Education:* Studied at Princeton and the Manhattan School of Music. *Career:* Debut: Berne, 1987 as Mozart's Count; Sang Mandryka in Arabella, Wolfram in Tannhäuser, Donizetti's Enrico, Germont, Nabucco and

Napoleon in Prokofiev's War and Peace, Karlsruhe Opera, 1989–92; Guest appearances as Verdi's Don Carlo, Marseilles; Paolo, Dresden, Marcello, 1994; Cologne, Iago, 1996; As Wolfram, Flanders Opera at Antwerp; Season 1998: as Scarpia at Cologne; Season 1999 as Scarpia at Cologne, Posa for the Komische Oper Berlin and Jokanaan in Salome for Glimmerglass Opera; Other roles include Riccardo in I Puritani, Eugene Onegin, Verdi's Renato and Ford, Don Giovanni and Belcore; Concerts include Schubert's Winterreise, Carmina Burana, Mahler's Wunderhorn Lieder, Cologne, 1996, and works by Bach and Stravinsky. *Address:* c/o Oper der Stadt Köln, Offenbachplatz, Pf 18024, 50505 Cologne, Germany.

BARTHA, Clarry; Singer (soprano); b. 1958, Sweden. *Education:* Studied at the Accedamia di Santa Cecilia, Rome, with Maria Teresa Pediconi and George Favaretto; Further study with Vera Rozsa in London. *Career:* Debut: Donna Anna at Drottningholm, Sweden, 1981; Has sung Donna Anna in Catania, at the Montepulciano Festival and at Brighton Festival with the Drottningholm Company; At Marseilles has sung Lisa in The Queen of Spades, Fiordiligi and Margherita in Mefistofele; Basle Opera as Agathe, Tatiana in Eugene Onegin and Mozart's Countess; Performances of Gluck's La Danza at Bologna, season 1986–87; Frankfurt Opera, 1987–88 as Iphigénie en Tauride, Desdemona and Fiordiligi; She sang Mozart's Countess at Rome in 1989; Sang Katya Kabanova at Basle, 1991; Season 1995–96 as Katya at Düsseldorf and Leipzig, Chrysothemis at Nice; Sang Tosca at Bonn, 2000; Concert commitments at the Prague Spring, Palermo and Ravello Festivals; Has sung with the Italian Radio, RAI, in Rome, Naples and Milan; Accademia di Santa Cecilia in Rome and the Maggio Musicale in Florence; Mozart's Vespers and Mendelssohn's Elijah in Stockholm; Tour of Israel with Gary Bertini. *Honours:* Prizewinner at the Beniamino Gigli and Vincenzo Bellini competitions. *Current Management:* Ingpen & Williams Ltd, 7 St George's Court, 131 Putney Bridge Road, London, SW15 2PA, England.

BARTKIEWICZ, Urszula; Harpsichordist; b. 28 Jan. 1952, Bielsko-Biała, Poland; m. Jerzy Kozub, 13 Sept 1987, 1 s. *Education:* Certificate of Maturity, 1971; Studies at the Academy of Music in Kraków headed by Kryzsztof Penderecki, 1971–75; Graduation with distinction; Studies at Conservatoire National de Bobigny, Paris, 1976–77; Harpsichord Class of Huguette Dreyfus; International Master Courses: with Zuzana Ruzickova, Rafael Puyana and Kenneth Gilbert; Doctor's Thesis in Musicology at Polish Academy of Sciences in preparation. *Career:* Numerous concerts in Poland, e.g. International Festivals, Warsaw Autumn; Wratislavia Cantans; Lancut Chamber Festival; Concerts in France, Czechoslovakia, Germany, Russia, Switzerland, Belgium, Austria, the United Kingdom and USA; Co-operation with the Polish National Philharmony, Jerzy Maksymiuk's Polish Chamber Orchestra; Several appearances on television and radio in Poland and USA; Masterclass and recital for students of Wayne State University, Department of Music, Detroit, Jan 1988. *Recordings:* Regular recordings for Polish Radio 1975–90; International and Polish harpsichord music from XVI–XX centuries, solo and chamber music; Records with Polish National Philharmony and Jerzy Maksymiuk's Polish Chamber Orchestra, basso continuo. *Address:* ul Bacha 10 m 301, 02-743, Warsaw, Poland.

BARTLETT, Clifford Alfred James; British musicologist and writer on music; b. 15 Aug. 1939, London, England; m. Elaine King 1975; one s. one d. *Education:* Dulwich Coll., Magdalene Coll., Cambridge. *Career:* Deputy Music Librarian, BBC, 1970–82; Keyboard Player for Ars Nova, 1969–75; Freelance Writer and Publisher, 1983–; Director, Early Music Centre Festival, 1987–88; Chairman, Eastern Early Music Forum; Member of the councils of the National Early Music Association and the Plainsong and Mediaeval Music Society. *Publications:* Under his own imprint, King's Music, has published editions of a large quantity of music, especially opera, by Monteverdi, Purcell, Handel and other baroque composers; Also edited Handel's Messiah, Coronation Anthems and other works for Oxford University Press; contrib. monthly surveys in Early Music News, 1977–94; Editor, chief writer and publisher of Early Music Review, 1994–; Editor, Brio, 1974–85; contrib. of numerous programme notes for major record companies and festivals. *Address:* Redcroft, Banks End, Wyton, Huntingdon, Cambridgeshire PE28 2AA, England. *E-mail:* clifford.bartlett@btopenworld.com.

BARTO, Tzimon; Pianist and Conductor; b. 1963, Florida, USA. *Education:* Studied piano and Conducting, Juilliard School. *Career:* Composed first opera aged 8; Began conducting at 14; Performer, Spoleto Festival, 1985; Numerous performances, major European capitals, USA and Japan; Salzburg Easter Festival, 1989; Salzburg Summer Festival, 1989; Many major festivals. *Recordings:* Prokofiev's Piano Concerto No.3; Ravel's Concerto in G Major; Chopin-Liszt-Schumann recital programme; Bartók's piano concerto No.2; Rachmaninov's Piano concerto No.3; Chopin piano concerto No. 2; Liszt piano concerto No. 2, Royal Philharmonic Orchestra. *Address:* Monckebergallee 41, 30453 Hannover, Germany.

BARTOLETTI, Bruno; Conductor; b. 10 June 1926, Sesto Fiorentino, Italy; m. Rosanna Bartoletti, 2 c. *Education:* Studied flute at Cherubini Conservatory, Florence; Received training in piano and composition. *Career:* Debut: Conducting, Dec 1953, with Rigoletto; Symphonic debut, Maggio Musicale Fiorentino, 1954, resident conductor, 1957–64; US Debut, Lyric Opera of Chicago, 1956; Played flute in orchestra of the Teatro Comunale, Florence; Assistant conductor from 1949, working with Rodzinski, Mitropoulos, Gui and Serafin; Led the premieres of Rocca's Antiche iscrizioni, 1955, and Malipiero's Il figluol prodigo and Venere prigioniera, 1957, at Florence; Mortari's La scuola delle mogli, 1959, at La Scala and Ginastera's Don Rodrigo at the Teatro Col ón Buenos Aires, 1964; Italian premieres of Egk's Der Revisor and The Nose by Shostakovich; Conducted Italian opera at The Royal Opera, Copenhagen, 1957–60; Artistic Director, 1965–69, Co-artistic Director, 1975–, Rome Opera; Artistic adviser 1986–87; Artistic Director, Teatro Comunale Florence, 1987–92, conducted Madama Butterfly and I Puritani in Florence, 1988–89; Lyric Opera, Chicago 1988–89 with La Traviata and Tancredi; Guest conductor with many opera houses in Europe, USA and South America; Grand Théâtre Geneva, 1991, Peter Grimes; Conducted I Quattro Rusteghi at Geneva, 1992; Norma at Genoa, 1994; Conducted Simon Boccanegra at Rome, 1996; Season 1998 with Wolf-Ferrari's Il Campiello at Bologna and Macbeth at Genoa. *Recordings:* Il Barbiere di Siviglia; Vivaldi's Gloria and Credo, Deutsche Grammophon; Manon Lescaut; Un Ballo in Maschera. *Address:* c/o Chicago Lyric Opera, 20 North Wacker Drive, Chicago, IL 60606, USA.

BARTOLI, Cecilia; Italian opera singer (coloratura mezzo-soprano) and recitalist; b. 4 June 1966, Rome; d. of Pietro Angelo Bartoli and Silvana Bazzoni. *Education:* Accademia di Santa Cecilia, Rome. *Career:* professional career began with TV appearance aged 19; US debut in recital at Mostly Mozart Festival, New York 1990; Paris debut as Cherubino in The Marriage of Figaro, Opéra de Paris Bastille 1990–91 season; debut, La Scala, Milan in Rossini's Le Comte Ory 1990–91 season; appeared as Dorabella in Così fan tutte, Maggio Musicale, Florence 1991; debut with Montreal Symphony Orchestra and Philadelphia Orchestra 1990–91 season; recitals in collaboration with pianist András Schiff since 1990; appeared in Marriage of Figaro and Così fan tutte conducted by Daniel Barenboim in Chicago Feb. 1992; debut at Salzburg Festival 1992; appeared in recital at Rossini bicentenary celebration at Lincoln Center, New York 1992; has appeared with many leading conductors including the late Herbert von Karajan, Claudio Abbado, Riccardo Chailly, Myung-Whun Chung, William Christie, Charles Dutoit, Adam Fischer, Nikolaus Harnoncourt, Christopher Hogwood, James Levine, Sir Neville Marriner, Zubin Mehta, Riccardo Muti, Giuseppe Sinopoli and the late Sir George Solti; particularly associated with the operas of Mozart and Rossini; highlights of the 2000–01 season included Cenerentola in Munich, Così fan tutte and Don Giovanni in Zurich, concert performances of Haydn's Orfeo with Hogwood in Birmingham, Amsterdam, Bremen and Paris, orchestral appearances with Harnoncourt and the Berlin Philharmonic in Berlin, Barenboim and the Chicago Symphony in Chicago and New York, Boulez and the London Symphony Orchestra in London and Amsterdam, Chailly and the Concertgebouw Orchestra in Amsterdam, all-Vivaldi concerts with the Giardino Armonico in Merano, Zurich, Paris, Lindau, Liechtenstein, New York, Vancouver, Los Angeles and San Francisco, baroque music concerts with the Akademie für Alte Musik in Oslo, Goteborg, Stockholm, Helsinki and Vienna. *Albums include:* Rossini Arias, Rossini Songs, Mozart Arias, Rossini Heroines, Chants d'amour, If You Love Me 1992, Mozart Portraits 1995, An Italian Songbook 1997, Cecilia Bartoli – Live Vivaldi Album 1999, Cecilia & Bryn, Turco in Italia, Mitridate, Rinaldo, Armida in Italy. *Honours:* Chevalier, Ordre des Arts et des Lettres; two Grammy Awards for Best Classical Vocal Album 1994, Deutsche Schallplatten Preis, La Stella d'Oro, Italy, Caecilia Award, Belgium, Diapason d'Or, France, Best Opera Recording of the Year for La Cenerentola, Japan, Classical BRIT award for best female artist 2004. *Current Management:* MusicArt Management AG, PO Box 123, 8702 Zollikon-Zurich, Switzerland.

BARTOLI, Sandro Ivo; concert pianist; b. 10 Feb. 1970, Pisa, Italy. *Education:* Florence State Conservatory, 1991; RAM, London, 1993; studied privately with Shura Cherkassky, London, 1994. *Career:* debut, Mozart's Concerto K 271 at The Imperial Theatre, San Remo, 1991; perfomed Respighi Toccata for piano and orchestra, BYCO (BBC recording debut); Bach Double Concertos with Alex Kelly at the Basilica di San Giovanni, Lucca, 1993; Mozart Concertos K 413, 414, and 415 at St John's, Smith Square, London, 1995; PBS live broadcast debut, Seeger Auditorium, Johnson City, TN, USA, 1995; Beethoven Concerto No. 5 at St James's, Piccadilly, London (BBC live recording), 1996; recitalist at Centre Georges Pompidou, Paris, 1996; performed Mozart concertos at Livorno Festival, 1997; Rachmaninov's Paganini Rhapsody at the Bridgewater Hall, Manchester, 1999; recitalist at Warwick and Leamington Festival, 1999; Troldhallen, Bergen, 2000; Nybrokayen Music Acad., 2000; Brighton Festival, England, 2000; Aix-en-Provence (radio broadcast), 2000; Ogier and Le Masurier International Piano

Festival, Jersey, Channel Islands, 2000; Fairfield Hall, London, 2001; performed Beethoven Concerto No. 5, Nordhausen, Germany, 2001; Shostakovich Concerto No. 1, Stockholm, 2001; performed at the Festival d'Avignon, France, 2001; recitalist, Teatro Carignano, Turin, Italy, 2002; Opera Holland Park, London, 2002; performed Rachmaninov Concerto No. 3, London, 2003; founded, directed and performed at Opera Etcetera, London, 2002. *Recordings:* Malipiero: Piano Music, 1995; Fugitives–Works by Casella, Grainger and Pabst, 1997; Casella: Piano Music, 1998; Opera Etcetera, 2003; Encores, 2003. *Honours:* Mary Elizabeth B'Stard Scholarship 1991–92; Royal Acad. Foundation Scholarship 1991–92; Gina Rosso Prize for Outstanding Work in the Arts, Lyric Club Renato Bruson, Turin, 2002. *Current Management:* Musikarte, Calle Palma 14, 07330 Consell, Islas Baleares, Spain.

BARTOLINI, Lando; Opera Singer (tenor); b. 11 April 1937, Casale di Prato, Florence, Italy; m. Deanna Mungai 1966, 2 d. *Education:* 5-year scholarship to Academy of Vocal Arts, Philadelphia, USA, 1968–73; Vocal instruction with Nicola Moscona; graduated, 1973. *Career:* debut, Iris of Mascagni at the Gran Liceo of Barcelona, Oct 1973; American debut in Cavalleria Rusticana, New York City Opera, 1976; Appeared at special events including: Concert with Philadelphia Orchestra; New Production of Ernani with Chicago Lyric; Manon Lescaut with Vienna State Opera in Tokyo; Simon Boccanegra at Festival d'Orange; New Production of Turandot at Munich State Opera; Turandot with La Scala, Milan; In Seoul during Olympic Games; Has sung in many other major venues around the world including La Scala, Arena di Verona, Paris Opéra, Metropolitan Opera, Covent Garden, Vienna, Budapest, Buenos Aires, Santiago del Chile, South Africa, Canada, Lisbon, Boston and Cleveland with Metropolitan Opera; Wide repertoire includes: Aida, Tosca, La Bohème, Il Trovatore, Don Carlo, Macbeth, Forza del Destino, Il Tabarro, Mephistopheles and Rigoletto; Sang Manrico in Il Trovatore at the Orange Festival, 1992; Radames for Opera Pacific, 1994; Sang Des Grieux in Manon Lescaut at Torre del Lago, 1996; Season 1996 as Radames at the Vienna Staatsoper and Verdi's Alvaro at Antwerp; Andrea Chénier at Monte Carlo, 1998; Season 1999–2000 as Radames at Florence and Puccini's Des Grieux at Catania. *Recordings:* I Cavalieri di Ekebu, with director Gianandrea Gavazzeni; Hungaroton, 1992; Respighi's La Semirama, 1st recording; Hungaroton, 1991 Solo Tenor Arias; Turandot Last Duet Alfano original, first time on record, 1990. *Publications:* La Follia Di New York, 1989; Orpheus Berlin, 1990; Das Opern Glas Germany, 1990; Opera News New York, 1991–93. *Current Management:* ICM Artists, New York. *Address:* Via Bargo 12, 50047 Casale di Prato, Florence, Italy.

BÄRTSCHI, Werner; Swiss pianist and composer; b. 1 Jan. 1950, Zürich, Switzerland; m.; two c. *Education:* Volksschule and Gymnasium Zürich; studied as pianist, composer and conductor in Zürich and Basel. *Career:* concerts in 35 countries on five continents; festival appearances include Yehudi Menuhin-Festival, Gstaad, Lucerne Festival, Zürcher Festspiele, Festival international de piano de la Roque d'Anthéron, Salzburger Festspiele; television appearances in various countries; film actor in Justiz, by Geissendörfer; initiation and realization of the Satie-Saison, 1980–81, and the Ives-Zyklus, 1985–86, both in Zürich; premiered works by John Cage, Klaus Huber, Wilhelm Killmeyer, Terry Riley, Dieter Schnebel, Wladimir Vogel and others; Pres., Music Committee of City of Zürich, 1990–92; Artistic Adviser of 1991 June Festival in Zürich; Artistic Dir of various concert series in Switzerland; performances of his own compositions in over 30 countries; several broadcasts and recordings; mem. Schweizerischer Tonkünstlerverein, Schweizerischer Musikpädagogischer Verband, Komponistensekretariat Zürich. *Compositions:* over 30 works of orchestral music, chamber music, vocal music, piano music; several transcriptions: Rossini, Fauré, Schoeck, Schnebel. *Recordings:* over 30 recordings, including music of over 40 composers; music for 10 films for Swiss television. *Publications:* Die unvermeidliche Musik des John Cage, 1969; Musik der Entfremdung – entfremdete Musik, 1981–82; Ratio und Intuition in der Musik, Kunst und Wissenschaft, 1984; Italian translation, 1989, Zu meinem Klavierstück in Trauer und Prunk, 1989; Leistung und Plausch im Musikunterricht, 1989; German editions of selected writings by Erik Satie, 1980 and Charles Ives, 1985; Music Editions of works by Zdenek Fibich, 1988, and Wladimir Vogel, 1989. *Honours:* Grand Prize, Académie du disque française, 1983. *Address:* Zolliker Strasse 97, 8702 Zollikon, Switzerland. *Telephone:* (52) 6204646 (home). *E-mail:* baertschi.w@rezital.ch (home).

BARTZ, Ingrid; Singer (Mezzo-Soprano); b. 20 March 1964, Aachen, Germany. *Education:* Studied in Cologne and Berne with Juliette Bise-Delnon, Edith Mathis and Brigitte Fassbaender. *Career:* Sang at Aachen Opera, from 1982, including Britten's Hermia; Opera-studio at Düsseldorf Opera, with Hänsel, 1986–87; Karlsruhe Opera, as Cherubino, Octavian, the Composer in Ariadne auf Naxos, Suzuki, Flora, Rosina, Mignon and Sesto in Handel's Giulio Cesare, from 1988; Guest appearances include major roles at Düsseldorf, Liège, Luxembourg, Strasbourg, Zürich, Lucerne, Frankfurt, Mannheim, Essen,

Vienna; Concert engagements with most German radio and television stations and abroad; Bonn Opera, 1993–, including several premieres and debuts: Nicklausse, Zerlina, Orlofsky, Fenena, from 1993; Bavarian State Opera Munich: since 1999, guest appearances; Season 1999–2000 as Suzuki in Butterfly at the Eutin Festival, Wellgunde in Götterdämmerung at Bonn and Ludmilla in The Bartered Bride for the Munich Staatsoper. *Recordings include:* Lieder by Mahler (Rückert and Wunderhorn Lieder), Brahms (Zigeunerlieder) and Wagner (Wesendoncklieder); Die Walküre, from Munich, 2002 (CD and DVD). *Address:* c/o NWB Apollon & Hermes, PR-Arts-Media Services Production, Im Flögerhof 12, 53819 Neunkirchen, Cologne, Germany.

BARYLLI, Walter; Violinist; b. 16 June 1921, Vienna, Austria. *Education:* Vienna Hochschule; Violin study with F von Reuter, Munich. *Career:* Debut: Munich, 1936; Concert tours throughout Europe and overseas; Member, Vienna State Opera Orchestra and Vienna Philharmonic, 1938–; Formerly, leader of both orchestras; Leader Barylli Quartet, 1945–; Professor of Violin, Vienna Conservatory, 1969–. *Honours:* Kreisler Prize (twice won). *Address:* Rennweg 4-14, 1030 Vienna, Austria.

BARZUN, Jacques Martin, AB, PhD, FRSA, FRSL; American writer and academic; *Professor Emeritus, Columbia University*; b. 30 Nov. 1907, Créteil, France; s. of Henri Martin and Anna-Rose Barzun; m. 1st Mariana Lowell 1936 (died 1979); two s. one d.; m. 2nd Marguerite Lee Davenport 1980. *Education:* Lycée Janson de Sailly and Columbia Univ. *Career:* Instructor in History, Columbia Univ. 1929, Asst Prof. 1938, Assoc. Prof. 1942, Prof. 1945, Dean of Graduate Faculties 1955–58, Dean of Faculties and Provost 1958–67, Seth Low Prof. 1960–67, Univ. Prof. 1967–75; Prof. Emer. 1975–; Literary Adviser, Scribner's 1975–93; fmr Dir Council for Basic Educ., New York Soc. Library, Open Court Publications Inc., Peabody Inst.; mem. Advisory Council, Univ. Coll. at Buckingham, Editorial Bd Encyclopedia Britannica 1979–; mem. Acad. Delphinale (Grenoble), American Acad. and Inst. of Arts and Letters (Pres. 1972–75, 1977–78), American Historical Asscn, Royal Soc. of Arts, American Arbitration Asscn, American Philosophical Soc., Royal Soc. of Literature, American Acad. of Arts and Sciences; Extraordinary Fellow, Churchill Coll., Cambridge 1961. *Publications:* The French Race: Theories of its Origins and their Social and Political Implications Prior to the Revolution 1932, Race: A Study in Modern Superstition 1937, Of Human Freedom 1939, Darwin, Marx, Wagner: Critique of a Heritage 1941, Romanticism and the Modern Ego (revised edn as Classic, Romantic, and Modern) 1943, Introduction to Naval History (with Paul H. Beik, George Crothers and E. O. Golob) 1944, Teacher in America 1945, Berlioz and the Romantic Century 1950, God's Country and Mine: A Declaration of Love Spiced with a Few Harsh Words 1954, Music in American Life 1956, The Energies of Art: Studies of Authors, Classic and Modern 1956, The Modern Researcher (with Henry F. Graff) 1957, Lincoln the Literary Genius 1959, The House of Intellect 1959, Science, the Glorious Entertainment 1964, The American University: How it Runs, Where it is Going 1968, On Writing, Editing and Publishing: Essays Explicative and Horatory 1971, A Catalogue of Crime (with Wendell Hertig Taylor) 1971, The Use and Abuse of Art 1974, Clio and the Doctors: Psycho-History, Quanto-History and History 1974, Simple and Direct: A Rhetoric for Writers 1975, Critical Questions 1982, A Stroll with William James 1983, A Word or Two Before You Go 1986, The Culture We Deserve 1989, Begin Here: On Teaching and Learning 1990, An Essay on French Verse for Readers of English Poetry 1991, From Dawn to Decadence: 500 Years of Western Cultural Life 2000, A Jacques Barzun Reader 2001; editor: Pleasures of Music 1950, The Selected Letters of Lord Byron 1953, New Letters of Berlioz (also trans.) 1954, The Selected Writings of John Jay Chapman 1957, Modern American Usage; translator: Diderot: Rameau's Nephew 1952, Flaubert's Dictionary of Accepted Ideas 1954, Evenings with the Orchestra 1956, Courteline: A Rule is a Rule 1960, Beaumarchais: The Marriage of Figaro 1961; contrib. articles to various scholarly and non-scholarly periodicals and journals. *Honours:* Chevalier Légion d'honneur, Presidential Medal of Freedom 2004. *Address:* 18 Wolfeton Way, San Antonio, TX 78218, USA.

BASELT, Franz (Bernhard); Professor of Musicology; b. 13 Sept. 1934, Halle, Saale, Germany; m. Elfried Kalisch, 3 Oct 1962, 1 s., 1 d. *Education:* Abitur, 1953; Hochschule für Musik Halle; Martin-Luther-Universität Halle, Dipl phil, 1958; Dr Phil, 1963; Dr sc phil, 1975. *Career:* Freeland, 1958–59; Assistant Professor, 1959–76; Professor of Musicology, 1977–82; Full Professor of Musicology, 1983; Chief Editor, Hallische Händel-Ausgabe, 1989; University Halle-Wittenburg; President, Georg-Friedrich-Händel-Gesellschaft, 1991; Editor, Händel-Jahrbuch, 1991. *Publications:* Händel-Handbuch vol. I–III, 1978–86; G. F. Händel, Leipzig, 1988; Editions of operas by G. P. Telemann, C. W. Gluck, G. F. Händel, 1967, 1969, 1970, 1988; Editions of Händel's Oreste, Kassel 1991; Telemann's Don Quixote, Madison, 1991. *Contributions:* Händel-Jahrbuch; Musical Times; Veroff der Intern; Händel-

Akademie Karlsruhe; Music and Letters. *Address:* Reilstrasse 83, 04020, Halle, Saale, Germany.

BASHFORD, Christina, BA, MMus, PhD, CertTHE; Musicologist and Lecturer; b. 20 Dec. 1961, Penryn, Cornwall; m. John Wagstaff. *Education:* King's Coll. London, Wadham Coll., Oxford. *Career:* Man. Ed., New Grove Dictionary of Opera 1988–92; Lecturer then Senior Lecturer, Oxford Brookes Univ. 1994–; mem. Royal Musical Asscn, British Assn of Victorian Studies. *Publications:* Music and British Culture 1785–1914: Essays in Honour of Cyril Ehrlich (ed. with Leanne Langley) 2000; contrib. to The New Grove Dictionary of Music and Musicians 2001. *Honours:* Jack Westrup Prize (Music and Letters) 1991. *Address:* Oxford Brookes University, Headington, Oxford, OX3 0BP, England (office). *Telephone:* (1865) 484985 (office). *E-mail:* cmbashford@brookes.ac.uk (office).

BASHMET, Yuri Abramovich; Russian musician (viola) and conductor; b. 24 Jan. 1953, Rostov-on-Don; m. Natalia Bashmet; one d. *Education:* Moscow State Conservatory. *Career:* concerts since 1975; gave recitals and played with maj. orchestras of Europe, America and Asia; played in chamber ensembles with Sviatoslav Richter, Vladimir Spivakov, Victor Tretyakov and others; restored chamber repertoire for viola, commissioned and was first performer of music by contemporary composers, including concertos by Alfred Schnittke, Giya Kancheli, Aleksander Tchaikovsky; first viola player to give solo recitals at leading concert halls including Tchaikovsky Hall, Moscow, Concertgebouw, Amsterdam, La Scala, Milan, Suntory Hall, Tokyo; Founder and Artistic Dir Chamber Orchestra Soloists of Moscow 1989–; Artistic Dir and Chief Conductor Young Russian Symphony Orchestra 2002–; f. Yuri Bashmet Int. Competition for Young Viola Players 1994–; Artistic Dir Dec. Nights Festival, Moscow 1998–; Founder and Artistic Dir Elba Music Festival 1998–; f. Yu. Bashmet Viola Competition, Moscow 1999–; f. Int. Foundation to award Shostakovich Prize annually. *Honours:* prize winner of int. competitions in Budapest 1975, Munich 1976; People's Artist of Russia 1986, State Prize of Russia 1993, Sonning Prize (Denmark) 1995. *Current Management:* ICM Artists Ltd, 40 West 57th Street, New York, NY 10019, USA. *Telephone:* (095) 561-66-96. *Address:* Briyusov per. 7, Apt. 16, 103009 Moscow, Russia (home). *Telephone:* (095) 229-73-25 (home).

BASS, Alexandra, ARCM, GRSM, PGCE; Flautist and Musician; b. 15 Dec. 1962, Funtington, England; m. Sebastian Toke-Nichols; one d. *Education:* Royal College of Music, 1980–84; Homerton College, Cambridge, 1984–85; Conservatoire Hector Berlioz and Ecole Normale, Paris, 1986–87; Guildhall School of Music and Drama 1999–2000. *Career:* led 1986 expedition to Peru and Bolivia to study the indigenous music of the Indians; orchestral player in BBC Symphony Orchestra, London Philharmonic Orchestra, Royal Philharmonic Orchestra, Liverpool Philharmonic, Hallé, and the orchestra of the Royal Opera House, Covent Garden; soloist and chamber music player; mem. Incorporated Society of Musicians, Musicians' Union. *Recordings:* Humoresque (Alibas flute and guitar duo), 2003. *Honours:* Chamber Music Prize, Royal College of Music, 1980; Prix Supérieur, Hector Berlioz Conservatoire, 1987. *Current Management:* Neil Chaffey Concert Promotions, 9 Munts Meadow, Weston, Herts SG4 7AE, England. *Website:* www.alibas.co.uk (home).

BASSETT, Leslie Raymond, BA, MMus, AMusD; composer; b. 22 Jan. 1923, Hanford, CA, USA; m. Anita Denniston 1949; two s. one d. *Education:* Fresno State College (now California State University, Fresno), University of Michigan, Ecole Normale de Musique, Paris, studied with Ross Lee Finney, Nadia Boulanger, Arthur Honegger, Roberto Gerhard. *Career:* Henry Russel Lecturer, Univ. of Michigan 1984; Albert A. Stanley Distinguished Univ. Prof. of Music Emeritus; mem. American Acad. of Arts and Letters. *Compositions:* Variations for Orchestra; Echoes from an Invisible World, orchestra; Concerto for Orchestra, 1991; From a Source Evolving, orchestra; Concerto Lirico, trombone and orchestra; Fantasy for Clarinet and Wind Ensemble; Sounds, Shapes and Symbols, band; Colors and Contours, band; Thoughts that Sing, Breathe and Burn for orchestra, 1995; Trio-Inventions for 3 cellos, 1996; Sextet for Piano and Strings; Fourth String Quartet, 1978; Arias for Clarinet and Piano; Dialogues for Oboe and Piano; Narratives for Guitar Quartet. *Honours:* Pulitzer Prize for Variations for orchestra, 1966; Rome Prize, American Academy in Rome, 1961–63; Koussevitsky Foundation Commissions, 1971, 1990; Guggenheim Fellow, 1973, 1980; Naumberg Recording Award, 1974; Distinguished Artist Award, State of Michigan, 1981. *Address:* 1618 Harbal Drive, Ann Arbor, MI 48105, USA.

BASTIAN, Hanns; Singer (Tenor); b. 30 Jan. 1928, Pforzheim, Germany. *Education:* Studied in Karlsruhe with Karl Hartlieb and in Coburg and Pforzheim. *Career:* Sang first in Pforzheim, 1946–53, then at Coburg; Engaged at Basel Opera, 1955–80, notably in premiere of Titus Feuerfuchs by Sutermeister, 1966, and in buffo and character roles; Guest appearances in Zürich, Berne, Darmstadt and Bregenz. Other roles included Florestan, Mozart's Pedrillo and Monostatos, David in Die Meistersinger, and many parts in operetta. *Address:* c/o Theater Basel, Theaterstrasse 7, 4010 Basel, Switzerland.

BATCHVAROVA, Vania (Petrova); Bulgarian opera director; *Associate Professor and Opera Stage Director, Cukurova University, State Conservatory, Adana, Turkey;* b. 22 May 1950, Pleven; m. Rusko Russkov 1985. *Education:* Studied Piano, Music High School, Russe, Bulgaria, 1965–69; Music Theory and Pedagogy, Bulgarian Academy of Music, Sofia, 1970–72; Musicology, Martin Luther University, Halle/Saale, Germany, 1972–73; Masters Degree, Opera and Stage Direction, Masters in Music (Piano), Hochschule für Musik 'Hanns Eisler', Berlin, Germany, 1973–78; Teatro alia Scata di Milano (Italy), 1986; St Petersburg (Russia), Simeon Ilitch Lapirov, 1989; Graduate courses in Effective Management, Managing Customer and Client Relations and Accounting for Managers from The Open University, UK, 1993–96; Computer Courses, Voice Pedagogy Courses, Music Semiotic Courses at NBU, Bulgaria, 1992–97. *Career:* Stage Director, Russe Opera House, 1979–82; Associate Professor, Opera Stage Directing and Opera Singing, Bulgarian Academy of Music, Sofia, 1982–97; Dean, Music and Performing Arts Department, New Bulgarian University, Sofia, Associate Professor, Opera Stage Directing and Opera Singing, 1992–98; Principal Stage Director, Plovdiv Opera House, 1996–97; Associate Professor, Cukurova University, State Conservatory, Turkey, 1998–; Directed works include Wagner's Götterdämmerung, Leipzig, 1976; Mussorgsky's Boris Godunov, Russe, 1979; Verdi's Falstaff, Sofia Opera House; Productions and directed works include: Dvořák, Rusalka, Plauen, Germany, 1978; Donizetti, L'Elisir d'amore, Stara Zagora, 1983; Puccini, Madama Butterfly, Sliven, 1986; Verdi, Nabucco, Burgas, 1987; Otto Nicolai's Die Lustige Weiber, Bulgaria, Moldova, Russia, 1989; Donizetti, Lucia di Lammermoor, Russe, 1995; Mozart, Le nozze di Figaro, New Bulgarian University, 1995; Verdi, Il Trovatore, Rigoletto, Nabucco, Plovdiv, Bulgaria, Seville, Spain and Palma de Mallorca, Menorca, 1996, etc.; Established Music Department in NBU and first education programme for opera stage directors in Bulgaria; Performances of children's musicals; performances for students in voice and opera education, Bulgaria (Academy of Music, NBU), Turkey (Cukurova University), guest in Vilnius, Lithuania and Moscow, Russian Fed.; Member of the organizing committee and of the jury of the following competitions in Bulgaria: Sv. Obretenov National Competition for singers and players; International Competition for Young Talented Musicians; G.Zl. Cherkin Natsonal Competition for Singers; Participated in International Festival for the Young 'Euro-art2004' in Bulgaria; Participated in and submitted papers to numerous symposia and international conferences in art, music education and semiotics; Workshops; Television opera productions; Piano and chamber concerts; Numerous radio programmes about opera. *Publications:* Libretto, Bulgarian Roses, musical for children; The Golden Donkey by Apulej, opera; Books: Educating the Singing Actor 1995; A View of Mozart's Philosophy through His Operas, 1997; Requiem for Dried Up Rivers, essays, 1998; The Dramaturgy of Opera, 1999; Contributions: Numerous articles in newspapers and magazines. *Address:* C.U. State Conservatory, 01330 Balcali/Adana, Turkey (office). *Telephone:* (322) 3386264 (office); (322) 2279886 (home); (532) 3011590 (office). *Fax:* (322) 3386265 (office). *E-mail:* vania@cu.edu.tr (office). *Website:* www.cu.edu .tr (office).

BATE, Jennifer Lucy, BA, FRCO, FRSA, LRAM, ARCM; British organist; b. 11 Nov. 1944, London; d. of Horace Alfred Bate and Dorothy Marjorie Bate. *Education:* Univ. of Bristol. *Career:* Shaw Librarian, LSE 1966–69; full-time concert career 1969–; has performed world-wide; has organized several teaching programmes; collaboration with Olivier Messiaen 1975–92; designed portable pipe organ with N. P. Mander Ltd 1984 and a prototype computer organ 1987; gives masterclasses world-wide and lectures on a wide range of musical subjects; mem. Inc. Soc. of Music; British Music Soc., vice-pres., Royal Philharmonic Soc., Royal Soc.. *Compositions:* Toccata on a Theme of Martin Shaw, Introduction and Variations on an Old French Carol, Four Reflections, Homage to 1685: Four Studies, The Spinning Wheel, Lament, An English Canon, Variations on a Gregorian Theme. *Recordings:* Complete Works of Messiaen, Complete Works of Franck, An English Choice, Virtuoso French Organ Music, Panufnik: Metasinfonia, Vivaldi Double and Triple Concertos, Jennifer Bate and Friends, Jennifer Plays Vierne, From Stanley to Wesley on period instruments, Reflections: the organ music of Jennifer Bate. *Television:* South Bank Show on Messiaen, La Nativité du Seigneur (Channel 4). *Publications:* Grove's Dictionary of Music and Musicians, Organist's Review. *Honours:* hon. Italian citizenship for services to music 1996; F.J. Read Prize, Royal Coll. of Organists, Young Musician 1972, voted Personnalité de l'Année, France 1989, one of the Women of the Year, UK 1990–97, Grand Prix du Disque (Messiaen), Diapason d'Or, Prix de Répertoire, France, Preis der deutschen Schallplattenkritik, Germany and MRA Award for 18th century series From Stanley to Wesley. *Address:* c/o PA Mrs Helen Harris, 35 Collingwood Avenue, Muswell Hill, London, N10 3EH,

England. *Telephone:* (20) 8883-3811. *Fax:* (20) 8444-3695. *E-mail:* jenniferbate@classical-artists.com (home). *Website:* www.classical -artists.com/jbate (home). *Current Management:* PVA Management Ltd, Hallow Park, Worcester, WR2 6PG.

BATES, Lucy; Singer (Soprano); b. 1973, Beverly, Yorkshire. *Education:* Royal Northern College of Music, with Sandra Dugdale; Masterclasses with Evelyn Tubb, Nigel Douglas and Robin Bowman. *Career:* Roles with RNCM included Mozart's Papagena and Blondchen, Ophelia, Catherine in La jolie Fille de Perth, Barena in Jenůfa and Sandrina in La finta giardiniera; Yum-Yum in The Mikado and Frasquita for Phoenix Opera, Rossini's Elvira for the Accademia Rossiniana, and Belinda in Dido and Aeneas; Glyndebourne Festival debut 2000, as Barbarina in Le nozze di Figaro. *Honours:* Peter Moores Foundation Scholar; Finalist, Frederic Cox Award Competition, 2000. *Address:* c/o Glyndebourne Festival Centre, Glyndebourne, Lewes, Sussex BN8 5UU, England.

BATIASHVILI, Elisabeth; violinist; b. 1979, Georgia. *Education:* Munich Musikhochschule with Ana Chumachenco, Mark Lubotsky in Hamburg. *Career:* Appearances in Mozart's Sinfonia Concertante K364, with Colin Davis, at Ravinia with the Chicago SO, recitals at the Wigmore Hall and Châtelet, Paris, and with the Cleveland Orchestra at the Blossom Festival; London Proms debut 2000; Further engagements with the City of Birmingham SO, Orchestre de Paris, Melbourne SO, NHK Symphony (Tokyo), Los Angeles PO, Philadelphia Orchestra and St Petersburg PO; engaged for New York Philharmonic (2005); Played Prokofiev's First Concerto with the CBSO at the 2002 London Proms; Philharmonic Orchestra in 2004; Chamber musician with Pierre-Laurent Aimard, Till Fellner, Alban Gerhardt and Steven Osborne. *Recordings include:* Brahms, Schubert and Bach recital (EMI); Brahms Double Concerto, with Alban Gerhardt (BBC Music Magazine). *Honours:* Prizewinner, 1995 Sibelius Competition, Helsinki; Leonard Bernstein Award in Schleswig Holstein, 2003. *Current Management:* Harrison/Parrott Ltd, 12 Penzance Place, London, W11 4PA, England. *Telephone:* (20) 7229 9166. *Fax:* (20) 7221 5042. *Website:* www .harrisonparrott.com.

BATIZ, Enrique; Pianist and Conductor; b. 4 May 1942, Mexico City, Mexico; m. 1965, divorced 1982, 1 s., 1 d. *Education:* Bachelor's Degree, Mexico University Centre, 1959; Southern Methodist University, Dallas, USA, 1960–62; Juilliard School of Music, New York, studied piano with Adele Marcus; Conducting with Jorge Mester, 1963–66; Postgraduate work, Warsaw Conservatory. *Career:* Debut: Mexico City, 1969; Founder-Conductor, Orquesta Sinfónica del Estado de México, 1971–73, 1990–; Appointed Guest Conductor, Royal Philharmonic Orchestra, London, England, 1984–; Guest Conductor with 150 orchestras world-wide; Conductor, Royal Philharmonic Orchestra tour in Mexico, 1988; mem, IAPA; Club de Clubes; Club Cambridge, Mexico City. *Compositions:* Es Tiempo de Paz, symphonic poem, 1976. *Recordings include:* Over 150 recordings including 41 with the Royal Philharmonic, 29 with the Orquesta Sinfónica del Estado de México and 19 with the Mexico City Philharmonic Orchestra. *Contributions:* Joaquin Rodrigo, His Life, in Epoca, 1993. *Current Management:* Mrs C A Ross, 6 Petersfield Crescent, Coulsdon, Surrey CR5 2JQ, England. *Address:* Plaza Fray Andres de Castro, Edif. 'C', Primer Piso, Toluca, Estado de Mexico CP 5000, Mexico.

BATJER, Margaret; Violinist; b. 17 Feb. 1959, San Angelo, TX, USA; m. Joel McNeely, 14 April 1985. *Education:* Interlochen Academy; Studied with Ivan Galamian and David Cerone at Curtis Institute of Music. *Career:* Debut: Solo appearance in Violin Concerto by Menotti with Chicago Symphony, aged 15; Appeared as Soloist with Philadelphia Orchestra at Academy of Music, with Dallas and Seattle Symphonies in Mendelssohn's Concerto at the St Louis Symphony; Chamber Orchestra of Europe; Prague Chamber Orchestra; Berlin Symphony Orchestra; New York String Orchestra at Carnegie Hall; Radio Telefis Dublin, with Prokofiev's 2nd Concerto; Concerts at the Marlboro Music Festival, Vermont and US tour with Music of Marlboro Ensemble; Tour of Germany, 1984. *Recordings:* Bach Concerto for Two Violins with Salvatore Accardo and the Chamber Orchestra of Europe; Mozart Concertone with Salvatore Accardo and the Prague Chamber Orchestra; Verdi and Borodin String Quartets, Mozart Complete Viola Quintets. *Honours:* Winner, G B Dealey Competition, Dallas, 1979. *Current Management:* Del Rosenfield Associates, 714 Ladd Road, Bronx, NY 10471, USA. *Address:* 5971 Lubao Ave, Woodland Hills, CA 91367, USA.

BATTEL, Giovanni (Umberto); Pianist; b. 11 Dec. 1956, Portoguaro, Venice, Italy; m. Mariangela Zamper, 15 June 1985. *Education:* Liceo in Classical Studies, 1975; Conservatory Tartini, Trieste, 1977; National Music Academy St Cecilia, Rome, 1984; Degree in Musicology, Bologna University. *Career:* S Remo Theatre, 1980; RAI Radio 3, 1981; Stresa Festival, 1981; With symphony orchestra, Auditorium RAI Rome, 1982; RAI 1, 1982, 1983, 1984; Alghero Festival, 1983; Mater Festival, 1983; Trondheim Symphony Orchestra, 1983; With Scarlatti Orchestra,

Auditorium RAI Naples, 1983; Trieste Theatre, 1985; Auditorium Cagliari, 1985; Musik Halle Hamburg, 1986; Lubeck, Bonn, 1986; Athens, Salonika, Greece, 1986; San Francisco, Los Angeles, USA; Paris, Nantes, Lille, France, 1987; Todi Festival, 1988; London, 1988; Director, Conservatory of Music 'Benedetto Marcello' in Venice; Artistic Director of piano competitions and of musical associations. *Recordings:* Miroirs and Valses Nobles et Sentimentales, Ravel; Busoni's Piano Concerto; E. Wolf-Ferrari, Piano Trios Op. 5 and Op. 7. *Honours:* 1st prize, national competitions: La Spezia, 1975; Trieste, 1978; Taranto, 1979; Albenga, 1979; International competition: 2nd prize, Vercelli, 1978; 2nd prize, Seregno, 1979; 4th prize, Bolzano, 1980; 1st prize, Enna, 1982. *Address:* Via Baratta Vecchia 253, 31022 Preganziol, Treviso, Italy.

BATTERHAM, Andrew (Bruce); Composer and Musician; b. 22 July 1968, Melbourne, Australia; m., 1 s., 2 d. *Education:* Bachelor of music, composition, University of Melbourne. *Career:* National Music Camp, Sydney, 1987, 1988; Australian Composers Orchestral Forum, 1997; Queensland Philharmonic, 1995; Perihelion, 1997; Tasmanian Symphony, 1997; Eliseon, 1988; Melbourne Symphony, 1999; Australian Chamber Orchestra, 1999; Melbourne Symphony, 2000, 2002; Member, Australian Performing Right Association; Musicians and Arrangers Guild of Australia; Melbourne Composer's League; Australian Music Centre, Sydney. *Compositions:* Thugine Legend; Cortege; Symphony No. 1, Off The Leash; Chiaroscuro; Organ Sonata; Maniacs and Broken Glass; Drum and Bass; The End of All Journeys, 2000. *Recordings include:* Melbourne Composers' League, 2000. *Honours:* Quantas Youth Award, 1994; Corbould Composition competition winner, 1995; Short-listed for Albert H Maggs Award (Commendation), 1999. *Address:* 26 Rosslyn Street, Blackburn, Melbourne, Australia, 3130.

BATTLE, Kathleen (Deanna); Singer (Soprano); b. 13 Aug. 1948, Portsmouth, Ohio, USA. *Education:* BMus, 1970; MMus 1971, University of Cincinnati-College Conservatory of Music; Studied with Franklin Bens and Italo Tajo. *Career:* Debut: Professional debut, soloist, Brahms Requiem, Spoleto Festival, 1972; Operatic debut as Rosina, Michigan Opera Theatre, Detroit, 1975; Metropolitan Opera, NY, 1978–1994; British debut at Glyndebourne, 1979, as Nerina in Haydn's La Fedeltà Premiata; Appearances with many other major opera houses of the world, including Covent Garden, debut 1985 as Zerbinetta in Ariadne auf Naxos; Soloist with leading orchestras; Recitalist at various music centres; Operatic roles include Susanna, Cleopatra, Zerbinetta, Sophie, Adina, Zerlina, Blonde, Nannetta and Despina; Sang Norina in Don Pasquale at Covent Garden, London, 1990; Contract at NY Met terminated, 1994; Career has centred on concert work from 1994. *Recordings:* For Deutsche Grammophon, Angel-EMI, Decca-London, Musicmasters, RCA and Telarc; In Mozart's Requiem, Così fan tutte, Coronation Mass, Don Giovanni and Die Zauberflöte; L'Italiana in Algeri; Ein Deutsches Requiem; Mahler 4th Symphony; Il Barbiere di Siviglia, Abbado; Handel Arias, Marriner; Semele; Videos of Il Barbiere di Siviglia and Die Zauberflöte from the Metropolitan, DGG. *Address:* c/o Columbia Artists Managements Inc, 165 West 57th Street, NY 10019, USA.

BATURIN, Sergei; Violinist; b. 1952, Moscow, Russia. *Education:* Studied at Moscow Conservatoire with Fjodor Druzhinin. *Career:* Co-founded Amistad Quartet, 1973, changed named to Tchaikovsky Quartet in 1994; Many concerts in former Soviet Union and Russia, with repertoire including works by Haydn, Mozart, Beethoven, Schubert, Brahms, Tchaikovsky, Borodin, Prokofiev, Shostakovich, Bartók, Bucci, Golovin and Tikhomirov; recent concert tours to Mexico, Italy and Germany; Series in commemoration of Tchaikovsky in Moscow. *Recordings:* Recitals for US-Russian company Arts and Electronics; By Tchaikovsky Quartet. *Honours:* With Amistad Quartet: Prizewinner at Béla Bartók Festival, 1976 and Bucchi Competition, Rome, 1990. *Current Management:* Sonata, Glasgow, Scotland. *Address:* 11 North Park Street, Glasgow G20 7AA, Scotland.

BAUDO, Serge; Conductor; b. 16 July 1927, Marseille, France; m. Madelein Reties, 16 June 1947, 1 s., 1 d. *Education:* Student, Conservatory of Paris. *Career:* Director, Radio Nice, France, 1957–59; Conductor, Paris Orchestra, 1968–70; Music Director, Opéra de Lyon, 1969–71; Music Director, Orchestra of Lyon, 1971–; Conductor of many international Orchestras including Tonhalle Orchestra, Zürich, Orchestre de la Suisse Romande, Berlin Philharmonic, Royal Philharmonic, London Philharmonic, NHR Orchestra, Leningrad Philharmonic, Stockholm Philharmonic, La Scala, Metropolitan Opera (debut 1970 Les Contes d'Hoffmann), Dallas Orchestra and Deutsche Oper, Berlin; Has conducted premieres of Messiaen's Et expecto at Chartres, 1965, and La Transfiguration at Lisbon, 1969; Milhaud's La Mère Coupable, Geneva, 1966; Dutilleux's Cello Concerto, Aix, 1970; Fastes de l'imaginaire by Nigg, 1974; Ohana's Le Livre des Prodiges, 1979; Daniel-Leseur's Dialogues dans le nuit, 1988; Founder, Berlioz Festival, Lyon, 1979; Conducted Roméo et Juliette at Zürich, 1990; Samson et Dalila at Zürich, 1996. *Honours:* Decorated, Chevalier Ordre National du Merité; Officer des Arts et des Lettres; Recipient, Grand Prix due Disque, 1976; Chevalier de la Légion d'Honneur Disque d'Or. *Address:* Orchestre National de Lyon, Hotel de Ville, 69000 Lyon, France.

BAUER, Hartmut; Singer (Bass); b. 1939, Kassel, Germany. *Education:* Studied at the Frankfurt Musikhochschule. *Career:* Sang at Augsburg Opera, 1965–68, Coburg, 1968–70, Wuppertal from 1970–90, notably as Creon in the 1972 German premiere of Milhaud's *Médée;* Bayreuth Festival, 1973–75, as Fafner and Hans Schwarz; Other appearances as Ariodeno in Cavalli's L'Ormindo, Mozart's Bartolo and Commendatore, Ramphis (Aida), Colline (La Bohème), Pimen, Schigolch (Lulu) and Cornelius' Abu Hassan; Guest at Cologne, Frankfurt, Barcelona and Hannover; Sang in the premiere of V D Kirchner's Erinys, Wuppertal, 1990; Gurnemanz in Parsifal, 1994; Season 1999 as Rocco in Fidelio at Eutin, Sarastro and Baron Ochs at Gelsenkirchen. *Address:* c/o Musiktheater im Revier, Kennedyplatz, pf 101854, 4650 Gelsenkirchen, Germany.

BAULD, Alison (Margaret); Composer; b. 7 May 1944, Sydney, New South Wales, Australia; m. Nicholas Evans, 4 April 1978, 1 s., 1 d. *Education:* Diploma, National Institute of Dramatic Art, Sydney; BMus, Sydney University; Composition Studies with Elisabeth Lutyens and Hans Keller; DPhil, York University, 1974; Studied Piano with Sverjensky, New South Wales Conservatorium. *Career:* Professional Actress, Shakespeare and Australian Television; Finalist, Radcliffe Competition, 1973; Musical Director, Laban Centre for Dance, Goldsmiths' College, University of London, 1975–78; Composer-in-Residence, New South Wales Conservatory, Sydney, 1978; Teaches part-time for University of Delaware, Hollins College and Pepperdine University, London; Works performed and broadcast, London, also Aldeburgh, York and Edinburgh Festivals, several European countries, Australia; mem, Association of Professional Composers; Musician's Union. *Compositions include:* On the Afternoon of the Pigsty for speaker and ensemble, 1971; Humpty Dumpty for tenor, flute and guitar, 1972; In a Dead Brown Land, music theatre, 1972; Mad Moll for solo soprano, 1973; Dear Emily, for soprano and harp, 1973; One Pearl for soprano and string quartet, 1973; Concert for piano and tape, 1974; Exiles, music theatre, 1974; Van Diemen's Land for choir, 1976; One Pearl II for soprano, flute and strings, 1976; I Loved Miss Watson for soprano, piano and tape, 1977; Banquo's Buried for soprano and piano, 1982; Richard III for voice and string quartet, 1985; Monody for solo flute, 1985; Copy Cats for violin and piano, 1985; Once Upon a Time, music theatre, 1986; Nell, Ballad opera, 1988; My Own Island for clarinet and piano, 1989; Farewell Already for string quartet, 1993; In Memoriam Uncle Ken for baritone and piano, 1997; Shakespeare Songs. *Recordings include:* Banquo's Buried; Farewell Already, string quartet and soprano. *Publications:* Play Your Way, piano and composition tutor, 1993; Shakespeare Songs for soprano and piano; Novel, Mozart's Sisters, 1997. *Honours:* Gold Medal, Piano, New South Wales, 1959; Paris Rostrum, composition, 1973. *Address:* 7 Suffolk Road, Barnes, London SW13, England.

BAUMANN, Ludwig; Singer (Baritone); b. 9 Nov. 1950, Rosenheim, Germany. *Education:* Studied in Munich, USA and Italy. *Career:* Sang bass roles at the Munich State Opera, 1970–72 including the premiere of Sim Tjong by Isang Yun; Baritone at the Coburg Opera, 1972–79 with many concerts elsewhere; Theater am Gärtnerplatz, Munich, 1979–85; Cologne Opera from 1985 with guest appearances at Lausanne, Valentin in Faust, 1986; Paris Châtelet, Gluck's Oreste, 1988; Turin, Hamlet by Thomas; Sang Kurwenal in Tristan, at Marseilles, 1992; Wolfram in Tannhäuser at Naples, 1998; Other roles include Rameau's Thesée, Opéra Comique, Paris; Rossini's Figaro at Nancy; Mozart's Papageno and Guglielmo. *Recordings:* La Bohème; Strauss's Daphne. *Address:* c/o Teatro San Carlo di Napoli, Via San Carlo, 80132 Naples, Italy.

BAUMEL, Herbert, DipMus; American violinist, conductor and composer; b. 30 Sept. 1919, New York, NY; m. 1st Rachael Bail 1949 (divorced 1970); one s. two d. (one deceased); m. 2nd Joan Patricia French 1971. *Education:* studied violin with Louis Persinger, Nathan Milstein; Mannes School of Music, Curtis Institute of Music, Santa Cecilia, Accademia Chigiana, Rome and Siena. *Career:* violinist, Concertmaster, Conductor, orchestras, chamber groups, Broadway shows, jazz ensembles, ballets, operas, world-wide, 1939–; Violin Soloist: Samuel Barber Violin Concerto, Curtis Symphony, Philadelphia Orchestra, 1939–40; New York City Ballet, Fort Wayne Philharmonic, WQXR Orchestra, Radio Italiana, Radio Nacional Venezuela, 1945–; 1st Violin, Philadelphia Orchestra, 1942–45; Member, Baumel-Booth Duo, 1968–; Baumel-Booth-Smith Trio, 1969–72; Violinist and Storyteller, 1969–; Concertmaster: Philadelphia, New York City and San Carlo Operas, Orquesta Sinfonica Venezuela, Broadway musicals including Fiorello, 1959, She Loves Me, 1963, Fiddler on the Roof, 1964, A Little Night Music, 1973; Presidential Gala Orchestra, Washington DC and New York, 1961–65; Conductor: Fort Wayne Civic and Corvallis Symphonies, Chamber Music Associates Orchestra, Alessandro Scarlatti Orchestra (Naples),

Oregon State University Chamber Players, 1945–; Commentator on National Public Radio's All Things Considered, 1999–. *Recordings include:* Selections from Fiddler on the Roof 2000. *Address:* Baumel Associates, 86 Rosedale Road, Yonkers, NY 10710, USA.

BAVERSTAM, Asa; Singer (Soprano); b. 1958, Sweden. *Education:* Studied at the Conservatory of Jutland in Århus, Denmark and at the Royal Opera Academy, Copenhagen. *Career:* Debut: Royal Opera in Copenhagen, 1990, as Despina; Has performed Susanna and Sophie in Der Rosenkavalier with the Opera Academy; Sang in the premiere of Life is a Bed of Roses by Arne Melinas, 1989; Theater Basel from 1990 as Xenia in Boris Godunov, Adina; Zerlina (1992); Has sung in masses and oratorios by Bach, Haydn, Handel, Mozart and Schubert in Denmark and Sweden; Concerts with the baroque orchestra La Stravaganza and as a member of the renaissance quartet Ensemble Charneyron; Season 2000 in Die schweigsame Frau, by Strauss, at Århus. *Honours:* Fourth round, Cardiff Singer of the World Competition, 1989. *Address:* Kaye Artists Management Ltd, Barratt House, 7 Chertsey Road, Woking, Surrey GU21 5 AB, England.

BAVICCHI, John (Alexander); Composer, Conductor and Teacher; b. 25 April 1922, Boston, Massachusetts, USA. *Education:* Studied Business Engineering and Administration, Massachusetts Institute of Technology, 1940–42; Civil Engineering, Newark College of Engineering, 1942–43; Cornell University, 1943; BM, New England Conservatory of Music, 1952; Studied composition with Carl McKinley, Francis Judd Cooke, Harvard University Graduate School, 1952–55; Theory with Archibald T Davison; Composition with Walter Piston; Musicology with Otto Gombosi. *Career:* Many teaching positions including: South End Music School, 1950–64; Boston Center for Adult Education, 1952–55; Cape Cod Conservatory of Music, 1956–58; Cambridge Center for Adult Education, 1960–73; Professor, Composition, Berklee College of Music, 1964–; Various conducting positions including: American Festival Ballet Company, 1962–65; Arlington Philharmonic Orchestra, 1968–82. *Compositions:* Orchestral: Concerto for clarinet and string orchestra, 1954; Suite No. 1, 1955; A Concert Overture, 1957; Fantasy for harp and chamber orchestra, 1959; Concertante for oboe, bassoon and string orchestra, 1961; Fantasia on Korean Folk Tunes, 1966; Caroline's Dance, 1974–75; Mont Blanc, overture, 1976–77; Music for small orchestra, 1981; Fusions for trombone and orchestra, 1984–85; Pyramid, 1986; Canto I for string orchestra, 1987; Songs of Remembrance, 1990; Quintet for Clarinet and String Quartet, 1995; Band: Summer Incident, 1959; Suite No. 2, 1961; Festival Symphony, 1965; JDC March, 1967; Spring Festival Overture, 1968; Suite No. 3, 1969; Concertante No. 2, 1972–75; Band of the Year, 1975; Symphony No. 2, 1975–77; Fantasy, 1979; Concord Bridge, 1982–83; Concerto for clarinet and wind ensemble, 1984; Large Ensemble: Suite No. 2 for clarinet ensemble, 1961; Fireworks, 1962; Music for mallets and percussion, 1967; Ceremonial Music, 1978–82; Concerto for 2 pianos and percussion, 1985; Concerto for Tuba and concert Band, 1988; Chamber Music; Piano Pieces; Organ Music; Choruses; Solo Songs. *Honours:* Award, National Institute of Arts and Letters, 1959; Featured composer, Cardiff Festival, Wales, 1981. *Address:* 26 Hartford Street, Newton, MA 02461, USA.

BAVOUZET, Jean-Efflam; concert pianist; b. 1962, France. *Education:* Paris Conservatoire with Pierre Sancan; masterclasses with Paul Badura-Skoda, Nikita Magaloff, Menahem Pressler, György Sandor. *Career:* Recitals in major concert halls world-wide, including the Kennedy Center, Lincoln Center, Kaufmann Hall, New York and the Salle Gaveau, Paris; Tours of Japan and USA; British engagements from 1987; Has appeared as concerto soloist with such conductors as Marek Janowski, Andrew Litton, Jorge Meste and Michel Plasson; Engagements in Germany, Netherlands, Japan, France and USA; Ravel's Left Hand Concerto with the Solingen Philharmonica and the Bournemouth Symphony, 1991; Has performed with many leading international orchestras including Gurzenich Orchestra of Cologne, Bournemouth Symphony, Hallé Orchestra, Manchester, Weimar Staatskapelle, Hong Kong Philharmonic, Calgary Philharmonic, Utah Symphony, Hungarian National Philharmonic and Symphony Nat. de Belgique; Debut with the Boston Symphony Orchestra under Ingo Metzmacher, 2002; Berliner Sinfonie Orchester under Jean-Claude Casadesus and Orchestre de Paris under Pierre Boulez, 2003; Season 2004–05 Appearances with London Symphony Orchestra; Concerto repertoire includes all the concerti of Bartók, Beethoven and Prokofiev, complete solo piano works of Ravel and Schumann. *Recordings:* Haydn 4 Sonatas and Fantaisie; Ravel's complete solo works for piano, MDG; Haydn and Schumann recitals for Harmonic Records; Debussy Etudes and an all-Chopin CD for Pony Canyon Classics. *Contributions:* Interview with Zoltan Kocsis for Le Monde de la Musique. *Honours:* Finalist at the 1987 Leeds International Competition; Prizewinner at the Young Concert Artists Competition, 1986, USA; Tomassoni-Beethoven Cologne, 1986; Special Jury Prize, Santander, Spain; Guilde Française des Artistes Solistes; First Prize, Paris Conservatoire, for Piano and Chamber Music; Chamber Music Prize, 1989; 'Choc' Award from Le Monde de la musique for Ravel complete solo works for piano and Haydn recordings; Diapason d'or for Ravel complete solo works for piano. *Current Management:* Robert Gilder & Co., Enterprise House, 59–65 Upper Ground, London, SE1 9PQ, England. *Telephone:* (20) 7928-9008. *Fax:* (20) 7928-9755. *E-mail:* rgilder@robert-gilder.com.

BAWDEN, Rupert; Composer, Conductor and Violinist; b. 1958, London. *Education:* Studied at Cambridge University with Robin Holloway. *Career:* Debut: Conductor at the 1986 Aldeburgh Festival; Plays violin and viola with various ensembles, including London Sinfonietta and the English Concert; Performances of works by Birtwistle, Goehr, Harvey, Weir and Hoyland, including several world premieres; Television recordings of works by Gruber, Holloway and Kagel; Michael Nyman's The Man who Mistook his Wife for a Hat for BBC radio; Engagements with the Bath, King's Lynn and London International Opera Festivals; BBC Symphony and Scottish Chamber Orchestra; Works have been performed in USA, Australia, Far East, the United Kingdom and France; 1989 performances by the London Sinfonietta and at the Promenade Concerts; Ballet commission from Munich Biennale 1990. *Compositions:* Railings for flute and piano 1980; Three-part Motet for soprano, mezzo, baritone and orchestra 1980; Passamezzo di Battaglia for oboe, horn and harpsichord, 1984; Sunless for ensemble 1984; Seven Songs from the House of Sand for brass quintet 1985; Le Livre de Fauvel for soprano, mezzo and ensemble 1986; The Angel and the Ship of Souls for 19 players 1983–87; Souvenirs de Fauvel for 2 pianos 1987; Dramatic Cantata on the Legend of Apollo and Daphne for violin, cello and 13 players 1989; Ultima Scena, Commissioned by Henry Wood Promenade Concerts 1989; Ballet Le Livre de Fauvel 1990. *Address:* c/o BMI, 79 Harley House, Marylebone Road, London, NW1, England.

BAX, Alessio; Italian pianist; b. 1977, Bari; m. Lucille Chung. *Education:* Bari Conservatory, Chigiana Acad., Siena, Southern Methodist Univ., Dallas with Joaquin Achucarro. *Career:* recitals throughout Europe, USA and Asia; concerts with London Philharmonic, City of Birmingham Symphony, Royal Liverpool Philharmonic, Royal Scottish Symphony Orchestra, Dallas Symphony, Houston Symphony, NHK Symphony, Tokyo Symphony, New Japan Philharmonic; tours of Japan (Suntory and Kioi Hall), Italy, Germany, UK, USA, Israel, Spain; worked with Sir Simon Rattle, Vernon Handley, Petr Altrichter, Owain Arwel Hughes, Sergiu Commissiona, Dmitry Sitkovetsky, Ken-ichiro Kobayashi; festivals include London Int. Piano Series, Bath, Harrogate, Ruhr Klavier Festivals, Beethoven Fest Bonn, Mecklenburg and the Snape Maltings Proms in Aldeburgh. *Recordings include:* Baroque Reflections, Piano and Organ music by Marcel Dupré, Brahms D minor Concerto with New Japan Philharmonic, Ligeti Two piano and four hands music with Lucille Chung, Beethoven Third Concerto with Hamamatsu SO. *Honours:* winner Hamamatsu Int. Piano Competition 1977, Leeds Int. Pianoforte Competition 2000. *Address:* c/o Warner Classics, 46 Kensington Court, London, W8 5DA, England. *Telephone:* (20) 7938-5632. *Fax:* (20) 7368-4903. *E-mail:* lucy.bright@warnerclassics.com. *Website:* www.alessiobax.com; www.warnerclassics.com.

BAYLEY, Clive; Singer, Bass; b. 15 Nov. 1960, Manchester, England; m. Paula Bradley, 15 July 1989. *Education:* Studied at the Royal Northern College of Music and at the National Opera Studio. *Career:* Debut: With Opera North; Sang in The Rape of Lucretia, Il Barbiere di Siviglia and as Claggart in Billy Budd, while at the RNCM; Professional debut as Schwarz in Die Meistersinger for Opera North, followed by the King in Aida, Colline in La Bohème, Don Basilio, Banquo, Bartolo in Le nozze di Figaro and in British premiere of Verdi's Jerusalem; English National Opera debut 1987, as Pietro in Simon Boccanegra, followed by appearances in Billy Budd, Un ballo in Maschera, Don Giovanni, Doctor Faust and The Return of Ulysses; Netherlands Opera 1989, as Trufaldino in Ariadne auf Naxos; December 1989 in a concert performance of Bernstein's Candide, conducted by the composer; Sang in the premiere of Birtwistle's Gawain at Covent Garden, May 1991; Concert repertoire includes the Verdi Requiem, Elgar's Dream of Gerontius and Apostles, the Brahms Requiem, Handel's Messiah, Israel in Egypt, the Choral Symphony, Rossini's Petite Messe Solennelle and Christus in the St Matthew Passion; Roles at ROH with parts in Fidelio, The Fiery Angel, Die Meistersinger, Colline in La Bohème; Further roles at Opera North include: Sparafucile, The Monk in Don Carlos and Raleigh in Gloriana; Sang Ferrando in Il Trovatore for Opera North, 1994; Mozart's Figaro for Opera North, 1996; Season 1998 as Kecal in The Bartered Bride and Verdi's Grand Inquisitor for the Royal Opera; Season 2000–01 as Debussy's Arkel for ENO, Alvise in La Gioconda for Opera North, Drago in Schumann's Genoveva at Garsington, and as Britten's Collatinus at Lausanne; Weber's Euryanthe at the London Proms, 2002. *Recordings:* Candide, DGG. *Honours:* Curtis Gold Medal for Singing; The Robin Kay Memorial Prize for Opera, RNCM. *Current Management:* Tom Graham, IMG Artists. *Address:* c/o IMG Artists, Lovell House, 616 Chiswick High Road, London W4 5RX, England.

BAYO, Maria; Singer (Soprano); b. 1964, Navarra, Spain. *Career:* Won prizes at the Francisco Vines and Maria Callas Competitions and has appeared from 1998 at Lucerne (Lucia di Lammermoor) and St Gallen (Amina in La Sonnambula); Sang Susanna at Madrid and Marseille (1990), Micaela at Monte Carlo (1991) and Musetta in La Bohème (debut role at La Scala, 1991); Season 1991/92 as Susanna at the Opéra Bastille, Paris, Norina in Don Pasquale at Hamburg, Amenaide in Tancredi at Schwetzingen and Rosina at Strasbourg; Season 1993–94 as Zerlina at Buenos Aires and Ensoleillad in Massenet's Chérubin at Covent Garden; Cavalli's Calisto at Brussels (1993); Berlin Staatsoper (1996) and Lyon Opéra (1999); Cherubino at Salzburg, 1998; Sang Liu in Turandot at the reopening of the Liceu Theatre, Barcelona, 1999; Season 2000–01 as Susanna at Salzburg, Manon at Madrid and Bizet's Leila for Marseilles Opera. Concert repertory includes Rossini's Stabat Mater and Mahler's 2nd Symphony. *Address:* c/o Opéra et Concert, 1 rue Volney, F–75002, Paris, France.

BAZOLA, François; singer (bass); b. 1965, Paris, France. *Education:* Paris Conservatoire with William Christie. *Career:* has sung with Les Arts Florissants in Lully's Atys (in Paris and New York), Rameau's Les Indes Galantes and Castor et Pollux, Purcell's Fairy Queen (Aix-en-Provence) and Charpentier's Le malade imaginaire; Sang Arcas in Médée by Charpentier in Paris, Lisbon and New York (1993) and Pan in King Arthur by Purcell (Paris and London, 1995); Assistant to William Christie with the choir of Les Arts Florissants, from 1994. *Address:* c/o Les Arts Florsissants, 10 rue de Florence, 75008 Paris, France.

BEACH, David (Williams); Professor of Music Theory and Administrator; b. 5 Sept. 1938, Hartford, CT, USA; m. Marcia Francesca Salemme, 20 June 1964, 1 s., 1 d. *Education:* BA, Brown University, 1961; MMus, 1964; PhD, 1974, Yale University. *Career:* Academic; Assistant Professor, Yale University, 1964–71; Assistant Professor, Brooklyn College, City University of New York, 1971–72; Associate Professor, 1974–85; Chairman, Theory Department, 1981–90, 1995–96; Professor, 1985–, Eastman School of Music; Chairman, Theory Department, 1981–90; University Dean of Graduate Studies, University of Rochester, 1991–1995; Professor and Dean, Faculty of Music, University of Toronto, 1996–; mem, Society for Music Theory, Executive Board, 1984–87; Chairman, Publications Committee, 1979–84; American Musicological Society. *Publications:* The Art of Strict Musical Composition by J P Kirnberger, translated by D Beach and J Thym with introduction and explanatory notes by Beach, 1982; Aspects of Schenkerian Theory, Editor, 1983; Music Theory in Concept and Practice, co-editor, 1997. *Contributions:* Acta Musicologia; Music Analysis; Journal of Music Theory; Music Theory Spectrum; Theory and Practice; Journal of Musicological Research; Integral; Journal of Music Theory Pedagogy. *Honours:* Deems Taylor Award ASCAP, 1983. *Address:* Faculty of Music, University of Toronto, 80 Queens Park, Toronto, Ontario M5S 2C5, Canada.

BEALE, Matthew; Singer (tenor); b. 1975, England. *Education:* Choral Scholar, New Coll., Oxford; Royal Coll. of Music, with Margaret Kingsley. *Career:* choral singing with the Tallis Scholars, The Sixteen and The Gabrieli Consort; Carmina Burana with the Liverpool Philharmonic Orchestra, Messiah at Worcester Cathedral and Bach's B Minor Mass at St John's Smith Square, 2000; opera roles include Mozart's Ferrando, Cimarosa's Paolino, Sir Philip and Narrator in Britten's Owen Wingrave and Sellem in The Rake's Progress; title role in the premiere of Francis Grier's St Francis of Assisi; Ugone in Flavio from the London Handel Festival, 2001; recitals in Japan, England and Wales; On Wenlock Edge by Vaughan Williams at St John's Smith Square, London, 2001. *Honours:* Sybil Tutton Award, RCM. *Current Management:* Caroline Phillips Management, The Old Brushworks, Pickwick Road, Corsham, Wiltshire, SN13 9BX, England. *Telephone:* (1249) 716716. *Fax:* (1249) 716717. *E-mail:* cphillips@caroline-phillips .co.uk. *Website:* www.caroline-phillips.co.uk/beale. *Address:* c/o Royal College of Music, Prince Consort Road, London SW7 2BS, England.

BEAMISH, Sally; Composer and Violist; b. 26 Aug. 1956, London, England; m. Robert Irvine 2 April 1988; two s. one d. *Education:* Trinity College of Music; studied at the Royal Northern College of Music; Staatliche Hochschule für Musik Detmold. *Career:* BBC Proms Debut, Viola Concerto, 1995; viola player until 1989; professional Composer from 1990; Composer-in-Residence Swedish Chamber Orchestra, 1998–2000; performances by Academy of St Martin, Nash Ensemble, London Philharmonic Orchestra, RSNO, BBC Scottish Symphony Orchestra, LMP, SCO; opera, Monster, premiered 2002; mem., SPNM, APC. *Compositions include:* Symphony No. 1, 1992; Tam Lin for oboe and orchestra, 1993; Magnificat, for 2 sopranos and ensemble, 1993; Violin Concerto, 1994; Monster, 1996; 1st Cello Concerto, 1997; Between Earth and Sea for ensemble, 1997; Symphony No. 2, 1998; The Imagined Sound of Sun on Stone (Saxophone Concerto), 1999; Knotgrass Elegy, oratorio (for BBC Proms), 2001. *Recordings include:* Tuscan Lullaby NMC in Dreaming; River (three concertos); The Imagined Sound of Sun on Stone (orchestral), with the Swedish Chamber Orchestra, conducted by Ola Rudner, 1999. *Honours:* GRNCM, 1978; Arts Council Composers Bursary, 1989; Paul Hamlyn Foundation Award, 1993; Scottish Arts

Council Bursary, 1999; Hon DMus, Glasgow Univ., 2001. *Current Management:* Scottish Music Information Centre, 1 Bowmont Gardens, Glasgow G12 9LR, Scotland.

BEARDSLEE, Bethany; Singer (Soprano); b. 25 Dec. 1927, Lansing, Michigan, USA; m. (1) Jacques-Louis Monod, (2) Godfrey Winham, 1956. *Education:* Michigan State University; Juilliard School. *Career:* Debut: New York, 1949; Concerts with Jacques-Louis Monod, giving the US premieres of works by Berg, Stravinsky, Webern, Krenek and Schoenberg; Concerts of Medieval and Renaissance music with the New York Pro Musica, 1957–60; Commissioned and performed Babbitt's Philomel 1964; Performed Schoenberg's Pierrot Lunaire with members of the Cleveland Orchestra 1972; Taught at Westminster Choir College from 1976; Partnership with pianist Richard Goode 1981; Professor of singing at University of Texas, Austin, 1981–82; Brooklyn College, City University of New York, from 1983. *Recordings:* Pierrot Lunaire, conducted by Robert Craft; Works by Babbitt, George Perle, Mel Powell, Bach, Haydn and Pergolesi. *Honours:* Laurel Leaf from American Composers Alliance, 1962; Ford Foundation Grant 1964; Honorary Doctorate, Princeton University, 1977.

BEAT, Janet Eveline, BMus, MA; composer; b. 17 Dec. 1937, Streetly, Staffordshire, England. *Education:* Birmingham Univ. *Career:* freelance horn player, 1962–65; Lecturer in Music, Madeley College of Education, 1965–67; Lecturer in Music, Worcester College of Education, 1967–71; Lecturer, Royal Scottish Academy of Music and Drama, 1972–96; Lecturer, Music Department (part-time), University of Glasgow, 1996–2002; mem. BACS. *Compositions include:* Brass: Hunting Horns are Memories, 1977; Fireworks in Steel, 1987; Chard Fanfare, 1992; Bold As Brass!, 1996; Vision Nocturne, 2003; Keyboard: Pentad, 1969; Piangam, 1978–79; Sonata No. 1, 1985–87; Cross Currents and Reflections, 1981–82; Alexa's Comet, 1984; Capriccios Vol 1, 1999–2002; Fanfare for Haydn, 2000; Dynamism, 2000; Sunsets and Lakes, 2003; Orchestra: Synchronism, 1977; Strings: Le Tombeau de Claude, 1973; The Leaves of My Brain, 1974; Circe, 1974; After Reading 'Lessons of War', 1977; 'Vincent' Sonata, 1979–80; A Willow Swept By Rain, 1982; Arabesque, 1985; Cat's Cradle for the Nemuri Neko, 1991; Convergencies, 1992; Scherzo Notturno, 1992; Joie de Vivre, 1994; Equinox Rituals, 1996; Violin Sonata No. 2, 1997; Concealed Imaginings, 1998; String Quartet No. 1, 1992–99; Violin Sonata No. 3, 1999; Summer Poem No. V, 1970; The Fiery Sunflower, 1972; Landscapes, 1976–77; Premiers Désirs, 1978; Mitylene Mosaics, 1983–84; Nomoi Aulodiki, 1984; Sylvia Myrtea, 1985; Aztec Myth, 1987; Aspara Music 1, 1994; Gedenkstück fur Kaethe, 2003; Woodwind: Apollo and Marysas, 1972–73; Inventions for Woodwind, 1974; Seascape With Clouds, 1978; Mitylene Mosaics, 1983–84; Two Caprices, 1998; Nomoi Aulodiki, 1984; En Plein Air, 2000–01; Electronic: Aztec Myth, 1987; A Springtime Pillow Book, 1990; Beating Around the Bush, 1990; Not Necessarily: As She Opened Her Eyes, 1990; Lydian Mix, 1990; Mandala, 1990; Memories of Java, 1990; The Song of The Silkie, 1991; Fêtes Pour Claude, 1992; Der Regenpalast, 1993; Strings: Mexican Night of the Dead, 2001; Harmony Opposites, 2002; Encounter, 2002; The Dream Magus, 2002. *Honours:* G. D. Cunningham Award, 1963; Honorary Research Fellow, Glasgow University, 1999. *Address:* The Scottish Music Centre, 1 Bowmont Gardens, Glasgow G12 9LR, Scotland. *E-mail:* info@scottishmusiccentre.com. *Website:* www .scottishmusiccentre.com/janet_beat.

BEATH, Betty, DipMus; Australian composer and pianist; b. 19 Nov. 1932, Bundaberg, Qld. *Education:* Queensland and New South Wales Conservatories. *Career:* lecturer and accompanist, Queensland Conservatory 1967–98. *Compositions include:* Strange Adventures of Marco Polo, 1 act opera, 1972; Francis, 1 act opera 1974; Songs from the Beasts' Choir for soprano and piano, 1978; Poems from the Chinese for soprano, clarinet, cello and percussion, 1979; Piccolo Victory, 1982; Black on White for piano left hand, 1983; Points in a Journey for soprano, flute and piano, 1987; Abigail and the Mythical Beast, music theatre, 1985; River Songs for soprano and piano, 1992; Lagu Lagu Manis for cello and piano, 1994; Asmaranda for orchestra, 1994; Journeys: An Indonesian Triptych for chamber orchestra, 1994; Indonesian Diptych, 1994; Golden Hours for chamber orchestra, 1995; Dreams and Visions, 1996; From a Quiet Place, 1997; Encounters for violin and cello, 1999; Lament for Kosovo, 1999; A Garland for St Francis for soprano, string quartet, flute, clarinet and percussion, 2002; Many national broadcasts include interview and performance of works to mark the 70th birthday, ABC Classic FM, 1996; Commissions from the Queensland Opera, 1973, Philharmonic, 1995 and Australian Broadcasting Corporation, 2002; Towards the Psalms (song cycle) 2004. *Recordings:* Indonesian Diptych on Music from Six Continents, 1995; Lagu Lagu Manis, Music from Six Continents, 1996; Dreams and Visions, 1997; River Songs, 1998; Lament for Kosovo, Music from Six Continents, 2001; Woman's Song, Music from Six Continents, 2001; From a Quiet Place, 2003. *Honours:* Perform/4MBS Award 2000.

BEAUCHAMP, Michael John; British opera director, theatre director and teacher; b. 2 June 1949, London, England. *Education:* University College, Durham, Glyndebourne Opera. *Career:* Staff Producer, Sadler's Wells and English National Opera, 1973–75; Resident Producer, Australian Opera, 1975–80; Freelance, 1980–; Productions: Happy End, Adelaide; Simon Boccanegra; HMS Pinafore; La Bohème; Australian Opera; La Bohème, National Opera of New Zealand and Glyndebourne Touring Opera; Rake's Progress, Brisbane and Sydney; Rigoletto, Perth, Western Australia and Melbourne; Lucia di Lammermoor, Tancredi, Wexford; The Happy Prince, Dunstan and The Devil, Morley Opera; Director, gala premieres for Australian Bicentennial, New South Wales Directorate; Teaching posts in Australia and England. *Address:* 40A Regents Park Road, London NW1 7SX, England.

BEAUDRY, Jacques, BA; symphony and opera conductor; b. 10 Oct. 1929, Sorel, QC, Canada; m. Pauline Bonneville. *Education:* Univ. of Montreal, Royal Conservatory of Music, Brussels, Belgium; studied with René Defossez, Paul Van Kempen, Willem Van Otterloo. *Career:* Prof. of Orchestral Conducting, University of Montreal; toured Europe as conductor with Montreal Symphony, Opéra Comique, Paris Opéra House, and New York Metropolitan Opera; radio broadcasts in Canada, Belgium, Netherlands, Italy, Czechoslovakia, Norway, Luxembourg and France; concerts in Russia, Poland, Guatemala, Switzerland, Greece, Monaco and USA; television appearances in Canada and France. *Honours:* Gold Medal of Quebec, Lieutenant Governor's Award 1958. *Current Management:* Beaudry Concerts, 235 Sherbrooke O P2, Montréal, QC H2X 1X8, Canada.

BEAUMONT, Adrian, BA, MMus, DMus, ARCM.; Composer and Lecturer; b. 1 June 1937, Huddersfield, England; m. Janet Price. *Education:* Univ. of Wales, Cardiff; composition with Nadia Boulanger (Fontainebleau). *Career:* appointed to staff of Music Department of University of Bristol, 1961; subsequently Reader in Composition until 2002; founder-conductor Bristol Bach Choir 1967–78. *Compositions:* include 3 Symphonies; Now Burns the Bright Redeeming Fire; Oboe Concerto; Summer Ecstasies; 2 string quartets; A Glimmer of Unshapen Dawn; Cello Sonata; three song cycles. *Publications:* Expectation and Interpretation in the Reception of New Music in Thomas, Composition, Performance, Reception (ed.). *Address:* 73 Kings Drive, Bishopston, Bristol, BS7 8JQ, England (home). *Telephone:* (117) 9248456 (home).

BECCARIA, Bruno; Singer (Tenor); b. 4 July 1957, Rome, Italy. *Career:* Debut: Bologna, 1986, as Edgardo in Lucia di Lammermoor; Sang at La Scala, Milan, 1986–87, as Ismaele and Pinkerton; Philadelphia Opera, 1986 and 1988, Vienna Staatsoper from 1987, New York Metropolitan debut, 1987, as Rodolfo; Verona Arena from 1988, as Enzo in La Gioconda, Radames and Turiddu; Teatro La Fenice Venice, 1990, as Ernani; Other roles include Gabriele Adorno (Catania, 1992), Andrea Chénier (San Francisco Opera), Faust, Don Carlos, and Maurizio in Adriana Lecouvreur. *Recordings include:* Beethoven's Mass in C (Decca). *Address:* c/o Metropolitan Opera, Lincoln Center, New York, NY 10023, USA.

BECERRA, Gustavo; Composer; b. 26 Aug. 1925, Temuco, Chile. *Education:* Studied at Santiago Conservatory, with Pedro Allende and with Domingo Santa Cruz. *Career:* Cultural Attaché to Chilean Embassy in Bonn, 1968–70; Freelance composer. *Compositions:* La Muerte de Don Rodrigo, opera, 1958; Three Symphonies, 1955, 1958, 1960; La Araucana and Lord Cochrane, oratorios, 1965, 1967; Violin Concerto, 1950; Flute Concerto, 1957; Concerto for piano with oboe, clarinet, bassoon and strings, 1970; Three Violin Sonatas; Viola Sonata; Three Cello Sonatas; Sonata for double bass and piano; Choral music. *Honours:* Premio Nacional de Arte, 1971. *Address:* Kurt Schumacher Str. 11, 26131 Oldenburg, Germany.

BECHLY, Daniela; Singer (Soprano); b. 1960, Hamburg, Germany. *Education:* Opera Diploma at the Hamburg Hochschule für Musik, 1984. *Career:* Debut: Vienna Kammeroper, 1984; Wexford Festival 1986, as Humperdinck's Goose Girl in Königskinder; Sang at Brunswick Opera, 1983–; Appeared in the Krefeld-Mönchengladbach company, 1985–87; Soloist at the Deutsche Oper Berlin, 1987–; Sang Susanna, Zerlina, Aennchen, Pamina, Anna in Die Lustige Weiber von Windsor, Gretel, Sandrina in La Finta Giardiniera, Elvira in Don Giovanni (Bern, 1991); Malwina in Der Vampyr by Marschner (Wexford, 1992) and Haydn's L'Incontro Improvviso; Rhinemaiden, Covent Garden, 1995; Cherubino, Deutsche Oper am Rhein, Düsseldorf, and Agathe at the Opera Festival at Zwingenberg, Germany, 1998; Recital, Women and Music, Villa Musica, Germany, 1999; Concert repertoire includes all major oratorio works, Mozart concert arias, Strauss 4 Last songs; Engagements in Ireland, Denmark, Norway, France, Italy, Austria. *Recordings:* Blumenmädchen in Parsifal recording under Barenboim; Ronnefeld Song Cycles. *Honours:* 1st prize, Hamburg Singing Contest, 1980; Finals Vienna Belvedere Competition, 1984; 2nd prize, Bordeaux Festival International de Jeunes Solistes. *Address:* Music International, 13 Ardilaun Road, London N5 2QR, England.

BECHT, Hermann; Singer (baritone); b. 19 March 1939, Karlsruhe, Germany. *Education:* Studied with E. Wolf-Dengel in Karlsruhe and with Josef Greindl. *Career:* Sang at Brunswick and Wiesbaden; Deutsche Oper am Rhein, Düsseldorf, from 1974; Roles include Strauss's Mandryka, Falstaff, Amfortas and Pfitzner's Borromeo; Bayreuth Festival from 1979, as Alberich and Kurwenal; Covent Garden Opera in The Ring; Sang Alberich at the Festival Hall, London in a concert performance of Das Rheingold; Guest appearances in New York, Stuttgart, Vienna and Staatsoper Munich (1986, in the premiere of V D Kirchner's Belshazzar); Waldner in Arabella, Teatro Liceo Barcelona, 1989; Sang Kurwenal at Nantes, 1989 and Alberich in Das Rheingold, Bonn, 1990; Sang in the premiere production of Mayer's Sansibar, Schwetzingen, 1994; Schigolch in Lulu at Dusseldorf, 2000. *Recordings:* Alberich in Ring cycle from Bayreuth. *Current Management:* Ingpen & Williams Ltd, 7 St George's Court, 131 Putney Bridge Road, London, SW15 2PA, England.

BECK, Jeremy; Composer; b. 15 Jan. 1960, Painesville, Ohio. *Education:* DMA, Yale University; MA Duke University; BSc, Mannes College of Music; Dagbe Drumming Institute, Ghana. *Career:* Debut: Carnegie Recital Hall, 1987; Associate Professor, University of Northern Iowa; Guest Lecturer in American Music, St Petersburg Conservatory, Russia; University of West Bohemia. *Compositions:* Death of a Little Girl with Doves, for soprano and orchestra, 1998; Laughter in Jericho, chamber opera, 1997; 3 sonatas for cello and piano, 1981, 1988, 1997; 3 string quartets, 1987, 1990 and 1994. *Recordings:* Four Pieces, 1995; Kopeyia for percussion ensemble, 1995; Songs Without Words, for flute and harp, 1997; Sonata No. 1, 1983; Toccata for piano solo, 1988. *Contributions:* Elliott Carter's Tonal Practice in the Rose Family, Essays in American Music Vol. II. *Address:* 2103 Walnut Street, Cedar Falls, IA 50613, USA.

BECKER, Andreas; Singer (Bass-baritone); b. 13 May 1940, Berlin. *Education:* Berlin Conservatory. *Career:* Debut: As Landgrave in Tannhäuser, Osnabruck, 1966; Repertoire of about 350 roles, opera, operetta and musicals; Appearances throughout Germany from 1966, notably at Krefeld, Bielefeld and Essen; Dortmund Opera from 1972, with guest appearances at Munich and elsewhere; Other roles have included Pizarro and Rocco in Fidelio, Wagner's Marke, Hunding and Fasolt, Verdi's Zaccaria and King Philip; Mozart's Osmin and Sarastro, Ochs (Rosenkavalier) and Alfonso, with further engagements at Munich, Hamburg, Paris, Netherlands and the Far East; Sang Mordred in Le Roi Arthus by Chausson at Dortmund, 1996; Doolittle in My Fair Lady and also appeared in The Merry Widow; Teacher, Dortmund Hochschule; Season 2000–01 at Dortmund as Kecal in The Bartered Bride and in the premiere of Wallenbeg by Erkki-Sven Tüür. *Address:* c/o Stadtische Buhnen Dortmund, Kuhstrasse 12, 4600 Dortmund, Germany.

BECKER, Günther (Hugo); Composer and Music Educator; b. 1 April 1924, Forbach, Baden, Germany. *Education:* Studied conducting with Gerhard Nestler, Badische Hochschule für Musik, Karlsruhe, 1946–49; Composition with Wolfgang Fortner, 1948–56; Choral conducting with Kurt Thomas, 1953–55, North West German Academy of Music, Detmold. *Career:* Music Teacher, Greek National School Anavryta, Athens, 1956–58; Music Adviser, Goethe Institute, Athens, 1957–68; Music Teacher, German Dörpfeld Gymnasium, Athens, 1957–68; Founded, Mega-Hertz, live electronic music group, Germany, 1969; Teacher, International Summer Courses for New Music, Darmstadt, 1967, 1968, 1970; Lecturer, Musikhochschule Rheinland, Robert Schumann Institute, Düsseldorf, 1973–74; Professor of Composition and Live Electronics, Hochschule für Musik, Düsseldorf, 1974–89; mem, International Society for Contemporary Music, President German Section, 1971–74. *Compositions:* Orchestral: Nachtund Traumgesänge for Chorus and Orchestra, 1964; Stabil-instabil, 1965; Correspondances I for Clarinet and Chamber Orchestra, 1966; Griechische Tanzsuite, 1967; Caprices concertants, 1968; Transformationen for Orchestra, Live Electronic Ensemble and Tape, 1970; Attitude, 1972–73; Konzert for Electronic Modulated Oboe and Orchestra, 1973–74; Ihre Bosheit wird die ganze Erde zu einer Wüste machen, sacred concerto for Speaker, Alto, Chorus, Organ, Instrumental Ensemble and Tape, 1978; Magnum Mysterium-Zeugenaussagen zur Auferstehung, scenic oratorio, 1979–80; Psychogramme for Trombone, Accordion and Percussion, 1993; Pieces for various instruments and electronics; 3 String Quartets, 1963, 1967, 1988; Befindlichkeiten for saxophone, cello and piano, 1997. *Address:* Arminiusstraße 41, 33175 Bad Lippspringe, Germany.

BECKER, Heinz; Musicologist and Music Educator; b. 26 June 1922, Berlin, Germany. *Education:* Trained in clarinet, piano, conducting and composition, Berlin Hochschule für Musik; PhD, Humboldt University, Berlin, 1951. *Career:* Assistant Lecturer, Institute of Musicology, 1956–66; Habilitation, 1961, University of Hamburg; Professor of Musicology, Ruhr-University, Bochum, 1966–87; mem, Gesellschaft für Musikforschung since 1951. *Publications:* Klarinettenkonzerte des 18. Jahrhunderts, 1957; Der Fall Heine-Meyerbeer, 1958; Edited,

Giacomo Meyerbeer: Briefwechsel und Tagebücher, 4 vols, 1960–85; Geschichte der Instrumentation, 1964; Beitrage zur Geschichte der Musikkritik, 1965; Studien zur Entwicklungsgeschichte der antiken und mittelalterlichen Rohrblattinstrumente, 1966; Beiträge zur Geschichte der Oper, 1969; Die Couleur locale in der Oper des 19 Jahrhunderts, 1976; Giacomo Meyerbeer in Selbstzeugnissen und Bilddokumenten, Reinbeck, 1980, Prague, 1996; Giacomo Meyerbeer: Ein Leben in Briefen, with G Becker, Wilhelmshaven 1983, Leipzig, 1987, English edition with supplements, 1989; With Gudrun Becker: Giacomo Meyerbeer. Weltbürger der Musik, Ausstellungskatalog zum 200 Geburtstag Meyerbeers; Im Auftrag de Staatsbibl. BLN; Preußischer Kulturbesitz, BLN 1991, Wiesbaden 1991; The 19th–century Legacy, Heritage of Music, Oxford, 1989; Johannes Brahms, 1993. *Contributions:* Articles in various music journals and other publications; über 400 Einzelveröffentlichungen. *Honours:* Festschrift published in honour of 60th birthday, 1982; G Meyerbeer–Musik als Welterfahrung, Festschrift in honour of 70th birthday, 1992, ed Sieghart Döhring and Jürgen Schläder. *Address:* Wohnstift Augustinum, App 1242, Sterleyer Str 44, 23879 Mölln, Germany.

BECKER, Rolf; Singer (Bass); b. 1935, Germany. *Career:* Sang with Cologne Opera, 1959–62, Hannover, 1962–92; Roles have included Mozart's Sarastro and Commendatore, Rocco, Daland, Fafner, Hunding, Gurnemanz, and Mephistopheles; Has also sung such modern repertory as Wesener in Die Soldaten by Zimmermann and buffo roles, including Basilio, Osmin, Kecal and Bartolo; Concert engagements in Spain, France and Italy. *Address:* c/o Niedersachsische Staatstheater, Opernhaus, Opernplatz 1, W-3000 Hannover 1, Germany.

BECKWITH, Daniel; Conductor; b. 1954, Chicago, USA. *Education:* Studied at Westminster Choir College, Princeton. *Career:* Opera Conductor; Recent engagements with Il Matrimonio Segreto, Falstaff, Die Entführung aus dem Serail and Il Barbiere di Siviglia at Wolf Trap, Così fan tutte for the Lyric Opera of Chicago, Grétry's Zemire et Azor at Houston; Giulio Cesare, The Rape of Lucretia and Turandot at Edmonton; The Coronation of Poppea and Mozart's Il Re Pastore for Canadian Opera; Lucia di Lammermoor in Cincinatti; Other appearances include Don Giovanni at the Metropolitan (1995, 1997), Figaro at Vancouver and Il Barbiere di Siviglia in Florida; L'Italiana in Algeri for Cleveland Opera; Season 1997 with Theodora at the Glyndebourne Festival, L'Elisir d'amore at Fort Worth, Handel's Xerxes in Seattle and Rinaldo for the Geneva Opera; The Crucible and The Magic Flute at Washington DC; Il Barbiere di Siviglia at Opera North, England, 1998; Further performances of Orphée et Eurydice in Utah; Platée (Rameau) New York City Opera; The Magic Flute, Seattle; Don Giovanni, San Francisco; Artistic Director of the Lake George Summer Opera Festival, 1999. *Address:* IMG Artists, 7th Avenue, 3rd Floor, New York, NY 10019, USA.

BECKWITH, John, BMus, MMus; Canadian composer, teacher, writer and pianist; b. 9 March 1927, Victoria, BC. *Education:* Univ. of Toronto, Royal Conservatory of Music, Toronto with Alberto Guerrero, studied composition with Nadia Boulanger in Paris. *Career:* Public Relations Dir, Royal Conservatory of Music, Toronto 1948–50; staff writer for radio music continuity, Canadian Broadcasting Corporation, Toronto 1953–55; freelance radio programmer and writer 1955–70; reviewer and columnist, Toronto Daily Star 1959–62, 1963–65; part-time special lecturer, Univ. of Toronto 1952–53, Lecturer 1954–60; Asst Prof. 1960–66; Assoc. Prof. 1966–70, Dean 1970–77, Prof. 1977–90; Dir, Inst. for Canadian Music 1984–90. *Compositions:* 4 songs to poems of e e cummings, 1950; Fall Scene and Fair Dance, 1956; Night Blooming Cereus, 1958; Concerto Fantasy, 1960; Flower Variations and Wheels, 1962; Jonah, 1963; The Trumpets of Summer 1964; Sharon Fragments, 1966; Circle, with Tangents, 1967; Canada Dash, Canada Dot, 1967; Gas!, 1969; Taking a Stand, 1972; All the Bees and All the Keys, 1973; Musical Chairs, 1973; Quartet, 1977; The Shivaree, 1978; Keyboard Practice, 1979; 3 Motets on Swan's China, 1981; Sonatina in 2 movements, 1981; A Little Organ Concert, 1981; Mating Time, 1981; 6 Songs to poems by E. E. Cummings, 1982; A Concert of Myths, 1983; Études, 1983; Arctic Dances, 1984; Harp of David, 1985; Crazy to Kill, 1988; Peregrine, 1989; Round and Round, 1992; Taptoo!, 1994; Eureka, 1996; Basic Music, 1998; Lady Wisdom, 2000; A New Pibroch, 2002. *Recordings:* Harp of David; Quartet; Keyboard Practice; Études; Arctic Dances; Sharon Fragments; Circle, with Tangents; 3 Motets on Swan's China; Stacey; Round and Round; A Concert of Myths; Synthetic Trios; The Trumpets of Summer. *Publications:* Gen. Ed., Canadian Composers Series, 1975–91; Canadian Consultant, The New Grove, London, 1980; Ed. or Co-ed., The Modern Composer and His World, 1961; Contemporary Canadian Composers, 1975; The Canadian Musical Heritage, Vol. 5, 1986, Vol. 18, 1995; Musical Canada, 1987; Author, Music Papers, 1997. *Honours:* five hon. doctorates, Member of the Order of Canada 1987. *Address:* 121 Howland Avenue, Toronto, M5R 3B4, Canada.

BECZALA, Piotr; Singer (Tenor); b. 1965, Poland. *Education:* Studied at the Katowice Music Academy and in Weimar, Kraków and Villecrose:

Sena Jurinac has been among his teachers. *Career:* Sang at the Linz and Salzburg Landestheater, as Mozart's Ferrando and Tamino, Gaston in Krenek's Schwergewicht, Cassio, Werther and Belmonte, 1992–; Zürich Opera debut as Rinuccio in Gianni Schicchi (company member from 1998), 1996; Further appearances as Alfredo, Lensky and Don Ottavio at Linz and as Alfred in Fledermaus; Concerts include Bruckner's Te Deum with the Vienna Philharmonic under Giulini and Schubert's E flat Mass under Muti; Further engagements at the Vienna Musikverein, and in Milan, Leipzig and Dresden; Théâtre de la Monnaie, Brussels, as Rinuccio, 1997; Season 2000–01 as the Duke of Mantua for Zürich Opera, and the Shepherd in Szymanowski's King Roger, at Amsterdam. *Address:* c/o Opernhaus Zürich, Falkenstrasse 1, 8008 Zürich, Switzerland.

BEDFORD, David, LTCL, ARAM; composer; b. 4 Aug. 1937, London, England; m. 1st Maureen Parsonage 1958; two d.; m. 2nd Susan Pilgrim 1969; two d.; m. 3rd Allison Powell 1996; one s. two d. *Education:* Royal Acad. of Music and Trinity College, London. *Career:* porter, Guy's Hospital, London 1956; teacher, Whitefield School, Hendon 1965; teacher 1968–80; composer-in-residence 1969–81, Queen's Coll., London; Assoc. Visiting Composer, Gordonstoun, Scotland 1983–86; composer in association, English Sinfonia 1987–; Chair., Asscn of Professional Composers 1991–93; Chair., Performing Right Soc. 2002–04; Chair., Performing Right Soc. Foundation 2000–01. *Compositions:* School operas: The Rime of the Ancient Mariner, 1975–76; The Death of Baldur, 1979; Fridiof's Saga, 1980; The Ragnarok, 1982–83; Symphony 1981; Sun Paints Rainbows on the Vast Waves, 1982; Snakes and the Giant, 1982; Star Clusters, Nebulae and Places in Devon for chorus and orchestra, 1971; Pancakes with Butter, Maple Syrup and Bacon and the TV Weatherman for brass quintet, 1973; instrumental music; Diafone, flute and vibraphone, 1986; Seascapes, string quintet and voices, 1986; For Tess, brass quintet, 1985; Into thy Wondrous House, soprano, chorus and orchestra, 1987; Gere curam mei finis, vocal soloists and harmonizer, 1987; Erkenne Mich, ensemble, 1988; Odysseus, children's opera, 1988; The Transfiguration: A Meditation, chamber orchestra, 1988; Fireworks, 1990; The OCD Band; The Minotaur, soprano and ensemble, 1990; Touristen Dachau, 1991; Allison's Concerto, 1992; The Goddess of Mahi River, 1993; A Charm of Grace, 1994; Recorder Concerto, 1995; Oboe Concerto, 1999; Percussion Concerto, 1999; The City and the Stars, 2001; Clothed in Robes of Music, 2002. *Recordings:* Numerous including: The Wind Music of David Bedford, 1998; 12 Hours at Sunset, 1999. *Honours:* Honorary Fellowship LTCL 1999. *Address:* 12 Oakwood Road, Bristol BS9 4NR, England (home). *Telephone:* (117) 9624202 (home). *E-mail:* dvbmus@aol.com (home).

BEDFORD, Steuart John Rudolf; Pianist and Conductor; b. 31 July 1939, London, England; m. (1) Norma Burrowes, 1969, (2) Celia Harding, 1980, 2 d. *Education:* BA, Lancing College, Oxford; Royal Academy of Music; FRCO; FRAM. *Career:* Debut: Oxford Chamber Orchestra, 1964; Glyndebourne Festival Opera, 1965–67; Debut with The Beggar's Opera, 1967; English Opera Group; English Music Theatre, Aldeburgh and London, 1967–73; At Aldeburgh conducted the world premieres of Britten's Death in Venice, 1973, and Phaedra, 1976; Artistic Director and Resident Conductor, English Music Theatre (British premiere of Britten's Paul Bunyan, 1976) and Aldeburgh Festival, 1975–; Chief Conductor, English Sinfonia Orchestra, 1981–90; Freelance Conductor at home and abroad, including Metropolitan Opera New York, Santa Fe, Buenos Aires, Rio de Janeiro, Canada, France, Germany, Austria, Australia and New Zealand; Royal Opera House Covent Garden, English National Opera, Welsh National Opera, Opera North; Conducted Noye's Fludde at Aldeburgh, 1994; Season 1997–98 with Billy Budd at the Met, A Midsummer Night's Dream for ENO and Martinů's Julietta for Opera North; Mozart's Lucio Silla at Garsington, 1998. *Recordings include:* Death in Venice; Phaedra; Beggar's Opera; Collins Britten series. *Honours:* Medal, Worshipful Company of Musicians; Organ Scholarship. *Current Management:* Harrison/Parrott Ltd, 12 Penzance Place, London, W11 4PA, England. *Telephone:* (20) 7229 9166. *Fax:* (20) 7221 5042. *Website:* www.harrisonparrott.com. *Address:* 76 Cromwell Avenue, London N6 5HQ, England.

BEECROFT, Norma; Composer; b. 11 April 1934, Oshawa, Ontario, Canada. *Education:* Studied with John Weinzweig in Toronto, 1952–58, at Tanglewood with Foss and Copland, at Darmstadt with Maderna and in Rome with Petrassi; Further studies in Electronic Music at the University of Toronto and Columbia-Princeton Electronic Music Center. *Career:* Worked in Toronto, 1965–73, Co-founding the New Music Concerts, 1971, President and General Manager until 1989. *Compositions include:* Improvisazioni Concertanti I–III, 1961, 1971, 1973; From Dreams of Brass for Narrator, Soprano, Chorus, Orchestra and Tape, 1964; Piece Concertante for Orchestra, 1966; Undersea Fantasy, Puppet Opera for Tape, 1967; The Living Flame of Love for chorus, 1967; Rasas I–III for Chamber Ensemble, 1968, 1973, 1974; Collage '76 for

Ensemble, 1976; Consequences for Five, 1977; Collage '78 for Bassoon, Piano, 2 Percussion and Tape, 1978; Hedda, Ballet for Orchestra and Tape, 1983; The Dissipation of Purely Sound, Radiophonic Opera for Tape, 1988; Accordion Play, 1989; Requiem Mass for Soloists, Chorus and Orchestra, 1990; Amp, String Quartet with Tape, 1992. *Address:* SOCAN (Canada), 41 Valleybrook Drive, Don Mills, Ontario M3B 2S6, Canada.

BEER, Birgit; Singer (Soprano); b. 1962, Lubeck, Germany. *Education:* Lubeck Musikhochschule. *Career:* Debut: Sang Tebaldo in Don Carlos at Augsburg; Sang at Saarbrucken, 1984–85; Lucerne, 1985–87; Vienna Volksoper, 1987–90; Further study with Renate Holm and Hanna Ludwig in Vienna; Theater am Gärtnerplatz, 1990–92 as Mozart's Blondchen, Offenbach's Olympia, Zerbinetta, and Adele in Die Fledermaus; Guest appearances at the Vienna Staatsoper, in Verona and Berlin and as Papagena at La Scala, Milan; Deutsche Oper Berlin as Rosina and Salzburg, 1994, as Frasquita in Carmen; Bonn Opera from 1992, as Puccini's Lauretta and Lisetta; Season 1996 as Papagena at Bonn and Marzelline in Fidelio at Liège; Sang Musetta at Essen, 1999. *Address:* c/o Oper der Stadt Bonn, Am Boeselagerhof 1, Pf 2440, 3111 Bonn, Germany.

BEESLEY, Mark; Singer (bass); b. 1961, Harrogate, Yorkshire, England. *Education:* Studied at Sussex University (MSc) and with Dennis Wicks and Laura Sarti. *Career:* Appearances with New Sussex Opera, the City of Birmingham Touring Opera, Opera North, Opera 80 and at the Batignano Festival; Member of the Royal Opera Covent Garden, 1989–, in Idomeneo (Voice of Neptune), Arabella, Fidelio, Capriccio, Samson et Dalila, Turandot (Timor), La Bohème (Colline), I Capuleti, Otello (Lodovico), and La Damnation de Faust (Brander, 1993); Other engagements in Poppea at the City of London Festival, Tosca (Angelotti) in Hong Kong and Midsummer Night's Dream (Theseus) at Aix-en-Provence; Sang in La Traviata and Don Carlos at Covent Garden, 1996; Concert repertoire includes the Verdi Requiem (at Seville) and Beethoven's Ninth (Brussels Philharmonic); Season 1999 with Schumann's Scenes from Faust at the London Prom concerts; Sang Sparafucile in Rigoletto for ENO, 1999; Season 2000–01 as Sarastro and Rossini's Basilio for ENO, and Drago in Schumann's Genoveva at Garsington. *Current Management:* Athole Still International Management, Forresters Hall, 25–27 Westow Street, London, SE19 3RY, England. *Telephone:* (20) 8771-5271. *Fax:* (20) 8768-6600. *Website:* www.atholestill.com.

BEESON, Jack Hamilton, BMus, MMus; composer, educator and writer; b. 15 July 1921, Muncie, Indiana, USA; m. Nora Beate Sigerist; one s. (deceased) one d. *Education:* Eastman School of Music, University of Rochester, Columbia University, studied privately with Béla Bartók. *Career:* debut ss actor in own opera, My Heart's in the Highlands, NET 1970. *Compositions:* over 60 published including: Jonah; Hello Out There; The Sweet Bye and Bye; Lizzie Borden; My Heart's in the Highlands; Captain Jinks of The Horse Marines; Dr Heidegger's Fountain of Youth; Cyrano; Sorry, Wrong Number, Practice in the Art of Elocution (operas); Symphony No. 1 in A. *Publications:* contrib. to journals and Grove's Dictionary (sixth edn). *Honours:* Hon. DMus (Columbia Univ.) 2002. *Address:* 404 Riverside Drive, New York, NY 10025, USA.

BEGG, Heather, OBE, DCNZM; singer (mezzo-soprano); b. 1 Dec. 1932, Nelson, New Zealand; d. of William James Begg and Johanna Swanson Begg (née Coghill). *Education:* National School of Opera, London, vocal studies with Dame Sister Mary Leo and Gertrude Narev in Auckland, Marianne Mathy in Sydney, Florence Wiese-Norberg in London. *Career:* debut, Auckland, New Zealand 1954, as Azucena in Il Trovatore; National Opera of Australia 1954–56; J. C. Williamson's Italian Opera, Australia 1955; Carl Rosa Opera, London 1960; resident, Sadler's Wells Opera, London 1961–64; New Zealand Opera 1964–67; English National Opera guest artist 1968–72; Royal Opera, Covent Garden, guest artist 1959–99, resident, 1972–76; Resident, Opera Australia, 1976–97, Guest Artist, 1997–; Guest Artist in Edinburgh, London, Salzburg and Orange Festivals, Strasbourg, Bordeaux, Milan, Vancouver, Chicago, San Francisco, San Diego, Singapore, Barcelona and Australasia; Concert Artist and Recitalist for radio and television in the United Kingdom, New Zealand and Australia; Operatic repertoire of over 100 principal mezzo-soprano roles, including most recently, Madame Armfeldt in Sondheim's A Little Night Music, 2004 with Canterbury Opera, New Zealand. *Recordings include:* Les Troyens; La Traviata; I Lombardi; La Sonnambula; Mefistofele; I Puritani; The Little Sweep; Die Fledermaus; Films of Die Fledermaus; Adriana Lecouvreur; Dialogues of the Carmelites; La fille du Régiment; The Mikado; Voss; Gipsy Princess; Patience; Le nozze di Figaro. *Honours:* Sydney Sun Aria Winner, 1955; Recipient, New Zealand Government Music Bursary, 1956; Countess of Munster Scholarship, 1959; Distinguished Companion of the New Zealand Order of Merit, 2000. *Address:* c/o Opera Australia, 480 Elizabeth Street, Surry Hills, Sydney, NSW 2010, Australia (office).

Telephone: (2) 9699-3184 (office). *Fax:* (2) 9699-3184 (office). *E-mail:* enquiries@opera-australia.org (office).

BEGLARIAN, Eve; Composer and Record Producer; b. 22 July 1958, Ann Arbor, Michigan, USA. *Education:* BA, Princeton University; MA, Columbia University. *Career:* Music performed at Washington Ballet, Kennedy Center, May 1991; Anthony de Hare, Kennedy Center, May 1990; New York New Music Ensemble, June 1988; Dinosaur Annex, Boston, 1989, 1990; Monday Evening Concerts, Los Angeles, 1990, 1991; Weill Recital Hall, April 1987. *Compositions:* Eloise (Electric Cello and Tape); The Beginning of Terror (Electronic Tape); Making Sense of It (flute, cello, violin, violoncello, pianoforte, percussion, tape); Miranda's Kiss (Piano solo); A Big Enough Umbrella (Viola, Tape); Elf Again for ensemble, 1998; Father/Daughter Dance, electro-acoustic, 1998; Non-Jew, 2 speakers, 1998. *Recordings:* Space 1986; Needful Things–Stephen King Audio Book, 1991; Born Dancin'/Eloise, 1991. *Publications:* Mikrokosmos, Bartók, corrected edition 1989.

BEGLARIAN, Grant; Composer and Consultant; b. 1 Dec. 1927, Tbilisi, Georgia, Russia; m. Joyce Ellyn Heeney, 2 Sept 1950, 1 s., 1 d. *Education:* BM, Composition, 1950, MM, Composition, 1951, DMA, 1958, University of Michigan, Ann Arbor, USA; Berkshire Music Center with Aaron Copland, 1960. *Career:* Director, Contemporary Music Project, The Ford Foundation, New York and Washington, 1960–69; Dean, Professor of Music, School of Performing Arts, University of Southern California, Los Angeles, 1969–82; President of National Foundation for Advancement in the Arts, Miami, 1982–91; Consultant in the Arts and Education, 1991–; International Co-ordinator, Think Quest, Amrenk, New York; mem, ASCAP; International Council of Fine Arts Deans. *Compositions include:* Duets for Violins, 1955; First Portrait for Band, 1959; Sinfonia for Orchestra, 1961; A Short Suite for String Orchestra, 1968; Fables, Foibles and Fancies for Narrator and Cellist, 1971; Diversions for Viola, Cello and Orchestra, 1972; To Manitou for Soprano and Orchestra, 1976; Partita for Orchestra, 1986. *Publications:* Film-Video as an Artistic Discipline, editor, 1978; The Arts in Shaping the American Experience, 1979; The Professional Education and Career Entry of Artists, 1982. *Honours:* George Gershwin Prize, 1959; Ysaye Medal, 1973; Distinguished Service Award, Music Teachers National Association, 1991. *Address:* 141 River Road, Scarborough, NY 10510, USA.

BEGLEY, Kim; Singer (Tenor); b. 23 June 1952, Wirral, Cheshire, England. *Education:* Guildhall School of Music, 1980–82; National Opera Studio, 1982–83. *Career:* Royal Opera House Covent Garden from 1983 as Andres in Wozzeck; Lysander in A Midsummer Night's Dream; The Prince in Zemlinsky's Florentine Tragedy; Achilles in King Priam and Froh in Das Rheingold; Other appearances include Boris in Katya Kabanova, Pellegrin in Tippett's New Year and Laca in Jenůfa for Glyndebourne Festival; Dancing Master in Ariadne and Male Chorus in Rape of Lucretia for ENO; Shuisky in Boris Godunov, Fritz in the British premiere of Der Ferne Klang, 1992, and Lohengrin and Alfred, Die Fledermaus in Frankfurt; Narraboth at the 1993 Salzburg Festival; Sang in Pfitzner's Palestrina at Covent Garden, Drum Major in Wozzeck at La Scala and Der Freischütz in Berlin, 1997; Sang Captain Vere in Billy Budd at the Opéra de La Bastille and Max in Der Freischütz at La Scala, 1998; Season 1999–2000 as Parsifal for ENO and Peter Grimes for Netherlands Opera; Wagner's Erik at Covent Garden, 2000; Season 2000–01 as Loge in Das Rheingold at Bayreuth and Florestan at Glyndebourne; Mendelssohn's Elijah at the London Proms, 2002; Drum Major in new production of Wozzeck at Covent Garden, 2003; Concert appearances include Die Fledermaus, Alfred, with André Previn at the Royal Philharmonic Orchestra; Elgar's Dream of Gerontius with the Philharmonia under Vernon Handley, Tippett's New Year with the London Philharmonic Orchestra and Janáček's From the House of the Dead with the BBC Symphony Orchestra. *Recordings include:* Florestan in Leonore with John Eliot Gardiner; Mephistopheles in Dr Faustus with Kent Nagano. *Address:* c/o IMG Artists Europe, Lovell House, 616 Chiswick High Road, London W4 5RX, England.

BEHAGUE, Gerard (Henri); Musicologist; b. 2 Nov. 1937, Montpellier, France. *Education:* Studied Piano and Composition at the National School of Music, University of Brazil, and at the Brazilian Conservatory of Music, Rio de Janeiro; Studied further at the Institute de Musicologie at the University of Paris, with Chailley; Musicology with Gilbert Chase at Tulane University, PhD 1966. *Career:* Joined faculty of University of Illinois and was appointed Professor of Music at the University of Texas, 1974; Associate Editor of the Yearbook for Inter-American Musical Research, 1969–75; Editor, Music Section of the Handbook of Latin American Studies, 1970–74; Editor of Ethnomusicology, 1974–78, and Latin American Music Review, from 1980; Editorial Adviser and major contributor to the New Grove Dictionary of Music and Musicians, 1970–80. *Publications include:* The Beginnings of Musical Nationalism in Brazil (Detroit 1971); Music in Latin America: An Introduction, 1977; Heitor Villa-Lobos: The Search for Brazil's Musical Soul, 1994. *Address:*

c/o New Grove Dictionary, 25 Ecclestone Place, Victoria, London WC1, England.

BEHLE, Renate; Austrian singer (dramatic soprano); *Professor, Hochschule für Musik und Theater, Hamburg;* b. 1946, Graz; one s. *Education:* University and Music Academy of Graz. *Career:* Sang as mezzo-soprano at Gelsenkirchen, 1979–82; Hanover State Opera, 1982–97, as Minnie, Mozart's Elettra, Leonore in Fidelio, Sieglinde, Tosca, the Marschallin and Ariadne; Other Strauss roles include the Dyer's Wife in Die Frau ohne Schatten, 1993–, and Chrysothemis (at Barcelona, 1997); Guest engagements at Hamburg, Cologne, La Scala Milan (as Salome) and Los Angeles (Isolde, 1997); 20th Century repertory includes Agave in Henze's Bassarids, Shostakovich's Katarina and Montezuma in Rihm's Die Eroberung vom Mexico, all at Hamburg; Katya Kabanova; New productions of Fidelio and Die Walküre at Stuttgart; Tristan und Isolde in Houston; Sieglinde and Senta in Hamburg; Dyer's Wife, Salome, Leonore and Isolde in Dresden and all three Brünnhildes in Cologne. Concerts include the Dvořák Requiem, the Shostakovich 14th Symphony in Leipzig and Beethoven's Ninth in Granada, 1997; Zemlinsky's Lyrische Sinfonie in Amsterdam and Munich; Mahler's Symphony No. 8 on tour with Michael Gielen and the Südwestfunk-Sinfonieorchester; Guest Visit to Carnegie Hall, New York with Bernd Alois Zimmermann's Requiem for a Young Poet; Fidelio in Valencia; Siegfried with the Bamberg Symphony Orchestra and Schoenberg's Gurrelieder at the Ravinia Festival; Further engagements include Die Walküre in Austin, Texas, and Die Frau ohne Schatten in Essen; Sang the Götterdämmerung Brünnhilde at Bonn 2000; Orfrud, Klytemänstra in Hamburg and Dresden 2005; Schönberg's Erwartung in Montreal and Glasgow 2005; Herodias in Cologne 2005; Prof., Hochschule für Musik und Theater, Hamburg 2000–. *Recordings include:* Zemlinsky's Der Kreidekreis and Spohr's Jessonda, Die Enberung o. Mexico (W. Ruhm, Penthesilea), Fidelio/Walküre DVD, Stuttgart. *Honours:* Kammersängerin Staatsoper Hannover 1987. *Address:* c/o Haydn Rawstron Ltd, 36 Station Road, London, SE20 7BQ, England (office).

BEHNKE, Anna-Katharina; Austrian singer (soprano); b. 1964, Wuppertal, Germany; d. of Georg Nowak; m.; one d. *Education:* Munich Musikhochschule. *Career:* debut, Vienna Kammeroper 1986, as Mozart's Susanna; wide repertoire includes roles as Aida, Desdemona, Elisabeth in Tannhäuser, Chrysothemis, Lulu (Basle 1994, Karlsruhe 1995, debut at Opera Bastille, Paris 1998), Shostakovich's Lady Macbeth (Karlsruhe 1996), Marschallin (Munich 1996), Bartók's Judith (Halle 1996–2000), Lucia di Lammermoor (Nat. Theatre, Prague 1998), Korngold's Violanta (Bergen 1998), Die Frau in Schoenberg's Erwartung (BBC Wales 1999), Gutrune and Senta (Trieste 2001), the Arabella (Paris 2002), Beethoven's Leonore (Kassel, Mainz, Graz, Wiesbaden and Antwerp 2002), Elsa in Lohengrin (Essen 2002) Marietta (Braunschweig 2003), Janacek's Fox (Cunning Little Vixen, La Scala, Milan 2003), Emila Marty in The Makropoulos Case (Braunschweig 2004) Salome in Bologna, Nuremberg, Hanover, Mannheim, Düsseldorf and La Scala, Milan (debut 2002), in Tokyo 2004, Senta (Moscow debut 2004, Rome debut 2004). *Current Management:* Herwald Artists Management, Strasse des Roten Kreuzes 64, 76228 Karlsruhe, Germany. *E-mail:* info@herwald-artists.com. *Website:* www.herwald-artists.com.

BEHR, Randall; Conductor and Pianist; b. 1958, USA. *Career:* Conducted Peter Hall's production of Salome at Los Angeles Music Center, 1989; Has returned to Los Angeles for La Traviata, Tosca (with Maria Ewing and Placido Domingo) and Peter Hall's production of Die Zauberflöte, 1993; Other repertory includes the Oliver Knussen double bill, Orfeo ed Euridice, Nixon in China, Così fan tutte, Die Frau ohne Schatten, La Bohème and Vivaldi's Orlando Furioso; Music Director of Long Beach Opera, California; Peter Brook's La Tragédie de Carmen on Broadway; Conducted La Traviata at the Liceu, Barcelona, 1992; Die Walküre in Valencia and Tancredi at Bilbao, with Marilyn Horne; Vienna Staatsoper debut, 1993–94, Madama Butterfly; Hansel and Gretel at Toronto, 1998; Appearance as pianist with Maria Ewing at Covent Garden and at the Teatro Comunale Florence, Théâtre du Châtelet Paris, the Vienna Konzerthaus and the Opéra de Lyon.

BEHRENS, Hildegard; Singer (Soprano); b. 9 Feb. 1937, Varel, Oldenburg, Germany; m. Seth Scheidman. *Education:* Freiburg Music Academy with Ines Leuwen. *Career:* Debut: Freiburg 1971, as Mozart's Countess; Sang in Düsseldorf and Frankfurt as Fiordiligi, Marie (Wozzeck), Agathe (Der Freischütz), Elsa and Katya Kabanova; Covent Garden debut 1976, as Leonore in Fidelio; Metropolitan Opera from 1976, as Giorgetta (Il Tabarro), Donna Anna, Tosca, Mozart's Electra and Wagner's Sieglinde, Isolde and Brünnhilde; Salzburg 1977, Salome; Guest appearances in Munich, Vienna and Lisbon; Bayreuth from 1983, sang Brünnhilde in a new production of The Ring, directed by Harry Kupfer, 1988 and in New York, 1988–90; Marie in Wozzeck, Metropolitan, 1990; Salome at Munich Concert and at Covent Garden, Sept 1990; Sang Elektra at Athens and the New York Metropolitan, 1991 and at Covent Garden, 1997; Isolde at the reopening of the Prinzregententheater, Munich, 1996; Brünnhilde at Birmingham, 1998; Leading role in premiere of Berio's Cronaca del Luogo, Salzburg, 1999; Engaged as Elektra at Baden-Baden, 2000; Season 2000–01 as Hanna Glawari at Munich and Cherubini's Médée at Montpellier (concert). *Recordings include:* Salome, conducted by Karajan (HMV); Fidelio (Decca); Les Nuits d'Eté and Ravel's Shéhérazade (Decca); Tristan und Isolde (Philips); Brünnhilde in The Ring, conducted by James Levine, also in Video; Video of Wozzeck, from Vienna conducted by Abbado (Virgin Classics). *Address:* c/o Royal Opera House (Contracts), Covent Garden, London WC2E 9 DD, England.

BEHRMAN, David; Composer; b. 16 Aug. 1937, Salzburg, Austria. *Education:* Studied privately in New York with Wallingford Riegger and at Princeton with Walter Piston; European studies with Henri Pousseur and Karlheinz Stockhausen. *Career:* From 1966 toured widely in the US with the Sonic Arts Union, giving performances of electronic music; Associated with John Cage, David Tudor and Gordon Mumma at the Merce Cunningham Dance Company, 1970–76; Formerly Artist-in-Residence at Mills College, Oakland, serving as Co-Director of the Center for Contemporary Music. *Compositions include:* Players with Curtains, 1966; Wave Train, 1966; Runthrough, 1967; For Nearly an Hour, 1968; A New Team Takes Over, 1969; Pools of Phase-locked Loops, 1972; Cloud Music, 1974–79; Figure in a Clearing, 1977; On the Other Ocean, 1977; Touch Tones, 1979; Indoor Geyser, 1979–81; Singing Stick, 1981; She's Wild, 1981; Sound Fountain, 1982; 6-Circle, 1984; Orchestral Construction Set, 1984; Interspecies Smalltalk, 1984; Installation for La Villett, 1985. *Recordings include:* Many albums of experimental music. *Address:* c/o ASCAP, ASCAP Building, 1 Lincoln Plaza, New York, NY 10023, USA.

BEILMAN, Douglas; Violinist; b. 1965, Kansas, USA. *Education:* Studied at Juilliard and the New England Conservatory, with Dorothy DeLay. *Career:* Co-founded the Sierra Quartet and performed at the Olympic Music Festival; Co-founded the New Zealand String Quartet, 1987, under the auspices of the Music Federation of New Zealand; Debut concert in Wellington, May 1988; Concerts at the Tanglewood School in USA, Banff International Competition in Canada and performances with the Lindsay Quartet at the 1990 International Festival of the Arts, Wellington; Soloist with New Zealand Symphony Orchestra and Artist-in-Residence at Victoria University, Wellington; Tour to Australia, 1990, for Musica Viva Australia; Tours of New Zealand, 1992, and concerts in New York, 1993. *Current Management:* Ingpen & Williams Ltd, 7 St George's Court, 131 Putney Bridge Road, London, SW15 2PA, England.

BEKKU, Sadao; Composer; b. 24 May 1922, Tokyo, Japan. *Education:* studied with Milhaud, Rivier and Messiaen at the Paris Conservatoire, 1951–54. *Career:* teacher in Tokyo; mem. Japanese branch of International Society for Contemporary Music (pres. 1968–73). *Compositions:* Operas: A Story of Three Women, Tokyo, 1965; Prince Arima, Tokyo, 1967; Aoi-no-ue, Tokyo, 1981; Two Japanese Suites, 1955, 1958; String Quartet, 1955; Two Prayers for Orchestra, 1956; Symphonies for Strings, 1959; Piano Sonatina, 1965; Kaleidoscope for Piano, 1966; Violin Sonata, 1967; Violin Concerto, 1969; Three Paraphrases for Piano, 1968; Sonata in Classical Style for Piano, 1969; Viola Concerto, 1972; Piano Concerto, 1981; 5 Symphonies, 1962, 1977, 1984, 1991, 1999; Cello Concerto, 1997. *Recordings:* works by Sadao Bekku: Symphony No. 3, Spring; Symphony No. 4, The Summer 1945; Symphony No. 5, piano concerto, violin concerto, cello concerto. *Publications include:* The Occult in Music 1972. *Address:* 8-4-18-503 Shimorenjaku, Mitakashi, Tokyo, Japan.

BELAMARIC, Miro; Composer and Conductor; b. 9 Feb. 1935, Sibenik, Dalmatia. *Education:* Studied with Milan Horvat and Stjepan Sulek at the Zagreb Academy of Music; Lovro von Matacic in Salzburg; Sergiu Celibidache in Siena. *Career:* Conductor of the Symphony Orchestra of Zagreb Radio from 1959; Chief Conductor of the Komedija Theatre and from 1978 Chief Conductor of Zagreb Opera; Assistant to Karajan at Salzburg Festival, 1965–68, to Karl Böhm, 1975–77. *Compositions include:* Operas: The Love of Don Perlimplin, Zagreb, 1975; Don Juan–ein Rebell für alle Zeiten, 1983. *Honours:* Winner, Vienna State Opera Competition for Don Juan, 1983. *Address:* c/o Vienna Staatsoper, Opernring 2, 1010 Vienna, Austria.

BELCOURT, Emile; Singer (Tenor); b. 1934, Saskatchewan, Canada. *Education:* Academy of Music, Vienna; Paris with Pierre Bernac and Germaine Lubin. *Career:* Early opera appearances in Germany and France; Paris Opéra Comique as Pelléas; Sang in Debussy's opera for Scottish Opera, 1962; Covent Garden 1963, as Gonzalez in L'Heure Espagnole; Sadler's Wells/English National Opera from 1963, in Die Fledermaus, Orpheus in the Underworld, Bluebeard, The Violins of St Jacques, Patience, Salome and Lucky Peter's Journey, Loge in The Ring; Sang in premieres of Bennett's A Penny for a Song, 1967; Hamilton's The Royal Hunt of the Sun, 1977; Blake's Toussaint l'ouverture, 1977; Lead in stage musicals Man of La Mancha and Kiss

me Kate; Canadian Opera debut in Heloise and Abelard, 1973; San Francisco, 1982, as Herod in Salome; Sang in the Covent Garden premiere of Berg's Lulu, 1981. *Recordings include:* Loge in The Ring Cycle, conducted by Reginald Goodall. *Address:* c/o English National Opera, London Coliseum, St Martin's Lane, London WC2N 4ES, England.

BELKIN, Boris; violinist; b. 26 Jan. 1948, Sverdlovsk, USSR. *Education:* violin studies aged six, Central Music School, Moscow, Moscow Conservatory with Yankelevitz and Andrievsky. *Career:* public appearances from 1955; emigrated 1974; debut in West, 1974 with Zubin Mehta and the Israel Philharmonic; orchestras with which he has appeared include Berlin Philharmonic, Concertgebouw, Israel Philharmonic, Los Angeles Philharmonic, Philadelphia, Cleveland; Season 1987–88, Pittsburgh, Royal Philharmonic and Tokyo Philharmonic Orchestras; conductors include Muti, Bernstein, Maazel, Haitink, Mehta, Ashkenazy and Steinberg. *Recordings:* Paganini Concerto No. 1 with the Israel Philharmonic; Tchaikovsky and Sibelius Concertos with the Philharmonia Orchestra; Prokofiev's Concertos with the Zürich Tonhalle Orchestra; Brahms Concerto with the London Symphony; Glazunov and Shostakovich Concerto No. 1 with the Royal Philharmonic; Brahms Sonatas with Dalberto. *Honours:* winner Soviet National Competition for Violinists 1972. *Current Management:* Terry Harrison Artists Management, The Orchard, Market Street, Charlbury, Oxfordshire OX7 3PJ, England. *Telephone:* (1608) 810330. *Fax:* (1608) 811331. *E-mail:* artists@terryharrison.force9.co.uk.

BELL, Christopher, BMus, MMus; British conductor; *Chorus Director, Grant Park Music Festival, Chicago*; b. 1961, Belfast, Northern Ireland. *Career:* Assoc. Conductor BBC Scottish Symphony Orchestra 1989–91; Chorusmaster Royal Scottish Nat. Orchestra Chorus 1989–2002; Artistic Dir Edinburgh Royal Choral Union 1993–94; Principal Guest Conductor State Orchestra of Victoria, Australia 1997–99; Founder and Music Dir Ulster Youth Choir 1999–2004; Chorus Dir Grant Park Festival, Chicago USA, Belfast Philharmonic Choir; Chorusmaster of RSNO Jr Chorus; Artistic Dir and Founder Nat. Youth Choir of Scotland and Children's Classic Concerts; conducted Royal Philharmonic, London Philharmonic, Ulster, Scottish Chamber, City of London Sinfonia, London Concert, RTE Nat. Symphony and Bournemouth Symphony Orchestras; overseas has worked with Duisburg Symphony Orchestra, Basel Symphony Orchestra, Dutch Radio Symphony, Brabants Orkest, Orquesta Filharmonica de Gran Canaria, Noord Nederlands Orkest, Philharmonie of Essen, New Zealand, Melbourne and Perth Symphony Orchestras;. *Honours:* Scotsman of the Year Award for Creative Talent 2001, Charles Grove Prize for his contrib. to cultural life in Scotland and rest of UK 2003. *Current Management:* Robert Gilder & Co., Enterprise House, 59–65 Upper Ground, London, SE1 9PQ, England. *Telephone:* (20) 7928-9008. *Fax:* (20) 7928-9755. *E-mail:* rgilder@robert-gilder.com.

BELL, Donald (Munro); Professor and Baritone; b. 19 June 1934, Burnaby, British Columbia, Canada. *Education:* Royal College of Music, 1953–55; Berlin, Private and in the Stadtische Oper Studio; Papers presented at: Phenomenon of Singing, Memorial University NFLD, Using Digital Technology in a Voice Lesson, 1997; XIV International Congress of Phonetic Sciences, co-author Dr Michael Dobrovolsky, Acoustic Characteristics of Vibrato Onset in Singing, San Francisco, 1999. *Career:* Debut: Wigmore Hall, 1958; Bayreuth, 1958, The Nightwatchman in Meistersinger, 1959–1960; the Herald in Lohengrin, the Steersman in Tristan and Isolde; CBC, BBC, NOS Holland, WDR, Nord Deutsche Rundfunk, Germany; Appeared at Luzern Festival with Thomas Beecham, 1959, Glyndebourne in 1963 as the Speaker in Die Zauberflöte; Grand Théâtre, Geneva, London Royal Festival Hall, Royal Albert Hall, by invitation at the opening of Lincoln Center, New York and Carnegie Hall with the Philadelphia Orchestra and many other venues; mem, Rotary Club; NATS. *Honours:* Recipient of various honours and awards. *Address:* University of Calgary, Department of Music, 2500 University Drive NW, Calgary, Alberta T2N 1N4, Canada.

BELL, Donaldson; Singer (Bass); b. 1958, Ayrshire, Scotland. *Education:* Royal Scottish Academy, Glasgow. *Career:* Company principal with the Royal Opera from 1978; Appearances in such operas as Werther, La fanciulla del West, Die Entführung, Der Rosenkavalier, Die Meistersinger (Night-Watchman), Die Zauberflöte, La Traviata, and Death in Venice; Royal Opera House education workshops: Oratorio and recital engagements in Britain and abroad. *Address:* c/o Royal Opera House (contracts), Covent Garden, London, WC2, England. *Telephone:* (20) 7240 1200. *Fax:* (20) 7212 9502.

BELL, Elizabeth, BA, BS; Composer; b. 1 Dec. 1928, Cincinnati, OH, USA; m. 1st Frank D. Drake 1953, three s.; m. 2nd Robert E. Friou 1983. *Education:* Wellesley Coll., Wellesley, MA, Juilliard School of Music, New York; studied with Peter Mennin, Vittorio Giannini, Paul Alan Levi. *Career:* performances throughout USA, also Russia, Ukraine, Bulgaria, Armenia, Japan, Australia, Canada, South America; four retrospective concerts in Ithaca, NY 1973, Cincinnati 1985, New York 1991, 1998, 2003; Music critic for Ithaca Journal, 1971–1975, now independent; radio and television interviews; mem., founder and officer, now Dir, New York Women Composers; mem. of the Board of Governors, American Composers' Alliance. *Compositions include:* Variations and Interludes for piano, 1952; String Quartet, 1957; Songs of Here and Forever, 1970; Fantasy-Sonata for cello and piano, 1971; Symphony No. 1, 1971; 2nd Sonata for piano, 1972; Soliloquy for solo cello, 1980; Loss-Songs for soprano and piano, 1983; Perne in a Gyre for clarinet, violin, cello and piano, 1984; Duovarios for 2 pianos, 1987; Millennium for soprano, clarinet and piano, 1988; Spectra for 11 instruments, 1989; Night Music for piano, 1990; River Fantasy for flute and string trio, 1991; Andromeda for piano, string orchestra and percussion, 1993; Les Neiges d'Antan, Sonata for violin and piano, 1998. *Recordings:* 2nd Sonata; Perne in a Gyre; Millennium; Andromeda; Night Music; Variations and Interludes; The Music of Elizabeth Bell (includes Andromeda, String Quartet, Perne in a Gyre, Symphony No. 1); Snows of Yesteryear (includes Spectra, Songs of Here and Forever, Duovarios, Les Neiges d'Antan); CDs on Classic Masters, North/South Records, Vienna Modern Masters, Master Musicians Collective. *Honours:* first prize, Utah Composers' Competition 1986, Grand Prize 1996; Delius Prize 1994; awards from Meet-The-Composer and New York Council for the Arts. *Current Management:* American Composers' Alliance. *Address:* 21 Beech Lane, Tarrytown, NY 10591-3001, USA. *Telephone:* (914) 631-4361. *Fax:* (914) 631-6444. *E-mail:* ebelfri@earthlink.net.

BELL, Emma; Singer (Soprano); b. 1970, Leamington Spa, England. *Education:* Royal Academy, London, with Joy Mammer. *Career:* Sang Handel's Radamisto and Salustia (Alessandro Severo) and Lia in Debussy's L'Enfant Prodigue at the RAM; Handel's Rodelinda for the Glyndebourne Tour 1998, and at the Festival 1999; Season 1999-2000 with Mozart's Exsultate Jubilate K165 at the Queen Elizabeth Hall and Elvira in Don Giovanni for Opera North; Sang Handel's Rodelinda at the Royal Festival Hall, 2002. *Honours:* Yamaha Music Foundation of Europe Scholarship; Dove Prize RAM; Kathleen Ferrier Award. 1988. *Current Management:* Askonas Holt Ltd, Lonsdale Chambers, 27 Chancery Lane, London, WC2A 1PF, England. *Telephone:* (20) 7400-1700. *Fax:* (20) 7400-1799. *E-mail:* info@askonasholt.co.uk. *Website:* www.askonasholt.co.uk.

BELL, Joshua; Violinist; b. 9 Dec. 1967, Bloomington, Indiana, USA. *Education:* Studied with Josef Gingold, 1980–89. *Career:* Debut: Concert with Philadelphia Orchestra, 1981; Season 1993–94, performed Nicholas Maw's Violin Concerto with the Philharmonia Orchestra, conducted by Leonard Slatkin, and at the Proms with London Philharmonic Orchestra and Roger Norrington, 1996; Season 1997–98, performances with orchestras such as New York Philharmonic, Boston Symphony, Cleveland Orchestra, Los Angeles Philharmonic, Pittsburgh and Dallas Symphony Orchestras and many European Orchestras; Performed at Salzburg Music Festival; Annual Joshua Bell Chamber Music Festival, Wigmore Hall, London, 1997–; Guest Professor, Royal Academy of Music, London, 1997–; Has worked with many conductors including Vladimir Ashkenazy, John Eliot Gardiner, Christoph von Dohnányi, Lorin Maazel, André Previn, Richard Hickox, Leonard Slatkin and Neville Marriner; Numerous appearances on television and video; Walton's Concerto at the 1999 London Prom concerts; Wigmore Hall concerts, 2000; Tchaikovsky Concerto at the Royal Festival Hall, 2001; Beethoven's Concerto in D major at the London Proms, 2002. *Recordings:* Nicholas Maw's Violin Concerto; Violin concertos of Mendelssohn and Bruch; Tchaikovsky's A Minor Trio; Lalo Symphonie Espagnole; Mozart, Concertos No. 3 and 5; Chamber music recitals with the Takacs Quartet; Film music for The Red Violin, John Williams' transcription of Porgy and Bess. *Current Management:* Astrid Schoerke. *Address:* c/o Monckebergallee 41, 30453 Hannover, Germany.

BELLING, Susan; Opera Singer (Soprano); b. 3 May 1943, Bronx, NY, USA. *Education:* Chatham Square Music School, 1958–60; Kathryn Long School, 1965–67; Metropolitan Opera Studio, 1964–67; Manhattan School of Music, 1960–63. *Career:* Masterclasses and workshops at Stanford University, California, 1978, University of Houston, 1978, and Manhattan School of Music, 1984; Faculty, New School of Social Research, 1986–; Over 100 American and world premieres; Sang title role in Reimann's Melusine for Santa Fe Opera, and Kirchner's Lily with New York City Opera; Performance of Arnold Schoenberg's Second Quartet with Erich Leinsdorf and the Boston Symphony; Sang Belinda in Dido and Aeneas for Metropolitan Opera's premiere season of the Forum Opera, Lincoln Center; Performed on numerous occasions with conductor James Levine in such roles as Zerlina in Don Giovanni at Hollywood Bowl, Papagena in Magic Flute with Cleveland Concert Associates, as soprano soloist in A Midsummer Night's Dream and the Mahler Fourth Symphony with the Chicago Symphony, and with Atlanta Symphony in The Marriage of Figaro; Debut in Europe, Baroque Festival of Venetian Music, Castelfranco, Veneto and Teatro

Olimpico, Italy, 1977; Numerous other performances include Haydn's Lord Nelson Mass with Minnesota Orchestra, Neville Marriner conducting, and Pamina in The Magic Flute. *Address:* c/o Allied Artists Bureau, Michael Leavitt, 195 Steamboat Road, Great Neck, NY 11024, USA.

BELLO, Vincenzo; Singer (Tenor); b. 1950, Mogliano, Treviso, Italy. *Career:* Debut: Manrico in Il Trovatore, Treviso, 1975; Appearances throughout Italy from 1975 and at Barcelona and Munich; Sang Manrico at Verona and the Metropolitan, New York, 1978; Festival engagements at Macerata as Alfredo, (1978); Orange as Verdi's Macduff and at Florence as Ismaele in Nabucco, 1977; Sang Donizetti's Edgardo and Rodolfo in La Bohème at Brescia, Ruggero in La Rondine at Venice; Venice and Trieste, 1990–91 as Edgardo, Rodolfo in Luisa Miller and Arturo in Bellini's La Straniera; Further appearances at Covent Garden, as Verdi's Riccardo, 1988 and at Lisbon, in Roberto Devereux. *Honours:* Winner, Toti dal Monte Competition, 1975. *Address:* c/o Teatro Comunale, Riva Novembre 1, 34121 Trieste, Italy.

BELLU, Cristina; Cellist; b. 7 Feb. 1968; m. James A Holzwarth, 29 Feb 1992. *Education:* Diploma, Violoncello, 1991; Chicago Musical College, Roosevelt University, 1994. *Career:* Member, Civic Orchestra of Chicago. Appearances with Orchestra da Camera Fiorentina, Orchestra Lirico-Sinfonica del Teatro del Giglio di Lucca, University of Chicago Symphony Orchestra; Chicago Chamber Orchestra; Orchestra del Maggio Musicale Fiorentino; Numerous performances world-wide; Co-founder, Operacion Tango group; Professor of Violoncello, Ecole Nationale de Musique, Mulhouse, France. *Recordings:* Operacion Tango en Concert, 1999. *Address:* 11 Avenue Marechal Foch, 68100 Mulhouse, France.

BELLUCCI, Giacomo; Composer; b. 20 Jan. 1928, Recanati, Italy. *Education:* Classical Studies Certificate, Lyceum; Studied at Rossini's Conservatory, Pesaro, with Giorgi and Rome's S Cecilia with Margola and Mortari; Diploma in Composition, 1961; Conducting with Ferrara. *Career:* Conductor of orchestra and choir (also in lyric stage and Polyphony), performing in Italy and abroad (Europe and USA); Founder and Director of Recanati's Gigli Music Institute, 1977–82; Professor at Rossini's Conservatory, Pesaro, 1965–98; Principal of various Italian conservatories, 1982–90. *Recordings:* RAI; ORF; Suisse Romande. *Compositions:* Coreographie (Ballet); Il Punto (opera ballet); 3 symphonies; 3 overtures; 3 suites; 16 concertos for solo instrument and orchestra; 16 string quartets; 7 trios; 5 oratorios; 2 psalms; other orchestral compositions; many chamber works for various instruments, voice, organ, and sacred music. *Publications:* Many articles, texts and essays on music, critical notes to concertos for dailies and periodicals. *Address:* 5 via Zanucchi, 61100 Pesaro, Italy.

BELLUGI, Piero; Conductor; b. 14 July 1924, Florence, Italy; m. Ursula Herzberger, 1954 (divorced), 5 c. *Education:* Conservatorio Cherubini, Florence; Accademia Chigiana, Siena; Akademie des Mozarteums, Salzburg and Tanglewood, MA, USA. *Career:* Musical Director, Oakland, California, Portland, Oregon Symphony Orchestras, 1955–61; Permanent Conductor, Radio Symphony Orchestra, Turin, 1967; Professor of courses for orchestral players and conductors, Italian Youth Orchestra, 1981–91; Guest Conductor including La Scala, Milan; debut 1961 with Handel's Serse; Vienna State Opera; Rome Opera; Aix-en-Provence Festival; Berlin Radio; Paris; Rome S Cecilia; Chicago; San Francisco Operas; Concert repertory includes music by Mahler, Berg, Schoenberg and Webern; Conducted the premieres of Milhaud's 10th Symphony, 1961, and Settimo Concerto by Petrassi, 1965; at present he is the general music director of the Teatro Massimo, Palermo, Italy. *Address:* Via della Montagnola 149, 50027 Strada in Chianti, Florence, Italy. *E-mail:* pierobellugi@tin.it.

BELOHLAVEK, Jiri; Conductor; b. 24 Feb. 1946, Prague, Czechoslovakia. *Education:* Studied at the Prague Academy of Arts with Sergiu Celibidache. *Career:* Assistant Conductor with the Czech Philharmonic; Conductor of the Brno State Philharmonic, 1971–77; Chief Conductor of the Prague Symphony Orchestra, 1977–90; Artistic Director and Principal Conductor of the Czech Philharmonic Orchestra from 1990–92; Extensive tours with the Prague Symphony and the Czech Philharmonic in Europe, the USA and Japan; Guest appearances with the Berlin Philharmonic, New York Philharmonic, the Boston, Toronto and Vienna Symphony Orchestras, Leipzig Gewandhaus, Stockholm Philharmonic, NHK Philharmonic (Tokyo) and the USSR State Symphony Orchestra; Edinburgh Festival, 1990, with the Prague Symphony Orchestra; Further British engagements with the City of Birmingham Symphony, the BBC Philharmonic, Scottish National, Royal Liverpool Philharmonic and BBC National Orchestra of Wales; Principal guest with the BBC Symphony Orchestra, 1995; Further concerts with the St Louis, Bavarian Radio, Washington National Dresden Philharmonic, Deutsche Kammerphilharmonie and Tonhalle (Zürich) Orchestras; Conducted the BBC Philharmonic in music by Brahms, Zemlinsky (Maeterlinck Songs) and Mahler (1st Symphony) at the 1993 Promenade Concerts. Season 1999 with Brahms 4th and Shostakovich 5th Symphonies at the London Proms; Conducted Dvořák's oratorio Saint Ludmilla at the 2002 Edinburgh Festival. *Recordings include:* Works by Martinů and Janáček, with the Czech Philharmonic. *Honours:* Finalist, Herbert von Karajan International Conducting Competition, 1971. *Address:* BBC, 50 Maida Vale Studios, Delaware Road, London W9 2 LG, England.

BELSKAYA, Nina; Violist; b. 1960, Moscow, Russia. *Education:* Studied at Moscow Conservatoire with Professor Strakhovos. *Career:* Member of the Prokofiev Quartet, founded at the Moscow Festival of World Youth and the International Quartet Competition at Budapest; Many concerts in the former Soviet Union and on tour to Czechoslovakia, Germany, Austria, USA, Canada, Spain, Japan and Italy; Repertoire includes works by Haydn, Mozart, Beethoven, Schubert, Debussy, Ravel, Tchaikovsky, Bartók and Shostakovich. *Current Management:* Sonata, Glasgow, Scotland. *Address:* 11 North Park Street. Glasgow G20 7AA, Scotland.

BELTON, Ian; Violinist; b. 1959, England. *Education:* Studied at the Royal Northern College of Music; Diplomas, BMus, Manchester University; GRNCM; PPRNCM. *Career:* Founder member of the Brodsky String Quartet; Resident at Cambridge University for 4 years and later residencies at Dartington International Summer School, Devon; Concert engagements include the Shostakovich Quartets at the Queen Elizabeth Hall in London and performances at the Ludwigsburg and Schleswig-Holstein Festivals; New York debut at the Metropolitan Museum; Tours of Italy, North America, Australia, Poland, Czechoslovakia, Istanbul and Japan; Complete quartets of Schoenberg for the BBC; French concerts include Théâtre du Châtelet, Paris; Concert in Amsterdam and performances at Berlin Festival, Carnegie Hall; Tour of Australia in 1993. *Recordings include:* Quartets of Elgar and Delius; Schubert A minor and Beethoven Op 74; Complete Quartets of Shostakovich; Borodin Quartet No. 2; Tchaikovsky Quartet No. 3; Collaboration with Elvis Costello entitled Juliet Letters. *Address:* c/o Brodsky Quartet, 21–22 Old Steine, Brighton BN1 1EG, England.

BELTRAN, Tito; Chilean singer (tenor); b. 1969. *Education:* Gothenburg Acad. and with Vera Rosza and Robin Stapleton, London. *Career:* roles include Nemorino, Ernesto, Edgardo, Rodolfo, Ruggero (La Rondine), Pinkerton, Rinuccio Italian Tenor (Der Rosenkavalier), Duca, Macduff, Ismaele, Alfredo, Tybalt, Tebaldo; has sung at Covent Garden (debut Rodolfo 1995), Opera North, Vienna (debut Nemorino 1997), Hamburg, Ludwigsfaafen, Bayerische Staatsoper Munich, Deutsche Oper Berlin, Leipzig, Mannheim, Opera Bastille (debut Der Rosenkavalier 2002), Toulouse, Bordeaux, La Scala (debut Der Rosenkavalier 2003), Genoa, Teatro Regio Torino, Parma, Arena di Verona, Roma, Lucca, Cosenza, Fenno, Monte Carlo, Geneva, Zurich, Gothenburg, Copenhagen, Norske Opera Oslo, Iceland, Menorca, Santiago Chile, Rio de Janeiro, Michigan (USA debut Rodolfo 1996), San Francisco, Orlando, Pittsburgh, Portland, New Nat. Theatre, Tokyo; numerous worldwide concerts and TV appearances; lives in Sweden. *Recordings:* four solo CD s for Suva Screen Classics: Tito, Romantica, A Tenor At The Movies, Amazing Grace; Celemin in La Dolores by Tomas Bretón (with Placido Domingo) for Decca. *Television:* sang Tybalt in Iambic Productions film of Romeo et Juliette (with Roberto Alagna and Angela Gheorghiu) (Channel 4) 2004. *Honours:* finalist, Cardiff Singer of the World Competition 1993, Opera Now Artist of the Year 1999. *Current Management:* c/o Penelope Marland Artists Management, 10 Roseneath Road, London, SW11 6AH, England. *Telephone:* (20) 7223-7319. *Fax:* (20) 7771-0675. *E-mail:* Penelope@marlandartists.fsnet.co.uk. *Website:* www.titobeltran.com.

BELYAEV, Yevegeni; Violinist; b. 1950, Crimea, Russia. *Career:* Co-Founder, Rachmaninov Quartet, 1974, under auspices of the Sochi State Philharmonic Society, Crimea; Many concerts in the former Soviet Union and from 1975–76 tours to Switzerland, Austria, Bulgaria, Norway and Germany; Participation in the 1976 Shostakovich Chamber Music Festival at Vilnius and in festivals in Moscow and St Petersburg; Repertoire has included works by Haydn, Mozart, Beethoven, Bartók, Schnittke, Shostakovich, Boris Tchaikovsky, Chalayev and Meyerovich. *Honours:* With the Rachmaninov Quartet: Prizewinner, First All-Union Borodin String Quartet Competition, 1987. *Current Management:* Sonata, Glasgow, Scotland. *Address:* 11 North Park Street, Glasgow G20 7AA, Scotland.

BEN-OR, Nelly; pianist and teacher; b. Warsaw, Poland. *Education:* Music High School Poland, Music Acad., Israel. *Career:* in Israel, awarded first prize in Mozart Competition, solo recitals, chamber music broadcasts, soloist with Radio Orchestra; in England, recitals in London, Queen Elizabeth Hall, Wigmore Hall, St John's, Smith Square for BBC and throughout the UK; recitals, broadcasts and masterclasses world-wide; teacher of the Alexander Technique 1963–; specialist in application of the Alexander Technique to piano playing; Prof., piano dept Guildhall School of Music 1975; mem. Incorporated Soc. of Musicians, European Piano Teachers' Asscn (UK founder cttee mem.),

Soc. of Teachers of the Alexander Technique. *Recordings:* Piano Variations (various composers) 1989, Beethoven Complete Bagatelles 1995, Beethoven Piano Quartet op 16, with Jerusalem String Trio 1990, Chopin Dances 1990, Debussy (Complete Images) 1997, Schubert Impromptus D899 and D935 1991, Dvorak/Fibch Piano Quartets, with Jerusalem String Trio 1990, Bach Toccata in D, Chopin (Mazurkas), Kinghorn piano sonata 2000. *Publications:* articles in various professional publications; contrib. to various professional publications on the application of the Alexander Technique to piano playing. *Address:* c/o Roger Clynes, 23 Rofaut Road, Northwood, Middlesex, HA6 3BD, England (office). *Telephone:* (1923) 822268 (office). *Fax:* (1923) 822268 (office). *E-mail:* roger.clynes@virgin.net (office). *Website:* www .pianocourseswithalexandertechnique.com (office).

BEN-YOHANAN, Asher; Israeli composer and music educator; b. 22 May 1929, Kavala, Greece; m. Shoshana Zwibel; one s. one d. *Education:* studied oboe and piano; composition studies with Paul Ben-Haim, Israel, Aaron Copland, USA and Luigi Nono, Italy; studies with Gustave Reese and Jan La Rue, New York Univ.; MMus, Univ. of Michigan. *Career:* compositions performed in Israel, Europe, USA, South America and Hong Kong; Head of Music Dept and Teacher of Theory, Thelma Yellin Music and Arts School, Tel-Aviv, Israel, 1966–75; Prof. of Music, Bar-Ilan Univ. 1973–96; mem. Israel Composers' League, Chair. 1989–92. *Compositions include:* Two Movements for Orchestra, 1959; String Quartet, 1962–64; Music for Orchestra, 1967; Chamber Music for 6, 1968; Quartetto Concertato, 1969; Mosaic, 1971; Concerto for String Orchestra, 1973; Four Summer Songs, 1974; Impressions for Piano, 1976; Soliloquy for Violin, 1977; Desert Winds for Flute, 1979; Three Songs without Titles, 1983; Episode for Trombone, 1984; Woodwind Quintet, 1985; Divertimento for Brass Trio, 1988–89; Hidden Feelings for Harp, 1990; Meditations for chamber orchestra, 1992, and other works. *Publications:* Music in Israel, A Short Survey, 1975; Music Notation, 1983. *Honours:* Morse Fellowship in Composition, Univ. of Cincinnati, USA 1971. *Address:* 4 Bloch Street, Tel-Aviv 64161, Israel (home).

BENACKOVA, Gabriela; Singer (Soprano); b. 25 March 1944, Bratislava, Czechoslovakia. *Education:* Bratislava Academy with Janko Blaho and Tatiana Kiesakova. *Career:* Debut: Prague National Theatre, 1970 as Natasha in War and Peace; Returned as Mimi, Marenka in The Bartered Bride, Jenůfa and Libuše in Smetana's opera, 1983; Appeared at Covent Garden in 1979 as Tatiana in Eugene Onegin, Cologne Opera in 1983 as Maddalena in Andrea Chénier, Vienna Staatsoper, 1985 as Marguerite in a new production of Faust directed by Ken Russell, San Francisco in 1986 as Jenůfa, Vienna Staatsoper in 1987 as Rusalka; Sang Desdemona at Stuttgart in 1990, Leonore at 1990 Salzburg Festival, Katya Kabanova at the Metropolitan in 1991; Season 1992 as Fidelio at Covent Garden; Sang Maddalena in Andrea Chénier at Zürich, 1994; Sang Wagner's Senta at Hamburg, 1996; Jenůfa at Zürich, 1998; Sang Desdemona at the New York Met, 1991, and Janáček's Emilia Marty at Brno, 2001. *Recordings:* Janáček's Jenůfa and The Cunning Little Vixen; The Bartered Bride; Libuše; Rusalka (Supraphon); Soloist in Janáček's Glagolitic Mass; Dvořák's Requiem. *Honours:* Prizewinner, Janáček Competition, Luhacovice in 1962; Winner, Dvořák Competition, Karlovy Vary in 1963; Czech National Artist in 1985. *Current Management:* Askonas Holt Ltd, Lonsdale Chambers, 27 Chancery Lane, London, WC2A 1PF, England. *Telephone:* (20) 7400-1700. *Fax:* (20) 7400-1799. *E-mail:* info@askonasholt.co .uk. *Website:* www.askonasholt.co.uk.

BENARY, Barbara; Composer and Gamelan Performer; b. 7 April 1946, Bay Shore, NY, USA. *Education:* BA, 1968, Sarah Lawrence College; PhD in Ethnomusicology, Wesleyan University, 1973. *Career:* Has played the violin and has performed on various stringed instruments of India, China and Bulgaria; In 1974 formed the Gamelan Son of Lion, an ensemble of Javanese instruments; Assistant Professor at Livingstone College, Rutgers University, New Jersey, 1973–80. *Compositions include:* Music Theatre: Three Sisters Who Are Not Sisters, 1967, The Only Jealousy Of Emer, 1970, The Interior Castle, 1973, The Gauntlet, 1976, Sanguine, 1976, The Tempest, 1981; Gamelan: Convergence, 1975, Braid, 1975, No Friends In An Auction, 1976, In Time Enough, 1978, Sleeping Braid, 1978, The Zen Story, 1979, In Scroll Of Leaves, 1980, Moon Cat Chant, 1980, Singing Braid, 1980, Solkattu, 1980, Sun Square, 1980, Exchanges, 1981, Hot-Rolled Steel, 1984; Dance Scores: Night Thunks, 1980, A New Pantheon, 1981, Engineering, 1981. *Address:* c/o American Music Center, 30 West 26th Street, Suite 1001, New York, NY 10010-2011, USA.

BENDER, Madeline; Singer (Soprano); b. 1970, USA. *Education:* Manhattan School of Music Opera Theater, Santa Fe Opera Apprentice Program. *Career:* Appearances as Ippolito in Traetta's Ippolito and Aricia at Montpellier, Mimi for Opera Birmingham, Ismene in Mitridate and Gluck's Eurydice at the Paris Châtelet; Tigrane in Handel's Radamisto at St Louis, Micaela in Carmen and Pannotchka in Rimsky's May Night for Sarasota Opera; Sister in Weill's Der Protangonist with the BBC

Symphony Orchestra; Further concerts with the Cincinnati, Toronto, Detroit, National and St Louis Symphonies; Glyndebourne Festival debut as Helena in A Midsummer Night's Dream, 2001; Violetta for Opera Birmingham, 2001–2002. *Recordings include:* Babes in Toyland by Herbert. *Address:* c/o Glyndebourne Festival Opera, Glyndebourne, Lewes, Sussex BN8 5UU, England.

BENEDICT, Roger; Violist; b. 1962, England. *Education:* Studied with Patrick Ireland and Eli Goren at the Royal Northern College of Music. *Career:* Principal violist of the Philharmonia Orchestra and soloist in Strauss's Don Quixote at the Edinburgh Festival and Festival Hall, London; Vaughan Williams Flos Campi with the New London Orchestra and premiere of Michael Berkeley's Concerto, with Philharmonia Orchestra, 1994; Also plays concerto works by Mozart, Bartók, Walton and Berlioz with Philharmonia, Royal Philharmonic, Ulster Orchestra; Member of the Bell'Arte Ensemble with performances at Symphony Hall, Birmingham; Performed with Wanderer Trio, Hagai Shaham and Noriko Ogawa at the Bastad Festival in Sweden; Al Bustan Festival, Beirut with flautist Patrick Gallois and harpist Fabrice Pierre, 1998; On leaving the Philharmonia became regular principal of English Chamber Orchestra; Appointed Prof. at the Royal Northern Collage of Music, 1998; International engagements include performances in South Africa, Scandinavia, the Middle East and Japan; In 2002 moved to Australia, Principal viola in the Sydney Symphony Orchestra; Artistic Director of James Fairfax Young Artists Program; Senior Lecturer at Sydney Conservatorium; solo tours of Japan, 2002; soloist with S.S.O. and other Australian Orchestras.. *Address:* 9 Alison Street, Roseville, NSW, 2069, Australia. *Telephone:* (2) 9880–7005. *E-mail:* rogerbenedict@dodo.com.au.

BENELLI, Ugo; Italian Singer (Tenor); b. 20 Jan. 1935, Genoa, Italy; m. Angela Maria Patrone; one s. one d.. *Education:* Studied with assistance of La Scala stipendium. *Career:* Debut: Piccola Scala, 1960; Guest appearances in Wiesbaden, Buenos Aires, Barcelona and Mexico City; appeared at Wexford Festival, 1966; Glyndebourne Festival, 1970 in Il Turco in Italia; Covent Garden debut in 1974 as Ernesto in Don Pasquale; Appeared in Turin in 1975 in Die drei Pintos by Weber/Mahler; Further engagements in Edinburgh, Moscow and San Francisco; appeared at Théâtre de la Monnaie, Brussels, in 1986 as Podestà in La Finta Giardiniera; Roles include Rossini's Almaviva, Lindoro, Don Ramiro , Bellini's Elvino, Donizetti's Nemorino, Ernesto and Tonio, Bizet's Nadir and Massenet's Des Grieux and Werther; Season 1992 as Conte Riccardo in I Quattro Rusteghi at Geneva, Don Anchise in La Finta Giardiniera and Le Nozze de Figaro at the Salzburg Festival and Mozart's Basilio at Florence; Sang Hauk in The Makropulos Case at Turin and Seu Cento, 1993; Season 2001–02 as Hans Styx in Orphée aux Enfers at Turin and Jack O'Brien in Mahagonny at Genoa. *Recordings include:* Il Barbiere di Siviglia and La Cenerentola; Don Pasquale and La fille du Régiment; Elisabeth Regina D'Inghilterra. *Address:* Viale Nazario Sauro, 6A Int. 4, 16145 Genoa, Italy. *Telephone:* (010) 311381. *Fax:* (010) 311381. *E-mail:* ugo.benelli@libero.it. *Website:* www.ugobenelli.com.

BENEŠ, Jiří, PhD; viola player and musicologist; b. 24 Sept. 1928, Komárno, Czechoslovakia; m. 1st; one s.; m. 2nd Zdenka Bubeníčkova; one d. *Education:* Univ. of Brno, Conservatory of Brno, Janáček Acad. of Musical Arts. *Career:* debut as viola player, Brno 1952; State Philharmonic Orchestra, Brno 1951–69; Moravian Quartet 1965–92; Dramaturg 1992–, including Brno Int. Music Festival (Moravian Autumn) 1993–; appearances on radio and television with Moravian Quartet, Czechoslovakia, Germany, Sweden, Italy; tours of most European countries; teacher, Janáček Acad. 1968–74, Conservatory of Brno 1969–82, Masaryk Univ. 2003–; mem. Czech Musical (Janáček) Soc.. *Publications:* contrib. to professional journals, radio programme notes, record sleeve notes. *Honours:* Italian Quartet Prize 1965, Janáček Medal 1978, Prize, Novecento Musicale Europeo, Naples 1988, Czech Music Council Award 2002. *Address:* Filipova 19, 63500 Brno, Czech Republic. *Telephone:* (546) 220204. *E-mail:* benesova@mujbox.cz.

BENESTAD, Finn; Music Educator and Musicologist; b. 30 Oct. 1929, Kristiansand, Norway. *Education:* violin lessons with Ernst Glaser, 1947–50; music courses at Univ. of Oslo; MA, 1953; PhD, 1961. *Career:* teacher, 1950–59; music critic, 1953–61; Prof. of Musicology at Univ. of Trondheim, 1961–64, Univ. of Oslo, 1965–98; Chair., Collected Works of Grieg. *Publications:* Johannes Haarklou: mannen og verket, 1961; Waldemar Thrane: en pioner i norsk musikkliv, 1961; Musikklaere, 1963, 5th edition, 1977; Musikkhistorisk oversikt, 1965, 3rd edition, 1976; Editor, Norsk musikk: Studier i Norge, vol. 6, 1968; Editor, Skolens visebok, 1972; Co-author, Edvard Grieg: Mennesket og kunstneren, 1980, English edition as Edvard Grieg: The Man and The Artist, 1988; Co-author, Johan Svendsen: Mennesket og kunstneren, 1990 and Edvard Grieg, Chamber Music, 1993; Edvard Grieg: Brev til Frants Beyer 1872–1907 (co-editor with Bjarne Kortsen), 1993; Edvard Grieg: Dagböker (Diaries) 1865, 1866, 1905, 1906, 1907, editor, 1993; Edvard Grieg: Briefwechsel mit dem Musikverlag C F Peters 1863–1907

(co-editor with Hella Brock), 1997; Edvard Grieg und Julius Röntgen. Briefwechsel 1883–1907 (co-editor with Hanna de Vries Stavland), 1997; Edvard Grieg: Brev i utvalg 1862–1907, vols I–II, 1998; Edvard Grieg: Letters to Colleagues and Friends, 2000; Edvard Grieg: Diaries, Articles, Speeches (co-editor with W. H. Halverson), 2001. *Contributions:* articles in various journals and other publications. *Honours:* Fulbright Scholar, Univ. of California, Los Angeles, 1968–69; elected mem., Norwegian Acad. of Sciences and Letters, 1979; Royal Danish Acad. of Sciences and Letters, 1991; Academia Europaea, 1992. *Address:* Agder allé 4A, 4631 Kristiansand, Norway.

BENGL, Volker; Singer (Tenor); b. 19 July 1960, Ludwigshafen, Germany. *Education:* Mannheim-Heidelberg Musikhochschule in Munich. *Career:* Staatstheater am Gartnerplatz, Munich; Guest, Vienna, Berlin, Wiesbaden; Sang at Saarbrucken from 1985; Dresden Semperoper; Guest appearances in Essen, Brunswick, Karlsruhe and Heidelberg; Sang Jenik in The Bartered Bride at Kaiserslautern, 1990; Other roles include Max in Der Freischütz, Tamino, Belfiore in La Finta Giardiniera, Don José, Pinkerton and parts in operetta; As concert singer appeared in New York, 1989, Berlin (Bruckner F minor Mass and Te Deum) and elsewhere in Europe; Other Repertoire includes Bach Christmas Oratorio and Dvořák Requiem; Sang Wilhelm Meister in Mignon at the Munich Gärtnerplaztheater, 2000. *Compositions:* Wiegenlied, words and music, 1997. *Recordings include:* Vorhang auf; Schön is die Welt. *Address:* Marschalls h-6, 80802 Munich, Germany.

BENGTSSON, Erling Blondal; Cellist; b. 1932, Copenhagen, Denmark; m. Merete Bengtsson 1958, two s. *Education:* Studied with Piatigorsky at Curtis Institute, USA. *Career:* Debut: First public concert at age 4; First concerto with orchestra at age 10; Professor of Cello, Curtis Institute, USA, the Royal Danish Conservatory, Copenhagen; the Swedish Radio's Music Academy, Stockholm and the State Academy in Cologne; Professor at the School of Music, University of Michigan, Ann Arbor, USA, 1990–; Masterclasses at Aldeburgh in England, Switzerland, Scandinavia and USA. Played with most of the world's leading orchestras with such conductors as Monteux, Sargent, Lutoslawski, Pritchard, Dorati, Groves, Ehrling, Berglund, Temirkanov and Yansons; Scandinavian first performances of cello-concertos by Britten, Barber, Khatchaturian, Delius, Lutoslawski and Walton. *Recordings:* Over 50 albums; Complete standard repertoire for cello and orchestra; Many contemporary concertos dedicated to him; Beethoven and Brahms Sonatas; Bach Suites for Solo Cello; Rachmaninov and Shostakovich sonata; Kodály Solo-sonata; Reger suites; Sonatas by Barber, Debussy, Prokofiev, 2001. *Contributions:* Edited Bach and Reger Solo Cello Suites for the Internet publishing company .SheetMusicNow.com. *Honours:* Honours and awards include: Knight, first class, of the order of Dannebrog, Denmark; Grand Knight of the order of the Falcon, Iceland; The English Hyam Morrison Gold Medal for cello; The title "Chevalier du Violoncelle" by Indiana University; Award of Distinction, The RNCM Manchester International Cello Festival, 2001. *Current Management:* Tivoli Artists, Copenhagen. *Address:* 1217 Westmoorland, Ypsilanti, MI 48197, USA. *Website:* www.erlingbb.com.

BENGUEREL, Xavier; Composer; b. 9 Feb. 1931, Barcelona, Spain. *Education:* Studied in Santiago and Barcelona with Cristobal Taltabull. *Compositions include:* 2 Violin Sonatas, 1953, 1959; String Quartet, 1955; Concerto for Piano and Strings, 1955; Concerto for 2 Flutes and Strings, 1961; Sinfonia Continua, 1962; Successions for Wind Quartet, 1960; Duo for Clarinet and Piano, 1963; Nocturno for Soprano, Chorus and Orchestra, 1963; Violin Concerto, 1965; Sinfonia Per A Un Festival, 1966; Sinfonia for Small Orchestra, 1967; Paraules De Cada Dia for Voice and Chamber Orchestra, 1967; Musica for 3 Percussionists, 1967; Sinfonia for Large Orchestra, 1969; Dialogue Orchestrale, 1969; Musica Riservata for Strings, 1969; Crescendo for Organ, 1970; Organ Concerto, 1971; Arbor, cantata, 1972; Verses for Guitar, 1973; Destructio for Orchestra. 1973; Capriccio Stravagante for Ensemble, 1974; Thesis for Chamber Group; Concerto for Percussion and Orchestra, 1976. *Honours:* Winner, Composition Prize of the Barcelona Juventudes Musicales, 1955; Represented Spain at ISCM Festival, 1960. *Address:* c/o SGAE, Fernando VI 4, Apartado 484, 28080 Madrid 4, Spain.

BENHAM, Hugh Raymond, BA, PhD, ARCO; teacher, examiner and organist; b. 14 Dec. 1943, Westbury, England; m.; one d. *Education:* Univ. of Southampton. *Career:* teacher 1968–97; examiner 1980–92, 1996–; organist 1965–; mem. Royal Musical Asscn, Incorporated Soc. of Musicians. *Publications:* Latin Church Music in England c.1460–1575; John Taverner (complete edition, Early English Church Music); John Taverner: his Life and Music (listening tests for students); contrib. to Music & Letters, The Musical Times, The Music Review, Early Music, Plainsong and Medieval Music, Music Teacher, Classroom Music, New Grove Dictionary of Music and Musicians 2001, Oxford Dictionary of Nat. Biography 2004. *Address:* 11 North End Close, Chandler's Ford, Eastleigh, Hants SO53 3HY, England (home). *E-mail:* hugh.benham@talk21.com (home).

BENINI, Maurizio; Conductor; b. 1968, Italy. *Education:* Bologna Conservatory. *Career:* Principal Conductor, Philharmonic Orchestra, Teatro Communale, Bologna, 1984; Opera debut at Bologna with Rossini's Il Signor Bruschino; Don Carlo and Rossini's Donna del Lago at La Scala, Milan; La Scala di Seta at Pesaro; Engagements in Paris at the Opéra Bastille and Palais Garnier; Principal Conductor, Wexford Festival Opera, 1995–97, with Pacini's Saffo, Donizetti's Parisina, 1996; Mercadante's Elena da Feltre, 1997; New York Met debut, 1998, L'Elisir d'amore; Royal Opera debut, 1999, with Un giorno di regno, Festival Hall; Other repertory includes Rossini's Zelmira, Lyon and Paris; Nabucco and Don Pasquale; 1999–2000 season: La Traviata, Deutsche Oper Berlin, La Sonnambula at La Scala and Faust at Opéra Bastille; Season 2002–03 at Covent Garden, with La Sonnambula and Madama Butterfly. *Recordings:* Elena da Feltre. *Address:* c/o La Scala Milan, Via Filodrammatici 2, 20121 Milan, Italy.

BENJAMIN, George; Composer, Conductor and Pianist; b. 31 Jan. 1960, London, England. *Education:* Peter Gellhorn, 1974–76; With Olivier Messiaen at the Paris Conservatoire, 1976–78; With Alexander Goehr at King's College, Cambridge, 1978–82; Research at IRCAM, Paris, 1984–87; Debuts: Redcliffe Concert, Purcell Room, London, 1979; Conducted Debussy's Pelléas et Mélisande, La Monnaie, Brussels, 1999. *Career:* Works performed and by such orchestras as London Sinfonietta, London Philharmonic, BBC Symphony, Concertgebouw, New York Philharmonic, Cleveland Orchestra, Boston Symphony, Ensemble Modern and Ensemble Intercontemporain; BBC television documentary profile, Omnibus, 1987; Artistic Director and Conductor of contemporary music festivals with San Francisco Symphony, 1992; Opéra Bastille, 1992; South Bank, 1993; Prince Consort Professor of Composition, Royal College of Music, 1985–2001; Henry Purcell Professor of Composition, King's College London, 2002–; Principal Guest Artist, Hallé Orchestra, 1993–96; Featured Composer, 1995 Salzburg Festival; Artistic Consultant, BBC Radio 3 Sounding the Century, 1997–99; Cheltenham Festival, 1998; Composer-in-Residence, Tanglewood, 1999, 2000; Festival of Music, By George, Barbican Hall, London, 2002; Featured composer, LSO, 2002–3. *Compositions:* Orchestral: Ringed by the Flat Horizon, 1979–80; A Mind of Winter, soprano and orchestra, 1981; At First Light, 1982; Jubilation, 1985; Antara (with electronics), 1985–87; Sudden Time, 1989–93; 3 inventions for chamber orchestra, 1995; Sometime Voices for baritone, chorus and orchestra, 1996; Palimpsest I, 2000; Palimpsest II, 2002; Olicantus, 2002; Chamber: Violin Sonata, 1976–77; Octet, 1978; Flight for flute, 1979; Duo for cello and piano, 1980; Piano Sonata, 1977–78; Sortilèges, 1981; 3 Studies for piano: Fantasy on Iambic Rhythm, Meditation on Haydn's Name, Relatively Rag, 1982–85; Upon Silence, mezzo and 5 viols, 1990; mezzo and string ensemble, 1991; Viola, Viola for viola duo, 1997; Shadowlines for piano solo, 2001; Three Miniatures for solo violin, 2001–2; Olicantus, for 17 players, 2002. *Recordings:* majority of works recorded. *Honours:* Lili Boulanger Award, Boston, 1985; Koussevitsky International Record Award, New York, 1987; Grand Prix du Disque Charles Cros, Paris, 1988; FRCM, 1994; Chevalier dans l'Ordre des Arts et Lettres, 1996; Edison Award, Amsterdam, 1998; Bavarian Academy of Arts, 2000; Schönberg Prize, Berlin, 2002. *Current Management:* Askonas Holt Ltd, Lonsdale Chambers, 27 Chancery Lane, London, WC2A 1PF, England. *Telephone:* (20) 7400-1700. *Fax:* (20) 7400-1799. *E-mail:* info@askonasholt.co.uk. *Website:* www.askonasholt.co.uk. *Address:* c/o Faber Music, 3 Queens Square, London, WC1N 3AU, England.

BENNETT, Elinor, LLB; Welsh harpist; *Artistic Director, William Mathias Music Centre;* b. 17 April 1943, Llanidloes, Wales; m. Dafydd Wigley 1967; three s. (two deceased) one d. *Education:* University College of Wales, Royal Academy of Music, London. *Career:* debut, Wigmore Hall, London; freelance harpist with London Symphony Orchestra, Philharmonia, English Chamber Orchestra, 1967–71; soloist and recitalist, BBC Radio 3; HTV, A Day in the Life of Elinor Bennett; BBC, At Home (Richard Baker); chamber music player; dir of festivals; dedicatee of many new works by contemporary composers, including Alun Hoddinott, Malcolm Williamson and John Metcalf; Artistic Dir, William Mathias Music Centre 2002–. *Recordings:* Two Harps; With Harp and Voice; The Harp of Wales; Portrait of the Harp, 1988; Nimbus: Images and Impressions, with Judith Hall (flute); Lorelt: Sea of Glass, 1994; Nimbus: Mathias, Santa Fe Suite and other 20th century classics, 1995; Sain: Harps and Songs, Portrait of the Harp, The Harp of Wales, Two Harps; Victorian Harp Music; John Thomas: 24 Welsh Melodies– The Complete Collection, 1998. *Publications:* Living Harp, Living Harp II 1998, John Thomas' Harp Duets 2000. *Honours:* Hon. Fellowships Univ. of Wales Aberystwyth, Cardiff Univ., Royal Welsh Coll. of Music and Drama. *Address:* Hen Efail, Bontnewydd, Caernarfon, Gwynedd LL54 7YH, Wales. *Telephone:* (1286) 830010. *E-mail:* elinor@elinorbennett.com. *Website:* www.elinorbennett.com.

BENNETT, Sir Richard Rodney, Kt; Composer; b. 29 March 1936, Broadstairs, Kent, England. *Education:* Royal Academy of Music,

London; French Government Scholarship to study with Pierre Boulez in Paris, 1957–59. *Career:* Commissioned to write 2 operas by Sadler's Wells, 1962; Professor of Composition at Royal Academy of Music, 1963–65; Vice-President of Royal College of Music, 1983–; International Chair of Composition at the Royal Academy of Music, London, 1995; Flute Concerto premiered at the 1999 London Prom concerts; mem, General Council, Performing Right Society, 1975–. *Compositions include:* The Approaches of Sleep, 1959; The Ledge, 1961; Nocturnes, 1962; Jazz Calendar, 1964; Symphony No. 1, 1965, No. 2, 1967, No. 3, 1987; Piano Concerto, 1968; Oboe Concerto, 1970; Guitar Concerto, 1971; Viola Concerto, 1973; Spells, choral in 1975; Violin Concerto, 1975; Serenade for Youth Orchestra, 1977; Acteon, for Horn and Orchestra, 1977; Sonnets To Orpheus, for Cello and Orchestra, 1979; Anniversaries, 1982; Sinfonietta, 1984; Love Songs, for Tenor and Orchestra, 1984; Moving Into Aquarius, 1984; Reflections On A Theme Of William Walton, for 11 solo strings, 1985; Clarinet Concerto, 1987; Saxophone Concerto, 1988; Percussion Concerto, 1990; Partita for orchestra, 1995; Flute Concerto, 1999; Partita, for solo cello, 2001; Chamber and incidental music; Opera: The Mines of Sulphur, 1964; A Penny For A Song, 1966; Victory, 1969; All The King's Men (for children), 1969; Isadora, ballet, 1981; Film and television music. *Honours:* Arnold Bax Society Prize for Commonwealth Composers, 1964; Anthony Asquith Memorial Award for Murder On The Orient Express film music, Society of Film and Television Awards, 1974. *Current Management:* Alice Gribbin, Clarion/Seven Muses, 47 Whitehall Park, London, N19 3TW, England. *Website:* www.c7m.co.uk.

BENNETT, William; Flautist; b. 7 Feb. 1936, London. *Education:* Guildhall School London, with Geoffrey Gilbert; Paris with Jean-Pierre Rampal, and with Marcel Moyse. *Career:* Former Principal Flautist with the London Symphony and Royal Philharmonic Orchestra, English Chamber Orchestra and Academy of St Martin-in-the-Fields; Many appearances as soloist in Britain and abroad in concerto repertory, including works dedicated to him by William Matthias and Richard Rodney Bennett; Contributed to world-wide development of flute manufacture tuned to William Bennett Scale; Teacher at Royal Academy, London, and transcriber of various works for flute. *Recordings:* Many albums in solo and chamber music repertory including works by Bach and Mozart. *Honours:* O.B.E., 1995. *Address:* c/o Royal Academy of Music, Marylebone Road, London, NW1 5HT, England.

BENNETT, Zon, BMus, MMus; Musicologist and Composer; b. 10 Aug. 1961, New York, NY, USA; m. Clare; two s. *Education:* Univ. of Michigan, USA, Univ. of Edinburgh, Univ. of Oxford. *Career:* Reader in Music, Durham Univ. 2000–; Senior Lecturer in Music, Hull Univ. 1994–2000; Tutor in Music, Univ. of Oxford 1990–94; Gen. Ed., Nineteenth-Century Music Review 2002–, Music in Nineteenth-Century Britain (book series) 1997–; mem. American Musicological Soc., Coll. Music Soc., Royal Musical Asscn. *Compositions:* Litany of the Sea for Orchestra 2000, Gothic Fragment 2000, Military Fanfare 1998, Communion Service 1995, Matins Responsary for Woman's Choir 1994. *Recordings:* The Gentlemen of St John's College Choir 1990. *Publications:* Music and Metaphor in Nineteenth-Century British Musicology 2000, The English Plainchant Revival 1992; contrib. to numerous publications and journals from 1989, including Nineteenth-Century British Music Studies, Music & Letters, Music & Liturgy, The Hymn Tune Index (ed. Nicholas Temperley), The Shorter Oxford Book of Carols, Early Music, New Dictionary of National Biography, The New Grove Dictionary of Music (second edn), Irish Musical Studies. *Honours:* Arts and Humanities Research Board Research Leave Grant 2003, Louise Dyer Award, Musica Britannica Trust 1992, Overseas Research Student Awards, CVCP 1990, 1991, Univ. of Hull Research Leave Award 1999. *Address:* University of Durham School of Music, Palace Green, Durham, DH1 3RL, England (office). *Telephone:* (191) 3343156 (office). *E-mail:* bennett.zon@durham.ac.uk (office). *Website:* www.dur.ac.uk/music (office).

BENNINGSEN, Lillian; Singer, (Contralto); b. 17 July 1924, Vienna, Austria. *Education:* Studied in Vienna with Anna Bahr-Mildenburg. *Career:* Debut: Salzburg Landestheater, 1948; Sang with Cologne Opera, 1950–52; Munich Staatsoper from 1951; As Eboli in Don Carlos, Fricka, Carmen, Amneris, Octavian and Dorabella; Marcellina in Le nozze di Figaro; Covent Garden, 1953 in the British premiere of Strauss's Die Liebe der Danaë, with the Munich Company; Salzburg Festival, 1955, in the premiere of Egk's Irische Legende; Schwetzingen Festival, 1961, in the premiere of Henze's Elegie für junge Liebende; Munich 1969 in the premiere of Aucassin and Nicolette by Bialas; Widely heard in recital and concert. *Recordings:* Le nozze di Figaro; Magdalene in Die Meistersinger conducted by Keilberth; Ariadne auf Naxos; Die tote Stadt by Korngold.

BENOIT, Jean-Christophe; Singer, (Bass-Baritone); b. 18 March 1925, Paris, France. *Education:* Studied at the Paris Conservatoire. *Career:* Sang in the French provinces, then at the Paris Opéra and Opéra-Comique; Guest appearances in Geneva for the premieres of Monsieur de Pourceaugnac by Martin, 1963; Milhaud's La Mère Coupable, 1966; Aix-en-Province Festival, 1954–57; Salzburg Festival, 1956; La Scala Milan, 1958; Further engagements at the Holland Festival, Monte Carlo and Brussels; Best known as Mozart's Guglielmo and Antonio; Rossini's Basilio; Raimbaud in Le Comte Ory; Somarone in Béatrice et Bénédict; Boniface in Le Jongleur de Notre Dame; Torquemada in L'Heure Espagnole; Brussels 1983, in the premiere of Le Passion de Giles by Philippe Boesmans; Professor of Singing at the Paris Conservatoire. *Recordings:* Carmen; Platée; Lakmé; Les Contes d'Hoffmann and Il Barbiere di Siviglia; Les Indes Galantes; Paer's Le Maître de Chapelle. *Address:* c/o Conservatoire National de Musique, 14 Rue de Madrid, 75008 Paris, France.

BENSON, Clifford (George); Concert Pianist; b. 17 Nov. 1946, Grays, Essex, England; m. 1 Sept 1973, 2 d. *Education:* ARCM Performance Diploma, 1964; Studied Piano with Lamar Crowson and Cyril Smith, Royal College of Music, London; Private Studies with George Malcolm, 1964–69; Studied Composition with Herbert Howells. *Career:* Debut: Royal Festival Hall, London, 1970; Performed Recordings and Broadcasts, BBC Radio 3, 1969–; Soloist, Royal Albert Hall Promenade Concerts, 1975; Travelled extensively playing at many major music festivals; Numerous recitals, solo and chamber music, also concertos; Duos with Thea King, William Bennett and Levon Chilingirian; mem, Incorporated Society of Musicians; Royal College of Music Union. *Compositions:* 3 Pieces for piano, 1983; Mozart Goes to Town (piano duet), 1985. *Recordings:* CRD; Deutsche Grammophon; CBS; Hyperion. *Honours:* Chopin Sonata Prize, Royal College of Music, 1966; Tagore Gold Medal, Royal College of Music, 1969; BBC Beethoven Duo Competition, 1969; Munich International Duo Competition, 1971 (with violinist Levon Chilingirian); Martin Musical Scholarship, NPO, 1968. *Address:* 76 Quarry Hill Road, Tonbridge, Kent TN 9 2PE, England.

BENSON, Joan; Clavichord Player, Fortepiano Player and Lecturer; b. 1935, St Paul, MN, USA. *Education:* MMus, Univ. of Illinois; protégée of Edwin Fischer, Switzerland; studies in clavichord music with Fritz Neumeyer, Germany, Santiago Kastner, Portugal; advanced study in Vienna, Paris, Italy and Germany. *Career:* concerts, lectures, appearances in festivals; television and radio appearances throughout USA, Europe, Near and Far East; Lecturer in Music, Stanford Univ., 1970–76; Asst Prof. of Music, 1976–82, Adjunct Prof., 1982–87, Univ. of Oregon. *Recordings:* Music by Kuhnau and C. P. E. Bach, 1988; Haydn and Pasquini, Boston Museum of Fine Arts clavichords, 1982; C. P. E. Bach on clavichord and fortepiano, 1972; Music for Clavichord, 1962. *Publications:* Haydn and the Clavichord, 1982; The Clavichord in 20th Century America, 1992; Bach and the Clavier, 1996. *Contributions:* articles: Haydn and the Clavichord, Vienna, 1982; Gulbenkian Society, Portugal; The Clavichord in 20th Century America, 1989; American Liszt Society Journal; Edwin Fischer, 1985; Clavier Magazine, Bach and the Clavier, 1990;. *Honours:* Performer's award, Univ. of Indiana; Kate Neal Award for Performance. *Current Management:* Marla Lowen. *Address:* 2795 Central Boulevard, Eugene, OR 97403, USA.

BENT, Ian (David); University Teacher; b. 1 Jan. 1938, Birmingham, England; m. Caroline Coverdale, 27 Aug 1979, 2 s., 1 d. *Education:* ARCO, 1958; St John's College, Cambridge, 1958–65; BA, 1st Class, Music Tripos, 1961; BMus, 1962; MA, 1965; PhD, 1969. *Career:* Lecturer in Music, King's College, University of London, 1965–75; Senior Consulting Editor, The New Grove Dictionary of Music, 1970–80; Professor of Music, University of Nottingham, 1975–87; Visiting Professor, Harvard University, USA, 1982–83; Visiting Professor, Columbia University, 1986–87; Professor, Columbia University, 1987–; mem, American Musicological Society; Royal Musical Association; Society for Music Theory; International Musicological Society. *Publications:* The Early History of the English Chapel Royal, 1066–1327, 1969; Source Materials and the Interpretation of Music; A Memorial Volume to Thurston Dart, 1981; Analysis, 1987; Music Analysis in the Nineteenth Century, 2 vols, 1994; Music Theory in the Age of Romanticism, ed., 1996. *Contributions:* Journal of the American Musicological Society; Music Analysis; Musical Times; Music and Letters; Proceedings of the Royal Musical Association; Theoria; General Editor, Cambridge Studies in Music Theory and Analysis. *Address:* Columbia University, New York, NY 10027, USA.

BENT, Margaret (Hilda); Musicologist; b. 23 Dec. 1940, St Albans, England; m. Ian Bent. *Education:* Studied at Girton College, Cambridge, PhD, 1969. *Career:* Taught at Cambridge, King's College London, 1965–75; Goldsmiths' College, from 1972; Teacher at Brandeis University, 1975–81; Princeton, from 1981; Researched Old Hall MS under Thurston Dart at Cambridge, published study with Andrew Hughes; President, American Musicological Society, 1983. *Publications:* The Old Hall Manuscript in the Corpus Mensurabilis Musicae series, XLVI, 1969–73; Dunstable, London, 1981; Articles on John Dunstable, Notation, Old Hall MS; Leonel Power and Square in the New Grove Dictionary of Music and Musicians, 1980; ed., Rossini's Il Turco in Italia,

for the Critical Edition, 1988; The Grammar of Early Music: Preconditions for Analysis, 1998. *Address:* All Souls College, Oxford, OX1 4AL, England. *E-mail:* margaret.bent@all-souls.oxford.ac.uk.

BENTLEY, Andrew; Composer and Computer Music Researcher; b. 30 June 1952, Fleetwood, England; m. Anna-Kaarina Kiviniemi, 9th Aug 1975, 2 s. *Education:* BA, Honours; DPhil, Composition, University of York, England. *Career:* Designer; Electronic Music Studio; Finnish Radio Experimental Studio, 1976–84; Teacher, Sibelius Academy, Helsinki, 1981–82; Studio Director, Helsinki University, 1982–84; Lecturer, Salford College of Technology, 1985–86; Director, Composers Desktop Project, York, 1986–; Leverhulme Computer Music Fellow, University of Nottingham, 1987–. *Compositions include:* Bowing, 1979; Portrait, 1979; Modulo, 1979; Contact with Bronze, 1979; Zoologic, 1980; Winter Winters, 1980; Aerial Views, 1981; Time for Change, 1981; Divertimento, 1983; Small Print, 1983. *Contributions:* Electronic Music for Schools, 1984; Professional Journals. *Honours:* Bourges International EAM Competition, 1979; Luigi Russolo Competition, 1979. *Address:* Leankatu 4 B 13, Helsinki 00240, Finland.

BENZA, Georgina; Singer (soprano); b. 1959, Russia (of Hungarian parentage). *Education:* Studied in Kiev and Budapest and in Munich with Wilma Lipp. *Career:* Has sung at the Munich Staatsoper from 1983, in such roles as Adina, Lauretta, Sophie, Pamina and Fiordiligi; More recent repertory includes Violetta, Tosca, Tatiana, Suor Angelica, Madama Butterfly, Marguerite and Aida; Guest engagements in Berlin (Deutsche Oper and Staatsoper), Frankfurt, Copenhagen, Leipzig, Bonn, Dresden and Barcelona; Bielefeld Opera as Tosca and Amelia in Un Ballo in Maschera; Sang Abigaille in Nabucco at Saarbrücken, 1999. *Honours:* Winner of Mozart Prizes in Vienna and Salzburg. *Current Management:* Athole Still International Management, Forresters Hall, 25–27 Westow Street, London, SE19 3RY, England. *Telephone:* (20) 8771-5271. *Fax:* (20) 8768-6600. *Website:* www.atholestill.com.

BENZI, Roberto; Conductor; b. 12 Dec. 1937, Marseilles, France; m. Jane Rhodes. *Education:* Studied music from age of 3; Baccalaureate, Sorbonne, Paris; Studied with André Cluytens, 1947–50;. *Career:* Debut: Bayonne, 1948; Conducted the Concerts Colonne in Paris. 1948; Appeared in films Prélude a la Gloire, 1949; L'Appel du Destin, 1950; Debut as opera conductor, 1954; Conducted Carmen at the Paris Opéra, 1959; Tours to Japan, 1961; Central Europe; North and South America; US Debut, 1971; Metropolitan Opera, 1972, Faust; Musical Director of the Orchestra Regional de Bordeaux-Aquitaine, 1973–87; Artistic Adviser of Gelders Orchestra, Arnhem, 1989. *Compositions:* Orchestrations of the Brahms Variations Op 23 and Op 24, 1970, 1973. *Recordings:* Many works with the London Symphony Orchestra, Lamoureux Orchestra, Paris Opéra, Hague Philharmonic and Budapest Philharmonic, including Beethoven and Rossini overtures; Chopin's 1st Piano Concerto with Magaloff, Bizet's Symphony, Liszt's Faust Symphony; Cello Concertos by Lalo and Saint-Saëns with Maurice Gendron. *Honours:* Chevalier de l'Ordre National; Chevalier de la Légion d'Honneur.

BERBIÉ, Jane; Singer (Mezzo-Soprano); b. 6 May 1934, Villefranche-de-Lauragais, Toulouse, France. *Education:* Studied at the Toulouse Conservatory. *Career:* After debut in 1958, sang at La Scala 1960, in L'Enfant et les Sortilèges, Glyndebourne Festival, 1969–71, 1983–84, as Despina in Così fan tutte; London Coliseum in the British premiere (concert) of Roussel's Padmavati, Aix-en-Provence, 1969–70; Salzburg Festival, 1974, as Marcellina in Le nozze di Figaro; Paris Opéra from 1975, as Zerlina and in Das Rheingold and Jenůfa; Guest appearances in Tokyo, Munich, London, Cologne and Milan, Rosina in Il Barbiere di Siviglia; Other roles include Concepcion in L'Heure Espagnole, Orsini in Lucrezia Borgia, Cherubino and Ascanio in Benvenuto Cellini; Salzburg Festival, 1988 as Mozart's Marcellina; Sang Annina in Der Rosenkavalier at the Théâtre des Champs Elysées, Paris, 1989; Teatro San Carlos, Lisbon, as the Marquise in La Fille du Régiment, 1989. *Recordings:* Benvenuto Cellini, conducted by Colin Davis; Così fan tutte; L'Enfant et les Sortilèges; Il Turco in Italia; Massenet's Cendrillon. *Honours:* Grand Prix; Toulouse Conservatory. *Address:* c/o Théâtre des Champs Elysées, 15 Avenue Montaigne, 75008, Paris, France.

BERCZELLY, Istvan; Singer (Baritone); b. 9 Sept. 1939, Budapest, Hungary. *Education:* Studied in Budapest. *Career:* Debut: Debrecen, 1967, as Don Giovanni; Sang at Debrecen until 1970; Budapest National Theatre from 1970, notably as Verdi's Renato, Basilio in La Fiamma by Respighi, Valentin (Faust), Bellini's Capulet, Wagner's Gunther, and the title role in Samson by Szokolay; Budapest, 1987, in the premiere of Szokolay's Ecce Homo; Premier of A Man from Venice by Ferenc Farkas, 1991; Sang Wagner's Hagen at Budapest, 1998. *Address:* c/o Hungarian State Opera, Nepoztarsasag utja 22, 1061 Budapest, Hungary.

BERDULLAS DEL RIO, Jorge; Composer; b. 20 Aug. 1960, Villagarcia de Arosa, Pontevedra, Spain. *Education:* conservatories in La Coruña, Santiago and Madrid; graduated as music teacher. *Career:* conducted choirs; became state music teacher/player 1985; founded contemporary music group, Talea 1986; founder mem., Galician Asscn of Composers 1987. *Compositions include:* El Paso, Op. 15a and 15b, for 6 and 12 percussionists and 2 conductors 1969, Biomecánicas (Letania para el día de los derechos del hombre), Op. 17, for piano and bass voice 1990, Proum (Homenaje a El Lissitzky) String Quartet No. 2, Op. 19 1991, Alogón (El dominio del caos), Op. 20, for string orchestra and 4 mixed voices 1991, Las estructuras del caos, Op. 23, methodology for a science of movement and simultaneous tempos in music 1995–96, Res Facta (Bajo el impulso de neoriel), Op. 24, for 5 orchestral groups (voice and instruments) situated in different places, and 5 conductors temporised by computer 1998–2000, El Apocalipsis según San Juan, Op. 25, for 12 orchestral groups (vocals and instruments) in different places, 12 speakers and 12 conductors 2001–. *Address:* Calle Rua Agriña No. 16 bajo derecha, 15705 Santiago de Compostela, Spain. *Telephone:* (981) 557225.

BERENS, Barbara; Singer (Soprano); b. 25 April 1966, St Ingbert, Germany. *Education:* Studied with Erika Köth and Josef Metternich, and in London with Vera Rozsa. *Career:* Sang with the Deutsche Oper am Rhein at Düsseldorf from 1988, notably as Susanna, Fiordigili, Pamina, Elvira in I Puritani, Liu and Hanna Glawari; Guest engagements in Cologne (as Gretel), Saarbrucken (Mme Cortese in Il Viaggio a Reims) and elsewhere in Germany; Also a noted recitalist. *Address:* c/o Deutsche Oper am Rhein, Heinrich Heine-Allee 16a, W-4000 Düsseldorf, Germany.

BERESFORD, Hugh; singer (baritone, tenor); b. 17 Dec. 1925, Birkenhead, England. *Education:* Royal Northern College of Music, Manchester, Vienna Music Academy; studied with Dino Borgioli and Alfred Piccaver. *Career:* debut, Linz, 1953, as Wolfram in Tannhäuser; Sang at Deutsche Oper am Rhein, Düsseldorf, from 1960; Sang in Graz, Augsburg and Wuppertal; Guest appearances at Covent Garden, Vienna, Munich, Stuttgart, Cologne, Brussels and Paris; Holland Festival, 1963, 1966; Venice, 1966, as Mandryka in Arabella; Sang further as Rigoletto, Posa in Don Carlos and Don Giovanni; Later career as tenor with Otello and Florestan at the Vienna Staatsoper, 1973; Tannhäuser at Bayreuth, 1972–73; Cologne Opera, 1981 as Florestan, and Erik in Der fliegende Holländer. *Address:* c/o Oper der Stadt Köln, Offenbachplatz, 5000 Cologne, Germany.

BEREZOVSKY, Boris; Concert Pianist; b. 4 Jan. 1969, Moscow, Russia. *Education:* Studied at the Moscow Tchaikovsky Conservatoire with Elisabeth Virsaladze. *Career:* Many concerts and recitals in Russia, Europe, Far East and the USA, 1990–; Appearances with the Royal Philharmonic and Philharmonia Orchestras, BBC Orchestra, London, the NDR Hamburg Symphony, the New York Philharmonic and the Moscow Philharmonic; Solo recitalist major international concert halls and festivals; Partnership with violinist Vadim Repin. *Recordings include:* Rachmaninov and Liszt Concertos; Chopin, Schumann, Ravel and Rachmaninov solos. *Honours:* Gold Medal, International Tchaikovsky Competition, Moscow, 1990. *Address:* c/o IMG Artists, Lovell House, 616 Chiswick High Road, London W4 5RX, England.

BERG, Nathan; Singer (Baritone); b. 1968, Saskatchewan, Canada. *Education:* Augustana University, Alberta; University of Western Ontario; Maitrise Nationale de Versailles; Guildhall School with Vera Rozsa. *Career:* Debut: Recital at Wigmore Hall, London; Sang Thésée in Rameau's Hippolyte, Peter Quince, Dr Falke and Eustachio in Donizetti's L'Assedio di Calais at the Guildhall School; Has sung professionally as Guglielmo, Masetto, Leporello, Figaro (Mozart), Schuanard, Various recordings and appearances with Abbado, Dohnányi, Salinnen, Shaw, Tilson Thomas; Leppard and William Christie among others. Various oratorio and recital work; Sang Abramane in Rameau's Zoroastre at Brooklyn Academy and on tour to Europe, 1998; Season 2000–01 in Handel's Theodora at the Salzburg Easter Festival, Masetto at Glyndebourne and Leporello for ENO. *Honours:* Prizewinner, Peter Pears, Kathleen Ferrier, Walter Gruner and Royal Overseas League Competitions. *Address:* c/o IMG Artists, Lovell House, 616 Chiswick High Road, London W4 5RX, England.

BERGAMIN, Peter; Conductor; b. 1965, Canada. *Career:* Appearances with the Toronto Symphony, Israel Chamber Orchestra, Royal Liverpool Philharmonic Orchestra, Scottish National Orchestra and Winnipeg Symphony; Music Director of the Vienna Taschenoper, 1994–97, with Maxwell Davies' Resurrection in Vienna and at Glasgow Mayfest. Further engagements with the Opéra National de Lyon, North Hungarian Symphony Orchestra and the King's Singers, London; Repertoire includes Mozart, Mahler, Beethoven, Wagner, Strauss and contemporary music. *Address:* c/o IMG Artists, Lovell House, 626 Chiswick High Road, London W4 5RX England.

BERGANZA, Teresa; Singer (Mezzo-Soprano); b. 16 March 1934, Madrid, Spain; m. (1) Felix Lavilla, 1957, (2) Jose Rifa, 1986, 1 s., 2 d. *Education:* Bachillerato, Conservatorio, Madrid. *Career:* Debut: Aix-en-Provence, France, 1957, as Mozart's Dorabella; Appeared in Così fan tutte and Le nozze di Figaro, Mozart; La Cenerentola, L'Italiana in

Algeri, Barbiere di Siviglia by Rossini; Carmen, Bizet; Werther, Massenet; Orfeo-Gluck; British debut Glyndebourne, 1958, as Mozart's Cherubino; At Covent Garden she appeared as Rossini's Rosina and Cenerentola and Bizet's Carmen; Sang in the opening concert of Bastille Opéra at Paris, 13 July 1989; Carmen at the Palais Omnisports, Paris, 1989; Sang Carmen at Madrid, 1992; Recital at the Wigmore Hall, London, 1997; Film, Don Giovanni, directed by Losey; Song recitals in Berlin and elsewhere from 1999; Paris, Opéra-Comique, 2003. *Recordings:* About 120 records by various record companies, including Le nozze di Figaro, Il Barbiere di Siviglia, Alcina, La Clemenza di Tito and L'Italiana in Algeri (HMV/EMI); La Finta Semplice by Mozart; Don Giovanni (CBS). *Publications:* Meditaciones de Una Cantante, Madrid, 1985. *Honours:* Medalla de Oro Merito Bellas Artes; Commandeur aux Arts et Lettres; Grand Prix du Disque, 6 times; Grand Prix Rossini; First Elected Woman and Singer in 250 years of the Spanish Royal Academy of Arts, 1995. *Current Management:* Musiepana, Calle Zurbamo, 34, 28101 Madrid, Spain. *Address:* Apdo 137, 28200 SLD Escorial, Madrid, Spain.

BERGASA, Carlos; Singer (Baritone); b. 1966, Spain. *Career:* Many engagements at opera houses in Spain and elsewhere in Europe, notably in Donizetti's La Favorita, Mozart's Così fan tutte (as Guglielmo) and Gounod's Faust (as Valentin); Also sings the Mörike-Lieder by Wolf; Contestant at the 1995 Cardiff Singer of the World Competition. *Address:* Fernan Gonzales 17, Madrid 28009, Spain.

BERGE, Sigurd; Composer; b. 1 July 1929, Vinstra, Norway. *Education:* Studied with Thorleif Eken at the Oslo Conservatory, also with Finn Mortensen, Course in Electronic Music, Stockholm, Utrecht. *Career:* First amanuensis in music at High School, Oslo; Tutor, Sagene College of Education, from 1959; Chairman, Norwegian composers Union, 1985–88. *Compositions:* Episode for violin, piano, 1958; Pezzo orchestrale, 1958; Tamburo piccolo for strings, percussion, 1961; Sinus for string and percussion, 1961; Chroma for Orchestra, 1963, A for Orchestra, 1965, B for Orchestra, 1966; Yang-Guan for wind quintet, 1967; Ballet for 2 dancers, percussion, 1968, 1970; Horncall, 1972; Between Mirrors for violin, chamber orchestra, 1977; Juvenes, amateur string orchestra, 1977; Music for Orchestra, 1978; Gudbrandsdalsspelet, music drama, 1980; Wind Ballet, 1981; Music for 4 horns, 1984; Horn Trio, 1987; Springar; Chorale for brass quintet, 1990; Horn Solo, 2000; Electronic pieces. *Recordings include:* Raga for Oboe and Orchestra, 1990; Springar; Chorale; Episode; Chroma; Flauto Solo; Horncall; Yang-Guan. *Publications include:* Viser og Blues, Books 1 and 2, 1999; Lydforming, 1999. *Address:* Norwegian Music Information Centre, Tollbugata 28, N–0157 Oslo, Norway.

BERGEL, Erich; Conductor; b. 1 June 1930, Rosenau, Romania. *Education:* Sibiu and Cluj Conservatories. *Career:* Debut: US Houston Symphony Orchestra, 1975; Played flute in the Sibiu Philharmonic Orchestra, 1945–48; Studied further in Cluj with Ciolan, 1950–55 and was conductor of the Oradea Philharmonic, 1955–59, Cluj Philharmonic, 1959–72; Musical Director of the Nordwestdeutsche Philharmonie, 1972–74; Principal Guest Conductor, Houston Symphony Orchestra, 1979–81; Directed the BBC National Orchestra of Wales at Cardiff and has been Professor of Conducting at the Berlin Hochschule für Musik. *Publications include:* Bach's Art of Fugue, vol. 1, Bonn, 1979. *Address:* c/o BBC National Symphony Orchestra of Wales, Broadcasting House, Landaff, Cardiff CF5 2YQ, Wales.

BERGEN, Beverly; Singer (Soprano and Mezzo-Soprano); b. 1950, New Zealand. *Education:* Studied at London Opera Centre. *Career:* Has appeared as guest artist at the Deutsche Oper Berlin, also in Hamburg, Düsseldorf and elsewhere in Germany; Sang in premiere of Maderna's Hyperion at Brussels; Operatic roles include Constanze, Jenůfa, Strauss's Countess, Katherina in Lady Macbeth of Mtsensk, Senta, Luisa Miller, Violetta, Musetta and Lucia di Lammermoor; Has performed throughout Australia in Messiah, Beethoven's Ninth and Das klagende Lied by Mahler; Other repertoire includes Mozart's Requiem, The Trojans, Bruckner's Te Deum, with the Sydney Symphony Orchestra and Judas Maccabaeus with St Hedwig's Cathedral Choir, Berlin; Changed to mezzo-soprano repertoire, 1989, appeared as Amneris in Aida; Engagements with Opera Factory, London.

BERGER, Roman; Composer; b. 9 Aug. 1930, Cieszyn, Poland; m. Ruth Strbova, 6 July 1968. *Education:* Academy of Musical Arts, Katowice, 1949–52; Academy of Musical Arts Bratislava, 1952–56, 1960–65. *Career:* Professor of Piano, Conservatoire, Bratislava, 1955–66; Fellow, television sound laboratory, 1966–67; Secretary, Union of Slovak composers, 1967–69; Lecturer on theory of composition, contemporary music and electronic music, Academy of musical arts, Bratislava, 1969–71, 1983–85; Contracted to Musicological Institute of the Slovak Academy of Sciences, 1977–91. *Compositions:* Transformations, 4 symphonic pieces, 1965; Memento for orchestra, 1974; Epitaph to Copernicus for electronics, 1973; De Profundis for bass, cello and electronics, 1980; Exodus 4 pieces for organ, 1982, 1997. *Publications:* Music and Truth, essays, 1997–87; Theory Wrongly Present, 1989; Velvet Revolution and Music, 1990; Permanent Conflict between Art and power, 1992; The Structure and Meaning of Heritage, 1996. *Address:* Bazovského 11/17, SR 841 01, Bratislava, Slovakia.

BERGER-TUNA, Helmut; Singer (bass); b. 7 May 1942, Vienna, Austria. *Education:* Hochschule für Musik und darstellende Kunst, Vienna, and with Franz Schuch-Tovini. *Career:* debut, first engagement with Kammeroper Wien; mem. Landestheater Linz 1969–72, Opernhaus-Graz 1972–77, Staatsoper Stuttgart (Germany) 1977–; 60 roles include Omin, Leporello, Sarastro, Rocco, van Bett, Falstaff (Nicolai), Kecal, Daland, Hunding, Fafner, Fasolt, Pogner, König Heinrich, Landgraf, Kaspar, Ramphis, Sparafucile, Baculus, Plumkett, Magnifico, Bartolo (Barbier), Don Pasquale, Baron Ochs (performed more than 100 times); operetta includes Ollendorf, Zsupan, Baron Webs, Frank); guest engagements in Staatsoper Hamburg, Berlin, Munich, Vienna, Teatro alla Scala, Deutsche Oper Berlin, Komische Oper Berlin, Opera House Zürich, Grande Opéra Paris, Royal Opera House Covent Garden London, Dresden, Düsseldorf, Cologne, Frankfurt, Barcelona, Lisbon, Madrid, Amsterdam, Oslo, Royal Opera House Copenhagen, Santa Cecilia Rome, Musikverein Vienna, Bruckner Haus Linz, Teatro la Fenice, Music Center Los Angeles, Seattle Opera; sang at the Salzburg Festival 1981, in the premiere of Cerha's Baal; other festivals include Bregenz and Mörbisch (Austria), Bergen (Norway). *Recordings:* Zar und Zimmermann; Die schweigsame Frau; Baal, K. A. Hartmann's Simplicius Simplissimus; Meistersinger von Nürnberg, Die Zigeunerbaron, Wolf's Der Corregidor, La faciulla des west, R. Schumann's Faust-Szenen. *Television:* appearances in Zar und Zimmermann, Martha, Der Vögelhandler, Der Zigeunerbaron. *Honours:* Kammersänger des Landes Baden-Württemberg 1985. *Address:* c/o Opéra et Concert, 1 rue Volney, 75002 Paris, France.

BERGLUND, Ingela; Singer (Soprano); b. 1959, Sweden. *Education:* Studied viola at Stockholm College of Music, 1974–79; State Opera School, Stockholm, 1985–88, with Kerstin Meyer and Elisabeth Söderströ m. *Career:* Debut: Royal Opera Stockholm, 1988, as Donna Anna; Member of Royal Stockholm Philharmonic Orchestra, 1979–84; Sang Mozart's Countess and the Woman in La Voix Humaine at Stockholm, 1988; Salzburg Landestheater, 1989–92 as Donna Anna, Musetta, Tatiana, Fiordiligi and Hanna Glawari in Die Lustige Witwe; Beatrice in Boccaccio by Suppé at Royal Opera, Stockholm; Guest appearances at Semper Opera, Dresden, and in Austria, USA, Spain and Japan. *Recordings:* Radio and television in Sweden. *Current Management:* IM Audio and Music AB, Stockholm. *Address:* Asogatan 67 VI, 118 29 Stockholm, Sweden.

BERGLUND, Paavo (Allan Englebert); Conductor; b. 14 April 1929, Helsinki, Finland; m. Kirsti Kiveskas, 1958, 1 s., 2 d. *Education:* Sibelius Academy, Helsinki. *Career:* Debut: 1965, Bournemouth Symphony Orchestra; Violinist, Finnish Radio Symphony Orchestra, 1949–56; Conductor, 1956–62; Principal Conductor 1962–71, Bournemouth Symphony Orchestra, 1972–79; Helsinki Philharmonic Orchestra, 1975–79; Principal Conductor of Stockholm Philharmonic Orchestra, 1987–91; Principal Conductor of Royal Danish Orchestra, 1993–96; Conducted the London Philharmonic at the Festival Hall, London, 1997; Maskarade by Nielsen at Copenhagen, 1996. *Recordings:* Complete Sibelius symphonies including first recording of Kullervo Symphony, 1971–77; Ma Vlast by Smetana, Shostakovich symphonies 5, 6, 7, 10, 11, and many other recordings including Mozart and Strauss Oboe Concertos with Douglas Boyd; Chamber Orchestra of Europe, ASV. *Publications:* A comparative study of the printed score and the Manuscript of the Seventh Symphony of Sibelius 1970. *Address:* Munkkiniemenranta 41, 00330 Helsinki 33, Finland.

BERGMAN, Erik (Valdemar); Composer; b. 24 Nov. 1911, Nykarleby, Finland; m. (1) Solveig von Schoultz, 7 July 1961, deceased, 3 Dec 1996, (2) Christina Idrenius-Zalewski, 26 Jan 2000. *Education:* Literature and Aesthetics, Musicology, University of Helsinki, 1931–33; Composition Diploma, Sibelius Academy, Helsinki, 1939; Studied Composition in Berlin with Heinz Tiessen and in Switzerland with Wladimir Vogel. *Career:* Debut: Helsinki, 1940; Conductor, Helsinki University Chorus, 1950–69; Professor of Composition at the Sibelius Academy, Helsinki, 1963–76; Concerts in Washington DC and New York, 1981, 1991, Paris, 1967, London, 1967, 1986, Leningrad, 1989, St Petersburg, 1992, Stockholm, 1993; Berlin, The singing Tree, opera, 1999; Works performed at several international festivals; mem, Academy of Finland, 1982. *Compositions:* The Singing Tree, opera (1995); The Journey, ballet, 1998–99; Works for orchestra, concertos for soloists and orchestra, works for soloists, choir and orchestra, works for solo instruments, chamber music. *Recordings:* The Singing Tree; Concerto for violin and Orchestra; Birds in the Morning, flute and orchestra; Concerto for Chamber Orchestra, 1997; Chamber works, works for piano, guitar, choral and vocal works; Musica Concertante for String Quartet, 1997. *Honours:* Pro Finlandia Medal, Sibelius International

Prize, 1965; DPhil, hc, 1978, 1982; Royal Swedish Academy of Music; Honorary Member, Society of Finnish Composers; Commander, Order of the White Rose of Finland; Commander, Order of the Lion of Finland; The State's Music Prize, 1989; The Nordic Council Music Prize, 1994; Finland Prize, 1997. *Address:* Berggatan 22 C 52, 00100 Helsinki, Finland.

BERGONZI, Carlo; Opera Singer (Tenor); b. 13 July 1924, Busseto, Parma, Italy; m. Adele, 2 c. *Education:* Parma Conservatory. *Career:* Debut (as baritone) as Figaro (Il Barbiere di Siviglia) at Lecce, 1949; Debut as Tenor in title role of Andrea Chénier, Teatro Petruzzelli, Bari, 1951; Subsequently appeared at various Italian opera houses including La Scala, Milan; US debut in Il Tabarro and Cavalleria Rusticana, Lyric Opera, Chicago, 1955; Appeared at Metropolitan Opera, New York in Aida (as Radames) and Il Trovatore (as Manrico), 1955–56; London debut Stoll Theatre, 1953 as Alvaro in La Forza del Destino; At Covent Garden he sang Verdi's Riccardo, Radames and Manrico and Puccini's Cavaradossi; Appeared at all the major opera houses in Europe and also in USA and South America; Repertoire included many Verdi roles as well as roles in operas by Donizetti, Boito, Leoncavallo and Mascagni; Sang Edgardo at Covent Garden, 1985; Metropolitan Opera 1956–83, in 249 performances of 21 roles, including Canio, Andrea Chénier, Cavaradossi, Riccardo, Nemorino, Macduff, Rodolfo, Alfredo, Pollione, Enzo and Manrico; Metropolitan Gala (25th anniversary), 4 Dec 1981; Sang Edgardo at the Vienna Staatsoper, 1988; Nemorino for New Jersey State Opera, 1989; Farewell Recital at Covent Garden, 1992; Retired 1994 with occasional appearances thereafter and became a vocal coach; Song recitals in Vienna and Zürich, 2000. *Current Management:* Askonas Holt Ltd, Lonsdale Chambers, 27 Chancery Lane, London, WC2A 1PF, England. *Telephone:* (20) 7400-1700. *Fax:* (20) 7400-1799. *E-mail:* info@askonasholt.co.uk. *Website:* www.askonasholt.co.uk.

BERINI, Bianca; Singer (Mezzo-Soprano); b. 20 Dec. 1928, Trieste, Italy. *Education:* Studied in Trieste and Milan. *Career:* Debut: Teatro Nuovo Milan, 1963 as Suzuki in Madama Butterfly; Has sung throughout Italy and in Vienna, Berlin, Amsterdam, Brussels, Marseilles, Nice, Toulouse and London; Metropolitan Opera debut in 1978 as Amneris, returning to New York until 1984 as Eboli, Amneris, Santuzza, Dalila, Ulrica, Azucena and Frederica in Luisa Miller; Further engagements in Dallas, Philadelphia, Baltimore, San Francisco, Lisbon, Barcelona and Zürich; Other roles include Adalgisa in Norma, Laura in La Gioconda, Ortrud in Lohengrin, Charlotte in Werther and Jane Seymour in Anna Bolena. *Recordings include:* Verdi's Requiem. *Address:* c/o Metropolitan Opera, Lincoln Center, New York, NY 10023, USA.

BERKELEY, Michael, FRAM, FRWCMD; Composer; b. 29 May 1948, London, England. *Education:* Westminster Cathedral Choir School; Royal Academy of Music; Further studies with Lennox Berkeley and Richard Rodney Bennett. *Career:* BBC Radio 3 Announcer, 1974–79; Programme Presenter, BBC 2 television; Composer-in-Residence, London College of Music, 1987–88; Opera, Baa Baa Black Sheep premiered at 1993 Cheltenham Festival; Artistic Director, Cheltenham International Festival of Music, 1995–2002; Co-Artistic Director, Spitalfields Festival, 1995–97; Board of Directors Royal Opera House, 1996–2002; Chairman Opera Advisory Board, Royal Opera House, 1998–2000; Chair. Bd of Govs, Royal Ballet 2003–; Associate Composer, BBC National Orchestra of Wales, 2001–. *Compositions:* Meditations for Strings, 1976; Oboe Concerto, 1977; Fantasia Concertante for Chamber Orchestra, 1977; String Trio, 1978; The Wild Winds for Soprano and Chamber Orchestra, 1978; Cello Sonata, 1978; Violin Sonata, 1979; Organ Sonata, 1979; At The Round Earth's Imagin'd Corners for Soprano, Baritone, Chorus and Organ, 1980; Uprising Symphony, 1980; Chamber Symphony, 1980; 4 String Quartets, 1981, 1984, 1988, 1995; Wessex Graves for Tenor and Harp, 1981; Flames for Orchestra, 1981; Suite, Vision of Piers The Ploughman, 1981; Gregorian Variations for Orchestra, 1982; Cello Concerto, 1982; Oratorio, Or Shall We Die?, 1982; Guitar Sonata, 1982; Clarinet Quintet, 1982; Songs of Awakening Love, 1986; Organ Concerto, 1987; Bastet, 1988; Music for a Ballet; Keening for Saxophone and Piano, 1988; Quartet Study, 1988; Coronach for String Orchestra, 1988; The Red Macula for Chorus and Orchestra, 1989; Fierce Tears for Solo Oboe, 1990; Stupendous Stranger for Chorus and Brass, 1990; Entertaining Master Punch for Chamber Orchestra, 1991; Opera, Baa Baa Black Sheep, 1992; Clarinet Concerto, 1992; Elegy for flute and strings, 1993; Viola Concerto, 1994; Secret Garden for orchestra, 1997; The Garden of Earthly Delights, 1998; Opera Jane Eyre, 1999, premiered 2000; Tristessa for cor anglais, viola and orchestra, 2003. *Address:* Repertoire Promotion Department, Oxford University Press, Music Department, 70 Baker Street, London W1M 1DJ, England. *E-mail:* repertoire.promotion.uk@oup.com.

BERKES, Kalman; Clarinettist; b. 1952, Budapest, Hungary. *Education:* Studied music from the age of 4; Béla Bartók Conservatory, 1966–70; Ferenc Liszt Academy of Music, 1977. *Career:* Principal Clarinettist, Budapest State Opera Orchestra and Budapest Philharmonic, 1972; Budapest Chamber Ensemble and Jeunesses Musicales Wind Quintet,

1973; Extensive Guest Performances throughout Europe including: Austria, France, Germany, Netherlands, Italy and Switzerland; Played Trios by Beethoven, Brahms and Zemlinsky at St John's, London, 1997. *Recordings:* Has made a number of records including Bartók's Contrasts. *Honours:* Silver Medal, Geneva International Musical Competition, 1972. *Address:* Franz Liszt Academy of Music, PO Box 206, Liszt Ferenctér 8, H–1391 Budapest VI, Hungary.

BERKOWITZ, Paul; Concert Pianist; b. 1 Oct. 1948, Montreal, Canada. *Education:* McGill University and Curtis Institute with Serkin and Horszowski. *Career:* Debut: London, 1973 (resident in London, 1973–93, Santa Barbara, California, 1993–); New York Solo Debut, Alice Tully Hall, 1978; Recitalist, Wigmore and Queen Elizabeth Halls, London; Tivoli, Copenhagen and throughout Europe and North America; Soloist with major orchestras in the United Kingdom and North America; Festival engagements in Belgium, Denmark, England, France, Italy, Scotland and Spain; Frequent solo radio broadcasts and recitals for BBC and CBC; Barcelona Festival with the Endellion Quartet and the Albion Ensemble; Beethoven duets with Richard Goode at the Wigmore Hall, 1990–91; Appearances with the BBC Scottish Symphony and English Sinfonia; Professor, Guildhall School, 1975–93; Professor, University of California, Santa Barbara, 1993–; Masterclasses at McGill University, University of British Columbia, Queens University, Royal Conservatory of Music, Toronto, in Canada and Yehudi Menuhin School and elsewhere in the United Kingdom, France and Barcelona; Repertoire includes sonatas and other major works by Schubert, Beethoven, Brahms, Mozart, Schumann, Chopin and Bartók; The Brahms Handel Variations and Klavierstücke op 76 and opp 116-119 and Schumann's Kreisleriana and C major Fantasy. *Recordings include:* Complete Sonatas of Schubert (7 vols); Schumann's Kreisleriana and Davidsbündlertänze, Brahms Piano Pieces Opp 116-118. *Honours:* Fellow of the Guildhall School of Music, 1988; Canada Council Grants, 1989–91; BBC Record Review and BBC Magazine First Choice Award for recording of Schumann's Kreisleriana, 1993. *Address:* Department of Music, University of California, Santa Barbara, CA 93106-6070, USA.

BERL, Christine; Composer; b. 22 July 1943, New York City, USA; 2 s. *Education:* BS in Piano, Mannes College of Music, 1961–64; MA in Composition, Queen's College, 1968–70. *Career:* Performances by Emanuel Ax in Highland Park, Ravinia, 1988; Commissioned by Peter Serkin for 1989–90, The Chamber Music Society of Lincoln Center for their 20th Anniversary Season with Frederica von Stade as guest artist, 1989; Cornell University Chorus, 1989; Concert devoted to Berl's works on Distinguished Artists Series of 92nd Street Y, 1990; Commissioned work for 2 pianos for Peter Serkin and Emmanuel Ax; Other participants: Patricia Spence, Matt Haimovitz, Richard Stoltzman, Richard Goode, Andre-Michel Schub, 1994; World premiere by French violinist Pierre Amoyal and Jeremy Menuhin of Masmoudi, a violin sonata commissioned by Radio France; New York premiere of Masmoudi at Merkin Concert Hall, 1994. *Compositions:* Elegy for Piano Solo, 1974; Three Pieces for Chamber Ensemble, 1975; Ab La Dolchor for Soprano, Female Chorus and Orchestra, 1979; Sonata for Piano, 1986–87; Dark Summer for Mezzo Soprano, Piano and String Trio; The Lord of the Dance, for Peter Serkin; The Violent Bear It Away for Orchestra, 1988; Cantilena for Cello and Piano, for Matt Haimovitz; Masmoudi for violin and piano, 1991. *Recordings:* Three Pieces for Chamber Ensemble, 1975, with Arthur Weisburg and members of the Contemporary Chamber Ensemble and Speculum Musicae, Ursula Oppens, Piano; Elegy, The Lord of The Dance; Piano Sonata by Edipan. *Address:* c/o ASCAP, ACAP Building, One Lincoln Plaza, New York, NY 10023, USA.

BERMAN, Boris, BA, MA; concert pianist and professor of piano; b. 3 April 1948, Moscow, Russia; m. Zina Tabachnikova 1975; one s. one d. *Education:* Moscow Tchaikovsky Conservatory. *Career:* debut in Moscow 1965; performances in over 30 countries, appeared with Concertgebouw, Philharmonia, Royal Scottish, Detroit, Minnesota, Houston, Atlanta, Toronto, Israel Philharmonic, Moscow Philharmonic, St Petersburg Philharmonic and many others; festivals include Bergen, Ravinia, Israel, Marlboro; numerous radio and television appearances around the world; former Prof. of Piano, Tel-Aviv University, Indiana University, Boston University, Yale School of Music; Music Dir, Music Spectrum concert series, Tel-Aviv 1975–84; Music Dir, Yale Music Spectrum, USA 1984–97; Dir, Summer Piano Institute at Yale 1990–92; Dir, International Summer Piano Institute, Hong Kong 1995–97; juror at various national, international piano competitions. *Recordings:* all solo piano works by Prokofiev in 9 vols, Stravinsky Concerto with Orchestre de la Suisse Romande, N Järvi, Prokofiev Concertos 1, 4, 5 with Concertgebouw Orchestra, N Järvi, Shostakovich, Scriabin all Sonatas in 2 vols; recitals or works by Debussy, Stravinsky, Shostakovich, Schnittke, Cage; numerous chamber recordings. *Honours:* Edison Classic Award, Netherlands 1990. *Current Management:* Askonas Holt Ltd, Lonsdale Chambers, 27 Chancery Lane, London, WC2A 1PF, England. *Telephone:* (20) 7400-1700. *Fax:* (20) 7400-1799. *E-mail:* info@ askonasholt.co.uk. *Website:* www.askonasholt.co.uk. *Address:* Yale School of Music, PO Box 208246, New Haven, CT 06520, USA.

BERMAN, Lazar; Pianist; b. 26 Feb. 1930, Leningrad, Russia; m. Valentina Berman, 28 Dec 1961, 1 s. *Education:* Graduated, Moscow Conservatory, 1953; Student of Masterclasses, 1953–57. *Career:* Debut: In concert, 1934; Orchestral debut, Moscow Philharmonic, playing Mozart's C major Concerto, K503, 1940; Professional Concert Pianist, 1957–; US debut at Miami University, Oxford, OH, also with American Orchestra, 1976; Appearances at Carnegie Hall with New Jersey Symphony Orchestra, 1971; Teacher at the Weimar Musikhochschule, 1995–; mem, Philharmonic Society of Moscow; Founder, Russia-Belgium Friendship Society. *Recordings:* Recording artist in music by Beethoven, Liszt, Prokofiev, Scriabin and Tchaikovsky's 1st Piano Concerto with Karajan, 1976. *Honours:* 1st Prize, International Youth Festival, East Berlin; 4th Place, Queen Elisabeth of Belgium Contest, Brussels, 1951. *Address:* c/o Concerto Winderstein Gmbtt, Leopoldstrasse 25, D–80802 München, Germany.

BERN, Jeni; Singer (soprano); b. 1973, Glasgow, Scotland. *Education:* Royal Scottish Academy; Royal College of Music, London. *Career:* Debut: Covent Garden Company 1998, as Mozart's Barbarina; Mozart's Susanna for English Touring Opera; Deidamia, and Sigismondo in Arminio for the London Handel Festival; Atalanta in Serse for the Early Opera Company; Dalinda in Ariodante for the Covent Garden Festival and Donizetti's Adina at Cambridge; Cristina in The Makropulos Case for Scottish Opera Go Round; Purcell's Belinda for Israel Chamber Orchestra and Jano in Jenůfa at Glyndebourne, 2000; Other roles include Britten's Titania, Janáček's Vixen and Narcissa in Haydn's Philemon and Baucis; Concerts include Messiah in Switzerland, Bruckner's Te Deum, a British tour with Vivaldi by Candelight and the premiere of Michael Torke's Book of Proverbs, Flowermaiden in Parsifal with the Royal Opera in concert. *Honours:* Countess of Munster Award. *Current Management:* Musicmakers International Artists Representation, Tailor House, 63–65 High Street, Whitwell, Hertfordshire SG4 8AH, England. *Telephone:* (1438) 871708. *Fax:* (1438) 871777. *E-mail:* musicmakers@compuserve.com. *Website:* www.operauk.com. *Address:* c/o Glyndebourne Festival Opera, Glyndebourne, Lewes, Sussex, BN8 5UU, England.

BERNARD, André; Conductor and Trumpeter; b. 6 April 1946, Gap, France. *Education:* Diplome Superieur of Conducting, Paris; 1st Place for Trumpet, Paris Superior Conservatory; Laureat International Trumpet Competition, Geneva, Switzerland, 1968; Studied German romantic repertory with Carlo Maria Giulini and Italian opera with Bruno Bartoletti, Siena, Italy. *Career:* Guest Conductor for many international orchestras including London Philharmonic, London Symphony Orchestra, and Mozarteum Salzburg; Opera conducting in Strasbourg, Lille, Siena, Geneva; Television appearances in France, Germany and Japan; Radio appearances in USA, Canada, Japan, Germany, Italy and France; Solo appearances including Salzburg Festival, Berlin Philharmonie, Carnegie Hall and Lincoln Center in New York, Paris, Tokyo, London, Rome, Prague, Madrid, Venice, and Washington; Appearances with world's leading orchestras; 31 Concerts on tour conducting Philharmonia Hungarica, including Carnegie Hall and Los Angeles, 1986; Contract for concert series in London, tours in France and Italy and recordings with New Symphony Orchestra of London and London Chamber Orchestra, 1982–87. *Recordings:* 20 with Academy of St Martin-in-the-Fields, English Chamber Orchestra, and Ensemble Instrumental de France. *Current Management:* Columbia Artists Management, NY, USA. *Address:* 19 Rue Joliot Curie, 93100 Montreuil, Paris, France.

BERNARD, Annabelle; Singer (Soprano); b. 11 Oct. 1934, New Orleans, Louisiana, USA. *Education:* Studies, Xavier University, New Orleans; The New England Conservatory. *Career:* Debut: Sang Susanna in Le nozze di Figaro, conducted by Boris Goldovsky, 1958; Appeared as Butterfly in Stuttgart, 1959; Lieder recitals with Hermann Reutter; Vienna Staatsoper debut as Aida, conducted by Karajan; Sang at the Deutsche Oper Berlin from 1962, debut as Aida; Salzburg Festival, 1973, as Electra in Idomeneo, conducted by Karl Böhm; Visits with the Deutsche Oper to Japan as Fiordiligi and in The Ring, 1987; Washington Opera, 1986, as Fiordiligi; New Orleans Opera as Maddalena in Andrea Chénier; Sang in the stage premiere of Mussorgsky's Salammbô at San Carlo, Naples; Modern repertory includes the premieres on Montezuma by Sessions, 1964 and Dallapiccola's Ulisse, 1968; Concert appearances with the Cleveland Orchestra conducted by Lorin Maazel at Carnegie Hall, the Berlin Philharmonic Orchestra. *Honours:* Berliner Kammersängerin, 1970; MD, Honoris Causa, Xavier University, 1976. *Address:* c/o Deutsche Oper Berlin, Richard Wagnerstrasse 10, 1000 Berlin, Germany.

BERNARDI, Mario; Conductor and Pianist; b. 20 Aug. 1930, Kirkland Lake, Ontario, Canada; m. Mona Kelly, 12 May 1962, 1 d. *Education:* Diplomas in Piano; Organ; Composition, B Marcello Conservatory,

Venice, 1947; Piano with Lubka Kolessa, Toronto. *Career:* Sadler's Wells Opera, 1963–69, with many performances of operas by Verdi; San Francisco Opera 1967, 1968, 1982; New York City Opera, 1970–86; Metropolitan Opera, 1984; Several major orchestras including Chicago, Pittsburgh, San Francisco, Toronto, Montreal, BBC; 13 years with National Arts Centre Orchestra, Ottawa, 1969–82, giving many premieres of works by Canadian Composers; Music Director, Calgary Philharmonic; Season 1987–88, with Cendrillon at Washington and Don Giovanni at Montreal; Conducted Lucia di Lammermoor at Washington 1989; Gave the Verdi Requiem at the 1988 Olympic Arts Festival; Conducted Fidelio at Toronto, 1991; Massenet's Chérubin at Covent Garden, 1994; Les Pêcheurs de Perles at Chicago, 1998; mem, Savage Club, London; Ranchmen's Club, Calgary. *Recordings:* Numerous recordings for EMI; RCA; CBC with Sadler's Wells Company; National Arts Centre Orchestra, Toronto, Vancouver Symphonies, CBC Radio Orchestra. *Recordings include:* Hansel and Gretel, with Sadler's Wells Company; Mozart Symphony K551 and Concerto K219, with Steven Staryk; Haydn arias and symphony No. 85; Brahms Serenade Op 11. *Honours:* Companion of the Order of Canada; Several honorary doctorates. *Current Management:* Columbia Artists Management, New York. *Address:* 248 Warren Road, Toronto, Ontario M4V 2S8, Canada.

BERNARDINI, Alfredo; Oboist; b. 30 Oct. 1961, Rome, Italy; 2 s., 1 d. *Education:* Studies, Royal Conservatory, The Hague, Netherlands, 1982–; Soloist diploma, 1987; Diploma, University of Oxford, 1985. *Career:* Performs with major European ensembles such as Hesperion XX, Les Arts Florissants, La Petite Bande, Capella Coloniensis, Amsterdam Baroque Orchestra, Collegio Strumentale Italiano, La Grande Ecurie, Concerto Armonico Budapest and Concerto Italiano. *Recordings:* With EMI, D&GM, Astrée and Bongiovanni. *Contributions:* Articles to Il Flauto Dolce; Early Music; Journal of the American Musical Instruments Society. *Address:* Via Sebenico 2, 00198 Roma, Italy.

BERNAS, Richard; conductor; b. 21 April 1950, New York, USA; m. 1st Deirdre Busenberg (divorced); m. 2nd Beatrice Harper; two s. *Career:* debut, as pianist, Kent University 1966, as conductor, London, England 1976; Warsaw Autumn Festival, 1977; Vienna Festival, 1984; Opéra de Lyon and Paris Opéra, 1985; London Sinfonietta, England, 1986; Edinburgh Festival, Scotland, 1986; The Royal Helsinki Philharmonic, 1988; Royal Ballet, Covent Garden, BBC Symphony Orchestra, 1989; Holland Festival, 1989; Aldeburgh Festival Opera, Suffolk, England, 1990; English National Opera, London, 1990; Netherlands Opera, Amsterdam and The Hague, 1991; Ars Musica Festival, Brussels, 1991; Orchestre National de Belgique, Brussels, 1993; Netherlands Radio Symphony Orchestra, 1994; Opéra de Bastille, 1995; Musique Oblique, Paris, 1995; Conductor, Saltarello Choir, 1976–80; Conductor, Music Projects, London, 1978–; Conductor in Residence, Sussex University, 1979–82. *Recordings:* Factory Classics; Virgin Classics; Continuum; NMC; Decca-Argo. *Current Management:* Robert Gilder & Co., Enterprise House, 59–65 Upper Ground, London, SE1 9PQ, England. *Telephone:* (20) 7928-9008. *Fax:* (20) 7928-9755. *E-mail:* rgilder@robert-gilder.com. *Address:* 73 Avenue Gardens, London, W3 8HB, England.

BERNASCONI, Silvano; Pianist and Composer; b. 16 Oct. 1950, Chiasso, Switzerland; m. Irene Cairoli Alessandra, 20 June 1984, 1 s. *Education:* Conservatoire de Lausanne; Piano with Francesco Zaza; Composition with Andor Kovach; Electronic music with Rainer Bosch; Conservatorio Santa Cecilia in Rome; Composition with Vieri Tosatti, Gregorian song with Domenico Bartolucci; Organ with Ferdinando Germani; Electronic music with Franco Evangelisti. *Career:* Debut: Rome, 1974; Pianist and composer, 1980–85; Executions of music commissioned by Musica Ticinensis, 1982 and Television; mem, Association of Swiss Musicians; European Composers Union. *Compositions:* Sounds and Crystals for two Vibraphones, 1982; Psallite, four lines for organ, 1974; Tourbillon, for violin and orchestra, 1993. *Recordings:* Sounds and Crystals, transparencies for two vibraphones and piano; Sounds Am Bach, for piano played by the composer. *Publications:* Didactics compositions in the European year of Music, 1985; Contributor to Musica & Teatro magazine. *Honours:* Invitation by UNCM to found a European Composers Union, 1991. *Address:* Casa Am Bach, 6803 Famignolo-Lugana, Switzerland.

BERNASEK, Vaclav; Violinist; b. 29 Oct. 1944, Kladno, Czechoslovakia; m. Milka Berskova, 13 July 1968, 1 d. *Education:* Academy of Music, Prague. *Career:* Debut: Principal Cello, Prague Symphony Orchestra; Founder, Member, Kocian Quartet, 1972–; Teacher, Docent, Chamber Music, Academy of Music, Prague; mem, Czech Music Society. *Recordings:* Bruckner, String Quartet in F major; Schubert, String Quintet in C major; Dvořák, String Quartets No. 10, 12, 13, 14; Mozart, String Quartets Nos 14–23; Brahms, String Sextets Op. 18 and Op. 36, with members of Smetana Quartet; Haydn, String Quartets op 20; Fibich, String Quartets; Tchaikovsky, Sextet; Schulhoff, Quartets and

duo for Violin and Cello. *Honours:* Grand Prix du Disque; Academie Charles Cros; Diapason d'Or. *Address:* Kanerova 312, 16400 Prague, Czech Republic.

BERNATHOVA, Eva; Concert Pianist and Senior Lecturer; b. 4 Dec. 1922, Budapest, Hungary; m. Joseph Bernath, 20 Feb 1947. *Education:* Gymnasium, Budapest; Professor Diploma, 1946; Performing Artist Diploma, 1947; Franz Liszt Academy of Music, Budapest. *Career:* Debut: Prague, 1948; Has toured in Europe, USA, Canada, Far East, India, Japan, Australia and New Zealand; Soloist with many world famous orchestras including Berlin Philharmonic, Czech Philharmonic, Orchestre de la Suisse Romande, Royal Philharmonic Orchestra, Gewandhaus Orchestra; Senior Lecturer at Trinity College of Music, London. *Recordings include:* Solo works by J H Voríšek, Franz Liszt, M Balakirev, J Suk, Mozart; Janáček's Concertino for Piano and Chamber Orchestra, Martinů's Concertino for Piano and Orchestra; Franck's Symphonic Variations; Ravel's Concerto in G; Bartók's Concerto No. 3; Chamber Music: Dvořák's Piano Quintet in A, Brahms' Piano Quintet in F minor, Franck's Piano Quintet in F minor, Shostakovich's Piano Quintet in G minor, Martinů's Piano Quintet. *Honours:* Grand Prix du Disque Francais, Paris for Janáček piano solo works; Grand Prix du Disque Academy Charles Cros, Paris for Franck's Piano Quintet with the Janáček Quartet. *Address:* 8 Purley Avenue, London NW2 1 SJ, England.

BERNEDE, Jean-Claude; Conductor and Violinist; b. 19 Sept. 1935, Angers, France. *Education:* Studied at the Paris Conservatoire with Pierre Dervaux and Igor Markevitch. *Career:* Soloist with the Ensemble de Musique Contemporain from 1958; Founded the Bernede string quartet, 1965, and was director of the Chamber Orchestra of Rouen, 1973–82; Artistic advisor of the Concerts Lamoureux from 1977 and director of the Rennes City Orchestra, 1981–85; Chief conductor of the Concerts Lamoureux from 1983 and professor of chamber music at the Paris Conservatoire, 1984. *Address:* c/o Association des Concerts Lamoureux, 252 Rue du Faubourg St Honoré, 75008 Paris, France.

BERNET, Dietfried; Conductor; b. 14 May 1940, Vienna, Austria; m. Johanna Lonsky. *Education:* Studied in Vienna at the Academy of Music and Performing Arts with Hans Swarowsky and Dimitri Mitropoulos. *Career:* Debut: Orchestral concerts in Austria; Conducted at major opera houses and guested with leading orchestras since 1962; Permanent Conductor at both Austrian State Opera Houses, 1964–; General Director of Music, City of Mainz and Conductor, Vienna State and Volksoper; Appearances with the Vienna and Chicago Symphonies, London Philharmonic and Philharmonia; RAI Orchestras in Italy, Berlin Philharmonic, Munich Radio and Philharmonia Hungarica; Festival engagements at Salzburg, Vienna, Spoleto, Glyndebourne, Budapest and Turin; repertoire includes works by Brahms, Bruckner, Mahler, Wagner, Verdi, Puccini and composers of the 20th century; Season 1991–92 with Die Meistersinger at Marseille, Don Giovanni at the Mozart Festival Schoenbrunn, Vienna; 1992–93 with Les Contes d'Hoffmann and Der Freischütz at the Volksoper; Idomeneo at Pretoria; 1994 concerts at Teatro Colón, Buenos Aires; Clemenza di Tito at Marseille; 1995 Tannhäuser at Copenhagen; Pearl Fishers at Leeds, with Opera North; Guest with Royal Danish Opera at Covent Garden with The Love of Three Oranges; Verdi Requiem with Royal Philharmonic Orchestra at Royal Albert Hall; Meistersinger at Torino; Chief Guest Conductor of the Royal Danish Opera, 1995–; 1996, Entführung at Geneva; House of the Dead, at Strasbourg; Arabella at Glyndebourne Festival; Don Giovanni at Covent Garden; 1997, Boris at Torino; Così fan tutte at Covent Garden (BBC live transmission); Mahler 3rd Symphony and Arabella at Copenhagen; Berlioz's Romeo and Juliette with Théâtre de la Monnaie, Brussels; Merry Widow with Royal Opera, London, 1998; Has also conducted opera at Munich, Hamburg, Cologne, Stuttgart, Naples, Barcelona, Venice, Palermo and Trieste; Conducted Martinů's Julietta at Bregenz, 2002. *Honours:* Winner, International Conductor's Competition at Liverpool, 1962; Granted title of Professor by the Austrian State President for merits for the republic of Austria, 1995. *Current Management:* Athole Still International Management, Forresters Hall, 25–27 Westow Street, London, SE19 3RY, England. *Telephone:* (20) 8771-5271. *Fax:* (20) 8768-6600. *Website:* www .atholestill.com.

BERNHEIMER, Martin; Music Critic; b. 28 Sept. 1936, Munich, Germany; m. (1) Lucinda Pearson, 30 Sept 1961, divorced 1989, 1 s., 3 d.; (2) Linda Winer, 27 Sept 1993. *Education:* BMus, 1958–59; MA, New York University, 1961; Studied musicology with Gustave Reese. *Career:* Teacher, New York University, 1959–62; Contributing critic, New York Herald Tribune, 1959–62; Contributing Editor, Musical Courier, 1961–64; Temporary Music Critic, New York Post, 1961–65; Assistant to the music editor, Saturday Review, 1962–65; Managing editor, Philharmonic Hall Programme, New York, 1962–65; New York correspondent 1962–65, Los Angeles Correspondent 1965–97; Opera; Music Editor and Chief Music Critic, Los Angeles Times, 1965–96; Teacher, University of Southern California, Los Angeles, 1966–71;

University of California at Los Angeles, 1969–75; California Institute of the Arts, 1975–82; California State University, Northridge, 1978–81; New York Music Critic for the Financial Times of London and guest Critic on Newsday, 1996–; Music Critic for New York Sidewalk (Microsoft), 1997–; Lecturer, Metropolitan Opera Guild, 1997–; mem, Pulitzer Prize Music Jury, 1984, 1986, 1989. *Contributions:* Articles in New Grove Dictionary of Music and Musicians; Articles and reviews in various journals; Liner notes for recordings; New Grove Dictionary of American Music; New Grove Dictionary of Opera; Regular panellist, moderator, essayist on Metropolitan Opera Broadcasts; Frequent guest on CBC broadcasts. *Honours:* Winner of Pulitzer Prize in Criticism, 1981.

BERNIUS, Frieder; Conductor; b. 1945, Ludwigshafen, Germany. *Education:* Studied in Stuttgart and Tubingen. *Career:* Founder, Stuttgart Chamber Choir, 1968; Regular appearances with the Stuttgart Baroque and Chamber Orchestras and German Chamber Philharmonic, Bremen; Suisse Romande Orchestra; Prague Philharmonic; Founder, International Festival of Early Music, Stuttgart, 1987; Professor, Mannheim Musikhochschule; Conductor, Haydn's Orfeo, London; Jommelli's Il Vologeso, Stuttgart, 1993; Demofoonte, Rome; Schwetzingen, 1995; Dresden Semperoper, Hasse's Olimpiade and Artemisia; Operas by Rameau including Hippolyte et Aricie at Bad Urach. *Recordings:* Il Vologeso. *Address:* c/o Kammerorchester Stuttgart, Heumadener Strasse 23, 7302 Ostfidern, Germany.

BERNSTEIN, Lawrence F.; Musicologist and University Professor; b. 25 March 1939, New York, NY, USA. *Education:* BS, Hofstra University, 1960; PhD, New York University, 1969. *Career:* Instructor, 1965–66; Assistant Professor, 1966–70; Music and Humanities, University of Chicago; Associate Professor 1970–81; Chairman Department of Music, 1972–73, 1974–77; Professor of Music, 1981–, University of Pennsylvania; Visiting Lecturer, Columbia University, Graduate School of Arts and Sciences, 1979; Visiting Associate Professor, Princeton University, 1980; Visiting Professor, Rutgers University, 1982–83; Supervising Editor, Masters and Monuments of the Renaissance, 1970–; Editor-in-Chief, Journal of the American Musicological Society, 1975–77. *Publications:* Ihan Gero; Madrigali italiani e canzoni francese a due voci, with James Haar, 1980; La Couronne et fleur des chansons a troys, 1984; The French Secular Chanson in the Sixteenth Century. *Contributions:* Articles in New Grove Dictionary of Music and Musicians, 1980; Articles and reviews in journals and other publications. *Address:* c/o Department of Music, University of Pennsylvania, 201 S 34th Street, Philadelphia, PA 19104-6313, USA.

BÉROFF, Michel; Pianist; b. 9 May 1950, Epinal, France. *Education:* Conservatories of Nancy and Paris, with Yvonne Loriod. *Career:* Debut: Paris, 1966; Has appeared on television and at Festivals in Portugal and Iran, 1967, also at Royal and Oxford Bach Festivals; Has lectured and given recitals and concerts in various European and South American countries; Appearances with the London Symphony Orchestra, Concerts Colonne, Orchestre de Paris, New York Philharmonic and BBC Symphony Orchestras; Toured Japan and South Africa. *Recordings include:* Prokofiev's Visions Fugitives; Messiaen's Quatuor pour la fin du Temps and Vingt Regards sur L'Enfant Jésus; Debussy's Préludes, Estampes and Pour le Piano; Music by Bartók, Stravinsky and Mozart. *Honours:* First Prize, Nancy Conservatory, 1962, 1963; First Prize, Paris Conservatory, 1966; First Prize, Olivier Messiaen Competition, Royan. *Address:* 114 rue de Dames, Paris 17, France.

BERONESI, Debora; Singer (Mezzo-soprano); b. 1965, Rome, Italy. *Education:* Accademia di Santa Cecilia, Rome. *Career:* Debut: Spoleto, 1988 as Eboli in Don Carlos; Appearances at Macerata and Treviso as Dorabella, Rossini's Isabella at Trieste and Meg Page in Falstaff at Enschede; Isaura in Rossini's Tancredi at Bologna; Palermo, 1993 in the premiere of Alice by Testoni; Salzburg Festival, 1993–94 as the Messenger in Monteverdi's Orfeo; Nero in Monteverdi's Poppea at La Scala, Milan and Antwerp; Frankfurt Opera, 1995 as Cecilio in Lucio Silla by Mozart and Idamante in Idomeneo; Sang Purcell's Dido at the 2001 Maggio Musicale, Florence. *Honours:* Winner, A Belli Competition, Spoleto, 1988. *Address:* c/o Frankfurt Opera, Untermainanlege 11, 6000 Frankfurt am Main, Germany.

BERTHOLD, Beatrice; Concert Pianist; b. 11 Sept. 1964, Wiesbaden, Germany. *Education:* Academies of Music, Vienna and Cologne; Academy of Music, Detmold. *Career:* Debut: Wiesbaden National Theatre, 1978 (C. M. von Weber, konzertstück); Television debut on ZDF/Eurovision, presented by singer Annelise Rothenberger (Liszt, piano concerto No. 2); Solo Recitals and Concerts with Renowned Orchestras in Europe: Lucerne Music Festival, Berlin (Philharmonie), Hamburg (Musikhalle), Cologne (Philharmonie), London, 1983–; US debut at the German American Piano Festival in Atlanta, 1995; Several Concert Tours to South America: Porto Alegre, (Teatro da Ospa), Caracas, (Teatro Teresa Careno) 1996–; Television and radio appearances with Beethoven Piano Concerto No. 5; Rachmaninov Piano Sonata

No. 1 and 2; Granados, Goyescas; Brahms, Fantasias op 116; Rhapsodies op 78; Scriabin, Fantasia op 28; Villa-Lobos, Ciclo Brasilieiro. *Recordings:* The Young Rachmaninov, 1990; Tchaikovsky/Rachmaninov/Scriabin: Early Piano Works, 1992; Granados: Goyescas + El Pelele, 1992; Hommage au Piano, 1994. *Current Management:* Konzertagentur Jens Gunnar Becker. *Address:* Grunstrasse 13, 58313 Herdecke, Germany.

BERTI, Marco; Singer (Tenor); b. 1961, Turin, Italy. *Education:* Studied at the Verdi Conservatory in Milan. *Career:* Sang widely in Italy as Jim in Mahagonny by Weill; Sang Pinkerton in Consenza, 1990, and Don Ottavio at Macerata, 1991; Frankfurt, 1991, as Guevara in a concert performance of Franchetti's Cristoforo Colombo; Strasbourg, 1992, as Alfredo; St Gallen, 1993, as Roberto Devereux; Season 1994–95 as Rodolfo and in Verdi's Stiffelio at La Scala; Season 1999–2000 as Foresto in Attila at Karlsruhe, Ismaele in Nabucco at the Deutsche Oper Berlin and Macduff at the Vienna Staatsoper; Riccardo (Ballo in Maschera) at the Bregenz Festival and Don José at Copenhagen; Sang Foresto at Montpellier, and made Covent Garden debut 2002, as Gabriele Adorno; Pinkerton, 2003. *Recordings include:* Cristoforo Colombo (Koch); Don Giovanni (Koch); Manon Lescaut (Sony). *Address:* c/o Opéra du Rhin, 19 Place Broglie, 67008 Strasbourg, France.

BERTIN, Pascal; Singer (countertenor); b. 1970, France. *Education:* Paris Conservatoire with William Christie. *Career:* Children's Choir of Paris, from age 11, with tours throughout the world; founder, Indigo, vocal jazz group, 1995; many concert and opera appearances with conductors Marc Minkowski, Christophe Rousset, John Eliot Gardiner, Sigiswald Kuijken and Philippe Herreweghe. *Recordings:* Oronte, Handel's Riccardo Primo; Caldara's Conversione di Clovedeo; The Three Countertenors and Pathways of Baroque Music–Cathedrals and Chapels; Orlando in Handel's Amadigi. *Honours:* First prize, Baroque vocal music, Paris Conservatoire. *Address:* c/o Harmonia Mundi UK, 45 Vyner Street, London, E2 9DQ, England. *Telephone:* (20) 8709-9525. *Fax:* (20) 8709-9501.

BERTINI, Gary; Composer and Conductor; b. 1 May 1927, Brichevo, Bessarabia, Russia; m. Rosette Berengole 1956; two c. *Education:* diploma, Tel-Aviv Conservatorio Verdi, Milan, 1948; diploma, Tel-Aviv Music Coll., 1951; Conservatoire National Superieur, Paris, 1954; Ecole Normale de Musique, 1954; Institut de Musicologie, Sorbonne, Paris, 1955; studied with Arthur Honegger and Olivier Messiaen. *Career:* Music Dir, Rinat Chamber Chorus 1955–72; Founder, Music Dir, Conductor, Israel Chamber Orchestra 1965–75; Principal Guest Conductor, Scottish National Orchestra 1971–81; Music Dir, Chief Conductor, Jerusalem Symphony Orchestra 1978–86; Chief Conductor, Cologne Radio-Symphony Orchestra 1983–91; Intendant and Gen. Music Dir, Frankfurt Opera 1987–90; Artistic Dir, Gen. Music Dir, New Israeli Opera, Tel Aviv 1987–1997; Music Dir, Tokyo Metropolitan Symphony Orchestra 1998–; guest conductor, principal orchestras and opera houses, Europe, USA, Japan; Artistic Adviser, Israel Festival 1976–83; conducted Dukas' Ariane et Barbebleue at the Paris Opéra in 1975; has given the premieres of four operas by Josef Tal, Ashmedai 1971, Masada 1967, (1973), Die Versuchung 1977 and Josef, 1995; Boris Godunov at the opening of the New Israel Opera 1994; Music Dir, Israel Opera from 1994; conducted Weber's Die drei Pintos at the 1997 Vienna Festival, Carmen at the Opéra Bastille, Paris, Peter Grimes at Genoa 1998, memorial concert for victims of 11 September 2001 terrorist attacks, Gedächtniskirche Berlin 2001, Saint-Saëns' Samson and Dalila (Placido Domingo as Samson), La Scala Milan; mem. Israel League of Composers. *Compositions:* Symphonic, Chamber, Incidental Music for theatre and radio. *Recordings include:* Berlioz Requiem and a complete Mahler cycle. *Publications:* contributor to musical journals of articles in the field of music. *Honours:* Recipient, Israel State Prize, 1978; Accademico Onorario, Accademia Nazionale di Santa Cecilia, Rome, Italy, 2002. *Address:* Konzertgesellschaft, PO Box, 4002 Basel, Switzerland. *Website:* www.konzertgesellschaft.ch.

BERTOLINO, Mario (Ercole); Singer (Bass-Baritone); b. 10 Sept. 1934, Palermo, Italy. *Education:* Studied in Palermo and with Mario Basiola in Milan; Giuseppe Danise in New York. *Career:* Debut: Teatro Nuovo Milan, 1955; Marcello in La Bohème; Sang at La Scala, in Rome, Palermo, Munich, Lyon and Mexico City; Moved to Forest Hills, NY, sang widely in the US at Boston, Cincinnati, Pittsburgh, San Antonio, Washington and New York City Opera; Roles have included Verdi's Amonasro, Renato, Macbeth, Iago, Germont and Luna; Donizetti's Dulcamara, Don Pasquale and Enrico; Gerard in Andrea Chénier; Puccini's Sharpless and Lescaut; Iago in Otello; Connecticut Opera 1987–88 as Don Pasquale and Dulcamara; Rome 1989, as Mozart's Bartolo; Also sang in concert.

BERTOLO, Aldo; Singer (Tenor); b. 22 Oct. 1949, Turin, Italy. *Career:* Debut: Sang Mozart's Ferrando at Susa, 1978; Many appearances in Italy; South America; Europe, in the lyric repertoire; Among his best roles are Donizetti's Edgardo, Tonie and Ernesto; Pylades, in Piccinni's

Iphigénie en Tauride; Rossini's Lindoro, Adalbert in Adelaide di Borgogna and Don Ottavio; Season 1985 sang Arturo in I Puritani at Martina Franca; Ramiro in La Cenerentola, in Santiago; At Valle d'Itria 1986, sang Thoas in the first modern revival of Traetta's Ifigenia en Tauride; Elvino in La Sonnambula at Piacenza, 1986; Teatro Carlo Felice, Genoa 1988, as Narciso in L'Italiana in Algeri; Other roles include the Fisherman in Guillaume Tell, Lorenzo in Fra Diavolo and Verdi's Alfredo; Season 1991, as Ernesto at Pisa and Narciso at Trieste. *Address:* c/o Teatro Carlo Felice, 16100 Genoa, Italy.

BESA, Alexander; Czech musician and violist; b. 28 Feb. 1971, Havana, Cuba; m.; one d. *Education:* Music School, Znojmo, Czech Republic, State Conservatory, Brno, International Menuhin Music Academy, Switzerland, Music Akademie Basel. *Career:* debut, Mozart Sinfonia Concertante K 364 with Moravian Chamber Orchestra, Brno, 1990; appeared as Viola Soloist with Camerata Bern, Kurphälzisches Kammerorchester, Camerata Lysy, Basle Symphony and Radio Orchestra, Janáček Philharmonic, Ostrava, B. Martinů Philharmonic, Zlin, Lucerne Symphony Orchestra, State Philharmonic, Kosice; Principal Violist. Lucerne Symphony Orchestra and Camerata Bern. *Recordings:* A Lysy, Camerata Lysy, Mendelssohn, 1992; T Zehetmair, Camerata Bern - Vivaldi, 1995; H Holliger, Camerata Bern, Bach, 1996; Ensemble Tiramisu, Quintets by Brahms and Herzogenberg, Octets by Mendelssohn and Gade, 1996, 1997; Viola Recital, 1997. *Honours:* Winner, Beethoven International Viola Competition, Czech Republic, 1994; Winner, H. Schaeuble Viola Competition, Lausanne, 1995; Morris Maddrell Prize, L. Tertis Viola Competition, Isle of Man, 1997; Best Recording of the Year, 1999 for 'Music for Viola and Piano'; Best recording of the year, 2002 for recording of Max Bruch's Concerto for Clarinet, Viola and Orchestra. *Current Management:* Central European Music Agency. *Website:* www.cema-music.com.

BESRODNY, Igor; Conductor and Violinist; b. 7 May 1930, Tbilisi, Russia. *Education:* Graduated Moscow Conservatoire, 1955. *Career:* Many appearances in Russia and elsewhere from 1948, after winning the Prague International Competition; Teacher at the Moscow Conservatoire from 1957 (professor, 1972); Debut as conductor, 1970, directing the Moscow Chamber Orchestra, 1977–83; Premiered the first Concerto by Kabalevsky, 1948. *Address:* c/o Moscow Conservatoire, ul Gertzena 13, 103009 Moscow, Russia.

BEST, Jonathan; Singer (Bass); b. 1958, Kent, England. *Career:* Debut: Sang Sarastro with Welsh National Opera, 1983; Many leading roles in the bass repertory, with Welsh National Opera, Scottish Opera, Dublin Grand Opera, Kent Opera and Opera North; Appearances at Covent Garden in Die Meistersinger, Otello, Don Carlos and King Arthur (as Grimbauld, with Les Arts Florissants, 1995); Season 1994–95 in The Rake's Progress at Salzburg, in The Queen of Spades at Glyndebourne and The Fairy Queen for English National Opera; Other roles include Don Alfonso in Così fan tutte (Opera North, 1997); Sang Trulove in The Rake's Progress for Welsh National Opera, 1996; Season 1998 with Cassandro in Mozart's Finta Semplice at Garsington and Garibaldo in Rodelinda for GTO at Glyndebourne; Season 1999–2000 as Leporello and Britten's Bottom for Opera North; St Magnus Festival 2000 in the premiere of Mr. Emmett takes a Walk, by Peter Maxwell Davies. *Address:* c/o Music International, 13 Ardilaun Road, London N5 2QR, England.

BEST, Matthew, MA; singer (bass-baritone) and conductor; b. 6 Feb. 1957, Farnborough, Kent, England; m. Rosalind Mayes 1983. *Education:* King's Coll., Cambridge, National Opera Studio, studied with Otakar Kraus, Robert Lloyd and Patrick McGuigan. *Career:* debut, Seneca in The Coronation of Poppea, Cambridge University Opera Society, 1978; Principal Bass, Royal Opera, 1980–86; regular guest artist with WNO, Opera North, Netherlands Opera, Scottish Opera, ENO; extensive concert career; Founder and Dir of the Corydon Singers 1973–, Corydon Orchestra 1991–; Principal Conductor of the Hanover Band 1998–99; has also worked frequently, as guest conductor, with English Chamber Orchestra, London Mozart Players, City of London Sinfonia, plus appearances with English Northern Philharmonia, Manchester Camerata, RTE Concert Orchestra, Royal Seville Symphony Orchestra; BBC National Orchestra of Wales; recent opera appearances (as singer) include Pizarro (Beethoven, Leonore) at the 1996 Salzburg Festival, BBC Proms, Lincoln Center Festival, New York, The Flying Dutchman, Jochanaan (Salome), King Mark (Tristan & Isolde) and Kutuzov (War and Peace) for ENO, Kurwenal (Tristan und Isolde), Amfortas (Parsifal) and Scarpia (Tosca) for Scottish Opera; sang Wotan in Das Rheingold (concert) for ENO 2001; Wotan in Das Rheingold and Die Walküre for Scottish Opera at the Edinburgh Festival 2000–01; Scarpia (Tosca) for Florida Grand Opera; sang the Wanderer in Siegfried at the 2002 Edinburgh Festival; complete Ring cycles (as Wotan) at the 2003 Festival. *Compositions:* Alice, opera, work performed Aldeburgh Festival 1979. *Recordings:* As singer: include, Beethoven, Leonore; Elgar, The Dream of Gerontius; Britten, Peter Grimes; Billy Budd; Berlioz, L'Enfance du Christ; Verdi, Don Carlo

(video); Vaughan Williams, Sir John in Love; As conductor include: Bruckner, Te Deum and Masses; Berlioz L'Enfance du Christ; Beethoven Mass in C and Emperor Cantatas; Fauré Requiem; Duruflé, Requiem; Vaughan Williams, Hugh the Drover; Rachmaninov Vespers; Works by Vaughan Williams, Britten, Finzi, Tchaikovsky, Mendelssohn, Simpson and others, all with Corydon Singers, Corydon Orchestra, English Chamber Orchestra, City of London Sinfonia. *Honours:* SE Arts Association; Friends of Covent Garden, Bursary, 1980; Decca-Kathleen Ferrier Prize, 1982. *Current Management:* IMG Artists, Lovell House, 616 Chiswick High Road, London, W4 5RX, England. *Telephone:* (20) 8233-5800. *Fax:* (20) 8233-5801. *E-mail:* artistseurope@imgworld.com. *Website:* www.imgartists.com.

BEST, Roger; Violist and College Professor; b. 28 Sept. 1938, Liverpool, England; m. Bronwen Naish, 5 c. *Education:* Royal Manchester College of Music. *Career:* Debut: Manchester 1955; With Hallé Orchestra, 1958–60; Principal Viola, Northern Sinfonia Orchestra, 1961–73; Gave world premieres of viola concertos by Malcolm Arnold, 1972 and Richard Rodney Bennett, 1973; Professor, Royal College of Music. *Honours:* Open Scholarship, RMCM, 1955; Hiles Gold Medal, 1958; Barber Trust Scholarship to Birmingham University, 1960. *Address:* 9 Granard Road, Wandsworth Common, London SW12, England.

BESUTTI, Paola; Musicologist; b. 18 April 1960, Mantua, Italy; m. Roberto Giuliani 1992. *Education:* Musicological studies at Parma University; Pianoforte at Conservatory of Music in Mantua. *Career:* Professor at Pesaro Conservatory of Music; Member of editorial staff of Rivista Italiana di Musicologia; Professor, Researcher, Institute of Musicology of Parma University, 1990–; mem, American Musicological Society; International Musicological Society; Società Italiana di Educazione Musicale; Società Italiana di Musicologia. *Recordings:* Collaborated with Parrott, Vartolo, Savall, Gini; BBC, RAI, Radio France, RSI. *Publications include:* La corte musicale di Ferdinando Carlo Gonzaga, Mantova Areari, 1989; Hildegard von Bingen, Ordo Virtutum, Sa musique et s. idée de théâtre, in Actes de la Societé Internationale pour l'étude du théatre médiéval, Barcelona, Institut del Teatro, 1997; Ave maris stella: la tradizione mantovana nuovamente posta in musica da Monteverdi in Claudio Monteverdi, Studi e prospettive, Firenze, Olschki, 1997; Tasso contra Guarini: una Rappresentazione con intermedi degli Intrichi d'amore (1606) in Torquato Tasso e la cultura estense, Firenze, Olschki, 1997; La figura professionale del cantante d'opera: Quaderni storici, XXXII n 2 agosto, 1997; Giostre e tornei a Mantova Parma e Piacenza fra Cinque e Seicento in Musica e tornei nel Seicento Italiano, Lucca, LIM. *Contributions:* Music reviews and publications including: Atlas Mondiale du Baroque, Dizionario degli Editori Musicali Italiani, The New Grove, The New Grove Dictionary of Opera. *Address:* Piazzale Vittorio Veneto 1, 46100 Mantova, Italy.

BEUDERT, Mark; Singer (Tenor); b. 4 June 1961, New York. *Education:* Studied at Columbia University and Michigan University. *Career:* Sang at Santa Domingo Opera from 1983; Grand Rapids Opera, 1985; At Philadelphia and the New York City Opera; Washington, 1986, as Pedrillo in Die Entfuhrung; Queensland State Opera at Brisbane as Pinkerton and Faust, 1987, 1991; Season 1988–89 as Candide by Bernstein for Scottish Opera and the Old Vic Theatre, London; Sam Kaplan in Weill's Street Scene for English National Opera. *Honours:* Winner, Pavarotti Competition at Philadelphia, 1985. *Address:* c/o New York City Opera, Lincoln Center, New York NY 10023, USA.

BEURON, Yann; Singer (Tenor); b. 1970, France. *Education:* Paris Conservatoire with Anna Maria Bondi. *Career:* Appearances as Belmonte, Strasbourg; Fernando at Bordeaux and in Rossini's Cenerentola at the Ascoli Festival; In Rameau's Hippolyte et Aricie, Paris Palais Garnier, Geneva, Opéra in Offenbach's Orphée, 1997; Concerts include the Evangelist in Bach's Passions; Soloist, Berlioz Te Deum. *Recordings:* Le Chevalier Danois, Gluck's Armide. *Address:* c/o Geneva Opéra, 11 Boulevard du Théâtre, 1211 Geneva 11, Switzerland.

BEVAN, Maurice (Guy Smalman); Singer; b. 10 March 1921, London, England; m. Anne Alderson, 1 d. *Education:* Magdalen College, Oxford; BMus Cantuar, 1990; FTCL; ARCM Hon. FGCM. *Career:* Vicar Choral, St Paul's Cathedral, 1949–89; Founder Member, The Deller Consort; Oratorio and Recitals, BBC; Soloist in the United Kingdom, Europe, USA, Israel and South America. *Recordings include:* Purcell's Fairy Queen; Handel's Acis and Galatea. *Publications:* Editions of English vocal music of the 17th and 18th Centuries. *Contributions:* Journal of the American Musicological Society; Die Musik in Geschichte und Gegenwart; Grove's Dictionary of Music and Musicians. *Address:* 45 Court Way, Twickenham, Middlesex TW2 7 SA, England.

BEYER, Frank Michael; Composer and Professor; b. 8 March 1928, Berlin, Germany; m.; two c. *Education:* studied sacred music, Berlin, composition with Ernst Pepping, Berlin Staatliche Hochschule für Musik. *Career:* Asst Prof., Berlin Kirchenmusikschule 1953–62; Asst Prof., Berlin Hochschule für Musik 1960–68, Prof. of Composition, 1968–93; Founder Dir, Musica Nova Sacra Concert Series, Berlin; Dir,

Contemporary Music Section, Berlin Akademie der Kunste; mem. Bayerische Akademie der Schönen künste. *Compositions:* Ballet: Geburt des Tanzes, 1987; Orchestral: Flute Concerto, 1964; Versi for Strings, 1968; Rondeau Imaginaire, 1972; Concertino a Tre for Chamber Orchestra, 1974; Diaphonie, 1975; Streicherfantasien to a Motive by J. S. Bach, 1977, also for String Quintet, 1978; Griechenland for 3 String Groups, 1981; Deutsche Tänze for Cello, Double Bass and Chamber Orchestra, 1982, arranged from Deutsche Tänze for Cello and Double Bass, 1980; Notre-Dame-Musik, 1983–84; Mysteriensonate for Viola and Orchestra, 1986; Architettura per Musica, 1989; Concerto for Oboe and Strings, 1986; Klangtore for orchestra; Liturgia for String Orchestra, 1996; Canto di giorno, concerto for violoncello and orchestra, 1998–99; Fuga fiammata for orchestra, 1999; Chamber: Biblische Szenen for soprano, tenor and 4 instruments, 1956; 3 String Quartets, 1957, 1969, 1985; Concerto for Organ and 7 Instruments, 1966–69, 1968; Chaconne for Violin, 1970; Wind Quintet, 1972; Sonata for Violin and Piano, 1977; De Lumine for 7 Players, 1978; Trio for Oboe, Viola and Harp, 1980; Fantasia Concertante for 2 Violins, 1982; Melos for Viola, 1983; Passacaglia Fantastica for Violin, Cello and Piano, 1984; Echo for Bass Flute, 1986; Sinfonien for 8 Players, 1989; Sanctus for Saxophone Quartet, 1989; Organ Music; Piano Pieces; Vocal: Major Angelis for Soprano, Women's Chorus and 6 Instruments, 1970; Canticum Mose et Agni for 8 Voice Double Chorus, 1976; Musik der Frühe for Violin and Orchestra, 1993; Persephone for orchestra, 1999; Et resurexit, 2003; Was Orpheus sah, Streichquartett, 2003. *Contributions:* Publications and contributions in several books and journals. *Honours:* Kunstpreis der Stadt Berlinlk. *Address:* Akademie der Künste, Hanseatenweg 10, 10557 Berlin, Germany. *Telephone:* (30) 833-8051.

BEZDUZ, Soner Bülen; Singer (tenor); b. 1970, Turkey. *Education:* Music Academy of Gazi University, Ankara; European Opera Centre, Manchester. *Career:* Debut: Mozart's Lucio Silla on tour with the European Opera Centre, 1999; State Opera of Mersin as Rodolfo in La Bohème, Edgardo (Lucia di Lammermoor) and the Duke of Mantua; Verdi's Alfredo at the Aspendos Festival; Cassio in Otello and roles in Benvenuto Cellini and Les Troyens in concert performances under Colin Davis; Season 2000–2001 as Alfredo in Nancy and Rennes, and Fenton in Falstaff for Opera de Lausanne. *Honours:* Prizewinner, Concours International de Chant de Paris, 1999. *Current Management:* Athole Still International Management, Forresters Hall, 25–27 Westow Street, London, SE19 3RY, England. *Telephone:* (20) 8771-5271. *Fax:* (20) 8768-6600. *Website:* www.atholestill.com.

BEZNOSIUK, Pavlo Roman; Irish/Ukranian violinist; b. 4 July 1960, London, England. *Education:* Guildhall School of Music and Drama. *Career:* Leader of Parley of Instruments 1984–7; founded Beethoven String Trio of London 1992; solo debut at Proms 1992; soloist and concertmaster with period-instrument orchestras, including The Acad. of Ancient Music, Amsterdam Baroque Orchestra, Orchestra of the Age of Enlightenment and the Hanover Band; Prof. of Baroque Violin, Koninklijk Conservatorium, The Hague. *Recordings include:* Bach Brandenburg Concertos with the New London Consort, Vivaldi's Op. 6 Concertos with Academy of Ancient Music, Schubert Octet with Hausmusik, Biber's Rosary Sonatas. *Address:* 170 Bow Common Lane, London, E3 4HH, England.

BEZUYEN, Arnold; Singer (tenor); b. 1965, Netherlands. *Education:* Studied in Alkmaar at International Opera Centrum Nederland. *Career:* Debut: Rodolfo in La Bohème, at Alkmaar; Sang at Augsburg and Bremen as Turiddu, Pinkerton, Alfredo in La Traviata, Ismael in Nabucco and Aegisthus in Elektra; Bayreuth Festival as Loge, and in Parsifal and Lohengrin; La Scala Milan in Die Frau ohne Schatten, under Giuseppe Sinopoli; Season 2001–2002 as the Berlioz Faust at Bremen, Shuisky in Boris Godunov at Kassel Wagner's Vogelgesang for Netherlands Opera and Beethoven's Florestan for Nationale Reis-opera. Other roles included Cassio in Otello, Idomeneo and Don José. *Recordings include:* Das Rheingold, conducted by Gustav Kuhn (Arte Nova). *Current Management:* Athole Still International Management, Forresters Hall, 25–27 Westow Street, London, SE19 3RY, England. *Telephone:* (20) 8771-5271. *Fax:* (20) 8768-6600. *Website:* www .atholestill.com.

BEZZUBENKOV, Gennady; Singer (Bass); b. 1955, St Petersburg, Russia. *Education:* Graduated St Petersburg Conservatoire 1979. *Career:* Appearances in opera throughout Russia; Kirov Opera from 1989; Roles have included Glinka's Ivan Susannin, Khan Konchak in Prince Igor, Gremin in Eugene Onegin, Pimen, Varlaam and Ivan Khovansky; Further engagements as Wagner's Gurnemanz and King Henry, Verdi's Grand Inquisitor and Mozart's Bartolo, and in London concert performances of The Legend of the Invisible City of Kitezh (Barbican Hall, 1994), Katerina Izmailova by Shostakovich and Parsifal (Royal Albert Hall, 1999); Sang Kutuzov in War and Peace and Dosifei in Khovanshchina with the Kirov Opera at Covent Garden, 2000; Sang Banquo at St Petersburg and the premiere of Gubaidulina's St John Passion, at Stuttgart, 2000; St John Passion at the London Proms, 2002.

Recordings include: War and Peace, The Gambler, The Maid of Pskov, Sadko and Ruslan and Lyudmilla (Phillips Classics). *Address:* c/o Kirov Opera, Mariinsky Theatre, Mariinsky Square, St Petersburg, Russia.

BIANCHI, Lino; Musicologist and Composer; b. 14 May 1920, Vedano Olona, Vasese, Italy; m. Gabriella Limentani. *Education:* Diploma in Composition, G Rossini Conservatory, Pesaro, 1945. *Career:* Artistic Director, Centro Oratorio Musicale, Rome, 1949–63; Edition de Santis, Rome, 1960–; GP da Palestrina Foundation, 1973–; Numerous broadcasts on Palestrina, Carissimi and other early composers; Italian radio and television, 1952–. *Compositions:* Il Principe Felice, one-act opera; Uruel, three-act dramatic commentary. *Recordings:* As conductor, works by Carissimi, Stradella, A Scarlatti and D Scarlatti. *Publications:* Editions of complete works of G Carissimi and GP de Palestrina; Complete oratorios of A Scarlatti, 1964–; A Stradella, 1969; Musical encyclopedias and journals. *Address:* Circonvallazione Clodia 82, 00195 Rome, Italy.

BIANCONI, Lorenzo (Gennaro); Musicologist; b. 14 Jan. 1946, Minusio/Muralto, Switzerland; m. Giuseppina La Face, 2 June 1979, 2 s. *Education:* PhD, University of Heidelberg, Germany, 1974; Studied Music Theory with Luciano Sgrizzi, Lugano, Switzerland. *Career:* Collaborator, Répertoire International des Sources Musicales, Italy, 1969–70; Member, German Institute, Venice, 1974–76; Guest Assistant, German Historical Institute, Rome, 1976; Guest Professor, Princeton University, USA, 1977; Professor of Musical Dramaturgy, Bologna University, Italy, 1977–; Professor of the History of Music, Siena University, Arezzo, Italy, 1980–83; Co-Editor, Rivista Italiana di Musicologia, 1973–79; Editor, Acta Musicologica, 1987–91; Head of Programme Committee, 14th International Musicological Congress, Bologna, 1987; Co-Editor, Musica e Storia, 1993–; Co-Editor, Il Saggiatore Musicale, 1994–; Editor, Historiae Musicae Cultores, 1999; Head of Music Department, Bologna University, Italy, 1998–2001; mem, Honorary Member, Accademia Filarmonica, Bologna; Corresponding Member, American Musicological Society. *Publications:* B Marcello, Sonates pour clavecin (editor with Luciano Sgrizzi), 1971; P M Marsolo, Madrigali a 4 voci (1614), 1973; A Il Verso, Madrigali a 3 e a 5 voci (1605–19), 1978; Il Seicento, 1982, English Edition, 1987; La Drammaturgia Musicale, 1986; Storia dell'Opera Italiana, 1987–, Anglo-American edition, 1998–; I Libretti Italiani di G F Händel (with G. La Face), 1992–; Il Teatro d'Opera in Italia, 1993; G Frescobaldi, Madrigali a 5 voci (with M. Privitera), 1996. *Honours:* Dent Medal of the Royal Musical Association, 1983; Premio Imola per la Critica, 1994. *Address:* via A Frank 17, 40068 San Lazzaro di Savena, Bologna, Italy.

BIANCONI, Philippe; Concert Pianist; b. 1960, France. *Career:* Many appearances in concerto repertory and recitals; Carnegie Hall debut recital 1987, followed by engagements with the orchestras of Cleveland, Los Angeles, Atlanta, Dallas, Pittsburgh and Montreal; BBC London Proms debut with the Orchestre de Paris and Semyon Bychkov; Other conductors include Lorin Maazel, Georges Prêtre, Jeffrey Tate, Kurt Masur, Edo de Waart and Christoph von Dohnányi; European recitals in London, Berlin, Vienna, Milan and Amsterdam; Chamber concerts with the Sine Nomine Quartet, Janos Starker and Gary Hoffman; Season 2000–01 with concerts in Budapest, Paris, Rome, Montreal, Mexico City; Rachmaninov 2nd Concerto at Palais Garnier, Paris; Recital debut at the Berlin Philharmonie, 2002; Season 2001–02: Concerts in Paris, New York, Reykjavik, Santiago do Chile, Tours in the USA, Germany and Spain, including with Berlin Philharmonic Orchestra. *Recordings include:* Ravel, Schubert and Schumann (Lyrinx); Brahms Piano Quintet (Clavos); Shostakovich and Prokofiev Cello Sonatas (Le Chant du Monde). *Honours:* Silver Medal, Seventh Van Cliburn International Competition. *Address:* c/o Musicaglotz, 11 rue Le Verrier, 75006 Paris, France.

BIBBY, Gillian; Composer; b. 31 Aug. 1945, Lower Hutt, New Zealand. *Education:* Studied at the University of Otago and at Victoria University with Douglas Lilburn; Further study in Berlin and Cologne, with Aloys Kontarsky, Kagel and Stockhausen. *Career:* Teacher in New Zealand, and editor of Canzona, 1982–84. *Compositions include:* Lest you be my enemy, ballet, 1976; Synthesis for tape, 1977; In Memoriam for 8 voices, organ and percussion, 1979; Marama Music, music-theatre, 1978; 11 Characters in Search of a Composer, for military band and percussion. *Address:* c/o New Zealand Music Centre, PO Box 10042, Level 13, Brandon Street, Wellington, New Zealand.

BICCIRE, Patrizia; Singer (Soprano); b. 1973, Porto San Giorgio, Italy. *Education:* Conservatorio Rossini and Accademia Rossiniana in Pesaro. *Career:* Debut: Rossini Festival at Pesaro 1992, as Protagonist in La Scala di Seta; Many appearances throughout Italy in bel canto and Mozart repertory; Glyndebourne Festival debut 2000, as Elvira in Don Giovanni; Season 2000–2001 as Nannetta in Falstaff at La Monnaie, Brussels, and Susanna in Le nozze di Figaro at Glyndebourne; Il turco in Italia at Grand Théâtre, Geneva. *Recordings include:* Albums for

EMI Classics. *Address:* c/o Glyndebourne Festival Opera, Glyndebourne, Lewes, Sussex BN8 5UU, England.

BICKERS, Helen; Singer (Soprano); b. 1959, Atlanta, Georgia, USA. *Career:* Sang at Bremerhaven Opera from 1986 as Amelia, Ballo in Maschera; Agathe in Der Freischütz; Vitellia in La Clemenza di Tito, Aida, Butterfly and Donizetti's Anna Bolena; Freiburg 1989–93 as Leonora in Il Trovatore; Elettra in Idomeneo, Ariadne, the Marschallin in Rosenkavalier and Janáček's Jenůfa; Dessau, 1993–95, as Anna Bolena and Lucrezia in I Due Foscari by Verdi; Guest appearances in London, Washington as Maria Stuarda; Düsseldorf, as Elisabeth in Don Carlos; Season 1995–96 as Amelia at the Deutsche Oper Berlin and Gioconda at Bremen; Season 2001–02 as Strauss's Ariadne and Chrysothemis, at Hannover. *Address:* c/o Staatstheater Hannover, Opernplatz 1, D-30159 Hannover, Germany.

BICKERSTAFF, Robert; Australian singer (baritone) and voice teacher; b. 26 July 1932, Sydney; m. Ann Howard. *Education:* New South Wales Conservatorium with Lyndon Jones, Melbourne Conservatorium with Henry Portnoj, Paris with Dominique Modesti. *Career:* debut, Marseilles 1962, as Thoas in Iphigénie en Tauride; Sang in Nice, Bordeaux and Marseille; Principal Baritone Sadler's Wells and English National Opera, 1964–70; Roles included: Amonasro, Escamillo, Macbeth, Boccanegra, Scarpia, Wotan, Mozart's Count and Eugene Onegin; Guest appearances with Pittsburgh Opera, Welsh National Opera and at Covent Garden; Over 60 roles in Opera; Other roles included Wagner's Dutchman, Ezio in Attila, Luna, Renato in Un Ballo in Maschera, Enrico in Lucia di Lammermoor and Massenet's Hérode; Boris in Lady Macbeth of Mtsensk by Shostakovich, Adelaide Festival; Oratorio and recital performances; Appearances on BBC radio and television; Previously Professor of singing at the Royal Academy in Music; London and Tutor of Singing at King's College, Cambridge. *Recordings:* La Juive, Raritas; Private Collection; Society of Musicians, London. *Honours:* Hon. ARAM. *Address:* 8 William Street, North Sydney, 2060, Australia.

BICKET, Harry; Conductor and Harpsichordist; b. 1960, Liverpool, England. *Education:* Royal College of Music and Oxford University. *Career:* Organist and harpsichordist with Academy of Ancient Music, The English Concert, Monteverdi Orchestra, Philharmonia and City of Birmingham Symphony Orchestra; Now Opera and Concert Conductor; Conducted Monteverdi's Orfeo and Combattimento di Tancredi e Clorinda and Handel's Ariodante, for English National Opera; Other productions include Gluck's Orfeo for Scottish Opera, Magic Flute for Opera North, The Return of Ulysses at Buxton Festival and for Opera North, and Werther for English Touring Opera; Conducted Storace's No Song, No Supper with BBC Scottish Symphony Orchestra; Conducted many British orchestras including Bournemouth Sinfonietta, City of London Sinfonia and Ulster Orchestra; Conducted Theodora at Glyndebourne, 1996; Season 1997–98 included Figaro at New York City Opera, Giulio Cesare for Australian Opera; Season 1998–99 with Rodelinda on Glyndebourne Tour, Orfeo with Royal Danish Opera and Semele with ENO; Further engagements include new opera productions for New York City Opera with Clemenza di Tito and Rinaldo, Bavarian State Opera with Rinaldo, and Opera North with Radamisto; in 2001–02 conducted Giulio Cesare with Los Angeles Opera, La Clemenza di Tito for WNO and Xerxes for ENO; Season 2002–03 included Messiah with WNO and Royal Liverpool Philharmonic Orchestra, Mathew Passion Rotterdam Philharmonic and Haydn Symphonies with Danish Radio Sinfonietta; Opera productions included Theodora for Glyndebourne Festival Opera, Tamerlano for Spoleto (USA) and debut with Chigaco Lyric Opera conducting Partnenope; Television work includes My Night with Handel for Channel 4, 1996. *Recordings:* Susan Graham and Orchestra of the Age of Enlightenment; David Daniels and OAE. *Current Management:* Askonas Holt Ltd, Lonsdale Chambers, 27 Chancery Lane, London, WC2A 1PF, England. *Telephone:* (20) 7400-1700. *Fax:* (20) 7400-1799. *E-mail:* info@askonasholt.co.uk. *Website:* www.askonasholt.co.uk.

BICKLEY, Susan; Singer (Mezzo-Soprano); b. 27 May 1955, Liverpool, England. *Education:* City University, London, and the Guildhall School of Music. *Career:* Debut: As Proserpina in Monteverdi's Orfeo, at Florence; Opera roles include Baba the Turk and Ulrica for Opera 80, Mozart's Marcellina and Elvira, Janáček's Kabanicha and Kostelnicka for the Glyndebourne Tour; Britten's Florence Pike, Hippolyta and Mrs Sedley at the Glyndebourne Festival; Dorabella and Andromache in King Priam for English National Opera, Feodor in Boris Godunov at Covent Garden; Further engagements as Kabanicha and a Flowermaiden at the Opéra Bastille (1997), Octavian at the Hong Kong Festival and Herodias in Salome at San Francisco; Concerts include Ligeti's Requiem at the 1994 Salzburg Festival and the Missa Solemnis on tour with Les Arts Florissants to Vienna and in France, 1995; Season 1995–96 with El Amor Brujo in Rome and Stravinsky's Faun and Shepherdess in Hong Kong; Further concerts with the London Symphony, Philharmonia, London Philharmonic Orchestra, London Sinfonietta, London Classical Players and Allegri and Brodsky Quartets; Season 1996–97 included Messiah with the Hallé Orchestra, Stravinsky with the BBC Symphony Orchestra and Das Lied von der Erde with the BBC National Orchestra of Wales; Premiere by a British company of Henze's The Prince of Homburg, 1996; Handel's Admeto at Beaune, 1998; Sang in the premiere of Louis Andriessen's Writing to Vermeer, Amsterdam 1999; Season 2000–01 as the Ghost in the premiere production of Birtwistle's The Last Supper, Berlin Staatsoper and Glyndebourne Touring Opera; Kostelnička in Jenůfa at Glyndebourne and in the premiere of David Sawer's From Morning to Midnight, for ENO; London Proms, 2002. *Recordings include:* Socrate by Satie, Monteverdi's Il Ballo delle Ingrate, Dido and Aeneas, and The Fairy Queen (EMI); Other labels include Hyperion, Nimbus and DGG. *Address:* Allied Artists, 42 Montpelier Square, London SW7 1JZ, England.

BIDDINGTON, Eric Wilhelm, BA, BSc, BMus, MA; New Zealand composer; b. 19 Oct. 1953, Timaru; m. Elizabeth Ann Biddington 1989. *Education:* Univ. of Canterbury, Christchurch. *Career:* debut, Christchurch Arts Centre, Christchurch; Major recitals of chamber music, Christchurch, 1985–97, Lower Hutt, 1988, Hamilton, 1989; Premiere performance of Concerto for Two Violins and String Orchestra at Tempe, Arizona, USA, 1989; mem. APRA. *Compositions:* Mainly chamber music and some orchestral works, including Suite for Violin and Piano, 1985; Three Pieces for Cello and Piano, 1986; Scherzetto, for Clarinet and Piano, 1986; Autumn Music for Viola and Piano, 1987; Flute Concerto, 1987; Music for Friends for piano trio, 1988; Suite for Oboe and Piano, 1989; Two Dances for Alto Saxophone and Piano, 1989; Four Piano Preludes, 1990; Three Bagatelles for Flute and Piano, 1990; Haere Ra–A Song for 2-part Treble Voices and Piano; Flute Concerto, 1991; Introduction for Clarinet and Piano, 1993; Concertos for Oboe, Alto Saxophone, Two Violins; Sinfonietta; Overtures; Sonatinas for Violin and Pianoforte, Tenor Saxophone and Piano, Oboe and Piano, Clarinet and Piano, Treble Recorder and Piano, Flute and Piano, Trumpet and Piano; Beauty and The Beast, ballet, 1994; Divertimento for Orchestra, 1996. *Recordings:* The Chamber Music of Eric Biddington; Music for Friends; Southern Melodies; Tunes and Airs, Chamber music by Eric Biddington; Flute Concerto and Chamber Music. *Publications:* 46 publs of chamber music, 10 with Nota Bene Music, 36 others; Pastorale for Clarinet and Piano, 1994; Introduction and Allegro for Alto Saxophone and Piano, 1994; Two Amourettes for Oboe and Piano, 1995. *Honours:* Award, Composers Association of New Zealand Trust Fund, 1989. *Address:* 27 Torrens Road, Hillmorton, Christchurch 2, New Zealand. *E-mail:* ebiddington@actrix.co.nz (home).

BIEITO, Calixto; Spanish opera and theatre director; b. 2 Nov. 1963, Miranda de Ebro, Catalonia; m. Roser Carni; one s. *Education:* Univ. of Barcelona, Drama School of Tarragona, Theatre Inst. of Barcelona. *Career:* opera productions include La Verbena de la Paloma (Zarzuela) at Edinburgh Festival 1997, Un Ballo in Maschera for ENO 2000, for Gran Teatre del Liceu, Barcelona 2001, Don Giovanni for ENO 2001, Così fan tutte for WNO 2002, Die Dreigroschenoper, Bobigny, Paris 2003, Il Trovatore at Staatsoper Hanover, Die Entführung aus dem Serail at Komische Oper, Berlin 2004, Il Trovatore at Edinburgh Festival 2004. *Honours:* Premio Ercillo for Life is a Dream 2000, Irish Times best director award for Barbaric Comedies, Glasgow Herald outstanding artist award 2003. *Address:* c/o Teatro Romea de Barcelona, Calle Hospital 51, Barcelona, Spain (office).

BIEL, Ann-Christin; Singer (Soprano); b. 1958, Sweden. *Education:* Studied at the Royal Music Academy, Stockholm with Birgit Sternberg and with Daniel Ferro, in New York. *Career:* Debut: Drottningholm 1981, as Cherubino; Has appeared at the Summer festival at Drottningholm, Stockholm, as Pamina 1982, 1989; Fiordiligi, 1984–85; Ilia, 1986, 1991; Susanna 1987; Serpetta in La Finta Giardiniera, 1988, 1990; Royal Opera Stockholm 1985, L'arbore di Diana by Martín y Soler; 1986 as Oscar in Un Ballo in Maschera; Sang Konstanze in the Berne, 1986, world premiere of Armin Schibler's Mozart und der graue Bote, Mozart's last days; Toured as Micaela in the Peter Brook version of Carmen, Paris, Hamburg, New York and Tokyo, 1982–86; Théâtre des Champs-Elysées, Paris 1986, as Barbarina in Le nozze di Figaro; Sang Julie in the world premiere of Miss Julie at Stockholm 1990; (music by Margareta Hallin, the part of Julie written for Ms Biel); Sang Gluck's Orpheus at Drottningholm, 1992; Concert appearances in Stockholm, New York, Paris, Amsterdam, Parma, Verona, Milan and Copenhagen: repertoire includes Bach's Passions, Die Schöpfung, Mozart's Vespers and Requiem, Monteverdi's Vespers and Ein Deutsches Requiem. *Recordings:* Videos of Mozart operas from Drottningholm, directed by Goran Järvefelt, conducted by Arnold Östman. *Address:* Drottningholms Slottsteater, PO Box 27050, 102 51 Stockholm, Sweden.

BIELAWA, Herbert; Composer; b. 3 Feb. 1930, Chicago, Illinois, USA. *Education:* BM; MM; BA at University of Illinois; DMA, University of Southern California; Studied with Gordon Binkerd, Burrill Phillips, Ingolf Dahl, Halsey Stevens, Ellis Kohs. *Career:* Professor of Music and

Director of Electronic Music Studio at San Francisco State University from 1966–91; Now retired. *Compositions:* A Bird in the Bush, Chamber Opera 1962; Spectrum for band and tape, 1965; Divergents, for orchestra, 1969; A Dickinson Album for choir, synthesized sound; piano; guitar, 1972; Dreams, for SSAA chorus, 1984; Rants, for SATB and violin, 1988; Song Cycles, The Snake and Other Creatures and Stone settings, song cycles, for soprano and piano, 1991; Quodlibet SF42569 for organ and tape, 1981; Duo for violin and harpsichord, 1984; Ants for soprano, violin and piano 1985; Through Thick and Thin, for flute, clarinet, viola and piano, 1991; Undertones, for organ, 1980; Monophonies, for organ, 1979; Organ Booklet for organ, 1992; Pentarcs, for piano, 1982; Expressions, for piano, 1992; Pipes and Brass for organ and brass quintet, 1997; Blurts for flute, clarinet and piano, 1997; Cyber for violin and cello, 1998; Feedback for organ and orchestra, 1999; Piano Concerto, 1999; Seque a Quattro for flute, clarinet, violin and cello, 1999; Earth, for flute, clarinet, violin, cello and piano, 2000. *Recordings* include: Pipe Organ Adventures. *Address:* 38 Sunset Drive, Kensington, CA 94707, USA.

BIERHANZL, Petr; Czech classical guitarist; b. 27 July 1952, Prague; m. Jana Bierhanzlova 1977; one s. *Education:* Conservatory of Prague, Czech Republic. *Career:* debut in Prague, 1975; Member, Guitar duo with Jana Bierhanzlova; Czech Republic, 1975–97; Poland, 1986, 1990, 1994; Germany, 1995, 1997, 1998; Lithuania, 1997; Radio: Poland, 1990; Czech Republic, 1992, 1993, 1995, 1996, 1997; Television: German television, 1978; Czech television, 1992, 1993, 1994, 1996, 1997; Repertoire includes: J Dowland's Lachrimae Pavan, Welcome Home, A Michna's Czech Lute, J. S. Bach's Preludes and fugues, Scarlatti's Sonata K 380, A Vivaldi's Concerto op 3 No. 6, A Soler's Sonatas, W A Mozart's Divertimento KV 439 b, F Sor's L'Encouragement op 34, F Carulli's Duo op 34 No. 2, E Granados' Danzas Espanolas; I Albeniz's Granada, Sevilla, A Dvořák's Sonatina op 100, Educational activity: Professor at the Jezek Conservatory of Prague, 1980–; Intergram, Prague; Lithuania, 2001; Spain, 2002. *Recordings:* The European Guitar Duets (Czech Guitar Duo), Scarlatti, Carulli, Sor and Truhlar (the first Czech recording of a guitar duo) 1992; English Renaissance Music (Czech Guitar Duo), Dowland, Byrd, Johnson and Bull; Czech Guitar Duo Plays Flamenco, 2001. *Address:* V Sareckem Udoli 2, 160 00 Prague 6, Czech Republic.

BILGRAM, Hedwig; Organist and Harpsichordist; b. 31 March 1933, Memmingen, Germany. *Education:* Studied with Karl Richter and Friedrich Wührer. *Career:* Teacher at the Munich Hochschule für Musik from 1961, Professor, 1964–; Many performances under Karl Richter in Munich and elsewhere, in the Baroque repertoire; Appeared also with trumpeter Maurice André; Premieres of works by André Jolivet, Henri Tomasi and Harald Genzmer. *Address:* c/o Hochschule für Musik, Areisstr 12, 8000 Munich 2, Germany.

BILINSKA, Jolanta; Musicologist; b. 1 March 1951, Rzeszów, Poland. *Education:* Diploma with Honours, Musicology Department, Jagiellonian University, Kraków, 1976. *Career:* Secretary of the Warsaw International Festival of Contemporary Music, 1979–95; Director of Polish Radio Music Recording Department. *Publications:* Opery Mozarta na scenach polskich w latach 1783-1830 (Mozart's Operas on Polish Stages from 1783–1830); Musikbiliothek und Musikleben am Hof der Fuerstin Izabella Lubomirska in Lancut 1791–1816, Musik des Ostens, Bd 11, 1989; Recepcja dziel Mozarta w Polsce 1783–1830 (Reception of Mozart's Works in Poland 1783–1830), 1991, German edition, 1992. *Contributions:* Ruch Muzyczny, a bi-weekly music magazine; Polish Music, quarterly. *Address:* Osowska 23 m 5, 04 312 Warsaw, Poland.

BILSON, Malcolm; Concert Pianist; b. 24 Oct. 1935, Los Angeles, CA, USA; m. Elizabeth Jármay 1961; two d. *Education:* BA, Bard Coll. 1957; Vienna State Acad., Reifezeugnis 1959; Ecole Normale de Musique, Paris, Licence Libre 1960; DMA, Univ. of Illinois, 1968. *Career:* Asst Prof., Cornell Univ. 1968, Assoc. Prof. 1970, Prof. 1975, Frederick J. Whiton Prof. of Music, 1990; specialises in repertoire of Viennese Classical School on period fortepianos; toured extensively in North America, Europe, the Far East and Oceania as soloist, chamber musician and soloist with orchestras, including the English Baroque Soloists, the Acad. of Ancient Music, Tafelmusik, Concerto Köln, Philharmonia Baroque and numerous modern-instrument orchestras; workshops and masterclasses world-wide, including the Sibelius Acad., Helsinki, Liszt Acad., Budapest, Kunitachi Coll., Tokyo, Griffith Conservatory, Brisbane, Jerusalem Music Centre, Scottish Acad. of Music and Dance, Glasgow, Royal Coll. of Music, London; Adjunct Prof., Eastman School of Music 1992–; mem. American Acad. of Arts and Sciences. *Recordings:* Complete Mozart Concertos for fortepiano and orchestra, with John Eliot Gardiner and the English Baroque Soloists; complete Mozart piano-violin sonatas with Sergui Luca; complete Mozart solo piano Sonatas; complete Beethoven piano sonatas (with other players), Claves; complete Beethoven cello-piano sonatas with Anner Bijlsma; complete Schubert piano sonatas (including unfinished

works); Schubert 4-hand piano works with Robert Levin. *Honours:* Hon. doctorate, Bard Coll., 1991. *Address:* c/o Department of Music, Lincoln Hall, Cornell University, Ithaca, NY 14853, USA.

BIMBERG, Siegfried (Wolfgang); Musicologist, Psychologist, Composer and Conductor; b. 5 May 1927, Halle, Saale, Germany; m. Ortrud Rummler, 19 June 1953, 1 s. *Education:* Musicology and Psychology, Martin Luther Univ., Halle; Diploma Degree, BA; PhD, 1953, Dr paed habil, 1956, DrSc phil, 1982. *Career:* Debut: Martin Luther Univ., Halle; Lecturer of Musicology, Halle Univ., 1952–1956; Lecturer in Musicology, Humboldt University, Berlin, 1956–62; Ordinary Prof. of Musicology and Music Education, 1964–92; Head of Dept for Musikdidatik, Martin Luther Univ., Halle-Wittenberg, 1962–90; Conductor and Leader, Chamber Choir, Halle Univ. Hallenser Madrigalisten, 1963–80; Concert tours throughout Europe; Records, radio and television; mem., Freie deutsche Akademie der Künste und Wissenschaften, Bonn; Landesverband Sachsen-Anhalt, Deutscher Komponisten; Verband deutscher Schulmusiker;. *Compositions include:* Opera, The Singing Horse, 1961; Eulenspiegels Brautfahrt, 1987; Cantatas; Songs; Ballads; Cantatas: Die Rosen schlafen nicht, 1990; Jonas und der Wal, 1996; Ohne Natur vergeht unser Leben, 1997; Vom Wind getragen, 1997; Mit Degen und Fagott, 1998; Verba nulla pretio emuntur, 1998; Zwischen Nil und Ninive; Recordings: Own compositions (choir works); Interpretation of own works and works of other composers. *Publications include:* Einfuehrung in die Musikpsychologie, 1957; Vom Singen zum Musikverstehen, 1957, 1969; Methodisch-didaktische Grundlagen der Musikerziehung, 1968, 1973; Handbuch der Musikaesthetik, editor and author 1979; Kontrast als musikaesthetische Kategorie, 1981; Handbuch der Chorleitung, editor and author 1981; Lieder lernen-Lieder singen, 1981; Ferruccio Busoni: Von der Macht der Toene, editor, 1983; Musik-Erleben-Lernen, 1995; Nachhall 1 and 2, 1996; Musikwissenschaft und Musikpädagogik Perspektiven für das 21 Jahrhundert, together with Guido Bimberg, 1997; Lieder von Wende zur Wende–das deutsche Gemeinschaftslied im 20 Jahrhundert, 1998. *Address:* Ernestusstrasse 24, 06114 Halle, Germany.

BIMBERG ZU LENNINGHAUSEN, Guido von, KBE; American musicologist, chair professor of music history and entertainment business executive; b. 14 March 1954, Halle, Germany; m. Christiane Bimberg 1981; one s. *Education:* studied musicology, music education, piano, literature, art history and theatre (Halle, Berlin, Tashkent, Moscow, Harvard, Stanford); business administration (Schwyz, Lausanne, Harvard); PhD 1979; Research Fellowship, Baltic, Central Asian, Caucasian, Russian, Siberian and Ukrainian Archives 1979–80; Habilitation 1981, Martin Luther Univ., Halle; MBA, Felchlin Business School, Schwyz-Lausanne/Harvard 1990. *Career:* Assoc. Prof. of Music History 1979–83, Chair Prof. of Musicology 1983–95, Martin Luther Univ., Halle; Chair Prof. of Music and Interdisciplinary Studies, Havana Univ. 1983–; Chair Prof. of Entertainment and Media Business, German Acad. of Humanities 1990–; Chair Prof. of Media Business, Washington Univ. 1992–; Chair Prof. of Entertainment and Media Business, Central Univ. of California Los Angeles 1995–; Hon. Prof. and Senator, Moscow Univ. 1995–; Chair Prof. of Musicology, Music Acad. of Dortmund 1995–; Chair Prof. of Entertainment Business, Int. School of Business Admin, Acad. of Sciences, Berlin 1997–; numerous visiting professorships, fellowships; Pres., German Acad. of Humanities, Bonn 1998–; Vice-Pres., Media Services Inc. 2000–, CCO Music Tourist Agency M.T.A. Inc., Nashville 2000–; mem. Bd Dirs, Digital Media Corp. 2000–, Entertainment Network Inc. 2001–, Tokyo Classics, Digital Media Corpn, New York 2001–; CEO, Music and Media Business Inc., Los Angeles 2001–; supervisory bd, MRI Inc. 2001–; bd mem., Int. Musical Congress and Festival, New York; media technical consultant world-wide; Hon. Consul to the Russian Federation 2002; Dir/Co-Dir, several music congresses and festivals, including Fasch Festival, Werckmeister Festival, Alicante Festival, Singapore Music Festival, Tokyo Classics, Los Angeles Hit Factory, Nashville Music Contest; Senator, German Acad. of Science and Arts, Westphalian Music Acad.; Pres., German Handel Society, German Music Research Foundation, Westphalian Music Soc., Int. Entertainment Business Soc.; Vice-Pres., German Musicological Soc., German Fasch Soc., Werckmeister Soc.; mem. bd dirs, Int. Soc. for Music Education; mem. of council, American Musicological Soc.; mem. assoc. bd, Coll. Music Soc.; mem. Int. Musicological Soc., Royal Music Asscn, Japanese Int. Musicological Soc.. *Publications include:* Opera in 18th Century Russia 1981, Dramaturgy of the Handel Operas 1985, Anatoli Lunacharsky: Essays on Music 1985, Schütz-Bach-Händel 1989, Mozart's Entführung aus dem Serail 1990, Music of Russian and German Composers 1990, Fasch and Music in 18th Century Europe 1995, Andreas Werckmeister: Die Musicalische Temperatur (co-author) 1996, Denkmäler der Musik in Mitteldeutschland (co-ed.) 1996, general edn and thematic catalogue of Fasch works (co-ed.) 1996, Music in 18th Century European Society 1997, Perspectives in Musicology and Education for the 21st Century 1997, Music in Canada/La Musique au Canada 1997, Music Sources from the Westphalian Music Archive 1997, Denkmäler der Musik in

Westfalen 1997, International Studies of Women in Music 1999, Women in Music in Westphalia 1999, Broadway on the Ruhr: The Musical Comedy in the New Millennium 2000, Music Technology 2001, Digital Music Business 2001, Leni Timmermann 2002, Baroque Music Recovered by the Telemann Orchestra Tradition (co-author) 2002; music books for children: The Wonderful Sound 1985 (in German, English, French, Spanish and Slovakian), La Musique en activité 1985, Music Theatre for Children (series ed.) 1987–94, Introducing Music 1989. *Contributions:* over 200 articles to professional international journals. *Honours:* Mussorgskij Medal 1990, American Musicology Award 1992, Canadian Govt Culture Prize 1992, Guido Adler Preis of German Musicology 1994, Gold Crown Medal, Hong Kong Music Asscn 1995, Prize Musica Westphalia 1997, Bundesverdienstkreuz 1998, CBE 1998, German Handel Prize 1998, German National Prize for Music and Musicology 2000, Innovation Prize for Music and Media Technology 2000, Grosse Bundes-Verdienstkreuz des Verdienstordens 2002, Dr hc, Univs of Moscow 2003, New York 2003, Order of Merit 2003; books in commemoration of 50th Birthday: No Limits (ed by Prof. Dr Hiroshi Watanabe) 2004, Festschrift Guido Bimberg/Ruediger Pfeiffer (ed by Dr Ching-Wah Wang) 2004. *Current Management:* German Academy for Humanities, Office of Prof. Dr Bimberg, Postfach 550133, 44209, Dortmund, Germany. *E-mail:* prof.dr.bimberg@crossoverstudies.com.

BINGHAM, Judith; Composer and Singer; b. 21 June 1952, Nottingham, England; m. Andrew Petrow, 20 Dec 1985. *Education:* Royal Academy of Music, London. *Career:* Studied with Hans Keller. Commissions from Peter Pears; King's Singers; BBC Singers; Songmakers' Almanac; Omega Guitar Quartet; New London Consort; Television and radio scores; Singing debut at penultimate night of the Proms, 1984 in Strauss's Deutsche Motette; Appearances with Taverner Consort, Combattimento; mem, ISM. *Compositions:* Cocaine Lil, soprano and piano, 1975; A Divine Image, Harpsichord, 1976; Chopin, piano, 1979; A Falling Figure for Baritone, clarinet, piano; BBC Commission, 1979; Mercutio for baritone, piano, 1980; Iago, bass-baritone, piano, 1980; Clouded Windows, mezzo, piano, 1980; The Ruin, SATB, 1981; A Midsummer Night's Dream, mezzo, piano, 1981; Into the Wilderness, organ, 1982; Pictured Within, piano, 1982; Ferrara, tenor, piano, 1982; A Hymn Before Sunrise in the Vale of Chamounix, 24 SATB-BBC Singers, 1982; Cradle Song of the Blessed Virgin, SSATB, 1983; Mass Setting; Sterna Paradisaea, SATB and Organ, 1984; A Winter Walk at Noon, 27 solo voices, BBC Commission, 1984; Just Before Dawn, SSAA, 1986; Chartres, Orchestra, 1987; Dove Cottage by Moonlight for 2 pianos, 1989; The Ghost of Combermere Abbey for chorus, 1993, Beyond Redemption for orchestra, 1995, The Temple at Karnak for orchestra, 1996; The Mysteries of Adad, children's theatre, 1996; The American Icons for wind band, 1997; The Snow Descends for brass ensemble; Passaggio, bassoon concerto, 1998; The Shooting Star, trumpet concerto, 1999; Walzerspiele for orchestra, 1999; Water Lilies for chorus, 1999; Shelley Dreams for violin and piano, 1999. *Recordings:* Cradle Song of the Blessed Virgin. *Honours:* Principal's Prize for Composition, 1971; BBC Young Composer, 1976. *Address:* c/o British Music Information Centre, 11 Stratford Place, London, W1, England.

BINI, Carlo; Singer (Tenor); b. 1947, Naples, Italy. *Education:* Studied at the Naples Conservatory. *Career:* Debut: Teatro San Carlo Naples, 1969, as Pinkerton; Sang in Italy and at the Deutsche Oper Berlin; State Opera Houses of Munich and Stuttgart; Hamburg Staatsoper, 1974, as Alfredo in La Traviata and Rodolfo; Sang further in Brussels, Paris, Marseille, Rio de Janeiro and New York City Opera; Metropolitan Opera, 1982, as Enzo in La Gioconda; La Scala, 1984, in I Lombardi; Sang Arrigo in I Vespri siciliani at Santiago, 1990; Avito in Montemezzi's L'amore dei tre re at Palermo, 1990; Other roles include, Rodolfo in Luisa Miller, Don Carlos, Gabriele Adorno, Don José, Laca in Jenůfa and Tchaikovsky's Vakula. *Recordings:* Verdi Requiem; Eine Nacht in Venedig; Video of I Lombardi. *Address:* c/o Teatro Massimo, 90100, Palermo, Italy.

BINNS, Malcolm; Concert Pianist; b. 29 Jan. 1936, Nottingham, England. *Education:* Bradford Grammar School, 1948–52; ARCM Royal College of Music, 1952–56; Chappell Medal, 1956. *Career:* Debut: London, 1957; Henry Wood Proms, 1960; Royal Festival Hall, 1961, in the first British performance of Prokofiev 4th Piano Concerto, with the Royal Philharmonic Orchestra; Appearances, London Philharmonic Orcherstra International series; Royal Festival Hall, 1969–; Concerts at the Aldeburgh Festival, Leeds Festival and Three Choirs Festival, 1975; Regular appearances at Promenade concerts; Formed a duo partnership with the violinist Manoug Parikian in 1966; Toured with Scottish National Orchestra and Limbourg Orchestra, 1988. *Recordings:* 1st complete recording of Beethoven piano sonatas on original instruments, 1980; Over 30 recordings for Decca, EMI and Chandos; Recordings of four concertos by William Sterndale Bennett with London Philharmonic Orchestra released on Lyrita, 1990. *Honours:* Recipient of Chappel Gold Medal; Medal of Worshipful Company of Musicians; Royal College of Music. *Current Management:* Melanie Turner Management. *Address:*

c/o Michael Harrold Management, 13 Clinton Road, Leatherhead, Surrey, KT 22 8NU, UK.

BINZER, Kim von; Singer (Tenor); b. 2 March 1952, Denmark. *Career:* Sang with the Choir of Danish Radio in Copenhagen; Soloist with Jutland Opera, Århus, 1979–87; Roles include Tamino in Zauberflöte, Ramiro in La Cenerentola, Alfred in Fledermaus, Piquillo in Offenbach's La Périchole, Goro in Madama Butterfly; Aix-en-Provence Festival, 1985, in Monteverdi's Orfeo; Royal Opera Copenhagen from 1987 as Count Almaviva in Il Barbiere, Tamino in Zauberflöte, Ferrando in Così fan tutte, Don Ottavio in Don Giovanni and Cassio in Otello; Opera productions for Danish Radio and Television; Frequent concert engagements; Stage Director, Royal Opera Copenhagen, 1994–; Head, Opera Academy, 1999–. *Recordings:* Fynsk Foraar by Nielsen; Kuhlau's Lulu. *Address:* c/o The Royal Opera, PO Box 2185, 1017 Copenhagen, Denmark.

BIONDI, Fabio; Italian violinist and conductor; b. 15 March 1961, Palermo. *Education:* studied with Salvatore Cicero and Mauro lo Guercio. *Career:* concerto debut with the Italian Radio Symphony Orchestra aged 12; formed Stendhal Quartet 1981; worked with Hesperion XX, Les Musiciens du Louvre, Musica Antiqua of Vienna, the Camerata di Lugano and the orchestra of the Due Dimensioni festival, Parma; founder ensemble, Europa Galante 1990; works as soloist and guest conductor with orchestras including the Santa Cecilia in Rome, Rotterdam Chamber Orchestra, the Opera of Halle, Zurich Chamber Orchestra, the Norwegian Chamber Orchestra, Orchestre Nationale de Montpellier, Orquesta Ciudad de Granada; Conductor, New York Collegium; directed European Union Baroque Orchestra 2002. *Recordings include:* Italian Violin Sonatas (Veracini, Locatelli, Mascitti, Geminiani, Tartini), J. S. Bach Arias and Cantatas with Ian Bostridge, Vivaldi's L'Estro armonico, String Quintets by Boccherini, Vivaldi's violin concertos Il cimento dell'armonia e dell'inventione (including The Four Seasons), Vivaldi Stabat mater, Scarlatti Concerti and Sinfonie. *Honours:* (with Europa Galante) Académie Charles Cros, Diapason d'Or de l'Année, Prix RTL and Grand Prix du Discophile. *Current Management:* Satirino Classical Music Agency, 59 rue Orfila, 75020 Paris, France. *E-mail:* ianmalkin@satirino.fr (office). *Website:* www.satirino.fr (office).

BIRET, Idil; Concert Pianist; b. 21 Nov. 1941, Ankara, Turkey. *Education:* Studied at the Paris Conservatoire with Alfred Cortot and Nadia Boulanger; Further studies with Wilhelm Kempff. *Career:* Debut: Played Mozart's Concerto K365 with Kempff in Paris, 1953; World-wide concerts with major orchestras including the conductors Monteux, Scherchen, Leinsdorf, Boult, Kempe, Sargent, Rozhdestvensky, Groves, Mackerras, Keilberth and Pritchard; US debut in 1962 playing Rachmaninov's 3rd Concerto with the Boston Symphony; London Symphony in 1963 under Monteux; Istanbul Festival in 1973 playing Beethoven's Violin Sonatas with Yehudi Menuhin; Frequent tours of Russia (with Leningrad Philharmonic 1984); Tours of Australia in 1980 and 1984; 85th Birthday celebration concert for Wilhelm Backhaus and 90th Birthday for Wilhelm Kempff; Festival engagements at Montreal, Persepolis, Royan, La Rochelle, Athens, Berlin and Gstaad; Symphonies of Beethoven arranged by Liszt at the Montpellier Festival in 1986; Ravel Gaspard de la Nuit and Beethoven's 6th Symphony at the Wigmore Hall in 1989; Member of juries at the Queen Elizabeth Competition, Belgium, the Van Cliburn in USA and the Busoni Competition, Italy. *Recordings include:* World premiere of Beethoven's Symphonies transcribed by Liszt, 1986; Complete works of Chopin, 1992; Complete piano solo works of Brahms, 1995. *Honours:* Lily Boulanger Memorial Fund, Boston, 1954, 1964; Harriet Cohen/Dinu Lipatti Gold Medal, London, 1959; Polish Artistic Merit Award, 1974; Chevalier de l'Ordre du Merité, France, 1976; State Artist of Turkey. *Address:* c/o M Sefik B Yuksel, 51 Avenue General de Gaulle, 1050 Brussels, Belgium.

BIRKELAND, Oystein; Cellist; b. 1958, Norway. *Education:* Norwegian State Academy of Music; Studied in Basel with Heinrich Schiff, in London with William Pleeth and Ralph Kirshbaum. *Career:* Has worked with Frans Helmersson, Arto Noras, Erling Blondal Bengtsson and Jacqueline du Pré; Member, 1982–, Principal Cellist, 1985–, Norwegian Chamber Orchestra; Performances as soloist, Norway, the United Kingdom, Germany, Switzerland, in concertos by Haydn, Boccherini, Vivaldi and others; Has played with Oslo Philharmonic, Trondheim Symphony Orchestra and Norwegian Radio Orchestra; Recent debut with Academy of St Martin-in-the-Fields, playing the Haydn Concerto in C major in Oslo, Helsinki and Stockholm; Recent festival appearances include Bergen International Music Festival, the Contemporary Music Festivals Platform, London, and Schleswig Holstein Music Festival; Plays a cello by Francesco Ruggiere (Cremona, 1680). *Recordings:* For BBC with pianist Joanna McGregor; With pianist Havard Gimse; 3 Russian sonatas with Ian Brown. *Current Management:* Diana Walters Artists Management, England. *Address:* c/o Diana Walters Artists

Management, Ivy Cottage, 3 Main Street, Keyham, Leicestershire LE7 9JQ, England.

BIRKS, Ronald; Violinist; b. 1945, England. *Education:* Studied at Royal Manchester College of Music with Béla Katona, Walter Jorysz and Alexander Moskovsky. *Career:* Member of the Lindsay String Quartet from 1971; Regular tours of Europe, the United Kingdom, USA, From 1974, quartet in residence at Sheffield University, then Manchester University, 1979; Premiered the 4th Quartet of Tippett at the 1979 Bath Festival and commissioned Tippett's 5th Quartet, 1992; Chamber Music Festival established at Sheffield, 1984; Regular concerts at the Wigmore Hall, including Haydn series, 1987; Plays Campo Selice Stradivarius of 1694. *Recordings:* Complete cycles of Bartók, Tippett and Beethoven quartets; Mozart Quintets; Haydn quartets Live from the Wigmore Hall, ASV; Second series of Beethoven quartets in preparation; All Haydn quartets from Op. 20 onwards. *Honours:* Gramophone Chamber Award for late Beethoven quartets, 1984; honorary degrees from Keele, Manchester, Leicester, Sheffield (two) and Sheffield Hallam Universities. *Current Management:* Ingpen & Williams Ltd, 7 St George's Court, 131 Putney Bridge Road, London, SW15 2PA, England. *Address:* 19 Gainsborough Road, Sheffield S11 9AJ, England.

BIRTWISTLE, Sir Harrison, Kt, CH; British composer; b. 1934, Accrington, Lancs.; m. Sheila Birtwistle 1958; three s. *Education:* Royal Manchester Coll. of Music and Royal Acad. of Music, London. *Career:* Dir of Music, Cranborne Chase School 1962–65; Visiting Fellow Princeton Univ. (Harkness Int. Fellowship) 1966; Cornell visiting Prof. of Music, Swarthmore Coll., Pa 1973–74; Slee Visiting Prof., New York State Univ., Buffalo, NY 1975; Assoc. Dir Nat. Theatre 1975–88; Composer-in-Residence London Philharmonic Orchestra 1993–98; Henry Purcell Prof. of Composition King's Coll., London Univ. 1994–2001; Visiting Prof., Univ. of Ala at Tuscaloosa 2001–02; Hon. Fellow Royal Northern Coll. of Music 1990; Dir of Contemporary Music, RAM 1996–2001; works have been widely performed at the major festivals in Europe including the Venice Biennale, the Int. Soc. of Contemporary Music Festivals in Vienna and Copenhagen, the Warsaw Autumn Festival and at Aldeburgh, Cheltenham and Edinburgh; formed, with Sir Peter Maxwell Davies, The Pierrot Players. *Operatic and dramatic works:* The Mark of the Goat (cantata) 1965, Punch and Judy (one-act opera) 1966, The Visions of Francesco Petrarca (sonnets for baritone and orchestra) 1966, Monodrama for soprano, speaker, ensemble 1967, Down by the Greenwood Side (dramatic pastoral) 1969, The Mask of Orpheus 1973, Ballet, Frames, Pulses and Interruptions 1977, Bow Down 1977, Yan Tan Tethera 1983, Gawain 1988, The Second Mrs Kong 1992, The Last Supper 1999. *Orchestral works:* Chorales for Orchestra 1962, Three Movements with Fanfares 1964, Nomos 1968, An Imaginary Landscape 1971, The Triumph of Time 1970, Grimethorpe Aria for Brass Band 1973, Melencolia I 1976, Silbury Air for small orchestra 1977, Still Movement for 13 solo strings 1984, Earth Dances 1985, Endless Parade for trumpet, vibraphone, strings 1987, Ritual Fragment 1990, Antiphonies for piano and orchestra 1992, The Cry of Anubis for tuba and orchestra 1994, Panic 1995. *Choral works and narration:* Monody for Corpus Christi for soprano and ensemble 1959, A Description of the Passing Year for chorus 1963, Entr'actes and Sappho Fragments for soprano and ensemble 1964, Carmen Paschale for chorus and organ 1965, Ring a Dumb Clarion for soprano, clarinet, percussion 1965, Cantata for soprano and ensemble 1969, Nenia on the Death of Orpheus for soprano and ensemble 1970, The Fields of Sorrow for 2 sopranos, chorus, ensemble 1971, Meridian for mezzo, chorus, ensemble 1970, Epilogue: Full Fathom Five for baritone and ensemble 1972, agm. for 16 solo voices and 3 instruments 1979, On the Sheer Threshold of the Night for 4 solo voices and 12-part chorus 1980, White and Light for soprano and ensemble 1989, Four Poems by Jaan Kaplinski for soprano and ensemble 1991, The Woman and the Hare, for soprano, reciter and ensemble 1999. *Instrumental works:* Refrains and Choruses for wind quintet 1957, The World is Discovered for ensemble 1960, Tragoedia for ensemble 1965, Three Lessons in a Frame 1967, Chorales from a Toyshop 1967, Verses for Ensembles 1969, Ut heremita solus, arr of Ockeghem 1969, Hoquetus David, arr of Machaut 1969, Medusa for ensemble 1970, Chronometer for 8-track tape 1971, For O For O the Hobby Horse is Forgot for 6 percussion 1976, Carmen Arcadiae Mechanicae Perpetuum for ensemble 1977, Pulse Sampler 1980, Clarinet Quintet 1980, Secret Theatre 1984, Words Overheard 1985, Fanfare for Will 1987, Salford Toccata for brass band and bass drum 1988, Nine Movements for string quartet 1991, An Uninterrupted Endless Melody for oboe and piano 1991, Five Distances for five instruments 1992, Tenebrae for soprano and ensemble 1992, Night for soprano and ensemble 1992, Movement for string quartet 1992, Slow Frieze for piano and 13 instruments 1996, Pulse, Shadows 1997, Harrison's Clocks for piano 1998, The Silk House Tattoo for 2 trumpets and percussion 1998, Three Niedecker Verses for soprano and cello 1998, Exody 1998, The Axe Manual 2000, The Shadow of Night 2001, Theseus Game 2002, The Io Passion 2004, Night's Black Bird 2004, The Story of 10 2004. *Theatre:* music for Hamlet, Nat. Theatre

1975, The Oresteia, Nat. Theatre 1986, The Bacchae, Nat. Theatre 2002. *Honours:* Chevalier des Arts et Lettres; Siemens Prize 1995; Grawemeyer Award (Univ. of Louisville, Ky) 1987. *Current Management:* Allied Artists Agency, 42 Montpelier Square, London, SW7 1JZ, England.

BISATT, Susan; Singer (Soprano); b. 1963, England. *Career:* Frequent festival engagements, including Almeida Contemporary Opera (Isabelle Rimbaud in The Man Who Strides the Wind by Kevin Volans) and Edinburgh (Salome in the opera by Strauss); Roles with Opera Restor'd in Britain and Abroad, in Dido and Aeneas, The Death of Dido (Pepusch) and Pyramus and Thisbe (Lampe); Other appearances with Opera North (as Papagena) and elsewhere as Violetta, Donna Elvira, Lucia di Lammermoor, Gilda, Norina and the soprano leads in Les Contes d'Hoffmann; Gluck's Eurydice, Mozart's Countess, and Rosina; Tours of the United Kingdom, Ireland and Finland with Opera Circus; Opera workshops with Opera North, Compact Opera, Théâtre de Complicité and the David Glass Ensemble; Television includes: The Singing Voice, for Channel 4. *Recordings include:* English Baroque Opera (Hyperion); Scenes from operas by Charles Dibdin; Purcell Songs (Naxos). *Address:* c/o C&M Craig Services Ltd, 3 Kersley Street, London SW11 4 PR, England.

BISCARDI, Chester; Composer and Teacher; b. 19 Oct. 1948, Kenosha, Wisconsin, USA. *Education:* BA, English Literature, 1970, MA, Italian Literature and Language, 1972, MM, Composition, 1974, University of Wisconsin, Madison; Studies at: Universita di Bologna; Conservatorio di Musica, G B Martini; MMA, 1976, DMA, Composition, Yale University School of Music, 1980. *Career:* Teacher, University of Wisconsin, 1970–74; Yale University, 1975–76; Music Faculty, Sarah Lawrence College, Bronxville, New York, 1977–; Director of Music Program, 1st William Schuman Chair in Music, Sarah Lawrence College, Bronxville, New York. *Compositions include:* Tartini, 1972; They Had Ceased to Talk, 1975; Trio, 1976, Di Vivere, 1981; Piano Concerto, 1983; Tight-Rope, chamber opera, 1985; Piano Sonata, 1986, revised, 1987; Traverso, for Flute and Piano, 1987; Netori, 1990; The Gift of Life, for Soprano and Piano, 1990–93; Music for an Occasion, for Brass, Piano and Percussion, 1992; Nel giardinetto della villa, for Piano 4 hands, 1994; Resisting Stillness for 2 guitars, 1996; Prayers of Steel, 1998; Recovering, 2000; In Time's Unfolding, 2000. *Recordings include:* Piano Sonata; Mestiere; Trasumanar; Traverso; The Gift of Life; Companion Piece; Incitation to Desire, tango; Tenzone; At The Still Point; Resisting Stillness. *Address:* ASCAP, ASCAP Building, One Lincoln Plaza, New York, NY 10023, USA.

BISCHOF, Rainer, PhD; Composer; b. 20 June 1947, Vienna, Austria. *Education:* Univ. of Vienna, studied composition privately with Hans Apostel. *Compositions:* Sonatine for Clarinet, 1969; Sonatine for Horn, 1970; Duo for Flute and Clarinet, 1970; Theme and 7 variations for Oboe and Cello, 1970; Quartet for Flute, Oboe, Horn and Bassoon, 1971; Grave for Violin and Piano, 1970–71; Deduction for Strings, 1973–74; Characteristic Differences for Violin and Piano, 1974; In Memoriam Memoriae, song cycle for Mezzo-soprano, Speaker, Vibraphone, Celesta, Bass, Clarinet and Cello, 1975–77; Orchesterstücke, 1976–82; Flute Concerto, 1978–79; Studies from the Flute Concerto for solo flute, 1978; Concerto for Violin, Cello and Orchestra, 1979–80; Variations for Organ, 1981; Viola Tricolor, 32 variations for Viola, 1982; Music for 6 Recorders, 1982–83; String Sextet, 1990; Studie in PP, 1991; Das Donauergeschenk, chamber opera, 1991; Quasi una fuga for orchestra, 1995; Sinfonia, 1995; Gesänge zur Kunst for chorus, 1996; Auf der Suche nach… for piano, 1996; Totentanz for orchestra, 1999; Der narrische Uhu, concerto for violin, 2001; Requiem fur Errol, 2003. *Address:* AKM, 111 Baumstr 8–10, 1031 Vienna, Austria.

BISPO, Antonio (Alexandre); Musicologist; b. 17 March 1949, São Paulo, Brazil (resident in Germany, 1974). *Education:* Diploma, Architecture, University of São Paulo, 1972; Licence Music Education, Institute Musical de São Paulo, 1972; Diploma in Composition and Directing, 1973; Postgraduate studies in Music Theory, 1975; PhD, 1979, Doctor. habil. 1997. *Career:* Director, Conservatorio Jardim America, São Paulo, 1971–72; Lecturer, Ethnomusicology and Aesthetics of Music, 1972–74; Researcher, Institut für Hymnologische und Musikethnologische Studien Maria Laach, Germany, 1979–; Councillor, Pontifical Association of Church Music, 1979–85; Director, Musikschule der Stadt Leichlingen, Germany, 1981–84; Director, Institut für Studien der Musikkultur des portugiesischen Sprachraumes e.V., 1989–; Lecturer, Musikwissenschaftliches Institut, University of Cologne; 1997–; Lecturer, Musikwissenschaftliches Seminar, University of Bonn, 2002–; Chairman, Ethnomusicology Section, Institute of Hymn and Ethnomusicology Studies, 1984–; President, Akademie Brasil-Europa. *Publications:* Numerous works, including, Die katholische Kirchenmusik in der Provinz São Paulo, 1979; Collectanea Musicae Sacrae Brasiliensis, 1981; Grundlagen christlicher Musikkultur in der aussereuropäischen Welt der Neuzeit, 1989; Leben und Werk von Martin Braunwieser, 1991–92; Christliche Volkstraditionen und

Synkretismus in Brasilien, 1989–90; Die Musikkulturen der Indianer Brasiliens, 1994–95; Christliche Musikanthropologie, 1999; Die Musikkulturen der Indianer Brasiliens II, 1999; Brasil/Europa & Musicologia, 1999, 2000; Die Musikkulturen der Indianer Brasiliens III, 2000; Brasil-Europa 500 Jahre: Musik und Visionen 2000; Die Musikkulturen der Indianer Brasiliens IV, 2002. *Honours:* National Order of Bandeirentos; Award of the Academia Paulistznade de Historia; Honour, Brazil Association of Folklore. *Address:* Theodor-Heuss-Ring 14, 50668 Cologne 1, Nordrhein-Westphalen, Germany. *E-mail:* bispo@netcologne.de.

BISSON, Yves; Singer (Baritone); b. 31 May 1936, Mostaganem, Algeria. *Education:* Studied at Paris Conservatoire with Renee Gilly-Musy and Louis Noguera. *Career:* Sung at the Paris Opéra, and the Opéra-Comique, notably in Manon, Faust, Platée, La Bohème, Werther, Roméo et Juliette, and Les Pêcheurs de Perles (all televised); Festival engagements at Aix-en-Provence as Rodolphe in Les Fêtes Vénitiennes by Campra, Avignon, Carpentras and Orange; Has sung in France, New York, Washington, Amsterdam, Brussels, Covent Garden London, Lisbon, Geneva, Zürich, Barcelona, Madrid, Vienna, Naples and Russia; Other roles include Lescaut in Auber's Manon Lescaut, Escamillo, Nilakantha in Lakmé, Mercutio, Sander in Zémire et Azor by Grétry, Massenet's Lescaut, Albert and Caoudal in Sapho, Mozart's Figaro and Masetto, Rangoni in Boris Godunov, Puccini's Marcello, Schaunard, Sharpless and Lescaut, Rameau's Oromases in Zoroastre and Citheron in Platée, Verdi's Posa, Germont and Ford; Sang François in Le Chemineau by Leroux at Marseilles, 1996. *Address:* c/o Opéra de Marseille, 2 Rue Molière, 1321 Marseille, Cédex 01, France.

BISWAS, Anup (Kumar); Composer and Concert Cellist; b. 1957, West Bengal, India. *Education:* Studied in India with Rev T Mathieson, at Royal College of Music; Further study with Pierre Fournier in Geneva, and Jacqueline du Pré in London. *Career:* Concerts throughout the United Kingdom, including St James and Lambeth Palaces; Elizabeth and Wigmore Halls; Grays Inn and Riverside Studios; Festival engagements at Cleveland; Belfast; Greenwich; Hereford; Masterclasses at the Dartington Summer School and concerts in Germany, Finland and Norway; JS Bach Tercentenary concerts in cathedrals and churches in the United Kingdom, featuring the suites for unaccompanied cello; Artistic Director of the Dante Alighieri Orchestra, from 1989; Royal Albert Hall, 1992, performing Celebration from his own ballet Ten Guineas under the Banyan Tree; Purcell Room Concert, 1993, playing Beethoven, Shostakovich, Walton and Brahms. *Compositions:* Music for Theatre Taliesin, Wales, 1986 production of Tristan and Essylt, featured by BBC Wales. *Address:* East West Arts Ltd, 93b Cambridge Gardens, London W10 6JE, England.

BJARNASON, Finnur; Singer (tenor); b. 1975, Reykjavík, Iceland. *Education:* Guildhall School and National Opera Studio, London. *Career:* debut, Male Chorus in the Rape of Lucretia for Icelandic Opera; sang Don Ottavio for Glyndebourne Touring Opera, 2000; appearances in Messiah throughout Britain and Beethoven's Ninth with the Icelandic Symphony Orchestra; recitals at St George's, Bristol, for the BBC and Wigmore Hall with Graham Johnson; Season 2001–2002 with Tebaldo in I Capuleti e i Montecchi for Grange Park Opera, Tamino with Icelandic Opera, and Don Ottavio at the 2002 Glyndebourne Festival. *Current Management:* Hazard Chase, Norman House, Cambridge Place, Cambridge CB2 1NS, England. *Telephone:* (1223) 312400. *Fax:* (1223) 460827. *Website:* www.hazardchase.co.uk.

BJERNO, Majken; Singer (Soprano); b. 29 May 1963, Århus, Denmark. *Education:* Studied in Copenhagen. *Career:* Debut: Opera Studio Copenhagen, 1989, as Pamina; Royal Opera Copenhagen from 1989 as Offenbach's Antonia, Mozart's Countess, Micaela, Mimi, Fiordiligi in Così fan tutte, Leonora in Nielsen's Maskarade and Mihail in Saul and David; Guest appearances at the Jutland Opera, Århus as Gutrune in Götterdämmerung and Mimi; Concert engagements in Bach's Passions; Beethoven's Ninth and Missa Solemnis; Requiems by Fauré, Brahms and Dvořák; Handel's Saul and Messiah; Masses by Mozart and Carmina Burana; Also sang recitals. *Recordings:* Mahler's 8th Symphony. *Address:* Tivoli Artists Management, 3 Vesterbrogade, DK-1630 Copenhagen, Denmark.

BJONER, Ingrid; opera and concert singer (soprano); b. 8 Nov. 1927, Kraakstad, Norway. *Education:* University of Oslo, Conservatory of Music, Oslo with Gudrun Boellemose, Hochschule für Musik, Frankfurt with Paul Lohmann; further study with Ellen Repp in New York. *Career:* Sang Third Norn and Gutrune in Norwegian radio recording of Götterdämmerung, 1956; Stage Debut, Oslo, 1957, as Donna Anna; Drottningholm Opera, 1957, as Handel's Rodelinda; Member, Wuppertal Opera, Germany, 1957–59; Deutsche Oper am Rhein Düsseldorf, 1959–61; Bayreuth Festival 1960, as Freia, Helmvige and Gutrune; Sang with Bayerische Staatsoper Munich from 1961, notably as the Empress in Die Frau ohne Schatten (1963) and as Isolde, in the centenary production of Tristan and Isolde, 1965; Metropolitan Opera

debut 1961, as Elsa in Lohengrin; Covent Garden from 1967, as Senta, Sieglinde and Leonore (Fidelio); Salzburg Festival, 1969–1970, Leonore; Sang the Duchess of Parma in the US premiere of Doktor Faust by Busoni, Carnegie Hall, 1974; Oslo and Copenhagen, 1985–86, as Elektra; Further appearances at La Scala, Vienna, Hollywood Bowl, Hamburg, Deutsche Oper Berlin, Cologne Opera, Warsaw and Vancouver; Season 1986–87 sang Isolde at Bayreuth and the Kostelnicka in Jenůfa at Karlsruhe; Staatsoper Munich 1988, as the Dyer's Wife in Die Frau ohne Schatten; Oslo Opera, 1989, Senta; The Dyer's Wife at Karlsruhe, 1990; Concert appearances world-wide, often in the songs of Grieg; Professor at Royal Academy of Music, Copenhagen, 1991–; Professor at Royal Academy of Music, Oslo, 1992–. *Recordings include:* Götterdämmerung, Decca; Die Frau ohne Schatten, DGG; Wagner's Wesendonck Lieder; Songs by Sibelius. *Honours:* Order of St Olav, Norway, 1964; Bavarian Order of Merit. *Address:* Gregers Grams vei 33, 0382 Oslo 3, Norway.

BJORLIN, Ulf; Composer and Conductor; b. 21 May 1933, Stockholm, Sweden. *Education:* Studied with Igor Markevitch in Salzburg and Nadia Boulanger in Paris. *Career:* Director of Royal Dramatic Theatre, Stockholm, 1963–68; Freelance Composer; Conductor of leading orchestras in Sweden and elsewhere in Scandanavia. *Compositions:* Pinocchio, children's musical, 1966; Ekon for orchestra, 1967; In Five Years, opera for actors and chamber ensemble, 1967; Epitaph for Lars Gorling, for orchestra, 1967; Of Melancholy, choreographic oratoria, 1970–; The Bit Theatre, opera, 1972; The Ballad of Kasper Rosenrod, opera, 1972; Karlekin till Belisa, radio opera, 1981; Wind Quintet, 1983; Tillfalle gor Tiufven, opera buffa, 1983; Den Frammande Kvinnan, opera, 1984. *Address:* c/o STIM, Sandhamnsgatan 79, PO Box 27372, 102 54 Stockholm, Sweden.

BJORNSSON, Sigurd; Singer (Tenor); b. 19 March 1932, Hafnarfjordur, Iceland. *Education:* Studied with Gerhard Husch in Munich. *Career:* Debut: Stuttgart, 1962, as Arturo in Lucia di Lammermoor; Sang at Stuttgart until 1968, Kassel, 1968–72, Graz, 1972–75, and Theater am Gärtnerplatz Munich until 1977; Among his best roles were Mozart's Belmonte, Ferrando and Tamino, Lionel in Martha, Nicolai's Fenton, Wagner's Froh and Steuermann, Bellini's Riccardo and Rinuccio in Gianni Schicchi; Guest appearances at the Deutsche Oper Berlin, Munich, Hamburg, the Vienna Volksoper and the Bregenz and Schwetzingen Festivals. *Address:* c/o Staatstheater am Gärtnerplatz, Gärtnerplatz 3, W-8000 Munich 5, Germany.

BLACK, Jeffrey; Singer (Baritone); b. 6 Sept. 1962, Brisbane, Australia. *Career:* Debut: European, Harlekin in Ariadne auf Naxos at Monte Carlo, 1986; Sang with Australian Opera from 1985 as Mercutio, Schaunard, Papageno, Dr Falke, Dandini, Rossini's Figaro and Ottone in Poppea; Glyndebourne Festival, from 1986, as Sid in Albert Herring, Demetrius and the Count in Figaro and Capriccio; Covent Garden appearances as well as engagements at Los Angeles as Guglielmo and Marcello, 1993, Opéra Bastille in Paris, Puccini's Lescaut, Geneva Opéra, Fieramosca in Benvenuto Cellini, San Francisco, Rossini's Figaro; Lyric Opera of Chicago and 1993 Salzburg Festival as Guglielmo, Teatro Col ón, (Buenos Aires) as Dandini, Don Giovanni in Antwerp, Count (Le nozze di Figaro) in Washington, Figaro (Barbiere) at the Met, New York and in Munich, Valentin (Faust) in Geneva and Eugene Onegin at San Diego; Returned to Australia to appear with Lyric Opera of Queensland and Victoria State Opera, Melbourne; Sang Britten's Demetrius for New Israeli Opera, 1994; Mozart's Count at the Metropolitan, and Onegin at Sydney, Australia, 1997; Tannhäuser at Sydney and Posa in Don Carlos for Opera North, 1998; Don Carlo in Australia in 1999; Concerts include tour of Australia with Geoffrey Parsons and the ABC Orchestras, Carmina Burana with the London Philharmonic and Christus in the St Matthew Passion under Franz Welser-Möst; Kiri Te Kanawa International Tour, 1999. *Recordings include:* Carmina Burana; Songs of the Wayfarer, Mahler. *Address:* c/o IMG Artists, Lovell House, 616 Chiswick High Road, London W4 5RX, England.

BLACK, Leo, BMus, MA; British writer, broadcaster, translator and pianist; b. 28 July 1932, London, England; m. Felicity Vincent. *Education:* Univ. of Oxford. *Career:* music publisher, Universal Edition, Vienna, London 1956–60; music programmes, BBC radio 1956–88, Producer 1960–71, Chief Producer 1971–82, Exec. Producer 1982–88; concerts as a song-accompanist; lecture-recital on Schubert's Arpeggioine Sonata, with cellist Felicity Vincent. *Publications:* Franz Schubert: Music and Belief, 2003; translations; contrib. to Über die Aufnahme der Musik Franz Schmidts, 1986; Franz Schmidt und das musikalische Hören, 1992; The Music of Hugh Wood; Heimito von Doderer, An English View, 1996; five major bicentenary articles on Schubert 1997, Schubert durch die Brille 2001; articles to Musical Times, The Listener, Opera Quarterly, Books and Bookmen. *Address:* 112 Chetwynd Road, London, NW5 1DH, England (home). *Telephone:* (20) 7485-1211. *E-mail:* leo.black@btinternet.com.

BLACK, Lynton; Singer (Bass-Baritone); b. 1960, England. *Education:* Studied at the Royal Academy of Music. *Career:* Debut: High Priest in Handel's Teseo, Covent Garden; Appearances with English Touring Opera, English Bach Festival, Garsington Festival Opera and Grange Park Opera; Principal Bass, D'Oyly Carte Opera, 1994–98; Debut at Salzburg Festival in Monteverdi's Orfeo, 1993; Debut at Paris Opéra as Notar in Der Rosenkavalier, 1996; Debut at Basle Opera as Achille in Handel's Giulio Cesare, 1998; Debut at Aix-en-Provence Festival as Achilles in La Belle Hélène, 1999; Debut at La Monnaie, Brussels, as Lesbo in Handel's Agrippina, 2000; Debut at Barcelona Opera as Achille in Giulio Cesare, 2001; Debut at Glyndebourne as Bartolo in Le nozze di Figaro, 2001; Other roles include Commendatore in Don Giovanni, Budd in Albert Herring, Don Alfonso in Così fan tutte, Frank in Die Fledermaus, Dick Deadeye in HMS Pinafore, The Mikado, Sultan in Haydn's L'Incontro Improvviso, Antonio in Le nozze di Figaro (Salzburg, 1995, 1996, 1998; Paris Opéra, 1999), Sciarrone in Tosca (La Monnaie, Brussels, 2000), Sagristano in Tosca (Paris, 2000), Hobson in Peter Grimes (Paris, 2001); mem, Equity; Savage Club; Sketch Club; Loophole Club; Curzon Club; President of D'Oyly Carte Dining Club; debut at Munich staatsoper as Father Trulove in The Rake's Progress 2002; other roles include BassI Israel in Egypt, Cadmus & Somnus in Handel's Semele. *Recordings:* Die Fledermaus (Frank); Rose of Persia (Gaoler). *Honours:* LRAM, 1981; DipRAM, 1983; ARAM, 1995. *Address:* 3 Temple Fortune Lane, London NW11 7UB, England. *E-mail:* lyntonbass@aol.com. *Website:* LyntonBlack.com.

BLACK, Virginia; Harpsichordist; b. 1950, England; m. Howard Davis. 2 s. *Career:* London concerts in the Wigmore Hall, Purcell Room and Queen Elizabeth Hall; Appearances at major festivals in the United Kingdom and Europe including the Prague Spring Festival; Recordings for the BBC and the Westdeutsche Rundfunk; Television performance of Bach's 5th Brandenburg Concerto, with the English Chamber Orchestra; Tours to Europe, the USA, Australia and New Zealand; Concerts with Howard Davis, violin; Other repertoire includes: Sonatas by Soler and Scarlatti; Bach's Chromatic Fantasy and Fugue, Concertos in E and C Minor, Fantasie and Fugue in A minor, Toccata in D and Partitas, Bach's Goldberg Variations; Pieces by Rameau, Dandrieu, Duphly and Forqueray; Falla's Harpsichord Concerto; Professor of Harpsichord at the Royal Academy of Music and Postgraduate Tutor since 1999; Chair of Postgraduate Diploma Studies at Royal Academy of Music from 2002. *Recordings:* 17 albums of harpsichord music including The Essential Harpsichord. *Honours:* Dip RAM, 1964; FRAM, 1988–89; Soler Sonatas, Critic's Choice in Gramophone, 1988; Goldberg Variations, Critic's Choice in Classic CD, 1991. *Address:* 123 Sheering Road, Old Harlow, Essex CM 17 0 JP, England.

BLACK, William (David); Concert Pianist; b. 23 Feb. 1952, Dallas, TX, USA. *Education:* BM, Oberlin College, 1974; MM 1976, DMA 1979, The Juilliard School. *Career:* Debut: New York, 1977; London, England, 1979; Solo and orchestral engagements across the USA, Canada, England, France, Netherlands, Belgium, Germany, Iceland, Japan, China and Italy; Television appearances in the USA and numerous USA and European radio broadcasts including world-wide broadcasts of the Voice of America; Bohemians, New York Musicians Club; European Piano Teachers' Association. *Recordings:* Works of David Diamond; World premiere recording of the original version of the 4th Piano Concerto of Sergei Rachmaninov; Hunter Johnson Piano Sonata; Gershwin, Rhapsody in Blue. *Contributions:* Keyboard Classics. *Honours:* Pi Kappa Lambda, 1974; Concert Artists Guild Award; Morris Loeb Award, The Juilliard School; Solo Recitalist Grant, National Endowment for The Arts, 1991.

BLACKBURN, Bonnie J., BA, MA, PhD; musicologist; b. 15 July 1939, Albany, NY, USA; m. 1st Edward E. Lowinsky 1971 (died 1985); m. 2nd Leofranc Holford-Strevens 1990. *Education:* Wellesley College, University of Chicago. *Career:* Research Assistant, Department of Music, 1963–76, Visiting Associate Professor, 1986, University of Chicago; Lecturer, School of Music, Northwestern University, 1987; Visiting Associate Professor, State University of New York, Buffalo, 1989–90; General Editor of Monuments of Renaissance Music, 1993–; mem, American Musicological Society; Royal Musical Association; International Musicological Society; Koninklijke Vereniging voor Nederlandse Muziekgeschiedenis; Plainsong and Mediaeval Music Society; Renaissance Society of America; Society for Renaissance Studies; Società Italiana di Musicologia. *Publications:* Music for Treviso Cathedral in the Late Sixteenth Century: A Reconstruction of the Lost Manuscripts 29 and 30, 1987; Josquin des Prez: Proceedings of The International Josquin Festival-Conference, 1976, edited with E Lowinsky; Edited Johannis Lupi Opera omnia, 3 vols, 1980–89; Edited, Music in the Culture of the Renaissance and Other Essays by Edward E Lowinsky, 1989; Editor with E Lowinsky and C A Miller, A Correspondence of Renaissance Musicians, 1991; The Oxford Companion to the Year (with Leofranc Holford-Strevens), 1999; Composition, Printing and Performance: Studies in Renaissance Music, 2000; Editor, with Reinhard

Strohm, Music as Concept and Practice in the Late Middle Ages (New Oxford History of Music, 3, 2nd edn, Part 1), 2001. *Contributions:* Musical Quarterly; Journal of The American Musicological Society; Musica Disciplina; Early Music History; The New Grove Dictionary of Music and Musicians; Early Music; Studi Musicali; Journal of Musicology; Die Musik in Geschichte und Gegenwart; Journal of the Royal Musical Association; Oxford Dictionary of National Biography. *Honours:* John Simon Guggenheim Memorial Foundation Fellowship, 1988–89. *Address:* 67 St Bernard's Road, Oxford OX2 6EJ, England. *E-mail:* bonnie.blackburn@wolfson.ox.ac.uk (office).

BLACKBURN, Olivia; Singer (Soprano); b. 1960, London, England. *Education:* Studied at Trinity College, London, and at the Pears-Britten School. *Career:* Regular concert on South Bank, London, in Die Schöpfung by Haydn, Vivaldi's Magnificat and Handel's Jephtha; German Requiem by Brahms at the Barbican with the Philharmonia and the St Matthew Passion with the Steinitz Bach Players; European performances in the Bach B Minor Mass, Haydn's Paukenmesse (Missa in tempore belli), Messiah and the Mozart Requiem; Opera debut in The Poisoned Kiss by Vaughan Williams at the Bloomsbury Theatre; Wexford Festival, 1987; With Cologne Opera has sung Naiad in Ariadne auf Naxos, Siebel in Faust, Sandrina (La Finta Giardiniera), Helena in A Midsummer Night's Dream and Pamina; Song recitals in Paris, Dublin, London, and Cambridge; Appearances with the Songmakers' Almanac in London and at the Nottingham and Buxton Festivals; Season 1989–90 in Ode to the West Wind by Arnell, Aci in Handel's Aci, Galatea e Polifemo with London Baroque at the Beaune Festival and Mendelssohn's Lobgesang conducted by Richard Hickox; Mozart's C Minor Mass in Scotland and in France with Malgoire and Portugal with Brüggen conducting; Covent Garden debut, 1992, as a Young Nun in The Fiery Angel; Television recording of Handel's Roman Vespers in Vienna. *Recordings include:* Bach B Minor Mass. *Address:* c/o Ron Gonsalves Management, 10 Dagnan Road, London SW12 9LQ, England.

BLACKHAM, Joyce; Singer (Soprano); b. 1 Jan. 1934, Rotherham, Yorkshire, England; m. Peter Glossop (divorced). *Education:* Studied at the Guildhall School of Music with Joseph Hislop. *Career:* Debut: Sadler's Wells Opera 1955, as Olga in Eugene Onegin; Covent Garden debut as Esmeralda in The Bartered Bride; Best known as Carmen, also sang Dorabella, Mimi, Norina, Rosina and roles in operettas by Offenbach, Johann Strauss and Lehar; Guest appearances Berlin, New York and New Zealand; With Welsh National Opera sang Rosina, Amneris and Cherubino; Sang Maddalena in Rigoletto at Covent Garden, 1974.

BLACKWELL, Harolyn; Singer (Soprano); b. 1960, Washington, District of Columbia, USA. *Education:* Studied at the Catholic University of America and with Carlo Bergonzi and Renata Tebaldi in Italy. *Career:* Has sung Jemmy in Guillaume Tell at the San Antonio Festival, Papagena in Cleveland, Oscar in Hamburg, Gilda with the Miami Opera, Sister Constance in Dialogues des Carmélites for Canadian Opera and Clara in Porgy and Bess at the 1986 Glyndebourne Festival; Symphonic engagements with the National Symphony, St Louis Philharmonic, Cincinnati Symphony, Minnesota Orchestra and Buffalo Philharmonic; Carnegie Hall as Xanthe in Die Liebe der Danaë by Strauss; Recitals in Buffalo, Denver, Dallas and New York (debut 1987); Season 1986–87 with debuts at Chicago as Oscar (Un Ballo in Maschera) and at the Metropolitan as Pousette in Manon; Xenia in Boris Godunov, conducted by James Conlon; Season 1987–88 with concert performance of Porgy and Bess under Simon Rattle, Nannetta in Falstaff at Nice and the Princess in L'Enfant et les Sortilèges at Glyndebourne; Season 1988–89 included Schubert's A-flat Mass in Detroit, Barbarina and Sophie (Werther) at the Met, Olga in Giordano's Fedora at Carnegie Hall and Zdenka (Arabella) at Glyndebourne; Season 1989–90 with Adele at the Met and Marie (La Fille du Régiment) in Seattle; Blondchen in Die Entführung at Aix-en-Provence; Season 1990–91 highlights were Oscar at the Met, Mahler's 4th Symphony in Florida and Charleston, Bach and Handel with the New York Chamber Symphony, Mozart's Il Re Pastore with the Nice Opera and Le nozze di Figaro (Susanna) in Toronto; Mozart's Zerlina at San Francisco, 1991; Sang Lakmé and Lucia di Lammermoor at Seattle, 2000. *Recordings include:* Porgy and Bess. *Address:* c/o Columbia Artists Management Inc, 165 West 57th Street, New York, NY 10019, USA.

BLACKWOOD, Easley; Composer, Pianist and Music Educator; b. 21 April 1933, Indianapolis, Indiana, USA. *Education:* Received piano training in Indianapolis; Studied composition, Berkshire Music Center, Tanglewood, Massachusetts, summers, 1948, 1949 (with Messiaen), 1950, with Heiden, Indiana University School of Music, Bloomington; With Hindemith, Yale University, MA, 1954, and with Boulanger in Paris, 1954–56. *Career:* Appeared as soloist with the Indianapolis Symphony Orchestra, 1947; Concerts throughout North American and Europe; Faculty member, 1958–68, Professor, 1968–, University of Chicago; Retired, 1997. *Compositions:* Orchestral: Symphony No. 1, 1954–55, No. 2, 1960, No. 3, 1964, No. 4, 1977, No. 5, 1992; Chamber

Symphony, 1954; Clarinet Concerto, 1964; Symphonic Fantasy, 1965; Oboe Concerto, 1965; Violin Concerto, 1967; Flute Concerto, 1968; Piano Concerto, 1970; Chamber: Viola Sonata, 1953; 2 string quartets, 1957, 1959; Concerto for 5 instruments, 1959; 2 violin sonatas, 1960, 1973; Fantasy for Cello and Piano, 1960; Pastorale and Variations for Wind Quintet, 1961; Sonata for Flute and Harpsichord, 1962; Fantasy for Flute, Clarinet and Piano, 1965; Symphonic Episode for Organ, 1966; Piano Trio, 1967; 12 Microtonal Etudes for Synthesizer, 1982; Piano pieces; Un voyage à Cythère for soprano and winds, 1966; 4 Letter Scenes from Gulliver's Last Voyage for mezzo-soprano, baritone and tape, 1972; Sonatina for Piccolo Clarinet and Piano, 1994; Sonata for Piano, 1996; Two Nocturnes for piano, 1996. *Recordings:* Piano works of Casella, Szymanowski; Ives, Copland, Prokofiev, Stravinsky, Berg, Nielsen and Alain. *Publications:* The Structure of Recognizable Diatonic Tunings, 1986. *Honours:* Fulbright Scholarship, 1954–56; 1st Prize, Koussevitzky Music Foundation, 1958; Creative Arts Award, Brandeis University, 1968; Several commissions. *Current Management:* Magna Carta Management, 3359 Kelly Lane SW, Roanoke, VA 24018, USA. *Address:* 5300 S Shore Drive #44, Chicago, IL 60615, USA.

BLADIN, Christer; Singer (Tenor); b. 1947, Stockholm, Sweden. *Education:* Studied in Freiburg and Stockholm. *Career:* Sang at the Freiburg Opera, 1972–76, Berne, 1976–78, Darmstadt, 1978–84, and at the Bonn Opera from 1986; Guest appearances at Perugia (Salieri's Les Danaides, 1984, Haydn's Orfeo, 1985) and Aix-en-Provence (Rossini's Armida, 1988); Other roles include Froh in Das Rheingold (Barcelona, 1986), Mozart's Belmonte and Tamino, Admète in Lully's Alceste and Ernesto in Don Pasquale; Has also appeared at La Scala, Milan, Nantes, Ghent and Marseille; Montpellier 1993–94, in operas by Philippe Hersant and René Koering. *Address:* c/o Oper der Stadt Bonn, Am Boeselagerhof 1, W-5300 Bonn, Germany.

BLÁHA, Ivo; Czech composer and teacher; b. 14 March 1936, Litomysl. *Education:* pupil of Ridky and Sommer, graduated 1958, postgraduate studies with Hlobil, 1965–70, Prague Acad. of Music; training in electronic music from Kabelac and Herzog, Plzeň Radio. *Career:* teacher, Prague Acad. of Music, 1964–; Docent, Film and TV Faculty, 1967–, Prof. 1999–, Head, Dept of Sound Design, FAMU; mem. Asscn of Czech Composers, Prague. *Compositions:* four string quartets: 1957, 1966, 1983, 'Curriculum vitae' 2000, Concerto for orchestra 1957, 3 Movements for violin and piano 1961, Spring Plays for wind quintet 1962, Concerto for percussion and orchestra 1964, Solitude, sonata for solo violin 1965, Music for wind quintet 1965, 3 Toccata Studies for piano 1967, Violin Concerto 1968, Duetto facile per violini 1970, Music to Pictures of a Friend for flute, oboe and clarinet 1971, Cello Sonata 1972, 2 Inventions for solo flute 1974, Duo for bass clarinet and piano 1975, Cet amour for speaker, wood instruments and tape 1975, Rays for piano 1976, Per archi: Sinfonia 1977, The Violin for violin solo 1979, Hymn for organ 1980, Sonata transparenta for flute and piano 1982, Moravian Lullabies: Musical pictures on folk songs, for soprano, flute and piano 1982, Something for Ear: 3 children's choirs with piano 1983, Zoolessons I for guitar 1984, II 1987, Vaults for organ 1986, Funny Things with Four Strings: 5 miniatures for 2–3 violins or violin ensemble 1986, Imaginations for violin and piano 1988, Sonata introspecta for viola 1989, Joy to Everyone, Christmas Cantata for children's choir and instrumental ensemble 1997, To Ancient Strings for children's choir a cappella 1998, Quasi Sonata for Harpsichord 1998, Welcome Spring! Little Cantata for choir of younger children and instruments 1998, Macrocosmos for piano 1998, Bergamasca: Symphonic Scherzo 2000, Soliloquy with Marimba for marimba and player's voice 2001, Living Water: songs for choir of younger children and piano 2001, 1 Plus Minus 1: musical scene for flautist-woman and violinist-man 2001, Hádes: ancient picture for contrabassoon and piano 2002, Ornaments for piano and orchestra 2003, Satyr's Circles for clarinet solo 2003, Missing Bow (Senza arco) for viola quartet 2004, Bear's Songs for children's choir and piano 2004, Quadrille: dance fantasy for viola foursome 2004. *Recordings:* 3rd and 4th String Quartets, Spring Plays for wind quintet, Solitude, sonata for solo violin, 3 Toccata Studies for piano, Violin Concerto, Duetto facile per violini, Cello Sonata, 2 Inventions for solo flute, Duo for bass clarinet and piano, Cet amour for speaker, wood instruments and tape, Rays for piano, Per archi: Sinfonia, The Violin for violin solo, Hymn for organ, Something for Ear: 3 children's choirs with piano, Zoolessons I for guitar, II, Vaults for organ, Imaginations for violin and piano, Sonata introspecta for viola, Joy to Everyone, Christmas Cantata for children's choir and instrumental ensemble, To Ancient Strings for children's choir a cappella, Quasi Sonata for Harpsichord, Macrocosmos for piano, Bergamasca: Symphonic Scherzo, Hádes: ancient picture for contrabassoon and piano, Ornaments for piano and orchestra, Satyr's Circles for clarinet solo. *Publication:* Sound Dramaturgy of Audio-visual Work 1995. *Honours:* Front position, Int. Rostrum of Composers, UNESCO 1991; Annual Prize of CHF Prague 1993. *Address:* FAMU, Smetanovo nábr. 2, 110 00 Prague 1, Czech Republic (office); Jablonecká 418, 190 00 Prague, Czech Republic.

E-mail: ivoblaha@seznam.cz (home). *Website:* www.famu.cz (office); members.sibeliusmusic.com/ivoblaha (home).

BLAHOVA, Eva; University Professor and Singer; b. 1 Dec. 1944, Skalica, Czechoslovakia; Divorced, 1 s., 1 d. *Education:* Music Academy, Bratislava, Slovakia, 1962–68; Music Academy, Vienna, Austria, 1968–71; Masterclass, Professor D Ferro and Erik Werba. *Career:* Debut: Slovak Philharmony, 1965; Sang in Concert Festivals: Music Festival, Bratislava, Slovakia; Kraków; Easter Festival, Poland; The Prague Spring Festival, Czech Republic; Carinthian Summer Festival, Ossiach, Austria; Ottawa, Montreal, Canada; Parma, Trento, Italy; Chartres, France; Vienna, Austria; Washington DC, New Jersey, USA; Hyundai Arts Center, Korea; Tokyo, Osaka, Japan; Professor of Singing, Music Academy, Bratislava, 1969–, European Music Foundation, 1992–98; Masterclasses in Netherlands and Czech Republic. *Recordings:* Nine German Arias, 1979; Haydn, Mozart, Beethoven Concert Arias, 1983; Romantic Songs, 1997. *Contributions:* Music Life; Slovak Reviews. *Address:* Lermontovova 16, 81105 Bratislava, Slovakia.

BLAHUSIAKOVA, Magdalena; Singer (Soprano); b. 1947, Czechoslovakia. *Education:* Studied in Sofia and Bratislava. *Career:* Member of the Brno Opera, 1969–82, notably as Santuzza, Aida, Donna Anna and Donna Elvira, Fiordiligi, Tatiana and Amelia (Simon Boccanegra and Un Ballo in Maschera); Guest appearances in Barcelona (1980), Genoa (as Jenůfa), and Lausanne (Rusalka); Sang Santuzza in Cuba (1987) and Yaroslavna in Prince Igor with the Slovak National Opera at Edinburgh, 1991; Concert engagements in The Spectre's Bride by Dvořák, Vienna, 1984, the Requiems of Dvořák and Mozart and Beethoven's Ninth; Concert tour of the USA, 1985. *Address:* c/o Janáček Opera, Dvořákoáva 11, 65770 Brno, Czech Republic.

BLAIR, James; Conductor; b. 1940, Stirling, Scotland. *Education:* Studied at Trinity College, London, and with Adrian Boult; Won Ricordi Conducting Prize and an Italian Government Scholarship to study with Franco Ferrara in Siena and Venice. *Career:* Artistic Director and Principal Conductor, Young Musicians' Symphony Orchestra, 1971–; Many performances of Mahler, Messiaen and Strauss; Engagements with all leading British orchestras and works with Opera North, Dublin Grand Opera and Athens Opera; US debut, 1984, with the Delaware Symphony; Later conducted Colorado Springs and Kansas City Symphony Orchestras; Many Young Musicians' Symphony Orchestra concerts given on BBC, including Mahler's 8th Symphony. *Recordings:* Late Romantic repertory.

BLAKE, David, BA, MA; composer and academic; b. 2 Sept. 1936, London, England; m. Rita Muir 1960; two s. one d. *Education:* Gonville and Caius Coll., Cambridge, Deutsche Akademie der Künste, Berlin, Germany. *Career:* Lecturer in Music 1964–71, Senior Lecturer 1971–76, Prof. of Music 1976–2001, Univ. of York, retired 2001. *Compositions include:* Variations for Piano, 1960; Three Choruses to Poems of Robert Frost, 1964; What is the Cause for Chorus; Fulke Greville, 1967; Nonet for Wind, 1971; Violin Concerto, BBC Proms, 1976; Toussaint, libretto Anthony Ward, premiere London Coliseum, 1977, opera in 3 acts, 1974–77; Clarinet Quintet, 1980; Scherzi ed Intermezzi for Orchestra, 1984; Seasonal Variants for 7 Players, 1985; Pastoral Paraphrase for Bassoon and Small Orchestra, 1988; The Plumber's Gift, libretto John Birtwhistle, premiere, London Coliseum, 1989; A Little More Night Music, for Saxophone Quartet, 1990; Mill Music for Brass Band, 1990; Cello Concerto, 1992; Three Ritsos Choruses, 1992; The Griffin's Tale for Baritone and Orchestra, text by John Birtwhistle, 1994; The Fabulous Adventures of Alexander the Great, for soloists, chorus and orchestra of young people, text by John Birtwhistle, 1996; Scoring a Century, an entertainment, text by Keith Warner, 1999; The Shades of Love for bass baritone and small orchestra, poems by C. P. Cavafy, 2000; String Quartet No. 4, 2003. *Recordings:* Violin Concerto, In Praise of Krishna; Variations for Piano; The Almanack. *Publications:* Hanns Eisler: A Miscellany 1995. *Address:* Mill Gill, Askrigg, Nr Leyburn, North Yorkshire DL8 3HR, England (home). *Telephone:* (1969) 650364 (home). *E-mail:* david.blake9@btopenworld.com (home).

BLAKE, Howard; Composer; b. 28 Oct. 1938, London, England. *Education:* Royal Academy of Music with Harold Craxton and Howard Ferguson. *Career:* Pianist, conductor, orchestrator and composer, London, 1960–70; From 1971 freelance composer; Benedictus performed at Manchester, Llandaff and St Alban's Cathedrals, Perth and Three Choirs Festivals, by the Bach Choir in London (1988) and with the Philharmonia RFH, 1989; Barbican concerts for children; Director of Performing Right Society and Executive Director, 1978–87; Visiting Professor of Composition at Royal Academy of Music, 1992; mem, MU; APC; Incorporated Society of Musicians; Garrick Club; Groucho Club. *Compositions:* The Station, comic opera, 1987; Orchestral: Toccata, 1976; The Annunciation (ballet); Concert Dances, 1984; Clarinet Concerto, 1984; Diversions for cello and orchestra, 1985; Three Sussex Songs, 1973; Two Songs of the Nativity, 1976; The Song of St Francis, 1976; A Toccata of Galuppi's for baritone and harpsichord, 1978;

Benedictus, dramatic oratorio, 1979; The Snowman for narrator, boy soprano and orchestra, 1982; Festival Mass for double choir a capella, 1987; Shakespeare Songs for tenor and string quartet, 1987; Instrumental: Piano Quartet, 1974; The Up and Down Man, children's suite, 1974; Penillion for violin and harp, 1975; Eight Character Pieces for piano, 1976; Dances for 2 pianos, 1976; Prelude for solo viola, 1979; Sinfonietta for 10 brass, 1981; Piano Concerto, Philharmonia commission to celebrate 30th birthday of HRH Princess of Wales, 1991; Violin Concerto, world premiere; Leeds City Council commission for their Centenary; The Snowman, ballet, 1993; Charter for Peace, commissioned for UN 50th Anniversary, 1995; A Midsummer Night's Dream, commissioned by RSC, 1996; Eva, ballet, 1996; The Bear, 1998; Stabat Mater, for soprano, narrators, chorus and orchestra, 2001; Also many scores for films, theatre, ballet. *Recordings:* Diversions for cello and orchestra, Toccata, 1991; Snowman; Benedictus; Clarinet and Piano Concertos; Granpa; Violin Concertos, The Snowman Ballet, A Midsummer Night's Dream. *Publications:* Many. *Honours:* Fellow, Royal Academy of Music, 1989; O.B.E., services to music, 1994. *Address:* Studio Flat 6, 18 Kensington Court Place, London W8 5BJ, England.

BLAKE, Rockwell (Robert); Singer (Tenor); b. 10 Jan. 1951, Plattsburgh, NY, USA; m. Deborah Jeanne Bourlier, 25 Aug 1973. *Education:* Studied voice with Renata Booth in high school; State University of New York, Fredonia; Catholic University of America, Washington DC. *Career:* Soloist: US Navy Band; Washington DC, Opera, 1976; Hamburg State Opera, 1977–79; Vienna State Opera, 1978; New York City Opera, 1979–81; Metropolitan Opera, New York, 1981–83, 1986, 1988, as Lindoro in L'Italiana in Algeri, Almaviva, Don Ottavio and Arturo in I Puritani; Chicago Lyric Opera, 1983, 1987; Rossini Opera Festival, Pesaro, 1983–85, 1987–88; San Francisco Opera, 1984; Paris Opéra, 1985; Naples San Carlo, 1985–88; Opéra-Comique, Paris, 1987; Bavarian State Opera, Munich, 1987; Rome Opera, 1988–89; Sang James V in La Donna del Lago at Bonn, 1990; Arturo in I Puritani at Barcelona, 1990; Tonio (La Fille du Régiment) at Santiago; Concert performance of Meyerbeer's Il Crociato in Egitto at the 1990 Montpellier Festival; Rossini cantatas at Martina Franca; Title role in Il Pirata at Lausanne, 1992; Season 1992 as Rossini's Almaviva at Genoa, Selim in Rossini's Adina at Rome, James V in La Donna del Lago at La Scala, Mozart's Ferrando at Dallas; Almaviva at the 1992 Caracalla Festival; Sang in Semiramide at the 1994 Pesaro Festival; Aix Festival 1996, as Jupiter in the French premiere of Handel's Semele; Ramiro in Cenerentola at Hamburg, 1998; Sang Oronte in Alcina at the Paris Palais Garnier and Lyric Opera of Chicago, 1999; Season 2000–01 as Libenskof in Il Viaggio a Reims at La Coruña, and as Idreno in Semiramide at Liège; Various concert engagements. *Recordings:* The Rossini Tenor; The Mozart Tenor; Encore Rossini; Alina la Regina di Golconda; Il Barbiere di Siviglia; Video of Rossini's Barber from the Metropolitan. *Honours:* First winner, Richard Tucker Award, 1978; National Opera Institute Grantee, 1975, 1976; Honorary DMus, State Orchestra. *Address:* c/o Columbia Artists Management Inc, 165 West 57th Street, New York, NY 10019, USA.

BLANC, Ernest (Marius Victor); Singer (Baritone); b. 1 Nov. 1923, Sanary-sur-Mer, France; m. Eliane Guiraud. *Education:* Studied at the Toulon Conservatory, 1946–49. *Career:* Debut: Marseille, 1950, as Tonio in Pagliacci; Paris Opéra from 1954, debut as Rigoletto; Sang in Paris until 1976, in operas by Puccini, Wagner, Offenbach and Verdi; Bayreuth Festival, 1958–59, as Telramund; La Scala Milan, 1960; Glyndebourne, 1960, as Don Giovanni and as Riccardo in I Puritani; Guest appearances in Naples, New York, Barcelona, Lisbon, Tel-Aviv, Florence and Amsterdam. Season 1986–87 as Des Grieux (père) at Nancy and Germont at Marseille. *Recordings:* Faust, Carmen, Iphigénie en Tauride, Les Contes d'Hoffmann, Les Pêcheurs de Perles.

BLANC, Jonny; Singer (Tenor); b. 10 July 1939, Lessebo, Sweden. *Education:* Studied at the Stockholm Conservatory with Kathe Sundstrom and with Clemens Kaiser-Breme in Essen. *Career:* Sang as baritone, 1962–67; Tenor debut, Stockholm, 1967, as Dmitri in Boris Godunov; Sang in the premieres of operas by Braein and Werle and as Florestan, Siegmund, Eisenstein in Die Fledermaus, Don Carlos, Don José, Cavaradossi and Riccardo in Un Ballo in Maschera; Sang in a revival of the Abbé Vogler's Gustaf Adolf och Ebba Brahe at Drottningholm, 1973; Sang Steva in the Stockholm Opera production of Jenůfa at the Edinburgh Festival, 1974; Guest appearances with Scottish Opera and in Malmö, Oslo, Frankfurt, Copenhagen, Miami, Lisbon and Helsinki; Well-known as concert singer; Artistic Manager, Malmö City Theatre, 1986; Opera Manager, Royal Opera Stockholm, 1991–; Principal, University College of Opera, Stockholm, 1994. *Address:* Dag Hammarskjölds väg 24, 11527 Stockholm, Sweden.

BLANCK, Kirsten; Singer (Soprano); b. 1965, Neumünster, Holstein, Germany. *Education:* Studied in Hamburg with Judith Beckmann and in Kiel and Lubeck. *Career:* Debut: Saarbrucken, 1986; Sang at the Lubeck and Kiel Operas from 1990, notably as Mozart's Queen of Night, and in Dresden, Berlin, Stuttgart and Frankfurt; Other roles include

Donna Anna (Kiel, 1991), Gilda (Hanover, 1993), Sophie in Der Rosenkavalier, Zerbinetta, and Lulu; Season 1992–93 at Kiel as Violetta and Donna Clara in Zemlinsky's Der Zwerg; Aminta in Die schweigsame Frau at Dresden, 1998; Season 2000–01 as Zerbinetta at La Scala, The Queen of Night at Dresden, Sophie in Der Rosenkavalier for San Francisco Opera and Constanze at Chemnitz; Many concert appearances. *Address:* c/o Buhnen der Hansestadt Lubeck, Fischergrube 5-21, W-2400 Lubeck Germany.

BLANCKE-BIGGS, Elizabeth; Singer (soprano); b. 1965, USA. *Career:* Appearances as Madama Butterfly and Liu in Turandot for Opera Grand Rapids, Nedda in Pagliacci for El Paso opera and the Trovatore Leonora for Augusta Opera; Micaela for Opera Colorado, Mimi at the Virginia Opera and Norma for the Di Capo Opera Theatre; European engagements as Donizetti's Maria Stuarda at Turin and in Honegger's Le Roi David at Nice; Other concerts include Beethoven's Ninth and Die Walküre in New Zealand; Fauré's Requiem, Mozart's C Minor Mass and Beethoven's Mass in C; Sang Mozart's Countess at the Aotea Centre, Auckland; Season 2001–2002 as Violetta for the Metropolitan Opera and Tosca for New York City Opera. *Current Management:* Athole Still International Management, Forresters Hall, 25–27 Westow Street, London, SE19 3RY, England. *Telephone:* (20) 8771-5271. *Fax:* (20) 8768-6600. *Website:* www.atholestill.com.

BLANK, Allan; Composer; b. 27 Dec. 1925, New York, NY, USA. *Education:* High School of Music and Art in New York; Juilliard, 1946–47, Washington Square College; MA, University of Minnesota, 1950; University of Iowa. *Career:* Violinist, Pittsburgh Symphony Orchestra, 1950–52; Teacher, Western Illinois University, 1966–68, Patterson State College, 1968–70, Lehmann College, 1970–77, and Virginia Commonwealth University at Richmond, 1978–; Music Director of the Richmond Community Orchestra, 1986–89. *Compositions include:* Operas Aria da Capo, 1960; Excitement at the Circus, children's opera, Patterson, 1969; The Magic Bonbons, 1983; The Noise, Richmond, 1986; Incidental music for Othello, 1983, and Measure for Measure, 1984; 5 String Quartets, 1958, 1981, 1989, 1998 (2); Concert Piece for band, 1963; Music for Orchestra, 1967; Wind Quintet, 1970; An American Medley, 1976; Music for Tubas, 1977; Divertimento for tuba and band, 1979; Kreutzer March for band, 1981; Concertino for bassoon and strings, 1984; Concert for 5 players, 1986; Concertino for string orchestra, 1987; Forked Paths, suite of 11 miniatures for trumpet, 1988; Overture for a Happy Occasion, 1986; Polymorphics, 1988; Concerto for clarinet and string orchestra, 1990; Songs from the Holocaust, 1996; Concerto for Violin and Orchestra, 1995; Concerto for Contrabass and String Orchestra, 1996; Songs; Concerto for piano and orchestra, 2001; Lines for Solo Contrabassoon, 2001; Three Tableaux for small orchestra, 2001; Concerto for Bassoon and Small Orchestra, 2002; Music for Multiply Violins, 2003; Becoming for Clarinet, Cello and Piano, 2003; Ensemble for Brass Quintet, 2003.. *Honours:* George Eastman Competition, 1983; National Endowment for the Arts, 1983; Virginia Music Teachers Association Commission, 1979, 1988, 1991. *Address:* 2920 Archdale Road, Richmond, VA 23235, USA.

BLANKENBURG, Heinz (Horst); Singer (Baritone) and Stage Director; b. 15 Oct. 1931, New York, NY, USA; m. (1) 2 s., 1 d., (2) Gayle Cameron-McComb, 14 Dec 1986. *Education:* Local universities, Los Angeles. *Career:* Debut: San Francisco Opera, 1955; Leading baritone, Glyndebourne Festival Opera, 1957–70, roles there included Mozart's Papageno and Figaro, Rossini's Raimbaud and Busoni's Arlecchino; Hamburg State Opera, 1959–73, San Francisco Opera, 1955–66; As Beckmesser, Schaunard, Fra Melitone (Forza del Destino) and Paolo in Simon Boccanegra; Sang with the Hamburg Staatsoper in the British premiere of Die Frau ohne Schatten, Sadler's Wells Theatre, 1966; Guest baritone with opera companies of Munich, Berlin, Vienna, Paris, Frankfurt, Metropolitan, Amsterdam, Rome, Brussels, Lausanne, Basle, Strasbourg, Naples, Venice, New Zealand, St Louis, Portland, Vancouver (1978), Seattle, Los Angeles; Faculty, University of California, Los Angeles and California State University, Los Angeles. *Recordings:* Discs, 2 labels; Television and radio recordings for BBC, RAI and ZDF. *Honours:* Kammersänger, Hamburg State Opera, 1966; Maori Welcome, New Zealand, 1971; Honorary Doctor of Performing Arts, California State University, Los Angeles, 1977, University of California, Los Angeles, 1986; Maori Welcome, New Zealand, 1971. *Address:* Opera Theatre, California State University, 5151 State University Drive, Los Angeles, CA 90032, USA.

BLANKENHEIM, Toni; Singer (Bass-baritone); b. 12 Dec. 1921, Cologne, Germany. *Education:* Studied with Paul Lohmann in Frankfurt and with Res Fischer in Stuttgart. *Career:* Debut: Frankfurt, 1947, as Mozart's Figaro; Sang at Frankfurt until 1950, then at Hamburg; Bayreuth Festival, 1954–59, as Kothner, Klingsor and Donner; Darmstadt, 1965–68; Stuttgart from 1968; Sang at Hamburg in the premieres of operas by Mihalovici, Martinů, Henze, Krenek, Von Einem, Goehr, Searle, Kelemen and Constant; Performances of works by Berg, Stravinsky, Liebermann and other modern composers; Sang Schigolch at the Paris Opéra in the 1979 premiere of Berg's Lulu (3 act version); Guest appearances in Vienna, Berlin, Munich, Milan, Paris, Mexico City, San Francisco and New York; Sang in the first local performance of The Birthday by Kalevi, at Hamburg, 1982; Many concert appearances. *Recordings:* Bastien et Bastienne by Mozart; Lulu; Donner in Das Rheingold, Bayreuth, 1957; Klingsor in Parsifal, Bayreuth, 1956.

BLANKENSHIP, Rebecca; Singer (Soprano); b. 24 March 1954, New York, USA. *Education:* Studied voice in New York with Judith Oas. *Career:* Sang two seasons at Ulm as a Mezzo Soprano; Sang Ariadne at Berlin Staatsoper, 1986; Appeared in Basle 1986–88 as Mozart's Elettra and First Lady, Leonora in Il Trovatore, Katharina in Lady Macbeth of Mtsensk; Season 1988–90: Martha, in Tiefland in Berlin and Vienna Volksoper, Leonore in Fidelio in Stuttgart and with Opera Forum in Netherlands, Elsa in Liège and Senta at Bregenz Festival; Marie in Wozzeck with Vienna Staatsoper, 1990–92; Regular appearances in Vienna, 1991–; Other roles include Female Chorus, in The Rape of Lucretia, Agathe in Der Freischütz, Hanna Glawari in Die Lustige Witwe; Sang Sieglinde at the San Francisco Opera, 1990, and at the Wiener Staatsoper, 1991, Marie in Wozzeck, La Fenice, Venice, 1992, Lady Macbeth of Mtsensk, Katarina at the Wiener Volksoper, 1992–, Erwartung by Schoenberg for Canadian Opera at Toronto, and Edinburgh Festival, 1993, Erwartung at the Le Grand Théâtre Genève, 1995. *Address:* Music International, 13 Ardilaun Road, London N5 2QR, England.

BLANZAT, Anne-Marie; Soprano; b. 24 Nov. 1944, Neuilly, France. *Education:* Studied in Paris. *Career:* Sang Yniold in Debussy's Pelléas et Mélisande at Aix-en-Provence, 1966, and Glyndebourne, 1969; Returned to Glyndebourne, 1976, as Mélisande, and sang the role many times in France and elsewhere (Nantes, 1974); Also successful as Susanna, Juliette (Strasbourg, 1983) and Manon; Strasbourg 1991 in La Voix Humaine by Poulenc; Sang also in modern repertory by Prodromidès, Poulenc and Prey, and in Rameau's Hippolyte et Aricie; Teacher in Conservatoire Municipal Maurice Ravel de Paris and Ecole Normale de Musique de Paris. *Honours:* Oscar de l'Art Lyrique, 1974; Officier des Arts et Lettres, 1998. *Address:* 2 Square Servan, 75011 Paris, France.

BLASI, Angela Maria; American singer (soprano); b. 16 Aug. 1956, Brooklyn, New York. *Education:* Loyola University, Los Angeles. *Career:* Ensemble mem., Hessen State Theater, Wiesbaden, 1982–85; Bavarian State Opera, Munich, 1985–88; Debut as Pamina at Salzburg Festival, Covent Garden, La Scala Milan; Guest appearances in European opera houses including Hamburg, Berlin, Vienna, Zürich, Florence; appeared as Liu in Turandot in the Forbidden City, Beijing with Zubin Mehta, 1998; Marguerite in Faust, Munich, 2000; New York Met debut as Pamina, 2000; Ellen Orford in Peter Grimes, Montpellier, France, 2001; Conception in L'Heure Espagnole, Brussels, Belgium, 2001; Nedda in Pagliacci, Brussels Monnaie, 2002; La Bohème at the Met, 2003; Agathe in Der Freischutz, Montpellier, 2003. *Film:* Comencini's film of La Bohème (Musetta), 1987. *Recordings:* Mozart's Requiem and Mahler's 4th Symphony. *Honours:* Bavarian Kammer-sängerin, 1994; Munich Merkur Prize, People's Choice Award for Interpretation of Marguerite in Faust at the Bavarian State Opera. *Address:* c/o Bayerische Staatsoper, Max-Joseph Platz, 80539 Munich, Germany. *Telephone:* (171) 3558875 (office). *Website:* www .angelamariablasi.com.

BLASIUS, Martin; Singer (Bass); b. 5 June 1956, Schwelm, Westphalen, Germany. *Education:* Studied at the Folkwang-Musikhochschule, Essen. *Career:* Sang at first in concert, notably for Austrian and Italian Radio, at the Bach-Woche Ansbach, the Göttingen Handel Festival and at the Frankurt Festival; Opera debut as Dulcamara, Gelsenkirchen, 1983; Moved to Hannover in 1987 and Düsseldorf in 1989; Guest appearances in opera and concerts throughout Germany; Appeared in a new production of Henze's The Bassarids, Duisburg, 1991 and sang the Grand Inquisitor in Don Carlos at Düsseldorf; Gärtnerplatztheater Munich 1992, as Mussorgsky's Ivan Khovansky; Bielefeld 1988, as Orth in Weill's Burgschaft; Season 1999–2000 as Wagner's Hunding at Münster, and Fafner in Siegfried. *Recordings include:* Der Traumgörge by Zemlinsky; Saint-Saëns's Christmas Oratorio; Golgotha by Martin; Kreutzer's Das Nachtlager von Granada. *Address:* c/o Deutsche Oper am Rhein, Heinrich Heine Allee 16, 4000 Düsseldorf, Germany.

BLATNÝ, Pavel; Czech composer, conductor, musician (piano) and musicologist; b. 14 Sept. 1931, Brno; m. Danuse Spirková 1982; one s. one d. *Education:* Brno Conservatory, Univ. of Brno, Berklee Coll. of Music, Boston, USA. *Career:* more than 2,000 recitals of piano music, often in a third-stream mode, mixing jazz and classical techniques; conductor of many concerts in the former Czechoslovakia; Chief of the Music Division, Czech television 1971–92; Prof., Janácek Acad. of Musical Arts, Brno 1979–90; Pres., Club of Moravian Composers. *Compositions include:* Music for Piano and Orchestra 1955, Concerto for Orchestra 1956, Concerto for Jazz Orchestra 1962–64, Twelfth Night

(based on Shakespeare's play) 1975, Forest Tales: The Well and Little House (television opera for children) 1975, The Willow Tree (cantata with orchestra) 1980, The Bells, symphonic movement 1981, Christmas Eve (cantata with orchestra) 1982, The Midday Witch (cantata with orchestra) 1982, Two Movements for Brasses 1982, Hommage à Gustav Mahler for orchestra 1982, Per organo e big band 1983, Prologue for mixed choir and jazz orchestra 1984, Ring a Ring o' Roses, for solo piano 1984, Signals for Jazz Orchestra 1985, Confrontation (written with his son, Marek Blatny), for rock group and symphony orchestra 1995, Play Rock, Play New Music (written with his son, Marek Blatny) 1997, Meditation 1999, Symphony Erbenia'da 2003; other music for wind instruments, for piano. *Recordings:* Pavel Blatny – Jazz in Modo Classico, 1980. *Honours:* Leoš Janáček Prize 1984, Anfiteatro d'Argento, Naples, Italy 1989, Lifetime Achievement Award, Brno 2000. *Address:* Absolonova 35, 62400 Brno, Czech Republic (home). *Telephone:* (5) 4122-3062.

BLATTERT, Susanne; Singer (Mezzo-soprano); b. 1966, Freiburg, Germany. *Education:* Studied in Hamburg with Judith Beckman. *Career:* Sang at Gelsenkirchen Musiktheater, 1990–93; Essen Opera from 1993; Further appearances at Hamburg, Cologne, the Bregenz Festival and in Budapest; Roles have included Mozart's Zerlina, Cherubino and Dorabella, Rossini's Rosina, Tancredi and Cenerentola; Essen, 1996 as Sesto in La Clemenza di Tito; Season 1997–98 as Wellgunde in Das Rheingold at Bonn; Season 2000–01 at Bonn as Dorabella, Wellgunde, and Micha in a staged version of Handel's Saul. *Honours:* Prizewinner, Concours International de Chant, Toulouse, 1992. *Address:* c/o Oper der Stadt Bonn, Am Boeselagenhof 1, Pf 2440, 5311 Bonn, Germany.

BLAUSTEIN, Susan (Morton); Composer; b. 22 March 1953, Palo Alto, California, USA. *Education:* Studied with Pousseur in Liège, and at Yale with Jacob Druckman and Betsy Jolas. *Career:* Former Junior Fellow at Harvard University; Assistant professor at Columbia University, New York, 1985–90. *Compositions include:* Commedia for 8 players, 1980; To Orpheus, 4 sonnets, 1982; String Quartet, 1982; Sextet, 1983; Concerto for cello and chamber orchestra, 1984; Song of Songs for mezzo, tenor and orchestra, 1985. *Honours:* Commissions from the Koussevitsky and Fromm Foundations. *Address:* c/o ASCAP, ASCAP House, 1 Lincoln Plaza, New York, NY 10023, USA.

BLAZE, Robin; singer (counter-tenor) and academic; *Professor of Vocal Studies, Royal College of Music*; b. 1971, England; m.; one s. *Education:* Magdalen Coll., Oxford, Royal Coll. of Music. *Career:* regular solo engagements in Europe, USA, South America and Asia with the King's Consort, the Acad. of Ancient Music, Bach Collegium Japan, Collegium Vocale, Gent, The English Concert, The Gabrieli Consort, Orchestra of the Age of Enlightenment, RIAS Kammerchor, Amsterdam Bach Orchestra, and The Sixteen; soloist with National Symphony Orchestra Washington, St Paul Chamber Orchestra, BBC Philharmonic, BBC National Orchestra of Wales, Hallé Orchestra, La Chapelle Royale, Scottish Chamber Orchestra, and Tafelmusik; appearances at festivals, including Edinburgh, BBC Proms, Bremen, Barossa, Boston, Schwetsingen, Istanbul, Potsdam, Leipzig, Flanders, Melbourne, Ambronay and Beaune; opera performances include Bertarido in Rodelinda (Glyndebourne Touring Opera and at the Göttingen Handel Festival), Anfinomo in Il Ritorno d'Ulisse in Patria (Teatro Sao Carlos, Lisbon), Arsamenes in Xerxes (ENO), Athamas in Semele (Royal Opera House, Covent Garden) 2003; chamber music concerts with Concordia, Fretwork, Sonnerie, Palladian Ensemble; recitals at the Wigmore Hall, BBC Radio 3, in Karlsruhe, Innsbruck, Göttingen, Halle and many UK festivals; Prof. of Vocal Studies, Royal Coll. of Music. *Recordings:* over 40 albums, including Bach Cantata Cycle with Bach Collegium Japan and recitals with lute player, Elizabeth Kenny. *Current Management:* Caroline Phillips Management, The Old Brushworks, 56 Pickwick Road, Corsham, Wiltshire SN13 9BX, England. *Telephone:* (1249) 716716. *Fax:* (1249) 716717. *E-mail:* cphillips@caroline-phillips.co.uk. *Website:* www.caroline-phillips.co.uk/blaze.

BLEGEN, Judith; American opera and concert singer (soprano); b. 27 April 1941, Missoula, MT; m. 1st Peter Singher 1976 (divorced 1975); one s.; m. 2nd Raymond Gniewek 1977. *Education:* Curtis Institute of Music, Philadelphia, PA, Music Academy of the West, Santa Barbara, CA. *Career:* leading soprano, Nuremberg Opera, 1965–68, as Donizetti's Lucia and Strauss's Zerbinetta; Staatsoper, Vienna, 1968–70; Metropolitan Opera, New York, 1970–, debut as Mozart's Papagena; Vienna roles include Zerbinetta (Ariadne auf Naxos), Rosina (The Barber of Seville), Aennchen (Der Freischütz), Norina (Don Pasquale); Numerous performances at Metropolitan include Marzelline (Fidelio), Sophie (Werther), Sophie (Der Rosenkavalier), Adina (L'Elisir d'amore), Juliette (Roméo et Juliette); Other appearances include Susanna (The Marriage of Figaro), San Francisco, title role in Manon, Tulsa Opera, Gilda (Rigoletto), Chicago, Despina (Così fan tutte), Covent Garden, Blondchen (Die Entführung), Salzburg Festival, Mélisande (Pelléas et Mélisande), Spoleto Festival, Susanna (The Marriage of Figaro),

Edinburgh Festival, Sophie, Paris Opéra; Has sung and played the violin in Menotti's Help, Help, the Globolinks! (premiere, Hamburg); Sang the Marschallin at the Paris Opéra, 1977; Adele in Die Fledermaus at Brussels, 1986. *Recordings:* Numerous including La Bohème (Puccini), Carmina Burana (Orff), Symphony No. 4 (Mahler), Harmonienmesse (Haydn), The Marriage of Figaro (Mozart), A Midsummer Night's Dream (Mendelssohn), Lord Nelson Mass (Haydn), Gloria (Poulenc), Peer Gynt Suite (Grieg), Lieder recital (Richard Strauss and Hugo Wolf), Baroque music recital. *Honours:* Fulbright Scholarship; Grammy Awards. *Address:* c/o Thea Dispeker, 59 East 54th Street, New York, NY 10022, USA.

BLINKHOF, Jan; Singer (Tenor); b. 10 July 1940, Leiden, Netherlands. *Education:* Studied in Amsterdam, with Joseph Metternich in Cologne and with Luigi Ricci in Rome. *Career:* Debut: With Netherlands Opera, 1971, as Arturo in Lucia di Lammermoor; Holland Festival, 1971, in the premiere of Spinoza by Ton de Kruyf; Amsterdam, 1974, in the premiere of Dorian Gray by Kox; Geneva Opera, 1985, as Tristan; Nice, 1986, as Herman in The Queen of Spades; Sang Laca in Jenůfa at the Zürich Opera, 1986; Other roles include Ismaele in Nabucco; Boris in Katya Kabanova, and roles in Wozzeck, The Rape of Lucretia, The Gambler by Prokofiev and Henze's Der Junge Lord; Sang Tristan at Nice, 1986–87, Laca at Covent Garden, 1988; Deutsche Oper Berlin, 1988, as Sergei in Lady Macbeth of the Mtsensk District; Sang Boris in Katya Kabanova at Geneva and Florence, 1989; Albert Gregor in The Makropulos Case at Berlin, 1990, followed by Sergei in Hamburg and Laca (Jenůfa) at Barcelona; Season 1994 as Florestan at Lisbon and Sergei at Florence; Season 1996 as Luca in From the House of the Dead at Nice and Florestan in Fidelio at Rome; Laca at Hamburg, 1998; Calaf at Barcelona, 1999; Sang the Drum Major in Wozzeck at the Vienna Staatsoper (2000), Janáček's Laca and Shuisky in Boris Godunov at Hamburg. *Address:* c/o Deutsche Oper Berlin, Richard Wagnerstrasse 10, 1000 Berlin, Germany.

BLOCH, Augustyn; Composer; b. 13 Aug. 1929, Grudziądz, Poland. *Education:* Studied composition with Tadeusz Szeligowski and organ with Felik Raczkowski at Warsaw Conservatory. m. Halina Lukomska. *Career:* Music Consultant to the Polish Radio Theatre from 1954; mem, Polish Composers Union. *Compositions include:* Opera: Jephtha's Daughter, 1968; Children's Opera-Pantomime: Sleeping Princess, 1974; Musical: Tale of The Violin Soul, 1978; Ballet: Voci, 1967, Gilgamesh, 1968, The Looking Glass, 1975; Orchestral: Meditations for Soprano, Organ and Percussion, 1961, Dialogues for Violin and Orchestra, 1963, Enfiando for Orchestra, 1970, A Poem About Warsaw for Narrator, Chorus and Orchestra, 1974, Oratorio for Organ, Strings and Percussion, 1982, Abide with Us, Lord, for Orchestra, 1986, Exaltabo Te for Mixed Choir, 1988, Ostra Brama Litany for Choir and Orchestra, 1989, Trio for Violin, violoncello and Piano, 1992, Upwards for Orchestra, 1993, Scared Out, song for Baritone, Viola, Cello and Piano to a text by Else Lasker-Schüler; Die Verscheuchte for baritone, viola, cello and piano, 1995; Hac festa die for chorus, organ, period instruments and orchestra, 1996. *Recordings:* Bloch Plays Bloch; Thou Shalt Not Kill; Chamber Music. *Honours:* Cavalier's and Officer's Cross of The Rebirth of Poland, 1969 and 1979; Polish Composers Union Prize, 1981; Brighton Festival Prize, 1989. *Address:* Wybieg 14, 00 788 Warsaw, Poland.

BLOCHWITZ, Hans Peter; Singer (Tenor); b. 28 Sept. 1949, Garmisch-Partenkirchen, Germany. *Education:* Studied at Darmstadt, Mainz and Frankfurt. *Career:* Sang at first in concert, notably as the Evangelist in the St Matthew Passion and in Lieder recitals (Die schöne Müllerin by Schubert); Opera debut Frankfurt 1984, as Lensky; Sang in the Scala-staged version of the St Matthew Passion at San Marco, Milan, 1985; Théâtre de la Monnaie, Brussels, and Geneva 1986, as Don Ottavio and Lensky; Guest appearances in Hamburg, Amsterdam and London (Ferrando in Così fan tutte, 1989); Aix-en-Provence Festival 1987–89, as Belmonte and Ferrando; Sang Idamante in Idomeneo at San Francisco, 1989; Don Ottavio at the Metropolitan Opera, 1990; Sang in the Choral Symphony at the 1993 Prom Concerts, London; Wilhelm in Henze's Der Junge Lord, Munich, 1995; Flamand in Capriccio at Dresden, 1996; Title role in Il ritorno d'Ulisse in Patria, Athens, 1997; Mozart's Titus at Glyndebourne, 1999; Teaches at Musikhochschule, Bern. *Recordings include:* Bach St Matthew Passion; Bach Christmas Oratorio; Bach B-Minor Mass; Mozart Requiem; Mozart Die Zauberflöte; Mozart Don Giovanni; Mozart Così fan tutte; Mozart La Finta Semplice; Mozart C-Minor Mass; Mozart Coronation Mass; Beethoven Missa Solemnis; Beethoven Fidelio; Handel Theodora; Handel Messiah; Haydn Schöpfung; Mendelssohn Lobgesang Symphony; Mendelssohn St Paul; Schubert and Die schöne Magelone by Brahms. *Current Management:* Peter G. Alferink, Artists Management Amsterdam B.V., Apollolaan 181, 1077 AT Amsterdam, Netherlands. *E-mail:* alferink@worldonline .nl.

BLOMSTEDT, Herbert Thorson; Swedish music director and conductor; b. 11 July 1927, Springfield, MA, USA; m. Waltraud Regina Petersen 1955; four d. *Education:* diplomas in Music Education, 1948, Organist/Cantor, 1950, Orchestra Conductor, 1950, Royal Acad. of Music, Stockholm; Philosophy, Univ. of Uppsala, Sweden, 1952. *Career:* Music Dir, Norrköping Symphony Orchestra, Sweden, 1954–61; Prof. of Conducting, Royal Acad. of Music, Stockholm, 1961–70; Permanent Conductor, Oslo Philharmonic, 1962–68; Music Dir, Danish Radio Symphony Orchestra, Copenhagen, 1967–77, Dresden Staatskapelle, 1975–85, Swedish Radio Symphony, 1977–82, San Francisco Symphony, 1985–95; Music Dir, NDR Symphony Orchestra, Hamburg, 1996–98, Leipzig Gewandhaus Orchestra, Leipzig, 1998–. *Recordings:* over 120 albums, including Bruckner's 4th and 7th Symphonies (Staatskapelle Dresden), Complete Nielsen Symphonies (San Francisco Symphony); Strauss Ein Heldenleben; Hindemith Mathis der Maler Symphony, Trauermusik and Metamorphoses. *Publications:* Till Känndomen om J. C. Bach Symfonier, dissertation, 1951; Lars Erik Larsson och hans concertinor (co-author), 1957; numerous articles; musical score of Franz Berwald's Sinfonie Singulière (ed.), 1965. *Address:* c/o Rosenheimer Str. 52, 81669 Munich, Germany.

BLOOMFIELD, Arthur John, BA; American music critic and food writer; b. 3 Jan. 1931, San Francisco, CA; m. Anne E. Buenger 1956; one s. two d. *Education:* Stanford Univ.. *Publications:* Fifty Years of the San Francisco Opera, 1972; The San Francisco Opera 1922–78, 1978; Arthur Bloomfield's Restaurant Book, 1987; Sunday Evenings with Pierre Monteux, 1997; The Gastronomical Tourist, 2002; music critic for San Francisco Examiner, 1965–79; San Francisco correspondent for Opera, 1964–89; program notes, Music and Arts records, 1996–. *Address:* 2229 Webster Street, San Francisco, CA 94115, USA.

BLOOMFIELD, Theodore (Robert); Conductor; b. 14 June 1923, Cleveland, Ohio, USA. *Education:* Studied conducting with Maurice Kessler, piano training, BM, 1944, Oberlin College Conservatory of Music; Conducting with Edgar Schenkman, Juilliard Graduate School, New York; Piano with Claudio Arrau; Conducting with Pierre Monteux. *Career:* Debut: New York Little Symphony Orchestra, 1945; Apprentice conductor to George Szell and Cleveland Orchestra, 1946–47; Conductor, Cleveland Little Symphony Orchestra, Cleveland Civic Opera Workshop, 1947–52; Music Director, Portland (Oregon) Symphony Orchestra, 1955–59, Rochester (New York) Philharmonic Orchestra, 1959–63; First Conductor, Hamburg State Opera, 1964–66; General Music Director, Frankfurt am Main, 1966–68; Chief Conductor, (West) Berlin Symphony Orchestra, 1975–82. *Recordings:* For several labels. *Address:* c/o Das Sinfonie Orchester Berlin, Kurfurstendamm 225, 1000 Berlin, Germany.

BLUMENTHAL, Daniel; American pianist; b. 23 Sept. 1952, Landstuhl, Germany. *Education:* University of Michigan and at Juilliard, New York, 1975–77. *Career:* many performances in Europe and elsewhere in the solo and chamber repertory, notably French and American music; with the Piano Trio of La Monnaie, Brussels, premiered the G minor Trio of Debussy, 1985; other partners include Pierre Amoyal, Barry Tuckwell and the Orlando Quartet; Prof. of Piano, Flemish Conservatory, Brussels, 1985–. *Current Management:* Helen Jennings Concert Agency, 2 Hereford House, Links Road, London, W3 0HX, England.

BLUNT, Marcus, BMus; British composer and teacher; b. 31 Dec. 1947, Birmingham; m. Maureen Ann Marsh 1988. *Education:* Univ. Coll. of Wales. *Career:* compositions performed in at least 10 countries and on BBC Radio 3 and Classic FM; woodwind teacher 1976–; mem. British Acad. of Composers and Songwriters, Performing Rights Soc., Inc. Soc. of Musicians. *Compositions:* Symphony, The Rings of Saturn for Orchestra, Piano Concerto, Once in a Western Island... for violin and orchestra, Concerto Pastorale for oboe d'amore and strings, Aspects of Saturn for strings, Capricorn for 12 winds, Venice Suite for brass ensemble, The Throstle-Nest in Spring for octet, Cerulean for wind quintet, two string quartets, A Celebration of Brahms and Joachim for piano trio, Lorenzo the Much Travel'd Clown for bassoon and piano, The Life Force for piano. *Address:* Craigs Cottage, Lochmaben, Lockerbie, Dumfriesshire, DG11 1RW, Scotland. *E-mail:* marcusblunt@argonet.co .uk. *Website:* www.scottishmusiccentre.com/marcus_blunt.

BLYTH, Alan, MA; British music critic and editor; b. 27 July 1929, London, England; m. Ursula Zumloh. *Education:* Univ. of Oxford. *Career:* contributor as critic, The Times, 1963–76; Associate Editor, Opera, 1967–84; Music Editor, Encyclopaedia Britannica, 1971–76; Critic, Daily Telegraph, 1976–89; mem, Critics' Circle; Garrick Club. *Publications:* The Enjoyment of Opera, 1969; Colin Davis, A Short Biography, 1972; Opera on Record (editor), 1979; Remembering Britten, 1980; Wagner's Ring: An Introduction, 1980; Opera on Record 2 (editor), 1983; Opera on Record 3 (editor), 1984; Song on Record (editor), Vol. 1, 1986, Vol. 2, 1988; Choral Music on Record, 1990; Opera on CD, 1992; Opera on Video, 1995; Entries on Singers in the New Grove Dictionary (1980 and 2000); contrib. to Gramophone, BBC. *Address:* 22 Shilling Street, Lavenham, Suffolk CO10 9RH, England.

BLYTHE, Stephanie; Singer (Mezzo-soprano); b. 1970, Mongaup Valley, New York. *Education:* Crane School of Music, Potsdam, New York. *Career:* Metropolitan Opera from 1994 in Parsifal, as Mistress Quickly in Falstaff, Baba the Turk in The Rake's Progress and Cornelia in Handel's Giulio Cesare, 1999; Mascagni's Mama Lucia on tour to Japan, 1997; Lincoln Center recital debut, 1997; Season 1999–2000 as Mistress Quickly at the Opéra Bastille, Paris, Fricka in The Ring for Seattle Opera, Carmen with Tulsa Opera and Rossini's Isabella at Philadelphia; Concerts include Mahler 8 with the San Francisco Symphony Orchestra, 1999; Beethoven 9 with the Boston Symphony Orchestra; Schumann's Scenes from Faust in Paris; Messiah with the Minnesota and Florida Orchestras, 1999–2000; Covent Garden debut 2003, as Mistress Quickly in Falstaff, followed by Ino in Semele. *Honours:* Richard Tucker Career Grants, 1995–96. *Address:* c/o IMG Artists, Lovell House, 616 Chiswick High Road, London W4 5RX, England.

BO, Sonia; Composer; b. 27 March 1960, Lecco, Italy. *Education:* Graduated, Milan Conservatory, 1985, and studied further with Donatoni in Rome. *Career:* Teacher of composition at the Piacenza Conservatory. *Compositions:* Concerto for chamber orchestra, 1984; Come un'allegoria for soprano and ensemble, 1986; D'Iride for ensemble, 1988; Polittico, five songs with ensemble, 1992. *Honours:* Winner, 1985 Guido d'Arezzo International Competition. *Address:* c/o SIAE, Via della Letteratura n 30, 00101 Rome, Italy.

BOATWRIGHT, McHenry; Singer (Bass-Baritone); b. 29 Feb. 1928, Tennille, GA, USA. *Education:* Studied at the New England Conservatory; BM, 1950–54. *Career:* Debut: Jordan Hall, Boston, 1956; New York Town Hall debut in 1958; New England Opera Theater, 1958 as Arkel in Pelléas et Mélisande; Concert appearances with Charles Munch, Leonard Bernstein and other leading conductors; Sang with the Hamburg Staatsoper in contemporary works, notably in the 1966 premiere of Schuller's The Visitation at the Metropolitan Opera, 1967; Concert tour of the Far East and Europe in 1966; Sang at the funeral of Duke Ellington, 1974; Well known in Negro Spirituals. *Recordings:* La Damnation de Faust; Porgy and Bess. *Honours:* Marian Anderson Award, 1953, 1954; Winner, Arthur Fielder Voice Contest; Winner, National Federation of Music Clubs Competition, 1957.

BOBESCO, Lola; Violinist; b. 9 Aug. 1921, Craiova, Romania. *Education:* Studied with her father, Professor Aurel Bobescu. *Career:* Many solo appearances from 1934, appearing with such conductors as Kempe, Klemperer, Böhm and Ansermet; Chamber musician, and until 1979 leader of the Eugene Ysaÿe string orchestra; Professor at the Brussels Conservatoire. *Honours:* Prizewinner at the 1937 Eugene Ysaÿe Competition. *Address:* Conservatoire de Musique, 30 Rue de la Régence, Brussels, Belgium.

BOCELLI, Andrea; Italian singer (tenor); b. 22 Sept. 1958, Lajatico, Pisa; m. Enrica Bocelli; two c. *Career:* fmr lawyer. *Recordings:* albums: various music: Bocelli 1995, Romanza 1997, Sogno 1999, Cieli di Toscana 2001; opera: Viaggio Italiano 1995, Aria 1998, Sacred Arias 1999, Verdi 2000, La Bohème 2000, Verdi Requiem 2001, Sentimento (Best Album, Classical BRIT Awards 2003) 2002, Tosca 2003; numerous singles. *Current Management:* MT Opera and Blues Production and Management, via Irnerio 16, 40126 Bologna, Italy. *E-mail:* mtorped@tin.it. *Website:* www.andreabocelli.org.

BOCHKOVA, Irina; Violinist; b. 2 Nov. 1938, Moscow, Russia. *Education:* Studied in Kazan and at the Moscow Conservatoire, 1957–62. *Career:* Many appearances in Russia and Europe from 1962, notably as chamber music partner with Vladimir Krainev (piano) and Natalia Gutman (cello); Teacher at the Moscow Conservatory from 1978. *Honours:* Silver Medal, 1962 Tchaikovsky Competition, Moscow; Winner, 1963 Long-Thibaud Competition, Moscow. *Address:* c/o Moscow Conservatory, ul Gertzena 13, 103009 Moscow, Russia.

BODE, Hannelore; Singer (soprano); b. 2 Aug. 1941, Berlin, Germany; m. Heinz Feldhof. *Education:* Studied with Ria Schmitz-Gohr in Berlin, at the Salzburg Mozarteum, Fred Husler, Lugano, and Karl-Heinz Jarius, Frankfurt. *Career:* Sang in Bonn from 1964; Basle, 1967–68; Deutsche Oper am Rhein, Düsseldorf, from 1968, notably as Weber's Agathe, Wagner's Elsa, Eva, Elisabeth and Sieglinde; Kammersängerin, Nationaltheater, Mannheim, 1971–; Appearances in London, Buenos Aires, Washington, Vienna, Munich, Berlin; Bayreuth, 1969–80, as Elsa, Eva and in The Ring; Sang at Mannheim 1996, in Hannas Traum by Harold Weiss and 1998 as Leocadia Begbick in Weill's Mahagonny. *Recordings:* Parsifal; Die Meistersinger conducted by Solti; Die Meistersinger, conducted by Varviso; Trionfo d'Afrodite by Orff. *Address:* c/o Nationaltheater Mannheim, Goethestrasse, 68161 Mannheim, Germany.

BODIN, Lars-Gunnar; Swedish composer; b. 15 July 1935, Stockholm, Sweden. *Education:* studied with Lennart Wenstrom, visited Darmstadt. *Career:* composer-in-residence, Mills College, Oakland 1972 and Dartmouth College 1990; teacher, Stockholm College of Music 1972–76;

Dir of the Electronic Music Studio, Stockholm 1979–89; collaboration with Bengt Emil Johnson in text-sound compositions; mem. Royal Swedish Academy of Music 1978–89. *Compositions include:* Dance pieces, Place of Plays, 1967, and... from one point to any other point, 1968; Music for brass instruments, 1960; Arioso for ensemble, 1962; Semi-Kolon: Dag Knutson in Memoriam for horn and ensemble, 1962; Calendar Music for piano, 1964; My World in Your World for organ and tape, 1966; Primary Structures for bassoon and tape, 1976; Enbart for Kerstin for mezzo and tape, 1979; Anima for soprano, flute and tape, 1984; Diskus for wind quintet and tape, 1987; Electronic: Winter Events, 1967; Toccata, 1969; Traces I and II, 1970–71; Memoires d'un temps avant la destruction, 1982; For Jon II Retrospective Episodes, 1986; Wonder-Void, 1990; Divertimento for Dalle, 1991; Best Wishes from the Lilac Grove, 1994; Bobb—The Life Manager, 1997; Jenseits von Licht und Dunkel, 2000; Lipton's Adventures, 2002; Text-sound pieces. *Recordings:* En Face, 1990; The Pioneers, 1992. *Honours:* Rosenberg Prize, 1984; The Stockholm City Award, 1986; Atterberg Award, 2004. *Address:* Helgalunden 17, 11858 Stockholm, Sweden. *Telephone:* (8) 642-52-44 (home). *E-mail:* bodin.l-g@swipnet.se (home).

BODLEY, Seoirse; Composer; b. 4 April 1933, Dublin, Ireland. *Education:* Studied at the Royal Irish Academy and in Stuttgart with Johann Nepomuk David. *Career:* Associate Professor of Music at University College, Dublin. *Compositions:* 5 symphonies, 1959, 1980, 1981, 1990, 1991; 2 chamber symphonies, 1964, 1982; Piano concerto, 1996; Sinfonietta, 1998; Violin sonata, 1957; Scintillae for 2 harps, 1968; Two String quartets, 1969, 1992; Choruses and incidental music; Pax bellumque for soprano and ensemble, 1997; News from Donabate for piano, 1999. *Address:* c/o University College, Faculty of Music, Dublin, Ireland.

BODOROVA, Sylvie; Composer; b. 31 Dec. 1954, Ceske Budejovice, Czech Republic; m. Jiri Stilec, 10 Aug 1984. *Education:* Studied in Brno, Bratislava and Prague; Further study with Franco Donatoni in Siena. *Career:* Performances of works in London, Dresden and at the Prague Spring Festival; Teaching in CCM Cincinnati, Ohio, 1995–96; Quattro, Prague. *Compositions include:* Passion Plays for viola and orchestra, 1982; Pontem video for organ, percussion and strings, 1983; Canzoni for Guitar and Strings, 1985; Messagio, violin concerto, 1989; Magikon for oboe and strings, 1990; Panamody for flute and strings, 1992; Vocal and instrumental music, including Una volta prima vera, violin sonata, 1992; Dona Nobis Lucem, 1995; Concerto dei Fiori, 1996; Terezin Ghetto Requiem, 1997; Concierto de Estio, 1999; Saturnalia, 1999; Shofarot-String Quartet, 2000; Juda Maccabeus, 2002; Mysterium druidum for harp and strings 2003. *Recordings:* Prague Guitar Concertos; Pontem Video; Terezin Ghetto Requiem; Concierto de Estío; Juda Maccabeus. *Address:* Lidická 990, 253 01 Hostivice, Czech Republic. *E-mail:* jistilec@arcodiva.cz. *Website:* www.bodorova.cz.

BODY, Jack; Composer and Ethnomusicologist; b. 7 Oct. 1944, Te Aroha, New Zealand. *Education:* University of Auckland. *Career:* Taught at Indonesian Music Academy, 1976–77, and at Victoria University, Wellington, from 1980. *Compositions include:* Orchestra: Melodies, 1983, Little Elegies, 1985, Pulse, 1995, Carmen Dances, 2002; Piano: Four Stabiles, 1968, Five Melodies, 1982, Three Rhythmics (duet), 1986, Sarajevo, 1996; Choir: Carol to St Stephen, 1975, Five Lullabies, 1988; Voice: Love Sonnets of Michelangelo for soprano and mezzo-soprano, 1982; String Quartet; Three Transcriptions, 1987, Arum Manis (with tape), 1991, Campur Sari (with Javanese musician), 1996, Saetas, 2002; Electro-acoustic: Musik dari Jalan (Music from the Streets), 1975; Musik Anak-anak (Children's Music), 1978, Fanfares, 1981, Jangkrik Genggong, 1985, Vox Humana, 1991; Ensemble: Turtle Time, 1968, The Caves of Ellora, 1979, Interior (with tape), 1987, The Garden, 1996; Homage to the Blues, 2004; Opera: Alley, 1997. *Recordings:* Composer Portrait: Jack Body; Sacred and Profane; Pulse. *Publications include:* Editor, Waiteata Music Press, 1980–; Recordings of traditional music of Indonesia and China. *Honours:* Officer, NZ Order of Merit 2002; Winner, Bourges Competition for Electronic Music 1976, Laureate, NZ Arts Foundation 2004. *Address:* c/o School of Music, Victoria University of Wellington, PO Box 600, Wellington, New Zealand. *Telephone:* (4) 463-5853 (office). *Fax:* (4) 463-5157 (office). *E-mail:* jack.body@vuw.ac.nz.

BOE, Alfred; Singer (tenor); b. 1974, Fleetwood, Lancashire. *Education:* Royal College of Music and National Opera Studio, London; Vilar Young Artists' Programme, Covent Garden, 2001. *Career:* Performances with D'Oyly Carte Company from 1994; Concerts include Verdi Requiem, Rossini Petite Messe and Stabat Mater, Puccini Messa di Gloria and Elijah; Season 1999–2000 as Ernesto for Scottish Opera-Go-Round and Rodolfo for Glyndebourne Touring Opera; Season 2001–2002 engagements as Roderigo in Otello at La Monnaie, Brussels, Ferrando for Grange Park Opera, First Night of London Proms (2001) and Albert Herring at the 2002 Glyndebourne Festival. *Honours:* Prizewinner, Lyric Tenor of World Competition, Munich; Winner, John McCormack Golden Voice, Athlone, 1998. *Current Management:* Askonas Holt Ltd,

Lonsdale Chambers, 27 Chancery Lane, London, WC2A 1PF, England. *Telephone:* (20) 7400-1700. *Fax:* (20) 7400-1799. *E-mail:* info@ askonasholt.co.uk. *Website:* www.askonasholt.co.uk.

BOEHMER, Konrad; composer; b. 24 May 1941, Berlin, Germany. *Education:* Cologne Univ. *Career:* scientific asst, Utrecht Institute of Sonology 1966–68; fmr music ed., Vrij Nederland; teacher, Royal Conservatory, The Hague 1971; Dir, The Hague Inst. of Sociology 1993. *Compositions include:* Dr Faustus, Paris Opéra, 1985; Woutertje Pieterse, Stadsschouwburg Rotterdam, 1988 (premiere); Kronos protos for ensemble, 1995; Un monde abandonée des facteurs for 4 mezzos, 1996; Logos Protos (electronic) 2000; Circe et Circenses for five sopranos and pianos 2001. *Publication:* Schoenberg and Kandinsky, a historic encounter (ed.) 1994. *Honours:* Rolf-Liebermann Opera Prize (Hamburg) 1983. *Address:* Royal Conservatory of Music and Drama, Juliana van Stolberglaan 1, 2595 CA The Hague, Netherlands (office). *Telephone:* (70) 315-1466 (office). *E-mail:* boehmer@koncon.nl (office). *Website:* www.koncon.nl (office).

BOESCH, Christian; Singer (Baritone); b. 27 July 1941, Vienna, Austria. *Education:* Studied at the Vienna Hochschule für Musik. *Career:* Debut: Berne in 1966; Sang in Saarbrucken, Lucerne and Kiel; Joined Vienna Volksoper in 1975; Sang at Salzburg Festival in 1978 as Papageno in Die Zauberflöte, Metropolitan Opera from 1979 as Papageno, Masetto and Wozzeck, and as Papageno at the Théâtre des Champs Elysées, Paris in 1987; Often heard in modern repertoire; Sang in Wolf-Ferrari's La Donne Curiose at the Cuvilliés Theatre in Munich, 1989; Sang Wozzeck at Buenos Aires in 1989. *Recordings:* Die Zauberflöte; Il Prigioniero by Dallapiccola; Haydn's Die Feuersbrunst. *Address:* c/o Volksoper, Wahringerstrasse 78, A 1090 Vienna, Austria.

BOESE, Ursula; Singer (Mezzo-Soprano); b. 27 July 1928, Hamburg, Germany. *Education:* Studied at the Musikhochschule, Hamburg. *Career:* Began career as concert soloist; Bayreuth Festival, 1958–65, in Parsifal and Der Ring des Nibelungen; Hamburg Opera from 1960, notably in Handel's Giulio Cesare, with Joan Sutherland, 1969; San Francisco, 1968, in Oedipus Rex; Guest appearances in Milan, Rome, Buenos Aires, London, Paris and New York; Opera roles have included Gluck's Orpheus, Handel's Cornelia, Dalila, Gaea in Daphne, Jocasta, Verdi's Ulrica and Azucena and Wagner's Fricka, Erda, Waltraute and Magdalene; Schwetzingen Festival 1982, in the premiere of Udo Zimmermann's Die wundersame Schustersfrau; Often sang Bach in concert. *Recordings:* Christmas Oratorio by Bach; Der Evangelimann by Kienzi; Salome and Lulu; Parsifal and The Devils of Loudun. *Honours:* Kammersängerin, 1969. *Address:* c/o Hamburgische Staatsoper, Grosse-Theaterstrasse 34, 20354 Hamburg, Germany.

BOESMANS, Phillipe; Composer; b. 17 May 1936, Tongeren, Belgium. *Education:* Studied composition with Froidebise and Pousseur at Liège Conservatory, 1954–62. *Career:* Music producer for Belgian radio from 1961; Worked at Liège electronic music studios, Centre de Recherches Musicales de Wallonie, from 1971; Pianist with the Ensemble Musique Nouvelle. *Compositions:* Etude I for piano, 1963; Sonance for 2 pianos, 1964; Sonance II for 3 pianos, 1967; Impromptu for 23 instruments, 1965; Correlations for clarinet and 2 instrumental groups, 1967; Explosives for harp and 10 instrumentalists, 1968; Verticles for orchestra, 1969; Blocage for voice, chorus and chamber ensemble, 1970; Upon La, Mi for voice, amplified horn and instrumental group, 1970; Fanfare for 2 pianos, 1971; Intervalles I for orchestra, 1972, II for orchestra, 1973, III for voice and orchestra, 1974; Sur Mi for 2 pianos, electric organ, crotale and tam-tam, 1974; Multiples for 2 pianos and orchestra, 1974; Element-Extensions for piano and chamber orchestra, 1976; Doublures for harp, piano, percussion and 4 instrumental groups, 1977; Attitudes, musical spectacle for voice, 2 pianos, synthesizer and percussion, 1977; Piano Concerto, 1978; Violin Concerto, 1979; Conversions for orchestra, 1980; La Passion de Gilles, opera, 1983; Ricercar for organ, 1983; Reigen, opera, 1993; Summer Dreams for string quartet, 1994; Ornamental Zone for clarinet, piano, cello and viola; Wintermärchen, opera after Shakespeare, 1999. *Honours:* Italia Prize, 1971. *Address:* SABAM, Rue d' Arlon 75–77, 1040 Brussels, Belgium.

BOETTCHER, Wolfgang; Cellist; b. 1940, Berlin, Germany. *Education:* Hochschule der Kunste, Berlin. *Career:* Soloist, Berlin Philharmonic until 1976; Co-founder, Brandis String Quartet, 1976, with chamber music appearances in Munich, Hamburg, Milan, Paris, London and Tokyo including concerts with the Wiener Singverein and the Berlin Philharmonic; Festival engagements at Salzburg, Lucerne, Vienna, Florence, Tours, Bergen and Edinburgh; Co-premiered Helmut Eder's Clarinet Quintet, 1984, the 3rd Quartet of Gottfried von Einem, 1981, and the 3rd Quartet of Giselher Klebe, 1983; Founding member of the Philharmonische Solisten, Berlin; Concerto appearances with such conductors as Celibidache, Fischer-Dieskau, Lutoslawski, Karajan and Menuhin; Professor at the Hochschule der Kunste, Berlin. *Recordings include:* Albums in the standard repertoire from 1978, recent releases include quartets by Beethoven, Weill, Schulhoff and Hindemith and the

String Quintet by Schubert. *Honours:* Prizewinner, International ARD Competition in Munich. *Address:* c/o Konzert-Direktion Hans Adler (Brandis Quartet), Auguste-Viktoria-Strasse 64, D–14199 Berlin, Germany.

BOEYKENS, Walter; Clarinettist; b. 6 Jan. 1938, Bornem, Belgium. *Education:* Studied at the Brussels Conservatoire. *Career:* From 1964 soloist with the Belgian Radio Symphony and has appeared with many other leading orchestras throughout Europe; Chamber engagements with the Amadeus, Grumiaux and Via Nova Quartets; Premiered Domains by Boulez and works by Philippe Boesmans and Marcel Poot; From 1969 Teacher at Conservatories in Anvers and Utrecht. *Address:* c/o Utrecht Conservatorium, Mariaplaats 28, 3511 LL Utrecht, Netherlands.

BOGACHEV, Vladimir; Singer (Tenor); b. 1960, Moscow, Russia; Many appearances at the Bolshoi, Moscow and in Europe as Radames, Cavaradossi, Don José, Dmitri in Boris Godunov and Otello; Lensky in Eugene Onegin and Herman in the Queen of Spades, Montreal, 1990; Season 1993 with Otello at Orlando, Florida, Radames in Liège and Don Carlos in Portland; sang in Tchaikovsky's Iolanta at Dresden, staged by Peter Ustinov; Sang Aeneas in Les Troyens with the London Symphony Orchestra under Colin Davis at the Barbican Hall, London, 1993, repeated at La Scala, 1996; Season 1996 as Otello in Amsterdam, Calaf at the Macerata Festival and in Khovanshchina at Brussels; Many appearances on Russian broadcasting services; Sang Otello for the Royal Opera at the Albert Hall and Calaf at Dallas, 1997–98. *Address:* c/o Dallas Opera, The Centrum, 3102 Oak Lawn Avenue, Suite 450, LB–130, Dallas, TX 75219, USA.

BOGACHEVA, Irina; Singer (Mezzo-Soprano); b. 1940, Russia. *Career:* Appearances with the Kirov Opera, St Petersburg, from 1963 as Verdi's Amneris, Azucena, Ulrica and Eboli; Marina in Boris Godunov, Hélène in War and Peace, Konchakovna in Prince Igor, Lyubava in Sadko and Clarice in The Love for Three Oranges; Further engagements as Carmen, Dalila, Charlotte in Werther, Naina in Ruslan and Lyudmila, Grandmother in The Gambler and the Sorceress in The Fiery Angel; Guest appearances at the Opéra Bastille, Paris, New York Met and La Scala, Milan; Sang with the Kirov in Summer season at Covent Garden, 2000. *Honours:* Honoured Artist of Russia. *Address:* c/o Kirov Opera, Mariinsky Theatre, Mariinsky Square, St Petersburg, Russia.

BOGART, John-Paul; Singer (Bass); b. 17 Sept. 1952, USA. *Education:* Studied at Princeton, Yale and the Juilliard School. *Career:* Sang as child in production of Die Zauberflöte at the Metropolitan Opera; Sang at Santa Fe, Miami and Philadelphia; Dallas Opera as First Nazarene in Salome; La Scala Milan as Basilio in Il Barbiere di Siviglia; Vienna Staatsoper as Ramphis, Sarastro, Raimondo, Sparafucile and Colline; Basle Opera, 1984–85 as Mozart's Figaro and as La Roche in Capriccio; Paris Opéra Comique in 1985 in The Stone Guest by Dargomyzhsky; Théâtre Châtelet, Paris, in I Masnadieri by Verdi; Chicago Lyric Opera as Masetto in Don Giovanni; Baltimore Opera as Gremin in Eugene Onegin; Sang in the premiere of Célestine by Maurice Ohana at the Paris Opéra in 1988; Milwaukee in 1989 as Gounod's Mephistopheles; Lodovico in Otello at Lisbon in 1989; Bonn Opera 1994, as Alonso in Il Guarany by Gomes; Also heard as concert singer. *Recordings:* Zuniga in Carmen; Turandot; Chichester Psalms; L'Esule di Roma by Donizetti.

BOGATSCHOVA, Irina; Singer (Mezzo-Soprano); b. 2 March 1939, Leningrad, Russia. *Education:* Studied at the Leningrad Conservatory. *Career:* Sang at the Kirov Theatre, Leningrad, from 1965, and guested at the Bolshoi, Moscow, and abroad as Marina (Boris Godunov) and in Prokofiev's War and Peace (San Francisco, 1991); Sang the Countess in The Queen of Spades at Hamburg (1990), La Scala, Théâtre des Champs Elysées, Paris, Barbican Hall (1999) and elsewhere; Sang Saburova in Rimsky's The Tsar's Bride at San Francisco, 2000. *Recordings:* Several issues on Melodiya. *Address:* c/o Kirov Theatre, St Petersburg, Russia.

BOGIANCKINO, Massimo; Opera Director; b. 10 Nov. 1922, Rome, Italy; m. Judith Matthias, 1950. *Education:* Conservatory of Music and Santa Cecilia Academy, Rome; University of Rome; PhD. *Career:* Musicologist and Concert Pianist; Director, Enciclopedia dello Spettacolo, 1957–62; Director, Accademia Filarmonica, Rome, 1960–63; Director, Teatro dell'Opera, Rome, 1963–68; Artistic Director, Festival of Two Worlds, Spoleto, 1968–71; Director of Concert Programmes, Accademia di Santa Cecilia, Rome, 1970–71; Artistic Director, La Scala, Milan, 1971–74; General Manager, Teatro Comunale, Florence, 1974–82; Adminstrator General, Paris Opéra, 1982–85; In 1985 became Mayor of Florence. *Publications:* L'arte clavicembalistica di D Scarlatti, 1956; Aspetti del Teatro musicale in Italia e in Francia nell'eta Barocca, 1968; Le canzonette e i madrigali di V Cossa, 1981. *Honours:* Bundesverdienstkreuz, Federal Republic of Germany. *Address:* Théâtre National d'Opéra, Paris, France.

BOGUSLAVSKI, Igor; Russian violist and viola d'amore player; b. 18 July 1940, Moscow; m. Anna Litvinenko 1969; one d. *Education:* Gnesin

Academy of Music and Moscow Tchaikovsky Conservatory with V. Borissovski. *Career:* debut as viola soloist with Symphony Orchestra, conducted by Y. Aranovich, Moscow Conservatory; Appearances with BSO on Russian radio and television playing concertos by Hindemith including viola d'amore chamber music, Bartók and Berlioz; Principal viola soloist, Bolshoi Theatre Orchestra, 1977–; Professor, Russian Gnesin Academy of Music, 1977–; Only active soloist to give concerts on viola d'amore; Played with numerous conductors including Rozhdestvensky, Blazhkov, Fedosseev, Lazarev and Simonov, Aranovich and Dudarova; Repertory includes Bach, Purcell, Vivaldi, Mozart, Paganini, Brahms, Glinka, Schumann, Bartók, Tchaikovsky, Britten, Hindemith, Martinů, Milhaud, Shostakovich, Prokofiev, Schnittke, Denisov; Several works specially composed for him; Viola teacher, giving masterclasses and participating in festivals in France, Taiwan, USA and Japan; Recently has given world premieres of concertos for viola and orchestra by A. Holminov, A. Baltin, S. Kallosc, J. Butzko, Y. Grinstein and V. Bibik; also premieres of Paganini's Sonata for viola and strings in C major (new version for orchestra); Martini's Plaisir d'amore for viola d'amore and strings; Shostakovitch's Viola Sonata (version for viola and strings by P. Lando); Stravinsky's Russian Song for viola and strings; Grinstein's Concerto in Retro Style for viola and strings; Performed in Tchaikovsky Conservatory Great Concert Hall and Russian Composers' Union Concert Hall, both in Moscow. mem, Viola d'Amore Society of America; Jury Member, Tchaikovsky Competition, Moscow, competitions in Geneva, Munich, Markneukirchen. *Recordings:* Hindemith, Kammermusik No. 5, Der Schwanendreher, for viola and orchestra; Strauss, Don Quixote; Brahms, Two Sonatas for Viola and Piano; J C Bach, Viola Concerto; Paganini, Sonata for Grand Viola and Strings; Graupner, Concerto for Viola d'Amore, viola and strings; Glinka, Sonata for Viola and Piano; Denisov, Variations on a Choral Theme by J. S. Bach; Three Pictures by Paul Klee, for viola and instrumental ensemble; Schnittke, Suite in the Old Style for viola d'amore, harpsichord and percussion; Igor Boguslavski plays the viola and viola d'amore with Bolshoi String Orchestra, conducted by Pavel Lando; Over 60 recordings on discs, CD and from radio. *Publications:* Alfred Shnittke, Suite in the Old Style, Ed. of score for viola d'amore solo, cembalo, companelli, vibratono, campane and marimba. *Address:* Build 2, Apt 5, 30 Studencheskaya Street, Moscow 121165, Russia.

BOHAC, Josef; Composer; b. 25 March 1929, Vienna, Austria. *Education:* Pupil of Petrzelka, Janáček Academy of Music, Brno, 1951–56. *Career:* Director, Panton publishing concern, 1968–71; Head, Department of Music Broadcasts, Czech Television; Secretary, Union of Czech Composers, 1979–; Rumcajs, 1985. *Compositions:* Operas: The Wooing, 1967; The Eyes, 1973; Goya, 1971–76; Golden Wedding, 1981; Hidden Tears, 1994; Orchestral: Symphonic Overture, 1964; Fragment, 1969; Elegy for Cello and Chamber Orchestra, 1969; Dramatic Suite for Strings and Kettledrums, 1969–70; Blue and White, suite, 1970; February Overture, 1973; Piano Concerto, 1974; Concerto for Violin and Chamber Orchestra, 1978; Concertino Pastorale for 2 Horns and Orchestra, 1978; Concerto for Orchestra, 1983; Dramatic Variants for Viola and Orchestra, 1983; Alfresco, violin concerto, 1996; Partita Concertante, 1997; Capriccio Sinfonico, 1997; Chamber: String Trio, 1965; Sonetti per Sonatori for Flute, Bass Clarinet, Harpsichord, Piano and Percussion, 1974; Sonata Giovane for Piano, 1983; My Lute Resounds, monodrama for Tenor, Soprano and Nonet or Piano, 1971; 2 cantatas, 1976, 1979; Sonata Lirica for Soprano, Strings and Vibraphone, 1982; Vokální Poéma for chorus and ensemble, 1987. *Address:* c/o OSA, Cs Armady 20, 160–56 Praha, 6–Bubenec, Czech Republic.

BOHAN, Edmund, MA; Singer (tenor) and Writer; b. 5 Oct. 1935, Christchurch, New Zealand; m. Gillian Margaret Neason 1968; one s. one d. *Education:* Canterbury Univ., New Zealand; singing with Godfrey Stirling, Sydney, Eric Green and Gustave Sacher London. *Career:* oratorio debut 1956, opera debut 1962, New Zealand; repertoire of over 170 operas and major works including opera, oratorio, concerts in England, Europe, Australasia and Brazil; opera, English Opera Group, Dublin Grand Opera, London Chamber Opera, State Opera of South Australia, Canterbury Opera New Zealand; Wexford Festival, New Zealand International Festival of the Arts, Aldeburgh Festival, Norwich Triennial, Adelaide Festival; National Opera of Wellington, New Zealand; television includes Australian Broadcasting, BBC Proms, ABC, and New Zealand Radio; film, Barber of Seville; venues include Royal Festival Hall, Queen Elizabeth Hall and other major halls with Royal Philharmonic Orchestra, London Concert, BBC Concert and Ulster Orchestras; oratorio soloist with British, Australian and New Zealand Choral Societies. *Recordings:* A Gilbert and Sullivan Spectacular; When Song is Sweet; Sweet and Low; Gilbert and Sullivan with Band and Voice; The Olympians (Bliss) Intaglo. *Publications include:* biogs: Edward Stafford – New Zealand's First Statesman; Blest Madman – FitzGerald of Canterbury; To Be A Hero Sir George Grey; history: The Story So Far – A Short Illustrated History of New Zealand; 7 novels including A Present for the Czar; The Irish Yankee; The Matter

of Parihaka; The Dancing Man; The Opawa Affair. *Address:* 5 Vincent Place, Opawa, Christchurch, New Zealand.

BÖHM, Ludwig; Music Archivist, Author and Editor; b. 5 July 1947, Munich, Germany. *Education:* Universities of Munich and Würzburg. *Career:* Secondary School Teacher, English, French, Spanish, Munich, 1981–83; Founder: Theobald Böhm Archives, 1980, and Theobald Böhm Society, 1990; Organiser, Commemorative Concerts, 1981 1994 and 2006 and first International Theobald Böhm Competition for Flute and Alto Flute, 2006, in Munich. *Publications:* Complete Musical Works for Flute by Theobald Böhm (editor), 15 vols, 2005; Documentation about Theobald Böhm in 10 vols, 2005, (author, Vols 1 and 4–7, editor, Vols 2, 3 and 8–10): Vol. 1, Commemorative Publication on the Occasion of Böhm's 200th Birthday; Vol. 2, Letters to and Articles about Böhm concerning Flute Construction; Vol. 3, Letters to and Articles about Böhm not concerning Flute Construction; Vol. 4, Catalogue of the Concerts by and with Böhm (ca 120); Vol. 5, Catalogue of the Musical Works of Böhm (37 works with opus numbers and 54 arrangements without opus numbers); Vol. 6, Catalogue of the still existing Flutes of Böhm, (ca 225); Vol. 7, Commemorative Writing on the occasion of the 125th Anniversary of Böhm's Death, Vol. 8, Complete Letters and Articles by Böhm; Vol. 9, Five Publications on Flute Construction by Böhm; Vol. 10, Biographies of Böhm by Karl von Schafhäutl, Marie Böhm and Karl Böhm. *Address:* Asamstrasse 6, 82166 Gräfelfing, Germany.

BOHMAN, Gunnel; Singer (Soprano); b. 4 March 1959, Stockholm, Sweden. *Education:* Studied at the Opera School, Stockholm. *Career:* Engaged by Lorin Maazel for the Vienna Staatsoper; Sang at the Mannheim Opera as Pamina, Fiordiligi and Marenka in The Bartered Bride; Sang Pamina at the Bregenz Festival and appeared further in Vienna, Zürich, Houston and Hamburg as Mozart's Countess, Agathe, Micaela, Mimi and Lola; Sang in the Jussi Björling Memorial Concert in Stockholm, 1985, with Birgit Nilsson, Elisabeth Söderströ m, Nicolai Gedda and Robert Merrill; Bregenz Festival, 1985–86, as Pamina, Vienna Volksoper from 1987 (as Fiordiligi), Staatsoper from 1988; Zürich and Parma, 1987, as Smetana's Marenka and Gluck's Euridice; Glyndebourne Festival, 1989, as the Countess in Figaro (also at the Albert Hall); Sang Elisabeth in Tannhäuser at the 1996 Savonlinna Festival; Luisa Miller and Hanna Glawari at Frankfurt, 1996; Weber's Agathe, 1998; Sang Jenůfa for Flanders Opera 1999; Season 2000–01 as Luisa Miller, and the Daughter in Hindemith's Cardillac, at Frankfurt; Concert repertoire includes Bach's Passions, B minor Mass and Christmas Oratorio; Ein Deutsches Requiem and Requiems of Mozart and Dvořák; Haydn Die Schöpfung and Die Jahreszeiten; Strauss Vier Letzte Lieder and Wagner Wesendonck Lieder. *Honours:* Jenny Lind Fellowship, 1978. *Address:* Jungfrugatan 45, S–114 44 Stockholm, Sweden.

BOIS, Rob du; composer; b. 28 May 1934, Amsterdam, Netherlands. *Education:* studied piano and jurisprudence. *Compositions:* Orchestral: Piano Concerto, 1960, revised, 1968; Cercle for Piano, 9 Winds and Percussion, 1963; Simultaneous, 1965; Breuker Concerto for 2 Clarinets, 4 saxophones and 21 strings, 1968; A Flower Given to My Daughter, 1970; Le Concerto pour Hrisanide for piano and orchestra, 1971; Allegro for strings, 1973; 3 Pezzi, 1973; Suite No. 1, 1973; Violin Concerto, 1975; Skarabee, 1977; Zodiak, 1977; Concerto for 2 violins and orchestra, 1979; Sinfonia da camera for wind orchestra, 1980; Luna, for alto flute and orchestra, 1988; Elegia for oboe d'amore and strings, 1995; Chamber: 7 Pastorales, 1960–64; Trio for flute, oboe and clarinet, 1961; Rondeaux pour deux for piano and percussion, 1962, 2nd series for piano 4-hands and percussion, 1964; Chants et contrepoints, for wind quintet, 1962; Espaces à remplir for 11 musicians, 1963; Oboe Quartet, 1964; String Trio, 1967; Symposium for oboe, violin, viola and cello, 1969; Trio Agitate for horn, trombone and tuba, 1969; Reflexions sur le jour ou Perotin le Grand ressuscitera for wind quintet, 1969; Fusion pour deux for bass clarinet and piano, 1971; Tracery for bass clarinet and 4 percussionists, 1979; Sonata for violin and piano, 1980; Elegia for oboe d'amore, violin, viola and cello, 1980; String Quartet No. 3, 1981; Sonata for Solo Viola, 1981; Ars aequi for 2 double basses and piano, 1984; Autumn Leaves for guitar and harpsichord, 1984; Hyperion for clarinet, horn, viola and piano, 1984; Forever Amber for 2 guitars, 1985; Das Liebesverbot for 4 Wagner tubas; On a Lion's Interlude for alto flute, 1986; Symphorine for flute and string trio, 1987; 4 String Quartets, 1960–90; Gàberbocchus for 4 pianos, 1994; Fleeting for clarinet and ensemble, 1997; Songs for violin, cello and piano, 1998; Die Gretchenfrage for flute and piano, 2004. *Address:* Spruitenbosstraat 21, 2012 LJ Haarlem, Netherlands.

BOISSEAU, Pierrick; Singer (Baritone); b. 1970, France. *Education:* Conservatoire National de Région de Versailles; Royal College of Music with Ryland Davies. *Career:* Sang with Paris Opéra Boys Choir as a child; Les Chantres de la Chapelle, Centre for Baroque Music at Versailles, under Jean-Claude Malgoire, Christophe Rousset and Ton Koopman; Oratorio soloist in Paris, Athens, Morocco, USA and Malta;

Handel's Julius Caesar and Alcindoro in La Bohème, with the Centre de Formation Lyrique de l'Opéra Bastille; Season 2000–2001 in the St John Passion at St John's Smith Square, under Peter Schreier, and Lotario in Flavio, with the London Handel Festival. *Honours:* Lavoisier Scholarship and Audrey Sacher RCM Scholarship. *Address:* c/o Royal College of Music, Prince Consort Road, London SW7 2 BS, England.

BOISSY, Nathalie; Singer (Soprano); b. 1963, Beaune, Côte d'Or, France. *Education:* Studied at Colmar, Strasbourg, Paris and the Oberlin Conservatory, USA. *Career:* Sang at the Linz Opera from 1988, as Frau Fluth (Nicolai), Marzelline, the Countess in Roméo et Juliette, Mimi, Romilda in Xerxes, Micaela, Leila in Les Pêcheurs de Perles and the Infantin in Der Zwerg by Zemlinsky; Sang Micaela at Bregenz (1991) and in Mendelssohn's Elijah at Linz, 1991; Donna Anna at the Munich Gärtnerplatztheater, 1999. *Address:* c/o Landestheater, Promenade 39, 4010 Linz, Austria.

BOKES, Vladimir; Composer; b. 11 Jan. 1946, Bratislava, Slovakia; m. Klara Olejárová 1970; two s. one d. *Education:* Secondary Music School, Konzervatorium 1960–65; Acad. of Music, Vysoka skola muzickych umeni, Bratislava 1965–70. *Career:* teacher in Conservatory, Bratislava, 1971–75; Asst. Acad. of Music, Bratislava 1975, Docent 1988, Prof. 1993; mem. Union of Slovak Composers (pres. 1995–99), Slovak section of Int. Soc. for Contemporary Music, International Festival of Contemporary Music Melos-Ethos Bratislava (pres. 1993–97). *Compositions:* Symphony No. 1, 1970, No. 2, 1978, No. 3, 1980, No. 4, 1982, No. 5, 1987; Piano Concerto No. 1, 1976, No. 2, 1984; String Quartet No. 1, 1970, No. 2, 1974, No. 3, 1982; Wind Quintet No. 1, 1971, No. 2, 1975, No. 3, 1982; Piano Sonata No. 1, 1973, No. 2, 1979, No. 3, 1980, No. 4, 1985; Vocal cycles, Sposob ticha, The way of silence, 1977, and Na svoj sposob, In its own way. 1978; Music for Organ and Wind Instruments, 1986; Preludes and Fugues for pPiano, 1989; Missa Posoniensis for 4 soli, choir, organ and orchestra, 1991; Variations on a Theme from Jan Egry for 8 wind instruments, 1995; Commedia dell'arte, aria for tenor and piano, 1995; Divertimento for 4 wind instruments, 2001. *Recordings:* Variations on a Theme from Haydn for Piano, 1975; 1st Piano Concerto, 1978; 3rd Symphony, 1989; Sonata for Viola and Piano, 1993; Cadenza II, 2000; Music for Piano (Preludes and Fugues, Sonata No. 2 an No. 4), 2001; Inquieto for Clarinet and Piano, 2003. *Contributions:* to Hudobny zivot, Bratislava: Biennale Zagreb, 1977; Communicativity in Music, 1988; Music of Defiance (interview), 1990; to Slovenska hudba, Bratislava: Cantate Domino Canticum Sacrum, 1991; Interview with Vladimir Bokes, 2001. *Address:* Svoradova 5, 811 03 Bratislava, Slovakia.

BOLCOM, William; Composer; b. 26 May 1938, Seattle, Washington, USA; m. (1) Fay Levine, divorced 1967, (2) Katherine Agee Ling, divorced 1969, (3) Joan Morris, 28 Nov 1975. *Education:* BA, University of Washington, 1958; MA, Mills College, 1961; Paris Conservatoire de Musique, 1959–61, 1964–65; DMusArt, Stanford University, 1964; Piano studies with Berthe Poncy Jacobson; Composition studies with John Verrall, Leland Smith, Darius Milhaud, George Rochberg. *Career:* Acting Assistant Professor of Music, University of Washington, 1965–66; Lecturer, Assistant Professor of Music, Queen's College, City University of New York, 1966–68; Visiting Critic in Music Theatre Drama School, Yale University, 1968–69; Composer in Residence, New York University, School of the Arts, 1969–71; Assistant Professor, 1973, Associate Professor, 1977, Professor, 1983–, Ross Lee Finney Distinguished Professor of Composition, 1993–, School of Music, University of Michigan; Board, American Music Center; Charles Ives Society; American Composers' Alliance. *Compositions include:* 4 Violin Sonatas, 1956–94; 6 Symphonies, 1957–97; Concertos for piano, 1975–76, violin, 1983, clarinet, 1990; 10 String Quartets, 1950–88; 12 New Etudes for piano, 1977–86; Sonata for Cello and Piano, 1989; Casino Paradise, musical, 1990; McTeague, opera, 1992; A View from the Bridge, opera, 1999; Songs of Innocence and of Experience, 1956–82; Many more chamber, choral and orchestral works including Suite for violin and cello, 1997. *Publications:* Reminiscing with Sissle and Blake, 1973. *Contributions:* Grove's Dictionary; Contributing Editor, Annals of Scholarship. *Honours:* Kurt Weill Award for Composition, 1963; Guggenheim Foundation Fellow; Rockefeller Foundation Awards; NEA Grants; Pulitzer Prize for Music, 1988; American Academy of Arts and Letters, 1993; Henry Russel Lectureship, 1997. *Current Management:* ICM Artists, 40 W 57th St New York, NY 10019, USA. *Address:* 3080 Whitmore Lake Road, Ann Arbor, MI 48105, USA.

BOLDYREV, Vladimir; Baritone; b. 1955, Ukraine. *Education:* Studied at the Kharkov Institute of Arts. *Career:* Principal at the Kharkov Opera from 1985, notably as Don Giovanni, Germont, Rossini's Figaro, Escamilo, Eugene Onegin, Yeletsky, Silvio and Samson; Further opera and recital engagements in the USA, Germany, France and Italy; Repertoire includes songs by Rachmaninov, Glinka and Tchaikovsky, and Lieder by Mahler, Schubert and Schumann. *Honours:* Prizewinner at the 1987 All-Union Glinka Song Competition. *Address:* Sonata Ltd, 11 North Park Street, Glasgow G20 7AA, Scotland.

BOLGAN, Marina; Singer (Soprano); b. 20 March 1957, Mestre, Venice, Italy. *Education:* Studied at Conservatories in Venice, Siena and Rome. *Career:* Debut: Sang Rosina in various Italian cities, 1981; Sang Nannetta in Falstaff at the Teatro della Zarzuela, Madrid, 1982, and Gilda at Toulouse; Adina in L'Elisir d'amore, Venice, 1984; Bellini's Elvira at the Bregenz Festival, 1985; Paisiello's Nina at Catania; Annetta in Crispino e la comare by the brothers Ricci at Teatro La Fenice, Venice, and Théâtre des Champs Elysées, Paris; Elvira and Lucia, Zürich Opera, 1987, 1989; at the Hamburg Staatsoper, sang Adina and elsewhere in Donizetti's La Romanziera and Betly; Further appearances at Bologna, Verona and the Vienna Staatsoper (Lucia, 1988); Sang Selinda in Vivaldi's Farnace at the Valle d'Istria Festival, Martina Franca, 1991; Gnese in Wolf-Ferrari's Il Campiello at Trieste (1991) and Mascagni's Lodoletta at Mantua, 1994.

BOLKVADZE, Eliso; Pianist; b. 2 Jan. 1967, Tbilisi, Georgia. *Education:* Special School of Music, Tbilisi, 1972–84; Conservatoire Superieur in Tbilisi, 1984–89; Worked with Michel Sogny in Austria, 1989–92. *Career:* Debut: Concert Hall, Tbilisi; Herkules Saal, Munich; Alt Oper, Frankfurt; Auditorium Louvre, Salles Pleyel and Gaveau, Paris; Pasadena Hall, Los Angeles; Concert Hall, Chicago; Teatro Mauzoni, Milan; Schubert Hall, Vienna. *Recordings:* 4 albums recorded with orchestra in Tbilisi, 1994–96; Saint Petersburg, 2 albums at Villa Schindler, Austria. *Honours:* International piano competitions: 1st prize, Lisbon Vianna de Motta, 1987; Van Cliburn competition, 1989; 3rd prize, Dublin, 1987. *Current Management:* Michel Sogny. *Address:* Villa Schindler, Obermarktstrasse 45, 6410 Telfs, Tirol, Austria.

BOLLIGER, Phillip John; Australian composer and classical guitarist; b. 2 May 1963, Sydney, NSW. *Education:* Vienna Hochschule, University of Sydney, studied in Siena and Basle, and with Peter Sculthorpe. *Career:* freelance guitarist and private teacher; composer of film music 1991–. *Compositions include:* Inventions for guitar, 1986; The Birds of My Gully for flute, 1988; Sailing Song for piano, 1990; Four Greek Dances for two guitars, 1990; Romance for flute and orchestra, 1990; Three Preludes for guitar, 1992; Benedictus Balaenarum for trombone and piano, 1993; Requiem Chernobyl for choir and orchestra, 1993; Zagorsk for string quartet and piano, 1993; Monsoon for flute, 1997. *Honours:* First Prize, City of Sydney Eisteddfod, 1987; First Prize, Warringah Eisteddfod, 1992. *Address:* c/o APRA, 1A Eden Street, Crows Nest, NSW 2065, Australia.

BOLOGNESI, Mario; Singer (Bass-baritone); b. 1957, Rome, Italy. *Career:* Sang Apollo in Gagliano's Dafne, London, 1981; Season 1983–84: in Gli Orazi e i Curiazi by Cimarosa at Savona and in Gluck's Alceste at Bologna; Further early repertory includes Albinoni's Il nascimento dell' Aurora, Venice, 1984; Jommelli's La Schiava liberata, Naples; Agenore in Mozart's Il re Pastore, Rome, 1989; Season 1989 in the premiere of Manzoni's Doktor Faust at La Scala and Rossini's Basilio at Glyndebourne; Season 1994–95 in Rossini's Maometo II at La Scala, Bardolph at Navarra and as Lucarno in Poppea by Monteverdi; Season 1997–98: As Pasqua in Wolf–Ferrari's Il Campiello at Bologna and Spoletta in Tosca at the Verona Arena; Season 2000–01 at La Scala and Palermo, in Adriana Lecouvreur and Tosca. *Address:* c/o Teatro Comunale di Bologna, Largo Respighi 1, 40126 Bologna, Italy.

BOLTON, Ivor; Conductor; b. 17 May 1958, Lancashire, England. *Education:* Clare College, Royal College of Music, National Opera Studio. *Career:* Conductor, Schola Cantorum of Oxford; Glyndebourne, 1982–92; Conductor, Gluck's Orfeo, Glyndebourne, 1989, has led Il Barbiere di Siviglia, Die Zauberflöte, The Rake's Progress and La Bohème for the Touring Company; Music Director, Glyndebourne Touring Opera, La Clemenza di Tito, 1993–94; Founded St James Baroque Players, 1984, and directs annual Lufthansa Festival of Baroque Music at St James, Piccadilly; Music Director of English Touring Opera, 1990–93, leading Don Giovanni, Figaro, Lucia di Lammermoor, Così fan tutte, Die Zauberflöte, La Cenerentola and Carmen; Così fan tutte at the Aldeburgh Festival; English National Opera debut, with Xerxes, 1992; La Gazza Ladra for Opera North and Monteverdi's Poppea in Bologna, 1993; Season 1997 with Giulio Cesare, Serse and Poppea at the Munich Festival; Chief Conductor of the Scottish Chamber Orchestra from Aug 1994, regular concerts with the London Mozart Players, English Chamber Orchestra, Scottish Symphony, Bournemouth Sinfonietta and BBC Symphony; Engaged for Die Entführung at Geneva, 2000; Handel's Saul and Rodelinda (new productions) for the Bayerische Staatsoper, 2003. *Recordings include:* Bach's concertos for Harpsichord; Purcell's Dido and Aeneas; Brahms and Mendelssohn Violin Concertos; Vivaldi's Stabat Mater; Handel's Ariodante, from Munich, 2000. *Current Management:* Ingpen & Williams Ltd, 7 St George's Court, 131 Putney Bridge Road, London, SW15 2PA, England.

BONALDI, Clara; Violinist; b. 9 March 1937, Dombasle-sur-Mourthe, France. *Education:* Studied at the Paris Conservatoire (first prize for violin, 1955). *Career:* Many appearances at major festivals in France and elsewhere in Europe; Has edited for performance the sonatas of Francoeur and Tartini and partnered harpsichordist Luciano Scrizzi (pianist Noel Lee from 1980). *Honours:* Prizewinner at the 1955 Long-Thibaud Competition and at the 1963 Munich International (as piano duettist). *Address:* c/o Noel Lee, 4 Villa Laugier, 75017 Paris, France.

BONAZZI, Elaine; Singer (Mezzo-Soprano); b. 1936, Endicott, New York, USA. *Education:* Studied at the Eastman School of Music, Rochester, and at Hunter College, New York. *Career:* Santa Fe Opera from 1959, notably as Meg Page in Falstaff and in the 1961 US premiere of Hindemith's Neues vom Tage; Appearances in Cincinnati, Houston, Dallas, Pittsburgh, Mexico City, Vancouver and New York (City Opera); Caramoor Festival New York in Semele, 1969; Often heard in operas by Rossini and in contemporary music; sang the Marquise in La Fille du Régiment at St Louis, 1990; Sang Linfea in La Calisto for Glimmerglass Opera, 1996; Many engagements as concert singer; Taught at Peabody Conservatory, Baltimore; mem, American Academy of Teachers of Singing; National Association of Teachers of Singing. *Recordings:* La Pietra del Paragone by Rossini; Le Rossignol by Stravinsky. Honours Sullivan Foundation Grant, 1960; Concert Artists Guild Award, 1960; Eastman Alumni Award, 1972; Directors Recognition Award, Peabody Academy, 1989. *Address:* c/o Opera Theater of St Louis, PO Box 13148, St Louis, MO 63119, USA.

BONCOMPAGNI, Elio; Conductor; b. 8 May 1933, Arezzo, Italy. *Education:* Violin and Composition, Florence and Padua; Conducting in Perugia and Hilversum. *Career:* Debut: Bologna, 1962, Don Carlos; Conductor at opera houses in Europe, including Théâtre de la Monnaie, Brussels, from 1974; British debut, 1983, Cherubini's Médée at the Barbican Hall, London; Un Ballo in Maschera for Opera Montreal, 1990; conducted José Carreras concert at the Scottish Exhibition Centre, Glasgow, 1991. *Honours:* Prize, Italian Radio International Competition, 1961, and Mitropoulos Competition, New York, 1967. *Address:* c/o Opéra de Montreal, 1157 Rue Sainte Catherine E, Montreal, Quebec H2L 2G8, Canada.

BOND, Graham; Conductor; b. 20 March 1948, Blackburn, Lancashire. *Education:* Piano, trombone and cello, Royal College of Music, London; Accademia Chigiana, Siena. *Career:* Repetiteur, London Opera Centre, 1969–70; Conductor, London Festival Ballet, 1970–1975; Principal Conductor, London Festival Ballet, 1975–80; Music Director, London Festival Ballet, 1980–94; Many British, European and other world tours, 1970–79; Theatres and orchestras in France, Spain, Italy, Germany, China, Yugoslavia, Greece, Venezuela and Turkey; Two extensive tours of Australia and two long seasons in Paris with Nureyev, 1975 and 1977; Guest performances, 1978–81, Royal Theatre, Copenhagen; Stuttgart Ballet Company; Capetown Ballet Company; Conducting staff, Royal College of Music, London 1984; Series of concerts, St John's Smith Square, 1984–95; Monte Carlo Opera, 1984; Tivoli Symphony Orchestra, Copenhagen, 1985; Stanislavsky Theatre, Moscow, 1987; Turin Opera; Granada Festival; Guest Conductor, Hong Kong Philharmonic Orchestra, Hong Kong Festival, 1987; Also Champs Elysées Theatre, Paris, and the Teatro Massimo, Sicily; Deutsche Oper, Berlin, 1990; Guest Conductor, Bolshoi Ballet, during tour of England, 1991; Guest engagement, Durban, South Africa, 1992; Opera House, Budapest; Guest Conductor, Sofia Opera Orchestra, Athens Festival, 1993; Palacio de Bellas Artes, Mexico City, 1993; Appointed Chief Ballet Conductor, Royal Danish Ballet, Royal Theatre, Copenhagen, 1994–; Guest performances in 1994 in Prague, Bratislava, Sicily and Orange County, USA; Conductor, Peter Maxwell Davies's Caroline Mathilde ballet, Royal Opera House, London, 1995; The Love of Three Oranges, Royal Theatre, Copenhagen and Bergen Festival, 1996; Guest Conductor, Dutch National and Netherlands Dance Companies, 1996–97; Deutsche Oper, Berlin, 1997–98; Conductor, Peter Grimes, Royal Theatre, Copenhagen, 1997; Guest Conductor, London Royal Ballet, 1998 and Far East tour, 1999; Guest, Teatro Real, Madrid, 1998; The Magic Flute and Madama Butterfly, Royal Danish Opera, 1998. *Honours:* Worshipful Company of Musicians Medal, 1969; Hon RCM, 1994. *Address:* 8 Calverley Park Crescent, Tunbridge Wells, Kent TN1 2NB, England.

BOND, Timothy M.; Concert Organist and Lecturer; b. 21 July 1948, Mullion, Cornwall, England. *Education:* BMus, FRCO, ARCM, Royal College of Music, London, England. *Career:* Debut: Westminster Cathedral, 1974; British Premiere, Schoenberg's Sonata Fragment, 1974; Premieres at Henry Wood Proms of: Ligeti–Two Studies, 1976; Schoenberg-Variations on a Recitative, 1979; Messiaen-L'Ascension, 1981; Schoenberg Festival, Royal Festival Hall, 1989; Appearances at Festivals including: Aldeburgh, Huddersfield, Southampton, City of London, Normandy; For television: Ceremonies and Rituals, broadcast of Messiaen's L'Ascension; Many broadcasts of Modern Organ Music including: Schoenberg, Messiaen, Stockhausen, Berio, Pousseur, Goehr; British Premiere of original version of Schoenberg's Variations on a Recitative, 1974; Commission and Premieres of works specially written: Uccelli by John Lambert, 1992; Echo Toccata by John Lambert, 1993;

The Grass is Sleeping by Avril Anderson, 1979; Concerto for Organ and Orchestra: Crossing The Great Water, by David Sutton-Anderson, 1992; Lecturer, Royal College of Music, London. *Recordings:* Messiaen: L'Ascension; Quatre Méditations Symphoniques. *Contributions:* Musical Times, 1978. *Honours:* SPNM Young Artists and Twentieth Century Music, 1975. *Address:* Spreekenhorst, 27321 Bahlum, Germany.

BOND, Victoria, MMA, DMA; American conductor, composer and music director; *Artistic Director, Welltone New Music, Inc.;* b. 6 May 1945, Los Angeles, California; m. Stephan Peskin 1974. *Education:* Univ. of Southern California, Juilliard School, New York with Sixten Ehrling, Herbert von Karajan, Roger Sessions, Darius Milhaud and Ingolf Dahl. *Career:* Assistant Conductor, 1972–77: Juilliard Orchestra; Juilliard Contemporary Music Ensemble; American Opera Centre; Cabrillo Music Festival, California, 1974; White Mountains Music Festival, New Hampshire, 1975; Aspen Opera, Colorado, 1976; Colorado Philharmonic, 1977; Exxon, Arts Endowment Conductor, Pittsburgh Symphony (Previn), 1978–80; Music Director: Pittsburgh Youth Symphony Orchestra, 1978–80; New Amsterdam Symphony, 1978–80; Southeastern Music Centre, Georgia, 1983–85; Empire State Youth Orchestra, Albany, 1982–86; Conducting staff, Albany Symphony, 1983–85; Artistic Director, Bel Canto Opera Company, New York City, 1982–88; Music Dir Roanoke Symphony Orchestra, Virginia, 1986–95; Artistic Dir Opera Roanoke, 1989–95; Artistic Adviser, Wuhan Symphony, China, 1997–2002; Artistic Dir Harrisburg Opera, Pennsylvania, 1998–2003; Adjunct Asst Prof., New York Univ. 2001–; currently Artistic Dir Welltone New Music, Inc.; Guest Conducting includes: Houston Symphony; Richmond Symphony; Anchorage, Alaska; Radio Telefis Eireann, Ireland; Shanghai Symphony, China; 1998: Honolulu Symphony; Louisville Symphony; Flagstaff Symphony; Greenville Symphony; Hudson Valley Symphony; 1999–2001: York Symphony; Lancaster Symphony; Music From Penn's Woods; 2001–04: Central Opera, Beijing, China; Dallas Symphony; Center for Contemporary Opera; Da Corneto Opera Company; Ann Arbor Symphony; Norwalk Symphony Orchestra; Cleveland Chamber Symphony. *Compositions include:* Mrs Satan, opera; A Modest Proposal, tenor and orchestra; Black Light, piano concerto; Old New Borrowed Blues for Chamber Ensemble; From an Antique Land for Voice and Piano; Molly Manybloom; Urban Bird, saxophone concerto; Thinking Like a Mountain for Narrator and Orchestra; Dreams of Flying for String Quartet; Variations on a Theme by Brahms, orchestra, 1997; 3 Chinese Folksongs for soprano, tenor and orchestra, 1998; Travels, opera, 1994; Modest Proposal for tenor and orchestra, 1998; Ancient Keys, piano concerto no. 2; Mrs. Satan, opera no. 2; A More Perfect Union, opera no. 3; Dancing on Glass, string trio; Breath; Art & Science; Sacred Sisters; Elevator Music; But on the Other Hand; Moli Hua. *Recordings include:* American Piano Concertos; Delusion of the Fury; Notes from Underground; An American Collage; Black Light; Live from Shanghai; Victoria Bond: Compositions; Yes. *Publications:* The Orchestra at the Time of Mozart, 1977; The Opera Brahms Never Wrote, Opera News; New Music's Scholarly Friend, 1983; Granting Money, 1984; Music at Calloway Garden, 1989; Double Life, 1996; Towards Creating a Composer-Friendly Environment. *Honours:* Dr hc (Washington and Lee Univ., Va) 1994, (Hollins Coll.) 1995, (Roanoke Coll.) 1995; Woman of the Year (Virginia) 1990, 1991. *Current Management:* c/o Stephan Peskin, 20 Vesey Street, New York, NY 10007. *Address:* 256 West 10th Street, Apt 3B, New York, NY 10014, USA (home). *Telephone:* (212) 964-1390 (office); (212) 691-6858 (home). *Fax:* (212) 608-4959 (office); (212) 627-4258 (home). *E-mail:* stephanpeskin@yahoo.com (office); victoriabond@earthlink.net (home). *Website:* www.victoriabond.com (home).

BONDARENKO, Alexander; Violinist; b. 1950, Crimea, Russia. *Career:* Co-Founder, Rachmaninov Quartet, 1974, under the auspices of the Sochi State Philharmonic Society, Crimea; Concerts in the former Soviet Union and from 1975–76 tours to Switzerland, Austria, Bulgaria, Norway and Germany; Participant in 1976 Shostakovich Chamber Music Festival at Vilnius, and in festivals in Moscow and St Petersburg; repertoire has included works by Haydn, Mozart, Beethoven, Bartók, Schnittke, Shostakovich, Boris Tchaikovsky, Chalayev and Meyerovich. *Honours:* Prize, First All-Union Borodin String Quartet Competititon with the Rachmaninov Quartet, 1987. *Current Management:* Sonata, Glasgow, Scotland. *Address:* 11 North Park Street, Glasgow G20 7AA, Scotland.

BONDE-HANSEN, Henriette; Singer (Soprano); b. 3 Sept. 1963, Funen, Denmark. *Education:* Opera School of Copenhagen Opera until 1991. *Career:* Appearances with Jutland and Royal Copenhagen Operas as Susanna and Barbarina in Figaro, Musetta, and Adele in Die Fledermaus; Season 1994–95 with Jutland and Oslo Operas as Woodbird in Siegfried; Opéra du Rhin Strasbourg and at Brussels in Mozart's Zaide, 1995; Season 1996 as Sophie in Der Rosenkavalier at Stuttgart and Mozart's C Minor Mass with the Academy of St Martin's on tour to Germany; Season 1999–2000 as Adina at Toronto, Gounod's Juliette at Strasbourg, Marzelline in Fidelio at La Coruña (concert); Other concert repertory includes Bach St John Passion; Haydn's Seasons; Brahms' Requiem; Poulenc's Gloria. *Recordings:* Mahler's 8th Symphony. *Address:* c/o The Royal Opera, Copenhagen, Denmark.

BONELL, Carlos Antonio; classical guitarist; b. 23 July 1949, London, England; m. Pinuccia Rossetti; two s. *Education:* Royal College of Music. *Career:* debut in Wigmore Hall, London; Soloist with all the major British orchestras and many orchestras overseas; Founded, Carlos Bonell Ensemble, 1983; Frequent broadcaster; mem. Musicians Union; ISM. *Compositions:* Spanish Folk Songs and Dances; 20 First Pieces, 1984. *Recordings:* Fandango, 1976; Rodrigo Concierto de Aranjuez with Montreal Symphony Orchestra and Charles Dutoit, 1981; 20th Century Music for Guitar, 1987; The Sea in Spring, 1997. *Publications:* Airs and Dances of Gasper Sanz, 1977; The Romantic Guitar and The Classical Guitar, 1983; Tarrega: Fantasia and Purcell: 3 Pieces from the Fairy Queen; Masterclass on Playing The Guitar, 1983; 3 Spanish Folk Songs for 3 Guitars, 1984; The Technique Builder, 1997; contrib. to Guitar Magazine. *Honours:* Honorary Associate, Royal College of Music, 1978; Nomination for Best Chamber Music Performance for Record, John Williams and Friends, American National Academy of Recording Arts and Sciences, 1978; Nominated for Grammy Award; Hon RCM. *Address:* Conciertos Vitoria SL, Calle Sagasta 3–5 ext. Izda, 28004 Madrid, Spain.

BONETTI, Antoni (Robert); Violinist and Conductor; b. 6 Nov. 1952, London, England; m. Ruth Back, 16 Mar 1974, 3 s. *Education:* AMusA, DSCM, New South Wales Conservatorium, 1973; ARCM, 1978. *Career:* Violinist, Principal 2nd Violin, 1968–72, Australian Youth Orchestra; Tour to Japan, 1970, South East Asia, 1974; Freelance Violinist, London, 1975–76, appearing with Royal Philharmonic Orchestra, New Philharmonia Orchestra, London Mozart Players; Concertmaster, Norrlands Opera Orchestra, Sweden, 1976–77; Stockholm Ensemble, 1977–78; Conductor, Musik Sällskap, Umeå, 1978; Baroque Violin with Gammerith Consort, Austria, 1978; Member of Kurpfalzisches Kammerorchester, 1979–81; Concertmaster, Queensland Theatre Orchestra, 1981–84; Lecturer, Queensland Conservatorium of Music, 1982–92; Head of Orchestral Studies, St Peter's Lutheran College, 1985–; Conductor, Baroque Orchestra of Brisbane, Brisbane Christian Chamber Orchestra, 1986–89, Concert Society Orchestra, 1987–90; Extensive tours with Divertimento Bonetti ensemble throughout Europe; Various conducting engagements with Redcliffe City Choir, Cleveland Symphony Orchestra, Ipswich Youth Orchestra, 1989; Director and Founder, Brisbane Sinfonia, 1990–; Adjudicator, various Eisteddfods. *Compositions:* Jacaranda for orchestra, 1992. *Honours:* Fellowship, Australian Council for the Arts, 1974.

BONFATTI, Gregory; Singer (Tenor); b. 1964, Italy. *Career:* Debut: Don Ramiro in La Cenerentola at Spoleto, 1991; Many appearances throughout Italy and elsewhere in Europe in the bel canto repertory; Ravenna Festival as Paolino in Cimarosa's Il Matrimonio Segreto, Tebaldo (I Capuleti e i Montecchi) and Lindoro in L'Italiana in Algeri; Festival della Valle d'Itria, Macerata, as Don Rodrigo in Mercadante's Caritea, regina di Spagna; Pubblio in Pacini's L'Ultimo Giorno di Pompei, 1996; Monte Carlo Opera 1996 in Pagliacci, with Leo Nucci and Placido Domingo. *Recordings include:* Caritea, regina di Spagna, and L'Ultimo Giorno di Pompei (Dynamic). *Honours:* Winner, Singing Competition of Teatro Belle, Spoleto, 1991. *Address:* c/o Teatro Arena Sferisterio, Piazza Mazzini 10, 62100 Macerata, Italy.

BONIG, Andrea; Singer (Mezzo-soprano); b. 1959, Bamberg, Germany. *Education:* Studied with Donald Grobe in Berlin and in Basle and Frankfurt. *Career:* Many concert engagements in Germany and elsewhere, including Liszt's Legend of St Elizabeth with the Bamberg Symphony Orchestra; Donizetti's Requiem with the Berlin Philharmonic; Teatro Liceo Barcelona, 1990 as Dryad in Ariadne auf Naxos; Rossweise in Die Walküre in Valencia and Bonn, 1991–92; Berlin Staatsoper from 1996, including Flosshilde in Das Rheingold; Season 1997–98 with Hippolyta in A Midsummer Night's Dream at the Vienna Volksoper; Further concert repertory includes Beethoven's Ninth and Saint-Saëns's Christmas Oratorio. *Address:* c/o Volksoper, Wahringerstrasse 78, 1090 Vienna, Austria.

BÓNIS, Ferenc, DMus; Hungarian musicologist; *President, Ferenc Erkel Society;* b. 17 May 1932, Miskolc; s. of Jószef Bónis and Ilona Kelemen; m. Terézia Csajbók. *Education:* Ferenc Liszt Academy of Music, Budapest. *Career:* Music Producer, Hungarian Radio, 1950–70; Scientific Collaborator, Musicological Institute of Hungarian Academy of Sciences, 1961–73; Professor, Musicological Faculty, Ferenc Liszt Academy of Music, 1972–86; Editor, Magyar Zenetudomány (Hungarian Musicology), 1959–; Editor, Magyar Zenetörténeti Tanulmányok (Studies on History of Hungarian Music), 1968–; Editor, Complete Edition of B Szabolcsi's Works, 1977–; Leader, Music Department for Children and Youth, Hungarian Radio, 1970–94; Leading Music Producer, Hungarian Radio, 1994–96; mem, Gesellschaft für Musikforschung; President, Hungarian Kodály Society 1993; President, Ferenc Erkel Society 1989–.

Recordings: Editor, Early Hungarian Chamber Music; Works by P Wranitzky and L Mozart; Béla Bartók–As We Saw Him (recollections); Zoltán Kodály–As We Saw Him (recollections). *Publications include:* Mosonyi Mihály, 1960; G Mahler und F Erkel, 1960; Béla Bartók, His Life in Pictures and Documents, 1980; Zoltán Kodály, A Hungarian Master of Neoclassicism, 1982; Tizenhárom találkozás Ferencsik Jánossal (Meeting J Ferencsik), 1984; International Kodály Conference (with E Szönyi and L Vikár), 1986; Kodály Zoltán Psalmus Hungaricusa, commented facsimile edition, 1987; Harminchárom óra ifjabb Bartók Bélával (33 hours with B Bartók Jr), 1991; Hódolat Bartóknak és Kodálynak (Devotion to Bartók and Kodály), 1992; Bartók-Lengyel, A csodálatos mandarin, 1993; Himnusz (Hungarian National Anthem), facsimile edition, 1994; Igy láttuk Kodályt (3rd enlarged edition), 1994; Igy láttuk Bartókot (2nd enlarged edition), 1995; A Himnusz születése és másfél százada (The Birth of the Hungarian National Anthem and its 150 Years), 1995; Das leidende Volk und die unterdrückte Nation auf der ungarischen Opernbühne, 1995; Ein städtisches Fest und die Idee der Vereinigung: Budapest 1923, 1996; Brahms und die ungarische Musik, 1996; Heldentum und Sehnsucht nach Freiheit. Zur Frage Beethoven und die ungarische Musik, 1998; The Dance Suite of Béla Bartók, facsimile edition, 1998; Szabolcsi, Kodály and the Bach-theory of Reverend Werker, 1999; From Mozart to Bartók, 2000; In Memoriam Ferenc Farkas, 2001; Die Ungarn im Finale der Symphonie No. 4 von Brahms, 2001; Üzenetek a XX. századból (Messages from the 20th Century), 2002; Mihály Mosonyi, 2002; Bartók-Lengyel, The Miraculous Mandarin, 2002; Gondolatok Bartók zenekari Concertójáról (On Bartók's Concerto for Orchestra), 2004; A Budapesti Filharmóniai Társaság százötven esztendeje (150 Years of the Budapest Philharmonic Society), 2005. *Honours:* Ferenc Erkel Prize, 1973; Officer's Cross of Order of the Hungarian Republic, 1992; Honorary Freeman of F. Erkel's native town Gyula, 1999; Doctor of the Hungarian Acad. of Sciences, 2003. *Address:* Belgrád rakpart 27.I.5, Budapest 1056, Hungary (office). *Telephone:* (1) 337-9975 (office). *Fax:* (1) 337-9975 (office).

BONNEMA, Albert; Singer (Tenor); b. 18 April 1953, Trummarum, Netherlands. *Education:* Sweelinck Conservatory, Amsterdam and with Nicolai Gedda. *Career:* Sang in operettas by Lehar and Offenbach at Amsterdam and Enschede; Guest appearances in Berlin, Salzburg and Klagenfurt (Cassio in Otello, 1989); Lensky in Eugene Onegin at Berne; Giovanni in Mona Lisa by Schillings at Kiel and Walther in Die Meistersinger at Amsterdam, 1995; Števa in Jenůfa at Dresden, 1996; Season 1997–98 as Lohengrin at Tokyo and Števa at Hamburg; Season 2000–01 at Dresden as Števa in Jenůfa, Wagner's Erik and Apollo in Strauss's Daphne; Florestan at the Komische Oper Berlin, the Götterdämmerung Siegfried at Stuttgart, and Dmitri in Boris Godunov at Hamburg;Modern repertory includes Goldschmidt's Der gewaltige Hahnrei and Judith by Siegfried Matthus, both at Berne; Frequent concert appearances. *Address:* c/o Netherlands Opera, Waterlooplein 22, 1011 Amsterdam, Netherlands.

BONNER, Tessa; Singer (Soprano); b. 1955, England. *Education:* Studied at Leeds University and the Guildhall School of Music. *Career:* Solo singer and consort member of such groups as the Tallis Scholars, the New London Consort, the Lute Group, Gabrieli Consort, Taverner Consort and the Early Opera Project; Frequent appearances with Musica Secreta, notably at the Early Music Centre Festival, the Lufthansa Festival of Baroque Music, and at the National Gallery; Early Music Network Tour of Britain, Nov 1991, with programme Filiae Jerusalem (sacred music for women's voices by Monteverdi, Carissimi, Cavalli, Viadna, Grandi and Marco da Gagliano); Other repertoire includes works by Marenzio, Luzzaschi, Wert, Luigi Rossi and the women composers Francesca Caccini and Barbara Strozzi; Participation in lecture-recitals and workshops on performance practice and ornamentation. *Address:* Robert White Management, 182 Moselle Avenue, London N22 6EX, England.

BONNER, Yvette; Opera Singer (soprano); b. 1 Aug. 1973, Epping, England. *Education:* Arts Education School, London, 1984–90; Royal Acad. of Music, 1995–98; postgraduate vocal course, graduated Dip-RAM for performance. *Career:* debut as Yniold in Pelléas and Mélisande, for ENO; performances include Jennie Hildebrand in Street Scene with Houston Grand Opera, 1994; Flora in Turn of the Screw for WNO 1995; Shepherd Boy in Tannhäuser for Opera North, 1997; Semele in Die Liebe der Danaë, 1999; First Maid in Die Agyptische Helena; Debut for Royal Opera (in concert) as Hermione in Strauss's Die Agyptische Helena, 1998; Esmeralda in The Bartered Bride, 1999; Flora in The Turn of the Screw for WNO, 2000; Season 2001–02, premiere of Alice in Wonderland, title role, for Nederlandse Opera; Esmeralda in The Bartered Bride for Royal Opera, Covent Garden; Genevieve in Siruis on Earth for Almeida Opera; El Trujaman in El Retablo De Maese Pedro, London Proms, 2002; Vixen in The Cunning Little Vixen, Aix en Provence Festival and tour 2002–03; concert work includes Les Illuminations, The Acad. of St Martin in the Fields, Carmina Burana, The Symphony Hall, Birmingham, Bach Magnificat and Vivaldi Gloria for The English Chamber Orchestra, Haydn's Nelson Mass at St John's, Smith Square. *Recordings:* Weill's Street Scene (Joan), with ENO, 1989; Emmie in Albert Herring, 1996; Die Liebe der Danae. *Honours:* Blyth-Buesst Operatic Prize, 1998; Emmy Destinn Award for Young Singers, for Czech opera and song, 2000. *Current Management:* Helen Sykes Artists Management, 100 Felsham Road, Putney, London SW15 1DQ, England.

BONNEY, Barbara; Singer (soprano); b. 14 April 1956, Montclair, New Jersey, USA; m. Hakan Hagegard (divorced). *Education:* Studied in Canada and at the Salzburg Mozarteum with Walter Raninger. *Career:* Debut: Darmstadt 1979, in Die Lustigen Weiber von Windsor; Sang at Darmstadt as Blondchen in Die Entführung, Cherubino in Le nozze di Figaro, Nathali in Henze's Der Prinz von Homburg and Massenet's Manon; Appeared at Frankfurt, Hamburg and Munich 1983–84; Covent Garden 1984 as Sophie in Der Rosenkavalier: Returned as Blondchen, 1987; La Scala Milan 1985, as Pamina; Schwetzingen Festival 1985 as Handel's Semele; Season 1987–88 as Sophie in Monte Carlo, Pamina at Geneva, Adina at Lausanne and Susanna at Zürich; Metropolitan 1989–90, as Adele in Fledermaus, Sophie in Der Rosenkavalier, 1991; Chicago Lyric Opera debut 1989, as Adele; Concert appearances include the Monteverdi Vespers at Copenhagen, 1990; Sang in Mozart Bicentenary Gala at Covent Garden, 1991; Mozart's Coronation Mass and Solemn Vespers at the 1993 Prom Concerts, London; Mozart's Susanna at the Metropolitan, 1997 and 2000; Soloist in centenary performance of the Brahms Requiem, Vienna Musikverein, 1997; Alphise in Les Boréades by Rameau at the 1999 London Prom concerts; masterclasses at Covent Garden, 2003. *Recordings:* Moses und Aron by Schoenberg and Haydn's Lord Nelson Mass; Lortzing's Zar und Zimmermann; Video of Messiah; Im Chambre Séparée 2003. *Current Management:* IMG Artists, Lovell House, 616 Chiswick High Road, London W4 5RX, England.

BONYNGE, Richard; Opera Conductor; b. 29 Sept. 1930, Sydney, New South Wales, Australia; m. Joan Sutherland, 1954, 1 s. *Education:* Trained as pianist; Specialist in bel canto repertoire. *Career:* Debut: As Conductor, with Santa Cecilia Orchestra, Rome, 1962; Conducted first opera, Faust, Vancouver, 1963; Has conducted in most world leading opera houses and at Edinburgh, Vienna and Florence Festivals; Has been Principal Conductor and Artistic/Musical Director of companies including Sutherland/Williamson International Grand Opera Company, 1965, Vancouver Opera, 1974–78, Australian Opera, 1976–86; Conducted Les Huguenots for Australian Opera, 1989 (Joan Sutherland's Farewell), Maria Stuarda at Sydney, 1992; Conducted La Fille du Régiment at Monte Carlo, 1996. Caterina Cornaro at the Queen Elizabeth Hall, 1998. *Recordings:* Opera including: Bellini's Beatrice di Tenda, Norma, I Puritani, La Sonnambula; Delibes' Lakmé; Donizetti's L'Elisir d'amore, La Fille du Régiment, Lucia di Lammermoor, Lucrezia Borgia, Maria Stuarda; Gounod's Faust; Handel's Alcina and Giulio Cesare; Léhar's Merry Widow; Leoni's L'Oracolo; Massenet's Esclarmonde, Le Roi de Lahore and Thérèse; Meyerbeer's Les Huguenots; Mozart's Don Giovanni; Offenbach's Les Contes d'Hoffmann; Puccini's Suor Angelica; Rossini's Semiramide; Strauss's Die Fledermaus; Thomas's Hamlet; Verdi's I Masnadieri, Rigoletto, La Traviata and Il Trovatore; Ballet including: Adam's Le Diable à Quatre, Giselle; Auber's Marco Spada; Burgmuller's La Péri; Chopin's Les Sylphides; Delibes' Coppelia, Sylvia; Massenet's Le Carillon, La Cigale; Offenbach's Le Papillon; Rossini-Respighi's La Boutique Fantastique; Strauss's Aschenbrödel; Tchaikovsky's The Nutcracker, Sleeping Beauty, Swan Lake; Recent recordings include: Le Domino Noir and Le Toréador (Adam), Paganini and Giuditta (Lehar), Carmelites, Lucrezia Borgia, Norma and Lakmé (all videos) and Cendrillon by Isouard; Others include recital with Sutherland, Tebaldi, Tourangeau and Pavarotti and many orchestral and ballet anthologies;. *Contributions:* Hard Work and Discipline (article on career) Opera Magazine, November 1998. *Current Management:* Ingpen & Williams Ltd, 7 St George's Court, 131 Putney Bridge Road, London, SW15 2PA, England.

BOOGAARTS, Jan; Dutch university lecturer, choir director, organist and composer; b. 10 May 1934, Helmond; m. Dorine Sniedt 1964; two s. one d. *Education:* Conservatory of Tilburg, Royal Conservatory, The Hague, Institute of Musicology, University of Utrecht. *Career:* radio recordings for BBC, various Dutch Radio stations, Sud Deutscher Rundfunk, ORTF, France, Culture France, Radio DDR, Radio Warsaw, Poland, Belgian Radio; Television: NOS KRO (Holland Festival), Warsaw Poland; Docent Choir Direction, Royal Conservatory, The Hague; Lecturer at University Utrecht; Visiting Professorships throughout Europe and America. *Recordings:* 30 including Plainsong, Holy Week, Ordo Missae Instauratus Concilii Vaticani II, Vespers, Compline; Missa Ambrosiana, Famous Hymni and Sequentiae; Renaissance Music: Madrigals and Chansons with texts by Petrach and Ronsard; Works of R White, Josquin, Lassus, Isaak, Senfl and others. *Publications:* Inleiding tot het Gregoriaans 1985; contrib. many articles to period Festschrift and small publications, magazines and journals.

Address: Havezate Die Magerhorst, Ploenstraat 48, Duiven, 6921 PN, Gelderland, Netherlands.

BOONE, Charles; Composer; b. 21 June 1939, Cleveland, Ohio, USA. *Education:* Pupil of Karl Schiske, Vienna Academy of Music, 1960–61; Received private instruction from Ernst Krenek and Adolph Weiss, Los Angeles, 1961–62; Studied theory at the University of Southern California, Los Angeles, BM, 1963 and composition at San Francisco State College, MA 1968. *Career:* Chairman, San Francisco Composers' Forum; Co-ordinator, Mills College Performing Group and Tape Music Center; Composer-in-Residence, Berlin, under the sponsorship of the Deutscher Akademischer Austauchdienst, 1975–77; Writer and Lecturer on contemporary music. *Compositions:* 3 Motets for Chorus, 1962–65; Oblique Formation for Flute and Piano, 1965; Starfish for Flute, Clarinet, 2 Percussions, 2 Violins and Piano, 1966; A Cool Glow of Radiation for Flute and Tape, 1966; The Edge of the Land for Orchestra, 1968; Not Now for Clarinet, 1969; Zephyrus for Oboe and Piano, 1970; Vermilion for Oboe, 1970; Quartet for Clarinet, Violin, Cello and Piano, 1970; Chinese Texts for Soprano and Orchestra, 1971; First Landscape for Orchestra, 1971; Vocalise for Soprano, 1972; Second Landscape for Chamber Orchestra, 1973, also for Orchestra, 1979; String Piece for String Orchestra, 1978; Streaming for Flute, 1979; Little Flute Pieces, 1979; Springtime for Oboe, 1980; Winter's End for Soprano, Countertenor, Viola da Gamba, and Harpsichord, 1980; Slant for Percussion, 1980; The Watts Tower for 1 Percussion, 1981; Trace for Flute and 10 Instruments, 1981–83; Solar One for Flute and Trumpet, 1985; The Timberline and Other Pieces for Carillon, 1987; Morphosis for 6 Percussion, 1997. *Honours:* National Endowment for the Arts Grants, 1968, 1975, 1983; Commissions. *Address:* 37003 Gravstark Street, Houston, TX 77006, USA.

BOOTH, Juliet; Singer (Soprano); b. 1961, London, England; m. William Symington, 1 June 1996. *Education:* Studied at Bristol University and the Guildhall School of Music. *Career:* Opera North from 1987, Frasquita (debut role), Ninetta in The Love for Three Oranges, Xenia in Boris Godunov; Pusette in Manon, Arminda in La Finta Giardiniera, Norina in Don Pasquale and Lauretta; Has also sung Mélisande in Aldeburgh, Virtu and Valletto in Opera London's L'Incoronazione di Poppea and Mozart's Countess for Welsh National Opera; Aix-en-Provence, 1991, as Helena in A Midsummer Night's Dream; Concert appearances at the South Bank and the Barbican, in France, Belgium and Singapore; Handel's Solomon in Berlin and Carmina Burana at the Edinburgh Festival under Neeme Järvi; Television appearances include Dennis O'Neill and Friends on BBC 2; Season 1990–91 with The Kingdom (Elgar), Haydn's Nelson Mass and Creation, Salieri's Prima la Musica with the City of London Sinfonia; Concert arias with the English Chamber Orchestra; Messiah; Gilda in Rigoletto, Opera North, 1992; Countess in Figaro, Glyndebourne Touring Opera, 1992; Morgana in Alcina, Covent Garden debut, 1992; Musetta and Mimi in La Bohème, Opera North, 1993; Alexina in Le Roi malgré Lui, 1994. *Recordings include:* L'Incoronazione di Poppea conducted by Richard Hickox (Virgin Classics); Bruckner Mass in F, Hyperion, 1992. *Honours:* Gold Medal for Singers, Schubert Prize for Lieder and the Ricordi Opera Prize, at the Guildhall School. *Current Management:* IMG Artists Europe. *Address:* c/o Opera North, Grand Theatre, 46 New Briggate, Leeds, Yorkshire, LS1 6NU, England.

BOOTH, Philip; Singer (Bass); b. 6 May 1942, Washington, DC, USA. *Education:* Sang with US Army Chorus, then studied further at the Eastman School of Music, with Julius Huehn, and with Todd Duncan in Washington. *Career:* Kennedy Center, Washington, 1971, in Ariodante; Many appearances as concert singer; Engagements at the opera houses of San Diego, Houston and San Francisco; Metropolitan Opera from 1973, as Pimen in Boris Godunov, Ramphis, Fasolt and Fafner in Der Ring des Nibelungen, Basilio and Osmin; Sang in the US premiere of Mascagni's Le Maschere, with Westchester Opera, 1989. *Address:* c/o Metropolitan Opera, Lincoln Center, New York, NY 10023, USA.

BOOTH-JONES, Christopher, ARAM; Singer (baritone); b. 4 Oct. 1943, Somerset, England; m. Leonora, 2 s., 1 step-s., 3 step-d. *Education:* Dover Coll., Royal Acad. of Music, London. *Career:* toured with Welsh National Opera for All as Mozart's Figaro and Rossini's Bartolo, 1972–73; Welsh National Opera, Figaro in Mozart's Marriage and Bohème; Glyndebourne Festival and Touring Opera; Phoenix Opera; English Music Theatre; London Musical Theatre Co; Narrator in Brecht's Caucasian/Chalk circle, Newcastle Festival; English National Opera from 1982 in Roméo et Juliette, Patience, Così fan tutte, Pagliacci, La Bohème, War and Peace, Osud, Akhnaten and Xerxes; Sang Claudio in a new production of Beatrice and Benedict, 1990; Mr Astley in a revival of The Gambler; English Music Theatre in Tom Jones, La Cenerentola and The Threepenny Opera; Die Zauberflöte; Opera North in Der Freischütz, A Midsummer Night's Dream, Beatrice and Benedict and Danilo in The Merry Widow; Kent Opera as Monostatos in Die Zauberflöte; Season 1992 with English National Opera in the premiere of Bakxai by John Buller and as the Music Master in Ariadne auf Naxos; Demetrius in A Midsummer Night's Dream, Count in The Marriage of Figaro and Schaunard in La Bohème, 1996; Season 1998 as Ford in Falstaff and Puccini's Sharpless for ENO; Germont Père in La Traviata, 1997, 1998, 1999; Sang Melot in Tristan und Isolde, Carmen and Die Frau Ohne Schatten (Strauss) for the Royal Opera in London, 2000. *Recordings:* Julius Caesar and Pacific Overtures; Tosca; Videos of The Gondoliers, Princess Ida, Rusalka, Xerxes, Billy Budd and Carmen. *Current Management:* Helen Sykes Artists Management, 100 Felsham Road, Putney, London SW15 1DQ, England.

BOOTHBY, Richard; British viola da gamba player and cellist; b. 1955, England. *Career:* Member of the Purcell Quartet, debut concert at St John's Smith Square, London, 1984; Extensive tours and broadcasts in France, Belgium, Netherlands, Germany, Austria, Switzerland, Italy and Spain; Tours of the USA and Japan, 1991–92; British appearances include 4 Purcell concerts at the Wigmore Hall, 1987, later broadcast on Radio 3; Repertoire includes music on the La Folia theme by Vivaldi, Corelli, C P E Bach, Marais, A Scarlatti, Vitali and Geminiani; Instrumental works and songs by Purcell, music by Matthew Locke, John Blow and Fantasias and Airs by William Lawes; 17th century virtuoso Italian music by Marini, Buonamente, Gabrieli, Fontana, Stradella and Lonati; J. S. Bach and his forerunners: Biber, Scheidt, Schenk, Reinken and Buxtehude; Member of Fretwork, debut concert at the Wigmore Hall, 1986; Appearances in the Renaissance and Baroque repertoire in Sweden, Austria, Belgium, Netherlands, France and Italy; Tour of Soviet Union, Sept 1989, Japan, June 1991; Gave George Benjamin's Upon Silence at the Queen Elizabeth Hall, 1990; Wigmore Hall concerts, 1990–91, with music by Lawes, Purcell, Locke and Byrd; Other repertory includes In nomines and Fantasias by Tallis and Parsons, dance music by Holborne and Dowland (including Lachrimae), London Cries by Gibbons and Dering, Resurrection Story and Seven Last Words by Schütz. *Recordings include:* With the Purcell Quartet: On the La Folia theme; Purcell Sonatas for 2 violins, viola da gamba and continuo; Sonatas by Vivaldi and Corelli; Series of 10 recordings with Fretwork. *Address:* Wigmore Hall (Contracts), Wigmore Street, London W1, England.

BOOZER, Brenda (Lynn); Singer (Mezzo-soprano); b. 25 Jan. 1948, Atlanta, Georgia, USA; m. Robert Martin Klein, 29 April 1973. *Education:* BA, Florida State University, Tallahassee, 1970; Postgraduate studies, Juilliard School, New York, 1974–77. *Career:* Chicago Lyric Opera, 1978; Festival of Two Worlds, Spoleto, Italy, 1978, 1979; Greater Miami Opera, 1979; Houston Grand Opera, 1979; Metropolitan Opera, New York, 1979–83, 1985, as Hansel, Meg Page, the Composer (Ariadne auf Naxos), Octavian and Orlofsky; Netherlands Opera, Amsterdam, 1981; Paris Opéra, 1982–83; Falstaff, at Covent Garden, 1983; Spoleto Festival, 1989, as Nicklausse in Les Contes d'Hoffmann; Concerts; Television appearances. *Honours:* Recording of Falstaff with the Los Angeles Philharmonic was nominated for a Grammy Award in 1984. *Address:* c/o Columbia Artists Management Inc, 165 West 57th Street, New York, NY 10019, USA.

BORDAS, Ricard; Singer (Countertenor); b. 1965 Barcelona, Spain. *Education:* Studied with Charles Brett at the Royal Academy of Music. *Career:* Proms debut in the St Matthew Passion under Joshua Rifkin, 1994; Carmina Burana at La Scala and the Granada Festival and Bach's Magnificat at the Barbican, London; London Handel Festival as Siroe and in Alexander's Feast; Ottone in Handel's Agrippina for Midsummer Opera and Scarlatti's Mitridate at the Schwetzingen Festival, 1996; Jonathan Miller's staged St Matthew Passion, tour of Dido and Aeneas in Mexico and Monteverdi's Poppea with Netherlands Opera; Season 1996–97 as Selino in Cesti's L'Argia at Innsbruck, the Monteverdi Vespers in Ripon Cathedral and Handel's Israel in Egypt at Bristol; Sang Valentiniano in Handel's Ezio at Halle, 1998. Music Director of Camerata Hispanica in London and the Group Vocal Odarum in Barcelona; Guest teacher at major London colleges. *Honours:* Shinn Fellowship, at the RAM.

BORETZ, Benjamin (Aaron); Composer, Music Theorist, Teacher and Writer on Music; b. 3 Oct. 1934, New York, NY, USA. *Education:* Piano and cello study; Training, conducting from Julius Rudel, harpsichord from Erwin Bodky; BA, Brooklyn College, 1954; Manhattan School of Music, New York; MFA, Brandeis University, 1957; Aspen Music School; University of California, Los Angeles; MFA, 1960, PhD, 1970, Princeton University; Composition teachers included Irving Fine, Harold Shapero, Arthur Berger, Darius Milhaud, Lukas Foss, Roger Sessions. *Career:* Consultant, Writer, Fromm Music Foundation, 1960–70; Founding Co-Editor, 1961–64, Editor, 1964–84, 1993–95, Perspectives of New Music; Music Critic, The Nation, 1962–70; Teacher, including New York University, 1964–69, Columbia University, 1969–72, Bard College, 1973–; Distinguished Visiting Professor, University of California, Los Angeles, 1991; Visiting Professor, University of California, Santa Barbara, 1991; Invited, Interdisciplinary Conference, Calgary, 1991; Co-Editor, The Open Space magazines, 1998–. *Compositions include:* Concerto grosso, string orchestra, 1956; Violin

concerto, 1956; Divertimento, 5 instruments, 1957; String Quartet, 1958; Group Variations I, orchestra, 1967, II, computer, 1971; Liebeslied, piano, 1974;. . . my chart shines high where the blue milk's upset. . ., piano, 1978; Passage for Roger Sessions, piano, 1979; Language, as a Music, 6 Marginal Pretexts for Composition, speaker, piano, prerecorded tape, 1980; Soliloquy I, piano, 1981; Soundscore works; Scores for Composing series, 1991–93; Music/Consciousness/Gender sound/video, 1995; Echoic/Anechoic, piano, 1997; Black/Noise I, II, III, (video and computer sound) 1997–98; Camille, video piece, 1997; UN (-) for orchestra, 1999. *Recordings include:* An Experiment in Reading, 1981; One (exercise) 8 piano solo sound sessions, Open Space, 1992; Open Space, 1993. *Publications include:* Edited with Edward T Cone: Perspectives on Schoenberg and Stravinsky, 1968, 2nd edition, 1972; Perspectives on American Composers, 1971; Perspectives on Contemporary Music Theory, 1972; Perspectives on Notation and Performance, 1976; If I am a Musical Thinker, 1981; Language as a Music, 1985; Music Columns from the Nation, 1962–1968, 1989 Open Space, 1991; Meta-variations: Studies on the Foundations of Musical Thought, 1994. *Contributions:* Professional magazines and journals. *Address:* 29 Sycamore Drive, Red Hook, NY 12571, USA.

BOREYKO, Andrey; Conductor, Composer and Teacher; b. 22 July 1957, St Petersburg, Russia; m. Julia Wolk 1990; one d. *Education:* conducting and composition with Elisabeta Kudriavzeva and Alexander Dimitriev, Rimski-Korsakov Conservatory. *Career:* debut as conductor, aged 20; founder, Dir, Res Facta early music group, Leningrad 1977, Barocco Consort, Leningrad 1984; Conductor, St Petersburg Theatre of Music 1985–86; Prin. Conductor, State Symphony Orchestra of Ulyanovsk, Russia, and Chamber Music Theatre 1987–89; Gen. Music Dir, Ural Philharmonic Orchestra, Yekaterinenburg 1990–92; Artistic Dir, Chief Conductor, Poznan Philharmonic Orchestra, Poland 1992–95; Prin. Assoc. Conductor, Russian Nat. Orchestra 1998–2001; Chief Conductor, Gen. Music Dir Jenaer Philharmonie, Prin. Guest Conductor Vancouver Symphony, 1998–2003; Music Dir, Winnipeg Symphony Orchestra 2001–02; Chief Conductor, Hamburger Symphoniker, First Guest Conductor, SWR Radio Symphony Orchestra, Stuttgart, 2004–05; int. guest performances and concerts with Deutsches Symphonie-Orchester Berlin, Gewandhausorchester Leipzig, Württembergisches Staatsorchester Stuttgart, SWR Radio Symphony Orchestra Stuttgart, Bamberger Symphoniker, NDR Symphony Orchestra Hamburg, Hamburger Symphoniker, Radio Symphony Orchestra Berlin, Radio Symphony Orchestra Frankfurt, Nationaltheater Orchester Mannheim, Dresdner Philharmonie, Symphony Orchestra of the MDR Leipzig, Cologne Gürzenich Orchester, Beethoven Orchester Bonn, Orchestre de la Suisse Romande, Basle Symphony Orchestra, Stockholm Royal Philharmonic, Malmö Symphony, Bergen Philharmonic, Trondheim Symphony Orchestra, Royal Flanders Philharmonic Orchestra, Belgian Nat. Orchestra, Philharmonia Orchestra, BBC Symphony Orchestra London, St Petersburg Symphony Orchestra, Prague Symphony Orchestra FOK, Orchestra del Maggio Musicale Fiorentino, Danish Nat. Orchestra, Oslo Philharmonic, Warsaw Philharmonic Orchestra, Polish Nat. Radio Orchestra, Symphony Orchestras of Montréal, Toronto, Detroit, San Diego, Sydney, Melbourne, Brisbane, Adelaide, Chamber Orchestra of the Kremerata Baltica, Amsterdam Sinfonietta, Royal Concertgebouw Orchestra Amsterdam, Berliner Philharmoniker, Chicago Symphony Orchestra, Münchner Philharmoniker, and others; guest at festivals in the Netherlands, Germany, Austria, Switzerland, Belgium, Italy, France and the USA; repertoire puts particular emphasis on contemporary Russian composers, including Sofia Gubaidulina, Gija Kantsheli, Valentin Silvestrov, Alexander Raskatov and Leonid Desyatnikov; engagements in 2004–06 include conducting the Chicago Symphony Orchestra, the Münchner Philharmoniker, the Pittsburgh Symphony Orchestra, the Vienna Radio Symphony Orchestra and the Gulbenkian Orchestra Lisbon, tours of the USA with the Czech Philharmonic, and of Germany with the Junge Deutsche Philharmonie, and the gala concert of the 70th anniversary of the Jenaer Philharmonie. *Recordings:* Silvestrov, Monadia, Sinfonie No. 4, 1992; Silvestrov, Sinfonie No. 5, 1992; A Ginastera, Ballettmusik, Philharmonie Poznan, 1993; Takemitsu, Nostalgie für Violine und Orchester, 1998. *Honours:* hon. conductor, Jenaer Philharmonie, best concert programme from Deutscher Musikverleger-Verband 1999–2000, 2001–02, 2002–03. *Current Management:* Monica Ott, Berliner Konzertagentur, Dramburger Str. 46, 12683 Berlin, Germany. *Telephone:* 5144858. *Fax:* 5142659. *E-mail:* BerlinKonzert.ott@t-online.de. *Website:* www.BerlinKonzert-ott.de.

BORG, Matti; Composer and Opera Singer (Baritone); b. 1956 Copenhagen, Denmark; Gitta-Maria Sjoberg, 1 July 1989, 1 s. *Education:* Theory of Music, University of Copenhagen, 1975–78; Diploma in Composition, 1983, Diploma in Solo Singing, 1987, Royal Conservatory of Denmark. *Career:* Debut: Copenhagen, 1987; Appeared as soloist in concerts in Scandinavia and on television and radio; Opera debut in Sweden, Norrlandsoperan; Works performed in Sweden, Norway, Denmark, Belgium, Spain and Canada; mem, Danish Composers' Society.

Compositions: Choral works, chamber music and songs, music for theatre, musicals; Symboise for mixed choir and solo instruments, 1979; Thirteen ways of looking at a blackbird, trio for soprano, flute and piano, 1981; Recollection, string quartet, 1983; Musicals: What are we dreaming of, 1986; Irene and her men, 1991; Fabliau, for female voice and 12 celli, 1995; Poems by Mörike, for mixed choir, 1997. *Address:* Obdams Allé 24, DK 2300 Copenhagen S, Denmark.

BORGIR, Tharald; Musicologist (Keyboard); b. 27 Dec. 1929, Gjerpen, Norway; m. 5 Sept 1951, 3 s., 1 d. *Education:* Music Conservatory, Oslo, 1951; MM, Yale University, USA, 1960; PhD, University of California, Berkeley, 1971. *Career:* Debut: Piano, Oslo, 1957; Teaching, 1967–93, Professor, 1987–, Chair, 1987–92, Oregon State University, Corvallis, USA; Numerous appearances on piano, harpsichord, fortepiano; mem, Greenberg Award Committee, American Musicology Society; College Music Society; Early Music America. *Publications:* The Performance of the Basso Continuo in Italian Baroque Music, 1987, paperback, 1988. *Address:* Department of Music, Oregon State University, Corvallis, OR 97331, USA.

BORISENKO, Vera; Singer (Mezzo-Soprano); b. 16 Jan. 1918, Goel, Russia. *Education:* Studied in Gomel and at the Minsk Conservatory; Further study in Kiev with Evtushenko and in Moscow and Sverdlovsk. *Career:* Sang at Sverdlovsk, 1941–45, Kiev, 1945–46, Bolshoi Theatre, Moscow, 1946–65, notably as Lyubava in Sadko, Lyubasha in The Tsar's Bride and Bonny Spring in The Snow Maiden; Other roles included Marfa in Khovanshchina and Carmen; Guest with the Bolshoi in Paris 1969, as Larina in Eugene Onegin; Gave concert performances from the 1960s. *Recordings include:* The Snow Maiden, Prince Igor, Dargomyzhsky's Rusalka, Tchaikovsky's The Enchantress, Rimsky's May Night, Carmen (title role) and Rigoletto (Maddalena). *Address:* c/o Bolshoi Theatre, Pr Marxa 8/2, 103009 Moscow, Russia.

BORISOVA, Rosa; Cellist; b. 1960, Moscow, Russia. *Education:* Central Music School, Moscow. *Career:* Co-Founder, Quartet Veronique, 1989; Concerts in Russia, including Russian Chamber Music Series and the 150th birthday celebrations for Tchaikovsky, 1990; Masterclasses at the Aldeburgh Festival, 1991; Concert tour of the United Kingdom in season, 1992–93; Repertoire includes works by Beethoven, Brahms, Tchaikovsky, Bartók, Shostakovich and Schnittke; Resident Quartet, Milwaukee University, USA, 1993–94. *Recordings include:* Schnittke's 3rd Quartet. *Honours:* With the Quartet Veronique: Winner, All-Union String Quartet Competition in St Petersburg, 1990–91; Third Place, 1991 International Shostakovich Competition at St Petersburg; Participated in Evian and London Quartet Competitions, 1994. *Current Management:* Sonata, Glasgow, Scotland. *Address:* 11 North Park Street, Glasgow G20 7AA, Scotland.

BORK, Robert; Singer (Baritone); b. 1959, Chicago, Illinois, USA. *Education:* Studied at Wheaton College, Illinois and at the Cologne Opera Studio. *Career:* Sang at Cologne from 1987, notably as Hummel in Reimann's Gespenstersonate, as Tarquinius in The Rape of Lucretia, Papageno, Belcore, Escamillo, Tsar Peter (Lortzing) and Schaunard in La Bohème; Dörfling in Der Prinz von Homburg by Henze, Cologne, 1992; Sang Donner in Das Rheingold at Toulouse and Redburn in Billy Budd at the Vienna Staatsoper, 2001; Concerts include The Raft of the Medusa by Henze, Bach's B Minor Mass and St Matthew Passion, Ein Deutsches Requiem and Mahler's 8th. *Address:* c/o Oper der Stadt Köln, Offenbachplatz, W-5000 Cologne 1, Germany.

BORKH, Inge; Singer (Soprano); b. 26 May 1917, Mannheim, Germany; m. Alexander Welitsch. *Education:* Studied first as an actress in Vienna; Vocal studies with Muratti in Milan, and at the Salzburg Mozarteum. *Career:* Debut: Lucerne in 1940 as Agathe; Sang in Switzerland until 1952, notably as Magda Sorel in The Consul by Menotti; Bayreuth in 1952 as Freia and Sieglinde; US debut at San Francisco in 1953 as Elektra; Guest appearances in Vienna, Hamburg, Stuttgart, Barcelona, Lisbon and Naples; Florence in 1954 as Eglantine in Euryanthe; Salzburg Festival in 1955 in the premiere of Irische Legende by Egk; La Scala Milan debut in 1955 as Silvana in La Fiamma by Respighi; Cincinnati in 1956 in Britten's Gloriana; Metropolitan Opera in 1958 and 1961 as Salome and Elektra; Covent Garden in 1959 and 1967 as Salome and the Dyer's Wife in Die Frau ohne Schatten; Academy of Music in New York 1968 in the US premiere of Orff's Antigonae; Other roles included Lady Macbeth by Verdi and Bloch, and Turandot; Resumed career as an actress in 1977 appearing at the Hamburg Schauspielhaus; Autobiography, Ich Komm' vom Theater nicht los, 1996. *Recordings:* Turandot; Antigonae; Die Frau ohne Schatten; Elektra; Salome; Das Rheingold; Euryanthe.

BORKOWSKI, Marian; Teacher and Composer; b. 17 Aug. 1934, Pabianice, Poland. *Education:* MA, Academy of Music, Warsaw, 1959–65; MM, Warsaw University, 1959–66; Postgraduate studies with Nadia Boulanger and Olivier Messiaen, Paris Conservatory; Musicology with Jacques Chailley and Barry S Brook, Paris University; Philosophy with Jean Hyppolite and Jules Vuillemin, Sorbonne and

Collège de France, 1966–68; Master's courses: International Courses of New Music, Darmstadt, 1972, 1974; Accademia Musicale Chigiana, Siena, 1973, 1975, studied with Franco Donatoni, Diploma with distinction, 1975. *Career:* Assistant Lecturer and Senior Assistant Lecturer, Department of Composition, 1967–71, Assistant Professor of Composition, 1971–76, Associate Professor, 1976–, Vice-Dean, Faculty of Composition, Conducting and Music Theory, 1975–78, Vice-Rector, 1978–81, 1987–, Artistic Director, Laboratory of New Music, 1985–, Chopin Academy of Music, Warsaw; Concert, radio and television performances; Performances at numerous international festivals. *Compositions include:* Spectra, 1980; Dynamics, 1981; Mater mea for mixed choir a cappella, to words by Krzysztof K Baczynski, 1982; Apasionate, 1983, Avante, 1984; Concerto, 1985–86; Pax in terra I, 1987, II, 1988. *Recordings:* Numerous. *Contributions:* Numerous critiques in magazines and newspapers. *Address:* ul Galczynskiego 5 m 17, 00-362 Warsaw, Poland.

BORNEMANN, Barbara; Singer (Mezzo-Soprano); b. 8 March 1955, Dingelstadt, Germany. *Education:* Studied in Weimar and at the Hanns Eisler Musikhochschule Berlin, with Hannelore Kuhse. *Career:* Debut: Halberstadt, 1978, as Olga in Eugene Onegin; Sang at Halberstadt until 1981, at Schwerin, 1981–86; Member of the Berlin Staatsoper from 1986; Further appearances in Dresden, Leipzig Czechoslovakia, Poland and Japan; Bayreuth Festival, 1990 as Mary in Der fliegende Holländer; Geneviève in Pelléas et Mélisande in Berlin, 1991; Sang Gaea in Strauss's Daphne (concert performance) Rome, 1991; Other roles include Mozart's Marcellina, Verdi's Ulrica and Mistress Quickly, Wagner's Magdalene and Fricka; Season 1994–95 as Cimarosa's Fidalma in Berlin and in Lulu at Salzburg; Housekeeper in Die schweigsame Frau at Dresden, 1998; Concert repertoire includes Bach's Christmas Oratorio and St John Passion, the Mozart and Verdi Requiems, Mendelssohn's Elijah and St Paul, Mahler's Kindertotenlieder. *Address:* c/o Deutsche Staatsoper Berlin, Unter den Linden 7, 1087 Berlin, Germany.

BÖRNER, Klaus; pianist, conductor, composer and academic; b. 22 June 1929, Senftenberg, Germany; m. Helga Kibat 1958; one s. one d. *Education:* Weimar Academy of Music, Lausanne Conservatoire de Musique, masterclasses with Alfred Cortot, Edwin Fischer, Wilhelm Kempff. *Career:* debut, Weimar, Mozart Piano Concerto E flat major K482, conductor Carl Ferrand, 1950; concerts as Pianist, 70 countries, solo recitals or with orchestra, Berlin, Düsseldorf, Bamberg, Lima, Guatemala, elsewhere; chamber music with Melos String Quartet, Mich-Goldstein, others; festivals include Berlin, Madrid, Bad Hersfeld, New Zealand; radio, television; taught, Düsseldorf Conservatory, 1956–69; founder, Acting Director, International Music Summer Camp, Sylt, Germany, 1959–89; Professor, Mainz University, 1969–97; Guest Professor, Hong Kong, Japan, Indonesia, New Zealand; Juror, national and international competitions. *Compositions:* Trio, horn, violin, piano, 1961; 3 Lieder, soprano, piano, 1990; Fantasie über eine Phantasie, Hommage à Mozart, piano 4 hands, 1993; Quartet, 4 bassoons, 1997. *Recordings:* Handel Chaconne G; J. S. Bach Partita E minor; Haydn Sonatas, C minor, C# minor; Beethoven Sonatas, A major op 2,2, G major op 31,1; Schumann Papillons op 2; Kreisleriana op 16. *Publications:* Klavierschulen für den Aufangsunterricht–Eine vergleichende Analyse 1978, Piano Duet Repertoire (ongoing). *Address:* Nibelungenstr 38, 41462 Neuss, Germany.

BORODINA, Olga; Singer (mezzo-soprano); b. 29 July 1963, St Petersburg, Russia. *Education:* Studied in St Petersburg and San Francisco. *Career:* Tours with the Mariinsky Opera, St Petersburg, to Europe and the USA, including Marfa in Khovanshchina and Konchakovna at the 1991 Edinburgh Festival and in Rome, 1992; Appearances at the Mariinsky Theatre, St Petersburg, in Boris Godunov and War and Peace, both televised in the West, as Carmen and as Lyubasha in Rimsky-Korsakov's The Tsar's Bride; Merida Festival, Spain, 1991, in Mussorgsky's Salammbô and in the final scene of Carmen, with Placido Domingo; Further engagements at San Francisco, as the Opéra Bastille, Paris, and in Bologna as Marina; Covent Garden, 1992–94, as Dalila, Marguerite in La Damnation de Faust and Cenerentola; Concert performances of Damnation de Faust with Valeri Gergiev in St Petersburg; Further engagements in Vienna, Berlin, Edinburgh and San Francisco; Engaged as Marina in Boris Godunov, Salzburg Festival and the Metropolitan, 1997–98; Verdi Requiem at the London Prom concerts, 1997; Sang in Berlioz Roméo et Juliette and La Damnation de Faust at the Royal Festival Hall, 1999; Further engagements include The Tsar's Bride, Samson et Dalila and L'Italiana in Algeri with San Francisco Opera and concert engagements at the Gulbenkian Foundation in Lisbon, Théâtre des Champs Elysées and Châtelet in Paris and the Musikverein in Vienna; Sang Amneris and Carmen at the New York Met, 2001; Mussorgsky's Songs and Dances of Death at the 2002 London Proms. *Recordings:* Songs by Tchaikovsky; Roméo et Juliette; Don Carlos; Arias; Samson and Delilah; La Forza del Destino; Verdi Requiem, conducted by Gergiev. *Current*

Management: Askonas Holt Ltd, Lonsdale Chambers, 27 Chancery Lane, London, WC2A 1PF, England. *Telephone:* (20) 7400-1700. *Fax:* (20) 7400-1799. *E-mail:* info@askonasholt.co.uk. *Website:* www .askonasholt.co.uk.

BORODINA, Tatiana; Singer; b. 1972, Perm, Russia. *Education:* graduated Perm Musical Coll. and St Petersburg Conservatoire, 1999. *Career:* Young Singers' Acad. of the Mariinsky Theatre, St Petersburg, 1998; repertoire has included Tchaikovsky's Tatiana and Iolanta, Marguerite in Faust, Mimi, Maria in Mazeppa and Wagner's Elsa and Freia; sang Elsa at Baden-Baden, 1999, Maria and Kupara in Rimsky-Korsakov's The Snow Maiden with the Kirov Opera at Covent Garden, 2000. *Honours:* prizewinner, New Voices of the West Competition, Rome 1997; prizewinner, International Rimsky-Korsakov Competition, St Petersburg. *Address:* c/o Kirov Opera, Mariinsky Theatre, Mariinsky Square, St Petersburg, Russia.

BOROWSKA, Joanna; Singer (Soprano); b. 1956, Warsaw, Poland. *Education:* Studied in Warsaw, and at the Opera Studio of Vienna Staatsoper, 1980–82. *Career:* Debut: Romilda in Serse and Micaela in Carmen at Warsaw, 1980; Member of Vienna Staatsoper from 1982, notably as Marenka in The Bartered Bride and as Mozart's Fiordiligi, Susanna and Marzelline, Gluck's Iphigénie en Aulide, (1987), Mimi, 1988, and Marguerite in Faust; Further engagements at Klagenfurt (Countess in Figaro), Bregenz (in Zeller's Der Vogelhändler, 1984), Barcelona and Covent Garden, London, Marenka at Bonn, 1991. *Recordings include:* Emma, in Khovanshchina, Vienna Staatsoper, 1989, and Maidservant in Elektra, conducted by Abbado. *Address:* c/o Oper der Stadt Bonn, Am Boselagerhof 1, 5300 Bonn, Germany.

BOROWSKI, Daniel; Singer (Bass); b. 1968, Lodz, Poland. *Education:* Chopin Academy of Music, Warsaw, with Teresa Zylis-Gara. *Career:* Roles at Warsaw and Poznan Operas have included the King in Aida, and in Penderecki's Ubu Rex, Ferrando in Il Trovatore and Rossini's Bartolo; Further engagements as the Commendatore at Strasbourg and Schwetzingen, the Monk in Don Carlos at the Amsterdam Concertgebouw, Colline in La Bohème at Frankfurt and Massimiliano in I Masnadieri for the Royal Opera in concert; Season 1998–99 with Pietro in Simon Boccanegra at Glyndebourne and Water Sprite in Rusalka for Vara Radio; Concerts include Bach's Christmas Oratorio, Messiah, and Mozart and Verdi Requiems. *Recordings include:* Die Zauberflöte. *Address:* c/o National Theatre, Warsaw, Place Teatring 1, 00–950 Warsaw, Poland.

BORRIS, Kaja; Singer (Mezzo-Soprano); b. 8 Jan. 1948, Den Haag, Netherlands. *Education:* Studied in Cologne and at the Opera Studio of the Deutsche Oper Berlin. *Career:* Member of the Deutsche Oper Berlin from 1973, singing Verdi's Mistress Quickly and Ulrica, Annina in Rosenkavalier, Azucena and Emilia (Othello), Geneviève in Pelléas et Mélisande, 1984, and Marthe in Faust, 1988; Appeared in the premiere of Reimann's Gespensteronate, 1984; Salzburg Easter Festival, 1982–83, as Mary in Fliegende Holländer; Further engagements at Munich, Hamburg, Vienna and Schwetzingen and in the concert hall; Sang the Sphinx in Enescu's Oedipe at the Deutsche Oper, 1996, and La Cieca in La Gioconda 1998; Season 2000–01 in Strauss's Die Aegyptische Helena (concert) and Mistress Quickly in Falstaff. *Recordings include:* Der fliegende Holländer; Feuersnot by Strauss; Die Lustige Witwe; Der Corregidor by Wolf; Schmidt's Notre Dame and Midwife in Zemlinsky's Der Kreidekreis. *Address:* c/o Deutsche Oper Berlin, Richard Wagnerstrasse 10, 1000 Berlin 10, Germany.

BORROFF, Edith; Composer and Musicologist; b. 2 Aug. 1925, New York, NY, USA. *Education:* Studied at the Oberlin Conservatory and the American Conservatory of Music in Chicago; PhD, University of Michigan, 1958. *Career:* Teacher at Milwaukee Downer College, 1950–54, Hillsdale College, Michigan, 1958–62, University of Wisconsin, 1962–66, Eastern Michigan University, 1966–72, and the State University of New York at Binghamton, 1973–92. *Compositions include:* String Trio, 1943; Clarinet Quintet, 1948; Sonata for cello and piano, 1949; Spring over Brooklyn, musical, 1954; IONS for flute and piano, 1968; The Sun and the Wind, musical fable, 1976; Game Pieces for woodwind quintet, 1980; Concerto for marimba and small orchestra, 1981; The Elements, sonata for violin and cello, 1987; Music for piano and organ; Choral music; Songs. *Recordings include:* Passacaglia (organ), 1946; Sonata for Horn and Piano, 1954; *Publications include:* Elisabeth Jacquet de la Guerre, 1966; The Music of the Baroque, 1970; Music in Europe and the USA, A History, 1971, 1989; Music in Perspective, 1976; Three American Composers, 1987; Music Melting Round: A History of Music in the United States, 1995. *Address:* 65 Forest at Duke Drive, Durham, NC 27705, USA.

BORST, Danielle; Singer (Soprano); b. 27 Jan. 1946, Geneva, Switzerland; m. Philippe Huttenlocher. *Education:* Studied at Geneva Conservatoire and with Juliette Bisse and Philippe Huttenlocher. *Career:* Former member of the Ensemble Vocale de Lausanne, under Michel Corboz; Opera appearances in Geneva, Lausanne, Biel-Solothurn, Aix-en-Provence, Montpellier and Vienna (Staatsoper); Paris Opéra, 1988, as Eurydice in Orphée aux Enfers; Mezières, 1988, as Gluck's Euridice; Sang Urbain in Les Huguenots at Montpellier, 1990; Hero in Béatrice et Bénédict at Toulouse, Pamina at Monte Carlo and Vitellia in Gluck's La Clemenza di Tito at Lausanne, 1991; Other roles include Mozart's Despina, Susanna, Sandrina and Illia, Gounod's Juliette, Dalinda (Ariodante), Rameau's Aricie, Micaela and Aennchen in Der Freischütz; Sang Mitrena in Vivaldi's Montezuma, at Monte Carlo, 1992; Gounod's Mireille at Lausanne, 1994; Sang Rosalinde at Lyon, 1995–96; Concerts include: Haydn's Schöpfung and Jahreszeiten, Berlioz L'Enfant du Christ, Honegger's Roi David, Passions and Oratorios by Bach, works by Monteverdi, Pergolesi, Handel and Mahler. *Recordings include:* Fauré's Pénélope, Armide by Lully, Monteverdi's Orfeo, Dido and Aeneas; Iphigénie en Tauride; Title role in L'Incoronazione di Poppea, conducted by René Jacobs. *Address:* c/o Opera de Lausanne, PO Box 3972, 1002 Lausanne, Switzerland.

BORST, Martina; Singer (Mezzo-Soprano); b. 13 Jan. 1957, Aachen, Germany. *Education:* Studied with Elsa Cavelti in Frankfurt and with Carla Castellani in Milan. *Career:* Sang at the National Theater Mannheim, from 1981, notably as Annius in La Clemenza di Tito, Cherubino, Dorabella, Rosina, Cenerentola, Orpheus and the Composer in Ariadne auf Naxos; Ludwigsburg Festival, 1982, 1984 as Annius and as Juno in Semele; Vienna Volksoper 1987, as Dorabella; Bregenz Festival, 1988 as Nicklausse in Les Contes d'Hoffmann; Liège and Nantes, 1989 as Bersi in Andrea Chénier; Sang Octavian at Hanover, 1990; Schwetzingen Festival, 1995 as Timante in Demofoonte by Jommelli; Sang Countess Geschwitz in Lulu at Mainz, 1999; Many concert hall appearances, including Mahler's Kindertotenlieder. *Recordings:* Così fan tutte, Harmonia Mundi.

BÖRTZ, Daniel; Composer; b. 8 Aug. 1943, Osby, Sweden. *Education:* Studied with Hilding Rosenberg, with Blomdahl and Lidholm at the Stockholm Music High School; Electronic Music, University of Utrecht. *Career:* Debut: Voces for orchestra, Concert Hall, Stockholm, 1968; Freelance Composer, 1968–; Opera Backanterna performed at the Royal Opera, Stockholm in production by Ingmar Bergman, 1991; Member, 1989–, President, 1998–2003, Royal Swedish Academy of Music. *Compositions include:* 2 string quartets, 1971, 1987; 10 Sinfonias, 1973–92; Concerto Grosso No. 2 for wind band, 1981; Violin Concerto, 1985; Oboe Concerto, 1986; 3 Cello concertos, 1981, 1985, 1996; Parodos for orchestra, 1987; Intermezzo for orchestra, 1989–90; Backanterna opera after Euripides, 1991; Songs about Death, for soprano and orchestra, 1992–94; Ballad for alto guitar, 1992–94; Strindberg Suite for orchestra, 1993–94; Variations and Intermezzi for strings, 1994; Sonata for piano, 1994; Songs and dances, trumpet concerto, 1994–95; Songs and Shadows, Violin concerto No. 2, 1995–96; Marie Antoinette, opera, 1996–97; Songs and Light, clarinet concerto, 1998; A Joker's Tales, recorder concerto, 1999–2000; Piano Trio, 2000; Songs, piano concerto, 2000–01; His Name was Orestes, oratorio, 2001–02. *Recordings include:* Parodos Symphonies Nos 1 and 7, Strindberg Suite with Stockholm Royal Philharmonic Orchestra and Gennady Rozhdestvensky; Symphony No. 6, chamber and choir works, with Stockholm Royal Philharmonic Orchestra, Hugh Wolff, Eric Ericson chamber choir; The Bacchae opera; Oboe Concerto; Marie Antoinette, opera; Songs and Dances, trumpet concerto; Sonata for Piano; A Joker's Tales; His Name was Orestes, oratorio. *Honours:* Christ Johnson Music Prize, Stockholm, 1987; International Rostrum of Composers, Paris, 1989; Litteris et Artibus, Stockholm, 1995. *Address:* c/o Carl Gehrmans, Box 6005, 10231 Stockholm, Sweden.

BORUP-JORGENSEN, Alex; Composer; b. 22 Nov. 1924, Hjorring, Denmark. *Education:* Studied Piano with Rachlew and Orchestration with Schierbeck and Jersild, Royal Conservatory, Copenhagen, 1946–51; Darmstadt, 1959, 1962. *Career:* Piano Teacher, Else Printz Music School, Copenhagen, 1950–64, then privately. *Compositions:* Partita viola, 1954; Improvisations quartet, 1955; Music for percussion and Viola, 1956; Duino Elegies by Rilke for mezzo, flute, violencello, 1956; Mikroorangisma Quartet, 1956; Sommasvit, string orchestra, 1957; Several songs with piano or other instruments, 1957–60; Sonatina, 2 violins, 1958; Winter Pieces, piano, 1961; Cantata, Rilke Herbsttag, alto, 7 instruments, 1963; Many songs for mezzo and piano, also for several voices, mostly Rilke and Th. Storm; Schlusztuck, Rilke, choir, 5 instruments, 1964; 5 String Quartets, 1950–65; Nordic Summer Pastoral small orchestra, 1964; Torso quartet and tape, 1965; Wintereleige, Holderlin, 3 voices, 9 instruments; Marin Orchestra, 1970; Mirrors; Soprano; Marimba; Guitar, 1974; Works for speaking choir, 1971–72; Tagebuch im Winter, flute, quartet, 1974; Praembula, guitar, 1976; Morceaux, guitar, 1974; Deja vu, concerto for guitar and string orchestra, 1983; Coast of sirens, 7 instruments and multivoice, tape, 1985; Thalatta, Piano, 1988; Raindrop Interludes for piano, 1994; Several works for recorder instruments, solo or with harpsichord. *Address:* Fredsholmvej 11, DK 3460 Birkerod, Denmark.

BOSABALIAN, Luisa; Singer (Soprano); b. 24 March 1936, Marseille, France. *Education:* Studied in Beirut, Milan, with Vittorio Ruffo. *Career:* Debut: Théâtre de la Monnaie, Brussels, as Micaela, 1964; Sang at Brussels as Mimi, Donna Anna, Donna Elvira, Desdemona, Giulietta and Antonia in Les Contes d'Hoffmann; Concert appearances at Edinburgh and the Holland Festival, conducted by Giulini; Metropolitan Opera, 1966, as Jenůfa; Guest appearances in London, Düsseldorf, Frankfurt, Rome, Moscow, Oslo, Milan and Vienna; Strasbourg 1974, in Les Indes Galantes by Rameau; Concert appearances in contemporary works; Music by Bach; Gave Lieder recital in Stuttgart, 1988; Concerts for Armenian relief at Munich, 1988–89; Sang at the Hamburg Staatsoper, 1965–73.

BOSCHKOVA, Nelly; Singer (Mezzo-Soprano); b. 1954, Bulgaria. *Education:* Studied in Sofia and with Ghena Dimitrova and Nicolai Ghiaurov. *Career:* Sang at the Sofia Opera from 1976, notably as Cherubino, Siebel, Olga, Marina, and Feodor in Boris Godunov; Komische Oper Berlin from 1981, as Baba the Turk and Monteverdi's Ottavia; Bremen Opera 1984–90, as Santuzza, Rosina, Amneris, Ortrud and Bellini's Romeo; Guest appearance at Zürich (Azucena, 1991), and the Vienna Staatsoper (Marfa in Khovanshchina, 1992); Season 1995–96, as Gertrude in Hamlet at the Vienna Volksoper and Madelon in Andrea Chénier at the Deutsche Oper, Berlin; Vienna Staatsoper 2000, as Mrs Sedley in Peter Grimes and Zita in Gianni Schicchi. *Address:* c/o Bremen Theater, Pf 101046, 2800 Bremen, Germany.

BOSE, Hans-Jurgen von; Composer; b. 24 Dec. 1953, Munich, Germany. *Education:* Hoch Conservatory, Frankfurt am Main, 1969–72; Pupil in composition of Hans Ulrich Engelmann; In piano of Klaus Billing, Hochschule für Musik Frankfurt am Main, 1972–75; Opera 63; Dream Palace performed at Munich, 1990; Slaughterhouse Five premiered at the 1996 Munich Festival. *Compositions:* Stage; Blutbund, chamber opera, 1974; Das Diplom, chamber opera, 1975; Die Nacht aus Blei, kinetic action, 1980–81; Die Leiden des jungen Werthers, lyrical scenes, 1986; 63: Dream Place, 1990; Slaughterhouse Five, 1995; Orchestra: Morphogenesis, 1975; Symphony No. 1, 1976; Musik für ein Haus voll Zeit, 1977; Songs for Tenor and Chamber Orchestra, 1977; Travesties in a Sad Landscape for Chamber Orchestra, 1978; Symphonic Fragment for Tenor, Baritone, Bass, Chorus; Orchestra, 1980; Variations for 15 strings, 1980; Idyllen, 1983; Sappho-Gesänge for Mezzo-Soprano and Chamber Orchestra, 1982–83; Labyrinth I, 1987; Oboe Concerto, 1986–87; 5 Children's Rhymes for Alto and 5 Instrumentalists, 1974; Threnos-Hommage à Bernd Alois Zimmermann for Viola and Cello, 1975; Solo Violin Sonata, 1977; Variations for Cello, 1978–79; Vom Wege abkommen for viola, 1982; Guarda el Canto for Soprano and String Quartet, 1982; Studie I for Violin and Piano, 1986; Lorca-Gesänge for Baritone and 10 instruments, 1986; Wind Sextet, 1986. *Address:* c/o GEMA, Herzog-Wilhelm Strasse 38, 8000 Munich 2, Germany.

BOSQUET, Thierry; stage designer and costume designer; b. 1932, Belgium. *Education:* National School of Architecture, Art and Design, Brussels. *Career:* from 1959 sets and costumes for more than 70 operas and ballets at the Théâtre Royale de la Monnaie, Brussels; Many other stagings in France, Italy, Switzerland, Germany, Canada, South America and Australia; Rigoletto and Otello in Liège, La Belle Hélène for Canadian Opera; New York City Opera with Werther, Die Zauberflöte and La Traviata; San Francisco Opera from 1980, with costumes for Aida, Carmen, Fledermaus and Capriccio; Realisations of original designs and costumes for Ruslan and Lyudmila (1995), Der Rosenkavalier (original Alfred Roller designs) and Tosca (San Francisco premiere, 1932); Pelléas et Mélisande at San Francisco, 1997. *Address:* c/o San Francisco Opera, War Memorial House, Van Ness Avenue, San Francisco, CA 94102, USA.

BOSTOCK, (Nigel) Douglas, BMus, MMus; conductor; b. 11 June 1955, Northwich, Cheshire, England. *Education:* Northern School of Music, University of Sheffield; private lessons with Adrian Boult, London; conducting masterclass with Prof. Dr Francis Travis; Freiburg Hochschule für Musik, Germany. *Career:* Musikdirektor, Konstanz, Germany, 1979–93; Regular Guest Conductor, Southwest German Philharmonic; Principal Conductor and Music Director, Karlovy Vary Symphony Orchestra, Czech Republic, 1991–98; Principal Guest Conductor, Chamber Philharmonic of Bohemia, 1991–; Permanent Guest Conductor, Munich Symphony Orchestra, 1997–; Music Director, Tokyo Kosei Wind Orchestra, 1999–; Principal Conductor, Aargau Symphony Orchestra Switzerland, 2001–; Guest conducting appearances with major orchestras throughout Europe, America and Japan; Conducted for television and radio; Guest artist at many international music festivals. *Recordings:* Dvořák, Fibich, Smetana, Novak, Mozart, Brahms, Bellini, other composers; Series of rare French music, 3 vols; Albums in Czech Republic, the United Kingdom with Royal Philharmonic, Germany, Japan, baroque music in Italy, Germany, Japan; Nielsen symphonies and other orchestral works with Royal Liverpool Philharmonic, 6+ vols; British Symphonic Collection with various orchestras: Bax, Delius, Vaughan Williams, Elgar, Holst, Butterworth,

Arnold Gregson, McCabe, Hoddinott etc, 9+ vols. *Publications:* Hans Pfitzner: The Last Romantic, 1979. *Current Management:* Hazard Chase Ltd, Norman House, Cambridge Place, Cambridge, CB2 1NS, England. *Telephone:* (1223) 312400. *Fax:* (1223) 460827. *Website:* www .hazardchase.co.uk. *Address:* Seestrasse 68, 78479 Reichenau, Germany.

BOSTRIDGE, Ian Charles, CBE; Singer (tenor); b. 25 Dec. 1964, London, England. *Education:* Cambridge and Oxford (doctorate 1990). *Career:* Wigmore Hall debut, 1993, Winterreise at the Purcell Room and Aldeburgh Festival concert, 1994; further concerts include the Bach B minor Mass in Ottawa under Pinnock, Handel's Resurrezione in Berlin, Britten's Serenade at the Schleswig-Holstein Festival, Schumann's Scenes from Faust with the London Philharmonic Orchestra and Hylas in Les Troyens under Colin Davis with the London Symphony Orchestra; opera debut, London, 1994, as Britten's Lysander; Covent Garden 1995 as Fourth Jew in Salome, ENO 1996 as Tamino and Lysander; Season 1995 with War Requiem in London and Hamburg, Britten's Spring Symphony at Aldeburgh, the St Matthew Passion under Charles Mackerras and Bach's Magnificat at the London Proms; sang Schubert's Schöne Müllerin in bicentenary concert at the Wigmore Hall, 1997; Vasek in The Bartered Bride for the Covent Garden Company at Sadler's Wells, 1998; Britten's Les Illuminations at the 1999 London Prom concerts; Premiere of Henze's Six Songs from the Arabic, 1999; Peter Quint in the Turn of the Screw, Covent Garden, 2002; Songs by Vaughan Williams (On Wenlock Edge), Schubert and Fauré (La bonne chanson) at the 2002 Edinburgh Festival. *Recordings include:* Rossini Messa di Milano, War Requiem and St Matthew Passion under Frans Brueggen; Purcell's Music for Queen Mary; Britten Holy Sonnets of John Donne. *Publications include:* Sorcery Shipwreck'd: Witchcraft and its Transformation c.1650–c.1750, 1997. *Current Management:* Askonas Holt Ltd, Lonsdale Chambers, 27 Chancery Lane, London, WC2A 1PF, England. *Telephone:* (20) 7400-1700. *Fax:* (20) 7400-1799. *E-mail:* info@askonasholt.co.uk. *Website:* www.askonasholt.co.uk.

BOTES, Christine; singer (mezzo-soprano); b. 1964, Kingston upon Thames, England. *Education:* with Frederic Cox at the Royal Northern College of Music and at the National Opera Studio. *Career:* Sang with Glyndebourne Chorus then with the RSC in The Tempest; Appearances with Scottish Opera as Iolanthe and Second Lady in The Magic Flute; Opera Factory as Diana in La Calisto, Thea in Knot Garden and Dorabella, also televised; Mozart roles include Cherubino at Sadler's Wells, Donna Elvira in the Netherlands and Belgium; With English National Opera has sung as Hansel on tour to Russia in 1990 and as the Fox in The Cunning Little Vixen, 1991; For ENO sang Cherubino in The Marriage of Figaro, 1991; Sang in the Mikado, 1991, Proserpina in Orfeo, 1992, Minerva in Return of Ulysses in 1992; Concert engagements with the Royal Philharmonic in Elgar's Sea Pictures and the London Sinfonietta, City of London Sinfonia and The Hanover Band; Bach's B Minor Mass in France and Poland and Messiah with the Orchestre de Liège and the City of Birmingham Choir; Concerts in Cologne and Lisbon with the Ensemble Modern of Frankfurt; Sang Herodias in Stradella's San Giovanni Battista, Batignano, 1996. *Current Management:* Robert Gilder & Co., Enterprise House, 59–65 Upper Ground, London, SE1 9PQ, England. *Telephone:* (20) 7928-9008. *Fax:* (20) 7928-9755. *E-mail:* rgilder@robert-gilder.com.

BOTHA, Johan; Singer (Tenor); b. 1965, Rustenberg, South Africa. *Education:* Studied in Pretoria. *Career:* Sang at Pretoria from 1988, in the premiere of Hofmeyer's The Fall of the House of Usher and other works; Europe from 1990 (concerts in Warsaw and Moscow); Kaiserslautern, 1991, as Gustavus in Un Ballo in Maschera, Dortmund Opera as the Prince in The Love for Three Oranges; Other roles include Max (Der Freischütz), Florestan (at Bonn), Pinkerton, Cassio (Otello), Pedro in Tiefland and Theo in Rautavaara's Vincent; Royal Opera, Covent Garden, 1995 as Rodolfo; Sang Turiddu at Bonn, and Pinkerton at La Scala, 1996; Season 1998 as Verdi's Arrigo at the Vienna Staatsoper; Season 2000–01 as Radames at Los Angeles and the Emperor in Die Frau ohne Schatten at Dresden. *Address:* c/o Stadtische Buhnen, Kuhstrasse 12, W-4600 Dortmund, Germany.

BOTT, Catherine; Singer (Soprano); b. 11 Sept. 1952, Leamington Spa, England. *Career:* Many appearances with leading early music ensembles, notably the New London Consort; Appearances at major concert halls in Europe, Latin America and USSR; British engagements include Early Music Network Tours; Festival concerts at Bath, Edinburgh and City of London; Mediaeval Christmas Extravaganza on the South Bank and concerts for the South Bank's 21st anniversary; Season 1988–89 with visits to Israel, Spain, Netherlands and Italy; French debut as Salome in Stradella's San Giovanni Battista at Versailles; Solo recitals at Flanders and Utrecht Festivals, Sadler's Wells Theatre and the King's Singers Summer Festival at the Barbican; Promenade Concert, London, 1990, with The Bonfire of the Vanities (Medici Wedding Celebration of 1539); Season 1991 with concerts and recordings in

France, recitals in Netherlands and Belgium and tour of Japan; Sang Mozart's Zaide at Queen Elizabeth Hall, 1991; Purcell's Dido at the Barbican, 1992; Sang in Michael Nyman concert on South Bank, 1996; Oswald von Wolkenstein concert, 1997. *Recordings include:* Monteverdi Vespers and Orfeo; Virtuoso Italian vocal music: de Rore, Rasi, Cavalieri, Luzzaschi, G and F Caccini, Gagliano, Marini, Rossi, Frescobaldi, Monteverdi, Barnardi and Carissimi (Il Lamento di Maria Stuarda); Cantigas de Amigo by Martin Codax and Cantigas di Santa Maria, anon (all with the New London Consort); Vaughan Williams Sinfonia Antarctica, with the London Symphony Orchestra; English canzonets and Scottish songs, with Melvyn Tan; English restoration theatre music: mad songs by Purcell and by Eccles and Weldon; Walton film music, with the Academy of St Martin-in-the-Fields.

BOTTI, Patrick; Conductor; b. 27 July 1954, Marseille, France; m. Catherine Fuller, 2 d. *Education:* Conservatoire National Supérieur de Musique, Paris; École Normale de Musique, Paris; Université de Paris, Sorbonne, Paris; New England Conservatory of Music, Boston, USA; Boston University, Boston; Conservatoire National de Marseille; Université de Droit et Sciences Politiques, Aix en Provence. *Career:* Debut: As a pianist, Palais des Festivals, Cannes, France, 1967; As a conductor, Marseille, 1974; Conducted in France, England, Italy, Canada, USA; Music Director, Concilium Musicum of Paris, 1977–82; Artistic Adviser and Principal Guest Conductor, Concilium Musicum of Paris, 1982–; Music Director, Conductor, French Symphony of Boston, since season 1984–85; Artistic Director, Conductor, New Hampshire Philharmonic Orchestra, since season 1993–94; Principal Guest Conductor, Central Massachusetts Symphony Orchestra, since season 1993–94; As Guest Conductor appearances included Colorado Springs Symphony Orchestra, Boston Philharmonic, New Hampshire Philharmonic Orchestra. *Address:* Conductor's Cooperative Management, 1208 Massachusetts Avenue, Suite #8, Cambridge, MA 02139, USA.

BOTTOMLEY, Sally Ann; Concert Pianist and Educator; b. 18 May 1959, Yorkshire, England. *Education:* Chetham's School of Music; Royal Northern College of Music, PPRNCM. *Career:* Debut: Concert debut with City of Birmingham Symphony, 1980; London recital debut, Purcell Room, 1981; Appearances with Royal Philharmonic, London Symphony, City of Birmingham, Hallé, Royal Liverpool Philharmonic Orchestra, Scottish National; Conductors include, Skrowaczewski, Järvi, Groves, Downes, Litton, Tortelier; Two Piano Partnerships with John Gough; Lecturer, Huddersfield University and Chetham's School of Music; Several television appearances and advertisements and radio performances. *Address:* c/o Chetham's School of Music, Long Millgate, Manchester, M3 1 SB, England.

BOTTONE, Bonaventura; Singer (Tenor); b. 19 Sept. 1950, England. *Education:* Studied at the Royal Academy of Music with Bruce Boyce. *Career:* Debut: Covent Garden, as Italian Singer in Der Rosenkavalier, conducted by Haitink; Returned in Capriccio by Strauss; US debut as Pedrillo in Die Entführung, at Houston Opera; Has sung with English National Opera as David in Die Meistersinger, the Duke of Mantua, Beppe, Nanki Poo in Jonathan Miller's production of The Mikado, Sam Kaplan in Weill's Street Scene, Truffaldino in the Love for Three Oranges, 1989 and Alfredo in La Traviata, 1990; Scottish Opera, 1989, as Governor General in Candide and Loge in Das Rheingold; Sang the Italian Tenor in Capriccio at Glyndebourne, 1990; Season 1992, as Verdi's Fenton at the London Coliseum and Conte di Libenskof in Il Viaggio a Reims at Covent Garden; Sang the Berlioz Faust with ENO, 1997; Season 1998, as Doctor Ox in the premiere of Gavin Bryar's opera and Rodolfo in La Bohème for ENO, debut at Santiago, Chile with Alfred in Die Fledermaus, and Italian Singer in Capriccio at Glyndebourne and the Metropolitan Opera; Frequent broadcaster in a wide range of BBC programmes; Sang in the Berlioz Te Deum, Royal Festival Hall, 2000; Season 2001 in Caruso and Mario Lanza tributes in Manchester and Dublin; Verdi's Riccardo for Atlanta Opera; Pinkerton at Santiago and Beethoven's Ninth in Germany; Season 2002–03 with Verdi's Duke in Milwaukee and roles with Chicago Lyric and Met Operas. *Recordings:* The Mikado; Orpheus in the Underworld. *Honours:* FRAM, 1998. *Address:* c/o Stafford Law Associates, 6 Barham Road, Weybridge, Surrey KT 13 9 PR, England.

BOUCHARD, Antoine, BA, LTh; Canadian organist and professor of organ; *Professor Emeritus, Faculty of Music, Laval University;* b. 22 March 1932, St Philippe-de-Neri, Quebec. *Education:* Laval Univ., Quebec. *Career:* concerts and festivals, Quebec City, Montreal, Paris, France; concerts in Canada and USA; radio performances, CBC and ORTF; series of concerts on 20 European historical organs, Radio Canada; Organ Prof. and Dir School of Music, Laval Univ., Quebec 1977–80, Prof. Emer. 1999–. *Compositions:* Prelude and In Paradisum, for organ, in Le Tombeau de Henri Gagnon. *Recordings:* Music by Dandrieu and Buxtehude, Noels français du 18e Siècle, Bach and Pachelbel, Anthologie de l'organiste, Vols I, II, III, The Early Pipe Organs of Quebec, Vols II, IV, VII, The 18 Chorals, by J.S. Bach, Oeuvres de Gaston Litaize, L'Orgue Français classique en Nouvelle-

France, 7 historical organs of north-western Germany, Nicolas Lebegue, Complete Pachelbel organ works. *Publications:* L'Organiste (three vols) 1982, Quelques réflexions sur le jeu de l'orgue 2003. *Contributions:* The Organ Yearbook, Netherlands, L'Orgue, Paris, Musicanada, L'Encyclopédie de la musique au Canada. Bulletin des Amis de l'Orgue. *Address:* 908 rue du Belvédère, St-Nicolas-Est, Quebec G7A 3V3, Canada. *E-mail:* antoinebou@videotron.ca.

BOUE, Georgi; Singer (Soprano); b. 16 Oct. 1918, Toulouse, France; m. Roger Bourdin, deceased 1973. *Education:* Studied at the Toulouse Conservatory, in Paris with Henri Büsser and Reynaldo Hahn. *Career:* Debut: Toulouse, 1935, as Urbain in Les Huguenots. Mireille in the opera by Gounod; Sang at Toulouse as Siebel in Faust, Hilda in Reyer's Sigurd, Mathilde in Guillaume Tell and Bizet's Micaela; Paris Opéra-Comique from 1938; Paris Opéra from 1942, notably in Les Indes Galantes by Rameau, 1953; Guest appearances in Arles, Brussels, Nice, Barcelona, Germany, Mexico City and Italy; La Scala Milan as Debussy's Mélisande; Tour of Russia as Tatiana in Eugene Onegin and Madama Butterfly; Théâtre de la Monniae Brussels, 1960, in La Belle Hélène; Die Lustige Witwe; Appeared as Malibran in the film by Sacha Guitry. *Recordings:* Thais, Urania; Faust conducted by Beecham; Les Contes d'Hoffmann; L'Aiglon; Founded the Centre Lyrique Populaire de France, Paris, 1966.

BOUGHTON, William Paul; Conductor; b. 18 Dec. 1948, Birmingham, England; m. Susan Ann Cullis 1981. *Education:* Guildhall School of Music, London; Prague Acad.; AGSM. *Career:* founder, Dir, English String Orchestra; Principal Conductor, English Symphony Orchestra and Jyvaskyla Sinfonia, Finland 1986–93; Artistic Dir, Malvern Festival 1983–88; guest conductor with Philharmonia, Royal Philharmonic Orchestra, London Philharmonic Orchestra and London Symphony Orchestra; mem. Royal Overseas League. *Recordings include:* first recordings of Finzi's Love's Labours Lost and Parry's 1st Symphony and Death to Life. *Honours:* Jyvaskyla City Award; Hon. DLitt; Hon. Assoc., Janáček Acad.. *Address:* c/o Eleanor Hope, 9 Southwood Hall, Wood Lane, London, N6 5UF, England.

BOUKOV, Yuri; French pianist; b. 1 May 1923, Sofia, Bulgaria. *Education:* studied in Bulgaria and at the Paris Conservatoire. *Career:* debut, Sofia, 1938; many appearances throughout Europe in post-war period, with tour to China, 1956; often heard in the sonatas of Prokofiev and premiered works by Menotti and Wissmer.

BOULEYN, Kathryn; Singer (Soprano); b. 3 May 1947, Maga Vita, Maryland, USA. *Education:* Studied at Indiana University and the Curtis Institute. *Career:* Debut: San Diego, 1978, as Nannetta in Falstaff; Miami, 1978, as Desdemona; New York City Opera from 1979; Spoleto Festival at Charleston in Haydn's La Vera Costanza, St Louis, 1981, in the US premiere of Fennimore and Gerda by Delius (as Fennimore); European debut, 1981, as Janáček's Fox (The Cunning Little Vixen) with Netherlands Opera; Other appearances as Gutrune at San Francisco (1985), Mozart's Countess at San Diego (1986), Tatiana in Eugene Onegin for Welsh National Opera (1988), Vitellia in La Clemenza di Tito (Scottish Opera), Donna Elvira, Elisabeth de Valois, Mimi, Manon Lescaut, Micaela and Venus in Tannhäuser; Seattle 1991 as Mozart's Countess. *Address:* c/o New York City Opera, Lincoln Center, New York, NY 10023, USA.

BOULEZ, Pierre; Composer and Conductor; b. 26 March 1925, Montbrison, France. *Education:* Paris Conservatoire, studied with Messiaen, Vaurabourg-Honegger and Leibowitz. *Career:* Director of Music to Jean-Louis Barrault Theatre, 1948; Aided by Barrault and Madeleine Renaud Barrault founded the Concerts Marigny which later became the Domaine Musical, Paris; Principal Guest Conductor, Cleveland Symphony Orchestra; Principal Guest Conductor, BBC Symphony Orchestra, 1971–75, with the orchestra gave many performances of music by Bartók, Berg, Messiaen, Debussy, Schoenberg and Stravinsky; Musical Director, New York Philharmonic, 1971–77; Director, Institute of Recherches et de Co-ordination Acoustique/ Musique, 1975–91; Conducted the centenary production of Wagner's Ring, Bayreuth, 1976–80; Conducted Pelléas et Mélisande for Welsh National Opera, 1992; 70th birthday concerts in London, Paris and New York, 1995; Inaugurated the BBC series Sounding the Century, Festival Hall, 1997, Stravinsky's Nightingale and The Rite of Spring; Series of 31 concerts in 11 countries to celebrate 75th birthday, 2000, including Barbican Centre, London; Conducted the BBC Symphony Orchestra at the London Proms, 2002; Engaged for new production of Parsifal at Bayreuth, 2004. *Compositions include:* Le Marteau sans Maître (cantata for voice and instruments to text by René Char); Structures (2 pianos), 1952–61; Third Piano Sonata, 1957; Improvisations sur Mallarmé (soprano and chamber ensemble); Poésie pour Pouvoir (orchestra), 1958; Pli selon Pli, 1957–89; Figures-doubles-prismes, 1963–68, Eclat and Eclat Multiples: Domaines, 1968; Livre pour quatuor, 1968; Cummings ist der Dichter, 1970; Explosante/Fixe, 1971–93; Memoriales, 1975; Rituel in Memoriam Bruno Maderna, for orchestra, 1975; Notations for orchestra, 1980; Répons, 1981; Dérive for ensemble, 1984; Anthèmes for violin solo and electronics, 1997; Sur incises, 1998. *Recordings include:* Numerous videos and professional recordings. DVD of 1976 Bayreuth Ring, released 2001. *Publications include:* Relevés d'apprenti (essay), 1996; Par volonté et par hasard, 1975; Points de repére; Jalons, 1989; Le pays fertile: Paul Klee, 1989; Correspondence P. Boulez/John Cage, 1991. *Honours:* Honorary Doctorate, Leeds, Oxford, Cambridge, Bristol and University of Southern California; Winner, Glenn Gould International Prize, 2002. *Address:* c/o IRCAM, 1 place Igor-Stravinsky, 75004 Paris, France.

BOULIN, Sophie; Singer (Soprano) and Composer; b. 1960, France. *Education:* Paris Conservatoire; Paris Opéra Studio. *Career:* Contemporary music concerts with Vinko Globokar, Diego Masson and Claude Prey; Baroque music with René Jacobs, Gustav Leonhardt, Jean-Claude Malgoire, Sigiswald Kuijken, William Christie and Philippe Herreweghe; Opera appearances in France and Germany, notably in productions by Herbert Wernicke of Monteverdi's Poppea, Gluck's Echo et Narcisse and Graun's Montezuma. *Compositions:* Le leçon de musique dans un parc, premiered under William Christie, 1982; Tou azimuts, given at Hamburg, Paris and Munich. *Recordings:* Echo in Echo et Narcisse; Rossane in Handel's Alessandro; Cantatas by Jacquet de la Guerre. *Address:* c/o SACEM, 225 Avenue Charles de Gaulle, 92521 Neuilly sur Seine, Cédex, France.

BOULTON, Timothy; British violist; b. 14 July 1960, England. *Career:* mem., Domus Piano Quartet, 1985–95, Raphael Ensemble, 1991–98, Vellinger String Quartet, 1998–2002; Prof. of Viola, Guildhall School of Music and Drama; Head of Strings, Junior Guildhall; founder of MusicWorks (Chamber Courses), running residential courses for teenagers; many international chamber music tours. *Recordings:* many recordings with the aforementioned groups. *Honours:* Gramophone Chamber Music Award, 1996. *E-mail:* tboulton@eurobell.co.uk.

BOUMAN, Hendrik; Harpsichordist, Fortepianist, Conductor and Professor; b. 29 Sept. 1951, Dordrecht, Netherlands; one s. *Education:* teaching certificate, 1977, Harpsichord solo performance diploma, 1978, Sweelinck Conservatorium, Amsterdam. *Career:* debut, conducting, Basilica of Notre Dame, Montréal, Canada, premiere of Tu me cherches by Alain Pierard; Mass for orchestra; several hundred Choristers; International Year of Youth, 1985; harpsichordist of Musica Antiqua Köln, 1976–83; extensive tours throughout Europe; festivals in Berlin, London, Netherlands, Flanders, Besancon, Festival de Paris; world tours of South America, 1980, North America, 1981, Asia, including India and Japan, 1982; regular radio recordings for all major European stations; founder, Dir, Ensemble Les Nations de Montréal, 1986; Prof., Univ. of Laval, Québec, 1987, Concordia Univ., 1985–; masterclasses and lectures, 1979–; mem., CAPAC. *Compositions:* several transcripts for harpsichord duo. *Publications:* Basso Continuo realisations for Marais; Sonnerie; Maresienne; Mancini; Recorder Concerto; Figured Bass and Harpsichord Improvisation. *Honours:* Diapason d'Or, 1982, for Giles; Diapason d'Or, 1982 for Monteverdi; Deutscher Schallplattenpreis, 1982; Early Music Award, 1982.

BOURGEOIS, Derek, MA, DMus; British director of music; b. 16 Oct. 1941, Kingston on Thames, England; m. Jean Berry 1965. *Education:* Magdalene College, Cambridge, Royal College of Music. *Career:* Lecturer in Music, Bristol University, 1971–84; Director of Music, National Youth Orchestra of Great Britain, 1984–93; Founder, National Youth Chamber Orchestra of Great Britain, 1989–93; Director of Music, St Paul's Girls' School, London, 1994–2002; mem, Vice-President of Composers Guild of Great Britain, Chairman, 1980–83. *Compositions include:* 206 works, including 20 symphonies; Concertos for double bass, clarinet, trombone (2), tuba, organ, euphonium, 3 trombones, percussion, trumpet and bass trombone, tenor horn, saxophone; 4 Concertos for Brass Band; 6 Symphonies for Wind Orchestra; Symphonic Fantasy: The Globe; 8 works for chorus and orchestra; 2 operas. *Recordings:* many of his original compositions. *Address:* La Tramuntana, Calle Orquidea No. 24 - Betlem, 07579 Arta, Mallorca, Balearics (home). *Telephone:* 971 589236 (home). *E-mail:* tramuntana@infoarta.com (home). *Website:* www.tramuntana.infoarta.com (home).

BOURGUE, Daniel; Horn Player; b. 12 Jan. 1937, Avignon, France. *Education:* Avignon Conservatoire and Paris Conservatoire. *Career:* soloist and chamber musician; concerts with the Musica wind quintet, 1961–67; horn soloist, Garde Republicaine Orchestra, 1963; at Concerts Pasadeloup, 1964; Opéra-Comique, 1967; Orchestre National de France; The Ensemble Intercontemporain; Ensemble Orchestral de Paris; Nouvel Orchestre Philharmonique; first horn soloist Paris Opéra Orchestra, 1964–89; mem., Paris Octet 1965–82; performed in Europe, Scandinavia, Africa, USA, Latin America, Canada, Japan; has premiered works by Messiaen (Appel Interstellaire), Francaix (Divertimento); Xenakis (Anaktoria, 1965), Pousseur, Jolas, Ballif, Constant and Delerue (Concerto); teaches at Versailles Conservatoire; lectures, masterclasses in France, Belgium, Germany, Italy, Bulgaria, USA,

Canada, Spain, Japan; organizes training sessions with the Spanish National Youth Orchestra three times a year 1987–; Dir, Editions Billaudot's Florilège Collection; Pres., Asscn Nat. des Cornistes Français. *Recordings:* music by Mozart, Handel, Rossini, Telemann, Haydn, Strauss, Saint-Saëns, Stamitz, Hoffmeister, Dukas, Chabrier, Corrette, Bréval, d'Indy, Gounod and others. *Publications:* five-volume teaching work Techni-cor (publr); Parlons du cor. *Address:* c/o Valmalè, 7 rue Hoche, 92300 Levallois Perret, Paris, France. *Address:* 12 rue Erik Satie, 94440 Santeny, France (home). *Telephone:* 1-43-86-04-61 (home). *E-mail:* danbourg@tele2.fr (home).

BOURGUE, Maurice; Oboist and Conductor; b. 6 Nov. 1939, Avignon, France. *Education:* Paris Conservatoire. *Career:* Principal of the Basle Orchestra, 1964–67, Orchestre de Paris 1967–79; Solo appearances with the Israel CO, I Solisti Veneti, I Musici, Lucerne Festival Strings and all the major French orchestras; British debut at the Wigmore Hall, 1979; Engagements with the ECO, Chamber Orchestra of Europe, Royal Philharmonic, and the London Symphony Orchestra under Abbado; Premieres have included Chemins IV by Berio (1974), Les Citations by Dutilleux (1991) and Messiaen's Concert à Quatre (1994); Founded the Ensemble à Vent Maurice Bourgue 1972 and has conducted the Oslo Philharmonic Orchestra, Ensemble Orchestral de Paris, Israel CO and Orchestras in Lyon, Montpellier, Nancy and the Auvergne; Tour of the United Kingdom with the Bournemouth Sinfonietta, 1995. *Honours:* Winner of Competitions at Birmingham (1985), Prague (1968) and Budapest (1970). *Current Management:* Ingpen & Williams Ltd, 7 St George's Court, 131 Putney Bridge Road, London, SW15 2PA, England.

BOUSKOVA, Jana; Czech harpist; b. 27 Sept. 1970, Prague; m. Jiri Kubita 1993; one s. *Education:* Prague Conservatory, Ostrava University, Indiana University, studied with Libuse Vachalova, Susann McDonald. *Career:* Concert Harpist, solo, chamber, concerts in USA, Japan, Germany, France, Italy, Spain, Greece, Canada, Czech Republic, Slovakia, Netherlands, Switzerland; Recital at Lincoln Center, 1993; Concert at the Berliner Philharmony Hall; International Music Festivals; Many recordings for television and radio; Teacher at the Prague Conservatory Concerts at the World Harp Congresses (Vienna, Paris, Copenhagen, Seattle, Prague); Concerts with Patrick Gallois, Mstislav Rostropovich; Artistic Chairman for the Seventh World Harp Congress in Prague, 1999. *Recordings:* Harp Recital (Scarlatti, Bach, Tournier, etc); Harp Recital (J L Dussek); Harp Recital (J F Fischer); Harp Concertos (Handel, Krumpholz, Boieldieu); Harp Concertos (J Ch Bach); Harp Concertos (J K Krumpholz Nos 1–6); Harp Recital (Bach, Fischer); Harp-Violin (Kreutzer-Nocturnos); Harp-Flute (Spohr, Ravel); Jana Bouskova Plays Virtuoso Encores (Chopin, Liszt, Falla); Solos for Harp (Ravel and Debussy); Harp Concertos (Dittersdorf, Wagenseil, Albrechtsberger). *Honours:* 1st Prize, Gold Medal, USA International Harp Competion, 1992; 2nd Prize, 11th International Harp Contest, Israel, 1992; 1st Prize, Grand Prix Concours International de Musique de Chambre de Paris, 1998; 1st Prize, TIM Torneo Internazionale di Musica, 1999; Harpa Award, 1999. *Address:* Oddechová 398, 15531 Prague 5, Lipence-Kazín, Czech Republic. *E-mail:* jana@bouskova.cz. *Website:* www.bouskova.cz.

BOVINO, Maria; Singer (Soprano); b. 1960, England. *Education:* Studied at Sheffield University and the Guildhall School of Music and Drama. *Career:* Debut: At King's College in London, as Bella in Schubert's Die Verschworenen; Sang Fiorella in Offenbach's Les Brigands with the Intermezzi Ensemble; Opera 80 from 1982 as Adele in Die Fledermaus, Despina in Così fan tutte and Elvira in L'Italiana in Algeri; Season 1984–85 as Emmie in Albert Herring at Glyndebourne and Titania in A Midsummer Night's Dream for Glyndebourne Tour; Sang First Boy in The Magic Flute for English National Opera in 1986 followed by the Queen of Night in 1988; With Scottish Opera from 1987 as Blondchen in Die Entführung and Papagena; English Bach Festival in Gluck's Orfeo and Dido and Aeneas in London, Granada and Athens; Covent Garden debut in 1989 in Albert Herring; Performances with Travelling Opera in season 1990–91 as Mimi and Gilda; Also sings Gilbert and Sullivan with the London Savoyards; Sang Susanna with Crystal Clear Productions in 1991; Sang Gilda with English Touring Opera, 1996; Queen of Night for Mid Wales Opera, 1998. *Address:* c/o Mid Wales Opera, 5 Llandaff Road, Cardiff, CF11 9NF, Wales.

BOWATER, Helen; Composer; b. 16 Nov. 1952, Wellington, New Zealand. *Education:* Studied with Gwyneth Brown and at Victoria University, Wellington. *Career:* Resident composer at Nelson School of Music, 1992; Mozart Fellow at University of Otago, 1993. *Compositions include:* Black Rain for soprano and cello, 1985; Songs of Mourning for baritone and string quartet, 1989; Stay Awake Ananda for 5 percussionists, 1990; The Bodhi Tree, string quartet, 1991; Witch's Mine for tape, 1991; Magma for orchestra, 1992. *Address:* c/o New Zealand Music Centre, PO Box 10042, Level 13, Brandon Street, Wellington, New Zealand.

BOWEN, Geraint Robert Lewis, BA, MA, MusB, FRCO; conductor and organist; *Organist and Director of Music, Hereford Cathedral*; b. 11 Jan. 1963, London, England; m. Lucy Dennis 1987; two s. *Education:* Univ. of Cambridge, Trinity College, Dublin, studied with Christopher Herrick, John Scott and Stephen Cleobury. *Career:* Organ Scholar, Jesus College, Cambridge, 1982–85; Television and radio broadcasts as organ accompanist and conductor, 1984–; Assistant Organist at Hampstead Parish Church, St Clement Danes Church, 1985–86, St Patrick's Cathedral, Dublin, 1986–89 and Hereford Cathedral, 1989–94; Assistant Conductor and Accompanist, Hereford Choral Society, 1989–94; Festival Organist at Hereford Three Choirs Festival, 1991, 1994; Appearances as conductor and recitalist in the United Kingdom, Ireland, USA and Australia; Organist and Master of the Choristers at St David's Cathedral, Wales, 1995–2001; Artistic Director, St David's Cathedral Festival, 1995–2001; Founder and Conductor, St David's Cathedral Festival Chorus, 1996–2001; Director of choral workshops in USA, 1997–; Organist and Director of Music, Hereford Cathedral, 2001–; Conductor, Hereford Choral Society, 2001–; Conductor at the Three Choirs Festival, 2002–; orchestras include Philharmonia, RPO, Bournemouth Symphony Orchestra. *Recordings:* Aeternae laudis lilium; The Psalms of David, vol. 1; Te Deum and Jubilate, vol. 3; The Sound of St David's. *Honours:* Selected for Gramophone Magazine's Critics' Choice, 1985. *Address:* 7 College Cloisters, The Close, Hereford, HR1 2NG, England.

BOWEN, John; Singer (tenor); b. 1968, England. *Education:* Royal College of Music. *Career:* appearances with Bath and Wessex Opera, Garsington Festival, City of Birmingham Touring Opera and Opera Factory Zürich; roles include Ugone in Flavio and Pan in La Calisto; concerts with the English Chamber Orchestra, Royal Liverpool Philharmonic Orchestra, London Mozart Players, and The King's Consort in The Indian Queen and Judas Maccabaeus; sang in the premiere of Tavener's Apocalypse at the London Proms in 1994 and tour of Bach's B minor Mass with René Jacobs; sang Soliman in Mozart's Zaide at the 1996 Covent Garden Festival. *Recordings include:* Rachmaninov's Vespers; Messiah; Monteverdi's Vespers. *Current Management:* Caroline Phillips Management, The Old Brushworks, Pickwick Road, Corsham, Wiltshire, SN13 9BX, England. *Telephone:* (1249) 716716. *Fax:* (1249) 716717. *E-mail:* cphillips@caroline-phillips .co.uk. *Website:* www.caroline-phillips.co.uk/bowen.

BOWEN, Kenneth (John); Singer (Tenor), Conductor, Teacher and Adjudicator; b. 3 Aug. 1932, Llanelli, Wales; m. Angela Mary Bowen, 31 Mar 1959, 2 s. *Education:* BA, University of Wales; MA, BMus, St John's College, Cambridge; Institute of Education, University of London. *Career:* Debut: Tom Rakewell, New Opera Company, Sadler's Wells, 1957; Flying Officer, Education Branch, RAF, 1958–60; Professor of Singing, 1967–, Head of Vocal Studies, 1987–91, RAM; Conductor of London Welsh Chorale, 1983–, and London Welsh Festival Chorus; Former concert and operatic tenor, retired in 1988; Appeared at Promenade Concerts, Aldeburgh, Bath, Swansea, Llandaff and Fishguard Festivals, throughout Europe, Israel, North America and the Far East; Performed at Royal Opera House, ENO, WNO, Glyndebourne Touring Opera, English Opera Group, English Music Theatre, Kent Opera, and Handel Opera Society; Frequent broadcasts, numerous first performances and many recordings. *Honours:* Prizes in Geneva, 's-Hertogenbosch, Liverpool and Munich International Competition (1st) and Queens Prize; Honorary RAM, John Edwards Memorial Award, GPWM. *Address:* 61 Queen's Crescent, London NW5 3QG, England.

BOWERS, Evan; Singer (tenor); b. 1960, New York, USA. *Career:* Sang Alfredo and Gounod's Tybalt for Texas Opera Theatre, Ernesto in San Francisco and for the Metropolitan Opera Guild; Ferrando and the Duke of Mantua for Israeli Vocal Arts Institute; European debut 1992, as Don Ottavio for the Wiener Kammeroper; Engagement with the Nuremberg Opera as Tamino, Oberon, Leopold in La Juive, Andres in Wozzeck and Rossini's Almaviva; Guest as Fenton at Innsbruck and Nemorino at the Salzburg Landestheater; Leipzig Opera from 1994, as Rodolfo, Lensky and Don Ottavio; Graz Opera debut as Tamino; Season 1996–97 as Beethoven's Jacquino, Don Ottavio at the Schönbrunn Festival and Gratiano in The Merchant of Venice for Portland Opera; Concerts include: The Missa Solemnis, Haydn's Creation and Seasons, Requiems of Verdi and Mozart; Venues include: France, Germany and the USA. *Current Management:* Athole Still International Management, Forresters Hall, 25–27 Westow Street, London, SE19 3RY, England. *Telephone:* (20) 8771-5271. *Fax:* (20) 8768-6600. *Website:* www .atholestill.com.

BOWERS-BROADBENT, Christopher (Joseph); Concert Organist and Composer; b. 13 Jan. 1945, Hemel Hempstead, England; m. Deirdre Cape, 17 Oct 1970, 1 s., 1 d. *Education:* Chorister, King's College Choir School, 1954–58; Berkhamsted School 1958–62; Royal Academy of Music, 1962–66. *Career:* Organ recitalist; Organist, West London Synagogue and Gray's Inn; Professor, Organ, Royal Academy of Music, 1976–92; mem, Royal College of Organists. *Compositions include:* The Pied Piper, children's opera; The Seacock Bane, teenagers' opera; The Last Man, comic opera; Worthy is the Lamb, oratorio; The Hollow Men, cantata; Te Deum; Collected Church Pieces, 1972; Collected Vocal Music, 1996; the Song at the Sea, organ and orchestra; 7 Words, Media Vital, Duets and Canons, organ solos; Mass for Gray's Inn, 1999. *Recordings:* Passio; Miserere; Trivium; Le Mystère; Duets and Canons, 2001. *Honours:* Fellow of the Royal Academy of Music, 1983. *Address:* 94 Colney Hatch Lane, London N10 1EA, England. *E-mail:* chris@ christopherbowers-broadbent.com. *Website:* www.christopherbowers -broadbent.com.

BOWLES, Edmund Addison, BA, PhD; American fmr musicologist and timpanist; b. 24 March 1925, Cambridge, MA; m. Marianne von Recklinghausen; one s. one d. *Education:* Swarthmore College, Yale University, Berkshire Music Center, Tanglewood, MA. *Career:* instructor in humanities, Mass. Institute if Technology 1951–55; Publicity Staff, Bell Telephone Laboratories, 1955–59 Senior Program Administrator, IBM Corporation, 1959–88; Consultant, Music Division, Library of Congress, 1955–; mem. American Musical Instrument Society; American Musicological Society, Fellowship of Makers and Researchers of Musical Instruments; The Galpin Society; Medieval Academy of America. *Publications:* Computers in Humanistic Research: Readings and Perspectives, 1967; Musikleben des 15. Jahrhunderts, 1976; Musical Performance in The Late Middle Ages (La Pratique Musicale au Moyen-Age), 1983; Musical Ensembles in Festival Books: An Iconographical and Documentary Survey, 1989; The Timpani: A History in Pictures and Documents, 2002; contrib. to various professional journals; Dictionary of the Middle Ages; Encyclopaedia Britannica; Garland Encyclopedia of Percussion; Several New Grove dictionaries; The New Harvard Dictionary of Music. *Honours:* Bessaraboff Prize, 1991 and Curt Sachs Award, 1997, American Musical Instrument Society. *Address:* 3210 Valley Lane, Falls Church, VA 22044, USA (home).

BOWLES, Garrett H.; Music Librarian; b. 3 Feb. 1938, San Francisco, CA, USA; 1 s., 1 d. *Education:* BA, Music, University of California, Davis, 1960; MA, Music Composition, San Jose State University, 1962; MLS, University of California, Berkeley, 1965; PhD, Musicology, Stanford University, 1978. *Career:* Head Music Cataloguer, Stanford University, 1965–79; Head Music Librarian, 1979–, Assistant Adjunct Professor of Music, 1980–, University of California, San Diego; Visiting Lecturer at University of Exeter, England, 1983. *Compositions include:* Festklang for Ernst Krenek, in Perspectives of New Music, 1985. *Recordings:* Handel's Messiah, 1984. *Publications:* Directory, Music Library Automation Projects, 1973, 1979; Ernst Krenek, Bio-bibliography, 1989; Editor, Ernst Krenek Newsletter, 1990–. *Contributions:* Journal of Association for Recorded Sound Collectors; Notes; Forte Artis Musicae. *Address:* Music Library 0175-Q, University of California at San Diego, 9500 Gilman Drive, La Jolla, CA 92093-0175, USA.

BOWMAN, James (Thomas); Singer (Counter-Tenor); b. 6 Nov. 1941, Oxford, England. *Education:* Cathedral Choir School; Kings School, Ely, Cambridgeshire; New College, Oxford; DipEd, 1964, MA (Oxon), History, 1967. *Career:* Sang with English Opera Group, 1967–, with debut as Britten's Oberon, and Early Music Consort, 1967–76; Operatic performances include: Sadler's Wells Opera, 1970–, Glyndebourne Festival Opera, 1970–, Opéra Comique, Paris, 1979–, Geneva, 1983, and Dallas and San Francisco Operas, USA; Operatic roles include: Endymion in La Calisto, The Priest in Taverner in the world premiere at Covent Garden in 1972, Apollo in Death in Venice, and Astron in The Ice Break in the 1977 premiere; Title roles include: Handel's Giulio Cesare, Tamerlano, and Scipione; Appearances include La Scala, Milan in 1980 as Jommelli's Fetonte, English National Opera in 1989 as Amphinomous in The Return of Ulysses, and Promenade Concerts in 1991 in Purcell's Ode for St Cecilia's Day; Sang Britten's Oberon at Aix-en-Provence in 1992, Barak in Handel's Deborah at 1993 Prom Concerts in London; Other roles include: Goffredo in Rinaldo, Lidio in Cavalli's Egisto, and Ruggiero in Vivaldi's Orlando; Sang Herod in Fux's La Fede Sacrilega in Vienna and Monteverdi's Ottone in Poppea at the Spitalfields Festival in London; Bach's St John Passion at St John's, London, 1997; Daniel in Handel's Belshazzar at the 1996 Göttingen Festival; Sang Britten's Oberon at the Barbican, 1998; Title role in Handel's Silla, Royal College of Music, 2000. *Recordings:* Oratorio; Mediaeval and Renaissance vocal music. *Address:* 19a Wetherby Gardens, London SW5 0 JP, England.

BOWYER, Kevin (John); Organist; b. 9 Jan. 1961, Essex, England; m. Ursula Steiner, 27 Aug 1981, 2 s., 2 d. *Education:* Royal Academy of Music with Douglas Hawkridge and Christopher Bowers-Broadbent, 1979–82; Studied with David Sanger. *Career:* Debut: Royal Festival Hall in 1984; Concerts throughout Europe and North America, specializing in unusual and contemporary repertoire; Performances of Kaikhosru Sorabji's Organ Symphony in London, 1987, Århus, 1988 and Linz in 1992; Broadcasts for BBC Radio 3 include works by Ligeti, Hugh Wood, Malcolm Williamson, Berio, Henze, Brian Ferneyhough, Charles

Camilleri, Niccolo Castiglioni; Numerous broadcasts for other networks. *Recordings:* A Late Twentieth Century Edwardian Bach Recital; Alkan Organ Works; Brahms Complete Organ Works; Reubke's 94th Psalm Sonata; Schumann's 6 Fugues on Bach; Organ Works by Dupré, Langlais, Hindemith, Pepping, Arnold Schoenberg; Complete Organ Works of J. S. Bach; Messiaen Organ Works, in 2 vols; Sorabji Organ Symphony No. 1; Works by Busoni, Ronald Stevenson, Alistair Hinton. *Publications:* Articles on Sorabji for The Organ and Organists Review. *Honours:* Grant, Countess of Munster Musical Trust; 1st Prize, St Albans International Organ Festival, 1983; 1st Prizes at international organ festivals in Dublin, Paisley, Odense and Calgary, 1990. *Address:* 2 Kingston Barn College, Kingston Farm, Chesterton, Leamington Spa CV 33 9LH, England. *E-mail:* kevinbowyer@cwcom.net.

BOYD, Anne (Elizabeth); Composer, University Music Teacher and Music Critic; b. 10 April 1946, Sydney, Australia; 1 d. *Education:* BA, 1st Class Honours, University of Sydney; DPhil, University of York; NSW Conservatorium of Music; Composition Teachers: Peter Sculthorpe, Wilfrid Mellers, Bernard Rands. *Career:* Debut: Adelaide Festival of Arts, 1966; Festival performances include: Adelaide in 1966, 1968, and 1976; Opening Season Festival of Sydney Opera House, 1973; Appearances at Edinburgh Windsor Festival, 1974, Aldeburgh Festival, 1980, Hong Kong Arts Festival, 1985, ISCM Festival, Hong Kong, 1986, 'Donne in Musica', Fiuggi, Italy, 1999 and Vale of Glamorgan Festival, Wales, 2001; Lecturer in Music, University of Sussex, 1972–77; Founding Head and Reader, Department of Music at University of Hong Kong, 1981–90; First Australian and first woman to be appointed Professor of Music at the University of Sydney, 1990–. *Compositions include:* Angklung, meditations for solo piano, 1974; Book of the Bells, for piano, 1980; String Quartets Nos 1 and 2; The Voice Of The Phoenix for solo piano, guitar, harp, harpsichord and full orchestra; As It Leaves The Bell for piano, 2 harps and 4 percussion; Goldfish Through Summer Rain, for flute and piano, 1979; Red Sun, Chill Wind, for flute and piano, 1980; Cloudy Mountain for flute and piano, 1981; Bali Moods No. 1 for flute and piano, 1987; Black Sun for orchestra, 1989; String Quartet No. 3, 1991; Grathwai, for orchestra, 1993; Ullaru Mourns, for cello, 1996; '. . . at the rising of the sun. . .', for orchestra, 2001; Choral: As I Crossed a Bridge of Dreams, 1975; The Little Mermaid, children's opera, 1978; The Death of Captain Cook, oratorio, 1978; Coal River, choral symphony, 1979; The Beginning of the Day, children's opera, 1979; The Last of His Tribe, 1980; Revelations of Divine Love, 1995; Dreams for the Earth, youth cantata, 1998; A Vision: Jesus Reassures His Mother, for vocal soloists, 1999; Song cycles for voice and chamber ensemble: My Name is Tian, 1979; Cycle of Love, 1981; Meditations on a Chinese Character, 1996; Last Songs of the Kamikaze, 1997. *Recordings include:* Meditations on a Chinese Character, 1997; Crossing a Bridge of Dreams, 1998.. *Contributions:* Founding Managing Editor, Music Now; Musical Times; Miscellanea Musicologica; Australian Journal of Music Education. *Honours:* AM in the Order of Australia, 1996; Hon. Doctor of the Univ. of York, 2003.. *Address:* c/o Department of Music, University of Sydney, Sydney, NSW 2006, Australia.

BOYD, Douglas; Oboist; b. 1 March 1959, Glasgow, Scotland. *Education:* Studied with Janet Craxton at the Royal Academy and with Maurice Bourgue in Paris. *Career:* Solo engagements in works by Strauss and Mozart, in Europe, The Far East and USA; Conductors have included Abbado, Berglund, Menuhin, Alexander Schneider and Michael Tilson Thomas; Co-Founder of the Chamber Orchestra of Europe as Principal Oboist, and leading member of the Wind Soloists of the Chamber Orchestra of Europe; Played in the Lutoslawski Concerto for Oboe and Harp, Glasgow, 1991; World premiere of Sally Beamish's Oboe Concerto written for him at the Queen Elizabeth Hall, London, 1993; During 1993–94 season performed with the Basle Radio Symphony Orchestra under Rudolph Barshai, National Arts Centre Orchestra of Ottawa under Nicholas McGegan, Hong Kong Philharmonic under David Atherton, BBC Scottish Symphony Orchestra under Alun Francis, and Budapest String Soloists; Has also appeared at the Bath and Boxgrove Festivals and Glasgow's Mayfest; Concertos with various orchestras and tours of the USA with Jeffrey Kahane and the Ridge Ensemble; Invitations to the Perth, Vancouver and Prague Autumn Festivals; In 1997 he made his first tour of Japan; Chamber Music with Andras Schiff, 1999; Developing conducting career, performances include: Scottish Chamber Orchestra, Manchester Camerata, Hong Kong Philharmonic, New Arts Philharmonic Orchestra, Pretoria, Orchestra National de Lyon, France, Upsalla Chamber Orchestra, Sweden. *Recordings:* Bach Concertos with Salvatore Accardo; Beethoven Music for Wind Instruments; Dvořák Serenade in D minor; Haydn Sinfonia Concertante; Vivaldi and Strauss Concertos; Mozart Concerto, Concertante K297b, Quartet K370, Serenades in E flat and C minor, Serenade (Gran partita), K361; Schumann recital with Maria Joâo Pires. *Address:* c/o Frank Salomon Associates, 201 W 54th Street, Suite 1C, NY 10019, USA.

BOYD, James; Violist; b. 1960, England. *Education:* Studied at the Yehudi Menuhin School, Guildhall School of Music and the Menuhin Academy in Gstaad. *Career:* Debut: South Bank, London premiere of Robert Simpson's 13th Quartet; BBC Radio 3 debut in 1991; Frequent tours with the Rafael Ensemble; Co-founder of Vellinger String Quartet in 1990; Participated in masterclasses with the Borodin Quartet at the Pears-Britten School, 1991; Concerts at the Ferrara Music Festival in Italy; Season 1992–93 concerts in London, Glasgow, Cambridge, Davos Festival, Switzerland and the Crickdale Festival in Wiltshire; Played at Wigmore Hall with works by Haydn, Gubaidulina and Beethoven, and at Purcell Room with Haydn's Seven Last Words. *Recordings include:* Elgar's Quartet and Quintet, with Piers Lane. *Honours:* Joint Winner of the Bernard Shore Viola Prize, 1988. *Address:* Vellinger String Quartet, c/o Georgina Ivor Associates, 66 Alderbrook Road, London SW12 8 AB, England.

BOYDE, Andreas; Pianist; b. 13 Nov. 1967, Oschatz, Germany. *Education:* Spezialschule and Musikhochschule, Dresden; Guildhall School of Music and Drama, London; masterclasses, Musikfestwochen Luzern. *Career:* debut with Berlin Symphony Orchestra, 1989; concerts with Dresden Philharmonic Orchestra, 1992, 1996; recital, Munich Philharmonic Hall, Gasteig, 1992; Festival La Roque d'Antheron, France, 1993; concert, Zürich Tonhalle with Zürich Chamber Orchestra, 1994; concerts with Freiburg Philharmonic Orchestra, 1994, 1997, 1999; Dresden State Orchestra, 1994, 1995; recitalist in Schumann Cycle, Düsseldorf, 1995; South American debut, recital in Teatro Municipal Santiago, Chile, 1996; concert, Munich Herkulessaal, with Munich Symphony, 1997; concert tour with Northwest German Philharmonic Orchestra, 1997; recital, Munich Prinzregenten Theatre, 1997; concert tour with Odessa Philharmonic Orchestra, including Cologne Philharmonic Hall and Stuttgart Liederhalle, 1997; recital, Dresdner Musikfestspiele, 1998; gave European premiere of piano concerto, Four Parables by Schoenfield with Dresdner Sinfoniker, 1998; concerts with Hallé Philharmonic, 1999; Schumann recital tour including own reconstruction of Schubert Variations in New York, Germany, London Wigmore Hall, 2000; premiere of piano concerto by John Pickard with Dresdner Sinfoniker, 2000; concerts with Konzertsaal KKL Lucerne with Lucerne Symphony Orchestra, 2000; concerts with Bamberger Symphoniker, 2000, 2001; concert tour with National Symphony Orchestra of Ukraine in the UK, 2001; concert with Bournemouth Symphony Orchestra, 2001; frequent broadcasts with most German radio stations. *Recordings include:* Schumann, Tchaikovsky, Mussorgsky, Ravel, Dvořák, Schoenfield and Brahms. *Publications:* Robert Schumann, Variationen über ein Thema von Schubert, reconstructed score by Andreas Boyde, 2000. *Current Management:* Clarion/Seven Muses, 47 Whitehall Park, London, N19 3TW, England.

BOYKAN, Martin, BA, MM; American composer; *Irving G. Fine Professor of Music, Brandeis University;* b. 12 April 1931, New York; m. Susan Schwalb 1983. *Education:* Berkshire Music Center, Tanglewood, Univ. of Zürich, Harvard Univ., Yale Univ. *Career:* composer-in-residence, Composer's Conference, Wellesley 1987, Warebrook Festival 1998, Abravanel Distinguished Composer, Salt Lake City 2001; Visiting Prof. of Composition, Columbia Univ. 1988–89, New York Univ. 1993, 1999–2000; currently Irving G. Fine Prof. of Music, Brandeis Univ.. *Compositions:* Psalm 126, 1965; String Quartets Nos 1, 1967, 2, 1972, 3, 1988; Concerto for 13 Players, 1971; Piano Trio, 1976; Elegy for soprano and 6 instruments, 1982; Epithalamion, 1985; Shalom Rav, 1987; Fantasy-Sonata for piano, 1987; Symphony No. 1, 1989; Piano sonata No. 2, Nocturne for cello, piano and percussion; Eclogue for 5 instruments, 1991; Echoes of Petrarch, for flute, clarinet and piano, 1992; Voyages for Soprano and piano, 1992; Sonata for cello and piano, 1992; Sea-Gardens for soprano and piano, 1993; Impromptu for violin solo, 1993; Three Psalms for soprano and piano, 1993; Pastorale for piano, 1993; Sonata for violin and piano, 1994; Maariv Settings for chorus and organ, 1995; City of Gold for flute solo, 1996; String Quartet No. 4, 1996; 3 Shakespeare's Songs for Women's Chorus, 1996; Piano Trio No. 2, 1997; Psalm 121, for soprano and string quartet, 1997; Usurpations for piano solo, 1998; Sonata for violin solo, 1998; Flume for clarinet and piano, 1999; Romanza for flute and piano, 1999; A Packet for Susan, 5 songs for voice and piano, 2000; Motet–Al Mishkavi for mezzo-soprano and consort of viols, 2001; Songlines for flute, clarinet, violin, cello; Concerto for violin and orchestra 2003; Second Chances, songs for mezzo-soprano and piano 2005. *Recordings:* String Quartets Nos 1 and 2; Elegy and Epithalamion; String Quartet No. 4; Piano Trio No. 2; City of Gold; Echoes of Petrarch; Sonata for violin and piano; Sonata for solo violin; A Packet for Susan; Flume. *Publications:* Quartets, Nos 1, 3, 4, 1987; Fantasy-Sonata, 1992; Piano Sonata No. 2, 1995; Sonata for cello; Echoes of Petrarch; Impromptu for violin solo; Sonata for violin and piano; City of Gold; Psalm 126; String Quartet No. 2; Piano Trio No. 1; Sonata for Solo Violin, 2000, Usurpations for Piano, 2004, Piano Trio No. 2; Silence and Slow Time: Studies in Musical Narrative, 2004. *Honours:* Rockefeller Award 1974, Fromm Foundation Commission Award 1976, National Endowment for the Arts Grant 1983, winner National Competition of International Society for Contemporary Music 1984, Guggenheim Fellowship 1984, Serge Koussevitzky Music Foundation Grant 1985, American Acad. and National Inst. of Arts and Letters Awards 1986, 1988, Sr Fulbright Lecturer Bar-Ilan Univ. (Israel) 1994. *Address:* Brandeis University, Waltham, MA 02454 (office); 10 Winsor Avenue, Watertown, MA 02472, USA (home). *Telephone:* (781) 736-3337 (office); (617) 926-0188 (home). *E-mail:* boykan@brandeis.edu (office).

BOYLAN, Orla; Singer (soprano); b. Sept. 1971, Dublin, Ireland. *Education:* Dublin and Milan (masterclasses with Leyla Gencer, Robert Kettleson and Renata Scotto). *Career:* Concerts include: Mozart's Requiem, Coronation Mass and Mass in C minor, Messiah, Verdi's Requiem and Rossini's Petite Messe; RTE production of Mendelssohn's A Midsummer Night's Dream and Strauss's Four Last Songs with the Wexford Symphonia; Song recitals at the Salle Cortot, Paris, and throughout Ireland; Season 1996–97 with Mozart's Fiordiligi in Milan, the C Minor Mass in Liverpool and Dublin and concerts with the RTE Concert orchestra; Season 1997–98, leading roles in Falstaff, Turn of the Screw, Nozze di Figaro, Eugene Onegin; Sang Celia in Mozart's Lucio Silla, Opera for Europe, 1998. *Honours:* Winner of Veronica Dunne Singing Competition, 1995; Prizewinner, European Operatic Singing Competition, La Scala, 1996; Belvedere International Singing Competition, Vienna, 1996. *Current Management:* Harrison/Parrott Ltd, 12 Penzance Place, London, W11 4PA, England. *Telephone:* (20) 7229 9166. *Fax:* (20) 7221 5042. *Website:* www.harrisonparrott.com.

BOYLAN, Patricia; Singer (Mezzo-Soprano); b. 1945, London, England. *Education:* Trinity College of Music; National Opera School; London Opera Centre. *Career:* English Opera Group with tours in Britten's operas under the composer to Russia; Appearances with Scottish Opera in Peter Grimes and Die Walküre, concerts and oratorios throughout the United Kingdom, including the Aldeburgh and Edinburgh Festivals; After raising her family returned to the concert hall in such works as Beethoven's Ninth and Mass in C, Mozart's C minor Mass and Requiem, the Verdi Requiem and Mahler's Kindertotenlieder; Sang in El Amor Brujo at the Manuel de Falla Festival in Seville; Operatic appearances as Larina in Eugene Onegin in Lisbon, Azucena in Madrid, Orpheus, Carmen and Amneris at Malaga; Sang Clytemnestra in Elektra for Welsh National Opera in 1992 and Auntie in Peter Grimes for Scottish Opera, 1993; Witch in Hansel and Gretel at Belfast, 1998. *Address:* c/o Opera Northern Ireland, 35 Talbot Street, Belfast, Northern Ireland, BT1 2LD.

BOZARTH, George S.; Historical Musicologist; b. 28 Feb. 1947, Trenton, New Jersey, USA. *Education:* MFA 1973, PhD 1978, Princeton University. *Career:* Professor of Music, University of Washington; Executive Director of the American Brahms Society; Director of Brahms Archive, Seattle, WA; Director of International Brahms Conference, Washington DC, 1983; Performer on historical pianos of late 18th through mid-19th centuries; Member of The Classical Consort; Co-Artistic Director of Gallery Concerts in Seattle. *Publications:* Editions: Johannes Brahms, Orgelwerke, The Organ Works, Munich, G Henle, 1988, J. S. Bach, Cantata, Ach Gott vom Himmel sieh darein, BWV2, Neue Bach Ausgabe, 1/16, 1981, 1984; The Brahms-Keller Correspondence, 1996; Facsimile editions of Brahms' manuscripts; Editor of Brahms Studies: Analytical and Historical Perspectives, 1990. *Contributions:* Numerous articles on Brahms' Lieder and Duets, the genesis and chronology of Brahms' works, Brahms' piano sonatas and First Piano Concerto, editorial problems and questions of authenticity, Brahms' pianos and piano music; performance practice in Brahms' late chamber music. *Address:* School of Music, Box 353450, University of Washington, Seattle, WA 98195-3450, USA. *E-mail:* brahms@u .washington.edu.

BOZIC, Darijan; Composer; b. 29 April 1933, Slavonski Brod, Yugoslavia. *Education:* Composition and Conducting, Ljubljana Academy of Music, 1958, 1961; Further study in London and Paris. *Career:* Conductor and Director of Studies, Slovene Opera, 1968–70; Conductor and Artistic Director, Slovenia Philharmonic, 1970–74; Professor, University of Ljubljana, 1980–94, University of Maribor, 1988–95; Director of SNG Opera, Ljubljana, 1995. *Compositions include:* Stage Works: La Bohème, 57, Opera, 1958; La Putain Respecteuse, Opera after Sartre, 1960; Iago, Happening for 8 performers and tape after Shakespeare, 1968; Ares-Eros Musical Drama after Aristophanes, 1970; Lysistrata 75, Operatic Farce after Aristophanes, 1985; Kralj Lear, Music Drama after Shakespeare, 1985; Telmah, Music Drama after Shakespeare, 1985; Bolt's A Man for All Seasons, 1990; 2 Symphonies, 1965, 1994; Concerto for Two, 1994; Piece of Music for Gerry Mulligan, for 5 saxophones and computer, 1996. *Address:* c/o Slovensko Narodno Gledaslisce, Zupanciceva 1, 61000 Ljubljana, Slovenia.

BRABBINS, Martyn; Conductor; b. 1959, England. *Education:* Goldsmiths' College, London, and Leningrad Conservatoire with Ilya Musin. *Career:* From 1988 appearances with most leading chamber and symphony orchestras in the United Kingdom, including all the BBC Orchestras (BBC Scottish at the 1997 Edinburgh Festival); Further festival engagements at Lichfield (Philharmonia Orchestra), Windsor, Cheltenham, Bath, Aldeburgh, Three Choirs and St Magnus Proms, annually since 1993; Guest with the St Petersburg Philharmonic Orchestra, North German Radio Symphony Orchestra and Orchestra of Gran Canaria; Tour with Australia Youth Orchestra, 1995; Tour of Russia with Sinfonia 21 (1996) and Contemporary Music Network tour of the United Kingdom, 1997; Opera includes Don Giovanni at the Kirov, Magic Flute for English National Opera, Schreker's Der ferne klang for Opera North, From Morning to Midnight for ENO and Alice in Wonderland for Netherlands Opera; Associate Principal Conductor of the BBC Scottish Symphony Orchestra, Principal Conductor of Sinfonia 21 and Conducting Consultant at the Royal Scottish Academy; Premiere recording of Die Kathrin by Korngold with BBC Concert Orchestra, 1997; Season 1999, with Elgar's Enigma Variations at the London Prom concerts; Conducted the BBC Symphony Chorus, the BBC Scottish Symphony Orchestra and Sinfonia 21 at the London Proms, 2002; Founder and director of the Orkney Conducting Course, annual event beginning 2003, and coinciding with the St Magnus Festival; Artistic Director of Cheltenham International Festival of Music, 2005–. *Honours:* Winner, 1988 Leeds Conductors' Competition. *Address:* Allied Artists, 42 Montpelier Square, London SW7 1JZ, England.

BRABEC, Lubomir; Czech classical guitarist; b. 21 May 1953, Plzeň. *Education:* Conservatoire Plzeň, Conservatoire Prague, Royal Academy of Music, Early Music Centre. *Career:* regular appearances with Prague Orchestras; Has performed throughout Europe, USSR, North and Latin America; Many television and radio appearances, including two one-hour television recitals; mem. SAI. *Recordings:* Baroque Music: Bach, Handel, Weiss, Jelinek; Spanish Music: Torroba, Falla, Albeniz; Turina, Rodrigo; A Vivaldi–Guitar Concertos with Prague Chamber Orchestra and with Violist L Maly and Guitarist M Myslivecek; Arrangements: Satie, Falla, Prokofiev; Transformation II–Bach, Janáček, Mussorgsky, Marcello; Lubomir Brabec Live at Prague Spring Festival–Dowland, Bach, Villa-Lobos; Viola and Guitar, Italian Music with Lubomir Maly. *Honours:* Title, Laureate of the Concours International de Guitare, Paris, 1974; H Villa-Lobos Medal, 1987, from Brazilian Government. *Current Management:* Pragokoncert, Maltezske nam 1, 11813 Prague 1, Czech Republic.

BRACANIN, Philip Keith, MA, PhD; Australian composer; *Professor and Head, School of Music, University of Queensland*; b. 26 May 1942, Kalgoorlie, Western Australia. *Education:* Univ. of Western Australia. *Career:* Faculty, Univ. of Queensland 1970–, Prof. and Head, School of Music 1997–; comms from Univ. of Queensland and Queensland Symphony Orchestra. *Compositions include:* With and Without for small orchestra 1975, Trombone Concerto 1976, Selections from the Omar Khayyam for choir and strings 1979, Heterophony for orchestra 1979, Rondellus for string orchestra 1980, Because We Have No Time, song cycle for low voice and orchestra 1981, Clarinet Concerto 1985, Concerto for Orchestra 1985, Throw Me a Heaven Around a Child, for baritone and chamber orchestra 1986, Concerto for Orchestra No. 2 1987, Dance Poem for chamber orchestra 1990, Guitar Concerto 1991, Symphony No. 2 for soprano, SATB choir and symphony orchestra 1995, Symphony No. 3 1995, Eternal Images for soprano, clarinet, horn and piano 1998, Windmills of Time for string orchestra 2000, Blackwoodriver Suite for guitar quintet 2001, Clocktower for orchestra 2002, Blackwood River Concerto for guitar and marimba/vibraphone 2002, Shades of Autumn, concerto for oboe and chamber orchestra 2003. *Recordings:* Guitar Concerto, Clarinet Concerto, Violin Concerto, Symphony No. 2, Symphony No. 3, Dance Gundah Concerto for Didjeridu and Orchestra, Under Yaarandoo for Didjeridu, Guitar and Orchestra. *Publications:* Symphony No. 2, 1998, Symphony No. 3, 1998. *Honours:* Australasian Performing Right Assen Award 1995. *Address:* c/o School of Music, University of Queensland, St Lucia, Queensland 4072 (office); 50/12 Bryce Street, St Lucia, Queensland 4067, Australia (home). *Telephone:* (7) 3365-3502 (office); (7) 3371-9889 (home). *Fax:* (7) 3365-4488 (office). *E-mail:* p.bracanin@uq.edu.au (office). *Website:* www .uq.edu.au/music (office); www.bracanin.com (home).

BRACEFIELD, Hilary Maxwell, MA, DipMus, DipTchg, LTCL; music lecturer and critic; b. 30 June 1938, Briggs, Dunedin, New Zealand. *Education:* Univ. of Christchurch. *Career:* teacher Brayfield High School, Dunedin; Lecturer Worcester Coll. of Education; Sr Lecturer and Head of Dept Univ. of Ulster; currently part-time lecturer Univ. of Ulster and Open Univ.; mem. Incorporated Soc. of Musicians, Royal Musical Assen (Convenor Irish Chapter), Int. Federation of Univ. Women. *Publications:* Contact Journal of Contemporary Music (part ed.), contrib. to Music and Musicians, Musical Times, Radio Times, BBC Radio. *Honours:* Blair Trust Travelling Fellowship 1970–73. *Address:* 103 Monkstown Road, Newtownabbey, County Antrim, BT37 0LG, Northern Ireland (home). *Telephone:* (28) 9086-9044 (home). *Fax:* (28) 9086-9044 (home). *E-mail:* HM.Bracefield@ulster.ac.uk (office).

BRACHT, Roland; Singer (Bass); b. 1952, Munich. *Education:* Studied at the Munich Musikhochschule; Studied at the Munich Music College, under Professor Blaschke. *Career:* Debut at the National Theatre in Verdi's Don Carlos; Sang at the Munich Opera Studio from 1971; Member of the Stuttgart Opera from 1973, notably as the Commendatore, in the production of Don Giovanni which reopened the Staatsoper, 1984; Ludwigsburg, 1978 as Masetto; Schwetzingen Festival, 1983, in the premiere of The English Cat by Henze; San Francisco, 1985 in Der Ring des Nibelungen; Debut in the War Memorial Opera House in San Francisco, June 1985; Debut at the Metropolitan Opera as King Heinrich, 1986; Sang Pogner in Die Meistersinger at the opening of the new Essen Opera, 1988; King Heinrich at Pretoria, 1989; Sang Colline in La Bohème at Stuttgart, 1991 and Mustafà in L'Italiana in Algeri, 1996; Season 1998 as Mozart's Osmin, and Rocco in Fidelio; Season 2000–01 at Stuttgart as Wagner's Hagen and Philip II in Don Carlos. *Recordings:* Don Giovanni; Die Entführung; Das Rheingold; Die Zauberflöte; Oedipus Rex; Alceste by Gluck; Die Feen by Wagner; Video of Der Freischütz. *Address:* c/o Staatstheater Stuttgart, Oberer Schlossgarten 6, 7000 Stuttgart, Germany.

BRADBURY, Colin; Clarinettist; b. 1935, England. *Education:* Studied at the Royal College of Music with Frederick Thurston, graduating in 1956. *Career:* Principal Clarinettist of the BBC Symphony, 1968–93; Performances of Concertos by Mozart, Weber, and Nielsen at the London Prom Concerts and director of the RCM Wind Ensemble; Duo partnership with pianist, Oliver Davies from 1978 with performances and recordings of Italian operatic fantasias, sonatas by Reger, Victorian music and The Art of The Clarinettist; Tutor with the National Youth Orchestra of Great Britain. *Address:* Manygate Management, 13 Cotswold Mews, 30 Battersea Square, London SW11 3 RA, England.

BRADLEY, Gwendolyn; Soprano; b. 12 Dec. 1952, New York City, USA. *Education:* North Carolina School of the Arts, Winston-Salem, North Carolina; Curtis Institute of Music, Philadelphia; Academy of Vocal Arts, Philadelphia. *Career:* Debut: Nannetta, Falstaff, Lake George Opera, New York, 1976; Metropolitan Opera debut, Nightingale, L'Enfant et les Sortilèges, 1981; Appearing as Blondchen, Gilda and Offenbach's Olympia; European debut, Corfu Festival, Greece, 1981; Guest appearances with opera companies in Cleveland, Philadelphia, Central City, Amsterdam, Glyndebourne, Hamburg, Berlin, Monte Carlo, Nice; Sang Rodelinda with Netherlands Opera, 1983–84 (also Sophie in Der Rosenkavalier); Paris Opéra 1986, Zerbinetta; Appeared as the Fiakermilli in Arabella at the 1987 Glyndebourne Festival; Deutsche Oper Berlin, 1989, as Musetta; Sang Gilda at the Wiesbaden Festival, 1990, with the company of the Deutsche Oper; Sang the Heavenly Voice in Don Carlos at the Deutsche Oper, 1992; Mozart's Blonde at Los Angeles, 1995; Season 1995–96 with Oscar and Nannetta at the Berlin Staatsoper; Pamina at Los Angeles, 1998; Deutsche Oper Berlin 2000, as Verdi's Oscar and Gilda; Many engagements as soloist with leading USA orchestras; Recitals. *Address:* c/o Columbia Artists Management Inc, 165 West 57th Street, New York, NY 10019, USA.

BRADSHAW, Claire; Singer (mezzo-soprano); b. 1970, Hull, England; m. Craig Ogden. *Education:* Royal Northern Coll. of Music, and with Barbara Robotham, David Pallard. *Career:* appearances, 1994– with Scottish Opera-Go-Round and Scottish Opera as Maddalena, Cherubino, Hansel and Dryad, and concert performances as Carmen for WNO; Spoleto Festival with Richard Hickox and in Vaughan Williams's The Poisoned Kiss with Hickox and the London Symphony Orchestra; concerts throughout the north of England at King's Coll., Cambridge (Messiah), with the Hallé Orchestra and in Western Australia and Provence; with Suzuki in concert (Royal Liverpool Philharmonic Orchestra) and recitals throughout the UK and Australia, 1997; sang Suzuki for WNO, 1998; Season 1999 included Lisetta in Il Mondo della Luna, 2nd Lady for WNO and a tour of South Africa with her husband, Australian classical guitarist Craig Ogden, in recital and appearing with major orchestras; sang St Matthew Passion with Aalborg Symphony Orchestra, Copenhagen; Mercédès with WNO, 2000; Varvara in Katya Kabanova with WNO, 2001. *Honours:* Webster Booth/ESSO Award; James Gulliver Prize, Scotland. *Current Management:* Harlequin Agency Limited, 203 Fidlas Road, Cardiff, CF14 5NA, England.

BRADSHAW, Murray Charles, MMus, PhD; academic; b. 25 Sept. 1930, Illinois, USA; m.; two s. one d. *Education:* American Conservatory of Music, University of Chicago. *Career:* Prof. of Musicology; mem. International and American Musicological Socs, American Guild of Organists. *Compositions:* several organ compositions in The Organists Companion. *Publications:* The Origin of the Toccata, 1972; The Falsobordone, 1978; Francesco Severi, 1981; Girolamo Diruta Il Transilvano, 1984; Giovanni Luca Conforti, 1985; Gabriele Fattorini, 1986; Emilio de'Cavalieri, 1990; Giovanni Luca Conforti: Breve et facile, 1999; contrib. to Journal of Musicology; Performance Practice Review; The Music Quarterly; The Music Review; Studi Musicali; Musica Antiqua; Musica Disciplina; Tijdschrift. *Honours:* American Philoso-

phical Soc. award 1987. *Address:* Department of Musicology, UCLA, Los Angeles, CA 90024, USA.

BRADSHAW, Richard (James); Conductor; b. 26 April 1944, Rugby, England; m. Diana Hepburne-Scott, 30 June 1977, 1 s., 1 d. *Education:* BA Honours, London University; Studied Piano and Organ; Conducting privately with Sir Adrian Boult; Calouste Gulbenkian Fellowship to work with Royal Liverpool Philharmonic under Sir Charles Groves. *Career:* Founder and Artistic Director, New London Ensemble; Chorus Director, Glyndebourne Festival, 1975–77; Resident Conductor, San Francisco Opera, 1977–89; Chief Conductor, Head of Music, 1989–94, Artistic Director, 1994–98; General Director, 1998–, Canadian Opera Company. *Recordings:* Canadian Broadcasting Corporation; Conductor: Rarities by Rossini and Verdi, plus chorus; French and Italian Arias, with Richard Margison; Soirée Française, with Michael Schade and Russell Braun; Recordings of Brahms, Bruckner, Verdi; Serata Italiana with Michael Schade and Russell Braun; Don Giovanni: Leporello's Revenge (Rhombus Media film soundtrack) with Dmitri Hvorostovsky. *Current Management:* Organisation Internationale Artistique, Paris, France. *Address:* Canadian Opera Company, 227 Front Street East, Toronto, Ontario M5A 1E8, Canada.

BRAEM, Thuering L. M.; Conductor and Composer; b. 10 April 1944, Basel, Switzerland. *Education:* Basel University; Heidelberg University; Piano Diploma, degree in Conducting, Academy of Music, Basel; MA, Composition, University of California, Berkeley; Studied Conducting, Curtis Institute of Music, Philadelphia. *Career:* Director, Music School, Basel, 1973–87; Director, Lucerne Conservatory, 1987–; Music Director, Radio-Choir, Basel and Junge Philharmonie Zentralschweiz; President, Jeunesses Musicales, Switzerland, 1984–90; Principal Guest Conductor, Bohemian Chamber Philharmony, Pardubic, and others. *Compositions:* Lettres de Cezanne; Alleluja for Voice; Ara for Flute Ensemble (all Nepomuk-Verlag, AARAU); Chamber Music, Choral Music; Ombra for Violin, viola and String Orchestra, 1991; Torrenieri for Horn and Strings, 1992; Concerto for Piano Trio and Orchestra, 1992. *Recordings:* Children's Songs of the American Indians; Fauré's Requiem; Music for cello and Orchestra by Martinů, Fauré, Dvořák and Tchaikovsky; Panton, Orchestral Music with Young Philharmonic of Central Switzerland. *Publications:* Musik und Raum, Basel, 1986; Series, Information und Versuche, 1975–90, 20 Issues; Bewahren and Oeffnen, Aarau, 1992; Research and Development in Future Institutions of Higher Learning in Music, 1997. *Contributions:* Articles in newspapers and journals. *Honours:* Edwin Fischer Prize, 1992. *Address:* Lerchenstr 56, 4059 Basel, Switzerland.

BRAININ, Norbert; Violinist; b. 12 March 1923, Vienna, Austria; m. Kathe Kottow, 7 April 1948, 1 d. *Education:* Studies with Professor Ricardo Odnoposoff, Konservatorium, Vienna; Professor Rosa Hochmann-Rosenfeld, Vienna; Carl Flesch and Max Rostal, London. *Career:* Debut with Amadeus Quartet and for forty years until 1987 all over the world; Professor of annual Amadeus Quartet Course at the Royal Academy of Music, London; Professor of Violin Playing at Scuola di Musica di Fiesole, 1980; Professor of Quartet Playing at Reichenau, Austria; Professor of Violin Playing at Hochschule für Musik Franz Liszt, Weimar, 1995; mem, Royal Academy of Music, London; Hochschule für Musik, Cologne. *Recordings:* Amadeus Quartet (predominantly with Deutsche Grammophon since 1960) of almost the entire classical and romantic repertoire for string quartet and/or strings and piano; Also works with clarinet, oboe and flute. *Honours:* O.B.E., 1961; DHC, University of York, 1968; University of London, 1983; Cross of Honour for Arts and Science, Federal Republic of Austria, 1972; Das Grosse Verdienstkreuz der Bundesrepublik Deutschlands, First Class, 1973; Goldenes Verdienstkreuz of the City of Vienna, 1999. *Address:* 19 Prowse Avenue, Bushey Heath, Hertfordshire, WD23 1JS, England.

BRAITHWAITE, Nicholas Paul Dallon, FRAM; musician and conductor; b. 26 Aug. 1939, London, England; m. Gillian Agnes Haggarty 1985; one s. one d. *Education:* Royal Academy of Music; Festival Masterclasses in Bayreuth and with Hans Swarowsky, Vienna. *Career:* Chief Conductor, Adelaide Symphony Orchestra, 1987–91; Principal Guest Conductor, 1977–84, Principal Conductor, 1984–91, Manchester Camerata; Chief Conductor, Tasmanian Symphony Orchestra; Permanent Guest Conductor, Norwegian State Radio Orchestra; Associate Conductor to Constantin Silvestri with Bournemouth Symphony Orchestra; Frequent Guest Conductor for all major orchestras in the United Kingdom; Toured Japan and Korea as Associate Conductor to Georg Solti with London Philharmonic Orchestra; Appearances with ORTF Orchestra, Paris; Oslo Philharmonic; Bergen Harmonien Symphony Orchestra; Odense Symphony Orchestra; New Zealand Symphony Orchestra; Melbourne Symphony Orchestra; Sydney Symphony Orchestra; Danish Radio Orchestra; Bergen Festival; Symphony Nova Scotia, Halifax; Musical Director and Chief Conductor, Stora Teater Opera and Ballet Companies, Gothenberg, 1981–84; Musical Director, Glyndebourne Touring Opera, 1976–80; Associate Principal Conductor, English National Opera Company, 1970–74; Dean of Music, Victorian

College of the Arts, 1988–91; Conducted Tosca at Elder Park, Adelaide, 1990; Francesca da Rimini for Chelsea Opera Group, 1994; Fledermaus for Scottish Opera, 1997; mem, ISM; MU. *Address:* Taringa Park, Mount Barker Road, Mahndorf, South Australia 5245.

BRAMALL, Anthony; Conductor; b. 6 March 1957; m. Elisabeth Werres. *Education:* Singing, Guildhall School of Music and Drama, London; postgraduate advanced conducting course. *Career:* Musical Dir, Southend Symphony Orchestra, Musical Dir, Southend Symphony Chorus, 1979–81; Asst to the Music Dir, Municipal Opera Pforzheim, Germany, 1981–85; House Conductor and Head of Music Staff, Municipal Opera Augsburg, 1985–89; Guest Conductor, Southwest German Chamber Orchestra, Vienna Chamber Orchestra, State Opera Brunswick, State Opera Darmstadt; Conductor, RIAS Radio Symphony Orchestra, and debut in the Berlin Philharmonie, 1988; Senior House Conductor, Coburg Opera, 1989; Senior House Conductor, State Opera Hanover, and Guest Conductor with the NDR Radio Symphony Orchestra, 1990–95; debut, Semper Opera, Dresden, 1992; Music Dir, Opera Krefeld and Principal Conductor, Niederrhein Symphony, 1995–2002; Music Dir and Principal Conductor, Badisches Staatstheater, Karlsruhe, 2002–; recent productions: La Bohème, La Cenerentola, La Clemenza di Tito (Dresden), Elektra, Turandot, Der Rosenkavalier, Madama Butterfly, Parsifal, Falstaff, Flying Dutchman, Figaro, Otello, Tosca, Wozzeck. *Recordings:* albums with Slovak Philharmonic and the Slovak Radio Symphony Orchestra; radio broadcasts with RIAS Berlin, NDR Hanover and WDR Cologne. *Honours:* Special Prize for 20th Century Music, Third International Hans Swarowsky Conducting Competition.

BRANDIS, Thomas; Violinist; b. 1935, Hamburg, Germany. *Education:* Studied with Eva Hauptmann at the Musikhochschule Hamburg, 1952–57 and with Max Rostal in London. *Career:* Leader, Berlin Philharmonic Orchestra, 1962–63; Co-Founder, Brandis Quartet, 1976; Many Chamber engagements in Europe and Tokyo, with the Wiener Singverein and the Berlin Philharmonic; Festival appearances at Salzburg, Florence, Vienna, Edinburgh, Tours and Bergen; Has co-premiered the Clarinet Quintet by Helmut Eder, 1984, and the 3rd Quartets of Gottfried von Einem and Giselher Klebe, 1981, 1983; Solo Concerto work under such conductors as Karajan, Böhm, Solti, Abbado, Schmidt-Isserstedt, Keilberth, Jochum, Tennstedt, and Albrecht. *Recordings:* As soloist: Albums with Karajan and Böhm; With the Brandis Quartet: Complete quartets of Schubert and Beethoven with other repertoire for the EMI/Electrola, Teldec, Orfeo, Nimbus and Harmonia Mundi labels. *Honours:* Prize, German Hochschulen Competition, 1946; International ARD Competition in Munich, 1947. *Address:* c/o Konzert-Direktion Hans Adler (Brandis Quartet), Auguste-Viktoria-Strasse 64, D–14199 Berlin, Germany.

BRANDSTETTER, John; Singer (Baritone); b. 2 Oct. 1949, Wayne, Nebraska, USA. *Education:* Studied at the University of Nebraska and with Richard Hughes in New York. *Career:* Debut: Minnesota Opera, 1976, as Ben in Conrad Susa's Black River; Sang at Minneapolis in the premiere of Argento's The Voyage of Edgar Allan Poe, 1976; Has also sung in the premieres of Bernstein's, A Quiet Place, 1983, repeated in Vienna, 1986, as Josuke in Miki's Joruri, St Louis, 1985, and in The Balcony by Di Domenica, Boston, 1990; Season 1986–87 appeared as Enrico (Lucia di Lammermoor) at Seattle, Silvio (Pagliacci) in Detroit and as the Beast in the US premiere of Stephen Oliver's Beauty and the Beast, at St Louis; Sang Egberto in Verdi's Stiffelio at Sarasota, 1990, and the High Priest in Alceste at the Chicago Lyric Opera; Other roles include Mozart's Almaviva and Papageno, Figaro, Germont and Falke; Has also appeared at Düsseldorf, the City Opera New York, Miami and Philadelphia.

BRANDT, Anthony; Composer; b. 23 June 1961, New York City; m., 1 s., 1 d. *Education:* Harvard University, BA, 1983; California Institute of the Arts, 1987. *Career:* Assistant Professor of Composition, Rice University, 1998–; Visiting Lecturership, Harvard University, 1993–97; Tufts University, 1996; MIT, 1997. *Compositions:* Septet-à-tête for seven players, 1993; String quartet, 1994; Hidden Motives for two pianos, 1996; Octopiece for eight players, 1996; Songs for soprano and string quartet, 1997; Turbulent Tones for orchestra, 1998; Breathing Room for soprano and string orchestra, 1998; Piéce de Résistance for three trombones, piano and percussion, 1998; Creeley Songs for soprano and piano, 1999; Roman à Clef for cello and piano, 2000; Crucible of the Millennium, documentary film score, 2001; Four Shadowings - String Quartet No.2, 2001–02; Express for orchestra, 2002; Handful for piano, 2002. *Contributions:* Editor-in-Chief, Soundout Digital Press. *Honours:* Fellow, MacDowell Colony, 1996 and 1998; Composer in Residence, International Music Festival of Morelia, Mexico, 1996; Fellow, Tanglewood Music Center, 1994; Fellow, Wellesley Composers, 1993. *Address:* 5206 Cheena Drive, Houston, TX 77096, USA.

BRANDUS, Nicolae, PhD; Romanian composer, pianist and musicologist; *Professor, National University of Music, Bucharest;* b. 16 April 1935, Bucharest; m. 1st Maria Cecylia Ostrowska 1969; m. 2nd Ioana Jeronim 1982; two s., one d. *Education:* Nat. Univ. of Music, Bucharest, Cluj-Napoca Acad. of Music. *Career:* debut: pianist, George Enescu Philharmony of Bucharest 1955, piano soloist 1958–75; concert performances in Romania and abroad; soloist, Ploiesti Philharmonic Orchestra 1959–69; Prof., Nat. Univ. of Music, Bucharest 1968–81, 1992–; Ed. Muzica Review, Bucharest 1981–; compositions printed, recorded, played and broadcast on radio and TV in Bucharest and abroad; mem. Romanian Composers' and Musicologists' Union, SACEM, Paris; Pres. Romanian Section, Int. Soc. of Contemporary Music 1992–2002; Visiting Composer and Lecturer in Europe, Asia and USA. *Compositions:* ed and recorded: Pieces for piano 1966, 1984, 7 Psalms 1969, 1981, Mamsell Hus 1977, 2002, Dialo(va)gos, concerto for piano and orchestra 1988–2002: ed: 8 Madrigals for choir a capella 1968, Sonata for 2 pianos 1978, The Betrothal (opera) 1981, Languir me fais 1986, Rhythmodia 1989, Oratorio on texts of the Gospel of Thomas 1996, Melopedia and Fuga for bassoon 1998, Ostinato for piano solo 2004. *Recordings include:* Vagues 1990, Kitsch-N 1984, Antifonia 1986, With the Gipsy Girls (opera) 1988, Dance in Rhythms, Ak-Sak 1998, European Parody 2001, Oratorio on texts of the Gospel of Thomas 2001, Phtora I – Durations 2001, 2nd Concerto for piano and orchestra 2002, Tabulatures 2002, Soliloque I 2004, Soliloque IV (Reverberations) 2004, Cnatus Firmus 2004, Match-Monodie and Polyphonie 2004. *Publications:* Interrelations (musical studies) 1984; numerous contribs to magazines and journals. *Honours:* Order of Cultural Merit (Bucharest) 1968, Officer 2004; Prize, Romanian Composers and Musicologists Union 1974, 2002, George Enescu Prize, Romanian Acad. 1977, prizes from Romanian radio and TV 1975, 1977. *Address:* Str. Dr Felix 101, Bl. 19 Sc. A Apt 42, 011036 Bucharest, Romania (home). *Telephone:* (21) 6507409 (home). *E-mail:* nbrandus@b.astral.ro (home). *Website:* www .cimec.ro/muzica/Pers/branduseng.htm (home).

BRANSCOMBE, Peter John; University Teacher and Musicologist; b. 7 Dec. 1929, Sittingbourne, Kent, England; m. Marina Elizabeth Riley 1967; two s. one d. *Education:* Dulwich Coll., London, 1944–48; MA, Worcester Coll., Oxford, 1956; PhD, Bedford Coll., London, 1977. *Career:* appearances on BBC radio and television, Austrian radio, Scottish television; Lecturer, German, 1959–69, Senior Lecturer, 1970–79, Prof. of Austrian Studies, 1979–, Emeritus Prof., 1996–, Univ. of St Andrews; Governor, Royal Scottish Academy of Music, 1967–73; mem. Scottish Early Music Consort (mem. of advisory cttee 1981–89), Royal Musical Association, MHRA, English Goethe Society, International Nestroy Society, Internationales Franz Schubert Institut, Schubert Institute (United Kingdom), Haydn Society of Great Britain, W. H. Auden Society, Scottish Arts Council (mem. music cttee 1974–81, mem. Council 1976–79), Conference of University Teachers of German in Scotland (Chair. 1983–85). *Publications:* Translator, Mozart and His World in Contemporary Pictures, 1961; Co-translator, Mozart, A Documentary Biography, 1965, revised 1966, revised third edition, 1990; Part Author, Co-Editor, Schubert Studies: Problems of Style and Chronology, 1982; Author, Mozart, Die Zauberflöte, 1991; Editor, Johann Sämtliche Werke: Stücke 35 (1998), 36 (2000), 37 (2001), 38 (1996). *Contributions:* New Grove Dictionary of Music and Musicians, approximately 120 articles, 1980 and 2001; New Grove Dictionary of Opera, approximately 120 articles, 1992; various professional journals. *Address:* 32 North Street, St Andrews, Fife KY16 9AQ, Scotland.

BRANT, Henry (Dreyfus); Composer; b. 15 Sept. 1913, Montreal, Quebec, Canada. *Education:* Studied at McGill Conservatorium, Montreal, 1926–29, the Institute of Musical Art and The Juilliard School in New York, 1932–34; Private study with Wallingford Riegger, Aaron Copland, George Antheil and Fritz Mahler. *Career:* Worked for Radio, Films, Jazz Groups and Ballets as Composer, Conductor and Arranger; Commercial music in Hollywood and Europe; Teacher at Columbia University, 1945–52, The Juilliard School, 1947–54 and Bennington College, 1957–80; Performer on Wind and Percussion Instruments; Music has employed spatial separation with variously contrasted instrumental and vocal groups. *Compositions include:* Antiphony I for 5 Orchestral Groups, 1953, revised 1968; Ceremony, Triple Concerto for violin, oboe and cello with voices, 1954; Labyrinth I (strings) and II for winds, 1955; The Grand Universal Circus, spatial opera, 1956; Conclave for Mezzo, Baritone and Instrumental ensemble, 1955; On the Nature of Things, for chamber orchestra, 1956; The Children's Hour for Voices, Brass, Organ and Percussion, 1958; Atlantis, Antiphonal Symphony, 1960; Violin Concerto with Lights, 1961; Fire in Cities, for 2 choirs and 2 instrumental ensembles, 1961; Odyssey–Why Not? for 2 Flutes and 4 small orchestral groups, 1965; Verticals Ascending for 2 wind ensembles, 1967; Windjammer for 5 Wind Instruments, 1969; An American Requiem, for wind orchestra, 1973; Divinity: Dialogues in the Form of Secret Portraits, spatial chamber music, 1973; Six Grand Pianos Bash Plus Friends, 1974; Solomon's Gardens for Voices, 24 Handbells and 3 Instruments, 1974; Homage to Ives, for baritone and orchestral groups, 1975; American Commencement for 2 Brass and percussion groups; Antiphonal

Responses, for 3 bassoons and orchestra, 1978; Cerberus, for double bass and piccolo, 1978; The $1,000,000 Confessions for 2 Trumpets and 3 Trombones, 1978; Trinity of Spheres for 3 orchestral groups, 1978; Orbits for 80 Trombones, Soprano and Organ, 1979; The Glass Pyramid, spatial fantasy, 1980; Inside Track, spatial piano concerto, 1980; The Secret Calendar, spatial chronicle, 1980; Horizontals Extending, for 2 wind ensembles and jazz drummer, 1982; Desert Forests for orchestral groups, 1983; Litany of Tides for Solo Violin, 2 orchestras and 4 Voices, 1983; Meteor Farm, spatial oratorio, 1983; Fire under Water, multiple improvisations, 1983; Burning Brant on the Amstel, mobile spatial aquatic spectacle, 1984; Western Springs for 2 orchestras, 2 choruses and 2 jazz combos, 1984; More recent compositions include: Pathways to Security, ambulant spatial cantata, 1990; Prisons of the Mind, spatial symphony for 8 orchestral groups, 1990; Skull and Bones, spatial oratorio, 1991; Hidden Hemisphere, spatial assembly for 4 concert bands, 1992; Fourscore, 4 spatial string quartet including tenor-cello, 1993; Homeless People, spatial string quartet with percussion inside piano, 1993; Trajectory, spatial cantata with silent film, 1994; Dormant Craters, for spatial percussion orchestra, 1995; Plowshares and Swords, total symphonic orchestral environment in 74 individual parts, 1995; Jericho for 16 trumpets and drums, 1996; Festive Eighty for concert band, 1997. *Address:* 1607 Chino Street, Santa Barbara, CA 93101-4757, USA.

BRAUCHLI, Bernard; clavichord player; b. 5 May 1944, Lausanne, Switzerland. *Education:* piano studies in Lausanne and Vienna, 1963–69; studied musicology at the New England Conservatory with Julia Sutton; researched Iberian keyboard music at Lisbon, 1977. *Career:* debut, Fribourg, Switzerland, 1972; US debut at Marlboro Coll., Vermont, 1973; numerous tours of Europe and North America with keyboard works of the 16th–18th Centuries, including works by Portuguese and Spanish composers; has given summer courses in Austria and Spain, 1978–83; Lecturer at the Boston Museum of Fine Arts, 1978–83; Prof. of Clavichord at the New England Conservatory 1983–92; founder and pres. of the Festival Musica Antica a Magnano; mem. of programme cttee, Festival International de l'Orgue Ancien de Valère; hon. life mem. Midwestern Historical Keyboard Society; mem. Het Clavichord, Netherlands. *Recordings include:* The Renaissance Clavichord; 18th Century Portuguese Keyboard Music; 18th Century Music for Two Keyboard Instruments; Keyboard Works of Carl Philip Emmanuel Bach. *Publications include:* The Clavichord (Nicholas Bessarabof Prize 1999), 1998; contributions to many professional journals. *Honours:* Julius Adams Stratton Prize for Cultural Achievement 1983. *Address:* Associazione Musica Antica a Magnano, via Roma 43, 13887 Magnano, Italy (office); 19a ave des Cerisiers, 1009 Pully, Switzerland (home). *Telephone:* (015) 679260 (office); (21) 728-5976 (home). *Fax:* (015) 679260 (office); (21) 728-7056 (home). *E-mail:* mam@bmm.it (office); bbrauchl@worldcom.ch (home). *Website:* www.mam.biella.com (office); www.bernardbrauchli.ch (home).

BRAUN, Lioba; Singer (Mezzo-Soprano); b. 1963, Germany. *Education:* Studied with Charlotte Lehmann. *Career:* Appearances in opera at Karlsruhe, 1987–89; Vienna Volksoper, 1989–90; Vienna Staatsoper 1992–93, notably in The Ring, conducted by Dohnányi; Mannheim Opera from 1993, as Wagner's Fricka, Venus and Brangaene; Countess Geschwitz in Lulu, Dalila, Carmen and Azucena; Bayreuth Festival as Brangaene in Tristan and Isolde, conducted by Barenboim; Further engagements at La Scala (The Ring, from 1994), Dresden, Zürich, Rome (Waltraute in Götterdämmerung) and Tokyo (season 1999–2000); Kundry in Parsifal at Mannheim, 2000, and Mahler's 8th Symphony in Berlin; Other concerts at Leipzig, Amsterdam, Munich and Rome (Gurrelieder by Schoenberg); Season 2001–02 in Das Rheingold at the Vienna State, the Brahms Alto Rhapsodie in Dresden, Mahler's 3rd in Munich and Waltraute at Bayreuth, Brangaene at Barcelona, 2002; Festival appearances include the Semperoper of Dresden, Opera Leipzig, the Opera House of Zurich, the State Theatre Stuttgart, in Genova, in Rome and La Scala, performing with the Munich Philharmonic, the Viennese and the Bamberg Symphony Orchestras, the Leipzig Gewandhaus Orchestra, the Concertgebouw Amsterdam and the conductors Blomstedt, Barenboim, Abbado, Maazel, Herreweghe, Levine, Muti, Sawallisch, Stein and Sinopoli. *Address:* c/o Theateragentur Dr G. Hilbert, Maximilianstr. 22, 80539 Munich, Germany. *E-mail:* schmidt@hilbert.de. *Website:* www.hilbert.de.

BRAUN, Russell; Singer (Baritone); b. 1968, Frankfurt, Germany. *Education:* Studied in Frankfurt and Toronto. *Career:* Appearances with Canadian Opera as Mozart's Guglielmo and Papagaeno, Rossini's Figaro and in concert performances of Henri VIII by Saint-Saëns and Massenet's Cendrillon; New York City Opera 1992, as Morales in Carmen, Pacific Opera 1993 as Britten's Demetrius; Concerts include Messiah in Montreal, Belshazzar's Feast with the Hartford Symphony Orchestra and at Salzburg in Mozart concert arias; Season 1995–96 as Mozart's Count in Monte Carlo and at the Paris Opéra-Comique; Sang Borilée in Rameau's Les Boréades at the 1999 London Prom concerts;

Season 2000–01 as Chorèbe in Les Troyens at Salzburg and Billy Budd in Toronto. *Address:* c/o Poilvé, 16 Avenue Franklin D. Roosevelt, F–75008 Paris, France.

BRAUTIGAM, Ronald; Pianist; b. 1 Oct. 1954, Haarlemmermeer, Netherlands; m. Mary Elizabeth Jane Cooper, 14 Dec 1995. *Education:* Sweelinck Conservatory, Amsterdam; RAM, London; Rudolf Serkin, USA. *Career:* Debut: Concertgebouw Amsterdam, 1979; Appearances with all major orchestras in the Netherlands; Foreign engagements include Oslo Philharmonic Orchestra, Bavarian Radio Symphony Orchestra Munich, English Chamber Orchestra; Salzburg Festival debut, 1992, with the Concertgebouw Orchestra under Frans Brüggen; mem, Ronald Stevenson Society, Edinburgh; Frank Martin Society, Netherlands. *Recordings:* Shostakovich, Concerto No. 1 (Concertgebouw Orchestra/Chailly, Decca); Hindemith, 2nd Kammermusik (Concertgebouw Orchestra/Chailly, Decca); Mendelssohn, piano concertos (Nieuw Sinfonietta Amsterdam, Markiz); Complete Piano Sonatas of W.A. Mozart and J. Haydn on fortepiano (Bis). *Honours:* Dutch Music Prize, 1984. *Current Management:* Marianne Brinks. *Address:* c/o Marianne Brinks, O.Z. Voorburgwal 72, 1012 GE Amsterdam Netherlands.

BRAY, Roger, MA, DPhil; British university teacher; *Professor of Music, Lancaster University;* b. 29 March 1944, Sheffield, England; m. Juliet Brown; one s. one d. *Education:* King's Coll. Choir School, Cambridge, King Edward's School, Birmingham, Magdalen Coll., Oxford. *Career:* Lecturer Univ. of Victoria, Canada 1968–70, Asst Prof. 1970; Lecturer in Music Manchester Univ. 1970–79; Prof. of Music Lancaster Univ. 1979–; mem. Royal Musical Assen. *Publications:* Blackwell History of Music in Britain II, The Sixteenth Century (ed.), Robert Fayrfax, complete works I and II (ed.), Early English Church Music 43 and 45 (ed.); contrib. to Music and Letters, Early Music, Musica Disciplina, Proceedings of the Royal Musical Association, RMA Research Chronicle, Journal of Plainsong and Medieval Music Society. *Address:* Department of Music, Lancaster University, Lancaster, LA1 4YW, England (office). *E-mail:* r.bray@lancaster.ac.uk (office).

BRAZDA, Josef; Czech horn player; b. 12 March 1939, Babice u Rosic, Brno; m. Vlasta Brázdová 1974; 2 d. *Education:* private artistic school, Brno, State Conservatoire, Brno, Janáček Acad. of Musical Arts, Brno. *Career:* debut: State Philharmonic Orchestra, Brno; Prague Academic Wind Quintet; Prague Chamber Orchestra; Musici d' Praga-Chamber Orchestra; Haydn Sinfonietta Vienna; Solo concertos and sonatas; horn instructor. *Compositions:* Instructive Compositions for 2, 3, 4 Horns. *Recordings:* Richard Strauss, Horn Concerto No. 2; Paul Hindemith, Horn Concerto; Franz Danzi, Horn Concerto E Major; Paul Hindemith, both Sonatas; Joseph Haydn, Horn Concerto D Major, Hob VII; Joseph Haydn, Divertimenti, Baritone Octets, with Haydn Sinfonietta Vienna. *Honours:* 2nd Prize, IX Int. Musikwettbewerb, Munich 1960, 1st Prize, XV Int. Prague Spring Festival 1962. *Address:* Roklanska 1095, 25101 Ricany u, Prague, Czech Republic.

BREAM, Julian, CBE, ARAM, FRCM, FRNCM; British classical guitarist and lutenist; b. 15 July 1933, London, England. *Education:* Royal College of Music. *Career:* debut, began professional career, Cheltenham 1947; Wigmore Hall, London, 1950; tours in Europe, America, Japan, Australia, India and Far East; Appeared at festivals at Aldeburgh, Bath, Edinburgh, Three Choirs, King's Lynn, Netherlands, Ansbach, Berlin and Stratford (Canada); Research into Elizabethan Lute Music which led to revival of interest in that instrument; Has encouraged contemporary English compositions for the guitar (including works by Britten, Walton and Tippett); Henze has composed Royal Winter Music (2 Sonatas after Shakespeare) for him; Formed Julian Bream Consort, 1960; Inaugurated Semley Festival of Music and Poetry, 1971; Season 1990–91 included concerts with Scottish Chamber Orchestra and tours of Italy and the United Kingdom (including 40th Anniversary Concert at the Wigmore Hall); Spring tours of Germany and the USA; Promenade Concerts, London with Malcolm Arnold's Guitar Concerto, 1991; Season 1992–93 included 60th Birthday Concert at the Wigmore Hall, Summer Festivals and BBC Proms. *Recordings include:* Villa-Lobos Concerto; Five Preludes and 12 Preludes. *Honours:* DUniv, Surrey, 1968; Exclusive Contract with EMI Classics since 1990; Villa-Lobos Gold Medal, 1976. *Current Management:* Hazard Chase, Norman House, Cambridge Place, Cambridge CB2 1NS, England. *Telephone:* (1223) 312400. *Fax:* (1223) 460827. *Website:* www.hazardchase.co.uk.

BRECKNOCK, John; Singer (Tenor); b. 29 Nov. 1937, Long Eaton, Derbyshire, England. *Education:* Birmingham Music School with Frederic Sharp and Dennis Dowling. *Career:* Debut: Alfred in Die Fledermaus, Sadler's Wells, London, 1967; Later repertoire includes Rossini's Almaviva and Comte Ory, Mozart's Belmonte and Ottavio and Verdi's Duke of Mantua; With the English National Opera at the London Coliseum sang in the British stage premieres of Prokofiev's War and Peace, 1972, and Henze's The Bassarids, 1974, and in the world premiere of Gordon Crosse's The Story of Vasco, 1974; Covent Garden debut 1974, as Fenton in Falstaff; Glyndebourne debut 1971; Has sung at the Metropolitan Opera and toured Canada in 1973; At the Teatro Regio Parma, 1985, sang Almaviva in Il Barbiere di Siviglia; Season 1985–86 sang Rossini roles in Paris. *Recordings include:* Alfredo in an English language Traviata, opposite Valerie Masterson. *Address:* c/o Teatro Regio Parma, Via Garibaldi 16, 43100 Parma, Italy.

BREDEMEYER, Reiner; Composer; b. 2 Feb. 1929, Velez, Colombia. *Education:* Studied with Karl Hoeller in Munich, 1949–53, and with Wagner-Regeny at the Akademie der Kunste in East Berlin, 1955–57. *Career:* Conductor of the German Theatre in East Berlin since 1961; Teacher, Akademie der Kuenste from 1978. *Compositions include:* Leben des Andres, Opera, 1971; Die Galoschenoper, 1978; Orchestral: Integration, 1961; Variante, 1962; Schlagstück 3, for Orchestra and 3 Percussion Groups; Bagatellen für B, for Piano and Orchestra, 1970; Piano und… 1970; Symphony, 1974; Double Concerto for Harpsichord, Oboe and Orchestra, 1974; Auftakte for 3 Orchestral Groups, 1976; Concerto for Oboe and Orchestra, 1977; 9 Bagatelles for Strings, 1984; Chamber includes: 4 Quintets, 1956, 1958, 1969, 1991; 3 String Quartets, 1962, 1968, 1983; 3 Septets, 1980, 1987, 1990; Aufschwung OST for piano, oboe, percussion and tuba, 1993; Cantata, 1961; Wostock for Choir and Orchestra, 1961; Karthago for Chorus and Chamber Ensemble, 1961; Zum 13.7 für Schoenberg, for Female Voice and Ensemble, 1976; Cantata 2 for 16 Voices and 16 Instruments, 1977; Das Alltaegliche for Soprano, Tenor and Orchestra, 1980; Die Winterreise for Baritone, Piano and Horn, 1984; Die Schoene Muellerin for Baritone, String Quartet and Horn Quartet, 1986; Operas: Candide, 1981–82; Der Neinsager, 1990; Songs; Piano Music. *Address:* GEMA, Postfach 80 07 67, 81607 Munich, Germany.

BREEDT, Michele; Singer (Mezzo-soprano); b. 1962, Johannesburg, South Africa. *Education:* Studied at Cape Town University. *Career:* Debut: Mozart's Cherubino in Cape Town; Performances in Cologne, Brunswick and Oldenburg as Adalgisa in Norma, Zerlina in Don Giovanni, Meg Page in Falstaff; Tchaikovsky's Pauline and Bellini's Romeo; Other roles include Emilia in Otello by Rossini; Verdi's Flora; Hansel, and Lola in Cavalleria Rusticana; Idamante in Idomeneo for Pretoria Opera; Season 1997–98 as Diana in Cavalli's Calisto for the Vienna Kammeroper and as Nicklausse in Les Contes d'Hoffmann at Cape Town; Many concert engagements in South Africa; Season 2000–01 as Magdalena at Bayreuth, Charlotte at Innsbruck and Nicklausse for the Vienna Staatsoper. *Address:* Opera of the Cape, PO Box 4107, Cape Town 8000, South Africa.

BREHM, Alvin; composer, conductor and double bass player; b. 8 Feb. 1925, New York, USA. *Education:* Juilliard with Zimmermann and Giannini; Columbia University, MA with Wallingford Riegger. *Career:* Played double bass with the Pittsburgh Symphony Orchestra, 1950–51; The Contemporary Chamber Ensemble, 1969–73; The Group for Contemporary Music, 1971–73; The Philomusica Chamber Music Society, 1973–83; The Chamber Music Society of Lincoln Center, 1984–89; Conductor of Contemporary Music from 1947; Founder-Conductor of the Composers' Theater Orchestra, 1967; Teacher, State University of Stony Brook, 1968–75; Manhattan School of Music, 1969–75; and SUNY at Purchase from 1982; Dean of Purchase, State University of New York Music Division, 1982–92; Head of Composition, Purchase, 1992–; Member of Fulbright Composition Panel, 1992–95. *Compositions include:* Divertimento for Trumpet, Horn and Trombone, 1962; Dialogues for Bassoon and Percussion, 1964; Brass Quintet, 1967; Cello Sonata, 1974; Concertino for Violin and Strings, 1975; Quarks for flute, Bassoon, String Quartet and Piano, 1976; Sextet for Piano and Strings, 1976; Piano Concerto, 1977; Double Bass Concerto, 1982; Tuba Concerto, 1982; Sextet for Woodwind Quintet and Piano, 1984; Children's Games for Flute, Clarinet, String Trio and Piano, 1985; Cialles for Russian Town, piano, 1993; Metamorphy, European Tour, piano; Lament for the Victims of AIDS for string quartet, 1996. *Recordings:* Cycle of Songs to Poems of Lorca, for soprano and 10 instruments; Quintet for Brass; Bassoon Quartet; 3 works for piano. *Contributions:* Clavier magazine, cover articles; American Record Guide, reviews. *Honours:* Grants: Naumburg Foundation, NEA, New York State Arts Council.

BRELL, Mario; German fmr singer (tenor); b. 1936, Hamburg. *Education:* studied at Hamburg. *Career:* sang operetta at Hof, 1963–65; Lucerne, 1965–67; Oldenburg, 1967–71; Krefeld, 1971–73; At Gelsenkirchen, 1973–82; Sang such repertory as Lohengrin, Parsifal, Zemlinsky's Zwerg, Hoffmann in Les Contes d'Hoffmann; Member of the Deutsche Oper am Rhein, Düsseldorf, from 1982, singing Diomedes in Penthesilea by Schoeck, 1986; Guest appearances in Zürich, Frankfurt, Karlsruhe, Milan, Barcelona and Berlin (both Die Fledermaus), Cologne, Hamburg and Bilbao (both Lohengrin), Gothenburg (Hoffmans Erzählungen) and Wiesbaden (premiere of Kirchner's Belshazar, 1986); Antwerp (Ariadne auf Naxos); Amsterdam, 1987, as Busoni's Mephisto and in Alexander von Zemlinsky's Kreidekreis; Bielefeld, 1990, as Bacchus in Ariadne auf Naxos; Other roles include the Count in

Schreker's Irrelohe and Max in Der Freischütz; Sang the major in Einem's Besuch der alten Dame, Gelsenkirchen 1991; Dortmund 1995, as Siegfried; broadcasts include Dessau's Lukullus, Smetana's The Kiss, Nestroy's Tannhäuser-Parodie, Mahagonny. *Recordings include:* Der Zar lässt sich photographieren by Weill, Tannhäuser-Parodie by Nestroy. *Address:* c/o Deutsche Oper am Rhein, Heinrich-Heine Allee 16, 40213 Düsseldorf (office); Siegener Str. 29, 47533 Kleve, Germany (home).

BREM, Peter; Violinist; b. 1948, Munich, Germany. *Education:* Graduate, Richard Strauss Conservatory, Munich, 1970. *Career:* Berlin Philharmonic Orchestra, 1970–76; Co-Founder, Brandis String Quartet, 1976, with concerts in Tokyo, London, Hamburg, Munich, Paris and Milan and engagements with the Wiener Singverein and the Berlin Philharmonic; Festival appearances at Salzburg, Edinburgh, Lucerne, Tours, Bergen, Florence and Vienna; Has Co-Premiered the 3rd Quartets of Gottfried von Einem and Giselher Klebe, 1981, 1983, and the Clarinet Quintet of Helmut Eder, 1984; Solo concerts with such orchestras as the Radio-Sinfonieorchester Berlin. *Recordings include:* Albums in the standard repertoire from 1978 with the EMI/Electrola, Teldec, Orfeo and Harmonia Mundi labels; Recent releases of Beethoven, Weill, Schulhoff and Hindemith and the Schubert String Quintet with Nimbus. *Honours:* Prizewinner at the Deutsche Hochschulewettbewerb. *Address:* c/o Konzert-Direktion Hans Adler (Brandis Quartet), Auguste-Viktoria-Strasse 64, D–14199 Berlin, Germany.

BREMERT, Ingeborg; Singer (Soprano); b. 1930, Germany. *Career:* Sang at Pforzheim, 1953–55, Zürich Opera, 1955–57; Member of the Munich Opera, 1960–67; Schwetzingen Festival, 1961, as Elizabeth in the premiere of Henze's Elegy for Young Lovers; Many guest appearances as Mozart's Arminda (La finta giardiniera) and Cherubino, Eva, the Composer (Ariadne auf Naxos), Isabella in Krenek's Karl V and Regina in Mathis der Maler by Hindemith. *Address:* c/o Bayerische Staatsoper, Max Joseph-Platz, W-8000 Munich 1, Germany.

BRENDEL, Alfred; Austrian pianist and writer; b. 5 Jan. 1931, Wiesenberg; s. of Ing. Albert and Ida (née Wieltschnig) Brendel; m. 1st Iris Heymann-Gonzala 1960 (divorced 1972); one d.; m. 2nd Irene Semler 1975; one s. two d. *Career:* studied piano under Sofija Deželić (Zagreb), Ludovika v. Kaan (Graz), Edwin Fischer (Lucerne), Paul Baumgartner (Basel), Edward Steuermann (Salzburg); studied composition under A. Michl (Graz) and harmony under Franjo Dugan (Zagreb); first piano recital Musikverein Graz 1948; concert tours through Europe, Latin America, North America 1963–; Australia 1963, 1966, 1969, 1976; has appeared at many music festivals, including Salzburg 1960–, Vienna, Edinburgh, Aldeburgh, Athens, Granada, Puerto Rico, London Proms and has performed with most of the major orchestras of Europe and USA, etc.; numerous recordings, including complete piano works of Beethoven, Schubert's piano works 1822–28; mem. Acad. of Arts and Sciences (USA). *Recordings:* extensive repertoire; Beethoven's Complete Piano Works, Beethoven Sonatas, Beethoven Concertos (with Vienna Philharmonic Orchestra and Simon Rattle) 1998. *Publications:* essays on music and musicians in Phono, Fono Forum, Österreichische Musikzeitschrift, Music and Musicians, Hi-Fi Stereophonie, New York Review of Books, Die Zeit, Frankfurter Allgemeine Zeitung, Musical Thoughts and Afterthoughts 1976, Nachdenken über Musik 1977, Music Sounded Out (essays) 1990, Musik beim Wort genommen 1992, Fingerzeig 1996, Störendes Lachen während des Jaworts 1997, One Finger Too Many 1998, Kleine Teufel 1999, Collected Essays on Music 2000, Alfred Brendel on Music 2001, Augerechnet Ich 2001 (English edn The Veil of Order: In Conversation with Martin Meyer 2002), Spiegelbild und Schwarzer Spuk (poems) 2003, Cursing Bagels (poems) 2004. *Honours:* Hon. RAM; Hon. RCM; Hon. Fellow, Exeter Coll. Oxford 1987; Commdr des Arts et des Lettres 1985, Hon. KBE 1989, Ordre pour le Mérite (Germany) 1991; Hon. DMus (London) 1978, (Oxford) 1983, (Warwick) 1991, (Yale) 1992, (Exeter) 1998, (Southampton) 2002, Hon. DLitt (Sussex) 1981, Dr hc (Cologne) 1995; Premio Città de Bolzano, Concorso Busoni 1949, Grand Prix du Disque 1965, Edison Prize (five times 1973–87), Grand Prix des Disquaires de France 1975, Deutscher Schallplattenpreis (four times 1976–84, 1992), Wiener Flötenuhr (six times 1976–87), Gramophone Award (six times 1977–83), Japanese Record Acad. Award (five times 1977–84, with Scottish Symphony Orchestra/Sir Charles Mackerras 2002), Japanese Grand Prix 1978, Franz Liszt Prize (four times 1979–83), Frankfurt Music Prize 1984, Diapason D'Or Award 1992, Heidsieck Award for Writing on Music 1990, Hans von Bülow-Medaille, Kameradschaft der Berliner Philharmoniker e. V., 1992, Cannes Classical Award 1998, Ehrenmitgliedschaft der Wiener Philharmoniker 1998, Léonie Sonnings Musikpris, Denmark 2002, Ernst von Siemens Musikpreis 2004. *Current Management:* Ingpen & Williams, 7 St George's Court, 131 Putney Bridge Road, London, SW15 2PA, England. *Telephone:* (20) 8874-3222. *Fax:* (20) 8877-3113.

BRENDEL, Wolfgang; Singer (baritone); b. 20 Oct. 1947, Munich, Germany. *Education:* Studied in Munich. *Career:* Sang Don Giovanni in

Kaiserslautern, 1970, then became a member of the Bayerische Staatsoper Munich; Roles include Papageno, Germont and Pelléas; Guest appearances in Hamburg, Düsseldorf, and Karlsruhe; Metropolitan Opera debut 1975, as Mozart's Count; Sang Verdi's Miller with the Chicago Lyric Opera, 1983; Bayreuth Festival, 1985, as Wolfram in Tannhäuser; Covent Garden debut 1985, as Luna in Il Trovatore; Eugene Onegin and Donizetti's Enrico, 1988; Metropolitan Opera and Bayreuth Festival, 1989, as Germont and Wolfram; Teatro, San Carlos, Lisbon, 1989, as Amfortas; Chicago 1990, as Eugene Onegin; Other roles include Puccini's Marcello and Strauss's Mandryka; Season 1991–92 as Amfortas in Parsifal at La Scala and as Count Luna at Munich; Sang Verdi's Renato, 1994; Wagner's Dutchman at the Deutsche Oper Berlin, 1997; Sang the Count in Capriccio at the New York Met, 1998; Season 2000–01 as Amfortas and the Dutchman at the Deutsche Oper, Berlin, Strauss's Mandryka at Zürich and Munich, Barak in Die Frau ohne Schatten at Essen. *Recordings:* Die Lustigen Weiber von Windsor, Paer's Leonora and Der Freischütz (Decca); Die Zauberflöte, La Bohème and Zar und Zimmermann (HMV); Ein Deutsches Requiem (Deutsche Grammophon); DVD of Die Meistersinger, Deutsche Oper 1995 (Arthaus). *Current Management:* Ingpen & Williams Ltd, 7 St George's Court, 131 Putney Bridge Road, London, SW15 2PA, England.

BRENER, Uri; Composer; b. 17 July 1974, Moscow; m. Ingrid Klüger, 19 Dec 1995, 1 s. *Education:* Central Special Music School, 1981–89; Gnessin College, Moscow, 1989–91; Robert Schumann Hochschule, Düsseldorf, 1991, 1994–96; Köln Hochschule, 1992–94; Sweelinck Conservatory, Amsterdam. *Career:* Concerts in Russia, Germany and Israel; Music to a short film; Form, Farbe und Licht, Fantasia for cello and piano, Reverie for piano, broadcast by Israeli classical music radio channel, 1998; Performances by the leading Israeli modern music performers as well as soloists; GEMA, 1996–; Israel Composer's League, 1997–. *Compositions:* Pieces for piano solo, Triptych, 1991; Aquarelles, 1990–97; Form, Farbe und Licht, 1995; Au debut et a la Fin, 1996; Aphorismes, 1997; Pieces for solo clarinet, Marimba, Cello, three vocal pieces, 1993; Sacrifice for soprano, violin and piano, 1990; Pieces for tuba, cello, clarinet and violin with piano; Chamber ensembles including string quartet, 1990; Wind quintet, 1991; Preludium, Fantasia und Fuga for 9 players, 1993; Three ballet scenes for 6 players, 1996; On The Other Side of Sound, 1998; Quartet for oboe, horn, cello and piano, 1998. *Recordings:* String quartet, 1997; Form, Farbe und Licht, 1998. *Publications:* IMC. *Honours:* Extraordinary Talented Composer, Special Committee of the Israeli Government, 1998. *Address:* Or Hachaim 1549/2, 87300 Ofakim, Israel.

BRENET, Thérèse; French fmr composer; b. 22 Oct. 1935, Paris; d. of Gen. François Brenet and Marguerite Warnier. *Education:* Paris Conservatoire. *Career:* Prof., Paris Conservatoire from 1970. *Compositions include:* La nuit de Maldoror, for female voice, piano and cello 1963; Pantomime, for flute 1974; Lyre d'Etoiles, for string trio with recitative 1979; Cristaux, for Celtic harp and mandolin 1982; Odi et Amo, for violin and orchestra 1992; Chimeres, for mandolin and orchestra 1993; Le Retour de Quetzalcoatl, for cello and orchestra 1995; Moires, for 6 ondes martenots and strings, 1985; Incandescence, for baritone, saxophone and piano, 1986; Vibration, for Celtic harp and strings, 1984; Oceanides, for piano left hand, 1986; Plus souple que l'eau, for ondes martenot and percussion, 1986; Au Vent de l'Ouest (To the West Wind), for piano 2000. *Honours:* Prix de Rome 1965. *Address:* c/o SACEM, 225 avenue Charles de Gaulle, 92521 Neuilly sur Seine Cédex, France (office).

BRENNEIS, Gerd; Singer (Tenor); b. 3 Jan. 1936, Nienhegen, Mecklenburg, Germany. *Career:* Debut: Essen, 1960, as Curzio in Figaro; Sang at Augsburg from 1965 as Verdi's Manrico and Gabriele Adorno, Idomeneo, Andrea Chénier, Lensky and Dmitri (Boris Godunov) and in operas by Wagner; Bayreuth Festival, 1973–74, as Walther and Siegmund; Deutsche Oper Berlin from 1974 as Wagner's Parsifal, Lohengrin and Tannhäuser, Strauss's Bacchus and the Emperor in Die Frau ohne Schatten; Huon in Oberon, 1986; Metropolitan Opera, 1976, as Walther; Has sung Tristan at Pretoria, South Africa, 1985, in Tokyo with the company of the Vienna Staatsoper, 1986, and Turin, 1987; Has also sung in Munich, Cologne, Florence and Milan; New York, 1976–81, as the Emperor; Nice Opera, 1988, as Siegfried; Television appearances include the title role in Wagner's Rienzi, with the Wiesbaden Opera; Deutsche Oper 1994, as Wagner's Erik. *Address:* Deutsche Oper Berlin, Richard Wagnerstrasse 10, 1000 Berlin, Germany.

BRESNICK, Martin; Composer; b. 13 Nov. 1946, New York, USA; 1 d. *Education:* BA in Music Composition, Hartt School of Music, University of Hartford, 1967; MA, 1968 and DMA, 1972 in Music Composition, Stanford University; Akademie für Musik, Vienna, Austria, 1969–70. *Compositions:* Trio for 2 Trumpets and Percussion, 1966; Introit, 1969; Ocean of Storms, 1970; Intermezzi, 1971; Musica, 1972; B's Garlands, 1973; Wir Weben, Wir Weben, 1978; Conspiracies, 1979; Der Signal, 1982; High Art, 1983; String Quartet No. 2 Bucephalus; One, 1986; Lady Neil's Dumpe, 1987; Trio, 1988; Pontoosuc, 1989; Musica Povera, Nos 1–12, 1991–1999; String Quartet No. 3, 1992; Cadillac Desert, 1996; GRACE, concerto for 2 marimbas and orchestra, 2000; Songs of the House People, 1999; For the Sexes: The Gates of Paradise, solo piano and DVD, 2001; My Twentieth Century, chamber music, 2002. *Recordings:* B's Garlands; Conspiracies; 3 Intermezzi; String Quartet No. 2 Bucephalus; Wir Weben, Wir Weben; Lady Neil's Dumpe; Piano Trio; Just Time. *Publications:* How Music Works. *Contributions:* Mosaic; Yale Journal of Music Theory. *Honours:* Charles Ives Living Award, American Academy of Arts and Letters. *Address:* Yale School of Music, PO Box 208246, New Haven, CT 06520, USA.

BRESNIG, Ulla; Singer (Mezzo-Soprano); b. 1939, Germany. *Education:* Studied at the Graz Conservatory. *Career:* Sang at the St Gallen Opera, 1964–65, Trier, 1967–69, and Kiel from 1969 (notably in the German premiere of Milhaud's La Mère Coupable); Hanover Opera, 1969–76; Among her best roles have been Mozart's Marcellina, Erda, the Countess in Lortzing's Der Wildschütz, Octavian, Verdi's Fenena and Azucena, and Orzse in Kodály's Háry Janos; Many concert appearances.

BRESS, Hyman; Violinist; b. 30 June 1931, Cap, Canada. *Education:* Studied at the Curtis Institute and with Heifetz at Tanglewood. *Career:* Soloist with the Montreal Symphony, 1956–60, and has given many concertos and solo engagements in North America and Europe; Bach's D Minor partita at the Wigmore Hall, London; Premiered the Virtuose Musik by Blacher, 1968. *Recordings include:* Solo violin works by Ysaÿe. *Publications include:* An Introduction to Modern Music.

BRETT, Charles; Singer (Countertenor); b. 27 Oct. 1941, Maidenhead, Berkshire, England; m. (1) Brigid Barstow, 1 Aug 1973, marriage dissolved, 1 s., 1 d., (2) Cecile Bourasset, 25 Sept 1999. *Education:* Choral scholar, King's College, Cambridge. *Career:* Leading performer with early and Baroque music ensembles led by Munrow, Harnoncourt, Leonhardt, Hogwood, Gardiner, Herreweghe and Malgoire; Recent engagements in US, France, Switzerland, Germany, Spain and Norway; Handel's Theodora, in Oslo; Israel in Egypt in Geneva; Bach's Christmas Oratorio in Versailles; Bach's St John Passion in Cambridge and London; B Minor Mass with Collegium Vocale Gent at Lourdes, Paris and Lyon; Many concerts with Le Grande Ecurie et la Chambre du Roy, conducted by Malgoire; Opera debut, 1984, in Angelica Vincitrice di Alcina by Fux, at Graz; Handel's Semele at Ludwigsburg; Tour of France with La Clemenza di Tito by Gluck; Aachen Opera, 1987, as Oberon; Founder and Director, Amaryllis Consort, vocal group specializing in Renaissance repertoire; Professor, Royal Academy of Music; Masterclass in Canada, Belgium, Germany, Spain, Mexico, France; Conductor: Performances of works by various composers in France; Dido and Aeneas for Cervantino Festival, Mexico, 1995; Visiting Professor, Toulouse Conservatoire; mem, ISM. *Recordings:* Handel's Dixit Dominus, Rinaldo, Messiah, The Triumph of Time and Truth; Bach's B Minor Mass; Lambert: Leçons des Ténèbres; Mozart Masses; Bach: Cantatas; Burgon: Canciones de Alma; Italian and English madrigals with Amaryllis Consort; Vivaldi's Nisi Dominus and Stabat Mater; Blow: Ode on the Death of Mr Henry Purcell. *Honours:* Hon RAM, 1991. *Address:* 34 Lebanon Court, Twickenham TW1 3DA, England.

BRETT, Kathleen; Singer (Soprano); b. 4 Sept. 1962, Campbell River, Canada. *Career:* Appearances with the Canada Opera Ensemble and elsewhere in Canada as Susanna, Bizet's Leila (Manitoba Opera), Adina (Calgary Opera) and Pamina (Edmonton Opera); European debut as Dorinda in Handel's Orlando at Antwerp, followed by Mozart's Barbarina at Covent Garden, Susanna at Monte Carlo and Amor in Gluck's Orphée et Euridice with L'Opera Française in New York; Other repertory includes Kristina in The Makropulos Case (San Francisco), Drusilla in Monteverdi's Poppea (Dallas Opera), Despina (Vancouver Opera), Zerlina, and Amarilli in Handel's Pastor Fido (at Toronto); Concerts include Messiah at Montreal, the Fauré Requiem with the Vancouver Symphony Orchestra, and A Midsummer Night's Dream by Mendelssohn; Season 1997–98 with Sophie in Der Rosenkavalier at Seattle, Pamina at Dallas, Nannetta in Falstaff at Los Angeles, Mozart's Servilia at Antwerp and Iris in Semele for Opera Pacific. *Honours:* Best Canadian Singer at the 1991 International Mozart Competition; Sullivan Award winner; Canadian Council Career Development Grant. *Address:* c/o Seattle Opera Association, PO Box 9248, Seattle, WA 98109, USA.

BREUL, Elisabeth; Singer (Soprano); b. 25 Aug. 1936, Gera, Germany. *Education:* Studied at the Musikhochschule of Gera and Dresden. *Career:* Debut: Gera 1958, as Donna Anna; Member of the Dresden Opera from 1960; Guest appearances in Berlin, Brussels, Brno, Łódź, Budapest, Genoa and Wiesbaden and music centres in Russia, France, Romania and Spain; Other roles include Tatiana in Eugene Onegin, Natasha in War and Peace, Marguerite, Tosca, Agathe, and Mozart's Countess and Susanna; Many appearances in the concert hall, in music by Bach and Handel; Teacher at the Musikhochschule of Dresden and Leipzig. *Honours:* Winner, Schumann Competition, Zwickau, 1973.

BREVIG, Per A., BA, DMus; Norwegian conductor and fmr trombonist; *Music Director, East Texas Symphony Orchestra*; b. 7 Sept. 1936, Halden; m. Berit Brevig 1959; two s. two d. *Education:* Juilliard School; conducting studies, Bergen, Norway 1963, 1964, Norrkoping, Sweden 1963, 1965, Hilversum, Netherlands 1964, The Juilliard School, New York, USA 1966–68, Leopold Stokowski Symposium for Young Conductors, New York 1966–68. *Career:* debut as soloist with Bergen Philharmonic Orchestra, 1961; principal trombonist, Detroit Symphony Orchestra 1966, Bergen Philharmonic Orchestra, Norway 1957–65, American Symphony Orchestra, New York 1966–70, Metropolitan Opera Orchestra, New York 1968–94; Music Dir and Conductor, Empire State Opera Company, New York 1990–; Conductor, Island Lyric Opera, New York 1993–2000; Music Dir, East Texas Symphony Orchestra; faculty mem., The Juilliard School, Manhattan School of Music, Mannes Coll. of Music, New York; Aspen Music Festival, Colorado; int. guest conductor for opera and symphonies; commissions and dedications include Roger Smith, Sonata for Trombone and Piano 1965, Alcides Lanza, Acufenos for Trombone and Four Instruments 1966, Egil Hovland, Concerto for Trombone and Orchestra, Noel Da Costa, Four Preludes for Trombone and Piano 1973, Vincent Persichetti, Parable for Solo Trombone 1978, Robert Starer, Serenade for Trombone, Vibraphone and Strings 1982, Paul Turok, Canzona Concertante No. 2 1982, Walter Ross, Trombone Concerto No. 2 for Trombone and Orchestra 1984, Melvyn Broiles, The Great Northern Posaune for Trombone and Brass Ensemble 1989, Arne Nordheim, Return of the Snark for Trombone and Electronic Tape 1989; Guest conducts orchestras worldwide; Music Director of East Texas Symphony Orchestra 2002–; founder and Pres. of the Edvard Grieg Society Inc., New York; mem. advisory boards of Medical Problems of Performing Artists and Musikphysiologie und Musik Medizin. *Publications include:* Avant Garde Techniques in solo Trombone Music, Problems of Notation and Execution, 1974; Losing One's Lip and Other Problems of Embouchure, 1990; Edvard Grieg and the Edvard Grieg Society, 1993; Medical Problems of Musicians, 1995. *Honours:* Koussevitsky Fellowship, Henry B Cabot Award, 3 Naumburg Fellowships, Neill Humfeld Award for excellence in teaching, Royal Medal of St Olav, presented by Norwegian King Olav V in recognition of his efforts on behalf of Norwegian music and culture in the USA 1990.

BREVIK, Tor; Composer, Conductor and Music Critic; b. 22 Jan. 1932, Oslo, Norway. *Education:* Studied violin, viola and theory, Oslo Conservatory; Also Sweden. *Career:* Founded Youth Chamber Orchestra, Oslo, 1958; mem, The Society of Norwegian Composers. *Compositions:* Opera, Da kongen kom til Spilliputt, 1973; Adagio and Fugue for Strings, 1958; Overture, 1958; Serenade for Strings, 1959; Chaconne for Orchestra, 1960; Concertino for Clarinet and Strings, 1961; Music for Violin, 1963; Canto Elegiaco for Orchestra, 1964; Contrasts, chamber ballet, 1964; Elegy for Soprano, Viola, Double bass and Percussion, 1964; Divertimento for wind quintet, 1964; Adagio Religioso for Horn, 1967; String de Quartet, 1967; Concertino for Strings, 1967; Music for 4 strings, 1968; Intrada for orchestra, 1969; Romance for Violin and Orchestra or Piano, 1972; Andante Cantabile for Violin and Strings, 1975; Septet, 1976; Fantasy for Flute, 1979; Light of Peace, Christmas play for children, 1980; Viola Concerto, 1982; Sinfonietta, 1989; Choral music; Songs; Sinfonia Brevik, 1991; The Singing Raft, cantata for soprano, mixed chorus, children's chorus and strings, 1992; Music for Orchestra, 1993; Serenade for 10 Winds, 1994; On Request!, music for band, 1994. *Recordings:* String Quartet, Divertimento for Wind Quintet; Septet and Elegy for Soprano. *Address:* Nebbaveien 53, NB 1433 Vinterbro, Norway.

BREWER, Aline; Harpist; b. 14 Sept. 1963, Shropshire, England. *Education:* Royal College of Music with Marisa Robles. *Career:* Debut: Wigmore Hall, 1990; Principal Harp with the Royal Philharmonic Orchestra; Former member of the European Community Orchestra and the Britten-Pears Orchestra; Solo appearances with the London Mozart Players, Primavera and the Britten-Pears Orchestra; Duo recitals with flautist Jennifer Stinton; Member of the Britten-Pears Ensemble, with performances throughout the United Kingdom and the USA. *Recordings include:* Romantic music for Flute and Harp; Mozart's Concerto K299, with Jennifer Stinton and the Philharmonia Orchestra. *Honours:* Joint Winner, South East Arts Young Artists Platform. *Address:* c/o Owen White Management, 14 Nightingale Lane, London N8 7QU, England.

BREWER, Bruce; Singer (Tenor); b. 12 Oct. 1941, San Antonio, Texas, USA; m. Joyce Castle. *Education:* Studied with Josephine Lucchese at University of Texas, Austin, and with Richard Bonynge in New York and London; Further study with Nadia Boulanger and Rosalyn Tureck. *Career:* Sang as first in concert, notably in Baroque and early music; Opera debut San Antonio 1970, as Don Ottavio; Camden Festival, London, in Donizetti's Torquato Tasso, 1974; Sang at Opera Houses in Boston, San Francisco, Berlin, Paris, Toulouse, Spoleto and London, Covent Garden 1979; Aix-en-Provence Festival in revival of music by Campra; La Scala Milan 1980, in L'Enfance de Christ by Berlioz;

Rossini's Le Comte Ory, 1991; Often heard in Bach and Mozart; Sang Lord Puff in Henze's English Cat in Paris, and in the premieres of Ballif's Dracula and Denisov's L'écume des jours; Paris Opéra, 1988, in the premiere of La Célestine by Maurice Ohana; Sang Fatty in Weill's Mahagonny at the Maggio Musicale, Florence, 1990; Truffaldino in Busoni's Turandot at Lyon, 1992. *Recordings:* Les Indes Galantes by Rameau; Rameau's Platée and Les Paladins; Messiaen's St François d'Assise; Rameau's Zoroastre; Boulevard Solitude by Henze; Beethoven's 9th Symphony; Berlioz's works for Soloists and Chorus; Les Nuits d'été; Gretry's L'Amant Jaloux; Liszt's Complete Songs for Tenor; Lully's Alceste; Offenbach's Orphée aux Enfers. *Address:* 1 rue du Courier, 53250 Couptrain, France.

BREWER, Christine; Singer (soprano); b. 1960, USA. *Education:* Studies in the USA with Birgit Nilsson. *Career:* Appearances with the Opera Theatre of St Louis as Ellen Orford in Peter Grimes, Ariadne, Donna Anna (also for Vancouver Opera, 1994); Sang Sifare in Mozart's Mitridate at the 1992 Mostly Mozart Festival in New York, Lady Billows in Albert Herring at San Diego and Vitellia in La Clemenza di Tito; Concert engagements include Szymanowski's Stabat Mater in Cleveland, the Vaughan Williams Benedicte in Louisville and Poulenc's Stabat Mater with the Leipzig Gewandhaus Orchestra; Beethoven's Ninth Symphony at Columbus and the Missa Solemnis at Washington DC and San Diego; Mendelssohn's Elijah with the Houston and Honolulu Symphonies; Recent engagements include the Mozart and Dvořák Requiems in Toronto, the Janáček Glagolitic Mass in Atlanta and at the Mann Music Center with the Philadelphia Orchestra under Charles Dutoit; Gretchen in Schumann's Faust at the Caramoor Festival; Donna Anna at Covent Garden, 1996; Strauss's Ariadne at Santa Fe, 1999; Schoenberg's Gurrelieder and Mahler's Symphony of a Thousand, at the London Proms, 2002; Sang in Le Roi Arthus by Chausson at the 2002 Edinburgh Festival; Sang Isolde in concert with the BBC SO, 2002–03. *Honours:* Winner, Metropolitan Opera National Council Auditions, 1989. *Current Management:* Askonas Holt Ltd, Lonsdale Chambers, 27 Chancery Lane, London, WC2A 1PF, England. *Telephone:* (20) 7400-1700. *Fax:* (20) 7400-1799. *E-mail:* info@askonasholt.co.uk. *Website:* www.askonasholt.co.uk.

BRIDEOAKE, Peter; Composer; b. 23 April 1945, Adelaide, South Australia. *Education:* MMus, Adelaide University, 1971; Study with Richard Meale, 1969–71. *Career:* Faculty Member, Elder Conservatory, 1975–; Commissions from the Australian Chamber Orchestra, Seymour Group and Victoria String Quartet. *Compositions include:* Composition for Winds, 1971; Music for Flute and Percussionists, 1972; Gedatsu for guitar, 1972; Chiaroscuro, 1978; String Quartet, 1980; Interplay for 2 clarinets and harp, 1981; Imagery for string orchestra, 1981; Shifting Reflections for chamber ensemble, 1982; Canto for Clarinet Alone, 1987; A Poet's Lament for soprano and piano, 1988. *Honours:* John Bishop Memorial Prize, 1976. *Address:* c/o APRA, 1A Eden Street, Crows Nest, NSW 2065, Australia.

BRIDGES, Althea; Singer (Soprano); b. 11 Jan. 1936, Sydney, Australia. *Education:* Studied at the Sydney Conservatory. *Career:* Member of the Australian Opera Company, 1961–64; Sang in Europe from 1964, at first in Austria (Graz); Vienna, Theater an der Wien, in the premiere of Hauer's Die schwarze Spinne, 1966; Stuttgart, 1968, in the premiere of Orff's Prometheus; Landestheater Linz, 1971–83; Sang Tosca at Frankfurt and Donna Anna at the Glyndebourne Festival; Bari, Italy, as Ortrud in Lohengrin; Other roles include Strauss's Elektra and Marschallin, Marguerite in Faust and Azucena in Il Trovatore; Sang in the premiere of Michael Kohlhaas by Karl Kögler at Linz, 1989; Season 2000 at Linz as Baba the Turk in The Rake's Progress and Auntie in Peter Grimes. *Address:* c/o Landestheater, Promenade 39, 4010 Linz, Austria.

BRIGER, Alexander; Conductor; b. 1965, Australia. *Education:* Sydney Conservatorium; Richard Strauss-Konservatorium, Munich. *Career:* Assistant to Charles Mackerras at Edinburgh Festival including Fidelio and Figaro; Engagements with Opera Australia in Jenůfa, Madama Butterfly and Il Barbiere di Siviglia; Conducted Eclat/Multiples by Boulez and works by Birtwistle with Ensemble Intercontemporain; Season 2001–2002 with the Birmingham Contemporary Music Ensemble, Danish Radio Sinfonietta, Sydney SO and Scottish Chamber Orchestra; The Cunning Little Vixen at the Aix-en-Provence Festival, 2002; 2002–03 with the Hanover Band, Philharmonic, LPO, and Swedish Radio Symphony Orchestra, BCMG; forthcoming operqa includes productions for Opera Australia, Royal Opera House and Glyndebourne; 2004 symphonic debuts include Deutschland Radio, Berlin & Frankfurt Radio, Orchestre de Paris. *Honours:* Winner International Workshop/Competition for Conductors, Czech Republic. *Current Management:* Askonas Holt Ltd, Lonsdale Chambers, 27 Chancery Lane, London, WC2A 1PF, England. *Telephone:* (20) 7400-1700. *Fax:* (20) 7400-1799. *E-mail:* info@askonasholt.co.uk. *Website:* www.askonasholt.co.uk.

BRIGGS, Sarah (Beth); Concert Pianist; b. 1972, England; m. 19 Nov 1994. *Education:* Studied with Denis Matthews at Newcastle, with John Lill, and Chamber Music with Bruno Giuranna at Blonay, Switzerland. *Career:* Debut: Fairfield Hall, Beethoven's 2nd Piano Concerto with New Symphony Orchestra; Many recitals and concerto performances throughout England and Scotland, Germany, Switzerland, Austria, France and USA; International radio and television recordings; Chester Summer Festival, 1989, with world premiere of posthumous pieces by Benjamin Britten; London concerto debut at the Barbican, 1989, playing Mozart K453; Also plays Mozart's 20 other original concertos; Further engagements with the Royal Liverpool Philharmonic, Northern Sinfonia, English Chamber Orchestra, Royal Philharmonic, Northern Chamber Orchestra, Ulster Orchestra, Scottish Chamber Orchestra, Manchester Camerata and the London Soloists Chamber Orchestra; US debut, July 1991, in the San Francisco Stern Grove Festival with the Midsummer Mozart Festival Orchestra, conducted by George Cleve; Further visits to USA for concertos and recitals; Returned to Midsummer Mozart Festival, 1993; Queen Elizabeth Hall debut, 1992, performing 2 Mozart piano concertos with Manchester Camerata; Chamber music concerts including recent series at the Royal College of Music, Manchester; Season 1997–98 included further concerts, Midsummer Mozart Festival, San Francisco, debuts with the Hallé and BBC Concert Orchestra; Formed Trio Melzi with leader and principal cellist of Manchester Camerata, 1999; Trio debut at Bridgewater Hall, Manchester, 2000; Trio featured on BBC Radio 3 and BBC 2. *Honours:* 1st Prize, Surrey Young Pianist of the Year Competition; 3rd Prize, BBC Young Musician of the Year, 1984; 1st Prize, Yorkshire Television Young Musicians' Awards, 1987; Hindemith Scholarship, 1987; Joint Winner, International Mozart Competition, Salzburg, 1988 (leading to engagement with Austrian Radio Symphony under Michael Gielen). *Address:* 86 The Green, Acomb, York YO26 5LS, England. *E-mail:* enquiries@sarahbethbriggs.co.uk. *Website:* www .sarahbethbriggs.co.uk.

BRIGHT, Colin (Michael); Composer and Music Lecturer; b. 28 June 1949, Sydney, New South Wales. *Education:* Studied with Mary Egan, Linden Sands, Christopher Nicols and Ton de Leeuw (composition, 1982). *Career:* Lecturer for High School Music Teachers, from 1987; Commissions from Synergy, Seymour Group, Southern Crossings and Sydney Symphony Orchestra. *Compositions include:* Percussion Quartet, 1980; Earth Spirit for orchestra, 1982; The Dreamtime for baritone and ensemble, 1982; Earth, Wind and Fire for saxophone quartet, 1982; Long Reef for string quintet and wind quintet, 1984; Midnight Tulips song cycle for soprano and large ensemble, 1985; The Sinking of the Rainbow Warrior, 1 act opera; Tulipstick Talk for percussion, 1985; Red Earth for 6 players, 1985; Music for contrabass octet and didjeridoo, 1986; Sun is God, string quartet, 1989; The Journey, opera, 1991; The Butcher's Apron for four percussion, 1991; Young Tree Green: Double Bass Concerto, 1993; War and Peace, vocal sextet, 1994; The Sinking of the Rainbow Warrior, one-act opera, 1994; Oceania, orchestral suite, 1999; The Wild Boys, 1997. *Honours:* 1 Act Opera Award, Australian Music Centre, 1986; Australian Music Centre, Best Composition, 1997. *Address:* c/o APRA, 1A Eden Street, Crows Nest, NSW 2065, Australia.

BRILIOTH, Helge; Singer (Tenor); b. 7 May 1931, Lund, Sweden. *Education:* Studied at the Royal Academy and the Opera School in Stockholm; Academia di Santa Cecilia, Rome; Mozarteum Salzburg. *Career:* In 1960 at Drottningholm sang the Baritone role of Bartolo in Paisiello's Il Barbiere di Siviglia; Bielefeld, 1962–64; Tenor debut as Don José, Stockholm, 1966; Bayreuth, 1969–75 as Siegmund and Tristan; Salzburg Easter Festival 1970 as Siegfried, under Karajan; Covent Garden 1970–, as Siegmund, Siegfried, Tristan and Parsifal; Metropolitan Opera debut 1971, as Parsifal; Glyndebourne 1971, as Bacchus in Ariadne auf Naxos; Drottningholm 1972, in the title role of Cavalli's Scipione Affricano; At the Royal Opera Stockholm, 1975 sang the Emperor in the Swedish premiere of Die Frau ohne Schatten; Sang at Stockholm in the 1986 premiere of Christina by Hans Gefors. *Recordings include:* Siegfried in Götterdämmerung. *Address:* Birger Jarlsgatan 79, 11356 Stockholm, Sweden.

BRILOVA, Elena; Singer (soprano); b. 9 Feb. 1961, Moscow, Russia. *Education:* Graduate, Moscow Conservatoire, 1986. *Career:* Sang in Concert, 1986–88; Bolshoi Opera Moscow from 1988 as the Queen of Shemakha, Antonida (A Life for the Tsar), Traviata, Rosina and other leading roles; Concert appearances as Constanze, Sophie, Oscar, Norina, Lucia, Amina and Leila (Les Pêcheurs de perles); Further engagements as the Queen of Night at Cologne and Vienna, Gilda in Oslo and Vienna; Palmide in Il Crociato in Egitto at the 1991 Ludwigsburg Festival; British debut, 1992, as the Queen of Shemakha with the London Symphony Orchestra; Season 1993 as Gilda at the Bergen Festival and in concert performances of Rigoletto at Tel-Aviv, conducted by Zubin Mehta; Concert engagements at Brussels and Frankfurt and with such conductors as Bashmet, Simonov, Rostropovich, Rozhdestvensky and Svetlanov; Sang in Berio's Outis at the

Théâtre du Châtelet, 1999, and as Rossini's Elvira at Dusseldorf, 2001. *Current Management:* Athole Still International Management, Forresters Hall, 25–27 Westow Street, London, SE19 3RY, England. *Telephone:* (20) 8771-5271. *Fax:* (20) 8768-6600. *Website:* www .atholestill.com.

BRINKMANN, Bodo; Singer (Baritone); b. 7 Dec. 1942, Binder, Brunswick, Germany. *Education:* Studied at the Berlin Musikhochschule with Karl-Heinz Lohmann. *Career:* Debut: Kaiserslautern, 1971; Member of the National Theatre Mannheim from 1974; Staatsoper Hamburg in Lohengrin; Munich Staatsoper, notably as Escamillo, 1984, and in the 1986 premiere of Reimann's Troades; Guest appearances in Berlin, Paris and Strasbourg; Deutsche Oper am Rhein 1987, as Telramund; Munich Olympia Hall, 1987, as Prince Igor; Bayreuth Festival 1987–92, Kurwenal, Donner and Gunther; Sang Jochanaan in Salome at Barcelona, 1989; Cologne Opera 1990, as Wotan in Die Walküre; Düsseldorf 1995–96, as Wolfram and Wotan; Season 2000–01 as the Wanderer in Siegfried at Münster and Meiningen. *Recordings include:* Video of The Ring from Bayreuth. *Address:* c/o Oper der Stadt Köln, Offenbachplatz, 5000 Cologne, Germany.

BRIZZI, Aldo; Conductor and Composer; b. 7 June 1960, Alessandria, Italy. *Education:* Bologna University; Milan Conservatorio. *Career:* Debut: 1st appearance as Conductor, 1978; Conducted concerts in Europe, Israel, USA, Central and South America; Principal performances with Berlin Philharmonic Chamber Ensemble, The Cluj Philharmonic Orchestra; Santa Cecilia Chamber Orchestra of Rome, The Haydn Orchestra of Bolzano; Musical Conductor of the Ensemble of Ferienkurse, Darmstadt; Permanent Conductor of E M Ferrari Orchestra, Alessandria and Akabthos Ensemble. *Compositions:* Works performed by numerous European orchestras, ensembles and soloists including, Ecyo, Danish Radio Orchestra, Montepulciano Festival Orchestra, New Philharmonic Orchestra of Paris, Ens de Cuivres et Percussion de l'Intercontemporain; Works broadcast by 21 European Radio Stations, 2 USA and Israeli State Radio. *Recordings:* Salabert conducting the Arditti String Quartet Consort; Electrecord conducting the Bacau Symphony Orchestra; Edipan with Composition of A Brizzi. *Publications:* Proposte Musicali, 1980; La Musica, Le Idée, Le Cose, 1981. *Contributions:* numerous magazines. *Honours:* Venezia Opera Prima, 1981; Stipendiendpreis, Darmstadt, 1984; Young Generation in Europe, Venice, Paris, Cologne, 1985; Franco Evangelisti, Rome, 1986; Young Composers' Forum, Cologne, 1989; Artistic Director of Scelsi Foundation, Rome. *Address:* Via Boves 6, 15100 Alessandria, Italy.

BRKANOVIC, Zeljko; composer, conductor and academic; b. 20 Dec. 1937, Zagreb, Croatia; m. Ivanka Brkanovic 1964; one s. one d. *Education:* Zagreb Music Academy, Skopje Music Academy, Academia Chigiana Siena, Italy, High School Stuttgart, Germany. *Career:* debut with first string quartet in Zagreb, 1974; Conductor, Croatian National Theatre Opera, Split and Zagreb, 1963–69; Musical Editor on radio and television, 1969–80; Professor, Music Academy Zagreb, 1980–; mem. Croatian Composers' Soc.. *Compositions:* Nomos, Suite for Strings, Ricercari, Two Symphonies; Concerto for Violin; Concerto for Piano and Orchestra (Josip Slavenski Award, 1983); Concerto for Violin, Violoncello and Orchestra; Lyrical Concerto for Piano and Orchestra; Concerto for Percussion and 3 Clarinets (Ministry of Culture Award, 1997); Concert Rondo for Piano, Wind and Brass Orchestra; also chamber, piano and organ music. *Recordings:* Tonal Sonata, 1977; Divertimento For Strings, 1977; Concerto for Piano and Orchestra, 1981; Concerto for Violin, 1983; Antependium, 1989; Second Symphony, 1991; Figures, 1995; Song Book, 1996; Author CDs, 1996 and 2002. *Publications:* Professor Dr E. Karkoschka, Stuttgart, 1991; Bulletin/Croatian Composers' Society, 1992; contrib. to Schweinfurtische Nachrichten, Vjesnik Zagreb, Vecernji list Zagreb, Slobodna Dalmacija Split, Piano Journal No. 49 London, p 46, 1992, Cantus Zagreb, 2003; Frankfurter Allgemeine Zeitung, 2003. *Honours:* Vladimir Nazor Concert Award 2003. *Address:* Zagreb Music Academy, Trg kralja Tomislava 18, 10000 Zagreb, Croatia. *Fax:* (1) 4922260. *E-mail:* ivanka.brkanovic@inet.hr.

BROAD, Daniel; Singer (Baritone); b. 1967, England. *Education:* Chetham's School, Manchester; Royal Northern College of Music, with Robert Alderson. *Career:* Glyndebourne Chorus from 1996; Keeper of the Madhouse in The Rake's Progress at the Festival, 2000; Sang Rossini's Figaro at Aix and for Castleward Opera, Yamadori in Butterfly for Clonter Opera, Marcello at Holland Park and Sid in Albert Herring at the Perth Festival; Further engagements in Béatrice and Bénédict for European Opera Union and Eugene Onegin in Baden Baden and Paris; Other roles include Mozart's Count, Tarquinius in The Rape of Lucretia and Ping in Turandot. *Recordings include:* Anthony in Sweeney Todd, for Opera North. *Honours:* Peter Moores Foundation Scholar. *Address:* c/o Glyndebourne Festival Opera, Glyndebourne, Lewes, Sussex BN8 5UU, England.

BROADBENT, Graeme; Singer (bass); b. 1962, Halifax, England. *Education:* Royal Coll. of Music with Lyndon Van der Pump; Moscow

Conservatoire with Evgeny Nesterenko. *Career:* performed in recital and oratorio throughout the UK and abroad, appearing at all the major London concert halls and at the Proms; repertoire encompasses 81 operatic roles and 47 oratorio and concert works, ranging from Monteverdi's Vespers to Schoenberg's Serenade Op 24; debut with Royal Opera, Covent Garden in Salome in 1997; sang in Palestrina at the Metropolitan Opera House on the Royal Opera's tour to New York; appeared with Royal Opera every season since; performed roles with ENO, Opera North and Scottish Opera; performed Judge/Hotel Manager/Duke in Powder her Face by Adès at the Aldeburgh and Almeida Festivals and Channel 4 television, Rossini's Stabat Mater with the Royal Liverpool Philharmonic Orchestra, Verdi's Requiem, at the Queen Elizabeth Hall, The Dream of Gerontius in Gloucester Cathedral; Beethoven's 9th Symphony at the Barbican; joined Royal Opera, Covent Garden as Principal Bass, 1999; roles for the Royal Opera include Nightwatchman in Meistersinger, Colline in La Bohème, Dr Grenvil in La Traviata, Angelotti in Tosca, Timur in Turandot, King Marke in Tristan, Leone in Atilla, Capellio in I Capuleti and King of Egypt in Aida; Glyndebourne Festival debut as Commendatore in 2000. *Current Management:* Askonas Holt Ltd, Lonsdale Chambers, 27 Chancery Lane, London, WC2A 1PF, England. *Telephone:* (20) 7400-1700. *Fax:* (20) 7400-1799. *E-mail:* info@askonasholt.co.uk. *Website:* www.askonasholt.co.uk.

BROADSTOCK, Brenton (Thomas); Composer; b. 12 Dec. 1952, Melbourne, Victoria, Australia; m., 3 c. *Education:* BA, Monash University, 1975. MMus, Memphis State University, USA; Diploma in Composition, University of Sydney; Composition with Peter Sculthorpe; AMusTCL, Trinity College of Music; DMus, University of Melbourne. *Career:* Tutor in Music, 1982–84, Senior Tutor in Music, 1984–87, Senior Lecturer in Music, 1989, then Associate Professor, Faculty of Music, University of Melbourne; Inaugural Composer-in-Residence, Melbourne Symphony Orchestra, 1988; Performances: Melbourne Summer Music Festival, 1985; Stroud Festival, England, 1985; Adelaide Festival, 1986; Spoleto Festival, Melbourne, 1986; Nova Festival, Brisbane, 1987; Music Today Festival, Tokyo, 1988; International Society for Contemporary Music World Days, Hong Kong, 1988, Oslo, 1990. *Compositions:* Symphony No. 3; 4 String Quartets; The Mountain for orchestra; Tuba Concerto; Piano Concerto; Battlements for orchestra; Woodwind Quartet; Aureole 104 for flute and piano; Solo Bass Clarinet; Oboe and Piano; Solo Piano; Beast from Air for trombone and percussion; Many works for brass band; Symphony No. 1, 1988; Symphony No. 2, 1989; Bright Tracks, soprano and string trio, 1994; Celebration for chamber ensemble, 1995; Saxophone Concertino, 1995; Dancing on a Volcano for orchestra, 1996; Catch the Joy, overture, 1998; I Touched Your Glistening Tears for oboe and piano trio, 1998. *Recordings:* Many works performed, recorded and broadcast by ABC; Fahrenheit 451, opera, 1992. *Honours:* Paul Lowin Prize, 1994. *Current Management:* G Schirmer, Australia. *Address:* 20 Simmons Street, Box Hill North, Victoria 3129, Australia.

BROADWAY, Kenneth; Duo Pianist; b. 1950, USA. *Education:* Studied at the Cleveland Institute of Music with Vronsky and Babin. *Career:* Formed Piano Duo partnership with Ralph Markham and has given many recitals and concerts in North America and Europe; BBC debut recital, 1979 and further broadcasts on CBC television, Radio France Musique, the Bavarian Radio and Radio Hilversum in Netherlands; Stravinsky's Three Dances from Petrushka at the Théâtre des Champs Elysées, Paris, 1984; Season 1987–88 included 40 North American recitals, concert with the Vancouver Symphony and New York debut on WQXR Radio; Season 1988–89 included the Concertos for Two Pianos by Mozart and Bruch in Canada and a recital tour of England and Germany; Recent performances of the Bartók Sonata for Two Pianos and Percussion, with Evelyn Glennie and a 1990–91 tour of North America, Europe and the Far East; Festival appearances include Newport USA 1988. *Recordings include:* Duos by Anton Rubinstein; Vaughan Williams Concerto for Two Pianos; Bartók Sonata for Two Pianos and Percussion. *Honours:* Young Artist of the Year, Musical America Magazine, 1989 (with Ralph Markham).

BROCHELER, John; Singer (Baritone); b. 21 Feb. 1945, Vaals, Limbourg, Netherlands. *Education:* Studied with Leo Ketelaars in Maastricht and with Pierre Bernac in Paris. *Career:* Sang at first in concert, notably in the Bach Passions, the Choral Symphony and the Brahms Requiem; Berlin Festival in the premieres of Die Erprobung de Petrus Hebraicus by Henri Pousseur, 1974 and Mare Nostrum by Kagel, 1975; San Diego Opera as Sharpless in Madama Butterfly, Ford in Falstaff, and in the 1979 premiere of Menotti's La Loca, with Beverly Sills; Netherlands Opera as Germont, Don Giovanni and Marcello, and in Donizetti's Maria Stuarda with Joan Sutherland; Frankfurt Opera 1983, as Amfortas in Parsifal; Glyndebourne 1984, as Mandryka in Arabella; Los Angeles Opera as Nabucco; La Scala Milan 1985, as Jochanaan in Salome and Golaud in Pelléas et Mélisande; Stuttgart 1985, in Henze's König Hirsch; Other appearances in Toronto, New

York and Paris, Vienna 1988 Goulaud in Pelléas et Mélisande, Bonn 1989; Wolfram, Tannhäuser, Munich 1989; Mathis der Maler, Hindemith; Sang Orestes in Elektra at Barcelona, 1990; Hindemith's Mathis and Von Einem's Danton at the 1990 Munich Festival; Sang Barak in Die Frau ohne Schatten for Netherlands Opera, 1992; Wozzeck, Stuttgart, 1993; Simon Boccanegra, Frankfurt, 1993; Wanderer in Siegfried, 1994; Dr Schön in Lulu, Salzburger Festspiele, 1995 and at the Berlin Staatsoper, 1997; Sang the Wanderer at Amsterdam, 1998; Season 1999–2000 as Dr Schön in Lulu at Salzburg and Amfortas in Munich; Hans Sachs at Covent Garden, 2002. *Recordings:* Dichterliebe; Handel's Dettinger Te Deum and Judas Maccabaeus; Kindertotenlieder, Mahler; Des Knaben Wunderhorn (Mahler); Lucrezia Borgia; Das Paradies und Die Peri. *Address:* c/o Bayerische Staatsoper, Postfach 745, 8000 Munich 1, Germany.

BROCK, Hannes; Singer (Tenor); b. 1 Nov. 1952, Stuttgart. *Education:* Studied in Berlin and Wuppertal. *Career:* Berlin Theater des Westens, 1978–79; Bach's St Matthew Passion with the Berlin Philharmonic, 1981; Sang at Opera at Hagen, Essen and Dortmund, 1981–95; Eutin Festival, 1986 in The Bartered Bride and Zeller's Der Vogelhändler; St Gallen Opera from 1995, with guest appearances at Mannheim, Düsseldorf, Dresden and Hamburg; Dortmund Opera 2001, in Wallenberg by Erkki-Sven Tüür, and as Monostatos; Roles have included Mozart's Tamino, Mime in Das Rheingold, Handel's Xerxes, Shuisky in Boris Godunov and Beppe in Pagliacci; Modern repertory includes the Captain in Wozzeck, Tom Rakewell, Steva in Jenůfa and Weill's Jim Mahoney. *Address:* c/o Stadttheater St Gallen, Museumstrasse 24, 9000 St Gallen, Switzerland.

BRODARD, Michael; Singer (Bass-Baritone); b. 1 April 1946, Fribourg, Switzerland. *Education:* Fribourg Conservatoire, 1965–74. *Career:* Concert Singer in France and Switzerland; Opera engagements at Geneva, Lausanne, Lucerne, Nancy and Metz; Further concerts at Brussels, Marseille, Frankfurt, Barcelona, Lisbon, Buenos Aires, Madrid and Warsaw; Repertoire ranges from Baroque to Modern Works. *Recordings include:* L'Enfant et les Sortilèges, Pelléas et Mélisande, Bach's Christmas Oratorio, Haydn's St Theresa Mass, Madrigals and Vespers by Monteverdi, Schubert's E-flat Mass and Vivaldi's Psalm 110; Stravinsky's Renard and Les Noces, Masses by Mozart. *Address:* Conservatoire de Musique, 228–A rue Pierre Aeby, CH–1700 Fribourg, Switzerland.

BRODERICK, Kathleen; Singer (Soprano); b. 1958, Vancouver, Canada. *Education:* Studied in Montreal, St Louis and New York. *Career:* Sang at Kaiserslautern, 1984–88; Saarbrucken, 1988–91; Berne 1990 as Dvořák's Rusalka; Other roles have included Mozart's Fiordiligi, Pamina, Countess Almaviva; Agathe in Der Freischütz, Violetta, Jenny in Mahagonny; Virginia Opera, Salome, 1993; Minnesota Opera as Turandot, 1994; Hamilton Opera, Canada, as Amelia in Un Ballo in Maschera, 1996; Orlando Opera, USA as Leonora in Il Trovatore, 1997; Season 1998 with Turandot for Florida Grand Opera, Turandot and Milada in Dalibor for Scottish Opera and Turandot for Flanders Opera at Antwerp; Long Beach Opera as Judith in Bluebeard's Castle, 1999; Lady Macbeth in the Scottish Opera Macbeth at the Edinburgh Festival, 1999; Turandot, Senta/Flying Dutchman, Elektra/title role at Nationaltheater Mannheim, 2000–03; Season 2000–01 as Lady Macbeth at Edinburgh, Bregenz, Vienna and Berlin (Deutsche Oper); Abigaille/Nabucco at Semperoper Dresden, 2001; Brünnhilde in English National Opera's Ring cycle (Valkyrie/Siegfried/Twilight of the Gods), 2002–05; Frequent concert appearances. *Address:* c/o Artists Management Zürich, Rutistrasse 52, 8044 Zürich-Gockhausen, Switzerland.

BROITMANN, Ruben; Singer (Tenor); b. 1959, Mexico City. *Education:* Mexico City and Juilliard, American Opera Center. *Career:* Early roles included Mozart's Ferrando and Don Ottavio; Rinuccio in Gianni Schicchi; Tour of Germany, Italy and Japan with the Peter Brook Carmen; Aix-en-Provence, 1987, as Pedrillo in Die Entführung; Guest appearances at Montevideo, Nancy, Puerto Rico and Frankfurt; Season 1992–93 as Alfredo at Graz, Don José at Freiburg and Ismaele in Nabucco at the Bregenz Festival; Vienna Staatsoper from 1993; Vienna Volksoper as Laertes in Hamlet, 1995; Raffaele in Verdi's Stiffelio, 1996; Sang Werther at Mannheim, 2001; Sings a varied concert repertoire. *Address:* c/o Vienna Staatsoper, Opernring 2, 1010 Vienna, Austria.

BROKAW, James Albert, II; Historical Musicologist; b. 4 Feb. 1951, Princeton, New Jersey, USA; m. Mollie Sandock, 27 June 1984. *Education:* BA, German Literature, Kenyon College, 1973; Studies in Music History and Theory, Baldwin Wallace Conservatory, 1977–78; PhD, Musicology, University of Chicago, 1986. *Career:* Assistant Professor of Music, Northeastern Illinois University, 1989–; Lecturer in Music, Chicago State University, 1986–; Lecturer in Music, University of Chicago Open Programme, 1986–; Advisory Board Member, Riemenschneider Bach Institute, 1982–86; Judge, Mu Phi Epsilon Music History Competition, 1988. *Publications:* The Genesis of the Prelude in C Major, in Bach Studies, Cambridge University Press,

1989; Techniques of Expansion in the Preludes and Fugues of Johann Sebastian Bach, dissertation; Programme Notes: The Chicago Symphony Orchestra/Performances for Peace, 1984–88; Music of the Baroque, 1984, 1987. *Contributions:* Reviews of scholarly editions of keyboard music of J. S. Bach, C P E Bach and Louis Couperin, in Notes, 1985, 1986, 1989; Recent Research on the Genesis and Sources of Bach's Well-Tempered Klavier, II, in Bach: The Quarterly Journal of the Riemenschneider Bach Institute, 1985. *Address:* Box 125 Ogden Dunes, Portage, IN 46368, USA.

BROKMEIER, Willi; Singer (Tenor); b. 8 April 1928, Bochum, Germany. *Education:* Studied in Mainz. *Career:* Debut: Stadttheater Mainz, 1952; Appearances in lighter operatic roles at the Deutsche Oper am Rhein Düsseldorf; Many engagements in operetta, notably at the Theater am Gärtnerplatz, Munich, and elsewhere in Germany; Cologne Opera, 1965, in the premiere of Zimmermann's Die Soldaten; Munich Festival, 1973, as Pedrillo in Die Entführung. *Recordings:* Gräfin Mariza; Lehar's Lustige Witwe and Land des Lächelns; Die Kluge by Orff; Korngold's Die Tote Stadt (RCA); Feuersnot by Strauss (Acanta).

BRONDER, Peter; Singer (Tenor); b. 22 Oct. 1953, Herefordshire, England. *Education:* Studied at the Royal Academy of Music with Joy Mammen and at the National Opera Studio. *Career:* Principal Tenor with the Welsh National Opera from 1986–90; Covent Garden debut as Arturo in Lucia di Lammermoor in 1986, also Major Domo in Der Rosenkavalier; Youth in Die Frau ohne Schlatten, 1992; First Jew in Salome, 1995; Sang Kudryash in Katya Kabanova in 1989 and Andres in Wozzeck in 1990 with the English National Opera; Shepherd in Oedipus Rex, 1991; Almaviva in 1992–93; Alfred in Die Fledermaus and Italian Tenor in Der Rosenkavalier, 1993; Further appearances include: Netherlands Opera as Ernesto, 1989 and the Prince in Les Brigands, 1992; Glyndebourne Festival, 1990; For Welsh National Opera performances in New York, 1989, Milan, 1989 and Tokyo, 1990; Debut at the Bavarian State Opera, Munich, as Mazal in The Adventures of Mr Brouček, also Narraboth, 1994; Invitations for Pedrillo in Die Entführung at Covent Garden, also Istanbul; Sang Pylades in Gluck's Iphigenia auf Tauris, Edinburgh, 1996; Alexander in Il Re Pastore for Opera North, 1998; Season 2000 as Mime for Longborough Festival, Loge at Edinburgh and in Dallapicolla's Il Prigioniero for ENO; Concert appearances in London, Paris, Vienna, Lisbon and for the Australian Broadcasting Company, Perth. *Recordings include:* Kiri Te Kanawa recital, Turco in Italia (Phonogram); Adriana Lecouvreur (Decca); Osud, Beethoven 9 (EMI); La Traviata, Ballo in Maschera (Teldec). *Honours:* Associate, Royal Academy of Music, 1989. *Current Management:* Allied Artists, London. *Address:* c/o Allied Artists, 42 Montpelier Square, London SW7 1JZ, England.

BRONFMAN, Yefim; Pianist; b. 10 April 1958, Tashkent, Russia. *Education:* Juilliard School of Music, New York, USA; Curtis Institute, Philadelphia, Pennsylvania; Private studies with Rudolf Serkin and Arie Vardi. *Career:* Debut: Israel Philharmonic with Kostalanetz, 1974; As Soloist with: Montreal Symphony Orchestra; Philadelphia; Los Angeles Philharmonic; New York Philharmonic; Minnesota Orchestra; Mostly Mozart Orchestra; English Chamber Orchestra; St Louis Symphony Orchestra; Scottish Chamber Orchestra; Vancouver Symphony Orchestra; Pittsburgh Symphony Orchestra; London Philharmonia; St Paul Chamber Orchestra; Houston Symphony Orchestra; Toronto Symphony Orchestra; Goteborg Symphony Orchestra; Royal Philharmonic; San Francisco Symphony Orchestra; Berlin Philharmonic; Chicago Symphony Orchestra; Baltimore Symphony Orchestra; Rotterdam Philharmonic; Bournemouth Symphony Orchestra; Cleveland Orchestra; National Symphony Orchestra; Rochester Philharmonic; Jerusalem Symphony Orchestra; Winnipeg Symphony Orchestra; Richmond Symphony Orchestra; New Jersey Symphony; Partnered Joshua Bell in Mozart-Tchaikovsky Festival at the Wigmore Hall, London, 1997; Bartók's Second Concerto at the London Proms, 1999; Bartók's Concerto No. 1 at the London Proms, 2002. *Recordings:* All Fauré; Prokofiev Violin Sonatas with Shlomo Mintz; Musical Heritage, Brahms Sonata in F minor and Scherzo Op 4; Mozart Sonatas for violin and piano with Robert Mann; Prokofiev Piano Sonatas 7 and 8; Mussorgsky, Pictures at an Exhibition, Stravinsky, 3 scenes from Petrushka; Rachmaninov: Piano Concertos 2 and 3, with Esa-Pekka Salonen and Philharmonia Orchestra, 1992; Prokofiev: Piano Concertos 1, 3 and 5, with Zubin Mehta and Israel Philharmonic, 1993. *Honours:* American-Israeli Cultural Foundation Scholarship, 1974; Winner of Avery Fisher Prize, 1991. *Current Management:* ICM Artists. *Address:* 40 West 57 Street, New York, NY 10019, USA.

BRONK, Stephen; Singer (Bass-baritone); b. 1958, Hyannis, MA, USA. *Education:* Studied at the Aachen Musikhochschule. *Career:* Debut: Justifiar in Kienzl's Evangelimann, Bregenz, 1984; Appearances in opera at Bremerhaven and Saarbrucken; Bonn Opera from 1993 as Mozart's Osmin, Figaro, Alfonso and Speaker in Die Zauberflöte; Grand Inquisitor in Don Carlos and King in Aida; Sang Pizarro in Fidelio at Bonn, 1995, and in Janáček's From the House of the Dead at Strasbourg,

1996; Other roles include Fasolt, Alberich and Hunding in The Ring; Concerts include Beethoven's Ninth at Bonn, 1994; Sang Pizarro in Fidelio and Don Alfonso at Dusseldorf, 1999–2000. *Address:* Bonn Opera, Am Boeselagerhof 1, Pf 2440, 5311 Bonn, Germany.

BROOK, Peter; stage director and film director; b. 21 March 1925, London, England. *Education:* Univ. of Oxford. *Career:* Director of productions at Covent Garden, 1948–50, with Boris Godunov, Salome (designs by Salvador Dali) and the premiere of The Olympians by Bliss, The Marriage of Figaro, 1949; Filmed The Beggar's Opera by Gay/Pepusch with Laurence Olivier, 1953; Metropolitan Opera, 1953 and 1957, Faust and Eugene Onegin; His reduction of Carmen, La tragédie de Carmen, was produced at the Paris Bouffes du Nord in the season 1981–82 and was seen on tour in Europe and the USA (New York), 1983; A much reduced version of Pelléas et Mélisande (Impressions of Pelléas) was performed in 1992–93; Directed Don Giovanni at Aix-en-Provence, 1998. *Address:* c/o Théâtre des Bouffes du Nord, 37 bis Bd de la Chapelle, 75010 Paris, France.

BROOKS, Darla; Singer (Soprano); b. 1957, West Virginia, USA. *Education:* Studied in the USA and at Graz. *Career:* Sang throughout the USA in opera and concert, notably in Chicago and Cincinnati; European debut with Lucerne Opera 1985, followed by engagements at Würzburg and Cologne; Roles have included Norina in Don Pasquale, Blondchen, Zerlina, Zerbinetta, Adele in Die Fledermaus and Adina in L'Elisir d'amore (at the Deutsche Oper Berlin); Other venues include the Teatro Liceu Barcelona, and the State Operas of Munich and Vienna; Schwetzingen Festival 1995 in Salieri's Falstaff. *Address:* c/o Deutsche Oper, Richard Wagner Strasse 10, D–10585 Berlin, Germany.

BROPHY, Gerard; composer; b. 7 Jan. 1953, Sydney, Australia. *Education:* masterclasses with Turibio Santos, 1976; Composition seminar, Mauricio Kagel, Basel, Switzerland; Studied with Richard Toop, NSW State Conservatorium of Music, 1981; Studied with Franco Donatoni, Italy; Graduated, Accademia Nazionale de Santa Cecilia, Rome, 1983; Composition course, Accademia Chigiana di Siena, 1983. *Career:* Composer in Residence, Musica Viva Australia, 1983; Australian Chamber Orchestra, 1986; Queensland Conservatorium of Music, 1987; Pittsburgh New Music Ensemble, 1988; Queensland Conservatorium of Music, 1989. *Compositions include:* Orchestral Works: Orfeo, 1982; Le Reveil de L'Ange, 1987; Matho, 1987; Ensemble Works: Lace, 1985; Mercurio, 1985; Spur, 1988; Head, 1988; Séraphita, 1988; Forbidden Colours, 1988; Frisson, 1989; Vocal Works: Flesh, 1987; Shiver, 1989; Instrumental Works: Chiarissima, 1987; Pink Chair Light Green Violet Violent FLASH, 1990; Vorrei Baciarti, for baritone and chamber ensemble, 1991; Tweak, for piccolo, 1991; Pluck It!, for solo guitar, 1992; Twist, for solo clarinet, 1993; Recent works include: Tudo Liquido, for wind and percussion, 1994; Colour Red... Your Mouth... Heart, for orchestra, 1994; Es, for solo flute, 1994; Bisoux, for english horn and bass clarinet, 1994; Umbigada, Obrigado!, for percussion quartet, 1995; Trip, for wind ensemble, 1996; Coil, 1996; Crimson Songs, for soprano and ensemble, 1997; Samba Mauve, 1997; Merge–a memoir of the senses for percussion quartet, large orchestra and sound design, commissioned by the Melbourne Symphony Orchestra, 1998; Hot Metallic Blues, for electric bass and ensemble, 1999; Ru B fogo, for ensemble, 1999; Birds of Paradise, for guitar orchestra, 1999; Body Map, for ensemble, 1999; Yo Yai Pakebi, Man Mai Yapobi, for African percussion and large orchestra, 1999; Heavy Metal Boyhood, for ensemble, 2000; Pink Edges, for six voices, 2000; Abraco, for solo piano, 2000; Sheer Nylon Dances, for violin, cello and piano, 2001; ...Vision Fugitive, for violin, cello and piano, 2001; Danses Veloutees, for solo viola and orchestra, 2001; ...Danse de l'Extase, for orchestra, 2001; Chorinho Pra Ela, for bass clarinet, 2002; Berceuse, for SATB motet, 2002; Pas de Deux, for clarinet and cello, 2002; Concerto in Blue, for guitar and orchestra, 2002; Trance Ripples, for solo marimba, 2002; Topolo-NRG, for baritone sax, double bass and piano, 2002; mFm, for soprano/baritone sax, bass guitar, marimba and piano, 2002; Chi's Cakewalk, for solo bass clarinet, 2002; Songo, for percussion quintet, 2002; Mantras, for orchestra, 2003; Brisbane Drumming, for percussion, 2003; Choro Pra Linos, for wind quintet, 2003; Phobia, for music theatre performers, 2003; Maracatu, for orchestra 2003; Songs of the North, for soprano and ensemble, 2004; Cancao, for wind quintet, 2004; Frevo, for wind quintet, 2004. *Recordings include:* Hydra, Synergy Percussion; Nadja, Sydney Symphony Orchestra; Shiver, Elision; Head, Het Trio; Nymphe-Echo Morphologique, Laura Chislett; November Snow, Music Box; Forbidden Colours, Queensland Symphony Orchestra; Angelicon, Lisa Moore; Breathless, Laura Chislett; Twist (Philippa Robinson, Floyd Williams, Roslyn Dunlop); Bisous (Barry Davis and Floyd Williams, Philippa Robinson, Roslyn Dunlop, Deborah de Graaff); Pluck It! (Ken Murray, Peter Constant); We Bop (Duo Contemporain, Margery Smith and Daryl Pratt); Charm, Marshall McGuire, Geoffrey Collins and Patricia Pollett; NRG, Henri Bok; Obsidian, Ex Novo Ensemble; Birds of Paradise, Guitarstrophy; Glove, six_new music ensemble; Crimson Songs, Perihelion; Pearl licks, pearl rub, pearl dub, Two

Complete Lunatics; the Room of the Saints, Patricia Pollett and Daryl Pratt; Chorinho pra Ela, Henri Bok. *Honours:* Numerous grants and fellowships including: Composer Fellowship, Australia Council Music Board, 1982, 1983; Italian Government Scholarship. *Address:* 26 Nott Street, Red Hill, Qld 4059, Australia. *E-mail:* g.brophy@griffith.edu.au.

BROS, José; Singer (tenor); b. 1965, Barcelona, Spain. *Education:* Barcelona Conservatory. *Career:* debut, Carmina Burana at Palma, 1987; many performances in leading roles at major opera houses, 1992–; Duke of Mantua at Palma and Nadir in Les Pêcheurs de Perles, followed by Percy in Anna Bolena, at Barcelona; leads in La Favorita at Las Palmas, Falstaff and I Capuleti at Lisbon, Lucia di Lammermoor at Zürich, Don Pasquale and Così fan tutte at Bilbao and L'Elisir d'amore (Nemorino, Covent Garden, 1997); further recent engagements at Hamburg, Vienna, Rome, Naples, Munich, Florence (Edgardo, under Zubin Mehta, at the Maggio Musicale), Bologna and Marseille; Nemorino at Barcelona and Madrid; Edgardo at Barcelona and Donizetti's Roberto Devereux at Hamburg (concert), 2000; recitals and concerts throughout Europe and in London. *Current Management:* Miguel Lerin, La Rambla 54, 2°, 1a, 08002 Barcelona, Spain.

BROSTER, Eileen; Pianist; b. 23 June 1935, London, England; m. R Chaplin, 6 May 1972, 1 s. *Education:* Studied with Frank Merrick and Cyril Smith at The Royal College of Music. *Career:* Debut: Wigmore Hall; Performed on BBC radio and television; Appeared in all South Bank Halls; Toured extensively as soloist in recitals and concerti; Performances at Wigmore Hall; mem, Incorporated Society of Musicians; EPTA. *Address:* 199 Beehive Lane, Gants Hill, Ilford, Essex, England.

BROTT, Alexander, OC, OQ, LicMus, DMus, LLD; Canadian musical director, conductor and professor of music; b. 14 March 1915, Montréal; m. Lotte Goetzel 1933; two s. *Education:* McGill University, Quebec Academy of Music, Juilliard School of Music, NY, Chicago University, Queen's University. *Career:* Professor and conductor-in-residence at McGill University since 1939; Concertmaster and Assistant Conductor, Montreal Symphony Orchestra; founder and Musical Director, McGill Chamber Orchestra; conductor of Montreal Pops Concerts; Conductor and Musical Director of Kingston Symphony Orchestra and Kingston Pops Concerts. *Compositions:* 18 Symphonies (13 Commissioned); 25 Solo and Chamber Music (12 Commissioned); 8 Vocal works (5 Commissioned), 1938–71; Songs and Orchestrations (11 Commissioned), 1971–78. *Recordings include:* many with McGill Chamber Orchestra including own compositions and works by Mozart, Haydn, Schubert and Bach; Alexander Brott's Compositions, 1994. *Honours:* Hon. Fellow, Royal Society of the Arts, London, 1960; Knight of Malta Order of St John of Jerusalem, 1985; Elected 'Great Montrealer' in 1994. *Address:* 5459 Earnscliffe Avenue, Montreal, QC H3X 2P8, Canada.

BROTT, Boris; Conductor; b. 14 March 1944, Montreal, Quebec, Canada; m. Ardyth Webster, 2 s., 1 d. *Education:* Conservatoire de Musique, Montreal; McGill University, Montreal; Studied conducting with Pierre Monteux, Igor Markevitch, Leonard Bernstein, Alexander Brott. *Career:* Debut: As violinist with Montreal Symphony, 1949; Founder, Conductor, Philharmonic Youth Orchestra, Montreal, 1959–61; Assistant Conductor: Toronto Symphony Orchestra, 1963–65; New York Philharmonic, 1968–69; Music Director: Northern Sinfonia Orchestra, England, 1964–69; Royal Ballet, Covent Garden, 1966–68, including the Covent Garden premiere of Stravinsky's The Soldier's Tale; Lakehead University, Thunder Bay, Ontario, 1967–72; Regina Symphony, 1970–73; Conductor, Music Director: Hamilton Philharmonic Orchestra, 1969–90; Ontario Place Pops Orchestra, 1983–91; Chief Conductor: BBC National Orchestra of Wales, 1972–77; CBC Symphony, 1976–83; President, Great Music Canada, 1977–; Artistic Director, Stratford Summer Music Festival, Ontario, 1982–84; Conductor, McGill Orchestra, Montreal, Quebec, 1989–; Artistic Director, Brott Music Festivals, Hamilton, Ontario, 1988–95; Conductor and MD, New West Symphony, Los Angeles, 1995–; Conductor and Music Director, Ventura Symphony, Ventura, California, 1990–95; Guest Conductor, All British orchestras, all major Canadian orchestras, USA, Korea, Japan, Germany, France, Sweden, Israel, Mexico, El Salvador, Italy, Denmark; Principal Guest Conductor and Music Adviser, Symphony Nova Scotia, 1981–; Co-conductor of McGill Chamber Orchestra, 1989; Music Director of the New West Symphony, California, 1992; Guest Conductor, Sadler's Wells Opera, Canadian Opera Company, Edmonton Opera; Writer, Host, Conductor, over 100 television programmes, the United Kingdom, USA, Canada; Appeared in film and radio; Conducted for Pope John Paul II at the Vatican, 2000. *Recordings:* Numerous for CBC, Sceptre-Mace, Mercury, including suites from operas by Handel; Dvořák's Serenade op 44; Symphonies by Richter, Holzbauer and Cannabich; Sibelius Pelléas; Ravel Le Tombeau de Couperin. *Address:* 301 Bay Street South, Hamilton, Ontario L8P 3JZ, Canada.

BROTT, Denis; Cellist; b. 9 Sept. 1950, Quebec, Canada; m. 27 Aug 1976, 1 s, 3 d. *Education:* Studied with Gregor Piatigorsky, University of Southern California, USA. *Career:* Festivals include Marlboro, Aspen, Hampden-Sydney, Orford and Sitka; Artistic Director, Festival of the Sound, Ontario, 1991; Faculty of the Music Academy of the West, Santa Barbara, 1993 and 1994 summer season, performing chamber music at festivals in Hampden-Sydney, Virginia and Sitka Alaska; Jury member, Evian International String Quartet Competition in France, also recitalist, chamber artist and soloist with orchestra; Professor of Cello and Chamber Music at Conservatoire de Musique de Montreal, Canada; In 1995 established a two-week Festival de Musique de Chambre de Montréal, a celebration of chamber music in the Chateau de Belvedere atop Mont Royal; On jury for the 1993 Evian International String Quartet Competition in France and the 1996 Munich String Quartet Competition; One of 3 invited guest lecturers for the Piatigorsky Seminar for Cellists, University of Southern California in Los Angeles, 1997. *Recordings include:* 20 chamber music works including the complete string quartets of Beethoven with the Orford String Quartet and Homage to Piatigorsky; Works of his father, Alexander Brott, featuring Arabesque for Cello and Orchestra, 1993. *Publications include:* Article, Schelome: The Message of King Solomon, Violoncello Society and Canadian Jewish News Viewpoints, 1993. *Current Management:* Davis Joachim, Les Concerts Davis Joachim Inc, 201 Brock Avenue North, Montreal, Quebec H4X 2G1, Canada. *Address:* 201 Brock Avenue North, Montreal, Quebec H4X 2G1, Canada.

BROUWER, Leo; Cuban composer and classical guitarist; b. 1 March 1939, Havana. *Education:* Juilliard School, New York with Stefan Wolpe and Vincent Persichetti, Hartt College with Isadore Freed. *Career:* debut 1956; Teacher at the National Conservatory, Havana, 1961–67; Director of experimental department of Cuban film music from 1967; Many tours as guitar soloist; Guitar Competition founded in his honour, Japan, 1984; Co-founded the Orchestra de Córdoba, Spain, 1992. *Compositions include:* Sonograms for prepared piano, 1963; Tropos for orchestra, 1967; Hexahedron for six players, 1969; Flute concerto, 1972; Homenaje a Lenin for electronics; 5 guitar concertos, 1972–92; Doble Concierto for violin, guitar and orchestra, 1995; Lamento for Rafael Orozco for clarinet and strings, 1996; Many smaller pieces for guitar. *Address:* c/o ACDAM, Calle 6 No. 313 entre 13 y 15, Vedado 10400, Havana, Cuba.

BROWN, Christopher (Roland); Composer; b. 17 June 1943, Tunbridge Wells, Kent, England; m. (1) Anne Smillie, 29 Mar 1969, 1 s., 1 d., (2) Fiona Caithness, 28 Dec 1985, 1 s. *Education:* Westminster Abbey Choir School, 1952–57; Dean Close School, Cheltenham, 1957–62; King's College, Cambridge, 1962–65; BA, 1965, MA, 1968; Royal Academy of Music, London, 1965–67; Hochschule für Musik, Berlin, Germany, 1967–68. *Career:* Freelance Composer, 1968–; Member, Professorial Staff, Royal Academy of Music, 1969–; Conductor, Huntingdonshire Philharmonic, 1976–91, 1994–95; Composer-in-Residence, Nene College, Northampton, 1986–88; Conductor, Dorset Bach Cantata Club, 1988–; Conductor, New Cambridge Singers, 1997–. *Compositions:* Regularly performed world-wide including: Triptych; The Sun: Rising; Organ Concerto; Festive Prelude; Festival Variations; 4 Operas; 2 String Quartets; Chamber Music for 5 instruments; Images; Ruscelli d'oro; La Légende de L'Etoile; Choral works include: David; A Hymn to the Holy Innocents; Three Medieval Lyrics; Magnificat; Chaunatecleer; The Vision of Saul; The Snows of Winter; Hodie Salvator Apparuit; Tres Canti Sacri; Landscapes; The Circling Year; Numerous songs, carols, church music; Mass for 4 voices, 1991; Christmas Cantata, 1992; The Ship of Fools, 1992; Star Song I, 1994; Summer Winds, 1995; Star Song III, 1996; Brown the Bear, 1997; Star Song IV, 1999; Invocation, 1999; To the Hills, 2000; Dance Variants, 2001. *Recordings include:* Laudate Dominum, Dean Close School Choir; Laudate Dominum, Canterbury Cathedral Choir; 'Tis Christmas Time, Huntingdonshire Philharmonic and Canticum; Seascape, British Chamber Choir and Brass Unlimited. *Publications:* Numerous. *Address:* 6 Station Road, Catworth, Huntingdon, Cambridgeshire PE28 0PE, England.

BROWN, David; Professor of Musicology, University Teacher, Writer on Music and Broadcaster; b. 8 July 1929, Gravesend, Kent, England; m. Elizabeth Valentine, 24 Dec 1953, 2 d. *Education:* Sheffield University, 1947–52, BA 1950, BMus 1951, DipEd 1952, MA 1960; PhD, Southampton University, 1971; LTCL. *Career:* Schoolmaster, 1954–59; Music Librarian, London University, 1959–62; Lecturer in Music, 1962–, Professor of Musicology, 1983–89, Southampton University; mem, Royal Musical Association; Royal Society of Arts; Member of Editorial Committee of Musica Britannica. *Publications:* Thomas Weelkes, 1969; Mikhail Glinka, 1973; John Wilbye, 1974; Tchaikovsky, 4 vols, vol. 1 1840–74, 1978, vol. 2 1874–78, 1982, vol. 3 1878–85, 1986 and vol. 4 1885–93, 1991; Tchaikovsky Remembered, 1993; Musorgsky, 2003. *Contributions:* Music and Letters; Musical Times; Music Review; Monthly Musical Record; Listener; Survey; etc.. *Honours:* Derek Allen Prize of The British Academy, for Tchaikovsky vol. 2, 1982; Yorkshire Post Music Book Award, for Tchaikovsky vol. 4, 1991. *Address:*

Braishfield Lodge West, Braishfield, Romsey, Hampshire SO51 0PS , England. *E-mail:* dandebrown@blwest.fsnet.co.uk.

BROWN, Donna; Singer (soprano); b. 15 Feb. 1955, Renfrew, ON, Canada. *Education:* studied with Edith Mathis in Salzburg. *Career:* opera debut in Paris as Michaela in Peter Brook's Tragedie de Carmen; has sung Pamina in Die Zauberflöte, Sophie in Der Rosenkavalier, Almirena in Rinaldo, Gilda in Rigoletto, Nanetta in Falstaff, Rosina in Il barbiere di Siviglia, Servillia in La Clemenza di Tito, Morgana in Alcina, and Michaela in Carmen; also appeared as Chimène in world premiere of Debussy's unfinished opera Rodrigue et Chimène; season 2003–04 concert tour and recording of Noel Coward and Ivor Novello songs, appearances with London Philharmonic, National Arts Centre Orchestra, San Francisco Symphony. *Recordings include:* Rodrigue et Chimène, Brahms' Requiem, Die Schöpfung, Lieder by Fanny Mendelssohn, Debussy Mélodies de jeunesse. *Address:* c/o Opéra et Concerts, 1 rue Volnay, 75002, Paris, France. *E-mail:* c.verset@opera-concert.com.

BROWN, Ian; Pianist and Conductor; b. 1955, England. *Career:* Originally began as a bassoonist, then became Pianist-in-Residence, Southampton University; Concerto soloist with many leading British orchestras including BBC Symphony Orchestra, BBC National Orchestra of Wales, Bournemouth Symphony Orchestra, performing in major European and Scandinavian countries, the Middle East, North and South America, Singapore, Hong Kong and Japan; Pianist with Nash Ensemble from 1978, playing in the annual Wigmore series and at all major British festivals; Has appeared in duo with Mstislav Rostropovich, Henryk Szeryng, Ruggiero Ricci, Elisabeth Söderströ m, Felicity Lott, Ralph Kirshbaum, György Pauk, James Galway and others; Soloist in Messiaen's Oiseaux Exotiques at the Proms; Toured Germany with BBC Philharmonic Orchestra in concerts celebrating Hans Werner Henze's 60th birthday; Recent appearances as conductor with Northern Sinfonia, the City of London Sinfonia, Scottish Chamber Orchestra and Bournemouth Symphony Orchestra and Sinfonietta; London conducting debut at the Barbican (Mahler's Resurrection Symphony with the Salomon Orchestra and London Choral Society). *Recordings:* Extensive recordings of chamber music from Haydn to the present day, with the Nash Ensemble. *Current Management:* Diana Walters Artists Management, England. *Address:* c/o Diana Walters Artists Management, Ivy Cottage, 3 Main Street, Keyham, Leicestershire LE7 9JQ, England.

BROWN, John; Violinist; b. 1943, Yorkshire, England. *Education:* Royal Manchester College of Music, with Endre Wolf and György Pauk, and at Salzburg Mozarteum. *Career:* Co-leader, 1968, Leader, 1973, London Symphony Orchestra; Leader of the Orchestra of the Royal Opera House, Covent Garden, 1976–96; Solo appearances with the BBC Scottish, BBC Symphony and London Symphony Orchestras; Plays a Stradivarius violin. *Honours:* Prizewinner of the BBC Violin Competition, 1966; O.B.E., 1987. *Address:* c/o London Symphony Orchestra, Barbican Centre, Silk Street, London, EC 2Y 8 DS, England.

BROWN, Justin; Conductor; b. 1962, England. *Education:* Studied at Trinity College, Cambridge, and at Tanglewood with Rozhdestvensky, Ozawa and Bernstein. *Career:* Appearances with the London Symphony Orchestra, Royal Philharmonic Orchestra, BBC Symphony Orchestra and Scottish Symphony Orchestra, Royal Liverpool Philharmonic Orchestra, Bournemouth Symphony Orchestra, Ulster Orchestra, Orchestre National du Capitole du Toulouse, Gothenburg Symphony Orchestra, Dresden Philharmonic Orchestra, Oslo Philharmonic, Sydney Symphony Orchestra St Petersburg Philharmonic Orchestra, Melbourne Symphony Orchestra and Orchestra Internazionale d'Italia; Engagements with English National Opera, Scottish Opera and at the Maggio Musicale, Santa Fe, Lisbon, Stuttgart, Strasbourg and La Monnaie (Brussels) opera houses; Season 1996–97 with debut at Norwegian and Nantes Opera; As Pianist, chamber music recitals in UK and Scandinavia, concertos (Beethoven, Mozart, Bach) directed from the keyboard UK, Malmö Symphony Orchestra, Israel Sinfonietta. *Recordings:* Bernstein, Candide, Scottish Opera; Tavener, The Protecting Veil, Wallfisch R. Philharmonic Orchestra; ,Koch, Orchestral Works, Odense Symphony Orchestra. *Honours:* Winner, London Mozart Players Best Young Conductor, 1990. *Address:* c/o IMG Artists, Lovell House, 616 Chiswick High Road, London W4 5RX, England.

BROWN, Paul; Stage Designer; b. 1960, Vale of Glamorgan, Wales. *Education:* Studied with Margaret Harris. *Career:* Designs for Monteverdi's Poppea at Bologna, Philidor's Tom Jones and Grétry's Zémire et Azor at Drottningholm; Royal Opera, Covent Garden with Mitridate, The Midsummer Marriage, I Masnadieri and Falstaff (2000); Lulu and Pelléas et Mélisande at Glyndebourne; Parsifal at the Opéra Bastille, Paris; Don Carlos for Opera Australia and Fidelio for English National Opera; Metropolitan Opera, New York, with Schoenberg's Moses und Aron and Lady Macbeth by Shostakovich; Designs for Purcell's King Arthur for the Châtelet, Paris, and Covent Garden, 1995; Season 2000–01 with Peter Grimes at the Bastille. *Address:* c/o Glyndebourne Festival Opera, Glyndebourne, Lewes, Sussex BN8 5UU, England.

BROWN, Rachel; Flautist and Recorder player; b. 1962, USA. *Education:* Royal Northern College of Music. *Career:* Principal Flautist with the King's Consort, the Hanover Band, Academy of Ancient Music and the Brandenburg Consort: Concerto performances on tour in Japan, Europe and America; Former Professor at RNCM, Manchester; Guildhall School, London and Royal College of Music, 2000–; Performances with the London Handel Festival 2001. *Recordings include:* Concertos by Vivaldi, Quantz, Handel, Telemann, JS and JC Bach; Sonatas by Schubert and Boehm (Chandos); Concertos by Quantz and CPE Bach (Hyperion). *Honours:* Winner, American National Flute Competition, 1984. *Address:* c/o Royal College of Music, Prince Consort Road, London SW7, England.

BROWNE, Sandra; Singer (Mezzo-Soprano); b. 27 July 1947, Point Fortin, Trinidad, West Indies. *Education:* BA Modern Languages, Vassar College, USA; Brussels Conservatory with Mina Bolotine; Royal Manchester College of Music with Frederic Cox. *Career:* Debut: With Welsh National Opera in Nabucco, 1972; Sang in the premiere of Alun Hoddinott's The Beach of Falsea, 1974; Kent Opera as Monteverdi's Poppea, English National Opera from 1974, as Octavian, Rosina, Monteverdi's Poppea, Dido and Carmen; Guest appearances in Toulouse, Marseille, Nancy and Florence as Carmen; Verona 1978, in a revival of Vivaldi's Orlando Furioso; La Scala Milan 1981 in Ariodante; Aix-en-Provence 1983, in Mozart's Mitridate; Other engagements in Pergolesi's Adriano in Siria (Florence), Dido and Aeneas (New York City Opera), Salome (Welsh National Opera), Radamisto and Ottone (Handel Opera Society); Concerts with most leading British orchestras, and in Norway, Portugal, France, Italy, Latin America and Australia; Regular Prom concert appearances. *Recordings:* Offenbach, Robinson Crusoe; Songs by Barber and Copland; Songs by Falla, Rodrigo, Granados and Montsalvatge; Rossini, Mosè in Egitto (Philips); Albinoni, Il Nascimento dell'Aurora (Erato); Vivaldi, Serenata a tre, Mio Cor Povero Cor (Erato). *Honours:* Kathleen Ferrier Memorial Scholarship 1971; RMCM Gold Medal for Voice 1972; Nominated for Laurence Olivier Award, 1991. *Address:* New Zealand Cottages, Barnham, Thetford, Norfolk IP24 2PL, England.

BROWNER, Alison; Singer (Mezzo-soprano); b. 22 Sept. 1958, Dublin, Ireland; m. Wilhelm Gries, 1 s., 1 d. *Education:* BA, Trinity College, Dublin; School of Music, Dublin; Private Studies, Hans Hotter, Munich. *Career:* Debut: Ludwigsburger Schloss Festspiele; National Theatre, Mannheim; Appeared at Bayreuth, Stuttgart, Zürich, Brussels, Antwerp, Covent Garden, Wexford Opera Festival, Staatsoper Berlin; Roles include La Cenerentola, Rosina (Barbiere), Cherubino, Hansel, Sesto, Idamante; Season 1995 as Rosina at Santiago and Cherubino at Antwerp; Season 1997–98 appeared at Melbourne and Brisbane Festivals; Extensive tour of Netherlands with St Matthew Passion and Sigiswald Kuikjen; Appeared at Madrid Opera, 1999; Engaged to tour in Poland and the Czech Republic with St John Passion also concert performances in Ireland of Messiah and Beethoven's Missa Solemnis, 2000. *Recordings:* Oberto (Verdi) Christmas Oratorio, B Minor Mass, St Matthew Passion (Bach), Hugo Wolf Orchestral Songs with Choir; Lo Speziale (Haydn opera); Mahler 4th Symphony; Konradin Kreutzer 'Faust'. *Current Management:* Music International. *Address:* Römer 9-11, 65549 Limburg, Germany.

BROWNRIDGE, Angela (Mary); Concert Pianist; b. 14 Oct. 1944, North Humberside, England; m. Arthur Johnson, 12 Oct 1968. 1 s. *Education:* Piano Scholar, Edinburgh University; Private study with Dorothy Hesse, Guido Agosti and Maria Curcio. *Career:* Debut: Wigmore Hall, London, 1970; Appearances in major London concert halls and with major orchestras in England and Abroad; Regular Broadcaster with Radio 3 and stations world-wide; Extensive recital tours in England, America, Canada, Far East and Europe; mem, Incorporated Society of Musicians; Musicians Union; EPTA; Beethoven Piano Society of Europe; Liszt Society. *Compositions:* Piano pieces, aged 7. *Recordings:* Solo piano repertoire by Camilleri, Satie, Barber Tchaikovsky, Scriabin, Schumann, Gershwin and Liszt; First ever completed collections of solo works by Barber, and Gershwin, Barber and Satie voted Records of the Month; Concertos with Royal Philharmonic, London Symphony and Hallé Orchestras. *Honours:* Scholarship to Edinburgh University, 1963; Tovey Prize for Performance, 1965; Frazer Scholarship, 1966; Vaughan Williams Trust Fund, 1972; Arts Council Award, 1972. *Current Management:* ManyGate Management, 13 Cotswold Mews, 30 Battersea Square, London SW11 3 RA. *Address:* 118 Audley Road, Hendon, London NW4 3HG, England.

BROZAK, Daniel; Composer, Theoretician and Violinist; b. 13 April 1947, Písek, Czechoslovakia. *Education:* Prague Conservatory; Royal Conservatory in the Hague; Institute for Sonology at Utrecht State University. *Career:* Debut: In Prague with own works for solo violin, 1973; Leader of Prague Chamber Studio until 1969; Musica Intuitiva until 1975; Theoretical research in the field of 12 tone harmony, 1975–84; Electronic and computer music, 1975–94; mem, IG-Komponisten Salzburg; SEAH Prague; SPNMS; SNH 39815; Artistic Initiative-EKVNM. *Compositions:* Les Voiles, 1977; Slunovrat, 1978; Equinox, 1978; The Seasons, 1981; Concerto da Chiesa, 1984; Diseased Society, 1988; Requiem, 1991. *Recordings:* Fresky, 1974; Rigorosum, 1975; Ave, 1978; In Manus Tuas, 1987; In A, 1988; In The Middle of Nowhere, 1989–90; Poetische Stunde, 1989; Dopisy Olze, 1990; Zbytecná Hudba, 1992; Necas Trhovcu, 1994; Katolické Radovánky, 1996; Privat Sky, 1997. *Publications:* Interval Keys, 1977; Structural Harmony, 1988; Pathology of Music, 1991; Zkazena Sul, 1997; Liturgie Zbabelych, 1998. *Contributions:* Interval Keys and Structural Harmony (with D Pandula) in Accademia Cristiana, Roma, Studie 110-11, 1987. *Honours:* Wieniawski Composition Competition (Sonata for solo violin, op 52), 1980. *Current Management:* Donemus, Amsterdam, Netherlands. *Address:* Paulus Potterstraat 16, 1071 CZ, Amsterdam, Netherlands.

BRUA, Claire; Singer (Soprano); b. 1970, France. *Education:* Studied with Albert Lance at the Nice Conservatoire; Paris Conservatoire with Rachel Yakar, Gundula Janowitz and William Christie. *Career:* Many performances in France and abroad with such conductors of Baroque music as René Jacobs and Jean-Claude Malgoire; Appearances with William Christie and Les Arts Florissants include Purcell's Dido, in Paris and Rome; Repertory includes Handel, Mozart and Rossini, and recitals of French song; Rinaldo in Jommelli's Armida abandonata at Beaune, 1994; Cavalli's Dido at the Paris Opéra Comique, 1998; Sang Pulcheria in Handel's Riccardo Primo, with Les Talents Lyriques under Christophe Rousset, Fontevraud, 1995; Mozart roles, Dorabella in Così fan tutte, Cherubino in Le nozze di Figaro, Zerlina in Don Giovanni, Annio in La Clemenza di Tito, Zweite Dame in Die Zauberflöte. *Recordings include:* Riccardo Primo. *Address:* 1 Rue de Chantilly, 75009 Paris, France.

BRUBAKER, Robert; Singer (Tenor); b. 1963, USA. *Career:* Sang Henri in Verdi's Vespri Siciliani at Carnegie Hall, New York, 1990; Canadian Opera at Toronto as Cassio in Otello; Season 1993 as Cavaradossi at Seattle and in the title role of Zemlinsky's Der Zwerg at the Spoleto Festival (USA and Italy) and Rome; Sang Pinkerton at Detroit (1994) and Rodolfo at Montreal, 1995; British debut for ENO 1991 as Weill's Jim Mahoney and Don José (returned 1999-2000, as Peter Grimes and as Mao in Nixon in China by John Adams); Washington Opera 1994 in the premiere of Argento's The Dream of Argento; Season 2000-01 as Pierre in War and Peace at the Opéra Bastille and Grimes at Aldeburgh; New York Met as Mephistopheles in Busoni's Faust and Albert Gregor in The Makropoulas Case; Covent Garden debut as Bacchus in Ariadne auf Naxos, 2002; Season 2002–03 in Boris Godunov at the Bastille, Schreker's Der Schatzgräber at Frankfurt and Peter Grimes at Toronto; Siegmund in Madrid, 2003. *Address:* IMG-Paris, 54 Ave Marceau, F–75008 Paris, France.

BRUCE, Margaret, ARCM; Canadian/British pianist; b. 28 June 1943, Vancouver, British Columbia, Canada; m. The Hon. H. L. T. Lumley-Savile 1972; three s. (triplets). *Education:* Scholar Toronto Conservatory of Music, Royal College of Music, London. *Career:* debut, Wigmore Hall, 1968; Performances at Wigmore Hall, 1968, 1979; Purcell Room, 1970, 1975, 1978, 1980, 1983; Barbican, 1983, 1985; Royal Concert Huddersfield, 1982; Italian debut, 1983; Tours: Czechoslovakia, 1968, 1981, Canada, 1984, 1987, 1989; Originator, new concert series at St John's, Smith Square, London, Canadians and Classics, 1986, 1988, 1989, 1990; Many other concerts at St John's, including solo and duet; With Royal Philharmonic Orchestra, Barbican, 1985; Bulgarian debut, 1992; Chomé Piano Trio debut, Barbican; Many concerts and recordings to follow, 1993; Bruce-Colwell Duo, Edinburgh Festival debut, 1994; Bruce/Lyttleton Duo recitals of poetry and piano solos, concerts USA, Canada, Italy, the United Kingdom, 1999; concerts Bermuda, Italy, Hebden Bridge Arts Festival 2004; works have been written for her by Herbert Howells, Lennox Berkeley, Jean Coulthard, Antonin Tucapsky. *Compositions:* CBC Recordings, Canada, 1969, 1982, 1984. *Recordings:* Premiere recording of Dvořák's From the Bohemian Forest, Op 68, with Peter Gellhorn; Solo recording, 1983; Divertimenti: 3 concerti written for her; Mozart Concerti K414 and K449, 2001. *Honours:* Royal College of Music, 1962; Sir James Caird Scholarship, 1966. *Address:* Via dei Pandolfini 27, 50122 Florence, Italy (office); Walshaw, Hebden Bridge, West Yorkshire HX7 7AX, England (home). *Telephone:* (777) 327-8477 (office); (1422) 842275 (home). *E-mail:* mls@musician.org (office); margaretbruce333@aol.com (home).

BRUCE, Neely; Composer, Pianist and Conductor; b. 21 Jan. 1944, Memphis, Tennessee, USA. *Education:* Studied Piano with Roy McAllister, University of Alabama; Piano and Composition with Soulima Stravinsky and Ben Johnston, University of Illinois. *Career:* Teacher, Wesleyan University, 1974–, and Conductor, American Music/Theater Group; Piano performances of much American music including premieres of works by Cage, Duckworth, Farwell, Brant; New York debut, 1968, at the Electric Circus; European debut, Warsaw, 1972, in songs by Ives; Directed scenes from American operas at Holland Festival, 1982; Member, Editorial Committee, New World Records,

1974–79; Chairman, New England Sacred Harp Singing, 1976, 1979, 1982; Senior Research Fellow, Institute for Studies in American Music, Brooklyn College, 1980. *Compositions include:* Pyramus and Thisbe, chamber opera, 1965; The Trials of Psyche, opera, 1971; Concerto for violin and chamber orchestra, 1974; Americana, or, A New Tale of the Genii, opera, 1983; The Blades O' Blue Grass Songbook, solo voices, piano, 1984–95; Atmo-Rag, chamber orchestra, 1987; Santa Ynez Waltz, chamber orchestra, 1990; Orion Rising, First Album for orchestra, 1991; Barnum's Band, large wind ensemble, 1992; Tanglewood, oratorio, 1993; Trio for Bands, 3 rock bands, 1994; Hugomotion, oratorio on texts of Hugo Grotius, 1995; Hansel and Gretel, opera, 1998; Instrumental, chamber, choral and vocal works. *Recordings:* Eight Ghosts, The Dream of the Other Dreamers, The Plague: A Commentary on the Work of the Fourth Horseman, composed for Electric Phoenix vocal quartet with electronics, 1992; Perfumes and Meaning, Illinois Contemporary Chamber Singers with William Brooks, conductor, 1992; Stanzas for Shep and Nancy, Linda Hirst, mezzo-soprano, composer at piano, 1992; For Tom Howell, John Fonville, flautist, 1992. *Current Management:* Jonathan Wentworth Associates, Mt Vernon, New York, USA. *Address:* 440 Chamberlain Road, Middleton, CT 06457, USA.

BRUCE-PAYNE, Sally; Singer (Mezzo-soprano); b. 1968, London. *Education:* Royal College of Music and with Felicity Palmer. *Career:* Concerts have included Bach's Choice of Hercules at the Göttingen Festival, the B Minor Mass on tour to Japan and Korea, English Baroque Soloists; Messiah with the Bach Choir and Bach Cantatas in the USA; Season 1998–99: With the St Matthew Passion on tour in Europe, Eryxene in Handel's Poro at Halle and Monteverdi's Ottavia in Japan; European tour of Messiah; Ottone in Handel's Agrippina at St John's Smith Square, Duruflé's Requiem at The Three Choirs Festival and Verdi Requiem with the Philharmonia conducted by David Willcocks; Works regularly with major British orchestras including Royal Liverpool Philharmonic Orchestra, Philharmonia, Bournemouth Symphony Orchestra and Scottish Chamber Orchestra; Season 2001–02 included title role in Offenbach's Dick Whittington at the City of London Festival, Elijah with the Philharmonia conducted by Wolfgang Sawallisch, Partenope at the Royal Opera House Linbury Theatre and the Buxton Festival and Messiah at the Lyon Festival. *Recordings:* Schubert's Mass in A flat and Haydn's Theresien and Nelson Masses conducted by John Eliot Gardiner; Vivaldi's operas Ottone in Villa, Tito Manlio and Giustino; Copland's In the Beginning. *Honours:* English Song Prize at the RCM; Muriel Kistner Prize. *Address:* c/o IMG Artists, Lovell House, 616 Chiswick High Road, London W4 5RX, England.

BRUDERHANS, Zdenek; Flautist and University Reader; b. 29 July 1934, Prague, Czechoslovakia; m. Eva Holubarova, 19 April 1962, 1 s., 1 d. *Education:* Baccalaureate, Akademicke Gymnasium, Prague; Distinction Diploma, Prague Conservatorium of Music; MMus, Prague Academy of Music. *Career:* Debut: Prague, 1957; Assistant Principal Flautist, Prague National Theatre, 1955–59; Principal Flautist, Prague Radio Symphony Orchestra, 1960–68; Represented Czechoslovakia at M.I.D.E.M in Cannes, France, 1968; Flute Professor, Sweden, 1969–73; Lecturer, Senior Lecturer, Reader, Dean of Music, 1987–88, Adelaide University, South Australia, 1973–97; Flute Soloist in 18 European Countries, USA, Australia and Asia on Radio; Recitals, concertos and in Festivals. *Recordings:* 16 recordings including recitals of works by Bach, Mozart, Haydn, Hindemith, Martinů, Messiaen, Berio, Debussy, Varèse, Ravel, Feld and Telemann; Zdenek Bruderhans Almanacs; Sonatas by Martinů, Feld, Prokofiev; 3 Flute Anthologies. *Publications:* Music, Tectonics and Flute Playing, 1997. *Contributions:* Miscellania Musicologica; The Instrumentalist; Pan and the Flute. *Honours:* Grand Prize, International Competition of Wind Instruments, Prague Spring Festival, 1959. *Address:* 2 McLaughlan Avenue, Brighton 5048, South Australia. *Telephone:* (8) 8298–3099. *E-mail:* flute@senet.com.au. *Website:* www.senet.com.au/~flute.

BRUEGGEN, Frans; Conductor and Musicologist; b. 30 Oct. 1934, Amsterdam, Netherlands. *Education:* Musieklyceum, Amsterdam; Recorder with Kees Otten; Awarded recorder diploma; Musicology at University of Amsterdam. *Career:* Many engagements as performer and conductor, in early and modern music; Played original 18th century flutes and recorders or copies; Member of avant-garde ensembles, including SourCream; Has commissioned many works (Berio's Gesti, 1966); Erasmus Professor of late Baroque music at Harvard University, 1972–73; Regent's Professor, University of California, Berkeley, 1974; Professor of recorder and early 18th century music at the Royal Conservatory, The Hague; Frequent concerts with cellist Anner Bylsma and harpsichordist Gustav Leonhardt; From 1981 has conducted symphonic music; Founder and Conductor of the Orchestra of the Eighteenth Century (concerts with the orchestra and Malcolm Bilson for the Mozart Bicentenary, 1991); Conducted Idomeneo for Netherlands Opera, 1991; Principal Guest Conductor of the Orchestra of the Age of Enlightenment from 1992, leading it at the 1993 Promenade Concerts in Haydn's London and Beethoven's Ninth Symphonies;

Gluck's Orfeo at Lyon, 1998. *Recordings include:* Mozart's Piano Concertos K466 and K491 (John Gibbons), Symphony K550 and Beethoven's 1st Symphony; Haydn Symphonies Nos 90 and 93; Rameau Suites from Dardanus and Les Boréades; Vivaldi Flute Concertos. *Publications:* Various editions of early music, published in London, Tokyo or Amsterdam. *Address:* c/o Orchestra of the Age of Enlightenment, 26 St Anne's Court, Dean Street, London W1V 3AW, England.

BRUHN, Siglind; Concert Pianist and Music Analyst; b. 11 Oct. 1951, Hamburg, Germany; m. Gerhold Becker, 20 Aug 1985. *Education:* MM, Piano Performance, Piano Pedagogy, Musikhochschule Hamburg and Stuttgart; MA, Romance Literature, Philosophy, University of Munich; Masterclasses with Wladimir Horzowski, Hans Leygraf, Nikita Magaloff; DrPhil, Music Analysis, Musikhochschule and University of Vienna, 1985. *Career:* Debut: 1965; Head of Community Music School, Munich, 1978–82; Head, Institute for Musical Interpretation, 1982–87; Director, Pianists' Academy, Ansbach, 1984–87; Director of Studies, University of Hong Kong, 1987–94; Guest Professor, Beijing Central Conservatory of Music, 1990; Visiting Scholar, University of Michigan, Ann Arbor, 1993–97; Permanent Research Associate, Institute for Humanities, University of Michigan, 1997–; Performances in all major West German cities, Zürich, London, Paris, Lisbon, Venice, Athens, Beirut, Rio de Janeiro, Quito, Johannesburg, Cape Town, Hong Kong, Manila, Beijing, Shanghai, Melbourne, Adelaide, Washington DC; Television and radio appearances on most German stations and for British, French, Swiss, Italian, Lebanese, South African, and Australian broadcasting corporations. *Recordings:* Ravel, Moussorgsky, 1984; Dvořák, 1986; Hindemith, duo sonatas, 1997; Hindemith, piano solo, 1997. *Publications:* Analysis and Interpretation in J. S. Bach's Well-Tempered Klavier, 1993; Musikalische Symbolik in Olivier Messiaens Weihnachtsvignetten, 1997; Images and Ideas in Modern French Piano Music, 1997; Alban Berg's Music as Encrypted Speech, editor, 1997; The Temptation of Paul Hindemith: Mathis der Maler as a Spiritual Testimony, 1998; Messiaen's Language of Mystical Love, editor, 1998; Signs in Musical Hermeneutics, editor, 1998; Musical Ekphrasis: Composers Responding to Poetry and Painting, forthcoming; Musical Ekphrasis in Rilke's Marien-Leben, forthcoming. *Contributions:* Scholarly journals, handbooks and collections in Europe, Asia and USA. *Address:* 1308 Broadway, Ann Arbor, MI 48105, USA.

BRUK, Fridrich; Composer; b. 18 Sept. 1937, Kharkov, Ukraine; m. Nadezhda Bruk 1959; one s. *Education:* Silver Medal, Kharkov Music Coll. of the Kharkov Conservatory 1956; diploma in composition, Conservatory Rimsky-Korsakov, Leningrad 1961. *Career:* debut, The Forty First (opera based on Boris Lavrenev's story) 1961; composer of opera, orchestral works and chamber music, music for theatre and film, popular songs; teaches pedagogue in various Finnish musical institutes; mem. Soc. of Finnish Composers, Finnish Composers' Copyright Bureau, Guild of Light Music Composers and Authors, Soc. of Russian Composers. *Compositions:* String quartet No.1 1983; music for children: Spring 1982, Snowdrop 1983, Sleigh Bells 1984, Summer 1985, Golden Autumn 1988, Winter 1988; Sunflecks, suite for orchestra 1987, Five duets for clarinet (B) and violoncello or bassoon 1983, Lyrical images, suite for piano 1985, Variations for piano on the Karelian song Strawberry 1985, Concert Variations on the old Kalevala song, for violoncello and piano 1985, The Steppe, suite for woodwind quartet, As Lace Against the Light, 7 songs for 3-voice choir 1986, Sonata for Cantele 1986, String quartet No.2 1987, Concertino for 2 violins and string orchestra or piano 1987, Sonata for 2 violins 1988, Sonata for violoncello 1989; Sonata for 2 trumpets 1989; music for television films 1988, 1989, Sonata for viola 1990, Sonata for clarinet (B) 1991, Sonata for piano 1994, Seven dialogues for oboe and viola 1995, Trio for clarinet (B), viola and violoncello 1996, Symphony No. 1 for orchestra and trombone solo 1998, Symphony No. 2 for orchestra and piano 1999, The Wander Singer, oratorio for baritone, soprano, mixed choir and orchestra (poetry by Oiva Paloheimo) 2000, Artist Chagall, Symphony No. 3 for orchestra and tenor 2000, Sounds of Spring, poem for orchestra 2000, Carelia, Symphony No. 4 for soprano, bass, drums, piano, harp and string orchestra (poetry from Kalevala and Eino Leino) 2001, Musik für Quartett 2001, The Hand of God, Christmas oratorio for narrator, soloists, children's choir and instrumental ensemble 2002, Sonata for Piano No. 2 2002, Symphony No. 5 for Orchestra 2002, Birds of Passage, Symphony No. 6 for baritone and orchestra (poetry by Viljo Kajava) 2001–03, The Cat's House (opera for children, libretto by Samuel Marshak) 2003. *Recordings:* Compositions by Fridrich Bruk 1993, Lyrical Images 1994, From Kalevala 1994, The Snowdrop 1996, Dialogues 1996, Artist Chagall, Symphony No. 3 for orchestra and tenor 2002, The Hand of God 2003, The Sunshine 2004. *Honours:* Cross of Merit of the Order of the Lion of Finland 1988, various Finnish grants and scholarships. *Address:* Papinkatu 18 A 41, Tampere, 33200 Suomi, Finland. *Telephone:* (3) 2144040. *Fax:* (3) 2144040.

BRUMAIRE, Jacqueline; Singer (Soprano); b. 5 Nov. 1921, Herbley, France. *Education:* Studied at the Paris Conservatoire. *Career:* Debut:

Paris Opéra-Comique, 1946, as The Countess in Le Nozze di Figaro; Sang in Paris as Mimi in La Bohème, Micaela, Manon, Antonia in Les Contes d'Hoffmann and Fiordiligi; Opéra-Comique 1951, in the premiere of Madame Bovary by Bondeville; Paris Opéra 1962, as Donna Elvira in Don Giovanni; Visited Peking 1981, to sing Carmen. *Recordings:* Opera arias, Philips; Milhaud's Les malheurs d'Orphée and Le Pauvre Matelot; Le Roi d'Yvetot by Ibert.

BRUMBY, Colin (James); Composer, Lecturer and Conductor; b. 18 June 1933, Melbourne, Victoria, Australia. *Education:* BMus, 1957; DMus, 1972; Conservatorium of Music, University of Melbourne. *Career:* Lecturer in Music, Kelvin Grove Teachers College, 1960–62; Head of Music Department, Greenford Grammar School, Middlesex, 1962–64; Lecturer in Music, 1964–65; Senior Lecturer, 1966–75; Associate Professor of Music, 1976–98; University of Queensland; mem, Australian Performing Right Association. *Compositions:* Flute Concerto; The Phoenix and the Turtle; Festival Overture on Australian Themes; Charlie Bubbles Book of Hours; Three Italian Songs for High Voice and String Quartet; Violin Concerto 1 and 2; Piano Concerto; South Bank Overture; Symphony No. 1 (The Sun); The Vision and The Gap (Cantata); Bassoon Concerto; Bassoon Sonata; Clarinet Sonatina; Flute Sonatina; Haydn Down Under (Bassoon Quintet); Victimae Paschali (SATB and Strings); Stabat Mater (Cantata); Piano Quartet; Christmas Bells, 1986; A Service of Rounds, 1985; Four Australian Christmas Carols, 1986; Operas: Fire on the Wind; Summer Carol; The Heretic, 1998–99; Borromeo Suite for flute and guitar; Viola Concerto, Tre aspetti di Roma; Trumpet Concerto; Clarinet Concerto, 1988; Canti pisani, 1989. *Publications:* Missa Canonica, 1991; Harlequinade, 1987; Of a Rose, a Lovely Rose, 1994; Organ Concerto, 1994; Cello Concerto, 1995; Toccata for Organ, 1995. *Honours:* Advance Australia Award (Music), 1981. *Current Management:* Australia Music Centre, PO Box N690 Grosvenor Place, Sydney, NSW 2000, Australia. *Address:* 9 Teague Street, Indooroopilly, Queensland 4068, Australia.

BRUMMELSTROETE, Wilke; Singer (mezzo-soprano); b. 1968, Netherlands. *Education:* Royal Academy, Hague; Britten-Pears School and Mozarteum, Salzburg. *Career:* Debut: Purcell's Dido, 1991; Netherlands Opera 1992, in Monteverdi's Poppea; Fortuna and Anfinomo in Monteverdi's Ulisse at Brussels, Vienna, Berlin and South Africa; Turno in Bononcini's Il Trionfo di Camilla at Utrecht, 1997: Teseo in Handel's Arianna at Göttingen 1999; Juno and Ino in Semele at San Francisco, 2000; Other roles include Andronico in Handel's Tamerlano, Carmen, and Clothilde in Norma; Concerts include Beethoven's Ninth in Lisbon, Mozart's Requiem in Japan and C minor Mass in Florence; Messiah in Vienna, Bach's Magnificat at the Barbican and Cantatas at the Queen Elizabeth Hall; Elgar's The Kingdom in Buenos Aires, Aldeburgh and Sydney; Season 2001–2002 with Ruggiero in Alcina at Göttingen, Dido with the Irish Chamber Orchestra and concert tour with Israel Camerata. *Current Management:* Askonas Holt Ltd, Lonsdale Chambers, 27 Chancery Lane, London, WC2A 1PF, England. *Telephone:* (20) 7400-1700. *Fax:* (20) 7400-1799. *E-mail:* info@ askonasholt.co.uk. *Website:* www.askonasholt.co.uk.

BRUNNER, Eduard; Clarinettist; b. 14 July 1939, Basle, Switzerland. *Education:* Studied in Basle and Paris. *Career:* Chamber musician in Germany and Switzerland, from 1959; Soloist with the Bavarian Radio Symphony Orchestra, from 1963; Collaborations with such musicians as violinist Gidon Kremer (at Lockenhaus), Heinz Holliger (oboe) and Aurèle Nicolet (flute); Has premiered works by Francaix and Isang Yun (Concerto, 1982, Quintet, 1984). *Address:* c/o Rundfunkorchester des Bayerischen Rundfunks, Rundfunkplatz: 1, W-8000 Munich 2, Germany.

BRUNNER, Evelyn; Singer (Soprano); b. 17 Dec. 1949, Lausanne, Switzerland. *Education:* Studied at the Lausanne Conservatory with Paul Sandoz, in Milan and with Herbert Graf in Geneva. *Career:* Sang with the Ensemble Vocal de Lausanne under Michael Corboz and with the Orchestre de Chambre de Lausanne under Victor Desrazens; Appearances at the Grand Théâtre de Genève as Micaela in Carmen, Marguerite in Faust and Cimarosa's Il Matrimonio Segreto, 1971; Sang Mozart's Countess at the Paris Opéra and in Hamburg and Berlin; Opéra du Rhin, Strasbourg, as Elsa in Lohengrin, 1986; Engagements at opera houses in Lyon, Toulouse, Avignon and Nantes; Other roles include Mozart's Fiordiligi and Donna Anna, Liu in Turandot and Verdi's Elisabeth de Valois and Violetta; Many concerts with the Collegium Academicum de Genève. *Recordings:* Rossini's Il Signor Bruschino, conducted by Robert Dunand.

BRUNNER, Heidi; Singer (Mezzo-soprano); b. 1965, Rothenburg, Switzerland. *Education:* Studied in Lucerne, Zürich and Basle. *Career:* Debut: Biel Opera, 1989 as Rossini's Cenerentola; Appearances at Biel as Isabella in L'Italiana in Algeri, Mozart's Zerlina and Dorabella; Ottavia in Poppea and Baba the Turk in The Rake's Progress; Guest appearances in Orontea by Cesti in Basle and Innsbruck; Landstheater Dessau fron 1993, as Giovanna in Anna Bolena and Pisaro in Verdi's

Due Foscari; Komische Oper Berlin, 1995 as Cenerentola and Massenet's Charlotte; Berlin Staatsoper, 1996 as Roggiero in Rossini's Tancredi; season 1998 as Messenger and Proserpina in Monteverdi's Orfeo at the Vienna Festival; Sang Gounod's Siebel at Munich, 2000. *Address:* c/o Bayerische Staatsoper, Max-Joseph-Platz, D–80539 Munich, Germany.

BRUNNER, Richard; Singer (Tenor); b. 1953, Ohio, USA. *Education:* Studied at the Opera School of Toronto and the Academy of Vocal Arts in Pittsburgh. *Career:* Sang Ramiro in Cenerentola with Philadelphia Opera (1978), Mime in Das Rheingold (Cincinnati and Dallas, 1981–82), Števa in Jenůfa at the Spoleto Festival, Florestan with Scottish Opera (1991) and roles such as Elemer (Arabella), Narraboth (Salome) and Cassio (Otello) at the Vienna Staatsoper; Denver Opera, 1992, as Walther von Stolzing; Other roles include Melot, Sellem (The Rake's Progress) and Eisenstein in Die Fledermaus; Bayreuth Festival 1994–96, as Wagner's Froh; Sang Narraboth in Salome at San Diego, 1998; Season 1999–2000 as Strauss's Emperor and Janáček's Albert Gregor at Darmstadt, Sam in Carlisle Floyd's Susannah for Washington Opera. *Address:* c/o Opera Colorado, 695 South Colorado Boulevard, Suite 20, Denver, CA 80222, USA.

BRUNO, Joanna (Mary); Singer (Soprano); b. 1944, Orange, New Jersey, USA. *Education:* Studied with Katherine Eastment in New Jersey, at the Juilliard School with Jennie Tourel and with Luigi Ricci in Rome. *Career:* Debut: Spoleto Festival 1969, in The Medium by Menotti; Sang in Santa Fe, Houston, Chicago, Fort Worth, City Opera, New York notably in the 1971 premiere of Menotti's The Most Important Man; European engagements in Trieste, Paris, Amsterdam and for Scottish Opera; Other roles include Mozart's Despina, Susanna and Pamina; Anne Trulove in The Rake's Progress, Micaela, Verdi's Nannetta; Puccini's Butterfly, Musetta and Mimi.

BRUSA, Elisabetta (Olga Laura); Italian Composer and Professor; *Professor of Composition and Orchestration, Conservatorio of Milan;* b. 3 April 1954, Milan, Italy; m. Gilberto Serembe, 3 May 1997. *Education:* Diploma, Composition, Conservatorio of Milan with Bruno Bettinelli and Azio Corghi, 1980; Further studies with Hans Keller, London. *Career:* Debut: First Composition performed, Piccola Scala, 1982; Television programme on Young Italian Composers, 1983; Various commissions, performances; Radio and television broadcasts in Italy, England, USA, Canada, Australia, Russia, France, Ukraine, Germany, Austria, Switzerland, Korea, and Albania with Orchestras such as the BBC Philharmonic, BBC Scottish Symphony Orchestra, CBC Vancouver Orchestra, St Petersburg Symphony Orchestra, National Symphony Orchestra of Ukraine, Philharmonisches Orchestra des Theatres Altenburg-Gera, Virtuosi of Toronto; Boris Brott Festival Orchestra, Radio and Television Symphony Orchestra of Tirana, London Chamber Symphony, New England Philharmonic, Tanglewood Music Center Orchestra, Alea III Ensemble, Contemporary Music Forum of Washington DC; Women's Philharmonic of San Francisco; Professor, Composition at: Conservatorio of Vicenza, 1980–82; Conservatorio of Mantova, 1982–84; Conservatorio of Brescia, 1984–85; Conservatorio of Milan, 1985–. *Compositions include:* Belsize String Quartet, 1981; Fables for chamber orchestra, 1983; Marcia Funebre for piano, 1984; Suite Concertante for orchestra, 1986; Sonata for piano, 1986; Nittemero Symphony for chamber orchestra, 1988; Symphony No. 1 for large orchestra, 1990; Sonata Rapsodica for violin and piano, 1991; La Triade for large orchestra, 1992; Firelights for large orchestra, 1993; Requiescat for mezzo-soprano and large orchestra, 1995; Fanfare for large orchestra, 1996; Adagio for string orchestra, 1996; Wedding Song for large orchestra, 1997; Florestan for large orchestra, 1997; Messidor for orchestra, 1998; Symphony No. 2 for large orchestra; Merlin, for large orchestra 2004. *Recordings:* Orchestral Works Vols. 1 and 2. *Honours:* 1st Prize Washington International Competition, 1982; Fellowship, Tanglewood Music Center, 1983; Fulbright Bursary, 1983; Fellowship, MacDowell Colony, 1988, 1989, 1990. *E-mail:* elisabetta.brusa@tiscali.it (office). *Website:* www.elisabettabrusa.it.

BRUSON, Renato; Singer (Baritone); b. 13 Jan. 1936, Este, Italy. *Education:* Studied in Padua, Italy. *Career:* Debut: Spoleto Festival, 1961; Has appeared at all major Italian Opera Houses including La Scala, Milan, Debut 1972; Specialising in Verdi and Donizetti operas in Attila, La Traviata, La Favorita and Lucia di Lammermoor; Other opera houses include Vienna, Hamburg, Berlin, Paris, Brussels etc; Covent Garden debut 1976, as Renato in Un Ballo in Maschera; Appearances in USA include Chicago, New York Metropolitan Opera and San Francisco; Debut as Enrico at the Metropolitan, 1969; Has sung at the Verona Arena 1975–76, 1978–82, 1985; Los Angeles and Covent Garden, 1982, as Falstaff; Also at Parma, 1986; Munich, 1985, as Macbeth; Sang Iago at La Scala, 1987; Don Giovanni at the Deutsche Oper Berlin, 1988; Carnegie Hall, New York, 1990, as Montfort in Les Vêpres Siciliennes; Sang Carlos in Ernani at Parma, 1990, Germont at Turin, Carlos at La Fenice, Venice; Sang Enrico in Lucia di Lammermoor at La Scala, 1992, Germont at the 1992 Macerata Festival and at Covent Garden, 1995;

Sang Macbeth at Monte Carlo, 1997; Germont at the 1999 Orange festival; Falstaff at Macerata, 1998; Season 2000–01 at the Vienna Staatsoper as Don Carlo in Ernani, and Iago. *Recordings:* Luisa Miller; Falstaff; Samson and Delilah etc. Films and television include Don Carlos, La Scala and Luisa Miller, Covent Garden. *Address:* Teatro Alla Scala, Via Filodrammatici 2, Milano, Italy.

BRUYNEL, Ton; Composer; b. 26 Jan. 1934, Utrecht, Netherlands. *Education:* Piano at Utrecht Conservatory. *Career:* Associated with Electronic Music Studio, University of Utrecht; Established own electronic music studio in 1957. *Compositions include:* Mostly with soundtracks; Resonance 1, ballet, 1960–62; Reflexes for Birma Drum, 1961; Relief for Organ, 1964; Mobile, 1965; Milieu, 1965–66; Mekaniek for Wind Quintet, 1967; Decor, ballet, 1967; Signs for Wind Quintet and Video Projection, 1969; Intra 1 for Bass Clarinet, 1971; Elegy for Female Voices, 1972; Looking Ears for Bass Clarinet and Grand Piano, 1972; Soft Song for Oboe, 1975; Dialogue for Bass Clarinet, 1976; Translucent ll for String Orchestra, 1978; From the Tripod for Loudspeakers, Women and Listeners, 1981; John's Lullaby for Chorus and Tape, 1985; Continuation for Chorus and Tape, 1985; Adieu petit Prince for Voice, 1983; Denk Mal das Denkmal for Man's Voice, 1984; Chicharras text, 1986; Toccare for Clavicembalo, 1987; Ascolta for Chorus and Soloist, 1989; Nocturnos en Pedraza for Flute and Soundtrack, 1988; Kolom for Organ, 1987; Non Sono un Cello for Tenor and Bass Baritone; La Dernière pavane for Small Mixed Choir, 1989; La Cadulta for Tenor Bass Baritone; Tropico for Tenor Bass Baritone, 1990; Dust for Small Organ, 1991; Tarde for Cello, 1992; Le Jardin for Alto Flute, Harpsichord and Woman's Voice, 1992; Ball'alla luce for strings, tape and percussion, 1997. *Address:* Fen Have 13, 7983 KD, Wapse Diever, Netherlands.

BRUZDOWICZ-TITTEL, Joanna; Composer and Music Critic; b. 17 May 1943, Warsaw, Poland. *Education:* Piano with Irena Protasewicz and Wanda Losakiewicz; Composition with Kazimierz Sikorski, MA, Warsaw Conservatory, 1966; Composition with Nadia Boulanger, Olivier Messiaen, Pierre Schaeffer, Paris, 1968–70. *Career:* Groupe de Recherches Musicales, French radio and television, Paris; Groupe International de Musique Electroacoustique de Paris; IPEM; Electronic studios, University of Ghent, Belgian radio and television; Founder, Jeunesses Musicales, Poland; Founder President, Frédéric Chopin and Karol Szymanowski Society, Belgium; Vice President, International Federation of Chopin Societies; Music criticism; Advocate of contemporary music; mem, SACD and SACEM (France), Society of Authors ZAiKS, ZKP, Poland, Honorary member of 'Donne in Musica' Italy. *Compositions:* Operas: In der Strafkolonie, or La Colonie Pénitentiaire, 1972, revised, 1986, 1995; Les Troyennes, 1973; The Gates of Paradise, 1987; Tides and Waves, opera, musical, 1992; Ballet: Le Petit Prince, 1976; Many film and theatre scores; Orchestral including: Piano Concerto, 1974; Symphony, 1975; Violin Concerto, 1975; Aquae Sextiae for winds, 1978; Double Bass Concerto, 1982; Four Seasons' Greetings, 4 concertos for violins, pianos, flute, marimba, string orchestra, 1989; The Cry of the Phoenix for cello and symphony orchestra, 1994; Chamber including: Trio dei Due Mondi for violin, cello, piano, 1980; Dum Spiro Spero for flute and tape, 1981; Para y contra for double bass and tape, 1981; Trio per Trio for flute, violin, harpsichord, 1982; Dreams and Drums for percussion, 1982; Oracle for bassoon and tape, 1982; Aurora Borealis for harp and organ, 1988; String Quartet No. 1, La Vita, 1983, No. 2, Cantus Aeterna with speaker, 1988; Spring in America, violin-piano sonata, 1994; Cantata: Urbi et Orbi for tenor, children's choir, 2 trumpets, 2 trombones, organ, 1985; The Cry of the Phoenix, cello concerto, 1994; Song of Hope and Love for cello and piano, 1997; The World–5 songs for soprano and piano, poetry by Czeslaw Milosz, 1995–6; Piano pieces; Organ music; Electronic and electro-acoustic pieces. *Recordings:* Several albums. *Honours:* 'Polonia Restituta', officer, highest distinction for achievement i.e. professional career, in Poland, 2001. *Address:* Mas Terrats, 66400 Taillet, France. *E-mail:* tibruz@wanadoo.fr.

BRYAN, John Howard, BA, BPhil; musician (early instruments) and academic; *Principal Lecturer in Music, University of Huddersfield;* b. 24 Feb. 1952, Ilford, Essex, England; one s. two d. *Education:* University of York. *Career:* debut, 1973; Co-Director, Landini Consort; Director, Rose Consort of Viols; Artistic Adviser, York Early Music Festival; Principal Lecturer, University of Huddersfield; Also plays with Consort of Musicke and Musica Antiqua of London; mem, North East Early Music Forum; National Early Music Association. *Recordings:* Nowell, Landini Consort; Songs and Dances of Fourteenth Century Italy, Landini Consort; The Play of Daniel, Landini Consort and Pro Cantione Antiqua; Elizabethan Christmas Anthems, Rose Consort of Viols; Dowland, Lachrimae, Rose Consort of Viols; Born is the Babe, Ah, dear Heart, Rose Consort of Viols; John Jenkins, Consort Music, Rose Consort of Viols; William Byrd, Consort music, songs and anthems, Rose Consort of Viols; Orlando Gibbons, Consort music, songs and anthems, Rose Consort of Viols; John Dowland, Dances and lute Songs, Purcell,

Fantasias and in Nomines, Rose Consort of Viols; Elizabethan Consort Music, Rose Consort; Alfonso Farrebosco I & II Consort Music, Rose Consort; John Ward Consort Music, Rose Consort; A Songbook for Isabella, Musica Antiqua of London; Music for Henry VIII's Six Wives, Musica Antiqua of London. *Contributions:* Music in Education; Compendium of Contemporary Musical Knowledge, 1992. *Address:* 28 Wentworth Road, Scarcroft Hill, York YO24 1DG, England. *E-mail:* j.h .bryan@hud.ac.uk.

BRYARS, Gavin, BA; British composer and professor of music; *Associate Research Fellow, Dartington College of Arts*; b. 16 Jan. 1943, Goole, Yorkshire; s. of Walter Joseph Bryars and Miriam Eleanor Bryars; m. 1st Angela Margaret Bigley 1971 (divorced 1993); two d.; m. 2nd Anna Tchernakova 1999; one s. one step d. *Education:* Goole Grammar School, Sheffield Univ., Northern School of Music and pvt composition study with Cyril Ramsey, George Linstead and Benjamin Johnston. *Career:* freelance double bassist 1963–66; Lecturer in Liberal Studies, North-ampton Coll. of Technology 1966–67; freelance composer/performer 1968–70; Lecturer in Music, Portsmouth Polytechnic 1969–70; Sr Lecturer, School of Fine Art, Leicester Polytechnic 1970–78, Sr Lecturer and Head of Music, School of Performing Arts 1978–85; Prof. of Music, De Montfort Univ. 1985–96; collaborations with artists, including Aphex Twin, John Cage, Brian Eno, Tom Waits; mem. Collège de Pataphysique, France 1974–; Ed. Experimental Music Catalogue 1972–81; British Rep. Int. Soc. for Contemporary Music Festival 1977; Visiting Prof. Univ. of Herts.; Arts Council Comms 1970, 1980, 1982, Bursary 1982. *Films:* Sea and Stars (Nat. Film Bd of Canada) 2003. *Radio:* I Send You This Cadmium Rec (BBC Radio 3, with John Berger and John Christie) 2002, Egil's Last Days (BBC Radio 3) 2004. *Television:* Last Summer (CBC TV, Dir Anna Tchernakova) 2000. *Compositions include:* The Sinking of the Titanic 1969, Jesus' Blood Never Failed Me Yet 1971, Out of Zaleski's Gazebo 1977, The Vespertine Park 1980, Medea (opera with Robert Wilson) 1982, My First Homage for two pianos 1978, Effarene 1984, String Quartet No. 1 1985, Pico's Flight 1986, By the Vaar for double bass and ensemble 1987, The Invention of Tradition 1988, Glorious Hill 1988, Cadman Requiem 1989, String Quartet No. 2 1990, Four Elements (dance piece) 1990, The Black River for soprano and organ 1991, The White Lodge 1991, The War in Heaven for chorus and orchestra 1993, Epilogue from 'Wonderlawn' for four players 1994, Three Elegies for Nine Clarinets 1994, The North Shore for solo viola and small orchestra 1994, After Handel's Vesper 1995, Cello Concerto 1995, The Adnan Songbook 1996, Doctor Ox's Experiment (opera) 1997, String Quartet No. 3 1998, The Porazzi Fragment for strings 1998, Biped (ballet) 1999, First Book of Madrigals 2000, Violin Concerto 2000, G (opera) 2001, Second Book of Madrigals 2001, Double Bass Concerto 2002, Book of Laude 2003, Writings on Water (ballet) 2003, Third Book of Madrigals 2003, Eight Irish Madrigals 2004, New York (percussion concerto) 2004, From Egil's Saga 2004. *Publications:* contrib. to Music and Musicians, Studio International, Art and Artists, Contact,The Guardian. *Address:* c/o Schott and Co. Ltd, 48 Great Marlborough Street, London, W1F 7BB, England (office). *Telephone:* (20) 7494-1487 (office). *Fax:* (20) 7287-1529 (office). *E-mail:* questions@gavinbryars.com (office). *Website:* www .gavinbryars.com (office).

BRYDON, Roderick; Conductor; b. 8 Jan. 1939, Edinburgh, Scotland. *Education:* Daniel Stewart's College, Edinburgh; BMus Edinburgh University; Chigiana Academy, Siena. *Career:* Debut: Covent Garden, 1984, with A Midsummer Night's Dream; Close association with Sadler's Wells Opera and Scottish Opera in operas by Janáček (From the House of the Dead), Stravinsky, Mozart, Puccini, Debussy and Cavalli, (L'Egisto); Formerly General Music Director Lucerne Opera, conducting Carmen, Don Giovanni, Albert Herring and Fidelio; Musical Director of Berne Opera, 1988–90, leading A Village Romeo and Juliet, Capriccio and Peter Grimes; Guest engagements in Hannover, Copen-hagen, Karlsruhe (Handel's Alcina); Bordeaux, (Così fan tutte) and Geneva (Death in Venice, The Rake's Progress and La Clemenza di Tito); Mozart's Mitridate and Rossini's Otello in Venice; Death in Venice at the 1983 Edinburgh Festival; La Traviata; The Rake's Progress with Opera North; Artistic Director of the Scottish Chamber Orchestra for the first 9 years of its existence including concerts at the Aix and Edinburgh Festivals; Promenade Concerts, 1982; Further concerts in Munich, Paris and Venice; Conducted Parsifal at the City Theatre Berne, 1989; Concert performances of The Cunning Little Vixen, 1990; Conducted Albert Herring at Los Angeles, 1992, followed by A Midsummer Night's Dream; The Rake's Progress, at the 1992 Aldeburgh Festival; Lucia di Lammermoor at Sydney, 1996; Catán's Florencia en el Amazones at Los Angeles, 1997; Handel's Serse at Geneva, 1998. *Address:* c/o Music International, 13 Ardilaun Road, London N5 2QR, England.

BRYN-JULSON, Phyllis; Singer (Soprano); b. 5 Feb. 1945, Bowdon, North Dakota, USA. *Education:* Studied singing at the Berkshire Music Center and at Syracuse University. *Career:* Debut: With the Boston

Symphony in Berg's Lulu Suite, 1966; Has given performances of works by George Crumb, David Del Tredici, Lukas Foss, Ligeti, Berg, Webern and Schoenberg (Pierrot Lunaire); Appearances at the Berlin, Edin-burgh, Lucerne and Aldeburgh Festivals; British debut 1975, in Pli selon Pli by Boulez, conducted by the composer; Boulez 60th birthday celebrations at Baden-Baden 1985; Orchestras with whom she has appeared include the New York Philharmonic, the Boston Symphony, Chicago Symphony, Berlin Philharmonic under Abbado; First operatic role as Malinche in Montezuma by Roger Sessions, US premiere, Boston 1976; Sang in Stravinsky's Nightingale and Ravel's L'Enfant et les Sortilèges at Covent Garden, season 1986–87; Tours of Australia, New Zealand, USSR and Japan with Boulez; Ensemble Intercontemporain; Tours of the US with the Los Angeles Philharmonic and of Europe with the BBC Symphony; Gave master classes at the Moscow Conservatoire in 1987 and took part in the 80th birthday celebrations for Olivier Messiaen and Elliott Carter, 1988; Sang in Carter's A Mirror on Which to Dwell, at London's Queen Elizabeth Hall, Feb 1991; Schoenberg's Erwartung at the Festival Hall, 1991; Premiered Marrying the Hang-man (one-woman chamber opera) by Ron Caltabiano in New York and San Francisco; Staged and televised opera Il Prigioniero by Dallapiccola in Tokyo, with Charles Dutoit conducting. *Recordings include:* A Mirror on which to Dwell; Le Visage Nuptial and Le Soleil des Eaux by Boulez, Erato; Il Prigioniero by Dallapiccola, Salonen, Swedish Radio Symph-ony; Erwartung by Schoenberg, Simon Rattle, City of Birmingham Symphony Orchestra; Schumann's Frauenliebe und Leben, with Leon Fleisher, piano. *Honours:* Distinguished Alumni Award, Syracuse University; Amphion Foundation Award. *Current Management:* Howard Stokar Management. *Address:* c/o Howard Stokar Manage-ment, 870 West End Avenue New York, NY 10025-4948, USA. *E-mail:* hstokar@stokar.com.

BRYSON, Roger; Singer (Bass); b. 1944, London, England. *Education:* Guildhall School, London; London Opera Centre with Walther Gruner and Otakar Kraus. *Career:* Glyndebourne Festival and Touring Opera from 1978 as Neptune in Il Ritorno d'Ulisse, Quince and Bottom in A Midsummer Night's Dream, Osmin in Die Entführung, Rocco in Fidelio and Leporello in Don Giovanni; Kent Opera in Rigoletto, Die Zauberflöte and Don Giovanni; English National Opera in the British premiere of Ligeti's Le Grand Macabre, 1982; Opera North in Die Meistersinger, Werther, La Fanciulla del West and Love of Three Oranges; Scottish Opera as Schigolch in Lulu and Don Alfonso in Così fan tutte; Sang at Nancy in the French premiere of Tippett's King Priam and on television in the Midsummer Marriage, 1989; As Alvise in La Gioconda for the Chelsea Opera Group, Mephistopheles in Faust for New Sussex Opera, 1989, Swallow in Peter Grimes, Don Pasquale for Opera North, Bartered Bride for New Tel-Aviv Opera; Sang in concert performances of Ligeti's Le Grand Macabre at the Festival Hall, 1989, Don Pasquale for Opera North, 1990, Premieres of Europeras 3 and 4 by John Cage at the 1990 Almeida Festival, London; Sang Quince in A Midsummer Night's Dream, Sadler's Wells, Dikoi in Katya Kabanova for Glynde-bourne Touring Opera, 1992, Flint in Billy Budd, 1992, Claggart in Billy Budd for Opéra de Nancy, 1993, Don Basilio in Barber of Seville for Opera Northern Ireland, Calandro in L'Incontro Improvviso by Haydn, for Garsington Festival, and Don Alfonso in Così fan tutte for ENO. *Address:* c/o Music International, 13 Ardilaun Road, Highbury, London, N5 2QR, England.

BUCHAN, Cynthia; Singer (mezzo-soprano); b. 1948, Edinburgh, Scot-land. *Education:* Royal Scottish Academy of Music, 1968–72. *Career:* Debut: Edinburgh 1968 in Monteverdi's Il Ballo delle Ingrate; Has appeared widely in the United Kingdom and Europe as Mozart's Cherubino and Dorabella, Massenet's Charlotte, Rossini's Rosina, Verdi's Preziosilla, Tchaikovsky's Olga and as Carmen; In 1987 sang in L'Enfant et les Sortilèges at Glyndebourne, Carmen for Opera North and Mistress Quickly in Peter Stein's production of Falstaff for the Welsh National Opera; Guest appearances in Madrid, Munich, Paris as Rosina, Frankfurt as Babette in Henze's English Cat, Adelaide, Hamburg as Miranda in Cavalli's L'Ormindo and Amsterdam as Varvara in Katya Kabanova; Glyndebourne 1989 as Hermia in A Midsummer Night's Dream; Sang Despina in Così fan tutte for New Israeli Opera, 1994; Maddalena in Rigoletto for WNO, 1997; Concert appearances in London, Munich, Paris and Lyon; Conductors include Gielen, Andrew Davis, Rattle, Ivan Fischer, Knussen, Del Mar, Bernstein and Bertini. *Recordings include:* Video of Bersi in Andrea Chénier, at Covent Garden in 1985.

BUCHANAN, Alison; Singer (Soprano); b. 1969, England. *Education:* Studied at the Guildhall School of Music and the Curtis Institute, Philadelphia. *Career:* Appearances as Clara in Porgy and Bess at the Barbican, in Messiah at Chichester Cathedral, Mozart's Requiem and Bach's Christmas Oratorio at Chelmsford Cathedral and Strauss's Four Last Songs at Curtis Hall; Debut with the San Francisco Opera with Western Opera Theatre as Mozart's Countess; Season 1995–96 at San Francisco as Mimi, Juliana in Argento's The Aspern Papers, and

Micaela; Season 1996–97 with Porgy and Bess excerpts in Bruges and Paris and appearances in Elektra, Death in Venice and Rigoletto at San Francisco; Other roles include Rosalinde, Mathilde in Guillaume Tell, Helena in A Midsummer Night's Dream and Madame Cortese in Il Viaggio a Reims; Sang Giunone in Cesti's Il Pomo d'Oro at Batignano, 1998. *Honours:* First Prize, Washington International Competition, 1995; Pavarotti Competition in Philadelphia, 1995. *Address:* c/o San Francisco Opera, Van Ness Avenue, San Francisco, CA, USA.

BUCHANAN, Dorothy (Quita); Composer; b. 28 Sept. 1945, Christchurch, New Zealand. *Education:* Graduated, University of Canterbury, 1967. *Career:* Founded music workshops at Christchurch, 1973; Music educationalist from 1977; Composer-in-Residence at New Zealand Film Archives, Wellington, 1984. *Compositions include:* Five Vignettes of Women for flute and female chorus, 1987, and other vocal music; Sinfonietta in 5 Movements, 1989; Due concertante for violin, cello and orchestra, 1991; Music for stage and screen; The Layers of Time for cello, women's voices and orchestra, 1995; Chamber music, including Echoes and Reflections for clarinet, guitar, violin and cello, 1993. *Address:* c/o SOUNZ, PO Box 10 042 Wellington, 39 Cambridge Terrace, Wellington, New Zealand.

BUCHANAN, Isobel (Wilson); Singer (Soprano); b. 15 March 1954, Glasgow, Scotland; m. Jonathan King (otherwise Jonathan Hyde, actor), 1980, 2 d. *Education:* Royal Scottish Academy of Music and Drama. *Career:* Debut: Glyndebourne, 1978 as Pamina; Vienna Staatsoper, 1978, as Micaela; Santa Fe, USA, 1979, as Zerlina and Adina; Chicago, 1979; New York, 1979; Cologne, Germany, 1979; Aix-en-Provence, France, 1981; Australian Opera Principal Singer, 1975–78; Freelance Singer, 1978–; Performances with Scottish Opera, Covent Garden, Munich Radio, Belgium, Norway and others; Other roles include Fiordiligi, Susanna and Donna Elvira; Sang Dorabella at the 1987 Glyndebourne Festival; In recent years has devoted career to concert appearances. *Recordings:* Various operatic and vocal recordings. *Current Management:* Marks Management Ltd, London. *Address:* 14 New Burlington Street, London W1X 1FF, England.

BUCHBINDER, Rudolf; Pianist; b. 11 Feb. 1946, Leitmeritz, Austria. *Education:* Studied piano with Bruno Seidlhofer. *Career:* Extensive repertoire of concert pieces, both classical and modern; Has performed works rarely played including The Diabelli Variations, a collection from 50 Austrian composers; Has performed a cycle of all 32 Beethoven Sonatas; Performances in many major cities in Europe, USA, South America, Australia and Japan; Regular guest at major music festivals; Has played with all important leading conductors. *Recordings:* The Diabelli Variations; Collection of Joseph Haydn piano works; Over 80 recordings. *Honours:* Grand Prix du Disque, for Haydn's piano works. *Current Management:* Astrid Schoerke. *Address:* c/o Monckebergallee 41, 30453 Hannover, Germany.

BUCHLA, Donald Frederick; Composer, Performer and Electronic Instrument Designer; b. 17 April 1937, Southgate, CA, USA. *Education:* BA, Physics, Univ. of California at Berkeley, 1961. *Career:* installed first Buchla synthesizer, San Francisco Tape Music Center, 1966; Founder of Buchla Assocs, Berkeley, 1966; designed and manufactured various electronic instruments; designed electronic music studios including Royal Academy of Music, Stockholm, and IRCAM, Paris; Co-Founder, Electric Weasel Ensemble, 1975; Co-Dir, Artists Research Collective, Berkeley, 1978–. *Compositions:* various pieces with electronic instruments including Cicada Music for some 2,500 Cicadas, 1963; 5 Video Mirrors for Audience of 1 or More, 1966; Anagnorisis for 1 Performer and 1 Voice, 1970; Harmonic Pendulum for Buchla Series 200 Synthesizer, 1972; Garden for 3 Performers and 1 Dancer, 1975; Keyboard Encounter for 2 Pianos, 1976; Q for 14 Instruments, 1979; Silicon Cello for Amplified Cello, 1979; Consensus Conduction for Buchla Series 300 Synthesizer and Audience, 1981. *Honours:* Guggenheim Fellowship, 1978; National Endowment for the Arts Grant, 1981. *Address:* c/o Buchla and Associates, PO Box 10205, Berkeley, CA 94709, USA. *Website:* www.buchla.com.

BUCHNER, Eberhard; Singer (Tenor); b. 6 Nov. 1939, Dresden, Germany. *Education:* Studied at the Carl Maria Von Weber-Musikhochschule, Dresden, 1959–64. *Career:* Debut: Schwerin in 1964 as Tamino; Staatsoper Dresden from 1966, and Staatsoper Berlin from 1968, notably in operas by Strauss, Mozart and Wagner; Sang Schubert's Die schöne m üllerin, in Vienna, 1972; Appeared at the Vatican in 1973 in a concert conducted by Bernstein; Sang at Metropolitan Opera in 1974, Covent Garden in 1975, Hamburg Staatsoper in 1983 in a revival of Armadis de Gaule by JC Bach, Théâtre de la Monnaie in Brussels, and Salzburg Festival in 1985 and 1990 as Flamand in Capriccio, and Royal Opera Copenhagen in 1986 as Wagner's Lohengrin; Sang Adolar in Euryanthe at the Berlin Staatsoper, 1986; La Scala Milan in 1988 as Erik in Der fliegende Holländer and sang Lohengrin at Lisbon in 1990; Sang Dionysus in The Bassarids at Hamburg, 1994 and as Der Alte in the premiere of

Schnittke's Historia von D Johann Fausten, 1995. *Recordings:* Die schweigsame Frau by Strauss; Froh in Das Rheingold; Bach Cantatas; Bach's B minor Mass; Sacred Music by Mozart; Beethoven's 9th Symphony.

BUCHT, Gunnar; Composer; b. 5 Aug. 1927, Stocksund, Sweden; m. Bergljot Krohn, 12 April 1958. *Education:* PhD, Musicology; Studied Composition with Karl Birger-Blomdahl, Carl Orff, Goffredo Petrassi, Max Deutsch; Piano with Yngve Flyckt. *Career:* Debut: Composer and Pianist, 1949; Chairman, Society of Swedish Composers, 1963–69; Teacher, Stockholm University, 1965–69; Vice President, International Society for Contemporary Music, 1969–72; Cultural Attache to the Swedish Embassy at Bonn, 1970–73; Professor of Composition, Royal College of Music, 1975–85, Director, 1987–93; mem, Royal Academy of Music. *Compositions include:* Opera, The Pretenders, after Ibsen, 1966; 12 Symphonies, 1952–97; 2 Cello Concertos, 1955–90; La fine della diaspora for tenor, chorus and orchestra (Quasimodo), 1957; Lutheran Mass, 1973; Journées oubliées, 1975; Au delá, 1977; Violin Concerto, 1978; The Big Bang–And After, 1979; Georgica, 1980; En Clairobscur for chamber orchestra, 1981; Fresques mobiles, 1986; Tönend bewegte Formen for orchestra, 1987; Chamber Music including String Quintet, 1950, 3 String Quartets, 1951, 1959, 1997, Sonata for piano and percussion, 1955, Symphonie pour la musique libérée for tape, 1969, Blad från mitt gulsippeänge for clarinet and piano, 1985; Partita for 2 violins, 2001; Unter Vollem Einsatz for organ and 5 percussionists, 1987; One Day I Went Out Into The World, novel for orchestra, 1983–84; Piano Concerto, 1994; Coup sur Coup for percussion, 1995; Concerto de Marle for viola and orchestra; Movements in Space for orchestra, 1996; Alienus' Dream for orchestra, 1999; Panta Rei for soli, chorus and orchestra, 1998–99; Den starkare (Strindberg), monodram for mezzo-soprano and orchestra, 2001; Superstrings for orchestra, 2002. *Recordings:* Symphony 7, Violin Concerto, Piano Concerto, Georgica, Cantata, Quatre pièces pour le pianiste; Coup sur Coup; Sections of One Day I Went Out Into The World; Odysseia (Kazantzakis), half-scenic oratorio for soli, chorus and orchestra, part one, 2000–2003. *Publications:* Electronic Music in Sweden, 1977; Europe in Music, 1996; Född på Krigsstigen (Born on the War Path), autobiography, 1997; Rum, rörelse, tid (Space, Movement, Time), 1999. *Contributions:* Swedish Journal of Musicology. *Honours:* Litteris et artibus, Royal Medal. *Address:* Burge Hablingbo, 62011 Havdhem, Sweden and Rådmansgatan 74, SE–113 60, Stockholm. *Telephone:* 08–736 60 31.

BUCK, Peter; cellist; b. 18 May 1937, Stuttgart, Germany. *Education:* Stuttgart Conservatory with Ludwig Hoelscher. *Career:* former mem. of Karl Munchinger's Stuttgart Chamber Orchestra in Heilbronn; co-founder of Melos Quartet of Stuttgart, 1965; represented Germany at the Jeunesses Musicales in Paris, 1966; international concert tours from 1967; bicentenary concerts in the Beethoven Haus at Bonn in 1970; toured Russia, Eastern Europe, Africa, North and South America, The Far East and Australia; British concerts and festivals from 1974; cycle of Beethoven quartets at Edinburgh Festival, 1987; played at Wigmore Hall, St John's Smith Square and Bath Festival in 1990; associations with Rostropovich in the Schubert Quintet and the Cleveland Quartet in works by Spohr and Mendelssohn; teacher at the Stuttgart Musikhochschule. *Recordings include:* Complete Quartets of Beethoven, Schubert, Mozart and Brahms; Quintets by Boccherini with Narcisco Ypes, and by Mozart with Franz Beyer. *Honours:* with Melos Quartet, Grand Prix du Disque and Prix Caecilia, from Academie du Disque in Brussels. *Current Management:* Ingpen & Williams Ltd, 7 St George's Court, 131 Putney Bridge Road, London, SW15 2PA, England.

BUCKEL, Ursula; Singer (Soprano) and Teacher; b. 11 Feb. 1926, Lauscha, Germany. *Education:* Studied with Hans Hoefflin in Freiburg and with Ria Ginster in Zürich. *Career:* Sang in Bach's St John Passion at Kreuzlingen, Switzerland; Based in Geneva from 1954; Many performances of cantatas and Passions by Bach, notably at the Bach-Festwochen at Schaffhausen and Ansbach; Tours of Switzerland, England, Finland, Austria, France, Germany and Italy; Far East tour with the Deutsche Bach-Solisten under Helmut Winschermann; Further tours to Athens and to Israel; Performances of music by Frank Martin; Sang Mozart's Donna Anna, 1970; Teacher of Voice at the Geneva Conservatory from 1971. *Recordings:* Mendelssohn's Elijah; Bach Cantatas; Christmas Oratorio by Schütz; L'Incoronazione di Poppea by Monteverdi.

BUCKLEY, Richard E(dward); Conductor; b. 1 Sept. 1953, New York City, USA. *Education:* BM, North Carolina School of the Arts, Winston-Salem, 1973; MMus, Catholic University of America, Washington DC, 1974; Aspen School of Music, Colorado, 1974; Salzburg Mozarteum, 1977. *Career:* Assistant Conductor and Chorusmaster, Washington Opera Society, 1973–74; Assistant to Music Director Seattle Opera, 1973–74; Assistant Associate, Resident, and Principal Guest Conductor at Seattle Symphony Orchestra, 1974–85; Music Director, Oakland Symphony Orchestra, California, 1983–86; Guest Conductor, New York Philharmonic Orchestra, Philadelphia Orchestra, Houston Symphony

Orchestra, San Antonio Symphony Orchestra, Oregon Symphony Orchestra, Los Angeles Philharmonic Orchestra, Minnesota Orchestra, Indianapolis Symphony Orchestra, BBC Symphony Orchestra, Royal Philharmonic Orchestra, Royal Liverpool Philharmonic Orchestra, Chicago Lyric Opera, Los Angeles Opera, New York City Opera, Houston Grand Opera, Canadian Opera, Netherlands Opera, and Hamburg State Opera, Covent Garden, Paris Opéra Bastille, Berlin Deutsche Oper, Royal Opera, Copenhagen, Teatro Bellini, Teatro San Carlos, Lisbon; Recent operatic premieres include Paulus' The Postman Always Rings Twice with Miami Opera and The Woodlanders at St Louis; US premiere of Sallinen's The King Goes Forth to France, for Sante Fe Opera; Other projects include Les Contes d'Hoffmann with Los Angeles Music Center Opera, Aida at Chicago and Rossini's Il Viaggio a Reims at St Louis; Conducted Il Barbiere di Siviglia for Miami Opera in 1990, and Dvořák's The Devil and Kate at St Louis; Season 1996 with Butterfly at Los Angeles and Aida at Philadelphia. *Honours:* Prizewinner, Besançon Competition in 1979; Rupert Foundation Competition in 1982. *Current Management:* Herbert Barrett Management Inc, 1776 Broadway, New York, NY 10019, USA. *Address:* 500 N Guadalupe Street, Ste G-896, Santa Fe, NM 87501, USA.

BUCQUET, Marie-Francoise; Pianist; b. 28 Oct. 1937, Montvilliers, France. *Education:* Studied at the Vienna Music Academy, The Paris Conservatoire and with Wilhelm Kempff, Alfred Brendel and Leon Fleisher. *Career:* Debut: Marguerite Long School in 1948; Attended course by Eduard Steuermann at Salzburg to study music of Schoenberg and followed courses by Pierre Boulez at Basle; Sylvano Bussotti, Betsy Jolas and Iannis Xenakis have written for her; Performs works by Bach, Haydn, Stockhausen, Schoenberg and standard repertory music; Professor of Accompaniment and Piano Pedagogy at the Paris Conservatoire from 1986. *Address:* c/o Conservatoire de Paris, 209 Avenue Jean Jaurès, Paris 75019, France.

BUCZYNSKI, Walter; Composer and Pianist; b. 17 Dec. 1933, Toronto, Canada. *Education:* Studied Composition with Milhaud, 1956 and Nadia Boulanger, 1960–62 at Toronto Conservatory. *Career:* Teacher of Piano and Theory at Royal Conservatory of Toronto, 1962, and Theory at University of Toronto from 1970. *Compositions include:* Piano Trio, 1954; Suite for Wind Quintet, 1955; Divertimento for Violin, Cello, Clarinet and Bassoon, 1957; Children's operas Mr Rhinoceros And His Musicians, 1957 and, Do Re Mi, 1967; Squares In A Circle for Flute, Violin, Cello and Strings, 1967; Four Movements for Piano and Strings, 1969; Zeroing In, 5 pieces for various vocal and instrumental groups, 1971–72; Three Against Many for Flute, Clarinet, Bassoon and Orchestra, 1973; Concerto for Violin, Cello and Orchestra, 1975; Olympics '75 for Brass Quintet; From The Buczynski Book Of The Dead, chamber opera, 1975; Naked At The Opera, 1979; Piano Concerto, 1979; Piano Quintet, 1984; The August Collection, 27 preludes, 1987; Litanies for Accordion and Percussion, 1988; Songs and piano music. *Address:* SOCAN, 41 Valleybrook Drive, Don Mills, Ontario M3B 2S6, Canada.

BUDAI, Livia; Singer (mezzo-soprano); b. 23 June 1950, Esztergom, Hungary. *Education:* Franz Liszt Academy Budapest with Olga Revheggi. *Career:* Debut: Sofia in 1973 as Carmen; Member of Hungarian State Opera, 1973–77; Concert appearances with the Hungarian Philharmonic and on Budapest Radio; Guest engagements in Austria, Bulgaria, Finland, France, Germany and Russia; Member of Gelsenkirchen Opera, 1977; Covent Garden debut in 1978 as Azucena, returning as Eboli in Don Carlos in 1983; US debut in San Francisco in 1979 as Eboli; Munich Staatsoper from 1980; Bologna in 1983 as Brangaene in Tristan und Isolde; Appearances in Berlin, Brussels, Vienna, Barcelona, Florence and Madrid as Elisabetta in Maria Stuarda, Marguerite in The Damnation of Faust, Wagner's Venus and Fricka, and Verdi's Amneris, Preziosilla and Azucena; Other roles include Gluck's Orfeo, Saint-Saëns's Dalila, Bartók's Judith and the Composer in Ariadne auf Naxos; Aix-en-Provence in 1987 as Mistress Quickly, Marseille in 1989 as Cassandre in Les Troyens; Sang Amneris at Bonn in 1990, Ortrud at Brussels, and the Princess in Adriana Lecouvreur for L'Opéra de Montréal; Appeared as Marfa in Dvořák's Dimitrij at Munich in 1992; Kundry in Parsifal with RAI at Turin in 1992; Sang Clytemnestra in Elektra at Frankfurt, 1994; Season 2000–01 as Jocasta in Oedipus Rex at Antwerp, Azucena for Budapest Opera and Kabanicha in Katya Kabanova at Lucerne. *Recordings:* Stabat Mater and Lange Mala Umbrae Terrores by Charpentier; Laura in La Gioconda. *Current Management:* Ingpen & Williams Ltd, 7 St George's Court, 131 Putney Bridge Road, London, SW15 2PA, England.

BUDD, Harold; Composer; b. 24 May 1936, Los Angeles, CA, USA; m. Paula Katzman, 26 June 1960, 2 s. *Education:* Los Angeles City College, 1957–59; BA, San Fernando State College, 1963; MM, University of Southern California, 1966. *Career:* Composition Faculty, California Institute of the Arts, 1971–76. *Compositions:* The Pavilion Of Dreams, 1978; The Plateaux Of Mirror, with Brian Eno, 1980; The Serpent (In Quicksilver), 1981; The Pearl, with Brian Eno, 1984; Abandoned Cities,

1984; The Moon And The Melodies, with The Cocteau Twins, 1986; Lovely Thunder, 1986; The White Arcades; Walk into my Voice, 1996. *Honours:* National Endowment for The Arts, Composer Fellowship, 1974, 1979. *Current Management:* Opal Ltd. *Address:* c/o Opal Ltd, 330 Harrow Road, London W9 2HP, England.

BUDDEN, Julian Medforth, OBE, BA, BMus, MA, FBA; musicologist and writer; b. 9 April 1924, Hoylake, Cheshire, England. *Education:* Queen's Coll., Oxford, Royal Coll. of Music, London. *Career:* music library clerk, BBC radio 1951, Music Presentation Asst 1955, Prod. for Music Programmes 1955–70, Chief Prod. for Opera 1970–76, Music Organizer for External Services 1976–83; editorial cttee mem. Critical Edition of the Works of G. Verdi; Pres., Centro Studi Giacomo Puccini, Lucca. *Publications:* The Operas of Verdi (three vols) 1973, 1978, 1981, Verdi 1985, Puccini 2002; contrib. to professional journals, including Music and Letters, Musical Times, The Listener. *Honours:* Yorkshire Post Award for Best Book on Music 1979, Derek Allen Prize, British Acad. 1980, Premio Diego Fabbri 1989. *Address:* 94 Station Road, Finchley, London, N3 2SG, England; via Fratelli Bandiera 9, 50137 Florence, Italy.

BUDIN, Jan; Clarinettist; b. 20 May 1950, Prague, Czechoslovakia; m. Vlasta Budínová, 5 July 1973, 1 s., 1 d. *Education:* Academy of Arts, Prague. *Career:* Concert performances in European countries; Television performances in the Czech Republic, Poland, Germany, Sweden, Denmark. *Compositions:* Some compositions for various chamber ensembles. *Recordings:* František Vincenc Kramár–Quartet B flat major, Op 21, No. 1; Quartet E flat major, Op 21, No. 2; Quintet B flat major, Op 95–Jan Budín with Panocha Quartet; Johannes Brahms–Quintet B minor, Op 115–Jan Budín with Panocha Quartet; František Vincenc Kramar–Symphonia Concertante E flat major, Op 70; Julius Fucik: Chamber music for two clarinets and bassoon; More recordings (especially early Czech music for Czech radio). *Contributions:* Editor-in-Chief of Musical Journal for Blind. *Honours:* First Prize in the International Competition of Blind Musicians, Prague, 1975. *Address:* 11 Dusní Street, 110 00 Prague 1, Czech Republic.

BUFFLE, Christine; Singer (Soprano); b. 1971, Switzerland. *Education:* Studied at Geneva Conservatoire; Guildhall School of Music and Drama, London; Opera Studio, Zürich. *Career:* Sang Ninetta in La Finta semplice and Doralice in Scarlatti's Trionfo dell' Onore, Geneva; Musetta, Naiad (Ariadne) Berlin Komische Opera; Coryphée, Gluck's Armide, Versailles; Queen of Night, Scottish Opera; Zürich Opera as Sicle in Cavalli's L'Ormindo, Papagena, High Priestess, Barbarina, Suor Angelica, Echo, Queen of Night and Donna Anna in Gazzaniga's Don Giovanni; Season 1999–2000 with Musetta and Naiad for the Komische Oper, Anna in Kurt Weill's Seven Deadly Sins in Geneva; Concerts include Handel's Samson and Haydn's The Seasons; Mozart's C Minor Mass and Requiem; Vivaldi's Gloria; Bach's Magnificat and St John Passion; Honegger's King David, Geneva, 2000. *Recordings:* Stravinsky's Les Noces and songs. *Address:* c/o Music International, 13 Ardilaun Road, London N5 2QR, England.

BUFKENS, Roland; Belgian singer (tenor) and academic; b. 26 April 1936, Ronse; m. Simone Deboelpaepe 1961; one d. *Education:* Brussels Conservatoire. *Career:* debut in Germany; German concerts specialising in Bach tradition and also the St John and St Matthew Passion; Performances with several German orchestras conducted by Kurt Thomas, Karl Richter, Kurt Redel and Nikolaus Harnoncourt; Berlioz's Romeo and Juliet in a tour of Japan and later in Paris' Théâtre des Champs Elysées, both conducted by Lorin Maazel; Other performances include: Stravinsky's Mavra, in the Concertgebouw of Amsterdam; Martin's Mystère de la Nativité, Madrid Teatro Real; All these performances were broadcast; Manuel de Falla's Vida Breve conducted by R. F. de Burgos in Palais des Beaux-Arts Bruxelles; Participated several times in the Holland Festival, Biennale of Zagreb, Festival of Lourdes, Schwetzinger Festspiele, Festival van Vlaanderen; Professor at Brussels Conservatoire and Lemmens Institute, Leuven. *Recordings:* Works by Schubert, Grétry, Gossec, Lully, Schütz, Bach, Dumont and Carl Orff; Compositions by Belgian composers André Laporte and Willem Kersters. *Publications:* contrib. to Lemmensinstitute Adem, articles for Dutch Singers Association ANZ. *Honours:* 1st Prize at Brussels Conservatoire, 1959; Chevalier de l'Ordre de la Couronne, 1978; Cecilia Prize, Belgium, 1974 for Zemire et Azor, F. M. Grétry. *Address:* 25 Avenue Georges Leclercq, 1083 Brussels, Belgium.

BUGHICI, Dumitru; Composer and Teacher; b. 14 Nov. 1921, Iasi, Romania. *Education:* Studied with Salmanov, Iasi Conservatory and with Schnittke, Leningrad Conservatory, 1950–55. *Career:* Faculty, Bucharest Conservatory; Israel resident from 1985. *Compositions include:* Orchestral: Simfonie-Poem, 1961, No. 3, Ecouri De Jazz, 1965–66, Simfonia Bucegilor, 1978–79, Simfonie Lirico-Dramatica-In Memoriam for String Orchestra, 1984, Simfonia Aspiratillor, 1985; Sinfoniettas: Simfonia Tinertii, 1958, Muzica De Concert, Simfonieta III, 1969; Filimon Sarbu, 1959, Poemul Bucuriei, 1962, Monumentul,

1964, Omagiu, 1967, Balada Concertana for Violin and Orchestra, 1969, Sinfonietta Da Camera, 1970, Cello Concerto, 1974, Trumpet Concerto, 1975, Jazz Concerto, 1982–83; Flute Concerto, 1985; Chamber: Suite for Violin and Piano, 1953, Scherzo for Cello and Piano, 1954, Fantasia for Trumpet and Piano, 1960, Violin Sonata, 1963, Fantasia Quartet, 1969, Six String Quartets, 1954–83, Fantasy for Xylophone and Double Bass, 1980; Flute Concerto, 1985; Bass Clarinet Concerto, 1986; Symphony of Gratitude, 1990; Piano Pieces. *Address:* Conservatorui de Muzica Ciprian Porumbescu, Str Stirbei Voda 33, 70732 Bucharest, Romania.

BUJARSKI, Zbigniew; Composer; b. 21 Aug. 1933, Muszyna, Poland. *Education:* Studied composition with Wiechowicz and conducting with Wodiczko at the Kracow State College of Music. *Compositions include:* Burning Bushes for Soprano and Chamber Ensemble, 1958; Triptych for String Orchestra and Percussion, 1959; Synchrony I for Soprano and Chamber Ensemble, 1959, II for Soprano, Chorus and Orchestra, 1960; Zones for Chamber Ensemble, 1961; Kinoth for Orchestra, 1963; Chamber Composition for Voice and Ensemble, 1963; Contraria for Orchestra, 1965; El Hombre for Vocal Soloists, Chorus and Orchestra, 1969–73; Musica Domestica for 18 Strings, 1977; Concert for Strings, 1979; Similis Greco, symphonic cycle, 1979–83; Quartet On The Advent, 1984; Quartet For The Resurrection, 1990; Pavane for the Distant One for strings, 1994; Lumen for orchestra, 1997; Five Songs for soprano and strings, 1997. *Address:* c/o Society of Authors ZAiKS, 2 Hipoteczna Street, 00 092 Warsaw, Poland. *Telephone:* (4822) 828 17 05. *Fax:* (4822) 828 13 47. *E-mail:* sekretariat@zaiks.org.pl. *Website:* www.zaiks.org.pl.

BUJEVSKY, Taras; Composer; b. 23 June 1957, Kharkiv, Ukraine; m. Jekaterina Tarakanova, 8 June 1991.one s. one d. *Education:* Composer, 1989; Postgraduate Course, Moscow State Conservatoire, 1991. *Career:* Musical Editor, Russian television, 1993–98; Lecturer, Russian Theatre Academy, 1995–97; His music is frequently heard on Russian radio and television, including 7 large broadcasts devoted to his life and music, 1991–99 mem. Moscow Composers Union, Russian Union of Cinematography. *Compositions:* Symphony, 1989; Repercussions of the Light for string orchestra, 1992; Foreshortenings, chamber symphony for percussion, trumpet, two pianos and mechanical devices, 1993; Post Scriptum for symphony orchestra, 1994; Breathing of Stillness for chamber orchestra, 1995; Eisenstein-Line, Suite for symphony orchestra, 1997; Music for Chamber Ensembles and Solo Instruments includes: Sensus Sonoris for flute and percussion, 1990; Silver Voices for four trumpets, 1991; Pathes of Phonosphere for clarinet; Voice of Loneliness for tenor saxophone, 1993; Mosaics, Suite for grand piano, 1994; Ciao Antonio for flute, oboe, violin, cello, harpsichord and tape; Für Isabella for sextet, 1995; Quartet for oboe, clarinet, bassoon and piano, 1996; Agnus Dei for mixed choir a capella, 1998; Electronic music, music for 30 films and television performances: Participant in international festivals: Moscow Autumn 1990–2003; 5 Capitals, Kiev, 1993; Festival of Contemporary Russian Music in Helsingborg, Sweden, 1994; Festival of Electronic Music, Synthesis-95, Bourges, France;Omen for symphony orchestra, 2000; Aria.ru-monoopera for actress, piano and tape, 2000; Music of Sovok for prepared dustpan and tape, 2000; Largo ricitare for violin and tape, 2001; Dolente cantabile for oboe d'amore, 2002; Das Kolophonium for 12 cellos, 2002; Choirs on poems by K. Vojtyla, 2003; Music for computer's games. *Publications:* Music for S Eisenstein's film The General Line, score for symphony orchestra, 1997; Repercations of the Light, score for string orchestra, 2003; Mosaics, Suite for grand piano, 2004; Collected verses, 2003; Essay About Death but more about Life, 2003. *Honours:* Russian TV TEFI, 1999. *Address:* Novoslobodskaja Str 67/69, Apt 113, Moscow 127055, Russia. *E-mail:* buyevsky@mtu-net.ru.

BUKOWSKI, Miroslaw Andrzej; Composer and Conductor; b. 5 Jan. 1936, Warsaw, Poland; m. Hanna Burzynska, 20 Aug 1966, 1 d. *Education:* MA, Composition, Academy of Music, Poznan, 1959; MA, Conducting, Academy of Music at Gdansk and Poznan, 1963. *Career:* Debut: Polish Students' Music Festival in Poznan, 1957; Assistant, 1963–67, Lecturer, 1967–80, Assistant Professor, 1980–88, Professor, 1988–, Academy of Music, Poznan; Conductor, Wielkopolska Symphony Orchestra, 1971–75; Professor, Pedagogical College in Zielena Gora, 1984–; mem, Association of Polish Composers, Society of Authors ZAiKS. *Compositions include:* Requiem for Solo Voices, Mixed Choir and Orchestra, based on Akhmatova's poem; Pastourelle, Interferences for Symphony Orchestra; Concerto for Cello and Orchestra; Ostinato and Mobile for Percussion Ensemble; Swinging Concerto; Symphonic Allegro for Symphony Orchestra; 4 Piano Sonatas; Sonatina for Piano; Expression for Piano; Three Sleepy Poems for Mixed Choir; 2 Cycles of Songs, Znikomosc, Stances. *Address:* Osiedle Pod Lipami 5-182, 61-632 Poznań, Poland.

BULCHEVA, Zlata; Singer (Mezzo-Soprano); b. 1970, St Petersburg, Russia. *Education:* Graduated St Petersburg Conservatoire 1995. *Career:* Appearances with the Kirov Opera from 1996, notably as Olga in Eugene Onegin, Konchakovna (Prince Igor), Carmen, Cherubino, and Erda in Das Rheingold; Further engagements as Ratmir (Ruslan and Lyudmilla), Nezhata (Sadko), Frasya in Prokofiev's Semyon Kotko and Fyodor in Boris Godunov; Concerts include Mahler 2nd and 3rd Symphonies; Sang with the Kirov Opera at Covent Garden, 2000. *Recordings include:* Boris Godunov. *Honours:* Prizewinner, Young Opera Singer's International Vocal, St Petersburg, 1996, International Rimsky-Korsakov Competition, 1998, and International Tchaikovsky, Moscow, 1999. *Address:* c/o Kirov Opera, Mariinsky Theatre, Mariinsky Square, St Petersburg, Russia.

BULJUBASIC, Mileva; Singer (Soprano); b. 17 Aug. 1937, Sarajevo, Yugoslavia. *Education:* Studied in Sarajevo, Italy and Austria. *Career:* Featured as Concert Artist since 1960; Stage career from 1970, with guest appearances in Italy, Germany, England, Russia, Japan and Czechoslovakia; Member of the Deutsche Oper am Rhein, Düsseldorf, from 1979; Sang at Seattle in 1975; Roles have included Butterfly, Mimi, Marenka in The Bartered Bride, Rusalka, Beethoven's Leonore and Verdi's Amelia in Ballo in Maschera and Leonora in Il Trovatore; Season 1992 as Butterfly at Hannover and Tosca at Düsseldorf. *Honours:* Prize for Interpretation; Modern Yugoslavian Musik Prize; Prix des Concours, Madama Butterfly, Japan, 1973. *Address:* Sertoriusring 7, 55126 Mainz, Germany.

BULJUBASIC, Sead; Singer (tenor) and Professor of Opera Singing; b. 10 Oct. 1942, Cazin, Bosnia; m. Mileva Buljubasic, 17 Feb. 1973. *Education:* BA, Italian Language and Literature; Musical Faculty of Art and Magisterium-Belgrade Conservatorio Giuseppe Verdi Milano; Mozarteum Salzburg. *Career:* Debut: National Theatre Opera Stage Belgrade, Eugene Onegin, Lenski; Opera Houses: Yugoslavia, Romania, Austria, Germany, USA; RTV Belgrade, RTV Sarajevo, until 1988, Duke of Mantua, Manrico, Alfred Germont, Rodolfo, Cavaradossi, Pinkerton, Calaf, Count Almaviva, Radames, Werther, Don José, Jenik, Prince (Rusalka), Lenski, Turiddu, Bluebeard, Faust, Edgardo. Recordings. Television and radio, Sarajevo, Belgrade, opera arias and songs; Concert Repertoire Songs: Schumann, Schubert, Strauss, Debussy, De Falla, Turina, Tchaikovsky, Rachmaninov. *Address:* Sertorius Ring 7, 55126 Mainz, Germany.

BULL, Edvard (Hagerup); Composer; b. 10 June 1922, Bergen, Norway; m. Anna Kvarme, 1955, 2 d. *Education:* Examination, Oslo University, 1944; Organ Diploma, Oslo Conservatory, 1947; Studied organ, composition and piano with Sandvold, Irgens Jensen, Brustad, Riefling and Wester; Pupil of Charles Koechlin, 1947–49; Composition with Darius Milhaud and Jean Rivier; Analysis with Olivier Messiaen; Diploma and Prize for Musical Composition, Conservatoire National Superieur de Musique, Paris, France, 1948–53; Pupil of Boris Blacher and Josef Rufer at Hochschule für Musik, Berlin, 1958–60. *Career:* Debut: Philharmonic Orchestra, Paris; Formerly Teacher of Theory, Oslo Klaverakademi and Oslo Musikkonservatorium; Performances in over 30 countries; Many commissions from French radio and television, Ministry of Culture, Quatuor Instrumental de Paris, Ensemble Moderne de Paris, Trio Daraux de Paris, Trio de France, Quatuor des Clarinettes de Belgique, Norske Blåse-Kvintett. *Compositions include:* 5 Symphonies, 1955–72; 6 Concertos; Le Soldat De Plomb, ballet, 1949; Portrait Münchhausen, ballet, 1961; Le Jeu Du Feu, one-act opera, 1974; Lamentation Pour Un Cygne Maudit, Hommage A Israel, opera, 1972–77; Chamber, instrumental and vocal works. *Recordings include:* Sonata Cantabile Op 35, 1988; 1Re Concerto pour Trompette et Orchestre Op 9, 1992; Trois Mouvements Symphoniques Op 16, 1992; Trois Bucoliques Op 14, 1992; Ad Ususm Amicorum Op 20, 1997; 6 Epigrammes Op 36, 1997; Rhapsody in Rag for trumpet and orchestra, 1998. *Address:* c/o TONO, 4 Galleri Oslo, Toyenbekken 21, Postboks 9171, Gronland, O134 Oslo 1, Norway.

BULLOCK, Susan, BMus, FRAM; British singer (soprano); b. 9 Dec. 1958, Cheshire. *Education:* Royal Holloway Coll., Univ. of London, Royal Acad. of Music and Nat. Opera Studio, London. *Career:* roles with ENO have included Donna Anna, Marguerite (Faust), Alice Ford, Butterfly, Ellen Orford, Princess Natalie (Henze's Prince of Homburg) 1996, Desdemona and Isolde; Glyndebourne debut as Jenůfa 1996, followed by Katya Kabanova and Lisa (Queen of Spades); guest appearances with New Israeli Opera and Flanders Opera (in Tippett's King Priam); American debut as Butterfly at Portland and title role in British premiere of Die Aegyptische Helena by Strauss at Garsington 1996; other important roles include Wagner's Isolde for Opera North, Oper Frankfurt, Rouen, Dusseldorf and Verona, Bninnhilde (Die Walküre) and Siegfried in Tokyo, and Gotterdammerung in Tokyo and at Perth Festival, Els (Schreker's Der Schatzgraber) Oper, Frankfurt, R. Strauss's Elektra in Brussels, Frankfurt, Dresden, Lady Macbeth (Bloch's Macbeth) in Vienna, Magda Sorel (Menotti's The Consul), Spoleto Festival, Italy and Teatro Colon, Buenos Aires, Argentina, Female Chorus (Britten's Lucretia), Mtinchen, Seville, Trittico in Charleston, and Tosca at Royal Albert Hall and debut Wigmore Hall recital; concerts include Berlioz's La Mort de Cleopatre with BBC Philharmonic Orchestra, Mahler's 4th Symphony with Royal Liverpool Philharmonic, Beethoven's Missa Solemnis with Les Arts Florissants,

Salome with Hong Kong Philharmonic Orchestra, and Messiaen's Poèmes pour Mi at the Proms 2004. *Recordings include:* Hindemith's Sancta Susanna, Menotti's The Consul and Britten's Albert Herring. *Honours:* Hon. Fellow, Royal Holloway Coll. 2004. *Current Management:* HarrisonParrott, 12 Penzance Place, London, W11 4PA, England. *Telephone:* (20) 7229-9166. *Fax:* (20) 7221-5042. *Website:* www .harrisonparrott.com.

BULYCHEV-OKSER, Michael; Pianist and Composer; b. 17 Feb. 1981, Moscow, Russia. *Education:* Moscow Central Music School for Gifted Children, Moscow State Conservatoire, 1988–96; Piano and Composition, Moscow State Conservatoire, 1990–96; Piano and Composition, Manhattan School of Music, 1996–98, Piano, College Division, 1998–. *Career:* Debut: Piano and Composition debut, Rachmaninov Recital Hall, Moscow Conservatoire, 1993; Tour, with group of Russian musicians, to Greece, Egypt, Israel and Turkey, 1993; Moved to USA, 1996; Performed in 33 different piano recitals; Scholarship, Summer Composition Program, La Schola Cantorum, Paris, France, 1998; Debut on New York radio on Robert Sherman's Young Artists Showcase series Soloist, Manhattan Philharmonic Orchestra, 1998; Spring Music Program concert, Oyster Bay, Long Island, New York, 1999; Solo Piano Recital, Italian Culture Centre of Long Island, 1999; Young Musicians Concert at Weill Recital Hall at Carnegie Hall, New York, 1999. *Compositions:* Sea Landscape; Near Ancient Jerusalem Walls; Kizi–the dying sacred place; Clouds are over Trinity-St Sergey Monastery; The Areadna's Thread, theme and variations; Lullaby for Violin and Piano; Prelude in C Major for Violin and Piano; Sonate in D Major for Cello and Piano; Old Moscow Houses, to words by Marina Zvetaeva. *Recordings:* Solo Piano Recital, 1996; Solo Original Composition Concert, 1997; Robert Sherman's Young Artist Showcase performance, 1998; Young Musicians Concert, 1999. *Address:* 499 East 8 Street, Apt 2C, Brooklyn, NY 11218, USA.

BULYCHEVA, Zlata; Singer (Mezzo-soprano); b. 1970, Russia. *Education:* Graduated St Petersburg Conservatory, 1995. *Career:* Appearances with the Kirov Opera from 1996, as Carmen, Olga, Fyodor in Boris Godunov, Cherubino, Konchakovna in Prince Igor and Ratmir in Ruslan and Lyudmilla; Froysa in Prokofiev's Semyon Kotko, Nezhata in Rimsky's Sadko, Polina (The Queen of Spades) and Erda in Das Rheingold; Mezzo roles in operas by Verdi, and Maria Bolkonskaya in War and Peace; Sang with the Kirov on tour to Covent Garden, London, 2001. Concerts include: Mahler's 2nd and 3rd Symphonies. *Recordings include:* Boris Godunov. *Honours:* Prizewinner, International Rimsky-Korsakov Vocal competition, St Petersburg, 1993 and International Tchaikovsky, Moscow, 1994. *Address:* c/o Kirov Opera, Mariinsky Theatre, 1 Theatre Square, St Petersburg, Russia.

BUMBRY, Grace; American singer (soprano, mezzo-soprano); b. 4 Jan. 1937, St Louis, MO. *Education:* Boston University, Northwestern University, Music Academy of the West with Lotte Lehmann, Paris with Pierre Bernac. *Career:* debut, Paris Opéra in 1960 as Amneris in Aida; Sang at the Stadttheater Basle until 1964; Bayreuth Festival, 1961–63 as Venus in Tannhäuser; Brussels Opera in 1961 as Carmen; Chicago Lyric Opera in 1963 as Ulrica in Un Ballo in Maschera; Covent Garden from 1963 as Eboli, Amneris, Salome and Tosca; Salzburg Festival, 1964–67 as Lady Macbeth and Carmen; Metropolitan Opera debut in 1965 as Eboli, later singing in New York as Carmen, Tosca, Venus, Gioconda and Gershwin's Bess in 1985; Has sung soprano roles from 1970 as Elisabeth de Valois, Santuzza in Vienna, 1970, Jenůfa at La Scala, 1974 and Ariane in Ariane et Barbe-Bleue by Dukas at Paris Opéra in 1975; Mezzo roles include Fricka, Azucena, Orpheus and Dalila; Appearances in Frankfurt, Budapest, Lisbon, Munich, Hamburg and Verona; Sang Aida at Luxor and Massenet's Herodiade at Nice in 1987; Marseilles in 1989 as Didon in Les Troyens; Sang Cassandre at the opening of the Opéra Bastille in Paris, 1990; Arena di Verona in 1990 as Carmen; Sang Cherubini's Medea at Athens, 1995; Concert performance as Massenet's Hérodiade, New York, 1995; Song recital at the Wigmore Hall, London, 2001; Engaged as Hérodiade (Massenet) at the Vienna Staatsoper, 2003. *Recordings include:* Israel in Egypt; Messiah; Don Carlos; Tannhäuser; Aida; Film of Carmen in 1968. *Honours:* Richard Wagner Medal, 1963; Honorary Doctorates from Rust College, Holy Spring, MS, Rockhurst College, Kansas City, University of Missouri at St Louis. *Address:* c/o J. F. Mastroianni Associates, Inc., 161 West 61st Street, Suite 17E, New York, NY 10023, USA.

BUNDSCHUH, Dieter; Singer (Tenor); b. 10 May 1940, Würzburg, Germany. *Career:* Sang in opera in Germany from 1965, Staadttheater Würzburg; Vienna Staatsoper, 1984–87 as Strauss's Matteo and Flamand; Belmonte in Die Entführung and Alfred in Die Fledermaus, Wiesbaden, 1981 in the premiere of Das Kalte Herz, by Kirchner; Guest appearances throughout Germany including Arnold in Guillaume Tell at Mannheim, 1987; Premiere of Hans Zender's Don Quichotte at Stuttgart, 1993; Sang Dr Caius in Falstaff at Bonn, 1998; Other roles include Zemlinsky's Zwerg, Vere in Billy Budd and the Captain in Wozzeck; Many concert and broadcast engagements. *Address:* c/o Bonn Opera, Am Boeselagerhof 1, Pf 2440, 5311 Bonn, Germany.

BUNDSCHUH, Eva-Maria; Singer (Soprano); b. 16 Oct. 1941, Brunswick, Germany. *Education:* Studied in Chemnitz and Leipzig. *Career:* Debut: Bernburg 1967, as Humperdinck's Hansel; Sang at Chemnitz, 1969–74, Potsdam, 1974–77; Associated with the Staatsoper Berlin from 1976, the Komische Oper from 1981; Sang first as mezzo, as Dorabella, Carmen and Eboli then soprano repertory from 1978; Olympia and Antonia in Les Contes d'Hoffmann, Wagner's Eva and Freia, Violetta, Musetta and Donna Anna; Recent Berlin Staatsoper roles have included the title part in the premiere of Judith by Siegfried Matthus, 1985, Jenůfa, 1986, and Isolde, 1988; Komische Oper, 1987–88, as Donna Anna and Salome; Bayreuth Festival, 1988, as Gutrune; Further engagements at Amsterdam (Shostakovich's Lady Macbeth, 1994), Salzburg, Wiesbaden, Bucharest and Moscow; Sang Chrysothemis in a new production of Elektra for Welsh National Opera, 1992; Elektra in a new production at Netherlands Opera, 1996; Gutrune in Götterdämmerung for Netherlands Opera, 1998. *Address:* c/o Welsh National Opera (Contracts), John Street, Cardiff, Wales CF1 4SP.

BUNNING, Christine; Singer (Soprano); b. 1960, Luton, England. *Education:* Guildhall School and with Irmgard Seefried, Vienna. *Career:* Appearances as Verdi's Lady Macbeth, Covent Garden and Edinburgh; Glyndebourne Festival in The Electrification of the Soviet Union (Nigel Osbourne), Katya Kabanova, and Berlioz's Hero for Opera North; Violetta, Mimi, Marenka in The Bartered Bride and Tosca for Welsh National Opera; Chelsea Opera Group in The Olympians by Bliss, as Chabrier's Gwendoline and as Elena in Mefistofele; Other roles include Suor Angelica; Donna Elvira for Opera Factory; Verdi's Abigaille; Medora, Il Corsaro; Amelia, Ballo in Maschera; Rosalinde, Die Fledermaus; English National Opera as Miss Jessel, Turn of the Screw and in Don Carlos, Street Scene and Trittico; Lady Macbeth for Opera Zuid, 1999; Florinda in Schubert's Fierrabras at the Buxton Festival, 2000. *Address:* Music International, 13 Ardilaun Road, London N5 2QR, England.

BUNTEN, Wolfgang; Singer (Tenor); b. 1968, Munich, Germany. *Education:* Studied in Munich at the Opera Studio in Bavarian State Opera. *Career:* Appearances with the Tolzer Knabenchor as a child; Sang widely in concerts and oratorios with appearances in France, Spain and Germany; Stage debut as Arturo in Lucia di Lammermoor at Munich; Innsbruck, 1992–94 as Fenton in Falstaff, Tom Rakewell, Nemorino and Rodolfo; Mozart's Tamino at Vienna, 1994; Stuttgart, Zürich, 1995 and Brussels, 1996; Season 1995–96, as Rodolfo at Basle; In Stravinsky's Rossignol at the Festival Hall, London; Percy in Anna Bolena at Bologna; US debut as Steva in Jenůfa, Cincinnati, 1998; Season 1999–2000 at Cologne, as Alfredo, Rinuccio in Gianni Schicchi and Froh in Das Rheingold. *Address:* c/o Opernhaus Zürich, Falkenstrasse 1, 8008 Zürich, Switzerland.

BURA, Corina, DMusicol; Romanian violinist and professor of music; *Professor, National University of Music*; b. 15 Feb. 1948, Cluj. *Education:* Lyceum Emil Racovitza, Cluj, Music Lyceum, Cluj, Conservatory of Music, Bucharest. *Career:* debut, soloist with The Philharmonia, Cluj 1967; recitals and concerts with orchestras in Romania; recitals in Germany; TV appearances; radio recordings of Bach, Handel, Telemann, Corelli, Pergolesi, Rameau, Tchaikovsky, Paganini, Szymanowski, Bartók and Romanian music; Prof., Nat. Univ. of Music, Bucharest; mem. Professorial Asscn of the Conservatory of Bucharest, Mihail Yora Foundation, Deutsche Gesellschaft für Musikphysiologie und Musikermedizin. *Recordings:* two albums of Handel music. *Publications:* The 20th Century Violin Concerto 2002; studies about modern music and aesthetics published in the Conservatory's publications; perm. column in Morning Star Literature Review 2001–. *Honours:* Diploma of Chief Promotion, The Music Lyceum 1965, 1966, 1967, Diploma of Chief Promotion, The Conservatory of Bucharest 1972. *Address:* Str. Ecaterina Teodoroiu No. 17, 010971 Bucharest, Romania. *Telephone:* (21) 6502721.

BURCHINAL, Frederick; singer (baritone); b. 7 Dec. 1948, Wichita, KS, USA. *Education:* Emporia State University, Juilliard School. *Career:* worked with the Metropolitan Opera Studio and made European debut in Floyd's of Mice and Men, at Amsterdam, 1976; Sang Scrooge in the 1979 premiere of Musgrave's A Christmas Carol, Virginia Opera; New York City Opera, State Theater, 1978–88; Metropolitan Opera from 1988 as Macbeth and Rigoletto; Other US appearances for the San Francisco Opera, Miami, Houston, New Orleans and San Diego Opera; Deutsche Oper am Rhein, Düsseldorf, from 1988; Title role in Simon Boccanegra with the Cologne Opera in 1990; Has also sung in London, Zürich, Berlin and Frankfurt; Other roles include Rossini's Figaro, Iago, Jack Rance, Tonio, Di Luna, Scarpia, Falstaff and Nick Shadow; Sang Posa in Don Carlos at Düsseldorf in 1991; Boccanegra at the Opéra Bastille, Paris, 1994; Sang Scarpia at Palermo, 2001.

BURCHULADZE, Paata; Singer (bass); b. 12 Feb. 1951, Tbilisi, Russia. *Education:* Studied at the Tbilisi Conservatory. *Career:* Debut: Tbilisi in 1975 as Mephistopheles in Faust; Sang in Russia and Milan; Studied further in Italy and began international career after winning competitions, 1981–82; Roles include Basilio in Il Barbiere di Siviglia, Leporello, King Rene in Iolantha, Gremin in Eugene Onegin and Boris Godunov; Guest appearances at the Bolshoi in Moscow; British debut in 1983 at the Lichfield Festival, in The Dream of Gerontius by Elgar; Covent Garden debut in 1984 as Ramfis in Aida; Salzburg Festival appearances as the Commendatore in Don Giovanni under Karajan; Sang Rossini's Basilio at the Metropolitan in 1989, and Khan Konchak in a new production of Prince Igor at Covent Garden in 1990; Sang Boris Godunov in a revival of Mussorgsky's opera, 1991, the Inquisitor in Prokofiev's The Fiery Angel in 1992; Sang King Philip in Don Carlos at Santiago, 1994; Sang Zaccaria in Nabucco at the Verona Arena and Konchak in Prince Igor at San Francisco in 1996; Walter in Luisa Miller for the Royal Opera at Edinburgh, 1998; Season 2000–01 at the Grand Inquisitor in Don Carlos at Washington, Boris Godunov at Hamburg, and Ramphis in Aida for San Francisco Opera. *Recordings include:* Scenes from operas by Mussorgsky and Verdi; Don Giovanni; Fiesco in Simon Boccanegra; Sparafucile in Rigoletto; Ramfis in Aida; Samson et Dalila. *Current Management:* Askonas Holt Ltd, Lonsdale Chambers, 27 Chancery Lane, London, WC2A 1PF, England. *Telephone:* (20) 7400-1700. *Fax:* (20) 7400-1799. *E-mail:* info@askonasholt.co.uk. *Website:* www.askonasholt.co.uk.

BURDEN, William; Singer (tenor); b. 1965, Florida, USA. *Education:* Studied at Indiana University. *Career:* Appearances with the San Francisco Opera as Belmonte, Count Lerma in Don Carlos and the title role in Bernstein's Candide; European debut as Rodolfo for Opera North (returned as Tamino); Further appearances as Rossini's Almaviva with Opera Northern Ireland, Janek in The Makropulos Case at San Francisco, Ali (L'Incontro Improvviso by Haydn) at Nice, Ramiro (Cenerentola) in South Africa and Ubalo in Haydn's Armida, at St Louis; Season 1995–96 with New York Met debut as Janek, and Tybalt in Roméo et Juliette; Mozart's La Finta Giardiniera for Glimmerglass Opera; Season 1997–98 as Tom Rakewell at Genoa, Tamino for Florida Opera, Ali in Bourdeaux and Cimarosa's Il Matrimonio Segreto in Lausanne; Sang Tybalt at the Met, 1998; Concert repertoire from Bach to Bernstein, with Messiah under William Christie. *Current Management:* Askonas Holt Ltd, Lonsdale Chambers, 27 Chancery Lane, London, WC2A 1PF, England. *Telephone:* (20) 7400-1700. *Fax:* (20) 7400-1799. *E-mail:* info@askonasholt.co.uk. *Website:* www.askonasholt .co.uk.

BUREAU, Karen; Singer (Soprano); b. 3 Feb. 1951, Glen Ellyn, Illinois, USA. *Education:* Opera School of the New York Metropolitan, 1981–84. *Career:* Debut: New York Met, 1982 as Lady in Waiting in Macbeth; Sang at Hannover Opera from 1985; As Leonore in Fidelio, Rezia in Oberon; Wagner's Senta, Freia, Elsa and Elisabeth; Leonora in La forza del Destino, Maddalena, Andrea Chenier, and Andromache in Troades by Reimann, 1987; Seattle Opera from 1986 as Gutrune and Elisabeth in Tannhäuser; Deutsche Oper Berlin, 1991 as Leonore; Brünnhilde in Wagner's Ring at Hannover; Wiesbaden and Flagstaff, Arizona Opera, 1996 and 1998; Other roles include Lady Macbeth, Heidelberg, 1995; Aida and the Dyer's Wife in Die Frau ohne Schatten, season 1997–98 at Kiel Opera; Elettra in Idomeneo; Donna Anna, Weber's Rezia and Euryanthe, Wagner's Eva and Isolde; Sang Abigaille in Nabucco at Hannover, 1999.

BURGANGER, Judith; Concert Pianist, Professor of Music and Artist-in-Residence; b. 1939, Buffalo, New York, USA; m., 3 d. *Education:* Artist Diploma, 1961, Graduate Certificate (MM), 1965, State Conservatory of Music, Stuttgart, Germany. *Career:* Debut: Solo recital, Buffalo; Orchestral, with Amherst Symphony; Early performances, 1946–60: Soloist with Buffalo Philharmonic, Toronto Symphony, National Symphony (Washington DC), Marlboro Festival (Vermont); Later performances, 1960–: Soloist, symphony orchestras throughout USA, Germany, Austria, Netherlands, Scandinavia, Italy, Switzerland, Thomas, Conlon, Akiyama; International guest performances, solo recitals and chamber music; Teaching: Artist Teacher, Cleveland Institute of Music; Associate Professor, Artist-in-Residence, Texas Tech Atlantic University; Artist Teacher, Carnegie Mellon University; Associate Professor, 1980, Professor, 1984–, Florida Atlantic University; Director of Conservatory Music, College of Liberal Arts, Florida Atlantic University; Created an annual Brahms Festival in 1983 performing all Chamber music compositions and works for 4 hands at 1 piano and songs include masterpieces from Friends of Brahms; Founder, FAU Chamber Soloists, 1987, ensemble performing subscription series throughout Florida and works for all combinations of instruments and voice; Collaborative artist with following string quartets: Cleveland, Emerson, Ridge, Shanghai, Lark, Cavani Alexander, Ciompi and Miami. *Recordings:* Burganger and Leonid Treer, The Art of Four Hands at One Piano, 1997. *Honours:* 1st Prizewinner of International

Piano Competition, Munich, Germany; 1st Prizewinner, Merriweather Post National Competition, Washington DC; Bronze Medal, Geneva International Piano Competition, Switzerland. *Address:* Conservatory of Music, 2912 College Avenue, Florida Atlantic University, Davie, FL 33314, USA.

BURGE, John, MMus, DMA, ARCT; Canadian composer; b. (David Byson), 2 Jan. 1961, Dryden, ON. *Education:* Royal Conservatory of Music, Toronto, Univ. of Toronto and Univ. of British Columbia. *Career:* Assoc. Prof. of Composition and Theory, Queen's Univ., Kingston, ON 1987–; Pres. Canadian League of Composers 1998–. *Compositions include:* Mass for Prisoners of Conscience 1989, Thank You God 1992, Divinum mysterium 1995, Symphony No. 1 1997. *Address:* Queen's University School of Music, Harrison-LeCaine Hall, Room 204, 39 Queen's Crescent, Kingston, ON K7L 3N6, Canada (office). *E-mail:* burgej@ post.queensu.ca (office). *Website:* www.queensu.ca/music (office).

BURGER, Ernst Manfred; German pianist and writer on music; b. 26 March 1937, Munich; m. Dorothea Maillinger 1972; one s. *Education:* Liberal Arts High School, Staatliche Hochschule für Musik, Munich, Künstlerische Staatsprüfung, Pädagogische Staatsprüfung. *Career:* writer on music and researcher on Chopin and Liszt. *Publications:* Franz Liszt, A Chronicle of His Life in Pictures and Documents, Munich, 1986, Paris, 1988, New York, 1989; Frédéric Chopin, A Chronicle of His Life in Pictures and Documents, Munich, 1990; Carl Tausig, Bonn, 1990; Robert Schumann, A Chronicle of His Life in Pictures and Documents, Mainz, 1998; Franz Liszt in Contemporary Photography, Munich, 2003; contrib. to Die Musik in Geschichte und Gegenwart (MGG) and Süddeutsche Zeitung; Music Journals; Articles about Jazz; Commentaries for recorded music. *Honours:* Grand Prix de Littérature Musicale, 1988; Ordre du Mérite en faveur de la culture polonaise, 1991; Robert Schumann Prize, Zwickau, 1999; Deutscher Musikeditions Prize for his book on Robert Schumann, 1999. *Address:* Erhardtstrasse 6, 80469 Munich, Germany.

BURGESS, Brio, BA; American composer, dramatist, poet and jazz singer; b. 27 April 1943, San Francisco, CA. *Education:* Russell Sage Coll. *Career:* various clerical positions at Federal, state, city and county agencies 1972–; performances in Saratoga Springs, NY, San Francisco, San Mateo, CA, Albany, NY, and Troy, NY, of music and words (original works) in various formats; presentation of Street Kids on Radio WRPI, NY and Play with Music, 1992, Radio Free America Broadcast. *Compositions:* Suite for Picasso; Escape, ballet, for Piano, Harp, Feet and Chains; Girl on a Ball, Children's Dance and Toys, piano tunes; Sound Dreams, piano music; Space Visions, including The Painter's Song; Hippy Children's Concentration Camp Blues, for Piano, Harp and Words; Tin Angel Blues, 1990; Purple Hood Suite, 1991–92. *Recordings:* Clear, 1978; Briomindsound, 1979; Ulysses Dog No. 9, 1980; Gathered Hear, 1980; Still, 1981; Ringade, 1982; Grate, 1982; Ether, 1982; Zen Meditations, 1987. *Publications:* poems in Poetalk Publications and BAPC Anthologies, 1989–95; Outlaw Blues, eight song-poems, 1992; Poem in Open Mic: The Albany Anthology, 1994; Street Kids and Other Plays, four opera-musical libretto, 1995. *Current Management:* Gail G. Tolley, 5 Cuyler Street, Albany, NY 12202, USA. *Address:* c/o ASCAP, ASCAP Building 1 Lincoln Plaza, New York, NY 10023, USA.

BURGESS, Grayston; Conductor and Countertenor; b. 7 April 1932, Cheriton, Kent, England; m. Katherine Mary Bryan, 3 d. *Education:* MA, King's College, Cambridge. *Career:* Sang with Westminster Abbey Choir, 1955–69; Sang Oberon in Britten's A Midsummer Night's Dream at Covent Garden; Dowland television programme; Performances with Handel Opera Society and the Henry Wood Promenade Concerts; Numerous radio broadcasts; Founder and Director of The Purcell Consort of Voices, 1963; Debut as Conductor at the 1963 Aldeburgh Festival; Concerts and recordings with the Purcell Instrumental Ensemble, the Elizabeth Consort of Voices, Musica Reservata, the London Sackbut Ensemble, the Philip Jones Brass Ensemble and the Jaye Consort of Voices. *Recordings include:* Josquin's Deploration sur la Mort de Johannes Ockeghem; Dunstable's Laudi; Ockeghem's Vive le Roy and Ave Maria; Machaut's La Messe de Notre Dame; William Byrd's Church Music; Richard Davy's St Matthew Passion; Music by Schütz, Schein and Scheidt; Doulce Memoire; 16th Century French Chansons; English Madrigals from the Reign of Queen Elizabeth; English Secular Music of the Late Renaissance; The Eton Choir Book; The Triumphs of Oriana; High Renaissance Music in England.

BURGESS, Sally; British singer (mezzo-soprano); b. 9 Oct. 1953, Durban, South Africa. *Education:* Royal Coll. of Music. *Career:* engaged by ENO and sang Zerlina (Don Giovanni), Cherubino, Pamina, Mimi, Micaela, the Composer in Ariadne, Massenet's Charlotte and Mrs Thatcher as Public Opinion in David Pountney's production of Orpheus in the Underworld; Covent Garden debut, 1983 as Siebel in Faust; Glyndebourne, 1983, in The Love of Three Oranges; Cavalli's Eritrea for the Camden Festival, 1985; sang Carmen in a new production by ENO, 1986; Amneris for Opera North; other roles include Sextus in Julius

Caesar and Orlofsky in Die Fledermaus; sang Minerva in The Return of Ulysses at the London Coliseum, 1989; Julie La Verne in Show Boat for RSC-Opera North (Gluck's Orpheus, 1990, Carmen, 1991); Fricka in Die Walküre for Scottish Opera, 1991; Amneris in Aida for Scottish Opera, 1992; sang Judith in new production of Duke Bluebeard's Castle at the Coliseum, 1991; sang in the premiere of Paul McCartney's Liverpool Oratorio, co-written by Carl Davis; sang Carmen at Bregenz, 1991–92, London Coliseum, 1993, Zürich and Berlin, 1994; sang Dalila at Nantes, 1994 and Carmen, New Zealand; sang Widow Begbick in Mahagonny by Kurt Weill, 1995, and Herodias in Salome from Richard Strauss, 1996, for the ENO; Carmen, The Met, New York, 1995; Isabella, The Voyage, Met, 1996; sang Dulcinée in Don Quixote (ENO), 1996 and Carmen in Munich; sang Ottavia in Poppea for Welsh National Opera, 1997; Eboli in Don Carlos for Opera North, 1998; sang Kabanova in Katya Kabanova at Munich Bayerische Staatsoper, Wagner's Ring Cycle at Geneva and in Carmen for the ENO, 1999; sang Mère Marie in Poulenc's The Carmelites for Welsh National Opera, 1999; sang Margareta in Genoveva for Opera North, 2000; On The Town with the BBC Concert Orchestra, 2000; appeared in Carmen and as Baba The Turk in The Rake's Progress for ENO, 2001; Fricka in Die Walküre at Geneva, and Azucena for ENO, 2000–01; Polinesso in Ariodonte for Houston Grand Opera, 2002–03; Fortunata in Satyricon in Antwerp and Nancy; Hanna Glawin in Merry Widow for the Metropolitan Opera, New York, 2003–04; concert appearances include Elgar's Dream of Gerontius; Verdi's Requiem; Songs of the Auvergne by Canteloube; Premiere of Twice Through the Heart by Mark-Anthony Turnage at the 1997 Aldeburgh Festival; one-woman show: Sally Burgess's Women, premiered at the Lyric Hammersmith, 1997; Tigrana in Edgar by Puccini for Chelsea Opera Group at the Queen Elizabeth Hall, 1999. Recordings include: The King and I; Five Irish Folk Songs, Howard Ferguson; Sally Burgess Sings Jazz; The Other Me; Happy Talk – Richard Rodgers. Current Management: AOR Management, PMB 221, 6910 Roosevelt Way NE, Seattle, WA 98103, USA. Telephone: (206) 729-6160. Fax: (206) 985-8499. E-mail: jennyrose@aormanagementuk.com. Website: www.aormanagementuk.com.

BURGON, Geoffrey (Alan); Composer; b. 15 July 1941, Hambledon, Hampshire, England; m. (1) Janice Elizabeth Garwood, 1963, marriage dissolved, 1 s., 1 d., (2) Jacqueline Krofchak, 1992, 1 s. Education: GGSM. Career: Composer, Trumpeter, 1964–71; Composer, Conductor, 1971–; As Trumpeter performed at Royal Opera House, with Northern Sinfonia Orchestra, Philomusica, London Mozart Players and others; Session work at theatres and jazz bands; As Conductor for film and television works. Compositions include: Many scores for dance including London Contemporary Dance Theatre, Ballet Rambert, London Festival Ballet and Royal Ballet; Over 40 scores for film, television and radio including: Tinker Tailor Soldier Spy, Brideshead Revisited, Bleak House, Life of Brian, Turtle Diary, The Chronicles of Narnia, The Children of The North, Martin Chuzzlewit, Silent Witness, Turning World, When Trumpets Fade, Cider with Rosie; Longitude; The Forsyte Saga; Choral and Orchestral Music: Gending, Acquainted With Night, Think On Dreadful Doomsday, Canciones Del Alma, Requiem, Veni Spiritus, The World Again, Revelations, Title Divine, The Trials Of Prometheus, Trumpet Concerto, 1993, Hard Times, opera, 1991; City Adventures for solo percussion and orchestra, Piano Concerto, 1997; Fantasia on REX for cello and orchestra; Almost Peace, Merciless Beauty, Recitativo, The Wanderer; String Quartet; A Different Dawn for orchestra, 1999; Alleluia Psallat, Shirtless Stephen, 2002; Three Mysteries, 2003. Recordings: Cathedral Music of Geoffrey Burgon; Brideshead Revisited; Music for Counter Tenor; The Fall of Lucifer; Merciless Beauty; Music for Dr Who. Publications: Over 40 scores. Contributions: Various professional journals. Honours: Prince Pierre of Monaco Award, 1969; Ivor Novello Awards, 1979, 1981; Gold Disc for Brideshead Revisited, 1982; British Academy nomination for Brideshead Revisited, 1982 and Martin Chuzzlewit, 1995; British Academy Award for Longitude, 2000, British Academy Award for The Forsyte Saga, 2003. Current Management: c/o Chester Music, 8–9 Frith Street, London W1V 5TZ, England.

BURMESTER, Pedro; Pianist; b. 9 Oct. 1963, Oporto, Portugal. Education: Oporto Musical Conservatory; Private studies with Helena Costa, Sequeria Costa, Leon Fleisher and Dmitri Paperno; Teaching, Oporto High School of Music. Career: Debut: 1972; Solo recitalist; Guest Soloist with orchestras in Portugal, Spain, Austria, France, Germany, Italy and USA; Television appearances in Portugal; Various musical festivals in Portugal and Macao; Radio appearances in Portugal and the USA. Honours: 1st Prize, 9th International Vianna da Mota Piano Competition, Lisbon, 1983; Jury Discretionary Award, 8th Van Cliburn International Piano Competition, Fort Worth. Current Management: Liliane Weinstadt, Bureau de Concerts, 59 avenue de Busleyden, 1020 Brussels, Belgium. Telephone: (2) 263-6565 (office). Fax: (2) 263-6566. E-mail: info@concerts-weinstadt.com. Website: www.concerts-weinstadt.com.

BURNETT, Yvonne; Singer (Mezzo-Soprano); b. 1965, Aberdeen, Scotland. Education: Royal Scottish Academy, Guildhall School and National Opera Studio. Career: Debut: Bianca in Les Brigands by Offenbach for Netherlands Opera; Sang Flosshilde in Das Rheingold at Nantes, Puccini's Suzuki and Olga in Eugene Onegin for Welsh National Opera; Lady Essex in Britten's Gloriana for Opera North; Appearances as Olga for Glyndebourne Touring Opera, 1994. Honours: Mary Garden International Prize; Sir James Caird Scholarship; Countess of Munster Scholarship. Address: c/o Glyndebourne Touring Opera, Glyndebourne, Lewes, Sussex BN8 5UU, England.

BURNSIDE, Iain; Pianist; b. 1950, Glasgow, Scotland. Education: Studied in Oxford, London and Warsaw. Career: Recital accompanist to Margaret Price, Victoria de Los Angeles, Sarah Walker, Nancy Argenta, Thomas Allen and Stephen Varcoe; Chamber Music performances with the Brodsky and Delmé Quartets, Douglas Boyd and Shmuel Ashkenasi; Appearances at the major British festivals and recitals in Europe, USA, Canada and Japan; Devised song series for Schoenberg, The Reluctant Revolutionary concert series on South Bank, London, 1988–89; Further contributions to the French Revolution Festival and Hermann Prey's Schubertiade, 1989; Artistic Director of series of vocal and chamber concerts at St John's Smith Square, London, 1989–; Recitals featuring Karol Szymanowski on South Bank. Recordings include: Gurney's Ludlow and Teme with Adrian Thompson and the Delmé Quartet. Address: c/o Ron Gonsalves, 10 Dagnan Road, London SW12 9LQ, England.

BURROUGHS, Bruce (Douglas); Singer (Operatic Baritone), Pedagogue and Writer; b. 12 Nov. 1944, Hagerstown, Maryland, USA. Education: AB, English Literature, University of California, Los Angeles, 1966; MM, Voice and Vocal Pedagogy, New England Conservatory of Music, 1971. Career: Debut: Papageno, in Magic Flute, Los Angeles Guild Opera, 1965; Metropolitan Opera debut in Einstein on the Beach, 1976; More than 40 roles including title roles of Monteverdi's Orfeo, Mozart's Don Giovanni, Busoni's Arlecchino, Menotti's Bishop of Brindisi; Editor-in-Chief, The Opera Quarterly; Music Critic, Los Angeles Times; mem, American Guild of Musical Artists. Recordings: Several. Publications: Author of biographical essays in International Dictionary of Opera, 1996; Author, Metropolitan Opera Guide to Opera on Video, 1997; Contributor, Collier's Encyclopaedia, 1998. Contributions: Articles, features and reviews to Music Journal and Opera News. Honours: Deems Taylor Award, American Society of Composers, Authors and Publishers, 1991. Address: 14832 Hart Street, Van Nuys, CA 91405, USA.

BURROWES, Norma Elizabeth; opera and concert singer (soprano); b. 24 April 1944, Bangor, Co. Down, Northern Ireland; m. Steuart Bedford 1969 (divorced 1980). Education: Queen's University, Belfast, Royal Academy of Music. Career: debut, Glyndebourne Touring Opera as Zerlina in Don Giovanni, 1969; Debut with Royal Opera House as Fiakermilli in Arabella, 1976; Roles included Blondchen in Die Entführung, Oscar in Un Ballo in Maschera, Despina in Così fan tutte, Woodbird in Siegfried, Sophie in Der Rosenkavalier, Cunning Little Vixen, Manon, Titania in Midsummer Night's Dream, Nannetta in Falstaff, Gilda in Rigoletto, Marie in Daughter of the Regiment, Juliet, Adina in L'Elisir d'amore, Susanna in Nozze di Figaro, and Lauretta in Gianni Schicchi; Sang regularly with Glyndebourne Opera, Scottish Opera, at Aldeburgh Festival, English National Opera, and Welsh National Opera among others; Sang at Salzburg, Paris, Aix-en-Provence, Avignon, Ottawa, Montreal, New York, Chicago and Buenos Aires; Metropolitan Opera from 1979 as Blondchen, Oscar and Sophie; Sang with all the principal London orchestras and on BBC radio and television, retiring in 1982. Recordings: Made numerous recordings including Die Schöpfung, The Fairy Queen, Hansel and Gretel, Acis and Galatea, Ariodante, Die Entführung, Haydn's Armida, Israel in Egypt and Semele, and Riders to the Sea by Vaughan Williams. Honours: Honorary DMus, Queen's University, Belfast; Order of Worshipful Company of Musicians.

BURROWS, Donald (Donwald) James, BA, CertEd, MA, PhD; academic, conductor, organist and harpsichordist; b. 28 Dec. 1945, London, England; m. Marilyn Jones 1971; three s. Education: Trinity Hall, Cambridge and Open University. Career: Director of Music, John Mason School, Abingdon, 1970–81; Lecturer in Music, Open University, 1982–89; Senior Lecturer in Music, 1989–95, Professor of Music, 1995–, Head of Music Department, 1991–2002; Conductor, Abingdon and District Music Society, 1972–83; Conductor, Oxford Holiday Orchestra, 1978–; Organist and Choirmaster, St Nicholas Church, Abingdon, 1972–82; Master of the Music, St Botolph's, Aspley Guise, 1985–95; Member, Redaktionskollegium, Hallische Händel-Ausgabe, 1984–; Founder Member, Handel Institute, 1985–, Chair Trustees and Council, 1998–; Member of Vorstand, Georg Friedrich Händel-Gesellschaft, 1987–, Vice-President, 1999–; Member of Advisory Board, Maryland Handel Festival, USA, 1988–2001; mem, Royal Musical Association; Royal College of Organists. Recordings: Insert notes for recordings include Handel's Water Music, Anthems, Utrecht Te Deum, Ode for St Cecilia's Day, Israel in Egypt, Organ Concertos and Messiah. *Publications include:* Handel Alexander's Feast; The Anthem on the Peace; Foundling Hospital Anthem, Violin Sonatas, Messiah, As Pants the Hart, Songs for Soprano and Continuo, Belshazzar, Imeneo, also Elgar pieces for violin and piano, (all as editor); A Catalogue of Handel's Musical Autographs; Handel (Master Musicians Biography); Handel's Messiah; The Cambridge Companion to Handel (as editor and author); Music and Theatre in Handel's World. *Contributions:* The Musical Times; Music and Letters; Early Music; Göttinger Händel-Beiträge. *Honours:* Studentship, Merton College, Oxford University, 1979; British Academy Research Grant, 1979; Vincent H Duckles Award, 1996; Händelpreis der Stadt Halle, 2000. *Address:* 126 High Street, Cranfield, Bedford MK43 0DG, England.

BURROWS, Stuart; Singer (tenor); b. 7 Feb. 1933, Pontypridd, Wales; m. Enid Lewis; one s. one d. *Education:* Trinity Coll., Carmarthen. *Career:* sang in concerts at first; stage debut with WNO in 1963 as Ismaele in Nabucco; Don Ottavio in Don Giovanni, Jenek in Bartered Bride, Ernesto in Don Pasquale, Rodolfo in Bohème; Athens in 1965 as Oedipus Rex with Stravinsky; Covent Garden from 1967 as Beppe in Pagliacci, Tamino in Magic Flute, Ottavio in Don Giovanni, Fenton in Falstaff, Elvino in La Sonnambula, Lensky in Onegin, Ernesto in Don Pasquale, Alfredo in Don Pasquale, Pinkerton in Butterfly, Alfredo in Traviata, Idomeneo, Titus in La Clemenza di Tito, Faust; US from 1967 as Tamino, Lensky, Pinkerton, Ottavio, Des Grieux; Vienna Staatsoper in 1970 as Tamino and Ottavio, Faust, Pinkerton, Salzburg Festival from 1970 in Mozart Roles; Metropolitan Opera from 1971 as Ottavio, Tamino, Pinkerton, Faust, Alfredo and Belmonte; Paris Opéra, 1975 Ottavio, Belmonte; appearances at Aix-en-Provence and Orange Festivals, and at Hamburg, Geneva, Houston, (Des Grieux), Santa Fe, (Tamino, Alfredo) and Boston; sang Mozart's Titus at Brussels, 1982 and Covent Garden, 1989; Mozart's Basilio at Aix, 1991; many concert appearances notably in music by Bach and Handel; BBC television films of Faust, La Bohème and Rigoletto; had own television series for eight years entitled Stuart Burrows Sings, also radio programmes; in demand as an adjudicator and singing teacher and for masterclasses. *Recordings:* Maria Stuarda by Donizetti; Die Zauberflöte; Beethoven's 9th Symphony; Eugene Onegin; La Clemenza di Tito; Don Giovanni; Die Entführung; many ballad recordings. *Honours:* Blue Riband, National Eisteddfod of Wales 1959; hon. doctorates, Carmarthen 1989, Univ. of Wales, Aberystwyth 1992; fellowships from Aberystwyth and Cardiff Univs and Trinity Coll., Carmarthen. *Address:* 29 Blackwater Grove, Fordingbridge SP6 3AD, England. *E-mail:* meryl@nicholls.f9.co.uk (office). *Website:* www.stuartburrows.f9.co.uk (office).

BURT, Francis, ARAM; composer and academic; b. 28 April 1926, London, England; m. Lina Burt. *Education:* Royal Academy of Music, Hochschule für Musik, Berlin. *Career:* Professor of Composition, Hochschule für Musik und darstellende Kunst, Vienna 1973–93. *Compositions include:* Iambics, for orchestra, Opus 5; Volpone, opera, Opus 9; Espressione Orchestrale, Opus 10; Der Golem, ballet, Opus 11; Fantasmasgoria, for orchestra, Opus 12; Barnstable, opera, Opus 13; Unter der blanken Hacke des Monds, for baritone and orchestra; Und Gott der Herr sprach, for solo voices, 2 choruses and orchestra; Morgana, for orchestra; Echoes, for 9 players; Hommage à Jean-Henri Fabre, for 5 players, 1994; 2 String Quartets, 1952, 1991; Blind Visions, for oboe and small orchestra, 1995; Bavarian Gentians, for chamber chorus and 6 players. *Recordings:* Classic Amadeo; Francis Burt: Unter der Blanken, Hacke des Monds, Echoes, Morsand, Der Golem; NMC: Und Gott der Herr Sprach for solo voices, two choruses and orchestra; Gramola: EXXJ, Hommage à Jean-Henri Fabre for five players; Creatives Centrum: Francis Burt zum 75 Geburstag (String Quartets 1 and 2). *Honours:* Mendelssohn Scholarship, 1954; Körner Prize, 1973; Würdigungspreis für Musik, Austrian Federal Ministry of Education and Art, 1978; City of Vienna Prize for Music, 1981; Grosses Silbernes Ehrenzeichen für Verdienste um die Republik Österreich, 1992. *Address:* Mayerhofgasse 12/20, 1040 Vienna, Austria.

BURT, Michael; Singer (Bass baritone); b. 1943, Farnham, Surrey, England. *Education:* Studied with Richard Federicks in New York. *Career:* Debut: Caracas, 1977, as Monterone and Sparafucile in the same performance of Rigoletto; Concert soloist in North America, including Bach's Christmas Oratorio and B minor Mass at Carnegie Hall; Covent Garden, London, 1979, as Second Armed Man in Die Zauberflöte; Further appearances at Frankfurt as Pizarro in Fidelio and at New Orleans as King Henry in Lohengrin; Zaccaria and the Hoffmann villains at Hannover, 1986–87; King Philip in Don Carlos and Wotan in Der Ring des Nibelungen at Graz, 1988; Adolfo in Schubert's Alfonso und Estrella, 1991; Sang Wagner's Dutchman at Montpellier, 1992, Jochanaan in Salome at Barcelona, 1991; Nuremberg 1995–96 as Gurnemanz, Orestes and Wotan; Aachen 1996, as Boris Godunov; Sang Wagner's Daland at Koblenz, 1999, and the Commen-

datore in Don Giovanni, 2000. *Address:* c/o Vereinigte Buhnen, Kaiser Josef Platz 10, 8010 Graz, Austria.

BURT, Robert; Singer (Tenor); b. 22 May 1962, England. *Education:* Graduated from the Guildhall School in 1989. *Career:* Appearances with Opera 80 as Monostatos and Don Ottavio, Dancing Master in Ariadne auf Naxos directed by Jonathan Miller with Chelsea Opera Group as Kleontes in Daphne and Mid-Wales Opera as Goro in Butterfly; Sang Don Jerome in the British premiere of Prokofiev's The Duenna, at the Guildhall School under Rostropovich, 1991; Glyndebourne Festival debut in 1992 as Tchaplitsky in The Queen of Spades, repeated at the Promenade Concerts, London; Sang Don Curzio in Figaro with Glyndebourne Touring Opera in 1992 and Janáček's From The House of the Dead, at the Barbican Hall, 1993; Young Servant in Elektra at opening night of BBC Proms, 1993; Recitals and oratorios include Carmina Burana at Snape, Vaughan Williams' Serenade to Music at the Barbican, and the Easter Oratorio by Bach and Mozart's Requiem in Munich; Festival engagements at Bath, Sully-sur-Loire and Dijon; Sang Iro in Monteverdi's Ulisse at Aix-en-Provence, 2000. *Address:* 8 Baranscraig Avenue, Brighton, Sussex BN1 8RE, England.

BURT, Warren Arnold, MA; composer; b. 10 Oct. 1949, Baltimore, Maryland, USA. *Education:* University of California at San Diego, studied with Robert Erickson and Kenneth Gaburo. *Career:* Australian Centre for Arts and Technology, 1994; Resident, Mills College, Oakland, 1995; Multi-Media Artist; Writer; Australia Council Composer's Fellowship, 1998–2000. *Compositions include:* (many with visuals and electronics) Nighthawk, 1973–76; Aardvarks IV, 1975; Moods, 1978–79; The Wanderer: Pocket Calculator Music II, 1983; Woodwind Quintet, 1985; Meditations, 1986; Voice, Tuning Fork and Accordion, 1986; Samples III, 1987; String Quartet No. 4, 1987; Chaotic Research Music, 1990; Some Kind of Seasoning, 1990–91; Dense Room, 1994; Music for Microtonal Piano Sounds, 1992–98; Diversity, 1998. *Recordings include:* Aardvarks V, 1978; Song Dawn Chords, 1981; Four Pieces for Synthesizer, 1981; Almond Bread Harmonies II, 1985; Chaotic Research Music, 1989–90; Three Inverse Genera, 1990; Parts of Speech, 1992; 39 Dissonant Etudes, 1996; Miss Furr and Miss Skeene, 1998; Diversity, multimedia theatre, 1998. *Publications:* Music Talks; 24 Pamphlets written of edited, 1982–85, Council of Adult Education, Melbourne; Writings from a Scarlet Aardvark–15 Essays on Music and Art; Critical Vices: The Myths of Post-Modern Theory (co-author with Nicholas Zurbrugg), 1999. *Honours:* Sounds Australian Award; Djerassi Residents Program, 1998. *Address:* PO Box 2154, St Kilda West, Victoria 3182, Australia. *Website:* www.emf.org/subscribers/burt.html.

BURTON, Amy; Singer (Soprano); b. 14 May 1958, USA. *Career:* Théâtre des Champs Elysées, Paris, as Woglinde and Woodbird in The Ring, 1987, also at Nice; Season 1988 as Adele in Die Fledermaus for Scottish Opera; As Douglas Moore's Baby Doe, for Colorado Opera at Central City; Sang Juliette at Zürich, 1990 and Nannetta in Falstaff at New Orleans; Sophie in Werther at Cincinnati, 1993; Season 1997–98, in Handel's Serse for New York City Opera and Ford's Wife in Falstaff for Glimmerglass Opera; Sang John Musto's Dove Sta Amore with Scottish Chamber Orchestra, 2000; Other roles include Luisa in The Duenna by Prokofiev; Governess in The Turn of the Screw, 2000; La Folie in Rameau's Platée, 2000; Concepcion in L'Heure Espagnole for New York City Opera, 2000; Liù in Turandot for Pittsburgh Opera, 2001. *Recordings:* Ernst Bacon Songs, 2001. *Address:* New York City Opera, Lincoln Center, New York, NY 10023, USA.

BURTON, Humphrey McGuire, BA (Cantab); British writer, academic and broadcaster; b. 25 March 1931, Trowbridge, England; two s. three d. *Education:* Univ. of Cambridge. *Career:* Head of Music and Arts, BBC Television, 1965–67, 1975–81; Editor, Presenter, Aquarius, ITV, 1970–75; Presenter, Concerts, Opera and Ballet, BBC, 1975–94; Presenter, Young Musician of the Year, 1978–94; Chair., EBU TV Music Working Party, 1976–86; Artistic Dir, Barbican Centre, 1988–90; Dir, Tender is the North, Festival of Scandinavian Arts, Barbican Centre, 1992; television dir, 1999–2002 including: Flight at Glyndebourne (Channel 4), Falstaff (BBC 2), The Return of Ulysses (Aix/DVD), 2002; broadcasting: Artist in Focus (BBC Radio 3), Walton and Menuhin series (Classic FM); Ada Vincent in Brixton (BBC4); conducted the Verdi Requiem at the Royal Albert Hall, 2001; mem., RPS; Hon. FCSD. *Recordings:* Mozart Harpsichord Duet K19d, with Erik Smith. *Publications:* Leonard Bernstein (biography), 1994; Menuhin (biography), 2000; Walton - The Romantic Loner, 2002. *Honours:* Hon. Fellow, Fitzwilliam Coll., Cambridge. *Address:* 13 Linden Road, Aldeburgh, Suffolk IP15 5JQ, England. *Telephone:* (1728) 452548. *Fax:* (1728) 451979.

BURTON, Stephen; Composer; b. 24 Feb. 1943, Whittier, California, USA. *Education:* Studied at the Oberlin Conservatory, 1960–62 Salzburg Mozarteum, 1962–65; Further study with Hans Werner Henze, 1966–67; Peabody Conservatory, 1972–73. *Career:* Director of the Munich Kammerspiel, 1963–64; Teacher, Heritage Chair in Music, George Mason University, Fairfax, VA, 1974–; Heritage Chair in Music, (endowed Chair for life), 1996–. *Compositions include:* Concerto Da Camera, 1963; Ode To A Nightingale for Soprano and Ensemble, 1963; Symphony No. 1, 1968; No Trifling With Love, opera, 1970; Stravinskiana for Flute and Orchestra, 1972; Dithyramb, 1972; 6 Hebrew Melodies, after Byron, 1973; String Quartet, 1974; Piano Trio, 1975; Songs Of The Tulpehocken for Tenor and Orchestra, 1976; Six Songs for Voice and 13 Instruments, 1977; Ballet Finisterre, 1977; The Duchess Of Malfi, opera after Webster, 1978; Symphony No. 2, after Sylvia Plath poems, for Mezzo, Baritone and Orchestra, 1979; Variations On A Theme Of Mahler for Chamber Orchestra, 1982; Violin Concerto, 1983; Aimee, opera, 1983; I Have A Dream, cantata for Narrator, Soprano and Orchestra, 1987; An American Triptych, 3 one-act operas after Crane's Maggie, Hawthorne's Dr Heidegger's Experiment and Melville's Benito Cereno, 1989; From Noon to Starry Night for chorus and chamber orchestra, 1989; Burning Babe, cantata, 1999; Brotherhood, Music Theatre, with Peter Burton, 1992; Restored film scores (with Gillian Anderson): Ben Hur, 1997, Passion of St Joan, 1998, Ten Commandments, 1998, Robin Hood, 1999. *Recordings:* Symphony No. 2 Ariel; Songs of the Tulpehocken. *Publications:* Orchestration, 1980. *Honours:* 30 major commissions and prizes. *Address:* GMU, 4400 University Drive, Fairfax, VA 22030, 4444, USA.

BURY, Alison (Margaret); Violinist; b. 20 Jan. 1954, Woking, England. *Education:* Studied with Sylvia Rosenberg and Frances Baines at the RCM, London; Sándor Végh and Nikolaus Harnoncourt, Salzburg, 1976–77. *Career:* Appearances with the Vienna Concentus Musicus, Academy of Ancient Music (1975–90), Taverner Players (1976–92), Amsterdam Baroque Orchestra, under Ton Koopman (1980–86) and the English Baroque Soloists under John Eliot Gardiner (leader from 1983); Leader of the Orchestra of the Age of Enlightenment, 1986–; Teacher and Director of the Baroque Orchestra, Royal College of Music, London; Chamber recitals with the Chandos Baroque Players, 1981–89, L'Ecole d'Orphée, 1982–89 and Geminiani Trio, 1983–90. *Recordings include:* Vivaldi's Four Seasons, with the Academy of Ancient Music and with the Taverner Players; Bach Double Concerto with Monica Huggett, and Elizabeth Wallfisch. *Address:* c/o Royal College of Music, Prince Consort Road, London SW7, England.

BURY, Grzegorz (Piotr Michal); Composer; b. 17 Nov. 1961, Katowice, Poland. *Education:* K Szymanowski Academy of Music, Katowice, Theory of Music, 1981–86, Composition, 1986–89, MA in Art, 1990. *Career:* Debut: Festival of Fascinating Music in Katowice, 1983. *Compositions include:* Solo instruments: Suite for Flute, Lament Songs (Treny) for Piano, Sonata With Air-Hammer for Piano, Little Prince, suite, for Piano, Echo, Clouds And Mountains for Piano: Pieces for solo instrument and piano: Walo, lullaby, for Viola and Piano, Gabeag, folk dance, for Violin and Piano, Polonaise, Golliwogs' War, Largo Cantabile e Finale for Bassoon and Piano, Sheheresade for Oboe and Piano; Symphonic: Crux, from texts from The Bible, for Boy Soprano, Tenor, Bass, Reciter, Mixed Choir and Orchestra, Concerto for Piano and Orchestra, Symphony for Jazz Band or Soloist improvising and Symphonic Orchestra, Missa Pro Defunctis, Requiem, for Voices, Choir and Orchestra; Chamber Music: Imitations for Flute, Oboe, Bassoon and Percussion, Oberek for Brass Quintet, In The Circus for 2 Pianos, Songs On The Lapse Of Time for Bass/Baritone/Oboe and Percussion, Classic Quartet for String, Black And White for 2 String Orchestras, Happy Sorrow for 5 Musicians, Rhapsody, in suite form, for Percussion, Piano and Percussion Group, Variations for Violin and Cello, Dialogues for Viola and Bassoon, Trio for Clarinet, Bassoon and Piano, Alarm for Voice, Dock and Chamber Ensemble, Elegia for Voice and Piano, 1993. *Address:* 40-866 ul Piastow 7-3, Osiedle 1000 Iecia, Katowice, Poland.

BUSCHING, Rainer; Singer (Bass); b. 1943, Halle/Saale, Germany. *Education:* Studied at the Felix Mendelssohn Bartholdy Academy of Music, Leipzig; Examination as opera and concert singer, 1972. *Career:* Guest appearances in Germany then engaged at Landestheater Dessau, 1973–85; Member of the Soloist ensemble at Dresden Staatsoper from 1985 notably as Wagner's Daland, Landgrave and King Henry, Verdi's Zaccaria, Ramphis and Padre Guardiano, Mozart's Sarastro and Commendatore, Weber's Lysiart and Kaspar, Basilio in Il Barbiere di Siviglia, Handel's Giulio Cesare and Gremin in Eugene Onegin; Guest appearances in Italy, Netherlands, Austria, Poland, Brazil and Russia; Sang Sarastro at Lubeck, 1992, at the reopening of the Chemnitz Opera; Season 2000 at the Semper Oper Dresden, as Sarastro and the Minister in Fidelio; Concert repertory includes St John and Matthew Passions by Bach, Messiah, Die Schöpfung and Jahreszeiten by Haydn, and Schubert's Winterreise. *Address:* c/o Dresden Staatsoper, 01069 Dresden, Germany.

BUSSE, Barry; Singer (Tenor); b. 18 Aug. 1946, Gloversville, NY, USA. *Education:* Studied at Oberlin College and the Manhattan School of Music. *Career:* Has sung as tenor from 1977 in Carlisle Floyd's Of Mice and Men at Houston; Created Bothwell in Musgrave's Mary, Queen of Scots for Virginia Opera in 1977 and repeated the role at the New York City Opera in 1980; Sang at Santa Fe in 1979 as Alwa in the US

premiere of the 3 act version of Lulu; European debut in 1982 as Don José for Netherlands Opera; Further appearances in Toulouse, San Francisco, Santa Fe and Miami; Seattle Opera in 1985 as Siegmund in Die Walküre; Sang Tichon in Katya Kabanova at Florence in 1988 and at Geneva in 1989; Sang Mephistopheles and Agrippa in Prokofiev's Fiery Angel at the Holland Festival in 1990; Other roles include Florestan, Cavardossi, Canio, Parsifal at Toulouse in 1987, Peter Grimes, Narraboth, Apollo in Daphne, Pollione and Massenet's Des Grieux; Created the title role in Nosferatu by Randolph Peters, Toronto, 1995; Sang Louis Sullivan in Daron Hagen's The Shining Bow, Chicago, 1998. *Recordings include:* Mary Queen of Scots. *Address:* c/o Seattle Opera Association, PO Box 9248, Seattle, WA 98109, USA.

BUSSI, Francesco; Musician and Musicologist; b. 14 Sept. 1926, Piacenza, Italy; m. Maria Villa, 20 July 1957, 1 s., 1 d. *Education:* Laurea in Lettere Classiche, 1948; Diploma di Pianoforte, 1949; Diploma di Paleografia Musicale, 1953; Diploma di Musica Corale, 1955. *Career:* Docente di Storia ed Estetica Musicale at Conservatorio di Parma, 1955–59; Docente di Storia ed Estetica Musicale at Conservatorio di Piacenza e Bibliotecario, 1959–; mem, SIDM; AIBM; AMS; Membro Effettivo della Deputazione di Storia Patria per le Province Parmensi; Socio Onorario del Rotary Club Piacenza-Farnese, 1993–. *Recordings:* Francesco Cavalli, Missa Pro Defunctis (Requiem) a 8 Voci, con il responsorio Libera me, Domine a 5 Voci, 1985; Gasparo Villani, Gratiarum Actiones a 20 Voci, 1993. *Publications:* Antifonario-Graduale di S Antonino in Piacenza; Umanità e Arte di G Parabosco; Catalogo dell' Archivio Musicale del Duomo di Piacenza; La Musica Sacra di F Cavalli in rapporto a Monteverdi; Storia, Tradizione e Arte nel Requiem di Cavalli; L'Opera Veneziana dalla Morte di Monteverdi alla Fine del '600; Tutti I Lieder di Johannes Brahms, 1999. *Contributions:* Jone di Chio; Il Cantore Spagnolo Pedro Valenzuela; Le 'Toscanelle' di Gabriele Villani; La Musica Strumentale di J Brahms; Tutti i lieder di J Brahms; Altro Cavalli Sacro Restituito; New Grove Dictionary of Music and Musicians; New Grove Dictionary of Opera; MGG; DEUMM and many others; Moderna Edizione Critica di Pezzi di Girolamo Parabosco, del Requiem di Cavalli, delle Toscanelle e delle Gratiarum Actiones di Villani, delle Composizioni Sacre di G. Allevi detto Piacenza;, di Altri Pezzi Sacri e dei 3 Vesperi di Cavalli; Edizione Italiana dei Voll 2, 4 and 5 della New Oxford History of Music; Storia di Piacenza, 1980, 1984, 1997. *Honours:* S Antonino d'oro, 1990; Premio internazionale L Illica, 1991–; Piacentino Benemerito, 1998. *Address:* Strada Guastafredda, 45-29100 Piacenza, Italy.

BUSSOTTI, Sylvano; Composer, Painter, Film Director and Stage Designer; b. 1 Oct. 1931, Florence, Italy. *Education:* Florence Conservatory, 1940–45, with Dallapiccola, Maglioni and Lupi; Private composition studies, 1949–56; Studied with Deutsch in Paris; Darmstadt courses with Cage; USA, 1964–65 on Rockefeller Foundation Grant. *Career:* Appearances at music festivals from 1958; Co-Founder of the exhibition Musica e Segno, seen in Europe and USA, 1962; Exhibited his own paintings in Italy, US, Japan, France and Germany; Director and Designer of stage works including his own; Professor of Music Drama at the L'Aquila Academy of Fine Arts Scuola di Musica di Fiesole, 1971–74; Director of the Teatro La Fenice, Venice, 1975; Director, The Puccini Festival, Torre del Lago, 1981–1985; Bussotti opera-ballet, Scuola Spettacolo, 1984–92; Designs and Production for La Bohème, Turandot, Trittico La Fanciulla del West (Puccini); Aida, Ballo in Maschera, Un giorno di regno, Rigoletto (Verdi); Ulisse (Dallapiccola); Otello, Barbiere (Rossini); Carmen (Bizet); Cavalleria Rusticana (Mascagni); Pagliacci (Leoncavallo) and La Gioconda, Genoa and Florence. *Compositions include:* Stage: Tema-Variazioni, Geographie Francaise, 1956, Raramente, mystery play, 1971, Bergkristall, ballet, 1974, Nottetempo, lyric drama, 1976, Le Racine, 1980, Fedra, lyric tragedy, 1988; L'Ispirazione, 1988; Satiresca, 1993, Tieste, 1993; Quartettino di Miniature, 1996; Concert: El Carbonero for 5 Voices, 1957, Breve for Ondes Martenot, 1958, Sette Fogli, 1959, Phrase A Trois for String Trio, 1960, Torso for Solo Voices and Orchestra, 1960–63, Rara for Guitar and String Trio, 1964–67, Julio Organum Julii for Speaker and Organ, 1968, I Semi Di Gramsci for String Quartet and Orchestra, 1962–71, Novelletta for Piano, 1962–73, Opus Cygne for Orchestra, 1979; Concerto a L'Aquila for piano and 9 instruments, 1986; Furioso, for mezzo and orchestra, 1994; Lingue Ignote for voices and chamber orchestra, 1994; Madrelingua, 1994; Modello for violin and orchestra, 1998. *Honours:* First Prize, Italian Section ISCM, 1965, 1972; DAAD, Berlin, 1972; Commandeur l'Ordre des Arts et des Lettres. *Address:* Via di Colle Marta 1, 2, 00030 Genazzano (RM), Italy.

BUSTERUD, James; Singer (Baritone); b. 1957, USA. *Career:* Sang Dandini in La Cenerentola at Philadelphia, 1986; Season 1987 as Malatesta in Don Pasquale and Mercutio in Roméo et Juliette at Washington; Santa Fe Opera as Sharpless in Butterfly, in Strauss's Friedenstag and Feuersnot; American premiere of Judith Weir's A Night at the Chinese Opera, 1989; Sang Don Ferdinand in Gerhard's The Duenna, Wexford, 1989; In Turandot for Miami Opera; Glimmerglass Opera, 1994 as Robert in Tchaikovsky's Iolanta and Portland Opera, 1996; As Bassiano in Le Marchand de Venise by Reynaldo Hahn. *Recordings:* Schaunard in La Bohème. *Address:* c/o Portland Opera Assn Inc, 1516 South West Alder Street, Portland OR 97205, USA.

BUSWELL, James Oliver, IV; Violinist, Conductor and Teacher; b. 4 Dec. 1946, Fort Wayne, IN, USA. *Education:* BA, Harvard College, 1970; Studied violin with Ivan Galamian at Juilliard School of Music, NY. *Career:* Debut: Violinist, St Louis in 1963; New York recital debut at Philharmonic Hall in 1967; Soloist with various orchestras, recitalist and chamber music player; Appearances as conductor; Visiting Professor at University of Arizona, Tucson, 1972–73; Teacher, Indiana University School of Music, Bloomington, 1974–86, and New England Conservatory of Music, Boston, 1986–; Former Member, Buswell Parnas Luvisi Trio; Television host for Stations of Bach on PBS Television. *Address:* c/o New England Conservatory of Music, 290 Huntington Avenue, Boston, MA 02115, USA.

BUTLER, Mark; Canadian/British violinist and chamber music coach; b. 5 Feb. 1949. *Education:* Royal Coll. of Music with Leonard Hirsch. *Career:* co-leader, Ulster Orchestra, 1970–71; BBC debut in 1971, London debut in 1972; solo recitals in the UK and Canada; Second Violinist of the Chilingirian Quartet, 1971–92; resident, Quartet of Liverpool Univ., 1973–76, Sussex Univ., 1978–92, and Royal Coll. of Music, 1986–92; annual series of concerts at the Queen Elizabeth Hall and Wigmore Hall; performances at the Edinburgh, Bath and Aldeburgh Festivals, Munich Herkulessaal, Amsterdam Concertgebouw, Zürich Tonhalle, Vienna Konzerthaus, and Stockholm Konserthuset; New York debut, 1976; tours of USA, Canada, Australia, New Zealand, South America and the Far East; represented the UK at the New York International Festival Quartet Series; television and radio appearances throughout Europe on national public radio in USA, and the BBC; mem., Acad. of St Martin-in-the-Fields, 1995–. *Recordings:* The Ten Great Mozart Quartets; Late Schubert Quartets; Debussy and Ravel Quartets; Elgar Quartet and Piano Quintet; Schubert Cello Quintet and Octet; Mozart Clarinet Quintet; Complete Quartets of Bartók and Dvořák; Bartók Piano Quintet. *Address:* c/o Academy of St Martin-in-the-Fields, Raine House, Raine Street, London, E1 9RG, England.

BUTLER, Martin, BMus, PPRNCM, MFA, FRNCM; British composer and professor of music; b. 1 March 1960, Hampshire, England. *Education:* Winchester School of Art, University of Manchester, Royal Northern College of Music, Princeton University, USA. *Compositions include:* From an Antique Land for ensemble, 1982; Concertino for chamber orchestra, 1983; Dance Fragments for ensemble, 1984; Cavalcade for orchestra, 1985; Tin Pan Ballet, 1986, arranged as Ballet con Salsa, 1987; Bluegrass Variations for violin, 1987; Piano Piano for 2 pianos and tape, 1988; Graffiti for tape, 1989; Jazz Machines for ensemble, 1990; O Rio, for full orchestra, 1990; Chaconne, for solo oboe, 1991; Down Hollow Winds, for wind quintet, 1991; Going with the Grain, for solo marimba and ensemble, 1992; On the Rocks, for solo piano, 1992; Still Breathing, for wind orchestra, 1992; Craig's Progress, opera, 1994; A Better Place, opera, 1999; Suzanne's River Song, for violin and piano, 1999. *Recordings:* Tin Pan Ballet; O Rio. *Publications:* Craig's Progress, 1994. *Address:* Repertoire Promotion Department, Oxford University Press, 70 Baker Street, London, W1U 7DN, England. *E-mail:* repertoire.promotion.uk@oup.com.

BUTT, John, MA, PhD, FRCO (CHM), FRSE, ADCM; Musician, Musicologist and University Professor; b. 17 Nov. 1960, Solihull, England; m. Sally; three s. one d. *Education:* Solihull School; King's College, Univ. of Cambridge. *Career:* Organ Scholar, King's College, Cambridge, 1979–82; Lecturer, University of Aberdeen, 1986–87; Research Fellow, Magdalene College, Cambridge, 1987–89; Professor of Music and University Organist, University of California, Berkeley, 1989–97; Lecturer, Univ. of Cambridge, Fellow of King's College, 1997–2001; Gardiner Professor of Music, University of Glasgow, 2001–; mem. Royal Society of Edinburgh, Royal Musical Association, Royal College of Organists, American Musicological Society. *Recordings:* 11 organ and harpsichord recordings for Hamonia Mundi; Telemann: Fantasies, 1999; Bach: Organ Toccatas, 2000; Elgar: Organ Works, 2002. *Publications include:* Cambridge Companion to Bach, 1997; Playing with History, 2002. *Honours:* W. H. Scheide Prize of the American Bach Society, 1991; Dent Medal, 2003. *Address:* University of Glasgow, 14 University Gardens, Glasgow, G12 8QQ, Scotland (office). *Telephone:* (141) 3304571 (office). *Fax:* (141) 3303518 (office). *E-mail:* j.butt@music.gla.ac.uk (office). *Website:* www.gla.ac.uk/department/music (office).

BUTTERFIELD, Adrian; violinist and viola d'amore player; b. 1965, England. *Career:* many appearances as soloist and director with modern and period-instrument ensembles; concert master and associate director of the London Handel Orchestra (London Handel and Tilford Bach Festivals); Engagements with the Brandenburg Consort, Parley of Instruments and Stuttgart Baroque Orchestra (Mozart's Concertante,

K364); Soloist in Bach's Concerto for two violins, with performances from Telemann to Mendelssohn, for BBC and on tour in Europe; Founder of London Handel Players, with concert at St George's Hanover Square, 2000; Concerto Accademico by Vaughan Williams, Three Choirs Festival 2001. *Recordings include:* String quartets by Boccherini and Donizetti. *Address:* c/o Royal College of Music, Prince Consort Road, London SW7, England.

BUTTERLEY, Nigel (Henry); Composer and Pianist; b. 13 May 1935, Sydney, Australia. *Compositions include:* Chamber Music: String Quartets No. 1, 1965, No. 2, 1974, No. 3, 1979, No. 4, 1995; Trio for Clarinet, Cello and Piano, 1979; Forest I for Viola and Piano, 1990; The Wind Stirs Gently, for flute and cello, 1992; Forest II, for trumpet and piano, 1993; Radiophonic: Watershore, 1978; Piano: Uttering Joyous Leaves, 1981; Lawrence Hargrave Flying Alone, 1981; Il Gubbo, 1987; Vocal: The True Samaritan, 1958; First Day Covers (with Barry Humphries), 1973; Sometimes with One I Love, 1976; The Owl, 1983; There came a Wind like a Bugle, Emily Dickinson, 1987; The Woven Light for Soprano and Orchestra, Kathleen Raine, 1994; Spring's Ending, Du Fu, 1997; Spell of Creation for choir, soloists and orchestra, 2000; Paradise Unseen for 6 solo voices, 2001; Orchestral: Meditations of Thomas Traherne, 1968; Violin Concerto, 1970; Fire in the Heavens, 1973; Symphony, 1980; Goldengrove, 1982; In Passing, 1982; From Sorrowing Earth, 1991; Poverty, 1992. Opera: Lawrence Hargrave Flying Alone, 1988. *Recordings include:* Violin Concerto; Meditations of Thomas Traherne; Goldengrove; From Sorrowing Earth; The Owl; Laudes; Letter from Hardy's Bay; Uttering Joyous Leaves; String Quartet No. 3; The True Samaritan; There came a Wind like a Bugle. *Honours:* Italia Prize for In the head the fire, 1966; Member of Order of Australia, 1991; Lowin Prize for Spell of Creation, 2001. *Current Management:* Tall Poppies Management, PO Box 373, Glebe, NSW 2037, Australia. *Address:* 57 Temple Street, Stanmore, NSW 2048, Australia. *E-mail:* nigelbut@bigpond.net.au.

BUTTERWORTH, Arthur Eckersley, MBE; British composer and conductor; b. 4 Aug. 1923, Manchester; m.; two d. *Education:* Royal Manchester College of Music. *Career:* trumpeter, Scottish National Orchestra, 1949–55; Hallé Orchestra, 1955–62; Conductor, Huddersfield Philharmonic Orchestra, 1962–93; Guest Conductor, various orchestras, 1965–. *Compositions:* Symphony No. 1, 1957; Symphony No. 2, 1965; Symphony No. 3, 1979; Symphony No. 4, 1986; Symphony No. 5, 2002; Violin Concerto; Viola Concerto; Cello Concerto; Concertos for organ, bassoon and trumpet; Piano Trio, 1983; String Quartet, 1998; Organ Sonata, 1999; Mist on the Marshes for soprano, piano and double bass, 1999; Haworth Moor, choral suite, 2000; Guitar Concerto, 2000; Various large scale and shorter orchestral works; Symphonic works for brass band, chamber music. *Recordings include:* Symphony No. 1 (Munich Symphony Orchestra), 1998; Romanza for Horn and Orchestra (CBC (Vancouver) Orchestra), 1998; The Path Across the Moors (Royal Ballet Sinfonia), 1999; Summer Music (Bassoon Concerto, Royal Ballet Sinfonia), 2001. *Address:* Comus Edition, Heirs House Lane, Colne, Lancashire, BB8 9TA, England (office); Pohjola, Dales Avenue, Embsay, Skipton, North Yorkshire, BD23 6PE, England.

BUTTERWORTH, Neil; British fmr composer, conductor, writer and broadcaster; b. 4 Sept. 1934, London; m. Anne Mary Barnes 1960; three d. *Education:* Univ. of London, Guildhall School of Music, London, Univ. of Nottingham. *Career:* Lecturer, Kingston Polytechnic, 1960–68; Head of Music, Napier College, Edinburgh, 1968–87; Conductor, Edinburgh Schools Choir, 1968–72; Glasgow Orchestral Society, 1975–83, 1989–2002, Edinburgh Chamber Orchestra, 1983–85; music critic, Times Educational Supplement 1993–97; mem. PRS, Incorporated Society of Musicians, Scottish Society of Composers. *Compositions:* 2 horn concertos; Overture Budapest; A Scott Cantata; Dunblane; In Memory Auschwitz; Partita; Dances for Dalkeith; Count Dracula (opera); many songs and instrumental works. *Publications:* Haydn, 1970; Dvořák, 1978; Dictionary of American Composers, 1984; Aaron Copland, 1985; Vaughan Williams, 1990; Neglected Music, 1991; The American Symphony, 1998; contrib. to Classic CD, Classical Music, Musical Opinion, The Scotsman, The Herald. *Honours:* Hon FLCM; Conducting prize, GSM, 1961; Churchill Travelling Fellowship, 1967. *Address:* The Lodge, 42 East High Street, Greenlaw, Duns, Berwickshire, TD10 6UF, Scotland (home). *Telephone:* (1361) 840408 (home).

BUWALDA, Sytse; Singer (Counter-Tenor); b. 28 Sept. 1965, Zuiderwoude, Netherlands. *Education:* Private studies; Sweelinck Conservatoire Amsterdam; Masterclasses. *Career:* Regular appearances in baroque and classical opera; Roles in 20th Century operas; Solo ensemble; Worked with some of the world's best known conductors and directors; Performs theatre shows; Performed at Festivals throughout Europe and Japan; Extensive oratorio and concert repertoire from the Renaissance to the present. *Recordings:* Over a hundred solo recordings; Most Bach Cantatas; Compilation albums of arias and songs by various composers; Work with ensembles. *Address:* Laan Nieuwer Amstel 34, 1182 JT Amstelveen, Netherlands.

BYBEE, Luretta; Singer (mezzo-contralto); b. 1965, Midland, Texas, USA. *Career:* Has sung widely in the USA and Europe as Isabella (Cologne and Dublin), Cherubino, Falliero in the US premiere of Rossini's Bianca e Falliero, Meg Page, Farnaces in Mozart's Mitridate at Wexford, Orlofsky, Nicklausse and Maddalena (New Orleans); Season 1993–94 as Dalila with Indianapolis Opera; Recent engagements as Carmen for Dayton Opera (following earlier appearances in Peter Brook's La Tragédie de Carmen), Amneris, Laura (La Gioconda), Venus and Waltraute; Concerts include the Verdi Requiem at Carnegie Hall, Messiah in Texas and the Mozart Requiem at Anchorage, Alaska. *Current Management:* Athole Still International Management, Forresters Hall, 25–27 Westow Street, London, SE19 3RY, England. *Telephone:* (20) 8771-5271. *Fax:* (20) 8768-6600. *Website:* www.atholestill.com.

BYCHKOV, Semyon; Conductor; b. 30 Nov. 1952, Leningrad, Russia; brother of Yakov Kreizberg; m. Tatiana Rozina 1973, 1 s., 1 d. *Education:* Diploma of Honour, Glinka Choir School, Leningrad, 1970; Studied with Ilya Musin and graduated from Leningrad Conservatory in 1974; Artistic Diploma, Mannes College of Music, New York, 1976. *Career:* Music Director, Bonch-Bruyevich Institute Chorus, Leningrad, 1970–72; Conductor of Leningrad Conservatory Symphony and Opera Orchestra, 1972–74; Associate Conductor, Music Director, Mannes College of Music Orchestra, 1976–80; Music Director, Grand Rapids Symphony Orchestra, 1980–85; Associate Conductor, 1980–81, Principal Guest Conductor, 1981–85, Music Director, 1985–89, Buffalo Philharmonic Orchestra; Music Director, Orchestre de Paris, 1989–1998; Guest Conductor with major world orchestras; Led the Orchestre de Paris at the 1991 Promenade Concerts in London; Conducted Beethoven's 5th Piano Concerto, 10th Symphony of Shostakovich and 2nd by Dutilleux, Dances of Galanta and Also Sprach Zarathustra; Parsifal at Florence, 1997, (Idomeneo, 1996); Principal Guest Conductor of the Orchestra of the Maggio Musicale Fiorentino, and of the St Petersburg Philharmonic Orchestra, 1992; Conducted Eugene Onegin at the Théâtre du Châtelet in 1992; Lady Macbeth of Mtsensk at Florence, 1994 and 1998; Tosca at the Munich Bayerische Staatsoper and concerts with the Munich Philharmonic, Staatskapelle Dresden and the Staatskapelle Berlin, 1998; 1998–99 tour of Japan with Cologne Radio Symphony Orchestra; Chief Conductor, Radio Symphony Orchestra of the West German Broadcasting Company in Cologne, 1999–; Chief Conductor of the Semperoper in Dresden, 1999–; Engaged for Strauss's Daphne at the Vienna Staatsoper, 2004. *Recordings:* More than 20 albums since 1985 with orchestras such as the Berlin Philharmonic, London Philharmonic and the Orchestre de Paris. *Honours:* 1st Prize, Rachmaninov Conducting Competition, 1973; Caecilia Award, Belgium, 1988; Echo Deutscher Schallplattenpreis, 1993. *Address:* c/o Pamela McCormick, 41A Stamford Road, London N1 4 JP, England.

BYERS, David; Composer; b. 26 Jan. 1947, Belfast, Northern Ireland. *Education:* Studied at Queen's University Belfast, 1965–67, and at the Royal Academy, London, 1968–71; Further study with Henri Pousseur in Liège, 1972–73. *Career:* Producer for BBC Northern Ireland, 1977–. *Compositions include:* Woyzeck, incidental music, 1986; Polyphony for ensemble, 1975; Dodecaphony, for two organs, 1980; At the Still Point of the Turning World, for string quartet, 1981; Caliban's Masque, for Wind Band, 1982; A Planxty for the Dancer, for orchestra, 1983; The Wren's Blether, for voices and ensemble, 1984; The Moon is Our Breathing for narrator and ensemble, 1985; Columba and the Crane, for tuba and tape, 1985; The Deer's Horn, for oboe and cello, 1988; The Journey of the Magi, for string quartet, 1990; Out of the Night, for orchestra, 1991; Medea, incidental music, 1991; Toccata: la morte d'Orfeo for Orchestra, 1996; Epigrams for piano, 1998. *Address:* c/o British Music Information Centre, 11 Stratford Place, London W1, England.

BYERS, Reginald; Singer (Tenor); b. 5 Dec. 1934, Sydney, Australia. *Education:* Sydney Conservatory and in Austria. *Career:* Debut: As Cavaradossi with Australian Opera at Sydney; Guest appearances in New York City Opera and with Scottish Opera in Glasgow; Many engagements with opera companies in Australia; Other roles have included Verdi's Radames, Ismaele in Nabucco, Gabriele Adorno, Riccardo, Alfredo and Don Carlos, Faust, Turiddu, Rodolfo, Dick Johnson, Calaf, Steva in Jenůfa and Bacchus in Ariadne auf Naxos; After retirement from stage, gave concerts and taught in Sydney. *Address:* c/o Sydney Opera House, Sydney, New South Wales, Australia.

BYLES, Edward; Singer (Tenor); b. 1935, Ebbw Vale, Wales. *Career:* Debut: Glyndebourne 1957, as Brighella in Ariadne auf Naxos; Toured with Opera For All and sang with major companies including Royal Opera and in Europe, Russia, Australia and Ireland; Joined English National Opera in 1974 with roles including Monostatos, Mime, Missail in Boris Godunov and Vitek in The Makropulos Case; Has sung in Tosca, War and Peace, Madama Butterfly, Orpheus in the Underworld and Pacific Overtures; In 1988 took part in the first British performance of Rimsky-Korsakov's Christmas Eve; Season 1992 with English National

Opera as the Broomstick-maker in Königskinder and Trabuco in The Force of Destiny; Spoletta in Tosca for ENO, 1994. *Address:* c/o English National Opera, London Coliseum, St Martin's Lane, London WC2N 4ES, England.

BYLSMA, Anner; Cellist and Teacher; b. 17 Feb. 1934, The Hague, Netherlands. *Education:* Studied with Carel Boomkamp, Royal Conservatory of Music, The Hague. *Career:* Principal Cellist, Concertgebouw Orchestra, Amsterdam, 1962–68; Toured throughout the world as Soloist with orchestras; Recitalist and Chamber-music player; British debut, Wigmore Hall, 1963; Many trio appearances with Frans Brueggen and Gustav Leonhardt; Teacher, Royal Conservatory of Music, The Hague; Sweelinck Conservatory, Amsterdam; Erasmus Scholar, Harvard University, 1982; Played Cello Suites by Bach, BBC Lunchtime Concert, 1992. *Recordings:* Numerous recordings including Angel-EMI; Das Alte Werk; Decca London; Harmonia Mundi; Philips; Pro Arte; RCA; Teldec; Telefunken. *Honours:* Winner, Pablo Casals Competition, Mexico City, 1959; Prix d'excellence, Royal Conservatory of Music, 1957. *Address:* c/o Byers Schwalbe & Associates Inc, One Fifth Avenue, New York, NY 10003, USA.

BYRNE, Connell; Singer (Tenor); b. 1936, Australia. *Education:* Studied in Australia, Italy and London. *Career:* Sang in such small London companies as Group Eight and Philiopera Circle, from 1961; Member of the Brunswick Opera, 1963–64, Mannheim Opera from 1965; Appearances at Graz and Berne from 1969 and at Bremen until 1980; Member of the Deutsche Oper am Rhein at Dusseldorf, 1976–82; Guest appearances at Sadler's Wells, London, 1968, as Walther in The Mastersingers, at Barcelona (Aegisthus, 1970), Turin (Tristan, 1976), the Vienna Staatsoper (Laca and Cavaradossi) and Dublin; Other roles include Erik, Lohengrin, Rienzi, Tannhäuser, Parsifal, Bacchus, Don Carlos and Don José. *Address:* c/o Deutsche Oper am Rhein, Heinrich-Heine-Allee 16a, D–40213 Dusseldorf, Germany.

BYRNE, Desmond; Singer (Bass-baritone); b. 1965, Montreal, Canada. *Education:* McGill University, Montreal, 1989. *Career:* Season 1989–90 as Leporello at Aldeburgh, under Steuart Bedford, Silvano (Un Ballo in Maschera) at Montreal and Melisso in Alcina at Vancouver; Season 1991–92 with Leporello at Seattle, Ravel/Poulenc double bill at the Paris Châtelet, The Dream of Gerontius with the Orchestre National de France, Masetto in Vancouver and Monterone (Rigoletto) at the Opéra Bastille; Further engagements in Lucia di Lammermoor at Tours, Massenet's Panurge in St Etienne and Gounod's Romeo in Toulouse (1993–1994). Sang in Gluck's Armide at Hamburg (1996), as Mozart's Figaro in Dublin and Massenet's Sancho Panza in Nantes (1997); Britten's Bottom in Strasbourg (1998), Créon in Enescu's Oedipe, in Paris and Bucharest, and Thoas in Iphigénie en Tauride at Nantes (1999); Season 2000–01 with Rangoni in Boris Godunov, and Balstrode in Peter Grimes at Tours. *Address:* c/o Musicglotz, 11 rue Le Verrier, 75006 Paris, France.

BYRNE, Elizabeth; Singer (Soprano); b. 1965, Lancashire, England. *Education:* Royal Northern College of Music and National Opera Studio, London. *Career:* Appearances with English National Opera as Oksana in the British premiere of Rimsky's Christmas Eve (1988), Amelia (A Masked Ball) and Madama Butterfly; Tosca, Bianca in Macmillan's Ines de Castro and Brünnhilde in Die Walküre (2001) for Scottish Opera; Aida for Welsh National Opera and Turandot for Mid-Wales Opera; Engagements with Lyric Opera Chicago as Tosca, Wagner's Gutrune, and Elena/Margherita in Mefistofele; Season 2000/2001 as Salome for Glimmerglass Opera, The Duchess of Parma in Busoni's Faust at the Met and Puccini's Minnie for Austin Lyric Opera; Sang Brünnhilde in Siegfried for Scottish Opera, 2002. *Address:* c/o Scottish Opera, 39 Elmbank Crescent, Glasgow, G2 4PT, Scotland.

BYRNE, Peter, ARCM, BMus, MMus; British musicologist and academic and director of music; b. 21 Nov. 1932, Grimsby; m. Anne J. Lavery; one s. two d. *Education:* Nat. Youth Orchestra of GB, Royal Coll. of Music, Goldsmiths Coll., London. *Career:* Dir of Music, Cardinal Wiseman School, Ealing 1959–64, Salvatorian Coll., Harrow 1965–79, Wimbledon Coll., Merton 1979–84; Prin. Lecturer, Goldsmiths Coll., London 1979–87; Academic Prof., Royal Mil. School of Music, London 1986–94; Organist and Choirmaster, Holy Ghost and St Stephen, Shepherds Bush 1960–63, St Benedict's Abbey, Ealing 1963–68; Musical Dir, Cecilians Operatic Soc., Ealing 1969–74; mem. Inst. of Advanced Musical Studies, King's Coll., London 1974–87; mem. Royal Musical Asscn. *Compositions:* Christopher Marlowe (opera) 1972. *Publications:* edn of seven works of Marc-Antoine Charpentier: H394 In Honorem Caeciliae Valeriani et Tiburtii canticum, H397 Caecilia virgo et martyr octo voc[ibus], H413 Caecilia virgo et martyr [I], H415 Caecilia virgo et martyr [II], H415a Prologue de la Ste Caecile après l'ouverture[:] Harmonia coelestis, H240 Motet: O sacrum [convivium] p[ou]r trois religieuses, H491 Dances from Medée [string orchestra]; Les Puys de musique d'Évreux. *Address:* Westgate House, Westgate, Louth, LN11 9YQ, England (home). *Telephone:* (1507) 354388/215 (home).

BYRNES, Garrett; Composer; b. 30 Dec. 1971, Bad Kreuznach, Rhein-land-Pfalz, Germany. *Education:* Bachelor of Music, Composition, Boston Conservatory, 1995; Master of Music, Composition, Peabody Conservatory of Music, 1999; DMA, Indiana University, in progress. *Compositions include:* Orchestral Music: Concertino for Two Cellos and String Orchestra, 1994; Concerto for Cello and Orchestra, 1997; Nordic Realms (Chamber Symphony No. 1), 1998; Episodes for String Orchestra, 1998; Flames of Imbolc, 1999; Dearg Gaelach for orchestra, 2000; Nor'easter: Study for Orchestra, 2001; Chamber Music: Wraps, music for ballet for oboe, 2 clarinets and string quartet, 1994; Impressions of the Ocean, for flute, violin and piano, 1995; Introduction and Scherzo for violin and cello, 1997; Three Pieces for flute and guitar, 1999; Visions in Twilight for solo harp, 2000; Vocal Music: Sketch of the Peternera, song cycle for soprano and guitar, text by Lorca, 1995; Two Poems of Robert Frost, for flute, soprano, vibraphone and cello, 1998; Twilight Night, for treble voice and piano, text by Christina Rossetti, 1999; Solo Instrumental Music: Three Pieces for Solo Flute, 1993; Sonata for solo violoncello, 1993; Sonata for Violin Solo, 1994; Nanna's Lament for solo viola, 1999; Piano Music: Fantasy for Piano, 1994; Piano Sonata, 1995; Suite for Piano, 1995; Miniature Pictures, 1996. *Address:* 3188 Braeside Drive, Bloomington, IN 47408, USA.

BYRNES-HARRIS, Aleicia; Singer (Soprano); b. 1950, Toronto, Ontario, Canada. *Education:* Studied in California, at Aspen and the San Diego Opera Studio. *Career:* Sang at first in San Diego and Los Angeles as Santuzza, Magda in The Consul and Mme Lidoine in The Carmelites; European engagements from 1981, notably at Oldenburg, Wiesbaden, Nürnberg and Hamburg as Butterfly, Desdemona, Marie in Wozzeck, Irene in Rienzi, Amelia in Ballo in Maschera, Leonore, the Dyer's Wife, Kundry and Isolde; Tosca, Senta, Elektra (Elektra), Ariadne, Rosalinde; Appeared at Zürich and Munich National Theatre; Title role in Aida by Verdi, Los Angeles Music Center Opera; Die Sängerin in Reigen by Boesmans, Vienna Modern Music Festival. *Address:* Zimmerstr. 12, 10969 Berlin, Germany.

BYRON, Michael, BA; composer; b. 7 Sept. 1953, Chicago, IL, USA. *Education:* California Institute of the Arts with Mario Guarneri, Thomas Stevens and Joe Higgins; York University, ON. *Career:* active on behalf of other US composers; works in collaboration with the performance art group, Maple Sugar. *Compositions include:* Song Of The Lifting Up Of The Head for Piano, 1972; Starfields for Piano 4 Hands, 1974; Morning Glory for Percussion, 1975; Marimbas, 1976; A Living Room At The Bottom Of A Lake for Orchestra, 1977; Music for 1 Piano, 1978; Three Mirrors for Percussion Ensemble, 1979; Music Of Steady Light; 158 Pieces for Strings, 1979–82; Tidal for Ensemble, 1981; Double String Quartet, 1984. *Honours:* Grants from York University, the Ontario Arts Council, The National Endowment for The Arts and The New York State Council of The Arts.

C

CABALLÉ, Monserrat; singer (soprano); b. 12 April 1933, Barcelona, Spain; m. Bernabé Marti, 1964, 1 s. *Education:* Conservatorio del Liceo; Studied under Eugenia Kemeny, Conchita Badia and Maestro Annovazi. *Career:* Debut: Mimi in La Bohème, State Opera of Basel, 1956; North American debut, Manon, Mexico City in 1964; US debut in Lucrezia Borgia at Carnegie Hall, 1965; Appeared at Glyndebourne Festival as the Marschallin in Der Rosenkavalier and the Countess in the Marriage of Figaro, 1965; Metropolitan Opera debut as Marguerite in Faust, 1965; Appeared frequently at Metropolitan Opera and other US opera houses; Has performed in most leading opera houses in Europe including Gran Teatro del Liceo, La Scala, Vienna Staatsoper, Paris and Rome Operas; Covent Garden debut in 1972 as Violetta; Had repertoire of over 40 roles; Sang Hypermestra in Salieri's Les Danaides at Perugia, 1983; Rome Opera in 1986 in title role of Spontini's Agnes di Hohenstaufen; Pesaro and Barcelona in 1987 as Rossini's Ermione and Pacini's Saffo; Vienna Staatsoper in 1988 as Mme Cortese in Il Viaggio a Reims; Barcelona in 1989 in La Fiamma by Respighi and the premiere of Cristobal Col ón by Balada; Sang Mme Cortese in a new production of Il Viaggio a Reims at Covent Garden in 1992; Vatican Concert 1994; Llangollen International Festival, 1997; Sang Catherine of Aragon in Henry VIII by Saint-Saëns at Barcelona, 2002. *Recordings:* Lucrezia Borgia; La Traviata; Salome; Aida. *Honours:* Most Excellent and Illustrious Dobna and Cross of Isabella the Catholic. *Current Management:* Columbia Artists Management Inc. *Address:* c/o Columbia Artists Management Inc, 165 West 57th Street, New York, NY 10019, USA.

CABLE, Margaret; Singer (Mezzo-Soprano); b. 1950, England. *Career:* Appearances in Europe, Scandinavia, Israel and the USA; Festival engagements at the Bath and Three Choirs Festivals; Promenade Concerts in London; Performances in Baroque repertoire with ensembles, using original instruments, including Bach's St Matthew Passion under Andrew Parrott and Messiah at the 1985 Lucerne Festival under Christopher Hogwood; Broadcasts include Handel's Belshazzar, Tippett's A Child of Our Time, works with orchestra by Arthur Bliss and Robin Holloway; Stage roles with Kent Opera included Mrs Grose in The Turn of The Screw, Dorabella, and Marcellina in Le nozze di Figaro, also at the 1986 Vienna International Festival; Sang Juno in Handel's Semele at York Early Music Festival in 1991; Sang in Bach's St John Passion at the Festival Hall, London, 1997. *Recordings include:* Haydn Masses with the Academy of Ancient Music; Madrigals directed by Peter Pears; Works by Mozart and Scarlatti directed by George Guest; Glazunov Songs and Lux Aeterna by William Mathias, with the Bach Choir; Handel's Carmelite Vespers and Messiah with Andrew Parrott and The Taverner Players.

CACHEMAILLE, Gilles; Singer (bass-baritone); b. 25 Nov. 1951, Orbe, Switzerland. *Education:* Lausanne Conservatoire. *Career:* concert hall appearances 1978–, at the Aix and Salzburg Festivals, at Paris, Lyon, Buenos Aires, Madrid, Strasbourg, Lisbon and Tokyo; repertoire has included the Passions of Bach, L'Enfance du Christ by Berlioz, Franck's Les Béatitudes, Haydn's Schöpfung and Jahreszeiten, works by Monteverdi and songs by Duparc, Poulenc, Schubert and Strauss; debut as mem. of the Lyon Opéra in the stage premiere of Rameau's Les Boréades at Aix, 1982; Lausanne Opéra as Guglielmo, Simone in La Finta Semplice, Mozart's Figaro and Papageno, and Belcore in L'Elisir d'amore, 1988; Mézières in 1988 at Gluck's Orpheus, Leporello at the Hamburg Staatsoper in 1987 and Vienna in 1989; sang in Martinů's Les Trois Souhaits at Lyon, 1990, and Leporello at Houston, 1991; sang Don Giovanni at Glyndebourne, 1994; Merlin in Chausson's Le Roi Arthus, at the Bregenz Festival, 1996; Leporello at Aix-en-Provence, 1998; sang Leporello at Toronto, Figaro (Mozart) at Barcelona and Don Alfonso for Opéra Lyon, 2000–01. *Recordings include:* L'Enfance du Christ; Chausson's Le Roi Arthus; Iphigénie en Aulide; Les Boréades; Gluck's La Rencontre Imprévue; Dominic in Arabella; Golaud in Pelléas et Mélisande; Guglielmo in Così fan tutte under Harnoncourt; Claudio in Béatrice et Bénédict. *Current Management:* Balmer & Dixon Management AG, Kreuzstrasse 82, 8032 Zürich, Switzerland. *Telephone:* (43) 244-8644. *Fax:* (43) 244-8649. *Website:* www.badix.ch.

CADDY, Ian Graham, LRAM, ARCM, ARAM; British singer (bass baritone); b. 1 March 1947, Southampton, England; m. Kathryn Dorothy Ash 1979 (divorced 1994); one s. two d. *Education:* Royal Acad. of Music. *Career:* debut in London 1974; sang with Opera For All, Kent Opera, New Opera Co., Phoenix Opera, Glyndebourne, Scottish Opera, WNO, Royal Opera Covent Garden, ENO, Houston Grand Opera, Nantes Opera, Vancouver Opera, Teatro la Fenice; opera, oratorio, festivals and recitals throughout the UK and in Austria, Brazil, Canada, at Wexford and Versailles Festivals, in Denmark, Ireland, France, Germany, Hong Kong, Iceland, Netherlands, Spain, USA and Yugoslavia; edited, published, performed and broadcast works by J. S. Mayr and Donizetti; staging dir of baroque opera in strict period style; numerous TV and radio broadcasts worldwide; runs own publishing title, Caddy Publishing; co-founder The Mayr-Donizetti Collaboration 1985–. *Recordings include:* L'Amor Coniugale by Mayr, Jigs, Reels and Songs of the Bottle by Holbrooke, Vivaldi's Dixit Dominus, Rameau's Princesse de Navarre and Nais, Schoeck's Notturno, Wallace's Maritana. *Video recordings:* Macbeth, The Beggar's Opera, La Fanciulla del West, Intermezzo, Sullivan's The Rose of Persia, Berners's Le Carosse du Saint-Sacrement. *Current Management:* Concert Directory International, Lyndhurst, Denton Road, Ben Rhydding, LS29 8QR, England; Music International, 13 Ardilaun Road, London, N5 2QR, England. *Address:* Convent Lodge, Andover Down, Hampshire SP11 6LR, England.

CADOL, Christine; Singer (Mezzo-Soprano); b. 1956, France. *Education:* Studied at the Paris Conservatoire, where she won a prize for her interpretation of Carmen. *Career:* Debut: 1978; Appearances from 1978 as Dalila at Nantes, Britten's Lucretia at Rouen, Anita in La Navarraise by Massenet at Marseilles, and Suzuki in Madama Butterfly; Further guest engagements at Liège, Limoges and Saint-Cere; Other roles include Meg Page, Waltraute and Marguerite in La Damnation de Faust; Many concert appearances. *Address:* 164 Avenue de la Capelette, 13010 Marseille, France.

CADUFF, Sylvia; Conductor and Professor of Conducting and Orchestral Studies; b. 7 Jan. 1937, Chur, Switzerland. *Education:* Studied at the Conservatoire of Lucerne; Further studies with Karajan at the Berlin Conservatory and with Kubelik, Matacic and Van Otterloo. *Career:* Debut: With the Tonhalle Orchestra, Zürich; Guest Conductor in all the European countries, USA, Japan, South Korea; Appearances with New York Philharmonic, Munich and Berlin Philharmonics, Radio Orchestra Berlin, Royal Philharmonic London; Assistant to Bernstein at the New York Philharmonic, 1966–67; As Music Director in Solingen, 1977–86, was first woman to be appointed Music Director in Europe; Taught conducting at the Berne Conservatory, 1972–77; mem, Swiss Musicians Association; Swiss Conductors Union. *Honours:* 1st Prize, Mitropoulos Competition, New York, 1966. *Address:* Belleriverstrasse 29, 6006 Lucerne, Switzerland.

CAETANI, Oleg; Conductor; b. 1956, Lausanne, Switzerland. *Education:* Studied with Nadia Boulanger, Igor Markevitch (his father), in Rome with Franco Ferrara, in Moscow with Kyrill Kondrashin and in Leningrad with Ilia Mussin. *Career:* Assistant to Otmar Suitner at the Staatsoper Berlin, 1981–84; Deutsche Nationaltheater Weimar, 1984–87; Kapellmeister at the St ädtische Buhnen Frankfurt am Main; Music Director at Wiesbaden, leading the Ring, Tristan und Isolde, La Forza del Destino, Otello, Rimsky's Invisible City of Kitezh and Bluebeard's Castle, 1992–95; Guest engagements with Semiramide in Vienna, Les Vêpres Siciliennes in Nice, Lucia di Lammermoor and Tosca at Trieste and Verdi's Falstaff at Stuttgart, in season 1996–97; Zürich Opera with Rigoletto, The Nutcracker, La Bohème and Norma; Led Tchaikovsky's Maid of Orleans at Strasbourg, 1998; Concert repertory includes music by Beethoven, Schubert, Schumann and Shostakovich, with soloists such as Martha Argerich, Viktoria Mullova, Shlomo Mintz and the late Sviatoslav Richter. *Honours:* Winner of the 1979 RAI Competition in Turin; Prizewinner at the 1982 Herbert von Karajan Competition. *Address:* c/o Opernhaus Zürich, Falkenstrasse 1, 8008 Zürich, Switzerland.

CAFORIO, Armando; Singer (Bass); b. 1956, Civitavecchia, Italy. *Education:* Studied in Alessandria and the USA. *Career:* Debut: Genoa, 1982, as Count Rodolfo in La Sonnambula; Florence, 1983, as Colline in La Bohème, Turin and Martina Franca from 1984; Guest appearances, 1984–85, in Dublin, Geneva, 1987; Torre del Lago and Maggio Musicale Festivals from 1987; Savona, 1990, in L'Ebreo by Apollini; Verona 1993, as Rodolfo in Catalani's Loreley; Other roles include Rossini's Don Magnifico and Basilio, the Grand Inquisitor, and Loredano in Verdi's Due Foscari; Sang Geronte in Manon Lescaut at Catania and Zaccaria in Nabucco at the Verona Arena, 2000. *Address:* c/o Teatro Comunale, Via Solferino 15, 50123 Florence, Italy.

CAHILL, Teresa (Mary); Singer (Lyric Soprano); b. 30 July 1944, Maidenhead, Berkshire, England; Divorced. *Education:* Associate, Guildhall School of Music, Piano; Licentiate, Royal Academy of Music, Singing. *Career:* Debut: Covent Garden, 1970, Barbarina in The Marriage of Figaro; Glyndebourne, 1970, First Lady in Die Zauberflöte; Glyndebourne, the English National Opera; Scottish and Welsh Opera; Covent Garden; Debut at Santa Fe Opera, 1972; La Scala, Milan, 1976, Philadelphia Opera, 1981, roles include Strauss's Sophie, Verdi's Alice Ford and Mozart's Donna Elvira; Sang at Covent Garden, 1970–77 as Zerlina, Sophie and Servilia, and in the 1976 premiere of Henze's We Come to the River; ENO, 1977, as Pauline Le Clerc in the premiere at

Toussaint L'ouverture by David Blake; Sang the title role in Strauss's Daphne, Chelsea Opera, 1990; Concerts include: Edinburgh Festival, Proms, Chicago Symphony Orchestra, Boston Symphony Orchestra, Vienna Festival, Berlin Festival, Hallé Orchestra, Frankfurt Radio Orchestra, Danish Radio Orchestra, Stockholm Philharmonic, BBC Orchestras, English Chamber Orchestra, Royal Liverpool Philharmonic, Houston Symphony Orchestra, Brussels Radio Orchestra, RAI Turin Orchestra, London Sinfonietta and Hamburg Philharmonie; Numerous television and radio performances; Professor, Trinity College of Music, London; Masterclasses, Lecturer and Private voice consultant; Examiner and Adjudicator at major vocal competitions including the National Mozart Competition, the Royal Overseas League, the Kathleen Ferrier Competition and the 'S-Hertogenbosch International Vocal Concours, 1998. *Recordings:* King Olaf by Elgar; Mahler's Eighth Symphony; Strauss Lieder Recital; Spirit of England and Coronation Ode by Elgar; Elgar War Music. *Address:* c/o Patrick Voullaire Artists Management, Park Offices, 121 Dora Road, London SW19 7JT, England.

CAHOVA, Monika; Singer (Soprano); b. 20 June 1966, Prague, Czechoslovakia. *Education:* The State Conservatory, Prague. *Career:* Debut: Sang Inez in Il Trovatore at the National Theatre, Prague, 1988; Many appearances at the Opera Theatre Liberec and also sings in the National Theatre of Prague; Roles in opera include: Marenka in Smetana's The Bartered Bride; Blazenka in The Secret; Vendulka in The Kiss; Titka in Dalibor; Dvořák's Rusalka, Terinka and Julie in Jakobin; Elisabeth de Valois in Don Carlo, Leonora in Il Trovatore, and Amelia in Simon Boccanegra; Mimi in La Bohème, and Tosca; Gioconda in La Gioconda; Marguerite in Faust; Micaela and Carmen in Carmen; Giulietta in Les Contes d'Hoffman and Hélène in La Belle Hélène; Donna Elvira in Don Giovanni and the Countess; Lisa in Tchaikovsky's Queen of Spades; Marica in Kalman's Die Gräfin Maritza; Liza in Das Land des Lächelns and Hana in Die Lustige Witwe; Also sang in Britten's War Requiem at the Summer Festival in Olomouc at Zagreb in The Days of Czech Opera, sang Dvořák's Rusalka and Marenka; Sang Donna Elvira with the National Theatre of Brno in Italy; Also appeared at the Teatro dell'Aquila, Fermo Teatro di Cita, Salerno; Dvořák's Stabat Mater at the Summer Festival in Marianskelazne; Sang Mozart's Requiem in Belgium and the Third Lady in Die Zauberflöte in Germany and in Tokyo; Regular guest appearances in Germany. *Address:* Nadrazni 7/294, Prague 5, Smichov 15000, Czech Republic.

CAILLARD, Jean-Philippe; Choral Director; b. 31 July 1924, Paris, France. *Career:* Formed first vocal ensemble, 1944, for the performance of then little heard Renaissance music; Recorded many albums, 1955–70, beginning with Josquin's Missa Pange Lingua; Associations with such conductors as Jean-François Paillard and Louis Frémaux in the performance of French Baroque music; Pedagogic and educational activities from 1951, and has researched early music performance. *Address:* c/o 23 Rue de Marly, 7860 Etang la ville, France.

CAINE, Rebecca; Singer (Soprano); b. 1962, Toronto, Canada. *Education:* Studied at the Guildhall School of Music, London. *Career:* North American debut in 1991 as Lulu for Canadian Opera, returning as Despina, Micaela and Pamina; Further appearances with New Sadler's Wells Opera, Handel Opera Society, Glyndebourne and Tulsa Opera; Created L A Lola in Mason's Playing Away with Opera North in 1994 (Munich and Leeds), and returned to Leeds in 1995 as Thomas' Ophelia; Opera Lyra Ottawa as Gilda and English National Opera as Pamina in 1995; Opéra de Nice in 1995 as Balkis in Haydn's L'Incontro Improvviso; Sang Violetta at Belfast, 1996; Season 1996–97 included Musetta and Susanna for English National Opera, Bernstein's Cunegonde for the BBC; Engaged as Martinů's Julietta for English National Opera, 1997–98; Sang Janáček's Vixen at Spoleto and Mozart's Aminta for Opera North, 1998; Fotis in the world premiere of The Golden Ass for Canadian Opera, 1999. *Honours:* Dora Mavor Moore Award, 1998. *Current Management:* Askonas Holt Ltd, Lonsdale Chambers, 27 Chancery Lane, London, WC2A 1PF, England. *Telephone:* (20) 7400-1700. *Fax:* (20) 7400-1799. *E-mail:* info@askonasholt.co.uk. *Website:* www.askonasholt.co.uk.

CAIRE, Patrice; Organist; b. 17 June 1949, Lyon, France. *Education:* Baccalaureate, 1968; Faculty of Law; Lyon Conservatory; Conservatoire National Superieur de Musique, Paris; Licence de Concert, Ecole Normale de Musique, Paris, 1975. *Career:* Organist, Sainte Croix Church, Lyon, 1973–83; Organist, St Bonaventure Sanctuary, Lyon, 1983–; Keeper, Grandes Orgues de l'Auditorium Maurice Ravel, Lyon, 1980–; Commissioner, International Improvisation Competition, 1982–83; Teacher, Conservatoire National Superieur de Musique, Lyon, 1979–; Recitals in France, Germany, England, Scotland, Switzerland, Sweden, Spain, Italy, Belgium, USA and Canada; Concert performances: Radio France; France Musique; France Culture; Radio Cando; Radio Suisse Romande; Spanish Radio Television; Sweden Radio; With orchestra under S Baudo, E Krivine, S Skrowaczewski, J Nelson and E Tchakarov; mem, Founder; Artistic Director, Les Grandes

Orgues de l'Auditorium Maurice Ravel, Lyon. *Recordings:* 2 recitals; Ch M Widor, Symphony No. 6; A Guilmant, Sonata No. 1 REM; 6 Pieces; Brass; Organ; Percussion; Busser; Litaize; Dupré; Vierne: Gigout, REM; N J Lemmens; Fanfare; Priere; Sonatas No. 1, 2, 3, REM; Lemmens, Lefebure Wely, REM; C Franck et l'orgue du Trocadero, REM; L Vierne, Finales of 6 Symphonies; Ch M Widor, Symphonies No. 4, 5,; Ch M Widor, Symphonies, No. 1 2; L Boellmann, Work for Grand Organ; C Franck, 12 Pieces for Grand Organ; Les Maitres du Trocadero; Guilmant; Widor; Lemmens; Franck; Dubois; Gigout; Saint-Saëns. *Current Management:* North America; Ph Truckenbrod, PO Box 69, West Hartford, CT 06107, USA. *Address:* 73 Rue Pierre Corneille 69006, Lyon, France.

CAIRNS, Christine; Singer (Mezzo-Soprano); b. 11 Feb. 1959, Ayrshire, Scotland. *Education:* Royal Scottish Academy of Music and Drama, Glasgow; Further study with Neilson Taylor. *Career:* Concerts with André Previn and the Los Angeles Philharmonic 1985; Prokofiev's Alexander Nevsky in Los Angeles and with the Cleveland and Philadelphia Orchestras; Royal Philharmonic Orchestra 1988, in Mahler's Kindertotenlieder; Tour of the US with Mahler's 4th Symphony; Festival Hall London, 1988, in Schoenberg's Songs Op 22; Promenade Concerts London, 1989, in Mozart's Coronation Mass, returned 1990; Guest appearances throughout the British Isles, Athens, Basle, Tokyo, Berlin, San Francisco and Dortmund; Touring throughout Spain; Guest engagements in Paris, Madrid, Rome, Zürich, Singapore and Rio de Janeiro; Staged performances of Monteverdi's Orfeo in Valencia; Concerts with Ashkenazy in Berlin and London, 1990; Mahler with Simon Rattle and Yuri Temirkanov in LA, 1991; Season 1996–97 with Beethoven's Mass in C at the Bath Mozart Festival and Elijah with the Ulster Orchestra. *Recordings:* Mendelssohn's Midsummer Night's Dream, Previn, Vienna Philharmonic; Prokofiev's Alexander Nevsky, Previn, LA Philharmonic; Die Erste Walpurgisnacht, Dohnányi, Cleveland Orchestra. *Current Management:* Carroll Artist Management. *Address:* c/o Carroll Artist Management, 11 Palmerston Place, Edinburgh EH1L 5 AF, Scotland.

CAIRNS, David (Adam); Critic and Writer; b. 8 June 1926, Loughton, Essex. *Education:* Oxford University, 1945–48; Princeton University, 1950–51. *Career:* Co-founded Chelsea Opera Group, 1950; Music Critic, Spectator, 1958–62; Financial Times, 1962–67; New Statesman, 1967–70; Sunday Times, 1973–; Succeeded Desmond Shawe-Taylor as chief music critic, 1983; Has also written reviews for the Observer, Evening Standard. *Publications include:* Translation of the Berlioz Memoirs, 1969, revised, 1977; Collection of essays, Responses, 1973–80; Biography of Berlioz, Vol. 1, 1989, Vol. 2, Servitude and Greatness, 1999. *Contributions:* Beethoven and Berlioz in Viking Opera Guide, 1993. *Honours:* C.B.E., 1997. *Address:* c/o Sunday Times, 1 Pennington Street, London EC 2, England.

CAIRNS, Janice; Singer (Soprano); b. 1955, Ashington, Northumberland, England. *Education:* Studied at the Royal Scottish Academy, with John Hauxvell and with Tito Gobbi in Rome. *Career:* Debut: Sang Verdi's Desdemona at the Thessaloniki Festival, directed by Gobbi; London debut as Odabella in Attila, for University College Opera; Appearances with Kent Opera as Alice Ford and Donna Anna; Manon Lescaut and Leonora in La Forza del Destino for Chelsea Opera Group; With English National Opera has sung Musetta, Ariadne, Eva, Maria in Mazeppa, Lisa, Maria Boccanegra, Tosca and Amelia; Scottish Opera as Rezia in Oberon, Leonara (Il Trovatore), Aida and Madama Butterfly; For Opera North has sung Aida, Leonore and Helen in the British stage premiere of Verdi's Jerusalem, 1989; Italian debut with Scottish Opera at La Fenice, Venice, as Rezia; Concert engagements include the Verdi Requiem with the London Symphony Orchestra, Odabella at the Concertgebouw, Rachmaninov's The Bells at the Proms and Britten's War Requiem at the Norwich Festival; English National Opera, 1992, as Anna in Street Scene and as Ariadne; Sang Turandot for Welsh National Opera, 1994; Tosca for English National Opera, 1996; Season 1997 with Korngold's Violanta for Opera North and at the London Proms; Foreign Princess in Rusalka for ENO, 1998. *Current Management:* Askonas Holt Ltd, Lonsdale Chambers, 27 Chancery Lane, London, WC2A 1PF, England. *Telephone:* (20) 7400-1700. *Fax:* (20) 7400-1799. *E-mail:* info@askonasholt.co.uk. *Website:* www.askonasholt.co.uk.

CAIRNS, Tom; British stage director and stage designer; b. 1950, England. *Career:* designed and directed premiere production of Birtwistle's Second Mrs Kong, for Glyndebourne Touring Opera at Glyndebourne, 1994; Other engagements include Tippett's King Priam for Opera North and Flanders Opera, La Bohème at Stuttgart, Don Giovanni for Scottish Opera and Un Ballo in Maschera at Munich; Stage Designs for Mozart's Apollo and Hyacinth at Batignano, Don Giovanni for Opera 80, The Midsummer Marriage, La Finta Giardiniera and Gianni Schicchi for Opera North; The Trojans for Scottish Opera, WNO and Opera North (also seen at Covent Garden): Billy Budd and Beatrice and Benedict for English National Opera; Samson et Dalila at the Bregenz Festival and Benvenuto Cellini by Berlioz for Netherlands

Opera. *Address:* c/o Glyndebourne Touring Opera, Glyndebourne, Lewes, Sussex BN8 5UU, England.

CALDWELL, John Anthony, BMus, MA, DPhil, FRCO; British lecturer, writer and composer; *Professor of Music, University of Oxford;* b. 6 July 1938, Bromborough, England; m. Janet; one s. one d. *Education:* Birkenhead School, Liverpool Matthay School of Music, Univ. of Oxford. *Career:* Asst Lecturer in Music, Bristol Univ. 1963–66; Lecturer in Music, Univ. of Oxford 1966–, Prof. 1999–; Fellow of Jesus Coll., Oxford 1999–: mem. Royal Musical Asscn, Plainsong and Mediaeval Music Soc. (mem. of council), Soc. for the Promotion of New Music. *Compositions:* Paschale mysterium trilogy: Good Friday 1998, The Word 2001, Pascha nostrum 2002; Divertimento for Orchestra 1999, The Story of Orpheus 2004. *Publications:* English Keyboard Music Before the Nineteenth Century 1973, Medieval Music 1978, Editing Early Music 1985, The Oxford History of English Music (two vols) 1991, 1999; contrib. to Early Music, Music and Letters, The New Grove Dictionary of Music and Musicians 1980, 2002, Early English Church Music (gen. ed.). *Address:* Faculty of Music, St Aldate's, Oxford, OX1 1DB, England (office). *Telephone:* (1865) 276131 (office). *Fax:* (1865) 276128 (office). *E-mail:* john.caldwell@music.ox.ac.uk (office).

CALDWELL, Sarah; Conductor; b. 6 March 1924, Maryville, USA; Opera Impresario; Opera Director. *Education:* University of Arkansas; Hendrix College; Violin with Richard Burgin, New England Conservatory of Music; Viola with Georges Fourel; Apprenticeship with Boris Goldovsky. *Career:* Assistant to Boris Goldovsky, Opera Dept, New England Conservatory of Music; Director, Boston University Opera Workshop, 1952–60; Founder; Director, Opera Group, Boston, 1958, which became Opera Company of Boston, 1965; Conducted or Produced the US Premieres of Prokofiev's War and Peace, Nono's Intolleranza, Schoewberg's Moses and Aron and Montezuma by Roger Sessions; Producer of the original versions of Boris Godunov and Don Carlos; Guest Conductor, Various orchestras including New York Philharmonic, Pittsburgh Symphony, Boston Symphony and Indianapolis Symphony. *Honours:* 1st Woman to appear as a Conductor with the Metropolitan Opera, New York, 1976, La Traviata. *Address:* c/o Opera Company of Boston, PO Box 50, Boston, MA 02112, USA.

CALLEO, Riccardo; Singer (Tenor); b. 1947, Endicot, New York, USA. *Education:* Studies at Yale, the Verdi Conservatory in Milan and at the Curtis Institute; Further study with Ken Neate in Stuttgart. *Career:* Sang at Bonn Opera, 1974–77, Innsbruck, 1977–79, and at the New York City Opera from 1979; Guest engagements at Cincinnati, Washington (Edgardo, 1983), Houston, Miami, Baltimore and Portland; Nantes Opera, 1989, Dorset Opera, 1991, as Boito's Faust; Other roles include Manrico, Turiddu, Radames, Rodolfo, Nemorino, Percy in Anna Bolena, the Duke of Mantua and Riccardo (Gustavus). *Address:* c/o New York City Opera, Lincoln Center, New York, NY 10023, USA.

CALLIGARIS, Sergio; composer, pianist and professor of piano; b. 1941, Rosario, Argentina. *Career:* concerts in Europe, the Americas, Asia and South Africa 1954–; Chair of Piano, Cleveland Institute of Music, OH, USA and California State Univ., Los Angeles 1969; teacher at conservatories in Italy from 1974; Arts Dir of American Acad. of the Arts in Europe; jury member of national and international piano competitions in Italy and abroad; musical profile as composer and pianist, Società Aquilana dei Concerti, 40th Anniversary Concert Cycle 1986; works performed on television internationally. *Compositions include:* published and recorded works: 24 Studi, 1978, 1979, 1980, Il Quaderno Pianistico di Renzo, for piano, 1978, Tre Madrigali, 1979; Published works: Scherzo, 1957, Sonata op 9, for cello and piano, 1978, Passacaglia, 1983, Due Danze Concertanti, 1986, Suite op 28 for solo cello, 1992, Suite da Requiem op 17a, for violin, horn and piano, 1983, Scene Coreografiche, op 30 for 2 Pianos (or Piano 4-Hands) and String Orchestra, 1994, Sonata Fantasia, op 31 for Trumpet and Piano, 1994, and op 32 for Solo Piano, 1994, Preludio, Corale e Finale, op 33 for Accordion, 1994; Clarinet Quartet No. 1, op 34, 1995; String Quartet No. 2, op 35, 1995; Toccata, Adagio and Fugue, op 36, for string orchestra, 1995; Double Concerto, op 37, for piano, violin and string orchestra, 1996; Sonata, op 38, for clarinet and piano, Sonata op 39, for viola and piano, Sonata op 40, for violin and piano, 1997; Double Concerto op 41, for two pianos and orchestra, 2000; Ave Verum op 42, for choir and piano, 2000; Ave Verum op 42a, for solo piano, 2000; Suite op 43, for two pianos and four drums, 2002; Preludio e Toccata op 44, for solo piano, 2002; Il Giorno, Suite for youth, op.45, for chorus, piano, or organ, violin or flute and percussion. Recorded works: Ave Maria, 1978, Symphonic Dances op 26, for large orchestra, 1990, Seconda Suite di Danze Sinfoniche, op 27 for Large Orchestra, 1990, Concerto for Piano and Orchestra, op 29, 1992. *Recordings include:* Concerts for Union Europeènne Radiodiffusion, 1977, 1985, 1987, 1994, 1999, 2001; Sergio Calligaris, recital; album dedicated to him of works by Chopin, Rachmaninov, Vitalini and Calligaris, 1993; Piano Concerto op 29, Second Suite of Symphonic Dances, op 27 and Sonata Fantasia for piano op 32, 1996; Clarinet Quartet No. 1 op 34, 1999; Double Concerto op 37

for violin, 1999; Piano and String Orchestra for the Union Europeenne Radio Diffusion, 1999; Shorts for Spot and Film, contemporary classical music by Sergio Calligaris. *Contributions:* CD Classica 1995, 1999; Piano Time, 1996, 2002; Musica, 1996, 2001; Amadeus, 1997; Il Giornale della Musica, 1997; Suonare News, 1999. *Address:* Viale Libia 76, 00199 Rome, Italy. *Website:* calligaris.carisch.it.

CALM, Birgit; Singer (Mezzo-soprano); b. 1959, Lubeck, Germany. *Education:* Studied in Lubeck and Hamburg. *Career:* Sang first at the Kiel Opera, then Osnabruck, 1984–85; Appearances at the Bayerische Staatsoper from 1984 have included Humperdinck's Hansel, Alkmene in Die Liebe der Danaë and Carlotta in Die schweigsame Frau; Guest appearances in concert and opera in Germany and abroad; Sang Rossweise and Flosshilde in The Ring at the Salle Pleyel, Paris, 1992. *Recordings:* Sacred music by Dittersdorf, Harmonia Mundi; Third Maid in Elektra, conducted by Sawallisch. *Address:* c/o Bayerische Staatsoper, Postfach 100148, 8000 Munich 1, Germany.

CAMANI, Adrianna; Singer (Mezzo-Soprano); b. 27 March 1936, Padua, Italy. *Education:* Studied at the Padua Conservatory with Sara Sforni Corti. *Career:* Debut: Naples 1968, as the Nurse in L'Incoronazione di Poppea; Has sung widely in Italy, notably in Genoa, Turin, Trieste, Venice and Naples; Sang in the Scala premiere of Dallapiccola's Ulisse; Major roles included La Cieca in La Gioconda, Ulrica in Un Ballo in Maschera, Eboli in Don Carlos and parts in Madama Butterfly, Andrea Chénier, Francesca da Rimini and Il Quattro Rusteghi. *Address:* c/o Conservatorio Statale di Musica Cesare Pollini, Via Eremitani 6, I–35121 Padua, Italy.

CAMBRELING, Sylvain; Conductor; b. 2 July 1948, Amiens, France. *Education:* Conservatoire National Superieur de Musique de Paris. *Career:* Assistant Conductor, Orchestre de Lyon, 1975–81; First Guest Conductor, Ensemble Intercontemporain, Paris, 1976–81; Musical Director, Théâtre de la Monnaie Brussels, 1981–92; Guest Conductor: Salzburg and Glyndebourne Festivals, Festival d'Aix-en-Provence. Hamburg Opera, La Scala Milan, Paris Opéra, Metropolitan Opera, New York, Grand Theatre at Geneva, Berlin Philharmonic, Munich State Orchestra, Vienna Symphony, Accademia Santa Cecilia Rome, Museum Orchestra at Frankfurt, Gurzenich Orchestra Cologne, Cincinnati Symphony, St Paul Chamber Orchestra, HaIIé Orchestra and Royal Liverpool Philharmonic; Conducted The Rake's Progress at the 1989 Glyndebourne Festival; Premiere of Des Glas in Kopf Wird Vom Glas by Eugeniusz Knapik at Antwerp, 1990; Lohengrin and From the House of the Dead at Brussels, 1990; New Production of Simon Boccanegra, 1990–91 season; Director of the Frankfurt Opera from 1993, Wozzeck, From the House of the Dead and Elektra; Lucio Silla at the 1997 Salzburg Festival and Katya Kabanova, 1998; Busoni's Faust at Salzburg, 1999. *Recordings:* La Clemenza di Tito, Lucio Silla, Louise-Charpentier, Semiramide, The Tales of Hoffmann, Le Sacre du Printemps; Sapho-Gounod; L'Histoire du Soldât, Requiem by Fauré and La Finta Giardiniera. *Address:* Allied Artists, 42 Montpelier Square, London, SW7 1JZ England.

CAMDEN, Anthony, FGSM, ARCM; British oboist; b. 26 April 1938, London, England; s. of Archie Camden and Jan Kerrison;; m. 1st Diane (divorced), one s. one d.; m. 2nd Lilly, one d. *Education:* Royal Coll. of Music, London. *Career:* founder mem., London Virtuosi 1972–; Prin. oboe, London Symphony Orchestra 1973–88; Chair. of Bd of Dirs, London Symphony Orchestra 1975–87; Prof., Dir and Provost of Queensland Conservatorium of Music 1988–93, (Griffith Univ.); Dean of Music, Hong Kong Acad. of Performing Arts 1993–2003, Fellow 2004–; Hon. Prof., Shanghai Conservatory, China. *Recordings:* 36 concertos recorded in London since 1995, including Bach Concerto for Violin and Oboe, with Yehudi Menuhin; 16 Albinoni Oboe Concertos for Naxos with London Virtuosi, Grace Williams Oboe Concerto London Symphony Orchestra; Mozart Oboe Quartet, Telemann Concerto for Flute and Oboe, with James Galway; Complete Handel Oboe Concertos; Italian Oboe Concertos, Vols 1 and 2; The Art of the Oboe; The Mozart Oboe Concerto; The Art of Anthony Camden. *Current Management:* Gerhild Baron International Artists Management: Dornbacher Strasse 41/III/2, 1170 Vienna, Austria. *Telephone:* (1) 489 61 54. *Fax:* (1) 485 67 11. *E-mail:* baron@via.at. *Website:* www.baronartistsmanagement.com. *Address:* Unit 9, River Gallery, 6, Merthyr Road, New Farm, Brisbane, Queensland, 4005, Australia (home). *Telephone:* (7) 3358-2368 (home). *Fax:* (7) 3358-6503 (home). *E-mail:* anthony@anthonycamden.com (home). *Website:* www.anthonycamden.com.

CAMERON, Fiona Mary, FRAM; Pianist; b. 4 March 1931, London, England; m. Derek Simpson, 10 April 1954, divorced, 2 s., 1 d. *Education:* Royal Academy of Music, London, with Harold Craxton; 2 months in Paris with Yvonne Léfebure. *Career:* Debut: Piano with Derek Simpson, cello, Recital Room, Royal Festival Hall, 24 June 1953; Broadcasting with Derek Simpson, cello, 1955–62, and Carl Pini, violin, 1962–64; Concerts at music clubs and Wigmore Hall until 1971, including Purcell Room with Diana Cummings, violin, April 1968;

Taught Piano, Royal Academy of Music 1974–86 and Royal Ballet School, 1963–86; Head of Piano, St Paul's Girls' School, London, 1987–92; mem, Incorporated Society of Musicians; Royal Society of Musicians. *Recordings:* Mendelssohn Sonata in D major for cello and piano, with Derek Simpson. *Honours:* Fellow, Royal Academy of Music, 1983. *Address:* Cremona, 19 Willowhayne Avenue, East Preston, Littlehampton, West Sussex BN16 1PE, England. *Telephone:* 01903 784629. *Fax:* 01903 784629. *E-mail:* fiona@cameron41.fsnet.co.uk.

CAMILLERI, Charles; Composer; b. 7 Sept. 1931, Hamrun, Malta; m. 22 Sept 1957, 1 s., 1 d. *Education:* Lyceum, Malta; Toronto University, Canada. *Career:* Conductor, CBC; Visiting Professor in numerous institutions; Professor, University of Malta, 1992–96. *Compositions:* Missa Mundi; Piano Concerto No. 1; Stone Island Within; Piano Trio; Taqsim; Piano Concertos Nos 2 and 3; Organ Concerto; Unum Deum, Cantata; Missa Brevis; 3 operas; Oratorio; Chamber Works; Flute Concerto, 1991; Cello Concerto, 1992; 2 Violin Concertos, 1960, 1996; Clarinet Sonata, 1995; Operas: Campostella, 1993, and The Maltese Cross, 1995; Piano Quintet, 1996; The Prayer of the Universe for organ, 1996; Trio for horn, violin and piano, 1998. *Publications:* The Music of The Mediterranean, 1986. *Address:* 24 Orchard Avenue, Finchley, London N3 3NL, England.

CAMILLETTI, Simonetta; Italian classical guitarist; b. 10 Feb. 1962, Civitavecchia, Rome. *Education:* Univ. La Sapienza, Rome, Conservatory A. Casella, L'Aquila, Music Acad., Chigiana, Siena. *Career:* winner selection, Castel Sant'Angelo's Friends, Rome 1987; performed for Radiotelevisione Italiana 1987–89, for Swiss television 1999; Prof. of Guitar, State Conservatory of Music 2003–. *Compositions:* Songs for voice and guitar: Eagles Fly; This Evening; Beethoven's Street, Look at the Sky; Bagatella; Aria; composed melodies to accompany poems. *Recordings:* Guitar Has a Soul. *Publications:* Oltre l'Azzurro (fiction), Attimi... (poems); articles in Heitor Villa Lobos and The Guitar; Editor, AFM Accord for Music; contributions to a biographical dictionary of Italians. *Honours:* Prize Bereshit International 1999. *Address:* Viale Eroi di Rodi 228, 00128 Rome, Italy.

CAMPANELLA, Bruno; Conductor; b. 6 Jan. 1943, Bari, Italy. *Education:* Studied Conducting with Piero Bellugi, Hans Swarowsky and Thomas Schippers; Composition with Dallapiccola. *Career:* Debut: Spoleto Festival, 1967; From 1971, has conducted 19th Century Italian opera at La Scala Milan, elsewhere in Italy and in Europe and North America; Conducted Rossini's Le Comte Ory at Montreal 1989; Don Pasquale at Covent Garden; Piccinni's La Cecchina at the 1990 Martina Franca Festival; Conducted L'Italiana in Algeri at the Teatro Regio Turin, 1992; 1992 at La Scala, Le Comte Ory and Fra Diavolo; Direttore stabile, Teatro Regio, Turin, 1992–; Conducted La Fille du Régiment in San Francisco and La Cenerentola in Florence 1993; Returned to Covent Garden for Cenerentola in 1994 and Houston in 1995; Season 1996–97 at Vienna State Opera with Linda di Chamounix by Donizetti, Don Pasquale and L'Italiana in Algeri; Rota's Italian Straw Hat at La Scala and La Cenerentola, L'Italiana in Algeri and I Capuleti e i Montecchi at the Paris Opéra, 1998; I Capuleti at Covent Garden, 2001. *Recordings:* Il Barbiere di Siviglia; La Fille du Régiment; DGG recording of bel canto arias with Kathleen Battle. *Address:* c/o Royal Opera House (Contracts), Covent Garden, London WC2E 9 DD, England.

CAMPBELL, David, GRSM, ARCM, LRAM; clarinettist; b. 15 April 1953, Hemel Hempstead, Hertfordshire, England; m. 1981; one s. *Education:* Barton Peveril, Hampshire, Royal College of Music. *Career:* debut at Wigmore Hall, April 1975; Solo clarinettist, recitalist and chamber music; Has played in 40 countries; Concertos with Royal Philharmonic Orchestra, English Chamber Orchestra, City of London Sinfonia, London Mozart Players, BBC Concert and BBC Scottish; BBC National Orchestra of Wales, BBC Philharmonic, Bournemouth Sinfonietta, Quebec Symphony, Bilbao Symphony and San Sebastian Symphony; Professor and Head of Woodwind, London College of Music; mem, Incorporated Society of Musicians; Clarinet and Saxophone Society. *Recordings:* Mozart Clarinet Concerto with City of London Sinfonia under Hickox on Pickwick; Steptoe Quintet and Complete Chamber Music for Clarinet by Brahms on Phoenix; Ravel Introduction and Allegro, Virgin Classics; Beethoven and Brahms Trios on Pickwick; Schubert Octet; Messiaen Quartet for the End of Time, Collins. *Publications:* Regular contributor to Allegro magazine. *Honours:* Mozart Memorial Prize, 1976; Martin Musical Scholarship, 1976. *Current Management:* c/o Janet Hughes, 76 Cross Oak Road, Berkhamsted, Hertfordshire HP4 3HZ, England. *Address:* 83 Woodwarde Road, Dulwich, London SE22 8UL, England.

CAMPBELL, Ian David, BA; Opera Director and Stage Director; b. 21 Dec. 1945, Brisbane, Qld, Australia; m. Ann Spira 1985; two s. *Education:* voice studies with Godfrey Stirling, Sydney 1964–72; Univ. of Sydney. *Career:* debut, Australian Opera, Sydney 1967; principal tenor, Australian Opera 1967–74; Senior Music Officer, Australia Council 1974–76; Gen. Man., State Opera of South Australia 1976–82;

Asst Artistic Administrator, Metropolitan Opera, New York 1982–83; Gen. Dir, San Diego Opera, CA 1983–; Producer and Host, At The Opera 1985–97, San Diego Opera Radio Program 1985–97, both on Radio KFSD-FM, San Diego; new series of San Diego Opera radio programme on X-BACH-AM 1997–2001; At the Opera on KPBS-FM 2002–; masterclasses, Music Acad. of the West, Santa Barbara, CA 1991–96; Stage Dir, La Bohème 1981, Les contes d'Hoffmann 1982, State Opera of South Australia; Cavalleria Rusticana/Pagliacci, Santa Barbara Grand Opera 1999; Falstaff 1999, Il Trovatore 2000, Tosca 2002 at San Diego Opera; Fellow, Australian Institute of Management; mem. Kona Kai Club, San Diego, Opera America (board mem. 1985–93, 1997–2001, chair. 2001–), San Diego Convention and Visitors' Bureau (board mem. 1997–2001). *Recordings:* War and Peace (television, opening of Sydney Opera House) 1973. *Honours:* Peri Award for services to California opera 1983, San Diego Press Club Headliner of Year 1991, Father of the Year, San Diego 1997, First Place for a Radio Series, Best of Show (Radio) for At the Opera with Ian Campbell 2003. *Address:* 18th Floor, Civic Center Plaza, 1200 Third Avenue, San Diego, CA 92101-4112, USA.

CAMPBELL, James (Kenneth); Clarinettist; b. 10 Aug. 1949, Leduc, Alberta, Canada. *Education:* Studied at Toronto University and with Yona Ettlinger in Paris. *Career:* CBS studio performances with Glenn Gould; Many appearances as concert soloist, including the Copland Concerto under the composer, 1978–79. Engagements with Allegri; Amadeus (until 1987) and Guarneri quartets, notably in Quintets by Mozart and Brahms; Quintets written for him by André Prevost and Ezra Laderman; Recitals with pianist John York, Toronto University 1978–87. Professor at Indiana University, 1987–. *Recordings include:* Duos with Glenn Gould and John York. *Honours:* Winner, CBC Talent Festival and Jeunesses Musicales, Belgrade, 1971. *Address:* Music Faculty, Indiana University, Bloomington, IN 47405, USA.

CAMPBELL, Margaret; British writer and lecturer on music; b. London, England; m. Richard Barrington Beare; two s. one d. *Education:* art scholarship, London. *Career:* talks and interviews on BBC radio; Cleveland Radio; Voice of America; USA; CBC Canada; BBC and Southern Television; Lectures at Cornell; Oberlin; Indiana; Oklahoma and Southern Methodist Universities; Manhattan School of Music, New York; Rice University; University of Texas at Austin; University of Southern California, USA; Cambridge, Guildford and Bath Universities; Guildhall School of Music and Drama; Purcell School, England; Festivals at Bergen and Utrecht, Netherlands; Editor, Journal of British Music Therapy, 1974–90; Member of Jury, International Cello Competition at Spring Festival, Prague, Czech Republic, 1994; Lectures at the Conservatoire and University of Sofia, Bulgaria, 1996; Member of Council (ESTA), 1996; Lectures at Sibelius Academy of Music, Helsinki, Finland, 1998; mem. Society of Authors; Royal Society of Literature; Royal Society of Arts; English Speaking Union; European String Teachers Association. *Publications:* Dolmetsch: The Man and His Work, London and USA, 1975; The Great Violinists, London and USA, 1981, Germany, 1982, Japan, 1983, and China, 1999; The Great Cellists, London 1988, Japan, 1996, China, 1999; Henry Purcell: Glory of His Age, London 1993; Married to Music, a biography of Julian Lloyd-Webber, 2001. *Contributions:* The New Grove Dictionary of Music and Musicians, 1980, 2000; The Independent; The Strad; The Cambridge Companion to the Cello, 1999; Collins Encyclopaedia of Classical Music, 2000; The Great Violinists and The Great Cellists, 2nd edition, 2004. *Honours:* Winston Churchill Memorial Travelling Fellowship, 1971; Fellow of the Royal Society of Arts, 1991. *Address:* 71 Shrublands Avenue, Berkhamsted, Hertfordshire HP4 3JG, England.

CAMPBELL, Richard; Violin Player; b. 1960, England. *Career:* Member of Fretwork, first London concert at the Wigmore Hall, London, July, 1986; Appearances in the Renaissance and Baroque repertoire in Sweden, France, Belgium, Netherlands, Germany, Austria, Switzerland and Italy; Radio broadcasts in Sweden, Netherlands, Germany and Austria; Televised concert on ZDF, Mainz, Tour of Soviet Union Sept 1989; Japan June 1991; Festival engagements in the United Kingdom; Repertory includes in Nomines and Fantasias by Tallis, Parsons and Byrd; Dance music by Holborne and Dowland, including Lachrimae; Six-part consorts by Gibbons and William Lawes; Songs and instrumental works by Purcell; Collaborations with vocal group Red Byrd in verse anthems by Byrd and Tomkins, London Cries by Gibbons and Dering; Resurrection Story and Seven Last Words by Schütz; Gave George Benjamin's Upon Silence at the Queen Elizabeth Hall, Oct 1990; Wigmore Hall concerts 1990–91 with music by Lawes, Purcell, Locke, Dowland and Byrd. *Recordings:* Heart's Ease, late Tudor and Early Stuart; Armada, Courts of Philip II and Elizabeth I; Night's Black Bird, Dowland and Byrd; Cries and Fancies, Fantasias, In Nomines and The Cries of London; Go Nightly Cares, Consort songs, dances and In Nomines by Byrd and Dowland; All on Virgin Classics Veritas label. *Address:* c/o Virgin Classics Ltd, 64 Baker Street, London W1M 1DJ, England.

CAMPION, Joanna; Singer (mezzo-soprano); b. 1968, England. *Education:* Choral Scholar, Trinity College, Cambridge, England; Royal College of Music, Guildhall School, Britten Pears School and the National Opera Studio. *Career:* Debut: Ursula in Beatrice et Benedict, for Cambridge Operatic Society; Other roles include title part in Prokofiev's The Duenna, Mrs Page in The Merry Wives of Windsor, Britten's Hermia for Singapore Lyric Opera, and Carmen (British Youth Opera, 1992); Baba the Turk in The Rake's Progress at Glyndebourne, Cenerentola and Hansel for Welsh National Opera and Rosina for English Touring Opera; Sang the Mother in Menotti's Amahl and the Night Visitors at the Spoleto Festival, later released on film directed by Menotti; Season 1998–99, engaged as Feodor in Boris Godunov for Welsh National Opera, Annina in Der Rosenkavalier for Scottish Opera and Sabina in Respighi's La Fiamma at the Wexford Festival; Concerts include Messiah on tour with Les Arts Florissants (1994), Mozart's C minor Mass at St Martin in the Fields, Bach's Passions at St John's Smith Square, Dream of Gerontius, Elijah and the Verdi Requiem at the Royal Albert Hall; Mahler Lieder, Elgar Sea Pictures and the Brahms Alto Rhapsody; Birthday celebrations for Yehudi Menuhin at Buckingham Palace, 1996. *Current Management:* Athole Still International Management, Forresters Hall, 25–27 Westow Street, London, SE19 3RY, England. *Telephone:* (20) 8771-5271. *Fax:* (20) 8768-6600. *Website:* www.atholestill.com.

CAMPO, Régis, BPhil; French composer; b. 6 June 1968, Marseilles; m. Kanako Abe 1997. *Education:* Aix-en-Provence, Marseilles Conservatory with Danielle Sainte-Croix,Georges Boeuf, Nice Conservatory with Jacques Charpentier, Conservatoire National Supérieur de Paris with Gérard Grisey, studied composition with Edison Denisov and Henri Dutilleux. *Career:* works have been commissioned by numerous international bodies and often played in many festivals or concert seasons world-wide by ensembles such as Nieuw Ensemble, Ensemble Intercontemporain, 2e2m, Orchestre national d'Ile de France. *Compositions include:* Fabel, for piano and ensemble, 1994; Commedia, for 19 musicians, 1995; Anima, for 6 musicians, 1996; Violin Concerto, 1997; Phantasmagoria, for orchestra, 1997; Les Jeux de Rabelais, 1998; Le Livre de Sonates for organ, 1997–99; Piano Concerto, 1998–99; Nova, for 12 voices, choir and large ensemble, 1998–99; Livre de fantaisies for cello, 1999; Faërie, for orchestra, 2000–01; First Book for Piano, 2000–02; Symphony No. 1 for orchestra, 2002–03. *Recordings:* numerous recordings and monographies. *Honours:* Gaudeamus Prize, 1996; First Prize, Special Young Composer Prize and Prix du Public of 3rd Dutilleux Competition, 1996; Dugardin Prize, SACEM, 1999; Pierre Cardin Prize, Institut de France, 1999; Residency, Villa Medici, Rome, 1999–2001. *Address:* c/o Les éditions Henry Lemoine, 41 rue Bayen, 75017 Paris, France.

CAMPORA, Giuseppe; Singer (Tenor); b. 30 Sept. 1923, Tortona, Italy. *Education:* Studied in Genoa and Milan. *Career:* Debut: Bari 1949, as Rodolfo in La Bohème. Career. La Scala Milan from 1951; Debut as Maurizio in Adriana Lecouvreur; Buenos Aires and Rio de Janeiro, 1952; Metropolitan Opera 1954, as Rodolfo; Guest engagements in Verona, Florence, Brussels, Paris, Hamburg, Lisbon, Zürich, Geneva, Monte Carlo, Baltimore and Cincinnati; La Scala 1952 in the premiere of Rocca's Uragano; Bregenz 1964, in Das Land des Lächelns; Italian television appearances as Radames, Pinkerton and Enzo in La Gioconda. *Recordings:* La Forza del Destino; La Gioconda; Madama Butterfly; Zazà by Leoncavallo; Scenes from Conchita by Zandonai. *Address:* c/o Conservatorio Giuseppe Verdi, Via del Conservatorio 12, I–20122 Milan, Italy.

CAMPOS, Anisia; Concert Pianist and Pedagogue; b. 1940, Brazil; m. Remus Tzincoca. *Education:* Graduate, Ecole Normale de Musique de Paris and Mozarteum Academy of Music, Salzburg, Austria; Studied with Alfred Cortot, Reine Gianoli and Claudio Arrau. *Career:* Recitals in Brazil, Portugal, Romania, France, Germany, England, Canada and Austria; Soloist with many orchestras including: Brazilian Symphony Orchestra in Rio de Janeiro, Brazil, the Bucharest George Enescu Philharmonic, Radio Television Orchestra in Bucharest, Cluj Philharmonic and Timisoara Philharmonic; Gave the first performance of Enescu's Sonata No. 1 in many cities; Collaborated with Remus Tzincoca in the discovery and reconstruction of the original version, in Romanian language, of Bartók's Cantata Profana, 1980s; Full Professor for Piano and Head of Clavier Section (Piano, Organ, Harpsichord), Conservatoire de Musique de Montreal (State Conservatory); Professor for Interpretation, Ecole Supérieure de Musique, Vincent d'Indy, Montreal, and University of Ottawa for several years; Held summer courses at the Orford Arts Centre; mem, Co-Founder, President, Canadian Enescu Foundation; Jury Member, Ecole Normale de Musique de Paris, France. *Address:* 632 Avenue Hervé-Beaudry, Laval, Quebec H7E 2X6, Canada.

CANARINA, John (Baptiste); Conductor; b. 19 May 1934, New York, USA. *Education:* BS, 1957; MS, 1958, Juilliard School; Conducting with Pierre Monteux and Jean Morel, Piano with Arthur Lloyd and Double Bass with Frederick Zimmermann. *Career:* Conductor, 7th US Army Symphony Orchestra, 1959–60; Assistant conductor, New York Philharmonic, 1961–62; Music Director, Jacksonville Symphony Orchestra, Florida, 1962–69; Director of Orchestral Activities, Drake University, 1973–; Guest Conductor: Royal Philharmonic; Philharmonia Orchestra; Bournemouth Symphony; BBC National Orchestra of Wales and BBC Scottish Symphony; Belgian Radio Orchestra; Slovak Radio Symphony Bratislava. *Publications:* Contributor to Tempo, High Fidelity, Opus and Keynote. *Address:* 3663 Grand Avenue, Apt 903, Des Moines, IA 50312, USA.

CANAT DE CHIZY, Edith; Composer; b. 26 March 1950, Lyon, France. *Education:* Studied with Maurice Ohana and Ivo Malec at the Paris Conservatoire, 1978–84. *Career:* Director of a conservatory in Paris from 1986. *Compositions include:* String sextet, 1982; Luceat for 10 solo violins, 1983; Livre d'heures for solo voices and ensemble, 1984; Yell for orchestra, 1985; Kyoran for ensemble, 1987; De noche for orchestra, 1991; Hallel for string trio, 1991; Siloël for strings, 1992; Canciones for 12 solo voices, 1992; Tombeau de Gilles de Rais, oratorio, 1993; Moïra, concerto for cello and orchestra, 1998. *Recordings:* Yell Hallel Canciones de Noche, 1994; Tombeau de Gilles de Rais, 1995; Exultet Siloël Moïra, 1999. *Honours:* Prix de la Tribune Internationale des Compositeurs, 1990. *Address:* c/o SACEM, 225 avenue Charles de Gaulle, 92521 Neuilly sur Seine Cédex, France.

CANIHAC, Jean-Pierre; Cornet Player; b. 16 April 1947, Toulouse, France; m. Michele Chauzy, 17 Aug 1968, 1 s., 1 d. *Education:* Baccalaureate, 1966; Conservatoire de Toulouse; Conservatoire de Versailles; Conservatoire National Superieur de Musique, Paris. *Career:* Founder, Saqueboutiers de Toulouse; Professor, CNR, Toulouse; Professor, Conservatoire National Superieur de Musique, Lyon; Member of Hesperion XX, La Grande Ecurie et la Chambre du Roi, La Chapelle Royale, Clemencic Consort. *Recordings:* L'Art de Cornet, Arion; Schütz, Symphoniae Sacrae, Erato; 7 Last Words of Christ, H Mundi; Siècle d'or à Venise, Adda; Six Marian Vespers of Monteverdi, Malgoire; and other music conducted by Parrott, Herreweghe and Corboz. *Contributions:* Brass Bulletin; Blue Brass. *Honours:* 1st Prize, Conservatoire de Toulouse, 1966; 1st prize, Conservatoire de Versailles, 1968; 1st prize Conservatoire National Superieur, Paris, 1970. *Address:* 8 rue Maran, 31400 Toulouse, France.

CANIN, Stuart V.; Violinist and Educator; b. 5 April 1926, New York City, USA; m. Virginia Yarkin, 8 June 1952, 2 s. *Education:* Juilliard School of Music, 1946–49. *Career:* Professor, Violin, State University of Iowa, 1953–60; Oberlin Conservatory of Music, 1960–66; Concertmaster, Chamber Symphony of Philadelphia, 1966–68; Concertmaster, San Francisco Symphony, 1970–80; Concertmaster, San Francisco Opera, 1969–72; Artist Faculty, Aspen Colorado Music Festival, 1960–63; Artist Faculty, Music Academy of the West, Santa Barbara, 1983–; Senior Visiting Lecturer, University of California, Santa Barbara, 1983–; Concertmaster, Casals Festival, San Juan, Puerto Rico, 1974–75; Mostly Mozart Festival, New York City, 1980. *Honours:* 1st Prize, Paganini International Violin competition, Genoa, 1959; Fulbright Professor to Freiburg, Germany Staatliche Hochschule für Musik, 1956–57. *Address:* 1302 Holmby Avenue, Los Angeles, CA 90024, USA.

CANINO, Bruno; Pianist and Composer; b. 30 Dec. 1935, Naples, Italy. *Education:* Studied at the Milan Conservatory with Calace and Bettinelli. *Career:* Piano Duo partner from 1953 with Antonio Ballista; Career as soloist from 1956, notably in works by Bussotti, Donatoni and Castiglioni; Professor of Music at the Milan Conservatory from 1961; Played in premieres of Rapsodia, by Davide Anzaghi, 1984; Played Ode by Castiglioni, 1966, Tableaux Vivants by Bussotti, 1964, Concerto for 2 Pianos and Orchestra by Berio, 1973; Member of the Trio di Milano; Accompanist to instrumentalists and singers including Cathy Berberian until 1983; Appearances with András Schiff include Schubert and Janáček Festival, London, 1995. *Compositions include:* Chamber and Instrumental Music. *Honours:* Prizes at Piano Competitions of Bolzano and Darmstadt, 1956–60. *Address:* Conservatorio Giuseppe Verdi, Via Conservatorio 12, 20122 Milan, Italy.

CANN, Antoinette, DipRCM; British pianist; b. 27 Sept. 1963, England; twin sister of Claire Cann. *Education:* studied piano with Phyllis Sellick at the Royal Coll. of Music, and with Anton Kuerti, Jean Paul Sevilla and Gilbert Kalish at the Banff School of Fine Arts. *Career:* duo piano player with twin sister; first major concert aged 13; many appearances in Europe, Canada, USA, New Zealand, Japan and the Middle East; extensive tours of the UK, including concerts at the Royal Festival Hall, Barbican Hall, Fairfield Halls, London, St David's Hall Cardiff, Glasgow Royal Concert Hall; concertos with the London Philharmonic, Royal Philharmonic, BBC Concert, London Mozart Players, English Sinfonia, Wren Orchestra, Glasgow Philharmonic; television engagements in the UK, Japan, USA, New Zealand; world premieres of Terry Winter Owens' Homage to Corelli and Pianophoria No. 3; Carey Blyton's Cinque

Ports; Michael Elliott's Geminae and Berceuse pour Deux; Timothy Blinko's two-piano concerto with English Sinfonia and Philip Ellis, 2003; South Bank premiere of the Max Bruch concerto for two pianos and orchestra, Royal Festival Hall. *Recordings:* albums: Gemini; La Danse; Rhapsody; Reflections; Fantasy; Complete Piano Duet Works of Carey Blyton. *Honours:* Gramophone Critic's Choice; Penguin Rosette Award; Classic FM Critic's Choice; Sound Sense Award; PLG Series; Countess of Munster Trust Awards; RCM President's Rose Bowl. *Current Management:* Appassionata, 5 Engleric, Chrishall, Royston Herts SG8 8QZ, England. *Telephone:* (1763) 261535. *E-mail:* twopianos@canntwins.com (home). *Website:* www.canntwins.com (home).

CANN, Claire, DipRCM; British pianist; b. 27 Sept. 1963, England; twin sister of Antoinette Cann. *Education:* studied piano with Phyllis Sellick at the Royal Coll. of Music, and with Anton Kuerti, Jean Paul Sevilla and Gilbert Kalish at the Banff School of Fine Arts. *Career:* duo piano player with twin sister; first major concert aged 13; many appearances in Europe, Canada, USA, New Zealand, Japan and the Middle East; extensive tours of the UK, including concerts at the Royal Festival Hall, Barbican Hall, Fairfield Halls, London, St David's Hall Cardiff, Glasgow Royal Concert Hall; concertos with the London Philharmonic, Royal Philharmonic, BBC Concert, London Mozart Players, English Sinfonia, Wren Orchestra, Glasgow Philharmonic; television engagements in the UK, Japan, USA, New Zealand; world premieres of Terry Winter Owens' Homage to Corelli and Pianophoria No. 3; Carey Blyton's Cinque Ports; Michael Elliott's Geminae and Berceuse pour Deux; Timothy Blinko's two-piano concerto with English Sinfonia and Philip Ellis, 2003; South Bank premiere of the Max Bruch concerto for two pianos and orchestra, Royal Festival Hall;. *Recordings:* albums: Gemini; La Danse; Rhapsody; Reflections; Fantasy; Complete Piano Duet Works of Carey Blyton. *Honours:* Gramophone Critic's Choice; Penguin Rosette Award; Classic FM Critic's Choice; Sound Sense Award; PLG Series; Countess of Munster Trust Awards; RCM President's Rose Bowl. *Current Management:* Appassionata, 5 Engleric, Chrishall, Royston, Herts SG8 8QZ, England. *Telephone:* (1763) 261535. *E-mail:* twopianos@canntwins.com (home). *Website:* www.canntwins.com (home).

CANNAN, Phyllis; Singer (Soprano); b. 22 Aug. 1947, Paisley, Scotland. *Career:* Sang as soprano with most major companies in the United Kingdom; Soprano repertoire from 1983; First Major role in Vivaldi's Griselda, Buxton Festival 1983; Sang Gluck's Alceste at the Queen Elizabeth Hall; Kostelnicka in Jenůfa and Katerina in The Greek Passion for Welsh National Opera; Santuzza, Tosca, Rusalka and Goneril, in the British premiere of Reimann's Lear, for English National Opera; Appearances in Der Rosenkavalier and King Priam at Covent Garden; Senta in Der fliegende Holländer at the 1987 Hong Kong Festival; Gerhilde in Die Walküre at the 1989 Promenade Concerts; Concert engagements include Britten's War Requiem in Belgium; Sang the Overseer in Elektra at the First Night of the 1993 London Proms. *Address:* c/o English National Opera, St Martin's Lane, London, WC2, England.

CANNE MEIJER, Cora; Singer (Mezzo-Soprano), Coach and Voice Teacher; b. 11 Aug. 1929, Amsterdam, Netherlands. *Education:* Amsterdam Conservatory with Jan Keizer and Re Koster; Studied further with Noemie Perugia in Paris and Alfred Jerger in Vienna. *Career:* Debut: With Netherlands Opera, Amsterdam, 1951; Glyndebourne, 1956, as Cherubino and in Die Zauberflöte and Cenerentola; Salzburg, 1959, in Haydn's Il Mondo della Luna; Zürich Opera, 1960–62; Regular appearances at the Holland Festival; Has sang at many major opera houses including, Vienna, Frankfurt, Brussels, Munich and Hamburg; Performed over 65 roles including: Dorabella, Isolier, Rosina, Isabella, Octavian, Marina in Boris Godunov and Carmen; Sang in world premiere of Milhaud's La Mère Coupable, Geneva, 1966; Was also widely in demand as Lied, concert and oratorio singer, repertory including works by Stravinsky and Berlioz, Bach's St Matthew Passion, Verdi's Requiem; Appeared on television as Carmen and Rosina; For over 20 years has taught at Amsterdam Sweelinck Conservatorium and giving master classes at home and abroad; Produced and Directed open air production of Mozart's Zauberflöte, summer 1989; Frequent Jury Member, International vocal competitions. *Recordings:* Les Noces by Stravinsky; Der Tag des Gerichts by Telemann; Comte Ory from Glyndebourne; Spanish Folksongs; French and Spanish Songs; Diary of One who Disappeared by Janáček. *Address:* Weteringstraat 48, 1017 SP Amsterdam, Netherlands.

CANNON, Philip; Composer; b. 21 Dec. 1929, Paris, France; m. Jacqueline Laidlaw, 1950, 1 d. *Education:* Dartington Hall Devon; Royal College of Music, London. *Career:* Lecturer in Music, Sydney University, 1958–60; Professor of Composition, Royal College of Music, 1960–95; mem, RMA; RPS; ISM; NFMS; PRS; MCPS. *Compositions:* 3 Operas, 2 Symphonies, including Son of Man commissioned by the BBC to mark the United Kingdom's entry to the EC; Choral works, Lord of Light, large scale requiem; Chamber Music, all broadcast and performed internationally; Piano quintet, 1998; Millennium Symphony, 1999. *Recordings:* Commissions: BBC; RF; BBC television; Three Choirs Festival; Gulbenkian Foundation; Chromatica USA; Phillip Cannon's Music performed by the Medici String Quartet, 1997. *Publications:* Biographical and critical articles in various magazines. *Honours:* Grand Prix; Critics Prize, Paris, 1965; FRCM, 1970; Te Deum, Commissioned by and dedicated to HM The Queen, 1975; Bard of Gorsedd Vernow, 1997. *Address:* Elmdale Cottage, Marsh, Aylesbury, Bucks., HP17 8SP, England.

CANONICI, Corrado; double bassist; b. 26 March 1961, Ancona, Italy. *Education:* Rossini Conservatory, Pesaro, double bass masterclasses with Franco Petracchi and Gary Karr, composition masterclasses with Hans Werner Henze and Brian Ferneyhough. *Career:* recitals in Italy, the United Kingdom, Ireland, USA, Luxembourg, Portugal, Spain, Switzerland, Sweden, Germany, Romania, Netherlands; Chamber music with Ensemble Modern, Music Projects/London, others; Appearances, Italian Radio, Romanian Television, German Radio, French Radio, Spanish Radio, USA Radio in Los Angeles; Masterclasses, New York University, Harvard University, Boston University, universities in Los Angeles and Manhattan School of Music, New York, Dartington International Summer Music courses; Double bass version of solo work by Stockhausen dedicated to Canonici and premiered in London, 4 Oct 1997; Artistic Director, Musica 2000 Festival, Italy; mem, Musicians Union. *Recordings:* Contrabass, including world premiere recording of Luciano Berio's solo bass piece, 1995; Cassandra, as a duo with clarinettist Roger Heaton, 1998; Sonage, as a duo with the former Mingus' trumpeter Jack Walrath, 2000. *Publications:* contrib. to New Notes magazine 1997, Double Bassist Magazine 1998. *Honours:* Xenakis Award, Paris, 1992; Darmstadt Award, 1992; International New Music Consortium Award, 1993, 1997, 1999; Performer in Residence, New York University, 1996. *Address:* World Concert Management, Unit 282, 95 Wilton Road, London, SW1V 1BZ, England.

CANONICI, Luca; Singer (Tenor); b. 22 June 1960, Montevarchi, Arezzo, Tuscany, Italy. *Education:* Studied in Rome with Tito Gobbi and at Pesaro. *Career:* Debut: Teatro Sociale Mantua, 1988, as the Duke of Mantua; Sang the Duke in Rome, 1986; Appearances in various Italian theatres, including Bologna and Florence, notably in the Italian premiere of Monteverdi's Ulisse in the version by Henze; Appeared as Rodolfo in the 1987 film version of La Bohème; Other roles include Nemorino and Ernesto, Fernando in Donizetti's Il Furioso all' isola di San Domingo; Frederico in L'Arlesiana; Almaviva and Werther; Bergamo 1990, in Mayr's La rosa bianca a la rosa rossa; Season 1991 as Fenton in Falstaff at Bonn; Pilade in Rossini's Ermione at Rome; Leading role in La Cambiale di Matrimonio at the Pesaro Festival; Sang Max in Leoncavallo's La Reginetta della Rosa, Palermo, 1992; ldreno in Semiramide at Zürich and Tonio in La Fille du Régiment at Rome; Season 1996 in the premiere of Berio's Outis at La Scala, as Bellini's Tebaldo at Genoa and Wolf-Ferrari's Filepeto at Parma; Sang Mascagni's Fritz at Naples, 1998; Season 1999–2000 as Conte Potioski in Donizetti's Gli Esilati di Siberia, at Montpellier, and Nemorino at the Vienna Staatsoper. *Address:* c/o Teatro dell'Opera, Piazza B Gigli 8, 00184, Rome, Italy.

CANTELO, April; Singer (Soprano), Singing Coach, Teacher and Adjudicator; b. 2 April 1928, Purbrook, Hampshire, England. *Education:* Studied at London with Julian Kimbell and at Dartington with Imogen Holst. *Career:* Debut: Sang Barbarina in Figaro and Echo in Ariadne auf Naxos with the Glyndebourne Company at Edinburgh, 1950; Glyndebourne Festivals, 1953, 1963, as Blondchen and Marzelline; English Opera Group, 1960–70, notably as Helena in the premiere of A Midsummer Night's Dream and as Emmeline in Purcell's King Arthur; At Sadler's Wells Theatre, 1962–66, sang in the premieres of Williamson's Our Man in Havana and The Violins of St Jacques; British premieres of Henze's Boulevard Solitude and Weill's Aufstieg und Fall der Stadt Mahagonny; Also created roles in Williamson's The Happy Prince, 1965, and Julius Cesar Jones, 1966; Directed Purcell's The Fairy Queen in New Zealand, 1972; made frequent broadcasts and concert appearances; mem, Equity; ISM; AOTOS. *Recordings:* The Indian Queen; Albert Herring and The Little Sweep; Béatrice et Bénédict; 18th Century Shakespeare Songs; Berlioz' Irelande; Haydn Masses with St John's College Choir, Cambridge. *Address:* 1 The Coalyard, All Saints Lane, Sutton Courtenay, Oxon OX14 4 AG, England.

CANTINI, Lorenza; Stage Director; b. Italy; m. *Education:* Accademia d'Arte Drammatica, Milan. *Career:* staged Boris Godunov, Florence 1993; Producer, I Due Foscari, Seoul, Leyle und Medjumn, Montepulciano 1993, Orfeo... Cantando Tolse, Favola di Orfeo 1994, L'Elisir d'Amore 1995, Gli Zoccoli in Villa 1996, Passione Secondo Giovanni 1997, La Forza del Destino, Athens, Il Campanello, Bologna 1998, La Serva Padrona, Florence, La Prova di un Opera Seria, Rome 1999, I Lombardi alla prima Crociata, Cremona 2001, La Serva Padrona, Florence 2001; Assoc. Producer at La Scala with work in Milan and on tour including Capuleti e i Montecchi, Covent Garden 2001, Adriana Lecouvrer, Moscow 2002. *Recordings:* La Forza del Destino 1997, La Serva Padrona 1999, I Lombardi alla Prima Crociata 2001. *Address:* c/o Fondazione Teatro La Scala, Via dell'Innovazione, 20100 Milan, Italy. *Telephone:* (2) 887-9326. *E-mail:* brianrichardearl@tiscali.it.

CANTRELL, Derrick (Edward); Cathedral Organist; b. 2 June 1926, Sheffield, England; m. Nancy Georgina Bland, 4 c. *Education:* MA; BMus, Oxford University; FRCO. *Career:* Organist, Manchester Cathedral, 1962–77; Lecturer, Royal Northern College of Music. *Recordings:* Manchester Cathedral Organ. *Honours:* Recipient of Sawyer and Limpus Prizes, Royal College of Organists. *Address:* 36 Parsonage Road, Manchester M20 9 PQ, England.

CAPOBIANCO, Tito; stage director, producer, set and lighting designer and educator; b. 28 Aug. 1931, La Plata, Argentina; m. Elena Denda; two s. *Career:* Producer and Technical Director, 1964, Producing Director, Technical Director and Set Designer, 1958, Teatro Colón, Buenos Aires; Artistic Director of Santiago Opera Festival; Stage Director of National Ballet of Chile; Professor of Acting and Interpretation at University of Chile, 1956; Stage Director and Lighting Designer of SODRE National Ballet and Opera; Stage Director of SODRE, Montevideo, Uruguay 1957; Artistic Director of Teatro Argentino; Producing Director and Stage Director of National Drama Company of Buenos Aires, 1959; Artistic Director, Cincinnati Opera and Summer Festival; Director of Opera Productions throughout the USA, 1961–65; Producer and Director, International Opera Festival, Mexico City, 1963–65; Founder and General Director of American Opera Centre, Juilliard School of Music, NY 1968–71; Created Opera Department of College of Performing Arts, Philadelphia, 1972; Artistic Director, 1975; General Director 1977; Created Verdi Festival 1978; Young American Conductor's Programme 1980; San Diego Opera; Vice-President and General Director, Pittsburgh Opera, 1983; Professor, Opera Department, Yale University 1983. *Compositions:* Libretto of Zapata. *Publications:* The Merry Widow, Franz Lehar, Translation. *Honours:* Cavaliere della Republica, Italy, 1979; Officier dans l'Ordre des Arts et Lettres, France, 1984; Doctor of Music, Duquesne University, 1988; Doctor of Letters, Indiana University of Pennsylvania, 1988; Doctor of Humane Letters, La Roche College, 1989. *Address:* Pittsburgh Opera, 711 Penn Avenue, Pittsburgh, PA 15222, USA.

CAPOIANU, Dumitru; Composer; b. 19 Oct. 1929, Bucharest, Romania. *Education:* Studied at the Bucharest Conservatory 1941–53. *Career:* Manager of the George Enescu Philharmonic Orchestra, 1959–73. *Compositions:* Wind Quintet, 1950; Viola Sonata, 1952; 2 Suites for orchestra, 1953, 1954; 2 String Quartets, 1954, 1959; Divertissement for string orchestra and 2 clarinets, 1956; Violin concerto 1957; Cosmos 60, ballet scene 1960; Cinematographic Variations for Orchestra, 1965; Steel, ballet 1965; String Trio 1968; Curte domneasca, The Princely Courtyard, spectacle of sound and light, 1969; Moto perpetuo for violin and orchestra, 1972; Chemari 77 for orchestra; Muzica de ambianta for orchestra 1980; Valses ignobles et sentimentales du tout for mezzo and strings, 1986; Three musicals, Dragostei Printesei, 1982, Censareasa 1984, and Tested Love, 1995; The Phoenix Bird for orchestra, 1994; Les verités de Dracula, suite for orchestra, 1995; Choral Music. *Address:* c/o UCMR-ADA, Calea Victoriei 141, Sector 1, Bucharest, Romania. *Telephone:* 21 212 7966. *Fax:* 21 210 7211. *E-mail:* ucmr@itcnet.ro.

CAPOLONGO, Paul; French conductor; b. 17 March 1940, Algiers, Algeria. *Education:* Algiers and Paris Conservatories. *Career:* Dir, Quito Symphony, 1963–67, Quito Conservatory, 1963–66; Asst to Leonard Bernstein at the New York Philharmonic, 1967–68; Conductor of Rhine Symphony Orchestra at Mulhouse, 1975–85. *Honours:* Mitropoulos Competition winner, 1967. *Address:* c/o Orchestre Symphonique du Rhin-Mulhouse, 38 Passage du Théâtre, 68100 Mulhouse, France.

CAPPELLETTI, Andrea; Violinist; b. 21 May 1961, Italy. *Education:* Diploma cum laude, Naples Conservatory, Parallel course, Liceo Linguistico. *Career:* 1st Violin, ECYO, 1977; Debut, Israel, 1984; Debut, RFH, 1986; Queen Elizabeth Hall, 1988; Regular appearances with leading orchestras, Italy; France; Germany; Scandinavia; Regular appearances in Europe; Australia; USA; Appointed Art Director, United Nations Concerts for the Disabled, 1990. *Recordings:* Exclusive contract, Koch International with 5 Mozart violin concertos, Italian Baroque Concerti, Respighi Concerti and Tartini sonatas for violin solo; For UNICEF Haydn Concerti. *Honours:* Vittorio Veneto, 1975; Kiefer Balitzel, 1977–78; Fordergemeinschaft, 1986. *Current Management:* Robert Kirp Corporation. *Address:* Via della Ripa 77, 50075 Montespertoli, Ripa F1, Italy.

CAPPUCCILLI, Piero; Singer (Baritone); b. 9 Nov. 1929, Trieste, Italy. *Education:* Studied in Trieste with Luciana Doaggio. *Career:* Debut: Teatro Nuovo Milan 1957, as Tonio in Pagliacci; Metropolitan Opera debut 1960, as Germont; La Scala Milan from 1964, debut as Ashton in Lucia di Lammermoor; Covent Garden debut 1967, as Germont;

Returned to London as Iago, Renato in Un Ballo in Maschera and as Simon Boccanegra, with the company of La Scala, 1976; Verona Arena 1968, 1970, as Posa in Don Carlos and as Luna in Il Trovatore; Chicago Lyric Opera 1969, in I Due Foscari; Salzburg Festival, 1975–77, as Posa and Boccanegra; Paris Opéra 1978; Arena di Verona, 1988, 1989, Amonasro and Nabucco; Stuttgart Opera, 1990, as Scarpia; Sang Simon Boccanegra at Barcelona, 1990; Luciano Pavarotti 30th Anniversary Gala, Reggio Emilia, 1991; Season 1991–92 as Nabucco at Verona and Rigoletto at Covent Garden; Other roles include Macbeth and Escamillo. *Recordings:* Lucia di Lammermoor, La Wally, I Puritani, Cavalleria Rusticana, Aida, Don Carlos, Il Pirata, Macbeth, Nabucco and Rigoletto, (Deutsche Grammophon); I Masnadieri, I Due Foscari.

CAPRIOLI, Alberto; Composer, Conductor and Musicologist; b. 16 Nov. 1956, Bologna, Italy. *Education:* Studied Composition with F Margola, C Togni (Parma Conservatory), B Schaeffer (Salzburg Mozarteum); Conducting with O Suitner, Vienna Academy of Music; Humanities with E Raimondi, C Ginzburg; U Eco (Bologna Univ.). *Career:* Guest Conductor, several European orchestras and new music festivals; Prof., Bologna Conservatory of Music; mem., Bd of Dirs, Italian Soc. for Comparative Literature, Florence; Centro Interdisciplinare Studi Romantici, Univ. of Bologna. *Compositions:* Frammenti dal diario, piano, 1974; Abendlied, soprano and orchestra, 1977; Sonata in memorian Alban Berg, piano, 1982; Sonetti di Shakespeare, child reciter and 10 instruments, 1983; Trio, piano, violin and cello, 1984; Del celeste confine, string quartet, 1985; Serenata per Francesca, 6 players, 1985; A la dolce ombra, piano trio, 1985; Dialogue, solo contrabass and 2 string quartets, 1986; Per lo dolce silentio de la notte, piano and computer music tape, 1987; Due Notturni d'oblio, 10 players, 1988; Symphoniae I, II, III, violin, 1988–89; Il vostro pianto aurora o luna, 5 players, 1989; Intermedio I, flute and computer music tape, 1989; Vor dem singenden Odem, quintet, 1990; Kyrie per Dino Campana, soloists, choir and 29 instruments, 1991; John Cage Variations, quintet, 1991; A quinze ans, cello, 1992; Anges, G-flute, viola and harp; Folâtre (Notturno di rosa), 2 guitars, 1993; L'ascesa degli angeli ribelli, reciter and 13 players, 1994; Dittico baciato, choir and orchestra, 1994; Elegia per Carlo Michelstaedter, oboe and 13 instruments, 1998; Canto, orchestra and reciter, 1998; Era, alto-saxophone and brass quintet, 1999; Fiori d'ombra, strings, 2001; Verweile... (danza notturna), reciter and 5 instruments, 2001; Gilles, violin and live electronics, 2002; Stelle assenti, chamber orchestra 2004. *Recordings:* five albums. *Publications include:* L'Italia nell'Europa Romantica, 1993; Luigi Nonos, A Carlo Scarpa, 1997; Pierre Boulez musicien-écrivain, 1998; La profezia del sacro in Hector Berlioz, 2000; Poesia romantica in Musica, 2004, 2005. *Contributions:* Comparatistica, 1989–98; Shakespeare Yearbook, 1994; Musica-Realtà, 1998; Giacomo Leopardi e la nuova musica, 1999. *Address:* D Guglielmini 7, 40137 Bologna, Italy. *E-mail:* alberto .caprioli@inwind.it. *Website:* www.cdmc.asso.fr/html/compositeurs/bio/ a_c/caprioli.htm; www.lingue.unibo.it/romanticismo/membri/caprioli/ caprioli.htm.

CAPRONI, Bruno; Singer (Baritone); b. 1960, England. *Education:* Studied at the Royal Northern College of Music and the National Opera Studio. *Career:* Sang in Menotti's The Consul, Madama Butterfly and Rigoletto while in college; Appearances with Opera Northern Ireland, Dublin Grand Opera, Wexford and Glyndebourne festivals; Royal Opera House Covent Garden from 1988 in Madama Butterfly, Don Carlos, Rigoletto, Der Freischütz, Otello, Die Meistersinger and Turandot; Sang Ezio in Verdi's Attila in a concert performance conducted by Edward Downes; Other roles include Marcello in La Bohème; Belcore; Ottokar in Der Freischütz; Verdi's Germont, Posa and Amonasro; Sang Schaunard in La Bohème at Covent Garden, 1996; Season 1998 as Ottokar in Der Freischütz, and Marcello at Cologne; Season 2000–01 as Nabucco for ENO, Rigoletto at Antwerp, Posa for the Vienna Staatsoper and Renato (Ballo in Maschera) at La Scala. *Honours:* Vaughan Williams; Frederick Cox award, 1987; Ricordi Prize for Opera 1988. *Address:* c/o Cologne Opera, Offenbachplatz, Pf. 180241, D–50505 Cologne, Germany.

CARBY, Catherine; Singer (Soprano); b. 1973, Australia. *Education:* Canberra School of Music, Australian National University; Royal College of Music, London. *Career:* Appearances with Victoria State Opera, Opera Queensland and Opera Australia. Roles have included Rosina, Mercédès (Carmen), Mallika in Lakmé and Jano in Jenůfa; English National Opera in 1999, as Kate in Madama Butterfly; Jerwood Young Singers Program, 2000; Season 2000–01 as Britten's Lucretia for British Youth Opera, title role in Muzio Scevola and Vitige in Flavio for the London Handel Festival. *Honours:* Winner, ABC Young Performer of the Year Awards, 1996; STA Australian National Aria Competition; Tait Memorial Trust Scholarships, RCM; Finalist, Kathleen Ferrier and Richard Tauber Awards. *Address:* c/o Royal College of Music, Prince Consort Road, London SW7, England.

CARD, June; Singer (Soprano); b. 10 April 1942, Dunkirk, New York, USA. *Education:* Studied at Mannes College, New York. *Career:* Sang on Broadway from 1959, with New York City Opera from 1963;

European engagements at Munich, two titles of Kammersängerin from Frankfurt and Munich; Gartnerplatztheater, from 1967; Member of the Frankfurt Opera 1969–; Appearances in Hamburg, London, Paris, Barcelona, Vienna, Cologne, Met New York, San Carlo (Naples); Over 140 roles, including Violetta, Jenůfa, Madama Butterfly, Minnie in La Fanciulla del West and Countess in Die Soldaten by Zimmermann; Has sung Janáček's Vixen, Katya and Emilia Marty, Magda in La Rondine, and roles in Schreker's Die Gezeichneten, Henze's Der Junge Lord and Bassarids and The Rake's Progress; Sieglinde and Katerina Izmailova; Frankfurt, 1988 in Poulenc's La Voix Humaine; Holland Festival in The Oresteia by Milhaud; Produced La Clemenza di Tito at Giessen, 1988; Fidelio, in France; Sang the Mother in Die Wände Adriana Hölsky at Frankfurt, 2000; Professor for Opera and Voice, University of Illinois, 1999–; Produced Mozart's Figaro and Così fan tutte, Weill's Street Scene. *Recordings:* Traviata, Gezeichneten. *Current Management:* Agentur Haase, 80802 Munich, Martiussti 3, Germany. *Address:* Arabellastrasse 5-1411, 81925 Munich, Germany.

CARDEN, Joan Maralyn, AO, OBE; Australian opera and concert singer; b. 9 Oct. 1937, Richmond, Vic.; d. of late Frank Carden and of Margaret Carden (née Cooke); m. William Coyne 1962 (divorced 1980); two d. *Education:* schools in Melbourne, language studies in London, Trinity Coll. of Music, London and London Opera Centre, voice studies with Thea Phillips and Henry Portnoj, Melbourne and Vida Harford, London. *Career:* debut, world premiere of Malcolm Williamson's Our Man in Havana, Sadler's Wells, 1963; joined Australian Opera (Opera Australia) 1971–; Royal Nat. Opera, Covent Garden as Gilda (Rigoletto) 1974; Glyndebourne as Anna (Don Giovanni) 1977; Scottish Opera as Constanze 1977; US debut at Houston as Amenaide (Tancredi) 1977, Metropolitan Opera Tour as Anna (Don Giovanni) 1978, Kennedy Center 1980, Miami Opera 1981; Singapore Festival 1983; Adelaide Festival 1984; other appearances include Victoria State Opera, Lyric Opera of Queensland, State Opera of South Australia; major roles include most Mozart heroines, Liu (Turandot), Marguerite (Faust), Gilda (Rigoletto), 4 heroines (Contes d'Hoffmann), Natasha (War and Peace), Tatyana (Onegin), Lakme, Leonora (Forza del Destino/Il Trovatore), Violetta (La Traviata), Alice (Falstaff), Mimi, Musetta (La Bohème), Madama Butterfly, Eva (Die Meistersinger), Feldmarschallin (Der Rosenkavalier), Elisabetta (Maria Stuarda), Medee, Tosca, Mother Abbess (Sound of Music); performs regularly in concert with SSO, MSO and QSO, and for Australian Broadcasting Corpn; concert repertoire includes Mozart Masses, concert arias, choral works, 4 Letzte Lieder (R. Strauss), works by Australian composers including Moya Henderson, Peter Sculthorpe. *Recordings:* Joan Carden Sings Mozart, Great Opera Heroines: Joan Carden. *Honours:* Dame Joan Hammond Award for Outstanding Service to Opera in Australia 1987, Australian Government Creative Fellowship 1993, DUniv (Swinburne Univ. of Technology, Melbourne) 2000. *Address:* Opera Australia, PO Box 291, Strawberry Hills, NSW 2012, Australia.

CARDY, Patrick Robert Thomas, BMus, MMA, DMus; Canadian composer and professor of music; b. 22 Aug. 1953, Toronto, ON. *Education:* University of Western Ontario, McGill University. *Career:* Professor, School for Studies in Art and Culture, Carleton University, Ottawa, 1977–; performances in Canada, USA and Europe. *Compositions include:* Golden Days, Silver Nights, 1977; Vox Humana, 1977; Jig, 1984; Mirages, 1984; Outremer: The Land Beyond the Sea, 1985; Mimesis, 1987; Qilakitsoq: The Sky Hangs Low, 1988; Tango!, 1989; Tombeau, 1989; The Little Mermaid, 1990; Avalon, 1991; Serenade, 1992; Chaconne, 1992; Autumn, 1992; 'Dulce et decorum est...', 1993; Danses folles et amoureuses, 1993; Et in Arcadia ego, 1994; Fhir a Bhata: The Boatman, 1994; Silver and Shadow, 1994; Te Deum, 1995; Dreams of the Sídhe, 1995; La Folia, 1996; Sans Souci, 1996; Bonavista, 1997; The Return of the Hero, 1997; '...and in the night the gentle earth is falling into morning...', 1998; Kalenda Maya, 1999; Zodiac Dances, 2000: Trabadores, 2000; Rhythm in Your Rubbish, 2001. *Recordings include:* Virelai; Éclat; Tango!; Tombeau; Dances Folles et Amoureuses; Sans Souci; Liesel, Suse, Ilze and Gerda; Jig; Numerous on major labels. *Address:* 29 Morgan's Grant Way, Kanata, ON K2K 2G2, Canada.

CARELLA, Giuiliano; Conductor; b. 1956, Milan, Italy. *Education:* Studied with Franco Ferrara at Siena. *Career:* Conductor of opera performances throughout Europe from 1986; Engagements at Verona, Munich and Hamburg Staatsoperas; Bologna, Salle Gaveau, Paris, Barcelona and Buenos Aires; L'Italiana in Algeri for the Bayerische Staatsoper; Festival of Martina Franca, with operas by Mercadante, and L'Ultimo Giorno di Pompei, by Pacini, 1996; La Morte di Didone at the Rossini Festival Pesaro, and the premiere of Lorenco Ferrero's La Nascite di Orfeo, at the Verona Teatro Filarmonico. *Recordings include:* Ernani; La Sonnambula by Bellini; Il Giuramento and Caritea regina di Spagna by Mercadante (Dynamic); L'Ultimo Giorno di Pompei (Dynamic). *Address:* c/o Accademia Chigiana, Via di Citta 69, 53100 Siena, Italy.

CAREWE, John (Maurice Foxall); Conductor; b. 24 Jan. 1933, Derby, England; 2 d. *Education:* Guildhall School of Music and Drama, London; Conservatoire National, Paris. *Career:* Founded Music Today, New Music Ensemble, 1958; Principal Conductor, BBC National Orchestra of Wales, 1966–71; Musical Director, Principal Conductor, Brighton Philharmonic Society, 1974–87; Principal Conductor, Fires of London, 1980–94; General Music Director of the Opera and the Robert Schumann Philharmonic, Chemnitz, 1993–96. *Recordings:* Stravinsky, Histoire du Soldat; Milhaud, Création du Monde; Bennett, Calendar; Maxwell Davies, Leopardi Fragments; Bedford, Music for Albion Moonlight; Debussy, Ibéria; Falla, Interlude and Dance, La Vida Breve; Bridge, Enter Spring and Oration; Colin Matthews, Landscape and Cello Concerto; Muller-Siemens, Under Neon Light I; Leyendecker, Cello Concerto; Debussy, Pelléas et Mélisande; Dvořák, Symphony No. 8; Brahms, Tragic Overture. *Honours:* Bablock Prize, 1960. *Current Management:* Jürgen Erlebach, Hamburg. *Address:* c/o Jürgen Erlebach, Grillparzerstrasse 24, 22085 Hamburg 76, Germany.

CAREY, Thomas; Singer (Baritone); b. 29 Dec. 1931, Bennetsville, Connecticut, USA. *Education:* Studied at the Henry Street Music School, New York, and with Rose Bampton; Further study at the Stuttgart Musikhochschule and with Hans Hotter. *Career:* Debut: Netherlands Opera, Amsterdam, as Germont, 1964; Sang in Lisbon, Nice, Paris, Stockholm, Basle, Zagreb, Venice and Belgrade; Guest singer at the State Operas of Munich, Hamburg, Stuttgart and Berlin; Covent Garden, 1970, as Mel in the premiere of Tippett's The Knot Garden; US engagements in Boston, Memphis and New Orleans; Many concert appearances; Teacher of Voice at the University of Oklahoma, Norman. *Recordings include:* The Knot Garden. *Address:* c/o University of Oklahoma, Catlett Music Center, Norman, OK 73019, USA.

CARIAGA, Marvellee; Singer (Mezzo-soprano); b. 11 Aug. 1942, California, USA. *Education:* Studied at California State University. *Career:* Sang with San Diego Opera from 1971; Fricka in performances of Der Ring des Nibelungen for Seattle Opera, 1975–81; Guest appearances at Vancouver, 1975–78, San Francisco, 1981, and Pittsburgh, Portland and Los Angeles, 1987–88; Rio de Janeiro, 1979, as Santuzza; Netherlands Opera, 1979 and 1982; Other roles have included Wagner's Venus, Ortrud, Waltraute, Brünnhilde (Siegfried), Isolde and Magdalene; Donna Anna, Amelia (Ballo in Maschera), Herodias and Kostelnicka in Jenůfa; Colorado, 1986, in the premiere of Pasatieri's The Three Sisters; Los Angeles Music Center Opera, 1991, as Mrs Grose in The Turn of the Screw; Mrs Herring at the Dorothy Chandler Pavilion, Los Angeles, 1992. *Recordings include:* The Three Sisters. *Address:* Los Angeles Music Center Opera, 135 North Grand Avenue, Los Angeles, CA 90012, USA.

CARIDIS, Miltiades; Greek Conductor; b. 9 May 1923, Danzig; m. Dr Sonja Dengel, 1 d. *Education:* Diploma in Conducting, Music Academy, Vienna, Austria, 1947. *Career:* Permanent Conductor, Opera in Graz, Cologne, Vienna (State Opera); Permanent Conductor, Danish Radio Symphony Orchestra, Copenhagen, 1962–69; Conductor in Chief, Philharmonia Hungarica, 1960–67; Artistic and Music Director, Philharmonic Society, Oslo, 1969–75; Conductor in Chief, Duisburg Symphony Orchestra, Germany, 1975–81; Artistic and Music Director, Tonkünstler-Orchester, Vienna, 1979–85; Guest Conductor to over 100 orchestras and 80 choirs since 1995; Artistic and Music Director, Radio Symphony Orchestra, Athens. *Address:* Himmelhofgasse 10, 1130 Vienna, Austria.

CARL, Eugene (Gene) Marion, Jr; Composer and Pianist; b. 8 Nov. 1953, Los Angeles, California, USA. *Education:* BA cum laude, Pomona College, USA, 1971–75; Freiburg im Breisgau, Germany, 1974; Institute for Sonology, Utrecht State University, Netherlands, 1975–76; Prize for Composition, Royal Conservatory, The Hague, 1976–81; Piano studies with John Ritter, 1971–74, Geoffrey Madge, 1976–81, master classes with Padolsky, Voorhies, Kontarsky; Composition with Karl Kohn, 1971–75, Konrad Lechner, 1974, Jan van Vlymen and Jan Boerman, 1976–81, master classes, Darmstadt, 1976. *Career:* Debut: Beethoven Piano Concerto No. 1, with Sepulveda Orchestra, 1968; Composition teaching; (Co-)Producer for special projects; Synthesizer programming and performance De Materie, L. Andriessen and Robert Wilson; Gene Carl band tours, 1995–96, 1996–97, 2000–01; Resident at the Djerassi Foundation near San Francisco, 1999. *Compositions include:* Scratch, violin solo, 1985; Gagarin for double orchestra, mixed choir, 2 solo voices, children's choir, synthesizers, tape, 1986–99; Leonardo, Leonardo for violin, electric guitar, tuba, drum kit, synthesizers, tape, voice, 1986; Hommage à Tarkovski for 2 saxophones, violin, synthesizers, percussion, tape, 1987; Claremont Concerto for B-flat clarinet, piano and string quartet, 1987; Roscoe Boulevard for 2 saxophones (doubling bass clarinet and clarinet) and ensemble, 1988; Pink Chinese Restaurants, a cantata for mezzo and 8 instruments, 1990; Laika for solo synthesiser, 1993; Nocturne for tuba, string trio and synthesizer, 1996; Tree of Time for 7 pianos, 1996; Below Paradise for 8 instruments, 1996; Wyoming Elegy, cantata for baritone and 8 instruments (in memoriam

Matthew Shepard), 1998–2000. *Recordings:* 2 albums as member of Hoketus Ensemble; Pianist with 5 UUs; Motor Totemist Guild; Balans, with Hoketus. *Contributions:* Co-editor, Ed., 1976–78, Journal of the Schoenberg Institute; Key Notes, Amsterdam; Cage's Sonatas and Interludes, catalogue, Antiqua Musica, Municiple Museum, The Hague, 1989. *Honours:* Djerassi Resident Artist Program, 1999. *Address:* c/o Donemus, Paulus Potterstraat 14, 1071 CZ Amsterdam, Netherlands.

CARL, Jeffrey; Singer (Baritone); b. 1961, Canada. *Education:* BMus, Hons, Voice Performance, McGill University; Diploma, University of Toronto, with Louis Quilico, at Siena and the Britten-Pears School. *Career:* Nick Shadow in Stravinsky's The Rake's Progress, Vancouver Opera; Ford in Falstaff at the Aldeburgh Festival; Verdi's Germont, di Luna, Macbeth; Puccini's Sharpless, Marcello, Scarpia; Tchaikovsky's Onegin, Mozart's Don Giovanni, Guglielmo; Donizetti's Enrico; Bellini's Riccardo, Gounod's Valentin, Thomas' Hamlet, Bizet's Escamillo as well as Henry VIII (Saint-Saëns), Genoveva (Schumann), Brandenburgers in Bohemia (Smetana) and Gershwin's Blue Monday, Italian debut in 1997; Concerts include: standard repertoire under David Willcocks with the Montreal Symphony, Simon Rattle with the Royal Liverpool Philharmonic and Michael Tippett: Messiah, Carmina Burana, Verdi's Requiem, Beethoven's Ninth, Bach Passions, The Creation, Belshazzar's Feast; Further engagements include: La Gioconda in Toronto, Carmen in Portugal, Child of Our Time in Singapore, Mascagni's Iris in Italy, Ballo in Maschera in Italy, Falstaff (Ford) in London, Mahler Eighth and Scarpia in Verona. *Recordings:* Weill's Firebrand of Florence with Thomas Hampson; La Bohème (Alagna, Ramey, Vaduva, Pappano conducting); The Czarevich with Hadley/Gustafson and Giuditta with Hadley/Riedel conducted by Richard Bonynge; Further recordings include: Caterina Cornaro, Donizetti, with Richard Bonynge. *Address:* c/o Franco Silvestri, Via Marconi 2, 37011 Bardolina, Italy.

CARLOS, Wendy, AB, MA; American synthesist, recording engineer and composer; b. (Walter Carlos), 14 Nov. 1939, Pawtucket, RI. *Education:* Brown Univ., Columbia Univ. *Career:* worked as a recording engineer, associating with Robert Moog in the development of the Moog Synthesizer 1964; pioneer in utilising the resources of the synthesizer; collaboration with Larry Fast in the development of a digital process of soundtrack restoration and surround stereo conversion, Digi-Surround Stereo Sound 1992–95; has delivered papers at New York Univ., Audio Engineering Soc. Digital Audio Conference, Dolby New York City Surround Sound demonstration and panel, and at other music/audio conferences; mem. Audio Engineering Soc., Soc. of Motion Picture and Television Engineers, Nat. Acad. of Recording Arts and Sciences. *Compositions include:* Noah (opera) 1964. *Recordings include:* albums as Walter Carlos: Switched-on Bach (three Grammy Awards) 1968, The Well-Tempered Synthesizer 1969, Timesteps 1970, Sonic Seasonings 1972, A Clockwork Orange (soundtrack) 1972, Pompous Circumstances 1974, Switched-on Bach II 1974, By Request 1975; albums as Wendy Carlos: Switched-on Brandenburgs 1979, The Shining (soundtrack) 1980, Tron (soundtrack) 1982, Digital Moonscapes 1984, Beauty In the Beast 1986, Land of the Midnight Sun 1986, Secrets of Synthesis 1987, Peter and the Wolf (with Al Yankovic) 1988, Woundings (soundtrack) 1998, Switched-On Bach 2000 1992, Tales of Heaven and Hell 1998, Switched-On Boxed Set 1999. *Address:* c/o Audio Engineering Society Inc., International Headquarters, 60 E 42nd Street, Room 2520, New York, NY 10165-2520, USA. *E-mail:* email@wendycarlos.com. *Website:* www.wendycarlos.com.

CARLSEN, Toril; Singer (Soprano); b. 1954, Oslo, Norway. *Education:* Studied in Oslo and Budapest. *Career:* Appearances at the National Theatre, Oslo, from 1979, notably as Fiordiligi, Pamina, Adina, Musetta, Micaela and Zdenka; Guest at the Berlin Staatsoper from 1989 (Mélisande, 1991); Many concert appearances. *Recordings include:* Peer Gynt by Grieg (Unicorn). *Address:* c/o Den Norske Opera, PO Box 8800, Youngstorget, 0028 Oslo, Norway.

CARLSON, Claudine; Singer (Mezzo-soprano); b. 26 Feb. 1950, Mulhouse, France. *Education:* Vocal training in California; Pupil of Gertrude Gruenberg, Jennie Tourel and Esther Andreas, Manhattan School of Music, New York. *Career:* Numerous appearances as soloist with major orchestras, including Boston Symphony, Detroit Symphony, New York Philharmonic, Minnesota Philharmonic, Los Angeles Philharmonic, St Louis Symphony, National Symphony, London Symphony Orchestra, Orchestre de Paris, Israel Philharmonic; Many festival appearances; Recitalist world-wide. *Recordings:* Various labels. *Honours:* 1st Prize, National Federation of Music Clubs Singing Competition; Martha Baird Rockefeller Award. *Address:* c/o ICM Artists Ltd, 40 West 57th Street, New York, NY 10019, USA.

CARLSON, Lenus (Jesse); Singer (Baritone) and Teacher; b. 11 Feb. 1945, Jamestown, North Dakota, USA; m. Linda Kay Jones, 20 Aug 1972. *Education:* BA, 1967; Postgraduate studies with Oren Brown, Juilliard School, 1970–73. *Career:* Apprentice Artist, Central City (Colorado) Opera, 1965–66; Debut as Demetrius, Midsummer Night's

Dream, Minnesota Opera, 1968; Sang with opera companies in Dallas, 1972–73, San Antonio, 1973, Boston, 1973, Washington DC, 1973, New York (Metropolitan Opera, debut as Berlioz's Aeneas, 23 Feb 1973), Amsterdam, 1974, others; British debut, Scottish Opera, Edinburgh Festival, 1975; Covent Garden debut, London, as Valentin, 1976; Sang at the Deutsche Oper Berlin as Paul in Die tote Stadt by Korngold, 1983; Nevers in Les Huguenots, 1987, Arcesias in Die toten Augen by d'Albert, 1987; Premiere of Oedipus by Wolfgang Rihm, 1988; Sang the Acrobat in Lulu at the Festival Hall, London, 1994; Creon in Enescu's Oedipe at the Deutsche Oper, 1996 and Klingsor in Parsifal, 1998; Season 1999–2000 at the Deutsche Oper as the Speaker in Die Zauberflöte, Strauss's Faninal and Kothner in Die Meistersinger; Various concert engagements; Teacher, Voice, Minneapolis, 1965–70, New York, 1970–. *Address:* c/o Columbia Artists Management Inc, 165 West 57th Street, New York, NY 10019, USA.

CARLYLE, Joan Hildred; singer (soprano); b. 6 April 1931, Wirral, Cheshire, England; two d. *Education:* studied with Bertha Nicklass Kempner. *Career:* debut, Covent Garden 1955, Frasquita; Principal Lyric Soprano, Covent Garden; Major roles sung in the United Kingdom include: Oscar, Ballo in Maschera, 1957–58; Sophie, Der Rosenkavalier, 1958–69; Glauce in Medea with Maria Callas; Nedda, Pagliacci, Zeffirelli production, 1959; Mimi, La Bohème, 1960; Titania, Midsummer Night's Dream, Britten (Gielgud production), 1960; Pamina, Magic Flute, 1962, 1966; Countess, Marriage of Figaro, 1963; Zdenka, Arabella (Hartmann production), 1964; Suor Angelica, 1965; Desdemona, Otello, 1965; Arabella, 1967; Marschallin, Der Rosenkavalier, 1968; Jenifer, Midsummer Marriage, 1969; Donna Anna, 1970; Reiza, Oberon, 1970; Adriana Lecouvreur, 1970; Rusalka, and Elisabetta in Don Carlos, 1975; Major roles sung abroad include Oscar, Nedda, Mimi, Pamina, Zdenka, Micaela, Donna Anna, Arabella, Elisabetta and Desdemona; Debuts at Salzburg, Metropolitan Opera, New York, and Teatro Colón, Buenos Aires, 1968; Teaching at home and privately in London, writing and promoting young singers and concerts; masterclasses. *Recordings include:* Karajan's production of Pagliacci as Nedda and Midsummer Marriage as Jenifer; Madama Butterfly duet (with Carlo Cossutta), Depuis le jour, Vissi d'Arte and Mahler's Fourth Symphony conducted by Britten (BBC), all 2000, Voice from the old House: includes VFOH 1/11, 12/29, 30/42 compilations, 43 Suor Angelica, 44/45 Otello, 46 La Bohème excerpts, 47/48 Arabella. *Address:* Laundry Cottage, Hanmer, Clywdd, SY13 3DQ, Wales. *E-mail:* joancarlyle@bt.click. *Website:* www.joancarlyle.co.uk.

CARMICHAEL, John Russell; Composer; b. 5 Oct. 1930, Melbourne, Victoria, Australia. *Education:* Mus Dip (Hons), University of Melbourne, 1951; Paris Conservatoire, 1954; Study with Arthur Benjamin 1955–57 and Anthony Milner, 1957–60; Commission from Friends of the Victorian Opera, 1995. *Compositions include:* Concierto Folklorico, for piano and strings, 1970; Trumpet Concerto, 1975; Fantasy Concerto for flute and orchestra, 1982; Lyric Concerto for cornet and piano, 1982; A Country Flair for clarinet and orchestra, 1989; Fêtes Champêtres for clarinet, 1989; Monotony for 2 pianos, 1990; When Will the Sun for soprano and piano, 1990; Bravura Waltzes for 2 pianos, 1990; Saxophone Concerto, 1990; Dark Scenarios for 2 pianos, 1994; From the Dark Side for piano, 1995. *Address:* c/o APRA, 1A Eden Street, Crows Nest, NSW 2065, Australia.

CARR, Colin (Michael); Cellist; b. 25 Oct. 1957, Liverpool, England. *Education:* Yehudi Menuhin School, 1966–74; Associate (Honours), Royal College of Music, 1972. *Career:* Soloist throughout Europe, North America, Australia and Far East with major orchestras including: The Royal Philharmonic Orchestra, Concertgebouw Orchestra, BBC Symphony, Philharmonic, Chicago Symphony, National Symphony Washington, English Chamber Orchestra, Scottish Chamber Orchestra, CBSO, Philadelphia Orchestra, Montreal Symphony; Recitals, London, Amsterdam, Paris, New York, Washington, Boston, Los Angeles, television and radio recordings, throughout both continents; Faculty Member, New England Conservatory, Boston, USA, 1983–89; Royal Academy of Music 1998–; State University of New York Story Brook, 2002–. *Recordings:* Sonatas by Debussy and Franck; Elegie, Romance and Papillon by Fauré; Complete Schubert works for Piano Trio; Complete Mendelssohn works for Piano Trio; Complete Brahms Trios with Golub, Kaplan, Carr Trio; Bach Solo Cello Suites; Brahms Sonatas. *Address:* c/o Caroline Baird Artists, 9 Onslow Gardens, London, N10 3JT, England.

CARR-BOYD, Ann; Composer; b. 13 July 1938, Sydney, New South Wales, Australia. *Education:* Studied at the University of Sydney (MA, 1963) and in London with Fricker and Goehr. *Career:* Teacher at the University of Sydney, 1967–73. *Compositions include:* Symphony, 1964; 2 string quartets, 1964, 1966; Vocal music, including Home Thoughts from Abroad for mezzo and ensemble, 1987; Instrumental pieces, including Dance Suite for woodwind quintet, 1984, and Theme and Variations for organ, 1989. *Address:* c/o APRA, 1A Eden Street, Crows Nest, New South Wales 2065, Australia.

CARRERAS, José; Singer (Tenor); b. 5 Dec. 1946, Barcelona, Spain; 1 s., 1 d. *Career:* Debut: Flavio (Norma), Gennaro (Lucrezia Borgia), Teatro Liceu, 1970–71; Appeared in La Bohème, Un Ballo in Maschera and I Lombardi, Teatro Reggio Parma, Italy, after winning 1972 Verdi singing competition; US debut as Pinkerton in Madama Butterfly, New York City Opera, 1972; Metropolitan Opera House debut, 1974, as Cavaradossi; Teatro alla Scala Milan debut, 1975, Riccardo in Un Ballo in Maschera; Appeared in film and video versions of Don Carlos, Andrea Chénier, I Lombardi, La Bohème, Verdi's Requiem Mass, Stiffelio, My Life (personal life story), Turandot, West Side Story (the recording); Other appearances include Teatro Col ón, Buenos Aires, Vienna Staatsoper, Royal Opera House, Covent Garden, London, Salzburg Easter and Summer Festivals, Lyric Opera House, Chicago, War Memorial Opera House, San Francisco, notably as Alfredo (La Traviata), Nemorino (L'Elisir d'amore), Andrea Chénier, Don José (Carmen), Radames (Aida), Werther, Edgardo (Lucia di Lammermoor), Alvaro (La Forza del Destino), Manrico (Il Trovatore); Returned to concert and stage after illness, 1987; Open air concert for audience of 150,000, 1988; Sang with 2 other tenors at World Cup Finals concert, Rome, 1990; appeared as Loris in Fedora at Covent Garden, 1994, and at La Scala, 1996; Sang Sly in the American premiere of Wolf-Ferrari's opera Washington, 1999; Founder, President, José Carreras International Leukaemia Foundation, 1988–. *Recordings:* Un Ballo in Maschera; Tosca; Turandot; Werther; Aida; La Bohème; Don Carlo; Requiem Mass (Verdi); West Side Story; South Pacific; La Forza del Destino; Carmen; Pagliacci. *Publications:* Singing with the Soul, autobiography, 1989. *Honours:* Winner, Laurence Olivier Award, 1993. *Current Management:* Carlos Caballé, Opera Caballé, Barcelona. *Address:* c/o Musicaglotz, 11 rue le Verrier, F~75006, Paris, France.

CARRINGTON, Simon (Robert); Musician, Bass Player and Music Director; b. 23 Oct. 1942, Salisbury, Wiltshire, England; m. Hilary Stott, 2 Aug 1969. 1 s., 1 d. *Education:* Christ Church Cathedral Choir School, Oxford; The King's School, Canterbury; King's College, Cambridge; New College, Oxford; MA (Cantab); Teaching Certificate (Oxon); Choral Scholar, King's College, Cambridge. *Career:* Co-Founder and Director of the King's Singers, 1968–93 with 3,000 performances world-wide and numerous concerts, radio and television appearances; Freelance Double Bass Player with all major British symphony and chamber orchestras; Since 1994 Professor, Artist in Residence and Director of Choral Activities at the University of Kansas; Monteverdi Vespers, 1994; Britten War Requiem, Tallis 40 part Motet, Tribute to Henry Purcell, 1995; Walton Belshazzar's Feast, Ligeti Lux Aeterna, Josquin Missa Gaudeamus, 1996; Mendelssohn Elijah (staged as an opera), Music from the time of the Mexican Viceroys, Bach Motets, 1997; Director of the Graduate Degree Programs in Choral Directing; Freelance Choral Workshop Director and Choral Competition Judge in the United Kingdom, USA, France, Germany, Netherlands and Hungary; Choral Conductor world-wide including Carnegie Hall performances, 1996 and 1997. *Compositions:* Numerous arrangements for The King's Singers. *Recordings:* Numerous with various labels internationally, 1971–93 including madrigals, motets, folk songs from five centuries. *Publications:* The King's Singers–A Self Portrait, 1981; Video: The Art of The King's Singers. *Address:* Department of Music and Dance, 332 Murphy Hall, University of Kansas, Lawrence, KS 66044, USA.

CARROLI, Silvano; Singer (Baritone); b. 22 Feb. 1939, Venice, Italy. *Education:* Studied at the Opera School of La Fenice, Venice. *Career:* Debut: Venice 1964, as Marcello in La Bohème; Sang widely in Italy and toured North America with the company of La Scala, 1976; Verona Arena from 1973, in Samson et Dalila, as Ezio in Attila (1985), Renato in Un Ballo in Maschera (1986) and as Amonasro (2000); Washington Opera 1977–78, as Cavaradossi; London, Covent Garden, as Iago and in La Fanciulla del West; Chicago Lyric Opera 1978; Brussels 1980, in a revival of Donizetti's Il Duca d'Alba; Barcelona 1983, as Escamillo; Paris Opéra 1984, as Nabucco and in Verdi's Jérusalem; Further appearances at the Metropolitan Opera and at the Deutsche Oper Berlin; Amonasro, Luxor, Egypt, 1987; Season 1988–89, Barnaba, Alfio at Verona, Michele in Il Tabarro at Florence, Puccini's Jack Rance at Caracalla Festival, Rome; Iago, Covent Garden, 1990; Scarpia, Arena di Verona; Season 1992, as Gerard in Andrea Chénier at Turin, Scarpia at Covent Garden, Amonasro at the Festival of Caracalla; Sang Scarpia at Hanover, 1994 and at Verona, 1998. *Recordings include:* Video of I Lombardi (Topaz). *Address:* c/o Stafford Law Associates, 6 Barham Close, Weybridge, Surrey KT 13 9 PR, England.

CARROLL, Joan; Singer (Soprano); b. 27 July 1932, Philadelphia, USA. *Education:* Studied in America, then with Margarethe von Winterfeldt in Berlin. *Career:* Debut: New York Opera Company 1957, as Zerbinetta; Appearances in North America and in Havana; Santa Fe 1963, as Lulu (US premiere of Berg's opera); European engagements in Belgium, France, Denmark, Switzerland and Netherlands; Sang Lulu in Hamburg, Munich and Zürich during the 1960s; Member of the Deutsche Oper am Rhein, Düsseldorf, from 1967; Sang Mozart's Constanze, Donna Anna and Queen of Night, as well as modern repertory, in Hanover, Berlin, Stuttgart, Cologne and Nuremberg. *Recordings include:* Works by Gorecki and Stravinsky.

CARRON, Elizabeth; Singer (Soprano); b. 12 Feb. 1933, New York, NY, USA. *Education:* Studied in New York. *Career:* Debut: New York City Opera, 1957, as Madama Butterfly; Sang in New York until 1977 and made guest appearances in Cincinnati, Chicago, Pittsburgh, San Francisco and New Orleans; Dallas, 1958, as Dirce in Cherubini's Médée, opposite Maria Callas; Edinburgh Festival, 1984, with the Washington Opera; Other roles have included Mozart's Constanze, Susanna and Zerlina, Violetta, Micaela, Mimi and Liu, Norina, Strauss's Salome and Daphne, Aithra in Die Ägyptische Helena and Birdie in Regina by Blitzstein. *Recordings include:* Regina. *Address:* c/o Washington Opera, Kennedy Center for the Performing Arts, Washington, DC 30566, USA.

CARSEN, Robert; stage director; b. 23 June 1954, Toronto, Canada. *Education:* Upper Canada College, York University, Toronto, Bristol Old Vic Theatre School. *Career:* Assistant Dir, Glyndebourne Festival Opera, 1982–85; Production of Boito's Mefistofele seen at Geneva 1988 and at San Francisco, Chicago, Houston, Washington and Metropolitan Operas, 1989–99; Aix-en-Provence Festival from 1991–96, with A Midsummer Night's Dream, Handel's Orlando, Die Zauberflöte, Semele (French premiere); Salome in Lyon; Bellini's La Straniera for Wexford, A Village Romeo and Juliet for Opera North, Mozart's Finta Semplice and Finta Giardiniera for the Camden Festival, London, and Cendrillon for Welsh National Opera; Metropolitan Opera debut with Eugene Onegin, European premiere of Blitzstein's Regina for Scottish Opera; Lucia di Lammermoor at Zürich and Munich, Katya Kabanova in Canada and Figaro for Bordeaux, Paris, Israel and Barcelona, 1997; seven-part Puccini cycle for the Flemish Opera, 1990–96; Otello, Falstaff and Macbeth in Cologne, Die Frau ohne Schatten and Verdi's Jérusalem in Vienna; Alcina, Lohengrin, Nabucco, Capuleti e i Montecchi and Manon Lescaut at the Opéra Bastille, Paris; Carmelites in Amsterdam, Semele at English National Opera and Antwerp; Tales of Hoffmann for the Paris Opéra, The Ring in Cologne, Jenůfa and Cunning Little Vixen in Antwerp, Dialogues of the Carmelites at La Scala; Capriccio for Paris Opera, Rosenkavalier at Salzburg, La Traviata at Teatro La Fenice, Venice, 2004; Elektra for Tokyo Opera Nomuri with Seiji Ozawa, Manon Lescaut at the Vienna Staatsoper and Il Trovatore in Bregenz 2005. *Honours:* Carl Ebert Award for directing, 1982; French Critics Prize, 1992; Chevalier des Arts et des Lettres, 1996; Grand Prix de la Presse Musicale Internationale, 1996. *Address:* Judy Daish Associates Ltd, 2 St Charles Place, London, W10 6EG, England.

CARSON, Clarice; Singer (Soprano); b. 23 Dec. 1936, Montreal, Canada. *Education:* Studied with Pauline Donalda and Jacqueline Richard in Montreal, with Julia Drobner in New York. *Career:* Debut: Montreal Opera 1962, in Menotti's Amahl and the Night Visitors; Many guest engagements in North America; New York City Opera 1965, as Mozart's Countess; Metropolitan Touring Opera 1967; European engagements in Barcelona, Rouen, Amsterdam and with Scottish Opera, Glasgow, 1969; Schwetzingen 1976, as Paer's Leonora; Other roles include Cassandre in Les Troyens; Mozart's Donna Anna, and Constanze; Verdi's Desdemona, Violetta, Aida, Elisabeth, Amelia and Leonora (Il Trovatore); Puccini's Tosca, Mimi, Liu, Butterfly and Musetta; Marguerite in Faust and the title role in Salome; Many concert performances. *Recordings include:* Leonora by Paer (MRF).

CARTER, Barbara; American singer (soprano); b. 1947, Columbus, Ohio, USA. *Education:* Studied at Capital University; University of Toronto with Louis Quilico; Musical Academy of the West with Martial Singher. *Career:* Sang Violetta and Musetta with the Canadian Opera Company on tour of the USA and Canada; European debut with the Essen Opera, then appeared as Queen of Night in Die Zauberflöte with the Covent Garden Opera on tour to the Far East; Further appearances in Berlin, Munich, Buenos Aires, Paris, Vienna, Amsterdam, La Scala, Milan, Venice, Barcelona, New York, Ottawa and Bregenz; Roles have included Lucia, Gilda, Marie in La Fille du Régiment, Zerbinetta, Sophie, Constanze, Zerlina, Rosina, Elvira in Puritani, Amenaide in Tancredi, Olympia, Nannetta and Gretel; Season 1990–91 as Constanze in Amsterdam and the Italian Singer in Capriccio at the Vienna Staatsoper; Concert appearances in works by Bach, Mozart, Haydn, Handel, Brahms, Orff, Schubert and Charpentier; Mahler's Symphonies 2, 4 and 8; Engagements with Giuseppe Sinopoli leading the Czech Philharmonic, the Philharmonia (London) on tour in Japan, the Accademia di Santa Cecilia in Rome and the Deutsche Oper Berlin (Fiakermilli in Arabella); Recital repertoire includes German Lieder and songs in Russian, French, English, Spanish, Italian and Portuguese. *Honours:* Life Achievement Award Capital Univ., Columbus, Ohio 1996. *Address:* Bruckerstrasse 7, 82284 Grafrath, Germany. *E-mail:* barbara.carter@soprano.de (home). *Website:* www.soprano.de (home).

CARTER, Elliott Cook, Jr; Composer and Teacher; b. 11 Dec. 1908, New York, NY, USA; m. Helen Frost-Jones, 6 July 1939, 1 s. *Education:* Piano, Longy School of Music; MA, Harvard University, 1932; Licence de contrepoint, Ecole Normale de Musique, Paris, Nadia Boulanger; Literature, languages, harmony and counterpoint with Walter Piston, orchestration, E B Hill. *Career:* Music Director, Ballet Caravan, 1937–39; Teacher, Music, Mathematics, Physics, Classical Greek, St John's College, Annapolis, 1939–41; Faculty: Peabody Conservatory of Music, 1946–48; Columbia, 1948–50; Yale, 1958–62; Composer in residence, American Academy, Rome, 1963; Professor at large, Cornell, 1967–68; Violin Concerto British premiere, Carter Festival, South Bank, London, 1991. *Compositions:* 2 ballets: Pocahontas, 1936, The Minotaur, 1947; Symphony No. 1, 1942, 1954; Chamber Elegy, cello, piano, 1943, arrangements, 1946, 1952, 1961; Holiday Overture, 1944, 1961; Sonata, cello, piano, 1948; Woodwind Quintet, 1948; 5 String Quartets, 1950–51, 1959, 1971, 1986, 1995; Elegy, strings, 1952; Sonata, 1952; Variations, orchestra, 1954–55; Double Concerto, harpsichord, piano, 2 chamber orchestras, 1961; Piano Concerto, 1964–65; Canon for 3: In Memoriam Igor Stravinsky, 3 equal instruments, 1971; Duo, violin, piano, 1973–74; Brass Quintet, 1974; A Symphony of 3 Orchestras, 1976; Night Fantasies, piano, 1980; Triple Duo, violin, cello, flute, clarinet, piano, percussion, 1982–83; Changes, guitar, 1983; Esprit rude-esprit doux, flute, clarinet, 1984; Penthode, 5 instrumental quartets, 1984–85; Oboe Concerto, 1987; Enchanted Preludes, flute, cello, 1988; Remembrance, 1988; Violin Concerto, 1990; Con leggerezza pensosa, clarinet, violin, cello, 1990; Anniversary, orchestra, 1991; Trilogy, harp, oboe, 1992; Quintet, piano, winds, 1992; Adagio Tenebroso, 1995; Clarinet Concerto, 1997; Symphonia, 1997; Luimen for ensemble, 1998; Piano Quintet, 1998; Opera, What Next?, premiered at the Berlin Staatsoper, 1999; Tempo e tempi, 1999; Asko Concerto, 1999–2000; Oboe Quartet, 2001; Boston Concerto, 2002; Incidental music; Choral and vocal works. *Honours:* Guggenheim Fellow, 1945, 1950; American Prix de Rome, 1953; Pulitzer Prize, Music, 1960, 1973; Various honorary doctorates; National Medal of Arts, 1985; Chevalier, Ordre des Arts et des Lettres, 1990; Commendatore, Italian Order of Merit; Prince Rainier Foundation Prize, Monaco, 1998. *Address:* c/o Boosey & Hawkes, 295 Regent Street, London W1R 8JH, England.

CARTER, Peter (John Burnett); Violinist; b. 30 Jan. 1935, Durban, South Africa; m. Sally Mackay, 20 Dec 1974, 1 s., 1 d. *Education:* Royal College of Music, London, 1952–55; Conservatoire Royale de Musique, Brussels, 1955–58; ARCM; LRCM; MMus Honoris Causa, University of Hull, 1987. *Career:* 2nd Violin, Dartington String Quartet, 1958–68; Director, Music, Natal Performing Arts Council, 1968–69; 1st Violin, Delmé String Quartet, Member ECO, 1969–74; Senior Lecturer, Cape Town, 1974–77; 1st Violin, Allegri String Quartet, Allegri Robles Ensemble, 1977, Melos Ensemble, 1984; mem, Incorporated Society of Musicians. *Recordings:* Complete Schubert Quartets, 1979–81; Brahms Quartets; Beethoven Quartets and Quintets; Ravel Septet; Stolen Gems, James Campbell, 1986; Leader Bath International Ensemble, 1988; Brahms Clarinet Quintet (James Campbell); Piano Quintet (Rian de Waal), 1992 CALA; Lombardini Sirman 6 Quartets, 1994; Bruch and Brahms 2 Viola Quintets, 1995; Schubert, Newbould, 1996; Haydn Op 33 No. 3, 1996; Ravel, 1996; Haydn, Shostakovich No. 3, 1996; Schubert, Newbould, Stravinsky, Mozart Clarinet quintet, 1997; Beethoven op 131, Britten No. 3, 1998; Romberg and Brandts Buys Quintets (with William Bennett, flute). *Honours:* Doctor of Music, Nottingham University, 1994; Doctor of Music, Southampton University, 1995; FRSA. *Current Management:* Biranda. *Address:* 35 Gartmoor Gardens, London SW19 6NX, England. *E-mail:* allegri@appleonline.net.

CARTER, Ronald; singer (tenor); b. 1961, Texas, USA. *Career:* sang first as baritone then appeared as Don José with New Rochelle Opera, Manrico for Long Island Opera and Canio for the Metro Lyric Opera of New Jersey; Has appeared with Augsburg Opera as Tichon (Katya Kabanova), Strauss's Emperor (1993), Turiddu and Cavaradossi; Guest appearances as Bacchus at Kaiserslautern and in Basle and Hanover; Sang Florestan at Krefeld, 2000. *Honours:* Awards from the Jugend in Wien competition, the Pavarotti Competition and the Liederkranz Foundation. *Current Management:* Athole Still International Management, Forresters Hall, 25–27 Westow Street, London, SE19 3RY, England. *Telephone:* (20) 8771-5271. *Fax:* (20) 8768-6600. *Website:* www.atholestill.com.

CARTERI, Rosanna; Singer (Soprano); b. 14 Dec. 1930, Verona, Italy. *Education:* Studied with Cuisnati and Nino Ederle. *Career:* Debut: Rome 1949, as Elsa in Lohengrin; La Scala debut 1951, in La Buona Figliuola by Piccinni; Sang in many concerts, notably in Donizetti's Requiem and in the premiere of Pizzetti's Ifigenia (Italian Radio 1950); Salzburg Festival 1952, as Desdemona, conducted by Furtwängler; Florence 1953, as Natasha in the premiere of Prokofiev's War and Peace; San Francisco 1954, as Mimi; Chicago Lyric Opera 1955, as Marguerite in Faust; Verona Arena 1958–59; Covent Garden 1960, Mimi; Sang in the premiere of Pizzetti's Calzare d'Argento, Milan 1961; Premiere,

Gilbert Bécaud's Opera d'Aran, Théâtre des Champs-Elysées, Paris, 1962. *Recordings include:* La Traviata (RCA); Falstaff, Guillaume Tell, Suor Angelica, La Bohème (Cetra); Solo in the Brahms Requiem, conducted by Bruno Walter.

CARVER, Anthony Frederick, BMus, PhD; University Teacher; b. 16 Nov. 1947, Brighton, England; m.; two s. one d. *Education:* Westlain Grammar School, Brighton and Birmingham Univ. *Career:* Lecturer in Music, Queen's Univ., Belfast 1973, Senior Lecturer 1974–; mem. Royal Musical Asscn, Asscn of Univ. Teachers. *Publications:* Cori Spezzati (two vols), Irish Church Praise (co-ed.), contrib. to ACTA Musicologica: Proceedings of the Royal Musical Association, Early Music. *Address:* School of Music, Queen's University, Belfast, BT7 1NN, Northern Ireland (office). *Telephone:* (28) 9097-5208 (office). *Fax:* (28) 9097-5053 (office). *E-mail:* a.carver@qus.ac.uk (office).

CARY, Tristram (Ogilvie); Composer, Writer and Teacher; b. 14 May 1925, Oxford, England; m. Doris E Jukes, 7 July 1951 (divorced 1978) 2 s., 1 d. *Education:* Christ Church, Oxford (Exhibitioner), 1942–43, 1946–47, interrupted by service in Royal Navy, BA, MA; Trinity College of Music, AMusTCL, LMusTCL, 1949–51; Hon RCM, 1972. *Career:* Debut: Wigmore Hall, London, 1949; Composing from age 14; Record Shop Assistant, 1951–54; 1st Electronic Music Studio, 1952; Self-employed, 1955–; Music for concerts, films, radio, television, theatre, musical directories; Founded Electronic Studio at Royal College of Music, 1967; Senior Lecturer 1974, Reader, Dean of Music 1982, University of Adelaide; Self-employed as Composer, Teacher, Writer, Computer Music Consultant. *Compositions:* 345, Narcissus, Trios, Sonata for Guitar Alone, Three Threes and One Make Ten, Arrangement of Bach's 6-part Ricercar, Continuum, Contours and Densities at First Hill, Peccata Mundi, Divertimento, The Songs Inside; Romantic Interiors, Steam Music, Two Songs from the Piae Cantiones, Nonet, Soft Walls, I Am Here, Family Conference, Seeds, Trellises, Strands, String Quartet II, Sevens, The Dancing Girls, Black White and Rose, Strange Places, Earth Holds Songs, Messages 1993, Inside Stories 1993, The Impossible Piano 1994, Suite–The Ladykillers 1996, Dublin Square for orchestra 1997, Through Glass 1998, Scenes From a Life 2000, Songs for the Adelaid Baroque 2004. *Recordings include:* Computer and orchestral music; Many radio, film, television score recordings; Quatermass and the Pit, the Film Music of Tristram Cary Vol. 1; The Ladykillers; Suite (music from Ealing Films); Soundings, electro-acoustic works, 1955–1996, 1999; The Hammer Quatermass Film Music Collection, 2000; Blood from the Mummy's Tomb, 2002; Devils' Planets – the Music of Tristram Cary for Dr Who, 2003. *Publications:* Illustrated Compendium of Musical Technology published in USA as Dictionary of Musical Technology, 1992. *Contributions:* Musical Times; Composer; The Electronic Music Review; The Guardian; Opera Australia; The Australian. *Honours:* Medal of the Order of Australia, (OAM), 1991. *Address:* 30 Fowlers Road, Glen Osmond, SA 5064, Australia.

CASADESUS, Jean-Claude; Conductor; b. 7 Dec. 1935, Paris, France; m. Anne Sevestre, 2 s., 1 d. *Education:* Harmony, Counterpoint, Fugue, Composition, Percussion (1st Prize), Paris National Conservatory, 1959; Conducting (1st Prize), Ecole Normale de Musique, Paris, 1965, with Pierre Dervaux; With Pierre Boulez, Basle, 1965. *Career:* Solo Timpanist, Concert Colonne, 1959–68; Percussion Soloist, Domaine Musicale with Pierre Boulez; Conductor, Paris Opéra, 1969–71; Co-Director, Orchestre Pays de Loire, 1971–76; Founder, Director, Lille National Orchestra, 1976–; Guest Conductor, USA, the United Kingdom, Moscow, St Petersburg, Prague, Leipzig, Dresden, Italy, Switzerland, Japan, elsewhere; Conducted Orchestra National de Lille in Revolution Revisited series, South Bank, London, 1989; Conducted Pelléas et Mélisande at Lille, 1996. Conducted Miami Orchestra, Philadelphia Orchestra, Berlin Symphony Orchestra, Utah Symphony Orchestra, Montreal Orchestra; President, Musique Nouvelle en Liberté. *Compositions include:* Music for theatre and films. *Recordings include:* Dutilleux, 1st Symphony; Berlioz, Symphonie fantastique; Ravel, Daphnis and Chloë, Bolero, La Valse, Concertos; Wieniawski, 2 violin concertos with Gitlis; Poulenc, Bal masqué, La Voix Humaine, Groupes des Six, Les Mariés de la Tour Eiffel; Bartók, Sonata for 2 pianos and percussion; Berio, Circles; Liszt, Préludes, Mephisto Waltz; Mozart, Funeral music, Clarinet Concerto, Double Concerto for flute and harp; Beethoven, 7th Symphony, 3rd Piano Concerto, Violin Concerto; Mahler, Symphonies Nos 1, 2, 4, 5, Kindertotenlieder, Rückertlieder, Des Knaben Wunderhorn; Stravinsky, Petrushka, Firebird; Bizet, Arlesienne, Clovis et Clothilde, Carmen Suites, Roma Symphony; Richard Wagner, Musical Extracts; Debussy, La Mer, La Damoiselle Élue, Nocturnes; Prokofiev, Alexander Nevsky; Debussy, Pelléas et Mélisande; Massenet, Werther; Berlioz, L'enfance du Christ; Poulenc, Concerts pour orgue, pour clavecin, Suite Française. *Publications:* Le plus court chemin d'un coeur à un autre (Edit Stock), 1997. *Honours:* 1st Recording Prize, Académie Charles Cros; Grand Prize, Record, European Year of Music, 1985; SACEM Grand Prix, 1985; Adviser to Prime Minister, 1981–84; General Secretary, Superior

Council of Music; Cross of Officer, Légion d'Honneur; Ordre des Palmes Académiques; Cross of Commander, Ordre des Arts et des Lettres; Cross of Officer, Order of Leopold; Commander: Order of Nassau, Ordre de Mérite National. *Current Management:* c/o IMG Artists, Lovell House, 616 Chiswick High Road, London. *Address:* 2 Rue de Steinkerque, 75018 Paris, France. *E-mail:* CDyer@imgworld.com.

CASAPIETRA, Celestina; Singer (Soprano); b. 23 Aug. 1938, Genoa, Italy; m. Herbert Kegel (deceased 1990). *Education:* Studied at the Milan Conservatory with Gina Cigna. *Career:* Debut: Teatro Nuovo, Milan, 1961, in Mese Mariano by Giordano; Sang in Genoa, San Remo, Pisa, Venice and Lyons; Sang at the Staatsoper Berlin from 1985, notably as Elsa, Constanze, Donna Anna, Agathe, Mimi, Micaela, Tatiana in Eugene Onegin and the title role in Daphne by Strauss; Salzburg Mozartwochen, 1984, as Vitellia in La Clemenza di Tito; Las Palmas, 1986, as Elisabeth in Tannhäuser; Guest engagements in London, Moscow, Helsinki, Copenhagen, Vienna and Prague; Zemlinsky's Der Kreidekreis, Hamburg, 1983, Amsterdam, 1989; Season 1994 as Tosca at Genoa and Ariadne at Lyon. *Recordings include:* Fiordiligi in Così fan tutte; Mozart's Masses; Orff's Trionfi. *Address:* c/o Deutsche Staatsoper, Unter den Linden 7, 1086 Berlin, Germany.

CASCIOLI, Gianluca; Concert Pianist; b. 1979, Turin, Italy. *Education:* Began piano studies 1986; Entered the Accademia Musicale in Imola, 1991; Composition classes at the Verdi Conservatory, Turin. *Career:* Many recital appearances throughout Italy specialising in classical and contemporary repertory, 1994–; Engagements with Orchestra della Scala, Orpheus Chamber Orchestra, Gustav Mahler Orchestra, Berliner Sinfonie-Orchestre, Orchestra Nazionale della RAI, Orchestra Sinfonica di Santa Cecilia, Orchester des Mozarteum, Salzburg; Work with the conductors Riccardo Muti, Claudio Abbado, Myung-Whun Chung; Concerts in Munich, Vienna, Berlin, Salzburg, Hannover, Frankfurt, Bremen, Hamburg, Paris, Barcelona, Lisbon, Athens, Tokyo, Peking; Further engagements in Paris and Athens and in International Piano Series at the Queen Elizabeth Hall, London; Named Star of the Year at Munich. *Recordings include:* Scarlatti; Beethoven; Debussy; Prokofiev; Boulez, Ligeti, Webern and Schoenberg, 1996. *Honours:* First prize, Umberto Micheli International Piano Competition, Milan, 1994. *Current Management:* Ingpen & Williams Ltd, 7 St George's Court, 131 Putney Bridge Road, London, SW15 2PA, England.

CASELLA, Elena; Conductor; b. 28 Jan. 1966, Milan, Italy; 1 d. *Education:* Diploma in Piano; Diploma in Composition; Diploma in Conducting, Milano Conservatorio di Musica G Verdi; Masterclasses in conducting with Ervin Acél, Italy and Hungary, Julius Kalmar, Vienna, Gustav Kuhn, Italy, Myung-Whun Chung, Italy. *Career:* Debut: Sala Verdi, Conservatorio in Milan with Orchestra Pomeriggi Musicali, Milan, 1994; Teacher of Orchestral Training, Hungary, 1995; Assistant of Gustav Kuhn, 1994–97; Numerous concerts with many orchestras including A Toscanini, Parma; Pomeriggi Musicali, Milan; Szegend Symphony, Hungary; Novi Musici, Naples; Serenade Ensemble, Trieste; Assistant of Ervin Acél in Wiener Musikseminar, 1998–. *Compositions:* Eos I and II, for solo guitar. *Honours:* Premio Internazionale, Sebetiater, for Music, Naples, 1997. *Address:* 26 Via Mose Bianchi, 20148 Milano, Italy.

CASHIAN, Philip John, DMus; British composer; b. 17 Jan. 1963, Manchester. *Education:* Univ. of Cardiff, Guildhall School of Music and Drama. *Career:* Northern Arts fellow-in-composition, Univ. of Durham 1993–96; Visiting Lecturer in Composition, Bath Spa Univ. 1997; composer-in-residence, Goldsmiths Coll., London 1999; co-founder and Dir, Oxford Festival of Contemporary Music. *Compositions include:* String Quartet 1988, Nightmaze 1991, Dark Inventions 1992, Chamber Concerto 1995, A Sea of Tales 1998, Night Journeys 1998, The Devil's Box 1999, Music for the Night Sky 1999, Tableaux 2003, Spitbite 2004, Three Pieces 2004. *Recordings:* String Quartet No. 1 (Bingham Quartet, NMC), Music for the Night Sky (Schubert Ensemble, NMC), Dark Inventions (BCMG, Asbury, NMC). *Honours:* Britten Prize 1991. *Address:* c/o British Music Information Centre, Lincoln House, 75 Westminster Bridge Road, London, SE1 7HS, England (office). *Website:* www.bmic.co.uk.

CASHMORE, John; Singer (baritone); b. 1960, Birmingham, England. *Education:* Studied at the Birmingham School of Music and the National Opera Studio, London. *Career:* Debut: Sang Guglielmo with Birmingham Music Theatre; Opera engagements with English National Opera, Scottish Opera-Go-Round, Wexford Festival, Batignano and the New D'Oyly Carte Opera Company; Guglielmo for Opera Forum in Netherlands, 1991, Figaro in a British tour of Mozart's opera, Marullo in Rigoletto for ENO, 1992, and roles from 1992 at Aachen including Lortzing's Zar and Don Giovanni; Opera galas at the Albert Hall, Festival Hall and in Glasgow; Oratorio engagements include Carmina Burana in Birmingham and Glasgow, Monteverdi Vespers at Coventry Cathedral and Victory's Ultima Rerum in Dublin. *Current Management:* Athole Still International Management, Forresters Hall, 25–27 Westow

Street, London, SE19 3RY, England. *Telephone:* (20) 8771-5271. *Fax:* (20) 8768-6600. *Website:* www.atholestill.com.

CASKEL, Christoph; Percussionist; b. 12 Jan. 1932, Greifswald, Germany. *Education:* Studied in Cologne, 1949–55. *Career:* Many performances of modern music at Darmstadt and elsewhere, notably with the brothers Kontarsky in Bartók's Sonata for two Pianos and Percussion; Collaborations with Stockhausen (premiere of Zyklus, 1959, and Kontakte), Mauricio Kagel and keyboard player Franz-Peter Goebels; Has performed with the Capella Coloniensis and given courses at Darmstadt and Cologne. *Address:* c/o Hochschule für Musik Rheinland, Dagoberstrasse 38, 5000 Cologne 1, Germany.

CASKEN, John; Composer; b. 15 July 1949, Barnsley, Yorkshire, England. *Education:* Birmingham University with Peter Dickinson and John Joubert, 1967–71; Warsaw Academy of Music (Polish Government Scholarship) with Andrzej Dobrowolski and consultations with Witold Lutoslawski, 1971–72. *Career:* Lecturer, Birmingham University, 1973–79; Research Fellow, Huddersfield Polytechnic, 1979–81; Lecturer, Durham University, 1981–92; Professor of Music at Manchester University, 1992–; Featured Composer, Bath Festival, 1980; Musica Nova, Glasgow, 1984; Huddersfield Contemporary Music Festival, 1986 and 1991; Southampton International New Music Week, 1989; Almeida Festival, 1989; Music Today, Tokyo, 1990. *Compositions include:* Orchestral: Tableaux des Trois Ages, 1977; Orion over Farne, 1984; Maharal Dreaming, 1989; Darting the Skiff for strings, 1993; Sortilège, 1996; Concertos: Masque for oboe, 1982; Erin for double bass, 1983; Cello Concerto, 1991; Violin Concerto, 1995; Distant Variations, concerto grosso for saxophone quartet and wind orchestra, 1997; Aprilès un silence for violin and small orchestra/large ensemble, orchestration of work for violin and piano, 1998; Ensemble: Music for the Crabbing Sun for 4 players, 1974; Amarantos for 9 players, 1978; Firewhirl for soprano and 7 players, 1980; String Quartet No. 1, 1982; Clarion Sea for brass quintet, 1985; Vaganza for large ensemble, 1985; Piano Quartet, 1990; String Quartet No. 2, 1994; Infanta Marina for cor anglais and 6 players, 1994; Instrumental: Thymehaze for treble recorder and piano, 1976; Salamandra for 2 pianos, 1986; A Spring Cadenza for solo cello, 1994; Aprilès un silence for violin and piano, 1998; Choral: To Fields We Do Not Know, 1984; Three Choral Pieces, 1990–93; La Orana, Gaugin for soprano and piano, 1978; Sharp Thorne for 4 solo voices, 1992; Still Mine for baritone and orchestra, 1992; Opera: Golem, 1986–88; God's Liar, opera after Tolstoy, 2000. *Honours:* First Britten Award for Composition, 1990; Gramophone Award, for Best Contemporary Recording, 1990; Northern Electric Performing Arts Award, 1990; Fondation Prince Pierre de Monaco Composition Prize, 1993; Northern Sinfonia Composer in Association, 1991–; Fellowship, Royal Northern College of Music, Manchester, 1996. *Current Management:* Schott Music Publishers. *Address:* 48 Great Marlborough Street, London W1V 2BN, England. *Website:* www.schott-music.com.

CASOLLA, Giovanna; Singer (soprano); b. 1944, Italy. *Education:* Conservatorio di San Pietro, Naples. *Career:* debut, Lisbon 1977, as Eboli in Don Carlos; sang at Turin 1978, 1982, Trieste 1979, Buenos Aires 1980, Detroit 1981; San Diego 1982, in the American premiere of Zandonai's Giulietta e Romeo; Metropolitan Opera 1984, as Zandonai's Francesca da Rimini, returned 1986, as Eboli; La Scala Milan 1983 and 1986, as Giorgetta in Il Tabarro; Verona Arena 1986 and 1988, as Maddalena in Andrea Chénier and La Gioconda; Caracalla Festival 1987, 1989, as Tosca; further guest appearances at Vienna and Miami 1988, Deutsche Oper Berlin 1989, Tosca, Stuttgart and Venice Eboli 1991; La Scala and Florence 1991, as Minnie in La Fanciulla del West and Santuzza; Puccini Festival, Torre del Lago 1991, as Giorgetta; other roles include Fedora, Amelia (Ballo in Maschera), Adriana Lecouvreur, Manon Lescaut, Silvana in Respighi's La Fiamma, Bartók's Judith, Maria in Tchaikovsky's Mazeppa and Elena Makropoulos; sang Santuzza at Florence 1996, and Gioconda 1998, Turandot at Barcelona 1999; season 2000 as Tosca at La Scala and Leonora (La Forza del Destino) at the Verona Arena; many concert appearances.

CASONI, Bianca-Maria; Singer (Mezzo-Soprano); b. 1 March 1932, Milan, Italy. *Education:* Studied at the Milan Conservatory with Bruna Jona and Mercedes Llopart. *Career:* Debut: Milan 1956, as Mercédès in Carmen; Sang widely in Italy after winning La Scala Competition; Salzburg 1960, as Giacinta in La Finta Semplice, 1960; Glyndebourne 1965, as Cherubino; Concert performance of Bellini's La Straniera, New York, 1969; Appearances at Covent Garden and the Festivals of Aix and Edinburgh; Monte Carlo, Geneva, Barcelona, Philadelphia and the Metropolitan Opera; Turin 1975, in the Italian premiere of Die drei Pintos, Mahler/Weber; Berlin Staatsoper 1981, as Cinderella. *Recordings include:* Mozart's Coronation Mass; La Straniera; Preziosilla in La Forza del Destino (EMI). *Address:* c/o Deutsche Staatsoper, Unter den Linden 7, 1086 Berlin, Germany.

CASSELLO, Kathleen; Singer (Soprano); b. 1958, Wilmington, Delaware, USA. *Education:* Dan Pressley, Delaware; Wilma Lipp, Salzburg;

Sesto Bruscantini, Italy. *Career:* European debut as Queen of Night in Hamburg, 1985; More than 200 Queen of Night performances since in Hamburg, 1986–88, Deutsche Oper and Staatsoper, Berlin, 1986–89, Moscow, 1987, Zürich, Geneva and Salzburg, 1988, Stuttgart, 1990; Staatstheater Karlsruhe Ensemble, 1987–89; Lucia in Karlsruhe, 1989–92, São Paulo, 1989, Marseille, San Sebastian and Zürich, 1990, Malaga, 1992, Treviso, Rome and Palermo, 1993; Traviata in Karlsruhe, 1987–92, Oviedo, 1991, Toulouse, 1992, Festival Orange and Rome, 1993, Tokyo, 1994, and Geneva; Elvira in Puritani at Marseille, 1991, Malaga, 1993; Gilda in Rigoletto at Marseille, 1992, Mexico City and Nice, 1993, La Scala with Riccardo Muti, 1994; Konstanze in Entführung in St Gallen, 1986–87, Vienna, 1988, Karlsruhe, 1989, Zürich, 1990, Munich National Theater, 1992, Avignon, 1993, Marseille and Hamburg, 1994–; Other roles include: Manon at the Met, 1990; Thaïs at Marseille, 1991; Pamina at Barcelona, 1991; Musetta at the Arena di Verona, 1992; Vitellia in La Clemenza di Tito in Toulouse, 1992, Athens, 1994; Amina in La Sonnambula at Messina, 1993; Elettra in Idomeneo at Venice, 1993; Giulietta in I Capuleti e i Montecchi at Parma, 1994; Amina at Rome, 1996; Season 2000 as Constanze and Donna Anna at Dresden, Donizetti's Maria di Rohan at Aachen. *Address:* c/o Mondial, 17 rue Brey, F–75017 Paris, France.

CASSIDY, Paul; Violist; b. 1959, Ireland. *Education:* Studied at the Royal College of Music, University of California at Los Angeles and Detmold, Germany. *Career:* Founder member of the Brodsky Quartet (name derives from violinist Adolph Brodsky, Principal of the Royal Manchester College of Music, 1895–1929); Resident at Cambridge University for 4 years and later residencies at the Dartington International Summer School, Devon; Concert engagements include the Shostakovich quartets at the Queen Elizabeth Hall, London, and performances at the Ludwigsburg and Schleswig-Holstein Festivals; New York debut at the Metropolitan Museum; Further tours of Italy, North America, Australia, Poland, Czechoslovakia and Japan; Complete quartets of Schoenberg for the BBC, 1992; French concerts include visit to the Théâtre du Châtelet, Paris. *Recordings include:* Quartets of Elgar and Delius; Schubert A minor and also Schubert D minor and Crumb, Black Angels; Beethoven Op 74; Complete quartets of Shostakovich. *Address:* c/o PRO Musicis (Brodsky Quartet), Ringstrasse 6, CH–6300 Zug, Switzerland.

CASSINELLI, Riccardo; Singer (Tenor); b. 27 Feb. 1936, Buenos Aires, Argentina. *Education:* Opera School of the Teatro Col ón, Buenos Aires. *Career:* Debut: Berne, 1968, as Amenofi in Rossini's Mosè in Egitto; Appearances at Geneva and Toulouse Operas; Théâtre des Champs Elysées, Paris, as Ferrando in Così fan tutte, Nicolai's Fenton, and Nemorino; Glyndebourne Festival, 1973, 1976; Opéra de Lyon, 1979 in Cavalli's Ercole Amante; Leading tenor at Buenos Aires until 1990; Salzburg Festival, 1986 as Mozart's Basilio; Geneva, 1987 in the premiere of Le Forêt by Liebermann; Festival engagements at Montpellier, Beziéres, Mozart's Monostatos, 1991, and Lausanne, Dr Caius in Falstaff, 1995; Nice Opéra, 1996 in From the House of the Dead by Janáček; Season 1998 as Brighella in Ariadne auf Naxos at Toulouse; Sang Malatestino in Zandonai's Francesca da Rimini at Buenos Aires, 2000. *Address:* c/o Toulouse Opera, Théâtre du Capitole, Place du Capitole, 31000 Toulouse, France.

CASSIS, Alessandro; Singer (Baritone); b. 1949, Italy. *Career:* Debut: Florence, 1971, in Un Ballo in Maschera; Sang in the Maggio Musicale, Florence, 1974, in La Fanciulla del West; Piccola Scala Milan in La Favola d'Orfeo by Casella; Sang Germont at Turin, 1977, Amonasro at the Verona Arena, 1982; La Scala Milan, 1983, as Michele in Il Tabarro, Sharpless in Butterfly, 1985; Returned to Verona in 1986 and 1988, as Gérard (Andrea Chénier) and Barnaba (La Gioconda); Further appearances at Naples, Genoa, Geneva, Palermo, Trieste and Lisbon; Baths of Caracalla, Rome, 1991, as Amonasro; Other roles include Carlo in La Forza del Destino and Verdi's Luna, Rigoletto and Renato; High Priest in Samson et Dalila; Sang Nabucco at Brescia, 1994 and Alfonso in La Favorita at Bergamo, 1995. *Recordings include:* I Lutuani by Ponchielli; Nerone by Boito. *Address:* c/o Teatro Donizetti, Piazza Cavour 4 I–24100 Bergamo, Italy.

CASSUTO, Alvaro (Leon); Conductor and Composer; b. 17 Nov. 1938, Oporto, Portugal. *Education:* Studied violin and piano as a child; Studied composition with Arthur Santos and Lopes Graca; Courses with Ligeti, Messiaen and Stockhausen, Darmstadt, summers 1960 and 1961; Studied conducting with Karajan, Pedro de Freitas Branco, Lisbon, and with Ferrara in Hilversum; PhD, Law, University of Lisbon, 1964; MA, Conducting, Vienna Academy of Music, 1965. *Career:* Assistant Conductor, Gulbenkian Orchestra, Lisbon, 1965–68; Little Orchestra, New York, 1968–70; Permanent Conductor, 1970–75, Music Director, 1975–89, National Radio Orchestra, Lisbon; Lecturer, 1974–75, Professor in Music, 1975–79, Conductor, Symphony Orchestra, University of California, Irvine; Music Director, Rhode Island Philharmonic Orchestra, Providence, 1979–85; National Orchestra Association, New York, 1981–87; Nova Filarmonia Portuguesa,

1988–93; Orquestra Sinfonica Portuguesa, 1993, Israel Raanana Symphony Orchestra, 2001. *Compositions:* In the Name of Peace, opera, 1971; Orchestral: Sinfonia breve No. 1, 1959, No. 2, 1960; Variations, 1961; Permutations for 2 orchestras, 1962; Concertino for piano and orchestra, 1965; Cro(mo-no)fonia for 20 strings, 1967; Canticum in Tenebris for soloists, chorus and orchestra, 1968; Evocations, 1969; Circle, 1971; To Love and Peace, symphonic poem, 1973; Homage to My People, suite for band, 1977; Return to the Future, 1985; The Four Seasons for piano and orchestra, 1986; Chamber: String Sextet, 1962; Song of Loneliness for 12 performers, 1972. *Recordings:* Various. *Honours:* Koussevitzky Prize, Tanglewood, Massachusetts, 1969. *Address:* Quinta do Mogo, Malveira Da Serra, 2750 Cascais, Portugal.

CASTEL, Nico; Singer (Tenor) and Educator; b. 1 Aug. 1931, Lisbon, Portugal. *Education:* Studied in Caracas, Milan, Frankfurt and the USA. *Career:* Debut: Santa Fe, 1958, as Fenton in Falstaff; New York City Opera, 1965, in The Fiery Angel by Prokofiev; Celebrated 30 years as Principal Artist, 1970–, Metropolitan Opera: Le nozze di Figaro; Hänsel und Gretel; Ariadne auf Naxos; Boris Godunov; Guillot, in the Sills recording of Manon; Appearances in Lisbon, Florence, Tel-Aviv, Caracas, Graz, Dresden, Frankfurt and the USA; Parallel career as diction and multi-lingual phonetics teacher and coach for singers at the Metropolitan, the Juilliard School, The Mannes College of Music and the International Institute of Vocal Arts in Israel, France and China; Staff Diction Coach, Santa Fe Opera, 2001–. *Recordings include:* La Bohème; Manon, Contes d'Hoffmann. *Publications:* The Nico Castel Ladino Song Book, 1983; A Singers' Manual of Spanish Lyric Diction, 1994; The Complete Puccini, Verdi and Mozart, Belcanto, Verismo French Opera Libretti, phoneticized and fully translated word by word, 1994. *Address:* 214 West 92nd Street, Apt 77E, New York City, NY 10025, USA.

CASTLE, Joyce; Singer (Mezzo-soprano); b. 17 Jan. 1944, Beaumont, Texas, USA. *Education:* Studied at the University of Kansas, the Eastman School and in New York. *Career:* Debut: San Francisco 1970, as Siebel in Faust; Debut, Metropolitan Opera, 1985; Die Fledermaus, Eugene Onegin; Puccini, Trittico; Wagner's Ring Cycle; Boris Godunov; Debut, New York City Opera, 1983, Ballad of Baby Doe, Sweeney Todd, Rake's Progress, Casanova; Regularly sang with Santa Fe Opera, Seattle Opera, Houston, Dallas, Washington, Montreal; Created role of Nazimova in Argento's Valentino, 1994, Kennedy Center; 1st performance of Bernstein's Arias and Barcarolles with Bernstein at the Piano; World premiere of Weisgall's Esther, 1993, New York City; Turin 1996 as Madame de la Haltière in Massenet's Cendrillon; Season 2000–01 as Orlovsky at Chicago, Herodias (Salome) in Antwerp and Augusta Tabor in The Ballad of Baby Doe for New York City Opera. *Recordings:* Candide, Old Lady, New York City Opera Recording; Grammy Winner, Sondheim Book of the Month Recording; Vocal Music of Stefan Wolpe; Vocal Music of Joseph Fennimore. *Current Management:* Janice Mayer & Associates. *Address:* 201 W 57th Street, New York, NY 10019, USA.

CASTRO, Carlos José; Costa Rican composer; b. 25 Jan. 1963, San José. *Education:* Castella Conservatory and Univ. of Costa Rica. *Career:* mem., Contemporary Music Centre, San José 1985–; teacher of music, Nat. Univ. School of Dance. *Compositions include:* Gobierno de alcoba (comic opera after play by Samuel Rovinsky), Mambrú se fue a la guerra (after play by Mario Vargas Llosa) 1992, La chunga 1995. *Honours:* Aquileo J. Echevarría Nat. Music Prize. *Address:* c/o Universidad Nacional, Centro de Arte, Segundo Piso, Heredia, Costa Rica (office).

CASTRO-ALBERTY, Margarita; Singer (Soprano); b. 18 Oct. 1947, San Juan, Puerto Rico. *Education:* Studied at the Pablo Casals Conservatory, Puerto Rico, the Accademia di Santa Cecilia, Rome, and at Juilliard, New York. *Career:* Debut: Santiago, 1978, as Amelia in Un Ballo in Maschera; Sang at the Teatro Col ón, Buenos Aires, 1979–80; European debut, 1980, in La Vida Breve by Falla; Carnegie Hall, 1981, as Lucrezia in I Due Foscari; Metropolitan debut, 1982, as Amelia; Festival d'Orange, 1983, as Aida; Guest engagements in Venice, Berlin, Vienna, Nancy, Rome and Toronto; Other roles include Donna Anna, Amelia Grimaldi, Nedda, Butterfly, Lucrezia Borgia, Elisabeth de Valois and the Trovatore Leonora; Sang at Marseilles, 1987. *Address:* c/o Opéra de Marseille, 2 Rue Molière, 13231 Marseille Cédex 01, France.

CASTRO-ROBINSON, Eve de; Composer; b. 9 Nov. 1956, London, England. *Education:* Studied at the University of Auckland (DMus, 1991). *Career:* Composer-in-Residence with the Auckland Philharmonic, 1991; Performances of her music with the Karlheinz Company in Auckland and with UNESCO in Paris. *Compositions include:* Stringencies for 11 solo strings, 1986; Peregrinations, piano concerto, 1987; Concerto for 3 clarinets, 1991; Instrumental pieces, including Tumbling Strains for violin and cello, 1992, and Tingling Strings for piano, 1993. *Address:* c/o New Zealand Music Centre, PO Box 10042, Level 13, Brandon Street, Wellington, New Zealand.

CASULA, Maria; Singer (Soprano); b. 1939, Cagliari, Sardinia, Italy. *Education:* Studied in Rome and Venice. *Career:* Sang with I Virtuosi di

Roma, in concert; Vienna Staasoper, 1967, as Vitellia in La Clemenza di Tito; Glyndebourne, 1969, Despina; Rome, 1978, in the Italian premiere of The Beggar's Opera, arranged by Britten; Cagliari, 1987, in Guillaume Tell. *Recordings include:* Il Barbiere di Siviglia, La Clemenza di Tito, Le nozze di Figaro, Leonora by Paer. *Address:* c/o Teatro Lirico, Viale Regina Margherita 6, 09100 Cagliari, Italy.

CATANI, Cesare; Singer (Tenor); b. 1970, Ascoli, Italy. *Education:* Studied at the Bergamo Conservatory. *Career:* Debut: Kochkarev in The Marriage by Mussorgsky, St Petersburg; Appearances in Moise et Pharaon at the Pesaro Rossini Festival, as Edoardo in Verdi's Un Giorno di regno at Parma and as Tebaldo in Bellini's I Capuleti e i Montecchi at Reggio Emilia; Wexford Festival, 1997 as Ubaldo in Mercadante's Elena da Feltre; Season 1998 as the Doge in Rossini's Otello at Pesaro and as Rodolfo in La Bohème at Toscana; Season 1999 sang Arrigo in Verdi's La battaglia di Legnano at Parma, Piacenza and Modena; Hindemith's Cardillac, as Il cavaliere, in Genova; Alfredo in La Traviata in Macerata and Gabriele Adorno in Verdi's Simon Boccanegra at Toscana; Concerts include Rossini's Petite Messe Solennelle, Salzburg and Rome; Mozart's Requiem, Turin. *Recordings:* Rossini Petite Messe; Elena da Feltre. *Address:* c/o Rossini Opera Festival, Via Rossini 37, 61100 Pesaro, Italy.

CATHCART, Allen; Singer (Tenor); b. 2 Aug. 1938, Baltimore, Maryland, USA. *Education:* Studied at the University of California and with Boris Goldovsky in New York. *Career:* Debut: Metropolitan Opera Studio, 1961, as Guglielmo in Così fan tutte; European engagements in Brussels, Rome, Zürich, Cologne, Stuttgart and Kiel; Welsh National Opera in Cardiff; Paris Opéra-Comique, in The Stone Guest by Dargomyzhsky, 1985; Paris Opéra as The Drum Major in Wozzeck; Other roles include Don José, Florestan, Cavaradossi, the Emperor in Die Frau ohne Schatten, Laca in Jenůfa and parts in operas by Wagner. *Recordings include:* Jason in Mayr's Medea in Corinto.

CATLING, Ashley; Singer (Tenor); b. 1975, England. *Education:* Guildhall School, with William McAlpine, and National Opera Studio, London. *Career:* Appearances in Friend of the People (premiere) by David Horne for Scottish Opera, Fenton and Ferrando for London Opera Players; Male Chorus in The Rape of Lucretia for The Other Theatre Company, Nemorino, and Steve Reich's video opera Three Tales on European and US tours; Concerts include St Matthew Passion at Westminster Cathedral and Carissimi's Jepthé at St John's Smith Square; Season 2001–2002 as Ferrando and Fenton in Guernsey, and Rossini's Petite Messe; Other roles include Sellem in The Rake's Progress, and Simon in Birtwistle's The Last Supper. *Address:* c/o National Opera Studio, Morley College, 61 Westminster Bridge Road, London, SE1 7XT, England.

CAUDLE, Mark; British bass violinist, bass violist and cellist; b. 1950, England. *Career:* Member of The Parley of Instruments; Frequent tours in the United Kingdom and abroad, including the British Early Music Network; Performances in Spain, France, Germany, Netherlands, Poland and Czechoslovakia; US debut in New York, 1988; Many concerts with first modern performances of early music in new editions by Peter Holman; Numerous broadcasts on Radio 3 and elsewhere; Repertoire includes Renaissance Violin Consort Music (Christmas music by Michael Praetorius and Peter Philips, music for Prince Charles I by Orlando Gibbons and Thomas Lupo); Baroque Consort Music by Monteverdi, Matthew Locke (anthems, motets and ceremonial music), Purcell (ayres for theatre), Georg Muffat (Armonico Tributo sonatas, 1682), Heinrich Biber (Sonate tam aris, quam aulis servientes, 1676), Vivaldi (sonatas and concertos for lute and mandolin, concertos for recorders) and J. S. Bach (Hunt cantata No. 208), with Crispian Steele-Perkins, trumpet, and Emma Kirkby, soprano, among others.

CAUSSE, Gérard; Violist; b. 26 June 1948, Toulouse, France. *Education:* Studied in Toulouse and at the Paris Conservatoire. *Career:* Violist of the Via Nova Quartet, 1989–71, Parrenin Quartet, 1972–80; Member of the Ensemble Intercontemporain from 1976; Professor at the Boulogne Conservatoire, 1980, Lyon, 1982, Paris, 1987; Chamber musician from 1982, notably with the Ivaldi Quartet; Season 2002–03 artistic director of the Toulouse National Chamber Orchestra, as conductor and as soloist; Concerto appearances include Radio France's Orchestre National, the Suisse Romande, Lille National Orchestra (Casadesus), Montpellier Philharmonic (Levi), Malaysia Philharmonic (Baakels), Luxembourg PO (Krivine) and Sao Paulo SO; Plays a Gasparo da Salo (1560); Professor at the Reina Sofia school in Madrid. *Address:* c/o Conservatoire National, 14 Rue de Madrid, 75008 Paris, France.

CAUSTON, Richard, BA, MA, ARCM (PG); British composer; *Fellow Commoner in the Creative Arts, Trinity College, Cambridge;* b. 12 March 1971, Whitechapel, London. *Education:* ILEA Centre for Young Musicians, London, Univ. of York, Royal Coll. of Music, Civica Scuola di Musica, Milan. *Career:* compositions written for performers such as BBC Symphony Orchestra, City of Birmingham Symphony Orchestra, London Sinfonietta and Evelyn Glennie; founded and runs the Royal Coll. of Music Gamelan programme; Fellow Commoner in the Creative

Arts, Trinity Coll., Cambridge 2003–; mem. Soc. for the Promotion of New Music. *Compositions:* Non mi comporto male, for piano 1993, The Peristence of Memory, for chamber ensemble 1995, Two pieces for Clarinet Duet 1995, Notturno for chamber ensemble 1998, rev. 2001, Millennium Scene for large orchestra 1998, rev. 2001, Concerto for Solo Percussion and Gamelan 2001, Seven States of Rain for violin and piano 2002 (British Composers Award, Best Solo/Duo 2004), Between Two Waves of the Sea, for orchestra with sampler, 2004, La Terra Impareggiabile, song cycle for baritone and piano 2005. *Publications:* contrib. to Tempo: Berio's Visage and the Theatre of Electroacoustic Music, The Guardian: Music of the Spheres, article on Concerto for solo percussion and gamelan, The Guardian: The God of Small Things, article on Jeremy Dale Roberts 2004. *Honours:* Fast Forward composition prize 1995, first prize of the Third International 'Nuove Sincronie' Composition Competition 1996, Mendelssohn Scholarship 1997, SPNM George Butterworth Award 1997, honourable mention in Large-scale Composition category of the Royal Philharmonic Soc. Awards 2000. *Current Management:* Oxford University Press, Repertoire Promotion Department, 70 Baker Street, London, W1U 7DN, England. *Telephone:* (20) 7616-5900 (office). *Fax:* (20) 7616-5901 (office). *E-mail:* repertoire .promotion@oup.co.uk (office). *Website:* www.oup.co.uk/music.repprom/ causton (office).

CAVA, Carlo; Singer (Bass); b. 16 Aug. 1928, Ascoli Piceno, Italy. *Education:* Studied in Rome. *Career:* Debut: Spoleto, 1955, in L'Italiana in Algeri; Netherlands Opera, Amsterdam, 1959; Glyndebourne, 1961–65, as Seneca in L'Incoronazione di Poppea, as Sarastro, Bartolo in Le nozze di Figaro, Basilio in Il Barbiere di Siviglia and Henry VIII in Anna Bolena; La Scala, 1973, as Boris Godunov; Appearances in Cairo, Amsterdam, Brussels, Frankfurt, Vienna, Munich, Berlin and Paris. *Recordings include:* Oroveso in Norma; Zaccaria in Nabucco; L'Incoronazione di Poppea; Il Barbiere di Siviglia; Linda di Chamounix. *Address:* c/o Teatro alla Scala, Via Filodrammatici 2, 21021 Milan, Italy.

CAVALLIER, Nicolas; singer (bass); b. 1964, France. *Education:* Royal Academy of Music and National Opera Studio, with Elisabeth Söderström and with Iris dell'Acqua. *Career:* debut, Nancy Opera, 1987, as Cascanda in The Merry Widow; Sang Achilles in Giulio Cesare conducted by Trevor Pinnock at the Royal Academy of Music; Season 1988–89 in Massenet's Thaïs for Chelsea Opera Group and roles in Les Malheurs d'Orphée (Milhaud), Renard (Stravinsky) and Geneviève de Brabant (Satie) at the Queen Elizabeth Hall; Season 1989–90 with Glass's Fall of the House of Usher in Wales, Henze's The English Cat in Berlin, Messiah with the Bournemouth Sinfonietta and John Metcalf's Tornrak at the Banff Centre in Canada; Sarastro in Die Zauberflöte at Glyndebourne; Sang Don Fernando (Fidelio) for the Glyndebourne Tour, 1990, Zuniga for Welsh National Opera and in Alcione by Marais for Les Arts Florissants in Paris; Masetto for Nancy Opéra; Other roles include Don Giovanni, Narbal in Les Troyens, Don Quichotte, Sparafucile and Mozart's Bartolo and Osmin; Season 1991–92 as Masetto at Nancy, Raleigh in Roberto Devereux at Monte Carlo and Celeus in Lully's Atys with Les Arts Florissants; 1992–93 in Hamlet by Thomas at Monte Carlo, Leporello at Metz and Mr Flint in Billy Budd at Nancy; Loredano in I Due Foscari by Verdi for Scottish Opera at the 1993 Edinburgh Festival; Sang Félix in Donizetti's Les Martyrs at Nancy, 1996; Sang Lord Sidney in Il Viaggio a Reims at Liège, 2000; Concert repertoire includes the Verdi and Mozart Requiems, A Child of our Time, Monteverdi Vespers and Die Schöpfung. *Honours:* Anne Lloyd Exhibition, Helen Eames Prize, Paton Award and Ricordi Award, Royal Academy of Music. *Current Management:* Robert Gilder & Co., Enterprise House, 59–65 Upper Ground, London, SE1 9PQ, England. *Telephone:* (20) 7928-9008. *Fax:* (20) 7928-9755. *E-mail:* rgilder@robert -gilder.com.

CAVE, Penelope, ARAM, GRSM, LRAM; harpsichordist; b. 17 April 1951, Guildford, Surrey, England; m. Michael Heale 1974; one s. one d. *Education:* Purcell School, Royal Acad. of Music, lessons and master-classes with Kenneth Gilbert, Colin Tilney, Ton Koopman and Gustav Leonhardt. *Career:* debut, Wigmore Hall 1980; solo recitals at major festivals in England and abroad; played at Purcell Room and Wigmore Hall and for BBC Radio 3, Belgian Radio and Classic FM; solo recitals at Edinburgh and Ryedale Summer Music Festivals 1995; regular tutor of harpsichord courses, masterclasses and workshops in England and abroad; mem. Incorporated Soc. of Musicians. *Recordings:* with the Camerata of London, Garth Hewitt and the Feinstein Ensemble; From Lisbon to Madrid (solo CD). *Publications:* contrib. to Harpsichord Fortepiano magazine, Music Teacher, Consort. *Honours:* Raymond Russell prize, winner Nat. Harpsichord Competition, Southport. *Address:* Betteridge House, 2 St Omer Ridge, Guildford, Surrey GU1 2DD, England. *E-mail:* penelope.cave@ntlworld.com. *Website:* www .impulse-music.co.uk/cave.htm.

CAZURRA, Anna; Composer and Musicologist; b. 1940, Barcelona; m., 1 s., 1 d. *Education:* Studied with Josep Soler, Barcelona Conservatoire; Doctorate, The Universitat Autonoma de Barcelona. *Career:*

Researcher, Universitat Autonoma, Barcelona; Researcher, Centre for 18th Century musical studies, University of Wales, College of Cardiff; Universitat Pompeu Fabra, Barcelona; Collaborations with Musical Associations and groups. *Compositions:* Poema Para Quinteto de Metal, for brass quintet; Cuatro Evolaciones, for piano; Postales de Viaje, for piano; String Quartets; El Grito, for soprano, flute, guitar and cello; Trio, for violin, cello and piano; Psalmus, for soprano and orchestra. *Recordings:* Poema Para Quintets de Metal, by 2111 Gothic quintet; El Grito. *Publications:* Introduccio a la Historia de la Musica, 1999; Les Obertures de Josep Doran, 1995; El Compositor Inestre de Capella Joan Rossell, doctoral thesis, 1993. *Contributions:* Some articles for the New Grove Dictionary, Diccionario de la Musica Espanola, Encyclopedia Catalana de la Musica. *Address:* Paseo Maragall, 315–317 Escalera A Entresvelo B, 08032 Barcelona, Spain.

CECCARINI, Giancarlo; Singer (Baritone); b. 19 July 1951, Pisa, Italy. *Education:* Studied in Pisa and Rome. *Career:* Debut: Spoleto 1975, as Belcore in L'Elisir d'amore; Has appeared widely in Italy as Marcello (La Bohème), Cimarosa's Maestro di Capella and Osmano in L'Ormindo by Cavalli (Venice 1976); Performances of Monteverdi's Combattimento at Terni, Bologna, Zürich, Mantua, Cremona and Frankfurt, 1980. *Recordings:* On Swiss Radio from 1977, including La Gazzetta by Rossini; At Genoa has sung Podestà in Docteur Miracle by Bizet, and Gianni Schicchi; San Remo, 1982, as Nabucco; Ping in Turandot at Helsinki, 1991; Records include I Pazzi per Progresso by Donizetti (UORC); Turandot (Nuova Era). *Address:* c/o Teatro La Fenice, Campo S Fantin 1965, 30124 Venice, Italy.

CECCATO, Aldo; Conductor; b. 18 Feb. 1934, Milan, Italy; m. Eliana de Sabata, 1966, 2 s. *Education:* Verdi Conservatory Milan, 1901–55; Studied conducting with Albert Wolff and Willem van Otterloo, the Netherlands, 1958; Berlin Hochschule für Musik, 1959–62. *Career:* Appearances as jazz and concert pianist; Assistant to Sergiu Celibidache, Accademia Musicale Chigiana, Siena, 1960; Guest conducting engagements throughout Italy and Europe; USA debut, Chicago Lyric Opera, 1969; Music Director, Detroit Symphony Orchestra, 1973–77; Generalmusikdirektor, Hamburg State Philharmonic Orchestra, 1975–83; Chief Conductor, Hannover Radio Orchestra, 1985–; Bergen Symphony Orchestra, 1985–; Conducted Maria Stuarda at Bergamo, 1989. *Recordings:* For ABC; Angel-EMI; Arabesque; Audio Fidelity; Klavier; Philips; Supraphon; La Traviata, Maria Stuarda, The Four Seasons, Mendelssohn's Piano Concertos (John Ogdon), Music by Ravel and Liszt. *Honours:* 1st Prize, RAI Conducting Competition, 1964. *Address:* c/o Rundfunkorchester Hannover, Rudolf von Bennigsen Ulfer 22, 3000 Hannover, Germany.

CECCHELE, Gianfranco; Singer (Tenor); b. 25 June 1940, Galliera Veneta, Italy. *Education:* Studied with Marcello del Monaco in Treviso. *Career:* Sang at Catania from 1964; Many appearances on the major Italian stages; Guest appearances in London, Paris, Barcelona, Hamburg, Munich, Nice, Chicago, Philadelphia and Montreal; Carnegie Hall New York 1968, as Zamoro in a concert performance of Verdi's Alzira; Best known in operas by Puccini and Verdi; Verona between 1967 and 1984; Rio de Janeiro, 1988, as Radames; Mercadante's La Vestale at Split, 1987; Season 1993–94 as Walter in Catalani's Loreley (Teatro Filarmonico) and Calaf at Viterbo. *Recordings include:* Aroldo by Verdi; Loreley by Catalani; Alzira; Title role in Rienzi by Wagner; Decio in Mercadante's La Vestale, Bongiovanni. *Address:* c/o Arena di Verona, Piazza Bra 28, 1-3 7121 Verona, Italy.

CECCHI, Gabriella; Composer; b. 3 Nov. 1944, Ricco del Golfo, La Spezia, Italy. *Education:* Studied at the Lucca Institute, Genoa Conservatory, 1974–77, in Siena with Franco Donatoni and in Sargiano-Arezzo with Brian Ferneyhough. *Career:* Performances of her music throughout Italy and elsewhere in Europe. *Compositions include:* Kite for chamber orchestra, 1981; In proiezione for orchestra, 1986; Riverberi for violin and harpsichord, 1988; Parvula for 10 flutes, 1990; Il gallo rosso, small chamber opera, 1992; Doppel atmung for 4 recorders and percussion, 1993; Grig Bian Ner, ballet, for piano, saxophone and percussion, 1994; Joueurs, for flute, clarinet, violin, cello, sax and double bass, 1995;... In un Mare..., for soprano, clarinet and piano, 1996. *Address:* via del Sempione 2, 19122 La Spezia, Italy.

CEELY, Robert (Paige); Composer; b. 17 Jan. 1930, Torrington, Connecticut, USA; m. Jonatha Kropp, 13 Jan 1962. *Education:* BMus, New England Conservatory, Boston, MA; MA, Mills College, CA; Graduate study at Princeton University, NJ; Major composition teachers include Darius Milhaud, Leon Kirchner, Roger Sessions and Milton Babbitt. *Career:* Faculty of Composition, Director of Electronic Music at New England Conservatory of Music, Boston, 1967. *Compositions:* String Trio, 1953; Woodwind Quintet, 1954; Composition for 10 Instruments, 1963; Stratti for Magnetic Tape, 1963; Elegia for Magnetic Tape, 1964; Vonce for Magnetic Tape, 1967; Modules for 7 Instruments, 1968; Logs for 2 Double Basses, 1968; Hymn for Cello and Bass, 1969; Beyond the Ghost Spectrum, ballet, 1969; Mitsyn for Computer-

Generated Tape, 1971; Slide Music for 4 Trombones, 1974; Rituals for 40 Flutes, 1978; Frames for Computer-Generated Tape, 1978; Lullaby for Trombone and Soprano, 1979; Flee, Floret, Florens for 15 Solo Voices, 1979; Piano Piece, 1980; Bottom Dogs for 4 Double Basses, 1981; Roundels for Large Wind Ensemble and Tape, 1981; Piano Variations, 1982; Totems for Oboe and Tape, 1982; Dialogue for Solo Flute, 1983; Giostra for Oboe and Tape, 1984; Minute Rag for Solo Piano, 1985; Pitch Dark for Jazz Ensemble, 1985; Synoecy for Clarinet and Tape, 1986; Timeshares for Percussion Ensemble, 1988; Special K Variations for Piano, 1989; Post hoc, ergo propter hoc for Solo Bass Clarinet, 1989; Harlequin for Solo Double Bass and Tape, 1990; Hypallage for Solo Trumpet and Tape, 1990; Asyndeton for Piano and Tape, 1993; Opera from Fernando Arrabal's The Automobile Graveyard, 1994; Group Sax, for five saxophones, 1996; Music for Ten, 1996; Enchanted Cycles, for computer-generated tape, 1996; Auros, for five instruments, 1997; Wieman's treibt, for bass clarinet and tape, 1997; Gymel, for two oboes, 1998; Triple Double for oboe, English horn, bassoon and tape, 1998; Mutual Implications for tape, 1999; Extensions for solo piano, 2000; Five Contemplative Pieces for chorus, 2000; Canons for alto flute, clarinet and bassoon, 2001; Seven etudes for piano, 2002; Three Satires for Orchestra, 2002. *Publications:* Electronic Music Resource Book, 1979. *Address:* 33 Elm Street, Brookline, MA, USA.

CEGOLEA, Gabriela; Singer, (Soprano); b. 1950, Moldova, USSR. *Education:* Studied in Bucharest and at the Benedetto Marcello Conservatory, Venice; Sang at the Taormina Festival, then studied further at the School of the Royal Opera, Stockholm. *Career:* Debut: Stockholm, 1977, as Tosca; Appearances as Tosca at Oslo and as Manon at Venice; La Scala Milan with Placido Domingo, conducted by Georges Prêtre; Further engagements in New York, Berlin, Stuttgart, San Francisco, Naples and Rome; Tours of Australia, Brazil and South Korea; Liège, 1989, as Maddalena in Andrea Chénier.

CELLI, Joseph; American Composer and Oboist; b. 19 March 1944, Bridgeport, Connecticut, USA. *Education:* BME, Hartt College of Music, Hartford, Connecticut, 1962–65; MM (major in oboe performance/ composition), Northwestern University, Chicago, 1970–72; Performance Seminar (2 summers), Oberlin Conservatory, Ohio, Private oboe/ English horn study with Ray Still (Chicago Symphony) Albert Goltzer (New York Philharmonic), Wayne Rapier (Boston Symphony Orchestra) John Mack (Cleveland Symphony Orchestra), 1970 and 1971; Fulbright Scholar, Korean Traditional Performing Arts Center, Seoul, Korea, 1991–93. *Career:* Composer, videomaker, performer throughout Europe, Asia, North and South America, 1972–; Gave US premieres of Stockhausen's Spiral and Solo for oboe; Executive Director, Real Art Ways (contemporary arts center), Hartford, Connecticut, 1975–86; CEO/ Executive Director, New Music America Miami Festival, Florida, 1987–89; Director of Cultural Programs, Miami-Dade Community College, Miami, Florida, 1989–90; Director, OO DISCS Inc Recording company (contemporary American music), 1991–; Founder/Director, Korean Performing Arts Institute, New York/Seoul, 1993–; Exec. Dir, Founder, Int. Performing Arts; Founder, multicultural Black Rock Art Center. *Compositions include:* World Soundprint: Asia for radio (with Jin Hi Kim), 1993; Pink Pelvis: Music For Dance for double reeds, Korean ajeng and Brazilian percussion, 1994; Sunny's piece: Music For Dance with double reeds, Komungo, percussion, 1994; Quintet: for Kayagum, Wx-7 and three kalimba, 1995. *Address:* Black Rock Art Center, 2838 Fairfield Avenue, Bridgeport, CT 06605 (office); 261 Groovers Avenue, Black Rock, CT 06605-3452, USA (home). *Telephone:* (203) 367-7917 (office); (203) 367-9061 (home). *Fax:* (203) 333-0603 (office). *E-mail:* oodiscs@connix.com (office). *Website:* www .InternationalPerformingArts.com (office).

CEMORE, Alan; Singer (Baritone); b. 1958, Wisconsin, USA; m. Dr Ursula Baumgartner. *Education:* BM, Vocal Performance, University of Northern Iowa, 1981; MMus, Indiana University, 1985; Hochschule für Musik, Frankfurt, 1981–82; Studied Voice with Margaret Harshaw and David Smalley. *Career:* Leading Baritone at the Wiesbaden Opera, 1986–88, Basel Opera, 1988–90, Graz Opera 1990–97, Bremen Theatre, 1998–; Spoleto Festival, 1984 in Die lustige Witwe, 1985, in La Fanciulla del West; Sang Tom in Henze's English Cat at Frankfurt (1986), at Turin and at the 1987 Edinburgh Festival; Wexford as Biagio in Gazzaniga's Don Giovanni and Pantalone in Busoni's Turandot, 1988; Radio and television appearances in Europe, Asia and USA; Over 50 opera roles in the USA and Europe; mem, Pi Kappa Lambda, Rotary International. *Recordings include:* Die grossmuetige Tomyris by Keiser; Oh wie verfuehrerisch, operatic selections from television show Happy Birthday George Gershwin!. *Honours:* Prizewinner, ARD International Music Competition, Munich, 1984; Rotary International Graduate Fellowship, 1981; Cole Porter Memorial Fellowship Winner, 1984. *Address:* Richard Wagner Str. 29, 28209 Bremen, Germany.

CEPICKY, Leos; Musician; b. 21 Aug. 1965, Pardubice, Czechoslovakia; m. Katerina Kus, 28 April 1985, 1 s., 1 d. *Education:* Prague Academy of Arts. *Career:* Debut: Prague Spring Quartet Competition, 1988;

Member, Wihan Quartet, Music Festivals in England, Austria, Germany, France, Italy, Belgium, Spain, Portugal, Singapore, USA, Japan, Rome and on Radio France. *Recordings:* Supraphon (Suk, Dvořák, Janáček); Haydn op 64, op 71; Mozart K168, K458, K465; Dvořák, Smetana 1; Janáček 1 and 2; Ravel and Britten 2; Beethoven op 59 1, 2, 3, op 14; Dvořák op 51 and op 106. *Contributions:* The Strad. *Honours:* Prize, Prague Spring Competition, 1988; Prize, London International String Quartet Competition. *Current Management:* Pragoart Music. *Address:* Archaeologicka 1884, 15000 Prague 5, Czech Republic.

CERAR, Maja; Violinist; b. 27 May 1972, Zürich, Switzerland. *Education:* Concert Diploma, Conservatory of Winterthur, 1995, studied with Aida Stucki-Piraccini; Student of Dorothy DeLay, New York; MA, Musicology, 1998, Doctoral studies in progress, Columbia University, New York. *Career:* Debut: Performed Mozart Violin Concerto K 218 with Symphony Orchestra of Zürich, Jiri Malat conducting, Zürich Tonhalle, 1991; Soloist with renowned conductors and orchestras, Europe; Collaboration with composers such as G Kurtag and B Furrer; Numerous premieres of contemporary music, USA, Europe; Lead roles in theatre and multimedia productions; Classical recital tours, Europe and USA, including Dame Myra Hess Memorial 'Concert Series, Chicago; Featured, news and portrait shows, Switzerland and Slovenia, and in film at Young Artists in Concert Festival, Davos; Member, Editorial Board, Musicology, 1998–. *Recordings:* Recollections, Sonata by U Krek, dedicated to her, 1996; Sonatas by Beethoven, Schubert, Brahms, with pianist Gérard Wyss, 1997; Violin Concerto by Samuel Barber, 2000. *Honours:* Supported by Swiss Study Foundation for Outstanding University Students, 1992–; Migros Foundation Study Grant Award, 1995–97; Fellowship, Columbia University, 1999. *Address:* 514 West 114th Street, Apt 23, New York, NY 10025, USA.

CERHA, Friedrich; Composer; b. 17 Feb. 1926, Vienna, Austria. *Education:* Studied at the Vienna Academy, 1946–51, with Vasa Prihoda (violin) and Alfred Uhl (composition) and at the university; DPhil. *Career:* With Kurt Schwertsik co-founded ensemble Die Reihe, 1958, with performances of contemporary music and works by the Second Viennese School; Completion of Act III of Alban Berg's Lulu performed at the Paris Opéra, 1979; Opera Baal premiered at the 1981 Salzburg Festival; Der Rattenfänger at Graz, 1987; British premiere of Cello Concerto at 1999 Prom concerts, London. *Compositions:* Espressioni fondamentali for orchestra, 1957; Relazioni fragili for harpsichord and chamber orchestra, 1956–57; Fasce for orchestra, 1959; Spiegel I–VII, 1960–61; Netzwerk, musical theatre, 1962–80, premiered Wiener Festwochen, 1981; Exercises for baritone and chamber ensemble, 1962–67; Langegger Nachtmusik I and II for orchestra, 1969, 1970, III, 1991; Double Concerto for violin, cello and orchestra, 1975; Baal-Gesänge for Baritone and orchestra, 1981; Keintate I, 1981–83, II, 1984–85, for voice and 11 instruments; Requiem für Hollensteiner for baritone, choir and orchestra, 1982–83; Eine Art Chansons for voice and 3 instruments, 1985–86; Phantasiestück for cello and orchestra, 1989; String-Quartett I, 1989, II, 1990, III, 1992; Impulse for orchestra, 1992–93; Concerto for viola and orchestra, 1993; Concertino for violin, accordion and ensemble, 1994; Requiem for choir and orchestra, 1994, completed 2003; Saxophon-Quartett, 1995; Acht Sätze nach Hölderlin-Fragmenten für Streichsextett, 1995; Jahr lang ins Ungewisse hinab für Ensemble, 1995–96; Concerto for Cello and Orchestra, 1996–97; Lichtenberg-Splitter, for baritone and ensemble, 1997; Der Riese vom Steinfeld, opera (libretto by Peter Turrini), 1999; Im Namen der Liebe for baritone and orchestra, 2000, premiered Staatsopen Wien, 2002; Hymnus for orchestra, 2000–01. *Recordings:* Spiegel I–VII; Baal; I Keintate, Eine letzte Art Chansons; String-Quartets 1–3; Acht Sätze nach Hölderlin-Fragmenten für Streichsextett; 12 CD Box From early works to the present, ORF Edition Zeitton 180. *Address:* Kupelwiesergasse 14, 1130 Vienna, Austria.

CERMÁKOVÁ, Vera; Czech composer, pianist and music teacher; b. 17 March 1961, Prague, Czechoslovakia; m. Josef Cermak 1984; one s. *Education:* Prague Conservatoire, Piano studies with Alena Polakova, 1977–83; Studied Composition with Oldrich Semerak, 1986–92. *Career:* teaches Piano and Composition at music school in Kladno; Interpretation of piano compositions; performs at festivals of classical and contemporary music; mem. Asscn of Composers, Prague; Atelier090; Music Studio N. *Compositions:* Free cycle for 3 String Quartets The Play of Lights, 1993; Fragments Nos 1–4 for Symphonic Orchestra, 1993; Seven Preludes for Guitar Solo, 1994; Three Bagatelles for Saxophone Quartet, 1996; Metamorphosis for Violoncello and Piano, 1997. *Recordings:* Prelude and Rhythmic Fantasia; Piano Solo, 1992; Fantasia (piano solo), 1993; Ostinato, Melodic No. 2 (piano solo), 1995; Kaleidoskop (piano solo), 1996; Seclusion of Clarinet solo, 1997; Reliefs for Chamber Orchestra, 1999; String Quartet No. 4, 2000; Genesis for Saxophone Quartet, 2000, Reflections and Meditations for Soprano, Tenor and Chamber Orchestra 2001, Solo for Soprano Saxophone 2002, Solo for Alto Saxophone 2002, Solo for Tenor Saxophone 2002, Solo for Baritone

Saxophone 2002, The Spectrum for String Orchestra 2004. *Honours:* Musica Iuvenis, Prague, 1997. *Address:* Karla Tomana 824, 27204 Kladno; Karla Tomana 824, 27204 Kladno, Czech Republic (home). *Telephone:* (312) 26-74-31 (home).

CERNY, Florian; Singer (Baritone); b. 4 Oct. 1946, Bavaria, Germany. *Education:* Studied in Australia, Vienna and Munich. *Career:* Solo debut with the Israel National Opera; Principal baritone of the Kiel Opera and has sung in Hamburg, Düsseldorf, Hanover and elsewhere in Europe; Geneva Opera as Biterolf in Tannhäuser; Season 1984–85 as Alfio and Tonio (Cav and Pag) with Opera North and Mozart's Figaro with English National Opera; Bayerische Staatsoper Munich 1986–, as Bretigny in Manon, Caliph in Der Barbier von Bagdad, Schaunard, and Dominic in Arabella; Other roles include Wagner's Dutchman and Kothner, Riccardo (I Puritani), Iago and Don Carlos (La Forza del Destino); Sang Wagner's Telramund at Leipzig, 1992; Season 1995–96 as Jochanaan at Dessau and Pizarro at Sydney; Sang Wotan in Das Rheingold at Braunschweig, 1999. *Address:* Music International, 13 Ardilaun Road, London N5 2QR, England.

CERNY, Pavel; Organist; b. 9 Oct. 1970, Prague, Czechoslovakia. *Education:* Academy of Music. *Career:* Live television recording, 1994; Several Czech radio recordings of historic Organ; Set of Historical Organ Recordings for the Dutch Radio (KRO) and Production; Prague Philharmony (Recital, 1995); Chartres, Padova, Verona (Recitals, 1996); Vienna, 1994; Salzburg, 1994. *Recordings:* Romantic Organ Repertoire for Four Hands and Four Legs, with Martin Rost (Germany), 1997; Jiri Ropek, Composer and Organist. *Publications:* Cooperation to International Organ Dictionary, Belgium. *Contributions:* Studies of significant Prague Organs, Hetorgel, 1997. *Honours:* 1st Prize, Opava (National), 1990; 1st Prize, Ljublja, 1992; 1st Prize, Prague, 1994. *Address:* Noutonice 10, 252 64 Velké Prilepy, Czech Republic.

CERQUETTI, Anita; Singer (Soprano); b. 13 March 1931, Montecorsaro-Macerata, Italy. *Education:* Studied at the Liceo Morlacchi in Perugia. *Career:* Debut: Spoleto 1951, as Aida; Sang Aida and the Trovatore Leonora at Verona, 1953; Chicago Lyric Opera, 1955–56, debut as Amelia in Un Ballo in Maschera; New York 1957, in Paride ed Elena by Gluck; Milan 1958 as Abigaille in Nabucco; Other roles included Norma, La Gioconda and Elena in I Vespri Siciliani. *Recordings:* La Gioconda (Decca); Reiza in Oberon; Mathilde in Guillaume Tell; Elvira in Verdi's Ernani; Zoraima in Les Abencérages by Cherubini (Cetra). *Address:* c/o Accademia Nazionale di Santa Cecilia, Vocal Faculty, Via Vittoria 6, I–00187 Rome, Italy.

CERVENA, Sona; Singer (Mezzo-Soprano); b. 9 Sept. 1925, Prague, Czechoslovakia. *Education:* Studied with Robert Rosner and Lydia Wegener in Prague. *Career:* Janáček Opera Brno, 1952–58, Staatsoper Berlin, 1958–61, Deutsche Oper Berlin, 1962–64, Opera Frankfurt, 1964–90; Title, Kammersaengerin Berlin and Frankfurt; Guest appearances, Prague, Vienna, Amsterdam, Brussels, Geneva, London, Milano, Paris, Barcelona, Lisbon, San Francisco, Los Angeles, Chicago; Festivals, Bayreuth 1960–66, Salzburg 1961, Glyndebourne 1963–64 as Clairon in Capriccio, Edinburgh 1966–78; Season 1987–88 at Frankfurt in Jenůfa and Schreker's Die ferne Klang. *Address:* Thalia Theater, Alstertor, 20095 Hamburg, Germany.

CERVENKA, Jan; Conductor; b. 1940, London, England. *Education:* Studied at the Royal College of Music and the Berlin Hochschule. *Career:* Assistant and Conductor at the Munster and Wiesbaden opera houses then returned to England to conduct Britten's Noye's Fludde; Guest with the BBC orchestras, in Venezuela with Nielsen's 4th Symphony, Netherlands, Bulgaria and Romania; Further concerts at the Albert and Festival Halls, London; Music Director of Worthing Borough Council from 1979; Guest Conductor with the Belgian Radio Symphony Orchestra and Choir from 1986. *Address:* c/o Orchestre Symphonique de la RTBF, Place Eugène Flagey 18, B–1050 Brussels, Belgium.

CERVETTI, Sergio; Composer and Teacher; b. 9 Nov. 1940, Dolores, Uruguay. *Education:* E Krenek and S Grove, Peabody Conservatory of Music, Baltimore, USA, 1963–67. *Career:* Composer in Residence, German Artists' Programme, West Berlin, 1969; Faculty, Tisch School of the Arts, New York University, 1970–; mem, Broadcast Music Inc. *Compositions:* String Trio, 1963; Piano Sonata, 1964; 5 Sequences for flute, horn, cello, electric guitar, piano, percussion, 1966; Orbitas, orchestra, 1967; El Carro de Heno, 1967; Zinctum, 1968; Peripetia, 1970; Plexus, 1971; Madrigal III, 1976; 4 Fragments of Isadora, 1979; Enclosed Time for electronics, 1985; Night Trippers, 1986; Leyenda, for soprano and orchestra, 1991; 4 string quartets, 1968, 1972, 1990, 1992; Concerto for harpsichord and 11 instruments, 1992; The Triumph of Death (song cycle for piano and soprano). *Recordings:* Compositions recorded on Composers' Recordings Inc and Periodic Music Inc; Candombe Alberada and Hard Rock for harpsichord, 1993; Candombe II for orchestra, 1998; Film Music, Segments of The Hay Wain used in Oliver Stone Natural Born Killers, 1994. *Honours:* Many commissions;

Grants for NEA, New York State Council for the Arts, and Meet the Composer. *Address:* 212 East Court Street, Doylestown, PA 18901, USA.

CHABRUN, Daniel; Conductor; b. 26 Jan. 1925, Mayenne, France. *Education:* Graduated Paris Conservatoire, 1954. *Career:* Many performances of modern music in France and elsewhere; Anton Webern festival with the ensemble Ars Nova, 1965, and premiere of Claude Prey's opera Jonas, 1966; Has also given works by Maurice Ohana, Lutoslawski, Xenakis, Barraud and Denisov; French premiere of Purcell's Indian Queen, 1966; Directed the orchestra of the Paris Conservatoire from 1972; Professor at the Montreal Conservatoire, 1975; Inspector with the French Ministry of Culture, 1980. *Address:* c/o Université de Montreal, Faculty of Music, 2900 Boulevard Edouard Montpetit, Montreal, Quebec H3C 3J7, Canada.

CHACHAVA, Vazha; Pianist and Accompanist; b. 20 April 1933, Tbilisi, Georgia. *Education:* Graduate, 24th Male School, Tbilisi, 1951; Study, Ruslaveli Theatre College, Tbilisi, 1953–57; Graduate, Central Music School, Tbilisi, 1952; Studies, Saradzhishvili Tbilisi Conservatory, 1958–62. *Career:* Debut: Solo Concert, Tbilisi Conservatory, 1952; Concerts and Recitals with E Obraztsova, I Archipova, V Chernov, V Lukiyanets in many Countries of Europe, America and Asia, Among them Recitals in La Scala, Lisbon, Maryinsky Theatre and Many Famous Concert Halls; Many Russian film, television and radio broadcasts and appearances. *Recordings:* Melodia; R Schumann, Romances, E Obraztsova, 1979; Tchaikovsky, Romances, E Obraztsova, 1979; G Rossini Petite Messe Solennelle, 1981; Lieder von Komitas with Hasmik Papian, 1996. *Publications:* Gerald Moore–Singer and Accompanist, 1987; Chamber-Vocal Music, Tchaikovsky Romances, 1988; G Sviridov Romances, Accompanist's Notes, 1995. *Address:* Bolshoi Nicolopescovsky per 3-16, Moscow 121002, Russia.

CHAILLY, Riccardo; Italian conductor; b. 20 Feb. 1953, Milan; s. of the late Luciano Chailly and of Anna Marie Motta; m. Gabriella Terragni 1987; two s. *Education:* Giuseppe Verdi and Perugia Conservatories and with Franco Caracciolo and Franco Ferrara. *Career:* Asst to Claudio Abbado, La Scala, Milan 1972–74; debut as Conductor with Chicago Opera 1974; debut, La Scala 1978, Covent Garden (operatic debut) 1979; concert debut with London Symphony Orchestra and Edin. Festival 1979; American concert debut, Los Angeles Philharmonic, CA 1980; Metropolitan Opera debut 1982; Prin. Guest Conductor, London Philharmonic Orchestra 1982–85; Chief Conductor Radio Symphony Orchestra, Berlin 1982–89; Vienna State Opera debut 1983; appearances Salzburg Festival 1984, 1985, 1986; Japan debut with Royal Philharmonic Orchestra 1984; New York Philharmonic Orchestra debut 1984; Music Dir Bologna Orchestra, Teatro Comunale 1986–93; Chief Conductor Royal Concertgebouw Orchestra, Amsterdam 1988–2004, Conductor Emeritus 2004–; Principal Conductor Giuseppe Verdi, Milan 1999–; Hon. mem. Royal Acad. of Music, London. *Honours:* Gramophone Award Artist of the Year 1998, Diapason d'Or Artist of the Year 1999; Grand' Ufficiale della Repubblica Italiana, Knight of Order of Netherlands Lion 1998, Cavaliere di Gran Croce (Italy) 1998, Abrogino d'Oro, Comune Milano (Italy). *Address:* c/o Royal Concertgebouw Orchestra, Jacob Obrechtstraat 51, 1071 KJ Amsterdam, Netherlands. *Telephone:* (20) 5730573 (office). *Fax:* (20) 6763331 (office). *Website:* www .concertgebouworkest.nl (office).

CHAITKIN, David; Composer; b. 16 May 1938, New York City, USA; m. Carol McCauley, 23 July 1960, 1 s. *Education:* BA, Pomona College, 1959; MA, University of California at Berkeley, 1965; Studied with Luigi Dallapiccola, Seymour Shifrin, Max Deutsch, Andrew Imbrie and Karl Kohn. *Career:* Early experience as a jazz pianist; Composed music for film, The Game; Commissions from Philadelphia Composers' Forum, Sylvan Winds, New Hampshire Music Festival, Da Capo Chamber Players/New York State Council on the Arts, Quintet of the Americas/ Chamber Music America; Gordon Gottleib; Pomona College, in honour of its Centennial; Anders Paulsson/Gotland (Sweden) Chamber Music Festival, Francesco Trio/Koussevitzky Music Foundation; Professor of Music, Reed College, 1968–69; New York University, 1969–76. *Compositions:* Symphony; Summersong, for 23 wind instruments; Etudes for piano; Concerto for flute and strings; Seasons Such as These for mixed chorus a cappella; Serenade for 7 players; Scattering Dark and Bright, duo for piano and percussion; Quintet, mixed chamber ensemble; Pacific Images, for chamber orchestra; Music in Five Parts, for septet; Nocturne for woodwind quintet; Impromptu for piano; Song Cycle for soprano and piano; Three Dances for piano; Rhapsody for cello and piano; Aria, for soprano saxophone and strings; Trio for violin, cello and piano. *Recordings:* Etudes for piano, David Burge pianist; Serenade, New York New Music Ensemble, Black; Seasons Such as These, Cantata Singers, Harbison; Summersong, for 23 wind instruments, Sylvan Winds, Weisberg; Scattering Dark and Bright. *Publications:* Etudes for piano; Summersong; Nocturne; Impromptu for piano; Quintet; Prelude and Dance, Piano Solo. *Honours:* National Endowment for the Arts, 1981; Guggenheim Fellowship, 1985; American Academy of Arts and Letters, 1980, 1994. *Current Management:* Music Publishing Services,

236 West 26th Street, Suite 11-S, New York, NY 10001, USA. *Address:* 160 West 87th Street, New York, NY 10024, USA.

CHALKER, Margaret; Singer (Soprano); b. 1958, Waterloo, New York, USA. *Education:* BME, Studied at Baldwin-Wallace College in Ohio; MM, Syracuse University. *Career:* Mostly Mozart Festival New York as Sifare in Mitridate and Giunia in Lucio Silla; Houston Opera as Pamina; Deutsche Oper am Rhein, from 1985, as Oscar (Ballo in Maschera), Gilda, Celia (Haydn's La Fedelta Premiata) and Lauretta in Gianni Schicchi; Zürich Opera from 1987, as Pamina, Gilda, Jemmy in Guillaume Tell, Sophie (Rosenkavalier) and Janáček's Vixen; Other roles include Mozart's Countess and Donna Anna, Micaela, Antonia in Les Contes d'Hoffmann and Helen in Gluck's Paride ed Elena; Season 1996 as Puccini's Lauretta at Zürich, Ariadne at Meiningen and the Marschallin in Prague; Season 1999 at Zürich as Viclinda in I Lombardi and Freia in Das Rheingold; Many concert appearances, notably in works by Bach and Composers of the 20th Century. *Address:* c/o Opernhaus Zürich, Falkenstrasse 1, 8008 Zürich, Switzerland.

CHALLENGER, Robert; singer (tenor); b. 1967, South Yorkshire, England. *Education:* Guildhall School of Music, studied with with Martin Isepp, Suzanne Danco and Hugues Cuenod at Aldeburgh. *Career:* concert appearances as the Evangelist in Bach's Passions, Handel's Messiah and Alexander's Feast; Mozart Requiem and C Minor Mass; Haydn Creation and Mass in Time of War; Britten Rejoice in the Lamb and Cantata Accademica; other concert repertory includes music by Palestrina, Byrd, Cage and Feldman; operatic roles include Beppe in Pagliacci, Brack Weaver in Weill's Down in the Valley and parts in La Jolie Fille de Perth, and Rossini's Il Viaggio a Reims, Covent Garden, 1992. *Honours:* Winner, Young Songmakers' Almanac Competition (recital at St John's Smith Square); Gramophone Prize for recording of Chamber Music, 1992.

CHALLIS, Philip; Pianist; b. 11 Aug. 1929, Huddersfield, Yorkshire, England; m. Mary J White, 19 Nov 1955. *Education:* Huddersfield College; Royal Manchester College of Music, studies with Herbert Fryer, Marguérite Long, Joszef Gat and Ilona Kabos. *Career:* Debut: BBC, London, 1943; Many broadcasts and television appearances in England, America and Canada; Innumerable concert tours in England, America and Canada, Europe, Scandinavia and the Far East; mem. Incorporated Society of Musicians, Chairman of Brighton Centre, 1983–86. *Recordings:* Mephisto Music, Liszt; Liszt-Beethoven, Piano Transcriptions; Sonatas of John Field; Selected Piano works, Moscheles; Second Piano Concerto, Josef Holbrooke. *Honours:* Fellow, Royal Manchester College of Music, 1972. *Address:* Balaton, 97 Alinora Crescent, West Worthing, Sussex BN12 4 HH, England.

CHALMERS, Penelope; Singer (soprano); b. 5 Oct. 1946, Worcester, England. *Education:* Bristol University. *Career:* Has sung such roles as the Marschallin (Der Rosenkavalier), Leonora (Trovatore), Turandot and Tosca with fringe opera companies; Title role in the British premiere of Bruch's Lorelei for University College Opera, Fiordiligi for Pavilion Opera and Rezia in Weber's Oberon at Haddo House, Scotland; London debut at the Prom concerts in Lambert's Rio Grande; Recent appearances as the Dyer's Wife in Die Frau ohne Schatten at Geneva, Helmwige and Ortlinde in Die Walküre at Covent Garden and Emilia Marty in The Makropulos Case at Hagen, Germany; Donna Anna and Lady Billows in Albert Herring for Opera 80, season 1991–92; Judith in Bluebeard's Castle, at the English National Opera, 1993; Sang title role in Salome with Scottish Opera; National Television debut as prima donna in BBC production of Stendhal's Le Rouge et le Noir, 1993. *Current Management:* Athole Still International Management, Forresters Hall, 25–27 Westow Street, London, SE19 3RY, England. *Telephone:* (20) 8771-5271. *Fax:* (20) 8768-6600. *Website:* www .atholestill.com.

CHAMBERS, Becky; Violist; b. 1975, England. *Education:* Royal College of Music, with Simon Rowland-Jones and Chillingirian Quartet. *Career:* Co-founded Tavec String Quartet at RCM, 1999; Performances given at London's National Gallery (Schubert's Octet, 2001), St Martin-in-the-Fields, Serpentine Gallery (BBC Proms) and Queen Elizabeth Hall; Music Society concerts throughout Britain and workshops and educational projects; Festival engagements at Lower Wye Valley Chamber Music Festival, 2000–2001; Association with the Piros Ensemble from 2000, giving large scale popular chamber works. *Honours:* Helen Just String Quartet Prize; Rio Tinto Ensemble Prize and NETA Music Prize, Bristol. *Address:* c/o Royal College of Music, Prince Consort Road, London, SW7 2 BS, England.

CHAMPNEY, Wendy; Violist; b. 23 Feb. 1958, USA. *Education:* Studied at Indiana University, the International Menuhin Academy in Gstaad. *Career:* Co-Founder and Violist of the Carmina Quartet, 1984; Appearances from 1987 in Europe, Israel, USA and Japan; Regular concerts at the Wigmore Hall from Oct 1987; Concerts at the South Bank Centre, London, Amsterdam Concertgebouw, the Kleine Philharmonie in Berlin, Konzertverein Vienna; Four engagements in Paris

1990–91, seven in London; Tours in Australasia, USA, Japan; Concerts at the Hohenems, Graz, Hong Kong, Montreux, Schleswig-Holstein, Bath, Lucerne and Prague Spring Festivals; Collaborations with Dietrich Fischer-Dieskau, Olaf Bär and Mitsuko Uchida. *Recordings:* Albums for Ex Libris, Bayer, Claves and Denon (from 1991). *Honours:* Joint winner (with members of Carmina Quartet) Paolo Borciani String Quartet Competition in Reggio Emilia, Italy, 1987. *Address:* c/o Intermusica Artists' Management, 16 Duncan Terrace, London N1 8BZ, England.

CHANCE, Michael; Singer (countertenor); b. 7 March 1955, Penn, Buckinghamshire, England. *Career:* Choral Scholar at King's College Cambridge; Appearances with the English Chamber Orchestra, Academy of Ancient Music, English Concert, Orchestra of St John's, Smith Square, and the Bournemouth Sinfonietta; Handel's Messiah at the Alice Tully and Avery Fisher Halls New York; Concerts with John Eliot Gardiner and the Monteverdi Choir in New York and at the Göttingen and Aix-en-Provence Festivals; Operatic roles include Apollo in Cavalli's Jason (Buxton Festival), 1983; Andronico in Handel's Tamerlano (Lyon Opéra), 1985; Otho in Handel's Agrippina (Bath Festival), Ottone in Monteverdi's L'Incoronazione di Poppea and the Military Governor in the world premiere of Judith Weir's A Night at the Chinese Opera (Kent Opera); Britten's Oberon and Voice of Apollo with Glyndebourne Opera; Paris Opéra debut 1988, as Ptolomeo in Handel's Giulio Cesare; Season 1992, as Amphinomous in Monteverdi's Ulisse for ENO, Julius Caesar for Scottish Opera and Britten's Apollo at Glyndebourne; Sang in the premiere of Birtwistle's Second Mrs Kong, 1994; Concerts include Bach cantatas at the Promenade Concerts, London, Messiah at King's College, Cambridge, Royal Albert Hall and in Edinburgh; Handel's Theodora at the Paris Opéra, 1987; Israel in Egypt in Stuttgart and at La Scala, Milan; Jephtha in London and Göttingen; Bach's St Matthew Passion in Spain and London, B Minor Mass with the Manchester Camerata; World premiere of Bennett's Ophelia, 1988; Apollo in Death in Venice with Glyndebourne Touring Opera at Norwich, 1989; The Fairy Queen with The Sixteen, Queen Elizabeth Hall, 1990; Promenade Concerts, London, Britten's Cantata Misericordium, Mozart's Credo Mass, 1991; Sang the title role in Gluck's Orpheus for ENO, 1997; Season, 1998 as Monteverdi's Ottone for WNO; Season 2000–01 as Gluck's Orpheus at Leipzig and soloist in the St Matthew Passion at La Scala; London Proms Chamber Music, 2002. *Recordings:* Bach's St John Passion, Christmas Oratorio and St Matthew Passion, Handel's Messiah (Deutsche Grammophon); Jephtha (Philips); Cavalli's Giasone (Harmonia Mundi); Bacco and other roles in The Death of Orpheus by Stefano Landi; Handel's Tamerlano, Orfeo settings by Monteverdi and Gluck. *Current Management:* Ingpen & Williams Ltd, 7 St George's Court, 131 Putney Bridge Road, London, SW15 2PA, England.

CHANCE, Nancy (Laird); Composer; b. 19 March 1931, Cincinnati, Ohio, USA; m. 7 Sept 1950, divorced, 3 s. *Education:* Magna cum laude, The Foxcroft School, 1945–49; Bryn Mawr College, 1949–50; Columbia University, part-time, 1959–68; Piano with William R Smith and Lilias McKinnon; Theory and Composition with Otto Luening and Vladimir Ussachevsky; Sundance Institute Film Composer Fellow, 1988. *Career:* Performances of her works by Philadelphia Orchestra, St Louis Symphony, The Jupiter Symphony, The American Composers Orchestra, The League ISCM, The Group for Contemporary Music, The New Music Consort, Da Capo Chamber Players, Relache, Continuum, The Goldman Memorial Band and numerous others; World premiere of Planasthai with the Cleveland Chamber Symphony. *Compositions:* Odysseus, solo voice, percussion and orchestra; String Quartet No. 1; Liturgy for orchestra; Elegy for string orchestra; Woodwind Quintet; Domine, Dominus: Motet for double chorus acapella; Duos III for violin and cello; Exultation and Lament for alto saxophone and timpani; Ritual Sounds, for brass quintet and percussion; Daysongs for alto flute and percussion; 3 Rilke Songs for soprano, flute, English horn and cello; In Paradisum, solo voice, mixed chorus, orchestra; Rhapsodia For Marimba Quartet; Ceremonial for Percussion Quartet; Planasthai, chamber orchestra, piano and percussion, 1992. *Recordings:* Daysongs, Ritual Sounds, Duos III and Lament. *Honours:* Winner: ASCAP Rudolph Missim Prize for Orchestral Compositions, 1982, 1984; NEA Composer Fellowships, 1981, 1983. *Address:* PO Box 96, Austerlitz, New York, NY 12017, USA.

CHANG, Sarah; Violinist; b. 10 Dec. 1980, Philadelphia, USA. *Education:* The Juilliard School. *Career:* Debut: New York Philharmonic, 1990; Live from Lincoln Center, New York Philharmonic; Berlin Philharmonic; Carnegie Hall, Montreal Symphony. Repertoire includes Tchaikovsky Concerto; Sibelius Concerto; Mendelssohn Concerto; Paganini Concerto no. 1; Vieuxtemps Concerto; Sibelius Concerto with the CBSO at the 1999 London Prom concerts; Also plays Bart ók's Second Concerto (BBC, 1999). *Recordings:* Paganini First Concerto with the Philadelphia Orchestra and Sawallisch; Lalo Symphonie Espagnole with the Royal Concertgebouw; Sibelius and Mendelssohn Concertos under Dutoit;

Berlin Philharmonic; Jansons, Simply Sarah. *Contributions:* New York Times; Washington Post; The Times; Life; People; The Strad; Strings. *Honours:* Gramophone, Young Artist of the Year, 1993; German Echo Schallplattenpreis, 1993; International Classical Music Award, Newcomer of the Year, 1994. *Current Management:* ICM Artists. *Address:* c/o IMG Artists, Lovell House, 616 Chiswick High Road, London, W4 5RX, England.

CHAPIN, Schuyler Garrison; American arts administrator; b. 13 Feb. 1923, New York, NY; m. 1st Elizabeth Steinway 1947 (died 1993); four s.; m. 2nd Catia Zoullas Mortimer 1995. *Education:* Longy School of Music. *Career:* Vice-Pres., Programs, Lincoln Center, New York, 1963–68; Exec. Producer, Amberson Productions, 1968–72; Gen. Man., Metropolitan Opera, New York, 1972–76; Dean, School of Arts, Columbia Univ., 1976–87; Dean Emeritus, 1987–; Vice-Pres., Worldwide Concert and Artist Activities, Steinway and Sons, 1990–92; Dir, Columbia Records, USA, Masterworks and later, Vice-Pres., Creative Services; recorded, among others, Bernstein and the New York Philharmonic; Ormandy, Philadelphia Orchestra; Szell, Cleveland Orchestra; Stern; Serkin; Francescatti; Casadesus; Fleisher; Tucker; Farrell; Gould; Juilliard Quartet; Budapest Quartet; Commr for Cultural Affairs for the City of New York, 1994–2002. *Publications:* Musical Chairs, 1978; Leonard Bernstein: Notes From a Friend, 1992; Sopranos, Mezzos, Tenors, Bassos and Other Friends, 1995. *Contributions:* New York Times, National Review, Prime Time, Horizons, and others. *Honours:* Chevalier Légion d'honneur 2002. *Address:* 655 Park Avenue, Apt 8C, New York, NY 10021, USA.

CHAPMAN, Janice; Singer (Soprano) and Teacher; b. 10 Jan. 1938, Adelaide, Australia. *Education:* Studied at the University of Adelaide and at the Royal College of Music in London and the London Opera Centre. *Career:* Sang leading roles with Sadler's Wells/English National Opera, Welsh and Scottish Operas and in many European houses; Toured Russia with the English Opera Group under Benjamin Britten and worked with the composer on the roles of Miss Jessel and Mrs Grose in The Turn of the Screw; Sang Mrs Julian in the stage premiere of Owen Wingrave at Covent Garden 1973; Other Britten roles have been Ellen Orford and Lady Billows, and she has sung in operas by Mozart, Wagner, Verdi and Puccini; Concert engagements with leading orchestras; Sang with her trio The Alexandra Ensemble at the Women's Music Festival at Beersheba in Israel, 1986; Appeared as Mrs Grose for New Israel Opera, 1990, conducted by Roderick Brydon; Professor of Voice at the London College of Music.

CHAPPLE, Brian, GRSM, ARAM, LRAM; composer; b. 24 March 1945, London, England. *Education:* Royal Academy of Music, London. *Career:* mem. Performing Right Society. *Compositions include:* Scherzos for four pianos, 1970; Trees Revisited, 1970; Praeludiana, 1971; Green and Pleasant, 1973; In Ecclesiis, 1976; Piano Concerto, 1977; Cantica, 1978; Venus Fly Trap, 1979; Little Symphony, 1982; Lamentations of Jeremiah, 1984; Piano Sonata, 1986; Magnificat, 1986; In Memoriam, 1989; Berkeley Tribute, 1989; Frink Tribute, 1990; Requies, 1991; Missa Brevis, 1991; Three Motets, 1992; Songs of Innocence, 1993; Ebony and Ivory, 1995; The St Paul's Service, 1996; A Bit of a Blow, 1996; Tribute for Jo Klein, 1997; Songs of Experience, 1998; Klein Tribute Quartet, 1998; Burlesque, 2000; The Cloud-Capped Towers, 2000; Ecce Lignum Crucis, Passiontide at St Paul's; A Bit of a Blow, English Quartets; Anthems, canticles, children's songs, piano music. *Honours:* BBC Monarchy 1000 Prize, 1973; UNESCO International Rostrum of Composers, 1976. *Address:* 3 Deer Park Crescent, Tavistock, Devon PL19 9HQ, England.

CHAPPUIS, Vincent; Composer; b. 26 Feb. 1960, Switzerland. *Education:* School of Music, Freiburg; Music Certificate, Lausanne; Composition sessions, France. *Career:* Numerous international festivals of contemporary music, mainly in Romania; Radio broadcast with Radio Canada, Quebec; Radio Belgium; France music and Swiss Espace 2; TU with Tele Europe Nova in Romania; mem, Founder and member of the Composers' Association Ici et Maintenant; Member of the Swiss Association of Musicians; Member of Forum Ircam, Paris. *Compositions:* Symphonie for big orchestra, 1991; Sinfonietta for chamber orchestra, 1992; Procession electro-acoustic piece, 1993; Dilemme trio for violin, double bass and piano, 1994; Fusions for 2 pianos and percussion, 1995; Quatuor for string quartet, 1996; Fusions II for piano and chamber orchestra, 1997; Rituels for piano, percussion and clarinet, 1998; Symphonie No. 2 for large orchestra and choir, 2001; Quatuor No. 2 for string quartet, 2002. *Recordings:* Quatuor; Trio Dilemme; Trio Rituels. *Honours:* Honorary member of the Percussion Ensemble of Cluj, Romania. *Address:* Rue Liotard 35, 1202 Geneva, Switzerland.

CHAPUIS, Gérard; Singer (Bass); b. 21 Oct. 1931, Lyon, France. *Education:* Studied at the Lyon Conservatory. *Career:* Sang with the Lyon Opéra, 1954–56; Paris Opéra, 1956–73; Among his best roles have been the Minister in Fidelio, Sparafucile, Ramphis, Raimondo (Lucia di Lammermoor), Pistol, Hector in Les Troyens, Sarastro (Die Zauberflöte), Commendatore (Don Giovanni), Osmin (Die Entführung), and in Un ballo in Maschera and Barbiere di Siviglia; Other appearances at the Paris Opéra-Comique; President, des Voix d'Or; President, Scene Française. *Honours:* Concours de Voix d'Or 1st Prize Caruso, 1956. *Address:* 5 rue Lyautey, 75016 Paris, France.

CHARBONNEAU, Pierre; Singer (Bass); b. 14 June 1949, Montreal, Canada. *Career:* Sang first in Canada, notably at Vancouver from 1974, and then with Canadian Opera at Toronto from 1978; Opéra de Montreal from 1983; Guest appearances with Washington Opera (1976), Opéra de Lyon from 1988; Sang Jupiter in Orphée aux Enfers at the Paris Opéra (1988), Don Pasquale at Rio de Janeiro, 1989; Carnegie Hall, 1991, in Boieldieu's La Dame Blanche; Other roles include Masetto, Sparafucile, Rocco, Raimondo, Hunding, Arkel, and Timur in Turandot. *Address:* c/o L'Opéra de Montréal, 260 de Maisonneuve Boulevard West, Montréal, Québec H2X 1Y9, Canada.

CHARD, Geoffrey; Singer (Baritone); b. 9 Aug. 1930, Sydney, Australia. *Education:* Studied at the New South Wales Conservatory. *Career:* Debut: Sydney 1951, in Carmen; Moved to England and became a member of the English National Opera; Other appearances with Welsh National Opera and the Glyndebourne and Edinburgh Festivals; Aldeburgh Festival 1967, 1968, in the premieres of Berkeley's The Castaway and Birtwistle's Punch and Judy; London Coliseum 1973–83, in the British premiere of Penederecki's The Devils of Loudun; Ginastera's Bomarzo and Ligeti's Le Grand Macabre; Roles in operas by Gluck, Mozart, Wagner, Britten, Orff, Menotti, Shostakovich, Janáček and contemporary British composers; Many engagements as concert singer; Sang Bartolo in Il Barbiere di Siviglia for Victoria State Opera, 1989; Germont in Traviata for the Ballarat Opera Festival, 1992, Balstrode (Peter Grimes) and Pizarro at Sydney; Tonio in Pagliacci at Sydney, 1996. *Address:* Victoria State Opera, 370 Nicholson Street, Fitzroy, VIC 3065, Australia.

CHARLTON, David; Musicologist; b. 20 June 1946, London, England. *Education:* BA, Nottingham University, 1967; Cambridge; PhD, 1974. *Career:* Lecturer, 1970, Reader, 1991, University of East Anglia; Reader, then Professor, Royal Holloway, University of London, 1995–. *Publications:* Many articles and reference works on French opera in the New Grove Dictionary of Music and the New Grove Dictionary of Opera; Grétry and the Growth of Opéra-Comique, 1986; French Opera 1730–1830: Meaning and Media, 2000; Editorial: ETA Hoffmann's Musical Writings, 1989; Hector Berlioz, Choral Works with Orchestra, 1993; Michel Sedaine 1719–1797: Theatre, Opera, Art, 2000; The Cambridge Companion to Grand Opera, 2003. *Address:* Department of Music, Royal Holloway, Egham, Surrey TW20 0EX, England. *E-mail:* D .Charlton@rhul.ac.uk.

CHARNOCK, Helen; Singer (Soprano); b. 1958, England. *Education:* Studied at the University of East Anglia, BA with Honours in Music and at Guildhall School with Laura Sarti. *Career:* Many performances with Opera Factory and London Sinfonietta, including the world premieres of Hell's Angels by Nigel Osborne and Birtwistle's Yan Tan Tethera, 1986; Sang in Weill's Mahagonny Songspiel, Ligeti's Aventures, Nouvelles Aventures and the British premiere of Reimann's Ghost Sonata; Workshops and performances in many venues with the London Sinfonietta's Education Programme, including Holloway Prison and the Huddersfield Contemporary Music Festival; Australian debut in 1986 as Clytemnestra in Iphigénie en Tauride; Sang in the premiere of Greek by Mark-Anthony Turnage at 1988 Munich Biennale, repeated at Edinburgh Festival in 1988 and English National Opera 1990; Has sung Britten's Governess and Mrs Coyle at Aldeburgh Festival and has appeared elsewhere as Semele, First Lady, Pamina, Micaela, Butterfly, Titania, Gretel, Adele, Despina and Musetta; Television appearances in works by Birtwistle, Ligeti and Turnage. *Recordings:* Greek by Turnage, 1993. *Honours:* The English Singers and Speakers Prize; 2 Royal Society of Arts Awards; Incorporated Society of Musicians Young Artists Award; Ian Fleming Bursary. *Address:* 21 Glengall Road, London SE15 6 NJ, England.

CHARTERIS, Richard; Musicologist, Writer and Editor; b. 24 June 1948, Chatham Islands, New Zealand. *Education:* BA, Victoria University, Wellington, New Zealand, 1970; MA with 1st class hons, University of Canterbury, 1972; PhD 1976, Universities of Canterbury and London. *Career:* Australian Research Council Chief Investigator, Music Department, University of Sydney, 1981–90; Australian Research Council Senior Research Fellow (Reader) 1991–94, Professor in Historical Musicology, Music Department, University of Sydney, 1995–. *Publications include:* Author of over 150 books and editions devoted to the music of Johann Christian Bach, Giovanni Bassano, John Coprario, Alfonso Ferrabosco the Elder, Domenico Maria Ferrabosco, Andrea and Giovanni Gabrieli, Adam Gumpelzhaimer, Hans Leo Hassler, Thomas Lupo, Claudio Monteverdi and others, and mostly in the series Corpus Mensurabilis Musicae, Musica Britannica, Recent Researches in the Music of the Baroque Era, Boethius Editions,

Fretwork Editions, King's Music Editions, Baroque and Classical Music Series; and books on composers, music and early sources in the series Boethius Editions, Thematic Catalogues Series, Musicological Studies and Documents and Altro Polo. *Honours:* Senior Scholar 1970–71, Mary Duncan Scholar 1975; Louise Dyer Award Royal Musical Association 1975; Australian Academy of Humanities Travelling Fellow 1979–80, Top Award Australian Hi Fi FM Classical Music Section 1988, Fellow of the Australian Academy of the Humanities 1990, Fellow of the Royal Historical Society (London) 2002, Australian Centenary Medal 2003. *Address:* Music Department, University of Sydney, NSW 2006, Australia.

CHASE, Roger; Concert Violist; b. 1958, London, England. *Education:* Studied at Royal College of Music with Bernard Shore and in Canada with Steven Staryk. *Career:* Debut: Solo with the English Chamber Orchestra, 1979; Performances internationally from 1976 with such ensembles as the London Sinfonietta, the Esterhazy Baryton Trio and the Nash Ensemble; Concerts with the chamber ensemble Hausmusik, featuring works by Mendelssohn, Schubert and Hummel; Modern repertoire includes a concerto by Richard Harvey, premiere at the Exeter Festival, 1991; Toured the USA with Hanover Band, 1992 playing Mozart's Sinfonia Concertante; Professor at the Guildhall School of Music and Drama. *Recordings include:* Works by Mendelssohn, Mozart's Concertante and Britten's Lachrymae. *Current Management:* Owen/White Management. *Address:* c/o Owen/White Management, 14 Nightingale Lane, London N8 7QU, England.

CHASLIN, Frédéric; Conductor and Pianist; b. 1963, Paris, France; pnr. Nancy Gustafson. *Career:* Assistant to Daniel Barenboim at the Orchestre de Paris 1987–89 and to Pierre Boulez at Ensemble Intercontemporain, 1989–91; Music Director of Rouen Opera and Symphonie 1991–94; Guest with the Orchestre National de France, from 1993, Orchestre de Paris (1994), Vienna Symphony Orchestra (1993–95), RAI Milan and orchestras of Nice, Marseilles, Lyon, Düsseldorf, Stuttgart and Toho Gakuen in Tokyo; Permanent Guest at the Bregenz Festival, 1993–, with Nabucco and Fidelio; Season 1994–95 with Lakmé at the Paris Opéra-Comique, followed by Der Ring des Nibelungen at Hanover; UK concert debut as guest with Manchester Hallé Orchestra, 1996; Season 1997–98 with Carmen and Manon at the Paris Opéra Bastille, Samson et Dalila for Scottish Opera; Season 1998 with La Favorita at Rome and La Traviata for New Israeli Opera; Concerts in Israel include Le Marteau sans Maître by Boulez; Chief conductor Jerusalem Symphony Orchestra 1999–2002; Tales of Hoffmann at Oper Leipzig 2001–02; Berlioz: Damnation de Faust for Opera North, 2003; La Traviata in Munich, 2003; Concerts with Royal Scottish National Orchestra devoted to Richard Strauss, with Nancy Gustafson, 2003. *Address:* Allied Artists, 42 Montpelier Square, London SW7 1JZ, England.

CHATEAUNEUF, Paula; British/American lutenist and early guitar player; b. 1958, USA. *Education:* Univ. of Connecticut, New England Conservatory, with Patrick O'Brien in New York; Fulbright Scholar, Guildhall School of Music, London with Nigel North. *Career:* moved to London, 1982; appearances with many early music ensembles, including the New London Consort, Orchestra of the Age of Enlightenment, English Concert, Sinfonye and the Gabrieli Consort; has worked extensively as soloist and continuo player, particularly in Baroque opera; involved in groups and projects devoted to improvisation and early dance music; tours of Europe, Australia and the Americas as soloist and ensemble player, performing at major festivals and recording for radio and TV; Tutor, Univ. of Birmingham Centre for Early Music Performance and Research. *Recordings include:* video, music for San Rocco, with the Gabrieli Consort; To the Unknown Goddess: A Portrait of Barbara Strozzi. *Address:* 170 Bow Common Lane, London, E3 4HH, England.

CHAUSSON, Carlos; Singer (Bass-Baritone); b. 17 March 1950, Zaragoza, Spain. *Education:* Studied in Madrid and at the University of Michigan. *Career:* Debut: San Diego, 1977, as Masetto; Appearances at Boston, Miami, New York City Opera and Mexico City (as Bartolo in Il Barbiere di Siviglia); Sang at Madrid from 1983, Barcelona from 1985; Vienna Staatsoper from 1986, as Paolo in Simon Boccanegra, and Don Alvaro in Il Viaggio a Reims, conducted by Abbado; Vienna Konzerthaus in Les Danaides by Salieri; Parma 1987, as Falstaff, Bologna, 1988–89, as Michonnet in Adriana Lecouvreur, Pantaleone in Le Maschere by Mascagni and Sharpless in Butterfly; Barcelona 1989, in the premiere of Cristobal Colon by Baladas, returned 1990, as Paolo; Modena 1990, as Geronte in Manon Lescaut; Sang Mozart's Figaro at Madrid, Masetto at the 1990 Vienna Festival; Grand Théâtre de Genève 1991, as Paolo; Madrid 1992, as Bartolo in the new production of Il Barbiere di Siviglia conducted by Alberto Zedda; Sang Don Magnifico in Cenerentola at the Palais Garnier, Paris, 1996; Giorgio in Paisiello's Nina at Zürich, and John Plake in Wolf-Ferrari's Sly, 1998; Season 2000–01 as Don Alfonso for Zürich Opera, Fra Melitone (La Forza del Destino) and in La

Cenerentola at Madrid. *Address:* c/o Gran Teatre del Liceu, Barcelona, Spain.

CHAUVET, Guy; Singer (Tenor); b. 2 Oct. 1933, Montlucon, Tarbes, France. *Education:* Studied with Bernard Baillour in Tarbes. *Career:* After winning prizes at Cannes, Toulouse and Paris, sang at the Paris Opéra 1959, as Tamino, returned as Faust, Cavaradossi, Florestan, Aeneas in Les Troyens and Jason in Médée; Holland Festival and Buenos Aires, 1961; Covent Garden debut as Cavaradossi, 1963; London Coliseum, 1969, in a concert performance of Roussel's Padmavati; Verona Arena 1971, as Radames; Has sung Parsifal in Brussels, Lohengrin in Berlin and Samson in Geneva; Vienna Staatsoper as Aeneas and Otello; Further appearances in New York, Metropolitan, as John of Leyden, Le Prophète, 1979; Monte Carlo, Lisbon and Dublin; Rio de Janeiro, Don José, 1981; San Francisco, Samson, 1983; Retired as singer 1985 and taught at Tarbes and Paris (Conservatoire). *Recordings:* Highlights from Werther and Hérodiade by Massenet; Scenes from Les Troyens; Sigurd by Reyer. *Address:* c/o San Francisco Opera, War Memorial Opera House, San Francisco, CA 94102, USA.

CHEDEL, Arlette; Singer (Contralto); b. 25 May 1933, Neuchâtel, Switzerland. *Education:* Studied in Neuchâtel and at the Vienna Musikakademie with Erik Werba. *Career:* Concert appearances in works by Schütz, Handel, Bach, Kodály, Frank Martin and Honegger; Radio Lausanne 1974, in the premiere of Trois Visions Espagnoles by Gerber; Montreux Festival, 1986, in Folie de Tristan by Schibler; Guest engagements in Vienna, Prague, Berlin, Rome and Besançon; Opera roles included Wagner's Erda, Magdalene and Mary, Mozart's Marcellina, Catherine in Jeanne d'Arc au Bûcher, the Nurse in Boris Godunov and Geneviève in Pelléas et Mélisande. *Recordings include:* L'Enfant et les Sortilèges and Les Noces by Stravinsky (Erato). *Address:* c/o Grand Théâtre de Genève, 11 Blvd du Théâtre, 1211, Genève 11, Switzerland.

CHEEK, John; Singer (Bass-Baritone); b. 17 Aug. 1948, Greenville, South Carolina, USA. *Education:* Studied at the North Carolina School of Arts and at the Accademia Chigiana in Siena with Gino Bechi. *Career:* Sang at the Festivals of Ravinia and Tanglewood and elsewhere in the USA, notably in music by Mozart; Metropolitan Opera debut 1977, as the Doctor in Pelléas et Mélisande: later appeared as Pimen, Ferrando in Il Trovatore, Klingsor, Panthée in Les Troyens, Monterone and Figaro; New York City Opera 1986, as Mephistopheles in Faust; Other roles include Wurm in Luisa Miller; Attila, New York, 1988; Padre Guardiano, Toronto; Metropolitan, La Bohème, 1989; Ramphis in Aida, Cincinnati Opera, 1990; Sang Don Pasquale at Cincinnati, 1996; Sang the Berlioz Mephistopheles at Helsinki, 2000; Television appearances and concerts. *Recordings include:* Tosca; Haydn Creation, Stravinsky The Rake's Progress, as Nick Shadow; Messiah; César Franck, Les Béatitudes (Satan), Hänssler. *Honours:* Doctor of Music (Honorary), 1985; North Carolina Prize, 1987. *Current Management:* Thea Dispeker Artist Representative, 59 E 54th Street, New York, NY 10022, USA. *Address:* Thea Dispeker Artist Representative, 59 E 54th St, New York, NY 10022, USA.

CHEN, Leland; Concert Violinist; b. 8 July 1965, Taiwan. *Career:* won the Yehudi Menuhin International Competition and made London concert debut with the London Philharmonia at the Barbican; further concerts with the London Philharmonic Orchestra and London Symphony Orchestra; tour of North America in 1985 with the Royal Philharmonic Orchestra; Royal Concert London in 1986 playing the Bach Double Concerto with Yehudi Menuhin; tours of Poland and the Netherlands and a 60-city recital tour of the USA; played Vivaldi's Four Seasons at Kennedy Center, Washington DC, televised by CBS; performances at Gstaad and Schleswig-Holstein festivals; performed throughout Europe with the Netherlands Philharmonic, Polish Chamber Orchestra, Warsaw Sinfonia and Chamber Orchestra of Europe; repertoire includes works by Bartók, Beethoven, Elgar, Mozart, Mendelssohn, Sibelius and Tchaikovsky. *Current Management:* Upbeat Classical Management, PO Box 479, Uxbridge, UB8 2ZH, England. *Telephone:* (1895) 259441. *Fax:* (1895) 259341. *E-mail:* info@upbeatclassical.co.uk. *Website:* www.upbeatclassical.co.uk.

CHEN, Pi-Hsien; Pianist; b. 1950, Taiwan. *Education:* Studied in Taiwan and at the Cologne Musikhochschule, Diploma 1970; further studies with Hans Leygraf and master classes with Wilhelm Kempff, Tatiana Nikolayeva and Geza Anda. *Career:* From 1972 has given performances in London (BBC Proms, South Bank, Barbican), Amsterdam, Zürich, Berlin, Munich, Barcelona and Tokyo; Festival appearances at Huddersfield, Lucerne, Schwetzingen, Hong Kong and Osaka; Orchestras include London Symphony, BBC Symphony, Royal Concertgebouw, Radio orchestras in Austria and Germany, the Züricher Kammerorchester, Tonhalle Orchestra and the Collegium Musicum Zürich; Conductors include Colin Davis, Bernard Haitink, Jean Martinon, the late Ferdinand Leitner, Bernhard Klee, Marek Janowski, the late Paul Sacher, Horst Stein and Peter Eötvös; Repertory ranges from Scarlatti to Boulez; Piano Duo performances with Pierre-Laurent Aimard.

Honours: Prizewinner, Concours Reine Elisabeth, 1972, Belgium; First Prize, Competition of the Rundfunkanstalten Munich, 1972. *Current Management:* Ingpen & Williams Ltd, 7 St George's Court, 131 Putney Bridge Road, London, SW15 2PA, England.

CHEN, Shih-hui, DMusA; Taiwanese composer; b. 6 Sept. 1962, Taibei. *Education:* Nat. Acad. of Arts. *Career:* resident in USA 1982–; currently Asst Prof. of Composition and Theory, Shepherd School of Music, Rice Univ.. *Compositions include:* String Quartet No. 1 1979, String Quartet No. 2 1987, Water Ink 1988, Mime 1988, 66 Times 1992, Moments 1995, Little Dragonflies 1996, String Quartet No. 3 1998, Fu (Ambush) I 1998, Fu II 1999, 'i' 2001, Jian (Gold) 2002, Twice Removed 2000–02, Shui 2003, Furl 2004, String Quartet No. 4 2004. *Honours:* American Acad. in Rome Prize 1999, Guggenheim Fellowship 2000, Barlow Commission 2001. *Address:* c/o Shepherd School of Music, MS 532, Rice University, PO Box 1892, Houston, TX 77251-1892, USA (office). *Telephone:* (713) 348-3742 (office). *Website:* www.ruf.rice.edu (office).

CHEN, Xieyang; Symphony Orchestra Conductor; b. 4 May 1939, Shanghai, China; m. Jian-Ying Wang 1973. *Education:* Piano student, Music Middle School, Shanghai Conservatory, 1953–60; Major in Conducting, Shanghai Conservatory, 1969–65; Musical study with Otto Mueller, Yale University, USA, 1981–82. *Career:* Debut: Shanghai; Conductor: Shanghai Ballet Orchestra, 1965–81; Aspen Festival, Group for Contemporary Music-New York, Brooklyn Philharmonia, Honolulu Symphony, Philippine State Orchestra, Hong Kong Philharmonic, Shanghai Symphony, Central Philharmonic-Beijing, 1981–83; Vilnius Symphony, Kaunas Symphony, Novosibirsk Symphony-USSR, 1985; Tokyo Symphony, Miyagi Philharmonic, Music Festival-Scotland, 1986–88; Music Director, Principal Conductor, Shanghai Symphony Orchestra; Resident Conductor, Central Philharmonic, Beijing. *Recordings:* Beethoven symphonies and Chinese composition for French recording company, 1983; Rachmaninov Symphony No. 2 and Szymanowski Violin Concerto No. 1, 1987; Chen Gang Violin Concerto The Butterfly Lovers and Beethoven's 9 symphonies, 1988. *Address:* 105 Hunan Lu, Shanghai, People's Republic of China.

CHEN, Yi; Composer and Violinist; b. 4 April 1953, Guangzhou, China; m. 1983. *Education:* BA, 1983, MA, 1986, Central Conservatory of Music, Beijing; DMA, 1993, Columbia University, NY, USA. *Career:* Concert Mistress, Beijing Opera Troupe Orchestra, 1970–78; Composer in Residence, The Women's Philharmonic, Chanticleer, San Francisco, 1993–96; Member of Composition Faculty, Peabody Conservatory, Johns Hopkins University, 1996–98; Cravens Millsap Missouri Distinguished Professor in Composition, University of Missouri, Kansas City Conservatory, 1998–. *Compositions:* Works performed and broadcast in Europe, USA and China, 1984–; Duo Ye No. 2, orchestra; Symphony No. 1; Xian Shi for viola and orchestra; Sprout for string orchestra; 3 Poems from Sung Dynasty for chorus; Woodwind Quintet; Near Distance, sextet for chamber ensemble; As in a Dream for soprano, violin and cello; Overture No. 1 and No. 2 for Chinese orchestra; Piano Concerto; Symphony No. 2; Sparkle for chamber ensemble, 1992; Song in Winter, two versions, 1993; Ge Xu (Antiphony) for orchestra, 1994; The Linear for orchestra, 1994; Shuo for string orchestra, 1994; Set of Chinese Folksongs for mixed choir or school choir and strings, 1994; Tang Poems Cantata, 1995; Chinese Myths Cantata, 1996; Qi for chamber ensemble, 1997; Golden Flute for flute and orchestra, 1997; Spring Dreams for mixed chorus, 1997; Fiddle Suite for erhu (Chinese fiddle) and string orchestra or full orchestra, 1997; Romance and Dance for string orchestra, 1997; Momentum for orchestra; Sound of the Five for cello and string quartet; Feng for woodwind quintet; Percussion Concerto for percussion and orchestra; Eleanor's Gift for cello and orchestra, 1998; Baban for piano solo; Chinese Poems for girls' chorus; Dunhuang Fantasy for organ and wind ensemble; Spring Festival for children's wind ensemble, 1999; Chinese Folk Dance Suite for violin and orchestra, 2001; Ba Yin for saxophone quartet and string orchestra, 2001; Chinese Mountain Songs for women's choir, 2001; Bright Moonlight for soprano and piano, 2001; Know You How Many Petals Falling for mixed choir, 2001; Ning for violin, cello and pipa, 2001; To the New Millennium for mixed choir, 2001; Wu Yu for chamber ensemble, 2002;... as like a raging fire... for chamber ensemble, 2002; Burning for string quartet, 2002; Singing in the Mountain for piano; Tu for full orchestra, 2002; At the Kansas City Chinese New Year Concert for string quartet; Chinese Fables for erhu, pipa, cello, percussion, 2002; Ballad, Dance and Fantasy for cello and full orchestra, 2003; Caramoor's Summer for chamber orchestra, 2003; Landscape for mixed choir, 2003; The West Lake for mixed choir, 2003; Two Chinese Folk Songs for mixed choir, 2003; Symphony No.3 for full orchestra, 2003. *Honours:* Ives Living Award (2001–04) from American Academy of Arts and Letters. *Address:* Theodore Presser Co, 4550 Warwick Blvd, Apt 1114, Kansas City, MO 64111, USA. *E-mail:* chenyi@aol.com. *Website:* www.presser.com/composers/chen.html.

CHEN, Zuohuang; Conductor, Pianist and Music Director; b. 2 April 1947, Shanghai, China; m. Zaiyi Wang 1969, 1 d. *Education:* High School Division, Central Conservatory, Beijing, 1960–65; Central

Conservatory, Beijing, 1977–80; MMus, 1982, DMA Orchestral Conducting, 1985, University of Michigan, USA. *Career:* Conductor, All China Trade Union Music and Dance Troupe, 1966–74; Conductor, China Film Philharmonic Orchestra, 1974–76; Associate Professor of Conducting, University of Kansas, USA, 1985–87; Conductor, Central Philharmonic Orchestra, Beijing, 1987–96; Led its US debut tour throughout America, 1987; Conductor of China Youth Symphony Orchestra, 1987–, leading its European Tour, 1987; Guest Conductor in over 20 countries with Zürich Tonhalle Orchestra, Vancouver Symphony Orchestra, Hungary State Symphony, Gulbenkian Orchestra, Tanglewood Music Festival Orchestra, Colorado Symphony Orchestra, Pacific Symphony Orchestra, Russian Philharmonic Orchestra, Haifa Symphony, Slovak Radio Symphony Orchestra, Hong Kong Philharmonic Orchestra, Pusan Philharmonic Orchestra, Mexico National and UNAM Symphony and the Taipei Symphony Orchestra; Music Director/Conductor, Wichita Symphony Orchestra, 1990; Music Director/Conductor, Rhode Island Philharmonic Orchestra, 1992–96; Artistic Director/Conductor, China National Symphony Orchestra, 1996–. *Recordings:* 5 albums with the China National Symphony Orchestra. *Current Management:* ICM Artists Ltd, 40 W 57th Street, New York, NY 10019, USA. *Address:* 10610 S Highland Lane, Olathe, KS 66061, USA.

CHÉREAU, Patrice; Opera Producer and Film Director; b. 2 Nov. 1944, Lezigne, Maine-et-Loire, France. *Career:* Co-Director of the Théâtre National Populaire, Paris, 1979–81; Director, Théâtre des Amandiers, Nanterre, from 1982; Opera Productions include Les Contes d'Hoffmann and Lulu, 1979, for the Paris Opéra and Der Ring des Nibelungen, Bayreuth, 1976; Has produced Lucio Silla by Mozart at La Scala, Milan; Produced Wozzeck at Paris (Châtelet), Berlin (Staatsoper) and the Lyric Opera, Chicago, 1992–93; Don Giovanni at Salzburg, 1994. *Recordings include:* Bayreuth Ring (DVD), 2001. *Address:* Festspielhaus, 8580 Bayreuth 1, Germany.

CHERICI, Paolo; Italian lute teacher; b. 26 March 1952, Naples. *Education:* Milan Conservatoire and Schola Cantorum of Basel. *Career:* concerts of Renaissance and Baroque music as lute soloist and in ensemble in Italy and abroad; appearances on radio and television in Italy and Switzerland; lute teacher at summer courses in Vicenza, Monza, Moneglia, Venice, Rocchetta Nevina, Trieste, Mercogliano; founder of the lute class at Milan Conservatoire; mem. The Lute Society, England, The Lute Society of America. *Recordings:* Collaborations with several recordings with music from the Renaissance to Baroque period. *Publications:* A Piccinini, Toccata per 2 liuti, 1977; J. S. Bach, Opere complete per liuto, 1980; A Vivaldi, Concerto per liuto e archi in D major, 1981; contrib. articles and reviews to Il Fronimo. *Honours:* Società Italiana del Liuto. *Address:* Via Ciro Menotti 7, 20129 Milan, Italy.

CHERNEY, Brian; Composer and Educator; b. 4 Sept. 1942, Canada. *Education:* BMus, 1964, MMus, 1967, PhD, Musicology, 1974, University of Toronto; ARCT Piano, 1961; Studied composition with Samuel Dolin and John Weinzweig. *Career:* Professor, Faculty of Music, McGill University, Montreal, 1972–; mem, Canadian League of Composers; Associate Composer, Canadian Music Center. *Compositions:* Chamber Concerto for viola and 10 players, 1974; String Trio, 1976; Dans le crépuscule du souvenir for piano, 1977–80; Adieux for orchestra, 1980; River of Fire for harp and oboe d'amore, 1983; In the Stillness of the Seventh Autumn for piano, 1983; Into the Distant Stillness for orchestra, 1984; String Quartet No. 3, 1985; In Stillness Ascending for viola and piano, 1986; Illuminations for string orchestra, 1987; Shekhinah for solo viola, 1988; Oboe Concerto, 1989; Transfiguration for orchestra, 1990; Et j'entends la nuit qui chante dans les cloches, for piano and orchestra, 1990; Apparitions, for cello and 14 musicians, 1991; Doppelganger for 2 flutes, 1991; In the Stillness of September 1942 for English horn and 9 solo strings, 1992; Like Ghosts from an Enchanted Feeling, for cello and piano, 1993; Die klingende Zeit, for flute and chamber ensemble, 1993–94; Et la solitude dérive au fil des fleuves, for orchestra, 1995; Tombeau, for piano, 1996; Echoes in the Memory for bass clarinet, cello and piano, 1997. *Recordings include:* Adieux; River of Fire: Into the Distant Stillness; Illuminations. *Publications:* Harry Somers, book, 1975; Compositions published, 1970–97. *Honours:* First Place, String Trio, International Rostrum of Composers, 1979; Jules Léger Prize for New Chamber Music, 1985. *Address:* 4362 Hingston Avenue, Montreal, Quebec H4A 2J9, Canada.

CHERNOMORTSEV, Victor; Singer (Baritone); b. 1950, Krasnodar, Russia. *Education:* Graduated Tchaikovsky Conservatoire, Moscow, 1973. *Career:* Many appearances throughout Russia in opera and concert; Mariinsky Theatre, St Petersburg, from 1994 as Mazeppa, Rigoletto, Prince Igor, Nabucco Tomsky in The Queen of Spades, Amonasro, Count Luna, Scarpia, Alberich in Das Rheingold and Grasnoi in The Tsar's Bride by Rimsky-Korsakov; Tours with the Kirov Opera throughout Europe and to the New York Metropolitan; Other roles include Robert in Iolanta and the Chinese Inspector in Stravinsky's The Nightingale; Sang Matreyev in War and Peace with the Kirov

Opera at Covent Garden 2000. *Honours:* Honoured Artist of Russia. *Address:* c/o Kirov Opera, Mariinsky Theatre, Mariinsky Square, St Petersburg, Russia.

CHERNOUSHENKO, Vladislav; Conductor; b. 14 Jan. 1936, Leningrad, Russia. *Education:* Studied at the Leningrad State Conservatoire. *Career:* Sang with the Boys Choir of the Glinka State Capella from 1944; Conducted the Karelia State Radio Orchestra, then the Leningrad Chamber Choir, 1962–74; Music Director of the Glinka State Capella, 1974–; Directed the premiere performance of Rachmaninov's complete Vespers, 1974; Re-established the Symphony Orchestra of the Glinka State Capella, 1988 and has toured with it to Germany, Netherlands, Switzerland, Ireland and France with a repertoire including Haydn, Shostakovich, Brahms, Bruckner, Schnittke and Mozart; Rector, Leningrad-St Petersburg State Conservatoire, 1979–. *Recordings include:* A wide repertoire. *Address:* c/o Sonata, 11 Northpark Street, Glasgow G20 7AA, Scotland.

CHERNOV, Vladimir; Baritone; b. 22 Sept. 1953, Russia. *Education:* Graduated Moscow Conservatory, 1981; Further study at La Scala, Milan. *Career:* Soloist with Kirov Theatre, Leningrad from 1984 as Rossini's Figaro, Germont, Valentin in Faust, Yeletzky in The Queen of Spades; Toured the United Kingdom and Ireland with the Moscow Radio Symphony Orchestra, 1985; US debut as Marcello in La Bohème with the Opera Company of Boston in 1989; In 1990 debuts with Scottish Opera as Don Carlo in La Forza del Destino, with Los Angeles Music Center Opera as Posa in Don Carlo, with Covent Garden as Figaro and Ezio in Attila and with Seattle Opera as Prince Andrei in War and Peace; Debuts in 1991 included Metropolitan Opera and Rome Opera as Miller in Luisa Miller; At Metropolitan has sung Germont, di Luna (Trovatore), Posa, Figaro, Stankar (Stiffelio) and title-role of Simon Boccanegra; San Francisco Opera debut as Ezio (Attila) in 1992; Debut with Vienna State Opera as Figaro in 1992; Since then has sung there almost his entire repertoire, including Ford (Falstaff) which also was his Salzburg Festival debut, 1993; Chicago Lyric Opera debut in 1992 as Renato in Ballo in Maschera; Deutsche Oper Berlin debut in 1993 as di Luna and Renato; Debuts in 1994 included Arena di Verona as Marcello and Posa and Paris Bastille Opéra as Simon Boccanegra; La Scala debut in 1995 as Stankar; Sang Francesco in Due Foscari at Covent Garden, 1995 and Eugene Onegin at the Met, 1997; Sang in Ernani at Marseilles, 1999; Rodrigo in Don Carlos at the Opéra Bastille, 1998; Belfiore, Verdi's Un giorno di Regno, for Covent Garden (concert), 1999; Season 2000–01 as Germont at the Met, Eugene Onegin for Opera Miami, Verdi's Miller at the Deutsche Oper Berlin and Renato in Munich; Nottingham in Donizetti's Roberto Devereux at Hamburg (concert). *Recordings include:* Rigoletto, DGG; Ballo in Maschera, Teldec; Several videos. *Honours:* Glinka Competition 2nd Prize, 1981; 3rd Prize, Tchaikovsky Competition, 1981; 2nd Prize, Voci Verdiani Competition, 1983; 1st Prize, Tito Gobbi Prize, Miriam Helin Competition, 1984. *Address:* CAMI, 165 West 57th Street, New York, NY 10019, USA.

CHERNYKH, Pavel; Singer (Baritone); b. 1960, Moscow, Russia. *Education:* Studied at Tchaikovsky Music School and with Yevgeny Nesterenko at the Moscow Conservatoire. *Career:* Debut: Stage Debut in season 1989–90 as Tchaikovsky's Onegin at the Bolshoi; Concerts and recordings with the Maly State Symphony, the St Petersburg Philharmonic and the Moscow Radio Orchestras, 1987–; Further performances as Silvio in Pagliacci, Robert in Tchaikovsky's Iolanta, Yeletsky in The Queen of Spades and Renato (Ballo in Maschera); Sang Onegin at the Paris Opéra Comique, 1987 and for the Vlaamse Opera in Antwerp, 1990; Stars of the Bolshoi Theatre concerts in Germany and Norway, 1990; Toured with the Bolshoi as Onegin to the USA, 1990 and sang at the Wolf Trap Theatre, Washington DC; Edinburgh Festival as Onegin, 1991; Sang Germont at St Petersburg, 1998. *Address:* c/o Sonata, 11 Northpark Street, Glasgow G20 7AA, Scotland.

CHESWORTH, David (Anthony); Composer and Sound Designer; b. 31 March 1958, Stoke, England. *Education:* BA (Hons), La Trobe University, 1979; National Young Composers School, 1986. *Career:* Sound Design School, 1987–92; Freelance Composer, 1993–; Commissions from Paris Autumn Festival, 1985; Melbourne Festival, 1990–91; Australian Broadcasting Corporation, 1993. *Compositions include:* Choral, for piano, 1982; Stories of Imitation and Corruption for orchestra and tape, 1986; Lacuna, chamber opera, 1992; Duet I for violin, cello and vibraphones, 1993; Exotica Suite for ensemble, 1993; The Soft Skin for cello, clarinet and piano, 1993; The Two Executioners, chamber opera, 1994; Focal Wall Soundscape, 1995; Cosmonart, opera commissioned by Opera Australia, 1997; Olympic Stadium Sound Environment, commissioned by the Olympic Co-ordination Authority, 1999. *Honours:* Prix Ars Electronica, Austria, 1993. *Address:* c/o APRA, 1A Eden Street, Crows Nest, NSW 2065, Australia.

CHEW, Geoffrey (Alexander); British university professor; b. 23 April 1940, South Africa; s. of James Alexander Chew and Florence Hilda

Chew; m. Jennifer Comrie, 22 July 1967, 1 s., 2 d. *Education:* Royal Coll. of Music, 1958–61; Caius Coll., Cambridge 1961–64; BA, 1963; MusB, 1964; PhD, Manchester Univ., 1968. *Career:* Univ. Lecturer: Johannesburg, 1968–70, Aberdeen, 1970–77, Royal Holloway, Univ. of London, 1977–05; mem, Royal Musical Asscn, American Musicological Soc., Gesellschaft für Musikforschung, International Musicological Soc., Soc. for Music Theory. *Contributions:* Journal of The American Musicological Society; Music Analysis; Musiktheorie; Cambridge Opera Journal. *Address:* Department of Music, Royal Holloway, University of London, Egham Hill, Egham, Surrey TW20 0EX (office); The Mount, Malt Hill, Egham, Surrey TW20 9PB, England (home). *Telephone:* (1784) 443537. *Fax:* (1784) 439441. *E-mail:* chew@sun.rhul.ac.uk.

CHI, Jacob; Music Director and Conductor; b. 9 Dec. 1952, Qingdao, Shandong, China; m. Lin Chang, 11 July 1987, 1 s. *Education:* BA, Music, magna cum laude, Siena Heights University, 1985; MM, Violin Performance, University of Michigan, 1987; DMA Orchestra Conducting, Michigan State University, 1996. *Career:* Conductor, Qingdao Opera, China, 1975–80; Music Director, Conductor, Pueblo Symphony, 1991–93, 1996–; Music Director, Conductor, Miami University Symphony Orchestra, 1993–97; Conductor, Colorado Music Festival, 1995–; Conductor, Echtenach International Music Festival, Luxembourg, 1996; mem, Conductors' Guild; American Symphony League; Music Teachers National Association. *Compositions:* Operetta, Apricot Field, 1976. *Recordings:* Festival International, Luxembourg; J C Bach Viola Concerto in C minor; Vivaldi, Four Seasons. *Honours:* First Prize, Fine Art Composition Contest, Shantung, China, 1976. *Address:* 516 W Golfwood Drive, Pueblo West, CO 81007, USA.

CHIARA, Maria; Singer (Soprano); b. 24 Nov. 1939, Oderzo, Italy. *Education:* Conservatorio Benedetto Marcello in Venice, with Antonio Cassinelli. *Career:* Debut: Venice Festival, 1965, as Desdemona in Otello; Sang widely in Italy, 1965–70, notably as Puccini's Liu at Verona, and Verdi's Odabella, Amelia (Ballo in Maschera) and Aida; Several debuts in Germany and Austria, 1970–71, including Munich and Vienna as Mimi and Butterfly; La Scala debut, 1972, as Micaela in Carmen; Covent Garden debut, 1973, as Liu in Turandot; Metropolitan Opera, 1977, as Violetta; Chicago Lyric Opera in Manon Lescaut; Appearances in Buenos Aires as Amelia (Simon Boccanegra) and Suor Angelica; Opened the 1985–86 season at La Scala as Aida; Australian Opera, Melbourne, 1986, in Un Ballo in Maschera; Aida at Luxor, Egypt, 1987; Amelia in Ballo in Maschera, at Bologna, Parma and Naples, 1989; Leonora in Forza del Destino, at the 1989 Spoleto and Verona Festivals; Aida at Turin, 1990; Other roles include Donizetti's Anna Bolena and Maria Stuarda, Verdi's Elisabeth de Valois and Giordano's Maddalena; Sang Leonora in Il Trovatore at Turin, 1991; Liu in Turandot at the Verona Arena, 1995. *Recordings include:* Aida; Madama Butterfly; Video of the Scala production of Aida.

CHIHARA, Paul (Seiko); Composer; b. 9 July 1938, Seattle, Washington, USA. *Education:* Studied with Robert Palmer at Cornell University, with Nadia Boulanger in Paris, Ernst Pepping in Berlin and with Gunther Schuller at the Berkshire Music Center. *Career:* Teacher, University of California, Los Angeles, 1966; Associate Professor, UCLA until 1974; Founded and Directed the Twice Ensemble; Andrew Mellon Professor, California Institute of Technology, 1975; Teacher, California Institute of the Arts, 1976; Composer-in-Residence, San Francisco Ballet, 1980; Commissions from the Boston Symphony Orchestra and the Los Angeles Philharmonic. *Compositions include:* Magnificat for 6 female voices, 1965; Driftwood for string quartet, 1967; Branches for 2 bassoons and percussion, 1968; Forest Music for orchestra, 1970; Windsong for cello and orchestra, 1971; Grass for double bass and orchestra, 1972; Ceremony III for flute and orchestra, 1973; Shinju, ballet, 1975; Missa Carminum, 1975; The Beauty of the Rose is in its Passing for ensemble, 1976; String Quartet (Primavera), 1977; 2 Symphonies, 1975, 1980; Misletoe Bride, ballet, 1978; Concerto for string quartet and orchestra, 1980; Sinfonia Concertante for 9 instruments, 1980; The Tempest, ballet, 1980; Saxophone concerto, 1981; Sequoia for string quartet and tape, 1984; Shogun the Musical, 1990; Forever Escher for saxophone quartet and string quartet, 1995; Sonata for viola and piano, 1997; Minidoka for chorus, percussion and tape, 1998; Concerto for violin, clarinet and orchestra, 1999; Film and television scores; Arrangements for musicals. *Address:* c/o ASCAP, ASCAP Bulding, 1 Lincoln Plaza, NY 10023, USA.

CHILCOTT, Robert (Bob) Lionel; composer; b. 9 April 1955, Plymouth, Devon, England; m. Polly Ballard 1981; one s. three d. *Education:* Royal College of Music, London. *Career:* mem. SPNM; Royal Society of Musicians. *Compositions:* Singing by Numbers, 1995; Fragments From His Dish, 1995; City Songs, 1996; Organ Dances, 1996; Friends, 1997; The Elements, 1997. *Address:* c/o Oxford University Press, New Music Promotion, 70 Baker Street, London W1M 1DJ, England.

CHILINGIRIAN, Levon, FRCM, OBE; Armenian/Cypriot violinist; b. 28 May 1948; m. Susan Paul Pattie; one s. *Education:* Royal Coll. of Music,

London. *Career:* debut, Purcell Room 1969; duo with Clifford Benson (piano), BBC radio and television, German and Swiss radio; Chilingirian Quartet formed 1971; Proms, Cheltenham, London, Aldeburgh, Bath, Paris, New York, Berlin and Adelaide Festivals; world-wide television and radio appearances; resident ensemble, Liverpool Univ. 1973–76, Sussex Univ. 1978–93, Royal Coll. of Music 1987–; Musical Dir, Camerata Nordica, Sweden; mem. ISM, Musicians' Union, ESTA, Royal Soc. of Musicians. *Recordings:* with quartet: works by Arriaga, Berwald, Korngold, Mozart, Haydn, Schubert, Beethoven, Schumann, Dvořák, Bartók, Debussy, Ravel, Panufnik, Tavener, Pärt, Wood, Stravinsky, Schnittke, Grieg, Chausson, Shostakovich, Borodin; solo: Tippett Triple Concerto; as duo: Schubert, Mathias, Ferguson and Finzi. *Publications:* Revised Grieg F Major Quartet 1891. *Honours:* First prize, BBC Beethoven Competition 1969, Munich Competition 1971; DMus, Sussex Univ., 1992; Cobbett Medal, 1993; Royal Philharmonic Society Chamber Music Award, 1995. *Address:* 7 Hollingbourne Road, London, SE24 9NB, England.

CHIN, Unsuk; South Korean composer; b. 1961, Seoul. *Education:* Nat. Univ. of Seoul, studied with György Ligeti in Hamburg. *Career:* work in electronic studio of the Technische Univ., Berlin 1988–; composer-in-residence, Deutsches Symphonie Orchester, Berlin 2001–02. *Compositions include:* Gestalten 1984, Troerrinnen 1986, Gradus ad infinitum 1989, Akrostichon-Wortspiel 1991, Santika Ekatala 1993, Fantaisie mécanique 1994, ParaMetaString 1996, Klavierkonzert 1996–97, Xi 1998, Miroirs des temps 1999–2000, six Piano Etudes 1999–2000, Kalà 2000, Violinkonzert 2001, Doppelkonzert 2002, snagS & Snarls 2003–04, Concerto for violin and orchestra (Grawemeyer Award for Music Composition) 2004. *Recordings:* Fantasie mécanique, Akrostichon-Wortspiel, Doppelkonzert and Xi performed by Ensemble Intercontemporain. *Address:* c/o Boosey & Hawkes, Komponisten Abteilung, Lützowufer 26, 10787 Berlin, Germany (office). *Website:* www.boosey.com.

CHINGARI, Marco; Singer (Baritone); b. 1963, Rome. *Career:* Sang at Busseto, Italy, 1987–88 in Verdi's Il Corsaro and La Forza del Destino; Appearances at Rome Opera, 1989 in Mascagni's Il Piccolo Marat; Season 1991–92: As Mathieu in Andrea Chénier at Turin and Escamillo in Carmen at Palma; Season 1994–95: As Max in Betly by Donizetti in Bergamo and in Zandonai's Francesca da Rimini at Palermo; Other roles include Michonnet in Adriana Lecouvreur and Verdi's Duke of Mantua; Season 2000 as Tonio in Pagliacci and Sharpless in Butterfly at Torre del Lago. *Recordings:* La Fanciulla del West; I Vespri Siciliani. *Honours:* Prizewinner, Voci Verdiane Competition, Busseto. *Address:* c/o Teatro Donizetti, Razza Cavour 14, 24100 Bergamo, Italy.

CHISSELL, Joan Olive, ARCM, GRSM; British musicologist; b. 22 May 1919, Cromer, Norfolk, England. *Education:* Royal Coll. of Music. *Career:* Lecturer in Music for Extra-Mural Depts, Univs of London and Oxford 1942–48; piano teacher, Jr Dept, Royal Coll. of Music 1943–53; Asst Music Critic, The Times 1948–79; regular broadcaster for BBC from 1943; reviewer for The Gramophone 1968–2003; jury mem., int. piano competitions including Milan, Leeds, Zwickau, Budapest, Dublin and Sydney, Australia; mem. Critics' Circle, Royal Coll. of Music Soc.. *Publications:* Robert Schumann 1948, Chopin 1965, Schumann's Piano Music 1972, Brahms 1977, Clara Schumann: A Dedicated Spirit 1983; contrib. to A Companion to the Concerto 1988, Benjamin Britten (A Symposium), Chamber Music, The Concerto, numerous journals and magazines, including Radio Times and The Listener. *Honours:* Robert Schumann Prize, Zwickau 1991.

CHITTY, Alison Jill, OBE; British stage designer; b. 1960, England. *Education:* St Martin's School of Art, Central School of Art and Design, London. *Career:* designs for premiere production of Tippett's New Year, at Houston and Glyndebourne 1989–90, premieres of Birtwistle's Gawain 1991, Goehr's Arianna at Covent Garden, Jenůfa in Dallas, Billy Budd in Geneva, Paris, Los Angeles and London, Giulio Cesare and Der fliegende Holländer in Bordeaux, Khovanshchina for ENO, Turandot in Paris, Otello in Munich, Tristan und Isolde at Chicago and Seattle, Die Meistersinger in Copenhagen, Aida in Geneva, Dialogues des Carmélites for Santa Fe Opera, premiere production of Birtwistle's The Last Supper at Berlin and Glyndebourne 2000–01; Dir, Motley Theatre Design Course. *Address:* c/o Glyndebourne Festival Opera, Glyndebourne, Lewes, Sussex BN8 5UU, England.

CHIUMMO, Umberto; Singer (Bass, Baritone); b. 1970, Italy. *Education:* Pescara Conservatoire. *Career:* Engagements as Dulcamara at Parma, Enrico in Anna Bolena at Washington and Raimondo in Lucia di Lammermoor for Welsh National and New Israeli Operas; Gounod's Mefistofele at Como, Frère Laurent at the Opéra Comique, Fenicio in Rossini's Ermione at La Monnaie, Brussels, and Alidoro in Houston; Don Giovanni at Sassari, Leporello in Turin and Publio in La Clemenza di Tito for Welsh National Opera; Count in Le nozze di Figaro for Rome Opera, and Bartolo at La Scala, Milan; Ariodate in Xerxes at Monaco and Ircano in Ricciardo e Zoraide at the Rossini Opera Festival, Pesaro;

Glyndebourne Tour 1994, 1996 as Rossini's Basilio and Mozart's Figaro; Garibaldo in Handel's Rodelinda at the Festival, 1998; Season 1998–99 as Raimondo in Toulouse, Leporello in Turin, and Ariodate for the Bayerische Staatsoper, Munich. *Address:* c/o Glyndebourne Festival Opera, Lewes, Sussex, BN5 5UU, England. *Telephone:* 01273 812321. *Fax:* 01273 812783.

CHLITSIOS, George; Conductor and Lecturer; b. 25 March 1969, Volos, Greece. *Education:* Studied Viola, Piano, Composition, Conducting, Epirotic Conservatory, Ioannina, Greece; Rotterdam Conservatorium and Royal (Koninklijk) Conservatorium, Hague, Netherlands; London College of Music; Thames Valley University. *Career:* Debut: Conductor, Tsakalof Youth Symphony Orchestra, 1989; Principal Conductor, Tsakalof Symphony Orchestra, 1993–97; Guest Conductor, LCM Symphony Orchestra, 1994; Guest Conductor, Athens State Orchestra, 1997; Principal Conductor, Epirus Opera House, Greece, 1997–; Music Director, Tsakalof Symphony Orchestra, 1997–; Concerts in Greece, France, England, Germany; Conducted many world premieres of symphonic works; Appearances in television and radio networks in Greece and abroad. *Honours:* Scholarship, Academy of Athens, 1993; Representative Conductor for Greece, VE-Day Celebrations, London, 1995; Medal, Mayor of Ioannina, Greece, 1995; Medal, Mayor of Kifisia, Greece, 1996. *Address:* c/o Tsakalof Symphony Orchestra, Platia G, Stavrou 5, 454 44 Ioannina, Greece.

CHMURA, Gabriel; Conductor; b. 7 May 1946, Wrocław, Poland; m. Mareile Chmura, 1 s., 1 d. *Education:* Diploma (Conducting), Vienna Academy of Music; Ecole Normale de Musique, Paris; MA, Piano and Composition, Tel-Aviv University. *Career:* Assistant to Karajan, 1971–73; Generalmusikdirektor, Aachen, 1974–82; Bochum Symphony Orchestra, 1982–87; Music Director-Designate, 1986–87, Principal Conductor, Music Director, 1987–90, National Arts Centre Orchestra, Ottawa, Canada; Guest Conductor: Berlin Philharmonic Orchestra; Vienna Symphony Orchestra; London Symphony Orchestra; Orchestre Nationale de France, Paris; Tonhalle Orchester, Zürich; North German Radio Symphony Orchestra, Hamburg; Bavarian Radio Symphony Orchestra, Munich; South German Radio Symphony Orchestra, Stuttgart; New York Philharmonic Orchestra; Paris Opéra; Bavarian State Opera, Munich; Conducted Werther at Parma, 1990; Music Director, Ottawa and American orchestras, 1991–97. *Compositions:* Pièce pour piano, 1968; 3 Songs for soprano and piano; Text James Joyce. *Recordings include:* Mendelssohn Overtures with London Symphony Orchestra; Schubert, Lazarus; Haydn Symphonies 6, 7, 8 with National Arts Centre Orchestra, Canada. *Honours:* Gold Medal, Guido Cantelli Conducting Competition, Milan, 1971; 1st Prize, Herbert von Karajan Conducting Competition, Berlin, 1971; Prix Mondial du Disque de Montreux, 1983. *Current Management:* TransArt (UK) Ltd, Cedar House, 10 Rutland Street, Filey, YO14 9JB, North Yorkshire, England. *Telephone:* (1723) 515819. *Fax:* (1723) 514678. *E-mail:* transartuk@transartuk.com. *Website:* www.transartuk.com.

CHODOS, Gabriel; Pianist and Teacher; b. 7 Feb. 1939, White Plains, New York, USA. *Education:* BA, Philosophy, 1959, MA, Music, 1964, University of California, Los Angeles; Diploma in Piano, Akademie für Musik, Vienna, 1966. *Career:* Debut: Carnegie Recital, New York City, 1970; Appearances throughout USA; Numerous tours of Europe, Israel and Japan; Solo performances with Chicago Symphony Orchestra, Radio Philharmonic, Netherlands, Jerusalem Symphony Orchestra and Aspen Chamber Symphony; Masterclasses at Aspen Festival, Rutgers Summer Festival, Chautauqua Festival, Hochschule für Musik, Leipzig, Toho Conservatory, Kunitachi Music University, Osaka University of Arts and elsewhere throughout Japan. *Recordings:* Schubert's Sonata in B-flat major and smaller works; Encore Favourites; Bartók's Sonata; Bloch's Visions and Prophecies; Franck's Prélude, Aria et Final; Berlinsky's Sonata for Violin and Piano; Beethoven's Sonata op. 111; Schubert's Moments Musicaux, Schubert's Sonata in G major, Brahms Klavierstücke op.76. *Address:* 245 Waban Avenue, Waban, MA 02468, USA.

CHOJNACKA, Elisabeth; Harpsichordist; b. 10 Sept. 1939, Warsaw, Poland. *Education:* Studied in Warsaw and with Aimée Van de Wiele in Paris. *Career:* Many performances of modern music throughout France and Europe, notably at the Domaine Musical and Ars Nova festivals; Has premiered works by Bussotti, Marius Constant, Donatoni, Gorecki, Christobal Halffter, Ligeti (Hungarian Rock, 1978) and Xenakis (Komboi, 1981). *Address:* c/o Ensemble Ars Nova, 16 Rue des Fossés St Jacques, 75008 Paris, France.

CHOO, David Ik-Sung; Conductor; b. 10 Sept. 1962, Seoul, Republic of Korea. *Education:* BMus, California State University, Northridge, 1981–88; MMus, Orchestral Conducting, University of Southern California, 1988–90; Doctor of Musical Arts in Orchestral Conducting, Peabody Conservatory of Music, 1998; Conducting studies Frederik Prausnitz, Violin studies with Manuel Compinsky, Miwako Watanabe and Kathleen Lenski; Piano studies with Nobuko Fujimoto. *Career:*

Debut: Guest Conductor, Aspen Concert Orchestra, 1988; Central Philharmonic Orchestra of China, Beijing, 1991; Conductor: US Chamber (assistant) and Symphony Orchestras (guest); Washington Central Choir and Central Orchestra; Los Angeles Orchestra; The Central Philharmonic Orchestra of China (guest); The Savaria Symphony Orchestra (guest), Hungary, 1992; Ploisti Philharmonic Orchestra (guest), Romania, 1994; St Petersburg Congress Orchestra (Guest), Russia, 1995; Hradec Kralove Philharmonic (guest), Czech Republic, 1995; St Petersburg Hermitage Orchestra (guest), 1997; Seoul Philharmonic Orchestra (guest), 1998; Savannah Symphony Orchestra (guest), 1998; Music Director of Columbia Camerata Musica Chamber Orchestra and Chesapeake Youth Symphony Orchestra; Bavaria Symphony Orchestra. *Publications:* Doctoral Dissertation on Franco Leoni's L'Oracolo: A Study in Orientalism, 1998. *Honours:* Prizewinner, Nicolai Malko Conducting Competition, Copenhagen, 1992. *Address:* 4808 Circling Hunter Dr #203, Columbia, MD 21045, USA.

CHOOKASIAN, Lili; Singer (Mezzo-Soprano); b. 1 Aug. 1921, Chicago, Illinois, USA. *Education:* Studied with Philip Manuel in New York and with Rosa Ponselle in Baltimore. *Career:* Debut: Chicago Symphony Orchestra conducted by Bruno Walter in Mahler, 1957; Stage debut Little Rock 1959, as Adalgisa in Norma; New York debut 1962, in Prokofiev's Alexander Nevsky; Metropolitan Opera debut 1962, as La Cieca in La Gioconda; Returned as Wagner's Erda and in Suor Angelica, Pelléas et Mélisande, IL Tabarro and Falstaff; New York City Opera 1963, The Medium by Menotti; Appearances at Salzburg, Bayreuth (Erda 1965), Mexico City, Hamburg and Buenos Aires; Created the Queen in Inès de Castro by Pasatieri (1976); Other roles include Amneris, Azucena, Mary in Der fliegende Holländer, Ulrica, and Madelon in Andrea Chénier; Concert engagements with major US orchestras. *Recordings:* Symphony No. 2 by Yardumian and Mahler's Das Lied von der Erde, with the Philadelphia Orchestra; Götterdämmerung; Mahler 2; Beethoven 9.

CHORZEMPA, Daniel (Walter); Pianist, Organist, Musicologist and Composer; b. 7 Dec. 1944, Minneapolis, Minnesota, USA. *Education:* University of Minnesota; Fulbright Scholar, Cologne, Federal Republic of Germany, 1965–66. *Career:* Former Church Organist, USA; Organ Instructor, University of Minnesota, 1962–65; Extensive Piano and Organ Recitals including Germany, Denmark, Italy and the United Kingdom, 1968–; in 1970 and 1971 played Beethoven's Diabelli Variations in Oxford and London. *Recordings:* For Philips including the major organ works of Liszt. *Address:* 5000 Cologne 1, Gross Budengasse 11, Germany.

CHOU, Wen-Chung; Composer; b. 29 July 1923, Chefoo, China. *Education:* Studied with Slonimsky, New England Conservatory, 1946–49; Columbia University with Otto Luening; Edgar Varèse, 1949–54. *Career:* Teacher at several American universities, including Columbia University, 1964; Editions of Amèriques and Octandre by Varèse, 1972, 1980; Tuning Up, 1998. *Compositions:* Landscapes for orchestra, 1949; The Fallen Petals for orchestra, 1954; Metaphors for wind orchestra, 1961; Pien, for piano, percussion and wind, 1966; Peking in the Mist for ensemble, 1986; Echoes from the Gorge, for percussion quartet, 1989; Windswept Peaks for violin, cello, clarinet and piano, 1990; Cello concerto, 1993; Clouds for string quartet, 1996. *Honours:* Guggenheim Fellowships, 1957, 1959; Elected to the Institute of the American Academy, 1982. *Address:* c/o ASCAP, ASCAP Building, 1 Lincoln Plaza, New York, NY 10023, USA.

CHOWNING, John (MacLeod); Composer and Teacher; b. 22 Aug. 1934, Salem, New Jersey, USA. *Education:* BM, Wittenberg University, Springfield, Ohio, 1959; Studied with Nadia Boulanger, Paris, 1959–62; PhD, Stanford University, 1966. *Career:* Teacher, 1966–, Director, Computer Music and Acoustics Project, 1966–74, Center for Computer Research in Music and Acoustics (CCRMA), 1975, Professor of Music, 1979, at Stanford University; Inventor of FM sound synthesis. *Compositions:* Pieces for computer-generated quadrophonic sound including: Sabelithe, 1971; Turenas, 1972; Stria, 1977; Phone, 1981. *Recordings:* Music with Computers, John Chowning. *Publications:* FM Theory and Applications, 1986. *Contributions:* The Simulation of Moving Sound Sources, 1972, The Synthesis of Complex Audio Spectra by Means of Frequency Modulation, 1973, both to Journal of the Audio Engineering Society. *Honours:* National Endowment for the Arts Grants; Commissions from Institut de Recherche et de Coordination Acoustique/Musique; Fellow, American Academy of Arts and Sciences, 1988; Awarded the Hooker Chair by the School of Humanities and Sciences at Stanford, 1993; Diplôme d'Officier dans l'Ordre des Arts et Lettres 1995. *Address:* c/o Center for Computer Research in Music and Acoustics, Music Department, Stanford University, Stanford, CA 94305-8180, USA.

CHRETIEN, Raphaël; Cellist; b. 17 Feb. 1972, Paris, France. *Education:* National Superior Conservatory. *Career:* Played, Europe: Barbican Hall, 1993, Théâtre des Champs Elysées, 1994; Basel Symphonic Hall,

1995; USA: Marlboro Music Festival, 1994, 1995; Japan: Touring Major Halls, 1994; Appearances with Prague Television and Radio, Philharmonic Orchestra, Dvořák, 1994, Basel Symphony Orchestra, Lalo, 1995, Cannes Philharmonic Orchestra, Tchaikovsky, 1994; Cello Teacher, Bordeaux National Conservatory. *Recordings:* Piatti, Caprices for Solo Cello; Brahms Trio Op.114; H Duparc and G Ropartz, Sonatas. *Honours:* 1st Prize Cello and Chamber Music, National Superior Conservatory, Paris; Vienna, 1993, Prague, 1994, Trapani and Belgrade, 1995, International Cello Competitions. *Current Management:* European Artistic Management, Paris. *Address:* 15 rue Hermel, 75018 Paris, France.

CHRIBKOVA, Irena, MgA; Czech organist; b. 22 July 1959, Bohumin. *Education:* Kromeriz Conservatory, Prague Academy of Music, Conservatoire National de Rueil-Malmaison, Paris, international organ masterclasses in Rotterdam, Biarritz, Porrentruy. *Career:* debut, Prague, 1981; solo organ recitals at int. festivals: Olomouc, Paris, 1985; Brno, Ljubljana, 1987; Paris 1988; Piran, Slovakia, 1992; Warsaw, Poland, Auxerre and Bourges, France 1993; Hamburg, Germany 1994; Prague, Czech Republic, Wisla, Warsaw, Fromborg, Poland 1995; Swedish Premiere of Faust, for Organ and Reciter by Peter Eben, 1995; Slovenia Premiere of Faust and Four Biblical Dances by Peter Eben, Ljubljana 1995; Berlin, Traunstein, Germany, Monte Carlo, Bourges, Prague, 1996; Berlin, Chartres, France, Serravalle Sesia, Italy, Hanover, Germany, 1997; TV broadcasts of concerts in Piran, 1992 and Warsaw, 1995; performed in Tokyo and Yokohama, Japan 2002; Czech Premiere of The Labyrinth of the World (organ and speaker) 2004; Dir, Int. Organ Festival, St James's Basilica, Prague; titular organist of St James's Basilica in Prague; mem. of juries at several int. organ competitions; Contrib. Organiste (periodical) 2002–. *Recordings:* Organs and Composing Organists of Prague St James's Basilica, 1996; Music of Paris Churches and Cathedrals, 2003. *Address:* Nádrazní 19, 150 00 Prague 5, Czech Republic. *Telephone:* (604) 20-84-90 (office). *E-mail:* auditeorganum@volny.cz (office); chribkova@seznam .cz (home). *Website:* www.audileorganum.cz (office); www .irenachribkova.cz (home).

CHRIST, Wolfram; Violist; b. 17 Oct. 1955, Hachenburg, Germany. *Education:* Studies at Freiburg. *Career:* Prizewinner ARD competition, Munich, 1976; Numerous solo concertos with conductors such as Abbado, Metha, Karajan, Maazel, Ozawa, Kubelik with Berlin Philharmonic, Munich Philharmonic, Hamburg Philharmonic, Czech Philharmonic and other orchestras throughout the world; Principal Violist, Berlin Philharmonic Orchestra, since 1978. *Recordings:* Bartók Viola Concerto, Ozawa, BPO; Berlioz Harold in Italy, Maazel, BPO; Hindemith Viola Concerto, Abbado, BPO; Mozart Sinfonia Concertante, Abbado, BPO; Plays regularly at international festivals as soloist and chamber musician. *Current Management:* Berlin Philharmonic Orchestra. *Address:* Matthäikirch st, 1000 Berlin, Germany.

CHRISTENSEN, Dieter; Professor of Ethnomusicology; b. 17 April 1932, Berlin, Germany; m. Nerthus Karger; one s. one d. *Education:* cello, Berlin State Conservatory, PhD, musicology, Free Univ., Berlin 1957. *Career:* debut, RIAS Radio, Berlin, 1949; taught at Univ. of Berlin and Hamburg, then at Wesleyan Univ., City Univ. of New York, USA and Universidade Nova, Lisbon, Portugal; Prof. and Dir, Center for Ethnomusicology, Columbia Univ., New York; Co-Dir, UNESCO project The Universe of Music: A History, –1993; Ed., UNESCO Collection of Traditional Music, 1994–2002. *Recordings:* Lappish folk songs; Kurdish folk music; Yugoslav folk music; Traditional Arts of Oman, 1993; A Wedding in Sohar, Oman, 1993. *Publications include:* Die Musik der Kate und Sialum, 1957; Die Musik der Ellice-Inseln (with G. Koch), 1964; Hornbostel Opera Omnia (co-ed.), 1974; Der Ring des Tlalocan, 1977; Musical Traditions in Oman, 1993; Shauqi's Dictionary of Traditional Music in Oman, 1994. *Contributions:* German and international professional journals; book review ed., Journal of Society for Ethnomusicology; Ed., Yearbook for Traditional Music. *Address:* Department of Music, Columbia University, New York, NY 10027, USA.

CHRISTENSEN, Jesper (Boje); Danish harpsichordist, professor and musicologist; *Professor, Schola Cantorum, Basel*; b. 3 Dec. 1944, Copenhagen, Denmark; 1 d. *Education:* Diploma, Composition, Theory, Pianoforte, Royal Danish Academy of Music, 1971. *Career:* numerous concerts and masterclasses at most major festivals and centres of Ancient Music; Prof. Schola Cantorum, Basel 1988–; Visiting Prof. Conservatoire Supérieur de Musique, Lyon 1989–2000, Centre de Musique Ancienne, Geneva 1989–98, Hochschule für Musik, Würtzburg 1992–95, Kunstuniversitat Graz (Abteilung Alte Musik 2004–05, Univ. de Basilicata, Potenza 2005–; mem. jury, Festival van Vlaanderen, International Harpsichord Competition 1992–; Founder and Musical Director ensemble Arcomelo 1997; recognized world-leading authority on basso continuo; also specializing in performance practice including romantic interpretation as documented on earliest historical recordings. *Recordings:* J. Mattheson, 12 Sonatas, for traverso and harpsichord; A. Corelli op 5 Sonatas, for violin and basso continuo; Corelli op 6 Concerti

Grossi; G. Muffat, Armonico Tributo; F. A. Bonporti, Invenzioni op 10, for violin and basso continuo; F. Geminiani, Six Sonatas for Violoncello and basso continuo; Timewave (world music, jazz, flamenco). *Publications:* Der Generalbass bei Bach und Händel 1985, Die Grundlagen des Generalbass-Spiels im 18 Jahrhundert 1992, French ed. 1994, English ed. 2002, Italian ed. 2003: 18th Century Continuo Playing, Generalbass, article in new MMG 1996, Zu einigen Heiligen Kühers des Generalbass-Spiels im 20 Jahrhundert 1995, Francesco Maria Veracini über das Dirigieren 2000. *Honours:* Carl Nielsen Prize, Copenhagen, 1971. *Address:* Schillerstrasse 29/13, A-8010 Graz, Austria.

CHRISTENSEN, Mogens; Composer and Assistant Professor; b. 7 April 1955, Laesoe, Denmark; m. Helle Kristensen. *Education:* Diploma in Music History and Music Theory, Royal Academy of Music, Århus, 1983; Teaching Certificate, Royal Academy of Music, Århus, 1983; Diploma in Composition, Royal Academy of Music, Århus, 1988; MMus, University of Århus, 1992; Soloist Diploma (PhD) in Composition, Royal Academy of Music, Copenhagen, 1993. *Career:* Debut: As a Composer, Denmark, 1982; His music has been performed in almost all European countries, in USA and South America. Being prizewinner at the UNESCO Composers International Rostrum, 1994, his piece Winter Light was broadcast all over the world; Composer-in-Residence (Copenhagen Philharmonic Orchestra); Teacher, Royal Academies of Music, Copenhagen and Århus, Academies of Music in Aalborg and Esbjerg and the Universities of Århus and Aalborg; Assistant Professor, Academy of Music, Esbjerg; mem, Danish Composers Society. *Compositions include:* Orchestral, Zurvan Akarana, 1986; Dreams within Dreams, 1st Violin Concerto, 1990; Las flores del mar de la muerte, 2nd Violin Concerto, 1993; Circulus Stellae, 1998; Crystalline Light, 1999; Chamber works, Orphian Fire Mountains, 1988; The Lost Poems of Princess Ateh, 1991; The Khazarian Mirrors, 1993; Vocal works, Hyperions Schicksalslied, 1982; Pessimisticum, 1993; Systema Naturae, chamber opera, 1998. *Recordings:* Mogens Christensen, Vocal and Chamber Music vol. I, 1991, vol. II, 1993, vol. III, 1995; Odriozola and Kristensen play Christensen and Odriozola (including Winter Light), 1995; 1994 Ensemble Nord (including The Lost Poems of Princess Ateh), 1992; Music for Solo Instruments, vol. I, 1998; Music for Recorder, 1999; Systema Naturae, 2001. *Publications:* Winter Light, 1994; 3 Works for Violin Solo, 1995. *Contributions:* Betrachtungen Über den Tonalitätsbegriff bei Edvard Grieg und Carl Nielsen (from Die Gratulanten kommen, 1993). *Honours:* Artist Prize of the County of Bergen, 1991; Artist Scholarship of the Danish State, 1993–95; Prizewinner, UNESCO Composers International Rostrum, 1994. *Address:* Stavnsholtvej 161, 3520 Farum, Denmark.

CHRISTESEN, Robert; Singer (Baritone); b. 15 Feb. 1943, Washington DC, USA. *Education:* Studied at the Manhattan School of Music and at Aspen School of Music with Aksel Schiotz and Jennie Tourel. *Career:* Debut: Henrik in Maskarade by Nielsen at St Paul, 1972; Sang with the Frankfurt and Dortmund Operas (1973–80) and appeared as guest Berlin (Komische Oper), Copenhagen, Budapest, Warsaw, Toulouse, Brno, Prague and in North and South America; Other roles have included Mozart's Count and Don Giovanni, Verdi's Ford, Germont and Luna, Eugene Onegin, Jochanaan, Rossini's Figaro, Kaspar in Der Freischütz and Lescaut in Henze's Boulevard Solitude.

CHRISTIE, Sir George William Langham, Kt, CH; British businessman; b. 31 Dec. 1934, Glyndebourne, England; m. Patricia Mary Nicholson 1958; three s. one d. *Career:* Asst to Sec., X Calouste Gulbenkian Foundation 1957–62; Chair., Glyndebourne Productions Ltd 1956–2000, and of other family cos; principal founder, Glyndebourne Touring Opera 1968–; instigated the rebuilding of the theatre at Glyndebourne (opened 1994); founder, Chair., London Sinfonietta; mem., Arts Council (Chair. of Music Panel). *Honours:* Dr hc (Sussex) 1990, (Keele) 1993, (Exeter) 1994; Deputy Lieutenant East Sussex, Hon. FRCM 1986, FRNCM 1986, hon. mem. Guildhall School of Music and Drama 1991. *Address:* Glyndebourne, Lewes, East Sussex, England.

CHRISTIE, Michael; American conductor; b. 30 June 1974, New York. *Education:* Oberlin College Conservatory of Music. *Career:* Conducting engagements with the Los Angeles and Buffalo Philharmonics, the Lahti Symphony and the Helsinki and Tampere (Finland) Philharmonics, Royal Scottish National Orchestra; United Kingdom debut with the City of Birmingham Symphony Orchestra, 1996; Season 1997–98, Assistant to Franz Welser-Möst, Zürich Opera; Apprentice Conductor, Chicago Symphony Orchestra, 1995–96; Music Dir, Colorado Music Festival, 2000–; Chief Conductor, The Queensland Orchestra, 2001–; Engagements with Swedish Radio Symphony; Netherlands Radio Symphony; Royal Liverpool Philharmonic; NDR Hannover; Czech Philharmonic; Orchestre Philharmonique de Luxembourg; DSO Berlin; Los Angeles Philharmonic; Dallas Symphony; Atlanta Symphony; Florida Philharmonic. *Honours:* Prize for Outstanding Potential at the First International Sibelius Conductors' Competition, Helsinki, 1995. *Current Management:* IMG Artists, 616 Chiswick High Road, London,

W4 5RX, England. *Telephone:* (20) 8233-5800. *Fax:* (20) 8233-5801. *E-mail:* artistseurope@imgworld.com. *Website:* www.imgartists.com.

CHRISTIE, Nan; Singer (soprano); b. 6 March 1948, Irvine, Scotland. *Education:* Royal Scottish Academy of Music; London Opera Centre. *Career:* Repertoire with Scottish Opera includes Britten's Tytania, Rimsky's Queen of Shemakha, The Queen of Night and Zerbinetta in Ariadne auf Naxos; Tours to Portugal, Poland, Switzerland and Germany; Sang in Mozart's La Finta Giardiniera and the premiere of Oliver's Tom Jones, with English Music Theatre; Tytania with Opera North; Isotta in Die schweigsame Frau and Despina in Così fan tutte, at the Glyndebourne Festival; Zdenka in Arabella, the Queen of Night and Offenbach's Eurydice with English National Opera; European engagements with Netherlands Opera, Despina; Opéra de Nancy as Pamina; Zürich Opera in the Ponnelle production of Lucio Silla and Frankfurt Opera as Zerbinetta, Marie in Die Soldaten and Susanna; Scottish Opera, 1990 as Despina in a new production of Così fan tutte; Birdie Hubbard in the British premiere of Blitzstein's Regina, Glasgow, 1991; Concerts at the Hong Kong Festival, Hallé Orchestra, BBC Symphony and London Symphony Orchestra, Nash Ensemble and the London Sinfonietta; Television appearances in Mozart's Schauspieldirektor and Ravel's L'Enfant et les Sortilèges; Italian debut in Mitridate by Mozart, La Fenice, Venice, and the Queen of Night in The Magic Flute for ENO, 1992; Premiere of Jonathan Harvey's Inquest of Love, English National Opera, 1993; Sang Third Official in the premiere of The Doctor of Myddfai, by Peter Maxwell Davies, Cardiff, 1996. *Recordings:* Videos of Glyndebourne Festival Così fan tutte; The Gondoliers, The Sorcerer and Princess Ida. *Current Management:* Askonas Holt Ltd, Lonsdale Chambers, 27 Chancery Lane, London, WC2A 1PF, England. *Telephone:* (20) 7400-1700. *Fax:* (20) 7400-1799. *E-mail:* info@askonasholt.co.uk. *Website:* www.askonasholt.co.uk.

CHRISTIE, Natalie; Singer (soprano); b. (Natalie Abrahamson), 17 Jan. 1975, Melbourne, Australia. *Education:* Victorian Coll. of the Arts, Guildhall School of Music and Drama, London, with Rudolf Piernay. *Career:* opera, La Bohème, British Youth Opera 1998, Carmen, Clonter Opera 1998, The Carmelites, WNO 1999, Orphee et Eurydice 2000, Der Rosenkavalier 2000, Le Nozze di Figaro 2001, The Magic Flute 2001, Leonore 2001, Adele in Die Fledermaus 2002; St John Passion (soloist), ENO (debut) 2000; Le Nozze di Figaro, Opera Australia 2000; Zerlina in Don Giovanni, Royal Opera House (debut), London 2002; soloist for BBC Nat. Orchestra of Wales, BBC Concert Orchestra, Tasmanian Symphony Orchestra; Roles for WNO 2002–03 Adele in Die Fledermaus, Adina in The Elixir of Love, Zerlina in Don Giovanni and Susanna in Le Nozze di Figaro. *Honours:* 20th Century Aria prize, Veronica Dunn Singing Competition 1997, Australian Music Foundation Award 1998, Sir John Moores Award, WNO 2000, Finalist Cardiff Singer of the World 2001. *Current Management:* Peter Bloor, Askonas Holt Ltd, Lonsdale Chambers, 27 Chancery Lane, London, WC2A 1PF, England. *Telephone:* (20) 7400-1700. *Fax:* (20) 7400-1799. *E-mail:* info@askonasholt.co.uk. *Website:* www.askonasholt.co.uk. .

CHRISTIE, William Lincoln; French harpsichordist, conductor and teacher; b. 19 Dec. 1944, Buffalo, New York, USA. *Education:* Studied harpsichord with Igor Kipnis, Berkshire Music Center, Tanglewood; BA, Harvard University, 1966; Harpsichord with Ralph Kirkpatrick; Organ with Charles Kribaum; Musicology with Claude Palisca and Nicholas Temperley; MMus, Yale University, 1970. *Career:* Teacher, Dartmouth College, 1970–71; Member, Five Centuries Ensemble, France, 1971–75; Concerto Vocale, 1976–80; Founder-Director, Les Arts Florissants, 1979–; Teacher, Innsbruck Summer Academy for Early Music, 1977–83; Professorship, Paris Conservatory, 1982–; Conducted Alcina at the Théâtre du Châtelet and Geneva, 1990; London debut of Les Arts Florissants at Greenwich, 1990, with Charpentier's Actéon, and Dido and Aeneas; Les Indes Galantes at Aix-en-Provence; Conducted Luigi Rossi's Orfeo at Vienna Konzerthaus, 1990; Season 1992 with Purcell's Fairy Queen at the Barbican Hall, London, Rameau's Castor et Pollux for the Baroque Festival at Versailles and Lully's Atys at Madrid; Purcell's King Arthur at Covent Garden, 1995; Handel's Theodora at Glyndebourne, 1996; Hippolyte et Aricie in Paris and Rameau's Les Fêtes d'Hébé at the Barbican, London, 1996; Lully's Thésée at the Barbican and Handel's Rodelinda at Glyndebourne, 1998; Season 1999–2000 with Rameau's Les Indes Galantes at the Palais Garnier, Paris; Claudio Monteverdi's Il Ritorno d'Ulisse in Patria, Aix-en-Provence, 2000; Engaged for Handel's Saul at Aix, 2004. *Recordings:* Masters of the French and Italian Baroque including Landi's Il Sant Alessio and Handel's Orlando, 1996–97; Rameau's Les Fêtes d'Hébé; d'India's Madrigals; Monteverdi's Operas and Handel's Alcina, 2000; Henry Desmarest's Les Grands Motets Lorrains, 2000; Jean-Philippe Rameau's La Guirlande and Zephyre, 2001; Albums of M. A. Charpentier for the Tercentenary, 2004 (Erato). *Honours:* Numerous awards including a number of Grand Prix du Disque of France and Prix Mondiale du Disque; First American to hold a Professorship at the Paris Conservatory; Awarded the French Légion

d'Honneur, 1993; Doctor honoris causa, State University of New York; Officier dans l'Ordre des Arts et des Lettres; Prix Grand Siècle Laurent Premier, 1997; Gramophone Award (Baroque Vocal category) for Handel's Acis and Galatea, 2000; Grammy Award for Best Opera Recording; Prix Arturo Toscanini de L'Academie du Disque Lyrique and Cannes Classical Awards (Baroque category), both for Handel's Alcina, 2001. *Address:* Les Arts Florissants, 2 rue de Saint-Petersburg, 75009, Paris, France.

CHRISTIN, Judith; Singer (Mezzo-Soprano); b. 15 Feb. 1948, Providence, Rhode Island, USA. *Education:* Studied at Indiana University. *Career:* Sang at first in concert, opera from 1980; Washington Opera from 1981 and at Santa Fe in the US premieres of Weir's A Night at the Chinese Opera, Penderecki's Schwarze Maske and Judith by Matthus; Los Angeles from 1983, San Diego, 1984, Philadelphia, 1986; New York Metropolitan from 1988, in Eugene Onegin, Faust, Die Zauberflöte, Luisa Miller and Le nozze di Figaro; European career from 1987 (Netherlands Opera); Roles have included Despina (Santa Fe, 1988–90), the Hostess in Boris Godunov, Suzuki in Butterfly and Carlotta in Die schweigsame Frau; Santa Fe 1996, as Suzuki and Baba the Turk in The Rake's Progress; Sang in the premiere of Carlisle Floyd's Cold Sassy Tree, Houston 2000. *Address:* c/o Metropolitan Opera, Lincoln Center, New York, NY 10023, USA.

CHRISTOFF, Dimiter, DrHabil; Bulgarian composer and academic; b. 2 Oct. 1933, Sofia. *Education:* State Music Acad., Sofia with M. Goleminov, study tours in Germany, USA, France, Netherlands. *Career:* teacher 1960–76, Prof. 1976–, State Music Acad.; Gen. Sec., Int. Music Council, UNESCO 1975–79; leader, Int. Composers' Workshop (a Bulgarian-Dutch initiative) 1977–; Ed.-in-Chief, Scientific Music Magazine, Bulgarian Musicology, Acad. of Sciences 1989–; publisher, Music, Yesterday, Today 1994; mem. Int. Soc. for Music Education, Bulgarian Composers' Union (vice-pres. 1972–85). *Compositions:* operas: The Game 1978, The Golden Fish Line 1984; orchestral: three piano concertos 1954, 1983, 1994, Sinfonietta for strings 1956, Poem 1957, three symphonies 1958, 1964, 1969, Overture 1961, Symphonic Episodes 1962, three violin concertos 1966, 1996, 1997, Chamber Suite for two piccolos, piano, percussion and strings 1966, Cello Concerto 1969, Concert Miniatures 1970, Overture with Fanfares 1974, Quasi una fantasia-gioco 1981, Game for cello and orchestra 1983, Perpetui mobili in pianissimi 1987, Groups Troupes 1988, Silent Adagio 1989, Cantilena Sopra due Toni 1990, Merry-go-round of the Suffering 1991, Collapse in the Silence 1992, Crash Down in the Mute 1992, Up High I Look for You 1993, It Streams It Runs Out 1994, I Rise in the Chaos 1995, I Set It Ajar, Peep In 1996, There High it Shines 1997, It Was for Millenniums Predicted 2000, Here is No Silent 2000; chamber: Suite for brass quartet 1953, Two Dances for trumpet and piano 1960, Sonata for solo cello 1965, Concerto for three small drums and five instruments 1967, String Quartet 1970, Quartet for flute, viola, harp and harpsichord 1973, Meditation of a Lonely Violoncello 1991, The Violoncello album dons the Right Hand of the Piano 1992, 16 piano sonatas, Blown Away from the Wind for string orchestra 1993, Await Your Pizzicatti 1994, Sad Silk Bows for violin and accompanying viola 1996, Give Me Solace 1993, piano ensemble music (duo, trio and quartet of piano players) Eroica Variations for piano eight strings 2002, Cool and Warm for strings 2002, eight etudes for harp 2002–03; choruses and songs. *Publications:* Theoretical Foundations of the Melodic Structure Vols 1–3 1973, 1982, 1989. *Address:* Mavrovets 7, 1415 Sofia-Dragalevtsi, Bulgaria. *Telephone:* 2-9672351.

CHRISTOPHERS, Harry; British conductor; *Conductor, The Sixteen Choir & The Symphony of Harmony and Invention;* b. 26 Dec. 1953, Goudhurst, Kent; m. Veronica Mary Hayward, 2 June 1979, 2 s., 2 d. *Education:* Canterbury Cathedral Choir School (Head Chorister), King's School Canterbury; BA, Honours, Music, Magdalen College, Oxford (Academical Clerk). *Career:* Founded The Sixteen 1977; Founded The Orchestra of The Sixteen 1986 (newly named The Symphony of Harmony and Invention 1997); South Bank debut 1983; Salzburg Festival debut 1989; BBC Prom debut 1990; Lisbon Opera debut 1994; Musikverein, Vienna debut 1998; Concertgebouw, Amsterdam debut 1999; English National Opera debut 2000; Orchestras conducted include: BBC Philharmonic, Academy of St Martins-in-the-fields, London Symphony Orchestra, Hallé, Royal Liverpool Philharmonic, English Chamber Orchestra, Northern Sinfonia, City of London Sinfonia; BBC National Orchestra of Wales, Scottish Chamber Orchestra, Avanti!, Tapiola Sinfonietta, Lahti Symphony Orchestra, Helsinki Philharmonic, Bergen Philharmonic; Tours with The Sixteen Choir and the Symphony of Harmony and Invention throughout Europe, Scandinavia, Israel, Japan, Australia, USA, Brazil; Conducted Messiah at the Barbican Hall, London 1999; Conducted Handel's Samson at the London Proms 2002. *Recordings include:* Taverner's Festal Masses, vols I–IV 1984–93 and Missa Gloria Tibi Trinitas 1989; Monteverdi's Masses 1987 and Vespers 1988; Handel's Messiah 1989, Chandos Anthems 1990, Alexander's Feast 1992, Esther 1996, Samson

1997, Italian Cantatas 1998; Byrds's Mass a 5 1989 and Mass a 4 1990; Poulenc's Figure Humaine 1990; Bach's St John Passion 1990, Christmas Oratorio 1993; B Minor Mass 1994; Eton Choir Book vols I–V 1991–95; Sheppard's Sacred Music vols I–IV 1990–92; Teixeira's Te Deum 1991; Britten's Choral Music 1992–93; Stravinsky's Symphony of Psalms 1995; Messiaen's Cinq rechants 1996; Scarlatti's Stabat Mater 1997; Victoria's Sacred Music vols I–III 1997–99; Video: Handel's Messiah in Dublin 1992, Tallis: Spem in Alium 2004, Handel Arias: Heroes and Heroines (with Sarah Connolly) 2004. *Honours:* Grand Prix du Disque for Messiah 1989; Gramophone, Early Music Award 1992; Deutschen Schallplattenkritik, Handel Alexander's Feast 1992; Diapason D'Or for Teixeira Te Deum 1992 and in 1995 for Symphony of Psalms. *Current Management:* The Sixteen, New Marston Centre, Jack Straw's Lane, Oxford OX3 0DL, England. *Telephone:* (1865) 793999. *Fax:* (1865) 793274. *E-mail:* info@thesixteen.org.uk (office). *Website:* www.thesixteen.com.

CHRISTOS, Marianna; Singer (Soprano); b. 1950, Beaver Falls, Pennsylvania, USA. *Career:* Sang with the New York City Opera, 1975–79, debut as Liu in Turandot; Has appeared widely in the USA at Pittsburgh, Washington, St Louis, Houston, Los Angeles and San Francisco; Roles have included Mimi, Gilda, Adina in L'Elisir d'amore, Margharita in Mefistofele, Donna Anna, Donna Elvira, Micaela, and Antonia in Les Contes d'Hoffmann; New Orleans 1985, as Bizet's Leila. *Address:* c/o New York City Opera, Lincoln Center, New York, NY 10023, USA.

CHRISTOU, Nicolas; Singer (Bass-baritone); b. 1940, Alexandria. *Education:* Studied in Brussels. *Career:* Sang at Brussels, 1966–81 as Golaud in Pelléas et Mélisande, Philip II in Don Carlos and Wagner's Wotan; Gunther and Kothner; Guest appearances throughout Europe, notably at Liège as the Father in Louise, Grandier in The Devils of Loudun and Pizarro in Fidelio, 1991–95; Festival engagements at Aix-en-Provence, as the Speaker in Die Zauberflöte and at Wexford; Deutsche Oper am Rhein, Düsseldorf, from 1991; Bremen Opera, 1996 as Boris Godunov; Other roles have included Mozart's Figaro and Leporello, Rossini's Basilio; Wagner's Telramund, Pogner, Amfortas and Dutchman; Mandryka in Arabella and Ramphis in Aida; Sang Dr Schön in Lulu at Liège, 1999. *Address:* c/o Bremen Opera, Pf 101046, 2800 Bremen, Germany.

CHU, Wang-Hua; Composer and Pianist; b. 5 Sept. 1941, Jiangsu, China. *Education:* BMus, Central Conservatory, Peking, 1963; MMus, University of Melbourne, 1985. *Career:* Piano Department, Central Conservatory of Music, Beijing, China, 1963–82; Freelance composer and pianist in Australia, 1982–; mem, The Australian Music Centre. *Compositions include:* Seven Piano Preludes, and Three Piano Variations, 1961–80; The Yellow River Piano Concerto (co-composer), 1970; The Spring Mirrored the Moon for piano, 1972; Sinjiang Capriccio for piano, 1977; Piano Sonata, 1981; String Quartet, 1983; Ash Wednesday for orchestra, 1984; The Borderland Moon for soprano and ensemble, 1984; Concerto for Chamber Orchestra, 1984; The Bamboo for piano and orchestra, 1986; Drinking Alone by Moonlight for soprano and chamber ensemble, 1985; 30 Chinese Folk Songs for piano, 1979–86; Barcarolle for piano, 1979; Autumn Cry for orchestra, 1988; Symphony, 1988; Sinfonia for chamber orchestra, 1988; The Ancient Battlefield for percussion solo, 1989; Piano Concerto, 1989; Fantasia Symphony: The Silk Road, 1990; Eva, Beloved Mother, for piano, 1993; Air and Variations for choral, 1998. *Recordings:* The Yellow River Piano Concerto, co-composer, 1970, 1980, 1990; Piano Sonata, 1986; A number of piano works, 1980, 1990. *Publications:* The Yellow River Piano Concerto, co-composer, 1975. *Honours:* 1st Prize, Albert Magg's Composition Competition, Australia, 1987. *Address:* 20 Bruce Street, Toorak, Vic 3142, Australia.

CHUCHROVA, Liubov; Singer (Soprano); b. 1971, Vilnius, Lithuania. *Education:* Studied at Vilnius, 1985–89; Guildhall School, London. *Career:* Sang Satirino in La Calisto and Maria in Krenek's Der Diktator at the GSM; Olga in Dargomyzhsky's Rusalka, 1997 Wexford Festival; Other roles include Anne Trulove, The Rake's Progress; Tatiana, Marguerite and Mozart's Vitellia, Vilnius Opera; Gorislava in Ruslan and Lyudmila for Dorset Opera; Spoleto Festival, 1999; War and Peace; Concerts include Vivaldi's Gloria; Bruch's Das Lied von der Glocke; Rossini's Petite Messe at Tel-Aviv; Mozart's Requiem at the Barbican, London. *Honours:* Winner, Maggie Teyte Competition, GSM. *Address:* c/o Music International, 13 Ardilaun Road, London N5 2QR, England.

CHUDOVA, Tatiana; Composer; b. 16 June 1944, Moscow, Russia. *Education:* Studied at the Moscow Central Music School and Conservatory, notably with Khrennikov. *Career:* Teacher in Moscow from 1970. *Compositions include:* Operas: The Dead Princess and the Seven Heroes, 1967, and To the Village, to Grandfather, 1978; 3 Suites for orchestra of folk instruments, 1980–82; Symphonic trilogy, 1981–82, and Symphony No. 4, 1988; Choral, solo vocal and instrumental music,

including 2 violin sonatas, 1974, 1987. *Address:* c/o RAO, Bolchaia Bronnai 6-1, Moscow 103670, Russia.

CHUNG, David Yu Sum, PhD, MPhil, LRSM, LTCL; Chinese university lecturer; *Assistant Professor and Performance Co-ordinator, Hong Kong Baptist University;* b. 10 April 1968, Hong Kong. *Education:* Guildhall School of Music and Drama, London; Univ. of Cambridge, Chinese Univ. of Hong Kong. *Career:* Asst Prof. and performance co-ordinator at Hong Kong Baptist Univ. 1998–; harpsichordist and musicologist, with performances in Europe, Asia and USA on a variety of historic and modern keyboard instruments; mem. British Clavichord Soc., Royal Musical Asscn, Southeastern Historical Keyboard Soc., American Musicological Soc.. *Recordings:* Stylus Phantasticus Works for Harpsichord 2003; contrib. to articles in Early Music 2003, Piano Artistry 2003, Early Keyboard Journal 2001. *Publications:* Jean–Baptiste Lully: 27 Opera Pieces Transcribed for Keyboard in the 17th and 18th Centuries, 2004. *Honours:* Christopher Kite Award 1997, Pres.'s Award for Outstanding Performance 2001. *Address:* Dept of Music and Fine Arts Hong Kong Baptist University, Kowloon Tong, Hong Kong (office). *Telephone:* 3411-7871 (office). *Fax:* 3411-7870 (office). *E-mail:* dchung@hkbu.edu.hk (office). *Website:* www.hkbu.edu.hk (office).

CHUNG, Kyung-Wha; South Korean violinist; b. 26 March 1948, Seoul; sister of Myung-Whun Chung and Myung-Wha Chung; m. Geoffrey Leggett 1984; two s. *Education:* Juilliard School, New York with Ivan Galamian. *Career:* started career in USA; European debut 1970; has played with maj. orchestras, including all London orchestras, Chicago, Boston and Pittsburgh Symphony Orchestra, New York, Cleveland, Philadelphia, Berlin, Israel and Vienna Philharmonics, Orchestre de Paris; has toured world; recordings for EMI; played at Salzburg Festival with London Symphony Orchestra 1973, Vienna Festival 1981, 1984, Edinburgh Festival 1981 and at eightieth birthday concert of Sir William Walton March 1982; with Hallé Orchestra, BBC Proms, London 1999. *Recordings:* Concertos by Bartók, Beethoven, Bruch, Mendelssohn, Stravinsky, Tchaikovsky, Vieuxtemps, Walton. *Honours:* winner of Leventritt Competition 1968. *Current Management:* Harrison Parrott Ltd, 12 Penzance Place, London, W11 4PA, England.

CHUNG, Mia; Concert Pianist and Assistant Professor of Music; b. 9 Oct. 1964, Madison, Wisconsin, USA. *Education:* BA magna cum laude, Harvard University, 1986; MM, Yale University, 1988; DMA, Juilliard School of Music, 1991. *Career:* Debut: Hall of the Americas, OAS Building, Washington DC, 1983; Assistant Professor of Music and Artist-in-Residence, Gordon College, 1991–; Appearances with Baltimore Symphony Orchestra, 1977, 1981; Performed with National Symphony Orchestra, 1983; Performed with National Gallery Orchestra, 1987; Performed with Fort Collins Symphony Orchestra, 1990; Performed with New Haven Symphony, 1989; Solo Recitals and Chamber Performances at OAS, Alice Tully Hall, National Gallery of Art, the Kennedy Center for Performing Arts, American Academy of Arts and Sciences and other venues; Records exclusively for Channel Classics Records. *Recordings:* Beethoven Bagatelles, Op 126 and Sonatas No. 16 in G major Op 31, No. 1 and No. 32 in C minor Op 111. *Honours:* First Prize in 1981 Johann Sebastian Bach International Competition in New York City, 1993. *Current Management:* Concert Artist Guild. *Address:* Fine Arts Department, Gordon College, Wenham, MA 01984, USA.

CHUNG, Myung-Wha; South Korean cellist; b. 19 March 1944, Seoul; sister of Myung-Whun Chung and Kyung-Wha Chung. *Education:* Juilliard School with Leonard Rose, Univ. of Southern California masterclass with Gregor Piatigorsky. *Career:* debut with the Seoul Philharmonic before study in New York; has appeared widely in Europe and North America 1971–, notably in England, Italy, Denmark, Germany, Spain, Sweden, Netherlands, Belgium, France, Switzerland, Portugal, Israel and Mexico; festival appearances at Lucerne, Flanders, Spoleto, Palma de Majorca, Birmingham, Evian and Dijon; television programmes in the USA, England, Germany and Switzerland; plays a 1731 Stradivarius cello known as Braga; Goodwill Ambassador for UN Drug Control Programme 1992–; faculty mem., Mannes Coll. of Music, New York and Korean Nat. Inst. of Arts. *Recordings include:* Tchaikovsky Rococo Variations with the Los Angeles Philharmonic under Charles Dutoit, Ten Piano Trio Works with the Chung Trio. *Honours:* First Prize Geneva Int. Music Competition 1971, Nat. Order of Cultural Merit, Republic of Korea 1992. *Address:* 315 West 70th Street, Suite 5G, New York, NY 10023, USA.

CHUNG, Myung-Whun; South Korean conductor and pianist; b. 22 Jan. 1953, Seoul; brother of Kyung-Wha Chung and Myung-Wha Chung. *Education:* Mannes Coll. of Music and Juilliard School, New York, USA. *Career:* asst to Carlo Maria Giulini as Assoc. Conductor, Los Angeles Philharmonic 1978–81; moved to Europe 1981, conducting Berlin Philharmonic, Munich Philharmonic, Amsterdam Concertgebouw, Orchestre de Paris, major London orchestras; Music Dir and Principal Conductor Radio Orchestra of Saarbrücken 1984–89; in USA has conducted the New York Philharmonic, Nat. Symphony Washington, the Boston Symphony, the Cleveland and Chicago Orchestras, Metropolitan Opera, San Francisco Opera 1986–; Guest Conductor, Teatro Comunale, Florence 1987; Musical Dir Opéra de la Bastille, Paris 1989–94; Covent Garden debut, conducting Otello 1997; Music Dir and Principal Conductor Orchestra of the Nat. Acad. of Santa Cecilia, Rome 1997–2005; conducted the Swedish Radio Symphony Orchestra at the London Proms, playing Beethoven's Fourth Piano Concerto and Nielsen's Fifth 1999; Musical Dir Radio France Philharmonic Orchestra 2000–; f. and Musical Dir Philharmonic Orchestra of Asia. *Honours:* Second Prize Tchaikovsky Competition, Moscow 1974, Abbiati Prize (Italian critics) 1987, Victoires de la Musique Best Conductor, Best Lyrical Production, Best French Classical Recording 1995. *Address:* c/o Accademia Nazionale di Santa Cecilia, Parco della Musica, L.go Luciano Berio 3, 00196 Rome, Italy.

CHURCH, Francis; Singer (Baritone); b. 1973, Liverpool, England. *Education:* Royal Scottish Academy, with Jeffrey Lawton, and National Opera Studio, London; Mozart and Britten roles with Thomas Allen at the Pears-Britten School. *Career:* Opera roles include Angelotti in Tosca, Benoit in La Bohème, Britten's Starveling and Sid, Guglielmo, and Sharpless in Madama Butterfly; Concerts include Elgar's Coronation Ode; Elijah by Mendelssohn, Messiah, A Child of our Time (Tippett) and Fauré's Requiem. *Honours:* Verdi Prize, National Mozart Competition and John Noble Competition, Scottish Opera. *Address:* c/o National Opera Studio, Morley College, 61 Westminster Bridge Road, London, SE1 7XT, England.

CHURGIN, Bathia (Dina); American/Israeli musicologist; b. 9 Oct. 1928, New York, NY, USA. *Education:* BA, Hunter Coll., New York City, 1950; MA, Radcliffe Coll., 1952; PhD, Harvard Univ., 1963. *Career:* Instructor to Full Prof., Vassar Coll. 1952–57, 1959–71; Prof., Founding Head of Dept, Bar-Ilan Univ., Ramat Gan, Israel, 1970–84; Visiting Prof., Harvard Summer School, Northwestern Univ., Univ. of North Carolina, Chapel Hill, CUNY, Queens Coll. and Graduate Center, Indiana Univ., Tel-Aviv Univ., The Hebrew Univ., Jerusalem, Rubin Acad. of Music, Jerusalem; Prof. Emer., Bar-Ilan Univ. 1996–; Festschrift published in her honour, JM XVIII, 2001; mem., Israel Musicological Soc. (Chair. 1994–95); American Musicological Soc., Int. Musicological Soc. *Publications:* The Symphonies of G B Sammartini, vol. 1: The Early Symphonies, 1968; Thematic Catalogue of the Works of Giovanni Battista Sammartini, Orchestral and Vocal Music (with Newell Jenkins), 1976; A New Edition of Beethoven's Fourth Symphony 1978; Israel Studies in Musicology II (Ed.), 1980; G B Sammartini, Sonate a tre stromenti, A New Edition with Historical and Analytical Essays, 1981; G B Sammartini: Ten Symphonies, 1984; Israel Studies in Musicology VI (Ed.), 1996; Beethoven's Fourth Symphony (Ed.), 1998. *Contributions:* Professional Journals: Francesco Galeazzi's Description (1796) of Sonata Form, JAMS XXI, 1968; Beethoven and Mozart's Requiem: A New Connection, JM V, 1987; Beethoven's Sketches for his String Quintet, Op 29, LaRue Festschrift, 1990; Harmonic and Tonal Instability in the Second Key Area of Classic Sonata Form, Ratner Festschrift, 1992; Sammartini and Boccherini: Continuity and Change in the Italian Instrumental Tradition of the Classic Period, Chigiana XLIII, 1993; The Andante con moto in Beethoven's String Quartet op 130: The Final Version and Changes on the Autograph, JM XVI, 1998; Beethoven and the New Development. Theme in Sonata-Form Movements, JM XVI, 1998; Exploring the Eroica: Aspects of the New Critical Edition, Tyson Festschrift, 1998, Stormy Interlude: Sammartini's Middle Symphonies and Overtures in Minor 2004, Recycling Old Ideas in Beethoven's String Quartet Op. 132 2005. *Address:* Department of Music, Bar-Ilan University, Ramat Gan, 52900, Israel (office). *Telephone:* (3) 531-8405 (office). *Fax:* (3) 635-6281 (office).

CHUSID, Martin; American musicologist and professor; b. 19 Aug. 1925, Brooklyn, New York; m. Anita B Chusid, 1 s. *Education:* BA, 1950, MA, 1955, PhD, 1961, University of California, Berkeley. *Career:* Teaching Assistant, 1953–55, Associate, 1955–57, University of California, Berkeley; Instructor, 1959–62, Assistant Professor, 1962–63, University of Southern California, Los Angeles; Associate Professor, 1963–68, Professor, 1968–, Acting Chairman, Music Department, 1966–67, 1981, 1986–87, New York University; Chairman, Music Department, Washington Square College of Arts and Sciences, 1967–70; Associate Dean, Graduate School of Arts and Sciences, 1970–72; Director, American Institute for Verdi Studies, 1976–; Visiting Professor of Music: Boston University, 1975, University of British Columbia, 1979, Southern Methodist University, 1980, Princeton University, 1981, Brigham Young University, 1982; Principal Editor, Verdi Newsletter, 1981–96. *Publications:* Schubert's Unfinished Symphony: A Monograph and Edition, 2nd edition, 1971; A Catalog of Verdi's Operas, 1974; The Verdi Companion (with W Weaver), 1979; Editions of works by Schubert and Verdi; Verdi's Middle Period, 1997; Schubert's Schwanengesang: Facsimiles and Reprint, 2000; A Companion to Schubert's Schwanengesang, 2000. *Contributions:* Articles on Verdi, Schubert, Mozart,

Haydn, Dvořák, Performance Practice, to various publications including The Cambridge Companion to Schubert, 1997. *Honours:* Honorary Doctor of Humane Letters, Centre College of Kentucky, 1977. *Address:* Department of Music, New York University, Washington Square, New York, NY 10003 (office); 4 Washington Square Village, New York, NY 10012, USA (home). *Telephone:* (212) 998-8305 (office); (212) 228-6215 (home). *Fax:* (212) 995-4147 (office). *E-mail:* mc4@nyu.edu (office).

CHYLINSKA, Teresa Wanda, MA; Polish musicologist, music editor and writer on music; b. 20 June 1931, Wojciechowice, Poland; m. 1957 (divorced 1960); one s. *Education:* Jagiellonian Univ., Kraków. *Career:* Chief, Dept of Polish Music, Polish Music Publications, Kraków, 1954–89; Lecturer, Jagiellonian Univ. and Acad. of Music, 1970s; Pres., The Karol Szymanowski Music Soc. 1979–80; mem., Scientific Bd, The Chopin Soc., Warsaw, 1982–88. *Publications include:* First critical edn of The Complete Works of Karol Szymanowski (26 vols Polish version, 17 vols German-English in co-edn with Universal Edition, Vienna); A Complete edn of Szymanowski's correspondence, Vol. 1, 1982, Vol. . 2, 1994, Vol. 3, 1997, Vol. 4, 2002; Szymanowski's Literary Writings, 1989; Szymanowski's Days at Zakopane, 1982, 4th edn; Szymanowski and His Music, popular monograph for young readers, 3rd edn, 1990; Karol Szymanowski, His Life and Works (in English), 1993; K Szymanowski: Lottery for Husbands, 1998. *Contributions:* New Grove Dictionary of Music and Musicians; Encyclopedia Muzyczna PWM; Pipers Enzyklopädie des Musik Theaters; Die Musik in Geschichte und Gegenwart. *Honours:* Jurzykowski Foundation Award, New York 1984, Polish Composers Union Award 1996, Karol Szymanowski Foundation Award 1997, Noweksiazki Award 2002. *Address:* ul Boguslawskiego 10.13, 31-038 Kraków, Poland (home). *Telephone:* (12) 422-30-18 (home). *E-mail:* TChylinska@interia.pl (home).

CIANNELLA, Giuliano; Singer (Tenor); b. 25 Oct. 1943, Palermo, Italy. *Career:* Debut: La Scala 1976, as Cassio in Otello; Metropolitan Opera from 1979, as Don Carlos, Des Grieux in Manon Lescaut, Rodolfo, Pinkerton, Alfredo and Macduff; Guest engagements in San Francisco, as Don José 1984 and Munich, Don Carlos, 1985; Covent Garden debut 1986, as Manrico in Il Trovatore; Verona Arena, 1983, 1986 and 1988; Bregenz Festival 1987, as Ernani; Cologne Opera, 1988, as Don José and Puccini's Des Grieux; Riccardo in Ballo in Maschera, at Parma, 1989; Season 1990–91 at the Vienna Staatsoper, as Riccardo (Ballo) and Manrico. *Address:* c/o Teatro Regio, Via Garibaldi 16, 43100 Parma, Italy.

CIARDI, Fabio Cifariello; composer; b. 1960, Rome, Italy. *Education:* Accademia S Cecilia, Rome, University of Bologna; postgraduate studies with Giacomo Manzoni, Tristain Murail and Phillipe Manoury in Paris at IRCAM, Franco Donatoni at Accademia Nazionale di S Cecilia, Rome. *Career:* Composer in Residence, EMS, Stockholm, 1995; Collaboration with Psychology Department of Rome University on recognition of sonic events; Teacher of Composition, Conservatorium of Perugia; Member of Edison Studio, association of composers for production of computer music, Director, 1999–; mem. Interuniversity Centre for Research on Cognitive Processing. *Compositions include:* Tre Piccoli Paesaggi, for tape, 1999; Frans van Mieris, for actor and bassoon, on a text by Edoardo Sanguineti, 1999; Canto di Festa, for actor, flute, clarinet, piano, violin, viola, cello, on a text by Luciano Violante, 1999; Piccolo Cantico, for choir, 1999; Future commissions include a work for viola and tape; Work for oboe and orchestra concerto; Work for tape. *Address:* via Coste di Fontana Conte 30, 00067 Morlupo, Rome, Italy.

CICCOLINI, Aldo; Concert Pianist; b. 15 Aug. 1925, Naples, Italy. *Education:* Studied with Paolo Denza at the Naples Conservatory. *Career:* Debut: Naples 1942, in Chopin's F Minor Concerto; Professor at the Naples Conservatory from 1947; Moved to France 1949; Professor at the Paris Conservatoire 1971–89; US debut 1950, with the New York Philharmonic, playing Tchaikovsky's 1st Concerto; Many concerts with the world's leading orchestras; Recital programmes include music by Fauré, Ravel, Liszt and Debussy. *Recordings:* Liszt, Années de Pelèrinage and Harmonies Poetiques et Religieuses; Complete piano works of Satie; Concertos by Saint-Saëns; Piano Concerto in D by Alexis de Castillon, conducted by Georges Prêtre. *Honours:* Santa Cecilia Prize, Rome, 1948; Marguérite Long-Jacques Thibaud Prize, Paris, 1949. *Address:* c/o Conservatoire National Superieur de Musique, 14 Rue de Madrid, 75008 France.

CICOGNA, Adriana; Singer (Mezzo-soprano); b. 1955, Este, Italy. *Education:* Studied in Padua with Gina Cigna. *Career:* Engagements from 1983 throughout Italy including Pizzetti's Fedra at Palermo; Donizetti's Sancia di Castiglia at Bergamo and Maddalena in Rigoletto at Florence; La Scala, 1987 as Suzuki in Madama Butterfly, also at Torre del Lago, 1995; Other roles include Fidalma in Il Matrimonio Segreto; Smeton in Anna Bolena and appearances in operas by Monteverdi, Rossini (La Gazzetta) and Mozart; Season 1998 at the Teatro Pergolesi, Jesi, as Metalce in a revival of Pergolesi's Il Prigionier superbo. *Recordings:* Requiem by Pacini. *Address:* c/o Teatro Comunale G Pergolesi, Piazza della Repubblica, 60035 Jesi, Italy.

CIESINSKI, Katherine; Singer (Mezzo-Soprano); b. 13 Oct. 1950, Newark, Delaware, USA. *Education:* Studies with Margaret Harshaw at Curtis Institute, Philadelphia. *Career:* Sang in the US premiere of Berg's 3 act Lulu; European debut 1976 at Aix-en-Provence; Later sang in Asia, Israel and elsewhere in Europe; In 1988 sang in premiere of Argento's The Aspern Papers at Dallas and La Celestine by Maurice Ohana, Paris; Metropolitan Opera debut 1988, as Nicklausse in Les contes d'Hoffmann, returning as Judith in Duke Bluebeard's Castle by Bart ók; Other roles include Waltraute in Götterdämmerung, Strauss's Composer and Octavian, Brangaene in Tristan and Isolde, Britten's Lucretia, Laura in La Gioconda and Barber's Vanessa; Cassandre in Les Troyens for Scottish Opera and at Covent Garden; La Favorite, title role, in revival of original French version, 1991; Santa Fe 1998, as Herodias in Salome. *Recordings:* War and Peace by Prokofiev, Dukas' Ariane et Barbe Bleue; Sapho by Massenet; Pauline in The Queen of Spades.

CIESINSKI, Kristine (Frances); Singer (Soprano); b. 5 July 1952, Wilmington, DE, USA; m. Norman Bailey, 1985. *Education:* Temple University, 1970–71; University of Delaware, 1971–72; BA in Voice, Boston University, 1974. *Career:* New York concert debut as Soloist in Handel's Messiah, 1977; European operatic debut as Baroness Freimann in Der Wildschütz at Salzburg Landestheater, 1979, singing there until 1981; Member of Bremen State Opera, 1985–88; Guest appearances at Cincinnati Opera, Florentine Opera, Milwaukee in 1983 and 1987, Cleveland Opera, 1985, Scottish Opera, 1985 and 1989, Canadian Opera, 1986, Opera North, Leeds, 1986 and 1988, Augsburg Opera, 1986, Mexico City, 1986, Welsh National Opera, 1987 and 1989, Bregenz Festival, 1987, Zagreb National Opera, 1988, Wexford Festival, 1988, English National Opera, 1989–93, Munich State Opera, 1989, Baltimore Opera, 1989, Winnipeg Opera, 1989 and 1991, Frankfurt State Opera, 1990 and 1993, New Orleans Opera, 1992, Leipzig Opera, 1992, and La Scala Milan in 1992; Roles include: Medea, La Wally, Eva, Senta, Donna Anna, Tosca, Aida, Ariadne, Salome, Verdi's Lady Macbeth, Shostakovich's Lady Macbeth of Mtsensk, Erwartung, Judith from Bart ók's Bluebeard, Berg's Marie, Beethoven's Leonora, Tchaikovsky's Tatiana and Salome, also many concert engagements in a repertory ranging from traditional works to contemporary scores; Sang Salome in a new production of Strauss's opera, ENO, 1996 and at Santa Fe, 1998; Season 1999–2000 as Wagner's Gutrune in San Francisco and Emilia Marty for Opera Zuid, Netherlands. *Recordings:* Several. *Honours:* Gold Medal, Geneva International Competition, 1977; 1st Prize, Salzburg International Competition, 1977. *Address:* c/o Trawick Artists Management Inc, 129 West 72nd Street, New York City, NY 10023-3239, USA.

CIOFI, Patrizia; Singer (Soprano); b. 1967, Casole d'Elsa, Siena, Italy. *Education:* Livorno Istituto Musicale; Siena and Fiesole, with Carlo Bergonzi, Alberto Zedda and Claudio Desderi. *Career:* Debut: Florence 1989, in Gino Negri's Giovanni Sebastiano; Appearances throughout Italy as Donna Anna, Gilda, Nannetta in Falstaff, Fulvia in Rossini's La Pietra del Paragone, and Violetta; Martina Franca 1994–96 as Amina in La Sonnambula, Dirce in Cherubini's Médée and Silvia in L'Americano by Niccolò Piccinni; Clorinda in La Cenerentola at Lima and Gilda at Savona and Palermo; Other venues include Parma, Trieste and Bologna; Concerts include Mozart's Mass in C minor; Covent Garden debut as Gilda, 2002. *Honours:* Winner, Giacomo Lauri Volpi Competition, 1998, and Ettore Bastianini Competition, Siena, 1991. *Address:* c/o Teatro Arena Sferisterio, Piazza Mazzini 10, 62100 Macerata, Italy.

CIONI, Renato; Singer (Tenor); b. 15 April 1929, Portoferraio, Elba. *Education:* Studied at the Florence Conservatory. *Career:* Debut: Spoleto 1956, as Edgardo in Lucia di Lammermoor; Italian television 1957, as Pinkerton; La Scala Milan from 1958; Spoleto 1959, in a revival of Donizetti's Il Duca d'Alba; Appearances in San Francisco and Chicago from 1961; Palermo 1963, in I Capuleti e i Montecchi by Bellini; Covent Garden 1964–65, as Cavaradossi, with Callas; The Duke of Mantua and Gabriele Adorno; Verona Arena 1966, as Cavaradossi; Engagements in Berlin, Prague, Paris, Berlin, Copenhagen, Buenos Aires, Bucharest and Edinburgh; Metropolitan Opera 1969–70; Sang Števa in Jenůfa at La Scala, 1974; Tours Opera 1979. *Recordings:* Rigoletto and Lucia di Lammermoor, with Joan Sutherland; Tosca, from Covent Garden.

CIORMILA, Mariana; Singer (Mezzo-Soprano); b. 1956, Romania. *Education:* Studied in Gelsenkirchen and sang there, 1982–84. *Career:* Appearances at Klagenfurt Opera, 1984–85, Houston Opera, 1986 (Marina in Boris Godunov), and Montpellier, 1987 (Orsini in Lucrezia Borgia); Has sung widely in Belgium as Adalgisa, Tancredi, Eboli and the Princess in Adriana Lecouvreur; Deutsche Oper Berlin, 1991, as Sextus in La Clemenza di Tito, Monte Carlo, 1992, as Dulcinée in Don Quichotte; Other roles include Dorabella, Isabella (Rossini) and Cenerentola; Deutsche Oper Berlin 1995–96, as Marina in Boris Godunov and the Countess in Andrea Chénier; Season 1997–98 in

Clemenza di Tito, L'Italiana in Algeri, Enescu's Oedipe and La Gioconda (as Laura); Season 2000 at the Deutsche Oper as Fenena in Nabucco, Merope in Enescu's Oedipe and Mercedes in Carmen. *Address:* c/o Opéra de Monte Carlo, Place du Casino, Monte Carlo.

CIUCIURA, Leoncjusz; Composer; b. 22 July 1930, Grodzisk Mazowiecki, Poland; m. Sylwia Grelich, 18 June 1967. *Education:* BA, Composition, Theory and Conducting, High School of Music, Warsaw, 1960. *Career:* Debut: Concert at High School of Music, Warsaw; Cofounder, Polish branch of Jeunesses Musicales movement, 1958–62; Founder, Editor, Carmina Academica Musical Publication; Editor, Musical Publication for Contemporary Music, 1989; Compositions performed world-wide, 1964–2003, including Festival ISCM World Music Days, International Festival of Music, Warsaw Autumn; Numerous international festivals of contemporary music world-wide; mem, Union of Polish Composers, Society of Authors ZAiKS. *Compositions:* Penetrations for Orchestral Groups, 4 Conductors and Composer, 1963; Emergenza for Choirs and Orchestra, 3 Conductors and Composer, 1963; In progress from 1963, Spiral Form. *Publications:* Spirale I per uno, Spirale II per uno e piu, 1964–2003; Creatoria I, II, 1964–2003; Intarsio, I, II, 1964–2003; Rencontre, I, II, 1964–2003; Incidenti I, II, 1964–2003; In Infinitum I, II, 1964–2003 (all for optional instruments and accompaniment). *Honours:* Laureate Prize, Ministry of Culture and Art, 1960; Prize, Polish Composers Union Competition for Canti al Fresco, 1961; Prize at International Composers Competition (Prague) for Concertino da Camera, 1962; Polish Broadcast and Television Prize for Ornamenti, 1963. *Address:* Zwirki and Wigury 5, 05-825 Grodzisk Mazowiecki, Poland.

CIULEI, Lenuta; Violinist; b. 25 May 1958, Bucharest, Romania; m. 2 s. *Education:* Bucharest Music Academy, and in Germany, Belgium and USA; Study with Stephan Gheorghiu, André Gertler, Raphael Druian and Ruggiero Ricci. *Career:* Debut: Romanian Television broadcast, 1967; Played concerts with orchestras, recitals as solo violinist and was leader of chamber music ensembles in 35 countries throughout Europe, North and South America, Asia; Performed at the UN Palais, Geneva, Bart ók Memorial House, Budapest, the Great Hall of the Tchaikovsky Conservatory, Moscow, the Lincoln Center's Alice Tully Hall and in Madrid for the Spanish Royal Family; Participated in many international festivals; Artistic Director Associate of Virtuosi de Caracas; Gives master classes at universities, international festivals and orchestras in the USA, Venezuela and Europe. *Honours:* First Prize, International Competitions; Pennsylvania Solo Recitalist Award; Order of Brazil for South American Music. *Current Management:* Gaiam International Arts Management. *Address:* PO Box 32239, Philadelphia, PA 19146, USA.

CIURCA, Cleopatra; Singer (Mezzo-Soprano); b. 1954, Romania. *Career:* Sang in Western Europe from 1981, notably at Reggio Emilio in Il Turco in Italia, at Dublin as Carmen, in Brussels as Eboli and at the Verona Arena as Laura in La Gioconda; New York Metropolitan from 1984, as Olga in Eugene Onegin, Marina, Maddalena and Eboli; Further engagements in San Francisco, Washington, Milan (Fenena in Nabucco), Paris and Detroit; Concert appearances include the Verdi Requiem in Vancouver (1986) and Adriana Lecouvreur (as the Princess) in London, 1987; Sang Carmen with Connecticut Opera, 1990. *Address:* c/o Metropolitan Opera, Lincoln Center, New York, NY 10023, USA.

CIURDEA, Teodor; Singer (Bass); b. 1957, Romania. *Education:* Studied in Bucharest. *Career:* Appearances at the National Opera, Bucharest from 1983; Sang Lothario in Mignon at the Wexford Festival, 1987; Prague State Opera, 1992; Vienna Staatsoper, 1987 as Mozart's Bartolo and Volksoper, 1991 as Achior in La Betulia Liberata by Mozart; Guest engagements at London, Basle and Bregenz; Sang Rossini's Basilio at Leipzig, 1993; Concerts and recitals in Vienna, Geneva and Paris. *Honours:* Prizewinner in competitions at Vienna, 1987. *Address:* c/o Leipzig Opernhaus, Augustusplatz 12, 1010 Leipzig.

CLAASSEN, René; Singer (Tenor); b. 1937, Helmond, Netherlands. *Education:* Amsterdam Conservatory, The Hague. *Career:* Debut: Maastricht, 1960; Sang at Bremerhaven from 1964, Kassel from 1968 as Wagner's Loge and Mime, Monostatos in Die Zauberflöte, Shuratov in From the House of The Dead, and the Villains in Les Contes d'Hoffmann; Appeared in Der Ring des Nibelungen, 1989 and sang Aschenbach in Death in Venice; Amsterdam 1986 in Zemlinsky's Der Kreidekreis and as Loge and Mime at Rotterdam, 1989; Sang Leonard in Nielsen's Maskarade at Kassel, 1994; Many concert appearances. *Address:* c/o Der Nederlandse Opera, Waterlooplein 22, 1011 PG Amsterdam, Netherlands.

CLAPTON, Nicholas; Singer (Counter-tenor); b. 1955, Worcester, England. *Education:* MA, Oxford, 1981; MA, London, 1982; Studied with David Mason and Diane Forlano. *Career:* Debut: Wigmore Hall, London, 1984; Aldeburgh Festival, 1985; London recital debut, 1986, Purcell Room; Since then numerous appearances throughout Europe and in the Far East; Operatic roles for ENO, Opera North, Channel 4 television, Batignano, EBF, ranging from Monteverdi and Handel to world premieres (Barry, Lefanu, Benedict Mason); Premieres of concert works by Helen Roe, Daryl Runswick, David Bedford, Simon Holt; Many recitals (Purcell, Rossini, Romantic song, etc) with Jennifer Partridge; Professor of Singing, RAM; Visiting Professor, Zeneakademia, Budapest; mem, ISM. *Recordings:* Purcell: Hail, Bright Cecilia; Duruflé: Requiem; Benedetto Marcello: Cantatas; Nicola Porpora: Cantatas. *Honours:* Winner, English Song Award, 1987; Winner, Heart of England International Competition for Singers, 1987; Two prizes, Concurso 'Francisco Viñas', Barcelona, 1985. *Address:* 4 Helen Road, Oxford OX2 0 DE, England.

CLARET, Lluis; Cellist; b. 10 March 1951, Andorra; m. Anna Mora, 1 s. *Education:* Liceo Conservatory, Barcelona; Conservatoire European, Paris; Bloomington School of Music, USA; Teachers include Enric Casals; Radu Aldulescu; Eva Janzer; György Sebok. *Career:* Debut: Boccherini Cello Concerto, Barcelona, 1968; Soloist concerts with National Symphony of Washington and Moscow Philharmonic; Orchestra National de France; English Chamber Orchestra; Czech Philharmonic, under Rostropovich, Pierre Boulez, Vaclav Neumman, Witold Lutoslawski; Played at closing ceremony of Barcelona 92 Olympics; mem, Barcelona Trio. *Recordings:* Bach: Complete Suites for cello solo, Auvidis Valois, 1999; Schubert: Sonata Arpeggione for cello and piano, Harmonia Mundi, 1992; Chopin: Sonata for cello and piano; Strauss: Sonata for cello and piano, Harmonia Mundi, 1991; Kodály: Sonata for cello, 1990; Schumann: Concerto for cello and orchestra, 1990; Haydn: Concerto No. 1 in C for cello and orchestra; Boccherini: Concerto No. 3 in G minor for cello and orchestra; Dvořák: Trio, Dumky, op. 90, Trio in F minor, 1992; Other works by Boulez, Mendelssohn and Ravel. *Honours:* First prize, Rostropovich Competition, 1977; Casals, 1978; Bologna Competition, 1975. *Current Management:* Carmen Netzel. *Address:* c/o Netzel, Pasaie Marimon, 10-4, 08021 Barcelona, Spain.

CLAREY, Cynthia; American singer (mezzo-soprano); b. 25 April 1949, Smithfield, Va, USA; m. Jake Gardner 1978 (divorced 2000), one s. *Education:* BMus, Howard Univ., Washington DC; Postgraduate Diploma, Juilliard School. *Career:* sang first with the Tri-Cities Opera Company; has sung in The Voice of Ariadne by Thea Musgrave with the New York City Opera; Boston Opera Company in the US premiere of Tippett's The Ice Break (1979) and The Makropulos Case (1986); Binghamton, New York, 1986, in the premiere of Chinchilla by Myron Fink; British debut at the Glyndebourne Festival, 1984, as Monteverdi's Ottavia, followed by Serena in Porgy and Bess (1986); Wexford Festival, 1985 and 1986, as Polinesso in Ariodante and Thomas's Mignon; has toured with Peter Brook's version of Carmen and appeared in the 1989–90 season in concert versions of Anna Bolena (Concertgebouw, as Jane Seymour), Weill's Lost in the Stars (Almeida Festival, London) and The Ice Break (as Hanna, at the Promenade Concerts, London); has also sung in operas by Cavalli, Mozart, Verdi, Puccini, Menotti and Offenbach; other roles include Monteverdi's Penelope, Cavalli's Diana (La Calisto), Handel's Rinaldo, Zerlina, Isoletta (La Straniera), Preziosilla, Dalila, Butterfly, Nicklausse and Octavian; sang Serena in the Covent Garden premiere of Porgy and Bess, 1992, and in Weill/ Grosz Concert at the 1993 London Proms; three roles in Berg's Lulu at the Festival Hall, London, 1994; sang Gershwin's Bess at Cape Town, 1996; sang Kristina in The Makropulos Case at Aix-en-Provence, 2000; has sung with major orchestras including: Chicago Symphony, Boston Symphony, Oakland Symphony, New York Philharmonic, BBC Symphony, City of London Sinfonia, Hallé Orchestra and Dallas Symphony; numerous concert appearances. *Recordings include:* Porgy and Bess; Tippett's The Ice Break; Duffy's A Time for Remembrance, Afrika Songs, Will: Lost in the Stars, Turnage: Somedays. *Current Management:* Herbert H Breslin, 132 Leroy Street, Binghamton, NY 13905, USA. *Telephone:* (607) 723-2235 (also fax) (home). *E-mail:* cclarey@ localnet.com (home).

CLARK, Derek (John); Conductor, Coach and Accompanist; b. 22 Aug. 1955, Glasgow, Scotland; m. Heather Fryer, 26 April 1980, 1 d. *Education:* Dumbarton Academy, 1967–72; Royal Scottish Academy of Music and Drama, 1972–76, Dip MusEd (hons), DipRSAM; University of Durham, BMus, hons 1st class, 1978; London Opera Centre, 1976–77. *Career:* Debut: Accompanist, Purcell Room, 1976; Conductor, Welsh National Opera, 1982; Staff Conductor, Welsh National Opera, 1976–97; Guest Conductor, Mid Wales Opera, 1989–92; Coach, Conductor, Welsh College of Music and Drama, 1992–97; Head of Music, Scottish Opera, 1997–; Guest Coach, RSAMD, 1998–; Conductor's repertoire includes: Tamerlano, Samson, Marriage of Figaro, Così fan tutte, Magic Flute, Die Entführung, La finta giardiniera, Lucia di Lammermoor, Don Pasquale, Count Ory, Beatrice and Benedict, Carmen, La Traviata, Rigoletto, La Bohème, Barber of Seville, Tosca, The Rake's Progress, Noye's Fludde and Maxwell Davies's Cinderella. *Compositions:* 3 One Act Operas for Young People: Hardlock House, 1988; The Witch of Mawddwy, 1993; The Forest Child, 1998 Songs, Choral Music and Arrangements. *Honours:* Worshipful Company of Musicians Silver

Medal, 1976. *Address:* Dalmally, 96 East King Street, Helensburgh G84 7DT, Scotland.

CLARK, Graham; Singer (tenor); b. 10 Nov. 1941, Littleborough, Lancashire, England; m. Joan Clark 1979, 1 step-d. *Education:* MSc, Loughborough University, 1969–70; Studied with Bruce Boyce, London, Bologna, Mantova. *Career:* Debut: with Scottish Opera, 1975; English National Opera, 1978–85 (over 150 performances); Sang with Royal Opera, Covent Garden, Welsh National Opera and Opera North, United Kingdom; Extensive international career, appearing at the Metropolitan Opera in New York for 13 seasons, 1985–2002; Bayreuth Festival, 1981–92, 2001–02 (over 100 performances); Appearances in Paris, Vienna, Berlin, La Scala Milan, Salzburg Festival, Hamburg, Brussels, Madrid, Aix en Provence, Dallas, Bilbao, Catania, Matsumoto, Yokohama, Tokyo, Chicago, San Francisco, Munich, Zürich, Barcelona, Turin, Nice, Rome, Toronto, Amsterdam, Stockholm, Bonn, Tel-Aviv, Vancouver; Has also sung in concert with many of the world's leading orchestras and at the festivals of Lucerne, Edinburgh, Brussels, Berlin, Paris, Chicago, Rome, Amsterdam, Washington, Cologne, Copenhagen, London Proms; Recorded with Philips, Sony, BMG, Decca, EMI, Erato, Teldec, The Met and BBC; Appears on several videos, including Bayreuth performances of Die Meistersinger, Der Fliegende Holländer and 1992 Ring des Nibelungen, as well as the Met's Ghosts of Versailles; Has sung over 300 Wagner performances including over 200 performances of Der Ring des Nibelungen (Loge and Mime). *Honours:* Olivier Award, 1986, for his portrayal of Mephistopheles in Busoni's Doctor Faust; Hon. DLitt, Loughborough University, 1999; Sir Reginald Goodall Prize, London Wagner Society, 2001. *Current Management:* Ingpen & Williams Ltd, 7 St George's Court, 131 Putney Bridge Road, London, SW15 2PA, England. *E-mail:* gclarkgb@aol.com. *Website:* www .grahamclark.org.

CLARK, J. Bunker; Musicologist; b. 19 Oct. 1931, Detroit, Michigan, USA; m. Marilyn Jane Slawson, 3 Aug 1964. *Education:* BMus 1954, MMus 1957, PhD 1964, University of Michigan. *Career:* Instructor of Organ and Theory, Stephens College, Columbia, Missouri, 1957–59; Lecturer in Music, University of California, Santa Barbara, 1964–65; Professor of Music History, University of Kansas, 1965–93; Emeritus, 1993–. *Publications:* Transposition in Seventeenth Century English Organ Accompaniments and the Transposing Organ, 1974; Editor, Anthology of Early American Keyboard Music, 1787–1830, 1977; Editor, Nathaniel Giles: Anthems, 1979; The Dawning of American Keyboard Music, 1988; Editor, American Keyboard Music through 1865, 1990; Series Editor, Bibliographies in American Music, 1975–84; Series Editor, Detroit Studies in Music Bibliography, 1985–; Series Editor, Detroit Monographs in Musicology/Studies in Music, 1990–. *Contributions:* American Organist; Choral Journal; Music and Letters; Musica Disciplina; Journal of the American Musicological Society; American Music. *Honours:* Citation for Distinguished Service, Sonneck Society, 1998. *Address:* 1618 Cypress Point Drive, Lawrence, KS 66047-1721, USA.

CLARK, Richard J.; Singer (baritone); b. 25 April 1943, Tucson, Arizona, USA. *Education:* Academy of Vocal Arts, Philadelphia, and Juilliard School, New York. *Career:* Debut: San Francisco, as Monterone in Rigoletto; Metropolitan Opera from 1981, as Verdi's Monterone and di Luna, Wagner's Amfortas and Kurwenal, Barnaba in La Gioconda, Michele in Il Tabarro and Gianciotto in Francesca da Rimini by Zandonai. *Address:* c/o Metropolitan Opera, Lincoln Center, New York, NY 10023, USA.

CLARKE, Adrian; Singer (baritone); b. 1953, Northampton, England. *Education:* Royal College of Music, London, and the London Opera Centre. *Career:* Appearances with Opera North in Die Fledermaus, The Mikado, Fanciulla del West, The Golden Cockerel, Faust and Carmen (as Escamillo); Don Ferdinand in the British stage premiere of Gerhard's The Duenna, 1994; Rossini's Barber for Scottish Opera and Dublin Grand Opera, Guglielmo and Taddeo in L'Italiana in Algeri for Opera 80; Nick Shadow in The Rake's Progress for New Sussex Opera; Contemporary music includes: Maxwell Davies's Martyrdom of St Magnus for Opera Factory, the premieres of Casken's Golem and Cage's Europera III (London, Berlin and Paris); Gerald Barry's Triumph of Beauty and Deceit for Channel 4 television, the British premiere of Mason's Playing Away (Opera North), Osborne's I am Goya and Rihm's Unsungen (Glasgow and Amsterdam); Season 1995–96 with Rossini's Barber for English Touring Opera, Rigoletto for Mid-Wales Opera and La Bohème for Glyndebourne Touring Opera; Season 2000 as Prince Afron in The Golden Cockerel at Bregenz and the title roles in the premiere of Mr. Emmett Takes a Walk by Peter Maxwell Davies, at Kirkwall. *Current Management:* Musicmakers International Artists Representation, Tailor House, 63–65 High Street, Whitwell, Hertfordshire SG4 8AH, England. *Telephone:* (1438) 871708. *Fax:* (1438) 871777. *E-mail:* musicmakers@compuserve.com. *Website:* www.operauk.com.

CLARKE, Karin; Singer (Soprano); b. 1963, New York, USA. *Education:* Tri-Cities Opera, New York, and International Opera Studio, Zürich. *Career:* Appearances at the Trier Opera as Giulietta in Hoffmann, Marguerite, Mozart's Countess and Anne Trulove; Further engagements at Hagen, Saarbrucken, Munster and Bielefeld notably as Fiordiligi, Saffi (Zigeunerbaron) and Rosalinde in Die Fledermaus; Guest at Brussels, Ghent, Liège and Linz, with concert appearances in New York and throughout Germany; Other roles include Agathe, Lady (Hindemith's Cardillac), Elvira in Ernani, Marenka in The Bartered Bride and the Marschallin; Sang the title role in a revival of Zemlinsky's Sarema, Trier Opera 1996 (first production 20th century). *Recordings include:* Sarema (Koch International). *Address:* c/o Theater der Stadt Trier, Am Augustinerhof, 5500 Trier, Germany.

CLARKE, Paul Charles; Singer (Tenor); b. 1965, Liverpool, England. *Education:* Royal College of Music with Neil Mackie. *Career:* Many performances throughout the United Kingdom including concerts with Bournemouth Sinfonietta, London Ensemble and Scottish Chamber Orchestra; Duke in Rigoletto, Fenton, the High Priest, Idomeneo and Rodolfo with Welsh National Opera, 1990–93; Paris debut, 1991 as Fenton at Théâtre des Champs Elysées; recent engagements as Dmitri in Boris Godunov and Rodolfo for Opera North, Alfredo and Nemorino for Scottish Opera, 1993–94; Covent Garden debut, 1994–95; Cassio in Otello; Tybalt in Roméo et Juliette; Alfredo in La Traviata; USA debut with Seattle Opera singing the Duke in Rigoletto, 1995; Engaged as Faust with Welsh National Opera and Rodolfo at Royal Opera House, Covent Garden, 1996; Season 1997–98 as Verdi's Macduff at Monte Carlo, Gabriele Adorno for WNO and the Duke of Mantua for Scottish Opera; Roméo at the Met and Rodolfo at Seattle; Sang Alfredo at Cincinnati and Pinkerton for WNO, 1998; Season 2000–01 as Verdi's Gabriele Adorno at Wellington, the Duke of Mantua for Santa Fe Opera and Massenet's Des Grieux at Dallas. *Honours:* Peter Pears Scholarship and Kathleen Ferrier Memorial Prize. *Current Management:* Askonas Holt Ltd, Lonsdale Chambers, 27 Chancery Lane, London, WC2A 1PF, England. *Telephone:* (20) 7400-1700. *Fax:* (20) 7400-1799. *E-mail:* info@askonasholt.co.uk. *Website:* www.askonasholt.co.uk.

CLARKE, Stephen (David Justin); Conductor; b. 21 July 1964, Thame, Oxon, England; m. Helen Victoria Morrison, 1 s. *Education:* New College, Oxford, 1977–82; MA, Music, Honours, Hertford College, organ scholarship, Oxford University; ARCO; Diploma, Guildhall School of Music and Drama. *Career:* Conductor, Oxford Philharmonia, 1983–85; Founder, St Michael's Sinfonia, 1981; Conductor, Oxford University Opera Club, 1983–85; Conductor, Schola Cantorum of Oxford, 1985–87; Guest Conductor, Oxford Pro Musica, 1985; Guest Conductor, St Endellion Festival Orchestra, 1987; Worked with Kent Opera, 1988, Geneva Grand Opera, 1988, Royal Scottish Academy of Music and Drama, 1988–89, British Youth Opera, 1988; Assistant Chorus Master, English National Opera, 1990; Head of Music, Scottish Opera, 1993. *Honours:* Ricordi Conducting Prize, 1985–86; Guildhall Diploma of Conducting, 1986. *Address:* 5 Crown Circus, Glasgow G12 9HB, Scotland.

CLAUSEN, Jeanne; Violinist; b. 16 Oct. 1944, Los Angeles, California, USA; m. John Cleveland, 2 July 1990, 1 d. *Education:* BA, Sarah Lawrence College, New York City; MMus, Cleveland Institute of Music, Ohio; Juilliard School of Music, New York City; Music Academy of the West, Santa Barbara, California; Meadowmount School of Music, New York City; Studied with Sascha Jacobsen, Dorothy DeLay, Donald Weilerstein, Sigiswald Kuijken and Ivan Galamian. *Career:* Founder and Leader of Ensemble La Cetra of Milan, Italy; Former Member of Amsterdam Baroque Orchestra, Netherlands, and California New Music Ensemble of Los Angeles; Performances on the Lira da Braccia; mem, International Lira Society. *Recordings:* Numerous. *Contributions:* Article on the Lira da Braccia. *Honours:* Coleman Chamber Music Auditions in Los Angeles, 1959, 1961; Scholarship, J M Kaplan Fund, New York, 1967. *Address:* c/o Amsterdam Baroque Orchestra, Meerweg 23, 1405 BC Bussum, Netherlands.

CLAYTON, Beth; Singer (Mezzo-soprano); b. 1970, Arkansas, USA. *Education:* Manhattan School of Music and with Mignon Dunn. *Career:* Sang Don Ramiro in La finta giardiniera at Washington, 1996; Cherubino at Caracas, Venezuela; Houston Opera in Roméo et Juliette and Virgil Thomson's Four Saints in Three Acts, also in New York and Edinburgh; Season 1998–99 with Cherubino and Nicklausse at Houston, Janáček's Fox at Toronto; Mère Marie in The Carmelites conducted by Seiji Ozawa and Mozart's Sesto in Israel; Season 1999–2000 with the premiere of Carlisle Floyd's Cold Sassy Tree at Houston and Carmen for Welsh National Opera; Concerts include Mahler's 8th Symphony with the Montreal Symphony Orchestra, 1999–2000; Messiah, Dallas Symphony Orchestra; A Midsummer Night's Dream; Sang in British premiere of Saariaho's L'amour de loin, Barbican Hall, 2002. *Address:* c/o Houston Grand Opera Association, 510 Preston Avenue, Houston, TX 77002, USA.

CLAYTON, Laura; Composer and Pianist; b. 8 Dec. 1943, Lexington, Kentucky, USA. *Education:* Studied with Milhaud at the Aspen School, Wuorinen at the New England Conservatory, and at the University of Michigan. *Compositions include:* Implosure for 2 dancers, slide and tape, 1977; Cree Songs for the Newborn for soprano and chamber orchestra, 1987; Panels for chamber ensemble, 1983; Sagarama for piano and orchestra, 1984; Clara's Sea for women's voices, 1988; Terra Lucida for orchestra, 1988. *Honours:* NEA awards and Guggenheim Fellowship. *Address:* c/o ASCAP, ASCAP House, 1 Lincoln Plaza, New York, NY 10023, USA.

CLEGG, John; British concert pianist; b. 7 Nov. 1928, London, England. *Education:* Jesus Coll., Cambridge, Royal Coll. of Music, studie piano with Herbert Fryer. *Career:* debut, Wigmore Hall, London 1951; has given recitals, concerts and broadcasts in most countries, with frequent tours of Africa, Middle East and Far East, and concerts in principal European centres; regular performer on BBC radio and television; pianist-in-residence, Lancaster Univ. 1981–93. *Recordings include:* Complete piano music by Alan Rawsthorne, 1996; Piano music of Milhaud, Koechlin, Ibert and Schmitt, 1998; Music by Chopin-Liszt; Poulenc and Adrian Self, 2000; Music by Fauré and Poulenc, 2002; Music by Howard Ferguson, William Mathias, Kenneth Leighton, 2002. *Honours:* Harriet Cohen Int. Award 1968. *Current Management:* J. Audrey Ellison, International Artists' Management, 135 Stevenage Road, Fulham, London, SW6 6PB, England. *Address:* Concord, 53 Marine Drive, Hest Bank, Lancaster, LA2 6EG, England (home). *Telephone:* (1524) 822357 (home). *E-mail:* jandjc@onetel.com (home).

CLEIN, Natalie; Concert Cellist; b. 1977, England. *Education:* Royal College of Music, Musik Hochschule (Heinrich Schiff), Vienna. *Career:* Debut: London Proms Concerts 1997 with Haydn's C major concerto; Appearances with Royal Philharmonic, English Chamber, Philharmonia London Philharmonic and City of Birmingham Orchestras; Elgar Concerto with LPO in Madrid and London; Lutoslawski Concerto with Hallé Orchestra; US Concerto debut with the California SO, with further engagements at Verbier, Delft and Divonne Festivals; Schwartzenberg Schubertiade, Kronberg; Manchester Cello Festival; Spannungen; Barbican Mostly Mozart; Chamber recitals at Wigmore Hall and Cheltenham and Bath International Festivals; Schumann Quintet with Martha Argerich; Dvořák Concerto at St Magnus Festival, 2001; Season 2000–2001 with Royal PO, BBC National Orchestra of Wales and tour of UK including Wigmore Hall recital; New Generation Artists concerts with BBC; Recital debuts: South America, Teatro Colon with Buenos Aires Philharmonic, 2003; US, New York Lincoln Centre, 2004. *Recordings:* Taverner, with the English Chamber Orchestra; Dvorat Sextet, with the Nash Ensemble; Recital disc (Brahms, Schubert), with Charles Owen, piano. *Honours:* BBC Young Musician of Year 1994; Winner, Eurovision Competition for Young Musicians, Warsaw, 1994; Ingrid zu Solms Cultur Preis, Kronberg Akad., 2003. *Current Management:* Askonas Holt Ltd, Lonsdale Chambers, 27 Chancery Lane, London, WC2A 1PF, England. *Telephone:* (20) 7400-1700. *Fax:* (20) 7400-1799. *E-mail:* gaetan.ledivelec@askonasholt.co.uk. *Website:* www.askonasholt.co.uk.

CLEMENCIC, René; composer, recorder player, harpsichordist, conductor and clavichord player; b. 27 Feb. 1928, Vienna, Austria; m. (1) 1 d., (2) Edda Rischka, 11 April 1968, 1 d. *Education:* PhD, University of Vienna, 1956; Old Music with J Mertin, Musical Theory with J Polnauer, Recorder with H U Staeps, L Höffer, V Winterfeld, W Nitschke, Harpsichord with Eta Harich-Schneider. *Career:* Clavichord player; Founder, Leader, early music ensemble Clemencic Consort, from 1968; Editor, mediaeval Carmina Burana; Baroque opera performances (1st modern including: Draghi's L'Eternita Soggetta al Tempo, Peri's Euridice, Leopold I's Il Lutto dell'Universo); Television play; Concerts world-wide; Soloist on the clavichord. *Compositions:* Maraviglia III and V; Sesostris II and III; Chronos II; Bicinia Nova; Music for Ariana Mnouchkine's film Molière; Musik zum Urfaust; Tolldrastische Szenen; Stufen; Musik zum Prinzen von Homburg; Missa Mundi; Unus Mundus; Requiem pro Vivis et Mortuis; Musica Hermetica; Drachenkampf; Strukturen Musica Instrumentalis; Revolution; Opus für Flöte und Streicher, 1991; Kabbala, 1992; Kammeroper, Der Berg, 1993; Apokalypsis, 1996; Klaviertrio Jeruschalajim, 1997; Emblemata, 1998; Reise nach Niniveh, 1999. *Recordings:* Over 100 as soloist on recorder and with consort; Numerous flute solos; Josquin: Missa Hercules Dux Ferrariae, Musica Sacra; Monteverdi: Missa da Capella, Il Combattimento, Messa a 4 voci; Mediaeval Carmina Burana; Dufay: Missa Ave Regina Coelorum, Missa Sine Nomine, Missa Caput, Missa Ecce Ancilla; Obrecht: Missa Fortuna Desperata; Ockeghem: Requiem; Marcello: Sonate a Flauto; Biber: Fidicinium; Fux: Dafne in Lauro; Carvalho: Testoride; Vivaldi: L'Olimpiade; Pergolesi: Stabat Mater; René Clemencic: Le Combat du Dragon; Kabbala; Apokalypsis; Fux: Requiem; Historic Tablatures: Johannes von Lubin; Dunstable: Sacred Music; Ockeghem: Missa sine Nomine. *Publications:* Alte Musikinstrumente,

1968; Carmina Burana, 1979. *Address:* Reisnerstrasse 26/7, 1030 Vienna, Austria.

CLEMENTI, Aldo; Composer; b. 25 May 1925, Catania, Italy. *Education:* Studied with Pietro Scarpini in Siena, at Catania and with Petrassi in Rome, 1952–54; Summer courses at Darmstadt, 1955–62. *Compositions:* Concertino in forma di variazioni, 1956; Tre Studi for chamber orchestra, 1957; 7 Scenes for chamber orchestra, 1961; Collage I–III, 1961–67; Informel I–III for various instrumental combinations, 1962–63; Variante A for chorus and orchestra and B for orchestra, 1964; Silben for female voice, clarinet, violin and 2 pianos, 1966; Concerto for wind orchestra and 2 pianos, 1967; Reticolo for string quartet, 1968; Concerto for piano and 7 instruments, 1970; Replica for harpsichord, 1972; Blitz, musical action for chamber ensemble, 1973; Sinfonia da camera, 1974; Concerto for piano, 24 instruments and carillons, 1975; Clessidra for 11 instruments, 1976; Reticolo for 12 strings, 1978; Collage Jesu meine Freude, action for 8 strings, 8 winds and tape, 1979; Es, rondeau in 1 act, produced at Teatro la Fenice, Venice, 1981; AEB for 17 instruments, 1983; Finale for 4 sopranos and orchestra, 1984; O du Selige for orchestra, 1985; Concerto for piano and 11 instruments, 1986; Romanza for piano and orchestra, 1991; Rapsodia for soprano, contralto and orchestra, 1994; Carillon, 1-act opera, 1996; Canone Perpetuo for 8 female voices and 9 instruments, 1996; Concerto for 2 harpsichords and strings, 1996; Passacaglia 2 for ensemble, 1997; Veni Creator for ensemble, 1997; Largo for strings, 1999; Von Himmel Hoch for 4 instruments, 1999. *Address:* SIAE (Sezione Musica), Viale della Letteratura n 30, 00144 Rome, Italy.

CLEMENTS, Joy; Singer (Soprano); b. 1931, Dayton, Ohio, USA. *Education:* Studied at University of Miami and in Philadelphia and New York. *Career:* Debut: Miami Opera 1956 as Musetta in La Bohème; Sang 1959–72 at New York City Opera and in Pittsburgh, Cincinnati, Baltimore, San Diego, Fort Worth, Hawaii; Appeared as Mary Warren in premiere of The Crucible by Robert Ward, New York, 1961; Appearances at Metropolitan from 1963; Guest engagements at Tel-Aviv 1963 and Brussels 1975; Other roles have included Mozart's Despina, Pamina and Susanna; Verdi's Violetta and Gilda, Gounod's Juliette, Manon, Martha, Gershwin's Bess; Many concert appearances. *Address:* c/o Metropolitan Opera, Lincoln Center, NY 10023, USA.

CLEMMOW, Caroline Anne, ARAM, LRAM, ARCM; British concert pianist; b. 10 Feb. 1959, London, England; m. Anthony Goldstone. *Education:* Walthamstow Hall School, Sevenoaks, Royal Acad. of Music. *Career:* leading piano duo with husband, Anthony Goldstone, appearing throughout British Isles and abroad, including USA; chamber music, including major tour of Russia, Ukraine; collaborations with percussionist Evelyn Glennie; occasional concerto soloist; mem. Incorporated Soc. of Musicians. *Recordings:* 25 piano duo recordings, seven chamber music recordings. *Address:* Walcot Old Hall, Alkborough, North Lincolnshire DN15 9JT, England (home). *E-mail:* carolineclemmow@aol.com (home).

CLEOBURY, Nicholas Randall; Conductor; b. 23 June 1950, Bromley, Kent, England; m. Heather Kay 1978, 1 s., 1 d. *Education:* Worcester College, Oxford University. *Career:* Assistant Organist, Chichester Cathedral, 1971–72; Assistant Organist, Christ Church, Oxford, 1972–76; Chorus Master, Glyndebourne, 1976–79; Assistant Director, BBC Singers, 1977–80; Freelance Conductor with all London and BBC orchestras, all major British orchestras; Extensive work in Europe, Scandinavia, USA and Australia, 1980–; Work with English and Welsh National Operas, Opera North and Flanders Opera; Principal Opera Conductor, Royal Academy of Music, 1980–87; Artistic Director, Broomhill, 1990–94; Artistic Director, Britten Sinfonia, 1991–; Artistic Director, Sounds New, 1997–; numerous broadcasts; Premiere of Symphony No. 5 by David Matthews at the 1999 London Prom concerts; mem. Savage Club; Lords Taverners. *Recordings:* Numerous for major recording companies. *Honours:* Fellow, Royal College of Organists, Limpus Prize, 1968; Honorary Member, Royal Academy of Music, 1985. *Current Management:* Connaught Artists Management Ltd, 2 Molasses Row, Plantation Wharf, London, SW11 3UX, England. *Telephone:* (20) 7738 0017. *Fax:* (20) 7738 0909. *E-mail:* classicalmusic@connaughtartists.com. *Website:* www.connaughtartists.com.

CLEOBURY, Stephen, BMus, MA, FRCM, FRCO; conductor and organist; b. 31 Dec. 1948, Bromley, Kent, England; two d. *Education:* St John's College, Cambridge. *Career:* organist, St Matthew's, Northampton, 1971–74; sub-organist, Westminster Abbey, 1974–78; Master of Music, Westminster Cathedral, 1979–82; Director of Music, King's College, Cambridge, 1982–; Conductor, CUMS, 1983–; Chief Conductor, BBC Singers, 1995–; many radio and TV appearances in UK and abroad with King's College Choir; conducted Bach's B Minor Mass at St John's, London, 1997; premiere of Havoc by Giles Swayne at the London Proms, 1999; Conducted BBC Singers and City of London Sinfonia at the London Proms, 2002; mem. Royal College of Organists (pres. 1990–92), Incorporated Society of Musicians. *Recordings:* a wide range of music

including that with King's College Choir and with the BBC Singers, and as organist at Westminster Abbey and King's College. *Publications:* carol arrangements. *Current Management:* Hazard Chase Ltd, Norman House, Cambridge Place, Cambridge, CB2 1NS, England. *Telephone:* (1223) 312400. *Fax:* (1223) 460827. *Website:* www.hazardchase.co.uk. *Address:* King's College, Cambridge CB2 1ST, England. *E-mail:* choir@kings.cam.ac.uk.

CLEVE, George; Conductor; b. 9 July 1936, Vienna, Austria. *Education:* Studied at Mannes College, New York, and with Pierre Monteux, George Szell, Franco Ferrara and Leonard Bernstein. *Career:* Debut: Salzburg Festival; Appearances with major American orchestras, including the New York Philharmonic and Symphony Orchestras of Chicago, Boston, Cleveland, Minnesota and San Francisco; Music Director of the San Jose Symphony and founder of the Midsummer Mozart Festival in San Francisco, 1974; Has conducted La Bohème, La Traviata, Le nozze di Figaro and Oedipus Rex; European engagements with the Northern Sinfonia, the Vienna Symphony Orchestra and the Orchestre National de France; Flanders Festival, 1990, Don Giovanni; Tour of Europe with the English Chamber Orchestra; Germany with the Stockholm Chamber Orchestra. *Honours:* Officier, Ordre des Arts et des Lettres, from the French Government; Silver Medal of Honour, City of Vienna. *Current Management:* Terry Harrison Artists Management, The Orchard, Market Street, Charlbury, Oxfordshire OX7 3PJ, England. *Telephone:* (1608) 810330. *Fax:* (1608) 811331. *E-mail:* artists@terryharrison.force9.co.uk. *Website:* www.terryharrison.force9.co.uk (office).

CLIBURN, Van (Harvey Lavan); Pianist; b. 12 July 1934, Shreveport, Louisiana, USA. *Education:* Studied with mother Rildia Bee Cliburn and at Juilliard School of Music. *Career:* Debut: Shreveport, 1940; Houston Symphony Orchestra, 1952; New York Philharmonic Orchestra, 1954, 1958; Concert pianist on tour, USA, 1955–56; USSR 1958; Appearances include Brussels, London, Amsterdam and Paris, notably in music by Tchaikovsky and Rachmaninov. *Honours:* Honorary HHD, Baylor University; Winner, 1st International Tchaikovsky Piano Competition, Moscow, USSR, 1958; In 1962 he established a Piano Competition in his name at Fort Worth, Texas; White House recital, 1987; Liszt and Tchaikovsky Concertos with the Philadelphia Orchestra, 1989; Concerts and soloist with the Houston Symphony Orchestra, 1989; Tour of USA with the Moscow Philharmonic Orchestra, 1994. *Current Management:* Shaw Concerts Incorporated, 1995 Broadway, New York, NY 10023, USA. *Address:* 455 Wilder Place, Shreveport, LA 71104, USA.

CLINGAN, Judith; Composer and Conductor; b. 19 Jan. 1945, Sydney, New South Wales, Australia. *Education:* Studied with Larry Sitsky at Canberra and at the Kodály Institute, Hungary. *Career:* Founded Gaudeamus, 1983, for the furtherance of music education. *Compositions include:* Children's operas Just Looking and Marco, 1991; Choruses, including The Birds' Noel, 1990, and Kakadu, 1990; A Canberra Cycle for soprano, baritone and ensemble, 1991; Songs of Solitude for soprano and ensemble, 1991. *Address:* c/o APRA, 1A Eden Street, PO Box 567, Crows Nest, NSW 2065, Australia.

CLOAD, Julia; Pianist; b. 6 Oct. 1946, London, England. *Education:* Royal College of Music, London; Liszt Academy, Budapest, Hungary; Further studies with Maria Curcio and Hans Keller. *Career:* Debut: Wigmore Hall; Concerto performances with Royal Philharmonic Orchestra, London Philharmonic Orchestra, Hallé Orchestra, Royal Liverpool Philharmonic Orchestra, under conductors including Bernard Haitink, John Pritchard, Adrian Boult, James Loughran, Christopher Seaman; Recitals, at the Wigmore Hall, Queen Elizabeth Hall, BBC and Budapest Spring Festival; Concertos: Royal Festival Hall and Radio 3. *Recordings:* Haydn Piano Sonatas; Schumann Sonatas. *Address:* 1/6 Colville Houses, Talbot Road, London W11 1JB, England.

CLOSE, Shirley; Singer (Mezzo-soprano); b. 1962, Oklahoma, USA. *Education:* University of Southern California. *Career:* Sang at the Augusta Opera from 1985; Amneris in Aida for Boston Opera; Mozart's Marcellina at Miami, 1988; Magdalena in Die Meistersinger at Nice, 1986; In Wagner's Ring at Orange, 1988; Cologne Opera, 1989–93 as Wagner's Fricka and Waltraute; Geneviève in Pelléas; Orlofsky in Die Fledermaus and Mary in Der fliegende Holländer; Guest appearances at Munich as Fenena in Nabucco; Bayreuth Festival, Waltraute, 1992 and the Deutsche Oper, Berlin; Sang Gluck's Alceste at Strasbourg, 1996. *Recordings:* Elektra; Die Walküre. *Address:* c/o Opéra du Rhin, 19 Place Broglie, 67008 Strasbourg Cédex, France.

CLOSTRE, Adrienne; Composer; b. 9 Oct. 1921, Thomery, France. *Education:* Studied at the Paris Conservatoire with Messiaen and Milhaud. *Compositions include:* Stage works: Nietzsche, 1975; Le secret, 1981; 5 scenes de la vie italienne, 1983; L'albatross, 1988; Annapurna, 1988; Melodramas: L'écriture du Dieu, 1991 and El Zaïr, 1992; Le Triomphe de la Vertu, 1995; Oboe concerto, 1970 and Concerto for flute, violin and chamber orchestra, 1972; Waves and Sun: Une lecture de Virginia Woolf, 1991; Le Zaire, sung melodrama, 1992. *Honours:* 1st Grand Prix de Rome, 1949; Grande Prix Musical Ville de Paris, 1955; Prix Florence Gould, 1976; Prix Musique de la SACD, 1987. *Address:* 15 Avenue Hoche, 75008 Paris, France.

CLOZIER, Christian (Robert Adrien); Composer and Director; b. 25 Aug. 1945, Compiègne, France; one d. *Education:* National Conservatory of Music, Paris; Practical School for Higher Studies, Paris. *Career:* Founder, Director, IMEB; Director, International Competition of Electro-acoustic Music, Bourges; Hon. President, International Confederation of Electro-acoustic Music (ICEM); Conceptor of Music Electro-acoustic Instruments. *Compositions include:* La Discordature; Opéra, A Vie; 22 août; Loin la Lune; Symphonie pour un enfant Seul; A la Prochaine, la Taupe; Quasars; Markarian 205; Par Pangloss Gymnopède; Le Bonheur, une idée neuve en Europe, Mon nom sous le soleil est France, le Temps scintille et le songs est savoir; Eleven spectacles multimedia;Démotique: De la grève, au loin; Clarissophone Ont été; Le père, le fils. *Recordings:* La Discordatura, Pathé Marconi; Lettre à une Demoiselle; Dichotomie, Pathé Marconi; Par Panglos Gymnopède; Le temps scintille et le songe est savoir; Le Clarissophone Symphonie pour un Enfant Seul, Edition IMED; Quasars, Le Chant du Monde. *Contributions:* Musique en Jeu No. 8, 1970; Faire 2–3, 1974; Faire 4–5, 1975; Poésie Sonore Internationale, Edition J.M. Place. *Address:* Institut International de Musique Electroacoustique, BP 39 Place Andre Malraux, 18000 Bourges, France. *E-mail:* administration@ ime-bourges.org. *Website:* www.imeb.net.

CLURMAN, Judith; Conductor; b. 11 March 1953, Brooklyn, New York, USA; m., 1 s. *Education:* Oberlin College, 1971–73; BMus, 1977; MMus, Juilliard School of Music, 1978. *Career:* Founder, Director, New York Concert Singers, 1988–; Director of Choral Activities, The Juilliard School, 1989–; Project Youth Chorus, 1996–; New York Chamber Symphony Chorus, 1996–98; Judith Clurman Choral Workshop, 1998–; Performed with New York Philharmonic, Boston Symphony, Orchestra of St Luke's, American Composers Orchestra, Mostly Mozart, Classical Band, Lincoln Center's Great Performers series; Musical Director, 92nd Street Y's Music of the Jewish Spirit, 1998–2001; Director of Choral Activities, TodiMusicFest, 2001–; Conducted numerous premieres including music by Leonard Bernstein, William Bolcom, John Corigliano, Philip Glass, Aaron Jay Kernis, Libby Larsen, David Diamond, Stephen Paulus, Ned Rorem, Christopher Rouse, Ellen Taaffe Zwilich, Tania Leon, Paul Schoenfield and Robert Beaser; mem, Chorus America; American Choral Directors Association. *Recordings:* Divine Grandeur; The Mask; A Season's Promise. *Honours:* First Prize, ASCAP; Chorus America Award, with New York Concert Singers, 1992. *Address:* 75 East End Avenue 9L, New York, NY 10028, USA.

COAD, Jonathan; Singer (Baritone); b. 1958, Crayford, Kent, England. *Education:* Studied at the Royal College of Music, London, England. *Career:* Many concert appearances, including tours with the Groupe Vocale de France throughout Europe and North America; Concert soloist in England and France; Sang Pooh-Bah in The Mikado for D'Oyly Carte Opera, and in Bernstein's Candide at the Old Vic, 1989; Engagements with the Royal Opera, Covent Garden, in Death in Venice, The Fiery Angel, Jenůfa, Tosca, Arabella, and La Bohème; Rigoletto 1997, as Court Usher, and sang Cross in Paul Bunyan for the Royal Opera, 1997–98. *Recordings include:* Albums with Groupe Vocale de France. *Address:* c/o Royal Opera House (Contracts), Covent Garden, London WC2E 9 DD, England.

COATES, Gloria; Composer; b. 10 Oct. 1938, Wausau, Wisconsin, USA. *Education:* BMus, Composition, Voice; BA, Art, Theatre; MMus, Composition, Musicology; Studied with Otto Luening and Alexander Tcherepnin. *Career:* Freelance Composer, Munich, Germany, 1969–; Organiser of German-American Contemporary Music Series, Munich and Cologne, 1971–84; Demonstrated work in vocal multiphonics, International Summer Course for New Music, Darmstadt, 1972; Taught for University of Wisconsin International Programs, Munich, 1975–83, London, 1976. Compositions widely performed, Europe, USA, India, including Warsaw Autumn Festival, 1978, Musica Viva Series in Munich, East Berlin Festival, 1979, Montepulciano, Dartington, Geneva Festivals; Radio recordings include for BBC-London, Suisse Romande, RAI Rome, Radio Poland, German Radio stations, Radio Johannesburg, Sweden, USA; Additional broadcasts, China, Finland, Spain, Portugal, Brazil, Canada, Belgium, Netherlands; Invited lectures, Harvard University, 1981, Max Mueller Bhavans, India, 1982. *Compositions include:* Music on Open Strings, 1974; String Quartet, commissioned by Kronos Quartet; Orchestral piece for New Music American Festival, New York, 1989; Piece for harp, flute and viola for Dresden Festival; 11 Symphonies, 1973–99; 5 String Quartets, 1966–88. *Recordings:* Bielefelder Catalog, Music on Open Strings, String Quartets I, II, III and IV; Symphonies 1, 2, 4, 7, Time frozen, Homage to Van Gogh, Tones in Overtones. *Honours:* Music on Open Strings cited as 1 of 12 most important recorded works by living composer, International Koussevitzky Panel, 1986; Yaddo Grants;

MacDowell Colony; UNESCO Grant, 1990. *Address:* Postfach 430363, 80733 Munich, Germany.

COATES, Leon; University Lecturer and Composer; b. 15 June 1937, Wolverhampton, England; m. 11 Sept 1976. *Education:* St John's College, Cambridge. *Career:* University Lecturer; Various radio appearances as pianist, harpsichordist, with Scottish Baroque Ensemble; Several broadcasts; Organist and Choirmaster, St Andrew's and St George's Church, Edinburgh; Lecturer, Edinburgh University, 1965–2002; mem, Scottish Society of Composers; Royal College of Organists; Guild of Professional Composers and Songwriters. *Compositions:* Song Cycle, North West Passage, 1994; Concertos for viola, 1979 and harpsichord, 1984; Music for Concert Band and Choir; Te Deum and Jubilate for choir and organ. *Recordings:* BBC Archive Recording of Music for 2 Harpsichords. *Publications:* Song Cycle North West Passage, 1994. *Contributions:* Tempo; Music in New Zealand; Short articles on relevant musical terms in The Oxford Composer Companions: J. S. Bach, 1999. *Address:* 35 Comely Bank Place, Edinburgh EH4 1ER, Scotland.

COATES, Oliver; British cellist; b. 19 May 1982, London, England. *Education:* Junior Academy of Music from 1992; Royal Academy of Music, studied with Colin Carr. *Career:* Debut at age 15 playing Haydn's C major Concerto at St John's Smith Square, 1999; Recitals and concertos in UK in Aldeburgh, Edinburgh and London, and across Europe and Asia including Japan, Holland, France and Norway: London Soloists' Chamber Orchestra Cello Festival, 2002; Paris Chopin Festival, 2003; Gala concert, Int. Cello Festival, Manchester 2004; Premieres of solo and chamber music by Elena Firsova, Stephane Altier, Dmitri Smirnov, Graham Williams; TV/radio: appearances on BBC1, Channel 5 and BBC Radio; mem., New Professionals Ensemble. *Honours:* Dame Ruth Railton chamber music prize at RAM; Winner, Douglas Cameron Cello Competition, May Mukle Cello Competition, Montefiore Prize, S&M Eyres Scholarship, Sir John Barbirolli Memorial Prize. *Address:* 169 Fordwych Road, London, NW2 3NG, England. *E-mail:* ollycoates@yahoo.com.

COBBE, Hugh Michael Thomas, OBE, MA; Librarian; b. 20 Nov. 1942, Farnham, England; m. Katherine Chichester 1982; two d. *Education:* St Columba's Coll., Dublin, Trinity Coll. Dublin. *Career:* Asst Keeper, Manuscript Dept, British Museum 1967–73 and British Library 1973–78; Head of Publications, British Library 1978–85, Head of Music Collections 1985–2001, Head of British Collections 2001–2002; mem. Royal Musical Asscn (pres. 2002–), Gerald Coke Handel Foundation (chair. 1996–); Fellow of Soc. of Antiquities. *Publications:* The Letters of Ralph Vaughan Williams; contrib. to Musical Times, Fontes Artis Musicae, New Grove Dictionary of Music and Musicians, Oxford Dictionary of National Biography. *Address:* Fox House, North End, Newbury, RG20 0AY, England (home). *Telephone:* (1635) 253190 (home). *Fax:* (1635) 253190 (home). *E-mail:* hugh.cobbe@pop3.hiway .co.uk (office).

COBURN, Pamela; Singer (soprano); b. 29 March 1955, Dayton, OH, USA. *Education:* De Pauw University, Eastman School and Juilliard. *Career:* Has sung at Munich Staatsoper from 1982. Vienna from 1984; Maggio Musicale Florence 1988 as Ellen Orford in Peter Grimes; Los Angeles 1990 as Ilia in Idomeneo; Sang Saffi in Der Zigeunerbaron at Zürich and Alice Ford in Falstaff for Miami Opera 1991; Salzburg and Munich Festivals 1991, as Mozart's Countess; Sang Ellen Orford in a production of Peter Grimes by Tim Albery, Munich, 1991; Engaged for Giulio Cesare and Das Rheingold at the 1997 Munich Festival; Other roles include Fiordiligi; Rosalinde in Die Fledermaus and Lauretta in Gianni Schicchi; Sang Hanna Glawari at the Deutsche Oper Berlin, 2000. *Recordings:* Honegger's King David; Siebel in Faust, Mozart's L'Oca del Cairo; Marzelline in Fidelio; Zemlinsky's Traumgörge; First Lady in Die Zauberflöte; Flowermaiden in Parsifal conducted by Barenboim. *Honours:* Prizewinner at ARD Competition, Munich 1980; Metropolitan Auditions of the Air 1982. *Current Management:* Ingpen & Williams Ltd, 7 St George's Court, 131 Putney Bridge Road, London, SW15 2PA, England.

COBURN, Robert (James); Composer and Educator; b. 29 Oct. 1949, Montebello, California, USA; m. Jeanne N Ashby, 12 May 1974, 1 s. *Education:* MA, Composition, University of California at Berkeley; BMus in Composition, University of the Pacific; PhD in Composition, University of Victoria. *Career:* Composition Commissions: Sun River Music Festival; San Francisco New Music Ensemble; Oregon Coast Music Festival; Sound-Art Environment Comm: City of Philadelphia Avenue of Arts, 1995; Oregon Convention Centre (landscape); Henry Gallery, Seattle; Performances: Festival of New Music, Roulette, New York; Forum '82 International Festival, New York; Electronic Music Plus Festival; mem, International Society for the Arts, Sciences and Technology; Computer Music Association; Founding Member, World Forum for Acoustic Ecology. *Compositions:* Traces (Star Map l) for viola and computer sound; Staursahng for live electronic music and visual images; Cantos for chamber orchestra; Bell Circles II, permanent sound environment, Oregon Convention Center; Luminous Shadows for cello, piano, and percussion, 1993; Songs of Solitude for chorus; Ellipse for solo flute; Shadowbox for clarinet, 1994. *Contributions:* Portland Review; Prologue; Leonardo Music Journal. *Honours:* Oregon Artists Fellowship, 1978; Eberhardt Research Fellowship, 1995. *Address:* Conservatory of Music, University of the Pacific, Stockton, CA 95211, USA.

COCCIANTE, Richard (Riccardo); composer, singer, musician (piano) and arranger; b. Saigon, Viet Nam; m. Catherine Boutet; one s. *Career:* composer, solo artist 1972–; world-wide television, radio appearances; tour venues include Gran Teatro La Fenice, Venice 1988, Sporting Club, Monaco 1988, 1990, 1995, Teatro dell'opera Caracalla, Rome 1991, Vina del Mar Festival, Chile 1994, Olympia, Paris 1994, 1996, Zenith, Paris 1994, Taj Mahal, Atlantic City 1995, Teatro Sistina, Rome 1988, 1993, 1995, 1997, Théâtre St Denis, Montréal 1994, 1996, Stadsschouwberg, Amsterdam 1995, Vienna Rathaus 1997; collaborated with producers, including Paul Buckmaster, Humberto Gatica, Ennio Morricone, James Newton-Howard, Vangelis; participated in album World War II, interpreting Michelle with London Symphony Orchestra; concert, Christmas in Vienna (with Placido Domingo, Sarah Brightman and Helmut Lotti) 1997. *Compositions:* Notre Dame de Paris (musical, Felix Award for Album of the Year, Canada) 1998–99, 2000 (Hymne pour la ville de Lyon) commissioned by Raymonde Barre, Mayor of Lyon, to celebrate the new millennium, Le Petit Prince (musical) 2002. *Recordings include:* albums: (in Italian) Mu 1972, Poesia 1973, Anima 1974, L'alba 1975, Concerto per Margherita 1976, Riccardo Cicciante: A Mano A Mano 1978, ...E Io Canto 1979, Cervo a Primavera 1981, Cocciante (Celeste Nostalgia) 1982, Sincerità 1983, Il Mare dei Papaveri 1985, La Grande Avventura 1987, Se Stiamo Insieme 1991, Eventi e Mutamenti 1993, Un Uomo Felice 1994, Innamorato 1997; in French: Atlanti 1973, Quand un Amour 1974, Concerto pour Marguerite 1978, Je Chante 1979, Au Clair de tes Silences 1980, Vieille 1982, Sincérité 1983, L'Homme qui vole 1986, Empreinte 1993, L'Instant Présent 1995; 10 albums in Spanish; three albums in English; film soundtracks: Tandem 1987, Storia di una capinera 1994, Toy Story 1996, Astérix and Obélix contre César 1999; international hit singles: Bella Senz' Anima (Italy)/Bella Sin Alma (Spain, Latin America) 1973, Quand un Amour (France, Belgium, Canada) 1974, Margherita (Italy)/Marguerite (France, Belgium, Canada)/Margarita (Spain, Latin America) 1976–78, Coup de Soleil (France, Belgium) 1980, Cervo a Primavera (Italy)/Yo Renascere (Spain, Latin America) 1980, Sincéritié (France)/Sincerità (Italy, Holland)/Sinceridad (Spain, Latin America)/Sincerity (USA) 1983, Questione di Feeling (duet with Mina, Italy)/Question de Feeling (duet with Fabienne Thiebeault, France, Belgium, Canada)/Cuestion de Feeling (duet with Melissa, Spain, Latin America) 1985–86, Se Stiamo Insieme (Italy, Belgium, Holland, Brazil) 1991, Pour Elle (France)/Per Lei (Italy, Brazil)/I'd Fly (Italy, France, Belgium, Holland)/Por Ella (Latin America)/Voorbij (Holland) 1993–95, Il ricordo di un istante (Italy, France, Belgium, Canada, Holland), Belle, Le Temps des Cathédrales, Vivre (excerpts from musical Notre Dame de Paris, France, Belgium, Canada) 1998–99. *Honours:* Rose d'Or Award (Greece) 1981, Rino Gaetano Award (Italy) 1982, winner, San Remo Festival (Italy) 1991, Telegatto (Italy) 1991, Medaille de la Ville de Paris (France) 1998, Victoire de la Musique Awards (France) for Song of the Year 1999, for Show of the Year 1999, Grande ufficiale della Repubblica Italiana (Italy) 1999, World Music Award (Monaco) for Best-selling French Artist/Group 1999, Rolf Marbot Award (France) for Song of the Year 1999, Felix Awards (Canada) for Song of the Year 1999, for Show of the Year 1999, for Best-selling Album 1999, for Album of the Year 1999. *Address:* Boventoon BV, Information Office, 4 rue Chauveau Lagarde, 75008 Paris, France.

COCHRAN, William; Singer (Tenor); b. 23 June 1943, Columbus, Ohio, USA. *Education:* Studies with Martial Singher at the Curtis Institute, Philadelphia and with Lauritz Melchior and Lotte Lehmann in California. *Career:* Sang Wagner roles in San Francisco and Mexico; Many appearances in Europe from 1967, notably in Hamburg and Frankfurt, roles include Max in Der Freischütz, Jason in Médée, Otello, Herod in Salome and Dmitri in Boris Godunov; Concert with the New York Philharmonic 1971; Covent Garden debut 1974, as Laca in Jenůfa; San Francisco 1977, as Tichon in Katya Kabanova; Appearances in operas by Busoni, Janáček, Zimmermann, Shostakovich and Stravinsky (Tom Rakewell at Frankfurt 1983); Sang Bacchus in Ariadne auf Naxos at the Metropolitan Opera 1985; Deutsche Oper Berlin, 1989 Schreker's Die Gezeichneten; Season 1988–89 at Düsseldorf; Sang Siegfried in Paris and Brussels, 1991; Zimmermann's Die Soldaten at Strasbourg and Tichon (Katya Kabanova), Los Angeles; The Councillor in The Nose by Shostakovich, Frankfurt City Opera; Title role, Otello for Welsh National Opera, May 1990; Season 1992 as Samson at Amsterdam and Schoenberg's Aron (concert performance) at the Edinburgh Festival; Sang Aegisthus in Elektra at the First Night of the 1993 London Proms; Herod in Salome at San Francisco, 1997; Season 1998 with Aegisthus at Catania and Peter Grimes at Madrid; Season 2000–01 as Aegisthus in

Elektra at Munich and Shuisky in Boris Godunov at Dusseldorf. *Recordings:* Mathis der Maler and Act I of Die Walküre; Doktor Faust by Busoni; Mahler's 8th Symphony. *Address:* c/o Welsh National Opera, John Street, Cardiff CF1 4SP, Wales.

COCKER, Jonathan; Stage Director; b. 1963, England. *Education:* Guildhall School of Music and Drama. *Career:* Productions of Purcell's Dido and Orfeo et Euridice for Jerusalem Studio Opera; Britten's Turn of the Screw for the Buxton Festival; Carmen and Orfeo for Northern Opera; Martinů's Comedy on the Bridge and Rimsky's Mozart and Salieri at the Ryedale Festival; Nielsen's Maskarade for the Opera North Tour, Purcell's Fairy Queen at festivals of Madrid, Athens and Valencia; Also for English Bach Festival at Linbury Theatre, Covent Garden, 2001; Further engagements with New Israel Opera, Opera North and Opera Studio; Musicals and Plays in the West End and on Tours to the United Kingdom and Europe.

CODREANU-MIHALCEA, Claudia; Singer (Mezzo-soprano); b. 1969, Romania. *Career:* Many concert and opera engagements in Romania and elsewhere in Europe; Repertory includes Mozart's Clemenza di Tito, Rossini's Cenerentola, and songs by Brahms and Mussorgsky; Contestant at the 1995 Cardiff Singer of the World Competition. *Address:* Bloc 3, SC 1, Apt 38, Sector 2, Str Doamna Ghieca nr 5, 72404 Bucharest, Romania.

COELHO, Elaine; Singer (soprano); b. 1950, Rio de Janeiro, Brazil. *Education:* Studied in Rio and Hanover. *Career:* Sang at Landestheater Detmold from 1974 as Verdi's Violetta and Nannetta, Mozart's Constanze, Zdenka in Arabella and Liu in Turandot; Stadttheater Bremen from 1976, as Norina in Don Pasquale, Mozart's Susanna, Euridice, Fiorilla in Il Turco in Italia and Lulu; Sang at Frankfurt am Main from 1984 and appeared as guest in Turin as Lulu; Further engagements at Aachen, the Vienna Volksoper and the Bregenz Festival, Giulietta in Les Contes d'Hoffmann, 1988; Sang Donna Anna in Don Giovanni at the Teatro Municipal, Rio de Janeiro, 1991; Vienna Volksoper 1992, as Abigaille in Nabucco; Season 1995–96 as Salomé in Hérodiade at the Vienna Staatsoper, Donna Elvira and Elettra in Idomeneo at the Munich Staatsoper; Season 2000–01 at the Vienna Staatsoper, as Elvira in Ernani and Offenbach's Giulietta.

COEN, Massimo; Violinist and Composer; b. 11 March 1933, Rome, Italy; m. Mirella Thau, 2 s., 1 d. *Education:* Law Degree, Rome University; Violin Diploma, St Cecilia Conservatory, Rome; Private Study, Chamber Music and Violin. *Career:* Founder, Chamber Music Groups; I Solisti di Roma, 1961 and Quartetto Nuova Musica, 1963, giving concerts and radio performances throughout Europe; Tour of USA and Canada as soloist with Cameristica Italiana, 1969; Founder, Music School, Rome; Teacher, National Academy of Dance; Discoverer, Editor and Performer of numerous ancient Italian musical MSS; mem, Professional Associations and Councils. *Compositions:* Quartetto II, 4 Temperamenti, 1987; Divertimento I, flute and strings, 1988; Divertimento II, La Marsigliese, 1989; Violin-Concerto, Saudades de Rio, 1991; C'Era una Volta, 1979; Integrazioni, 1980; Dosilado, 1983; Nascite, 1983; Peav Suite, 1983; Didone, 1983; La Donna Senz'ombra, 1984; Il Rovescio della Medaglia, 1984; Sophitour, 1985; Introduzione e Valzer in Do, 1985; Quartetto per Archi No. 1, 1986; Quartetto per Archi No. 2, 1987; Concerto Grosso per Orchestra D'Archi, 1988; 2 Divertimenti, 1988–89; Fantasia Per Oboe e Quartetto D'Archi, 1993; 3 Liriche Per Soprano and Violin, 1994; Maternidade, As Palabras, A Obra per soprano e violino su poesie di M. L. Verdi, 1994; Crysolith D 12 per violino e fisarmonica, 1996; Lolly, per quartetto d'archi e danza, 1996; Le Opere e i Giorni per due violini, 1996; L'Anima Negli Occhi per violino e viola, 1996; O' Mazzamauriello per violino e violoncello, 1996; Tenores per sax soprano e quartetto d'archi, 1997; Mneme per soprano, sax soprano e quartetto d'archi; Transcrizioni da Handel, Haydn, Mozart, Donizetti per voce e quartetto d'archi, 1998; Accelerazioni, Serpentine e Itaca per quartetto d'archi, 1999; Mediterraneo per violino, flauto, clarinetto e sassofono, 2000; Nascita di Afrodite for Violin, clarinet, Sax alto, dance, 2000; Cosi 'Fan Tutti for violin and actor; Accelerazioni II for violin, percussion and dance, 2001; Lo Sforzo Umano for violin, percussion, actor and dancers, 2002; Moby Dick for violin, bass clarinet, percussion and actor, 2003; Zampe, Zampette — Ninna Nanna for string quartet and Bell 2003; Kleines Quartettsatz for strings, 2003. *Recordings:* Baroque and Contemporary Music; Massimo Coen works Edipan Rome; Massimo Coen Live Portrait, 2002. *Contributions:* Mondo Operaio. *Honours:* Member, International Jury, Gaudeamus Foundation Competition, Rotterdam, 1976; 2002 Carsulae Award. *Address:* Via Ipponio 8, 00183 Rome, Italy.

COERTSE, Mimi; Singer (Soprano); b. 12 June 1932, Durban, South Africa. *Education:* Studied in Johannesburg and in Vienna, with Josef Witt. *Career:* Debut: With the Vienna Staatsoper in Naples, as a Flowermaiden in Parsifal, 1955; Basle 1956, as the Queen of Night; Tour of South Africa; Appearances at the Salzburg Festival as Constanze in Die Entführung, 1956; Glyndebourne Festival 1957, as Zerbinetta; Sang at the Vienna Staatsoper from 1957; Salzburg 1960, as the Queen of Night; Mahler's 8th Symphony; Guest Appearances in London, Cologne, Brussels, Frankfurt and Munich; Sang Mozart's Countess in Pretoria, South Africa, 1989. *Recordings:* Fiakermilli in Arabella.

COGEN, Pierre; Organist, Composer and Music Professor; b. 2 Oct. 1931, Paris, France; m. Michèle Vermesse, 5 July 1986. *Education:* Cathedral Music School for Children, 1944–51; Higher studies in Philosophy, Paris, 1957–59; Organ study with Jean Langlais, Schola Cantorum; Certificate of Competence as Professor of Organ at National Conservatories; CAPES, Music Education (Secondary). *Career:* Liturgical Organist, 1945–94; Director of Boys' Choir, 1952–65; Concert Organist, 1959–; Professor of Organ and Music Education, 1961–93; Assistant to Jean Langlais, Sainte Clotilde and Schola Cantorum, 1972–76; Organist, Basilique Sainte Clotilde, 1976–94. *Compositions include:* Pieces for Organ, published in Das neue Orgelbaum II, 1986; Pieces for Organ, in Pedals Only, 1988; Offrande, 1990; Nocturne, 1992; Deux Chorals, 1992; Cortège, 1996; Various unpublished works. *Recordings:* Organ works of Jean Langlais, 3 recordings; Sept Chorals-Poémes pour les Sept Paroles du Christ, de Charles Tournemire. *Honours:* Recipient, prizes for organ and for composition, Président de la Fédération Francophone des Amis de l'Orgue F.F.A.O., 2003. *Address:* 12 rue Saint-Saëns, 75015 Paris, France.

COGHILL, Harry MacLeod, ARMCM; British opera and concert singer (bass); b. 14 April 1944, Edinburgh, Scotland; m. Anna Sweeny 1970; one s. one d. *Education:* Royal Manchester College of Music, studied singing with Frederick Cox, with Yvonne Rodd-Marling. *Career:* debut with English National Opera, as Seneca in Monteverdi's L'Incoronazione di Poppea, 1971; Concert tour of North America, 1965; Member of Glyndebourne Festival Chorus, 1970, 1971; Principal Bass, English National Opera, 1971–79; Created several roles in contemporary operas; Extensive repertoire in all periods of opera and oratorio; Freelance appearances with English Music Theatre, Handel Opera, Kent Opera, Opera 80 and other English companies, 1979–; Appearances in festivals at Aldeburgh, Belfast, Dortmund, Exeter, Munich, Vienna; Founder, A Song for Ockenden, concert series for The Ockenden Venture, in aid of refugee children, 1980; Lecturer in Singing, School of Music, University of Auckland, New Zealand, 1987. *Contributions:* Educational supplements. *Address:* Derryheen, Hook Heath Road, Woking, Surrey GU22 0LB, England.

COGNET, André; Singer (Bass-baritone); b. 1967, France. *Education:* Marseille Conservatoire; Studio of the Paris Opéra. *Career:* Sang Puccini's Schaunard at Toulouse, in Stravinsky's Pulcinella at the Théâtre des Champs Elyseés, Escamillo in Peter Brook's version of Carmen, baritone roles in Les Contes d'Hoffmann and Mozart's Figaro; Wexford Festival appearances as Gaveston in La Dame Blanche and Donizetti's L'Assedio de Calais; Further engagments as Zuniga in Carmen at Munich, Guglielmo at Karlsruhe, Hamlet at Rouen and Zurga for Opera North; Captain in Gulitt's Wozzeck at Rouen, 1997; Season 1997/98 with Les Noces by Stravinsky under Marek Janowski, L'Enfance du Christ by Berlioz in Madrid, and the title role in Paisiello's Il Re Teodoro a Venezia, at the Teatro La Fenice; Verona Arena 1999 as Escamillo in Carmen; Season 2000–2001 as Puccini's Lescaut, with the Israel Philharmonic and Ravel's L'Enfant et les Sortilèges in Berlin; US debut as Gounod's Mephistopheles for Florida Grand Opera, 2002. *Address:* c/o Musicaglotz, 11 rue Le Verrier, 75006 Paris, France.

COGRAM, John; singer (tenor); b. 1967, Sussex, England. *Education:* Royal College of Music, National Opera Studio and with Janice Chapman; masterclasses with Birgit Nilsson and Luigi Alva. *Career:* Ulm Opera 1994–96, as M. Triquet in Eugene Onegin, Wenzel in The Bartered Bride, Steersman in Fliegende Holländer, Remendado (Carmen) and Bajazet in Handel's Tamerlano; Other roles include Alfredo in La Traviata at Clonter Farm, Pinkerton with English Festival Opera and Rodolfo with English Touring Opera; Oronte in Handel's Alcina in concert performances at Cologne; Basle Opera from 1996, as Pedrillo (Entführung) and Pang in Turandot; Recitals include: Die schöne Müllerin and Dichterliebe. *Honours:* Cuthbert Smith Award, RCM.

COHEN, Arnaldo; Concert Pianist; b. 22 April 1948, Rio de Janeiro, Brazil; 1 s., 2 step-c. *Education:* Engineering University of Rio de Janeiro; Graduate in Piano and Violin, School of Music, Federal University of Rio de Janeiro. *Career:* Debut: Royal Festival Hall, London, 1977; Appearances at Albert Hall, Barbican, Queen Elizabeth Hall and Wigmore Hall in London, La Scala in Milan, Concertgebouw in Amsterdam and Musikverein in Vienna; Performed in the Amadeus Piano Trio, 1988–92; Fellow of RNCM, Manchester, 1992–; Served on the Jury of the Busoni, Liszt and Chopin Competitions; Concerts under Menuhin, Tennstedt, Sanderling and Masur; Masterclasses in Europe, USA and South America; Currently teaching at the Royal Academy of Music, London. *Recordings:* Brasiliana, Three Centuries of Music from Brazil; Chopin 2nd Scherzo, 4th Ballade, Allegro de Concert, Largo and Bolero; Liszt B Minor Sonata, Dante Sonata, Scherzo and March.

Schumann Fantasie op 17, Arabesque op 18, Brahms Handel variations; Liszt Sonata. *Recordings:* For television and radio, BBC, Dutch, German, Italian and others. *Honours:* 1st Prize, Beethoven Competition, 1970; 1st Prize, Busoni Piano Competition, Italy, 1972; Broadwood Fellow in Piano studies at Royal Northern College of Music, 1991; Appointed to the Broadwood Trust Fellowship, Royal Northern College of Music, 1992; Fellow, Royal Northern College of Music honoris causa, 2000. *Telephone:* (20) 7723 7787 (home). *E-mail:* arnalddocohen@ compuserve.com (home). *Current Management:* Arts Management Group, Mr William Capone, St James Building, 1133 Broadway, Suite 1025, New York, 10010, USA. *Fax:* (20) 7738 0909.

COHEN, David; Belgian concert cellist; b. 14 June 1980, Tournai. *Education:* Conservatoire Royal de Bruxelles, 1991–93; Yehudi Menuhin School, 1994–98; Guildhall School of Music and Drama, London, 1998–2002, with Oleg Kogan; Masterclasses with Rostropovich, Natalia Gutman, William Pleeth, Steven Isserlis, Bernard Greenhouse and Boris Pergamenschikov. *Career:* Played in Rostropovich's cello sextet at age 17 and tour in Germany with Saint-Petersburg Philharmonic Orchestra; Int. soloist from age 11 with Belgian, French, Swiss, UK and Polish orchestras including the Polish Philharmonic under Menuhin (Tchaikovsky's Pezzo Capriccioso) and Philharmonia Orchestra, Royal Festival Hall, London (Shostakovitch Concerto) under Sir Charles Mackerras; Youngest Ever Principal Cellist of the Philharmonia Orchestra, 2001. *Recordings:* Lalo Cello Concerto, with the Liège Philharmonic (Cyprès); Lutowslasky pieces with Forlane; Jeunes solistes francophones. *Honours:* numerous grants and awards including First Prize, Int. Music Competition, Wathrelos, France, 1995; 1st Grand Finalist, Audi Int. Competition, UK, 1995; Winner, Geneva Int. Cello Competition, Patrick F. Liechti Special Prize, 2000; Guildhall Gold Medal, 2002; Young Soloist of the Year, Community of French speaking Radios of the World (CRPLF), 2003; Radio Suisse Romande Award, Hattory Foundation, 2003. *Address:* c/o Philharmonia Orchestra, 1st Floor, 125 High Holborn, London, WC1V 6QA, England. *Telephone:* (20) 7274-6116 (home). *Fax:* (7887) 649026 (office). *Website:* www .davidcohen.be.

COHEN, Isidore (Leonard); Violinist and Teacher; b. 16 Dec. 1922, New York, NY, USA; m. Judith Goldberg, 1 s., 1 d. *Education:* Studied violin with Ivan Galamian; Chamber music with Felix Salmond and Hans Letz; BS, Juilliard School of Music, 1948. *Career:* Schneider String Quartet, 1952–55; Juilliard String Quartet, 1958–66; Beaux Arts Trio, 1968–; Appearances as soloist with orchestras and as a recitalist; Associated with Marlboro (Vermont) Music School and Festival, 1957–; Teacher: Juilliard School of Music, 1957–65; Mannes College of Music, 1970–88. *Recordings:* As member of Beaux Arts Trio. *Honours:* Various awards as member of Beaux Arts Trio; Career highlighted in N Delblanco's book The Beaux Arts Trio: A Portrait, 1985. *Address:* c/o Columbia Artists Management Inc, 165 West 57th Street, New York, NY 10019, USA.

COHEN, Joel; Conductor, Lutenist, Writer and Lecturer; b. 23 May 1942, Providence, Rhode Island, USA. *Education:* BA, Composition, Musicology, Brown University, 1963; MA, Harvard University, 1965; Studied theory and composition with Nadia Boulanger, Paris, 1965–67. *Career:* Director, Boston Camerata, 1968–; Guest conductor at various music festivals (Aix-en-Provence, Strasbourg, Tanglewood); Lecturer, Early Music Performance at US and European universities and conservatories; Specialist in Mediaeval, Renaissance and Baroque music. *Recordings:* With Boston Camerata and Cambridge Consort; Johnny Johnson by Weill (Erato). *Honours:* Grand Prix du Disque, 1989. *Address:* c/o The Aaron Concert Management, 729 Boylston Street, Suite 206, Boston, MA 02116, USA.

COHEN, Raymond; Violinist; b. 27 July 1919, Manchester, England; m. 8 Mar 1953, 1 s., 1 d. *Education:* Fellow, Royal Manchester College of Music. *Career:* Debut: As a child; International soloist, having played with major orchestras in many parts of the world; Leader of many orchestras, including Royal Philharmonic Orchestra, 1959–65; Violinist, Cohen Trio; Soloist on BBC radio and television; mem, Incorporated Society of Musicians. *Recordings:* Violinist, Delius's Double Concerto, with Royal Philharmonic Orchestra; Soloist, Robert Farnon's Rhapsody; Saint-Saëns's Introduction and Rondo Capriccioso; Vivaldi's Concerto for 2 violins and orchestra. *Honours:* 1st Prizewinner, Carl Flesch International Competition, 1945; Honorary Member, Royal College of Music. *Address:* 6 Alvanley Gardens, London NW6 1 JD, England.

COHEN, Robert; Concert Cellist; b. 15 June 1959, London, England; m. Rachel Smith 1976. *Education:* Guildhall School of Music, 1975–77; Cello studies with William Pleeth, André Navarra, J Du Pré, M Rostropovich. *Career:* Royal Festival Hall debut, Boccherini Concerto, age 12; London recital debut, Wigmore Hall, age 17; Invited to Tanglewood Festival, USA, 1978; First tour of USA, 1979; Concerts in Europe and Eastern Europe, 1979; Concerts world-wide with major orchestras and eminent conductors, 1980; Many television appearances and radio broadcasts; Visiting Professor, Royal Academy of Music, 1996–; Performs on Bonjour Stradivarius cello dated 1692; mem, Incorporated Society of Musicians; Patron, Beauchamp Music Club; Fellow, Purcell School of Music. *Recordings:* Elgar Cello Concerto; Dvořák Cello Concerto; Grieg Sonata; Rodrigo Concierto en Modo Galante; Virtuoso Cello Music; Beethoven Triple Concerto; Dvořák Complete Piano Trios with Cohen Trio; Schubert String Quintet with Amadeus Quartet; Tchaikovsky Rococo Variations; Franck Sonata. *Honours:* Suggia Prize, 1967–72; Young Concert Artists, New York, 1978; Piatigorsky Prize, 1978; UNESCO Prize, Czechoslovakia, 1980.

COHN, James (Myron); Composer, Musicologist and Inventor; b. 12 Feb. 1928, Newark, New Jersey, USA; m. Eileen B Wions, 3 Sept 1979. *Education:* BS, 1949, MS, 1950, Juilliard School of Music; Postgraduate study in Electronic Music, Hunter College, New York; Study of Musical Composition with Roy Harris, Wayne Barlow and Bernard Wagenaar. *Career:* Musicologist, American Society of Composers, Authors and Publishers, 1954–84; Inventor of various patented control devices for electronic musical instruments; mem, American Federation of Musicians; American Society of Composers, Authors and Publishers; Songwriters' Guild of America. *Compositions include:* Published works: Symphonies Nos 3–8; A Song of the Waters; Variations on The Wayfaring Stranger; Variations on John Henry; The Little Circus; Sonata for Flute and Piano; Statues in the Park, choral; 2 Concertos for Clarinet and String Orchestra. *Recordings include:* Concerto da camera; Quintet for Winds; Little Overture; Sonatina for clarinet and piano; Sonata for flute and piano; Serenade for flute, violin and cello; Trio for piano, violin and cello; Mount Gretna Suite for chamber orchestra; Homage, Tone poem for orchestra; Concerto for piano and orchestra; Concerto for trumpet and strings; Concerto for concertina and strings; Evocations Concerto No. 2 for clarinet and strings; Concerto No. 1 for clarinet and strings; A song of the Waters, Tone poem for orchestra, (Variations on Shenandoah). Recordings for radio, television and films. *Contributions:* Book reviews to Library Journal. *Honours:* Queen Elisabeth of Belgium Prize for Symphony No. 2, 1953; AIDEM Prize for Symphony No. 4. *Address:* 38-62 240th Street, Little Neck, NY 11363, USA.

COHRS, (Benjamin) Gunnar; conductor, music researcher and publicist; b. 1965, Hameln, Germany. *Education:* Jugendmusikschule Hameln, 1972–85; Hochschule für Künste Bremen, 1989–94; University of Adelaide, 1994–95 (as DAAD Scholar); High Distinction Degrees in Conducting, Flute and Voice, 1994; Diploma in Musicology, 1996. *Career:* Conductor of the Jugendstreichorchester Hameln, 1985–90; Bremen String Orchestra, 1991–95; Several choirs; Conducting assistances and appearances; International conducting debut, Russian National Orchestra, Moscow, 2000; Japanese Debut: Royal Flanders Philharmonic, Tokyo, 2001; Principal Guest Conductor of the New Queen's Hall Orchestra, London, 2002; mem, Internationale Bruckner Gesellschaft Wien. *Compositions include:* Chamber Music: amour perdu for Piano, 1994, arranged for small orchestra, 1999. *Publications:* Bruckner, IX Symphony, Finale, (completed performing version), 1993; Frank Martin: Sonata da Chiesa, arranged for flute and strings, 1995; Bruckner, Studienband zum 2. Satz der IX Sinfonie, 1998: Bruckner Two discarded Trios for the IX Sinfonie, completed performing versions, 1998; Bruckner, IX Sinfonie, (new critical edition and report), 1999. *Contributions:* Radio Bremen; Fono Forum; Klassik Heute; BREMER-Die Stadtillustrierte; Weserkurier; Programme notes; CD booklets; essays; articles; papers at international conferences. *Current Management:* Arte Music, Bettina Braun-Angott, Maximilian-Wetzger-Str. 6, 80636, Munich. *Address:* Postfach 107507, 28075 Bremen, Germany. *E-mail:* artiumbremen@yahoo.de.

COKER, Paul; Pianist; b. 1959, London, England. *Education:* Began piano studies aged 5 and entered Yehudi Menuhin School, 1967, piano with Louis Kentner. *Career:* Won National Federation of Music Societies' Concert Award, 1978, and soon gave several London recitals, as well as concerts in France, Germany, Belgium, Netherlands, the USA, Canada and India; Further study at Tanglewood, USA, from 1980, winning the Jackson Master Award there; Has played with most leading British orchestras and with the Berlin Philharmonic; The Grieg Concerto with the Belgian National Symphony; Many recitals with Yehudi Menuhin in Europe, the USA, Far East and Australia.

COKU, Alexandru; Singer (Soprano); b. 1963, USA. *Education:* Studied with Margaret Harshaw at Indiana University. *Career:* Has sung in Europe from 1988, notably as Euridice to the Orpheus of Jochen Kowalski at Covent Garden and as Pamina at the rebuilt Frankfurt Opera, 1991; Further engagements as Pamina at Vienna, Munich and Düsseldorf; Amsterdam, 1992, as Ismene in Mozart's Mitridate; US appearances as Anne Trulove in The Rake's Progress at Chicago (1990) and Cecilio in Lucio Silla at San Francisco (1991); Season 1995–96 as Mozart's Elektra, Offenbach's Antonia and Constanze at Düsseldorf, Romilda in Handel's Xerxes at Cologne, 1998; Giulietta in Les Contes

d'Hoffmann; Season 2000–01 as Mozart's Countess in Cologne, Ellen Orford at Nancy and Handel's Agrippina for Glimmerglass Opera. *Address:* c/o Cologne Opera, Offenbachplatz, Pf. 180241, D–50505 Cologne, Germany.

COLAIANNI, Domenico; Singer (Baritone); b. 1964, Italy. *Education:* N. Piccinni Conservatory, Bari. *Career:* Early appearances as Mengotto in Piccinni's La Cecchina, Papageno and Schaunard in La Bohème; Enrico in Donizetti's Il Campanello and Slook in Rossini's La Cambiale at Bologna; Cimarosa's Maestro di Capella at Parma, Ping in Turandot at Lecce and Bizet's Don Procopio in Novara; Further engagements in Australia, in Paisiello's Il Barbiere di Siviglia, Rossini's Il Signor Bruschino in Tokyo and Osaka, and Donizetti's Olivio e Pasquale in Germany; Operas by Salieri, Vivaldi and Hasse in Budapest; Sang in the first modern performance of I Rantzau, by Mascagni, at Livorno; Festival of Martina Franca in Leo's Amor vuol sofferenza, and as Lisandro in Piccinni's L'Americano, 1996. *Recordings include:* L'Americano (Dynamic).

COLBERT, Brendan; Composer; b. 11 Sept. 1956, Ballarat, Victoria, Australia. *Education:* Studied with Brenton Broadstock, 1983–86 Riccardo Formosa 1986–88; National Orchestral Composers School, 1991, 1995. *Compositions include:* Passages for alto saxophone, electric guitar, piano and percussion, 1987; Murderers of Calm for ensemble, 1987; Agite II for mandolin, 1989; Fourplay for viola, cello, clarinet and piano, 1991; Agite I for flute, 1991; Parallaxis for ensemble, 1993; Agite II for piano, 1993–95; Mirror, Picture, Echo, Shadow, Dream for cello, flute, percussion and piano, 1994; Entfernt for string orchestra, 1994; Sphinx for ensemble, 1995; Sanctuary for orchestra, 1995. *Honours:* Warringah Eisteddfod Young Composers Competiton, 1985. *Address:* c/o APRA, 1A Eden Street, Crows Nest, NSW 2065, Australia.

COLD, Ulrik; Singer (Bass); b. 15 May 1939, Copenhagen, Denmark. *Education:* As Singer, privately educated in Copenhagen and Århus; Bachelor of Laws from Copenhagen University. *Career:* Sang in concert from 1963, then in opera in Copenhagen; Engaged at Kassel, 1969–71; Komische Oper Berlin, 1971, as Massenet's Don Quixote; Sang Sarastro in the Bergman film version of Die Zauberflöte; Intendant of the Royal Opera Copenhagen, 1975–77; Baroque repertory concerts in France, Germany, Netherlands, Switzerland and Scandinavia; Operatic roles include: Wagner's Marke, Landgraf and Gurnemanz; Verdi's Padre Guardiano and Zaccharia; Roles in works by Handel, Monteverdi and Rameau; US debut, San Francisco, as Sarastro, 1980; Alazim in Zaide, Wexford Festival, 1981; Sang at Teatro Comunale Bologna, 1987; The General in The Gambler by Prokofiev, English National Opera, 1991; Saul in a concert version of Nielsen's Saul and David, London, 1992. *Recordings:* Armide by Lully; Admeto by Handel; Rameau's Hippolyte et Aricie and Handel's Xerxes; L'Incoronazione di Poppea; St Matthew Passion by Bach; Ulrik Cold Sings Carl Nielsen; Schnittke's Faust Cantata. *Address:* c/o Allied Artists Agency, 42 Montpelier Square, London SW7 1JZ, England.

COLDING-JORGENSEN, Henrik; Composer, Organist, Pedagogue and Choir Leader; b. 21 March 1944, Riisskov, Denmark; m. (1) Birgit Nielsen, 1966–87, (2) Mette Bramso, 1992–99, 1 d. *Education:* Organist, 1966, Organ Pedagogue, Royal Danish Conservatory. *Career:* Organ teacher; Teacher of Musical Theory; Organist; Choir Leader; Producer of radio and television programmes; Composer; Chairman of Board, Holstebro Electronic Music Studio, 1977–85; Member, Musical Committee, Roskilde County, 1979–87; Member, Committee of Representatives of State Music Council, 1981–91; Member, Committee of Representatives of State Art Council, 1981–85; Member, Danish Arts Council, 1981–84; mem, Danish Composer Society, Board, 1981–91; Danish ISCM, Board until 1982; Danish Organist and Cantor Society, Board, 1992–95; Danish Choirleaders, 1996. *Compositions include:* Ave Maria, 1974; Balances, 1974; To Love Music, 1975; Victoria Through the Forest, 1975; Boast, 1980; Dein Schweigen, 1982; Recitativ and Fuga; An Die Nachgeborenen ll, 1984; Du Sollst Nicht, 1984; Sic Enim, 1985; Nuup Kangerlua, 1985; Partita, aria e minuetto, 1986; Le Alpi Nel Cuore, 1988; 2 Songs by Keats, 1988; Nunc Est, 1989; The Soul and The Butterfly, 1990; Babylon, 1991; As a Traveller, 1992; Krystal; Metamorfose for string quartet, 1993; Discourse with Time, 1996; Sourires, 1997; Four British Songs, 1997; Duo Viri in Vestibus Albis, 1999; Dolori, 2000; Elegie-Wiegenlied, 2000; Englens Hånd, 2001; Primavere, 2002; Kyrie Agnus Dei, 2002. *Honours:* Various bursaries, prizes and commissions; Concours International de Composition Musicale Opera et Ballet, Geneva, 1985. *Address:* Kildehuset 3, 3.tv, 2670 Greve, Denmark. *E-mail:* mail@hc-j.dk. *Website:* www.hc-j.dk.

COLE, Rosamund; Singer (Soprano); b. 1968, England. *Education:* Royal Northern College of Music; National Opera Studio, London; Cologne Opera Studio. *Career:* Appearances with British Youth Opera, 1992 and 1993, as Susanna in Le nozze di Figaro and Ninetta in La Gazza Ladra; With Opera North in 1996 as Barbarina; At Cologne Opera, 1996–98, as Ännchen in Der Freischütz, Priestess in Aida, Johanna in Sondheim's

Sweeney Todd, Barbarina, Despina, Zerlina and Gretel in Hänsel und Gretel; Darmstadt Staatstheater, 1998–2000, as Serpetta in La Finta Giardiniera, Hannchen in Der Vetter aus Dingsda, Frasquita in Carmen, Valencienne in Die Lustige Witwe and Gretel; Concert appearances include Wigmore Hall recital in 1994 and Flowermaiden in Parsifal with the Cologne Philharmonie with James Conlon. *Honours:* Countess of Munster Award; Sybil Tutton Prize; Wolfson Prize Grant. *Address:* Music International, 13 Ardilaun Road, London N5 2QR, England.

COLE, Steve; Singer (Tenor); b. 1954, USA. *Career:* Sang with Washington Opera from 1981, Aix-en-Provence (as Monostatos), 1982, and in Paris, Avignon (Henze's Boulevard Solitude), and Nice; New York Metropolitan debut, 1987, as Brighella in Ariadne auf Naxos; San Francisco Opera from 1990; Other modern repertory includes the premieres of Medea by Gavin Bryars (Lyon, 1984) and La Noche Triste by Prodromidès (Nancy, 1989); Other buffo and character roles include Bardolph in Falstaff, Pong in Turandot and Sellem in The Rake's Progress; Sang John Styx in Orphée aux Enfers, Geneva, 1998; Season 1999–2000 as Monostatos in Barcelona and Osmin in Haydn's l'Incontro Improvviso at Eisenstadt. *Address:* c/o San Francisco Opera, War Memorial House, Van Ness Avenue, San Francisco, CA 94102, USA.

COLE, Tobias; Singer (Countertenor); b. 1969, Australia. *Education:* BMus (Hons) University of Sydney, 1993, ARCM, Royal College of Music, 1994. *Career:* Appearances included Medoro in Handel's Orlando for West Australian Opera, Eustazio in Rinaldo for Opera Australia and Ulisse in Deidamia for the London Handel Festival; Title role in Rinaldo for Abbey Opera; Other roles include Farnace in Mitridate and Handel's Julius Caesar; Oratorios include St Matthew Passion for City of Bath Bach Choir, Messiah for Queensland and Adelaide Symphonies, Bernstein's Chichester Psalms with the Sydney Phiharmonia and Handel's Brockes Passion for the London Handel Festival, 2000–2001; Sang in Purcell's Fairy Queen for the English Bach Festival at the Linbury Theatre, Covent Garden, 2001.

COLE, Vinson; Singer (Tenor); b. 21 Nov. 1950, Kansas City, Kansas, USA. *Education:* Studied at the Curtis Institute, Philadelphia. *Career:* Debut: Sang Werther in the opera by Massenet while still a student, 1975; Sang in the premiere of Jubilee by Ulysses Kay at Jackson, Mississippi, in 1976; European debut, 1976, with Welsh National Opera, as Belmonte in Die Entführung aus dem Serail; Later appearances in Stuttgart, Naples, Salzburg, Paris and Marseilles; St Louis, 1976–80, as Tamino and Rossini's Comte Ory; New York City Opera, 1981, as Fenton in Die lustigen Weiber von Windsor; Other roles include Gennaro in Lucrezia Borgia, Nadir in Les Pêcheurs de Perles, Lenski in Eugene Onegin, Gluck's Orfeo and Gounod's Faust; Sang in Mozart's Requiem under Georg Solti at Vienna, 1991; Sang Donizetti's Edgardo at Detroit, Ferrando at Seattle, 1992; Nadir in Les Pêcheurs de Perles in Seattle, 1994; Sang Jason in Cherubini's Medea, Athens 1995; Don Carlo in the French version of Verdi's opera, Brussels, 1996; Renaud in Gluck's Armide, to open the 1996–97 Season at La Scala; Season 1999–2000 as Mozart's Titus at Covent Garden (house debut); Season 2000–01 as Gerald in Lakmé at Seattle, the Berlioz Faust at Edinburgh and Cavaradossi in Sydney. *Address:* c/o Seattle Opera Association, PO Box 9248, Seattle, WA 98109, USA.

COLEMAN, Tim; Stage Director; b. 30 Oct. 1949, Eastbourne, Sussex, England. *Education:* Cambridge and Amsterdam Conservatory, composition. *Career:* Wrote incidental music for over 30 plays, then Chief Dramaturg of Netherlands Opera; Debut as Director with Opera Northern Ireland in Die Fledermaus, 1990, returned 1991 for Le nozze di Figaro and 1992 Rigoletto; United States debut with The Beggar's Opera for the Manhattan School of Music; Season 1991–92, Tosca for Minnesota Opera and Opera Omaha, Tamerlano for Dublin Opera Theatre, and The Merry Wives of Windsor for the Guildhall School of Music; Season 1992–93, L'Italiana in Algeri for Dublin Grand Opera/Opera Ireland, Così fan tutte in Oklahoma City; Season 1993–94, Rigoletto in Hong Kong, L'Isola disabitata in New York, Tosca in Indianapolis, Le nozze di Figaro for the Kirov Opera in the Mariinsky Theatre, St Petersburg; Festivals of Mikkele, Finland, Schleswig-Holstein, Germany, and Beth Shean (Israel) Season, 1994–95; Un Giorno di Regno, Dorset Opera; La Traviata, Hong Kong; Le nozze di Figaro, The Hague, Netherlands. *Current Management:* Athole Still International Management, Forresters Hall, 25–27 Westow Street, London, SE19 3RY, England. *Telephone:* (20) 8771-5271. *Fax:* (20) 8768-6600. *Website:* www.atholestill.com.

COLEMAN-WRIGHT, Peter; Singer (baritone); b. 1958, Australia; m. Cheryl Barker. *Education:* Studied in London with Otakar Kraus, Joan Hammond, Paul Hamburger and Geoffrey Parsons. *Career:* Has sung at Glyndebourne as Guglielmo, Demetrius, Dandini, Morales in Carmen and Sid in Albert Herring; English National Opera as Niels Lyhne in Fennimore and Gerda, Rossini's Barber, Schaunard, Billy Budd and Don Giovanni; Australian Opera as Mozart's Count; Covent Garden,

Dandini, then Don Alvaro in Rossini's Il Viaggio a Reims and Papageno; Bordeaux Opera, Guglielmo, Masetto; Victoria State Opera, Wolfram, Papageno, Valentin in Faust; Further engagements with Netherlands Opera, the Fenice Venice and the Australian Opera; Grand Théâtre Genève; Other roles include Eisenstein and Falke in Die Fledermaus, Masetto, Rossini's Figaro, Wolfram in Tannhäuser, Zurga and the Soldier/Brother in Busoni's Doctor Faust; Lieder recitals at the South Bank, Covent Garden, Théâtre du Châtelet in Paris and the Aix and Spoleto Festivals; Brahms Requiem and Mahler Kindertotenlieder in Austria; Concerts in Netherlands, Spain, Germany, Finland, Iceland and for the Australian Broadcasting Commission; Premiere of Inquest of Love by Jonathan Harvey, English National Opera, 1993; Wigmore Recital, 1993; Bordeaux, Count Almaviva, 1993; Australian Opera, Don Giovanni, 1993; Staatsoper Munich, Don Giovanni; Marcello, Grande Théâtre Genève and Covent Garden in Eugene Onegin, ENO and Lyric Opera Queensland; Billy Budd, Covent Garden; Chorèbe in Les Troyens, Australian Opera; Sang Escamillo in Carmen at the Opéra Bastille, Paris, 1997; Sang in premiere production by a British company of Strauss's Die Liebe der Danaë, Garsington, 1999; Concerts with BBC Symphony including the British premiere of Hindemith's Mörder Hoffnung der Frauen; Season 2000–01 with The Prisoner (ENO), Don Giovanni (Vancouver) and Die Liebe der Danaë (New York). *Recordings include:* Oedipus Rex by Stravinsky, EMI; Mass of Life; Fennimore and Gerda by Delius; Saint Paul by Mendelssohn; Paul Bunyan, The Pilgrim's Progress. *Honours:* Glyndebourne Touring Prize. *Current Management:* Harrison/Parrott Ltd, 12 Penzance Place, London, W11 4PA, England. *Telephone:* (20) 7229 9166. *Fax:* (20) 7221 5042. *Website:* www.harrisonparrott.com.

COLES, Samuel; Flautist; b. 1964, England. *Education:* Studied with James Galway, at the Guildhall School of Music and at the Paris Conservatoire with Jean-Pierre Rampal. *Career:* Solo and chamber music performances in the United Kingdom and Europe in Holland Concertgebouw and The Hague, with the Bordeaux Symphony, the Monte Carlo Orchestra and the London Soloists Chamber Orchestra; Mozart Concerto K313 with the Orchestre de Paris at Rampal's Gala Concert, Paris; Chamber recitals with members of the European Community Youth Orchestra and duet partnership with harpist Isabelle Courret; Concerto engagements with Kenneth Montgomery, Aldo Ceccato and Alain Lombard; As orchestral player has performed under Simon Rattle, Claudio Abbado and Pierre Boulez. *Recordings include:* Mozart Concerti with the English Chamber Orchestra under Yehudi Menuhin. *Honours:* Premier Prix at the Paris Conservatoire, 1987; Winner, Scheveningen International Flute Competition, Netherlands, and National Flute Association Young Artists' Competition, San Diego, USA. *Address:* c/o Guildhall School of Music, Barbican, London, EC 2Y 8DT, England.

COLETTI, Paul; Concert Violist and Professor; b. 1959, Scotland. *Education:* Studied at Royal Scottish Academy, International Menuhin Academy, Banff Center and Juilliard School; Teachers included Alberto Lysy, Sándor Végh and Don McInnes. *Career:* Solo concerts at the Queen Elizabeth Hall, Geneva, Buenos Aires, Edinburgh, Assisi, Toulon and Harrogate Festivals; Recitals at Toronto, Chicago, Cincinnati, Belgrade and Los Angeles; NY debut recital in 1983; Member of the Menuhin Festival Piano Quartet; Chamber performances with Menuhin in Paris, London and Gstaad; Member of Chamber Society of Lincoln Center, NY; Further engagements with Camerata Lysy Ensemble and playing Bartók's Viola Concerto in Berlin; Former Professor of Viola and Chamber Music at Menuhin Academy; Former Head of Viola Department at Peabody Conservatory, Baltimore; Head of String Department at University of Washington, Seattle; Guest conducted the New Japan Philharmonic in Tokyo. *Compositions:* From My Heart, 1994; Viola Tango, 1994; Dream Ocean, 1995. *Recordings:* Chamber pieces by Mozart, Strauss and Mendelssohn; 20 albums recorded. *Current Management:* Tom Parker Artists. *Address:* c/o University of Washington, Music Department (Strings Faculty), Seattle, Washington, USA.

COLGRASS, Michael (Charles); Composer; b. 22 April 1932, Chicago, Illinois, USA; m. Ulla Damgaard, 25 Nov 1966, 1 s. *Education:* BMus, University of Illinois, 1956; Composition with Lukas Foss, Berkshire Music Center, Tanglewood, summers 1952, 1954; Darius Milhaud, Aspen, Colorado Music School, summer 1953; Wallingford Riegger, 1958–59, Ben Weber, 1959–62, New York. *Career:* Freelance solo percussionist, various New York groups, 1956–67. *Compositions include:* Stage: Virgil's Dream, music theatre, 1967; Nightingale Inc, comic opera, 1971; Something's Gonna Happen, children's musical, 1978; Orchestral: Auras, harp, orchestra, 1973; Concertmasters, 3 violins, orchestra, 1975; Letter from Mozart, 1976; Déjà vu, 4 percussionists, orchestra, 1977; Delta, violin, clarinet, percussion, orchestra, 1979; Memento, 2 pianos, orchestra, 1982; Demon, amplified piano, percussion, tape, radio, orchestra, 1984; Chaconne, viola, orchestra, 1984; The Schubert Birds, 1989; Snow Walker, Organ, orchestra, 1990; Arctic Dreams, symphonic band, 1991; Chamber: Wolf, cello, 1976; Flashback, 5 brass; Winds of Nagual: A Musical Fable, wind ensemble, 1985; Strangers, Variations, clarinet, viola, piano, 1986; Folklines, string quartet, 1987; Piano pieces; The Earth's a Baked Apple, chorus, orchestra, 1969; New People, mezzo-soprano, viola, piano, 1969; Image of Man, 4 solo voices, chorus, orchestra, 1974; Theatre of the Universe, solo voices, chorus, orchestra, 1975; Best Wishes USA, 4 solo voices, double chorus, 2 jazz bands, folk instruments, orchestra, 1976; Beautiful People, chorus, 1976; Mystery Flowers of Spring, 1978; Night of the Raccoon, 1979. *Recordings:* Chaconne; Variations for 4 Drums and Viola; The Earth's a Baked Apple; New People; Déjà vu; Light Spirit; As Quiet As; Fantasy Variations; Concertmasters; Night of the Raccoon; Three Brothers; Many others. *Contributions:* Articles to New York Times. *Honours:* Guggenheim Fellow, 1964, 1968; Rockefeller Grant, 1968; Ford Foundation Grant, 1972; Pulitzer Prize in Music, 1978; Emmy Awards, 1982, 1988; Jules Léger Chamber Music Prize. *Address:* 583 Palmerston Avenue, Toronto, Ontario M6G 2P6, Canada.

COLIBAN, Sorin; Singer (Bass); b. 1971, Romania. *Education:* Studied at the Bucharest Conservatory. *Career:* Debut: Bart ók's Bluebeard at Bucharest, 1993; Season 1995–96 with Don Giovanni at Athens, Royal Opera debut as Alvaro in a concert performance of Verdi's Alzira, and the Monk in Don Carlos at the London Proms; Season 1996–97 included Colline at Royal Opera House, Covent Garden; In 1997 debut at San Francisco Opera as Mozart's Bartolo; Season 1998–99 Alidoro (La Cenerentola) at Palais Garnier; Capelio in I Capuleti e i Montecchi (Bastille-Paris) and Zuniga at Monte Carlo; 1999–2000 Capulet (Roméo et Juliette) at Covent Garden, Raimondo (Lucia) at San Francisco; Other roles include Procida (Les Vêpres Siciliennes) and Fiesco (Simon Boccanegra). *Honours:* Winner of Don Giovanni Competition in Athens and national competitions in Romania. *Address:* c/o Theateragentur Erich Seitter, Opernring 8/13, 1010 Vienna, Austria.

COLIN, Georges; Composer; b. 15 June 1921, Schaerbeek, Brussels, Belgium; m. Albertine De Clerck, 17 Mar 1948, 2 s., 2 d. *Education:* Royal Conservatory of Music, Brussels; Harmony, 1943; Counterpoint, 1948; Fugue, 1949; History of Music, 1959. *Career:* Teacher, Athenee and Ecole Normale de Schaerbeek, 1976; Headmaster, Academy of Music, Anderlecht, 1976–81; mem, SABAM; CeBeDeM. *Compositions:* Symphonie breve for orchestra, 1950; Cinq Poèmes français de R M Rilke for voice and piano, 1952; Woodwind Quartet, 1955; Concertstuck La Folia, for contrebasse and orchestra, 1964; Cinq Croquis d'eleves, for piano, 1962; Sonatine for violin and piano, 1962; Sonate for flute and piano, 1965; La Porte de pierre, poem of André Doms, for baritone solo, mixed choir and orchestra, 1969; Phantasme for harp, 1977; Sequences for violin and piano, 1978; Pièces brèves for piano, 1996; Lithos, atmosphères pour 14 intruments, 1997; Never More, for cello, marimba and piano, 1999; Femme de Meuse–7 poèmes d'André Doms, for mezzo, flute and piano, 2000; Cinq Eclats D'"Illuminee"–poèmes d'André Doms, for soprano (or tenor), oboe, clarinet and cello, 2000; Five Short Pieces for string quartet, 2000; Never More, Cathie, 2nd version, for cello, marimba and piano, 2000; With Jeanne Colin: Le Tombeau d'André Jolivet for 2 pianos, 1975; Short Pieces for harps, 1976; Flute Quartet, 1976; Two Pieces for flute and harp, 1979; Cantate Pour Le Vif Des Temps, poems of André Doms, tryptique profane pour soprano and baritone solos, mixed choir and orchestra; Ryoan-Ji, 1986; Corps de feu, 1991. *Publications:* 9 Chants Populaire, Chants and Danses Populaires; Doucle France, flauto dolce; La Flute à bec alto (méthode en 3 vols). *Honours:* Médaille Commemorative de la Guerre, 1940–45; Prix de Composition de la Province de Brabant, 1964; Lettres à un jeune compositeur, 1996. *Address:* Haut du Village 40, 5600 Sautour, Philippeville, Belgium.

COLLARD, Jean-Philippe; Concert Pianist; b. 27 Jan. 1948, Mareuil-sur-Ay, France; 3 s., 1 d. *Education:* Studied at the Paris Conservatoire, 1959–64. *Career:* Performances throughout France and in Russia, Japan, Spain, Italy, Germany, Switzerland and the Netherlands; US debut in a series of concerts with the San Francisco Symphony under Seiji Ozawa; Regular appearances with the New York Philharmonic; British engagements with the London Symphony, Royal Philharmonic, Philharmonia, Hallé, City of Birmingham Symphony, Scottish Chamber and BBC Symphony, Welsh and Philharmonic Orchestras; Conductors include Dorati, Previn, Mehta, Lombard, Skrowaczewski, Loughran, Rattle, Maksymiuk, Dutoit and Pritchard; Tour of Britain, 1991, with the Orchestre de Paris under Semyon Bychkov; Season 1992–93 included concerts with the New York Philharmonic under Previn, the Philadelphia Orchestra and the Royal Scottish Orchestra; Played Rachmaninov's 1st Concerto at the London Proms, 1993; Poulenc's Concerto for Two Pianos, with Pascal Rogé at the 1999 Proms; Opened the Wigmore Hall's Chopin Series, 1999; Season 1999–2000 engaged to play with the Philharmonia and the Royal Scottish National Orchestra. *Recordings:* Over 50 including Rachmaninov Etudes Tableaux; Brahms Hungarian Dances, with Michel Béroff; Ravel Concertos with the

Orchestre National de France; Saint-Saëns Complete Concertos with André Previn and the Royal Philharmonic; Franck and Magnard Violin Sonatas with Augustin Dumay; Chopin Ballades and 3rd Sonata. *Honours:* Premier Prix du Conservatoire de Paris; Grand Prix du Concours National des Artistes Solistes; Prix Albert Roussel; Grand Prix du Concours International Marguérite Long/Jacques Thibaud; Record of the Year, USA, 1978, 1979; Prize, French Recording Academy, 1978, 1981, 1982; Chevalier des Arts et des Lettres. *Current Management:* Sulivan Sweetland. *Address:* c/o Sulivan Sweetland, 28 Albion Street, London W2 2AX, England.

COLLIER, Gilman (Frederick); Composer, Conductor, Pianist and Teacher; b. 14 April 1929, New York, NY, USA. *Education:* AB, Harvard University, 1950; Yale School of Music, 1950–51; Mannes Music School, 1951–53; Studied theory and composition with Walter Piston, Paul Hindemith, Bohuslav Martinů, conducting with Carl Bamberger, Leonard Bernstein and Pierre Monteux, piano privately with Nadia Reisenberg. *Career:* Music Director, Conductor, the Monmouth Symphony Orchestra, 1964–72; Faculty Member, New School for Social Research, New York City, 1953–60; Faculty Member, Westchester Conservatory of Music, White Plains, New York, 1954–74; Faculty Member, 1969, Assistant Director, 1975–95, Monmouth Conservatory of Music. *Compositions:* 3 piano sonatas and many shorter works for piano solo; Sonata for 1 piano, 4 hands; Duo sonatas for flute, oboe, English horn, clarinet, French horn, trumpet, violin, viola and cello with piano; String Quintet; Fantasy for double-reed ensemble; Trios for flute, violin, piano, violin, cello, piano and oboe, English horn and piano; 2 String Quartets; Piano quintet; 4 Chicago Psalms, SSAA; Concerto Grosso for string orchestra and piano; Almande Smedelyn and Divertimento for double reed ensemble; Two Song Cycles for voice and orchestra or piano; Sinfonietta for classical orchestra, 1997. *Address:* 65 Larchwood Avenue, Oakhurst, NJ 07755, USA.

COLLINS, Anne, ARCM, LRAM; British opera and concert singer (contralto); b. 29 Aug. 1943, Durham, England. *Education:* Royal College of Music, London. *Career:* debut as Governess in The Queen of Spades, SWO, Coliseum; English National Opera; Covent Garden; Welsh National Opera Company; Glyndebourne Festival; Scottish Opera; Grand Théâtre Genève; Canadian Opera Company; Théâtre de la Monnaie Brussels; Châtelet Paris; Opéra Bastille, Paris; Hamburg Staatsoper; La Scala Milan; Roles included Erda, Waltraute, Mrs Herring and Ulrica; Mistress Quickly, Florence Pike, Auntie, Mrs Sedley, Baba the Turk, Marcellina; Beroe and Akhrosimova in the British stage premieres of The Bassarids and War and Peace; Sosostris (Midsummer Marriage) and Anna in Les Troyens, (Covent Garden debut, 1977), Scottish Opera, Opera North; BBC Promenade Concerts; Recordings and song recitals; Concerts with major orchestras and choral societies in the United Kingdom and Europe; Toured Australia for ABC; Video films of Gilbert and Sullivan operas, Gondoliers, Mikado, Iolanthe, Patience and Princess Ida, 1983; Sang the Angel of Death in the premiere of MacMillan's Inès de Castro, Edinburgh, 1996. *Recordings:* Erda, Rhinegold and Siegfried (English National Opera, Goodall); Janáček Glagolitic Mass, Kempe; Vivaldi Cantatas; Elgar Coronation Ode; Third Lady in Die Zauberflöte; Mrs Peachum in Britten's version of The Beggar's Opera; Dame Carruthers in Yeomen of the Guard; Mrs Sedley in Peter Grimes; Mrs Herring in Albert Herring; Empress Persicaria in The Poisoned Kiss. *Current Management:* Askonas Holt Ltd, Lonsdale Chambers, 27 Chancery Lane, London, WC2A 1PF, England. *Telephone:* (20) 7400-1700. *Fax:* (20) 7400-1799. *E-mail:* info@askonasholt.co.uk. *Website:* www.askonasholt.co.uk.

COLLINS, Kenneth; Singer (Tenor); b. 21 Oct. 1935, Birmingham, England. *Education:* Studied with Charles Dean and Ettore Campogaliani. *Career:* Debut: Camden Festival 1970, as Marcello in the British premiere of Leoncavallo's La Bohème; Has sung with Welsh National Opera, Scottish Opera, Covent Garden, Aldeburgh Festival, English National Opera, Paris Opéra, NY City Opera, Colon/Buenos Aires, the Australian Opera, Strasbourg, Cologne, Granada, Valence, Madrid, Florence, Los Angeles; Repertoire includes Calaf, Manrico, Alvaro, Don Carlos, Radames, Gustavus, Dick Johnson, Andrea Chénier, Ernani and Cavaradossi; Season 1994–95 with Australian Opera as Canio and Ismaele (Nabucco); Cavaradossi, 1998. *Honours:* Awarded Australia Medal 1993 for services to opera. *Current Management:* Jenifer Eddy Artists' Management, 11/596 St Kilda Road, Melbourne 3004, Australia.

COLLINS, Michael; Clarinettist; b. 27 Jan. 1962, London, England. *Education:* Began clarinet studies aged 10; Royal College of Music with David Hamilton; Further studies with Thea King. *Career:* BBC television Young Musician of the Year while still at school; Other awards include Frederick Thurston Prize, 1st Prize in Leeds National Competition and Concert Artists' Guild of New York Amcon Award, 1983; Carnegie Hall debut, 1984; BBC Promenade Concert debut, 1984, with Thea Musgrave's Concerto; 1985 Proms season played the Copland Concerto and was soloist in Bernstein's Prelude, Fugue and Riffs; Appointed youngest ever Professor at the Royal College of Music, 1985;

Played the Finzi Concerto with the City of London Sinfonia in 1987; Performances of Weber's 2nd Concerto conducted by Stanislaw Skrowaczewski and Esa-Pekka Salonen; Appointed principal clarinet of the Philharmonia Orchestra, 1988; Associated with the Takacs Quartet, the Nash Ensemble and the pianists Noriko Ogawa and Kathryn Stott in chamber music; Recital partnership with Mikhail Pletnev, piano; Played Malcolm Arnold's 2nd Concerto at the Last Night of the London Proms, 1993; Stravinsky's Ebony Concerto at South Bank, London, 1999; Messiaen's Quartet for the End of Time at the 1999 London Prom concerts. *Recordings:* Finzi's Concerto; Bernstein's Prelude, Fugue and Riffs and Stravinsky's Ebony Concerto; Quintets by Mozart and Brahms with the Nash Ensemble. *Address:* c/o Clarion/ Seven Muses, 64 Whitehall Park, London N19 3 TN, England.

COLLINS, Michael (Augustus); Conductor and Pianist; b. 16 Oct. 1948, Sydney, Australia; m. Lynette Kay Jennings, 24 Nov 1971, 2 s. *Education:* CBHS, St Mary's Cathedral, Sydney (Leaving Certificate, 1965); Performers and Teachers Diploma in Piano, New South Wales State Conservatorium of Music, 1965–68; Conducting Hochschule für Musik, Vienna, 1973–74. *Career:* Repetiteur and Conductor, Australian Opera, 1970–73; Repetiteur, Vienna Staatsoper, 1974–77; Repetiteur and Conductor, Württembergische Staatsoper, Stuttgart, 1977–79; Musical Director, Stuttgart Ballet, 1979–84; Conductor, Bayerische Staatsoper, Munich, 1984–90; 1 Kapellmeister Staatstheater Braunschweig, Guest Conductor, Deutsche Oper, Berlin, 1990. *Address:* c/o Deutsche Oper Berlin, Richard Wagnerstrasse 10, 1000 Berlin, Germany.

COLLINS, Michael B.; Professor of Musicology; b. 26 July 1930, Turlock, California, USA. *Education:* BA, 1957, MA, 1958, PhD, 1963, Stanford University. *Career:* Eastman School of Music, 1964–68; School of Music, University of North Texas, Denton, 1968–2001, retired; mem, American Musicological Society. *Publications:* Editor, Alessandro Scarlatti's Tigrane, 1983; Co-Editor, Opera and Vivaldi, 1984; Editor, Gioachino Rossini's Otello, 1994. *Contributions:* Dramatic Theory and the Italian Baroque Libretto, Cadential Structures and Accompanimental Practices in Eighteenth-Century Italian Recitative, Brazio Bracciolo's Orlando furioso: A History and Synopsis of the Libretto, in Opera and Vivaldi; The Performance of Sesquialtera and Hemiolia in the 16th century, 1964; The Performance of Triplets in the 17th and 18th Centuries, 1966, A Re-examination of Notes inégales, 1967, In Defence of the French Trill, 1973, The Literary Background of Bellini's I Capuleti e i Montecchi, 1982, in Journal of the American Musicological Society; A reconsideration of French Over-dotting, Music and Letters, 1969. *Honours:* Fulbright-Hays Grant for research in Italy, 1963–64. *Address:* College of Music, University of North Texas, Denton, TX 76203, USA. *E-mail:* mbc0019@unt.edu.

COLLOT, Serge; Violinist; b. 27 Sept. 1923, Paris, France. *Education:* Studied at the Paris Conservatoire, 1944–48 (composition with Arthur Honegger). *Career:* Co-founder and member of the Parrenin Quartet, 1944–57; French String Trio from 1960; Violist with the Domaine Musical Concerts, 1953–70, and premiered the Sequenza for viola by Berio; Teacher at the Paris Conservatoire from 1969 and violist with the orchestra of the Paris Opéra until 1986. *Address:* c/o Conservatoire National, 14 Rue de Madrid, 75008 Paris, France.

COLOMBARA, Carlo; Singer (Bass); b. 1964, Bologna, Italy. *Career:* Sang at Teatro Donizetti, Bergamo, 1985, in a Young Singers Concert; Teatro dell'Opera Rome as Silva in Ernani and Wurm in Luisa Miller; Creon in Oedipus Rex by Stravinsky at Venice, Banquo in Macbeth and Oroveso in Norma in Tokyo; Guest appearances at Vienna Staatsoper, Bolshoi Moscow, London, Berlin, Buenos Aires, Brussels and San Francisco; La Scala debut, 1989, as Procida in I Vespri Siciliani, and appeared in Moscow with the company of La Scala in Turandot and I Capuleti e i Montecchi; Verdi Requiem at Festival Hall, London, 1990; Sang Assur in Semiramide at Venice, 1990, Rodolfo in La Sonnambula; Engagements with such conductors as Giulini, Colin Davis, Gianandrea Gavazzeni, Maazel, Sawallisch and Solti; Sang Raimondo in Lucia di Lammermoor at Munich, 1991, Padre Guardiano at Cremona and Colline at 1992 Verona Arena Festival; Attila in Verdi's opera at Macerata, 1996; Season 1996 as Verdi's Oberto at Montpellier, Oroveso at Houston and Enrico (Anna Bolena) at Bologna: Moor in I Masnadieri for the Royal Opera at Edinburgh, 1998; Season 2000–01 as Genoa as Verdi's Attila and Roger (Jérusalem), at Madrid, as Silva in Ernani, and at Zürich as King Philip in Don Carlos; Television appearances include Aida and Lucia di Lammermoor from La Scala. *Recordings:* Colline in La Bohème; Verdi Requiem; Handel's Rinaldo. *Honours:* Winner, GB Viotti International Competition, Vercelli, 1985. *Address:* c/o Teatro alla Scala, Via Filodrammatica 2, 20121 Milan Italy.

COLONELLO, Attilio; stage director and stage designer; b. 9 Nov. 1930, Milan, Italy. *Education:* studied architecture with Gio Ponti and Ernesto Rogers in Milan. *Career:* Designed Traviata for 1956 Florence Festival, Mefistofele at La Scala, 1958; Returned to Milan for Don Pasquale, 1965 and 1973, and the premiere of Pizzetti's Clitennestra, 1965; US debut at Dallas, 1962, Otello and L'Incoronazione di Poppea, 1963; Metropolitan Opera, New York, with designs for Lucia di Lammermoor, 1964, Luisa Miller, 1968, and Il Trovatore, 1969; Designs and productions at San Carlo, Naples, 1964–88, for Roberto Devereux, Adriana Lecouvreur, Samson et Dalila, Carmen, La Gioconda and I Puritani; Verona Arena, 1962–84, with Nabucco, Cavalleria Rusticana, La Bohème, Rigoletto, La Forza del Destino, Aida, Un Ballo in Maschera and I Lombardi; Teatro Margherita, Genoa, 1991, Andrea Chénier; Directed the Italian premiere of Rossini's Le Siège de Corinthe at Genoa, 1992, Turandot at 1992 Caracalla Festival.

COLONNA, Monica; Italian singer (soprano); b. 1970. *Career:* appearances as Donizetti's Adina, Modena, 1995 and as Mimi and Carolina in Il Matrimonio Segreto, Spoleto; Season 1996 in Rota's Notte di un nevrastenico at Cosenza; Cimarosa's Le astuzie femminili at Ferrara and Donizetti's Parisina, Wexford; Mercadante's Elena da Feltre, 1997 Wexford Festival; Donna Anna, Cologne and Aix, 1998; Sang Mercadante's Elena da Feltre at Lugo, 1999; season 2000–01 as Fiordiligi at Detroit, Donna Elvira for Scottish Opera and Britten's Lucretia at the Teatro Goldoni, Florence. *Recordings include:* Elena da Feltre. *Honours:* Winner, Modena Competition, 1995; Finalist, Lauri-Volpi Competition, 1993; Pavarotti Competition, 1995. *Current Management:* Ornella Cogliolo, Via del Babuino 76, 00187 Rome, Italy. *Telephone:* 6 3207627. *Fax:* 6 3207628. *E-mail:* cogliolo@cogliolo.it. *Website:* www .cogliolo.it.

COLPOS, Mariana; Singer (Soprano); b. 1965, Romania. *Education:* Bucharest Academy. *Career:* Appearances at Bucharest and throughout Europe as Tosca, Aida, Butterfly, Norma, Lucia di Lammermoor and Ariadne auf Naxos; Leonora in Il Trovatore, Marguerite, Donna Elvira, Elisabeth de Valois and Mimi; Season 1998 with Norma and Micaela on tour in the United Kingdom with the Moldovan Opera; Atelier Lyrique, Paris as Butterfly; Concerts include Mozart, Verdi and Britten's Requiems; Mahler 2nd, 4th and 8th symphonies; Beethoven's 9th; Radio and television appearances. *Address:* Music International, 13 Ardilaun Road, London N5 2QR, England.

COLZANI, Anselmo; Singer (Baritone); b. 28 March 1918, Budrio, Bologna, Italy. *Education:* Studied with Corrado Zambelli in Bologna. *Career:* Debut: Bologna, 1947, as the Herald in Lohengrin; Verona Arena from 1952; La Scala from 1954, notably in the stage premiere of Milhaud's David; US debut, 1956, as Count Luna at San Francisco; Metropolitan Opera debut, 1960, as Boccanegra; Returned to New York for 16 seasons in 201 performances, including Verdi's Falstaff and Amonasro, Puccini's Scarpia and Jack Rance, Gerard in Andrea Chénier and Ashton in Lucia di Lammermoor; Sang Amonasro for Houston Grand Opera, 1966. *Recordings:* La Gioconda; La Forza del Destino; Maria di Rohan by Donizetti; Iphigénie en Tauride, with Callas; Agnese di Hohenstaufen by Spontini, Florence, 1957; Zandonai's Francesca da Rimini. *Address:* c/o Metropolitan Opera, Lincoln Center, New York, NY 10023, USA.

COMENCINI, Maurizio; Singer (Tenor); b. 1958, Italy. *Education:* Studied at the Verona Conservatory and the Scala Opera Milan. *Career:* After winning prizes at the Toti del Monte and Maria Callas Competitions has sung widely in Italy, notably as Fenton in Falstaff at Parma (1986), in Monteverdi's Ulisse (Florence, 1987) and as Belfiore in Mozart's Finta Giardiniera (Alessandria, 1991); Further engagements at Palermo in Auber's Fra Diavolo, at Genoa in 1992 as Neocles in Rossini's Siège de Corinthe and at Lucca as Donizetti's Nemorino; Season 1994–95 as Nemorino and Elvino at Genoa, Rossini's Lindoro at Brescia and Almaviva at the Vienna Staatsoper; Many radio and other concert engagements. *Address:* c/o Teatro Comunale, Via 1 Frugoni 1516, 16121 Genoa, Italy.

COMES, Liviu; Composer, Musicologist and Professor; b. 13 Dec. 1918, Serel-Transylvania, Romania; m. 1st Valeria 1943; one s. one d.; m. 2nd Alice 1992. *Education:* Composition, Cluj-Napoca Acad. of Music, 1950. *Career:* Prof., Harmony, Counterpoint and Musical Forms, 1950–69, Pro-Rector, 1963–65, Rector, 1965–69, Cluj-Napoca Music Academy; Professor, Counterpoint, 1969–81, Pro-Rector, 1971–74, Bucharest Music Academy. *Compositions:* Sonatas for Piano, 1951; For Violin and Piano, 1954; For Clarinet and Piano, 1967; Wind Quintet, 1964; Wind Trio, 1981; A Song in Stone, oratorio, 1978; Salba for Orchestra, 1969; Maguri for Orchestra, 1986; Transylvanian Offer, cantata, 1987; Vocal and Choral music; String Quartet, 1989; Byzantine Mass, 1990; Sonatina for oboe and piano, 1992; Sonata for violin, 1995. *Publications:* The Melody of Palestrina, 1971, Italian translation, 1975; Treatise on Counterpoint, 1986; The World of Polyphony, 1984. *Contributions:* Articles and papers to Romanian Press. *Honours:* Order of Labour, 1965; Order of Cultural Merit, 1969; Prize of the Romanian Academy, 1974; Honorary Citizen of Cluj, 1994 and Bistritza, 1995; Doctor honoris causa, Cluj Music Academy, 1998. *Address:* Str Spatarului No. 42, 70241 Bucharest, Romania.

COMISSIONA, Sergiu; Conductor; b. 16 June 1928, Bucharest, Romania; m. Robinne Comissiona, 16 July 1949. *Education:* Studied violin, piano, horn; Voice and conducting with Silverstri and Lindenberg, Bucharest Conservatory. *Career:* Debut: Conducted Gounod's Faust, Sibiu, 1945; Violinist, Bucharest Radio Quartet, 1946–47; Violinist, 1947–48, Assistant Conductor, 1948–50, Music Director, 1950–55, Romanian State Ensemble; Principal Conductor, Romanian State Opera, 1955–59; Music Director, Haifa Symphony, 1960–66; Founder, Music Director, Ramat Gan Chamber Orchestra, 1960–67; Music Director, Göteborg Symphony, 1966–77; Music Adviser, Northern Ireland Orchestra, Belfast, 1967–68; Music Director, Baltimore Symphony, 1969–84; Chautauqua (NY) Festival Orchestra, 1976–80; Music Adviser, Temple University Festival, 1977–80; American Symphony Orchestra, New York, 1977–82; Artistic Director, 1980–83; Music Director-Designate, 1983–84, Music Director, 1984–88, Houston Symphony, Chief Conductor, Radio Philharmonic Orchestra, Hilversum, 1982–; Music Director, New York City Opera, 1987–88; Chief Conductor, Helsinki Philharmonic, Music Director, Vancouver Symphony, Chief Conductor, Orquesta Sinfonica, RTVE, Madrid, 1990; Guest conductor, orchestras and opera companies throughout world. *Recordings include:* Roussel's Sinfonietta and Stravinsky's Apollon Musagète; Chopin's 2nd Piano Concerto, Nights in the Gardens of Spain (Alicia de Larrocha); Britten's Les Illuminations and Diversions; Mendelssohn's 3rd Symphony; Liszt's Works for Piano and Orchestra (Jerome Lowenthal); Rachmaninov's Symphonic Dances. *Address:* c/o Vancouver Symphony, 601 Smithe Street, Vancouver, British Columbia V6B 5G1, Canada.

COMMAND, Michele; Singer (Soprano); b. 27 Nov. 1946, Caumont, France. *Education:* Studied at the Conservatories of Grenoble and Paris. *Career:* Debut: Lyon, 1967, as Musetta in La Bohème; Toulouse 1968, as Fiordiligi; Sang in Paris, at the Opéra and the Opéra-Comique, as Mozart's Donna Elvira and Fiordiligi, Gounod's Mireille, Mélisande and Portia in the premiere of Reynaldo Hahn's Le Marchand de Venise; Paris Palais des Sports 1989, as Micaela in Carmen; Sang Gounod's Sapho at Saint-Etienne, 1992 (Adriana Lecouvreur and Massenet's Chimène, 1994–95); Compiègne 1996, as Cherubini's Médée. *Recordings:* Pelléas et Mélisande; Ariane et Barbe-Bleue and Fauré's Pénélope; Don Quichotte by Massenet; Orphée aux Enfers by Offenbach, Siebel in Faust; Harawi by Messiaen.

COMPARATO, Marina; Singer (Mezzo-soprano); b. 1970, Perugia, Italy. *Education:* Florence Conservatory. *Career:* Appearances as Rossini's Rosina Sesto in La Clemenza di Tito, and Siebel in Faust at Spoleto; Teatro Comunale, Florence, as Isolier in Le Comte Ory, and roles in Elektra, Rimsky's The Tale of Tsar Salten, Orfeo ed Euridice and Les Troyens, 2001; Glyndebourne Festival debut 2000, as Cherubino; Further engagements as Annio in La Clemenza di Tito at Ferrara, La Cenerentola and Il Viaggio a Reims at Pesaro, Monteverdi's Ulisse in Athens and Boris Godunov at Rome; Flowermaiden in Parsifal at the Opéra Bastille, Paris; Concert engagements throughout Europe. *Recordings include:* Vivaldi's Juditha Triumphans (Opus 111). *Address:* Teatro Comunale, Via Solferino 15, 50123 Florence, Italy.

CONANT, Robert (Scott); Harpsichordist; b. 6 Jan. 1928, Passaic, New Jersey, USA; m. Nancy Lydia Jackson, 10 Oct 1959, 1 s., 1 d. *Education:* BA, Yale University, 1949; Juilliard School, 1949–50; MM, Yale School of Music, 1956; Piano with Sascha Gorodnitzki; Harpsichord with Ralph Kirkpatrick. *Career:* Debut: Town Hall, New York, 1953; Wigmore Hall, London, England, 1958; Major recital series and ensemble engagements in USA and Europe, 1956–; Chicago, Denver and Philadelphia Symphony Orchestras; Founded annual Festival of Baroque Music, now held in Saratoga Springs and Greenfield Center, New York, 1959–; Assistant Professor, Yale School of Music, 1961–66; Associate Professor, Professor, 1967–86, Professor Emeritus, 1986–, Chicago Musical College, Roosevelt University; Harpsichordist with: Viola da Gamba Trio of Basel; The Robert Conant Baroque Trio, with Terry King on baroque cello and Kenneth Goldsmith on baroque violin, 1986–; Nova/Antiqua, with James Ketterer, percussion, and Brian Cassier on double bass, 1986–. *Recordings:* Solo on old harpsichords, Yale Collection of Musical Instruments, vol. 1; Robert Conant, Harpsichord, Foundation for Baroque Music; Ensemble performances on several labels. *Publications:* Twentieth Century Harpsichord Music: A Classified Catalog (with Frances Bedford), 1974. *Address:* 163 Wilton Road, Greenfield Center, NY 12833, USA.

CONDO, Nucci; Singer (Mezzo-soprano); b. 15 Jan. 1938, Trieste, Italy. *Education:* Studied in Rome. *Career:* Sang in Vivaldi's Juditha Triumphans at the Queen Elizabeth Hall, London, 1972; New York Kennedy Center, 1972; Glyndebourne Festival, 1972–79, in Le nozze di Figaro, Falstaff, Il Ritorno d'Ulisse and Der Rosenkavalier; Cologne, 1984, as Lucia in La Gazza Ladra; La Scala, 1985, in a revival of Rossi's Orfeo; Guest appearances with Netherlands Opera and at the Prague and Dubrovnik Festivals; Sang as Ida in Gemma di Vergy at the Teatro Donizetti, Bergamo, 1987; Sang Mozart's Marcellina at the Teatro La Fenice, Venice, 1991; Concert tours of Yugoslavia, Austria and the USA. *Recordings include:* La Gazza Ladra: Rossini's Otello; Il Ritorno d'Ulisse; Mefistofele by Boito; Video of Le nozze di Figaro, Glyndebourne, 1973. *Address:* c/o Teatro Donizetti, Piazza Cavour 14, 241 Bergamo, Italy.

CONLON, James (Joseph); Conductor; b. 18 March 1950, New York, NY, USA. *Education:* High School of Music and Art, New York; BM, Juilliard School, New York 1972; Studied conducting with Jean Morel. *Career:* Debut: Formal debut conducting with Boris Godunov, Spoleto Festival, 1971; Conductor, Juilliard School, 1972–75; Youngest conductor to lead a subscription concert, New York Philharmonic Orchestra, 1974; Metropolitan Opera debut, New York, with Die Zauberflöte, 1976; Guest conductor with major orchestras and opera companies in USA and Europe, including Chicago, Boston, Philadelphia, Cleveland, Pittsburgh and National Symphony Orchestras; Music Director, Cincinnati May Festival, 1979–; Chief Conductor, Rotterdam Philharmonic Orchestra, 1983–91; Principal Conductor, Cologne Opera, 1989–96; General Music Director of the City of Cologne, 1991–96; Principal Conductor, Opéra National de Paris, 1996–; London, Covent Garden debut with Don Carlo, 1979; Opéra de Paris debut with Il Tabarro and Pagliacci in 1982, Maggio Musicale Fiorentino debut with Don Carlo, 1985, Chicago Lyric Opera debut in 1988 with La Forza del Destino, Milan La Scala debut with Oberon in 1993 General Music Director, City of Cologne; Led Pelléas et Mélisande at the Palais Garnier, Paris, 1997; Music Director of the Opéra National de Paris, 1997, (Tristan and Don Carlos, 1998); Music Director of LA Opera, 2006–. *Recordings:* For 2 recording companies. *Address:* c/o Opéra Bastille, 120 Rue de Lyon, 775012 Paris, France.

CONNELL, Elizabeth, BMus; Irish singer (soprano); b. 22 Oct. 1946, Port Elizabeth, South Africa. *Education:* London Opera Centre with Otakar Kraus; Maggie Teyte Prize, 1972. *Career:* debut: Varvara in Katya Kabanova at the 1972 Wexford Festival; appeared with Opera Australia including War and Peace at opening of Sydney Opera House 1973, and sang mezzo roles with English National Opera 1975–80, notably Verdi's Eboli and Herodias in Salome; Covent Garden debut 1976, as Viclinda in I Lombardi; Bayreuth debut 1980, as Ortrud in Lohengrin; sang Lady Macbeth in Hamburg, Mozart's Vitellia at Covent Garden and Wagner's Kundry and Venus with Netherlands Opera; soprano roles from 1983; season 1984–85 as Electra in Idomeneo at Salzburg, Norma in Geneva and Vitellia in a new production of La Clemenza di Tito at the Metropolitan; season 1985–86, Leonora (Trovatore) and Beethoven's Leonore at Covent Garden; Electra at Glyndebourne 1985; appearances at La Scala in Macbeth and I Lombardi; sang Electra in new production of Idomeneo, Covent Garden 1989; Lady Macbeth, Bonn 1990, and Cologne 1992; sang Fidelio at Sydney, Odabella in Attila at Geneva 1992, Senta in Der fliegende Holländer at the Bayreuth Festival; concert performances of Mendelssohn's 2nd Symphony under Abbado and the Missa Solemnis in Paris; sang Isolde at the Festival Hall, London 1993 and at the Coliseum theatre 1996; Elektra at San Francisco 1997; Isolde 1998; season 2000–01 as Senta at the Vienna Staatsoper, Isolde in Madrid, Brünnhilde in Götterdämmerung at Sydney (concert) and Elektra at Bordeaux; recent engagements include Brunnhilde, the Kostelnicka, Ortrud and Ariadne in Australia, Ortrud, Fidelio and Isolde in Berlin, Senta in Hamburg and Berlin, Elektra in Berlin, Madrid, Bordeaux, Tokyo and Montreal, Ortrud in Mannheim and the Färberin (Die Frau ohne Schatten) in Frankfurt; sings Elektra in Oviedo and Berlin, Isolde in Hamburg, Abigaille in Hamburg and Sydney and Norma for Opera Australia. *Recordings:* Rossini's Guillaume Telle, MAhler's Eighth Symphony, Mendelssohn's Second Symphony, Franz Schreker's Die Gezeichneten, Donizetti's Poliuto, Verdi's I Due Foscari, Schönberg's Gurrelieder, Wagner's Lohengrin, Schubert Lieder (with Graham Johnson); video of Covent Garden production of Luisa Miller. *Current Management:* Askonas Holt, Lonsdale Chambers, 27 Chancery Lane, London, WC2A 1PF, England. *Telephone:* (20) 7400-1700 (office). *Fax:* (20) 7400-1799 (office). *E-mail:* peter.bloor@askonasholt.co.uk (office). *Website:* www.askonasholt.co.uk (office).

CONNELL, John; Singer (Bass); b. 11 March 1956, Glasgow, Scotland. *Education:* Studied at Royal Northern College of Music and at National Opera Studio. *Career:* Debut: English National Opera; Roles at Royal Opera, Covent Garden: Titurel in Parsifal, the Monk in Don Carlos, Sparafucile in Rigoletto (1985) and as Ramphis in Aida; With English National Opera has sung the Commendatore, Colline, the Monk in Don Carlos, Ferrando in Trovatore, Leporello in The Stone Guest, Pogner, Basilio, Banquo and Sarastro; Televised appearances in Billy Budd and Lady Macbeth by Shostakovich; Season 1990–91 in new productions of Pelléas et Mélisande and Peter Grimes, as Arkel and Swallow; Sang Banquo at the Bolshoi, Moscow, and Kirov St Petersburg, 1990, on tour with English National Opera; Welsh National Opera, Sarastro in The Magic Flute and Silva in Ernani; Opera North in Salome, The Barber of Seville and La Bohème; Other engagements as Hunding in Spain and

France; Concert engagements in the Verdi Requiem at The Barbican and as Pimen in Boris Godunov; Windsor Festival, 1987, as Fidelio; Season 1992 as Padre Guardiano in The Force of Destiny and as Sarastro for English National Opera; The Hermit in Der Freischütz, with the New York Philharmonic and in Peter Grimes with the London Symphony Orchestra and Rostropovich; Swallow in Peter Grimes at La Monnaie, Brussels and Don Basilio for Garsington Opera, 1994; Dansker in Billy Budd for Royal Opera House, Covent Garden, 1995; Don Fernando in Fidelio, ENO, 1996; Season 1997 with Mozart's Bartolo and Wagner's Daland for ENO; Count des Grieux in Manon, 1998. *Recordings include:* Elijah (Philips); Serenade to Music by Vaughan Williams (Hyperion). *Current Management:* Askonas Holt Ltd, Lonsdale Chambers, 27 Chancery Lane, London, WC2A 1PF, England. *Telephone:* (20) 7400-1700. *Fax:* (20) 7400-1799. *E-mail:* info@askonasholt.co .uk. *Website:* www.askonasholt.co.uk.

CONNOLLY, Justin (Riveagh); Composer; b. 11 Aug. 1933, London, England. *Education:* Royal College of Music with Peter Racine Fricker and Adrian Boult. *Career:* Harkness Fellowship, 1963–65, studying with Mel Powell; Taught at Yale University, 1963–66; Professor of Theory and Composition at the Royal College of Music from 1966–89; mem, Association of Professional Composers; Liveryman, Worshipful Company of Musicians. *Compositions include:* Sonatina in 5 Studies for Piano; Antiphonies for orchestra; Cinquepaces for brass quintet; Poems of Wallace Stevens I and II for soprano and instruments, 1967, 1970; Anima for violin and orchestra, 1974; Diaphony for organ and orchestra, 1977; Chamber music series with titles Obbligati, Triads and Tesserae, 1966–89; Ceilidh for 4 violins, 1976; Waka for mezzo-soprano and piano, 1981; Sestina A and B for ensemble, 1978; Verse and Prose for a cappella chorus Fourfold, from The Garden of Forking Paths for 2 pianos, 1983; Ennead (Night Thoughts) for piano, 1983; Spelt from Sibyl's Leaves for 6 solo voices and ensemble, 1989; Nocturnal, flutes with piano, percussion, double-bass, 1990; Cantata, soprano and piano, 1991; Symphony, 1991; Sapphic for soprano and 7 instruments, 1992; Gymel A for flute and clarinet, 1993; Gymel B for clarinet and cello, 1995; Studies from the Garden of Forking Paths for piano, 2000; Piano Trio, 2000. *Honours:* Collard Fellowship, The Musicians' Company, 1986. *Address:* c/o Novello & Co Ltd, Lower James Street, London W1, England.

CONNOLLY, Sarah; British singer (mezzo-soprano); b. 1963, County Durham, England; m. Carl Talbot 1998; one d. *Education:* Royal Coll. of Music and with David Mason and Gerald Martin Moore. *Career:* concert engagements include Mozart's Requiem under Neville Marriner, Bach's B Minor Mass with Philippe Herreweghe, at Berlin Philharmonia and Honegger's Jeanne d'Arc au Bûcher with the Royal Liverpool Philharmonic, Prom Concerts, London 1997; Wigmore Hall Recital debut with Julius Drake; opera debut as Annina in Der Rosenkavalier for WNO 1994; further roles include the Messenger in Orfeo and the Fox in The Cunning Little Vixen (ENO), Charlotte in Massenet's Werther for English Touring Opera and the Musician in Manon Lescaut at the Glyndebourne Festival 1997; season 1997–98 for ENO as Handel's Xerxes, Meg in Verdi's Falstaff; Eduige in Rodelinda for Glyndebourne Touring Opera 1998; world premiere of Rime D'Amore by Matteo D'Amico conducted by Giuseppe Sinopoli in Rome 1998; Ariodante for New York City Opera 1999; Ruggiero in Handel's Alcina, ENO 1999; the roles of the Queen of Sheba and Second Woman with Ivor Bolton in Handel's Solomon for Maggio Musicale 1999; world premiere of Mark Anthony Turnage's The Silver Tassie, ENO 2000; sang Juno and Ino with San Francisco Opera in Handel's Semele, conducted by Charels Mackerras; role of Nerone in L'Incoronazione di Poppea at Maggio Musicale 2000; further concerts include Bach's St Matthew Passion with the Gabrieli Consort in Spain and with Herreweghe 1998; The Dream of Gerontius in Sydney and Mark Anthony Turnage's Twice Through the Heart, with Markus Stenz in Rome and London; Ravel's L'Heure espagnole at the London Proms 2002; Carnegie Hall debut, Pergolesi Stabat Mater 2003; sang Dido in Dido and Aeneas at the Proms 2003; Annio in La Clemenza di Tito at the New York Met 2003–04; engaged to sing the title role in Giulio Cesare at the Glyndebourne Festival 2005. *Recordings include:* Bach Cantatas with Philippe Herreweghe, Les Fêtes d'Hebé by Rameau with Les Arts Florissants and Juditha Triumphans, Vivaldi with the King's Consort. *Honours:* Prizewinner, opera section of the 's-Hertogenbosch Competition, Netherlands 1994, Gramophone Award for Baroque Opera 1998. *Current Management:* Askonas Holt Ltd, Lonsdale Chambers, 27 Chancery Lane, London, WC2A 1PF, England. *Telephone:* (20) 7400-1700. *Fax:* (20) 7400-1799. *E-mail:* info@askonasholt.co.uk. *Website:* www.askonasholt.co.uk.

CONRAD, Barbara; Singer (Mezzo-soprano); b. 11 Aug. 1945, Pittsburg, Texas, USA. *Education:* Studied at the University of Texas, Austin. *Career:* Metropolitan Opera from 1982, as Verdi's Preziosilla and Maddalena, Annina in Der Rosenkavalier and Maria in Porgy and Bess; European engagements at Frankfurt, Vienna, Brussels and Munich; Sang at Greater Miami Opera, 1989; Other roles include Wagner's

Fricka and Verdi's Azucena and Eboli. *Recordings include:* Hamlet (Thomas) and Porgy and Bess. *Address:* c/o Bess Pruitt and Associates Inc, 819 East 168th Street, Bronx, NY 10459, USA.

CONSOLI, Marc-Antonio; Composer, Conductor and Editor; b. 19 May 1941, Italy. *Education:* BMus, 1966; MMus, 1967; DMA, 1976; Studied with Ernst Krenek, Gunther Schüller, George Crumb. *Career:* Commissioned by Fromm and Koussevitsky Foundations, the Royan in France, Steirischer Herbst of Austria (Festivals); Works performed at International Festivals including International Society for Contemporary Music in Helsinki, 1978, Belgium, 1981; New York Philharmonic and Los Angeles Philharmonic; mem, Broadcast Music Association; American Composers' Alliance. *Compositions include:* Sciuri Novi; Interactions I, II, III, IV, V, 1970–71; Isonic, 1971; Lux Aeterna, 1972; Profile, 1973; Music for Chambers, 1974; Sciuri Novi II, 1974; Canti Trinacriani, 1976; Memorie Pie, 1976; Tre Canzoni, 1976; Odefonia, 1976; Tre Fiori Musicali, 1987; Vuci Siculani, 1979; Naked Masks, 1980; Orpheus Meditation, 1981; The Last Unicorn, 1981; Afterimages, 1982; String Quartet, 1983; Ancient Greek Lyrics, 1985; Musiculi II, 1985–86; Reflections, 1986; Eyes of the Peacock, 1987; Cello Concerto, 1988; Greek Lyrics, 1988; String Quartet II, 1989; Arie Mutate, 1990; Musiculi IV, 1990, 1992; Musiculi III, 1992, 1994; Games for 2, 3 and 4, 1994, 1995; Cinque Canti, 1995; Varie Azioni, 1995; Di-ver-ti-mento, 1995; Collected Moments, 1996; Sciuri novi III, 1996; Pensieri Sospesi, 1997; Rounds and Relays, 1997; Varie Azioni II, 1998; Varie Azioni III, 1999. *Honours:* Guggenheim Memorial Fellowships, 1971, 1979; Fulbright Scholarship to Poland, 1972–74; National Endowment for the Arts Grants, 1976, 1979; Prize, Competition, Monaco. *Address:* c/o ASCAP, ASCAP Building, One Lincoln Plaza, New York, 10023, USA.

CONSTABLE, John Robert, FRAM; Piano Accompanist and Harpsichordist; b. 5 Oct. 1934, Sunbury-on-Thames, Middlesex, England; m. Katharine Ingham; two d. *Education:* studied with Harold Craxton, Royal Acad. of Music, London. *Career:* repetiteur, Royal Opera House, Covent Garden, London, 1960–72; principal keyboard player, London Sinfonietta, since its formation; principal harpsichordist, Acad. of St Martin-in-the-Fields, 1984–; Prof., Royal Coll. of Music, 1985–; mem. Incorporated Society of Music, Musicians' Union. *Recordings:* many with London Sinfonietta and Acad. of St Martin-in-the-Fields, playing harpsichord continuo for operas and as accompanist on recital records. *Address:* 13 Denbigh Terrace, London, W11 2QJ, England.

CONSTANT, Marius; Composer and Conductor; b. 7 Feb. 1925, Bucharest, Romania; 1 s. *Education:* Bucharest Conservatory of Music; National Conservatory of Music, Paris. *Career:* Musical Director, French Radio, 1952–; Musical Director, Roland Petit Ballet and Paris Opéra Ballet, 1973–78; Conductor, Ars Nova Ensemble; Regular guest conductor of leading orchestras in Europe, Canada, USA and Japan; Teaches composition at Stanford University, USA, and conducting at Hilversum, Netherlands. *Compositions:* Operas: Le Souper, 1969; Jeu de Sainte Agnés, 1974; La Tragédie de Carmen, (version of Bizet), 1981; Impressions de Pelléas, (version of Debussy), 1992; Sade/Teresa (original), 1996; Oratorios, Des Droits de l'Homme, 1989, and Chants de Retour, 1995; Ballets: Cyrano de Bergérac, 1959; Eloge de la Folie, 1966; Paradis Perdu, 1967; Candide, 1970; Septentrion, 1975; Nana, 1976; L'Ange Bleu, 1985; Orchestral: 24 Preludes, 1959; Twilight Zone, signature tune, 1961; Turner; Chants de Maldoror, 1962; Chaconne et Marche Militaire, 1968; Candide for harpsichord and orchestra, 1971; Concerto Gli Elementi for trombone and orchestra, 1977; Symphony for Winds, 1978; Concertante for alto saxophone and orchestra, 1978; Nana-Symphony, 1980; 103 Régards dans l'Eau, 1981; Pelléas et Mélisande-Symphony, 1983; L'Inauguration de la Maison for wind band, 1985; Choruses and Interludes for French Horn and Orchestra, 1990; Hameenlinna: An Imaginary Landscape, for orchestra, 1991; Brevissima Symphony, 1992; Symphonie Concertante for 6 pianos and orchestra, 1994; Winds, 1968; 14 Stations for percussion and 6 instruments, 1970; Traits, Cadavre Exquis, aleatoric, 1971; Chamber music. *Recordings:* Music by Satie, Xenakis, Debussy, Varèse, Messiaen and Constant. *Honours:* 1st Prize for Composition, Paris Conservatory; Officier, Légion d'Honneur; Grand Officier, Ordre du Mérite; Prix Italia, 1952; Member of the Académie de Beaux-Arts, 1993. *Address:* 16 rue des Fosses St Jacques, 75005 Paris, France.

CONSTANTIN, Rudolf; Singer (Baritone); b. 16 Feb. 1935, Paris, France. *Education:* Studied in Paris and Zürich. *Career:* Sang at Rheydt, 1958–59, Aachen, 1959–60, Berne, 1960–63, Graz, 1963–67, Cologne, 1967–69; Frankfurt am Main, 1969–83; Guest appearances at Dresden, Berlin, Amsterdam, Brussels, Vienna (Volksoper), Paris and Copenhagen; Sang Ruprecht in The Fiery Angel at Zürich, Gunther in Götterdämmerung at Covent Garden and the Villains in Les Contes d'Hoffmann at the Salzburg Festival; Other roles have included Mozart's Don Giovanni, Count and Guglielmo, Verdi's Amonasro, Luna, Germont, Nabucco, Simon Boccanegra, Rigoletto, Macbeth, Posa and Iago; Wagner's Telramund, Dutchman, Wolfram, Amfortas and Wotan (Die Walküre); Strauss's Orestes, Jochanaan, Mandryka and

Faninal; Golaud in Pelléas et Mélisande and Mittenhofer in Elegy for Young Lovers by Henze: Further engagements at Geneva, Marseille, Monte Carlo, Prague and Edinburgh; Many concert appearances; Tchaikovsky Festival at Prague, 1993.

CONSTANTINE, Andrew; Conductor; b. 1964, England. *Education:* Studied in Siena, at the Turin Opera and the St Petersburg Conservatoire. *Career:* Engagements from 1991 with the London Philharmonic in Prokofiev's 5th Symphony, the Hallé and English Chamber Orchestras, the Royal Philharmonic Orchestra and London Mozart Players; Assistant Conductor of English National Opera's Madama Butterfly and Principal Conductor of the Sinfonia of Birmingham; Further appearances with the St Petersburg and Sofia Philharmonics and the Komische Opera, Berlin; Led Das Rheingold at Leicester, 1998. *Honours:* Winner in 1991 of the Donatella Flick Conducting Competition, London. *Address:* Patrick Garvey Management, Top Floor, 59 Lansdowne Place, Hove, East Sussex, BN3 1 FL, England.

CONSTANTINESCU, Dan; Composer; b. 10 June 1931, Bucharest, Romania. *Education:* Composer's Diploma, Bucharest Conservatory of Music. *Career:* Debut: Jassy Philharmonic, 1957; Lecturer in Harmony and Composition, Bucharest Conservatory; mem, Romanian Composers' Union. *Compositions include:* Divertissement for string orchestra; Ballad for orchestra; Chamber Symphony; Symphony Concertante; Concerto for piano and string orchestra; Concerto for 2 pianos and small orchestra; 4 Sonatas for 2 instruments; Trio for violin, clarinet, piano and percussion; 5 Quartets; Symphony for string orchestra; Symphony for wind instruments; Concerto for harpsichord, harp and wind instruments; String sextet; Symphony for 32 voices; 5 cycles of piano music. *Recordings:* Piano part, various works. *Honours:* Georges Enescu Prize, Romanian Academy, 1968. *Address:* Strada Corneliu Botez 3, Bucharest 9, Romania.

CONSTANTINESCU, Mihai; Violinist and Professor; b. 22 Aug. 1926, Chisinau, Russia; m. Corina Bura 1981; one d. *Education:* Bachelorship, Matel Basarab High School, diploma, Conservatoire of Music, Bucharest. *Career:* debut, Radio Bucharest 1941; recital, Dalles Hall, Bucharest 1943; soloist, George Enescu Philharmonic, Bucharest; radio and television appearances; tours of Russia, Czechoslovakia, Korea, China, Germany, Viet Nam, Poland, Bulgaria, France, Belgium, Luxembourg, Hungary, Yugoslavia, Italy, Cuba, Spain, Venezuela, Chile, Argentina, Ecuador and elsewhere; Prof., Conservatoire of Music, Bucharest. *Compositions:* Cadenzas for Mozart's Third Concerto for violin and orchestra and Haydn's First Concerto for violin and orchestra. *Recordings:* works by Mozart, Beethoven, Pergolesi, Handel, Sabin Dragoi, Livui Comes, Wilhelm Berger (Romanian music), two Handel recordings, and Rameau 1986. *Address:* Str Ecaterina Teodoriou 17, 010971 Bucharest 1, Romania.

CONTE, David; Composer and Teacher; b. 20 Dec. 1955, Denver, Colorado, USA. *Education:* BM, Bowling Green State University, Ohio; MFA, DMA, Cornell University; Private study with Nadia Boulanger, 2 years. *Career:* Faculties, Cornell University, Colgate University, Interlochen Centre for the Arts, San Francisco Conservatory of Music; mem, ASCAP. *Compositions:* Invocation and Dance for male chorus and orchestra; Requiem Triptych (im memoriam Nadia Boulanger) for male chorus and orchestra; Piano Fantasy; The Masque of the Red Death; Ballet for orchestra; Of a Summer's Evening, guitar duo; The Dreamers; 2 act Chamber Opera; Pastorale and Toccata for organ; Piano Quintet; In Praise of Music, SATB and orchestra; Ave Maria; The Gift of the Magi, one-act chamber opera; Songs of Consolation, soprano and organ. *Honours:* Fulbright Scholarship, 1976; Meet the Composer Grant, 1983, 1986, 1987; Ralph Vaughan Williams Fellowship. *Current Management:* E C Schirmer Music Co, 138 Ipswich Street, Boston, MA 02215, USA. *Address:* San Francisco Conservatory of Music, 1201 Ortega Street, San Francisco, CA 94122, USA.

CONTI, Nicoletta; Orchestral Conductor and Teacher; b. 12 July 1957, Bologna, Italy. *Education:* Bologna Conservatory of Music; Milan Conservatory. *Career:* Debut: Liszt Academy, Budapest, 1984; Aspen Music Festival, 1984; Tanglewood Music Center, 1985; Appearances with Orchestra Sinfonica di Bari, Orchestra Regionale Toscana, Orchestra Simphonia Perusina, Orchestra Sinfonica Abrudiese, Orchestra Pro Musica Riminia, Danish Radio Orchestra; mem, American Symphony Orchestra League. *Honours:* Concorso da Camera Stresa, 1981; Malko Competition for Young Conductors, 1986. *Address:* Via Palestro 7, 40123 Bologna, Italy.

CONTIGUGLIA, John and Richard (twins); Pianist; b. 13 April 1937, Auburn, New York, USA. *Education:* Received advice from Percy Grainger; Studied with Jean Wilder and Bruce Simonds, Yale University; Dame Myra Hess, London. *Career:* Debut: Duo recital at age 6; Professional debut, London, 1962; Performed throughout the world as a virtuoso duo; Repertoire includes works from the past to

contemporary scores; Special emphasis on the piano transcriptions of Liszt; Premiere of Liszt's Grosses Konzertstück über Mendelssohns Lieder ohne Worte, Utrecht, 1986. *Recordings:* Several. *Honours:* Ditson Fellowship. *Address:* c/o ICM Artists Ltd, 40 West 57th Street, New York City, NY 10019, USA.

CONVERY, Robert; Composer; b. 4 Oct. 1954, Wichita, Kansas, USA. *Education:* Studied at Westminster Choir College, Curtis Institute and Juilliard, New York; David Diamond, Vincent Persichetti and Ned Rorem were among his teachers. *Career:* Resident Composer with Phillips Exeter Academy, 1988, 1991, Dickinson College, 1989–90, and the New York Concert Singers, 1991–93. *Compositions:* The Lady of Larkspur, opera in 1 act after Tennessee Williams, 1980; Pyramus and Thisbe, 2 scenes after Shakespeare, 1983; The Blanket, opera in 1 act, produced at Spoleto Festival, Charleston, 1988. *Honours:* Charles Miller-Alfredo Casella Award; Charles E Ives Award for The Blanket. *Address:* c/o ASCAP, ASCAP Building, 1 Lincoln Plaza, New York, NY 10023, USA.

CONWELL, Julia; Singer (Soprano); b. 1954, Philadelphia, Pennsylvania, USA; m. Giancarlo del Monaco. *Education:* Studied at Curtis Institute of Music and with Margaret Harshaw. *Career:* Sang in various US opera houses, notably as Musetta in La Bohème for Michigan Opera; European debut with Munich Staatsoper as Musetta; Further appearances as Nedda in Pagliacci, Liu in Turandot, Düsseldorf, 1982, and Oscar in Ballo in Maschera, Frankfurt, 1984; Sang Charpentier's Louise at Nice and Zerlina at Rome, 1984; Other roles have included Paolina in Poliuto by Donizetti, Rome, 1986; Gilda and Salome at Augsburg, 1988, and Diana in Iphigénie en Tauride, Deutsche Oper Berlin; Member of the Stuttgart Staatsoper from 1985. *Recordings:* Sandrina in La Finta Giardiniera; Euridice in Orfeo by Gluck; Works by Henze. *Address:* c/o Stuttgart Staatstheater, Oberer Schlossgarten 6, 7000 Stuttgart, Germany.

CONYNGHAM, Barry (Ernest); Composer; b. 27 Aug. 1944, Sydney, New South Wales, Australia. *Education:* MA, University of Sydney; Postdoctoral Studies Certificate, University of California, San Diego; D.Mus, University of Melbourne. *Career:* Part-time Lecturer, Tutor, University of New South Wales and National Institute of Dramatic Art, 1968–70; Senior Tutor, University of Western Australia, 1971; Postdoctoral post, University of California, San Diego, 1972–73; Visiting Fellow, Princeton University, 1973–74; Composer and Researcher in residence, University of Aix-Marseille, 1974–75; Lecturer, 1975–79, Senior Lecturer, 1979–84, Reader, 1984–89, University of Melbourne; Dean, Creative Arts, University of Wollongong, 1989–94; Vice-Chancellor, Southern Cross University, 1994–; Board, Playbox Theatre Company; Deputy Chair, Opera Australia, 1995–. *Compositions:* Crisis: Thoughts in a City, 1968; The Little Sherriff, 1969; Five Windows, 1969; Three, 1969; Five, 1970; Water. . . Footsteps. . . Time, 1970; Ice Carving, 1970; Edward John Eyre, 1971–73; Six, 1971; Playback, 1972; Without Gesture, 1973; From Voss, 1973; Snowflake, 1973; Ned, 1974–77; Mirror Images, 1975; Sky, 1977; Apology of Bony Anderson, 1978; Mirages, 1978; Bony Anderson, 1978; Concerto for double bass, 1979; Basho, 1980; Journeys, 1980; Viola, 1981; Imaginary Letters, 1981; Horizons: Concerto for orchestra; Southern Cross: Concerto for violin and piano, 1991; Dwellings, 1982; Fly, 1982–84; Voicings, 1983; Cello Concerto, 1984; Preview, 1984; Antipodes, 1984–85; The Oath of Bad Brown Bill, 1985; Generations, 1985; Recurrences, 1986; Vast I The Sea, II The Coast, III The Centre, IV The Cities, 1987; Glimpses, 1987; Bennelong, 1988; Matilda, 1988; Streams, 1988; Monuments: Piano Concerto, 1989; Waterways: Viola Concerto, 1990; Cloudlines: Harp Concerto, 1990; Decades for orchestra, 1993; Alterimages for koto and orchestra, 1994; Dawning, 1996; Nostalgia, 1997; Passing, 1998; Yearnings, 1999; String Quartet 2, 1999. *Recordings:* Many. *Publications:* Scores published by major publishers. *Honours:* 4 Fellowships: Churchill, 1970, Harkness, 1972–74, Australia Council, 1975, Fulbright Senior, 1982; Member, Order of Australia. *Address:* c/o Boosey and Hawkes, Locked Bag 188, Artarmon, NSW 1570, Australia.

COOK, Brian (Robert) Rayner; Singer (Baritone); b. 17 May 1945, London, England; m. Angela Mary Romney, 24 Aug 1974, 1 s., 1 d. *Education:* BA, Music, University of Bristol, 1966; Postgraduate Studies, Royal College of Music, London; ARCM, Honours, Singing Performance; Studied privately with Alexander Young (vocal studies) and Helga Mott (repertoire). *Career:* Debut: Major conducting debut, opera, 1966; Professional solo singing debut, 1967; Church Organist and Choir Master at age of 15; First concert at major London venue, Royal Albert Hall, conducted by John Barbirolli, 1969; Appearances as Solo Singer, oratorio, recitals and opera throughout the United Kingdom, Western and Eastern Europe, USA, Canada, South America, Middle East, Far East, North Africa; Frequent broadcasts British and European radio and television; Many first performances and broadcasts particularly works created for him by various distinguished composers; Visiting Tutor in Vocal Studies, Birmingham Conservatoire, England, 1980–99, and formerly Welsh College of Music and Drama, Cardiff;

Postgraduate Examiner, Birmingham Conservertoire –1999; Specialist University Music Assessor, Higher Education Funding Councils of England and of Wales, 1994–95; Has directed a number of Singers' Workshops, taught at summer schools, served on juries of international singing competitions and given specialist adjudications. *Recordings include:* Opera, oratorio and works from Schütz, Charpentier, Adam, Fauré, Dvořák, Nielsen and Orff to Parry, Elgar, Delius, Vaughan Williams, Ferguson and Walton; Song recitals including Vaughan Williams, Butterworth, Elgar, Poston, Coates, Cruft, Holst, Rubbra, Williamson, Havergal Brian, Camilleri. *Contributions:* Royal College of Music Magazine, Music and Musicians. *Honours:* Kathleen Ferrier Memorial Scholarship, 1969; All RCM major singing prizes, 1967–69. *Address:* The Quavers, 53 Friars Avenue, Friern Barnet, London N20 0XG, England.

COOK, Deborah; American opera and concert singer (soprano) and cantor; b. 6 July 1948, Philadelphia, PA; m. Ronald Marlowe 1985; one s. *Education:* studied with Irene Williams. *Career:* debut, Operatic-Glyndebourne and Covent Garden; Glyndebourne Touring Opera, 1971, as Zerbinetta; 3 years principal soprano in Bremen, 2 years Munich National Theatre; Sang in Sydney, Melbourne, Barcelona, Edinburgh, Geneva, Rome, Paris, Los Angeles, San Francisco, Leipzig, East Berlin; Appeared at Covent Garden Opera House, Hamburg State Opera (from 1981), Deutsche Oper Berlin, Frankfurt Opera, Stuttgart Opera, Deutsche Oper am Rhein; Bonn Opera, 1984–85; Roles include Verdi's Gilda, Strauss's Zerbinetta, Donizetti's Lucia and Mozart's Queen of Night and Constanze; Created role of Rachel in Henze's We Come to the River, Covent Garden, 1976, and Angel of Bright Future in Rochberg's The Confidence Man; Sang Lucia di Lammermoor at the Buxton Festival, 1979. *Recordings:* Dinorah; Ariadne auf Naxos; L'Etoile du Nord. *Address:* c/o Opera Rara, 25 Compton Terrace, London N1 2UN, England.

COOK, Edward; Singer (Tenor); b. 30 June 1954, Oxnard, California. *Education:* Studied at New England Conservatory, Boston and at Bloomington; Further study with James King. *Career:* Sang Gianni Schicchi, Rossini's Figaro and other baritone roles; Froh in Das Rheingold at the Metropolitan; Miami Opera as Siegmund in Die Walküre, 1990; Further Wagner roles include Parsifal at Wuppertal and Schwerin, 1994–95; Siegfried at Essen, 1996; Siegmund and Siegfried at Karlsruhe, 1994–95; Further engagements at Rome and Turin as Gluck's Orestes and Festival Hall, London, as Florestan; Other roles include Idomeneo and Strauss's Bacchus. *Address:* c/o Karlsruhe Opera, Baumeisterstrasse 11, Pf1449, 7500 Karlsruhe, Germany.

COOK, Jeff (Holland); Music Director, Conductor and Composer; b. 21 Aug. 1940, Chicago, Illinois, USA; m. Kate Young, 12 May 1974, 1 d. *Education:* BM, Northwestern University, 1962; MA, Ohio State University, 1964; MM, New England Conservatory of Music, 1966; Studied with Pierre Boulez, John Barbirolli, Jean Fournet, Bruno Maderna, Herbert von Karajan, Erich Leinsdorf, Karlheinz Stockhausen, György Ligeti. *Career:* Music Director, Conductor, Wheeling Symphony Orchestra, 1973–85; Music Director, Conductor, Mansfield Symphony Orchestra, Ohio, 1976–; Associate Conductor, Pittsburgh Ballet Theatre, 1987–91; Conductor, Louisville Ballet, Kentucky, 1990–; Guest Conductor: Anchorage Symphony, Eastern Music Festival, Rhode Island Philharmonic, North Carolina Symphony, Orquesta Sinfonica Nacional (Santo Domingo), Ballet of Ljubljana (Slovenia); North Bay Music Festival (Ontario). *Compositions:* Euripides Electra, 1972. *Recordings:* Broadcasts on West Virginia Public Radio, Ohio Public Radio, Canadian Broadcasting Corporation. *Address:* 649 Robinwood Drive, Pittsburgh, PA 15216, USA.

COOK, Terry; Singer (Bass); b. 9 Feb. 1956, Plainville, Texas, USA. *Education:* Studied at Texas University. *Career:* Sang with the Chicago Lyric Opera from 1980, at Santa Fe (Festival) from 1982, and at the Metropolitan from 1983; Roles have included Dr Grenvil in Traviata, Ferrando, the King in Aida, Oroe in Semiramide and Gershwin's Porgy; Further engagements at Seattle (1985), Théâtre Châtelet, Paris (in Handel's Rinaldo), at the Grand Opéra Paris as Colline in La Bohème and the Opéra-Comique as the Speaker in Die Zauberflöte; Other roles include Achillas in Giulio Cesare, Raimondo in Lucia di Lammermoor and the Minister in Fidelio; Sang Oroe in Semiramide at Dallas, 1993; Sang Crown in Porgy and Bess at Munich, 2000; Many concert appearances. *Address:* c/o Metropolitan Opera, Lincoln Center, New York, NY 10023, USA.

COOK-MacDONALD, Linda; singer (soprano); b. 22 Sept. 1947, Twin Falls, Idaho, USA. *Education:* studied in Cincinnati and Mainz. *Career:* debut, Krefeld, 1971, as Fiordiligi; Sang at such German houses as Krefeld, Wuppertal, Essen and Darmstadt; US appearances at Memphis, Cincinnati, Pittsburgh and Portland; Sang in New York at City Opera; Roles have included Mozart's Constanze, Pamina, Queen of Night and Zerlina, Agathe, Alice Ford, Marguerite, Musetta and Zdenka; Modern repertory has included Thalmar in Leben des Orest

by Krenek and Philippe in Penderecki's The Devils of Loudun; Many concert appearances.

COOKE, Arnold Atkinson; Music Professor and Composer; b. 4 Nov. 1906, Gomersal, Yorkshire, England. *Education:* BA (Cantab), 1928; BMus (Cantab), 1929; DMus, 1948; Staatliche Akademische Hochschule für Musik, Berlin, Germany, 1929–32; student of Paul Hindemith. *Career:* Prof., Harmony, Counterpoint and Composition, Royal Manchester Coll. of Music, 1933–38; Prof., Harmony, Counterpoint and Composition, Trinity Coll. of Music, London, 1947–78; mem., Composers' Guild of Great Britain (Chair. 1953), Incorporated Society of Musicians, Performing Right Society, MCPS, Dolmetsch Foundation (Governor), Tonbridge Music Club (pres.). *Compositions:* various chamber works, choral works, songs and song cycles, concertos, orchestral works including Symphonies Nos 1–6, 1946–84, operas including Mary Barton, The Invisible Duke, Jabez and the Devil, ballet. *Recordings include:* Symphony No. 3 and Suite from Jabez and the Devil; Song Cycle, The Seamew, Suite in C for piano; Quartet for oboe and string trio; Concerto for clarinet and string orchestra, 1982; Concerto for Orchestra, 1986. *Contributions:* Music Survey. *Honours:* Third Prize for Overture, Daily Telegraph, 1934. *Address:* c/o Mrs J. F. Earnshaw, 94 Totley Brook Road, Sheffield S17 3QT, England. *Website:* www.musicweb.uk.net/cooke/.

COOKE, Mervyn John, BA, MPhil, MA, PhD; composer and musicologist; b. 29 Aug. 1963, Dover, Kent, England. *Education:* Royal Academy of Music and King's College, Cambridge. *Career:* Research Fellow, Fitzwilliam College, Cambridge 1987–93; Lecturer in Music, University of Nottingham 1993; Head of Music Department, University of Nottingham 1998; Professor of Music, University of Nottingham 2000. *Compositions:* Symphonic Poem Messalina, Broadcast, BBC Concert Orchestra, Radio 3 1979, Horn Sonata, Broadcast, BBC Radio 3 1986; compositions performed in the Purcell Room 1979, Festival Hall 1980, Queen Elizabeth Hall 1986; incidental scores for Cambridge Greek Plays 1983 and 1989. *Publications:* Britten and the Gamelan, in D Mitchell, Death in Venice 1987, Britten: Billy Budd 1993, Britten: War Requiem 1996, The Chronicle of Jazz 1997, Britten and the Far East 1998, Jazz 1998, The Cambridge Companion to Benjamin Britten 1999, The Cambridge Companion to Jazz 2002, Selected Letters of Benjamin Britten Vol. 3 2004; contrib. to Musical Times, Journal of Musicological Research, Journal of Royal Musical Association, Music and Letters, Journal of the American Musicological Soc., Music Analysis. *Address:* Department of Music, University of Nottingham, Nottingham, NG7 2RD, England.

COOKE, Richard; Conductor; b. 1958, England. *Education:* Chorister at St Paul's Cathedral; Choral scholar at King's College, Cambridge, under David Willcocks. *Career:* Conducted various University orchestras; Led the chamber ensemble in the War Requiem at the Festival Hall, 1984; Trained the London Philharmonic Choir in Mahler 8 and for The Kingdom by Elgar; Has conducted concerts at the Albert and Festival Halls and throughout South East England; Gothenburg Symphony Orchestra from 1989 in Belshazzar's Feast, the Glagolitic Mass, Dvořák 6 and the Sea Symphony by Vaughan Williams; Has also conducted the Brahms Requiem, A Child of our Time, Monteverdi's Vespers and St Nicolas in Sweden; Verdi Requiem at the Uppsala International Festival (1990) and in Boulogne and Canterbury; Conductor of the Chalmers Music Weeks in Sweden and Artistic Director of the St Columb Festival in Cornwall. *Recordings include:* Mahler 8th Symphony and The Kingdom, with the London Philharmonic Choir.

COOP, Jane Austin; Concert Pianist; b. 18 April 1950, Saint John, NB, Canada; m. George Laverock 22 Feb. 1984; one d. *Education:* Art diploma, 1971, BMus, Performance, 1972, University of Toronto; MM, Peabody Conservatory, Baltimore, 1974. *Career:* Debut: St Lawrence Centre, Toronto, Canada; Wigmore Hall, London, England; Carnegie Recital Hall, New York, USA; Soloist with all major Canadian Orchestras; Recitals and Concerts in Canada, USA, England, France, Poland, Netherlands, Yugoslavia, Hungary, Czechoslovakia, Russia; Major Tours of Hong Kong, China, Japan. *Recordings:* The Romantic Piano; Beethoven–Eroica variations and Sonatas Op 109 and Op 111; Bach, English Suite No. 3 and Partita No. 5; Haydn, 4 Sonatas; Mozart, The Piano Quartets, with members of the Orford Quartet; Piano Pieces; Piano Variations (Schumann, Schubert, Brahms); Piano Concerti, (Bartók and Prokofiev). *Honours:* 1st Prize, Washington International Piano Competition, 1975; Finalist, Munich International Competition, 1977; Killam Award for Career Excellence, 1989. *Current Management:* Joyce Maguire Arts Management, 3526 West 5th Avenue, Vancouver, British Colombia, Canada.

COOPER, Anna; Singer (Mezzo-soprano); b. 1965, England. *Education:* Studied at the Royal Academy of Music, and at La Fenice, Venice. *Career:* Many appearances with leading British opera companies, including Glyndebourne, English National Opera and English Opera Group; Roles have included parts in Albert Herring, Die Walküre, Die

Zauberflöte, L'Italiana in Algeri and Dido and Aeneas; Appearances with the Royal Opera, Covent Garden, as Flora, Lola, the Madrigal Singer (Manon Lescaut), Kate Pinkerton, Grimgerde, Countess Ceprano (Rigoletto) and Annina; Glasa in Katya Kabanova, 1997; Further engagements in Brussels, Saarbrucken, Milan, Athens, Korea, Strasbourg, Japan and the USA. *Honours:* Winner, Kathleen Ferrier Award; Scholarship to La Fenice, Venice. *Address:* c/o Saarbrücken Opera, Schillerplatz, D–66111 Saarbrücken, Germany.

COOPER, Barry Anthony Raymond, MA, DPhil, FRCO; university professor; b. 2 May 1949, Westcliff-on-Sea, Essex, England; m. Susan Catherine Baynes 1973l four c. *Education:* University College, Oxford, studied organ with John Webster, composition with Kenneth Leighton. *Career:* Lecturer in Music, St Andrews University, 1973; Research Officer, 1974, Lecturer in Music, 1978, Senior Lecturer in Music, 1989, University of Aberdeen; Senior Lecturer in Music, 1990, Reader in Music, 2000, Professor of Music, 2003, University of Manchester; mem, Royal Musical Association; Royal College of Organists. *Compositions:* Oratorio, The Ascension; Song-Cycle, The Unasked Question; Wind Band, Mons Graupius; Choral, Organ and Chamber Music. *Publications include:* G. B. Sammartini, Concerto in G (Ed OUP) 1976; J. C. Schickhardt, Sonata in D (Ed OUP) 1978; Catalogue of Early Printed Music in Aberdeen Libraries, 1978; Englische Musiktheorie im 17 und 18 Jahrhundert (in Geschichte der Musiktheorie, Band 9, 1986); Beethoven's Symphony No. 10, First Movement (Realisation and Completion), Universal Edition, 1988; English Solo Keyboard Music of the Middle and Late Baroque, 1989; Beethoven and the Creative Process, 1990; L. van Beethoven, Three Bagatelles (Ed Novello), 1991; The Beethoven Compendium (Ed), 1991; Beethoven's Folksong Settings, 1994; J. Blow, Complete Organ Music (Ed Musica Britannica), 1996; D. F. Tovey, A Companion to Beethoven's Pianoforte Sonatas (Ed), 1999; Beethoven (Master Musicians), 2000. *Contributions:* Musical Times; Music and Letters; Music Review; RMA Research Chronicle; Proceedings/Journal of RMA; Recherches sur la Musique Française Classique; Early Music; Acta Musicologica; Beethoven Journal; BBC Music Magazine; Welsh Music History; Irish Musical Studies; Bulletin of the John Rylands University Library of Manchester; New Grove Dictionary of Music and Musicians, Ad Parnassum. *Honours:* Osgood Prize, 1972; Halstead Scholarship, 1972–74; RSE Research Fellow, 1986–87. *Address:* Martin Harris Building (Music), University of Manchester, Coupland Street, Manchester M13 9PL, England.

COOPER, Imogen; Concert Pianist; b. 28 Aug. 1949, London, England; m. John Alexander Batten, 1982. *Education:* Paris Conservatoire (Premier Prix). *Career:* Pianist, regular performer at Proms since televised debut 1975; First British pianist and first woman to appear in South Bank Piano Series, 1975; Regular performer with all major British orchestras; Orchestral engagements with: Berlin Philharmonic, Vienna Philharmonic, Boston Symphony, New York and Los Angeles Philharmonic Orchestras; International tours include Austria, Italy, Germany, Australasia, Netherlands, France, Scandinavia, Spain, USA, Japan; Co-commissioned with Cheltenham Festival and premiered Traced Overhead by Thomas Adès, 1996. *Recordings include:* Schubert Piano Works: The Last 6 Years, Schubert and Schumann with Wolfgang Holzmair; Mozart: Double and triple piano concertos, with Alfred Brendel; Schubert Trios and Arpeggione Sonata with Raphaël Oleg and Sonia Wieder-Atherton; Eichendorf Lieder with Wolfgang Holzmair; Rachmaninov/Franck/Fauré with Sonia Wieder-Atherton. *Current Management:* Askonas Holt Ltd, Lonsdale Chambers, 27 Chancery Lane, London, WC2A 1PF, England. *Telephone:* (20) 7400-1700. *Fax:* (20) 7400-1799. *E-mail:* info@askonasholt.co.uk. *Website:* www.askonasholt.co.uk.

COOPER, Kenneth; Harpsichordist, Pianist, Musicologist, Conductor and Educator; b. 31 May 1941, New York City, USA; m. Josephine Mongiardo, 1 June 1969, 1 s. *Education:* High School of Music and Art, New York City; BA, 1962, MA, Graduate faculties, 1964, PhD, Graduate Faculties, 1971, Columbia University; Harpsichord Study with Sylvia Marlowe, Mannes College of Music. *Career:* Debut: Wigmore Hall, 1965; Alice Tully Hall, USA, 1973; Academic Instructor, Barnard College, 1965–71; Adjunct Assistant Professor, Brooklyn College, 1971–73; Professor of Harpsichord, Director of Collegium, Mannes College, 1975–85; Visiting Specialist in Performance Practice, Montclair State College, 1977–92; Artist-in-Residence, Columbia University, 1983–; Graduate seminars in Baroque Performance Practice, Manhattan School of Music, 1984–; Director, Baroque Aria Ensemble, Manhattan School of Music; Graduate Workshops in Performance Practice, Peabody Conservatory of Music, 1987–90; Graduate workshops at New England Conservatory, 2001; Many residencies and guest appearances and lectures; Performance: Premieres of works by Seymour Barab, Noel Lee, Ferruccio Busoni, Paul Ben-Haim, Ernst Krenek and others; Dozens of modern day revivals; Guest appearances and festivals; Harpsichordist and Pianist, Grand Canyon Chamber Music Festival, 1985–; Director, Berkshire Bach Ensemble, 1991–; Chairman, Harpsichord Department,

Manhattan School of Music, 1984–. *Recordings:* Numerous including: soundtracks, Van Gogh Revisited; Every Eye Forms Its Own Beauty; Valmont; Louis Cat Orze; Bach: 6 Brandenburg Concerti; Gamba-Harpsichord Sonatas, with Yo-Yo Ma; Flute-Fortepiano Sonatas with Susan Rotholz; Silks and Rags; Mother Goose and More; Bach Goldberg Variations. *Publications include:* Three Centuries of Music in Score. *Contributions:* Professional journals. *Address:* 425 Riverside Drive, New York, NY 10025, USA.

COOPER, Lawrence; Singer (Baritone); b. 14 Aug. 1946, Los Angeles, California, USA. *Education:* Studied at the San Fernando State College. *Career:* Sang with the San Francisco Opera from 1977 and at the City Opera New York from 1983; Wexford Festival, 1981, as George in Moore's Of Mice and Men, Houston Opera, 1982, as Wozzeck; Guest engagements in Los Angeles, Chicago (Lyric Opera), Seattle and Detroit (1988); Other roles include Ford in Falstaff, Marcello in La Bohème, Valentin (Faust) and Germont; Frequent concert appearances. *Address:* c/o New York City Opera, Lincoln Center, New York, NY 10023, USA.

COOTE, Alice; British singer (mezzo-soprano); b. 10 May 1968, Frodsham, Cheshire, England. *Education:* Guildhall School of Music and Drama, London, Royal Northern Coll. of Music and Nat. Opera Studio. *Career:* concerts include oratorio with London and Liverpool Philharmonic Orchestras, Bergen Philharmonic, London Mozart Players, appearances at the BBC Proms 1997, 2002, 2003, recitals at Cheltenham and Edinburgh Festivals, on BBC Radio 3, and at the Wigmore Hall, London; roles include Cherubino in Figaro, Dorabella in Così fan tutte, Penelope in The Return of Ulysses, Kate Pinkerton in Madama Butterfly, Suzy in La Rondine, the Page in Salome, Glycère in Cherubini's Anacréon ou l'amour fugitif, Fortuna and Valletto in Poppea, Hanna Kennedy in Mary Stuart; season 1998–99 included her debut at Opéra Bastille in Parsifal, the title role in Rape of Lucretia at Nantes, Tamyris in Il Re Pastore for Opera North, Ruggiero in Alcina at Stuttgart; season 2002–03 included Covent Garden debut as Dryade in Ariadne auf Naxos, Ruggiero in Alcina at San Francisco, Octavian in Der Rosenkavalier for ENO, Strauss' Composer in Chicago, Dido in Les Troyens for San Francisco Opera, Turnspit in Rusalka and Orlando at Covent Garden; 2004 appearances include Rinaldo at Göttingen, Der Komponist in Ariadne auf Naxos for WNO. *Recordings include:* Vaughan Williams' Hugh the Drover 1994, Rossini's Ricciardo e Zoraide 1997, Great Operatic Arias 2002, Verdi's Falstaff 2002, Handel: The Choice of Hercules 2002, Songs 2003. *Honours:* Brigitte Fassbaender Award for Lieder Interpretation, Decca-Kathleen Ferrier Prize 1992. *Current Management:* IMG Artists, Lovell House, 616 Chiswick High Road, London, W4 5RX, England. *Telephone:* (20) 8233-5800. *Fax:* (20) 8233-5801. *E-mail:* smardo@imgworld.com. *Website:* www.imgartists.com.

COPE, David (Howell); Composer, Writer and Instrument Maker; b. 17 May 1941, San Francisco, California, USA. *Education:* Studied at Arizona State University and with Halsey Stevens, Ingolf Dahl and George Perle at the University of Southern California. *Career:* Teacher at Kansas State College, 1968–69, California Lutheran College, the Cleveland Institute, Miami University of Ohio and the University of California, Santa Cruz, from 1977; Editor of The Composer, 1969–81. *Compositions include:* Tragic Overture, 1960; 4 Piano Sonatas, 1960–67; 2 String Quartets, 1961, 1963; Variations for piano and wind, 1965; Contrasts for orchestra, 1966; Music for brass and strings, 1967; Iceberg Meadow for prepared piano, 1968; Streams for orchestra, 1973; Spirals for tuba and tape, 1973; Requiem for Bosque Redondo, 1974; Arena for cello and tape, 1974; Re-Birth for concert band, 1975; Rituals for cello, 1976; Vectors for 4 percussion, 1976; Tenor Saxophone Concerto, 1976; Threshold and Visions for orchestra, 1977; Glassworks for 2 pianos and tape, 1979; Piano Concerto, 1980; The Way for various instruments, 1981; Corridors of Light for various instruments, 1983; Afterlife for orchestra, 1983. *Address:* c/o ASCAP, ASCAP Building, 1 Lincoln Plaza, New York, NY 10023, USA.

COPLEY, John Michael Harold; Opera Director and Producer; b. 12 June 1933, Birmingham, England. *Education:* Sadler's Wells Ballet School; Diploma, honours in Theatre Design, Central School of Arts and Crafts, London. *Career:* Stage Manager: Opera and ballet companies, Sadler's Wells in Rosebery Avenue, 1953–56, musicals, plays and so on, London West End; Deputy Stage Manager, 1960–63, Assistant Resident Producer, 1963–65, Associate Resident Producer, 1966–72, Resident Producer, 1972–75, Principal Resident Producer, 1975–88, Covent Garden Opera Company, productions including: Suor Angelica, 1965, Così fan tutte, 1968, 1981, Le nozze di Figaro, 1971, Don Giovanni, 1973, Faust, 1974, Benvenuto Cellini, 1976, Ariadne auf Naxos, 1976, Maria Stuarda, Royal Silver Jubilee Gala, 1977, La Traviata, Lucrezia Borgia, 1980, Semele, 1982; Other productions include: Numerous operas, London Coliseum, Athens Festival, Netherlands Opera, Belgian National Opera, Wexford Festival, Dallas Civic Opera (US debut, 1972, Lucia di Lammermoor), Chicago Lyric Opera, Greek National Opera, Australian Opera, English Opera North, Scottish Opera, English

Opera Group; Vancouver Opera; Ottawa Festival, San Francisco Opera, Metropolitan Opera (New York), Santa Fe Opera, La Bohème, 1990; Houston Grand Opera, Washington Opera, San Diego Opera, London West End; Dallas production of Hansel and Gretel seen at Los Angeles, 1992; Directed local premiere of Britten's A Midsummer Night's Dream, Houston, 1993; Season 1996 with La Rondine at St Louis and Madama Butterfly at Santa Fe; Appearances include: Apprentice, Britten's Peter Grimes, Covent Garden, 1950; Soloist, Bach's St John Passion, Bremen, Germany, 1965; Co-director with Patrick Garland, Fanfare for Europe Gala, Covent Garden, 1973. *Current Management:* Hazard Chase, Norman House, Cambridge Place, Cambridge CB2 1NS, England. *Telephone:* (1223) 312400. *Fax:* (1223) 460827. *Website:* www .hazardchase.co.uk. *Address:* 9D Thistle Grove, London SW10 9RR, England.

CORAL, Giampaolo; Composer; b. 22 Jan. 1944, Trieste. *Education:* Diploma at the Conservatory of Music B Marcello, Venice. *Career:* Founder and Art Director of International Contemporary Music Festival, Trieste Prima; Art Director of International Competition for musical composition, Prize Town of Trieste. *Compositions include:* Stage Works, Mr Hyde, opera in one act; Schwanengesang, chamber opera in one act; Favola, romantic pantomime in one act; Orchestral Works, Magnificat for soprano and orchestra, Amras for violin and orchestra, Kubin Zyklus for orchestra, Tout a coup et comme par jeu for flute and orchestra, Requiem for orchestra; Chamber music, Osservando Paul Klee for violin, cello, piano, Trakl Lieder for soprano and piano, Seconda Sonata for piano, Klavieralbum I–III, Raps I–XI for ensemble, Damonen und Nachtgesichte von A. Kubin for ensemble, Modulazioni for piano (four hands), Aloe for vocal ensemble and five brass. *Publications:* Editio Musica, Budapest; Suvini Zerboni, Milano; Sonzogno, Milano; Curci, Milano; Edipan, Roma; Dictionary: Riemann Musik Lexikon, Utet. *Address:* Via Ponchielli 3, 34122 Trieste, Italy.

CORAZZA, Remy; Singer (Tenor); b. 16 April 1933, Revin, Ardennes, France. *Education:* Studied at the Toulouse and Paris Conservatories. *Career:* Debut: Opéra-Comique, Paris, as Beppe in Pagliacci, 1959; Sang Gonzalve in L'Heure Espagnole at the Paris Opéra, 1960; Many performances in Paris and elsewhere in France as Pinkerton, Rodolfo, Hoffmann, Nadir and in Mozart roles; Opéra du Rhin, Strasbourg, from 1974, Salzburg from 1978, as Monostatos and the Hoffmann buffo roles; Professor at the Paris Conservatory, 1985; Glyndebourne debut, 1987, as Torquemada in L'Heure Espagnole; Nantes Opera 1990 in Le Pré aux clercs by Hérold and Le Roi l'a dit by Delibes. *Address:* c/o Conservatoire National, 14 Rue de Madrid, 75008 Paris, France.

CORBELLI, Alessandro; Singer (Baritone); b. 21 Sept. 1952, Turin, Italy. *Education:* Studied with Giuseppe Valdengo. *Career:* Debut: Bergamo, 1974, as Marcello in La Bohème; Many appearances in the buffo repertory at opera houses in Italy, Vienna, Paris and Germany; Rossini roles include Pacuvio in La Pietra del Paragone (Picco Scala and Edinburgh, 1982), Dandini in La Cenerentola (Glyndebourne, 1985) and Gaudenzio in Il Signor Bruschino (Paris, 1986); Rome Opera, 1985–86, as Belcore (L'Elisir d'amore) and Marcello; Covent Garden debut, 1988, as Taddeo in L'Italiana in Algeri; Season 1989–90 in Pergolesi's Lo frate' nnamorato at La Scala, conducted by Muti, as Don Alfonso at the Salzburg Festival and as Germano in La Scala di Seta at Schwetzingen; Other roles include Papageno (Ravenna, 1986), Guglielmo, Escamillo, Malatesta and the Figaros of Mozart, Rossini and Paisiello; Fabrizio in Crispino e la Comare, Pantaleone in The Love of Three Oranges and Monteverdi's Ottone; Season 1992 as Belcore at Parma, Rossini's Martino and Gormano at Cologne, the Paris Opéra-Comique and the Schwetzingen Festival; Sang Leporello at Lausanne, 1996 and Alfonso at Covent Garden, 1997; Dandini in Cenerentola at Pesaro and Dulcarmara at Madrid, 1998; Season 2000–01 as Rossini's Dandini and Taddeo at the New York Met. Leporello at Glyndebourne and Belfiore in Verdi's Un giorno di regno, at Bologna; Dandini at Covent Garden, 2003. *Recordings include:* La Cenerentola, conducted by Abbado; L'Italiana in Algeri; Paisiello's Barbiere di Siviglia and La Buona Figliuola by Piccinni. *Address:* c/o Teatro alla Scala, Via Filodrammatici 2, 20212 Milan, Italy.

CORBETT, Sidney; Composer; b. 26 April 1960, Chicago, Illinois, USA. *Education:* BA with high distinction in Music Composition, 1982, further studies, 1978–82, University of San Diego, California; Studied composition principally with Pauline Oliveros, Bernard Rands, Joji Yuasa, Jean-Charles François; MM, 1984, MMA, 1985, DMA, 1989, Yale School of Music; Principal composition teachers include Jacob Druckman and Martin Bresnick; Thesis on Metaphor Structures in Contemporary Music; DAAD Fellow and member of G Ligeti Seminar, Hamburg, Germany, 1985–87. *Career:* Compositions performed in USA and Europe, including radio broadcasts; Active as composer in Germany, 1985–. *Compositions:* Arien, violin solo, 1983; Pastel Nos 1 and 2, trombone quartet, 1984, 1988; Ghost Reveille for orchestra, 1984; For Pianos, for 4 pianos, 1984; Bass Animation for contrabass with 2 percussions, 1985; Arien IV: Solo Music for guitar, 1986; Kandinsky

Romance for chamber ensemble, 1986; Cactus Flower for solo flute, 1988; Pianos' Dream, piano duo, 1989; Concerto for trombone and wind orchestra, 1989; Lieder aus der Dunkelkammer for soprano, harp and chamber orchestra, 1990; Symphony No. 1 Tympan, 1991–92; Hamlet Variations (in memoriam John Coltrane) for solo euphonium, 1992; Gloucester Epiphonies for chamber ensemble, 1993. *Address:* Vogelsangstrasse 55, 7000 Stuttgart 1, Germany.

CORBOZ, Michel; Conductor; b. 14 Feb. 1934, Marsens, Switzerland. *Education:* Studied at Ecole Normale in Fribourg. *Career:* Chorus Master at Notre-Dame in Lausanne from 1954, leading such works as the Fauré Requiem; Accompanied singers at the organ and worked at various Lausanne churches; Founded the Ensemble Vocal et Instrumental de Lausanne, 1961, giving notable performances of Monteverdi's Orfeo; Conductor of the choirs of the Gulbenkian Foundation in Lisbon from 1969, leading works by Bach, Monteverdi and Vivaldi; Conducted Monteverdi's Il Ritorno d'Ulisse at Mézières, 1989. *Recordings:* Monteverdi's Orfeo and Vespers, Bach's B minor Mass, Cavalli's Ercole Amante, Charpentier's David et Jonathas, works by Vivaldi and Giovanni Gabrieli. *Address:* c/o Conservatoire de Musique, 228-Arue Pierre Aeby, CH–1700 Fribourg, Switzerland.

CORDERO, Roque, BA; Panamanian composer, conductor and educator; b. 16 Aug. 1917, Panama City; m. Elizabeth L. Johnson 1947; three s. *Education:* Hamline Univ., studied composition with Ernst Krenek, conducting with Dimitri Mitropoulos, Stanley Chapple and Leon Barzin. *Career:* Dir and Prof., Nat. Inst. of Music, Panama 1950–64; conductor, Nat. Orchestra of Panama 1964–66; guest conductor in Colombia, Brazil, Chile, Argentina, Puerto Rico, USA, El Salvador and Guatemala; Prof. of Music and Asst Dir, Latin American Music Center, Indiana Univ., USA 1966–69; Prof. of Music, Illinois State Univ. 1972–. *Compositions:* over 20 published including Cinco Mensajes para Cuatro Amigos for guitar, 1983; Cantata for Peace for solo baritone, choir and orchestra, 1979; Fourth Symphony, Panamanian, 1986; Serenata, for flute, viola, clarinet and harp, 1987. *Recordings:* Violin Concerto and 8 Miniatures with Detroit Symphony; 2nd Symphony; Duo, 1954; Dodecaconcerto; Cinco Mensajes para Cuatro Amigos for Guitar; Sonatina Ritmica; Permutaciones 7; Quinteto; Four Messages for flutes and piano; 8 Miniatures (Chicago Sinfonietta); Second Symphony, The Louisville Orchestra. *Publications include:* Curso de Solfeo, Argentina 1963, Mexico 1975; The Music of Panama: Four Messages for flutes and piano, 1992; Fanfarria Jubilosa for orchestra, 1994; Duos for oboe and bassoon, 1996; Centennial Symphonic tribute for orchestra, 1997; contrib. to Buenos Aires Musical; Revista Musical Chilena; Journal of Inter-American Studies; Grove's Dictionary of Music. *Address:* Music Department, Illinois State University, Normal, IL 61790-5660, USA.

CORDIER, David John, MA; singer (countertenor); b. 1 May 1959, Rochester, Kent, England; m. Ursula Cordier 1990; one s. one d. *Education:* King's College, Cambridge, Royal College of Music, London. *Career:* debut at Wigmore Hall, 1989; Darmstadt (Lear by Reimann), 1990; Handel Opera, Göttingen; Halle and Karlsruhe Festivals; Recital Berlin Philharmonic, 1996; Opera in Amsterdam, Munich, Düsseldorf, Dresden; Innsbruck, Salzburg and Bern; Season 1998 with Ezio at the Halle Handel Festival and Bertarido in Rodelinda for GTO; sang Handel's Radamisto at Halle, 2000; Teacher at Hanns Eisler Hochschule in Berlin (countertenor). *Recordings include:* Bach Matthew Passion, conducted by Gustav Leonhardt; Solo recitals English song. *Address:* Lindlarer Str 98, 51491 Overath, Germany.

CORGHI, Azio; Composer; b. 9 March 1937, Cirie, Turin, Italy. *Education:* Studied at Turin Conservatory, Piano Diploma, 1961, and with Bruno Bettinelli at Milan Conservatory. *Career:* Freelance composer and teacher of composition at Conservatorio Giuseppe Verdi, Milan. *Compositions:* Music theatre pieces: Symbola, 1971, and Tactus, 1974; Ballets with voices: Actus III, 1978, and Mazapegul, 1986; Opera Gargantua after Rabelais, produced at Teatro Regio, Turin, 1984; Opera Blimunda, produced at Teatro Lirico, Milan, 1990; Opera Divara, produced at Städtischen Bühnen Münster, 1993; Version of Handel's Rinaldo at Catania, 1997; Isabella, after Rossini, Pesaro, 1998. *Publications:* Critical editions of L'Italiana in Algeri and Tosca. *Address:* Conservatorio Giuseppe Verdi, Via del Conservatorio 12, 20122 Milan, Italy.

CORIGLIANO, John Paul; Composer and Teacher; b. 16 Feb. 1938, New York, NY, USA. *Education:* BA, Columbia University, 1959; With Otto Luening, Vittorio Giannini, Manhattan School of Music; Privately with Paul Creston; Honorary doctorates from Manhattan School of Music, 1992 and Ithaca College, 1995. *Career:* Music Programmer, WQXR-FM and WBAI-FM, New York, 1959–64; Associate Producer, Musical Programmes, CBS-TV, 1961–72; Music Director, Morris Theatre, New Jersey, 1962–64; Teacher of Composition: College of Church Musicians, Washington DC, 1968–71; Manhattan School of Music, 1971–; Lehman College, City University of New York, 1973–, Distinguished Professor, 1986–; Composer-in-Residence, Chicago Symphony Orchestra, 1987–89;

Symphony No. 1 premiere, Boston Symphony, also New York Philharmonic, Chicago Symphony, Seattle Symphony; The Ghosts of Versailles premiere, Metropolitan Opera, 1991; Fanfares to Music, Cincinnati Symphony, 1995; mem, American Society of Composers, Authors and Publishers. *Compositions:* Kaleidoscope, 2 pianos, 1959; Sonata, violin, piano, 1963; Elegy, orchestra, 1965; The Cloisters, 4 songs, voice, piano, 1965, voice, orchestra, 1976; Christmas at the Cloisters, chorus, organ or piano, 1966; Tournaments Overture, 1966; Piano Concerto, 1968; Poem in October, tenor, 8 instruments, 1970, tenor, orchestra, 1976; The Naked Carmen, mixed-media opera, 1970; Creations, 2 scenes from Genesis, narrator, chamber orchestra, 1972; Gazebo Dances, band, 1973; Aria, oboe, strings, 1975; Oboe Concerto, 1975; Poem on His Birthday, 1976; Etude Fantasy, piano, 1976; Voyage, string orchestra, 1976, flute, string orchestra, 1983; Clarinet Concerto, 1977; Pied Piper Fantasy, Flute Concerto, 1981; 3 Hallucinations, 1981; Promenade Overture, 1981; Echoes of Forgotten Rites: Summer Fanfare, 1982; Fantasia on an Ostinato, piano, 1985, orchestra, 1986; Symphony No. 1, 1989–90; Opera, The Ghosts of Versailles, 1991; Phantasmagoria (on Themes from The Ghosts of Versailles), cello and piano, 1993; How Like Pellucid Statues, Daddy, 1994; Amen, for double a cappella chorus, 1994; String Quartet, 1996; Chiaroscuro, 1997; Fancy on a Bach Air, 1997; The Red Violin, Chaconne for violin and orchestra, 1998; Troubadours, variations for guitar and orchestra, 1999; Vocalise, 1999; A Dylan Thomas Trilogy, chorus, soloists and orchestra (1960–76; rev. 1999); The Mannheim Rocket, 2000; Phantasmagoria: Suite from The Ghosts of Versailles, orchestra, 2000; Symphony No. 2, 2000; Mr. Tambourine Man: Seven Poems of Bob Dylan, 2000; Incidental music for plays; Film scores. *Recordings:* Symphony No. 1, Chicago Symphony/Barenboim; Pied Piper Fantasy; Fantasia on an Ostinato; Of Rage and Remembrance–Symphony No. 1, 1996; String Quartet, 1996; Video of The Ghosts of Versailles (DGG); Phantasmagoria (The Fantasy Album). *Honours:* Guggenheim Fellow, 1968–69; NEA Grant, 1976; Award, 1990, Member, 1991, American Academy and Institute of Arts and Letters; L. Grawemeyer Award, 1991; Musical American Composer of the Year Winner, 1992; Grammy Award, Classical Album of the Year, 1996; Grammy Award, Composition of the Year, 1996; George Washington University Presidential Medal of Honor, 1996. *Current Management:* Jay K. Hoffman & Associates, 136 East 57th Street, New York, NY 10017, USA. *Address:* 365 West End Avenue, New York, NY 10024, USA.

CORNWELL, Joseph; Singer (tenor); b. 1959, England. *Education:* BA in Music, York University. *Career:* Sang originally with such early music groups as the Consort of Musicke and the Taverner Consort; Promenade Concert debut, 1982, in Monteverdi's Vespers under Andrew Parrott; Tours of Netherlands and France in the Bach Passions; Verdi's Requiem at the Albert Hall, conducted by David Willcocks; Bruckner's Te Deum at the Festival Hall; Appearances at the Paris, Bruges, Flanders, Three Choirs and Brighton Festivals; Conductors include Trevor Pinnock, Stephen Cleobury, Ton Koopman and Roger Norrington; Bach's B minor Mass with the London Bach Orchestra at the Barbican, Nov 1990; Has sung on ITV, Swiss television and BBC television; Opera roles include Fenton in Falstaff, Frederic in Mignon, Jove in The Return of Ulysses (Kent Opera) and parts in Mahagonny and Let's Make an Opera; Sang title role in Monteverdi's Orfeo for Oslo Summer Opera, conducted by Andrew Parrott, and in 1993 for Boston Early Music Festival; Also sang Lurcanio in Handel's Ariodante for St Gallen Opera, in Switzerland; Arretro in Peri's Euridice in Rouen, 1992–93; Sang in King Arthur with The Sixteen, Lisbon, 1996. *Recordings include:* Monteverdi Christmas Vespers; Handel's Messiah; Albums for several labels; Monteverdi Vespers with Parrott; Rossini's Petite Messe Sollenelle with Jos Van Immerseel. *Current Management:* Hazard Chase Ltd, Norman House, Cambridge Place, Cambridge, CB2 1NS, England. *Telephone:* (1223) 312400. *Fax:* (1223) 460827. *Website:* www.hazardchase.co.uk.

CORP, Ronald; British conductor and ecclesiastic; b. 4 Jan. 1951, Wells, Somerset, England. *Education:* MA (Oxon); Dip Theol (Southampton). *Career:* librarian, producer and presenter, BBC Radio 3, 1973–87; Founder Conductor, New London Orchestra, 1988 and New London Children's Choir, 1991; Musical Dir, The London Chorus Soc. and Conductor, Highgate Choral Soc.; broadcasts for BBC with BBC Singers, BBC Concert Orchestra, Ulster Orchestra, New London Orchestra and New London Children's Choir; Promenade Concert debut, 1990 with Britten's Noye's Fludde and further Proms with New London Orchestra in 1991, 1995, 1998, 1999 and with BBC Concert Orchestra, 1996 and 1997; Ordained Deacon in the Church of England 1998, Priest 1999–; mem. Asscn of British Choral Dirs (ABCD), Nat. Fed. of Music Socs (NFMS); Vice Pres. Sullivan Soc.; Trustee Musician's Benevolent Fund and Chair. of the Education Cttee. *Compositions:* And All the Trumpets Sounded, 1989; Laudamus, 1992; Four Elizabethan Lyrics, 1994; Jubilate Deo, 1995; Cornucopia, 1997; Piano Concerto, 1997; A New Song, 1999; Mass 'Christ Our Future', 2000; Mary's Song, 2001; Adonai Echad, 2001; Other choral works. *Recordings:* 18 albums with New London Orchestra, including British Light Music Classics I–

IV, Kaleidoscope 2002, Dover Beach (BBC Singers Commission) 2003, Forever Child 2004; Poulenc, Satie, Milhaud, Prokofiev and Virgil Thomson; Britten recording with New London Children's Choir;. *Publications:* The Choral Singer's Companion, 1987. *Address:* 76 Brent Street, London NW4 2ES, England. *Telephone:* (208) 202-8123. *Fax:* (208) 203-4134. *E-mail:* ronald.corp@btconnect.com. *Website:* www.ronaldcorp.com.

CORSARO, Frank (Andrew); Opera Director; b. 22 Dec. 1924, New York, NY, USA. *Education:* Studied at the City College of New York, the Yale University School of Drama and the Actors' Studio. *Career:* Debut: New York City Opera, 1958, Floyd's Susanna; City Opera productions have included Rigoletto, La Traviata, Pelléas et Mélisande, Prince Igor, Faust, Don Giovanni, A Village Romeo and Juliet and Janáček's Makropulos Case and Cunning Little Vixen, 1981; For Houston Opera has produced premiere productions of Pasatieri's The Seagull, 1974, and Scott Joplin's Treemonisha, 1975; Premieres of Floyd's Of Mice and Men (Seattle, 1970) and Hoiby's Summer and Smoke (St Paul, 1971); At the Glyndebourne Festival has produced Prokofiev's The Love of Three Oranges; Metropolitan Opera, 1984, Handel's Rinaldo; Season 1992 with the US stage premiere of Busoni's Doktor Faust, New York City Opera; New production of Faust for the Chicago Lyric Opera, 1996; Hansel and Gretel for Canadian Opera Company and Houston Opera, 1998. *Address:* c/o New York City Opera, Lincoln Center, New York, NY 10023, USA.

CORTE, Miguel; Singer (Tenor); b. 1952, Mexico. *Education:* Studied in Monterrey and New York. *Career:* Debut: Metropolitan Opera, 1981, as Alfredo; Sang with Kentucky Opera as the Duke of Mantua, Rodolfo, Pinkerton, Fenton and Jacquino; European engagements as the Duke at Zürich (1984), Alfredo at Trieste (1985) and Werther in Mexico City (1985); Has also sung in Salzburg (Alfredo, 1983), San Francisco (as Pinkerton) and in the Verdi Requiem (at Seattle). *Address:* c/o Kentucky Opera, 631 South Fifth Street, Louisville, KY 40202, USA.

CORTES, Gardar; Conductor and Singer (tenor); b. 1950, Reykjavík, Iceland. *Education:* Studied at Royal Academy of Music and Trinity College of Music in London. *Career:* Has conducted choirs in Iceland and founded the Reykjavík Symphony Orchestra, 1985, leading it on a tour of Denmark; With Icelandic Opera has conducted Orpheus in the Underworld, Pagliacci and Die Fledermaus, Noye's Fludde at the International Festival in Reykjavík; Appearances as singer with Oslo Opera, Royal Swedish Opera, Seattle Opera, Windsor Festival, Opera North and Belfast Festival; Intendant of the Gothenburg Opera, Sweden; Roles have included Eisenstein, Tamino, Hoffmann, Radames, Cavaradossi, Florestan and Otello.

CORTEZ, Luis Jaime; Mexican composer and musicologist; b. 1963, Morelia, Michoacán. *Education:* Univ. of Mexico. *Career:* Dir, Centro Nacional de Investigación, Documentación e Información Musical 1987–1994; Dir, Conservatorio de las Roses, Morelia 1996–. *Compositions include:* Formas demasiado lejos 1985, Canto por un equinoccio 1989, Lluvias (Symphony No. 1) 1992, En blanco y negro (Symphony No. 2) 1995, Las tentaciones de San Antonio (opera) 1996. *Address:* Conservatorio de las Roses, Santiago Tapia No. 30, Col. Centro, Morelia, CP 58000, Mexico (office).

CORTEZ, Viorica; Singer (Mezzo-soprano); b. 22 Dec. 1935, Bucium, Romania; m. Emmanuel Bondeville, 1974 (deceased 1987). *Education:* Studied at the Iasi and Bucharest Conservatories. *Career:* Debut: Iasi Opera, 1960, as Dalila; Sang Dalila at Toulouse, 1965; Bucharest Opera, 1965–70; Covent Garden debut, 1968, as Carmen; Italian debut, 1969, as Amneris at Naples; La Scala Milan, 1970, as Dalila; US debut, Seattle Opera, 1971; Metropolitan Opera from 1971, as Carmen, Amneris, Giulietta in Les Contes d'Hoffmann, Adalgisa in Norma and Azucena; Chicago debut, 1973, in Maria Stuarda; Sang in the premiere of Bondeville's Antoine et Cléopatre, Rouen, 1974; Paris Opéra, 1980, in Bluebeard's Castle, Oedipus Rex and Boris Godunov; Sang La Cieca in La Gioconda at the Verona Arena and Barcelona, 1988; Gertrude in Hamlet, Turin, 1990, and the title role in the premiere of La Lupa by Marco Tutino at Livorno; Season 1992 as Ulrica at Genoa; Montpellier 1995, as Uta in Reyer's Sigurd; Sang Rosa in Cilea's L'Arlesiana at Montpellier, 1996; Season 2000–01 as the Marquise in La Fille du régiment at Strasbourg, and as Lia in Magnard's Bérénice at Marseilles. *Recordings:* Carmen; Aida; Il Trovatore; Verdi's Oberto; Donizetti's Requiem; Rigoletto; Video of Rigoletto. *Address:* c/o Opéra de Montpellier, 11 boulevard Victor Hugo, 34967 Montpellier, France.

CORY, Eleanor; Composer; b. 8 Sept. 1943, Englewood, NJ, USA. *Education:* Studied with Charles Wuorinen and others at Columbia University in New York. *Career:* Has taught at Yale University, Manhattan School of Music, and Sarah Lawrence College among others. *Compositions include:* Waking for soprano and ensemble, 1974; Octagons for ensemble, 1976; Tapestry for orchestra, 1982; String Quartet, 1985; Of Mere Being for chorus and brass quintet, 1987; Fantasy for flute, guitar and percussion, 1991; Canyons for chamber orchestra, 1991. *Address:* c/o ASCAP, ASCAP Building, 1 Lincoln Plaza, New York, NY 10023, USA.

COSMA, Octavian (Lazar); Musicologist, Professor and Doctor; b. 15 Feb. 1933, Treznea, Salaj, Romania; m. Elena, 15 Nov 1958, 1 s., 1 d. *Education:* Rimsky Korsakov Conservatory, St Petersburg, Russia, 1959. *Career:* Debut: Muzica, 1954; Councillor, Ministry of Culture and Education, 1959–63; Assistant Lecturer, Professor, Academy of Music, Bucharest, 1959–; Secretary, 1990, Vice President, 1992, Romanian Union of Composers and Musicologists; Editor-in-Chief of journal, Mizica, 1990; mem, Romanian Union of Composers; American Musicological Society. *Publications:* The Romanian Opera, 2 vols, 1962; Enescu's Oedipus, 1967; The Chronicle of Romanian Music, vols I 1973, II 1974, III 1975, IV 1976, V 1983, VI 1984, VII 1986, VIII 1988, IX 1991; The Universe of Romanian Music, 1995. *Contributions:* Various professional journals. *Honours:* Ciprian Porumbescu Prize, Romanian Academy, 1962; Prize, Romanian Union of Composers, 1968. *Current Management:* Conservatorul Ciprian Porumbescu, Bucharest. *Address:* Cotroceni 5–7, Bucharest 76528, Romania.

COSMA, Viorel; Musicologist and Professor; b. 30 March 1923, Timisoara, Romania; m. Coralia Cosma. *Education:* Municipal Conservatory, Timisoara; Academie of Music, Bucharest. *Career:* Debut: As conductor in 1944; Musicologist and Music Critic from 1946; Professor from 1950. *Publications:* Historiographic Works: Two Millenia of Music, in English, 1982, Musicological Exegeses, 1984; Lexicography: Romanian Musicians, Lexicon, 1970, Musicians of Romania (A-C), Lexicon, 1989; Monographs: Ion Vidu, 1956, Ciprian Porumbescu, 1957, Elena Teodorini, 1960, Nicolae Filimon, 1966, The George Enescu Philharmonic, 1968, The Madrigal Choir, 1971, Enescu Today, 1981, Dinu Lipatti, 1991; Epistolography: Bartók, 1955, Enescu, 2 vols, 1974 and 1981; Romanian Performers: Lexicon, 1996. *Honours:* Prize, Romanian Composers, 1970, 1972, 1978, 1983, 1988, 1991; Prize, Academy of Romania, 1971. *Address:* Str Luterana 3, Bucharest, Romania.

COSSA, Dominic; Singer (Baritone) and Teacher; b. 13 May 1935, Jessup, Pennsylvania, USA; m. Janet Edgerton, 26 Dec 1957, 1 s., 1 d. *Education:* BS, University of Scranton, 1959; MA, University of Detroit, 1961; LhD, University of Scranton; Detroit Institute of Musical Arts, Philadelphia Academy of Vocal Arts; Principal vocal teachers: Anthony Marlowe, Robert Weede and Armen Boyajian. *Career:* Debut: Operatic debut as Morales, Carmen, New York City Opera, 1961; Leading baritone roles, New York City Opera; Metropolitan Opera debut, New York, as Silvio in Pagliacci, 1970–76; Other Met roles were Masetto, Rossini's Figaro, Marcello and Puccini's Lescaut; Opéra du Rhin, Strasbourg, 1976; Sang M. Triquet in Eugene Onegin at Florence, 2000; Faculty Manhattan School of Music, New York; Chair, Voice/ Opera, University of Maryland, College Park. *Recordings:* For Decca-London; New World Records; RCA-Victor including Achilles in Giulio Cesare, conducted by Julius Rudel. *Honours:* Inducted into Hall of Fame for great American Singers, Philadelphia Academy of Vocal Arts, 1993. *Address:* 845 Stonington Way, Arnold, MD 21012, USA.

COSSOTI, Max-René; Singer (Tenor); b. 1950, Italy. *Career:* Debut: Siena, 1973, in Gazzaniga's Don Giovanni; Genoa, 1974, Ernesto at Spoleto (1975) and Glyndebourne from 1976, as Fenton, Ferrando, Almaviva, Eurymachos in Monteverdi's Ulisse and Fileno in Haydn's La Fedeltà Premiata; Further engagements at Innsbruck, 1983, in Cesti's II Tito; Lisbon, 1985, as the Prince in Cenerentola and Trieste, 1992, as Zemlinsky's Zwerg; Other roles include Elvino in La Sonnambula, Alfredo, Gerald in Lakmé, Werther, and Alfred in Die Fledermaus; Sang L'incredible in Andrea Chenier at Rome, 1996; Dagobert in Lehar's Eva at Naples, 1998; Sang Mozart's Basilio at Klagenfurt, 2001. *Recordings include:* Videos of Ulisse, Falstaff and Il Barbiere di Sivigila from Glyndebourne. *Address:* c/o Teatro Comunale G Verdi, Riva Novembre 1, 34121, Trieste, Italy.

COSSOTTO, Fiorenza; Singer (Mezzo-soprano); b. 22 April 1935, Crescentino, Italy; m. Ivo Vinco, 1958. *Education:* Turin Conservatory; Study with Ettore Campogalliani. *Career:* Debut: La Scala Milan, 1957, in the premiere of Poulenc's Les Dialogues des Carmélites; Returned to Milan until 1973, notably as Verdi's Eboli, Amneris and Azucena, and in La Favorite, Les Huguenots, Il Barbiere di Siviglia and Cavalleria Rusticana; Sang Jane Seymour in Anna Bolena at Wexford in 1958; Covent Garden debut, 1959, as Neris in Cherubini's Médée; Chicago Lyric Opera, 1964, in La Favorite; Metropolitan Opera debut, 1968, as Amneris, returning for Laura in La Gioconda, Adalgisa, Norma, Carmen and Mistress Quickly (Falstaff); Sang, Verona Arena, 1960–89, notably as Amneris, which she sang at the Metropolitan, 1989; Sang Dalila at Newark, New Jersey, 1989, the Princess in Adriana Lecouvreur, Rome; Sang Santuzza, Piacenza, 1990; Ulrica at Lisbon and Amneris at Buenos Aires; Sang Ulrica at Genoa, 1992. *Recordings:* Roles in Andrea Chénier, Norma, Madama Butterfly, La Sonnambula, Macbeth, Don Carlos, Cavalleria Rusticana, Médée and Il Trovatore.

Address: c/o Teatro Comunale, Opera de Genova, Passo al Teatro 4, Italy.

COSTA, Mary; Singer (Soprano); b. 5 April 1932, Knoxville, Tennessee, USA. *Education:* Studied with Mario Chamlee at Los Angeles Conservatory and with Ernest St John Metz. *Career:* Sang in concert and took small roles in opera, then appeared as Susanna at Glyndebourne, 1958; San Francisco Opera from 1959, notably in the US premiere of A Midsummer Night's Dream, 1961; Royal Opera House, 1962, as Concepcion in L'Heure Espagnole and Violetta; Metropolitan Opera from 1964, as Violetta, Vanessa, Gilda, Despina, Alice Ford, Manon, Rosalinde and Musetta; Sang at the Bolshoi Theatre, Moscow, 1970, and appeared in the film The Great Waltz, 1972; Founded the Knoxville Tennessee Opera Company, 1978, and established the Mary Costa Scholarship at the University of Tennessee, 1979; Many concert appearances. *Recordings:* La Bohème. *Address:* c/o Knoxville Opera Company, PO Box 16, Knoxville, TN 37901, USA.

COSTANZO, Giuseppe; Singer (Tenor); b. 1958, Catania, Italy. *Career:* Debut: Bari, 1983, as Arturo in Lucia di Lammermoor; Macerata Festival, 1984, as Almaviva; Bergamo, 1984, as Ernani, Trieste and Tel-Aviv, 1985, as Pinkerton; La Scala debut, 1988, as Conte Alberto in L'Occasione fa il ladro; Cologne, 1991, as Gabriele Adorno in Simon Boccanegra; Other roles include Ernesto, Rinuccio in Gianni Schicchi, Edgardo, and Alfredo (Lisbon, 1987); Many concert engagements. *Address:* c/o Teatro Nacional San Carlos, Rua Serpo Panto no G, 1200 442 Lisbon, Portugal.

COSTINESCU, Gheorghe, DMus; composer, conductor, pianist, musicologist and educator; b. 12 Dec. 1934, Bucharest, Romania; m. Silvelin von Scanzoni 1971. *Education:* Bucharest Conservatory, Darmstadt and Cologne, Juilliard School, Columbia University, studied composition with Mihail Jora in Romania, Luciano Berio in USA; studied with Nadia Boulanger, Karlheinz Stockhausen, Henry Pousseur, Mario Davidovsky and Chou Wen-chung, conducting with Harold Faberman, Maurice Peress and Dennis Russell Davies in USA and with Sergiu Celibidache in Germany. *Career:* debut as composer and pianist, Sonata for Violin and Piano at Shiraz-Persepolis Festival, Iran, 1967; debut as conductor, The Washington premiere of Peter Maxwell Davis' Miss Donnithorn's Maggot at the Corcoran Gallery of Art, 1979; Professor Emeritus, Lehmann College, City University of New York; Premieres: Evolving Cycle of Two-Part Modal Inventions for piano, Romanian Broadcast, 1964; Past Are The Years for tenor and vocal ensemble with Juilliard Chorus, Lincoln Center, New York City, 1970; Jubilus for soprano, trumpet and percussive body sounds, commissioned and broadcasted by National Public Radio, USA, 1981; Premiere of Stage work: The Musical Seminar at Tanglewood Festival, 1982; German premiere at State Opera of Stuttgart, 1989; British premiere with Paragon Opera Project at Royal Scottish Academy of Music, Glasgow, 1992; Premiere of Pantomime for chamber orchestra at the Romanian National Opera Bucharest, 1998; Premiere of Paragon 2000 for chamber orchestra, with the Paragon Ensemble of Scotland, Glasgow, 2000, full orchestra version with the Concerto Orchestra, Bucharest, 2001; first retrospective concert, The Ensemble Sospeso at Miller Theatre, New York, 2002. *Recordings:* Composers Recordings Inc, USA; Published works: Evolving Cycle for piano, 1964; Song to the Rivers of My Country, vocal symphonic work, 1967; Sonata for Violin and Piano, 1968. *Publications:* Treatise on Musical Phonology 1968; studies and articles on contemporary music, essays on comparative aesthetics. *Address:* 120 Riverside Drive, Apt 6E, New York, NY 10024, USA. *Telephone:* (212) 877-3494. *E-mail:* g.s.costinescu@rcn.com.

COTRUBAS, Ileana; opera and concert singer (soprano); b. 9 June 1939, Galati, Romania; m. Manfred Ramin 1972. *Education:* Conservatorul Ciprian Porumbescu, Bucharest. *Career:* debut, Yniold in Pelléas et Mélisande, Bucharest Opera, 1964; Frankfurt Opera, 1968–70; Glyndebourne Festival, 1968; Salzburg Festival, 1969; Royal Opera House, Covent Garden, London, 1971, as Tchaikovsky's Tatiana; Lyric Opera of Chicago, 1973; Paris Opéra, 1974; La Scala, Milan, 1975; Metropolitan Opera, New York, 1977, as Mimi in La Bohème; Operatic roles included Susanna, Pamina, Norina, Gilda, Traviata, Manon, Antonia, Tatiana, Mimi, Mélisande; Concerts with all major European orchestras; Lieder recitals at Musikverein Vienna, Royal Opera House Covent Garden, Carnegie Hall, New York, La Scala; Manon, 1988; Sang Elisabeth of Valois, Florence, Marguerite at Hamburg, 1985, Amelia Boccanegra, Naples, 1986; Monte Carlo, 1987, as Alice Ford, Barcelona, 1988, as Desdemona; Sang Mélisande, Florence, 1989; Retired, 1990. *Recordings:* Bach Cantatas; Mozart Masses; Brahms Requiem; Mahler Symphonies Nos 2 and 8; Complete Operas including Le nozze di Figaro, Die Zauberflöte, Hansel and Gretel, Calisto, Louise, L'Elisir d'amore, Les Pêcheurs de Perles, La Traviata, Rigoletto, Alzira. *Honours:* 1st Prize, International Singing Competition, 's-Hertogenbosch, Netherlands, 1965; 1st Prize, Munich Radio Competition, 1966; Austrian Kammersängerin, 1981; Great Officer of the Order Sant Iago da Espada (Portugal), 1990.

COTTELI, Honorat; Violinist; b. 4 Jan. 1941, Banska Bystrica, Czechoslovakia; m. 2 s., 2 d. *Education:* Conservatory of Music, Bratislava, Slovakia, 1955–60. *Career:* Debut: Diplom Concert, 1960; Radio Symphony Orchestra, Bratislava, 1959; Slovak Philharmonic Orchestra, 1960–67; Concert Master, State Opera Orchestra, Banska Bystrica, 1964; Concertmaster, Opera Orchestra, Sankt Gallen, Switzerland, 1967–70; Conservatory of Music, Zürich, 1976; Opera Orchestra, Zürich, 1970; mem, Swiss Musicians Union. *Compositions:* Trio burlesco, 1994; Intrada for strings, 1989; Impressions for strings, 1993; Bagatellen for solo instruments, strings, 1991; Orchestino, concertino for grand orchestra, 1996; Capriccio for violin and piano, 1996; Preludi for violin and piano, 1995; Fantasticherie, 1995; Episodi, 1996; Fantasia gioccosa, 1997; Partita Slovacca, 1997; Brass Quintet, 1997; Musica per Contrabbassi, 1997; Swing Part for strings, 1995; Favole Slovacche, 1998; Suit per tre, 1998; Racconti di Faust, 1996; 5 songs for voice, 1996–98; Music of Stadent, 1987. *Honours:* Second prize, Composition Competition, Bratislava, Slovakia, 1996. *Address:* Poststrasse 29, CH 8957, Spreitenbach, Switzerland.

COUROUPOS, Yorgos; Composer; b. 1 Jan. 1942, Athens, Greece. *Education:* Studied the piano at Athens Conservatory, and composition with Messiaen in Paris, 1968–72. *Career:* Administrative posts at National Lyric Theatre, Athens; Director of Kalamata Municipal Conservatory from 1985. *Compositions:* Music theatre works, notably: Dieu le Veut, 1975; Grisélidis, 1977; Pylades, opera in 1 act with libretto by G Himonas after Sophocles and Euripides, performed at the Athens Concert Hall, 1992; Odyssey, ballet, 1995: The Runaways of the Chessboard, opera, 1998. *Address:* c/o AEPI, Fragoklisias and Samou Street 51, 151 25 Amarousio, Athens, Greece.

COUROUX, Marc; Pianist, Lecturer and Writer; b. 1970, Montreal, Canada. *Education:* Humanities and Mathematics; Studies with Louis-Philippe Pelletier, McGill University, 1989–94. *Career:* Repertory includes Night Fantasies by Elliott Carter, Euryali by Iannis Xenakis, 14 Etudes by György Ligeti, Other Works by Ambrosini, Cage, Donatoni, Lindberg, Messiaen, Nancarrow, Rzewski, Schoenberg, Stockhausen, Szymanowski and Tippett, along with Canadian Composers Brégent, Cherney, Gonneville, Tremblay and Vivier; Premieres of Envolée by Sean Ferguson and Variations by James Harley, 1994; Soloist, McGill Symphony Orchestra in the North American Premiere of Bengt Hambraeus' Concerto for Piano and Orchestra, 1995; Recital of Canadian and Belgian Works, ARS Musica Festival Brussels, 1995; Performed, Concerto for piano and orchestra by György Ligeti with CBC Vancouver Orchestra, 1996; Performed Piano Solo Pieces, Nouvel Ensemble Moderne, 1996; Artist-in-Residence, Banff Centre for the Arts, Princeton and Rutgers Universities, Domaine Forget Summer Course for New Music, St-Irénée, Quebec; Lecturer, Universities of New York, Stony Brook, and Buffalo. *Publications:* Several articles in professional journals. *Address:* c/o Latitude 45, Arts Promotion Inc, 109 St Joseph Blvd West, Montreal, Quebec H2T 2P7, Canada.

COURTIS, Jean-Philippe; Singer (Bass); b. 24 May 1951, France. *Education:* Studied at the Paris Conservatoire. *Career:* Sang first at the Paris Opéra (from 1980), then the Opéra-Comique (1983); Appearances at the Aix Festival in Werther, Semiramide, and Ariadne auf Naxos, and guest engagements throughout Europe as Henry VIII in Anna Bolena (Amsterdam, 1989), Don Giovanni (Strasbourg, 1990) and Arkel (Vienna Staatsoper, 1991); Sang Méphistophélès in Faust at the Paris Opéra, 1988, and appeared in the 1990 opening of the Opéra Bastille (Les Troyens); Other roles include the Commendatore in Don Giovanni, Don Quichotte, and Frère Bernard in Messiaen's St François d'Assise (premiere, 1983); Season 1994–95 as Falstaff in Le Songe d'une nuite d'été by Thomas, Creon in Cherubini's Médée at Martina Franca and Gounod's Frère Laurent at Houston; Isménor in Rameau's Dardanus at Lyon, 1998; Sang Somarone in Béatrice et Bénédict at Amsterdam, 2001; Many concert engagements. *Address:* c/o Opéra de la Bastille, 12 Rue de Lyon, 75012 Paris, France.

COVELL, Roger (David); Musicologist, Critic, Conductor and Composer; b. 1 Feb. 1931, Sydney, Australia; m. Patricia Anne Brown, 10 May 1975, 3 s., 1 d. *Education:* BA, Queensland; PhD, New South Wales. *Career:* Chief Music Critic, Sydney Morning Herald, 1960–2001; Senior Lecturer, Head, Music Department, University of New South Wales, 1966; Associate Professor, 1973; Personal Chair, 1984; Head, School of Music and Music Education, 1993–96; Emer. Prof., Dir, Music Performance Unit, 1997–; Visiting Professor, Education, 1997–; mem, Australia Council, 1977–83; Australia Society for Music Educators; Musicological Society of Australia; Senior Music Writer, 2002–. *Compositions:* Theatre Music and Choral Works. *Recordings:* Barry Conyngham's Edward John Eyre, 1974. *Publications:* Australia's Music: Themes of a New Society, 1967; Music in Australia, Needs and Prospects, 1970; Edward Geoghegan's Currency Lass, 1976; Folk Songs of Australia, 1987. *Contributions:* Studies in Music; Australian Encyclopedia; New Grove Dictionary of Opera, 1992. *Honours:* Fellow, Australian Academy of the Humanities, 1983; Order of Australia, 1986;

Geraldine Pascall Prize for music criticism, 1993. *Address:* 9 Kubya Street, Blackheath, NSW 2785, Australia.

COVEY-CRUMP, Rogers; Singer (Tenor); b. 1944, England. *Education:* Royal College of Music, London; BMus, London University. *Career:* Concert, broadcasting and commercial recording engagements as a solo artist and as a member of the Hilliard Ensemble, Gothic Voices, the Deller and Taverner Consorts and Singcircle (Stockhausen's Stimmung); Promenade Concerts, 1984–99, Purcell's Odes, Pärt's Miserere, Bach's St Matthew Passion; and premiere of MacMillan's Quickening; Performances of Bach, Haydn and Pärt in Finland and Estonia, 1985–96, Bach's St John Passion in Vancouver, 1997, Bach's Matthew passion in Stockholm for Swedish Radio with Tonu Kaljuste, 1997; Tours of the United Kingdom, 1988, 1992 and 1998, with Contemporary Music Network in Pärt's Passio, Miserere and Litany; Summer Schools with the Hilliard Ensemble in Lewes, Cambridge, Finland, Germany and Austria since 1984; Residencies in California and Pennsylvania 1988 and 1992; Lecturer and writer on aspects of vocal ensemble singing. *Recordings include:* Bach's B Minor Mass and St John Passion, Monteverdi's Vespers and Purcell with Andrew Parrott and the Taverner Players; Bach's St Matthew Passion with Roy Goodman and the choir of King's College, Cambridge; Bach's St Mark Passion with the European Union Baroque Orchestra; Pärt's Passio, Miserere and Litany; Lute Songs, with Paul O'Dette and with Jakob Lindberg; Hilliard Ensemble collaboration with Norwegian saxophonist, Jan Garbarek in the albums Officium and Mnemosyne. *Address:* 4 Garland Court, Victoria Street, St Albans, AL 1 3SY. *Website:* www.hazardchase .co.uk.

COVIELLO, Roberto; Singer (Baritone); b. 1958, Italy. *Career:* Debut: Naples, 1983; Sang Guglielmo at Bari, 1984, and Paisiello's Figaro at the 1986 Spoleto Festival; La Scala Milan from 1987, as Don Giovanni and other major baritone roles; Pesaro Festival, 1988–89, in La Scala di Seta and La Gazza Ladra; Other roles include Mozart's Figaro, Belcore, Malatesta, Valentin, Mercutio (Roméo et Juliette), Valentin and Ford in Falstaff; Season 1990–91 in opera at Bonn, Santiago, Bergamo and Trieste. *Address:* c/o Teatro alla Scala, Via Filodrammatici 2, 20121 Milan, Italy.

COWAN, Richard; Singer (bass-baritone), Composer and Artistic Director; b. 24 Dec. 1957, Euclid, OH, USA. *Education:* degree in Vocal Performance and Composition, Indiana Univ. *Career:* debut, Chicago Lyric, 1983, in Lady Macbeth of the Mtsensk District by Shostakovich; has sung frequently in Chicago (Escamillo 1991, Anthony and Cleopatra 1991, Simon Boccanegra 1995, The Consul 1996) and guested in Los Angeles, Detroit, Toronto, Vancouver and numerous other locations world-wide; Maggio Musicale, Florence, 1985, as the Animal Tamer in Lulu, Aix Festival, 1986, as Masetto and Théâtre du Châtelet, Paris, 1988–89, in Der Freischütz and Fidelio; La Scala Milan debut, 1989; Metropolitan, New York from 1990, as Schaunard, Don Giovanni and Guglielmo; Bartók's Bluebeard at Geneva, 1995; sang in The Consul by Menotti in Chicago, 1996; best known as Don Giovanni (Avignon, Marseilles, Strasbourg, Santa Fe, Metropolitan Opera, Toronto, Rio de Janeiro, Detroit, St Etienne); founder, Artistic Dir Festival Lyrique de Belle Ile en Mer, Brittany 1998–. *Recordings:* Sharpless in Madama Butterfly (film and recording), 1994, Ravel's Brain, 2000. *Honours:* Grand Prize, Paris Int. Singing Contest 1986, George London Award 1986. *Address:* Chateau Fouquet, BP 80, Belle Ile en Mer, 56360, France.

COWAN, Sigmund; Singer (baritone); b. 4 March 1948, New York, NY, USA. *Education:* University of Miami; University of Florida; New York Institute of Finance; Scholarship, Juilliard School; Fellowship, Manhattan School of Music. *Career:* Appearances: New York City Opera, Deutsche Oper am Rhein; Spoleto Festival, Kennedy Center, Miami Opera, Basel, Essen, Wiesbaden, Vienna Festival, Berlin Staatstheater, Brussels, Amsterdam (Opera and Concertgebouw), Carnegie Hall, Mexico City, Dublin, and Calgary and Edmonton (Canada), Rotterdam (VARA television), Utrecht (Radio KRO), Amsterdam (VARA Radio), Italy (RAI), USA (NBC television), Austria (ORF television), Germany (3rd Channel); Sang with Rochester Philharmonic, National Symphony, Baltimore Symphony and at Flagstaff Festival; Appeared with National Orchestra, Mexico City, Canadian Opera, L'Opera de Montreal, Baltimore Opera; Television Live from Lincoln Center PBS Tonio in Pagliacci; Roles in Nabucco, Rigoletto, Macbeth, Il Trovatore, I Due Foscari, Un Ballo in Maschera, La Forza del Destino, La Traviata; Sang Rigoletto at Toronto, 1996; Engaged for debut in Marseille, France, as Germont in La Traviata, 2000. *Recordings include:* Die Gezeichneten with Edo de Waart. *Current Management:* Athole Still International Management, Forresters Hall, 25–27 Westow Street, London, SE19 3RY, England. *Telephone:* (20) 8771-5271. *Fax:* (20) 8768-6600. *Website:* www.atholestill.com. *Address:* c/o Dorothy Cone, 150 W 55th Street, New York, NY 10019, USA.

COWIE, Edward; Composer, Painter, Natural Scientist, Writer and Film-maker; b. 17 Aug. 1943, Birmingham, England; m. Heather Jean Johns, 1995, 2 d. by second marriage. *Education:* BEd, London University; BMus, D.Mus, Southampton University; PhD, Lancaster University. *Career:* Senior Lecturer, Lancaster University, 1973–83; Professor, Creative Arts, University of Wollongong, New South Wales, Australia, 1983–89; Granada Composer/Conductor, Royal Liverpool Philharmonic Orchestra, 1983–86; Professor, Creative Arts, James Cook University, Queensland, Australia, 1989–95; Professor and Director of Research, Dartington College of Arts, Devon, England, 1995–; Artist in Residence with the Royal Society for the Protection of Birds, 2002–2005; Associate Composer BBC Singers, 2002–2005; mem, British Ornithologists Union; Fellow, Royal Society of Arts. *Compositions include:* Commedia, opera, 1979; Concerto for Orchestra, 1982; 5 string quartets, 1974–95; Symphony (American), 1983; Choral Symphony, 1984; Ancient Voices 1 and 2, 1983, 1991; Cello Concerto; 1992; Water, Stone, Wood and Breath, for chorus and percussion, 1996; Between Two Waves for 12 voices, 1999; Oboe Concerto, 1999; From Moment to Moment for chamber orchestra, 2000. *Recordings:* many compositions recorded. *Publications:* Music published in London; 41 exhibitions as painter; Birds Talk, 2001. *Honours:* Many prizes won as composer. *Address:* c/o Dartington College of Arts, Totnes, Devon TQ9 6EJ, England. *Website:* www.edward-cowie.com; www.ump.co.uk/cowie.htm.

COX, Jean; Singer (Tenor); b. 16 Jan. 1922, Gadsen, Alabama, USA. *Education:* University of Alabama and the New England Conservatory; With Wally Kirsamer in Frankfurt, Luigi Ricci in Rome and Max Lorenz in Munich. *Career:* Debut: New England Opera Company, 1951, as Lensky in Eugene Onegin; Spoleto, 1954, as Rodolfo; Sang at Brunswick, 1955–59, Mannheim from 1959; Bayreuth Festival, 1956–75, as the Steersman, Erik, Lohengrin, Parsifal, Siegfried and Walther; Hamburg Staatsoper, 1958–73; Guest appearances in Berlin, Vienna, Munich, Stuttgart and Frankfurt; Bregenz Festival, 1961, in Fra Diavolo; Chicago Lyric Opera, 1964, 1970, 1973; Paris Opéra, 1971, as Siegmund; Covent Garden, 1975; Siegfried; Metropolitan Opera debut, 1976, as Walther; Further engagements in Lisbon, Stockholm, Geneva, Zürich, Mexico City, Houston and Pittsburgh; Other roles included Strauss's Herod and Bacchus; Alvaro in La Forza del Destino, Max in Der Freischütz and the Cardinal in Mathis der Maler by Hindemith; Siegfried and Walther von Stolzing, Bayreuth Festival, 1983–84; Sang Captain Vere in Billy Budd at Mannheim, 1989. *Recordings include:* Die Meistersinger; Jean Cox sings Wagner. *Address:* Nationaltheater, Postfach 102362, 6800 Mannheim, Germany.

COXON, Richard; Singer (Tenor); b. 25 Aug. 1968, Nottingham, England. *Education:* Royal Northern College of Music, with John Mitchinson. *Career:* Debut: Flavio in Norma for Scottish Opera, 1993; Further roles with Scottish Opera have included Narraboth in Salome, Jacquino, Nemorino, Alfred in Die Fledermaus, Barbarigo in Verdi's Due Foscari, Don Ottavio, Alfredo, and Jiri in The Jacobin by Dvořák; Guest appearances for Opera Northern Ireland, Opera Zuid in Maastricht, Glyndebourne Festival Opera, Nationale Reisoper Holland and English National Opera; Concerts include Mendelssohn's St Paul with the Scottish National Orchestra, Messiah with the Bergen Philharmonic Orchestra and engagements with the Hallé Orchestra, BBC Concert Orchestra, BBC Scottish Symphony Orchestra and London Pops Orchestra; Fenton in Falstaff and Young Convict in From the House of the Dead, Painter in Lulu and Nick in The Handmaid's Tale for English National Opera; Mr By-Ends in Pilgrim's Progress for Royal Opera, in concert; Brighella in Ariadne auf Naxos for Scottish Opera at the Edinburgh Festival and on tour; Edgardo in film version of Lucia di Lammermoor, directed by Don Boyd; Squeak in Billy Budd, Gastone in La Traviata for Royal Opera; Italian Tenor in Der Rosenkavalier for Opera North and at the Spolete Festival, Italy; Kudjas in Katya Kabanova for Opera de Montreal, Florida Grand Opera and Scottish Opera. *Honours:* Webster Booth/Esso Award; Clonter Opera Prize; Ricordi Opera Prize. *Address:* c/o IMG Artists, Lovell House, 616 Chiswick High Road, London W4 5RX, England.

CRAFT, Robert Lawson, BA; Conductor and Writer on Music; b. 20 Oct. 1923, Kingston, NY, USA. *Education:* Juilliard School of Music, New York, Berkshire Music Center, Tanglewood; studied conducting with Pierre Monteux. *Career:* Conductor, Evenings-on-the-Roof and Monday Evening Concerts, Los Angeles, 1950–68; Assistant to, later closest associate of Igor Stravinsky, 1948–71; Collaborated with Stravinsky in concerts and in preparing several books; Conducted first performances of various later works by Stravinsky; Conducted works ranging from Monteverdi to Boulez; US premiere of Berg's Lulu (2 act version) Santa Fe, 1963. *Recordings include:* works of Stravinsky, Webern, and Schoenberg, Schoenberg series 1998. *Publications:* With Stravinsky: Conversations with Igor Stravinsky, 1959; Memories and Commentaries, 1960; Expositions and Developments, 1962; Dialogues and a Diary, 1963; Themes and Episodes, 1967; Retrospections and Conclusions, 1969; Chronicle of a Friendship, 1972; Prejudices in Disguise, 1974; with Vera Stravinsky, Stravinsky in Photographs and Documents, 1976; Current Convictions: Views and Reviews, 1977; Present Perspectives, 1984; Translator and Editor, Stravinsky's Selected Correspondence, 2 vols, 1982, 1984; Stravinsky: Glimpses of a Life, 1992; The Moment of Existence: Music, Literature and the Arts, 1996; An Improbable Life 2003. *Contributions:* articles in various journals and other publications. *Address:* 1390 South Ocean Blvd, Pompano Beach, FL 33062, USA.

CRAFTS, Edward (James); Singer (Bass-Baritone); b. 11 Nov. 1946, New York, NY, USA. *Education:* Studied at Curtis Institute and Indiana University. *Career:* Has sung widely in the USA from 1982, notably at Houston Opera (as Dulcamara), St Louis and the City Opera New York (as Escamillo); Santa Fe, 1984, in the US premiere of Zemlinsky's Eine Florentinische Tragödie; La Scala Milan, 1984, in Bernstein's Trouble in Tahiti; Seattle, 1987, as Iago; New Jersey, 1983, in the US premiere of Wagner's Liebesverbot; Further appearances at La Scala, Covent Garden, Cleveland and Chicago; Other roles include Falstaff, Scarpia and Mephistopheles; Sang Wotan in The Ring for Arizona Opera at Flagstaff, 1996. *Address:* c/o New York City Opera, Lincoln Center, New York, NY 10023, USA.

CRAGG, Elizabeth; Singer (Soprano); b. 1970, England. *Education:* Royal Holloway College, London; Royal College of Music, with Elisabeth Robson. *Career:* Solo engagements in Messiah, at St John Smith's Square, Bach's B minor Mass in Singapore, St Matthew Passion with the English Concert and recital at the Victoria and Albert Museum, London; Season 2000–01 as Celia in the British premiere of Handel's Silla, and Orazio in Muzio Scevola, for the London Handel Festival; Choral Singer with The Sixteen, BBC Singers, The Choir of the Enlightenment and the English Concert Choir. *Recordings include:* Handel's Silla. *Honours:* Dorothy Silk Prize, RCM. *Address:* c/o Royal College of Music, Prince Consort Road, London SW7, England.

CRAIG, Jon; Singer (Tenor); b. 30 Oct. 1923, St Louis, Missouri, USA. *Education:* Studied in Washington, at Juilliard and with Paul Althouse. *Career:* Debut: Sang Pinkerton in 1948; Sang at New York City Opera, 1952–65, notably in the 1954 premiere of The Tender Land by Copland and in US premieres of Der Prozess, 1953, Der Revisor by Egk, 1960, and The Fiery Angel, 1965; Metropolitan Opera from 1953, San Francisco from 1957; Further engagements at Pittsburgh, Chicago, Philadelphia, Mexico City and New Orleans; Other roles have included the Duke of Mantua, Fenton and Alfredo by Verdi, Cavaradossi, Don José, Turiddu, Rodolfo, Erik in Der fliegende Holländer, Dimitri, Boris Godunov and Walton's Troilus; Fort Worth Opera 1970, in Die Fledermaus. *Recordings:* Highlights from Les Contes d'Hoffmann.

CRAIG, Russell; Stage Designer; b. 1948, New Zealand. *Education:* Studied in New Zealand and moved to London in 1974. *Career:* Designs for Scottish Opera with Savitri, Hedda Gabler, Rossini double bill, Oberon and L'Elisir d'amore, 1981–94, Welsh National Opera with Barber of Seville, Die Entführung, Ariadne and Le Comte Ory, 1986–91, and English National Opera with The Rape of Lucretia and Ariadne auf Naxos, 1983; Designs for Opera North include Così fan tutte, The Magic Flute, A Village Romeo and Juliet, Acis and Galatea, Showboat, and Oberto, 1983–94; La Bohème for Glyndebourne Touring Opera in 1991. *Address:* c/o Jeffrey Campbell, 11a Grey Stone Court, South Street, Eastbourne BN21 4LP, England.

CRANE, Louise; Singer (Mezzo-Soprano); b. 1965, England. *Education:* Studied at the Guildhall School of Music, 1982–86, and at the Royal Northern College of Music with Barbara Robotham. *Career:* Sang in Opera Factory's Don Giovanni and Dialogues des Carmélites for Opéra de Lyon; Further engagements as Third Lady and Mistress Quickly with English Touring Opera, in The Siege of Corinth and The Nightingale for Chelsea Opera Group, Stravinsky's Mother Goose at Aldeburgh and Mozart's Marcellina for European Chamber Opera; English National Opera debut, 1993 in the premiere of Harvey's Inquest of Love; Sang Rita in Zampa for Opera Omnibus, 1996; Concert engagements in Rossini's Stabat Mater, Messiah, Beethoven's Ninth and Missa Solemnis, The Dream of Gerontius and Das Lied von der Erde; Touring performances of Gilbert and Sullivan. *Address:* Helen Sykes Artists Management, 100 Felsham Road, Putney, London SW15 1DQ, England.

CRASS, Franz; Singer (Bass-baritone); b. 9 Dec. 1928, Wipperfurth, Germany. *Education:* Studied at the Cologne Musikhochschule with Clemens Glettenberg. *Career:* Debut: Krefeld, 1954, as the King in Aida; Sang at Hanover, 1956–62; Bayreuth Festival, 1959–73, as King Henry, the Dutchman, Fasolt, Wolfram, King Marke and Gurnemanz; La Scala, 1960, as Rocco and the Commendatore; Salzburg Festival as Sarastro; London, 1960, 1964, in the Missa Solemnis and Mozart's Requiem, conducted by Klemperer; From 1964 sang in Hamburg, Munich, Frankfurt and Vienna; With Hamburg Opera sang Barak in the British premiere of Die Frau ohne Schatten, Sadler's Wells Theatre, 1966;

Other roles included Philip II, Nicolai's Falstaff, Duke Bluebeard and the Hermit in Der Freischütz (Frankfurt, 1980); Often heard in sacred music by Bach. *Recordings include:* Der fliegende Holländer; Lohengrin; Ein Deutsches Requiem; Die Zauberflöte; Fidelio; Parsifal; Giulio Cesare by Handel; Der Freischütz; Speaker, Second Armed Man and Second Priest in Die Zauberflöte, conducted by Klemperer, recording issued 1989. *Address:* EMI Classics (Artists' Contracts), 30 Gloucester Place, London W1A 1ES, England.

CRAWFORD, Bruce; Manager; b. 16 March 1929, West Bridgewater, Massachusetts, USA; m. Christine Crawford, 1958. *Education:* BS, University of Pennsylvania, 1952. *Career:* Entered advertising, 1956; Chief Executive Officer, BBDO International, 1977–; President, Batten, Barton, Durstine and Osborn, 1978–; Joined Board of Metropolitan Opera, 1976, serving on Executive Committee, 1977–, Vice-President, 1981, President, May 1984, General Manager, Metropolitan Opera, 1985–89. *Address:* c/o Metropolitan Opera, Lincoln Center, New York, NY 10023, USA.

CRAWFORD, John (Charlton); Composer and Educator; b. 19 Jan. 1931, Philadelphia, USA; m. Dorothy Lamb, 25 June 1955, 1 s., 1 d. *Education:* BMus, 1950, MMus, 1955, Yale School of Music; PhD at Harvard University, 1963. *Career:* Instructor of Music, Amherst College, 1961–63; Assistant Professor, Wellesley College, 1963–70; Associate Professor of Music, 1970–75, Professor of Music, 1975–94, University of California, Riverside; mem, ASCAP; American Musicological Society; American Music Center. *Compositions include:* Magnificat, 1959; Ash Wednesday, 1968; Three Shakespeare Songs, 1970; Psalm 98, 1971; Don Cristobal and Rosita, 1979; Two Shakespeare Madrigals, 1980; Prelude, Fugue and Meditation for String Quartet, 1993; Concerto for viola and orchestra, 1995. *Recordings:* String Quartet No. 2, Sequoia Quartet, 1993. *Publications:* Translator and Essayist, Arnold Schoenberg, Wassily Kandinsky: Letters, Pictures and Documents, 1984; Co-author with Dorothy L Crawford of Expressionism in 20th Century Music, 1993. *Contributions:* Musical Quarterly; Journal of Arnold Schoenberg Institute. *Honours:* Boott Prize in Choral Composition, Harvard University, 1956; ASCAP Serious Music Award, 1969–74 and 1994–2004. *Address:* 203 Lexington Avenue, Cambridge, MA 02138, USA.

CRAWFORD, Timothy (Terry); Lutenist and Musicologist; b. 11 July 1948, Farnham, Surrey, England; m. Emilia de Grey, 18 April 1975, 2 s., 1 d. *Education:* University of Sussex, 1966–69; Royal College of Music, 1971–75; Arts Council Research Grant for Continental Travel, 1976. *Career:* Founder Member of early music ensembles Ars Nova and Parley of Instruments; Frequent appearances with English Baroque Soloists, London Philharmonic Orchestra; Assistant Editor, Early Music Magazine, 1984–85; Music Co-ordinator for Royal Academy of Arts; Research Fellow, King's College London, 1989–; Projects include: Electronic Corpus of Lute Music (ECOLM), Online Music Recognition and Searching (OMRAS); mem, Lute Society, Committee 1975–87; National Early Music Association, Committee 1985–86; RMA; Musicians' Union. *Recordings:* Orfeo (Conductor: J E Gardiner); Il Ritorno d'Ulisse (Conductor: R Leppard); Sacred Music of Monteverdi (with Parley of Instruments and Emma Kirkby, Ian Partridge and David Thomas). *Publications:* Editor: Lute Society Journal and The Lute, 1979–87; Silvius Leopold Weiss, The Moscow Manuscript, 1995; S. L. Weiss, Complete Works, The Dresden Manuscript, 2000. *Contributions:* Frequently to The Lute, Early Music, Chelys, Journal of the Lute Society of America. *Address:* 40 Albion Drive, Hackney, London E8 4LX, England.

CREECH, Philip; Singer (Tenor); b. 1 June 1950, Hempstead, New York, USA. *Education:* Studied at Northwestern University. *Career:* Sang with Chicago Symphony Chorus, 1973–75; Metropolitan Opera, debut 1979 as Beppe in Pagliacci; Other roles at the Metropolitan have been Mozart's Pedrillo, Edmondo in Manon Lescaut, Brighella in Ariadne auf Naxos, Hylas in Les Troyens and Rinuccio in Gianni Schicchi; Premiere of The Voyage by Philip Glass at the Met, 1996; Many concert appearances. *Recordings:* Carmina Burana. *Address:* c/o Metropolitan Opera, Lincoln Center, NY 10023, USA.

CREED, Kay; Singer, Voice Teacher, Opera Coach and Lecturer; b. 19 Aug. 1940, Oklahoma City, USA; m. Carveth Osterhaus, 5 Oct 1975, 1 d. *Education:* BMus, MPA, Oklahoma City University; Study in Munich, Germany, 1965. *Career:* Debut: New York City Opera, 1965; Created role of Fortuna in Don Rodrigo by Ginastera; Mrs Danton in Danton's Death; Opera roles include Carmen, Cenerentola, Dorabella, Hansel, Giulietta, Sextus in Julius Caesar, Ulrica, Urbain (Les Huguenots); Solo Performances with New York Philharmonic, Chicago Symphony, Philadelphia Orchestra, Carnegie Hall, Les Huguenots; Dallas Symphony; Naumberg Orchestra, Oklahoma City Symphony; Board of Directors, Cimarron Circuit Opera, 1985; Lecturer in Opera and Voice, Cantor Classes for Catholic Litugy; Founding Member, Oklahoma City Guild of Tulsa Opera; Founding Member, Oklahoma Opera and Musical

Theater Company; Founding Director, Edmond Central Historical Opera. *Address:* 415 W Eubanks, Oklahoma City, OK 73118, USA.

CREFFELD, Rosanna; Singer (Mezzo-Soprano); b. 1945, England; m. Richard Angas. *Education:* Royal College of Music with Flora Nielsen; Paris with Pierre Bernac; Further study with Vera Rosza in London. *Career:* Debut: Glyndebourne 1969, as Second Lady in Die Zauberflöte; Glyndebourne Touring Opera 1969–70, as Dorabella, and as Olga in Eugene Onegin; Appearances at Aix-en-Provence, Amsterdam, Strasbourg, Lyon and Bremen; Scottish Opera Glasgow as Dorabella and Cherubino; Monteverdi's Orfeo with the English National Opera; Paris Opéra as Cherubino and as Lucretia in The Rape of Lucretia by Britten; Engagements in San Diego 1984, and Pittsburgh 1986; Lausanne 1986, in Honegger's Antigone. *Recordings include:* Matilde in Rossini's Elisabetta Regina d'Inghilterra (Philips). *Address:* c/o English National Opera, St Martin's Lane, London WC2N 4ES, England.

CRESHEVSKY, Noah; Composer; b. 31 Jan. 1945, Rochester, New York, USA. *Education:* Studied at the Eastman School, Rochester, 1950–61 and at the Juilliard School with Berio, 1966; Further study with Nadia Boulanger in Paris and with Virgil Thomson. *Career:* Teacher, Juilliard and Hunter College, New York; Brooklyn College from 1969; Visiting Professor, Princeton University, 1987–88 Director, centre for Computer Music, Brooklyn College, 1992–. *Compositions include:* Vier Lieder, stage piece, 1966; Three pieces in the Shape of a Square for 4 performers and tape, 1967; Monogenesis for voices, chamber orchestra and tape, 1968; Variations for 4 pianists and tape, 1969; Mirrors for dancers and tape, 1970; Circuit for tape, 1971; Broadcast, 1973; Chaconne for piano or harp, 1974; Guitar, 1975; In Other Words: Portrait of John Cage, 1976; Great Performances for any 2 instruments and tape, 1977; Great Performances, 1978; Portrait of Rudy Perez, 1978; Highway, 1979; Sonata, Nightscape and Celebration for tape, 1980–83; Strategic Defense Initiative, 1986; Electric String Quartet, 1988; Talea, 1991; Private Lives, 1993; Coup d'état; Gone Now, 1995; Who, 1995; Sha, 1996; Electric Fanfare, 1997. *Honours:* National Endowment of the Arts Grant, 1981. *Address:* c/o ASCAP, ASCAP Building, 1 Lincoln Plaza, NY 10023, USA.

CRESPIN, Regine; Singer (Soprano); b. 23 Feb. 1927, Marseille, France. *Education:* Paris Conservatoire with Suzanne Cesbron-Viseur and Georges Jouatte. *Career:* Debut: Mulhouse 1950, as Elsa; Sang Elsa at the Paris Opéra, 1950; Sang Desdemona, Marguerite, the Prioress in Dialogues des Carmélites and Reiza in Oberon; Paris, Tosca, Ballo in Maschera; Iphigénie en Tauride; Die Walküre; Tannhaüser; Bayreuth Festival 1958–61, as Kundry and Sieglinde; La Scala Milan 1959, as Pizzetti's Phaedra; Glyndebourne 1959–60, as the Marschallin; Covent Garden from 1960, as Tosca, Elsa and Leonore in Fidelio; US debut Chicago 1962, as Tosca, Marschallin; Metropolitan Opera from 1962, the Marschallin, Senta, Amelia in Un Ballo in Maschera, Sieglinde, Brünnhilde in Die Walküre, Charlotte, Santuzza and Carmen; Teatro Col ón, Buenos Aires from 1962, as Fauré's Pénélope, Didon and Cassandre in Les Troyens, Gluck's Iphigénie (en Tauride), and in Parsifal, Der Rosenkavalier; Werther; Damnation de Faust; Carmen; Various concerts and recitals; Salzburg Festival 1967, as Brünnhilde in Die Walküre, conducted by Karajan; Mezzo-Soprano roles from 1971, including title roles, Offenbach's La Grand Duchesse de Gerolstein and Menotti's The Medium, San Francisco, 1983, 1986; Sang Mme de Croisy at the Metropolitan, Dialogues des Carmélites, 1987; Retired 1989 after singing the Countess in The Queen of Spades, Paris; Recitalist in Poulenc, Wolf and Offenbach; Concert repertoire included Ravel's Shéhérazade and Nuits d'Eté by Berlioz. *Recordings include:* Les Dialogues des Carmélites (EMI); Sieglinde in Die Walküre, Der Rosenkavalier, Don Quichotte by Massenet (Decca); Brünnhilde in Die Walküre (Deutsche Grammophon); Tosca; Iphigénie en Tauride; Pénélope; Damnation de Faust; Carmen; Les Troyens; La Grande Duchesse de Gérolstein; La Perichole; La Vie Parisienne; Poulenc's Stabat Mater. *Address:* Music International, 13 Ardilaun Road, London N5 2QR, England.

CRESSWELL, Lyell Richard; Composer; b. 13 Oct. 1944, Wellington, New Zealand; m. Catherine Mawson, 4 Jan 1972. *Education:* BMus, Honours, Victoria University of Wellington, New Zealand, 1968; MMus, University of Toronto, Canada, 1970; PhD, Aberdeen University, 1974. *Career:* Music Organiser, Chapter Arts Centre, Cardiff, 1978–80; Forman Fellow in Composition, Edinburgh University, 1980–82; Cramb Fellow in Composition, 1982–85; Glasgow University, 1985–; Freelance Composer; mem, British Academy of Composers and Songwriters Composers Association of New Zealand. *Compositions:* Ylur, 1990–91; Voices of Ocean Winds; The Pumpkin Massacre; Il Suono di Enormi Distanze; A Modern Ecstasy; Cello Concerto; O!; Salm; Speak for Us, Great Sea; Passacagli; O Let the Fire Burn, Concerto for String Quartet and Orchestra (premiered 1997); Kaea, Trombone Concerto, 1997 (premiered, 1998); The Voice Inside, concerto for violin and soprano (premiered 2002); Of Smoke and Bickering Flame, concerto for Chamber Orchestra (premiered 2003); Shadows Without Sun (premiered 2003),

Ara Kopikopiko (premiered 2005). *Recordings:* Numerous. *Honours:* Ian Whyte Award, 1978; APRA Silver Scroll, 1980; Creative Scotland Award, 2001; Honorary D.Mus Victoria University of Wellington, New Zealand, 2002; Inaugural Elgar Bursary, 2002. *Address:* 4 Leslie Place, Edinburgh EH4 1NQ, Scotland.

CRICHTON, Ronald (Henry); Writer and Music Critic; b. 28 Dec. 1913, Scarborough, Yorkshire, England. *Education:* Radley College, 1927–31; BA, MA, Christ Church, Oxford, 1932–36. *Career:* Programme Organiser, Anglo-French Art and Travel Society, London, 1937–39; Army Service, 1940–46; British Council: Greece, Belgium, West Germany, London, 1946–67; Music Criticism, Financial Times, 1967–78; Freelance, 1979; Governing Body, British Institute of Recorded Sound, 1973–77; Arts Council Sub-Committees: Dance Theatre, 1973–76, Opera, 1976–80; mem, Critics Circle, Society of Authors. *Publications:* Joint Editor, A Dictionary of Modern Ballet, 1959; Manuel de Falla: A Descriptive Catalogue of His Works, 1976; Falla, BBC Music Guide, 1982; The Memoirs of Ethel Smyth, 1987, edited and abridged by Ronald Crichton. *Contributions:* The New Grove Dictionary of Music and Musicians; Heritage of Music, 1989; Newspapers, reviews, periodicals, in England and abroad. *Address:* c/o David Higham Associates Ltd, 5–8 Lower John Street, London W1R 4HA, England.

CRIDER, Michele; Singer (Soprano); b. 1963, Illinois, USA. *Career:* Debut: Leonora in Il Trovatore at Dortmund, 1989; Appearances from 1991 at La Scala, Covent Garden, Deutsche Oper Berlin and the State Operas of Hamburg, Vienna, Munich, Stuttgart and Wiesbaden; Further appearances at Florence, Zürich and Barcelona; Roles have included Aida, Luisa Miller, Butterfly, the Trovatore and Forza Leonoras, Odabella (Attila), Lucrezia (Due Foscari) and Amelia (Un Ballo in Maschera); US debut as Butterfly for San Diego, followed by Elisabeth in Don Carlos and the Trovatore Leonora at the Metropolitan; La Scala 1995 as Elena and Margherita in Mefistofele; Opéra Bastille, Paris as Madama Butterfly; Engaged as Aida for Netherlands Opera, 2000; Season 2000–01 as Verdi's Odabella at Genoa, the Trovatore Leonora at the New York Met and Aida at San Francisco; Concert engagements at Salzburg, Maggio Musicale Florence, Orange and Ravinia Festivals, Salle Pleyel Paris and London Barbican. *Recordings include:* Un Ballo in Maschera, under Carlo Rizzi; Elena and Margherita in Mefistofele, conducted by Muti; Verdi Requiem, under Richard Hickox. *Honours:* Finalist, 1988 Pavarotti Competition; Prizewinner, 1989 Geneva International Music Competition. *Address:* c/o Metropolitan Opera, Lincoln Center, New York, NY 10023, USA.

CRILLY, David Robert, DPhil, MA, LTCL, LLCM; British lecturer; b. 3 June 1959, Birkenhead. *Education:* City of Leeds Coll. of Music, Univ. of Southampton, Univ. of London RHBNC, Univ. of Oxford. *Career:* Sr Lecturer in Music, Dir of Research, composer and performer; Artistic Dir, annual Cambridge Shakespeare Festival. *Compositions:* In that quiet earth, for symphony orchestra, voice and narrator 2000, Leap of faith, for chamber orchestra and voices 2003. *Publications:* Is the application of the principles of semiology to music analysis founded upon a philosophical mistake?, in European Journal for Semiotic Studies 2002, Wiggenstein, Music Language – Games, The Open Space issue no. 2, Spring 2002, Elastic form and concrete structure: the analysis of improvised music, in Nikos Mastorakis ed. Mathematics and Computers in Modern Science 2002, Perception of Mathematical Structure and Architectural Design: Form and Forming in Music, in ISAMA 1999 International Society of the Arts, Mathematics and Architecture, The Problem of Form in Analytical Discussions, in Ideas and Production, a journal in the history of ideas Vol. XI. *Address:* Music Department, Anglia Polytecnic University, East Road, Cambridge, CB1 1PT, England (office); 6a Fair Street, Cambridge, CB1 1HA, England (home). *Telephone:* (1223) 363271 (office); (1223) 321984 (home). *E-mail:* d.crilly@apu.ac.uk (office); Bartok2571@msn.com (home). *Website:* www .apu.ac.uk/music (office).

CRIST, Richard, MM; American singer (bass) and vocal instructor; b. 21 Oct. 1947, Harrisburg, PA. *Education:* New England Conservatory, Boston. *Career:* debut in Berlioz's Les Troyens, Opera Company of Boston, 1972; Appearances with Opera Companies including: Santa Fe, Boston, Philadelphia, San Francisco, Memphis, Mobile, Orlando, Lake George and the Virginia and Goldovsky Opera Theatres; European debut with Opéra de Lyon in the French creation of Die Soldaten by Zimmermann (1982) under Ken Russell and Serge Baudo; Opera and Oratorio appearances throughout USA and with various orchestras; Canadian debut with Toronto Mendelssohn Choir, 1984; Operatic Repertoire of over 75 roles and nearly 100 Oratorio and Symphonic Works; Opera Performance of Tchaikovsky's The Queen of Spades, filmed for PBS television, Philadelphia, 1984; Debut in La Traviata, Metropolitan Opera, 1985; Sang in Semiramide, Fidelio, Meistersinger, Der Freischütz and Ballo in Maschera, Hamburg State Opera, 1985; Debut in Contes d'Hoffmann, San Diego Opera, 1985; Debut in Pelléas and Mélisande, Philadelphia Orchestra, 1986; Appearances in Henze's The English Cat, Alte Opera, Frankfurt, Germany and Turin, Italy,

1986; First Performance in USA of Mayr's Requiem, Alice Tully Hall 1986; Sang with the Company of the Bolshoi, Moscow, at Boston, 1988 in Shchedrin's Dead Souls; premiere of The Balcony by Di Domenica, Boston, 1990; other roles include Mozart's Leporello, Osmin, and Sarastro; Rocco in Fidelio, Gremin in Eugene Onegin and Samuel in Un Ballo in Maschera; Season 1991/2 in Gluck's La Rencontre Imprévue at Wexford, as Mozart's Bartolo in Dublin and in the Rossini Birthday Gala at the Barbican Hall; Svetlovsk Philharmonic Orchestra, 1993; mem, American Guild of Musical Artists. *Current Management:* Thea Safimm, Ludvig Brunner, 250 W 57th Street, New York, NY 10107, USA. *Address:* c/o New England Conservatory of Music, Vocal Faculty, 290 Huntington Avenue, Boston, MA 02115, USA.

CROCKETT, Donald; Composer, University Professor and Conductor; b. 18 Feb. 1951, Pasadena, California, USA; m. (1) divorced, 1 d., (2) Vicki Ray, 6 June 1988. *Education:* BM, 1974, MM, 1976, University of Southern California; PhD, University of California, Santa Barbara, 1981. *Career:* Conductor, USC Contemporary Music Ensemble; Guest Conductor with Monday Evening Concerts; Cleveland Chamber Symphony; Pittsburgh New Music Ensemble; Regional and national premieres of music by Lutoslawski, Davies, Musgrave, Gruber, Ruders, et al; Composer-in-Residence, Pasadena Chamber Orchestra (conductor Robert Duerr), 1984–87; Professor, University of Southern California; Composer-in-Residence, Los Angeles Chamber Orchestra (conductor Christof Perick), 1991–97; Conductor, Xtet (Los Angeles based new music ensemble). *Compositions:* Lyrikos (tenor and orchestra), 1979; The Pensive Traveller (high voice and piano), 1982; Vox in Rama (double chorus and orchestra), 1983; Melting Voices (orchestra), 1986; The 10th Muse (soprano and orchestra), 1986; Occhi dell'alma mia (high voice and guitar), 1977; Array for String Quartet, commissioned by the Kronos Quartet, 1988; Pilgrimage for piano solo, 1988; Still Life with Bell, 14 players, commissioned by the Los Angeles Philharmonic, 1989; Celestial Mechanics, oboe and string quartet, 1990; String Quartet No. 2, commissioned by the Stanford String Quartet, 1993; Roethke Preludes (orchestra), commissioned by the Los Angeles Chamber Orchestra, 1994; Island for concert band, 1998; The Falcon's Eye for solo guitar, 2000. *Recordings:* Melting Voices, orchestra, Orchestra of the Americas, Paul Freeman, conductor; Celestial Mechanics (oboe and string quartet), Los Angeles Chamber Orchestra; Array, String Quartet No. 2, to be sung on the water, Stanford String Quartet, 1998; Pilgrimage: Vicki Ray, Pianist, 1999. *Publications include:* Still Life With Bell, 14 players, Celestial Mechanics, oboe and string quartet; Roethke Preludes for orchestra; Island for concert band; The Falcon's Eye. *Address:* School of Music, University of Southern California, Los Angeles, CA 90089-0851, USA.

CROFT, Richard; Singer (Tenor); b. 1959, Cooperstown, New York, USA. *Career:* Sang Nemorino at Washington and Ramiro in La Cenerentola at St Louis, season 1986–87; European engagements include Mozart's Belfiore, Achille in Gluck's Iphigénie en Aulide and Belmonte at Drottningholm; Strasbourg and Nice, 1990–91, as Don Ottavio and Ferrando; Welsh National Opera, 1989, as Belmonte (repeated at the Metropolitan, 1991); Glyndebourne, 1991, Don Ottavio; Septimus in Handel's Theodora at Glyndebourne, 1996 and Tom Rakewell at Santa Fe; Season 1999 with Debussy's Pelléas at Glyndebourne and the London Prom concerts. *Recordings include:* Video of Die Entführung (Virgin). *Address:* c/o Metropolitan Opera, Lincoln Center, New York, NY 10023, USA.

CROLL, Gerhard; Musicologist; b. 25 May 1927, Düsseldorf, Germany. *Education:* Studied at University of Gottingen, doctorate 1954. *Career:* Assistant Lecturer, University of Munster, 1958; Chair of Musicology, Salzburg from 1966; President, International Gluck-Gesellschaft from 1987. *Publications:* Editions of Steffani's Tassilone and Die Entführung aus dem Serail; Gluck's Le Cinesi for the complete edition, 1958, (Editor-in-Chief from 1960) and Alceste 1988; Entries on Gluck and Weerbecke in The New Grove Dictionary of Music; Articles on Mozart discoveries Larghetto and Allegro in E-flat for two pianos and string quartet arrangement of a Bach fugue, K405; Gluck in Wien (1762), 1997; Rossini in Neapel, 1998; Member of Zentralinstitut für Mozart-Forschung and contributor to the Neue-Mozart-Ausgabe. *Address:* c/o New Grove Dictionary, 4 Porter's South, Crinian Street, London, N1 9XW, England.

CRONIN, Stephen (John); Composer; b. 2 Sept. 1960, Brisbane, Queensland, Australia. *Education:* PhD, University of Queensland, 1995; Studied with Colin Brumby, 1978–81. *Career:* Faculty Member, University of Queensland, 1984, Queensland Conservatory, 1986; Commissions from Seymour Group 1993, Synergy 1993; Australian Chamber Orchestra, 1995. *Compositions include:* In Moments Unseen for string quartet, 1984; Requiem, for chorus, percussion, 2 pianos and harp, 1985; Duo Concertante, for clarinet, viola and strings 1986; The Drover's Wife for narrator and orchestra, 1987; Piano Concerto, 1989; The Snake Pit for ensemble, 1990; Eros and Agape for chamber ensemble, 1990; House Songs for tenor and ensemble, 1991; Eros Reclaimed, for ensemble, 1992; Carmina Pu for chorus, 1992; Cries and

Whispers, for orchestra, 1993; Even Love can Wield a Stealthy Blade, for bass clarinet and percussion, 1993; Blow for wind octet, 1994; Kiss, for percussion quartet, 1994; Apriès Nuages for string orchestra, 1995. *Honours:* Vienna Modern Masters Recording Project, 1992. *Address:* c/o APRA, 1A Eden Street, Crows Nest, NSW 2065, Australia.

CROOK, Howard; Singer (Tenor); b. 15 June 1947, New Jersey, USA. *Education:* Studied at State University, Illinois, and appeared at first in concert. *Career:* Sang at the Seattle Opera, then appeared as Pelléas and Belmonte at Amsterdam; Paris Opéra-Comique, 1987, as Lully's Atys, Aix-en-Provence, 1987, as Vulcan in Lully's Psyche; Schwetzingen, 1988, in Salieri's Tarare, Versailles, 1988, in Rameau's Pygmalion; Albert Hall, London, 1989, in Daniel Purcell's The Judgement of Paris; Sang in Cesti's Orontea at the 1990 Innsbruck Festival, Rameau's Castor et Pollux at Aix (1991) and Lully's Alceste at the Théâtre des Champs-Elysées, Paris; Sang with Les Musiciens du Louvre in Lully's Acis et Galatée at Beaune, 1996. *Recordings include:* St Matthew Passion and Messiah (DGG); Scylla et Glaucus (Erato); Bach Magnificat and Pygmalion (Harmonia Mundi). *Address:* c/o P.G. Alferink Artists BV, Apollolaan 181, NL-1077AT, Amsterdam, Netherlands.

CROOK, Paul; Singer (Tenor); b. 1943, Blackburn, England. *Education:* Studied in Geneva and London. *Career:* Appearances with Geneva Opera and English National Opera; Royal Opera, Covent Garden, from 1975 as Mozart's Monostatos, Mime in Der Ring des Nibelungen and Herod in Salome; Other roles in Ariadne auf Naxos, Falstaff, Hoffmann, Die Meistersinger, Tosca, Don Pasquale and Turandot; Guest appearances for Deutsche Oper Berlin and San Francisco Opera (as Mime) and in Naples, Warsaw, Paris and Buenos Aires. Tours of Japan and South Korea with the Royal Opera; Sang Pfeifer in English Stage premiere of Hindemith's Mathis der Maler, Covent Garden 1995. *Recordings include:* Otello, Werther, La fanciulla del West and Les Contes d'Hoffmann. *Address:* c/o San Francisco Opera, War Memorial House, Van Ness Avenue, San Francisco, CA, USA.

CROOM, James; Singer (Tenor); b. 1960, North Carolina, USA. *Education:* Studied with James Schwabacher. *Career:* Appeared for two seasons as apprentice artist with Santa Fe Opera; Has sung twenty roles with Scottish Opera, the Glasgow Grand Opera (Calaf, 1990), Western Opera Theatre and San Francisco Opera; Appearances in Simon Boccanegra, Manon Lescaut, Die Zauberflöte (Monostatos) and Die Meistersinger for Scottish Opera; Other roles include Arbace (Idomeneo), Goro (Madama Butterfly) and Mephistopheles in Busoni's Doktor Faust. *Recordings include:* Video of L'Africaine, from San Francisco Opera. *Honours:* Regional finalist, Metropolitan Opera Auditions; Regional Winner, National Association of Teachers of Singing Competition. *Address:* c/o War Memorial Opera House, Van Ness Avenue, San Francisco, CA 94102, USA.

CROPPER, Peter; Violinist; b. 1945, England. *Education:* Studied with Sidney Griller at the Royal Academy of Music, at the University of Keele and with Vilmos Tatrai in Budapest. *Career:* Founder Member, Lindsay String Quartet, 1986 (now The Lindsays); Regular tours of Europe, England and the USA; From 1972 quartet in residence at Sheffield University, then Manchester University (1978); Premiered the 4th Quartet of Tippett at the 1979 Bath Festival and commissioned Tippett's 5th Quartet, 1992; For the Chamber Music Festival established at Sheffield, 1984; Regular concerts at the Wigmore Hall, including Haydn series, 1987. *Recordings include:* Complete cycles of Bartók, Tippett and Beethoven; Haydn quartets Live from the Wigmore Hall (ASV). *Honours:* Prizewinner (with members of Lindsay Quartet) at Liège International Competition, 1969; Gramophone Chamber Award for late Beethoven Quartets, 1984; Plays Stradivarius from the Golden Period. *Current Management:* Ingpen & Williams Ltd, 7 St George's Court, 131 Putney Bridge Road, London, SW15 2PA, England.

CROSS, Gregory; Singer (tenor); b. 1960, USA. *Career:* European debut, 1992, as Renaud in Gluck's Armide at Versailles, under Marc Minkowski; Further appearances as Rossini's Almaviva for Opéra de Nancy, Ferrando at Strasbourg, Tamino for Greater Miami Opera, Lurcano in Ariodante for Welsh National Opera and in Messiah at San Francisco; Sang Iopas in Les Troyens under Colin Davis and Leukippos in Daphne under André Previn, both with the London Symphony Orchestra; Further concerts include Haydn's Seasons and Mozart's Requiem in Canada, and the Saint Matthew Passion and Mozart's C minor Mass at the Kennedy Center, Washington DC; Sang Don Ottavio at Fort Lauderdale, 1997. *Recordings include:* Les Troyens, under Charles Dutoit. *Current Management:* Askonas Holt Ltd, Lonsdale Chambers, 27 Chancery Lane, London, WC2A 1PF, England. *Telephone:* (20) 7400-1700. *Fax:* (20) 7400-1799. *E-mail:* info@askonasholt.co .uk. *Website:* www.askonasholt.co.uk.

CROSSE, Gordon; Composer; b. 1 Dec. 1937, Bury, Lancashire, England. *Education:* Oxford University with Wellesz; Accademia di Santa Cecilia, Rome with Petrassi. *Career:* Birmingham University 1964–69, as Tutor in Extra Mural Department and in Music Department; Fellow in Music,

University of Essex, 1969–76; Visiting Professor in Composition, University of California, 1977; Freelance Composer, from 1978; Commissions from the BBC Symphony Orchestra, Royal Philharmonic Orchestra, London Symphony Orchestra and Festivals of Aldeburgh, Cheltenham and Edinburgh; The Story of Vasco premiered at the London Coliseum. *Compositions:* Stage Purgatory, 1-act opera after Yeats, 1966; The Grace of Todd, comedy, 1969; Wheel of the World, entertainment on Chaucer's The Canterbury Tales, 1972; The Story of Vasco, opera in 3 acts, 1974; Potter Thompson, 1-act music drama, 1975; Orchestral: Elegy, 1959; Concerto da Camera, 1962; Symphony No. 1, 1964; Ceremony, 1966; 2 Violin Concertos, 1962, 1970; Some Marches on a Ground, 1970; Ariadne for oboe and ensemble, 1972; Symphony No. 2, 1975; Epiphany Variations, 1976; Wildboy, 1977; Thel for ensemble, 1978; Symphony for chamber orchestra, 1976; Dreamsongs, 1979; Cello Concerto, 1979; Array for trumpet and orchestra, 1986; Quiet, for wind band, 1987; Vocal: Changes for soprano, baritone, chorus and orchestra, 1965; The Covenant of the Rainbow for chorus and organ; For the Unfallen for tenor, horn and strings, 1963; Memories of Morning Night for mezzo and orchestra, 1971; The New World, poems by Ted Hughes for voice and piano, 1978; Harvest Songs for chorus and orchestra, 1980; Dreamcanon I, for chorus, 2 pianos and percussion, 1981; Sea Psalms for chorus, children's voices and orchestra, 1990; Chamber: String Quartet, 1980; Trio for Clarinet, Cello and Piano, 1981; Wave Songs for cello and piano, 1983; Piano Trio, 1986; Meet My Folks, 1964, and Holly from the Bongs, 1974, all for children. *Address:* Brants Cottage, Blackheath, Wenhaston, Halesworth, Suffolk IP19 9EX, England.

CROSSLEY, Paul; Pianist; b. 17 May 1944, Dewsbury, Yorkshire, England. *Education:* Organ Scholar at Mansfield College, Oxford; Piano with Fanny Waterman; Study with Messiaen and Yvonne Loriod in Paris. *Career:* Won 1968 Messiaen Piano Competition at Royaun; 1973 premiered Tippett's 3rd Sonata (Bath) and Maw's Personae (London); Jan 1985 premiered Tippett's 4th Sonata in Los Angeles; 1986 presented series of six programmes for Channel 4 television, Sinfonietta, featuring major 20th century composers; Programmes on Liszt and Ravel for BBC television and Poulenc for Hessischer Rundfunk, Germany; Piano Soloist in British stage premiere of Janáček's Diary of One Who Disappeared, London Coliseum, 1986; Artistic Director of the London Sinfonietta, 1988–94; Season 1993–94, Debussy recital tour of Japan; Engagements with Hallé, BBC Scottish, Netherlands Radio Philharmonic and Los Angeles Orchestras; Played in the British premiere of Henze's Requiem at the 1993 London Proms; Ravel recital at the South Bank, London, 1997; Season 1999 with Poulenc's Aubade at the London Prom concerts. *Recordings:* Diapason d'Or for the complete solo works of Ravel and Tippett; Prix Caecilia for the Berg Chamber Concerto with the London Sinfonietta; Grand Prix de l'Académie Française for the Fauré Violin sonatas, with Arthur Grumiaux; Recently recorded Franck and complete Debussy piano works, and Franck's Symphonic Variations with Vienna Philharmonic under Carlo Maria Giulini; One of the first musicians to feature on the Internet. *Honours:* C.B.E., 1993. *Current Management:* Connaught Artists Management Ltd, 2 Molasses Row, Plantation Wharf, London, SW11 3UX, England. *Telephone:* (20) 7738 0017. *Fax:* (20) 7738 0909. *E-mail:* classicalmusic@connaughtartists .com. *Website:* www.connaughtartists.com.

CROSSMAN, (Wallace) Bruce, BMus, MMus, MPhil,; composer; b. 2 Nov. 1961, Auckland, New Zealand; m. Colleen Anne Guild 1986; one s. *Education:* Otago University, Dunedin, York University, England, 1990; Doctor of Creative Arts, University of Wollongong. *Career:* New Zealand Queen Elizabeth II Arts Council Grants, 1983–93; Composer-in-Residence, Nelson School of Music, New Zealand, 1987; Fellow in Composition, Pacific Composers Conference, Japan, 1990; Mozart Fellow, Otago University, New Zealand, 1992; Visiting Lecturer in Music, Waikato University, 1994; mem, Composers Association of New Zealand; Australian Music Centre. *Compositions:* Piece Number Two for orchestra, 1984; Pezzo Languendo for solo piano, 1984; Expression in Blue for violin and piano, 1988; Dual for two violins, 1988; Dialogue for Jerusalem for clarinet and piano, 1989; A Peace in Time for 2 pianos, 1989; City of Broken Dreams for orchestra, 1989; Timbres for guitar, 1991; Colour Resonances and Dance for orchestra, 1996; Rituals for soprano and string quartet, 1996. *Recordings:* Expression in Blue on A Violin and Piano Recital: Mark Menzies and Dan Poynton, The Waiteata Collection of New Zealand Music: Vol. I. *Honours:* Corbould Composition Competition Prize, 1996; Australian Postgraduate Award, 1996–99. *Address:* c/o Faculty of Creative Arts, University of Wollongong, Northfields Avenue, Wollongong, NSW 2522, Australia.

CROW, Todd, BA, MS; pianist and music professor; b. 25 July 1945, Santa Barbara, CA, USA; m. Linda Goolsby 1967; one s. one d. *Education:* University of California, Juilliard School, Music Academy of the West. *Career:* debut in London, 1975; New York, 1981; London orchestral debut, London Philharmonic Orchestra, 1986; Has given numerous concerts in USA, Europe and South America; Mount Desert Festival of Chamber Music, Maine; Maverick Concerts, Woodstock, New York,

Music Mountain, Connecticut; Radio appearances on BBC, National Public Radio and New York City Stations; Professor of Music, Department of Music, Vassar College, Poughkeepsie, New York; New York orchestral debut with American Symphony Orchestra, 1992; Additional festivals include: Casals Festival and Bard Music Festival; Music Director, Mount Desert Festival of Chamber Music, Maine; Performances with St Luke's Chamber Ensemble. *Recordings:* Schubert Piano Sonatas; The Artistry of Todd Crow; Mozart Piano Concerto K467; Liszt E flat Piano Concerto; Berlioz/Liszt Symphonie Fantastique; Complete music for cello and piano by Mendelssohn (with Mark Shuman, cellist); Piano Works by Taneyev; Ernst Toch Piano Concerto No. 1; Haydn Piano Sonatas; Piano Works by Dohnányi. *Publications:* Bartók Studies 1976; contrib. to Journal of the American Liszt Society. *Honours:* University of California Distinguished Alumni Award 1986. *Address:* Department of Music, Vassar College, Poughkeepsie, NY 12604, USA. *E-mail:* tocrow@vassar.edu.

CROWN, David; Singer (Bass Baritone); b. 1965, England. *Education:* Purcell School of Music; King's College, Cambridge; Masterclasses with Graham Johnson, and Roger Vignoles; Training as Baritone with David Pollard. *Career:* Early roles (as bass) included Don Giovanni, Leporello, Uberto in La Serva Padrona and Mefistofele; Companies included Broomhill Opera, Covent Garden and Batignano Festivals, and Pavillion Opera; Concerts as baritone include Messiah at Durham Cathedral, Elijah at Truro, Beethoven's Mass in C, Tippett's A Child of our Time and Fauré's Requiem; Season 2000 with Bach's Magnificat and Handel's Israel in Egypt with the Whitehall Choir at St John's Smith Square. *Honours:* Wagner Society Bayreuth Bursary and National Federation of Music Societies Award, 1997. *Address:* c/o Whitehall Choir, St John's Smith Square, London, W1, England.

CROWTHER, John Victor, BA, MA, DipEd, PhD; university lecturer; b. 3 Sept. 1937, Todmorden, England; m. Valerie; one d. *Education:* Grammar School, Todmorden, Univ. Coll. Durham, Nottingham Univ. *Career:* music teacher at secondary schools in Leeds 1959–66; Lecturer/ Principal Lecturer in Music Education at Loughborough Coll. of Education 1966–77; Dir of the Music Centre at Loughborough Univ. 1977–97; Ed. and Musical Dir of Cesti's opera 'Orontea' Vicenza 1969; public lectures and conference papers at Siena, Modena, Dublin, Durham, Edinburgh, Nottingham; mem. Royal Musical Asscn, Commissione Scientifica, Edizione Nazionale Dell' Opera Omnia Di Alessandro Stradella. *Publications:* The Oratorio in Modena 1992, The Oratorio in Bologna 1650–1730 1999, editions of 17th-century Italian oratorios by Vitali, Ferrari, Stradella, Freschi and Colonna, critical edition of Alessandro Stradella's oratorio 'La Susanna' Opera Omnia, Ser. III, Vol. I; contrib. to The Music Review, Music and Letters, Victorian Studies, Irish Musical Studies, Alessandro Stradella e Modena. *Address:* 21 Priory Road, Loughborough, Leicestershire, LE11 3PW, England (home). *Telephone:* (1509) 215533 (home).

CROXFORD, Eileen; Cellist; b. 21 March 1924, Leighton Buzzard, Bucks, England; m. David Parkhouse, (deceased 1989), 2 s. *Education:* Royal College of Music; Studied with Effie Richardson, Ivor James, Pablo Casals. *Career:* Debut: London, Wigmore Hall; BBC Promenade Concerts, Royal Albert Hall; Recitalist world-wide with husband, Concert Pianist, David Parkhouse; Concertos with leading orchestras; Trio with David Parkhouse and High Bean; Acclaimed in 1987 as world's longest standing Trio; Tours of East and West Europe, North and South America, Far East, Middle East, China and North Africa; Professor of Cello, Royal College of Music for 40 years; Founder, Member with David Parkhouse of Music Group of London. *Recordings:* Beethoven, Ghost and Archduke Trios, Irish Songs; Schubert, Trout Quintet; Trios by Bush, Mendelssohn and Ravel; Cello and piano sonatas by Dohnányi, Barber, Rachmaninov, Kodály, Debussy; Vaughan Williams, 2 Quartets, On Wenlock Edge, Studies on Folk Songs; Warlock, The Curlew; Lennox Berkeley, Sextet; Elgar, String Quartet. *Honours:* Alexander Prize, 1945; Queen's Prize, 1948; Boise Foundation Award, 1949; Fellow, Royal College of Music, 1983; Cobbett Medal of the Worshipful Co of Musicians for services to Chamber Music, 1991; Founder, Parkhouse Award, The International Chamber Music Award for Piano based groups in memory of David Parkhouse. *Address:* 11 Roehampton Court, Queens Ride, London SW13, England.

CRUDELI, Marcella; Concert Pianist, State Music Conservatory Director and Teacher; b. 16 April 1940, Gondar, Ethiopia; 1 s. *Education:* Language School; Mozarteum, Akademie für Musik, Salzburg, Austria; Hochschule, Akademie für Musik, Wien, Austria; State Conservatory G Verdi, Milan, Italy. *Career:* Debut: Rome, 1955; Over 2,000 concerts in 85 countries; Director, State Conservatory 'L. D'Annunzio' of Pescara; Teacher at the Ecole Normale de Musique de Paris 'Alfred Cortot' and at the Academia Pescarese. *Recordings include:* D Cimarosa, 62 Sonatas; B Galuppi, 12 Sonatas; R Schumann, Concerto A Minor, with Symphony Orchestra of Taipei; Glinka, variations on theme of Sonnambula, with Orchestra Rias of Berlin; Beethoven, Sonata Op 81; Mozart, Sonata K576; Schubert, Impromptus

Op 90; E Grieg, Concerto A Minor, with Symphony Orchestera of Taipei. *Publications:* D Cimarosa, Revision of 62 Sonatas; B Galuppi, Revision of 12 Sonatas. *Honours:* Appointed by the President of the Republic 'Cavaliere al Merito Della Repubblico Italiana'. *Address:* Via Pierfranco Bonetti 90, 00128 Rome, Italy.

CRUM, Alison, BA, LTCL, LRAM, MTC (London); Viol Player and Teacher; *Professor of Viol, Trinity College of Music;* b. 23 Nov. 1949, Derby, England; m. Roy Marks. *Education:* Shrewsbury High School for Girls, Reading Univ., London Univ.; studies with Wieland Kuijken and Jordi Savall. *Career:* solo viol player, consort player and teacher, with numerous world-wide performances since 1975; Prof. of Viol Trinity Coll. of Music 1987–; Visiting Specialist W Dean Coll. 1987–; mem. Incorporated Soc. of Musicians, Musicians' Union, Viola da Gamba Soc. of Great Britain (pres. 1997–). *Recordings:* over 80 recordings with many British early music groups, notably with Rose Consort of Viols, Musica Antiqua of London; Consort of Musicke, Dowland Consort, four solo recordings of Bach, Marais, Rogniono, Dalla Casa. *Publications:* Play the Viol 1989, seven books of music for viols 1989–; contrib. to Chelys, Early Music Today. *Address:* 87 Olive Road, London, NW2 6UR, England (home). *Telephone:* (20) 8452-3254 (home). *Fax:* (20) 8452-3254 (home). *E-mail:* alison@alisoncrum.co.uk (home). *Website:* www.alisoncrum.co.uk (home).

CRUMB, George, BM, MM, DMA; American composer; *Annenberg Professor, University of Pennsylvania;* b. 24 Oct. 1929, Charleston, WV; s. of George Henry and Vivian Reed; m. Elizabeth Brown 1949; two s. one d. *Education:* Mason Coll. of Music, Univ. of Illinois, Univ. of Michigan, Hochschule für Musik (Berlin). *Career:* Prof., Univ. of Colorado 1959–63; Creative Assoc., State Univ. of New York at Buffalo 1963–64; Prof. of Composition, Univ. of Pa 1971–, Annenberg Prof. 1983–. *Compositions include:* Four Processionals for orchestra, Ancient Voices of Children, Black Angels for electric string quartet, Eleven Echoes of Autumn 1965, Songs, Drones and Refrains of Death, Vox Balaenae for three masked musicians 1971, Makrokosmos vols I–V 1972–79, Music for a Summer Evening, Five Pieces for Piano, Night of the Four Moons, Night Music I, Echoes of Time and the River (Pulitzer Prize for Music) 1968, Four Nocturnes for violin and piano, Dream Sequence for violin, cello, piano and percussion 1976, Star-Child for soprano, children's chorus and orchestra 1977, Celestial Mechanics, Apparition, Whitman for soprano and piano 1979, A Little Suite for Christmas 1979, Gnomic Variations for piano 1981, Pastoral Drone for organ 1982, Processional for piano 1983, A Haunted Landscape for orchestra 1984, The Sleeper, An Idyll for the Misbegotten, Federico's Little Songs for Children for soprano, flute and percussion 1986, Zeitgeist for two amplified pianos 1987, Quest for guitar and ensemble 1990, Easter Dawning for carillon 1991, Mundus Canis for guitar and percussion 1998, Eine Kleine Mitternachtmusik 2002, Unto the Hills 2002, Otherworldly Resonances 2002. *Honours:* Koussevitsky Int. Recording Award 1971, UNESCO Int. Rostrum of Composers Award 1971, Prince Pierre de Monaco Prize 1989, Edward MacDowell Colony Medal, Peterborough 1995. *Address:* Music Building, University of Pennsylvania, PA 19104 (office); 240 Kirk Lane, Media, PA 19063, USA. *Telephone:* (215) 565-2438.

CRUZ DE CASTRO, Carlos; Composer, Professor and Production Manager; b. 23 Dec. 1941, Madrid, Spain. *Education:* Studied Law and Social Sciences at Universidad Central de Madrid; Studied music at Royal High Conservatory of Music, Madrid, composition with Gerardo Gombau and Francisco Calés, conducting with Enrique García Asensio and composition with Milko Kélemen at Hochschule Robert Schumann in Düsseldorf and with Gunther Becker and Antonio Janigro. *Career:* Participant at the VII Biennial in Paris, representing Spain with his pieces, Menaje for Non-Conventional Instruments and, Pente for Wind Quintet, 1971; Co-Founder with Mexican pianist and composer, Alicia Urreta of the Spanish-Mexican Festival of Contemporary Music, 1973; Took part in Premio Italia representing Spanish National Radio with his work, Mixtitlan in 1975 and at the Composers' International Tribune in Paris in 1979; With 6 other composers he established the Spanish Association of Symphonic Composers in 1976; Professor of Composition, Counterpoint, Chamber Music, Musical Forms and Aesthetics at the Conservatory at Albacete, 1983; Production Manager of Radio Clásica for Spanish National Radio; mem, Spanish Association of Symphonic Composers. *Compositions include:* Theatre: El Momento De Un Instante II, 1973–74; Ballet: Carta A Mi Hermana Salud, 1985; Instrumental: Imagenes De Infancia for piano; There And Back for guitar; Concerto for orchestra, 1984, Suite for guitar No. 1, 1993; Toccata Vieja En Tono Nuevo; 4 string quartets, 1968, 1975, 1994, 1998; Saxophone Concerto, 1997; Symphony 'Canarias', 1998; Barcarola for piano, 1999; La Sombra del Inquisitor, opera, 1999. *Recordings include:* Ida Y Vuelta; Concierto Para Guitarra Y Orquesta De Cuerda; Menaje; Morfologia Sonora No. 1. *Honours:* Music Prize by Mexican Union of Theatre and Music Chroniclers, 1977. *Address:* Clara Del Rey 46, 28002 Madrid, Spain.

CRUZ-ROMO, Gilda; Opera Singer (Soprano); b. 12 Feb. 1940, Guadalajara, Mexico. *Education:* Mexico City Conservatory, with Angel Esquivel. *Career:* Debut: Mexico City 1962, in Die Walküre; Metropolitan Opera from 1970 as Madama Butterfly, Puccini's Tosca, Manon and Suor Angelica; Verdi's Leonora (Trovatore and La Forza del Destino), Elisabeth de Valois, Aida, Amelia (Ballo in Maschera) and Violetta; Season 1972–73 at Covent Garden and La Scala Milan, as Aida; Appearances in Australia, South America and the Soviet Union and at the Vienna State Opera, Rome Opera, Paris Opéra, New York City Opera and Chicago Lyric Opera; Concert appearances in Canada, Mexico, USA, Japan, Israel and Soviet Union; Vienna Staatsoper, 1979 as Leonora in La Forza del Destino; New Jersey and Connecticut, 1988 as Donna Anna and Cherubini's Medea; Ars Musica Chorale and Orchestra, Englewood, New Jersey, as Santuzza and Matilda in the US premiere of Mascagni's Silvana, 1988–89. *Recordings include:* Rossini's Stabat Mater; Video of Aida at 1976 Orange Festival. *Honours:* 1st Prize, Metropolitan Opera National Award, 1970. *Address:* c/o Connecticut Grand Opera, 61 Atlantic SE, Stamford, CT 06901, USA.

CSAPO, Gyula; Composer; b. 26 Sept. 1955, Papa, Hungary; m. Eva Botai, 10 Oct 1980, 1 s. *Education:* Béla Bart ók Conservatory; Diploma in Composition and Music Theory, Franz Liszt Academy of Music, Budapest, 1981; Institut pour la Recherche et Coordination Acoustique/ Musique, Paris, 1982; PhD, Composition, State University of New York, Buffalo, 1989. *Career:* Member, New Music Studio, Budapest; Extensive concert performances, radio recordings and broadcasts with, or without the Studio in Budapest, Warsaw, Toruń (Poland), Vienna, Darmstadt, Milan, Rotterdam, London, Frankfurt am Main, Edmonton (Alberta, Canada), Buffalo, New York; Film music scores; Associated with Protean Forms Collective, New York City. *Compositions include:* Krapp's Last Tape, After Beckett, 1974–75; Tao Song, 1:1/2, 1974–77; Fanatritraritrana, 1977–81; Handshake After Shot, 1977; Hark, Edward..., 1979–81; Na'Conxypan, 1978–88; Phedre's Hymn to the Sun, 1981; Yagul, 1987; Infrared Notes, No.1 (Prismed Through Darkness), 1986–88; Remnants in White, tape, 1989; Choral in Perfect Time for keyboard and bass drum, 1993; Phèdre: une tragédie en musique, 1996–. *Address:* 182 Graham Avenue, Apt No. 3, Brooklyn, NY 11206, USA.

CSENGERY, Adrienne; singer (soprano); b. 3 Jan. 1946, Bavaria, Germany. *Education:* Bartók Conservatory, Budapest, Franz Liszt Acad. with Eva Kutrucz. *Career:* early engagements at the Budapest State Opera and in Monteverdi's Vespers, conducted by Lovro von Matacic; Engagements in Zagreb, Dubrovnik and Palermo; Marzelline in Fidelio at the 1974 Munich Festival; Hungarian State Opera Budapest as Marguerite, Lulu and Anne Trulove; Mozart roles at Munich; Susanna, Pamina, Fiordiligi and Zerlina; Appearances at Hamburg, Bayreuth, Cologne, Amsterdam and Bern with Sawallisch, Pritchard, Haitink, Lopez-Cobos, Michael Gielen and Roderick Brydon; Glyndebourne Festival 1976–77 as Susanna and Zerlina, in productions directed by Peter Hall; Wigmore Hall recital 1980, with English Canzonettas by Haydn; Gave the world premiere of Kurtag's Messages of the Late Miss RV Troussova, with the Ensemble Intercontemporain conducted by Boulez, 1981; Later performances of the work in La Rochelle, Milan, Venice, Florence, Budapest, Bath, Edinburgh and London; Gave the British premiere of Kafka Fragments by Kurtag at the 1989 Almeida Festival, London. *Recordings include:* Wigmore Hall Recital 1980 (Hungaroton); Messages of the late RV Troussova (Erato). *Honours:* Gramophone Record Prize, 1983; Gramophone Contemporary Music Award, 1985.

CUBAYNES, Jean-Jacques; Singer (Bass-baritone); b. 14 Feb. 1950, Toulouse, France. *Education:* Studied at the Toulouse Conservatory and the Paris Opéra studio. *Career:* Sang at the Toulouse Opera from 1978, notably as Zuniga, Mephistopheles, Colline and Monterone; Paris Opéra debut 1987, as Publio in La Clemenza di Tito; Opéra Bastille as the Old Hebrew in Samson et Dalila, Samuel in Ballo in Maschera and Zuniga in Carmen, 1991–95; Artistic Director, The Festival Déodat de Severac, Toulouse, France, 1994–; Guest appearances throughout France and in Dublin, Perugia, Liège, Bonn, Karlsruhe, Regensburg and Seville; Other roles have included Don Giovanni in 1988, Lothario in Thomas's Mignon, 1989, Arkel in Pelléas et Mélisande, Gessler in Guillaume Tell, Sparafucile, Daland, and Rodolfo in La Sonnambula; Bregenz Festival 1991, as Zuniga in Carmen; Sang Melcthal in Guillaume Tell at Liège, 1997 and Ramfis in Aida in 1998. *Recordings include:* Gounod's Mireille and Roussel's Padmavati. *Current Management:* Living Art Impresariat, 9 Boulevard Montmartre, 75002 Paris, France. *Address:* 40 Rue Alsace-Lorraine, 31000 Toulouse, France.

CUBERLI, Lella (Alice), BMus; American concert and opera singer (soprano); b. 29 Sept. 1945, Austin, TX; m. Luigi Cuberli 1972. *Education:* Southern Methodist University. *Career:* Debut: European Violetta in La Traviata in Hungary, 1975. Sagra Musicale Umbria in the oratorio La Betulia Liberata by Mozart, 1975; Spoleto Festival concerto da camera with music by Schubert and Beethoven, 1977; Debut at La Scala in Milan in Mozart's Abduction, 1978; Since then regular appearances in operas such as Mozart's Re Pastore, 1979, Handel's Ariodante, 1981 (Opera taken on tour by La Scala to the Edinburgh Festival, 1982), Mozart's Lucio Silla, 1984; Le nozze di Figaro, 1987 and Orfeo by Gluck, 1989; Debut at Festival Woche in Berlin with the Beethoven Missa Solemnis, conductor Herbert von Karajan, 1985, also performed in the Beethoven 9th, 1986, and the Brahms Requiem, 1987, again with Karajan conducting; 1986 debut at Salzburg Festival with Le nozze di Figaro (role of Countess) with James Levine conducting with repeats in 1987 and 1988; 1986 debut at the Mozart Festival in Paris again in Figaro with Daniel Barenboim conducting; 1987, new production of Traviata made especially for her at the Monnaie in Brussels; 1988 debut at Vienna Staatsoper in Viaggio a Reims, Claudio Abbado conducting; 1989 concert at Pesaro Opera, Festival of Beethoven's Schottische Lieder, Pianist Maurizio Pollini; Sang Mozart's Countess at Orchestra Hall, Chicago, 1992; Antonia in Les Contes d'Hoffmann at the Opéra Bastille, the Countess with the Royal Opera in Japan and at Florence, 1992; Sang Donna Anna at the 1996 Salzburg Festival. *Recordings include:* Beethoven, Missa Solemnis, Deutsche Grammophon (Karajan), 1985; Mozart, Da Ponte operas, Erato (Barenboim) Berlin Philharmonic, 1990. *Honours:* Franco Abbiati Italian Critics Award, 1981 and Premio Jorio, 1984; Le Grand Prix du Disque conferred by the Academy of France in Paris and Prix Rossini of Paris and the Maschera d'argento award in Campione d'Italia, 1986; Premio Paisiello in Taranto, Italy, 1987. *Address:* c/o Oldani, Viale Legioni Romane 26, 20147 Milan, Italy.

CUCKSTON, Alan; British harpsichordist, pianist, conductor and lecturer; b. 2 July 1940, Horsforth, Yorkshire, England; m. Vivien Broadbent, 16 Nov 1965, 2 s., 3 d. *Education:* Kings College, Cambridge, BMus 1963, MA 1965. *Career:* debut: Wigmore Hall 1965; BBC recitalist 1964; solo concerts in Europe, the USA; keyboard accompanist with Academy of St Martin in the Fields and Pro Cantione Antiqua; Conductor The Alan Cuckston Singers 1961–. *Recordings:* Solo Piano Music of Alan Rawsthorne, William Baines, Eugene Goossens, Edward German, John Field, Sterndale Bennett, Stanford, Corder; Solo Harpsichord Music of Burnett, Kinloch, Farnaby, Tallis, Byrd, Handel, Couperin, Rameau; Conductor, English Northern Philharmonia in K. Leighton, M. Hurd, J. Gardner, Conductor City of Bradford Orchestra in Rawsthorne. *Publications:* chapters in William Walton – Music and Literature 1999, Arthur Bliss – Music and Literature 2002. *Address:* Turnham Hall, Cliffe, Selby, North Yorkshire YO8 6ED, England (home). *Telephone:* (1757) 638238 (office). *E-mail:* alancuckston@email.com (home).

CUENOD, Hugues; Singer (Tenor); b. 26 June 1902, Corseaux-sur-Vevey, Switzerland. *Education:* Studied at the Conservatories of Geneva and Basle and in Vienna. *Career:* Debut: Paris 1928, in the French premiere of Krenek's Jonny spielt Auf; Sang in Geneva 1930–33, Paris 1934–37; Concert tour of North America with Nadia Boulanger, 1937–39; Professor at the Geneva Conservatory, 1940–46; Widely known in French songs and in early music; Lieder recitals with Clara Haskil; Sang in the premiere of Honegger's Le Danse des Morts, Basle, 1940; Performances as the Evangelist in Bach's St Matthew Passion; Created Sellem in The Rake's Progress, Venice, 1951; Covent Garden, 1954, as the Astrologer in The Golden Cockerel; Glyndebourne, 1954–, notably as Don Basilio, in Cavalli's L'Ormindo and La Calisto, and in Le nozze di Figaro (50th Anniversary Season, 1984); Metropolitan Opera debut 1987, as the Emperor in Turandot; Geneva Opera 1989, as Monsieur Taupe in Capriccio. *Recordings:* St Matthew Passion (Nixa); L'Enfant et les Sortilèges, Ariadne auf Naxos, Oedipus Rex, Les Contes d'Hoffmann, La Calisto (Decca); Le nozze di Figaro (EMI); Early Music for Erato. *Address:* c/o Glyndebourne Festival Opera, Lewes, Sussex BN8 5UU, England.

CULLAGH, Majella; Irish singer (soprano); b. 1963, d. of Tom Cullagh and the late Mrs Cullagh. *Education:* Cork School of Music; National Opera Studio, London. *Career:* Appearances with the Royal Danish Opera as Donizetti's Adina, Adèle in Le Comte Ory with the Glyndebourne Tour, Isabella in Wagner's Das Liebesverbot at Wexford and Mozart's First Lady for Opera North; Melissa in Handel's Amadigi at the Covent Garden Festival and New York, and the title role in Medea by Gavin Bryars; Concerts include Huit scènes de Faust by Berlioz in Venice, and engagements in the USA; Season 2000–01 with Fiordiligi in the Canary Islands, Micaela in Carmen and Countess for Opera North, Donna Anna in Regensburg and Tatiana in Eugene Onegin for Grange Park Opera; Manon for Opera New Zealand; Ninetta in Lagazza Ladra and Arminda in La Finta Giardiniera for Opera North; Violetta in La Traviata and Musetta in La Bohème for Glyndebourne on tour; Nedda in I Pagliacci, Bérénice in L'Occasione Fa Il Ladro and Ghita in Der Zwerg for Opera North. *Recordings include:* Mendelssohn 2nd Symphony (Naxos); Donizetti's Zoraida di Granata and Rossini's Bianca e Falliero (Opera Rara); Don Giovanni (Chandos), Donizetti's Pia de Tolomei, Rossini's Elisabetta Regina d'Inghilterra and Mercadante's Zaira, The

Thieving Magpie and The Magic Flute. *Current Management:* Athole Still International, Foresters Hall, 25–27 Weston Street, London, SE19 3RY, England. *Telephone:* (20) 8771-5271. *Fax:* (20) 8771-8172. *E-mail:* scott@atholestill.co.uk. *Website:* www.atholestill.com; www .majellacullagh.com (home).

CULLEN, Bernadette; Singer (Mezzo-soprano); b. 1949, Australia. *Career:* Appearances from 1981 with Australian Opera as Maffio Orsini in Lucrezia Borgia, Nicklausse and Giulietta in Hoffman, Cherubino in Figaro, Angelina in Cenerentola, Ottavia in Poppea, the Secretary in The Consul, Charlotte in Werther and Rosina in Il Barbiere di Siviglia; Further performances include Brangaene in a new production of Tristan, Sesto in Clemenza di Tito, Donna Elvira in Don Giovanni, also for Lyric Opera of Queensland; Eboli in Don Carlos and Adalgisa in Norma for Victoria State Opera; Vitellia in concert under Christopher Hogwood, Gala Concert with Joan Sutherland and Richard Bonynge in Perth, Dorabella at Hong Kong and British debut as Isolier in Le Comte Ory for Welsh National Opera; Sang Donna Elvira at the reopening of the Tyl Theatre, Prague, under Charles Mackerras, Leonara in La Favorita for WNO in Cardiff and at Covent Garden, Dido in Dido and Aeneas in Palermo (1994), Cassandre in La Prise de Troie for the Australian Opera, Brangaene in Tristan and Isolde for Scottish Opera; Venus in Tannhäuser at Sydney, 1998; Concert repertoire includes Mahler's 8th under Charles Dutoit; Rossini Stabat Mater and Petite messe Solennelle; Verdi Requiem in Sydney under Carlo Rizzi and with the Hallé Orchestra, Liverpool Oratorio under Carl Davis, Dream of Gerontius with the Ulster Orchestra and Beethoven's Ninth; Season 2000–01 as Eboli at Melbourne and Azucena at Sydney. *Recordings:* Pulcinella with the Australian Chamber Orchestra; The Bohemian Girl, conducted by Richard Bonynge. *Honours:* Vienna State Opera Award, Opera Foundation Australia, 1995. *Address:* c/o Braden Arts Management Ltd, Station House, 790 George Street, Sydney, NSW 2000, Australia.

CULLIS, Rita; Singer (Soprano); b. 25 Sept. 1952, Ellesmere Port, Cheshire, England. *Education:* Royal Manchester College of Music. *Career:* Joined the chorus Welsh National Opera, 1973; Principal on Contract, Welsh National Opera, 1976; Roles include Leila (Pearl Fishers), the Countess (Figaro), Tytania (Midsummer Night's Dream), Pamina (Magic Flute), Ellen (Peter Grimes), Donna Anna (Don Giovanni) and Lenio in Martinů's Greek Passion; Buxton Festival 1981, as Elisetta in Cimarosa's Il Matrimonio Segreto; Opera North 1985, as Jenifer in The Midsummer Marriage and as Christine in Strauss's Intermezzo; Season 1986–87 sang the Countess of Tel-Aviv Opera, Ariadne for Opera Northern Ireland and Donna Anna for her debut at the English National Opera, returned for The Fox in Janáček's Cunning Little Vixen; Concert engagements with RAI Milan, Hallé Orchestra, Ulster Radio, Royal Liverpool Philharmonic and the Bournemouth Symphony; Netherlands Opera, Freischütz, 1989–90; Other engagements as the Composer and Fiordiligi, English National Opera, the Fox in The Cunning Little Vixen, Scottish Opera, and the Countess and Donna Anna, debuts with the Canadian Opera Company and San Diego Opera, 1992; Season 1992–93 as the Composer in Ariadne for ENO and Covent Garden debut as Janáček's Fox; Sang Third Norn in Götterdämmerung at Covent Garden, 1995; Bach's St Matthew Passion at the Festival Hall, 1997; Season 1997–98 with Elisabeth in Tannhäuser for Opera North, Senta for ENO, Ellen Orford and Sieglinde for Royal Opera; Season 1999 as Hecuba in King Priam for ENO, Mozart's Countess at Hamburg and Creusa in the premiere of Param Vir's Ion, at Aldeburgh. *Address:* c/o P.G. Alferink Artists BV, Apollolaan 181, NL–1077AT, Amsterdam, Netherlands.

CULMER-SCHELLBACH, Lona; Singer (Soprano); b. 4 Feb. 1954, Miami, Florida, USA. *Career:* Prizewinner at the 1985 Mozart Competition, Salzburg, and appeared in the 1986 premiere of Penderecki's Schwarze Maske, at Salzburg; Also sang the role of Europa in Die Liebe der Danaë at the Vienna Staatsoper and at Santa Fe, 1988; Sang in the premiere of Patmos by Wolfgang von Schweinitz at Munich (1990) and appeared at Kassel from 1989; Lady Macbeth by Shostakovich, 1996; Further appearances in Essen, Paris, Berlin and Dresden, as Marie in Wozzeck, Shostakovich's Lady Macbeth, Elsa, Donna Elvira and Ariadne; Season 2000–01 as Aida at Heidenheim, Marina in Boris Godunov and Tosca at Kassel, Santuzza for Frankfurt Opera; Frequent concert engagements. *Address:* c/o Staatstheater Kassel, Friedrichplatz 15, W-3500 Kassel, Germany.

CULVER, (David) Andrew, MM; composer and performer; b. 30 Aug. 1953, Morristown, NJ, USA. *Education:* composition with Bengt Hambaeus; McGill University. *Career:* Founder Member of SONDE, Canadian music design and performance group; Has worked at Yellow Springs Institute for Contemporary Studies, New Music Concerts Toronto, Staten Island Children's Museum, 1983 and the Children's Museum of Manhattan, 1989–91; Collaborations with John Cage 1981–92, including computer assistance with the premiere of Europeras 1 and 2 at the Frankfurt Schauspielhaus, 1987; Founder, Anarchic

Harmony Foundation; mem, SOCAN. *Compositions:* Stage works Viti 1981; Music with Tensegrity Sound Source No. 5, 1983; Hard Lake Frozen Moon, 1989; Quasicrystals, sound sculpture, 1989; Ocean 1-95, 1994; From Zero (film), 1995; Architonic Space, 1996. *Address:* 127 Willowbrook Road, Clinton Corners, NY 12514, USA.

CUMBERLAND, David; Singer (Bass-baritone); b. 1945, Ohio, USA. *Education:* Studied at the Juilliard School, New York. *Career:* Debut: Sang Pizarro in a concert performance of Fidelio under Leonard Bernstein at Lincoln Center; Has appeared widely at German opera houses, notably in Frankfurt, Gelsenkirchen, Wiesbaden, Cologne, Leipzig and Freiburg; Repertoire has included Hans Sachs, the Landgrave in Tannhäuser, King Phillip in Don Carlo and the Dutchman; Has sung at the opera of Marseille and appeared in La Serva Padrona and Bastien and Bastienne at Clermont-Ferrand; Linz Opera in Der fliegende Holländer; US engagements at the Kentucky Opera, Philadelphia Opera; National Grand Opera and in Dallas; San Francisco and New York (City Opera); Spoleto Festival as Rodolfo in La Sonnambula; British debut with Opera North, 1988 as the Dutchman; Concert appearances at the Carnegie Hall, in Boston, at the Vienna Musikverein and in Santiago; Francesco Cenci in the world premiere of Beatrice Cenci, by Berthold Goldschmidt, 1994; Sang King Lycomedes in the world premiere of Wolfgang Andreas Schultz's Achill und der zehn Mädchen, Kassel, Germany, in 1997, Pogner in Die Meistersinger von Nürnberg at the reopening of the opera house in Magdeburg, Germany and sang Alberich in Wagner's Rheingold in Magdeburg and in further performances of Wagner's Ring in 1998. *Address:* Weinmarkt 5, CH 6004, Luzern, Switzerland.

CUMMINGS, Claudia; Opera Singer (Soprano); b. 12 Nov. 1941, Santa Barbara, California, USA; m. (1) H W Cummings, 12 June 1962, (2) Jack Aranson, 26 May 1973, 1 d. *Education:* BA, Vocal Performance, San Francisco University, 1963. *Career:* Debut: San Francisco Opera, 1971; San Francisco, New York City, Houston, Seattle, San Diego, Minnesota, Miami, Charlotte Opera Companies; Netherlands Opera; Stuttgart Opera premiere of Satyagraha by Philip Glass, 1980; Canadian Opera; Sang Countess de la Roche by B A Zimmermann, 1991 at New York City Opera; Other roles have included Violetta, Rosalinda, Lucia di Lammermoor, Lulu, Marguerite, 3 Heroines in the Tales of Hoffmann, Countess in The Marriage of Figaro. *Recordings:* Satyagraha, Philip Glass. *Address:* PO Box 4306, New Windsor, NY 12553, USA.

CUMMINGS, Conrad, BA, DMA; American composer, conductor and musician (keyboard); b. 10 Feb. 1948, San Francisco, CA. *Education:* Yale Univ., State Univ. of New York, Stony Brook, Columbia Univ., Tanglewood, Computer Music Project, Stanford, IRCAM, Paris. *Career:* teacher Columbia-Princeton Electronic Music Center 1974–76; Electronic Music Co-ordinator, Brooklyn College CUNY 1976–79; Assoc. Prof., Dir Music and Media Program Oberlin Conservatory 1980–91; Vice-Pres. CFO Hyperspace Cowgirls (children's interactive media co.), New York 1995–2002; mem. composition faculty (evening div.) The Juilliard School 2003–; commissions from the Smithsonian Inst., Oberlin Coll., San Francisco Opera Center, Cleveland Chamber Orchestra, Canadian Brass, Opera Delaware, Brandywine Baroque, Avian Orchestra; panelist Nat. Endowment for the Arts Opera Music-Theatre Div. 1993, 1994. *Compositions include:* Fragments from 'The Golden Gate' for mezzo soprano, tenor and piano 1985, I Wish They All Could Be... for instrumental octet 1986, Where I Live for soprano, baritone and baroque ensemble 1987, Positions 1956 for amplified voices and instruments 1988, Insertions for amplified voices and instruments 1988, Photo-Op opera 1992, Scenes from Tonkin for voices and chamber orchestra 1990, Dénouement for large orchestra 1992, There Is No Hope For Art for soprano, piano and double bass 1992, Tonkin (opera in three acts) 1993, Barnar Venet: Lignes (film score) 1995, 1996, Pierrette Bloch, Boucles (film score) 1997, 1998, Shakespeare in Loves for soprano and baritone voices and baroque ensemble 2000, In Memoriam Marge Laszlo for chamber ensemble 2004. *Honours:* MacDowell Colony Fellowships 1981, 1986, Djerassi Foundation Fellowship 1985, grants from the Nat. Endowment for the Arts 1981, 1992, Martha Baird Rockefeller Fund 1980, Opera America 1992, The Rockefeller Foundation 1992. *Address:* 415 W 23rd Street Apt 11–D, New York, NY 10019, USA (office). *Telephone:* (212) 741-1559 (office). *E-mail:* conrad@conradcummings.com (office). *Website:* www.conradcummings.com (office).

CUMMINGS, Diana, ARAM; Violinist; b. 27 April 1941, Amersham, Buckinghamshire, England; m. Luciano Jorios; two s. one d. *Education:* recital diploma, RAM. *Career:* debut, Wigmore Hall; has toured throughout the UK as soloist and chamber musician; numerous television and radio broadcasts; formerly leader of English Piano Quartet; mem., Cummings String Trio; with Trio gave Haydn's Op 53 No. 1, Martinů's trio and Beethoven's Op 9 No. 1, for the BBC 1991; mem. Musicians' Union, ISM. *Recordings include:* Complete String Trios of Beethoven. *Honours:* Prizewinner, International Paganini Competition, Genoa 1963, International Competition A, Curci, Naples

1967. *Address:* 2 Fairhazel Mansions, Fairhazel Gardens, London, NW6, England.

CUMMINGS, Douglas; Cellist; b. 5 Oct. 1946, England; m. two s. *Career:* Principal Cellist of the London Symphony Orchestra, 1969–92. *Recordings:* 2 Bach Suites for unaccompanied cello (Abbey); Swan Lake duet, with Ida Haendl (violin) and the London Symphony Orchestra; Schubert Quintet in C, with the Lindsay Quartet; Trout Quintet, Schubert with Dame Moira Lympani and Principals of LSO. *Honours:* FRAM, 1977. *Address:* 7 Yerbury Road, London N19 4RN, England.

CUMMINGS, Laurence; Harpsichordist and Conductor; b. 1968, Sutton Coldfield, England. *Education:* Studied at Oxford University (Organ scholar at Christ Church) and the Royal College of Music. *Career:* Has performed with the Orchestra of the Age of Enlightenment, The Sixteen, The Gabrieli Consort; conducted Esther (1732), Alexander Balus, Agrippina for the London Handel Festival; Theodora for Glyndebourne on Tour; Ariodante for English Touring Opera , Autumn 2003; Future plans include La Spinalba, Casa da Musica, Porto; Semele English National Opera, Autumn 2004; Giulio Cesare, Glyndebourne Festival, 2005; Musical Director of London Handel Society 2002–; Musical Director Tilford Bach Society 2002–; Head of Historical Performance, Royal Academy of Music 1997–. *Recordings include:* Louis and Francois Couperin keyboard music. *Address:* 81 Chetwynd Road, Dartmouth Park, London NW5 1DA, England. *E-mail:* laurence@chetwynd.clara.co.uk.

CUNNINGHAM, Thomas (Tom); composer and conductor; b. 24 March 1946, Edinburgh, Scotland; m. Alison Hannah 1972; two d. *Education:* George Heriot's School, Edinburgh, Univ. of Edinburgh, Morley Coll., London. *Career:* Musical Dir, Brussels Gilbert & Sullivan Soc. 1978–82, Brussels Choral Soc. 1984–2002, Hot Air 2003, Con Spirito 2003–05; composer of choral music and editor of choral music; mem. Asscn of British Choral Dirs. *Compositions:* Merry Christmas Jazz, Esta Noche, Rock O my Soul, Sweet was the Song, The Good-bye Jazz. *Recordings:* Joseph Jongen: Mass op. 130, Christmas Concert 1988, Festive Joy 2000. *Publications:* Choral scores of Gustav Mahler: Symphony Nos 2 and 3, Jongen: Mass op. 130, Deus Abraham, Quid sum Miser, and Three Sacred Songs (ed.). *Address:* 7 Lauder Road, Edinburgh, EH9 2EW, Scotland. *Telephone:* (131) 667-8614. *E-mail:* europa@cflat.co.uk.

CUPER, Philippe; Clarinettist; b. 25 April 1957, Lille, France. *Education:* Studied at the Paris Conservatoire with Guy Deplus, Henri Druart, Guy Dangain, Jacques Lancelot and Gilbert Voisin and with Stanley Drucker at Juilliard, New York. *Career:* Soloist with the Concerts Lamoureux, 1978–87; Orchestra of the Paris Opéra from 1984; Many appearances as concert soloist and as chamber musician with the Paris Wind Octet, pianists Paul Badura-Skoda and Michel Dalberto and violinist Augustin Dumay. *Recordings:* 25 albums. *Contributions:* Clarinette magazine; International Clarinet Society magazine; Band Journal, Tokyo; Clarinet and Saxophone Society Magazine, London. *Honours:* Prizewinner, Munich International Competition, 1982, Geneva, 1979, and Prague, 1986; 1st Prize, Prague, 1986. *Address:* c/o Association des Concerts Lamoureux, 252 Rue du Faubourg St Honoré, 75008 Paris, France.

CUPIDO, Alberto; Singer (Tenor); b. 19 March 1948, Portofino, Italy. *Education:* Studied at the Giuseppe Verdi Conservatory, Milan and at the Accademia Chigiana in Siena. *Career:* Debut: Genoa 1977 as Pinkerton; Sang widely in Italy and in Strasbourg, Vienna and Frankfurt; Glyndebourne 1978 as Rodolfo; Munich Staatsoper 1982 as Faust; US debut San Francisco 1983; Florence 1983 as Rinuccio in Gianni Schicchi; La Scala debut 1984 as Edgardo in Lucia di Lammermoor; Returned 1986 as Orontes in I Lombardi; Wiesbaden 1986 in Giulietta e Romeo by Zandonai; Further appearances in Cologne, Hamburg, Berlin and Montreal; Other roles include Alfredo, Fenton, the Duke of Mantua, Fernando in La Favorita and Rodolfo in Luisa Miller; Sang Edgardo at Monte Carlo, 1987; Faust at Geneva, 1988; Teatro Comunale Florence, 1989; As Faust in Mefistofele, Rodolfo at Rome, 1990; Gabriele Adorno in a new production of Simon Boccanegra at Brussels, 1990; Debut at the Verona Arena as Cavaradossi; Season 1991–92 as Boito's Faust at the Lyric Opera Chicago and as Don Carlo at Verona; Season 1994–95 as Rodolfo and Don José at Verona, Reyer's Sigurd and Cavaradossi at Marseille and Graz, 1995; Enzo in La Gioconda at Berlin, 1998; Also heard in the concert hall; Season 2000–01 as Hoffmann in Vienna, Pollione in Norma at Florence and Calaf at the Deutsche Oper Berlin. *Honours:* Prizewinner at Competitions in Parma, 1975 and Busseto, 1976. *Address:* Stafford Law Associates, 6 Barham Close, Weybridge, Surrey KT 13 9 PR, England.

CURA, José; Singer (tenor), Conductor and Composer; b. 5 Dec. 1962, Rosario, Santa Fe, Argentina; m. Silvia Ibarra 1985; two s. one d. *Education:* composition and conducting studies, Univ. of Rosario; vocal studies at the School of Arts of the Teatro Colón, Buenos Aires; vocal studies with Horacio Amauri in Argentina and Vittorio Terranova in

Italy. *Career:* international appearances at leading opera houses from 1992; Season 1993–94 included Albert Gregor, in The Makropulos Case, in Turin; Le Villi, Martina Franca; Season 1994–95, sang Loris in Fedora in Chicago; Stiffelio at Covent Garden; Season 1995–96, sang in Iris, in Rome, Samson at Covent Garden and in the Puccini Spectacular in Australia; Season 1996–97 included Don José with San Francisco Opera; Stiffelio and Samson at Covent Garden; Mascagni's Turiddu in Ravenna; Bellini's Pollione in Los Angeles; Don José in San Francisco; Cavaradossi with the Vienna Staatsoper, in Milan as Enzo in Gioconda; In Verona with Don José; Amsterdam Concertgebouw in Pagliacci; Otello in Turin; Season 1997–98 with Night of the Stars Royal Opera Gala at the Albert Hall, London, Loris in Fedora at the Vienna Staatsoper, Samson at Turin, and Radames in Tokyo; further concert engagements include Puccini Arias at the Barbican Centre, London, 1998; Puccini Documentary on BBC 2 in Great Composers series, 1998; appearances at opera houses throughout Germany, 1997–98, including Hamburg, Stuttgart, Cologne, Mannheim; further roles include Puccini's Des Grieux, and Manrico in Il Trovatore; Debut as Verdi's Otello, 1997, conducted by Claudio Abbado (also televised); sang Otello with the London Symphony Orchestra under Colin Davis at the Barbican Hall, 1999 and at Covent Garden, 2001; Samson in concert performances at the London Barbican, 2002. *Recordings include:* Le Villi; Iris; Argentine Songs; Puccini Arias; Samson and Delilah; Otello; Pagliacci; Manon Lescaut; Verismo. *Honours:* Premio Abbiatti Italian Critics' Award; Premio Carrara Cultura Millenaria, 1997; XII Premio Internazionale di Arte e Cultura Cilea, 1997; Opera Now Artist of the Year 1997–98. *Address:* JC International, Avda Machupichu 26, Apt 111, 28043 Madrid, Spain. *Telephone:* (91) 3000134. *Fax:* (91) 7599577. *E-mail:* jcproductions@cuibar.com. *Website:* www.josecura.com; www.cuibar.com.

CURLEY, Carlo; Concert Organist; b. 24 Aug. 1952, USA. *Education:* North Carolina School for the Arts; Privately with Virgil Fox, Robert Elmore (Philadelphia), Arthur Poister (Syracuse University) and Sir George Thalben-Ball (Temple Church, London). *Career:* Organist-Choirmaster and Teacher of Music, Girard College, Philadelphia; Director of Music, Druids Hills Baptist Church, Atlanta, Georgia; Artist-in-Residence, Fountain Street Church, Grand Rapids, Michigan; Organist, Alexandra Palace, London; Performances and Masterclasses at National Music Camp, Interlochen, Michigan; Frequent appearances on radio and television in USA, England, Australia, Canada, Japan and Denmark; Organ Consultant and Designer. *Recordings:* The Emperor's Fanfare, Brightly Shining, Organ Fantasia, Organ Imperial, Bach Organ Favourites, Bach Great Organ Works; The World of Carlo Curley (all for Decca). *Honours:* Patron, Holbrook Music Society (the United Kingdom); Patron and Organ Consultant to the City of Melbourne. *Address:* c/o PVA Management Ltd, Hallow Park, Worcester WR2 6PG, England.

CURNYN, Christian; Conductor; b. 1965, England. *Education:* York University; Guildhall School, London. *Career:* Founded Early Opera Company, 1994: productions of Purcell, M. A. Charpentier and Handel's Orlando, Queen Elizabeth Hall; Monteverdi Ballets for the York Early Music Festival, L'Orfeo and L'Incoronazione di Poppea; Charpentier's La Descente d'Orphée aux Enfers, for the Spitalfields Festival, and Médée; Handel's Rinaldo for the Guildhall School; Cesti's Il Pomo d'Oro and Handel's Aci, Galatea a Polifermo for the Batignano Festival, Italy. Season 2000–01 with Acis and Galatea and Purcell's Fairy Queen at the Wigmore Hall; Messiah in Tokyo and Handel's Partenope for the Covent Garden Festival. *Current Management:* Hazard Chase, Norman House, Cambridge Place, Cambridge CB2 1NS, England. *Telephone:* (1223) 312400. *Fax:* (1223) 460827. *Website:* www.hazardchase.co.uk. *Address:* c/o Wigmore Hall, Wigmore Street, London, W1, England.

CURPHEY, Margaret; Singer (Soprano); b. 27 Feb. 1938, Douglas, Isle of Man. *Education:* Studied with John Carol Case in Birmingham and with David Galiver and Joan Cross in London. *Career:* Debut: Sadler's Wells Opera 1965, as Micaela in Carmen; Sang with Sadler's Wells/English National Opera in operas by Mozart, Wagner, Verdi and Puccini; Sang Eva in new production of The Mastersingers, conducted by Reginald Goodall, Sieglinde in The Valkyrie and Gutrune in The Twilight of the Gods; Camden Theatre 1967, in the British premiere of Mozart's Lucio Silla, Guest engagements in Sofia and elsewhere in Europe; Sang Brünnhilde at the London Coliseum, 1977; Brünnhilde at Santiago and Seattle 1978; Season 1981–82 as Rezia in Oberon for Opera North and Jaroslavna in Prince Igor; Many appearances as concert singer. *Recordings:* The Ring of the Nibelung, conducted by Reginald Goodall. *Honours:* Prizewinner at 1970 International Competition, Sofia. *Address:* c/o Opera North, Grand Theatre, 46 New Briggate, Leeds, Yorkshire, LS1 6NU, England.

CURRAN, Alvin; Composer and Performer; b. 13 Dec. 1938, Providence, Rhode Island, USA. *Education:* BA, Brown University, 1960; Studied composition with Ron Nelson (Brown) and Elliott Carter (Yale), Yale University, 1963. *Career:* Co-Founder, Musica Elettronica Viva Group,

Rome, 1966; Solo performances in major festivals (new music), 1973–; Large-scale environmental works for chorus, orchestra, ship's horns and foghorns, 1980–; Milhaud Professor of Music Composition, Mills College, 1992–. *Compositions:* Songs and Views from the Magnetic Garden; Light Flowers, Dark Flowers; Canti Illuminati; For Cornelius; Maritime Rites, 1979–1992 (Music on Water); 1985 A Piece for Peace, 3 choruses, 3 speakers, 3 percussion, cello, violin, saxophone, 3 accordions, 1984; Electric Rags II, saxophone quartet, 1989; Notes from Underground/Floor Plan, sound installation, 1991; Animal Behaviour, solo performance live electronics, 1992; Schtyx, piano, violin, percussion, 1993; Inner Cities, 1994; The Twentieth Century, 1996; Endangered Species, 1996; Caged Notes, 1993–96; Erat Verbatim, 6 part sound work for radio, 1989–97; Pittura Fresca, violin concerto and small ensemble, 1997; Rose of Beans, double trio, 1998–99; Theme Park x 4, percussion quartet, 1998; Toto Donaueschingen, computer-generated sound installation in large Baroque Park, 1999. *Publications:* Maritime Rites, the book, 1984; Maritime Rites: The Lake, 1989; Music from the Centre of the Earth, 1994; Featured Composer in Musik Texte, 1994. *Honours:* National Endowment for the Arts Grants, 1977, 1983; Prix Italia for Radio Works, 1985–A Piece for Peace; DAAD Resident Composer in Berlin, 1986; Ars Acoustica International, 1989; Prix Italia (Special Award), 1988; Fromm Foundation, 1998. *Address:* Mills College, Department of Music, Oakland, California 94613, USA.

CURRY, Diane; Singer (mezzo soprano); b. 26 Feb. 1942, Clifton Forge, Virginia, USA. *Career:* Sang at the City Opera, New York, from 1972, Spoleto Festival from 1975 and at Graz in 1977; Other European engagements at the Deutsche Oper Berlin (1984–88), Hamburg Staatsoper, Köln, Bonn, Brussels, Geneva, Marseille, Nice, Teatro di Bologna and Maggio Musicale di Firenze, Arena di Verona (Amneris); Teatro di Roma; Teatro La Fenice Venice and Théâtre du Châtelet, Paris; Returned to the USA at the Metropolitan, New York (Nurse in Die Frau ohne Schatten, 1990), San Francisco and Seattle, the Chicago Lyric Opera; Other roles include Ulrica, Azucena, Laura and Cieca in La Gioconda, Fricka, Waltraute, Brangaene, Herodias, Clytemnestra, Mère Marie in Dialogues des Carmelites; Additions to her repertoire in 1999 included: Erda in Das Rhinegold and Siegfried, the Old Prioress in Dialogues des Carmelites and La Principessa in Suor Angelica; Many concert appearances, notably the Mahler Symphonies and the Verdi Requiem; Recorded Verdi Requiem for Telarc. *Honours:* Grammy Award, Gramophone Award, 1988. *Address:* c/o Metropolitan Opera, Lincoln Center Plaza, New York, NY 10023, USA.

CURTIN, Phyllis; Singer (Soprano); b. 3 Dec. 1921, Clarksburg, West Virginia, USA. *Education:* BA, Wellesley College; Studied at Wellesley College with Olga Avierino; Opera study with Boris Goldovsky at New England Conservatory and Tanglewood. *Career:* Debut: With New England Opera Theater, 1946 as Countess in The Marriage of Figaro and Lady Billows in Albert Herring; Sang at New York City Opera from 1953, notably in Von Einem's Der Prozess, Salome and in the premieres of Floyd's Susannah and The Passion of Jonathan Wade; Also sang Cressida in Walton's Troilus and Cressida, Giannini's The Taming of The Shrew and Poulenc's Les Mamelles de Tirésias; Sante Fe in 1958 in premiere of Floyd's Wuthering Heights; Glyndebourne in 1959 as Donna Anna; Metropolitan Opera from 1961 as Fiordiligi, Rosalinde, Eva, Mozart's Countess, Violetta and Ellen Orford in Peter Grimes; New York concert performances of Pelléas et Mélisande, 1962; Guest appearances in Vienna, Buenos Aires, Frankfurt, Milan, Glasgow, Paris and Trieste; Other roles included: Salome and Alice Ford in Falstaff; Sang Rosine in the premiere of Milhaud's La Mère Coupable, Geneva, 1966; Ellen Orford at Edinburgh Festival, 1968; Retired from public singing in 1984; Teacher at Aspen School of Music and the Berkshire Music Center; Artist-in-Residence at Tanglewood, 1964–; Guest Teacher, Central Conservatory, Beijing, 1987 and Moscow Conservatory, 1989; Recitalist across USA, Canada, Australia, New Zealand and South America; Soloist with major orchestras of US and other countries; US premieres of Britten's War Requiem with Boston Symphony and Shostakovich's Symphony No. 14 with the Philadelphia Orchestra; Dean Emerita and Professor of Voice and Artistic Director at Opera Institute in Boston University School for the Arts; Head of Vocal Program at Tanglewood; mem, Formerly served on National Council of The Arts. *Honours:* Ambassador for The Arts by US Government. *Address:* 9 Seekonk Road, Great Barrington, MA 01230-1558, USA.

CURTIS, Alan; Harpsichordist, Conductor and Musicologist; b. 17 Nov. 1934, Mason, Michigan, USA. *Education:* BM, Michigan University, 1955; PhD, University of Illinois, 1963; Amsterdam with Gustav Leonhardt, 1957–59. *Career:* Joined Faculty of University of California at Berkeley, 1960; Professor, 1970–; Active as keyboard player and conductor in the USA and Europe; Productions of L'Incoronazione di Poppea, staged and designed by Filippo Sanjust, in Amsterdam, Brussels, Innsbruck, Spoleto and Venice; Handel's Ariodante at La Scala, 1980, Later productions in Innsbruck and Turin; Conducted Rameau's Dardanus at Basel, 1981; Il Sant'Alessio by Stefano Landi at

Rome Opera, 1981; La Schiava Liberata by Jommelli for Netherlands Opera, 1982, and at the San Carlo, Naples, 1984; Cesti's Il Tito at Innsbruck, 1983, and Venice and Turin 1984; First production since 1707 of Handel's Rodrigo, Innsbruck, Madeira and Lisbon, 1984; Conducted a new production of Gluck's Armide, to open the restored Bibiena Theatre in Bologna, 1984; Gluck's Paride ed Elena at Vicenza, 1988; Conducted Cimarosa's Gli Orazi e i Curiazi at Rome, 1989, to mark the 200th anniversary of the French Revolution; Handel's Floridante with the Tafelmusik Baroque Orchestra at Toronto, 1990; Revival of Gli Orazi at Lisbon, 1990; Collector of early keyboard instruments by Martin Skowroneck. *Recordings:* Cavalli's Erismena; L'Incoronazione di Poppea (Fonit Cetra); Handel's Admeto and Rodrigo (Erato); La Schiava Liberata (Erato); La Susanna by Stradella; Goldberg Variations by Bach; CPE Bach's Rondos nebst eine Fantasie for Fortepiano; Buova d'Antona by Traetta. *Publications:* Sweelinck's Keyboard Music: A Study of English Elements in Seventeenth Century Dutch Composition, 1969, 1972; Edition of Jommelli's La Schiava Liberata and L'Incoronazione di Poppea, Novello, 1990. *Current Management:* Music International, 13 Ardilaun Road, Highbury, London N5 2QR, England.

CURTIS, Mark; Singer (Tenor); b. 1958, Hertfordshire, England. *Education:* Studied at the Royal Northern College of Music and at the National Opera Studio; Italy with Maestro Campogalliani. *Career:* Appearances with Glyndebourne Touring Opera in Die Zauberflöte and as Fenton and Jacquino; At Covent Garden in Alceste, Pagliacci (Beppe), Manon Lescaut and Fidelio; Kent Opera as Don Ottavio and Monostatos and in King Priam and Carmen; With Opera North has sung The Steersman, Vasek, Stroh (Intermezzo), Don Basilio (Le nozze di Figaro) and Arv in the British premiere of Nielsen's Maskarade; English National Opera as Amenophis in Mosè, and Don Ottavio, and in the world premiere of Birtwistle's The Mask of Orpheus, 1986; Other roles include Hylas in Les Troyens, the Madwoman in Curlew River and Nadir in Les Pêcheurs de Perles; Sang in the Mozart pasticcio The Jewel Box and King Priam (Hermes) for Opera North, 1991; Has also sung at Bath Abbey and the South Bank Halls and in Dublin, Brussels, Hanover, Berlin, Rome, Palermo, Seville, Hong Kong, Jerusalem, Helsinki and Edinburgh; Many concert appearances with English National Opera, Hilarion in Princess Ida and at Théâtre Royal de la Monnaie, Brussels, Der Soldat in world premiere of Philippe Boesmans, Reigen, 1993; English National Opera in King Priam (Hermes), 1995; Sang Goro in Butterfly for Opera North, 1996; Season 1997–98, sang M. Triquet in Eugene Onegin and Eumeus in The Return of Ulysses for Opera North; Nadir in The Pearl Fishers for English National Opera; Sang with Wiener Symphoniker in Vienna, Hamburg Philharmonic (L'Enfance du Christ), the Bamberg Symphoniker (Beethoven's 9th Symphony) and the Schwetzinger Festival (Beethoven's Missa Solemnis) under Roger Norrington; Sang Don Basilio in Le nozze di Figaro, Garsington Festival Opera, 1999; Goro in Opera Ireland's Madama Butterfly; Rev. Horace Adams in Tours production of Peter Grimes, France; Season 1999–2000 as Hermes in King Priam for ENO, Mozart's Basilio at Garsington and Goro in Butterfly at Dublin. *Recordings include:* Trabuco in La Forza del Destino and Yamadori in Madama Butterfly; Simpleton in Boris Godunov for Opera North conducted by Paul Daniel. *Address:* c/o Music International, 13 Ardilaun Road, Highbury, London N5 2QR, England.

CURTIS-SMITH, Curtis; Composer and Pianist; b. 9 Sept. 1941, Walla Walla, Washington, USA. *Education:* Studied piano, Northwest University, 1965; Composition with Bruno Maderna, Tanglewood, 1992. *Career:* Piano soloist and concerts, 1968–; Western Michigan University, 1968–. *Compositions:* 3 string quartets, 1964, 1965, 1980; Winter pieces for chamber orchestra, 1974; Belle du Jour for piano and orchestra, 1975; Music for handbells, 1977; Plays and Rimes for brass quintet, 1979; The Great American Symphony for orchestra, 1981; Songs and cantillations for guitar and orchestra, 1984; Float Wild Birds; Sleeping for orchestra, 1988; Gold are My Flowers, cantata, 1992; African Laughter, sextet, 1994; Violin concerto, 1994. *Honours:* Koussevitsky prize, 1972. *Address:* c/o ASCAP, ASCAP Building, 1 Lincoln Plaza, New York, NY 10023, USA.

CURTIS-VERNA, Mary; Singer (Soprano); b. 9 May 1927, Salem, Massachusetts, USA. *Education:* Studied at Hollis College, Virginia and with Ettore Verna. *Career:* Debut: Teatro Lirico Milan, 1949 as Desdemona; Appearances in Vienna, Paris, Munich, Stuttgart and Florence; Returned to USA 1951 and sang in Philadelphia; San Francisco 1952, Aida and Donna Anna; New York City Opera 1954 as Donna Anna; La Scala Milan 1954 as Desdemona; Metropolitan Opera from 1957 as the Trovatore Leonora, Tosca, Amelia in Un Ballo in Maschera, Santuzza, Aida, Turandot, Elisabeth de Valois and Violetta; Sang Desdemona at Baltimore, 1969; Further engagements in Buenos Aires and at the Verona Arena. *Address:* c/o Metropolitan Opera, Lincoln Center, NY 10023, USA.

CURZI, Cesare; Singer (Tenor); b. 14 Oct. 1926, San Francisco, USA. *Education:* Studied privately. *Career:* Debut: San Francisco 1947 as Pinkerton; Sang in San Francisco and elsewhere in North America; Moved to Europe 1955 and appeared at opera houses in Kiel, Nuremberg and Frankfurt (Alfredo 1957); Salzburg Festival 1959, in Il Mondo della Luna by Haydn; Further engagements in Stuttgart, Hamburg, Berlin and Cologne; Maggio Musicale Florence, 1959 and 1973–74; Member of the Deutsche Oper am Rhein Düsseldorf from 1965 and sang at Nuremberg until 1986; Other roles included Rodolfo, Ferrando in Così fan tutte, Ernesto and the Duke of Mantua. *Recordings:* Rigoletto (Electrola); Eine Nacht in Venedig; Die Fledermaus. *Address:* c/o Deutsche Oper am Rheim, Heinrich-Heine Allee 16, 0-4000 Düsseldorf, Germany.

CVEJIC, Biserka; Singer (Mezzo-soprano); b. 5 Nov. 1923, Krilo-Jesenice, Split, Yugoslavia. *Education:* Studied at Belgrade Music Academy. *Career:* Debut: Belgrade Opera 1950, as Maddalena in Rigoletto; Sang at Belgrade 1954–60, notably as Charlotte in Werther and as Amneris on tour to Vienna 1959; Metropolitan Opera debut 1961, as Amneris; Vienna Staatsoper 1959–79, Zagreb Opera 1975–78; Further appearances at Covent Garden, Verona Arena, La Scala and Buenos Aires; Sang in Massenet's Marie-Magdalene at Paris, 1977; Other roles have included Eboli, Azucena, Carmen and Delilah; Retired 1990. *Recordings:* Eugene Onegin, The Queen of Spades, Prince Igor, Boris Godunov, The Snow Maiden; War and Peace; Zigeunerbaron. *Address:* c/o Vienna Staatsoper, Opernring 2, Vienna, Austria.

CYNAN JONES, Eldrydd; Soprano; b. 1965, Wales. *Career:* Concerts and recitals throughout Europe, with opera in Wales and England; Repertory includes Handel's Giulio Cesare, Turandot and Adriana Lecouvreur; Also sings songs by Strauss and Duparc; Contestant at the 1995 Cardiff Singer of the World Competition. *Address:* 1 Hermon Street, Treorchy, Rhondda, Mid Glamorgan CF42 6PW, Wales.

CZAPO, Eva; Singer (Soprano) and Teacher; b. Nov. 1944, Budapest, Hungary. *Education:* Studied at Bart ók Conservatory, Budapest, in Basel and with Elsa Cavelti. *Career:* Sang with Trier Opera 1968–69;

Guest appearances in concert and opera at Basel, Zürich, Lucca, 1981, Bologna and Spoleto 1981; Appearances at the Salzburg, Lausanne, Lucerne, Lugano, Schwetzingen, Helsinki and Granada festivals; Concert repertoire has included Bach's B minor Mass, Beethoven's Ninth, Messiah, Elijah and St Paul by Mendelssohn, Haydn's Schöpfung and Jahreszeiten, Mozart's Requiem and C minor Mass and works by Schoenberg, Nono, Dallapiccola, Stravinsky, Szymanowski, Messiaen and Hindemith; Further engagements at Berlin, Hamburg, Munich, Milan, Rome, Turin, Parma and Lisbon; Voice Teacher at Basel and Founder of the Divertimento Vocale, Basel, 1987. *Recordings:* Bach Cantatas and Cavalieri's Rappresentazione di anima e di corpo; Schoenberg's Moses und Aron, conducted by Gielen; Schubert Masses; Davidde Penitente by Mozart and Carissimi's Dives malus. *Address:* c/o Musik-Akademie der Stadt Basel, Leonhardsstrasse 6, 4501 Basel, Switzerland.

CZYZ, Henryk; Conductor and Composer; b. 16 June 1923, Grudzjdz, Poland; m. Halina Buczacka. *Education:* Studied Law and Philosophy in Torun; Conducting and Composition at the Music High School, Poznan. *Career:* Conducting debut with Polish National Radio Orchestra, 1948; Art Director and Chief Conductor, Philharmonic Orchestra of Łódź, 1957–60 and 1974–80 and Kraków, 1964–68; Gave triple bill of works by Debussy, Honegger and Stravinsky at the Warsaw Opera in 1962; Conducted the premieres of Penderecki's St Luke Passion (Munster 1966) and The Devils of Loudun (Hamburg 1969); US debut 1973, with the Minnesota Orchestra; Conducted the Düsseldorf Orchestra, 1971–74; Professor at Warsaw Academy, 1980–95. *Compositions:* Etude for orchestra, 1949; Symphonic Variations, 1952; Comic Opera, The Dog Lover's Dilemma, 1967; Ingrid Bartsch, musical, 1982. *Recordings include:* St Luke Passion, Dies Irae and other works by Penderecki, Szymanowski's 2nd Symphony and excerpts from King Roger; Schumann's Das Paradies und die Peri. *Publications:* Writer, 7 books edited, 1973–85; Editor, 3 biographical books, 1993, 1995. *Address:* Moliera 2-21, Warsaw 00076, Poland.

D

DA SILVA, Miguel; Violist; b. 1960, France. *Education:* Studied at the Paris Conservatoire with Jean-Claude Pennetier and with members of the Amadeus and Alban Berg Quartets. *Career:* Member of the Ysaÿe String Quartet from 1984; Many concert performances in France, Europe, America and the Far East; Festival engagements at Salzburg, Tivoli (Copenhagen), Bergen, Lockenhaus, Barcelona and Stresa; Many appearances in Italy, notably with the 'Haydn' Quartets of Mozart; Tours of Japan and the USA 1990 and 1992. *Recordings:* Mozart Quartet K421 and Quintet K516 (Harmonia Mundi); Ravel, Debussy and Mendelssohn Quartets (Decca). *Honours:* Grand Prix Evian International String Quartet Competition, May 1988, special prizes for best performances of a Mozart quartet, the Debussy quartet and a contemporary work; 2nd Prize, Portsmouth International String Quartet Competition, 1988. *Address:* c/o 12/13 Richmond Buildings, Dean Street, London W1V 5AF, England.

D'ACCONE, Frank Anthony, BMus, MMus, MA, PhD; musicologist and academic; b. 13 June 1931, Somerville, MA, USA. *Education:* Boston University, Harvard University; studied with Karl Geiringer, Gardner Read, Nino Pirrotta, A. Tillman Merritt and Walter Piston. *Career:* Assistant, Associate, Professor of Music, State University of New York, Buffalo, 1960–68; Visiting Professor, 1965–66, Professor of Music, 1968–, University of California, Los Angeles; Editor, Music of the Florentine Renaissance, Corpus Mensurabilis Musicae series XXXII, 1966–; mem. American Musicological Soc.. *Publications:* Alessandro Scarlatti's Gli equivoci nel sembiante: The History of a Baroque Opera, 1985; The Civic Muse: Music and Musicians in Siena during the Middle Ages and the Renaissance, 1997; contrib. articles in many journals and publications including The New Grove Dictionary of Music and Musicians. *Honours:* Guggenheim Fellowship, 1980–81; International Galileo Galilei Prize of the Rotary Club of Italy, 1997. *Address:* c/o Music Department, University of California, Los Angeles, CA 90024, USA.

DADÁK, Jaromír; Composer and Conductor; b. 30 May 1930, Znojmo, Czechoslovakia; m. Ludmila Zapletalová; one s. three d. *Education:* Janáček Acad. of Art, Brno, 1956. *Career:* Conductor, Ostrava Radio Orchestra, 1960–63, Brno Radio Orchestra, 1953–90, Bratislava Radio Orchestra, 1982–91; Sec., Czechoslovak Composer Federation, 1967–69; Dir, Olomouc State Symphony Orchestra, 1969–71; political dissident, 1972–89; mem., Society of Czech Composers (pres. 1993–98), Asscn of Music Artists and Scientists, Society of Czech Composers, Society for New Music, Přítomnost (founder mem.). *Compositions:* Orchestral: Never More for symphony orchestra, 1959; Concerto-Symphony for piano and symphony orchestra, 1959; Concertino for dulcimer and orchestra, 1965; Concerto for piano 4-hands and symphony orchestra, 1972; Concerto for alto (viola) and small orchestra, 1976; Sonata corta for string orchestra, 1977; Concerto for tuba and small orchestra, 1982; Four Scanty Honours for bassoon and string orchestra, 1991; Ludi for string quartet and symphony orchestra, 1991; Benedictum for symphony orchestra, 1996; Chamber music: Three studies for piano 4-hands and percussions, 1965; Partita for violin, clarinet and piano, 1965; Four concert studies for dulcimer, 1967; Per aspera ad astra for organ, 1971; Four miniatures for dulcimer, 1975; Musica gioccosa for violin, clarinet, violoncello and piano, 1980; Sonata for dulcimer, 1980; Concerto for alto (with piano), 1983; Sonata for violin and piano, 1989; Sonata for violoncello, 1992; Transformations for hautboy, clarinet, bassoon and piano, 1994; Sonata for piano, 1994; Double-sonata for violoncello and piano, 1995; Capriccio for piano, 1997; Ballad for piano, 1998; Small terzet for two for basclarinet and piano with percussions, 1998; Exclamatio ad astra for organ, 2000. *Publications:* Our Folk Song, 1991. *Honours:* National Prize, 1960; CMF Prize, Prague, 1972; Grand Prix Radio Bratislava, 1981. *Address:* Kubelíkova 43, 130 00, Prague 3, Czech Republic.

DAGGETT, Philip; Singer (Tenor); b. 1962, Chesterfield, England. *Education:* Studied in Chesterfield and at Guildhall School of Music, 1985–. *Career:* Songman at York Minster, 1981–85; Concert appearances include Bach's Actus Tragicus in Paris and the St John Passion throughout Spain; Has sung in Mozart's C Minor Mass and Requiem; Mendelssohn's Lobgesang (Queen Elizabeth Hall debut) and Elijah; Britten's Cantata Misericordium and St Nicolas; Operatic roles include Paris in La Belle Hélène, Beppe in Pagliacci and Mozart's Ferrando; Premiere of Birtwistle's Gawain at Covent Garden, May 1991; Also sings Count Almaviva in Il Barbiere di Siviglia; Sang Tamino with Opera Lirica at the Holland Park Theatre, 1992; Premiere of Maxwell Davies's The Doctor of Myddfai, 1996; Sang Boyar in Boris Godunov for Welsh National Opera, 1998. *Recordings include:* The Fairy Queen with Harry Christophers and The Sixteen; A Festal Mass at the Imperial Court of Vienna and Charpentier's Vespers for the Feast of St Louis with the Yorkshire Baroque Soloists and Peter Seymour. *Address:* c/o Simply Singers, 23 Freke Road, London SW11 5PU, England.

DAHL, Tracy; Singer (Soprano); b. 1964, Winnipeg, Manitoba, Canada. *Education:* Studied with the Merola Opera Program. *Career:* Sang in the USA from 1986, notably as Offenbach's Eurydice at Houston, Olympia at Chicago (1987), Serpetta in La Finta Giardiniera at St Louis (1988) and Oscar in Ballo in Maschera at San Francisco (1990); Also appeared as Oscar at the New York Metropolitan, 1990, returning 1991 in the premiere of The Ghosts of Versailles by Corigliano (repeated, 1995); Toronto Opera, 1992, as Nannetta, Sophie in Werther and Zerbinetta, 1995; Season 1999–2000 as Verdi's Oscar and as Lucia di Lammermoor, Servilia in La Clemenza di Tito at New York City Opera. *Address:* c/o Metropolitan Opera, Lincoln Center, New York, NY 10023, USA.

DAHLBERG, Stefan; Singer (Tenor); b. 3 May 1955, Sweden. *Education:* Studied at the State Academy of Music and the State College of Musical Drama in Stockholm. *Career:* Concerts and Broadcasts throughout Scandinavia; Operatic roles include Rustighello in Lucrezia Borgia by Donizetti, Tamino, Beppe, Count Almaviva, King Charles in The Maid of Orleans by Tchaikovsky and Sextus in Giulio Cesare; Royal Opera Stockholm as Tamino, Sextus, Ferrando and Don Ottavio; Drottningholm 1987, as Titus in La Clemenza di Tito; Visited Brighton with the Drottningholm Company, 1987; Season 1988–89 with concert performance of Haydn's Armida in Amsterdam; Grand Théâtre Geneva as Jacquino in Fidelio, conducted by Jeffrey Tate; Gounod's Faust at the Stockholm Opera; Concertgebouw Amsterdam, 1989, as Ubaldo in Rossini's Armida; Drottningholm, 1989, as Tamino; Sang Calaf in Busoni's Turandot at Lyon, 1992; Leading tenor role of Vicente Martin y Soler's Una Cosa Rara; Alfredo in Verdi's La Traviata, Stockholm Royal Opera, 1993; Haydn's Orlando at Drottningholm, 1994; Concert repertoire includes Suter's Der Abwesende Gott, Die Schöpfung by Haydn, Le Roi David by Honegger, Messiah, Puccini's Messa di Gloria and works by Thomas Jernefelt and Sven-David Sandström. *Recordings:* Videos of La Clemenza di Tito, Die Zauberflöte and Don Giovanni, from Drottningholm. *Address:* c/o Drottningholms Slottstheater, PO Box 27050, 10251 Stockholm, Sweden.

DAIKEN, Melanie (Ruth); Composer; b. 27 July 1945, London, England. *Education:* Studied at the Royal Academy and at the Paris Conservatoire with Loriod and Messiaen. *Career:* Deputy Head of Composition at the Royal Academy from 1986. *Compositions include:* Operas: Eusebius, 1968, and Mayakovsky and the Sun, Edinburgh, 1971; Viola Sonata, 1978; Attica for Orchestra, 1980; Requiem for Piano, 1983; Der Gärtner for 13 Solo Strings and Piano, 1988; Song settings of poems by Lorca, Beckett, Trakl and Baudelaire. *Address:* c/o PRS Ltd, 29–33 Berners Street, London W1P 4AA, England.

DALAYMAN, Katarina; Singer (Soprano); b. 1968, Sweden. *Education:* Studied at the Stockholm Royal College of Music. *Career:* Debut: Stockholm Royal Opera 1991, as Amelia in Simon Boccanegra; Stuttgart Opera from 1993, as Marie in Wozzeck, Desdemona, Eva in Die Meistersinger and Elisabeth in Tannhäuser (1997); Further appearances as Mimi and Marietta in Die tote Stadt at Stockholm, Strauss's Ariadne at the Brussels Opera (1997) and Marie at the Maggio Musicale, Florence (1998); Season 1998/99 with Parisian debut at the Opéra National as Marie; Season 1999/2000 included Ariadne auf Naxos, Tannhäuser and The Queen of Spades in Munich, Dr Faustus at the Met and the Salzburg Festival, Bluebeard's Castle at the Royal Opera House, Covent Garden; Concerts include Mahler's 8th Symphony with the London Symphony Orchestra, Sibelius's Kullervo Symphony, under Colin Davis, and Penderecki's Requiem, conducted by the composer; Wagnerian Gala Evening in San Diego and La Damnation de Faust with the Munich Philharmonic and James Levine, 1999; Appeared with the London Symphony Orchestra and Simon Rattle in concert performances of Ariadne auf Naxos, 2000; Engagements for 2001–02 included Wozzeck at the Metropolitan Opera, New York, and the Royal Opera House, Covent Garden; Brangäne (Tristan and Isolde) at the Met; Ariadne and Kundry (Parsifal) at the Paris Opéra Bastille; Die Walküre and Lady Macbeth at Covent Garden; Tannhäuser in Brussels; Engaged for title role in Shostakovich's Lady Macbeth of Mtsensk at Covent Garden, 2003–04; Pique Dame and Walküre at The Met, 2004; Tosca in Stockholm, 2004; Tannhauser in Munich, 2004. *Address:* Artistsekretariat Ulf Törnqvist, Sankt Eriksgatan 100, 2 tr, S-1133 31 Stockholm.

DALBERG, Evelyn; Singer (Mezzo-Soprano); b. 23 May 1939, Leipzig, Germany. *Education:* Studied with Parry Jones at Guildhall School of Music, Annelies Kupper in Munich and with her father, Frederick Dalberg, at Cape Town and Mannheim. *Career:* Debut: Koblenz 1964, as

Venus in Tannhäuser; Sang at various provincial German Opera Houses and in South Africa, notably Cape Town and Johannesburg; Other roles have included Verdi's Ulrica, Amneris, Eboli and Mistress Quickly, Nancy in Martha, Giulietta in Les Contes d'Hoffmann, Judith in Bluebeard's Castle, the Witch in Hansel and Gretel and Prince Orlofsky in Die Fledermaus. *Address:* c/o Johannesburg Operatic and Dramatic Society, PO Box 7010, Johannesburg 2000, Transvaal, South Africa.

DALBERTO, Michel (Jean Jacques); Pianist; b. 2 June 1955, Paris, France. *Education:* Paris National Conservatory, 1972. *Career:* Debut: Paris; Appearances, major European Centres; Festivals: Edinburgh, Lucerne, Aix-en-Province, Montreux; Tours in Japan, Canada; Radio and television performances; Paris debut with the Orchestre de Paris, 1980; Partnerships with Henryk Szeryng, Augustin Dumay and Viktoria Mullova, Violin, and Nikita Magaloff, Piano. *Recordings:* Works of Schubert, Schumann, Brahms, Beethoven, Mozart. *Honours:* Clara Haskil Prize, 1975; First Prize, Leeds International Competition, 1978; Grand Prix Academie Charles Cros, 1980. *Current Management:* Opera Et Concert, Paris, France. *Address:* c/o IMG Ltd, Lovell House, 616 Chiswick High Road, London, W4 5RX, England.

DALBY, Martin; Composer; b. 25 April 1942, Aberdeen, Scotland. *Education:* Studied at the Royal College of Music from 1960, with Herbert Howells (composition) and Frederick Riddle (viola); Further study in Italy. *Career:* BBC Music Producer in London, 1965–71; Cramb Research Fellow in Composition at Glasgow University, 1972; Head of Music, BBC Scotland, 1972–93; Chairman Composers' Guild of Great Britain, 1995–98; mem, PRS; MCPS; ISM; British Academy of Composers and Songwriters. *Compositions:* Several compositions for cello, piano and string instruments 1965–79; More recent compositions include: Man Walking, octet for wind and strings, 1980; Antoinette Alone for mezzo and piano, 1980; Chamber Symphony, 1982; Nozze di Primavera for orchestra, 1984; A Plain Man's Hammer for symphonic wind ensemble, 1984; Piano Sonata No. 1, 1985; De Patre ex Filio octet for wind and strings, 1988; Piano Sonata No. 2, 1989; The Mary Bean for orchestra, 1991; Path for brass band, 1992; Sarabande for St Kevin, for organ, 1992, Butterfly Music for brass quintet, 1993; Variations for a Fair Maid of Perth for orchestra, 1993; Cantata: John Clare's Vision for soprano and strings, 1993; The White Maa for orchestra, 1994; String Quartet, 1995; Piano Sonata No. 3, 1998; A Wheen in Doric for symphony orchestra, 2000. *Honours:* Sony Gold Award for Best Classical Music Programme, 1993; BASCA Gold Badge Award, 1998. *Current Management:* Scottish Music Information Centre, Glasgow; Novello and Co, London. *Address:* 23 Muirpark Way, Drymen, Glasgow G63 0DX, Scotland.

DALE, Clamma; Singer (Soprano); b. 4 July 1948, Chester, Pennsylvania, USA. *Education:* BMus 1970, MS 1975, Juilliard School, New York; Studied Voice, Philadelphia Settlement Music School. *Career:* Debut: Operatic debut as Antonia, Les Contes d'Hoffman, New York City Opera, 1975; Sang with numerous Opera Companies; Toured as Concert Singer; Roles include: Pamina, Countess Almaviva, Nedda, Musetta, Gershwin's Bess at the Theater des Westens, Berlin, 1988; Deutsche Oper Berlin, 1989, as Liù in Turandot. *Recordings:* For Deutsche Grammophon; RCA. *Address:* c/o New York City Opera, Lincoln Center, New York, NY 10023, USA.

DALE, Laurence; Singer (Tenor); b. 10 Sept. 1957, Pyecombe, Sussex. *Education:* Studied at the Guildhall School of Music, 1976–80 and at the Mozarteum, Salzburg. *Career:* Debut: With English National Opera as Camille in The Merry Widow, 1981; Covent Garden debut 1982, as Second Noble in Lohengrin; Sang Don José in Peter Brook's La Tragédie de Carmen in Paris, 1981 and on Broadway, 1983; in 1983 sang Gounod's Romeo at Basle and Ramiro at Glyndebourne; Visited Los Angeles with the Royal Opera, 1984, singing Pong in Turandot; English National Opera 1988, as Monteverdi's Orfeo; For Welsh National Opera has sung Mozart's Ottavio and Ferrando and Eisenstein in Die Fledermaus; With Opera North as Mozart's Tamino and Belmonte and Jenik in The Bartered Bride; Further appearances in Lyon, Paris, Hamburg, Amsterdam, Aix, Geneva, Brussels (Tamino and Idomeneo) and Zürich; Other roles include Tchaikovsky's Lensky, Jacquino in Fidelio, Méhul's Joseph and Gonzalve in L'Heure Espagnole; Concert engagements include Mozart's C Minor Mass and Haydn's St Cecilia Mass with the London Philharmonic; Bach's Christmas Oratorio with the Los Angeles Philharmonic; Britten's Spring Symphony at the Festival Hall; The Dream of Gerontius and Liszt's Faust Symphony at the Brighton Festival; Messiah in Vienna, Stravinsky's Pulcinella and Rossini's Stabat Mater; Appearances on television in the United Kingdom and Europe; On 27 January 1991 sang Tamino in Die Zauberflöte at the Landestheater Salzburg, to inaugurate the Mozart Bicentenary; Season 1991/92 as Ferrando at Stuttgart and Belfiore in La Finta Giardiniera at the Salzburg Festival; Sang Don Ottavio at Genoa, 1993; Pelléas at Brussels, 1996; Season 1999 as Chevalier de la Force in Les Dialogues des Carmélites at the London Prom concerts;

Season 1999–2000 as Monteverdi's Orfeo in Amsterdam and Chicago. *Recordings:* La Tragédie de Carmen; Videos of Princess Ida, Die Zauberflöte from Aix and Cenerentola from Glyndebourne; Mozart's C Minor Mass. *Address:* c/o Théâtre Royal de la Monnaie, 4 rue Leopold, B–1000 Brussels, Belgium.

DALIS, Irene, AB, MS, MA; American singer (mezzo-soprano) and professor of music; *General Director, Opera San Jose;* b. 8 Oct. 1925, San Jose, CA; m. George Loinaz 1957; one d. *Education:* San Jose State University, Columbia University Teachers' College, studied voice with Edyth Walker in New York, Paul Althouse, Otto Mueller in Milan, Italy. *Career:* debut with Berlin State Opera 1955; Metropolitan Opera, New York 1957; leading dramatic mezzo-soprano, Metropolitan Opera 1957–77 as Eboli, Amneris, Santuzza, Azucena, Lady Macbeth and Dalila, 22 roles in 232 performances; first US born Kundry to open Bayreuth Festival 1963; opened the Met opera season as Amneris in Aida 1963; premiered Dello Joio's Opera, Blood Moon 1961 and Henderson's Opera, Medea 1972; sang The Nurse in Die Frau ohne Schatten at Sadler's Wells Theatre 1966; Prof. of Music, San Jose State Univ. 1984–; founder and Gen. Dir, Opera San Jose 1984–. *Honours:* Fulbright Scholar 1951, Distinguished Service Award Columbia University 1961, Wagner Medallion 1963, Tower Award San Jose State University 1974, California Public Educators Hall of Fame 1985, Award of Merit People of the City of San Francisco, Honoured Citizen of San Jose 1986, Hon. DMus (Santa Clara Univ.) 1987, Hon. DFA (California State Univ.) 1999. *Address:* Opera San Jose, 2149 Paragon Drive, San Jose, CA 95131, USA. *E-mail:* dalis@operasj.org. *Website:* www.operasj.org.

DALLAPOZZA, Adolf; Singer (Tenor); b. 14 April 1940, Bozen, Austria. *Education:* Studied with Elisabeth Rado in Vienna. *Career:* Sang in the chorus of the Vienna Volksoper while a student; Solo debut 1962, as Ernesto in Don Pasquale; Sang at the Volksoper until 1972, and guested in Munich, Hamburg, Milan, Brussels and Cologne; Bregenz Festival, 1972–84; Many roles in works by Mozart, Italian Opera and in Operas of the Baroque; Many appearances in Operettas; Wilhelm Meister in Mignon at the Vienna Volksoper, 1988; Season 1990 in Strauss's Intermezzo at Bologna and as Lensky at the Volksoper; Sang Dr Caius in Falstaff at the Volksoper, 2000. *Recordings:* Die Fledermaus, Der Vogelhändler; Idomeneo; Intermezzo; Fidelio; Die Meistersinger; Königskinder by Humperdinck. *Address:* c/o Volksoper, Währingerstrasse 78, 1090 Vienna, Austria.

DALLEY, John; Violinist; b. 1 June 1935, Madison, Wisconsin, USA. *Education:* Studied at Curtis Institute, Philadelphia, with Ivan Galamian. *Career:* Member of the Oberlin Quartet, formerly teacher at Oberlin Conservatory, Performed in Chamber Music with Rudolf Serkin at the Marlboro Festival and prompted by Alexander Schneider to co-found the Guarneri String Quartet, 1984; Many tours in America and Europe, notably appearances at the Spoleto Festival, 1965, to Paris with Arthur Rubinstein and London 1970, in the complete quartets of Beethoven; Noted for performances of the Viennese Classics, and works by Walton, Bartók and Stravinsky; Season 1987–88 included tour of Japan and concerts at St John's Smith Square and the Queen Elizabeth Hall, London; On faculty of the Curtis Institute, Philadelphia, and at the University of Maryland. *Recordings:* Mozart's Quartets dedicated to Haydn; Complete Quartets of Beethoven; With Arthur Rubinstein, Piano Quintets of Schumann, Dvořák and Brahms; Piano Quartets by Fauré and Brahms. *Honours:* Edison Award for Beethoven recordings 1971. *Current Management:* Ingpen & Williams Ltd, 7 St George's Court, 131 Putney Bridge Road, London, SW15 2PA, England.

DALL'OLIO, Gabriella; Harpist; b. 7 May 1965, Bologna, Italy. *Education:* Harp Studies, Conservatories of Bologna and Verona, with Anna Loro, Diploma with Honours, 1978–87; Graduated, honours, Liceo Scientifico, Bologna, 1984; Masterclasses with Pierre Jamet, Jacqueline Borot and Fabrice Pierre in Italy and France, 1986–90; Ecole Normale Supérieure de Paris with Fabrice Pierre (harp) and Michael Hentz (chamber music), Diplôme Supérieur de Harpe and Diplôme Supérieur de Musique de Chambre, 1988–90; Meisterklassdiplom, Hochschüle für Musik, Würzburg, 1993–94. *Career:* Recitals and solo appearances with orchestras and chamber music ensembles throughout Europe and The Middle East; Live recordings on radio and television in Europe; Contemporary music workshops; Appearances with several leading chamber ensembles including Kontraste and Holst Singers; Regular appearances as Guest Principal Harpist with numerous orchestras since 1987 including Chamber Orchestra of Europe, BBC Symphony and Concert Orchestras, Royal Opera House, Bavarian Radio Orchestra, English Chamber Orchestra and numerous regional and festival orchestras; Worked under many leading conductors; Harp Teacher, Trinity College of Music, London. *Recordings include:* Tema y Variaciones by Joaquin Turina; Two Recitals for Harp with works including Rossini, Handel, Fauré, Bach, Britten, Ginastera, Hindemith, and Roussel; Donatoni; Jean Francaix; Wandering Winds, flute and harp works with Wissam Boustany; Chamber Music Works by Marek;

Harp Concerto by Villa-Lobos. *Honours:* Victor Salvi Competition, Italy; Scholarships from French and German Governments; Prizes, National Competitions in Alessandria and Latina, Italy. *Address:* 16 Elspeth Road, Wembley, Middlesex, HA0 2BW. *Telephone:* (20) 8900-0593. *Fax:* (20) 8900-0593. *E-mail:* gabrielladallolio@hotmail.com.

DALTON, Andrew; Singer (Countertenor); b. 29 Sept. 1950, Melbourne, Australia. *Education:* Studied in Brisbane. *Career:* Debut: Sang at Vadstena, Sweden in Provenzale's La Stellidaura vendicata; Has sung in Baroque Opera at Venice, Innsbruck, Munich, Berne and Amsterdam; Appeared with Scottish Opera in Cavalli's Egisto and at the 1987 Buxton Festival as Fernando in Conti's Don Chisciotte in Sierra Morena; Season 1988–89 in Jommelli's Fetonte at La Scala, Milan, in Monteverdi's Ulisse with Opera de Lausanne at Mézières, and as Apollo in Death in Venice with Australian Opera at Sydney; Engagements in Germany and Switzerland as Britten's Oberon, and has sung in Monteverdi's Orfeo, Handel's Agrippina and Ariodante, and Jommelli's La Schiava Liberata; Sang in Purcell's Indian Queen at the Barossa Festival, Australia, 1995. *Address:* Australian Opera, Sydney Opera House, New South Wales, Australia.

DAM-JENSEN, Inger; Danish singer (soprano); b. 13 March 1964, Copenhagen; m. Morten Ernst Lassen. *Education:* Royal Danish Acad. of Music, Danish Opera School, studied with Kirsten Buhl Møller. *Career:* started career 1992, winner Cardiff Singer of the World Competition 1993; roles include Zdenka (Arabella), Ophelia (Hamlet), Norina (Don Pasquale), Sophie (Der Rosenkavalier), Adina (L'elisir d'amore), Susanna (Le Nozze di Figaro), Musetta (La Bohème), Gilda (Rigoletto), Cleopatra (Giulio Cesare), Despina (Così fan Tutte), Lisa (La Sonnambula), Blöndchen (Die Entführung aus dem Serail), Sifare (Mitridate); concert appearances with numerous orchestras, including Danish Radio Symphony, New York Philharmonic, Berlin Philharmonic, Czech Philharmonic and Gabrieli Consort; performed closing scene from Strauss' Daphne, London Proms 1999; has performed at Edin. Festival. *Recordings:* Mahler's Fourth Symphony, Grieg's Peer Gynt, Brahms' Ein Deutsches Requiem. *Current Management:* Harrison/Parrott Ltd, 12 Penzance Place, London, W11 4PA, England. *Telephone:* (20) 7229-9166. *Fax:* (20) 7221-5042. *Website:* www.harrisonparrott .com. *E-mail:* inger@danlassen.dk.

DAMARATI, Luciano; Composer, Conductor and Organist; b. 6 Feb. 1942, Lucca, Italy. *Education:* Diplomas: Piano, 1965; Composition, 1970; Organ, 1971; Orchestral Conducting, 1975; Studies: Organ with Alessandro Esposito and Fernando Germani; Orchestral Conducting with Franco Ferrara; Choral Conducting with Nino Antonellini; Musicology at Chigiana Academy of Music, Siena. *Career:* Many concerts as Organist and Orchestral Conductor; Broadcasts as Composer, Orchestra Conductor and Choir Conductor on Italian Radio and Television; mem, Italian Society of Musicology. *Compositions:* Impressioni (viola and piano), 1968; Fuga (organ), 1970; Preludio (organ), 1978; Immagini (piano), 1980; Contrasti (piano), 1980; Preghiera semplice (voice, choir and orchestra), 1986; I due fanciulli (voice and piano), 1986; Inno di lode a Dio (voice, choir of mixed voices, violin and organ), 1988; Le Ciaramelle (voice, violin and piano), 1988; La voce (voice, violin and piano), 1989; A Silvia (voice and piano), 1991; Mottettone (choir of mixed voices, 2 trumpets, trombone, tam-tam, kettledrums and organ), 1995. *Contributions:* La Provincia di Lucca, 1974; Actum Luce, 1980; Rivista di Archeologia Storia e Costume. *Honours:* 2nd Prize for Composition, Rodolfo del Corona, Leghorn. *Address:* Piazza S Francesco 14, 55100 Lucca, Italy.

DAMASE, Jean-Michel; Composer and Pianist; b. 27 Jan. 1928, Bordeaux, France. *Education:* Conservatoire National Superieur de Paris. *Career:* US debut 1954, as Pianist and Composer in a New York Concert. *Compositions:* Quintet for Flute, Harp and String Trio, 1947; Interludes for Orchestra, 1948; Rhapsody for Oboe and String Orchestra, 1948; Trio for Flute, Harp and Cello, 1949; Piano Concerto, 1950; Ballet La Croqueuse de Diamants, 1950; Violin Concerto, 1956; La Tendre Eleonore, Opéra-Bouffe, Marseilles, 1962; Colombe, Comedie Lyrique, Bordeaux, 1961; Eugene Le Mysterieux, Feuilleton Musical, Paris, 1964; Madame de Roman, Musical, Monte Carlo, 1970; Eurydice, Comédie Lyrique, Bordeaux, 1972; L'heritiere, Opera in 4 Acts after Washington Square by Henry James, Nancy, 1974; Quartet for Flute, Clarinet and Piano, 1992; Concerto for Flute and Orchestra, 1993; Variations, Mozart: for Piano and Orchestra, 1994; Four Facettes for flute and guitar, 1997. *Honours:* Prix de Rome, 1947. *Address:* c/o PRS Ltd, Member Registration, 29–33 Berners Street, London W1P 4AA, England.

DAMIANI, Davide; Singer (Baritone); b. 1966, Pesaro, Italy. *Career:* Recital, concert and opera appearances throughout Italy and Europe; Contestant at the 1995 Cardiff Singer of the World Competition; Repertory includes Le nozze di Figaro and Don Carlo, Lieder by Strauss and Schumann; Seasons 1995–99 as house-baritone at the Vienna State Opera; Welsh National Opera 1996, as Don Giovanni; Season 2000–01

as Don Giovanni at Toronto and Britten's Tarquinius at Florence. *Address:* c/o Miss Elin de Kat, Stage Door Management, Via Giardini 941/2, 41040 Saliceta San Giuliano (Modena), Italy.

DAMISCH-KUSTERER, Sieglinde; Singer (Soprano); b. 1951, Amsterdam, Netherlands. *Education:* Studied at the Salzburg Mozarteum and in Vienna with Hilde Konetzni. *Career:* Sang at the Vienna Staatsoper from 1979, Salzburg Festival, 1981 (Das Buch mit sieben Siegeln by Schmidt); Further engagements at Augsburg and elsewhere in Germany as Fiordiligi, Elisabeth de Valois, Tatiana, Jenůfa, Mimi and Pamina; Sang Jenůfa at Mönchengladbach, 1991; Frequent concert appearances. *Address:* c/o St ädtische Buhnen Augsburg, Kasernstrasse 4–6, Pf 111949, Augsburg, Germany.

DAMONTE, Magali; Singer (Mezzo-Soprano); b. 30 June 1960, Marseilles, France. *Education:* Studied in Marseilles. *Career:* Debut: Sang Zulma in L'Italiana in Algeri at Marseilles in 1978; Many appearances in France with operas by Rossini, Cimarosa and Gounod; Paris Opéra 1980, as Iphise in Rameau's Dardanus; Aix-en-Provence Festival from 1981, as Rosina, Cenerentola and Isaura in Tancredi; At the Opéra de Lyon has sung Aloès in L' Etoile (visit with the company to the Edinburgh Festival, 1985); Marseilles 1987, as Fidalma in Il Matrimonio Segreto, Théâtre des Champs Elysées, Paris 1989, as Hedwige in Guillaume Tell; Other Rossini roles include Isabella, Ragonde (Le Comte Ory) and Marie (Moise); Sang Carmen at Covent Garden, 1994, and at Vancouver, 1996. *Recordings:* L'Etoile, conducted by John Eliot Gardiner. *Address:* c/o Opéra de Lyon, 9 Quai Jean Moulin, 89001, France.

DANBY, Graeme; Singer (Bass); b. 1955, Durham, England. *Education:* Royal Academy of Music. *Career:* Sang with Scottish Opera until 1995; Appearances with English National Opera in Salome, Boris Godunov, Semele, Rigoletto, Damnation of Faust (Brander), Figaro, Peter Grimes, Poppea and Manon Lescaut; Further engagements with Mid Wales Opera in Aida and Garsington Opera in Le nozze di Figaro; Glyndebourne Tour in Die Entführung and Music Theatre Wales in The Rape of Lucretia and Birtwistle's Punch and Judy; Royal Opera debut 2001, as Marquis d'Obigny in La Traviata; Concerts include Will Todd's oratorio St Cuthbert, at Durham Cathedral, 2001. *Address:* c/o English National Opera, St Martin's Lane, London, WC2, England.

DANCEANU, Liviu; Romanian composer; *Professor of Composition, University of Music, Bucharest;* b. 19 July 1954; m. Rodica Danceanu 1976. *Education:* Academy of Music C. Poroumbescu, Bucharest, composition with Stefan Niculescu. *Career:* debut, Academy of Music, C. Porumbescu, 1978; Concerts in Bucharest and other musical centres, London, Paris, Rotterdam, Turin, Munich, Warsaw, Prague, Moscow, New York, Salzburg, Vienna, Valencia, Porto, Geneva; Appearances on Romanian Radio and Television, BBC London, Radio France, Bayerisches Rundfunk, Suisse Romande, RAI Turin; Recordings with Electrecord Recording House, Bucharest; Leader and Conductor, The Workshop for Contemporary Music ARCHAEUS, 1985–; Professor of Composition, History of Music and Music Aesthetic, Nat. Univ. of Music, Bucharest 1990–; Visiting Lecturer at the Academies of Music in Lyon, Munich, Alcoi, Cleveland, Munster, Carbondale, Chisinau, Moscow, Oldenburg, Turin and Dijon. *Compositions:* Les Heros, op 1, 1978; La Rocade De Janus, op 2, 1978; Allegorie, op 3, 1979; Sonate pour Basson, op 4, 1980; In Memoriam Lucian Blaga, op 5, 1981; Angulus Ridet, op 7, 1981; A Cache-Cache, op 8, No. 1, 1982; Steps to Melody, op 8, No. 2, 1982; Ossia, op 9, 1982; To Peace, op 10, 1982; Quasifuga, op 11, 1983; Quasiconcerto, op 12, 1983; Quasisymphonia (Symphony No. 1), op 13, 1983; Quasiricercare, op 14, 1984; 3 Chansons Infantiles, op 15, No. 1, 1984; 6 Stop-Cadres, op 15, No. 2, 1984; Quasipreludiu, op 16, 1984; Florilège, op 17, 1985; Protocantus, op 18, 1985; Quasipostludiu (Addenda), op 19, 1985; Glass Music, op 20, 1985; Quasitoccata, op 21, 1985; Rhymes for Archaeus, op 22, 1986; Quasiopera, op 38, 1986; Concerto for bassoon, op 49, 1989; Hexaphonic Melody, op 50, No. 1, 1988; The Great Union, op 50, No. 2, 1988; Trochos, op 51, 1989; L'Effetto Doppler, op 52, 1989; Quasisonata, op 53, 1989; Palimpseste de Couternon, op 54, 1954; Palimpseste 1 &2, op 55, 1990; Seven Days, op 56, 1992; Syntiphoniy, op 57, 1991; Concertino Sintoboe, op 58, 1991; Symphony No. 2, op 59, 1992; Saxas, op 60, 1992; Opus 61, 1993; Feast Music, op 62, 1993; Aliquote, op 63, 1994; Andamento, op 64, 1994; Game, op 65, 1994; Climax, op 66, 1995; Chinonic, op 67, 1995; Parallel Musics No. 1, op 68, 1995; Parallel Musics No. 2, op 69, 1996; Sega-Nomia, op 70, 1997; History 1, op 71, 1997; Bas-soon, op 72, 1997; Sifflet en Scène, op 73, 1997; L'Abîme de Pascal, op 74, 1998; History 2, op 75, 1998; Micro-Pseudo-Requiem, op 76, 1999; Domestic Music, op 77, 1999; History-Rhapsody, op 78, 1999; Opus 79, 2000; Opus 80, 2000; Tachycardia, op 81, 2000; Panta rei, op 82, 2001; Baclamo, op 83, 2001; Beverdillini, op 84, 2001; Dance by Dance, op 85, 2002; Superbia, op 86, 2002; Lili-Acul, op 87, 2002; One Day of D.G.'s Life, op 88, 2002; Ira, op 89, 2002; Prayer, op 90, 2002; Luxuria, op 91, 2003; Vocabule, op 92, 2003; Tachycardia Again, op 93, 2003; Pietas, op 94, 2003. *Publications:* Angulus ridet; Symphony No. 1; Symphony No. 2;

Aliquote4; Quasipreludiu; Quasifuga; Quasipostludiu; Quasiopera; Books: Implosive Essays I, 1998; Introduction in the Epistemology of Music, 1999; Implosive Essays II, 2001 Book with Instruments, 2002; Book with Dances, 2002, Seasons of Music – An Elliptic and Didactic History of Music, 2003. *Honours:* Romanian Culture Order 2004; Studieen de Toulouse Prize, France 1986, ATM Prize 1987, ACIM Prize 1988, Union of Romanian Composers Prize 1988, 1990, 1994, 2000, 2003, Romanian Acad. Prize 1989, SOROS Prize 1997. *Address:* Calea Vacaresti No. 276, Bl 63, Apt 49, Sector 4, 040062 Bucharest, Romania. *E-mail:* liviud@itcnet.ro.

DANCUO-PEHARDA, Mirjana; Singer (Soprano); b. 16 Jan. 1929, Karlovac, Croatia; m. Zdenko Peharda. *Education:* Studied in Zagreb. *Career:* Debut: National Opera, Zagreb 1945, as Giannetta in L'Elisir d'amore; Sang Belgrade, Sofia, Brno and elsewhere in Eastern Europe; Guest appearances at Teatro Liceo Barcelona, The Vienna Volksoper, Den Norske Opera, Oslo, Stockholm and Gothenburg in Sweden; Herodias in Salome (Strauss); Other roles have included Mozart's Countess and Donna Anna, Verdi's Amneris, Amelia in Ballo in Maschera and Trovatore Leonora, La Gioconda, Margherita in Mefistofele, Yaroslavna in Prince Igor, Leonore in Fidelio, Marina in Boris Godunov, Wagner's Sieglinde and Elisabeth, the Marschallin in Der Rosenkavalier, Tosca and Desdemona; Kostelnicka in Jenůfa, Lady Billows in Albert Herring; Teacher at the Operatic High School in Oslo, 1994–; mem, Norwegian Opera Singers Association. *Honours:* Oslo City Culture Prize, 1978. *Address:* Jerikoveien 89B, 1052 Oslo, Norway.

DANEL, Mark; Violinist; b. 1965, England. *Education:* Studied in London and with Feodor Droujinin, violist of Russia's Beethoven Quartet. *Career:* Many concerts throughout the United Kingdom, notably at the Aldeburgh Festival with Quartet in Residence, Huddersfield, Andover and Middle Temple; Repertoire includes quartets by Shostakovich and Fauré and English works. *Honours:* As member of Danel Quartet: Prizewinner in competitions at Florence, St Petersburg, Evian and London, 1991–94. *Address:* c/o Irene Witmer Management, Liedesgracht 42, NL–1016 AM Amsterdam, Netherlands.

DANEMAN, Sophie; British singer (soprano); b. 1968, England; m. Simon Robson 2001; one s. *Education:* Trained at the Guildhall School of Music and Drama. *Career:* Works with Christie, Hogwood, Marriner, Lesne, Malgoire, Herreweghe, King, Daniel, Hickox, McGegan, Ivor Bolton, Kraemer and Rattle; Has Sung with RIAS Kammerchor, Philharmonische Staatsorchester Halle, Freiburg Baroque Orchestra, Les Arts Florissants, Scottish Chamber Orchestra, Berlin Philharmonic and Orchestra of the Age of Enlightenment; Regular appearances at the South Bank Centre, Wigmore Hall, Maggio Musicale Fiorentino, Lufthansa Festival of Baroque Music, Edinburgh, Belfast and Saintes Festivals; Title role in Handel's Arianna in Creta at Göttingen, 1999; Rameau's La Guirlande (concert) at Cologne, and in Handel's Theodora and Acis and Galatea, at Salzburg, 2000, Eileen in Wonderful Town 2004; Repertoire includes: Despina, Susanna, Frasquita, Mélisande and Euridice; recitalist at Wigmore Hall, Queen Elizabeth Hall, Carnegie Hall, Concertgebouw, Vienna Concerthaus, Schwarzenberg. *Recordings include:* Handel's Rodelinda; Rameau's Grand Motets (Gramophone Award) and Castor and Pollux; Montéclaire's Jephté, Dido and Aeneas; Charpentier's Médée and La Descente D'Orphée, Mendelssohn and Schumann Lieder, Handel's Acis and Galatea (Gramophone Award), Handel's Theodora (title role), Giovanni Pergolesi's Marian Vespers; Jean-Baptiste Lully's Divertissement de Versailles, Noel Coward (with Ian Bostridge). *Address:* 29 Christchurch Road, London, SW14 7AQ. *Telephone:* (7710) 829-948 (home). *E-mail:* sophdane@dircon.co.uk (home).

DANGAIN, Guy; musician (clarinet); b. 12 July 1935, Sains-en-Gohelle, France; one d. *Education:* Conservatoire National Superieur de Musique, Paris, studied clarinet with Prof. Ulysse Deleclute, chamber music with Prof. Ferrand Oubradous. *Career:* clarinet soloist with National Orchestra of France 1963–93; Prof., Ecole Normale, Paris, Conservatoire National Superieur du Musique, Paris; Dir, International Festival, Haut Bugey. *Compositions:* over 50 collections of compositions. *Recordings:* Brahms Sonata; Debussy, Rhapsody; Rhapsody with National Orchestra of Martinon; Repertoire from young clarinettist H. Mundi; Creation du Monde, du Bernstein; Hommage à Louis Ca Huzoc; Guisganolerie: Hommage à Guisganol; Quinette et Two Songs. *Publications:* Prestige de la clarinette, 1987; A propos de la clarinette, 1991. *Honours:* Chevalier des Arts et des Lettres. *Address:* 14 Ruelle à Potier, 95590 Nerville la Forêt, France.

D'ANGELO, Gianna; Singer (Soprano); b. 18 Nov. 1929, Hartford, Conneticut, USA. *Education:* Studied at the Juilliard School, New York, and in Italy with Toti dal Monte. *Career:* Debut: Rome 1954, as Gilda; Glyndebourne 1955–56 and 1962, as Rosina, Clorinda in La Cenerentola and Zerbinetta in Ariadne auf Naxos; Brussels Opera 1956; Metropolitan Opera from 1961, as Gilda, Amina in La Sonnambula, Lucia di Lammermoor, Rosina and Zerbinetta; 8 Seasons with 36 Performances

in 7 roles; Guest appearances in Milan, Paris and London. *Recordings:* Rigoletto; La Bohème; Il Barbiere di Siviglia; Les Contes d'Hoffmann. *Address:* c/o Metropolitan Opera, Lincoln Center, New York, NY 10023, USA.

D'ANGELO, James, BMus, MMus, PhD; American teacher, composer and pianist; b. 17 March 1939, Paterson, NJ; m. Georgina Joysmith 1970; two d. *Education:* Columbia Univ., New York Univ., Manhattan School of Music, studied with Gunther Schuller, William Russo, John Lewis (MJQ), Jan Gorbaty and Jean Catoire. *Career:* debut, Carnegie Recital Hall, New York 1966; Prof. of Music, CUNY 1970–86; Lecturer, Goldsmiths' Coll., London 1987–; workshop leader in the Psychology of Musical Performance and Theraputic Voice Work 1992–; mem. advisory bd, Caduceus Journal 1993–; as composer, works performed at various colls in USA 1968–75, and at various London venues 1985–; song cycle debuted at Carnegie Recital Hall 1971; as pianist, London concerts of own music 1986–; featured composer, Planet Tree Music Festival London 1998, 2000; guest presenter at Findhorn Foundation, Scotland. *Compositions:* Tintinnabulations song cycle for soprano, Toccata for solo percussionist, Songs on poems by e e cummings, The Way of the Spiritual Warrior 1989, The Elements 1990, The Great Happiness 1991, Fool and Angel Entering a City 1993, Fools (three movement suite for flute and percussion) 1997, The Song of Solomon 1998, The Holy City 1998, Tenebrae Factae Sunt 2001, Pater Noster for baritone and string quartet 2003. *Recordings:* Fast Cats and Mysterious Cows (including Krishna Portraits) 1999, Suite of Ten Third Stream Songs 2004. *Publications:* Healing with the Voice 2000, The Healing Power of the Human Voice 2005; contrib. to International Dictionary of Opera, Hindemith Jahrbuch, Contemporary Music Review. *Address:* 33 Morpeth Street, Gloucester, Gloucestershire G41 4TN, England (home). *Telephone:* (1594) 517-333 (office). *E-mail:* healingvibes@soundspirit.co .uk (office); james.dangelo@lineone.net (home). *Website:* www .soundspirit.co.uk.

DANIEL, Nicholas Jeremy Gordon; oboist, conductor and teacher; b. 9 Jan. 1962, Liss, Hampshire, England; m. Joy Farrall 1986; two s. *Education:* chorister Salisbury Cathedral School, Purcell School, London, Royal Academy of Music. *Career:* debut, South Bank 1982; Concerto and recital appearances, at home and abroad; Proms debut, 1990, four subsequent appearances; Founder and Director, Haffner Wind Ensemble, 1990; Daniel-Drake Duo 1980–; Regular broadcasts of wide repertoire, more than 30 recordings; Tours include USA, Japan, Australia, Scandinavia, Netherlands, Italy, Bulgaria, Spain, France, Switzerland, Germany, South America; Performances with Brodky, Allegri, Brindisi, Vanbrugh, Lindsay String Quartets; Professor, Guildhall School of Music and Drama, 1984–97; Professor of Oboe, Bloomington, Indiana, 1997–99; Prince Consort Prof. of Oboe, Royal College of Music, London, 1999–2002; Prof. Hochschule für Musik und Kunst, Trossingen, Germany, 2004–; Artistic , Osnabruck Kammermusiktage, 2001–; Founder mem. and Assoc. Artistic Dir, Britten Sinfonia, 2002–; Artistic Dir, Leicester Symphony Orchestra, 2001–, Leicester Int. Music Festival, 2004; Regional Council mem., Arts Council England, East; Artistic Dir, Barbirolli Isle of Wight Int. Oboe Competition, 2005. *Honours:* BBC Young Musician of the Year, 1980; Gillet Young Artists Prize, Graz, 1984 and Munich Competition, 1986; Associate, 1986, Fellow, 1997, Royal Academy of Music; Honorary Fellow, Purcell School, 1988; Fellow, The Guildhall School, 1996. *Address:* Hedgerow House, 48 Station Road, Warboys, Cambridgeshire, PE28 2TH, England. *E-mail:* SoloOboe@aol.com.

DANIEL, Paul; Conductor; b. 1 July 1958, Birmingham, England. *Education:* sang in choir of Coventry Cathedral and read music at King's Coll., Cambridge; Guildhall School, London, with Franco Ferrara in Italy, and with Adrian Boult and Edward Downes. *Career:* engagements with the Royal Philharmonic, City of Birmingham Symphony, Scottish National Orchestra, Rotterdam Philharmonic, London Symphony, London Philharmonic, Philharmonia, Minneapolis Orchestra, Rochester Philharmonic, New York, London Sinfonietta and Ensemble Inter Contemporain, Paris, and Munich Philharmonic, RSO Berlin, ORF Vienna, Hallé, Manchester; principal conductor of the English Northern Philharmonica; US debut, 1988, with the London Sinfonietta at the Pepsico Summer Fair; Music Dir, Opera Factory, 1987–90; The Beggar's Opera, Cavalli's La Calisto, Birtwistle's Punch and Judy, Così fan tutte and a triple bill of works by Maxwell Davies, Ligeti and Weill; productions for ENO include Ligeti's Le Grand Macabre, Glass's Akhnaten, Dargomyzhsky's Stone Guest, Birtwistle's The Mask of Orpheus and the British premiere of Reimann's Lear (1989); for Nancy Opéra conducted the French premiere of Tippett's King Priam, 1988; Music Dir, Opera North, 1990–96; Music Dir, ENO, 1997–(2005); productions for Opera North include British Stage Premiere of Jérusalem, Ariane et Barbe-bleue, Dukas, Verdi's Attila, Tippett's King Priam, 1991, British première of Schreker's Der ferne Klang, Rigoletto, Boris, Don Carlos, Wozzeck, Il Trovatore, Pelléas and Mélisande, Luisa Miller, Medea, 1993; La Monnaie, Brussels, from

1994, with Così fan tutte, Khovanshchina and Béatrice et Bénédict, 1997; premiere of Bose's Slaughterhouse Five at Munich, 1996; Season 1998 with Hoffmann, Manon, Falstaff and Otello for ENO; premiere of The Silver Tassie by Mark Anthony Turnage, 2000; initiated ENO Wagner Ring Cycle with The Rhinegold (concert), 2001 and The Valkyrie, 2002; conducted the Bournemouth Symphony Orchestra at the London Proms, 2002; engaged with Siegfried and The Twilight of the Gods for ENO at the Barbican, 2002–03; staged productions of The Ring for ENO at London Coliseum 2003–04, 2004–05. *Address:* c/o Ingpen & Williams Limited, 7 Saint George's Court, 131 Putney Bridge Road, London, SW15 2PA, England.

DANIELS, Barbara; Singer (soprano); b. 7 May 1946, Granville, OH, USA. *Education:* BA, Ohio State Univ., MA, Univ. of Cincinnati. *Career:* debut, West Palm Beach, FL, as Susanna 1973; sang in Europe from 1974, notably in Innsbruck as Violetta and Cologne as Alice Ford, Rosalinda, Mozart's Countess and Manon Lescaut; appeared in the Michael Hampe productions and films of Agrippina and Il Matrimonio Segreto; Covent Garden from 1978 as Musetta, Donna Elvira, Rosalinde and Alice Ford; Washington DC 1979, as Donizetti's Norina; San Francisco from 1980, as Zdenka in Arabella and as Violetta, Liu and Micaela; Zürich Opera as the Comtesse, in the Ponnelle production of Le Comte Ory; Metropolitan Opera from 1983, as Musetta, Violetta, Rosalinde, Marguerite and the title role in Les Mamelles de Tirésias; Musetta at Rome 1987; Teatro Regio Turin as Violetta 1988; Rosalinde in Fledermaus at the Metropolitan and Chicago 1990; Jenůfa at Innsbruck 1990; Minnie in La Fanciulla del West at the Metropolitan 1991; sang Senta at Cincinnati 1996; Alice Ford at Baltimore 1997; sang Puccini's Minnie at Nice 2000; concert appearances in Rossini's Mosè at Perugia; Boito's Mefistofele at the Zürich Tonhalle, Schumann's Scenes from Faust with the Berlin Philharmonic and the Missa Solemnis under Giulini at the Maggio Musicale Florence; Prof. of Voice, Salzburg Mozarteum and Innsbruck Conservatory. *Recordings include:* Scenes from Faust, La Bohème (conducted by Bernstein), Mad About Puccini, Fanciulla de West (video), Il Matrimonio Segreto (video), Agrippina (video). *Honours:* Dr hc, Cincinnati Univ. 1992. *Address:* c/o Opéra et Concert, 1 rue Volney, 75002, Paris, France.

DANIELS, Charles; Singer (tenor); b. 1960, Salisbury, England. *Education:* Choral Scholar at King's College, Cambridge; Royal College of Music, with Edward Brooks. *Career:* Many appearances in the UK, Europe, Canada and USA; Handel's La Resurrezione in Oslo; Saul in Göttingen; Solomon in Halle; L'Allegro at Handel's Church in London; Mendelssohn's Elijah and Puccini's Messa di Gloria under Michel Corboz; Bach St Matthew Passion for De Nederlandse Bach Vereniging; Christmas Oratorio in St Gallen, Lugano, Dublin; regular appearances at the BBC Promenade Concerts; Elgar's Dream of Gerontius; Luigi Nono's Canti di Vita e Amore (Edinburgh Festival); Britten's War Requiem (Canterbury Festival); Cavalieri's Anima e Corpo (Schwabische Gmund); Schubert Mass in E Flat with London Phiharmonic Orchestra; Handel's Esther in Hebrew and English in New York; Monteverdi's Orfeo and Purcell's King Arthur in Toronto; the premiere of Wojciech Kilar's Missa Pro Pace with the Warsaw Philharmonic. *Recordings include:* Handel Messiah and Schütz Christmas Story, with Paul MacCreesh; Bach's Easter Oratorio, with Andrew Parrott; Dowland songs, with David Miller; Senfl tenorlied, with Fretwork; Peachum in The Beggar's Opera; The Fairy Queen, under William Christie; many Purcell albums, with the King's Consort; Haydn's St Cecilia Mass; Charpentier Vêpres aux Jésuites, under Michel Corboz. *Honours:* Hubert Parry Prize at the GKN English Songs Awards, 1986. *Current Management:* Hazard Chase, Norman House, Cambridge Place, Cambridge CB2 1NS, England. *Telephone:* (1223) 312400. *Fax:* (1223) 460827. *E-mail:* info@hazardchase.co.uk. *Website:* www.hazardchase .co.uk.

DANIELS, Claire; Singer (Soprano); b. 1963, England. *Education:* Studied at the Royal Northern College of Music and in Paris with Janine Reiss. *Career:* Appearances include: Jennie Hildebrand in Street Scene; A Nymph, in Rusalka; Niece, in Peter Grimes for English National Opera; Amor, in Orfeo ed Euridice for Opera North; Zerlina for Kent Opera; Sang in Purcell's King Arthur at the Buxton Festival; Rossini's L'Occasions fa il ladro and L'Italiana in Algeri and Grétry's Le Huron; Vespina, in Haydn's L'Infedeltà Delusa for Garsington Opera; Nannetta, in Falstaff for Opera Zuid in Netherlands; Mozart's Susanna and Servilia and Adina in L'Elisir d'amore for Scottish Opera (1993); The Girl, in Nigel Osborne's Sarajevo, for Opera Factory; Serpetta in La finta giardiniera by Mozart for Klagenfurt Opera in Austria; Concert appearances throughout Germany and at Aix-en-Provence, Barcelona and Gothenberg; Mozart's Mass in C Minor with Charles Mackerras; Les Nuits d'Été at Perth Festival; Carmina Burana in Valencia; Sang in Peter Grimes with the London Symphony Orchestra under Rostropovich; Mozart's Exultate Jubilate for concert tour of Great Britain with the Stuttgart Philharmonic Orchestra. *Address:* c/o Marks Management, 14 New Burlington Street, London W1X 1FF, England.

DANIELS, David; Singer (Counter-tenor); b. 12 March 1966, Spartanburg, SC, USA. *Education:* Studied with George Shirley at the University of Michigan. *Career:* Debut: Sang Nero in L'Incoronazione di Poppea at the Glimmerglass Opera Festival, 1994; Handel's Tamerlano at Glimmerglass in 1995; Followed by Arsamenes in Xerxes with the Boston Lyric Opera Season 1995–96; in Israel in Egypt at the Vienna Musikverein, Messiah in Boston and Handel's Saul with the Philharmonia Baroque Orchestra; Salzburg Festival debut, as Hamor in Handel's Jephtha, 1996; Sang Didymus in Theodora at the Glyndebourne Festival, 1996; Opened the 1996–97 season with English National Opera as Oberon in A Midsummer Night's Dream; London and New York recital debuts, at the Wigmore Hall and Lincoln Center, 1996; Engaged for Monteverdi's Ulisse at Los Angeles Opera, as Sesto in Handel's Giulio Cesare for the London Royal Opera, 1997; The same role at the Metropolitan, 1999; Sang Handel's Rinaldo at the London Barbican, 2000 and at Bavarian State Opera, 2001; Other roles include Monteverdi's Nero (San Francisco 1998) and Arsace in Handel's Partenope (Glimmerglass 1998); Engaged as Giulio Cesare at the Palais Garnier, Paris, 2002. *Recordings include:* Video of Handel's Theodora. *Current Management:* Askonas Holt Ltd, Lonsdale Chambers, 27 Chancery Lane, London, WC2A 1PF, England. *Telephone:* (20) 7400-1700. *Fax:* (20) 7400-1799. *E-mail:* info@askonasholt.co.uk. *Website:* www.askonasholt.co.uk.

DANILEVSKI, Alexander; Composer and Lutenist; b. 4 Sept. 1957, St Petersburg, Russia; m. Emilia, 9 Sept 1990, 3 s., 2 d. *Education:* Composition, Leningrad Conservatoire, 1974–80; Lute, Scola Cantorum Basilensis, 1991–93. *Career:* Debut: The I Sonato for Violin, St Petersburg Philharmonic 1981 and Lute Recital; 90 Solo Recitals and Concerts throughout Russia; Festivals, Recitals and Concerts in Europe (early music); Founder, 'Syntagma' (ensemble of early music); Performances of Lauda, Antiphones, Sonata for Cello in Grand Festival des Musiques Slaves, Paris, 1996, 1997; More than 30 concerts of early music given by Syntagma; mem, American Lute Society. *Compositions:* Sonatas for Violin, Violoncello and Piano; Missa for Choir and Orchestra; Seven Words of Christ on the Cross; Strophes enfilees (nai kai); Concerto for Organ, Harpsichord and Piano; Quatuors 1-4, Chamber Music; Lauda, for voice and ensemble; Antiphones-I, for recorder quartet; Antiphones-II, for string quartet; Revelation, for cello, 1997; Sonatos 1–3 for piano; Concert and Night Music for 2 pianos; Seven Words for soprano and ensemble. *Recordings:* Guillaume Dufay and Music of His time, with Ensemble Pro Anima, St Petersburg; Medieval and Renaissance Music with the same; Johannes Ciaconia and His Time; Solo; Francesco da Milano, Fancies and Ricercars, St Petersburg. *Publications:* Works for Piano, 1997–98; 20 Russian Barocco Songs. *Address:* 30 Rue de la Marne, 57000 Metz, France.

DANON, Oskar; Conductor and Composer; b. 7 Feb. 1913, Sarajevo, Yugoslavia. *Education:* Studied at Prague Conservatory and University. *Career:* Conducted Opera and Concerts in Sarajevo from 1938; Director and Conductor of Belgrade Opera, 1945–60; Led performances of The Bartered Bride in Prague, then Prince Igor and Don Quichotte with the Belgrade Company on tour to Paris, 1958; Wiesbaden Festival, 1959; The Love for Three Oranges, Paris Opéra 1960, with Boris Godunov; Edinburgh Festival, 1962, leading Don Quichotte, Prince Igor and the British premieres of Prokofiev's The Gambler and The Love for Three Oranges; Prince Igor at the Chicago Lyric Opera, 1962; Further engagements with Tristan und Isolde at Barcelona, 1969, and Arabella at Amsterdam, 1970; Opened the restored National Theatre Belgrade, 1990 with The Prince of Zeta by Konjovic. *Recordings:* Prince Igor and A Life for the Tsar with the Belgrade Company. *Address:* National Theatre, Belgrade, Croatia.

DANZ, Ingeborg; Singer (Contralto); b. 1961, Witten, Germany. *Education:* Studied in Detmold. *Career:* Frequent appearances from 1987 as concert and oratorio singer; Tours of North and South America, USA, Japan, Russia and Europe, with Neville Marriner, Herreweghe, Harnoncourt and Helmuth Rilling; Season 1996 with Bach's St John Passion at the Amsterdam Concertgebouw and Handel's Jephtha with the Bamberg Symphony Orchestra at the Salzburg Festival; Other festival engagements at Stuttgart, Oregon, Ludwigsburg, Schwetzingen and Tanglewood; Recital tour with Juliane Banse and Thomas Quasthoff, 1997. *Recordings include:* Mozart Masses with Nikolaus Harnoncourt, St Matthew Passion with Helmuth Rilling. *Honours:* Scholarship from Richard Wagner Federation. *Address:* c/o Kunstler Sekretariat am Gasteig, Rosenheimerstrasse 52, 81669 Munich, Germany.

DAO; French (b. Vietnamese) composer; b. (Nguyen-Thien Dao), 16 Dec. 1940, Hanoi, Viet Nam; m. Hélène Latapie 1963. *Education:* Olivier Messiaen's class, Paris Conservatory. *Career:* debut at Festival de Royan 1969. *Compositions include:* The 19, female voices, ensemble, 1969; Nho, soprano, cello, 5 double basses, 1970; Khoc To Nhu, mixed voices; Koskom, orchestra, 1971; Bai tap, ondes Martenot, piano, 1974; Camatithu, 6 percussions, 1974; Framic, bass flute, 1974; Mau va hoa, orchestra, 1974; Bao gio, 2 percussions, 2 pianos, 1975; Mua, harpsichord, 1976; A Mi K giao tranh, double bass, 1976; Giai phong, orchestra, electro-acoustics, 1977; Bay, percussions, 1977; Mai Sau, violin, strings, 1977; Phu Dong II, 4 (2) percussions, 1977; Noi Xa, 2 ondes Martenot, electric guitar, percussion, 1977; My-chau Trong-thuy, opera, 1978; Hoang Hon, soprano, orchestra, 1979; Ecouter/Mourir, opera, 1980; Concerto Ten Do Gu, percussion, orchestra, 1980; Chuong gam song, organ, 1981; Tuon Han, soprano, clarinet, 1982; Than Mong, cello concerto, 1982; Poussière d'empire, soprano, mixed voices, percussion, 1983; Tay-Son, percussion, 1984; L'Aube est une oeuvre, children's or female choir, string quartet, percussion, 1984; Piano concerto, 1984; Cimes murmerées, string trio, 1985; La mer pétrifiée, opera, 1986–87; Tim Lua, piano, 1987; Pli-ombre, bass clarinet, 1987; Temps songe, 7 percussionists (165 instruments), 1987; VV2, bassoon, 1987; Concerto, Thien Thaï, violin, orchestra, 1988; Concerto l'Envol, flute, strings, 1988; Symphonie pour pouvoir, symphony orchestra, soprano, 1989; Concerto 1989, string sextet, orchestra, 1989; 1789 l'aurore, string sextet; Voie-Concert, ensemble, 1990; Quatuor à Cordes No. 1, 1991; Les Enfants d'Izieu, opera-oratorio, 1991–93; Les Perseides, 1992; Feuillets pour quatuor et perc, 1994; Hoa-Tau 1995, for string orchestra, 1995; Giao-Hoa Sinfonia, for orchestra, 1996; Khai-Nhac, for orchestra, 1997; Hon-Non-Nuoc for soloists, choir and orchestra, 1998, Khai Minh Prelude, small orchestra 1999, Scherzovivo 1999, Song Hon, orchestra 2000, Arco Vivo, solo cello 2000, Kosmofonia, orchestra and choir 2000, Chuyen Coi, small orchestra 2001, Song Nhat Nguyen, Concerto pour Monocorde, cello and orchestra 2002, Song Nhac Truong Chi, ballet 2003, Quatre Lyriques de Ciel et de Terre, opéra de chambre 2003, Song Than, orchestra, bass and choir 2004, Khoi Truong Chi, monocorde vietnamien solo 2004, Khoi Song, cithare vietnamien solo 2005. *Recordings:* Les Enfants d'Izieu. *Honours:* Chevalier, Ordre des Arts et des Lettres, Médaille de la Résistance (Viet Nam), Médaille de la Culture (Viet Nam); Prix Gian Carlo Menotti for recording of Les Enfants d'Isieu, Prix Olivier Messiaen de Composition Musicale de la Fondation Erasme (Netherlands), Prix André Caplet de l'Académie des Beaux Arts. *Address:* 28 rue Madame, 75006 Paris, France. *Telephone:* 1-42-22-18-91 (home). *Fax:* 1-42-22-18-91 (home). *E-mail:* nguyenthien .dao@wanadoo.fr (home). *Website:* www.nguyenthiendao.com (home).

DARA, Enzo; Singer (Bass); b. 13 Oct. 1938, Mantua, Italy. *Education:* Studied with Bruno Sutti in Mantua. *Career:* Debut: Fano 1960, as Colline in La Bohème; Reggio Emilia 1966, as Dulcamara in L'Elisir d'amore; La Scala Milan debut 1970, as Bartolo in Il Barbiere di Siviglia; Sang Bartolo on his New York (1982) and Covent Garden (1985) debuts; Pesaro 1984, in a revival of Rossini's Il Viaggio a Reims; Guest appearances in Naples, Bologna, Moscow, Brussels, Venice, Palermo and Rome; Returned to Covent Garden 1987, as Dulcamara; Pesaro Festival, 1988, in Il Signor Bruschino; Don Pasquale at Venice, 1990; Teatro de la Zarzuela Madrid, 1990, in Il Turco in Italia; Sang Bartolo at the Verona Arena, 1996; Sang Geronio in Il Turco in Italia and Don Magnifico in Cenerentola at Buenos Aires and Munich, 2000. *Recordings:* Il Barbiere di Siviglia and Il Viaggio a Reims; L'Italiana in Algeri; La Buona Figliuola by Piccinni; Donzetti's L'ajo nell' imbarazzo; Il Turco in Italia.

DARBELLAY, Jean Luc; composer, conductor and clarinettist; b. 2 July 1946, Berne, Switzerland; m. Elsbeth Darbellay-Fahrer 1971; one s. one d. *Education:* Diploma as Physician, Berne University, 1971; Berne Conservatory, 1974–79; Studies in composition with Theo Hirsbrunner, Cristobal Halffter, Dimitri Terzakis; Lucerne Conservatory with Edison Denisov and Klaus Huber; Foundation Ludus Ensemble Berne, 1978; Conducting studies with Pierre Dervaux and Franco Ferrara. *Career:* Concerts throughout Europe as Conductor of various orchestras including: Ludus Ensemble, Landesjugendchor Niedersachsen and Quaderni Perugini di Musica Contemporanea; Ensemble Contre-champs, MDR Kammerphilharmonie; John Cage Festival, Perugia. *Compositions include:* Glanum, 1981; Amphores, 1983; C'est un peu d'eau qui nous separe, 1989; Cello Concerto (Radio France recording) in Paris with Ensemble Denosjours, dedicated to Siegfried Palm, 1989; Interférences, 1991; Before Breakfast, film music, 1991; Pranam III, command of the Quaderni Perugini and Siegfried Palm, 1992; Cantus, command of the Altenburger Orgelkonzerte, 1993; Itinéraires, for St Petersburg Festival, 1994; Elégie, 1994; Incanto (Horn Concerto), Plauen, 1995; A la recherche, creation in Moscow; PRANAM IV (Cello Concerto for Siegfried Palm), in Halle. *Recordings:* Leading the Sächsisches Kammerorchester Leipzig: Mozart Divertimento, K251, Violin Concerto, K218, Haydn's Horn Concerto No. 2 and Symphony No. 1, Mozart's Serenade in C minor, K388, Darbellay's Espaces, Sept Poèmes Romands and Wind Octet; Aube Imaginaire with Choeur Novantiqua Sion; Album with pieces for violoncello and horn, with Olivier Darbellay, 1997. *Address:* Editors Editions Tre Media, Amalienstrasse 40, 76133, Karlsruhe, Germany.

D'ARCANGELO, Ildebrando; Singer (bass-baritone); b. 1969, Pesaro, Italy. *Education:* Studied with Maria Vittoria Romano and in Bologna. *Career:* Engagements in La Bohème at Chicago, I Capuleti by Bellini at the Berlin Staatsoper, Rossini's Armida and Guillaume Tell at Pesaro and as Mozart's Masetto at the New York Met, Figaro at Salzburg, 1996; Don Giovanni in Bonn and Leporello at the Bayerische Staatsoper; Banquo in Macbeth at Bologna and Colline in La Bohème at Covent Garden, 1996; Season 1997–98 as Figaro in Rome, Paris and New York, Enrico in Lucia di Lammermoor at the Edinburgh Festival and Leporello in Vienna; Leporello at the Theater an der Wien, 1999; Sang Rossini's Mosè at Monte Carlo, 2000. *Recordings include:* Rigoletto and I Lombardi under James Levine; Otello under Myung Wha Chung; Semiramide; Le nozze di Figaro; Don Giovanni (as Leporello, under John Eliot Gardiner); Don Carlos; Lucia di Lammermoor (with Mackerras); Don Giovanni (with Abbado). *Honours:* Winner, Concorso Internazionale Toti dal Monte, Treviso. *Current Management:* Askonas Holt Ltd, Lonsdale Chambers, 27 Chancery Lane, London, WC2A 1PF, England. *Telephone:* (20) 7400-1700. *Fax:* (20) 7400-1799. *E-mail:* info@askonasholt.co.uk. *Website:* www.askonasholt.co.uk.

DARLINGTON, Jonathan; Conductor; b. 1962, England. *Career:* Engagements with the Teatro San Carlo, Naples, Hamburg State Opera, Lausanne Opéra and Bordeaux Opera; Principal Guest Conductor at the Deutsche Oper am Rhein, Düsseldorf, and concerts with the Orchestra Sinfonia di San Carlo and Swedish Chamber Orchestra; Repertoire includes works by Mozart, Beethoven, Mendelssohn, Schubert and Brahms; Season 2001–2002 with the Bochum Symphony, Orchestre Philharmonique de Strasbourg, Orchestre National de L'Ile de France and China Philharmonic Orchestra at the Peking Music Festival; Further opera work at the Théâtre des Champs Elysées, Paris, and Vancouver Opera: repertoire includes 200 works; Choral repertoire includes the Bach Passions and B minor mass, Haydn's Creation, Requiems of Dvorák and Mozart and the Glagolitic Mass by Janáček. *Address:* c/o IMG Artists, Lovell House, 616 Chiswick High Road, London, W4 5RX.

DARLINGTON, Stephen Mark, MA, DMus, FRCO; organist and tutor in music; *Organist and Tutor in Music, Christ Church, Oxford;* b. 21 Sept. 1952, Lapworth, Warwickshire, England; m. Moira Ellen Hill 1975; three d. *Education:* Christ Church, Oxford. *Career:* Assistant Organist, Canterbury Cathedral, 1974–78; Master of the Music, St Alban's Abbey, 1978–85; Artistic Director, International Organ Festival, St Albans, 1979–85; Organist and Tutor in Music, Christ Church, Oxford, 1985–; Choragus, Univ. of Oxford 1998–; President, Royal College of Organists, 1998–2000; council mem. Royal College of Organists. *Recordings include:* Masses by Byrd, Esteves, Lassus, Martin, Palestrina, Poulenc, Taverner, Victoria; Choral works by Haydn, Mathias, Pygott, Tippett, Vaughan Williams, Vivaldi, Walton, Weelkes; Choral Works by Britten, Haydn, Janacek, Goodall; Masses by Aston and Ashwell. *Address:* Christ Church, Oxford OX1 1DP, England. *Website:* www.chchchoir.org.

DARLOW, Denys, FRCM, FRCO, FLCM; British conductor, composer, organist and academic; b. 13 May 1921, London, England; m. Sophy Margaret Guillaume. *Career:* Founder, Tilford Bach Festival, 1952, London Handel Festival, 1976, BBC Third Programme; Prom Concert; Appearances in Sweden, Germany, Austria, Netherlands, Belgium, France, America, New Zealand; Concerts and radio; Professor at Royal College of Music; Conducted Handel's Alessandro Severo at the RCM, 1997; Radamisto, 1998; First modern performance of Silla, 2000; 80th Birthday Concert with Handel's L'Allegro, St George's, London, 2001; World Premier of staged performance Handel's Brockes Passion, 2002; mem, Royal Society of Musicians. *Compositions include:* Te Deum; Stabat Mater; Requiem; Music for Holy Week. *Recordings:* The Triumph of Time and Truth; Oratorio, Handel; Aminta e Fillide; Cantata, Handel; Silla, Opera, Handel; Il Duello Amoroso, Cantata, Handel. *Honours:* FRCO, 1946; FLCM, 1980; FRCM, 1984. *Address:* The Coach House, Drury Lane, Redmarley D'Abitot, Glos GL19 3JX, England. *Telephone:* (1531) 650616.

D'ASCOLI, Bernard; Pianist; b. 18 Nov. 1958, Aubagne, France. *Education:* Marseille Conservatoire, 1973–77; private teachers. *Career:* Paris debut (Salle Cortot), 1981; London debut at Queen Elizabeth Hall and Royal Festival Hall, 1982; Australian debut at Sydney Opera House, 1983; Amsterdam Concertgebouw, 1984; US debut in Houston, 1985; Vienna debut at Musikverein, 1986; Tokyo debut at Casals and Bunka Kaikan Halls, 1988; orchestral engagements include appearances with Royal Philharmonic Orchestra, London Philharmonic, Philharmonia, BBC Symphony Orchestra, Chamber Orchestra of Europe, Amsterdam Philharmonic, Houston Symphony Orchestra, Orchestra National de Toulouse, Boston Symphony Orchestra, under such conductors as John Pritchard, Kurt Sanderling, Yehudi Menuhin, Sergiu Commissiona, Ivan Fischer, Michel Plasson, Tadaaki Otaka; played Ravel and Gershwin at the Royal Festival Hall, London, 1997; regular television and radio broadcasts. *Recent recordings include:* Schumann with Nimbus, 1989; Chopin. *Honours:* Most Talented French Artist of the Year, Megève, 1976; First Prize, Maria Canals Competition, Barcelona, Spain, 1978; Third Prize, Leeds International Piano Competition, England, 1981. *Current Management:* TransArt (UK)

Ltd, Cedar House, 10 Rutland Street, Filey, YO14 9JB, North Yorkshire, England. *Telephone:* (1723) 515819. *Fax:* (1723) 514678. *E-mail:* transartuk@transartuk.com. *Website:* www.transartuk.com. *Current Management:* c/o Van Walsum Management, 4 Addison Bridge Place, London W14 8XP, England.

DASZAK, John; Singer (Tenor); b. 24 Feb. 1967, Ashton-under-Lyne, England. *Education:* Guildhall School, London, and the Royal Northern College of Music, with Robert Alderson. *Career:* Opera roles have included Števa in Jenůfa, Jack in Mahagonny and Pang in Turandot, for English National Opera; The Duke of Mantua and Mozart's Ferrando in Italy, Peter Grimes for English Touring Opera and Rustighello in Donizetti's Lucrezia Borgia at the Martina-Franca Festival; Concerts include Otumbo in Verdi's Alzira at Covent Garden, Don Ottavio for the Liverpool Mozart Orchestra, Britten's Serenade and Rossini's Petite Messe at the Buxton Festival; Verdi's Requiem at Chester Cathedral and the Manchester Free Trade Hall, Messiah in Blackburn Cathedral and St John's Smith Square, London; Season 1997–98 with Skuratov in From the House of the Dead and Dmitri in Boris Godunov for English National Opera; Peter Grimes and Dmitri for Welsh National Opera; Števa in Jenůfa, 1998; Roles in Mahagonny at Lausanne; Weber's Euryanthe at the London Proms, 2002. *Address:* c/o IMG Artists, Lovell House, 616 Chiswick High Road, London W4 5RX, England.

DATYNER, Harry; Pianist; b. 4 Feb. 1923, La Chaux-de-Fonds, Switzerland; m. Bluette Blum, 14 June 1954, 1 s. *Education:* Etudes Conservatoire National in Paris with Marguerite Long and later with Edwin Fischer. *Career:* Concerts in Europe, northern and southern Africa, North and South America; Soloist with orchestras: Suisse Romande, Lausanne, Montreal, Bucharest, Montevideo, Baden-Baden, Madrid, Bruxelles National, London Philharmonic, Prague, Barcelona, Paris; Masterclass, Conservatoire de Musique de Genève; Festival appearances at Montreux, Lausanne, Montevideo, Salzburg, Ascona, Prague, Espagne and Portugal; Member of Jury at International Competitions at Genève, Cologne, Athens, Berlin, Mallorca, Lisbon; Conductors: Ansermet, Prêtre, Dutoit, Sawallisch, Stein, Jordan, Matacic, Carvalho, Dervaux, Groves; Cours d'Interpretation: Suisse, Television Suisse, Espagne, Canada. *Honours:* 1st Prize a l'unanimite Concours d'éxécution musicale, Geneva; Prix de l'institut Neuchatelois, 1973. *Address:* 1245 Collonge-Bellerive, Switzerland.

DATZ, Irene; Singer (Soprano); b. 14 April 1963, Zhytomyr, Ukraine. *Education:* Studied at the Kiev State Conservatoire from 1980. *Career:* Sang with the Kiev State Radio Orchestra, 1985 and made her debut with Kiev National Opera in 1986, at first as Mezzo-Soprano; At Kiev and Bolshoi Operas has sung Donna Anna, Mimi, Tosca, Nedda, Cherubino, Marguerite, Marfa in The Tsar's Bride, and Iolanta; Tours of North America from 1991 with appearances at the Metropolitan Opera as Tatiana; Solo recitals in Chicago, Philadelphia, Illinois and Washington; Sang Wagner's Elsa at the Kiev Opera in 1994. *Address:* Sonata Ltd, 11 North Park Street, Glasgow G20 7AA, Scotland.

DAUGHERTY, Michael; Composer; b. 28 April 1954, Cedar Rapids, Iowa, USA. *Education:* Studied at North Texas State (BM) and the Manhattan School of Music (MA, 1976); Jacob Druckman, Roger Reynolds, Bernard Rands and Gil Evans at Yale University, DMA, 1986; Further study at IRCAM, Paris, 1979–80, and with Ligeti at the Hamburg Musikhochschule, 1982–84. *Career:* Faculty of Oberlin Conservatory, 1986–91; Full Professor of Composition, University of Michigan, Ann Arbor. *Compositions include:* Piano Plus, 1985; Snap–Blue Like an Orange for 16 players, 1987; Strut for string orchestra, 1989; Beat Boxer for string quartet and pre-recorded DAT tape, 1991; Firecracker for oboe and 6 players, 1991; Flamingo for chamber orchestra, 1991; Desi, Bizarro, and Niagara Falls for symphonic wind band, 1991–92; Sing Sing: J Edgar Hoover for string quartet and tape, 1992; Dead Elvis for bassoon and 6 players, 1993; Metropolis Symphony (premiered Carnegie Hall), 1988–93; Le Tombeau de Liberace, for piano and ensemble, 1994; Paul Robeson Told Me for string quartet and tape, 1994; Motown Metal for brass ensemble and percussion, 1994; Lounge Lizards for 2 pianos and 2 percussion, 1994; What's That Spell? for 2 amplified sopranos and 16 players, 1995; Jackie's Song, for cello, 1996; Jackie O, chamber opera in 2 acts (premiere Houston Opera), 1997; Route 66 for orchestra, 1998; Spaghetti Western for English horn and orchestra, 1998; Sunset Strip for chamber orchestra, 1999; UFO for percussion solo and orchestra, 1999; Hell's Angels for bassoon quartet and orchestra, 1999. *Recordings:* Numerous for major labels. *Address:* c/o Faber Music, 3 Queen Square, London WC1N 3AU, England.

DAUSGAARD, Thomas; Conductor; b. 1963, Denmark. *Education:* Studied in Scandinavia. *Career:* Assistant Conductor to Seiji Ozawa at the Boston Symphony Orchestra, 1993–96; Beethoven's Missa Solemnis with the Swedish Radio Symphony Orchestra and Chorus, 1993; Further concerts with the Danish National Radio Symphony Orchestra; Season 1996–97 with the Oslo, St Petersburg and Royal Philharmonic Orchestras and the Montreal Symphony; Principal Guest Conductor

with Danish Radio Symphony Orchestra from 1997 (tour of Germany, 2001); Conducted the Danish National Symphony Orchestra at the London Proms, 2002; Music Dir of the Swedish Chamber Orchestra, 1997–; Prin. Guest Conductor 2001–04, and Chief Conductor 2004– of the Danish National Symphony Orchestra; Guest conductor to the Bayerischer Rundfunk, Dresden Philharmonic, Frankfurt Radio Symphony and Leipzig Gewandhaus Orchestras in Germany and the Orchestre Philharmonique de Radio France in Paris; Recent engagements include conducting the Netherlands Philharmonic Orchestra, the RSB Berlin, the Stockholm and Oslo Philharmonic Orchestras, St Petersburg Philharmonic Orchestra , RAI Turin and La Scala Philharmonic Orchestras. *Recordings include:* Zemlinsky's Seejungfrau and Sinfonietta (Chandos); Beethoven Symphony Nos 1, 2, 4, 5 and 7 and Piano Concertos No 1, 2 and 3 and the Triple Concerto; Other comnposers include Berwald, Brahms, Grieg, Hamerik, Hartmann, Kunzen, Langgaard, Ligeti, Liszt, Mozart, Nørgård, Riisager, Sibelius, Sinding, Stenhammar, Svendson and Wiren.. *Honours:* Music Critics' Circle Prize, Denmark, 1993; Prizewinner at International Competitions. *Address:* c/o IMG Artists, Lovell House, 616 Chiswick High Road, London W4 5RX, England.

D'AVALOS, Francesco; Teacher, Composer and Conductor; b. 11 April 1930, Naples, Italy. *Education:* Studied Classics at college, Naples; Philosophy, Naples University; Started Piano study with Vicenzo Vitale at age 12, then Composition with Renato Parodi; Diploma in Composition, San Pietro a Majella Conservatory, Naples; Accademia Chigiana, Siena, with Franco Ferrara and Sergiu Celibidache. *Career:* Debut: Concert as Conductor, RAI, Rome, 1964; Has appeared with Philharmonia Orchestra, London, 1987–; Has taught at several Italian conservatories; Holds Chair of Fugue and Advanced Composition and Chair of Conducting, San Pietro a Majella Conservatory, Naples. *Compositions:* Hymne an die Nacht, 1958, conducted by H W Henze, Hessischer Rundfunk; Studio Sinfonico, 1982, conducted by d'Avalos, Lugano; Symphony for Orchestra and Soprano, premiered Norddeutscher Rundfunk, Hamburg; Qumran, study for orchestra, La Scala with Eliahu Inbal; Maria di Venosa-Gesualdo, musical drama in 2 acts, 1992; Die Stille Stadt for soprano, timpano and strings, 1994; Qumran, musical drama in 3 parts, 2001; Other orchestral works, works for voice, chamber music. *Recordings:* Over 30 including: Brahms, complete orchestral works; Martucci, complete orchestral works; Wagner, overtures; Bruckner, Symphony No. 7; Mendelssohn, complete orchestral works; Clementi, complete orchestral works; Maria di Venosa with Philharmonia Orchestra and Chorus, soloists, madrigalists, 1994. *Honours:* Premio Marzotto for Composition; Grand Prix International du Disque for Martucci's Symphonies, Académie Charles Cros, Paris, 1990; MRA Award for Raff's Symphony No. 3, Im Walde, 1993. *Address:* 50 via dei Mille, Naples, Italy.

DAVENPORT, Glyn; Singer (bass-baritone); b. 3 May 1948, Halifax, Yorkshire, England; m. Jane Keay 1972; two s. *Education:* Royal Coll. of Music, London, 1966–70; ARCM, viola, LRAM, singing; Staatliche Musikhochschule, Hamburg, Germany, 1970–73. *Career:* debut, Wigmore Hall, London, England, 1973; opera appearances with English Opera Group, English Music Theatre, Scottish Opera, Royal Opera House, Kent Opera, Wexford Festival Opera, Opera Factory, Zürich; recitals for BBC Radio 3, Songmakers' Almanac, British Council in Near and Middle East; oratorio in major London venues and BBC, Switzerland, Germany and Iceland. *Recordings:* The English Cat, Hans Werner Henze. *Honours:* winner, Kathleen Ferrier Memorial Competition, 1972. *Current Management:* Musicmakers International Artists Representation, Tailor House, 63–65 High Street, Whitwell, Hertfordshire SG4 8AH, England. *Telephone:* (1438) 871708. *Fax:* (1438) 871777. *E-mail:* musicmakers@compuserve.com. *Website:* www.operauk.com. *Address:* Wendover, Horsell Rise, Horsell, Woking, Surrey GU21 4BD, England. *E-mail:* glyndavenport@boltblue.com.

DAVID, Avram; Composer, Teacher and Pianist; b. 30 June 1930, Boston, Massachusetts, USA; m. Leslie, 3 Dec 1977. *Education:* BA Music, 1955; MA Music, 1956; DMA Musical Composition, 1964; Boston University; Berkshire Music Center, Tanglewood, Summer 1948; Kranichsteiner Musikinstitut, Darmstadt, West Germany, Summer 1961 and 1966; Private Study of Piano and Philosophy of Performance and Composition with Margaret Chaloff and Composition with Francis Cooke, Harold Shapero, Karlheinz Stockhausen, Pierre Boulez. *Career:* Private Teaching, 1960–64; Chairman, Composition Department, Composer-in-Residence, Boston Conservatory of Music, 1964–73; Director, Avram David Studio, 1973–77; Director, Margaret Chaloff Studio, 1977–; Lecturer, Harvard University and New England Conservatory of Music; Appearances as solo pianist in concert and on television and radio. *Compositions:* Composer of 133 works including: 2 Orchestral Works including 1 Symphony; 21 works for Chamber Ensembles; 6 String Quartets; 2 Solo Violin Sonatas; 43 works for Solo Piano including 5 Sonatas; 24 works for Solo Winds; 8 Choral works. *Recordings:* Sonata for Horn Solo, Opus 101. *Address:* c/o ASCAP, ASCAP Building, One Lincoln Plaza, New York, NY 10023, USA.

DAVIDOVICH, Bella; Concert Pianist; b. 16 July 1928, Baku, USSR; m. Julian Sitkovetsky (deceased), 1 s. (Dmitri Sitkovetsky, q.v.). *Education:* Moscow Conservatory. *Career:* Recitalist, Orchestral Soloist, Chamber Musician, in all major music centres internationally; Duo recitals with s. (violinist Dmitry Sitkovetsky); Professor of Piano: Moscow Conservatory, USSR, 16 years; Juilliard School of Music, New York, USA, 1983–; Engaged 1997–98 with the Rotterdam Philharmonic, Ulster Orchestra and Stuttgart Symphony Orchestra. *Honours:* 1st Prize, Chopin International Piano Competition, Warsaw, Poland, 1949. *Address:* c/o Agnes Bruneau, 155 West 68th Street, No. 1010, New York, NY 10023, USA.

DAVIDOVICI, Robert; Violinist and Professor of Violin; b. 1 Oct. 1946, Sutu-Mare, Romania; m. Tamara Golan, 8 Mar 1973, 2 s., 2 d. *Education:* School of Music No. 1, Bucharest, 1958–62; Conservatorium of Music High School, Sydney, Australia, 1962–63; Performers and Teacher Diploma, 1st Class Honours, 1966; Juilliard School of Music, USA, 1967–73; Postgraduate Diploma, 1970. *Career:* Debut: Alice Tully Hall, New York, USA, 1972; mem, College Music Society; American String Teachers Association; Violin Society of America. *Recordings:* Recital with Steven DeGroote of works by Copland, Gunther Schuller, Walter Piston, Hugh Aitken and Paul Schonfield. *Honours:* 1st Prize, Carnegie Hall International American Music Competition, 1983; 1st Prize, Naumberg Competition, New York, 1972; Flaggler Award, 1973. *Current Management:* Shaw Concerts Incorporated.

DAVIDOVSKY, Mario; American composer and teacher; b. 4 March 1934, Buenos Aires, Argentina; m. Elaine Davidovsky. *Education:* received violin lessons in childhood; Studied composition and theory with Guillermo Graetzer, Buenos Aires; Studied with Theodore Fuchs, Erwin Leuchter and Ernesto Epstein; Completed training with Aaron Copland and Milton Babbitt, Berkshire Music Center, Tanglewood, 1958. *Career:* Associated with Columbia-Princeton Electronic Music Center, 1960–; Teacher, University of Michigan, 1964; Di Tella Institute, 1969–70; City College of the City University of New York, 1968–80; Columbia University, 1981–; Director, Columbia-Princeton Electronic Music centre, 1981–94; Professor of Music, Harvard University, 1994–; mem, Elected to Institute of American Academy of Arts and Letters, 1982. *Compositions include:* Synchronisms No. 1 for flute and electronics, 1963, No. 2 for flute, clarinet, violin, cello and electronics, 1964, No. 3 for cello and electronics, 1965, No. 4 for men's or mixed chorus and electronics, 1967, No. 5 for percussion ensemble and electronics, 1969, No. 6 for piano and electronics, 1970, No. 7 for orchestra and electronics, 1973, No. 8 for woodwind quintet and electronics, 1974; No. 9 for violin and electronics, 1988; No. 10 for guitar and electronics, 1992; Orchestral: Concertino for percussion and strings, 1954; Planos, 1961; Divertimento for cello and orchestra, 1984; Concertante for string quartet and orchestra, 1990; Concertino for violin and chamber orchestra, 1995; Chamber: 4 String Quartets, 1954, 1958, 1976, 1980; Flashbacks for ensemble, 1995; Tape: Electronic Study No. 1, 1961, No. 2, 1962, No. 3, 1965. *Honours:* Guggenheim Fellowships, 1960, 1971; Rockefeller Fellowships, 1963, 1964; American Academy of Arts and Letters Award, 1965; Pulitzer prize in Music, 1971; Naumberg Award, 1972; Guggenheim Award, 1982; Various commissions. *Address:* Music Department, Harvard University, Cambridge, MA, USA.

DAVIDSON, Cheyne; Singer (Baritone); b. 1965, USA. *Education:* Studied at the Cleveland Institute of Music and the Manhattan School of Music. *Career:* Tour of Europe, Japan and Israel, as Escamillo in Peter Brook's version of Carmen, La Tragédie de Carmen; Zürich Opera as the Speaker in Die Zauberflöte, Massenet's Hérodiade, Marcello, David in L'Amico Fritz, Sharpless, and Ramiro in L'Heure Espagnole (1996); Guest appearances at Stuttgart as Sharpless and the Speaker, 1994; Escamillo at Hamburg; In Francesca da Rimini at the Bregenz Festival; Season 1996–97 as the Messenger in Robert Wilson's production of Oedipus Rex at the Paris Théâtre du Châtelet, and Schaunard in La Bohème at Zürich; Premieres include Ein Narrenparadies by Ofer Ben-Amot, at Vienna, and the song cycle with orchestra Vom Unvergänglichen by Franz Thurauer, at Bregenz; Season 2000 as Escamillo, Donner in Das Rheingold and Tomsky in The Queen of Spades at Zürich. *Address:* c/o Opernhaus Zürich, Falkenstrasse 1, 8008 Zürich, Switzerland.

DAVIDSON, Joy; Singer (Mezzo-Soprano); b. 18 Aug. 1940, Fort Collins, Colorado, USA. *Education:* Studied in Los Angeles, at Florida State University and with Daniel Harris. *Career:* Debut: Miami, 1965 as Rossini's Cenerentola; Sang at the opera houses of Dallas, Houston, New Orleans and San Francisco; Santa Fe 1969, in the US premiere of Penderecki's The Devils of Loudun; Appearances with the Welsh National Opera and at Lisbon, Sofia, Vienna, Munich, Milan and Florence; Other roles include Carmen, Charlotte in Werther, Dalila, Verdi's Eboli and Preziosilla and Gluck's Orpheus; Also heard as concert

Singer; Sang Baba the Turk in The Rake's Progress at the State Theatre, New York, 1984.

DAVIDSON, Robert; Composer; b. 17 Dec. 1965, Brisbane, Queensland, Australia. *Education:* BMus (Hons), University of Queensland, 1987; Further study with Terry Riley and LaMonte Young, 1995. *Career:* Freelance Composer; Performer in orchestra, including Queensland and Sydney Symphony Orchestras. *Compositions include:* Dodecahedron for string orchestra, 1985; Eight, for ensemble, 1986; Stained Glass for 2 violins, 2 cellos, 2 clarinets, 2 pianos, 1986; Zemar for piano, 1987; Sound Panels, for flute, string quartet and double bass, 1988; Triptych for orchestra, 1988; Tapestry, for viola, cello, clarinet and piano, 1989; Refrains, for double bass and piano, 1989; Adeney Cycle, for violin and viola, 1990; Strata for mixed ensemble, 1990; Variations and Episodes, for piano, 1990; Arch for 3 violins, 1992; Conversations, for viola, cello and clarinet, 1993; Mesh, for double bass and piano, 1993; Violin Concerto, 1994; Three Grounds, for ensemble, 1994; Chaconne for orchestra, 1994; Boombox Pieces for multiple cassette players, 1995. *Address:* c/o APRA, 1A Eden Street, Crows Nest, NSW 2065, Australia.

DAVIDSON, Tina; Composer and Pianist; b. 30 Dec. 1952, Stockholm, Sweden; m., 1 d. *Education:* BA, Piano and Composition, Bennington College, 1972–76; Composition Studies with Henry Brant, Vivian Fine, Louis Calabro. *Career:* Associate Director, RELACHE, The Ensemble for Contemporary Music, 1978–89; Piano Instructor, Drexel University, 1981–85; Residencies: Chamber Music Conference and Composers' Forum; Milay Colony for the Arts, October 1981; Yellow Springs Fellowship of the Arts, May 1982; Charles Ives Center, 1986; Composer-in-Residence, Orchestra Society of Philadelphia, 1992–94; Composer-in-Residence, Opera Delaware Symphony Orchestra and YWCA of Wilmington Delaware, 1994–97; Fleisher Art Memorial Composer in Residence, 1997–99. *Compositions include:* Inside And Out, piano and 2 players, 1974; Recollections of Darkness, string trio, 1975; Two Beasts From The Forest Of Imaginary Beings, narrator and orchestra, 1975, commissioned by Sage City Symphony, student commission, 1976; Five Songs from The Game of Silence, soprano and viola, 1976; Billy and Zelda, music theatre (8 singers, 1 actress, string quartet and percussion), 1977; Piano Concerto, piano and orchestra, 1981; Unicorn/Tapestry, mezzo-soprano, violoncello and tape, 1982; Other Echoes, 2 violins, 1982; Wait For The End Of Dreaming, 2 baritone saxophones, Double Bass, 1983–85; Shadow Grief, soprano (or alto saxophone), 1983; Day of Rage, and I Am The Last Witness, piano solo, 1984; Blood Memory: A Long Quiet After The Call, cello and orchestra, commissioned by Sage City Symphony, 1985; Bleached Thread Sister Thread, 1992; Fire on the Mountain, marimba, vibraphone and piano, 1993; They Come Dancing for full orchestra, 1994; Over Salt River, soprano, 1995; Star Fire, for youth orchestra, 1996; It Is My Heart Singing, string sextet, 1996; Of The Running Way, for clarinet (or alto saxophone) and piano, 1996; Lost Love Songs, for solo cello, 1997. *Recordings:* Cassatt, 1994; I Hear the Mermaids Singing, 1996. *Honours:* Pennsylvania Council Fellowship, 1983–96; PEN Fellowship, 1992–94. *Address:* 508 Woodland Terrace, Philadelphia, PA 19104, USA.

DAVIES, Arthur; Singer (Tenor); b. 11 April 1941, Wrexham, Wales. *Education:* Studied at the Royal Northern College of Music. *Career:* Has sung with Welsh National Opera as Nemorino, Albert Herring, Nadir in Les pêcheurs de Perles, Rodolfo, and Don José; Covent Garden debut 1976, in the world premiere of We Come to the River by Henze: has returned in Lucia di Lammermoor, and as Alfredo, the Italian Tenor in Der Rosenkavalier, Števa in Jenůfa, and Pinkerton; Scottish Opera at the Edinburgh Festival as the Fox in The Cunning Little Vixen, and David in Die Meistersinger; Appearances with English National Opera as the Duke of Mantua, Alfredo, the Gounod Faust, and Werther; Opera North as Jenik in The Bartered Bride, Pinkerton, Don José and Nadir; Foreign engagements in Chicago, Cincinnati, Connecticut, Ghent, Leipzig, Lisbon, New Orleans, Moscow, Santiago and New York (Metropolitan House with the ENO company); Sang Faust with ENO, Jan 1990; Gaston, British stage premiere of Verdi's Jérusalem, Opera North; Cavaradossi and Pinkerton for Scottish Opera; Cincinnati Opera, July 1990 as Faust; Edinburgh Festival, 1990 as Yannakos in The Greek Passion by Martinů; Sang Cavardossi for Opera Pacific at Costa Mesa, 1992; Don José at San Diego and the Duke of Mantua for ENO; Sang Verdi's Foresto at Buenos Aires, 1993; Samson at Metz, 1996; Concerts include the Verdi Requiem at the Festival Hall, London, conducted by Giulini. *Recordings:* Rigoletto (EMI; also on video); The Dream of Gerontius, with the London Symphony Orchestra (Chandos); Elijah; Rossini's Stabat Mater; The Kingdom of Elgar. *Address:* c/o Stafford Law Associates, 6 Barham Close, Weybridge, Surrey KT 13 9 PR, England.

DAVIES, David (Somerville); Conductor and Artistic Director; b. 13 June 1954, Dunfermline, Scotland; m. Virginia Henson, 15 Sept 1986. *Education:* Royal Scottish Academy of Music, University of Edinburgh; Salzburg Mozarteum; Conservatoire National De Marseille. *Career:* Assistant Principal Flute, Scottish National Orchestra, 1975–80;

Principal Flute, Scottish Opera, 1980–85; Freelance Conductor, 1985–, working with BBC Scottish Symphony Orchestra, Scottish Chamber Orchestra, Royal Scottish National Orchestra, Royal Liverpool Philharmonic Orchestra in England; l'Orchestre Philharmonique de Radio France, l'Opéra de Marseille, l'Orchestre Philharmonique de Marseille in France; Ensemble Caput in Iceland and the Stadtorchester Winterhur in Switzerland; Conductor and Artistic Director, Paragon Ensemble, Scotland, Paragon Opera Projects, Scotland, 1985–; Lecturer, Royal Scottish Academy of Music and Drama, 1991–. *Recordings:* Two vols of world premiere recordings of Scottish Contemporary music, 1991 and 1993. *Address:* c/o Paragon Ensemble Ltd, 2 Port Dundas Place, Glasgow G2 3LB, Scotland.

DAVIES, Dennis Russell; Conductor and Pianist; b. 16 April 1944, Toledo, OH, USA. *Education:* BMus, 1966, MS, 1968, DMA, 1972, Juilliard School of Music, New York; Studied piano with Berenice B MacNab, Lonny Epstein and Sascha Gorodnitzki; Conducting with Jean Morel and Jorge Mester. *Career:* Teacher, Juilliard School of Music, 1968–71; Co-founder with Luciano Berio, Conductor, Juilliard Ensemble, 1968–74; Music Director, Norwalk (Conn) Symphony Orchestra, 1968–73; St Paul (Minn) Chamber Orchestra, 1972–80; Cabrillo (Calif) Music Festival, 1974–92; American Composers Orchestra, NY, 1977–; Generalmusikdirektor, Wurttemberg State Theatre, Stuttgart, 1980–87; Principal Conductor and Director of Classical Music Programming, Saratoga, NY, Performing Arts Center, 1985–88; Generalmusikdirektor, City Theatre and Beethoven Hall Orchestra, Bonn, 1987–95; Guest Conductor with various opera companies and orchestras in North America and Europe; Champion of Contemporary Music; Conducted premieres by: Luciano Berio, John Cage, Hans Werner Henze, Philip Glass (Akhnaten, 1984), Mauricio Kagel, William Bolcom, Joan Tower, Pauline Oliveros, Lou Harrison, Kurt Schwertsik; Conducted the premiere of William Bolcom's Songs of Innocence and Experience, Stuttgart, 1984; Music Director, Brooklyn Academy of Music, 1991–93; Principal Conductor, Brooklyn Philharmonic, 1991–95; Conducted the premiere of Manfred Trojhan's Enrico, Schwetzingen Festival, 1991; Chief Conductor: Stuttgart Chamber Orchestra, 1995–, Vienna Radio Symphony Orchestra from 1996; Led Thomson's Four Saints in Three Acts at the 1996 Lincoln Center Festival. Season 1998 with Lulu at the Opéra Bastille and Weill's Mahagonny at Salzburg; Chief Conductor, Linz Opera (Landstheater), Austria, 2002–; Chief conductor and Music Director, Bruckner Orchester Linz, 2002–. *Recordings:* Many for various labels including Philip Glass, Heroes Symphony, 1997. *Honours:* Alice M Ditson Award for Conductors, 1987. *Address:* c/o Columbia Artists Management Inc, 165 West 57th Street, New York, NY 10019, USA.

DAVIES, Eirian; Singer (soprano); b. 22 May 1954, Llangollen, Wales; 1 s. *Education:* BA, Music, University College of Wales at Aberystwyth, Postgraduate course for performers, Royal Academy of Music, London. *Career:* Debut: Vivaldi's Griselda, Buxton Festival, and Gounod's La Colombe, 1983; Welsh National Opera: Rhinemaiden, in Das Rheingold and Götterdämmerung; Gerhilde, in Die Walküre; Lisa in La Sonnambula; Aenchen in Der Freischütz; English National Opera: Pamina in The Magic Flute; Frasquita in Carmen; Orpheus in the Underworld; Opera North Mimi in La Bohème; Christine in Robert Saxton's Caritas (world premiere); Glyndebourne: world premiere of Nigel Osborne's Electrification of the Soviet Union; Garsington: Rezia in L'Incontro Improvviso, by Haydn; Music Theatre Wales: Dotty in world premiere of Hardy's Flowers; Edinburgh Festival: World premiere of Macmillan's Tourist Variations and Craig Armstrong's Anna; Semur en Auxois Festival; Mozart's Constanze; More recent performances include: Princess Natalie in Der Prinz von Homburg, in Cologne; Gepopo in Le Grand Macabre and Aventures et Nouvelles Aventures, by Ligeti in Zürich; World premiere of Kubo's Rashomon in Graz; Salzburg Festival debut, 1997, in Feldman's Neither, also Wien Moderne Festival in Rihm's Frau Stimme; Appearances on television for BBC and HTV, and for BBC Radio 3. *Recordings:* Le Grand Macabre; Caritas by Robert Saxton. *Honours:* Catherine and Lady Grace James Award; Winner, Francisco Vinas International Competition, Barcelona, 1984. *Current Management:* Athole Still International Management, Forresters Hall, 25–27 Westow Street, London, SE19 3RY, England. *Telephone:* (20) 8771-5271. *Fax:* (20) 8768-6600. *Website:* www.atholestill.com.

DAVIES, Joan; Singer (Mezzo-Soprano); b. 1940, Swansea, Wales. *Education:* Royal College of Music, London. *Career:* Sang with the Glyndebourne Chorus, then with Sadler's Wells until 1969, notably as Offenbach's Hélène and in the premiere of Bennett's A Penny for a Song, 1965; Debut with Welsh National Opera as Meg Page in Falstaff; Sang Meg Page at Covent Garden and appeared in La Traviata and the premiere of Henze's We Come to the River, 1976; Other engagements in Munich and Berlin and with Scottish Opera, Opera North, Pheonix Opera, Basilica Opera and Dublin Grand Opera; New Sadler's Wells Opera from 1983 in The Mikado, The Count of Luxembourg, The Merry Widow and works by Gilbert and Sullivan (also in New York);

Appearances at the Wexford Festival in The Devil and Kate, and Gazzaniga's Don Giovanni (1987); Other roles include Mme Popova in Walton's The Bear (Lisbon), Auntie in Peter Grimes at the Royal Opera, Ghent, and Mozart's Marcellina in Bordeaux and Rouen; Television appearances as Meg Page, Marcellina and Mary in Der fliegende Holländer; Concert engagements with the Royal Liverpool Philharmonic and the Ulster Orchestra. *Address:* Music International, 13 Ardilaun Road, London N5 2QR, England.

DAVIES, John Lloyd; Stage Director and Designer; b. 1950, Wales. *Career:* New production and revivals for ENO, with Carmen, Rusalka, Carmen and Madama Butterfly; The Cunning Little Vixen and Les Troyens for Scottish Opera; Don Giovanni, Die Zauberflöte and Rigoletto for the Vienna Kammeroper; Wozzeck and Rimsky-Korsakov's May Night in London; Un Ballo in Maschera at Klagenfurt, Zar und Zimmermann at Aachen and Danton's Death by Einem at Brighton; Tosca in Malmö. Reimann's Das Schloss in Vienna; Albert Herring at Aldeburgh and Tchaikovsky's The Enchantress for New Sussex Opera; Director of Productions at Musik Werkstatt Wien and New Sussex Opera; Season 2001–2002 with Les Contes d'Hoffmann in Nuremberg. *Honours:* Josef Kainz Medal, Austria. *Current Management:* Athole Still International Management, Forresters Hall, 25–27 Westow Street, London, SE19 3RY, England. *Telephone:* (20) 8771-5271. *Fax:* (20) 8768-6600. *Website:* www.atholestill.com.

DAVIES, Menai; Singer (Mezzo-soprano); b. 17 Nov. 1939, Wales. *Education:* Studied with Gwilyn Gwalchmai Jones and Valetta Jacopi. *Career:* Taught music for 14 years; Engaged with Welsh National Opera 1974–86, in repertory from Monteverdi to Britten, to the premiere of Metcalf's The Journey (1981); Mamma Lucia in Cavalleria Rusticana, 1995; Glyndebourne Touring Opera from 1987 (debut in L'Enfant et les Sortilèges) and Festival from 1989, as Grandmother in Jenůfa, Auntie in Peter Grimes and Cleaner in The Makropulos Case (1995); Other appearances with Scottish Opera, English National Opera and Opera North's Gloria, H K Gruber; Britten's Mrs Herring at Rome and Reggio Emilia, Mrs Grose in Peter Grimes at Cologne, Schwetzingen and Dresden; Théâtre du Châtelet, Paris, in Jenůfa and in premieres of operas by Fenelon and Philippe Manoury; The Makropulos Case at Barcelona and New York; Ideally suited for older roles in modern works.

DAVIES, (Albert) Meredith, CBE; conductor; b. 30 July 1922, Birkenhead, England; m. Betty Hazel Bates 1949; three s. one d. *Education:* Keble College, Oxford, Royal College of Music, Accademia di S Cecilia, Rome, Italy. *Career:* Organist, Hurstpierpoint College, Sussex, 1939; Served World War II, 1939–45, Royal Artillery, 1942–45; Conductor, St Alban's Bach Choir, 1947; Organist and Master of Choristers, Cathedral Church of St Alban, 1947–49; Musical Director, St Alban's School, 1948–49; Organist and Choirmaster, Hereford Cathedral, and Conductor, 3 Choirs Festival, Hereford, 1949–56; Organist and Supernumerary Fellow, New College, Oxford, 1956; Associate Conductor, 1957–59, Deputy Music Director, 1959–60, City of Birmingham Symphony Orchestra; Conductor, City of Birmingham Choir, 1957–64; Musical Director, English Opera Group, 1963–65; Musical Director, Vancouver Symphony Orchestra, Canada, 1964–71; Chief Conductor, BBC Training Orchestra, 1969–72; Conductor, Royal Choral Society, 1972–85; Conductor, Leeds Philharmonic Society, 1975–84; Principal, Trinity College of Music, 1979–88; President, Incorporated Society of Musicians, 1985–86. *Recordings:* Delius: Violin Concerto, Double Concerto, Village Romeo and Juliet and Fennimore and Gerda; Vaughan Williams: Riders to the Sea and Sir John in Love. *Address:* 10 Mallard Close, New Alresford, Hampshire, SO24 9BX, England.

DAVIES, Neal; Singer (Baritone); b. 1965, Newport, Gwent, Wales. *Education:* Studied at King's College, London, The Royal Academy of Music and the International Opera Studio, Zürich. *Career:* Many roles at the Coburg Opera, Germany, including Papageno in a Brigitte Fassbaender production of Die Zauberflöte; Concerts at the Edinburgh Festival include Prokoviev's Hamlet, Janáček's Sarka, Schubert's Die Freunde von Salamanca, Leonore and Ninth Symphony by Beethoven, and the Scenes from Faust by Schumann, 1992–; Further opera includes Starveling in Midsummer Night's Dream with the London Symphony Orchestra, Handel's Radamisto at Marseilles and Orlando at the City of London Festival, La Bohème with the Oslo Philharmonic Orchestra and Masetto in Don Giovanni for Welsh National Opera; Season 1996–97 as Schaunard for WNO, in Stravinsky's Rossignol under Pierre Boulez for the BBC, Elijah with the Liverpool Philharmonic Orchestra and Messiah with the Gabrieli Consort under Paul McCreesh; Debut with the Royal Opera in Rameau's Platée (also at Edinburgh), 1997; Sang Mozart's Figaro and Handel's Achilla with the Royal Opera, 1998; Season 1999 with Nielsen's Springtime on Funen at the London Prom concerts; Revueltas's la noche de los mayas at the London Proms, 2002; Many recital engagements. *Recordings include:* A Midsummer Night's Dream; Classics; Elijah; Messiah; Henri Dutilleux Songs with orchestra; Vivaldi Cantatas with Robert King. *Honours:* Winner, Lieder Prize at the Cardiff Singer of the World Competition, 1991. *Current Manage-*

ment: Askonas Holt Ltd, Lonsdale Chambers, 27 Chancery Lane, London, WC2A 1PF, England. *Telephone:* (20) 7400-1700. *Fax:* (20) 7400-1799. *E-mail:* info@askonasholt.co.uk. *Website:* www.askonasholt .co.uk.

DAVIES, Noel; Conductor; b. 1945, London, England. *Education:* Royal College of Music, with Richard Austin and Adrian Boult. *Career:* Conducting Staff, Sadler's Wells Opera, then Resident Conductor, English National Opera, 1974–; Many performances of the standard repertory, including operas by Mozart, Verdi and Puccini; Collaborations with Janet Baker, Ann Murray, Thomas Allen, Rosalind Plowright and Felicity Lott; Guest Conductor with Rigoletto for the Bergen Festival, Giulio Cesare at Houston and Gloriana at the Metropolitan, New York; Xerxes, Giulio Cesare and Don Giovanni, 1997, Bavarian State Opera, Il Trovatore at Dublin and Giulio Cesare for the Covent Garden company at the Barbican, season 1997–98; Performing editions with Charles Mackerras of operas by Handel, including Xerxes for English National Opera. *Current Management:* Athole Still International Management, Forresters Hall, 25–27 Westow Street, London, SE19 3RY, England. *Telephone:* (20) 8771-5271. *Fax:* (20) 8768-6600. *Website:* www.atholestill.com.

DAVIES, Sir Peter Maxwell, Kt (see Maxwell Davies, Sir Peter)

DAVIES, Ryland, FRMCM; opera and concert singer (tenor); b. 9 Feb. 1943, Cwym, Ebbw Vale, Wales; m. 1st Anne Howells (divorced 1981); m. 2nd Deborah Rees 1983; one d. *Education:* Royal Manchester College of Music. *Career:* debut as Almaviva, Barber of Seville, Welsh National Opera, 1964; Glyndebourne Chorus, 1964–66; Soloist and Freelance, Glyndebourne and Sadler's Wells, Royal Opera House, Covent Garden, Welsh National Opera, Scottish Opera, Opera North; Performances in Salzburg, San Francisco, Chicago, New York, Hollywood Bowl, Paris, Geneva, Brussels, Vienna, Lyon, Amsterdam, Mannheim, Rome, Israel, Buenos Aires, Stuttgart, Berlin, Hamburg, Nice, Nancy, Philadelphia; Sang Lysander in A Midsummer Night's Dream at Glyndebourne, 1989, Tichon in Katya Kabanova at the 1990 Festival; Other roles have included Mozart's Ferrando and Don Ottavio, Ernesto, Fenton, Nemorino, Pelléas, (Berlin 1984), Oberon, (Montpellier, 1987); Tamino, Lensky, Belmonte and Enéas in Esclarmonde; Sang Podestà in Mozart's Finta Giardiniera for Welsh National Opera, 1994; Arbace in Idomeneo at Garsington, 1996; Season 1998 with Mozart's Basilio at Chicago; Sang Alcindoro in Bohème at Covent Garden and Basilio at Glyndebourne, 2000; Monostatos at Covent Garden, 2003; Concert appearances at home and abroad; Radio and television broadcasts; Appeared in films including: Capriccio, Entführung, A Midsummer Night's Dream; Trial by Jury, Don Pasquale. *Recordings:* Die Entführung; Les Troyens; Saul; Così fan tutte; Monteverdi Madrigals, Messiah, Idomeneo, Il Matrimonio Segreto, L'Oracolo (Leoni), Lucia di Lammermoor, Thérèse, Judas Maccabaeus, Mozart Requiem, Credo Mass, Mozart Coronation Mass and Vêspres Solennelle. *Honours:* Boise and Mendelssohn Foundation Scholarship, 1964; Ricordi Prize, 1964; Imperial League of Opera Prize, 1964; John Christie Award, 1965. *Address:* 71 Fairmile Lane, Cobham, Surrey KT11 2WG, England.

DAVIES, Wyn; conductor; b. 8 May 1952, Gowerton, Wales; m. Jane Baxendale 1975. *Education:* Christ Church, Oxford. *Career:* appearances in concert with BBC National Orchestra of Wales, BBC Scottish Orchestra, Bournemouth Symphony Orchestra, English Chamber Orchestra, Scottish Chamber Orchestra, City of Birmingham Symphony Orchestra, Northern Chamber Orchestra, Orchestra of Opera North, Manchester Camerata, Halle, Northern Sinfonia, Auckland Philharmonia, Belgrade Philharmonic; Guest Conductor, Opera North, English National Opera, Scottish Opera, New Sadler's Wells Opera, Welsh National Opera, Carl Rosa Opera, New Zealand Opera. Assistant Conductor, Metropolitan Opera, New York, USA, 1985–86; one-man cabaret show, Just Wyn. *Current Management:* Performing Arts, 6 Windmill Street, London W1P 1HF, England. *Address:* Springmount, Lidgett's Lane, Rainow, Cheshire SK10 5TG, England.

DAVIS, Sir Andrew Frank, Kt; Conductor; b. 2 Feb. 1944, Ashridge, Hertfordshire, England; m. Gianna, 1 s. *Education:* BMus (Organ Scholar), King's College, Cambridge; MA (Cantab), 1967; With Franco Ferrara, Rome, 1967–68; DLitt, York University, Toronto, 1984. *Career:* Debut: BBC Symphony Orchestra, 1970; Pianist, Harpsichordist, Organist, St Martin-in-the-Fields Academy, London, 1966–70; Assistant Conductor, BBC Scottish Symphony Orchestra, Glasgow, 1970–72; Appearances, major orchestras and festivals internationally including Berlin, Edinburgh, Flanders; Conductor, Glyndebourne Opera Festival, 1973–; Music Director, 1975–88, Conductor Laureate, 1988–, Toronto Symphony; Conductor, China, USA, Japan and Europe tours, 1983, 1986; Principal Guest Conductor, Royal Liverpool Philharmonic Orchestra, 1974–77; Associate Conductor, New Philharmonic Orchestra, London, 1973–77; Conducted: La Scala Milan, Metropolitan Opera, Covent Garden, Paris Opéra; Music Director, Glyndebourne, 1988–; Chief Conductor, BBC Symphony Orchestra, 1989–2000; Now Con-

ductor Laureate; Conducted La Clemenza di Tito, Chicago, Oct 1989; Szymanowski King Roger, Festival Hall, London, 1990; Katya Kabanova and Tippett's New Year, (1990) Glyndebourne Festival; Opened 1991 Promenade Concerts, London, with Dream of Gerontius; Glyndebourne, 1992, Gala and The Queen of Spades; Conducted Elektra, at First Night, 1993 London Proms; Berg's Lulu, Festival Hall, 1994, returned 1997, for Stravinsky's Oedipus Rex, Persephone and The Rakes's Progress; Hansel and Gretel, 1996–97, and Capriccio, 1997–98, for the Met; Philadelphia, Chicago and Boston Orchestras, New York Philharmonic, and other leading American and European orchestras; Music Director and Principal Conductor of the Chicago Lyric Opera, 2000; Season 1999 with a new production of Pelléas et Mélisande at Glyndebourne and Tippett's The Mask of Time at the London Prom concerts; Conducts the BBC Symphony Orchestra annually at the London Proms; Britten War Requiem, City of London Festival and London Symphony Orchestra, 2002; Queen's Golden Jubilee Concert, 2002; Lohengrin at Bayreuth Festival, 2002/3; Cunning Little Vixen, La Scala Milan, 2003. *Compositions:* La Serenissima (Inventions on a Theme by Claudio Monteverdi); Chansons Innocentes. *Recordings include:* All Dvořák Symphonies, Mendelssohn Symphonies, Borodin Cycle; Enigma Variations, Falstaff, Elgar; Overtures: Coriolan, Leonore No. 3, Egmont, Fidelio, Beethoven; Symphony No. 10, Shostakovich, and violin concertos; Canon and other digital delights, Pachelbel; Cinderella excerpts; The Young Person's Guide to the Orchestra; Concerto No. 2, Rachmaninov; The Planets, Gustav Holst; Symphony No. 5, Horn Concerto, Piano Concerto No. 2, Hoddinott; Brahms piano concertos; Nielsen Symphonies Nos 4 and 5; The British Line series with the BBC Symphony Orchestra including the Elgar Symphonies and Enigma Variations, Vaughan Williams, Delius, Britten and Tippett; Operatic releases including Glyndebourne productions of Katya Kabanova, Jenůfa, Queen of Spades, Lulu and Le Comte Ory. *Honours:* 2 Grand Prix du Disque Awards, Duruflé's Requiem recording with Philharmonic Orchestra; Gramophone of Year Award, 1987, Grand Prix du Disque, 1988, Tippett's Mask of Time; Royal Philharmonic Society/ Charles Heidsieck Award, 1991; Royal Phiharmonic Society Award, Best musical opera performance of 1994, Eugene Onegin, on behalf of Glyndebourne Festival Opera, 1995; Gramophone Award for Best Video for Lulu; 1998 Award for Best Contemporary recording of Birtwistle's Mask of Orpheus; Critics Choice Award for Elgar/Payne Symphony No. 3; Artistic Adviser, Pittsburgh Symphony Orchestra 2005–. *Current Management:* Askonas Holt Ltd, Lonsdale Chambers, 27 Chancery Lane, London, WC2A 1PF, England. *Telephone:* (20) 7400-1700. *Fax:* (20) 7400-1799. *E-mail:* info@askonasholt.co.uk. *Website:* www .askonasholt.co.uk.

DAVIS, Carl; Composer and Conductor; b. 28 Oct. 1936, New York. *Education:* Studied composition with Hugo Kauder and with Per Norgaard in Copenhagen. *Career:* Conductor, New York City Opera and with the Robert Shaw Chorale; Incidental music for BBC and Royal Shakespeare Company; Ballets for Northern Ballet and London Contemporary Dance Theatre; Collaboration with Paul McCartney on the Liverpool Oratorio. *Compositions:* Symphony Lines on London, 1980; Clarinet Concerto, 1984; Fantasy for Flute, Strings and Harpsichord, 1985; The Most Wonderful Birthday of All for soprano and orchestra; Ballets, A Simple Man, 1987; Lippizaner, 1989; Christmas Carol, 1992; Savoy Suite ballet for orchestra, 1993; Alice in Wonderland ballet with music by Tchaikovsky and additional music by Carl Davis, 1995; Film scores and suites including music for silent films Ben Hur and Napoleon; The French Lieutenant's Woman; Champions; Topsy-Turvy; For television: World at War; Pride and Prejudice. *Address:* c/o Faber Music, 3 Queen Street, London WC1N 3AU, England. *Website:* carldavis.filmmusic.com.

DAVIS, Sir Colin Rex, Kt; British conductor; b. 25 Sept. 1927, Weybridge, Surrey, England; m. 1st April Cantelo 1949; one s. one d.; m. 2nd Ashraf Naini 1964; three s. two d. *Education:* Royal Coll. of Music. *Career:* Conductor Assoc., Kalmar Orchestra and Chelsea Opera Group; Asst Conductor, BBC Scottish Orchestra 1957–59; Conductor, Sadler's Wells Opera House (ENO) 1959, Principal Conductor 1960–65, Musical Dir 1961–65; Artistic Dir, Bath Festival 1969; Chief Conductor, BBC Symphony Orchestra 1967–71, Chief Guest Conductor 1971–75; Musical Dir, Royal Opera House, Covent Garden 1971–86; Guest Conductor, Metropolitan Opera, New York 1967 (Peter Grimes), 1970, 1972; Principal Guest Conductor, Boston Symphony Orchestra 1972–84; Principal Guest Conductor, London Symphony Orchestra 1975–95; conducted the premieres of Tippett's The Knot Garden 1970, and The Ice Break 1977; British premiere of Berg's Lulu, three-act version 1981; Bayreuth Festival, first British conductor 1977 (Tannhäuser); Vienna State Opera debut 1986; Music Dir and Principal Conductor, Bavarian State Radio Orchestra 1983–92; Hon. Conductor, Dresden Staatskapelle 1990–; Principal Conductor, London Symphony Orchestra 1995; premiere of Tippett's The Rose Lake 1995; Principal Guest Conductor, New York Philharmonic Orchestra 1998–2003; has worked regularly with many orchestras in Europe and America; season

1999 with the Choral Symphony at the London Prom concerts and Benvenuto Cellini and Les Troyens at the Barbican Hall, both with the London Symphony Orchestra; new production of Don Giovanni at Covent Garden 2002. *Recordings:* extensive recording with Boston Symphony Orchestra, London Symphony Orchestra, Dresden Staatskapelle, Bavarian Radio Symphony Orchestra. *Honours:* Hon. DMus (Keele) 2002, (Royal Acad. of Music) 2002; Audio Award 1975, Evening Standard Opera Award 1976, Medal of the Finland Sibelius Soc. 1977, Grand Prix (France and Belgium) 1977, Grosse Deutscher Schallplattenpreis 1978, Grammy Award for Opera Recording of the Year 1980, Int. Soc. of Performing Arts Admins. Amb. Foundation Int. Award 1990, Bayerischen Verdienstorden 1992, Freedom of the City of London 1992, Royal Philharmonic Soc. Gold Medal 1995, Distinguished Musician Award Inc. Soc. of Musicians 1996, Grammy Award for Best Orchestral Recording 1997, Maximiliansorden of the Federal Land of Bavaria 2000, Grammy Award for Best Classical Recording and Best Opera Recording 2002, three BRIT Awards 2002, Gramophone Award Opera Category 2002, South Bank Show Award 2004; Commendate of the Repub. of Italy 1976, Commdr's Cross of the Order of Merit, Germany 1987, Commdr, Ordre des Arts et des Lettres 1990, Commdr First Class, Order of the Lion of Finland 1992, Bavarian Order of Merit 1993, Officier, Légion d'Honneur 1999. *Current Management:* Columbia Artists Management Ltd, 28 Cheverton Road, London, N19 3AY, England. *Address:* c/o Alison Glaister, 39 Huntingdon Street, London, N1 1BP, England (office). *Telephone:* (20) 7609-5864 (office). *Fax:* (20) 7609-5866 (office). *E-mail:* aglaister@rexx.demon.co.uk (office).

DAVIS, Howard; Musician; b. 9 April 1940, Wolverhampton, England; m. Virginia Black 1965; two s. *Education:* Royal Academy of Music. *Career:* Leader, Alberni String Quartet; World-wide tours with many broadcasts and television appearances; Professor, Royal Academy of Music, London. *Recordings:* Many including complete chamber music of Beethoven, Mozart, Schumann and complete quartets of Benjamin Britten. *Honours:* FRAM; FRSAMD; FRSA. *Address:* The Garden Flat, 74 Harley Street, London, W1G 7HQ England. *Telephone:* (20) 7323 0559. *E-mail:* hwrddvs2@aol.com.

DAVISLIM, Steve; Singer (Tenor); b. 1967, Australia. *Education:* Studied with Joan Hammond and John Modenos. *Career:* Engaged with the Zürich Opera, as Rossini's Almaviva, the Narrator in The Rape of Lucretia and Ferrando in Così fan tutte; Further appearances at Hamburg and Berlin as Almaviva, at the Salzburg Festival in Concerts, First Prisoner under Solti, as Don Curzio (Figaro) under Harnoncourt and Athens as Don Ottavio, 1996, Ludwigsburg Festival as Tamino, 1998–; Fenton under Abbada in Ferrara and Berlin; Concerts include Liszt's Faust Symphony, Beethoven's Missa Solemnis (with Roger Norrington, in London) and Matthew Passion (Bach), with Riccardo Chailly; Concerts with orchestras such as Chicago Symphony, Tonhalle Orchestra, Zürich, Cleveland Symphony, Wiener Philharmoniker, San Francisco BBC Symphony, Camerata Bern. *Recordings include:* Beethoven's 9th, Schumann's Manfred, Broadway Songs; Masses of Johann Zach; Bertoni's Orfeo; Holliger's Schneewittchen, opera world premiere. *Honours:* Australia Arts Council Grant; Queen Elizabeth II Silver Jubilee Scholarship. *Address:* c/o Opernhaus Zürich, Falkenstrasse 1, 8008, Zürich, Switzerland.

DAVITASHVILI, Shalva; Composer; b. 1 Jan. 1934, Telavi, Georgia; m. Nino Zabukidze, 6 Nov 1959, 1 s., 1 d. *Education:* Tbilisi State Conservatoire. *Career:* Debut: The Tiger and the Young Man, symphonic poem, Tbilisi State Conservatoire, 1960; Director, music school, Akhalnalexi. 1966–68; Georgian television, 1968–70; Teacher at musical college, 1970–; Director, Polioshvili Museum, 1992–; mem, Georgian Union of Composers, 1980–96. *Compositions:* 2 symphonies; 3 symphonic poems; 2 ballets; 3 cantata; 5 concertos; 2 vocal-symphonic cycles; Choral works; Pieces for piano; Pieces for other instruments; Incidental music; Film scores; Songs. *Recordings:* 3 concertos for clarinet and orchestra; 9th April, symphonic poem; Vocal cycles; Parts of ballets; Sakartveloze, cantata; Songs. *Publications:* Concerto No. 1, 1972; Concerto No. 2, 1981; Concerto No. 3, 1988; 9th April, 1990; Symphony No. 2, 1992. *Contributions:* Vladimir Kremen, Premier of Zviadauri in Kutaisi, Sovijetski balet, 1987. *Honours:* Merited Artist of Georgia, 1982. *Address:* Gorgasali str 39, app 21, 380014 Tbilisi, Georgia.

DAVY, Gloria; Singer (Soprano) and Professor of Voice; b. 29 March 1937, Brooklyn, NY, USA. *Education:* Studied at the Juilliard School with Belle Julie Soudant and in Milan with Victor de Sabata. *Career:* Sang the Countess in the US premiere of Strauss's Capriccio (Juilliard) 1954; World tour with Porgy and Bess; Recital and oratorio appearances before returning to NY in concert performance of Anna Bolena, at the Metropolitan as Pamina, Aida, Nedda and Leonora in Il Trovatore from 1958; Sang in Vienna in Aida, Covent Garden debut, 1959–60, as Aida, Deutsche Oper Berlin from 1961 with Wieland Wagner and Karl Böhm, as Aida, Amelia, Butterfly, Fiordiligi, Donna Anna, Donna Elvira and Salome; Guest engagements 1963–69 in Hamburg, Munich,

Geneva, Paris, Madrid, Brussels and London; Sang in the premiere of Henze's Nachtstücke und Arien, 1957, Stockhausen's Momente, 1972, Vortrag über Hu, 1974; Concert tours of Germany, Switzerland, Italy, and France, 1975–85; Debut recital at Wigmore Hall, London, 1983; Professor of Music in Voice at Indiana University School of Music, Bloomington, from 1985; Sang Berg's Sieben Frühe Lieder, Lulu and Der Wein, with the conductors Otmar Suitner and Kurt Masur, 1981–85; New Year's Eve in Milan, Dortmund, 1988–89; Other repertoire included Handel's Acis, Gluck's Iphigénie, Mozart's Countess and Pamina, Strauss's Daphne and Anaide in Mosè by Rossini, Bach St Matthew Passion, Beethoven Missa Solemnis, Handel's Deborah, Schoenberg Erwartung and Shostakovich 14th Symphony. *Recordings include:* Aida; Il Trovatore; Cavalleria Rusticana; Stockhausen's Momente; Zandonai's Conchita; Verdi's Requiem; Dido and Aeneas. *Address:* c/o Dortmund Opera, Kuhstrasse 12, 4600 Dortmund, Germany.

DAWIDOFF, Mikhail; Singer (Tenor); b. 1960, Russia. *Education:* Russian Academy of the Theatrical Arts, Moscow. *Career:* Many appearances with the Bolshoi Opera and elsewhere in Russia; Lucerne Opera as Don José, Pedro in Tiefland and Don Carlos; Radames and Vaudemont in Tchaikovsky's Iolanta at St Gallen; Further engagements as Cavaradossi for Palm Beach Opera, Manrico at Antwerp, Don Carlos in Netherlands and Calaf for Basle Opera; Bolshoi Opera as Alfredo, Lensky, Vladimir in Prince Igor and Verdi's Riccardo, Radames at the Deutsche Opera, Berlin, and Verona; Sang Des Grieux in Manon Lescaut at Glyndebourne, 1999. *Honours:* Prizewinner, 1994 Tchaikovsky Competition, Moscow. *Address:* c/o Glyndebourne Festival Opera, Lewes, Sussex BN8 5UU, England. *Telephone:* 01273 812321. *Fax:* 01273 812783.

DAWKINS, Timothy; Singer (Baritone); b. 1965, England. *Education:* Royal College of Music. *Career:* Appearances with Glyndebourne as Dominik in Arabella and Captain in Eugene Onegin; Leporello at the Batignano Festival, Italy, Mozart's Figaro in the South of France and Switzerland, and the Speaker in Die Zauberflöte on tour to USA; Budd in Albert Herring and Dr Bombasto in Busoni's Arlecchino at Aldeburgh; Colline in La Bohème for European Chamber Opera and roles in Goehr's Arianna; English Bach Festival in Dido and Aeneas, and in The Fairy Queen at the Linbury Theatre, Covent Garden, 2001; Further engagements with Scottish Opera, Opera North Wexford Festival Opera and Chelsea Opera Group. *Honours:* Erich Vietheer Memorial Award, Glyndebourne. *Address:* c/o English Bach Festival, Linbury Theatre, Royal Opera House, London WC2E 9 DD, England.

DAWNEY, Michael William, BA, MLitt, MPhil; music journalist, teacher, pianist, organist and arranger and composer; b. 10 Aug. 1942, Romford, Essex, England. *Education:* Durham University; Lincoln College, Oxford, under Edmund Rubbra and Egon Wellesz; Institute of Dialect and Folk Life Studies, Leeds University; London International Film School, under Richard Arnell; Bournemouth University. *Compositions:* A Carolan Suite for harpsichord or strings; Five Irish Dances for orchestra; A Christmas Greeting for choir; Now Welcome Summer for choir; Christmas Morn for choir and orchestra; The Cattery, song cycle; Echoes for brass; Lions in Heraldry for brass; The Punk's Delight for brass; An Easter Improvisation, Fantasia, Finale, Veni Emmanuel, In Paradisum, Prelude and Fugue, Adeste Fidelis, Veni Creator Spiritus, Fuga Spirituale for organ; Good King Wenceslas Lets His Hair Down; three songs for junior choir; many arrangements for organ of works by Saint-Saëns, Humperdinck, Purcell, Verdi, Fauré, Franck, others. *Recordings:* Hail Holy Queen; Hail Holy Queen in film The House of Mortal Sin; Reap Me the Earth, Hymns for Celebration. *Publications:* Folksong books for English Folk Dance and Song Society; Doon the Wagon Way, 1973; The Iron Man, 1974; The Ploughboy's Glory, 1976; contrib. to Dictionary of Christian Biography 2001. *Honours:* Jt First Prize, Cork Int. Choral Festival 1976, First Prize, Queen's Silver Jubilee Competition, Trent Park Music Centre 1977. *Address:* 29A West Rd, Bournemouth, BH5 2AW, England.

DAWSON, Anne; Singer (Soprano); b. 9 Feb. 1959, Stoke, England. *Education:* Studied at the Royal Northern College of Music. *Career:* Sang Angelica in Handel's Orlando at the Bath Festival, 1978, Grenoble Festival, 1979; Recital tours throughout the United Kingdom; With Glyndebourne Touring Opera has sung Eurydice, Susanna and Micaela; Welsh National Opera as Gilda and Pamina; Marguerite, Gilda and the title role in The Cunning Little Vixen with English National Opera; Covent Garden debut in Don Carlos, 1988; Overseas engagements include Gilda in Frankfurt, the Vixen in Vancouver, and appearances with the Netherlands and Lausanne Operas; Sang Hero in Beatrice and Benedict, London Coliseum, 1990; Susanna for Welsh National Opera; Season 1992 as Ninetta in The Thieving Magpie for Opera North, Anne Trulove for Glyndebourne Touring Opera and Chloe in The Queen of Spades at the Festival; Mimi in La Bohème for GTO, 1995; Cecilio in Mozart's Lucio Silla for Garsington Opera, 1998; Sang Polly in The Beggar's Opera at Strasbourg, 2000; Concert repertoire includes

Schubert's Fierrabras, at South Bank conducted by Jeffrey Tate, Carmina Burana, and Mozart's Exsultate Jubilate (Fishguard Festival). *Recordings include:* Songs by English composers. *Honours:* John Ireland Festival Centenary Competition and the Gerald Finzi Song Award Competition, 1981; Soprano prize at the 1981 International Singing Competition, 's-Hertogenbosch; Kathleen Ferrier Memorial Scholarship, 1982. *Address:* 50 Great Portland Street, London W1N 5AH, England.

DAWSON, Lynne; Singer (Soprano); b. 3 June 1956, York, England. *Education:* Studied at the Guildhall School of Music, London. *Career:* Appearances from 1985 with Trevor Pinnock and the English Concert; John Eliot Gardiner, the Monteverdi Choir and English Baroque Soloists and Christopher Hogwood and the Academy of Ancient Music; Further concerts with Barenboim, Davis, Rattle, Mackerras, Ashkenazy, and Giulini; Tours of Europe and the USA; Opera debut as the Countess with Kent Opera, 1986; Monteverdi's Orfeo at Florence, 1988; Festival engagements at Aldeburgh, Edinburgh, Salzburg, Bruges, Aix-en-Provence, Paris, Vienna and Promenade Concerts; Opera career includes Zdenka in Arabella at the Châtelet, Pamina, Berlin Staatsoper; Appearances as Fiordiligi at Naples, Constanze Brussels, Teresa in Benvenuto Cellini for Netherlands Opera, 1991; Other roles include, Xiphares in Mitridate (Châtelet, Paris, 1991), Amenaide in Rossini's Tancredi, Berlin Staatsoper, 1994; Shéhérezade at the 1995 London Proms; Sang Nitocris in Belshazzar at the 1996 Handel Festival, Göttingen; Opera North 1996 as Gluck's Iphigénie (en Aulide); Sang Libera Me from Verdi's Requiem at the funeral of Diana, Princess of Wales, 1997; Sang Dido in Dido and Aeneas at Vlaamse Opera, 1998; Engaged for premiere of Elliott Carter's opera What Next?, Berlin, 1999; Season 2000 at Lyon and Graz, in Handel's Hercules and Agrippina. *Recordings:* Over 60 including: Bach B Minor Mass, Monteverdi Orfeo, Purcell, Dido and Aeneas; Messiah; Mozart C Minor Mass; Purcell Timon of Athens and Dioclesian, Iphigénie en Aulide; Jephtha; Vespers by Mozart; Mozart's Requiem; Gluck's La Recontre Imprévue; Mozart's Elvira and Constanze, Beethoven 9, Midsummer Night's Dream, Acis and Galatea; Ginevra in Ariadonte; Norina in Don Pasquale; Zaide. *Address:* c/o IMG Artists, Lovell House, 616 Chiswick High Road, London W4 5RX, England.

DAWSON, Ted, BMus, BEd, MMA, PhD; Canadian composer and teacher; b. 28 April 1951, Victoria, BC. *Education:* Victoria School of Music, University of Victoria with Brian Cherney and Rudolf Komorous, McGill University with Bengt Hambraeus and Alcides Lanza, University of Toronto, State University of New York at Buffalo with Charles Wuorinen, Peter Otto, Jan Williams, Jeremy Noble and Martha Hyde. *Career:* Lecturer at Concordia University, 1974–78 and Vanier College in Montreal, 1978–80; Assistant Professor at Queen's University, Kingston, Ontario, 1987–88; Assistant Professor at Brock University, St Catherines, Ontario, 1988–90; Founder of the ComPoster Project to promote Canadian music through education; Artistic Director of Canadian Music Days Festival of Contemporary Canadian Music, held in Estonia, 1993; Organiser, The True North Festival, in Taiwan, 12 concerts of Canadian music and a major contemporary art exhibition, 1998. *Compositions:* Pentad for string quartet, 1971; Concerto Grosso 1 for tape with/without amplified viola, bassoon, trombone, and percussion, 1972–74; Chameleon for amplified flute, 1975; The Land of Nurr, 1975; The Clouds of Magellan for tape and slides, 1976–77; Binaries for 4 dancers, amplified piano and percussion, 1978–80; Joint Actions for solo female dancer and male double bass player, 1981; Phantasms for solo piano, 1986–87; Portraits in a Landscape for tape, 1988; Traces in Glass for orchestra, 1986–92; Symphony 1 for orchestra, 1992–94; Topographical Sonata for amplified piano and tape, 1992–96; Dragon Songs, for bass baritone voice and orchestra, 1995–98; Piano Concerto Wisteria, 2002. *Recordings:* True North Festival in Taiwan, including Symphony 1 and Dragon Songs performed by the Taipei Symphony Orchestra conducted by Victor Feldbrill. *Publications:* Teacher's Guide to Canadian Music 1991. *Honours:* SOCAN Prize for Orchestral Composition, Winnipeg New Music Festival's Canadian Composers Competition. *Address:* 3420 Bayview Avenue, Toronto M2M 3S3, Canada.

DAYMOND, Karl; Singer (Baritone); b. 1965, England. *Education:* Studied at Guildhall School with Thomas Hemsley and at National Opera Studio, sponsored by Glyndebourne. *Career:* Appeared at Glyndebourne Festival, 1992; Sang Valentin for Opera Northern Ireland; Season 1993 as Schaunard for Welsh National Opera and Mountjoy in Gloriana for Opera North; Claudio in Beatrice and Benedict for WNO, Hamlet, Marcello, Papageno, Opera North; Dandini in Cenerentola at Garsington; For Vlaamse Opera in Il Trittico and Un Ballo in Maschera; Anthony in Sweeney Todd for Opera North and Hector in Antheil's Transatlantic for Minnesota Opera; Appeared as Purcell's Aeneas for BBC 2 television, 1995; Marcello in La Bohème for Opera North, 1996; Sang Paride in Cesti's Pomo d'Oro at Batignano, 1998; Season 1999 in Bernstein's Wonderful Town, at the BBC Prom

concerts, London; Sang Kopernikus in the premiere of Rêves d'un Marco Polo by Claude Viviers for Netherlands Opera, 2000. *Recordings:* Méhul's Stratonice with Les Arts Florissants; Wonderful Town; Dido and Aeneas; Weir's A Night at the Chinese Opera, 1999. *Honours:* British Song Prize, 1987; Polonsky Foundation Award, 1989. *Current Management:* Askonas Holt Ltd, Lonsdale Chambers, 27 Chancery Lane, London, WC2A 1PF, England. *Telephone:* (20) 7400-1700. *Fax:* (20) 7400-1799. *E-mail:* info@askonasholt.co.uk. *Website:* www.askonasholt.co.uk.

DAZELEY, William; Singer (Baritone); b. 1966, England. *Education:* Studied at Guildhall School, London. *Career:* Season 1990–91 as Onegin with British Youth Opera; Season 1991–92 as Schaunard with British Youth Opera and Don Giovanni for Opera North; British premiere of Schreker's Der Ferne Klang, 1992; Season 1992–93 with Opera North in Billy Budd and as Mozart's Count and Schaunard, also as Don Giovanni for English Touring Opera; Season 1993–94 as Mowgli in world premiere of Michael Berkeley's Baa Baa Black Sheep for Cheltenham Festival, also as Mowgli for Opera North, Harlekin for Broomhill and Papageno for Opera North; Season 1994–95 as Rossini's Figaro for Glyndebourne Touring Opera, as Demetrius for Teatro Regio, Turin, and as Pelléas for Opera North; Mozart's Count for GTO at Glyndebourne, 1996; Soldier in Busoni's Faust at Salzburg, 1999; Sang Mercutio in Gounod's Roméo et Juliette at Covent Garden, 2000; Sang Christ in the premiere of Birtwistle's The Last Supper, Berlin, 2000; London Proms, 2002. *Recordings include:* Billy Budd; Doktor Faust (Erato); La Bohème. *Honours:* Decca-Kathleen Ferrier Prize, 1989; Richard Tauber Prize; Winner, Walter Gruner International Lieder Competition, 1991. *Current Management:* Askonas Holt Ltd, Lonsdale Chambers, 27 Chancery Lane, London, WC2A 1PF, England. *Telephone:* (20) 7400-1700. *Fax:* (20) 7400-1799. *E-mail:* info@askonasholt.co.uk. *Website:* www.askonasholt.co.uk.

DE BEENHOUWER, Jozef; Belgian concert pianist; b. 26 March 1948, Brasschaat. *Education:* Pharmacy, University of Louvain; Graduate, Chapelle Musicale Reine Elisabeth Argenteuil, 1974; Higher Diploma, Royal Flemish Conservatory, Antwerp, 1975. *Career:* Concert Pianist, with orchestras and solo recitals; Chamber Music: Vienna, (Musikverein, Konzerthaus with Vienna Symphony), Amsterdam, (Concertgebouw), Lisbon (Foundation Gulbenkian), London, Berlin, (Schauspielhaus), Dresden, (Semper-Oper), Rheinisches Musikfest, Flanders Festival, Estival de Paris and USA; Professor of Piano, Royal Flemish Conservatory, 1983–; Artistic Dir of Brussels Lunchtime Concerts, 1990; member of jury in international piano competitions. *Recordings include:* Schumann Op 12; Ravel's Gaspard de la Nuit, 1982; Peter Benoit's Contes et Ballades and Sonata, 1984; Joseph Ryelandt's Piano Works, 1986; Clara Schumann's Complete Piano Works, 1991; Robert Schumann's Op 16, 111 and 133, 1994; Robert Schumann's Dichterliebe with Robert Holl, 1994; Belgian Piano Music by P Benoit, L Mortelmans, J Jongen, M de Jong and V Legley, 1997; Cello Sonatas by A De Boeck and J L Nicodé (with M Van Staalen), 1998; Songs and piano music by Lod Mortelmans, 1999; Johannes Brahms, Klavierstücke, Op 76, 118 and 119, 2000; Ludwig Schuncke, Piano Sonata etc. 1986–2000; Hans Pfitzner, Klaviertrios (with Robert Schumann Trio), 2001; Peter Benoit: Liefdedrama – Uit Henriette's Album, 2002; Marinus de Jong: Piano Concerto no. 1, piano music, 2003; Songs by Wagner, Nystroem and De Boeck (with Nina Stemme) 2004; Robert Schumann: Carnaval, Waldszenen and Kinderszenen 2005. *Publications:* Robert Schumann, Concertsatz 1839, 1987; Clara Schumann, Concertsatz 1847, 1994. *Honours:* Robert Schumann Prize (Zwickau) 1993. *Address:* Frilinglei 45, 2930 Brasschaat, Belgium (office). *Telephone:* (3) 654-97-72 (home). *E-mail:* jozef.de.beenhouwer@pandora.be (home).

DE CANDIA, Roberto; Singer (Baritone); b. 1968, Molfetta, Bari, Italy. *Education:* Studied singing with Sesto Bruscantini. *Career:* Debut: Sang in Puccini's Messa di Gloria (concert) at the Santa Cecilia, Rome, and in Massenet's Manon at Parma; Engagements as Gianni Schicchi at Turin; Marcello at the Verona Arena, Taddeo (L'Italiana in Algeri) and Masetto in Don Giovanni at the Salzburg Festival; Other roles include: Rossini's Figaro (Paris Opéra-Comique), Parmenione in L'Occasione fa il ladro (Pesaro) and Alcandro in Pacini's Saffo (Wexford Festival); La Scala, Milan, 1996–97, as Ubalde in Gluck's Armide and Poeta (Il Turco in Italia); Glyndebourne Festival 1997, as Lescaut in a new production of Manon Lescaut; Season 1997–98 as Massenet's Lescaut at the Metropolitan, Dandini, and Belcore (L'Elisir d'amore); Season 1998–99 La Bohème; Gala Concert with Luciano Pavarotti at the Metropolitan Opera in New York; Sang in La Forza del Destino and Il Barbiere di Siviglia at La Scala; Season 2000–01 as Rossini's Dandini at Pesaro, Falstaff at Modena and Massenet's Lescaut at the Met. *Recordings:* Saffo; Mascagni's Messa di Gloria; Il turco in Italia with Riccardo Chailly; La Bohème with Riccardo Chailly. *Current Management:* Prima International Artists Management. *Address:* c/o Prima International Artists Management, Palazzo Zambeccari, Piazza de'Calderini 2/2, 40124 Bologna, Italy.

DE CAROLIS, Natale; Opera Singer (Bass-Baritone); b. 25 July 1957, Anagni, Italy. *Education:* Pont Institute of Vatican State, studied with Renato Guelfi and Maria Vittoria Romano. *Career:* Debut: 1983; La Scala, Milan; Metropolitan Opera, New York; La Fenice, Venice; Maggio Musicale, Florence; Salzburg Festival; La Zarzuela, Madrid; Sydney Opera House; Rossini Opera Festival; Pesaro Teatro Comunale; Bologna Opera; Zürich Opera; Teatro Massimo, Palermo; Teatro Bellini, Catania; Buenos Aires; Paris; Macerata; S Carlo, Napoli and Bonn; Sang Don Parmenione in a Rossini double bill at Cologne and Schwetzingen, 1992; Count Robinson in Il Matrimonio Segreto at the 1992 Ravenna Festival; Vienna, Musikverein, Staatsoper, Konzerthaus; Frankfurt, Don Giovanni, Figaro, Guglielmo, Belcore; Rome, Teatro Dell'Opera; Hamburg, Berlin, Lausanne, Montpellier, Aix-en-Province, Lisbon, Touloun, Oviedo; Sang Donizetti's Belcore at Covent Garden, 1997; Season 1998 with Guglielmo for the Royal Opera London, and Fernando in Rossini's Gazza Ladra at Venice; Season 2000–01 as Don Giovanni at Glyndebourne and Don Alfonso at Detroit. *Recordings:* Signor Bruschino, Scala di Seta (Rossini); Don Giovanni (Mozart); Rinaldo (Handel); Mozart Recital; L'Occasione fa Il Ladro and L'Inganno Felice (Rossini); Le nozze di Figaro (Mozart); La Ninfa Pazza per Amore (Paisiello); Mozart Recital; Don Giovanni, Così fan tutte, Le nozze di Figaro, Highlights. *Honours:* Spoleto; Baroque Festival Viterbo; Toti Dal Monte (Treviso); Lauri Volpi. *Current Management:* Askonas Holt Ltd, Lonsdale Chambers, 27 Chancery Lane, London, WC2A 1PF, England. *Telephone:* (20) 7400-1700. *Fax:* (20) 7400-1799. *E-mail:* info@askonasholt.co.uk. *Website:* www.askonasholt.co.uk.

DE CLARA, Roberto; Conductor; b. Hamilton, Ontario, Canada; m. Anna Colangelo, 1 Oct 1983, 1 s. *Education:* BMus, Summa Cum Laude, McMaster University, Canada; Wiener Meisterkurse; Vienna Mozarteum; Salzburg Sommerakademie; Accademia Chigiana, Siena; Aspen Music School; University of Toronto; Royal Conservatory, Toronto. *Career:* Debut: Hamilton Philharmonic, 1981; Assistant Conductor, Opera Hamilton, 1979–84; Assistant Conductor, Hamilton Philharmonic, 1981–82; Music Director, Prince George Symphony, 1984–87; Music Director, York Symphony, 1990–; Israel Vocal Arts, Tel-Aviv, 1994–95; Musical Director, Oakville Symphony, 1997–; European Opera debut with Così fan tutte, National Theatre Prague, 1998; mem, American Federation of Musicians; Opera America. *Honours:* Heinz Unger Conducting Prize, Toronto, 1978; Canada Council Scholarships, 1979, 1980; Hans Haring Conducting Prize, Salzburg Mozarteum, 1984; Canada-Israel Cultural Foundation Grant, 1994. *Address:* 129 Sirente Drive, Hamilton, Ont L9A 5H5, Canada.

DE GRANDIS, Renato; Composer; b. 24 Oct. 1927, Venice, Italy. *Education:* Studied Musicology and Composition with Malipiero in Venice; Masterclasses in Siena. *Career:* As Composer, has been concerned with dodecaphonic and aleatory techniques; Resident in Darmstadt, 1959–81, then Venice. *Compositions:* Unperformed Operas, La Fanciulla del Lago, Il Gave and Il Pastore, 1951–54; Il Cierco di Hyuga, 1959 (Staged Bonn, 1969), Gloria al Re, 1962 (Staged Kiel, 1967); Eduard und Kunigunde, Wiesbaden, 1971; Das Wahrhaftige ende des Don Giovanni, Bonn, 1973; Die Schule Der Kahlen, Karlsruhe, 1976. *Honours:* Italian Radio Prize, 1945; National First Prize for Composition, 1953. *Address:* SIAE (Sezione Musica), Viale della Letteratura n.30, 00144 Roma (EUR), Italy.

DE GROOTE, Philip; Cellist; b. 25 Dec. 1949, South Africa. *Career:* Co-Founder and Cellist of the Chilingirian Quartet, 1971; Resident Quartet of Liverpool University, 1973–76; Resident Quartet of Sussex University, 1978–; Resident Quartet of Royal College of Music, 1986–; Annual Series of Concerts at the Queen Elizabeth Hall and Wigmore Hall; Performances at the Edinburgh, Bath, Aldeburgh Festivals; Munich Herkulessaal, Amsterdam Concertgebouw, Zürich Tonhalle, Vienna Konzerthaus, Stockholm Konserthuset; New York debut 1976; Annual coast-to-coast tours of the USA and Canada; Represented the United Kingdom at the New York International Festival quartet series; Tours of Australia, New Zealand, South America, the Far East; Television and Radio throughout Europe, National Public Radio in the USA, the BBC. *Recordings:* All Great Mozart Quartets; Late Schubert Quartets; Debussy and Ravel Quartets; Elgar Quartet and Piano Quintet; Schubert Cello Quintet and Octet; Mozart Clarinet Quintet; Complete Quartets of Bartók and Dvořák; Bartók Piano Quintet. *Address:* c/o Intermusica Artists Management, 16 Duncan Terrace, London N1 8BZ, England.

DE JONG, Conrad (John); Composer and Professor; b. 13 Jan. 1934, Hull, Iowa, USA. *Education:* BM, Music Education and Trumpet, North Texas State University, Denton, 1954; MM, Music Theory with B Heiden and Brass Instruments, Indiana University School of Music, 1959; T de Leeuw, Amsterdam, 1969. *Career:* Professor of Music, University of Wisconsin, River Falls, 1959–. *Compositions:* Prelude and Fugue for Brass Trio, 1958; 3 Studies for Brass Septet, 1960; Music for 2 Tubas, 1961; Essay for Brass Quintet, 1963; String Trio, 1964; Fun and Games for Any Woodwind, Brass or String Instrument(s) and Piano,

1966, revised 1970; Peace On Earth for Chorus and Organ, 1969; Aanraking (Contact) for Trombone, 1969; Hist Whist for Voice, Flute, Viola and Percussion, 1969; Grab Bag for Tuba Ensemble, 1970; The Silence of the Sky in My Eyes for 1/2 Track Stereo Tape, Musicians, Light and Optional Dance and Audience Participation, 1973; A Prayer for Chorus, Piano, Brass Wind Chimes and Optional Audience, 1975; Ring! My Chimes for Chimes, 1/2 Track Stereo Tape and Slides, 1977; 3 Short Variation Fanfares for Brass Quintet, 1980; La Dolorosa for English Horn, 1982. *Address:* c/o Music Department, University of Wisconsin at River Falls, River Falls, WI 54022, USA.

DE KANEL, Vladimir; Singer (Bass-baritone); b. 1940, Shanghai, China. *Career:* Debut: Colombia, 1962, as Rossini's Bartolo; Frankfurt Opera from 1969, as Mozart's Leporello, Don Alfonso and Papageno, Oroveso in Norma and Rossini's Basilio; Guest appearances throughout Germany and France; Schumann's Genoveva in Paris and Rameau's Castor et Pollux for Frankfurt Opera; Liège Opera, 1985–92, as Gounod's Mephistopheles and Rodolfo in La Sonnambula; Wagner's Daland at Rio de Janeiro, 1987; Frankfurt, 1996, as Wurm in Luisa Miller; Concerts of Russian songs.

DE LA MORA, Fernando; Singer (Tenor); b. 1958, Mexico City. *Education:* Studied in Mexico City, New York, Tel-Aviv and at North Carolina University. *Career:* Debut: Sang Borsa in Rigoletto at Mexico City; Has appeared widely in Mexico as Pinkerton, Cavaradossi and Alfredo; San Francisco Opera, 1988–89, as Gounod's Romeo, and Rodolfo; Alfredo at Vienna Staatsoper and the Deutsche Oper Berlin 1989; Faust at Cologne and the Verdi Requiem on tour to Moscow with the ensemble of La Scala; Milan debut 1990, as Alfredo, which he sang also at the Santa Fe Festival, 1991; Barcelona 1992 as Nemorino; Season 1995–96 as Rodolfo at Buenos Aires and Werther for Miami Opera; Season 2000 as Don José at Miami, Rodolfo for Santa Fe Opera, Alfredo in Baltimore, Roberto Devereux for New York City Opera and Macduff at Montpellier. *Address:* c/o Opéra et Concert, 1 rue Volney, F–75002 Paris, France.

DE LAET, Joris (Maurits); Professor; b. 12 July 1947, Antwerp, Belgium; m. Maria Vervoort, 11 Aug 1774, 1 d. *Education:* Basic music theory at Academies of Antwerp; Autodidact in electronic and computer music and recording techniques, computer information and composition, first performances in International Cultural Centre, Antwerp, 1974. *Career:* Tape music composition, Parametric; Live electronics, video-art at festivals in Europe, Canada and Brazil; Many radio appearances since 1973; International seminars and lectures; Concert Organiser of experimental and electronic music and video-art; Director of SEM; Manager of sound studio of the Antwerp Music Conservatory and Professor of Electronic Music Composition; Producer, monthly radio programme dedicated to electro-acoustic music, 1992–; Co-founder and Vice President of BeFEM/FeBeMe, Belgian Federation of Electro-acoustic Music, 1994. *Compositions include:* Metrokunst, 1989; Water-toren-Installatie, 1989; Transparent Bodies, 1991; Commissioned works: Naderen, 1988, Blamis, 1990, Penetration, 1992, Irreversible, New Environment, 1992, Aural Silver, 1993, The Shift, 1994; Bruit Noir, 1995; Soleil Silencieux, 1996; Pigeon Piégé, 1997; Pièce de Résistance, 1998. *Recordings:* All music and video-art, including concerts of the SEM Ensemble. *Publications:* Editor, SEM magazine, 1975–79; Editor and part author, Documenta Belgicae II, 1985; Author of syllabus in use at Conservatory of Antwerp on Analogue Synthesis techniques, 1979; Various articles in newspapers and magazines. *Address:* Kapel Straat 44, 3140 Keerbergen, Belgium.

DE LANCIE, John; Oboist and Stage Director; b. 26 July 1921, Berkeley, CA, USA. *Education:* Curtis Institute, Philadelphia. *Career:* played oboe in Pittsburgh Symphony Orchestra, 1940–42; played with Philadelphia Orchestra from 1946, Principal Oboist 1954–74; teacher, Curtis Institute 1954–74, Dir 1977–85; commissioned and gave the premieres of Jean Francaix' Horloge de Flore in Philadelphia in 1961, and the Concerto by Benjamin Lees in 1963; Dir, New World School of Music 1987. *Recordings include:* Strauss Oboe Concerto 1987. *Current Management:* Harwood Management Group Inc., 509 W 110 Street, New York, NY 10025, USA. *Telephone:* (212) 864-0773. *Fax:* (212) 663-1129. *E-mail:* jim@harwood-management.com. *Website:* www.harwood-management.com.

DE MAIN, John (Lee); Conductor; b. 11 Jan. 1944, Youngstown, Ohio, USA. *Education:* BM 1966, MS 1968, Juilliard School of Music, New York; Studied Piano with Adele Marcus; Conducting with Jorge Mester. *Career:* Associate Conductor, St Paul (Minn) Chamber Orchestra, 1972–74; Music Director, Texas Opera Theater, 1974–76; Houston Grand Opera, 1979–94; Opera/Omaha, 1983–; Conducted the local premiere of Britten's A Midsummer Night's Dream, Houston, 1993; L'Elisir d'amore at Seattle, 1998. *Recordings:* For Composers' Recordings Inc; RCA. *Honours:* Julius Rudel Award, 1971; Grammy Award, 1977; Grand Prix de Disque, 1977. *Address:* c/o Houston Grand Opera, 510 Preston Avenue, Houston, TX 77002, USA.

DE MEY, Guy; Singer (Tenor); b. 4 Aug. 1955, Hamme, Belgium. *Education:* Studied at Brussels Conservatory and at Amsterdam with Erna Spoorenberg; Further study with Peter Pears and Eric Tappy. *Career:* Has appeared in Baroque Opera at such centres as Berlin, Hamburg, Strasbourg and Spoleto; Lully's Atys under William Christie in Paris, Florence and New York; Alidoro in Cesti's Orontea at Innsbruck 1986, returning for Aegus in Cavalli's Giasone, 1988; Rameau's Hippolyte at Regio Emilia and Eurymachus in Il Ritorno d'Ulisse at Mézières, 1989, conducted by Michel Corboz; London 1986 as Monteverdi's Orfeo; Brussels 1988, as the Painter in Lulu; Sang Don Polidoro in Mozart's La Finta Semplice at Innsbruck, 1991; Lully's Alceste at Opéra Comique, Paris, 1992; Further engagements at Utrecht Early Music Festival, Zürich, Venice and Bologna; Sang in the French version of Don Carlos at Brussels (1996) and Orpheus by Monteverdi for the English National Opera; Season 2000–01 as Carrado in A. Scarlatti's Griselda, at Innsbruck, M. Triquet in Eugene Onegin at Brussels and the Schoolmaster in The Cunning Little Vixen, for Netherlands Opera; Concert Repertoire includes the Evangelist in Bach's Passions. *Recordings:* Le Cinesi by Gluck; A Scarlatti's La Giuditta; Lully's Atys; Der Geduldige Sokrates by Telemann, Monteverdi's Orfeo and Poppea; Cavalli's Xerse and Giasone, Alessandro by Handel, Orontea and Rameau's Platée. *Address:* Théâtre Royale de la Monnaie, 4 Leopoldstrasse, 1000 Brussels, Belgium.

DE MOOR, Chris; Singer (Bass); b. 22 June 1946, Antwerp, Belgium. *Education:* Studied at the Brussels Conservatory. *Career:* Sang throughout Belgium and France, notably as Massenet's Don Quichotte, at Antwerp; Claudius in Hamlet by Thomas and Gounod's Frère Laurent at Antwerp, 1996; Zaccaria in Nabucco and Arkel in Pelléas. *Recordings:* Messiah; Mireille by Gounod. *Honours:* Vercelli and Barcelona, 1984. *Address:* Antwerp Opera, Ommeganchstrasse 59, 2018 Antwerp, Belgium.

DE PALMA, Sandro; Pianist; b. 14 Feb. 1957, Naples, Italy. *Education:* Classical studies in Latin, Greek; Studied Piano privately with Vincenzo Vitales, Naples. *Career:* Debut: Naples; Appeared ORF, Vienna, 1977; Carnegie Hall, New York, 1978; Other appearances include: Dvořák Hall, Prague; Interforum, Budapest; Gewandhaus, Leipzig; Dresden; East Berlin; Performances with major Italian Orchestras: RAI, Rome; San Carlo; Fenice Venice; Milan; Tours, France; Italy, Switzerland, USSR. *Recordings:* Liszt; 1st recording of Muzio Clementi's Gradus ad Parnassum, with Fonit Cetra. *Honours:* 1st Prize, Casella Competition, Naples, 1976; 1st Prize, Bruce Hungerford, New York, 1977. *Current Management:* Patrizia Garrasi, Via Manzoni 31, 20121 Milan, Italy. *Address:* Via del Colosseo 23, Rome, Italy.

DE PEYER, Gervase (Alan); Clarinettist and Conductor; b. 11 April 1926, London, England; m. (1) Sylvia Southcombe, 1950, divorced 1971, 1 s., 2 d. . m. (2) Susan Rosalind Daniel, 1971, divorced 1979. m. (3) Katia Perret Aubry, 1980. *Education:* Studied with Frederick Thurston at the Royal College of Music and with Louis Cahuzac in Paris. *Career:* International Soloist, 1949–; Co-founded the Melos Ensemble, 1950; First clarinet with the London Symphony, 1955; Teacher at the Royal Academy of Music from 1959; As soloist has given the premieres of works by Arnold Cooke, Musgrave, Horovitz, Hoddinott and Sebastian Forbes; Joined the Chamber Music Society of the Lincoln Center, New York, 1969: performances with Barenboim, Rostropovich, Menuhin, Perlman, and the Amadeus Quartet; Has conducted the English Chamber Orchestra, London Symphony and the Melos Sinfonia; Director, London Symphony Wind Ensemble; Associate Conductor, Haydn Orchestra of London; Conductor-in-Residence of the Collegium Musicum, in Assisi and Rome; Tour of the USA, 1988 with Quatuor pour le fin du Temps by Messiaen; Gives recitals and master classes throughout the world; Wigmore Hall concert with Gwenneth Pryor and the Allegri Quartet, 1989; Commissioned and premiered the Clarinet Quartet by Berthold Goldschmidt, 1994. *Recordings include:* Melos Ensemble; French, English and German music for clarinet and piano, Brahms Sonatas, with Gwenneth Pryor (Chandos). *Publications:* Edition of Mendelssohn Sonata in E flat. *Honours:* Worshipful Company of Musicians Gold Medal, Royal College of Music, 1948; Charles Gros Grand Prix du Disque, 1961, 1962; Plaque of Honour from Academy of Arts and Sciences of America for recording of Mozart Concerto, 1962. *Address:* c/o Michael Harrold Management, 13 Clinton Road, Leatherhead, Surrey, KT 22 8NU, England. *Telephone:* 01372 375728. *E-mail:* management@angelus.co.uk.

DE PONT DAVIES, Rebecca; singer (mezzo-soprano); b. 3 July 1962, London, England. *Education:* Guildhall School of Music and Drama. *Career:* debut, Death in Venice, Glyndebourne Touring Opera, 1989; Gaea in Strauss's Daphne at Garsington Festival, 1995; La Zia Principessa/Zita in Puccini's Il Triticco at Broomhill, 1995; Contemporary works by Judith Weir, Jonathan Dove, Henze, in the United Kingdom and Europe; Concert Appearances at major British venues, Canada and Columbia; 3rd Lady in The Magic Flute, Opera Factory, 1996; Die Muschel in the British premiere of Strauss's Die Agyptische Helena at Garsington, 1997; Moksada in Snatched by the Gods (Param Vir) for Scottish Opera, 1998; Emilia in Verdi's Otello for English National Opera, 1998; Leda in Strauss's Die Liebe der Danaë for Garsington, 1999; Martha/Pantalis in Boito's Mephistopheles, Annina in Der Rosenkavalier and Mrs Sedley in Peter Grimes all for English National Opera, 1999; Geneviève in Pelléas et Mélisande and 3rd Secretary to Chairman Mao in Adams's Nixon in China for English National Opera, 2000; Schwertleite, Die Walküre BBC Proms, 2000; For English National Opera: Flosshilde, Das Rheingold, 2001; Mistress Quickly, Falstaff, 2001; Princess Marya Bolkonskaya, War and Peace, 2001; Ulrica, Un Ballo in Maschera, 2002; Theatre Dresser/School Boy/Groom, Lulu, 2002. *Recordings:* Antigone; Fleurs Jetées; Falstaff, 2001. *Honours:* Many educational prizes including award from Countess of Munster Musical Trust; AGSM; PDVT; Violet Openshaw Memorial Prize for Contraltos; Dorothy Openshaw Prize for Melodie. *Current Management:* Robert Gilder & Co., Enterprise House, 59–65 Upper Ground, London, SE1 9PQ, England. *Telephone:* (20) 7928-9008. *Fax:* (20) 7928-9755. *E-mail:* rgilder@robert-gilder.com.

DE PONTES-LEÇA, Carlos; Portuguese writer on music and music manager; b. 26 Nov. 1938, Coimbra. *Education:* Coimbra University, University of Navarra, Spain, Music Conservatories of Lisbon and Coimbra. *Career:* Assistant Director, Music Department, Calouste Gulbenkian Foundation; Associate Editor (for Music and Dance) of the cultural magazine Coloquio-Artes, Lisbon, 1971–96; Artistic Director of the Leiria Music Festival; writer of music programmes on Portuguese TV and radio, essays on the history of music and music aesthetics, and programme notes for Gulbenkian Foundation, San Carlos Theatre (Lisbon National Opera) and recordings; commentator of opera performances on radio and television; founder mem. Portuguese Music Council. *Publications:* contrib. The New Grove Dictionary of Music and Musicians, London; Gulbenkian Dictionary of Portuguese Music and Musicians, Lisbon; Verbo Encyclopedia, Lisbon. *Address:* Calouste Gulbenkian Foundation, 1067-001 Lisbon, Portugal.

DE SALAS, Sergio; Singer (Bass-Baritone); b. 1947, Spain. *Education:* Studied in Madrid, Barcelona and Milan. *Career:* Sang at Opera Houses in Spain from 1971; Appeared as Rigoletto in Valencia and sang in Paris, Marseilles, Bologna and Seville; Liège 1987–88 as the four villians in Les Contes d'Hoffmann; Teatro Real Madrid, 1989, as Gerard in Andrea Chénier; Liège 1990, as Canio; Other roles include Wagner's Dutchman, Athanael in Thais, Mephistopheles in La Damnation de Faust and parts in operas by Verdi. *Honours:* Prizewinner at Beniamino Gigli Competition Macerata and the Voci Verdiane at Parma, 1974.

DE SARAM, Rohan; British cellist; b. 9 March 1939, Sheffield, Yorkshire, England; m.; two c. *Education:* studied in Ceylon, in Florence with Gaspar Cassals, in Puerto Rico with Casals, further study with John Barbirolli. *Career:* from age 11 gave recitals and concerts in Europe; US debut with New York Philharmonic, Carnegie Hall 1960; further concerts in Canada, USSR, Australia and Asia; as a soloist, in addition to standard repertoire has worked personally with Kodály, Walton, Shostakovich; premieres of works by Pousseur and others; has taught at Trinity Coll. of Music; mem., Arditti Quartet, with repertoire including works by Boulez, Carter, Ferneyhough, Henze, Ligeti and many other living composers, and premiers of works by Bose, Britten, Bussotti, Cage, Davies, Glass, Gubaidulina, Hindemith, Kagel, Nancarrow, Rihm and Schnittke; as soloist has given the British premieres of Kottos for solo cello by Xenakis and Ligeti's solo cello sonata; has given the world premiere of Pousseur's Racine 19, Xenakis' Epicycles for cello and ensemble and Roscobeck for cello and double bass, Dillon's Eos for solo cello, and Berio's Sequenza XIV for cello; founder, De Saram Clarinet Trio and a duo with his brother, Druvi; interested in the music of his native Sri Lanka and plays the Kandyan drum. *Honours:* Suggia Award 1957, Ernst Von Siemens Prize 1999. *E-mail:* rosiedesaram@hotmail.com.

DE SIMONE, Bruno; Singer (baritone); b. 1957, Naples, Italy. *Education:* Studied with Sesto Bruscantini. *Career:* Debut: Spoleto, 1980, as Valentin in Faust and Albert in Werther; La Scala Milan debut, 1990, in Pergolesi's Lo frate 'nnammurato; Teatro San Carlo, Naples, from 1991, in Pergolesi's Flaminio, Don Giovanni and Paisiello's L'Idolo cinese; Has also sung at Florence in Paisiello's Barbiere di Siviglia and Pergolesi's Livietta e Tracollo; Macerata, 1992, as Malatesta, Naples, 1994, in Haydn's Mondo della Luna; Other roles include Rossini's Figaro, Taddeo, Dandini, Magnifico, Rimbaud and Germano, Mozart's Figaro, Alfonso, Guglielmo, Count and Leporello, Donizetti's Dulcamara, Belcore and Sulpice; Sang Geronimo in Il Matrimonio Segreto at Rome, 1996; Season 2000–01 as Rossini's Bartolo at Zürich, Taddeo at Padua and in Cimarosa's Il marito disperato, at Naples. *Current Management:* Athole Still International Management, Forresters Hall, 25–27 Westow Street, London, SE19 3RY, England. *Telephone:* (20) 8771-5271. *Fax:* (20) 8768-6600. *Website:* www.atholestill.com.

DE SMET, Raoul; Belgian fmr academic and composer; b. 27 Oct. 1936, Antwerp; m. Marisa Seys, 26 May 1962, 1 s., 3 d. *Education:* MPhil, Catholic University of Louvain; Postgraduate Diploma in Spanish Literature, University of Salamanca, Spain; Music Academy, Deurne; Composition with A Verbesselt and Ton de Leeuw, electronic music with L Goethals, Ipem Gent. *Career:* Debut: Darmstadt Ferienkurse Neue Musik; Professor of Spanish Linguistics and Translation, Kath Vlaamse Hogeschool, Antwerp, 1969–97; Founder of Orphische Avonden playing concerts of new chamber music, 1974; Publisher, EM-Reeks, new music of Flemish Composers, 1981; Foundation of Orpheus-Prijs Contest for interpretation of new chamber music, 1987; mem. SABAM; Unie Belgische Componisten; Stichting Orpheus; CeBeDeM; Music Council of Flanders. *Compositions:* Chamber Opera: Ulrike 1979, 1988, Vincent, 1990; Concerto for Alto Sax, Strings, Accordion and Percussion, 1992; Concerto for Violin and Symphonic Orchestra, 1993; 2 Symphonies, 1960, 1995; 2 String Quartets; Clarinet and String Quartet; Octopus for 8 Bass Clarinets; Track-Sack-Fantasy for 10 accordions; Logbook 1, cello suite; Gnomons 2 for 4 Trombones and Stereotape; Soledad Sonora for Alto Sax; Concerto for accordion and string orchestra, 2000. *Recordings:* Publications: Chamber music. Numerous. *Honours:* Fuga Trophy 1995. *Address:* Ruytenburgstraat 58, 2600 Berchem, Belgium. *Telephone:* (32) 300-466 (office). *E-mail:* orpheusprys@belgacom.net (office).

DE VAUGHN, Paulette; Singer (Soprano); b. 8 Aug. 1951, California, USA. *Education:* Studied with Martial Singher at Santa Barbara, at Juilliard School and in Vienna. *Career:* Debut: As Elisabeth de Valois at Paris Opéra; Appearances at National Theatre Prague from 1980, as Tosca, the Trovatore Leonora, Mimi, Amelia, Ballo in Maschera, Lady Macbeth, Turandot, Violetta and Abigaille; Sang Tosca at Stockholm 1988 and in season 1989–90 appeared as Savonlinna, as Tosca at Graz, as Mozart's Electra at Mannheim, Manon Lescaut, Staatsoper Berlin, Elena in I Vespri Siciliani and Komische Oper Berlin, Dresden and Sofia; Saarbrucken as Aida, Salome, Senta, Elsa and Leonore in Fidelio; Sang Aida at Royal Opera Copenhagen, 1991, at the Montpellier Festival 1992 and Alexandria, Egypt, 1995; Concerts and Lieder recitals in Austria, Germany and Sweden. *Address:* c/o Det Kongelige Teater, Box 2185, 1017, Copenhagen, Denmark.

DE VOL, Luana; Singer (Soprano); b. 30 Nov. 1942, St Bruno, San Francisco, California, USA. *Education:* San Diego University with Vera Rozsa in London and with Jess Thomas. *Career:* Debut: San Francisco 1983, as Ariadne auf Naxos; European debut Stuttgart 1983, as Leonore in Fidelio; Sang the Forza Leonora at Seattle 1983 and appeared at Aachen and Amsterdam; Member of Mannheim Opera from 1986; Appearances in Berlin, Staatsoper and Deutsche Oper from 1986 as Euryanthe, Agathe, Rezia in Oberon, Leonore and Senta; Staatsoper, Hamburg 1989, as Irene in Rienzi, Zürich and Vienna 1989 as Ellen Orford in Peter Grimes and Eva in Schreker's Irrelohe; Further engagements in Bologna, Dortmund, Gelsenkirchen and Frankfurt and at Bregenz and Orange Festivals; Sang Amelia in Ballo in Maschera at Stuttgart and Leonore in a concert performances at Festival Hall 1990; Gutrune in Götterdämmerung concert in Rome and Elsa in Lohengrin at Taormina, both conducted by Sinopoli 1991; Sang Marina in Dvorák's Dimitrji at Munich, Leonore at Zürich and Andromache in Reimann's Troades at Frankfurt, 1992; Sang Strauss's Empress at the Paris Châtelet. 1994; Season 1995-96 as Maria in Friedenstag, Amelia (Ballo) and Wagner's Elsa and Isolde at Dresden; Brunswick 1996 and Ghent 1998 as Isolde; Season 2001–02 as the Dyer's Wife in Die Frau ohne Schatten, at Dresden, and Isolde at Antwerp; Other roles include Donna Anna, Isolde, Elisabeth de Valois and Elisabeth in Tannhäuser, Brünnhilde and the Marschallin; Concert reperoire includes the Britten War Requiem and Shostakovich's 14th Symphony. *Recordings include:* Eva in Schreker's Irrelohe (Sony). *Address:* c/o Opéra et Concert, 1 rue Volney, F–75002 Paris, France.

DE WAAL, Rian; concert pianist; b. 1958, Netherlands. *Education:* Sweelinck Conservatory, Amsterdam; masterclasses with Rudolf Serkin and Leon Fleisher. *Career:* Regular concert appearances with the Concertgebouw Orchestra, Rotterdam and Stuttgart Philharmonics, Polish and Radio Chamber Orchestra and the State Orchestra of Lithuania; Further concerts and recitals in Boston, Washington, DC, Atlanta and Montreal and on tour to Poland; Performs works by Godowsky, Balakirev and Tausig, as well as contemporary Dutch composers, in addition to the standard repertoire. *Honours:* Prizewinner at Vianna da Motta Competition, Lisbon, 1979, and the Queen Elisabeth Competition in Brussels, 1983. *Current Management:* Robert Gilder & Co., Enterprise House, 59–65 Upper Ground, London, SE1 9PQ, England. *Telephone:* (20) 7928-9008. *Fax:* (20) 7928-9755. *E-mail:* rgilder@robert-gilder.com.

de WAART, Edo; Dutch conductor; *Artistic Director, Hong Kong Philharmonic Orchestra;* b. 1 June 1941, Amsterdam; s. of M. de Waart and J. Rose; one s. one d. *Education:* Amsterdam Music Lyceum with Haakon Stotijn, Hilversum with Franco Ferrara. *Career:* co-prin. oboe Amsterdam Philharmonic 1961, Concertgebouw Orchestra 1963; Asst Conductor, New York Philharmonic 1965–66, Concertgebouw Orchestra, Amsterdam 1966; Musical Dir Netherlands Wind Ensemble 1966; Conductor, Rotterdam Philharmonic 1967, Musical Dir and Prin. Conductor 1973–79; Prin. Guest Conductor, San Francisco Symphony Orchestra 1975–77, Music Dir 1977–85; Music Dir Minn. Orchestra 1986–95; Artistic Dir Dutch radio organization, Nederlandse Omroep Stichting; Chief Conductor, Netherlands Radio Philharmonic Orchestra 1989–; Prin. Guest Conductor, Santa Fe Opera 1991–92; Artistic Dir and Chief Conductor, Sydney Symphony Orchestra 1993–2003; Artistic Dir Hong Kong Philharmonic Orchestra 2004–; guest conductor with leading orchestras and at leading venues in the USA and Europe, and at festivals including Spoleto, Bayreuth and Holland. *Honours:* First Prize Dimitri Mitropoulos Competition, New York 1964. *Current Management:* Harrison/Parrott Ltd, 12 Penzance Place, London, W11 4PA, England. *Telephone:* (20) 7229-9166. *Fax:* (20) 7221-5042. *Website:* www .harrisonparrott.com. *Address:* c/o Hong Kong Philharmonic Orchestra, Level 8 Administration Building, Hong Kong Cultural Centre, Tsim Sha Tsui, Kowloon, Hong Kong (office). *Telephone:* 2721 2030 (office). *Fax:* 2311 6229 (office). . *Website:* www.hkpo.com.

DEACON, Nigel; British composer; b. 6 Jan. 1957, Leicester, England. *Education:* studied piano and composition. *Career:* Chemistry Educator, Wyggeston and Queen Elizabeth College, Leicester, 1979–; Energy Research, GEC Alsthom, 1978–98; Alstom Energy, 1998–; Composer, 1979–; est. Diversity Website; mem. Association of Teachers and Lecturers 1979–, Vintage Radio Programme Collectors' Circle. *Compositions:* For piano: Five Fugues, 1986; Five French Nursery Tunes, 1986; Three Diversions, 1986; Six Folktune Settings, 1986; Six Miniatures, 1987; Twelve Folktune Settings, 1987; Three Chorales, 1987; Six More Miniatures, 1988; Five Sonatas, 1989; 24 Folktune Settings, 1995; Three Scottish Airs, 1995; Twelve Folktune Preludes, 1996; Six preludes, 1996; Three irregular preludes, 1997; Welsh Folktune Preludes, 1998–, "Voi che Sapete?", 2000; Two Slovak Folktunes, 2002; Marigold, 2002; L'Invitation au voyage, 2003; and arrangements for piano solo. *Publications:* Scientific Articles, School Science review, 1984–98; Technical publications, 1978–2001; contrib. reviews for International Talking Machine, Vintage Radio Programme Collectors' Circle magazine. *Address:* 56 Arbor Road, Croft, Leicestershire LE9 3GD, England. *Telephone:* (1455) 284096. *Fax:* (870) 1331412. *E-mail:* suttonelms@ukonline.co.uk. *Website:* web.ukonline.co.uk/suttonelms.

DEAK, Csaba; Swedish Composer and Teacher; b. 16 April 1932, Budapest, Hungary. *Education:* Studied Clarinet and Composition, Bela Bart ók Conservatory, Budapest, 1949–55; Composition with Ferenc Farkas, Budapest Academy of Music, 1955–56, with Hilding Rosenberg, Sweden; Composition, Clarinet, Conducting, Ingesund School of Music, Arvika; Teacher's Certificate Stockholm Musikhögskolan, 1969. *Career:* Teacher: Swedish State School of Dance, Stockholm, 1969–; University of Göteborg, 1971–74. *Compositions:* Jubilemus Salvatori, chamber cantata, 1958; 2 string quartets, 1959, 1967; Duo Suite for flute and clarinet, 1960; The Fathers, chamber opera, 1968; 121 for winds, percussion, double bass, 1969; Etude on Spring, 1970; Trio for flute, cello, piano, 1971; Andante och Rondo for wind quintet, 1973; Lucie's Ascent into Heaven, astrophonic minimelodrama, 1973; Verbunk for brass sextet, 1976; Bye-bye, Earth, A Play About Death, 1976–77; Hungarian Dances for Wind Quintet, 1977; Octet for wind quintet and string trio, 1977; Eden for symphonic band, 1978; The Piper's Wedding for wind quintet and symphonic band, 1979; Herykon for brass quintet, 1981; Vivax for orchestra, 1982; 5 Short Pieces for symphonic band, 1983; Farina Pagus for symphonic band, 1983; Massallians for trumpet, trombone, brass ensemble, percussion, 1985; Saxophone Quartet, 1986; Quintet for alto saxophone and string quartet, 1988; Concerto Maeutro for trumpet, euphonium, marimba, symphonic band, 1989; Quartet for tubas, 1990; Ad Nordiam Hungarica for chamber ensemble, 1991; Concerto for clarinet and wind orchestra, 1992; Anémones de Felix for symphonic band, 1993; Magie Noire for clarinet and string quartet, 1993; Novem for saxophone quartet and brass quintet, 1994; Memento Mare for mixed choir and wind orchestra, 1995; Symphony for wind orchestra, 1995; Gloria for mixed choir, 1996; Octet for saxophone quartet and string quartet, 1998; Mayinka for symphony orchestra, 1999; Brassonance for brass band, 2000; Piano pieces; Choruses; Songs; Symphony No 2 for wind orchestra, 2001; Recollection for wind ensemble, 2003, Concerto for Flute and String Orchestra 2004. *Honours:* Atterberg Music Prize, 1992,Gustavus Adolphus Fine Art Award 1989. *Address:* Döbelnsgatan 56, 113 52 Stockholm, Sweden. *Telephone:* 46-8-16-02-17 (home). *Fax:* 46-8-16-02-17 (home). *E-mail:* csaba.deak@chello.se.

DEAN, Brett; Composer and Violist; b. 23 Oct. 1961, Brisbane, Queensland, Australia; m. Heather Betts, 2 d. *Education:* Queensland Conservatorium of Music; Hochschule der Künste, Berlin. *Career:* Debut: As Violist: Hindemith Concerto with Melbourne Symphony Orchestra (ABC Concerto Competition), 1981; As Composer: Ariel's Music with Queensland Symphony Orchestra, 1995; As Violist: Member of Berlin Philharmonic Orchestra, 1985–; Soloist with Berlin Philharmonic Orchestra under Abbado, 1995; Chamber music at major European festivals including Bath, Aldeburgh and Salzburg; As Composer: One of a Kind, music for Jiri Kylian Ballet, 1998; Carlo, with Berlin Philharmonic under Simon Rattle, 1999; His works performed throughout Europe, Japan, USA and Australia. *Compositions:* Voices of Angels, written for Imogen Cooper, 1996; 12 Angry Men, for the 12 cellos of Berlin Philharmonic Orchestra, 1996; Carlo, for the Australian Chamber Orchestra, 1997; Beggars and Angels, for Melbourne Symphony Orchestra, 1999. *Recordings:* Hindemith: Viola d'Amore Concerto, with Frankfurt Radio Symphony Orchestra and Albert; Frankel: Viola Concerto, with Albert; Brahms and Bruckner: String Quintets, with Brandis Quartet; Dean: Music for 'One of a Kind', with Pieter Wispelwey, cello. *Honours:* 1st Prize at ABC Concerto Competition, 1981; Queensland Conservatorium Medal for Excellence, 1982; Honoured as Selected Work at Unesco International Rostrum of Composers, Paris, 1999. *Current Management:* Boosey & Hawkes, Berlin.

DEAN, Robert; conductor and vocal coach; b. 4 Sept. 1954, Surrey, England. *Education:* Durham University, Royal College of Music, Royal Northern College of Music, National Opera Studio. *Career:* debut, as Baritone, Musica Nel Chiostro, Alidora, in Cesti's Orontea 1979, as Conductor, Batignano Festival, Leonora 1987; Appearances with Covent Garden, ENO, Glyndebourne Festival and Touring, Scottish Opera, Opera North, Welsh National Opera, 1979–86; Scottish Opera Music Staff, 1988–, Head of Music, 1990–; Conducted Over 100 Performances, 1993–; Freelance: Canadian Debut, Edmonton Opera, 1993; US debut, Kentucky Opera 1995, conducted Die Zauberflöte there 1998. *Recordings:* Coronation Anthems; Video, Rossini Barbiere di Siviglia from Glyndebourne. *Current Management:* Robert Gilder & Co., Enterprise House, 59–65 Upper Ground, London, SE1 9PQ, England. *Telephone:* (20) 7928-9008. *Fax:* (20) 7928-9755. *E-mail:* rgilder@robert-gilder.com. *Address:* 51 Lyndhurst Drive, Leyton, London, E10 6SB, England.

DEAN, Roger (Thornton); Composer and Double Bass Player; b. 6 Sept. 1948, Manchester, England. *Education:* BA, Cambridge University, 1970, MA, PhD, 1973; DSc, Brunel University, 1984. *Career:* Professor, Brunel University, 1984–88; University of Sydney, 1988–. *Compositions include:* Destructures, for trumpet and large ensemble, 1979; Breaking Worlds, for violin, clarinet and double bass, 1980; Heteronomy 1–4 for ensemble, 1982; BA and BA for brass quintet, 1985; Timestrain, for clarinet and piano, 1989; Reel Choice for ensemble, 1989; Time Dance Peace, for dancers and 8 instruments, 1991; It Gets Complicated, for speaking pianist, 1992; Poet Without Language, for voices and electronics, 1992; Nuaghic Echoes, for voice and electronics, 1993; Elektra Pulses for string quartet and tape, 1993; Three Bagatelles for piano, 1994; Sonopetal for orchestra, 1995. *Honours:* Development Fellowships from the Arts Council of Great Britain. *Address:* c/o APRA, 1A Eden Street, Crows Nest, NSW 2065, Australia.

DEAN, Stafford; singer (bass); b. 20 June 1937, Kingswood, Surrey, England; m. 1st Carolyn Joan Lambourne; four s.; m. 2nd Anne Elizabeth Howells; one s. one d. *Education:* Epsom College, Royal College of Music, studied with Gordon Clinton, Howell Glynne and Otakar Kraus. *Career:* toured with Opera For All, 1962–63 and 1963–64; Glyndebourne debut as Lictor in L'Incoronazione di Poppea, 1964, also as Le Bailli in Werther, Rochefort in Anna Bolena, Leporello, Don Alfonso, Swallow in Peter Grimes and Trulove in The Rake's Progress; With Sadler's Wells Opera/ENO, ENO, 1964–70 with debut, Zuniga, also as Count Ribbing in Masked Ball, Plutone in Orfeo, Private Willis in Iolanthe, Sam Breeze in A Penny for a Song, Colline, Daland, Padre Guardiano, Sarastro, Leporello; Covent Garden debut as Masetto, 1969; also as Nightwatchman in Meistersinger, Narbal in The Trojans, He-Ancient in Midsummer Marriage, Alfonso d'Este in Lucrezia Borgia, Figaro, Leporello, Don Alfonso, Speaker, Rangoni, Bottom, Prime Minister in The King Goes Forth to France, Gessler in William Tell, Prof. Bieganski in Sophie's Choice; Guest appearances at many international venues including: Metropolitan Opera, New York, Chicago Lyric Opera, San Francisco Opera, Toronto, Stuttgart, Staatsoper Munich, Hamburg, W. Berlin, Cologne, Bonn, Frankfurt, Vienna, Prague, Paris, Aix-en-Provence, Madrid, Barcelona, Turin, Florence, Genoa, Amsterdam, Geneva and Zürich; Concert appearances include: Beethoven's 9th Symphony and Missa Solemnis, Verdi Requiem; Haydn's Creation, Berlioz's L'Enfance du Christ, and Romeo et Juliette, Shostakovich 14th Symphony, Bass Soloist in world premiere of Penderecki Requiem, Stuttgart, 1984; Television appearances: Sparafucile in Rigoletto; Daland in The Flying Dutchman for BBC; Rocco in Fidelio for Welsh Nat. Opera; Don Alfonso in Così fan tutte at Glyndebourne; King of Portugal in Ines de Castro with Scottish Opera; Alfonse d'Este in Lucrezia Borgia; 300th performance as Leporello in Don Giovanni and Prof. Bieganski in Sophie's Choice for Covent Garden; Other roles include: Osmin, Seneca, Don Basilio, King

Phillip, Ferrando, Banquo, King of Egypt, Don Pasquale, Raimondo (Lucia di Lammermoor), Dulcamara, Lord Cecil (Maria Stuarda), Timur, Don Fernando, Titurel, Arkel, Prince Gremin, Kecal, Count Villem (The Jacobin), Dansker (Billy Budd). *Recordings:* Idomeneo, I Lombardi; The Burning Fiery Furnace; The Midsummer Marriage; Monteverdi Madrigals; Anna Bolena; Oedipus Rex; The Rake's Progress; The Beggar's Opera; Orfeo; Beethoven's 9th Symphony; L'Enfance du Christ; A Village Romeo and Juliet; Yeomen of the Guard; Mikado; Don Giovanni; Mozart Requiem; Lucrezia Borgia; Peter Grimes. *Current Management:* IMG Artists, Lovell House, 616 Chiswick High Road, London, W4 5RX, England.

DEAN, Timothy; Conductor; b. 1956, England. *Education:* Studied at Reading University and at the Royal College of Music. *Career:* Has worked with Opera North, the Buxton Festival Opera and the Royal Opera House, Covent Garden; Kent Opera, 1983–90, conducting Così fan tutte, Agrippina, The Magic Flute, La Traviata, Carmen, Le Comte Ory and Don Giovanni on the company's visit to the Singapore Festival; Conducted Martin's Le Vin Herbé for the London Music Theatre Group and the British premiere of Legrenzi's Guistino for the Chichester Festival; Vivaldi's Juditha Triumphans at the Camden Festival; Acis and Galatea for the English Bach Festival in Italy; Music Director of British Youth Opera, conducting Don Giovanni and The Marriage of Figaro in London and on tour; Music Director of the London Bach Society from 1988, appearing with them at Chichester and City of London festivals and on the South Bank; Season 1990–91, Assistant Music Director of New D'Oyly Carte Opera Company (conducting in the United Kingdom and USA); English National Opera debut, 1991, with Bluebeard's Castle and Oedipus Rex; Scottish Opera debut, 1991, with Barber of Seville; Music Director of The Opera Company, Tunbridge Wells, 1991–94; Also with British Youth Opera, conducting Così fan tutte (1998), Eugene Onegin, La Bohème, Carmen and La Gazza Ladra; In 1994 conducted Kent Opera in The Prodigal Son at major British festivals and for the BBC; Since Sept 1994 Head of Opera at the Royal Scottish Academy of Music and Drama, Glasgow; (L'Assedio di Calais by Donizetti, 1998); Conducted British Youth Opera in Albert Herring, 1996; appointed artistic director British Youth Opera, 2001. *Address:* c/o RSAMD, School of Music, 100 Renfrew Street, Glasgow G2 3 DB, Scotland.

DEAN, Winton (Basil); Author and Musicologist; b. 18 March 1916, Birkenhead, England; m. Hon Thalia Mary Shaw (deceased 2000), 4 Sept 1939, 1 s., 3 d. (2 deceased, 1 adopted). *Education:* MA, Classics and English, King's College, Cambridge, 1940. *Career:* Translated Libretto of Weber's Opera Abu Hassan, Arts Theatre, Cambridge, 1938; War Service, Naval Intelligence, 1944–45; Music Panel, Arts Council, 1957–60; Ernest Bloch Professor of Music, University of CA, Berkeley, USA, 1965–66; Regent's Lecturer, 1977; Matthew Vassar Lecturer, Vassar College, 1979; Editor, with Sarah Fuller, Handel's Opera Julius Caesar, 1977, published 1999; Trustee and Member Committee, The Handel Institute, 1987; mem, Royal Musical Association, Council, 1965–, Vice President, 1970–98; Honorary Member, 1998; G F Händel Gesellschaft, Halle, Member of Vorstand, 1979–, Vice President, 1991–99, Honorary Member, 1999; Göttinger Händel Gesellschaft, Member of Curatorium, 1981–97, Honorary Member, 1997; International Musicological Society. *Publications include:* The Frogs of Aristophanes, 1937; Bizet, 1948, 3rd revised edition, 1975; Carmen, 1949; Introduction to The Music Of Bizet, 1950; Franck, 1950; Handel's Dramatic Oratorios and Masques, 1959; Shakespeare and Opera, 1964; Georges Bizet, His Life and Work, 1965; Beethoven and Opera, 1971; Editor, E J Dent, The Rise of Romantic Opera, 1976; The New Grove Handel, 1982; Handel's Operas 1704–1726 (with J M Knapp), 1987, revised edition, 1995; Essays on Opera, 1990, revised edition, 2000; Production Style in Handel's operas (in the Cambridge Companion to Handel), 1997. *Contributions:* Grove's Dictionary of Music and Musicians; Music and Letters; Musical Times; Opera. *Honours:* Honorary Member, Royal Academy of Music, 1971; Fellow, British Academy, 1975; Corresponding Member, American Musicological Society, 1989; City of Halle Handel Prize, 1995; Honorary Doctor of Music, Cantab, 1996. *Address:* Hambledon Hurst, Godalming, Surrey GU8 4HF, England.

DEATHRIDGE, John; Musicologist; b. 21 Oct. 1944, Birmingham, England. *Education:* Studied at Oxford University with Egon Wellesz and Frederic Sternfeld. *Career:* Lived in Germany during 1970s working as Conductor, Organist and Broadcaster; Fellow of King's College, Cambridge, 1983–96; Visiting Professor, Princeton University, USA, 1990–91; University of Chicago, 1992; King Edward Professor of Music, King's College London, 1996; mem, Royal Musical Association; American Musicological Society. *Publications:* Study of Wagner's Sketches for Rienzi, 1977; New Grove Wagner, with Carl Dahlhaus, 1984; Verzeichnis der musikalischen Werke Richard Wagners und ihrer Quellen, with Martin Geck and Egon Voss, 1986; Editor, The Wagner Handbook; Essays on Wagner's Life and Work, 1992; Editor, Family Letters of Richard Wagner, 1991; Critical edition of Wagner's Lohengrin, 3 vols,

1996–2000. *Contributions:* Cambridge Opera Journal; New German Critique; Times Literary Supplement; Programme notes for Covent Garden, Lohengrin and Der Freischütz 1997–98. *Address:* King's College London, School of Humanities, Department of Music, Strand, London WC2R 2LS, England.

DECKER, Franz-Paul; German conductor; b. 22 June 1928, Cologne; m. Christa Terka; two d. *Education:* Studied with P Jarnach and E Papst, Cologne Hochschule für Musik; Studied with E Bucken and K Fellerer, Univ. University of Cologne. *Career:* Music Dir, Krefeld, 1946–50; 1st Conductor, State Opera Wiesbaden, 1953–56; Municipal Music Dir, Wiesbaden, 1953–56; Generalmusikdirektor, Bochum, 1956–64; Chief Conductor, Rotterdam Philharmonic Orchestra, 1962–68; Music Dir, Montreal Symphony Orchestra, 1967–75; Prin. Guest Conductor and Music Adviser, Calgary (Alberta) Philharmonic Orchestra, 1975–77; Artistic Adviser, Winnipeg Symphony Orchestra, 1981–82; Prin Guest Conductor, New Zealand Symphony Orchestra, Wellington, 1980–89; Music Dir, Barcelona Symphony, 1986–92; Chief Conductor, New Zealand Symphony, 1990–99; Prin. Guest Conductor, National Arts Centre Orchestra, Ottawa, 1991–99; Conducted the Ring-Cycle by Wagner at the Teatro Colón in Buenos Aires, 1995–98; Guest conductor worldwide since 1960 including opera performances in Ottawa, Montreal, Houston Opera, Dallas Opera, Lyric Opera Chicago and Tulsa Opera; regular Guest Conductor with the Teatro Colón in Buenos Aires since 1961, presented complete Mahler works and two Wagner Ring Cycles 1991–98. *Recordings:* Various. *Honours:* Dr hc; Bundesverdienstkreuz 1st Class, Germany; Herscheppend Schep ik Roquette Pinto Medal, Brazil; Medal, Netherlands; Queen Elizabeth II Jubilee Medal, Canada. *Address:* Kronenburgerstrasse 2, 50935 Cologne, Germany; Also: 486 B Mount Pleasant Avenue, Westmount, QC, Canada. *Fax:* (221) 439197 (home).

DECKER, Richard; Singer (Tenor); b. 1958, USA. *Education:* Studied at the Manhattan School of Music (master classes with Judith Raskin and Nan Merriman); Further study at the Zürich Opera studio. *Career:* Sang with Zürich Opera from 1985 and made guest appearances in Saarbrucken, at the Aix and Macerata Festivals (Ferrando in Così fan tutte) and at the Vienna Staatsoper (in Zimmermann's Soldaten); Other roles include Alwa in Lulu (at Aachen) and has made frequent concert appearances, in Germany and Switzerland; Season 1995–96 at Heidelberg as Thomas' Wilhelm Meister and Wagner's Erik at Eutin; Berg's Alwa at Mannheim, 1998; Season 2000–01 as Alwa at Dusseldorf and Melot in Tristan at Amsterdam. *Address:* c/o Opernhaus Zürich, Falkenstrasse 1, 8008 Zürich, Switzerland.

DECKERT, Hans Erik; Cellist and Conductor; b. 11 Jan. 1927, Hamburg, Germany. *Education:* Diploma in Cello, Conducting, Musical Theory, Royal Danish Conservatory of Music, Copenhagen; Further study under Pablo Casals, Maurice Gendron, Igor Markevitch and Sergiu Celibidache. *Career:* Debut: Solo debut (cello), Royal Conservatory of Music, Copenhagen, 1952; Cellist, Royal Chapel, Denmark; Docent, Cello, Conducting, Chamber Music, Ingesunds Academy of Music, Sweden; Docent, Cello, Chamber Music, Esbjerg Academy of Music, Denmark; Docent, Cello, Conducting, Jutland Academy of Music, Århus, Denmark; Initiator of the Cello Academy, a 12-part cello ensemble of young European musicians; mem, Honorary President and Founder of ESTA (Danish section), 1981; Danish Soloists' Union. *Compositions:* Canzona Per Dodici Violoncelli and numerous compositions for choir. *Recordings:* Frequent radio broadcasts as cellist and conductor in Germany and Denmark. *Publications:* Cello School, Wilhelm Hansen, 1964; Ed, Mogens Heimann String Quartet Studies, 1995. *Honours:* Much in demand throughout Europe and Latin America as Lecturer, Masterclass Teacher and Chamber music Animator. *Address:* Norsmindevej 170, 8340 Malling, Denmark. *Telephone:* 0045 86931585. *Fax:* 0045 86931555. *E-mail:* hed@os.dk.

DECOUST, Michel; Composer; b. 19 Nov. 1936, Paris, France; m. Irene Jarsky, 1969, 1 d. *Education:* Studied Paris Conservatory under Louis Fourestier, Olivier Messiaen, Darius Milhaud; Studies with Stockhausen and Pousseur, Cologne, 1964, 1965, conducting studies with Boulez, Basle, 1965. *Career:* Professor of Composition, Dartington College summer school, England, 1967–69; Set up regional French orchestra, Pays de la Loire, 1967–70; In charge of musical activities, Maisons de la Culture, Rennes and Nevers, 1970–72; Founder, Director, Pantin Conservatory, 1972–76; Head, Education Department IRCAM, 1976–79; Chief Inspector for Musical Research, Ministry of Culture and Communications, 1979–; His music performed at various festivals, Europe, Israel, New York, also broadcast on radio, Italy, Germany, Spain, England, Greece, Switzerland, Poland, USA; President, ISCM France. *Compositions:* Orchestral, small ensemble, wind band and vocal works; instrumental solos and duos, electro-acoustic music, etc; Si et Si Seulement, orchestra, 1972; L'application des Lectrices aux Champs, soprano and orchestra, 1977; Eole, flute quartet, 1985; Sept Chansons Erotiques, settings of poems for soprano and piano, 1986; Bleus, text Blaise Cendrars, soprano and piano, 1986; De la Gravitation Suspendue

des Memoires, orchestra, 1986; Je qui d'Autre, 3 voices and ensemble, 1987; Sinfonietta, 1983, for 10 instruments; Sonnet, 1985 for 15 instruments; One plus One Equals Four, Piano Percussion, 1988; Spectre for Wind Band, 1978; Interphone, Magnetic Tape; Les Galeries de Pierre, Alto Solo, 1984; Le Cygne, flute Solo, 1982; Lierre, 12 Cordes, 1986; Cafe-theatre, Chant-piano, 1985; Violin Concerto, 1990; Ligne for clarinet and string quartet, 1992; Cent Phrases pour Eventail for six voices and ensemble, 1996. *Recordings:* Releve d'Esquisse, Le Cygne, sinfonietta, Harmonia Mundi France, HMC 5152-HM57. *Publications:* Cahiers Perspectives, 1987. *Address:* 35 Rue de Clichy, 75009 Paris, France.

DECSENYI, Janos; Composer; b. 24 March 1927, Budapest, Hungary. *Education:* Studied composition with Rezsö Sugar, Budapest Conservatory, 1948–52; Endre Szervanszky, Budapest Academy of Music, 1952–56. *Career:* Hungarian Radio, Budapest, 1952–92, latterly as Head, Department of Serious Music and Director, Electronic Music Studio; Script Editor, Department of Serious Music, 1992–. *Compositions:* Stage includes: An Absurd Story, ballet, 1962; Orchestral: Divertimento for Harpsichord and Chamber Orchestra, 1959; Csontvary Pictures, 1967; Melodiae Hominis for Chamber Orchestra, 1969; Thoughts by Day, by Night, 1971; Commentaries on Marcus Aurelius for 16 Solo Strings, 1973; Double for Chamber Orchestra, 1974; Variations for Piano and Orchestra, 1976; Concerto Boemo, 1976; Concerto Grosso for Chamber Orchestra, 1978; Who Understands the Speech of Crickets?, for Chamber Orchestra and Tape, 1983; Cello Concerto, 1984; The Third One for 15 Solo Strings, 1985; I Symphony, 1986; II Symphony, 1993; Keepsake Album, audiovisual oratorio for soprano, bass, chamber choir, chamber ensemble, electronic and projected images, 1998; Vocal: Love for Soprano and Orchestra, 1957; Metamorfosi for Soprano and Piano, 1964; Shakespeare Monologues for Bass and Piano, 1968; The Plays of Thought, cantata for Soprano and Chamber Orchestra, 1972; Roads, etudes for Soprano and Piano, 1979; Twelfth Symphony of S.W. for Soprano and Percussion, 1980; 2 Symphonies, 1988, 1993; Keepsake Album, audio-visual oratorio, 1997; Chamber: String Trio, 1955; Sonatina Pastorale for Flute and Piano, 1962; String Quartet No 1 1978; String Quartet No 2 2003; Old Hungarian Texts, for Soprano, Bass and Chamber Ensemble, 1992; Frauengesänge, on German Poems, 1998; The Tiger, the Donkey and the Lemmings, 1998; Choral Music: Incidental music for theatre, films and radio; Electronic: Stones, 1987; Prospero's Island, 1989; Birds of the Cathedral, 1991; Book of Verses, five electro-acoustic sound poems. Pedagogical pieces;Farewell to a Far-Away Century — oratorio 2001; Des Dichters R M Rilke Begegnung mit dem Tod — Song Cycle 2001; From the Distance to the Nowadays — cantata to lines from the poems of E Ady 2003; Four Preludes to Saint-Exupéry, with choir 2003. *Recordings:* Several compositions recorded. *Honours:* Merited Artist, Hungary; Bart ók-Pásztory Prize, 1999. *Address:* Wesselenyi u.65, 1077 Budapest, Hungary.

DĚD, Jan; Composer; b. 22 June 1936, Plzeň, Czechoslovakia. *Education:* Plzeň Conservatory. *Career:* mem., Music Centre of West Bohemia, Plzeň, Czech Music Society, Prague. *Compositions:* Four songs on the words of folk poetry, chorus, op 1, 1962; Wistful Variations, small ballet for 5 dancers, 5 musicians and reciter, op 38; Short Czech Mass for combined chorus and symphonic orchestra, op 42; Sonatine for Solo Viola, op 43; Great Czech-Latin Mass to Our Lady for combined chorus, soloists, symphonic orchestra and organ, op 44, 1992; Concerto of a serenade in E flat for clarinet in B and piano, op 51, 1996; Christmas Songs for combined chorus and chamber orchestra, op 60, 2002. *Address:* Zelenohorská 2, 32600 Plzeň, Czech Republic. *E-mail:* j.ded@cbox.cz.

DEDEN, Otto; Composer, Conductor, Organist and Choirmaster; b. 19 Nov. 1925, Amsterdam, Netherlands; m. S.A.M van Dijk, 4 c. *Education:* Studied Composition with Henk Badings. *Career:* Appearances in Church Services on radio and television; Choral Concerts with various male, female and mixed choirs. *Compositions:* 29 Masses; 50 Motets; Te Deum; Hymns; Ballads; Oratorios; Arrangements of Folk Songs (commissions), Dirge, Soprano with Organ, 1993; 5 two ballads, 1992; Mysteria; Kain; 4 Cantatas for mixed choir and orchestra and solo; Magnificat for mixed choir, organ, flute and alto solo; Several Cantatas for choir and orchestra preludes and fugas for great organ; Requiem for a Killed Soldier. *Recordings:* Ballade v.d. Bezemsteel (male voices), Maastricht, 1958; Raamconcerto, 1973; Otto Deden Musica Collecta (collection of recent works). *Honours:* Royal Order of Knighthood of Oranje Nassau, 1982; Order of Knighthood of Gregorius Magnus, Vatican; Medal of Honour of the City of Dordrecht, Netherlands. *Address:* Polluxhof 16, 3318 BJ Dordrecht, Netherlands.

DEERING, Richard, FTCL, GTCL, LRAM, ARCM, PGCA; Concert Pianist; b. 15 July 1947, London, England; four c. *Education:* Trinity Coll. of Music. *Career:* debut Wigmore Hall, London 1973, piano recitals and broadcasts in over 90 countries 1975–; founder mem. of piano 40 (8 hands at 2 pianos); premières of several works, with many composers writing and dedicating works to Richard Deering; examiner world-wide for Trinity Coll. London 1979–; mem. Incorporated Soc. of Musicians, Adjudicators' Council of British and Int. Federation of Festivals (vice-chair. 2000–02). *Recordings:* Beatles Concerto with Tokyo Symphony Orchestra, English Piano Music, Mediterranean Inspired (Music of Charles Camilleri), Piano 40. *Publications:* ed. of Music Sales 'Composer' series and 'Century of Piano Music' series; contrib. to Classical Music magazine. *Honours:* Royal Philharmonic Soc. award for distinguished services to British Music 1981. *Address:* 55 Dalmally Road, Croydon, CR0 6LW, England (home). *Telephone:* (20) 8656-6222 (home). *Fax:* (20) 8655-1770 (home). *E-mail:* richard@malacca.demon.co.uk (home). *Website:* www .impulse-music.co.uk/deering.htm (office).

DEGRADA, Francesco; Musicologist, Professor, Writer and Music Editor; b. 23 May 1940, Milan, Italy. *Education:* Diploma, Piano, 1961, Composition Diploma, 1965, Conducting, Milan Conservatory; Arts Degree, University of Milan, 1964. *Career:* Teacher, Bolzano Conservatory, Brescia Conservatory; Lecturer, 1964–76, Professor of Music History, 1976–, Director of the Arts Department, 1983–, University of Milan; Teacher, Milan Conservatory, 1966–73; Founder-Director and Harpsichordist, Complesso Barocco di Milano, 1967–76; Consultant to the Publisher, G Ricordi, 1971–; Member, Editorial Boards of Critical Editions of Vivaldi, Pergolesi and Verdi; mem. Accademia Nazionale di Santa Cecilia, Roma; Academia Europaea, London. *Publications:* Al Gran Sole Carico d'Amore, Per Un Nuovo Teatro Musicale, 1974 2nd edition, 1977; Sylvano Bussotti e il Suo Teatro, 1976; Antonio Vivaldi da Venezia all'Europa, 1977; Il Palazzo Incantato, Studi Sulla Tradizione del Melodramma dal Barocco al Romanticismo, 2 vols, 1979; Vivaldi Veneziano Europeo, 1980; Illusione e disincanto. Mozart e altri percorsi settecenteschi, 2000; Edited Studi Pergolesiani/Pergolesi Studies, 4 vols, 1986, 1988, 1999, 2000; Andrea Gabrieli e il Suo Tempo, 1988. *Contributions:* Many articles in scholarly journals. *Address:* Via Gaudenzio Ferrari 3, 20123 Milan, Italy.

DEKANY, Bela; Violinist; b. 22 April 1928, Budapest, Hungary; m. Dorothy Browning, 22 June 1961, 1 s., 1 d. *Education:* Franz Liszt Academy, Budapest with Professor Weiner; Academy for Music, Vienna, Austria, with Professor E Morawec. *Career:* Debut: Budapest, 1947; Has given recitals and broadcast performances; soloist with orchestras in Hungary, Austria, Switzerland, Australia and the United Kingdom; Formed Dekany String Quartet, Netherlands, 1960–68; Leader, BBC Symphony Orchestra, London, England, 1969–92. *Recordings:* Haydn String Quartets with Dekany String Quartet. *Address:* 68 Woodside Avenue, London N6, England.

DEKLEVA, Igor; Slovenian academic and pianist; *Professor of Piano and Piano Duet, Academy of Music, Ljubljana;* b. 30 Dec. 1933, Ljubljana; m. Alenka Dekleva; two s. *Education:* Piano, Acad. of Music, Ljubljana; further studies in Siena, Salzburg, and Musical Acad., Munich; PhD in Music. *Career:* concerts, recitals, performances with orchestras in Slovenia and abroad, with repertoire including baroque, romantic and contemporary works; frequent appearances as piano duo with Alenka Dekleva, including first appearance at Opatija Tribune, 1967; several concert tours with violinist Michael Grube; directed masterclasses in piano in several countries; author, leader and performer, two television series about piano masterpieces throughout history, and Slovene piano works; Prof. of Piano and Piano Duet, Acad. of Music, Ljubljana 1998–; mem., Asscn of Musical Artists (vice-pres.), Kiwanis Int., European Piano Teachers' Asscn of Slovenia (pres.), numerous hon. memberships and fellowships. *Compositions:* many works for piano, chamber orchestra and choirs. *Recordings:* some 30 albums. *Publications:* Slovene National Piano School (eight vols). *Honours:* Dr hc (World Univ. Arizona) 1987; Betetto Prize 1980; Fellowship for Distinguished Service to Music, Madras Philharmonic and Choral Soc. 1984, Grand Ambassador of International Achievement 1990, Award of Excellence, Lisbon 2001, Capital City of Ljubljana Award 2004. *Address:* Hruševo 77, 1356, Dobrova, Slovenia. *Telephone:* (1) 3649075 (home). *Fax:* (1) 2427320 (office); (1) 3649075 (home).

DEL BIANCO, Tito; singer (dramatic tenor); b. 3 July 1932, Trieste, Italy; one s. one d. *Education:* studied with Augusta Rapetti Bassi in Trieste, with Renata Cotogni in Rome. *Career:* debut, New York, USA in Stabat Mater by Rossini, director Thomas Schippers, 1965; in Italy as Otello by Verdi, 8th Festival of Two Worlds, Spoleto, 1965; Title role of Otello, Teatro Regio Parma, 1966–71; Bayerische Staatsoper Munchen, 1973; May Festival Wiesbaden, 1970; Festival Szeged, Hungary, 1971; Festival Varna Bulgaria, 1972; Maggio Musicale Florence, 1980; Sang Calaf in Turandot at Naples, 1965, Bologna, 1969, Parma Regio, 1970; Pollione in Norma, Genoa, 1967; Faone in Pacini's Saffo, Naples, 1967; Radames in Aida at Naples, 1968; Ismaele in Nabucco, Trieste, 1969; Canio in Pagliacci, Parma Regio, 1969; Festival Torre del Lago Puccini, 1971; Director of Studies Centre A Rapetti Bassi, Trieste; Professor of Music Academy, Conservatorio in Trieste; Director of Studies Centre Augusta Rapetti Bassi. *Recordings include:* Rossini's Stabat Mater; Pacini's Saffo; Tito Del Bianco: Opera Arias, 2000. *Publications:* A

Festival for Giuseppe Verdi in Prima Pagina, Parma, Italy, 1981; La Voce Cantata: Tecnica Vocale ed Espressione dell' Anima, 1981; Il Canto e la Psiche, 1990; L'Approccio al canto come Terapia, 1991; Il Festival Verdiano a Parma, 1999; La Forza del Destino e Altre Storie, 1999; Verdi e i Segni dei Tempi, 2000; contrib. to La Scuola di Canto di Augusta Rapetti Bassi, 1988; L'Espressione del Canto Nella Lezione di Reynaldo Hahn, 1993; La Parabola di Tristan und Isolde, 1993; Misticismo in Musica: Bruckner, Schoenberg e Brahms, 1994; Lo Strumento voce: Aspetti, Didattici e docimologici, in Capriccio di Strauss, 1996. *Honours:* Gold Medal, Giuseppe Verdi Prize, Parma, 1967; Commendatore of the Italian Republic, 1998; Medal, City of Trieste, 2003. *Address:* c/o Centro Studi A. Rapetti Bassi, CP 2159-TS11, 34123 Trieste, Italy. *E-mail:* csarbeit@libero.it.

DEL CARLO, John; Singer (Bass-baritone); b. 21 Sept. 1951, USA. *Career:* Sang in The Love for Three Oranges at San Diego (1978) and appeared with Western Spring Opera, 1980–81; European career from 1980, in Donizetti's Olivo e Pasquale at Barga; member of the Cologne Opera from 1987, and Rossini's Cambiale di Matrimonio at the 1987 Schwetzingen Festival; San Francisco Opera from 1982, as Alidoro in Cenerentola and Wagner's Kothner; Sang Donner and Gunther in Ring cycles for Seattle Opera, 1984–92; Other roles include the Wanderer in Siegfried (Cologne, 1990), Mustafà, Don Alfonso, Dulcamara and Simon Boccanegra; Sang Dulcamara at Santiago, 1996; Sang Baron di Kelbar in Verdi's Un Giorno di Regno at the Festival Hall, London for the Royal Opera, 1999; Sang Rossini's Bartolo at Chicago, 2001. *Recordings include:* La Gioconda (Decca), La Cenerentola (Philips) and La Cambiale di Matrimonio (Warner video). *Address:* c/o Seattle Opera Association, PO Box 9248, Seattle, WA 98109, USA.

DEL MAR, Jonathan (Rene); Conductor and Musicologist; b. 7 Jan. 1951, London, England. m. Annabel Teh Gallop, 5 Sept 1992, two s. *Education:* MA, Music, Christ Church, Oxford, 1969–72; ARCM Diploma, Royal College of Music, 1976; Teatro La Fenice, Venice, 1976–77; Accademia S. Cecilia, Rome, 1977. *Career:* Debut: London Symphony Orchestra, Barbican, 1984; Conductor, performed with many British orchestras also throughout Europe; mem Dvořák Society. *Publications:* Indicatore Anagrafico di Venezia, 1996; New Bärenreiter Urtext Edition of Beethoven Symphonies 1–9, 1996–2000; Beethoven Cello Sonatas, 2004. *Contributions:* Tempo; BBC Music Magazine; Beethoven Journal; Das Orchester; Beethoven Forum; Early Music. *Honours:* Prize, Imperial Tobacco International Conductors' Award, 1978; Prize, Nikolai Malko Competition, 1980; Prize, First Leeds Conductors' Competition, 1984. *Address:* Oakwood, Crescent Lane, London SW4, England. *Telephone:* (20) 7622-2000. *Fax:* (20) 7622-2000.

DEL MONACO, Giancarlo; Stage Director; b. 27 Dec. 1943, Treviso, Italy. *Education:* Studied music and languages at Lausanne. *Career:* Debut: Siracusa, 1964, Samson and Delilah; Assistant to Gunther Rennert, Wieland Wagner and Walter Felsenstein at Stuttgart, 1965–68; Personal assistant of the General Director Vienna Staatsoper, 1968–70; Principal Stage Director at Ulm, 1970–73; Intendant at Kassel, 1980–82; Director, Macerata Festival, 1986–88; Staged Les Huguenots at Montpellier, 1990, and at Barcelona, Roberto Devereux, the first of a projected trilogy of Donizetti's Tudor Operas; L'Elisir d'amore at Helsinki, 1991, followed by Metropolitan Opera debut with La Fanciulla del West; Intendant and Principal Producer at Bonn, 1992–97; Further guest engagements at Bayerische Staatsoper, Zürich Opera and Vienna Staatsoper; Staged Montemezzi's L'Amore dei tre re at Kassel, 1992 and Otello at Reggio Emilia; Staged at the Metropolitan Madama Butterfly and Simon Boccanegra, 1994–95; La Forza del Destino, 1995–96; Verdi's Stiffelio, 1997. *Honours:* Bundesverdienstkreuz, 1st Class, 1987; Cavaliere Ufficiale della Repubblica, 1987; Commendatore Dell' Ordine al Merito della Repubblica Italiana, 1993; Chevalier des arts et lettres, France, 1995; Cruzeiro del Sul, Brazil, 1995. *Current Management:* Zemsky/Green Division, Columbia Artists Management inc, 165 West 57th Street, New York, NY 10019, USA. *Address:* c/o Oper der Stadt Bonn, Am Boselagerhof 1, 53111 Bonn, Germany.

DEL POZO, Rodrigo; Singer (Tenor); b. 1969, Chile. *Education:* Studied lute, guitar and singing; Scholarship to study with Jacob Lindberg, 1992; Continuation of studies with Nigel Rogers and David Mason. *Career:* Sang with most leading groups specialising in Baroque repertoire, including St James' Baroque Players, BBC Proms, 1996; Concerto Palatino, Bruges; Sang with The King's Consort in Purcell and Blow Anthems and Odes, Bratislava Cantans Festival; Purcell with Tafelmusik, Toronto; Sang with Orchestra of the Age of Enlightenment, English Bach Festival Orchestra; Ensemble Baroque de Limoges; Performed and recorded Mondonville Motets and Draghi, Mondonville Festival, Versailles; Performed Rameau's Anacréon with Les Musiciens du Louvre, Cité de la Musique; Sang Monteverdi Madrigals, BBC Proms, Royal Albert Hall, and on tour in USA; Performed with the Harp Consort, Wigmore Hall; Baroque opera performances have included Oslo Sommeropera and Boston Early Music Festival with Andrew

Parrott; Pastore I, in Monteverdi's L'Orfeo, Beaune Festival and the Festtage Alter Musik, Stuttgart, with Tragicomedia and Stephen Stubbs; Arcetro, in Peri's Euridice, Drottningholm Theatre and the London Lufthansa Baroque Festival with Combattimento; Solo roles in Indian Queen with the King's Consort, Schwetzinger Festspiele; Concerts and recordings in France, Germany, Austria, Portugal, Netherlands, Spain and Belgium with the Gabrieli Consort; The King's Consort, BBC Prom; The Harp Consort, Teatro Lirico; Tragicomedia, Le Parlement de Musique; L'Ensemble Baroque de Limoges, Versailles and on tour in France; Performed, Purcell Odes, Les Arts Florissants, 1999; Tour with King Arthur, Gabrieli Consort and the King's Consort. *Recordings:* Many recordings for leading recording companies as well as for BBC Radio 3 and television and radio stations in America and Europe; Live recital for BBC Radio 3. *Address:* 11 Sunnymead, Hernes Road, Oxford OX2 7PX, England.

DEL TREDICI, David (Walter); Composer and Teacher; b. 16 March 1937, Cloverdale, California, USA. *Education:* Studied Piano as a youth; Took courses in composition with Seymour Shifrin, Andrew Imbrie and Arnold Elston, University of California, Berkeley, BA, 1959, and with Earl Kim and Roger Sessions, Princeton University, MFA, 1963. *Career:* Debut as Piano Soloist with the San Francisco Symphony Orchestra at age 16; Pianist, Aspen (Colorado) Music Festival, 1958, Berkshire Music Center, Tanglewood, 1964, 1965; Composer-in-Residence, Marlboro (Vermont) Music Festival, 1966, 1967; Teacher, Harvard University, 1966–72; State University of New York at Buffalo, 1973, Boston University, 1973–84, City College and Graduate School of the City University of New York, 1984–; Composer-in-Residence, New York Philharmonic Orchestra, 1988–; Professor, the Juilliard School, 1993–96; Professor, Yale University, 1999. *Compositions:* String Trio, 1959; I Hear an Army for soprano and string quartet, after James Joyce, 1963–64; Night Conjure-Verse, after James Joyce, 1965; Syzygy for soprano, horn and chamber ensemble, after James Joyce, 1966; The Last Gospel for soprano, chorus, rock group and orchestra, 1967, revised 1984; Pop-Pourri for amplified soprano, mezzo-soprano ad libitum, chorus, rock group and orchestra, 1968, revised 1973; An Alice Symphony, after Lewis Carroll, 1969–75; Adventures Underground, after Lewis Carroll, 1971, revised 1977; Vintage Alice: Fantascence on A Mad Tea Party for amplified soprano, folk group, and orchestra, after Lewis Carroll, 1972; Final Alice for amplified soprano and orchestra, after Lewis Carroll, 1977–81; March to Tonality for orchestra, 1983–85; Haddock's Eyes for soprano and chamber ensemble, 1985–86; Ballad in Yellow, for piano. 1997; Dracula, for soprano and ensemble, 1998–99; Gay Life for voice and orchestra, 2000. *Recordings:* Various Compositions recorded. *Address:* c/o Fine Arts Management Inc, 75 Lafayette Avenue, Brooklyn, NY 11217, USA.

DEL VIVO, Graziano; Singer (Bass); b. 1 Nov. 1937, Florence, Italy. *Education:* Studied at Florence University and Conservatory. *Career:* Debut: Spoleto, 1961, as Ramphis in Aida; Teatro Regio Parma, as Onofrio in Galuppi's I tre amanti ridicoli, 1964, and as Achillas in Handel's Giulio Cesare and Sparafucile in Rigoletto; Florence, 1965, in Billy Budd and Katerina Izmailova, returning in Robert le Diable by Meyerbeer, 1968, and Spontini's La Vestale, 1970; La Scala Milan as Pluto in Casella's Orfeo; Edinburgh Festival, 1969 and 1972; Sang in The Nose by Shostakovich at Rome and at Genoa and Naples in the Verdi Requiem; Pisa, 1973, in a centenary concert for Titta Ruffo.

DELACOTE, Jacques; Conductor; b. 16 Aug. 1942, Remiremont, France; m. Maria Lucia Alvarez Machado. *Education:* Paris Conservatory; Studied with Hans Swarowsky, Vienna Academy of Music; Assistant to Darius Milhaud and Leonard Bernstein. *Career:* Debut: New York Philharmonic Orchestra; Guest conductor with the Cleveland Orchestra, San Francisco Symphony, Orchestre de Paris, Orchestre National de France, Scottish National Orchestra, Berlin Radio Symphony Orchestra, Bavarian Radio Orchestra, Cologne Radio Symphony Orchestra, Südfunk Stuttgart; Vienna Philharmonic Orchestra; Vienna Symphony Orchestra; BBC London, London Philharmonic, Vienna State Opera; London debut with the London Symphony Orchestra 1973, Mahler's Third Symphony; Théâtre Musical de Paris with Massenet's Cendrillon (1981) and Verdi's Ernani (1982); Conducted the Royal Opera in Otello at the Albert Hall, 1998; Royal Opera House, Covent Garden London, including Far East tour to South Korea and Japan, Paris Opéra, Hamburg State Opera; Deutsche Oper Berlin; National Orchestra of Belgium, Scottish Chamber Orchestra, English Chamber Orchestra, Yomiuri Nippon Symphony Orchestra, Danish Royal Orchestra, Copenhagen, Tokyo Philharmonic Orchestra, Bavarian State Opera, Munich, Pittsburgh Opera, Chicago Lyric Opera; Israel Philharmonic Orchestra, Teatro Liceo, Barcelona, Teatro Real, Madrid, Teatro Colón, Buenos Aires, Théâtre de La Monnaie, Brussels, Opera House, Zürich, Scottish Opera, Glasgow, Welsh National Opera, Cardiff, English National Opera, Coliseum and La Fenice, Venice; Festivals at Flandres, Macerata, Blossom; Klangbogen in Vienna; Festival of Inverness; Wiesbadner Festspiele, Dresdener Festspiele,

Pablo Casals Festival, 1999. *Recordings:* With Royal Philharmonic, Royal Opera House, Covent Garden Orchestra, Bavarian Radio Orchestra, London Philharmonic; Carmen and Traviata, Royal Opera House, London; Samson et Dalila, Hérodiade, Roméo et Juliette, Teatro Liceo, Barcelona; Turandot and Carmen, Royal Opera House, London, video. *Honours:* Gold Medal and 1st Prize, Dimitri Mitropoulos Competition, New York, 1971.

DELAMBOYE, Hubert; Singer (Tenor); b. 1945, Valkenburg, Netherlands. *Career:* Sang in opera at Bielefeld and Wiesbaden, 1974–76; Cologne Opera from 1979; Seattle, Paris and Metropolitan, New York, 1986–88, as Mimi in The Ring; Wiesbaden from 1991 in Katya Kabanova and as Wagner's Loge, Siegmund, Siegfried and Tristan; Salzburg Festival, 1993 as Mozart's Lucio Silla; Frankfurt from 1994 as Cornelius's Nureddin, Loge and Samson; Brussels 1995 as Herod in Salome; Other roles include Verdi's Otello; Season 1997–98 as Paul in Die Tote Stadt at Wiesbaden, Florestan at the Théâtre des Champs-Elysées, Paris and Tichon in Katya Kabanova at Salzburg; Season 2000–01 as Tristan for Reisopera, Netherlands, Lancelot in Le Roi Arthus by Chausson at Edinburgh (concert), in Schoenberg's Die Jakobsleiter at the Vienna Staatsoper and as Tannhäuser at Wiesbaden; Concert and broadcast engagements. *Address:* c/o Hepsisches Staatstheater, Christian Zais Strasse 33-5, 6200 Wiesbaden, Germany.

DELDEN, Lex (Alex) Van; Actor and Singer (tenor); b. 21 June 1947, Amsterdam, Netherlands; s. of composer Lex van Delden and actress Jetty van Dijk. *Education:* Drama School, Amsterdam, 1966–67; Private singing lessons with Jan Keizer, Marianne Blok and Andrew Field. *Career:* Debut: 1967; Opera: Gianni Schicchi (G Puccini); Turandot (F Busoni); Die Fledermaus (Johann Strauss); Il Ritorno d'Ulisse (Claudio Monteverdi); Ariadne auf Naxos (Richard Strauss); and others; also extensive stage, film and TV work. *Compositions include:* Active as composer for theatre: Romeo and Juliet (W Shakespeare); Dance of Death (A Strindberg); The Spanish Brabantine (Bredero). *E-mail:* lexvandelden@onetel.net.uk.

DELGADO, Alexandre; Portuguese violist and composer; b. 8 June 1965, Lisbon. *Education:* Fundação Musical dos Amigos das Crianças, Lisbon, Conservatório de Música, Lisbon and Nice Conservatoire. *Career:* conductor, Fundação Musical dos Amigos das Crianças string orchestra 1981–86; mem., European Community Youth Orchestra 1988–99; musical asst, Rádio de Portugal 1989–91; mem., Gulbenkian Orchestra 1991–95; founder mem., Lacerda String Quartet; guest composer, Maastricht Festival 2001. *Compositions include:* Prelúdio 1982, Turbilhão 1987, Flute Concerto 1988, Antagonia 1990, String quartet 1991, Langará 1992, O doido e a morte (chamber opera) 1994, Tresvariacões 1999, Viola Concerto 2000. *Recordings include:* recital with Bruno Belthoise, Arditti String Quartet. *Publications:* Luis de Freitas Branco e o 1º modernismo português 1990, A Sinfonia em Portugal. *Honours:* Young Musicians Award, Lisbon 1987, João de Freitas Branco Award 1992. *Address:* Av. Luís Bivar 38, 5º esq., 1050-145 Lisbon, Portugal. *Telephone:* 213 571 711. *E-mail:* alexandre.delgado@mail.telepac.pt.

DELLA CASA, Lisa; Singer (Soprano); b. 2 Feb. 1919, Burgdorf, Switzerland; m. Dragan Debeljevic. *Education:* Studied with Margarete Haeser in Zürich. Debut; Solothun-Biel, 1941, as Madama Butterfly. *Career:* City Theatre, Zürich, 1943–50, as Pamina, Gilda and Serena in Porgy and Bess, and in the premiere of Willy Burkhard's Die schwarze Spinne; Joined Vienna Staatsoper, 1947; Salzburg Festival from 1947, as Zdenka in Arabella, the Countess in Capriccio, Mozart's Donna Elvira, Countess and Pamina, Ariadne, Chrysothemis, Octavian, the Marschallin and in the premiere of Von Einem's Der Prozess, 1953; Glyndebourne Festival, 1951, as the Countess in Le nozze di Figaro; Bayreuth, 1952, as Eva in Die Meistersinger; Covent Garden and La Scala Milan from 1953; Metropolitan Opera, 1953–68, as Mozart's Countess, Donna Elvira, Arabella, Eva, the Marschallin and Octavian (155 performances); Sang Arabella in a new production of Strauss's opera at Covent Garden, 1965; Guest appearances at Paris, Chicago, Buenos Aires, Munich and Rome; Retired, 1974. *Recordings:* Le nozze di Figaro; Don Giovanni; Così fan tutte; Arabella; Orfeo ed Euridice; La Vie Parisienne. *Honours:* Ehrenmitglied at the Vienna Staatsoper, 1985. *Address:* c/o Staatsoper, Opernring 2, 1010 Vienna, Austria.

DELLER, Mark Damian; singer (counter-tenor); b. 27 Sept. 1938, St Leonards-on-Sea, England; m. Sheelagh Elizabeth Benson; three s. *Education:* chorister at Canterbury Cathedral, choral scholar at St John's College, Cambridge. *Career:* Lay Vicar, Salisbury Cathedral, 1960–68; founder and Director, Guildhall Winter Concerts, 1962; Artistic Director, first festival of the arts, Salisbury, 1967; Vicar-Choral, St Paul's Cathedral, 1969–73; Choral Conductor; began recording with father Alfred Deller, 1962; joined Deller Consort in early 1960s; has toured extensively in Europe, USA, Canada and South America, as member of Deller Consort and as a solo singer; Director, Deller Consort, 1979–; Director, Stour Music, 1976–, Canterbury Festival, 1988–2003. *Recordings:* as member of Deller Consort, the Vanguard, Argo and

Nonesuch labels; Purcell's The Fairy Queen, King Arthur and The Indian Queen (Harmonia Mundi). *Honours:* Hon. DMus (Univ. of Kent) 1995. *Address:* 2 Rural Terrace, Wye, Ashford, Kent, England.

DELLO JOIO, Justin, BM, MM, DMA; American composer; *Faculty Composer-in-Residence, New York University;* b. 18 Oct. 1960, New York, NY; s. of Norman and Grayce Dello Joio; one d. *Education:* Juilliard School of Music, New York. *Career:* Prof. of Composition, New York University, currently Faculty Composer-in-Residence; works performed by Detroit Symphony Orchestra, Juilliard Orchestra with Sixten Ehrling, members of the Mendelssohn String Quartet, and Primavera String Quartet; Piano Sonata premiered in National Gallery of Arts, Washington, District of Columbia (also broadcast); Collaborated with American novelist John Gardner on opera The Holy Sinner. *Compositions:* Works for orchestra, chamber orchestra, string quartet, vocal music and solo piano. *Recordings:* String Quartet No. 1, Primavera String Quartet, Music of Justin Dello Joio (Horacio Gutierrez, piano). *Publications:* Sonata for Piano, 1986; Musica Humana, Symphonic Poem for Orchestra, Two Concert Etudes, Music for Piano Trio. *Honours:* Charles Ives Scholarship, National Institute and American Academy of the Arts; Grants: New York State Council on the Arts, 1983; National Endowment for the Arts, 1985; New York Foundation for the Arts, 1986; J. Guggenheim Fellowship. *Address:* c/o ASCAP, ASCAP House, 1 Lincoln Plaza, New York, NY 10023; 400 E 89th Street, New York, NY 10128, USA (home). *Telephone:* (212) 427-8182. *Fax:* (212) 427-8182. *E-mail:* jnd1@nyu.edu.

DELOGU, Gaetano; Italian conductor; b. 14 April 1934, Messina. *Education:* Studied music, University of Catania; Law degree, 1958; Studied conducting with Franco Ferrara, Rome and Venice. *Career:* Guest Conductor, Italian Radio, Rome, Milan, Turin and Naples, London Symphony Orchestra, BBC Orchestra, Royal Opera Covent Garden, Orchestre National de France, Japan Philharmonic, Czech Philharmonic; New York Philharmonic Orchestra and National Symphony Orchestra, Washington DC, USA, 1968–69; Conductor, Teatro Massimo, Palermo, Italy, 1975–78; Music Dir and Conductor, Denver Symphony, USA 1978–87, Prague Symphony Orchestra 1995–2000, apptd Hon. Dir 2000. *Recordings include:* Bruckner's Seventh Symphony, Schubert's Great C Major Symphony, Orff's Carmina Burana, Haydn's Symphonies Nos 83 and 101; Mahler's 1st Symphony; Hindemith's Symphonic Metamorphoses and Nobilissima Visione, Smetana's Ma Vlast 2001. *Honours:* 1st Prize, Young Conductors' Competition, Florence, 1964; Dimitri Mitropoulos Competition, New York, 1968. *Current Management:* Connaught Artists Management Ltd, 2 Molasses Row, Plantation Wharf, London, SW11 3UX, England. *Telephone:* (20) 7738 0017. *Fax:* (20) 7738 0909. *E-mail:* classicalmusic@connaughtartists.com. *Website:* www.connaughtartists .com.

DELUNSCH, Mireille; Singer (Soprano); b. 1962, Mulhouse, France. *Education:* Studied with Evelyn Brunner, Strasbourg Conservatoire. *Career:* Sang at Opera du Rhin and in Schoenberg's Moses und Aron, Théâtre du Châtelet, Paris; Pamina at Lyon and Mimi at Bordeaux; Rameau's Hippolyte et Aricie, Palais Garnier; Gluck's Armide, Nice, Amsterdam and Paris; Season 1998 with Gluck's Eurydice at Bordeaux and Venus in Rameau's Dardanus at Lyons; Season 1999–2000 as La Folie in Rameau's Platée, at Antwerp, and Poppea at Aix and Vienna (Theater an der Wien). *Recordings:* French Cantatas; Lully's Acis et Galatée; Gluck's Armide and Iphigénie en Aulide, under Marc Minkowski. *Address:* c/o Opéra de Lyon, 1 Place de la Comedie, 69001 Lyon, France.

DELVAUX, Albert; Director and Music Professor; b. 31 May 1913, Louvain, Belgium; m. Fernande Tassignon, 4 April 1945, 2 s., 1 d. *Education:* Royal Conservatory, Liège (Diploma of Virtuosity on Violoncello); Higher Diploma, Chamber Music; 1st Prize, Harmony, Counterpoint and Fugue and History of Music. *Career:* Head, Counterpoint, Royal Conservtory, Liège, 1945; Professor, Conservatory of Louvain and Tirlemont Academy until 1945; Honorary Director, St Nicolas Academy, 1945–78; Honorary Professor, Brussels Royal Conservatory until 1978. *Compositions include:* Symphony orchestra: Scherzo; Poème; Symphonique Suite; Variations; Miniatures; Sinfonia II; Sinfonia Burlesca I; Mouvement Symphonique; Sinfonie III; Concerto I and II for violin; Sinfonia IV; Capriccio for orchestra; Chamber orchestra: Esquisses; Concerto da Camera I and II; 5 Bagatelles; Introduttione e allegro; Sinfonia Concertante for violin and alto; Concerto for violin and violoncello; Concerto I and II for violoncello; Prelude for flute; Concerto for viola. *Recordings:* Sinfonia Burlesca; Esquisses; Trio No. 2; Sonata a quattro; Concerto for oboe, clarinet, bassoon and flute. *Honours:* 1st Prize Queen Elizabeth Symphonisch Music; 3rd Prize, Queen Elizabeth Chamber Music. *Address:* Kwadeplas 3, 9180 Belsele, Belgium.

DEMARINIS, Paul; Composer; b. 8 Oct. 1949, Cleveland, Ohio, USA. *Education:* Studied at Antioch College, Ohio, and with Robert Ashley at

Mills College, Oakland. *Career:* Taught composition and computer at Mills College, 1973–78; Wesleyan University, 1979–81, San Francisco State University, 1987–89; Collaborations as a performer with Robert Ashley and David Tudor in New York and Paris and at New Music America Concerts, 1980–85; Computer audio-graphic systems installed at Museum of Contemporary Art, Chicago and the Wadsworth Atheneum; Audio installations at the Exploratorium San Francisco and the Children's Museum, Boston. *Compositions:* Computer-processed speech works Kokole, 1985, and I Want You, 1986; Installations Pygmy Gamelin, Paris, New York and Los Angeles, 1976–80; Music Room, Faultless Jamming, San Francisco and Boston, 1982–; Laser Disk, Eindhoven, Netherlands, 1989. *Address:* c/o San Francisco State University, Music Department, 1600 Holloway Avenue, San Francisco, CA 94132, USA.

DEMBSKI, Stephen (Michael); Composer and Professor; b. 13 Dec. 1949, Boston, Massachusetts, USA. *Education:* Diploma, Phillips Academy, Andover, 1967; Clifton College, Bristol, England, 1967–68; Ecole Normale de Musique, Paris, 1971; BA, Antioch College, 1973; MA, State University of New York, Stony Brook, 1975; MFA, 1977, PhD, 1980, Princeton University. *Career:* Professor, Director of Advanced Composition Programme, School of Music, University of Wisconsin, Madison; Music presented by: UNESCO, Denmark, 1978; 5th International Festival of Electronic-Acoustic Music, Bourges, France, 1976; International Society for Contemporary Music, Bonn, 1976; New York New Music Ensemble; American Composers' Orchestra; Huddersfield Festival, England; Alan Feinberg; Ursula Oppens; Fred Sherry; Robert Black; Christopher Kendall, Jonathan Faralli, Mauro Castellano, Daniel Druckman, Bert Turetsky, Gregory D'Agostino. *Compositions:* Recorded: Pterodactyl for piano, 1974; Tender Buttons for piano, 1977; Trio, 1977; Digit for clarinet and computer synthesized tape, 1978; Stacked Deck for large chamber ensemble, 1979; Alba for chamber ensemble, 1980; Alta for piano, 1981; Spectra for orchestra, 1985; Sonata for violin and piano; Of Mere Being for soprano and large orchestra; Sonotropism, for saxophone, piano, electric guitar, 1996; Recorded as conductor: 48 Motives by Scott Fields. Published: Sunwood for guitar, 1976; Sonata for violin and piano, 1987–88; The Show, 1986; Fantasy for solo flute, 1988; On Ondine for piano, 1991–2000; Three Scenes from Elsaveta, opera, 1992; Memory's Minefield, 1994; At Baia, 1994; Out of my System, 1995; For Five, 1996; Brass Attacks, 1997; Le Monde Merengue, 1998; Another Day, 2001; Only Yesterday, 2002; Contemplations, 2002; Pied Beauty, 2002; Respite from the Roast, 2002. *Publications:* International Musical Lexicon, 1980; Milton Babbitt–Words About Music (with Joseph N Straus), 1987. *Address:* 96 Perry Street B-22, New York, NY 10014, USA.

DEMETEROVA, Gabriela; Violinist; b. 17 May 1971, Prague, Czechoslovakia. *Education:* Prague Conservatory, The Academy of Music in Prague. *Career:* Debut: In Prague, concert in the 100th season the Czech Philharmonic Orchestra; Czech Radio, interviews, solo performances; Solo concerts in the Czech Republic, England, France, USA, Netherlands, Germany, Austria; Various television and video recordings; mem, Friends of the Prague Spring Festival. *Recordings:* The Old Czech Masters, HIF Biber, Mystery Sonatas I and II, Violin recital–Mozart, Beethoven, Brahms. *Publications:* The Strad, The Yehudi Menuhin, violin competition, 1993. *Contributions:* All major Czech magazines and journals. *Honours:* All major prizes, J Kocian Violin Competition, 1980–90; Prague Spring Violin Competition, 1992; All major prizes, Yehudi Menuhin International Violin Competition, 1993. *Current Management:* Ars/Koncert Brno, Uvoz 39, 602 00 Brno, Czech Republic. *Address:* Bilkova 21, Prague 1, 110 00 Czech Republic.

DEMIDENKO, Nikolai; Concert Pianist; b. 1 July 1955, Anisimova, Russia; m. (1), 1 s., (2) Julya Dougyallo, 15 Aug 1994. *Education:* Studied at Moscow Conservatoire with Dmitri Bashkirov. *Career:* Debut: British debut with Moscow Radio Symphony Orchestra, 1985; Has performed in Russia and abroad in concert and recital from 1976; Frequent tours of Japan and concerts with Bolshoi Symphony, Polish National Radio Orchestra, London Philharmonic, BBC Philharmonic and BBC Scottish Symphony, London Proms debut 1992 with Rachmaninov's 4th Concerto; Resident in the United Kingdom from 1990, teacher at Yehudi Menuhin School; Season, 1992–93 in concerts with the St Petersburg Philharmonic and the Philharmonia Orchestra; Recitals in Paris, Milan and the Concertgebouw, Amsterdam; Two-Piano recital with Dmitri Alexeev at Wigmore Hall, March 1993, to mark the 50th Anniversary of Rachmaninov's death; Six Piano Masterworks solo recitals at Wigmore Hall, January to June 1993 recreating concerts given by Alkan and Rubinstein in the 19th Century: The Classicists, The Age of Beethoven, The Early Romantics, The High Romantics, The Baroque Revival and Legacies and Prophecies, Liszt, Berg, Gubaidulina and Messiaen; Returned to London for German Romantic concerts, 1997. *Recordings:* Albums of Bach-Busoni, Chopin and Liszt; Medtner 2nd and 3rd Concertos with BBC Scottish Symphony Orchestra, Medtner and Chopin Concertos with Philharmonia; Live recordings at Wigmore Hall Masterworks series. *Honours:* Medallist, 1976 Concours International de Montreal and 1978 Tchaikovsky International Competition, Moscow. *Address:* c/o Georgina Ivor Associates, 28 Old Devonshire Road, London SW12 9RB, England.

DEMITZ, Hans-Jürgen; Singer (Baritone); b. 1946, Hanover, Germany. *Career:* Sang in opera throughout North Germany from 1976; Hanover, 1983, as Wagner's Dutchman and Marschner's Hans Heiling; Bayreuth, 1983, as Donner; Season 1985 with the premieres of Boehmer's Dr Faustus in Paris and Sutermeister's Le Roi Berenger in Geneva; Spoleto Festival, 1987, as Amfortas, Cerha's Der Rattenfänger at the Vienna Staatsoper; Other roles include as Wagner's Kurwenal at Trieste and Gunther at Lisbon. *Recordings include:* Zemlinsky's Florentinische Tragödie. *Address:* c/o Staatsoper, Opernring 2, 1010 Vienna, Austria.

DEMPSEY, Gregory; Singer (Tenor); b. 20 July 1931, Melbourne, Victoria, Australia. *Education:* Studied in Australia with Mavis Kruger and Annie and Heini Portnoj. *Career:* Debut: National Opera of Victoria, 1954, as Don Ottavio; Sang with Sadler's Wells/English National Opera from 1962, notably as Wagner's Mime and David, Don José, Peter Grimes, Tom Rakewell, and in the premiere of Bennett's The Mines of Sulphur (1965); Sang in the first local productions of Janáček's The Makropulos Case (1966) and The Excursions of Mr Brouček (1979); Other roles include the Drum Major in Wozzeck, Dionysius in The Bassarids by Henze (British stage premiere), Aeneas in Les Troyens and the Shepherd in Szymanowski's King Roger (New Opera Company); US debut, San Francisco, 1966, in The Makropulos Case; Aldeburgh Festival, 1967, in the premiere of Musgrave's The Decision; Covent Garden debut, 1972, as Laca in Jenůfa; Sang Bob Boles in Peter Grimes, Sydney, 1986; Prince Populescu in Countess Maritza at Melbourne, 1986. *Recordings include:* Billy Budd; The Ring of the Nibelung, conducted by Reginald Goodall.

DEMPSTER, Stuart (Ross); Trombonist, Professor and Composer; b. 7 July 1936, Berkeley, California, USA; m. Renko Ishida, 19 Dec 1964, 2 s. *Education:* BA, Performance, 1958, MA, Composition, 1967, San Francisco State College; Private Trombone lessons with AB Moore, Orlando Giosi and John Klock. *Career:* Principal Trombonist, Oakland Symphony Orchestra, California, 1962–66; Member, Performing Group, Mills College, 1963–66; Tours as Soloist, 1962–; Teacher, San Francisco Conservatory of Music, 1961–66; California State College, Hayward, 1963–66; Assistant Professor 1968–78, Associate Professor 1978–85, Professor 1985–98, Emeritus Professor, 1998–, University of Washington, Seattle; Masterclasses, International Trombone Workshop, 1974–. *Compositions:* Sonata for bass trombone and piano, 1961; Adagio and Canonic Variations for brass quintet, 1962; Chamber Music 13 for voice and trombones, 1964; The Road Not Taken for Voice, chorus and orchestra, 1967; Ten Grand Hosery, Mixed Media Ballet, 1971–72; Pipedream, Mixed Media Piece, 1972; Life Begins at 40, Concert Series and Musical Gallery Show, 1976; Standing Waves for trombone, 1976; Didjeridervish for didjeridu, 1976; Monty for trombone, 1979; Fog Calling for trombone and didjeridu, 1981; Harmonic Tremors for trombone and tape, 1982; Hornfinder for trombone and audience, 1982; Roulette for trombone and audience, 1983; Aix en Providence for trombones, 1983; JDBBBDJ for didjeridu and audience, 1983; Don't Worry, It Will Come for garden hoses and audience, 1983; Sound Massage Parlor for didjeridu, garden hoses, shell and audience, 1986; SWAMI (State of Washington as a Musical Instrument), an Acoustic Guide to the State of Washington for the State's Centennial, 1987–89; Milanda Embracing for unspecified mixed ensemble, 1993–94; Underground Overlays for conches, chanters and trombone, 1994–95; Caprice for unicycle riding trombonist, 1995; Time Piece for solo of mixed ensemble, 1998; Alternate Realities for solo flute; Various co-composed compositions with Pauline Oliveros, others in the Deep Listening Band, 1988–. *Recordings:* Numerous for major labels. *Publications:* The Modern Trombone: A Definition of Its Idioms, 1979. *Address:* c/o School of Music 353450, University of Washington, Seattle, WA 98195, USA.

DEMUS, Jörg (Wolfgang); Pianist; b. 2 Dec. 1928, St Pölten, Austria. *Education:* Vienna State Academy of Music, Austria, 1939–45; Studied Piano with Walter Kerschbaumer, Organ with Karl Walter, Composition with Joseph Marx, Conducting with H Swarowsky and Joseph Krips; Diploma of the State Academy, Vienna; Studies with Yves Nat (Paris), W Gieseking, W Kempff, A Benedetti-Michelangeli, Edwin Fischer. *Compositions:* Franckiana, 6 Little Pieces for piano. *Recordings:* Has made 350 records, notably of music by Bach, Beethoven and Schubert, often in partnership with pianist Paul Badura-Skoda, accompanist to leading musicians including Dietrich Fischer-Dieskau, Edith Peinemann and Antonio Janigro. *Publications:* Die Klaviersonaten L van Beethoven, 1974; Abenteuer der Interpretation, 1976. *Honours:* Premio Busoni, Bolzano, 1956; Honorary Professor of Austria, 1977; Edison Prize, Amsterdam; The Harriet Cohen Bach Medal, 1977; Beethoven Ring, Vienna, 1977; Mozart Medal, Vienna Mozartgemeinde, 1979. *Current Management:* Mr Roland Sölder, Vienna, Austria.

Address: c/o Mr Roland Sölder, Döblinger Haupstrasse 77a, 1190, Vienna, Austria.

DENCH, Chris; Composer; b. 10 June 1953, London, England; m. Diana Palmer, 1 d. *Career:* Commissioned by Elision resulting in Driftglass, 1990–91, which represented Australia at '92 International Rostrum of Composers in Paris; The French Ministry of Culture; The ABC; The BBC; The Arditti String Quartet; austraLYSIS; Synergy; and others. His works have been performed by Ensemble Accroche Note of Strasbourg, the Berlin Radio Symphony Orchestra, Ensemble Exposé, Ensemble Intercontemporain, London Sinfonietta, Music Projects, London, the Xenakis Ensemble and such soloists as Andrew Ball, Laura Chislett, James Clapperton, Rolf Hind, Stephanie McCallum, and many others; He has had works presented at such events as the Brighton Festival, Darmstadt Ferienkurse für Neue Musik, the Hong Kong ISCM World Music Days, Insel Musik Berlin, many Festivals in France and Italy, the Sydney Spring Festival and the Venice Biennale. *Compositions:* Four large-scale solo flute works for Laura Chislett, including Sulle Scale della Fenice; Tilt for solo piano; several large ensemble pieces, including Enoncé and Afterimages, quattro frammenti and planetary allegiances; chamber music; atsiluth, heterotic strings; Propriocepts for four voices and orchestra; 4 Symphonies, 1980, 1982, 1987, 1997; flesh and the mirror for Elision; beyond status geometry for Synergy, 1995; The heart's algorithms for piano, 1999. *Recordings:* Numerous recordings. *Honours:* Kranichsteiner Musikpreis, 1984. *Address:* c/o Australian Music Centre, PO Box N690, Grosvenor Place, Sydney 2000, Australia.

DENE, Joszef; Singer (Bass); b. 31 March 1938, Budapest, Hungary. *Education:* Studied in Budapest; Sang at the Hungarian State Opera, notably as Alberich in Das Rheingold. *Career:* Many performances at the Zürich Opera, in works by Monteverdi, Berg, Verdi, Janáček and Wagner; Berlin Komische Oper, 1975, as Mozart's Figaro; Further engagements at La Scala, Bayreuth, San Francisco and the Metropolitan (Wagner's Alberich, 1981); Paris Opéra, 1982 and 1985, as Gloucester in Reimann's Lear and as Trithemius in the premiere of Boehmer's Docteur Faustus; Opéra du Rhin Strasbourg and Barcelona, 1985–96, as Des Grieux in Manon; Season 1987 at Graz as the Hangman in the premiere of Cerha's Rattenfänger and as Taddeo in L'Italiana in Algeri at the Schwetzingen Festival; Graz Opera, 1988–89, as Alberich in Siegfried and Götterdämmerung; Sang Mesner in Tosca at Zürich, 2000; Other roles include Mozart's Alfonso and Papageno, Don Pasquale, Pizarro, Kurwenal, Klingsor, Leporello and Handel's Claudius (Agrippina). *Recordings:* Don Giovanni, Boito's Nerone and Judita Triumphans by Vivaldi; Il Ritorno d'Ulisse, Zürich, 1982.

DENES, Istvan; Conductor and Composer; b. 1950, Budapest, Hungary. *Education:* Piano, Conducting and Composition, Franz Liszt Academy, Budapest; Vienna Musikhochschule (Scholarship from Georg Solti). *Career:* Conductor, Budapest State Opera and Lecturer in Harmony, Franz Liszt Academy, 1980–84; Principal Conductor, Bremen Opera, 1987–95; Salieri's Axur, re d'Ormus at Verona and Salome at Montpellier; Further engagements at Prague, Essen, Stuttgart, Jena, Berlin, Darmstadt, Vienna Volksoper and Bregenz Festival; Conducted the first production this century of Zemlinsky's first opera, Sarema (Trier Opera, 1996). *Compositions include:* Logarithmische Rhythmen for percussion; Trio in Memoriam Bela Bartók for piano, cello and violin; Mohacs 1526, Hommage à Beethoven; Funerailles for orchestra. *Recordings include:* Sarema (Koch International). *Address:* c/o Theater der Stadt Trier, Am Augustinherhof, 5500 Trier, Germany.

DENÈVE, Stéphane; Conductor; b. 1972, France. *Education:* Graduated Paris Conservatoire, 1995. *Career:* Assistant to Georg Solti for Bluebeard's Castle with Orchestre de Paris, 1995, and Don Giovanni at the Paris Opéra, 1996; Conducted Die Zauberflöte at the Deutsche Oper am Rhein, Dusseldorf, 1997 (Permanent Conductor from 1999); Engagements with Cologne Opera for Dialogues des Carmélites, Così fan tutte, La Traviata and Die Zauberflöte, 1998–2000; Pelléas et Mélisande for Cincinnati Opera; Season 2000–01 with St Petersburg Philharmonic, Orchestre de Paris and Washington National Symphony Orchestra; Music Director of the Royal Scottish National Orchestra, 2004–. *Honours:* First Prize in Conducting, Paris Conservatoire, 1995. *Address:* c/o IMG Artists, Lovell House, 616 Chiswick High Road, London W4 5RX, England.

DENIZ, Clare (Frances); Concert Cellist and Teacher; b. 7 April 1945, England. *Education:* Private piano study from age 5; Private cello study with Madeleine Mackenzie from age 11; Won Junior Exhibition to Royal Academy of Music after only one years tuition; Teachers: Lilley Phillips and Derek Simpson, gaining LRAM; Further study with Christopher Bunting, Jacqueline du Pré and Antonia Butler; Masterclasses with Paul Tortelier then became a pupil. *Career:* Debut: Purcell Room, London, 1983; Former Principal Cellist with Royal Ballet Orchestra and sub-principal cellist with English National Opera; Many recitals specializing in British and French music as well as standard repertoire;

Appeared at: Cambridge Festival, Cheltenham Lunchtime Concerts, Fairfield Hall Centenary Concert for Arnold Bax; Concertgebouw Amsterdam debut 1987, an unaccompanied Bach recital, returning in 1990; Recording for BBC Radio Oxford, 1987 and recorded a recital of French music in 1991; Invited to take part in Counterpoint II recital series by Incorporated Society of Musicians, 1990; 3 Concerts of first performances for the Wessex Composers Group, 1990, conceived by Incorporated Society of Musicians; Children's concerts and workshops; Played Haydn's C Major Concerto in 1990 and gave a Virtuoso Recital in 1992 for the Jacqueline du Pré Appeal Fund; Solo recitals given in Amsterdam, 1990 and 1992 and in Paris, 1993; Concert given for the EEC Brussels Commission, 1994. *Honours:* Elected Fellow of The Royal Society of Arts, 1990. *Address:* 31 Friday Street, Henley-on-Thames, Oxfordshire RG9 1AN, England.

DENIZE, Nadine; singer (mezzo-soprano); b. 6 Nov. 1943, Rouen, France. *Education:* studied with Marie-Louise Christol and Germaine Lubin in Paris. *Career:* debut, Paris Opéra, 1965, as Marguerite in La Damnation de Faust; Paris Opéra-Comique, as Charlotte in Werther; appearances in Marseille, Lyon, Nice and Orange; member of the Deutsche Oper am Rhein, Düsseldorf, from 1971; Strasbourg, 1974–77; guest engagements at the Hamburg Staatsoper, Vienna Staatsoper and at La Scala Milan, the Met; Paris Opéra as Octavian and Jenůfa; Other roles include Cassandre in Les Troyens, Eboli in Don Carlos, Wagner's Kundry and Honegger's Antigone; Opéra du Rhin, Strasbourg, 1986, as Ortrud; Teatro Colón, Buenos Aires, 1988, as Marguerite by Berlioz; Opéra-Comique, Paris, 1988, as Marina in Boris Godunov; Sang Brangaene in Chicago, 1985; Anna in Les Troyens, 1990, opening production of Opéra Bastille, Paris; Season 1999 as Madame de Croissy in Les Dialogues des Carmélites at Strasbourg and London (Prom concerts); Season 2000–01 as Geneviève in Pelléas at the New York Met and Clytemnestra in Elektra at Bordeaux; Katia Kabanova in Geneva, 2003; Pique Dame in Lyon, 2003; Hamlet in Trieste, 2004; Pelléas at Glyndebourne Festival, 2004. *Recordings:* Carmen; Herodiade, Beatrice and Benogret; Guercoeur, Faust; Beethoven Cantatas; Mort de Cléopâtre, Berlioz. *Address:* c/o Mariano Horak, Agentur Caecilia, Rennweg 15, 8001 Zürich, Switzerland.

DENLEY, Catherine; Singer (Mezzo-Soprano); b. 1954, Northampton-shire, England; m. Miles Golding, 3 s. *Education:* Studied at Trinity College of Music, London. *Career:* Sang 2 years with the BBC Singers; Solo performances with major orchestras and conductors throughout Europe and as far afield as the USA, Canada, China, Japan and the Ukraine; US appearances at the Tanglewood Festival with the Boston Symphony Orchestra; San Francisco concerts with John Eliot Gardiner; Performances of Messiah with the Hallé Orchestra, City of Birmingham Symphony, the English Concert in Belgium and The Sixteen in Finland and Poland; Mozart's Requiem in Salzburg and Innsbruck; Elgar's The Music Makers and the Bliss Pastoral at South Bank; Bach B Minor Mass at Aldeburgh and York; Beethoven's Missa Solemnis at the Windsor Festival; Staged performances of L'Incoronazione di Poppea at Spital-fields; Operatic roles include: Olga in Eugene Onegin at the Aldeburgh Festival; Nutrice in Monteverdi's Poppea; Handel Operas: Giustino and Radamisto; Mrs Noah in Noye's Fludde; Radio and television recordings in the United Kingdom and Europe; Television recordings include appearances in Channel 4's Maestro series and Mahler's 8th Symphony from Dublin; Sang Third Lady in Die Zauberflöte, 1990; Promenade Concerts; Sisera in Handel's Deborah at the 1993 Proms; Mahler 2 in Kiev and Odessa; Tucapsky Stabat Mater in the Czech Republic; Haydn Stabat Mater in Madrid and Handel Judas Maccabaeus in Berlin and Halle; Season 1999 with Mozart's Requiem and Schumann's Scenes from Faust at the London Prom concerts. *Recordings:* Monteverdi's L'Orfeo and L'Incoronazione di Poppea; Handel's Semele, Hercules, Il Duello Amorosa and Messiah; Vivaldi's Gloria; Requiem by Bruckner; In the Beginning by Copland; Die Zauberflöte. *Honours:* G.T.C.L.; F.T.C.L. *Address:* CDI, Lyndhurst, Denton Road, Ben Rhydding, Ilkley, West Yorkshire, LS29 8QR, England.

DENNER, Bettina; Singer (Mezzo-soprano); b. 5 Jan. 1960, Weimar, Germany. *Education:* Studied at the Leipzig Musikhochschule, notably with Hans Christian Polster. *Career:* Sang at the Leipzig Opera from 1983, as Zerlina, Carlotta in Die schweigsame Frau, and Nicklausse in Les Contes d'Hoffmann; Guest at the Berlin Staatsoper from 1987, as Cherubino and on tour to Japan; Other roles have included Dorabella, Idamante, Massenet's Charlotte, Hermia in A Midsummer Night's Dream and Orlovsky; Sang the Hostess in Boris Godunov at Leipzig, 1993; Many concert engagements, notably at the Leipzig Thomasschule and the Gewandhaus. *Address:* c/o Deutsche Staatsoper Berlin, Unter den Linden 7, 1060 Germany.

DENNING, Angela; Australian singer (soprano); b. 1952, Sydney, NSW. *Education:* New South Wales Conservatory. *Career:* sang with the State Opera of South Australia from 1976 and with the Australian Opera at Sydney from 1979; English National Opera, 1982–83, Deutsche Oper Berlin, 1984, and the Staatsoper, 1988; Sang Clorinda in La Cener-

entola at Salzburg, 1988–89, and Dalila in Handel's Samson at the 1988 Göttingen Festival; Other roles include Donna Anna and Meyerbeer's Marguerite de Valois (both in Berlin), Lucia di Lammermoor, Gilda, Nannetta, the Queen of Night and Fiordiligi. *Recordings include:* La Cenerentola (video).

DENNIS, Elwyn; Composer; b. 10 Aug. 1941, Los Angeles, USA. *Education:* BA, University of California, 1965. *Career:* Sculptor, Lecturer, Department of Architecture, University of Melbourne, 1974–75; Lecturer, Ballarat University, 1990–92; Manager of Clouds, a nature conservation area. *Compositions include:* Evidence of Origin, performance with sculpture, 1982; Particle Flow, 1983; Space of Concern, 1983; Clouds Are, 1984; Wimmera, 1986; A Mother's Day, 1987; Time Again, 1987; Invention for Guitar, 1988; Details of a Morning, 1988; Dry Country, 1992; Waiting Winter Out, tape with harpsichord, 1994; Commissions Association of Australia and The Listening Room, ABC-FM. *Honours:* Caulfield Arts Centre Purchase Prize, 1979. *Address:* c/o APRA, 1A Eden Street, Crows Nest, NSW 2065, Australia.

DENNISON, Robert; Concert Pianist; b. 10 June 1960, Philadelphia, USA. *Education:* Studied in Philadelphia Music Academy, at Temple University and the Peabody Conservatory; Further Study with Claude Frank and Horszowski. *Career:* Debut: Philadelphia, with the Shosta-kovich Second Concerto, 1971; Concerts and recitals in Washington, Boston, Cleveland, Los Angeles, St Louis and Chicago; Russian Tours with concerts in Kiev, St Petersburg, Vilnius, Moscow and Novosibirsk, 1991–93; Further engagements at Chicago, New Jersey, Colorado, San Francisco, Boston, Essen, Berlin, Hamburg Music Festival, Lucerne Festival and in Hungary, Romania and Czechoslovakia, 1992–93; Repertoire includes contemporary works by American composers as well as the standard classics. *Address:* c/o Sonata, 11 Northgate Street, Glasgow G20 7AA, Scotland.

DENNISTON, Patrick; Singer (Tenor); b. 1965, New York, USA. *Education:* Studied at Syracuse University and the Lyric Opera Center, Chicago. *Career:* Engagements with the San Francisco Opera, Houston Grand Opera, New York City Opera, Opera Pacific, Kentucky Opera, New Israeli Opera, Bonn Opera and at the Spoleto Festival; Further appearances throughout Canada; Roles have included Pinkerton, Don Carlos, Don José, Edgardo, Dmitri, Lensky and Alfredo; Glyndebourne Festival 1997, as Des Grieux in a new production of Manon Lescaut; Season 1997–98 with Pinkerton and Ismaele in Nabucco at Chicago, Erik in Der fliegende Holländer, and Radames at Houston; Cavaradossi at Madison. *Address:* c/o Lyric Opera Chicago, 20 North Wacker Drive, Chicago, IL 60606, USA.

DEPLUS, Guy Gaston Simon; clarinettist; b. 29 Aug. 1924, Vieux Condé, France; m. Yvette Vandekerkhove 1946, one s. *Education:* Conservatoire National Superieur du Musique de Paris. *Career:* Guard Republican Band and Orchestra, 1947; Concerts Colonne, 1950; Domaine Musical, with Pierre Boulez, 1953; Ars Nova, with Marius Constant, 1963; Paris Octet, 1965; Opéra Comique, 1968; Opera, 1973; Professor, Chamber Music, Paris Conservatory, 1974; Concerts in Berlin, Salzburg, Vienna, 1977; Professor, Clarinet, Paris Conservatory, 1978; Judge, International Competitions; Professor Ecole Normale de Musique de Paris, 1991; mem. International Clarinet Asscn (French chair.). *Recordings:* Mozart, Concerto, Trio, Quintet; Weber, 1st Clarinet Concerto, Concertino, Grand Duo; Rossini, Introduction, Theme and Variations; Beethoven Septet; Brahms 2 sonatas and trio; Messiaen Quartet. *Contributions:* The Clarinet. *Honours:* Quoted by Stravinsky in Memories and Commentaries, 1959; 4 Prix de l'Academie du Disque Francais; Lifetime Achievement Award, International Clarinet Association for Outstanding Performance, Teaching, Research and Service to the Clarinet, 1999. *Address:* 37 Square Saint Charles, 75012 Paris, France.

DEPOLTOVA, Eva; Singer (soprano); b. 5 Aug. 1945, Bratislava, Czechoslovakia. *Education:* Univ. of Music Arts, Prague, with Zdenka Zika and Elena Obraztsova. *Career:* debut, Prague National Theatre 1974; sang in concert with Czech Philharmonic Orchestra, Vienna Symphony Orchestra and other major orchestras, in Prague, Vienna, Salzburg, Linz, Copenhagen, Vienna, Lyon, Switzerland, Italy, Japan, Germany, Tehran, Istanbul, Taiwan; Dvořák Requiem and Stabat Mater, Janáček Glagolitic Mass, Beethoven, The Ninth Symphony, 1976; roles include Lady Macbeth, Marenka, The Bartered Bride, Violetta, La Traviata, Aida, Donna Anna and many others; sang Krasava in Libuše by Smetana at the National Theatre, Prague, 100th Anniversary re-opening 1983. *Recordings:* Fibich-Sarka, Foerster's Eva; Smetana, Dalibor, Libuše and The Kiss, Mozart, Don Giovanni, Martinů's The Miracles of Our Lady and Gilgamesh. *Honours:* Prix Caecilia, Union de la Presse 1985. *Address:* NA Prikope 12, 110 01 Prague, Czech Republic.

DEPREIST, James Anderson; Conductor; b. 21 Nov. 1936, Philadel-phia, PA, USA; m. 1st Betty Louise Childress 1963; two d.; m. 2nd

Ginette Grenier 1980. *Education:* BS 1958, MA 1961, Univ. of Pennsylvania; studied with Vincent Persichetti, Philadelphia Conservatory of Music, 1959–61. *Career:* conductor, Contemporary Music Guild, Philadelphia, 1959–62; specialist in music, US State Dept, 1962–63; Conductor, Bangkok, Thailand, 1963–64; Asst Conductor, New York Philharmonic Orchestra, 1965–66; Principal Guest Conductor, Symphony of the New World, 1968–70; European debut, Rotterdam Philharmonic Orchestra, 1969; Assoc. Conductor, 1971–75; Principal Guest Conductor, National Symphony Orchestra, Washington DC, 1975–76; Music Dir, L'Orchestre Symphonique de Québec, 1976–83, Oregon Symphony Orchestra, Portland, 1980–, Malmö Symphony Orchestra, 1991–94, Philharmonique De Monte-Carlo, 1994–98; Guest Conductor with major orchestras in North America and Europe; engaged for Andrea Chénier at Monte Carlo. *Publications:* Book of Poems, This Precipice Garden, 1987; The Distant Siren (poems), 1989. *Honours:* First prize, Dimitri Mitropoulos International Conducting Competition, New York, 1964. *Current Management:* TransArt (UK) Ltd, Cedar House, 10 Rutland Street, Filey, YO14 9JB, North Yorkshire, England. *Telephone:* (1723) 515819. *Fax:* (1723) 514678. *E-mail:* transartuk@transartuk.com. *Website:* www.transartuk.com.

DERENZI, Victor; American conductor; *Artistic Director, Sarasota Opera.* *Career:* Artistic Dir and principal conductor, Sarasota Opera 1981–; conductor with Lyric Opera of Chicago, St Louis, Toledo, New Orleans and New York City operas, and Opéra du Montréal, Un Ballo in Maschera in Canary Islands, and Spoleto Festival; responsible for Sarasota Opera Verdi Cycle, a multi-year project to present all of Verdi's music. *Address:* Sarasota Opera, 61 N Pineapple Avenue, Sarasota, FL 34236, USA (office). *Telephone:* (941) 366-6645 (office); (941) 955-5571 (home). *E-mail:* info@sarasotaopera.org (office). *Website:* www .sarasotaopera.org (office).

DERNESCH, Helga; singer (soprano, mezzo-soprano); b. 3 Feb. 1939, Vienna, Austria; m. Werner Kramm. *Education:* Vienna Conservatory. *Career:* debut, Berne Opera 1961, as Marina in Boris Godunov; Sang Antonia in Les Contes d'Hoffmann, Fiordiligi and Wagner roles; Wiesbaden, 1963–65; Cologne Opera, 1965–69; Bayreuth from 1965, as Freia, Gutrune and Eva; Scottish Opera from 1968, as Gutrune, Leonore, Brünnhilde, Isolde and the Marschallin; Salzburg Easter Festival from 1969, as Brünnhilde, Isolde and Fidelio; Covent Garden debut, 1970 as Sieglinde, followed by Chrysothemis in Elektra, the Dyer's Wife and the Nurse in Die Frau ohne Schatten, and Adelaide in Arabella, 1986; Debuts at Chicago, 1971 and Vienna, 1972 as Leonore in Fidelio; Created Fortner's Elisabeth Tudor, Berlin 1972, Goneril in Reimann's Lear, Munich 1978 and Hecuba in Reimann's Troades, Munich 1986; San Francisco from 1982, as Herodias in Salome, and Erda and Fricka in Der Ring des Nibelungen, 1984–85; Metropolitan Opera debut 1985, as Marfa in Khovanshchina; Tour of Japan with the Bayreuth ensemble, 1967 and with the Hamburg Staatsoper, 1984; Metropolitan 1989, as Fricka and Waltraute in the Ring and The Nurse in Die Frau ohne Schatten; Sang Mistress Quickly in Falstaff at Los Angeles, 1990; Fricka in the Ring at San Francisco; Covent Garden, in the Ring, 1991; Sang Clytemnestra in Elektra at San Francisco, 1991, and at the Opéra Bastille, Paris, 1992; Electress in Henze's Der Prinz von Homburg at the 1992 Munich Festival; Frau von Luber in Weill's Silbersee at the 1996 London Proms; Kabanicha in Katya Kabanova at Glyndebourne, 1998; Sang title role in premiere of Reimann's Bernada Albas Haus, Munich 2000. *Recordings:* Fidelio and Tristan und Isolde; Der Ring des Nibelungen, conducted by Karajan, DGG; Elisabeth in Tannhäuser; Cassandre in Les Troyens, Vienna, 1976. *Address:* Salztorgasse 8/11, 1013 Vienna, Austria.

DEROUBAIX, Jeanne; Singer (Mezzo-soprano); b. 16 Feb. 1927, Brussels, Belgium. *Education:* Studied in Brussels. *Career:* Sang in ensemble Pro Musica, under the direction of Safford Cape (1947–53); Toured widely in Europe with repertoire specialising in music of 13th–16th centuries; Lieder recitals and programmes of French chansons; Often heard in contemporary music; Sang in the first performances of Stravinsky's Threni (Venice 1958) and A Sermon, a Narrative and a Prayer (Basle 1962); Also heard in Schoenberg's Pierrot Lunaire and works by Boulez; Professor at the Musikhochschule Detmold from 1957. *Recordings:* Lieder by Brahms; Beethoven's Missa Solemnis; Monteverdi's Orfeo; Le Marteau sans Maître by Boulez.

DES MARAIS, Paul (Emile); Composer and Professor; b. 23 June 1920, Menominee, Michigan, USA. *Education:* Studied with Leo Sowerby, Chicago, 1937–41; Nadia Boulanger, Cambridge, 1941–42 and Paris, 1949; BA, 1949, MA, 1953, Harvard University. *Career:* Teacher, Harvard University, 1953–56; University of California, Los Angeles, 1956–. *Compositions:* Stage: Epiphanies, chamber opera, 1968; Incidental music to Dryden's A Secular Masque, 1976; Shakespeare's A Midsummer Night's Dream, 1976; Sophocles's Oedipus, 1978; G B Shaw's St Joan, 1980; Dryden's Marriage à la Mode, 1981; Shakespeare's As You Like It, 1983; G Etherege's The Man of Mode, 1984. Dance: Triplum for organ and percussion, 1981; Touch for 2 pianos,

1984. Chamber: 2 piano sonatas, 1947, 1952; Theme and Changes for harpsichord, 1953; Capriccio for 2 pianos and percussion, 1962; 2 Movements for 2 pianos and percussion, 1972 revised and enlarged as 3 Movements, 1975; The Baroque Isles for 2 keyboard percussionists, 1986; Orpheus, theatre piece for narrator and instruments, 1987; The French Park, for two guitars, 1988. Choral: Six-part Mass for double chorus, 1947; Motet for mixed voices, cellos and double basses, 1959; Psalm 121, 1959; Organum 1–6 for chorus, organ and percussion, 1972, revised and enlarged, 1980; Brief Mass for chorus, organ and percussion, 1973; Seasons of the Mind for chorus, piano 4-hands and celesta, 1980–81. Vocal: Reflections on Faure for voice and piano, 1972; Late Songs for voice and piano, 1978; Slowsong for voice and piano, 1987; The French Park for two guitars, 1988. *Publications:* Harmony, 1962. *Contributions:* Articles in Perspectives of New Music. *Address:* c/o Music Department, University of California at Los Angeles, Los Angeles, CA 90024, USA.

DESCHÉNES, Bruno; Composer; b. 12 Oct. 1955, Cap-Chat, Quebec, Canada; m. Shizuko Toguchi, 18 April 1981. *Education:* BMus, Composition, McGill University, Montréal, 1979; Master in Composition, University of Montréal, 1983; Research on Music Perception, Listening and Teaching. *Career:* Performing and Conducting on Radio and Concerts, 1980–; Compositions performed in France, USA, Venezuela, Brazil and Montréal, 1979–; Gives lectures, workshops and writes articles on Music Perception and Music Listening in Canada, USA and Europe. *Compositions:* Improvised Music: Expansion, Horizon, Pyramide, Chakras; Electronic Music: Murmures for tape and percussion; Different Chamber Groups: Dimension, Innerance, Prisme, Poemes Luminescence, Calme En Soi, Double Jeu; Choir: Ondes, Ondes et Particules; Les Vagues for narrator and tape, 1994; Le Monde est une Bulle d'air, tape, 1994. *Contributions:* The Perceptions of Colour Through Music, Musicwork 26, 1984; Regularly publishes articles in the bulletin of the Centre Québécois de la Couleur. *Address:* 5565 Rue Clark, Montréal, QC H2T 2V5, Canada.

DESDERI, Claudio; Singer (Baritone) and Conductor; b. 9 April 1943, Alessandria, Italy. *Education:* Studied at the Florence Conservatory. *Career:* Sang as first in concert; Opera debut as Guadenzio in Il Signor Bruschino at the 1969 Edinburgh Festival, with the Maggio Musicale; Has sung widely in Italy and in Munich, Salzburg, Paris, Amsterdam, Chicago, Philadelphia, and Vienna; Best known in opera by Verdi, Berlioz, Monteverdi, Nono, Rossini, Bellini, Mozart, Donizetti and Massenet; Regular appearances in the United Kingdom from 1981; Glyndebourne Festival (as Figaro and Alfonso), Promenade and Festival Hall concerts; Covent Garden debut as Mozart's Figaro, 1987; Alfonso in Così fan tutte, 1989; Conducts Chamber Orchestras in Italy; Masterclasses at Musica di Fiesole; Conducted Così fan tutte and Le nozze di Figaro at Turin, 1989, Piacenza, 1990, Royal College of Music, London, 1990; Sang Don Magnifico in La Cenerentola at Covent Garden, 1990; Glyndebourne Festival as Falstaff, Maggio Musicale Florence as Leporello; Met debut 1995, as Rossini's Bartolo; Los Angeles 1995, as Don Pasquale; Sulpice in La Fille du Régiment at Rome, 1998. *Recordings include:* Così fan tutte and Le nozze di Figaro, conducted by Haitink. *Address:* c/o Poilvé, 16 Avenue de Franklin D. Roosevelt, F–75008, Paris, France.

DESIMONE, Robert A.; Stage Director, Arts Administrator and Conductor; b. 1940, USA; m. Angela Carol Bonica, 21 July 1974, 1 s., 1 d. *Education:* Performance Certificate, Music Academy of the West; BM, MA, University of Southern California; Diploma International Opera Centre, Zürich, Switzerland; DMA, University of Washington, USA. *Career:* Debut: As Stage Director, Rome, Italy; Director of Opera, University of Texas, Austin; Director of Opera, College Conservatory of Music, Cincinnati; Assistant Director, School of Music, University of Washington; Executive Director, Visual Arts Center, Anchorage, Alaska; Administrative Co-ordinator, Music Center Opera Association, Los Angeles; Director: City of the Angels Opera, Los Angeles; John F Kennedy Center for the Performing Arts, Washington DC; Lincoln Center for the Performing Arts, New York; Seattle Opera Association, Seattle, Washington; Stage Director: Teatro del' Opera, Rome; Teatro Goldini, Rome; Opernhaus, Zürich, Switzerland; Resident Stage Director, Seattle Opera Association, Seattle, Washington; Guest Director, theatres in Germany, Switzerland, Italy, USA; mem, National Opera Association; Metropolitan Opera Guild; College Music Society; Central Opera Association. *Address:* 3601 72nd Avenue SE, Mercer Island, WA 98040, USA.

DESJARDINS, Michaël (Anthony); Pianist; b. 2 Dec. 1959, Boston, Massachusetts, USA. *Education:* National Conservatory of Nice; National Superior Conservatory of Paris; Mozarteum, Salzburg; Cleveland Institute of Music. *Career:* Debut: Piano recital at Princess Grace Theatre, Monte Carlo, 1983; Has performed in major halls and festivals in France, Germany, Italy, Switzerland, Thailand, elsewhere; Appearances as Soloist with French, Russian and Polish orchestras, such as Philharmonic Orchestras of Nice, Cannes and Czestochowa, Chamber

Orchestra of Haute-Normandie, The Moscow Soloists; Television appearances: J Martin's Le Monde est à vous, on France 2, A Duault's Portée de Nuit, on France 3, on TV 5 Bangkok, and numerous programmes on Télé Monte-Carlo; Major radio broadcasts on France Musique, France Inter, Radio Nostalgie, Radio Monte-Carlo; Founder and Director of various musical festivals. *Recordings:* Voyage Musical. *Honours:* Honours Medal, City of Cannes, 1971; Grand Prix, City of Nice, 1975; Honours Medals, City of St-Jean-Cap-Ferrat, 1996, 1999; Lys d'Or Honorary Medal, 1996; Honours Medal, J Rodrigo Anniversary, 1999; Decorated by Srinakharinwirot University, Bangkok, 1999. *Current Management:* B P Com. *Address:* 37 rue Hoche, 06 400 Cannes, France.

DESSAY, Natalie; Singer (Soprano); b. 19 April 1965, Lyon, France. *Education:* Studied at the Bordeaux Conservatory and in Paris. *Career:* After winning the 1990 Mozart Competition in Vienna sang in Bizet's Don Procopio at the Paris Opéra-Comique and at Montipellier in Ariadne auf Naxos; Liège and Nantes, 1990, in Si j'étais Roi by Adam and Le Roi l'a dit by Delibes; Lyon Opéra from 1991, in Mozart's Schauspieldirektor and as Blondchen; Opéra Bastille, Paris, 1992, as Olympia in Les Contes d'Hoffmann; Mozart concert at the 1992 Aix-en-Provence Festival; Met debut 1995, as Fiakermilli in Arabella; Sang Lakmé at Nimes, 1996; Season 2000–01 as Olympia at the Opéra Bastille, Ophélie at the Châtelet, the Queen of Night in Vienna, Constanze at Geneva Opera and Strauss's Aminta at the Bastille. *Recordings include:* Lucia di Lammermoor, in French, 2002. *Address:* c/o Cédelle, 78 Boulevard Malesherbes, F–75008 Paris, France.

DESSI, Daniela; Singer (Soprano); b. 14 May 1957, Genoa, Italy. *Education:* Studied in Parma and Siena. *Career:* Sang at first in concert and made stage debut at Savona, in Pergolesi's Serva Padrona; Mozart roles have included the Countess and Fiordiligi (at La Scala and Genoa), Donna Elvira (at Florence) and Vitellia in Desdemona (to the Otello of Placido Domingo), Amelia Bocanegra (at Vienna, Venice, and Hamburg) and Elizabeth de Valois (notably with Pavarotti at La Scala, 1992); Sang Alice Ford at Boston and Amsterdam; Made debuts as the Trovatore Leonora and Violetta at Rome and Tokyo, 1993; Nedda in Pagliacci at Philadelphia and the New York Met, Mathilde (Guillaume Tell) at Pesaro and Mascagni's Iris in Rome; Zürich Opera as Aida (season 1996–97), Mimi, Donna Elvira, Desdemona and Ginerva in Giordano's La Cena della Beffe; Sang in Salieri's Danaides at Verona, 1996, Madama Butterfly in Florence and Tosca in Tokyo, 1997; Season 1998 as Dolly in Wolf Ferrari's Sly at Zürich and Tosca at the Verona Arena; Season 2000–01 as Butterfly at Verona, Lucia di Lammermoor at Geneva, Adriana Lecouvreur for La Scala, Maddalena in Andrea Chénier at Nice and Tosca for Chicago Lyric Opera. *Recordings include:* Video of Don Carlos, from La Scala. *Address:* c/o Opernhaus Zürich, Falkenstrasse 1, 8008 Zürich, Switzerland.

DESYATNIKOV, Leonid Arkadievich; Russian composer; b. 1955, Kharkov, Ukraine. *Education:* Leningrad State Conservatory. *Career:* mem. Composers' Union 1979–. *Works include:* opera: Poor Lisa; ballet: Love Song in Minor; tango-operetta: Astor Piazzola's Maria de Buenos Aires (Grammy Award); symphony: Sacred Winter; film scores: Sunset 1990, Lost in Siberia 1991, Capital Punishment 1992, Touch 1992, Moscow Nights 1994, Katia Izmailova 1994, Hammer and Sickle 1994, Giselle's Mania 1995, The Prisoner of the Mountains 1996, The One Who is More Tender 1996, Moscow 2000, His Wife's Diary 2000. *Honours:* Golden Sheep Prize 2000. *Address:* Nepokorennykh prosp. 16, korp. 1, apt 177, 195220 St Petersburg, Russia (home). *Telephone:* (812) 545-20-98 (home).

DEUSSEN, Nancy (Bloomer); Composer; b. 1 Feb. 1931, New York, NY, USA; m. (1) Charles J Webster, 1952. m. (2) John H Bloomer, 1962. m. (3) Gary R Deussen, 1982, 1 s., 2 d. *Education:* Juilliard School of Music, 1949–51; Manhattan School of Music, 1951–53; BM, Composition, University of Southern California, School of Music, 1957–59; BM Music Education; Graduate Studies in Composition, UCLA, University of Southern California, Long Beach State University, San Jose State University. *Career:* Original ballet music The Little Hill performed New York City, 1952; Reflections on the Hudson for orchestra, 1955; Missa Breve premiere, Redlands, California, 1957; Suite for clarinet and piano, 1959; Woodwind Quintet premiere, 1985; Concert of original chamber music and orchestra premiere of Three Rustic Sketches, 1989; mem, American Music Center; Mu Phi Epsilon; NACUSA; American Composers Forum, BMI. *Compositions:* Little Fugue and Harvest Suite, for recorders, 1956; Missa de Angelis, 1957; Suite for clarinet and piano, 1959; The Serpent, Cantata, 1965; Woodwind Quintet, 1983; Three Rustic Sketches, for orchestra, 1987; Prelude and Cascades for piano, 1987; Fanfare and Andante for winds, 1988; The Long Voyage, for soprano and recorders, 1988; Trio for violin, clarinet and piano, 1988; Two Pieces for violin and piano, 1990; Trio for violin, cello and piano, 1993; Peninsula suite for string orchestra, 1994; Concerto for clarinet and small orchestra, commissioned by Richard Nunemaker, clarinettist, premiered 1995 by Consortium of 5 orchestras; Musings: Circa 1940 for

solo piano, 1995; Canticles for brass, 1997; Parisian Caper, 1997; Ascent to Victory, for orchestra, 1997; The Pegasus Suite for flute and piano, 1998; Tribute to the ancients for brass quintet, 1998; A Silver, Shining Strand, suite for orchestra, 2001; Celebration Octet, 2002; Et in Terra Pax (SATB/pf), 2002; Tico (Orchestra), 2004. *Recordings:* San Andreas Suite; One of Nature's Majesties; Two Pieces for violin and piano; The Pegasus Suite; Reflections on the Hudson. *Honours:* First Prize, Britten-on-the-Bay, 1996; Mu Phi Epsilon Composition Competition, 1999; Marmor Chamber Music Composition Competition, 2002. *Address:* 3065 Greer Road, Palo Alto, CA 94303, USA. *Website:* nancybloomerdeussen .com.

DEUTEKOM, Cristina; Opera Singer (Soprano); b. 28 Aug. 1932, Amsterdam; Netherlands; Debuts: Amsterdam, 1962, as the Queen of Night which she also sang on her Covent Garden debut; Appeared at Munich State Opera, 1996. *Career:* Vienna Festwochen, 1996; Sang at Metropolitan Opera, New York, 1967; Sang in all major opera houses in Europe, especially Italy and also in USA: specialised in bel canto operas by Rossini, Bellini and Donizetti and the great Verdi operas; Among her roles were Mozart's Fiordilgi and Constanze, Bellini's Norma and Elvira, Rossini's Armida and Verdi's Odabella and Giselda; Sang Elvira at Amsterdam, 1984, Norma at San Diego, 1985. *Recordings:* Various. *Honours:* Grand Prix du Disque, 1969, 1972. *Address:* c/o H R Rothenberg, Johannisthaler Chaussee 421, 1000 Berlin 47, Germany.

DEUTSCH, Helmut; Pianist; b. 1945, Vienna, Austria. *Education:* Studied piano, composition and musicology in Vienna. *Career:* Chamber musician and accompanist to leading singers; Former partners include Irmgard Seefried, Rita Streich, Ileana Cotrubas, Hans Hotter and Hermann Prey; Recent recital partners include Olaf Bär, Anne Sofie von Otter, Ruth Ziesak, Peter Schreier, Bernd Weikl, Barbara Bonney, Dietrich Henschel, Juliane Banse, Angelika Kirchschlager and Bo Skovhus; Many major festival appearances; Teacher at the Vienna Music Academy, 1967–79; Munich Hochschule für Musik, 1979–; Masterclasses in Europe and Japan. *Honours:* Vienna Composition prize, 1967. *Address:* c/o IMG Artists, Lovell House, 616 Chiswick High Road, London W4 5RX, England. *E-mail:* hedeutsch@yahoo.com.

DEVIA, Mariella; Singer (Soprano); b. 1948, Imperia, Italy. *Education:* Studied at the Accademia di Santa Cecilia, Rome. *Career:* Debut: Spoleto 1972, as Despina in Così fan tutte; Rome Opera 1973, as Lucia di Lammermoor; Guest appearances in Italy and at Munich, Hamburg and Berlin; Has sung Donizetti's Adina in Dallas and Verdi's Oscar in Chicago; Metropolitan Opera from 1979, as Gilda, Constanze in Die Entführung, Nannetta in Falstaff; Concert performance of Lakmé in New York; Sang title role in Donizetti's Elisabetta al Castello di Kenilworth at Bergamo, 1989; Elvira in I Puritani at Rome and Madrid, 1990; Maggio Musicale Florence, 1990 as Donizetti's Parisina; Rossini roles include Adele in Le Comte Ory, Amenaide in Tancredi and Semiramide; Pesaro Festival 1995, Zelmira; Sang Lucia di Lammermoor at Florence, 1996; at Teatro alla Scala: Capuleti e Montecchi, Lodoïska (Cherubini), Lucia di Lammermoor, Die Entführung, La fille du régiment, Turco in Italia 1990–97; Covent Garden: Die Zauberflöte, 1988; Rigoletto, 1990; Season 1999–2000 at Covent Garden as Desdemona in Rossini's Otello; Season 2000–01 as Donizetti's Adelia at Carnegie Hall, Bellini's Amina and Elvira at Florence, Lucrezia Borgia in Bologna. *Recordings include:* Rossini Adelaide di Borgogna, Donizetti Elisabetta al Castello di Kenilworth, Bellini La Sonnambula and I Puritani (Fonit Cetra); L'Elisir d'amore; Lucia di Lammermoor, with Zubin Mehta. *Address:* c/o R Lombardo Inc, One Harkness Plaza, 61 West 62nd Street, Suite 6F, New York, NY 10023, USA.

DEVICH, Janos; Cellist and Professor; b. 3 April 1938, Szeged, Hungary; m. Sara Veslelszky, 12 Aug 1974, 3 s. *Education:* Liszt Ferenc Academy for Music, Budapest. *Career:* Concerts regularly in almost all the countries in Europe, USA (five times), Australia, Japan (seven times), China, South Korea; Festivals in Besançon, Bath, Estoril, Prague, Warsaw, Babilin, Como, Chamonix, Amiens, Devon; President, Magyar Zenemüvezeti Társaság; Vice President, Magyar Muzsikus Forum. *Recordings:* Kodály, Mozart, Dohnányi, Contemporary composers string quartet; String Quartets (Debussy, Ravel, D'Indy); Piano Quintets (Brahms, Schumann, Schubert); Complete Quartets (Schubert, Haydn). *Honours:* Franz Liszt Prize, 1970; Merited Artist of Hungary, 1990; Bart ók-Pasztory Prize, 1996. *Address:* Budapest, Pusztaszeri-ut 30, Hungary 1025.

DEVINU, Giusy; Singer (Soprano); b. 1960, Cagliari, Italy. *Education:* Studied at the Cagliari Conservatory. *Career:* Debut: Sang in 1982; Has sung Violetta at La Scala under Riccardo Muti and at other Italian centres; Further engagements in Rigoletto at Bologna, 1990, Rossini's L'Occasione fa il ladro at Pesaro, 1989, and in Don Pasquale and as the Countess in Le nozze di Figaro at the Teatro La Fenice Venice, 1990-91; Sang in the Seven Stars concert at the Baths of Caracalla, 1991; Trieste 1991 as Lucieta un Wolf-Ferrari's Il Campielo, Rome 1992 as Marie in La Fille du Régiment; Macerata Festival 1992 as Traviata; Sang

Bellini's Giulietta at Genoa, 1996; Season 1998 with Lehar's Eva at Naples and Liu in Turandot at Turin; Sang Elcia in Rossini's Mosè in Egitto at Monte Carlo, 2000. *Address:* c/o Teatro La Fenice, Campo S Fantin 1965, 30124 Venice, Italy.

DEVLIN, Michael (Coles); Singer (Bass-Baritone); b. 27 Nov. 1942, Chicago, Illinois, USA. *Education:* BMus, Louisiana State University, 1965; Vocal training with Treigle, Ferro, and Malas, New York. *Career:* Debut: Operatic debut as Spalanzani, Les Contes d'Hoffmann, New Orleans, 1963; First appearance with New York City Opera as the Hermit in US premiere of Ginastera's Don Rodrigo, 1966; On roster until 1978; British debut as Mozart's Almaviva, Glyndebourne Festival, 1974; Royal Opera Covent Garden, London, 1975, 1977, 1979; European debut, Holland Festival, 1977; Frankfurt Opera and Bavarian State Opera, Munich, 1977; Metropolitan Opera debut in New York as Escamillo, 1978; San Francisco Opera, 1979; Hamburg State Opera and Paris Opéra, 1980; Miami Opera and Monte Carlo Opera, 1981; Dallas Opera, 1983; Chicago Lyric Opera, 1984; Los Angeles Opera, 1986; Other roles have been Don Giovanni, Eugene Onegin, Golaud, Don Alfonso, Ford, Wotan and the villains in Les Contes d' Hoffmann; At Santa Fe has sung Altair in Strauss's Die Aegyptische Helena and the Commandant in Friedenstag; Sang Pizarro in Fidelio at Los Angeles, 1990; Jochanaan in Salome at Covent Garden, 1992; Sang Escamillo at Los Angeles, 1992 followed by Boris Godunov, 1994; Amsterdam 1995, in Schoenberg's Moses und Aron; The Doctor in Wozzeck at the Metropolitan, 1997; Season 1998 as Dikoy in Katya Kabanova at St Louis; Sang in Miss Havisham's Fire by Argento at Saint Louis, 2001; Numerous appearances as soloist with major orchestras. *Current Management:* New Century Artist Management. *Address:* c/o Opera Theatre of Saint Louis, PO Box 191910, 539 Garden Avenue, Saint Louis, MO 63119, USA.

DEVOS, Louis; Singer (Tenor); b. 15 June 1926, Brussels, Belgium. *Education:* Vocal studies in Graz, Austria. *Career:* Founded Ensemble Musica Polyphonica 1950, for the performance of early music; Sang in the first performance of Stravinsky's Cantata, Brussels 1952, and in the premiere of the radio opera Orestes by Henk Badings, 1954; Concerts with the Munich Philharmonic from 1956, under the direction of Pierre Boulez and Hermann Scherchen; Sang in the premieres of Martin's Mystère de la Nativité (Geneva 1959) and Pilatus (Rome 1964); Cologne 1972, in Penderecki's Utrejna; Vienna Staatsoper 1974, as Aron in Schoenberg's Moses und Aron; Guest appearances in London, Milan, Amsterdam and Brussels. *Recordings:* Vocal music by Lully; Der Tod Jesu by Graun; Zelenka's Magnificat; Les Indes Galantes by Rameau; Lutoslawski's Paroles tissées; Moses und Aron; Rousseau's Le Devin du Village. *Address:* c/o Staatsoper, Opernring 2, 1010 Vienna, Austria.

DEVOYON, Pascal; Pianist; b. 6 April 1953, Paris, France; m. 29 Feb 1992, 2 s. *Education:* French Baccalaureate Mathematics section; Ecole Normale de Musique Conservatoire de Paris. *Career:* Has played with major orchestras from 1975 including the Philharmonia, Leningrad Philharmonic, NHK Tokyo; Broadcasts over radio and television with Orchestre de la Suisse Romande, Orchestre National d'Espayne, Rotterdam, Stuttgart Philharmonic and RAI of Milan; Debussy Sonatas and Fauré's D Minor Trio for the London Prom concerts at the Victoria and Albert Museum; Professor at the Paris Conservatoire, 1991; Berlin Hochschule für Musik, 1995. *Recordings:* Ravel, Liszt, Tchaikovsky, Bach, Franck, Fauré, Schumann, Grieg, Saint-Saëns. *Honours:* Second Prize, Viotti, 1973; Busoni, 1974; Third Prize, Leeds, 1975; Second Prize, Tchaikovsky, 1978. *Current Management:* Charles Finch, 11a Queens Road, Wimbledon, London SW19 8NG, England. *Address:* 50 Avenue de la Paix 93270 Sevran, France.

DEW, John; Stage Director; b. 1 June 1944, Santiago de Cuba, Cuba. *Education:* Studied in Germany with Walter Felsenstein and Wieland Wagner. *Career:* Debut: The Rake's Progress, at Ulm, 1971; Directed Mozart and Wagner cycles at Krefeld in the 1970s; Head of Production at Bielefeld from 1981, with Maschinist Hopkins by Brand, Schreker's Irrelohe and Der Singende Teufel, Hindemith's Neues vom Tage, Der Sprung über den Schatten and Zwingburg by Krenek; Bakchantinnen by Wellesz, Fennimore and Gerda, Nixon in China and Boito's Nerone; Season 1987–88 at the Deutsche Oper Berlin with Les Huguenots and the premiere of Los Alamos by Neikrug; Les Huguenots seen at Covent Garden, 1991; Other productions include La Juive at Bielefeld and Nuremberg, Clemenza di Tito at Zürich, Death in Venice at Nuremberg, 1992; Aida at Hamburg, 1993; Puritani, Vienna, 1994; Andrea Chénier, Berlin; Leipzig production of Le nozze di Figaro seen at the Israel Festival, 1992; Appointed Artistic Director of the Theatres of the City of Dortmund, 1995; Directed the premiere of Schnittke's Historia von D Johann Fausten, Hamburg, 1995; Floyd's Susannah at the Deutsche Oper, Berlin, 1997; Season 1998 with Die Königin von Saba at Dortmund and Lehar's Paganini in Vienna. *Current Management:* Athole Still International Management, Forresters Hall, 25–27 Westow Street, London, SE19 3RY, England. *Telephone:* (20) 8771-5271. *Fax:* (20) 8768-6600. *Website:* www.atholestill.com.

DEWIS, Michael; Singer (Baritone); b. 1970, England. *Education:* Guildhall School and National Opera Studio. *Career:* Appearances as Marcello for the Mananan Festival, Escamillo at Dartington and Renato (Un Ballo in Maschera) for Opera Holland Park; Season 1997–98 in Don Carlos and The Golden Cockerel for the Royal Opera; Other roles include Papageno, Jack Rance (La Fanciulla del West) and Don Alfonso; Concerts include Messiah at the Albert Hall, Beethoven's Ninth, Mendelssohn's Elijah, Verdi's Requiem and The Dream of Gerontius. *Honours:* Guildhall Schubert Prize. *Address:* c/o Harlequin Agency Ltd, 203 Fidlas Road, Cardiff CF4 5NA, Wales.

DEXTER-MILLS, Christopher John, BA, MMus, PGCE; Teacher and Musicologist; b. 11 Dec. 1956, Boston, England; m. Suzanne; one s. *Education:* Dartington Coll. of Arts, Durham Univ. School of Education, Goldsmiths Coll., London, Univ. of East Anglia. *Career:* assistant teacher of music, Ernulf Community School 1980–85; organist, St Mary's Parish Church, St Neots 1981–83; Head of Music, Soham Village Coll. 1986–94; conductor, Ely Choral Soc. 1992–2000; Dir of Music, The Netherhall School, Cambridge 1995–; mem. Royal Musical Asscn. *Publications:* Dandriem: Les Caractères de la Guerre.

DEYOUNG, Michelle; Singer (Mezzo-Soprano); b. 1969, Colorado, USA. *Education:* Apprentice with the Santa Fe Opera and the Israel Arts Vocal Institute; Met Opera Young Artists' Program, appearing in Carmelites, Aida and Die Zauberflöte, 1993-94. *Career:* Concert appearances with the San Francisco Symphony in Beethoven's Ninth, Mahler's Third and Das klagende Lied, with the Boston Symphony in Mahler 2, the Houston Symphony in Schoenberg's Gurrelieder and the New York Philharmonic (David Del Tredici premiere); Other Repertory includes the Verdi Requiem, Ravel's Sheherazade and Wagner's Wesendonck Lieder, in London, Amsterdam and Paris; Jocasta in Oedipus Rex, in Paris, season 1996; Engaged as Fricka at Seattle and Chicago, 1997-98; Sang Brangaene at Seattle and Fricka for the Royal Opera at the Albert Hall, 1998; Engaged for Mahler 3 at Los Angeles, 2003. *Honours:* Winner, Marilyn Horne Foundation Wings of Song; Marian Anderson Award. *Current Management:* Askonas Holt Ltd, Lonsdale Chambers, 27 Chancery Lane, London, WC2A 1PF, England. *Telephone:* (20) 7400-1700. *Fax:* (20) 7400-1799. *E-mail:* info@askonasholt.co.uk. *Website:* www.askonasholt.co.uk.

DI BELLA, Benito; Singer (Baritone); b. 1942, Palermo, Sicily, Italy. *Education:* Studied at the Palermo Conservatory and in Pesaro. *Career:* Sang at Spoleto and elsewhere in Italy before La Scala Milan debut, 1971, as Marcello in La Bohème; Sang further in Naples, Genoa, Venice and Palermo; Amonasro at the 1989 Verona Arena, Jack Rance at the 1985 Macerata festival; Further appearances throughout North and South America as Verdi's Luna, Germont, Pietro (Simon Boccanegra) and Rigoletto, Gerard in Andrea Chenier, the Herald in Lohengrin and Escamillo; Taormina Festival, 1990. *Address:* c/o Arena di Verona, Pizza Bra 28, 3 Verona, Italy.

DI BONAVENTURA, Anthony; Pianist; b. 12 Nov. 1930, Follensbee, West Virginia, USA. *Education:* Studied at the Curtis Institute with Vengerova. *Career:* Debut: With the NY Philharmonic in 1943, playing Beethoven's C minor Concerto; Beethoven cycle under Otto Klemperer with the London Philharmonic, 1959; Has performed widely in the US with major orchestras in the standard repertory and in works by contemporary composers; Vincent Persichetti, Luciano Berio (Points on a Curve to Find), Alberto Ginastera and Milko Kelemen have written works for him; Teacher at the School of Music, Boston University, from 1973. *Recordings:* Works by Scarlatti, Chopin, Debussy and Prokofiev, Eighth Sonata.

DI CESARE, Ezio; Singer (Tenor); b. 1939, Rome, Italy. *Education:* Studied in Rome. *Career:* Sang with a vocal sextet and made tours of Italy; Stage debut, 1975, in Bellini's Beatrice di Tenda; Many appearances in Italy and elsewhere in Europe as Alfredo, Rodolfo, and Tom Rakewell in The Rake's Progress; La Scala Milan, 1980, 1984, in Vivaldi's Tito Manlio and Idomeneo; Arvino, in Verdi's I Lombardi; Appearances in Netherlands and at the Verona Arena; Sang at Rome, 1986, in Spontini's Agnese di Hohenstaufen; Teatro Liceo, Barcelona, 1987, in the Spanish premiere of Mozart's Lucio Silla; Pesaro Festival, 1988, as Iago in Rossini's Otello; Sang Carlo in Pergolesi's Lo Frate Innamorato at La Scala 1989; Gabriele Adorno at Cremona; Rome Opera, 1990, in Franco Mannino's Il Principe Felice; Season 1992 as Iarba in Jommelli's Didone Abbandonata at the Teatro Rossini, Lugo; Season 1994 as Ismaele in Nabucco at Verona; La Scala 1995, as Raffaela in Verdi's Stiffelio; Jesi 1998, as Sostrate in Pergolesi's Il Prigionero Superbo; Sang the High Priest in Idomeneo at Florence, 1996; Season 2000-01 as Offenbach's Orphée at Turin and the Prince in Lulu at Palermo. *Recordings:* Verdi's Stiffelio; La Finta Giardiniera; Alfano's Cyrano de Bergerac. *Address:* c/o Arena di Verona, Piazza Bra 28, 37121, Verona, Italy.

DI DOMENICA, Robert Anthony, BS; flautist, teacher and composer; b. 4 March 1927, New York, NY, USA. *Education:* New York University.

Career: New York City Opera Orchestra; Freelance Flautist, New York Philharmonic Orchestra; Various engagements as solo artist; Faculty Member, 1969–, Associate Dean, 1973–76, Dean, 1976–78, New England Conservatory of Music, Boston. *Compositions include:* Operas: The Balcony, 1972, The Scarlet Letter, 1986; Beatrice Cenci, 1993; The Cenci, 1995; Francesco Cenci, 1996; Orchestral: Symphony, 1961, Concerto for violin and chamber orchestra, 1962, Concerto for wind quintet, strings and timpani, 1964, Music for flute and string orchestra, 1967, Variations on a Theme by Gunther Schuller for 13 instruments, 1983, Dream Journeys, 1984; Variations Soliloquies, 1988; Gone are the Rivers and Eagles, 1992; Chamber: Sonata for flute and piano, 1957, Sextet for woodwind quintet and piano, 1957, Quartet for flute, violin, viola and cello, 1960, Quintet for clarinet and string quartet, 1965, Sonata for violin and piano, 1966, Saeculum aureum for flute, piano and tape, 1967, Sonata for saxophone and piano, 1968; Piano Pieces, Vocal: Wind Quintet for soprano and woodwind quintet, 1963, Songs from Twelfth Night for tenor, flute, viola da gamba and harpsichord, 1976, Hebrew Melodies for soprano, violin and piano, 1983. *Recordings:* Leona Di Domenica in live first performance of the Solo Piano Music of Robert Di Domenica; Three Orchestral Works by Robert Di Domenica conducted by Gunther Schuller and the Radio Philharmonic of Hannover. *Publications:* Dream Journeys for Orchestra, 1984. *Honours:* Guggenheim Fellowship, 1972; Opera The Balcony premiered by the Opera Company of Boston, 1990 and Moscow's Bolshoi Theater, 1991.

DI FRANCO, Loretta; Singer (Soprano); b. 28 Oct. 1942, New York, NY, USA. *Education:* Studied with Maud Webber and Walter Taussig in New York. *Career:* Sang in the chorus of the Metropolitan Opera until 1965; Solo appearances in New York in The Queen of Spades, Don Giovanni (Zerlina), Un Ballo in Maschera (Oscar), Gianni Schicchi (Lauretta), Le nozze di Figaro (Marcellina) and Lucia di Lammermoor (title role); Returned to Met 1990, as Marthe in Faust. *Address:* c/o Metropolitan Opera, Lincoln Center, New York, NY 10023, USA.

DI GIUSEPPE, Enrico; Singer (Tenor); b. 14 Oct. 1932, Philadelphia, PA, USA. *Education:* Studied with Richard Bonelli at Curtis Institute of Music, Philadelphia, with Hans Heinz at Juilliard School of Music, NY. *Career:* Debut: Operatic debut as Massenet's Des Grieux, New Orleans, 1959; Toured with Metropolitan Opera National Company; NY City Opera debut as Michele in The Saint of Bleecker Street, 1965; On roster, 1967–81; Metropolitan Opera debut in NY as Turiddu, 1970; Sang at the Met until 1985 as Pinkerton, Rossini's Almaviva and Lindoro, Mozart's Ferrando, Alfredo, the Duke of Mantua and Rodolfo; Guest appearances with opera companies in Baltimore, Boston, Cincinnati, Dallas, Houston, Ottawa, Philadelphia, Pittsburgh, San Francisco, Toronto and other cities; Various engagements as concert artist. *Recordings:* Several recordings. *Address:* c/o Metropolitan Opera, Lincoln Center, New York, NY 10023, USA.

DI LOTTI, Silvana; Composer; b. 29 Nov. 1942, Aglie Canavese, Turin, Italy. *Education:* Studied in Turin and Salzburg, with courses at Siena notably with Berio and Boulez. *Career:* Teacher at the Turin Conservatory; Performances of her music in Italy and elsewhere. *Compositions include:* Aragorn for clavicembalo and 5 strings; Contrasti for 2 clarinets, 1981; Capriccio for violin and piano, 1981; Duo In Eco for violin and guitar, 1982; Conversari for orchestra, 1982; Serenata for chamber orchestra, 1982; Groups for piano. 1983; In Nomine Domini for orchestra, 1983; Intonazione for saxophone and piano, 1983; Rapsodia for 2 chitarre, 1984; Surfaces for organ, 1985; Aura for piano, 1985; Piano Trio, 1986; C'est Pour Toi Seule for coro misto, 1987; Mattutino for harp, 1990; A Solo for clarinet and ensemble, 1991; Arabesque for cello, 1991; E Nessun Tempo Ha Memoria Di Echi Svelati for bass clarinet and harp, 1992; Musica per Giocare for piano, 1994; Terre Rare for orchestra, 1995. *Recordings:* Haide for violin, cello and piano. *Address:* c/o Viale Ovidio 5, 10090 Gassino, Fr Bardassano, (TO) Italy.

DI PIANDUNI, Oslavio; Singer (Tenor); b. 1939, Montevideo, Uruguay. *Education:* Studied in Montevideo. *Career:* Appeared at Montevideo 1961–65 as Rinuccio in Gianni Schicchi and Lionel in Martha; Klagenfurt 1968–70 and Alfredo, Riccardo, Hoffmann, Don José, Pinkerton and Calaf at Bielefeld, 1970–75; Further engagements at the Theater am Gärtnerplatz, Munich, 1975–76, Vienna Volksoper, 1976–78 and Kiel 1979–82; Bremen 1982–84, Zürich 1988 as Edmund in Reimann's Lear; Hanover 1989, as Andrea Chénier; Other roles include Luigi in Il Tabarro, Hermann in The Queen of Spades and Otello, Oslo, 1999; Has also sung in operettas by Lehar, Johann Strauss and Offenbach; Many concert appearances and Lieder recitals. *Address:* c/o Niedersachische Staatstheater, Opernplatz 1, 3000 Hannover, Germany.

DI PIETRO, Rocco; Composer; b. 15 Sept. 1949, Buffalo, New York, USA; m. Juli Douglass, 28 May 1973, 1 s. *Education:* BPS, State University of New York, 1985; Studied with Hans Hagen, Lukas Foss and Bruno Maderna. *Career:* Lecturer on Modern Music; Performances of his compositions have been played in major cities of Europe and USA by such Musicians and Ensembles as Christiane Edinger, Christobal Halffter, Lukas Foss, Bruno Maderna, Bavarian Radio Orchestra, Brooklyn Philharmonic, St Paul Chamber Orchestra. *Compositions:* Overture to Combats for History, for percussion orchestra, 1980–81; Melodia Arcana for percussion and tarot cards, 1980–83; Aria Grande for violin and orchestra, 1980; Tratto Bizzaro, opera, 1984; Beauty and the Beast, incidental music for theatre, 1986; Annales after Tasso for madrigal voices and percussion, 1987. *Publications:* Melodia Nera for Timpani, AM Percussion Publications, 1985. *Current Management:* Sheldon Soffer, New York. *Address:* c/o American Percussion Publications, PO Box 436, Lancaster, NY 14086, USA.

DI VIRGILIO, Nicholas; Singer (Tenor); b. 1937, New York, USA. *Education:* Studied at the Eastman School and in New York. *Career:* Debut: Sang Pinkerton with Chautauqua Opera, 1961; Sang at Baltimore from 1956, San Francisco, 1966–67, Cincinnati, New Orleans, 1969–70, San Diego, Pittsburgh and the New York City Opera, 1964–71; Metropolitan Opera from 1970, as Pinkerton and as Edgardo in Lucia di Lammermoor; European engagements at Brussels, Amsterdam and Lyon, 1968–70; London, 1978, in the Verdi Requiem; Other roles have included Mozart's Idomeneo, Don Ottavio and Ferrando, Verdi's Alfredo, Fenton and Riccardo, Faust, Rodolfo, Hoffmann, Don José, Laca in Jenůfa and Cavaradossi. Voice Teacher at the University of Illinois.

DIADKOVA, Larissa; Singer (Mezzo-soprano); b. 1954, Zelenodolsk, Russia. *Education:* Studied at the St Petersburg Conservatory. *Career:* Sang with the Kirov Opera, St Petersburg, and elsewhere in Russia as Ratmir in Ruslan and Lyudmilla, Konchakovna in Prince Igor, Tchaikovsky's Olga and Pauline and the Duenna in Prokofiev's Betrothal in a Monastery; Guest appearances at the Bregenz and Edinburgh Festivals; Florence, 1995 as Verdi's Ulrica, Bolshoi and Metropolitan, 1996 as Marfa in Khovanshchina and Madelon in Andrea Chénier; Lyon and Savonlinna Festival, 1996 as the Countess in The Queen of Spades and Liubov in Mazeppa; Season 1998 as Ulrica at Monte Carlo, in Tchaikovsky's Mazeppa at the New York Met and Marfa with the Kirov Opera at La Scala; Season 2000–01 as Ulrica at the Vienna Staatsoper, Mistress Quickly at Salzburg, Azucena at Verona and Amneris for San Francisco Opera; Jezibaba in Rusalka at Covent Garden (concert) 2003. *Recordings:* Rimsky's Sadko; Mazeppa by Tchaikovsky. *Address:* Kirov Opera, 1 Theatre Square, St Petersburg, Russia.

DIAMOND, David (Leo); Composer; b. 9 July 1915, Rochester, New York, USA. *Education:* Cleveland Institute of Music, 1927–29; Eastman School of Music, University of Rochester, 1930–34; American Conservatory, Fontainebleau, France, summer 1937, 1938; New Music and Dalcroze Institute, New York City, 1934–36. *Career:* Teacher, composition, Metropolitan Music School, New York City, 1950; Lecturer, American music, Seminar in American Studies, Schloss Leopoldskron, Salzburg, Austria, 1949; Fulbright Professor, University of Rome, Italy, 1951–52; Slee Professor of Music, University of Buffalo, New York, 1961, 1963; Professor, Chairman, Department of Composition, Manhattan School of Music, New York City, 1965–67; Visiting Professor, University of Colorado, 1970; Composer-in-residence, American Academy in Rome, 1971–72; Lamont School, University of Denver, 1983; Juilliard School of Music, 1973–97; mem, American Academy of Arts and Letters. *Compositions include:* 11 Symphonies, 1941–92, concertos for violin, flute, piano and violoncello, string quartet with orchestra, 11 string quartets, 1940–68, chamber music, 52 preludes and fugues for piano, sonatas, choral music and songs, scores for motion pictures and other forms of instrumental music; Night Thoughts for orchestra, 1996; Composer, Conductor, original score, Margaret Webster production, The Tempest, 1944–45; Incidental music, Tennessee Williams' Rose Tattoo, 1950; Ballets, Tom, Dream of Audubon; Opera, The Noblest Game. *Recordings include:* Music for albums, Romeo and Juliet, The Tempest Overture, 4th Symphony, 4th String Quartet; 5 vols Symphonies. *Honours:* Edward MacDowell Gold Medal Award, 1991; Gold Medal, American Academy of Arts and Letters, 1993; Gold Medal, National Medal of the Arts. *Address:* 249 Edgerton Street, Rochester, NY 14607, USA.

DIANDA, Hilda; Composer; b. 13 April 1925, Cordoba, Argentina. *Education:* Studied with Malipiero and Scherchen; Further study at Milan Electronic Music Studios and in Darmstadt. *Career:* Teacher at Cordoba until 1971; Performances of her music in Europe and North America; Educator and Lecturer. *Compositions include:* Requiem, 1984; Cantico, after St Francis of Assisi, 1985; Trio for clarinet, cello and piano, 1985; Encantanientos for tape, 1985; Viola Concerto, 1988; Paisaje for 4 percussion, 1992; Mitos for percussion and strings, 1993; Pitiales for marimba, 1994. *Honours:* Cultural Merit Medal, Italy. *Address:* c/o SADAIC, Lavalle 1547, Apartado Postal Number 11, Sucursal 44-B, 1048 Buenos Aires, Argentina.

DIAZ, Justino; Singer (Bass-Baritone); b. 29 Jan. 1939, San Juan, Puerto Rico. *Education:* Studied at the University of Puerto Rico, at the New England Conservatory and with Ralph Errolle and Frederick Jagel. *Career:* Debut: Puerto Rico, 1957, in Menotti's The Telephone; Metropolitan Opera from 1963, as Monterone and Sparafucile in Rigoletto, Figaro, Rossini's Maometto II and Colline; Festival Casals, Puerto Rico, 1964–65; Spoleto Festival, 1965; Salzburg Festival, 1966, as Escamillo; Created A y in Barber's Antony and Cleopatra, New York Met, 196 S ala, ilan, 1969, in Rossini's L'Assedio do Corinto; New York C Opera, 1973, in Ginastera's Beatrix Cenci; Covent Garden, 1976, as Escamillo; Guest appearance in Hamburg, Vienna, Mexico City, Chicago and San Francisco; San Francisco and Milan, 1982, as Scarpia and Asdrubalo in La Pietra del Paragone; Sang Attila at Cincinnati, 1984, Iago at Covent Garden, 1990; Michele in Il Tabarro at Miami, 1989, Iago and Scarpia at Los Angeles; Sang Escamillo at Rio de Janeiro, 1990; Debut as Amonasro at Cincinnati, 1990; Sang Iago in Zeffirelli's film version of Otello, 1987; Greater Miami Opera, 1992 as Franchetti's Cristoforo Colombo; Sang Puccini's Jack Rance at Covent Garden, 1994, Scarpia in 1995 (and for Opera Pacific, 1998); Sang Iago for Washington Opera, 2000. *Recordings:* Medea and La Wally; Thais by Massenet; L'Assedio di Corinto and Otello; Semele; Videos of Zeffirelli's Otello, and Meyerbeer's L'Africaine, from San Francisco Opera. *Address:* c/o Stafford Law Associates, 6 Barham Close, Weybridge, Surrey KT 13 9 PR, England.

DIBAK, Igor; Composer; b. 5 July 1947, Spisska Nova Ves, Czechoslovakia; m. Katarina Ormisova, 31 Jan 1970. *Education:* Piano study, Conservatorie Zilina, 1962–66; With Professor Jan Cikker, Department of Composition, University of Arts, Bratislava, 1966–71; Magister. *Career:* Editor, Musical Department, Czech television, 1969–79; Editor-in-Chief, Musical Department, Czech Radio, Bratislava, 1979–87; Editor-in-Chief, Musical Department, Czech television, Bratislava, 1987–90; Director of Music School, 1990; mem, Slovak Music Union, Bratislava; Slovak Protective Union of Authors, Bratislava. *Compositions:* Opera Candlestick; New Year's Eve Part; Ballet Portrait; Symphonic works including Accordion Concerto, 1996; Chamber compositions; Compositions for children. *Recordings:* Moments musicaux 1, Fantasy for Viola and Orchestra, Divertimento for Strings, Opera Candlestick, New Year's Eve Part, Ballet Portrait, Czech television; Symphonic and Chamber works, Czech Radio Bratislava. *Publications:* Methodics of Piano Improvisation, 1981. *Contributions:* Hudobny zivot (Music Live). *Honours:* Jan Levoslav Bella Award, 1979; Union of Slovak Music Composers Award, 1987. *Current Management:* Music Information Centre, Fucikova 29, 811 02 Bratislava, Slovakia. *Address:* Bajzova 10, 821 08 Bratislava, Slovakia.

DIBBLE, Jeremy (Colin); Professor in Music; b. 17 Sept. 1958, Epping, Essex, England; m. Alison Jane Manning, 4 Aug 1984. *Education:* Trinity College, Cambridge, 1977–80; BA, Univ. of Cambridge, 1980; Doctoral work, 1980–86, PhD, 1986, Univ. of Southampton. *Career:* Lecturer in Music, Univ. College, Cork, Ireland, 1987–93, Lecturer in Music, 1993–98, Reader in Music, 1998–2003, Prof. of Music, 2003–; mem. Society of Fellows, Knott/Christopherson Fellowship, from October 2004; Univ. of Durham; Administrator and Secretary to Turnbull Memorial Trust; mem. Oxford and Cambridge. *Recordings:* Consultant, Editor and Sleeve-note Writer for many recordings of works by Parry, Stanford and others. *Publications:* Books: C Hubert H Parry: His Life and Music, 1992, revised edition, 1998; Nineteenth-Century British Music Studies (with Zon), 2002; Charles Villiers Stanford: Man and Musician, 2002; Parry Sonatas for violin and Piano, Musica Britannica Trust, Vol. LXXX, 2003. *Contributions:* Essays on Vaughan Williams in Perspective; Irish Musical Studies II: Studies in Church Music; King Arthur and Music; Music and British Culture 1785–1914; Constructions of Nationalism; Nineteenth Century British Music Studies Vols I and II; Articles in Journal of the British Institute of Organ Studies; Brio; Journal of the Ralph Vaughan Williams Society; New Grove 2, New Dictionary of National Biography; Thoemmes Dictionary of Nineteenth Century British Philosophers; Musik in Geschichte und Gegenwart; Dictionary of Irish Biography; New Oxford Companion to Music; Grolier's Encyclopaedia of the Victorian Era; Musical Editor to Dictionary of Hymnology; Reviews in Music and Letters, Notes and journal of Victorian Studies. *Address:* 69 Beechfield Rise, Coxhoe, Durham DH 6 4 SD, England. *E-mail:* jeremy.dibble@durham.ac.uk.

DICHTER, Misha; Concert Pianist; b. 27 Sept. 1945, Shanghai, China; m. Cipa Dichter, 21 Jan 1968, 2 s. *Education:* BSc, Juilliard School of Music, USA. *Career:* Performs in Recital and with major orchestras and in Chamber Music concerts world-wide; Performances with Chicago Symphony, Los Angeles Philharmonic, Philadelphia Orchestra, Israel Philharmonic Orchestra; Performs in duo-piano programmes with wife, Cipa Dichter. *Recordings include:* Beethoven Sonatas No. 14 in C Sharp Minor, Op 27 No. 2, Moonlight; No. 8 in C Minor, Op 13, Pathetique; No. 28 in A Major, Op 101; Brahms Piano Concerto No. 1 in D Minor; Brahms Piano Concerto No. 2 in B Flat Major Op 83; Gershwin Rhapsody in Blue; Addinsell Warsaw Concerto; Litolff, Scherzo from Concerto Symphonique Op 102; Works by Liszt, including: Liszt complete Hungarian Rhapsodies; Fantasy on the Waltz from Gounod's Faust; Etudes de Concert; Schumann Symphonic Studies, Op 13 and Fantasie in C Major; Brahms: Variations and Fugue on a theme by Handel, Op. 24; Fantasias Op. 116; Waltzes, Op. 39; Stravinsky, Piano Concerto. *Contributions:* New York Times; Ovation; Keyboard. *Honours:* Silver Medal, International Tchaikovsky Competition, Moscow, 1966; Grand Prix International du Disque Liszt, 1998. *Address:* Shuman Associates, 120 West 58th Street, New York, NY 10019, USA.

DICK, James Cordell, BMus,; concert pianist; b. 29 June 1940, Hutchinson, Kansas, USA. *Education:* University of Texas at Austin, Royal Academy of Music, London; studied with Dalies Frantz, Clifford Curzon. *Career:* debut, Carnegie Hall, New York City, USA; performs professionally throughout the USA and abroad in orchestral, chamber and solo repertoire; performed with conductors Kondrashin, Barbirolli, Ormandy, Maazel, Levine, Comissiona, Lombard, Schwarz, Fleisher, de Priest, Fiedler, Foster, Robert Spano and Christopher Hogwood among others; has performed on radio in England, Germany, France, Netherlands, Switzerland, Mexico and US Commissions new music for piano and orchestra; founder and Artistic Director of International Festival-Institute at Round Top, Texas. *Compositions:* Etudes for piano and orchestra, by Ben Lees, gave world premiere, 1975; Shiva's Drum, by Dan Welcher, gave world premiere in 1994; Krishna, from Malcolm Hawkins (England), world premiere in 1996; Rising Light by Chinary Ung. *Recordings:* Beethoven's Concerto No. 4; Tchaikovsky Concerto No. 1; Chopin Concerto No. 1; Prokofiev Concerto No. 3; Saint-Saëns Concerto No. 2; Rachmaninov Rhapsody. *Honours:* Prize, Tchaikovsky Competition, Russia, 1965; Prize, Leventritt Competition, New York City, 1965; Prize, Busoni Competition, Italy, 1965; Chevalier des Arts et des Lettres, 1996; Texas State Musician, 2003. *Current Management:* Alain Declert & Associates, PO Box 89, Round Top, TX 78954, USA. *Address:* Festival Hill, Round Top TX 78954-0089, USA.

DICKIE, Brian; Opera Administrator; b. 23 July 1941; m. 1st Victoria Teresa Sheldon 1968; two s. one d.; m. 2nd Nancy Gustafson 1989. *Education:* Haileybury; Trinity Coll., Dublin. *Career:* Admin. Asst, Glyndebourne Opera, 1962–66; Admin., Glyndebourne Touring Opera, 1967–81; Opera Man., Glyndebourne Festival Opera, 1970–81, Gen. Admin., 1981–89; Artistic Dir, Wexford Festival, 1967–73; Artistic Adviser, Theatre Music de Paris, 1981–87; Chair., London Choral Society, 1978–85; Vice-Chair., TNC, 1980–85 (Chair., TNC Opera Cttee, 1976–85); Vice-Pres., Theatrical Management Asscn, 1983–85; Gen. Dir, Canadian Opera Company, 1989–93. *Address:* 405 Edgemere Way North, Naples, FL 33999, USA.

DICKIE, John; Singer (Tenor); b. 5 Sept. 1953, London, England. *Education:* Studied at the University of Music, Vienna and the Vienna Academy. *Career:* Engaged in Wuppertal, 1979–82, Mannheim, 1982–85; Hamburg Staatsoper from 1985–87; Bregenz Festival, 1981–86, in L'Incontro Improvviso, Lucia di Lammermoor, Der Vogelhändler and Die Zauberflöte; Member of the Wiener Staats and Volksoper since 1987; Guest appearances at Covent Garden, Deutsche Oper Berlin, Staatsoper Berlin, Geneva, Düsseldorf among others; Other roles include Mozart's Belmonte, Don Ottavio, Ferrando, Tito and Belfiore, Lionel in Martha, Nemorino in L'Elisir d'amore, Berlioz's Benedict, Lensky in Eugene Onegin and Wagner's Steuermann and Froh; Sang Don Fabrizio in the world premiere of Schnittke's Gesualdo, Vienna, 1995; Title role in Leopold I's Il figliol prodigo, Vienna, 1997; Season 2000–01 at the Vienna Staatsoper in Die Jakobsleiter by Schoenberg, as Monostatos and as Red Whiskers in Billy Budd; Also heard as concert singer. *Recordings:* Mozart Tenor Arias; Così fan tutte (complete);, Fledermaus, Eisenstein (complete); Apollo und Hyazinth, Mozart (complete); Television production of Gluck's Orpheus et Euridice (Paris version); Album of own songs, Timeslip, 1987. *Address:* c/o Vienna Staatsoper, Opernring 2, A1010 Vienna, Austria.

DICKINSON, Meriel; Singer (Mezzo-Soprano); b. 8 April 1940, Lytham St Anne's, England; m. Robert J.H. Gardner, 1991. *Education:* GRSM; ARMCM; Piano and Singing Performer's Diploma with Honours; Vienna Academy, Austria. *Career:* Debut: London, 1964; Frequent radio programmes; 2 BBC television documentary films; Recital programmes with composer Peter Dickinson (brother) throughout Europe; mem, Park Lane Group; Incorporated Society of Musicians. *Recordings:* Contemporary British Composers (Crosse, Berkeley, Dickinson); Erik Satie Songs and Piano Music; Brecht-Weill series with London Sinfonietta; Singing teacher and Adjudicator. *Honours:* Countess of Munster Musical Trust Scholarship, 1964–66. *Address:* The Old Bakery, Grendon Underwood, Aylesbury HP18 0SW, England.

DICKINSON, Peter; Composer, Pianist and Writer; b. 15 Nov. 1934, Lytham, Lancashire, England; m. Bridget Jane Tomkinson, 2 s. *Education:* LRAM; ARCM, Piano Performance; Organ Scholar Queens'

College, Cambridge; MA Music; ARCO Sawyer Prize; FRCO; Stewart of Rannoch Scholar; Juilliard School of Music, New York, USA; D Mus (London). *Career:* Various teaching posts in New York, London and Birmingham; First Professor of Music, 1974–84, Emeritus, 1984–, Keele University; Professor, 1991–97, Emeritus professor, 1997–, Goldsmiths' College, University of London; Head of Music, Institute of United States Studies, University of London; Performances and recordings as Pianist, mostly with sister Meriel Dickinson (mezzo), radio and television in the United Kingdom and abroad. *Compositions include:* Orchestral works (Merseyside Echoes, 1985), concertos (Piano, 1984, Violin, 1986), chamber music, choral works, songs, keyboard music, church music. *Recordings:* Piano Concerto; Outcry; Organ Concerto; Song cycles (Auden, Dylan Thomas, Cummings, Heath-Stubbs, Lord Berners); Rags, Blues and Parodies (Burns, Corso, Lord Byron, Stevie Smith, Satie etc); American Trio; organ and piano works. *Publications:* Editor: 20 British Composers, 1975; The Complete Songs and Piano Music of Lord Berners, 1982; The Music of Lennox Berkeley, 1989, new edition 2003; Marigold: The Music of Billy Mayerl, 1999; Ed. Copland Connotations: Studies and Interviews, 2002. *Contributions:* Various books and journals including book chapters and dictionaries. *Honours:* Hon D.Mus, Keele University, 1999. *Address:* c/o Novello & Co, 8–9 Frith Street, London W1V 5TZ, England.

DICKMAN, Stephen (Allen); Composer; b. 2 March 1943, Chicago, Illinois, USA. *Education:* Studied composition with Jacob Druckman at Bard College, and theory and composition with Arthur Berger and Harold Shapero at Brandeis University; Further study with Ernst Krenek at Berkshire Music Center and with Golfredo Petrassi in Rome. *Career:* Has travelled widely in order to study the music of Asia and the Middle East. *Compositions include:* Rabbi Nathan's Prayer, soprano and violin, 1995; The Violin Maker, musical in progress; Theatre Pieces King Arthur, 1996, and Cyrano, 1997; Duets, for 2 singers a capella, 1992–98; Four for Tom, piano and baritone, 1997; The Music of Eric Zann, baritone solo, on a story by H P Lovecraft, 1998. *Recordings:* The Music of Eric Zann; Who Says Works; Four For Tom; Indian Wells; If There Were No. Birds and Rabbi Nathan's Prayer, forthcoming; Trees and Other Inclinations; The Wheels of Ezekiel; The Song of the Reed, My Love Makes Me Lonely, Love, the Hierophant. *Honours:* CAP Award, 1987, 1990; NEA/Artist as a Producer of New American Works Award, 1989; Meet the Composer, 1995; SOS Grant, East End Arts Council and New York Foundation for the Arts, 1995, 1998, 1999; Meet the Composer Fund Award, 1990, 1995, 1996; Timeline Suffolk Decentralization Grant, 1998; American Composers Forum Commission, 1998. *Address:* 73 Squaw Road, East Hampton, NY 11937, USA.

DICKSON, Grant; Singer (Bass); b. 1940, New Zealand. *Career:* Debut: New Zealand Opera, 1962; Appearances with Australian Opera as Mozart's Sarastro and Bartolo; Don Basilio, Don Pasquale and Baron Ochs; Rocco, Mephistopheles and Trulove for New Zealand Opera; European engagements from 1991, including the Commendatore in Dresden, Pluto in Telemann's Orpheus at Berlin and Boris Godunov for Welsh National Opera; Season 1998–99 with Schigolch in Lulu for De Vlaamse Opera and King Mark in Tristan for WNO; Season 1999–2000 in The Greek Passion and La Bohème at Covent Garden; Concerts include the Verdi Requiem at the Albert Hall. *Address:* c/o Harlequin Agency Ltd, 203 Fidles Road, Cardiff CF4 5NA, Wales.

DICKSON, Joan; Cellist and Teacher; b. 21 Dec. 1921, Edinburgh, Scotland. *Education:* LRAM; ARCM; Studied in Paris and Rome. *Career:* Solo Cellist with major British Orchestras; Appearances at the London Promenade Concerts, Cheltenham Festival, Edinburgh Festival; Tours abroad; Regular Broadcaster; Television appearances; Professor of Cello, Royal College of Music, London; Teacher of Cello, Royal Scottish Academy of Music, Glasgow; Short Talks, BBC radio. *Recordings:* Iain Hamilton Cello Sonata; Cesar Franck Sonata. *Contributions:* Incorporated Society of Musicians Magazine. *Honours:* Fellow, Royal College of Music; Fellow, Royal Scottish Academy Music and Drama; Cobbett Gold Medal for services to Chamber Music.

DIDONATO, Joyce; Singer (Mezzo-soprano); b. 1970, Prairie Village, Kansas, USA. *Education:* Academy of Vocal Arts, Philadelphia and the Houston Opera Studio. *Career:* Sang Ino in Handel's Semele at Spoleto, Italy, 1996; Houston Grand Opera, 1996–97 as Siebel in Faust, Fyodor in Boris Gudonov and Grace Kelly in the premiere of Jackie O; Season 1998–99 as Nicklausse in Les Contes d'Hoffmann and Cherubino at Houston; Premiere of Tod Machover's Resurrection, after Tolstoy; Rosina for Kentucky Opera; Engaged for Cherubino at Santa Fe and Dorabella at Houston, 2001; Rossini's Isabella and Angelina for New Israeli Opera; Rosina at the Paris Opéra, 2002; Covent Garden debut at the Fox in The Cunning Little Vixen, 2003. *Honours:* District winner, Met Opera Auditions, 1996. *Address:* c/o IMG Artists, Lovell House, 616 Chiswick High Road, London W4 5RX, England.

DIDONE, Rosanna; Singer (Soprano); b. 13 Feb. 1952, Galliera, Veneta, Italy. *Education:* Studied at the Benedetto Marcello Conservatory

Venice. *Career:* Debut: Padua 1978, as Serpina in La Serva Padrona; Appearances at Venice in Idomeneo, as Rosette in Manon and Bianca in La Rondine; Clarice in Il Mondo Della Luna at Turin and Frasquita in Carmen at Padau, 1982; At Trieste (from 1982) has sung Gnese in Il Campiello, Amor (Orpheus ed Euridice), Barbarina, and a Naiad in Ariadne auf Naxos; Rome Opera 1982 and 1988 in Don Carlos and as Mme Silberklang in Der Schauspieldirektor by Mozart; Other roles include Musetta, Marie-Louise in Kodály's Háry János, Biancofiore in Francesca da Rimini, Gilda, Susanna, Carolina (Il matrimonio segreto), Norina (Don Pasquale), Oscar, Nannetta, Laura and Despina; Guest appearances in Netherlands and Bulgaria. *Recordings:* Egloge in Mascagni's Nerone, and Francesca da Rimni (Bongiovanni).

DIEMER, Emma Lou; Composer, Organist and University Professor; b. 24 Nov. 1927, Kansas City, Missouri, USA. *Education:* BM, 1949, MM, 1950, Yale School of Music; PhD, Eastman School of Music, 1960. *Career:* Pianist; Organist; Composer-in-Residence, Santa Barbara Symphony, 1990–92; Professor of Composition, University of California, Santa Barbara, 1971–91; Organist, First Presbyterian Church, Santa Barbara, 1984–2000. *Compositions:* Over 100 published compositions; 10 listings in Schwann Catalogue, 17 works recorded; Concerto for marimba, 1990; Concerto for piano, 1991; Sextet, 1992; Four Biblical Settings for organ, 1992; Kyrie, 1993; Fantasy for piano, 1993; Gloria, 1996; Psalms for organ and flute, Psalms for organ and trumpet, Psalms for organ and percussion, 1998; Mass, 2000; Piano Trio, 2000; Homage to Tchaikovsky, 2001. *Recordings:* 10 including Declarations for organ; Toccata and Fugue for organ; Toccata for piano; Summer of 82 for cello and piano; Quartet for piano, violin, viola and cello; Sextet for woodwind quintet and piano; Youth Overture; Encore for piano, 1991; Sextet, 1993; Concerto in One Movement for piano, 1995; String Quartet No. 1, 1995; Santa Barbara Overture, 1997; Concerto in One Movement for piano, 1998; Fantasy for piano, 1998; Suite of Homages, for orchestra 1999; Four Chinese Love Poems, 1999; Piano Concerto, 2000; Suite of Homages, 2001, Santa Barbara Overture, 2001. *Publications:* Over 100 including: Toccata for marimba, 1956; Sonata for violin and piano, 1968; Sextet for woodwind quintet and piano, 1968; Anniversary Choruses for chorus and orchestra, 1970; Concerto for flute, 1973; Symphony No. 2, 1976; Toccata for piano, 1979; Suite of Homages for orchestra, 1985; String Quartet No. 1, 1987; Choral–A Feast for Christmas, 1992; Marimba Concerto, 1994; Organ Works, 1957–2002; Kyrie and Gloria, 1997; Psalms for flute and organ, 1999; Psalms for percussion and organ, 1999; Mass, 2000; Piano Sonata No. 3, 2001. *Honours:* Kennedy Center Friedheim Award, for Concerto in One Movement for piano, 1995; American Guild of Organists Composer of the Year, 1995; Honorary Doctorate of Letters, Central Missouri State University, 1999. *Address:* 2249 Vista del Campo, Santa Barbara, CA 93101, USA. *E-mail:* eldiemer@cox.net.

DIENER, Melanie; Singer (Soprano); b. 1967, Germany. *Education:* Studied with Sylvia Geszty in Stuttgart and with Rudolf Piernay in Mannheim; Further study at Indiana University. *Career:* Concerts include the Brahms Requiem in Paris and Zürich, Mendelssohn's St Paul under Philippe Herreweghe and Mahler's 2nd Symphony at Linz; Recitals in Stuttgart and Bonn; Opera debut as Mozart's Ilia at Garsington, England, 1996; Season 1996–97 with Elijah at the Berlin Philharmonie, Fiordiligi at Covent Garden and in Paris, First Lady in Die Zauberflöte at the Salzburg Festival; Asberta in Holzbauer's Gunther von Schwarzburg under Ton Koopman at the Amsterdam Concertgebouw; The Strauss Four Last Songs at Turin and the Verdi Requiem at St Gallen; Season 1997–98 with Korngold's Kathrin for the BBC, Agathe in Der Freischütz for the Royal Opera in concert and Donna Elvira at Aix; Elsa in Lohengrin at Bayreuth, 1999; Covent Garden as Donna Elvira, 2002, returned to London 2003, as Elsa. *Honours:* Prizewinner, International Mozart Competition, Salzburg, 1995; Winner, Kirsten Flagstad Prize, Oslo, 1995. *Current Management:* Balmer & Dixon Management AG, Kreuzstrasse 82, 8032 Zürich, Switzerland. *Telephone:* (43) 244-8644. *Fax:* (43) 244-8649. *Website:* www.badix.ch.

DIESSELHORST, Jan; Cellist; b. 1956, Marburg, Germany. *Education:* Studied in Frankfurt and with Wolfgang Boettcher in Berlin. *Career:* Joined the Berlin Philharmonic Orchestra, 1979; Co-founded the Philharmonic Quartet Berlin, giving concerts throughout Europe, the USA and Japan; British debut, 1987, playing Haydn, Szymanowski and Beethoven at Wigmore Hall; Bath Festival, 1987, playing Mozart, Schumann and Beethoven (Op. 127); Other repertoire includes quartets by Bart ók, Mendelssohn, Nicolai, Ravel and Schubert; Quintets by Brahms, Weber, Reger and Schumann. *Address:* c/o Berlin Philharmonic Orchestra, Philharmonie, Matthäuskirchstrasse 1, 1000 Berlin 30, Germany.

DIETRICH, Karl; Composer and Teacher; b. 9 July 1927, Wachstedt/ Eichsfeld, Germany; m. Gerda Lins, 29 April 1952, 2 d. *Education:* Matriculation and Study, University Jena and High School of Music, Franz Liszt, Weimar. *Career:* Professor for Composition, High School of

Music, Franz Liszt, Weimar; mem, Ordentliches Mitglied Deutscher Komponisten-Interessenverband. *Compositions:* Seven Symphonies, 1969–92; Operas: Die Wette des Serapion, 1984; Pervonte, 1989; Orchestral: 3 Divertimenti for Orchestra, 1972–76; Piano Concerto 1964; Concerto for orchestra, 1969; Dramatic Scenes for 3 flutes (1 Soloist), and large orchestra, 1974; Violoncello Concerto 1982; Concertino giocoso for string orchestra, 1962; Konzert-Suite for string orchestra, 1967; Memorial for string orchestra in connection with the choral of J. S. Bach, Vergiá mein Nicht, 1994; Konzertantes Präludium für Orchestra, 1996; Chamber Music: Prokofiev-Variationen für Klavier 4-händig, 1970; Anregungen für Klavier, 1974; Etude capricieuse für Cello-Solo, 1993; Ton-triage für Flöte-Solo, 1986; 3 Liederzyklen für Singstimme und Klavier; 3 Bläserquintette; 6 Dialoge für 2 Oboen; Divertimento für Flöte und Streichtrio. Organ: Groáe Fantasie für Orgel, 1981; Vision für Flöte und Orgel, 1984; Rupert-Mayer-Reflexionen für Orgel. Church Music: Psalm 49, Die Vergänglichkeit des Menschen, für Bariton und Orgel, 1994; Deutsche Messe für Männerchor a cappella, 1995; Schöndorfer Messe, lateinischer Text, für mittlere Singstimme und Orgel, 1996, und Kirchenmusikalische Kompositionen diverser Art für Chöre und Soli. *Recordings:* Symphony No. 4, contra bellum, SSO Thüringen, Conductor Lothar Seyfarth; Dramatic Szenes, Rundfunk-Sinfonieorchestra Leipzig, Conductor Herbert Kegel; Symphony No. 7, Philharmonie Erfurt, Conductor Wolfgang Rögner. *Publications:* Opéra Comique Pervonte nach Ch M Wieland; Violoncello Concerto; Symphony No. 4; Vision for flute and organ; Konzertsuite for string orchestra; Concertino giocoso for string orchestra; Three Cheerful Stories, cappella choir; Prokofiev-Variationen für Klavier 4-händig. *Honours:* Kunstpreis des FDGB, 1971; Kunst Preis der DDR, 1975; Kunstpreis der Stadt Weimar, 1983. *Address:* Auf dem Dürbache 10, 99438 Legefeld/Stadt Weimar, Germany.

DIETSCH, James (William); Opera Singer (Baritone); b. 21 March 1950, Kansas City, Missouri, USA; m. Susan Kay Schell, 23 Aug 1980, 1 s. *Education:* BME, 1972, MMus Voice, 1975, University of Missouri, Kansas City; Juilliard School of Music American Opera Center, 1979–82; Vienna Academy of Music, Austria. *Career:* Debut: Fargo-Moorhead Civic Opera, 1975; New York Town Hall, 1981; Carnegie Hall, 1982; Leading artist with numerous opera companies and concert appearances in USA and abroad, including: San Francisco Opera, New York City Opera, English Opera North, Karlsruhe Badisches Staatstheater; Saarbrucken Saarländiches Staatstheater; Michigan Opera, Milwaukee Opera, Deutsche Oper am Rhein, Minnesota Opera, Hawaii Opera, Staatstheater Essen, Santa Fe Opera, Spoleto Festival USA, New York Philharmonic, Mexico City Philharmonic; Season 1992 as Scarpia at Costa Mesa, (Opera Pacific) and Nabucco at Montreal. *Recordings:* Il Corsaro by Verdi, Historical Recording Incorporate, 1981. *Address:* c/o Robert Lombardo Associates, 62 West 62nd Street, Suite 6F, New York, NY 10023, USA.

DIJKSTRA, Hebe; Singer (Mezzo-Soprano); b. 4 Sept. 1941, Tvijzelerheide, Netherlands; m. Jan Alofs. *Education:* Studied at the Hague Conservatory. *Career:* Debut: Sang Gluck's Orpheus at Enschede, 1975; Sang Mistress Quickly at Enschede, and appeared in Rimsky's Sadko at Bonn, 1976; Engaged at Detmold, 1976–79, Saarbrucken 1979–80, Freiburg, 1981–83; Krefeld, 1982–85, Wuppertal, 1987–89; Amsterdam, 1989, in Der Kreidekreis by Zemlinsky; Member of the Staatstheater am Gärtnerplatz, Munich from 1989; Sang Rossweise in Die Walküre at Bayreuth, 1988–91; Ulrica at Amsterdam 1992; Mary in Der fliegende Holländer at the 1992 Bayreuth Festival; Other roles include Carmen, Fricka, Waltraute, the Nurse in Boris Godunov, and La Comandante in I Cavalieri di Ekebù by Zandonai; Sang Margret in Wozzeck at Amsterdam, 1994; Witch in the premiere of Robert Heppener's Een Ziel van Hout, 1998; Sang Hecuba in Troades by Reimann at Berlin and Berne, 2000. *Address:* c/o Staatstheater am Gärtnerplatz, Gärtnerplatz 3, 8000 Munich, Germany.

DILBÈR, MA; singer (lyric coloratura soprano); b. 1960, Finland. *Education:* Music Academy, Beijing. *Career:* debut as Gilda in Rigoletto with Finnish National Opera; Performed with major Chinese ensembles while at school and at the music academy; Numerous engagements throughout Europe and the rest of the world; Repertoire includes Adina, Haydn's Orlando Paladino, Blondchen, Despina, Elvira, Gilda, Lakmé, Nannetta, Olympia, Rosina, Sophie in Der Rosenkavalier, Zerbinetta and Zerlina; Performances with major orchestras including the Symphony Orchestra of Beethovenhalle, Bonn, Radio Orchestras of Denmark, China, Finland, Frankfurt; Mitteldeutschen Rundfunk, Århus, Malmö, Helsinki; Performed in the major opera venues worldwide; Subject of documentaries with Swedish, Finnish and Chinese television. *Recordings:* Five albums in China; Coloratura arias; Folk Songs; Lieder with piano; Nannetta in Falstaff; Lisa in La Sonnambula; The Art of Coloratura with Malmö Opera Orchestra. *Honours:* Second Prize, International Mirjam Helin Singing Competition, Helsinki, 1984; Birgit Nilsson Prize, twice. *Address:* Bågängsvägen 53, 21620 Malmö, Sweden.

DILKES, Neville; Conductor; b. 28 Aug. 1930, Derby, England; m. (1) D Pamela Walton, deceased 1979, 4 d., (2) Christine M Allen, 12 April 1986. *Education:* Private and master classes; Netherlands Radio Union International Conductors' course; Fellow Trinity College, London; Fellow Royal College Organists. *Career:* Founder conductor of Kettering Symphony Orchestra; Founder conductor of Opera Da Camera; Founder conductor English Sinfonia; Associate conductor Philomusica of London; International radio and television; mem, Royal Society of Musicians of Great Britain. *Recordings:* English and French music, Bax, Butterworth, Moeran, Honegger, Ibert and Jolivet. *Honours:* Watney, Sargent Award for Conductors, 1963. *Address:* La Graineterie, 23 Rue Des Huttes, 85370 Nalliers, France.

DILLON, James; Composer; b. 29 Oct. 1950, Glasgow, Scotland. *Education:* Glasgow School of Art, 1967–68; Polytechnic of Central London, 1972–73; Polytechnic of North London, 1973–76. *Career:* Works performed and featured at festivals throughout the world including: Antidogma (Turin), Bath, Darmstadt, Gulbenkian (Lisbon), Huddersfield, ISCM (Toronto), La Rochelle, Musica Nel Nostro Tempo (Milan), Music of Eight Decades (London), Paris d'Automne, Warsaw, Zig-Zag (Paris), Châtelet (Paris), Donaueschingen (Germany), Musica Nova (Glasgow), Musica (Strasburg), Ars Musica (Brussels), Ultima (Oslo), Venice Biennale, Sydney Spring, ISCM World Music Days (Toronto, Stockholm, Seoul and Manchester); Guest Lecturer at the Universities of Keele, London, New York, Nottingham, Oxford also Universities of Central England and Gothenburg; Guest Composer at the 1982, 1984, 1986 Darmstadt Fierenkurse; jury member of Gaudeamus Composers Competition, 1985, ISCM International, 1988 and Besancon International Competition, 1990. *Compositions:* Spleen, 1980; Once Upon a Time, 1980; Come Live With Me, 1981; Parjanya-Vata, 1981; East 11th Street, 1982; String Quartet, 1983; Sgothan, 1984; La Coupure, 1986; Helle Nacht, 1987; Del Cuarto Elemento, 1988; L'Ecran parfum, 1988; Shrouded Mirrors, 1988; La Femme Invisible, 1989; L'Oeuvre au noir, 1990; Blitzschlag, 1991; String Quartet No. 2, 1991; ignis noster, 1991–92; Siorram, 1992; Vernal Showers, 1992; L'Evolution Du Vol, 1993; Viriditas, 1993; Traumwerk Book I, 1995; Redemption, 1995; Oceanos, 1996; Todesengel, 1996; The Book of Elements Vol. I, 1997; String Quartet No. 3 1998; Hyades, 1998; Eos, 1998–99; residue..., 1999; Vapor, 1999; La coupure, 2000; Via Sacra, 2000; Violin Concerto, 2000; Book of Elements (III), 2000; La Navette, 2000–01; Book of Elements (II), 2001; Two Studies, 2001; Two Studies, 2001; Traumwerk (book 2), 2001; Traumwerk (book 3), 2001–02; Book of Elements (IV), 2002; Book of Elements (V), 2002; Piano Quintet, 2002; New Work, 2002–03; The Rape of Philomela, 2002–04. *Recordings:* helle Nacht; ignis noster; Come Live with me; A Roaring Flame; Sgothan; Ti re-Ti Ke-Dha; Evening Rain; Crossing Over; Spleen; Del Cuarto Elemento; East 11th Street, NY 10003; La femme invisible; Windows and Canopies; Dillug Kefitsah. *Publications:* Problemas Discursivos en La Muska Contemporanea, Valencia, 1989; Speculative Instruments: Timbre, Métaphore pour La Composition, 1991. *Honours:* Kranichsteiner Musikpreis, Federal Republic of Germany, 1982; Classical Music Personality of the Year, London Times, 1989; Royal Philharmonic Society Award, 1997. *Address:* c/o Peters Edition Ltd, 10–12 Baches Street, London N1 6DN, England.

DILLON, James; Composer; b. 29 Oct. 1950, Glasgow, Scotland. *Education:* Glasgow School of Art, 1967–68; Polytechnic of Central London, 1972–73; Polytechnic of North London, 1973–76. *Career:* Works performed and featured at festivals throughout the world including: Antidogma (Turin), Bath, Darmstadt, Gulbenkian (Lisbon), Huddersfield, ISCM (Toronto), La Rochelle, Musica Nel Nostro Tempo (Milan), Music of Eight Decades (London), Paris d'Automne, Warsaw, Zig-Zag (Paris), Châtelet (Paris), Donaueschingen (Germany), Musica Nova (Glasgow), Musica (Strasburg), Ars Musica (Brussels), Ultima (Oslo), Venice Biennale, Sydney Spring, ISCM World Music Days (Toronto, Stockholm, Seoul and Manchester); Guest Lecturer at the Universities of Keele, London, New York, Nottingham, Oxford also Universities of Central England and Gothenburg; Guest Composer at the 1982, 1984, 1986 Darmstadt Ferienkurse; Jury member of Gaudeamus Composers Competition, 1985, ISCM International, 1988 and Besancon International Competition, 1990. *Compositions:* Spleen, 1980; Once Upon a Time, 1980; Come Live With Me, 1981; Parjanya-Vata, 1981; East 11th Street, 1982; String Quartet, 1983; Sgothan, 1984; La Coupure, 1986; Helle Nacht, 1987; Del Cuarto Elemento, 1988; L'Ecran parfum, 1988; Shrouded Mirrors, 1988; La Femme Invisible, 1989; L'Oeuvre au noir, 1990; Blitzschlag, 1991; String Quartet No. 2, 1991; ignis noster, 1991–92; Siorram, 1992; Vernal Showers, 1992; L'Evolution Du Vol, 1993; Viriditas, 1993; Traumwerk Book I, 1995; Redemption, 1995; Oceanos, 1996; Todesengel, 1996; The Book of Elements Vol. I, 1997; String Quartet No. 3 1998; Hyades, 1998; Eos, 1998–99; residue..., 1999; Vapor, 1999; La coupure, 2000; Via Sacra, 2000; Violin Concerto, 2000; Book of Elements (III), 2000; La navette, 2000–01; Book of Elements (II), 2001; Two Studies, 2001; Two Studies, 2001; Traumwerk (Bk 2), 2001; Traumwerk (Bk 3), 2001–02; Book of Elements (IV), 2002;

Book of Elements (V), 2002; Piano Quintet, 2002; New Work, 2002–03; The Rape of Philomela, 2002–04. *Recordings:* helle Nacht; ignis noster; Come Live with me; A Roaring Flame; Sgothan; Ti re-Ti Ke-Dha; Evening Rain; Crossing Over; Spleen; Del Cuarto Elemento; East 11th Street, NY 10003; La femme invisible; Windows and Canopies; Dillug Kefitsah. *Publications:* Problemas Discursivos en La Muska Contemporanea, Valencia, 1989; Speculative Instruments: Timbre, Métaphore pour La Composition, 1991. *Honours:* Kranichsteiner Musikpreis, Federal Republic of Germany, 1982; Classical Music Personality of the Year, London Times, 1989; Royal Philharmonic Society Award, 1997. *Address:* c/o Peters Edition Ltd, 10–12 Baches Street, London N1 6DN, England.

DIMITROVA, Anastasia; Singer (Soprano); b. 16 Nov. 1940, Pernik, Bulgaria. *Education:* Studied at State Conservatory, Sofia and in Zagreb. *Career:* Debut: Sang in Nabucco at Skopje, 1965; Many Appearances at Opera Houses in Bulgaria and Yugoslavia, notably, Belgrade, Sofia, Zagreb and Rijeka; Roles have included Verdi's Elisabetta and Leonora (Trovatore), Mimi, Yaroslavna (Prince Igor), Tatiana in Eugene Onegin, Marenka (Bartered Bride), Rusalka, Micaela, Euridice and Marguerite. *Honours:* Winner, Francisco Vinas (Barcelona 1969) and Bussetto Competitions. *Address:* c/o Sofia State Opera, Boulevard Dondoukov 58, 1000 Sofia, Bulgaria.

DIMITROVA, Ghena; Singer (Soprano); b. 6 May 1941, Beglej, Bulgaria. *Education:* Studied with Professor Christo Brumbarov in Sofia. *Career:* Debut: Sofia, as Abigaille in Nabucco; Sang widely in Bulgaria. From 1970 sang in Italy and at Strasbourg, Karlsruhe, Mannheim and Stuttgart; US debut, 1982, as Elvira in Ernani at Dallas; Verona Arena and La Scala Milan, 1982, 1983, as Turandot; Barcelona, 1984, as Verdi's Odabella; Salzburg Festival, 1984, as Lady Macbeth; Covent Garden debut, 1984, Turandot, returned, 1990; New York debut as Abigaille, 1984; Guest appearances in Buenos Aires, Vienna, Paris, Düsseldorf and Berlin; Other roles include Aida, Norma, Leonora in Il Trovatore and La Gioconda; Sang Norma in Houston, 1987, and Paris; Aida at Luxor, Egypt, 1987; Verona Arena, 1988, as Turandot; Sang Santuzza at Covent Garden and the Metropolitan, 1989; Season 1992 at the Festival of Caracalla and Tosca at Torre del Lago; Season 1993–94 included Aida and Cavalleria Rusticana at Arena di Verona and La Fanciulla del West at the Metropolitan Opera House, New York; Season 1994–95 as Turandot at Torre del Lago, Metropolitan Opera House, Caracas and Pasadena; Tosca with Rome Opera on tour to Nagoya, Japan, and recitals in Tenerife and Athens; Sang Lady Macbeth in Athens, 1997; Abigaille in Nabucco at Rome and Verona, 1998; Sang Abigaille and the Forza Leonora at Verona, 2000. *Recordings:* Nabucco; Aida; La Gioconda; I Lombardi and Oberto by Verdi; Video of Turandot. *Address:* c/o Stafford Law, 6 Barham Close, Weybridge KT 13 9 PR, England.

DINDO, Enrico; Cellist; b. 16 March 1965, Turin, Italy. *Education:* Conservatorio G Verdi, Turin; Mozarteum Salzburg, with Antonio Sangro. *Career:* Debut: 1st Cellist with La Scala Orchestra, 1988; Soloist in Beethoven Triple Concerto at La Scala, 1996; Worked with conductors Roberto Abbado, Aldo Cecato, Gunter Neuhold, Peter Maag, Gianandrea Noseda, Riccardo Chailly, Riccardo Muti, Mstislav Rostropovich; Played with Orchestre Nationale de France, St Petersburg Philharmonic Orchestra, Orchestra Sinfonica Nazionale RAI, Chicago Symphony and Kirov Chamber Orchestra. *Recordings:* Brahms, Cello Sonatas; Haydn, Cello Concerti. *Honours:* 1st Prize, Rostropovich Cello Competition, Paris, 1987. *Current Management:* AMP, Milan. *Address:* V Mercadante 8, 20124 Milan, Italy.

DINESCU, Violeta; German composer; *Professor of Applied Composition, University of Oldenburg;* b. 13 July 1953, Bucharest, Romania. *Education:* Bachelor's Degree, College Georghe Lazar, Bucharest, 1972; Master's Degree, 1977, Special Diploma and study year for composition, 1978, Conservatory Ciprian Porumbescu. *Career:* Instructor at George Enescu Music School, Bucharest, 1978–82; Instructor at Conservatory for Church Music, Heidelberg, Germany, 1986–90; Lecturer at various universities in Germany, RSA and USA, 1986–; Instructor for Harmony and Counterpoint at Hochschule, Frankfurt, 1989–90; Instructor of Theory, Harmony and Counterpoint at the Academy of Church Music, Bayreuth, 1990–94; Professor of Applied Composition, University of Oldenburg, 1996–. *Compositions include:* Orchestral and Vocal Compositions; Chamber Music; Solos, Duos, Trios, Quartets, Quintets, Sextets, and Septets; Works for Chamber Ensemble; 4 Operas; Children's Opera; 2 Ballet Music; Film Music; Experimental Music. *Honours:* Recipient of over 50 international prizes, distinctions and selections from several countries including: Romania, Germany, Canada, USA, Italy, England, Columbia, RSA, Hungary, Poland and Austria. *Address:* University of Oldenburg, FK III/Music, Pf 2503, 26111 Oldenburg (office); Presuhnstrasse 39, 26133 Oldenburg, Germany (home). *Telephone:* (441) 7982027 (office); (441) 42979 (home). *Fax:* (441) 7984016 (office); (441) 9490455 (home). *E-mail:* violeta.dinescu@uni-oldenburg.de (office). *Website:* www.dinescu.net.

DINITZEN, Kim Bak; Cellist; b. 24 Oct. 1963, Haderslev, Denmark; m. Ursula Smith, 8 May 1993. *Education:* Studied at Royal Danish Conservatoire of Music with Erling Blondal Bengtsson; Private studies in London with Ralph Kirshbaum. *Career:* Debut: Copenhagen, 1986; Weill Recital Hall at Carnegie Hall, New York, 1988; Wigmore Hall, London, 1991; Soloist with all Danish symphony orchestras; Recitals and chamber music concerts throughout Europe; Member of Chamber Orchestra of Europe, 1990–; Teacher at Royal Northern College of Music, Manchester, England, 1996–. *Recordings:* Benjamin Britten: Complete Works for Cello; G Fauré: Complete Works for Cello and Piano, with Elisabeth Westenholz, piano; Prokofiev and Schnittke Sonatas, with Paul Coker, piano; Niels W Gade: String Quintet, Sextet and Octet with the Johannes Ensemble. *Honours:* Victor Borge Prize, Denmark, 1987; 1st Prize for Cello, Washington International Competition, 1988; East and West Artists' Prize for New York debut, 1988; 3rd Prize, Gaspar Cassapo International Cello Competition, Florence, 1990. *Current Management:* Tivoli Artists' Management. *Address:* Flat 1, 3 Randolph Place, Edinburgh EH3 7TQ, Scotland.

D'INTINO, Luciana; Singer (Mezzo-Soprano); b. 1959, San vito al Tagliamento, Pordenone, Italy. *Education:* Studied at the Benedeto Marcello Conservatory, Venice. *Career:* Debut: Sang Azucena in Il Trovatore, 1983; Appearances as Rossini's Rosina in Marcerata and Naples, 1984, 1986; Aida at Cagliari and Trieste; La Scala Milan from 1987 in Nabucco, Guillaume Tell; Jommelli's Fetonte, Adriana Lecouvreur and as Luggrezia in Pergolesi's Lo Frate 'nnamorato; Sang Frederica in Luisa Miller at Rome, 1990 and on Metropolitan Opera Debut, 1991; Turin 1990 as Eboli in Don Carlos and Savona 1991 as Arsace in Rossini's Auerliano in Palmira; Sang Preziosilla in Forza del Destino at Naples, Sara in Roberto Devereux at Bologna, 1992; Preziosilla at the 1992 Maggio Musicale, Florence; Amneris in Aida at Covent Garden, 1994, and at Buenos Aires, 1996; Sang Eboli at Bologna, 1998; Season 2000–01 as Rossini's Isabella at Turin and Eboli for Zürich Opera; Verdi Requiem at Florence, Palermo, Rome and Saõ Paulo, 2001. *Recordings include:* Lo Frate 'nnamorato, conducted by Riccardo Muti. *Honours:* Winner, Spoleto Singing Competition, 1993. *Address:* c/o Teatro alla Scala, Via Filodrammatici 2, 20121 Milan, Italy.

DIVALL, Richard Sydney Benedict, OBE, FRAS, FRNS; Australian conductor; b. 9 Sept. 1945, Sydney, NSW. *Education:* Univ. of Melbourne, Conservatorium of Music, Sydney. *Career:* debut, Handel's Xerxes, Sydney; Producer of Music, ABC 1960–70; Musical Dir, Queensland Opera 1971–; guest conductor, ABC 1972–; Music Dir, Victoria State Opera 1972–95, Prin. Conductor 1995–97; Assoc. Prof. of Music, Univ. of Melbourne 1992–; Prin. Resident Conductor, Opera Australia 1997–2002; edited 18th-century symphonies, series of eight vols. of colonial Australian repertoire music and 15 operas; Chair. of Marshall-Hall Trust. *Recordings include:* repertoire of over 140 operas, Early Australian Music Vol. 1. *Publications:* Music of Carl Linger, 1998; Complete Music of Henry Handel Richardson, 1999; New Publications of 3 volumes of Music of Frederick Septimus Kelly; Volume of music of Dom Rosendo Salvado, Alfred Hill, GW Marshall-Hall, Alberto Zelman, Australia's First Piano Music; 2 Symphonies and 2 String Quartets of Charles Edward Horsley, 1 Symphony and String Quartet of Fritz Hart; 6 volumes of early Maltese Music; Pergolesi "Stabat Mater" (Wignacourt ms). *Honours:* D Artes e Cul (Hon. SP), 1987; KM, 1989; Commendatore al Merito, 1989; D Lett (Hon Monash), 1992; Australian Centenary Medal, 2003; Senior Fellowship Inst. for Studies in Australian Music Melbourne Univ.; Fra' n The Order of Malta (Cav n di Giustizia); Doc Univ. (Hon Aust Cath U.); Sr Fellow, State Library of Victoria 2003–04; Sir Bernard Heinze Award 2005. *Current Management:* Jenifer Eddy, 11/596 St Kilda Road, Melbourne, 3004, Australia. *Address:* 301 Arcadia, 228 The Avenue, Parkville, Vic. 3025, Australia. *Telephone:* 3 9381 0789 (home). *Fax:* 3 9381 0790 (home). *E-mail:* maestro@spin.net .au.

DIVES, Tamsin; Singer (Mezzo-Soprano); b. 1968, England. *Education:* Studied at the Guildhall School. *Career:* Opera appearances with Glyndebourne Festival, English National Opera, Opera North, Chelsea Opera and Edinburgh and Harrogate Festivals; Roles include Fidalma in Il Matrimonio Segreto and Mrs Grose in The Turn Of The Screw; Concerts with the Hallé Orchestra, Northern Sinfonia and The Nash Ensemble; Sang in the British Premiere of Korngold's Die tote Stadt, Queen Elizabeth Hall, 1996. *Recordings include:* Davies' The Martyrdom of St Magnus; Macmillan's Visitatio Sepulchri.

DIVOKY, Zdenek; Horn Player; b. 1954, Brno, Czechoslovakia. *Education:* Studied at the Janáček Academy in Brno with Frantisek Socl. *Career:* Wind Section of the State Philharmonic Orchestra in Brno; Czech Philharmonic, 1979; Solo peformer in concert and member of such chamber ensembles as the Prague Brass Trio, the Horn Quartet of the Czech Philharmonic, the Collegium Musicum Pragense and the Stamic Quartet; Solo engagements in Germany, Australia, England, Spain and Canada; Repertoire includes concertos by M and J Haydn, Telemann, Mozart, Punto, Rosetti, Schumann, Weber and Strauss; Recitalist in

Beethoven, Mozart, Reicha, Brahms, Britten, Hindemith and Bur-ghauser; Tours with the Czech Philharmonic and with various chamber ensembles to Europe, the USA and Japan. *Honours:* Prizewinner at Prague Spring International Festival and competitions in Munich and Markneukirchen.

DIXON, James; Conductor; b. 26 April 1928, Estherville, Iowa, USA. *Education:* Studied at the University of Iowa and with Dimitri Mitropoulos, 1949–60. *Career:* Conducted the US 7th Army Band in Germany; Led the University of Iowa Symphony, 1954–59; New England Conservatory Symphony in Boston, 1969–61; Conductor of the Tri-City Symphony in Davenport, Iowa, and Rock Island, Illinois; Associate Conductor of the Minneapolis Symphony, 1961–62; Guest Conductor with the National Orchestra of Greece in Athens, the Norddeutscher Rundfunk, Hamburg, the Westdeutscher Rundfunk, Cologne, the Tanglewood Orchestra, the Chicago Civic Symphony and the Chicago Symphony (1972); Conducted a student group at the International Society for Contemporary Music Festival in Boston, 1976; Has led the premieres of Charles Wuorinen's Piano Concerto and works by T J Anderson and William Matthews. *Honours:* Gustav Mahler Medal, 1963.

DJIOEVA, Irina; Singer (Soprano); b. 1971, Magadan, Russia. *Education:* St Petersburg Conservatoire. *Career:* Appearances with the Kirov Opera from 1996, as Verdi's Violetta, Leonora (La Forza del Destino) and Elisabeth de Valois, Glinka's Lyudmilla, and Marfa in Rimsky's The Tsar's Bride; Mozart's Queen of Night, Susanna and Donna Anna, Woglinde in Das Rheingold, Stravinsky's Nightingale and Lucia di Lammermoor; Further roles at the Mariinsky Theatre, St Petersburg, include Amina (La Sonnambula), Volkhova in Rimsky's Sadko, and Mimi; Sang in the Verdi season with the Kirov Opera at Covent Garden, 2001; Further tours to Italy and the New York Met; Sang Flowermaiden in Parsifal at Salzburg, 1998. *Honours:* Prizewinner, 1995 Mario del Monaco Competition and Rimsky-Korsakov International, 1996. *Address:* c/o Kirov Opera, Mariinsky Theatre, 1 Theatre Square, St Petersburg, Russia.

DJUPSJÖBACKA, Gustav (Mikael); Pianist; b. 21 Dec. 1950, Borgå, Finland; m. Lena von Bonsdorff, 15 July 1977, 1 s., 1 d. *Education:* Sibelius Academy, 1969–73; Musical Academy, Prague, 1973–74; Hochschule für Musik, Vienna, 1975–77. *Career:* Debut: Helsinki, 1978; Keyboard Player, Radio Symphony Orchestra of Finland, 1977–87; Lecturer in Lied Music, Sibelius Academy, 1987–; Mainly lied recitals in Europe, North and South America with Ritva Auvinen, Monica Groop, Tom Krause, Jorma Hynninen, others; mem, Yrjö Kilpinen Society; Madetoja Foundation; Académie Francis Poulenc; Nordic Music Committee; Member of Rimski Korsakov Singing Contest Jury, St Petersburg, 2002. *Recordings:* Winterreise and Sibelius Songs with Tom Krause; Sibelius Songs with Ritva Auvinen; Complete Madetoja Songs with Gabriel Suovanen and Helen Juntunen. *Publications:* Yrjö Kilpinen's Morgenstern Songs, 1992; Aaree Merikanto Songs, 2000; Kilpinen Songs, 2002; Guide on Finnish Art Songs, 2001. *Honours:* Sylvi Kekkonen Scholarship, 1975, 1976. *Address:* Töölöntorinkatu 3 A 2, 00260 Helsinki, Finland.

DMITRIEV, Alexander; Conductor; b. 1935, Leningrad, USSR; m., 1 s. *Education:* Leningrad Conservatory, under Kudriavtseva, Tiulin, Rabinovitch. *Career:* Conductor Karelian Radio and Television Symphony Orchestra, 1961, Principal Conductor, 1962–71; Assistant of Leningrad Philharmonic Orchestra under E. Mravinsky, 1970–71; Chief Conductor, Maly Opera and Ballet Theatre, Leningrad, 1971–7; Chief conductor and music director Symphony Orchestra, Leningrad (now St Petersburg) Philharmonic society, 1977–; Chief conductor Stavanger Symphony Orchestra, Norway, 1990–98. *Recordings include:* Miaskovsky's Violin Concerto; Balakirev's Piano Concerto; Medtner's Piano Concerto No. 1; Tchaikovsky Symphony Nos 4, 5, 6; Rachmaninov, Symphony No. 2; Beethoven Symphony Nos 1–9; Schubert Symphony Nos 1-9; Handel Messiah, Haydn Schöpfung; Debussy 3 Nocturnes, Ravel Valses nobles et sentimentales, Ma Mère l'Oye; Saeverud Peer Gynt, Symphony dolorosa; Rachmaninov Piano Concerto No. 3; Britten Violin Concerto. *Honours:* Prize, 2nd USSR Competition for Conductors, 1966. *Current Management:* Amdre Wider, Brussels. *Address:* Symphony orchestra St Petersburg Philharmonic society, Mikhailovskaja str 2, St Petersburg 091011, Russia. *E-mail:* dmitriev@mail.spbnit.ru or alexanderdmitriev@hotmail.com.

DOBBER, Andrzej; Singer (Baritone); b. 26 May 1961, Wiecbok, Poland. *Education:* Studied in Warsaw (making his debut as Gremin while a student) and in Nuremberg. *Career:* Sang at Nuremberg Opera, 1987–91, debut as Tonio in Pagliacci; Frankfurt Opera from 1991, as Nardo in La finta giardiniera, Luna, the Herald in Lohengrin, Gremin and Marcello; Guest at the Vienna Staatsoper as Escamillo (1992) and frequent concert appearances; Cologne from 1995, as Eugene Onegin and Mozart's Count; Sang Fyodor in The Invisible City of Kitezh at the Komische Oper, Berlin, 1996; Season 2000-01 in Berlin as Danilo in Die

Lustige Witwe at the Deutsche Oper, and as Orestes in Elektra at the Komische Oper. *Address:* c/o Alfernik, Apollolaan 181, NL–1077 AT Amsterdam, Netherlands.

DOBBS, Mattiwilda, BA, MA; American singer (coloratura soprano); b. 11 July 1925, Atlanta, GA; d. of John Wesley Dobbs and Irene Thompson Dobbs; m. 1st Luis Rodríguez García 1953 (died 1954); m. 2nd Bengt Janzon 1957 (died 1997). *Education:* Spelman Coll., Atlanta and Columbia Univ. *Career:* studied with Lotte Leonard 1946–50; Marian Anderson scholarship, soloist at Mexico Univ. Festival 1947; studied at Mannes Music School and Berkshire Music Center 1948, with Pierre Bernac, Paris 1950–52; debut La Scala, Milan in L'Italiana in Algeri 1953; sang at Glyndebourne 1953, 1954, 1956, 1961, Royal Opera House, Covent Garden, London 1953, 1954, 1955, 1956, 1959, San Francisco Opera 1955, Metropolitan Opera, New York 1956–64, Stockholm Royal Opera 1957–71, Hamburg State Opera 1961–63, Norwegian and Finnish Opera 1957–64; concert appearances in USA, Australia, New Zealand, Israel, USSR, Netherlands, France, Sweden, Mexico; Visiting Prof., Univ. of Texas at Austin 1973–74; Prof., Univ. of Illinois 1975–76, Univ. of Georgia 1976–77, Howard Univ., Washington, DC 1977–91. *Honours:* 1st Voice Prize, Geneva Int. Competition 1951; Order of the North Star (Sweden). *Address:* 1101 South Arlington Ridge Road, Apt. 301, Arlington, VA 22202, USA. *Telephone:* (703) 892-5234.

DOBRÉE, Georgina, FRAM; British clarinettist, basset hornist, teacher and editor; b. 8 Jan. 1930, London, England. *Education:* Royal Academy of Music, studied with Gaston Hamelin in Paris. *Career:* member of Chamber Music Ensembles; Recitals, broadcasts, lecture recitals and masterclasses in Europe and USA; Many premieres and recipient of numerous dedications; Professor, Royal Academy of Music, 1967–86; Director, Chantry Records, 1975–84, mainly of 19th and 20th Century works and own performances; mem. RMA; International Clarinet Association; CASS; RAM Club; Royal Society of Musicians; PAMRA. *Publications:* Chantry Publications formed 1988, editions of mainly 19th century music for clarinet and/or basset horn, assigned June 2000 to Emerson Edition Ltd; Editions of other works with clarinet for MR, OUP, Schott, Chester and Nova. *Honours:* French Government Scholarship, 1949; First Prize, Darmstadt, 1953. *Address:* 58 Ninesprings Way, Hitchin, Hertfordshire SG4 9NR, England.

DOBRONRAVOVA, Svetlana; Singer (Soprano); b. 1957, Taganrog, Russia. *Education:* Studied at the Rostov on Don Conservatoire. *Career:* Debut: Lvov State Opera in 1982 as Tosca; Sang with the Lvov Opera until 1989 notably as Santuzza, Yaroslavna and Gioconda; National Opera Kiev from 1989 as Abigaille, Elisabeth de Valois, Aida, Desdemona, Leonora in Forza del Destino, Elsa, Tatiana and Maria in Mazeppa; Guest engagements in Canada and throughout Europe, including concerts of the Mozart and Verdi Requiems; British debut in 1996 with the Perm Opera as Abigaille. *Address:* Sonata Ltd, 11 North Park Street, Glasgow G20 7AA, Scotland.

DOBSON, John; Singer (Tenor); b. 1930, Derby, England. *Education:* Guildhall School of Music, with Norman Walker; Study in Italy with Giovanni Inghilleri. *Career:* Debut: Bergamo 1957, as Pinkerton; New Opera Company 1958, in Sir John in Love and A Tale of Two Cities; Glyndebourne Festival 1959, in Der Rosenkavalier; Engagements with English National Opera, Welsh National Opera and Scottish Opera; Deutsche Oper am Rhein, Düsseldorf, Orange Festival and Maggio Musicale, Florence; Covent Garden, 1959–95, in 100 roles and 2000 performances: roles include Wagner's David, Mime, Loge and Melot, Beethoven's Jacquino and Mussorgsky's Shuisky; Sang Paris in the premiere of Tippett's King Priam, Coventry, 1962; Sang Luke in the 1977 premiere of Tippett's The Ice Break; With the Royal Opera at La Scala Milan, 1976 and the Far East, 1979, 1986 and 1992; Sang Mime in the first Japanese performances of Wagner's Ring with the Deutsche Oper, 1987; Sang in the British Premiere of Berio's Un Re in Ascolto, 1989; Borsa in Rigoletto; Inn Keeper in a new production of The Cunning Little Vixen, 1990, the Emperor in Turandot; Director of Young Singers Ensemble at Covent Garden; Sang Mime in Siegfried, 1991, Jakob Glock in a new production of Prokofiev's Fiery Angel, 1992; Sang Altoun in Turandot at Covent Garden, 1994; Freelance Singer from 1995; Abbate in Andrea Chénier with the Royal Opera at the Festival Hall, 1998; Retired from singing in 1998 after a performance of the Rector (Peter Grimes) with the Royal Opera House at the Savonlinna Festival. *Recordings include:* Videos of Peter Grimes, Otello, Samson et Dalila and La Fanciulla del West. *Honours:* O.B.E., 1985. *Address:* c/o Royal Opera House (Education), Covent Garden, London WC2E 9 DD, England.

DODD, Geraint; Singer (Tenor); b. 1958, Rhosllanerchrugog, Wales. *Education:* Royal Northern College of Music, with Joseph Ward. *Career:* Appearances with Welsh National Opera as the Duke of Mantua, Pinkerton and Macduff; Florestan, Werther and Rodolfo for English Touring Opera; Don José in concert for WNO, 1988, and Radames for Mid Wales Opera; Other roles include Pollione in Norma (Neath Opera),

Calaf, Cavaradossi in Tosca and Captain Vere in Billy Budd; Concerts include Messiah, the Verdi Requiem and The Dream of Gerontius. *Address:* Harlequin Agency Ltd, 203 Fidlas Road, Cardiff CF14 5NA, Wales.

DODERER, Gerhard, PhD; musicologist and organist; b. 25 March 1944, Kitzingen, Germany; m. C. Rosado Fernandes 1970. *Education:* Univ. of Würzburg, Staatskonservatorium of Würzburg. *Career:* organ recitals since 1970 in Europe and elsewhere; Prof. of Musicology, Universidade Nova de Lisboa, Portugal 1981–; mem. American, Spanish, Portuguese and German Musicological Socs. *Recordings:* albums of historical Portuguese organs. *Publications:* Portuguese Clavichords of the 18th Century 1971, Organa Hispanica (nine vols) 1971–84, Orgelmusik und Orgelbau in Portugal 1976, Domenico Scarlatti: Libro di Tocate 1991, The Organs at Braga Cathedral 1992, J. de la Té y Sagau: Cantatas Humanas a Solo (1723) 1999, L. Giustini di Pistoia: Sonate de Cimbalo di piano e forte 2002, Portugese String Keyboard Instruments of the 18th Century: Clavichords, Harpsichords, Piano and Spinets (with J. H. van der Meer) 2004. *Address:* Rua do Borja 133-B, 3A, Lisbon 1350-046, Portugal. *E-mail:* gdoderer@mail.telepac.pt.

DODGE, Charles; Composer; b. 5 June 1942, Ames, Iowa, USA; m. Katharine Schlefer, 1 July 1978, 1 s., 1 d. *Education:* BA, University of Iowa; MA, DMA, Columbia University; Studied composition with Richard Hervig, Darius Milhaud, Philip Bezanson, Gunther Schuller, Otto Luening, computer music with Godfrey Winheim. *Career:* Major performances: Tanglewood, 1965, 1973, 1986; Warsaw Autumn Festival, Poland, 1978, 1985, 1986; New Music, New York Festival, USA, 1979; Stockholm Festival of Electronic Music, Sweden, 1980, 1982; Venice Biennale, Italy, 1981; Calarts Festival, USA, 1983; Olympic Arts Festival, Los Angeles, 1984; New York Philharmonic, 1984; Los Angeles Philharmonic, 1984. *Compositions:* Folia; Changes: Earth's Magnetic Field; Speech Songs; Extensions; The Story of Our Lives; In Celebration; Cascando; Any Resemblance Is Purely Coincidental; The Waves; The One and the Other for chamber orchestra, 1993; That Which I Should Have Done!... for organ and tape, 1996; Just Harmonies–for Christian Wolff, 1996. *Recordings:* Earth's Magnetic Field, Nonesuch; Charles Dodge-Synthetic Speech Music. *Publications:* Computer Music; Synthesis, Composition and Performing (with Thomas A Jerse), 1985. *Contributions:* Musical Fractals, Byte Magazine, 1986. *Address:* Conservatory of Music, Brooklyn College, City University of New York, NY 11210, USA.

DOESE, Helena; Singer (soprano); b. 7 Aug. 1946, Göteborg, Sweden. *Education:* Studied in Göteborg, with Luigi Ricci in Rome, with Erik Werba and Gerald Moore in Vienna and with Vera Rozsa in London. *Career:* Debut: Göteborg 1971, as Aida; Bern Opera 1972–75, as Jenůfa, Micaela and Donna Anna; Royal Opera Stockholm from 1973 as Liu in Turandot, Mimi, Katya Kabanova and Eva in the Friedrich production of Die Meistersinger; Glyndebourne debut 1974, as Mozart's Countess: Fiordiligi 1975; Covent Garden from 1974 as Mimi, Gutrune in Götterdämmerung, Agathe in Der Freischütz and Amelia in Simon Boccanegra; Tatiana in Eugene Onegin for Scottish Opera; Guest appearances in Marseilles (Elisabeth de Valois), Sydney, (Aida), Paris Opéra, (Fiordiligi), Hamburg, (Agathe), San Francisco, (Countess) and Zürich (Sieglinde); Member of Frankfurt Opera: has sung title roles in Ariadne auf Naxos, Jenůfa and Iphigénie en Tauride, Countess in Capriccio, the Marschallin, and Chrysothemis in Elektra; Deutsche Oper Berlin, 1987, as Agathe followed by the Marschallin at Copenhagen; Sydney, 1988, as Eva in Die Meistersinger; Sang Rosalinde at Oslo, 1988, Tosca 1989; Season 1991/92 as Fidelio at Toronto, Elsa at Frankfurt and Ariadne at Stuttgart; Season 1994–95 sang Chrysothemis at Frankfurt, and Sieglinde; Strauss's Ariadne auf Naxos at the Teatro Colón, Buenos Aires, 1995 and Elisabeth in Tannhäuser by Wagner at Sau Paulo in 1996. *Recordings include:* Videos of Glyndebourne Così fan tutte and Covent Garden Bohème.

DOGHAN, Philip; Singer (tenor); b. 1949, London, England. *Education:* BA, Durham University. *Career:* Sang as a boy in premiere of Tippett's King Priam, 1962; Sang in chorus at Glyndebourne and with the English Opera Group and English Music Theatre; English National Opera in Orfeo, the premiere of The Plumber's Gift and The Return of Ulysses; Has sung with Opera Factory in the premiere of Birtwistle's Yan Tan Tethera, 1986, La Calisto, The Knot Garden and Reimann's The Ghost Sonata; Appearances in Il Matrimomio Segreto and Les Pêcheurs de Perles in Rennes; Tom Rakewell at Cologne Opera, Alessandro in Il Re Pastore at the Théâtre des Champs Elysées; Mignon, La Straniera, La Cena delle Beffe, Elisa e Claudio and Gazzaniga's Don Giovanni at the Wexford Festival; Don Juan in The Stone Guest for the Berlin Kammeroper; Così fan tutte in Tours and Idomeneo in Metz; Concert engagements include Stravinsky's Threni for Italian Radio and appearances with Janowski, Hager, Rattle, Malgoire and Hogwood in Netherlands, Germany, Italy, Belgium and France; Sang several roles in the ENO revival of Busoni's Doctor Faust, 1990; Regular broadcasts for the BBC, Radio France and RAI; Orpheo in

Lord's Masque by Castiglioni at La Fenice; Paris Opéra debut as Le Duc in Offenbach's Les Brigands, 1993; Royal Opera House, Basilo in Figaro, 1994; Cologne Opera 1995, as Tom Rakewell; Sang Britten's Aschenbach at Lubeck and in Die Wände by A.Hölszky at Frankfurt, 2000. *Honours:* Winner, Premier Grand Prix at Toulouse, 1980. *Current Management:* Athole Still International Management, Forresters Hall, 25–27 Westow Street, London, SE19 3RY, England. *Telephone:* (20) 8771-5271. *Fax:* (20) 8768-6600. *Website:* www.atholestill.com.

DOHMEN, Albert; Singer (Bass-Baritone); b. 1955, Krefeld, Germany. *Education:* Studied in Cologne and with Gladys Kuchta, 1977–84. *Career:* Sang at the Deutsche Oper am Rhein, Düsseldorf, 1983–85; Wiesbaden from 1986, Hamburg, 1986–87, Vienna Volksoper, 1987–90; Guest appearances at Stockholm (Assur in Semiramide, 1988), Catania (Kaspar in Der Freischütz) and Cairo, in Haydn's La Vera Costanza; Sang in the premiere of Bose's Die Leiden des Jungen Werthers at Ludwigsburg, 1986 and in the German premiere of La Princesse de Cleve by Jean Francaix; Sang Don Giovanni in festivals at Prague and Macerata, 1991; Returned to Macerata 1992, as Don Parmenione in Rossini's L'Occasione fa il Ladro. Other roles include Mozart's Count and Alfonso, Don Magnifico, the Grand Inquisitor and Verdi's Procida and Paolo, Scarpia and Gianni Schicchi; Wagner's King Henry, Biterolf, Wotan, Donner, Gunther and Amfortas; Sang Simone in Zemlinsky's Eine Florentinische Tragödie at Florence, 1996; Season 1998, as Weber's Kaspar at Rome and Jeremiah in Weill's Propheten at the London Proms; Season 2000–01 as the Wanderer at Trieste, Wotan in Die Walküre at Geneva, Scarpia for Covent Garden and the Rheingold Wotan at the Vienna Staatsoper; Concert repertoire includes the Verdi Requiem and Zemlinsky's Sieben Sinfonische Gesänge. *Recordings:* Spirit Messenger in Die Frau ohne Schatten, conducted by Solti. *Address:* c/o Volksoper, Wahringerstrasse 78, 1090 Vienna, Austria.

DOHNÁNYI, Christoph von (see von Dohnányi, Christoph)

DOHNÁNYI, Oliver von; Conductor; b. 2 March 1955, Trencin, Czechoslovakia; m. Natalia Melnik, 23 Jan 1996, 1 d. *Education:* Konzervatorium in Bratislava (Violin, conducting and composition), Academy of Music Prague, Hochschüle für Musik, Vienna (both conducting). *Career:* Conductor of the Radio Symphony Orchestra, Bratislava, 1979–86; Principal Conductor of the Slovak National Opera House in Bratislava, conducted new productions of Borodin's Prince Igor, Puccini's Tosca, Rossini's Il Barbiere di Siviglia, Smetana's The Bartered Bride, Verdi's Rigoletto, Gounod's Faust; Conductor, Slovak Philharmonic Orchestra; Istropolitana Chamber Orchestra; Music Director of the National Theatre in Prague, 1993–96; Conducted Smetana's Libuše, Gounod's Romeo and Juliet, Puccini's La Bohème, Verdi's Rigoletto, Prokofiev's Cinderella, and two Mozart operas; Don Giovanni and The Marriage of Figaro, which toured Japan, 1995, 1997; Regular guest conductor Czech National Symphony Orchestra, Prague, Yomiuri Nippon Symphony Orchestra in Tokyo, Hungarian State Philharmonic, Portugal State Symphony Orchestra, Northern Philharmonic in Leeds, Kosice State Philharmonic, Brno State Philharmonic and Slovak Sinfonietta, Zilina; Also conducts at the Danish Royal Opera House, Copenhagen, National Theatre, Brno, Teatro San Carlo, Naples, the Royal Liverpool Philharmonic, English National Opera, English Chamber Orchestra, London Mozart Players, Northern Philharmonic in Leeds, BBC Belfast and Irish National Symphony Orchestra; Conducted Verdi's Falstaff and a new production of Boito's Mephistopheles for English National Opera, 1999. *Recordings:* Smetana's Libuše and My Country (with National Theatre of Prague); Famous Russian Masterpieces; Bach's St John Passion; Works by F Mendelssohn-Bartholdy. *Current Management:* Music International (UK). *Address:* Renoirova 2A, 152 00 Prague 5, Czech Republic. *E-mail:* o.v.dohnanyi@volny.cz.

DOIG, Christopher; Singer (Tenor); b. 4 April 1948, New Zealand. *Education:* Studied in New Zealand and with Anton Dermota at the Vienna Music Academy. *Career:* Sang at the Vienna Staatsoper from 1976 as David, Jacquino, Steuermann, Dr Caius and Remendado in Carmen; Linz Opera from 1980 as Don Ottavio, Tamino, Lionel in Martha, Fenton, Nemorino and the Duke of Mantua; Guest engagements in Vienna and at La Scala and the Salzburg Festival; Debut with Australian Opera, 1988, as Nerone in L'Incoronazione di Poppea; Sang David in Meistersinger at Sydney, conducted by Charles Mackerras; Hamburg Opera 1991, as Elemer in Arabella; Director of the New Zealand International Festival of Arts; Also sang in Jenůfa at Sydney, 1992; Maurizio in Adriana Lecouvreur, Sydney, 1992; Don José in Carmen and Erik in Fliegende Holländer, Cologne, 1992; Wozzeck, Stuttgart; Salome, Melbourne and Don José in Barcelona; Walther von Stolzing at Sydney, 1994; Sydney 1995, as Boris in Katya Kabanova. *Current Management:* Haydn Rawstron Ltd, London. *Address:* c/o Opera Australia, PO Box 291, Strawberry Hills, NSW 2012, Australia.

DOLEZAL, Karel; Czech viola player; b. 16 Jan. 1948, Prague; m. 1974; two s. *Education:* High School of Music, studied with Profs Cerny and Maly. *Career:* debut in Knights Hall of The Waldstein Palace, Prague

1973; solo performances at Prague Spring Festival 1976, Bratislava Music Festival 1977; music festival performances at Brno, Karlovy Vary, T Teplice, Poland, GDR, Romania; solo concert, BBC, TV Prague and 12 concerts for Radio Prague; made biographical film with the Dolezal String Quartet (Czech Film Corpn), programmes for TV Prague, Radio NY 1981; performances at Wigmore Hall, London, Birmingham, Dublin, Prague Spring Festival, Paris Festival, Bretagne, Tonhalle Zürich, Berlin, Halle; concert tours of Austria, Spain, Scandinavia, Hungary, Tunisia etc.; radio and television programmes for Hamburg, Bremen, Frankfurt, Wiesbaden, Saarbrucken; concert tour of USA 1980; with quartet, concert tours of Japan 1993, Spain 1997, Kangasniemi Festival, Finland 1997; Prof., Prague Conservatoire 1993; concert tour in BRD 1998–99; masterclasses in Seoul, Daegu, Republic of Korea 2000. *Recordings:* 2 String Quartets by Dvořák, 1983; 2 String Quartets by Leoš Janáček, 1984; 5 albums of works by Mozart, Dvořák, Janáček, Martinů, Shostakovich, and others; Solo: Viola and piano works by: Bloch, Rubinstein, Hindemith, Matousek, 1995, Mendelssohn, Reger, Weber, 1997; Quartet: Quartets by Janáček, 1992; 2 Quartets by Dvořák, 1994; Quartets by Smetana, Fibich, 1996. *Address:* Milesovska Street 6, 130 00 Prague 3, Czech Republic. *E-mail:* dolezalkin@volny.cz.

DOLLARHIDE, Thomas; Composer and Musicologist; b. 30 Aug. 1948, Santa Rosa, California, USA. *Education:* MA and PhD, University of Michigan; Study with Leslie Bassett and William Bolcom. *Career:* Faculty of La Trobe University, 1981–89. *Compositions include:* Shadows, wind quintet, 1973; Theme and Variations, for 2 cellos, flute, clarinet and 2 speaking voices, 1976; Other Dreams, Other Dreamers, for orchestra, 1976; Shoestrings for flute and clarinet, 1977; Pluriels for orchestra, 1979; Punk for piano, 1980; By Thunder Mill Pond by trombone, 1981; Ragings of a One Pot Screamer, for piano, 1982; A Back Street for violin, 1983; Two Pieces, for piano, 1984; Madness in Paradise, for violin, viola, double bass, clarinet, guitar, mandolin and percussion, 1986; Aria for cello and piano, 1990; The Dark Horse for orchestra, 1992. *Honours:* Broadcast Music Award to Young Composers, USA, 1975–76. *Address:* c/o APRA, 1A Eden Street, Crows Nest, NSW 2065, Australia.

DOLMETSCH, Jeanne-Marie; Recorder Player and Treble Viol Player; b. 15 Aug. 1942, Hindhead, Surrey, England. *Education:* violin and piano, Royal Acad. of Music, 1961–64; LRAM. *Career:* Debut: Queen Elizabeth Hall, London, 1973; toured USA, Colombia, Germany, France, Ireland and Sweden with the Dolmetsch Ensemble; recorder soloist and Asst Dir, Haslemere Festival; appearances at Bath Festival, English Bach Festival; numerous radio broadcasts and television programmes. *Recordings:* collections of early music with the Dolmetsch Ensemble. *Address:* Jesses, Grayswood Road, Haslemere, Surrey, England.

DOLMETSCH, Marguerite Mabel, LRAM; British recorder player and viola da gamba player; b. 15 Aug. 1942, Hindhead, Surrey, England; m. Brian E. Blood. *Career:* travelled widely with the Dolmetsch Ensemble and the Dolmetsch Concertante, touring America, France, Germany, Sweden, South Africa, Colombia; Has performed at the Three Choirs Festival, Bath Festival and Haslemere Festival; Has also appeared at Queen Elizabeth Hall, Purcell Room and Wigmore Hall; Radio broadcasts and television programmes in the United Kingdom, Germany, South Africa and South America. Recitals: Various recitals with the Dolmetsch Ensemble; Director of the Dolmetsch Summer School and Dolmetsch Musical Instruments; Assistant Director, Haslemere Festival; mem. National Federation of Decorative and Fine Arts Societies. *Recordings:* Choice Consorts for Recorders; A Christmas Tapestry, in Words and Music; A Chest of Viols. *Address:* Heartsease, Grayswood Road, Haslemere, Surrey GU27 2BS, England.

DOLTON, Geoffrey; Singer (Baritone); b. 30 Dec. 1958, Shrewsbury, England. *Education:* Studied at the Royal Academy of Music with Joy Mammen; Also at NOS and in Milan with Peter Moores Foundation. *Career:* Debut: With Opera North, as Guglielmo in Così fan tutte, 1983; Further roles with Opera North as Mozart's Count, Lescaut in Massenet's Manon Lescaut and Henrik in the British premiere of Nielsen's Maskarade; With Opera Factory has sung Guglielmo (also televised) and Orestes in Gluck's Iphigenia operas; Manoel Theatre Malta, Figaro in Il Barbiere di Siviglia; Season 1992 as Hector in Tippett's King Priam at Antwerp, Monteverdi's Otho for Opera Factory, in Krenek's What Price Confidence? at the Almeida Festival and as Alan in Birtwistle's Yan Tan Tethera; Other roles include Papageno for Welsh National Opera and Opera Northern Ireland; Schaunard in La Bohème for Scottish Opera; Hector in King Priam for Opera North, Malatesta in Don Pasquale for New Israeli Opera and the title role in Grétry's Le Huron at the Buxton Festival, 1990; Sang Guglielmo in Così fan tutte for ENO, 1990; Recitals with the pianist Nicholas Bosworth; Season 1994, ENO Eisenstein in Die Fledermaus; Opera Northern Ireland, Figaro in the Barber of Seville; Castleward Opera Dandini in La Cenerentola; Sang in La Traviata for GTO at Glyndebourne, 1996; Season 2000, Caseyflood in John Lunn's Zoë for Glyndebourne and Channel 4; First Mate in Billy Budd in Venice; Dr Malatesta in Don

Pasquale for Opera Zuid. *Recordings:* Donizetti's Emilia di Liverpool, with the Philharmonia Orchestra (Opera Rara). *Honours:* Peter Pears Prize for Recital Singing at the RAM; Honorary ARAM, 1992. *Address:* Allied Artists Agency, 42 Montpelier Square, London SW7 1JZ, England.

DOMANINSKA, Libuse; Singer (Soprano); b. 4 July 1924, Brno, Czechoslovakia. *Education:* Studied at the Prague Conservatory with Hana Pirkova and Bohuslav Sobesky. *Career:* Debut: Brno 1946, as Vendulka in The Kiss by Smetana; Sang at Brno in operas by Smetana and Janáček (Jenůfa, Katya Kabanova and the Vixen); Prague National Opera, 1955–85; Visited Edinburgh with the company in 1964, as Milada in Dalibor; Komische Oper Brelin 1956, Vienna Staatsoper, 1958–68; Holland Festival 1959, as Katya Kababova; Roles in Russian operas and in Mozart, Puccini and Verdi; Marenka in The Bartered Bride, Smetana's Libuše, Jenůfa, Aida, Elisabeth de Valois, Euridice and Foerster's Eva; Many concert appearances, notably in Janáček's Glagolitic Mass at La Scala; Retired 1985. *Recordings:* Glagolitic Mass, The Cunning Little Vixen, The Devil's Wall by Smetana (Supraphon). *Honours:* Artist of Merit, 1966; National Artist, 1974. *Address:* c/o National Theatre, PO Box 865, 11230 Prague 1, Czech Republic.

DOMANSKY, Hanus; Composer; b. 1 March 1944, Novy, Hrozenkov, Czechoslovakia. *Education:* Studied piano with Jaroslav Shanel; Composition with Jan Duchan, Brno Conservatory; Composition with Dezider Kardos, graduated 1970, Bratislava Academy of Musical Arts. *Career:* Associated with Czech Radio; Bratislava. *Compositions:* Concerto piccolo for Orchestra, 1970; Symphony, 1980; Piano Concerto, 1984; Music for Trumpet, Flute and Bass Clarinet, 1966; Musica giocosa for Violin and Piano, 1971; Dianoia for Violin, 1976; Piano pieces; Organ music; About Winter, cantata for Narrator, Children's Choir and Orchestra, 1968; Fiat lux, oratorio for Narrator, Soprano, Chorus and Orchestra, 1970; Versifying for Chorus and Percussion, 1972; Recruiting Songs for Men's Chorus, 1978; Solo Songs. *Honours:* Slovak Composers Award, 1983. *Address:* c/o Czech Radio, Bratislava, Slovakia.

DOMINGO, Plácido, FRCM; Spanish opera singer; b. 21 Jan. 1941, Madrid; s. of the late Plácido and Pepita (Embil) Domingo; m. Marta Ornelas; three s. *Education:* Nat. Conservatory of Music, Mexico City. *Career:* operatic début at Monterrey, Mexico 1961; with Israel Nat. Opera for over two years; début at Metropolitan Opera, New York 1968; British début in Verdi's Requiem at Festival Hall 1969; Covent Garden début in Tosca 1971, returned to sing in Aida, Carmen 1973, La Bohème 1974, Un Ballo in Maschera 1975, La Fanciulla del West; has taken leading roles in about 120 operas; with New York City Opera 1965–; Artistic Dir Washington Opera 1994–, LA Opera 2000–; Artistic Adviser and Prin. Guest Conductor Los Angeles Opera; Fellow, Royal N Coll. of Music; recent engagements include Tosca (conducting), Romeo and Juliet at Metropolitan Opera, New York, NY, Aida, Il Trovatore in Hamburg, Don Carlos in Salzburg, I vespri siciliani and La forza del destino in Paris, Turandot in Barcelona, Otello in Paris, London, Hamburg and Milan, Carmen in Edin., Turandot at the Metropolitan; New York stage début in My Fair Lady 1988 (213 performances by 2000); Luigi in Il Tabarro at the Met 1989; Otello at Covent Garden 1990, Lohengrin at Vienna Staatsoper, Don José at Rio de Janeiro, Otello at the Met and Barcelona; Don Carlos at Los Angeles, Dick Johnson at Chicago, Riccardo in Un Ballo in Maschera at the 1990 Salzburg Festival; debut as Parsifal at the Met 1991 and 2001, Otello at Covent Garden 1992, Siegmund in Die Walküre at the Vienna Staatsoper 1992; 1997 season included Don José and Siegmund at the Met and Gabriele Adorno in Simon Boccanegra at Covent Garden; 1999 season Herman in the Queen of Spades at the Met, and at Covent Garden 2002; concert performance of Verdi's Battaglia di Legnano with the Royal Opera 2000; Canio in Pagliacci at Covent Garden 2003; Nero in premiere of Monteverdi's Poppea in Los Angeles 2003; Rasputin in premiere of Deborah Drattell's Nicholas and Alexandra, Los Angeles 2003; opened 2002/03 Los Angeles Opera Season in Puccini's Fanciulla des West. *Films include:* Madame Butterfly with Von Karajan, La Traviata 1982, Carmen 1984, Otello 1986. *Recordings:* has made well over 100 recordings, including Aida, Un Ballo in Maschera, Tosca, Tannhäuser 1989, Die Frau ohne Schatten 1993, Gounod's Roméo et Juliette 1996, Merlin by Albeniz 2000; has made more than 50 videos. *Publications:* My First Forty Years (autobiog.) 1983, My Operatic Roles 2000. *Honours:* Dr hc (Royal Coll. of Music) 1982, (Univ. Complutense de Madrid) 1989; Hon. DMus (Oxford Univ.) 2003; Commdr Légion d'honneur; Hon. KBE 2002; Medal of Freedom; nine Grammy Awards. *Current Management:* Vincent and Farrell Associates, Suite 740, 481 8th Avenue, New York, NY 10001, USA.

DOMINGUEZ, Guillermo; Singer (Tenor); b. 1961, Caracas, Venezuela. *Education:* Studied with José Castro in Caracas, then at Rome and Turin. *Career:* Debut: Treviso, 1984, as Rodolfo; Sang Rodolfo at Paris, Amiens and Munich; Zürich Opera as Don Ottavio and Ferrando and in Guillaume Tell; Appearances at Monte Carlo as Edgardo in Lucia di

Lammermoor and at Innsbruck as Cavaradossi and the Duke of Mantua, 1988; National Theatre Mannheim as Alfredo and Puccini's Edgar with the Dresden Staatskapelle; Engagements in Spain as the Duke of Mantua; Many concert appearances. *Address:* c/o National Theater, Am Goetheplatz, 6B00 Mannheim, Germany.

DOMINGUEZ, Oralia; Singer (Contralto); b. 15 Oct. 1927, San Luis, Potosi, Mexico. *Education:* Studied at the Mexican National Conservatory. *Career:* Sang in Debussy's La Demoiselle Elue while a student; Stage debut Mexico City 1950, appeared as Amneris in 1951; Sang in Europe from 1953, London debut at the Wigmore Hall; La Scala Milan 1953 in Adriana Lecouvreur; Covent Garden 1955, as Sosostris in the premiere of The Midsummer Marriage by Tippett; Glyndebourne Festival 1955–64, as Mistress Quickly, Isabella, and Arnalta in the Leppard-Monteverdi L'Incoronazione di Poppea; Venice 1960, in Alcina, with Joan Sutherland; Sang at the Deutsche Oper am Rhein, Düsseldorf, from 1960; Guest appearances in Buenos Aires, Vienna, Frankfurt, Paris, Rome, Naples, Florence, Chicago, Dallas and New Orleans; Stuttgart Opera 1972–76; Mexico City concert, 1973. *Recordings:* Erda in The Ring, Mozart's Coronation Mass, Verdi Requiem (Deutsche Grammophon); Il Tabarro, La Gioconda (Decca). *Address:* c/o Deutsche Oper am Rhein, Heinrich-Heine Allee 16, 4000 Düsseldorf, Germany.

DOMINGUEZ, Ruben; Singer (Tenor); b. 4 Sept. 1940, Caracas, Venezuela. *Education:* Studied in Milan. *Career:* Debut: As Cavaradossi, Mexico City, 1967; Sang throughout the USA and in Venezuela as Donizetti's Edgardo, The Duke of Mantua, Alfredo, Riccardo in Un Ballo in Maschera, Rodolfo and Andrea Chénier; Cincinnati, 1985–86 as Radames and Manrico; Milwaukee, 1988 as Calaf; Opera North, 1986 as Ramirez in La Fanciulla del West; Teatro Col ón Buenos Aires, 1992 as Cavaradossi; Other roles include: Pollione in Norma, Opéra Nancy. *Address:* c/o Opera de Caracas, Museo del Teclado, Parque Central, Edif, Tacaqua, Mezzanina, Caracas 1010, Venezuela.

DONADINI, Giovanna; Singer (soprano); b. 1964, Italy. *Education:* Studied in Venice and Ancona. *Career:* Debut: Monteverdi's Selve Morale e Spirituale, at La Fenice Venice; Mozart's Countess and Fiordiligi at Treviso, 1990–91; Season 1994 with Pamela Nubile by Farinelli at Treviso, and Camilla in Leo's Amor vuol Sofferanza at Martina Franca; Donna Elvira in Switzerland, and Galuppi's Le Nozze at Vicenza, 1996; Rossalane in Cimarosa's I Turchi Amanti at Citta di Castello, Fiordiligi in Tokyo and Mozart's Susanna at the Teatro Verdi, Sassari; Concerts include Pergolesi's Stabat Mater, Bach's Magnificat, Haydn's Stabat Mater, Beethoven's Ninth and the Four Last Songs at Treviso and Toulouse. *Honours:* 1994 Concorso Internazionale, Bilbao. *Current Management:* Athole Still International Management, Forresters Hall, 25–27 Westow Street, London, SE19 3RY, England. *Telephone:* (20) 8771-5271. *Fax:* (20) 8768-6600. *Website:* www .atholestill.com.

DONAT, Zdislava; Singer (Soprano Coloratura); b. 4 July 1939, Poznań, Poland. *Education:* Studied with Zofia Bregy in Warsaw and Gino Bechi in Siena, Italy. *Career:* Debut: Poznan 1964, as Gilda from 1971 in Teatr Wielki, Warsaw; Theater am Gärtnerplatz, Munich, as Queen of Night; Bayerische Staatsoper Munich, Hamburg; Vienna Staatsoper; London Covent Garden; La Scala, Milan; Met-Opera, New York; Teatro Col ón Buenos Aires; Deutsche Oper, Berlin; San Francisco Opera; Opera in Moscow, Naples, Zürich, Frankfurt and many others; Festivals in Salzburg, 1979–87; Bregenz, Orange, Munich, Tokyo, Athens, Wroclaw and others; Roles include: Lucia di Lammermoor, La Sonnambula, Giulia in Capuleti, Norina, Constanze, Blonde, Zerlina, Olympia, Gilda, Violetta, Manon (Massenet), Martha, (Flotow), Queen in Golden Cockerel, La Princesse and Le Feu in L'Enfant at les Sortilèges by Ravel, Hanna (Moniuszko), Marzelline (Beethoven), Adele (Johann Strauss) and others; Warsaw 1991, as Giulia in I Capuleti e i Montecchi; Television productions, recitals and appearances with symphony orchestras. *Recordings include:* Die Zauberflöte, RCA, conductor J Levine; Operatic Arias, Polski Nagrania, conductor J Dobrzanski; Requiem by R Maciejewski, conductor, T Strugala. *Honours:* Grand Prix in Toulouse; Kammersängerin, Munich, 1977. *Address:* Teatr Wielki, Moliere 3, 00 076 Warsaw, Poland.

DONATH, Helen; Singer (Soprano); b. 10 July 1940, Corpus Christi, Texas, USA; m. Klaus Donath, 10 July 1965, 1 s. *Education:* Del Mar College, Corpus Christi, Texas; Paolo Novikova; Maria Berini. *Career:* Debut: Cologne Opera as Inez in Il Trovatore, 1960; Hannover Opera; Bavarian State Opera, Munich; Salzburg Festival; Vienna State Opera; Deutsche Oper, Berlin; La Scala, Milan; Royal Opera, Covent Garden; Lisbon; Hamburg; Bayreuth Festival, San Francisco Opera; Paris Opéra; Sang Pamina at the 1970 Salzburg Festival; US debut as Sophie at San Francisco, 1971; Covent Garden debut as Anne Trulove in The Rake's Progress, 1979; Other roles include: Mozart's Zerlina, Ilia and Susanna, Micaela, Mélisande, Mimi, Oscar and Aennchen; Sang Eva in Die Meistersinger at Seattle, 1989; Season 1993–94 as Eva in Dresden

and Agathe at the Berlin Staatsoper; Season 1996 as Mimi at Detroit and Mozart's Countess for Florida Grand Opera; Countess at Seattle 1997–98; Season 2000 as Despina at Miami, the Marschallin in Detroit and Desdemona at Schwerin. *Recordings:* Beethoven, Fidelio (Angel); Britten, Turn of the Screw (Philips); Handel, Messiah (Deutsche Grammophon); Mozart, Requiem (Angel and Philips); Pfitzner, Palestrina (Deutsche Grammophon); Strauss, Arabella (Angel); Strauss, Der Rosenkavalier (London). *Honours:* Pope Paul Medal, 1967; Grand Prix du Disque, Deutsche Schallplatten Preis, 1990, Bavarian Kammersängerin; Culture Prize of Lower Saxony. *Current Management:* Shaw Concerts, 1900 Broadway, New York, NY 10023, USA. *Address:* Bergstrasse 5, 3002 Wedemark 1, Germany.

DONATI, Walter; Singer (Tenor); b. 4 Sept. 1938, Potsdam, Germany. *Career:* Sang in Italy from 1983, notably at Treviso as Erik in Der fliegende Holländer, at La Scala in Tannhäuser, I Lombardi and Macbeth; Sang Don Carlos at Dublin (1985), Radames at Avignon (1986), and Dick Johnson at Buenos Aires; Further appearances at Venice as Foresto in Attila, at Florence as Dimitri in Boris Godunov, Paris Opéra as Raimbaut in Robert le Diable (1985), returning as Pollione (1988); Manrico at Covent Garden (1990); Baritone from 1995 (Nabucco at Lonigo near Verona); Amonasro at Earl's Court, London, 1998; Sang Gleb in Giordano's Siberia at Wexford, 1999, and Nabucco at St Margreth 2000. *Address:* c/o Théâtre National de l'Opéra, 8 Rue Scribe, 75009 Paris, France.

DONCEANU, Felicia; Composer; b. 28 Jan. 1931, Bacau, Romania. *Education:* Bucharest Conservatory. *Career:* former Ed. of Editura Musicala, Bucharest. *Compositions include:* Spinet Sonata 1983, Moldavian Echoes, suite for Strings 1985, Three Symphonic Sketches 1982, The Clever Bell, chorus 1986, Inscription On A Mast, for Harp 1989, The Music Lesson, song 1992. *Honours:* Composition Prize, Romanian Composers' Union. *Address:* GEMA, Postfach 301240, 10722 Berlin, Germany.

DONGEN, Maria van; Singer (Soprano); b. 23 March 1928, Netherlands. *Career:* Sang Mozart's Countess and Pamina at Amsterdam; Member of the Zürich Opera, 1959–65, debut as the Forza Leonora; Guest appearances at Frankfurt, London, (Countess at the Albert Hall), Bologna, Parma (Elisabeth, 1963), and Pisa (Elsa); Amsterdam 1963–67, as Donna Elvira; Munich from 1964, Vienna from 1967 as Ariadne, Fiordiligi, Senta and Desdemona; Munich Opera 1967, as Strauss's Danae, and as Irene in Rienzi; Further engagements at Barcelona and Hamburg (as Leonora in Fidelio), Graz, the Deutsche Oper Berlin, Piccola Scala Milan and the Salzburg Festival (First Lady in Die Zauberflöte, 1963–64); Sang Leonore at the Landestheater Salzburg, 1971; Frequent concert engagements. *Address:* c/o Vienna State Opera, Opernring 2, 1010 Vienna, Austria.

DONNELLY, Malcolm (Douglas); Opera Singer (Baritone); b. 8 Feb. 1943, Sydney, Australia; m. Dolores Ryles. *Education:* Sydney Conservatory and Opera School; London Opera Centre. *Career:* Debut: Australian Opera, 1966; Australian Opera, Scottish Opera, English National Opera, Opera North, Netherlands Opera, Victoria State Opera, State Opera South Australia, Welsh National Opera, Royal Opera House, Covent Garden, English National Opera Tour, Moscow, Leningrad, 1991, Adelaide Festival 1991; Appearances at Edinburgh Festival, 1975, 1976; Wexford Festival, 1977, 1978; Glyndebourne, 1979, 1981, 1985; Hong Kong Festival, 1987; Brighton International Festival, 1988; Roles include, Macbeth, Simon Boccanegra, Rigoletto, Pizarro (Fidelio); Sang Kurwenal in Tristan und Isolde for Australian Opera, 1990, Macbeth with ENO on tour to Russia, Scarpia with Scottish Opera and Shishkov in From the House of the Dead for Welsh National Opera, 1990; Season 1992 in Ovations concert by ENO at the Barbican Hall, Don Carlos in Ernani for Welsh National Opera and Ford in Falstaff for the English National Opera; Boccanegra and Iago in Australia; Sharpless, Royal Opera House, Covent Garden; Kurwenal for Australian Opera, Macbeth and Telramund (Lohengrin) ENO, 1993; Di Luna (Il Trovatore) Victoria State Opera, Kurwenal (Tristan und Isolde) Scottish Opera; Verdi Requiem, Guildford Cathedral, 1994; Scarpia, Lyric Opera of Queensland; Nabucco, Australian Opera; Falstaff, State Opera South Australia, 1995; Sang Iago at Sydney, 1996; Janáček's Forester, 1997; Butterfly, Royal Albert Hall, Australian Opera, Alberich in Wagner's Ring Cycle, State Opera of South Australia, 1998. *Recordings:* Videos of Lucia di Lammermoor and Un Ballo in Maschera, Australian Opera. *Honours:* Sydney Sun Aria Competition, 1969; Australian Opera Auditions Scholarship, 1970. *Current Management:* Jenifer Eddy, Melbourne. *Address:* PO Box 464, Ryde 2112, New South Wales, Australia.

DONNELLY, Patrick; Singer (Bass-Baritone); b. 15 March 1955, Sydney, Australia. *Education:* Studied at the Conservatorium of Music, Sydney and at the Guildhall School of Music, London. *Career:* Concert debut at Sydney Opera House in Belshazzar's Feast by Walton; Also appeared at Tiresias (Oedipus Rex) and in the Monteverdi Vespers;

Sang with Glyndebourne Chorus on the 1983 Tour, solo debut as Theseus in A Midsummer Night's Dream, 1985; Festival and Tour appearances in Idomeneo (Neptune), Don Giovanni (Masetto), La Traviata, Le nozze di Figaro (Bartolo) and L'Incoronzione di Poppea; Other roles include Mozart's Figaro for Opera 80, First Minister in Cendrillon at the Wexford Festival and Bart ók's Bluebeard at the Barbican; Sang Polyphemus in Acis and Galatea on tour in France, Hayden in the premiere of 63 Dream Palace by Jurgen Bose in Berlin, 1990, and the Herald in Lohengrin for Australian Opera, October 1990; Licone and Caronte in Haydn's Orlando Paladino at Garsington, Oxford; Mozart's Figaro at Grange Park, 1998; Concerts at most major London centres, including Stravinsky's Renard at the Queen Elizabeth Hall. *Recordings:* Renard with the Matrix Ensemble; Pergolesi's La Serva Padrona (Meridan).

DONOHOE, Peter Howard; Pianist and Conductor; b. 18 June 1953, Manchester, England; m. Elaine Margaret Burns 1980, 1 d. *Education:* Chetham's School of Music, Manchester, 1961–71; Leeds University, 1971–72; Royal Manchester College of Music, 1972–73; Royal Northern College of Music, 1973–76; Paris Conservatoire, 1976–77; Diplomas: ARCM; GRNCM; BMus. *Career:* Concert Appearances throughout the world as Recitalist, Soloist with Major Orchestras and Chamber Musician, including USA, Canada, Japan, Australia, USSR, Continental Europe, the United Kingdom; Annual appearances at Henry Wood Promenade Concerts, 1979–; Regular appearances at South Bank, London, Broadcasts on television and radio; Appearances at several major festivals including Edinburgh, Cheltenham, Bath, Hollywood Bowl, La Roche d'Arraignon, Prague; Guest Conductor including Ulster Orchestra, City of Birmingham Symphony Orchestra, Royal Liverpool Philharmonic Orchestra, Hallé Orchestra, Moscow Chamber Orchestra; Played Tippett's Piano Concerto at the 1991 Promenade Concerts, London; Tchaikovsky's Second Concerto at the 1993 Proms; Played the Britten Concerto at the Barbican, 1997. *Recordings include:* Stravinsky, Three Movements from Petrushka; Prokofiev, Sonata No. 6; Tchaikovsky, Complete Works for Piano and Orchestra; Messiaen, Turangalila Symphony; Rachmaninov Concerto No. 3 and Etudes Tableaux and Preludes; Muldowney Concerto; Gershwin Rhapsody in Blue on The Jazz Album, with Simon Rattle. *Honours:* Dayas Gold Medal, Royal Manchester College of Music, 1977; Liszt-Bartók Competition, Budapest, 1976; Finalist Leeds International Piano Competition, 1981; Winner, 7th International Tchaikovsky Competition, Moscow, 1982; Honorary Fellow, Royal Northern College of Music, 1983. *Current Management:* Hazard Chase, Norman House, Cambridge Place, Cambridge CB2 1NS, England. *Telephone:* (1223) 312400. *Fax:* (1223) 460827. *Website:* www.hazardchase.co.uk.

DONOSE, Ruxandra; Singer (Mezzo-Soprano); b. 2 Sept. 1964, Bucharest, Romania. *Education:* Academy of Music, Ciprian Porumbescu, Bucharest. *Career:* Debut: Bellini's Romeo and Varvara in Katya Kabanova at Basle, 1991; Rossini's Rosina at Vienna, Hamburg, Toulon and São Paulo; Carmen at Vienna, Leipzig and Prague; Mozart's Cherubino at Dresden, Dorabella in Vienna and Sesto at Covent Garden; Offenbach's Nicklausse and Monteverdi's Poppea at San Francisco; Appearances as Varvara in Vienna, Feodor (Boris Godunov) at the Salzburg Festival, Annio in La Clemenza di Tito at Glyndebourne (1998) and Covent Garden (2000); Season 1999 with Strauss's Composer at Minneapolis and L'Enfant et les Sortilèges at Carnegie Hall; Sang Mozart's Sesto at Glyndebourne, 1999, Annio at Covent Garden and Mèlisande at Cincinnati, 2000; Engaged as Charlotte in Werther at Covent Garden, 2004. *Recordings:* Das Lied von der Erde and Bach's B minor Mass. *Honours:* Best Young Singer of Romania, 1989; ARD Competition, Munich, 1990; Marian Anderson Vocal Arts Competition, Special Prize, 1991. *Current Management:* Columbia Artists, New York. *Address:* Hebragasse 4/10, 1090 Vienna, Austria.

DOOLEY, Jeffrey (Michael); Singer (Counter-Tenor) and Choral Conductor; b. 7 Oct. 1945, Milwaukee, Wisconsin, USA. *Education:* Milton College, Milton, Wisconsin; BA, Wisconsin Conservatory, 1968; Apprenticeship with Mark Deller, Deller Consort, Canterbury, England, 1974. *Career:* Debut: Carnegie Hall, 1977; Regular appearances in Early Music scene, New York: Basically Bach (Lincoln Center), Clarion Concerts, Amor Artis Ensemble, Waverly Consort, Boston Early Music Festival Orchestra, Milwaukee Symphony Orchestra, Connecticut Symphony; Recital-lecture presentations, The Art of the Counter-Tenor, duo with Richard Kolb, lutenist, founder of The Gotham Consort; Founder, Director, The Stuyvesant Singers, Toronto, Canada; Ongoing appearances with the following Baroque Orchestras: Tafelmusik, Toronto, Ars Musica, Michigan, Levin Baroque Ensemble, Amor Artis Ensemble, Concert Royal, ARTEC Ensemble, New York; European appearances, Madeira Bach Festival, 1981; Stour Music, England, 1985; Amor Artis tour, Switzerland and Italy, 1991; Specialist in the Handel Oratorio, frequently giving masterclasses in interpretation of the arias, and performing; mem, Early Music, America; International Society of Early Music Singers. *Recordings:* Henry Purcell: Airs and Duets,

Nonesuch; J. S. Bach: Mass in B Minor, Nonesuch; Johannes Ockeghem: Masses, Nonesuch; G Dufay: Masses, Nonesuch; J. S. Bach: St John Passion, Newport Classic; G F Handel: Acis and Galatea, Newport; H Schütz: St Matthew Passion, Newport. *Contributions:* The Counter-Tenor Voice Defined, 1977; The Counter-Tenor's Roles in Music, 1982. *Current Management:* Melody Bunting International, 127 West 72nd Street, Suite 2-R, New York 10023, USA. *Address:* 229 East 11th Street, New York, NY 10003, USA.

DOOLEY, William; Singer (Baritone); b. 9 Sept. 1932, Modesto, California, USA. *Education:* Studied at the Eastman School of Music and in Munich with Viktoria Prestel and Hedwig Fichtmuller. *Career:* Debut: Heidelberg 1957, as Posa in Don Carlos; Sang at Bielefeld 1959–62; Member of the Deutsche Oper Berlin from 1962, notably in the premieres of Montezuma by Sessions (1964), Gespenstersonate by Reimann (1984) and Rihm's Oedipus, 1987; Salzburg Festival 1964, as Lucio Silla and 1966 in the premiere of The Bassarids by Henze; Metropolitan Opera from 1964, as Amonasro, Eugene Onegin, the villains in Les Contes d'Hoffmann, Telramund, Orestes (Elektra) and Mandryka; Hamburg Staatsoper 1967, as Iago and 1979 in the premiere of Jakob Lenz by Wolfgang Rihm; Guest appearances at the Royal Opera Stockholm from 1967; Other roles include: Berg's Wozzeck and Dr Schön, Pizarro, Kothner, Macbeth, Escamillo, Nick Shadow, Captain Mary (Die Soldaten) and Goryanchikov in From the House of the Dead; Sang Eagle in the premiere of Los Alamos by Marc Neikrug at Berlin, 1989; Santa Fe 1991, as Tiresias in Oedipus by Wolfgang Rihm. *Recordings include:* Telramund in Lohengrin (RCA); Jakob Lenz (Harmonia Mundi). *Address:* c/o Deutsch Oper Berlin, Richard Wagnerstrasse 10, 100 Berlin, Germany.

DOONER, Daniel; Stage Director; b. 1955, Ottawa, Canada. *Education:* Universities of London and Toronto. *Career:* Associate director with many British opera companies; Revivals of Rigoletto, Così fan tutte and La Traviata (2001) for the Royal Opera; Janáček's The Makropulos Case at the Brooklyn Academy for Glyndebourne Festival; Lucia di Lammermoor for Welsh National Opera at Malaga and The Magic Flute for English Touring Opera: Rigoletto, Cav and Pag, Donizetti's Betly, Il Barbiere di Siviglia and Puccini double bill for Opera Europa at Holland Park, London. *Current Management:* Athole Still International Management, Forresters Hall, 25–27 Westow Street, London, SE19 3RY, England. *Telephone:* (20) 8771-5271. *Fax:* (20) 8768-6600. *Website:* www.atholestill.com.

DOORNBUSCH, Paul; Composer and Sonologist; b. 30 Dec. 1959, Melbourne, Australia. *Education:* BMus, University of Melbourne, 1984; Postgraduate degree, Computer Science, University of Melbourne, 1990; Postgraduate studies in Sonology, Electronic Music, and Composition, Royal Conservatory of Holland, 1993, 1994. *Career:* Staff member, Royal Conservatory of Holland, 1995; Sound installation, Alive, International Computer Music Conference, 1996; Compositional residency for Strepidus Somnus, STEIM, Amsterdam; Member, EU Committee to implement centre for aural art, Macedonia, 1998; Senior Sonologist, I-Cubed Virtual Reality Centre, RMIT University, 2000; Research Fellow, Department of Computer Science, University of Melbourne, 2000; mem, International Computer Music Association. *Compositions:* Continuity 2, for recorder, quartet and electronics; Continuity 1, for electronics; Strepidus Somnus, for voices and electronics; Oxidization, for percussion and electronics; Corrosion, for percussion and electronics; Lorenz, for piano; ACT 5, for bassoon and percussion; G4, for electronics; MFPG, for electronics; Structured Luck, for bassoon and electronics; Asfixiation, for flute and electronics; On The Fence, medium ensemble and electronics; Iceberg, for electronics; Preludes, for 4 voices; M1 and M2, for soloist and electronics. *Recordings:* Corrosion, The Works of Paul Doornbusch. *Publications:* The Frog Peak Collaboration Project, 1998; Corrosion, 2001; Book: The Music of CSIRAC, 2001; Computer software. *Contributions:* Numerous newspaper articles; Several for The Age. *Address:* 5 Newton Street, Glenroy, VIC 3046, Australia.

DORDI, Patrizia; Singer (Soprano); b. 1956, Italy. *Education:* Studied at the Accademia di Santa Cecilia, Rome. *Career:* Debut: Rome, 1979, in Schumann's Manfred; Opera debut in Handel's Ariodante at La Scala, 1980; Guest at La Fenice, Venice, as Lisa in La Sonnambula and Mathilde in Guillaume Tell; Naples as Elmira in Jommelli's La schiava liberata and at Catania as Amor in Orfeo ed Euridice; Other repertory includes Micaela, Sabina in Cimarosa's Gli Orazi ed i Curiazi, Pamina (Ravenna Festival), Mimi and Musetta; Zürich Opera 1992, as Mathilde in Guillame Tell.

DORFMÜLLER, Joachim, DrPhilHabil; academic; b. 13 Dec. 1938, Wuppertal, Germany; m. Ursula Petschelt, 14 May 1976, 1 s., 2 d. *Education:* Universities of Cologne and Marburg; Studied piano and organ with father; Musikhochschule, Cologne. *Career:* Teacher, Music, Mathematics and Latin, Gymnasium, 1969–78; University of Duisburg, 1978–84; University of Münster 1984–, and Music Academy, Cologne,

1984–98; Founder, Artistic Director, Wuppertaler Orgeltage, 1973–2002; Over 2,800 concerts on organ and piano in 21 countries including the USA and Japan; mem, Humboldt-Akademie der Wissenschaften, 1990, Norwegian Agder Acad. of Sciences and Letters 2004; President, Deutsche Edvard Grieg-Gesellschaft, 1993; Research Group of the Norwegian Academy of Science and Letters, 1997. *Recordings include:* Virtuoso organ music of the Romantic period; Famous Organ works by Saint-Saëns; Piano works by Grieg; Meditations: Bach, Bernstein and Messiaen; Bach to Rachmaninov; Bach to Ligeti. *Publications include:* Norweg Klaviermusik 1900–1950, 1968; Zeitgenöss Orgelmusik 1960–84, 1985; 300 Jahre Orgelbau im Wuppertal, 1988; Geschichte des Sinfonieorchesters Wuppertal, 1991; Wuppertaler Musikgeschichte, 1995; Geistl. Musik von Grieg, 2000; Geschichte der Orgelmusik, 2006. *Contributions:* More than 500 articles for Herder-Musiklexikon, Rheinische Musikerbiographien; Musik in Geschichte und Gegenwart; National and international journals. *Honours:* Director of Church Music, 1990; Cultural Prize of the Rhineland, 1993, Bundesverdienstkreuz 2004. *Address:* Ringelstraße 22, 42289 Wuppertal, Germany.

DORFMÜLLER, Kurt, DPhil; German musicologist and librarian; b. 28 April 1922, Munich; m. Liselotte Laubmann; two s. *Education:* Univ. of Munich. *Career:* Bavarian State Library 1954–84, including Head of Music Collection 1963, Head of Acquisitions Division 1969–, Vice-Dir 1972; hon. mem. Int. Asscn of Music Libraries, Int. Inventory of Musical Sources. *Publications:* Studien zur Lautenmusik in der ersten Hälfte des 16 Jahrhunderts, 1967; Beiträge zur Beethoven-Bibliographie, 1977; Bestandsaufbau an wissenschaftlichen Bibliotheken, 1989; Musik in Bibliotheken, 1997; New ed. (with Norbert Gertsch) of Das Werk Beethovens...von Georg Kinsky and Hans Halm, vol.1, 2005; contrib. musicology and library science articles to journals, Festschriften and library exhibition catalogues. *Honours:* Ars Jocundissima Festschrift für Kurt Dorfmüller 1984. *Address:* Gabriel-von-Seidl-Strasse 39, 82031 Grünwald, Germany.

DORING, Ute; Singer (Mezzo-soprano); b. 4 June 1963, Berlin. *Education:* Studied in Berlin with Luisa Bosabalian. *Career:* Sang in opera at Kassel, 1990; Ulm, 1991–95; Roles have included Mozart's Cherubino and Idamante, Rossini's Rosina and Angelina and Octavian in Der Rosenkavalier; Schubertiade concerts at Feldkirch from 1995; Season 1995–96 as Flower Maiden in Parsifal at Bayreuth and roles in Eugene Onegin, Die Zauberflote, Otello and Figaro, Cologne; Frequent concert engagements; Nicklausse in Les Contes d'Hoffmann at Cologne; 1994–1997 Schubertiade Concerts Feldkirch, 1999 Wiener Klangbogen: Lieder-Recital and Sycorax in Faust by Spohr; Marie in Wozzeck: 1997 at Wuppertal, 2000 at Osnabrück and at Bonn, 1998 at Milan Scala as 2. Dame in Zauberflöte and in 2000 as Margret in Wozzeck, 2002 Debut in U.S.A, San Francisco Opera as Varvara in Kat'a Kabanova; 1999 and 2000 as Hansel in Frankfurt, 2001 as Leonore in Fidelio at Osnabrück; Season 2003 as Orlofsky at Cologne, Wozzeck - Marie at Wiesbaden and Gutrune (Götterdämmerung) at Cologne. *Current Management:* Balmer & Dixon Management AG, Kreuzstrasse 82, 8032 Zürich, Switzerland. *Telephone:* (43) 244-8644. *Fax:* (43) 244-8649. *Website:* www.badix.ch.

DORNBUSCH, Hans; Singer (Tenor); b. 1946, Gothenburg, Sweden. *Education:* Studied at the Stockholm Academy and at the School of the Royal Opera. *Career:* Debut: Stockholm, 1969, as Calaf; Member of the Royal Opera Stockholm from 1970, notably as Manrico, Otello, Pinkerton, Turiddu, Andres in Wozzeck and the Steuermann in Fliegende Holländer; Sang Pope Alexander VII in the premiere of Christina, by Hans Gefors, 1986; Character roles in Albert Herring and Hansel und Gretel; Guest appearances in England and Germany; Frequent concert engagements. *Address:* c/o Stockholm Music Academy, Valhallavägen 103–109, s–115 31 Stockholm, Sweden.

DOROW, Dorothy; Singer (Soprano); b. 1930, London, England. *Education:* Studied at Trinity College, London. *Career:* Sang in London from 1958, notably in BBC Invitation Concerts (Webern conducted by John Carewe, and the British premiere of Herzgewächse by Schoenberg, 1960); Has sung in the premieres of works by Birtwistle, Nono, Maderna, Dallapiccola, Bussotti, Ligeti, Boulez, Goehr and Bennett (The Ledge, Sadler's Wells, 1961); Sang Hilde Mack in the British premiere of Henze's Elegy for Young Lovers, Glyndebourne 1961; Lived in Sweden 1963–77, Netherlands from 1977: Professor of Voice at the Conservatoire of Amsterdam and The Hague; Masterclasses in Europe and Scandinavia; Concerts and opera in Italy, at La Scala, Venice, Rome, Florence and Bologna (Le Grand Macabre by Ligeti); Repertoire from Monteverdi to the 20th Century; Covent Garden debut 1983, as Stravinsky's Nightingale.

DOSS, Mark; Singer (Bass); b. 1960, Chicago, USA. *Career:* Sang Merlin in Purcell's King Arthur at St Louis, 1989; Season 1990 as Sarastro at the Glyndebourne Festival and Mozart's Publio at Chicago; New Orleans, 1991, as Rossini's Basilio, and Britten's Collatinus at San Diego; Season 1992 as Sparafucile in Rigoletto with Canadian Opera,

Toronto, and in the premiere of Alice by Anthony Davis, at Philadelphia; Escamillo in Carmen at Brussels; Nourabad in Les Pêcheurs de perles and Water Spirit in Rusalka at San Diego, 1993–95; Other roles include Hercules in Gluck's Alceste at Chicago; Season 1998 as Frère Laurent in Roméo et Juliette at San Diego, Escamillo at San Francisco and High Priest in Samson et Dalila for Cincinnati Opera; Sang Escamillo at Chicago and Ravenna, Rossini's Mustafà at Turin, 2000. *Honours:* Winner, George London Competition, Washington, 1987. *Address:* San Diego Opera, PO Box 988, San Diego, CA 92112, USA.

DOUFEXIS, Stella; singer (mezzo-soprano); b. 1968, Frankfurt am Main, Germany. *Education:* Hochschule der Künste, Berlin, studied with Anna Reynolds, masterclasses with Dietrich Fischer-Dieskau and Aribert Reimann. *Career:* debut in Dido and Aeneas, Berlin, 1992; concert engagements in Schubert's Lazarus, under Fischer-Dieskau, Pergolesi's Stabat Mater (Konzerthaus, Berlin), Ravel's Shéhérazade, under Ashkenazy, and Janáček's Glagolitic Mass; Season 1995–96 at the Heidelberg Opera, as Cherubino, Hansel, Nicklausse, Gluck's Orfeo and in the German premiere of Birtwistle's Second Mrs Kong; British debut at the Wigmore Hall in the International Songmakers series; Season 1996–97 in Provenzale's La Stellidaura Vendicata and Second dame in Die Zauberflöte at La Monnaie, Brussels; Rosina at Heidelberg; Schubert Lieder in Berlin and Lucerne, the Masses with the Deutsches Symphony Orchestra; Season 1998–99 with Der Rosenkavalier for Scottish Opera, Falstaff under Claudio Abbado in Ferrara, Berlin and the Salzburg Easter and Sumer Festival, 2001; with Berlioz's Les Troyens and Janacek's Da schlaue Füchslein, Munich Staatsoper, 2002; debut Liceu Barcelona in Felipe Pedrell's Els Pirineus, 2003. *Recordings include:* Webern, Dessau, Blacher and Fortner Lieder; Glagolitic Mass; Schumann series with Graham Johnson; Orchestra Songs of Joseph Marx with Steven Sloane. *Current Management:* Künstlersekretariat amGasteig, Rosenheimer str. 52, 81669 Munich, Germany.

DOUGLAS, Barry; Pianist; b. 23 April 1960, Belfast, Northern Ireland; m. Deirdre O'Hara, 2 s., 1 d. *Education:* Belfast School of Music; Royal College of Music, London, 1978–82; Diploma RCM (Performance); Private study with Maria Curcio in London and Yvgeny Malinin (Moscow Conservatoire) in Paris. *Career:* Debut: First Recitals in Belfast in 1977–78; London Philharmonic, RFH, 1983; Wigmore Hall, London, 1981;Berlin Philharmonic, 1987; New York recital debut Carnegie Hall, New York, 1988; Royal festival Hall with London Philharmonic, 1983; Subject of BBC documentary film Rhapsody in Belfast and film After the Gold; Appeared in John Schlesinger's film Madame Sousatska; Played Rachmaninov 2 with London Symphony Orchestra and Michael Tilson-Thomas in television series Concerto; Broadcasts, BBC Radio 3, Radio Ulster, Radio London, BBC television; Live performances with orchestras and recorded concerts; Performed for Thames television; Concerts, USA, Japan, France, Germany, the United Kingdom, Denmark, Sweden, Netherlands, Italy, Greece, Ireland, USSR, Australia, New Zealand; Performed with all major British orchestras; Played Beethoven's 4th Concerto at the Festival Hall, London, 1997; Concerts throughout North and South America, and in Europe, 2000–01; City of London Festival, 2002; Commissions new works from young Irish composers. *Recordings:* Tchaikovsky Concerto No. 1 with London Symphony Orchestra/Slatkin; Brahms Concerto No. 2 with London Symphony Orchestra; Mussorgsky, Liszt and Beethoven solo works; Liszt Concertos 1 and 2 and Hungarian Fantasy with London Symphony Orchestra/Hirokami; Prokofiev Solo Sonatas 2, 7 and Cinderella; Berg and Liszt Sonatas; Brahms Quintet with Tokyo Quartet; Tchaikovsky 2, 3 and Concert Fantasy; Rachmaninov 2 coupled with some Rachmaninov Preludes; Corigliano Concerto with St Louis Symphony under Slatkin; Reger Piano Concerto Op 114, Marek Janowski and Orchestre Philharmonique de Radio France, coupled with Strauss Burleske; Britten Piano Concerto Op 13, Marek Janowski and Orchestre Philharmonique de Radio France, coupled with Debussy Fantasie pour piano et orchestre and Debussy Pour le Piano. *Honours:* Medal, Worshipful Company of Musicians; 1st Prize, classified, Paloma O'Shea Piano Competition, Spain, 1980; Concert Artists' Guild Award of New York, 1982; Silver Medal, Arthur Rubinstein Piano Master Competition, Israel; Gold Medal, Tchaikovsky Competition, Moscow, 1986; Honorary D.Mus, Queens University, Belfast, 1987; Honorary FRCM, Royal College of Music, London, 1988; O.B.E, 2002. *Current Management:* IMG Artists. *Address:* c/o IMG Artists, Lovell House, 616 Chiswick High Road, London W4 5RX, England.

DOUGLAS, James, LRAM, ARCM; composer, organist and accompanist; b. 4 July 1932, Dumbarton, Scotland; m. Helen Torrance Fairweather 1968; two s. one d. *Education:* Heriot Watt College, Edinburgh, Conservatoire, Paris, Hochschule, Munich, Mozarteum, Salzburg. *Career:* debut at Wienersaal, Salzburg, 1951; Dir, Eschenbach Editions, Caritas Records, Caritas Voices and Caritas Ensemble; Professor, Académie des Sciences Humaines Universelles, Paris, 1992–; mem. MPA, PRS, MCPS, PPL, BPI, British Academy of Composers and Songwriters. *Compositions:* 15 symphonies, 15 string quartets, 20 orchestral works, 200 songs, organ works, piano and organ works, flute works, chamber and instrumental works; 4 operas: Mask, The King, Molière, Cuthbert; choral works. *Recordings:* A Vision, 2000; Cloud of Unknowing, 2001; Visions of Glory, 2001; Cry of the Deer, 2001; 8 CDs in the "Caritas Live" series, 2002–04. *Publications:* The Music of Hermann Reutter 1966. *Address:* c/o Eschenbach Editions, 28 Dalrymple Crescent, Edinburgh EH9 2NX, Scotland. *E-mail:* eschenbach@caritas-music.co.uk. *Website:* www.caritas-music.co.uk.

DOUGLAS, Nigel; Singer (Tenor), Director, Writer, Broadcaster and Lecturer; b. 9 May 1929, Lenham, Kent, England; m. Alexandra Roper, 21 July 1973, 1 s., 2 d. *Education:* Magdalen College, Oxford University; Musikakademie, Vienna, Austria. *Career:* Debut: Rodolfo in La Bohème, Vienna Kammeroper, 1959; Leading roles in opera houses and festivals, Aldeburgh, Antwerp, Barcelona, Basel, Berne, Brussels, Buenos Aires, Covent Garden, Düsseldorf, Duisburg, Edinburgh, English National Opera, Garsington, Glyndebourne, Hamburg; Sadler's Wells, Scottish Opera, Venice, Lisbon, Vienna Volksoper, Welsh National Opera, Wexford, Zürich, Tokyo, Catania, Paris-Bastille, Seoul, New York and others; Repertoire of 80 roles including Peter Grimes, Captain Vere (Billy Budd), Aschenbach (Death in Venice), Eisenstein (Fledermaus), Danilo (Merry Widow), Loge (Rheingold), Herod (Salome), Captain (Wozzeck), Hauk-Sendorf (Makropulos Case); Has written and presented over 300 programmes on opera and operetta for BBC Radio 2, 3, 4 and World Service; Regular television appearances in the United Kingdom and Europe; Directed numerous productions for Sadler's Wells, Australian Opera, Royal Flemish Opera. *Recordings:* Owen Wingrave; Salome; Zigeunerbaron; Various recitals. *Publications:* English versions of Die Csardasfürstin (Kalman), 1982, Gräfin Mariza (Kalman), 1983, Merry Widow (Lehar), 1983; Legendary Voices, 1992; More Legendary voices, 1994; The Joy of Opera, 1997; Lectures on various aspects of opera and operetta in London, Edinburgh, Zürich, Vienna, New York, Cleveland, Los Angeles, Sydney, Canberra, Brisbane. *Contributions:* Numerous articles to Times Literary Supplement; Opera Magazine; BBC Music Magazine. *Honours:* Nominated for Royal Philharmonic Society Book Prize 1993, Worshipful Company of Musicians' Sir Charles Santley Memorial Prize 2003. *Current Management:* Music International, UK. *Address:* Eythorne House, Eythorne, Dover, Kent CT 15 4 BE, England.

DOUSA, Eduard, PhD; Czech composer and teacher; b. 31 Aug. 1951, Prague; m. 1976; two s. *Education:* gymnasium, Charles Univ., Prague, Acad. of Musical Arts, Prague. *Career:* teacher of theory of music, Conservatoire, Prague; teacher of theory of music, Philosophical Faculty, Prague 1986–; Conservatoire Prague 1995–; mem. Soc. of Czech Composers, Collegium (soc. for contemporary music) (chair. 2003–). *Compositions include:* Sonata for Organ; Variations on a Baroque Theme for Strings; Miniatures for Piano (for children); Sonatine for clarinet and piano (for children); Rhapsody for Clarinet and Piano; Three short suites for guitar (for children); Concerto for four saxophones and orchestra, 1993; Romantic Fantasy for two pianos, 1995; Fantasia for trumpet and organ, 1995; Uno per quattro per flauto, oboe, chittern ed violoncello, 1996; Imaginations for violin and guitar, 1997; Motorico for violin solo, 1997; Summer Sonatine for soprano saxophone and piano, 1999; Sonata drammatica for piano, 2001; Sonata brevis accordion 2001; Concerto for violin, accordion, guitar and strings, 2000; Concert music for violoncello, 2000; Concerto for violin and chamber orchestra, 2003; Concert music for violoncello and brass instruments, 2003. *Recordings:* Rhapsody for clarinet and piano, 1989; Variations on a Baroque Theme for strings, 1988; Miniatures for flute, violin, violoncello and harpsichord, 1990; Concerto for four saxophones, 1995; Many compositions were recorded for Czechoslovak Radio: Concertino for trumpet and orchestra, Sonata for piano, String-quartet, Romantic Phantasy for violin and piano, Rhapsody for clarinet and piano, Dialogue for oboe and piano and many compositions for children, musical fairy tales, songs, choirs; theoretical work on the history of Czech music for children. *Address:* Tenisová 9, 102-00 Prague 10, Czech Republic.

DOW, Dorothy; Singer (Soprano); b. 8 Oct. 1920, Houston, Texas, USA. *Education:* Juilliard School, New York. *Career:* Sang in and directed various choirs in New York, 1938–44; Sang Santuzza in a Concert Performance of Cavalleria Rusticana, Buffalo, 1944; Columbia University, New York, in the premiere of the Mother of us All, by Thompson, 1947; Sang with the Zürich Opera, 1948–50; La Scala from 1950, as Elisabeth, Marie (Wozzeck), Danae by Strauss, Chrysothemis, Gioconda and Walton's Cressida; Sang Erwartung in the US premiere of Schoenberg's monodrama, with the New York Philharmonic, 1951; Glyndebourne Festival, 1952–53; Lady Macbeth and Ariadne; Carnegie Hall, New York, 1952, in the US premiere of Christophe Colombe by Milhaud; Florence 1953, Agnese di Hohenstaufen by Spontini; Sang Renata in the stage premiere of Prokofiev's Fiery Angel, Venice, 1955.

DOWLING, Richard William; American concert pianist; b. 6 Sept. 1962, Houston, TX. *Education:* BM, Summa Cum Laude, University of

Houston, 1985; MM, Yale University, 1987; DMA, Piano Performance, University of Texas, Austin, 1990; Principal Teacher, Abbey Simon; Additional Studies with Jeanne-Marie Darre at Le Conservatoire de Musique, Nice and at Ecole Normale de Musique, Paris, France; Yale Norfolk Summer School and Music Festival, Connecticut, USA. *Career:* Debut: With Fort Worth Symphony, Texas, 1981; Solo Recitals throughout USA; PBS television solo recital programme debut aired nationally, 1986; Recital tour, France, 1991; Concerto appearances with Oklahoma Symphony, Houston Civic Symphony, Shreveport (Louisiana) Symphony, Midland-Odessa (Texas) Symphony, Brazos Valley (Texas) Symphony, Yale Trumbull Symphony, Arkansas Symphony; Concerto appearances with Jupiter Symphony, Tully Hall, Lincoln Center, New York City, 1992; 1st Holder of Walles Chair in the Performing Arts, Lamar University, 1989–90; Artist Faculty (Piano), The Harid Conservatory of Music, Boca Raton, Florida, USA; Recitals: Austria, Australia, South Africa, 1992; 2nd Tour of France, 1992; Gina Bachaeur Festival, Salt Lake City, Utah, 1993; Paris Recital Debut: Salle Cortot, 1994; Recitals in Singapore, Kuala Lumpur, Hong Kong, 1997. 1998: Solo recital, Weill Recital Hall, Carnegie Hall, New York, 1998; 5th tour of France, 1998; 6th tour of France, 1999; 1998–99 performed all piano solos and works with orchestra by George Gershwin for centennial celebration with West Virginia Symphony; mem, Artist Roster; The Piatigorsky Foundation, 1994–. *Recordings:* Richard Dowling Plays Chopin, 1997; A Frog He Went A Courting: Pairs of Pieces with cellist Evan Drachman, 1999; Sweet and Low-Down, Richard Dowling Plays George Gershwin, 2001; Richard Dowling Plays Chopin, Vol. II, 2003; World's Greatest Rags, 2004. *Publications:* New critical edition of Maurice Ravel's Trio for Piano, Violin and Cello, 1990; Critical edns of complete solo piano works of Ravel, nocturnes of Fauré, and sonatas of Hummel; Transcriptions of Gershwin solo piano works. *Honours:* Chevalier of the Company of Musketeers of Armagnac, Gascony, France in recognition of dedication to French musical arts, 1996; Grand Prix, French Piano Inst., 1993. *Current Management:* Joseph H. Conlin Concert Management, 853 Seventh Avenue, New York, NY 10019, USA; Parker Artists, Thomas F. Parker, 382 Central Park West, Suite 9G, New York, NY 10025, USA. *Website:* www.parkerartists.com. *Address:* 261 West 71st Street, No. 3, New York, NY 10023, USA. *E-mail:* PianistNYC@aol.com (home). *Website:* www.Richard-Dowling.com (home).

DOWNES, Andrew, BA, MA; composer and lecturer; b. 20 Aug. 1950, Handsworth, Birmingham, England; m. Cynthia Cooper 1975; two d. *Education:* St John's College, Cambridge, Royal College of Music, studied singing with Gordon Clinton, composition with Herbert Howells, Sir Lennox Berkeley. *Career:* debut, Wigmore Hall, 1969; Established Faculty of Composition, 1975, Head of School, 1990, Professor, School of Composition and Creative Studies, 1992–, Birmingham Conservatoire; Chaired Symposium on Music Criticism, Indian Music Congress, University of Burdwan, 1994; Performances of own works include: Vienna, 1983, 1998, 2001, 2002; Israel Philharmonic Guest House, Tel-Aviv, 1989; Berlin Kaiser Willhelm Gedächtniskirche, 1990; New York, 1996, 2003; Calcutta School of Music, 1994; Paris, 1995, 1996, 1997, 1998, 2001; University of New Mexico, 1995, 1997; Barletta, Italy, 1996; Bombay and Delhi, 1996; Eugene Oregon, 1996; Chicago, 1997; Caracas, Venezuela, 1997; Phoenix, Arizona, 1998; Rudolphinum, Prague, 1998, 2001, 2002; Genoa, 2002; Washington, 2002; Colorado, N Carolina, Michigan, 2003; Dublin, 2003; BBC Radio 2, 3 and 4; French Radio; France Musique; Austrian Radio; Czech Radio; Dutch Radio; Italian television. *Compositions include:* Sonata for 8 Horns Opus 54, University of New Mexico commission, 1994, subsequently performed by the Horns of the Czech Philharmonic Orchestra, 1997, 1998, 2001; Sonata for 8 Flutes, premiered at the USA National Flute Association Convention in New York, 1996; Songs From Spoon River, performed in New York, at Tanglewood Festival and on Radio 3; Towards A New Age, performed by the Royal Philharmonic Orchestra in Symphony Hall, Birmingham, 1997; New Dawn, oratorio based on American Indian texts, performed in Birmingham, 2000, and King's Chapel, Cambridge, 2001; Runnymede Service, St George's Chapel, Windsor and Chapel of Royal Holloway, University of London, 2000; Sonata for 8 Pianists, Birmingham, 2000 and Genoa, 2002; Sonata for Horn and Piano and Suite for 6 Horns for the Vienna Horn Society; Concerto for 4 Horns and Symphony Orchestra for the Czech Philharmonic Orchestra, 2002; 5 Dramatic Pieces for 8 Wagner Tubas for The Horns of the Czech Philharmonic Orchestra, 2003; Songs of Autumn, commissioned by Symphony Hall, Birmingham, for 1200 children with players from the CBSO. *Recordings include:* Sonata for 8 Horns by Horns of Czech Philharmonic Orchestra; Concerto for 2 Guitars and Strings, with Simon Dinnigan, Fred T. Baker and Strings from the City of Birmingham Symphony Orchestra; The Marshes of Glynn, commissioned for Royal Opening of the Adrian Boult Hall, Birmingham; Centenary Firedances, commissioned for the Centenary of the City of Birmingham; Sacred Choral Music, performed by the Chapel Choir of Royal Holloway, University of London; Flute Choir music by

USA Flute Choirs; Music for Horns and Piano by the Vienna Horn Society; Sonata for Oboe and Piano; Sonata for Violin and Piano; Sacred Mass for Solo Violin; 3 Song Cycles; O Vos Omnes, motet, Cantamus commission; Sonata for 2 Pianos; Fanfare for a Ceremony, commission for Open University; Shepherd's Carol; The Souls of the Righteous, anthem. *Publications:* 86 works including 5 symphonies, 5 choral works, 2 double concertos, 3 string quartets, 6 works for brass ensemble, 5 song cycles, 7 anthems, 5 works for flute choir, 3 works for horn ensemble, sonatina and 2 sonatas for piano, and 7 sonatas for solo instrument with piano. *Address:* c/o Lynwood Music, 2 Church Street, West Hagley, West Midlands DY9 0NA, England. *E-mail:* downlyn@globalnet.co.uk. *Website:* www.users.globalnet.co.uk/~downlyn.

DOWNES, Craig; Singer (Tenor); b. 1960, South Africa. *Education:* Studied at University of Cape Town Opera, 1988–89. *Career:* Studio Soloist, CAPAB Opera, Cape Town; Junior soloist, CAPAB Opera, 1991; Productions of opera, operetta and musicals; Sang in venues throughout South Africa and Mauritius, 1994; Appeared regularly in oratorio, concerts and cabaret; Involved in the development of opera in rural areas of South Africa; Performances included Ismaele, Eisenstein and Alfredo in La Traviata; Welsh National Opera, 1995; Performed as High Priest of Neptune, Pinkerton in Madama Butterfly and Borsa in Rigoletto; Sang Lensky for performances of Eugene Onegin, Holland Park Festival; Erik, The Flying Dutchman, English National Opera; Lensy, ENO; Skuratov, From The House of The Dead; Sang leading tenor role, Carlo in Masnadieri, Amici di Verdi; Pinkerton, Madama Butterfly, Royal Albert Hall; Taken part in several opera gala concerts; Alfredo, La Traviata, Castleward Opera; Concert performances of Candide, London Symphony Orchestra, Barbican Hall; Beethoven's Missa Solemnis, Chelmsford; The First Knight, Parsifal, English National Opera, 1999; Alfredo, Castleward Opera, Ireland, 1999; Performed Dvořák Requiem, Rochester Cathedral, 1999; Don José for Co-opera, Ireland, 1999. *Address:* 6 The Hop Gardens, Thornwell, Chepstow, Gwent NP6 5RX.

DOWNES, Sir Edward Thomas, Kt; Conductor; b. 17 June 1924, Birmingham, England. *Education:* Studied at University of Birmingham and Royal College of Music (Composition and Horn); Further study with Hermann Scherchen. *Career:* Carl Rosa Opera, 1950–52; Covent Garden from 1952, notably Der Freischütz (1954), Les Contes d'Hoffmann, Katerina Izmailova (1963), Der Ring des Nibelungen (1967), Hamlet by Searle (1969), Victory (1970) and Taverner (1972); Many performances of operas by Verdi, British premiere of The Bassarids by Henze, BBC, 1968; Conducted the premieres of Birtwistle's Chorales 1967, and Brian's Symphonies Nos 14 and 21, 1970; Musical Director of Australian Opera, 1972–76, conducting Prokofiev's War and Peace at opening of Sydney Opera House, 1973; Welsh National Opera 1975, Der fliegende Holländer; Conducted first performance of Prokofiev's opera Maddalena, BBC, 1979; Conducted first modern performance of Tchaikovsky's Vakula the Smith, BBC, 1989; Led Revivals of Otello and Il Trovatore at Covent Garden, 1990, new production of Attila; Principal Conductor, BBC Philharmonic from 1980; with the orchestra recorded a studio performance of Jérusalem by Verdi; Promenada Concerts 1989, with music by Bax, Walton, Strauss, John McCabe and Sibelius; Prokofiev's Symphonies in the Russian Spring series at the Festival Hall, 1991; Promenade Concerts, 1991, with the first Russian language performance of Prokofiev's Fiery Angel in the United Kingdom; Appointed Associate Music Director and Principal Conductor at Covent Garden, 1991; New Production of Verdi's Stiffelio, 1993; Season 1996–97 at Covent Garden with Tosca. Concert Performance of Norma for the Royal Opera, 2000; Led first Covent Garden performance of Verdi's I Masnadieri, 2002. *Publications:* Translations of Jenůfa, Katerina Izmailova and Khovanshchina. *Current Management:* Ingpen & Williams Ltd, 7 St George's Court, 131 Putney Bridge Road, London, SW15 2PA, England.

DOWNEY, John Wilham, BM, MM, DèsL; composer and academic; b. 5 Oct. 1927, Chicago, Illinois, USA. *Education:* De Paul University, Chicago Musical College, Paris Conservatoire, Sorbonne, Univ. of Paris. *Career:* teacher, De Paul University, Chicago City College; Roosevelt University; Professor of Composition and Composer-in-Residence, University of Wisconsin, 1964–; founder, Wisconsin Contemporary Music Forum. *Compositions:* Ageistics, ballet, 1967; Incidental music to Shakespeare's Twelfth Night, 1971; Orchestral: La Joie de la paix, 1956; Chant to Michelangelo, 1958; Concerto for harp and chamber orchestra, 1964; Jingalodeon, 1968; Symphonic Modules, 1972; The Edge of Space for bassoon and orchestra, 1978, Discourse for oboe, harpsichord and strings, 1984; Double Bass Concerto, 1987; Declamations, 1985; Symphony (in two movements), 1992; Chamber: String Trio, 1953; For Those Who Suffered, for chamber orchestra, 1995; Violin Sonata, 1954; Wind Octet, 1954; 2 string quartets, 1964, 1976; Cello Sonata, 1966; Crescendo for 13 percussionists, 1977; Agort for woodwind quintet, 1967; Almost 12 for wind quintet, string quintet and percussion, 1970; Ambivalences I for any chamber combination, 1972; High Clouds and

Soft Rain for 24 flutes, 1977; Duo for oboe and harpsichord, 1981; Portrait No. 1 for piano solo, 1980 Portrait No. 2 for clarinet and bassoon, 1983 and Portrait No. 3 for flute and piano, 1984; Piano Trio, 1984; Prayer for violin, viola and cello, 1984; Recombinance for double bass and piano, 1985; Solo Pieces: Tabu for Tabu, 1967; Lydian Suite for cello, 1975; Silhouette for double bass, 1980; Call for Freedom for symphonic winds, 1990; Ode to Freedom, orchestral, 1991; Rough Road for flute and guitar, 1995; Angel Talk for eight cellos, 1995; Piano pieces: Adagio Lyrico for two pianos, 1953; Eastlake Terrace for solo piano, 1959; Edges, piano solo, 1960; Pyramids, piano solo, 1961; Portrait No. 1, piano solo, 1980; Yad Vashem–An Impression, solo piano, 1991; Memories, piano solo, 1991; Vocal music, including Tangents, jazz oratorio, 1981; Choral works: What If? for choir, brass octet and solo timpani, 1973; Suite of Psalms for a cappella choir, 1989; Ghosts, for twelve violins, 1996; Setting of Psalm 90 for choir, organ, brass octet, timpani and soprano soloist, 1997; Mountains and Valleys, solo piano, 1999; Irish Sonata, violin and piano, 1999. *Recordings:* The Edge of Space; Cello Sonata on CRI; String Quartet No. 2; John Downey Plays John Downey; A Dolphin Octet for Winds, What If?; Adagio Lyrico and Agort; John Downey played by the London Symphony Orchestra: Declamations, Discourse, Jingalodeon, Concerto for Double Bass and Orchestra. *Publications:* Eastlake Terrace, 1959; Pyramids, 1960; Cello Sonata, Agort, Jingalodeon, Billaudot in Paris; Prayer, Silhouette, Portrait No. 3, 1984; Theodore Presser; La musique populaire dans l'oeuvre de Bela Bartók, 1966; Lydian Suite, 1976; Discourse, 1984; Soliloquy, 1997. *Address:* 4413 N Prospect Avenue, Shorewood, WI 53211, USA.

DOYLE, Grant; Singer (Baritone); b. 1971, Australia. *Education:* Elder Conservatorium, Adelaide; Royal College of Music, London; Vilar Young Artist Programme, Covent Garden, 2001. *Career:* Appearances with State Opera of South Australia and Opera Australia as Luiz in The Gondoliers and as Yarmadori in Madama Butterfly; Mozart's Count and Britten's Owen Wingrave at RCM; Season 2001–2002 as Purcell's Aeneas with the Irish Chamber Orchestra, and concerts with Orlando PO, Florida; Enrico in Donizetti's Il Campanello for Les Azuriales Opera, France, and Forester in The Cunning Little Vixen with Deutsches SO, Berlin, under Kent Nagano, for BBC TV. *Honours:* Royal Overseas League Trophy and National Mozart Competition for Singers, 2000, prize-winner. *Address:* c/o Vilar Young Artists, Royal Opera House, Covent Garden, London, WC2, England. *Telephone:* (20) 7240 1200. *Fax:* (20) 7212-9502.

DRABOWICZ, Wojciech; Singer (Baritone); b. 1963, Poznán, Poland. *Education:* Studied at the Poznán Academy, 1984–89. *Career:* Won prizes at the 1990 Tchaikovsky Competition, Moscow, and the Belvedere, Vienna; Member of the Poznán Opera from 1989 (debut as Eugene Onegin) and sang Morales at the 1991 Bregenz Festival; Other roles include Mozart's Guglielmo and Pagageno, Malatesta in Don Pasquale and other lyric repertory; Recitalist in songs by Schumann, Chopin and Schubert; La Monnaie, Brussels, 1992; European tour Theatre du Nord, Paris, 1992–93; Il Barbiere di Siviglia and Figaro, directed by Jerome Savary at Warsaw Opera House, 1993; Eugene Onegin at Glyndebourne Opera Festival including a BBC Prom, 1994; Così fan tutte at Monnaie, Brussels, 1994; Pelléas et Mélisande, Kiel State Opera, 1995; The Queen of Spades at Glyndebourne Opera Festival, 1995; Further engagements include King Roger by Szymanowski at Théâtre des Champs Elysées, 1996, Eugene Onegin at Glyndebourne Opera Festival in 1996 and Figaro in Le nozze di Figaro 1997; Season 1998 as Vershinin in the premiere of Three Sisters by Peter Eötvös at Lyon, and Eugene Onegin at Barcelona; Sang King Roger at Warsaw, 2000. *Address:* c/o Poznán Grand Theatre, Fredry 9, 60-967 Poznán, Poland.

DRAGONI, Maria; Singer (Soprano); b. 1958, Procida, Naples, Italy. *Education:* Studied in Naples. *Career:* Debut: Sang Imogene in Il Pirata at Naples, 1984 (Teatro di Jesi); Appeared in the title role of Pergolesi's Il Flamino at the Teatro San Carlo Naples, 1984; Season 1988–89, as Fenena in Nabucco at La Scala, Turandot at Nancy and Ravenna and Aida at Marcerata; Mathilde in Guillaume Tell and Bellini's Norma at the Théâtre des Champs Elysées and Mulhouse, 1989; Season, 1990–91, as Elisabeth de Valois at Turin and Donna Anna at the Teatro dell' Opera at Rome; Sang Mimi at Naples and Elisabeth de Valois at the Verona Arena, 1992; Other roles include Paolina in Poliuto by Donizetti, Donna Anna, and La Gioconda; Sang Aida at Florence, 1996; Season 1995–96 as Norma at Zürich and Elvira in Verdi's Ernani at Strasbourg; Season 1999–2000 at Jesy as Ines de Castro in the opera by Persiani, as Elvira in Ernani at Genoa and as Norma at Savona.

DRAHEIM, Joachim, PhD; German musicologist and pianist; b. 26 July 1950, Berlin-Schmargendorf. *Education:* University of Heidelberg, studied piano with Ursula Draheim, violoncello with Annlies Schmidt-de Neveu. *Career:* concerts as solo, chamber music and lieder pianist in Germany, Austria and Switzerland; Freelance, many recordings of lieder and piano pieces, Süddeutscher Rundfunk Karlsruhe and

Heidelberg, (Südwestrundfunk, Studio Karlsruhe) 1973–; Freelance, several German and foreign music publishers including Breitkopf and Härtel, Wiesbaden, and Wiener Urtext Edition, and recording companies, 1974–; Numerous editions including Brahms und seine Freunde-works for piano, works by Mozart, Beethoven, Loewe, Fanny Hensel, Liszt, Mendelssohn, Robert and Clara Schumann, Chopin, Carl Reinecke, Woldemar Bargiel, Brahms, Busoni, others; First editions: Mendelssohn: Albumblatt in A major, Sonata in D major and Sonata movement in G minor for two pianos; Brahms: Die Müllerin; Schumann: Der Korsar, Piano accompaniment to Bach's Suite in C major for solo cello, Violin setting of Schumann Cello Concerto in A minor op 129, Variations on a nocturne by Chopin for piano, others; Teaching at Lessing Gymnasium, Karlsruhe, 1978–; Works for the Neue Schumann-Gesamtausgabe, the Neue Weber-Gesamtausgabe, the Neue Mendelssohn-Gesamtausgabe and the new MGG. *Honours:* Robert Schumann Preis der Stadt Zwickau 2003. *Address:* Sophienstrasse 165, 76185 Karlsruhe, Germany.

DRAHOS, Béla; Flautist and Conductor; b. 1955, Kaposvar, Hungary. *Education:* Studied with Henrik Prohle at the Györ Conservatory and with Lorant Kovacs at the Ferenc Liszt Academy, Budapest, graduated, 1978; From 1991 studied conducting with Professor Carl Osterreicher in Vienna. *Career:* Solo Flautist with the Budapest Symphony Orchestra from 1976, including many foreign tours; Solo Flautist with the Hungarian State Orchestra, 1990; Solo Career in Austria, Bulgaria, Belgium, Czechoslovakia, England, Finland, France, Soviet Union, Switzerland and Germany; Concerts with the New Zealand Symphony Orchestra, 1988; West Berlin Philharmonie, 1989; Leader and Founder Member, Hungarian Radio Wind Quintet; Music Director, Kaposvar Symphony Orchestra, 1990; Assistant Conductor, Hungarian State Symphony Orchestra, 1993; Guest Conductor of leading orchestras in Hungary; Conducts operas and concerts in Austria and Germany. *Recordings:* Mozart Concerto K314; Paganini 24 Caprices; Bach 4th Brandenburg Concerto and Concerto for Two Flutes in F; Vivaldi Concertos (Hungaroton); 16 Haydn Symphonies for Naxos; Beethoven's Symphonies 1–9 and Overtures, Naxos. *Address:* c/o Hungarian Symphony Orchestra, 10–12 Pava utca, H–1094 Budapest, Hungary.

DRAKE, George (Warren James), PhD; lecturer in music and musicologist; *Associate Professor, School of Music, University of Auckland;* b. 4 Aug. 1939, Auckland, New Zealand; m. Carla Maria Driessen, one s., one d. *Education:* Univ. of Auckland; , Univ. of Ill., USA. *Career:* Assoc. Prof. 1976–, Univ. of Auckland; Dean, Faculty of Music, 1985–88; Head of the School of Music, 1988–91; Founding Pres., New Zealand Musicological Soc., 1982–85; Musicological Soc. of Australia; Int. Musicological Soc. *Publications:* Liber Amicorum John Steele: A Musicological Tribute, editor, 1997; Petrucci, Motetti B (Monuments of Renaissance Music XI, Chicago) 2002. *Address:* c/o School of Music, University of Auckland, Auckland, , New Zealand. *E-mail:* w.drake@auckland.ac.nz. *Website:* www.music.auckland.ac.nz.

DRAKE, Julius; Pianist; b. 1959, England; m., two d. *Career:* many appearances world-wide collaborating with leading performers; Recitals with singers Thomas Allen, Victoria de los Angeles, Olaf Bär, Barbara Bonney, Felicity Lott, Lorraine Hunt, Edith Mathis, Ian Bostridge, Hughes Cuenod, Gerald Finley, Wolfgang Holzmair, Simon Keenlyside, Angelika Kirchschlager, Thomas Quasthoff and Joan Rodgers; Festival engagements at Kuhmo (Finland), Saintes (France) and Perth, with Michael Collins (clarinet), Natalie Clein (cello), Nicholas Daniel, Steven Isserlis, Ernst Kovacic, Christian Poltera, Christian Altenburger (violin) and Robert Cohen (violin) and Belcea, Maggini and Szymanowski Quartets; Performances of Hans Werner Henze's Songs from the Arabian, with Ian Bostridge, 2000–01; Artistic Director, Perth International Music Festival, Australia, 2001–2003; Season 2001–2002 with piano trio concerts in Spain, accompanied by Robert Cohen and Massimo Quarta, tours of USA and Japan with Ian Bostridge, Wigmore Hall with Gerald Finley and Amsterdam Concertgebouw with Thomas Quasthoff; London Proms Chamber Music, 2002; Recent appearances include concerts at Edinburgh, Salzburg, Schubertiade Festivals and in Amsterdam, London, Paris, Vienna, NY, Tokyo and Washington. *Recordings include:* French chansons, with Hugues Cuenod; English Songbook, Schubert and Schumann Lieder, Britten Canticles and Henze's Songs from the Arabian, with Ian Bostridge (EMI); Sibelius Songs with Katarina Karneus; Mahler, Haydn and Schumann with Alice Coote; Britten Canticles with Ian Bostridge, David Daniels, Christopher Maltman. *Current Management:* IMG Artists, Lovell House, 616 Chiswick High Road, London, W4 5RX, England. *Telephone:* (20) 8233-5800. *Fax:* (20) 8233-5801. *E-mail:* artistseurope@imgworld.com. *Website:* www.imgartists.com.

DRAKULICH, Stephen; Singer (Tenor); b. 1958, Iowa, USA. *Education:* Studied at Southern Illinois University; Apprentice at the Lyric Opera of Chicago; Study with Norman Gulbranson at Northwestern University. *Career:* Sang in The Turn of the Screw, The Rake's Progress and Lucia di Lammermoor at Chicago; Wuppertal Opera as Mozart's

Ferrando and Tamino, Rodolfo in Bohème and Britten's Albert Herring, Janáček's Fox, Ramiro (Cenerentola), Lensky, Steuermann in Fliegende Holländer and Jacquino, at Bremen Opera, 1982–89; Sergei in Lady Macbeth of the Mtensk District, Peter Grimes, Captain Vere (Billy Budd) and Jimmy in Mahagonny, Freiburg Opera, 1989–92; Guest appearances as Arkenholz in Reimann's Gespenstersonate at Stuttgart and Hamburg; Sergei on tour to Japan with Cologne Opera; Tom Rakewell in Switzerland and Peter Grimes at the Glyndebourne Festival, 1992; Adam in the premiere of Der Garten by Josef Tal, 1988; Season 1996–97 in D'Albert's Tiefland and Wolf-Ferrari's Sly, in Germany; Essex in Roberto Devereux for Blackheath Opera, 1998. *Honours:* Award winner at the Metropolitan Opera National Council Auditions. *Address:* c/o Freiburg Opera, Bertoldstrasse 46, 79098 Freiburg in Breisgau, Germany.

DRAN, Thierry; Singer (Tenor); b. 17 Aug. 1953, Bordeaux, France. *Education:* Studied at the Bordeaux Conservatory and in Paris with Michel Sénéchal. *Career:* Appearances at the Paris Opéra-Comique, the Berlioz Festival at Lyon (as Benedict), Rouen (Nadir, and in Les Indes Galantes); Marseille (in Capuleti e i Montecchi) and Lyon, as Fenton in Falstaff; Grand Théâtre Geneva, in Offenbach's Les Brigands and Barbe Bleue; Sang in the Ravel double bill at Glyndebourne, 1987–88; Paris Opéra as Don Ottavio and as Mercure in Orphée aux Enfers; Guest appearances at Bordeaux, as Jean in Le Jongleur de Notre Dame and Liège (Ernesto, the Duke of Mantua and Rossini's Count Almaviva); Frequent concert engagements. *Recordings:* Messager's Fortunio and Duc de Mantoue in Les Brigands. *Address:* c/o Opéra Royal de Wallonie, 1 rue des Dominicains, B–4000 Liège, Belgium.

DRASKOVIC, Milimir; composer, conductor, multimedia artist, producer and publisher; b. 5 June 1952, Sarajevo, m. Biljana Vasilievic. *Education:* Belgrade Music Acad., Belgrade Opera with Borislav Pascan. *Career:* Composer of music for numerous ensembles, for film and television, video, performance installation and for graphics and multimedia packages; Performances of work includes Gaudeamus, Utrecht, 1978; Festival international des musiques experimentales, Bourges, 1982; Radio biennale, Paris, 1982; Esquiss' Art, Almada, Portugal, 1982; BITEF, Belgrade 1982; Die Glockenspielen, Essen, 1983; New Art in Italia, Beograd-Zagreb-Pristina 1983; Video C.D. Ljubljana 1983; European Minimal Music Project, Belgrade, 1983; Planum '84, Budapest, 1984; Different New Music, Belgrade, 1984–86; Yugoslav Documentary and Short Film, Belgrade, 1986–2000; Festival of Alternative Film, Split, 1987; Aut Art Alternativa, Grisignana 1989; Computer Art, Belgrade, 1991; Byzanz und Danach, Berlin, 1992–95; Eight Weeks, Belgrade 1995; Eine Kleine Geschichtsmusik, Goethe Institut, Belgrade, 1996; Oktoih, Belgrade 1997; From the New World, Belgrade 1999; Triosonata, Belgrade, 2000; Serbian Music, Kol hamuzika Jerusalim 2001; Draskovic-Oktoïh, Outaut, Toronto 2002; Images of Notations, Ljubljana 2003; Open October Salon, Toronto 2003–04; music at numerous film festivals throughout Europe, and for radio and television. *Compositions include:* D'orchestra 1–5; Musica linea 1–10; HPSCHD 1–6; Eine Kleine Geschichtmusik; Octoechos; Eight Weeks; From the New World; Opera, Orgelwerke, Unfinished Symphony. *Recordings:* Opus 4, 1981; Ensemble for Different New Music, 1981; Film Music, 1989; Serbian Music for Harpsichord, 1 and 2, 1996; Oktoih/Milimir Draskovic's Eight Weeks, 1997; From the New World, 1999; Triosonata, 2000; From the New Old World 2001. *Publications:* Dirigent, 1981; Portrait of a Young Musician, 1983; Examples of Ideosemas, 1983; Music Design, 2000; Opus 4 2001. *Contributions:* Beorama. *Address:* Brace Srnic 23, 11050 Belgrade, Serbia and Montenegro. *E-mail:* milimir.draskovic@EUnet.yu.

DRATH, Janina (Nina) Irena Drath-Nowicka; pianist; b. 14 Oct. 1954, Katowice, Poland; m. Jerzy Bogdan Nowicki 1981; one s. *Education:* Acad. of Music, Warsaw. *Career:* debut with Silesian Philharmonic Orchestra 1968, with WOSPRIT (Great Symphony Orchestra of Radio and Television) 1968; first recital, Katowice 1963; first recital abroad, Ostrava, Czechoslovakia 1965; regular concerts (solo and with orchestra) from age 14; concert tours and performances in Poland, Spain, Italy, Germany, Belgium, France, USA, Mexico, Czechoslovakia; many radio and television performances; guest artist, Annual Chopin Workshops, Texas A&M Univ., USA 1981–94; artist-in-residence, Central State Univ., OK 1985–87; debut at Carnegie Hall, NY New York 1998; founder and Pres., Fryderyk Chopin Soc. of Texas 1990, Int. Chopin Piano Competition, Corpus Christi 1993, Sonata and Sonatina Int. Youth Piano Competition, Corpus Christi 1994; Artistic Dir and founder, Virtuoso Piano Performance Studies; jury mem., int piano competitions. *Recordings:* with Vandor Music Group: works of Haydn, Chopin, Petroff and Mozart; three albums of piano music by P. Petroff. *Address:* 4610 Abner Drive, Corpus Christi, TX 78411, USA.

DRESHER, Paul (Joseph); Composer; b. 8 Jan. 1951, Los Angeles, California, USA; m. 8 Mar 1986. *Education:* BA, Music, University of California, Berkeley, 1977; MA, Composition, University of California, San Diego, 1979; Private studies: North Indian Classical Music with

Nikhil Banerjee, 1974–77; Ghanaian Drumming with C K and Kobla Ladzekpo, 1975–79: Javanese and Balinese Gamelan. *Career:* Composer, Performer throughout USA, Canada, Europe; Works performed at New York Philharmonic, San Francisco Symphony, Minnesota Opera, Brooklyn Academy of Music, Cal Arts Festival, New Music America, 1981, 1983, 1985, London International Festival of Theatre, Munich State Opera, Festival d'Automne, Paris; Commissions include Nonsuch Commission Award from American Music Center, and radio composition for Olympic Arts Festival; Founder, Artistic Director, Paul Dresher Ensemble (electro-acoustic chamber ensemble), 1993–, premiere on six-city tour of Japan, and performing at Lincoln Center; mem, BMI; American Music Center, Board of Directors; Opera America; Chamber Music America. *Compositions:* This Same Temple, 1977; Channels Passing, 1981; Night Songs, 1981; Liquid and Stellar Music, 1981; The Way of How, opera, 1981; Dark Blue Circumstance, electronic, 1982–84; Reaction, 1984; See Hear, opera, 1984; Other Fire, electronic, 1984; Slow Fire, opera, 1985–86; Water Dreams, electronic, 1986; Power Failure, opera, 1989; Double Ikat, trio, 1989; Cornucopia, chamber orchestra, 1990; Pioneer, opera, 1991; The Gates, 1993; Din of Iniquity, 6 instruments, 1994; Stretch, 6 instruments, 1995; Blue Diamonds for solo piano, 1995; Violin Concerto, 1996–97; Elapsed Time, violin and piano duo, 1998. *Recordings:* Liquid and Stellar Music, This Same Temple; Slow Fire, complete opera, 1992; Opposites Attract, 1992; Double Ikat, Channels Passing, Dark Blue Circumstance, Night Songs, 1993; Casa Vecchia, 1995. *Contributions:* Sounding Eleven. *Honours:* Commissioned by Saint Paul Chamber Orchestra and Meet the Composer; Commission from the Library of Congress, 1997–98. *Current Management:* Bernstein Artists Inc, Brooklyn, New York. *Address:* 51 Avenida Drive, Berkeley, CA 94708, USA.

DREW, David; Writer on Music, Publisher, Producer, Editor and Dramaturg; b. 19 Sept. 1930, London, England; m. Judith Sutherland, 1960. *Education:* BA, Cambridge University, 1953. *Career:* Freelance writer, with part-time consultancy and editorial duties, The Decca Record Company, 1955–59; Producer, BBC Music Department, 1960; Music Critic, New Statesman, 1960–67; Music Consultant to the Calouste Gulbenkian Foundation, UK Branch, and Artistic Director of the Foundation's recording series, Music Today, EMI/Argo, 1961–75; European Representative and Adviser, The Kurt Weill Foundation for Music, 1971–76; Editor, later Advisory Editor, of Tempo, 1971–92; BBC Music Advisory Committee and Arts Council Music Panel, 1971–80; Adviser to the Holland Festival, 1971, Berlin Festival, 1974–75; Director, Contemporary Music, Boosey & Hawkes Music Publishers, 1975–92; Programme Committee of Mürztal Music Workshop, Austria, 1983–91; Executive Committee of Les amis du compositeur Igor Markevitch, Lausanne and London, 1988–95; Trustee, Britten-Pears Foundation, Director of Britten Estate Ltd, 1989–99; Artistic Director, Largo Records, Cologne, 1993–98; Editorial Board, The Kurt Weill Edition, 1992–; Artistic Adviser, South Bank Centre, Weill Centenary Series, 1999–2000; Dramaturg, Broomhill Opera, 1999–2000; Editorial Advisory Board, Tempo, 2003–; Editions of many stage and concert works by Kurt Weill, notably Cry the Beloved Country, Carnegie Hall, 1988; Performing Edition of Roberto Gerhard's opera, The Duenna, Madrid, Barcelona, Opera North, 1992. *Publications:* Über Kurt Weill, 1975; Weill, Ausgewählte Schriften, 1975; Essays on the Philosophy of Music, 1985; The Kurt Weill Handbook, 1987. *Contributions:* Numerous articles on 20th Century Composers, such as Stravinsky, Messiaen, Gerhard, Spinner, Gorecki; Der Weg der Verheissung and the Prophecies of Jeremiah, 1998. *Address:* 12 Favart Road, London SW6 4 AZ, England.

DREW, James; Composer, Playwright, Pianist and Director; b. 9 Feb. 1929, St Paul, Minnesota, USA; m. Gloria Kelly, 26 Mar 1960, 1 s., 1 d. *Education:* Certificate, New York School of Music, 1956; MA, Tulane University, 1964; Private study with Wallingford Riegger, 1956–69 and Edgard Varèse, 1956. *Career:* Composer for concert hall, theatre and film; Composer, Northwestern University, 1964–66, Yale University, 1966–73, Tanglewood, Lennox, MA, summer 1973, LSU, 1973–75; Director, Ghost Puppet Theatre, 1970–; Visiting Composer, California State University, 1976–77, University of California at Los Angeles, 1977–78; Director of American Music Theatre, 1978–, Mysterious Travelling Cabaret, 1980–, No Sleep Theatre, 1984–, and Greywolf International, 1993–; Director, Blast Operatheater, 1996–. *Compositions include:* Symphonies; Concerto for small percussion orchestra; Mysterium, opera; Faustus–an Epilogue for 2 pianos, solo viola and chamber ensemble; The Orangethorpe Aria; Five O'Clock Ladies, stage work; Last Dance, video work; Whisper, video; Cantobosolo for contrabass solo; Cantobosolo for percussion and orchestra; Live From the Black Eagle, video work; Cello Concerto; In This Place of Half Lights, Gloria… Sotto Voce, a monodrama; In Memoriam of Gloria Kelly Drew, 1990; Piano Concerto, Formingreforming, 1991; Easter Concerto for violin grand and orchestra, 1992; Celestial Cabaret for piano and chamber orchestra, 1993; Inaudible Answers for orchestra, 1994; Book of Lights, 1994; Elephants Coming for string quartet, 1994; Walden

Songs for chamber orchestra, 1995; Sacred Dances of the Tunnel Saints, 1995; Hypothetical Structures, 1996; Survivors in Pale Light, 1996; Viola Concerto (Cellar-Lise's Alléluias); Giggles, ballet, 1996–98; With Closed Eyes Danced the Raven, 1998; The Ringing Hour for voices, percussion, orchestra, 1998; Contrabass Concerto, chanber version, 1999. *Recordings:* Sonata Appassionata for Cello and Piano (Cello America vol. 2), 1994; Cantolobo Solo (monodrama); Contoloboso (monodrama). *Honours:* Guggenheim Fellow, 1973–74. *Current Management:* Cooke Associates, Nicolaistraat 17, 2517 SX Den Haag, Netherlands. *Address:* Greywolf Arts Institute, 10830 So 1000 East, Sandy, Utah 84094, USA.

DREYFUS, George; Musician and Composer; b. 22 July 1928, Wuppertal, Germany. *Education:* Vienna Academy of Music, Austria, 1955–56. *Career:* Orchestral Musician, Australian Broadcasting Commission, 1953; Formed New Music Ensemble, Melbourne, 1958; Freelance Composer, 1965–; Foundation Member, Musical Director, International Society for Contemporary Music, Melbourne, 1965; Formed George Dreyfus Chamber Orchestra, Melbourne, 1970; Musica Viva Outback tour, 1974; One-man show, Melbourne, Sydney and various country centres, 1977–78; Composer-in-Residence, Rome, 1976, Jerusalem, 1980, Tianjin, 1983, Shanghai, 1986, and Nanjing, 1991. *Compositions include:* Galgenlieder, 1957; Songs, Comic and Curious, 1959; Music in the Air, 1961; The Seasons, 1963; Quintet for wind instruments, 1965; Garni Sands, two-act opera by Frank Kellaway, 1965–66; Symphony No. 1, 1967; Reflections in a Glasshouse, 1969; The Gilt-Edged Kid, one-act opera by Lynne Strahan, 1970; Sextet for didjeridu and wind instruments, 1971; The Lamentable Reign of Charles the Last, one-act pantopera by Tim Robertson, 1975; Symphony No. 2, 1976; Symphonie Concertante, 1978; An Australian Folk Mass, 1979; The Ballad of Charles Rasp; The Sentimental Bloke, 1985; Rathenau, opera by Volker Elis Pilgrim, 1993; Die Marx Sisters, opera by Volker Elis Pilgrim, 1995; Film and television scores. *Recordings:* Rush and the Adventures of Sebastian the Fox; Film Music of George Dreyfus; Serenade for small orchestra; Quintet, After the Notebook of J-G Noverre; The Marvellous World of George Dreyfus, Vols I and II; Song of the Maypole; George Dreyfus Chamber and Orchestral Music, Symphonies 1 and 2, Sextet for didgeridu and wind instruments; Larino, Safe Haven; Rush (Australian Fantasy); one-hour documentary film, Life is Too Serious. *Publications:* The Last Frivolous Book, autobiography; Being George–and liking it!, 1998. *Honours:* Order of Australia; Bundesverdienstkreuz 1. Klasse. *Address:* 3 Grace Street, Camberwell, Victoria 3124, Australia.

DREYFUS, Huguette (Pauline); Harpsichordist; b. 30 Nov. 1928, Mulhouse, France. *Education:* Diplomas, Piano, Harmony, Counterpoint, Ecole Normale de Musique, Paris; Conservatoire National Supérieur de Musique, Paris; Advanced studies, Harpsichord, Chigiana Academy, Siena. *Career:* Soloist, ORTF and various other radio and television networks in France, South Africa, Germany, Belgium, Canada, the United Kingdom, Switzerland, Austria, Brazil, Colombia, Denmark, Ecuador, Hungary, Italy, Luxembourg, Peru, Sweden, Czechoslovakia, Yugoslavia, Japan, USA; Harpsichord Teacher, Conservatoire National Supérieur de Musique de Lyon and Conservatoire National de Région de Rueil-Malmaison. *Recordings:* J. S. Bach: 6 English Suites, 6 French Suites; Rameau: Pièces de Clavecin; Couperin: Pièces de Clavecin; Scarlatti: Chronological Anthology of 70 Sonatas; Seixas: 14 Sonatas; Bartók: Pieces from Mikrokosmos; Chamber music by J. S. Bach, Leclair, Rameau, Haydn, Vivaldi, Corelli, C P E Bach, W A Mozart; J. S. Bach: Italian Concerto, Chromatic Fantasy and Fugue, Inventions and Sinfonias, 6 Partitas, French Overture, 4 Duetti, Praeludium, Fuga and Allegro in E flat major Goldberg variations; Wilhelm-Friedemann Bach: 9 Fantasien; J. S. Bach Harpsichord Transcriptions of 16 Concerti by various composers; J. S. Bach: The Well-Tempered Klavier, vol. I; Henri Dutilleux: Les Citations, Diptyque for oboe, harpsichord, double bass, percussion; JS Bach: The Well-Tempered Klavier, Vol. II. *Honours:* 1st Medal, Harpsichord, International Competition, Geneva, 1958; Prix du Président de la République, Académie Charles Cros, 1985; Officier, Ordre National du Mérite, 1987; Grosse Ehrenzeichen für Verdienste um die Republik Österreich, 1992; Chevalier dans l'Ordre de la Légion d'Honneur, 1995; Officier dans l'Ordre Arts et des Lettres, 1999; Numerous Grand Prix for recordings. *Address:* 91 Quai d'Orsay, 75007 Paris, France.

DRISCOLL, Loren; Singer (Tenor); b. 14 April 1928, Midwest, Wyoming, USA. *Education:* Studied at Syracuse and Boston University. *Career:* Debut: As Caius in Falstaff, Boston, 1954; New York City Opera debut, 1957, as Timur in Turandot; Sang Tom Rakewell in The Rake's Progress at Santa Fe, 1957; Deutsche Oper Berlin from 1962, notably as Fenton, Pinkerton, Flamand (Capriccio), Don Ottavio and The Painter in Lulu; Sang in the premieres of Henze's Der junge Lord (1965) and Ulisse by Dallapiccola (1968); Glyndebourne Festival, 1962, Ferrando; Salzburg Festival, 1966, as Dionysos in the premiere of The Bassarids by Henze, repeating the role at La Scala and Santa Fe, 1968; Metropolitan Opera from 1966, as David, and Alfred in Die Fledermaus; Schwetzingen

Festival, 1971, as the Architect in the premiere of Reimann's Melusine, repeated at Edinburgh; Brussels, 1973, in the premiere of Love's Labour's Lost by Nabokov; Santa Fe, 1977, in the US premiere of Boulevard Solitude by Henze; Rome, 1982, with the company of the Deutsche Oper, in Undine by Lortzing; Further appearances in Hamburg, Cologne and Edinburgh. *Recordings:* Der junge Lord and Lulu; Oedipus Rex, Renard and The Nightingale, conducted by Stravinsky. *Address:* c/o Deutsche Oper Berlin, Richard Wagnerstrasse 10, 1000 Berlin, Germany.

DRIVALA, Jenny; Singer (Soprano); b. 4 July 1965, Greece. *Education:* Studied at the Athens and Bremen Conservatories. *Career:* Appearances at the Vienna Staatsoper, La Scala Milan and in Naples, Rome, Melbourne, Paris Châtelet, Florence and Pretoria; Repertoire includes Donizetti's Lucia, Maria Stuarda and Lucrezia Borgia, Violetta, Thais and Mélisande; Sang title role in Gluck's Armide for ORF television, Strauss's Daphne and Salome for Greek Radio and Glauce in Médée by Cherubini; Season 1994–95 as Massenet's Thais at St Gallen and Glauce in Athens; Strauss concert with Charles Mackerras; Sang Anna Bolena at Athens, 2000.

DRIVER, Danny, MA, (Cantab.), PGDipRCM, ARCM; pianist; b. 1977, London. *Education:* Cambridge Univ., Royal College of Music. *Career:* solo recitals in London at Wigmore Hall, Queen Elizabeth Hall, Purcell Room, Fairfield Hall; recital and concerto appearances in UK, USA, Canada, Israel, Norway and Germany; Teacher, junior dept of Royal Acad. of Music; Assistant to Head of Keyboard, Royal College of Music. *Honours:* BBC Radio 2 Young Musician of the Year, 2001; Royal Overseas League Coutts Bank Award for Keyboard, 2001; Royal College of Music Amerada Hess Junior Fellowship, 2001; Eric Falk Trust Award, 2002. *Address:* 146a Audley Road, London, NW4 3EG, England. *Website:* www.dannydriver.co.uk.

DROBKOVA, Drahomira; Czech singer (mezzo-soprano); b. 1935. *Career:* sang at Ostrava Opera, 1966–83; Roles have included Verdi's Ebol, Amneris and Azucena; Wagner's Ortrud and Adriano; Octavian and Marina, Boris Godunov; Dorabella; Prague Nat. Theatre, from 1983 in operas by Puccini, Smetana, Janáček, Strauss, Verdi and Dvořák; Savonlinna Festival, 1991, as the Witch in Rusalka; Concerts at Prague and elsewhere in music by Zelenka, Janáček and Mozart. *Recordings:* Janáček's Glagolitic Mass; Dvořák's Rusalka, Supraphon; Dvořák's American Flag; Marfa in Dimitrij, Mass D Dur, Spiritual Songs – Ave Maria; B. Martinu, The Prophecy of Isaiah, Hymn to St. James, Supraphon; The Drahomira Drobkova Album. *Honours:* Thalia 1993, Verdi's Ebol. *Address:* Antošovicka 178, Ostrava 2-Koblov, 71100, Czech Republic.

DRUCKER, Eugene; Violinist; b. 17 May 1952, Coral Gables, Florida, USA. *Career:* Co-leader of the Emerson String Quartet from its foundation in 1976–77; Public debut at Alice Tully Hall, New York in March 1979, playing works by Mozart, Smetana and Bartók; Quartet-in-Residence at the Smithsonian Institution, Washington, from 1980 and the Hartt School of Music, 1981–2002, the Aspen Music Festival from 1983, State University of New York at Stony Brook, 2002–; Member of the faculty at SUNY Stony Brook, 2002–; European debut at the Spoleto Festival, 1981; Noted for performances of the quartets of Bartók, including all six works in a single evening; Has given the premieres of works by Mario Davidovsky, Gunther Schuller, Richard Wernick, John Harbison, Wolfgang Rihm and Maurice Wright; with Emerson Quartet 100 concerts annually in major musical capitals of Europe, US and Canada; Tours of Japan and Australia; Resident Quartet of Chamber Music Society of Lincoln Center, 1982–89. *Recordings:* with the Emerson Quartet: Bartók complete Quartets, Mozart 6 Quartets dedicated to Haydn, Schubert Cello Quintet with Rostropovich, Ives and Barber Quartets, Prokofiev Quartets and Sonata for 2 violins, Complete Beethoven Cycle, 1997, Ned Rorem's Quartet No. 4 and Edgar Meyer's Quintet for String Quartet and Double Bass, 1998; Mozart and Brahms Clarinet Quintets with David Shifrin, 1999, the complete Shostakovich Quartets, 2000; Bach's Art of the Fugue, 2003; As soloist: Bach Sonatas and Partitas for violin and complete Duos and Sonatas by Bartók. *Honours:* Naumburg Award for Chamber Music, 1978; Gramophone Magazine: Best Chamber Music Record and Record of the Year for Bartók Quartets, 1989; Grammy for Best Chamber Music and Classical Record of the Year, also for Bartók, 1990; Grammy Award for Best Chamber Music Album for Beethoven Quartets, 1998; Gramophone Magazine Award for Best Chamber Music Record for Shostakovich Quartets, 2000; Grammy Awards for Best Chamber Music and Classical Record of the Year for Shostakovich Quartets, 2001. *Current Management:* IMG Artists. *Address:* c/o IMG Artists, 825 7th Avenue, New York NY 10019, USA.

DRUIETT, Michael; Singer (bass); b. 23 Jan. 1967, London. *Education:* European Opera Centre, Belgium, Scuola Superiore, Italy and the National Opera Studio, London. *Career:* Appearances with English National Opera in The Love for Three Oranges, Wozzeck, Gianni

Schicchi, Salome, Cunning Little Vixen, Rigoletto, Ariodante, Don Carlos, Masked Ball, Orfeo and Lohengrin; Wozzeck in Paris under Barenboim; Principal Bass with the Royal Opera, Covent Garden, from 1993–97; Season 2000–01 as Donner in Das Rheingold and Ferrando in Il Trovatore for Scottish Opera; Further performances Paris Bastille, Toulouse, Bordeaux, Lyon, Dublin, Brussels, Tel-Aviv, Welsh National Opera; Performs regularly with major symphony orchestras. *Recordings:* Floyd's Susannah, with the Opéra de Lyon; Puccini Experience with the Orchestra of the Royal Opera/Downes. *Current Management:* Hazard Chase, Norman House, Cambridge Place, Cambridge CB2 1NS, England. *Telephone:* (1223) 312400. *Fax:* (1223) 460827. *Website:* www.hazardchase.co.uk.

DRUMM, Imelda; Singer (mezzo-soprano); b. 1969, Ireland. *Education:* Dublin City University; Leinster School of Music with Dr Veronica Dunne; National Opera Studio, London, 1996–97. *Career:* Roles with Glyndebourne Opera include Cherubino, 1994, Isolier in Le Comte Ory, 1997, Dorabella in Così fan tutte, 1995, Tisbe in La Cenerentola for Opera Ireland and Theodata in Handel's Flavio for OTC Dublin; Season 1998 as Cenerentola for English Touring Opera and Abaces in a revival of Artaserses by Terradellas at Barcelona. *Honours:* Richard Lewis/Jean Shanks Award and Esso Touring Award, Glyndebourne Opera.

DRUMMOND, Sir John Richard Gray, Kt; Arts Administrator; b. 25 Nov. 1934, London, England. *Education:* Trinity College, Cambridge; MA, Cantab. *Career:* BBC radio and television, 1958–78, as Writer, Director, Producer and Editor; Member, Music Panel, Arts Council, 1970–78; Member, Dance Committee, Arts Council from 1974–80; Director, Edinburgh International Festival, 1978–83; Controller, BBC Music from 1985–92, BBC Radio 3, 1987–92; Director, Promenade Concerts, 1992–95; mem, Scottish Arts Club. *Address:* 61C Campden Hill Court, London W8 7HL, England.

DU, Ming Xin; Composer and Music Educator; b. 19 Aug. 1928, Qian Jiang County, Hubei Province, China; m. 1 Sept 1966, 1 s., 1 d. *Education:* Yu Cai Music School, 1939; Tchaikovsky Music Conservatory, 1954–58. *Career:* Debut: Piano Solo Concert, Shanghai, 1948; Participated in the Asian Composers' Conference and Music Festival, Hong Kong, 1981; Two concerts, Hong Kong Philharmonic Orchestra of works by Du Mingxin, 1982, 1988, composed for the film Wonderful China; Travelled to USA in 1986 for performance of Violin Concerto in John F Kennedy Center and gave lectures in some famous music institutes; mem, Executive Director and General Secretary, Chinese Musicians Association. *Compositions:* Ballet Suite, The Mermaid; The Red Detachment of Women; Symphonic Picture, The South Sea of My Mother Land; Symphonic Fantasia, The Goddess of the River Luo; Symphony, Youth; 2 Violin Concertos, 2 Piano Concertos, Great Wall Symphony; Flapping! the Flags of Army. *Recordings:* The Mermaid; The Red Detachment of Women; The South Sea of My Mother Land; The Goddess of the River Luo; Youth; Great Wall Symphony; 1st Violin Concerto; 1st Piano Concerto. *Address:* Central Conservatory of Music, 43 Bao Jia Street, Beijing 100031, People's Republic of China.

DU BOIS, Mark; Singer (Tenor); b. 9 Nov. 1953, Toronto, Canada. *Education:* Studied in Toronto. *Career:* Debut: Canadian Opera Company, Toronto; Don Curzio in Le nozze di Figaro, 1976; Opera roles in Canada and elsewhere have included Tamino, Ramiro in Cenerentola, Fenton, Laerte in Hamlet and Rossini's Almaviva; La Scala, Milan, 1982 in Stravinsky's Mavra; Belfast Opera, 1983 as Tonio in La Fille du régiment; San Diego Opera, from 1987 notably as Ernesto in Don Pasquale; Concerts in London and elsewhere. *Address:* San Diego Opera, PO Box 988, San Diego, CA 92112, USA.

DU PLESSIS, Christian; Singer (Baritone); b. 2 July 1944, Vryheid, South Africa. *Education:* Studied with Teasdale Griffiths and Esme Webb in South Africa and Otakar Kraus in London. *Career:* Debut: With the PACT Opera in Johannesburg, as Yamadori in Madama Butterfly, 1967; Sang in a 1970 concert performance of Andrea Chénier in London and appeared as Valentin in Faust at Barcelona, 1971; Member of the Sadler's Wells/English National Opera, 1973–81, notably as Cecil in Maria Stuarda, and Verdi's Germont and Posa; Guest appearances in Barcelona, Johannesburg and elsewhere; Concert performances for London Opera Society and Opera Rara in L'Etoile du Nord by Meyerbeer, Gli Orazi ed i Curiazi by Mercadante, Donizetti's Torquato Tasso, Maria di Rudenz, Rosmonda d'Inghilterra and Maria Padilla, and Bellini's Il Pirata; Retired, 1988. *Recordings:* Germont in an English-Language Traviata conducted by Charles Mackerras; Maria Stuarda; Meyerbeer's Dinorah; L'Assedio di Calais by Donizetti.

DUBÉ, Jean; Pianist; b. Dec. 1981, Canada. *Career:* Debut: Italian Women's Society Gala, Edmonton, Alberta, Canada, 5 years of age; Mozart Concerto No. 5 with Radio France Philharmonic Orchestra, Mozart Bicentenary Gala, Paris, 9 years of age; World-wide recitalist, chamber musician and soloist with orchestra in Japan, Canada, Latvia, France, Ireland, Germany, Belgium, Switzerland, Netherlands, Hungary, Czechoslovakia, Italy and Romania, 1988; Canadian television,

1988; French television and radio; Japanese television, Fuji; Concert Châtelet, 1991; Toured with orchestra, south of France, 1992; Salle Gaveau, France Musique; Toured Germany with orchestra, NDR radio, 1993; Japanese television, NHK, 1995; Toured Canada, Japan, 1996; Invalides, Bagatelle (Paris), Chimay (Belgium), 1997; Toured Western Europe; Czech television, 1998; French and German television, 1999; Hungarian Institute, Musée d'Orsay, Paris and Tokyo, 2000; Festivals: Messiaen Festival, Dublin, Riga, BBC Radio 3, Orléans, Nice, Utrecht and Dietzenbach, 2001; Bayreuth, St Petersburg; performed Sain-Saëns Concerto No. 2, Concertgebouw, Amsterdam, 2003. *Recordings:* Samuel Barber, Sonata for piano; Conservatory of Paris-Meyer Foundation records: XXth century piano music: Ginastera, Bartók, Mochizuki, Messiaen, Komulainen, Prokofiev; Videotape: 8 productions for French and European cable television (Grieg Piano Concerto and Saint-Saëns Concerto for piano No. 4) with Orchestra Le Sinfonia de Lyon, conducted by Jean-Claude Guerinot, recorded live in Cathedral of St John, Lyon, France; also recordings of Liszt, Franck, Sibelius, Ciurlionis and others. *Honours:* First Prize, 'Young Prodigies Mozart', Paris National Competition, 1991; Youngest graduate ever, Nice Conservatory, 1992; First Prize, National Superior Conservatory of Paris, 1996; First Prize, Francis Poulenc, 1997; First Prize, Jeunesses Musicales, Bucharest, 1998; Yvonne Lefèbure Scholarship Orléans XXth Century, 2000; Second Grand Prize, Olivier Messiaen, Paris, 2000; Second Prize, Takasaki, 2000; Best Show of the Year, for Turangalila concert, 2001; First Prize, Franz Liszt Piano Competition, 2002. *Current Management:* Marie Méli, 30 rue du Moulin Joly, 75011 Paris, France.

DUBINBAUM, Gail; Singer (Mezzo-Soprano); b. 1958, New York, USA. *Education:* Studied with Herta Glaz and with the Metropolitan Young Artists Program. *Career:* Sang at the Metropolitan from 1982, debut in L'Enfant et les Sortilèges; Appearances in New York and elsewhere in the USA as Rossini's Rosina and Isabella and as Mozart's Dorabella; Engagements at the Vienna Staatsoper 1986–88; Suzuki in Butterfly for Opera Pacific at Costa Mesa and again at Detroit, 1991; sang in the Jeremiah Symphony with Leonard Bernstein conducting Boston Symphony, Los Angeles Philharmonic and the Pittsburgh Symphony (40th Anniversary of premiere), sang Suzuki and Bach Magnificat with Zubin Mehta and Israel Philharmonic; sang Nefertiti in Akhnaten by Philip Glass at Chicago, 2000; sang Nefertiti with the Boston Lyric Opera, Suzuki with Arizona Opera and Maddalena with Montreal Opera. *Address:* 2430 W Barbie, Phoenix, AZ 85085, USA. *E-mail:* DuMass315@aol.com.

DUBOSC, Catherine; Singer (Soprano); b. 12 March 1959, Lille, France. *Education:* Studied at Strasbourg Conservatory, Ecole National in Paris from 1980 with Denise Dupleix and Hans Hotter; Further study with Eric Tappy at Lyon. *Career:* Sang at Lyon Opéra, 1985–87, as Mozart's Despina, Pamina and Susanna, Nannetta, Blanche in Dialogues des Carmélites and Marzelline (Fidelio); Sang Gretel at Geneva, 1987 and Isipile in Cavalli's Giasone at Utrecht, 1988, and the Théâtre des Champs Elysées, Paris, 1990; Appearances at Montpellier (Pamina, 1991), Avignon, Nancy, Edinburgh and Strasbourg; Sang Mélisande at Lausanne, 1992 and at Frankfurt, 1994; Sang Blanche in the Danish premiere of Poulenc's Carmelites, Copenhagen, 1997. *Recordings include:* Giasone, The Love for Three Oranges, Campra's Tancrède, Scylla et Glaucus by Leclair and Darande in Gluck's La Rencontre Imprevue (Erato).

DUBROVAY, Laszlo; Composer and Teacher; b. 23 March 1943, Budapest, Hungary. *Education:* Bart ók Conservatory, Budapest; Graduated, Academy of Music, Budapest, 1966; Principal Teachers: Istvan Szelenyi, Ferenc Szabo, Imre Vincze; Completed training in Germany with Karlheinz Stockhausen, Composition and Electronic Music from Hans-Ulrich Humpert, 1972–74. *Career:* Teacher of Music Theory, Budapest Academy of Music, 1976–; Residence in Berlin, 1985; Professor of Theory, Franz Liszt Academy of Music, Budapest, 1998–; mem, Hungarian Arts Academy. *Compositions include:* Stage music: The Ransom, opera in one act, 1991; The Sculptor, dance-play in one act, 1993; Faust the Damned, dance-play, 1998; Orchestral: 2 concertos for piano, 1982, 1998; Concertos for: strings, 1979, flute, 1981, trumpet, 1981, violin, 1991, cimbalom, 1994; Triple concerto for trumpet, trombone and tuba, 1989; 4 suite of Faust the Damned, 1989; Hungarian Symphony, 1997; Cantata Aquilarum, 1999; Timbre Symphony, 2000; Concert for Hungarian folk instruments, 2000; Symphonic band music: Deserts, 1987; March, 1990; The Ransom, 1992; Buzzing Polka, 1993; The Death of Faust, 1996; Ballet Suite, 1996; Festive Music, 2000; Chamber music: 3 string quartets, 1970, 1976, 1983; 2 wind quintets, 1968, 1972; 3 brass quintets, 1971, 1980, 1998; Brass Septet, 1980; 13 solos for different instruments, 1975–2000; Paraphrasis for piano, 1999; choruses, tape, live electronic and computer music pieces. *Address:* c/o ARTISJUS, Meszaros u. 15–17, H–01539 Budapest 114, PoB 593, Hungary.

DUDDELL, Joe, FRAM; composer; b. 1972, England. *Education:* Salford Univ.; with Steve Martland at Royal Acad. of Music,. *Career:* commis-

sions include London Sinfonietta, BT Scottish Ensemble, ViVA! and the BBC, including three works for the Proms; works performed at Bath, Chester, Huddersfield, Spitalfields, Lichfield, Lucerne and Brisbane Festivals, South Bank and Barbican Centres in London, New York and Moscow, and at tours in Scotland and Taiwan; Lecturer in Composition, Exeter Univ. *Compositions include:* Circle Square, saxophone quartet 1997; Parallel Lines, tuned percussion and piano, 1999; The Realside, soprano, tenor, chorus and optional brass, 1999; Computation, counter-tenor and ensemble, 1999; Vaporize, piano 4 hands, 2000; Snowblind, percussion and strings, 2001; Ode to English, unaccompanied voices, 2002; Ruby, percussion and orchestra, 2002–03; Shadowplay, cello and chamber orchestra, 2003; Temporal Keys, solo organ, 2003, New Dawn Fades, string orchestra 2004, Mnemonic, flute, harp and strings 2004, Freaky Dancer, vibraphone and guitar quartet 2003, Arbor Low, string quartet 2004. *Current Management:* Schott Co Ltd, 48 Great Marlborough Street, London, W1F 7BB, England. *Telephone:* (20) 7494-1487. *Fax:* (20) 7287-1529. *Website:* www.schott-music.com.

DUDZIAK, Francis; Singer (Baritone); b. 1959, France. *Education:* Studied at the Paris Conservatoire. *Career:* Sang at the Opéra du Rhin, Strasbourg, 1982–85; Lyon Opéra, 1985–88; Guest appearances throughout France in Monteverdi's Orfeo and Ulisse as Mozart's Masetto and Guglielmo, Ramiro in L'Heure Espagnole and in operetta; Saint-Cere Festival, 1985 in Dalayrac's L'Amant statue and Maison à vendre; Strasbourg, 1991 as Papageno; Many concerts in Paris and elsewhere. *Address:* 8 Rue Charles Nodier, 75018 Paris, France.

DUESING, Dale; Singer (baritone); b. 26 Sept. 1947, Milwaukee, USA. *Education:* Began studies in Milwaukee as a pianist; Vocal studies at Lawrence University in Wisconsin. *Career:* San Francisco Opera as Britten's Billy Budd and Donizetti's Belcore; Seattle Opera as Wagner's Wolfram and Tchaikovsky's Eugene Onegin; Glyndebourne debut 1976, as Olivier in Capriccio; later sang Guglielmo in Così fan tutte, conducted by Bernard Haitink; Ottone in L'Incoronazione di Poppea, Lysander in A Midsummer Night's Dream, 1989, and Figaro, 1989; Metropolitan Opera debut 1979, as Harlekin in Ariadne auf Naxos; Concert engagements with the New York Philharmonic, Berlin Philharmonic, Boston Symphony, Concertgebouw Orchestra, BBC Symphony and Santa Cecilia of Rome; Conductors include Giulini, Levine, Leppard, Ozawa, Sawallisch, Dohnányi and Previn; Opera engagements include Ariadne at La Scala, Billy Budd and Peter Grimes at the Metropolitan, Die Meistersinger in Brussels and Così fan tutte at Santa Fe; Sang Figaro at Seattle, 1989; Goryanchikov in From the House of the Dead, at Brussels, 1990; Guglielmo at Barcelona and Olivier at the 1990 Glyndebourne Festival; Solo recitalist in the USA and Europe; World Premiere: Wade in Jonathan Wade by Carlisle Floyd, Houston Opera; Così fan tutte at Liceo, Barcelona; Marriage of Figaro, Glyndebourne Opera under Rattle; Metropolitan Opera, New York, Pelléas and Papageno; Season 1991/92 as Mozart's Count at Brussels, 'T' in the premiere of Schnittke's Life with an Idiot at Amsterdam and Nardo in La Finta Giardiniera at the Salzburg Festival; Prodocismo in Il Turco in Italia at Théâtre du Champs-Elysées, Paris, 1996; Brussels 1997, in Orphée aux Enfers; Season 1998 as Bill in Mahagonny at Salzburg and Toby Belch in the premiere of Trojahn's Was ihr Wollt at Munich; Sang Leontes in the premiere of Wintermärchen by Boesmans, Brussels 1999; Narrator in the premiere of Sophie's Choice at Covent Garden, 2002. *Recordings include:* Don Giovanni and Zemlinsky's Lyric Symphony; Così fan tutte; Arias and Barcaroles, Leonard Bernstein. *Current Management:* Askonas Holt Ltd, Lonsdale Chambers, 27 Chancery Lane, London, WC2A 1PF, England. *Telephone:* (20) 7400-1700. *Fax:* (20) 7400-1799. *E-mail:* info@askonasholt.co.uk. *Website:* www .askonasholt.co.uk.

DUFFIELD, Alan, FTCL, LRAM, ARCM, ABSM; singer (tenor); b. 1952, Ripon, England. *Education:* Birmingham School of Music, Nat. Opera Studio, London. *Career:* concerts include Bach's St John Passion and B minor Mass (Lufthansa Festival, London), Handel's Joshua, High Priest in Idomeneo, under Simon Rattle, and Britten's Serenade for tenor, horn and strings (CBSO); Mozart's Requiem and Haydn's Nelson Mass with the London Mozart Players, BBC recital of John Joubert songs; appearances at Glyndebourne in Orfeo (ENO), and as Don Basilio and Don Curzio (Le nozze di Figaro); roles in La Bohème, Madama Butterfly, Der Rosenkavalier, Death in Venice, Samson; Mathis der Maler (Hindemith) for the Royal Opera. *Honours:* Dr hc (Birmingham Conservatoire). *Address:* c/o Royal Opera House, Covent Garden, London, WC2, England.

DUGDALE, Sandra; Singer (Soprano); b. 4 Jan. 1946, Pudsey, Yorkshire, England. *Education:* Studied in Leeds and at the Guildhall School, London. *Career:* Debut: With Glyndebourne Touring Opera as Despina in Così fan tutte; Has sung with English National Opera in operas by Mozart, Janáček and Strauss; Welsh National Opera in The Greek Passion by Martinů; Four principal roles with the Handel Opera Society; Handel roles with the English Bach Festival; Covent Garden debut 1983 as Fire and The Nightingale in the Ravel/Stravinsky double bill; returned 1985, as Adele in Die Fledermaus; Festival appearances include Hong Kong, Camden, Batignano, Wexford and Vienna; Frequent broadcasts with the BBC, including the Much Loved Music Show and Lo Speziale by Haydn (ITV); Sang Adele for Opera Northern Ireland at the Grand Opera House, Belfast, 1990; Sullivan's Angelina for D'Oyly Carte at Bournemouth, 1990; Concert engagements with most major British orchestras, under the batons of Charles Mackerras, Roderick Brydon, Charles Groves, David Atherton, Philip Ledger, Mark Elder, John Eliot Gardiner and Vernon Handley; Regular visits to the USA. *Recordings include:* Videos of operettas by Gilbert and Sullivan; Series, 100 Years of Italian Opera, with the Philharmonia Orchestra. *Address:* c/o Music International, 13 Ardilaun Road, London, N5 2QR, England.

DUHAMEL, Antoine; Composer; b. 30 July 1925, Valmondois, France. *Education:* Studied with Messiaen and Liebowitz in Paris. *Career:* Club d'Essai, 1950–52; Discophiles Français, 1954–57 (Yves Nat, Lily Kraus, studios A Charlin); Film music from 1961 for such directors as J D Pollet, J L Godard, Fr Truffaut, B Tavernier, and now F Trueba and P Leconte. Wrote the orchestral music with Pierre Jansen for D W Griffith's Intolérance, 1985; Founder, Ecole de Musique de Villeurbanne, 1980; mem, SACEM; Honorary President, Syndicat national des Auteurs et Compositeurs; Vice-President, Fondation Beaumarchais. *Compositions:* Operas and other works for stage: L'Ivrogne, (Baudelaire), 1953, staged Tours, 1984 as Le scieur de long; Lundi, Monsieur, vous serez riche (Forlani), Paris 1969; L'Opéra des Oiseaux (Aristophane), Lyon, 1971; Ubu a L'Opera (Jarry), Avignon, 1974; Gambara (Balzac), Lyon, 1978; Les Travaux d'Hercule, Vaise 1981, Adelaide, 1983 and Brisbane, 1998; Le Transsiberien (Cendrars), Paris, 1983; Requiem de Jean Cocteau, Milly la Forêt, 1989; Quatrevingt-treize (Hugo), Fourvières, 1989; Carmenmania, ballet, Nice, 1994. *Recordings:* Many albums of film music. *Publications:* Gambara, a book of the collection Avant-Scène Opéra. *Honours:* Prix Georges Enesco, 1977; Grand Prix Sacem, 1998. *Address:* 243 rue Georges Duhamel, 95760 Valmondois, France.

DUMAY, Augustin; Concert Violinist; b. 17 Jan. 1949, Paris, France. *Education:* Studied at the Paris Conservatoire from 1959 with Roland Charmy. *Career:* Debut: Théâtre des Champs Elysées, Paris, 1963; Studied further with Arthur Grumiaux, 1962–67, then played regularly in public; Partnerships with Jean-Philippe Collard and Michel Beroff; Concert with Karajan and the Berlin Philharmonic 1979 followed by Bartók's 2nd Concerto conducted by Colin Davis; Further engagements with L'Orchestre National de France, Suisse Romande Orchestra, London Symphony and English Chamber, and at the Montreux, Bath, Berlin, Lucerne, Monaco, Aix, Leipzig and Montpellier festivals; Other conductors include Ozawa, Dutoit, Sanderling, Sawallisch, Fruhbeck de Burgos and Skrowaczewski; Chamber music collaborations with Maria Joao Pires, Michel Dalberto, Lynn Harrell, Jean-Bernard Pommier, Yo-Yo Ma and Richard Stoltzmann; Gave the premiere of Berio's Sequenza 9, for solo violin, and the premieres of the concertos by Marius Constant and Isang Yun; Director of the National Chamber Orchestra of Toulouse from 1988; Played a 1721 Stradivarius, formerly belonging to Fritz Kreisler, then a 1744 Guarneri instrument. *Recordings:* Lalo's Symphonie Espagnole, conducted by Michel Plasson, and Chausson's Concerto for piano, violin and string quartet, with Collard and the Muir Quartet; Mozart, Complete Violin Concertos; Tchaikovsky and Mendelsohn, Violin Concertos, London Symphony Orchestra; Mozart, Piano and Violin Sonatas; Brahms, Complete Violin and Piano Sonatas with Maria Joâo Pires. *Current Management:* TransArt (UK) Ltd, Cedar House, 10 Rutland Street, Filey, YO14 9JB, North Yorkshire, England. *Telephone:* (1723) 515819. *Fax:* (1723) 514678. *E-mail:* transartuk@transartuk.com. *Website:* www.transartuk.com. *Address:* Granjinha Do Meio, Excalos De Baixo, 6005 Alcains, Portugal.

DUMITRESCU, Iancu (Ioan); Composer, Music Critic, Conductor and Pianist; b. 15 July 1944, Sibiu, Romania; m. (1) Cristina Dumitrescu, 10 May 1979, (2) Ana-Maria Avram, Sept 1988. *Education:* High School of Music, Bucharest; Piano with Cici Manta; Composition with Alfred Mendelssohn, Stefan Niculescu, Aurel Stroe, and with Sergiu Celibidache, Trier, Germany. *Career:* Founder, Leader and Conductor, chamber music ensemble Hyperion; Pianist specialising in avant garde music; Compositions performed on television and radio, Romania, Austria, Netherlands, France, Italy, 1970–; Commands: Radio France, Paris; Commande d'Etat, Minister of Culture, France; Kronos Quartet, San Francisco and G Enescu Philharmonic Orchestra; World premieres: Amsterdam, Berlin, Bremen, Bucharest, Cluj, Paris (Radio France), London (Royal Festival Hall), Royan, Warsaw, Vienna, Lisbon (Gulbenkian Foundation), Milan (Piccola Scala), Rome, Boston, New York, San Francisco; Head, Radio France, Paris. *Compositions include:* Alternances, I, II, string quartet, 1968; Multiples, 3 groups of percussion, 1972; Apogeum for orchestra, 1973; Reliefs for two orchestras and piano, 1975; Orion I and II, for three groups of percussion, 1978; Perspectives au Movemur, string quartet 1979;

Zenith, percussion, 1980; Nimbus, 3 trombones, percussion, tape, 1980; Cogito-Trompe L'oeil for ensemble, 1981; Grande Ourse for ensemble, 1982; Aulodie Mioritica, double bass, orchestra, 1984; Haryphonies (alpha, beta, gamma), double bass, percussion, harryphono, piano prépara, 1985; Holzwege, viola solo, 1986; Reliefs for orchestra; Harryphonies (epsilon), large orchestra, 1986; Monades (gamma and epsilon), for 6 monocords and harryphone, 1988; Gnosis, for double bass and string ensemble, 1988–97; L'Orbite D'Uranus; Astrée Lointaine, bass saxophone, orchestra, 1991; L'Empire des Signes, 1992; Au De La De Movemur; Clusterum, percussion, 1993; Galaxy, 3 harryphones, 3 percussions, micro-processor, 1993; 5 Impulsions, large orchestra, 1993; A Priori, chamber ensemble, 1994; Mythos, chamber ensemble, 1994; Kronos/Holzwege, string quartet; Impuls, bass flute, percussion, 1994; Mnemosyne, chamber ensemble, 1994; Pulsar Perdu for Kronos Quartet, string quartet, 1995; Fluxus, for tapes and large orchestra, 1996; Sirius Kronos Quartet, for string quartet and tape, 1996; Meteorites, electronic music, 1997; Ouranos, for distorted spectral sounds, string orchestra and electronic tape, 1997; La Chute dans le Temps, for six groups of instruments, new distorted spectral sounds and tape, 1997; New Meteors, Oiseaux célestes and Colossus, 2000. *Recordings:* Opera Omnia. *Address:* 16 Dr Draghiescu nr 16, sector 5, 76224 Bucharest, Romania.

DUNCAN, Martin; Stage Director; b. 1960, London. *Education:* LAMDA, London. *Career:* Stagings of Die Zauberflöte and Ariadne auf Naxos for Scottish Opera; Serse and La Clemenza di Tito in Munich; The Barber of Seville for English Touring Opera; L'Heure Espagnole, Gianni Schicchi, The Thieving Magpie and Iolanta for Opera North; Artistic Director of Nottingham Playhouse, 1994–99; British premiere production of Birtwistle's The Last Supper for Glyndebourne, 2000–01; Season 2001–2002 with The Rake's Progress and Die Entführung for the Bayerische Staatsoper, Munich. *Address:* c/o Glyndebourne Festival Opera, Glyndebourne, Lewes, Sussex BN8 5UU, England.

DUNDAS-GRANT, Deirdre; Bassoon Player; b. 28 May 1927, Ewell, Surrey, England; d. of James H. Dundas-Grant and Katherine Galloway; 1 d., 1 s. *Education:* Royal Acad. of Music. *Career:* Debut: Bournemouth Municipal Orchestra as Second, then Principal Bassoon; Principal Bassoon with BBC Concert Orchestra, 1961–69; Principal, London Bach Orchestra; Monteverdi Orchestra; Steinitz Bach Players; Menuhin Festival Orchestra; Solo recitals and chamber music with BBC and music clubs; Sessions and engagements with all major orchestras; Founder member, National Youth Orchestra and Portia Wind Ensemble; currently retd from public performing, engaged in examining, adjudication and consultation; mem, RAM Guild; Chairman, British Double Reed Society 1999–2002; Royal Society of Musicians. *Recordings:* Bach Art of Fugue; Christmas Music from Venice with John Eliot Gardiner; Philip Jones Brass and Ensemble; Bach's B minor Mass with Academy of St Martin in the Fields; Many orchestral recordings. *Publications:* Arrangements of Bach Trios for Woodwind; Liszt Quintet; contrib. to British Double Reed Notes; numerous articles. *Honours:*- Fellow, Royal Academy of Music, 1989, Mem. Court of Assts, Royal Soc. of Music 2004; Bach, Beethoven Scholarship, Royal Academy of Music, 1947–49. *Address:* 24 Dora Road, London SW19 7 HH, England.

DUNK, Roderick; Conductor; b. 1959, Birmingham, England. *Education:* Studied at the Birmingham Conservatory. *Career:* Played double bass in the BBC Symphony Orchestra and BBC Concert Orchestra, 1978–90; From 1990 regular guest conductor with the BBC Concert, Royal Philharmonic, London Symphony and Halle Orchestras; Since 1996 conducted London Symphony Orchestra, Royal Philharmonic, Philharmonia, London Philharmonic, Vienna Symphony and Prague Symphony orchestras in several series of Compact Discs; Arranger and Music Director for BBC television, conductor of the London production of Carmen Jones and music director for Travelling Opera; Directed numerous performances with London City Ballet and Birmingham Royal Ballet; In 1986 formed the London Palm Court Orchestra, giving performances of Edwardian and Victorian music. *Address:* c/o Travelling Opera, 114 St Mary's Road, Market Harborough, Leicestershire, LE16 7DT, England.

DUNKI, Jean-Jacques; Pianist and Composer; b. 28 Feb. 1948, Aarau, Switzerland; m. Christine Baader, 6 Aug 1994, one d. *Education:* Music Education, Aarau, Switzerland; Piano, Conducting, Musicology, Basel, Berlin, Paris, London, Baltimore, New York. *Career:* Debut: As Pianist, 1963; Composer, 1978; Performing in most European Countries, USA, 1979–, Japan, 1993–; Latin America, 1997; 1999– international career as fortepianist. *Compositions:* Lutezia, 1978; Tú... no tienes imaginación, 1979; Prokrustes, 1982; Tetrapteron O–IV, 1991; Pessoa, 1993; Nulla dies, 1994; Figures, 1997; Kammerstück I–VIII, 1985–99. *Recordings:* Piano Music of Berg, Webern and Zemlinsky; Chamber Music of Grieg, Reger, Schumann; Own music. *Publications:* Several articles on Schoenberg, Schumann, Reger and Webern. *Honours:* 1st Prize, Arnold Schoenberg Piano Competition, 1981. *Address:* Bruderholzallee 12, 4059 Basel, Switzerland.

DUNN, Mignon; Singer (Mezzo-soprano); b. 17 June 1931, Memphis, Tennessee, USA; m. Kurt Klippstatter, 24 July 1972. *Education:* Southwestern University; University of Lausanne; Vocal studies with Karin Branzell and Beverly Johnson, New York. *Career:* Debut: Operatic debut as Carmen, New Orleans, 1955; New York City Opera debut, 1956, on roster until 1957, then 1972 and 1975; Metropolitan Opera debut, New York, as Nurse in Boris Godunov, 1958, regular appearances in over 50 major roles including Ortrud, Mother Marie (Carmélites), Amneris, Azucena, Marina, Fricka, Herodias and Anna (Les Troyens); Guest appearances with opera companies in Chicago, San Francisco, Boston, Miami, Berlin, Hamburg, Vienna, Florence and other cities; Sang the Kostelnicka in Jenůfa at the 1988 Spoleto Festival; Season 1988–89 as the Witch in Rusalka at Philadelphia and Amneris in Chicago; Created Madame Irma in the premiere of The Balcony by Di Domenica, Boston, 1990; Clytemnestra in Nuria Espert's production of Elektra at Barcelona, 1990; Mistress Quickly in Falstaff for New York City Opera, 1996; Soloist with orchestras in USA and Europe; Faculty, University of Illinois, 1990. *Recordings:* For several labels. *Honours:* Honorary D.Mus, Southwestern University, 1974.

DUNN, Susan, BA; American singer (soprano); b. 23 July 1954, Malvern, AR. *Education:* Hendrix Coll. and Indiana Univ. *Career:* debut as Aida at Peoria (IL) Opera Co. 1982; subsequent appearances at La Scala (Milan, Italy), Carnegie Hall, Lyric Opera (Chicago, IL), Vienna Staatsoper, Australian Opera, Washington Opera, San Diego Opera (CA), Teatro Communale Bologna, Metropolitan Opera (New York), Sydney Opera House (Australia); has performed with leading orchestras, including New York Philharmonic, Chicago Symphony, Boston Symphony, Orchestre de Paris, Concertgebouw Orchestra (Netherlands); roles include Aida, Sieglinde in Die Walküre, Elena in I Vespri Siciliani, Elisabeth de Valois in Don Carlo, Leonora in La Forza del Destino, Leonora in Il Trovatore, Amelia in Un Ballo in Maschera, Amelia Boccanegra. *Honours:* Nat. Metropolitan Opera Council Award 1981, winner Philadelphia Opera Co./Pavarotti Int. Vocal Competition 1981, winner WGN-III Opera Competition 1983, Dallas Morning News-Dallas Opera G. B. Dealey Prize 1983, Richard Tucker Award 1983. *Current Management:* Herbert H. Brelin Inc, 119 W 57th Street, New York, NY 10019, USA.

DÜNNEBACH, Ulrich; Singer (Bass-baritone); b. 21 April 1946, Limbach, Germany. *Career:* Debut: Hagen Opera, 1969; Sang in opera at Aachen, 1975–80, Detmold, 1980–85, Nuremberg from 1985; Guest appearances at Munich as the Hermit in Der Freischütz, 1995, and at Liège and Rome, 1996, as Rocco in Fidelio; Sang Wagner's Daland at Bologna and Liège, 2000–01; Other roles have included Mozart's Figaro, Leporello, Alfonso and Sarastro; Oroveso in Norma, the Doctor in Wozzeck, King Philip in Don Carlos, Banquo and Zaccaria (Nabucco); Concerts include Penderecki's Polish Requiem, conducted by the composer. *Address:* Nuremberg Opera, Richard-Wagner Platz 2-10, 90443 Nuremberg, Germany.

DUNSBY, Jonathan (Mark); Musician and Professor of Music, University of Reading; b. 16 March 1953, Wakefield, Yorkshire, England; m. (1) Anne Davis, 7 Sept 1974, 1 d., (2) Esther Cavett, 25 May 1983, 1 d. *Education:* ARCM, 1968; BA, Honours, New College, Oxford, 1973; PhD, Leeds University, 1976; Harkness Fellow, 1976. *Career:* Debut: Piano, Wigmore Hall, 1972; Bronze Medal, Geneva International Competition, 1970; Jury Prize, Munich International Competition, 1970; Winner, Commonwealth Competition, 1974; Regular appearances with Violinist, Vanya Milanova; Professor of Music, University of Reading. *Publications:* Structural Ambiguity in Brahms, 1981; Founding Editor of Journal of Music Analysis, 1981; Music Analysis in Theory and Practice (with Arnold Whittall), 1987; Schoenberg, Pierrot Lunaire, 1992; Performing Music, 1995. *Contributions:* Music and Letters; The Musical Quarterly; Journal of Music Theory; Perspectives of New Music; Journal of the Arnold Schoenberg Institute. *Address:* University of Reading, Department of Music, 35 Upper Redlands Road, Reading, Berkshire RG1 5JE, England.

DUPHIL, Monique; Pianist; b. 24 April 1936, France; m. Jay Humeston, 2 d. *Education:* Studied privately with Marguérite Long and at Paris Conservatoire National Supérieur de Musique with, Jean Doyen, Rose Lejour, Joseph Calvet and Pierre Pasquier. *Career:* Debut at 15: At Paris Théâtre des Champs Elysées with L'Orchestre des Concerts du Conservatoire (now Orchestre de Paris); Solo recitals in over 50 countries; Performances with orchestras in Europe, South America, Asia (Taiwan, Hong Kong, Japan, China, Korea), Australia, USA under conductors including Eugene Ormandy, George Hurst, Charles Dutoit, Maag, Sanderling, Verbitsky, Benzi, Akiyama, de Priest; Has performed with Pierre. Fournier, H. Szeryng, R. Ricci, J. P. Rampal, Michel Debost, K. Leister, the St Petersburg and American String Quartets and the Geistag and Mozarteum String Trios; Member of the Amici and Villa Lobos Trios; Prof. of Piano, Oberlin Music Conservatory, OH, USA. *Recordings:* JS Bach's French Suites; Piano Music by A Liadov; H Villa Lobos' Piano Trios Nos 1, 2 and 3 and Piano and Cello Sonata No. 2.

Current Management: New Fine Arts (solo); Mariedi Anders (Amici Trio), San Francisco. *Address:* Oberlin College, Music Conservatory, Oberlin, OH 44074, USA. *E-mail:* mduphil@oberlin.edu.

DUPONT, Stephen; Singer (Bass); b. 29 July 1958, Houston, Texas, USA. *Education:* Studied at Memphis State University and the American Opera Center, New York. *Career:* Sang in La Bohème at New York and appeared in operas by Menotti at Spoleto and Palermo, 1984; Guest appearances at Venice in the Verdi Requiem and Don Carlos, in Paris and San Francisco; Mozart's Commendatore at La Scala, 1989, Colline and Ramphis at the Metropolitan, 1986–87; Sang Gremin at Strasbourg, 1990, Sparafucile at Bonn and Banquo for Miami Opera (1992). *Address:* c/o Metropolitan Opera, Lincoln Center, New York, NY 10023, USA.

DUPRÉ, Heather; Pianist; b. 30 March 1949, Channel Islands. *Education:* Licenciate, Recital Diploma, Royal Academy of Music, 1967–72. *Career:* Debut: Wigmore Hall, 1976; Solo Pianist, Recitals in the United Kingdom including several appearances at Edinburgh Festival Fringe, Wigmore Hall and Purcell Room; Broadcast on Radio London, 1974; Junior Professor, Royal Academy of Music, 1973–76; Examiner, Associated Board of Royal Schools of Music, 1979–2000; mem, Solo Performers Section, Incorporated Society of Musicians. *Address:* 19c Abercorn Place, St Johns Wood, London NW8 9DX, England.

DUPUY, Martine; Singer (Mezzo-Soprano); b. 10 Dec. 1952, Marseilles, France. *Career:* Debut: Aix-en-Province 1975, as Eurydice in Campra's Le Carnaval de Venise; Has sung in the coloratura mezzo repertoire in Europe and North and South America; Marseilles Opera 1985, as Bellini's Romeo and as Isabella in L'Italiana in Algeri; Paris Opera 1985, as Neocles in Le Siège de Corinthe; Other Rossini roles include Malcolm (La Donna del Lago) at Nice 1985 and Bonn 1990, Cenerentola (Lausanne) and Arsace in Semiramide at Valle d'Itria and Nice, 1985; Metropolitan Opera debut 1988, as Sextus in Giulio Cesare; Sang in the opening concert at the Bastille Opera, Paris, 13 July 1989; Season 1990-91 as Mère Marie in Les Dialogues des Carmélites for Lyon Opera, Jane Seymour (Anna Bolena) at Marseilles and Madrid and Armando in a concert performance of Meyerbeer's Il Crociato in Egitto at Montpellier; Other roles include Monteverdi's Nero and Penelope; Mozart's Cecilio (Lucio Silla) and Sextus (La Clemenza di Tito); Adalgisa in Norma and Donizetti's Maffeo Orsini (Lucrezia Boria) and Ada (Il Diluvio Universale); Has also sung in Buenos Aires, Salzburg and Lausanne; Brussels 1996, as Eboli in the French version of Don Carlos; The Prince in Cendrillon at Turin; Cenerentola at Tel-Aviv, 1998; Sang the Mother in Charpentier's Louise at Toulouse 2000. *Honours:* Winner, International Singing Competition, Peschiera del Garda, 1975; Grand Prix 1985 from Opera International, France. *Address:* c/o Opéra de Lyon, 9 Quai Jean Moulin, F-69001, Lyon, France.

DURMULLER, Jorg; Singer (Tenor); b. 28 Aug. 1959, Berne, Switzerland. *Education:* Studied at Wintherthur and Hamburg and with Christa Ludwig and Hermann Prey. *Career:* Appeared with the company of the Hamburg Staatsoper at the 1986 Schwetzingen Festival, in the premiere of Die Lieden des Jungen Werthers by Hans-Jurgen von Bose; Member of the Bielefeld opera from 1987, notably as Mozart's Ferrando and Tamino, Verdi's and Nicolai's Fenton, and Chateauneuf in Zar und Zimmermann; Sang Ramiro in Cenerentola, 1989; Tour of Russia and Spain, 1989, guest appearances in concert and opera in Brussels, Paris, Pesaro, Geneva and Mannheim; Innsbruck Early Music Festival, 1991, as Fracasso in Mozart's La Finta Semplice, conducted by René Jacobs; Komische Oper Berlin, 1996 as Mozart's Ferrando; Sang Wagner's Steuermann at Strasbourg, 2001. *Recordings:* Bruckner's Missa Solemnis in F. *Address:* St ädtisches Buhnen, Brunnenstrasse 3, 4800 Bielefeld 1, Germany.

DÜRR, Alfred; Musicologist, Writer on Music and Editor; b. 3 March 1918, Charlottenburg, Germany. *Education:* PhD, Musicology, University of Göttingen, 1950. *Career:* Member 1951–83, Assistant Director, 1962–81, Johann-Sebastian-Bach-Institute, Göttingen; Editor, Bach-Jahrbuch, 1953–74; Editor of works for Bach Neue Ausgabe sämtlicher Werke. *Publications:* Studien über die frühen Kantaten Johann Sebastian Bachs, 1951, 2nd Edition, revised 1977; Zur Chronolgie der Leipzigir Vokalwerke J Bachs (revised reprint from Bach-Jahrbuch 1957), 1976; Johann Sebastian Bach, Weihnachts Oratorium, 1967; Die Kantaten von Johann Sebastian Bach, 1971, 7th edition, revised, 1999; Johann Sebastian Bach: Seine Handschrift-Abbild seines Schaffens, 1984; Im Mittelpunkt Bach: Ausgewählte Aufsätze und Vorträge, 1988; Die Johannes-Passion von Johann Sebastian Bach: Entstehung, Überlieferung, Werkeinführung, 1988, 3rd edition, 1999; Bachs Werk vom Einfall bis zur Drucklegung, 1989; Johann Sebastian Bach–Das Wohltemperierte Klavier, 1998. *Contributions:* Articles in scholarly journals. *Honours:* Member, Akademie der Wissenschaften, Göttingen, 1976–; Festschrift published in honour of 65th birthday, 1983; Honorary doctorate, Baldwin-Wallace College, Berea, Ohio, 1982 and Oxford, 1995; Corresponding member, American

Musicological Society, 1988–. *Address:* Charlottenburger Strasse 19, 37085, Göttingen, Germany.

DÜRR, Karl Friedrich; Singer (Bass-baritone); b. 1949, Stuttgart, Germany. *Education:* Studied German Literature and Political Science, receiving his PhD in 1978. *Career:* Debut: Sang Antonio in Le nozze di Figaro at Ludwigsburg; Studied further with Gunther Reich and sang with the Stuttgart Staatsoper from 1980, notably as Rihm's Jakob Lenz, Mozart's Figaro, Leporello, Don Alfonso, Klingsor (Parisifal) and Biterolf (Tannhäuser), Alfio (Cavalleria), Monterone, Zuniga in Carmen, Krishna in Satyagrapha by Philip Glass, Faninial (Rosenkavalier); Animal trainer and Athlete in Lulu by Berg; Kothner in Die Meistersinger; Appearances at the Ludwisburg and Schwetzingen Festivals and with the ensemble of the Stuttgart Staatsoper on tour to Russia (Zimmermann's Die Soldaten); Further engagements as Kaspar in Der Freischütz, Kurwenal, and Wozzeck; Concerts in Kassel, Trieste, Berlin and New York; 1989; Vienna Festival 1990, as Krenek's Diktator and as the Boxer in Schwergewicht; Sang Don Alfonso at Stuttgart, 1991; Also in Paris, Bastille Opera (Die Soldaten) and Semper-Oper, Dresden (Leporello) and other German opera houses such as Düsseldorf and Bonn; Sang in Debussy's Chute de la Maison Usher at Stuttgart, 1996; Sacristan in Tosca and Bartolo in Il Barbiere di Siviglia at Stuttgart, 1998; Appointed Kammersänger at Stuttgart Staatstheater, 1998; Season 2000–01 as Offenbach's Crespel at Stuttgart, and in Donizetti's Le Convenienze and I Pazzi per progetto. *Recordings:* Eisenhardt in Die Soldaten. *Address:* c/o Staatstheater Stuttgart, Oberer Schlossgarten 6, 7000 Stuttgart, Germany.

DÜRR, Walther; Musicologist; b. 27 April 1932, Berlin, Germany; m. Vittoria Bortolotti 1960; two d. *Education:* PhD, Tübingen Univ., 1956. *Career:* Lecturer, Bologna Univ., Italy, 1957; Asst, Tübingen Univ., Germany, 1962; Gen. Ed., Neue Schubert-Ausgabe, 1965; Hon. Prof., Tübingen Univ.; broadcasts for radio stations Deutsche Welle, Cologne, Südwestfunk, Baden-Baden; mem. Society for Musical Research, International Musicological Society. *Publications:* Rhythmus und Metrum im italienischen Madrigal insbesondere bei Luca Marenzio, 1956; Serie IV (Lieder) of Neue Schubert Ausgabe, 1966; Franz Schuberts Werke in Abschriften; Liederalben und Sammlungen, 1975; Der Kleine Deutsch (with Werner Aderhold and Arnold Feil), 1983; Das Deutsche Sololied im 19 Jahrhundert, 1984; Franz Schubert (with Arnold Feil), 1991; Zeichen Setzung Aufsätze zur Musikalischen Poetik, 1992; Musik und Sprache, 1994; Schubert Handbook, editor with Andreas Krause, 1997; Schubert und das Biedermeier, Festschrift Walther Dürr, 2002, ed. Michael Kube, Werner Aderhold, Walburga Litschauer. *Contributions:* Die Musikforschung; Archiv für Musikwissenchaft; Österreichische Musikzeitschrift; 19th Century Music; MGG; New Grove Dictionary of Music and Musicians; numerous hon. anniversary works and reviews. *Address:* Hausserstrasse 140, 72076 Tübingen, Germany.

DUSSAUT, Thérèse; Pianist; b. 20 Sept. 1939, Versailles, France; m. Claude Lemaréchal. *Education:* Conservatoire National Supérieur, Paris; Musikhochschule, Stuttgart. *Career:* Debut: 1951, Salle Gaveau, Paris, with orchestra conducted by Georges Tzipine; Regular concert appearances, both solo and orchestral; Has undertaken several world tours including one for the Ravel centenary, 1975; Professor at Toulouse Conservatory; mem, Juries of International Competitions: Tchaikovsky, Moscow; Munich; Szymanowski, Poland; Horowitz, Ukraine; Kraïnev, Ukraine; Member of Summer Music Academy, Kiev; Arts-Sciences-Lettres, Paris; Triptyque, Paris. *Compositions:* Rameau Pièces en Concert by Billaudot; Rameau Fêtes d'Hébé by Billaudot. *Recordings:* Rameau Complete Works; Works by Ravel, Tchaikovsky and Shostakovich. *Contributions:* French Pianism–an Historical Perspective, Charles Timbrell. *Honours:* First Prize, International Piano Competition, Munich. *Current Management:* Liegner, New York, USA. *Address:* 14 rue Saint Victor, 75005 Paris, France.

DUSSEK, Michael; Concert Pianist; b. 1958, England. *Career:* Chamber musician throughout Europe, Japan and Australia, and Canada, notably with such soloists as Cho-Liang Lin, Anne Akiko Meyers, Kurt Nikkanen and Ofra Harnoy; Recent recitals in the Amsterdam Concertgebouw, Tokyo, Madrid, Milan and Vienna; Engagements throughout the United Kingdom with the cellist Alexander Baillie, oboist Douglas Boyd and violinist Lorraine McAslan; Concerto soloist with the London Mozart Players at the Festival Hall and work for BBC Radio 3 as chamber musician and accompanist; Purcell Room recital 1993 with Markus Stocker, featuring music by Schumann, Brahms, Liszt and Martinů. *Recordings:* Brahms Piano Trios and Horn Trio with the Dussek Trio, contemporary Finnish music with the Edymion Ensemble, cello sonatas with Ofra Harnoy and cello sonatas by Reger; Professor, Royal Academy of Music.

DUSSELJEE, Kor-Jan; Singer (Tenor); b. 1965, Netherlands. *Education:* Graduated Dutch Academy of Arts, 1988; Masterclasses with Schwarzkopf and Hartmut Holl. *Career:* Concerts throughout the Netherlands, from 1988; Besançon and Savonlinna Festivals, Switzerland and Germany; Opera engagements in Germany as Wilhelm Meister, Tamino, Don Ottavio, Lancelot in Purcell's King Arthur and Leopold in La Juive; Architect in Reimann's Melusine at Dresden and Munich; Season 1998–99 as First Jew in Salome and Francesco in Benvenuto Cellini, both with Rotterdam Philharmonic under Gergiev; Further appearances with the Scottish CO, Dresden Staatskapelle and Bamberg Symphony Orchestra. *Address:* c/o Netherlands Opera, Waterlooplein 22, 1011 Amsterdam, Netherlands.

DUTILLEUX, Henri; French composer; b. 22 Jan. 1916, Angers; s. of Paul and Thérèse (née Koszul) Dutilleux; m. Geneviève Joy 1946. *Education:* Conservatoire Nat. de Musique, Paris. *Career:* Dir Service Créations Musicales Radiodiffusion Française 1945–63; Prof. of Composition Ecole Normale de Musique, Paris 1961–, Pres. 1969–74; Assoc. Prof. Conservatoire Nat. Supérieur de Musique, Paris 1970–71; fmr mem. UNESCO Music Council; assoc. mem. Royal Acad. of Music, Belgium. *Compositions:* Sonata for Piano 1948, First Symphony 1951, Le Loup (Ballet) 1953, Second Symphony (Le Double) 1959, Métaboles (for orchestra) 1964, Cello Concerto: Tout un monde lointain 1970, Figures de Résonances (for two pianos) 1971, Preludes for Piano 1974, Ainsi la Nuit (for string quartet) 1976, Timbres, Espace, Mouvement (for orchestra) 1978, 3 Strophes sur le nom de Sacher (for cello) 1981, L'Arbre des Songes (violin concerto) 1985, Le Jeu des contraires (for piano) 1988, Mystère de l'instant (for 24 strings and cimbalom) 1989, Les Citations (for oboe, harpsichord, double-bass and percussion) 1991, The Shadows of Time (for orchestra) 1997, Sur le même accord for violin and orchestra 2002, Correspondances for song and orchestra 2003. *Publications:* Mystère 1997, Mémoire des sons 1997. *Honours:* hon. mem. American Acad. and Inst. of Arts and Letters, Accad. di Santa Cecilia, Rome, RAM, London; Grand Prix de Rome 1938, Grand Prix du Disque 1957, 1958, 1966, 1968, 1976, 1978, 1984, Grand Prix Nat. de la Musique 1967, Prix de la Ville de Paris 1974, Koussevitzky Int. Recording Award 1976, World Record Award (Montreux) 1983; Prix Int. Maurice Ravel 1987, Grand Prix, Music Council UNESCO 1987, Praemium Imperiale Japan 1994; Grand Officier, Légion d'honneur, Grand-Croix de la Légion d'honneur 2004, Commdr Ordre Nat. du Mérite, des Arts et des Lettres, du Mérite Culturel de Monaco. *Address:* 12 rue St-Louis-en-l'Isle, 75004 Paris, France. *Telephone:* 1-43-26-39-14.

DUTOIT, Charles E., OC; Swiss conductor and music director; b. 7 Oct. 1936, Lausanne; s. of Edmond Dutoit and Berthe Dutoit (née Laederman); one s. one d. *Education:* Conservatoire of Lausanne and Geneva, Accademia Musicale Chigiana, Siena, Italy, Conservatorio Benedetto Marcello, Venice, Italy and Berks. Music Center, Tanglewood, USA. *Career:* Assoc. Conductor Berne Symphony Orchestra 1964, Principal and Artistic Dir 1966–78; Associate Conductor Tonhalle Orchestra Zurich 1966; Conductor and Artistic Dir Zurich Radio Orchestra 1964; Artistic Dir Nat. Symphony Orchestra of Mexico and Göteborg Symphony Orchestra 1977–2002; Artistic Dir Montreal Symphony Orchestra 1977–2002; Prin. Guest Conductor Minn. Orchestra 1983–84, 1985–86; Artistic Dir and Prin. Conductor Philadelphia Orchestra summer season, Mann Music Center 1991–2001, Saratoga Springs 1991–; Music Dir Orchestre Nat. de France 1990–2001; Prin. Guest Conductor NHK Symphony Orchestra, Tokyo 1996–, Music Dir 1998–; over 125 recordings since 1980, winning over 40 int. awards; operatic début Covent Garden (conducting Faust) 1983; Principal Conductor 1996 and Music Dir, NHK Symphony Orchestra, Tokyo 1998–2003; Guest Conductor of all major orchestras in USA, Europe, South America, Far East Asia, Australia and Israel. *Recordings:* 120 discs with various orchestras including Falla's Three Cornered Hat and El amor Brujo, The Planets, Tchaikovsky's 1st Piano Concerto, Saint-Saëns 3rd Symphony, Bizet's L'Arlesienne and Carmen Suites, Gubaidulina Offertorium with Boston Symphony, Symphonies by Honegger, Roussel's Symphonies with French Nat. Orchestra, Saint-Saëns Piano Concertos, Suppé Overtures, Berlioz' Les Troyens. *Honours:* Honorary Citizen of the city of Philadelphia; Commdr Ordre des Arts et des Lettres, Honorary Officer of the Order of Canada, Grand Prix du Président de la République (France); DMus hc (Montreal) 1984, (Laval) 1985; Grand Prix de l'Académie du disque français, High Fidelity Int. Record Critics' Award, Montreux Record Award, Japan Record Acad. Award, Artist of the Year (Canada Music Council) 1982. *Address:* POBox 5088 St Laurent, Montréal, QC H4L 4Z7 Canada.

DUTT, Hank; Violist; b. 4 Nov. 1952, Muscatine, Iowa, USA. *Career:* Joined the Kronos String Quartet, 1977; Many performances of contemporary music, including the premieres of works of John Cage (30 Pieces for string quartet), Pauline Oliveros (The Wheel of Time) and Terry Riley (G-Song, Sunrise of the Planetary Dream Collector and Cadenzas on the Night Plain); Formerly Quartet-in-Residence at Mills College, Oakland; From 1982 resident quartet at the University of Southern California; Appearances at the Monterrey Jazz Festival, Carnegie Recital Hall, San Quentin Prison and London's South Bank; New York debut 1984; Noted for 'cross-over' performances of jazz and popular music in arrangement. *Address:* c/o UCLA Music Department, University Park, Los Angeles, CA 90089, USA.

DUTTON, Brenton (Price); Composer and Tubist; b. 20 March 1950, Saskatoon, Canada; 2 s., 1 d. *Education:* BM, MM, Oberlin Conservatory of Music. *Career:* Tubist with Cleveland Orchestra, 1968–74; L'Orchestra Symphonique de Quebec, 1971–74, San Diego Symphony, 1980–; Solo Recital appearances throughout Canada, USA, Europe; Professor of Music, San Diego State University, 1980–, California Institute of the Arts, 1981–84; Brass Coach for the Jeunesses Musicales World Orchestra, in Europe, North and South America, 1986–1992; Tubist and Artistic Director of Westwind Brass, 1993–. *Compositions:* Over 100 including Symphony No. 2, 1972; Symphony No. 3, 1974; Song of the Moon, solo flute; On Looking Back, Brass Quintet; December Set, Woodwind Quintet; Dialogues of the sybarites, 3 trumpets and organ; Circles; Chinese Reflections; A Rolling Silence; Songs of Love, all song cycles for baritone and chamber ensemble; Additional Works: Ecq theow Variants, brass quintet; On A Darkling Plain, brass quintet; Song of the Sun, solo viola; Hotel Europejski Suite, violin, piano; Gilgamesh, opera in 3 acts, 1977–78. *Recordings:* Symphony No. 5 Dark Spirals, 1985; Character Dances and proud Music of the Storm, 1986; Carnival of Venice, brass quintet, 1983; Olympic Entrance, Tuba Suite, 1984; The Siren of Urak for viola and brass quintet, 1998; Tuba Concerto I and II, 1998; many radio and television broadcasts; Kraków, Summer; Quebec, Spring, both for string orchestra. *Publications:* Over 70 including, Sonata in Fact for Trumpet, Piano; Resonances for Tuba Quartet; Madrigals, Book I, 1998; Tuba Concerto II, 1998; And the Halls Resound, 1998. *Address:* School of Music and Dance, San Diego State University, San Diego, CA 92182, USA.

DUTTON, Lawrence; Violist; b. 9 May 1954, New York, USA. *Career:* mem., Emerson String Quartet, 1976–; premiere concert at Alice Tully Hall, New York, 1977, with works by Mozart, Smetana and Bartók; European debut at Spoleto, Italy in 1981; Quartet-in-Residence at Smithsonian Institute, Washington, 1980–, at the Hartt School, 1981–, and at Spoleto and Aspen Festivals, 1981–; first resident quartet at Chamber Music Society of Lincoln Center, season 1982–83; tour of Japan and Australia 1987; many performances of works by Bartók, including all six quartets in a single evening, and contemporary works; premieres include Mario Davidovsky's 4th Quartet and works by Maurice Wright and George Tsontakis; Bartók's 4th quartet and Brahms' C minor, London, 2001. *Recordings:* Walter Piston's Concerto for string quartet, winds and percussion; works by Andrew Imbrie, Henry Howell, Roy Harris and Gunther Schuller; Bartók's Six Quartets.

DUVAL, Denise; Singer (Soprano); b. 23 Oct. 1921, Paris, France. *Education:* Studied at the Bordeaux Conservatory. *Career:* Debut: Bordeaux 1943, as Lola in Cavalleria Rusticana; Sang at the Folies Bergères, Paris, 1944; Paris Opéra from 1947, notably as Salomé in Hérodiade by Massenet, and as Blanche in the French premiere of Dialogues des Carmelites, 1947; Sang at the Opéra-Comique Paris in the 1947 premiere of Poulenc's Les Mamelles de Tiresias: returned 1959 for the premiere of La Voix Humaine (repeated at La Scala 1960); Paris 1949, in the premiere of Le oui des jeunes Filles, by Hahn-Busser; Other roles were Thais, the Princess in Marouf by Rabaud, Concepcion, and Portia in La Marchande de Venise by Hahn; Edinburgh Festival with the Glyndebourne company in 1960, as Elle in La Voix Humaine; Glyndebourne Festival 1962–63, as Mélisande; Guest appearances in Milan, Vienna, Brussels, Amsterdam and Buenos Aires; Retired 1965 and became Professor at the Ecole Française de Musique in Paris. *Recordings:* L'Heure Espagnole, Les mamelles de Tirésias (Columbia); Dialogues des Carmélites (HMV).

DUVILLIER-WABLE, Laurent, LLL; French composer; b. 7 Oct. 1947, Nîmes; m. Françoise Gripois 1975; one s. one d. *Education:* studied piano with Suzanne Joly, composition with Michel Puig, René Leibowitz and Arnold Schoenberg. *Career:* began composing, self-taught, 1960; Professor of Music, Ecole de l'Abbaye au Bois, Paris, 1966–68; Joined the Board, 1969, Director-General, 1981–97, Société des Gens de Lettres; Director-General, Société Civile des Auteurs Multimédia, 1981–; SACEM, Paris. *Compositions include:* Possibilités I for 2 pianos, 1971; Possibilités II for 2 tenor instruments, Possibilités III for violoncello and piano, Possibilités IV, Le chant de l'Unsui, for soprano and piano, 4 hands, Possibilités V, violoncello solo, Possibilités VI for piano, 4 hands, recorded by ORTF, broadcast on France-Culture, 1973; Approche I for flute and violin, Approche II for soprano and flute, Variable I for 2 pianos, 1973; Variable I, piano solo version, 1974; Rite, music for mime and dance, 1975; Parcours, film music, 1977; Sonata for flute and percussion, 1992; Concertino pour neuf, A mon ami musicien Jean Villatte, commission, recorded by Radio France, 1993; Sonata II, De la forêt des stèles, 1996. *Publications:* Sonata II, De la forêt des stèles. *Address:* 150 rue de Tolbiac, 75013 Paris, France.

DUYKERS, John; Singer (Tenor); b. 1941, Canada. *Career:* Seattle Opera from 1966 (Masetto in Don Giovanni, 1968); Vancouver Opera from

1968, Edmonton from 1969; Sang Mao Tse-tung in premiere productions of Nixon in China by John Adams at Houston, San Francisco and Edinburgh, 1987; St Louis, 1989, and Philadelphia, 1992, in the premieres of Under the Double Moon and Tania, by A Davis; Chicago and Long Beach Opera, 1994, in The Gambler by Prokofiev; Sellem in The Rake's Progress at the Théâtre du Châtelet, Paris, 1996; Season 2000–01 in the premiere of In the Penal Colony by Philip Glass, at Seattle, as Strauss's Herod at Philadelphia, and Weill's Fatty at Genoa; Other roles include Strauss's Herod and Aegisthus. *Address:* c/o Long Beach Opera, 6372 Pacific Coast Highway, Long Beach, CA 90803, USA.

DVORACEK, Jiri; Composer, Professor and Music Administrator; b. 8 June 1928, Vamberk, Czechoslovakia. *Education:* Studied organ, Prague Conservatory, 1943–47; Studied composition with Ridky and Dobias, Prague Academy of Music, 1949–53. *Career:* Teacher 1953–67, Senior Lecturer 1967–78, Professor of Composition and Head, Composition Department 1979–90, Prague Academy of Music; President, Union of Czech Composers and Concert Artists, 1987–89. *Compositions:* Opera: Aphrodite's Island, 1967; Orchestral: 2 Symphonies, 1953, 1986; Symphonic Suite, 1958; Concertante Suite, 1962; Ex Post for piano and orchestra, 1963; Quattro Episodi, 1971; I am Living and Singing, cantata for soloists, choir, reciter, children's choir and orchestra, 1978; Giubilo, 1983; Concert for violin and orchestra, 1989; Chamber: Sonata Capricciosa for violin and piano, 1956; Invention for trombone and piano or small orchestra, 1961; Meditations for clarinet and percussion, 1964; Music for harp, 1970; Due per duo for horn and piano, 1970; Dialogues for flute and piano, 1973; Brass Quintet, 1973; Music for viola and piano, 1976; Sonata for trumpet and piano, 1977; Organ Sonata, 1979; Accordion Sonata, 1979; Theme and Variations for trombone and piano, 1980; Prague Transformations for wind quintet, 1981; Clarinet and Piano Play, 1982; Violin and Organ Play, 1984; Partita for oboe and bassoon, 1986; Partita Piccola, for violin, guitar and harmonica, 1987; Three Movements for string quartet, 1990; Trio for clarinet, violin and piano, 1994; Choral music; Songs. *Recordings:* Various compositions recorded. *Address:* Antala Staska 1015/43, 140 00 Prague 4, Czech Republic.

DVORÁKOVÁ, Ludmila; Singer (Soprano); b. 11 July 1923, Kolin, Czechoslovakia; m. Rudolf Vasata, deceased 1982. *Education:* Studied with Jarmila Vavrdova at The Prague Conservatory. *Career:* Debut: Ostrava 1949, as Katya Kabanova; Sang in Ostrava as Rusalka, Elisabeth de Valois, Countess Almaviva and Aida; Sang in Bratislava and at the Smetana Theatre, Prague, from 1952; Member, Prague National Opera, 1954–57 as Milada in Dalibor, Elisabeth, Leonore, Senta, and in Czech operas; Sang Leonore at the Vienna Staatsoper, 1956; Sang at Berlin Staatsoper, 1960–84 as Brünnhilde, Venus, Elisabeth de Valois, Kundry, Isolde, Ortrud, Tosca and the Marschallin; Karlsruhe 1964 as Isolde; Bayreuth Festival, 1965–71 as Gutrune, Brünnhilde, Venus, Ortrud and Kundry; Covent Garden, 1966–71 as Brünnhilde, Isolde and Leonore; Metropolitan Opera, 1965–68; Paris Opéra, 1966; Elektra, Graz 1973; Opera München, La Scala, Opera Roma, San Francisco, Buenos Aires, Deutsche Oper am Rhein Düsseldorf, 1973–74; Vienna Staatsoper, 1964–85; Salome, Herodias, Berlin, 1979–; Jenůfa, Kostelnicka, 1980; Visited Japan, 1983, 1984, with the State Operas of Berlin and Hamburg; Jenůfa, Vienna, 1984; Other roles included: Katerina Izmailova, (Vienna, 1965), Ariadne and The Dyer's Wife in Die Frau ohne Schatten. *Recordings:* Gutrune in Götterdämmerung, from Bayreuth; Wagner Recital. *Address:* 16200 Prague 6, Na Orechovce 14, Czech Republic.

DVORSKY, Miroslav; Singer (Tenor); b. 1960, Partizánske, Czechoslovakia. *Education:* Studied in Bratislava and Milan. *Career:* Debut: Bratislava, 1983, as Nemorino; Sang in the 1987 premiere of Cikker's The Insect May and guested at Edinburgh, 1990, as Gounod's Faust; Theater am Gärtnerplatz, Munich, from 1994, notably as Des Grieux in Manon; Rome, 1994, as the Prince in Rusalka and Rodolfo in La Bohème; Toronto, 1996, as the Duke of Mantua; Many appearances in operettas by Lehar and Johann Strauss; Season 2000–01 as Smetana's Jenik at Toronto, Ismaele in Nabucco at the Vienna Staatsoper, Oronte in I Lombardi at Marseille and a production of the Verdi Requiem at the Deutsche Oper, Berlin; Rodolfo in Florence and the Dvořák Requiem with the Orchestre de Paris; Sang Števa in Jenůfa at Hamburg, 2000, Laca for Washington Opera; President, Alzheimer Foundation, Slovakia. *Recordings include:* Das Land des Lächelns; Miroslav Dvorsky-Arias. *Current Management:* Austroconcert International. *Address:* c/o Austroconcert International, Gluckgasse 1, 1010 Vienna, Austria.

DVORSKÝ, Peter; Opera Singer (Tenor); b. 25 Sept. 1951, Partizanske, Czechoslovakia; m. Marta Varsova, 19 July 1975, 2 d. *Education:* Graduated, Conservatory Bratislava, 1973; Studied at La Scala, Milan, 1975–76. *Career:* Debut: Slovak National Theatre, Bratislava, in Onegin, 1973; 5th Prize, Tchaikovsky Competition (Laureate), Moscow, 1974; 1st Prize, Geneva, 1975; La Traviata, Metropolitan Opera, 1977; Rigoletto, Covent Garden London, 1978; Traviata, Rigoletto at the Bolsov Theatre, Moscow, 1978; La Bohème, La Scala, Milan, 1979; Elisir

D'Amore, Vienna State Opera, 1980; La Bohème, La Scala, 1981; Manon, with Vienna State Opera, 1984; La Bohème, La Scala, 1985; Adriana Lecouvreur, 1989; Verdi Operatic Festival with Sherrill Milnes, Tokyo, 1992; Puccini Operatic Festival, 1994; Regular appearances in: Bratislava, Prague, Budapest, Moscow, Vienna, Milan, London, New York, Munich, San Francisco, Chicago, Frankfurt; Sang at Covent Garden from 1978, as Alfredo 1986, and Lensky and Riccardo 1988; Metropolitan New York and Barcelona, 1987, as Rodolfo and Edgardo; Salzburg Festival 1989, as Cavaradossi; Sang Des Grieux at Modena and Barcelona, 1990; Maggio Musica Florence, 1992, as Don Alvaro in La Forza del Destino; Ballo in Maschera, Buenos Aires, 1994; Concerts with Caballé and Milnes, 1996; Tosca, La Bohème and concert, Japan, 1997; Puccini, Manon Lescaut at Vienna, 1986, Barcelona, 1990 and Modena, 1990 with M Freni; Season 1999 in Suchon's Whirlpool at Bratislava and Janáček's Jenůfa at the National Theatre, Prague; mem, President and Founder, Harmony Foundation, health and rehabilitation centre. *Recordings:* Janáček: Makropulos Case, Jenůfa, Kata Kabanova, all with Charles Mackerras; Verdi: Otello, Cassio with Georg Solti, La Bohème, Bartered Bride, Madama Butterfly, Elisir d'amore; Traviata; Dvořák: Stabat Mater, Requiem; Recital 1, 2, 3; La Bohème; Gounod: Faust; E Suchon: The Whirlpool; Manon Lecsaut; P Mascagni: Cavalleria Rusticana; J Massenet: Werther; G Donizetti: Elisir d'amore; G Verdi: Requiem. *Honours:* People's Artist, CSSR Music-Piano. *Current Management:* Slovkoncert, Slovak Artistic Agency, Bratislava, Slovakia. *Address:* J. Hronca 1a, 841 02 Bratislava, Slovakia.

DWORCHAK, Harry; Singer (Bass-baritone); b. 1947, Hershey, Pennsylvania, USA. *Education:* AVA, Philadelphia, 1970. *Career:* Sang first at the Barcelona Opera (from 1970), then throughout North America, with a 1982 debut at the New York City Opera; Théâtre du Châtelet, Paris, 1982, as Banquo; Welsh National Opera, 1985, as Oroveso; Sang Ferrando in Trovatore at the Metropolitan in 1988, at the Munich Staatsoper, 1992; Der fliegende Holländer, Frankfurt, 1991, Washington DC, 1995; Scarpia, Covent Garden, 1996; Bayerische Staatsoper, 1997; Sang Jochanaan (Salome), Austin, Texas, 1999; Season 2000–01 engaged as Wotan in Rheingold; Season 2001–02, Metropolitan Opera as Count Waldner in Arabella and Geisterbote in Die Frau ohne Schatten; Der Landgraf in Tannhäuser for Tulsa Opera, 2001; Other roles include the Commendatore, Monteverdi's Seneca, Bellini's Capulet, Mephistopheles (Faust), Don Quichotte, Daland, Wagner's Dutchman, and Dosifey in Khovanshchina; Further engagements as Wotan, Rheingold, Augsburg; Wotan, Walküre, Augsburg; Der Wanderer; Pizarro in Fidelio, Buenos Aires, entire Ring Cycle. *Recordings:* Das

Schloss, Bayerische Staatsoper, Munich; Don Alfonso in Così fan tutte, European Television Broadcast. *Honours:* Richard Tucker Award, 1987; Carnegie Hall Concert, 1987. *Current Management:* John J. Miller, New York. *Address:* 15 West 72nd Street, New York, NY 10023, USA.

DYACHKOV, Yegor; Cellist; b. 1974, Moscow, Russia. *Education:* Studies with Alexander Fedorchenko, Moscow Conservatory, Radu Aldulescu, Rome, André Navarra, Vienna, Yuli Turovsky, Montreal, Boris Pergamenschikow, Cologne. *Career:* Numerous Recitals in the Former Soviet Union, Italy, Latin America, Taiwan, USA, Canada; Guest Soloist with Montreal Symphony Orchestra, Metropolitan Orchestra of Montreal, Orchestre Symphonique de Quebec, National Arts Centre Orchestra in Ottawa, I Musici de Montreal; Concert Performances in Quebec, Ontario, New Brunswick; Performances at the Lanaudiere International Music Festival, Domaine Forget International Music Festival, Chamber Music Festival in Ste-Pétronille, Orford International Music Festival, Scotia Festival of Music, Mozarteum in Caracas; Vancouver Chamber Music Festival; Evian Festival, 1999. *Recordings:* Glazunov's Concerto Ballata; Strauss and Pfitzner Sonatas. *Current Management:* Latitude 45 Arts Promotion Inc. *Address:* c/o Latitude 45, Arts Promotion Inc, 109 St Joseph Blvd West, Montreal, Quebec H2T 2P7, Canada.

DYAKOVSKI, Lubomir; Singer (Tenor); b. 1 March 1950, Dupnitza, Bulgaria; m. Rossitza Ivanova Dyakovska, 1 s., 1 d. *Education:* Graduated from Vocal Faculty, Bulgarian Musical Academy, 1973. *Career:* Debut: Ernesto in Don Pasquale by Donizetti, 1970; Permanently engaged in Russe and Pleven; Numerous performances throughout Europe; Over 40 tenor solo performances in Masses, Oratorios and Requiems including Lensky in Eugene Onegin, Nadir in the Pearl Fishers by Bizet and Almaviva in Il Barbiere di Siviglia by Rossini; Sang with all major symphony orchestras and choruses in Bulgaria; Performances with major Bulgarian and European television and radio companies; Sang in studio recording of The Suffering of Jesus for Radio Zagreb; Participated in opening of Summer Music Festival in Dubrovnik, 1991; Soloist for Bolshoi Don Kosaken Ensemble, performing throughout Switzerland, Austria and Germany; mem, Rotary International; Union of Musicians in Bulgaria. *Recordings:* Russian songs and arias; Songs of Petrarca by Liszt, St Matthew Passion, Night of Walpurgis and Bach's Magnificat; The Golden Cockerel, Rimsky-Korsakov; Eugene Onegin; Prince Igor by Borodin; Evangelist in Christmas Oratorio by J. S. Bach; Handel's Messiah. *Honours:* Numerous Government and state awards. *Address:* c-x Storgozia, bl 72, entr A, ap 15, 5800 Pleven, Bulgaria.

E

EAGLE, David Malcolm, BMus, MMus, PhD; composer, flautist and teacher; b. 21 Dec. 1955, Montreal, QC, Canada; m. Hope Lee 1980. *Education:* McGill Univ., studied flute with Cindy Shuter, composition with Bengt Hamnbraeus, Donald Steven, Hochschule für Musik, Freiburg with Klaus Huber and Brian Ferneyhough, Univ. of California at Berkeley. *Career:* freelance composer; works played, Canada, Holland Festival, 1985, Germany, Switzerland; Broadcasts on CBC Radio Canada, BBC, Hessischer Rundfunk, Swiss Radio, KRO (Netherlands); invited Guest Composer, Boswil Kunstlerhaus, Switzerland, 1985; commissions from Montreal Chamber Orchestra, Array-Music, Toronto Consort, many individuals; co-ordinator, Electro-acoustic Music Studio, Assistant Professor, Composition, Theory, University of Calgary, 1990–. *Compositions:* Zhu Fong, string quartet, 1978; Strata-Vari for 14 strings, 1980; Within for solo cello, 1982; Strahlen for organ, 1983; Aura for septet, 1984; Renew'd at ev'ry glance for variable instruments, 1985; Toccare for harpsichord, 1986; Luminous Voices for early music ensemble and tape, 1987–88; Crossing Currents for orchestra, 1991; Hsuan for guzheng and tape, 1992; Nohocki for flute and cello, 1993; Music for AXIO, Open This Door, for AXIO (midi-controller), 1993; Sounding after Time for violin, cello, piano, computer, synthesizer, 1993. *Address:* 27 Stradwick Rise SW, Calgary, Alberta T3H 1G6, Canada.

EAGLEN, Jane; British singer (soprano); b. 4 April 1960, Lincoln, England. *Education:* Royal Northern Coll. of Music; studies with Joseph Ward. *Career:* debut, ENO in Patience, 1984; engagements with ENO as Leonora in Il Trovatore and Elizabeth I in Mary Stuart; Western Australia Opera, Perth, as Tosca; Lyric Opera of Queensland, Brisbane, as Madama Butterfly; Scottish Opera, as Donna Anna; London Promenade Concert debut, 1989, as Sieglinde in Act III of Die Walküre; sang Brünnhilde, 1991; Tosca for ENO, 1990; Donna Anna and Amelia (Ballo), Bologne, 1991; sang Mathilde in Guillaume Tell at Covent Garden, Geneva, 1992; Scottish Opera as Norma in a new production of Bellini's opera; Tosca, Buenos Aires, 1993, then Donna Anna in Don Giovanni, Vienna State Opera, and title role in Norma, Seattle Opera; Brünnhilde in Die Walküre, Opera Pacific, California, and Vienna State Opera, 1994; Norma with Riccardo Muti, Ravenna Festival, 1994; title role in Ariadne, with ENO, 1994; Brünnhilde in Die Walküre, La Scala, Milan, 1994, and with Lyric Opera of Chicago, 1995; Amelia in Un Ballo in Maschera, Opéra de Paris Bastille, 1995; La Gioconda, Chicago, and Tristan and Isolde at Seattle, 1998; concert appearances at the Wigmore Hall, Festival Hall and the Barbican Centre; Verdi Requiem and Mahler 8th Symphony; recitals for the Wagner Societies of London, New York and Buenos Aires; sang Isolde and Turandot at the New York Met 2000, 2003, and in Puerto Rico 2004; Turandot at Covent Garden 2001; complete Ring Cycle for Seattle Opera 2001, Met and Lyric Opera of Chicago 2001–05; London Proms, 2002; sang La Vestale for ENO 2003, Ortrud in Lohengrin, and Ariadne, in Seattle 2004. *Recordings:* Die Flammen; Medea in Corinto; Norma, with Muti; Tosca; Turandot; Mozart and Strauss; Bellini and Wagner; Song Cycles by Strauss, Berg and Wagner; Der fliegende Holländer, conducted by Barenboim, 2002, Tannhauser 2002 (Gramophone Award for best complete opera). *Honours:* Peter Moores Foundation Scholarship; Countess of Munster Award; Carl Rosa Trust Award. *Current Management:* AOR Management Inc., 6910 Roosevelt Way NE, PMB 221, Seattle, WA 98115, USA. *Telephone:* (206) 729-6160 (office). *Fax:* (206) 985-8499 (office). *E-mail:* jennyrose@aormanagementuk.com (office). *Website:* www.aormanagementuk.com (office).

EARLE, Roderick; British singer (baritone); b. 29 Jan. 1952, Winchester, England; s. of Dennis and Fenella Earle; 1 s., 1 d. *Education:* Chorister, Winchester Cathedral; St John's College, Cambridge; Royal College of Music, London; Further study with Otakar Kraus. *Career:* With English National Opera, 1978–80; debut Royal Opera Covent Garden as Antonio in Le Nozze di Figaro, 1980; joined Royal Opera, sung over 60 roles including Schaunard, Abimelech, Orestes, Monterone, the Bonze, Brander, Harasta (Cunning Little Vixen), Kothner, the Philosopher (Cherubin), King Fisher, (Midsummer Marriage), Alberich, Siegfried and Götterdämmerung; Has appeared with all major British companies, toured to Japan, South Korea, Greece and Finland with the Royal Opera and appeared in festivals at Edinburgh, Buxton, Israel, Athens, Flanders; Has sung Kothner, Rangoni and Abimelech at Teatro Regio, Turin, and Altair in British premiere of Strauss's Die Ägyptische Helena and Ford at Garsington; other appearances include A Midsummer Night's Dream and Turandot (Rome Opera), Der Fliegende Hollander (Opera de Massy), Amonasro, Alfio and Tonio (Royal Albert Hall), Germont and Scarpia (Holland Park Opera), Ford and the Count Figaro (New Zealand Opera), Rigoletto (Opera Zuid) and Monterone (ENO); Sang Melchior Amahl and the Night Visitors at Sadler's Wells. *Recordings include:* Ferneyhough's Transit; Rossini's Stabat Mater with

Richard Hickox; Les Troyens with Sir Colin Davis. *Films:* appeared in videos of La Fanciulla des West, Manon Lescaut, Andrea Chenier, Der Rosenkavalier (Solti), Carmen (Mehta), Salome (Downes), Otello and Traviata (Solti); soundtrack of film Meeting Venus. *Honours:* Musician of the Year Award, Greater London Arts Asscn;; various Grammy Awards. *Current Management:* Musichall, Vicarage Way, Ringmer, BN8 5LA, England. *Address:* St Raphael, 155 Maldon Road, Colchester . CO3 3BJ (home). *Telephone:* (1206) 574476 (home). *E-mail:* earle@ukonline.co.uk (home).

EAST, Leslie Charles, BMus, MMus, FGSM; Music Publisher; b. 8 July 1949, Doncaster, England; m. Lilija Zobens; two d. *Education:* Kingsbury County Grammar School, London, King's Coll. London. *Career:* visiting lecturer and concert organizer, City of London 1973–75; Dir of Music, Guildhall School of Music and Drama, London 1975–87; Publishing Dir, Novello and Co Ltd 1987–98; Man. Ed. 1998–99 and then Dir of Publishing, Associated Board of the Royal Schools of Music (Publishing) Ltd 1999–; Chair., Soc. for the Promotion of New Music 1978–83; Arts Council Panel mem. 1988–92; Chair., New Macnaughten Concerts 1989–99, Early Music Centre and Network 1994–2001, City Music Soc. 1998–; mem. Worshipful Company of Musicians, Royal Soc. of Musicians, Royal Philharmonic Soc., Asscn of British Choral Directors, Royal Overseas League, Royal Musical Asscn, The Peter Warlock Soc.. *Honours:* Freeman of the Musicians' Company 1998. *Address:* ABRSM (Publishing) Ltd, 24 Portland Place, London, W1B 1LU, England (office). *Telephone:* (20) 7467-8234 (office). *Fax:* (20) 7467-8833 (office). *E-mail:* leslieeast@abrsm.ac.uk (office).

EASTBURN, Susanna de Martelly, BA, MPhil; Festival Director; b. 6 Jan. 1969, Truro, England. *Education:* Penair School, Cornwall, Millfield School, Somerset, King's Coll. Cambridge. *Career:* International Promotions Man., Chester Music/Novello & Co. Ltd 1994–2001; Artistic Dir, Huddersfield Contemporary Music Festival 2001–; non-exec. positions include Yorkshire Regional Arts Council 2002–; mem. British Arts Festivals Asscns (exec. bd mem.), Réseau Varèse (exec. bd mem.), Soc. for Promotion of New Music (vice-chair.), Int. Soc. for Contemporary Music (chair., British Section). *Address:* Huddersfield Contemporary Music Festival, Department of Music, Huddersfield University, Huddersfield, HD1 4TY, England (office). *Telephone:* (1484) 425082 (office). *Fax:* (1484) 472957 (office). *E-mail:* info@hcmf .co.uk (office). *Website:* www.hcmf.co.uk (office).

EATHORNE, Wendy; Singer (Soprano) and Teacher; b. 25 Sept. 1939, Four Lanes, Cornwall, England; 1 d. *Education:* Studied at the Royal Academy of Music, 1959–65; ARAM; LRAM; ARCM; JP; Hon FCSM; FTCL; FRSA. *Career:* West End production, Robert and Elizabeth, 1965–67; Numerous concert appearances including Promenade Concerts, London; Engagements with the London Bach Choir, London Symphony Orchestra, Hallé Orchestra and other leading British orchestras; Repertoire includes works by Handel (Susanna and Belshazzar), Liszt (Missa Solemnis) and Haydn (The Creation); Appearances with Welsh National Opera, English National Opera and Royal Opera, Covent Garden; Glyndebourne, 1969–71, as Sophie in Werther, First Boy in Die Zauberflöte and Atalanta in The Rising of the Moon; Italian debut in Ariadne auf Naxos; Repertoire also includes Julia in La Vestale by Spontini and Marguerite in Faust; Festival Adjudicator; Many recitals with the pianist Geoffrey Pratley, programmes include groups of songs by Purcell to modern pieces; Head of Vocal Studies, Opera and Music Theatre at Trinity College of Music, 1989–94; Senior Lecturer, Trinity College of Music. *Recordings:* Masses by Bach; A Village Romeo and Juliet; Monteverdi Madrigals Libro IV; A Scarlatti Clori e Zeffiro and St Cecilia Mass, Schubert Mass in A flat; Vaughan Williams The Pilgrim's Progress and Sir John in Love; Bridge, The Christmas Rose. *Address:* 23 King Edward's Road, Ruislip, Middlesex HA4 7AQ, England.

EATON, John C.; Composer; b. 30 March 1935, Bryn Mawr, USA; m. Nelda Nelson, 31 May 1973, 1 s., 1 d. *Education:* AB, MFA, Princeton University. *Career:* Columbia Artists in USA, Hamburg Opera, Maggio Musicale, Venice Festival, Los Angeles Philharmonic, Tanglewood, many more. *Compositions:* Operas performed: The Tempest, 1985; The Cry of Clytaemnestra, 1980; Danton and Robespierre; The Lion and Androcles; Myshkin; Herakles; Don Quixote, 1996; Travelling with Gulliver, 1997; King Lear, 2000; 2 Symphonies; Duo, mixed chorus; Mass, 1997; Blind Man's Cry; Concert Music for Solo Clarinet; Piano Variations; Microtonal Fantasy; Piano Trio; Concert Piece. *Recordings:* Danton and Robespierre; The Music of John Eaton; Microtonal Fantasy; Electro Vibrations. *Publications:* New Music Since 1950, 1974. His work was reviewed in, Time; New Yorker; London Financial Times; New York Times; High Fidelity; Opera News. *Honours:* Prix de Rome, 1959–61; Guggenheim, 1962, 1965; Fromm Commission, 1966; Koussevitzky

Commission, 1970; Citation, NIAL, 1972; Composer in Residence, AAR, 1975; PBC Commission, 1970; Peabody Award, 1973; National Music Theater Award, 1988; MacArthur Fellow, 1990. *Address:* c/o ASCAP, ASCAP House, 1 Lincoln Plaza, New York, USA.

EBBECKE, Michael; Singer (Baritone); b. 8 Dec. 1955, Wiesbaden, Germany. *Education:* Studied at the Richard Strauss Conservatory Munich and with Josef Metternich in Cologne. *Career:* Debut: Stuttgart 1982, as Mozart's Figaro; Member of the Stuttgart Staatsoper from 1982, notably as Belcore, Giulio Cesare, Eugene Onegin, Silvio, and Don Fernando in Fidelio; Guest appearances at the Berlin Komische Oper (Guglielmo, 1984) and Deutsche Oper (Orestes in Iphigénie en Tauride, 1988); Appearances at Karlsruhe, Paris, Lyon (Wolfram in Tannhäuser) and La Scala Milan (Scherasmin in Oberon, 1989); Sang Stolzius in Die Soldaten at Stuttgart, 1987, Papageno and Escamillo in Season, 1990–91, Guglielmo, 1991–92; Season 1995–96 as Pantaleone in The Love for Three Oranges at Stuttgart; Melisso in Handel's Alcina, 1998; Sang Verdi in the premiere of Adriana Hölszky's Giuseppe Sylvia, Stuttgart 2000; Concert engagements include Bach's St John Passion at Amsterdam, 1987. *Recordings:* Die Soldaten. *Address:* c/o Stuttgart Staatsoper, Oberer Schlossgarten 6, 700 Stuttgart, Germany.

EBEN, Petr; Composer, Pianist and Lecturer; b. 22 Jan. 1929, Zamberk, Czechoslovakia; m. Sarka Hurnikova-Ebenova, 3 c. *Education:* Academy of Music, Prague. *Career:* Debut: Pianist, Prague 1952; Composer, Concerto for organ and orchestra, Prague, 1954; Music Director, TV Prague, 1954; Lecturer, Institute for Musicology, Charles University, Prague, 1955–; mem, Union of Composers, Prague; Chairman, Creative Section, Czechoslovakian Music Society. *Compositions:* Sunday Music for Organ; Concerto, piano and orchestra; Apologia Sokratus, oratorio; Vox Clamantis, orchestra; Maidens and Swallows, female choir; Unkind Songs; Vespers, choir and organ; Pragensia; Greek Dictionary, cycle, female choir and harp; Nachtstunden (Night Hours), symphony, wind quintet and chamber orchestra; Faust, organ; Windows After Chagall, trumpet and organ; Mutationes, commissioned, Cardiff Festival; String Quartet; Il Concerto, organ and Orchestra, commissioned, ORF, Vienna; Ballet, Curses and Blessings, commissioned, Nederlands Dans Theater; Prague Nocturne, orchestra, 1983; Improperia for orchestra, 1995; Jeremias, church opera, 1997; Tabulatura nova, guitar; Cantata, In Honorem Caroli, men's choir and orchestra. *Recordings:* Most compositions recorded, plus: Missa Adventus; Vespers. *Publications:* Cteni a hra partitur, co-author. *Contributions:* Various journals. *Honours:* 1st prize, Gold Medal, 6 love songs, Moscow, 1957; 1st prize, The Lovers Magic Spell, cantata, Jihlava Vocal Festival, 1959; 1st prize, 10 children's duets, Jirkov, 1966; 2 prizes, Laudes, Kassel, 1965. *Current Management:* Pragokoncert, Prague 1. *Address:* Union of Czech Composers, Prague 5, Czech Republic.

EBERHARDT, Cornelius; Conductor; b. 3 Jan. 1932, Oberaudorf, Germany; m. Ursula Schade 1957; one d. *Education:* Univs of Munich and Hamburg, 1950–53; State Acad. of Music, Munich, 1953–56; Accademia Chigiana, Siena, Italy, 1958. *Career:* Chorus Master of Municipal Opera, Ulm, Germany, 1956–60; Assoc. Conductor, Munich State Theatre, 1960–69; Music Dir, Regensburg Symphony and Opera, 1969–77; founder of Regensburg Music School; co-founder of Bavarian Festival of Modern Composers, 1973; Music Dir of Corpus Christi Symphony, TX, USA, 1975–2000; Prof. of Opera and Conductor, State Acad. of Music, Munich, Germany, 1977–97; Music Dir of American Institute of Musical Studies, Dallas, TX, 1978–; Visiting Prof., 1979–80, Prof. and Music Dir, 1984–87, Univ. of Texas, Austin; Visiting Prof., Corpus Christi State Univ., 1981–82; Guest Conductor in Europe and North and South America; Music Dir, Mozart Festival International, 1991; Pres., State Acad. of Music, 1991–95; Principal Guest Conductor, Munich Symphony, 1996–2002. *Publications:* Das Regensburger Orchester, 1972; Der Dirigent in Handbuch der Musikberufe, 1987; Volksmusik und Kunstmusik in Südosteuropa, 1988. *Honours:* Bavarian State Award for Young Artists, 1969; Order of Merit, Germany, 1996. *Address:* Darmstaedterstrasse 11-7, 80992 Munich, Germany.

EBRAHIM, Omar; Singer (Baritone); b. 6 Sept. 1956, London, England. *Education:* Studied at the Guildhall School of Music, London. *Career:* Appearances with the Opera Factory in Punch and Judy, The Beggar's Opera, The Knot Garden, and La Calisto; Sang in the premieres of Birtwistle's Yan Tan Tethera, South Bank, 1986 and Nigel Osborne's The Electrification of the Soviet Union, Glyndebourne, 1986; Glyndebourne Touring Opera in Il Barbiere di Siviglia and La Bohème; Has sung Hector in King Priam for Kent Opera; With Scottish Opera has appeared in Mahagonny, Die Fledermaus and Iolanthe; Covent Garden, 1989, in the British premiere of Un Re in Ascolto by Berio; Sang Don Giovanni with Opera Factory at the Queen Elizabeth Hall, 1990, Parkhearst in the premiere of Bose's 63: Dream Palace at the 1990 Munich Biennale; The Fool in the premiere of Birtwistle's Gawain, Covent Garden, May 1991; Sang the Voice of Goya in the premiere of Osborne's Terrible Mouth, Almeida Festival, 1992; Created Vermeer in Birtwistle's The Second Mrs Kong, Glyndebourne, 1994; Sang Horace

Tabor in the British premiere of Moore's The Ballad of Baby Doe, Bloomsbury Theatre, 1996; Momo in Cesti's Il Pomo d'Oro at Batignano, 1998. Television appearances include Yan Tan Tethera, by Birtwistle, The Kiss by Michael Nyman and the title role in a BBC version of Marschner's Vampyr, 1992; Concert repertoire includes Morton Feldman/Beckett Words and Music, Aventures, Nouvelles Aventures (Ligeti), Enoch Arden (Strauss) and Ode to Napoleon Bonaparte (Schoenberg). *Address:* c/o Allied Artists, 42 Montpelier Square, London SW7 1JZ, England.

ECHOLS, Paul (Clinton); Opera Director, Musicologist and Editor; b. 13 Feb. 1944, Santa Monica, California, USA. *Education:* BA, Magna Cum Laude, Duke University, Durham, North Carolina, USA, 1966; MA, Musicology, New York University, 1968. *Career:* Deputy Chairman, 1971–75, Assistant Professor of Music, 1971–75, Department of Music, Brooklyn College, New York; Editorial Co-ordinator, The Charles Ives Society, 1976–82; International Director, Concert Music Division, Peer Southern Music Publishers, New York, 1982–85; Director, Historical Performance Programme, 1980–84; Director, Opera Program, 1988–, The Mannes College of Music, New York; Vice-President and Director of Publishing, G Schirmer/Associated Music Publishers Inc. New York, 1986–87; Editor, Historical Performance; The Journal of Early Music America, 1987–; mem, Board of Directors, The Charles Ives Society, Inc; Early Music America, Inc; American Musicological Society; Sonneck Society, and others. *Publications:* Numerous Articles for scholarly journals and other publications including New Grove Dictionary of Music in America; Numerous editions of music including Renaissance and Baroque Choral Music and The Orchestral Works of Charles E Ives. *Address:* The Mannes College of Music, 150 West 85th Street, New York, NY 10024, USA.

ECKHARDT, Mária; Hungarian musicologist and choral conductor; *Director, Liszt Frenec Memorial Museum and Research Centre*; b. 26 Sept. 1943, Budapest. *Education:* Liszt Ferenc Acad. of Music. *Career:* Librarian and Research Worker, Music Dept, Nat. Széchényi Library, Budapest, 1966–73; Research Worker, Inst. of Musicology, Hungarian Acad. of Sciences, Budapest, 1973–87; Dir, Liszt Ferenc Memorial Museum and Research Centre at Liszt Acad. of Music, Budapest, 1986–. *Publications:* Franz Liszt und sein Kreis in Briefen und Dokumenten aus den Beständen des Burgenländischen Landesmuseums, with Cornelia Knotik, 1983; Liszt Ferenc Memorial Museum Catalogue, 1986; Franz Liszt's Estate at the Budapest Academy of Music, 1, Books, 1986; Franz Liszt's Music Manuscripts in the National Széchényi Library, 1986; Liszt Ferenc válogatott levelei 1824–1861, (selected letters 1824–1861), Budapest, 1989; Franz Liszt's Estate at the Budapest Academy of Music, II, Music, 1993; Franz Liszt's Weimarer Bibliothek (with Evelyn Liepsch) 1999. *Contributions:* Books on Liszt, Schubert, Chopin and Schumann, 1996–2002; Studies on Liszt and 19th-Century musical life and composers in: Studia Musicologica, Magyar Zene, The New Hungarian Quarterly, Journal of The American Liszt Society, Muzsika and others; exhibition catalogues, forewords to Liszt editions by Henle (Munich). *Honours:* Award of Excellence, American Liszt Soc., 1985; Erkel Prize, 1987, Szaboksi Prize 2004, MAOE Musical Grand Prize 2004. *Address:* Vörösmarty atca 35, 1064 Budapest (office); Ruszti ut 11, 1022 Budapest, Hungary (home). *Telephone:* (1) 342 7320 (office). *Fax:* (1) 413 1526 (office). *E-mail:* eckhardt@lib.liszt.hu (office). *Website:* www.lisztmuseum.hu (office).

ECKHART, Janis (Gail); Opera Singer (Mezzo Soprano); b. 21 July 1953, CA, USA. *Education:* BA, magna cum laude, Phi Beta Kappa 1973, Sec Teaching Credential, 1974, University of California, Los Angeles; Academia Real de Musica, Madrid, Spain, 1974. *Career:* Debut: New York City Opera, 1981; Numerous roles at New York City Opera including: Nabucco, 1981, Rigoletto, 1981, 1984, 1988 and 1989, Carmen, 1986 and 1988; In Rigoletto at Opéra de Monte Carlo, 1983, and Aida, Opera Delaware, 1984; Sang in Il Trovatore, 1987, and in Un Ballo in Maschera, 1986, both at National Grand Opera; Carmen, Seattle Opera, 1982; Samson et Dalila, National Philharmonic of the Philippines, 1980; Les Contes D'Hoffmann at the Opera Metropolitana, Caracas, 1981; Nabucco, Rigoletto, Teatro de Opera, Puerto Rico, 1988; Rigoletto, Opera Carolina, 1990; Carmen, Metro Lyric Opera, 1992; Carmen, Cairo Opera, Egypt, 1992; Mahler's Kindertotenlieder and Songs of a Wayfarer, Nashville Symphony, Verdi's Requiem, New York Chorale Society and Plymouth Church of the Pilgrims; Concert tour, Instituto Technológico de México, 1992; Kismet, Taipei Symphony, 1993; Ambassadors of Opera, Far East Concert Tour, 1993; Middle East Concert Tour, 1993; Cavalleria Rusticana, Hong Kong, 1994; Carmen, Madrid, Lisbon, 1995; Aida, Cairo Opera, 1996; Beethoven's 9th Symphony, Avery Fisher Hall, 1997; Amneris in Aida, Dicapo Opera Theatre tour, 2001; Carmen in Florida, 2001, 2003. *Address:* 15 W 72nd Street, New York, NY 10023, USA.

EDDY, Jenifer; Singer (Coloratura Soprano); b. 1933, Melbourne, Australia; m. David Beamish, one s. *Education:* Studied in Melbourne with Henri Portnoj and in London with Bertha Nicklauss Kempner and

Roy Henderson. *Career:* Frequent Guest Soloist with Australian Broadcasting Corporation in Concerts, Studio Broadcasts and on Television and Major Choral Groups, 1953–58; Professional stage debut, 1954, as Mascha in The Chocolate Soldier, Princess Theatre, Melbourne; Opera debut, 1956, as Nedda in Pagliacci; Elizabethan Opera Company, 1956–57 as Mozart's Susanna, Despina, Papagena and as Polly Peachum, Beggar's Opera; Covent Garden, 1959–69, roles including Xenia (Boris Godunov), Amor (Gluck's Orpheus), Fiakermilli (Arabella), Olympia (Tales of Hoffmann), Sophie (Der Rosenkavalier), Tytania (A Midsummer Night's Dream); Guest appearances with Sadler's Wells Opera, English National Opera, Welsh National Opera, Scottish Opera, English Opera Group, Bordeaux Opera, Maggio Musicale, Edinburgh, Leeds, Bath and Schwetzingen Festivals; Roles include, Despina, Rosina, Norina, Blondchen, Madame Herz (The Impressario), Musetta, Zerbinetta, Adele (Die Fledermaus); Appearances for BBC on radio, television and in concert; Managing Director, Jenifer Eddy Artists' Management, Melbourne, 1975–; Director, Lies Askonas Ltd, London, 1982–97; Consultant Askonas Holt Ltd, 1998–. *Recordings include:* Die Entführung, Gypsy Baron, Hansel and Gretel. *Honours:* Medal, Order of Australia, 1997. *Address:* Jenifer Eddy Artists' Management, Suite 11, The Clivedon, 596 St Kilda Road, Melbourne 3004, Victoria, Australia. *Telephone:* (3) 9529-5410 (office). *Fax:* (3) 9529-5410 (office). *E-mail:* info@jeam.com.au (office).

EDDY, Timothy; Violoncellist; b. 1930, USA. *Education:* Studied with Bernard Greenhouse. *Career:* Duo recitals with pianist Gilbert Kalish and soloist with orchestras at Denver, Dallas, and the Maggio Musicale, Florence; Concerts with the Bach Aria Group and festival engagements at Santa Fe, Marlboro, Florida and at SUNY Stony Brook; Cellist with the Orion String Quartet, including appearances throughout the USA and at the Wigmore Hall, London; Further European appearances at the Lockenhaus and Turku (Finland) Festivals; Collaborations with Rudolf Serkin, Pablo Casals, and members of the Végh, Budapest and Guarneri Quartets; Professor of Cello at SUNY, Stony Brook. *Recordings:* Albums with Columbia, Angel Vox, Vanguard, Nonesuch, New World and Delos. *Current Management:* Orion String Quartet, c/o Ingpen & Williams Ltd, 7 St George's Court, 131 Putney Bridge Road, London, SW15 2PA, England.

EDELMANN, Peter; singer (baritone); b. 1962, Vienna, Austria. *Education:* Vienna Musikhochschule. *Career:* Sang Mozart's Figaro on tour in Europe; Member of the Koblenz Opera from 1985, notably in the title role at the premiere of Odysseus by Klaus Arp, 1989; Guest appearances in Mannheim, Dortmund, Wuppertal and Krefeld, as Mozart's Don Giovanni and Guglielmo, Marcello, the Forester in Cunning Little Vixen, Rossini's Figaro, Posa and Lord Tristan in Martha; Lieder recitals and concerts in Vienna, Budapest, Salzburg and Wexford; Member of the Deutsche Oper Berlin from 1990 (Papageno 1991); Sang in the premiere of Desdemona und ihre Schwestern by Siegfried Matthus, Schwetzingen 1991; Theseus in Enescu's Oedipe, Berlin, 1996; Albert in Werther, Berlin (concert), 1998; Sang Morales in Carmen, Gounod's Valentin and Melot in Tristan at the Deutsche Oper, 2000. *Honours:* Winner, 1989 Belvedere Competitions, Vienna. *Current Management:* Robert Gilder & Co., Enterprise House, 59–65 Upper Ground, London, SE1 9PQ, England. *Telephone:* (20) 7928-9008. *Fax:* (20) 7928-9755. *E-mail:* rgilder@robert-gilder.com.

EDELMANN, Sergei; Pianist; b. 22 July 1960, Lvov, Russia. *Education:* Studied with father, Head Piano Department, Lvov Conservatory; Studied with Rudolf Firkusny, Juilliard School, New York, 1979 with Claude Frank, Aspen (Colorado) Music School. *Career:* Debut: First public appearance as soloist, Beethoven Piano Concerto No. 1 with Lvov Philharmonic Orchestra, 1970; More than 50 concerts throughout Russia; Toured widely in Europe and North America as soloist with leading orchestras and as a Recitalist. *Recordings:* For RCA. *Honours:* Gina Bachauer Memorial Scholarship Award, 1979. *Address:* c/o Arien Arts & Music B.V.B.A., de Boeystraat 6, B–2018 Antwerp, Belgium.

EDER, Claudia; Singer (Mezzo-soprano); b. 7 Feb. 1948, Augsburg, Germany. *Education:* Studied at Munich and Frankfurt, with Marianne Scheck. *Career:* Debut: Bielefeld, 1973, as Offenbach's Nicklausse; Sang at Wiesbaden and Gärtnerplatz Theater, Munich from 1975; Vienna Volksoper from 1982, notably in Christoph Rilke by Matthus; Salzburg Festival, 1993, as Octavian, Düsseldorf, 1995, as Carmen; Other roles include Dorabella, Cenerentola, Meg Page and Hansel; Concert engagements throughout Austria and Germany. *Address:* c/o Deutsche Oper am Rhein, Heinrich-Heine Alle 16a, 40213 Düsseldorf, Germany.

EDER, György; Cellist; b. 2 Feb. 1949, Budapest, Hungary. *Education:* Franz Liszt Academy, Budapest, 1969–73; Yale University, 1978; The Banff Centre, 1983; University of Wisconsin, 1984. *Career:* Founding Member, Eder String Quartet, 1973–96; Member, Kodály String Quartet, 1998–; Concert tours world-wide; Principal Cellist, Budapest Symphony Orchestra, and later Budapest Festival Orchestra, several years. *Recordings:* Over 40 albums. *Honours:* Prizewinner, Evian Competition, 1976; Prizewinner, Munich Competition, 1977. *Address:* Galoca utca 15, 1028 Budapest, Hungary.

EDER, Helmut; Composer and Teacher; b. 26 Dec. 1916, Linz, Austria. *Education:* Linz Conservatory; Training in composition from Hindemith in Salzburg, 1947, Orff in Munich, 1953–54, J N David in Stuttgart, 1954. *Career:* Teacher, Linz Conservatory, 1950–, co-founding its electronic music studio, 1959; Teacher, Salzburg Mozarteum, 1967, now Emeritus Professor Composer; mem, Programme Organiser, International Stiftung Mozarteum; Rotary Club, Salzburg-Nord. *Compositions:* Operas: Oedipus, 1958; Der Kardinal, 1962; Die weisse Frau, 1968; Konjugationen 3, 1969; Der Aufstand, 1975; Georges Dandin oder Der betrogne Ehemann, 1978–79; Mozart in New York, 3-act opera, Salzburg Festival, 1991; Ballets: Moderner Traum, 1957; Anamorphose, 1963; Die Irrfahrten des Odysseus, 1964–65; Orchestral: Symphony No. 1, 1950, No. 2, 1962, No. 3, 1969, No. 4, Choral Symphony, 1973–75, No. 5, Organ Symphony, 1979–80; Musica semplice, flute, harpsichord, strings, 1953; Music for 2 trumpets and strings, 1955; Concerto for piano, 15 wind instruments, double basses, percussion, 1956; Pezzo Sereno, 1958; Concerto semiserio, 2 pianos and orchestra, 1960; Oboe Concerto, 1962, 2 Violin Concertos, 1963, 1964; Danza a solatio, 1963; Concerto a dodici per archi, 1963; Nil admirari, 1966; Syntagma, 1967; Concerto for bassoon and chamber orchestra, 1968; L'Homme armé, concerto for organ and orchestra, 1968–69; Metamorphosen, flute, oboe, string quartet, orchestra, 1970; Melodia-ritmica, strings, 1973; Pastorale, strings, 1974; Divertimento, soprano, orchestral group, 1976; Jubilato, chamber orchestra, 1976; Serenade, 6 horns, 46 strings, 1977; Double Concerto, cello, double bass, orchestra, 1977–78; Cello Concerto, 1981; Concerto No. 3, violin and orchestra, 1981–82; Concerto A B, chamber orchestra, 1982; Notturno, flute, oboe, strings, 1983, revised, 1984; Haffner Concerto, flute and orchestra, 1984; Concertino, classical orchestra, 1984; Pièce de concert, strings, 1984; Duetto-Concerto, 2 flutes and orchestra, op 95; Symphony No. 6, 1994; Oboe Concerto, 1996; Chamber: String Quartet, 1948; Szene for 6 horns, 1977; Suite with Intermezzo for 11 winds, 1979; Quintet, clarinet, 2 violins, viola, cello, 1982; Quartet, flute, string trio, 1983; String Quartet No. 4, op 94, 1991; Trio for clarinet, viola and piano, 1994; Piano pieces; Organ music; Choral works. *Recordings:* Numerous. *Honours:* Several prizes; Various commissions. *Address:* c/o AKM, Baummanstrasse 10, 1031 Vienna, Postfach 259, Austria.

EDGAR-WILSON, Richard; Singer (Tenor); b. 1963, Ipswich, Suffolk, England. *Education:* Studied at Christ's College, Cambridge (choral exhibition); The Royal College of Music with Edward Brooks. *Career:* Opera includes: Albert Herring, Tamino (Magic Flute), Quint (Turn of the Screw), Beauty (The Triumph of Beauty and Deceit, Gerald Barry, C4 television); Concert repertoire includes Messiah, Bach's B minor Mass, the Monteverdi Vespers, Mozart's Coronation and C minor Masses and Carissimi's Jephtha; Works by Kodály, Stainer, Vaughan Williams, Berio and Britten; Solo appearances all over England and North America, France, Norway and Germany; Operatic roles include Handel's Acis and The Mad Woman in Britten's Curlew River; Work with conductors, Trevor Pinnock, Richard Hickox, Charles Mackerras, Robert King. *Recordings:* Purcell's Dioclesian, Pinnock; Stradella, San Giovanni Battista, Minkowski (winner Gramophone Award 1993); Schubert, Die schöne Müllerin. *Current Management:* Ron Gonsalves Management.

EDLUND, Mikael; Swedish composer; b. 19 Jan. 1950, Tranås; two d. *Education:* Univ. of Uppsala, State Coll. of Music, Stockholm with I. Lidholm and A. Mellnäs. *Career:* Producer at Fylkingen, Stockholm 1979; teacher in composition, State Coll. of Music, Gothenburg 1985–87; Pres., Swedish Section of ISCM 1996–98; mem. Soc. of Swedish Composers, Swedish Performing Right Soc., Int. Soc. for Contemporary Music (Swedish Section), Fylkingen. *Compositions:* The Lost Jugglery for mezzo-soprano, cello, piano and 2 percussionists, 1974–77; Trio Sun for clarinet, bassoon and piano, 1980; Leaves for 8 female voices, acoustic piano, electric piano, harp and 7 percussionists, 1977–81; Brains and Dancin' for string quartet, 1981; Fantasia on a City for piano, 1981–86; Jord for 5 percussionists, 1982; Små Fötter, a miniature for guitar, 1982; Music for double wind quintet, 1984; Orchids in the Embers for piano, 1986; Ajar for orchestra, 1988–91; Blue Garden for piano trio, 1992–94; Dissolved Window for 21 strings, 1986–96; Fanfara, trumpet solo, 1995; Un punto nel cortile for flute, 1997; Solo for violin, 1998–99; Così ballano; Cinghiali for flute, violin, violoncello and piano, 2000; Mannen och flugan from male choir, 2002. *Recordings:* Brains and Dancin'; Trio Sun; Orchids in the Embers; Små Fötter; Leaves; Fantasia on a city. *Honours:* Christ Johnson 1985. *Address:* Backvägen 2, 19135 Sollentuna, Sweden. *E-mail:* edlund@minpost.nu.

EDWARDS, George Harrison; Composer; b. 11 May 1943, Boston, Massachusetts, USA; m. Rachel Hadas, 22 July 1978. *Education:* BA, Oberlin College, 1965; MFA, Princeton University, 1967. *Career:* Theory Faculty, New England Conservatory of Music, 1968–76; Assistant Professor of Music, 1976–86, Associate Professor of Music, 1986–93,

Professor, 1993, Columbia University. *Compositions:* String Quartet, 1967; Kreuz und Quer, 1971; Monopoly, 1972; Giro, 1974; Exchange-Misere, 1974; Draconian Measures, 1976; Gyromancy, 1977; Veined Variety, 1978; Northern Spy, 1980; String Quartet 2, 1982; Moneta's Mourn, 1983; Suave Mari Magno, 1984; A Mirth but Open'd, 1986; Heraclitian Fire for string quartet and string orchestra, 1987; Piano Concerto, 1990; Plus ça change... for ensemble, 1992; The Isle is Full of Noises for 6 instruments, 1995; Trio for clarinet, viola and piano, 1996. *Address:* 838 West End Avenue, Apt 3A, New York, NY 10025, USA.

EDWARDS, Joan; Singer (Mezzo-soprano); b. 1944, London, England. *Education:* Studied at the London Opera Centre. *Career:* Debut: Schwertleite in Die Walküre at Covent Garden; Sang with the English Opera Group in Britain and abroad, often with Benjamin Britten conducting; Opera North from 1978 as Marcellina in Le nozze di Figaro, Third Lady (Magic Flute), Mother in Hansel and Gretel, Juno and Minerva in Orpheus in the Underworld, Berta in Il Barbiere di Siviglia and Mary in The Flying Dutchman; Many concert performances; Appeared on BBC television in La Traviata.

EDWARDS, Owain Tudor; Musicologist; b. 10 Nov. 1940, Ruabon, Wales; m. Grete Strand 1965; one s. two d. *Education:* BMus 1962, MMus 1964, PhD 1967, Univ. of Wales, Bangor. *Career:* Asst Lecturer 1965, Lecturer 1967, Music Dept, Univ. Coll. of Wales, Aberystwyth; Lecturer in Music, Open Univ. 1970; Lecturer in Music, Liverpool Univ. 1973; Reader and Head of Music History 1974, Prof. 1985–, Norges Musikkhogskole, Oslo, Norway; organist, Kroer Church, 1980–; mem. Norwegian Acad. of Science and Letters. *Compositions:* Adventsgudst-jeneste 1986, 155 orgelsatser til gudstjeneste bruk 1992, Processional Music for brass 1995. *Publications:* Joseph Parry 1841–1903 1970, Beethoven 1972, People, Instruments and the Continuo 1974, Suite, Sonata and Concerto 1974, Matins, Lauds and Vespers for St David's Day 1990, The Penpont Antiphonal 1997, English Eighteenth-Century Concertos – an Inventory and Thematic Catalogue 2005. *Contributions:* New Grove Dictionary of Music and Musicians, The Music Review, The Musical Quarterly, Proceedings of the Royal Musical Association, Revue Bénédictine, Cantus Planus, Studia Musicologica Norvegica, Svensk tidskrift för musikforskning, Modern Asian Studies and Flerstemmige Innspill. *Address:* Norges Musikkhøgskole, Gydasv 6, Postboks 5190, Majorstua, 0302 Oslo 3, Norway. *Telephone:* 23-36-70-63 (office). *E-mail:* owain.edwards@nmh.no (office).

EDWARDS, Ross; Australian Composer; b. 23 Dec. 1943, Sydney, NSW; m. Helen Hopkins 1974; one s. one d. *Education:* New South Wales State Conservatory of Music, Univ. of Sydney; MMus, Univ. of Adelaide, 1970. *Career:* International Society of Contemporary Music Festivals, Stockholm, 1966, Basel, 1970; mem., numerous professional organisations. *Compositions:* Sonata for 9 instruments, Quem Quaeritis (children's nativity play) 1967, Etude for orchestra 1969, Monos I (cello solo), Monos II (piano solo) 1970, Mountain Village in a Clearing Mist for orchestra, Antifon for voices, brass ensemble, organ and percussion, 5 Little Piano Pieces, The Tower of Remoteness, Concerto for piano and orchestra, Christina's world (chamber opera), Shadow D-Zone 1977, The Hermit of Green Light 1979, Ab Estasis Foribus 1980, Maninya I 1981, II for string quartet, III 1985, IV 1985–86, V 1986, Kumari (solo piano), Laikan I and II, Ten Little Duets 1982, Marimba Dances 1982, Etymalong 1984, Reflections 1985, Flower Songs 1986, Maninyas for violin and orchestra 1988, Varrageh for solo percussion and orchestra 1989, Aria and Transcendental Dance for horn and string orchestra 1990, Sensing (dance piece) 1993, Guitar Concerto 1994, Veni Creator Spiritus (double string quartet) 1994, Enyato III for orchestra 1995, Binyang for clarinet and percussion 1996. *Contributions:* Music Now, Australian Contemporary Music Quarterly.

EDWARDS, Sian; Conductor; b. 27 May 1959, West Chiltington, Sussex, England. *Education:* Studied at the Royal Northern College of Music and with Charles Groves, Norman Del Mar and Neeme Järvi; Further study with Ilya Alexandrovitch Musin at the Leningrad Conservatoire, 1983–85. *Career:* Concert engagements with the London Philharmonic, Royal Philharmonic, London Sinfonietta, Scottish National Orchestra, City of Birmingham Symphony, Hallé, BBC Philharmonic, BBC Scottish Symphony and the Royal Liverpool Philharmonic; Opera debut with Scottish Opera, 1986, Mahagonny by Weill; Glyndebourne Festival, 1987, La Traviata, L'Heure Espagnole and L'Enfant et les Sortilèges; Katya Kabanova with Glyndebourne Touring Opera, 1988; Covent Garden, 1988, as the first woman to conduct opera there (The Knot Garden by Tippett); Conducted the world premiere of Greek by Mark Anthony Turnage at the 1988 Munich Biennale (repeated at the Edinburgh Festival); Season 1989–90 included concerts with the London Philharmonic and the BBC Symphony at the Festival Hall; Rigoletto at Covent Garden; French debut with the Orchestre de Paris and US concerts with the San Francisco Symphony; The Gambler by Prokofiev for English National Opera; Conducted Il Trovatore at Covent Garden, 1990, Carmen, 1991; Music Director of English National Opera, 1993–95; Led the Docklands Sinfonietta in London Proms debut, 1993,

with music by Britten, Dallapiccola and Mozart (K551); Engaged for Eugene Onegin at ENO, 2000. *Honours:* British Council Scholarship, 1983; Winner, Leeds Conductors' Competition, 1984. *Current Management:* Ingpen & Williams Ltd, 7 St George's Court, 131 Putney Bridge Road, London, SW15 2PA, England.

EDWARDS, Terry; choral director; b. 1939, London, England. *Career:* formed and directed such groups as London Sinfonietta Voices, Electric Phoenix and London Voices; concerts and recordings with radio choirs, choral societies and choruses world-wide; Season 1988 with the BBC Singers and Choral Society at the Festival Hall, Bach's B minor Mass at Glasgow; concerts with the London Sinfonietta in the Prom Concerts and festival appearances in Berlin, Geneva and Turin; Chorus Master for Georg Solti in three Verdi concerts in Chicago; directed the chorus at the Michael Vyner Memorial at Covent Garden, 1990; Chorus Dir, Royal Opera, Covent Garden 1992–2004; concerts with the Danish Radio Choir, 1991 and works by Erik Bergmann in Finland; directed Sinfonietta Voices in Stockhausen's Stimmung at the Queen Elizabeth Hall, 1997. *Recordings include:* Messiaen Cinq Rechants, Rachmaninov and Tchaikovsky Vespers, A Boy was Born by Britten; Verdi Choruses and Otello; La Bohème; Ligeti-A-Capella Music; Holliger; Die Jahres-zeiten; Don Carlos; Curlew River.

EDWARDS, Warwick (Anthony); University Lecturer and Performer on Early Instruments; b. 22 April 1944, Dewsbury, England; m. Jacqueline Freeman, 2 d. *Education:* King's College, University of Cambridge; MA; BMus; PhD. *Career:* Lecturer, 1971–, Senior Lecturer, 1986–, Glasgow University; Director, Scottish Early Music Consort, 1976–; Director, Glasgow International Early Music Festival, 1990–. *Recordings:* Mary's Music: Songs and Dances from the time of Mary Queen of Scots, Scottish Early Music Consort, W Edwards Director, 1984. *Publications:* Editor: Music for Mixed Consort (Musica Britannica 40), 1977; W Byrd: Latin Motets (from manuscript scores) (The Byrd Edition 8), 1984. *Contributions:* Grove's Dictionary, 6th edition; Music and Letters; Proceedings of the Royal Music Association; Early Music; The Consort; British Book News. *Address:* 22 Falkland Street, Glasgow G12 9 PR, Scotland.

EDWORTHY, Joanne Elizabeth, GMus, RNCM; British singer (mezzo-soprano) and singing teacher; b. 24 July 1970, Epsom, Surrey; m. Robert Allen; one s. one d. *Education:* Royal Northern Coll. of Music. *Career:* debut as Hansel, WNO 1995; Siebel in Faust, WNO 1996; Glyndebourne co. mem. 1996–2000; opera roles include Hansel and Meg Page at QEH, Xerxes, Ramiro and Amadigi at New Coll., Oxford 1998–2003, Cheubino in Mozart's Figaro at Edinburgh Festival 2002; recitals and oratorio include St Martin in the Fields, St John's, Smith Square, Royal Festival Hall, Sheldonian Theatre, Christchurch Cathedral; radio and television role of Siebel in Gounod's Faust for WNO 1996; vocal tutor at St Paul's Girls' School, Hammersmith, London. *Honours:* Wingate Foundation Scholarship, Countess of Munster Award, Thurston Memorial Award (RNCM), Oncken Song Prize (RNCM). *Address:* 83 Arundel Road, Sands, High Wycombe, Buckinghamshire, HP12 4ND, England (home). *Telephone:* (1494) 521969 (home). *E-mail:* jo@jedworthy.co.uk (office). *Website:* www.jedworthy.co.uk.

EENSALU, Marika; Singer (Mezzo-soprano); b. 20 Sept. 1947, Tallinn, Estonia. *Education:* Studied at Tallinn and with Irina Arkhipova in Moscow. *Career:* Sang at the Estonia Theatre, Tallinn, from 1980, as Rosina, Carmen, Dorabella, Bradamante in Alcina, Marfa and Ulrica; Savonlinna Festival, 1987, with guest appearances in Moscow and throughout Germany, Denmark and Hungary; Concert engagements in works by Estonian composers. *Address:* c/o Estonian State Opera, Estonian Boulevard, 20001 Tallinn, Estonia.

EEROLA, Aulikki; Singer (Soprano); b. 1947, Tuusula, Finland. *Education:* Studied at the Sibelius Academy, Helsinki, and with Hilde Zadek and Erik Werba in Vienna. *Career:* Debut: Sang in concert at Helsinki, 1975; Savonlinna Festival, 1977, as Pamina in Die Zauber-flöte, and has appeared widely in Germany, Austria, England, France and North America as concert soloist. *Address:* c/o Finnish National Opera, Bulevardi 23-27, 00180 Helsinki 18, Finland.

EEROLA, Lasse Olavi; Composer and Music Teacher; b. 24 Sept. 1945, Kuusankoski, Finland; m. Päivi Irmeli, 27 August 1983, 2 s. *Education:* Sibelius Academy, Helsinki, Finland, 1970–77. *Career:* Clarinet and Saxophone Player, 1967–74; Teacher of Theory and Clarinet, 1969–; Composer, 1975–; mem, Society of Finnish Composers; The Finnish Clarinet Society. *Compositions:* Variations for wind orchestra, 1975, recorded 1980 and 1992; Variations for orchestra, 1977; Metamorphoses for orchestra, 1979; Suite for Orchestra, 1980–81; Music for clarinet and piano, 1980–82; Miniature for orchestra, 1982; Chamber Music, 1983–84; Aino, 1984–85; Ceremonial Fanfare for Kouvola, 1984, recorded 1988; Fantasy for orchestra, 1985; Two Pieces for orchestra, 1985–86; Syksyisia Kuvia, 1986; Fantasia for clarinet and wind orchestra, 1986; Brass Quintet, 1987. *Recordings include:* Quintet for Brass, 1992; Scenes from Northern Carelia, 1990; Suite for wind orchestra, recorded 1995; Music for tuba and orchestra, 1991; Rose Red Music for brass and percussion instruments, 1994; Three Pieces for wind quintet, 1994; Amordus Play for tuba and piano, 1994–95; Three Pieces for tuba and piano, 1993–94. *Honours:* Province of North Karelia Art Prize, 1986 and 1995. *Address:* Suutarinkatu 12, 80100 Joensuu, Finland.

EETVELT, Francois van; singer (bass-baritone); b. 23 May 1946, Bornem, Belgium. *Education:* Brussels and Antwerp Conservatories and in Italy and Germany. *Career:* Sang Amfortas in Parsifal at Antwerp in 1976 and has sung there and in Brussels, Prague, Leipzig, Bratislava, Dresden and Helsinki as Don Giovanni, Wagner's Donner, Gunther, Wolfran and Kurwenal; Sang Apollo in Monteverdi's Orfeo, Jochanaan and Tarquinius in The Rape of Lucretia; Sang in the premiere of Das Schloss by André Laporte at Brussels in 1986; Festival engagements at Flanders and Aldeburgh; Television appearances include Monteverdi's Orfeo. *Honours:* Winner, Belcanto Competition, Ostend in 1978. *Address:* Theatre Royal de la Monnaie, 4 Leopold-strasse, 1000 Brussels, Belgium.

EFRATY, Anat; Singer (soprano); b. 28 June 1966, Tel-Aviv. *Education:* Studied at the Rubin Academy, Tel-Aviv, and with Walter Berry in Vienna. *Career:* Debut: Mahler's 2nd Symphony, with the Israel Symphony, 1993; New Israeli Opera from 1993, as The Bird in Farber's The Journey to Polyphonia, Britten's Helena, Ninetta in The Love for Three Oranges and other roles; US debut, San Diego, 1995, in Vivaldi's Gloria; German debut, Stuttgart, 1995, as Flaminia in Haydn's Mondo della luna; Théâtre du Châtelet, Paris, 1995, as Tebaldo in Don Carlo; Other roles include Frasquita, Sophie in Werther, Nannetta and Despina; Season 2000–01 as Lulu and Sophie at the Vienna Staatsoper, Lulu at Palermo. *Current Management:* Athole Still International Management, Forresters Hall, 25–27 Westow Street, London, SE19 3RY, England. *Telephone:* (20) 8771-5271. *Fax:* (20) 8768-6600. *Website:* www.atholestill.com.

EFREMOV, Alexander; Pianist; b. 8 July 1962, Tomsk, Siberia, Russia. *Education:* Far Eastern Institute of Arts, Vladivostok; Pianist, solo-ensembleist, accompanist, Tchaikovsky Conservatory, Moscow; Piano, Aesthetics, Masters degree, Postgraduate studies with Professor Dimitri Bashkirov. *Career:* Debut: Far Eastern Philharmonic, solo concert, 1985; Far East television, Russia, 1980–85; Radio ORF, 1997–; American Broadway music concerts, Tonhalle, Zürich, 1993; Concert in tribute to Geza Anda, Geza Anda House, Zürich, 1993; Solo Concert at Grossmünster, 1993; Concert with Bruckner Orchester, Linz, 1995; Chamber concert at Gasteig, Munich, 1996; Concert with Yevgeny Nesterenko at Vienna Konzerthaus, 1996; Concert with the Vienna Symphonic Orchestra at the Bregenz Festival, 1996; Concert in Theatre de St Quentin en Yvelines, Paris, 1997; Répétiteur and solo pianist, Porgy and Bess with the Vienna Symphony Orchestra, Bregenz, 1998. *Publications:* Schumann and the Aesthetics of German Romanticism, Lenin State Library, Moscow, 1990. *Address:* c/o Vienna Symphony Orchestra, Lehargasse 11, A–1060 Vienna, Austria.

EGERTON, Francis; Singer (tenor); b. 14 July 1930, Limerick, Republic of Ireland. *Career:* Early appearances with Scottish Opera, the Glyndebourne Festival and at Sadler's Wells; Covent Garden from 1972 as Iopas in Les Troyens, Beppe, Flute, the Captain in Wozzeck and roles in Carmen, Les Contes d'Hoffmann and La Fanciulla del West; Has sung Mime in Siegfried for Scottish Opera and in San Francisco; Other roles include, Pedrillo, Strauss's Scaramuccio at Nice, Italian Tenor at Glasgow and Monsieur Taupe in Capriccio at Glyndebourne, Bardolfo in Falstaff at San Francisco, in concert at Chicago and at Los Angeles, conducted by Giulini; Sang Il Conte in Cimarosa's Il Fanatico Burlato at Drottningholm, the Captain in Wozzeck at Edinburgh and Los Angeles; Season 1990–91 with Mr Upfold in Albert Herring at San Diego, the four tenor roles in Hoffmann in Paris, Goro in Madama Butterfly and Eumaus in Il Ritorno d'Ulisse in Los Angeles; Appearances in Prokofiev's The Fiery Angel at the Proms and Covent Garden, 1991–92, as the Doctor; Season 1995–96 as M le Comte in La Belle Vivette, after Offenbach, for English National Opera; M. Taupe in Capriccio at Glyndebourne, 1998; Other recent roles in Falstaff at the Oper der Stadt in Cologne, Billy Budd at the Bastille, Goro in Los Angeles and Missail for Washington Opera; Sang the Emperor in Turandot at Covent Garden, 2002. *Current Management:* Athole Still International Management, Forresters Hall, 25–27 Westow Street, London, SE19 3RY, England. *Telephone:* (20) 8771-5271. *Fax:* (20) 8768-6600. *Website:* www.atholestill.com.

EGMOND, Max van; Singer (Baritone); b. 1 Feb. 1936, Semarang, Indonesia. *Education:* Studied in Netherlands with Tine van Willigen-de Lorme. *Career:* After winning prizes in Netherlands, Brussels and Munich made many appearances as concert singer, notably in Baroque music, Netherlands, England, Brazil, Germany, Austria, Italy, Poland, Belgium, USA and Canada; Engagements at most leading music festivals and centres; Radio and television broadcasts; Teacher of

singing at the Amsterdam Musieklyceum from 1973. *Recordings:* St Matthew and St John Passions by Bach; Bach Cantatas conducted by Gustav Leonhardt and Nikolaus Harnoncourt; Der Tag des Gerichts by Telemann; Reger's Requiem; Il Ritorno d'Ulisse, Orfeo and Il Combatti-mento by Monteverdi; St Luke Passion by Schütz; Schubert's Schwa-nengesang; Lully's Alceste. *Honours:* Winner, 's-Hertogenbosch Competition, 1959; Edison Awards for Gramophone Recordings, 1969, 1971. *Address:* Willemsprakweg 150-1, Amsterdam 1007, Netherlands.

EGRI, Monika; Pianist; b. 17 Oct. 1966, Budapest, Hungary; m. Attila Pertis, 28 June 1991. *Education:* Bart ók Conservatory, Budapest; Music Academy, Vienna. *Career:* Performances, Hungarian Days, London, 1989, Musikverein, Vienna, 1991, Budapest Spring Festival, Carinthian Summer Festival, Austria; Television and radio recordings, Hungary, Austria, Italy; Founded Egri and Pertis Piano Duo, 1980s. *Recordings:* For Hungarian Radio and ORF, Austria; Journey Around the World, 1995; Liszt: Opera Fantasies and Transcriptions for 2 pianos, 1997–98. *Contributions:* Die Presse; Kronen Zeitung; Piano Journal. *Honours:* Magistra Artium, 1994; Grand Prix Internationale du Disque Liszt, 1998; Prizewinner, many international competitions. *Current Management:* Annart Artists Management, Barkacs utca 7, 1221 Budapest, Hungary; J A Ellison, International Artists Management, 135 Stevenage Road, Fulham, London SW6 6PB, England; Künstle-rmanagement Till Dönch, Weimarer Str 48, 1180 Vienna, Austria. *Address:* Kaltwasserstrasse 1, 3413 Unterkirchbach, Austria.

EHDE, John Martin; Swedish cellist and conductor; b. 25 April 1962, Stockholm. *Education:* Royal Academy of Music, Århus, Denmark, Hochschule für Musik, Vienna. *Career:* debut recital, Royal Academy, Copenhagen, 1987; first appeared on Swedish Radio aged 11; recitals and concertos with orchestras throughout Europe and Canada; radio and television appearances in Scandinavia, Iceland, Italy, Viet Nam, Hong Kong, Canada; Solo Cellist, Helsingborg Symphony Orchestra, Sweden 1989–99; speciality, performing the music of Frederick Delius; Cello Concerto, sonata; Young People's Concerts with most Swedish and Danish symphony orchestras (speaker, cellist, conductor); freelance soloist and chamber musician, with tours in Canada, Hong Kong, Viet Nam, Singapore 2000–; mem. Leopold Stokowski Soc., London, Frederick Delius Soc., England. *Recordings:* numerous with The Lin Ensemble and with the pianist Carl-Axel Dominique (Sonatas by Alkan, Debussy and Delius) 1997; Cello Concerto by Olof Lindgren 1997. *Honours:* 1st Prize in many Swedish Youth Competitions; Cultural Grant, Malmö Lions Club 1974; 1-year Grant for studies in Vienna, Swedish Institute for Science and Art 1987; Awarded Scholarship from Foundation of Legendary Swedish Conductor Sten Frykberg 1990. *Address:* Mansasvej 22, 2500 Valby, Denmark. *E-mail:* john@ehde.dk (office). *Website:* www.ehde.dk.

EHRLING, Sixten; Conductor; b. 3 April 1918, Malmö, Sweden; m. Gunnel Lindgren, 2 d. *Education:* Studied at the Royal Academy of Music, Stockholm. *Career:* Debut: Royal Opera Stockholm, 1940; Assistant to Karl Böhm at Dresden, 1941; Music Director of the Royal Opera Stockholm, 1953–60; Visited Edinburgh and London with the premiere production of Blomdahl's Aniara, 1959; Director of Salzburg Mozarteum course for conductors, 1954; Music Director, Detroit Symphony Orchestra, 1963–73; Head of the conducting department at the Juilliard School, New York, from 1973; Metropolitan Opera, 1973–77, Peter Grimes, Der Ring des Nibelungen, Il Trittico, Simon Boccanegra, Bluebeard's Castle; Principal Guest Conductor, Denver Symphony Orchestra 1979–85. *Recordings include:* Symphonies by Berwald with the London Symphony Orchestra; Music by Blomdahl with the Stockholm Philharmonic. *Honours:* Knight Commander, Order of the White Rose, Finland (for championing the works of Sibelius). *Address:* c/o Juilliard School, Lincoln Plaza, NY 10023, USA.

EIRIKSDOTTIR, Karolina; Composer; b. 10 Jan. 1951, Reykjavík, Iceland; m. Thorsteinn Hannesson, 1 Aug 1974, 1 d. *Education:* Graduated, Reykjavík College, 1971, Reykjavík College of Music, 1974; MMus Music History and Musicology, 1976, MMus Composition 1978, University of Michigan, USA. *Career:* Major performances of works: Iceland Symphony Orchestra (4 works), at Nordic Music Days in Helsinki 1980, Oslo 1982, Copenhagen 1984; At Scandinavia Today, Washington DC 1982; Opera, Nagon har jag sett in Vadstena in Sweden, 1988, Reykjavík, 1989; Sinfonietta performed by the BBC Scottish Symphony Orchestra during Breaking the Ice Festival in Glasgow, 1992; Six Movements for String Quartet performed by the Arditti String Quartet, London, 1992; Three Paragraphs for Orchestra performed by the Malmö Symphony Orchestra at Stockholm New Music Festival, Stockholm, 1993; Performances at Nordic Music Festival, Göteborg, 1991; Dark Music Days Festival in Reykjavík, 1993 and Kuhmo Festival in Finland, 1993; Commission, Icelandic State television, work for symphony orchestra, 1985; Several performances, Iceland and abroad; Opera, I Have Seen Someone (1988) given British premiere by Lontano, 1996; mem. Society of Icelandic composers. *Compositions include:* Notes, Sonans, Sinfonietta, for orchestra; 5 pieces for chamber orchestra; 6 movements for string quartet; Rondo and Rhapsody for piano; In Vultu Solis, violin; Trio, violin, cello, piano; 6 poems from the Japanese, and Some Days, voice and instruments; All pieces in manuscript at Iceland Music Information Centre, Reykjavík; Orchestral pieces, Notes, Sonans, Sinfonietta, Klifur, Three Paragraphs, Opera: Nagon har jag sett, chamber orchestra: Five pieces and Rhapsody in C; Land possessed by poems for baritone and piano, solo pieces for clarinet, harpsichord and guitar and chamber music; Concerto for clarinet and orchestra, 1994; Living by the sea: a Collection of Songs, 1997; Man Alive, chamber opera, 1999; Solos for cello and violin. *Recordings:* Sinfonietta, Iceland Symphony Orchestra, conductor Paul Zukofsky; Other works recorded by Iceland State Broadcasting Service; Karolina Eiriksdottir–Portrait; Icelandic Chamber Music. *Address:* Blatun 6, 225 Bessastadahreppur, Iceland.

EISMA, Will Leendert; Composer and Violinist; b. 13 May 1929, Sungailiat, Indonesia; m. Wilhelmina A Reeser, 30 Nov 1960, 1 s., 1 d. *Education:* Conservatory of Rotterdam; Composition, Accademia di Santa Cecilia, Rome; Institute for Sonology, Utrecht. *Career:* Violinist: Rotterdam Philharmonic, 1953–59, Chamber Orchestra, Società Corelli, 1960–61, Chamber Orchestra, Radio Hilversum, 1961–89; Member of electro instrumental group ICE; Director, Studio for Electronic Music, Five Roses. *Compositions:* 4 Concerti for orchestra, 1 for 2 violins and orchestra, 1961; Taurus-A, 1963; Volumina for orchestra, 1964; Concerti for oboe, horn, 1973; Chamber and electronic music, 1970; Concerto for string trio and orchestra, 1974; Concerto for percussion, 1979; Concerto for English horn, 1981; Concerto for 5 violas, 1982; Du dehors–Du dedans, 1983; Silver Plated Bronze, 1986; Te Deum, 1988; Passo del Diavolo, 1988; Mawar jiwa for gamelan, 1992; Uguisu for gamelan, 1997. *Address:* Oude Amersfoortsweg 206, Hilversum 1212 AL, Netherlands.

EJSING, Mette; Singer (Mezzo-soprano); b. 9 Nov. 1954, Silkeborg, Denmark. *Education:* Studied in Copenhagen with Ulrik Cold and Ingrid Bjoner. *Career:* Sang with the Stuttgart Staatsoper, 1991–95; St Gallen, 1992, as the Countess in The Queen of Spades; Erda in Wagner's Ring at Karlsruhe, Århus, Vienna Staatsoper (1995) and La Scala, Milan (1996); Staatsoper Berlin, 1995, in Der Rosenkavalier, Die Zauberflöte and Der fliegende Holländer; Bayreuth Festival in Parsifal and Die Walküre; Sang Erda in Siegfried at Helsinki, 1998; Season 1999–2000 as Erda in Siegfried at Sydney and Trieste, Erda and First Norn at Bayreuth; Concerts in San Francisco, Berlin and elsewhere. *Address:* c/o Finnish National Opera, PO Box 176, Helsingkatu 58, 00251 Helsinki, Finland.

EK, Harald; Tenor; b. 1936, Jonkoping, Sweden. *Education:* Studied in Gothenburg with G Kjellertz and R Jacobson. *Career:* Debut: Gothenburg in 1966 in Die Lustige Witwe; Sang at Drottningholm in 1967 as Almaviva in Paisiello's Il Barbiere di Siviglia, Stadtstheater Berne, 1969–72, and Bayreuth Festival in 1971 in Der fliegende Holländer and Das Rheingold; Member of the Staatsoper Hamburg, 1972–75, and Zürich Opera from 1975; Sang Don José at Gothenburg in 1988; Other roles include Don Ottavio, Tamino, Hoffmann, Comte Ory, Cavaradossi, Tom Rakewell and Alfred in Die Fledermaus. *Recordings include:* Der fliegende Holländer. *Address:* School of Theatre and Opera, University of Göteborg, Box 5439, 40229 Göteborg, Sweden.

EKLÖF, Marianne; Singer (Mezzo-soprano); b. 15 March 1956, Sweden. *Education:* Studied in Stockholm, at Juilliard (New York) and in London with Vera Rozsa. *Career:* Sang in opera at Malmö from 1985, as Carmen and in the premiere of Werle's Midsummer Night's Dream; Stockholm Folkoperan from 1990, in Samson et Dalila and Les Contes d'Hoffmann; Jutland Opera, Århus, 1995, as Waltraute in Götterdämmerung; Sang Mme de la Motte in the British premiere of Marie Antoinette by Daniel Börtz, at Brighton; Many concert engagements. *Recordings include:* Grieg's Peer Gynt and Sigurd Josalfar. *Address:* c/o Folkoperan, Hornsgatan 72, 11721 Stockholm, Sweden.

EKLUND, Anna; Soprano; b. 1964, Sweden. *Education:* Studied at the Stockholm College of Music and the State Opera School. *Career:* Debut: Stockholm Royal Opera as Papagena; Sang in staged version of Carmina Burana at Stockholm in 1991; Roles have included Isamene in Haeffner's Elektra at Drottningholm, Novis Elisabeth in Forsell's Riket ar Ditt, the Queen of Night and Serpetta in La Finta Giardiniera; Season 1991–92 in the St Matthew Passion under Philippe Herreweghe in Sweden, Barcelona and Madrid, Betty in Salieri's Falstaff at Drottningholm; Season 1992–93 as Zémire in Grétry's Zémire et Azor at Drottningholm, and the leading female role in the premiere of Amorina by Lars Runsten at the Royal Opera Stockholm. *Address:* Nordic Artists Management, Sveavagen 76, 11359 Stockholm, Sweden.

EKLUND, Hans; Composer and Professor; b. 1 July 1927, Sandviken, Sweden. *Education:* Studied with Lars-Erik Larsson, Stockholm Musikhogskolan, 1949–52; Ernst Pepping, Berlin, 1954; Rome, 1957. *Career:* Professor of Harmony and Counterpoint, Stockholm Musikhogskolan, 1964–. *Compositions include:* Opera: Mother Svea, 1972;

Orchestral: Symphonic Dances, 1954, Musica da Camera, No. 1, 1955, No. 2, 1956, No. 3, 1957, No. 4, 1959, No. 5, 1970, No. 6, 1970; Symphonies: No. 1, Sinfonia Seria, 1958, No. 2, Sinfonia Breve, 1964, No. 3, Sinfonia Rustica, 1967–68, No. 4, Hjalmar Branting in memoriam, 1973–74, No. 5, Quadri, 1978, No. 6, Sinfonia Senza Speranza, 1983, No. 7, La Serenata, 1984, No. 8, Sinfonia Grave, 1985, No. 9, Sinfonia Introvertita, 1992, No. 10 'Sine Nomine', 1994, No. 11, Sinfonia piccola, 1995, No. 12, Freschi, 1996; Other: Toccata, 1966, Concerto for trombone, winds and percussion, 1972, Requiem Per Soli Coro Ed Orchestra, 1977–78, Horn Concerto, 1979, Concerto for tuba and brass orchestra, 1980, Divertimento, 1986; Chamber: 2 Sonatas for solo violin, 1956, 1982, 3 Preludes for piano, 1990, 2 Pastoral Songs for choir, 1993; Various solo pieces, piano music and organ works and choruses. *Honours:* Member, Royal Swedish Academy of Music, 1975–; Awarded degree, Litteris et Artibus from the King of Sweden, 1985; Christ Johnson Fund Music Prize, 1989. *Address:* Bjornskogsgrand 63, 162 46 Vallingby, Sweden.

EL-DABH, Halim Abdul Messieh, MM, MFA; American composer and teacher; b. 4 March 1921, Cairo, Egypt. *Education:* Sulcz Conservatory, Cairo, University of Cairo, Berkshire Music Center, Tanglewood with Aaron Copland and Irving Fine, New England Conservatory of Music, Boston, Brandeis University. *Career:* teacher, Haile Selassie University, Addis Ababa 1962–65, Howard University 1966–69; teacher 1969–, Co-Dir 1979–, Center for the Study of World Musics, Kent State University. *Compositions include:* 3 Symphonies, 1950–56; String Quartet, 1951; Fantasia-Tahmeel for darabukka or timpani and strings, 1954; Bacchanalia for orchestra, 1958; Juxtaposition No. 1 for percussion ensemble, 1959; Black Epic, opera-pageant, 1968; Opera Files, 1971; Drink Of Eternity, opera-pageant, 1981; Concerto for darabukka, clarinet and strings, 1981; Tonography III for 5 winds, 1984; Piano pieces and choruses. *Publications:* The Derabucca: Hand Techniques in The Art of Drumming, 1965. *Honours:* Fulbright Scholarship; two Guggenheim Fellowships. *Address:* c/o Center for the Study of World Musics, Kent University, Kent, OH 44242, USA.

ELCHLEPP, Isolde; Singer (Mezzo-soprano); b. 1952, Strasbourg, France. *Education:* Opera School of the Bavarian State Opera. *Career:* Sang first at Bremen, notably as The Woman in Schoenberg's Erwartung, 1985; Wiesbaden from 1986 as Wagner's Venus, Fricka and Waltraute, and Azucena in Il Trovatore; Hanover Opera as Carmen, Ortrud, Santuzza, Octavian, the Composer, Amneris and Kundry; Deutsche Oper Berlin, 1990, as Ortrud; Guest appearances in Düsseldorf, Mannheim, Brunswick, Karlsruhe, Basle (Herodias in Salome) and Brussels; Concert repertory includes Schoenberg's Pierrot Lunaire, which she has sung in Paris and Nuremberg; Guest in Tokyo in Erwartung; Also sang Elektra with the Oslo Philharmonic; Troades, Frankfurt Opera; Fricka in Das Rheingold and Die Walküre at Hanover, 1992 as well as Hostess in the premiere of Reimann's Das Schloss, Deutsche Oper Berlin; Debut at Bayreuth Festival as Ortrud in 1993; Sang the Woman in Erwartung in a Pierre Audi production for Netherlands Opera; Season 1996 at Hanover as Lady Macbeth and Orff's Antigonae; Marie in Wozzeck at Turin, 1998; Sang Brünnhilde at Hannover, 1999, and Elektra at the Komische Oper Berlin, 2001. *Current Management:* Haydn Rawstron Ltd, London. *Address:* c/o Staatstheater Hannover, Opernhaus, Opernplatz 1, D–30159 Hannover, Germany.

ELDER, Mark Philip, CBE, MA; British conductor; *Music Director, Hallé Orchestra*; b. 2 June 1947, Hexham, England; s. of John Elder and Helen Elder; m. Amanda Jane Stein 1980; one d. *Education:* Bryanston School and Corpus Christi Coll., Cambridge. *Career:* music staff Wexford Festival 1969–70; Chorus Master and Asst Conductor Glyndebourne 1970–71; music staff Royal Opera House, Covent Garden 1970–72; Staff Conductor Australian Opera 1972–74; Staff Conductor ENO 1974–77, Assoc. Conductor 1977–79, Music Dir 1979–93; Prin. Guest Conductor London Mozart Players 1980–83, BBC Symphony Orchestra 1982–85, City of Birmingham Symphony Orchestra 1992–95; Music Dir Rochester Philharmonic Orchestra, NY 1989–94, Hallé Orchestra 2000–. *Honours:* Dr hc (Royal Acad. of Music) 1984, Hon. Fellow Royal Northern Coll. of Music; Olivier Award for Outstanding Contribution to Opera 1990. *Address:* c/o Ingpen & Williams Ltd, 7 St George's Court, 131 Putney Bridge Road, London, SW15 2PA, England.

ELIAS, Brian David; composer; b. 30 Aug. 1948, Bombay, India. *Education:* Royal Coll. of Music, studied with Elisabeth Lutyens. *Career:* freelance ed., arranger and copyist; clerk and statistician assistant, 1972–78; composer, full-time with some teaching commitments; mem. British Acad. of Composers and Songwriters. *Compositions include:* La Chevelure for soprano and chamber orchestra; Somnia for tenor and orchestra; L'Eylah for orchestra, commissioned by BBC for Promenade Concerts, 1984; Tzigane for solo violin; Peroration for solo soprano; Geranos for chamber ensemble, commissioned by The Fires of London, 1985; 5 songs to Poems by Irina Ratushinskaya for mezzo-soprano and orchestra commissioned by BBC for Winter Season, 1989–;

The Judas Tree, ballet score commissioned by The Royal Ballet choreographed by Kenneth MacMillan, 1992; Fanfare, Royal Ballet, choreographed by Matthew Hart, 1993; Laments for mezzo-soprano, 6 female voices and orchestra (commissioned by BBC for the Cheltenham Festival, 1998); The House That Jack Built for orchestra commissioned by the BBC for Winter Season 2001–2002; Three Songs (Christina Rosetti); A Talisman for bass-baritone and chamber orchestra (commissioned by Cheltenham Int. Festival of Music. *Recordings:* Peroration by Irina Ratushinskaya; The Judas Tree; Laments, Moto Perpetuo. *Honours:* jt second prize for Proverbs of Hell, Radcliffe Music Award, 1977. *Address:* c/o Chester Music, 8–9 Frith Street, London, W1D 3JB, England (office). *Telephone:* (20) 7434-0066 (office). *E-mail:* promotion@musicsales.co.uk (office). *Website:* www.chesternovello.com (office).

ELIAS, Jorge; Singer (Tenor); b. 1973, Spain. *Education:* Queen Sofia School of Music, Madrid with Alfredo Kraus. *Career:* Appearances throughout Spain from 1995, including Oviedo Opera, Il Barbiere di Siviglia, Bilbao and Madrid; Edgardo in Lucia di Lammermoor at Bergamo, 1997; Verdi's I Masnadieri at Piacenza, Don Carlos at the Santander Festival; Rodolfo in La Bohème at Lucca; Season 1999–2000 with Bruckner's Te Deum at the Teatro Comunale in Florence under Zubin Mehta; Other concerts include Donizetti's Requiem at Bergamo. *Honours:* Placido Domingo Trophy; 1st Prize, Ciudad de Logzaño Opera Contest; 2nd Prize, Francisco Slouso International Opera Contest. *Address:* c/o IMG Artists, Lovell House, 616 Chiswick High Road, London W4 5RX, England.

ELIAS, Rosalind; Singer and Opera Director; b. Lowell, MA, USA. *Education:* New England Conservatory, Boston, Accademia di Santa Cecilia, Rome; further study with Daniel Ferro in New York. *Career:* sang with New England Opera 1948–52; Metropolitan Opera from 1954 as Cherubino, Dorabella, Rosina and Hansel, and in the premieres of Barber's Vanessa, and Antony and Cleopatra; Scottish Opera in 1970 as Rossini's La Cenerentola; Vienna Staatsoper in 1972 as Carmen; Glyndebourne Festival in 1975 as Baba the Turk in The Rake's Progress; other appearances in Hamburg, Monte Carlo, Barcelona, Lisbon and Aix-en-Provence; other roles included Verdi's Amneris and Azucena, Massenet's Charlotte and Giulietta in Les Contes d'Hoffmann; sang Herodias in Salome at Houston in 1987; produced Carmen at Cincinnati in 1988 and Il Barbiere di Siviglia for Opera Pacific, Costa Mesa, in 1989; sang Mistress Quickly in Falstaff at Boston, 1996; Italian debut as Old Lady in Bernstein's Candide, Turin, 1997; sang the Baroness in Vanessa at Monte Carlo, 2001. *Recordings:* La Gioconda, La Forza del Destino, Il Trovatore, Falstaff, Madama Butterfly, Rigoletto, Der fliegende Holländer. *Address:* c/o Opera Pacific, 3187 Red Hill Avenue, Costa Mesa, CA 92626, USA.

ELIASSON, Andreas; Composer; b. 3 April 1947, Borlange, Sweden. *Education:* Studied with Ingvar Lilholm and Gyorgy Ligeti. *Compositions:* Hymn, for mens' voices; Winds and Percussion, 1970; Melos for String Quartet, 1970; Picnic for Wind Quintet, 1972; Glasdans for orchestra, 1973; En avoss, church opera, 1974; Disegno for string quartet, 1975; Canti in Iontananza for chamber orchestra, 1977; Impronta for orchestra, 1978; Turnings for orchestra, 1978; Ombra for clarinet and string quartet, 1980; Backanterna, incidental music, 1982; Symphony, 1988; Fantasia for orchestra, 1988; Sinfonia concertante, 1989; Farfalle e ferro for horn and strings, 1992; Stammor for string quartet, 1992; Clarinet Concerto, 1992; Violin Concerto, 1992; Kimmo for trumpet and 6 percussion, 1996; Bass Clarinet Concerto, 1996; Oratorio, 2000. *Honours:* Royal Swedish Academy Prize, 1983. *Address:* c/o STIM, Sankhamnsgaten 79, 102 54 Stockholm, Sweden.

ELIASSON, Sven Olaf; Singer (Tenor); b. 4 April 1933, Boliden, Sweden. *Education:* Royal Music Academy, Stockholm. *Career:* Sang at Oslo from 1961, Stockholm from 1965; Guest appearances at the Hamburg Staatsoper, 1968–74; Further engagements at Zürich, Düsseldorf and Frankfurt; Glyndebourne in 1967 as Don Ottavio; Drottningholm Opera in 1967 as Belmonte in Die Entführung; Zürich Opera in 1968 and 1975 as Pfitzner's Palestrina and in the premiere of Klebe's Ein Wahrer Held; Stockholm Opera in 1970 in the premiere of Rosenberg's Hus Med Dubbel Ingang; Sang Schoenberg's Aron with the Hamburg Staatsoper in Israel in 1974; Other roles included Don José, Riccardo in Un Ballo in Maschera, Peter Grimes and Tom Rakewell in The Rake's Progress; Director of Oslo Opera from 1983; Sang Siegmund at Århus, 1987. *Recordings include:* Il Ritorno d'Ulisse in Patria by Monteverdi; Video of Swedish Opera production of Die Meistersinger. *Address:* c/o Jutland Opera, Thomas Jensens Alle, DK-8000 Århus, Denmark.

ELKINS, Margreta; Singer (Mezzo-Soprano); b. 16 Oct. 1932, Brisbane, Australia. *Education:* Studied with Ruby Dent in Brisbane, with Pauline Bindley in Melbourne and Vera Rozsa in London; Further study with Campogalliani in Milan. *Career:* Debut: Brisbane Opera Company in 1955 as Azucena; Joined the Royal Opera, London in 1958 and sang Octavian, Adalgisa in Norma, Amneris and Marina in Boris Godunov; Sang Helen in the premiere of Tippett's King Priam, with the Royal Opera at Coventry in 1962; Sadler's Wells Theatre in 1963 in Giulio Cesare by Handel; Many appearances with Joan Sutherland; Guest engagements in Genoa, Naples, Barcelona, Boston, New Orleans and Philadelphia; Sang at Amsterdam in 1974 in Handel's Rodelinda; Sang with Australian Opera, Sydney from 1975, and sang Amneris at Brisbane in 1988 and Azucena in 1990; Repertoire ranges from Monteverdi to Wagner; Many concert appearances. *Recordings include:* Many opera sets; With Joan Sutherland: I Puritani, La Sonnambula, Faust, Shield's Rosina, Giulio Cesare and Griselda by Bononcini. *Address:* c/o Lyric Opera of Queensland, PO Box 677, South Brisbane, Queensland 4101, Australia.

ELLIOTT, Alasdair; Singer (tenor); b. 1954, Hamilton, Scotland. *Education:* Royal Scottish Acad., Glasgow; Guildhall School of Music; Pears-Britten School of Advanced Musical Studies; National Opera Studio. *Career:* sang with Kent Opera; Curzio (Nozze di Figaro), Flich (Beggar's Opera); English Touring Opera: Ramiro (La Cenerentola), Belmonte (Entführung), also for Glyndebourne Touring Opera; Opera Northern Ireland: Leicester (Maria Stuarda), Pedrillio (Entführung); Scottish Opera: Squeak (Billy Budd), Basilio (Nozze di Figaro), Iopas (Les Troyens), Rector (Peter Grimes), Benda (The Jacobin); ENO: Jew (Salome), Priest (Christmas Eve), Andrés (Wozzeck), Servant (The Bacchae, John Buller, world premiere); Brighella (Ariadne auf Naxos), Vova (Life with an Idiot); Royal Opera House: Fisherman (Guillaume Tell), Gelsomina (Il Viaggio a Reims), Vogelgesang (Die Meistersinger von Nürnberg), Priest (Die Zauberflöte), Junger Diener (Elektra); Pong (Turandot), Don Curzio (Nozze di Figaro); CBTO: Calasis (Les Boréades, Rameau); Covent Garden Festival Opera: Tamino (Die Zauberflöte); Edinburgh International Festival: Gerry (Tourist Variations, James Macmillan, world premiere); Netherlands Opera: Host (Benvenuto Cellini); Drottningholm Court Theatre: Armida (Haydn); Opéra Comique: Azeste (Ascanio in Alba); concerts in Spain, Switzerland, Netherlands, Canada, Trevor Pinnock and the English Concert, London Mozart Players, Jane Glover (including the first performance of The Vessel, Stephen Oliver); recent roles include Roderigo in Otello and Gastone in Traviata, for the Royal Opera, Pong in Turandot at the Teatro Real in Madrid, David in Die Meistersinger at The Staatstheater, Stuttgart, Palestrina at the Metropolitan Opera, New York and Eurimachus in Il Ritorno d'Ulisse at Lisbon, Mime in The Ring for Scottish Opera, Vasek in The Bartered Bride at Glyndebourne, Valzacchi in Der Rosenkavalier for Frankfurt Opera, Nick in Fanciulla del West in the Netherlands, Andres in Wozzeck for ROH; Monostatos in The Magic Flute for ENO, Brighelle in Ariadne for ROH, Bardolph in Falstaff for ENO; recitals: Queen's Hall, Edinburgh, Jubilee Hall, Aldeburgh, Purcell Room, Wigmore Hall, Royal Opera House, London. *Recordings include:* various Baroque repertoire with Janiculum. *Current Management:* AOR Management Inc., 6910 Roosevelt Way NE, PMB 221, Seattle, WA 98115, USA. *E-mail:* jennyrose@aormanagementutc.com.

ELLIOTT, Alasdair; Singer (tenor); b. 1954, Hamilton, Scotland. *Education:* Royal Scottish Acad., Glasgow; Guildhall School of Music; Pears-Britten School of Advanced Musical Studies; National Opera Studio. *Career:* sang with Kent Opera; Curzio (Nozze di Figaro), Flich (Beggar's Opera); English Touring Opera: Ramiro (La Cenerentola), Belmonte (Entführung), also for Glyndebourne Touring Opera; Opera Northern Ireland: Leicester (Maria Stuarda), Pedrillio (Entführung); Scottish Opera: Squeak (Billy Budd), Basilio (Nozze di Figaro), Iopas (Les Troyens), Rector (Peter Grimes), Benda (The Jacobin); ENO: Jew (Salome), Priest (Christmas Eve), Andrés (Wozzeck), Servant (The Bacchae, John Buller, world premiere); Brighella (Ariadne auf Naxos), Vova (Life with an Idiot); Royal Opera House: Fisherman (Guillaume Tell), Gelsomina (Il Viaggio a Reims), Vogelgesang (Die Meistersinger von Nürnberg), Priest (Die Zauberflöte), Junger Diener (Elektra); Pong (Turandot), Don Curzio (Nozze di Figaro); CBTO: Calasis (Les Boréades, Rameau); Covent Garden Festival Opera: Tamino (Die Zauberflöte); Edinburgh International Festival: Gerry (Tourist Variations, James Macmillan, world premiere); Netherlands Opera: Host (Benvenuto Cellini); Drottningholm Court Theatre: Armida (Haydn); Opéra Comique: Azeste (Ascanio in Alba); concerts in Spain, Switzerland, Netherlands, Canada, Trevor Pinnock and the English Concert, London Mozart Players, Jane Glover (including the first performance of The Vessel, Stephen Oliver); recent roles include Roderigo in Otello and Gastone in Traviata, for the Royal Opera, Pong in Turandot at the Teatro Real in Madrid, David in Die Meistersinger at The Staatstheater, Stuttgart, Palestrina at the Metropolitan Opera, New York and Eurimachus in Il Ritorno d'Ulisse at Lisbon, Mime in The Ring for Scottish Opera, Vasek in The Bartered Bride at Glyndebourne, Valzacchi in Der Rosenkavalier for Frankfurt Opera, Nick in Fanciulla del West in the Netherlands, Andres in Wozzeck for ROH; Monostatos in The Magic Flute for ENO, Brighelle in Ariadne for ROH, Bardolph in Falstaff for ENO; recitals: Queen's Hall, Edinburgh, Jubilee Hall, Aldeburgh, Purcell Room, Wigmore Hall, Royal Opera House, London. *Recordings include:* various Baroque repertoire with Janiculum. *Current Management:* AOR Management Inc., 6910 Roosevelt Way NE, PMB 221, Seattle, WA

98115, USA. *Telephone:* (206) 729-6160 (office). *Fax:* (206) 985-8499 (office). *E-mail:* jennyrose@aormanagementuk.com. *Website:* www .aormanagementuk.com.

ELLIOTT, Anthony; Conductor and Concert Cellist; b. 3 Sept. 1948, Rome, New York, USA; m. Paula Sokol, 9 June 1975, 4 d. *Education:* Rome Free Academy, Rome, New York, USA; Performers Certificate, 1969, School of Music, Indiana University; Bachelor of Music with Distinction, 1970, Indiana University. *Career:* Debut: St Lawrence Centre of Performing Arts, Toronto, Ontario, Canada; Soloist with Detroit Symphony, New York Philharmonic, CBC Toronto Orchestra, Minnesota Orchestra, Vancouver Symphony, Colorado Philharmonic; Recitals broadcast on NET, NPR and CBC, including premiere performances of 20th century compositions; Former Musical Director, University Symphony Orchestra, Western Michigan University; Former Assistant Music Director, Marrowstone Music Festival; Former Professor of Cello, University of Houston; Former Music Director of the Houston Youth Symphony and Ballet; Visiting Professor, Eastman School of Music, Indiana University; Presently Professor of Cello, University of Michigan. Chamber music: Appeared with present and former concertmaster of Berlin Philharmonic, Concertgebouw Orchestra, Philadelphia Orchestra, Chicago Symphony, Minnesota Orchestra, Toronto Symphony, Montreal Symphony, and with members of Juilliard, Emerson, and Concord String Quartets. Also appeared with members of Chamber Music Society of Lincoln Center, and with Quarter Canada. *Recordings:* Solo cellist: Ravel, Mother Goose (complete ballet) (2); Ravel, La Valse and Alborada del Gracioso; Rimsky-Korsakov, Russian Easter Overture; Holst, The Planets; Koch International Classics Series, Music by Slav Composers; Lamentations Suite by Coleridge Taylor; Sonata for cello and piano Op No. 3 by Paul Hindemith; Cello music by Rachmaninov, 2002; recordings available at cdbaby.com, Slavic Music for Cello, French Music for Cello. Music for Cello and Piano by African—American Composers and an all Rachmaninoff CD. *Honours:* Gold Medalist, Feuermann Memorial International Cello Solo Competition. *Address:* School of Music, University of Michigan, Ann Arbor, MI 48109-2085, USA. *E-mail:* aelliot@umich.edu.

ELLIOTT, Marie; Singer (Soprano); b. 1970, Devon, England. *Education:* Guildhall School, with Johanna Peters; Royal Academy of Music; Further study with Janet Baker, Sarah Walker and Brigitte Fassbaender. *Career:* Solo oratorio appearances in Mozart's Requiem at Gloucester Cathedral. The Apostles by Elgar at Wells, Mendelssohn's Elijah, Pergolesi's Stabat Mater at St Martin-in-the-Fields, and Bach's Christmas Oratorio; Opera debut as Teodata in Flavio, for the London Handel Festival, 2001; Other roles include Dorabella, Rosina, Britten's Lucretia, and Isolier in Le Comte Ory; solo recital at St James's Piccadilly and Verdi Requiem at Bedford, 2001. *Honours:* Lucille Graham Award and Isabel Jay Prize, RAM, London. *Address:* c/o Royal College of Music, Prince Consort Road, London SW7, England.

ELLIOTT, Paul; Singer (Tenor) and Teacher; b. 19 March 1950, Macclesfield, Cheshire, England; m. Wendy Gillespie, 1982, 2 s. *Education:* Chorister at St Paul's Cathedral, London, 1959–62; The King's School, Canterbury, 1964–69; Choral Scholar, Magdalen College, Oxford, 1969–72; BA 1973, MA 1977, University of Oxford; Principal voice teachers: David Johnston and Peter Pears. *Career:* Vicar choral, St Paul's Cathedral, 1972–75; Member of John Alldis Choir, 1972–76; Cantores in Ecclesia, 1972–76, Schütz Choir of London, 1972–78; Monteverdi Choir, 1973–78; Founder member of Hilliard Ensemble, 1974–78; London Early Music Group, 1976–79; Vocal consort member of various consorts; Tours of Europe and USA as solo concert artist; Operatic engagements include: Handel's Acis in St Gallen, 1984, Mozart's Belmonte, Indiana University, 1988, and Mozart's Arbace in Chicago, 1988; Artist-in-Residence at Washington University, St Louis, 1984–85; Visiting Lecturer, Indiana University School of Music, Bloomington, 1985–87; Associate Professor of Music, 1987–92, Professor of Music, 1992–, Early Music Institute, Indiana University School of Music; Member of Theatre of Voices, 1991–; Various workshops and seminars; Pres., McClosky Inst. of Voice, Boston, USA, 2003 (Certified McClosky Voice Technician, 2000); mem, National Early Music Association; Early Music America; National Association of Teachers of Singing, America; American Association of University Professors. *Recordings:* As member of various vocal ensembles; As soloist with works by Bach, Handel, Purcell. *Honours:* US Citizenship, 1999. *Address:* School of Music, 1201 E Third Street, Bloomington, IN 47405-2200, USA. *Telephone:* (812) 855-8254 (office). *E-mail:* elliottp@ indiana.edu. *Website:* mypage.iu.edu/~elliottp.

ELLIS, Brent; Singer (Baritone); b. 20 June 1944, Kansas City, MO, USA. *Education:* Studied with Daniel Ferro in New York and with Luigi Ricci in Rome. *Career:* Debut: Washington DC in 1967 in the premiere of Ginastera's Bomarzo; Santa Fe Opera from 1972 notably as Mozart's Figaro, in the 1982 premiere of Rochberg's The Confidence Man and as Kunrad in Strauss's Feuersnot; New York City Opera debut in 1974 as Ottone in L'Incoronazione di Poppea; Glyndebourne from 1977 as Ford

in Falstaff, Marcello, Don Giovanni and Germont in the Peter Hall production of La Traviata; Metropolitan Opera from 1979 as Silvio in Pagliacci, Rossini's Figaro and Donizetti's Belcore; Opera North, Leeds as Scarpia and Macbeth; Welsh National Opera as Zurga in Les Pêcheurs de Perles; Cologne Opera from 1984 in La Gazza Ladra, Wozzeck, Rigoletto and Eine Florentinische Tragödie by Zemlinsky; Appearances in the premieres of Pasatieri's Washington Square for Michigan Opera and The Seagull for Seattle Opera; Sang Germont at Glyndebourne, 1987, Santa Fe, 1989, also Kunrad in Feuersnot, 1988; San Francisco in 1989 as Iago, followed by Rigoletto at Covent Garden; Season 1992 as Amonasro at Seattle; Sang Dandini in Cenerentola at Toronto, 1996; Sang Macbeth for New Israeli Opera, 2000; Concert appearances in Mahler's 8th Symphony with the Chicago Symphony and with orchestras in San Francisco, Minnesota, Baltimore, Houston and Denver; Great Woods Festival with Michael Tilson Thomas. *Address:* c/o New York City Opera, Lincoln Center, New York, NY 10023, USA.

ELLIS, David; singer (baritone); b. 1970, England. *Education:* Royal Northern College of Music. *Career:* debut as Silvio in Pagliacci with Iceland Opera; Appearances as Don Giovanni with English Touring Opera, and Marcello and Donizetti's Talbot for Scottish Opera; Member of Covent Garden Opera from 1994 in Carmen, Die Meistersinger, Un Ballo in Maschera, Peter Grimes, Fanciulla del West, Salome and Billy Budd; Other roles include Belcore, Guglielmo and Posa in Don Carlos.

ELLIS, David; Composer; b. 10 March 1933, Liverpool, England. *Education:* Royal Manchester College of Music, 1953–57; FRNCM; ARMCM. *Career:* Music Producer, 1964–77, Head of Music, 1977–86, BBC; Artistic Director, Northern Chamber Orchestra, 1986–94; Associate Director, Orquestra Sinfónica Portuguesa, 1994–. *Compositions:* Sinfonietta, 1953; String Trio, 1954; Dewpoint for soprano, clarinet and strings, 1955; Piano Sonata; Diversions on a theme of Purcell for strings, 1956; Violin Concerto, 1958; Piano Concerto, 1961; Opera Crito, 1963; Magnificat and Nunc Dimittis for choir and organ, 1964; Elegy for orchestra, 1966; Fanfares and Cadenzas for orchestra, 1968; Carols for an Island Christmas, 1971; Symphony No. 1, 1973; Solus for strings, 1973; L for orchestra, 1977; Sonata for solo double bass, 1977; String Quartet No. 1, 1980; Berceuse for clarinet and piano, 1981; Aubade for horn and piano, 1981; Suite Française for strings, 1987; Contra-provisations, 1994; Symphony No. 2, 1995; String Quartet No. 2, 1996; Four Songs, 1998; A Little Cantata, 1998; Three Note Variables for Piano, 1998; Symphony No. 3 1998–99; Shadows in Blue, 1999; Epiphany Nocturne, 1999; Island Seascape, 1999; Old Willows, 2000; Attleborough Tuckets, 2000; Rondo in Blue Minor for brass band, 2001; Contra Partita per Bassi, 2001; String Quartet No. 3, 2002; Concerto for bassoon and strings, 2002; Vetrate di Ricercata for organ, 2002. *Recordings:* An Image of Truth, 1999; Fast Forward, 1999; Old City: New Image, 2002. *Honours:* Royal Philharmonic Prize, 1956; Royal College of Music Patrons' Award, 1956; Theodore Holland Award, 1957; Silver Medal, Royal Manchester Institution, 1957; Ricordi Prize, 1957. *Address:* Vassaras, 14 Patch Lane, Bramhall, Cheshire, England. *E-mail:* delliscomposer@aol.com. *Website:* www.davidellis-composer.co .uk (office).

ELLIS, Gregory (Charles); Violinist; b. 3 Nov. 1960, Preston, Lancashire, England; m. Leslie Gail Toney, 22 Dec 1985, 1 s., 2 d. *Education:* Royal Academy of Music, London; DipRAM, 1983; ARAM, 1989; With Shmuel Ashkenasi at Northern Illinois University; Also student of Carmel Kaine and Frederick Grinke. *Career:* Debut: Wigmore Hall, London; Violinist and Leader, Vanbrugh String Quartet, resident to Radio Telefis Eireann since 1986; Frequent tours, the United Kingdom, Europe, Far East North and South America; Broadcasts on Radio 3, BBC World Service, Radio Telefis Eireann television and radio, Sky Channel (Arts), US and Canadian Radio, French television, Brazilian and Mexican television. *Recordings:* Several labels. *Honours:* Vanbrugh String Quartet 1st British string quartet to win the London/Portsmouth International String Quartet Competition, 1988. *Current Management:* Christa Phelps. *Address:* Vanbrugh House, Castle Treasure, Douglas, Co Cork, Ireland.

ELLIS, James (Antony); Composer and Conductor; b. 5 March 1954, Ashton-under-Lyne, England; m. Fiona Anne Johnson, 25 Feb 1978, 4 d. *Education:* Music Scholar, King's College, Cambridge, 1972–75; MA (Cantab); MMus, King's College, London, 1982. *Career:* Violinist Member of the Royal Philharmonic Orchestra, 1977–80, and Philharmonia, 1980–81; Assistant Tutor, King's College, London, 1982–84; Lecturer in Music, University of Keele, 1984–86; Composer-in-Residence, National Centre of Orchestral Studies, Goldsmiths' College, London, 1986–87; Lecturer in Music, City University, 1989–; Conductor for Thames Chamber Players, Oxford Haydn Players and appearances with National Centre of Orchestral Studies, European Community Youth Orchestra, Capricorn. *Compositions include:* Chamber: String Quartet No. 1, Summer Song; Works for Piano: Sonata No. 1, Autumn Tale; Serenata; Variations for Orchestra, 1979; Festive Fanfare;

Prelude, Dream Sequence and the Song Of The Washerwoman, from the opera Yerma; Appearances; The Name Of The Rose; Summer Cycle including Summer Night; Summer's Apotheose; String Quartet No. 2, L'Eveil Au Désir; Canti Cantici, Libro 1. *Contributions:* Editorial Assistant, Music Analysis; Various reviews. *Address:* 2 Stanley Avenue, Chesham, Buckinghamshire HP5 2JF, England.

ELLIS, Osian (Gwynn); Harpist; b. 8 Feb. 1928, Fynnongroew, Flint, Wales; m. Rene Ellis Jones, 1951, 2 s. *Education:* Royal Academy of Music. *Career:* Numerous radio and television broadcasts; Recitals and concerts world-wide; Shared poetry and music recitals with Dame Peggy Ashcroft, Paul Robeson, Richard Burton, C Day-Lewis among others; Member of Melos Ensemble; Solo harpist with London Symphony Orchestra; Professor of Harp at Royal Academy of Music, 1959–89; Works written for him include Harp Concertos by Hoddinott, 1957, Mathias, 1970, Jersild, 1972, Gian Carlo Menotti, 1977, and William Schuman, 1978; From 1960 worked with Benjamin Britten who wrote for him Harp Suite in C, Opus 83, and Canticle V for performance with Peter Pears, Birthday Hansel, and folk songs; With Peter Pears on recital tours to Europe and USA, 1974–; mem, Former Member, Music and Welsh Advisory Committees, British Council. *Recordings include:* Concertos, recitals and folk songs. *Publications:* The Story of the Harp in Wales, 1991. *Honours:* Paris Award for film, The Harp; Grand Prix du Disque; French Radio Critics Award; FRAM, 1960; Honorary D.Mus, University of Wales, 1970; C.B.E., 1971. *Address:* Arfryn, Ala Road, Pwllheli, Gwynedd LL53 5BN Wales.

ELMING, Poul; Singer (tenor); b. 21 July 1949, Aalborg, Denmark. *Education:* Studied at the Conservatories in Aalborg and Århus, and with Paul Lohmann in Wiesbaden. *Career:* Debut: Sang in recital from 1978; Performed baritone roles with Jutland Opera, Århus, from 1979; Royal Opera Copenhagen from 1984 in many roles including Mozart's Count, Eugene Onegin, Malatesta and Verdi's Germont and Posa; Further private studies at Royal Danish Music Conservatory and the Juilliard, New York; Made his tenor debut as Parsifal at the Royal Opera, Copenhagen in 1989; Has sung Erik in Der fliegende Holländer and Spalanzani in Les Contes d'Hoffmann; Bayreuth Festival, Covent Garden, Deutsche Oper Berlin and the Vienna Staatsoper; Hannover and Mannheim from 1990 as Siegmund in Die Walküre and Parsifal; Many recitals and concerts including appearances with the Danish Radio Symphony Orchestra in Copenhagen; Sang Siegmund at Covent Garden, 1994; Parsifal at the 1996 Bayreuth Festival; Lohengrin at Copenhagen, 1998; Season 2000–1 as Siegmund at the New York Met, Parsifal at Bayreuth and Covent Garden, and as Luke in the premiere of The Handmaid's Tale by Poul Ruders, at Copenhagen. *Recordings include:* Video of Parsifal from the Berlin Staatsoper, 1995. *Current Management:* Ingpen & Williams Ltd, 7 St George's Court, 131 Putney Bridge Road, London, SW15 2PA, England.

ELMS, Lauris; Singer (Contralto); b. 20 Oct. 1931, Melbourne, Australia. *Education:* Studied with Katherine Wielaert in Melbourne and Dominique Modesti in Paris. *Career:* Principal contralto, Covent Garden, 1957–59 before returning to Australia; Soloist with ABC and NZBC Orchestras; Principal contralto Sutherland-Williamson Opera Co, 1965, principal contralto Elizabethan Opera and Australian Opera, 1966–87. Soloist Musica Viva Australia, Royal Philharmonic, Israel Philharmonic Orchestras; Chamber Music Federation, New Zealand; Royal Command Performances, 1958, 1959, 1964, 1970, 1973; Royal Opening Concert, Sydney Opera House, 1973 and opening opera season, 1973; Toured Israel, 1958, 10th Anniversary of the Israeli State, 9 performances of Beethoven 9th Symphony; Korea, 1973; China, 1983, 2000; Principal operatic roles: Amneris, Azucena, Ulrica, Principessa, Lucretia, Judith, Sesto, Orfeo, Mrs Sedley. *Recordings:* Peter Grimes, Britten; Highlights from Graun's Montezuma (title role); Bononcini's Griselda (title role), Bonynge; Debussy and Beethoven song recitals; Brahms and Berg songs with Geoffrey Parsons; Schubert Lieder with John Winther; Liszt songs with David Miller; Elgar Sea Pictures; Chausson, Poème de L'amour; Operatic Arias with SSO and WASO; Video: Il Trovatore from Sydney Opera House, Sutherland, Bonynge. *Honours:* O.B.E., 1973; AM, 1982; Hon D Mus (Syd). *Address:* c/o Opera Australia, Sydney Opera House, New South Wales, Australia.

ELMS, Roderick (James Charles); Pianist and Organist; b. 18 Oct. 1951, Ilford, England. *Education:* Licentiate, Guildhall School of Music, 1965; Licentiate, Royal Academy of Music, 1970; Fellow, Royal College of Organists, 1974. *Career:* Debut: Wigmore Hall and Purcell Room, 1976; Regular Recitalist on organ and piano; Participant in recordings and public concerts given by all major symphony orchestras, some broadcast on radio or television; Member of GNAFF Ensemble, which made successful television debut, Dec 1982. *Compositions:* Many arrangements and original compositions performed and broadcast by BBC; Original Music to Love is a Gift; 4 Season Nocturnes for horn and orchestra, 1999. *Recordings:* Numerous works recorded with orchestras and choirs including many solo recordings with London Symphony, London Philharmonic and Royal Philharmonic Orchestras; Organ

Music of Percy Whitlock, album; Solo piano album; Christmas arrangements recorded on Christmas Gift; Magnificat; In Dulci Jubilo; Original Music to Love is a Gift recorded on Just For Today; Frank Martin Ballade for piano and orchestra, London Philharmonic Orchestra/Bamert, 1995. *Honours:* ARAM. *Address:* 23 Bethell Avenue, Cranbrook, Ilford, Essex IG1 4UX, England.

ELOY, Jean-Claude; Composer; b. 15 June 1938, Mount Saint Aignan, Seine Maritime, France. *Education:* Studied with Milhaud, Martenot and Boulez, 1950–61. *Career:* Cologne Electronic Music Studio with Stockhausen, 1972–73; Producer for Radio France, 1971–87. *Compositions:* Symphony no 1, 1962; Equivalences for 18 instruments, 1963; Poly-chronies I and II for wind and percussion, 1964; Faisceaux-Diffractions, for 28 instruments, 1970; Kamakela for 3 ensembles and 3 choruses, 1971; Vers l'etendue for orchestra, 1974; Fluctuante Imnnuable for orchestra, 1977; Reverberation for 4 tapes and percussion, 1980; Anahata for soloists and ensemble, 1986; Sapho Hiketis for women's voices and electronics, 1989; Gaia for soprano and electronics, 1992. *Address:* c/o SACEM, 225 Avenue Charles de Gaulle, 92521 Neuilly sur Seine Cédex, France.

ELSNER, Christian; Singer (Tenor); b. 1965, Freiburg im Breisgau, Germany. *Education:* Studied in Frankfurt am Main. *Career:* Lensky in Eugene Onegin at Oper Heidelberg, Tichon in Katya Kabanova, Pedrillo in Entführung, Macduff in Macbeth at Staatstheater Darmstadt and Idomeneo at Norwegian State opera in Oslo; Concerts include Lieder recitals at the Schubertiade Feldkirch and throughout Europe; Mahler's Lied von der Erde in Munich and at the Wiener Festwochen, Bruckner's Te Deum at the Salzburg Festival, Beethoven's Ninth in London and Schumann's Faustszenen in Tokyo with conductors such as Giulini, Jordan, Herreweghe, Nelson, Blomstedt and Honeck. *Recordings include:* Schumann's Dichterliebe; Mahler's Lieder eines fahrenden Gesellen; Schubert Songs, and Mahler's Lied von der Erde. *Honours:* Winner, International Walter Gruner Lieder Competition, London, 1993; Second Prize, International ARD competition, Munich, 1994. *Address:* Kunstler Sekretariat am Gasteig, Rosenheimerstrasse 52, 81669 Munich, Germany.

ELSTE, (Rudolf Otto) Martin, DPhil; German musicologist, discologist and music critic; *Curator, Staatliches Institut für Musikforschung;* b. 11 Sept. 1952, Bremen. *Education:* University of Cologne, Rheinische Musikschule, Cologne, King's College, London, England, Technische Universität, Berlin. *Career:* Curator, Staatliches Institut für Musikforschung Preussischer Kulturbesitz, 1982–; Review Editor, IASA Phonographic Bulletin, 1982–93; Panel member, German Record Critics Award, 1983–; Chairman, IASA Discography Committee, 1992–96; Vice President, IASA, 1996–99; Consulting Musicologist, Bach-Tage Berlin, 1986–87; Advisory Board Member, CIMCIM, 1995–2001; Editorial Advisory Board Member, Music in Performance, 1997; Vice-President, Verein f. Musik Archiv-Forschung, 1998–2001; President, German Record Critics Award, 2000–; Consulting Editor, Die Musik in Geschichte und Gegenwart; Bd mem. RIdIM Commission Mixte 2004–. *Publications:* Internationale Heinrich Schütz Diskographie 1928–72, 1972; Verzeichnis deutschsprachiger Musiksoziologie, 1975; Bachs Kunst der Fuge auf Schallplatten, 1981; Co-contributor, Musikinstrumenten Museum Berlin, 1986; Co-contributor, Handwerk im Dienste der Musik, 1987; Co-contributor, 100 Jahre Berliner Musikinstrumenten Museum, 1988; Kleines Tonträger-Lexikon, 1989; Co-contributor, Kielklaviere, 1991; Co-contributor, Musikalische Interpretation, 1992; Modern Harpsichord Music: A Discography, 1995; Editor/Translator, Baines, Lexikon der Musikinstrumente, 1996; Co-contributor, Bach-Handbuch, 1999; Meilensteine der Bach-Interpretation, 2000; editor: Ausgezeichnet! 2004. *Contributions:* New Grove; Fono Forum; Fanfare; Die Musikforschung; Basler Jahrbuch für Historische Musikpraxis; Jahrbuch des Staatlichen Instituts für Musikforschung; Jahrbuch Preussischer Kulturbesitz; Klassik heute; Musik in Geschichte und Gegenwart; Frankfurter Allgemeine Zeitung; Die Zeit; Neue Zeitschrift für Musik, Hindemith-Jahrbuch. *Honours:* ARSC Award for Excellence in Historical Recorded Sound Research 2001. *Address:* SIMPK, Tiergartenstrasse 1, 10785 Berlin, Germany (office). *Telephone:* (30) 25481132 (office). *Fax:* (30) 25481172 (office). *E-mail:* elste@sim.spk-berlin.de (office). *Website:* www.martin-elste.de (home).

ELWES, John; Singer (Tenor); b. 1946, England. *Education:* Studied with George Malcolm at Westminster Cathedral; Further study at the Royal College of Music. *Career:* Chorister at Westminster Cathedral; Soloist in Britten's Missa Brevis and Abraham and Isaac; Frequent broadcaster for the BBC; Repertoire includes Baroque, Lieder and Contemporary Music on the concert platform and operas by Gluck, Handel, Mozart and Monteverdi on stage; Sang Orfeo in Monteverdi's opera with Phillippe Herreweghe and La Chapelle Royale at the Montpellier opera house and with Flanders Opera, Antwerp, 1989–90. *Recordings include:* Orfeo in The Death of Orpheus by Stefano Landi, with Tragicomedia directed by Stephen Stubbs.

EMMERLICH, Gunther; singer (bass); b. 18 Sept. 1944, Thuringia, Germany. *Education:* Studied in Weimar and Dresden and with Pavel Lisitsian. *Career:* debut, sang the Peasant in Die Kluge by Orff at the Dresden Staatsoper in 1978; Appeared as Kuno in Der Freischütz at the reopening of the Semper Oper, Dresden, and has sung with the Dresden Ensemble at the Vienna Volksoper and in Amsterdam as Don Alfonso in 1988; Other roles include Osmin in Die Entführung, Geronimo in Matrimonio Segreto, Rocco, Dulcamara and the Hermit in Der Freischütz; Many concert appearances. *Recordings:* Der Freischütz; Eugene Onegin.

ENCINAS, Ignacio; Tenor; b. 1958, Spain. *Education:* Studied with Enzo Costantini and in Madrid; Masterclasses with Gianni Poggi and Gino Bechi. *Career:* Sang in Trovatore and La Favorita at the Santander Festival; Rigoletto at the Zarzuela Theatre in Madrid and appeared further in Oviedo, Valladolid and Malaga; At Dijon has sung in Pollione in Norma, Alfredo in Traviata, Rigoletto, and Riccardo in Un Ballo in Maschera; Season 1989–90 as Maurizio in Adriana Lecouvreur at Liège, returning as Turiddu and Rodolfo in La Bohème; Sang in Verdi's Attila at the Teatro Romano of Benevento and as Macduff in a concert performance of Macbeth at the 1990 Gstaad Festival and at Naples, 1998; Performances of Nabucco in Nimes, and as Arturo at Marseille, 1990–91; Sang Rodolfo in Luisa Miller for the Royal Opera at Edinburgh, 1988; Season 2000–01 as Turiddu at Buenos Aires, Calaf at Liège and Cavaradossi at the Deutsche Oper, Berlin. *Honours:* Winner of numerous international competitions. *Address:* c/o Mondial Musique, 17 rue Brey, F–75017 Paris, France.

ENDERLE, Matthias; Violinist; b. 16 June 1956, Switzerland. *Education:* Studied at the Winterhur Conservatory, in Indiana, and at the University International Menuhin Academy in Gstaad. *Career:* Co-Founder and Leader of the Carmina Quartet, 1984; Appearances from 1987 in Europe, Israel, Japan and USA; Regular concerts at the Wigmore Hall from 1987; Concerts at the South Bank Centre, London, Amsterdam Concertgebouw, the Kleine Philharmonie in Berlin, and Konzertverein Vienna; Four engagements in Paris, 1990–91, and seven in London; Tours of Australasia, the USA and Japan; Concerts at the Hohenems, Graz, Hong Kong, Schleswig-Holstein, Montreux, Bath, Lucerne, and Prague Spring Festivals; Collaborations with Dietrich Fischer-Dieskau, Olaf Bär and Mitsuko Uchida. *Recordings:* Various. *Honours:* Joint Winner, with members of Carmina Quartet, Paolo Borciani String Quartet Competition in Reggio Emilia, Italy, 1987; Gramophone Prize for Best Chamber Music Recording, 1992. *Address:* c/o Intermusica Artists' Management, 16 Duncan Terrace, London N1 8BZ, England.

ENDO, Akira; Conductor; b. 16 Nov. 1938, Shido, Japan. *Education:* Studied violin with Vera Barstow, Eudice Shapiro, and Jascha Heifetz; BM, MM, 1962, University of Southern California, Los Angeles. *Career:* Violinist, Trojan String Quartet, 1960–62; 2nd Violinist, Pacific String Quartet, 1962–69; Conductor, Long Beach Symphony Orchestra, California, 1966–69, and West Side Symphony Orchestra, Los Angeles, 1968–69; Music Director, American Ballet Theatre, NY, 1969–79; Resident Conductor of Houston Symphony Orchestra, 1974–76; Music Director, Austin Symphony Orchestra, TX, 1975–82 and Louisville Orchestra, 1980–83.

ENGEL, Karl; Concert Pianist; b. 1 June 1923, Basle, Switzerland; m. Barbara Wackernagel, 26 Oct 1976, 1 s., 1 d. *Education:* Humanistisches Gymnasium Basle; Basle Conservatory with Paul Baumgartner; Ecole Normale Paris with Alfred Cortot. *Career:* International career as concert pianist since 1948; Cycles of all Mozart piano concertos in Paris, Berlin, Munich, Salzburg, Vienna and Zürich; Cycles of all Beethoven piano sonatas in West Germany and Tel-Aviv; Series of all Mozart piano sonatas in Salzburg; Concert tours in Europe, USA and Japan; Guest of all major music festivals in Europe; Chamber music with Pablo Casals (Prades), Menuhin, Tortelier and Fournier; Lieder recitals with Dietrich Fischer-Dieskau, Hermann Prey and Peter Schreier; Professor of Piano at Hochschule für Musik Hanover, 1959–86; Masterclass at Berne Conservatory; mem, Schweizerischer Tonkunstlerverein. *Recordings:* Complete piano works of Schumann; Complete Mozart piano concertos with the Mozarteum Orchestra conducted by Leopold Hager; Complete solo piano music by Mozart; Chamber music and Lieder. *Honours:* Prize, Queen Elisabeth Competition in Belgium, 1952. *Address:* Chemin du Closalet Nr. 2, 1822 Chernex (VD), Switzerland.

ENGELMANN, Hans Ulrich; Composer and Professor; b. 8 Sept. 1921, Darmstadt, Germany. *Education:* Studied composition with Fortner, Heidelberg, 1945–49; With Leibowitz and Krenek, Darmstadt, 1948–50; Musicology with Gennrich and Osthoff, Philosophy with Adorno, University of Frankfurt am Main, PhD, 1952. *Career:* Music Adviser, Hessischen Landestheater, Darmstadt, 1954–61; Lecturer, 1969–73; Professor, 1973–, in composition, Hochschule für Musik, Frankfurt am Main; Music Adviser, Theater Bonn, 1972–73; President, Work-Commission, GEMA; President, German Composers' League. *Compositions include:* Stage Works: Doktor Fausts Hollenfahrt, 1949–50; Verlorener Schatten, 1960; Der Fall Van Damm, 1966–67; Magog, 1956–57; Serpentina, 1962; Ophelia, 1969; Revue, 1972–73; Orchestral Works: Music for strings, brass and percussion, 1948; Impromptu, 1949; Partita, 1953; Strukturen, 1954; 5 Orchestra Pieces, 1956; Polyfonica, 1957; Nocturnos, 1958; Ezra Pound Music, 1959 Trias for piano, orchestra and tape, 1962; Shadows, 1964; Sonata for jazz orchestra, 1967; Sinfonies, 1968; Capricciosi, 1968; Sinfonia da camera, 1981; Chamber: Cello Sonata, 1948; String Quartet, 1952; Integrate for saxophone and piano, 1954; Choir and Orchestra: Incanto, 1959; Missa Popularis, 1980–83; Stele for chorus soloists, symphony orchestra, 1987; Choral music including cantatas; New Works: Dialogue Piano Percussion, 1991; Clarinota, 1991; Tastenstück, 1991; Essay, 1992; Modus, 1992; Ciacona for chamber orchestra, 1993; Per Luigi, 1996. *Recordings include:* 99 Bars for Cembalo; Commedia Humana; Monographie "H.U.E. und sein Werk", 1985; Portrait Hans Ulrich Engelmann, 1999. *Publications:* Bela Bartók's Mikrokosmos, doctoral thesis; Autobiography: Vergangenheitsgegenwart, 2001. *Contributions:* Melos; Neue Zeitschrift für Musik; Musik und Bildung. *Honours:* Scholarship, Harvard University, 1949; Goethe Medaille, 1986; Kreuz der BRD, 1992; Hessischer Verdienstorden, 1997. *Address:* Park Rosenhohe, Engelweg 15, 64287 Darmstadt, Germany. *Telephone:* (6151) 77979. *Fax:* (6151) 77979.

ENGERER, Brigitte; French pianist; b. 27 Oct. 1952, Tunis, Algeria. *Education:* Paris Conservatory, studied piano with Lucette Descaves in Paris, Moscow Conservatory with Stanislav Neuhaus. *Career:* soloist with many leading orchestras including Orchestre de Paris, Berlin Philharmonic Orchestra, London Symphony Orchestra, Vienna Symphony Orchestra, Chicago Symphony Orchestra with Daniel Barenboim, Czech Philharmonic Orchestra, Minnesota Orchestra, Los Angeles Philharmonic Orchestra and Toronto Symphony; Numerous recitals world-wide; Many festival and television appearances; Professor, Paris Conservatoire, 1994–; Video with Switzerland Orchestra with Strauss Burlesque. *Honours:* 6th Prize, Long-Thibaud Competition, 1969; 6th Prize, Tchaikovsky Competition, Moscow, 1974; 3rd Prize, Queen Elisabeth of Belgium Competition, 1978; Grand Prix du Disque with Schumann Carnaval. *Current Management:* ICM Artists Ltd, 40 West 57th Street, New York, NY 10019, USA.

ENGERT, Ruth; Singer (Mezzo-Soprano); b. 9 Oct. 1946, Frankfurt-am-Main, Germany. *Education:* Studied at the Frankfurt Musikhochschule and with Josef Metternich in Cologne. *Career:* Sang at Koblenz, Freiburg and Hannover, 1969–79; Member of the Deutsche Oper Berlin from 1979, notably as Mozart's Cherubino and Dorabella, Verdi's Eboli and Meg Page, Wagner's Fricka, Brangaene and Waltraute, Octavian, Nicklausse in Les Contes d'Hoffmann and Charlotte in Die Soldaten; Guest appearances at Turin in Clytemnestra in 1987, at Venice as the Composer in Ariadne auf Naxos and at Genoa, Madrid and Lisbon; Bayreuth Festival in 1989 as Venus in Tannhäuser; Sang Kundry at the Spoleto Festival in Italy and in Charleston, USA, 1986–90, and Octavian in Rosenkavalier at Catania in 1992; Sang Kundry for Flanders Opera, 1996; Clytemnestra in Elektra at Catania, 1998; Sang Herodias in Salome at Gelsenkirchen 1999. *Recordings:* Strauss's Feuersnot; Parsifal at Bayreuth, 1985; Die Walküre at Bayreuth, 1987; Eugene Onegin; Funeral Cantata by Cherubini. *Address:* c/o Musiktheater im Revier, Kennedyplatz, Pf 101854, 4650 Gelsenkirchen, Germany.

ENGLICHOVA, Katerina; Harpist; b. 13 June 1969, Prague, Czechoslovakia. *Education:* Conservatoire, Prague; Curtis Institute of Music, Philadelphia. *Career:* Debut: New York, Weill Recital Hall at Carnegie Hall, 1998 Paris, 2000; Modern Art Museum, Los Angeles, 1996; Paris, France, 1994, 1996, 1998, Hong Kong, 1998, 2001, Boston 1999, England 1999; The VII World Harp Congress, Prague, 1999; Festivals: Pacific Music Festival, Japan; Music by the Red Sea, Israel; Tanglewood Music Festival, USA; Rencontres Musicales d'Evian, France; Prague Autumn, Czech Republic; Repertoire includes Ravel, Introduction and Allegro; Ginastera Concerto etc; mem, World Harp Society. *Recordings:* Britten, Voice and Harp; Hindemith, Sonata; Harmonia Mundi, A Roussel, with Czech Nonet; Panton, M Ravel, C Debussy, Solo and Chamber Recital; Koch, Discover, C Saint-Saëns, L Spohr, P Hindemith, with Josef Suk, Violin; Petr Eben, Music for Harp; Rossetti Sonatas, 2000; Granados-Danzas Espagnolas, Supraphon, 2002. *Honours:* Prize, E Herbert Hobin Harp Competition, USA, 1993; 1st Prize Concerto Soloists Competition, 1994; 1st Prize, Pro Musicis International Award, New York, 1995; European Broadcast Competition, 1997; International Music Competition, Vienna, 1999; Tim Competition, Italy, 2002. *Website:* www.englichova.cz.

ENGLISH, Gerald; Singer (Lyric Tenor), Educator and Administrator; b. 6 Nov. 1925, England; m. (1) Jennifer Ryan, 1954, 2 s., 2 d., (2) Linda Jacoby, 1974, 1 s. *Education:* Royal College of Music. *Career:* After war service began career as lyric tenor, subsequently travelling USA, and Europe; Appeared at Sadler's Wells, Covent Garden and Glyndebourne;

Often heard in operas by Mozart and Monteverdi, and concert music by Bach, Stravinsky, Fauré and Dallapiccola; Professor, Royal College of Music, 1960–77; Director, Opera Studio, Victorian College for the Arts, Melbourne, Australia, 1977–89; Sang the title role in Andrew Ford's Sigmund Freud, Adelaide 2000. *Recordings:* Schumann Song Cycles with Roger Smalley Piano; Whispers music by Andrew Ford and vocal music of Peggy Glanville Hicks. *Honours:* D.Mus honoris causa, Sydney University, 1989; Australian Creative Artist Fellowship, 1994. *Address:* PO Box 4177, Geelong, Victoria 3220, Australia.

ENGLISH, Jon Arthur, BM; composer, trombonist, percussionist and double bass player; b. 22 March 1942, Kankakee, Illinois, USA; m. Candace Natwig. *Education:* University of Illinois with Kenneth Gaburo. *Career:* member of the Harry Partch Ensemble, 1961–62, the Illinois Contemporary Chamber Players, 1963–66 and the Savannah Symphony Orchestra, 1967; Associate Artist of the University of Iowa Center for New Music and New Performing Arts until 1974; has worked from Cologne since 1976; Performances in Europe as soloist, with Candace Natwig, singer, and in new music groups. *Compositions include:* 404 1-2 East Green Street for Tape, 1965; Sequent Cycles for 6 players, 1968;... Whose Circumference Is A Nowhere, 1970; Used Furniture Sale for Tape, 1971; Summerstalks for Performer and Tape, 1973; Shagbolt for Trombone, 1978; Electrotrombonics, 1979; Foursome, 1979; Dog Dreams, 1982; Harmonies For Charlie Mingus, 1983.

ENS, Phillip; Singer (Bass); b. 1962, Canada. *Career:* Debut: Manitoba Opera, 1985 as the Marchese in La Forza del Destino; Many appearances throughout Canada as Sarastro, Masetto and Figaro, for Pacific Opera Verdi's Sparafucile and Banquo and Gounod's Frère Laurence; Canadian Opera Company debut, 1989 as Don Fernando in Fidelio; US debut in 1992 as Sparafucile with Philadelphia Opera; Stuttgart Opera, 1993 as Sparafucile, Sarastro, Banquo in Macbeth, Mozart's Commendatore and Pimen in Boris Godunov; Carontes in Monteverdi's Orfeo at Munich and Claggart in Welsh National Opera's Billy Budd; Season 1999–2000 as Padre Guardiano in La Forza del Destino at the Deutsche Oper Berlin, Hunding at the Metropolitan Opera; Sarastro in Hamburg and Gremin in Eugene Onegin at Brussels; Season 2002–03 as Fafner and Hunding in The Ring at Stuttgart; Ramfis in Brussels; Wurm in the Metropolitan Opera's new prodution of Luisa Miller; Hunding with the Lyric Opera of Chicago; Concerts include the Missa Solemnis in Brussels and Paris, and the Mozart Requiem at Salzburg and the BBC Proms. *Address:* c/o IMG Artists, Lovell House, 616 Chiswick High Road, London W4 5RX, England.

ENSTRÖM, Rolf; Composer; b. 2 Nov. 1951, Södertälje, Sweden; m. Karin Enströ m-Salomonsson, 3 May 1980, 2 s., 1 d. *Education:* Engineer, studied Musicology and Philosophy at the universities in Stockholm and Gothenburg; Studied Music in Örebro, Musicology in Gothenburg; Composition self-taught. *Career:* Debut: With multimedia piece Myr at the International Society for Contemporary Music Festival, Athens, 1979; As multimedia artist has collaborated with artists in adjacent fields, including photographer Thomas Hellsing; His music performed world-wide; Directions played at International Society for Contemporary Music, Athens, 1979; Teaching at EMS, Stockholm; Summer courses at Nordens Biskops Arnö, near Stockholm; Participant, DAAD cultural exchange programme, 1991, then Composer-in-Residence, Berlin. *Compositions:* Tape music, music for instruments and electronics and multimedia works, including: Slutförbannelser, text by Elsa Grave, 1981; Fractal, multimedia piece (with Thomas Hellsing); Tjidtjag och Tjidtjaggaise, based on Lapp joik, 1987; Skizzen aus Berlin, 1991; Asylum, multimedia piece (with Thomas Hellsing); Vigil, saxophone quartet, 1994; In Ice, Mirror, 1995; Spin, 1995; Charm, 1996; Io, intermedia, 1996; Open Wide, piano, percussion, tape, 1997; Strange, 1997; Rama, mixed choir and tape, 1998; Kairos, 1999; Up, 1999. *Recordings:* Directions, Final Curses, Tjidtjag och Tjidtjaggaise; Fractal; Dagbrott, Sequence In Blue, Tonal Nagual, Tsentsaks; In Ice, Mirror. *Address:* c/o STIM, Box 27327, 10254 Stockholm, Sweden.

ENTREMONT, Philippe; Conductor and Pianist; b. 7 June 1934, Rheims, France. *Education:* Studied under Jean Doyen at Paris Conservatoire. *Career:* Debut: Barcelona at age 15; US debut at National Gallery, Washington DC and with National Orchestral Association, NY, 1953; Appearances as recitalist and guest artist with major orchestras world-wide; Music Director, Conductor and Pianist with Vienna Chamber Orchestra; Has conducted many leading orchestras including Royal Philharmonic Orchestra, Ensemble Orchestral de Paris, Mostly Mozart, Dallas Orchestra, and Montreal Orchestra; Appeared in many major summer festivals including Schleswig-Holstein and Carinthian Festivals; World tour with Vienna Chamber Orchestra for Bicentennial of Mozart's death, 1991; Former President of Ravel Academy and Juror for international piano competitions; Permanent Conductor for Netherlands Chamber Orchestra, 1993. *Recordings include:* Works by Chopin, Mozart, Schubert, Stravinsky, Bernstein, Milhaud, and Debussy's Printemps, and Ravel's Bolero. *Honours:* 1st Laureate, Grand Prizewinner, Marguérite Long-

Jacques Thibaud Competition; Grand Prix du Disque; Edison Award, Netherlands; Knight, Legion of Honour; 1st Class Cross of Honour for Arts and Sciences, Austria. *Current Management:* ICM Artists. *Address:* c/o ICM Artists, 40 West 57th Street, New York, NY 10010, USA.

EÖSZE, László; Former Art Director; b. 17 Nov. 1923, Budapest, Hungary; m. (1) 2 c., (2) 24 September 1983. *Education:* PhD, Aesthetics and Literature. *Career:* Music Teacher and Pianist; Concerts in Hungary and Europe, 1946–51; mem, Co-President, F Liszt Society; Executive Secretary, 1975–95, International Kodály Society; Hungarian Musicological Society, 1996–. *Publications:* 16 books including, Zoltán Kodály élete és munkássága (Life and Work of ZK), 1956; Zoltán Kodály élete képekben (K's Life in Pictures), 1957; Az opera utja (History of Opera), 1960; Giuseppe Verdi, 1961, 2nd edition, 1966; Enlarged, 1975; Zoltán Kodály, His Life and Work, English, 1962, in German, 1965; Zoltán Kodály, 1967; Kodály, His Life in Pictures and Documents, 1971, English and German; Richard Wagner, 1969; Richard Wagner, Eine Chronik seines Lebens und Schaffens, 1969; Zoltán Kodály, életének krónikája, 1977; 119 római Liszt dokumentum, 1980; Selected Studies on Z Kodály, 2000; Essays and articles in various languages. *Contributions:* The New Grove Dictionary of Music and Musicians; Brockhaus Riemann Musiklexikon; Numerous professional publications. *Honours:* Erkel Prize, 1977; Gramma Award, 1978; Medium Cross of the Order of the Hungarian Republic, 1998; Medal for Merit of the Pres. of the Repub., 2003; Grand Prize of the Nat. Soc. of Creative Artists, 2003. *Address:* Attila ut 133, 1012 Budapest, Hungary.

EÖTVÖS, Peter; Composer and Conductor; b. 2 Jan. 1944, Hungary. *Education:* Budapest Academy of Music, 1958–65; Cologne Musikhochschule, 1966–68. *Career:* Music Director, Ensemble Intercontemporain, Paris, 1979–91; Principal Guest Conductor, BBC Symphony Orchestra, 1985–88, leading the premiere of Birtwistle's Earth Dances, 1987; First Guest Conductor, Budapest Festival Orchestra, 1992–95; Chief Conductor, Radio Kamerorkest Hilversum, 1994–; Conducted first performances of pieces by Birtwistle, Boulez, Donatoni, Kurtag, Reich, Stockhausen and Xenakis; Operas include premiere of Stockhausen's Donnerstag and Montag aus Licht at Milan Scala and Covent Garden; Engaged by most major festivals in Europe as Conductor and Artistic Adviser; Professor, Hochschule für Musik, Karlsruhe, Hochschule für Musik, Cologne, Bart ók Seminar, Szombathely; Founder and President, International Eötvös Institute for Young Conductors; mem, Akademie Der Künste, Berlin; Szechenyi Academy of Art, Budapest. *Compositions include:* For orchestra: Chinese Opera, Shadows, Psychokosmos Zero Points, Atlantis; Two Monologues, Replica; For ensemble: Intervalles-Interieurs, Windsequenzen, Brass the Metalspace, Steine, Triangel; For string quartet: Korrespondenz; For music theatre and opera: Harakiri; Radames; As I Crossed a Bridge of Dreams; For vocal ensemble: 3 comedy madrigals; Endless Eight; For solo: Psalm 151 for percussion; Two Poems for violoncello; Thunder for timpani Kosmos for piano; Multimedia: Der Blick; Three Sisters, Le Ballon, Angels in America. *Recordings:* Moro Lasso, 1963; Mese, 1968; Cricket-music, 1970; Intervalles-Interieurs, 1974–81; Sequences of the Wind, 1975; Chinese Opera, 1986; Trois Soeurs, 1998; Atlantis, 1998; Psychokosmos, 1998; Shadows, 1998; Hochzeitsmadrigal, 1998. *Recordings:* Three Sisters; Atlantis; Bartók, Kurtag, Eötvös; Chinese Opera; Percussion Pieces. *Honours:* Commandeur de l'Ordre des Arts et des Lettres, France, 1986; Bart ók Award, Budapest, Hungary, 1997; Prix Claude-Rostand, Grand Prix de la Critique, 1997, 1998, Paris; Kaske Musikpreis, Munich, 2000;Kossuth Prize, Hungary, 2002. *Current Management:* Harrison-Parrott. *Address:* c/o Harrison-Parrott, 12 Penzance Place, London W11 4 PA, England.

EPSTEIN, David M.; Composer, Conductor, Theorist and Professor; b. 3 Oct. 1930, New York, NY, USA; m. Anne Merrick, 21 June 1953, 2 d. *Education:* AB, Antioch College, 1952; MMus, New England Conservatory of Music, 1953; MFA, Brandeis University, 1954; PhD, Princeton University, 1968. *Career:* Guest conductor of well known orchestras, Germany, Austria, Czechoslovakia, Poland, Israel, France, Belgium, Mexico, USA and others; Member, Herbert von Karajan Musikgespräche, Salzburg, 1983–88; Board of Directors, The Conductors Guild; Alumni Board and Board of Trustees, Antioch College. *Compositions include:* String Trio; Sonority–Variations for Orchestra; Fantasy Variations for Solo Viola or Violin; The Seasons; String Quartet, 1971; The Concord Psalter, 1978; Music for theatre, film and television. *Recordings include:* Bloch, Concerto Grosso No. 2, Czech Radio Orchestra; Tillis, Festival Journey, The New Orchestra of Boston; Kurt Weill–Suite from Der Silbersee, MIT Symphony Orchestra; Copland–Dance Symphony, Piston–Incredible Flautist, MIT Symphony. *Publications:* Beyond Orpheus, Studies in Musical Structure, 1979; Shaping Time: Music, The Brain and Performance, 1995; Various articles and music arrangements. *Address:* Department of Music, Massachusetts Institute of Technology, Cambridge, MA 02139, USA.

EPSTEIN, Matthew A.; Opera Impresario and Consultant; b. 23 Dec. 1947, New York, NY, USA. *Education:* BA, European History,

University of Pennsylvania, 1969. *Career:* Manager Representative with extensive list of operatic artists; Consultant to opera companies and symphony orchestras on production concepts and casting, USA and Europe; Formerly Artistic Director of BAM Opera at the Brooklyn Academy of Music and Artistic Consultant for a Concert Opera series at Carnegie Hall, SONY Classical, 1991–94; General Director, Welsh National Opera, 1993–94; Vice-President, Columbia Artists Management Incorporated; Artistic Adviser to Lyric Opera of Chicago and Artistic Consultant to Santa Fe Opera. *Current Management:* Columbia Artists, 165 W 57th Street, New York, NY 10019, USA.

EQUILUZ, Kurt; Singer (Tenor); b. 13 June 1929, Vienna, Austria. *Education:* Studied in Vienna with Adolf Vogel. *Career:* Sang as chorister in Vienna from 1945; Solo career at the Vienna Staatsoper from 1957, notably as Mozart's Pedrillo, Beethoven's Jacquino and in operas by Strauss; Sang at the Salzburg Festival in the premieres of Liebermann's Penelope, 1954, Martin's Le Mystère de la Nativité, 1960 and Wagner-Régeny's Das Bergwerk zu Falun, 1961; Performed the Narrator in Schnittke's Historia von D. Johann Fausten, Vienna, 2001; Many concert appearances as Lieder singer and in religious music; Professor, Graz Musikhochschule, 1971–; Professor of Lieder and Oratorio, Academy for Music in Vienna, 1982–. *Recordings:* Monteverdi's Orfeo and Il Ritorno d'Ulisse; Cantatas by Bach and the St John and St Matthew Passions (Telefunken); Cavalieri's La Rappresentazione di Anima e di Corpo (Deutsche Grammophon). *Address:* Schwenkgasse 8/4, 1120 Vienna, Austria.

ERB, Donald James, BS, MM, DMus,; American composer and music educator; b. 17 Jan. 1927, Youngstown, OH; m. Lucille Hyman 1950; one s. three d. *Education:* Kent State Univ., Cleveland Inst. of Music, Indiana Univ. School of Music, studied with Harold Miles, Kenneth Gaburo, Marcel Dick, Bernhard Heiden in USA, Nadia Boulanger in Paris. *Career:* teacher 1953–61, composer-in-residence 1966–81, Prof. of Composition 1987–, Cleveland Inst. of Music; composer-in-residence, Dallas Symphony Orchestra 1968–69; staff composer, Bennington Composers' Conference, VT 1969–74; Visiting Prof. 1975–76, Prof. of Music 1984–87, Indiana Univ. School of Music; Meadows Prof. of Composition, Southern Methodist Univ. 1981–84; composer-in-residence, St Louis Symphony Orchestra 1988–90. *Compositions include:* orchestral: Chamber Concerto for piano and strings 1958, Symphony of Overtures 1964, Stargazing for band and tape 1966, Christmasmusic 1967, Autumnmusic for orchestra and electronic sounds 1973, Music for a Festive Occasion for orchestra and electronic sounds 1975, Trombone Concerto 1976, Cenotaph (For EV) for symphonic band 1979, Sonneries 1981, Contrabassoon Concerto 1984, The Dreamtime 1985, Concerto for brass and orchestra 1986, Ritual Observances for orchestra 1991, Violin Concerto 1992, Evensong for orchestra 1993, Suddenly It's Evening for electronics and cello 1997, Dance You Monster for trumpet 1993, Three Pieces for double bass 1999; chamber music, choral works and piano pieces. *Publications:* contrib. article on orchestration to Encyclopaedia Britannica (15th edn) 1974. *Honours:* Aaron Copland Award 1993, 1996. *Address:* 4073 Bluestone Road, Cleveland Heights, OH 44121, USA.

ERBE, Teresa; Singer (Soprano); b. 1958, Oberschesien, Germany. *Education:* Studied in Katowice. *Career:* Sang at Gdansk from 1981; Bremerhaven Opera, 1986–87, and Bremen, 1987–92, as Salome, Arabella and Elisabeth de Valois; Essen from 1992, as Bartók's Judith, the Marschallin and Giulietta in Les contes d'Hoffmann (1996); Season 1999–2000 as Salome at Freiburg, and Natasha in Three Sisters by Peter Eötvös; Further appearances in Rusalka, and operetta; Guest engagements in Prague, Stockholm, Copenhagen and St Petersburg. *Address:* Essen Opera, Rolandstrasse 10, 4300 Essen 1, Germany.

ERBEN, Valentin; Cellist; b. 14 March 1945, Austria. *Education:* Studied in Vienna, Munich and Paris. *Career:* Co-Founder and Cellist of the Alban Berg Quartet from 1971; Many concert engagements worldwide, including complete cycles of the Beethoven Quartets in 15 European cities, 1987–88 and 1988–89 seasons; Bartók/Mozart cycle in London, Vienna, Paris, Frankfurt, Munich, Geneva and Turin, 1990–91; Annual concert series at the Vienna Konzerthaus and festival engagements world-wide; Associate Artist at the South Bank Centre in London; US appearances in Washington DC, San Francisco and at Carnegie Hall in New York; Professor, Musikhochschule, Vienna and Cologne. *Recordings include:* Complete Quartets of Beethoven, Brahms, Berg, Webern and Bartók; Late Quartets of Mozart, Schubert, Haydn and Dvořák; Quartets by Ravel, Debussy and Schumann; Live recordings from Carnegie Hall playing Mozart and Schumann, Konzerthaus in Vienna, and Opéra-Comique in Paris, playing Brahms. *Honours:* Grand Prix du Disque; Deutsche Schallplatenpreis; Edison Prize; Japan Grand Prix; Gramophone Magazine Award. *Address:* Intermusica Artists' Management, 16 Duncan Terrace, London N1 8BZ, England.

ERBSE, Nebrio; Composer; b. 27 Feb. 1924, Rudolstadt, Germany. *Education:* Studied at the Musikhochschule of Weimar and Berlin, with

Boris Blacher. *Career:* Debut: Conducted in Berlin in 1961; Freelance Composer; Has conducted and directed opera; Moved to Salzburg in 1957, with his opera, Julietta, being performed there in 1959. *Compositions:* Stage: Juliena, opera, 1957, Ruth, ballet, 1958, Der Herr In Grau, comic opera, 1966; Orchestral: Symphony in 4 Movements, 1964, Das Hohelied Salomons, 1969, for string and wind players, 1971, Symphony No. 2, 1970, Triple Concerto, 1972; Chamber music and music for chorus. *Honours:* Beethoven Prize, Bonn, 1961; Appreciation Award for Music, Austrian Ministry for Education and Art, 1973. *Address:* c/o GEMA, Postfach 80 07 67, 81607 Munich, Germany.

ERDÉLYI, Csaba; Viola Player and Conductor; b. 15 May 1946, Budapest, Hungary; m. Ju-Ping Chi, 8 Oct 1989, 3 s. *Education:* Artist and Teacher Diplomas, Franz Liszt Academy of Music, 1970; Influential teachers: Pál Lukács, Yehudi Menuhin, Bruno Giuranna. *Career:* Franz Liszt Chamber Orchestra, 1968–72; Eszterházy Baryton Trio, 1973–78; Principal Viola, Philharmonia Orchestra, London, 1974–78; Professor of Viola, Guildhall School of Music, London, 1980–87; Chilingirian String Quartet, 1981–87; Professor of Viola: Indiana University, Bloomington, 1987–91; Rice University, Houston, TX, 1991–95; Soloist in RFH, Promenade Concerts; Frequent Partner with Yehudi Menuhin; Masterclasses world-wide including: RAM London, Aldeburgh, Alaska, Beijing, Mexico, Budapest, USA; Annual summer classes in Gubbio Festival, Italy; Jury Member of BBC Young Musician of The Year and Lionel Tertis Viola Competition, Isle of Man; First US performance of Brahms/Berio Sonata for Viola and Orchestra; Opening recital at International World Viola Congress in Redlands, CA, 1989, and Vienna, 1992; mem, Institute for the Development of Intercultural Relations through the Arts, Geneva. *Recordings:* Hoddinott, Viola Concerto; Strauss Songs with Jessye Norman. *Publications:* Bartók: Viola Concerto; Bach: Suite Pour La Luth for Viola; Hummel: Fantasia; Mozart: Sinfonia Concertante KV 364 for String Sextet; Arrangement of Brahms' Sonata Op 78; Viola part to Schubert's Arpeggione Sonata. *Contributions:* Music and The Fear of Violence in Classical Music. *Honours:* 1st Prize, Carl Flesch Competition, 1972. *Address:* 2420 Boston Road, Bloomington, IN 47401, USA.

ERDING-SWIRIDOFF, Susanne; Composer; b. 16 Nov. 1955, Schwabisch Hall, Germany; m. Paul Swiridoff, 11 Mar 1988. *Education:* Stuttgart University, 1975–77; Oxford and Cambridge, England in summers, 1976–80; Yale University, USA, 1976; Universite de Montreal, Canada, 1978; Studied music, piano and composition with Milko Kelemen, Stuttgart Academy of Music, 1974–79 and composition with Dieter Acker, Munich, 1980; Seminars on composition at Buenos Aires, 1981; International Summer School of Music with Peter Maxwell Davies, Dartington, England, 1985; Composition with Agosto Benjamin Rattenbach, Buenos Aires, 1985. *Career:* Many television appearances, 1983–88. *Compositions include:* Orchestra: Yellan, 1981, Event, 1985, Il Visconte Dimezzato, 1994; Concertos: Konzert, 1983, Tierra Querida, 1986; Operas: Joy, chamber opera, 1983, Die Wundersame Geschichte Des Peter Schlemihl, marionette opera, 1991; Ballet: Yellan, 1981; Piano: Klaviersuite, 1982, Maske Und Kristall IV, 1992; Chamber Music: Grotesques Arabesques, 1980, Rotor, 1982, Homage To The City Of Dresden, 1985, Variations Serieuses, Fayence, 1986, Labirinto Del Sole, 1987, Gioielli Rubati, 1987, Blumen Und Blut, 1988, Zeitstimmen, 1993; Vocal: Okteondo, 1979, Initialen, 1986, Maske Und Kristall X, 1993, XII, 1994. *Address:* Am Postgutle 14, Post Box 620, 74506 Schwabisch Hall, Germany.

ERICKSON, Kaaren; Singer (Soprano); b. 9 Feb. 1953, Seattle, USA. *Education:* Studied at Western Washington University, Bellingham, WA, 1970–74 and the Music Academy of the West with Martial Singher and Maurice Abravanel. *Career:* Sang Gilda in 1982 and won 1st prize 1982 Munich Competition; Sang at the Deutsche Oper Berlin and the Munich Staatsoper; Piccola Scala 1983, in Les Pélerins de la Mecque; US engagements at Seattle, San Francisco, Houston, Cincinnati and the City Opera New York; Metropolitan Opera from 1985 as Susanna in new production of Le nozze di Figaro; Appears in the Met videos of Wagner's Ring, Parsifal and Elektra; Blanche in Dialogues of the Carmelites, as Zerlina in Don Giovanni and a Flowermaiden in a new production of Parsifal (1991); Other roles have included Mozart's Pamina and Fiordiligi, Micaela, Contessa, Ellen Orford and Marschallin in Der Freischütz; Sang in the premiere of The Voyage by Philip Glass, Metropolitan, 1992; Many Lieder recitals and concert appearances; mem, National Association of Teachers of Singing. *Recordings:* Le Cinesi by Gluck; The White Election by Gordon Getty; Messiah (Handel) with the Atlanta Symphony, Robert Shaw; Dvořák Stabat Mater with NJ Symphony, Zdenek Macal. *Current Management:* Thea Dispeker Artist Management. *Address:* c/o Thea Dispeker Artists Management, 59 E 54th St, NY 10022, USA.

ERICSDOTTER, Siw; Singer (Soprano); b. 9 Feb. 1919, Norrkoping, Sweden. *Education:* Studied in Stockholm with Nanny Larsen-Todsen. *Career:* Member of the Royal Opera Stockholm, 1951–54; Sang with the Hamburg Staatsoper, 1954–59; Appeared in Berlin from 1959 notably as

Wagner's Elsa, Eva and Sieglinde; Guest appearances in Vienna, Paris and in Italy; Stuttgart Opera, 1962–70; Other roles include Leonore, Amneris, Tosca and the title role in Judith by N Berg. *Recordings include:* Herodias in Salome and Der Evangelimann by Kienzl.

ERICSON, Barbro; Singer (Mezzo-Soprano); b. 2 April 1930, Halmstad, Sweden. *Education:* Studied in Stockholm with Arne Sunnegard. *Career:* Debut: Stockholm in 1956 as Eboli in Don Carlos; Guest appearances in London, Berlin, Hamburg, Edinburgh, Helsinki, France, Netherlands and Italy; Sang at Paris Opéra in 1964 as Venus in Tannhäuser, Bayreuth Festival from 1964 as Kundry and Venus, and Salzburg Easter Festival in 1967 in Die Walküre under Karajan; Metropolitan Opera debut in 1968 as Fricka, returning to New York in 1976 as Herodias in Salome; Sang in the premiere of Ligeti's Le Grande Macabre, 1978. *Recordings include:* Die Walküre; Requiem and other works by Ligeti.

ERKOREKA, Gabriel, DipRAM, MA, ARAM; Composer; *Teacher, Musikene, Basque Country Conservatoire*; b. 27 Feb. 1969, Bilbao, Spain. *Education:* Conservatorio Superior de Música, Bilbao, Royal Acad. of Music, London. *Career:* performances include Festival International de Alicante, Auditorio National de Musica (Madrid), Wigmore Hall, ICA and South Bank Centre, London, ISCM World Music Days 1998 in Manchester, Musikverein in Vienna, Chicago, New York, Amsterdam, Paris, Rome, Sydney, Tokyo; teacher of composition Musikene Basque Country Conservatoire. *Compositions:* over 40 pieces, including Kantak for piccolo and chamber ensemble, Bizitiza for mezzo soprano and ensemble, Izaro for piano quintet, Afrika for solo marimba and orchestra, Océano for symphony orchestra. *Recordings:* Kantak, Krater, Nubes, Cuatro Diferencias for accordion. *Honours:* SGAE prize 1996, INAEM prize 2001, Rome prize awarded by the Spanish Acad. in Rome 2001. *Current Management:* Repertoire Promotion Department, Oxford University Press, 70 Baker Street, London, W1U 7DN, England. *Telephone:* (20) 7616-5900 (office). *Fax:* (20) 7616-5901 (office). *E-mail:* repertoire.promotion@oup.com (office). *Website:* www.oup.co.uk/music/repprom (office).

EROD, Ivan; Composer, Professor and Pianist; b. 2 Jan. 1936, Budapest, Hungary; m. Marie-Luce Guy, 11 April 1969, 3 s., 2 d. *Education:* Academy of Music, Budapest, 1951–56; Academy of Music, Vienna, 1957–61. *Career:* Debut: Budapest; Coach for Vienna State Opera, 1962–64; Concert Pianist on 5 continents; Appearances include: Salzburg Festival, and Vienna Philharmonic with Karl Bohm; Full Professor for Composition and Music Theory at Hochschule für Musik und Darstellende Kunst, Graz, Austria, 1971–89, and Hochschule für Musik, Vienna, 1989–. *Compositions:* 2 Operas; Orchestral works, Concertos, Chamber Music, Cantatas, Lieder, Chorus works. *Recordings:* As pianist, 10 records with Rudolf Schock, tenor; Pierrot Lunaire (Die Reihe, Vienna), recordings in 10 countries; As composer, with various labels; Numerous radio recordings for BBC. *Contributions:* Articles in Osterreichische Musikzeitschrift. *Honours:* Several Austrian State Prizes; Bart ók Pasztory Prize, 1993. *Current Management:* Verlag Doblinger, Vienna, Austria. *Address:* Gumpendorfer Strasse 9-13, 1060 Vienna, Austria.

ERÖS, Peter; conductor; b. 22 Sept. 1932, Budapest, Hungary; m. 1st Georgia Weiser 1956; two s.; m. 2nd Jasmin Fay Roberts 1985 (divorced). *Education:* Franz Liszt Music Academy, Budapest; studies with Zoltan Kodály, Leo Weiner, Laszlo Somogyi. *Career:* Assistant to: George Szell (Cleveland Orchestra), Otto Klemperer (Holland Festival), Ferenc Fricsay, Assistant to Bayreuther Festival, 1957–60; Associate Conductor, Amsterdam Concertgebouw Orchestra, 1960–65; Music Director, Malmö Symphony Orchestra, Sweden, 1966–68; Principal Guest Conductor, Melbourne Symphony Orchestra, 1968–70; Music Director, San Diego Symphony Orchestra, Music Director, La Jolla Chamber Music Society, 1972–80; Principal Conductor, Western Australia Symphony Orchestra, Perth, 1975–79; Music Director, Peabody Symphony and Opera, Baltimore, USA, 1982–85; Music Director, Aalborg Symphony Orchestra, Denmark, 1983–89; Music Director, University of Washington Symphony Orchestra and Opera Department, 1989–; Numerous guest engagements with leading orchestras throughout the United Kingdom, Europe and the USA. *Recordings:* Siegfried Wagner, Orchestral Works; Gabriel von Wayditch, Jesus before Herod; Many recordings for Australian Broadcasting Commission and Swedish Radio. *Publications:* contrib. to various professional journals and newspapers. *Address:* c/o University of Washington, Department of Music, Seattle, WA 98195, USA.

ESCHENBACH, (Ringmann) Christoph; pianist and conductor; b. 20 Feb. 1940, Breslau, Germany. *Education:* Piano studies with foster mother at age 8, with Eliza Hansen and studied conducting with Wilhelm Bruckner-Ruggeberg, Hamburg Conservatory. *Career:* London debut in 1966; Gave the premiere of Henze's 2nd Concerto at Bielefeld in 1968; USA debut as soloist with Cleveland Orchestra in 1969; Many world tours both as soloist with leading orchestras and as recitalist;

Many duo piano appearances with Justus Frantz; Debut as opera conductor with La Traviata at Darmstadt in 1978; Generalmusikdirektor, Rheinland-Pflaz State Philharmonic Orchestra, 1979–81; 1st Permanent Guest Conductor, 1981–82, Chief Conductor, 1982–85, Tonhalle Orchestra, Zürich; Covent Garden debut in 1984 with Così fan tutte; Music Director of Houston Symphony Orchestra, 1988–; Barbican Hall, London, concert 1997 (Emperor Concerto and Bruckner's 4th Symphony); Conducted Robert Wilson's production of Parsifal in 1992; Engaged for Parsifal at Bayreuth, 2000; Conducted the BBC Symphony Orchestra at the London Proms, 2002; Guest Conductor with many major orchestras of the world. *Recordings include:* Schumann's Violin Concerto and Fantasie in C, with Thomas Zehetmair and the Philharmonia. *Honours:* 1st Prize, Steinway Piano Competition in 1952; 2nd Prize, Munich International Competition in 1962; 1st Prize, Clara Haskil Competition, Montreux in 1965; Recording Prizes. *Address:* c/o Houston Symphony Orchestra, 615 Louisiana Street, Houston, TX 77002, USA.

ESCHKENAZY, Vesko; Violinist; b. 3 Dec. 1970, Sofia, Bulgaria. *Education:* Studied with Yfrah Neaman in London, Pierre Amoyal in Lausanne and at the Bulgarian Conservatory, leaving with an Honours degree. *Career:* Leader, Pioneer Youth Philharmonic Orchestra in Sofia, 1979, touring France, Italy, Germany and Brazil; Solo performances with the English Chamber Orchestra, Royal Philharmonic Orchestra, Sofia Philharmonic, Bulgarian Festival Symphony, Monte Carlo Symphony, City of London Sinfonia, Philharmonia and London Philharmonic (Beethoven Concerto, 1992); Festival engagements in Sofia, Varna, Cannes, Montpellier and Nantes, with tours to the former Soviet Union, throughout Europe, India, Brazil and China; Repertoire includes concertos by Bach, Brahms, Mozart, Prokofiev, Sibelius and Shostakovich; Sonatas by Tartini, Bach, Mozart, Beethoven, Franck and Schumann. *Recordings include:* Bruch and Mendelssohn Concertos, conducted by Emil Tchakarov; Brahms Violin Concerto with Sofia Philharmonic Orchestra and Emil Tabakov conducting. *Honours:* Winner of various competitions in Europe and China. *Address:* World Wide Artists Ltd, 6 Petersfield Crescent, Coulsdon, Surrey CR5 2JQ, England.

ESCHRIG, Ralph; Singer (Tenor); b. 2 April 1959, Dresden, Germany. *Education:* Studied at the Musikhochschule Dresden. *Career:* Sang at the Dresden Staatsoper 1984–87, notably in the local premiere of The Nose by Shostakovich; Lyric Tenor at the Berlin Staatsoper from 1987, notably as Mozart's Ottavio, Belmonte, Tamino and Ferrando, Fenton by Nicolai and in the Singspiels Erwin und Elmire by Reichardt and Zar und Zimmerman by Lortzing; Concert appearances as the Evangelist in Bach's Passions, Lieder by Schubert and Schumann and The Diary of One who Disappeared by Janácek; Engagements with the Dresden Kreuz Choir and Chorus of St Thomas's Leipzig and broadcasting stations in Germany and Finland. *Recordings include:* Mendelssohn Motets and Bastien und Bastienne by Mozart. *Honours:* Prizewinner, 1984 International Bach Competition; 1987 Mozart Competition at Salzburg. *Address:* c/o Berlin Staatsoper, Unter den Linden 7, 1086 Berlin, Germany.

ESCOBAR, Roberto B.; University Professor and Musician; b. 11 May 1926, Santiago, Chile; m. Marta Cruchaga, 19 Mar 1950, 2 s. *Education:* MA, Philosophy, Catholic University, Valparaiso; Conservatorio Nacional and Escuela Moderna de Musica, Santiago; Manhattan School of Music, New York. *Career:* Composer; Conductor, Chilean Modern Music Ensemble, 1973–78; Musicologist; President, Chilean Composers' Association, 1974–78; President, Sociedad Chilena de Filosofia, 1985–88. *Compositions:* Over 60 works performed publicly, including: Laberinto, 1971, first performed in USA, 1976; Symphonia de Fluminis, 1987, first performed in USA, 1992; Tower of the Winds, first performed in USA, 1989; Sinfonia Andres Bello, 1992, first performed in Chile, 1993; Prometheus, first performed in Chile, 1996; Cantos Cecilianos, first performed in Chile, 2000. *Recordings:* Preludios Franceses; Homenaje a Amengual; Talagante; Cuarteto Estructural, Cuarteto Funcional, Macul, La Granja, Elegia, Quinteto La Paloma. *Publications:* Catalogue of Chilean Music, 1969; Chilean Musicians and Their Music, 1971; Study in Black and White, 1973; Chilean Composers, 1997. *Contributions:* Various journals. *Honours:* Goethe Prize for Composition, 1982; Honorary Professor, University of Missouri, 1989; Claudio Arrau Prize, Chile, 1993, Distinguished Professor (Life Appointment) Universidad de Chile 1997. *Address:* PO Box 16360, Santiago 9, Chile.

ESCOT, Pozzi; Composer, Teacher and Writer on Music; b. 1 Oct. 1933, New York, NY, USA. *Education:* BS, 1956, MS course, 1957, Juilliard School of Music, New York; Studied with Philipp Jarnach at Hamburg Hochschule für Musik, 1957–61. *Career:* Teacher at New England Conservatory of Music, Boston, 1964–67, 1980–81, and Wheaton College, Norton, MA, 1972–; Professor, Graduate School, New England Conservatory, Boston, 1964–; Wheaton College, Norton, Massachusetts, 1972–; Editor, Sonus Journal, 1980–; Lecturer at University of Peking and University of Shanghai, 1984; Lecturer, Harvard, Princeton,

Chicago, Stanford, Berkeley, Illinois, Northwestern Universities. *Compositions:* 5 Symphonies, 1952–57; 5 String Quartets; A Trilogy for chamber ensembles; Concerto for piano; Diverse chamber and solo works; 3 Poems of Rilke for narrator and string quartet, 1959; 3 Movements for violin and piano, 1959–60; Lamentus, Trilogy No. 1 for soprano and 8 players, 1962; Visione, Trilogy No. 3 for soprano, speaker and 5 players, 1964; Sands... for orchestra, 1965; Neyrac Lux for 2 guitars and electric guitar, 1978; Eure Pax for violin, 1980; Concerto for piano and chamber orchestra, 1982; Trio In Memoriam Solrac for violin, cello and piano, 1984; Jubilation for string quartet, 1991; Mirabilis III for low voice, 3 flutes and 3 violins, 1995; Visione 97 for chorus, 1997; Piano pieces and pieces for instrument and tape. *Publications:* Sonic Design: The Nature of Sound and Music, with Robert Cogan, 1976, 1981; Sonic Design: Practice and Problems, 1981. *Contributions:* Mystics Quarterly; Interface; New York Theory Society Music and Practice; Edinburgh University Musical Praxis; Perspectives of New Music; Stanford University Humanities Review; University of Leuven, Belgium. *Address:* 24 Avon Hill, Cambridge, MA 02140, USA.

ESCRIBANO, María; Composer and Pianist; b. 24 Jan. 1954, Madrid, Spain. *Education:* Studied, Real Conservatorio Superior de Musica de Madrid, 1963–73; Study with Rodolfo Halffter, Curso Internacional de Musica Manuel de Falla de Granada, 1971; Studied techniques of contemporary composition with Cristobal Halffter, Tomas Marco and Carmelo A Bernaola, Real Conservatorio Superior de Musica de Madrid; Also complete courses in the analysis of contemporary music and attended the Darmstadt International Courses, 1974–76. *Career:* Premiere of first work for instrumental ensemble, 1975; Resided in France as member of the Roy Hart Theatre, worked as composer, actress and pianist, 1978–80; Toured France, Belgium and Spain, 1980; Co-founder Theatrical Group, Agada, 1983; Composition and Music Teaching, 1989–; mem, Society of Authors. *Compositions include:* Muñecas de mimbre, 1974; Sin Seso, 1978; Concierto para Imma, 1976; L'histoire d'un s., 1978; Cuentos y canciones de la media lunita, 1987; Madrid de noche 1992; El sonido viajero, 1992; Memoria del viento, 1992; Desde la otra orilla, 1993; Sortilegio, 1993; Solar, 1994. *Publications:* Dictionary of Iberoamerica Music–dos mujeres en la musica/Historia de la musica española. *Honours:* Several scholarships. *Address:* c/o SGAE, Fernando VI 4, Apartado 484, 28080 Madrid 4, Spain.

ESHAM, Faith; singer (soprano); b. 6 Aug. 1948, Vanceburg, Kentucky, USA. *Education:* Studied at Juilliard School with Jennie Tourel and Beverly Johnson. *Career:* Debut: New York City Opera in 1977 as Cherubino; European debut as Nedda in Nancy; Sang Cherubino at Glyndebourne in 1981 and at La Scala in 1982; Vienna Staatsoper in 1984 as Micaela in Carmen; Geneva Opera in 1984 as Mélisande; New York City Opera as Pamina in Die Zauberflöte, Leila in Les Pêcheurs de Perles, Marguerite in Faust and Massenet's Cendrillon; Washington DC as Zerlina in Don Giovanni; Pittsburgh Opera as Gilda; Las Palmas as Antonia in Les Contes d'Hoffmann; Metropolitan Opera debut in 1986 as Marzelline in Fidelio; Season 1990–91 as Musetta at Cologne, Pamina for Washington Opera and Susanna at Fort Lauderdale; Micaela for Cincinnati Opera, Butterfly at St Louis and Cherubino at the Dallas Opera, 1992; Sang Butterfly for Welsh National Opera, 1995; Concert appearances at the Mostly Mozart Festival, New York, Requiem and Schubert's A flat Mass, and Fauré's Requiem with the Pittsburgh Symphony under Charles Dutoit. *Recordings include:* La nozze di Figaro conducted by Haitink; Video of Carmen, with Domingo. *Honours:* Young Artists Award from the National Opera Institute, 1978–79; Concours International de Chant de Paris Prize, 1981.

ESHPAI, Andrey (Yakoulevitch); Composer and Pianist; b. 15 May 1925, Kozmodemiansk, Russia; m. Alexandra Stempnevski, 2 s. *Education:* Studied with Miashoveky, Sofronitsky and Khachaturian at the Moscow Conservatory. *Career:* Regular television and radio appearances; Secretary, Union of Russian Composers; First Secretary, Union of Composers of RSFSR. *Compositions include:* 4 Symphonies, 1959–82; 2 Violin Sonatas, 1966, 1970; Concerto for orchestra, 1967; Festival Overture, 1970; The Circle, ballet, 1981; Oboe Concerto, 1982; Symphony No. 5, 1985–86, No. 6, (Liturgy) 1988–89, No. 7, 1991; Concerto for soprano saxophone and orchestra, 1986; Viola Concerto, 1988; Cello Concerto, 1989; Cello-Sonate, 1990; Violin Concerto No. 3, 1990; Hungarian Tunes for viola and orchestra. 1953; Symphonic Dances, 1949; 2 Piano Concertos; Violin Concerto No. 4, 1991; String Quartet (Concordia Discordans), 1992–95; Flute Concerto, 1994; Concerto for trumpet and trombone with symphony orchestra; Horn Concerto, 1995; Four Poems for orchestra, 1998; I Loved You for low voice and piano, 1999; Chamber Music includes: Rondeau-Etude for 4 saxophones; Music for over 60 films. *Address:* Apartment No. 121, Studentcheskaya st 44/28, 121 165 Moscow, Russia.

ESPERIAN, Kallen; Singer (Soprano); b. 8 June 1961, Waukegan, Illinois, USA. *Education:* Studied at the University of Illinois. *Career:* Sang in various opera houses and concert halls in the USA then won the

1985 Pavarotti Competition and toured with the tenor to China, singing Mimi in La Bohème; Further appearances as Mimi at the Berlin and Vienna Staatsopers in 1986, the Lyric Opera of Chicago and the Metropolitan, NY, 1989; Returned to the Metropolitan as Elena in I Vespri Siciliani; Has sung Verdi's Luisa Miller in Vienna, 1986, Verona and Geneva, 1993; Sang Desdemona at the Opéra Bastille in Paris and Reggio Emilia, 1992, Mozart's Countess at St Louis, the Trovatore Leonora at Chicago and Nedda for Connecticut Grand Opera; San Francisco in 1991 as Donna Elvira in Don Giovanni; Sang Desdemona at Covent Garden, 1997, and Amelia in the original version of Simon Boccanegra; Season 1999–2000 as Alice Ford in Falstaff at Chicago and Elisabeth de Valois at Munich. *Address:* c/o Grand Théâtre de Geneve, 11 Boulevard du Théâtre, 1211 Geneva 11, Switzerland.

ESPERT, Nuria; Stage Director; b. 1935, Barcelona, Spain; m. Armando Moreno 1954. *Career:* performed as actress with Compania Titular Infantil del Teatro Romea, in Barcelona 1947–52; formed theatre company with husband and acted in performances in Spain, France, Germany, Iran and the United Kingdom (World Theatre season at the Aldwych); first production, The House of Bernarda Alba by Lorca at the Lyric, Hammersmith 1986; staged Madama Butterfly for Scottish Opera and at Covent Garden, La Traviata for Scottish Opera in 1989, seen at the Teatro La Zarzuela, Madrid 1990 and Elektra at Barcelona in 1990; returned to Covent Garden for Rigoletto in 1988 and Carmen in 1991 (also at the Seville Expo 1992); staged Elektra at Frankfurt 1994, Turandot for the reopening of the Teatre Liceu, Barcelona 1999.

ESPINOSA, Pedro; Pianist; b. 13 Oct. 1934, Galdar, Gran Canaria, Canary Islands. *Education:* Teachers: His mother (Juana Lorenzo) Alfred Cortot, Marguérite Long, Edward Steuermann, Witold Malcuzynski, David Tudor. *Career:* Debut: Teatro Perez-Galdos, Las Palmas de Gran Canaria, 16 Nov 1949; Has played at Venice and Paris Biennials and Enescu Festival, Bucharest; Other festivals include Darmstadt, Granada, Santander and San Sebastian; Has appeared with the Orquesta Sinfónica de Bilbao, Orquesta de RTVE and Orquesta Sinfónica de Madrid; Spanish premiere of Messiaen's Les Oiseaux Exotiques, with the Orquesta Nacional, 1963; Other notable performances include Bart ók's Sonata for 2 pianos and percussion (1955), complete works for piano of Schoenberg, Berg and Webern (1956), 2nd and 3rd Sonatas by Boulez (1961, 1967), Stockhausen's Klavierstück VI (1972) and first complete performance of Mompou's Música callada (1980); Lecture-concerts with Theodor Adorno; Professor at the Royal Conservatories of Madrid, Pamplona and Guadalajara; Classes at Lyon, Freiburg and Geneva Conservatories and various Spanish institutions; Piano works dedicated to him by many distinguished composers; mem, Royal Academy of Fine Arts of the Canary Islands; Hijo Predilecto of City of Galdar. *Recordings:* For many European broadcasting companies; Records in Germany and Spain, notably the complete Klavierstücke of Stockhausen. *Honours:* Kranichstein Prize, Kranichsteiner Musikinstitut, Darmstadt; 1st Prize, Real Conservatorio de Madrid; Fine Arts Award for interpretation of 20th century piano music, Fundación March, 1965; 1 of 3 Most Distinguished Interpreters of Ravel's Concerto for left hand, Ravel Academy, 1975; Annual Piano Competition in Galdar named after him, 1988. *Address:* c/o Rafaela Bonilla 19, 28028 Madrid, Spain.

ESPOSITO, Valeria; Singer (soprano); b. 10 April 1961, Naples, Italy. *Education:* Salerno Conservatoire. *Career:* Debut: Teatro del Giglio in Lucca as Zerlina in Don Giovanni in 1986; Appeared in concert productions at La Scala of Riccardo III by Flavio Testi and Berg's Lulu; Amsterdam in 1987 as Nausicca in Ulisse by Dallapiccola; Lucca in 1987 in Domenico Puccini's Il Ciarlatano; Teatro Lirico Milan as Sophie in Werther; US debut at Houston in 1988 in Werther; Teatro San Carlo Naples in 1988 as Amor in Orfeo e Euridice; La Scala in 1989 in Pergolesi's Lo Frate Innamorato; Radio France in 1989 in the title role of Linda di Chamounix by Donizetti; Welsh National Opera in 1989 as Amina in La Sonnambula; Sang Ippodamia in Paer's Achille at Lugo di Romagna in 1988; Sang Amina at the 1992 Macerata Festival and at Rome 1996; Season 1995–96 as Adina at Rome, Rossini's Fiorilla at Catania and Constanze at the Vienna Staatsoper; Offenbach's Olympia at Catania, 1998; Lucia di Lammermoor at Toulouse, 1998; Sang Gilda at St Gallen and the Queen of Night at Barcelona, 2000; Featured Artist, Opera Now Magazine, 1992. *Honours:* Winner, Aslico Competition, Milan, 1987; Winner, Cardiff Singer of the World Competition, 1987. *Current Management:* Athole Still International Management, Forresters Hall, 25–27 Westow Street, London, SE19 3RY, England. *Telephone:* (20) 8771-5271. *Fax:* (20) 8768-6600. *Website:* www .atholestill.com.

ESSER, Hermin; Singer (Tenor); b. 1 April 1928, Rheydt, Germany. *Education:* Studied at the Schumann Conservatory Düsseldorf with Franziak Martiensen-Lohmann. *Career:* Debut: Krefeld 1954; Sang at Gelsenkirchen, the Komische Oper Berlin and Wiesbaden; member of the Deutsche Oper am Rhein, Düsseldorf, 1964–; Bayreuth Festival from 1966, as Froh, Erik, Tristan, Tannhäuser, Siegmund and Loge;

Sang Tristan at Monte Carlo in 1973 and Parsifal at Rome in 1974; Sadler's Wells Opera 1973, with Scottish Opera as Tristan; Guest appearances in Paris, Moscow, Warsaw, Brussels, Zürich, Chicago, Geneva and Zürich; Sang Herod in Salome at the Staatsoper Berlin, 1988. *Recordings:* Das Rheingold; Der fliegende Holländer. *Address:* c/o Deutsche Staatsoper, Unter den Linden 7, 1086 Berlin, Germany.

ESSWOOD, Paul; singer (countertenor) and conductor; b. 6 June 1942, Nottingham, England; m. 1st Mary L. Cantrill 1966; m. 2nd Aimee D. Blattmann 1990; three s. one d. *Education:* Royal College of Music. *Career:* operatic debut at Berkeley University of California, 1968; Concert: BBC Messiah, 1965; Lay Vicar, Westminster Abbey, 1964–71; Professor: RCM, 1977–80; Baroque Vocal Interpretation, RAM, 1985–; European operatic debut, Basle in title role of Il Tigrane, A Scarlatti; World premieres: Lyric Opera, Chicago, Paradise Lost by Penderecki, 1979, Stuttgart State Opera in Title role of Akhnaten by Philip Glass, 1984; Major performances in: Zürich, Cologne, Stuttgart, Milan, Covent Garden; Performed in major centres and festivals including: Edinburgh, Leeds Triennial, English Bach, Three Choirs, Vienna, Salzburg, Zürich, Naples, Israel, Netherlands, Wexford; Zürich Opera 1996, in the premiere of Schlafes Bruder, by Herbert Willi; Debut as Conductor, Chichester Festival, 2000; Co-Founder, Pro Cantione Antiqua, a capella male voice ensemble for performance of early music, 1967; mem, Incorporated Society of Musicians. *Recordings:* Most of Bach's Cantatas; Bach: Matthew Passion, Christmas Oratorio; Handel: Jephtha, Saul, Belshazzar, Messiah, Il Pastor Fido, Rinaldo, Xerxes; Chamber Duets; Monteverdi: Poppea, Ulisse (also on film), Vespers 1610; Solo recordings of Songs to My Lady, Lute songs, Music for a While, Purcell Songs, Schumann Liederkreis, Op 39 and Dichterliebe; Britten, Folksongs and Canticle II. *Honours:* ARCM, Teachers and Performers, 1964; Honorary RAM, 1990; German Handel Prize, 1992. *Address:* Jasmine Cottage, 42 Ferring Lane, Ferring, West Sussex BN12 6QT, England.

ESTEP, Craig; Singer (Tenor); b. 1962, USA. *Career:* Sang Rinuccio in Gianni Schicchi at Charlotte Opera, 1987; San Francisco Opera as Ferrando in Così fan tutte, Alfredo, Nemorino, and Noburo in the 1991 US premiere of Henze's Das verratene Meer; Washington Opera, 1992–95, as Nemorino, and Tonio in La fille du Régiment; Calgary Opera, 1994, as Edgardo; Cologne, 1995, as Anfinomo in Monteverdi's Ulisse; Other roles include Pong in Turandot, Cassio in Otello and Ernesto in Don Pasquale. *Address:* c/o Washington Opera, John F. Kennedy Center, Washington DC, 20566, USA.

ESTES, Simon; Singer (Bass-Baritone); b. 2 March 1938, Centreville, IA, USA. *Education:* Studied with Charles Kellis at the University of Iowa and at the Juilliard School, NY. *Career:* Sang at various German opera houses from 1965 with debut at the Deutsche Oper Berlin as Ramfis in Aida; Member of Zürich Opera, 1976; Metropolitan Opera from 1976 in roles including Oroveso in Norma, La Scala in 1977 as Arkel in Pelléas et Mélisande, Hamburg Staatsoper in 1978 as King Philip in Don Carlos, Bayreuth Festival from 1978 as the Dutchman and Amfortas, Geneva Opera in 1984 as Jochanaan in Salome, and Covent Garden debut in 1986 as Wagner's Dutchman; Sang Wotan in new productions of Der Ring des Nibelungen at Berlin, 1984–85 and the Metropolitan, 1986–88; Appearances at San Francisco, Glyndebourne Festival, Paris Opéra, Munich and Vienna; Other roles include the Villains in Les Contes d'Hoffmann, Escamillo, King Mark, Mephistopheles, the Pharoah in Rossini's Moses and Boris Godunov; Concert engagements include the US premiere of the 14th Symphony by Shostakovich with the Philadelphia Orchestra; Other concerts with the New York Philharmonic, Chicago Symphony, Boston Symphony and the Berlin Philharmonic; London Promenade concerts debut in 1989 in Act III, Die Walküre; Sang title role in the musical King, in London in 1990; Season 1992 included Macbeth for Greater Miami Opera and Wotan at Bonn; Sang Zaccaria in Nabucco at the 1994 Orange Festival, Porgy at Cape Town, 1996. *Recordings include:* Simon Boccanegra; Oberto by Verdi; Mahler's 8th Symphony; Fauré's Requiem.

ETHUIN, Paul; Conductor; b. 24 Sept. 1924, Bruay-sur-Escaut, France. *Education:* Studied at the Paris Conservatoire, 1943–46. *Career:* Professor of flute at the Rheims Conservatoire, 1944–51; Second Conductor at the Rheims Opéra, 1948, Principal from 1955; Capital Théâtre, Toulouse, 1955–61; Opéra d'Avignon, 1962–66, Director of music at the Théâtre des Arts, Rouen, 1966, Paris Opéra and Opéra-Comique, 1968–71; Led the premiere of Bondeville's Antony and Cleopatra, 1974, and returned to Rouen, 1984–89.

EULER, Christian; Violist; b. 12 May 1956, Kassel, Germany; m., 1 s. *Education:* Bachelor and Master of Music degrees, Juilliard School of Music. *Career:* Philadelphia Orchestra, under Riccardo Muti, 1984–91; Member of Philadelphia Chamber Ensemble; Professor for Viola and Chamber Music at Universität für Musik und darstellende Kunst, Graz, Austria, 1991–; Solo and chamber music appearances in Europe. *Address:* Clemensstr 8, 80803 Munich, Germany.

EVAN, Allan; Singer (Baritone); b. 1941, Macon, Georgia, USA. *Education:* Studied at Juilliard and in Munich, Salzburg and Vienna. *Career:* Sang at Trier and elsewhere in Germany from 1968, as Crown in Porgy and Bess; Bremen Opera, 1973–76, Zürich, 1976–79, Basle 1977–87, Mannheim from 1987; Other roles have included Escamillo and Pizarro (at Graz), Don Giovanni, Amonasro (Wiesbaden, 1996), Wotan, Amfortas and Scarpia in Tosca (Mannheim, 1994); Strauss's Barak and D Schnyder's The Tempest, Berne, 1996; Sang Dr Schön in Lulu at Mannheim, 1998. *Address:* c/o Nationaltheater Mannheim, Mozartstrasse 9, 68161 Mannheim, Germany.

EVANGELATOS, Daphne; Singer (Mezzo-Soprano); b. 1952, Athens, Greece. *Education:* Studied in Athens, Munich and Vienna. *Career:* Sang first at the Bayerische Staatsoper, Munich then in Vienna, Cologne, Frankfurt, Hamburg and Vienna; Théâtre de la Monnaie Brussels in 1982 in La Clemenza di Tito; Hamburg Staatsoper in 1984 in Cavalli's L'Ormindo; Salzburg Festival in 1985 in Henze's version of Monteverdi's Il Ritorno d'Ulisse, as Melanto; Cologne in 1986 as the Prince in Massenet's Cendrillon; Other roles include Octavian in Der Rosenkavalier, Mozart's Cherubino, Sextus and Annius, Preziosilla in La Forza del Destino, the Composer in Ariadne auf Naxos and Wagner's Waltraute; Sang Tisbe in La Cenerentola at the 1988 Salzburg Festival; Wolf-Ferrari's Le Donne Curiose at the 1990 Munich Festival; Has also appeared in Campra's Tancrède, at Aix, Ramiro in La Finta Giardiniera, Orpheus, Mozart's Annius and Sextus, Fricka, Waltraute, and Varvara in Katya Kabanova. *Address:* c/o Music International, 13 Ardilaun Road, London N5 2QR, England.

EVANGELIDES, Petros; Singer (Tenor); b. 1949, Limasol, Cyprus. *Education:* Studied in Athens and Vienna. *Career:* Sang at Klagenfurt, 1973–74 and as Ernesto on tour in Switzerland, Germany and Netherlands, 1974; Stadttheater Berne, 1976–82, National Theatre Mannheim, 1982–84, Glyndebourne Festival in 1983 as Pedrillo in Die Entführung, Deutsche Oper Berlin as Monostatos and Pedrillo; Further appearances in Stuttgart, Amsterdam and Berlin, returned to Glyndebourne, 1984–91, in L'Incoronazione di Poppea, Falstaff, Die Entführung and Carmen; Vienna Staatsoper from 1984 notably in 1986 tour to Japan in Manon Lescaut and Tristan und Isolde; La Scala debut in 1986 as Monostatos; Sang Johannes in the premiere of Der Rattenfänger by Friedrich Cerha, Graz in 1987; Guest engagements at Hamburg as Brighella in Ariadne, Bonn, Zürich as Singer in Rosenkavalier, Strasbourg and Vichy. *Recordings include:* Video of L'Incoronazione di Poppea. *Address:* c/o Staatsoper, Opernring 2, 1010 Vienna, Austria.

EVANS, Dame Anne; Singer (soprano); b. 20 Aug. 1941, London, England. *Education:* Royal College of Music, London; Conservatoire de Musique, Geneva. *Career:* Principal Soprano, English National Opera, 1968–78; Debut as Mimi in La Bohème, then Mozart's Fiordiligi, Verdi's Violetta, Strauss's Marschallin, Wagner's Elsa and Sieglinde and Smetana's Mlada; With Welsh National Opera sang Strauss's Chrysothemis, Empress and Dyer's Wife, Beethoven's Leonore, Mozart's Donna Anna; Has sung extensively in Germany, Italy, France and America including Brünnhilde in Berlin, Nice, Paris, Turin, Zürich, Vienna, Buenos Aires and at the 1989–92 Bayreuth Festivals; Isolde in Brussels, 1994, Berlin, 1996, Dresden, 1997 and Paris 1998; Sieglinde in San Francisco; Elsa in Buenos Aires; Leonore in Stuttgart; Made Metropolitan debut with Elisabeth in Tannhäuser in 1992 and returned for Leonore in Fidelio in 1993; Recitals at Edinburgh Festival 1993 and Wigmore Hall, 1995; Sang Brünnhilde in Siegfried, 1995, and Götterdämmerung, 1996 at Covent Garden; Ariadne in Ariadne auf Naxos (original version), Edinburgh Festival, 1997; Madame Lidoine in Les dialogues des Carmélites, Glimmerglass Opera Festival, 2002. *Recordings:* Helmwige and Third Norn in ENO Ring under Goodall; Brünnhilde's Immolation scene; Brünnhilde in Der Ring des Nibelungen from Bayreuth; Mrs Grose in The Turn of the Screw. *Honours:* D.B.E., 2000. *Current Management:* Ingpen & Williams Ltd, 7 St George's Court, 131 Putney Bridge Road, London, SW15 2PA, England.

EVANS, (D.) John O.; Broadcaster and Musicologist; *Head of Music Programming, BBC Radio 3b.* 17 Nov. 1953, Morriston, South Wales. *Education:* Univ. Coll., Cardiff, 1972–78; ATCL Piano, 1974; BMus, 1975; MA, 1976; PhD, Univ. of Wales, 1984. *Career:* First Research Scholar, Britten-Pears Library and Archive, Red House, Aldeburgh, England 1980–85; Music Producer, BBC Radio 3 1985–89, Chief Producer (series) 1992–93, Head of Music Dept 1993–97, Head of Classical Music 1997–2000, Head of Music Programming 2000–; Postgraduate Music Tutor, Univ. Coll., Cardiff, Wales 1986–87; Artistic Dir, Volte Face Opera Project 1986–89; Exec. Trustee of The Peter Pears Award 1989–92; Artistic Dir of Covent Garden Chamber Orchestra 1990–93; Guest Lecturer for National Film Theatre, ENO, Fairfield Halls, Croydon, Britten-Pears School, Aldeburgh Festival, Royal Coll. of Music, Goldsmiths' Coll., Univ. of London, Hull Univ., Camden Festival, Bath Festival, International Brown Symposium on Benjamin Britten at Southwestern Univ., Georgetown, TX, USA; Chair. Royal Philharmonic Soc. Awards Opera Jury; Juror International Conductors' Competition,

Lisbon 1995, Kondrashin Conducting Competition 1998, BBC Singer of the World Competition, Cardiff 2003–, Tosti Int. Singing Competition; Dir of the Britten Estate; Trustee of the Britten Pears Foundation; Chair. of the Concentric Circles Theatre Bd. *Publications:* Benjamin Britten: Pictures from a Life 1943–1976 (with Donald Mitchell) 1978, Benjamin Britten: His Life and Operas (ed.) 1982. *Contributions:* A Britten Companion 1984, A Britten Source Book 1987, ENO, Royal Opera and Cambridge Opera Guides on Britten's Peter Grimes, Gloriana, The Turn of the Screw, Death in Venice; articles in magazines including Opera Quarterly. *Honours:* Prix Italia and Charles Heidsieck Award 1989, Royal Philharmonic Soc. Award 1994, Sony Radio Award 1997, Vienna TV Award 2004. *Address:* Room 4126, Broadcasting House, Portland Place, London W1A 1AA, England. *Telephone:* (20) 7765-0481 (office). *Fax:* (20) 7765-0546 (office). *Website:* www.bbc.co.uk/radio3 (office).

EVANS, Damon; Tenor; b. 1960, Baltimore, MD, USA. *Education:* Studied at the Interlochen Arts Academy on a Reader's Digest Foundation Scholarship. *Career:* Sang Amon in Akhnaten by Philip Glass at the New York City Opera in 1985; Virginia Opera Association in 1985 as Benji in the premiere of Musgrave's Harriet: The Woman Called Moses; Glyndebourne Festival in 1986 as Sportin' Life in Porgy and Bess; Has also sung Sportin' Life at Charleston, Boston, London with Philharmonic Orchestra and Moscow with the Finnish National Opera in 1988; Concert engagements include Beethoven's Ninth and Pulcinella, conducted by Simon Rattle; Bernstein's West Side Story at the Usher Hall in Edinburgh and a Bernstein Celebration at Alice Tully Hall in New York; Sang in the British premiere of Blitzstein's Airborne Symphony with the London Symphony, A Child of Our Time at the City of London Festival and Weill's 3 Concert Suites at the Almeida Festival; Carnegie Hall debut in 1989 in the premiere of a suite from Weill's Lost In The Stars; Has also sung Janáček's Diary of One Who Disappeared with Matrix at the Queen Elizabeth Hall; Sang Don José in Carmen Jones in London, 1991; Sang in Porgy and Bess at Covent Garden in 1992 and in the Weill/Grosz concert at the 1993 London Proms; Sang Sporting Life at Costa Mesa, CA, 1996. *Address:* c/o Opera Pacific, 9 Executive Circle, Suite 190, Irvine, CA 92714, USA.

EVANS, Edgar; Opera Singer (Tenor); b. 9 June 1912, Cardiganshire, Wales; m. Nan Walters, 1 s. *Education:* Private study with Dawson Freer, London, and Luigi Ricci, Rome Opera. *Career:* Debut: London, 1947 at Covent Garden in Massenet's Des Grieux; Professor of Singing, Royal College of Music; Founder Member and Principal Tenor, Royal Opera House, from 1946, as Don José, Alfredo, Mussorgsky's Dimitri, Calaf, Captain Vere, Tchaikovsky's Herman and Janáček's Laca; Numerous radio and television programmes; Sang Andres in the British stage premiere of Wozzeck (1952), Števa in the first British Jenůfa (1956) and Helenus in the first Covent Garden Troyens by Berlioz (1957); Narraboth in the Brook/Dali production of Salome and Zinovy in the British premiere of Katerina Izmailova by Shostakovich (1963), Herman in The Queen of Spades; Invited to Covent Garden 2002 as guest at Tchaikovsky's opera, in his 90th year; mem. Incorporated Society of Musicians. *Recordings:* Tristan und Isolde; Albert Herring. *Honours:* Honorary RCM, 1977. *Address:* The White House, 110 Preston Hill, Harrow, Middlesex HA3 9 SJ, England.

EVANS, Joseph; Singer (Tenor); b. 13 Aug. 1945, Brookhaven, Missouri, USA. *Career:* Sang with the New York City Opera, 1976–, in Les Pêcheurs de Perles, Maria Stuarda, Don Giovanni, The Love of Three Oranges, Attila and La Traviata; Appearances with the Opera Company of Boston in Don Pasquale, Rigoletto, Benvenuto Cellini, War and Peace, I Capuleti e i Montecchi, Ruslan and Lyudmila, Die Soldaten by Zimmermann, Montezuma by Sessions and Orphée aux Enfers; Has also sung with Houston Grand Opera and with opera companies in San Diego, Palm Beach, Cincinnati, Cleveland, Hawaii, Fort Worth and Colorado; Sang in The Love of Three Oranges in Geneva, The Prodigal Son in Venice, Persephone by Stravinsky at Nancy, and Guidon in Rimsky's Tsar Saltan at La Scala; Season 1988–89 with The Devil and Kate and Marschner's Der Templar und die Jüdin at Wexford; Sang Alwa in Lulu for the Opéra de Nantes, and Max in Der Freischütz for Welsh National Opera; Concert engagements with Bernstein and the New York Philharmonic, Lukas Foss and the Brooklyn Philharmonic and with Julius Rudel and Michael Tilson Thomas; Has also sung with the Pittsburgh, Atlanta and Indianapolis Symphony Orchestras and appeared in concerts with the Orchestre de l'Ile de France; Sang Lucas Wardlaw in Floyd's Passion of Jonathan Wade, Santa Fe, 1996; Sang Captain Vere in Billy Budd at Seattle, 2001. *Address:* Music International, 13 Ardilaun Road, London N5 2QR, England.

EVANS, Peter; Singer (Tenor); b. 1962, England. *Education:* Studied at the Royal Northern College of Music and the Royal Scottish Academy. *Career:* South Bank debut as Purcell's Aeneas with the English Chamber Orchestra, 1988; Further concerts with the Bournemouth Sinfonietta, London Bach Orchestra and Royal Liverpool Philharmonic; Repertory has included Elijah, Messiah (at Gdańsk, Poland), Mozart's

Requiem (Aix Festival), Purcell's King Arthur with the English Concert and Hindemith's Das Nusch-Nuschi with the BBC Symphony Orchestra, 1995; Sang Monteverdi's Orfeo at the Aldeburgh festival, 1993; First Shepherd with ENO, 1996; Covent Garden Festival as Mozart's Schauspieldirektor and Lurcanio in Handel's Ariodante, 1996–97; Concert venues include the Queen Elizabeth Hall, St John's Smith Square and the Wigmore Hall. *Honours:* NFMS Concert Artists Award, 1987.

EVANS, Peter Angus; Musicologist; b. 7 Nov. 1929, West Hartlepool, England. *Education:* Studied with Arthur Hutchings and A E Dickinson at Durham University, 1947–51, BA in 1950; FRCO, 1952; BMus, Durham, 1953; MA, 1953; DMus, 1958. *Career:* Music Master, Bishop Wordsworth's School, Salisbury, 1951–52; Lecturer, Durham University, 1953–61; Professor of Music, Southampton University, 1961–90. *Publications include:* Articles on Britten and Jonathan Harvey in Tempo and The Musical Times; Chapter: The Vocal Works in Michael Tippett: A Symposium, 1965; The Music of Benjamin Britten, 1979; Articles on Britten and Rawsthorne in The New Grove Dictionary of Music and Musicians, 1980; Instrumental Music, chapter in Blackwell History of Music in Britain, 20th century volume, 1995. *Honours:* Honorary Member, Guildhall School of Music, 1998. *Address:* Pye's Nest Cottage, Parkway, Ledbury, Herefordshire HR8 2JD, England.

EVANS, Peter Geoffrey, BMus, ARCM; British pianist, teacher and conductor; b. 13 Jan. 1950, Redhill, Surrey, England. *Education:* University of Edinburgh, Hochschule für Musik, Vienna, Austria. *Career:* performances as solo pianist and in various duos and ensembles throughout the United Kingdom, including Aldeburgh and Edinburgh Festivals, London's South Bank and Wigmore Halls, St John's Smith Square, also in Austria, Germany, France, Poland, Ireland, USA, former USSR and Japan, 1974–; Appearances on Scottish, Tyne-Tees and BBC television, including BBC 2 Beethoven cello/piano sonata series; Recordings for French and Swedish Radio and Radio 3; Soloist with all major orchestras in Scotland; Principal Conductor, Edinburgh's Meadows Chamber Orchestra, 1972–; Conducting debut in Spain at Festival of Torroella de Montgri, Catalonia, 1986; Close association with International Musicians Seminar, Cornwall, 1982–93; Masterclasses, Oberlin College, Ohio, USA, 1980, Deal Summer Music Festival, 1985–88; Membership of London-based Premiere Ensemble, 1990–; Artistic Co-Director of Hebrides Ensemble, 1991–2003. *Recordings:* Brahms and Martinů sonatas for cello and piano, with Steven Isserlis, cello; Cello and piano recital, with Alexander Baillie, cello, 1988; Solo piano in Britten's Young Apollo, with Scottish Chamber Orchestra, Serebrier, 1990; Recital of French music for cello and piano; Works by Webern, Lutoslawski and Rachmaninov for cello and piano, with William Conway; Over 70 for BBC, including large number for Radio 3. *Address:* 49 Spottiswoode Road, Edinburgh, EH9 1DA, Scotland. *Telephone:* (131) 4476414. *Fax:* (131) 4476414. *E-mail:* peterevans49@hotmail.com.

EVANS, Rebecca (Ann); Singer (Soprano); b. 19 Aug. 1963, Neath, Wales. *Education:* Guildhall School of Music and Drama, London. *Career:* Debut: As Gretel in Hansel and Gretel, Welsh National Opera in 1990; Has appeared in television series, Encore and Rebecca Evans; Roles include Ilia in Idomeneo, Oscar in Un Ballo in Maschera, Inez in La Favorita, the title role in Massenet's Cendrillon, and the Countess in Rossini's Count Ory; Season 1994 as Strauss's Sophie and Berlioz's Hero for Welsh National Opera, Marzelline in Leonore at the Edinburgh Festival; Janáček's Vixen with Scottish Opera, 1997; Season 1998 as Susanna for the Royal Opera, Massenet's Cendrillon at Ghent and Nannetta at the London Proms; Season 2000–01 as Anne Trulove at San Francisco and Sophie at Munich (also Susanna, and Zdenka in Arabella); Sang Zerlina under Abbado at Covent Garden, 2002, Nannetta in 2003. *Recordings:* Mabel in The Pirates of Penzance; Belinda in Dido and Aeneas; Barbarina in Le nozze di Figaro; Nannetta in Falstaff conducted by John Eliot Gardiner; Italian Song Recital; Delius, Requiem; Finzi, Dies Natalis. *Honours:* Prizewinner, BP Peter Pears, 1990; Young Welsh Singer of the Year, 1991; Honorary Doctorate, University of Glamorgan. *Current Management:* Harlequin Agency Ltd. *Address:* 203 Fidlas Road, Llanishen, Cardiff CF14 5NA, Wales.

EVANS, Tecwyn; New Zealand chorus master and conductor; b. 1970, Auckland. *Education:* University of Otago, University of Kansas with Brian Priestman. *Career:* debut, Dunedin Sinfonia, 1997; Led Die Fledermaus for Kansas University Opera; Chorus Master at Glyndebourne Festival, from 1999; Glyndebourne Festival from 2000, with youth opera Zoë, and La Bohème for the Tour; Engagements with Netherlands Radio Choir, and choral workshops in New Zealand, USA and England; Assistant Conductor at Glyndebourne 2001 for Otello (Festival) and Le nozze di Figaro (Tour); Fidelio at the Paris Châtelet, 2000. *Honours:* Fulbright Fellowship.

EVANS, Wynne; Singer (Tenor); b. 1972, Carmarthen, Wales; m. Tanwen, 1999, 1 d. *Education:* Studied at the Guildhall School and the National Opera Studio, London. *Career:* Opera performances for Welsh National Opera include Liberto in Poppea, 1997, Tamino in the Magic Flute, 1998, Le Chevalier in Dialogues of the Carmelites, 1999, Alfredo in La Traviata, 2000–01, Rodolfo in La Bohème, 2001, Jaquino in Leonore, 2001, 1st Jew in Salome, 2001, Schoolmaster in The Cunning Little Vixen, 2001 and Alfred in Die Fledermaus, 2002; Roles for Opera North include Fenton in Falstaff, 1999, Prunier in La Rondine, 2000, and Paulino in The Secret Marriage, 2003; Roles for Scottish Opera include Tamino in the Magic Flute, 1998 and the Italian Tenor in Der Rosenkavlier, 1999; Other roles include Peacock in Broken Strings for the Almeida Opera and BBC Radio 3, 1996, Fracasso in La Finta Semplice for the Classical Opera Company, 1999, and Arvino in Lombardi for Chelsea Opera, 2001; Concert work includes Tippett's A Child of Our Time in Besançon; Charpentier's Orphée; Messiah in Handel Hall, Halle, Royal Albert Hall, London and St David's Hall, Cardiff; Verdi Requiem in the Royal Albert Hall, London; Wigmore Hall recital; BBC Proms Debut 2001; Operas for television: Salome & The Little Sweep and Rodolfo in the BBC drama The Beggar Bride. *Address:* c/o Doreen O'Neill, Harlequin Agency Ltd, 203 Fidlas Road, Cardiff CF4 5NA, Wales. *Telephone:* 02920 750821. *E-mail:* wynne@wynneevans.co.uk.

EVERETT, Paul (Joseph); Lecturer in Music; b. 6 May 1955, London, England; m. Margaret Mary Bernadette McLoughlin, 21 July 1979, 1 s. *Education:* BMus (Hons), Sheffield University, 1976; PhD, Liverpool University, 1984. *Career:* Lecturer in Music, Liverpool University, 1980–81; Lecturer in Music, University College, Cork, 1981–; mem, RMA. *Publications:* Editor of various modern editions of music by D Purcell, J C Schickhardt, J B Loeillet and several works by Vivaldi for the Istituto Italiano Antonio Vivaldi; Scholarly articles on Italian sources, especially those of Vivaldi's music; The Manchester Concerto Partbooks, 2 vols, 1989. *Contributions:* Music and Letters; Musical Times. *Address:* Music Department, University College, Cork, Ireland.

EVROVA, Katia (Ekaterina); Pianist; b. 5 Oct. 1947, Sofia, Bulgaria. *Education:* Diploma of Excellence in Piano and Musical Pedagogy, Bulgarian Superior Conservatoire of Music, Sofia, 1971; Diploma of Excellence in Chamber Music, Debussy Conservatoire, Paris, 1982. *Career:* first appearance with aunt Yova Kallova, teacher of piano, Sofia, 1952; concerts as member of violin and piano duo and trio with piano, 1976–81; concerts as violin and piano duo with Vladimir Lazov, 1983–89, performances including cycle of Schubert sonatas, 1987, cycle of 19 sonatas for piano and violin by Mozart, 1989; concert tours, Europe and Asia; piano teacher, Chaumont, France, 1989; founded the Mezzo-Forte Ensemble (piano, flute, classical guitar) with Franck Douvin and Gérard Montaudoin, 1989; Piano and Chamber Music Teacher at School of Music, Pays de Langres, 1990; concerts with the Mezzo-Forte Ensemble at Chaumont and 4th European Congress of Jewish Studies, Troyes, 1990; debut, cycle of Mozart works for piano and violin as duo with Svetoslav Marinov, 1990; tours of Brazil and Mexico, 1991, France, 1992, 1993, Brazil, 1993; concerts in France in duo with Svetoslav Marinov, 1994, 1995–; concerts, 1996, and the integral of Beethoven's sonatas for piano and violin, duo with S. Marinov, 1997; concert tour as soloist with Orchestral Ensemble of the Sofia Philharmonia in 1998 at Sofia; concert tours in France as Duo Amadeus 91 (with S. Marinov) at Arc-en-Barrois, 1999, 2002, Chaumont and Joinville, 2000; Concert tour with Vocalys Ensemble in the Rossini's Petite messe solennelle, France, 2003; mem., Former Dramaturgist, Sofia Weeks of Music, Bulgarian International Festival, RBA of ABI. *Address:* 28 rue du Château Paillot, 52000 Chaumont, France.

EVSTATIEVA, Stefka; Singer (Soprano); b. 7 May 1947, Rousse, Bulgaria. *Education:* Sofia Conservatoire with Elena Kiselova. *Career:* Member of Rousse Opera, 1971–79; Roles have included Verdi's Amelia, Elisabeth de Valois, Aida and Desdemona, Margarita in Mefistofele, Yaroslavna in Prince Igor, Puccini's Mimi and Suor Angelica; Member of Bulgarian National Opera in Sofia from 1978; Guest appearances in Vienna, Frankfurt, Munich, Hamburg, New York, Berlin, Milan, Verona, Madrid and Paris; Roles include, Leonora in Il Trovatore, Elvira in Ernani, Madeleine de Coigny in Andrea Chénier, Donna Elvira in Don Giovanni and Lisa in Queen of Spades; Royal Opera debut in Manchester as Desdemona in Otello; London 1983 as Elisabeth de Valois; Metropolitan debut in 1983 as Elisabeth de Valois; San Francisco in 1984 and 1986 as Aida; Toronto, 1989–90 as Tosca, Mimi, Leonora in La Forzo del Destino and Desdemona; Appeared at Nimes in 1986 as Medora in the French premiere of Verdi's Il Corsaro; Sang at the Savonlinna Festival in 1990 as Aida; Season 1991–92 as Amelia in Ballo in Maschera at Antwerp, Tosca at Buenos Aires and the Forza Leonora at Florence; Sang Giordano's Maddalena at Buenos Aires, 1996; Elisabeth de Valois at Trieste, 1997; Many engagements as concert singer. *Recordings:* Rimsky-Korsakov's Boyartinya Vera Sheloga and The Maid of Pskov; 2 Recitals of Italian arias. *Address:* c/o San Francisco Opera, War Memorial Opera House, San Francisco, CA 94102, USA.

EWENS, Craig R. R.; English pianist and piano teacher; b. 26 March 1966, Wokingham, England. *Education:* Royal Coll. of Music Jr Dept, 1979–84; Guildhall School of Music and Drama, 1984–90. *Career:* debut, St John's Smith Square, London, 1988; many recitals for nat. music socs and in London; solo recitals at St John's Smith Square, Barbican Centre, St Martin in the Fields, St James's Piccadilly, St Bride's Fleet Street, Purcell Room; mem., Incorporated Soc. of Musicians, European Piano Teachers' Asscn; Fellow, Guild of Musicians and Singers. *Recordings:* Prokofiev 2nd Piano Concerto; Beethoven Sonatas op 57, 81a, 109, 110; Mozart Sonata K.457; Chopin Ballades; Schubert Wanderer Fantasy; Schumann Fantasy op 17; Prokofiev Sonatas Nos 2, 3 and 6; Berg Sonata op 1; Liszt Variations on Weinen, Klagen, Sorgen, Zagen; Ravel Scarbo. *Honours:* AGSM, Concert Recital Diploma (Premier Prix) GSMD 1988, Teresa Carreno Memorial Piano Prize 1984. *Address:* Flat 16, Howitt Close, Howitt Road, London NW3 4LX, England. *Telephone:* (20) 7483-4405. *E-mail:* craigewens@onetel.com.

EWING, Alan; Singer (Bass); b. 1959, Northern Ireland. *Education:* Read Music at University of East Anglia; Choral Scholar, Norwich Cathedral Choir; Guildhall School of Music with Rudolf Piernay, 1980–84. *Career:* Roles at the Guildhall School of Music include Sarastro, Colline, Bottom, Collatinus in The Rape of Lucretia, and Falstaff in The Merry Wives of Windsor; Has sung widely with Renaissance and Baroque groups, notably with the Consort of Musicke at major festivals in the USA, Australia, Japan, Israel and Europe; Has sung in oratorios throughout Europe and with the 1989 Young Songmakers' Almanac Concert; Appearances in The Rape of Lucretia at the Aldeburgh Festival and as the Voice of Neptune in Idomeneo with Rattle at the Queen Elizabeth Hall; Sang Trulove in The Rake's Progress conducted by John Lubbock and in Kopernicus by Claude Vivier in a Pierre Audi production at the Almeida Festival; Sang Osmin in Die Entführung at the 1991 Buxton Festival; Sang Rocco in Fidelio for Opera Northern Ireland, 1996; Season 1998 as the Priest in The Cunning Little Vixen at Spoleto and Vengeance in Rameau's Zoroastre on tour with Les Arts Florissants; Season 2000–01 in the premiere of Rêves d'un Marco Polo, at Amsterdam, as Handel's Polyphemus at the Salzburg Easter Festival, and as Britten's Collatinus at Florence. *Recordings:* Various albums with the Consort of Musicke. *Address:* Allied Artists Agency, 42 Montpelier Square, London SW7 1JZ, England.

EWING, Maria Louise; Singer (soprano); b. 27 March 1950, Detroit, MI, USA; m. Peter Hall 1982 (divorced 1990); one d. *Education:* Piano studies with Mabel Barel and Gizo Santo; Studied singing with Marjorie Gordon, Eleanor Steber, Jennie Tourel and Otto Guth; Music Scholarship, Cleveland Institute of Music. *Career:* Debut: Meadow Brook Festival, 1968; Debut as Cherubino at the Metropolitan Opera in 1976 and at La Scala in Pelléas et Mélisande; Particularly known for her interpretations of Dorabella in Così fan tutte, Susanna and Cherubino in Figaro and the title roles in La Périchole and La Cenerentola; Roles at Glyndebourne include Carmen, Poppea and Ariadne; In 1988 gave Covent Garden debut as Salome; Season 1988–89 included Carmen at Earls Court in London; Sang Carmen in a new production at Covent Garden in 1991 and sang Salome there in 1992, filmed for television; Sang Messiaen Poèmes Pour Mi with Philharmonia under Boulez in London and Paris in 1993, and sang the closing scene from Salome at 1993 London Proms; Season 1993–94 in premiere of new works by Michael Tilson Thomas, with London Symphony Orchestra, Tosca and Madama Butterfly at the Vienna State Opera and The Trojans with Levine at the Metropolitan Opera; Season 1995 with Tosca at Covent Garden and Purcell's Dido for BBC television; Marie in Wozzeck at the Met, 1997; Sang Fedora at Los Angeles, 1997. *Recordings:* Andrea Chénier; Don Giovanni; Mozart's Requiem under Bernstein, 1988; Lady Macbeth of Mtensk, title role, with Bastille Opéra, 1993; Shéhérazade under Simon Rattle; Pelléas et Mélisande under Abbado.

EWINGTON, John, OBE, MA, FGCM, ACertCM, DipChMus, FGMS; British director of music; *General Secretary, Guild of Church Musicians;* b. 14 May 1936, Goodmayes, Essex; m. Hélène Mary Leach; two s. *Education:* South East Essex County Technical School, Lambeth, Goldsmiths' Coll. Univ. of London. *Career:* national service in RN 1954–56; Admin Asst, Inst. of London Underwriters 1953–67; Underwriting Asst, PCW Agencies Lloyd's 1967–86; senior broker, HSBC Gibbs 1986–97; Dir of Music and organist, Blechingley Parish Church 1966–97; Dir of Music, City Singers, London 1968; Dir of Music, St Mary Woolnoth 1970–93; Gen. Sec. Guild of Church Musicians 1979–; organist and Dir of Music, St Katherine Cree, London 1998–; Conjoint Sr Lecturer Conservatorium School of Music and Drama Univ. of Newcastle, NSW 2004–; Gov. De Stafford School, Surrey 1979–84, Oxted School 1984–2005, Vice Chair. 1995–2005; mem. Friday Club, City Livery Club, Lloyds of London Three Rooms Club. *Compositions:* Hillbrow (hymn tune). *Publications:* Landmarks in Christian Worship and Church Music (with Canon Arthur Dobb); contrib. to magazines, journals, Church Times. *Honours:* Freeman City of London 1980, Hon. FFCM 1993, Hon. FCSM 1990, Hon. mem. RSCM 2002, Liveryman Worshipful Co. of Musicians 2001,

Hon. Fellow Univ. of Newcastle, NSW 2004; Order of St Lazarus of Jerusalem 2002. *Address:* Hillbrow, Godstone Road, Blechingley, RH1 4PJ, England (home). *Telephone:* (1883) 743168 (home). *Fax:* (1883) 743168 (home). *E-mail:* JohnMusicsure@orbix.co.uk (office). *Website:* www.churchmusicians.org (office).

EYSER, Eberhard; Swedish composer and violist; b. 1 Aug. 1932, Marienwerder, Prussia, Germany. *Education:* Akademie für Musik und Theater, Hanover, Mozarteum, Salzburg, Accademia Chigiana, Siena, Italy. *Career:* violist, Royal Swedish Opera Orchestra. *Compositions:* about 360 works, including chamber and orchestral music, vocal and electronic music, computer music; Operas and chamber operas include Molonn, 1970, The Death of a Bird, 1971, A Man's Dream, 1972, Last Voyage, 1973, King of Hearts, 1973, Abu Said, 1976, Summer's Day, 1979, The Deep Water, 1980, Bermuda Triangle, 1981, Via Gravis, 1981, The Ravens, 1982, Roses and Ruins, 1982, The Last Day on Earth, 1982, The Red Book Mystery, 1984, Twilight in Granada, 1984, It Was Raining Yesterday, 1985, The Picture of Dorian Gray, 1986; The Aspern Papers, 1989; 5 saxophone quartets, orchestral works, Itabol, Metastrophy, Macbeth Overture; Charley McDeath, chamber opera, 1992. *Recordings:* King of Hearts, Last Voyage, The Deep Water, Overture, Circus Overture, Duo 3 G The Bard. *Address:* Karlbergsv 71B, 11335 Stockholm, Sweden. *Telephone:* 46 8308425. *E-mail:* eyser.eb@swipnet .se. *Website:* www.sami.se/art/eyser/home.htm.

EZZAT, Mohammed Amin; Iraqi *Conductor, Baghdad Symphony Orchestra. Compositions include:* Three Fragments. *Address:* Iraqi National Symphony Orchestra, Baghdad Convention Center, Green Zone, Baghdad, Iraq.

F

FABBRI, Franca; Italian singer (soprano); b. 28 May 1935, Milan. *Education:* studied in Milan with Adelina Fiori, Adelaide Saraceni and Giuseppe Pais. *Career:* debut, Spoleto in 1963 as Violetta; Has sung widely in Italy and in Berlin, Hamburg, Cologne, Budapest, Warsaw, San Francisco and Aix-en-Provence; Sang in the premieres of L'Idiota and Riva delle Sirti by Chailly, Orfeo Vedevo by Savino and Al Gran Sole Carico d'Amore by Nono, 1975; Repertoire included Lucia di Lammermoor, Musetta, Nedda, Fiordiligi, Gilda, Marguerite de Valois in Les Huguenots, the Queen of Night and Pamira in L'Assedio di Corinto by Rossini; Roles in operas by Britten, Shostakovich, Maderna and Malipiero. *Address:* c/o Conservatorio Giuseppe Verdi, Via del Conservatorio 12, 20122 Milan, Italy.

FABBRICINI, Tiziana; Singer (Soprano); b. 1961, Asti, Piemont, Italy. *Education:* Studied in Milan and other centres in Italy. *Career:* Won various singing competitions, 1982–85, and sang minor roles in provincial Italian opera houses; Made La Scala debut in 1990 as Violetta; Season 1991 in La Traviata at Naples and Elvire in a revival of La Muette di Portici by Auber at Ravenna; Sang Lucia di Lammermoor at La Scala in 1992 and at Houston, 1994, Fiorilla in Il Turco in Italia at the Théâtre des Champs-Elysées, 1996; Sang Tosca at Savona, 1997; Season 1999–2000 at Genoa as Arianna in Nasso, in the opera by Porpora and as Tosca at the Balbeck Festival. *Address:* c/o Théâtre des Champs Elysée, (Artist Contracts), 15 Avenue Montaigne, F–75008 Paris, France.

FABER, Lothar; Oboist; b. 7 Feb. 1922, Cologne, Germany. *Education:* Studied at the Cologne Musikhochschule and at the Paris Conservatoire. *Career:* Played with the WDR Orchestra, Cologne, from 1946, and has made many appearances at festivals throughout Europe: Berlin, Venice, Warsaw, Netherlands and Darmstadt; Has premiered works by Maderna, K Mayer, Baird, Fortner, Schuller and Zimmermann; Has given summer courses at Darmstadt and Siena, 1972–77. *Address:* c/o WDR Sinfonie-Orchester, D 50600 Koln, Germany.

FABIAN, Marta; Dulcimer Player; b. 1946, Budapest, Hungary. *Education:* Started playing the dulcimer at age 8; Studied at Béla Bart ók Conservatory, 1960–64 and Ferenc Liszt Academy of Music, Budapest, 1967. *Career:* Soloist with Budapest Chamber Ensemble; Has made numerous guest performances in Austria, Belgium, Bulgaria, Czechoslovakia, Finland, France, Germany, the United Kingdom, the Netherlands, Italy, Latin America, Mexico, Poland, Russia, Spain, Sweden, Switzerland, Turkey, USA and Yugoslavia and appeared at the Bratislava, Darmstadt, Netherlands, Lucerne, IGNM (SIMC) of Athens and Graz Festivals, Warsaw Autumn Festival of Modern Music, the Witten Festival and the Zagreb Biennial Festival of Modern Music. *Recordings include:* Cimbalom Recital. *Honours:* Grand Prize, French National Record Academy, 1977; Liszt Prize.

FAERBER, Jorg; Conductor and Composer; b. 18 June 1929, Stuttgart, Germany. *Education:* Studied at the Hochschule für Musik, Stuttgart. *Career:* Theatre conductor and composer in Stuttgart and Heilbronn, 1952–60; Founded Württemberg Chamber Orchestra, 1960; Tours to Austria, the United Kingdom, France, Italy, USA and South Africa; Many performances in the Baroque repertory; Appearances with the European Community Chamber Orchestra, various BBC Orchestras, the Bournemouth Sinfonietta, the Thames Chamber Orchestra, and the Northern Sinfonia; Festival engagements at Swansea and with the English Bach Festival. *Recordings:* Bach Brandenburg Concertos; Boyce Symphonies; Vivaldi Four Seasons and other concertos; Bassoon Concertos by Weber, Graun, J C Bach, K Stamitz, Boismortier and Mozart; Concertos for cello, clarinet, viola and flute by Stamitz; Trumpet concertos by Torelli, Albinoni, Biber, Stölzel and Manfredini; Mozart piano concertos K413 and K450, violin concertos K218 and K219, flute concertos, Sinfonia Concertante K297b and overtures. *Address:* Postfach 3730, 7100 Heilbronn/Neckar, Germany.

FAGÉUS, Kjell; Clarinettist; b. 25 July 1949, Lönneberga, Sweden; m. Lena Fagéus, 23 Aug 1993, 2 s. *Education:* University study in Mathematics, 1 year; Student, 1970–74, Solo Diploma and Pedagogical Examination, 1974, Royal Music Academy, Stockholm; Studied with Stanley Drucker, Juilliard School of Music, New York, 1975–76. *Career:* Debut: Waldemars udde, Stockholm, 1974; Principal Clarinet, Royal Opera, Stockholm, 1976–90; Chamber music and solo performances throughout the world; Coach in Mental Training, Royal Academy, Stockholm, and for professional musicians at SAMI; mem, SYMF; SAMI, Sweden. *Recordings:* 3 albums with Stockholm Wind Quintet; Mozart Clarinet Concerto and Swedish Concertos with Royal Opera Orchestra; Mozart and Brahms Clarinet Quintets. *Publications:* Lek på fullt allvar, 1998. *Contributions:* Visions of Excellence, for International Society for Mental Training and Excellence. *Honours:* Swedish Government Scholarship, 10 years. *Address:* Skvattramstigen 19, 14264 Trångsund, Sweden.

FAGGIONI, Piero; Opera Producer; b. 12 Aug. 1936, Carrara, Italy. *Education:* Worked under Jean Vilar and Luchino Visconti in Italy. *Career:* Debut: La Bohème at Venice in 1964; Produced Alceste at La Scala in 1972, La Fanciulla del West in Turin in 1974 and at Covent Garden, Norma at Vienna in 1977, Carmen at Edinburgh in 1977, Macbeth at Salzburg in 1984, Francesca da Rimini at Metropolitan Opera in 1984 and production of Boris Godunov at Barcelona; Staging of Massenet's Don Quichotte seen at Paris Opéra in 1986, and Florence and Monte Carlo in 1992; Produced Il Trovatore at Covent Garden in 1989; Principal Guest Producer at Covent Garden until 1990; Don Quichotte at the Rome Opera, 1997. *Address:* c/o Teatro dell Opera, Piazza B Gigli 00184 Rome, Italy.

FAHBERG, Antonia; Singer (Soprano); b. 19 May 1928, Vienna, Austria. *Education:* Studied at the Vienna Music Academy. *Career:* Sang at Innsbruck from 1950, and Munich from 1952; Opera engagements in Hamburg, Vienna, Brussels and Amsterdam; Radio and television engagements; Noted interpreter of works by Rossini (Stabat Mater), Beethoven (Christ at the Mount of Olives), Bruckner (Te Deum) and Bach. *Recordings include:* St Matthew Passion and Cantatas by Bach; Alexander Balus by Handel; Il Ritorno d'Ulisse and L'Incoronazione di Poppea; Diana in Gluck's Iphigénie en Tauride. *Address:* c/o Bayerische Staatsoper, Postfach 745, 8000 Munich 1, Germany.

FÄHNDRICH, Walter; Swiss musician and composer; b. 1 April 1944, Menzingen; one d. *Education:* studied in Lucerne. *Career:* international activities as Viola Player, Composer and Improviser; Solo Concerts; Music Installations, Music For Spaces; Improvisation; Professorship for Improvisation, Basel; Since 1990 organisation of the International Congresses for Improvisation, Lucerne; mem, Schweizerischer Tonkünstler-Verein. *Compositions:* Works for viola solo; Music For Spaces; Musical landscape projects; Chamber music; Electro-acoustic music; Music for radio plays, theatres, ballets. *Recordings:* Viola, ECM; Spaces, UNIT; Music For Spaces, Reihe Cantz; Various radio and television recordings. *Publications:* Improvisation, 1992; Improvisation II, 1994; Improvisation III, 1998; Zur geschichte und gegenwart der Elektronischen Musik, 1999; Improvisation IV, 2001; Improvisation V, 2003; Various publications on Music and Space. *Current Management:* Katherin Fähndrich, Piodina 20, 6614 Brissago, Switzerland.

FAIRBAIRN, Clive (Stuart); Conductor; b. 21 April 1946, London, England; m. Nicola Swann, 18 Aug 1979, 1 d. *Education:* Royal Academy of Music, London. *Career:* Debut: St Johns, Smith Square, London, 1977; Principal Conductor, New Mozart Orchestra, 1977–; Principal Conductor, Lindstrom Philharmonic Orchestra, 1984–; Guest appearances include London Symphony Orchestra, London Philharmonic, Philharmonia, and Wren Orchestra; Has broadcast with New Mozart Orchestra, London Symphony Orchestra, and Wren Orchestra; Conducted in Germany, Switzerland, Turkey and Portugal; mem, Incorporated Society of Musicians.

FAIX-BROWN, Winifred; Singer (Soprano); b. 1954, USA. *Education:* Studied in Illinois. *Career:* Sang in Europe from 1980, at Gelsenkirchen until 1984, Deutsche Oper Berlin, 1985–86; Guested as Lucia di Lammermoor at Mexico City, 1981, and at Chicago as Musetta (1987); Portland, 1983, as Fiordiligi, Miami, 1984 (Lucia), Milwaukee, 1989 (Donna Anna); Other roles include Elettra in Idomeneo (Miami, 1990), Leonora (Forza del Destino), Desdemona and the Marschallin (Los Angeles, 1984); Nice 1991, as Fiordiligi. *Current Management:* Robert Lombardo Associates. *Address:* 61 West 62nd Street, Suite 6F, New York, NY 10023, USA.

FALCON, Ruth; singer (soprano); b. 2 Nov. 1946, Residence, LA, USA. *Education:* studies in New Orleans, and Italy with Tito Gobbi and Luigi Ricci. *Career:* debut, New York City Opera in 1974 as Micaela in Carmen; Title role in Mayr's Medea in Corinto, Bern, 1975; Bayerische Staatsoper Munich, 1976–80 as Leonora in Trovatore and La Forza del Destino, and Mozart's Countess and Elettra; Guest artist in New York, Canada, Germany and France as Puccini's Manon Lescaut and Weber's Agathe; Paris Opéra debut in 1981 as Mozart's Donna Anna; Covent Garden and Vienna Staatsoper in 1983 as the Trovatore Leonora; Sang Anna Bolena at Nice in 1985; Nancy Opéra in 1986 as Norma; Aix-en-Provence Festival as Ariadne; Covent Garden in 1987 and Metropolitan in 1989 as the Empress in Die Frau ohne Schatten; Buenos Aires 1993 as Turandot; Sang the Trovatore Leonora at New Orleans, 1997; Concert repertory includes Mahler's 8th Symphony, Beethoven's Missa Solemnis, Verdi's Requiem and works by Handel, Mozart, Brahms, Dvořák and Strauss. *Recordings include:* Die Walküre; Götterdämmerung. *Current Management:* Robert Gilder & Co., Enterprise House,

59–65 Upper Ground, London, SE1 9PQ, England. *Telephone:* (20) 7928-9008. *Fax:* (20) 7928-9755. *E-mail:* rgilder@robert-gilder.com.

FALEWICZ, Magdalena; Singer (Soprano); b. 11 Feb. 1946, Lublin, Poland. *Education:* Studied at the Warsaw Conservatory with Olga Olgina and Maria Kuninska-Opacka. *Career:* Member of the Warsaw Chamber Opera, 1971–72; Solo debut as Oscar in Un Ballo in Maschera at the Komische Oper Berlin in 1973; Sang Madama Butterfly with Welsh National Opera in 1978 and for ENO at the London Coliseum in 1986; Member of the Staatsoper Berlin from 1984 with guest appearances in Frankfurt and Leipzig, and in the USA, Bulgaria, Finland and Netherlands; Dresden Staatsoper in 1985 as the Countess in the premiere of Siegfried Matthus' Weise von Liebe und Tod des Comten Christoph Rilke; Mozart's Countess at Dresden, 1988. *Recordings include:* Schubert's Alfonso und Estrella; Amor in Gluck's Orfeo ed Euridice; Die Kluge by Orff. *Address:* c/o Deutsche Staatsoper, Unter den Linden, 1086 Berlin, Germany.

FALIK, Yuri; Composer, Conductor and Cellist; b. 30 July, 1936, Odessa, Russia; m. Valentina Papkova, 19 Mar 1957, 1 s., 1 d. *Education:* Central Special Music School, Odessa, 1945–55; Cello, Leningrad Conservatory of Music, 1955–60, Postgraduate, 1960–63, Composition, 1960–64; Teachers included Shtrimer (Cello), Rostropovich (Cello), Arapov (composition); Masterclasses with Shostakovich (composition) and Rabinovich (conducting). *Career:* Teacher, Leningrad Special Music School, 1960–71; Chief Conductor, Leningrad Conservatory Chamber Orchestra, 1964–68; Professor of Cello, 1965–81, Professor of Composition and Instrumentation, 1981–, Leningrad Conservatory; Visiting Profesor, Northwestern University, 1991–92; Guest Conducting appearances throughout Russia and: Chicago Symphony Orchestra, 1990; Northwestern University Chamber Orchestra, 1991; St Petersburg Philharmonic Orchestra 1998–2000; Baltimore Symphony Orchestra, 2000; Moscow Philharmonic Orchestra, 2000; Saratov Symphony Orchestra, 2000; Nizhny Novgorod Symphony Orchestra, 2001; mem, Composers' Union; ASCAP. *Compositions:* Stage works:; Oresteia, Choreographic Tragedy, 1968; Les Fourberies de Scapin, opera, 1984; Polly and the Dinosaurs, opera, performed in Concert in Chicago, 1990; Orchestral: Concertino, oboe and chamber orchestra, 1961; Symphony, string orchestra and percussion, 1963; Concerto for orchestra, 1967; Music for strings, 1968; Easy Symphony, 1971; Concerto for violin and orchestra, 1971; Concerto for orchestra No. 2, Symphonic Etudes, 1977; Concertino for bassoon and strings, 1987; Concerto della Passione for cello and orchestra, 1988; Vivat Chicago Symphony, Overture for orchestra, 1991; Symphony No. 2 (Kaddish), 1993; Chamber: 8 String Quartets, 1955–2001; Trio for oboe, cello and piano, 1959; Wind Quintet, 1964; Concerto for 6 winds and percussion (Buffoons), 1966; English Divertimento, flute, clarinet and bassoon; Introduction and 3 Canzones for flute, bassoon, violin, cello and piano, 1995; Vocal Music including Solemn Song, Cantata, 1968; Winter Songs, 1975; Autumn Songs, 1970 for a capella chorus; Estonian Watercolours, Suite for women's chorus, 1976; 4 Concertos for chorus a capella, 1979, 1987, 1988, 1998; Russian Orthodox Liturgical Chants for mixed chorus and soloists, 1990–92; 2 concertos for chorus a capella, 1998, 2001; Mourning Mass for Igor Stravinsky, for 16 strings and 4 trombones, 1975; Mass for soloists, mixed chorus and chamber orchestra, 1996; Elegies- Concerto from Soprano solo and chorus a capella, 2001; Lyrical concertino for cello and orchestra, 2002. *Publications:* E Ruchievskaja, Yuri Falik, The Composer and His Works, 1981. *Honours:* Prize, Second Tchaikovsky International Competition, 1962; First Prize, Helsinki International Cello Competition, 1962. *Address:* St Petersburg N Rimsky Korsakov Conservatory, Teatralnaya Pl 3, 190001 St Petersburg, Russia.

FALKMAN, Carl Johan; Singer (Baritone); b. 24 July 1947, Stockholm, Sweden. *Education:* Studied in Stockholm, and with Gino Bechi in Florence. *Career:* Debut: Stockholm, 1973, in the premiere of Werle's Tintomara; Drottningholm Festival from 1973, as Guglielmo, Pacuvio in Kraus's Proserpina; Guest engagements in Scandinavia and elsewhere as Dandini in La Cenerentola, Mozart's Figaro and Masetto, Eugene Onegin and Marcello; Don Giovanni at the Prague bicentenary performances, Prague, 1987; Grétry's Zémire et Azor at Drottningholm, 1993; Sang Wozzeck and Papageno at the Royal Opera Stockholm, 2000. *Address:* c/o Drottningholms Slottstheater, PO Box 270505, 10251 Stockholm, Sweden.

FALLETTA, JoAnn; Conductor; b. 27 Feb. 1954, New York, NY, USA. *Education:* Studied at Juilliard, Queens College and Mannes College. *Career:* Soloist with orchestras on classical guitar, lute, mandolin; Has conducted leading orchestras at Denver, Indianapolis, Phoenix, St Paul, Richmond, Toledo, Tucson and Columbus; European engagements in Italy, France, Switzerland and Denmark; Music Director of the Long Beach Symphony Orchestra, 1989; Music Director of the Virginia Symphony Orchestra, 1991, with guest appearances with the Symphony Orchestras of San Francisco, Savannah, Delaware, Hamilton and Antwerp; German debut with the Mannheim National Theatre Orchestra, in works by Barber, Gershwin and Brahms; Music Director

of the Buffalo Philharmonic, 1998–. *Honours:* Winner of Stokowski, 1985, Toscanini, 1985, and Bruno Walter Awards, 1982–87. *Current Management:* ICM Artists. *Address:* 40 West 57th Street, New York, NY 10019, USA.

FALLOWS, David Nicholas, BA, MMus, PhD, FBA; British musicologist; *Professor of Music, University of Manchester;* b. 20 Dec. 1945, Buxton, England; m. Paulène Oliver 1976 (separated); one s. one d. *Education:* Jesus Coll., Cambridge, King's Coll., London, Univ. of California at Berkeley. *Career:* Asst. Studio der Frühen Musik, Munich 1967–70; Lecturer in Music, Univ. of Wisconsin at Madison 1973–74; Lecturer in Music, Univ. of Manchester 1976–82, Sr Lecturer 1982–92, Reader in Music 1992–97, Prof. of Music 1997–; Reviews Ed., Early Music 1976–95, 1999–2000; Visiting Assoc. Prof., Univ. of N Carolina at Chapel Hill 1982–83; founder and Gen. Ed., Royal Musical Asscn Monographs 1982–98; Visiting Prof. of Musicology, École Normale Supérieure, Paris 1993; corresponding mem. American Musicological Soc. 1999–; mem. Int. Musicological Soc. (vice-pres. 1997–2002, pres. 2002–(07)), Royal Musical Asscn (vice-pres. 2000–). *Publications:* Dufay 1982, Chansonnier de Jean de Montchenu (co-author) 1991, Companion to Medieval and Renaissance Music (ed. with T. Knighton) 1992, The Songs of Guillaume Dufay 1995, Oxford Bodleian Library MS Canon Misc. 213: Late Medieval and Early Renaissance Music in Facsimile, Vol. 1 (ed.) 1995, Songs and Musicians in the Fifteenth Century 1996, The Songbook of Fridolin Sicher 1996, A Catalogue of Polyphonic Songs 1415–1480 1999; contrib. to reference works, scholarly books and professional journals, including Gramophone, The Guardian, Early Music, New Grove Dictionary of Music and Musicians 1980, 2001. *Honours:* Ingolf Dahl Prize in Musicology 1971, Dent Medal 1982; Chevalier, Ordre des Arts et des Lettres 1994. *Address:* 10 Chatham Road, Manchester, M16 0DR, England. *E-mail:* david.fallows@man.ac.uk.

FALVAY, Attila; Violinist; b. 7 Sept. 1958, Budapest, Hungary; m. Maria Farnadi, 28 June 1983, two d. *Education:* Liszt Ferenc Academy of Music, Budapest with Professor Semyon Snitkowsky and Vienna Music Academy with Professor Josef Sivo. *Career:* 1st Violinist of Kodály Quartet, 1980–; Leader of Budapest Symphony Orchestra, 1989–. *Recordings include:* Complete Haydn Quartets; Complete Beethoven Quartets; Complete Schubert Quartets; Ravel; Debussy; d'Indy Quartets 1,2; Schumann; Brahms Piano Quintet; Schubert Forellen QUintet; Hofstetter Quartets 1–6; Mozart; Brahms Clarinet Quintet; Kodály Quartets 1,2; Mendelssohn Octet; Motzart Horn Quintet; Oboe Quartet; Musical Joke. *Honours:* Szigeti Competition, Budapest 2nd Prize 1978, Hubay Prize, 1980, Merited Artist of Hungary 1990; Bartók-Pásztory Prize 1996. *Current Management:* Budapest Artists, Gergely Arts,. *Address:* 1121 Budapest, Kázmér utca 40, 1121, Budapest, Hungary. *E-mail:* falvay@axelero.hu. *Website:* www.kodalyquartet.org.

FALVO, Robert; Percussionist; b. 27 Aug. 1963, New York City, USA. *Education:* BM, Music Education, Performer's Certificate, State University of New York, Fredonia, 1985; MM, Percussion Performance, 1987; DMA, Percussion Performance, Manhattan School of Music; Studied with Fred Hinger, Christopher Lamb, James Presiss, Claire Heldrich, Lynn Harbold, and Theodore Frazeur among others. *Career:* Performances with The New Music Consort, New York City, 1987–, NOA, Carnegie Hall, New York City, 1988–, English Chamber Orchestra with US tour in 1988, Pierre Boulez and the Scotia Festival Orchestra, Nova Scotia, Canada, 1991, Frick Hawkins Dance Company Orchestra with tour to Tokyo, Shanghai, Hong Kong and throughout USA, 1991–, and Tokyo Symphony with world tour in 1991; Has also appeared with Erie Chamber Orchestra, Hudson Valley Symphony Orchestra, and New Music Orchestral Project; Xylophone Soloist with Fredonia Symphony Orchestra; Many contemporary music recitals in New York area including Carnegie Hall, Merkin Hall, Miller Hall, Hubbard Hall and Town Hall; Has conducted the Manhattan School of Music Contemporary and Percussion Ensembles; Frequent lectures on contemporary composition techniques for percussion instruments; Assistant Professor of Music, teaching percussion at School of Music, Appalachian State University in North Carolina. *Recordings:* Various. *Address:* PO Box 368 DTS, Boone, NC 28607, USA.

FANDREY, Birgit; Singer (Soprano); b. 1963, Vorpommern, Germany. *Education:* Studied at the Carl Maria von Weber Musikhochschule in Dresden. *Career:* Associated with the Opera Studio of the Dresden Staatsoper, then appeared with the main company from 1987 notably as Mozart's Susanna, Papagena, Pamina and Zerlina, Euridice, Mimi, Gretel, Sophie Scholl in Udo Zimmermann's Die Weisse Rose and in parts in operas by Siegfried Matthus; Sang Handel's Galatea at the Halle Festival in 1987, Amor in Orfeo ed Euridice at the Leipzig Gewandhaus, Mozart's Constanze at Amsterdam and Pamina at St Gallen; Constanze at Munich, 1993; Lieder recitals in works by Schubert, Schumann, Brahms and Strauss; Concert repertoire includes Beethoven's Mass in C at Amsterdam Concertgebouw, Bach's St John

Passion, Messiah and Mozart's Exsultate Jubilate. *Address:* c/o Dresden Staatsoper, 8012 Dresden, Germany.

FANNING, David John, BMus, PhD, GNCM; Academic and concert pianist; *Professor of Music, Manchester University*; b. 5 March 1955, Reading, Berkshire, England; m. 1st 26 July 1975 (divorced 1994), 1 s., 2nd 1994 (divorced 2004). *Education:* Manchester Univ., Royal Northern Coll. of Music 1973–77. *Career:* fmr Reader Manchester Univ., now Prof. of Music 2004–; mem. Royal Musical Asscn. *Publications:* The Breath of the Symphonist: Shostakovich's Tenth 1988, Carl Nielsen Symphony No. 5 1997, Shostakovich: String Quartet No. 8 2004. *Contributions:* Gramophone, Music and Letters, The Daily Telegraph, The Musical Times. *Address:* c/o School of Music and Drama, Coupland Street, Manchester M13 9PL, England. *Telephone:* (161) 275-4989. *Fax:* (161) 275-4994. *E-mail:* david.fanning@manchester.ac.uk. *Website:* www.arts .machester.ac.uk/subjectareas/music/academicstaff/davidfanning.

FANSHAWE, David Arthur; British composer, explorer, sound recordist and ethnomusicologist, writer, photographer and record producer; b. 19 April 1942, Paignton, Devon, England; m. 1st Judith Grant 1971; one s. one d.; m. 2nd Jane Bishop 1986; one d. *Education:* St George's Choir School, Stowe, Royal College of Music. *Career:* debut as composer and cantor soloist, Queen Elizabeth Hall, London 1970; composer for BBC, ITV, British Film Inst., documentaries, feature films and private commissions; multi-media presenter on indigenous and traditional music and own compositions 'One World One Music', active promoter and participant in concerts of own works world-wide; researcher and founder of The Fanshawe Collections 1965–94, with 3,000 tapes of traditional music from Arabia, Africa South-East Asia and the Pacific; publishing, copying and cataloguing The Pacific Collections, establishing The World Music Foundation, completing major work, Pacific Odyssey for world premiere at Sydney Opera House; BBC autobiographical documentaries include African Sanctus, Musical Mariner and Tropical Beat. *Compositions include:* African Sanctus, Dover Castle, Requiem For The Children Of Aberfan, The Clowns' Concerto, Arabian Fantasy, The Awakening;. *Television music includes:* When the Boat Comes In (BBC), Tarka the Otter, Flambard (ITV). *Recordings include:* African Sanctus, Dona Nobis Pacem, Salaams; ethnic compilations include Music of the River Nile, Spirit of Polynesia, Micronesia and Melanesia, Music of the South Pacific, Music of Kenya Tanzania, Music of Thailand and Laos, Heiva I Tahiti, Pacific Chants; contribs to many other albums. *Address:* PO Box 574, Marlborough, Wiltshire SN8 2SP, England. *E-mail:* music@fanshawe.com.

FARBACH, Kent; Composer; b. 2 Aug. 1961, Southport, Queensland, Australia. *Education:* BMus, 1989, MMus, 1995, Queensland Conservatory. *Career:* Senior Teacher, Forte Music School; Queensland Conservatory, 1992–. *Compositions include:* Mini Overture with Fanfares, for brass Septet and organ, 1989; Beneath the Forest Canopy, for ensemble, 1989; Life Stratum for orchestra, 1990; Tears for string orchestra, 1991; 1845: An Irish Elegy, for orchestra, 1992; From Quiet Places, for violin, cello, flute, clarinet, wind chimes, percussion and piano, 1993; Into the Landscape, for orchestra, 1994; Commissions from the Melbourne and Sydney Symphony Orchestras (1992), Queensland Symphony Orchestra (1994) and Sydney Philharmonia Choir (1995). *Honours:* Adelaide Chamber Orchestra Prize, 1992. *Address:* c/o APRA, 1A Eden Street, Crows Nest, NSW 2065, Australia.

FARBERMAN, Harold; Conductor and Composer; b. 2 Nov. 1929, New York City, USA; m. Corinne Curry, 22 June 1958, 1 s., 1 d. *Education:* Scholarship student, diploma, Juilliard School of Music, NY, 1951; BS, 1956, MS, 1957, New England Conservatory of Music, Boston. *Career:* Percussionist, Boston Symphony Orchestra, 1951–63; Conductor, New Arts Orchestra, Boston, 1955–63, Colorado Springs Philharmonic Orchestra, 1967–68, Oakland Symphony Orchestra, CA, 1971–79; Principal Guest Conductor, Bournemouth Sinfonietta, 1986–; Founder, First President, Conductors' Guild, 1975; Founder, Conductors' Institute, University of West Virginia, 1980, relocated to University of South Carolina in 1987. *Compositions include:* Opera: Medea, 1960–61; Mixed-Media, If Music Be, 1965; Ballets, film scores; Orchestral: Concerto for bassoon and strings, 1956; Timpani Concerto, 1958; Concerto for alto saxophone and strings, 1965; Violin Concerto, 1976; War Cry on a Prayer Feather, 1976; Shapings for English horn, strings and percussion, 1984; Concerto for cello and orchestra, 1998–99; Chamber: Variations for percussion and piano, 1954, Music Inn Suite for 6 percussion, 1958, Quintessence for woodwind quintet, 1962, Images for 5 brass, 1964, Alea for 6 percussion, 1976; Concerto for flute and chamber orchestra, 1996; Little Boy and the Tree Branch, 1998. Vocal works. *Recordings include:* Symphonies by Mozart, Schumann and Beethoven; Bartók's Divertimento and Sonata for two pianos and percussion; Schoenberg/Handel Concerto; Bassoon Concertos by Weber and Hummel; Mahler, 1, 2, 4, 5, 6, 10; 22 Michael Haydn Symphonies; Glière No. 3, Bournemouth Symphonietta. *Publications include:* The Art of Conducting Technique: A New Perspective, 1997. *Honours:*

Winner Belgium's St Helena award for best recording of the year. *Address:* 176 E 71st Street 7C, New York, NY 10021, USA.

FARINA, Franco; Singer (Tenor); b. 1957, Connecticut, USA. *Career:* Sang widely in opera in USA from 1986; Tamino at Cincinnati, Pinkerton at Pittsburgh (1989); Houston, Chicago and New Orleans; European engagements at the Paris Opéra (Pollione in Norma at the Bastille, 1996), Glyndebourne (Stravinsky's Tom Rakewell, 1989) and Frankfurt (Duke of Mantua, 1990); Metropolitan Opera from 1990 as Rodolfo, Alfredo and Pinkerton (1995); Toulouse, 1993, as Lensky in Eugene Onegin, Deutsche Oper Berlin, 1995, as Riccardo; Season 1998 as Manrico at Geneva, Cavaradossi in Cincinnati and Carlo in Verdi's Masnadieri for the Royal Opera at Baden-Baden, Edinburgh and Savonlinna; Cavaradossi at the NY Met, 2002; Season 2002–03 as Carlo in I Masnadieri at Covent Garden, Manrico at the Met, Radames at Barcelona and Gabriele Adorno for the Vienna Staatsoper. Concerts include the Verdi Requiem and Beethoven's Missa Solemnis. *Address:* Metropolitan Opera, Lincoln Center, New York, NY 10023, USA.

FARKAS, Andras; Conductor; b. 14 April 1945, Budapest; m. Francoise Viquerat, 23 June 1973, 1 s., 1 d. *Education:* Béla Bart ók Academy, Budapest; Franz Liszt Academy, Budapest; Orchestra conducting with Hans Swarowsky, and horn at Akademie für Musik und Darstellende Kunst, Vienna. *Career:* Debut: Budapest, 1973; Settled in Switzerland in 1974 and performed in concerts throughout Europe; Invited Conductor, Orchestra of Hungarian Radio, Budapest Philharmonic, Orchestre de la Suisse Romande, Orchestre de Chamber de Lausanne, Orchestra of Slovakian Radio, Bratislava, Orchestra of Pilzn Radio, and Orchestre de Seville; Artistic Director and Founder, Nouvel Orchestre de Montreux, 1987; mem, Swiss Musicians Association; Centre Europeen de la Culture, Geneva. *Recordings:* Several for Hungarian and Swiss television and radio. *Contributions:* Swiss Musical Review, 1975–77. *Honours:* Vermeil Medal, Arts, Sciences et Lettres, Paris, 1990. *Address:* Chemin des Bouvreuils 12. 1009 Pully, Switzerland.

FARKAS, Andrew; Librarian and Educator; b. 7 April 1936, Budapest, Hungary; Divorced. *Education:* Eötvös Lóránd University of Law, Budapest, 1954–56; BA, Occidental College, Los Angeles, 1959; MLS, University of California, Berkeley, 1962. *Career:* Gift and Exchange Librarian, Chief Bibliographer and Assistant Head, Acquisitions Department, University of California, Davis, 1962–67 and Assistant Manager, Walter J Johnson Inc, New York City, 1967–70; Director of Libraries and Professor of Library Science, University of North Florida, Jacksonville, FL, 1970–2003; Contributing Editor, The Opera Quarterly (OUP), 1993–; Current title Director of Libraries Emeritus; mem, American Library Association. *Publications:* Music Editor to newspaper, Daily Democrat, Woodland, CA, 1965–67; Advisory Editor: 42 vol. series, Opera Biographies, 1977; Titta Ruffo: An Anthology, 1984; Opera and Concert Singers: An Annotated International Bibliography, 1985; Editor: Lawrence Tibbett, Singing Actor, 1989; Enrico Caruso: My Father and My Family, joint author with Enrico Caruso Jr, 1990; Jussi, joint author with Anna-Lisa Björling, 1996; Series Editor, Opera Biographies, for Amadeus Press, 1989–; Librarians' Calendar and Pocket Reference, annual since 1984; Adviser and Contributor: International Dictionary of Opera, 1993. *Address:* Director of Libraries, University of North Florida, 4567 St John's Bluff Road South, Jacksonville, FL 32224, USA.

FARKAS, Katalin; Singer (Soprano); b. 5 Jan. 1954, Budapest, Hungary. *Education:* Studied in Budapest. *Career:* Has sung at the Hungarian State Opera from 1982 as Rosina, Sophie (Werther), Sophie (Der Rosenkavalier), Mozart's Blondchen, Belinda, Nannetta (Falstaff), Oscar, Norina and Flotow's Martha; Glyndebourne Festival debut in 1985 as Zdenka in Arabella; Season 1986–87 in Liszt's Don Sanche at Naples and Amaryllis in Il Pastor Fido at the Göttingen Festival; Other roles include Beethoven's Marzelline, Donizetti's Gianetta (L'Elisir d'amore) and Serafina (Il Campanello), Zerbinetta; Göttingen 1990 in Handel's Floridante. *Recordings include:* World premiere recordings with Hungaroton; Handel: Terpsicore-Erato (conductor Nicholas McGegan, with Derek Lee Ragin); Handel: Atalanta, title role (conductor Nicholas McGegan); Telemann: Der geduldige Socrates-Erato (conductor Nicholas McGegan, with Paul Esswood, Guy de Mey); Don Sanche (Liszt, under Tamás Pál); Other important recorded roles are Serpina (Pergolesi: La serva padrona); Amarilli (Handel: Il pastor fido, also with Esswood and McGegan). *Address:* Hungarian State Opera House, Andrassy ut 22, 1061 Budapest, Hungary.

FARLEY, Carole; Singer (soprano); b. 29 Nov. 1946, Le Mars, Iowa, USA; m. José Serebrier 1969, 1 d. *Education:* BMus, Indiana University, 1968; Fulbright Scholar, Hochschule für Musik, Munich, 1968–69. *Career:* Debut: Town Hall, New York, 1969; Paris, National Orchestra, 1975; London, Royal Philharmonic Society, 1975; South America, Teatro Colón Philharmonic Orchestra, Buenos Aires, 1975; Soloist with major American and European symphonies, 1970–; Soloist, Linz Opera, 1969, Welsh National Opera, 1971 (Lulu in 1st production by British company of Berg's opera), 1972, Cologne Opera, 1972–75, Brussels Opera, 1972, Philadelphia Lyric Opera, 1974, Strasbourg Opera, 1975, Lyon Opéra, 1976, 1977, New York City Opera, 1976, as Offenbach's Hélène, New Orleans Opera, 1977, Cincinnati Opera, 1977, Metropolitan Opera Company, 1977–, Zürich Opera, 1979, Canadian Opera, 1980, Düsseldorf Opera, 1980, 1981, 1984, Chicago Lyric Opera, 1981, Palm Beach Opera, 1982; Théâtre Municipale, Paris, 1983, Théâtre Royale de la Monnaie, Brussels, 1983, Teatro Regio, Turin, 1983, Nice Opera, 1984; Cologne Opera in Salome, conductor John Pritchard, 1985; Firenze Maggio Musicale, Teatro Comunale, 1985, as Lulu; La Voix Humaine, television film, ABC Australia; Marie in Wozzeck at Buenos Aires, 1989; Metropolitan Opera premiere of Shostakovich Lady Macbeth of Mtensk, 1994; Wozzeck at Opéra du Capitole de Toulouse, 1995; mem, American Guild of Musical Artists; Repertoire also includes Monteverdi's L'Incoronazione di Poppea, Massenet's Manon, Mozart's Idomeneo and Johann Strauss' Die Fledemaus; Performed a series of concerts with the Bamberger Symphoniker and the BBC Symphony Orchestra to celebrate the centennial of Kurt Weill. *Recordings include:* Final Scenes from Daphne and Capriccio by Strauss, Belgian Radio Orchestra, conductor José Serebrier; Songs, Prokofiev and Weill; Britten Les Illuminations; Poulenc, La Voix Humaine, Menotti The Telephone; Tchaikovsky Opera Arias; Milhaud Songs; Strauss Songs with Orchestra; Kurt Weill; Delius; Carole Farley Sings Grieg Songs with Orchestra (London Philharmonic Orchestra/Philharmonia); Beethoven Ninth Symphony with the Royal Philharmonic under Antal Dorati for Deutsche Grammophone; Vienna Dances for CBS under Kostelanetz; Gubtram on BBC; Marschner's Der Vampyr on Foni-Cetra with the RAI Rome Orchestra. *Honours:* Abbiati Prize, Best Opera Production (Lulu, Lyubimov, Turin Opera); Grand Prix du Disque, France, 1996; Diapason d'Or, France, 1997; Deutsche Schallplatten Critics Award for French Songs with Orchestra on ASV. *Current Management:* Robert Lombardo Management, New York; 270 Riverside Drive, New York, NY 10025, USA (home).

FARMAN, Raphaëlle; Singer (soprano); b. 1965, France. *Education:* Paris Conservatoire, 1985–1990; Opera School of the Opéra Bastille, 1990–92. *Career:* Debut: Mozart's Susanna, 1989; Gilda in Rigoletto and Bellini's Elvira for Radio France; Appearances in The Queen of Spades and Carmen (as Frasquita) at the Opéra Bastille; Arminta in La Finta Giardiniera at Nantes, Gluck's Euridice at Lille, Mozart's Countess in Rennes, Poulenc's Blanche in St Etienne, and Micaela for Opera La Havana, Cuba (2001); British debut as Massenet's Esclarmonde, for Chelsea Opera Group, London; Engagements as Offenbach's Antonia, and the Countess, at Tours, Anna in La Dame Blanche, Poulenc's Thérèse and Donna Anna for the Opéra Comique, Paris; Season 2001–2002 as Venus in Cherubini's Anacreon in Venice, Donna Anna at Toulon, and Mozart's Sandrina at the Opéra Comique; Concerts with Armin Jordan, Charles Dutoit, Michel Plasson and Myung Whun Chung. *Current Management:* Athole Still International Management, Foresters Hall, 25–27 Westow Street, London, SE19 3RY, England. *Telephone:* (20) 8771-5271. *Fax:* (20) 8768-6600. *Website:* www.atholestill.com.

FARNCOMBE, Charles Frederick; Conductor; b. 29 July 1919, London, England; m. Sally Mae Felps, 23 May 1963, 1 d. *Education:* BSc in Engineering, London University, 1940; Royal School of Church Music, 1947–48; Royal Academy of Music, 1948–51; LRAM, 1952. *Career:* Musical Director, Handel Opera Society, 1955–85; Conducted first modern British performances of Rinaldo, Alcina and Deidamia, Rodelinda, Radamisto, Riccardo Primo, Scipione, Ottone, Atalanta, Ariodante, Ezio, Giustino and Rodrigo; Artistic Director Llantilio Crossenny Festival, 1962–; Chief Conductor, Royal Court Theatre, Drottningholm, Sweden, 1970–79; Guest Conductor, London Chamber Opera, 1974–; Chief Guest Conductor of Badisches Staatstheater, Karlsruhe, 1979–95; Musical Director, London Chamber Opera, 1983–95; Musical Director, Malcolm Sargent Festival Choir, 1986–; Guest Conductor Komische Oper in Berlin, 1995–98; Artistic Director Madley Festival, 1996–; Fellow, Royal Swedish Academy, 1972. *Recordings:* Rameau's Castor and Pollux; Great Handel Choruses; Drottningholm Music; Handel's Rodrigo; Handel Highlights, 1993. *Honours:* Royal Gold Medal of Drottningholm, 1971; C.B.E., 1977; Order of the Royal Northern Star, Sweden, 1982; Gold Medal from the Handel Academy in Karlsruhe, 1992. *Current Management:* Werner Kühnly, Wörthstrasse 31, 70563 Stuttgart, Germany. *Address:* 32 Trinity Court, 170A Gloucester Terrace, London W2 6HS, England. *Telephone:* (711) 7802764 (office). *Fax:* (711) 7804403 (home). *E-mail:* kuehnly@aol.com (office).

FARNES, Richard; Conductor; b. 1964, England. *Education:* King's College, Cambridge; National Opera Studio; Royal Academy of Music; Guildhall School (Rossini's Journey to Rheims). *Career:* Music Staff, Glyndebourne and with Scottish Opera and Opera Factory; English Touring Opera, with Falstaff, La Bohème and The Barber of Seville; Gloriana, Figaro, Giovanna D'Arco, La Traviata, The Nightingale's to

Blame (Simon Holt) and The Secret Marriage for Opera North; Bastien und Bastienne and La Serva Padrona for European Chamber Opera; Macbeth for City of Birmingham Touring Opera; Season 1997–98 with The Makropulos Case at Glyndebourne, Die Entführung, Figaro and La Bohème for Glyndebourne Touring Opera; The Magic Flute, Param Vir double bill and world premiere of David Horne's Friend of the People, 1999, for Scottish Opera; Also Nabucco for New Israeli Opera, Tel-Aviv, Albert Herring at Guildhall School, 1998 and The Rake's Progress in Dublin, 1999; Founded Equinox 1992, for the performance of modern chamber ensemble pieces. *Honours:* Henry Wood and Philharmonia Chorus conducting scholarships at the RAM. *Current Management:* Ingpen & Williams Ltd, 7 St George's Court, 131 Putney Bridge Road, London, SW15 2PA, England.

FARNON, David Graham, MA, DipMus; composer, conductor and producer; b. 12 Oct. 1956, London, England; m. Susie Best 1989; two s. *Education:* Univ. of Cambridge, Royal Academy of Music, Royal College of Music, Trinity College of Music, London. *Career:* performances at The Barbican, Royal Festival Hall, London Palladium, the Queen Elizabeth Hall with orchestras including, London Symphony Orchestra and London Philharmonic Orchestra; numerous television and radio appearances. *Compositions:* approximately 400 for KPM, Chappell, Carlin, Destiny and Kanda Music Libraries; 2 Pieces for Orchestra, 1980; Overture: London By Day, 1981; Musical, Songs for Loving Swingers, 1991; Beyond The Furthest Star, for the Royal Choral Society, 1993; Pastourelle for violin and orchestra, 1993; 10 Pieces for wind band, 1989–94; 30 Pieces for woodwind ensemble, 1988–94; Various shows, television and radio commissions. *Recordings:* Conducting with the Royal Philharmonic Orchestra, including Holst, Elgar, Strauss, Albinoni and various operatic arias; First performance of Robert Farnon's Piano Concerto, Cascades to the Sea, with the Bratislava Radio Symphony Orchestra. *Address:* Les Villets Farm, Les Villets, Forest, Guernsey GY8 0HP. *Telephone:* (1481) 265712. *E-mail:* david@farnon.co.uk.

FARNON, Robert (Joseph); Musician and Composer; b. 24 July 1917, Toronto, Canada; m. Patricia Mary Smith, 13 Aug 1963, 4 s., 1 d. *Education:* Broadus Farmer School of Music, 1930–32; Humberside College, 1932–34; Toronto Technical College, 1934–35. *Career:* Principal Trumpet, CBC Concert Orchestra, 1936–38; Musical Director, CBC, 1939–42; Conductor for BBC television and radio, 1946–; Served with the Canadian Army, 1943–46; Member, BBC Music Advisory Committee; Guest Conductor for various international orchestras. *Compositions include:* Symphony No. 1, 1939, No. 2, 1941; Film music in the United Kingdom, Canada and US from 1946; Canadian Impressions Suite, 1952; Rhapsody for Violin and Orchestra, 1956; Prelude And Dance for Harmonica and Orchestra, 1969; Saxophone Triparte, 1974; Cascades to the Sea for piano and orchestra, 1998; Hollywood Stars, and Scenic Wonders, 1998, for orchestra. *Honours:* 5 Ivor Novello Awards for Composition, 1960–85; Tesco Citation for Services to British Music, 1995; Grammy Award for best Orchestral Arrangements; Order of Canada for Services to Music, 1998; Millennium Fanfare for CI Celebrations, 1999. *Address:* c/o Warner Chappell Music Ltd, Griffin House, 161 Hammersmith Road, London W6 8 BS, England.

FARQUHAR, David (Andross); Composer; b. 5 April 1928, Cambridge, New Zealand; m. Raydia d'Elsa, 2 June 1954, 1 s., 1 d. *Education:* BMus, University of New Zealand; MA, Cambridge University; Guildhall School of Music. *Career:* Lecturer, 1953–; Professor of Music, Victoria University of Wellington, New Zealand, 1976–93; mem, Composers Association of New Zealand, Founding President; New Zealand Music Centre, Board Member. *Compositions:* And One Makes Ten; Anniversary Duets, (2 sets); Concertino for piano and strings; Evocation; Suite for guitar; Five Scenes for guitar; On Your Own; Partita; Ring Round the Moon, dance suite; Three Pieces for double bass; Three Scots Ballads; Concerto for Wind Quintet; Three Pieces for Violin and Piano; Three Improvisations; Six Songs of Women; Three Songs of Cilla McQueen; Eight Blake Songs; Three Echoes, String Quartets Nos 1, 2, and 4; Waiata Maori; Ode for piano; Five Canons for two clarinets; Symphony No. 1; Symphony No. 2; Symphony No. 3; Scherzo for orchestra; Folksong Trio (recorders); In Despite of Death. *Recordings:* Concerto for wind quintet; Symphonies nos 1–3; Three Improvisations; Three Pieces for violin and piano; Concertino for piano and strings; Evocation; Partita; Ring Round the Moon; Three Scots Ballads; In Despite of Death; Scherzo for orchestra; Magpies and Other Birds, Echoes and Reflections; String Quartet No. 1; Suite for guitar; Auras, 1998; Anniversary Suite No. 2, 1998; Homage to Stravinsky, 1998; Serenade for Strings; Six Songs of Women; Eight Blake Songs, Writing in the Sand, Three Medieval Carols, Three Songs of Cilla McQueen, Five Songs of e e cummings. *Honours:* Companion New Zealand Order of Merit, 2004. *Address:* 15 Nottingham Street, Wellington, New Zealand.

FARR, Gareth, BMus; New Zealand composer and percussionist; b. 29 Feb. 1968, Wellington. *Education:* Victoria Univ., Weelington, Auckland Univ., Eastman School of Music. *Career:* composer-in-residence,

Chamber Music New Zealand. *Compositions include:* Pembukaan 1990, works for Javanese gamelan, including Kebyar moncar and Reongan, Lilith's Dream of Ecstasy 1995, From the Depths Sound the Great Sea Gongs 1996, Hikoi 1998, Concerto for four percussionists 2005. *Recordings include:* album: Ruaumoko, Beowulf, Orakau, Rangitoto and Te Papa played by New Zealand Symphony Orchestra. *E-mail:* gareth@drumdrag.com. *Website:* www.garethfarr.com.

FARRELL, Eibhlis; Composer; b. 27 July 1953, Rostrevor, County Down, Ireland. *Education:* Studied at Queen's University, Belfast and at Bristol University. *Career:* Deputy Principal at the College of Music, Dublin Institute of Technology, 1983. *Compositions include:* Concerto Grosso, 1988; Sinfon for orchestra, 1990; Exultet, oratorio, 1991; Exaudi Voces and A Garland For The President for solo voices and chorus, 1991; Soundshock for concert band, 1993; Solo vocal music including, The Silken Bed for mezzo, violin, cello and harpsichord, 1993; Caritas Abundar for 2 sopranos and chorus, 1995; Island of Women for orchestra, 1996; Chamber and instrumental pieces including, Earth-shine for harp, 1992. *Address:* c/o IMRO, Pembroke Row, Dublin 2, Ireland.

FARREN-PRICE, Ronald (William); Pianist and University Academic; b. 2 July 1930, Brisbane, Australia; m. Margaret Lillian Cameron, 15 Jan 1982, 3 s., 2 d. *Education:* Diploma in Music, University of Melbourne, 1951; Studies with Claudio Arrau on a personal scholarship donated by him, 1952–55, London and New York. *Career:* Debut: Melbourne Symphony Orchestra, Concerto, 1947; Wigmore Hall, London, 1955; Has played in over 50 countries including 12 concert tours of the former USSR and many performances at London's Wigmore Hall, Queen Elizabeth Hall, Purcell Room and St John's Smith Square; Performances at Carnegie Recital Hall, New York, National Gallery, Washington, and Tchaikovsky Hall, Moscow; Reader in Music, 1975, Dean, Faculty of Music, 1986–90, Head of Keyboard, 1991–97, Associate Professor, 1989–, Senior Associate of the Faculty, 1998–, Fellow of Queen's College, 1991–, Council Member of Queen's College, 1986–, Music Patron, Trinity College Music Foundation, University of Melbourne; Patron St Paul's Cathedral Old Christians Association; Director, Australian National Academy of Music, 1999; Federal Examiner for the Australian Music Examinations Board, 1984–85, 1994–97; Has performed concertos with many leading conductors including Antal Dorati, Ferdinand Leitner, Eugene Goossens, Charles Groves, Willem van Otterloo, John Hopkins and Harry Blech; Has broadcast recitals in many countries and also appeared in television recitals; mem, Melbourne Club, University House, University of Melbourne. *Current Management:* Impresaria Pty Ltd. *Address:* Faculty of Music, University of Melbourne, Parkville, Victoria 3052, Australia.

FARRER, John; Conductor; b. 1950, USA. *Career:* Many performances with leading orchestras in the USA, notably with the San Francisco Symphony Orchestra and as guest conductor elsewhere; Music Director of the Roswell Symphony Orchestra in New Mexico; Faculty Member of the Conducting Workshops of the American Symphony Orchestra League; London debut in 1986 with the London Philharmonic; Senior Guest Conductor with the English Sinfonia and further concerts with the Royal Philharmonic Orchestra and the Bournemouth Symphony Orchestra. *Recordings include:* Tchaikovsky album with the London Philharmonic, Dvořák with the RPO and Copland and Gershwin with the Bournemouth Symphony Orchestra. *Address:* c/o Bournemouth Symphony Orchestra, 2 Seldown Lane, Poole, Dorset, BH15 1UF, England.

FARULLI, Piero; Professor of Viola; b. 13 Jan. 1920, Florence, Italy. *Education:* Conservatorio di Stato Luigi Cherubini, Florence, under Gioacchino Maglioni. *Career:* Professor of Viola, 1957–77; For 34 years a member of Quartetto Italiano; Has also collaborated with Amadeus and Berg Quartets; Appeared with Trio di Trieste, 1978–; Has lectured at Accademia Chigiana di Siena, 1978–, and at Salzburg Mozarteum; Member of judging panel at several international competitions such as the Tchaikovsky Competition in Moscow and Tertis in London and has been active in many aspects of musical life and education in Italy, notably in Fiesole, where he founded the well-known Scuola di Musica di Fiesole in 1974 and is its Director. *Recordings:* With Quartetto Italiano: all String Quartets of Mozart, Beethoven, Schumann, Brahms and Webern; With Melos Quartet: Mozart Quintets K 593 and K 614. *Honours:* Medaglia della Cultura e dell'Arte; Premio Edison; Premio Viotti; Premio Abbiati, 1981; Premio Massimo Mila; Accademia Nazionale di Santa Cecilia; Grand 'Ufficiale della Repubblica, 1994. *Address:* Via G d'Annunzio 153, Florence, Italy.

FASHAE, Alycia; Singer (soprano); b. 1970, England. *Education:* Royal Northern College of Music, with Ryland Davies and Honor Shepherd; L'Opéra National de Paris. *Career:* Appearances in Paris as Mozart's Servilia, Pamina and Fiordiligi; Adina in L'Elisir d'Amore, Lucia di Lammermoor, Gounod's Juliette, Micaela, Bizet's Leila, Massenet's Sophie and Cendrillon, Violetta, Gilda and Nannetta; Engagements on

tour of Britain as Violetta, with European Chamber Opera and Pamina with Diva Opera; Leila in The Pearl Fishers for English National Opera; Season 2001–2002 as Donna Anna and Offenbach's Antonia with Diva Opera, Frasquita in Carmen for ENO and Gilda for European Chamber Opera; Tour of USA as Hanna Glawari in the Merry Widow. *Current Management:* Athole Still International Management, Forresters Hall, 25–27 Westow Street, London, SE19 3RY, England. *Telephone:* (20) 8771-5271. *Fax:* (20) 8768-6600. *Website:* www.atholestill.com.

FASSBAENDER, Brigitte; Intendant, Stage Director and Singer (Mezzo-Soprano); b. 3 July 1939, Berlin, Germany. *Education:* Studied in Nuremberg with her father, Willi Domgraf-Fassbaender. *Career:* Debut: Munich in 1961 as Nicklausse in Les Contes d'Hoffmann; Has sung in Germany and Milan as Eboli, Sextus, Hansel, Carlotta in Die schweigsame Frau, Clarice in La Pietra del Paragone, Marina and the Countess Geschwitz in Lulu; San Francisco in 1970 as Carmen, Covent Garden debut in 1971 as Octavian, Paris Opéra in 1972 as Brangaene, Salzburg Festival, 1972–78 as Dorabella in Così fan tutte; Metropolitan Opera debut in 1974 as Octavian, returning to New York in 1986 as Fricka; Vienna Staatsoper in 1976 in the premiere of Kabale und Liebe by Von Einem; Countess Geschwitz in the Vienna premiere of Berg's Lulu; Sang at Bayreuth Festival, 1983–84, La Scala Milan in 1986 in Die Frau ohne Schatten, Metropolitan Opera in 1986 as Fricka, Salzburg Festival in 1989 as Clytemnestra in Elektra; Produced Der Rosenkavalier at Munich in 1989, La Cenerentola at Coburg in 1990, Der Ferne Klang for Opera North in 1992, Hansel and Gretel in Augsburg in 1992, A Midsummer Night's Dream in Amsterdam in 1993 and Susannah in Vienna in 1995; Sang Clairon in Capriccio at the 1990 Glyndebourne Festival; Concert artist in works by Bach and Mahler, and song recitalist; Masterclasses at the 1992 Brereton International Symposium; Directed Opera for Europe in Mozart's Lucio Silla, 1998; Directed over 30 operas world-wide since 1990; Opera Director, Braunschweig Opera, 1995–97; Intendantin, Tiroler Landestheater, Innsbruck, 1999. *Recordings include:* Over 150 since 1964 including Lulu, Die Fledermaus, Bach's St John Passion, Messiah, Mozart's La Finta Giardiniera, Bach's Christmas Oratorio; Video of Elektra (as Clytemnestra), under Abbado. *Address:* c/o Sekretariat, Haiming, 83119 Obing, Germany.

FAST, George Allen, BMusA; Canadian singer (countertenor), voice professor and writer on music; b. 27 March 1954, Leamington, ON. *Education:* University of Western Ontario. *Career:* debut with Waverly Consort, Kennedy Center, Washington DC, USA, 1979; Soloist with Tafelmusik Baroque Orchestra, The Bach Ensemble, National Arts Centre Orchestra (Ottawa), CBC Vancouver Orchestra, Smithsonian Chamber Players, New York Oratorio Society, Oregon Symphony, Opera Atelier (Toronto), Casals Festival, Madeira Bach Festival, Wratislavia Cantans, Pacific Opera Victoria, Les Violons du Roy, Studio de Musique Ancienne de Montréal, L'Orchestre de la Nouvelle France, Edmonton Symphony, Louisville Bach Society and others; Assistant Professor of Early Music Voice, Director of Cappella Antica, McGill University. *Recordings:* The Christmas Story, The Waverly Consort, CBS Masterworks, 1983; Renaissance Favorites, The Waverly Consort, CBS Masterworks, 1985; Bach Cantatas 8, 78 and 99, Bach Ensemble, Joshua Rifkin, Decca, 1989; Complete Alto Cantatas of Buxtehude, McGill Records, 1989. *Current Management:* Colwell Arts Management, RRNo. 1, New Hamburg, ON, Canada. *Address:* 263 Bourchemin Ouest, St Hugues, QC J0H 1N0, Canada.

FATH, Karl; German singer (bass); b. 1941. *Career:* Sang at Giessen, 1963–67, Koblenz, 1968–72, Brunswick, 1972–74 and Saarbrucken, 1974–77; Engaged at Gelsenkirchen from 1977 and has made guest appearances at Stuttgart, Karlsruhe, Frankfurt, 1984–86 and Cologne, 1987–88; Tour of Brazil in 1982 singing in Jakob Lenz by Wolfgang Rihm; Appeared as Don Magnifico in La Cenerentola at Bielefeld, 1989, Lunardo in I Quattro Rusteghi by Wolf-Ferrari at Hannover in 1991; Sang Truffaldino in Ariadne auf Naxos at Hannover, 2000; Many lieder recitals and concert appearances. *Recordings:* Petite Messe Solennelle by Rossini. *Address:* c/o Niedersachsiche Staatstheater, Opernplatz 1, 3000 Hannover, Germany.

FAULKNER, Julia; Singer (Soprano); b. 1962, St Louis, Missouri, USA. *Education:* Studied with Margaret Harshaw at Bloomington. *Career:* Sang Arminda in Mozart's Finta Giardiniera at Lyon, returning for Alice Ford in Falstaff; Mozart and Strauss roles at the Munich Staatsoper (Marschallin, 1995); Vienna, 1993–95, as Arabella and the Countess in Capriccio; Miami Opera, 1991, as Fiordiligi; Sang Marianne in Der Rosenkavalier at the Met, 2000; Other roles include Ariadne and Wagner's Gutrune (Vienna Staatsoper); Further engagements at Hamburg, Amsterdam, Geneva and Stockholm. *Recordings include:* Die Zauberflöte and Pergolesi's Stabat Mater. *Address:* c/o Bayerische Staatsoper, Max-Joseph-Platz, 80539 Munich, Germany.

FAUST, Isabelle; German violinist; b. March 1972, Esslingen. *Education:* Colleges of Music in Saarbrücken, Detmold and Berlin. *Career:*

Played with major orchestras: Hamburg Philharmonic, Yehudi Menuhin conducting, Württemberg Chamber Orchestra, Württemberg Philharmonic, Stuttgart Radio Symphony, Stuttgart Philharmonic, State Philharmonic of Rheinland-Pfalz, Bremen Philharmonic, Orchestra of Padua, West German Radio Symphony of Cologne, Stockholm Sinfonietta; US debut with Utah Symphony in 1995, Paganini Concerto No. 1; Has toured: Germany, Israel, Spain, Italy, Japan; Chamber Music with: B Giuranna, B Pergamenschikow, N Brainin, J Goritzki, N Gutman, J Silverstein, L Hokanson, Ph Hirschorn; Played at festivals of: Schleswig-Holstein, Bad Kissingen, Colmar, Lyon, Berlin, Sarasota. *Recordings:* Radio: Bartók's Solo Sonata for Violin; Mozart's Violin Concerto in A Major; Prokofiev's Concerto No. 1; Dvořák's Violin Concerto in A Minor; Mendelssohn's Violin Concerto in E Minor; Bruch's Violin Concerto in G Minor; Several recitals. *Honours:* 1st Prize, International Leopold Mozart Competition for Violinists, Augsburg, 1987; Premio Quadrivio Award in Rovigo, Italy for Outstanding Musical Achievement, 1990; 1st Prize in Paganini Competition in Genoa, Italy, 1993; Prize for Highly Talented Young Artists in Nordhein-Westfalen, 1994. *Current Management:* Hazard Chase, 25 City Road, Cambridge CB1 1DP, England. *Telephone:* (1223) 312400. *Fax:* (1223) 460827. *Website:* www.hazardchase.co.uk. *Address:* Lontelstrasse 19, 70839 Gerlingen, Germany.

FAUST, Michael; Flautist; b. 16 Jan. 1959, Cologne, Germany; m. Debora Bendocchi Alves, 30 Dec 1985, 1 s., 1 d. *Education:* Hochschule für Musik, Hamburg. *Career:* Principal Flautist with the Santa Cecilia Orchestra in Rome, the Hamburg Philharmonic (conductor C v. Dohnányi), Stuttgart Opera (conductor D R Davis), Munich Philharmonic (conductor S Celibidache), and Cologne Radio Symphonie (conductors Gary Bertini, Hans Vonk and Semyon Bychkov); Major Solo Concerts in New York, St Louis, Boston, Tokyo, Moscow and Paris; Ibert-concerto with the Moscow Symphony, conductor V Fedossejew, 1985; Gunther Schuller's Flute-concerto with the St Louis Symphony Orchestra, 1998; Premiere of Mauricio Kagel's flute concerto Das Konzert, 2003; Founding member of Ensemble Contrasts Köln; Professor for flute, Robert-Schumann-Hochschule Düsseldorf. *Recordings:* H W Henze El Cimarron; J. S. Bach to Mozart; 20th Century Flute Concertos, Ibert, Bernstein, Nielsen, Elliott Carter, French Flute Music. *Honours:* Prizes and Awards at Competitions in Bonn, Rome, Prague, New York. *Current Management:* Rolf Sudbrack, Hamburg. *Address:* Worringer Strasse 21, 50668 Köln, Germany. *Website:* www.mfaust.de.

FEATHERSTONE, Gary Maxwell; Composer and Performer; b. 2 Sept. 1949, Sydney, Australia. *Education:* piano and music education, Sydney Conservatorium. *Career:* debut, Radio 2CH, Sydney, aged 15; performances in England, France, Poland, Germany and Australia; recordings for ABC Radio and 2MBS, FM Radio, Sydney. *Compositions:* Piano Concerto No. 1, Piano Concerto No. 2, Rhapsody on Original Theme for Piano and Orchestra, Serenade for Strings 1999, Symphonic Fantasia – Peter Ibbetson (full orchestra) 2000. *Recordings:* Serenade for Strings (Nevsky Quartet, St Petersburg, Russia), Symphonic Fantasia (Peter Ibbetson, Slovak Radio Orchestra), Australian Piano Music (three compositions), Barcarolle (for ABC-FM, Australian Composers Concert) 1995. *Publications:* Piano Pieces for Children 1989, Idyll, for flute and piano 1990, Prelude in E Flat major, for piano 1990, Improvisation, for piano 1993, Pieces for Musical Children 1993, I Need Love, for voice and piano 1995, Four Nocturnes 1995, The Waltzes, for piano 1995, Barcarolle, for piano 1995, Berceuse, for piano 1996, Scherzo, for piano 1996, Two Dance Songs, piano 1997, 24 Preludes, piano 1999, Romance for Violin and Piano 2001, Dance in the Moonlight, for oboe and piano 2002.

FEDDERLY, Greg; Singer (tenor); b. 1961, California, USA. *Education:* Studied at the University of Southern California. *Career:* Appearances with the Los Angeles Opera have included Britten's Albert Herring, Mozart's Monostatos, Pinkerton, Hylas in Les Troyens and Arturo in Lucia di Lammermoor, 1988–; European debut as Tom Rakewell at the Aldeburgh Festival, 1992; Engagements at the Théâtre du Châtelet, Paris, in Die Frau ohne Schatten and Moses und Aron; Philidor's Tom Jones at the Drottningholm Festival, 1995; Gluck's Orpheus, 1996; Further roles include Mozart's Ferrando, Alfredo in La Traviata, Washington, 1996, Rossini's Almaviva, Seattle, 1997 and David in Die Meistersinger at Los Angeles, season 1997–98; Sang in the premiere of Florencia of the Amazons, at the Houston Opera, 1996; Tamino at Los Angeles, 1998; Season 1999–2000 included Telemaco in Ulisse at Glimmerglass; Concerts of The Creation in Barcelona; Alfredo in La Traviata at Los Angeles Opera and Pinkerton in Madama Butterfly in Santa Barbara. *Recordings include:* The Rake's Progress, for Swedish Television. *Honours:* First recipient of the Marilyn Horne Scholarship at UCLA. *Current Management:* Askonas Holt Ltd, Lonsdale Chambers, 27 Chancery Lane, London, WC2A 1PF, England. *Telephone:* (20) 7400-1700. *Fax:* (20) 7400-1799. *E-mail:* info@askonasholt.co.uk. *Website:* www.askonasholt.co.uk.

FEDER, Donn-Alexandre; Concert Pianist and Teacher; b. 23 June 1935, Philadelphia, PA, USA; m. Janet Landis, 26 Aug 1960, 1 d. *Education:* BS, 1958, MS, 1959, DMA, 1973, Juilliard School of Music; Studies with Rosina Lhevinne, Kabos and Gorodnitzki; Study at Eastman and with Jorge Bolet. *Career:* Debut: New York Town Hall in 1963; Extensive concerting throughout Europe, Mexico, Canada and USA, and for NBC and ABC television and BBC, England; Appearances with major European and American orchestras; Faculty, Philadelphia College of Performing Arts, 1971–81; Piano Faculty, Manhattan School of Music, 1978–; Member of 2-piano team, Feder and Gilgore; Co-director of Musicisti Americani Festival and Institute, Rome and Sulmona, Italy; Artist-Teacher, Taiwan International Festival, China, 1988 and 1989. *Recordings:* With the Netherlands Radio Philharmonic under Allers and Van Otterloo. *Recordings include:* Szymanowski Piano Music, Excursions for Two Pianos, Music of Barber, Copland and Gershwin (with Elisha Gilgore), Bartók Sonata for 2 Pianos and Percussion, Stravinsky's Concerto for 2 Solo Pianos, with Elisha Gilgore. *Address:* c/o Manhattan School of Music, Piano Faculty, 120 Claremont Avenue, New York, NY 10027, USA.

FEDIN, Alexander; Singer (Tenor); b. 11 Sept. 1954, Russia. *Career:* Sang at first in concert, then appeared at the Bolshoi, Moscow, from 1986, notably as Werther, Rossini's Almaviva and the Holy Fool in Boris Godunov; Guested with the Bolshoi at Glasgow, 1990, as the King in Tchaikovsky's Maid of Orleans, and at Rome, 1989, in a concert performance of Rachmaninov's Aleko; Berlin Staatsoper, 1991, as the Duke of Mantua; Further appearances at the Vienna Staatsoper, in Dortmund and at the Teatre Liceu, Barcelona; Cologne Opera 1995–96 as Tamino, Steuermann and Cassio; Season 2000–01 as Faust at Essen, Wagner's Erik at Freiburg and the Prince in The Love for Three Oranges at Cologne. *Address:* c/o Bolshoi Opera, 103009 Moscow, Russia.

FEDOSEYEV, Vladimir (Ivanovich); Conductor; b. 5 Aug. 1932, Leningrad, Russia; m. Olga Ivanovna Dobrohotova. *Education:* Moscow Musical Institute; Moscow State Conservatory. *Career:* Debut: With Mravinsky Orchestra at the Leningrad Philharmonic Concert Hall; Principal Conductor for Academic Orchestra of Russian Folk Instruments, TV-Radio, Russia, 1957–74; Principal Conductor for Moscow Radio Symphony Orchestra, 1974–; Appeared regularly with RAI Milano Symphony Orchestra and French National Orchestra; Recent appearances with Munich Symphony Orchestra, Vienna Philharmonic Orchestra, Hamburg Radio Symphony, La Scala Opera, Istanbul and Ankara Symphony Orchestras, Antwerp Symphony Orchestra, Tokyo Philharmonic Orchestra, NHK Orchestra, and Osaka Symphony Orchestra, Japan; Conducted the Vienna Symphony Orchestra in La Damnation de Faust at the 1992 Bregenz Festival; Conducted Carmen at Vienna Staatsoper in 1993 and 3 performances of Verdi's Requiem with Luciano Pavarotti and World Festival Choir in Oslo, Stockholm in 1992 and Munich in 1993; Conducted Elektra at Rome, 1997; Montemezzi's L'Amore dei tre Re at the 1998 Bregenz Festival. *Recordings:* About 100 with the Grand Moscow Radio Symphony Orchestra. *Honours:* 2nd Prize for Record of the Year, Tchaikovsky's 6th Symphony, Tokyo, 1983; Crystal Award, International Music Awards, Osaka, 1988; Silver Award for Best Concert of Season, Osaka, 1989; Golden Orpheus Award, French National Academy for recording of the opera, May Night. *Current Management:* Moscow Radio Symphony Orchestra. *Address:* Moscow Radio Symphony Orchestra, Piatnitskaia Str 25, 113326 Moscow, Russia.

FEENEY, Angela; Singer (Soprano); b. 19 Oct. 1954, Belfast, Northern Ireland. *Education:* Studied at Belfast, Dublin and Munich. *Career:* Debut: Irish National Opera, 1977, as Cherubino; English National Opera from 1978, as Micaela, Marenka in The Bartered Bride, Nedda, and Donna Elvira (1986); Munich Staatsoper, 1983–86, as Papageno, Gretel, and Ingrid in Egk's Peer Gynt; Deutsche Oper Berlin, 1985, as Butterfly, Dublin Grand Opera, 1986, as Gluck's Euridice; Wexford Festival, 1986, as Giulietta in Verdi's Un giorno di Regno; Other roles include Mimi and the Trovatore Leonore. *Address:* c/o Opera Theatre Company, 18 St Andrew Street, Dublin 2, Ireland.

FEGRAN, Espen; Singer (Baritone); b. 1960, Oslo, Norway. *Education:* Studied at the Oslo Academy with Nicolai Gedda. *Career:* Sang at the Norwegian National Opera in Oslo as Papageno (1987), Marcello, Guglielmo, Mozart's Count and similar repertory; Wiesbaden Opera from 1988, as Eugene Onegin, Belcore, Beckmesser, and in Henze's Verratene Meer; Bonn, 1992, in Jakob Lenz by Rihm; Leipzig 1996, in Greek by Turnage. *Address:* c/o Hessisches Staatstheater, Christian Zeds-Strasse 3–5, W-6200 Wiesbaden, Germany.

FEIGIN, Joel; American composer; *Associate Professor of Composition, University of California, Santa Barbara;* b. 23 May 1951, New York, NY; m. Severine Neff, 7 June 1986. *Education:* BA, Columbia University; DMA, The Juilliard School; Studied with Nadia Boulanger, Fontainebleau; Mellon Fellowship, Cornell University; Aaron Copland-American

Society of Composers, Authors and Publishers Fellowship, Tanglewood Music Center. *Career:* Professor of Music, University of California at Santa Barbara; Senior Fulbright Scholar at Moscow Conservatory, Russia, 1998–99. *Compositions:* Mysteries of Eleusis, opera; Twelfth Night, opera; Elegy, in Memoriam Otto Luening for orchestra; Echoes from the Holocaust for chamber ensemble; Mosaic in Two Panels for strings; Transience for oboe and percussion; Nexus for flute and piano; Four Poems of Linda Pastan for soprano and ensemble; Five Ecstatic Poems of Kabir for soprano and ensemble; Veränderungen for violin and piano; Variations on a Theme by Arnold Schoenberg for piano; Festive Overture for orchestra 1996; Six Sonnets to Orpheus (Rilke) for mezzo and piano, 1996; Music for 'Mountains and Rivers', 1996; Tapestry, for French horn, violin and piano, 1998; Meditations on Dogen for Piano 1998. *Recordings:* Transience (2-CD set) includes 10 chamber and vocal works. *Publications:* Transience for oboe and percussion, 1997. *Contributions:* Stil oder Gedanke? Die Schoenberg-Nachfolge in Europa und Amerika; Roger Sessions Newsletter, Vol. I; Perspectives of New Music, Vol. 12. *Address:* c/o Rosalie Calabrese Management, Box 20580 Park West Station, New York, NY 10025-1521, USA. *Telephone:* (212) 663-6620. *Fax:* (212) 663-5941. *E-mail:* rcmgt@yahoo.com. *Website:* www.joelfeigin.com.

FEIGIN, Sarah; Israeli Composer; b. 1 July 1928, Riga, Latvia. *Education:* Studied at the Riga Music Academy. *Career:* Emigrated to Israel in 1972 and was director of the Music Conservatory at Holon from 1973. *Compositions include:* The Golden Tree, ballet, 1956; The House Of The Cat, children's opera, 1959, revised 1988; Violin Sonata, 1968; The Storm, ballet, 1969; Music for piano and organ, for educational use. *Current Management:* c/o ACUM Ltd, 9 Tuval Street, Ramat-Gan 52117, Israel.

FEJER, András; Cellist; b. 1950, Hungary. *Education:* Studied with András Mihaly at the Franz Liszt Academy, with the Amadeus Quartet and Zoltán Szekeley. *Career:* Founder Member of the Takacs Quartet in 1975; Many concert appearances in all major European centres and the USA; Tours include New Zealand, Japan, England, Sweden, Belgium and Ireland; Bart ók Cycle for festival at South Bank in 1990, and at the Théâtre des Champs-Elysées in 1991; Great Performers Series at Lincoln Center and Mostly Mozart Festival at Alice Tully Hall, NY; Visits to Japan in 1989 and 1992; Mozart Festivals at South Bank, Wigmore Hall and Barbican Centre in 1991; Beethoven cycles at the Zürich Tonhalle, in Dublin, at the Wigmore Hall and in Paris, 1991–92; Plays Amati cello made for the French Royal Family and loaned by the Corcoran Gallery, Washington DC. *Recordings:* Schumann Quartets, Opus 41, Mozart String Quintets with Denes Koromzay, 6 Bartók Quartets, Schubert's Trout Quintet with Zoltán Kocsis, Haydn, Opus 76, Brahms, Opus 51, Nos 1 and 2, Chausson Concerto with Joshua Bell and Jean-Yves Thibaudet; Works by Schubert, Mozart, Dvořák and Bartók. *Honours:* Winner, International Quartet Competition, Evian, 1977, and Portsmouth International Quartet Competition, 1979. *Address:* Artists Management International, 12–13 Richmond Buildings, Dean Street, London W1V 5 AF, England.

FELCIANO, Richard (James); Composer and Teacher; b. 7 Dec. 1930, Santa Rosa, California, USA. *Education:* Pupil of Milhaud, Mills College, Oakland, California, MA, 1955; Continued studies with Milhaud and Ple-Caussade, Paris Conservatory, 2 diplomas, 1955; Private studies with Dallapiccola, Florence, 1958–59, with Bezanson, University of Iowa, PhD, 1959. *Career:* Composer-in-Residence, National Center for Experiments in Television, San Francisco, 1967–71, City of Boston, 1971–73; Chairman of Music Department, Lone Mountain College, San Francisco, 1959–67; Professor, University of CA, Berkeley, 1967–; Founder, Center for New Music and Audio Technologies, University of CA, Berkeley, 1987. *Compositions include:* Chamber Opera: Sir Gawain and The Green Knight, 1964; Orchestral: Mutations, 1966, Galactic Rounds, 1972; Orchestra 1980; Concerto for organ and orchestra, 1986; Symphony for strings, 1993; Overture Concertante for clarinet and orchestra, 1995; Chamber: Evolutions for clarinet and piano, 1962, Glossolalia for baritone, organ, percussion and tape, 1967, Chod for violin, cello, double bass, piano, percussion and live electronics, 1972, Alleluia to The Heart of Stone for reverberated recorder, 1984, Shadows for flute, clarinet, violin, cello, piano and percussion, 1987, Palladio for violin, piano and percussion, 1989, Responsory for solo male voice and live electronics, 1991, Camp Songs for chamber orchestra (15 instruments), 1992, Cante Jondo for bassoon, clarinet and piano, 1993, String Quartet, 1995; Piano pieces and various choral works. *Recordings:* Conducted own works; In Celebration of Golden Rain, for Indonesian gamelan and organ, 1977; Concerto for organ and orchestra, 1986. *Publications:* Analysis and commentary on sketches for Edgard Varèse's Poème électronique in Space Calculated in Seconds (Treib), 1997. *Honours:* Fulbright Fellowship, 1958; Guggenheim Fellowship, 1969; American Academy of Arts and Letters Award, 1974; Various grants and commissions; Library of Congress Kousse-

vitzky Commission, 1999. *Address:* c/o Music Department, University of California, Berkeley, CA 94720, USA.

FELD, Jindrich; Composer and Music Teacher; b. 19 Feb. 1925, Prague, Czechoslovakia; m. Helena Feldova, 22 July 1955, 1 d. *Education:* Prague Conservatoire, 1945–48; Academy of Music, Prague. 1948–52; PhD, Charles University, Prague, 1952. *Career:* Composer; Music Teacher; Viz Composer-in-Residence, University of Adelaide, Australia, 1968–69; Professor, Conservatoire of Prague, 1972–86; Head, Department of Music, Czechoslovak Radio Prague, 1990–92; Guest lectures in Germany, Denmark, Norway, France, UK, several univs in the USA and Japan. *Compositions include:* Orchestral: Three Frescoes for symphony orchestra, 1963; Symphony No. 1, for symphony orchestra, 1967; Dramatic Fantasy, The Days of August, for symphony orchestra, 1968–69; Symphony No. 2, for symphony orchestra, 1983; Cosmae Chronica Boemorum, oratorio-cantata for Soloists, mixed chorus and symphony orchestra, 1988; Symphony No. 3, Fin de Siècle, for symphony orchestra, 1994–98; Sinfonietta for symphony orchestra, 2001; Solo concertos: Flute concerto, 1954; Violoncello Concerto, 1958; Piano Concerto, 1973; Violin Concerto, 1977; Saxophone Concerto, 1980; Concertino for flute, piano and orchestra, 1991; American Concertino for soprano, saxophone and chamber orchestra, 2002; Chamber solos: Sonatas for flute and piano, 1957; Piano, 1972; Cello and Piano, 1972; Violin and piano, 1985; Saxophone and piano, 1990; Concert Music for viola and piano, 1983; Partita concertante, for violoncello solo, 1991; Chamber Ensembles: 6 string quartets, 1949–93; Chamber Suite for nonet, 1960; Wind Quintet No. 2, 1968; Brass Quintet, 1970; String Quintet, 1972; Saxophone Quartet, 1981; Concerto da camera, for two string quartets, 1987; Flautarchia, Music for Flute and String Quartet, 2000; Vocal music: Three Inventions for mixed chorus, 1966; Gloria cantus, mixed chorus on Latin text, 1984; Laus Cantus for soprano and string quartet, 1985; Stage work: A Postman's Tale, children's opera, 1956. *Publications:* Numerous compositions published and recorded. *Contributions:* Hudebni Rozhledy (Musical Review), Prague. *Address:* Peckova 17, 186 00 Prague 8, Karlin, Czech Republic.

FELDBUSCH, Eric; Composer and Cellist; b. 2 March 1922, Grivegnee, Belgium. *Education:* Studied at the Liège Conservatory, 1934–40. *Career:* Active as concert cellist and teacher; Professor de Violoncello, 1953–63, Director, 1963–73, Mons Conservatory; Director, Brussels Conservatory, 1974–87; mem, Membre de l'Académie Royale des Sciences des Lettres et des Beaux Arts de Belgique, 1982. *Compositions include:* Opera: Orestes, 1969, Ballet El Diablo Cojuelo, 1972; Orchestral: Contrastes, 1956, Les Moineaux De Baltimore, suite, 1958, Mosáique for cello solo, 1961, Three Lorca Poems for voice and orchestra, 1964, Violin Concerto, 1967, Fantaisie–Divertissement, 1967, Cantique Des Cantiques for soprano and orchestra, 1970, Piccola Musica for strings, 1971, Triade for chamber orchestra, 1977, Concertante for 2 pianos and orchestra, 1986, Cello Concerto, 1988; Chamber: Violin Sonata, 1957, 4 String Quartets, 1955–71, Duo for flute and piano, 1959, Trio for flute, cello and violin, 1961, Septet for soprano and ensemble, 1969, Cheminement for violin and strings ensemble, 1984; Remembrance pour deux violons et piano, 1995; Mirages for orchestra, 2001; Quartet No. 5, 2002; Piano music and incidental music for plays. *Address:* Rue Vergot 29/4, 1030 Brussels, Belgium.

FELDERER, Ingeborg; Singer (Soprano); b. 28 Nov. 1933, Innsbruck, Austria. *Education:* Studied in Vienna and Milan. *Career:* Engaged at the Basle Stadttheater, 1955–59, notably in the premiere of Titus Feuerfuchs by Sutermeister and the local premiere of The Fiery Angel by Prokofiev, 1957, Wuppertal, 1959–62, Karlsruhe, 1962–65, and Basle, 1962–67; Sang minor roles at the Bayreuth Festival, 1961–63, and made guest appearances in Copenhagen, Frankfurt, Barcelona, Brussels, Zürich and Paris; Metropolitan Opera, NY, 1967–70 as Santuzza and the Trovatore Leonora; Vienna Staatsoper as Senta, Chrysothemis in Elektra and Woglinde; Barcelona in 1969 as Elisabetta in Maria Stuarda; Other roles include Hecuba in King Priam with the German premiere at Karlsruhe in 1963, Tosca, Katya Kabanova and the Duchess of Parma in Doktor Faust by Busoni; Frequent concert appearances. *Address:* c/o Bayerische Staatsoper, Postfach 100148, 8000 Munich 1, Germany.

FELDHOF, Gerd; Singer (Baritone); b. 29 Oct. 1931, Radvormwald, Cologne, Germany. *Education:* Studied in Detmold. *Career:* Debut: Essen in 1959 as Mozart's Figaro; Guest engagements at Buenos Aires in 1960; Sang at St ädtische Oper Berlin and Frankfurt Opera from 1961 and Metropolitan Opera from 1961 with debut as Kaspar in Der Freischütz; Further appearances in Helsinki, Hamburg, Copenhagen, Amsterdam, Montreal, Mexico City, Japan and Korea; Bayreuth Festival 1968–78, notably as Amfortas; Also sings Barak in Die Frau ohne Schatten (Karlsruhe, 1992); Deutsche Oper Berlin, 1996, as Wagner's Kurwenal. *Recordings include:* Lulu; Kothner in Die Meistersinger; Beethoven's 9th Symphony; Jonny Spielt Auf by Krenek;

Hindemith's Mathis der Maler. *Address:* Festspielhaus, 85008 Bayreuth, Germany.

FELDHOFF, Heinz; Singer (Bass); b. 1939, Radvormwald, Cologne, Germany. *Career:* Sang at Essen, 1964–66, Bremen, 1966–70, Mannheim, 1970–87; Bayreuth Festival, 1967–78, as Hans Ortel, Reinmar and Fafner; Other roles have included Leporello, Baculus in Lortzing's Wildschütz, Ochs, and Riedinger in Mathis der Maler; Guest at Lisbon (1981) Antwerp (1983) and Dublin (1984); Sang Schigolch in Lulu at Heidelberg, 2000. *Address:* c/o Nationaltheater Mannheim, Am Goetheplatz, D-6800 Mannheim, Germany.

FELDMAN, Barbara (Monk); Canadian Composer and Theorist; b. 18 Jan. 1953, Quebec, Canada; m. Morton Feldman, 6 June 1987. *Education:* McGill University, Montreal, studied with Bengt Hambraeus; PhD, Composition, State Univ. of NY, Buffalo, 1987, studied with Morton Feldman. *Career:* Compositions performed by the Arditti Quartet, Clarinettist Roger Heaton, pianists Yvar Mikhashoff, Ursula Oppens, Frederic Rzewski, Aki Takahashi, percussionists Stven Schick, Robyn Schulkkowsky and Jan Williams, and cellist Frances-Marie Uitti; her music has been premiered at Darmstadt and festivals including Inventionen in Berlin, Nieuwe Muziek in Middelburg, Other Minds in San Francisco, Toronto New Music and in the Rotonda in Tokyo; Faculty, Internationale Ferienkurse für Neue Musik, Darmstadt, 1988, 1990; guest lectured at Hochschule der Künste in Berlin; Founder, Artistic Dir, Time Shards Music Series, Georgia O'Keefe Museum, Santa Fe, 2001–. *Compositions:* Trio for violin, cello and piano, 1983; Variations for six string instruments, 1986; Variations for string quartet and chorus, 1987; Duo for piano and percussion, 1988; The I and Thou for solo piano, 1988; Two Pianos, 1989; The Immutable Silence for instrumental ensemble, 1990; Pure Difference for instrumental ensemble, 1991; Infinite Other for choir and instruments, 1992. *Compositions include:* Orchestral: Design for String Orchestra, 1980 The Northern Shore for Piano, Percussion and Orchestra or Chamber Orchestra, 1997; Chamber music: Movement for Solo Viola, 1979; Trio for violin, cello and piano, 1984; Pure Difference, clarinet, bassoon, violin, piano, synthesizer, percussion, 1990; Shadow, string quartet, 1991; Verses for Five, flute, bass clarinet, French horn, piano (and celesta), percussion, 1996; Proche et lointaine...la femme, bass clarinet, accordion, 2001; Choral: Variations for String Quartet and Chorus (text by Ludwig Wittgenstein), mixed chorus, string quartet, 1987; Infinite Other (text by Homer), 2 sopranos, mixed chorus, flute, clarinet, string quartet, piano, film adlibitum (by Stan Brakhage), 1992; Piano: The I and Thou, 1988; Two Pianos, 1989; Clear Edge, 1993; In the Small Time of a Desert Flower, 2000. *Publications:* Article, All Things Being Unmeasured, in New Observations, 1989. *Honours:* Edgard Varese Fellowship, SUNY Buffalo, 1984–87. *Address:* c/o SOCAN, 41 Valleybrook Drive, Don Mills, Ontario M3B 2S6, Canada.

FELDMAN, Jill; Singer (Soprano); b. 21 April 1952, Los Angeles, CA, USA. *Education:* Studied at San Francisco, Basle and Paris; Studied Musicology at the University of California at Santa Barbara. *Career:* Has sung in Europe and the USA in many performances of early music; US opera debut in 1979 as Music in Monteverdi's Orfeo; European opera debut in 1980 as Clerio in Cavalli's Erismena at Spoleto; Concerts with William Christie include Charpentier's Médée at the Salle Pleyel, Paris in 1984; Edinburgh Festival 1985, as Artheuse in Charpentier's Actéon and Priestess in Rameau's Anacréon; Sang Vita in the first modern revival of Marco Marazzolli's La Vita Humana, at the Tramway, Glasgow, with the Scottish Early Music Consort, 1990. *Recordings:* Rameau's Anacreon; Cesti's Orontea; Cavalli's Xerse; Charpentier's Médée, Acteon and Les Arts Florissants; Incidental music for Molière's Le Malade Imaginaire, Purcell's Orpheus Britannicus and Harmonia Sacra; Solo Recital, Udite Amanti; Italian trecento, Ensemble Mala Punica; Van Eyck: French and English Lute Songs. *Address:* Località Campodalti, 52020 Pergine Valdarno, (AR) Italy.

FELENCHAK, Vladimir; Singer (Tenor); b. 1972, Yalta, Russia. *Education:* Graduated Glinka Academic Choir School 1990, St Petersburg Conservatoire 1998. *Career:* Young Singers Academy at the Mariinsky Theatre, St Petersburg, from 1998; Appearances with the Kirov Opera as Mozart's Basilio, the Duke of Mantua, Alfredo, the Indian Merchant in Sadko and Rimsky-Korsakov's Kaschchei and Berendai (The Snow Maiden); Sang Tamino and Monostatos in Die Zauberflöte in Midia, Lithuania, 1998; Other roles include the Simpleton in Boris; Sang with the Kirov Opera in summer season at Covent Garden, 2000. *Address:* c/o Kirov Opera, Mariinsky Theatre, Mariinsky Square, St Petersburg, Russia.

FELIX, Václav; Composer, Musicologist and Educator; b. 29 March 1928, Prague, Czechoslovakia; m. Danuse Felixová, 1 s., 2 d. *Education:* Graduate, Musical Faculty, Academy of Musical Arts, Prague, 1953; PhD and Candidate of Science, Charles University, Prague. *Career:* Editor, Hudební Rozhledy, Prague, 1959–61; Assistant, Musical Faculty, 1951–54, Special Assistant, 1960–73, Docent in Music Theory,

1973–84, Professor, Composition and Music Theory, 1985–92, Dean of Musical Faculty, 1985–90; mem, Association of Musical Artists and Scientists, 1990. *Compositions include:* Sonata Capricciosa for flute and piano, 1981; Concerto for trumpet and orchestra, 1984; Symphony No. 1 for female voice and orchestra, 1974; The Advertisement, chamber mini-opera, 1977; Sonata Lirica for oboe and piano, 1978; Double Concerto for violoncello, piano and string orchestra, 1978; Quartetto Amoroso for string quartet, 1979; Symphony No. 2 for small orchestra, 1981; Mariana, Opera in 4 acts, 1982; Sonata Poetica for piano solo, 1988; Sonata Concertante for viola and piano, 1989; Sonata Melodiosa for English horn and piano, 1993; Concerto for violoncello and orchestra, 1990; Symphony No. 3 for mixed choir and large orchestra, 1986; Symphony No. 4 for large orchestra, 1987; Symphony No. 5 for chamber orchestra, 1987; Symphony No. 6 for large wind orchestra, 1990; Sententiae Nasonis for mixed choir, 1995; Numerous other published compositions. *Publications:* Janáček's Sonata Style, 1980; The Fundamental Problems of Musical Forms, 1983. *Contributions:* Hudební Rozhledy; Zivá hudba. *Address:* K Betáni 1099, 148 00 Prague 4-Kunratice, Czech Republic.

FELLER, Carlos; Singer (Bass); b. 30 July 1922, Buenos Aires, Argentina. *Education:* Opera Studio of Teatro Col ón. *Career:* Debut: Sang the Doctor in Pelléas et Mélisande, Buenos Aires, 1946; Sang widely in South America and toured Europe with Argentinian Chamber Orchestra, 1958; Resident in West Germany from 1958, notably at Cologne Opera where he has sung Don Pasquale, Dulcamara, Dr Bartolo, Leporello and Don Alfonso; Glyndebourne Festival, 1959–60, as Don Alfonso, Figaro, the Speaker in Die Zauberflöte and Dr Bombasto in the British premiere of Busoni's Arlecchino; Appearances at the Salzburg, Edinburgh and Holland Festivals and in most major opera houses in Europe and the Americas; Metropolitan Opera debut, 1988 as Don Alfonso, followed by Dr Bartolo, 1990; Buenos Aires and Santiago, 1990–91; Other roles in Il Matrimonio Segreto, Venice and Washington; Wozzeck at Seattle; Zar und Zimmermann, Der Rosenkavalier, La Cambiale di Matrimonio and Il Signor Bruschino at Cologne; Season 1992 as Don Alfonso in performances of Così fan tutte in Paris and Lisbon conducted by John Eliot Gardiner; Season 1992–93, Nozze di Figaro on tour with John Eliot Gardiner to Lisbon, Paris, London; La Bohème, Opéra Nationale, Paris, 1995; Season 1995–96, sang Alcindoro/Benoit in La Bohème, Opéra Nationale in Paris, also for season, 1996–97; Season 1997–98 included Le nozze di Figaro, La Traviata and Lulu, Opéra National, Paris, and from 1998–99 performances of Nozze di Figaro at the Brussels Opera and further performances of La Bohème in Paris; Sang Schigolch in Lulu, Opéra Bastille, 1998; Season 2000–01 included La Nozze di Figaro at the Brussels Opera, Merry Widow at the Teatro Col ón in Buenos Aires and La Bohème in Florence; Season 2001–02: Engaged to sing Tales of Hoffmann in Geneva. *Recordings:* Don Alfonso and Mozart's Bartolo with the Drottningholm Ensemble, conducted by Arnold Oestmann; Videos of Il Barbiere di Siviglia, Il Matrimonio Segreto, La Gazza Ladra and Agrippina. *Current Management:* Haydn Rawstron Ltd, London. *Address:* c/o Haydn Rawstron UK Ltd, 36 Station Road, London SE20 7BQ, England.

FELLINGER, Imogen; Musicologist; b. 9 Sept. 1928, Munich, Germany. *Education:* University of Munich and Tübingen; PhD, University of Tübingen, 1956. *Career:* Research Collaborator, International Inventory of Musical Sources, RISM, Federal Republic of Germany, 1957–62; Chairman, Research Department for Music Bibliography, 19th Century, Institute of Musicology, University of Cologne, 1963–70; Chairman, Music Archive of the 19th Century State Institute for Music Research, Prussian Culture Collection, Berlin, 1970–93; Head of Library, 1971–93; Scientific Councillor, 1974, Scientific Super Councillor, 1983. *Publications:* Über die Dynamik in der Musik von Johannes Brahms, 1961; Verzeichnis der Musikzeitschriften des 19 Jahrhunderts, 1968; Periodica Musicalia 1789–1830, 1986; Editor, Klavierstücke op 118 and 119 von J Brahms, 1974; Richard Fellinger, Klänge um Brahms, Erinnerungen, new edition, 1997; Periodica Musicalis 1831–1850, 2000. *Contributions:* MGG Edition 1–2; Riemann Musik Lexikon; Neue Deutsche Biographie; Die Musikforschung; Studien zur Musikgeschichte des 19 Jahrhunderts; Beiträge zur rheinischen Musikgeschichte; Beiträge zur Beethoven-Bibliographie, 1978; The New Grove Dictionary of Music and Musicians, 1980, 2000; Fontes Artis Musicae; Mozart-Jahrbuch, 1978–79, 1980–83; Alban Berg Studien, vol. 2, 1981; Acta Musicologia, 1983–84; Bruckner-Symposium, Linz, 1983–85; Hamburger Jahrbuch für Musikwissenschaft, vols 7–8; Brahms-Studien, 1981, 1983, 1985; Brahms 1–2, Cambridge, 1983, 1987; Jahrbuch des Staatlichen Instituts für Musikforschung, 1971, 1987–88; The New Grove Dictionary of Opera; The New Grove Dictionary of American Music. *Address:* 10 St Anna-Platz, 80538 Munich, Germany.

FELLNER, Till; Austrian concert pianist; b. 1972, Vienna. *Education:* Vienna Conservatory with Helene Sedo-Stadler, studied with Alfred Brendel and Oleg Maisenberg. *Career:* performances with a number of leading orchestras, including Acad. of St Martin in the Fields, BBC Symphony Orchestra, Camerata Academica Salzburg, Chicago Symphony Orchestra, City of Birmingham Symphony Orchestra, Los Angeles Philharmonic, Orchestre de Paris, Vienna Philharmonic, Vienna Symphony, London Philharmonia; has worked under many noted conductors, including Claudio Abbado, Andrew Davis, Nikolaus Harnoncourt, Heinz Holliger, Leonard Slatkin, Neville Marriner and Kent Nagano; chamber work with Thomas Zehetmair, Alban Berg Quartet, Heinrich Schiff and the Virtuose Bläser Wien; solo recitals and concerts in many cities, including Amsterdam, Berlin, London, Moscow, Munich, New York, Paris, Salzburg and Vienna; appearances at Schubertiade Feldkirch, Wiener Festwochen, Mostly Mozart in New York, Tanglewood Festival, Edinburgh Festival, Festival d'Antheron, Festival Montreaux-Vevay, Klavier-Festival Ruhr, Salzburg Festival and others; season 1997–98, solo cycle of three concerts with works by Schubert, Berg, Schoenberg and Webern, with performances in London, Paris, Vienna and Vevey; tour of Japan with the Alban Berg Quartet, the USA with the Mozarteum Orchestra Salzburg, and Australia, performing with the Symphony Orchestras of Melbourne, Queensland, Sydney and Tasmania 1998–99; season 1999–2000, three-concert cycle playing Book 1 of The Well-Tempered Klavier by J. S. Bach and the five last piano sonatas of Beethoven in Brussels, London Wigmore Hall, Lyon, Rome, Paris, Vienna and many other cities; season 2003–04 played J. S. Bach's The Well-Tempered Clavier Book 2 and works by Brahms, Liszt, Kurtág, Ligeti, Franck and Messiaen, performing in Vienna, London, Vevay, Amsterdam, Barcelona, Milan and Vancouver. *Recordings include:* Schubert: Four Impromptus for Piano, Schoenberg: Suite für Klavier op 25, Beethoven: Piano Sonata in F minor, opus 57, Mozart: Piano Concerto K482, Rondo in A minor, K511, Beethoven: Piano Sonata in C minor op 10, Schumann: Kreisleriana op 16, Reubke: Sonata in B minor, Schubert: Sonata in A minor op 143, Mozart: Piano Concertos No. 25, K503 and No. 19, K459, J. S. Bach: The Well-Tempered Clavier Book 1. *Honours:* first prize Clara Haskil Int. Competition 1993, Mozartinterpretationspreis of the Mozartgemeinde Wein 1998. *Address:* c/o Künstlermanagement Till Dönch, Rögergasse 24–26/G2, 1050 Vienna, Austria. *Website:* www.doench.at.

FELTSMAN, Vladimir; Pianist and Teacher; b. 8 Jan. 1952, Moscow, Russia. *Education:* Piano lessons from age 6 with mother; Studied at Central Music School Moscow and with Yakov Flier at Moscow Conservatory. *Career:* Debut: Soloist with Moscow Philharmonic in 1963; Toured Russia and Eastern Europe from 1971; Played in Japan in 1977 and France in 1978; Emigrated to USA in 1987; Performed at The White House in 1987; New York recital debut at Carnegie Hall in 1987; Professor, State University of New York, New Paltz, 1987–. *Recordings:* Various. *Honours:* 1st Prize, Prague Concertino Competition, 1967; Joint 1st Prize, Marguérite Long-Jacques Thibaud Competition, Paris, 1971. *Address:* c/o Music Department, State University of New York, New Paltz, NY 12561, USA.

FENNELLY, Brian; Composer, Theorist, Pianist and Professor of Music; b. 14 Aug. 1937, Kingston, New York, USA; m. 1st, one s.; m. 2nd Jacqueline Burhans Baczynsky. *Education:* Bachelor of Mechanical Engineering, 1958, BA, 1963, Union College; MMus, Yale School of Music, 1965, PhD, Yale University Graduate School, 1968. *Career:* USAF, 1958–61; teacher, Union College and Yale University Faculty 1962–68; Professor 1968–97, Professor Emeritus 1997–, New York University; Editor, Contemporary Music Newsletter 1969–77; Composers' Forum 1968; Performances, USA, Europe, Canada, South America and International Society for Contemporary Music International Festival 1973, 1980, 1981, 1984; commissions from Koussevitzky Foundation 1983, 1999, Fromm Music Foundation 1999; Rockefeller Foundation Bellagio Center residency 1999; Camargo Foundation residency 2002; Copland House residency 2004. *Compositions:* numerous including: SUNYATA, 1970; String Quartet in 2 Movements, 1971–74; Tesserae I–IX, 1971–80; In Wildness is the Preservation of the World, 1976; Quintuplo, 1977–78; Tropes and Echoes, 1981; Canzona and Dance, 1982–83; Thoreau Fantasy No. 2, 1985; Corollaries I–IV, 1986–2000; Brass Quintet, 1987; Keats on Love, 1988–89; Lunar Halos, 1990; A Sprig of Andromeda, 1991–92; On Civil Disobedience, 1993; Locking Horns, Brass Quintet No. 2, 1993–94; Skyscapes I–III, 1996–2002; Chrysalis, 1997; Sonata Serena, 1997–98; Velvet and Spice, Brass Quintet No. 3, 1999; Three's Company, 2000; Arias and Interludes (String Quartet No. 2), 2001, Quincunx 2003, Sasquatch 2003–04; others recorded. *Recordings:* Wind Quintet; Evanescences; String Quartet in 2 movements; In Wildness Is The Preservation Of The World; Sonata Seria; Scintilla Prisca; Prelude and Elegy; Empirical Rag; Tesserae VII; For Solo Flute; Concerto for saxophone and string orchestra; Tesserae VIII; Tesserae II; Fantasy Variations; Two Poems of Shelley; On Civil Disobedience; A Sprig of Andromeda; Paraphrasis; Chrysalis, Thoreau Fantasy No.2, Concert Piece for Trumpet and Orchestra, Lunar Halos, Reflections/Metamorphoses. *Contributions:* Dictionary of Contemporary Music, 1974; New Grove Dictionary of Music and Musicians; Perspectives of New Music; Journal of Music

Theory. *Honours:* Nat. Endowment for the Arts Composer Fellowships 1977, 1979, 1985, Guggenheim Foundation Fellowship 1980, First Prize Louisville Orchestra Competition 1986, American Acad. of Arts and Letters Lifetime Achievement Award 1997. *Address:* 2 Schryver Court, Kingston, NY 12401, USA. *E-mail:* Brian.Fennelly.MUS.65@aya.yale.edu (office); FennellyBL@aol.com (home). *Website:* sai-national.org/phil/composers/bfennell.html.

FENOUILLAT, Christian; Set Designer; b. 1940, Grenoble, France. *Career:* Stage designs include Fidelio and Gluck's Orpheus for Welsh National Opera; Bellini's I Capuleti at Lisbon, Gluck's Armide and Mozart's Clemenza di Tito at the Théâtre des Champs Elysées and Jenůfa at Spoleto; Wozzeck, Hamlet by Thomas, Der Rosenkavalier and Wagner's Ring, for Geneva Opera; Pelléas et Mélisande at Brussels and Ariane et Barbe-Bleue by Dukas for Opéra de Lyon; Designs for La Cenerentola at Covent Garden, Hamlet at Barcelona and Lucia di Lammermoor for Chicago Lyric Opera (2001–2002 season). *Address:* c/o Opéra de Lyon, 1 place de la Comédie, F–69001 Lyon, France.

FERGUS-THOMPSON, Gordon; British pianist; b. 9 March 1952, Leeds; s. of the late George Thompson and Constance Webb. *Education:* Temple Moor Grammar School, Leeds and Royal Northern Coll. of Music. *Career:* debut, Wigmore Hall 1976; has appeared as soloist with orchestras, including Orchestra of the Hague, Gothenburg Symphony Orchestra, Royal Liverpool Philharmonic, The Philharmonia, City of Birmingham Symphony, Hallé, BBC Symphony; extensive tours in Europe, N America, Australia, Far East and S Africa; Prof. of Piano, Royal Coll. of Music 1996–; Gulbenkian Foundation Fellowship 1978. *Recordings include:* The Rachmaninoff Sonatas 1987, Balakirev and Scriabin Sonatas 1987, Complete Works of Debussy (five vols), Complete Works of Scriabin (five vols) 1990–2001, Rachmaninoff's Etudes-Tableaux 1990, Bach Transcriptions 1990, Complete Works of Ravel (two vols) 1992, Headington: Piano Concerto 1997. *Honours:* MRA Prize for Best Instrumental Recording of the Year 1991, 1992. *Address:* 12 Audley Road, Hendon, London, NW4 3EY, England (home). *Telephone:* (20) 8202-5861 (home).

FERMANI, Simone; Conductor; b. 1954, Italy. *Education:* Studied at the Perugia Conservatory, Santa Cecilia Conservatory Rome and with Franco Ferrara; Assistant to Leonard Bernstein and the Vienna Philharmonic Orchestra, 1986; Mozart repertory in Bologna, Padua, Venice and Milan; Artistic Director, 1991–, Orchestra Sinfonica Del Sacro Cuore, Milan; Further concerts in Rome, Würzburg, Bangkok, Montreal, Canada, and Il Barbiere di Siviglia at Marseille; Other opera repertory includes works by Mozart, Wagner, Bizet, Rossini, Puccini and Verdi; *Honours:* Perrenoud Prize, 1995 Conductor's Competition, Vienna. *Current Management:* Athole Still International Management, Forresters Hall, 25–27 Westow Street, London, SE19 3RY, England. *Telephone:* (20) 8771-5271. *Fax:* (20) 8768-6600. *Website:* www.atholestill.com.

FERNANDEZ, Nohema; Pianist; b. 23 May 1944, Havana, Cuba; 1 d. *Education:* Diploma, Conservatorio Internacional, Havana, 1960; BMus, DePaul University, USA, 1965; MMus, Northwestern University, 1966; DMA, Stanford University, 1983; Piano studies with Jorge Bolet, Adolph Baller, and duo-pianists Vronsky and Babin. *Career:* Debut: Havana in 1960; New York debut at Carnegie Recital Hall in 1983; Appearances at Festival de Musica Latino-Americana, Mexico City, Cabrillo Festival, and Sunriver Festival and recitals in Glasgow, Edinburgh, Vienna, Amsterdam, New York, Miami and San Francisco; Radio broadcasts in Mexico City, New York and San Francisco and television appearances in Chicago and San Jose; Soloist with orchestras in US, Seoul; Recitals in Cuba, USA, Canada, Europe, South America; Member, Jaffe-Fernández Duo (cello and piano); Radio broadcasts in Mexico, USA, Korea; Television appearances. *Recordings:* Various including Latin-American music for the Saarländisches Rundfunk. *Contributions:* Articles in Piano Quarterly and Latin American Music Review. *Honours:* NEA Solo Recitalist Award, 1990–91; Distinction of Honour, La Rosa Blanca, Los Angeles, 1996. *Current Management:* Joanne Rile Artists Management. *Address:* c/o Joanne Rile Artists Management, 801 Old York Road, Noble Plaza, Suite 212, Jenkontown, PA 19046-1611, USA.

FERNANDEZ, Wilhelmenia; Singer (Soprano); b. 5 Jan. 1949, Philadelphia, Pennsylvania, USA. *Education:* Studied at Philadelphia, 1969–73, and at the Juilliard School. *Career:* Debut: Houston Opera, 1977, as Gershwin's Bess; Sang in Porgy and Bess on tour in the USA and Europe; Pa ris Opéra, 1979, as Musetta in La Bohème; Appearances at the New York City Opera, in Boston and Michigan, and at Toulouse as Aida; Opéra du Rhin, Strasbourg, and Liège, 1987–88, as Marguerite; Theater des Westens, Berlin, 1988, as Bess; Bonn Opera, 1989, as Aida; Sang the title role in Carmen Jones, London, 1991; Winner of the Evening Standard Award for Best Actress in a Musical; National Indoor Arena, Birmingham, 1992; 1994–96, Aida at Deutsche Oper Berlin; Other roles include Mozart's Countess and Donna Anna, Purcell's Dido and the title role in Luisa Miller; Concert engagements include Beethoven's Ninth; Recital at Kensington Palace in the presence of HRH Princess of Wales; Regular recitalist throughout Europe and USA; Appeared in the film Diva. *Address:* c/o Marks Management Ltd, 14 New Burlington Street, London W1X 1FF, England.

FERNANDEZ-GUERRA, Jorge; Composer; b. 17 July 1952, Madrid, Spain. *Education:* Studied at the Madrid Conservatory. *Career:* From 1970 has worked as musician, composer and actor in the Independent Theatre Movement; Opera, Sin Demonio No Hay Fortuna, based on the Faust legend and performed at Madrid's Sala Olimpia in 1987. *Compositions include:* Sin Demonio No Hay Fortuna, opera; Incidental music to plays by Aeschylus, Wilde, Beckett, Brecht and others; Chamber and orchestral music. *Address:* c/o SGAE, Fernando VI 4, Apartado 484, 28080 Madrid 4, Spain.

FERNEYHOUGH, Brian (John Peter); Composer; b. 16 Jan. 1943, Coventry, England; m. Stephany Jan. *Education:* Birmingham School of Music, 1961–63; Royal Academy of Music with Lennox Berkeley, 1966–67; Amsterdam Conservatory with Ton de Leeuw, 1968–69; Basle Academy with Klaus Huber, 1969–71. *Career:* Emigrated to Switzerland in 1969; Lecturer at Freiburg Musikhochschule, 1973–86; Lecturer, Darmstadt Summer Courses, 1976–96; Accademia Chigiana, 1980–81; Composition Masterclasses at Civica Scuola di Musica di Milano, 1983–86; Composition Teacher at Royal Conservatoire, The Hague, 1986–87; Professor of Music, University of California, San Diego, 1987–99; Fondation Royaumont, 1990–; Terrain performed at the 1993 Prom Concerts in London; William H Bonsall Professor of Music, Stanford University, 1999–; mem, Akademie der Künste, Berlin, 1996. *Compositions include:* Sonatina for 3 clarinets and bassoon, 1963; Coloratura for oboe and piano, 1966; Sonata for 2 pianos, 1966; Prometheus for wind sextet, 1967; Epicycle for 20 strings, 1968; Firecycle Beta for orchestra, 1969–71; Sieben Sterne for organ, 1970; Time and Motion Study I for bass clarinet, II for cello and electronics, III for 16 voices, percussion and electronics, 1971–77; Transit, for 6 voices and large ensemble, 1975; La Terre Est Un Homme for orchestra, 1976–79; Carceri d'Invenzione, 1980–86; Superscriptio for piccolo, 1981; Adagissimo for string quartet, 1983; Mnemosyne for bass flute and tape, 1986; Quartet No. 4, 1990; Trittico per GS for double bass, 1989; Terrain for solo violin and ensemble, 1992; On Stellar Magnitudes, 1995; Allgebrah, 1996; Flurries, 1997; Unsichtbare Farben for violin, 1998; Maisons Noires for 22 instruments, 1998. *Recordings include:* Superscriptio; Intermedio Alla Ciaconna; Etudes Transcendantales; Mnemosyne; La Chute D'Icare; String Quartets played by the Arditti Quartet; Chamber Works, 1987; Terrain, Kurze Schatten II, 4th String Quartet, ASKO Ensemble, 1996; Carceri d'Invenzione III and other works, Ensemble Contrechamps, 1996. *Publications:* Collected writings, 1996. *Contributions:* Darmstaedter Beitraege, Musiktexte, Contemporary Music Review; Brian Ferneyhough: Collected Writings, 1994. *Honours:* Mendelssohn Scholarship, 1968; Koussevitsky Prize, 1977; Visiting Artist, Academic Exchange Service, Berlin, 1976–77; Chevalier dans l'Ordre des Arts et des Lettres, Paris, 1984; Royal Philharmonic Prize, 1995; Fellow, Birmingham Conservatoire, 1997; Fellow, Royal Academy of Music. *Address:* Braun Music Center, Stanford, CA 94305-3076, USA.

FERRAND, Emma; Cellist; b. 1 Oct. 1948, London, England; m. Richard Deakin, 6 Sept 1969, 3 c. *Education:* International Cello Centre, London, 1965–66; Royal Academy of Music, London; Pupil of Pierre Fournier, Geneva. *Career:* debut: Wigmore Hall 1974; solo concerts; BBC recordings; BBC television with Elgar Concerto 1975; chamber music concerts; member, Deakin Piano Trio and Deakin Chamber Players; Senior Lecturer, Royal Northern College of Music, Manchester 1983–; Artist in Residence, Stowe Summer School and Lake District Summer Music 1999–2004; Visiting Professor, Eastman School of Music, NY, USA, 1994; Jury Member, South Africa International String Competition; appearances on BBC 2, Radio 3; tour and masterclasses in USA 2001; concerts throughout Canada and UK 2003. *Recordings:* C Hubert Parry's complete piano trios, piano quartet; Parry's Chamber Works with Piano; Bach Suites for Solo Cello Vol. I. *Honours:* Associate of RAM. *Address:* Ings Cottage, Berrier, Nr Penrith, Cumbria CA11 0XD, England. *Website:* www.emmaferrand.co.uk.

FERRANDIS, Bruno; Conductor; b. 1960, France (Algiers). *Education:* Guildhall School, London, and Juilliard School, New York; Further study with Leonard Bernstein and Franco Ferrara. *Career:* Associate Conductor, Juilliard Opera Center, –1993; Resident Conductor, Canadian Opera Company, Toronto, 1993–; repertoire: Lulu, Pelléas, Jenůfa, Katya Kabanova, Erwartung, Fidelio, and works by Verdi, Puccini and Strauss; Dir, New York ensemble Music Mobile, –1996; Contemporary Opera Training in Banff, –2001; Symphonic repertoire with BBC Northern, Polish Radio, Monte Carlo and Jerusalem Symphony, Hong Kong and Seoul Philharmonics, Madrid RTVE, French orchestras particularly Radio France Philharmonique; Specialist in Gurlitt's Wozzeck and Die Soldaten. *Honours:* Grand Prix de la Critique, 1997. *Address:* c/o Musicaglotz, 11 rue le Verrier, 75006 Paris, France.

FERRARI, Elena; Singer (Soprano); b. 1970, England. *Education:* National Opera Studio, London. *Career:* Appearances with Opera North as Musetta (1996) and Bice in Korngold's Violanta (also at the 1997 London Proms); Mozart's Countess for English Touring Opera 1997 and Fiordiligi for Opera North, 1997–98; Other roles include Adina (L'Elisir d'amore) Violetta, Donna Elvira, Marguerite, Mélisande, Cherubini's Medea and Polly Peachum in The Threepenny Opera; Jenny in Weill's Mahagonny Songspiel at the London Proms, 1997; Season 1998, as Cinna in Mozart's Lucio Silla for Garsington Opera; Other concerts include the Verdi Requiem, Elijah, Italian Songs and French Melodies. *Honours:* Gerald McDonald Award, National Opera Studio. *Address:* c/o Opera North, Grand Theatre, New Briggate, Leeds, Yorks, LS1 6NU, England.

FERRARINI, Alida; Singer (Soprano); b. 9 July 1946, Villafranca, Verona, Italy. *Education:* Studied at the Verona Conservatory and in Venice. *Career:* Debut: Trevisto in 1974 as Mimi; Appearances at the Verona Arena from 1975 as Mércédes and Micaela in Carmen, Oscar and Gilda; Further performances in Rigoletto at Parma in 1987, Paris Opéra in 1988 and Bilbao in 1990; Sang Micaela and Adina at La Scala, Milan; Other roles have included Xenia in Boris Godunov and Liu in Turandot at Verona, Norina, Euridice, Ines in La Favorita at Bregenz, Nannetta and Lauretta in Gianni Schicci; Season 1984 sang Gilda at Covent Garden, and made American debut as Adina at San Francisco; Appeared as Marie in La Fille du Régiment at the Paris Opéra and the Teatro São Carlos in Lisbon, 1988–89; Sang Pergolesi's Serpetta at Reggio Emilia, Micaela at Genoa and Liu at the Festival of Caracalla, 1992; Verona Arena 1996, as Micaela; Verdi's Oscar, 1998. *Address:* c/o Arena di Verona, Piazza Bra 28, 37121 Verona, Italy.

FERRÉ, Susan (Ingrid); Concert Organist and Harpsichordist; b. 5 Sept. 1945, Boston, Massachusetts, USA; d. of Gustave A. Ferré and Dorothy Fredericks Ferré; m. Kenneth Charles Lang 18 June 1980; one s. *Education:* BA, Philosophy and Music Literature, BMus, Texas Christian University, 1968; Diplome d'Orgue et Improvisation, Schola Cantorum, Paris, France, 1969; MMus, Eastman School of Music, New York, USA, 1971; DMA, North Texas State University, 1979; Studies with Jean Langlais, Marcel Dupré in France and David Craighead, USA. *Career:* Formerly Adjunct Faculty Member, North Texas State University, Denton and Southern Methodist University, Dallas; Musical Director, Texas Baroque Ensemble, 1980–2001; Director of Early Music at Round Top Festival, 1986–2000; Organ and Harpsichord performances in North and South America, Europe and Scandinavia; Featured Artist, Lahti Organ Festival, Finland and at the World Council of Churches, Switzerland; Recitals at the Cathedral of Notre-Dame, Paris, France; Numerous radio broadcasts, USA; Visiting Assistant Professor of Music and University Organist, Pacific Lutheran University, Tacoma, Washington, 2001–2002; Board Pres., Westfield Center for Keyboard Studies, 1999–2004; Board mem., Jehan Alain Soc., 2002–04; Past Dean, Dallas Chapter, American Guild of Organists, 1991–93. *Compositions:* Numerous compositions published and recorded by Avant Quart Company, France. *Recordings:* Works of Langlais on the Cavaillé organ at Ste Clotilde, Paris; Messe Solennelle by Louis Vierne (VQR Digital Recordings); Preludes & Postludes for the year beginning 9-11-2001; Recordings for national radio and television, France, Hungary, Sweden, Finland, USA; Works by Karg-Elert, Langlais, Alain, Duruflé, Fanny Mendelssohn, Liszt, Ethel Smyth, Tournemire, Messiaen and Bolcom. *Honours:* Fulbright Scholar, 1968–69; Distinguished Alumna Award, Univ. of N Texas School of Music, 2001. *Current Management:* Independent Concert Artists, Garland, Texas, USA. *E-mail:* iconcertartists.com. *Address:* HC 72, Box 199, Kingston, OK 73439, USA. *E-mail:* susanferre@earthlink.net (home). *Website:* home.earthlink.net/~susanferre/ (home).

FERRERO, Lorenzo; composer; b. 17 Nov. 1951, Turin, Italy. *Education:* studied with Massimo Bruni and Enore Zaffiri at Bourges (electronic resources), Turin Univ. *Career:* collaboration with the Musik Dia Licht Galarie in Munich from 1974, producing multimedia works; Artistic Consultant at the Puccini Festival at Torre del Lago, 1980–84; Artistic Director of the Arena di Verona 1991–94; Works to attempt a reconciliation between opera and pop/rock music. *Compositions:* Piano Concerto, 1991; Paesaggio con figura for orchestra, 1994; Tempi di quartetto, 1996–98; Three Baroque Buildings, concertino for trumpet, bassoon and strings, 1997; Theatre pieces, Rimbaud, Avignon, 1978; Marilyn, Rome, 1980; La Figlia del Mago, Montepulciano, 1981; Charlotte Corday, Rome, 1989; Le Bleu-blanc-rouge Et Le Noir, Paris, Centre George Pompidou, 1989; Nascita di Orfeo, Verona Filharmonico, 1996. *Address:* Via Lanfranchi 17, 10131 Turin, Italy.

FERREYRA, Beatriz Mercedes; composer; b. 21 June 1937, Cordoba, Argentina. *Education:* studied with C. Bronstein in Buenos Aires, with Nadia Boulanger, Edgardo Canton, in Darmstadt with György Ligeti and Earle Brown, Groupe de Recherches Musicales (GRM), Paris and Radiotelevisione Italiana (RAI) with Pierre Schaeffer. *Career:* debut with Groupe de Recherches Musicales (GRM), Paris 1964; Asst Prof.,

GRM 1965–70, Groupe de Musique Experimentale de Bourges (GMEB) 1973; B. Baschet Musical Instrument Development 1971; Music Therapy 1973–76, 1989; Dartmouth Coll. Computer System 1975; jury mem. at fourth Int. Music Competition, GMEB 1976, second Int. Radiophonic Competition Phonurgia Nova, Arles 1987, Royal Conservatory of Music, Mons, and at the 'Metamorphoses' 2000–01. *Compositions:* Demeures Aquatiques 1967, Médisances 1968, L'Orvietan 1970, Etude aux sons flegmatiques 1971, Le Récit 1971, Antartide (film score) 1971, Siesta Blanca 1972, Mutations (film score) 1972, A la lueur de la lampe (ballet) 1973, Canto del Loco 1974, Homo Sapiens (for television) 1975, Tierra Quebrada 1976, Echoes 1978, La Baie St James (for television) 1980, Jeux des Rondes 1980–84, Musiques en Feu (for television) 1981, Cercles des Rondes 1982, La Calesita 1982, Boucles, rosettes et serpentines 1982, Bruissements 1983, Arabesque autour d'une corde raide 1984, Passacaille déboitée pour un lutin 1984, Petit Poucet Magazine 1985, The UFO Forest 1986, L'Autre... ou le chant des marécages 1987, Souffle d'un petit Dieu distrait 1988 (definitive version 1997), Brise sur une fourmillère 1988, Tata, tocame la toccata 1990, Remolinos 1990, Mirage Contemplatif? 1991, Ríos de Sueño: No. 1 Río de los pájaros 1999, No. 2 Río de los pájaros escondidos 1999–2000, No. 3 Río de los pájaros azules 1993, 1998, Jazz't for Miles 2001, La Ba-balle du chien-chien à la mé-mère 2001, Cantos de antes 2002, Les Chemins du vent des glaces 2002, Murmureln 2003, Le Solfegiste solfeté 2003. *Publications:* Pierre Schaeffer, Solfège de l'Objet Sonore (co-author) 1967, Souffle d'un petit Dieu distrait 1997, Chrysopée electronique 1998; contrib. to Petit Poucet Magazine. *Address:* 600 Chermin des Logis, 76270 Nesle Hodeng, France.

FIALA, George; Composer, Pianist and Conductor; b. 31 March 1922, Kiev, Ukraine, Russia. *Education:* Tchaikovsky State Conservatory, 1939–41; Studied composition with Hansmaria Dombrowski and conducting with Wilhelm Furtwängler, Akademische Hochschule für Musik, Berlin, 1942–45, and with Leon Jongen at Conservatoire Royal de Musique. *Career:* Active member of well-known Seminaire des Arts Brussels, participated in many musical events as composer, pianist and conductor; Settled in Montreal, Canada, in 1949 and active as composer, pianist, organist and teacher; Producer for Radio Canada International. *Compositions include:* Soloist with orchestra: Capriccio, 1962, Divertimento Concertante, 1965, Musique Concertante, 1968, Sinfonietta Concertata, 1971; Voices with orchestra: Canadian Credo, 1966; Orchestral: Autumn Music, 1949, Symphony No. 4, 1973, Overtura Buffa, 1981, The Kurelek Suite, 1982; Flute Concerto, 1991; Sinfonico II, 1992; Chamber music: Cantilena and Rondo, 1963, Duo Sonata for Violin and Harp, 1971, Concertino Canadese, 1972, Partita Concertata, 1982, Quintet, 1982; Musique à 7, 1992; Voice: Four Russian Poems, 1968, My Journey, 1982; Requiem, 1995; Piano solos and duos. *Recordings:* Chamber Music for Five Wind Instruments; Montreal; Concertino; Suite Concertante; Three Movements; Sonata Breve; Sonata l for Two Pianos; Duo Sonata; The Kurelek Suite; Quartet No. 2 for Saxophones; Sinfonietta Concertata. *Address:* PO Box 66, Station B, Montreal, Quebec, H3B 3J5, Canada.

FIALKOWSKA, Janina; Pianist; b. 1951, Canada. *Education:* Baccalaureate and Maîtrise, University of Montreal; Studies in Paris with Yvonne Lefébure; At the Juilliard School with Sasha Gorodnitzki and privately with Arthur Rubinstein. Has performed with all major North American orchestras and most major European orchestras. Recitals World-wide. Premiered Liszt's Concerto No. 3 opus posthumus with Chicago Symphony, 1990. Premiered the Andrzej Panufnik Concerto; Renowned for Chopin and Liszt interpetations and promotes 20th century Polish and Canadian music; Founder of Piano 6, a group of internationally renowned Canadian Pianists who are committed to a programme that affordably brings important recitals to areas throughout Canada where classical music performances are a rarity. *Recordings:* Musicaviva: Moszkowski Concerto; Szymanowski solo piano works; Chopin 24 Etudes; Paderewski, Piano and orchestra works. *Honours:* Top Prizewinner, A Rubenstein Piano Competition, 1974; Opus Award, 1998; Awarded with the Officer of the Order of Canada, 2002. *Current Management:* Ingpen & Williams Ltd, 7 St George's Court, 131 Putney Bridge Road, London, SW15 2PA, England.

FIDDES, Ross Ashley; Composer and Conductor; b. 20 Nov. 1944, Newcastle, New South Wales, Australia. *Education:* AMusA, 1971; Dip Law, 1968. *Career:* Solicitor, 1968–95; Musical Director, Novocastrian Arts Orchestra, 1991–95; Principal Conductor, Opera Hunter, 1992–95; Conductor and Musical Director, The Sound Construction Company, 1988–94. *Compositions include:* Four Ceremonies, for piano, 1982; Never Again, for male chorus, 1984; White Birds Flying, for female chorus, 1984; Children, for chorus, 1984; The Proposal, 1 act chamber opera, 1985; Combination Permutations, for piano duet, 1985; Suite for Brass Quintet, 1985; Trumpet Sonata, 1985; Ceremony, for symphonic wind band, 1987; Image and Refraction, for clarinet, bassoon, horn and string quintet, 1987; Bird Song, song cycle for soprano and clarinet, 1991; Abelard and Heloise, 2-act musical, 1997–. *Honours:* Festival of

Emerging Composers, USA, 1995; City of Newcastle Drama Award (CONDA), for outstanding achievement in Newcastle Theatre, for Abelard and Heloise, 1997. *Address:* PO Box 375, New Lambton, NSW 2305, Australia.

FIELD, Helen; Singer (soprano); b. 14 May 1951, Awyn, North Wales. *Education:* Royal Northern College of Music; Royal College of Music. *Career:* Has sung with Welsh National Opera as Poppea, Musetta, Mimi, Tatyana, Butterfly, Marenka, Jenůfa, Marzellina, Vixen and Desdemona; Appeared with Opera North in first British production of Strauss's Daphne in 1987 and Massenet's Manon; Appeared with English National Opera as Nedda, Pamina, Donna Anna, Violetta, Jenifer in Midsummer Marriage, and Gilda (also at Metropolitan, NY); Sang Jo-Ann in the premiere of Tippett's New Year at Houston in 1989, and Glyndebourne in 1990 as the Governess in The Turn of the Screw for Netherlands Festival and Cologne and Montpellier Operas, Butterfly at Deutsche Oper Berlin, Katya for Scottish Opera and Emma in Khovanshchina for Royal Opera, Covent Garden; Sang Pearl in the premiere of The Second Mrs Kong, Glyndebourne, 1994; Sang the title role in the premiere of MacMillan's Inès de Castro, Edinburgh, 1996; Concerts with all major British orchestras; Butterfly and Liu sung in concert at Gewandhaus with Kurt Masur; Strauss's Vier Letzte Lieder with Gunther Wand, Norddeutscher Rundfunk and the BBC Symphony Orchestra at the Proms; Sang as Salome at Los Angeles and Santa Fe, 1998; Sang Katerina Izmailova at Dublin, 2000. *Recordings:* Gilda; Village Romeo and Juliet; Rossini's Stabat Mater, and Petite Messe Solennelle; Hiawatha; Janáček's Osud. *Current Management:* Athole Still International Management, Forresters Hall, 25–27 Westow Street, London, SE19 3RY, England. *Telephone:* (20) 8771-5271. *Fax:* (20) 8768-6600. *Website:* www.atholestill.com.

FIELDSEND, David; Singer (tenor); b. 1947, Yorkshire, England. *Education:* Guildhall School of Music and Drama. *Career:* Debut: Vanja in Katya Kabanova at the 1972 Wexford Festival; Appearances with Scottish Opera as Jacquino in Fidelio, Arturo (Lucia di Lammermoor) and Rossini's Almaviva; Further engagements with the D'Oyly Carte Opera, Opera North, Travelling Opera, Chelsea Opera Group and Dorset Opera; Covent Garden debut, 1983, in Der Rosenkavalier, Bardolph (Falstaff) in Paris and Borsa (Rigoletto) at Jerusalem; Concerts and oratorios with orchestras and choral societies throughout the United Kingdom and Europe; Season 1996 included gala concert with the Royal Philharmonic and Gilbert and Sullivan evening at the Albert Hall. *Recordings include:* Five operetta albums with the D'Oyly Carte Opera. *Honours:* Gold Medal at the GSMD, London. *Current Management:* Musicmakers International Artists Representation, Tailor House, 63–65 High Street, Whitwell, Hertfordshire SG4 8AH, England. *Telephone:* (1438) 871708. *Fax:* (1438) 871777. *E-mail:* musicmakers@compuserve.com. *Website:* www.operauk.com.

FIERENS, Guillermo; classical guitarist; b. 1940, Argentina. *Education:* studied with Andres Segovia. *Career:* debut in Spain 1963; US debut in 1965 with concert tour of Mexico in 1967; Regular engagements in the United Kingdom with the London Symphony Orchestra, Hallé Orchestra, English Chamber, Royal and London Philharmonics, Philharmonia and Orchestra of the Welsh National Opera; Played at Queen's Hall in Edinburgh in 1983 and festival appearances at Norwich, St Andrews, Harrogate, Lichfield, Newbury and Belfast; Further concerts in Netherlands, Switzerland, Spain, Hong Kong, Czechoslovakia, USA, Italy and Canada. *Recordings:* Music by Castelnuovo-Tedesco, Albeniz, Turina, Sor and Villa-Lobos. *Honours:* Caracas International Guitar Competition 1967; Citta d'Alessandria Competition in Italy; Gold Medal, Villa-Lobos Competition, Rio de Janeiro, 1971.

FIFIELD, Christopher George, MusB, ARCO, ARMCM; British conductor and writer on music; *Music Director, Lambeth Orchestra*; b. 4 Sept. 1945, Croydon, Surrey, England; m. Judith Weyman 1972 (divorced); three c. *Education:* Manchester Univ., Royal Manchester Coll. of Music, Guildhall School, Cologne Musikhochschule. *Career:* fmrly Asst Dir of Music Capetown Opera, music staff Glyndebourne for 12 years, Music Dir London Contemporary Dance Theatre, Dir Northampton Symphony Orchestra, Central Festival Opera, Reigate and Redhill Choral Soc. and Jubilate Choir; frequent conductor at Trinity Coll. of Music; Dir of Music, Univ. Coll. London 1980–90; fmrly chorus master Chelsea Opera Group; currently Music Dir and Conductor, Lambeth Orchestra. *Publications:* Max Bruch: His Life and Works 1988, Wagner in Performance 1992, True Artist and True Friend: A Biography of Hans Richter 1993, Letters and Diaries of Kathleen Ferrier 2003; contrib. to reference books and journals, including Viking Opera Guide, International Opera Guide, New Grove Dictionary of Opera 1992, Grove 7, Dictionary of National Biography, Oxford Companion to Music. *Address:* 162 Venner Road, London, SE26 5JQ, England. *E-mail:* christopherfifield@ntlworld.com. *Website:* www.lambeth-orchestra.org.uk.

FIGUERAS, Montserrat; Singer (Soprano); b. 7 March 1940, Barcelona, Spain. *Education:* Studied in Barcelona and Basle. *Career:* Performances with Ars Musicae and research into early singing techniques; Has worked with the Schola Cantorum Basiliensis and sung with members of the ensemble Hesperion XX and the Capella Reial; Sang in Martin y Soler's Una Cosa Rara at the 1997 Vienna Festival (Grosser Saal).

FIGUEROA, Rafael; Cellist; b. 27 March 1961, San Juan, Puerto Rico; m. Irma I. Justicia 1987. *Education:* BM and Performer's Certificate, Indiana Univ. School of Music; violoncello studies with Janos Starker and Gary Hoffman. *Career:* recital debut at Terrace Theater, Kennedy Center for The Arts, Washington DC; recitals in major concert halls including Library of Congress, Kennedy Center, National Gallery of Art, Jordan Hall, Shriver Hall, Merkin Hall, Caslas Hall in Tokyo, Carnegie Recital Hall; numerous radio broadcasts on national public radio. *Recordings:* F. Mendelssohn's Concerto for Violin and Piano with Orpheus Chamber Orchestra, 1989; Schoenberg's Verklärte Nacht, 1990; Strauss's Le Bourgeois Gentilhomme and Divertimento Op 86, 1992; Weber's Clarinet Concertos and Rossini's Variations, 1992. *Contributions:* The Strad Magazine, Strings Magazine.

FILATOVA, Ludmila; Singer (Mezzo-soprano); b. 1935, Russia. *Career:* Many appearances in concert and opera throughout Russia and Europe; Kirov Opera, St Petersburg, from 1958 as Charlotte in Werther, Amneris, Azucena, Carmen, and Lyubasha in The Tsar's Bride by Rimsky-Korsakov; Duenna in Prokofiev's Betrothal in a Monastery, Mrs Sedley in Peter Grimes and Filipyevna in Eugene Onegin; Sang Semyon's mother in Semyon Kotko by Prokofiev at Covent Garden with the Kirov Opera, 2000 (British premiere); Other roles include Plushkin in Dead Souls and Aksinya in Quiet Flows the Don. *Honours:* Winner, Glinka All-Union Competition; People's Artist of Russia. *Address:* c/o Kirov Opera, Mariinsky Theatre, Mariinsky Square, St Petersburg, Russia.

FILIANOTI, Giuseppe; Singer (Tenor); b. 1973, Italy. *Education:* With Alfredo Kraus in Milan and at the academy of La Scala. *Career:* Debut: Sang in Donizetti's Dom Sébastien at Bologna; Appearances at La Scala in Gluck's Armide and Paisiello's Nina and as Donizetti's Edgardo at Turin; Alfredo at Florence, Tokyo and Covent Garden (2001); Engagements in Rossini's Le Siège de Corinthe and Tancredi at Pesaro, Un giorno di regno by Verdi at Bologna and La Favorita at Las Palmas, 2001; Season 2001–2002 as Tamino and Rinuccio in Gianni Schicchi at Rome, and Fenton in Falstaff at Bologna. *Honours:* Winner, Francisco Viñas and Placido Domingo Operalia Competitions. *Address:* c/o Teatro Comunale di Bologna, Largo Respighi 1, 40126 Bologna, Italy.

FILIP, Ana Felicia; Singer; b. 1959, Romania. *Education:* Studied at the Bucharest Academy. *Career:* Debut: As Antonia in Les Contes d'Hoffmann, with Romanian Opera; Sang at first at Brasov, then at the National Opera in Bucharest (debut, 1986, as Antonia in Les Contes d'Hoffmann); Guest appearances in Basle (as Violetta, 1991), Frankfurt and elsewhere including Covent Garden, 1994; Nancy 1998, as Violetta; Season 2000–01 as the Trovatore Leonora at Dortmund and Contessa de Folleville in Il Viaggio a Reims, at Liège and Bologna; Many concert engagements. *Address:* c/o Stafford Law Associates, 6 Barham Close, Weybridge, Surrey KT 13 9 PR, England.

FILIPOVA, Elena; Singer (Soprano); b. 2 Dec. 1957, Pasardjk, Bulgaria. *Education:* Sofia Music High School; Piano and oboe at Sofia Music Conservatory. *Career:* Debut: Marenka in Bartered Bride, Bad Staatstheater Karlsruhe, 1981; Badisches Staatstheater, 1981–86; Sang at Salzburg Festival in 1983; Guest performances at Hamburg, Frankfurt, Barcelona, Luxemburg, Hannover as Violetta in 1988, Bern, Vienna, and Nuremberg; Has also sung Donna Anna, Amelia Boccanegra and Tatiana, and sang Aida at Hanover in 1990; Concerts in Germany, Austria, France, Italy, and Switzerland, and television appearances on ORF Salzburg Festival in 1983, ZDF, Berlin in 1983, SWF, Baden Baden in 1985 with Mozart and Handel Arias; Sang Manon Lescaut at Sydney, 1998; Sang Puccini's Minnie at Toronto, 2001. *Honours:* 1st Prize, Karajan Foundation, Salzburg Festival, 1982. *Address:* Staatstheater, Opernplatz 1, 3000 Hannover, Germany.

FILIPOVIC, Igor; Singer (Tenor); b. 18 April 1951, Ljubljana, Slovenia. *Education:* Studied in Ljubljana and in Italy. *Career:* Debut: Sang Ernesto in Don Pasquale, 1976; Member of the Vienna Kammeroper, 1976–77, Lucerne Opera, 1977–78; Guest appearances in Europe, the USA and Canada as Rossini's Amenofi in Mosè in Egitto and Arnoldo in William Tell, Arturo in I Puritani, Edgardo in Lucia di Lammermoor, Enrico in Maria di Rudenz, Tonio in La Fille du Régiment, the Duke of Mantua in Rigoletto, Alfredo in La Traviata, Riccardo in Un Ballo in Maschera, Rodolfo in Luisa Miller, Cavaradossi in Tosca, and Don José at Bregenz Festival in 1992; Also sang at Prague, Venice, Milan, Rome, Turin, Palermo, Vienna Staatsoper and Volksoper, Stuttgart, Mannheim, Frankfurt, Brussels, Chicago and New York at the City Opera; Verdi's Riccardo at Ljubljana, 1998; Broadcasting engagements

throughout Europe. *Address:* c/o Opernhaus Dortmund, Kuhstrasse 12, 44137 Dortmund, Germany.

FINCKEL, David; Cellist; b. 6 Dec. 1951, Kutztown, Pennsylvania, USA. *Career:* Member of the Emerson String Quartet from 1977; Premiere concert at Alice Tully Hall in New York, 1977, with works by Mozart, Smetana and Bart ók; European debut at Spoleto, Italy in 1981; Quartet-in-Residence at the Smithsonian Institute, WA, from 1980, at the Hartt School from 1981 and at the Spoleto and Aspen Festivals from 1981; First resident quartet at the Chamber Music Society of Lincoln Center, season 1982–83; Many performances of works by Bart ók including all six quartets in a single evening, and contemporary works; Premieres include Mario Davidovsky's 4th Quartet and works by Maurice Wright and George Tsontakis, Beethoven series at South Bank, London, 1996; Haydn, Beethoven, Razumovsky Quartets, 2001. *Recordings include:* Walter Piston's Concerto for String Quartet, Winds and Percussion; Works by Andrew Imbrie, Henry Cowell, Roy Harris and Gunther Schuller; Bartók's Six Quartets.

FINDLAY, Jane; Singer (mezzo-soprano); b. 1960, England. *Education:* Royal Northern Coll. of Music and with Peter Harrison and Paul Hamburger. *Career:* sang with the Glyndebourne Festival Chorus, then as Hermia and Dorabella with the Touring Opera, and Third Boy in Die Zauberflöte at the Festival; sang Dorabella with the Northern Ireland Opera Trust in Belfast and with Opera 80 in tour; appearances at the Wexford Festival and with Opéra Nancy; sang in Margot-la-Rouge at the Camden Festival in 1984 and in Monteverdi's L'Orfeo at Florence under Roger Norrington; tour of Germany with the Monteverdi Choir in 1985, including Irene in Handel's Tamerlano at the Göttingdon Festival and concert performances in Cologne; Season 1987–88 in Opera 80's Cenerentola and appearances in The Gondoliers and La Belle Hélène for New Sadler's Wells Opera; WNO debut in 1989 in La Traviata and Covent Garden debut in 1990 as Magdalena in Die Meistersinger; concert repertoire includes The Dream of Gerontius, Shéhérazade by Ravel, Bach's Christmas Oratorio and Messiah. *Honours:* South East Arts Award; Miriam Licette Award, 1985.

FINE, Wendy; Singer (Soprano); b. 19 Dec. 1943, Durban, South Africa. *Education:* Studied with John van Zyl in Durban and with Christian Mueller, Erik Werba and Maria Hittorf at the Vienna Music Academy. *Career:* Debut: Stadttheater Berne as Madama Butterfly; Appearances at opera houses in London, Hamburg, Munich, Stuttgart, Berlin, Lisbon, Vienna and Geneva; Sang at Bayreuth Festival in 1971; Roles include Nedda, Micaela, Marguerite, Mimi, Sophie in Der Rosenkavalier, Desdemona, Fiordiligi, Donna Elvira, Pamina, Luise in Der Junge Lord (British premiere in 1965), Ophelia in Szokolay's Hamlet, and Maria in The Miracles of Our Lady by Martinů; Sang at Covent Garden, 1971–77 as Musetta, Gutrune, Donna Elvira, Fiordiligi and Jenůfa, and at La Scala Milan in 1977 as Berg's Marie.

FINGERHUT, Margaret; Pianist; b. 30 March 1955, London, England. *Education:* Royal College of Music, London; Peabody Conservatory, Baltimore. *Career:* Performed in the United Kingdom, America, Europe, Scandinavia, Africa, India, Turkey and Israel; Played with London Symphony, Royal Philharmonic, London Philharmonic and Philharmonia Orchestras; Broadcasts for BBC radio and WFMT, Chicago; Appeared on film and television; Professor of Piano, Royal Northern College of Music, 1998–. *Recordings:* Chandos Records; Several with the London Philharmonic and London Symphony Orchestras, including world premiere recording of Arnold Bax's Winter Legends; Has also recorded music by Grieg, Dukas, Falla, Howells, Suk, Stanford and Moeran; Collections of Russian and French Composers. *Honours:* Hopkinson Gold Medal, 1977; Boise Foundation Scholarship, 1977; Greater London Arts Association, Young Musician of the Year, 1981. *Current Management:* Helen Houghton. *Address:* 9 Cromwell Road, Burgess Hill, Sussex RH15 8QH, England.

FINK, Bernarda; Argentine singer (mezzo-soprano); b. 29 Aug. 1955, Buenos Aires; m.; two c. *Education:* Instituto Superio de Arte del Teatro Colón, Buenos Aires and with Michel Corboz in Europe. *Career:* sang Rossini's Cenerentola at Buenos Aires 1986; concerts of Baroque music with Michel Corboz as conductor in Paris, Geneva, Berlin, Lisbon and Tokyo; sang Penelope in Monteverdi's Ulisse at Innsbruck 1993, Montpellier and Barcelona (also the Messenger in Orfeo); Amsterdam as Proserpina in Orfeo 1995; Cenerentola at the Berlin Staatsoper 1994; season 2000 as Dorabella at Aix-en-Provence and European tour as Gluck's Orpheus, with René Jacobs; recitals at Carnegie and Wigmore Halls, Paris, Vienna and Sydney Opera Houses. *Recordings include:* Rossini's Zelmira and Handel's Amadigi, Handel's Giulio Cesare and Flavio, Monteverdi's Orfeo and Ulisse, Messiah. *Current Management:* Impulse Art Management, PO Box 15401, MK Amsterdam, Netherlands. *Telephone:* (20) 626 69 44. *Fax:* (20) 622 71 18.

FINK, Manfred; Singer (Tenor); b. 15 April 1954, Frankfurt am Main, Germany. *Education:* Studied in Frankfurt. *Career:* Chorus of the Cologne Opera, 1979–81 then soloist with the Mainz Opera from 1981 with debut as Tamino; Deutsche Oper am Rhein, Düsseldorf, from 1982 as Mozart's Ferrando, Belmonte and Don Ottavio; Guest appearances from 1984 at Buenos Aires, Venice, Rome, Nice, Florence as David in Die Meistersinger in 1985, Frankfurt and Vienna; Other roles have included Edgardo in Lucia di Lammermoor, Des Grieux in Manon Lescaut, Rinuccio and Nemorino; Sang the Steuermann in Der fliegende Holländer for Cologne Opera in 1991, and Pedrillo in Die Entführung at the Schwetzingen Festival in 1991; Sang Verdi's Macduff at the Komische Oper, Berlin, 1997. *Recordings:* Handel Dettingen Te Deum. *Address:* c/o Komische Oper, Behrenstrasse 55–57, D–10117 Berlin, Germany.

FINK, Michael (Jon); Composer and Teacher; b. 7 Dec. 1954, Los Angeles, USA. *Education:* Studied at the California Institute of the Arts with William Kraft, Harold Budd, Barney Childs and Mel Powell (MFA 1980). *Career:* Performances with the Negative Band and Stillife; Composer-in-Residence, North Michigan University, 1985; Teacher at California Institute of the Arts from 1982. *Compositions include:* Two pieces for piano, 1983; Work for chamber orchestra, 1986; Living to be Hunted by the Moon, for clarinet, bass clarinet, electronics, 1987; A Temperament for Angels, electronics and keyboards, 1989; Sound Shroud Garden, with Jim Fox, 1989; Epitaph, bass clarinet, 1990. *Recordings include:* Album vocalise. *Publications include:* Business Music in Contemporary Life, 1989. *Address:* c/o ASCAP, ASCAP Building, 1 Lincoln Plaza, NY 10023, USA.

FINK, Myron S.; composer; b. 19 April 1932, Chicago, USA. *Education:* Juilliard School with Bernard Wagenaar and Castelnuovo-Tedesco, Burrill Phillips at the University of Illinois, Cornell University with Robert Palmer and in Vienna. *Career:* former teacher at Alma College, Hunter College New York, the Curtis Institute and the City University of New York; Opera, The Conquistador, premiered at San Diego, 1997. *Compositions:* Operas: The Boor, after Chekhov, 1955, Susanna And The Elders, 1955, Jeremiah, 1962, Judith And Holofernes, 1978, Chinchilla, 1986, The Island Of Tomorrow, 1986; The Conquistadors, 1997. *Honours:* Woodrow Wilson Memorial Fellowship 1954.

FINK, Richard-Paul; Opera Singer (Dramatic Baritone); b. 23 March 1955, USA. *Education:* Kent State University; Oberlin College. *Career:* Worked and performed with the Houston Symphony, Pops, Houston Ballet; Other productions include Falstaff, Boris Godunov, Eugene Onegin at Houston Opera, Scarpia at Bremer Stadt Theater in Germany, 1988, Jokanaan in Salome, Enrico in Lucia di Lammermoor and Tchelio in The Love for Three Oranges at Bremen Opera, 1988–89, Kaspar in Der Freischütz, 1988–89, Escamillo in Carmen and as Rigoletto for Welsh National Opera, 1990–91, the Water Gnome in Rusalka and Klingsor in Parsifal at Houston Grand Opera, 1991–92; 1992–93 season opened as Sid in Albert Herring with the Atlanta Opera, Kurwenal in Tristan, Count di Luna in Il Trovatore, Pizarro in Fidelio and Sebastiano at the Washington Opera Kennedy Center's staging of D'Albert's Tiefland; Sang Wagner's Dutchman at Sydney, 1996; The Forester in The Cunning Little Vixen at Toronto, 1998; Alberich in Wagner's Ring Cycle (Met, Dallas, Seattle), 1999, 2000, 2001; Title role in Flying Dutchman in Sydney, Toronto and Mexico City; Leading roles with Metropolitan Opera, New York, Opéra Bastille, Paris, Seattle, Dallas, Los Angeles and others; Engaged for Rigoletto for Opéra du Montreal, 2003. *Current Management:* Columbia Artists Management, Inc. (Zemsky-Green Division), 165 West 57th Street, New York, NY 10019. *Address:* 1310 Bridle Spur Lane, Houston, TX 77055, USA.

FINK, Walter; Singer (Bass); b. 1949, Vienna, Austria. *Education:* Studied at the Vienna Conservatory. *Career:* Sang at the Vienna Staatsoper from 1977 (Baron Ochs, 1982); Bregenz Festival, 1989–95, as Daland, and Rocco in Fidelio; Brussels, 1992, in Rossini's La Donna del Lago; Vienna, 1991–95, as Mozart's Osmin and Pogner in Die Meistersinger; Other roles include Kaspar in Der Freischütz, Wagner's Landgrave and Hunding, Sarastro, Ramphis (Aida), Orestes and La Roche in Capriccio; Season 1997–98 as the Father in Leopold I's Il Figliol Prodigo at the Vienna Redoutensaal and Colonna in Rienzi at the Staatsoper; Season 2000–01 as General Polkan in The Golden Cockerel at Bregenz and as Sarastro at Antwerp. *Recordings include:* Fafner in Das Rheingold. *Address:* c/o Vienna Staatsoper, Opernring 2, 1010 Vienna, Austria.

FINKE, Martin; Singer (Tenor); b. 1948, Rhede bei Bocholt, Germany. *Education:* Studied with Hilde Wesselman at the Folkwang Hochschule Essen. *Career:* Sang first at opera houses in Augsburg, Cologne Stuttgart; and at Bayreuth Festival, 1975; Sang at Barcelona in 1983 as Jacquino in Fidelio and Bregenz Festival in 1984; Sang David in Die Meistersinger at the Théâtre de la Monnaie in Brussels, 1985 and at Salzburg Festival in 1986 in the premiere of Penderecki's Die schwarze Maske; Other roles include Mozart's Pedrillo and Monostatos and Mime in Der Ring des Nibelungen, Nice Opéra, 1988; Cologne Opera 2000, as Hauk in The Makropulos Case and Mime in Das Rheingold; Concert singer in the Passions of Bach, Messiah and the Missa Solemnis.

Recordings: Pagliacci, Intermezzo and Ariadne auf Naxos; Die Verschworenen by Schubert; Operettas by Lehar. *Address:* c/o Oper der Stadt Köln, Offenbachplatz, 5000 Cologne, Germany.

FINKO, David; Composer and Conductor; b. 15 May 1936, Leningrad, Russia. *Education:* Studied at the Leningrad School of Performing Arts, 1950–58 and Leningrad Conservatory, 1960–65. *Career:* Emigrated to the USA in 1979; Visiting Lecturer, University of Pennsylvania, 1979–81; Lecturer and Composer-in-Residence, University of Texas, El Paso, 1981. *Compositions:* Polinka, after Chekhov, 1965; In A Torture Chamber Of The Gestapo, 1970; The Enchanted Tailor, 1983; Orchestral: 6 Tone Poems, 1965–78, Symphony No. 1, 1969, Piano Concerto, 1971, Viola Concerto, 1971, Symphony No. 2, 1972, Double Concerto for Violin, Viola and Orchestra, 1973, Double Concerto for Viola, Double Bass and Orchestra, 1975, Harp Concerto, 1976, Concerto for 3 Violins and Orchestra, 1981, Pilgrimage To Jerusalem, 1983; Hear, O Israel for soloists, chorus and orchestra, 1987; Violin Concerto, 1988; Chamber: Piano Sonata, 1964, Mass Without Words for Violin and Organ, 1968, Lamentations of Jeremiah for Violin, 1969, Fromm Septet, 1983. *Honours:* Grants and fellowships, ASCAP, The Fromm Foundation and the Memorial Foundation of Jewish Culture. *Address:* Music Department, University of Texas, El Paso, TX, USA.

FINLEY, Gerald; Singer (Baritone); b. 30 Jan. 1960, Montreal, Canada; m. Louise Winter, two s. *Education:* Studied at King's College, Cambridge, the Royal College of Music, the National Opera Studio and The Britten-Pears School. *Career:* Wide range of opera, concert and recitals; Debut role: Papageno with Roger Norrington, Mozart Experience, 1989; Debuts: Sid in Albert Herring at Glyndebourne, 1989; Der Graf in Capriccio at Chicago; Figaro (Le Nozze), Covent Garden, 1995; Paris Valentin, 1997; Papageno, Metropolitan Opera, New York, 1998; Appeared in title role in Tobias Picker's Fantastic Mr Fox in Los Angeles, 1998; Has sung Papageno, Figaro, Don Giovanni and Sharpless at the Paris Opéra, Papageno and Marcello at the Met, 2000; Jaufré Rudel in Sariaaho's L'Amour de Loin, 2000; Harry in the world premiere of Mark Anthony Turnage's The Silver Tassie at the English National Opera; Premieres at Paris, Théâtre du Châtelet, Santa Fe Opera, 2002; Appearances worldwide as Don Giovanni; Engaged as Janáček's Forester at Covent Garden, 2003; Don Giovanni at Royal Opera House; Guglielmo, Cosi Fan Tutte in Salzburg, 2004; Olivier, Capriccio at the Paris Opera, 2004; Jaufre Rudel, L'Amour de Loin, Saariaho in Helsinki, 2004. *Recordings:* Extensive radio recording with the BBC and CBC; Die Zauberflöte (Papageno); Così fan tutte (Guglielmo); Don Giovanni (Masetto); Pilgrim's Progress (Pilgrim); Albert Herring (Sid); Dido and Aeneas (Aeneas); Songs of Travel; Songs of Frank Bridge; Die Schöpfung; Nelson Mass; Theresienmesse; Das Paradies und Die Peri; Webern Kantate No. 2; L'Enfance du Christ; Britten Canticle No. IV; Maxwell Davies's Resurrection; Brahms Requiem. *Honours:* ARCM, 1980; Friends of Covent Garden Award, 1986; John Christie Award, Glyndebourne, 1989; Juno Award, Canadian Recording Academy for Songs of Travel, 1999; Royal Philharmonic Society Award for Singers 2000; Olivier Award Nomination 2000. *Current Management:* IMG Artists, Europe. IMG Artists, New York (USA and Canada). *Address:* c/o IMG Artists, Lovell House, 616 Chiswick High Road, London W4 5RX, England.

FINNIE, Linda; Singer (mezzo-soprano); b. 9 May 1952, Paisley, Scotland. *Education:* Royal Scottish Acad. of Music with Winifred Busfield. *Career:* debut, Scottish Opera, Glasgow in 1976; sang widely in Europe including Paris Opéra and Madrid and Welsh National Opera from 1979; roles with the ENO have included Eboli, Amneris and Ortrud in Lohengrin; guest appearances in The Ring at Covent Garden; sang in Mahler's 8th Symphony at the Promenade Concerts and under Claudio Abbado in Verdi's Requiem in Chicago, 1986; 1987 season included Prokofiev's Alexander Nevsky at the Proms, Messiah in San Francisco and Elgar's Sea Pictures; Frankfurt and Nice debuts in 1987 as Amneris and as Waltraute in Götterdämmerung, and Bayreuth debut in 1988 in a new production of The Ring under Daniel Barenboim; sang Fricka, Siegrune and Second Norn at the 1990 Festival; concert season 1992–93 with the New Japan Philharmonic, Orchestra National de France, Berlin Symphony, Czech Philharmonic and the Santa Cecilia Orchestra, Rome; sang Ortrud in Lohengrin at Bayreuth, 1993–94 and at Tokyo, 1997. *Recordings:* Alexander Nevsky and the Choral Symphony; Elgar Sea Pictures with London Philharmonic Orchestra under Thomson; Ravel's Shéhérazade under P. Tortelier; Respighi Il Tramonto under Vasary; La Rondine with London Philharmonic Orchestra under Maazel; L'Enfant et Les Sortilèges with London Symphony Orchestra under Previn; Eugene Onegin; Prokofiev's Ivan the Terrible with Philharmonia under Järvi. *Honours:* Kathleen Ferrier Prize, 1977.

FINNILA, Birgit; Singer (Contralto); b. 20 Jan. 1931, Falkenberg, Sweden; m. Allan Finnila, 2 s., 3 d. *Education:* Studied in Goteborg with Ingalli Linden and at Royal Academy of Music with Roy Henderson. *Career:* Concerts in Sweden from 1963; London debut in 1966 followed by concerts in Berlin, Hamburg, Hanover, Stuttgart and

Düsseldorf; Tours of USA, Australia, Russia and Israel from 1968; Opera debut at Goteborg in 1967 as Gluck's Orpheus; Guest appearances at La Scala Milan and the Munich Staatsoper; Salzburg Easter Festival, 1973–74 as Erda in The Ring, under Karajan; Sang Brangaene in Tristan und Isolde at the Paris Opéra in 1976. *Recordings:* Cimarosa's Requiem; Mozart's Betulia Liberata; Bach's Magnificat; Bruckner's Te Deum; Dvořák's Requiem; Strauss's Aegyptische Helena; Bach's B minor Mass; Vivaldi's Tito Manlio. *Honours:* Grand Prix du Disque for Juditha Triumphans by Vivaldi. *Address:* c/o Svensk Konsertdirektion AB, Box 5076, 40222 Goteborg, Sweden.

FINNISSY, Michael Peter; Composer; b. 17 March 1946, London, England. *Education:* Royal Coll. of Music, London. *Career:* Dir of Music, London School of Contemporary Dance, 1969–74; Lecturer, Chelsea Coll., Chelsea School of Art, Dartington Summer School; guest artist, The Victorian Coll. of The Arts, Melbourne, 1982–83; composition teacher, Winchester Coll., 1987–, Sussex Univ., 1989–2000; Chair in Composition, Univ. of Southampton, 1999–; Sr Fellow, KBC-Chair in New Music, Catholic Univ. of Leuven, 2000–02; Royal Acad. of Music, 1991–2001; Chair., British Section ISCM, 1989–90; Pres., ISCM, 1991–96; Exec. Councillor, ISCM, 1990–96; hon. mem., International Society for Contemporary Music. *Compositions:* World, 1968–74; Folk-Song Set, 1969–70; Tsuru Kame, 1971–73; Mysteries, 1972–79; Cipriano, 1974; seven piano concertos, 1975–81; Offshore, 1975–76; Mr Punch, 1976–77; English Country-Tunes, 1977; Alongside, 1979; Sea and Sky, 1979–80; Kelir, 1981; Dilok, 1982; Whitman, 1981–2005; Vaudeville, 1983; Ngano, 1983–84; String Quartet, 1984; Cabaret Vert, 1985; The Undivine Comedy, Stage Work, 1988; Red Earth, 1987–88; Gershwin Arrangements and More Gershwin, 1975–90; Obrecht Motetten, 1988–; Unknown Ground, 1989–90; Thérèse Raquin, stage work, 1992–93; Folklore, 1993–95; Shameful Vice, Stage Work, 1994; Liturgy of Saint Paul, 1995; The History of Photography in Sound, 1995–2001; Onbevooroordeeld Leven, 2000–01; four organ symphonies 2002–; Verdi Transcriptions 1972–2005. *Current Management:* Oxford University Press Repertoire Promotion Department, 70 Baker Street, London, W1U 7DN, England. *Telephone:* (20) 7616 5900. *Fax:* (20) 7616 5901. *Website:* www.michaelfinnissy.info.

FINSCHER, Ludwig; Musicologist and Professor; b. 14 March 1930, Kassel, Germany. *Education:* Pupil of Rudolf Gerber, PhD, University of Göttingen, 1954; PhD h. c., University of Athens, 2002; Completed Habilitation, University of Saarbrücken, 1967. *Career:* Editor, 1961–68, Co-editor, 1968–74, Die Musikforschung; Professor of Musicology, University of Frankfurt am Main, 1968–81; University of Heidelberg, 1981–95, now retired; mem, Honorary Member, International Musicological Society; Honorary Foreign Member, Royal Musical Association, London, 1978–; Mainz Academy of Sciences; Heidelberg Academy of Sciences; Academia Europaea. *Publications include:* Loyset Compère (c 1450–1518): Life and Works, 1964; Studien zur Geschichte des Streichquartetts: l, Die Entstehung des klassischen Streichquartetts: Von den Vorformen zur Grundlegung durch Joseph Haydn, 1974; Editor, Renaissance-Studien: Helmuth Osthoff zum 80 Geburtstag, 1979; Editor, Quellenstudien zur Musik der Renaissance: l, Formen und Probleme der Überlieferung mehrstimmiger Musik im Zeitalter Josquins Desprez, 1981; Editor, Ludwig van Beethoven, 1983; Editor, Claudio Monteverdi: Festschrift Reinhold Hammerstein zum 70 Geburtstag, 1986; Editor, Die Musik des 15 und 16, Jahrhunderts, Neues Handbuch der Musikwissenschaft, vol. 3/1–2, 1989–90; Editor, Die Musik in Geschichte und Gegenwart, 2nd edition, 1994–. *Contributions:* Edited complete musical works of Gaffurius, 1955, 1960; The Collected Works of Compère, 1958–72; With, K. von Fischer, The Collected Works of Hindemith, 1976–; Edited works for Neue Mozart-Ausgabe and the complete works of Gluck; Bach's Posthumous Role in Music History, 1998; Joseph Haydn, 2000. *Honours:* Order Pour le Mérite, 1994; Great Order of Merit, Germany, 1997; PhD hc, Univ. of Zürich, 2003. *Address:* Am Walde 1, D–38302 Wolfenbüttel, Germany.

FINSTERER, Mary; Composer; b. 25 Aug. 1962, Canberra, Australia. *Education:* Studied with Brenton Broadstock and Riccardo Formosa in Melbourne and Louis Andriessen in Amsterdam; BMus, MMus, Melbourne University, undertaking a PhD in composition. *Career:* Lecturer at various universities including Montreal, Dusquene in Pittsburgh, Wollongong, Melbourne and Victorian College of Arts, Australia; Her work has been performed at major festivals and concerts Throughout the world including New York, Paris, Amsterdam, Pittsburgh, Los Angeles, Montreal, Zürich, Essen, Berlin, Frankfurt, Manchester, London, Sydney and Melbourne; Many commissions and performances from leading ensembles in Australia, Europe, Canada and the USA including the Queensland, Melbourne and Sydney Symphony Orchestras, Australian Chamber Orchestra, Le Nouvel Ensemble Modern, Ensemble Modern, Arditti String Quartet and Ensemble Intercontemporain. *Compositions include:* Scat, for chromatic harmonica and orchestra, 1992; Catch, for soprano saxophone, bass clarinet and piano, 1992; Omaggio alla Pieta, for 6 voices, double bass (optional)

and percussion, 1993; Tract for solo cello, 1993; Constans, violin concerto, 1995; Nyx, concerto grosso, 1996; Magnet, for solo tuba and tape, 1997; Ether, for solo flute, 1998; The Door in the Wall for solo piano with multimedia, 1999; Pascal's Sphere, for chamber orchestra and multimedia, 1999. *Honours:* Le Nem Forum, 1991; Paris Rostrum, 1992; Has represented Australia in 4 ISCM World Music Day Festivals: Switzerland, 1991; Germany, 1995, England, 1997 and Romania, 1998.

FIORILLO, Elisabetta; Singer (Mezzo-soprano); b. 1960, Naples, Italy. *Career:* Appeared as Ulrica at Naples, Musetta in Leoncavallo's Bohème at Venice and Azucena at Zürich, Macerata, Turin, Verona, and Parma, 1984–; Guest appearances in Berlin, Hamburg, Verona and Philadelphia as Amneris in Aida, 1993–96; Preziosilla in La Forza del Destino at Barcelona, Azucena at Munich, Eboli in Turin and Fenena in Nabucco at Naples; Sang Eboli at Trieste, 1997; Concert repertory includes the Verdi Requiem and song recitals; Further engagements at the Vienna Staatsoper and the Caracalla Festival, Rome. *Honours:* Winner, Mattia Battistini Competition, 1983; Prizewinner, Voci Verdiane Competition Busseto and the Vincenzo Bellini Competition, 1984. *Address:* c/o Opernhaus Zürich, Falkenstrasse 1, 8008 Zürich, Switzerland.

FIRSOVA, Elena Olegovna; Russian composer; b. 21 March 1950, Leningrad (now St Petersburg); d. of Oleg Borisovich Firsov and Victoria Evgenievna Firsova; m. Dmitri Smirnov 1972; one s. one d. *Education:* Moscow Conservatory with Alexander Pirumov and Yury Kholopov, also studied with Edison Denisov. *Career:* mem. Composers' Union, Russia 1976–; British debut with Petrarch's Sonnets 1980; moved to UK 1991; freelance composer 1991–; Prof., composer-in-residence, Keele Univ. 1993–; Tutor in Composition, Royal Northern Coll. of Music, Manchester 1999–2001; featured composer, Park Lane Group Jan. 2004. *Compositions include:* String Quartet No. 1 1972, String Quartet No. 2 1974, Violin Concerto No. 1 1976, Chamber Concerto for flute and strings 1978, String Quartet No. 3 Misterioso 1980, Chamber Concerto for cello and orchestra 1982, Violin Concerto No. 2 1983, Earthly Life cantata for soprano and ensemble 1984, Fantasie for violin solo 1985, Chamber Concerto for piano and orchestra 1985, Music for 12 1986, Piano Sonata 1986, Forest Walks for soprano and ensemble 1987, Chamber Concerto for horn and ensemble 1987, Augury for orchestra and chorus 1988, Autumn Music 1988, Monologue for bassoon 1989, Nostalgia for orchestra 1989, String Quartet No. 4 Amoroso 1989, Stygian Song for soprano and ensemble 1989, Odyssey for seven performers 1990, Verdehr-Terzett for violin, clarinet and piano 1990, The Nightingale and the Rose (chamber opera after Wilde) 1991, Seven Haiku for voice and lyre 1991, Far Away saxophone quartet, Sea Shell for voice and ensemble 1991, Whirlpool for voice, flute and percussion 1991, Silentium for voice and string quartet 1991, String Quartet No. 5 Lagrimoso 1992, Secret Way for orchestra and voice 1992, Distance for voice and ensemble 1992, Meditation in the Japanese Garden for flute, viola and piano 1992, You and I for cello and piano 1992, Starry Flute 1992, Vigilia for violin and piano 1992, Otzvuki for flute and guitar 1992, Cassandra for orchestra 1992, Phantom for four viols 1993, The Night Demons for cello and piano 1993, Crucifixion for cello and bayan 1993, Hymn to Spring for piano 1993, Monologue for solo saxophone 1993, The Enchanted Island 1993, Album Leaf for cello and piano 1993, Piano Trio No. 2 Mad Vision 1993, Insomnia for four singers 1993, Before the Thunderstorm for soprano and ensemble 1994, String Quartet No. 6 1994, String Quartet No. 7 Compassione 1995, String Quartet No. 8 The Stone Guest 1995, String Quartet No. 9 The Door is Closed 1996, Chamber Concerto for cello and orchestra 1996, Temple of Mnemosyne chamber concerto for piano and orchestra 1996, The River of Time for mixed chorus and chamber orchestra 1997, The Secrets of Wisdom for soprano, flute, recorder and percussion 1997, The Sound of Time Passing for orchestra 1997, The Captivity for wind orchestra, Leaving for strings, Equinox for choir, The Scent of Absence for bass, harp and flute 1998, String Quartet No. 10 La Malinconia 1998, Frozen Time for piano quartet, Winter Elegy for counter-tenor and string trio, The Singing Forest for four recorders and strings, Das Erste ist vergangen for soprano, bass, mixed choir and chamber orchestra, Vernal Equinox for violin and piano 1999, Perpetual Return for ensemble 2001, The Rest is Silence for cello (from poem by Mandelstam), Epitaph for string trio, Romantische Fragmente for ensemble, Prrok (Prophet) for baritone, chorus and accordion, Euphonisms for euphonium and piano 2003, Requiem on Anna Akhmatova Poem 2003. *Current Management:* Boosey & Hawkes PLC, First Floor, Aldwych House, 71–91 Aldwych, London, WC2B 4HN, England. *Telephone:* (20) 7299-1919. *Fax:* (20) 7299-1991. *Website:* www.boosey.com/firsova.

FIRTICH, Georgy (Ivanovich); Composer; b. 20 Oct. 1938, Russia; Divorced, 2 s. *Education:* Leningrad Music College; Leningrad Conservatoire. *Career:* Debut: Leningrad in 1953 as composer and musician; Composer of symphonies, film scores, and music for radio and theatre; Chairman of St Petersburg Association of Modern Music; Professor, Music Faculty, St Petersburg State Pedagogical University; mem, Composers' Union of St Petersburg; Association of Modern Music, St

Petersburg. *Compositions include:* 7 Sonatas for Piano and for Viola and Piano, 1960–90; Bug, 1961 and Return, 1964, ballets; About Motherland, symphony, 1963; Baths, opera, 1971; Concerto-Symphony, 1986; Vocal Cycle for Baritone, 1988; Vocal Cycle for Soprano and Piano, 1990; Choral works include: Leningrad, cantata in 6 movements, for Soprano, Baritone, Chorus and Symphony Orchestra, 1976; 10 Sonatas for Piano and for flute and piano, 1996–99; Concerto Fanasia for 2 pianos, 1997; Quintet-fantasia Music Therapy, 1999; Young Ignoramus, musical play, 1999; The Reminiscences of Mikhailovskoye, symphonic poem, 1999. *Recordings include:* Adventures of Captain Vrungel, 1986; Edwards; Sonata No. 4 for piano, 1985; Concerto-symphony for piano and symphony orchestra, 1986; Doctor Aibolit, 1999. *Honours:* Laureate of Leningrad Competitions; Honoured Worker of Arts, Russia, 1993. *Address:* Novoalexandrovskaya St 11-29, St Petersburg 193012, Russia.

FISCH, Asher; Conductor; b. 1965, Jerusalem, Israel. *Career:* Engagements with Don Giovanni at Munich, Tristan and La Forza del Destino at Copenhagen and Katya Kabanova at Houston; British and US debuts 1995–1996, with Der fliegende Holländer at Los Angeles and Gala with the Royal Opera; Music Director of Vienna Volksoper until 2000, with Die Meistersinger and Zemlinsky's Der König Kandaules; Vienna Staatsoper performances include Parsifal, Tosca, and Eugene Onegin; Metropolitan Opera debut 2000, The Merry Widow; Season 2001–2002 with Parsifal for Seattle Opera, Les Contes d'Hoffmann in Berlin and The Ring in Adelaide (2004–2005); Music Director of New Israeli Opera, Tel-Aviv (Otello, Aida and Norma, 2001–2002); Concerts with the Munich, Israel and Radio France Philharmonics, Detroit Symphony, Philharmonica Hungarica and NHK SO, Japan. *Current Management:* Askonas Holt Ltd, Lonsdale Chambers, 27 Chancery Lane, London, WC2A 1PF, England. *Telephone:* (20) 7400-1700. *Fax:* (20) 7400-1799. *E-mail:* info@askonasholt.co.uk. *Website:* www.askonasholt.co.uk.

FISCHER, Adam; Conductor; b. 9 Sept. 1949, Budapest, Hungary; m. one s. one d. *Education:* Kodály School, Budapest; conducting in Budapest, Vienna, Rome. *Career:* won Milan Cantelli Competition, 1973; Gen. Music Dir, Graz Opera, Karlsruhe, Friburg; conducted Fidelio at the Bavarian State Opera, followed ny Dvořák's Rusalka; US debut, San Francisco Opera with Don Giovanni, 1981; conducted new production of Macbeth for Chicago Lyric Opera, 1981; US symphonic debut with Boston Symphony Orchestra, 1984; Paris Opéra debut with Der Rosenkavalier, 1984; first Japanese tour, 1984; led Hungarian State Symphony Orchestra's US tour, 1985; La Scala, Milan, debut with Zauberflöte, 1986; Artistic Dir, Austro-Hungarian Haydn Festival, 1987–; Musical Dir, Kassel Opera, 1987–92; Royal Opera House debut with Die Fledermaus, 1989; Presenter and Conductor, first Gustav Mahler Festival, 1989; ENO debut, 1991; conducted opening of Vienna Konzerthaus with Vienna Chamber Orchestra, 1991; Bluebeard's Castle with ENO, 1992–93; debut, Metropolitan Opera, New York, with Otello, 1992–93; Austro-Hungarian Haydn Orchestra debut, BBC Proms, London, 1993, and Lincoln Center, New York, 1994; Barber of Seville, 1995–96; Aida, 1996–97; led Hungarian State Symphony Orchestra in Athens with Verdi's Macbeth, 1997; Mostly Mozart Festival, New York, 1997; regular productions with the Vienna State and Zürich Operas; Haydn's L'Isola disabitata at Eisenstadt, 1998; guest conducting in 2002 included Maggio Musicale, Hamburg, Bamberg, Vienna Opera House; Ring Cycle, Bayreuth Festival, 2002–04; Principal Conductor, Danish Radio Sinfonietta; Music Dir National Theater Mannheim, conducts operas and concerts throughout the season. *Recordings:* Haydn's Complete Symphonies with Austro-Hungarian Haydn Orchestra; Queen of Sheba (first recording), 1982; Hungarian repertoire (especially Bartók) with Hungarian State Symphony; Lucio Silla and Des Knaben Wunderhorn, Danish Radio Sinfonietta, 2002. *Honours:* BBC television recording of Duke Bluebeard's Castle with London Philharmonic Orchestra won Italia Prize, 1989; Grand Prix du Disque for Queen of Sheba, 1982. *Current Management:* Askonas Holt Ltd, Lonsdale Chambers, 27 Chancery Lane, London, WC2A 1PF, England. *Telephone:* (20) 7400-1700. *Fax:* (20) 7400-1799. *E-mail:* info@askonasholt.co.uk. *Website:* www.askonasholt.co.uk.

FISCHER, György; Conductor, Pianist and Harpsichordist; b. 12 Aug. 1935, Budapest, Hungary. *Education:* Franz Liszt Academy, Budapest; Salzburg Mozarteum. *Career:* Assistant to Karajan at the Vienna State Opera where he conducted Die Zauberflöte and Die Entführung; Principal Conductor at the Cologne Opera, notably in a Mozart cycle produced by Jean Pierre Ponnelle; Bavarian State Opera with Don Giovanni, Idomeneo and Die Zauberflöte in South America, and Cimarosa's Le Astuzie Femminili at Wexford; British debut with the Welsh National Opera in 1973 returning for Così fan tutte and Le nozze di Figaro; London debut in 1979 with the British premiere of Mozart's Mitridate at the Camden Festival; English Chamber Orchestra from 1980; Debut with Australian Opera, 1987–88, conducting Così fan tutte in 1990; Don Giovanni for Vancouver Opera in 1988; Season 1992 with Le nozze di Figaro at Sydney; Accompanist to leading singers including

his former wife, Lucia Popp. *Recordings include:* Mozart Arias for soprano voice with Kiri Te Kanawa, Teresa Berganza and Cecilia Bartoli.

FISCHER, Hanne; Singer (mezzo-soprano); b. 1968, Denmark. *Education:* Royal Danish Acad. of Music, Copenhagen, studied with Ingrid Bjoner and Vagn Thordal. *Career:* debut, Royal Opera, Copenhagen 1993, as Cherubino in Le Nozze di Figaro; engaged as member of the ensemble at the Opera in Kiel, Germany 1993–97, where she sang Siebel (Faust), Second Lady (The Magic Flute), Dorabella (Così fan tutte), Cherubino (Le Nozze di Figaro), Hänsel (Hänsel and Gretel), Angelina (Rossini's La Cenerentola) and Idamante (Idomeneo); guested at the Royal Opera, Copenhagen, singing Rosina (The Barber of Seville) 1993, 1994, Dorabella (Così fan tutte) 1995, and Zerlina (Andreas Homoki's staging of Don Giovanni) 1996; debut at the Glyndebourne Festival as Annio (Nicholas Hytner's staging of La Clemenza di Tito) 1995, she was reinvited there to sing Isolier (Le Comte Ory) 1997, 1998; further engagements at the Flemish Opera, Antwerp, as Annio 1997, Idamante (Idomeneo) 1998; member of the ensemble at the Royal Opera, Copenhagen 1997–, where she has sung Suzuki (Madama Butterfly), Idamante (Idomeneo), Der Komponist (Ariadne auf Naxos), Dorabella (Così fan tutte), Cherubino (Le Nozze di Figaro), Offred's Double (The Handmaid's Tale), Pauline (Queen of Spades), Amando (Le Grand Macabre) and Marchesa Melibea (Il Viaggio a Reims); numerous concerts all over Europe, several of which broadcast on radio and TV, including the title role in Offenbach's Perichole and the final gala concert at Euromusicale, Munich; soloist in the first performance of Vølvens Spaadom by Andy Pape, with Copenhagen Philharmonic Orchestra 2000; soloist in the Philharmonie Berlin with the RSO Berlin in the performance of Franz Léhar's opera Tatjana 2001; season 2000–01 at the Flemish Opera, Antwerp and Gent, singing The Fox in Robert Carsen's staging of The Cunning Little Vixen by Janáček, also guested at the Staatsoper Hamburg and the Opera in Bonn; season 2002–03, debut at the Théâtre des Champs-Elysées, Paris as The Fox (The Cunning Little Vixen), at the Flemish Opera singing Dorabella (Guy Joosten's staging of Così fan tutte), with both the Copenhagen Philharmonic and the Danish National Radio Symphony Orchestra as soloist in Mahler's Rückert-Lieder, and with the Royal Opera, Copenhagen singing Waltraute (Kasper Holten's new production of Die Walküre); season 2003–04 debut as Sextus (David McVikar's new La Clemenza di Tito), and performances in Il Viaggio a Reims, Das Rheingold, and The Handmaid's Tale at the Royal Opera, Copenhagen. *Recordings:* Tatjana (with the RSO, Berlin) 2001, The Handmaid's Tale 2000, Archipel and les solitudes (with the Danish National Radio Symphony Orchestra and Leif Segerstam) 2000, Des Sänger's Fluch (with the Danish National Radio Symphony Orchestra and Michael Schönwandt) 1999, Vom Pagen und der Königstochter (with the Danish National Radio Symphony Orchestra and Michael Schönwandt) 2000. *Honours:* Noilly Prat Music Prize. *Address:* Opern- und Konzertagentur Kursidem & Tschaidse, Am Tal 28, 80331 München, Germany. *Telephone:* (89) 29 16 16 61. *Fax:* (89) 29 16 16 67. *E-mail:* kursidem@opern-agentur.com.

FISCHER, Ivan; Conductor; b. 20 Jan. 1951, Budapest, Hungary; 2 c. *Education:* Studied cello and composition in Budapest; Conducting studies with Hans Swarowsky, Vienna, and Nikolaus Harnoncourt, Salzburg. *Career:* Premio Firenze, 1974; Many engagements with British orchestras from 1976; Music Director of the Northern Sinfonia of England, 1979–82; Toured the United Kingdom with London Symphony Orchestra, 1980; Founded Budapest Festival Orchestra, 1983; Music Director of Kent Opera, 1984–89, conducting Agrippina, L'Incoronazione di Poppea, Die Entführung aus dem Serail, Le nozze di Figaro, Carmen, La Traviata, Die Zauberflöte, Il Re Pastore, Le Comte Ory, Fidelio, Don Giovanni and Peter Grimes; Season 1987–88 directed Die Zauberflöte for English National Opera and La Gazza Ladra at the Paris Opéra; Season 1988–89 conducted Don Giovanni at the Vienna Staatsoper, returning for Le nozze di Figaro and Die Entführung; US engagements with orchestras in Pittsburgh, San Francisco, Los Angeles, Chicago and Cincinnati (Principal Guest Conductor of the Symphony Orchestra); Also conducts St Paul Chamber Orchestra and in Montreal and Toronto; Recent engagements with the Royal Concertgebouw, Amsterdam, and Berlin and Israel Philharmonics; Toured Switzerland, 1989, with Budapest Festival Orchestra and pianist Zoltan Kocsis, ending with a visit to the Barbican Hall, London; First Guest Conductor, Cincinnati Symphonic Orchestra, 1990–95; Conducted the Orchestra of the Age of Enlightenment in Zaide at the Queen Elizabeth Hall, 1991; Bluebeard's Castle at the 1992 Proms; Tour of Paris, Cologne, Vienna and New York with Bartók's Stage Works, 1996; Season 1999 with Dvořák's Violin Concerto and Bartók's Concerto for Orchestra at the London Prom concerts; Bayreuth 2001, The Ring. *Recordings include:* Symphonies by Schubert, Mahler, Mozart and Mendelssohn, the Brahms Violin Concerto (with Boris Belkin and London Symphony Orchestra) and Don Pasquale, Bartók Concertos with Budapest Festival Orchestra and Zoltan Kocsis. *Honours:* 1st

Prize, Firenze International Concours, 1976; Winner, Rupert Foundation Competition, 1976; MUM Prize in USA and ERASMUS Prize in Netherlands for Bartók recordings. *Address:* c/o Budapest Festival Orchestra, Vorosmarty Tek 1, 1062 Budapest, Hungary.

FISCHER, Jan F.; Composer; b. 15 Sept. 1921, Louny, Czechoslovakia; m. 1969, 1 d. *Education:* Studied at the Prague Conservatory, 1940–45; Master School for Composers, with Jaroslav Rídky, Prague University, 1945–48. *Career:* Committee member of the Pritomnost Association for Contemporary Music, 1945–49, and of the Union of Czechoslovak Composers, 1949–70; mem, Guild of Czech Composers, Presidium, 1959–67l VP FIAF, 1964–66; Society Present Time, 1991–97, chairman, 1997–98. *Compositions include:* Operas: The Bridegrooms, Brno, 1957; Romeo, Juliet and Darkness, 1962; Oh, Mr Fogg (after Around the World in 80 Days), 1971; The Miracle Theatre, Radio Prague, 1973; Dekameron, 1977; Copernicus, 1983; The Bridge for Klara, television 1988; The Rites, 2001; Ballets: Marionetteer, 1980; Battallion, 1997; Orchestral: Symphony, 1959; Clarinet concerto, 1963; Harp concerto, 1973; Commemoration, 1973; Night Music for strings, 1973; Concerto for orchestra, 1980; Partita for string orchestra, 1983; Piano Quintet, 1949; Conversations with Harp for string trio, harp and flute, 1979; Brass Quintet, 1983; Sextet for harp and wind quintet, 1993; Concertos for two harps and string orchestra, 1997; Arietti for soprano and harp, 1996; Armonioso for violin and piano, 1998; Concerto for flute, harp and string orchestra, 1999; Chamber operas: Excitement, 1996; Guard, 1996. *Recordings:* Prague Preludes for 5 harps; Suite for Flute and Harp; Etudes for harp solo; Monologues for harp solo; 130 works for theatre, music for film and television; Songs. *Honours:* State Award, Laterna Magica, Brussels, 1959; Prize, City of Prague, 1966; Prize, Guild of Composers, 1986. *Address:* 147 00 Prague 4, Jasna 18, Czech Republic.

FISCHER, Klaus Peter; Musicologist; b. 16 Jan. 1937, Breslau, Silesia, Germany. *Education:* Diploma in School Music, Franz-Liszt Hochschule, Weimar, 1958; PhD, Cologne University, 1970. *Career:* German Historical Institute, Rome, Italy, 1970–72; German Research Association, 1972–76; Scientific Collaborator, Institute for Hymnological and Ethnological Studies, Cologne-Maria Laach, Germany, 1977–78; Lecturer, 1982–87, Associate Professor, 1988–, University of Pavia, Italy; mem, Gesellschaft für Musikforschung; International Musicological Society; Società Italiana di Musicologia; Associazione fra Docenti Universitari Italiani di Musica. *Publications:* Die Psalmkompositionen in Rom um 1600 (ca 1570–1630), 1979. *Contributions:* Analecta Musicologica; Archiv für Musikwissenschaft; Studi Musicali; Die Musikforschung; New Grove's Dictionary of Music and Musicians, 6th edition; Kirchenmusikalisches Jahrbuch; Die Musik in Geschichte und Gegenwart (MGG), 2nd edition; Congress Reports; Articles in: The New Grove Dictionary of Music and Musicians, second edition, 2001. *Address:* Via Villa Glori 5, 26100 Cremona, Italy.

FISCHER, Miroslav; Stage Director and Opera Regisseur; b. 6 Dec. 1932, Slovakia; m. (1) Olga Hanakova, 17 Oct 1977, (2) Jitka Saparova, 19 Oct 1977, 1 s., 1 d. *Education:* School of Musical Arts, Bratislava, 1955. *Career:* Debut: Traviata, at Slovak National Theatre, Bratislava, 1955; More than 130 operas and operettas performed in Bratislava, Banska, Bystrica, Kosice, Brno, Plzeň, Ankara, Bilbao, Brussels, most notably: The Consul, 1956; Fliegende Holländer, 1957; Pelléas et Mélisande, 1958, Fidelio, 1960; Midsummer Night's Dream, 1963; La Forza del Destino, 1964; The Greek Passion, 1969; Salome, 1976; Lohengrin, 1976; Falstaff, 1978, Elektra, 1980; Don Carlos, 1981; Katarina Izmailova, 1984; Un Ballo in Maschera, 1985; Wozzeck, 1985; Donizetti's Caterina Cornaro at Bratislava, 1997. *Address:* Dankovskeho 14, 811 03 Bratislava, Slovakia.

FISCHER, Norman; Cellist; b. 25 May 1949, Plymouth, MI, USA. *Education:* Studied at the Interlochen Arts Academy and with Richard Kapuscinski at the Oberlin College Conservatory. *Career:* Member of the Concord String Quartet from 1971; Nationwide performances in a wide repertory, including many works by American composers; George Rochberg has written his Piano Quintet, String Quintet and String Quartets Nos 3–7 for the ensemble; Other composers who have been premiered include Lukas Foss (Third Quartet), Ben Johnston (Crossing) and Jacob Druckman (Third Quartet); Quartet in Residence at Dartmouth College, New Hampshire, from 1974. *Recordings include:* Fourth, Fifth and Sixth Quartets by George Rochberg. *Honours:* Naumburg Award, 1971. *Address:* c/o Music Department, Dartmouth College, Hanover, NH 03755, USA.

FISCHER-DIESKAU, Dietrich; German singer (baritone) and conductor; b. 28 May 1925, Berlin; s. of Dr Albert Fischer-Dieskau and Dora Klingelhöffer; m. 1st Irmgard Poppen 1949 (died 1963); three s.; m. 2nd Ruth Leuwerik 1965 (divorced 1967); m. 3rd Kristina Pugell 1968; m. 4th Julia Varady 1978. *Education:* high school in Berlin, singing studies with Profs Georg Walter and Hermann Weissenborn. *Career:* mil. service 1943–45; POW in Italy until 1947; First Lyric and Character Baritone, Berlin State Opera 1948–; mem. Vienna State Opera Co. 1957–; Prof. of Singing Musikhochschule Berlin 1981–; numerous concert tours in Europe, USA and Asia; has appeared at a number of festivals: Bayreuth, Salzburg, Lucerne, Montreux, Edin., Vienna, Holland, Munich, Berlin, Coventry, etc.; best-known roles in Falstaff, Don Giovanni, The Marriage of Figaro, etc.; first performances of contemporary composers Britten, Henze, Tippett, etc.; mem. Akad. der Künste, Bayerische Akad. der Schönen Künste, Munich, Int. Mahler-Gesellschaft (Vienna) and German Section, Int. Music Council, High School for Music and Theatre, Munich 1999. *Publications:* Texte deutscher Lieder 1968, Auf den Spuren der Schubert-Lieder 1971, Wagner und Nietzsche, der Mystagoge und sein Abtrünniger 1974, Franz Schubert, ein Portrait 1976, Robert Schumann—Wort und Musik 1981, Töne sprechen, Worte klingen-Zur Geschichte und Interpretation des Gesanges 1985, Nachklang 1987, Wenn Musik der Liebe Nahrung ist: Künstlerschicksale im 19 Jahrhundert 1990, Johann Friedrich Reichardt: Kapellmeister dreier Preussenkönige 1992, Claude Debussy und seine Welt 1994, Schubert und seine lieder 1998. *Honours:* Hon. mem. Wiener Konzerthausgesellschaft 1963, RAM (London), Royal Acad. (Stockholm), Deutschen Oper, Berlin 1978, Royal Philharmonic Soc.; Bundesverdienstkreuz 1st Class 1958, Grosses Verdienstkreuz des Verdienstordens der Bundesrepublik Deutschland 1974, Chevalier Légion d'honneur 1990, Hon. DUniv (Oxford) 1978, Hon. DMus (Paris-Sorbonne) 1980, (Yale) 1980; Int. Recording Prizes almost every year since 1955, Berlin Kunstpreis 1950, Mantua Golden Orpheus Prize 1955, Edison Prize 1960, 1962, 1964, 1965, 1967, 1970, President's Prize Charles Gros Acad., Paris 1980, Förderungspreis der Ernst-von-Siemens-Stiftung 1980, Mozart Medal 1962, Golden Orpheus 1967, Grammy Award (several times), Prix Mondial Montreux (several times), Ernst-Reuter-Plak 1993, Polar Music Prize 2004. *Address:* c/o Deutsche Verlanganstalt, Stüttgart, Germany (office).

FISCHER-MÜNSTER, Gerhard; German composer, conductor, musician (piano, clarinet) and lecturer; b. 17 Nov. 1952, Münster-Sarmsheim; m. Bettina Fischer-Münster 1979; one s. one d. *Education:* Peter Cornelius Konservatorium, Mainz; Staatliche Musikhochschule und Johannes Gutenberg Universität, Mainz; Staatsexamen (lecturer, soloist), 1974; seminar for conducting, Bingen. *Career:* first compositions in 1965; concerts as soloist (piano, clarinet); concerts as conductor of a number of orchestras and ensembles; radio and television performances and recordings in Germany, Italy, Austria, Switzerland, France, Belgium, USA, and Japan; guest conductor with the European Symphony Orchestra, Luxembourg, 1993; performances at international festivals; jury member of music competitions; guest lecturer at Universität Mainz and various institutions; founder of wind chamber ensemble, 1981; founder of Symphonic Wind Orchestra of Mainz Conservatory, 1991; lecturer at Peter Cornelius Konservatorium, Mainz (clarinet, improvisation, composition, symphonic wind orchestra, wind chamber ensemble) 1975–. *Compositions include:* symphonies: Psychodrom; Im Anfang war das Wort; Daliphonie; Haiku-Lieder; Psalm 99; Schizophonie; Geldschein-Sonate; Piano Concertino; Symphonic Pictures; Sonatas, lieder, and orchestral works. *Recordings include:* Haiku-Lieder; Philosophie eines Filous; Musique de table; Süd-Freak-Idyll; Adoration and more. *Publications:* Harmonie aus dem Einklang; Lehrplan Klarinette; Kreativ Üben; Lexikon Komponisten der Gegenwart; Lexikon des Blasmusikwesens; Wer ist Wer Deutschland. *Honours:* numerous prizes from Germany, Switzerland, UK, USA. *Address:* Auf den Zeilen 11, 55424 Münster-Sarmsheim, Germany. *Telephone:* (6721) 46727 (home). *E-mail:* fischer-muenster@gmx.de (home). *Website:* www.fischer-muenster.de.

FISHER, Gillian; Singer (Soprano); b. 1955, England; m. Brian Kay. *Education:* Studied with John Carol Case at the Royal College of Music and with Jessica Cash. *Career:* Appearances in the world's leading concert halls, including Albert, Festival and Barbican Halls, London; Amsterdam Concertgebouw, Lincoln Center, New York and Suntory Hall, Tokyo; Handel Festivals in London and in Maryland, USA; Frequent broadcasts with repertoire ranging from Baroque music to the vocal symphonies of Milhaud; Featured in Central Television series Man and His Music; Sang in Theodora and other works by Handel for tercentenary year, 1985; Sang in Messiah with Ton Koopman and the Amsterdam Baroque Orchestra, Japan, 1987; Appearances in Italy, Japan and Australia with vocal group The Sixteen; Gluck's Euridice at Covent Garden, 1989. *Recordings include:* Purcell's King Arthur and Dioclesian with John Eliot Gardiner and the Monteverdi Choir; The Triumph of Time and Truth by Handel with Denys Darlow and the London Handel Orchestra; Great Baroque Arias and Pergolesi's Stabat Mater with the King's Consort and Michael Chance; Purcell's Fairy Queen and Bach cantatas with The Sixteen and Harry Christophers and Handel duets with the King's Consort and James Bowman. *Current Management:* Magenta Music. *Address:* c/o Brian Kay, Radio 3, BBC Broadcasting House, Portland Place, London W1A 1AA, England.

FISHER, Jonathan; Singer (Baritone); b. 1963, England. *Education:* Guildhall School, London, with Bernard Dickerson, and Cologne Musikhochschule. *Career:* Appearances for the Royal Opera, Covent Garden, in The Pilgrim's Progress and La Battaglia di Legnano (concert), Chérubin by Massenet, Der Rosenkavalier, Simon Boccanegra and The Midsummer Marriage; Henry Higgins in My Fair Lady for the Covent Garden Festival; Associated with Royal Opera House education projects. *Recordings:* The Pilgrim's Progress, Peter Grimes, Christmas from Covent Garden. *Publications:* By George, musical about the Gershwins. *Honours:* Painter prize, Guildhall School. *Address:* c/o Royal Opera House (contracts), Covent Garden, London, WC2, England. *Telephone:* (20) 7240 1200. *Fax:* (20) 7212-9502.

FISHER, Norma; Concert Pianist; b. 11 May 1940, London, England; m. Barrington Saipe, 3 Sept 1967, 2 s. *Education:* Guildhall School of Music with Sidney Harrison, 1951–57 and privately with Ilona Kabos, 1957–68 and Jacques Fevrier, Paris, 1962. *Career:* Debut: Wigmore Hall, 1956; Proms, Royal Albert Hall, 1963; Performances throughout the United Kingdom, Europe, USA, Canada and Israel in recitals, concertos and chamber music; Regular performer for BBC, London; Represented the United Kingdom twice at International Jeunesses Musicales Congress; Jury Member of many major international piano competitions; Invited to give Masterclasses world-wide; Founded London Masterclasses in 1988. *Honours:* 2nd Prize, Busoni International Piano Competition, Italy, 1961; Piano Prize (Joint holder with Vladimir Ashkenazy), Harriet Cohen International Awards, 1963. *Current Management:* J. Audrey Ellison, International Artists Management, London, England. *Address:* 5 Lyndhurst Gardens, Finchley, London N3 1TA, England.

FISHER, Stephen (Carey); Musicologist; b. 18 May 1948, Norfolk, Virginia, USA. *Education:* BA, University of Virginia, 1969; PhD, University of Pennsylvania, 1985. *Career:* Assistant Professor, Widener University, 1985–87; Lecturer, University of Pennsylvania, 1989–; mem, American Musicological Society; International Musicological Society; Music Library Association. *Publications:* The Symphony 1720–1840, series B, vol. IX, 1983; Joseph Haydn Werke, series 1, vols 9, Sinfonien um 1777–79, 2002,. *Contributions:* Haydn-Studien; Mitteilungen der Internationalen Stiftung Mozarteum; Current Musicology; Haydn Studies, 1975; The Haydn Yearbook; The Eighteenth Century: A Current Bibliography; Eighteenth Century Studies; Journal of Musicology; New Grove Dictionary of Opera; Notes; Journal of the American Musicological Society; New Grove Dictionary of Music. *Honours:* Fulbright-Hays Grant, 1976–77. *Address:* Department of Music, University of Pennsylvania, 201 South 34th Street, Philadelphia, PA 19104-6313, USA. *E-mail:* docsfisher@aol.com (home); fisher@pobox.upenn.edu (office).

FISICHELLA, Salvatore; Singer (Tenor); b. 1948, Italy. *Education:* Studied in Catania and Rome. *Career:* Debut: Spoleto Festival, as Werther; Sang in Rigoletto and I Puritani at the Rome Opera and appeared widely in Europe and America as Arturo, Arnoldo (Guillaume Tell) and Gualtiero (Il Pirata); New York Met debut as Arturo, opposite Joan Sutherland; Engagements at the Zürich Opera under Nello Santi in I Puritani, Il Pirata and Guillaume Tell; Further leading roles in such operas as Traviata, Butterfly, La Favorita, Roberto Devereux, Faust, Mefistofele and Attila; Season 1996–97 as the Duke of Mantua at Zürich, Pinkerton and Alfredo at Palermo, Edgardo (Luci di Lammermoor) at La Scala and Fernando (La Favorita) at Catania; Further roles in Rossini's Mosè in Egitto and Otello, I Capuleti e i Montecchi, and The Two Widows; Season 2000–01 as the Duke of Mantua at St Gallen and Gualtiero in Bellini's Pirata at Catania. *Honours:* Premio Bellini d'Oro in Catania; Premio Internazionale Giacomo Lauri Volpi, at Rome. *Address:* c/o Opernhaus Zürich, Falkenstrasse 1, 8008 Zürich, Switzerland.

FISK, Eliot Hamilton, BA, MA; American classical guitarist and professor of music; b. 10 Aug. 1954, Philadelphia, PA. *Education:* Yale University, Aspen Music School with Oscar Ghiglia, studied with Andres Segovia, Ralph Kirkpatrick, Albert Fuller. *Career:* solo recital debut, Alice Tully Hall, New York, 1976; Toured throughout the world as soloist with orchestras, as recitalist and chamber music performer; Teacher, Aspen Music School, 1973–82; Yale University, 1977–82; Mannes College of Music, 1978–82; Professor, Cologne Hochschule für Musik, 1982–89; Professor, Mozarteum, Salzburg, 1989–; Prepared transcriptions of works by Bach, Scarlatti, Mozart, Paganini, Mendelssohn, E Halffter, I Albeniz, E Granados, for guitar; New works for guitar composed for him by Robert Beaser, Luciano Berio, Cristóbal Halffter, Nicholas Maw, Xavier Montsalvatge, George Rochberg. *Recordings:* First recordings of Paganini Caprices Op 1; Rochberg, Caprice Variations; Balada, Concierto Magico; Segovia, Canciones Populares; Berio, Sequenza XI; Beaser, Mountain Songs. *Publications:* Transcriptions of Bach, Frescobaldi, Scarlatti, Paganini; Editions of Beaser, Berio, Rochberg, Halffter, Montsalvatge, Maw and others. *Honours:* International Classical Guitar Competition, Gargnano, Italy 1980. *Current Management:* ICM Artists Ltd, 40 W 57th Street, New York, NY 10019, USA.

FISSORE, Enrico; singer (bass-baritone); b. 23 Jan. 1939, Piemonte, Italy. *Education:* Milan and Turin Conservatories. *Career:* debut, Teatro Nuovo Milan 1964, as Don Giovanni; Many appearances in Europe and North America in Italian operas of the 17th and 18th centuries; Glyndebourne debut 1967, as Schaunard in La Bohème; USA debut at San Francisco, as Rossini's Bartolo; La Scala Milan 1979, in Vivaldi's Tito Manlio; Further engagements as Verdi's Melitone and Dulcamara in L'Elisir d'amore at the Metropolitan, Don Magnifico (La Cenerentola) with Florida Opera and Leporello at Portland (season 1997–98); Other appearances at the Chicago Lyric Opera, Vienna Staatsoper, Opéra Bastille, Salzburg Festival and Munich; Glyndebourne 1997, as Bartolo in Le nozze di Figaro, followed by Puccini's Trittico in Brussels. *Current Management:* Robert Gilder & Co., Enterprise House, 59–65 Upper Ground, London, SE1 9PQ, England. *Telephone:* (20) 7928-9008. *Fax:* (20) 7928-9755. *E-mail:* rgilder@robert-gilder.com.

FITKIN, Graham; British composer; b. 19 April 1963, Crows-an-Wra, Cornwall. *Education:* Univ. of Nottingham, Koninglijk Conservatorium, The Hague. *Career:* co-founder piano ensemble, The Nanquidno Group 1985; Programme Dir, Soc. for the Promotion of New Music 1993; PRS Composer in Education 1995, 1996, 1998; composer-in-residence, Royal Liverpool Philharmonic Orchestra 1994–96; founder sextet, Graham Fitkin Group 1996; composer-in-residence, The Harbourside Centre, Bristol 1997–98; featured composer for Park Lane Group and at Presteigne Festival 1999, at Mixing Music Festival 2000, at Int. Guitar Festival 2001; composer-in-residence, The Lemon Tree, Aberdeen 2000, 2001; various collaborative projects with different organizations, including The Geography Project, Scotland 1999–. *Compositions include:* Drum (music theatre) 1989, Loud 1989, Log 1990, Line 1991, Nasar 1992, Ghosts (opera) 1993, Huoah 1994, Length 1994, Metal 1995, Henry 1995, Granite 1995, Bebeto 1995, North 1998, Bob 1998, Timber 2000, Ending 2000, Ascendant 2001, Circuit concerto for two pianos 2002. *Honours:* Int. Grand Prix Music for Dance Video Award 1994. *Address:* c/o G. Ricordi & Company, Bedford House, 69–79 Fulham Street, London, SW6 3JW, England (office). *E-mail:* info@fitkin.com. *Website:* www.fitkin.com.

FITZGERALD, Daire; Concert Cellist; b. 1966, Dublin, Ireland. *Education:* Studied with Rostropovich, at the Menuhin School with William Pleeth and the Menuhin Academy with Radu Aldulescu. *Career:* Concerts throughout Western Europe, China, India, Israel and Czechoslovakia, while a student at the Society of Lincoln Center, New York, and concerts with such orchestras as the Royal Philharmonic, Warsaw Sinfonia, Central Philharmonic of Peking, Hallé and Berlin Radio Symphony; Soloist with the Camerata Lysy Gstaad on tour to Japan and Canada; Berlin debut with the Saint-Saëns A minor concerto; New Year's Concert for Finnish television, tour of USA playing chamber music with Menuhin and participation on Julian Lloyd Webber's Cellothon at South Bank, London.

FLAGELLO, Ezio; Singer (Bass); b. 28 Jan. 1931, New York, NY, USA. *Education:* Studied with Friedrich Schorr and John Brownlee at the Manhattan School of Music; Further study with Luigi Ricci in Rome. *Career:* Debut: Concert performance of Boris Godunov at Carnegie Hall, 1952; Sang Dulcamara in Rome, 1956; After winning Metropolitan Auditions of the Air (1957) appeared in New York until 1987, as Leporello, Fiesco in Simon Boccanegra, Pogner, Philip II and Rossini's Basilio; Sang Enobarbus in the inaugural production of the Metropolitan Opera at Lincoln Center, Antony and Cleopatra by Barber (1966); Guest appearances in San Francisco, Dallas, Houston, Milan, Vienna, Berlin, Prague and Florence; Screen debut, Francis Ford Coppola's Godfather II; Sang Sarastro for Pennsylvania Opera Theater, 1991. *Recordings include:* Così fan tutte; Lucrezia Borgia; Lucia di Lammermoor; Un Ballo in Maschera; Ernani; Luisa Miller; Rigoletto; La Forza del Destino; Alcina; I Puritani; Don Giovanni. *Address:* 2005 Samontee Road, Jacksonville, FL 32211, USA.

FLANAGAN, Leslie John; Singer (Baritone); b. 1969, Rockhampton, Australia. *Education:* Studied in Australia and at the Scottish Academy of Music. *Career:* Appearances at the Mananan Festival as Schaunard in La Bohème and as Malatesta in Don Pasquale for Clonter Opera; Junior Principal with English National Opera, 1999–2000 season; Other roles include Papageno, Demetrius (A Midsummer Night's Dream), Don Giovanni and Escamillo; Concerts include the Fauré and Brahms Requiems, Mendelssohn's St Paul, Elgar's Apostles and Puccini's Messa di Gloria. *Honours:* Marianne Mathy Award, 1996. *Address:* Harlequin Agency, 203 Fidlas Road, Cardiff CF4 5NA, Wales.

FLECK, William; Singer (Bass); b. 28 Aug. 1937, Tyrone, Pennsylvania, USA. *Education:* Studied at the Eastman School and at the Manhattan School of Music. *Career:* Sang widely in the USA, at first as guest in Boston, Minneapolis and Hawaii; Metropolitan Opera from 1980, in Die Zauberflöte, Tannhäuser, Traviata, Bohème and Tosca; Sang Rocco at Mexico City, 1983; Sang in the US premiere of Ruslan and Lyudmilla at

Boston and elsewhere as Leporello, Alfonso, Don Magnifico, and Morosus in Die schweigsame Frau; Baron Ochs in Der Rosenkavalier, directed by Jonathan Miller, New York City Opera debut, 1996. *Current Management:* Sardos Artists Management Corp, 180 West End Avenue, New York, NY 10023. *Address:* 24 Riverside Drive, Ridgefield, CT 06877, USA.

FLEET, Marlene (Rose); Concert Pianist; b. 13 Feb. 1942, Grimsby, South Humberside, England; m. Harry Terence Harvey Taylor, 5 June 1972. *Education:* LRAM, ARCM, Grimsby Technical College; Royal Academy of Music, 1960–65. *Career:* Debut: Wigmore Hall, 1964; Numerous concerts in the United Kingdom, Europe and America; Appearances at Wigmore Hall, Purcell Room, Queen Elizabeth Hall, Royal Festival Hall, London; Plays regularly for BBC and has performed on BBC television; Played with most of the leading British orchestras and with many distinguished conductors. *Recordings:* Numerous recordings for BBC Radio 3. *Honours:* Winner of most of solo pianist prizes, Royal Academy of Music, 1960–65; Countess of Munster Scholarship; Martin Musical Scholarships. *Address:* 22 Fairefield Crescent, Glenfield, Leicester LE3 8EH, England.

FLEISCHER, Tsippi; Composer; b. 20 May 1946, Haifa, Israel. *Education:* Studied at the Tel-Aviv and New York Universities and the Rubin Academy of Music; PhD, Musicology, Bar Ilan University, Ramat Gan, Israel, 1995. *Career:* Teacher at the Tel-Aviv and Bar-Ilan Universities; Professor, Music Department Levinsky Institute, Tel-Aviv. Member, Levinsky Institute Pedagogical Committee. *Compositions include:* A Girl Named Limonad, music theatre, 1977; Girl-Butterfly-Girl, song cycle, for soprano and ensemble, 1977; Lamentation for soprano, women's chorus, 2 harps and percussion, 1985; In The Mountains Of Armenia for children's chorus, 1988; Cantata, Like Two Branches, 1989; Oratorio 1492-1992, 1992; Four Old Winds, 4 multi-medias in ancient Semitic languages), 1993–96; Medea, chamber opera, 1995; Salt Crystals, 1st Symphony, 1995; The Train Symphony, 2nd Symphony, 1998; Regarding Beauty, 3rd Symphony, 1998; A Moving Shadow, 4th Symphony (incl. folk wind and percussion), 2000; An Israeli-Jewish Collage, 5th Symphony 2002–2003; Ethnic Silhouettes, 1988–98; Lead Life (song cycle), 2001Opera: Medea, 1995; Cain and Abel, 2001; Victoria, 2003–2004;. *Recordings include:* Tsippi Fleischer Vocal Music, 1992; Tsippi Fleischer Art Music Settings of Arab Poetry, 1993; Around the World with Tsippi Fleischer, 1997; Israel at 50 a Celebration of the Music of Tsippi Fleischer, 1999. *Honours:* ACUM prize for Music, 1994; Prime minister's Award for Composers, 50th Anniversary of the State of Israel, 1998; ACUM Prize for life time achievement in composition for the concert hall, 2002. *Address:* PO Box 8094, Haifa 31080, Israel.

FLEISHER, Leon; Pianist and Conductor; b. 23 July 1928, San Francisco, California, USA. *Education:* Studied piano with Artur Schnabel, 1938–48; Conducting with Pierre Monteux. *Career:* First public recital, 1934; Played Liszt's A Major Concerto with the San Francisco Symphony, 1942; Brahms D Minor Concerto in San Francisco and New York, 1943, 1944; International career from 1952; Gave concerts with George Szell and the Cleveland Orchestra; Joined faculty of the Peabody Conservatory of Music, Baltimore, 1959; Premiered Leon Kirchner's Concerto, Seattle, 1963; Lost use of right hand, 1965, and later played Piano Left Hand repertoire; Co-Director of the Theatre Chamber Players, Washington DC, 1968; Associate Conductor of the Baltimore Symphony Orchestra, 1973–78; Guest engagements as conductor with leading orchestras in the USA; Resumed bimanual solo pianist career, 1982; Artistic Director of the Tanglewood Music Center, 1986–97. *Address:* ICM Artists Ltd, 10 Barley Mow Passage, London, W4 4PH, England.

FLEMING, Renée, MMus; American opera singer (soprano); b. 14 Feb. 1959, Indiana, PA; d. of Edwin Davis Fleming and Patricia (Seymour) Alexander; m. Richard Lee Ross 1989 (divorced 2000); two d. *Education:* Potsdam State Univ., Eastman School of Music of Univ. of Rochester, Juilliard School American Opera Center. *Career:* debuts Houston Grand Opera (Marriage of Figaro) 1988, Spoleto Festival, Charleston and Italy 1987–90, New York City Opera (La Bohème) 1989, San Francisco Opera, Metropolitan Opera, Paris Opera at Bastille, Teatro Colon, Buenos Aires (all Marriage of Figaro) 1991, Glyndebourne (Così fan tutte) 1992, La Scala Milan (Don Giovanni) 1993, Vienna State Opera (Marriage of Figaro) 1993, Lyric Opera of Chicago (Susannah) 1993, San Diego Opera (Eugene Onegin) 1994, Paris Opera 1996, Massenet's Thais at Nice and Gounod's Marguerite at the Met 1997, Floyd's Susannah at the Met 1999, Louise at Barbican Hall, London and the Marschallin at Covent Garden 2000; premiered Previn's A Streetcar Named Desire 1998; recital tour with Jean-Yves Thibaudet 2001–02; London Proms 2002, Dvořák's Rusalka in concert at Covent Garden 2003, Bellini's Il Pirata at the Met 2003; Fulbright Scholar to Germany 1984–85. *Honours:* George London Prize 1988, Richard Tucker Award 1990, Solti Prize, Acad. du Disque Lyrique 1996, Vocalist of the Year, (Musical America) 1997, Prize Acad. du Disque Lyrique 1998, Grammy Awards 1999, 2002,

creation of the dessert 'La Diva Renée' by Master Chef Daniel Boulud 1999, Classical BRIT Award for top-selling female artist 2003, Classical BRIT outstanding contribution to music award 2004. *Current Management:* M. L. Falcone Public Relations, 155 West 68th Street, Apt. 1114, New York, NY 10023-5817, USA. *Telephone:* (212) 580-4302. *Fax:* (212) 787-9638.

FLETZBERGER, Matthias; Pianist; b. 24 Aug. 1965, Vienna, Austria. *Education:* Hochschule für Musik, Vienna. *Career:* Musikverein Wien; Mozarteum Salzburg Festival; Festivals, Puerto Rico, Lockenhaus, Athens, Naples; Soloist, Israel Philharmonic, Orchestre de Bordeaux, R Schumann Philharmonie, Hochschulorchester Vienna, Orquesta Sinfonica de Chile; Recitals in Europe, America, Australia; Musical Assistant to Elisabeth Schwarzkopf and Renata Tebaldi; Musical Director and Principal Conductor of the Superstiltheater in Vienna. *Recordings:* Production of video clips for ORF; Radio and television recordings; Conductor of the television production of The Magic Flute at the Vienna Festival, 1991. *Honours:* Recipient, various prizes and awards. *Address:* Alban Bergweg 11, A 1130 Vienna, Austria.

FLIMM, Jürgen; Stage Director; b. 17 July 1941, Giessen, Germany. *Education:* Cologne University. *Career:* From 1971 has directed classic theatre productions throughout Germany; Opera debut with Al Grand Sole, Carico d'Amor by Luigi Nono, Frankfurt 1978; Further engagements with Così fan tutte, Don Giovanni, and Haydn's Orfeo, with Cecilia Bartoli (1995); Monteverdi's Poppea at the 1993 Salzburg Festival and Der Ring des Nibelungen at the Bayreuth Festival, 2000; Schubert's Alfonso und Estrella at the Wiener Festwochen, 2001, Wozzeck at La Scala, Der ferne Klang and Gounod's Roméo et Juliette for the Vienna Staatsoper; Season 2001–2002 with Fidelio at the New York Met and Haydn's Orfeo at Covent Garden; Intendant of Salzburg Festival, 2006–. *Honours:* Medaille für Kunst und Wissenschaft, Hamburg, 1991; Bundesverdienstkreuz, 1992; Konrad-Wolf-Preis, Berlin, 1995. *Address:* c/o Theateragentur Dr G. Hilbert, Maximilianstrasse 22, 80539 Munich, Germany.

FLOR, Claus Peter; Conductor; b. 16 March 1953, Leipzig, Germany; m. Sabine, 1985, 1 s. *Education:* Robert Schumann Conservatory, Zwickau, age 10; Franz Liszt Institute for Music, Weimar, 1966; Mendelssohn Bartholdy High School of Music, Leipzig, under Rolf Reuter; Studied with Rafael Kubelik and Kurt Sanderling. *Career:* Principal Conductor, Suhler Philharmonic, 1981; Guest Conductor, Gewandhaus Orchestra, Leipzig, Dresden Staatskapelle, Berlin Symphony Orchestra; Principal Conductor, Artistic Adviser, 1984, General Music Director, 1985, Berlin Symphony Orchestra, with world tour, 1988, at Edinburgh Festival, 1990; US debut, Los Angeles Philharmonic, 1985; Berlin Philharmonic debut, 1988, and concerts, Berlin Festival, 1993; Vienna Symphony Orchestra, 1991; New York Philharmonic debut, Principal Guest Conductor, Philharmonic, London, Principal Guest Conductor, Artistic Adviser, Tonhalle Orchestra, Zürich, 1991; Conducted Philharmonia at 1993 London Proms, Mendelssohn's 5th and Szymanowski's 3rd Symphonies, Bart ók's 3rd Piano Concerto; Regularly with Munich Philharmonic, Bayerische Rundfunk Symphony, Radio Symphony Orchestras of Frankfurt, Hamburg, Cologne and Berlin, Orchestre de Paris (debut with Bruckner's 7th Symphony), Royal Concertgebouw Amsterdam, Rotterdam Philharmonic Orchestra; Recent guest engagements include Israel Philharmonic, NHK Symphony, Tokyo; Has worked with Boston, St Louis, Dallas, Montreal, Cincinnati and London Symphonies, Minnesota and Philadelphia Orchestras, Royal Philharmonic; Opera engagements, Deutsche Oper Berlin, Bayerische Staatsoper, Semper Oper Dresden; Regular visitor, Berlin Staatsoper, recently conducting La Traviata, Der Freischütz, Lohengrin; Conducted new Schaaf production of Entführung at Staatsoper Hamburg, 1992–93; Toured Japan with Vienna Symphony Orchestra, 1997; Appearances at major European festivals, 1997; Die Zauberflöte at Cologne Opera, 1997. *Recordings include:* Mendelssohn: A Midsummer Night's Dream; Martinů symphonies; Cherubini Requiem; New Year's Day concert of popular classics; Franck Symphony in D minor, Dvořák Symphony No. 8, Royal Philharmonic; Mozart's Coronation Mass, Philharmonia; Shostakovich: 10th Symphony, Royal Concertgebouw. *Honours:* Mendelssohn Scholar, 1979; 1st Prizes, competitions, Poland, Denmark. *Address:* c/o Intermusica Artists Management, 16 Duncan Terrace, London N1 8BZ, England.

FLÓREZ, Juan Diego; Peruvian singer (tenor); b. 1973, Lima. *Education:* studied in Lima and at the Curtis Inst., Philadelphia. *Career:* debut in Matilde di Shabram at the Rossini Opera Festival, Pesaro 1996; signed exclusive contract with Decca Music Group 2001; appearances include La Scala, Milan (in Armide, Falstaff, Cappello di Paglia di Firenze, Barbiere di Siviglia, Nina Pazza per Amore, La Sonnambula), Comunale, Firenze (in Le Comte Ory, Falstaff), Covent Garden, London (in Elisabetta by Donizetti, Otello by Rossini, La Cenerentola), Konzerthaus, Vienna (in La Semiramide), Carlo Felice, Genoa (in La Cenerentola, Le Comte Ory), Rossini Opera Festival, Pesaro (in Matilde di Shabram, Il Signor Bruschino, Petite Messe Solennelle, La Cenerentola, Viaggio a Reims), Regio, Turin (in La Sonnambula, Maria Stuarda), La Maestranza, Seville (in Donizetti's Alahor in Granata), Filarmonico, Verona (in Italiana in Algeri), Vienna Staatsoper (in Barbiere di Siviglia, Italiana in Algeri, Gianni Schicchi), Opera di Roma (in Barbiere di Siviglia), Las Palmas (in Italiana in Algeri), Vienna Musikverein (in Stabat Mater), Bayerische Staatsoper (in Italiana in Algeri), Gran Teatro del Liceo, Barcelona (in Stabat Mater), Opera National, Paris (in Italiana in Algeri), Bilbao (in Barbiere di Siviglia); engaged at La Scala, Opéra Bastille, Covent Garden, Opera Châtelet, New York Met, Salzburg Festival and San Francisco Opera until 2005. *Honours:* Abbiati Prize 2000, Rossini d'Oro (Pesaro) 2000. *Current Management:* Ernesto Palacio, Via Donizetti 11, Lurano, Italy. *Telephone:* (35) 800623. *Fax:* (35) 4877812. *E-mail:* ernesto palacio .com. *Website:* www.ernesto palacio.com.

FLOROS, Constantin; Musicologist; b. 4 Jan. 1930, Salonika, Greece. *Education:* Studied composition and conducting, Vienna Music Acad. and musicology at Vienna University. *Career:* Professor of Musicology, Univ. of Hamburg, 1972–. *Publications:* 22 books including 3 vols on medieval notations; 3-vol. treatise on Gustav Mahler; 2 vols on Johannes Brahms; 2 vols on Alban Berg; Der Mensch, die Liebe und die Musik, 2000. *Address:* Schlangenkoppel 18, Hamburg, Germany.

FLOWERS, Kate; Singer (soprano); b. 1950, Cheshire, England. *Education:* Studied at the Northern School of Music and the Royal Northern College of Music; Further study in Paris. *Career:* Glyndebourne Festival from 1976, as Despina, Isotta in Die schweigsame Frau, Norina in La Fedeltà Premiata and the title role in The Cunning Little Vixen; Appearances with Opera North as Gretel, Despina, Susanna, Zerlina, Aennchen in Der Freischütz and Thérèse in Les mamelles de Tirésias; Polly Peachum in The Beggar's Opera for Scottish Opera; Micaela, Marenka and Jenůfa for the Welsh National Opera; Concert engagements in Europe, and on London's South Bank with the Philharmonia, the English Chamber Orchestra, Royal Philharmonic, Hallé Orchestra, London Philharmonic and the Academy of St Martin in the Fields; Sang Jenny in The Threepenny Opera for Opera North, 1990; Sang Mrs Ford in Falstaff with City of Birmingham Touring Opera, 1995; Sang Marianne in Der Rosenkavalier at Covent Garden, 2000. *Honours:* John Christie Award and Royal Society of Arts Scholarship, 1977. *Current Management:* Musicmakers International Artists Representation, Tailor House, 63–65 High Street, Whitwell, Hertfordshire SG4 8AH, England. *Telephone:* (1438) 871708. *Fax:* (1438) 871777. *E-mail:* musicmakers@compuserve.com. *Website:* www.operauk.com. *Address:* c/o The Grand Theatre, 46 New Briggate, Leeds LS1 6NH, England.

FLOYD, Carlisle; Composer; b. 11 June 1926, Latta, South Carolina, USA. *Education:* Studied at Converse College, Spartenberg, and with Ernest Bacon at Syracuse University (BA, 1946, MA, 1949); Piano with Rudolf Firkusny and Sidney Foster. *Career:* Teacher at Florida State University, 1947–76; M D Anderson Professor of Music at the University of Houston, 1976–; Susannah given New York Met premiere 1998. *Compositions:* Operas: Slow Dusk, 1949; Susannah, 1951; Wuthering Heights, 1958; The Passion of Jonathan Wade, 1962; The Sojourner and Mollie Sinclair, 1963; Markheim, 1966; Of Mice and Men, 1969; Bilby's Doll, 1976; Willie Stark, 1981; Cold Sassy Tree, 2000; Pilgrimage, song cycle, 1956; Piano Sonata, 1957; The Mystery, song cycle, 1960; Flower and Hawk, monodrama for soprano and orchestra, 1972; Citizen of Paradise, song cycle, 1983; A Time to Dance for baritone, chorus and orchestra, 1994. *Address:* c/o ASCAP, ASCAP Building, 1 Lincoln Plaza, New York, NY 10023, USA.

FLURY, Urs Joseph; Composer, Violinist, Conductor; b. 25 Aug. 1941, Bern, Switzerland. *Education:* Musicology, Art and Philosophy, Bern and Basel Universities; Conservatory Biel and Basel. *Career:* Stage, television and radio appearances in Switzerland and other European Countries. *Compositions:* Chamber Music: Fantasia and Sonata for violin solo; 2 Suites for violin and piano; Variations and Duo for violin and viola; Wind Quintet; Quartet for oboe, violin, viola and cello; Lieder; Orchestral Works: Vineta (Symphonic Poem); 3 Suites, The Little Mermaid, Concerto di carnevale for rag band and orchestra; 3 Fantasies on Carols for organ and strings; Instrumental Concertos: Concertino Veneziano for violin and strings; Concerto for violin in D; Cello Concerto; Vocal Music: Christmas Oratorio, 3 masses, salve regina. *Recordings:* As Violinist and Conductor: Cello Concerto; Concertino Veneziano, Concerto for violin in D, Sonata for Violin Solo; Suite Nostalgique, Christmas Oratorio, The Little Mermaid; Vineta; Lieder; Quartet for oboe, violin, viola and cello; Duo for violin and viola. *Publications:* Pahlen Kurt: Oratorien der Welt, 1985; Pahlen Kurt, Neue Musikgeschichte der Welt, 1990; Hartnack Joachim: Grosse Geiger unserer Zeit, 1983; Schweizer Chorkomponisten, 1999; Musik in Geschichte und Gegenwart, 2000. *Contributions:* Several professional journals and magazines. *Honours:* Music Prize, Canton Solothurn, 1993. *Address:* Zelglistrasse 5, 4562 Biberist, Switzerland. *Website:* www.urs-joseph-flury.ch.

FOCILE, Nuccia; Singer (Soprano); b. 25 Nov. 1961, Militello, Sicily, Italy. *Education:* Turin Conservatory. *Career:* Season 1986–87, as Oscar in Ballo in Maschera at Turin and Philadelphia, Thalia in Rameau's Platée at Spoleto, Elvira (L'Italiana in Algeri) at Schwetzingen and Mistress Ford in Salieri's Falstaff at Peralade; Further engagements at Buenos Aires as Musetta, Valencienne in The Merry Widow at Venice and Nannetta at Covent Garden, 1988; Rio de Janeiro in 1989 as Rossini's Rosina, and Oscar at Naples, and Ascanio in Pergolesi's Lo frate 'nnamorato at La Scala; Returned to Milan in 1990 as Servilia in La Clemenza di Tito and appeared at Bergamo as Eleanora in Donizetti's L'Assedio di Calais; Pesaro Festival, 1990, as Giulia in La Scala di Seta, Teatro Valle Rome as Countess in Paisiello's Don Chisciotte; Returned to Philadelphia, 1991, as Norina, sang Mozart's Susanna at Houston and appeared at the Opéra Bastille, Paris, as Ilia in Idomeneo; Barcelona and Dallas, 1992, as Adina in L'Elisir d'amore, Oscar at the Opéra Bastille, Paris, Tatiana at the Théâtre du Châtelet and Carolina (Matrimonio Segreto) at the 1992 Ravenna Festival; Sang Gounod's Juliette at the Paris Opéra-Comique, 1994; La Traviata for WNO, 1995; Season 1996–97 with Mozart's Ilia at Florence, Liù and Susanna for the Royal Opera, Mimi in Paris and Tel-Aviv, and Amelia Boccanegra for WNO; Season 2000–01 as Amelia Grimaldi at Wellington, Susanna for WNO and Mimi at the Met. *Recordings include:* Lo frate 'nnamorato (Pergolesi) and L'Assedio di Calais (Donizetti); Le nozze di Figaro, Così fan tutte and Don Giovanni with Charles Mackerras. *Honours:* Turin International Competition, 1983; Pavarotti Competition, Philadelphia, 1986. *Current Management:* Askonas Holt Ltd, Lonsdale Chambers, 27 Chancery Lane, London, WC2A 1PF, England. *Telephone:* (20) 7400-1700. *Fax:* (20) 7400-1799. *E-mail:* info@ askonasholt.co.uk. *Website:* www.askonasholt.co.uk.

FODOR, Eugene Nicholas, Jr; Violinist; b. 5 March 1950, Turkey Creek, Colorado, USA. *Education:* Studied with Harold Wippler, Denver; Ivan Galamian, Juilliard School of Music, New York, 1966–68; Josef Gingold, Harry Farbiman and William Primrose, Indiana University School of Music, diploma 1970; Jascha Heifetz, University of Southern California at Los Angeles, 1970–71. *Career:* Debut: Soloist at age 10 with Denver Symphony Orchestra; Soloist with major orchestras, 1974–; Recitalist, Performed at the White House, Washington DC 1974, 1986. *Honours:* 1st Prize, Merriweather Post Competition, 1967; Paganini Competition, Genoa, 1972; Co-2nd Prize, Tchaikovsky Competition, Moscow, 1974. *Current Management:* Hillyer International Inc, 888 Seventh Avenue Suite 300, New York, NY 10106, USA.

FOLAND, Nicolle; Singer (Mezzo-soprano); b. 1968, Des Moines, USA. *Education:* University of Northern Iowa. *Career:* Appearances with the Western Opera Theater on tour and in San Francisco as Adele and Rosalinda (1993), Donna Anna, and Tina in Argento's The Aspern Papers (Opera Center); San Francisco Opera, 1995–, as Kate Pinkerton, Clorinda (La Cenerentola), Gerhilde, Musetta, multiple roles in the premiere of Harvey Milk, and High Priestess in Aida; Guest with Indianapolis Opera as Adina in L'Elisir d'amore; Season 1996–97 as Micaela with Cincinnati Opera, Musetta with Los Angeles Music Center Opera and Seattle Opera; Micaela at San Francisco, 1998; Concerts include Placido Domingo special at San Francisco. *Address:* c/o San Francisco Opera, War Memorial Opera House, Van Ness Avenue, San Francisco, CA 94102, USA.

FÖLDES, Imre; Musicologist and Professor of History; b. 8 March 1934, Budapest, Hungary; m. Dr Zsuzsa Vadász, 1 d. *Education:* Graduate in composition, Ferenc Liszt Academy of Music, Budapest. *Career:* Musicologist, Professor of Music History and Theory, Ferenc Liszt Academy of Music, Department of Teachers Training Institute; Educational Lecturer on Music for the general public and radio; mem. Hungarian Musicians Association; Society for Propagating Sciences and Arts; Hungarian Ferenc Liszt Society; Hungarian Kodály Society; Lajos Bárdos Society. *Publications:* Harmincasok, Beszélgetések magyar zeneszerzökkel (Generation of The Thirties–Talks with Hungarian Composers), 1969; Life and Works of J. S. Bach, 1976; The Melody Dies Irae, 1977. *Contributions:* Az ének-zene tanítása; Muzsika; Parlando. *Honours:* Art Prize for Socialist Culture, 1974; Art Prize, National Council of Trade Unions, 1975; Szabolcsi Prize, 1977; Ferenc Erkel Prize, 1986. *Address:* Kresz Géza utca 26, 1132 Budapest, Hungary.

FOLDI, Andrew (Harry); Opera Director and Singer (Bass); b. 20 July 1926, Budapest, Hungary; m. Marta Justus, 19 May 1977, 1 s., 1 d. *Education:* MA, Musicology, 1948, PhD, Philosophy, 1945, University of Chicago. *Career:* Debut: La Bohème, 1950; Director of Music, Department of Adult Education, University of Chicago, 1949–61; Chairman of the Opera Department, DePaul University, 1951–57; Adviser, Netherlands Opera, 1977–80; Chairman and Artistic Director, Opera Department, Cleveland Institute of Music, 1981–91; Director, Chicago Lyric Opera Center for American Artists, 1991–95; Stage direction includes: The Barber of Seville (Atlanta Opera), 1989; The Merry Wives of Windsor, (Chicago Opera Theatre), 1990; La Tragédie de Carmen (Lyric

Opera Center, Chicago), 1992; Television performances of Il Barbiere di Siviglia, 1967, The Merry Widow, 1977, Elixir of Love, 1978, and Lulu, 1980; Other performances include: Alberich in the Ring and Schigolch in Lulu at the Metropolitan Opera, Bartolo in Il Barbiere de Siviglia, Vienna Staatsoper and San Francisco, Cardillac at La Scala; mem, American Musicological Society. *Recordings include:* Fiddler on the Roof, 1974; A Modern Psalm, 1975. *Publications:* Articles in Opera News, Alban Berg Society. *Address:* Chicago Opera Theater, 20 East Jackson Boulevard, Suite 1400, Chicago, IL 60604, USA.

FOLWELL, Nicholas, ARAM; singer (baritone); b. 1953, England. *Education:* Studied with Raimund Herincx; Royal Academy of Music and London Opera Centre. *Career:* Sang with Welsh National Opera from 1978 as Mozart's Figaro and Leporello, Pizarro, Melitone, Escamillo, The Poacher in The Cunning Little Vixen, Alberich in The Ring of the Nibelung (also at Covent Garden with Welsh National Opera, 1986) and Wagner's Melot and Klingsor; As guest with other British companies has sung the Villians in The Tales of Hoffmann, Tonio, Beckmesser, Schaunard, Creon and The Messenger in Oedipus Rex, Alberich and Papageno (English National Opera 1990); Sang in Weill's Seven Deadly Sins with the London Sinfonietta, 1988; Debuts in France, Italy, Austria and West Germany, 1987–90; Created Koroviev in York Höller's Master and Margarita in Paris, 1989; Covent Garden and Glyndebourne, 1990, as The Poacher (conducted by Simon Rattle) and Beethoven's Pizarro; Sang in The Weill Event at the 1990 Almeida Festival; Promenade Concerts, 1991, in Prokofiev's The Fiery Angel; Alberich in Rheingold (Opéra de Nantes), 1992; Mozart's Figaro for Glyndebourne Touring Opera at Sadler's Wells; Cecil, Maria Stuarda, Buxton Festival, 1993; Alberich in Siegfried at the Opéra de Nantes, 1993; Sang Sancho Panza in Don Quichotte for ENO, 1996; Van Tricasse in the premiere of Dr Ox's Experiment by Gavin Byars, ENO, 1998; Alberich in The Ring at the Longborough Festival, 2000–02. *Recordings:* Tristan and Isolde and Parsifal, conducted by Reginald Goodall; Poacher (Cunning Little Vixen); Pish-Tush (The Mikado). *Current Management:* Robert Gilder & Co., Enterprise House, 59–65 Upper Ground, London, SE1 9PQ, England. *Telephone:* (20) 7928-9008. *Fax:* (20) 7928-9755. *E-mail:* rgilder@robert-gilder.com.

FONDA, Jean (Pierre); Concert Pianist; b. 12 Dec. 1937, Boulogne-sur-Seine, Paris, France. *Education:* Virtuosity Prize, Piano Instrumentation, Geneva Conservatory, Switzerland. *Career:* Debut: Germany, 1958; Concert tours in Europe, South America, USA, Japan, Middle East, Turkey, elsewhere; Television in Paris, Munich; Major European Summer Festivals including Lucerne, Montreux, Edinburgh and Monte Carlo. Compositions; Cadenzas for various piano concertos. *Honours:* Recipient, Harriet Cohen Medal, London, 1968; Chevalier des Arts et des Lettres, awarded by French Minister of Culture, 1980. *Current Management:* Ingpen & Williams Ltd, 7 St George's Court, 131 Putney Bridge Road, London, SW15 2PA, England. *Address:* 20 Parc Château Benquet, Geneva, Switzerland.

FONDRAY, Alain; Singer (Baritone); b. 1932, Bangolet, France. *Education:* Studied in Paris. *Career:* Debut: Tonio in Pagliacci, Cherbourg, 1968; Sang in many provincial French opera houses in 1970s; Appearances at the Paris Opéra, 1985 and 1991, in Jerusalem by Verdi and as the High Priest in Samson et Delila; Royal Opera House, Covent Garden, in La Fanciulla del West, La Scala Milan as Amonasro, Metropolitan Opera in Cavalleria Rusticana; Sang Scarpia at San Francisco, returning in 1990 as Renato in Un Ballo in Maschera; Vienna Staatsoper and Barcelona, 1991, as the High Priest and Scarpia; Festival engagements include Orange, 1992, as Count Luna, and Bregenz, 1993, as Nabucco; Sang Massenet's Sancho Panza at Toulouse, 1992, and Count Luna at Orange; La Scala, 1993, as Scarpia; Sang in Massenet's Thais at Nice, 1997; Season 2000–01 as Iago at Brussels, Comte de Toulouse in Verdi's Jérusalem at Genoa, and in the premiere of Cecilia by Charles Chayne at Monte Carlo; Amonasro at Maastricht and Massenet's Hérode at St Etienne. *Recordings include:* Sancho Panza in Don Quichotte, conducted by Michel Plasson. *Address:* c/o Opéra de La Bastille, 120 Rue de Lyon, F-75012 Paris, France.

FONSECA, Regina; Singer (Mezzo-soprano); b. 1932, Portugal. *Career:* Sang at Düsseldorf, 1958–59, Bremen, Saarbrucken, Mainz, Kiel and Kassel, 1959–69; Engaged at the Mannheim National Theatre, 1969–81, Gelsenkirchen, 1981–82, Dortmund, 1983–84; Guest appearances at Cologne and Nuremberg, Naples, Hamburg (Brangaene in Tristan und Isolde, 1967), Monte Carlo and the Deutsche Oper Berlin, 1975; Sang Kundry at the 1976 Bayreuth Festival and the Composer in Ariadne auf Naxos at the Vienna Staatsoper; Deutsche Oper am Rhein, Düsseldorf, 1983; Other roles have included Wagner's Venus, Ortrud, Waltraute and Fricka, Strauss's Clytemnestra and Nurse, Countess Geschwitz in Lulu, Verdi's Eboli, Lady Macbeth and Azucena, Zenobia in Handel's Radamisto and the Countess in Zimmermann's Die Soldaten.

FONTANA, Bill; Composer, Sound Sculptor and Radio Producer; b. 25 April 1947, Cleveland, Ohio, USA. *Education:* Studied at John Carroll University and at the New School for Social Research; BA, 1970; Private study with Louis Lane and Philip Corner. *Career:* Composer-in-Residence and music director for the Toronto Free Theater, 1972–73; Compiled archive of natural sounds for the Australian Broadcasting Commission, 1975–78; Natural sound archive for the Oakland Museum in California, 1979; Assembled material for series of 365 programmes broadcast in San Francisco, 1983, as Soundscapes; Composer, sound sculptor and radio producer on various broadcasting stations. *Compositions include:* Phantom Clarinets, 1975; Handbell Sculptures, 1977; Wave Spiral, 1977; Music for a Resonant Space, 1977; Music for Carillon; Standing Wave Sculpture, 1978; Piano Sculpture, 1978; Ocarina Sculpture; Sound Sculpture for Brass Band; Space between Sounds, 1980; Flight Paths out to Sea; Grid Projections; Landscape Sculpture with Foghorns, 1981; Oscillating Steel Grids along the Brooklyn Bridge, 1983; Sound Recycling Sculpture, 1983; Soundscapes, 1983; Metropolis Köln, 1985; Vertical Water, 1991; Earth Tones, 1992; Spiralling Sound Axis, 1993; Sound Island, 1994; Wave Trains, 1996; Acoustical Visions of Venice, 1999; Wave Memories, 1999; Music Information Network Lyon, 2001. *Address:* c/o ASCAP, ASCAP Building, 1 Lincoln Plaza, Lincoln Center, New York, NY 10023, USA.

FONTANA, Gabriele; Singer (Soprano); b. 1958, Innsbruck, Austria. *Education:* Studied with Ilse Rapf at the Vienna Musikhochschule. *Career:* Sang Echo in Ariadne and Lauretta in Gianni Schicchi at the Opera Studio of the Vienna Staatsoper; Sang Pamina at Frankfurt; Hamburg Staatsoper from 1982, as Susanna, Servilia in La Clemenza di Tito and Sophie in Der Rosenkavalier; Sang in the premiere of Udo Zimmermann's Die Weisse Rose, revised version; Guest appearances in Bremen and Hanover; Glyndebourne, 1984, as the Countess in Le nozze di Figaro; Bregenz Festival, 1985, as Pamina; Vienna Staatsoper and Glyndebourne Festival, 1987, as Fiordiligi; Sang in Die weisse Rose at Innsbruck, 1989; Lieder recitals in London, Berlin, Brussels and Vienna; Season 1996–97 with First Lady in Die Zauberflöte at Amsterdam; Bruckner's Mass in F Minor, with Radio Symphony Orchestra of Leipzig, and with Düsseldorf Sinfoniker, 1997; Season 2000–01 at Hannover as Martinů's Katerina, Poppea, and Ursula in Mathis der Maler; Countess in Capriccio at Amsterdam. *Recordings include:* Schubert Lieder and Bach Cantatas; Idomeneo, Arabella; Gluck's Paride ed Elena; Die grossmütige Tomyris by Reinhard Keiser; Rheintochter in Das Rheingold with Dohnányi and the Cleveland Symphony Orchestra. *Address:* c/o Tiroler Landestheater, Rennweg 2, 6020 Innsbruck, Austria.

FONTANA, Sergio; Singer (Bass); b. 14 Feb. 1950, Berne, Switzerland. *Education:* Studied in Milan and with Mario del Monaco. *Career:* Stage career from 1972, with appearances in Geneva, Bologna, Florence, Milan, Metz and Berne; Roles have included Verdi's Zaccaria and Sparafucile, Wurm in Luisa Miller, Rodolfo in La Sonnambula, Sarastro, Timur in Turandot, Zuniga in Carmen and Biterolf in Tannhäuser. *Recordings include:* Macbeth; Madama Butterfly.

FONTYN, Jacqueline; Composer; b. 27 Dec. 1930, Antwerp, Belgium; m. Camille Schmit, deceased, 2 c. *Education:* Studied piano with Ignace Bolotine; Studied theory and composition with Marcel Quinet; Studied in Paris with Max Deutsch and in Vienna with Hans Swarowski. *Career:* Professor of Composition, Conservatoire Royal de Bruxelles, 1971–90; Has given lectures and seminars around the world; mem. Royal Academy of Belgium. *Compositions include:* Symphony Orchestra: Evoluon, 1972; Quatre Sites, 1977; In the Green Shade, 1991; On a Landscape by Turner, 1992; L'Anneau de Jade, 1996; Goeie Hoop, 1998; Au Fil des Siecles , 2000; Chamber or String Orchestra: Galaxie, 1965; Pour 11 Archets, 1971; Evoluon, 1972; Per Archi for string orchestra, 1973; Solo and Orchestra: Mouvements Concertants for 2 pianos and strings, 1957; Violin Concerto, 1974; Quatre Sites, 1976; Halo for harp and 16 instruments, 1978; Colinda, for cello and orchestra, 1991; Vent d'Est for classical accordion and strings; Es ist ein Ozean, concerto for flute, harpsichord and string orchestra, 1999; Symphonic Band: Frises, 1975; Creneaux, 1983; Aratoro, 1992; Blake's Mirror, 1993; Vocal Music: Psalmus Tertius for baritone, choir and orchestra; Ephemeres for mezzo-soprano, and orchestra, 1979; Alba for soprano, clarinet, cello, harp or percussion, piano, 1981; Pro and Antiverb(e)s for soprano and cello, 1984; Cheminement for soprano and 8 players, 1986; Rosa, Rosae for soprano, contralto, clarinet, violin, harp and piano, 1986; In the Green Shade, 1988; Rose des Sables for mezzo-soprano, speaker, female choir and orchestra, 1990; On a Landscape by Turner, 1992; Sieben Galgenlieder for soprano or mezzo-soprano, oboe or clarinet, cello and piano, 1994; L'anneau de Jade, 1996; Ich Kannte Meine Seele Nicht for 6 mixed voices or 6 female voices, 1997; Goeie Hoop, 1998; Au Fil des Siecles, 2000; Naïra for mezzo and piano, 2000; Solos and Duos: piano solo: Capriccio, 1954; Ballade, 1963; Le Gong, 1980; Aura, 1982; Spirales for 2 pianos, 1971; Six Climats for cello and piano, 1972; Controverse for bass clarinet and percussion, 1983; La Deviniere for violin and piano, 1987–88; Polissonnerie for percussion and piano, 1991; La Quinta Stagione for violin solo, 1991; Analecta for 2 violins, 1981; Instrumental and Chamber Music: Piano Trio, 1957; Horizons for string quartet, 1977; Zones for flute, clarinet, cello, percussion and piano, 1979; Meglio Tardi for flute, bass clarinet and piano, 1994; La Fenêtre Ouverte for traverso, gamba and harpsichord, 1996; Aube for flutes, guitar and piano, 1998; En luminures for organ, 2000; Koba, for violin and piano, 2000; Ein (Kleiner) Winternachtstraum, 2002; Battements D'ailes, 2001; Rivages Solitaires, 1989; Virus Alert, opera, 2002;. *Recordings:* Concerto pour violon et orchestre, Michaël Bezerchny, Orchestre National de Belgique, Georges Octors, DGG; Spirales, Ballade, AUa, Capriccio, Le Gong, Mosaici, Bulles, Robert Groslot and Daniel Blumenthal, CD Duchesne; Ephemeres, Per Archi, Halo, Psalmus Tertius, Koch Schwann/ Aulos; Créneaux, Blake's Mirror, Aratoro, Frises, Grand Orchestre d'Harmonie "Musique Royale des Guides", Norbert Nozy, WWM; Alba, Intermezzo, Mime 5, Fougeres, Filigrane sul Cuor Della Terra, Compagnon de la Nuit, Ottavo Records; Pro and Antverb(e)s, Sieben Galgenlieder, Le Gong, Six Climats, Mosaïques, Musica a Quattro, Mime 2, Cyprès. *Honours:* Prix Arthur Honegger de the Fondation de France, 1988; Awarded title of Baroness by the King of Belgium in recognition of her artistic merits; Commission from the Serge Koussevitzky Music Foundation, Library of Congress Washington; Awarded the title Baroness by the King of Belgium. *Address:* Rue Léon Dekaise 6, B1342 Limelette, Belgium. *E-mail:* performourmusic@wanadoo.com.

FORBES, Elizabeth; Critic, Writer on Music and Translator; b. 3 Aug. 1924, Camberley, Surrey, England. *Education:* Autodidactic. *Career:* Freelance Music Critic, Financial Times, 1970–80. *Publications:* Opera from A to Z, 1977; Observer's Book of Opera, 1982; Mario and Grisi, 1985; Old Scores, detective story; Translations for Nottingham University of Spontini's La Vestale, Auber's La Muette de Portici, Meyerbeer's Robert le Diable and Berwald's Queen of Golconda; Translations for Radio 3: Schubert's Claudine von Villa Bella, Brand's Maschinist Hopkins and Wagner-Régeny's Die Bürger von Calais. *Contributions:* Opera Now/The Independent; Encyclopedia of Opera, 1976; New Grove Dictionary of Music and Musicians, 1980, 2001; The Performing Arts, 1980; New Grove Dictionary of American Music, 1986; Whitaker's Almanack, 1991–2004; New Grove Dictionary of Opera, 4 vols, 1992; Viking Opera Guide, 1993; New Dictionary of National Biography, and The Collins Classical Music Encyclopedia, 2001. *Address:* Flat 3, 1 Bryanston Square, London W1H 2 DH, England.

FORBES, Elliot; American professor of music (retd); b. 30 Aug. 1917, Massachusetts, USA; m. Kathleen Brooks Allen, 7 June 1941, 3 d. *Education:* BA, 1941, MA, 1947 Harvard; Mozarteum, Salzburg, 1937; Westminster Choir College, 1946. *Career:* Debut: Conductor, Harvard Glee Club and Radcliffe Choral Society, 1958; Teacher at Cate School, California, 1941–43, Belmont Hill School, Massachusetts, 1943–45; Assistant Professor, 1947–54, Associate Professor, 1954–58, Princeton University; Professor of Music at Harvard University, 1958–84; mem, AAAS; American Musicological Society; College Music Association. *Publications:* Editor: Thayer's Life of Beethoven, 1964, Beethoven's Fifth, 1971, A History of Music at Harvard to 1972, 1988, A Report of Music at Harvard, 1972–90, 1993. *Contributions:* Articles in American Choral Review and Music Quarterly. *Honours:* Phi Beta Kappa; Signet Society Medal, 1985; Harvard Medal, 1991; Hon D.Mus, New England Conservatory, 1996, Harvard Univ., 2003. *Address:* 975 Memorial Drive, Apt 210, Cambridge, MA 02138, USA. *Telephone:* (617) 864-6787.

FORBES, Rupert Oliver; Singer (Tenor), Conductor and Stage Director; b. 27 Jan. 1944, London, England; m. Elisabeth Burnett, 10 July 1976, 2 s. *Education:* St John's College, Cambridge University; With Pierre Bernac, Paris, and Luigi Ricci, Rome; Opera Studio, Zürich; Arturo Merlini, Milan. *Career:* Sang at the Zürich Opera 1970–75; Engaged at the Stadttheater Basel from 1975, singing Mozart's Monostatos and Pedrillo, Jacquino in Fidelio, Tybalt in Roméo et Juliette, Lindoro, (Haydn's La Fedeltà Premiata), the comic roles in Les contes d'Hoffmann, Wagner's Steuermann, Hauptmann in Wozzeck (Berg) and Lord Barrat in Der Junge Lord; Guest appearances in Mannheim, Wiesbaden, Kassel, Bremen and Freiburg; Since 1990, freelance singer with Covent Garden, Scottish Opera, Glyndebourne, Rome, Wexford; Stage Director, Of Mice and Men (Carlisle Floyd) Opéra de Nantes; Many engagements in concert and oratorio, notably in works by Bach. *Recordings:* As tenor: Visitatio Sepulchri by James MacMillan; Salome by Strauss; Conductor: Fauré Requiem, Opera Choruses, My Fair Lady, Fiddler on the Roof, Oliver, Carmen. *Address:* 10 Mount Vernon Road, Edinburgh EH16 6BW, Scotland. *Telephone:* 0131 6643030.

FORBES, Sebastian; Composer and University Professor; b. 22 May 1941, Amersham, Buckinghamshire, England; m. (1) Hilary Spaight Taylor, 2 d., (2) Tessa Brady, 24 Sept 1983, 1 s., 1 d. *Education:* Royal Academy of Music, 1958–60; Kings College, Cambridge University, 1960–64; MA, Cantab; BMus, Cantab; D.Mus, Cantab; LRAM; ARCO; ARCM. *Career:* Treble Soloist, 1953–56; BBC Producer, 1964–67; Organist, Trinity College, Cambridge, 1968; Lecturer, Bangor University, 1968–72; Conductor, Aeolian Singers, 1965–69; Seiriol Singers,

1969–72; Horniman Singers, 1981–90; Lecturer, University of Surrey, 1972–; Professor of Music, 1981–; Compositions and commissions: Essay for clarinet and orchestra, Proms, 1970; Symphony, Edinburgh Festival, 1972; Sinfonia I–III, 1979, 1989, 1990; 8 ensemble sonatas, 1976–2001; Much organ and piano music including Sonata-Rondo for piano, 1996; Much chamber music including 5 string quartets, 1969, 1979, 1982, 1996, 2000; Numerous works of church music; mem, Performing Right Society. *Recordings:* String Quartet No. 1, 1971; Capriccio for organ, 1980; Bristol Mass, 1992; Hymn to St Etheldreda, 1996. *Publications:* String Quartet No. 1, 1970; Organ sonata, 1970; Violin Fantasy No. 2, 1980; Seasonal Roundelay, 1985; Numerous choral pieces, Cathedral Music. *Honours:* McEwen Memorial Prize, 1962; Clements Memorial Prize, 1963; Radcliffe Music Award, 1969; SPNM Carl Flesch Prize, 1980; ARAM, 1990; FRSA, 1997. *Address:* Octave House, Boughton Hall Avenue, Send, Woking, Surrey GU23 7 DF, England. *Website:* www.sebastianforbes.com.

FORBES-LANE, Andrew; Singer (Tenor); b. 1960, Walton-on-Thames. *Education:* Manchester University; Royal Northern College of Music, with Nicholas Powell. *Career:* Appearances with Opera North, City of Birmingham Touring Opera, and Crystal Clear Opera; English National Opera 1993, in the premiere of Jonathan Harvey's Inquest of Love; Roles have included Don José, Alfredo, Tamino, Pinkerton, Lensky, Jenik in The Bartered Bride, Ferrando, Rodolfo, and Tichon in Katya Kabanova; Glyndebourne Festival and Tour debut 1999, as Ringmaster in The Bartered Bride; Don Curzio in Le nozze di Figaro, 2000; Concerts with the RTE, Dublin, Hanover Band, London Proms, Salisbury Festival and in Antwerp. *Address:* c/o Glyndebourne Festival Opera, Glyndebourne, Lewes, Sussex BN8 5UU, England.

FORD, Andrew; Composer, Conductor, Writer and Broadcaster; b. 18 March 1957, Liverpool, England. *Education:* Graduated with honours, Composition, University of Lancaster, 1978; Composition study with Edward Cowie and John Buller; Doctor of Creative Arts, University of Wollongong, 1994. *Career:* Fellow in Music, University of Bradford, 1978–82; Founder, Music Director, Performer, Big Bird Music Theatre, 1982; Lecturer, Faculty of Creative Arts, University of Wollongong, New South Wales, Australia, 1983–95; Many world and Australian premieres with the Faculty's contemporary music ensemble SCAW, 1984–90, including Stockhausen's Stimmung, 1986; Conductor, Australia Ensemble, Seymour Group, Magpie Musicians, Australian Chamber Orchestra; Composer in residence, Bennelong Programme, Sydney Opera House, 1985; Own works played in Australia, Europe, America, South East Asia; Commissions; Writer and broadcaster on music; Featured composer, many festivals, including Aspekte, Salzburg, 1984, Ferrara 1985, Istanbul, Buffalo, Up-Beat to The Tate, Liverpool, Aspen, 1988; Composer in residence, Australian Chamber Orchestra, 1993–94, also Conductor. *Compositions:* Music theatre: Songs for the Lady Pan, 1981–83; From Hand to Mouth, 1984–85; Poe, opera, 1981–83; Whispers, 1990; Casanova Confined, 1995; Children's opera: The Piper's Promise, 1986–87; The World Knot, 1987–88; Orchestral: Concerto for Orchestra, 1980; Prologue, Chorale and Melodrama, 1981; Epilogue to an Opera, 1982; The Big Parade, 1985–86; Imaginings, piano and orchestra, 1991; The Widening Gyre, chamber orchestra, 1993; The Great Memory, cello and orchestra, 1994; The Furry Dance, 1999; Chamber ensemble: Sonata for 4 Instruments, 1978; Chamber Concerto No. 1, 1979, No.2 Cries in Summer, 1983; Bright Ringing Morning, 1981, Pit, 1981; Boatsong, 1982; Rant, 1984, Pea Soup, 1984; Four Winds, saxophone quartet, 1984; Foolish Fires, 1985; String Quartet, 1985; Deep Blue, 1986; On Canaan's Happier Shore, 1987; The Art of Puffing, 1989; Parabola, 1989; Ringing the Changes, 1990; Pastoral, 1991; Clarion, 1991; Dance Maze for large ensemble, 1996; Tattoo for 12 timpani and 4 pianos, 1998; The Unquiet Grave for viola and ensemble, 1998; Solo instruments: Les débris d'un rêve, piccolo and reverb, 1992; Portraits, piano, 1981; Like Icarus Ascending, violin, 1984; A Kumquat for John Keats, piano, 1987; Swansong, viola; Several vocal works; The Laughter of Mermaids, vocal ensemble; Insomnia, chorus and ensemble; Vocal: Harbour, tenor and strings. *Address:* c/o The Music Show, ABC Radio National, GPO Box 9994, Sydney, NSW 2001, Australia.

FORD, Anthony Dudley, BMus; British musician; b. 19 Sept. 1935, Birmingham; m. Diane Clare Anwyl; one s. one d. *Education:* Birmingham Univ. *Career:* Sr Lecturer in Music, Univ. of Hull 1964–99; conductor, Hull Bach Choir 1969–; freelance harpsichordist and pianist; mem. Royal Musical Asscn, Asscn of Univ. Teachers. *Compositions:* various songs and choral pieces. *Publications:* editions: Giovanni Bononcini: When Saul was King, Aeterna Fac, Arias from the Vienna Operas; Purcell: Fantazias and In Nomines; contrib. to The Musical Times, Proceedings of the Royal Musical Association, Current Musicology, Die Musik in Geschichte und Gegenwart, Dictionary of National Biography. *Honours:* Barber Post-graduate Scholarship in Music 1957. *Address:* 199 Victoria Avenue, Hull, HU5 3EF, England (home). *Telephone:* (1482) 343199 (home).

FORD, Bruce Edwin; American singer (lyric tenor); b. 15 Aug. 1956, Lubbock, TX; m. Hetty Ypma 1982; one s. *Education:* West Texas State University, Texas Tech University and the Houston Opera Studio. *Career:* debut, Houston Grand Opera, 1981; sang with Wuppertal Opera from 1983, as Belmonte, Rameau's Dardanus, Nureddin (Der Barbier von Bagdad) and Ramiro; Bordeaux 1985, as Almaviva; Minnesota Opera, 1985, as Tamino; Mannheim Opera from 1985, as Fenton, Tamino, Ferrando and Ramiro; Appeared at the 1986 Wexford Festival as Argirio in Rossini's Tancredi; Ferrando at the Salzburg Festival, 1993, and the Royal Opera House, Covent Garden, 1995; Sang Rinaldo in Armida by both Haydn and Rossini for VARA (Dutch Broadcasting), 1989; Berlioz's Lelio for the Düsseldorf Symphonic; Sang Agorante in Ricciardo e Zoraide at Pesaro, 1990; Also in Pesaro: Otello (Rossini), 1991; Almaviva, 1992; Antenore (Zelmira), 1995; Also heard as Uberto in La Donna del Lago at Düsseldorf and Rodrigo (Rossini Otello) for San Francisco Opera, 1994; Covent Garden debut 1991, Almaviva; La Donna del Lago (Uberto) at La Scala with Muti, 1992; Mitridate (title role) at Covent Garden, Amsterdam and Salzburg, 1991, 1993, 1997; Ernesto (Don Pasquale), Chicago Lyric Opera, 1995; Almaviva, Met debut, 1997; Season 1999–2000 as Otello in a new production of Rossini's opera at Covent Garden; Sang arias from Rossini's Zelmira and Elisabetta, Edinburgh Festival, 2002, Season 2002–03 as Mozart's Tito at Covent Garden and Idomeneo in Florence; mem. ISM, AGMA. *Recordings include:* Adriano in Crociato in Egitto by Meyerbeer; Giasone in Medea in Corinto by Mayr; Enrico in Rosmonda d'Inghilterra by Donizetti; Agorante in Ricciardo e Zoraide, Rossini; Solo album, Romantic Heroes; Horace in Le Domino Noir, Auber; Edgardo in Lucia di Lammermoor; Messiah, Imene in Bertoni's Orfeo; Ghernando in Rossini's Armida; Enrico in Donizetti's Maria de Rudenz; Fenimoore in Pacini's Maria Regina d'Inghilterra; An English language recording of The Barber of Seville; Solo album of arias. *Current Management:* Athole Still International Management, Forresters Hall, 25–27 Westow Street, London, SE19 3RY, England. *Telephone:* (20) 8771-5271. *Fax:* (20) 8768-6600. *Website:* www.atholestill.com.

FORD, Trevor, ARAM, ARSCM, FRSA; Music Administrator, Editor and Flautist; b. 28 Nov. 1951, London, England; m. Marianne Barton, 8 Dec 1979, 2 s. *Education:* Recital Diploma, Royal Academy of Music 1972–76. *Career:* orchestral flautist 1976–; Personnel Man. English Sinfonia 1979–2003; Orchestral Man. Philomusica of London 1981–2002, Midland Philharmonic 1982–96, Ambache Chamber Orchestra 1984–89; Gen. Man. English Festival Orchestra 1984–; Bd Dirs Asscn of British Orchestras 1985–88, mem. of Council 2004–; Dir of Music, St John's Church, Palmers Green 1992–2003; Chair. Organists' Working Party 1993–95; Treasurer Inc. Soc. of Musicians 1996–2003; mem. of Council and Exec., Under-Treasurer Royal Coll. of Organists 1995–2004; Prof. Guildhall School of Music and Drama 1996–; Prof. Birmingham Conservatoire 1999–2004; mem. of Council Royal School of Church Music 2001–; mem. Musicians' Union, Inc. Soc. of Musicians, Asscn of British Choral Dirs, Church Music Soc.. *Publications:* editor: The Musician's Handbook 1986, 2nd edition 1991, 3rd Edition 1996, The Art of Auditioning 1988, Church Music Quarterly 1989–2000. *Honours:* Hon RCO. *Address:* 151 Mount View Road, London N4 4JT, England.

FORRESTER, Maureen; Singer (Contralto); b. 25 July 1930, Montreal, Quebec Province, Canada. *Education:* Studied with Barnard Diamant in Montreal. *Career:* Debut: Sang in concert at Montreal, 1953; Alto solo in Mahler's 2nd Symphony at New York Town Hall, conducted by Bruno Walter, 1956; Many concert appearances with leading US orchestras in Boston, San Francisco, Philadelphia and elsewhere; Tours to Netherlands, Germany, France, Belgium, Spain and Scandinavia; Sang Gluck's Orpheus in Toronto, 1961, and appeared as Cornelia in Giulio Cesare to open New York City Opera's first season in Lincoln Center (1966); San Francisco debut, 1967, as La Cieca in La Gioconda, Metropolitan Opera, 1975, as Erda in Das Rheingold; Covent Garden, 1971, as Fricka in Der Ring des Nibelungen; Paris, 1981, in Massenet's Cendrillon; Has also sung at opera houses in Canada and South America; Other roles have included Mistress Quickly, Monteverdi's Arnalta, Brangaene (Tristan and Isolde), Ulrica, and the Witch in Hansel and Gretel; Sang with the Bach Aria Group, 1964–74, and toured the USA with the Montreal Symphony, 1982, with Les Nuits d'Été by Berlioz; Pittsburgh Opera, 1989, as Clytemnestra in Elektra; Sang at San Diego and La Scala Milan, 1990, as Mme de Croissy in Dialogues des Carmélites and the Countess in The Queen of Spades; mem, Chairman of the voice department at the Philadelphia Academy, 1966–71; Chairman of the Canada Council, 1984. *Recordings:* Giulio Cesare; Beethoven's 9th and the Alto Rhapsody; Handel's Serse and Rodelinda; Elektra. *Address:* c/o Pittsburgh Opera Inc, 711 Penn Avenue, 8th Floor, Pittsburgh, PA 15222, USA.

FORSBERG, Bengt; Pianist; b. 1950, Sweden. *Education:* Gothenburg Music Academy; London, with Peter Feuchtwanger; Copenhagen with Herman D. Koppel. *Career:* Chamber musician, and accompanist to leading soloists; Chamber Music Society of Lincoln Center, New York; concerts 1999–2000 with Anne Sofie von Otter, featuring music by Korngold; Further engagements at the Wigmore Hall, London, Lisbon, Paris Châtelet, Graz and Gothenburg; Season 1999–2000 with Stravinsky's Piano Concerto and Medtner's 2nd Concerto, with the Royal Philharmonic, in Stockholm; Other repertoire includes Mozart and Martinů Concertos, Bach's Well-Tempered Klavier, and works by Grieg, Sibelius, Fauré and Franck. *Recordings include:* Songs by Stenhammar and Sibelius, with Anne Sofie von Otter; Schumann's Frauenliebe und Leben, Lieder by Berg, Korngold, Strauss and Schubert; Songs by Grieg and Weill; Albums with Mats Lidström, cello. *Address:* c/o IMG Artists, Lovell House, 616 Chiswick High Road, London, W4 5RX.

FORSBERG, Roland; Director of Music and Organist; b. 18 Sept. 1939, Stockholm, Sweden; m. (1) Margaretha Widlund, 1967–91, (2) Lisbeth Carlborg, 1992, 2 s., 1 d. *Education:* Professor of Music, Royal Academy of Music, Stockholm, 1961; Higher Organist Exam, 1963; Higher Cantor Exam, 1964; Diploma, Organist, 1968. *Career:* Director of Music: Norrmalm Church, Stockholm, 1964–89; Organists, Immanuel Church, Stockholm, 1989–; Musical Expert, Swedish State Psalm Committee, 1976–86; mem, Kammarmusikföreningen Samtida Musik; Föreningen Svenska Tonsättare, Stockholm. *Compositions include:* Liten Svit for organ, 1959; Passacaglia for organ, 1960; Verbum Christi, vocal, 1963; 12 Sacred Songs, 1964; Musica solenne for organ, 1965; Orgeljojk for 2 organs, 1975; Sicut Cervus Organ Symphony, 1977; Sonata lapponica for violin and piano, 1980; Sonatina da cappella for violin and organ, 1983; 3 piano sonatas; Concertos for flute and oboe; Sacred concertos for solo voices and organ; Songs; Hymns; Motets; Cantatas; Oratorios; Masses and other choral works; 8 organ suites; Psalm sonata for mixed chorus (English words), 1984; Credo Triptych for organ, 1988; Memoria for violin and piano or organ, 1988; Symphonic Pictures for Archipelago for organ and brass orchestra, 1995; Missa in Millennium Immanuel, 1998–99. *Recordings:* Kärlekens musik; Tre orglar i Västervik; En gång blir allting stilla; Sjögrens Legender; Autography, Swedish Composers play their own works; Orgelmusik i Sjövik; Skärgårdsorgel, Archipelago the Mid-Eighteenth Century Organ of Utö. *Publications:* Editions: Sjung svenska kanon, 1977; Fader wår (Gustaf Duben), 1980; Seven Sacred Songs (Anders Bond), 1981; Organ Fantasy (Otto Olsson), 1983; Two Organ Pieces (Anders Bond), 1985; 88 Preludes (Anders Bond); Organ Preludes I–III; Concerto grosso g-moll transcription for organ (Archangelo Corelli); Sinfonia IB26 transcription for organ solo (Johan Helmich Roman); Sinfonia in G Major, 1994. *Honours:* Numerous including Composers Scholarships, STIM, Stockholm, 1974, 1981, 1985; Föreningen Svenska Tonsättare, 1996. *Address:* Dalarö Prästgård, 13054 Dalarö, Sweden.

FORST, Judith; Singer (Mezzo-soprano); b. 7 Nov. 1943, British Columbia, Canada. *Education:* Studied with Bliss Hebert in New York and with Robert Keyes in London. *Career:* Debut: Vancouver, 1967, as Lola in Cavalleira Rusticana; Sang at the Metropolitan Opera from 1968, as Hansel, Siebel and Lola; San Francisco debut, 1974, as Suzuki; Appearances at New Orleans, Santa Fe, Miami (Donna Elvira, 1988), Detroit and Toronto, 1987, as Preziosilla; Seattle, 1991, as Dorabella and Jane Seymour in Anna Bolena; Returned to the Met, 1991, as Donna Elvira; Other roles include Mozart's Cherubino, Olga (Eugene Onegin), Maddalena, Octavian, Carmen and Cenerentola; Sang Andromaca in the first British performance (concert) of Rossini's Ermione, Queen Elizabeth Hall, 1992; Sang Gertrude in Thomas' Hamlet at San Francisco, 1996; Kostelnicka in Jenůfa at Cincinnati, 1998; Season 2000 as Clytemnestra in Elektra at Santa Fe and Augusta Tabor in The Ballad of Baby Doe, at San Francisco; Season 2001–2002 performances in Strauss's Arabella and Humperdinck's Hansel und Gretel at the Met and Tchaikovsky's Pique Dame with the Canadian Opera, 2002; Season 2003 engagements include performances with Sante Fe, Pittsburgh, Dallas, San Diego and New York Opera Companies. *Honours:* Winner, Metropolitan Auditions; Juno Award for best classical recording of the year for a CD of Modern Canadian Music, 2001; Hon. DLitt from Univ. of BC, 1991; Hon. DMus from the Univ. of Victoria, 1995; Inducted into the Order of Canada, 1992; Inducted into the Order of BC, 2001; Freeman of the City of Port Moody, BC. *Address:* c/o Metropolitan Opera, Lincoln Center, New York, NY 10023, USA.

FORSTER, Andreas; Singer (Baritone); b. 17 Sept. 1949, Naumberg, Germany. *Education:* Studied in Berlin and in Essen with Gladys Kuchta. *Career:* Debut: Detmold, 1974, as Schaunard in La Bohème; Sang at Kaiserslautern, 1975–76, Saarbrucken, 1976–78, Nuremberg, 1978–88; Staatstheater Hanover from 1988; Guest appearances at the Staatsoper Berlin, Düsseldorf, Cologne, Dortmund, Stuttgart, Munich, Wiesbaden and Orlando, Florida, USA; Roles have included Verdi's Nabucco, Rigoletto, Macbeth and Simon Boccanegra, Germont, Renato, Iago and Amonasro, Rodrigo, Luna, Donizetti's Enrico, Belcore and Dulcamara, Gerard, Escamillo, Eugene Onegin, Wolfram, Amfortas, Marcello, Olivier in Capriccio and Mozart's Don Giovanni and Count; Concert engagements in works by Bach, Handel, Beethoven, Brahms, Mahler and Penderecki; Lieder recitals and broadcast concerts in

Germany, France and Italy; Sang Grigoris in The Greek Passion and Telramund in Lohengrin at Hannover, 2000. *Address:* Niedersachische Staatstheater, Opernplatz 1, 30159 Hannover, Germany.

FORSYTH, Malcolm (Denis); Composer and Conductor; b. 8 Dec. 1936, Pietermaritzburg, South Africa; m. (1) Lesley Eales, 1965, divorced 1984, one d. *Education:* BMus, 1963, MMus, 1966, D.Mus, 1972, University of Cape Town; Conductors class, Canford Summer School of Music, 1980–84. *Career:* Conductor: Chamber Choir and Orchestra, University of Cape Town, 1962–64; St Cecilia Orchestra, 1977–86; Edmonton Wind Sinfonia, 1978–79; West Wind Chamber Ensemble, 1980–83; Chamber Choir, University of Witwatersrand, 1983; Guest Conductor: Cape Town, CAPAB and Edmonton Symphony Orchestras, Alberta Ballet Orchestra, National Orchestra, SABC, Johannesburg; As Trombonist: Assistant Principal Cape Town Symphony Orchestra, 1961–67; Co-Principal, CAPAB Symphony Orchestra, 1971–72; Principal, Edmonton Symphony Orchestra, 1973–80; Junior Lecturer, College of Music, University of Cape Town, 1967; Assistant Professor, 1968–71, Associate Professor, 1971–77, Professor of Music, 1977–, Division Chairman, Concert Activity Chairman, 1984–86, Artistic Director, Music Department, 1987–89, McCalla Professor, 1990–91, University of Alberta, Edmonton, Canada; Visiting Professor, Cape Town and Witwatersrand Universities; Composer-in-Residence: Banff Centre, 1975–78; Festival of the Sound, 1991; University of Alberta, 1997; Juror; Commissions include Canada Council, CBC and University of Cape Town; Fellow of the Camargo Foundation, Cassis, France, 1993; Composer-in-Residence, University of Alberta, 1996–; Saskatchewan New Music Festival, 1997. *Compositions:* Works for orchestra, band, ensembles, piano, vocal solos and choir including Valley of a Thousand Hills for orchestra, 1989; These Cloud Capp'd Towers for trombone and orchestra, 1990; Electra Rising for cello and chamber orchestra, 1995. *Recordings:* Electra Rising, 1997; Soaring with Agamemnon. 1998. *Honours:* Composer of the Year, Canada, 1989; JUNO Winner for Best Classical Composition, 1987, 1995, 1998; Queen's Jubilee Medal 2003; Order of Canada 2003. *Current Management:* BMG Ariola, Counterpoint Musical Services. *Address:* 9259 Strathearn Drive, Edmonton, Alberta T6C 4E1, Canada.

FORTE, Allen; Music Theorist; b. 23 Dec. 1926, Portland, Oregon, USA. *Education:* Studied at Columbia University, MA, 1952. *Career:* Taught at Teachers' College of Columbia, 1953–59; Member of theory faculty at Mannes College, 1957–59; Yale University from 1959, Professor from 1968; Editor of the Journal of Music Theory, 1960–67; President of the Society for Music Theory, 1977. *Publications include:* Schenker's Conception of Musical Structure, 1959; Bartók's 'Serial' Composition, 1960; The Compositional Matrix, 1961; Tonal Harmony in Concept and Practice, 1962; A Theory of Set-complexes for Music, 1964; A Program for the Analytical Reading of Scores, 1966; Computer-implemented Analysis of Musical Structure, 1966; Music and Computing the Present Situation, 1967; The Structure of Atonal Music, 1970; The Harmonic Organization of The Rite of Spring, 1978; The Atonal Music of Anton Webern, 1998; Olivier Messiaen as Serialist, 2002. *Address:* c/o Yale University, Music Department, New Haven, CT 06520, USA.

FORTE, Cinzia; Singer (Soprano); b. 1968, Italy. *Career:* Appearances at La Scala Milan as Lisette in La Sonnambula, as Pamina at La Coruña, Gilda (Rigoletto) in Venice and Lucia di Lammermoor; Teti in Rossini's Le nozze di Teti e di Peleo at Pesaro, Traviata in Modena and Lisette in Puccini's La Rondine at Covent Garden (2002); Baroque repertory includes Vivaldi's Farnace (at Madrid), Messiah, Te Deum by Charpentier and Pergolesi's Stabat Mater; Season 2002–03 as Corina in Rossini's Il viaggio a Reims in Oviedo, Lucia in Tokyo and Adina in L'elisir d'amore at Venice; Other roles include Susanna and Musetta. *Address:* c/o Ouverture, Via Braccianese Claudia 44, 1–00062, Bracciano, Rome, Italy.

FORTIN, Lyn; Singer (Soprano); b. 28 April 1962, Quebec, Canada. *Education:* Studied in Quebec and with Martial Singher. *Career:* Sang with Canada Piccola Opera from 1985; Quebec Opera, 1987 and 1989, Susanna and Gilda; Montreal Opera from 1990, as Offenbach's Olympia, Sophie in Der Rosenkavalier, Gounod's Juliette and Leila in Les pêcheurs de perles (1996); Philadelphia, 1991, as Norina in Don Pasquale, Portland Opera, 1994, as Micaela in Carmen; Season 1998 as Donizetti's Adina at Seattle and Mozart's Countess at Montreal; Sang Donna Anna with Scottish Opera, 2001; Frequent concert appearances. *Address:* c/o L'Opéra de Montréal, 260 de Maisonneuve Boulevard West, Montréal, Quebec H2X 1Y9, Canada.

FORTIN, Viktor; Austrian composer and academic; b. 14 May 1936, Fohnsdorf, Steiermark; m.; one s. *Education:* Steiermarkisches Landes Konservatorium; University of Vienna; Academie für Musik und Kunst, Graz. *Career:* mem. President of Steirischer Tonkunstlerbund; Osterreichischer Komponistenbund. *Compositions include:* Appalachian sonata for flute and piano 1970, Happy Suite for strings, piano and percussion 1978, Maja's Orchestra for strings and piano, Ohhh Pinocchio!, Opera House, Graz 1994–95, Tartu, Estonia 1999, Kraków, Poland 2005, Concerto for speaker and orchestra, with texts from Mozart letter, Graz 1994, Lublin 1997, Quito, Ecuador 1998, Archibalds Adventures for 2 speakers and orchestra 1997, 1998, Cairo and Graz 1999 5 Love Songs with texts from Erich Fried, Marginals to the Spring 1986, Der Kleine Klabautermann, Blacksmith Variations, Concerto for soprano recorder and strings, Hafer Quartet. *Recordings include:* Ohhh Pinocchio! 1994, Viktor Fortin and Friends 1996, Archibald's Adventure 2000, Missa duri montis 2003, Concertino for bassoon & strings 2004, Concert amusant (flute & strings) 2004. *Publications:* Doblinger, Vienna, Concert for soprano recorder and string orchestra, 1992, Brass Light, Not Easy, Moeck Germany, Lambsborner Nuesse for recorder-orchestra, 1997. *Contributions:* Musik aus Osterreich, 1998. *Honours:* Goldenes Ehrenzeichen des Landes Steiermark 1995. *Address:* 8054 Graz, Halmweg 13, Austria (home). *Telephone:* (316) 296207 (home). *E-mail:* fortin@aon.at (home). *Website:* www.fortin.at (home).

FORTUNATO, D'Anna; Singer (Mezzo-soprano); b. 21 Feb. 1945, Pittsburgh, Pennsylvania, USA. *Education:* Studied with Frederick Hagel and Gladys Miller at the New England Conservatory, 1965–72; Further study with Phyllis Curtin at the Berkshire Music Center. *Career:* Concert appearances in Pittsburgh, Detroit, Louisville, Atlanta and Minnesota; Recitals with the Chamber Music Society of Lincoln Center and with the Boston Musica Viva ensemble; Taught at Longy School of Music, Cambridge, 1974–82; Member of the Liederkreis Ensemble; European debut, Paris, 1980, as Purcell's Dido with the Boston Camerata; Sang in the premiere of John Harbison's opera Full Moon in March, New York, 1979; New York recital debut, 1981; New York City Opera debut, 1983, as Ruggiero in Handel's Alcina. *Honours:* Co-winner, Naumburg Chamber Music Prize, 1980. *Address:* c/o New York City Opera, Lincoln Center, New York, NY 10023, USA.

FORTUNE, George; American singer (baritone) and voice teacher; b. 13 Dec. 1935, Boston, Massachusetts. *Education:* Brown University, Providence, Boston University; vocal studies with Todd Duncan. *Career:* debut: Ulm 1960, as Fluth in Die Lustigen Weiber von Windsor; guest appearances in Bordeaux, Brussels, Strasbourg, Hamburg and Munich; Glyndebourne 1964, as the Count in Le nozze di Figaro; Santa Fe 1967, in the US premiere of Henze's Boulevard Solitude; Member of the Deutsche Oper Berlin from 1967; roles include Mozart's Figaro and Guglielmo, Rigoletto, Giulio Cesare, Iago, Amonasro, Posa, Scarpia, Gerard and Wolfram; further appearances in Dusseldorf, Frankfurt, Milan and Zürich; debut at the Metropolitan Opera New York in 1985 with Tonio, further parts include Jack Rance and Alfio; sang Scarpia at the Teatro San Carlos, Lisbon 1988, the High Priest in Samson et Dalila at the Deutsche Oper Berlin 1989; Barnaba in La Gioconda 1998; season 2000–01 as Scarpia at the Prague State Opera, Gounod's Capulet at Strasbourg, Count Luna for the Deutsche Oper; many concert engagements. *Recordings include:* Thérèse by Massenet, Olympie by Spontini, Christus by Liszt, Armida by Dvorak. *Address:* c/o Konzert-Direktion Hans Alder, Auguste-Viktoria-Strasse 64, D-14199 Berlin; Keithstrasse 12, D- 12307 Berlin, Germany (home). *E-mail:* fortune@p-soft.de (home).

FORTUNE, Nigel (Cameron); Musicologist; b. 5 Dec. 1924, Birmingham, England. *Education:* Studied Music and Italian at Birmingham University (BA, 1950) and researched Italian monody at Cambridge under Thurston Dart (PhD, 1954). *Career:* Music Librarian at London University, 1956–59; Lecturer in Music at Birmingham University, 1959–69, Reader in Music from 1969; Secretary of the Royal Musical Association, 1957–71, Vice-President, 1991; Member of editorial committee, Musica Britannica, 1975–77; Senior member, editorial committee, New Grove Dictionary of Music and Musicians, 1970–80; Editorial work for the New Oxford History of Music. *Publications include:* Continuo Instruments in Italian Monodies, 1953; Italian Secular Song from 1600 to 1635, 1954; Italian 17th Century Singing, 1954; Purcell's Autographs (with F B Zimmerman), 1959; A New Purcell Source, 1964; Philip Rosseter and his Songs, 1965; Editor, with Denis Arnold, The Monteverdi Companion, 1968, and The Beethoven Companion, 1971; Opera and Church Music, 1630–1750 (editor with Anthony Lewis), 1975; Editions of John Dowland and sacred music by Purcell (with Thurston Dart and Anthony Lewis).

FOSS, Lukas; American composer, conductor and pianist; b. 15 Aug. 1922, Berlin, Germany; m. Cornelia Brendel, 1950, 1 s., 1 d. *Education:* Studies, Curtis Institute of Music (piano, composition, conducting), Yale University (composition), Berkshire Music Center (composing and conducting). *Career:* Pianist, Boston Symphony Orchestra 1944–50, (premiered Hindemith's Four Temperaments 1944), Professor of Conducting and Composition, University of California 1953–62; Music Director, Ojai Festival, Buffalo Philharmonic Orchestra 1963–70; Founder-Director, Center for Creative and Performing Arts, SUNY, Buffalo 1963; Music Director, Brooklyn Philharmonic 1971–90; Conductor, Jerusalem Symphony Orchestra 1972–76; Music Director, Milwaukee Symphony Orchestra 1981–86; Composer in Residence,

Tanglewood, summers 1989, 1990; Professor, Boston University 1992–; mem. American Academy of Arts and Letters. *Compositions:* over 120 including operas The Jumping Frog 1949 and Griffelkin 1955; Solo for piano 1982, 4 Symphonies, No. 3 1991, No. 4 1995, Renaissance concerto for flute and orchestra 1986; chamber: 4 string quartets 1947, 1973, 1975, 1997, Brass Quintet 1978, Percussion Quartet 1983, Tashi for clarinet, string quartet and piano 1986; piano pieces; choral music; War and Peace for organ 1996. *Recordings:* over 30 works recorded, some of which were also conducted by Foss. *Publication:* A Bio-bibliography, USA 1991. *Honours:* New York Music Critics Circle Awards 1944, 1954; Guggenheim Fellowships 1945, 1960; Fellow, American Academy, Rome 1950–51; Fulbright Grant 1950–52; Brandeis University, Creative Arts Award 1983; 11 Honorary Doctorates. *Address:* 1140 Fifth Avenue, New York, NY 10128, USA (home). *Telephone:* (212) 722-8003.

FOSTER, Anthony; Composer; b. 11 April 1926, Gravesend, Kent, England; m. Barbara Foster, 26 July 1952, deceased 1991, 1 d. *Education:* LRAM, ARCO; Piano with Anne Collins, Arthur Tracy Robson, Organ with John Cook, John Webster, Composition with Gordon Jacob, Richard Arnell. *Career:* Composed many works, secular and sacred for solo and choral voices, solo instruments and orchestra; Composed incidental music for BBC productions; mem, The British Academy of Composers and Songwriters; The Performing Right Society. *Recordings:* Jonah and the Whale, Harrow School of Young Musicians, Royal Albert Hall, London, 1983; A Child is Born, 1987, Christ the Lord is Risen Again, 1997, Child of Heaven, 1999, Chichester Cathedral Choir, directed by Alan Thurlow; Jubilate Deo for Organ, Alan Thurlow, Organist, Chichester Cathedral, 1988; Magnificat, Blessed Virgin Mary Service, Carlisle Cathedral Choir, directed by Jeremy Suter 2000. *Publications:* 55 published works (including all the above-mentioned titles). *Honours:* Honorary Vice-President, Brighton Schools Music and Drama Association, 1977. *Address:* 1 Cawley Road, Chichester, West Sussex PO 19 1UZ, England.

FOSTER, Catherine; Singer (Soprano); b. 1975, Nottingham, England. *Education:* Studied at Royal Northern College of Music and the National Opera Studio. *Career:* Appearances as Britten's Governess in Nottingham, Donna Anna at Dartington and Musetta for the Mananan Festival; Welsh and English National Operas with the Queen of Night; Concerts include Mozart's Requiem and C Minor Mass, Schubert's Mass in G, Elijah, the Brahms Requiem and Haydn's Theresienmesse, 1999–2000 season. *Honours:* Dame Eva Turner Award, 1997; Mario Lanza Opera Prize. *Address:* Harlequin Agency, 203 Fidlas Road, Cardiff CF4 5NA, Wales.

FOSTER, Donald H.; American professor emeritus; b. 30 April 1934, Detroit, Michigan, USA. *Education:* BS, Wayne State University, 1956; MMus, 1960, PhD, 1967, University of Michigan. *Career:* Music Faculty, Olivet College, Michigan, 1960–67; Professor of Musicology, College-Conservatory of Music, University of Cincinnati, Ohio, 1967–99; mem, American Musicological Society; American Association of University Professors. *Publications:* L'histoire de la femme adultère by Louis-Nicolas Clérambault, 1974; Louis-Nicolas Clérambault 1676–1749: Two Cantatas for Soprano and Chamber Ensemble, 1979; Symphonies concertantes of Jean-Baptiste Davaux; Overtures of Franz Beck; Jean-Philippe Rameau: A Guide to Research, 1989; Sourcebook for Research in Music (co-author) 1993, revised edn 2005. *Contributions:* Symphony Orchestras of the USA: Selected Profiles, 1986; Opera Quarterly; Recherches sur la musique française classique; The Diapason; Acta Musicologica; Current Musicology; L'orgue–cahiers et mémoires. *Honours:* Fulbright Grant, 1962. *E-mail:* dfoster@fuse.net. *Address:* 393 Amazon Avenue, Cincinnati, OH 45220, USA.

FOSTER, Jillian; Singer (Soprano); b. 1970, England. *Education:* Studied at the Royal Academy of Music. *Career:* Has sung with Kent Opera, Wexford Festival, Dublin Grand Opera and the Richard Strauss Society; Roles have included Tosca, Mimi, Donna Elvira, Violetta, Agathe and Arabella; Sang Garsenda in Francesca da Rimini with the Chelsea Opera Group and Messiah and Beethoven's Ninth with the Tokyo Philharmonic. *Honours:* Winners' Concert at the 1992 Pavarotti Competition. *Address:* Helen Sykes Artists Management, 100 Felsham Road, Putney, London SW15 1DQ, England.

FOSTER, Lawrence Thomas; Conductor; b. 23 Oct. 1941, Los Angeles, California, USA. *Education:* Studied conducting with Fritz Zweig, Los Angeles; Attended the Bayreuth Masterclasses and the Berkshire Music Center, Tanglewood, Massachusetts. *Career:* Debut: Young Musicians' Foundation Debut Orchestra, Los Angeles, 1960; Assistant Conductor, Los Angeles Philharmonic Orchestra, 1965–68; Chief Guest Conductor, Royal Philharmonic Orchestra, London, 1969–74; Conductor-in-Chief, Houston Symphony Orchestra, 1971–78; Revised version of Walton's Troilus and Cressida at Covent Garden, 1976; Chief Conductor, Opéra de Monte Carlo and Orchestre National (renamed Orchestre Philharmonique) de Monte Carlo, 1979–91; General Music Director, Duisberg, 1981–88; Music Director, Lausanne Chamber Orchestra, 1985–;

Jerusalem Symphony Orchestre, 1988–; Conducted new production of Hamlet by Ambroise Thomas at Monte Carlo, 1993; Music Director, Aspen Music Festival, 1991–96; Music Director, City of Barcelona Symphony, 1996–; Has premiered Birtwistle's Triumph of Time (1972) and Goehr's Piano Concerto, 1972; Conducted the Orquesta Simfónica de Barcelona at the London Proms, 2002. *Recordings:* For various labels. *Honours:* Koussevitzky Prize, 1966. *Current Management:* Harrison/Parrott Ltd, 12 Penzance Place, London, W11 4PA, England. *Telephone:* (20) 7229 9166. *Fax:* (20) 7221 5042. *Website:* www.harrisonparrott.com.

FOTEK, Jan; Composer; b. 28 Nov. 1928, Czerwinsk nad Wisla, Poland. *Education:* Studied with Stanislav Wiechowicz in Kraków and Szeligowski in Warsaw. *Compositions:* Operas: The Sea of Recovered Unity, Polish Radio, 1967; Galileo, 1969; The Spoons and the Moon, 1973–76; The Woodland Princess, opera-ballet, Warsaw, 1978; Man and Angels, misterium sacrum, 1982; Vir sapiens dominabitur astris, after Dante, Copernicus, St Francis and Michelangelo, Polish Radio, 1983; Opus Concertante for organ, piano and percussion, 1959; Gregorian Hymn for chorus and orchestra; A Cycle of Verses for children's chorus and orchestra, 1963; Epitasis for orchestra, 1967; The Last War for narrator, chorus and orchestra, 1971; Partita for 12 bassoons and 3 double bassoons, 1973; Musica Chromatica for strings, 1982; Sonata for tuba and piano, 1984; Czarnolas Suite for strings, 1986; Ecloga for counter-tenor and ensemble, 1987. *Address:* c/o Society of Authors ZAiKS, 2 Hipoteczna Street, 00 092 Warsaw, Poland. *Telephone:* (4822) 828 17 05. *Fax:* (4822) 828 13 47. *E-mail:* sekretariat@zaiks.org.pl. *Website:* www.zaiks.org.pl.

FOU, Ts'ong; Pianist; b. 10 March 1934, Shanghai, China. *Education:* Studied in China with Mario Paci and at the Warsaw Conservatory with Zbigniew Drzewiecki. *Career:* Debut: With the Shanghai Municipal Orchestra, playing Beethoven's Emperor Concerto, 1951; Gave 500 concerts in Eastern Europe while studying in Poland; Moved to London, 1958; Solo appearances in Europe, Scandinavia, the Far East, Australia and New Zealand, North and South America. *Recordings include:* Concertos by Beethoven, Haydn, Chopin, Mozart; Solo recitals of Chopin, Debussy, Bach, Handel, Mozart, Beethoven, Schubert, Scarlatti, Schumann; Chopin: Mazurkas (complete); Chopin: Nocturnes and Solo Piano works. *Honours:* 3rd Prize, Bucharest Piano Competition, 1953; 3rd Prize, International Chopin Competition, Warsaw, 1955. *Address:* 62 Aberdeen Park, London N5 2BL, England.

FOUCHECOURT, Jean-Paul; Singer (Tenor); b. 10 Aug. 1958, Blanzy, France. *Education:* Trained as conductor and saxophone player; Vocal studies under the influence of Cathy Berberian. *Career:* Many appearances with such early music groups as Les Arts Florissants, and Les Musiciens du Louvre; Rameau's Les Indes Galantes, Les Fêtes d'Hébé and Zoroastre, Lully's Atys and Charpentiers's David et Jonatas under the direction of William Christie, Concerts in France and on tour throughout Europe, America and Japan; Rameau's Hippolyte et Aricie and Lully's Phaëton under Marc Minkowski; Further engagements in Purcell's Fairy Queen at the Aix Festival, Monteverdi's Orfeo under René Jacobs at Salzburg, L'Incoronazione di Poppea with Christophe Rousset for Netherlands Opera and Monteverdi's Ulisse with Michel Corboz at Geneva; Other repertory includes the Berlioz Roméo et Juliette (with John Eliot Gardiner), Offenbach's Orphée aux Enfers, Mozart's Nozze di Figaro and Poulenc's Les Mamelles de Tiresias with Seiji Ozawa, (on tour to Japan, 1996); Season 1997–98 in the title role of Rameau's Platée with the Royal Opera and at Edinburgh; L'Enfant et les Sortilèges at Florence, 1998; Debut at the Met in New York with Tales of Hoffmann; Season 1999–2000 included Golden Cockerel at Covent Garden, Madama Butterfly with Boston Symphony Orchestra, Poppea at Aix en Provence Festival and Platée at the Bastille; Engaged as Arnalta in Poppea for Netherlands Opera, 2001; Ravel's L'Heure Espagnole at the London Proms, 2002. *Recordings include:* Lully's Atys and Phaëton; Mondonville's Titon et L'Aurore and Les Fêtes de Paphos; Rameau's Les Indes Galantes, Pygmalion and Hippolyte et Aricie; Socrate by Satie; Les Mamelles de Tiresias. *Current Management:* Askonas Holt Ltd, Lonsdale Chambers, 27 Chancery Lane, London, WC2A 1PF, England. *Telephone:* (20) 7400-1700. *Fax:* (20) 7400-1799. *E-mail:* info@askonasholt.co.uk. *Website:* www.askonasholt.co.uk.

FOUNTAIN, Ian; British pianist; b. 15 Oct. 1969, Welwyn Garden City, England. *Education:* chorister at New Coll., Oxford, Winchester Coll., Royal Northern Coll. of Music with Sulamita Aronovsky. *Career:* has performed widely in the UK, in major London recital halls and in Europe and the USA from 1986, with recitals at festivals including Sintra, Stresa, Montpellier, Davos, Kuhmo, Berlin, Schleswig-Holstein, Prague Spring and Ravello; worked with leading orchestras, including the London Symphony Orchestra, Czech Philharmonic, Israel Philharmonic, City of Birmingham Symphony Orchestra, Philharmonic Orchestra, Bournemouth Symphony Orchestra, English Chamber Orchestra, Royal Liverpool Philharmonic Orchestra, Britten Sinfonia, Deutches Symphonie-Orchester, Singapore Symphony Orchestra, Polish Nat. Radio Symphony, Slovak Philharmonic and Jerusalem Symphony; Prof.

of Piano, Royal Acad. of Music, London. *Recordings:* Beethoven: Diabelli Variations, Non-Beethoven Diabelli Variations. *Honours:* winner Viotti-Valsesia Int. Piano Competition (Italy) 1986, jt winner Arthur Rubinstein Int. Piano Competition 1989. *Current Management:* Connaught Artists Management Ltd, 2 Molasses Row, Plantation Wharf, London, SW11 3UX, England. *Telephone:* (20) 7738-0017. *Fax:* (20) 7738-0909. *E-mail:* classicalmusic@connaughtartists.com. *Website:* www.connaughtartists.com.

FOUNTAIN, Primous, III; composer; b. 1 Aug. 1949, St Petersburg, Florida, USA. *Education:* DePaul University in Chicago. *Career:* freelance composer from 1968, including association with the Arthur Mitchell Dance Theatre of Harlem. *Compositions include:* Manifestations for orchestra, 1969; Grudges for orchestra, 1972; Ritual Dance of the Amaks for orchestra, 1973; Duet for flute and bassoon, 1974; Cello Concerto, 1976; Ricia for violin, cello and piano, 1980; Harp Concerto, 1981; Symphony No. 1, Epitome of the Oppressed, 1984. *Honours:* BMI Composition Award, 1968; Guggenheim Fellowships, 1974, 1977; Award, American Academy and Institute of Arts and Letters.

FOURNET, Jean; Conductor; b. 14 April 1913, Rouen, France. *Education:* Studied with Philippe Gaubert at the Paris Conservatoire. *Career:* Debut: Rouen, 1936; Conducted in Rouen and Marseilles until 1944; Music Director of the Opéra-Comique, Paris, 1944–57; Conducting courses at Ecole Normale, Paris, 1944–62; Conducted Pelléas et Mélisande in Tokyo, 1958; Conductor of the Netherlands Radio Orchestra, 1961–68; Chicago Lyric Opera, 1965; Principal Conductor of the Rotterdam Philharmonic from 1968–73; Guest conductor in Europe, South America, USA and Israel; Metropolitan Opera debut, 1987, Samson et Dalila; Conducted Les Dialogues des Carmélites at Seattle, 1990. *Recordings include:* Berlioz Grande Messe des Morts, 1943; Louise by Charpentier, Pelléas et Mélisande and Les Pêcheurs de Perles; Mignon; d'Indy Symphonie; Saint-Saëns Piano Concertos; Fauré Requiem; Franck Symphonic Poems; Debussy La Damoiselle élue (Janine Micheau), Nocturnes, Ibéria and Prélude. *Address:* c/o Seattle Opera Association, PO Box 9248, Seattle, WA 98109, USA.

FOURNIER, Brigitte; Singer (Soprano); b. 14 June 1961, Nendaz, Switzerland. *Education:* Studied in Berne, Essen and Lausanne. *Career:* Sang in concert in works by Bach, Handel, Mozart, Schubert, Rameau and Honegger; Concert and lieder venues at the Aix and Montpellier Festivals, and throughout Switzerland; Sang Musetta in La Bohème at Biel/Solothurn, Naiad in Ariadne auf Naxos at Lausanne and Zerbinetta at Klagenfurt (1991); Toulouse, 1995, as Constance in Dialogues des Carmélites, Geneva, 1996, as Mozart's Blondchen; Season 2000–01 as Lucia in The Rape of Lucretia at Lausanne and the Woodbird in Siegfried at Geneva. *Recordings include:* Zelenka Requiem.

FOURNILLIER, Patrick; Conductor; b. 26 Dec. 1954, Neuilly-sur-Seine, France. *Education:* Studied with Louis Fourestier and Pierre Dervaux in Paris; Strasbourg Conservatoire with Jean-Sebastian Bereau, Salzburg Mozarteum with Leopold Hager, and with Franco Ferrara at the Accademiana Chigiana, Siena. *Career:* Assistant Conductor to Jean-Claude Casadesus at L'Orchestre National de Lille, 1983–85, Artistic Director, until 1986; Music Director, Nouvel Orchestre de St Etienne, 1988–, and Director, Sinfonietta d'Amiens, 1989–92; Music Director, Massenet Festival, St Etienne, 1988–; Important revivals of such neglected Massenet operas as Amadis, Thérèse, Cléopâtre, Esclarmonde and Grisélidis; Le Roi de Lahore by Massenet, 1997; Premieres have included Quatre-Vingt-Treize by Antoine Duhamel, 1989. *Honours:* Hans Haring Prize, Salzburg, 1982; Second Prize, Besancon International Conductors Competition, 1984; Prizewinner, Vaclav Talich Competition Prague, 1985; Second Prize, Grzerorz Fitelberg Competition at Katowice, 1987.

FOWKE, Philip (Francis); Concert Pianist; b. 28 June 1950, Gerrards Cross, England; m. Elizabeth Turnbull, 1999. *Education:* Began piano studies with Marjorie Withers, 1957; Scholarship to Royal Academy of Music, London, to study with Gordon Green, (Piano Performance) 1967–74; LRAM (Piano Performance); ARCM (Piano Performance); Dip RAM. *Career:* Debut: Wigmore Hall, 1974; British Concerto debut with Royal Liverpool Philharmonic, 1975; Royal Festival Hall debut, 1977; BBC Promenade Concert debut, 1979; US debut 1982; Debuts in Denmark, Bulgaria, France, Switzerland, Hong Kong, Belgium and Italy, 1983; Austrian debut at Salzburg Mozart Week, 1984; New Zealand debut, 1994; Has appeared regularly with all the leading orchestras in the United Kingdom and gives recitals and concerto performances for BBC radio; Professor, Royal Academy of Music, 1984–91; Professor Welsh College of Music and Drama, 1994; Head of Keyboard Department Trinity College of Music, London, 1995–99; Senior Fellow of Keyboard Department, 1998; Recitalist and piano tutor at the Dartington International Summer School, 1996, 1997 and 2000; Concerto appearances with the Hallé and in the USA, 1997; 50th Birthday Concert at Wigmore Hall, 2000; BBC Proms, 2001. *Recordings:* Bliss; Britten; Chopin; Delius; Finzi; Rachmaninov, Ravel; Tchaikovsky;

Hoddinott Piano Concerto; Film scores including the Warsaw Concerto with the RTE Concert Orchestra and Proinnsías O Duinn, 1998. *Current Management:* Patrick Garvey, 59 Lansdowne Place, Hove, East Sussex, BN3 1 FL. *Address:* 15A Tredegar Terrace, London, E3 5AH, England. *E-mail:* philipfowke@aol.com.

FOWLER, Bruce; Singer (Tenor); b. 1965, West-Monroe, Louisiana, USA. *Career:* Chicago Opera from 1990, notably as Nemorino in L'Elisir d'amore; Lindoro in Il Turco in Italia at Cleveland and Tonio in La Fille du régiment at Toronto (1994); Pesaro Festival, 1993, as Carlo in Rossini's Armida, and as Ferrando in Così fan tutte at Catania; Bonn Opera, 1995–96, in La Rondine and as Rossini's Almaviva; Sang Ferrando for Palm Beach Opera, 1998; Season 2000–01 as Rossini's Lindoro at the Deutsche Oper Berlin, Idreno in Semiramide at St Paul and Ramiro in Cenerentola at Cincinnati; Alfredo for Finnish National Opera. *Recordings include:* Armida.

FOWLER, Jennifer; Composer; b. 14 April 1939, Bunbury, Western Australia, Australia. *Education:* BA Hons, 1961, Dip Ed, 1962, BMus, 1967, University of Western Australia; Further study, Studio for Electronic Music, Utrecht, 1968–69. *Career:* Resident, London, 1969–; Music Teacher, schools, 1962–72; Freelance Composer; mem, Women in Music; International Alliance for Women in Music; Sonic Arts Network; British Academy of Composers and Songwriters. *Compositions include:* Hours of the Day, 4 mezzos, 2 oboes, 2 clarinets, 1968; Chimes, Fractured, ensemble, 1971; Veni Sancte Spiritus, chamber choir, 1971; Chant with Garlands, orchestra, 1974; Voice of the Shades, soprano, ensemble, 1977; Piece for EL, solo piano, 1981; The Arrows of St Sebastian, II, bass clarinet, cello, tape, 1981; Line Spun with stars, piano trio, 1983; When David Heard. . ., choir, piano, 1983; Echoes from an Antique Land, ensemble, 1983; Threaded Stars, solo harp, 1983; Blow Flute, solo flute, 1983; Letter from Haworth, mezzo, clarinet, cello, piano, 1984; Answer Echoes, 4 flutes, 1986; Lament, baroque oboe, bass viol, 1987; Restless Dust, cello, piano, 1988; And Ever Shall Be, mezzo, ensemble, 1989; Reeds, Reflections. . ., oboe, string trio, 1990; Plainsong for Strings, string orchestra, 1992; Lament for Mr Henry Purcell, ensemble, 1995; Singing the Lost Places, soprano and orchestra, 1996; Lament for Dunblane, chamber choir, 1996; Eat and Be Eaten, 6 singers and harp, 2000; Magnificat 2, soprano, flute, cello and harp, 2000; Freewheeling, solo harp, 2001; Echoes. . ., flute, cello, violin, cello and piano, 2001; Magnificat & Nunc Dimittis, 2002; Hymn for St Brigid, for SATB, 2002; Apparas Flying, 3 recorders, cello and harpsichord, 2003; Towards Release, violin, marimba and guitar, 2003. *Recordings:* Chimes Fractured on Australian Festival of Music Vol. 10; Blow Flute on The Flute Ascendant; Threaded Stars on Awakening; Echoes from an Antique Land on Mizu to Kori; Veni Sancte Spiritus on Sydney Dreaming. *Contributions:* New Music Articles, Vol. 4, 1985; Contemporary Music Review, Vol. II, 1995. *Honours:* Prize for Hours of the Day, Berlin Academy of the Arts; Radcliffe Award, 1971; 1st Prize, Chamber Music, International Contest for Women Composers, Mannheim, 1974; Miriam Gideon Prize, 2003. *Address:* 21 Deodar Road, London SW15 2NP, England. *E-mail:* 100611.2060@compuserve.com. *Website:* www .impulse-music.co.uk/fowler.htm.

FOWLER, John; Singer (Tenor); b. 1956, USA. *Career:* Sang in the USA as Edgardo in Lucia di Lammermoor, and in Norma; European engagements from 1983, including Rodolfo at Cologne and Hoffmann at Liège, 1985; Vienna Staatsoper, 1984–85, as Des Grieux, Leicester in Maria Stuarda and Arturo in I Puritani; Hamburg Staatsoper, 1984–85, in Rosenkavalier, Traviata and La Bohème; Welsh National Opera, 1986–87, as Edgardo and as Tonio in La Fille du Régiment; Further appearances in New Orleans, Houston (as Faust), Miami (Hoffmann, 1989), with Edmonton Opera (Duke of Mantua) and Liège (Gounod's Romeo, 1988); Concert showings in works by Respighi, Verdi (Requiem) and Mendelssohn (Elijah); Sang Percy in Anna Bolena at Barcelona and Donizetti's Edgardo at Dublin, 1991; Sang Hoffmann at Cincinnati, 1992; Gounod's Faust at Saint Louis, 1998. *Honours:* Winner, Metropolitan Opera Auditions, 1981. *Address:* c/o Herbert Barrett Management, 1776 Broadway, Suite 1610, New York, NY 10019, USA.

FOWLES, Glenys; Singer (Soprano); b. 4 Nov. 1946, Perth, Western Australia, Australia. *Education:* Studied with Margarita Mayer in Sydney, Kurt Adler in New York and Jani Strasser in London. *Career:* Debut: Sang Oscar (Ballo in Maschera), Australian Opera in Sydney, 1969; Sang in the USA, 1974–81, notably at the New York City Opera as Poppea, Susanna, Mélisande, 1976, Mimi and Micaela; European engagements have included Ilia in Idomeneo at Glyndebourne (1974), Sophie and Titania for Scottish Opera (Midsummer Night's Dream); Other roles include Gounod's Juliette, Mozart's Zerlina and Pamina, Marzelline, Marguerite (Faust), Nannetta, Anne Trulove, Mimi and Lauretta; Sang Liu in Turandot for Australian Opera, 1991; Marschallin, 1992. *Address:* Australian Opera, Sydney Opera House, Sydney, New South Wales, Australia.

FOX, Donal Leonellis; American composer and jazz and classical musician (piano); b. 17 July 1952, Boston, MA. *Education:* New England Conservatory of Music, Berklee Coll. of Music, Berkshire Music Center, Tanglewood; theory and counterpoint with Avram David, composition and harmony with T. J. Anderson, composition and orchestration with Gunther Schuller. *Career:* debut, premiere of Refutation and Hypothesis II for chamber orchestra, Festival of Contemporary Music at Tanglewood 1983; piano and improviser, world premiere of Oliver Lake's Movements Turns and Switches for violin and piano, Library of Congress, Washington 1993; piano and improviser, world premiere, The Demon, Int. Ottawa Jazz Festival, Nat. Gallery of Canada 1995; piano and improviser, world premiere of Anthony Kelley's Africamerica for piano and orchestra 1999; publisher and writer, BMI 1993–; Pres., Leonellis Music 1994–, Harry Fox Agency Inc 1996–; mem. Massachusetts Cultural Council (educational collaborative 1984–). *Television:* Donal Fox and David Murray in Session 1993, The Fox/Troupe Project (PBS) 1993, Say Brother (WGBH) 1993. *Compositions:* Refutation and Hypothesis I: a Treatise for piano solo 1981, Dialectics for two grand pianos 1988, Variants on a Theme by Monk for alto saxophone and piano 1990, Jazz Sets and Tone Rows for alto saxophone and piano 1990, Vamping with T. T. for bass clarinet and piano 1993, T-Cell Countdown for voice, piano and double bass 1993, River Town Packin House Blues, The Old People Speak of Death, Following the North Star Boogaloo for piano and poet 1993, Gone City: Ballet in Three Movements for clarinet, piano and double bass 1994. *Recordings include:* Boston Duets 1992, Videmus 1992, Ugly Beauty 1995, Donal Fox: Mellow Mood 1996, Donal Fox: Gone City 1997. *Honours:* Meet the Composer/Rockefeller Foundation/NEA grant 1991, Guggenheim Fellowship in Music Composition 1997, Bogliasco Fellowship in Music Composition 1998, Djerassi Foundation Fellowship in Music Composition 1999. *Current Management:* Leonellis Music, 14 Highland Park Avenue, Roxbury, MA 02119, USA.

FOX, Erika; Composer; b. 3 Oct. 1936, Vienna, Austria; m. 1961, 1 s., 1 d. *Education:* ARCM, Royal College of Music, London; Also private study with Jeremy Dale Roberts and Harrison Birtwistle. *Career:* Numerous commissions from leading contemporary music groups; Works performed at London's South Bank, Canada, Greece, Turkey, Czechoslovakia, festivals and broadcasts; Rehearsed orchestra at Menuhin School; Teaching includes Centre for Young Musicians, Pimlico; Junior Department, Guildhall School of Music and Drama; Composition workshops in various schools and privately; Sometime ballet pianist for Arts Educational Schools. *Compositions include:* Lamentations for Four, 1973; The Slaughterer, chamber opera, 1975; Paths Where the Mourners Tread, 1980; Litany for Strings, 1981; Movement for String Sextet, 1982; Shir, 1983; Kaleidoscope, 1983; Quasi Una Cadenza, 1983; Nick's Lament, 1984; Osen Shomaat, 1985; Silver Homage, 1986; Rivka's Fiddle, 1986; On Visiting Stravinsky's Grave at San Michele, 1988; Hungarian Rhapsody, 1989; The Bet, puppet music drama, 1990; The Dancer Hotoke, chamber opera, Garden Venture commission, 1992 (Olivier Award Nomination); The Moon of Moses, 1992; Davidsbündler Lieder for flute and piano, 1999; David Singt vor Saul for piano and ensemble, 2000; Piano concerto commissioned by Julian Jacobson, 1993; Tuned Spheres, 1995. *Current Management:* Elinor Kelly, Westbrook Farm Cottage, Boxford, Nr Newbury, Berkshire RG16 8DL, England. *Address:* 78 Peterborough Road, London SW6 3EB, England.

FOX, Fred(erick Alfred); Composer; b. 17 Jan. 1931, Detroit, Michigan, USA. *Education:* Studied at Wayne State University, The University of Michigan, Indiana University, Bloomington with Bernhard Heiden. *Career:* Teacher at Franklin College, Indiana and Sam Houston University, Huntsville; Worked in Minneapolis; Assistant, Contemporary Music Project, Washington DC; Teacher, California State University, Hayward, 1964–74 and at Indiana University, 1974–97, Chairman of Composition Department, 1980–97; mem, ASCAP; American Music Center; Composers' Forum. *Compositions include:* A Stone, A Leaf, an Unfound Door for soprano and ensemble, 1966; BEC for chamber ensemble, 1968; The Descent for chorus and percussion, 1969; Violin Concerto, 1971; Matrix for cello, strings and percussion, 1972; Ternion for oboe and orchestra, 1973; Variables No. 5 for orchestra, 1974; Variables Nos 1–4 and 6 for instruments, 1976; Time Excursions for soprano, speaker and instruments, 1976; Beyond Winterlock for orchestra, 1977; Ambient Shadows for 8 instruments, 1978; Night Ceremonies for orchestra, 1979; Sonaspheres Nos 1–5 for chamber ensemble, 1980–83; Nilrem's Odyssey for baritone, speaker and chorus, 1980; Tracings for orchestra, 1981; Bren for 13 brass, 1982; Januaries for orchestra, 1984; Shaking the Pumpkin for saxophone, piano and percussion, 1988; Auras for chamber ensemble, 1989; Nightscenes for strings and percussion, 1989; Devil's Tramping Ground for chamber ensemble, 1991; Echo Blues for orchestra, 1992; Dreamcatcher for 13 players, 1994; Impressions for orchestra, 1995; When the Thunder Speaks for saxophone and piano, 1998. *Recordings:* Music of Frederick Fox; Music of Frederick Fox, Volume 2; Shaking The Pumpkin. *Address:* 711 South Clifton Street, Bloomington, IN 47401, USA.

FOX, Leland Stanford; Music Professor and Administrator; b. 25 Jan. 1931, Worcester, MA, USA; m. Wanda R. Nelson 1 March 1955; one s. one d. *Education:* BM, 1956, MM, 1957, Baylor Univ.; PhD, Florida State Univ., 1962. *Career:* Hearst Publications, New York, 1948–51; Graduate Asst, 1956–57, Instructor of Music, 1957–60, Baylor Univ.; Graduate Asst, Florida State Univ., 1960–62; Principal Tenor, Asolo Festival, 1962; opera and oratorio performances; Instructor in Music, Pensacola Junior Coll., 1962–63; Assoc. Prof. of Music, Univ. of Oklahoma, 1963–66; Assoc. Prof. to Prof., Dir of Opera Theater, 1966; Editor, The Opera Journal, 1968–88; Assoc. Dean of Graduate School, Univ. of Mississippi, 1986–. *Publications include:* Index of Italian Opera 1900–1970; Opéra Comique: A Vehicle for Classic Style, 1964; From Out of the Ashes: Santa Fe Opera's New Theater, 1968; La Belle Arsène 1773 by Pierre Alexandre Monsigny, 1969; The State of Opera: A Dialogue Between Boris Goldovsky and Carlisle Floyd, 1971; ed. of numerous books. *Contributions:* New Grove Dictionary of Music and Musicians; Opera Quarterly.

FOX, Malcolm; Composer; b. 13 Oct. 1946, Windsor, England; m. Pauline Elizabeth Scholz, 5 April 1980, 1 s. *Education:* Royal College of Music, University of Lndon; ARCM 1966; BMus (Hons), 1967; MMusRCM, 1968. *Career:* Music Director, Cockpit Theatre, London, 1972–74; Lecturer in Music, 1974–79, Senior Lecturer, 1980–, University of Adelaide, South Australia; mem, Australasian Performing Right Association; Australia Music Centre; Fellowship of Australian Composers; Association of Professional Composers (UK). *Compositions:* Sid the Serpent, opera, 1976; Six Miniatures, violin and piano, 1977; Violin Concerto, 1980; The Iron Man, opera, 1987; Pathways of Ancient Dreaming, string orchestra, 1990; Ten Thousand Years Goodbye, soprano, piano and clarinet, 1992. *Publications:* Music Education in South Education (1836–1986), chapter in From Colonel Light into the Footlights–The Performing Arts in South Australia from 1936 to the present, 1988. *Contributions:* Siegfried's Death, 1989; The Swan Knight in Wagner's Lohengrin, 1989; Wotan's Spear, 1993. *Address:* 13 Whinham Street, Fitzroy, Adelaide, South Australia 5082, Australia.

FOX, Sarah; Singer (Soprano); b. 1973, Yorkshire, England. *Education:* Studied with Margaret H Clark at London University and at Royal College of Music (graduated Opera School, 1999). *Career:* Debut: Wigmore Hall recital with Roger Vignoles, 1998; St John's Smith Square recital, March 1999, with Malcolm Martineau; Recitals for BBC Radio 3; Concerts and Festival engagements throughout the United Kingdom; Tour of Sweden, 1999, with the King's Consort; Appearances with the Classical Opera Company, notably as Rosina in Mozart's La Finta Semplice at Covent Garden (Linbury Theatre), 2000; Sang in Bach's B minor Mass at St John's, London, with the Rodolfus Choir and the Orchestra of the Age of Enlightenment, 2000; Covent Garden, February 2000, with the Classical Opera Company, opera arias by Haydn and Mozart; Sang Iphis in Handel's Jephtha at the Edinburgh Festival, 2002. *Recordings include:* Boccherini's Stabat Mater with the King's Consort. *Honours:* Thomas Allen Opera Scholarship, 1997, Queen Elizabeth Rose Bowl, 1998, at the RCM; Winner, Kathleen Ferrier Award, 1997. *Current Management:* Askonas Holt Ltd, Lonsdale Chambers, 27 Chancery Lane, London, WC2A 1PF, England. *Telephone:* (20) 7400-1700. *Fax:* (20) 7400-1799. *E-mail:* info@askonasholt.co .uk. *Website:* www.askonasholt.co.uk.

FOX, Tom; Singer (Baritone); b. 1950, USA. *Education:* Studied at the College Conservatory of Music in Cincinnati Opera Company. *Career:* Appeared with Texas Opera Theater, 1974, then with Houston Grand Opera; Resident member of Cincinnati Opera, 1976–80; Frankfurt Opera from 1981 as Orestes (Elektra), Amonasro, Don Pizarro, Escamillo, Klingsor, Ford, Figaro and Nick Shadow in The Rake's Progress; Wiesbaden, 1981, as Don Giovanni; Hamburg Staatsoper, 1983, as Arcalems in Amadis de Gaule by J C Bach; Has sung with Canadian Opera as Orestes, Jochanaan and Escamillo; Welsh National Opera, 1985, as Escamillo; Other roles include Iago (Teatro Col ón, 1986), Claudius in Hamlet by Thomas (Pittsburgh), Alberich in The Ring for Nice Opera, at the Théâtre des Champs Elysées and in San Francisco; Gessler in Guillaume Tell in Nice; Dutchman, Amonasro, the villains in Hoffmann and Scarpia (Pittsburgh); Giovanni (Francesca di Rimini) in Turin; Barnaba in La Gioconda with Rome Opera; Invited to San Francisco for the US premiere of Henze's Das Verratene Meer; Season 1992/93 with debut in Washington as Iago, the role of Vesco di Blois in Massenet's Esclarmonde in Palermo, Telramund in Montpellier; Debut at the Metropolitan Opera, New York as Alberich, Jochanaan in San Francisco; 1993/94, Prus (Makropulos Case) in San Francisco and Bologna, his debut at the Lyric Opera of Chicago as Scarpia, his debut as Wotan at the Santiago Opera in Chile, Klingsor in a new production of Parsifal at the Munich Staatsoper and Kurwenal in a new production of Tristan at La Monnaie in Brussels; Sang Pizarro in Fidelio at the 1996 Salzburg Festival; Sang Scarpia at Cincinnati, 1998; Season 2000–01 as Kurwenal and Klingsor for San Francisco Opera and Prus in The Makropulos Case at the New York Met. *Address:* Kaye Artists

Management Ltd, Barratt House, 7 Chertsey Road, Woking GU21 5 AB, England.

FRACCARO, Walter; Singer (Tenor); b. 1968, Italy. *Career:* Many appearances at leading opera houses from 1993; Season 1994–95 as Ismaele in Nabucco at Barcelona, Cavaradossi at Valencia and Lisbon, and Raffaele in Stiffelio at Madrid; Further engagements as Alfredo at Lisbon, Radames at Pittsburgh, Riccardo in Ballo in Maschera at Tenerife and Marseilles; Alfredo and the Verdi Requiem at the International Festival of Peralada in Spain; Season 1996–97 as Faust in Mefistofele at Pittsburgh, Radames at San Francisco, Pinkerton at the Metropolitan Opera and Verdi's Macduff in Hamburg; Don José at San Francisco, 1998. *Honours:* Winner, 1993 Concorso di Vorallo Valesia (Jury Prize from Carlo Bergonzi); Placido Domingo Prize at the 1993 Concorso Internazionale di Canto Francisco Vinas, Barcelona. *Address:* c/o Metropolitan Opera, Lincoln Center, New York, NY 10023, USA.

FRACKENPOHL, Arthur Roland; American composer and professor; b. 23 April 1924, Irvington, New Jersey. *Education:* studied with Bernard Rogers, Eastman School of Music, BA 1947, MA 1949; Darius Milhaud, Berkshire Music Center, Tanglewood, summer 1948; Nadia Boulanger, Fontainebleau 1950; D.Mus, McGill University, Montreal 1957. *Career:* Teacher 1949–61, Professor 1961–85, Crane School of Music, State University of New York at Potsdam; mem. ASCAP. *Compositions:* chamber opera: Domestic Relations (To Beat or Not to Beat) 1964; orchestral: A Jubilant Overture 1957, Largo and Allegro for Horn and Strings 1962, Short Overture 1965, Concertino for Tuba and Strings 1967, Suite for Trumpet and Strings 1970, Concerto for Brass Quintet and Strings 1986; band music: Brass Quartet 1950, 5 Brass Quintets 1963, 1972, 1986, 1994, 1997, Trombone Quartet 1967, Brass Trio 1967, String Quartet 1971, Breviates for Brass Ensemble 1973, Suite for Brass Trio and Percussion 1973, Trio for Oboe, Horn and Bassoon 1982, Tuba Sonata 1983; Concerto for bassoon and band 1998; choral works: Te Deum 1962, Gloria 1968, Mass 1990; piano pieces; song cycles; solo songs. *Recordings:* The Art of Brass, with Potsdam Brass Quintet, The Art Collection: Caroline Brass. *Publications:* Harmonization at the Piano 1962, 6th edition 1991. *Address:* c/o 13 Hillcrest Drive, Potsdam, NY 13676, USA (home).

FRANCESCH, Homero; Concert Pianist; b. 6 Dec. 1947, Montevideo, Uruguay. *Education:* studied in South America and with Ludwig Hoffmann at the Munich Acad. *Career:* many appearances as concert soloist throughout Europe, notably with the Ravel concertos and in the premiere of Henze's Tristan, London 1974; frequent radio and television appearances. *Current Management:* Concerto Winderstein GmbH, Postfach 44 04 46, 80753 München, Germany. *Telephone:* (89) 38 38 46. *Fax:* (89) 33 79 38. *E-mail:* artists@winderstein.de. *Website:* www .concerto.de.

FRANCESCHETTO, Romano; Singer (Bass-baritone); b. 1957, Italy. *Education:* Studied at the Parma Conservatory. *Career:* Has sung widely in Italy from 1981, notably at La Scala in Milan, Rome, Verona, Venice, Turin, Palermo, Bologna, Trieste and Catania; Further engagements in Hamburg, Dresden, St Petersburg, Bordeaux, Tel-Aviv, Rio de Janeiro, Seoul and elsewhere; Has performed all the major buffo roles such as Don Bartolo, Dulcamara, Don Magnifico; Leporello; Geronimo; Don Pasquale; Gianni Schicchi; Also leading roles in many baroque and classical operas. *Recordings include:* Morlacchi's Barbiere di Siviglia (Bongiovanni); Paisiello's Don Chisciotte; Rossini's Adina; Salieri's Falstaff. *Current Management:* Alberto Mirri, Rome. *Address:* Via Fornio 6/C, 43036 Fidenza, Italy.

FRANCI, Carlos; Composer, Conductor; b. 18 July 1927, Buenos Aires, Argentina. *Education:* Studied at the Rome Conservatory and with Fernando Previtali at The Academy of St Cecilia. *Career:* Conducted symphonic music at first, then Hänsel und Gretel at Spoleto in 1959; Appearances at many opera houses in Italy and abroad, including the Vienna Staatsoper; led the Company of Rome Opera in Rossini's Otello at the NY Metropolitan, 1968, returning as guest, 1969–72; Other repertoire includes: Spontini's Fernand Cortez and Verdi's Nabucco, Berne, 1990; Conducted the Seven Stars concert at the Baths of Caracalla, 1991; Verdi's I Masnadieri at Piacenza, 1998. *Compositions include:* L'Imperatore, Opera, produced at Bergamo, 1958. *Address:* c/o Teatro dell Opera di Roma, Piazza B Gigli 8, 00184 Rome, Italy.

FRANCI, Francesca; Singer (Mezzo-soprano); b. 1962, Rome, Italy. *Education:* Studied with Rodolfo Celletti and Tito Gobbi. *Career:* Debut: Sang Mahler's Lieder eines fahrenden Gesellen at Verona, 1984; Appeared as Maddalena in Rigoletto at Genoa and Naples, Rosina at Bari and Suzuki in Bologna, 1988; Festival della Valle d'Itria 1988 in Donizetti's Maria di Rohan, as Armando; Edvige in Guillaume Tell at La Scala, Milan, returning as Fatima in Oberon; Sang Ernestina in Rossini's L'Occasione fa il Ladro at Pesaro; Further engagements at Rome and Naples (from 1987), Florence, Monteverdi's Otho, 1992, Paris and Wiesbaden; France 1992 as Stephano in Gounod's Roméo et

Juliette; Season 1996 as Contessa d'Arco in Rossini's Matilde di Shabran at Pesaro and Fenena in Nabucco at the Verona Arena; Season 1998 as La Cieca in La Gioconda at Genoa, Fenena at Rome and Beppe in L'Amico Fritz at Naples; Sang Verdi's Preziosilla at Verona Arena and Adalgisa in Norma at Catania, 2000. *Recordings include:* Maria di Rohan. *Address:* c/o Teatro Alla Scala, Via Filodrammatici 2, 20121 Milan, Italy.

FRANCIS, Alun; Conductor; b. 1943, Kidderminster, England. *Education:* Royal Manchester College of Music, 1960–63. *Career:* Played the horn in Hallé and Bournemouth Symphony Orchestras; From 1966 has conducted more than 60 orchestras in over 20 countries; Guest conductor at the Vienna Festival, Hong Kong Arts Festival with the BBC Scottish Symphony, Arhus Festival in Denmark with the Philharmonia Hungarica, Promenade Concerts, London, with the Royal Philharmonic, and Festival Hall, 1983, in Henryk Szeryng Golden Jubilee concert; Chief Conductor and Artistic Director of the Ulster Orchestra, 1966–67, and the Northern Ireland Opera Trust, 1974–84; Director, Northwest Chamber Orchestra in Seattle, 1980–85; Director and Artistic Adviser, Overijssells Philharmonic in Netherlands, 1985–87; Chief Conductor of the NordwestDeutsche Philharmonie and Principal Conductor of Berlin Symphony (from 1989); Repertoire includes Bel Canto opera (1978 revival of Donizetti Gabriella di Vergy, premiere of revised version, at Belfast) and 20th century music ranging from Berio to Stockhausen; Has composed music for the concert hall, films and theatre. *Recordings:* Donizetti's Ugo, Conte di Parigi, with the Philharmonia Orchestra; Offenbach's Christopher Columbus, with the London Mozart Players (Opera Rara); Other albums with the London Symphony, Royal Philharmonic, English Chamber and Northwest Chamber Orchestras. *Address:* c/o London Artists, 10 Guild Street, Stratford-upon-Avon, CV 37 6RE, England.

FRANCIS, Jeffrey; Singer (Tenor); b. 1958, Poplar Bluff, Missouri, USA. *Education:* Studied in Seattle. *Career:* Sang at the Berlin Staatsoper from 1990, as Lentolo in Graun's Cleopatra e Cesare, Tamino, Paolino in Il Matrimonio Segreto, Jupiter in Semele (1996) and in Gassmann's L'Opera Seria; Rossini Festival at Pesaro, 1993–95, as Gernando in Armida and Rodolphe in Guillaume Tell; Season 1993–94 as Evander in Alceste at Vienna, Argirio in Rossini's Tancredi in Berlin and Rossini's Almaviva at Santa Fe; Season 1998 with Rossini's Ramiro in Tel-Aviv and Chapelou in Le Postillon de Lonjumeau at the Berlin Staatsoper; Season 2000 in Roméo et Juliette by Berlioz at Salzburg and as Almaviva at the Vienna Staatsoper. *Recordings include:* Armida.

FRANCIS, Sarah (Janet); Oboist; b. 1939, London, England; m. Michael D C Johnson, 2 d. *Education:* ARCM, Scholar, Royal College of Music, London; French Government Scholarship, Paris; Boise Foundation Scholarship to study with Pierre Pierlot, Paris. *Career:* Debut: BBC, 1959; Principal Oboe, BBC National Orchestra of Wales; BBC Recitalist; Soloist, Chamber Music and Orchestral Player; Professor, Royal College of Music, London; Director, London Harpsichord Ensemble, Dedicatee of many concert and chamber music works; Masterclasses in Amsterdam, Cologne, Geneva, Moscow and Stockholm Conservatoires; mem, British Music Society; Royal Society of Musicians; Incorporated Society of Musicians; Former Chairman, British Double Reed Society. *Compositions:* Seven Dedications: Gordon Jacob, Seven Bagatelles, 1971; Gordon Crosse, Ariadne, for solo oboe and 12 players, 1972; Phyllis Tate, The Rainbow and the Cuckoo, oboe quartet, 1975; Crosse, Little Epiphany Variations for oboe and cello, 1977; Anthony Payne, Concerto, 1980; William Mathias, Oboe Concerto, 1989; Stephen Dodgson, Oboe Quartet, 1994. *Recordings:* Britten Metamorphoses, Quartet, Crosse Ariadne; Boccherini Quintets; Crusell, Reicha Quintets; Howells, Rubbra Sonatas; Rutland Boughton Oboe Concerto, RPO; Mozart and Krommer Concertos, LMP; Britten complete oboe music; Bax, Holst Quintets; Moeran, Jacob Quartets, Chandos; Complete Albinoni, Handel and Telemann Concertos LHE, Unicorn-Kanchana; Vanhal Quartets. *Publications:* Going Solo, Faber, 1995; Oboe Music to Enjoy, 1996. *Contributions:* Joy Boughton: A Portrait; Double Reed News. *Honours:* Somerville Prize for Wind instruments, RCM, 1959; FRCM, 2001. *Address:* 10 Avenue Road, London N6 5DW, England.

FRANCK, Mikko; Conductor; b. 1979, Helsinki, Finland. *Education:* Sibelius Academy (violin and conducting), 1992–97; New York, Israel and Sweden. *Career:* Children's chorus member at the Finnish National Opera; Appeared as the young Sibelius at the Helsinki Swedish Theatre, 1992; Conductor with such Finnish orchestras as the Vaasa, Lappeenranta, Pori and the Chamber Orchestra of the Sibelius Academy, Helsinki; Season 1997–98 with the Turku Philharmonic, Tapiola Sinfonietta, Tampere Philharmonic and Netherlands Radio Philharmonic; Japanese tour with the Sibelius Academy Symphony Orchestra; Conductor, The Magic Flute, at the Finnish National Opera; US debut at the Aspen Festival; Season 1999–2000 included return visits to the Stockholm Philharmonic, Finnish Radio Symphony, Swedish Radio Symphony, Bergen Philharmonic and a tour of Japan with the Bamberg Symphony in 2000; Season 2002–03 appointed Music Director and Chief

Conductor of the Orchestre National de Belgique, debuts with Chicago, San Francisco Symphony and Berlin Philharmonic orchestras and a tour of Japan with the Orchestre National de Belgique; Concerts with the Scottish Chamber, BBC National Orchestra of Wales, Hessischer Rundfunk, Stuttgart Opera and Tokyo Symphony Orchestras; Engaged for the premiere of Rautavaara's Rasputin, Helsinki, 2003; Chief Conductor, Finnish Nat. Opera 2006–. *Recordings:* Sibelius En Saga and Lemminkainen Legends with the Swedish Radio Symphony; Tchaikovsky's Sixth Symphony. *Honours:* Nominated for a Grammy Award (Best Orchestral performance) in 2001. *Current Management:* Harrison/Parrott Ltd, 12 Penzance Place, London, W11 4PA, England. *Telephone:* (20) 7229 9166. *Fax:* (20) 7221 5042. *Website:* www .harrisonparrott.com.

FRANDSEN, John; Composer and Organist; b. 13 March 1956, Aalborg, Denmark; m. Kirsten Grove, 5 Jan 1985, 1 d. *Education:* Aalborghus Statsgymnasium; MA in Music at Århus University; Composition and Organ at Royal Academy of Music, Århus. *Career:* Teacher at Århus University, 1979–83 and The Royal Academy of Music, Århus, 1980–; Organist at Ellevang Church, 1982–84 and Holy Ghost Church, Århus, 1984–; Conductor of Cantilena Choir, 1983–; mem, Chairman of Young Nordic Music, Danish Section, 1983–87; Chairman of Århus Unge Tonekunstnere, 1983–; Danisher Composers' Society. *Compositions:* String Song for String Quartet, 1980; Wo Immer Wir Soielen for Mixed Choir, 1982; Songs of Innocence for Soprano and Guitar, 1984; Amalie Lever, opera, 1984; Avers/Revers for Wind Quintet, 1985; Deux Poèmes Sur Le Temps for Mixed Choir, 1985; Amalie Suite for Chamber Orchestra, 1985; Stabat Mater for Tenor and Organ, 1986; Petite Suite for Guitar, 1986; De/Cadences for Wind Quintet, 1987. *Recordings:* Songs of Innocence with soprano Ellen Lunde and guitarist Erling Moldrup. *Contributions:* Organistbladet; Dansk Mussiktidsskrift. *Address:* Odinsvej 7, 8230 Aabyhoj, Denmark.

FRANK, Claude; Pianist; b. 24 Dec. 1925, Nurnberg, Germany; m. Lilian Kallir 1959, one d. (Pamela Frank). *Education:* studied in France and USA with Artur Schnabel, K. U. Schnabel. *Career:* debut, New York Philharmonic 1959; appearances with most major orchestras, including New York Philharmonic, Boston Symphony, Chicago Symphony, Cleveland Orchestra, Philadelphia Orchestra, Berlin Philharmonic, Concertgebouw, London Symphony, Royal Philharmonic; performed with conductors, including Bernstein, Giulini, Leinsdorf, Mehta, Szell; tours of Australia, Africa, Israel, Taiwan; appearances at most major music festivals; New York memorial concert for Artur Schnabel 1981. *Recordings:* 32 Beethoven Piano Sonatas, Mozart Concertos, Beethoven Trios, numerous other works. *Publications:* contrib. to Piano Quarterly, Keynote Magazine. *Honours:* Beethoven Society Award 1979. *Current Management:* Columbia Artists Management LLC, 165 West 57th Street, New York, NY 10019-2276, USA. *Telephone:* (212) 841-9500. *Fax:* (212) 841-9744. *E-mail:* info@cami.com. *Website:* www.cami.com.

FRANK, Pamela; Violinist; b. 20 June 1967, New York, USA; d. of Claude Frank and Lillian Kallir. *Education:* studied with Szymon Goldberg and Jaime Laredo; Graduated Curtis Institute, Philadelphia, 1989. *Career:* debut, Carnegie Hall, New York, with the New York String Orchestra, conducted by Alexander Schneider 1985; many appearances with leading orchestras world-wide, including Boston Symphony, Cleveland Orchestra, Tonhalle Orchestra (Zürich) and Orchestre de Paris; Soloist with the Academy of St Martin-in-the-Fields, London, and leader of Academy Chamber Ensemble; engagements with chamber musicians, including Peter Serkin and Yo-Yo Ma and frequent recital tours with her father; contemporary repertoire includes music by Takemitsu, Ellen Taafe Zwilich and Aaron Jay. *Recordings include:* albums with the Academy of St Martin-in-the-Fields. *Current Management:* IMG Artists, Lovell House, 616 Chiswick High Road, London, W4 5RX, England. *Telephone:* (20) 8233-5800. *Fax:* (20) 8233-5801. *E-mail:* artistseurope@ imgworld.com. *Website:* www.imgartists.com.

FRANK, Susanne; Violinist; b. 2 Nov. 1962, Switzerland. *Education:* Studied at the Winterthur Conservatory in Paris and the International Menuhin Academy. *Career:* 2nd violin of the Carmina Quartet since 1987; Appearances from 1987 in Europe, Israel, Japan and the USA; Regular concerts at the Wigmore Hall from Oct 1987; Concerts at the South Bank Centre, London, Amsterdam Concertgebouw, the Kleine Philharmonie in Berlin, Konzertverein Vienna; Four engagements in Paris, 1990–91, seven in London; Tours to Australasia, USA, Japan, and concerts at the Hohenems, Graz, Hong Kong, Montreux, Schleswig-Holstein, Bath, Lucerne and Prague Spring Festivals; Collaborations with Dietrich Fischer-Dieskau, Olaf Bär and Mitsuko Uchida. *Recordings:* Albums for several labels (from 1991). *Honours:* Joint winner (with members of Carmina Quartet), Paolo Borciani String Quartet Competition in Reggio Emilia, Italy, 1987; Gramophone prize for best recording of chamber music, 1992. *Address:* c/o Intermusica Artists' Management, 16 Duncan Terrace, London N1 8BZ, England.

FRANKE-BLOM, Lars-Åke (Harry); Composer; b. 4 April 1941, Norrköping, Sweden; m. Gunilla Marie-Louise Dalin 1965, 1 s., 2 d. *Education:* Master's degree, Romance Languages, University of Uppsala, 1965; Logopede, Karolinska Institute, Stockholm, 1967; Composition with Nils Eriksson and Daniel Börtz. *Career:* Debut: With orchestral work Motions, 1975; Active in Norrköping, collaborating with the local symphony orchestra on several occasions; The troll battle commissioned and performed by the Folkopera, Stockholm, 1979; The well of the virgins, ballet, commissioned by Swedish Television, 1982; The web of yearning commissioned by Norrköping Symphony Orchestra, 1984, presented on Swedish Television, 1988; HP, opera commissioned by the Royal Theatre, Stockholm, 1990, first performance, 2001; mem, Association of Swedish Composers, 1978. *Compositions:* Motions for orchestra, 1973; Music for mobile for orchestra, 1975–77; Concertos for violoncello, 1977, viola, 1980, contrabasso, 1983; The troll battle, opera for children, 1979; 3 symphonies, 1982, 1993, 1994; Web of yearning, symphonic poem, 1984; Impossible reality, chamber music, 1986; HP, opera in 2 acts, 1990–95; Music for art, chamber music, 1991; The 3rd Symphony Fire on the Earth, commissioned and performed by the Swedish Radio Symphony Orchestra in 1998; Music for the film, Bathers, presented on Swedish television, 1999, A Mansion Tale opera 2004. *Recordings:* Endymion; Music for mobile; Web of yearning, music and television film; Music for art; Several radio recordings. *Honours:* Prizewinner, International New Music Composers' Competition, 1989–90. *Address:* Mastgatan 15, 60385 Norrköping, Sweden.

FRANKL, Peter; British concert pianist; b. 2 Oct. 1935, Budapest, Hungary; s. of Tibor and Laura Frankl; m. Annie Feiner 1958; one s. one d. *Education:* High School, Franz Liszt Acad. of Music, Budapest. *Career:* began career in late 1950s, London debut 1962, New York debut with Cleveland Orchestra under George Szell 1967; has performed with world's major orchestras, including Berlin Philharmonic, Amsterdam Concertgebouw, Israel Philharmonic, Leipzig Gewandhaus and all the London and major American orchestras, under conductors, including Abbado, Boulez, Colin Davis, Antal Dorati, Haitink, Herbig, Leinsdorf, Maazel, Masur, Muti, Rozhdestvensky, Salonen, Sanderling and Georg Solti; Visiting Prof. of Piano Yale Univ., USA 1987. *Recordings include:* complete works for piano by Schumann and Debussy, a solo Bartók and Chopin album, a Hungarian Anthology, Mozart concertos with mems of the English Chamber Orchestra, Brahms piano concertos nos 1 and 2, the complete four-hand works by Mozart with Tamás Vásáry, the three Brahms violin sonatas with Kyung Wha Chung, Brahms, Schumann, Dvořák and Martinů recordings, quintets with the Lindsay Quartet. *Honours:* won first prize in several int. competitions; Officer's Cross Order of Merit (Hungary) 1972. *Address:* 5 Gresham Gardens, London, NW11 8NX, England. *Telephone:* (20) 8455-5228. *Fax:* (20) 8455-2176. *Website:* www.peterfrankl.co.uk (home).

FRANKLIN, James (Jim), PhD; Lecturer in Music Technology; b. 14 Feb. 1959, Sydney, NSW, Australia. *Education:* Univ. of Sydney; Shihan (master performer), International Shakuhachi Research Centre, Japan, 1996; studies with Peter Sculthorpe 1978–81, Milko Kelemen 1982–85, Ton de Leeuw 1985–86, Riley Lee 1988–98, Katsuya Yokoyama 1996; PhD Univ. of Sydney, 1998. *Career:* Univ. of Sydney, 1987–93; Lecturer in Music Technology, Univ. of Western Sydney 1994–2003; founder mem., OHM, Electronic Music Group. *Compositions include:* Corno Inglese, for choir, 1979; Talisman, for piano, 1980; Three Glimpses of Aquilon, for piano, 1980; Across the Swan's Riding, for piano and orchestra, 1981; The Unliving Seed, chamber opera, 1983; Boundaries for the Child of Flame, for string quartet, 1984; Fragments of a Broken Land, for orchestra, 1984; Triptych, for 8 voices and ensemble, 1984; Dream Within a Dream, for tape, 1988; Raising Dust, for synthesizer, 1988; The Hours of the Sea-Bird, for voices, keyboard, synthesizer, sampler and sequencer, 1988; Fountain of Light, for Shakuhachi and electronics, with Riley Lee, 1991; Middle Dance, for voices and ensemble, 1992; Naratic Visions, dance theatre, 1993; Heart, for Shakuhachi, voice and live electronics, 1994; Three Treasures: Columns and Webs, for koto quartet, percussion, Shakuhachi and electronics, 1996; Peace Bell, for 3 shakuhachi and collaged prerecorded bells, 1996; Songs for the Not-Born #1, for shakuhachi and live electronics, 1996; Water Spirits, for koto, shakuhachi and electronics, with Satsuki Odamura, 1994–96, Thoughts of Distant Clouds for koto and shakuhachi 1998, Butsuga for shakuhachi 1999, Moon Road to Dawn (with Antony Wheeler) 1999, Abundance (with Michael Atherton) 2001, Flötenspiel for shakuhachi 2002, Songs for the Not-Born #2 2002 and #3, 2003 for shakuhachi, theremin and live electronics; A Lattice of Winds, for shakuhachi and koto, 2003; Aurora, with Michael Atherton, for shakuhachi, koto, ruined piano, guitars, marimba and double bass, 2003. *Honours:* Munich International Multi-Media Festival, Best Original Soundtrack, 1990. *Address:* PO Box 179, Springwood, NSW 2777, Australia. *E-mail:* dr_jim_franklin@hotmail.com.

FRANKLIN, Peter (Robert); University Teacher; b. 19 Dec. 1947, London, England. *Education:* BA, DPhil, University of York, 1966–72. *Career:* Teacher of Music and German, Harlaxton College, Lincolnshire, 1974–79, and at William Jewell College, Liberty, Missouri, USA, 1979; Lecturer, Department of Music, University of Leeds, 1980–1995. *Publications:* Natalie Bauer-Lechner–Recollections of Gustav Mahler (editor, annotator), 1980; The Idea of Music, Schoenberg and Others, 1985. *Contributions:* Many journals including The Music Review, Music and Letters, Opera (1992), The Musical Quarterly and The Musical Times, on Mahler and Schreker; Programme Notes (e.g. Pfitzner's Palestrina at Covent Garden, 1997); Article on Mahler in New Grove Dictionary, 2001. *Address:* c/o St Catherine's College, Oxford, OX1 3UJ.

FRANOVA, Tatiana; Pianist; b. 3 Aug. 1945, Czechoslovakia; m. Eduard Ihring, 20 Aug 1966, 1 d. *Education:* Bratislava Conservatoire, 1959–64; Academy of Music and Dramatic Arts, Bratislava, 1964–69; Music Academy, Vienna, 1969–73; Postgraduate studies in Bratislava, 1980–83. *Career:* Concert tours in Austria, Brazil, Cuba, Egypt, France, Germany, Hungary, India, Italy, Luxembourg, Poland, Romania, Spain, Gran Canaria, Switzerland, Sweden, USSR; Professor, Academy of Arts, Cairo, Egypt, 1983–87; Professor of Piano, Academy of Music Arts, Bratislava, 1987–; mem, Slovak Music Union. *Recordings:* Brahms: Sonata in F sharp minor Op 2, 1975; Rachmaninov: Sonata in B minor Op 36, 1975; Etudes–Chopin, Liszt, Scriabin, Rachmaninov, 1978; Rachmaninov: Concerto No. 1 in F sharp minor, 1982; De Falla: Nights in the Gardens of Spain, 1982; Complete works of Glazunov, 1991. *Honours:* 1st Prize in Radio Competition, Young People's Studio, 1964; Silver Medal at International Festival, Bordeaux, 1974; F Kafenda Prize, 1980. *Current Management:* Slovkoncert. *Address:* Gorkeho 7, 81101 Bratislava, Slovakia.

FRANTZ, Justus; Pianist; b. 18 May 1944, Hohensalza, Germany. *Education:* Hamburg Hochschule für Musik, with Eliza Hansen; Wilhelm Kempff in Positano. *Career:* European concerts from 1960; Mozart concerto series with Karajan and the Berlin Philharmonic; US debut, 1975, in the Dvořák Concerto with the New York Philharmonic under Bernstein; later performances in New York and Washington with Kempe, Giulini and Haitink; 1983 tour of USA, Japan and Europe with pianist Christoph Eschenbach; Prof., Hamburg Musikhochschule, 1985–; founded Schleswig-Holstein Music Festival, 1986 and directed until 1994; performed the Beethoven concerti, 1988; performed complete cycle of Mozart concerti in several European cities, season 1987–88. *Recordings:* Concerti by Dvořák and Schumann under Bernstein; Duos by Mozart and Schubert with Eschenbach; Bach concerti, 1985; Mozart concerti for 2 and 3 pianos with Eschenbach, Helmut Schmidt and the London Philharmonic. *Address:* c/o Opéra et Concert, 1 rue Volney, 75002 Paris, France.

FRANZEN, Olov (Alfred); Composer, Cellist and Recitalist; b. 22 Jan. 1946, Umeå, Sweden; m. Ingeborg Axner, 12 Nov 1977. *Education:* Stockholm Music Academy, 1966–73; Music Teacher Examination, 1970; Cello with Gunnar Norrby, 1966–72; Composition with Ingvar Lidholm, 1969–73. *Career:* Debut: As composer, A Wind Quintet in Lund, 1963; As Cellist, Nyströ m, 1971; Cellist in Norrkoping Symphony Orchestra, 1971–72; Harpans Kraft, Stockholm, 1971–77; Swedish television Film, Sundcreme with Harpans Kraft, 1976; Freelance in Härnösand and Founder, HND Ensemble, 1977–92; Cellist, Sundsvall Chamber Orchestra, 1983–90; Teacher of Composition, Kapellsberg Music School, Härnösand, 1983–92; In 1986 started Faimo Edition for publishing music scores and recordings; Freelance in Skokloster, 1992–; hundreds of solo recitals throughout Sweden, 1993–; Has played with Harpans Kraft and HND in Sweden, Finland, Austria on radio; Composition played in all Nordic countries and abroad; Cellist, Duo Franzén, 1978–; Skokloster Chamber Soloists, 1994–97; Trio Concordia, 1999–. *Compositions include:* Cytoplasma for song and piano, 1968; Fiesta for percussion ensemble, 1982; Har for soprano and harp, 1983; The Vacuum State for symphony orchestra, 1983; From The Junction Point for bassoon and live electronics, 1985; Suite for 3 flutes, 1986; Agnim for symphony orchestra, 1987; It's Getting Sunny for brass band, 1988; Gaps for violin and piano, 1990; Apmel for flute, clarinet, percussion, piano and string quartet, 1992; The Unseen Present for cello and reciter, 1993; Opus NN for mezzo soprano, guitar and cello, 1994; Clouds on Blue Sky for symphony orchestra, 1995; Organic music No. 2 for cello solo, 1995; String Quartet, 1996; Lamentode, for soprano, bass clarinet and piano, 1997; Autumn Duo for 2 violins, 1997; Four Realities for reciter and symphony orchestra, 1998; La terza via for cello solo, 2000; In Fondo for mezzosoprano, flute and cello, 2001; Organic Music No. 4 for string sextet, 2002; Strigi Aluconi Gratias for saxophone quartet, 2003. *Recordings:* Beyond, with 6 Pieces for winds and piano, 1991; Gaps, 1997; Four Realities, 2000; La Terza Via, four pieces for solo cello, 2002. *Address:* Abbotvägen 18, 74695 Skokloster, Sweden.

FRASER, Malcolm (Henry); Opera Director; b. 1 Aug. 1939, Kingston-upon-Thames, England; m. 25 April 1964, 4 s. *Career:* Assoc. Dir, Lincoln Repertory, 1966–68; Resident Dir, Welsh National Opera Company, 1968–76; Senior Lecturer, Royal Northern College of Music, 1976–87; Founder, Artistic Dir, Buxton Int. Festival, 1979–87; J Ralph Corbett Distinguished Prof. of Opera, Univ. of Cincinnati, 1986–2003; Guest Dir, London Opera Centre, New Sadler's Wells Opera, Portland Opera, Seattle Opera, Calgary Opera, Edmonton Opera, Virginia Opera, Arkansas Opera, until 1990; Permanent Guest Dir, Arkansas Opera, 1988–; Associate Artistic Dir, Buxton International Festival, 1988–; Florentine Opera of Milwaukee; Artistic Dir, Opera Theatre of Lucca, 1996–; Directed World Premiere of Hermann's Wuthering Heights for Portland Opera, as well as Falstaff with Sir Geraint Evans and Don Giovanni with James Morris for the same company. *Honours:* Churchill Fellow, 1969; Prize for Mise-en-Scène, Prague International Television Festival, 1975; Kodály Medal, Hungarian Government, 1982; 14 times winner, National Opera Association Prize for best college production in USA; Manchester Evening News Award and Sunday Times (London); Prof. Professor Emeritus of the University of Cincinnati. *Address:* Madeira House, Tideswell, Derbyshire SK17 8NU.

FREDMAN, Myer, LRAM; British conductor and author; b. 29 Jan. 1932, Plymouth, Devon, England; m. Jeanne Winfield, 26 Aug 1954, 2 s. *Education:* Dartington Hall; The Opera School, London. *Career:* debut: Cork; Glyndebourne Festival with operas by Mozart, Verdi, Maw and Von Einem; Glyndebourne Touring Opera 1968–74; State Opera of South Australia; Seymour Group; Guest Conductor throughout Europe, America and Australia; BBC television; Wexford, Perth and Adelaide Festivals also at Hong Kong Fest; Conductor in Poland, Belgium, Romania and Germany; Conducted Cavalli's L'Ormindo at Brussels in 1972, Bizet's Carmen in Hamburg 1973 and Il Barbiere di Siviglia in Sydney 1974; season 1992 with La Bohème for the Canadian Opera Company, Toronto and Le nozze di Figaro in Sydney; Head of Opera at the New South Wales Conservatorium 1981–92 including the premiere of Lawrence Hargrave by Nigel Butterfly in 1988; Associate Artist of The Australian Opera 1991–99; concert debut South America 1992 at Montevideo and Buenos Aires; conducted Australian premieres of Midsummer Marriage, Death in Venice and One Man Show; Dialogues des Carmélites 1997. *Recordings:* Bax Symphonies 1 and 2, London Philharmonic Orchestra, No. 3 with Sydney Symphony; H Brian Symphonies 16 and 22 with London Philharmonic Orchestra; Delius Paradise Garden with London Philharmonic Orchestra; Benjamin Overture to an Italian Comedy; Respighi Sinfonia Drammatica, Piano Concerto with Sydney Symphony; Puccini Le Villi with Adelaide Symphony; Britten and Delius recordings. *Publications:* The Conductor's Domain 1999, From Idomeneo to Die Zauberflöte 2002 The Drama of Opera 2003. *Honours:* Bronze Medal by Italian Government 1965. *Address:* 18A Nietta Road, Lindisfarne, Tasmania 7015 (home). *Telephone:* (3) 6243-1368. *E-mail:* mfredman@netspace.net.au. *Website:* www.netspace.net.au/~mfredman.

FREDRIKSSON, Karl-Magnus; Singer (Baritone); b. 6 Feb. 1968, Stockholm, Sweden. *Education:* Music High School; Opera High School, 1989–91; Masterclass with D Fischer-Diskau, 1991. *Career:* Debut: Stockholm Royal Opera, 1996; Recital at Wigmore Hall, 1994, 1995; Recitals at Helsinki Opera Stage, 1996; and in Stockholm Opera Stage, 1997; Die Lustige Weiber von Windsor, Stockholm Opera, 1997; Radio Opera in Swedish Radio, 1997; Several tours with Eric Ericson in Europe; Figaro in Il Barbiere di Siviglia, Royal Opera Stockholm, 1998; mem, The Swedish Theatre Order. *Recordings:* Kullervo (Sibelius) with Colin Davis; Die Lustige Witwe (Lehar) with John Eliot Gardiner; Nordic Romances (solo recording); Summer Night, 1999. *Honours:* Major soloist prize from the Swedish Royal Music Academy, 1993; Miriam Helin Competition in Helsinki. *Current Management:* Scandinavian Artists Management AB. *Address:* Vastmannag 76, 113 26 Stockholm, Sweden.

FREEDMAN, Gertrud; Singer (Soprano); b. 1933, Germany. *Education:* Studied at the Augsburg Conservatory. *Career:* Sang at Passau and Mainz, 1957–60, Munich Staatsoper, 1960–80; Guest appearances at Lisbon and Barcelona as Sophie and Blondchen, Komische Oper Berlin as Rosina in Paisiello's Barbiere di Siviglia; Other roles include Mozart's Papagena and Despina, Anna in Intermezzo, Zdenka, Oscar, Musetta, and Adele in Die Fledermaus. *Address:* c/o Bayerische Staatsoper, Max-Joseph-Platz, D-80539 Munich 1, Germany.

FREEDMAN, Harry; Composer; b. 5 April 1922, Lódz, Poland; m. Mary Louise Freedman, 15 Sept 1951, 3 d. *Education:* Winnipeg School of Art, 1936–40; Royal Conservatory of Music, Toronto, 1945–50; Tanglewood Music Centre, 1949. *Career:* English Horn for Toronto Symphony Orchestra, 1946–70; Host of Junior Round-Up, Music Segment CBC television, 1958–60; Host, CBC Thursday Music, 1967–69; Many guest appearances on Television and Radio. *Compositions:* Tableau; Images; 3 Symphonies; 9 Ballets; 2 String Quartets; Numerous orchestral works, chamber works, choral works, song cycles; Scores for films, television, theatre and radio; 1 act opera, Abracadabra; Sonata for Winds, 1990; Spirit Song, soprano and string quartet, 1993; Indigo, string orchestra, 1994; Viola Concerto, 1996; Borealis, orchestra and 4 choirs, 1997;

Dances, solo harp, 1997; Voices, choir, 1998; Graphic 8, string quartet, 2000; Graphic 9: for Harry Somers, 16 solo strings, 2000; Duke (memento of Duke Ellington), orchestra, 2001; Phoenix for string quartet, 2003; Spanish Skies for soprano and piano, 2003. *Recordings include:* Images with Toronto Symphony, Ozawa; Tangents with Vancouver Symphony; The Flame Within with Festival Singers; Poems of Young People, Maureen Forrester; Town, Esprit Orchestra; Touchings, Nexus (percussion) with Esprit Orchestra; Variations, Baroque Trio of Montreal; Tableau, CBC Vancouver Orchestra; The Sax Chronicles, Gerry Mulligan with the Houston Symphony Orchestra. *Address:* 616 Avenue Road, Apt 503, Toronto, Ontario M4V 2K8, Canada. *E-mail:* freedman@nobelmed.com.

FREEMAN, David; Stage Director; b. 1 May 1952, Sydney, New South Wales, Australia; m. Marie Angel. *Career:* Founded Opera Factory in Sydney, 1973, and in Zürich, 1976, with 20 Swiss productions; Productions for Opera Factory in London 1981–98 included The Knot Garden, Punch and Judy, The Beggar's Opera, Cavalli's La Calisto, Birtwistle's Yan Tan Tethera (world premiere 1986); Eight Songs for a Mad King by Peter Maxwell Davies, Ligeti's Adventures/Nouvelles Aventures and Reimann's The Ghost Sonata; Mozart's 3 Da Ponte operas presented at the Queen Elizabeth Hall as part of the bicentenary celebrations; Has also produced Osborne's Hells Angels; Founded Opera Factory Films in 1991; Directed Prokofiev's The Fiery Angel for Marinsky Theatre, St Petersburg, Covent Garden and Metropolitan, New York; Operas by Birtwistle, Maxwell Davies, Ligeti and Mozart have been shown on BBC and Channel 4 television; For English National Opera has produced Orfeo, Akhnaten by Glass (British premiere), The Mask of Orpheus (world premiere) and The Return of Ulysses; Productions elsewhere have included: La Bohème for Opera North, Manon Lescaut at the Opéra-Comique, Paris, and work in Germany, Houston and New York; The Magic Flute, for Opera Factory, 1996; Butterfly and Tosca, Raymond Gubbay (1998–2001). *Honours:* Chevalier, l'Ordre des Arts et Lettres, 1985. *Current Management:* Allied Artists. *Address:* c/o English National Opera, St Martin's Lane, London WC2N 4ES, England.

FREEMAN-ATTWOOD, Jonathan, BMus, MPhil; British educator, musician (trumpet), producer and writer; *Vice-Principal, Royal Academy of Music*; b. 4 Nov. 1961, Woking, England; m. Henrietta Parham; one s. one d. *Education:* Univ. of Toronto, Christ Church, Oxford. *Career:* Dean of Undergraduate Studies, RAM 1991–95, Vice-Principal and Dir of Studies 1995–; Prof., Univ. of London 2001–. *Recordings:* 70 recordings as producer for independent labels (ASV, BIS, Channel Classics, Naxos, Avie, Simax, GNN, Chandos); recordings as trumpet soloist: Albinoni Sonatas and Concertos with Ian Simcock, Bach Connections with Colm Carey, Rheinberger with John Wallace and Colm Carey. *Publications:* contrib. to New Grove (2nd edn), Music and Letters, Musical Times, Early Music, Gramophone. *Honours:* Hon. RAM; Diapason d'or and Gramophone Awards as producer 1997, 2001, 2003. *Address:* Royal Academy of Music, Marylebone Road, London, NW1 5HT, England (office). *Telephone:* (20) 7873-7351 (office). *Fax:* (20) 7873-7451 (office). *E-mail:* K.McKiernan@ram.ac.uk (office).

FREIBERG, Christine; Singer (soprano); b. 1966, England; m., two c. *Education:* Royal College of Music, with Marion Studholme and in Paris with Bruce Brewer. *Career:* Clori in Cavalli's L'Egisto for St James's Opera; First Niece in Peter Grimes in Nantes and Cologne; Cherubino for Reisopera in Netherlands; Appearances with Opéra de Nantes in Ariadne auf Naxos; Kullervo by Sallinen; Götterdämmerung and Parsifal; Season 1998–99: Flower Maiden in Parsifal for Reiseopera, Netherlands; Italian Singer in Capriccio for Opera Nantes; Nele in Till Eulenspiegel for Nantes, 1999; Fyodor in Boris Godunov for Opera Ireland, 1999; Il re pastore: Aminta, for Musiek theater, Transparant, Belgium, 2002 and 2003 Tour; Many concert appearances. *Address:* Music International, 13 Ardilaun Road, London N5 2QR, England. *Telephone:* 01727 766432. *E-mail:* pc.raymond@virgin.net.

FREIER, Jurgen; Singer (Baritone); b. 3 Feb. 1943, Danzig, Germany. *Career:* Debut: Dresden Staatsoper, 1973, as Silvio in Pagliacci; Dresden until 1980, as Papageno, Rossini's Figaro and Belcore; Guest appearances throughout eastern Europe; Berlin Staatsoper from 1980, notably as Lysiart in Weber's Euryanthe, in the title role of Graf Mirabeau by Matthus (premiere, 1989) and Eugene Onegin; Düsseldorf, 1991, in Schreker's Die Gezeichneten; Hamburg, 1995, in the premiere of Schnittke's Historia von Dr Johann Fausten, Munich, 1996, in the premiere of Bose's Schlachthof 5; Komische Oper Berlin as Pizarro and Cologne Opera as Kurwenal, 1998; Season 1999–2000 as Wagner's Donner and Gunther at Hamburg, Kurwenal for Cologne Opera, and Alberich at Chemnitz. *Address:* Berlin Komische Oper, Behrenstrasse 55-57, 10177 Berlin, Germany.

FREIRE, Nelson; Brazilian pianist; b. 18 Oct. 1944, Boa Esperança. *Education:* studied with Nise Obino and Lúcia Branco in Brazil, with Bruno Seidlhofer in Vienna. *Career:* debut at Vienna Acad. of Music, performing Brahms' Sonata in F sharp minor 1959; duo partner Martha Argerich 1959–; has appeared with orchestras, including the Berlin Philharmonic, Munich Philharmonic, Royal Concertgebouw, Rotterdam Philharmonic, Vienna Symphony, London Symphony, Royal Philharmonic, Orchestre de Paris; signed exclusive recording contract with Decca 2001. *Recordings include:* Chopin 24 Preludes; Piano duos with Martha Argerich. *Honours:* prizewinner Int. Piano Competition of Rio de Janeiro 1957, First Prize Vianna da Motta competition, Lisbon 1972, Dinu Lipatti medal, London, Edison Prize for Chopin recording. *Address:* c/o Decca Classics, Universal Music (UK) Ltd, Elsinore House, 77 Fulham Palace Road, London, W6 8JA, England.

FREITAG, Erik; Composer and Violin Teacher; b. 1 Feb. 1940, Vienna, Austria. *Education:* Studied at the Vienna Hochschule für Musik and with Karl-Birger Blomdahl, Stockholm. *Career:* Violinist Swedish Radio, 1964–66; Philharmonic Orchestra, Stockholm, 1967–1970; Section Leader, Conservatory of Vienna; Composer-in-Residence at the University of North Western Michigan in association with the International Festival Earth/Arts Traverse, Michigan, 1996; mem, Austrian Society of Composers; ISCM Austrian Section; Ensemble Wiener Collage (adminstration). *Compositions:* Quintet for clarinet, horn, violin, cello and piano; Circuits magiques for string quartet; Limericks–5 songs for medium voice and 6 instruments; Immagini for violin solo, flute, oboe, violin, viola, cello, double bass and piano. *Recordings:* Helle Nacht for strings, 1990; Sonata for cello and piano, 1990; Triaphonie I for horn, violin and piano, 1995; Soul-Sky for violin solo, 1995; El retablo de la catedral de Tarragona for chamber ensemble, 1992; Radio: Yoziguanatzi for Orchestra, 1994; Triaphonie II for saxophone, violin and piano; Passages in the Wind, Poems by John Gracen Brown for baritone and 7 instruments; Reflections in Air for string trio; 3 pieces for string quartet; Strindburg-ljus och skugga for chamber orchestra; Idun for violin and piano; Sonata Nachtstücke for violin and viola. *Honours:* Competition Prize Nordelbische Tage, Hamburg, 1975; Prize, Austrian Ministry of Education. 1975; Prize, City of Vienna, 1979; Theodor Körner Prize, 1981. *Address:* Schippergasse 20, 1210 Vienna, Austria.

FRÉMAUX, Louis Joseph Félix; Orchestral Conductor; b. 13 Aug. 1921, Aire-sur-Lys, France; m. (1) Nicole Petibon, 1948, 4 s., 1 d., (2) Cecily Hake, 1999. *Education:* Conservatoire National Supérieur de Musique, Paris. *Career:* Musical Director and Permanent Conductor of Orchestre National de l'Opéra de Monte Carlo, Monaco, 1955–66; Principal Conductor, Rhônes-Alpes Philharmonic Orchestra, Lyon, 1968–71; Principal Conductor and Musical Director, City of Birmingham Symphony Orchestra, 1969–78; Created City of Birmingham Symphony Orchestra Chorus, 1974; Particularly known for performances of Berlioz; Chief Conductor, Sydney Symphony Orchestra, 1979–81; Principal Guest Conductor, 1982–85; Guest appearances in Austria, Belgium, Netherlands, France, Italy, New Zealand, Norway, Switzerland, South America and Germany; Has premiered Panufnik's Sinfonia Sacra, 1964, McCabe's 2nd Symphony, 1971, and Columbia Falls by Nicola le Fanu, 1975. *Recordings include:* French Baroque music by Gilles, De La Lande, Rameau, Campra, Mouret and Charpentier; Poulenc Stabat Mater and La Bal Masqué; Berlioz Grande Messe des Morts and overtures, Bizet Symphony, Saint-Saëns 3rd Symphony; Poulenc Les Biches, Piano Concerto and Gloria; Symphonie Fantastique; Rimsky's Schéhérazade. *Honours:* Croix de Guerre, 1945, 1947; Order of Cultural Merit, Monaco, 1965; Chevalier de la Légion d'Honneur, 1969; 8 Grand Prix du Disque Awards; Koussevitsky Award, 1973; The Music Trades Association Awards, 1976; Hon D Music, Birmingham, 1978; Honorary Member Royal Academy of Music, London, 1978. *Address:* 25 Edencroft, Wheeley's Road, Birmingham, B15 2LW, England.

FRENI, Mirella; Singer (soprano); b. 27 Feb. 1935, Modena, Italy; m. (1) Leone Magiera, 1955, 1 d., (2) Nicola Ghiarouv. *Career:* Debut: 1955 at Modena, as Micaela; Glyndebourne Festival, 1961; Royal Opera House, Covent Garden, 1962, as Zerlina in Don Giovanni; Metropolitan Opera House, New York, 1965; Appearances at Vienna State Opera and Salzburg Festival and in leading opera houses throughout the world; Major roles include Nannetta in Falstaff, Mimi in La Bohème, Zerlina in Don Giovanni, Susanna, Adina in L'Elisir d'amore, Violetta in La Traviata, Desdemona in Otello, centenary performance at La Scala, 1987; Grand Opera, Houston, 1987, as Aida; Marked 35th anniversary of debut in 1990 at Modena, as Manon Lescaut; Gala concert with the Boston Opera/Boston Symphony, 1990; Gran Teatro del Liceo, Barcelona, 1989, as Tatyana and Adriana Lecouvreur, Manon Lescaut, 1990; La Scala Milan, 1990, as Lisa in The Queen of Spades; Sang Alice Ford at the Metropolitan, 1992; Rome Opera and Barcelona, 1992, as Mimi; Sang Giordano's Fedora at Covent Garden, 1994 and at the New York Met, 1997; Tatiana at Turin, 1998; Sang Fedora at Genoa, 2000; Tchaikovsky's Maid of Orleans in Paris, 2002. *Recordings include:* Carmen; Falstaff; La Bohème; Madama Butterfly including video; Alcina; Tosca; Guillaume Tell; Verdi Requiem; Simon Boccanegra; Don

Carlos; Aida; Faust; Turandot; L'Amico Fritz; Don Giovanni; L'Elisir d'amore; Le nozze di Figaro.

FRENI, Rose; Singer (Mezzo-soprano); b. 1941, USA. *Career:* Sang at Wuppertal, Düsseldorf and Karlsruhe, 1965–75; Schwetzingen, 1969, in the premiere of Klebe's Das Märchen; New York City Opera from 1977, debut as Santuzza; Boston Opera from 1982, in the US premiere of Zimmermann's Die Soldaten, and Adalgisa in Norma; Giessen Opera, 1993, as Ariadne; Other roles have included Maddalena in Rigoletto, Jocasta in Oedipus Rex and the Witch in Dido and Aeneas. *Address:* c/o New York City Opera, Lincoln Center, New York, NY 10023, USA.

FRENKLOVA, Jana; Pianist; b. 17 Sept. 1947, Prague, Czechoslovakia; 1 d. *Education:* Prague Conservatoire, 1962–67, Honours Graduate; Leningrad Conservatoire, 1967–68 (studies curtailed after Russian invasion of Czechoslovakia). *Career:* Debut: Prague, 1956; Pianist in Residence, Lancaster University, 1975–79; Pianist in Residence, University College of North Wales, 1979–; Recording Artist for BBC Radio 3, 1977–. *Honours:* Numerous first prizes in Czechoslovakia up to 1968; Finalist, Alfredo Casella Competition, Naples, 1970; Winner, Dudley Competition, 1971. *Current Management:* Encore Concerts. *Address:* Maen Hir Bach, Dwyran, Anglesey, Gwynedd LL61 6UU, North Wales.

FRETWELL, Elizabeth; Operatic Soprano (retired), Adjudicator and Vocal Consultant; b. 13 Aug. 1920, Melbourne, Australia; m. Robert Simmons, 1 s., 1 d. *Career:* Joined National Theatre, Melbourne, 1950; Came to the United Kingdom in 1955; Joined Sadler's Wells, 1956 and Elizabethan Opera Company, Australia, 1963; Tours: West Germany, 1963; USA, Canada and Covent Garden, 1964; Europe, 1965; Guest Soprano with Cape Town and Durban Opera Companies, South Africa, 1970; Joined Australian Opera, 1970; Roles included Violetta, in La Traviata, Leonore in Fidelio, Ariadne in Ariadne auf Naxos, Senta in Flying Dutchman, Minnie in Girl of the Golden West, Leonora in Il Trovatore, Aida, Ellen Orford in Peter Grimes, Leonora in Forza del Destino, Alice Ford in Falstaff, Amelia in Masked Ball, Giorgetta in Il Tabarro, opening season, Sydney Opera House, 1973; Has sung in BBC Promenade Concerts and on television; mem, Music Board, Australian Opera Foundation, 1982–. *Recordings:* Il Trovatore; Land of Smiles, by Lehar. *Honours:* Order of the British Empire, 1977. *Address:* c/o Australian Opera, Sydney Opera House, Sydney, NSW, Australia.

FREUD, Anthony, LLB; British opera administrator and barrister; *General Director, Welsh National Opera;* b. 30 Oct. 1957, London; s. of the late Joseph Freud and Katalin Freud (née Löwi). *Education:* King's Coll. School, Wimbledon and King's Coll., London. *Career:* trained as barrister before joining Sadler's Wells Theatre Co. 1980–84; Co. Sec., Welsh National Opera 1984, Head of Planning 1989–92, Gen. Dir 1994–; Exec. Producer, Opera, Philips Classics 1992–94. *Honours:* Hon. Fellowship of Cardiff Univ. 2002. *Address:* Welsh National Opera, John Street, Cardiff, CF10 5SP, Wales (office). *Telephone:* (29) 2046-4666 (office). *Fax:* (29) 2048-3050 (office). *E-mail:* anthony.freud@wno .org.uk (office). *Website:* www.wno.org.uk (office).

FREUDENTHAL, Otto; Composer, Pianist and Violist; b. 29 July 1934, Gothenburg, Sweden; 1 s. *Education:* TCL, England; Studied piano with Ilona Kabos. *Career:* Debut: (as pianist) Wigmore Hall, London; Recitals and Concerts in England, Germany, Switzerland, Netherlands, Scandinavia, Japan, China, USA; Broadcasts; Teacher, Royal College of Music, Manchester; Assistant to Dr Otto Klemperer to 1973; mem, Swedish Society of Composers, STIM. *Compositions:* Chamber music, viola concerto, concert piece for trombone and orchestra; In Highgate Cemetery for strings; Chamber opera; A BankoMat cantata; The Song About Our Town; A cantata to Linkopings 700 year jubilee; Symphony, 1989; String Quartet, 1991; Saxophone concert, 1992. *Recordings:* Coliseum records, BBC, Swedish Radio; Wir Wandelten, with Cheryl Jonsson, soprano. *Publications:* (essay) Music and Equity (with Irene Lotz); Chamber Music with Wollenweber Edition, Munich, Plucked String Music. *Honours:* Harriet Cohen Memorial Medal for interpretation of Beethoven; Swedish State Cultural Stipend, 1977, 1987. *Address:* Bäckfall, 590 41 Rimforsa, Sweden (office); 6 Hillsborough, Corris Uchaf, Powys, SY20 9RG, Wales (home). *Telephone:* (1654) 761405. *E-mail:* otto@cooptel.net (home).

FREY, Alexander (James); Organist, Pianist, Music Director and Conductor; b. 5 Oct. 1961, Chicago, Illinois, USA. *Education:* BMus (honours), organ, piano, conducting, 1984, MMus (honours), organ, conducting, 1986, University of Michigan, Ann Arbor; Teachers include Gavin Williamson (piano), Robert Glasgow (organ), Gustav Meier (conducting); Dietrich Fischer-Dieskau (opera and lieder accompanying), Berlin. *Career:* Appeared as Pianist and Organist with Berlin Philharmonic Orchestra, Hollywood Bowl Orchestra, Deutsches Sinfonie Orchester, Rundfunk-Sinfonie Orchester Berlin, Brandenburg Chamber Orchestra (also Guest Conductor, 1993–94), Ars Longa Chamber Orchestra of Germany (also Principal Guest Conductor, 1991–94), Ensemble Europa (also Conductor, 1995), members of

Chicago Symphony Orchestra, (under Mauceri, Abbado and others); Annual world-wide recital tours; Music Director, Hamburg Kammerspiele Theater, 1992–93, Berliner Ensemble, 1992–95, collaborating with Peter Zadek; Music Director, Antony and Cleopatra at Edinburgh Festival, Vienna Festwochen, Holland Festival, Berlin, 1994, Das Wunder von Mailand, Venice Festival, 5th European Festival, Berlin, 1995, Ich bin das Volk, Heidelberg Festival, Berlin, 1995; Conducted Ensemble Europa, Israel, Berlin, to commemorate end of WW II, 1995; Chamber music with Ruggiero Ricci, Vermeer Quartet and Donald McInnes; Featured pianist or organist in 3 films; Television and radio, USA, Canada, Europe including Germany. Principal Conductor, Philharmonia Orchestra of Berlin, 1995–; Principal Conductor, Artist-in-Residence and Artistic Adviser, Festival Ruidoso, 1995–. *Current Management:* Artist Recitals, 3427 Fernwood Avenue, Los Angeles, CA 90030, USA.

FREY-RABINE, Lia; Dramatic Soprano; b. 12 Aug. 1950, Crosby, Minnesota, USA; m. Eugene Rabine, 27 June 1976, 1 s. *Education:* BMus, MMus, Indiana University, Bloomington; Private vocal studies with Eugene Rabine (Founder and Director of the Rabine Institute for Functional Voice Pedagogy, Bonstadt, Germany). *Career:* Debut: Municipal Theatre, Bern, Switzerland, 1973; Principal Singer, Bern, 1973–75, Flensburg, Germany, 1975–77, Nürnberg, 1977–79, Hagen, 1979–84, Frankfurt, 1984–; Guest appearances in numerous other German, Austrian and Swiss theatres and in Barcelona, Ghent, Rome, Naples, Vienna State Opera and other European cities; Sang the Siegfried Brünnhilde at Dortmund, 1991; and Elektra there, 1996. *Honours:* Metropolitan Opera Auditions National Finalist, 1971; Outstanding Musician of 1983, State of Nordrhein-Westfalen. *Current Management:* Kühnly Agency, Stuttgart, Germany. *Address:* Kleinstrasse 6, 61194 Niddatal-2, Germany.

FREYER, Achim; Stage Director and Theatre Designer; b. 30 March 1934, Berlin, Germany. *Education:* Studied at the Akademie der Kunste, East Berlin. *Career:* Debut: Designed sets and costumes for the Ruth Berghaus production of Il Barbiere di Siviglia at the Berlin Staatsoper, 1967; Emigrated to the West, 1973, and created designs for Cardillac and Pelléas et Mélisande at the Cologne Opera 1973–75; Directed and designed Iphigénie en Tauride at the Munich Staatsoper 1979 (seen at Amsterdam and Basle, 1990); Philip Glass's Satyagraha and the premiere of Akhnaten at the Stuttgart Staatsoper (1981, 1984); Orfeo ed Euridice at the Deutsche Oper Berlin, 1982, Die Zauberflöte at Hamburg (seen at the Vienna Festival 1991); Iphigénie en Tauride at the Deutsche Staatsoper, 1994; Die Zauberflöte for Salzburg, 1997 and Don Giovanni 1998, at Schwetzingen. *Address:* c/o Deutsche Staatsoper, Unter den Linden 7, 1086 Berlin, Germany.

FRIED, Anneliese; Singer (Mezzo-soprano); b. 1962, Germany. *Education:* Studied in Karlsruhe. *Career:* Sang at Aachen Opera, 1985–91; Munster, 1991–93, Cologne from 1993; Guest appearances at Düsseldorf (Mistress Quickly in Falstaff, 1995), Dresden (Fidalma in Il Matrimonio Segreto, 1996), Paris, Zürich and Geneva; Other roles have included Mary in Der fliegende Holländer, Ericlea in Monteverdi's Ulisse, Mrs Sedley in Peter Grimes, and Orlofsky in Die Fledermaus; Professor at the Cologne Musikhochschule from 1995. *Address:* c/o Staatliche Hochschule fur Music, Vocal Faculty, Dagobertstrasse 38, D–50668, Germany.

FRIED, Joel (Ethan); Conductor; b. 22 April 1954, California, USA; m. Mary Anne Massad, 9 Dec 1990, 1 step-d. *Education:* BMus, 1973; MMus, Piano Performance, DMA, University of Southern California, 1979. *Career:* Debut: Hidden Valley Opera, 1978; European debut, Heidelberg Castle Festival, 1981; Assistant Conductor, New York City Opera, 1980–82; Resident Conductor, Heidelberg Castle Festival, 1981–; Studienleiter, Saarland State Theatre, 1983–86; Chorus Master, Cleveland Opera, 1990–92; Chorus Master and Music Administrator, Pittsburgh Opera, 1992–; Conducting appearances with Zürich Opera, Fort Worth Opera and Cleveland Opera. *Honours:* 2nd Prize, American Conductors Competition, 1978; Special Prize for Contemporary Music, Hans Swarowsky International Conducting Competition, Vienna, 1984. *Address:* c/o Pittsburgh Opera, 711 Penn Avenue, Pittsburgh, PA 15222, USA.

FRIED, Miriam; Violinist; b. 9 Sept. 1946, Satu-Mare, Romania. *Education:* Rubin Academy of Music, Tel-Aviv; Graduate Studies, Europe and USA (Juilliard School, Ivan Galamian). *Career:* Debut: Carnegie Hall, New York, 1969; Royal Festival Hall, England; Appearances, orchestras world-wide including, Los Angeles Philharmonic; Philadelphia, Cleveland, Chicago, Boston Symphonies; New York Philharmonic; Berlin and Munich Philharmonics; Vienna Symphony; Zürich Tonhalle; Orchestre Nationale de France; Recent appearances include Stuttgart Radio Orchestra (conducted Neville Marriner); Danish Radio (Kurt Sanderling); Jerusalem Symphony at Berlin Festival; Orchestre Nationale, Belgium; Philharmonic Orchestras, Monte Carlo, Stuttgart, Nuremburg; Nouvel Orchestre Philharmonique, Paris; Opened Helsinki Festival (with Helsinki Philharmonic conducted by Gennadi Rozhdestvensky), 1988; Hollywood Bowl (Yuri Temirkanov), 1988; Cleveland Orchestra (Mariss Jansons), 1989; Santa Cecilia (Temirkanov), 1989; Orchestre de Paris (Kurt Sanderling), 1989; American engagements for 1994–95, Chicago Symphony Orchestra, Cleveland Orchestra, Boston Symphony Orchestra, Philadelphia Orchestra; Frequent engagements, Royal Philharmonic Orchestra; BBC television and Promenade Concerts; Edinburgh Festival; Scottish National Orchestra; Bournemouth Symphony; Numerous recitals. *Recordings:* Recital album, Deutsche Grammophon; Solo Violin Works, Bach; Sibelius Violin Concerto, Helsinki Philharmonic (Okko Kamu), 1988. *Honours:* Scholarship, overseas studies, American Israel Cultural Foundation; 1st Prizes, Paganini International Competition, Genoa Italy, 1968, Queen Elisabeth Competition, Belgium, 1971. *Current Management:* Agence de Concerts et Spectacles Caecilia. *Address:* c/o Mauroy Concerts, 19 rue des Primevères, L–2351, Luxembourg.

FRIEDE, Stephanie; Singer (Soprano); b. 1959, New York, USA. *Education:* Studied at the Juilliard School and the Oberlin Conservatory. *Career:* Debut: Houston Opera, 1985, as Siebel in Faust; Sang further at Houston as Zerlina, Micaela and Manon; European debut as Stuttgart 1987, as Adina; Amsterdam, 1987, as Massenet's Cendrillon; Season 1991 as Donna Anna at Munich and Elettra in Idomeneo at Glyndebourne; Liège, 1992, as Salome in Herodiade by Massenet; Further engagements at the Buxton Festival as Eleanore d'Este in Torquato Tasso by Donizetti, at Cologne as Violetta and elsewhere in Europe as Gounod's Juliette, Anne Trulove, and Mimi; Season 2000–01 as Giulietta at Antwerp, Salome and Sieglinde for Zürich Opera, and Amelia (Ballo in Maschera) at Hamburg. *Address:* c/o Oldani, Viale Legioni Romane 26, 1–20147 Milan, Italy.

FRIEDEL, Martin (Kurt); Composer; b. 3 Aug. 1945, Warwateil, Germany. *Education:* BSc (Hons), 1967, PhD, 1972, University of Melbourne. *Career:* Fellowships and Residences in Australia and Germany, 1976–95; Commissions from theatres in Australia, and the Adelaide Festival of the Arts, 1992. *Compositions include:* Sin, 7 act opera for 4 voices and orchestra, 1978; Two Songs, for soprano and ensemble, 1982; South of North, 1 act chamber opera, 1985; Conversations Before the Silence, cantata, 1989; Foxy, 1 act chamber opera, 1991; The Heaven Machine and Seduction of a General, 1 act operas for soprano and electronics, 1991; Four Choral Fragments for Walter Benjamin, 1992; Songs from the Astronauts, for soprano, baritone and ensemble, 1994; The Third Planet, oratorio, 1995; Three Night Pieces, string quartet, 1995. *Honours:* Best Score, Chicago International Film Festival, 1994. *Address:* c/o APRA, 1A Eden Street, Crows Nest, NSW 2065, Australia.

FRIEDERICH, (Albert) Matthias; oboist, recorder player and composer; b. 16 June 1954, Heidelberg, Germany; m. Margaret Joy Stone 1980; one s. *Education:* Cologne Music College with G. Hoeller, H. Hucke and A. Meidhof. *Career:* debut, recorder soloist, Vivaldi's Sopranini Recorder Concerto in C major, Heidelberg, 1966; Concerts with George Malcolm, Amadeus Quartet, Mozarteum Quartet, Munich String Trio, and Sinfonia Varsovia, Poland; Since 1988, member of Pifferari di Santo Spirito Trio, Heidelberg (with Margaret Friederich and Peter Schumann); Concerts, Berlin, Paris, Dallas and Tokyo; mem, International Double Reed Society. *Compositions:* Happy Birthday Variations, 1989; Highstreet Dixie, 1990; Enigma Blues for FGB, 1991; Jubilee Stomp, 1992; Amusement, 1994. *Recordings:* Music for Fun, 1991; Pifferari Safari, 1993. *Contributions:* Article, Jazz on the oboe and the cor anglais, to Rohrblatt. *Address:* Floringasse 2, 69117 Heidelberg, Germany.

FRIEDLI, Irene; Singer (Mezzo-soprano); b. 1965, Rauchlisberg, Switzerland. *Education:* Studied with Kurt Widmer at the Basle Music Academy and attended master classes with Dietrich Fischer-Dieskau and Brigitte Fassbaender. *Career:* Shepherd and Hope in Monteverdi's Orfeo and Dryad in Ariadne auf Naxos, Lucerne Opera, 1993–94; Zürich Opera as Gertrude in Roméo et Juliette, Suzuki, Third Lady in Die Zauberflöte, Mercédès (Carmen) and the title role in L'Enfant et les Sortilèges, 1994; Opera and concert engagements with such conductors as Helmuth Rilling, Horst Stein, Michel Corboz and Neeme Järvi; Has appeared widely as guest in Switzerland and abroad, notably in contemporary concert music. *Honours:* Prizewinner at the Hugo Wolf (Stuttgart), Schubert (Graz) and Othmar Schoeck (Lucerne) Competitions. *Address:* c/o Opernhaus Zürich, Falkenstrasse 1, 8008 Zürich, Switzerland.

FRIEDMAN, Gérard; Singer (Tenor); b. 3 April 1926, Paris, France. *Education:* Studied at the Paris Conservatoire with Roger Bourdin and Charles Panzera. *Career:* Sang Don Curzio in Don Giovanni at the 1955 Aix Festival, Théâtre des Champs Elysées, Paris, 1954, in the premiere (concert) of Prokofiev's Fiery Angel; Sang widely in France until 1988 as Spalanzani in Les Contes d'Hoffmann, a Brahmin in Padmâvatí by Roussel and Torquemada in L'Heure Espagnole by Ravel; Professor at the Metz Conservatory from 1970. *Recordings include:* Auber's Manon Lescaut, Samson et Dalila, Fauré's Pénélope and Chausson's Le Roi Arthus, Te Deum by Lully, Masses by M A Charpentier and songs by Fauré. *Address:* c/o Conservatoire National de Région Metz, 2 Rue Paradis, 57036 Metz, France.

FRIEDMAN, Leonard (Matthew); Violinist; b. 11 Dec. 1930, London, England; m. twice, 2 s., 3 d. *Education:* Guildhall School of Music and Drama. *Career:* Debut: Central Hall, 1938; Conway Hall, 1949; Joint Founder, Haydn Orchestra and Cremona Quartet; Member, Adolph Busch Chamber Orchestra, English Chamber Orchestra, Rostal, Hurwitz, Bath Festival; Founder Leader, Northern Symphony; Deputy Leader, Royal Philharmonic Orchestra and Leader, Bremen Philharmonic; Leader, Westphalia Symphony; Founder, Scottish Ensemble; Guest Leader, Scottish Chamber; London Festival; Member, Melos of London; Duo with Allan Schiller, and with son Richard Friedman; Director, Friedman Ensemble; mem, Honorary Member, Royal Overseas; Scottish Arts; New Club. *Recordings:* Director, Music at Hopetoun; Director, Music at Drumlanrig; Scandinavian Serenade; String Orchestra Music by Mozart; Baroque Cello Concertos; English Serenade; Schubert String Quintet; Bach Concertos; Tribute to Kreisler. *Honours:* Gold Medal, Guildhall School of Music, 1953; Royal Patronage of Duke of Edinburgh, 1975; Citizenship Prize of Edinburgh, 1980–81; Founder/Director, Camerata of St Andrew, 1988. *Address:* 17a Dublin Street, Edinburgh EH1 3PG, Scotland.

FRIEDRICH, Reinhold; Trumpet Player; b. 14 July 1958, Weingarten, Baden, Germany; m. Annette Friedrich, 2 s. *Education:* Studies with Edward Tarr, Pierre Thibaud, Paris, 1979–83. *Career:* Debut: Berlin Philharmony; Swiss television in Zürich, 1995; Television and Live Broadcasting of the EBU Opening Concerto with B A Zimmermann's Nobody Knows De Trouble I See, Biennale Berlin 1997 Trumpet Concerto by Benedict Mason; mem, International Trumpet Guild. *Compositions:* B. A. Zimmermann, Nobody Knows De Trouble I See, 1994; Hummel, First Recordings of the Concerto in E Major with the Historical Keyed Trumpet, 1996. *Recordings:* B A Zimmermann, Nobody Knows De Trouble I See; Hummel and Puccini, Recordings with the Historical Keyed Trumpet; Orchestra, Wiener Akademie; Sequenza X by Berio; Gubaidulina's Trio. *Contributions:* Frankfurter Allgemeine Zeitung. *Honours:* 1st Prize, German Music Competition, 1981; Winner, ARD Competition, Munich, 1986. *Current Management:* Astrid Schoerke, Hannover. *Address:* Badener Str 49a, 76229 Karlsruhe, Germany.

FRIEND, Caroline; Singer (Soprano); b. 1950, England. *Career:* Concert appearances in the United Kingdom, Switzerland, Belgium, France, Germany and the Netherlands; Repertoire includes Handel's Oratorios, Bach's Oratorios and Cantatas, Schubert's A flat Mass, Britten's War Requiem under Stephen Cleobury in King's College, Vaughan Williams' Sea Symphony, Howells' Hymnus Paradisi, Rossini's Stabat Mater, Dvořák's Stabat Mater; Mahler's 4th Symphony and Les Nuits d'Eté with the Netherlands Philharmonic under Franz-Paul Decker; Appearances with the Songmakers' Almanac in England and Ireland, performing Robin Holloway's Women in War; Sang Diane in Rameau's Hippolyte et Aricie for the English Bach Festival under Jean-Claude Malgoire in Athens and Versailles and at Covent Garden; Other roles include Mozart's Donna Anna, Susanna, Pamina, Countess and Fiordiligi (Pavilion Opera), Rosalinde (Die Fledermaus), Norina (Don Pasquale), Hannah in The Merry Widow, Tosca and Mimi, (Puccini), Berta in The Barber of Seville and performances of Balfe's The Siege of Rochelle; Engagements in all the major London concert halls and with many choral societies; Conductors include Adrian Boult, John Eliot Gardiner and Charles Mackerras. *Address:* 33 Wetherby Mansions, Earls Court Square, London SW5 9BH, England.

FRIEND, Lionel, LRAM, ARCM; conductor; b. 13 March 1945, London, England; s. of Norman A. C. Friend and Moya Lilian Friend; m. Jane Hyland 1969, one s. two d. *Education:* Royal College of Music, London, London Opera Centre. *Career:* debut, Welsh National Opera, 1969; Welsh National Opera, 1968–72; Glyndebourne Festival Opera, 1969–72; Staatstheater, Kassel, Germany, 1972–75; Staff Conductor, English National Opera, 1976–89; Musical Director, Nexus Opera, 1981–; Musical Director, New Sussex Opera, 1989–96; Guest Conductor: BBC Symphony; Philharmonia; Swedish Radio; Orchestre National de France; Hungarian Radio; Opera National, Brussels; Many international festivals. *Recordings:* Works by Anthony Milner, Havergal Brian (BBC Symphony Orchestra), Alan Rawsthorne (BBC Scottish Symphony Orchestra), Nicholas Maw, Anthony Payne, Bliss, Poulenc, Colin Matthews, Debussy, Simon Holt, Schoenberg (Nash Ensemble), Stravinsky (Scottish Chamber Orchestra); Has conducted over 100 world premiere performances including Birtwistle's The Woman and the Hare, 1999. *Address:* 136 Rosendale Road, London, SE21 8LG, England (home). *Telephone:* (20) 8761-7845.

FRIGERIO, Ezio; Stage Designer; b. 16 July 1930, Como, Italy. *Education:* Studied architecture at Milan Polytechnic. *Career:* Costume Designer, Giorgio Strehler's Piccolo Teatro d'Arte from 1955; Collaborations with Strehler, Eduardo de Filippo and other directors in Italy and elsewhere; Designed Don Pasquale at the Edinburgh Festival, 1962, Tosca at Cologne, 1976, and Carmen at Hamburg, 1988; Collaborations with Nuria Espert for Madama Butterfly and Traviata at Scottish Opera (1987 and 1989), Rigoletto at Covent Garden, 1988, and Elektra at Barcelona, 1990; La Scala Milan, 1990, with Fidelio and The Queen of Spades; Designs for Il Turco in Italia and Anna Bolena at Madrid, season 1990–91; Andrea Chénier for Buenos Aires, 1996; Aida at Palermo, 1998; Frequent associations with costume designer Franca Squarciapino. *Address:* c/o Royal Opera House (Contracts), Covent Garden, London WC2E 9 DD, England.

FRIMMER, Monika; Singer (Soprano); b. 1955, Marburg, Germany. *Education:* Studied in Hanover. *Career:* Staatstheater, Hanover, 1981–93, notably in operas by Mozart and the Baroque repertory; Herrenhausen Festival, 1981, as Morgana in Handel's Alcina; Hanover, 1989, as Matilde in a revival of Steffani's Enrico Leone; Deutsche Oper Berlin, 1991–92; Sang in Handel's Radamisto at Göttingen, 1993; Concert engagements throughout Europe, and in the USA and Israel. *Recordings include:* Messiah, Mozart Masses and Pergolesi Stabat Mater; Radamisto. *Address:* c/o Göttingen Handel Festival (contracts), Augustplatz 8, 7010 Leipzig, Germany.

FRISCH, Walter M.; Professor of Music; b. 26 Feb. 1951, New York, NY, USA; m. Anne-Marie Bouché 1981, 2 s. *Education:* BA, Yale University, 1973; MA, 1977, PhD, 1981, University of California, Berkeley. *Career:* Assistant Professor of Music, 1982–88, Associate Professor, 1988–94, Professor, 1994–, Columbia University; Research in music of 19th and 20th centuries, especially the Austrian tradition (Schubert, Brahms, Schoenberg); mem, American Musicological Society; American Brahms Society. *Publications:* Brahms' Alto Rhapsody (editor, facsimile edition), 1983; Brahms and the Principle of Developing Variation, 1984; Schubert: Critical and Analytical Studies (editor), 1986; The Early Works of Arnold Schoenberg, 1993. *Contributions:* Co-editor, 19th Century Music, 1984–92. *Honours:* Winner, American Society of Composers, Authors and Publishers-Deems Taylor Award for outstanding book on music, 1985, 1995. *Address:* Department of Music, Columbia University, New York, NY 10027, USA.

FRISELL, Sonja; Stage Director; b. 5 Aug. 1937, Richmond, Surrey, England. *Education:* Studied piano and acting at the Guildhall School. *Career:* Associated with Carl Ebert at the St ädtische Oper Berlin and at Glyndebourne; Staff Producer, La Scala, solo producer in North and South America and Europe; Directed La Favorite at the 1977 Bregenz Festival, Vivaldi's Tito Manlio at La Scala, 1979, and Handel's Agrippina at Venice, 1985; Marriage of Figaro, San Francisco, 1982; Directed Carmen at Buenos Aires, 1985, Aida at the Metropolitan, 1988; Lyric Opera of Chicago, 1989–90; Don Carlos: Khovanshchina at San Francisco, 1990; Don Giovanni, Capetown, 1991; Directed: Die Zauberflöte for Washington Opera at Kennedy Center, 1991 (revived 1998); Forza del Destino at San Francisco, 1992; Otello at Washington, 1992; Ballo at Chicago, 1992; Rigoletto at Gothenburg, 1993; Trovatore at Chicago, 1993; Lucia at Calgary, 1994; Eugene Onegin, Calgary, 1996; La Gioconda, La Scala, 1997; Elena da Feltre, by Mercadante, Wexford, 1997; Turandot, Seville, 1998 and Trieste, Cagliari, Santander and Cordoba, 1999; Eugene Onegin, Phoenix, 2000; Otello, Washington, 2000; Eugene Onegin with Arizone Opera, 2000; La traviata in Rio de Janeiro, 2001; Don Carlos, Washington, 2001; Carmen, Iceland, 2001; LaTraviata, Rio de Janeiro, 2001; Otello, Tokyo, 2002; Otello in Tokyo, 2002; Salome with Arizona Opera, 2003; Turnadot in Helsinki, 2004mem, AGMA. *Current Management:* CAMI New York, USA. *Address:* Quinta do Refugio, Pincho 8600-090 Bensafrim, Algarve, Portugal.

FRITH, Benjamin; Concert Pianist; b. 11 Oct. 1957, Sheffield, England; m. Donna Sansom, April 1989, 3 d. *Education:* Private study with Fanny Waterman since childhood; BA (Hons) 1st Class, Music, Leeds University, 1979. *Career:* Debut: Official London debut in recital at Wigmore Hall, 1981, sponsored by Countess of Munster Trust; Performing career of recitals, concertos and participation in chamber music ensembles in London and the Provinces including South Bank, Wigmore Hall, Usher Hall Edinburgh, Aldeburgh, Harrogate and many major festivals; Television and radio appearances; Concerts in Italy, Spain, Germany, Poland, Israel and America; mem, Incorporated Society of Musicians. *Recordings:* Diabelli and 32 variations by Beethoven; Chamber music; Schumann piano music, Davidsbündlertänze (opus 6), Fantasiestücke (opus 12); Martin Ellerby, piano and chamber works, and Collage, French and English, clarinet and piano music with Linda Merrick; Mendelssohn, complete solo piano works and complete works for piano and orchestra; Messiaen, Visions de l'Amen, with Peter Hill, Malcolm Arnold, complete piano works. *Honours:* Joint Top Prizewinner, Busoni International Pianoforte Competition, 1986–;

Gold Medallist and joint 1st Prizewinner, Arthur Rubenstein International Piano Masters Competition, 1989. *Current Management:* Modena International Music, Italy; Rosalia Heifetz, Israel. *Address:* 6 Carisbrook Road, Carlton in Lindrick, Nottinghamshire S81 9 NJ, England.

FRITTOLI, Barbara; Singer (Soprano); b. 1967, Milan, Italy. *Education:* Studied at the Giuseppe Verdi Conservatory, Milan. *Career:* Sang first at the Teatro Comunale, Florence, and has appeared as Mozart's Countess under Abbado, Fiordiligi in Vienna and Ravenna, 1996; Donna Elvira at Naples; Desdemona with Antonio Pappano at Brussels and with Abbado at the Salzburg Easter Festival, 1996; New York Met and Covent Garden debuts as Mimi and Micaela; Medora in Verdi's Il Corsaro, Turin, 1996; Concerts include Strauss's Vier Letzte Lieder in Milan, Rome and London, Rossini's Stabat Mater, Ein Deutsches Requiem and the Verdi Requiem; Sang Fiordiligi in Così fan tutte at Covent Garden and Glyndebourne, 1998; Season 1999–2000 in new production of Falstaff at Covent Garden; Season 2002–03 as Donizetti's Maria Stuarda at Edinburgh (concert) and Vitellia in La Clemenza di Tito at Covent Garden, returning for Luisa Miller. *Recordings include:* Il Trittico, with Mirella Freni; Il Barbiere di Siviglia; Pergolesi's Stabat Mater, with Riccardo Muti. *Honours:* Winner of several international competitions. *Current Management:* Askonas Holt Ltd, Lonsdale Chambers, 27 Chancery Lane, London, WC2A 1PF, England. *Telephone:* (20) 7400-1700. *Fax:* (20) 7400-1799. *E-mail:* info@askonasholt.co .uk. *Website:* www.askonasholt.co.uk.

FRITZ, Rebekka, BA, MA, PhD, LRSM; Musicologist; b. Berlin, Germany. *Education:* Trinity Coll., Dublin Univ., Ireland. *Career:* Lecturer in Musicology, Trinity Coll., Dublin 1994–97, Conservatory of Music, Dublin 1996–97; violin teacher, Lüchow-Dannenberg 1997–98; Lecturer in Musicology, Univ. of Paderborn 1998, Münster Univ. 1999–; mem. of editorial bd for Die Musik in Geschichte und Gegenwart 2001–; mem. Royal Musical Asscn, Gesellschaft für Musikforschung, ACMP. *Publications:* Text and Music in German Operas of the 1920s 1998, Denen Kennern... Winifried Schlepphorst zum 65. Geburtstag 2002, Die Sammlung Nordkirchen: Kammermusik 2004; contrib. to Die Musik in Geschichte und Gegenwart. *Honours:* Trinity Postgraduate Award 1992–95. *Address:* Musikwissenschaftl. Seminar, Schossplatz 6, 48149 Münster, Germany (office). *Telephone:* (251) 8324560 (office). *E-mail:* fritzr@uni-muenster.de (office). *Website:* www.uni-muenster.de/ Musikwissenschaft (office).

FRITZSCH, Johannes; Conductor; b. 1960, Meissen, Germany. *Education:* Studied with his father and at Dresden Hochschule für Musik from 1975. *Career:* Second Kapellmeister, Rostock Opera, 1982–87; Conducted Il Barbiere di Siviglia and Il Matrimonio Segreto at the Semper Opera Dresden, 1987; Nearly 200 performances at the Dresden Staatsoper with the Dresdener Staatskapelle; Guest Conductor, Royal Swedish Opera in Stockholm; Regular orchestra concerts in former East Germany; West German debut October 1990 with Beethoven's Fifth Piano Concerto and the New World Symphony with the National Theatre Orchestra, Mannheim; Danish debut, October 1991 with the Orchestra of Danish Radio at Copenhagen; Also engaged for Don Giovanni, Royal Opera, Stockholm, 1991; Rialto Theatre, Copenhagen, 1991; Entführung, Nozze di Figaro and Don Giovanni, Royal Opera Stockholm, 1991; La Traviata, Hanover, 1991; Hansel and Gretel at Sydney, with Australian Opera, 1992; Die Bassariden at Freiburg, 1993; Music Director, 1993–; Der Freischütz at Cologne, 1997. *Address:* c/o Freiburg Opera, Bertoldstrasse 46, 79098 Freiburg im Breisgau, Germany.

FROBENIUS, Wolf; Musicologist; b. 1 June 1940, Speyer/Rhein, Germany. *Education:* Studies in Musicology, History of Art and History, Freiburg i/Br, Germany and Paris, France; PhD, Freiburg i/Br, 1968; Habilitation, Freiburg i/Br, 1988. *Career:* Staff Member, Handwörterbuch der musikalischen Terminologie, Akademie der Wissenschaften und der Literatur, Mainz, 1968–88; Teacher, University of Freiburg i/ Br, 1971–88; Professor, University of Saarbrücken. *Publications:* Hohannes Boens Musica und seine Konsonanzenlehre, 1971. *Contributions:* Handwörterbuch der Musikwissenschaft; The New Grove; Die Musik in Geschichte und Gegenwart. *Address:* Akazienweg 56, 66121 Saarbücken, Schafbrücke, Germany.

FRONTALI, Roberto; Singer (Baritone); b. 1963, Italy. *Career:* Sang at the Rome Opera from 1986, in Spontini's Agnese di Hohenstaufen, Valentin in Faust and Massenet's Albert; Season 1992–93 as Belcore at Dallas and Ford in Falstaff at La Scala; Sang Rossini's Figaro at Florence and Naples, 1993; San Francisco, 1993, as Riccardo in I Puritani; Season 1995–96 with Marcello in La Bohème at the Metropolitan; Florence, 1996, as Enrico in Lucia di Lammermoor; Other roles include Nottingham in Roberto Devereux by Donizetti, Verdi's Miller and Puccini's Sharpless; Season 1998 with Alphonse in La Favorite at Rome and Rossini's Figaro at Genoa and for the Royal Opera, London; Season 2000–01 as Count Luna at the New York Met, Eugene Onegin at Florence, Germont for the Opéra Bastille, Falstaff at

Frankfurt and Ernesto in Il Pirata by Bellini at Catania. *Recordings include:* Falstaff; L'Elisir d'amore. *Address:* c/o Teatro dell Opera di Roma, Piazza B. Gigli 8, 00184 Rome, Italy.

FROUNBERG, Ivar; Composer; b. 12 April 1950, Copenhagen, Denmark; m. Inge Sínderskov Madsen, 1 s. *Education:* Organist and Choirleader, 1976; MA, Composition, State University of New York, USA, 1981; Royal Danish Academy of Music, 1986. *Career:* Lecturer, Electroacoustic Music, 1986–90, Assistant Professor, Musical Composition, 1991–, The Royal Danish Academy of Music; Board of the Danish Composers' Society, 1982–94; Board of KODA, 1988–94; Music Coordinator at the 1994 ICMC; Chairman ISCM Festival, 1996; Chairman, DIEM, 1998–; Councillor at the Danish Arts Council, 1999–; Prof., Norwegian State Acad. of Music, Oslo, 2000–. *Compositions:* Drei-Klang, 1982; Henri Michaux preludes, 1985; Embryo, 1985; Multiple Forms, 1986; A Dirge: Other echoes inhabit the Garden, 1988; What did the Sirens sing as Ulysses sailed by?, 1989; A Pattern of Timeless Motion, 1989; Time and the Bell, 1990; SHâTaLè, 1991; World Apart 1992–94;... to arrive where we started, 1993; Hydra, 1996; Droemmespor, 1997; The Anatomy of a Point, 1990–95/97; Hoodoos 1997; Quasi una sonata, 1998; Cancion, no cantado, 1998; Voyelles, 1999; SAXO, 2000; Prélude-Voyage-Jotunheim, 2002; Logographes, 2003. *Recordings:* A Pattern of Timeless Motion; What did the Sirens Sing as Ulysses sailed by?, A Dirge: Other Echoes Inhabit the Garden, Multiple Forms; Other Echoes Inhabit the Garden (solo version); Worlds Apart;... to arrive where we started. *Publications:* Theory and Praxis in the compositional methods of Iannis Xenakis–an exemplification; Komponisten Pierre Boulez, 1985; Ein Schwebender Stein... Positionen 37. *Contributions:* Dansk Musiktidskrift; Nutida Musik. *Honours:* The Ancker Grant, 1994; 3 Year Grant of the Danish State Arts Council, 1994–96; Prize in Honour of Carl Nielsen, 1995; The Poul Schierbeck Prize of Honour, 1998. *Address:* POB 5190, Gydasvei 6, Majorstua, 0302, Norway (office); Melchiorsvej 1, 3450 Alleríd, Denmark. *Telephone:* 23-36-71-08 (office). *E-mail:* if@nmh.no (office).

FRUGONI, Orazio; Pianist; b. 28 Jan. 1921, Davos, Switzerland. *Education:* Graduated Milan Conservatory, 1939; Attended master classes of Alfredo Casella at the Accademia Chigiana, Siena, and Dinu Lipatti at the Geneva Conservatory. *Career:* Played in concerts in Italy from 1939 and in the USA from 1947; Piano professor at the Eastman School, Rochester, until 1967; Director, 1967–72; Teacher of piano at the Luigi Cherubini Conservatory at Florence from 1972. *Recordings include:* Beethoven's E flat concerto of 1784 (premiere recording); Mendelssohn's Piano Concerto. *Honours:* Prix de Virtuosité, Geneva Conservatory, 1945. *Address:* Conservatorio di Musica L Cherubini, Piazzetta delle Belle Arti, Florence, Italy.

FRÜHBECK DE BURGOS, Rafael; Conductor; b. 15 Sept. 1933, Burgos, Spain; m. Maria Carmen Martinez, 1959, 1 s., 1 d. *Education:* Music Academies in Bilbao, Madrid and Munich and University of Madrid. *Career:* Chief Conductor, Municipal Orchestra, Bilbao, 1958–62; Music Director and Chief Conductor, 1962–78, Honorary Conductor, 1998, Spanish National Orchestra. Madrid; Music Director of Düsseldorf and Chief Conductor, Düsseldorf Symphoniker, 1966–71; Musical Director, Montreal Symphony Orchestra, 1974–76; Principal Guest Conductor, National Symphony Orchestra, Washington, USA, 1980–90; Principal Guest Condcutor, Yomiuri Nippon Symphony Orchestra, Tokyo, 1980–90; Honorary Conductor, Yomiuri Nippon Symphony Orchestra, Tokyo, 1991; Conducted opening concert of 1989 Edinburgh Festival, Falla's Atlantida and La Vida Breve; Chief Conductor of the Vienna Symphony Orchestra, 1991–96; Music Director, Deutsche Oper, Berlin, 1992–97; Principal Guest Conductor Dresden Philharmonic Orchestra, Germany, 2003–04; Conducted Carmen at Genoa, 1992; Don Carlos in Berlin; Chief Conductor, Rundfunk Sinfonieorchester Berlin, Germany, 1994–2000; Led new production of Faust at Zürich, 1997; Der fliegende Holländer in Berlin; Conducted Wolf-Ferrari's Sly at Zürich; Chief Conductor RAI National Symphony Orchestra, Turin, 2001–. *Compositions:* Orchestration of the Suite Espagñola, by I Albéniz, 1965; Orchestration of Tema y Variaciones by J Turina, 1985. *Recordings include:* Falla El amor brujo; La vida breve, Nights in the Gardens of Spain and L'Atlantida; Mozart Requiem and Schumann 3rd Symphony; Mendelssohn Elijah and St Paul; Orff, Carmina Burana, Le Sacre du Printemps, Prokofiev Violin Concertos, Mendelssohn Violin Concerto; Beethoven's Symphonies and the complete works of Falla, with ballets by Stravinsky and Bartók with the London Symphony Orchestra, for Collins Classics. *Honours:* Dr hc (Univ. of Navarra, Pamplona, Spain) 1994, Dr hc (Univ. of Burgos) 1998; Fundación Guerrero Prize of Spanish Music 1996, Int. Gustav Mahler Soc. Gold Medal, Vienna 1996, Gold Memorah (equivalent hon. mem.) Israel Philharmonic Orchestra 1999; Gold Medal of the City of Vienna, Austria 1995, Gold Medal of the Civil Merit of the Austrian Republic, Vienna 1996, Gold Medal of the State of Vienna 2000, Big Cross of the Civil Merit of the Federal Republic of Germany 2004. *Current Management:* Muscipána, Madrid. *Address:* Avenida del Mediterráneo 21, Madrid 28007, Spain.

FRYKBERG, Susan; Composer; b. 10 Oct. 1954, Hastings, New Zealand. *Education:* Studied at the University of Canterbury; University of Otago; Simon Fraser University. *Career:* Freelance Composer; Teacher in Vancouver, the University of Auckland and Simon Fraser University; mem, Canadian Music Centre; New Zealand Music Centre. *Compositions include:* Electro-acoustic music theatre pieces: Saxarba, 1985, Caroline Herschel Is Minding The Heavens, 1988, Woman And House, 1990, Mother Too, 1991; Birth/Rebirth/Bearing Me, 1991; Insect Life, 1993; Audio-Birth Project, 1996–97; Sue and Kathy Telecompose Across the Country, 1997. *Recordings:* Astonishing Sense of Being Taken Over by Something Far Greater Than Me; Harangue 1. *Publications:* Acoustic Dimensions of Communication, Study Guide; Simon Fraser University. *Address:* c/o New Zealand Music Centre, PO Box 10042, Level 13, Brandon Street, Wellington, New Zealand.

FU, Haijing; Singer (baritone); b. 1960, China. *Education:* Studied in London and New York. *Career:* Concert engagements include Mozart's Requiem with the Montreal Symphony Orchestra, Zemlinsky's Lyric Symphony, Beethoven's Ninth, Carmina Burana with the Pacific Symphony and the Cleveland Orchestra, Verdi's Requiem in Geneva; Mendelssohn's Erste Walpurgisnacht with the Boston Symphony and Mozart's C minor Mass with the Cincinnati Orchestra; Metropolitan Opera debut 1990, as Germont, followed by Sir Richard Forth in I Puritani; Renato with Atlanta Opera, Enrico and Verdi's Miller at Philadelphia and Filippo in Bellini's Bianca e Fernando at Catania, Italy, 1992; Appearances as Rigoletto with the San Diego and Edmonton Opera companies; Other roles include Marcello in La Bohème, and Posa in Don Carlos; Sang Germont at Philadelphia, 1992; Season 1998 as Germont at Miami and in Stiffelio at the New York Met. *Honours:* Second Prize, Benson and Hedges Gold Award International Competition, London, 1987; Winner, Metropolitan Opera National Council Competition, 1988. *Address:* c/o Metropolitan Opera House, Lincoln Center, New York, NY 10023, USA.

FUCHS, Barbara; Singer (Soprano); b. 1959, Zürich, Switzerland. *Education:* Studied at Frankfurt and Zürich, with masterclasses by Erik Werba, Sena Jurinac and Elisabeth Schwarzkopf. *Career:* Sang at the Ulm Opera, 1983–85, as Blondchen, Adele, Olympia, Rosina and Susanna; Gelsenkirchen, 1985–87, as Sophie, the Queen of Night and Annina in Eine Nacht in Venedig; Frankfurt from 1990, as Zerbinetta, Helena in Reimann's Troades and other coloratura roles; Guest appearances throughout Germany and frequent concert engagements.

FUCHS, Olivia; Opera Director; b. 15 Aug. 1963, London, England; m. Nigel Robson; one s. one d. *Education:* BA, German and Drama, Westfield Coll., Univ. of London; Postgraduate Diploma, Drama Studio, London. *Career:* debut, Johnny Johnson by Kurt Weill for Opera Factory Zürich, 1992; Britten's Turn of the Screw, for Bath Theatre Royal, 1993; Handel's Arminio for the London Handel Society, 1996; Mozart's Marriage of Figaro at the Queen Elizabeth Hall, 1996; La Bohème, 1997, and Il Trovatore, 1998, both for Opera South, Ireland; Mozart's Apollo and Hyacinth for the Classical Opera Company, 1998; Premiere of John Lunn's The Maids for ENO/Lyric Theatre, Hammersmith, 1998; Britten's The Turn of the Screw for the Brighton Festival, 2000; Verdi's La Traviata for English Touring Opera, 2001–02; Janáček's Osud and Sarka for Garsington Opera, 2002; Beethoven's Fidelio for Opera Holland Park, 2003; Wolf's Italian Songbook for Royal Opera House, 2003; Dvorak's Rusalka for Opera North, 2003; Tchaikovsky's Cherevichki for Garsington Opera 2004; Verdi's Luisa Miller for Opera Holland Park 2004; Peter Sellar's Theodora for Opera du Rhin 2004; Don Giovanni for Opera North 2005 fmr Assoc. Dir, Glyndebourne and Opera Factory; mem., Directors' Guild of Great Britain. *Current Management:* Music Hall, Vicarage Way, Ringmer, BN8 5LA, England. *Telephone:* (1273) 814240 (office). *Fax:* (1273) 813637 (office). *E-mail:* info@musichall.co.uk (office).

FUGE, Katharine; Singer (Soprano); b. 1968, Jersey. *Education:* Studied in London. *Career:* Engagements with the English Bach Soloists, notably on the Bach Cantata Pilgrimage tour, 2000, throughout Europe and in New York; St Matthew Passion with De Nederlande Bachvereniging, 2001; Handel and Zelenka with Collegium Vocal Gent, Handel's Athalia with Frieder Bernius in Göttingen, Acis and Galatea in Denmark; Season 2000-01 in Britain at Symphony Hall, Birmingham, Wigmore Hall, and Liverpool and Southwark Cathedrals; Repertory includes Poulenc's Gloria, Stabat Mater by Stanford and Pergolesi, and Messiah; Sang First Mermaid in Weber's Oberon at the Barbican Hall, London 2002. *Recordings include:* Albums in DG Archiv collection, Bach Cantata Pilgrimage; Vivaldi Gloria and Handel Dixit Dominus (Philips Classics); Dvořák Mass in D. *Address:* c/o English Baroque Soloists, 57 Kingswood Road, London, SW19 3 ND, England.

FUGELLE, Jacquelyn; Singer (Soprano); b. 1949, London, England; m. George Johnston, 1975, 1 d. *Education:* Studied at Guildhall School of Music; Vienna Academy and in Rome. *Career:* Debut: Wigmore Hall, London, 1975; Extensive repertoire in oratorio, recital and opera;

Appearances in England, Canada and Europe; Television and radio appearances in the Netherlands, Sweden and for the BBC; Debut at Royal Opera House, Covent Garden, 1991 as Arbate in Mozart's Mitridate; Other roles at Royal Opera House include Falcon, in Die Frau ohne Schatten; Debut with Scottish Opera, 1993; Major oratorio performances include Elijah with London Philharmonic Orchestra, conducted by Kurt Masur; Broadcasts include Messiah in Norway, Mendelssohn's 2nd Symphony in Paris and B Minor Mass in Iceland; mem, ISM; Equity. *Recordings:* Operatic Favourites with Joan Sutherland, Luciano Pavarotti; Music by Bottesini with Tomas Martin on double bass and Anthony Halstead on piano. *Honours:* Silver Medal, Worshipful Company of Musicians; Countess of Munster; Royal Society of Arts Scholarships; 2nd Prize, Kathleen Ferrier Competition. *Address:* 38 Wadham Road, Portsmouth, Hampshire, PO 2 9EE, England.

FUJIKAWA, Mayumi; Violinist; b. 27 July 1946, Asahigawa City, Japan. *Education:* Toho Conservatoire, Tokyo; Antwerp Conservatory, Belgium; further study with Leonid Kogan in Nice. *Career:* concerts with leading orchestras in South America, Australia, Israel, Asia, Japan and Europe; American orchestras in Philadelphia, Boston, Chicago, Pittsburgh and Cleveland; festival engagements at Aldeburgh with Previn, Edinburgh with the Concertgebouw Orchestra and Kondrashin; other conductors include Barenboim, Dutoit, Foster, Haitink, Levine, Ormandy, Sanderling and Rattle; television appearances playing the Mozart Concertos with the Scottish Chamber Orchestra; Promenade Concerts, London, 1991, in Mozart's Sinfonia Concertante. *Recordings:* Mozart Concertos with the Royal Philharmonic conducted by Walter Weller; Beethoven's Kreutzer and Franck's Sonata with Michael Roll; Tchaikovsky and Bruch Concertos with the Rotterdam Philharmonic; Sonatas by Prokofiev and Fauré. *Honours:* Second Prize, Tchaikovsky International Competition, Moscow, 1970; First Prize, Henri Vieuxtemps Competition, Verviers, Belgium, 1970. *Current Management:* Terry Harrison Artists Management, The Orchard, Market Street, Charlbury, Oxfordshire OX7 3PJ, England. *Telephone:* (1608) 810330. *Fax:* (1608) 811331. *E-mail:* artists@terryharrison.force9.co.uk.

FUJIOKA, Sachio; Conductor; b. 1962, Tokyo, Japan. *Education:* Studied in Japan with Kenichiro Kobayshi and Akeo Watanabe; Royal Northern College of Music, 1990–. *Career:* Assistant Conductor of the BBC Philharmonic, 1994; Season 1995–96 as Conductor of the Japan Philharmonic and Principal Conductor of the Manchester Camerata; Season 1996–97 with Royal Philharmonic Bournemouth, Norwegian Radio, Stavanger and Singapore Symphony Orchestras; Royal Liverpool and Guildford Philharmonics, the Ulster Orchestra and the Orchestra National du Capitole de Toulouse. *Recordings include:* Album with the BBC Philharmonic, 1996. *Honours:* Charles Grove Conducting Fellowship, 1993. *Address:* c/o IMG Artists, Lovell House, 616 Chiswick High Road, London W4 5RX, England.

FUKAI, Hirofumi; Violist; b. 10 Feb. 1942, Saitama, Japan. *Education:* Studied with Ivan Galamian at Juilliard, at the Toho School, Tokyo, and the Basle Conservatory. *Career:* Soloist with the Berne Symphony and the Hamburg Philharmonic, 1970–87; NDR Symphony from 1988; Concert performances throughout Europe, notably in the premieres of works by Zimmermann, Rihm and Henze (Compases para preguntas ensimismadas); Professor at the Hamburg Musikhochschule from 1974. *Address:* Hochschule für Musik, Harvesthuderweg 12, 2000 Hamburg 12, Germany.

FUKASAWA, Ryoko; Pianist; b. 22 June 1938, Togane City, Chiba Prefecture, Japan; m. Tomoyuki Fukasawa, 2 Oct 1967, deceased. *Education:* Hochschule für Musik und darstellende Kunst, Vienna, 1956–59. *Career:* Debut: Recital in Tokyo with Tokyo Symphonia Orchestra, 1953; Recital in Vienna, 1959; Regular concerts with Tonkünstler Orchester conducted by E Merzendorfer, Musikverein, 1960; NHK Symphony Orchestra conducted by S Ozawa in Tokyo, 1963; Wiener Kammer Orchester conducted by A Quadri, 1965; NHK Symphony Orchestra, conducted by L von Matacic, 1966; Concert tours of Switzerland, Hungary and Japan, 1965–68; Concert tours in Europe, South America and Asia; Television and radio appearances in Japan and Europe; Numerous premieres of contemporary music in Japan and Europe. *Recordings:* Encore Album, 1988; Piano Recital, 1989; Beethoven Violin Sonata, 1991; Schubert and Beethoven, 1992; Trout Quintet with Wiener Kammer Ensemble, 1992; Moments Musicaux, 1997; Mozart Recital, 1999. *Publications:* Diary for the Piano, 1955; Diary from Vienna, 1957; Schubert and Vienna, pocketbook on music, 1980; The Piano and Me, 1991. *Honours:* 1st Prize at the Student Music Competition in Japan, 1950; 1st Prize, Japan Music Competition organised by NHK and Mainich, Newspaper, 1953; Top Prize, Geneva International Music Competition, 1961. *Address:* 2-18-1 Chome, Tamagawa Denenchofu, Setagaya-ku, Tokyo 158-0085, Japan.

FULGONI, Sarah; Mezzo-Soprano; b. 1970, London, England. *Education:* Studied at the Royal Northern College of Music. *Career:* Has sung with the Welsh National Opera from 1994 as Prince Charming in Cendrillon and Beatrice in Beatrice and Benedict; Season 1995 as Dorabella with English National Opera, Strauss's Composer at Broomhill Opera, Celia in Haydn's Fedeltà Premiata at Garsington and Hyppolita in A Midsummer Night's Dream at the Ravenna Festival; Further engagements at the Harrogate and Schleswig-Holstein Festivals, at La Scala in Elektra and in Berlin in Mahler's Third Symphony; Sang Carmen with Welsh National Opera, 1997 and Ino in Semele for Flanders Opera, 1998; Engaged in Carmen at Santa Fe; Other roles include Charlotte in Werther (at Tel-Aviv), Monteverdi's Penelope (Geneva) and Leonora in La Favorita (Nice); Sang Berlioz's Béatrice for WNO and Netherlands Opera, 2001; Covent Garden debut as Federica in Luisa Miller, 2003. *Honours:* Frederic Cox Award, Curtis Gold Medal, Runner-up in 1993 Kathleen Ferrier Awards. *Address:* c/o IMG Artists, Lovell House, 616 Chiswick High Road, London, W4 5RX, England.

FULKERSON, James Orville, MM; composer and trombonist; b. 2 July 1945, Manville, Illinois, USA. *Education:* Illinois Wesleyan University, University of Illinois. *Career:* Fellow at the Center for Creative Performing Arts, State University of New York at Buffalo, 1969–72; Residencies at the Deutscher Akademischer Austauschdienst in Berlin, 1973, and the Victorian College of the Arts, Melbourne, 1977–79; From 1981 resident at Dartington College, South Devon. *Compositions include:* Guitar Concerto, 1972; To See a Thing Clearly for orchestra, 1972; Co-ordinative systems Nos 1–10, 1972–76; Orchestral Piece, 1974; Music for Brass Instruments Nos 1–6, 1975–78; Raucasity and the Cisco Kid or, I Skate in the Sun, theatre piece, 1978; Concerto for amplified cello and chamber orchestra, 1978; Vicarious Thrills for amplified trombone and pornographic film, 1979; Symphony, 1980; Force Fields and Spaces for trombone, tape and dancers, 1981; Cheap Imitations IV for soloist, tape and films, 1982; Put Your Foot Down Charlie for 3 dancers, speaker and ensemble, 1982; Rats Tale for 6 dancers, trombone and ensemble, 1983; Faust for tape, 1992; Antigone, tape, 1993; Eden, electronics, 1992; Wood-Stone-Desert for trumpet, live electronics and tape, 1996; Mixed-media works, television and film music; Various instrumental pieces under the titles Space Music, Patterns, Metamorphosis and Chamber Musics.

FULLER, Albert; Harpsichordist and Conductor; b. 21 July 1926, Washington DC, USA. *Education:* Studied organ with Paul Callaway at the national Cathedral in Washington; Peabody Conservatory; Georgetown, Johns Hopkins and Yale Universities (Ralph Kirkpatrick and Paul Hindemith); Studied French Baroque Keyboard Music in Paris. *Career:* Performer on the harpsichord in New York from 1957, Europe from 1959; Repertoire includes French music and the sonatas of Scarlatti; Professor of Harpsichord at the Juilliard School from 1964; President and Artistic Director of the Aston Magna Foundation (for the study of Baroque music), 1972–83; Summer Academies at Great Barrington, Massachusetts; Conductor of Rameau's Dardanus and Les Sauvages (Les Indes Galantes); Handel's Acis and Galatea and Xerxes, 1978, 1985; Assoc. Prof. Yale Univ., 1977–80; Founder, 1985, Helicon Foundation. *Publications include:* Edition of the harpsichord music of Gaspard Le Roux. *Address:* c/o Juilliard School of Music, Lincoln Plaza, NY 10023, USA.

FULLER, David Randall, AB, AM, PhD; American musicologist, organist and harpsichordist; b. 1 May 1927, Newton, MA. *Education:* Harvard Univ.; studied organ with E. Power Biggs, William Self and André Marchal, harpsichord with Albert Fuller. *Career:* Instructor, Robert Coll., Istanbul 1950–53; Asst Prof., Dartmouth Coll. 1954–57; Prof. of Music, State Univ. of New York, Buffalo 1963–98; John Knowles Paine Travelling Fellowship, Harvard 1960–61; Nat. Endowment for the Humanities Sr Fellowship 1976–77; CIES-Fulbright Research Award (Western European Regional Research Programme) 1985; mem. American Musicological Soc., American Guild of Organists, Soc. for Seventeenth-Century Music. *Recordings:* music by Armand-Louis Couperin (with William Christie), organ music of Widor, Reubke, Liszt, Stehle and others. *Publications:* A Catalogue of French Harpsichord Music 1699–1780 (with Bruce Gustafson) 1990, edns of keyboard works by Armand-Louis Couperin and Handel; contrib. numerous articles on French baroque music and historical performance to The New Grove Dictionary of Music and Musicians 2001, The New Harvard Dictionary of Music 1986, Early Music and others. *Honours:* Westrup Prize of the Music and Letters Trust 1997. *Address:* c/o State University of New York, Buffalo, NY 14260, USA.

FULLER, Louisa; Violinist; b. 1964, England. *Education:* Studied at the Royal Academy of Music with Emanuel Hurwitz; Further study with David Takeno. *Career:* Extensive tours of Europe as Principal second Violin of the Kreisler String Orchestra, winner in 1984 of Jeunesses Musicales Competition in Belgrade; Co-founder and Leader of the Duke String Quartet, 1985–, performing throughout the United Kingdom, with tours of Germany, Italy, Austria and Baltic States and South Bank series, 1991 with Mozart's early quartets, made the soundtrack for Ingmar Bergman documentary, The Magic Lantern, for Channel 4 television, 1988, BBC debut feature, features for French television,

1990–91 playing Mozart, Mendelssohn, Britten and Tippett works, Brahms Clarinet Quintet for Dutch radio with Janet Hilton, Live Music Now series with concerts for disadvantaged people, The Duke Quartet invites... at the Derngate Northampton, 1991 with Duncan Prescott and Rohan O'Hora, Resident Quartet of the Rydale Festival in 1991, Residency at Trinity College, Oxford, with tours to Scotland and Northern Ireland and a concert at Queen Elizabeth Hall in 1991, appeared on Top of the Pops and Radio 1, Number 1 album in 1993 with, Little Angels, featured on BBC Def ll and in German television documentary, String parts for Lloyd Cole, Blur, the Cranberries and Pretenders, 1994–95 and extensive work with choreographers, Bunty Mathias, Union Dance and Rosas, 1994–95. *Recordings include:* With Duke Quartet: Quartets by Tippett, Shostakovich and Britten, Dvořák (American) Barber Quartet and Kevin Volans Works, 1995. *Honours:* Poulet Award from RAM; Top 3 Newcomers Cannes Classical Music Award, for Duke's American disc, 1994. *Current Management:* Scott Mitchell. *Address:* 81B Sarsfeld Road, London SW12 8HT, England.

FULTON, Thomas; Conductor; b. 18 Sept. 1949, Memphis, Tennessee, USA. *Education:* Studied with Eugene Ormandy at the Curtis Institute, Philadelphia. *Career:* Has conducted at the Hamburg Staatsoper and the San Francisco Opera: Metropolitan Opera on tour; New York performances from 1981, including Manon Lescaut, Madama Butterfly and works by Verdi; Paris Opéra, 1979, Robert le Diable by Meyerbeer; Deutsche Oper Berlin, 1986, Macbeth; Conducted La Voix Humaine and Il Tabarro for Miami Greater Opera, 1989, Billy Budd at the Metropolitan and Nabucco at the Orange Festival, France; Don Carlos, 1990. *Address:* c/o Greater Miami Opera Association, 1200 Coral Way, Miami, FL 33145, USA.

FURLANETTO, Ferruccio; Singer (Bass); b. 16 May 1949, Pordenone, Sicily, Italy. *Education:* Studied with Campogaliani and Casagrande. *Career:* Sang at Vicenza in 1974 as Sparafucile in Rigoletto; Trieste, 1974, as Colline in La Bohème, with José Carreras and Katia Ricciarelli; Appearances at La Scala, Banquo, Turin, Leporello, and San Francisco as Alvise in La Gioconda; Metropolitan Opera, 1980; Salzburg Festival from 1986, as Philip II and Leporello, 1990, conducted by Riccardo Muti; San Diego and Covent Garden, 1988, as Mephistopheles and Leporello; In 1989 sang Mozart's Figaro at Geneva and Fernando in La Gazza Ladra at the Pesaro Festival; Season 1991–92 included Le nozze di Figaro in Paris, London, Salzburg and New York; Sang in Semiramide and Don Giovanni at the Metropolitan; Concert performances of Mozart's Da Ponte operas with the Chicago Symphony; Other roles include Philippe II, Don Giovanni, Leporello with Karajan, Figaro (Salzburg), Figaro, Bastille, Procida in Vespri Siciliani, Scala; Festival appearances 1996 at Salzburg (Don Giovanni) and Florence (Orestes); Philip II in Don Carlos for the Royal Opera at Edinburgh, 1998; Season 2000–01 as Don Giovanni at Salzburg, Gremin in Eugene Onegin at Florence, Leporello for the New York Met and Attila at Trieste; mem, Ambassador of Honour of the United Nations. *Recordings include:* Don Alfonso in Così fan tutte, conducted by James Levine; Roles in Mozart's Da Ponte operas, conducted by Daniel Barenboim; Videos of Don Carlos, Metropolitan and Salzburg, Rigoletto, Metropolitan, Vespri Siciliani at La Scala, and Don Giovanni at the Metropolitan and Salzburg; Also many films. *Address:* Musicaglotz, 11 Rue de Verrier, 75006 Paris, France.

FURLANETTO, Giovanni; Singer (Bass-baritone); b. 1958, Italy. *Career:* Sang in Italian opera houses from 1982; Trieste, 1989, in Donizetti's Linda di Chamounix, Florence, 1989, as Mozart's Figaro; Philadelphia Opera as Wurm in Luisa Miller; Season 1990 as Leporello at Trieste and Ircano in Rossini's Ricciardo e Zoraide at Pesaro; Salzburg Festival, 1995, as Masetto; Season 1995–96 as Escamillo at Nice and Wurm in Santiago; Mozart's Figaro at San Francisco, 1997; Season 1998 as Nonancourt in Rota's Italian Straw Hat, at La Scala; Sang Mozart's Figaro at Hamburg and Leporello in Baltimore, 2000. *Address:* c/o Teatro alla Scala, Via Filodrammatici 2, 20121 Milan, Italy.

FURMANSKY, Abbie; Singer (Soprano); b. 1969, USA. *Education:* Juilliard School, New York; Santa Fe Opera School. *Career:* New York City Opera from 1993, as Micaela, Musetta, Janáček's Fox, and Lisette in La Rondine; Engagements with Canadian Opera, and at Frankfurt, Washington (Esmeralda in The Bartered Bride) and New Jersey; Deutsche Oper Berlin from 1995, as Pamina, Zerlina, Sophie in Werther, Gretel, and Junge Mädchen in Schoenberg's Moses and Aron (season 1999–2000). Concerts include Elijah, Haydn's Lord Nelson Mass, Mahler's 4th Symphony, Beethoven's Missa Solemnis and Mozart's Requiem and Vespers; Schoenberg's 2nd Quartet and Rossini's Petite Messe. *Recordings include:* Ines in La Favorite by Donizetti. *Honours:* Prizewinner, 1999 Francesco Vinas Competition, Barcelona. *Address:* c/o Theateragentur Dr G. Hilbert, Maximilianstrasse 22, 80539 Munich, Germany.

FURRER-MÜNCH, Franz; Composer; b. 2 March 1924, Winterthur, Switzerland; m. Cécile Brosy. *Education:* 1st artistic training, Zürich

and Basel; Studied Flute, Piano, Harmony, Counterpoint and Composition, Basel Konservatorium; Scientific studies, ETH, Zürich; Musicology with K von Fischer and P Müller, Zürich University; Study visits: Federal Republic of Germany including Studio für elektronische Musik, Freiburg i Br, and USA including the State University of New York at Stony Brook for research work with Professor G W Stroke at the Electro-optical Sciences Center and the University of Bennington, Vermont. *Compositions include:* intarsia, for cello solo, 1972; Silben for organ, 1977; Von Dort nach Dort for 4 percussion, piano, tape and film, 1981–82; L'Oiseau en papier–Vier Versuche, Ikarus zu begreifen for solo cello, string orchestra and piano, 1984–85; Souvenir mis en scène for two cellos, 1988–89; Trio for violin, cello and piano, 1991–92; Skizzenbuch for chamber ensemble, 1992–93;... hier auf dieser Strasse, von der sie sagen, dass sie schön sei, for voice, flute, cello and 4 timpani, 1993; Erwarten im Flachland, Nebengesänge für Violine solo, 1994; Wort Jahr Stunde for alto flute in G, cello and piano, 1995–96; adagio, adagio cantabile for solo cello, for P. Sacher, 1997/98; Gesänge vom schwebenden Turm for flute, oboe, violin and cello, for the 60th birthday of Heinz Holliger, 1999; Von weit/schreiben ins meer, for chamber- and percussion-ensemble and voice, 1999–2000; ans ungereimte verdingt, for tenor sax solo, 2000; eng/weit/lento I-XII, 2001 for bass fl., fl. in G, 2 gramcassa and some perc. instruments; Symphonische Bläller for string orchestra, 2002; Auftrags werk der schweizer kulturstiflung pro Helretia und Prasid. Dep. Stadt Zurich; Kunstpreis Zollikon 2002. *Recordings include:* Dialogue for oboe and clarinet, 1972; Timbral Variations, 1973; Images sans cadres, for voice and clarinet quartet, 1982, 1990; Souvenir mis en scène, for 2 cellos, Thomas and Patrick Demenga, 1988–89; Skizzenbuch for ensemble, 1993; Erwarten in Flachland for violin, 1994; Canti Velati for flute and cello, 1998; Portrait-CD Franz Furrer-Münch, 1999. *Publications:* Zur Semiotik graphischer Notation (Walter Gieseler), 1978; Instrumentation in der Musik des 20. Jahrhunderts (W Gieseler. L. Lombardi and R. D. Weyer), 1985; Harmonik in der Musik des 20. Jahrhunderts (Walter Gieseler), 1996. *Address:* Hohfurristrasse 4, 8172 Niederglatt, Switzerland.

FÜRST, Janos; Conductor; b. 1935, Budapest, Hungary. *Education:* Studied at the Liszt Academy, Budapest, and in Brussels. *Career:* Formed Irish Chamber Orchestra, 1963; London debut, 1972, with the Royal Philharmonic Orchestra; Appearances with all major London orchestras; Engagements in Finland, Sweden, Denmark, Germany, Spain, Italy and Israel; Tours of Australia and New Zealand; Chief Conductor of Orchestra of Malmö, Sweden, 1974–78; Music Director of the Aalborg Symphony Orchestra, Denmark, 1980–83; Music Director of the Opera and Philharmonic Orchestra in Marseille; Former Conductor of the Irish Radio Orchestra in Dublin; Music Director of the Stadtorchester Winterthur, Switzerland; Has conducted opera in Stuttgart, Gothenburg and Copenhagen and for English National Opera and Scottish Opera; Elektra at Marseille, 1989; Creator and leader of the International Conductors' Course for the Dublin Masterclasses, 1982–89; Mahler series with the RTE Orchestra, 1988–89; US debut, 1990, with the Indianapolis Symphony Orchestra. *Recordings include:* Salome by Peter Maxwell Davies; Numerous with Swedish companies; Mahler's Lieder eines fahrenden Gesellen and Kindertotenlieder, with the RTE Orchestra. *Honours:* Premier Prix at the Brussels Conservatory; Swedish Gramophone Prize, 1980. *Address:* c/o EMI Classics, 30 Gloucester Place, London W1A 1ES, England.

FUSCO, Laura de; Concert Pianist; b. 1950, Catellammare di Stabia, Italy. *Education:* Studied at the Conservatorium San Pietro a Maiella in Naples. *Career:* Many concert appearances from 1966, notably in Europe, USA, South America and Japan; Orchestras have included the Detroit Symphony, Philadelphia, Orchestra National de Paris, Budapest Philharmonic, Santa Cecilia Rome, Moscow Symphony, Residentie Den Haag and the Yomiuri Nippon Symphony; Conductors have featured Muti, Mehta, Ceccato, Chailly, Inbal, Maag, De Burgos and Fedoseyev; Marlboro Festival concerts at the invitation of Rudolf Serkin; Debut with the BBC Philharmonic, Feb 1991.

FUSSELL, Charles C(lement); Composer, Conductor and Teacher; b. 14 Feb. 1938, Winston-Salem, North Carolina, USA. *Education:* Piano with Clemens Sandresky, Winston-Salem; BM, Composition, 1960, with Thomas Canning, Wayne Barlow and Bernard Rogers; Piano with José Echaniz; Conducting with Herman Genhart, Eastman School of Music, Rochester, New York; Pupil of Boris Blacher, Berlin Hochschule für Musik, 1962; MM, Eastman School, 1964. *Career:* Teacher, Theory, Composition, University of Massachusetts, 1966, Founder-Director of its Group for New Music, 1974, later renamed Pro Musica Moderna; Teacher, Composition, North Carolina School of the Arts, Winston-Salem, 1976–77; Boston University, 1981; Conductor, Longy School Chamber Orchestra, Cambridge, Massachusetts, 1981–82; Artistic Director, New Music Harvet/Boston, Boston's first city-wide contemporary music festival, 1989. *Compositions:* Orchestral: Symphony No. 1, 1963, No. 2, 1964–67, No. 3, Landscapes, 1978–81; 3 Processionals, 1972–73; Northern Lights, chamber orchestra, 1977–79; 4 Fairy Tales,

1980–81; Dance Suite, 5 players, 1963; Ballades, cello and piano, 1968, revised, 1976; Greenwood Sketches: Music for String Quartet, 1976; Free-fall, 7 players, 1988; Julian, drama, 1969–71; Voyages, soprano, tenor, women's chorus, piano, winds, recorded speaker, 1970; Eurydice, soprano and chamber ensemble, 1973–75; Resume, song cycle, soprano and 3 instruments, 1975–76; Cymbeline, drama, soprano, tenor, narrator, chamber ensemble, 1984; The Gift, soprano and chorus, 1986; 5 Goethe Lieder, soprano or tenor and piano, 1987, for soprano or tenor and orchestra, 1991; A Song of Return, chorus and orchestra, 1989; Wilde, symphony No. 4, baritone and orchestra; Last Trombones, 5 percussionists, 2 pianos, 6 trombones, 1990; Symphony No. 5, for large orchestra, 1994–95; Night Song, for piano solo, 1995; Specimen Days, a cantata, for baritone solo, chorus and orchestra, 1993–94; Being Music (Whitman) for baritone solo and string quartet, 1993; Venture, four songs for baritone and piano, 2001; Right River for cello solo and string orchestra, 2001; Infinite Fraternity for baritone solo, chorus, flute and viola, 2002; High Bridge, a choral symphony, 2003–04.. *Recordings:* Goethe Lieder; Specimen Days; Being Music; Symphony No. 5; The Astronaut's Tale, chamber opera. *Honours:* Ford, Fulbright, Copland Grants and commissions. *Address:* ASCAP, ASCAP House, 1 Lincoln Plaza, New York, NY 10023, USA.

FUSSELL, Louis; British music teacher and composer; b. 8 Oct. 1925, Manchester. *Education:* English and German studies; Trinity College of Music, London; Fellowship, 1954. *Career:* Debut: Bamberg, 14 July 1998; Teacher, stringed instruments, various schools; mem, Incorpo-

rated Society of Musicians, 1974–84. *Compositions include:* Bamberg Festive Overture, 1998; Overture for the Year 2000, 2000; Symphony No. 1, 2001; Symphony No. 2, 2001; Symphonies No 3 and No 4, 2002–03; overtures, concerto for trumpet and orchestra, chamber music; concerto for flute and orchestra; Symphony No 5, Romanian. *Recordings include:* Bamberg Festliche Ouverture, 1998; Symphonies 1, 2, 3, 4, 5 and 6 2000–04), 4 overtures, 3 string quartets, 2 concertos. *Address:* 35 Rutland Road, Bedford, MK40 1DG, England. *Telephone:* (1234) 307520 (home).

FUTRAL, Elizabeth; Singer (Soprano); b. 1968, Louisville, USA. *Education:* Studied at the Opera Center of Chicago Opera. *Career:* Debut: New York City Opera, 1992, as Gilda; Sang Bella in The Midsummer Marriage, and Lakmé at the City Opera; Season 1995–96 as Gounod's Juliette at Miami, Valencienne in The Merry Widow at the City Opera and Lucia di Lammermoor at Florence; Rossini's Matilde di Shabran at Pesaro, Musetta at Covent Garden and Catherine in Meyerbeer's Etoile du Nord, at Wexford, 1996; Other roles include Tytania in A Midsummer Night's Dream; Season 1999 with Gounod's Juliette at Chicago, Gilda at Pittsburgh and Brussels, Susanna at Munich and Strauss's Zerbinetta at Santa Fe; Season 2000–01 as Donizetti's Adina for Chicago Opera, Gilda at Santa Fe, Nannetta in Munich and Baby Doe in the Opera by Douglas Moore for the New York City Opera; Lucia di Lammermoor at New Orleans. *Address:* c/o IMG Artists, Lovell House, 616 Chiswick High Road, London W4 5RX, England.

GABOS, Gábor; Hungarian pianist; b. 4 Jan. 1930, Budapest; m. Ingeborg Sandor 1951; one s. one d. *Education:* Performer's Diploma, Ferenc Liszt Academy of Music, Budapest. *Career:* debut, Budapest, 1952; Festival Hall, London; Musikverein, Vienna; Châtelet, Paris; Palais des Beaux-Arts, Brussels; Further appearances in Italy, Russia, Japan, Germany, Sweden, Greece, Switzerland, Peru, South America and throughout Europe. *Honours:* Liszt Ferenc Award of Hungarian Government, 1959; Lauréat du Concours International Reine Elisabeth, Brussels, 1960; 1st Prize, International Liszt-Bartók Competition, 1961; Top Award for the Japan Record Academy, 1968; Merited Artist of the Hungarian People's Republic, 1976. *Address:* Nyul utca 10, 1026 Budapest, Hungary.

GADD, Stephen; singer (baritone); b. 18 Sept. 1964, Berkshire, England. *Education:* St John's College, Cambridge; Royal Northern College of Music. *Career:* Ping in Turandot at Covent Garden; Yeletsky in Queen of Spades for Scottish Opera; Count in Marriage of Figaro for Scottish Opera; Marcello (La Bohème), Peking Festival; Escamillo (Carmen) for BBC; Other appearances at Geneva Opera, Châtelet (Paris), Opéra Comique (Paris), New Israeli Opera and Opéra du Rhin; Concert repertoire includes: Britten, War Requiem; Walton, Belshazzar's Feast; Mendelssohn, Elijah. *Recordings include:* Mozart's Coronation Mass; Purcell's Dioclesian for DGG with Trevor Pinnock and the English Concert; La Bohème and Madama Butterfly (excerpts) with RPO; Hamish Maccun Works. *Honours:* Kathleen Ferrier Memorial Scholarship.

GADDES, Richard; Opera Administrator; b. 23 May 1942, Wallsend, England. *Education:* Studied at Trinity College of Music, London. *Career:* Co-founded Wigmore Hall Lunchtime Concerts, 1965; Emigrated to USA, 1969; Artistic Administrator of Santa Fe Opera, 1969–76, Gen. Dir, 2000–; Founded Opera Theater of St Louis, 1976, Gen. Dir, 1976–85; Production of Britten's Albert Herring for WNET and BBC television, 1978; Visited Edinburgh with the St Louis Company in 1983, with Fennimore and Gerda by Delius and The Postman Always Rings Twice by Stephen Paulus, the first American opera to be performed at the Edinburgh International Festival; American premiere of Saariaho's L'Amour de loin, 2002; world premiere of Sheng's Madame Mao, 2003; mem, Board of Directors, Pulitzer Foundation for the Arts; William Matheus Sullivan Foundation. *Honours:* Honorary Doctor of Musical Arts, St Louis Conservatory, 1983; Honorary DFA, University of Missouri, St Louis, 1984; Honorary DA, Webster University, 1986. *Address:* Santa Fe Opera, PO Box 2408, Santa Fe, NM 97504-2408, USA.

GADENSTÄTTER, Clemens; Austrian composer, conductor and flautist; b. 26 July 1966, Zell am See. *Education:* Universität für Musik und darstellende Kunst, Vienna with Erich Urbanner, Musikhochschule Stuttgart with Helmut Lachenmann. *Career:* founder (with Florian Müller), Ensemble Neue Musik, Vienna 1990; Lecturer, Darmstadt Ferienkurse für Neue Musik 1994; teacher, Universität für Musik und darstellende Kunst, Vienna 1995–, and in Graz 1998–; Ed. bi-annual journal, Ton 1995–2000. *Compositions include:* Trio 1990, Musik für Orchesterensembles 1990–94, Versprachlichung: dreaming of a land an arm's length away – die arie des vogelnestaushebers (with film installation by Joseph Santarromana) 1992–94 (version without film entitled Versprachlichung) variationen und alte themen 1996, Ballade L 1997, Polyskopie 2000–01, Wir müssen einzelne irgendwann bitten, alle jetzt aufzupassen (electroacoustic) 2001, Comic sense 2002–03. *Recordings:* Polyskopie, Streichtrio II, Variationen und alte themen, Comic sense, Versprachlichung, schniTt, Musik für Orchesterensembles. *Publications:* tag day. ein schreibspiel (with Lisa Spalt) 2000; contrib. to Stellwerk I 2002. *Honours:* winner Forum junge Komponisten competition, WDR 1992, Publicity-Preis of the SKE-Fond 1997, Vienna Förderungspreis 1997, first prize 2003. *Address:* 2. Bez, Gr. Sperl-G. 32-34, 1020 Vienna, Austria. *E-mail:* mailport@aon.at.

GAEDE, Daniel; violinist; b. 25 April 1966, Hamburg, Germany; m. Xuesu Liu 1992. *Education:* Studienstiftung des Deutschen Volkes and Abbado European Musicians Trust, studied with Thomas Brandis in Berlin, Max Rostal in Switzerland, Josef Gingold in the USA. *Career:* regular performances as soloist and chamber musician in Europe, Asia, N and S America; soloist with Philharmonia Orchestra, London, City of London Sinfonia, Vienna Philharmonic Orchestra; leader, Vienna Philharmonic Orchestra 1994–. *Honours:* 1st Prize, German National Competition, Jugend musiziert, 1983; Prizewinner, Carl Flesch Competition, London and Artist International Competition, New York; Eduard Söring Prize, 1987; Joseph Joachim Prize, 1989. *Address:* Mariahilferstrasse 49-1-14, 1060 Vienna, Austria.

GAETA, Luis; Singer (Baritone); b. 1953, Buenos Aires, Argentina. *Education:* Studied in Buenos Aires and with Tito Gobbi. *Career:* Many appearances at the Teatro Col ón, Buenos Aires, notably as Verdi's Rigoletto, Posa (1996) and Germont, Marcello, Jack Rance (La Fanciulla del West), Valentin and Rossini's Figaro; Prus in The Makropulos Case, Mozart's Count and the Villains in Les Contes d'Hoffmann; Premieres of works by local composers and guest appearances throughout South America; Season 1998 as Malatesta in Don Pasquale; Many concert engagements; Season 2000 as Puccini's Sharpless at Buenos Aires and Donizetti's Enrico at Córdoba. *Address:* Teatro Col ón, Buenos Aires, Argentina.

GAGE, Irwin; Pianist; b. 4 Sept. 1939, Cleveland, Ohio, USA. *Education:* Studied with Eugene Bossart at the University of Michigan; Yale University with Ward Davenny; Vienna Akademie with Erik Werba, Klaus Vokurka and Hilde Langer-Rühl. *Career:* Accompanist to leading singers, including Hermann Prey, Dietrich Fischer-Dieskau, Christa Ludwig, Gundula Janowitz, Jessye Norman, Elly Ameling, Lucia Popp, Brigitte Fassbaender, Tom Krause, Arleen Auger, Anna Reynolds, René Kollo, Peter Schreier and Edita Gruberova plus younger singers François Le Roux, Cheryl Studer, Thomas Hampson, Siegfried Lorenz and Francisco Araiza; Festival appearances at every major festival in the world; Professor at the Zürich Conservatory and master classes throughout the world; Anniversary concerts of Brahms, Ravel, Schubert and Mendelssohn, 1997. *Recordings:* Over 50 recordings, some of which have won prizes such as the Gramophone Award (3 times), Grand Prix du Disque, Deutsche Schallplatten Preis (5 times), Edison Prize, recording prizes from Spain, Belgium, Finland and Japan and the Ovation-MUMM Awards in USA. *Address:* Kunstler Sekretarat am Gasteig, Rosenheimer StraSSe 52, 81669 Munich, Germany.

GALAS, Diamanda, BA, MA; singer and composer; b. 29 Aug. 1955, San Diego, CA, USA. *Education:* University of California, San Diego. *Career:* Lead role in Globokar's Un Jour Comme Une Autre, Avignon Festival, 1979; Sang her solo works at Théâtre Gérard Philippe St Denis, Paris, also festivals throughout Europe; US and Central American premieres of works by Iannis Xenakis and Vinko Globokar with L'Ensemble Intercontemporaire, Musique Vivante and Brooklyn Philharmonic; Solo performances, New York Philharmonic's Horizons Festival, Pepsico Festival, Brooklyn Philharmonic's Meet the Moderns, 1982, 1983, 1984, San Francisco Symphony's New and Unusual Music, 1984, Creative Time's Arts in the Anchorage, many others; Appeared in film Positive Positive; Solo tours, Australia, Sweden, Yugoslavia, Netherlands, Italy, Spain, Bavaria, 1988; British premiere of Masque of the Red Death, Queen Elizabeth Hall, London, 1989, then Lincoln Center, New York; Plague Mass performed, 1990, Berlin, Basel, Barcelona, Olympic Festival, Helsinki Festival, world premiere of newest section at St John the Divine Cathedral, New York, then 1991 Athens Festival; World premiere of Vena Cava, the Kitchen, New York City, 1992; Opened 1993 Serious Fun! Festival, Lincoln Center, with electro-acoustic work Insekt; 1993 world tour included USA, Spain, Netherlands, Austria, Slovenia, Switzerland, Belgium, Norway; Director, Intravenal Sound Operations, New York. *Compositions include:* Published: Tragouthia ap to Aima Exoun Iona, 1981; The Litanies of Satan, 1981; Panoptikon, 1982; Wild Women with Steak Knives, 1982; Eyes without Blood, 1984; Free Among the Dead, 1985; Deliver Me from Mine Enemies, 1986; Masque of the Red Death, 1989; Insekta, electro-acoustic monograma, 1993; Malediction and Prayer for low voice and piano, 1996; Nekropolis for low voice, 1999; Recorded: The Litanies of Satan, 1982; Diamanda Galas, 1984; The Divine Punishment, 1986; Saint of the Pit, 1987; You Must Be Certain Of The Devil, 1988; The Masque of the Red Death, 1985, trilogy, 1989; The Singer, 1992; Vena Cava, 1993; Film music; The Sporting Life, 1994; Schrei X, 1996; Malediction and Prayer, 1998. *Address:* 584 Broadway, Suite 1008, New York, NY 10012, USA.

GAGNE, Marc; Professor and Composer; b. 16 Dec. 1939, Saint Joseph de Beauce, Quebec, Canada; m. Monique Poulin, 27 Dec 1969, 1 s., 2 d. *Education:* Doctor of Letters, University Laval, Quebec, 1970; 3 years at School of Music, University Laval with Jacques Hétu, José Evangélista and Roger Matton. *Career:* Symphonie de chants paysans created at Moncton Choralies Internationals, 1979; His Symphonie-itineraire was principal work by Quebec Symphony Orchestra at Festival marking 375th anniversary of the discovery of Canada; L'opéra Menaud was given on television in the form of a scenic Cantata, May 1992. *Compositions:* Les Chansons de la tourelle, in the folklore mode, 1975; Jeu a deux faces, Piano Sonata No. 1; Ceremonial d'orgue pour la fete du Tres Saint-Sacrement, 1976; Deux chorals pour le temps de la Passion for organ, 1976; Les Jeunes Filles a marier, suite for a capella choir on folklore themes, 1977; Short Mass, Du Peuple de Dieu, 1981; Messe, Des enfants de Dieu, 1993; Sonate du roi Renaud for alto saxophone and piano, 1983; Vari-anes et moulin-ations for solo marimba, 1983; Symphonie-itineraire, 1983–84; Menaud, opera in 3 acts and a prologue, 1984–86; Évangéline et Gabriel, opera in 2 acts, 1987–90; Le Père Noël, la sorcière et l'enfant, conte de Noël for chamber orchestra, choir and soloists, 1993; Les Verdi (opera in 3 acts), 1999; Trio with piano No. 1 (Le rossignol y chante), 1999; Trio with piano No. 2 (Au bois du rossignolet), 1999; Horn Sonata (The Winter), 1999. *Address:* 677 Avenue du Chateau, Sainte-Foy, QC G1X 3N8, Canada.

GAGNON, Alain; Composer; b. 1938, Trois-Pistoles, Québec, Canada. *Education:* Ecole de Musique, Laval University; Graduate degree in Composition studying under Jeanne Landry, Jocelyne Binet and Roger Matton; Studied with Henri Dutilleux, Ecole Normale de Musique, Paris; Studied with Olivier Alain, Ecole César-Franck, Paris; Studied composition and orchestration with André-François Maresconi, Geneva Conservatory; Initiated into electro-acoustic music at University of Utrecht. *Career:* His works have been performed in France, Switzerland, Germany, Latin America and Canada and several have been recorded or published; Sat on several juries including Competition for Young Composers, 1980, with Murray Schafer, Barbara Pentland and Toru Takemitsu; Teacher, Techniques of Composition, Ecole de Musique, Laval University, 1967–; Director of Composition Programme, Laval University, 1977–. *Compositions include:* Works for orchestra, chamber music, string quartets and piano; Trio pour flûte, violon et violoncello; Septuor; Les oies sauvages; Prélude pour orchestra, 1969; Ballet score, 1983. *Honours:* Received Prix d'Europe, 1961; Association de musique actuelle de Québec honoured him by performing 3 of his works including Incandescence. 1982.

GAHL, Dankwart (Arnold); Cellist and Professor; b. 18 Dec. 1939, Korbach, Germany; m. Irmgard Schuster (deceased 1996), 23 May 1964, 1 s., 1 d. *Education:* Private cello and viola da gamba instruction (with Johannes Koch/Kassell); Summer class with Casals, 1959; Entry to the Akademie für Musik und darstellende Kunst, Vienna, Oct 1959; Student of Wilfried Boettcher; Theory with Erwin Ratz; Pedagogics Diploma, 1963; Final Concert Diploma with 1st class honours. *Career:* Foundation member of the Vienna Soloists, 1959, touring with this formation all over the world, participating in many famous festivals, for example playing with Casals at Prades Festival; Originating from this same ensemble is the Alban Berg Quartet and the Austrian String Quartet, of which he has been a member since 1972; Quartet in residence at Mozarteum, Salzburg, 1972–, holder of the cello class, 1972–; Foundation member of the piano trio Trio Amade, Salzburg, 1979; Ordinary Professor at the Hochschule, 1984–; Concerts in the USA and several tours to the Far East; Guest classes in South Korea on many occasions; Has given classes with the Quartet at Salzburg Summer Academy, Mozarteum for many years; Invited jurist of international chamber music competitions on many occasions; mem, Vienna Symphony Orchestra. *Honours:* Scholarship, Studienstiftung des Deutschen Volkes. *Address:* Carl Storch-Strasse 10, Salzburg, Austria.

GÄHMLICH, Wilfried; Singer (Tenor); b. 14 July 1939, Halle, Germany. *Education:* Studied at the Musikhochschule Freiburg and with Alfred Pfeifle in Stuttgart. *Career:* Debut: Giessen, 1968, as Pedrillo in Die Entführung; Sang at Wuppertal, 1973, in the premiere of Blacher's Yvonne, Prinzessin von Burgund; Appearances in Düsseldorf, Zürich, Vienna, Stuttgart, Wiesbaden and London; Salzburg, 1983, in Dantons Tod by Von Einem; Other roles include Florestan, the Drum Major in Wozzeck, Tamino, Andrea Chénier, Don José and Max in Der Freischütz; Bregenz Festival, 1987–88, in Les Contes d' Hoffmann; Sang Pedrillo in Die Entführung at the Theater an der Wien, Vienna, 1989; The Sailor in Krenek's Orpheus und Eurydike for the Austrian Radio; Salzburg Festival, 1992, as The Hunchback in Die Frau ohne Schatten; Valzacchi in Der Rosenkavalier at the Opéra Bastille; Sang in the premiere of K... by Philippe Manouri at the Opéra Bastille, 2001. *Recordings:* Dantons Tod; Die Entführung; Video of Elektra conducted by Abbado (as the Young Servant). *Address:* c/o Staatsoper, Ringstrasse, Vienna, Austria.

GAJEWSKI, Jaromir (Zbigniew); Conductor, Musician and Composer; b. 2 April 1961, Pryzyce, Poland. *Education:* MA, Academy of Music, Poznan. *Career:* Debut: Poznan, 1986; Teacher of Conducting, Composition and Harmony, 1988–; Founder of Academy Orchestra, 1991–; mem, Polish Composers' Society; Polish Society for Contemporary Music. *Compositions:* Altana–Songs for voice and piano, 1986; 2 String Quartets, 1986, 1988; Penetration for symphony orchestra, 1989; From Dawn to Dusk for orchestra, 1989; In Cage, opera, 1990; Overture, 1993; 3rd string quartet, 1995; Requiem Symphony, 1997; Fantasy, 1998; Why Has Thou Forsaken Me?, 1999. *Recordings:* Altana–Songs; 2 String Quartets. *Address:* ul Boguslawa 24/3, 79-200 Pyrzyce, Poland.

GAL, Zahava; Singer (Mezzo-soprano); b. 29 Aug. 1948, Haifa, Israel. *Education:* Piano, Rubin Academy, Jerusalem; Voice, Opera, Juilliard School with Jennie Tourel and Daniel Fero. *Career:* Feodor in Boris Godunov, La Scala, 1979; Salzburg Easter Festival production of Parsifal, 1980; Angelina in La Cenerentola, Netherlands Opera, Amsterdam, 1980; Feodor in Boris Godunov, Carmen, Paris Opéra, 1981; Sang Carmen in Peter Brook's Carmen, Hamburg, Zürich; Rosina in Barber of Seville, Washington DC (2 seasons), Glyndebourne Festival Opera, at Santiago de Chile, Scottish Opera in Lyon, Avignon, Nantes, Dario Fo's Amsterdam production, Frankfurt Opera (2 seasons); Isolier in Le Comte Ory, Pesaro, Italy; Cherubino in Marriage of Figaro at Monte Carlo, Vienna Staatsoper and Santa Fe Festival; Ariodante in Nancy, Paris, Lausanne, Dejanira in Hercules, title role in Teseo, Covent Garden, Siena, Athens Summer Festival, Handel Year, 1985; Nicklausse, Rosina, Carmen with New Israeli Opera, 1988–89; Rinaldo, Paris; Elmira in Floridante with Tafel Baroque Orchestra in Toronto, San Francisco; Zerlina in Don Giovanni, Nancy; Concert repertoire includes Schéhérazade, L'Enfant et les Sortilèges (Ravel), Songs of a Wayfarer, 3rd and 4th Symphonies (Mahler), Romeo and Juliet (Berlioz), Requiem, C-minor Mass (Mozart), Bruckner's Te Deum, Beethoven's 9th, Pergolesi's Stabat Mater; Has sung with Mehta and Israel Philharmonic, Barenboim and New York Philharmonic, Abbado with La Scala Orchestra and Chicago Symphony, Armin Jordan and Orchestre de la Suisse Romande, Mata with Pittsburgh and Dallas Symphonies; Television appearances in Switzerland, Italy, France, Israel. *Recordings include:* Mussorgsky's choral works with Abbado; Amaltea in Moses in Egypt; L'Incoronazione di Poppea; Duet selection; Donizetti cantata. *Honours:* Grand Prix, 1st Prize, Mélodie Française Concours International de chant, Paris; Top Prize, Lieder, Munich International Competition; 1st Place, Kathleen Ferrier Young Artists Award. *Current Management:* Robert Lombardo. *Address:* c/o Robert Lombardo, 61 West 62nd Street 6F, New York, NY 10023, USA.

GAL, Zoltan; Violist; b. 1960, Hungary. *Education:* Studied at the Franz Liszt Academy, Budapest, and with Sandor Devich, György Kurtág and András Mihaly. *Career:* Member of the Keller String Quartet from 1986, debut concert at Budapest, Mar 1987; Played Beethoven's Grosse Fuge and Schubert's Death and the Maiden Quartet at Interforum 87; Series of concerts in Budapest with Zoltán Kocsis and Deszo Ranki (piano) and Kalman Berkes (clarinet); Further appearances in Nuremberg, at the Chamber Music Festival La Baule and tours of Bulgaria, Austria, Switzerland, Italy (Ateforum 88, Ferrara), Belgium and Ireland; Concerts for Hungarian Radio and Television. *Recordings:* Albums (from 1989). *Honours:* 2nd Prize, Evian International String Quartet Competition, May 1988. *Address:* c/o SullivSweet, 28 Albion Street, London, W2 2AX, England.

GALANTE, Inessa; Singer (Soprano); b. 1959, Riga, Latvia. *Education:* Studied at the Riga conservatory. *Career:* Sang at the Riva National Opera, 1982–91, notably as Gilda, Adina, L'Esilir d'Amore, Rosina, Micaela, Rimsky's Snow Maiden, Marguerite, Lucia di Lammermoor and Olympia in Les Contes d'Hoffmann; Guest appearances at St Petersburg as Lucia and Marguerite; Mannheim Opera from 1991 as Pamina, Nedda, Freia in Das Rheingold, Mimi, and Gluck's Euridice; Sang Micaela at Frankfurt, 1993 and Donna Elvira at Düsseldorf, 1996; Violetta at Nancy, 1998; Sang Mimi for Miami Opera, 1999; Concert repertory in Russia, Germany and North America includes Requiems by Brahms, Faure, Verdi and Mozart; Beethoven Ninth. *Address:* c/o Opera de Nancy, 1 Rue St Catherine, 54000 Nancy, France.

GALE, Elizabeth; Singer (Soprano); b. 8 Nov. 1948, Sheffield, Yorkshire, England. *Education:* Studied at the Guildhall School of Music, London, with Winifred Radford. *Career:* Debut: With the English Opera Group, in Purcell's King Arthur; Appeared in The Turn of the Screw with the EOG; Scottish Opera (Glasgow) as the Queen of Shemakha in The Golden Cockerel and Despina and Tytania; Welsh National Opera (Cardiff) as Blondchen in Die Entführung; Glyndebourne, 1973–86, as Barbarina, Papagena, Susanna, Nannetta, Zerlina, Marzelline in Fidelio, Drusilla in L'Incoronazione di Poppea, Titania (A Midsummer Night's Dream, 1984) and Miss Wordsworth (Albert Herring, 1985) also Amor in Orfeo; Marzelline at the Paris Opéra and the Vienna Staatsoper; Covent Garden as Zerlina and as Adele in Die Fledermaus, also as Woodbird (Siegfried) and Xenia (Godunov); Zürich Opera as Susanna, Ilia (Idomeneo), Ismene (Mitridate), Nannetta, Drusilla and Marzelline; Frankfurt, 1980, in Castor et Pollux by Rameau also as Aennchen (Freischütz) and Marzelline; Guest appearances in Amsterdam, Geneva and Cologne; Sang at San Diego, in La Voix Humaine by Poulenc, 1986, US debut; Appeared with Chelsea Opera Group at the Queen Elizabeth Hall, 1989, as Massenet's Thais; Glyndebourne Festival, 1990, as Miss Wordsworth, repeated at Los Angeles, 1992; Sang in Owen Wingrave at Glyndebourne, 1997; Season 1998 as Alice Ford at Garsington and Despina for Glyndebourne Touring Opera; Sang Susanna, Tytania and Oscar in Ballo at Hong Kong Festival; Despina in Los Angeles and Donna Elvira in Belfast; Sang Despina at Glyndebourne, 2000; Many concert engagements, in particular in works by Handel; Guest, Opera Houses, Vienna and Paris. *Recordings include:* Le nozze di Figaro and Don Giovanni; Amor in Orfeo ed Euridice; Israel in

Egypt; Handel's Messiah, Saul, and Jephtha conducted by Harnoncourt; Dido and Aeneas; Semele in Die Liebe der Danaë, in a BBC recording of Strauss's opera; Recital of Bliss Songs with Nash Ensemble. *Honours:* John Christie Award, Glyndebourne, 1973. *Address:* c/o Musichall, Vicarage Way, Ringmer, East Sussex, BN8 5 LA, England.

GALIMIR, Felix; Violinist; b. 20 May 1910, Vienna, Austria; m. Suzanne Hirsch, 18 Feb 1945. *Education:* Pupil of Adolf Bak, Vienna Conservatory, Diploma, 1928; Carl Flesch, Berlin and Baden-Baden, 1929–30. *Career:* Founder, Galimir String Quartet, Vienna, 1929; US debut, Town Hall, New York, 1938; Founder, reconstituted Galimir String Quartet, New York, 1938; First Violinist, NBC Symphony Orchestra, New York, 1939–54; Concertmaster, Symphony of the Air, New York, 1954–56; Teacher-Performer, Marlboro (VT Festival and Music School, 1954–); Teacher, Juilliard School of Music, New York, 1962; Head, Chamber Music Department, Curtis Institute of Music, Philadelphia, 1972–; Teacher, Mannes College of Music, New York, 1977–. *Recordings:* Various. *Honours:* Grand Prix du Disque, 1937, 1938; Honorary D.Mus, New School of Music, Philadelphia, 1984 and Mannes College of Music, 1987. *Address:* 225 East 74th Street, New York, NY 10021, USA.

GALINDO, Juan; Singer (Baritone); b. 1947, San Sebastian, Spain. *Education:* Studied at the San Sebastian Conservatory and at La Scala Milan with Giuseppe di Stefano. *Career:* Debut: Barcelona, 1973, as Enrico in Lucia di Lammermoor, with Pavarotti; Has sung widely in Italy as Carlos in Forza del Destino, Rigoletto, Macbeth and Iago; Guest appearances in Liège, Berne, Zürich, Graz, Copenhagen and Munich, notably as Marcel in Puccini's Il Tabarro; Season 1984–85 as Iago and Nabbucco at St Gallen, Rigoletto at Zürich. *Address:* c/o Teatro alla Scala, Via Filodrammatici 2, 20121 Milan, Italy.

GALL, Hugues R.; French opera house director; b. 18 March 1940, Honfleur; s. of Max Gall and Geneviève Carel. *Education:* Inst. des Sciences Politiques, Sorbonne. *Career:* fmr official, Ministries of Agric., Educ. and Culture; Sec.-Gen. Réunion des Théâtres Lyriques 1969–73; Deputy Dir-Gen. Paris Opéra 1973–80; Dir-Gen. Grand Theatre, Geneva 1980–94; Dir-Gen. Paris Opéra 1995–2004; elected mem. Acad. des Beaux-Arts, Inst. de France 2002. *Honours:* Prix Montaigne 1996, Prix Grand Siècle-Laurent Perrier 1999; Officier Légion d'honneur, Ordre nat. du Mérite, des Palmes académiques, Chevalier du Mérite agricole, Commdr des Arts et des Lettres.

GALL, Jeffrey Charles, BA, MPhil; American singer (countertenor); b. 19 Sept. 1950, Cleveland, OH; m. Karen Rosenberg 1978. *Education:* Princeton University, Yale University with Blake Stern, Arthur Burrows. *Career:* member, Waverly Consort, 1974–78; Debuts: Brooklyn Academy of Music in Cavalli's Erismena, Spoleto Festival, Italy, 1980, La Scala, 1981, Edinburgh Festival, 1982, San Francisco Opera, 1982, La Fenice, 1984, Teatro di San Carlo Naples, 1984, Canadian Opera, 1984, Handel Festival at Carnegie Hall, 1984, Chicago Lyric Opera, 1986, Sante Fe Opera, 1986, and Metropolitan Opera, 1988; Has sung in operas by Jommelli, Lully, Pergolesi, Cesti, Purcell, Scarlatti and Mozart; Television appearances include the title role in Handel's Giulio Cesare; Season 1992 included Britten's Oberon at Los Angeles and in Conti's Don Chisciotte at the Innsbruck Festival of Early Music; Performed Oberon in Britten's Midsummer Night's Dream with the Frankfurt Opera, Ottone in Monteverdi's Poppea for the Cologne Opera, David in Handel's Saul with the Boston Caecelia Society, 1993; Returned to Metropolitan Opera in Britten's Death in Venice in 1994; Sang Medieval Carmina Burana for Clemencic Consort, Oberon in for the New Israeli Opera and Ottone for the Dallas Opera, repeated at Amsterdam, 1996. *Recordings include:* Flavio conducted by René Jacobs. *Honours:* First Prize, Bodky Award for Performance of Early Music, 1977. *Current Management:* William Knight, 309 Wood Street, Burlington, NJ 08016, USA.

GALLA, Jan; Singer (Bass); b. 21 Dec. 1955, Nova Zahky, Czechoslovakia. *Education:* Studied at the Bratislava Conservatory. *Career:* Member of the National Theatre Bratislava, in the Italian and Slavonic opera repertory; Guest appearances in Rio de Janeiro (as Ramphis in Aida, 1986), the Paris Opéra and Opéra-Comique, and Opera North, Leeds; Sang Verdi's Attila with the Bratislava company at Edinburgh, 1990; Season 1992–93 as Donizetti's Raimondo in Dublin and the Commandant in From the House of the Dead at the Barbican Hall; Bratislava 1995, as Massenet's Don Quichotte. *Address:* c/o Slovak National Theatre Opera, Gorkého 4, 815 06 Bratislava, Slovakia.

GALLARDO-DOMAS, Cristina; Singer (Soprano); b. 1968, Santiago, Chile. *Education:* Studied in Santiago and at Juilliard, New York. *Career:* Sang at Santiago Opera as Butterfly, Nedda, Mimi and Liu in Turandot; Spoleto Festival, 1993 as Suor Angelica; Rome Opera 1994 as Traviata; Hamburg, 1995; Detroit, 1994 and La Scala, 1994–95 as Antonia in Les Contes d'Hoffmann; Season 1995–96 as Mimi at the Metropolitan, at the Opéra Bastille, Paris and Hamburg; Season 2000–01 as Violetta and Mimi at the Met, Amelia Grimaldi for Munich

Opera and Liu in Turandot at Covent Garden (debut); Returned to London 2003, as Madama Butterfly; Other roles include Marie in La fille du Régiment and Magda in La Rondine by Puccini; Many concert engagements. *Address:* c/o Metropolitan Opera, Lincoln Center, New York, NY 10023, USA.

GALLEGO, Maria; Singer (Soprano); b. 1962, San Fernando, Spain. *Education:* Studied in Cadiz and at the Barcelona Conservatory. *Career:* Debut: Barcelona, 1985 as Sidonie in Gluck's Armide; Appearances at Barcelona as Celia in Mozart's Lucio Silla, Monica in Respighi's La Fiamma and in Strauss's Capriccio; Telemaco by Gluck, 1987; Guest appearances in Bologna and Ravenna as Rosaura in Le Maschere by Mascagni, 1988; Pisa and Madrid; Bonn Opera, 1991–92; Other roles include Betty in Salieri's Falstaff. *Address:* c/o Bonn Opera, Am Boeselagerhof 1, 53111 Bonn, Germany.

GALLI, Dorothea; Singer (Soprano); b. 11 Nov. 1951, Zürich, Switzerland; m. Rudolf Bamert. *Education:* Studied with Elsa Cavelli and Elisabeth Schwarzkopf and at the Salzburg Mozarteum. *Career:* Sang at the Zürich Opera, 1976–78, Kaiserlautern, 1978–79, Gelsenkirchen, 1979–82; Guest appearances at the Deutsche Oper am Rhein Düsseldorf, Karlsruhe, Mannheim, Dortmund, Heidelberg and Amsterdam; Roles have included Mozart's Donna Elvira, Fiordiligi and Ramiro (La Finta Giardiniera), Leonore, Marguerite, Mimi, Tatiana, the Marschallin, Arabella, Emilia Marty and Giorgietta in Gianni Schicchi; Many Lieder recitals and performances of oratorio. *Address:* c/o Opernhaus Zürich, Falkenstrasse 1, 8008 Zürich, Switzerland.

GALLO, F. Alberto; Professor of History of Music; b. 17 Oct. 1932, Verona, Italy. *Education:* LLD; PhD. *Publications include:* Antonii Romani Opera, 1965; Mensurabilis Musicae Tractatuli, 1966; Il Codice Musicale 2216 della Biblioteca Universitaria di Bologna, 1968–70; Franchini Gafurii Extractus Parvus Musicae, 1969; Petrus Picardus Ars Motettorium Compilata Breviter, 1971; Johannes Boen Ars Musicae, 1972; La Prima Rappresentazione al Teatro Olimpico, 1973; Italian Sacred Music, 1976; Storia della Musica: Il Medioevo, 1977; Il Codice Musicale Panciatichi 26 della Biblioteca Nazionale di Firenze, 1981; Geschichte der Musiktheorie, 1984; Music of the Middle Ages, 1985; Musica e Storia tra Medio Evo e Età Moderna, 1986; Italian Sacred and Ceremonial Music, 1987; Musica nel castello Bologna, 1992; Il Codice Squarcialupi, Firenze, 1992. *Address:* L Alberti 34, 40137 Bologna, Italy.

GALLO, Lucio; Singer (Bass-baritone); b. 1958, Taranto, Italy. *Education:* Studied in Turin. *Career:* Sang Marcello to Pavarotti's Rodolfo in Peking, China; Escamillo in Turin and Leporello at the Vienna Staatsoper, 1989; Returned to Vienna as Valentin in Faust, Marcello, and Paolo in Simon Boccanegra; Further appearances at the Hamburg Staatsoper as Mozart's Count (also at Covent Garden), Dandini in Cenerentola at Bologna and Don Alvaro in Il Viaggio a Reims at Pesaro; Metropolitan Opera New York debut, 1991, as Guglielmo; Mozart's Figaro, 1992, with the Covent Garden company on tour to Japan; Sang Dallapiccola's Prigioniero at Florence, 1996; Puccini's Lescaut at La Scala, 1998; Season 2000–01 at the Deutsche Oper Berlin as Eugene Onegin and Macbeth at the Staatsoper; Amonasro at Macerata, Mozart's Count at Munich and Ford in Falstaff for the Salzburg Easter Festival; Covent Garden 2001 and 2003, Dandini and Sharpless; Concert repertory includes Les Béatitudes by Franck, Winterreise, and Lieder by Wolf. *Recordings include:* Bartolo in Il Barbiere di Siviglia. *Address:* c/o Staatsoper, Opernring 2, 1010 Vienna, Austria.

GALSTIAN, Juliette; Singer (soprano); b. 1970, Armenia. *Education:* Graduated, Piano and Voice, Yerevan Conservatoire, 1995. *Career:* Appearances in Armenia as piano recitalist and concert soloist; From season 1996 engagements at leading opera houses, including Mimi in the centenary production of La Bohème at Turin; Zerlina in Don Giovanni at La Fenice, Susanna in Le nozze di Figaro and Xenia in Boris Godunov at Turin, Flowermaiden in Parsifal at the Opéra Bastille, Paris, Valencienne in The Merry Widow at with the Royal Opera, London. *Honours:* Laureate, Maria Callas Grand Prix, Athens; Winner, Viotti International Competition; Prizewinner, Jose Carreras Competition at Pamplona. *Current Management:* Athole Still International Management, Forresters Hall, 25–27 Westow Street, London, SE19 3RY, England. *Telephone:* (20) 8771-5271. *Fax:* (20) 8768-6600. *Website:* www.atholestill.com.

GALTERIO, Lou, BA; American opera director and administrator; b. 29 Nov. 1942, New York, NY. *Education:* Marquette University, Milwaukee. *Career:* worked as an actor and theatre director; Opera productions for the Opera Theater of St Louis include Così fan tutte, Le nozze di Figaro, Albert Herring, Ariadne auf Naxos and the US premiere of Prokofiev's Maddalena, 1982; Director of opera production at the Manhattan School from 1977; Santa Fe Opera, Il Barbiere di Siviglia and Hindemith's Neues vom Tage, 1981; Kennedy Center, Washington, Argento's Postcard from Morocco, 1979; New York City Opera, 1980, La Cenerentola; Chicago Opera Theater, 1984, Don Giovanni; Staged Don

Giovanni at Santa Fe, 1992. *Address:* c/o Santa Fe Opera, PO Box 2408, Santa Fe, NM 87504, USA.

GALUZIN, Vladimir; Singer (Tenor); b. 1957, Novosibirsk, Siberia, Russia. *Education:* Studied at Novosibirsk Conservatoire. *Career:* Sang at the Novosibirsk Opera, 1988–90, Kirov Theatre St Petersburg, 1990–; Tours with the Kirov to Spain, Italy, France and the Edinburgh Festival; Appearances as Otello in St Petersburg and as Guest in Stuttgart, Dresden, Amsterdam, Brussels and Japan; Grishko in the Kupfer production of Rimsky's Invisible City of Kitezh (Bregenz, 1995), and Sergei in the Graham Vick production of Lady Macbeth of the Mtsensk District, at the Metropolitan, 1996; Season 1996–97 as Pinkerton at Cologne and Alexei in The Gambler by Prokofiev at La Scala; Many engagements at the Vienna Staatsoper (debut as Hermann in The Queen of Spades); Season 1997–98 with Otello at Brussels and for the New Israeli Opera, Lensky in Eugene Onegin at Buenos Aires; Other roles include Radames, Don Carlos, Calaf, Cavaradossi, Chevalier des Grieux, Andrei in Tchaikovsky's Mazeppa and Vladimir in Prince Igor; Season 1998 as Khovansky in Khovanshchina at La Scala and Calaf at Madrid; Returned to Madrid 2000, for Alvaro in La Forza del Destino; Season 2000–01 as Pinkerton, Shostakovich's Sergei and Alexei in The Gambler by Prokofiev at the New York Met; Cavaradossi at Orange, Radames at the Verona Arena and Hermann in The Queen of Spades at Covent Garden. *Recordings include:* Video of title role in Rimsky's Sadko (Philips). *Address:* Bureau de Concert Maurice Werner, 7 Rue Richerance, 75008 Paris, France.

GALVANY, Marisa; Singer (Soprano); b. 19 June 1936, Paterson, New Jersey, USA. *Education:* Studied with Armen Boyajian. *Career:* Debut: Seattle Opera, 1968, as Tosca; New York City Opera from 1972, as Elizabeth I in Maria Stuarda, Anna Bolena, Médée, Santuzza and Violetta; Mexico City and San Francisco, 1972–73, Aida; New Orleans, 1974, as Rachel in La Juive; Guest appearances in Philadelphia, Warsaw, Prague, Belgrade and Rouen; Metropolitan Opera from 1979, as Norma, Ortrud, and the Kostelnicka in Jenůfa; Other roles include Verdi's Hélène, Abigaille and Elvira, Turandot, Mozart's Countess, Massenet's Salomé and Tchaikovsky's Iolanta; Sang Verdi's Ulrica in New York Central Park, 2000. *Recordings include:* Title role in Medea in Corinto by Giovanni Simone Mayr. *Address:* c/o Metropolitan Opera, Lincoln Center, New York, NY 10023, USA.

GALVEZ-VALLEJO, Daniel; Singer (Tenor); b. 1967, Spain. *Education:* Studied in Spain and Italy. *Career:* Many appearances in Italy as Alfredo and Rodolfo in La Bohème; Montpellier Festival, 1991–95, as Igor in Bizet's Ivan IV, and in Sacchini's Oedipe a Colone; Riccardo in Verdi's Oberto; Sang in Les Brigands by Offenbach at the Paris Opéra, Bastille, 1994; Season 1995 as Hoffmann at Lyon and Don José at Lille; Other roles include Pollione in Norma and Wagner's Steersman. *Recordings:* Samson et Dalila. *Address:* c/o Opera de Montpellier, 11 Boulevard Victor Hugo, 34000 Montpellier, France.

GALWAY, Sir James, Kt, KBE, FRCM, FRCO, FGSM; British flautist and conductor; b. 8 Dec. 1939, Belfast; s. of James and Ethel Stewart Galway (née Clarke); m. 1st 1965; one s.; m. 2nd 1972; one s. two d. (twins); m. 3rd Jeanne Cinnante 1984. *Education:* Mountcollyer Secondary School, Royal Coll. of Music, Guildhall School of Music, Conservatoire National Supérieur de Musique, Paris. *Career:* first post in Wind Band of Royal Shakespeare Theatre, Stratford-on-Avon; later worked with Sadler's Wells Orchestra, Royal Opera House Orchestra, BBC Symphony Orchestra; Prin. Flute, London Symphony Orchestra and Royal Philharmonic Orchestra; Prin. Solo Flute, Berlin Philharmonic Orchestra 1969–75; int. soloist 1975–; soloist/conductor 1984–; Prin. Guest Conductor, London Mozart Players 1997–; performances worldwide include appearances in The Wall, Berlin, and at the Nobel Peace Prize Ceremony, 1998; as conductor, toured Germany with Wurttembergisches Kammerorchester and Asia with Polish Chamber Orchestra, 2000–01; has premiered many contemporary flute works commissioned by and for him; numerous recordings; James Galway Rose named after him by David Austin. *Film music:* flute soloist, soundtrack of Lord of the Rings – Return of the King. *Publications:* James Galway: An Autobiography 1978, Flute (Menuhin Music Guide) 1982, James Galway's Music in Time 1983, Flute Studies – Boehm 12 Grand Studies 2003. *Honours:* Hon. MA (Open Univ.) 1979; Hon. DMus (Queen's Univ., Belfast) 1979, (New England Conservatory of Music) 1980; (St Andrew's Univ.); Officier des Arts et des Lettres 1987; Grand Prix du Disque 1976, 1989; Pres. Merit Award, Nat. Acad. Recording, Arts & Sciences, 2004. *Address:* c/o Lisa Baglieri, Benzeholzstr. 11, CH-6045 Meggen, Switzerland. *E-mail:* lisabag@earthlink.net (office). *Website:* www.superflute.com (home).

GAMBA, Piero; Conductor; b. 16 Sept. 1936, Rome, Italy. *Education:* Studied piano and score reading with his father. *Career:* Conducted Beethoven's 1st Symphony at the Rome Opera House, aged 8; Tours of Europe and North and South America whilst a child; British debut 1948, conducting Beethoven and Dvořák in London; Moved to Madrid in 1952;

Guest engagements in London, 1959–63 often with the London Symphony Orchestra; Musical Director of Winnipeg Symphony Orchestra, Canada, 1970–81; Principal Conductor, Adelaide Symphony Orchestra from 1982–88. *Recordings include:* Rossini's Overtures with the London Symphony Orchestra; Beethoven's Piano Concertos with Julius Katchen as soloist.

GAMBA, Rumon; Conductor; b. 1970, England. *Education:* Royal Academy of Music, with Colin Metters. *Career:* Associate conductor of the BBC PO, from 1998; Music Director of the Iceland SO, 2002–; Appearances with all the BBC Orchestras, City of Birmingham SO, Britten Sinfonia, Bournemouth SO and Royal Scottish National Orchestra; Season 2001–02 with Munich PO (Shostakovich 8th Symphony) Toronto SO, Bergen PO, London PO, Melbourne and Dusseldorf Symphonies and NDR Hannover; Season 2002–03 with US debut (Florida PO), New York PO youth series concerts and 2003 Sydney Festival (most leading Australian orchestras); Further engagements with Barcelona and Basle Symphonies, Orquesta de Valencia and Singapore SO; Blue Peter concerts with the BBC PO at the London Proms, 2002. *Recordings include:* Malcolm Arnold Symphonies and music by Vaughan Williams, Auric, Bliss, Alwyn and Richard Rodney Bennett (film music) (Chandos). *Current Management:* Harrison/Parrott Ltd, 12 Penzance Place, London, W11 4PA, England. *Telephone:* (20) 7229 9166. *Fax:* (20) 7221 5042. *Website:* www.harrisonparrott.com.

GAMBERONI, Kathryn; Soprano; b. 11 June 1955, Pennsylvania, USA. *Education:* Studied at the Curtis Institute. *Career:* Debut: St Louis in 1981 as Gerda in the US premiere of Fennimore and Gerda by Delius; Sang with the St Louis Company at the Edinburgh Festival in 1983 as Margot la Rouge by Delius; Seattle Opera from 1985 as Adina, Despina, Adele, Juliette, Zerbinetta and Marzelline, 1991; Santa Fe in 1985 in the US premiere of The English Cat by Henze, returning in 1989 in Judith Weir's A Night At The Chinese Opera and as Satirino in La Calisto; Guest appearances in Paris, Dallas, Cologne, Chicago and Melbourne; Other roles include Mozart's Blondchen, Susanna and Papagena, and Fanny in Rossini's La Cambiale di Matrimonio; Sang Rosina in Paisiello's Il Barbiere di Siviglia for Long Beach Opera in 1989 and the title role in The Cunning Little Vixen at the New York City Opera in 1991. *Address:* c/o New York City Opera, Lincoln Center, New York, NY 10023, USA.

GAMBILL, Robert; Tenor; b. 11 March 1955, Indianapolis, Indiana, USA. *Education:* Studied at the Hamburg Musikhochschule with Hans Kagel. *Career:* Debut: Milan 1981 as Michael in the premiere of Stockhausen's Donnerstag aus Licht; Sang at Frankfurt from 1981 notably in Die Gezeichneten by Schreker; Sang at Wiesbaden as Ernesto, Tamino, Don Ottavio and Nicolai's Fenton; Glyndebourne in 1982–85 as Almaviva in Il Barbiere di Siviglia and Don Ramiro in La Cenerentola, La Scala Milan in 1982, Teatro La Fenice, Venice as Ferrando in Così fan tutte in 1983; Sang David in Die Meistersinger at the renovated Zürich Opera in 1984; Geneva and Aix-en-Provence in 1984 as Rossini's Lindoro and Almaviva; Season 1987–88 as Belmonte at Buenos Aires and the Steersman in Fliegende Holländer at La Scala, also at the Metropolitan in 1989; Schwetzingen Festival in 1987 as Rossini's Almaviva, Theater an der Wien Vienna in 1988 in Schubert's Fierrabras, sang Almaviva at Munich in 1990 and Wagner's David at Covent Garden; Other roles include Mozart's Ferrando, Renaud in Armide, Verdi's Fenton and Iopas in Les Troyens; Sang in Rossini double bill at Cologne and Schwetzingen in 1992; Sang Offenbach's Barbe-bleue at Stuttgart, 1996; Season 1997–98 with Max at Frankfurt and Florestan at Stuttgart; Sang Tannhäuser at Dresden, 2001; London Proms, 2002; Engaged as Tristan at Glyndebourne (2003). *Recordings include:* Rossini's Stabat Mater; Evander in Gluck's Alceste ed Euridice; Tenor Solo in Messiah. *Address:* c/o Staatstheater Stuttgart, Oberer Schlossgarten 6, 7000 Stuttgart 1, Germany.

GAMMON, Philip (Greenway); Pianist and Conductor; b. 17 May 1940, Chippenham, Wiltshire, England; m. Floretta Volovini, 1963, 2 s. *Education:* Royal Academy of Music, 1956–61; Pupil of Harold Craxton; Badische Musikhochschule, 1961–64; Pupil of Yvonne Loriod. *Career:* Joined Royal Ballet, Covent Garden, 1964; Ballet for All Principal Pianist, 1968–71; Teaching appointments at Watford School of Music and Trinity College; Returned to Royal Ballet, 1972; Solo Pianist for many ballets including Elite Syncopations, A Month in the Country and Return to the Strange Land; Conducting debut with Ballet for All at Richmond Theatre, 1970; At Covent Garden, 1978, Sleeping Beauty; Radio 3 broadcasts in recitals as soloist and accompanist; Debut Festival Hall and Barbican Hall in 1984 as Piano Soloist; Solo pianist for Rhapsody, Mr Worldly Wise, Ballet Imperial, Concerto, La Fin du Jour, Winter Dreams; The Concert, Margaurite and Armand; Guest conducting with the English National Ballet, Hong Kong Ballet, 1996 and National Ballet of Portugal, 1997 and 1998; Principal Pianist and Conductor of the Royal Ballet, 1999–; Presents a lecture-recital, Music and Reminiscence, A Pianist's Life with the Royal Ballet. *Recordings:* Elite Syncopations, with musicians from the Covent Garden Orchestra;

A Month in the Country, Chopin/Lanchbery; Winter Dreams; DVD of Margaurite and Armand (Liszt Sonata), 2004. *Publications:* First orchestral arrangement of La Chatte Metamorphosée en femme, premiered in 1985 at the Royal Opera House. *Honours:* Recital Diploma, 1960; MacFarren Gold Medal, 1961; Karlsruhe Culture Prize, 1962; Badische Musikhochschule Diplom, 1963; ARCM (Performers), 1969; ARAM, 1991; FRAM, 2002. *Address:* 19 Downs Avenue, Pinner, Middlesex HA5 5AQ, England.

GANASSI, Sonia; Singer (Mezzo-soprano); b. 1967, Reggio Emilia, Italy. *Career:* Debut: Spoletto, 1991 as Rossini's Cenerentola; Rome Opera from 1992, as Rossini's Isabella and Rosina; Season 1995 as Rosina at Venice, Adalgisa in Norma at Bologna, Carmen at Monte Carlo and Emma in Zelmira at Pesaro; US debut Washington, 1993 as Cenerentola; Season 1996 as Isabella at Genoa; Giovanna in Anna Bolena at Bologna and as Mascagni's Zanetta at Florence; Season 1997–98 as Rosina for the Royal Opera in London; Bellini's Romeo at Reggio Emilia and Maffeo Orsini in Lucrezia Borgia at La Scala; Other roles include Elisabetta in Maria Stuarda, Dorabella, Nicklausse in Les Contes d'Hoffmann and Massenet's Charlotte; Season 2001–02 as Cenerentola, and Romeo in I Capuleti e i Montecchi at Covent Garden; Adalgisa at Turin, Donizetti's Leonora at Bologna, Cenerentola in Madrid, Milan and San Francisco, Elisabetta in Barcelona; London Proms, 2002. *Recordings:* Il Barbiere di Siviglia; Rossini's Sigismondo. *Address:* c/o Grand Teatre Liceu, La Rambla 51–59, 08002 Barcelona, Spain.

GANTER, Martin; Singer (Baritone); b. 15 May 1965, Freiburg, Germany. *Education:* Studied in Berlin, Germany. *Career:* Debut: Mozart's Count at Coblenz, 1989; Sang in the premiere of Henze's Das verratene Meer, Berlin, 1990; Appearances at the Bavarian State Opera, Munich, from 1991, as Ned Keene in Peter Grimes, Schaunard (La Bohème), Papageno, Silvio and Malatesta; Guglielmo (Così fan tutte) in Basle, Barcelona and Dresden (1997); Don Giovanni at Hof and Rossini's Figaro at Baden-Baden (1985), Dandini in La Cenerentola at the Dresden Staatsoper, 1996. *Honours:* Winner, VDMK Competition, Berlin, 1988. *Address:* c/o Haydn Rawstron Ltd, 38 Station Road, London SE20 7BQ, England.

GANZAROLLI, Wladimiro; Singer (Bass); b. 9 Jan. 1932, Venice, Italy. *Education:* Studied at the Bendetto Marcello Conservatory in Venice. *Career:* Debut: Teatro Nuovo in Milan in 1958 as Mephistopheles in Faust; Sang at La Scala Milan from 1959, notably as Falstaff and as Bottom in the local premiere of Britten's A Midsummer Night's Dream, Spoleto in 1959 in a revival of Il Duca d'Alba by Donizetti, Monte Carlo in 1960, Vienna Staatsoper from 1964, Teatro Col ón Buenos Aires in 1966 as Leporello in Don Giovanni and as a guest in the USA, notably in San Francisco, Chicago, Dallas and at the Metropolitan Opera in 1968; Sang at Teatro Regio, Turin, 1955–82. *Recordings:* Le nozze di Figaro; Così fan tutte; Don Giovanni, conducted by Colin Davis; La Vera Costanza by Haydn under Antal Dorati; Un Giorno di Regno and Stiffelio by Verdi; Les Huguenots by Meyerbeer; Luisa Miller. *Address:* c/o Teatra alla Scala, Via Filodrammatici 2, Milan, Italy.

GARAVANTA, Ottavio; Tenor; b. 26 Jan. 1934, Genoa, Italy. *Education:* Studied with Rosetta Noli and Vladimiro Badiali. *Career:* Debut: Milan in 1954 as Don Ottavio; Sang major roles in Italy at La Scala and in Rome, Florence and Verona; Guest engagements in Vienna, Buenos Aires, Berlin, Marseilles, Brussels, Chicago, San Francisco, Lisbon and Belgrade; Glyndebourne Festival in 1967 as Rodolfo in La Bohème; Has often appeared in revivals of neglected Italian operas; Sang at Théâtre de la Monnaie, Brussels, in 1980 in Donizetti's Il Duca d'Alba, Genoa in 1985 as Cadmo in Donizetti's Il Diluvio Universale and sang Carlo in a concert performance of Verdi's Giovanna d'Arco with Margaret Price at Festival Hall in London, 1989; Sang at Teatro Regio Turin in 1990 as Radames; Livorno 1992, as Giorgio in I Rantzau by Mascagni. *Recordings:* Scenes from Rossini's Otello with Virginia Zeani; Mosè in Egitto by Rossini; Admeti in Dejanice by Catalani. *Honours:* Winner of the Verdi Competition at Bussetto and competitions at Genoa and Modena. *Address:* c/o Teatro di Torino, Piazza Castello 215, 10124 Turin, Italy.

GARAZZI, Peyo; Tenor; b. 31 March 1937, St Jean Pied de Port, Basses Pyrenees, France. *Education:* Studied in Bordeaux and Paris. *Career:* Sang first at the Théâtre de la Monnaie in Brussels; Sang at Royal Opera Ghent in 1962 as Nadir in Les Pêcheurs de Perles, Paris, 1977 in Gwendoline by Chabrier and guest appearances in Bordeaux, Munich and Berlin; Covent Garden Opera in 1983 as Don Carlos in a French language revival of Verdi's opera; Other roles include Florestan, Aron in Moses und Aron by Schoenberg and parts in operas by Delibes, Donizetti, Offenbach and Puccini. *Recordings include:* Don Quichotte by Massenet.

GARCIA, Jose; Singer (Bass); b. 1959, USA. *Career:* Season 1987 as Sarastro for Pennsylvania Opera and the Commendatore in a Peter Sellars production of Don Giovanni; Season 1988–89 as the Grand Inquisitor in Don Carlos at Bologna; Polidoro in Rossini's Zelmira at

Venice; Gounod's Frère Laurent at Seattle; Season 1990 as Roger in the British premiere of Verdi's Jérusalem for Opera North; Sarastro for Glyndebourne Touring Opera. *Recordings:* Zelmira. *Address:* Opera North, Grand Theatre, 46 New Briggate, Leeds LS1 6NU, England.

GARCIA, Navarro Luis; Conductor; b. 30 April 1941, Chiva, Valencia, Spain. *Education:* Studied at Valencia and Madrid Conservatories and in Italy with Franco Ferrara and at Vienna Academy with Hans Swarowsky. *Career:* Founded the Spanish University Orchestra in 1963; Permanent Conductor of the Valencia Symphony, 1970–74; Musical Director of San Carlos Theatre at Lisbon, 1980–82; Principal Guest Conductor of the Radio Symphony Orchestra, Stuttgart, 1984–87, the Vienna State Opera, 1987–91, and the Tokyo Philharmonic Orchestra, 1992–; Generalmusikdirektor of the Stuttgart State Opera, 1987–91; Musical and Artistic Conductor of the Barcelona Symphony Orchestra, 1991–93; Permanent Guest Conductor at Deutsche Oper Berlin, 1992–; Appearances in most major international opera theatres including Covent Garden La Bohème in 1979 and Tosca in 1983, La Scala Milan, Madama Butterfly in 1987 and Vienna State Opera, Falstaff, La Bohème, Tosca, La Forza del Destino and Andrea Chénier; Has also conducted many leading orchestras including the Vienna Philharmonic, London Symphony and Philharmonia, Leningrad Philharmonic, Chicago Symphony, Pittsburgh Symphony, and Los Angeles Philharmonic; mem, Royal Academy of San Carlos, Spain. *Recordings:* Several. *Honours:* 1st Prize, Madrid Conservatory, 1963; Prizewinner, International Competition Besançon, 1967; Gold Medal, Paris City, 1983. *Address:* Conciertos Vitoria, Amaniel 5-50-2, 28015 Madrid, Spain.

GARCIA-ASENSIO, Enrique; Conductor; b. 22 Aug. 1937, Valencia, Spain. *Education:* Master's degree, Violin, Harmony, Counterpoint, Fugue, Chamber Music, Composition, Royal Conservatory of Music, Madrid; Orchestra Conducting, Munich Higher School of Music, with Professors Lessing, Eichhorn and Mennerich; Further study, Accademia Chigiana, with Sergiu Celibadache. *Career:* Has conducted all leading Spanish orchestras; Music Director, Conductor: Las Palmas Philharmonic, Canary Islands, 1962–64, Valencia Municipal Orchestra, 1964–65, Spanish Radio and Television Orchestra, Madrid, 1966–84; Assistant Conductor, National Symphony Orchestra, Washington DC, season 1967–68; Principal Guest Conductor, Valencia Orchestra; Conductor, Madrid Municipal Symphonic Band, 1994–98; Music Director and Conductor of the Radio and Television Symphony Orchestra, 1998–; Led orchestras in Canada, USA, Mexico, Dominican Republic, Brazil, Uruguay, Argentina, Portugal, France, Italy, England, Belgium, Russia, Japan, Northern Ireland, Israel, Netherlands, Greece, Denmark, Romania, Puerto Rico, Austria, Germany, Bulgaria, Switzerland, Iceland; Turkey, Luxemburg, South Africa, Slovakia and the Czech Republic; Symphonic and operatic repertory; Assistant to Celibadache at master classes, Bologna, Munich; Professor of Conducting, Royal Conservatory of Music, Madrid, 1970–; International master classes, Netherlands, Dominican Republic; Presenter, The World of Music educational television programme, 4 years. *Recordings:* Numerous including: Zarzuela, Teresa Berganza and English Chamber Orchestra, 1976; Ernesto Halffter, English Chamber Orchestra, 1991. *Address:* Gavilan 8, 28230 Las Rozas, Madrid, Spain.

GARCISANZ, Isabel; Singer (Soprano); b. 29 June 1934, Madrid, Spain. *Education:* Studied with Angeles Ottein in Spain and with Erik Werba in Vienna. *Career:* Debut: Vienna Volksoper in 1964 as Adèle in Le Comte Ory; Sang in Paris at the Opéra and the Opéra-Comique; Guest appearances in Bordeaux, Marseille, Nancy, Nice, Cologne, Barcelona and Miami; Glyndebourne, 1966–68, 1970 as Concepcion in L'Heure Espagnole, Nerillo in L'Ormindo and Zaida in Il Turco in Italia; Toulouse, 1972–73 in the premieres of operas by Casanova and Nikiprowetsky; Strasbourg in 1974 in the premiere of Delereue's Medis et Alissio; Engagements with French Radio, Paris, in the first performances of works by Mihalovici; Was the first singer of Hahn's Sybille; Sang in the premiere of Le Château des Carpathes, by Philippe Hersant, Montpellier, 1993; mem, Acanthes; Union des Femmes Artists Musiciennes. *Recordings:* L'Ormindo; Le Maître de Chapelle by Paer; Le Roi Malgré Lui by Chabrier; Cantigas; Sybille; Mass by Ohana; 3 Centuries of Spanish Melodies; Spanish Songs by Rodrigo, Falla, and Garcia. *Current Management:* Agence Thérèse Cedelle, 78 Boulevard Makesherres, 75008 Paris, France. *Address:* c/o Opéra du Rhin, 19 Place Broglie, 67008 Strasbourg Cédex, France.

GARD, Robert; Singer (Tenor); b. 7 March 1927, Cornwall, England. *Education:* Studied with Dino Borgoli, Walter Hyde at the Guildhall School of Music and Kaiser Breme in Bayreuth. *Career:* Debut: English Opera Group in Lennox Berkeley's Ruth, 1957; Sang for Welsh Opera then at Aldeburgh and in Australia as Britten's Peter Quint in the Turn of The Screw, Albert Herring, Male Chorus and Aschenbach; Sang Anatol in War and Peace at the opening of the Sydney Opera House in 1973, appearing on television in this production, and Charpentier's Louise and Manon; Sang Aschenbach in a film version of Britten's Death in Venice in 1981, commissioned by the Britten Foundation; Other roles included Aegisthus, Herod, Loge, Siegmund, Tamino, Števa in Jenůfa, Peter Grimes, Tom Rakewell, and Le Mesurier in the premiere of Meale's Voss, 1986; Sang Mr Upfold in Albert Herring at Sydney, 1996. *Honours:* O.B.E., 1981. *Address:* c/o Australian Opera, Sydney Opera House, Sydney, NSW, Australia.

GARDINER, Sir John Eliot, Kt, CBE, MA, FRSA; British conductor and musical director; b. 20 April 1943, Fontmell Magna, Dorset; s. of late Rolf Gardiner and of Marabel Gardiner (née Hodgkin); m. 1st Cherryl Anne Ffoulkes 1971 (divorced 1981); m. 2nd Elizabeth Suzanne Wilcock 1981 (divorced 1997); three d.; m. 3rd Isabella de Sabata 2001. *Education:* Bryanston School, King's Coll., Cambridge, King's Coll., London, and in Paris and Fontainebleau with Nadia Boulanger. *Career:* f. and Artistic Dir Monteverdi Choir, 1964, Monteverdi Orchestra 1968, English Baroque Soloists 1978, Orchestre Révolutionnaire et Romantique 1990; concert debut Wigmore Hall, London 1966; youngest conductor Henry Wood Promenade Concerts, Royal Albert Hall 1968; operatic debut Sadler's Wells Opera, London Coliseum 1969; Prin. Conductor CBC Vancouver Orchestra 1980–83; Musical Dir Lyon Opera 1982–88, Chef fondateur 1988–; Artistic Dir Göttingen Handel Festival 1981–90, Veneto Music Festival 1986; Prin. Conductor NDR Symphony Orchestra, Hamburg 1991–94; residency at the Châtelet, Paris Oct. 1999–; Bach Cantata Pilgrimage, with performances throughout Europe 2000; conducted Handel's Israel in Egypt at the London Proms 2002, The Cunning Little Vixen at Covent Garden 2003; regular guest conductor with major orchestras in Amsterdam, Paris, Brussels, Geneva, Frankfurt, Dresden, Leipzig, London, Vienna, Berlin; appearances at European music festivals, including Aix-en-Provence, Aldeburgh, Bath, Berlin, Edinburgh, Flanders, Netherlands, London, Salzburg, BBC Proms; over 200 recordings. *Publications:* Claude le Jeune Hélas, Mon Dieu (ed.) 1971, contrib. Gluck's Orfeo 1980. *Honours:* Hon. Fellow King's Coll., London 1992, Royal Acad. of Music 1992; Dr. hc (Univ. Lumière de Lyon) 1987; Commdr Ordre des Arts et des Lettres 1997 (Officier 1988); 15 Gramophone awards including Record of the Year 1991, Artist of the Year 1994, Edison Awards 1982, 1986, 1987, 1988, 1989, 1996, 1997, Grand Prix du Disque 1978, 1979, 1980, 1992, Prix Caecilia 1982, 1983, 1985, Arturo Toscanini Music Critics' awards 1985, 1986, Deutscher Schallplattenpreis 1986, 1994, 1997. *Address:* Gore Farm, Ashmore, near Salisbury, Wiltshire, SP5 5AR, England (home).

GARDNER, Jake; singer (baritone); b. 14 Nov. 1947, Oneonta, NY, USA; m. Cynthia Clarey 1978; one s. *Education:* State University of New York, Potsdam, Syracuse University. *Career:* spent first 10 years of career studying and performing with the tri-Cities Opera, Binghamton, New York; Sang Valentin in Faust at Houston, 1975; Carnegie Hall, 1976, in a concert performance of Le Cid by Massenet; Sang James Stewart in premiere of Thea Musgrave's Mary, Queen of Scots at 1977 Edinburgh Festival, and repeated the role at Norfolk, Virginia, 1978 and elsewhere; Appeared with Boston Opera in 1979 US premiere of Tippett's The Ice Break and has sung at opera houses in Washington, Detroit, San Diego, San Francisco, New Orleans and St Louis; Has sung Mozart's Guglielmo and Figaro with Netherlands Opera, Escamillo in Peter Brook's version of Carmen throughout Europe and at Lincoln Center; Wexford Festival debut 1987 as Valdeburgo in La Straniera; Has also sung the title role of Il Ritorno d'Ulisse conducted by Nicholas McGegan for Long Beach Opera and in the premiere of Musgrave's Incident at Owl Creek Bridge, for BBC Radio 3; Principal baritone at Cologne Opera from 1989, as Valentin, Nardo in La Finta Giardiniera, Mozart's Count, Puccini's Lescaut and Marcello, Belcore in L'Elisir d'amore; Concert performances of Figaro and the Glagolitic Mass, conducted by Simon Rattle; Glyndebourne Festival debut 1991, as Guglielmo; Other roles in Shostakovich The Nose for Cologne Opera and title role in Don Giovanni for Dresden Opera, 1994; Ned Keene in Peter Grimes, Châtelet, 1995; Schwetzingen Festival, 1995, in Salieri's Falstaff; Sang Kolenaty in The Makropulos Case at Aix, 2000. *Recordings include:* El Cid, Mary, Queen of Scots. *Current Management:* Askonas Holt Ltd, Lonsdale Chambers, 27 Chancery Lane, London, WC2A 1PF, England. *Telephone:* (20) 7400-1700. *Fax:* (20) 7400-1799. *E-mail:* info@askonasholt.co.uk. *Website:* www.askonasholt.co.uk.

GARDNER, John Linton, CBE, BMus; British composer; b. 2 March 1917, Manchester, England; m. Jane Margaret Mary Abercrombie 1955 (died 1998); one s. two d. *Education:* Exeter College, Oxford. *Career:* Music Staff, Royal Opera House, 1946–52; Tutor, Morley College, 1952–76 (Director of Music 1965–69); Professor, Royal Academy of Music, 1956–86; Deputy Chairman, PRS, 1983–88; Chairman, 1963, Composers' Guild; Honorary Member, Royal Philharmonic Society, 1998. *Compositions:* 5 operas, including The Moon and Sixpence, 1957; 3 symphonies; 3 string quartets; 3 piano sonatas, concertos for piano, trumpet, organ, oboe and flute; Brass Chamber Music; 12 major Cantatas for chorus and orchestra, including The Ballad of the White Horse; Music for smaller groups; Concerto for flute and strings, 1994;

Sextet for piano and wind, 1995; Much unaccompanied choral music. *Recordings:* A Latter-Day Athenian Speaks; Theme and Variations for brass; Quartet for saxes; Tomorrow Shall Be My Dancing Day; Ecossaises; Burns Sequence; Flute Concerto; Third Symphony; Oboe concerto; 2nd Oboe Sonata. *Publications:* contrib. to Schumann, A Symposium; Musical Companion; Journals including Listener, Musical Times, RAM Magazine, Tempo, Dublin Review. *Honours:* Gold Medal, Bax Society, 1958. *Address:* 20 Firswood Avenue, Epsom, Surrey KT19 0PR, England.

GARDOW, Helrun; Singer (Mezzo-soprano); b. 8 Jan. 1944, Eisenach, Germany. *Education:* Studied in Berlin and Milan and with Josef Metternich in Cologne. *Career:* Sang at the Bonn Opera, 1969–76, and Zürich Opera, 1976–87 in various roles including Orpheus and Dorabella; Appeared in the premieres of Kelterborn's Ein Engel Kommt nach Babyon, 1977 and Der Kirschgarten in 1984; Guest appearances at Copenhagen, Düsseldorf, Edinburgh, Berlin, Dresden, Munich, Milan and Vienna; Concert engagements at Frankfurt, Madrid, Amsterdam, Cologne and Naples; Active in Seoul, Korea from 1987 as singer and director of Art-Com, in computer visual art and music. *Recordings:* Minerva in Il Ritorno d'Ulisse; L'Incoronazione di Poppea; Dido and Aeneas; Bach Cantatas and Magnificat; Haydn's Theresa Mass; Mozart's Missa Brevis in D. *Address:* c/o Opernhaus Zürich, Falkenstrasse 1, 8008 Zürich, Switzerland.

GARETTI, Helene; Singer (Soprano); b. 13 March 1939, Roanne, Loire, France. *Education:* Studied at the Paris Conservatoire and with Regine Crespin. *Career:* Sang first at Nice then Paris Opéra from 1968 as Marguerite, Iphigénie en Tauride, Médée, Chrysothemis in 1987 and Desdemona in 1988; Sang Massenet's Grisélidis at Strasbourg in 1986; Appearances at the Paris Opéra-Comique as Mimi, Butterfly, Katya Kabanova and Donna Elvira in 1988; Sang Sieglinde at Rouen and elsewhere in France; Other roles have included Leonore, Ariadne and Marguerite in Damnation de Faust.

GARIBOVA, Karine; Violinist; b. 1965, Moscow, Russia. *Education:* Studied at the Central Music School, Moscow. *Career:* Co-Founder, Quartet Veronique, 1989; Many concerts in the former Soviet Union and Russia, notably in the Russian Chamber Music Series and the 150th birthday celebrations for Tchaikovsky, 1990; Masterclasses at the Aldeburgh Festival, 1991; Concert tour of the United Kingdom in season 1992–93; Repertoire includes works by Beethoven, Brahms, Tchaikovsky, Bartók, Shostakovich and Schnittke. *Recordings include:* Schnittke's 3rd Quartet. *Honours:* Winner, All-Union String Quartet Competition, St Petersburg, 1990–91; Third Place, International Shostakovich Competition at St Petersburg, 1991, both with the Quartet Veronique. *Address:* c/o Sonata (Quartet Veronique), 11 Northpark Street, Glasgow G20 7AA, Scotland.

GARILLI, Fabrizio; Pianist and Composer; b. 29 July 1941, Monticelli d'Ongina, Placenza, Italy; m. Anna Paola Rossi, 8 Sept 1968, 1 s. *Education:* Diploma in Piano, Composition and Choral Music; Teaching qualification. *Career:* Debut: Piano Soloist with orchestra, Beethoven's 3rd Concerto, Teatro Municipale, Piacenza; Concerts as solo pianist with orchestra and chamber music; Conservatory Director. *Compositions:* Fantasie for Piano; Cantico delle Creature for Soloists, Choir and Organ; Contrappunti Su Temi Gregoriani for Organ and Orchestra; Metamorfosi for 2 Pianos and Percussion; Laude for Female Choir, Narrator and Orchestra. *Recordings:* Music of 17th Century Italians, Ciampi, Galuppi and Scarlatti, and JS Bach Well-Tempered Klavier, 2 records. *Publications:* Studi per Pianoforte; La Cartellina; Pezzi Per Cordo di Voci Bianche; Pezzi per Organo. *Honours:* 1st Prize, FM Neapolitano Composition Competition, Naples; 2nd Prize, Pedrollo, Milan; 1st Place, Assisi Prize; Various compositions commended in other composition competitions. *Address:* Via A da Sangallo 22, 29100 Piacenza, Italy.

GARINO, Gerard; Singer (Tenor); b. 1 June 1949, Lancon, Provence, France. *Education:* Studied at the Bordeaux Conservatoire and in Italy. *Career:* Debut: Bordeaux, 1977 as Rossini's Almaviva; Appearances at Bordeaux as Gerald in Lakmé and in La Dame Blanche and Gounod's Mireille; Further engagements as Mozart's Ferrando at Toulouse and Nadir in Les Pêcheurs de Perles at Aix; Paris Opéra and Liège 1981, in Il Matrimonio Segreto and Don Pasquale (Ernesto); Returned to Liège 1982 and 1987, as Idomeneo and in Grétry's Zemire; Portrait de Manon, Monte Carlo 1989; Season 1991, as Nadir at the Opéra-Comique, Paris, Pylades in Iphigénie en Tauride by Piccinni at Rome and Masaniello in La Muette de Portici at Marseille; Other roles include Tonio (La Fille du Régiment), Macduff, Ismaele (Nabucco) and Nicias (Thais); Traviata and Romeo and Juliette at Liège, Bohème at Toulouse, Thérèse (Massenet) at Monte Carlo, 1989; Manon (Massenet) at Bordeaux, Anna Bolena at Marseille, 1990; Werther at Festival Massenet and Festival de La Coruna, Spain, 1993; St Gallen 1994, as Nicias in Thais by Massenet. *Recordings:* L'Abandon d'Arianne by Milhaud; Don Sanche by Liszt; Messiaen's St François d'Assise; Il Pitor Parigino by

Cimarosa; Video of Carmen (as Remendado); La Mort d'Orphée, Berlioz. *Honours:* Winner, 1973 Enrico Caruso Competition. *Address:* Teatro dell'Opera, Piazza B Gigli, 00184 Rome, Italy.

GARNER, Françoise; singer (soprano); b. 17 Oct. 1933, Nerac, Lot-et-Garonne, France. *Education:* Paris Conservatoire, Accademia di Santa Cecilia, Rome and in Vienna. *Career:* debut, Paris Opéra-Comique in 1963 in the premiere of Menotti's Le Dernier Sauvage; Sang in Paris as Rosina, Leila, Lakmé and Olympia; Paris Opéra as Gilda and Lucia di Lammermoor, and Aix-en-Provence Festival in 1971 as the Queen of Night in Die Zauberflöte; Sang Marguerite in Faust at La Scala Milan in 1977, and at Verona Arena as Butterfly and Gounod's Juliette, 1977–79; Many performances in France and Italy in operas by Bellini; Metropolitan Opera 1986 as Elvira in I Puritani. *Address:* c/o Teatro alla Scala, via Filodrammatici 2, 20121 Milan, Italy.

GARO, Edouard; Chorus Master and Composer; b. 6 July 1935, Nyon, Switzerland; m. Verena Rellstab, 2 April 1963, 1 s., 1 d. *Education:* Arts, History, Philology, University of Lausanne; Composition, Singing, Academy of Lausanne; Studies, Pierre Mollet and Maroussia Le Mar Hadour, Geneva and Sylvia Gähwiller, Zürich. *Career:* Founder, Conductor, Ensemble Choral de la Côte; Music Master, Gymnase Cantonal de Nyon; Professor, Séminaire Pédagogique de l'enseignement secondaire, Lausanne; mem, ASM; SUISA; SSA. *Compositions:* Prospectrum, piano and tape, 1971; Les Sept contre Thèbes, 8 female voices and percussion, 1978; Incantation a 3, clarinet solo and tape, 1980; Agamemnon, opera, 1982; Le Masque blanc sur fond rouge, opera-ballet, 1984; Un Instant seul, 1989; Petra cantat, 1994; Joutes, 1996; La Grande Eclipse, 1996; String Quartet No. 1, 1993–97, No. 2, 1995–97, No. 3, 1998; Violin Concerto, 1999; Joutes rhapsodiques, cello, clarinet, piano, 2001; Requiem, S.T.B. solo; boy's choir, choir, instr. ensemble, 2001. *Publications:* Invention for Music Teaching: SOLMIPLOT. *Honours:* Grand Prix UFAM, with Medal from Ville de Paris, 1972; Silver Medal, International Exhibition of Inventions and New Techniques, Geneva, 1974. *Address:* 16 rue de la Porcelaine, 1260 Nyon, Switzerland.

GARRARD, Don; Singer (Bass); b. 31 July 1929, Vancouver, Canada. *Education:* Studied at the Toronto and Vancouver Conservatories and Opera School, Toronto; Music Academy of the West at Santa Barbara with Lotte Lehmann; Final 2 years study in Milan. *Career:* Debut: Toronto in 1952 as the Speaker in Die Zauberflöte; Sang Don Giovanni for Canadian television; Sadler's Wells Opera London from 1961 as Attila, Sarastro, Rocco, Raleigh in Gloriana, Trulove in The Rake's Progress and in the British premiere of Pizzetti's L'Assassinio nella Cattedrale in 1962; Scottish Opera in 1963 in the British premiere of Dallapiccola's Volo di Notte; Aldeburgh Festival in 1964 in the world premiere of Curlew River by Britten; Glyndebourne Festival, 1965–76 as Rochefort in Anna Bolena, Gremin, Pastor in the local premiere of Von Einem's The Visit of The Old Lady, Trulove and Arkel in Pelléas et Mélisande; Hamburg Staatsoper debut in 1968 as Padre Guardiano in La Forza del Destino and Covent Garden debut in 1970 as Ferrando in Il Trovatore followed by Prince Gremin in E Onegin, 1971–72; English National Opera as Sarastro; Mephisto (Faust); Rocco (Fidelio); Beckett in Murder in the Cathedral; Attila; Guardiano (Forza); Daland in Flying Dutchman; The Wanderer in Siegfried; Guest appearances in Santa Fe, Johannesburg, Toronto, Ottawa, Washington and Edinburgh; Sang the Grand Inquisitor in Don Carlos at Toronto in 1988, Daland in Der fliegende Holländer for Pacific Opera at Victoria BC, in 1989; Sang King Mark in Tristan und Isolde for Capab Opera at Cape Town in 1992; Season 1994–95, as Rocco and Sarastro; Crespel in Les Contes d'Hoffmann, 1998; many concert appearances. *Recordings include:* The Rake's Progress. *Honours:* 1st Prize Singing, Stars of Tomorrow and NOS Futures Etoiles, Canada, 1953, 1954; Vercelli Concours, 1961; Queen's Jubilee Medal, 1977. *Address:* The Villa, 18 Van Der Poll Avenue, Tokai 7945, Cape Town 8000, South Africa.

GARRETT, David; Concert Violinist; b. 1981, USA. *Career:* Appearances with the Chamber Orchestra of Europe under Abbado and the Munich Philharmonic under Mehta; British debut at the 1993 Brighton Festival with the Bournemouth Symphony, returned in 1994 with the London Philharmonic under Matthias Bamert and in 1995 with City of Birmingham Symphony Orchestra under Stefan Sanderling; US debut with the Los Angeles Philharmonic in 1994 under Zubin Mehta. *Recordings include:* Exclusively for Deutsche Grammophon, Recital and Concerto albums. *Current Management:* Askonas Holt Ltd, Lonsdale Chambers, 27 Chancery Lane, London, WC2A 1PF, England. *Telephone:* (20) 7400-1700. *Fax:* (20) 7400-1799. *E-mail:* info@askonasholt.co.uk. *Website:* www.askonasholt.co.uk.

GARRETT, Eric; Singer (Bass-baritone); b. 1935, Yorkshire, England. *Education:* Studied at the Royal College of Music in London and with Eva Turner and Tito Gobbi. *Career:* Debut: Covent Garden in 1962 in La Bohème; Many character roles at Covent Garden from 1962; Appearances with Scottish Opera and the Welsh National Opera, Brussels and

Ghent, 1978–79 as Bartolo in Il Barbiere di Siviglia, Dulcamara in L'Elisir d'amore and in Adriana Lecouvreur; Antwerp, 1981 as Baron Ochs in Der Rosenkavalier; Sang Mustafà in L'Italiana in Algeri at Covent Garden in 1988, Ceprano in Rigoletto in 1989, Skula in a new production of Prince Igor in 1990, followed by Don Pasquale and Alcindoro; Other roles at Covent Garden include Gianni Schnicci, Don Fernando, Sacristan, Swallow, Varlaam and Frank; Has also sung Falstaff, Melitone, Scarpia, Ochs, Kecal, Schigolch in Lulu and Rocco; Guest appearances include San Francisco, Los Angeles, Marseilles, Montpellier and Munich; Flemish Deputy in Don Carlos at Covent Garden, 1996; Mozart's Antonio with the Royal Opera, 1998. *Recordings include:* La Fanciulla del West; Billy Budd. *Address:* Stafford Law Associates, 6 Barham Close, Weybridge, Surrey KT 13 9 PR, England.

GARRETT, Lesley, CBE; Singer (soprano); b. 10 April 1955, Thorne, Doncaster, England. *Education:* Royal Acad. of Music, and with Joy Mammen. *Career:* appearances include that with the Glyndebourne Festival and Touring Co and with Opera North; numerous European engagements include Servillia in La Clemenza di Tito in Geneva, The Fairy Queen at Maggio Musicale, Florence and a Schoenberg cabaret song recital at the Pompidou Centre in Paris; ENO from 1984 as Bella in The Midsummer Marriage, Valencienne in The Merry Widow, Atalanta in Xerxes (also televised) and Yum-Yum in Jonathan Miller's production of The Mikado for Thames television; many other successful performances including Oscar in a new production of A Masked Ball and Princess Ninetta in The Love For Three Oranges, 1989, Susanna at ENO in 1990, Atalanta on tour to Russia and Brazil, Papagena in a revival of The Magic Flute; Season 1991–92 as Adele in Die Fledermaus, Rose in Weill's Street Scene and Zerlina at the Coliseum; sang Euridice in a new production of Gluck's Orpheus for ENO 1997; Rossini's Rosina at ENO 2001. *Recordings include:* Diva 1992, Prima Donna 1993, A Soprano Inspired 1998, The Soprano's Greatest Hits 1997, A Soprano in Love 1999, I Will Wait for You 2000, Travelling Light 2001, The Singer 2002, So Deep Is The Night 2003. *Honours:* Winner, Kathleen Ferrier Memorial Competition, 1979. *Current Management:* The Music Partnership Ltd, Suite 6, Riverside House, 27–29 Vauxhall Grove, London, SW8 1BH, England.

GARRISON, Jon; Tenor; b. 11 Dec. 1944, Higginsville, Missouri, USA. *Career:* Has sung widely in North America notably at opera houses in Houston, Montreal, Santa Fe and San Diego; Metropolitan Opera from 1974 in Death in Venice, Manon Lescaut, Così fan tutte as Ferrando and Die Zauberflöte as Tamino; New York City Opera from 1982 as Adméte in Alceste, Don Ottavio, Rodolfo, Nadir, the Duke of Mantua, Tom Rakewell, Tamino and Nicholas in the premiere of Reise's Rasputin in 1988; Sang Prince Edmund in the premiere of Stewart Copeland's Holy Blood and Crescent Moon at Cleveland, 1989, and sang Shuratov in the US stage premiere of From The House of The Dead, in New York, 1990; Sang the title role in Oedipus Rex at the Festival Hall, London, 1997; Idomeneo at the 1996 Garsington Festival. *Address:* c/o New York City Opera, Lincoln Center, New York, NY 10023, USA.

GARRISON, Kenneth; Singer (Tenor); b. 6 Dec. 1948, West Monroe, Louisiana, USA. *Education:* Studied at the Salzburg Mozarteum and with Hans Hopf in Munich. *Career:* Debut: Regensburg, 1977, as Mozart's Basilio; Sang at Regensburg until 1980, Oldenburg, 1980–82, Karlsruhe, 1982–84 (Wagner's Mime and Steersman); Munich Staatsoper from 1984, as Luzio in Wagner's Das Liebesverbot, Dvořák's Dimitri, the Prince in Love for Three Oranges, Max and Narraboth; Guest engagements as Strauss's Emperor at Karlsruhe, Radames at Saarbrucken and Parsifal at Brunswick and Essen; Mainz, 1990, as Otello; Season 1993 at Brunswick as Strauss's Emperor, Strasbourg 1996 in From the House of Death; Many concert appearances, notably in Beethoven's Ninth and Rossini's Stabat Mater; Season 2000–01 as Mime in Siegfried at Mannheim and Tannhäuser at Cape Town. *Address:* c/o Bayerische Staatsoper, Max-Joseph-Platz, Pf 100148, W-8000 Munich 1, Germany.

GASCO, Daniel; Singer (Tenor); b. 1961, Valencia, Spain. *Education:* Studied in Valencia and with Waldemar Kmentt in Vienna. *Career:* Appearances in Vienna as Nicolai's Fenton and Mozart's Ferrando and in Rossini's Il Viaggio a Reims; Bregenz Festival, 1989–93 as Rossini's Ramiro and Lindoro, Fenton, and in Rossini's Stabat Mater; Berne, 1993 as Daniel in Judith by Matthus; Season 1994 as Ferrando at Lubeck and Verdi's Fenton at Brunswick. *Address:* c/o Staatsoper, 1010 Vienna, Austria.

GASDIA, Cecilia; Soprano; b. 14 Aug. 1960, Verona, Italy. *Education:* Studied classics and piano in Verona. *Career:* Debut: Florence in 1982 as Giulietta in I Capuleti e i Montecchi by Bellini; La Scala in 1982 as Anna Bolena in the opera by Donizetti; Perugia and Naples in 1982 in Demophoon by Cherubini and as Amina in La Sonnambula; Paris Opéra debut in 1983 as Anais in Moise by Rossini; Pesaro in 1984 in a revival of Il Viaggio a Reims by Rossini; US debut in Philadelphia in 1985 as Gilda in a concert performance of Rigoletto; Chicago Lyric Opera and

Metropolitan Opera in 1986 as Giulietta and as Gounod's Juliette; Other roles include Violetta, Liu in Turandot, Hélène in Verdi's Jérusalem and Mrs Ford in Salieri's Falstaff; Sang Rosa in Fioravanti's Le Cantatrici Villane, Naples, 1990; Season 1991–92 as Adina at Chicago, Mimi at Bonn, Nedda at Rome, Elena in La Donna del Lago at La Scala and Rosina at the Festival of Caracalla; Pesaro Festival 1994, as Semiramide; Zürich 1997, as Gounod's Marguerite; Season 1998 as Euridice at Florence, Giulietta in Un Giorno di Regno at Parma, Handel's Cleopatra at Glimmerglass, New York, and Suzel in L'Amico Fritz at Naples; Season 2000–01 as Jean in Le Jongleur de Notre Dame by Massenet in Rome, Elcia in Rossini's Mosè in Egitto at Verona and as Suzel in Mascagni's L'Amico Fritz. *Recordings include:* Catone in Utica; Motets by Vivaldi; Il Viaggio a Reims; Video of Turandot; Rossini's Armida and Ermione. *Address:* c/o Teatro San Carlo, Via San Carlo 98F, 80132 Naples, Italy.

GASSIEV, Nikolai; Singer (Tenor); b. 1950, St Petersburg, Russia. *Education:* Graduated St Petersburg Conservatory, 1980. *Career:* Appearances with Kirov Opera, 1990; As Missail and the Simpleton in Boris Godunov, Finn in Ruslan, Agrippa in The Fiery Angel, Mozart's Basilio, Indian Guest in Sadko and Cassio in Otello; Jerome in Prokofiev's Duenna, Monostatos, Yeroshka in Prince Igor; Tours of Europe and USA, New York Met with the Kirov; Season 1998: Rachmaninov's Miserly Knight at Venice and St Petersburg; Trabucco in La Forza del Destino; Sang Fieramosca in Benvenuto Cellini with Rotterdam Philharmonic Orchestra under Valery Gergiev, London, 1999; Season 2000–01 as Bomelius in Rimsky's The Tsar's Bride, at San Francisco, and the Marquis in The Gambler by Prokofiev at the New York Met; Mussorgsky's Boris Godunov at the London Proms, 2002. *Recordings:* Operas by Rimsky-Korsakov, Mussorgsky and Prokofiev. *Address:* c/o Kirov Opera, 1 Theatre Square, St Petersburg, Russia.

GASTEEN, Lisa; Soprano; b. 1957, Queensland, Australia. *Education:* Studied at the Queensland Conservatorium with Margaret Nickson and in San Francisco and at the London Opera Studio. *Career:* Debut: Lyric Opera of Queensland in 1985 as the High Priestess in Aida and Diana in Orpheus in The Underworld; Appearances with Australian Opera as Miss Jessel in The Turn of the Screw, Frasquita, Madame Lidoine in Carmelites, both Leonoras, Elsa, Donna Elvira and Leonore in Fidelio; Victorian State Opera as Elisabeth in Tannhäuser, Elisabeth de Valois and Desdemona, Leonora Trovatore, 1993; Season 1991–92 as the Trovatore and Forza Leonoras for Scottish Opera, Amelia in Un Ballo in Maschera for Welsh National Opera and Washington Opera, Donna Anna in Prague and Fidelio Leonore in Stuttgart; Concert repertoire includes Rossini's Stabat Mater and Elijah for the Sydney Philharmonia, Beethoven's Ninth in Sydney, Melbourne and Tasmania, Tokyo Philharmonic; Sang Verdi's Requiem for Hungarian Radio in 1993, Maddelena in Andrea Chénier for Deutsche Oper Berlin in 1994 and Aida for Australian Opera in 1995; Sang the Trovatore Leonora at Sydney, 1996; Sang the Empress in Die Frau Ohne Schatten for Melbourne Festival, 1996; Season 1999–2000 as Brünnhilde in Siegfried at Stuttgart, Verdi's Elisabeth de Valois and Strauss's Chrysothemis at Sydney; Season 2001–2002 all three Brünnhilde at Meiningen and Isolde for Opera Australia in Melbourne; Engaged as Brünnhilde at Covent Garden, 2005. *Honours:* Winner, Metropolitan Opera, NY, Competition, Australian Regional Finals, 1982; Covent Garden Scholarship, 1984; First Australian Recipient of Metropolitan Opera Educational Fund Grant; Received Advance Australia Award, 1991; Winner, Cardiff Singer of The World Competition in 1991; Helpmann Award for role as Isolde with Opera Australia. *Address:* c/o Jenifer Eddy Artists' Management, Suite 11, The Clivedon, 596 St Kilda Road, Melbourne 3004, Victoria, Australia.

GASZTECKI, Marek; Singer (Bass); b. 1953, Poland. *Career:* Debut: Poznan, 1977, as Theseus in A Midsummer Night's Dream; Sang at Poznan until 1980, then with Darmstadt Opera as Don Magnifico in Cenerentola, the Water Spirit in Rusalka and many other roles; Many guest appearances elsewhere in Germany, notably as Cecil in Donizetti's Maria Stuarda and in The Lighthouse by Maxwell Davies; Has also sung in contemporary works by Klebe and Cerha and has sung in concert in works by Bach, Handel and Haydn; Season 1994–95 in Prokofiev's Fiery Angel at Kassel and as Lothario in Mignon by Thomas at Heidelberg; Season 1999–2000 in Busoni's Faust at Salzburg and in Szymanowski's King Roger for Netherlands Opera. *Address:* c/o Oper der Stadt Bonn, Am Boeselagerhof 1, Pf 2440, W-5300 Bonn, Germany.

GASZTOWT-ADAMS, Helen (Catriona); Soprano; b. 29 Sept. 1956, Geelong, Victoria, Australia. *Education:* Victorian College of The Arts, Melbourne; National Opera Studio, London, 1989; Studied with Audrey Langford and Janice Chapman. *Career:* Debut: Pamina in Die Zauberflöte, State Opera of South Australia, 1983; Sang in Don Giovanni, Manon, Countess Maritza, and Figaro for State Opera of South Australia, 1985–86; Debut with Australian Opera as Nanetta in 1986 then in Suor Angelica, Il Tabarro, Médée, Poppea, and Carmen; London debut, Anna Bolena at National Opera Studio Showcase, Queen

Elizabeth Hall in 1989; BBC Cardiff Singer of the World finals in 1989; European concert debut, Grusse aus Wien, Robert Stolz Club, recorded for Belgian radio and television, 1990; Sang Gilda in Rigoletto, Australian Opera in 1990; English National Opera debut as Donna Elvira in 1991; Other appearances include Rossini's Petite Messe Solennelle, Netherlands and Belgian tour, Strauss's Vier Letzte Lieder, Koninklijk Ballet van Vlaanderen, Antwerp, Belgium, Mozart's Requiem, English String Orchestra, Bath Mozart Festival, and as Pamina in Die Zauberflöte, Victoria State Opera, Melbourne; Extensive radio and television recital and concert work including Handel's Messiah, Mendelssohn's Elijah, A Midsummer Night's Dream, Orff's Carmina Burana, and Vier Letzte Leider; Performed with Melbourne and Sydney Symphony Orchestras, Australian Chamber Orchestra, and opera and concert performances in the United Kingdom, Barbados, Australia, France and Spain. *Address:* c/o English National Opera, St Martin's Lane, London WC2N 4ES, England.

GATES, Crawford; Conductor and Composer; b. 29 Dec. 1921, San Francisco, California, USA; m. Georgia Lauper 1952; two s. two d. *Education:* BA, San Jose State Coll.; MA, Brigham Young Univ.; PhD, Music, Eastman School of Music, Univ. of Rochester; conducting studies with Eleazar de Carvalho and Hans Swarowsky. *Career:* debut, Stanford Univ., as composer, 1938; Utah Symphony, as conductor; Chair., Music Dept, and Conductor, Symphony Orchestra and Opera, Brigham Young Univ., 1960–66; Artist-in-Residence, Prof., Chair of Music Dept, Beloit Coll., Beloit, Wisconsin, 1966–89; Music Dir, Beloit Janesville Symphony, 1966–1999, Quincy Symphony, 1969–70, Rockford Symphony Orchestra, 1970–86. *Compositions include:* six stage works, seven symphonies, Tone Poems, Suites, Concertos, numerous choral arrangements, four major choral works, trumpet concertino and horn sonata; Pentameron for piano and orchestra (commissioned by Grant Johannesen); over 100 titles published including Suite for String Orchestra. *Recordings:* Symphony No. 2, Orchestral Setting of Beloved Mormon Hymns, included on Philadelphia Orchestra Album; The Lord's Prayer and A Jubilant Song; Music to the New Hill Cumorah Pageant, 1988; Promised Valley. *Address:* 2108 Scenic Drive, Salt Lake City, UT 84109, USA. .

GATI, Istvan; Tenor; b. 29 Nov. 1948, Budapest, Hungary. *Education:* Studied at the Franz Liszt Academy, Budapest. *Career:* Member of the Hungarian State Opera from 1972 notably in the premieres of Csongor and Tunde by Attila Bozay in 1985 and Ecce Homo by Sandor Szokolay, 1987; Appearances at the Vienna Staatsoper from 1986; Sang Don Giovanni at Liège in 1988, Nick Shadow at the Deutsche Oper Berlin in 1989 and Antonio in Le nozze di Figaro at the 1991 Vienna Festival; Season 1999–2000 as Ruggiero in Halévy's La Juive and Marco in Gianni Schicchi; Guest appearances in Italy, France, Poland, Spain, Netherlands and Austria and concert engagements in works by Bach, Handel, Mozart, Beethoven and Liszt. *Recordings include:* Cantatas by Bach, Don Sanche and The Legend of St Elisabeth by Liszt; Salieri's Falstaff; Paisiello's Barbiere di Siviglia; Don Pasquale; Simon Boccanegra; Telemann's Der Geduldige Sokrates; Balthazar and Jonas by Carissimi; Ein Deutsches Requiem; Mahler's Lieder eines Fahrenden Gesellen; Oronte in Handel's Floridante. *Honours:* Competition Winner at Salzburg, Vienna, Trevisto and Moscow at Tchaikovsky International in 1974. *Address:* c/o Hungarian State Opera, Nepoztarsasag utja 22, 1061 Budapest, Hungary.

GATTI, Daniele; Italian conductor; b. 6 Nov. 1961, Milan; m. Silvia Chiesa 1990. *Education:* Giuseppe Verdi Conservatory, Milan. *Career:* conducted Verdi's Giovanna d'Arco 1982; appearances with the Maggio Musicale Fiorentino Orchestra, Milan Angelicum, Bologna Municipal Orchestra, regional orchestras of Italian radio; f. Stradivari Chamber Orchestra 1986; debut at La Scala, Milan with Rossini's L'occasione fa il Ladro 1987–88 season; US debut with American Symphony Orchestra, Carnegie Hall, New York 1990; Covent Garden debut with I Puritani 1992; Music Dir Accad. di Santa Cecilia, Rome 1992–; Prin. Guest Conductor, Royal Opera House, Covent Garden 1994–96; debut at Metropolitan Opera, New York with Madama Butterfly 1994–95 season; debut with Royal Philharmonic Orchestra 1994, Music Dir 1995–; debut with New York Philharmonic 1995; Music Dir Teatro Communale, Bologna 1997–; has led many orchestras in Europe and USA, including the Bavarian Radio Symphony, London Philharmonic, Cleveland Orchestra, Boston and Chicago Symphonies and the Accademia Santa Cecilia, Rome; has conducted at many of the world's leading opera houses; conducted the RPO at the London Proms 1999, 2002. *Current Management:* Columbia Artists Management Ltd, 28 Cheverton Road, London, N19 3AY, England. *Telephone:* (20) 7272-8020. *Fax:* (20) 7272-8991. *E-mail:* info@cami.co.uk. *Address:* Via Scaglia Est 134, 41100 Modena, Italy (office); c/o Royal Philharmonic Orchestra, 16 Clerkenwell Green, London, EC1R 0DP, England.

GATTI, Giorgio; Singer (Bass-Baritone); b. 1 April 1948, Poggio a Caino, Italy. *Education:* Studied in Florence and Rome. *Career:* Opera engagements throughout Italy in operas by Pergolesi, A Scarlatti,

Salieri, Anfossi, Piccinni, Morlacchi and Sacchini, Florence, 1994 in La Bohème; Opera and concert appearances in France, Germany, Switzerland, Japan and North America; Member of group Recitar Cantando, 1980–90. *Recordings:* Il Barone di Rocca antica by Anfossi; Fioravanti's La Servascaltra. *Address:* c/o Teatro Comunale, Via Solferino 15, 50123 Florence, Italy.

GAUCI, Miriam; Maltese opera singer; b. 3 April 1957, Vittoriosa, Gozo; d. of Carmel Cutajar and Rosette Tabone; m. Michael Laus 1987; one d. *Education:* Conservatorio G. Verdi and Centro di Perfezionamento Artisti Lirici, Milan, Italy. *Career:* soprano, debut at La Scala, Milan, Italy in La Sonnambula, L'Orfeo, Die Frau ohne Schatten; debut in USA in Madame Butterfly at Santa Fe 1987; appeared in La Bohème with Placido Domingo, Los Angeles, USA, Hamburg, Germany; appeared in La Traviata, Geneva, Switzerland, Dresden, Germany; also sang in Madrid, Lisbon and Berlin, Manon at Vienna Staatsoper 1996 and in Boito's Mefistofele; in Falstaff at the Hamburg Staatsoper 1997, Mimi at the New York Met 2001; 1st prize in various int. competitions including Treviso, Bologna, Milan, Italy 1979. *Video:* Carmen 1989. *Recordings include:* Madame Butterfly 1992, Manon Lescaut, Pagliacci (Naxos), La Bohème, Deutsches Requiem, Verdi's Requiem, Egmont, Operatic Arias. *Address:* c/o Grand Théâtre de Genève, 11 Boulevard du Théâtre, 1211 Geneva, Switzerland; Villa No. 5, Salini Street, Marsascala, Malta. *Telephone:* 820033. *Fax:* 690477.

GAVANELLI, Paolo; Singer (Baritone); b. 1959, Monselice, near Padua, Italy. *Career:* Debut: Sang Leporello at the Teatro Donizetti, Bergamo in 1985; Season 1988–89 as Mephistopheles at Barcelona and Marcello in La Bohème in Madrid; Further engagements as Marcello at Venice, Bologna and the State Operas of Munich and Vienna in 1991; Sang Luna in Trovatore at the Metropolitan in 1990 returning in Puritani and as Germont in 1992; Sang Gerard in Andrea Chénier at San Francisco and Stuttgart, Renato in Un Ballo in Maschera at Chicago and Verdi's Falstaff at the Rome Opera; Festival appearances at Pesaro as Germano in La Scala di Seta, 1990 and the Arena Verona; Has also appeared at La Scala from 1991 and Genoa as Renato; Other roles include Rossini's Figaro and Verdi's Iago, Rigoletto and Amonasro; Festival appearances 1996 at Ravenna (as Alfio) and Rome (Gerard); Renato (Ballo in Maschera) at Verona, 1998; Season 2000–01 at the Munich State Opera as Riccardo in I Puritani, Germont, and Posa; Nabucco at Verona, Falstaff at Covent Garden and Simon Boccanegra for San Francisco Opera; Germont for the Royal Opera, 2002. *Recordings:* Marcello in La Bohème. *Address:* c/o Metropolitan Opera House, Lincoln Center, New York, NY 10023, USA.

GAVAZZI, Ernesto; Singer (Tenor); b. 7 May 1941, Seregno, Monza, Italy. *Education:* Studied at the Milan Conservatoire with Bruno Carmassi and at the Scuola della Scala with Vladimiro Badiali. *Career:* Debut: Treviso in 1971 as Nemorino in L'Elisir d'amore; Many appearances in Italy and elsewhere in Europe as Elvino in La Sonnambula, Paolina in Il Matrimonio Segreto and Rossini's Almaviva, Don Ramiro, Giocondo in La Pietra del Paragone, Edward Milfort in Il Cambiale di Matrimonio, Rodolphe in Guillaume Tell and Don Eusebio in L'Occasione fa il Ladro; Has sung at Pesaro and La Scala in several Rossini revivals including Zefirio in Il Viaggio a Reims, 1984–85; Sang Goro in Madama Butterfly and Chekalinsky in The Queen of Spades at La Scala, 1990–97; Normanno in Lucia di Lammermoor at La Scala, 1997; Season 2000–01 at La Scala in Tosca, Rigoletto, Il Trovatore and Falstaff. *Recordings include:* Il Viaggio a Reims; Captain in Simon Boaccanegra; Borsa in Rigoletto; Uldino in Attila; Guillaume Tell under Riccardo Muti. *Address:* c/o Teatro alla Scala, Via Fildrammatici 2, 20121 Milan, Italy.

GAVIN, Julian; Singer (Tenor); b. 1965, Melbourne, Victoria, Australia. *Education:* Studied in Melbourne (BMus) and at the National Opera Studio, London. *Career:* Has appeared widely in the United Kingdom and Ireland as Alfredo, Des Grieux, Nemorino, Rodolfo, Tamino, Don José and the Duke of Mantua; Further appearances in Franck's Hulda, Alvaro in La Forza del Destino, Ismaele in Nabucco, Arrigo in Verdi's Battaglia di Legnano, Pinkerton, and Laca in Jenůfa (Opera North, 1995); Pollione in Norma at Lucerne, 1996; Steersman in The Flying Dutchman, Alfredo in La Traviata for Australian Opera, 1996, 1997; Concert repertoire includes Messiah, Rossini's Stabat Mater, The Dream of Gerontius, the Verdi Requiem with David Willcocks, Mahler's 8th Symphony at the Festival Hall; Tippet, A Child of Our Time, Ulster Orchestra; Sang Beaumont in Maw's The Rising of the Moon for the BBC; Season 1996–97 as the Duke of Mantua, Alfredo and Pinkerton for ENO; Sang Hoffmann, 1998; Carlo VII in Verdi's Giovanna d'Arco for Opera North, Don Carlos in Leeds, at the Edinburgh Festival and for the Royal Opera, 1998 with Haitink, and for Opera Australia, 1999; Season 1999–2000, Roméo in Gounod's Roméo et Juliette and Don José in Carmen, Puccini's Des Grieux at Genoa, with the ENO Rodolfo in La Bohème and the title role in Ernani; Pinkerton for Opera North; Concert performances of Kodály's Psalmus Hungaricus with the BBC Symphony Orchestra and Berlioz Roméo et Juliette with the Sydney Symphony

Orchestra; Manrico for ENO 2001; mem, International Society of Musicians. *Recordings:* Godvino in Verdi's Aroldo; Don José in Carmen; Roméo et Juliette; Les Contes d'Hoffmann. *Honours:* Lady Turner Prize, University of Melbourne, 1978; L Mus A, 1985. *Address:* c/o English National Opera, St Martin's Lane, London, WC2, England.

GAVRILOV, Andrei; Pianist; b. 21 Sept. 1955, Moscow, Russia. *Career:* Debut: Recital Festival, Salzburg, 1974; Appeared with all major London Orchestras; Recitals, Queen Elizabeth Hall, Barbican, Royal Festival Hall, London; Also in Austria, Belgium, France, Germany, Netherlands, Spain, Switzerland, Italy, Japan, Canada, New Zealand; Festivals in Salzburg, Roque d'Antheron, Schleswig Holstein, New Zealand, 1986; Regular visits to USA include concerts with Philharmonic Orchestra, with Muti and Frühbeck de Burgos; Other conductors include, Abbado, Haitink, Muti, Ozawa, Svetlanov and Tennstedt. *Recordings include:* EMI, Scriabin, Chopin; Rachmaninov, Concerto No. 2 and 3, Paganini Variations; Stravinsky and Concerto, Rite for Spring, with Vladimir Ashkenazy; Chamber recordings, Shostakovich; Violin Sonata; Gavrilov/Kremer; Britten, The Golden Vanity, Friday Afternoons, with Vienna Knabenchor, solo pieces; Romeo and Juliet, Goldberg Variations. *Honours:* 1st Prize, Tchaikovsky Piano Competition, 1974; Contract with EMI, 1976–90; Musical Prize, Gramophone, for Prokofiev's Piano Concerto No. 1 with Simon Rattle and London Symphony Orchestra, 1978; Musical Prize, Deutscher Schallplattenpreis for Prokofiev recording, Sonata No. 8, 1981; Grand Prix International du Disque de l'Acadèmie Charles Crois, for Scriabin recording, 1985; High Fidelity International Record Critics Award, for EMI Scriabin, 1985; Grand Prix International du Disque de l'Academie Charles Crois, for Rachmaninov solo recording, 1986; Siena, Premio Internationale Academie Musicale Chigiana, best pianist of the world, 1989; Man of the Year, Board of International Research, ABI, 1995; Gold Record of Achievement; World Lifetime Achievement Award. *Address:* Am Walberstück 7, 65520 Bad Camberg, Germany.

GAWRILOFF, Saschko; Violinist; b. 20 Oct. 1929, Leipzig, Germany. *Education:* Early studies with his father; Leipzig Conservatory, 1942–44 with Gustav Havemann and Martin Kovacz in Berlin, 1945–47. *Career:* Leader of the Dresden Philharmonic, 1947–48, Berlin Philharmonic, 1948–49, Berlin Radio Symphony, 1949–53, Museum Orchestra of Frankfurt am Main, 1953–57, and Hamburg Radio Symphony, 1961–66; Teacher at the Nuremberg Conservatory, 1957–61; Professor at the North-West German Music Academy, 1966–69, at the Folkwanghochschule in Essen from 1969; Head of masterclasses for violin at the Cologne Musikhochscule; Appearances with leading orchestras include Germany and the United Kingdom and concerts in Vienna, Milan, Madrid, Rome, Paris, India and Japan; Conductors include Boulez in Berg Concerto, Solti, Dohnányi, Gielen and Inbal; Has given the premieres of works by Maderna, Dieter Kaufmann and Schnittke; Formed a trio with Alfons Kontarsky and Klaus Storck in 1971; Member of the Robert Schumann Trio with Johannes Goritzki and David Levine; Contemporary music with Siegfried Palm and Bruno Canino. *Honours:* Winner, International Competitions at Berlin and Munich in 1953; Genoa Paganini Competition and City of Nuremberg Prize, 1959. *Current Management:* Ingpen & Williams Ltd, 7 St George's Court, 131 Putney Bridge Road, London, SW15 2PA, England.

GAYER, Catherine; Soprano; b. 11 Feb. 1937, Los Angeles, California, USA. *Education:* Studied in Los Angeles. *Career:* Sang in the premiere of Nono's Intolleranza in 1960, at Venice in 1961, Covent Garden in 1962 as the Queen of Night, Deutsche Oper Berlin from 1963 notably as Hilde Mack in Henze's Elegie für Junge Liebende, Berg's Lulu and Marie in Zimmermann's Die Soldaten and Nausicca in the 1968 premiere of Dallapiccola's Ulisse, and Scottish Opera from 1968 as Susanna, Hilde Mack, the Queen of Shemakha in The Golden Cockerel and in the 1975 premiere of Orr's Hermiston; Sang at Schwetzingen Festival in 1971 in the premiere of Reimann's Melusine, at Edinburgh Festival in 1972 with the company of the Deutsche Oper Berlin in Die Soldaten; Sang the leading role in the premiere of Joseph Tal's Der Versuchung at Munich in 1976; Other roles include Ulisse at La Scala, Zerbinetta, Gilda and Mélisande, sang the Woman in Schoenberg's Erwartung at the Komische Oper Berlin in 1988, songs by Reimann and Szymanowski at the 1990 Aldeburgh Festival, Berlin Kammeroper in 1991 with Berio's Sequenza III, Tal's Die Hand, The Medium by Maxwell Davies and Weisgall's The Stronger; Sang at Stuttgart in 1992 as the Grand-Mother in Dinescu's Eréndira and in Rag Time, an arrangement of Joplin's Treemonisha at the 1992 Schwetzingen Festival and in 2 productions of Schoenberg's Pierrot Lunaire; Sang in Manon at the Deutsche Oper, 1998. *Recordings:* Woodbird in Siegfried; Elegie für Junge Liebende; Die Israeliten in Der Wüste by CPE Bach; Il Giardino d'Amore by Scarlatti. *Honours:* Winner, San Francisco Opera Auditions, 1960 and Berlin Kammersängerin in 1970. *Address:* c/o Deutsche Oper, Richard Wagnerstrasse 10, Berlin, Germany.

GAYFORD, Christopher; Conductor; b. 1963, Wilmslow, England. *Education:* Royal Coll. of Music with Christopher Adey, John Forster and Norman del Mar. *Career:* repetiteur at Graz Opera, 1987; Jr Fellow in Conducting at the Royal Northern Coll. of Music, 1988; conducted Don Carlos and A Midsummer Night's Dream at the Royal Northern Coll. of Music, 1990; debut with the London Mozart Players at the Barbican Hall, 1990, in L'Elisir d'amore for Royal Northern Coll. of Music and Don Giovanni for Opera North; Asst Conductor to Royal Liverpool Philharmonic Orchestra, 1992–93; conducted Così fan tutte for British Youth Opera at Sadler's Wells, 1992. *Honours:* Besançon International Competition for Young Conductors, 1989.

GEBHARDT, Horst; Singer (tenor); b. 17 June 1940, Silberhausen, Germany. *Education:* Studied in Weimar and Berlin. *Career:* Debut: Schwerin in 1972 as Chateauneuf in Lortzing's Zar und Zimmermann; Sang at Leipzig, the Staatsoper Dresden and Berlin; Member of the Leipzig Opera from 1985 including role as Erik in Fliegende Holländer in 1989, and has made guest appearances in France, Italy, Spain, England, Yugoslavia, Russia, Poland, Japan and Cuba; Other roles have included Max, Mozart's Belmonte, Ottavio, Titus, Tamino and Ferrando, Lensky, Fenton, Strauss's Narraboth and Flamand, Jacquino in Fidelio, David in Die Meistersinger, Alfredo and Sextus in Giulio Cesare; Kiel Opera 1991, in Vincent by Rautavaara. *Recordings:* Idomeneo; Parsifal; Palestrina; Alfonso und Estrella. *Honours:* Prizewinner, International Bach Competition, Leipzig and National Opera Competition, Germany, 1972. *Address:* St ädtische Theatre, 7010 Leipzig, Germany.

GEDDA, Nicolai; Singer (tenor); b. 11 July 1925, Stockholm, Sweden. *Education:* Musical Academy Stockholm. *Career:* Debut: Stockholm in 1952; Concert appearances in Rome, 1952, Paris, 1953 and 1955, Vienna, 1955, Aix-en-Provence and Rome, 1953, Paris, London and Vienna, 1954, Salzburg Festival, 1957–59, and Edinburgh Festival, 1958–59; With Metropolitan Opera, NY from 1957, created role of Anatol in Barber's Vanessa in 1958; World-wide appearances in opera, concerts and recitals; First London recital in 1986 and in concert performances of Bernstein's Candide at the Barbican Hall in London, 1989; Sang Christian II in the first modern performance of Naumann's Gustaf Wasa at Stockholm in 1991; Sang Patriach Abdisu of Assyria in Pfitzner's Palestrina at Covent Garden, 1997; 75th birthday song recital in Vienna, 2000. *Recordings include:* Les Contes d'Hoffmann; Boris Godunov; Il Barbiere di Siviglia; Il Turco in Italia; I Capuleti e i Montecchi; La Damnation de Faust; Carmen; Les Pêcheurs de Perles; Faust; A Life for The Tsar; Louise; Fra Diavolo; Lady Macbeth of Mtensk; Manon; Thais; Così fan tutte; Die Zauberflöte; Don Giovanni; Roussel's Padmâvati; Bach's St Matthew Passion; Rossini's Petite Messe Solennelle; La Bohème; Carmen with Callas; Werther; Der Barbier von Bagdad; Der Rosenkavalier; Capriccio; Die Fledermaus; Rigoletto; Vanessa; Benvenuto Cellini; War and Peace; Pfitzner's Palestrina; Schubert's Die Zwillingsbrüder; Weber's Abu Hassan; Der Freischütz; Gluck's Le Cadi Dupé; Die Entführung; Lortzing's Undine. *Current Management:* Askonas Holt Ltd, Lonsdale Chambers, 27 Chancery Lane, London, WC2A 1PF, England. *Telephone:* (20) 7400-1700. *Fax:* (20) 7400-1799. *E-mail:* info@askonasholt.co.uk. *Website:* www.askonasholt.co.uk. *Address:* Valhallavagen 110, 114 41 Stockholm, Sweden.

GEDGE, Nicholas (Paul Johnson); Singer (Bass-baritone); b. 12 March 1968, Brecon, Wales; m. Kate Robinson, 16 Sept 1995, 1 d. *Education:* St John's College, Cambridge, 1987–90; MA, Law, University of Cambridge; Royal Academy of Music, 1990–94. *Career:* Debut: Theseus in Midsummer Night's Dream, Covent Garden Festival, 1994; Sang Leporello at Royal Academy of Music, Charon at Batignano, Dr Bartolo and Don Magnifico with English Touring Opera; Concerts with London Philharmonic Orchestra, Ulster Orchestra, CLS; Recitals, Buxton Festival and Wigmore Hall. *Honours:* Queen's Commendation for Excellence, Royal Academy of Music. *Address:* 28 Vestry Road, London SE5 8NX, England.

GEERTENS, Gerda; Composer; b. 11 Aug. 1955, Wildervank, Netherlands. *Education:* Studied with Klaas de Vries, 1981–85. *Career:* Performances of works at the Concertgebouw in Amsterdam, in Darmstadt, Israel, Ireland and the US. *Compositions include:* Mexitli for mixed choir and ensemble, 1982; Trope for cello, 1987; As En Seringen for ensemble with percussion, 1988; String Trio, 1990; Contrast for saxophone quartet, 1990; Heartland for symphony orchestra, 1994; Transitions for flute trio, 1998; New Era, electronic music, 2001. *Address:* c/o Vereniging Buma, PO Box 725, 1180 AS Amstelveen, Netherlands.

GEFORS, Hans; Composer; b. 8 Dec. 1952, Stockholm, Sweden. *Education:* Studied composition with Per-Gunnar Alldahl and Maurice Karkoff; Pupil of Ingvar Lidholm at Stockholm Academy of Music, 1972; Per Norgård at Jutland Conservatory of Music, Diploma in 1977. *Career:* Active as composer, music critic and editor; Professor of Composition at Malmö College of Music, 1988; Der Park premiere at the 1992 Wiesbaden Festival; Clara, premiere at the 100th anniversary of the Opéra Comique, Paris, 1998; mem, STIM; Royal Academy of Music. *Compositions:* Operas: The Poet And The Glazier, 1979, Christina, 1986, Der Park, 1991; Vargen Kommer, 1997; Clara, 1998; Music Theatre: Me Morire En Paris, 1979, The Creation No. 2, 1988; Orchestral: Slits, 1981, Christina Scenes, 1987, Twine, 1988, Die Erscheinung Im Park, 1990; Lydias Sånger for mezzo and orchestra, 1996; Njutningen for soprano, baritone, choir and orchestra, 2002; The Knight of the Boy's Gaze, 2003; Chamber: Aprahishtita, 1970–71, La Boîte Chinoise, 1976, L'Invitation Au Voyage for Voice, Guitar and Violin, 1981, Krigets Eko for Percussionist, 1982, Tjurens Död, 1982, Flickan Och Den Gamle, 1983, Galjonsfiguren, 1983, One Two, 1983; A Hunting for the Wind for organ, 1994; Vocal: Singer On Förtröstan for Voice and Guitar, 1970, Whales Weep Not! for 16 Part Choir, 1987, En Obol, sonnets, for Voice, Clarinet, Cornet, Cello and Piano, 1989; Total Okay, 1992. *Recordings:* Scenes from Christina; Vargen Kommer. *Honours:* Christ Johnson Fund Prize, 1994, 2002. *Address:* STIM, Sandhamnsgatan 79, PO Box 27327, 102 54 Stockholm, Sweden.

GEIGER, Ruth; pianist; b. 30 Jan. 1923, Vienna, Austria. *Education:* studied in Vienna with Hans Gal and Julius Isserlis, Juilliard School, New York with Josef Lhevinne. *Career:* debut at the Town Hall, New York, 1944; recitals and appearances with orchestras in USA; radio and television broadcasts in New York; annual concert tours of Europe from 1957; orchestras include Suisse Romande, New Philharmonia, English Chamber Orchestra; BBC Series, My Favourite Concertos; appearances on BBC solo recital series at St Johns Smith Square, London; numerous live broadcasts; live concerto broadcasts with Glasgow BBC Orchestra; Complete Schubert Sonatas for Basle Radio; Toured Sweden, Netherlands, Belgium, Switzerland, Austria, England; Masterclasses at University of Sussex, 1971; Chamber Music with the Allegri Quartet; Concert and teaching week's residency at Yale University, USA; Most recent appearances on Live BBC Concert series; Lunchtime Recital at St David's Hall, Cardiff, 1992; Live Broadcast of Lunchtime Recital at St John's Smith Square, London, 1992; 1995 includes recital on Sunday Morning Coffee Concerts, Wigmore Hall, London; Masterclass and Recital, Newton Park College, Bath; Recital in Tours, France; Solo recitals in Tours, France, 1995, 1997, also collaboration in Tours with French mezzo-soprano in Lieder by Schubert and Brahms. *Recordings include:* Schubert Sonatas for Critics Choice Records. *Honours:* Naumburg Award, New York, 1943; Finalist, Leventritt Competition, 1944 and Rachmaninov Competition, 1948. *Address:* 160 W 73 Street, New York, NY 10023, USA.

GELB, Peter; American business executive and film and television producer; *President, Sony Classical;* b. 1959, s. of Arthur Gelb. *Career:* fmr man., Vladimir Horowitz; Pres. Sony Classical USA 1993–95, Pres. Sony Classical Int. Operations 1995–; Man. Dir Metropolitan Opera, New York 2005–. *Honours:* Emmy Awards for Outstanding Classical Program in the Performing Arts 1987, 1990, 1991, Emmy Awards for Outstanding Individual Achievement in Int. Programming 1991, Int. Documentary Asscn Award 1991, Grammy Award 2002. *Address:* Sony Classical USA, 550 Madison Avenue, New York, NY 10022, USA (office). *Website:* www.sonyclassical.com (office).

GELIOT, Michael, BA; British opera director and theatre director; b. 27 Sept. 1933, London, England; m. Diana Geliot; two c. *Education:* Univ. of Cambridge. *Career:* Staged first British production of Liebermann's School For Wives, while at Cambridge in 1958; Sadler's Wells from 1960; Burt's Volpone for the New Opera Company in 1961 and Weill's Mahagonny in 1963; Resident Producer then Director of Productions with Welsh National Opera, 1965–78; Productions for Scottish Opera, Kassel, Zürich, Barcelona, Wexford, Amsterdam, Ottawa, Lausanne, Netherlands Opera with Wozzeck in 1973, and Munich Opera with Fidelio in 1974; Staged the premiere of Maxwell Davies's Taverner at Covent Garden in 1972; Translations of Mozart's Zauberflöte and Nozze di Figaro; Stagings at Kassel Opera include Le nozze di Figaro in 1980; Collaborations with the designer, Ralph Koltai. *Honours:* Critics' Prize, Barcelona 1974.

GELLMAN, Steven D.; Composer, Pianist and Professor of Music; b. 16 Sept. 1947, Toronto, Canada; m. Cheryl Gellman, 18 Oct 1970, 1 s., 1 d. *Education:* Juilliard School of Music, New York, USA; Conservatoire de Paris. *Career:* Soloist with CBC Symphony Orchestra in own Concerto for Piano and Orchestra, aged 16; Compositions performed in USA, Canada, France, Europe, South America and Japan; European tour with Toronto Symphony, 1983; Gellman's Awakening performed 10 times throughout Europe; Universe Symphony, Inaugurated the International Year of Canadian Music, 1986; From 1994 appointed Full Professor of Composition and Theory, Faculty of Music, University of Ottawa; mem, Associate of Canadian Music Centre; Canadian League of Composers. *Compositions include:* Orchestral: Odyssey, 1971, Symphony No. 2, 1972, Chori, 1976, The Bride's Reception, 1983; Jaya Overture, 1995; Chamber Music: Mythos ll for flute and string quartet, recorded, 1968, Wind Music for brass quintet, recorded, 1978, Dialogue for solo horn, 1978, Transformation, 1980, Chiaroscuro, 1988, Concertino for guitar and string quartet, 1988, Red Shoes, 1990, Musica Eterna for string quartet, 1991, Child-Play for chamber orchestra, 1992, Sonata for cello and piano, 1995; Piano: Melodic Suite, 1972, Poeme, recorded, 1976, Waves and Ripples, 1979, Keyboard Triptych for piano-synthesizer, 1986; Orchestra: Love's Garden for soprano and orchestra, 1987, Piano Concerto, 1988–89; Canticles of St Francis for choir and orchestra, 1989; Opera: Gianni, 1996–99. *Publications:* Album for Piano, 1994. *Honours:* Named Composer of The Year, 1987. *Address:* c/o Music Department, Stewart Street, University of Ottawa, Ottawa, Ontario, K1N 6N5, Canada.

GELMETTI, Gianluigi; Conductor; b. 11 Sept. 1945, Rome, Italy. *Education:* Studied at the Accademia di Santa Cecilia in Rome with Franco Ferrera, with Sergiu Celibidache and in Vienna with Hans Swarowsky. *Career:* Musical Director of Pomeriggi Musicale of Milan, and teacher at the Conservatory until 1980; Artistic Director of RAI Symphony Orchestra at Rome, 1980–84; Musical Director of Rome Opera, 1984–85; Chief Conductor of the South German Radio Symphonie Orchestra, 1989; Musical Director, Orchestre Philharmonique de Monte Carlo in 1990; Has conducted the first performances of Castiglioni's Sacro Concerto in 1982, Donatoni's In Cauda in 1983 and Henze's 7th Symphony in 1984; Conducted Tosca at La Fenice in Venice, 1989 and a double bill of Rossini's La Cambiale di Matrimonio and Il Signor Bruschino at the 1989 Schwetzingen Festival, Rossini's La Gazza Ladra with Katia Ricciarelli at Pesaro in 1989 and Salieri's Les Danaides at the 1990 Ravenna Festival; Season 1992 with Tancredi at Bologna, Rossini double bill at Schwetzingen and Il Matrimonio Segreto at the Ravenna Festival; Conducted Mascagni's Iris at Rome, 1996; Royal Opera premiere of Rossini's Otello, Covent Garden, 2000; Returned to Covent Garden for La Rondine and Turandot, 2002; Chief Conductor and Artistic Director, Sydney SO, 2004. *Recordings include:* Telerecording of Rossini double bill; La Gazza Ladra; Il Barbiere di Siviglia. *Address:* Symphonie Orchester des Suddeutsche Rundfunk, Neckarstrasse 230, Postfach 837, 7000 Stuttgart, Germany.

GELT, Andrew (Lloyd); Composer, Conductor and Performer; b. 2 Feb. 1951, Albuquerque, New Mexico, USA. *Education:* BM, cum laude with distinction, Music Theory, University of New Mexico, 1973; MM, Clarinet Performance, University of Southern California, 1975; DMA, Theory and Composition, University of Miami, 1978; Studied at University of Denver; Clarinet student of Mitchell Lurie; Studied with Stanley Drucker. *Career:* Professor of several Universities and Colleges including University of Miami, University of North Carolina, Richmond Technical College, Temple University, Princeton University; Specialises in the analysis of microprocessor devices as applied to music; Main expertise in theory and composition of music in the eclectic vein. *Compositions:* Symphony No. 1, Op 34, The Art of Eclecticism, premiered by Frederick Fennell, second performance by the Orchestra Society of Philadelphia; Lamento for strings, Op 22; Homage to Gesualdo, Op 33; Suite Eclectique, Op 35; Concerto-Quintet for five clarinets assorted, Op 19; Sonatina Veehemente, Op 26; Armageddon; Works housed at the American Music Center in New York. *Current Management:* The American Music Center, 30 West 26th Street, Suite 1001, New York, NY 10010-2011, USA. *Address:* PO Box 922, Hollywood, FL 33022, USA. *E-mail:* andrew@gelt.net. *Website:* www.gelt.net.

GEMERT, Theo Van; Singer (Baritone); b. 20 Oct. 1940, Kerkrade, Netherlands. *Education:* Studied at the Maastricht Conservatory. *Career:* Professional Footballer, including Dutch National Team, before career as a singer; Sang at Aachen, 1970–71 as Germont and Jochanaan, and at Wuppertal from 1973 as Wotan and Gunther in The Ring, Creonte in Médée, Rigoletto, Iago, Nabucco, Count Luna, Simon Boccanegra, Telramund, Amfortas and Orestes; Guest appearances in Germany, France, Netherlands and Barcelona; Sang Hindemith's Cardillac at Wuppertal, 1991 and the Grand Inquisitor in Don Carlos, 1996; Season 2000–01 at Eutin and Hagen, in Der Freischütz and Der Kuhhandel by Weill. *Address:* c/o St ädtische Buhnen, Spinnstrasse 4, 5600 Wuppertal, Germany.

GEMROT, Jiri; Composer; b. 15 April 1957, Prague, Czechoslovakia; m. 16 Oct 1982. *Education:* Prague Conservatorium, 1972–76; Graduated in Composition, Academy of Musical Arts, Prague, 1981; Master Composers Course with Franco Donatoni, Accademia Chigiana, Siena, Italy, 1981. *Career:* Producer of Radio Prague, 1982–86, 1990–; Editor, Panton Publishing House, 1986–90. *Compositions:* Published: Sonata for piano No. 1, 1981; Tributes for orchestra, 1983; 5 Lyrical Songs To Poems by Ingeborg Bachmann for soprano and piano, 1984; Inventions for violin and viola, 1984, Sonata for piano No. 2, 1985; Maxims for 15 strings, 1986; Rhapsody for bassoon and piano, 1986; Preludium and Toccata for harpsichord, Rhapsody for oboe and piano, 1988; Sonatina for violin and piano, 1990; Inventions for cello and double bass, 1991; Concerto for flute and orchestra, 1992; Psalmus 146 for mixed chorus and orchestra, 1992;' Lauda, Sion, for baritone and wind orchestra,

1994; Schalmeiane for 6 oboes, 1996; IV Sonata for piano, 1996; The American Overture, 1996; Concertino for orchestra, 1997; Bachman lieder for soprano and orchestra, 1998; Concertino for harp and orchestra, 1998; V sonata for piano, 1999; Quintet for piano and strings, 2001; Sonata for cello and piano, 2001; Trio for violin, cello and piano, 2001; Concertino for flute, timpani, bagpipe and orchestra, 2002; Double-Concerto for cello, piano and orchestra, 2002; Sapporiana for flute and guitar, 2003, Piano Concerto, 2003. *Recordings:* Tributes; Dances And Reflections; Cello Concerto; Sonata for harp; Bucolic for string quartet; Meditation for viola and Organ; Invocation for Violin and Organ; Sonatina for flute and piano; Maxims for 15 strings; Piano Sonatas. *Address:* Na Valech 32, Prague 6, Czech Republic.

GENCER, (Ayse) Leyla; singer (soprano); b. 10 Oct. 1924, Istanbul, Turkey. *Education:* Istanbul Conservatory; Further study with Giannina Arangi Lombardi and Apollo Granforte. *Career:* debut Ankara, 1950 as Santuzza; Teatro San Carlo Naples, 1954 as Madama Butterfly; and soon after in opera houses of Europe and USA; Palermo and Trieste as Violetta in La Traviata, 1955; Trieste, as Agata in Il franco cacciatore, 1956; San Francisco as Francesca da Rimini, 1956; with La Scala Milan, 1956–1980: notably in the premieres of Poulenc's Dialogues des Carmélites, 1956, soloist in Verdi's Requiem to Toscanini's Funeral, Milan Cathedral; Leonora in La Forza del Destino, Cologne; Paolina in Poliuto, 1960; Elisabetta in Don Carlos and Lisa in La Dama di Picche, 1961; Aida, 1963; Lady Macbeth, 1964; Norma, 1965; Amelia in Simon Boccanegra, 1966; Ottavia in Incoronazione di Poppaea, 1967; Elettra in Idomeneo, 1968; Lucrezia Borgia, Elena in I vespri siciliani, 1970; Gluck's Alceste, 1972; Performances elsewhere include La Fenice, Venice, as Lucrezia in I due Foscari, 1957; Florence as Lida in La battaglia di Legnano, 1959; Rome as Donna Elvira in Don Giovanni, 1960; Salzburg Festival as Amelia in Simone Boccanegra, 1961; Covent Garden, London as Elisabetta in Don Carlos and Donna Anna in Don Giovanni, 1962; Glyndebourne Festival as The Countess in Figaro's Hochzeit and Donizetti's Anna Bolena, 1962–63; Verona as Amelia in Un ballo in maschera, 1962, Aida, 1963, Norma, 1965, Leonora in Il trovatore, 1968; Edinbrugh Festival as Donizetti's Maria Stuarda, 1969, and Rossini's Elisabetta Regina d'Inghilterra, 1972; Further appearances in Vienna, Munich, Moscow, Warsaw, Oslo, Buenos Aires and Rio de Janeiro; Pioneer of Donizetti and Bellini renaissance; Artistic Dir, Teacher, Singing and interpretation Acad. of La Scala Theatre, 1997–; Istanbul Int. Singing Competition Leyla Gencer named after her, 1995. *Recordings include:* Mozart's Don Giovanni, Nozze di Figaro; Idomeneo; Donizetti's Anna Bolena, Maria Stuarda, Roberto Devereux, Lucrezia Borgia; Belisario, Lucia di Lammermoor; Caterina Cornaro, Les Martyrs, Messa di Requiem for Bellini; Bellini's I Puritani, Norma, Beatrice di Tenda; Pacini's Saffo; Spontini's La Vestale; Verdi's Il Trovatore, Erneni, Macbeth, La Forza del Destino, Aida, Attila, I due Foscari, La Battaglia di Legnano, Gerusalemme, Simon Boccanegra, Don Carlos, Un Ballo in Maschera, Rigoletto; Massenet's Werther; Zandonai's Francesca da Rimini; Ponchielli's La Gioconda; Rossini's Elisabetta Regina d'Inghilterra; Poulenc's Dialoghi delle Carmelitane; Pizzetti's Assassinio nella Cattedrale; Tschaikovsky's La Dama di Picche; Songs: Chopin, Bellini, Donizetti; Schumann-Liszt. *Honours:* Over 50 int. awards including: Commendatore della Repubblica italiana, 1967; Ambrogino d'Oro, Milan, 1988, Renowned Artist of Repub. of Turkey, 1989; Dr hc, University of Istanbul, 1989. *Address:* c/o Viale Majno 17A, 20122 Milan, Italy.

GENS, Veronique; Singer (Soprano); b. 19 April 1962, Orleans, France. *Education:* Studied at the Paris Conservatoire. *Career:* Has sung with Les Arts Florissants from 1986; Solo engagements include Mozart's Cherubino and Vitellia, under Jean-Claude Malgoire, the Countess with Opéra de Lyon, 1994, and Donna Elvira, at Tourcoing; Sang Venus in King Arthur with Les Arts Florissants in Paris and at Covent Garden, 1995; Mozart's Idamante in Lisbon, 1995; Has also worked with such conductors as William Christie, Marc Minkowski and René Jacobs; Season 1996 with Les Talens Lyriques at the Versailles Baroque Days as Venus in Les Fêtes de Paphos by Mondonville, Beaune Festival with Les Musiciens du Louvre as Lully's Galatée; Solo engagements include Fiordiligi with Vlaamse Opera, Belgium, 1997 and Donna Elvira at Aix-en-Provence, Milan, La Monnaie and Tokyo with Claudio Abbado and Peter Brook, 1998–99; As Vitellia (Clemenza di Tito) in Madrid, 1999 and engaged as Fiordiligi there in 2002; Wigmore Hall, London, recital 2000; Aluria in Hamburg, 2002; Donna Elvira in Don Giovanni, Glyndebourne, 2002 and Liceu Barcelona, 2003. *Recordings:* Dido and Aeneas; Les Arts Florissants, William Christie; Hippolyte et Aricie by Rameau; Les Musiciens du Louvre, Marc Minkowski; Campra Motets, Requiem and Te Deum; Charpentier David et Jonathas, Miserere and Missa Assumpta Est; Jommelli Armida Abbandonata and Lamentations; Lully Acis et Galatée, Alceste, Armide, Atys, Phaeton; Marais, Alcyone; Mondonville Les Fêtes de Paphos; Mozart's Così fan tutte and Don Giovanni; Purcell King Arthur and Fairy Queen; Rameau Castor et Pollux, Dardanus and Platée; Mozart Arias; Handel's Cantatas; Cosí fan Tutte with Jacobs; French Songs with Roger Vignoles; Berlioz: Les

Nuits d'Eté. *Honours:* Revelation Musicale de l'année, 1995; Artiste Lyrique of the Year, 1999. *Address:* c/o Hilbert Agentur, Maximillianstrasse 22, D–80539, Munich, Germany.

GENTILE, Ada; Composer; b. 26 July 1947, Avezzano, Italy; m. Franco Mastroviti, 2 July 1972. *Education:* Diploma in Piano, 1972 and Composition in 1974, S Cecilia Conservatoire, Rome; Advanced course with Goffredo Petrassi, Accademia di Santa Cecilia, 1975–76. *Career:* Participant in international composition competitions; Her works performed throughout Europe, Canada, USA, China, Japan and Australia; Invited to festivals of contemporary music including Huddersfield, Århus, Zagreb, Warsaw, Alicante, Bacau and Kassel; Commissions from RAI, French Ministry of Culture, Opera theatre in Rome and Accademia di Santa Cecilia; Artistic Director, G Petrassi Chamber Orchestra, 1986–88, and Nuovi Spazi Musicali Festival, Rome; Teacher at S Cecilia Conservatoire and presenter of contemporary music festivals for RAI-Radiotre. *Compositions:* About 60 published works and several recorded works. *Recordings:* 12 titles. *Address:* Via Divisione Torino 139, 00149 Rome, Italy. *E-mail:* ada.gentile@tin.it.

GENTILE, Louis; Singer (Tenor); b. 2 Sept. 1957, Connecticut, USA. *Education:* Studied in New York. *Career:* Guest appearances in opera and broadcasting houses in Europe and the USA; Sang at Darmstadt, 1983–86; Krefeld, 1986–88 as Alfredo, among other roles; Netherlands Opera at Amsterdam, 1988, in Fidelio, Berlin Staatsoper, 1986, in Judith by Siegfried Matthus; Appeared at the Deutsche Oper Berlin 1990, as Schwalb in Mathis der Maler; Pedro in Tiefland at the Theater am Gärtnerplatz, Munich, 1991; Sang Don José at Oslo, 1991; Other roles include Tamino, Rossini's Almaviva, Boris in Katya Kabanova, Cavalli's Ormindo, Rodolfo, and Erik in Der fliegende Holländer; Sang Bibalo's Macbeth for Norwegian Opera at Oslo, 1992; Season 1995 at Bielefeld in the premiere of Der Sturz des Antichrist by Ullmann and at Leipzig as Boris in Katya Kabanova; Wagner's Tristan at Ghent, 1998; Sang Max at Bonn and Tristan in Antwerp, 2001. *Honours:* Winner Young Talent Presents, Competition, 1981. *Address:* c/o Deutsche Oper Berlin, Richard Wagnerstrasse 10, 1000 Berlin, Germany.

GEORG, Mechthild; Singer (Mezzo-soprano); b. 1956, Germany. *Education:* Studied in Düsseldorf with Ingeborg Reichelt: and at the Cologne opera studio. *Career:* Sang at first in concert, then at the Essen Opera from 1989; Guest engagements throughout Germany as Monteverdi's Octavia and Penelope, Cherubino, the Composer in Ariadne auf Naxos, Flosshilde (Hamburg, 1992) and Henrietta in Graf Mirabeau by Matthus; Concerts in Belgium, Austria and Switzerland; Sang Atalanta in Handel's Serse at Copenhagen, 1996; Magdeburg Telemann Festival 1996, in Der Neumodische Liebhaber Damon. *Recordings:* Suor Angelica and Gianni Schicchi; Messiah and Schumann Requiem; Udolin in Schubert's Die Verschworenen. *Address:* c/o Theater Essen, Rolandstrasse 10, D-4300 Essen 1, Germany.

GEORGE, Alan Norman, MA; violist; b. 23 Dec. 1949, Newquay, Cornwall, England; m. Lesley Schatzberger; one s. two d. *Education:* King's College, Cambridge. *Career:* debut as member of Fitzwilliam Quartet, Purcell Room, London, 1973; Member, Fitzwilliam Quartet, 1969–, Quartet in Residence, University of York, 1971–74, 1977–86, University of Warwick, 1974–77, Fitzwilliam College, Cambridge, 1998–; Lecturer, University of York, 1986–88, Finchcocks Quartet, 1992–96; Participant, 1st performance of Quartets, No. 2 by Sebastian Forbes, Edward Cowie, David Blake, Cuaderna by Bernard Rands, No.1 by Michael Blake, Rachel Stott, Matthew King; Long Hidden by Jackson Hill; Clarinet Quintet by David Blake; Michael Blake Clarinet Quintet, 1st British performances, Shostakovich Quartets 13, 14, 15; Alfred Schnittke, Canon in Memory of I F Stravinsky; Fitzwilliam Quartet, affiliate artists at Bucknell University, Pennsylvania, USA, 1978–86, 1998–; Tutor in Viola, Royal Northern College of Music, 1998–; Principal Viola, English Baroque Soloists, Orchestre Révolutionnaire et Romantique; Member, New London Consort, Lumina contemporary music group; 1st performances,... et Quart by John Paynter, Clarinet Trio by William Sweeney; Concerts and recordings, London Classical Players, Age of Enlightenment, Academy of Ancient Music, English Baroque Soloists, New London Consort, King's Consort, Hanover Band, Yorkshire Baroque Soloists. *Recordings:* Shostakovich Quartets Nos 1–15; Franck Quartet in D; Borodin Quartets Nos 1 and 2; Delius Quartet; Sibelius Voces Intimae; Brahms Clarinet Quintet; Wolf Italian Serenade; Schubert String Quintet; Beethoven Quartets ops 127, 130, 132, 133, 135; Shostakovich Piano Quintet with V Ashkenazy; Mozart Clarinet Trio with A. Hacker and K. Evans; Schumann Piano Quintet and Piano Quartet with R. Burnett; Mozart Clarinet Quintet with L. Schatzberger; Chamber version of Beethoven's Piano Concerto No. 4, with R Levin; Haydn Seven Last Words from the Cross; Chamber versions of Mozart Piano Concertos K413, K415 and Piano Quartet K452a, with Richard Burnett; Haydn Quartets Op 1/6, 71/2, 77/2. *Publications:* Shostakovich Chamber Music; Performing Haydn's Quartets, 2001; Russian and Soviet Quartets in the 20th Century, 2001. *Address:* 10 Bootham Terrace, York YO30 7DH, England.

GEORGE, Donald; Singer (Tenor); b. 13 Sept. 1955, San Francisco, USA. *Education:* Studied at Louisiana State University in Berlin and with Josef Metternich in Munich. *Career:* Sang lyric tenor roles at the Theater am Gärtnerplatz, Munich, Brussels and the Vienna Staatsoper, 1986, in the premiere of Das Schloss by André Laporte and as Belmonte; Deutsche Oper Berlin, 1988–89, as Bernstein's Candide and as Fenton in Die Lustigen Weiber von Windsor; Guest appearances at Madrid in the local premiere of Lulu, Würzburg (as Belmonte), Komische Oper Berlin (Tamino); Leopold in La Juive (Bielefeld 1989); Giessen (Mozart's Titus) and Bregenz (Steuermann in Der fliegende Holländer); Other roles include Faust, Ferrando, Leukippos (Daphne), Jason in Médée and Jenik in The Bartered Bride; Sang Antonio in Prokofiev's The Duenna at the 1989 Wexford Festival; Title role in Rossini's Aureliano in Palmira at Bad Wildbad, 1996; The Prince in The Love for Three Oranges, Komische Oper Berlin, 1998; Season 1999–2000 as Mozart's Ferrando at Naples and Bob Boles in Peter Grimes at La Scala; Concerts at the Barbican Hall, London; Other repertoire includes works by Bach, Handel, Orff and Vaughan Williams. *Recordings include:* Alzira by Verdi. *Address:* c/o Deutsche Oper Berlin, Richard Wagnerstrasse 10, 1000 Berlin, Germany.

GEORGE, Michael; Singer (Baritone); b. 10 Aug. 1950, Thetford, England. *Education:* Chorister at King's College Cambridge; Royal College of Music, London. *Career:* Debut: The Maltings, Snape, in Handel's Saul, 1972; Solo engagements and as member of leading early music ensembles in the United Kingdom and Europe; Sang in Handel's L'Allegro at the 1988 Promenade Concerts, Brahms Requiem with the London Symphony Orchestra and Kurt Sanderling, Haydn's Creation in Madrid, Beethoven's Missa Solemnis and Choral Symphony with the Hanover Band, Purcell's Dioclesian with John Eliot Gardiner, and performances of Messiah with The Sixteen in London, Italy, Spain, Poland and France; Engagements at the Three Choirs Festival, Royal Festival Hall, Oslo, Brussels and tour of Austria, Germany and Yugoslavia with the Orchestra of St John's; Twentieth century repertoire includes Threni by Stravinsky for the BBC, A Child of Our Time with the Bournemouth Symphony Orchestra, the premiere of John Metcalf's The Boundaries of Time for the BBC at the Swansea Festival and Christus in the St John Passion by Arvo Pärt during a tour of the United Kingdom with the Contemporary Music Network; Sang in 3 Promenade Concerts in 1990, and in Bach's Cantata Herz und Mund und Tat und Leben, Bonfire of the Vanities and Janáček's Glagolitic Mass; Sang Abinoam in Handel's Deborah at the 1993 Proms; Grimbald in Purcell's King Arthur at Rome, 1996; Sang in Oswald von Wolkenstein concert at the Purcell Room, London, 1997; Sang in staged version of Bach's St John Passion for ENO, 2000; Handel's Samson at the London Proms, 2002. *Recordings include:* Medieval Carmina Burana; Monteverdi's Vespers of 1610 and Orfeo; At The Boar's Head by Holst; Purcell's St Cecilia Ode; Handel's Ottone; Complete Purcell Odes with the King's Consort. *Current Management:* IMG Artists. *Address:* c/o IMG Artists Europe, Lovell House, 616 Chiswick High Road, London W4 5RX, England.

GEORGIADIS, John (Alexander); Violinist and Conductor; b. 1939, Rochford, Essex, England. *Education:* Royal Liberty; RAM, London. *Career:* Concertmaster, CBSO, 1962–65; Concertmaster, London Symphony Orchestra, 1965–79; Music Director, London Virtuosi, 1972–; Bristol Sinfonia, 1982–84; 1st violin Gabrieli Quartet, 1987–90; Music Director, Bangkok Symphony Orchestra, 1994–96; Website Builder, 1996–; mem, RAM Guild. *Recordings:* London Symphony Orchestra, Chandos and Pickwick; Gabrieli Quartet, Chandos; Various Naxos. *Honours:* FRAM, 1968; FGSM, 1969; Honorary Doctorate, Essex University, 1990; Dove Prize 1960; Gulbenkian Award 1961. *Address:* Shoreline House, Wellington Parade, Walmer, Deal, Kent CT14 8AB, England. *E-mail:* johngeorgiadis@musicgallery.co.uk (home). *Website:* www.johngeorgiadis.com.

GEORGIAN, Karine; Cellist; b. 5 Jan. 1944, Moscow, Russia; m. Anthony Philips, 15 Dec 1990, 1 s. *Education:* Gnessin School, Moscow, 1950–61; Private studies with Armen Georgian, father, 1949–61; Moscow Conservatory with Mstislav Rostropovich, 1961–68. *Career:* Regular appearances with leading Soviet, European and American orchestras and festivals; Debut tour in 1969 at Carnegie Hall with Chicago Symphony, returning in 1970 in a performance of Khatchaturian Cello Rhapsody; Recital at Prague in 1970; Played with Berlin Philharmonic Orchestra in 1970, Leningrad Philharmonic Orchestra in 1973, and Royal Philharmonic Orchestra in 1982; Professor of Cello at Staatliche Hochschule für Musik since 1984; Played at BBC Proms, Henry Wood Promenade Concerts in 1985 and 1990, and with Philadelphia Orchestra in 1990. *Recordings:* Brahms Trio in B with Dmitri Alexeyev and Liane Isakadze; Denisov Concerto in C with Moscow Philharmonic and Dmitri Kitayenko; Khatchaturian Cello Rhapsody with Bolshoi Radio Symphony and Aram Khatchaturian; Sonatas by Shostakovich and Locatelli, Aza Amintayeva; Couperin Music for 2 Cellos with Natalia Gutman; Brahms Trio in A minor with Thea King and Clifford

Benson. *Honours:* 1st Prize, All Union Music Competition, 1966; 1st Prize and Gold Medal, Tchaikovsky International Competition, Moscow, 1966. *Address:* c/o Olivia Ma Artists' Management, 65 Campden Street, London W8 7EL, England.

GERBER, Steven (Roy); Composer and Pianist; b. 28 Sept. 1948, Washington, USA. *Education:* BA, Haverford College, 1969; MFA, Princeton University, 1971; Composition with Robert Parris, Milton Babbitt, JK Randall, Earl Kim; Piano with Robert Parris, Agi Jambor, Irwin Gelber. *Career:* Received 3 commissions; World premiere of his compositions Symphony No. 1 and Serenade for String Orchestra during tour of Russia in 1990, returning in 1991 to perform several more concerts of his orchestral and chamber works including a concert at Tchaikovsky Hall in Moscow, since then has returned numerous times; US premiere of Symphony No. 1 by Louisville; mem, Several professional organizations. *Compositions include:* Dirge and Awakening for Orchestra premiered by the Russian National Orchestra under Mikhail Pletnev; Violin Concerto written for the American violinist Kurt Nikkanen who premiered it in Moscow and Novosibirsk in 1994 and playing it again at Kennedy Center in Washington with National Chamber Orchestra, 1995. *Recordings:* Many of his compositions have been recorded including Une Saison en Enfer. *Honours:* Fellowship, Princeton University; Winner of competitions held by The New Music Consort with String Quartet No. 2 and Musicians' Accord with Concertino; Duo in 3 Movements for Violin and Piano won The American Composers' Alliance 50th anniversary recording award. *Address:* 639 West End Avenue 10D, New York, NY 10025, USA.

GERELLO, Vassily; Singer (Baritone); b. 1950, Chernivtsi, Ukraine. *Education:* Studied at the St Petersburg Conservatory. *Career:* Sang as professional while a student, and with the Kirov Opera as Verdi's Germont and Posa, Valentin (Faust), Napoleon in War and Peace, Balearalz in Mussorgsky's Salammbô and the Venetian Guest in Rimsky's Sadko; On tour to Edinburgh Festival, 1991; Season 1993–94 as Papageno and Mozart's Figaro in St Petersburg, Rossini's Figaro with Netherlands Opera; Season 1994–95 as Paolo in Simon Boccanegra at the Bastille Opéra and Covent Garden; Eugene Onegin for Toronto Opera and the Vienna Staatsoper, 1998; Yeletsky in The Queen of Spades at Buenos Aires and Posa at the São Paulo Opera; Season 1995–96 with Bohème, Giulio Cesare and Boccanegra at the Bastille Opéra; New York Met debut, as Alfio in Cavalleria Rusticana, 1997; Rachmaninov's Aleko at the 1999 London Proms. *Recordings include:* Dr Pustrpalk in Salatán by Pavel Haas; Tchaikovsky's Moscow Canatata. *Current Management:* Askonas Holt Ltd, Lonsdale Chambers, 27 Chancery Lane, London, WC2A 1PF, England. *Telephone:* (20) 7400-1700. *Fax:* (20) 7400-1799. *E-mail:* info@askonasholt.co.uk. *Website:* www.askonasholt.co.uk.

GERGALOV, Alexander; Singer (Baritone); b. 1960, Russia. *Career:* Performances at the Kirov Opera, St Petersburg from 1990 including Eugene Onegin; Robert in Tchaikovsky's Iolanta; Yeletsky in The Queen of Spades; Andrei in War and Peace; Germont; Yeletsky at Lyon Opéra, 1996; Other roles include: Figaro in Il Barbiere di Siviglia; Don Carlo in La Forza del Destino; Renato in Un Ballo in Maschera; Papageno; Rodrigo in Don Carlos; Many guest engagements in Europe with the Kirov Company; Numerous concert appearances. *Recordings:* The Queen of Spades; Rimsky's Sadko; War and Peace (Bolkonsky); Betrothal in the Monastery (Ferdinand); Kashchey the Immortal (Ivan Korolevich). *Address:* c/o Kirov Opera, Theatre Square 1, St Petersburg, Russia.

GERGIEV, Valery; Conductor; b. 2 May 1953, Moscow, Russia. *Education:* Studied piano and conducting in Ordzhonikidze, later at Leningrad Conservatory; Whilst a student won the All Union Conductors Competition Prize in Moscow and the Karajan Competition in Berlin. *Career:* Conductor at Kirov Opera, 1977–, and chief conductor of the Armenian State Orchestra; Appeared with the Russian State Symphony Orchestra in France in 1987; Guest engagements with the Berlin Philharmonic, L'Orchestre de France and Dresden Philharmonic; London debut in 1988 with the London Symphony Orchestra at the Barbican, with later engagements with the City of Birmingham Symphony Orchestra, Royal Liverpool Philharmonic, Bournemouth Symphony and BBC Philharmonic; Succeeded Yuri Temirkanov as music director of Kirov Opera and Ballet Theatre in 1988; Conducted Welcome Back St Petersburg at the Kirov Gala at Covent Garden in 1992, with debut in opera there in Eugene Onegin in 1993; Conducted Boris Godunov at the Helsinki Fair Centre, Khovanschina at Rome in 1992, Kirov Opera at the Metropolitan in 1992 in The Fiery Angel, The Queen of Spades and Boris Godunov; Prince Igor at Caesarea in Israel and Otello at the Metropolitan in 1994; Principal Guest Conductor at the Met; Season 1994/95 with Rimsky's Invisible City of Kitezh in London and Edinburgh; Conducted Lohengrin at Covent Garden (1997) and Parsifal at the 1997 Savonlinna Festival; Staged new production of Semyon Kotko in the 1999 White Knights Festival; Conducted Rotterdam Philharmonic Orchestra and Philharmonia at the Festival

Hall, 1999; Roméo et Juliette, Benvenuto Cellini and La Damnation de Faust by Berlioz; Two-month season with Kirov Opera and Ballet at Covent Garden, 2000 and 2001; Conducted a trio of concerts by the Kirov Orchestra at the London Proms, 2002. *Address:* c/o Kirov Opera, 1 Theatre Square, St Petersburg, Russia.

GERGIEVA, Larissa; pianist; b. 1959, Beltsy, Moldova. *Education:* Vladikavkas with Zarama Lolaeva. *Career:* Repetituer at the Vladikavkas Opera, then at the Tchaikovsky Opera House Perm, 1987–; Russian recitals at Moscow and St Petersburg and partnerships with leading singers in Italy, Germany, USA and the United Kingdom (Edinburgh, Wigmore Hall and Queen Elizabeth Hall); Season 1994–95 included recitals at the Edinburgh Festival with Olga Borodina and Galina Gorchakova, and at the Wigmore Hall in the Wigmore/Kirov series; Coaching engagements have included The Fiery Angel and Ruslan and Ludmila with the San Francisco Opera, 1994–95; Accompanied Kirov artists in Shostakovich Songs for the BBC, 1995; Masterclasses for singers at Perm, and general director of Rimsky-Korsakov Competition for singers at St Petersburg. *Recordings include:* Tchaikovsky Songs, and the Mighty Handful, with Olga Borodina. *Honours:* First prize at the Kazan and Tallinn National Competitions. *Current Management:* Askonas Holt Ltd, Lonsdale Chambers, 27 Chancery Lane, London, WC2A 1PF, England. *Telephone:* (20) 7400-1700. *Fax:* (20) 7400-1799. *E-mail:* info@askonasholt.co.uk. *Website:* www.askonasholt.co.uk.

GERINGAS, David; Concert Cellist and Conductor; b. 29 July 1946, Vilna, Russia; m. Tatiana Schatz. *Education:* Studied with Rostropovich at the Moscow Conservatoire, 1963–71. *Career:* Concert tours of Germany in 1970 and Hungary in 1973; Resident in Germany from 1976; Many recitals with pianist, Tatiana Schatz; Played in the orchestra of the North German Radio and has given solo performances of works by Honegger, Milhaud, Hindemith and Kabalevsky; Premiered the Sonata for Solo Cello by Gottfried von Einem in 1987; Piano trio performances with Gerhard Oppitz and Dmitri Sitkovetsky; Also plays the baryton and has formed the Trio Geringas with the violinist, Vladimir Mendelssohn and the cellist, Emil Klein; Concerts with the Berlin PO, Vienna SO, Montreal SO, Philadelphia Orchestra, Chicago Symphony, NHK SO (Tokyo), London PO, Philharmonia and Israel PO, with conductors such as Ashkenazy, Gerd Albrecht, Eschenbach, Kondrashin, Leitner, Rattle, Rostropovich, Sawallisch and Tilson Thomas; as conducor performances include with North German Radio Symphony, Orchestra da Camera di Padova and the Forum Philharmonic in Netherlands; currently guest conductor of the South-West German CO in Pforzheim and the Lithuanian CO; Active career in chamber music working with his wife pianist Tatjana Geringas and British pianist Ian Fountain; Commissioned works from composers including Sofia Gubaidulina, Peteris Vasks, Erkki Sven Tüür, and was a pioneer in introducing the music of many Russian avant-garde composers to the west, including Gubaidulina, Denisov and Schnittke; Professor of Cello at the Musikhochschule in Lübeck, 1980–2000 and at the Hochschule für Musik "Hanns Eisler", 2000–. *Recordings include:* Gubaidulina Offertorium with the Boston Symphony under Dutoit; Concertos by Boccherini and Pfitzner. *Honours:* Winner, Tchaikovsky International Competition, 1970; Preis der Deutschen Schallplattenkritik, 1994. *Current Management:* Connaught Artists Management Ltd, 2 Molasses Row, Plantation Wharf, London, SW11 3UX, England. *Telephone:* (20) 7738 0017. *Fax:* (20) 7738 0909. *E-mail:* classicalmusic@connaughtartists.com. *Website:* www.connaughtartists.com.

GERMAIN, Alan; Stage Director; b. 1948, France. *Education:* Studied Music, Choreography and Architecture in Paris. *Career:* Founded dance and theatre company, 1972, for historically authentic performances throughout France; Productions include Mozart's Requiem at the Opéra Comique, 1995; Opéra Côté Costume at the Palais Garnier, 1995; Le Triomphe de la Vertu at the Musée National du Moyen Age, 1999; Cesti's Il Tito at the Opéra du Rhin, Strasbourg, with Les Arts Florissants; Lehar's The Merry Widow at the Opéra de Saint-Etienne, Opéra de Vichy, 1999/2003, Opéra de Massy, 2003; Productions for the English Bach Festival include Gluck's Iphigénie en Tauride at the Royal Opera and for Athens Festival; Rossini's Le Siège de Corinthe in Madrid and Oresteia by Xenakis at the Linbury Studio Theatre, Covent Garden, 2000; Lully/Molière Bourgeois Gentilhomme at the Château de Chambord 1995, and at the Linbury, 2001, Château de Blois and Grand Théatre de Reims, 2002; Gluck's Telemaco at the Covent Garden and the Athens Festival, 2003; Exhibition, Costumes de scène en liberté, Grand Théâtre de Reims, 2001. *Publications:* Le Tour du Monde en 80 Langues, 1995; Les Origines de l'Homme, 1997; La Ville Invisible, 1999; Les Grenouilles de Saint-Pierre, 2001 L'Affaire Callas, 2002; Meurtre à la Française, 2004. *Address:* 29 rue de Paradis, 75010 Paris, France. *E-mail:* compagnie@alaingermain.com. *Website:* www.alaingermain.com.

GESSENDORF, Mechthild; Soprano; b. 6 June 1937, Munich, Germany; m. Ernö Weil. *Education:* Studied at the Munich Musikhochschule and with Joseph Metternich in Cologne. *Career:* Sang with the Vienna

Kammeroper from 1961 then at Bremen and Bonn, Staatsoper Munich from 1981 as Aida, the Empress in Die Frau ohne Schatten, Rosenkavalier, Don Carlos and in The Turn of the Screw, at Salzburg Festival in 1981 as Amelia Boccanegra and Bregenz Festival in 1983 as Agathe; US debut in 1983 as the Marschallin, in Rosenkavalier at Tulsa, at Philadelphia in 1985 as Ariadne, Metropolitan Opera debut in 1986 as the Marschallin returning in 1989 as the Empress in Die Frau ohne Schatten, and Senta in 1990; Sang at Vienna State Opera, Oper Köln, Düsseldorf, Deutsche Opéra Berlin, Staatsoper Hamburg, Grand Opéra Paris, at Covent Garden in 1987 in Tannhäuser and Lohengrin in 1988, La Scala as Senta in 1988, at the Savonlinna Festival, Edinburgh Festival, Aix-en-Provence, Lyric Chicago, Toronto, Montreal and Detroit; Sang Sieglinde in Die Walküre for Greater Miami Opera in 1989, Ariadne at Lyon and Barcelona, the Marschallin in Paris and Agathe in Der Freischütz at Monte Carlo; Sang in Beethoven's Choral Symphony at the 1989 Promenade Concerts, as Elsa in Lohengrin at Lisbon in 1990, and the Marschallin at the Metropolitan in 1991; Season 1994–95, as Sieglinde with Pacific Opera, Wagner's Elisabeth at Buenos Aires and the Marschallin at the Met; Sang Leokadia Begbick in Mahagonny at Hamburg, 2000. *Recordings include:* Die Lustige Witwe; Penthesilea by Schoeck. *Address:* c/o Kaye Artists, Barratt House, 7 Chertsey Road, Woking GU21 5 AB, England.

GESSI, Romolo; Conductor; b. 25 March 1960, Trieste, Italy; m. Alessandra Carani, 4 Mar 1995, 1 d. *Education:* Conducting studies at the State Conservatoire, St Petersburg, with Kukuskin; Wiener Meisterkurse, Vienna, with Kalmar; Accademia Musicale, Pescara, with Renzetti. *Career:* Debut: Symphonic, Teatro Rossetti, Trieste, 1991; Opera, Teatro Lirico di Spoleto, with Puccini's La Bohème, 1995; Music Director, Chamber Orchestra of Friuli Venezia-Giulia, 1991–, and Serenade Ensemble, 1994–2000; Professor of Conducting, State Conservatoire, Milan, 1995; Professor of Chamber Music, State Conservatoire, Trieste, 1997–; Professor, European Masterclass in Spoleto; Conductor, Orchestra del Teatro Lirico di Spoleto; Guest Conductor with Milano Classica, Filarmonia Veneta; Numerous concerts in Italy, Austria, Spain, Hungary, Russia, Sweden, Switzerland, Slovenia and Croatia. *Recordings:* Rimsky-Korsakov, Dvořák, Strauss and Music in the 20th Century, with Serenade Ensemble. *Honours:* Second Prize, Gusella Conducting Competition, Pescara, 1993; First Prize, Austrian-Hungarian International Conducting Competition, Vienna and Pécs, 1994; Best Classified, Opera Conducting Competition, Caserta, 1994. *Address:* Via Brunner 9, 34125 Trieste, Italy.

GESZTY, Sylvia; Singer (Soprano); b. 28 Feb. 1934, Budapest, Hungary. *Education:* Studied at the Budapest Conservatory and the Budapest Music Academy with Erszébet Hoor-Tempis. *Career:* Sang at the Berlin Staatsoper from 1961 with debut as Amor in Orfeo ed Euridice, Komische Oper Berlin, 1963–70, and Hamburg Staatsoper, 1966–72; Covent Garden and Salzburg Festival debuts in 1966 and 1967 as the Queen of Night; Sang at Stuttgart Opera from 1971, Glyndebourne Festival, 1971–72 as Zerbinetta and Constanze, Luzern Festival in Paisiello's Barbier, Los Angeles in 1973 with the company of the New York City Opera as Sophie in Der Rosenkavalier and Schwetzingen Festival in 1976 as Gismonda in Cimarosa's Il Marito Desperato; Sang Rosina in Haydn's La Vera Costanza at Vienna in 1984, also televised; Guest appearances in Buenos Aires, Vienna, Paris, Amsterdam, Moscow, Cairo, Helsinki, Stockholm, Lisbon, Venice, Rome; Many concert appearances. *Recordings include:* Ariadne auf Naxos; Die Israeliten in der Wüste by CPE Bach; Cantatas by JS Bach; La Rappresentazione di Anima e di Corpo by Cavalieri; Die Zauberflöte; Così fan tutte; Barbier von Bagdad by Cornelius; Mozart's Die Schuldigkeit des Ersten Gebotes; Handel's Imeneo; Mozart's Kolatur-Konzertarien; Songs by Debussy, Ravel, Kodály, Bartók; Dessau Lieder; Beethoven's Christus am Ölberg; Television productions: Hoffmann's Erzählunen; Barbier von Bagdad; Eine Nacht in Venedig. *Honours:* Since 1988, biennial International Coloratura Singing Competition held in her name. *Address:* c/o Secretary ICSC, PO Box 1163, 75390, Gechingen, Germany.

GEYER, Gwynne; Singer (Soprano); b. 1965, USA. *Career:* Season 1991 as Tatiana in Eugene Onegin at St Louis; Rosalinde in Die Fledermaus at Toronto and Nedda at the New York City Opera; Season 1993–94 as Rusalka at the Metropolitan Opera; Smetana's Marenka at Toronto and Mimi in Geneva; Sang in Kalman's Gräfin Mariza at Santa Fe, 1995; Musetta at the Opéra Bastille, Paris and the title role in Landowski's Galina at Lyon; Sang Jenůfa at Cincinnati, 1998; Many concert appearances. *Address:* c/o Cincinnati Opera, Music Hall, 1241 Elm Street, Cincinnati OH 45210 USA.

GHAZARIAN, Sona; Singer (Soprano); b. 2 Sept. 1945, Beirut, Lebanon. *Education:* Studied at the Armenian College in Beirut; Psychology at the American University in Beirut; Masterclasses in Music at the Accademia Chigiana, Siena, and at the Accademia Santa Cecilia in Rome. *Career:* Member of the Vienna Staatsoper from 1972 notably as

Oscar in Un Ballo in Maschera and as Violetta in La Traviata, during the same period appeared in the title role in Lucia di Lammermoor at the Grand Théâtre of Geneva; Bregenz Festival in 1983 as Aennchen in Der Freischütz; Guest appearances in Hamburg, Paris, Brussels, Geneva and Salzburg; Sang at Verona Arena in 1985, Barcelona in 1988, and Metropolitan Opera in 1989 as Musetta in La Bohème; Sang in JC Bach's Adriano in Siria for Austrian Radio, conducted by Charles Mackerras; Susanna in Paisiello's Nina at Zürich, 1998. *Recordings:* Il Re Pastore by Mozart; Marzelline in Fidelio; Un Ballo in Maschera; Mozart Gala in Tokyo; Beethoven's Missa Solemnis–Live Concert at the Vatican. *Honours:* Many International Prizes. *Current Management:* Dr Raab and Dr Böhm, Plankengasse 5, 1010 Vienna, Austria. *Address:* c/o Vienna State Opera House, Opernring 2 1010 Vienna, Austria.

GHEORGHIU, Angela; Singer (soprano); b. 7 Sept. 1965, Adjud, Romania; m. Roberto Alagna 1996. *Education:* Studied at the Bucharest Academy. *Career:* Debut: Bucharest 1983, as Solveig in Grieg's Peer Gynt; Appearances from 1992 at Covent Garden as Zerlina, Mimi, Nina in Massenet's Chérubin and Violetta; Met debut 1993 as Mimi; Further engagements as Adina in Vienna, Liu and Micaela at the Metropolitan and Gounod's Juliette at Washington; Sang Donizetti's Adina at Covent Garden, 1997; Suzel in Mascagni's L'Amico Fritz at Monte Carlo, 1999; Engaged as Juliette at Covent Garden, 2000 and as Magda in Puccini's La Rondine, 2002; Sang in Verdi Requiem under Claudio Abbado, Berlin, 2001; Engaged as Nedda in new production of Pagliacci at Covent Garden 2003 and as Gounod's Marguerite, 2005. *Recordings include:* videos of La Traviata from Covent Garden and L'Elisir d'amore from Lyon. *Address:* c/o Stafford Law Associates, 6 Barham Close, Weybridge, Surrey, KT13 9PR, England.

GHEORGHIU, Stefan; Romanian violist; b. 13 Aug. 1951, Constanta; m. Cornelia Gheorghiu 1975; two s. *Education:* Music High School, Bucharest, Music Academy, Bucharest. *Career:* debut recital, 1973; first concert as soloist (Arad) 1975; soloist with George Enescu, Philharmonic Orchestra, 1976; mem. of George Enescu Philharmonic Orchestra 1974–, First Viola 1985–; solo career in Romania and Italy; founder member of Romantica String Trio; Professor at Darmstadt Summer Courses for Contemporary Music 1986–; Professor at the Music Academy, teaching viola 1993–; President, Romanian Federation on the Musicians Union; President, Union of Interpretative Creation of Romanian Musicians. *Recordings:* 1975–95 recordings as Soloist and Chamber Music at Romanian Radio and Television Broadcasting System; 1984, Mozart-Sinfonia Concertante for violin and viola. *Honours:* Medal, Markneukirchen (DDR), 1977; Special Prize for Interpretation of a French Piece, Evian, France, 1979; Prize, Darmstadt, Germany, 1984. *Address:* Str Frumoasa 52, et 4, ap 18, 78116 Bucharest, Romania.

GHEZZO, Dinu; Composer and Conductor; b. 2 July 1941, Tuzla, Romania; m. Marta Ghezzo, 3 Oct 1961, 1 d. *Education:* State Diploma in Education, 1964, in Composition, 1966, Romanian Conservatory; PhD, University of California, Los Angeles, 1973. *Career:* Program Director, Composition, Director, Professor of Composition, New York University; Director, George Enescu International Composition Competition; Co-Director, New Repertory Ensemble of New York. *Compositions include:* Aphorisms; Structures; Sketches, recorded; Breezes Of Yesteryear; Sound Shapes l and ll; From Here To There; Two Prayers for Soprano and Tape; A Book Of Songs; Ostrom; Doina; Five Village Scenes for chamber ensemble, 1995; Checkmate for John Cage, for ensemble and dancers, 1995; Wind Rituals, 1995; In Search of Euridice for saxophone, piano and tape, 1995; Five Corrado Songs for bass and tape, 1996; Italian Love Songs, 1997; Sound and Etchings for clarinet, 1997; Imaginary Voyages for clarinet, cello and percussion, 1997. *Recordings:* Several. *Publications:* Most works published. *Contributions:* Tomis; Living Musician. *Address:* New York University, Music Department, 35 West 4th Street, New York, NY 10003, USA.

GHIGLIA, Lorenzo; Stage Designer; b. 26 Nov. 1936, Florence, Italy. *Education:* Studied in Florence. *Career:* Worked at the Bergamo Festival in 1958 then designed the premiere of Pizzetti's Il Calzare d'Argento at La Scala in 1961 for director Margherita Wallmann; Has also collaborated with Franco Enriquez, Mario Missiroli and Filippo Crivelli; Designed La Bohème at Palermo in 1961, Attila at Florence in 1962 and Petrassi's Il Cordovano at Turin in 1966; US commissions include Pagliacci and Rigoletto for Houston Opera and Samson et Dalila at Dallas; Glyndebourne, 1965–66 with Anna Bolena and Dido and Aeneas; Further designs at Florence with Le Villi and Busoni's Arlecchino in 1972 and 1975, La Scala and Suor Angelica in 1973 and Catania with Médée in 1977. *Address:* c/o Teatro alla Scala, Via Filodrammatici 2, 20121 Milan, Italy.

GHIGLIA, Oscar; classical guitarist; b. 13 Aug. 1938, Livorno, Italy; m. Anne-Marie d'Hautesserre 1966; one d. *Education:* Conservatory Santa Cecilia, Rome. *Career:* concert tours in North America, 1965–; Performed with Juilliard, Tokyo, and Emerson String Quartets, Julius

Baker, Victoria de Los Angeles, and Jean Pierre Rampal; Performances world-wide include Turkey, Israel, Japan, Australia and New Zealand; Artist in Residence at Hartt School of Music, University of Hartford, USA, and Musik Akademie de Stadt, Basel; Summer Instructor at Aspen, Colorado Music Festival, 1969, Academia Musicale Chigiano, Siena, Italy, 1976 and Banff Centre for The Arts, Canada, 1978–. *Recordings include:* Paganini Sonata; The Guitar In Spain; The Spanish Guitar of Oscar Ghiglia. *Current Management:* 197 South Quaker Lane, West Hartford, CT 06119, USA. *Address:* Helfenberg Strasse 14, Basel, 4059, Switzerland.

GHINDIN, Alexander; Concert Pianist; b. 1977, Moscow. *Education:* Tchaikovsky State Conservatory, Moscow. *Career:* Concert and recital engagements in Russia, USA and Europe, from 1994; Festival apearances in Stockoholm, Luxembourg, Moscow and Brussels; Soloist with the Moscow Virtuosi, the London Philharmonic Orchestra under Ashkenazy, Philharmonic de Liège, St Petersburg Camerata and Philharmonia, London; Season 2001–2002 with the Monte Carlo Philharmonic, Munich Philharmonic and the London Philharmonica at Lincoln Center (Rachmaninov's 3rd Concerto); Recitals under the auspices of UNESCO, for the Pope and English Royalty. *Recordings include:* Albums for Decca and Harmonia Mundi. *Honours:* Prizewinner, 1994 Tchaikovsky International and 1999 Queen Elisabeth Competition. *Address:* c/o Musicaglotz, 11 Rue le Verrier, 75006 Paris, France.

GHIUSELEV, Nicola; Singer (bass); b. 17 Aug. 1936, Pavlikeni, Bulgaria; m.; two s. one d. *Education:* Acad. of Fine Arts, Sofia. *Career:* debut, Sofia 1961, as Timur in Turandot; sang at the Vienna Opera, Salzburg Festival, Metropolitan, Paris Opéra, La Scala and Covent Garden (debut 1976, as Pagano in I Lombardi); further appearances at Naples, San Francisco, Buenos Aires, Chicago, Madrid, Barcelona, Athens, Moscow, St Petersburg, Berlin, Bonn, Hamburg, Geneva, Zürich, Tokyo, Yokahama, Turin, Houston, San Diego, San Paulo, Tehran and Verona Arena; roles include Verdi's Philip II, Attila, Zaccaria, Ramfis, Pagano, Silva (Ernani) and Banquo; Mussorgsky's Dosifei, Pimen and Boris Godunov; Mozart's Don Giovanni, Leporello and Sarastro; Mephistopheles of Gounod and Boito; Rossini's Don Basilio and Mustafà; Lindorf and Dr Miracle in Hoffman, Enrico in Anna Bolena, Puccini's Colline, Creonte in Medea, Ivan Khovansky in Khovanshchina and Rimsky's Ivan the Terrible; sang Arkel in Pelléas at Bologna, 2000. *Recordings:* opera sets for various record companies. *Honours:* honours in Bulgaria, Italy and France; Grand Prize, Second International Music Competition 1963. *Address:* Villa Elpida-Boyana, Sofia 1616, Bulgaria.

GIACOMINI, Giuseppe; Tenor; b. 7 Sept. 1940, Veggiano, Padua, Italy. *Education:* Studied with Elena Fava Ceriati in Padua, Marcello del Monaco in Treviso and Vladimiro Badiali in Milan. *Career:* Debut: In 1966 as Pinkerton in Madama Butterfly; Sang in Berlin and Vienna from 1972, Hamburg from 1973, La Scala debut in 1974, Paris Opéra debut in 1975, and US debut at Cincinnati Opera from 1976 as Alvaro in La Forza del Destino, Verdi's Macduff, Don Carlos and Manrico, Puccini's Cavaradossi and Canio in Pagliacci; Further appearances in Barcelona, Boston, Budapest, London, Munich and Tokyo; Sang Verdi's Otello at San Diego in 1986; Season 1992 as Alvaro at Naples, Canio at Rome and Radames at the festival of Caracalla; Other roles include Puccini's Calaf, Luigi, Rodolfo and Des Grieux, Pollione in Norma, Turiddu in Cavalleria Rusticana, Giordano's Andrea Chénier, Verdi's Radames in Aida, and Ernani; Sang Radames at the Verona Arena, Manrico at the Vienna Staatsoper and Calaf at Covent Garden, 1996; Season 2000–01 as Canio in Pagliacci at the Vienna Staatsoper and Cavaradossi at Covent Garden. *Recordings include:* Norma; Fausta by Donizetti; Manon Lescaut; Cavalleria Rusticana; Il Tabarro and Tosca, both new editions, recorded in Philadelphia under Riccardo Mutio. *Honours:* Prizewinner in competitions at Naples, Vercelli and Milan. *Address:* c/o Patricia Greenan, 19b Belsize Lane, London NW3 4DU, England.

GIAIOTTO, Bonaldo; Singer (Bass); b. 25 Dec. 1932, Ziracco, Udine, Italy. *Education:* Studied in Udine and with Alfredo Starno in Milan. *Career:* Debut: Teatro Nuovo Milan in 1957; Sang widely in Italy then appeared as Rossini's Bartolo at Cincinnati in 1959; Metropolitan Opera debut in 1960 as Zaccaria in Nabucco and has sung in New York for 25 years in 300 performances, notably as Ramphis, Raimondo and Timur; Further engagements in Paris, London, Bordeaux, Rome, Geneva, Vienna, Hamburg and Madrid; Concert tour of South America in 1970; Season 1985 as Banquo in Zürich, Attila at the Verona Arena and in a revival of Donizetti's Il Diluvio Universale at Geneva, as Noah; La Scala Milan debut in 1986 as Rodolfo in La Sonnambula; Season 1988–89 as Ramphis in Aida at Chicago, Fiesco in Simon Boccanegra at Piacenza and Padre Guardiano in Miami and Verona; Sang Timur in Turandot at Turin in 1990; Season 1992 as Alvise in La Gioconda at Rome and Philip II and Ramphis at the Verona Arena; Sang in the French version of Don Carlos at Brussels, 1996. *Recordings:* Ferrando in Il Trovatore; Brogni

in La Juive; Luisa Miller; Aida; La Traviata; Turandot; La Cieco in Massenet's Iris conducted by Patanè. *Address:* c/o Arena di Verona, Piazza Bra 28, 37121 Verona, Italy.

GIBAULT, Claire; Conductor; b. 1955, Le Mans, France. *Education:* Studied at the Le Mans Conservatory and in Paris. *Career:* Staff Conductor and Assistant to John Eliot Gardiner at the Lyon Opera, 1983–89, leading Pelléas et Mélisande, La Finta Giardiniera, Il Barbiere di Siviglia and Iphigénie en Tauride; For Nice Opéra has conducted Mitridate, Rossini's Donna del Lago, La Traviata and Die Zauberflöte, and Idomeneo at Liège; Assistant to Claudio Abbado at the Vienna Staatsoper in 1986 and engaged there in 1988; Debut with the Royal Opera at Covent Garden in 1993 in Pelléas et Mélisande; Le Comte Ory at Glyndebourne, 1997; Led Wolfgang Rihm's Jakob Lenz at Lyon, 1998. *Address:* c/o OWM, 14 Nightingale Lane, London N8 7QU, England.

GIBB, James; Pianist, Teacher and Professor Emeritus; b. 7 March 1918, Monkseaton, Northumberland. *Education:* Merchiston Castle School, Edinburgh, Scotland; Taught piano by Mabel Lander, a pupil of Leschetizky. *Career:* Debut: Promenade Concert 1949 in Royal Albert Hall; Concerto Soloist, Berlin Philharmonic Orchestra and North-West German Radio Orchestra under Hans Schmidt-Isserstedt; Extensive tours in Central America and the Caribbean; Concert with BRNO State Radio Symphony Orchestra, conducted by Carlo Maria Giulini, Prague Spring Festival. Schubert Piano Sonatas for Meridan; mem. Incorporated Society of Musicians. *Publications:* Article in Penguin's Keyboard Music edited by Denis Matthews (later issued by David and Charles). *Honours:* Professor Emeritus, Guildhall School of Music and Drama, 1995; Fellow, Guildhall School of Music and Drama, 1967. *Current Management:* Anthony Purkiss. *Address:* 35 Fonthill Road, Hove, E Sussex BN 3 6HB, England.

GIBBONS, Jack; Pianist; b. 2 March 1962, England. *Career:* Debut: London Solo Debut, 1979; Numerous solo and concert appearances from the age of 10; Annual solo concert at the Queen Elizabeth Hall, London, since 1990; Performances at the Barbican, London; Symphony Hall, Birmingham; New York and Washington DC Debuts, 1994; Debut, Lincoln Center, New York, 1997; Many appearances on BBC radio, television and Classic FM radio, and with various orchestras. *Compositions:* Solo piano arrangements of Gershwin's Concert Works and Overtures, and transcriptions of Gershwin's original piano improvisations from recordings and piano-rolls. *Recordings:* For series of solo piano albums; The Authentic George Gershwin vols 1, 2, 3 and 4; Alkan's Complete Opus 39 Etudes, vols 1 and 2; Lambert's Rio Grande with the English Northern Philharmonica, Opera North, conductor David Lloyd-Jones. *Honours:* First Prize, Newport International Pianoforte Competition, 1982; MRA Award for best solo instrumental recording for The Authentic George Gershwin, 1993. *Current Management:* Carolyn Sachs, Trillium Productions Inc, New York, USA. *Address:* c/o Carolyn Sachs, Trilium Productions Inc, 345 Riverside Drive, Suite 6A, New York, NY 10025, USA.

GIBIN, Joao; Singer (Tenor); b. 1929, Lima, Peru. *Education:* Studied in Lima and at the Scuola della Scala, Milan, Italy. *Career:* Sang first in Italy then guested with the Netherlands Opera in Amsterdam as Andrea Chénier and Calaf; Vienna Staatsoper from 1958; Covent Garden 1959, as Edgardo opposite Joan Sutherland's Lucia; leading roles at La Scala from 1960; New York City Opera and Maggio Musicale, Florence, 1961, as Radames and Don Carlos. *Recordings:* Fanciulla del West, with Birgit Nilsson (Columbia); Lucia di Lammermoor, with Sutherland. *Honours:* Winner, MGM South American Caruso Competition, 1954. *Address:* c/o Teatro alla Scala, Via Filodrammatici 2, 20121 Milan, Italy.

GIBSON, Jon (Charles); Flautist, Saxophonist and Composer; b. 11 March 1940, Los Angeles, California, USA. *Education:* Studied at Sacramento and San Francisco State Universities. *Career:* Co-founded the New Music Ensemble in 1961; Associated with minimalist group of composers including participation in the premiere of Terry Riley's In C, 1964, and membership from 1968 of the Philip Glass Ensemble; Visual arts involved in compositions, some of which written for dancers; Solo appearances as instrumentalist in the USA and Europe. *Compositions include:* Opera: Voyage Of The Beagle, 1985; Who Are You, Vocal and Tape Delay; Visitations: An Environment Soundscape And Radioland for Tape, 1966–72; Instrumental: Multiples, 1972, Song I–IV, 1972–79, Melody I–IV, 1973–75, Cycles for Organ, 1973, Recycle l and ll, 1977, Call, 1978, Return, and Variations both for Small Ensemble, 1979–80, Extensions, dance score, 1980, Relative Calm, dance score, for Small Ensemble and Tape, 1981, Interval for Video Tape, 1985; Southern Climes for ensemble, 1993; Chorales from Relative Calm for ensemble, 1993; Chrome, 1995; Lines, for ensemble, 1996; Unfinished Business I for small ensemble, 1997; A Rose It Isn't, solo instrument, 1997. *Recordings include:* Einstein On The Beach, with the Philip Glass Ensemble. *Honours:* Grantee, Creative Artist Public Service Program,

1974, 1981 and Rockefeller Foundation, 1982. *Address:* c/o ASCAP, ASCAP Building, 1 Lincoln Plaza, New York, NY 10023, USA.

GIEBEL, Agnes; Singer (Soprano); b. 10 Aug. 1921, Heerlen, Netherlands; m. Herbert Kanders, 1 s., 2 d. *Education:* Studied at the Folkwang-Schule Essen with Hilde Wesselmann. *Career:* Gave first public concert in 1933 with Lieder by Strauss and Reger; Adult career from 1947 giving many concerts and recitals in Europe and North America; Bach Cantatas series with Karl Ristenpart for Berlin Radio, 1950–51; Church concerts in Cologne until 1982, Duet concert there; 1989; Repertoire included 20th century works, Mozart arias and much Baroque music. *Recordings include:* Bach's Christmas Oratorio; St Matthew Passion; St John Passion; Beethoven's Missa Solemnis; Die Schöpfung; Bach Cantatas; Ein Deutsches Requiem; Song recitals, and album with Hermann Prey and Celibidache. *Address:* c/o Cologne Musikhochschule, Dagoberstrasse 38, D–50668 Cologne, Germany.

GIELEN, Michael (Andreas); Conductor; b. 20 July 1927, Dresden, Germany; m. Helga Augusten, 20 May 1957, 1 s., 1 d. *Education:* Dresden, 1936; Berlin, 1937; Vienna, 1940; After emigration in 1940 studied music in Buenos Aires with Dr Erwin Leuchter. *Career:* Coach, Teatro Col ón, Buenos Aires, 1947–50; Conductor, Vienna State Opera, 1950–60; Chief Conductor with Stockholm Royal Opera, 1960–65; Freelance Conductor, Cologne, Germany, 1965–68; Conducted the premiere of Zimmermann's Die Soldaten, 1965; Music Director, Belgian National Orchestra, Brussels, 1969–73; Chief Conductor of Netherlands Opera, 1973–75; Music Director and General Manager of Frankfurt Opera House, 1977–87; Music Director, Cincinnati Symphony Orchestra, USA, 1980–86; Chief Conductor of SWR Symphony Orchestra, Baden-Baden, Germany, 1986–1999; Professor of Conducting at Mozarteum in Salzburg, 1987–; Television Series in 6 parts with SWR SO, Orchester-Farben, 1993; Salzburg Festival debut 1995, Berg's Lulu; Conducted Lulu at the Berlin Staatsoper, 1997 and Fidelio at Stuttgart, 1998; Permanent Guest Conductor of the SWR SO, 1999–. *Compositions:* 4 Gedichte von Stefan George, 1958; Variations for 40 Instruments, 1959; Un dia sobresale, 1963; Die glocken sind auf falscher spur, 1969; Mitbestimmungs Modell, 1974; String Quartet, 1983; Pflicht und Neieune for ensemble, 1988; Rückblick, trio for 3 cellos, 1989; Weitblick, sonata for solo cello, 1991. *Recordings include:* Schoenberg's Moses und Aron and Piano and violin Concertos with Alfred Brendel and Wolfgang Marschner; Zimmermann's Die Soldaten; Ligeti's Requiem and Cello Concerto (Siegfried Palm); Stockhausen's Carré; Werle's Dreaming of Thérèse, with the Royal Stockholm Orchestra; Recordings with Cincinnati Symphony Orchestra, Gielen Edition with SWR SO. *Address:* c/o South West German Radio, 76530 Baden-Baden, Germany.

GIERHARDT, Heike; Singer (Soprano); b. 8 Aug. 1964, Frankfurt, Germany. *Education:* Studied at the Frankfurt Musikhochschule. *Career:* Sang at the Mannheim Opera, 1987–92; Essen from 1992; Roles have included Nicolai's Frau Fluth, Mozart's Constanze, Donna Anna, Pamina and Fiordiligi; Marenka in The Bartered Bride, Freia in Das Rheingold and Saffi in Der Zigeunerbaron; Guest engagements at Dresden, Frankfurt, Dortmund and Weimar; Season 1998 as Mme Lidoine in Les Dialogues des Carmélites at Essen; Season 1999 as the Empress in Die Frau ohne Schatten at Essen and Barcelona; Numerous concert appearances. *Address:* Essen Opera, Rolandstrasse 10, 4300 Essen 1, Germany.

GIERLACH, Robert; Polish singer (bass-baritone); b. 1965. *Education:* Chopin Conservatoire, Warsaw. *Career:* appearances in title role of Szymanowski's King Roger at Carnegie and Festival Halls and at Salzburg Festival; Rossini's Basilio and Alidoro for Rome Opera; Mozart's Count in Venice and Trieste, Faraone in Rossini's Mosè in Egitto at Verona, Don Giovanni at Amsterdam and Don Profondo in Il Viaggio a Reims at Bologna; Stravinsky's Oedipus Rex (as Creon) in Paris, and Pulcinella; Mozart's Figaro at Glyndebourne (debut, 2001), Florida, Geneva and Detroit. *Honours:* Winner, Viotti Contest at Vercelli and Alfredo Kraus Competition, Las Palmas. *Current Management:* Pinnacle Arts, Thierschstrasse 11, 80538 Munich, Germany. *Telephone:* 49-89-340-8630. *Fax:* 49-89-3408-6310. *Website:* www.pinnaclearts.com.

GIERSTER, Hans; Musical Director; b. 12 Jan. 1925, Germany. *Education:* Musikhochschule, Munich; Mozarteum, Salzburg. *Career:* Formerly Musical Director of Freiburg-im-Breisgau Municipal Theatres; General Musical Director, Nuremberg, 1965; Director, Musiktheater Nuremberg, 1971; Conductor at Munich Staatsoper; Guest Conductor at State Operas of Hamburg, Munich and Vienna; Guest appearances at festivals in Munich, 1964, Edinburgh with Bavarian State Opera in Così fan tutte in 1965, Glyndebourne with Magic Flute in 1966, Zürich in 1971 and Vienna in 1972; Concerts with Philharmonic Orchestras of Bamberg, Berlin, Munich, Vienna, London, and Mexico City. *Address:* Musiktheater Nürnberg, 8500 Nuremberg, Hallerweisse 4, Germany.

GIERZOD, Kazimierz; Polish pianist; b. 6 Aug. 1936, Warsaw; m. Jolanta Zegadlo 1974. *Education:* Warsaw Frederic Chopin Acad. of Music with Prof. Margerita Trombini-Kazuro, Accademia Chigiana, Siena, Italy with Prof. Guido Agosti. *Career:* regular recitals and concerts in Europe, Canada, China, Japan, USA, South America, Australia and Kuwait from 1964; Tutor 1969–73, Assistant Professor 1973–86, Professor 1986–, Dean of Piano Dept 1975–87, F. Chopin Academy of Music in Warsaw, elected as Rector of F. Chopin Academy of Music 1987, 1990–93; lectures on musical interpretation, masterclasses in Poland, Japan, USA, Venezuela, China, Germany, Taiwan and Cyprus; radio and television commentator during International F. Chopin Piano Competition in Warsaw 1985, 1990; radio and television interviews and interviews for local and foreign press; Visiting Professor Soai University, Osaka, Japan 1988–; Chief of Piano Chair 1999–; mem. Jury Member of the Piano Competititon, Europe, Japan and Venezuela; President, F. Chopin International Foundation, Warsaw, Poland 1992–99; Pres. F. Chopin Society, Warsaw 2002. *Recordings:* archival recordings for Polish radio of Polish music, recordings for American, Cypriot, Polish and Japanese radio and television, album released in Poland and Germany. *Address:* ul Sygietynskiego 36, 05-805 Otrebusy, Poland.

GIETZ, Gordon; Singer (Tenor); b. 1968, Canada. *Education:* Studied in Calgary, Toronto and New York. *Career:* Artist en Residence with Opera de Montréal; Recent engagements: Sang Don Ottavio in Don Giovanni, Opéra National de Paris; Števa in Jenůfa, Grand Théâtre de Genève; Tamino in Die Zauberflöte, De Nederlandse Opera; Idamante in Idomeneo, Chevalier in Dialgoues des Carmélites and Benedict in Beatrice and Benedict, all with Santa Fe Opera; Sam Polk in Susannah, Grand Théâtre de Genève; Tom Rakewell in The Rake's Progress, Edmonton Opera, Duke in Rigoletto, Hennessy Opera, Beijing and Hanoi; Fenton in Falstaff, New York City Opera; Alfredo in La Traviata, Opera Company of Philadelphia; Hoffmann in Les Contes d'Hoffmann and Tamino in Die Zauberflöte, l'Opéra de Montréal; Roméo in Roméo et Juliette, Western Australia Opera; Danceny in Dangerous Liaisons, Washington Opera; Recent concert engagements: Sang Števa in Jenůfa, Philadelphia Orchestra, Carnegie Hall; Das Lied von der Erde, Mainly Mozart Festival; Klaus-Narr, Gurre lieder, Ravinia Festival; Beethoven's Ninth Symphony, Houston Symphony and at BBC Proms, Royal Albert Hall; Jacquino in Fidelio, New York Philharmonic; Schubert's Mass in E Flat, Philadelphia Orchestra; Mahler's Eighth Symphony, Winnipeg Symphony; Frère Mass ée in Saint François d'Assise, VARA Radio Orchestra, Concertgebouw; Season 2000–01: Lysander in Britten's A Midsummer Night's Dream, Glyndebourne Festival Opera; Carmina Burana, Tanglewood Festival; Engaged to sing Jack in The Midsummer Marriage, Royal Opera House, Covent Garden; Valinace in Arshak II, San Francisco Opera; Števa in Jenůfa, Théâtre du Châtelet; Camille in Thérèse Raquin, Dallas Opera; Rinuccio in Gianni Schicchi, De Vlaamse Opera; Duke in Rigoletto, Edmonton Opera; Covent Garden debut as Stingo in the premiere of Sophie's Choice, 2002. *Recordings include:* L'Enfance du Christ and Berlioz's Lelio; Les Mamelles de Tirésias. *Address:* c/o IMG Artists, Lovell House, 616 Chiswick High Road, London W4 5RX, England.

GIFFORD, Anthea; British classical guitarist; b. 17 Feb. 1949, Bristol, England; m. John Trusler 1970; one s. one d. *Education:* Accademia Musicale Chigiana, Siena, Italy, Royal College of Music, London. *Career:* debut, Purcell Room, London; Many solo recitals and over 30 programmes on BBC Radio 3 with violinist, Jean-Jacques Kantorow; Recitals at the Purcell Room, Wigmore Hall, Fairfield Hall, Barbican Centre, Queen Elizabeth and Festival Halls; Television appearances on Channel 4, BBC 2, and TSW among others, frequent chamber music recitals with Delmé String Quartet and adjudicator for Overseas League; Performances in Italy, France, Spain and Germany; Director of Droffig Recordings; mem, Incorporated Society of Musicians; Overseas League. *Recordings:* Paganini and his Contemporaries by Kantorow-Gifford Duo, 1991; Solo Recital, 1991; Paganini Ensemble, 1991; Kantorow-Gifford Violin and Guitar Duos, 1993; Dodgson Duo Concerto with Northern Sinfonia, 1994. *Publications:* contrib. to Guitar International. *Honours:* Young Musician of the Year, Greater London Arts Association Award. *Address:* 24 Donovan Avenue, London, N10 2JX, England.

GIFFORD, Helen; Composer; b. 5 Sept. 1935, Melbourne, Australia. *Education:* BMus, Melbourne University Conservatorium of Music, 1958. *Career:* Composer in Residence, Melbourne Theatre Company, 1970–; Commissions from Melbourne Chorale, Astra Chamber Music Society, Australian Broadcasting Commission, Australian Percussion Ensemble. *Compositions include:* Chamber Music: Fantasy for Flute and Piano, 1958, Skiagram for Flute, Viola and Vibraphone, 1963, String Quartet, 1965, Canzone for Chamber Orchestra, recorded, 1968, Sonnet for Flute, Guitar and Harpsichord, 1969, Overture for Chamber Orchestra, 1970, Images For Christmas for Speaker, Electric Guitar, Small Organ with Percussion, Celesta and Effects for 5 Players, 1973;

Point of Ignition for mezzo and orchestra, 1997; The Western Front, World War I, for choir and ensemble, 1999; Piano: Piano Sonata, 1960, Waltz, 1966, Cantillation, 1966; Orchestral: Phantasma for String Orchestra, recorded, 1963, Imperium, 1969; Vocal, Choral: As Dew In Aprille, Christmas carol for Boy or Female Soprano, Piano or Harp or Guitar, 1955, Vigil, a cappella, 1966, Bird Calls From An Old Land for 5 Soprano Soloists, a Cappella Female Choir, 1971; Brass: Company Of Brass for Ensemble, 1972; Theatre: Incidental music and songs, Jo Being, 1-act opera, 1974; Music for the Adonia, theatre, 1992. *Address:* c/o J Albert and Son, 139 King Street, Sydney, New South Wales 2000, Australia.

GILAD, Jonathan; Concert Pianist; b. 1981, Marseilles, France. *Education:* Marseilles Conservatory, and with Dimitri Bashkirov in Colmar and Madrid. *Career:* Concerts with the Israel Philharmonic under Zubin Mehta, Monte Carlo Philharmonic Orchestra, The Ulster Orchestra and Lausanne Chamber Orchestra; US debut, 1996 with the Chicago Symphony Orchestra, returned 1997 with the Chopin E minor Concerto; Berlin recital debut, 1988; Season 1998–99 included USA tour with the St Petersburg Philharmonic Orchestra; Boston Symphony Orchestra concerts, appearances with the Israel Philharmonic Orchestra and at the Maggio Musicale, Florence; Schumann Concerto with the Chicago Symphony Orchestra in Berlin under Daniel Barenboim; Wigmore Hall debut, 2000. *Recordings:* Numerous. *Honours:* Prizes at the Paris Mozart Competition, 1991; Salzburg Mozarteum Competition, 1992. *Address:* c/o Konzertdirektion Hörtnagel Berlin GmbH, Oranienburger Strasse 50, D–10117 Berlin, Germany.

GILBERT, Alan; conductor; b. 23 Feb. 1967, New York, USA. *Education:* Harvard Univ., Curtis Inst. of Music, Juilliard School. *Career:* Chief Conductor and Artistic Adviser, Royal Stockholm Philharmonic Orchestra 2000–; Music Dir, Santa Fe Opera 2003–; Principal Guest Conductor, NDR Hamburg Symphony Orchestra 2003/04 season; guest conducting engagements include performances with the Bayerischer Rundfunk, Orchestre de Paris, Tonhalle, New York Philharmonic, Los Angeles Philharmonic, NHK Symphony, Royal Concertgebouw Orchestra (debut June 2003), BBC Proms debut with the Mahler Chamber Orchestra (Aug. 2003) and debut with Zurich Opera (Oct. 2003). *Honours:* First Prize in the International Competition for Musical Performance, Geneva, 1994; Seaver/National Endowment for the Arts Conductors Award, 1997. *Current Management:* Serena Eveans, IMG Artists, Lovell House, 616 Chiswick High Road, London, W4 5RX, England. *Telephone:* (20) 8233-5800. *Fax:* (20) 8233-5801. *E-mail:* sevans@imgworld.com.

GILBERT, Anthony; Composer; b. 26 July 1934, London, England; 2 s., 1 d. *Education:* MA, D.Mus, University of Leeds; Composition with Anthony Milner, Matyas Seiber, Alexander Goehr and Gunther Schuller; Conducting with Lawrence Leonard, Morley College, London. *Career:* Lecturer in Composition, Goldsmiths' College, 1968–73; Composer in Residence, University of Lancaster, 1970–71; Lecturer in Composition, Morley College, 1972–75; Senior Lecturer in Composition, Sydney Conservatorium, Australia, 1978–79; Composer in Residence, City of Bendigo, Victoria, 1981; Head of School of Composition and Contemporary Music, Royal Northern College of Music until 1999; mem, Society for the Promotion of New Music; Performing Right Society; Mechanical Copyright Protection Society; British Academy of Composers and Songwriters. *Compositions:* Operas: The Scene-Machine, 1971, The Chakravaka-Bird, 1977; Orchestra: Symphony; Sinfonia; Ghost and Dream Dancing; Crow Cry; Towards Asavari; On Beholding a Rainbow (violin concerto), 1997; Another Dream Carousel; Wind orchestra: Dream Carousels; Chamber: 4 string quartets; Saxophone Quartet; Quartet of Beasts; Nine or Ten Osannas; Vasanta With Dancing; Instrumental: Ziggurat; Reflexions, Rose Nord; Moonfaring; Dawnfaring; 3 Piano Sonatas; Spell Respell; The Incredible Flute Music; Treatment of Silence; Osanna for Lady O; Vocal: Certain Lights Reflecting; Love Poems; Inscapes; Long White Moonlight; Beastly Jingles; Music Theatre: Upstream River Rewa, 1991; Handles to the Invisible, chorus, 1995; Vers de Lune, 1999; String Orchestra: Another Dream Carousel; Sheer; Palace of the Winds. *Recordings:* Moonfaring; Beastly Jingles; Nine or Ten Osannas; Towards Asavari; Dream Carousels; Igorochki; Quartet of Beasts; Six of the Bestiary; Farings; Another Dream Carousel. *Honours:* Fellow of Royal Northern College of Music, 1981. *Current Management:* University of York Music Press. *Address:* 4 Oak Brow Cottages, Altrincham Road, Styal, Wilmslow, Cheshire SK9 4JE, England. *E-mail:* anthonygilbert@anthgilbert .demon.co.uk.

GILBERT, Jane; Singer (mezzo-soprano); b. 1969, New York, NY, USA; m. John Hancock. *Education:* Studied at the Juilliard Opera Center. *Career:* Season 1993–94 at Cenerentola at Kansas City, Varvara in Katya Kabanova for Canadian Opera, Britten's Lucretia at the Brooklyn Academy and Ragonde in Comte Ory at Spoleto Festival, USA; Season 1994–95 as Bartók's Judith at Melbourne (also at Edinburgh), Olga in Eugene Onegin at Toronto, (1996), Cuniza in

Oberto for Opéra de Nice and Federica in Luisa Miller for Washington Opera; Concert repertoire includes the Berlioz Mort de Cléopâtre. *Current Management:* Athole Still International Management, Forresters Hall, 25–27 Westow Street, London, SE19 3RY, England. *Telephone:* (20) 8771-5271. *Fax:* (20) 8768-6600. *Website:* www .atholestill.com.

GILBERT, Kenneth; Harpsichordist and Organist; b. 16 Dec. 1931, Montreal, Canada. *Education:* Honorary, D.Mus, McGill University. *Career:* Professor of Harpsichord, Hochschule für Musik, Stuttgart and the Mozateum, Salzburg; Summer courses at Accademia Chigiana, Siena; Professor at the Salzburg Mozarteum, 1989. *Recordings include:* Complete Harpsichord Works of François Couperin, and Rameau; Bach's English and French Suites and Well-Tempered Klavier; Goldberg Variations, 1987; Music by Lully, 1988, Bach English Suites, 1988, Couperin's Four Books for Harpsichord, 1989; Music by Frescobaldi, Byrd, Froberger, Purcell, Handel, Rameau, Bach, Couperin and Scarlatti, 1988. *Publications:* Complete Harpsichord Works of Rameau, François Couperin, D'Anglebert, Bach's Goldberg Variations, Frescobaldi Toccatas; Complete Keyboard Sonatas of Scarlatti in 11 vols. *Honours:* Canada Council Arts Fellowship, 1968, 1974; International Calouste Gulbenkian Foundation Award, 1970; Artist of The Year, Canada, 1978; Officer, Order of Canada, 1986; Professor of Harpsichord, Paris Conservatoire, 1988–1996. *Address:* 11 Rue Ernest-Psichari, 75007 Paris, France.

GILCHRIST, Diana; Soprano; b. 1970, Canada. *Education:* Studied at Banff School of Fine Arts and in Los Angeles and London. *Career:* Founded Opera Lyra at Ottawa and sang at Koblenz Opera from 1989, notably as Susanna, Janáček's Vixen and Gilda; Sang Mozart's Blondchen with Mainz Opera, followed by Zerbinetta; Bielefeld in 1991 as Grétry's Zemire, Vienna Volksoper in 1992 as the Queen of Night, returning as Offenbach's Olympia; Concerts in Canada and Germany have included Orff's Carmina Burana. *Address:* Helen Sykes Artists Management, 100 Felsham Road, Putney, London SW15 1DQ, England.

GILCHRIST, James; Singer (tenor); b. 1970, England. *Education:* Chorister at New College, Oxford; Choral Scholar, King's College, Cambridge. *Career:* Concerts include: Haydn's Creation at the Queen Elizabeth Hall, London, Elijah at St David's Cathedral, Solomon in Buxton and Mozart's Requiem at the Barbican with the English Chamber Orchestra; Engagements with the King's Concert in Purcell Odes at the Wigmore Hall, and Bach's B minor Mass at the Queen Elizabeth Hall, 2000; Messiah in Oslo, Bach's Magnificat with The Sixteen in Spain and the Christmas Oratorio in Italy; Opera includes Mozart's Ferrando and Strauss's Scaramuccio, under Richard Hickox, and Gomatz in Mozart's Zaide in Istanbul; Season 2000–01 with the Britten War Requiem in King's College Chapel, Monteverdi Vespers and Messiah with The Sixteen, Bach Passions with the Australian Chamber Orchestra and various Bach touring projects, notably with the Monteverdi Choir and Orchestra. *Current Management:* Hazard Chase, Norman House, Cambridge Place, Cambridge CB2 1NS, England. *Telephone:* (1223) 312400. *Fax:* (1223) 460827. *Website:* www .hazardchase.co.uk.

GILES, Alice; concert harpist; b. 9 May 1961, Adelaide, Australia. *Education:* studied with June Loney and Alice Chalifoux. *Career:* extensive concert performances in Australia, the USA, Israel and Germany; Festival engagements at Schleswig-Holstein, Bayreuth (International Youth Festival) and Düsseldorf New Music Festivals, Adelaide (Britten's Canticles with Barry Tuckwell and Gerald English), Sydney, Marlboro Music Festival (USA), and Bath Mozartfest; New York Merkin Hall debut, 1983, 92nd Street 'Y' Concert, 1988; Wigmore Hall debut, June 1989, and tour with Luciano Berio; Featured Soloist at festivals including Salzedo Centennial, Austin, Texas, World Harp Congress, Copenhagen, and World Harp Festival, Cardiff, Wales; Frankfurt Hochschule, 1990–98; School of Music at Canberra, Australia, 1999–; Concertos with Collegium Musicum Zürich, Badische Staatskapelle Karlsruhe, English Symphony Orchestra, all major symphony orchestras in Australia and tour of North and South America with Australian Youth Orchestra; Chamber concerts with violinist Thomas Zehetmair and pianist Arnan Wiesel; mem, Co-Founder, Director, EOLUS–International Salzedo Society. *Recordings include:* Recital, Fauré's Impromptu in D flat major, 2 Preludes of Debussy, Tournier's 2nd Sonatine, 5 Preludes of Salzedo; Recital of works for solo harp by Carlos Salzedo; Chamber music for flute and harp with Geoffrey Collins, flute. *Honours:* Churchill International Fellowship, 1980; Winner, International Harp Competition, Israel, 1982. *Current Management:* Robert Gilder & Co., Enterprise House, 59–65 Upper Ground, London, SE1 9PQ, England. *Telephone:* (20) 7928-9008. *Fax:* (20) 7928-9755. *E-mail:* rgilder@robert-gilder.com.

GILFEDDER, John (Francis); Composer; b. 27 Jan. 1925, Melbourne, Victoria, Australia. *Education:* BMus, 1958, BEd (Hons), 1962,

University of Melbourne. *Career:* Faculty Member, Queensland Conservatorium, 1970–; Concert Presenter and Producer. *Compositions include:* The Trojan Doom for speaking voice, string quartet, flute, cor anglais and horn, 1972; Orbits About a Theme for piano, 1981; Colours of the Cosmos, for percussion ensemble, 1985; The Legend of Tibrogargan, for orchestra, 1986; Raga of the Morning for cello, 1989; Reedy Rivers, for woodwind, 1992; Transparencies in Violet, for viola and string orchestra, 1994; Conversazione Pastorale, for saxophone quartet, 1994; Te Deum in Montage, for choir, 1995; Commissions from the Queensland Philharmonic (1994) and others. *Address:* c/o APRA, 1A Eden Street, Crows Nest, NSW 2065, Australia.

GILFRY, Rodney; Singer (Baritone); b. 11 March 1959, California, USA. *Career:* Sang in opera at Los Angeles as Guglielmo, Mozart's Figaro, the Villains in Contes d'Hoffmann and Ford in Falstaff, 1990; European engagements as Figaro at Hamburg, Tel-Aviv and Zürich; Frankfurt Opera from 1989, as Gounod's Mercutio, Ernesto (Il Pirata) and Massenet's Herod; Geneva, 1988, as Lescaut in Manon, Santa Fe, 1991, in the US premiere of Oedipus by Rihm; Concert engagements include Bach's B minor Mass in Paris and at La Scala, Milan; Season 1992 as Guglielmo in Barcelona and at the Holland Festival, Don Giovanni at the Opéra de Lyon; Sang Sharpless in Butterfly at Los Angeles, 1996; Guglielmo at Covent Garden, 1997; Met debut as Demetrius in A Midsummer Nights Dream, 1997; Season 1998 as the Count in Capriccio at Glyndebourne and Stanley in the premiere of Previn's A Streetcar Named Desire at San Francisco; Season 2000–01 as Billy Budd and Dandini at Los Angeles, Valentin in Faust at Munich and Guglielmo for the New York Met; Nathan in the premiere of Sophie's Choice, Covent Garden, 2002. *Recordings:* Ein Deutsches Requiem; Così fan tutte. *Address:* c/o Opéra de Lyon, 9 Quai Jean Moulin, 69001 Lyon, France.

GILL, Timothy; Cellist; b. 1960, England. *Career:* Co-founded the Chagall Piano Trio at the Banff Centre for the Arts in Canada, resident artist; Debut concert at the Blackheath Concert Halls in London in 1991; Further appearances at the Barbican's Prokofiev Centenary Festival, the Warwick Festival and the South Place Sunday Concerts at the Conway Hall in London; Purcell Room London recitals in 1993 with the London premiere of piano trios by Tristan Keuris, Nicholas Maw and Ethel Smyth (composed in 1880); Premiere of Piano Trio No. 2 by David Matthews at the Norfolk and Norwich Festival in 1993; Engaged for the Malvern Festival in 1994. *Address:* Chagall Trio, South Bank Centre, Press Office (Pamela Chowham Management), London SE1, England.

GILLES, Marie-Louise; Singer (Mezzo-Soprano); b. 1937, Duren, Germany. *Education:* Studied at the Folkwang-Hochschule Essen with Hilde Wesselmann. *Career:* Wiesbaden Opera from 1962 as Octavian, Dorabella and the Composer in Ariadne auf Naxos; Staatsoper Munich, 1964–66, Bremen, 1966–68 and from 1968 at Hannover notably as Azucena, Brangaene, Eboli, Waltraute, Fricka, Ortrud, Berg's Marie and Countess Geschwitz, and Santuzza; Bayreuth Festival, 1968–69, appearances at the Dubrovnik and Salzburg Easter Festivals and concert engagements in Washington, New York, Vienna, Paris and Lisbon; Professor at the Hannover Musikhochschule from 1982. *Recordings:* Petite Messe Solennelle by Rossini; Bach Cantatas; Hans Heiling by Marschner. *Address:* Hochschule für Musik und Theater, Emmichplatz 1, 3 Hannover, Germany.

GILLESPIE, Neil; Singer (Tenor); b. 1968, Glasgow, Scotland. *Education:* Royal Scottish Academy, with Duncan Robertson; Britten-Pears School and European Centre for Opera and Vocal Studies, Belgium; further studies with Nicolai Gedda. *Career:* Appearances with Opéra de Lyon, New Israeli Opera and English National Opera; Royal Opera, Covent Garden in Mathis der Maler by Hindemith, Verdi's Il Corsaro, Luisa Miller, Paul Bunyan and The Pilgrim's Progress; Giuseppe in La Traviata, 2001; Other roles include Bacchus in The Olympians by Bliss, Rossini's Almaviva, Tamino, and Sailor in Dido and Aeneas. *Address:* c/o Royal Opera House (contracts), Covent Garden, London. WC2, England. *Telephone:* (20) 7240 1200. *Fax:* (20) 72129502.

GILLESPIE, Rhondda (Marie); Concert Pianist; b. 3 Aug. 1941, Sydney, New South Wales, Australia; m. Denby Richards, 1973. *Education:* New South Wales Conservatory, Sydney, with Alexander Svergensky; the United Kingdom with Denis Matthews and Louis Kentner. *Career:* Recitals and concerto appearances throughout the world, including the United Kingdom, USA, Australia, Far and Near East, Europe and Scandinavia; BBC television series on Liszt's Christmas Tree; From 1984 many tours with Robert Weatherburn as Duo, Two's Company; mem, Lansdale Club. *Recordings:* Duets (with Robert Weatherburn); Sonatas by Bliss and Lambert; Concertos by Usko Meriläinen; Sonata, 2 Ballads and Christmas Tree Suite by Liszt; Works by Camilleri. *Honours:* New South Wales Concerto Prize, 1959; Harriet Cohen Commonwealth Medal, 1966. *Address:* 2 Princes Road, St Leonards-on-Sea, East Sussex TN 37 6EL, England.

GILLESPIE, Wendy; Viol Player; b. 1950, New York, USA. *Career:* Member of Fretwork with first London concert at the Wigmore Hall in 1986; Appearances in the Renaissance and Baroque repertoire in Sweden, France, Belgium, Netherlands, Germany, Austria, Switzerland and Italy; Radio broadcasts in Sweden, Netherlands, Germany and Austria and a televised concert on ZDF, Mainz; Tour of Russia in 1989 and Japan in 1991; Festival engagements in the United Kingdom; Repertory includes In Nomines and Fantasias by Tallis, Parsons and Byrd, dance music by Holborne and Dowland including Lachrimae, six-part consorts by Gibbons and William Lawes, songs and instrumental works by Purcell; Collaborations with vocal group, Red Byrd in verse anthems by Byrd and Tomkins, London Cries by Gibbons and Dering, Resurrection Story and Seven Last Words by Schütz; Gave George Benjamin's Upon Silence at the Queen Elizabeth Hall in 1990; Wigmore Hall concerts, 1990–91 with music by Lawes, Purcell, Locke, Dowland and Byrd. *Recordings:* Heart's Ease, late Tudor and early Stuart; Armada, courts of Philip II and Elizabeth II; Night's Black Bird by Dowland and Byrd; Cries And Fancies (fantasias, In Nomines and The Cries Of London by Gibbons); Go Nightly Cares, consort songs, dances and In Nomines. *Address:* c/o OWM, 14 Nightingale Lane, London N8 7QU, England.

GILLETT, Christopher; Singer (Tenor); b. 1958, London, England. *Education:* Studied at the Royal College of Music with Robert Tear and Edgar Evans; National Opera Studio, London. *Career:* Debut: Sadler's Wells as Edwin in The Gypsy Princess, 1981; sang with New Sadler's Wells Opera in Gilbert and Sullivan; Has appeared with Glyndebourne Touring Opera as Ferrando and Albert Herring; Hermes in King Priam for Kent Opera; Royal Opera House Covent Garden from 1984 as Flute in Midsummer Night's Dream, Roderigo in Otello, Dov in Knot Garden, Pang and Hermes and in Parsifal, Un Re in Ascolto and Idomeneo; Sang Nooni in The Making of the Representative for Planet 8 by Glass at the London Coliseum and in Amsterdam; Season 1990–91 with the Martyrdom of St Magnus by Maxwell Davies in London and Glasgow; Mozart's Ferrando at Garsington Manor and Arbace with the English Bach Festival at Covent Garden and in the Vichy Festival, France; Pysander in Netherlands Opera Ulisses; Sang Musil in the premiere of Broken Strings by Param Vir, Amsterdam, 1992; Tichon in Katya Kabonova for Glyndebourne Touring Opera and Britten's Flute at the 1992 Aix-en-Provence Festival; Concert engagements include Elgar's The Kingdom with the London Philharmonic, Tippett's Mask of Time with the Hallé; Bach's St John Passion in Hong Kong, Cambridge and Greenwich and Elijah with the Bach Choir; Season 1997 with Britten's Flute and Pirzel in Die Soldaten for English National Opera and M Triquet for Netherlands Opera; Season 1999 as Britten's Flute in Rome and in the premiere of Rêves d'un Marco Polo by Claude Vivier at Amsterdam; Oliver Knussen's Where the Wild Things Are and Higglety, Pigglety, Pop! at the London Proms, 2002. *Honours:* Winner, Grimsby Singing Competition, 1980; Countess of Munster Award, 1981. *Address:* c/o IMG Artists, Lovell House, 616 Chiswick High Road, London, W4 5RX, England.

GILLIES, Malcolm (George William); Professor of Music; b. 23 Dec. 1954, Brisbane, Australia. *Education:* BA, hons. Australian National University, 1977; DipEd, University of Queensland, 1978; Royal College of Music, 1973; BA, 1980, MA, 1984, Cambridge University; MMus, London University, 1981; PhD, 1987; LMus A. *Career:* Tutor in Music, University of Melbourne, 1981–83; Lecturer, Music, Victorian College of Arts, 1983–86; Lecturer, Music, 1986–90, Senior Lecturer, 1991–92, University of Melbourne; Professor of Music, 1992–99, University of Queensland; Executive Dean, Humanities and Social Sciences and Pro-Vice-Chancellor, University of Adelaide, 1999–; Fellow, 1992, President, 1998–, Australian Academy of the Humanities; President, National Academies Forum, Australia, 1998–. *Publications include:* Bartók in Britain, 1989; Notation and Tonal Structure in Bartók's Later Works, 1989; Bartók Remembered, 1990; Bartók im Spiegel Seiner Zeit, 1991; Editor: The Bartók Companion, 1993; Halsey Stevens's The Life and Music of Béla Bartók, 3rd edition, 1993; The All-Round Man: Selected Letters of Percy Grainger, co-editor, 1994; Northern Exposures, 1997; Grainger on Music, co-editor, 1999; General Editor, series, Oxford Studies in Musical Genesis, Structure and Interpretation. *Address:* Faculty of Humanities and Social Sciences, University of Adelaide, SA 5005 Australia.

GILLINSON, Clive, CBE, ARAM, FRAM, FRNCM; British cellist; *Executive and Artistic Director, Carnegie Hall;* b. 1946, Bangalore, India; m. Penny; three c. *Education:* Frensham Heights School, Royal Acad. of Music. *Career:* played in Nat. Youth Orchestra of Great Britain 1963–65, Philharmonia Orchestra –1970, London Symphony Orchestra 1970–84; elected to Bd of Dirs London Symphony Orchestra 1976–79, 1983–, Finance Dir 1979, Man. Dir 1984–2005; Exec. and Artistic Dir Carnegie Hall, New York 2005–; owned an antique shop, Hampstead, London 1978–86; Chair. Asscn of British Orchestras 1992–95; Gov. and mem. of Exec. Cttee Nat. Youth Orchestra 1995–; founding pnr

Masterprize 1997–; founding trustee Nat. Endowment for Science, Technology and the Arts 1998–; mem. Int. Music Council of the Children's Hearing Inst., New York 1998–. *Honours:* Dr hc (City Univ.) 1995; Royal Acad. of Music May Mukle Cello Prize, ABSA Garrett Award 1992, Hon. GSMD 1992, Freeman of the City of London 1993. *Address:* c/o Carnegie Hall, 881 Seventh Avenue, New York, NY 10019-3210, USA.

GILMORE, Gail; Singer (Mezzo-soprano); b. 21 Sept. 1950, Washington, District of Columbia, USA. *Education:* Xavier University, New Orleans; MMus, Indiana University, Bloomington. *Career:* Sang at Krefeld, Germany, 1975–79; Appearances at Giessen, Enschede (Netherlands) and the Vienna Staatsoper; Staatsoper Wiesbaden, 1979–82; Deutsche Oper am Rhein, Duesseldorf, 1981–82, returning in 1986 (Penthesilea by Schoeck); New York City Opera, 1981–82; Teatro La Fenice, Venice, 1983–84, as Kundry in Parsifal; Sang at the Verona Arena, 1983–86, as Carmen and as Ulrica (Un Ballo in Maschera); Further engagements in Frankfurt, Nice, Cologne, Nuremberg, Barcelona and Hannover; Other roles include Cassandre (Les Troyens), Octavian, the Composer, Eboli, Gluck's Orpheus, Fricka, Brangaene, Cenerentola, Begonia (Der junge Lord) and Venus; Teatro Fenice Venice, 1987, as Ortrud; Metropolitan Opera debut, 1987, as Fricka in Das Rheingold; Zürich Opera, 1990, as Azucena; Season 1992–93 as Amneris at San Juan and the Festival of Caracalla, and premieres in Prague as Salome, in Buenos Aires as the Countess in Lulu, and in Bergen (Norway) and Tel-Aviv as Delilah in Samson and Delilah; Sang Leonore in Fidelio at Schwerin 1999; Concert performances of Schoenberg's Gurrelieder, Passions by Bach, Brahms Alto Rhapsody, Les nuits d'été (Berlioz), La voix humaine (Poulenc) and works by US composers such as Barber, Joplin, Arlen, Bernstein and Gershwin. *Recordings:* Famous opera arias, 1992; Gershwin songs with Royal Philharmonic Orchestra, London, 1993; Complete Opera Fosca with Carlos Cornes, 1997; Arias, with Staatsorchestre Frankfurt, 1999. *Address:* c/o Gilmore Music Productions, Apollolaan 125, 1077 AP Amsterdam, Netherlands. *E-mail:* info@gilmore.nl.

GILMOUR, Russell (Scott); Composer; b. 21 May 1956, Penrith, New South Wales, Australia. *Education:* BA, University of New England, 1986; Australian Chamber Orchestra's Composer Workshop, 1987, 1993. *Career:* Faculty Member, All Saints College, Bathurst, 1987–90; Canterbury College, Queensland, 1990–; Commissions from Bathurst City and Chamber Orchestras, 1987, 1989. *Compositions include:* A Peaceable Kingdom, for chamber orchestra, 1987; Mud, for tuba, 1989; Songlines, for orchestra, 1989; Edge, for flute, 1990; Wood Dance, for marimba, 1991; Point II, for recorder, 1991; Blowpipes, for flute quartet, 1993; Cantate Domino, for choir, 1993; String Quartet: The Art of Reckoning, 1993; A Way Along, for choir and marimba, 1994. *Contributions:* Sounds Australian (Spring 1992). *Address:* c/o APRA, 1A Eden Street, Crows Nest, NSW 2065, Australia.

GILVAN, Raimund; Singer (Tenor); b. 1938, Manchester, England. *Education:* Studied at the Cologne Musikhochschule. *Career:* Sang at the Mainz Opera from 1961, Mannheim, 1963–74; Among his best roles have been Capito in Mathis der Maler, Lensky, Henze's Junge Lord, Adrasto in Traetta's Antigone, David in Die Meistersinger and Pfitzner's Palestrina; Many concert appearances. *Recordings:* Beethoven Missa solemnis, Bach B minor Mass, Lieder by Wolf.

GIMENEZ, Eduardo; Singer (tenor); b. 2 June 1940, Mataro, Barcelona. *Education:* Studied with Carmen Bracons de Clomer and Juan Sabater in Barcelona and Vladimiro Badiali in Rome. *Career:* Debut: Reggio Emilia in 1967 as Nemorino in L'Elisir d'amore; Has sung widely in Italy and at the Teatro Liceo, Barcelona; Holland Festival in 1970 in La Fedeltà Premiata by Haydn; Guest appearances in Brussels, Nice, Monte Carlo, Venice, Budapest, Bordeaux, Tel-Aviv, Seattle and Washington; Sang at Pesaro and La Scala Milan, 1984–85 in a revival of Rossini's Il Viaggio a Reims; Well known in operas by Cimarosa, Bellini, Paisiello, Galuppi, Mozart, Verdi and Puccini; Has sung in Paisiello's Il Barbiere di Siviglia at Leningrad, and at Barcelona in 1988 in the premiere of Libre Vermell by Xavier Benguere, returning as Ferrando in Così fan tutte in 1990; Covent Garden debut 1990, as Ernesto; Season 1992 as Rossini's Don Ramiro at the Semper Oper Dresden and in Barcelona. *Recordings include:* Elvino in La Sonnambula; Don Pasquale; L'Atlantida by Falla; Rossini's Armida.

GIMENEZ, Raul; Tenor; b. 14 Sept. 1950, Argentina. *Education:* Studied in Buenos Aires. *Career:* Debut: Teatro Col ón Buenos Aires in 1980 as Ernesto in Don Pasquale; Sang in concert and opera throughout South America before his European debut as Filandro in Cimarosa's Le Astuzie Femminili at the 1984 Wexford Festival; Sang in Paris and Venice as Roderigo in Rossini's Otello and appeared as Elvino in La Sonnambula in 1989 at the Théâtre des Champs-Elysées; Season 1987 sang at the Pesaro Festival in Rossini's L'Occasione fa Il Ladro, at Amsterdam as Ernesto and as Alessandro in Il Re Pastore at Rome; Aix-en-Provence in 1988 as Gernando and Carlo in Rossini's Armida; Toronto and Zürich in 1989 as Almaviva; US debut at Dallas as Ernesto,

Lisbon in 1989 as Tonio in La Fille du Régiment and Covent Garden 1990–93 as Almaviva, Ernesto and Ramiro; Season 1990 with appearances as Argirio in Tancredi at Geneva, Così fan tutte at Buenos Aires and Salieri's Les Danaides at the Ravenna Festival as Lyncée; Debuts at Vienna State Opera in 1990 as Almaviva, La Scala in 1993 as Argirio in Tancredi, and at Florence in 1993 in La Cenerentola; Further guest appearances in Munich, Rome Geneva, Naples, Bologna, Verona, Turin, Frankfurt, Toulouse, Monte Carlo, Lausanne, Schwetzingen Festival and Brussels; Season 1996 sang Appio in Pacini's L'Ultimo giorno di Pompei, Martina Franca; Lindoro in L'Italiana in Algeri at the Vienna State Opera, 1996; Season 1998 debut at Paris Opéra Bastille as Tebaldo in Capuleti ed i Montecchi and Edgardo in Lucia di Lammermoor, as Il Turco in Italia at Monte Carlo and Almaviva at Geneva; Season 2000 as Don Ottavio at La Coruña and as Ramiro in La Cenerentola at the Met and in Madrid. *Recordings include:* Arias by Mozart, Rossini, Bellini and Donizetti; Les Danaides; L'Occasione fa il Ladro conducted by Michelangelo Veltri; Il Turco in Italia; Rossini's Messa di Gloria, 1992; Il Barbiere di Siviglia; Viaggio a Reims; La Cenerentola; L'italiana in Algeri; L' Inganno Felice; Rossini's Stabat Mater; La Sonnambula. *Address:* c/o Patricia Greenan, 19b Belsize Park, London NW3 4DU, England.

GIMSE, Havard; Pianist; b. 15 Sept. 1966, Kongsvinger, Norway. *Education:* Norway State Academy of Music; Bergen Music Conservatory; Mozarteum, Salzburg; Musikhochschule, Berlin. *Career:* Debut: Trondheim Symphony Orchestra, 1981; Soloist with Major Scandinavian orchestras, such as Oslo Philharmonic, Bergen Philharmonic, Helsinki Radio, since 1981; Concerts in Europe and North and South America; Played with conductors including Kitajenko, Talmi, Schonwandt, Iona Brown; Several chamber music appearances; Oslo Philharmonic Tour of the United Kingdom, 1995–96; Schleswig-Holstein Festival, 1997; Valdemossa Chopin Festival, 1997. *Recordings:* Liszt: Piano Sonata; Chopin: Piano Music; Grieg: Piano and chamber music; Tveitt: Piano Music. *Honours:* Princess Astrid's Music Prize, 1985; Robert Levin Festival Prize, 1986; Jugend Musiziert Frankfurt, 1987; Steinway Prize, Berlin, 1995; Grieg Prize, Norway, 1996. *Current Management:* Pro Arte International Management. *Address:* Fosswinchelsrt 9, N5007 Bergen, Norway.

GINKEL, Peter van; Singer (Bass-baritone); b. 10 March 1933, Eindhoven, Netherlands. *Education:* Studied at the Quebec Conservatory and with Kurt Herbert Adler in San Francisco. *Career:* Debut: Woodstock, New York, as Colonel Ibbetson in Peter Ibbetson by Deems Taylor; Has appeared at most Canadian opera houses and in Chicago in the premiere of Penderecki's Paradise Lost in 1978; German engagements at Cologne, Dortmund, Stuttgart, Mannheim, Düsseldorf and Nuremberg; Roles have included Mozart's Figaro and Alfonso, Verdi's Iago and Rigoletto, Caspar, Wagner's Dutchman, Wotan and Alberich, Escamillo, Wozzeck and Jochanaan; Engaged at Basle Opera, 1979–80; Many concert appearances. *Recordings include:* Lieder by Beethoven and Wolf. *Address:* c/o Stadtische Buhnen, Richard Wagner-Platz 2-10, 8500 Nuremberg, Germany.

GINTY, Eugene; Singer (Tenor); b. 10 Dec. 1965, London, England. *Education:* BA Hons Degree in Music, Durham University; Studies under Ian Barr. *Career:* Debut: Japan and France, 1994; Don Jose, 1997; Cavaradossi, for Midwales Opera, 1997; Don Ramiro for English Touring, 1997; Sandy, The Lighthouse, 1998; Tonio, La Fille du Régiment for English Touring Opera, 1998; 4 appearances on BBC Radio 2's Friday Night is Music Night; Numerous appearances on BBC Radio 3 including Rossini's Petite Messe Solennelle; 1 appearance on Radio 4, Seeds of Faith; Concert Repertoire: Evangelist (St John), Sheffield Cathedral (St Matthew), Durham Cathedral and St Anne's, Belfast; Britten's Abraham and Isaac, Eton College, 1994; Bach Cantata 191 at Queen Elizabeth Hall, 1995; Schubert's Mondschein at Wigmore Hall under Stephen Cleobury; Britten's Serenade for Tenor, Horn, and Strings, Cleveland Chamber Orchestra, 1996; Elgar's Dream of Gerontius, Guildford Civic Hall, 1998; mem, Equity; Pamra. *Recordings:* Psalms and Part Songs, BBC Singers/Jane Glover; Pärt and Tormis, BBC Singers/Bo Holton; Richard Strauss, BBC Singers/Stephen Cleobury. *Current Management:* O.C.A. *Address:* 270 Shrub End Road, Colchester, Essex CO3 4RL.

GINZER, Frances; Singer (Soprano); b. 19 Sept. 1955, Calgary, Alberta, Canada. *Education:* Studied at Calgary, North Texas State and Toronto Universities. *Career:* Debut: Canadian Opera Toronto, as Clothilde in Norma; Sang Antonia in Les Contes d'Hoffmann at Toronto, followed by the Verdi Requiem, Messiah, Beethoven's Ninth and Die Schöpfung; European opera debut Karlsruhe, 1983 as Antonia; Engaged at Düsseldorf from 1987 and has made guest appearances at Hamburg, Stuttgart, Cologne, Bonn, London (English National Opera), Munich State Opera, Frankfurt, Zürich, Warsaw, Maastricht, Vancouver, Calgary, Edmonton, Winnipeg and USA debut in Dallas, Texas; Welsh National Opera 1991, as Violetta; Duisburg 1991, as Frau Fluth in Die Lustige Weiber von Windsor; Washington Opera 1995, as Senta;

Brünnhilde in Siegfried at Düsseldorf, 1996; Elsa in Lohengrin at Tokyo, 1997; Early roles included Micaela, Constanze, Donna Anna and Mozart Countess; Lucia, Cleopatra, Sophie in Der Rosenkavalier, Aminta (Die schweigsame Frau), Jenůfa, Leila (Les Pêcheurs des perles) and Mimi; Present Repertoire includes Turandot, Ariadne, Senta and Tosca; Sang Brünnhilde for San Francisco and Dallas Opera, 1999–2000; Turandot at Covent Garden, 2002. *Recordings include:* Handel's Rodrigo; Adriana Lecouvreur. *Address:* c/o Welsh National Opera, John Street, Cardiff CF1 4SP, Wales.

GIORDANI, Marcello; Singer (Tenor); b. 1963, Catania, Sicily. *Career:* Debut: Spoleto Festival 1986, as Duke of Mantua; La Scala debut 1988, as Rodolfo, and US debut at Portland, as Nadir; Season 1991 in Live from Lincoln Center (New York) concert and debut at the Verona Arena, as the Duke; Recent engagements as Nemorino, Rodolfo and Alfredo at the Metropolitan (season 1996–97), Pinkerton, Edgardo and Gounod's Roméo at Houston, Alfredo at Covent Garden under Georg Solti, Tonio (La Fille du Régiment) and Hoffmann at Portland and Faust at the Opéra Bastille, Paris; Further engagements at San Francisco Seattle, Chicago, Vienna (in Rosenkavalier and I Puritani), Hamburg, Munich and Berlin; Season 1997–98 as Werther at the Metropolitan, in Lucrezia Borgia at La Scala, L'Elisir d'amore in Dallas and as Pinkerton at San Francisco; Season 2000–01 as Faust at Los Angeles, Gabriele Adorno for San Francisco Opera, Rodolfo at the Met, Cavaradossi for Chicago Opera and Raoul in Les Huguenots at Carnegie Hall. *Address:* c/o Metropolitan Opera, Lincoln Center, New York, NY 10023, USA.

GIOVANINETTI, Christoph; Violinist; b. 1960, France. *Education:* Studied at the Paris Conservatoire with Jean-Claude Pennetier and with members of the Amadeus and Alban Berg Quartets. *Career:* Member of the Ysaÿe String Quartet from 1984; Many concert performances in France, Europe, America and the Far East; Festival engagements at Salzburg, Tivoli in Copenhagen, Bergen, Lockenhaus, Barcelona and Stresa; Many appearances in Italy notably with the Haydn Quartets of Mozart; Tours of Japan and the USA in 1990 and 1992. *Recordings:* Mozart Quartet K421 and Quintet K516; Ravel, Debussy and Mendelssohn Quartets. *Honours:* Grand Prix Evian International String Quartet Competition, 1988; Special prizes for best performances of a Mozart quartet, the Debussy quartet and a contemporary work; 2nd Prize, Portsmouth International String Quartet Competition, 1988. *Address:* c/o Phelps, Ysaÿe Quartet, 6 Malvern Road, London, E8 3LT, England.

GIRAUD, Suzanne; Composer; b. 31 July 1958, Metz, France. *Education:* Studied at the Strasbourg and Paris Conservatoires; Further study with Tristan Murail and Brian Ferneyhough. *Compositions include:* Tentaive-Univers for percussion, 1983; String Quartet, 1983; Terre Essor for Orchestra, 1984; Ergo Sum for 15 Instruments, 1985; L'Offrande a Venus for 8 instruments, 1985; Le Rouge Des Profondeurs for 6 Instruments, 1990; L'Oeil Et Le Jour for Percussion, 1990; String Trio, 1991; Envoûtements 1 for violin, 1996; Petraca for 6 voices. 1996; Envoûtements 4 for string quartet, 1997; Ton Coeur sur la Pente du Ciel for orchestra, 1998; To One in Paradise for mezzo-soprano and orchestra, 1999; Zéphyr for piano, 1999; Au Commencement était le Verbe, for 16 voices and 6 percussionists, 2002; Le Bel été for baritone and piano, 2002; Envoûtements V for guitar and string quartet, 2001; Duos pour Prades for clarinet and cello, 2002; Envoûtements VI for 6 percussionists, 2003; Le Vase de Parfums, opera, 2004. *Recordings:* To One in Paradise; Envoûtements I, II, III and IV. *Honours:* First Prizes at the Paris Conservatory; Diploma from the Accademia Chigiana in Sienna for Composition; In residence at the Villa Medici, Rome; Chosen for performance by the ISCM (Budapest, Manchester). *Address:* 125 Avenue du General de Gaulle, 94500 Champigny-sur-Marne, France. *Website:* www.resmusica.com/suzanne/.

GIROLAMI, Renato; Baritone; b. 1959, Amelia, Torino, Italy. *Education:* Studied in Germany with Ernst Haefliger and Dietrich Fischer-Dieskau and in Italy with Sesto Bruscantini. *Career:* Sang Mozart's Figaro and Leporello at Passau, Germany, St Gallen, Switzerland and at Salzburg Landestheater, 1987–89; From 1989 with ensemble at Vienna Volksoper singing Figaro, Leporello and Guglielmo in Così fan tutte; From 1991 member of Vienna Staatsoper where he added Bartolo in Barber of Seville, also in Stuttgart, 1992–94, Belcore in L'Elisir d'amore, Sharpless in Madama Butterfly and Taddeo in L'Italiana in Algeri; Other roles include Somarone in Béatrice et Bénédict with Neville Marriner in London, 1990, Papageno at Barcelona in 1991, the Count in Le nozze di Figaro at Bari, 1991, Schaunard in La Bohème at Naples in 1992 and at Tokyo in 1993, and Enrico in Lucia di Lammermoor at Marseilles in 1994; Sang at Essen 1999–2000 as Don Alfonso and Don Pasquale. *Address:* Friedgasse 57-2, 1190 Vienna, Austria.

GISCA, Nicolae; Conductor and Professor of Conducting and Orchestration; b. 30 Sept. 1942, Tibirica, Romania; m. Elena Gisca, 28 Jan 1965, 1 d. *Education:* Music Conservatory George Enescu, Iasi, Romania, 1960–65. *Career:* Debut: Conductor with Conservatory Choir, 1962;

Conductor of over 900 choral, chamber and symphony concerts with Conservatory Symphony and Chamber Orchestras, Conservatory Choir and Chamber Choir, Bacau and Botosani Philharmonic Orchestras; Performances and tours of concerts in Romania, Austria, Germany, Belgium, Luxembourg, Switzerland, Wales, France, Italy and Spain with Chamber Choir, Cantores Amicitae; Television and radio appearances; Professor of Conducting at George Enescu Arts Academy; Doctor in Music, 2002. *Compositions:* Arrangements and choral processing of European, American, African and Asian Folksongs for Choir; 145 Musical pieces. *Recordings:* The Tour of The World in 16 Melodies; Winter Songs From Everywhere; The Festival of Political Song; Christmas Carols from Romania and From the World; Romanian Choral Music; Cantores Amicitae Sings the World; Christmas Carols from Everywhere; Kripenspiel; P. Constantinescu: The Byzantine Oratorio for Christmas; Negro Spirituals; The Liturgies of the World. *Publications:* The Conductor's Art, 1982; The Treaty of Instruments Theory, 1987, Vol. II, 1998; The Chorus Conductor's, 1992; The Phenomenology of choral music interpretation, 2003. *Address:* Str Gr Ureche, No. 1, B1 Maracineanu et 9, ap 33, 6600 Iasi, Romania.

GITECK, Janice; Composer and Pianist; b. 27 June 1946, New York, USA. *Education:* Studied at Mills College with Darius Milhaud and Morton Subotnick; Paris Conservatoire with Olivier Messiaen, 1969–70; Aspen School with Milhaud and Charles Jones; Has also studied electronic music, Javanese gamelan and West African percussion. *Career:* Teacher at Hayward State University, the University of California at Berkeley, 1974–76, and Cornish Institute, Seattle from 1979; Co-Director of the Port Costa Players, 1972–79. *Compositions include:* Piano Quintet, 1965; 2 String Quartets; How To Invoke A Garden, cantata, 1968; Traffic Acts for 4-track tape, 1969; Sun Of The Center, cantata, 1970; Magic Words, 1973; Messalina, 1973; Helixes for ensemble, 1974; A'gita, opera, 1976; Sandbars On The Takano River, 1976; Thunder Like A White Bear Dancing, 1977; Callin' Home Coyote, burlesque, 1978; Far North Beast Ghosts The Clearing, 1978; Peter And The Wolves for trombone with actor and tape, 1978; Breathing Songs From A Turning Sky, 1980; When The Crones Stop Counting for 60 flutes, 1980; Tree, chamber symphony, 1981; Hopi: Songs Of The Fourth World, 1983; Loo-Wit for viola and orchestra, 1983. *Honours:* Grants from The California Arts Council, 1978 and The National Endowment For The Arts, 1979 and 1983; Commissions from soloists and ensembles. *Address:* c/o ASCAP, ASCAP Building, 1 Lincoln Plaza, New York, NY 10023, USA.

GITLIS, Ivry; Concert Violinist; b. 22 Aug. 1922, Haifa, Israel; m. Paule Deglon. *Education:* Studied at the Ecole Normale de Musique, Paris, and with Flesch, Enescu and Thibaud. *Career:* First played in public at age 8 in Israel; Worked in British Troop entertainment during the War; Debuts with the London Philharmonic, BBC Symphony and other British orchestras during the 1940s; Paris debut in 1951, Israel debut in 1952 and US debut in 1955; Many recitals and concert appearances with leading orchestras; Often heard in works by 20th century composers. *Recordings include:* Concertos by Berg, Stravinsky, Bartók and Tchaikovsky. *Honours:* Winner, Thibaud Prize, 1951.

GIULINI, Carlo Maria; Conductor and Former Music Director; b. 9 May 1914, Barletta, Italy; m., 3 s. *Education:* Accademia di Santa Cecilia, Rome. *Career:* Debut: As conductor, Rome 1944; Formed the Orchestra of Milan Radio, 1950; Principal Conductor at La Scala, 1953–55; Associated with Callas and conducted her in La Traviata and Gluck's Alceste; Debut in the United Kingdom conducting Verdi's Falstaff at the Edinburgh Festival in 1955; Closely associated with Philharmonia Orchestra from 1955; Debut at Royal Opera House Covent Garden in Don Carlos, 1958; Principal Guest Conductor of Chicago Symphony Orchestra, 1969–78; Music Director, Vienna Symphony Orchestra, 1973–76, and Los Angeles Philharmonic Orchestra, 1978–84, often heard in music by Verdi, Bach, Mozart and Beethoven; Conducted new production of Falstaff in Los Angeles and at Covent Garden in 1982, after 14 years absence from opera (co-production by Los Angeles Philharmonic, Covent Garden and Teatro Communale); Conducted Schumann's Third Symphony and Brahms' Fourth at the 1996 Rhineland Festival. *Recordings include:* Brahms' Violin Concerto with Chicago Symphony, Perlman; Le nozze di Figaro and Don Giovanni with Philharmonia; Mozart Arias; Schubert's 8th Symphony with Philharmonia; Schumann's 3rd with Los Angeles Philharmonic; Don Carlos with Covent Garden Orchestra. *Honours:* Honorary Member, Gesellschaft der Musikfreunde, Vienna, 1978; Honorary DHL DePaul University, Chicago, 1979; Gold Medal, Bruckner Society; Una Vita Nella Musica. *Address:* c/o Robert Leslie, 53 Bedford Road, London SW4, England.

GIURANNA, Bruno; Violist; b. 6 April 1933, Milan, Italy. *Education:* Studied at the Santa Cecilia Conservatory in Rome. *Career:* Founder Member of the ensemble, I Musici, with tours of Europe, North and Central America; Solo career from 1954 with the premiere of Ghedini's Concerto; Appearances with the Berlin Philharmonic, Concertgebouw

Orchestra and Orchestra of La Scala; Artistic Director of the Padova Chamber Orchestra, 1983–92 and Professor at the Berlin Hochschule, 1983–98. *Recordings include:* Mozart's Sinfonia Concertante with Henryk Szeryng, Franco Gulli and Anne-Sophie Mutter, Vivaldi Concerti, Mozart Piano Quartets and complete Beethoven String Trios. *Address:* Via Bembo 96, 31011 Asolo TV, Italy. *Website:* www.giuranna .com.

GIZBERT STUDNICKA, Bogumila; Harpsichordist; b. 16 March 1949, Kraków, Poland; 1 s. *Education:* MMus with honours, Academy of Music, Kraków, 1973; Study with Jos Van Immersel, Conservatoire Royal, Antwerp, Belgium; Diploma with special honours, Conservatoire Royal, 1979; Masterclasses with Zuzana Ruzickova, Kenneth Gilbert, and Ton Koopman. *Career:* Numerous concert appearances including with Polish Orchestra of Wojciech Rajski, Poland and other European countries; Active participant in many chamber music ensembles; Assistant Professor, Department of Harpsichord and Early Instruments and Department of Chamber Music, Academy of Music, Kraków; mem, Polish Society of Musicians. *Recordings:* Concertos of Antonio Vivaldi, JS Bach's transcriptions, Polskie Nagrania Musa; Recordings for Polish and Belgian radio and television and Dutch radio. *Honours:* Prize, Polish Piano Festival, Slupsk, 1974; Prize with Distinction, International Harpsichord Competition, Bruges, Belgium, 1977. *Address:* ul Meissnera 4 m 66, 31462 Kraków, Poland.

GJEVANG, Anne; Singer (Contralto and Mezzo-soprano); b. 24 Oct. 1948, Oslo, Norway. *Education:* Studied in Oslo, the Accademia di Santa Cecilia in Rome and with Erik Werba, Music Academy in Vienna. *Career:* Debut: Klagenfurt in 1972 as Baba the Turk in The Rake's Progress; Sang in Ulm from 1973, and Bremerhaven, 1977–79; Staatstheater Karlsruhe, 1979–80 as Carmen, Ulrica and Orpheus, Bayreuth, 1983–86 as Erda in Der Ring des Nibelungen and again for a new production of the Ring in 1988, 1989 and Erda and First Norn in 1990; Zürich Opera, 1985–90 as Maddelena in Die Meistersinger, Carmen, L'Italiana in Algeri, Ulrica and Erda; Many concert appearances notably in Messiah in Chicago in 1984 and the Missa Solemnis, Lied von der Erde; Lieder recitals in Germany and Austria; La Scala in 1987 in Beethoven's Missa Solemnis and Salome; Metropolitan Opera in a new production of Der Ring des Nibelungen in 1988 and 1990; Sang Lady Macbeth in the premiere of Bibalo's Macbeth at Oslo in 1990 repeated in 1992; Covent Garden in 1991 as Erda in the Ring; Sang Clytemnestra in Elektra at Amsterdam, and Brangaene in Tristan at Bologna, 1996; Season 1998 as Wagner's Erda and Waltraute in Amsterdam, Fricka at Helsinki; Sang Clytemnestra at Baden Baden and Amsterdam, 1999–2000. *Recordings:* Tiefland; Norn in Götterdämmerung; Messiah; Schumann's Das Paradies und die Peri; Ponchielli's La Gioconda; Solo Recitals in works by Wolf, Sibelius, Liszt, Grieg and de Falla; Video of Mitridate by Mozart as Farnace. *Address:* c/o Den Norske Opera, Storgarten 23, 0184 Oslo 1, Norway.

GLANVILLE, Mark; Singer (bass); b. 24 May 1959, London, England. *Education:* Studied at Oxford University and the Royal Northern College of Music. *Career:* Debut: Sang the 2nd Soldier in Les Troyens and the Doctor in Macbeth for Opera North, 1987; Has sung Nourabad (Les Pêcheurs de Perles), the King (Aida), the King of Clubs in The Love for Three Oranges, Hobson in Peter Grimes and Betto di Signa in Gianni Schicchi for Opera North; Scottish Opera debut, 1988, as the Commendatore in Don Giovanni; Radio Vara, Amsterdam, as Lord Rochefort in Anna Bolena; Omaha Opera as Ferrando in Il Trovatore; Sang Iago at Haddo House, 1996; Concert engagements include Bruckner's Te Deum for the Hallé Orchestra and Messiah with the Royal Liverpool Philharmonic; Opera: King (Oranges) in Lisbon, 1991; Father (Jewel Box) for Opera North, 1991; New Israeli Opera, 1992; Concerts of Beethoven 9 (Ulster Orchestra conducted by Tortelier and Netherlands Philharmonic, conducted by Menuhin; Mozart Requiem, Bournemouth Sinfonietta conducted by Menuhin, City of London Orchestra conducted by Judd, Stravinsky's Oedipus (RAI Milano conducted by Gatti). *Recordings include:* Donizetti's L'Assedio di Calais (Opera Rara); Schubert's Mass in G. *Honours:* Scholarships from the Peter Moores Foundation and the Countess of Munster and Ian Fleming Trusts; Ricordi Opera Prize and Elsie Sykes Fellowship, Royal Northern College of Music. *Current Management:* Athole Still International Management, Forresters Hall, 25–27 Westow Street, London, SE19 3RY, England. *Telephone:* (20) 8771-5271. *Fax:* (20) 8768-6600. *Website:* www.atholestill.com.

GLANVILLE, Susannah; Singer (Soprano); b. 1964, England. *Education:* Studied with Margaret Field at the Birmingham Conservatoire and with Margaret Kingsley at the Royal College of Music; Further study at the National Opera Studio. *Career:* Season 1994–95 with Glyndebourne Touring Opera singing Musetta in La Bohème; Mimi for English Touring Opera; Luisa Miller at Opera North; European debut in Nice as Mozart's Countess. Season 1996–97 Fiordiligi in Così fan tutte for Opera North and Mozart's Pamina for English National Opera; Season 1998–99 sang Verdi's Giovanna D'Arco for Opera North;

American debut as Blanche Dubois in André Previn's Streetcar Named Desire with San Francisco Opera; Title role in Strauss's Arabella for Opera North and Vitellia in Mozart's La Clemenza di Tito for Glyndebourne Touring Opera; Concert Appearances include Britten's War Requiem with the Bournemouth Symphony Orchestra, Hindemith's Das Nusch-Nuschi and Mörder, Hoffnung der Frauen with the BBC Symphony Orchestra and Andrew Davies;Verdi's Requiem with the English Northern Philharmonia and Paul Daniel and Blanche Dubois in Streetcar Named Desire Suite with André Previn at the Tanglewood Festival; Sang Schumann's Genoveva for Garsington Opera, 2000: First Lady in Die Zauberflöte at Covent Garden 2003. *Current Management:* Askonas Holt Ltd, Lonsdale Chambers, 27 Chancery Lane, London, WC2A 1PF, England. *Telephone:* (20) 7400-1700. *Fax:* (20) 7400-1799. *E-mail:* info@askonasholt.co.uk. *Website:* www.askonasholt.co.uk.

GLASER, Werner (Wolf); Composer, Pianist and Conductor; b. 14 April 1910, Cologne, Germany; m. Renée Glaser, 4 c. *Education:* University; Pupil of: Abendroth; Dahmen; Jarnach; Hindemith. *Career:* Debut: Pianist, 1918; Conductor, Opera of Chemnitz, 1929–31; Teacher in Denmark; Teacher, Västerås, Sweden, 1945–; Composer; Critic; Soloist; Various programmes at the Swedish Broadcasting Service; Series of recitals; Conferences; Vice Director, Town Music School, Västerås. *Compositions:* 13 Symphonies; 5 Operas; 14 String Quartets; Col Legno, German Recital; Chamber Music; 2 Ballets; Cantatas; Work for solo instruments; Concertos; Stage Work Performances at: Stockholm; Gothenberg; Västerås. *Recordings:* Phono Suecia, Linnea rezza for Solo; Opus 3: for duo; Fermat, for duo; Coronet, for saxophone quartet; Caprice, for trio. *Publications:* Trumma och triangel, 1946; Den sköna leken, 1947; Poems 1–7, 1969–77; Poems, 1981; Poems, 1992. *Honours:* Medal of the Swedish Royal Academy of Music, 1993. *Address:* Djäknegatan 16, 722 15 Västerås, Sweden.

GLASS, Beaumont; Opera Coach, Stage Director, Recital Accompanist, Author and Lecturer and University Professor; b. 25 Oct. 1925, New York, NY, USA; m. Evangeline Noël Young, 7 June 1958, 1 d. *Education:* BS, US Naval Academy, Annapolis, 1949; Graduate studies, San Francisco State College and University of California at Berkeley, 1955; Private music study in Piano, Violin and Theory. *Career:* Debut: As Stage Director, Northwest Grand Opera, Seattle, 1956; Northwest Grand Opera, 1956–57; Assistant to Lotte Lehmann, Music Academy of the West, 1957–59, 1961; Coach, New York City Opera, 1959; Coach, Studienleiter, Zürich Opera, 1961–80; Accompanist, Grace Bumbry Recital Holland Festival, 1965; Accompanist, Grace Bumbry Brahms Lieder Recital, Salzburg Festival, 1965; Coach, Harpsichordist, Recital Accompanist, Festival of Aix-en-Provence, 1974, 1976–78; Director of Opera, University of Iowa, 1980–98; Stage Director, Utah Opera Company, autumn 1988; Stage Director, Cedar Rapids Symphony opera productions, 1987–2001; 3 week residency Mason Gross School of the Arts, Rutgers University, 1999; Masterclasses, Indiana University, 2000; Coach, opera and lieder, AIMS, Graz, Austria, 2000–; Stage Director, Maine Opera Company, 2000–. *Publications:* Biography of Lotte Lehmann, 1988; Schubert's Complete Song Texts, Vol. I, 1996, Vol. II, 1997; Brahms' Complete Song Texts, 1999; Hugo Wolf's Complete Song Texts, 2000; Robert Schumann's Complete Song Texts, 2001. *Contributions:* Contributing and consulting editor, The Opera Quarterly, 1983–89. *Honours:* University of Iowa Presidential Lecturer, 1988. *Address:* The Steeples, 2 Mountain Street, Camden ME 04843-1649, USA.

GLASS, Paul Eugène, BMus; Composer; b. 19 Nov. 1934, Los Angeles, CA, USA; m. Penelope Margaret Mackworth-Praed 1977. *Education:* piano, trombone, composition, theory from early age; Univ. of Southern California; composition with Boris Blacher, Ingolf Dahl, Hugo Friedhofer, Goffredo Petrassi (Accademia di Santa Cecilia), Roger Sessions (Princeton Univ.), Witold Lutoslawski (Warsaw). *Career:* first public performance of compositions 1956; composer of concert music, film and television music; Prof., Conservatorio di Musica della Svizzera Italiana and Franklin Coll., Switzerland. *Compositions:* (all works published) orchestral works include: Sinfonia No. 3 1986, No. 4 1992, Lamento dell'acqua 1990, Quan Shi-qu 1994, Corale per Margaret 1995, Omaggio for piano 1995, How to Begin, for orchestra 1995, Sinfonia No. 5 ad modum missae 1999; chamber works include: Quartet for flute, clarinet, viola, violoncello 1966, Wie ein Naturlaut for 10 instruments 1977, Saxophone Quartet 1980, String Quartet No. 1 1988; vocal works include: 3 Songs for baritone and piano 1954, 5 chansons pour une Princesse errante for baritone and piano 1968, baritone and orchestra 1992, Sahassavagga, for children's chorus (text from the Dhammapada) 1976, Un sogno, for children's chorus (text Alberto Nessi) 1981, Deh, spiriti miei, quando mi vedete for chorus (text Guido Cavalcanti) 1987, Pianto de la Madonna for soprano, baritone, chorus, orchestra (text Jacopone da Todi) 1988; film scores include: The Abductors 1957, Lady in a Cage 1962, Bunny Lake is Missing 1965, Catch My Soul 1972, Overlord 1974, The Late Nancy Irving 1983, Die Abzocker 2000,

Kakapo, ballet pour enfants 2001, Soggetti migranti for three percussionists and orchestra 2002, Prisma for solo dancer and jazz ensemble 2002, Sinfonia No. 6: quinto giorno 2003. *Recordings:* Portrait Paul Glass; Sinfonia No. 3, Quartetto I, 5 pezzi per pianoforte, Lamento dell'acqua; Jan Fryderyk, 2 concerts, Cologne; Concerto per pianoforte estemporaneo e orchestra; I Cantori della Turrita, Guilys; Sahassa-vagga; many for Swiss radio. *Address:* Presso Conservatorio della Svizzera Italiana, via Soldino 9, 6900 Lugano-Besso, Switzerland.

GLASS, Philip; American composer; b. 31 Jan. 1937, Baltimore, MD; s. of Benjamin Glass and Ida Glass (née Gouline); m. 1st JoAnne Akalaitis (divorced); m. 2nd Luba Burtyk (divorced); one s. one d.; m. 3rd Candy Jernigan (died 1991); m. 4th Holly Critchlow 2001; two s. one d. *Education:* Peabody Conservatory, Baltimore, Univ. of Chicago and Juilliard School of Music. *Career:* Composer-in-Residence, Pittsburgh Public Schools 1962–64; studied with Nadia Boulanger, Paris 1964–66; f. Philip Glass Ensemble 1968–, concert tours USA and Europe; f. record co. Chatham Square Productions, New York 1972, Dunvagen Music Publrs, Orange Mountain Music record co. 2002; mem. ASCAP. *Film scores include:* North Star 1977, Koyaanisqatsi 1983, Mishima 1985, Powaqqatsi 1987, The Thin Blue Line 1988, Hamburger Hill 1989, Mindwalk 1990, A Brief History of Time 1991, Anima Mundi 1991, Candyman 1992, The Voyage 1992, Orphée 1993, Candyman II: Farewell to the Flesh 1994, Monsters of Grace 1998, Bent 1998, Kundun 1998, The Hours (BAFTA Anthony Asquith Award 2003, Classical BRIT Award for contemporary music 2004) 2002. *Compositions include:* String Quartets (1–4), Violin Concerto, Low Symphony, The Palace of the Arabian Nights, The Fall of the House of Usher, Einstein on the Beach 1976, Madrigal Opera: The Panther 1980, Satyagraha 1980, The Photographer 1982, The Civil Wars: A Tree Is Best Measured When It Is Down 1983, Akhnaten 1983, The Juniper Tree 1985, A Descent Into The Maelstrom 1986, In The Upper Room 1986, Violin Concerto 1987, The Light for Orchestra 1987, The Making of the Representative for Planet 8 1988, The Fall Of The House Of Usher 1988, 1,000 Airplanes on the Roof (with David Henry Hwang) 1988, Mattogrosso 1989, Hydrogen Jukebox (with Allen Ginsberg) 1989, The White Raven 1991, Orphée, chamber opera after Cocteau 1993, La belle et la bête, after Cocteau 1994, Witches of Venice (ballet) 1995, Les enfants terrible (dance opera) 1996, The Marriages Between Zones Three, Four and Five 1997, Symphony No. 5 1999, Symphony No. 6 (Plutonian Ode) 2000, In the Penal Colony (theatre) 2000, Tirol Concerto, piano and orchestra 2000, Concerto Fantasy for two timpanists and orchestra 2000, Voices for Organ, Didgeridoo and Narrator 2001, Concerto for Cello and Orchestra 2001, Danassimo 2001, The Man in the Bath 2001, Passage 2001, Diaspora 2001, Notes 2001, Galileo Galilei (opera) 2002. *Publications:* Music by Philip Glass 1987, Opera on the Beach 1988. *Honours:* BMI Award 1960, Lado Prize 1961, Benjamin Award 1961, 1962, Ford Foundation Young Composer's Award 1964–66, Fulbright Award 1966–67, Musical America Magazine Musician of the Year 1985, New York Dance and Performance Award 1995. *Current Management:* Dunvagen Music, 632 Broadway, Suite 902, New York, NY 10012, USA. *Telephone:* (212) 979-2080 (office). *Fax:* (212) 473-2842 (office). *E-mail:* info@dunvagen.com (office). *Website:* www.philipglass.com.

GLASSMAN, Allan; Singer (Tenor and Baritone); b. 1950, Brooklyn, New York, USA. *Education:* Studied at Hartt College of Music and Juilliard School. *Career:* Sang as a baritone at Michigan Opera from 1975, then at Philadelphia, Washington and the City Opera, New York; Roles have included Dandini in La Cenerentola, Rossini's Figaro, Belcore, Enrico in Lucia di Lammermoor, Ford and Schaunard; Studied further in New York and sang tenor roles at the Metropolitan from 1985 with debut as Edmondo in Manon Lescaut; Further appearances in USA and at Frankfurt as Tybalt in Roméo et Juliette, Cassio, Bacchus, Alfredo, Hoffman, Faust and Eisenstein; Sang Tichon in Katya Kabanova at the Metropolitan in 1991, Marcello in Leoncavallo's La Bohème at St Louis, Dimitri in Boris Godunov at Pittsburgh in 1991, and Arrigo in I Vespri Sicilani at Nice in 1992; Season 1995–96 as Kardinal Albrecht in Mathis der Maler, and Cavaradossi at the New York City Opera, Bacchus in Ariadne auf Naxos for Miami Opera; Tichon at Dallas, 1998; Sang Boris in Katya Kabanova at Montreal, 2000. *Address:* 1704 Garnet Lane #3002, Ft Worth, TX 76112, USA.

GLAUSER, Elisabeth; Mezzo-Soprano; b. 1 June 1943, Interlaken, Switzerland. *Education:* Studied in Berne, Stockholm and Italy. *Career:* Sang in Pforzheim, 1971–73, Freiburg, 1973–75, Dortmund, 1975–82, and Staatsoper Stuttgart, 1982–88; Sang Rossweise at Bayreuth Festival, 1976–80, Adelaide in Arabella at Glyndebourne Festival in 1985; Guest appearances at Rome Opera as Herodias in Salome in 1988 and Komische Oper Berlin in Düsseldorf, Zürich, Bologna, Venice, Cologne, Lisbon, Hanover and Schwetzingen Festival; Other roles have been Marcellina, Maddalena, Kundry, Fricka, Waltraute, Octavian, Clytemnestra and the Countess Geschwitz in Lulu; Concert soloist in works by Bach, Handel, Mozart, Brahms, Beethoven and Liszt; Teacher,

Berne Conservatory, 1988–. *Address:* c/o Hochschule für Musik und Theater, Papiermüthlestr 13, CH–3000 Bern, Switzerland.

GLAZER, Gilda; Pianist; b. 1949, New York, NY, USA; m. Robert Glazer. *Education:* BA, Music, Queens College, City University of New York; MA, Music, Columbia University; Piano student of Nadia Reisenberg. *Career:* Debut: Kaufman Concert Hall, New York; Resident Keyboardist, Chicago Symphony; Resident Keyboardist, St Louis Symphony; Guest Soloist, Chicago, St Louis, North Carolina Symphonies; Resident Soloist, New York String Symphony; Pianist, Glazer Duo, 1970–; Pianist, New York Piano Quartet; Guest Pianist with Mendelssohn Quartet; World premieres of works by Leo Ornstein, David Ott; Piano Faculties: Hartt College of Music; Chicago Musical College; Extensive solo tours; Appearances in Lincoln Center, Carnegie Hall and Ravinia Festival; Pianist, New Friends of Chamber Music, New York. *Recordings:* Piano solos and chamber music of Leo Ornstein, Joaquin Turina, Easley Blackwood and David Amram. *Publications:* Album of works for Piano and Viola, edited, 1980; Schubert Arpeggione Sonata, edited 1993. *Contributions:* American Piano Magazine. *Honours:* Judge, Heida Hermanns International Competition. *Current Management:* Robert M Gewald Management. *Address:* Prestige Concerts International, 14 Summit, Englewood, NJ 07632, USA.

GLAZER, Robert; Violist and Conductor; b. 1945, Anderson, Indiana, USA; m. Gilda Glazer. *Education:* BMus, MMus, Chicago Musical College; Studied Viola with William Primrose, Conducting with Franco Ferrara. *Career:* String Faculty, Columbia University; Member, Chicago Symphony; Co-Principal Viola, St Louis Symphony; Violist, Hartt String Quartet; Music Director, New York String Symphony; Violist of Glazer Duo, 1970–; Guest Soloist: St Louis Symphony, Louisville Orchestra, Hartford Symphony; Guest Violist with Lenox Quartet, Manhattan and Mendelssohn Quartets; Extensive solo tours; World premieres of works by David Epstein and Leo Ornstein; Conductor, American Chamber Orchestra, Brevard Music Festival. *Recordings:* Soloist, Morton Gould Viola Concerto with Louisville Orchestra; Violist, Lyric by George Walker; Works by Joaquin Turina and Easley Blackwood. *Publications:* Editor: Album for Viola and Piano, 1980; Schubert Arpeggione Sonata, 1993. *Contributions:* Conductors Guild Journal; Instrumentalist. *Honours:* Tanglewood Award; Judge, Washington International Competition; Judge, Primrose Memorial Competition; Robert Glazer Viola Award created at Chicago Musical College of Roosevelt University. *Current Management:* Robert M Gewald Management. *Address:* Prestige Concerts International, 14 Summit, Englewood, NJ 07632, USA.

GLENN, Bonita; Singer (soprano); b. 1960, Washington, USA. *Education:* Philadelphia Academy of Music. *Career:* sang with the Vereingen State Orchestra under Eugene Ormandy, the Oakland Symphony, Toronto Symphony and Rochester Orchestra; recitals at Carnegie Hall, Avery Fisher Hall, Tully Hall, and Kennedy Hall and in Canada and Costa Rica; sang in La Bohème with Philadelphia Grand Opera and in Turandot at the Salzburg Landestheater under Leopold Hager; sang Manon in Houston and Pamina with Santa Fe Opera; appeared as Musetta, Suppé's Galatea, and Corilla in Viva La Mamma at Berne and St Gallen in Switzerland; concert engagements in Europe, Canada and the USA, in Germany with the Nuremberg Symphony Orchestra, the Stuttgart Symphony in Four Last Songs under Neville Marriner, and the Bavarian Radio Symphony Orchestra; sang Clara in Porgy and Bess with the Royal Liverpool Philharmonic conducted by Libor Pešek and with the Scottish Chamber Orchestra under Carl Davis, 1989–90. *Honours:* Winner, Philadelphia Orchestra Vocal Competition.

GLENNIE, Evelyn Elizabeth Ann, OBE, GRSM, FRAM, FRCM, FRNCM; British timpanist and percussionist and composer; b. 19 July 1965, Aberdeen, Scotland; d. of Isobel Glennie and Herbert Arthur Glennie. *Education:* Ellon Acad., Aberdeenshire, Royal Acad. of Music, London. *Career:* solo debut at Wigmore Hall, London, 1986; concerto, chamber and solo percussion performances worldwide; gave Promenade concerts' first-ever percussion recital 1989; numerous TV appearances, including three documentaries on her life; composer of music for TV and radio; many works written for her by composers, including Bennett, Rouse, Heath, Macmillan, McLeod, Muldowney, Daugherty, Turnage and Musgrave; f. Evelyn Glennie Nat. Music Scholarship; Munster Trust Scholarship 1986. *Films:* wrote and played music for The Trench. *Plays:* Playing from the Heart. *Recordings include:* Rhythm Song, Dancin', Light in Darkness, Rebounds, Veni Veni Emmanuel, Wind in the Bamboo Grove, Drumming, Her Greatest Hits, The Music of Joseph Schwantner, Sonata for Two Pianos and Percussion (Bartók), Last Night of the Proms – 100th Season, Street Songs, Reflected in Brass, Shadow Behind the Iron Sun, African Sunrise, Manhattan Rave, UFO, Bela Fleck-Perpetual Motion, Oriental Landscapes, Fractured Lines. *Television includes:* music for Trial and Retribution 1–5 (Yorkshire TV), music for Mazda commercial Blind Ambition, Survival Special (Anglia) and others. *Publications:* Good Vibrations (autobiog.) 1990, Great Journeys of the World, Beat It!. *Honours:* Hon. DMus (Aberdeen)

1991, (Bristol, Portsmouth) 1995, (Leicester, Surrey) 1997, (Queen's, Belfast) 1998, (Exeter, Southampton) 2000; Hon. DLitt (Warwick) 1993, (Loughborough) 1995, (Salford) 1999; Hon. LLD (Dundee) 1996; Hon. DUniv (Essex, Durham) 1998; Hon. Fellow Welsh Coll. of Music and Drama; many prizes and awards, including Shell/LSO Music Gold Medal 1984, Queen's Commendation Prize at RAM 1985, Grammy Award 1988, Scotswoman of the Decade 1990, Charles Heidsieck Soloist of the Year, Royal Philharmonic Soc. 1991, Personality of the Year, Int. Classical Music Awards 1993, Young Deaf Achievers Special Award 1993, Best Studio Percussionist, Rhythm Magazine 1998, 2000, Best Live Percussionist, Rhythm Magazine 2000, Classic FM Outstanding Contribution to Classical Music 2002, Walpole Medal of Excellence 2002, Musical America 2003. *Current Management:* IMG Artists Europe, Lovell House, 616 Chiswick High Road, London, W4 5RX, England. *Telephone:* (20) 8233-5800. *Fax:* (20) 8233-5801. *E-mail:* info@imgartists.com. *Website:* www.imgartists.com. *Address:* PO Box 6, Sawtry, Huntingdon, Cambridgeshire PE17 5YF, England (office). *Telephone:* (1480) 891772 (office); (1480) 891772 (office). *Fax:* (1480) 891779 (office). *E-mail:* carla@evelyn.co.uk (office). *Website:* www.evelyn.co.uk (office).

GLENNON, Jean; Singer (Soprano); b. 1960, USA. *Career:* Professional career from 1983 when she was a winner of the Metropolitan Opera Auditions; Many appearances with opera companies in Miami, Virginia and New York; Season 1993 gave her British concert debut with the Academy of St Martin in the Fields and further concerts at Düsseldorf, Brescia and Montreux; Season 1994 with Musetta at Antwerp, Aida at Würzburg, and Mimi in Dortmund; Concerts of the Verdi Requiem at Bordeaux and Beethoven's Ninth in Strasbourg; Season 1995–96 as Tosca at St Gallen, Butterfly at Malmö and Donna Anna for New Zealand Opera. *Recordings include:* Floyd's Susannah, with Opéra de Lyon; Sang Turandot at Auckland, 1997. *Address:* Helen Sykes Artists Management, 100 Felsham Road, Putney, London SW15 1DQ, England.

GLICK, Jacob; American violist, viola d'amore player, mandolinist and educator; b. 29 Jan. 1926, Philadelphia, PA; m. Lilo Kantorowicz 1949; two d. *Education:* New School of Music, Philadelphia, Peabody Conservatory, Baltimore, MD, Yale Summer School of Music, Norfolk, CT, Kneisel Hall, Blue Hill, MN. *Career:* debut at Carnegie Recital Hall, New York City, 1962; Town Hall recital, New York City, 1964; Performance of Hindemith's Schwanendreher Concerto with Clarion Orchestra, Avery Fisher Hall, Lincoln Center, 1965; Soloist in Vivaldi's Concerto for Mandolines with New York Philharmonic under Bruno Maderna, 1972; Performance of Schoenberg's Serenade with Boulez at New York Philharmonic Rug Concert, 1974; Guest Faculty at Shanghai Conservatory, 1985–86. *Compositions:* Mandolinear, 1965; Octet–Four Hands, 1968; Row for Lou, 1992. *Recordings:* Variazioni Sopra Una Melodia, by Robert Moevs; Aldebaran, by Jean Eichelberger Ivey; Serenade, Op 24, by Arnold Schoenberg; Various with Contemporary Quartet and Beaux-Arts Quartet; contrib. to Contemporary Music Newsletter; Record Album Notes, CRI-SD 135; Concertante for Piano and Orchestra, 1944, Vivian Fine. *Address:* RR! Box 80-S, North Bennington, VT 05257, USA.

GLICK, Srul (Irving); Composer; b. 8 Sept. 1934, Toronto, Canada; m. 18 Sept 1957, 1 s., 2 d. *Education:* BMus, 1955, MMus, 1958, University of Toronto; Continued studies with Darius Milhaud, Louis Saguer and Max Deutch. *Career:* Teacher of Theory and Composition, Royal Conservatory of Music and York University; Composer-in-Residence at Beth Tikvah Synagogue, Toronto, 1969–. *Compositions include:* Chamber music, orchestral, works for solo instruments with orchestra, vocal, choir with instruments, and piano; Violin concerto, 1976; Divertimento for strings, 1987; String Quartet No. 1, 1984, and No. 2, 1994; Cello sonata, 1989; The Reawakening for orchestra, 1991; Piano Concerto, 1992; Piano Quintet; Piano Sonatina, 1996. *Recordings:* 4 Preludes for piano; Petite Suite for solo flute; Suite Hebraique No. 1; Songs from The Sabbath Festivals and High Holy Days; I Never Saw Another Butterfly; Gathering In, a symphonic concept for strings; Suite Hebraique No. 2; 2 Landscapes for tenor and piano; Music for Passover; Suite Hebraique No. 4; Prayer and Dance for cello and piano; String Quartet No. 1; Violin Concerto; Anthology including 17 works including Northern Sketches and Fantasy for Violin and Orchestra (Vision of Ezekiel).

GLOBOKAR, Vinko; Composer and Trombonist; b. 7 July 1934, Anderny, Meurthe et Moselle, France; m. Tatjana Kristan, 27 June 1963, 2 s. *Education:* Diploma, Ljubljana Conservatory, 1954; Trombone at Conservatoire National de Musique, Paris, 1954–59; Composition and Conducting with René Leibowitz, 1959–63; Composition with Berio, 1965; University Physics, 2 years. *Career:* Trombone Soloist; Conductor; Played with group for new music, Buffalo University, 1966; Teacher of Trombone, Staatliche Hochschule für Musik, Cologne, 1968–76, and Composition, New Music Courses, Cologne; Founder, New Phonic Art Quartet, 1969; Director of Department for Instrumental and Vocal Research, IRCAM, Paris, 1973–79; Professor, Scuola di Musica, Fiesole-

Florenna, 1983–; Solo performer of works written for him by Stockhausen, Berio, Kagel and others; British premiere with Heinz Holliger of Gemeaux by Toru Takemitsu, Edinburgh, 1989; Played his Kolo at Dartington Summer School, 1992. *Compositions include:* Accord for soprano and ensemble, 1966; Concerto Grosso for 5 instruments, chorus and orchestra, 1970; Laboratorium for ensemble, 1973; Les Emigres, 1982–86; Labour, 1992; Blinde Zeit for ensemble, 1993; Dialog Über Feuer, 1994; Dialog Über Erde, 1994; Dialog Über Wasser, 1994; Dialog Über Luft, 1994; Masse, Macht und Individuum, 1995. *Recordings include:* Les Emigrées; Vinko Globokar; Globokar by Aulos. *Publications:* Vzdih-Izdih; Einatmen-Ausatmen Komposition und Improvisation by Vinko Globokar. *Contributions:* About 30 articles in musical magazines. *Honours:* 1st Prize: Trombone, Paris, 1959, Gaudeamus, Composition, 1968 and Radio Yugoslavia, 1973. *Address:* 2 rue Pierre et Marie Curie, 75005 Paris, France.

GLONTI, Felix (Phillip); Composer and Professor; b. 8 Nov. 1927, Batumi, Georgia; m. Eteri Ahvlediani, 1 s. *Education:* Conservatory of St Petersburg. Debut; World premiere of Dawn, a ballet in 2 acts, libretto and staging by V Chabukiani, in Tbilisi, 29 Oct 1967. *Career:* World premiere in Brussels Symphony No. 1 Romantic (Horizons du Monde), 1966; Symphony No. 6 Vita Nova, world premiere, Tbilisi, 1979; Symphonic Meditations on a theme by Francesco Petrarca, world premiere in Prague, 1980; Symphony No. 7, Fiat Lux, world premiere, Tbilisi, 1981; Symphony Concertante, Wanderjahre for pianoforte and full symphonic orchestra, world premiere Tbilisi, 1983; Symphony No. 10, Pax Humana, world premiere Tbilisi, 1987. *Compositions:* Symphonies: No. 6, Vita Nova, 1979, No. 7, Fiat Lux, 1981, No. 8, Symphonic Groups, 1982, No. 10, Pax Humana, 1984, No. 1, Romantic, 1986, No. 11, The Open World, 1987, No. 12, Symfoniya-Liturgiya for soprano, baritone, chorus and orchestra, 1989; Sinfonia Concertante for cello and orchestra, 1990; Concertante for violin and orchestra, 1993; Concertante for piano and orchestra, 1997; Opera, Kleopatra, after Shakespeare, 1976, revised 1994; Three Sonnets for vocal soloists and piano, 1997. *Recordings:* Romantic Symphony No. 1; Vita Nova, Symphony No. 6; Symphonic Meditations on a theme by Francesco Petrarca; Marienbadische Elegie (Symphonic Concerts); Wanderjahre (Symphony concertante); Symphony Concertante for pianoforte and full symphony orchestra, 1998; Ode to Life Happiness and Love, words by Plato and Shakespeare, for soloists, chorus and organ. *Publications:* The Anthropology of Post-Serial Musical Thinking for Characterization of Conceptual Paradigm, 2000. *Contributions:* Georgian Literature, 1981; Soviet Music, 1983. *Address:* Alexander Kazbegi str No. 20/9, Tbilisi 380077, Georgia.

GLOSSOP, Peter; British opera singer (baritone) (retd); b. 6 July 1928, Sheffield, England; s. of Cyril Glossop and Violet Elizabeth Wright; m. 1st Joyce Blackham 1955 (divorced 1976); m. 2nd Michelle Yvonne Amos 1977 (divorced 1987); two d. *Education:* High Storrs Grammar School, Sheffield. *Career:* joined Sadler's Wells Opera 1952, notably singing Rigoletto, di Luna, Silvio, Scarpia and Eugene Onegin; with Covent Garden Opera Co 1962–66, notably in Verdi roles of Amonasro, Iago, di Luna, Posa, Renato, Rigoletto, Simon Boccanegra, and in the title role of Billy Budd; sang Verdi roles each season at La Scala, Milan 1965–72, notably Rigoletto; freelance singer 1966–86; Iago at Salzburg with Herbert von Karajan 1970; sang at Metropolitan Opera 1971–86, notably as Scarpia, Don Carlo in La forza del destino, Wozzeck and Falstaff; Flying Dutchman at Opera North 1979; Mandryka at ENO 1980. *Films:* Tonio in I Pagliacci, conducted by Herbert von Karajan, Iago in Otello, conducted by Karajan. *Television includes:* Billy Budd (BBC) 1966, Rigoletto (BBC) 1972, Otello (BBC) 1973. *Recordings:* Billy Budd, conducted by the composer, Chorebus in Les Troyens, conducted by Sir Colin Davis, Macbeth. *Publications:* autobiography 2004. *Honours:* First Prize Bulgarian First Competition for Young Opera Singers 1961; Hon. DMus (Sheffield) 1970; 'Amici di Verdi' Gold Medal 1965, Verdi Gold Medal of Parma 1967, Silver Cross of St George 1996. *Address:* End Cottage, 7 Gate Close, Hawkchurch, Axminster, Devon, England.

GLOVER, Jane (Alison); Conductor; b. 13 May 1949, Helmsley, Yorkshire, England. *Education:* BA, MA, DPhil, St Hugh's College, Oxford University. *Career:* Debut: Oxford University Opera Club in 1971 with Le Nozze di Figaro; As professional conductor at Wexford Festival in 1975 with Cavalli's Eritrea; Lecturer in Music at St Hugh's College, 1976–84, St Anne's College, 1976–80, and Pembroke College, 1979–84; Musical Director, London Choral Society, 1983–98, and Huddersfield Choral Society, 1989–96; Artistic Director, London Mozart Players, 1984–91; Music Dir, Music of the Baroque (Chicago), 2002–; Senior Research Fellow, 1982–91, Honorary Fellow, St Hugh's College, 1991–; Operas and concerts for BBC, Musica Nel Chiostro, English Bach Festival, Glyndebourne Festival Opera (Musical Director, Touring Opera, 1982–85), Covent Garden (debut in 1988), English National Opera (debut in 1989), Royal Danish Opera, Glimmerglass Opera, New York and Australia Opera; Conductor with many orchestras including

London and Royal Philharmonic Orchestras, English Chamber Orchestra, Royal Scottish National Orchestra, Bournemouth Symphony City of Birmingham Symphony, BBC Symphony and Philharmonic Orchestras, and many orchestras in Europe, USA, Australia and New Zealand; Appearances in documentaries and presentation for BBC and LWT, especially the Orchestra and Mozart series; Conducted Mozart's Requiem at St Paul's Cathedral in 1991 and Britten's War Requiem at the 1995 Proms; Gluck's Iphigénie en Tauride at the 1997 Glimmerglass Festival (La Calisto there, 1996); Orpheus for ENO, 1997; Orphée et Eurydice at Bordeaux 1997; Handel's Ariodante for New York City Opera, 1999; Opera Australia in Giulio Cesare, 2000; Così fan tutte, Chicago, 2002; Agrippina, New York City Opera, 2002; Turn of the Screw, Chicago, 2003; Cenerentola, Opera Australia, 2003. *Recordings:* Series of Haydn and Mozart Symphonies. *Publications:* Cavalli, 1978. *Contributions:* Music and Letters; Musical Times. *Honours:* Several hon. degrees; Fellow, Royal College of Music; ABSA/Daily Telegraph Arts Award, 1990; C.B.E., 2003. *Address:* c/o Askonas Holt Ltd, Lonsdale Chambers, 27 Chancery Lane, London WC2A 1PF, England.

GLUBOKY, Pyotr; Singer (Bass); b. 1947, Gordiyenki, near Volgograd, Russia. *Education:* Studied at the Moscow Conservatoire and the Bolshoi Theatre. *Career:* Appearances at the Moscow Bolshoi from 1975, as Rossini's Bartolo and Basilio, Leporello and Alfonso, Pimen, King Philip, Mendoza in Prokofiev's Betrothal in a Monastery and parts in his War and Peace; Guested with the Bolshoi at the 1991 Edinburgh Festival as Panas in Rimsky-Korsakov's Christmas Eve; Concert appearances in Greece, England, Canada, USA, Australia, France, Italy and Japan. *Address:* c/o Bolshoi Theatre, 10309 Moscow, Russia.

GLUSHCHENKO, Fedor; Conductor; b. 1944, Rostov-on-Don, Russia. *Education:* Studied at the Rostov Musical Academy and the Moscow and Leningrad Conservatories. *Career:* Chief Conductor of the Karelian Radio and Television Symphony Orchestra, Finland, 1971; Formerly Chief Conductor of the Ukranian State Symphony Orchestra; Regular Guest Conductor with the Moscow Philharmonic, the Russian State Symphony Orchestra, the Moscow Symphony and the Ministry of Culture Orchestra, and orchestras in Riga, Vilnius, Sverdlovsky, Tbilisi and Tashkent; Season 1989–90 with appearances at the Soviet Contemporary Music Festival, Cheliabinsk and at the Athens Festival with the Athens Broadcasting Orchestra; Concerts with the Prague Symphony Orchestra and visits to Belgium, Greece and Istanbul; British debut in 1989 with the BBC Scottish Symphony returning to appear with Royal Liverpool Philharmonic and the Scottish Chamber Orchestra. *Honours:* Diploma of Distinction at the Soviet Concourse of Conductors; People's Artist of the Ukranian SSR. *Address:* c/o Scottish Chamber Orchestra, 4 Royal Terrace, Edinburgh, EH7 5 AB, Scotland.

GLYNN, Gerald, BA, MA; composer; b. 3 Sept. 1943, Brisbane, Qld, Australia. *Education:* University of Queensland, University of Sydney, electronic studios of French Radio, studied with Peter Maxwell Davies, Olivier Messiaen, Larry Sitsky, composition seminars with Iannis Xenakis and Henri Pousseur. *Career:* NSW Conservatory, 1981; Commissions from Seymour Group (1982) and Symeron (1992). *Compositions include:* Masses, for organ, 1972; Chanson de Ronsard, for soprano, countertenor and percussion, 1974; Changes, for cello, 1975; Syntheses, for string quartet, 1977; Interplay for cello and piano, 1980; William Blake Triptych for chorus, 1981; Chamber Concerto, 1982; Love's Coming, song cycle for medium voice and piano, 1986; Toccata-Sonata, for piano, 1989; Filigrees 1, 2 and 3, for piano, 1981–91; The Rose of Amherst, song cycle for medium voice and piano, 1991; Strata for violin and piano, 1994; Filigrees 4 for piano, 1997. *Address:* 13 Rue Chaligny, 75012 Paris, France.

GNAM, Adrian; Conductor, Music Director and Oboist; b. 4 Sept. 1940, New York, NY, USA; m. Catharine Dee Morningstar, 16 Aug 1983, 1 s., 1 d. *Education:* BMus, 1961, MMus, 1962, College Conservatory of Music, Cincinnati; BS, D.Mus, ABD, University of Cincinnati, 1962. *Career:* Debut: Carnegie Recital Hall and Town Hall, New York, 1962; Principal Oboe: American Symphony Orchestra under Stokowski, Cleveland Orchestra under Szell; Heritage Chamber Quartet, Carnegie Wind Quintet, Chamber Arts Ensemble; Faculty: University of Cincinnati College-Conservatory of Music, 1967–76, Ohio University, 1969–76; Distinguished Artist in Residence, Mercer University 2001; Guest Conductor throughout the USA; Orchestras in Romania, Yugoslavia, Venezuela, Mexico City, Japan, Italy, Brazil, Spain; Congress of Strings, Temple and Georgetown Universities, Peabody Conservatory, Universities of Michigan, Georgia and Houston, Colorado Philharmonic; Assistant Music Director, 1976–82, Music Director, 1982–84, National Endowment for the Arts; Principal Guest Conductor, Philadelphia Concerto Soloists Chamber Orchestra, 1977–88; Music Director: Midland Symphony, Michigan, 1982–86, Macon Symphony, Georgia, 1983–, Eugene Symphony, Oregon, 1985–89, Tuscaloosa Symphony, Alabama, 1993–96; Music Director, Macow Sinfonia 2000; President, Conductors' Guild; AFM; American Symphony Orchestra

League. *Recordings:* For several labels. *Address:* 85440 Appletree Court, Eugene, OR 97405, USA.

GOBLE, Theresa; Singer (Mezzo-soprano); b. 1970, England. *Education:* Studied at the Guildhall School, National Opera Studio, Britten-Pears School and European Opera Centre, with Vera Rozsa and Nicolai Gedda. *Career:* Concert repertoire includes the Verdi Requiem, Rossini Stabat Mater and Petite Messe, Messiah, Dvořák Stabat Mater and Tippett's Child of Our Time; Created the Aunt in Param Vir's Snatched by the Gods, for ENO Contemporary Opera Studio; Sang Flosshilde in Das Rheingold for Scottish Opera, and appeared as Baba the Turk in The Rake's Progress at the Queen Elizabeth Hall (1997); Ulrica (Ballo in Maschera) for Opera Holland Park; Other roles include Dorabella, Verdi's Amneris, Eboli and Mistress Quickly, Charlotte (Werther), Carmen, Adalgisa, Leonora (La Favorita) and Laura in La Gioconda. *Address:* c/o Karen Durant Management, 298 Nelson Road, Whitton, Middlesex, TW2 7BW, England.

GOCKLEY, David; Administrator; b. 13 July 1943, Philadelphia, Pennsylvania, USA. *Education:* Studied at Brown and Columbia Universities and New England Conservatory, Boston. *Career:* Sang at first in opera and became House Manager at Santa Fe Opera, 1968; Assistant Managing Director at Lincoln Center, New York, 1970; General Director, Houston Opera, 1972 presiding over premieres of Pasatieri's The Seagull, 1974, Floyd's Bilby's Doll, 1976, Willie Stark, 1981 and revised version of The Passion of Jonathan Wade, 1991 and Harvey Milk by Stewart Wallace and Michael Korie; Also Glass's Akhnaten, 1984, and The Making of The Representative for Planet 8, (1988), Nixon in China by John Adams, (1987), Tippett's New Year, (1989), Meredith Monk's Atlas, (1991) and Robert Moran's Desert of Roses, 1992; Has introduced surtitles and educational programmes and initiated the touring Texas Opera Theatre. *Honours:* Honorary Doctorate of Humane Letters, University of Houston, 1992; Honorary Doctorate of Fine Arts at Brown University, 1993; Opera Magazine feature, People: 222, July 1996. *Address:* c/o Houston Grand Opera Association, 510 Preston Avenue, Houston, TX 77002, USA.

GODAR, Vladimir; Composer; b. 16 March 1956, Bratislava, Czechoslovakia. *Education:* Bratislava Conservatory; Academy of Music and Drama, 1980. *Career:* Editor, OPUS Publishing House. *Compositions include:* Trio for oboe, violin and piano, 1973; Fugue for string orchestra, 1975; Three Songs, 1977; Overture for symphony orchestra, 1978; Symphony, 1980; Wind Quintet, 1980; Trio for violin, clarinet and piano, 1980; Ricercar, 1980; Melodarium, 20 dances, 1980; Melodarium, 72 duets, 1981; Lyrical Cantata, 1981; Partita, 1983; Talisman, 1983; Grave Passacaglia for piano, 1983; Four Serious Songs, 1984; Orbis Sensualium Pictus, oratorio, 1984; Concerto Grosso Per Archi e Cembalo, 1985; Sonata In Memoriam Viktor Shklovski, 1985; Symphony No. 2, 1992; Via Lucis for orchestra, 1994; Déploration sur la mort de Witold Lutoslawski, piano quintet, 1994; Tombeau de Bartók for orchestra, 1995. *Honours:* Jan Levoslav Bella Prize, Slovak Music Fund. *Address:* SOZA, Kollarova nam 20, 813 27 Bratislava, Slovakia.

GODFREY, Daniel Strong, BA, PhD; Composer and Music Professor; b. 20 Nov. 1949, Bryn Mawr, PA, USA; m. Diana Carol Bottum 1976; one s. *Education:* Yale Univ.; Yale School of Music, 1975; Univ. of Iowa, 1982. *Career:* Dir, Yale Russian Chorus, including tours of USA and USSR, 1969–72; Visiting Asst Prof., Music Composition and Theory, Univ. of Pittsburgh, PA, 1981–93, Asst Prof., 1983–88, Assoc. Prof., 1988–93, Prof., 1993–, Dir, 1997–99; Composer in Residence, Syracuse Univ. School of Music, Syracuse, NY, 2002–. *Compositions:* String Quartet, 1974; Progression, 1975; Trio, 1976; Five Character Pieces for viola and piano, 1976; Celebration for solo piano, 1977; Music for marimba and vibraphone, 1981; Scrimshaw for flute and violin, 1985; Concentus for small orchestra, 1985; Intermedio for string quartet, 1985; Dickinson Triptych for soprano and piano, 1986; Three Marian Eulogies for high voice, viola and piano, 1987; Mestengo for orchestra, 1988; Numina for 6 instruments, 1991; Clarion Sky for orchestra, 1992; String Quartet No. 2, 1993; Two Scenes in Chiaroscuro for 10 performers, 1994; Serenata Ariosa for clarinet, viola and piano, 1995; Festoons for piano solo; From a Dream of Russia, for clarinet, violin and piano, 1996; Jig, for wind ensemble/concert band, 1996; Sinfonietta for string orchestra, 1996; Lightscape for orchestra, 1997; Symphony in Minor, 1999; String quartet No. 3, 2000, revised, 2001; Shindig for solo horn and wind ensemble, 2000, revised 2001; Breath and Shadow for bassoon and string quintet, 2001; Romanza for string quartet, 2001; Concerto for piano and chamber winds, 2003; Pomp and Revelry for wind quintet, 2004. *Recordings:* String Quartet No. 3; String Quartet No. 2; Romanza; Lightscape for orchestra; Jig; Festoons; Scrimshaw; Trio; Five Character Pieces; Celebration; String Quartet No. 1; Progression; Music for Marimba and Vibraphone; Intermedio. *Publications:* Music Since 1945, Elliott Schwartz (co-author),. *Contributions:* Elliott Carter's String Quartet No.3: A Unique Vision of Musical Time, in Sonus, Vol. 8, No. 1. *Honours:* New York Foundation for the Arts Award, 1991; Winner, Spirit of Today's West Competition, 1991; Indiana State University

Festival Award, 1992; American Acad. of Arts and Letters, 1998; Barlow Endowment for Music Composition, 1999; Big Ten Band Directors Association, 1999; Koussevitzky Music Foundation Award, 2000; J. S. Guggenheim Foundation Award, 2001–02. *Current Management:* American International Artists. *E-mail:* cynthia@artists.com. *Address:* 222 Kensington Place, Syracuse, NY 13210, USA. *E-mail:* dsgodfre@syr .edu.

GODFREY, Victor; Singer (Bass-baritone); b. 10 Sept. 1934, Deloraine, Canada. *Education:* Studied with Gladys Whitehead in Winnipeg and Joan Cross in London; Further study with Hans Hotter in Munich and with Giovanni Inghilleri. *Career:* Debut: Covent Garden in 1960 as the Doctor in Macbeth; Appeared with the Covent Garden Company at Coventry in 1962 in the premiere of King Priam by Tippett, and Aldeburgh Festival in 1966 in the premiere of The Burning Fiery Furnace by Britten; Guest appearances at Drottningholm and at opera houses in Glasgow with Scottish Opera, Edinburgh, Florence, Naples, Berlin, Düsseldorf, Montreal, Nice and Amsterdam; Other roles included Scarpia, Amonasro, Zaccaria in Nabucco, Wotan, Wolfram, Orestes and Jochanaan; Also sang in operas by Busoni, Dallapiccola and Hindemith; Many concert engagements.

GODSON, Daphne; Violinist; b. 16 March 1932, Edinburgh, Scotland. *Education:* LRAM; ARAM; Royal Academy of Music, London; Brussels Conservatoire. *Career:* Principal Soloist for Scottish Baroque Ensemble, 1969–87; Principal for Scottish Chamber Orchestra, 1974–76; Member of Bernicia Ensemble, Scottish Early Music Consort; Leader, Edinburgh Bach Players; Soloist with BBC Scottish, Scottish National Orchestra and the Bournemouth Symphony Orchestra; Teacher, RSAMD, City of Edinburgh Music School; mem, Incorporated Society of Musicians; Soroptimist International. *Recordings:* Various. *Honours:* Premiere Prize, Brussels Conservatoire, 1956; ARAM, 1988. *Address:* 48-11 Learmonth Avenue, Edinburgh, EH4 1HT, Scotland.

GODZISZEWSKI, Jerzy, MA; pianist; b. 24 April 1935, Wilno, Poland. *Education:* Superior Music School, Warsaw; summer masterclasses in piano with Benedetti Michelangeli, Arezzo, Italy. *Career:* regular appearances as soloist and with orchestras in Poland and abroad; performed complete piano works of Maurice Ravel 1975, of Karol Szymanowski 1982; chamber music appearances; teacher of piano, Superior Music School, Wroclaw 1967–77; teacher of piano 1978–, Prof. 1988–, Acad. of Music, Bydgoszcz; appearances in int. music festivals, including Warsaw Autumn, Chopin festivals; mem. Polish Artists' and Musicians' Asscn. *Recordings:* piano works of Chopin, Szymanowski, Debussy, Ravel, Prokofiev and others for Polish radio and television, and for Muza and Wifon record companies; Complete Piano Works of K. Szymanowski. *Honours:* Distinction, Sixth Chopin Int. Piano Competition, Warsaw 1960, Szymanowski Memorial Foundation Award 1998, Fryderyk Prize for Best Solo Record for Complete Piano Works of K. Szymanowski 1998. *Current Management:* Maria Blaszczak Artists' Management, ul. Ogrody 13/246, 85-870 Bydgoszcz, Poland. *Telephone:* (52) 3713211. *Fax:* (52) 3713211. *Address:* ul. W. Lokietka 54, 85-200 Bydgoszcz, Poland. *E-mail:* iamb@lazi.pl.

GOEBBELS, Heiner; Composer; b. 17 April 1952, Neustadt, Germany. *Education:* Studied in Frankfurt. *Career:* Co-founded Duo Heiner Goebbels Alfred Harth, 1976–88; Music Director, Frankfurt Schauspiel, 1978–88; Founded performance group Cassiber, 1982. *Compositions include:* Tränen des Vaterlands, ballet, 1987; Red Run, ballet, 1988–91; Befreiung for narrator and ensemble, 1989; Newtons Casino, music theatre, 1990; Black on White, music theatre, 1995; Surrogate Cities for orchestra, 8 movements, 1995; Industry and Idleness, for chamber orchestra 1996; Roman Dogs, radio play, 1996; Nichts Weiter, for orchestra, 1996. *Honours:* Prix Italia 1996; for Roman Dogs. *Address:* c/o German Music Information Centre, Weber str. 59, 53113 Bonn, Germany.

GOEBEL, Reinhard; Violinist; b. 31 July 1952, Siegen, Westphalia, Germany. *Education:* Studied in Cologne and Amsterdam; Teachers include Maier, Gawriloff and Leonhardt. *Career:* Founder of Musica Antiqua Köln in 1973 for the performance of early music, touring in Europe, North and South America, the Far East and Australia; London debut at the Queen Elizabeth Hall, 1978; Played in a concert at the 1989 York Festival in England with music by Legrenzi, Schmelzer and Biber; Season 1996 with Gluck's Orphée et Eurydice at Drottningholm and Handel's Serse at Copenhagen. *Recordings include:* Bach's Art of Fugue and Musical Offering; Biber's Mensa Sonora and Solo Violin Sonata in A; Orchestral Suites by Telemann. *Address:* Brüsseler Str. 94 50672 Köln, Germany.

GOEBELS, Franzpeter; Pianist, Harpsichordist and Professor; b. 5 March 1920, Mülheim-Rhur, Germany; m. Gertraud Kockler, 1 s., 1 d. *Education:* Univs of Cologne and Berlin. *Career:* Debut: 1940; Solo Pianist, Deutschanlandsenderm, Berlin; Docent, Robert Schumann Konservatorium, Düsseldorf; Professor, Hochschule für Musik, Detmold; mem, VDMK. *Compositions:* (as Angfied Traudger) Dependances

for Harpsichord and Strings, 1970; Byrd-Boogy, 1971; Bach: Goldberg Variations for Harpsichordist and Strings. *Recordings include:* 6 Sonatas by Bach and Bach Concertos for Harpsichord, Publications: Das Sammelsurium, 1968; Handbuch der Pianistik. 1973. *Contributions:* Melos; Musica; Musik und Bildung. *Honours:* Honourable Professor, University of Barcelona; IAM; Ruhr Preis für Kunst und Wissenschaft, 1969. *Address:* An Der Pyramideneiche, (Privatzufahrt: Clara Schumann Weg), Postfach 4023, 493 Detmold 14, Germany.

GOEHR, Alexander; Composer and Professor of Music; b. 10 Aug. 1932, Berlin, Germany. *Education:* Royal Manchester College of Music; Paris Conservatoire. *Career:* Lecturer, Morley College, 1955–57; Music Assistant, BBC, 1960–67; Winston Churchill Trust Fellowship, 1968; Composer-in-Residence, New England Conservatory, Boston, USA, 1968–69; Associate Professor of Music, Yale University, 1969–70; West Riding Professor of Music, Leeds University, England, 1971–76; Artistic Director, Leeds Festival; Professor of Music, University of Cambridge, 1976–99, Emeritus Professor, 1999; Visiting Professor, Peking Conservatoire of Music, 1980; Board of Directors, Royal Opera House, London, 1982–87; Composer-in-Residence at Tanglewood Music Center, 1993; Opera Arianna premiered at Covent Garden, 1995. *Compositions include:* 4 string quartets, 1957–90; Fantasia, Op 4; Violin Concerto; Little Symphony; Pastorals; Romanza for cello; Symphony in 1 Movement, Op 29; Sutter's Gold, cantata; The Deluge, cantata; Arden Must Die, opera, 1967; Piano Concerto, 1970; Concerto for Eleven, 1972; Metamorphosis/Dance, 1973; Lyric Pieces, 1974; Konzertstuck, 1974; Kafka Fragments, 1979; Sinfonia, 1980; Deux Etudes, 1981; Behold the Sun, opera, 1985; Symphony with Chaconne, 1986; Eve Dreams in Paradise, mezzo, tenor and orchestra, 1988; Carol for St Steven, 1989; Sing, Ariel, mezzo, 2 sopranos and 5 instruments, 1989–90; Still Lands, 3 pieces for small orchestra, 1990; Variations on Bach's Sarabande from the English Suite in E minor for wind instruments and timpani, 1990; Death of Moses, 1992; Colossus or Panic for orchestra, 1993–95; Arianna, opera, 1995; Schlussgesang for viola and orchestra, 1997; Idées fixes for ensemble, 1997; Sur terre en l'air for viola, 1998; In memoriam Olivier Messiaen for ensemble, 1998; Duos, for violin and two violas, 1998; Kantan and Damask Drum, opera, premiered Dortmund, 1999. *Recordings:* Cello Romanza, Symphony in 1 Movement, 1993; Sing Ariel, 1993; The Death of Moses, 1994; Piano Concerto, Symphony in 1 Movement, 1995; Arianna, 1999. *Publications include:* Finding the Key, selected writings, 1998. *Honours:* Honorary FRMCM; Honorary FRAM, 1975; Honorary FRNCM, 1980; Honorary FRCM, 1981; Honorary Vice-President, SPNM, 1983–; Honorary D.Mus: Southampton, 1973, Manchester, 1989, Nottingham, 1994, Sienna, 1999, Cambridge, 2000; Foreign Member, American Academy of Arts and Letters, 1992; Honorary Professor Beijing Central Conservatoire, 2001. *Address:* Faculty of Music, 11 West Road, Cambridge CB 3 9DP, England.

GOEKE, Leo; Tenor; b. 6 Nov. 1936, Kirksville, Missouri, USA. *Education:* Studied at Louisiana State University, State University of Iowa with David Lloyd and New York with Hans Heinz and Margaret Harshaw. *Career:* Debut: Metropolitan Opera in 1971 as Gaston in La Traviata; Sang Tamino, Edgardo, Alfredo, the Duke of Mantua, Ferrando and Don Ottavio in New York; Glyndebourne Festival, 1973–78 as Flamand in Capriccio, Idamante, Tom Rakewell, Don Ottavio and Tamino; Stuttgart in 1981 in the German premiere of Satyagraha by Philip Glass, repeated in 1990; Other roles include Ernesto in Don Pasquale, Almaviva, Rodolfo, Belmonte, Pinkerton and Massenet's Des Grieux; Guest engagements at the New York City Opera and in Seattle, Strasbourg, Baltimore and Amsterdam; Television appearances include Gandhi in the Stuttgart production of Satyagraha in 1983. *Address:* Staatstheater Stuttgart, Oberer Schlossgarten 6, 7000 Stuttgart 1, Germany.

GOENNENWEIN, Wolfgang; Conductor and Educator; b. 29 Jan. 1933, Schwabisch-Hall, Germany. *Education:* Studied music in Stuttgart, and philosophy at Heidelberg and Tubingen Universities. *Career:* Director of the South German Madrigal Choir at Stuttgart, 1959; Tours throughout Europe from 1964 and to South America in 1971; Director of the Cologne Bach Choir, 1969–73; Repertoire has included Palestrina, Bach, Schütz and Stravinsky; Chair of Choirmastership at Stuttgart Musikhochschule, 1968; Artistic Director at the Ludwisburg Castle Festivals from 1972 conducting Die Zauberflöte, Fidelio and Der Freischütz, 1972–89; Principal of the Hochschule für Musik und Darstellende Kunst at Stuttgart, 1973; Has also conducted the Bach Passions and Christmas Oratorio, Haydn Oratorios and Masses by Mozart and Bruckner; General Director, Staatstheater Stuttgart in opera, ballet and theatre, 1985, and at Ludwigsburg Festival in 1990 with Die Entführung; Conducted L'elisir d'amore at the 2002 Ludwigsburg Festival. *Recordings include:* Bach Cantatas, St Matthew Passion and Magnificat; Mozart's Requiem, with the Consortium Musicum; Handel's Dettinger Te Deum; Haydn's Creation and Seasons, with the Ludwigsburg Festival Orchestra; Mozart's Mass in C minor; Beethoven's Missa

Solemnis, with the Collegium Aureum; Brahms' Ein Deutsches Requiem; Bruckner's E minor Mass. *Address:* Staatstheater Stuttgart, Oberer Schlossgarten 6, 7000 Stuttgart 1, Germany.

GOERGEN, Viviane; Pianist; b. 17 June 1948, Paris, France. *Education:* Studied French and German, Nancy University; Graduated, Conservatoire de la Ville de Luxembourg, 1965; Graduated, Conservatory of Nancy, France, 1967; Licence de Piano, Paris Conservatory and Ecole Nationale de Musique, Paris. *Career:* Debut: Luxembourg; First appeared, Paris, 1971; London, 1973; Zürich, 1974; Bonn, 1975; Brussels, 1976; Prague, 1978; Vienna, 1979; Frankfurt, 1982; Madrid, 1983; Berlin, 1991; Since 1978 has taken part in regular foreign tours; Numerous radio appearances; first performances of works, partly especially composed for her; Devotes attention to the music of Claude Debussy and to reviving pianoworks of forgotten composers; mem, Founded the Center for the Mental Training of Musical Performers, 1994. *Recordings:* Schumann: Davidsbündlertänze, Drei Romanzen Op 28; Johannes Brahms: Sonata Op 5 and Sonata Op 38; César Franck: Sonata in A Major; Ludwig van Beethoven: Sonatas Op 5; Dimitri Shostakovich: Sonata Op 40.; Lyonel Feiniger, The Piano Works, 1994; Kurt Dietmar Richter, Feiniger Impulse, 1994; Claude Debussy, Images, 1997; Erwin Schulhoff, 3rd Sonata for piano, 1997; Ernst Toch, 10 recital and 10 concert studies (op 56 and 55), Burlesques (op 31), 1999. *Honours:* Order of Merit, for artistic achievements, Luxembourg, 1993. *Address:* Nelkenstr 1, 63322 Rödermark, Germany.

GOERNE, Matthias; German singer (baritone); b. 31 March 1967, Karl-Marx-Stadt. *Education:* studied with Hans Beyer, Elisabeth Schwarzkopf, Dietrich Fischer-Dieskau. *Career:* Bach St Matthew Passion under Kurt Masur launched his reputation 1990, followed by opera debut with the title role in Henze's Der Prince von Homburg, Cologne 1992; Wigmore Hall recital 1994; performances with Dresden Staatsoper 1997; Salzburg debut 1997, Metropolitan Opera debut 1998, both as Papageno; Edinburgh Festival performance of Schubert's Winterreise with Alfred Brendel 1998; Wozzeck in Zürich 1999, at Covent Garden 2002; created role of Kasim in Henzes L'Upupa 2003, repeated in Teatro Real, Madrid 2004; tour of USA, including performances with Philadelphia Orchestra, Los Angeles Phiharmonic and the Nat. Symphony Orchestra, Washington, as well as Lieder evenings with Alfred Brendel in Los Angeles and with Christoph Eschenbach in Carnegie Hall 2004; sang Bluebeard in Bartók's Duke Bluebeard's Castle in concert performance with the Berliner Philharmoniker 2005; returned to Metropolitan Opera as Papageno 2005. *Recordings include:* Bach Cantatas, Schubert's Winterreise with Alfred Brendel, Dichterliebe, Schumann's Heine and Eichendordd Leiderkreise and Kerner songs, German operatic arias, Schubert songs, Mahler songs with the Concertgebouw Orchestra, Schumann Lieder. *Honours:* winner Hugo Wolf Competition 1990. *Current Management:* Michael Kocyan Artists Management, Wielandstr. 37, 10629 Berlin, Germany. *E-mail:* info@matthiasgoerne.de. *Website:* www.matthiasgoerne.de.

GOERNER, Stephan; Cellist; b. 23 Oct. 1957, Switzerland. *Education:* Studied at the Winterhur Conservatory, at Juilliard and the International Menuhin Academy in Gstaad. *Career:* Co-Founder and Cellist of the Carmina Quartet, 1984 with appearances from 1987 in Europe, Israel, Japan and USA; Regular concerts at the Wigmore Hall from 1987 and at the South Bank Centre in London, Amsterdam Concertgebouw, the Kleine Philharmonie in Berlin, and Konzertverein Wien in Vienna; Four engagements in Paris, 1990–91, seven in London and tours to Australasia, USA, and Japan with concerts at the Hohenems, Graz, Hong Kong, Montreux, Schleswig-Holstein, Bath, Lucerne, and Prague Spring Festivals; Collaborations with Dietrich Fischer-Dieskau, Olaf Bär and Mitsuko Uchida. *Recordings:* Various. *Honours:* Joint winner with members of Carmina Quartet, Paolo Borciani String Quartet Competition in Reggio Emilia, Italy, 1987. *Address:* c/o Intermusica Artists' Management, 16 Duncan Terrace, London N1 8BZ, England.

GOERTZ, Harald; Conductor, Musicologist, Pianist and Manager; b. 31 Oct. 1924, Vienna, Austria; m. Carola Renner, 1 s., 1 d. *Education:* PhD, University of Vienna, 1947; Advanced studies of piano with Wührer and conducting with Reichwein, Krips and Swarowsky, Academy of Music, Vienna. *Career:* Assistant to von Karajan, Scala di Milano, Lucerne and others; Music Director, opera and concerts, Ulm, Germany, 1955–63; Guest Conductor, Stuttgart, Vienna, Berlin and others; Teacher, Academy of Music, Stuttgart and Salzburg Mozarteum; Professor, Leader of Conductor's Class, Opera Section, Hochschule für Musik, Vienna and seminars for interpretation; Chorus Director, Vienna Opera to 1991; President, Austrian Society of Music, 1963–97; Writer and Commentator, Austrian Television and Salzburger Festspiele. *Publications:* Editor, Osterreichisches Musikhandbuch, Dictionary of Contemporary Austrian Composers, Vienna, 1989, new editions, 1993, 2003; Author, Mozart's Dichter Lorenzo da Ponte, 1988; Gerhard Wimberger, monography, 1990; Österreichische Komponisten der Gegenwart, Editor, 1994; Hanns Eisler Symposion (Ed), 2000; Verdi für Opernfreunde, 2001. *Contributions:* Grove Dictionary of Music and Musicians. *Honours:* Officer of the British Empire; Bundesverdienst-Kreuz, Germany. *Address:* Wiedner Hauptstrasse 40, 1040 Vienna, Austria.

GOETHALS, Lucien (Gustave Georges); Composer; b. 26 June 1931, Ghent, Belgium; m. Maria De Wandelaer, 12 July 1958, 1 s. *Education:* Royal Conservatory of Ghent; Studied composition with Norbert Rosseau and modern technics with Godfried Michael Koenig. *Career:* Organist, 1958–62; Producer, IPEM, 1962; Professor, Analysis, Royal Conservatory, Ghent; Producer, BRT 3, 1964. *Compositions:* Cellotape for cello, piano and electronic music, 1969; Endomorfie for violin, piano and electronic music, 1969; Contrapuntos, electronic music, 1974; Llanto por Salvador Allende for trombone solo; Klankstrukturen organ solo; Triptiek, violin and harpsichord; Sinfonia en Grismayor, 2 orchestras and electronic music, 1966; Many electronic compositions, chamber music and compositions for orchestra; Concerto for Orchestra, 1972; Concerto for 2 clarinets and orchestra, 1983; Concierto de la luz aj las tinublas, for organ and orchestra, 1989; 2 string quartets, 1967, 1992. *Publications:* Lucien Goethals, Le Constructivisne Bifuntionel by Dr H Sabbe; Lucien Goethals, Composer, by H Sabbe. *Contributions:* Professional journals. *Honours:* Mathieu Prize, 1956; Provincial Composition Prize, 1960; Koopal Prize, 1977; Culture Prize, City of Ghent, 1981. *Address:* Verschansingsstraat 32, Mariakerke, 9030 Ghent, Belgium.

GOLAN, Itamar; Pianist; b. 1970, Vilnius, Lithuania. *Education:* Studied in Israel with Lara Vodovoz and Emmanuel Krasovsky; Further study in Boston, 1985–88. *Career:* Recitals and chamber music performances in Israel and the USA 1977–; Collaborations with Mischa Maisky, Ivry Gitlis and the Aurora Piano Quartet; Appearances at the Ravinia, Edinburgh, Besançon, Ludwigsburg and Wyoming Festivals; Concert partners have included Maxim Vengerov, Shlomo Mintz and Tabea Zimmerman; Trio formation with Mintz and Mat Haimovitz (violin and cello); Solo engagements with the Israel Philharmonic under Zubin Mehta and the Jerusalem Symphony Orchestra with David Shallon; Faculty member of the Manhattan School of Music, 1991–; Paris Conservatoire, 1994–. *Current Management:* Askonas Holt Ltd, Lonsdale Chambers, 27 Chancery Lane, London, WC2A 1PF, England. *Telephone:* (20) 7400-1700. *Fax:* (20) 7400-1799. *E-mail:* info@askonasholt.co.uk. *Website:* www.askonasholt.co.uk.

GOLANI, Rivka; violist; b. 22 March 1946, Tel-Aviv, Israel. *Education:* University of Tel-Aviv with Oedon Partos. *Career:* one of the world's most highly acclaimed soloists, giving concerts throughout the world in both traditional and contemporary repertoire; Inspired over 200 works, of which 25 are concerti; Examples, Viola concerti by Holloway (the United Kingdom); Hummel (Germany); Fontajn (Belgium); Colgrass (USA); Vagn Holmboe (Denmark); Yuasa (Japan); Turner (Canada) and others; Solo works by Holliger (Switzerland); Holmboe (Denmark). *Recordings include:* Rubbra Viola Concerto and Elgar Cello Concerto (arr Tertis) and Bax Phantasy with Vernon Handley and the Royal Philharmonic Orchestra; Bartók Viola Concerto in Hungary with András Ligeti and the Budapest Symphony Orchestra; Martinů Rhapsody Concerto with Peter Maag and the Bern Symphony; Arnold Viola Concerto; Viola and Piano, Brahms Sonatas, Otto Joachim (Conifer Records); Contemporary recordings include Colgrass Chaconne (CBS), Viola Nouveau and Prouesse and others. *Publications:* Birds of Another Feather (drawings). *Honours:* Grand Prix du Disque for Viola Nouveau, 1985. *Address:* c/o Werner Concerts, 17 rue du Quatre Septembre, 75002 Paris, France.

GOLDBERG, Reiner; Singer (Tenor); b. 17 Oct. 1939, Crostau, Germany. *Education:* Carl Maria von Weber Hochschule für Musik, Dresden, with Arno Schellenberg. *Career:* Debut: As Luigi in Il Tabarro at Dresden in 1966; Dresden State Opera, 1973–77 and Deutsche Staatsoper East Berlin from 1977; Roles include Florestan, Turiddu, Cavaradossi, Hermann in The Queen of Spades, Aron in Schoenberg's Moses und Aron, and Sergei in Katerina Izmailova; Guest appearances in Leipzig, Leningrad, Vienna, Prague and Italy; Toured Japan with Dresden Company in 1980; Covent Garden debut in 1982 as Walther in Die Meistersinger; Paris 1982 in a concert performance of Strauss's Die Liebe der Danaë, Bayreuth Festival in 1988 in a new production of The Ring produced by Harry Kupfer, New York debut in 1983 in a concert performance of Strauss's Guntram, La Scala Milan in 1984 as Tannhäuser, and Teatro Liceo, Barcelona in 1985 as Siegfried; Sang Walther at Covent Garden in 1990, Erik in Der fliegende Holländer at Bayreuth in 1990 and Bayreuth Festival in 1992, Florestan and Tannhäuser at the Metropolitan in 1992; Aegisthus in Elektra at Florence, 1996; Tannhäuser at the Berlin Staatsoper, 1999; Season 2000–01 as Max in Der Freischütz at the Berlin Staatsoper and Walther von Stolzing in Madrid. *Recordings:* Drum Major in Wozzeck; Parsifal in the film version of Wagner's opera by Syberberg, with role mimed by a woman; Max in Der Freischütz; Guntram; Siegmund in Haitink's recording of Die Walküre. *Address:* c/o Allied Artists Ltd, 42 Montpelier Square, London SW7 1JZ, England.

GOLDENTHAL, Elliot; American composer; b. 2 May 1954, New York, NY. *Education:* Manhattan School of Music with John Corigliano. *Career:* freelance composer of theatre, film and choral music; collaborations with Yo-Yo Ma, Julie Taymor and Neil Jordan; mem. ASCAP. *Compositions include:* Brass Quartet 1983, The Transposed Heads (musical after Thomas Mann) 1987, Pastime Variations for chamber orchestra 1988, Shadow lay Scherzo for orchestra 1988, Juan Darien, A Carnival Mass 1988, Fire Water Paper: A Vietnam Oratorio 1995, Concerto for trumpet and piano 1996, Othello (for San Francisco Ballet) 2003, incidental music for A Midsummer Night's Dream, The Taming of the Shrew, The Tempest, Titus Andronicus. *Film scores:* Cocaine Cowboys 1979, Blank Generation 1980, Drugstore Cowboy 1989, Pet Cemetery 1989, Grand Isle 1991, Alien 3 1992, Demolition Man 1993, Interview with the Vampire 1994, Golden Gate 1994, Cobb 1994, Voices 1995, Batman Forever 1995, Heat 1995, Michael Collins 1996, A Time to Kill 1996, Batman & Robin 1997, The Butcher Boy 1998, Sphere 1998, In Dreams 1998, Titus 1999, Final Fantasy: The Spirits Within 2001, Frida (Golden Globe for Best Score 2003) 2002, The Good Thief 2002, S.W.A.T. 2003. *Television music:* Criminal Justice 1990, Fool's Fire 1992, Behind the Scenes (series) 1992, Roswell 1994. *Current Management:* Gorfaine/Schwartz Agency Inc., 13245 Riverside Drive, Suite 450, Sherman Oaks, CA 91423, USA.

GOLDING, Robin Mavesyn, MA (Oxon); British writer and editor; b. 4 June 1928, London, England; m. 1st Claire Simpson 1956 (divorced); one d.; m. 2nd Felicity Lott 1973 (divorced). *Education:* Christ Church, Oxford (Westminster Scholar). *Career:* freelance writer on musical subjects; experience of local journalism (The Kensington News), the record industry (Vox), music and general publishing (George Rainbird); Librarian, Boyd Neel Orchestra 1953–56; Admin. Asst 1961–65, Registrar 1966–87, Royal Acad. of Music; Ed., Royal Acad. of Music Magazine 1963–87; mem. Savage Club, Garrick Club, Chelsea Arts Club, Royal Musical Asscn, Royal Soc. of Musicians, Royal Philharmonic Soc., Critics' Circle. *Publications:* Ernest Closson's History of the Piano (revised from 1947 edn); Editor, Royal Academy of music Magazine, 1963–87; compiled innumerable programme notes 1953–; contrib. to Gramophone, CRC, Classical Record Collector, Musical Times, Music and Musicians, Records and Recording, The Strad, Arts Review. *Honours:* Hon. ARAM 1965, Hon. RCM 1971, Hon. RAM 1976. *Address:* 33 Prentice Street, Lavenham, Sudbury, Suffolk CO10 9RD, England. *Telephone:* (1787) 247817. *Fax:* (1787) 248485.

GOLDMANN, Friedrich; Composer and Conductor; b. 27 April 1941, Siegmar-Schönau, Chemmitz, Germany. *Education:* Darmstadt, with Karlheinz Stockhausen; Dresden Musikhochschule, 1959–62; Akademie der Künste, Berlin, 1962–64; Humboldt University, 1964–68. *Career:* President of German section of ISCM, 1990–97; Professor of Composition, Hochschule der Künste, Berlin, 1991–. *Compositions include:* Essays for orchestra, I–III 1963, 1968, 1971; Oedipus Tyrann for chorus and orchestra, 1969; 4 Symphonies 1973, 1973, 1986, 1988; Concertos for Trombone (1977), Violin (1977), Oboe (1979), Piano (1979); 2 string quartets, 1975, 1997; Zusammenstellung, wind quintet 1976; Piano Trio, 1978; Piano Sonata 1987; Wind Quartet, 1991; Klangszenen I and II for orchestra, 1990, 1992; Fast erstarrte Unruhe for ensembles, I–III, 1991, 1992, 1995; Ketten for flute, 1997; Schubert Heine Lieder, arranged for baritone and orchestra, 1997; Trio for oboe, cello and piano, 1998. *Honours:* Sächsische Akademie der Künste, Dresden, 1995. *Address:* c/o German Music Information Centre, Weber Str. 59, 53113 Bonn, Germany.

GOLDSMITH, Barry; Concert Pianist; b. 4 June 1959, New York, USA. *Education:* Peabody Conservatory of Music; Johns Hopkins University, BM, DMA, Piano Scholarship; MM, Piano, Indiana University School of Music; Piano Scholarship, Manhattan School of Music. *Career:* Debut: Carnegie Recital Hall, New York City, 1982; Solo Recitals in USA, Canada and Europe; Cities include, New York, Philadelphia, Washington DC, Baltimore, San Francisco, Vancouver, London, Oslo, The Hague, Brussels, Milan; Performed in Major Concert Halls: Carnegie Recital Hall, New York City; Wigmore Hall, London; Diligentia Hall, The Hague; University Hall, Oslo; Solo Recitals at Interlochen Arts Academy; Guest Appearances at Universities on the East Coast and Midwest, USA; Soloist with Peabody Symphony, The Queensborough Symphony and Orchestras in New York; Live Performances on WNYC FM Radio in New York City; Taped Performances on National Public Radio, USA; Solo recitals in Edinburgh (Scotland) and with orchestras in New York's Town Hall (USA); Professor of Piano at Queensborough Community College in New York. *Compositions:* Works for Piano, Voice or Violin and Piano; The Heritage, Suites for Violin and Piano. *Recordings:* Recording Artist with CRS Records; Piano Concerti by Russian-Jewish composers with Royal Scottish Nat. Orchestra, David Amos conducting (Helicon). *Current Management:* International Artists Alliance. *Address:* 75-07 171 Street, Flushing, NY 11366, USA.

GOLDSTEIN, Malcolm; Composer and Violinist; b. 27 March 1936, Brooklyn, New York, USA. *Education:* Studied at Columbia University with Otto Luening. *Career:* Has taught at Columbia-Princeton Electronic Music Center, 1959–60, Columbia University, 1961–65, New England Conservatory, 1965–67, Goddard College, Vermont, 1972–74, and Bowden College, Brunswick, Maine, 1978–82; Co-Director of the concert series, Tone Roads, 1967–69, giving performances of works by Ives, Varése and Cage; Director of the New Music Ensemble and Collegium at Dartmouth College, 1975–78; Has toured Europe and North America as violinist. *Compositions include:* Emanations for violin and cello, 1962; Ludlow Blues for wind and tape, 1963; Overture To Fantastic Gardens, 1964; Majority for string trio, 1964; Sirens For Edgard Varése, 1965; Sheep Meadow for tape collage, 1967; Frog Pond At Dusk, 1972; Upon The Seashore Of Endless Worlds, 1974; Yosha's Morning Song Extended, 1974; Hues Of The Golden Ascending for flute and ensemble, 1979; On The First Day Of Spring There Were 40 Pianos, 1981; A Breaking Of Vessels, Becoming Song, flute concerto, 1981; The Seasons, Vermont, 1980–82; Of Bright Mushrooms Bursting In My Head for ensemble, 1984; Cascades Of The Brook (Bachwasserfall) for orchestra, 1984; Through the deserts of time, string quartet, 1990; Aparicion con vida, theatre piece, 1993; Regarding the Tower of Babel, for speaker and ensemble, 1997; Divisions of Ground for woodwind instruments, piano and percussion, 1998. *Publications include:* Edition of the 2nd Symphony by Ives; From Wheelock Mountain, scores and writings, 1977. *Address:* c/o ASCAP, ASCAP Building, 1 Lincoln Plaza, New York, NY 10023, USA.

GOLDSTONE, Anthony (Keith); Concert Pianist; b. 25 July 1944, Liverpool, England; m. Caroline Clemmow, 26 July 1989. *Education:* Royal Manchester College of Music. *Career:* Debut: Wigmore Hall, London, 1969; Appearances throughout England with all major symphony orchestras and in recital; Many festivals; Several London Promenade Concerts including the Last Night in 1976; Very frequent broadcaster; Tours, North and South America, Africa, Asia, Europe, Australasia; Flourishing piano duo with wife Caroline Clemmow and numerous chamber activities including founding Musicians of the Royal Exchange in 1978; mem, Incorporated Society of Musicians. *Recordings:* Solo piano: Schubert, Lyapunov, Arensky, Glière, Parry, Elgar, Holst, Lambert, Moussorgsky, Britten, Bridge, A Moyzes and others; Chamber: Beethoven, Sibelius, Mendelssohn, Holst, others; Piano Duo: Two-piano works by Holst (Planets), Brahms (Sonata), Gál, Britten, George Lloyd, Soler, others; Piano duets by Schubert (complete), Rimsky-Korsakov, Tchaikovsky, Stravinsky, Elgar, virtuoso variations, romantic sonatas, others; Concertos: Beethoven (from London Promenade Concerts), Alkan, Saint-Saëns Pitfield. *Honours:* International Piano Competitions, Munich, Vienna, 1967; BBC Piano Competition, 1968; Gulbenkian Fellowship, 1968–71; Fellow, Royal Manchester College of Music, 1973. *Address:* Walcot Old Hall, Alkborough, North Lincolnshire DN15 9JT, England.

GOLDTHORPE, (John) Michael, MA; singer (tenor); b. 7 Feb. 1942, York, England. *Education:* Trinity College, Cambridge; Certificate of Education, King's College, London; Guildhall School of Music and Drama, London. *Career:* Debut: Purcell Room, London, January 1970; Paris debut, 1972; Opera Royal, Versailles, 1977; Royal Opera, Covent Garden and BBC television, 1980; Regular Broadcaster, BBC radio; US debut, Miami Festival, 1986; Appearances in Singapore, Iceland, most countries Western Europe; Concertgebouw, Amsterdam, 1986; Directed Medieval Concert in Rome, 1987; Noted Bach Evangelist and exponent of French Baroque; Lucerne Festival's performance of Frank Martin's Golgotha, 1990; Series of concerts for the Sorbonne, Paris, 1992; Examiner, Trinity College of Music and Royal College of Music, London; Lecturer, Teacher, Univ. of Surrey, Roehampton, London; Founder and Artistic Dir, specialist Victorian music group and charity, The Bold Balladiers, 1995; mem, Hon Fellow, Cambridge Society of Musicians, 1993; Member of the Royal Society of Musicians of Great Britain, 1999. *Recordings include:* Rameau: Hippolyte et Aricie, La Princesse de Navarre and Pygmalion; Charpentier: Missa Assumpta est Maria; Mondonville Motets; Cavalli: Ercole Amante; Delius: Irmelin; Monteverdi: L'Incoronazione di Poppea, Madrigali; Blanchard: Cantatas; Stuart Ward: St Cuthbert of Lindisfarne and Other Songs. *Honours:* Choral Exhibition, Cambridge, 1961; Lieder Prize GSM, 1967; Greater London Arts Asscn Young Musicians Award, Inc. Soc. of Musicians Young Musicians Award, Park Lane Group's Young Musicians Award, early 1970s; Wingate Scholarship, 1994; SEDA accreditation as Teacher in Higher Education, 2000. *Address:* 23 King Edward's Road, Ruislip, Middlesex HA4 7AQ, England. *E-mail:* mgoldthorpe@tiscali.co.uk. *Website:* www.balladiers.freeserve.co.uk/mg/.

GOLESORKHI, Anooshah; Singer (Baritone); b. 1962, Tehran, Iran. *Education:* Studied in California. *Career:* Debut: Opera Pacific Costa Mesa, 1988 as Amonasro in Aida; Sang Escamillo at Bergen Opera, Norway; Iago on tour with the Company in Israel, 1993; Connecticut Opera 1991 as Garriso in Massenet's Navarriase; San Jose Opera as Rossini's Figaro and Marcello in La Bohème; St Gallen 1993 as Barnaba in La Gioconda and Canterbury Opera, New Zealand as Scarpia; Other roles include Verdi's Nabucco, Renato, Luna and Macbeth and Gerard in Andrea Chénier. *Address:* c/o Opera Bergen, Kommediebakan 9, 5016 Bergen, Norway.

GOLIGHTLY, David Frederick, BA, AMusM; British composer; b. 17 Nov. 1948, Co. Durham, England. *Education:* Huddersfield University; Guildhall School of Music and Drama; Leeds University; Nottingham University. *Career:* Composer. *Compositions include:* The Eye, a Chamber Opera premiered 1992; Symphony No. 1; Rites of Passage and The St Petersburg Mass premiered 1994 in the State Capella Hall, St Petersburg, Russia; Frontiers (Five arrangements of American folk songs for male voice choir); Songs of the Cliff Top for baritone and piano; Star Flight, Northumbrian Fantasy, Crimond arrangement, and A Weardale Portrait for brass band; Septet for brass; Little Suite for brass quintet; Three Pieces for tombone quartet (Vol. 1 and 2); Concert Fanfare for brass and percussion; Four Preludes for flute and guitar; Three Shadow Portraits for piano; Piano Sonata No. 1; Flute concerto; Trumpet concerto; Concerto for strings; Three Pan Love Songs for solo flute; Piano Trio Letter of Regret; Dances for Showgirls for piano trio; Music for the Theatre and Film. *Current Management:* Modrana Music Promotions Ltd, 41 Parklands Way, Poynton, Cheshire SK12 1AL, England. *Telephone:* (1625) 875389. *E-mail:* info@modranamusicpromotions.com.

GÖLLNER, Theodor; Musicologist and Administrator; b. 25 Nov. 1929, Bielefeld, Germany; m. Marie Louise Martinez, 1 s., 1 d. *Education:* PhD, University of Heidelberg, 1957; Phil habil, University of Munich, 1967. *Career:* Lecturer, 1958–62, Assistant, 1962–67, Associate Professor, 1967, Professor, 1973–, Chair in Musicology and Director, Institute of Musicology, 1973–97, Dean, Division of History and Fine Arts, 1975–77, University of Munich; Associate Professor, 1967–71, Professor, 1971–73, University of California, Santa Barbara, USA; Member, Bavarian Academy of Sciences, 1982–; European Academy of Sciences and Arts, 1991–; mem, International Musicological Society; Gesellschaft für Musikforschung; Gesellschaft für Bayerische Musikgeschichte, President 1981–2001. *Publications:* Formen früher Mehrstimmigkeit, 1961; Die mehrstimmigen liturgischen Lesungen, 2 vols, 1969; Die Sieben Worte am Kreuz bei Schütz und Haydn, 1986; 'Et incarnatus est' in Bachs h-Moll-Messe und Beethovens Missa Solemnis, 1996; Pausa, Farewell (lecture) to Munich University, 1998; Editor: Münchener Veröffentlichungen zur Musikgeschichte, 1977–; Münchener Editionen zur Musikgeschichte, 1979–. *Contributions:* Various publications. *Address:* Musikwissenschaft Institut, University of Munich, Geschw Scholl Platz 1, 80539 Munich, Germany.

GOLOVIN, Andrei; Composer and Conductor; b. 11 Aug. 1950, Moscow, Russia. *Education:* Moscow Conservatoire, 1971–76; Postgraduate Course, 1977–79. *Career:* Teacher of Composition at Gnesins' State Musical College, 1975–, and Gnesins' Russian Academy of Music, 1989–; mem, Russian Composers' Union. *Compositions:* Published: Cadence and Ostinato for 5 timpani, bells, tam-tam and piano, 1979, Concerto Symphony for viola, cello and symphony orchestra, 1980, Sonata for oboe and cembalo, 1980, Sonata for piano, 1981, Duet for violin and piano, 1981, Duet for viola and cello, 1981, Sonata Breve for viola and piano, 1982, Japanese edition, 1992, 2 Pieces for piano, 1982, Sonata for cello solo, 1983, 2 Pieces for flute and piano: Portrait, and, Landscape, 1983, Prelude for vibraphone, 1984, Legend for piano, 1984, 3 Easy Pieces for piano, 1985, 1st Quartet for 2 violins, viola and cello, 1986, Music for string quartet, 1986, Sonatina for piano, 1986, Japanese edition, 1991, Fairy-Tale for horn and piano, 1987, Concert Symphony for viola, piano and orchestra, 1988, Symphony for full symphony orchestra, 1990, Elegy for cello solo, 1990, Poeme Nocturne for viola and piano, 1991, Plain Songs: Canata to Verses by N Rubtsov for mezzo-soprano, bass, piano and chamber orchestra, 1991, Remote Past for piano, 1991; Symphony No. 4, for cello and orchestra, 1992; On the Hills of Georgia, chorus, 1992; Spring Song for trombone and piano, 1993; First Love, opera after Turgenev, 1996. *Recordings:* Simple Songs: Cantata, Elegy for cello solo; Sonata Breve for viola and piano; Elegy for cello solo; Concert Symphony for viola, piano and orchestra; Quartet for 2 violins, viola and cello; 2 Pieces for flute and piano; Music for strings. *Address:* Shumkin St 3, k2, Ap 45, Moscow 107113, Russia.

GOLTZ, Christel; Singer (Soprano); b. 8 July 1912, Dortmund, Germany; m. Theodor Schenk. *Education:* Studied with Ornelli-Leeb in Munich and with Theodor Schenk. *Career:* Sang first at Plauen as Eva, Santuzza and Octavian; Sang at the Dresden Staatsoper from 1936 notably as Reiza in Oberon, in the premiere of Sutermeister's Romeo und Julia in 1941 and in the local premiere of Orff's Antigonae in 1950; Sang in Berlin from 1947, then in Munich and Vienna as Salome, Elektra, the Countess in Capriccio, Tosca and Leonore; Covent Garden, 1951–52 as Salome and as Marie in the local stage premiere of Wozzeck; Salzburg Festival from 1954 in the premiere of Liebermann's Penelope and as Elektra and Leonore, and as Salome at the Metropolitan Opera in 1954; Guest engagements in Paris, Brussels and Milan; Sang at the State Operas of Munich and Vienna until 1970. *Recordings:* Salome; Die Frau

ohne Schatten. *Honours:* Ehrenmitglied of the Dresden Staatsoper, 1996. *Address:* c/o Vienna State Opera, Ring Strasse, Vienna, Austria.

GOLUB, David; Pianist and Conductor; b. 22 March 1950, Chicago, USA. *Education:* Studied with Alexander Uninsky in Dallas and with Beveridge Webster at the Juilliard School, New York; Graduated, 1974. *Career:* Debut: With Dallas Symphony Orchestra, 1964; Appeared with orchestras in Philadelphia, Cleveland, Dallas, St Louis, Pittsburgh, Cincinnati, Chicago, Minnesota, Washington and Atlanta; Solo appearances also with orchestras of Toronto, Ottawa, Edmonton, Montreal, Calgary and Vancouver; Has performed at all major North American music festivals; International appearances with such conductors as Maazel, Mata, Horst Stein, Zinman, Conlon, Chailly, Levine, Dutoit, Bychkov, DeWaart, Foster, Skrowaczewski and Albrecht; European engagements with orchestras in London, Rome, Paris, Milan, Geneva, Florence, Rotterdam, Amsterdam and Prague; Appeared in film From Mao to Mozart, which documented tour to China in 1979 with Isaac Stern and formed a piano trio with Colin Carr and Mark Kaplan. *Recordings:* Gershwin and Rachmaninov with London Symphony Orchestra and complete piano trios of Schubert, Mendelssohn and Brahms; Haydn's L'Isola Disabitata, as conductor; The Complete Trios of Dvořák, Rachmaninov with Golub-Kaplan-Carr Trio. *Current Management:* Herbert Barratt Management. *Address:* 1776 Broadway, New York, NY 10019, USA.

GOMBRICH, Carl; Singer (Bass); b. 1975, England. *Education:* Guildhall School, and National Opera Studio, London, with Neil Howlett; King's College, London and Morley Opera. *Career:* Early roles included Ribbing (Ballo in Maschera), Gounod's Mephistopheles, Sparafucile (Rigoletto) and Guglielmo; Appearances as the Commendatore in Don Giovanni for Pavilion Opera and on Japanese Tour; Don Pasquale for Opera Italiana and Blansac in La Scala di Seta at the 1999 Wexford Festival; The Monk in Don Carlos, Oroveso (Norma) and Mozart's Osmin, for British Youth Opera, Linbury Studio Theatre, Covent Garden. *Address:* c/o National Opera Studio, Morley College, 61 Westminster Bridge Road, London, SE1 7XT, England.

GOMEZ, Jill, FRAM; British opera and concert singer (soprano); b. 21 Sept. 1942, New Amsterdam, British Guiana. *Education:* Royal Acad. of Music, Guildhall School of Music. *Career:* operatic début as Adina in L'Elisir d'Amore with Glyndebourne Touring Opera 1968 and has since sung leading roles with Glyndebourne Festival Opera incl. Mélisande, Calisto and Ann Truelove in The Rake's Progress; has appeared with The Royal Opera, English Nat. Opera and Scottish Opera in roles including Pamina, Ilia, Fiordiligi, the Countess in Figaro, Elizabeth in Elegy for Young Lovers, Tytania, Lauretta in Gianni Schicchi and the Governess in The Turn of the Screw; cr. the role of Flora in Tippett's The Knot Garden, at Covent Garden 1970 and of the Countess in Thea Musgrave's Voice of Ariadne, Aldeburgh 1974; sang title role in Massenet's Thaïs, Wexford 1974 and Jenifer in The Midsummer Marriage with Welsh Nat. Opera 1976; cr. title role in William Alwyn's Miss Julie for radio 1977; performed Tatiana in Eugene Onegin with Kent Opera 1977; Donna Elvira in Don Giovanni, Ludwigsburg Festival 1978; cr. title role in BBC world premiere of Prokofiev's Maddalena 1979; Fiordiligi in Così fan tutte, Bordeaux 1979; sang in première of the Eighth Book of Madrigals in Zürich Monteverdi Festival 1979; Violetta in Kent Opera's production of La Traviata, Edin. Festival 1979; Cinna in Lucio Silla, Zurich 1981; The Governess in The Turn of the Screw, Geneva 1981; Cleopatra in Giulio Cesare, Frankfurt 1981; Teresa in Benvenuto Cellini, Berlioz Festival, Lyon 1982, Leila in Les Pêcheurs de Perles, Scottish Opera 1982–83; Governess in The Turn of the Screw, English Nat. Opera 1984; Helena in Glyndebourne's production of Britten's A Midsummer Night's Dream; Donna Anna in Don Giovanni, Frankfurt Opera 1985 and with Kent Opera 1988; Rosario in Goyescas by Granados 1988, Helena in Midsummer Night's Dream, London Opera 1990; cr. role of Duchess of Argyll in Thomas Adès's Powder Her Face, Cheltenham Int. Music Festival and London 1995; regular engagements including recitals in France, Austria, Belgium, Netherlands, Germany, Scandinavia, Switzerland, Italy, Spain and the USA; Festival appearances include Aix-en-Provence, Spoleto, Bergen, Versailles, Flanders, Netherlands, Prague, Edin. and BBC Promenade concerts; masterclasses Pears-Britten School, Aldeburgh, Trinity Coll. of Music, London, Dartington Summer Festival, Meridian TV. *Recordings include:* Vespro della Beata Vergine 1610 (Monteverdi), Acis and Galatea (Handel), A Child of Our Time (Tippett), three recital discs of French, Spanish and Mozart songs, Quatre Chansons Françaises (Britten), Trois Poèmes de Mallarmé (Ravel), Chants d'Auvergne (Canteloube), Les Illuminations (Britten), Bachianas Brasileiras No. 5 (Villa Lobos), Cabaret Classics with John Constable, Knoxville-Summer of 1915 (Barber), South of the Border (Down Mexico Way...) arranged by Christopher Palmer for Jill Gomez, Britten's Blues (songs by Britten and Cole Porter); première recordings of Cantiga – The Song of Inês de Castro commissioned by her from David Matthews, Seven Early Songs (Mahler), A Spanish Songbook (with John Constable), The Knot Garden

(Tippett), Miss Julie (William Alwyn), Powder Her Face (Thomas Adés). *Address:* 16 Milton Park, London, N6 5QA, England. *Telephone:* (20) 8348-4193 (home); (1954) 267353 (home). *Fax:* (20) 8348-4193 (home). *E-mail:* jillgomez@btopenworld.com (home).

GOMEZ-MARTINEZ, Miguel-Angel; Conductor and Composer; b. 17 Sept. 1949, Granada, Spain. *Education:* Studied at the Granada and Madrid Conservatories, in USA and Vienna with Hans Swarowsky. *Career:* Conducted opera in Lucerne, Berlin, Frankfurt, Munich and Hamburg, at Covent Garden in London, Paris, Geneva, Berne, Houston, Chicago, Florence, Rome, Venice and Palermo; Resident Conductor for Berlin Deutsche Oper, 1973–77, and Vienna Staatsoper, 1977–82; Festivals in Berlin, Vienna, Munich, Macerata in Italy, Granada, Santander, San Sebastián, Savonlinna in Finland and Helsinki; Repertoire of over 50 operas including works by Mozart, Puccini, Rossini, Verdi and Wagner; Conductor for Radiotelevision Española Orchestra, 1984–87; Artistic Director and Chief Conductor, Teatro Lirico Nacional Madrid, 1985–91; General Musikdirektor, Nationaltheater Mannheim and Chief Conductor of the Nationaltheater Orchestra, 1990–93; Chief Conductor of Hamburg Symphony, 1992–, and General Music Director of the Finnish National Opera, Helsinki, 1993–; Concerts with most major orchestras in Europe, Far East and America; Chief Conductor, Orchestra of Valencia. *Compositions include:* Suite Burlesca; Sinfonia del Descubrimiento, first performed in 1992, at Mozart Saal, Rosengarten, Mannheim; Five Canciones sobre poemas de Alonso Gamo, for soprano and orchestra, first performed Grosse Musikhalle, Hamburg, 1996. *Current Management:* Balmer & Dixon Management AG, Kreuzstrasse 82, 8032 Zürich, Switzerland. *Telephone:* (43) 244-8644. *Fax:* (43) 244-8649. *Website:* www.badix.ch.

GONDA, Anna; Singer (Mezzo-soprano); b. Jan. 1950, Miskole, Hungary. *Education:* Studied at Franz Liszt Academy in Budapest and in Berlin. *Career:* Debut: Sang Gluck's Orpheus in Berlin, 1976; Sang at Rostock, 1976–78, Vienna Staatsoper from 1981 notably on tour to Japan in 1986 and at Salzburg Festival in 1984 in the premiere of Un Re in Ascolto by Berio; Appeared in Zigeunerbaron at Zürich Opera conducted by Nikolaus Harnoncourt in 1990; Lieder recitals and concerts in Austria, France and Switzerland; Other roles include Verdi's Azucena, Ulrica, Mistress Quickly, Amneris, Maddalena and Preziosilla, Wagner's Erda and Brangaene, Marina in Boris Godunov, Clytemnestra and Penelope in Il Ritorno d'Ulisse; Vienna Staatsoper 1995–96 as Erda, Ulrica and Zulma in L'Italiana in Algeri. *Recordings include:* Zulma in L'Italiana in Algeri; Margret in Wozzeck. *Address:* c/o Opernhaus Zürich, Falkenstrasse 1, 8008 Zürich, Switzerland.

GONDEK, Juliana (Kathleen); Singer (Soprano); b. Pasadena, California, USA; 1 d. *Education:* Violin study; BM, 1975, MM, 1977, University of Southern California School of Music; Britten-Pears School of Advanced Musical Studies, Aldeburgh, England. *Career:* Debut: San Diego Opera; Sang Contessa in Le nozze di Figaro with Netherlands Opera in 1986, Heroines in The Tales of Hoffmann in 1986, Alcina in 1987 at Opera Theatre of St Louis, title role in Bianca e Falliero at Greater Miami Opera in 1987, Fiordiligi in Così fan tutte at Hawaii Opera in 1989, Vitelia in La Clemenza di Tito for Scottish Opera in 1991, title role in Beatrice di Tenda in 1991, Elvira at Seattle Opera in 1991 and Gismonda in Othone, 1992; Zenobia in Radamisto, 1993; Title role in Esther, 1994; Ginevra in Ariodante at the Handel Festival, Göttingen, 1995; Aspasia in Mozart's Mitridate, 1993; Leyla in Bright Sheng's The Song of Majnun with San Francisco Symphony, 1992; Triple role of Diane Feinstein/Harvey's Mama/The Hooker in world premiere of Harvey Milk with Houston Grand Opera, New York City Opera and San Francisco Opera, 1995–96; Ela in world premiere of Dreamkeepers by David Carlson with Utah Opera, 1996; Title role in the world premiere of Hopper's Wife by Stewart Wallace and Michael Korie, 1997; Ginevra in Ariodante with Dallas Opera, 1998; Sang Mozart's Countess at Cologne, 2000; Appeared in concert in Canada, USA and in Europe; Appeared as soloist in Edinburgh, Caramoor, Marlboro, Mostly Mozart, Newport, Lincoln Center, Göttingen and Avignon Festivals and as recitalist in USA and Europe; Sang as soloist with New York Philharmonic, Minnesota Orchestra, symphonies of St Louis, San Francisco, Montreal, Toronto, Detroit, Dallas, Seattle, Indianapolis and Baltimore; Philharmonia Baroque and Freiburger Barock Orchestras; Professor of Voice and Opera Studies, University of California at Los Angeles, 1997–. *Recordings:* As Gismonda in Handel's Ottone, 1992; Video, Live From The Met, as 1st Lady in Die Zauberflöte with Metropolitan Opera, 1992; As Zenobia in Handel's Radamisto, 1993; Fortuna in Handel's Giustino, 1994; Ginevra in Handel's Ariodante, 1995; Premiere recording of Harvey Milk with San Francisco Symphony Orchestra and Chorus under Donald Runnicles. *Current Management:* Colbert Artists Management Inc. *Address:* c/o Colbert Artists Management Inc, 111 West 57th Street, New York, NY 10019, USA.

GONG, Dong-Jian; Opera Singer (bass); b. 1 Dec. 1957, Nanchang, China. *Education:* Shanghai Conservatory of Music, China, 1980–84;

Artist Diploma, Indiana University, USA, 1988–90; Opera music Theatre International, USA, 1991. *Career:* Debut: Colline in La Bohème, Vienna Staatsoper, 1991; Colline, Opera de Nice, France, Sparafucile in Rigoletto, Bilbao, Spain, Ramfis in Aida with Palm Beach Opera, Giorgio in I Puritani with Opera Malaga, Spain and as Timur with the Teatro Municipal in Santiago, 1992–93; Asdrubila, an opera premiered at 1993 Barcelona Summer Festival; Zaccaria in Nabucco with the Opera de Bellas Artes in Mexico City, Ferrando in Il Trovatore with Minnesota Opera, Raimondo in Lucia di Lammermoor with the New Jersey State Opera, Il Frate in Don Carlos in Bilbao, 1993–94; Sparafucile in Rigoletto, Timur in Turandot and Colline in a new production of La Bohème, he also appeared with the Virginia Opera as Basilio in Il Barbiere di Siviglia, performed the Boatsman in Bruch's Odysseus with the American Symphony Orchestra at Avery Fisher Hall, soloist in the Verdi Requiem with the Kennedy Opera, 1995–96; Returned to Vancouver Opera as Zaccaria in Nabucco, concert appearances included a performance of Beethoven's Missa Solemnis with the Richmond Symphony, 1994–95; Performances of Philip II in Don Carlos with the Kentucky Opera, the Grand Inquisitor in Don Carlos with Opéra de Lyon and Opéra de Nice, Ramfis with Oper der Stadt Köln and performances in Munich, Amsterdam and Hong Kong in the role of Kublai Khan in Marco Polo, 1996–97; Oper der Stadt Köln for performances of Ramfis in Aida, 1997–98; Ramfis at the Deutsche Oper Berlin, performances of Beethoven's Symphony No. 9 with the Columbus Symphony Orchestra, Biterolf in Tannhäuser in Seville, Oroveso in Norma with Opera Memphis, soloist in the Verdi Requiem with the Nashville Symphony, 1998–99. *Recordings:* Marco Polo by Tan Dun as Kublai Khan. *Current Management:* Pieter G. Alferink Artists Management Amsterdam BV, Apollolaan 181, 1077 AT Amsterdam, Netherlands.

GONLEY, Stephanie; violinist; b. 1966, England. *Education:* Chetham School of Music, Guildhall School of Music, with Dorothy DeLay at Juilliard School and in Berlin. *Career:* Mozart Concertos with Manchester Camerata, Mendelssohn, Walton, Brahms and Bruch with Royal Philharmonic, Walton with the London Philharmonic Orchestra and Beethoven in the Netherlands with Adrian Leaper; Further engagements with English Chamber Orchestra in 1990, Philharmonia and Halle, at Montpellier Festival and in Hong Kong, Belgium and Canada, played Vivaldi's Four Seasons with English Chamber Orchestra at Festival Hall in 1993; Prom Debut in 1995 with BBC Scottish Symphony Orchestra; Leader, English Chamber Orchestra; (Masterclasses at Banff, Canada, Aspen, USA and Prussia Cove, Cornwall, England); Co-Founded the Vellinger String Quartet in 1990; (Particpated in master classes with the Borodin Quartet, Pears-Britten School in 1991); Concerts at Ferrara Musica Festival in Italy and debut on South Bank with the London premiere of Roberts Simpson's 13th Quartet; BBC Radio 3 debut in 1991; Season 1994–95 with concerts in London, Germany, Spain, USA, Italy at Sweden, Paris, at Davos Festival, Switzerland; Played at Wigmore Hall several times (with Haydn Op 54 No. 2, Gubaidulina and Beethoven Op 59 No. 2), and at the Purcell Room with Haydn's Seven Last Words. *Recordings include:* Elgar's Quartet and Quintet with Piers Lane. *Honours:* Winners of 1994 London International String Quartet Competition. *Current Management:* Robert Gilder & Co., Enterprise House, 59–65 Upper Ground, London, SE1 9PQ, England. *Telephone:* (20) 7928-9008. *Fax:* (20) 7928-9755. *E-mail:* rgilder@robert-gilder.com.

GONNEVILLE, Michel; Lecturer and Composer; b. 1950, Montreal, Canada. *Education:* Studied piano at an early age; Studied at Ecole de Musique Vincent-d'Indy, 1968–72; BMus, 1972; Doctorate in Composition, University of Montreal. *Career:* Composer, studying analysis and composition with Giles Tremblay at Conservatoire de Musique de Montreal, 1973, obtaining first prizes in Analysis and Composition in 1974 and 1975; Attended Stockhausen's seminars in Darmstadt in 1974 and his composition classes in Cologne for three semesters, also working in the Electronic Studio at Cologne Musikhochschule; Student and Personal Assistant to Henri Pousseur at Liège; His professors included Frederic Rzewski and Joh Fritsch; Returning to Canada in 1978 he lectured on analysis and composition at Montreal and Rimouski Conservatories and at the Universities of Montreal and Ottawa; Professor of Composition and Analysis, Conservatoire de Musique de Montreal. Composed works for Louis-Philippe Pelletier, Michael Laucke, Robert Leroux, Gropus 7, L'Ensemble d'Ondes de Montreal, the SMCQ and a recent work premiered by the Orchestre des Jeunes du Quebec; His works have been performed in Montreal, Quebec, Toronto, Metz, Cologne, Bonn, Liège and Paris and several have been recorded including Adonwe and broadcast by CBC and WDR in Cologne. *Compositions include:* Chute/Parachute for piano and band, 1989; Adonwe for piano and orchestra, 1994; Attirévers le haut par le menu for alto solo, 1995; Le Cheminement de la baleine, 1998. *Address:* 6812 20th Avenue, Montreal, Quebec, H1X 2J7, Canada.

GONZAGA, Otoniel; Singer (Tenor); b. 1944, Philippines. *Career:* Has appeared at opera houses in Europe and North America, 1967–; Engaged at Trier, 1973–77, Frankfurt am Main, 1977–88; Member of Cologne Opera, 1988–; Guest engagements at Stuttgart, Munich (Theater am Gärtnerplatz), Vienna (Volksoper), Barcelona, Berne and Genoa; Sang Otello at Aachen, Edgardo in Lucia di Lammermoor at Cincinnati, 1990; Other roles have included Ferrando, Faust, Almaviva and Luigi in Il Tabarro; Season 1993–94 as Calaf at Bergen and Manrico at Cincinnati; Many concert appearances. *Address:* c/o Stadttheater, Theaterstrasse 1–3, 5100 Aachen, Germany.

GONZALES, Dalmacio; Singer (Tenor); b. 12 May 1945, Olot, Spain. *Education:* Studied in Barcelona and at the Salzburg Mozarteum with Arleen Auger and Paul Schilharsky; Further study with Anton Dermota in Vienna. *Career:* Debut: Teatro Liceo Barcelona in 1978 as Ugo in Parisina by Donizetti; New York City Opera and San Francisco in 1979 as Alfredo and in Rossini's Semiramide and Tancredi; Metropolitan Opera from 1980 as Ernesto in Don Pasquale and later as Almaviva, Fenton and Nemorino; Sang at La Scala Milan and Aix-en-Provence in 1981 in Ariodante and Tancredi, at Pesaro and La Scala, 1984–85 in a revival of Rossini's Il Viaggio a Reims and further appearances in Rome, Los Angeles, Chicago, Berlin, Zürich, Trieste and London; Sang Ford in Salieri's Falstaff at Parma in 1987 and at Munich Festival in 1990 as Catullus in Catulli Carmina by Orff; Sang Ugo at the 1990 Maggio Musicale, Florence; Other roles include Rossini's Argiro in Tancredi, Idreno in Semiramide, Lindoro, James V in La Donna del Iago and Rinaldo in Armida; Season 1992 as Nemorino at Barcelona and Demetrio in Rossini's Demetrio e Polibio at Martina Franca; Madrid 1995, as Stravinsky's Oedipus; Sang Calaf in Turandot at the reopening of the Teatre Liceo, Barcelona, 1999. *Recordings:* Verdi's Requiem, Falstaff and Il Viaggio a Reims; La Donna del Lago by Rossini. *Address:* c/o Teatre alla Scala, Via Filodrammatici 2, 20121 Milan, Italy.

GONZALEZ, Carmen; Singer (Mezzo-soprano); b. 16 April 1939, Vallodid, Spain. *Career:* Studied at the Madrid Conservatory and with Magda Piccarolo and Rodolfo Celetti in Milan. *Recordings:* Orlando Furioso by Vivaldi; Anacreon by Cherubini. *Address:* c/o Netherlands Opera, Waterlooplein 22, 1011 PG, Amsterdam, Netherlands.

GONZALEZ, Manuel; Singer (Baritone); b. 30 April 1944, Madrid, Spain. *Education:* Studied at the Madrid Conservatoire. *Career:* Debut: Théâtre de la Monnaie Brussels in the lyric baritone repertoire at opera houses in Brussels, Antwerp, Ghent and Liège; Guest engagements in Dortmund, Essen, Frankfurt, Hamburg, Stuttgart and Mannheim; Barcelona, Lisbon, Paris, Nice, Marseilles and Geneva, and at the Vienna Volksoper; Sang roles in operas by Donizetti, Bizet, Mozart, Puccini, Rossini, Massenet and Verdi; Wagner's Wolfram von Eschenbach and Tarquinius in Britten's The Rape of Lucretia; Wexford Festival 1973, in Donizetti's L'Ajo nell'imbarazzo (The Tutor in a Fix); Many concert appearances. *Address:* c/o Théâtre de la Monaie, 4 Leopoldstrasse, 1000 Brussels, Belgium.

GOODALL, Howard (Lindsay); Composer and Broadcaster; b. 26 May 1958, London, England. *Education:* Chorister, New College, Oxford; ARCO, 1975; Music Scholar, Christ Church, Oxford (MA Hons). *Career:* Composer TV themes and scores: Blackadder, Mr Bean, Vicar of Dibley, The Gathering Storm, The Borrowers, Red Dwarf; Composer and Performer in: Rowan Atkinson in Revue, the United Kingdom Tours 1977–87, World Tour 1982, West End, 1981, 1986, Broadway, 1986; TV programmes (writer and presenter); Howard Goodall's Big Bangs; Howward Goodall's Oragn Works; Howward Goodall's Chorla Works; Howward Goodall's Great Dates; BBC Choir of the Year; mem, BASCA; Liberal Club; PRS; MU; European Movement; Liberal Club. *Compositions:* Musicals: The Hired Man, with Melvyn Bragg, 1984; Girlfriends, 1987; Days of Hope, 1991; Silas Marner, 1991, The Kissing-Dance, 1999, The Dreaming, 2001; Choral: In Memoriam Anne Frank; Missa Aedis Christi; Psalm 23; Dover Beach, Jubilate Deo, I am not I, Marlborough Canticles, Salisbury Canticles. *Honours:* Ivor Novello Award, Best Musical, 1985; BAFTA Huw Weldon Award, 2001; Peabody Award for Journalism & Mass Communication; IMZ TV Best Arts Documentary Award; British Television Advertising Craft Award Best Original Music. *Current Management:* PBJ Management. *Address:* 7 Soho Square, London, W1D 3DQ, England. *Telephone:* (20) 7287-1112. *Website:* www.howardgoodall.co.uk.

GOODALL, Valorie; Singer (Soprano), Voice Teacher and Opera Director; b. 23 Sept. 1936, Waco, Texas, USA; m. William P Mooney, 21 Jan 1962, 2 s. *Education:* BM cum laude, Baylor University, 1958; MM, University of Colorado, 1959. *Career:* Debut: Graz Opera House, Austria; Leading Lyric Soprano, roles of Mimi, Micaela, Mélisande, Zdenka, Composer, Fiordiligi, Cherubino, Graz Opera; Performances at opera houses of Graz, Geneva, Bern, Theater an der Wien in Vienna, Prague; Star/producer, State museum tour of Venus and Adonis with early instruments, New Jersey, USA, 1981; Founder/director of Opera at Rutgers; Performer in oratorio, song recital and musical theatre;

Resident Stage Director: New England Lyric Operetta, Stamford, Conn. *Recordings:* Land des Lächelns by Lehar, opposite Giuseppe di Stefano, London Records. *Address:* Voice Department, Mason Gross School of the Arts, Rutgers University, New Brunswick, NJ 08903, USA.

GOODE, Richard Stephen, DipMus, BSc; American pianist; b. 1 June 1943, New York, NY; m. Marcia Weinfeld 1987. *Education:* Mannes Coll. of Music, Curtis Inst., studied with Nadia Reisenberg and Rudolf Serkin. *Career:* debut, New York Young Concert Artists 1962; Carnegie Hall recital début 1990; founding mem., Chamber Music Soc. of the Lincoln Center; mem. Piano Faculty, Mannes Coll. of Music 1969–; concerts and recitals in USA, Europe, Japan, South America, Australia, Far East; has played with Baltimore, Boston, Chicago, Cleveland, New York, Philadelphia, Berlin Radio, Finnish Radio and Bamberg Symphony Orchestras, New York, Los Angeles, Baltimore, Orpheus, Philadelphia, ECO and Royal Philharmonic Orchestras. *Honours:* Young Concert Artists Award, First Prize Clara Haskil Competition 1973, Avery Fischer Prize 1980, Grammy Award (with clarinettist Richard Stoltzman). *Current Management:* Frank Salomon Associates, 201 W 54th Street, Apt 1C, New York, NY 10019, USA. *Address:* 12 East 87th Street, Apt 5A, New York, NY 10128, USA (office).

GOODING, Julia; Singer (Soprano); b. 1965, England. *Education:* Studied at the Guildhall School. *Career:* Opera appearances at the Innsbruck Festival and the Opéra-Comique, Paris; Dido and Aeneas in Mexico; Concerts with such conductors as Malgoire, Minkowski, Leonhardt, Bruggen and Mackerras in Europe, North America and the Far East. *Recordings include:* King Arthur; Handel's Belshazzar; Handel's Teseo; Purcell Odes; Monteverdi's Orfeo; Blow Venus and Adonis. *Address:* c/o Ron Gonsalves Management, 7 Old Town, Clapham, London, SW4 0JT, England.

GOODLOE, Robert; Singer (Baritone); b. 5 Oct. 1936, St Petersburg, Florida, USA. *Education:* Studied at Simpson College Indianola (Iowa) and with Harvey Brown and Armen Boyajian. *Career:* Debut: Des Moines, Iowa, 1963, as Mozart's Figaro; Has sung principally at the Metropolitan Opera, also in Hartford, Baltimore, Philadelphia and San Francisco; Roles include Puccini's Scarpia, Michele and Marcello; Enrico (Lucia di Lammermoor); Mercutio in Roméo et Juliette; Germont in La Traviata and Paolo in Simon Boccanegra. *Address:* c/o Metropolitan Opera, Lincoln Center, NY 10023, USA.

GOODMAN, Alfred; Composer and Musicologist; b. 1 March 1920, Berlin, Germany; m. Renate Roessig, 14 July 1966, 1 s. *Education:* BS, Columbia College, New York; MA, Composition, Musicology, Columbia University; PhD, Technische Universität, Berlin. *Career:* Editor, Westminster Records, New York City; Composer, Movietone, New York City; Music Editor, Bavarian Broadcasting Commission; Lecturer, Academy of Music, Munich Service, 1971–; Lecturer, Academy of Music, College of Music, Munich, 1976–. Gave lecture at Arnold Schoenberg Symposium, Duisburg, Germany, 1993. *Compositions:* Psalm XII; The Audition, opera in 1 act; Pro Memoria for orchestra; Individuation, symphonic work; Chamber works, songs, choral compositions, television and film scores, orchestral works; The Lady and the Maid, opera in 1 scene; Across the Board for brass ensemble (for Locke Brass Consort, London); Brassology for Eleven (for Brunn Brass Ensemble, Czechoslovakia); Works for organ and brass; Timpani; Works for organ and saxophone, organ and flute or trumpet; Universe of Freedom-Orchestrology, 1991; Orchestrette in 7 parts, 1992; Orchesterology, 1994; Reflections: Manhattan Survey, for orchestra, 1997. *Publications:* Musik im Blut; Lexikon: Musik von A-Z; Die Amerikanischen Schuler Franz Liszts; Dictionary of Musical Terms, 1982. *Address:* Bodenstedt Strasse 31, 81241 Munich, Germany.

GOODMAN, Craig (Stephen); Flautist, Conductor and Educator; b. 6 July 1957, Pittsburgh, Pennsylvania, USA. *Education:* BA, Yale University, 1978; MM, Yale School of Music, 1979; Private study with Marcel Moyse and theory with Narcis Bonet. *Career:* Debut: Konzerthus, Vienna, Austria, 1975; Solo Flutist, Opera Company, Philadelphia, 1978–79; Freelance, American Symphony, New York City Ballet, St Luke's Chamber Orchestra, Musica Aeterna, 1979–86; Solo engagements, Australia, Europe, USA; Musical Director, The Players of the New World, New York; Chamber Music performances with L'Ensemble, New York City, Bach Aria Group, New York City and Ensemble i, Vienna, Austria; Solo videos of Bach and Gossec, WYNC Television, New York; Featured artist on Sunday Morning with Charles Kuratt, CBS television. *Recordings:* Bach Aria Group, Bach Brandenburg Concerto No. 4 with James Buswell, Samuel Baron and Festival Strings, Ensemble I recording, Bach Trio Sonata in G for 2 flutes and continuo; Musical Heritage Society recording, Morton Gould's Concerto for wind quartet, piano and violin.

GOODMAN, Erica; Harpist; b. 19 Jan. 1948, Toronto, Canada. *Education:* Royal Conservatory of Music, Toronto; National Music Camp, Interlochen, Michigan; Univ. of Southern California, Los Angeles; Curtis Institute of Music, Philadelphia. *Career:* debut, Alice Tully Hall-

Lincoln Center, New York, 1972; child prodigy, accompanied opera singer Teresa Stratas on national television at the age of 13, 1961; played for Pres. Kennedy at the White House, 1962; youngest musician ever to join the Toronto Musicians' Asscn, 1962; mem. of Toronto and CBC Symphony Orchestras, 1962–66; conducted by Igor Stravinsky, 1964; soloist, Philadelphia Orchestra, 1968; toured Japan with flautist Robert Aitkin at invitation of Toru Takemitsu to perform his work, 1995; performed at the Royal Palace in Stockholm with horn player Sören Hermansson, 1996; one of the most active studio harpists on the continent and played on numerous scores of films, television and radio productions. *Recordings include:* Erica Goodman In Concert; Erica Goodman And Friends; The Virtuoso Harp; Flute and Harp; Erica Goodman Plays Canadian Harp Music; Horn And Harp Odyssey; Trio Lyra. *Address:* 9 York Ridge Road, Toronto, ON M2P 1R8, Canada. *E-mail:* erigo78@hotmail.com. *Website:* www.ericagoodman.tripod.com.

GOODMAN, Roy; Conductor, Director and Violinist; b. 26 Jan. 1951, Guildford, Surrey, England. *Education:* Chorister, King's College, Cambridge, 1959–64; Royal College of Music, 1968–70; Berkshire College of Education, 1970–71. *Career:* From 1971 successively: Head of Music at two comprehensive schools, Senior String Tutor for Berkshire, Director of Music at University of Kent and Director of Early Music at Royal Academy of Music; Co-Director of the Parley of Instruments, 1979–86; Principal Conductor of the Hanover Band, 1986–94; Seven tours of USA, 1988–94 including Lincoln Center and Carnegie Hall; Musical Director of the European Union Baroque Orchestra, 1988–; Guest Conductor with Finnish and Swedish Radio, Lahti, Tampere, Ulster, Norrköping, Reykjavík and Stavanger Symphony Orchestras, Royal Liverpool and Rotterdam Philharmonic Orchestras, English Northern Philharmonia, Orchestre de Bretagne, New Queen's Hall Orchestra, Scottish, English, Swedish, Netherlands Radio, Netherlands, Geneva, Lausanne and Manitoba Chamber Orchestras, City of London Sinfonia, Västerås Sinfonietta, German Handel Soloists, Freiburg Baroque Orchestra, Netherlands Wind Ensemble and the Amsterdam Bach Soloists; Conducted complete Beethoven Symphonies in Hannover, Handel's Tamerlano in Paris and Aldeburgh and with Opera North in Leeds, Scipione, Tamerlano, Ezio and Amadigi in Karlsruhe, Mozart's Bastien and Bastienne in Portugal, Don Giovanni in Belfast, La Clemenza di Tito for Flanders Opera, Gluck's Orfeo for English National Opera at the London Coliseum and Trädgården by Jonas Forssell at the Drottningholm Court Theatre in Sweden; Revival of Arne's Artaxerxes, London 1995; Appointed Principal Conductor of Umeå Symphony Orchestra from July 1996; Conducted the New Queen's Hall Orchestra at the Barbican Hall, 1997; La Clemenza di Tito at Antwerp, 1997. *Recordings:* As conductor, violinist and keyboard player, has directed some 100 recordings for various labels of repertoire ranging from Monteverdi to Holst, including major orchestral works by Purcell, Corelli, Bach and Handel, and the symphonies of Haydn, Beethoven, Schubert, Weber, Berwald and Schumann. *Address:* 217 Birchanger Lane, Birchanger, Bishops Stortford, Herts CM23 5QJ, England. *Telephone:* (1279) 647467. *Fax:* (1279) 647467. *E-mail:* roy@roygoodman.com. *Website:* www.roygoodman.com.

GOODWIN, (Trevor) Noël, BA; critic and writer on music and dance; b. 25 Dec. 1927, Fowey, Cornwall, England; m. Anne Mason Myers 1963; one step-s. *Career:* Assistant Music Critic: News Chronicle, 1952–54; Manchester Guardian, 1954–55; Music and Dance Critic, Daily Express, 1956–78; Associate Editor, Dance and Dancers, 1958–; Executive Editor, Music and Musicians, 1963–71; London Dance Critic, International Herald Tribune, Paris, 1978–83;Music Reviews, The Times, 1978–98; London Correspondent, Opera News, New York, 1980–91; Overseas News Editor, 1985–91, Editorial Board, 1991–99, Opera; Planned and presented numerous radio programmes of music and records for BBC Home and World Services since 1954; Frequent contributor to music and arts programmes on Radios 3 and 4. *Publications:* London Symphony, portrait of an orchestra, 1954; A Ballet for Scotland, 1979; A Knight at the Opera (with Geraint Evans), 1984; Royal Opera and Royal Ballet Yearbooks (editor), 1978, 1979, 1980; New Grove Dictionary of Music and Musicians (area editor, writer), 1980; A Portrait of the Royal Ballet (editor), 1988. *Contributions:* Numerous journals and magazines; Encyclopaedica Britannica, 15th edition, 1974; New Grove Dictionary of Music, 1980, 2000; Encyclopaedia of Opera, 1976; New Oxford Companion to Music, 1983; Pipers Enzyklopädie des Musiktheaters, 1986–91; New Grove Dictionary of Opera, 1992; Viking Opera Guide, 1993; International Dictionary of Ballet, 1993; Metropolitan Opera Guide to Recorded Opera, 1993; International Encyclopedia of Dance, 1998; Larousse Dictionnaire de la Danse, 2000; New Dictionary of National Biography, forthcoming. *Address:* 76 Skeena Hill, London SW18 5PN, England.

GOODWIN, Paul; Conductor and Oboist; b. 2 Sept. 1956, England. *Education:* City of London School, Temple Church Choir, Nottingham University; Guildhall School of Music; Vienna Hochschule für Musik. *Career:* Associate Director of the Academy of Ancient Music; Director,

Dartington Festival Baroque Orchestra and the Royal College of Music Baroque Orchestra; Principal Guest Conductor of the English Chamber Orchestra, 1998–2003; Guest engagements with Ulster Orchestra, Hallé, BBC Symphony Orchestra, Scottish Chamber Orchestra, RTE Dublin, CBSO, English Chamber Orchestra, Swedish Chamber Orchestra, Comiische Oper Berlin, Lyon opera Orchestra, Nurenburg Philharmonic, SWR Rundfunk Orchester, Hessiche Rundfunk Orchester, Orchestra National de Lille, European Baroque Orchestra, and in the USA with the Portland Baroque Orchestra and St Pauls Chamber Orchestra; Conducted staged production of the Bach St Matthew Passion in collaboration with Jonathan Miller; Opera productions include Karlsruhe Opera, Opernhaus Halle and Opera North and at the Megaron, Athens; Conducted Handel's Poro at Halle and Il Re Pastore at Leeds, 1998; London Proms 1999, with Haydn's 64th Symphony and excerpts from Handels Triumph of Time and Truth; Featured at the London Proms 1999, 2002 and 2004 with the Academy of Ancient Music. *Recordings:* Solo recordings on the oboe: (Bach, Telemann, Albinoni, Vivaldi, Haydn, Mozart); As a Conductor with the AAM (Mozart, Handel, Schütz and Tavener). *Current Management:* Askonas Holt Ltd, Lonsdale Chambers, 27 Chancery Lane, London, WC2A 1PF, England. *Telephone:* (20) 7400-1700. *Fax:* (20) 7400-1799. *E-mail:* info@askonasholt.co.uk. *Website:* www.askonasholt.co.uk.

GORBENKO, Pavel; Violinist; b. 1956, Moscow, Russia. *Education:* Studied at Gnessin Music Institute with Dr Kiselyev. *Career:* Co-founder, Amistad Quartet, 1973, now Tchaikovsky Quartet; Many concerts in Russia with repertoire including works by Haydn, Mozart, Beethoven, Schubert, Brahms, Tchaikovsky, Borodin, Prokofeiv, Shostakovich, Bart ók, Barber, Bucci, Golovin and Tikhomirov; Recent concert tours to: Mexico; Italy; Germany. *Recordings include:* Recitals for a US-Russian company. *Honours:* Winner with Amistad Quartet: Bela Bart ók Festival, 1976; Bucchi Competition, Rome, 1990. *Address:* c/o Sonata (Tchaikovsky Quartet), 11 Northpark Street, Glasgow G20 7AA, Scotland.

GORCHAKOVA, Galina; Singer (Soprano); b. 1 March 1962, Novokuznetsk, Russia. *Education:* Novosibirsk Academy and Conservatory. *Career:* Appearances with Sverdlovsk Opera, 1988–, as Tatyana, Butterfly, Yaroslavna in Prince Igor, Santuzza, Katerina (Lady Macbeth of Mtsensk), Liu, Militrissa (The Legend of Tsar Saltan), Tamara (The Demon by Rubinstein), and Clara in Prokofiev's The Duenna; Guest appearances elsewhere in Russia, notably as the Trovatore Leonora, Yaroslavna and Lisa in The Queen of Spades at Maryinsky Theatre; Sang Renata in The Fiery Angel by Prokofiev at 1991 Promenade Concerts (British debut), at St Petersburg, and at Covent Garden (British stage premiere of the opera in the original Russian), 1992; Sang Natalya in concert performance of Tchaikovsky's The Oprichnik Edinburgh, 1992, Renata at the Metropolitan, New York; Season 1995 as Tosca at Covent Garden and Butterfly in New York, returned to London as Tosca, 1997; Leonora in La Forza del Destino at St Petersburg, 1998 and Munich 1999; Australian debut at 1999 Sydney Festival; Season 2000 as Tosca at Washington, Santuzza at Buenos Aries and Tatiana in Florence. *Honours:* Prizewinner, Mussorgsky and Glinka Competitions. *Current Management:* Askonas Holt Ltd, Lonsdale Chambers, 27 Chancery Lane, London, WC2A 1PF, England. *Telephone:* (20) 7400-1700. *Fax:* (20) 7400-1799. *E-mail:* info@askonasholt.co.uk. *Website:* www.askonasholt.co.uk.

GORDEI, Irina; Singer (Soprano); b. 1968, Russia. *Education:* Graduated Byelorusia State Academy 1991. *Career:* Ekaterinburg Opera and Ballet Theatre from 1993, as Tosca, Aida, Amelia (Un ballo in Maschera), Lisa (The Queen of Spades) and Verdi's Elisabeth and Lady Macbeth; Teatro Comunale, Floreance, 1994 as Amelia (repeated at Vienna Staatsoper 1995); Appearances with Kirov Opera, St Petersburg, from 1999, including Verdi season at Covent Garden, 2001; Concert repertoire includes Verdi Requiem and works by Shostakovich (Festival Medal, 1997). *Honours:* Prizewinner, International F. Vignas Competition, Barcelona, 1993. *Address:* c/o Kirov Opera, Mariinsky Theatre, 1 Theatre Square, St Petersburg, Russia.

GORDIEJUK, Marian (Stanislaw Wlodzimierz); Composer, Music Theory Lecturer, Music Journalist and Musicologist; b. 9 Feb. 1954, Bydgoszcz, Poland; m. 2 July 1977, 1 s., 2 d. *Education:* State College of Music, Łódź, Pedagogic studies with Assistant Professor Antoni Kedra, 1976; Studies in Music Theory under Professor Franciszek Wesolowski, 1977; Studies in conducting vocal-instrumental groups with Professor Zygmunt Gzella, 1978; Studies in Composition, with Professor Jerzy Bauer, 1979. *Compositions include:* Suite, Birds, for two transverse flutes (Łódź) 1976, published: Edition Agencja Autorska Warszawa, 1986, Contemporary Polish Music, Series of Chamber Music Compositions; Games for flute and harp (Gdansk) 1987, recorded: Polskie Radio, Gdansk, 1987; Children's Quart Miniature for Oboe or Flute and Piano (Łódź) 1987, recorded: Telewizja Polska, Łódź, 1987; String Quartet (with amplifier) Gdansk, 1991. *Address:* ul Tczewska 12, 85-382 Bydgoszcz, Poland.

GORDON, Alexandra; Singer (Soprano); b. 1945, Dannevirke, New Zealand. *Education:* Studied at London Opera Centre and with Walter Midgley. *Career:* Debut: Sang First Boy in Die Zauberflöte and Despina in Così fan tutte for New Zealand Opera, aged 19; Sang with Opera for All at Glyndebourne and with Scottish Opera, notably as the Queen of Night and Flotow's Martha, and in The Nightingale by Stravinsky; Many concert appearances and radio broadcasts; Sang Delia in new production of Rossini's Il Viaggio a Reims, Covent Garden, 1992. *Honours:* Friends of Covent Garden Scholarship, at London Opera Centre. *Address:* c/o New Zealand National Opera, State Opera House, PO Box 6588, Tel Aro, Wellington, New Zealand.

GORDON, David Jamieson; American concert and opera singer (tenor); b. 7 Dec. 1947, Philadelphia; m. Barbara Bixby 1969. *Education:* College of Wooster, McGill University, Conservatoire de Quebec, Canada. *Career:* debut with Lyric Opera of Chicago, 1973; frequent appearances with North American and European orchestras and opera companies, including Metropolitan Opera, Lyric Opera of Chicago, San Francisco Opera, Hamburg Staatsoper, Boston Symphony, Philadelphia Orchestra, Cleveland Orchestra, Los Angeles Philharmonic; Specialist in music by J. S. Bach; Also appears regularly as master class teacher and lecturer; Bach Festivals of Bethlehem, Carmel, Oregon and Winter Park (USA) Stuttgart, Tokyo. *Recordings:* Bach Magnificat–R Shaw/Atlantic Symphony; Acis and Galatea, Seattle Symphony; Pulcinella, St Paul Chamber Orchestra; other recordings on Telarc, London Decca, Delos, RCA Red Seal and Nonesuch/Electra. *Current Management:* Thea Dispeker Inc, 59 East 54 Street, New York, NY 10022, USA. *Address:* 84 South Clinton Street, Doylestown, PA 18901, USA.

GORECKI, Henryk Mikolaj; Polish composer; b. 6 Dec. 1933, Czernica, near Rybnik; m. Jadwiga Gorecki 1959; two c. *Education:* Katowice State Higher School of Music, under B. Szabelski. *Career:* docent, Faculty of Composition, Rector 1975–79, Extraordinary Prof. 1977–, State Higher School of Music, Katowice; mem. Council of Higher Artistic Education, Ministry of Culture and Arts. *Compositions:* Symphony No. 1, for strings and percussion, 1959; Scontri for orchestra, 1960; Concerto for 5 Instruments and String Quartet, 1957; Genesis for instrumental ensemble and soprano, 1963; Cantata for organ, 1968; Canticum Graduum for orchestra, 1989; Ad matrem for soprano, chorus and orchestra, 1971; Symphony No. 2 Copernican, 1972, No. 3 Lamentation Songs, 1976; Beatus Vir for baritone, chorus and orchestra, 1979; Harpsichord Concerto, 1980; Lullabies and Dances for violin and piano, 1982; O Domina Noztra for soprano and organ, 1985/90; Already it is Dusk, String Quartet, 1988; Good Night, for soprano and ensemble, 1990; 2 string quartets, 1988, 1991; Little Requiem for a Certain Polka, for piano and 13 instruments, 1993; Three Fragments for voice and piano, 1996; Little Fantasia for violin and piano, 1997. *Honours:* 1st Prize, Young Composers' Competition, Warsaw for Monologhi, 1960; 1st Prize, Parish Youth Biennale, for 1st symphony, 1961; Prize, UNESCO International Tribune for Composers for Refrain, 1967; for Ad Matrem, 1973; 1st prize, Composers Competition, Szczecin for Kantata, 1968; Prize, Union of Polish Composers, 1970; prize, Committee for Polish Radio and Television, 1974; Prize, Minister of Culture and Arts, 1965, 1969, 1973; State Prize 1st Class for Ad Matrem and Nicolaus Copernicus Symphony, 1978. *Address:* U1 Feliksa kona 4 m 1, 40-133 Katowice, Poland.

GORMLEY, Clare; Soprano; b. 1969, Australia. *Career:* Frequent concert and recital appearances throughout Australia and in Europe; Repertory includes Lieder by Mozart and Schumann, Bach's St Matthew Passion and Goyescas by Granados; Contestant at the 1995 Cardiff Singer of the World Competition; Season 1995–96 as Alexandra in the premiere of The Eighth Wonder, at Sydney and Gretel at Brisbane (also at the Met); Debut with Royal Opera, London, as Despina (1998, also at the New York Met). *Honours:* Winner, Metropolitan Opera Auditions. *Address:* c/o Jennifer Eddy Artists' Management, Suite 11, The Clivedon, 596 St Kilda Road, Melbourne, Victoria 3004, Australia.

GÖRNE, Matthias; Singer (Baritone); b. 1966, Cheminitz, Germany. *Education:* Studied in Liepzig from 1985, then with Fischer-Dieskau and Elisabeth Schwarzkopf. *Career:* Performed with the children's choir at Chemnitz Opera; Sang in Bach's St Matthew Passion under Kurt Masur, Leipzig, 1990; Appearances with Hanns Martin Schneidt and Munich Bach Choir and with NDR Symphony Orchestra Hamburg; Further engagements under Horst Stein, with Bamberg Symphony and in Hindemith's Requiem under Wolfgang Sawallisch; Concerts at Leipzig Gewandhaus under Helmuth Rilling and in Amsterdam and Paris; Lieder recitals with pianist Eric Schneider; Sang title role in Henze's Prinz von Homburg, Cologne, 1992, Marcello in La Bohème at Komische Oper Berlin, 1993; Wolfram in Tannhäuser at Cologne, 1996; Die schöne Müllerin at Bath, 1997; Engaged for Die Zauberflöte at the 1997 Salzburg Festival; Season 1999–2000 as Papageno at Salzburg, Wozzeck for Zürich Opera and Bach's St John Passion in New York; Covent Garden debut 2002, as Wozzeck. *Recordings include:* Winterreise, 1997; Entartate Musik. *Address:* c/o KuenstlerSekretariat am Gasteig, Lothar Schacke, Rosenheimer Str. 52, 81669 Munich, Germany.

GOROKHOVSKAYA, Yevgena; Singer (Mezzo-soprano); b. 1944, Baku, Russia. *Education:* Studied at Leningrad Conservatory. *Career:* Debut: Maly Theatre, Leningrad, as Lehl in The Snow Maiden by Rimsky-Korsakov, 1969; Member, Maryinsky Opera Leningrad (now St Petersburg), 1976–; Roles have included Lubasha in The Tsar's Bride by Rimsky, Eboli (Don Carlos) and Azucena; Guest appearances, Germany, Romania, Spain, France, Greece, USA, Switzerland, Czechoslovakia; On Tour to the United Kingdom, 1991, sang Mme Larina in Eugene Onegin at Birmingham and Marfa in Khovanshchina at Edinburgh Festival; Salzburg Easter Festival 1994 as the Nurse in Boris Godunov. *Recordings:* Several albums. *Address:* c/o Maryinsky Opera and Ballet Theatre, St Petersburg, Russia.

GORR, Rita; Singer (Mezzo-soprano); b. 18 Feb. 1926, Zelzaete, Belgium. *Education:* Studied in Ghent and at the Brussels Conservatory. *Career:* Debut: Antwerp 1949, as Fricka in Die Walküre; Strasbourg Opera 1949–52, as Orpheus, Amneris and Carmen; Paris Opéra-Comique and Opéra debuts 1952, as Charlotte (Werther) and as Magdalene in Die Meistersinger; Bayreuth Festival 1958, as Ortrud and Fricka; La Scala Milan 1960, as Kundry; Covent Garden 1959–71, debut as Amneris; Edinburgh Festival 1961 in Iphigénie en Tauride, with the Covent Garden company; Metropolitan Opera from 1962, as Amneris, Eboli, Santuzza, Azucena and Dalila; London Coliseum 1969, in a concert performance of Roussel's Padmavati (British premiere); Other roles have included Margared (Le Roi d'Ys), Massenet's Hérodiade, the title role in Médée by Cherubini and Didon in Les Troyens by Berlioz; Sang the Mother in Louise by Charpentier at Brussels, 1990; First Prioress in Dialogues des Carmélites at Lyon, 1990 followed by Herodias in Salome; Toronto 1997, in The Carmelites; Sang the Nurse in Eugene Onegin at Barcelona, 1998; Countess in Queen of Spades at Munich, 2001. *Recordings:* Pelléas et Mélisande; Dialogues des Carmélites, Iphigénie en Tauride; Aida, Lohengrin; Louise by Charpentier. *Honours:* Winner, Competition at Verviers, 1946; Winner, Lausanne International Singing Competition, 1952. 21. *Address:* c/o Opéra de Lyon, 9 Quai Jen Moulin, 69001 Lyon, France.

GORRARA, Riccardo (Richard), DipMus; classical guitarist, lutenist and conductor; b. 29 May 1964, Metz, France. *Education:* studied in Italy and England, Guildhall School of Music, Royal Academy of Music, Paris Music College. *Career:* debut in Genoa Cathedral, Italy; appeared in most European halls and festivals, Milan, Rome, Turin, London, Paris, Madrid; Paris Festival, Edinburgh Festival; mem, Royal Philharmonic Society; National Early Music Association; Lute Society; Dutch Lute Society; Brussels Philharmonique Society. *Compositions:* Varied; Music for guitar and lute from 15th Century to present, including Dowland, Frescobaldi, Ferrabosco, Couperin, Weiss, Bach, Sor, etc. *Recordings:* Various major recordings for guitar and lute, particularly works from 15th Century to 20th Century rarely played; 7 Gramophone recordings, also for radio broadcasting; Various national radio stations in Italy, Denmark, Switzerland. *Publications:* contrib. various reviews of Guitar and lute method, technique, interpretation for Italian guitar and music magazines.

GORTON, Susan; Singer (Mezzo-soprano); b. 1946, Cheshire, England. *Education:* Studied at the Royal Manchester College of Music. *Career:* Debut: Feklusha in Katya Kabanova for the Glyndebourne Tour, 1992; Further appearances with GTO, as Filippyevna in Eugene Onegin and Marcellina in Le nozze di Figaro; Glyndebourne Festival 1995–97, as the Chambermaid in The Makropulos Case; Further engagements as Mistress Quickly and Mrs Sedley in Peter Grimes, for English National Opera; Florence Pike in Albert Herring for English Touring Opera, Martha in Faust and Mamma Lucia in Cavalleria Rusticana for Welsh National Opera; Premieres include Julian Grant's A Family Affair for the Almeida Festival and The House of Crossed Desires by John Woolrich for Music Theatre Wales, 1996; Season 1997–98 as the Hostess in Boris Godunov and Grandmother in Jenůfa for WNO, and Mrs Sedley for the Lyric Opera, Chicago. Season 1998–99 Mrs Sedley in Peter Grimes and Mamma Lucia in Cavalleria Rusticana for Welsh National Opera and Chambermaid in The Makropulos Case for Gran Teatre del Liceu; Grandmother Burja in Jenůfa and Auntie in Peter Grimes for Glyndebourne Festival Opera, 2000; Countess in The Queen of Spades, Welsh National Opera, 2000; Mary in Der fliegende Holländer, Lyric Opera of Chicago, 2001; Mrs Herring, Glyndebourne Festival Opera, and Florence Pike, GTO, in Albert Herring, 2002. *Address:* c/o Harlequin Agency Ltd, 203 Fidlas Road, Cardiff CF4 5NA, Wales.

GORTSEVSKAYA, Maria; Singer (Mezzo-soprano); b. 1965, Russia. *Career:* Many appearances in solo recitals in France, Belgium, Germany and Spain; Mariinsky Theatre, St Petersburg, from 1990, as Siebel in Faust, Fyodor in Boris Godunov, Rossini's Rosina, Bizet's Mercédès and roles in The Fiery Angel and War and Peace; Sang Adjutant to Marshal Murat in War and Peace with the Kirov Opera at Covent Garden, 2000;

Appearances as guest with the Kirov in Japan and the USA (Metropolitan Opera). *Address:* c/o Kirov Opera, Mariinsky Square, St Petersburg, Russia.

GORZYNSKA, Barbara, MA; Polish violinist; b. 4 Dec. 1953, Cmielow; d. of Zygmunt and Janina (née Nowak) Gorzynski; m. Ryszard Rasinski 1982; one s. *Education:* Acad. of Music, Łódź. *Career:* debut with Great Symphony Orchestra of Polish Radio 1969; performances as soloist with London Philharmonic Orchestra, Royal Philharmonic Orchestra (UK), Staatskapelle Dresden (Germany), Warsaw Philharmonic Orchestra, English Chamber Orchestra, Halle Orchestra (Germany) 1981–; London debut Royal Festival Hall 1981; Prof. of Violin Acad. of Music, Łódź; Visiting Prof. Hochschule für Musik und Darstellende Kunst, Graz, Austria; recordings with Le Chant du Monde, WIFON, Polskie Nagrania. *Recordings include:* Chopin's Trio in G Minor 1986, Wieniawski's Pieces for Violin and Piano 1988, Mozart's Violin Concerto in D 1991. *Honours:* First Prize and Henryk Szeryng Special Prize Zagreb Int. Violin Competition 1977, First Prize Carl Flesch Int. Violin Competition 1980. *Current Management:* Tennant Artists, Unit 2, 39 Tadema Road, London, SW10 0PZ, England. *Telephone:* (20) 7376-3758. *Fax:* (20) 7351-0679. *E-mail:* info@tennantartists.demon.co.uk. *Address:* Sienkiewicza 101–109 m 48, 90-301 Łódź, Poland.

GOSMAN, Lazar; Violinist and Conductor; b. 27 May 1926, Kiev, USSR; m. Eugenia Gosman, 16 April 1950, 1 s. *Education:* Central Music School, Moscow, 1934–44; Diploma, Honours, Tchaikovsky Conservatory of Music, Moscow, 1945–49. *Career:* Violinist, Leningrad Philharmonic Orchestra; Music Director, Leningrad Chamber Orchestra, 1962–77; Associate Concertmaster, St Louis Symphony, USA, 1977–82; Music Director, Tchaikovsky Chamber Orchestra, formerly Soviet Emigré Orchestra; Professor, Violin, State University of New York, Stonybrook. *Recordings:* Over 40 with Leningrad Chamber Orchestra; Two records with Tchaikovsky Chamber Orchestra. *Current Management:* Herbert Barrett Management, New York. *Address:* 3 East Gate Street, Setauket, NY 11733, USA.

GOSSETT, Philip; Music Professor; b. 27 Sept. 1941; m. 2 c. *Education:* BA, Amherst College, 1958–61, 1962–63; Columbia University, 1961–62; MFA, Princeton University, 1963–65; Research in France and Italy, 1965–67; PhD (1970) Princeton University, 1967–68. *Career:* Teacher, University of Chicago, 1968–, Robert W Reneker Distinguished Service Professor; Radio Programmes for Metropolitan Opera, New York and for WFMT, Chicago; Lectures for Metropolitan Opera, Lyric Opera of Chicago, Chicago Symphony Orchestra, Philadelphia Orchestra, Chicago Chamber Choir, Houston Grand Opera, Teatro la Fenice, Venice, Teatro Communale in Florence, Rossini Opera Festival in Pesaro, Acad. di Santa Cecilia in Rome, colleges and universities; Consultant for National Endowment for Humanities, IL Humanities Council, Social Sciences and Humanities Research Council of Canada and various University Presses; Board of Directors, Chicago Symphony Orchestra; Dean, Division of the Humanities, University of Chicago, 1989–99; Gauss Seminars, Princeton University, 1991; Vocal ornamentation and stylistic advisor for various opera houses and recording companies including: Metropolitan Opera, Teatro dell'Opera in Rome, Rossini Opera Festival in Pesaro, Miami Opera; Fellow, American Academy of Arts and Sciences, 1989–; 'Consulenza musicologica', Verdi Festival, Parma, 2000–; Hambro Visiting Professor of Opera, Oxford University, 2001; President, American Musicological Society, 1994–96; President, Society for Textual Scholarship, 1993–95. *Publications include:* Many books and articles, programme notes for various organisations; General Editor of Edizione critica delle opere di Gioachino Rossini and Works of Giuseppe Verdi and various editorial boards; Critical Edition Rossini Tancredi, 1983, Rossini Ermione with P Brauner, 1995, and Semivanide with A. Zedda, 2001. *Honours:* Honorary member, Academia Filarmonica di Bologna, 1992; DHL, Amherst College, 1993; Grand ufficiale della Repub Italy, 1997; Cavaliere di gran croce, Italy, 1998; Order of Rio Branco, Brazil, 1998; Accademico Onorario, Accademia di Santa Cecilia, Rome, 2003. *Address:* 5810 South Harper Avenue, Chicago, IL 60637, USA.

GOTHONI, Ralf; Pianist, Conductor and Composer; b. 2 May 1946, Rauma, Finland; m. Elina Vähälä, 2 s. *Education:* Sibelius Academy, Helsinki; Folkwang-Hochschule, Essen. *Career:* Soloist with leading orchestras worldwide, guest at major festivals; Debut: Jyvaskyla Festival; Principal Guest Conductor, Turku Philharmonic, 1994–2000; Principal Conductor, English Chamber Orchestra, 2000–; Music Dir Northwest Chamber Orchestra, Seattle, 2001–; Prof. for chamber music, Musikhochschule Hamburg, 1986–96; Hanns Eisler-Hochschule Berlin, 1996–2000; Sibelius-Acad. Helsinki, 1992–; Guest Prof., Royal College of Music, London, 2000–. *Compositions:* 3 chamber operas, chamber music and songsr. *Recordings:* 80 recordings including music by Britten; Piano concerto, Rautavaara; 2 piano concertos, Villa Lobos; Chorus XI Schubert; Chamber music and piano sonatas, Brahms; Piano quartets. *Publications:* Book, The Moment of Creativity, 1997, Does the Moon Rotate, 2001, Piano book, 2003. *Honours:* Gilmore Award, 1994; Pro

Finlandia medal, 1992; Schubert medal, 1977. *Address:* Joachim Friedrichstr 19, 10711, Berlin.

GOTSINDER, Mikhail; Violinist; b. 1950, Moscow, Russia. *Education:* Studied at Moscow Conservatoire with David Oistrakh. *Career:* Co-founder, Amistad Quartet, 1973, now Tchaikovsky Quartet; Many concerts in Russia with repertoire including works by Haydn, Mozart, Beethoven, Schubert, Brahms, Tchaikovsky, Borodin, Prokofiev, Shostakovich, Bartók, Barber, Bucci, Golovin and Tikhomirov; Recent concert tours to: Mexico; Italy; Germany. *Recordings include:* Recitals for a US-Russian company; All Tchaikovsky's quartet works. *Honours:* Winner with Amistad Quartet: Bela Bartók Festival, 1976; Bucchi Competition, Rome, 1990. *Address:* c/o Sonata (Tchaikovsky Quartet), 11 Northpark Street, Glasgow G20 7AA, Scotland.

GOTTLIEB, Gordon; Percussionist, Conductor and Composer; b. 23 Oct. 1948, Brooklyn, NY, USA. *Education:* total musicianship with James Wimer, 1961–71; High School of Performing Arts, 1966; timpani and percussion with Saul Goodman, 1966–71; BMus, 1970, MMus, 1971, Juilliard School of Music. *Career:* extensive performing with New York Philharmonic, including solo appearances in 1974 and 1986; commissioning and performing new works for piano and percussion with brother Jay, active in contemporary music and has played with Contemporary Chamber Ensemble, Speculum Musicae, the Juilliard Ensemble, the Group for Contemporary Music and others; as conductor performed the New York premiere of Vesalii Icones by Peter Maxwell Davies and made his Carnegie Hall debut conducting William Walton's Facade with Anna Russell narrating, 1981; conducted Histoire du Soldât of Stravinsky with L'Ensemble and Shaker Loops of John Adams at the Santa Fe Chamber Musical Festival, 1986; performed with Stevie Wonder, Ray Charles, Patti LaBelle, Tony Bennett, Paula Abdul, Michael Bolton, Bette Midler, Sarah Vaughan, Quincy Jones, Al Jarreau, Paul Winter; mem. Percussive Arts Society, NARAS, Recording Musicians' Asscn. *Compositions:* Graines gemellaires, improvisation 1; Traversées, improvisation 2, Saudades do Brasil; The River Speaker; Improvisations with Jay Gottlieb; Ritual Dancer; Fanfare, with Paul Winter; various jingles. *Recordings:* History, Michael Jackson; Kingdom of the Sun, film with Sting; Bulletproof Heart, with Grace Jones; A Secret Life, with Marianne Faithfull; Romulus Hunt, My Romance, with Carly Simon; Sostice Live!, Prayer for the Wild Things, with Paul Winter; Pete, Pete Seeger; many films and jingles; Bartók, Sonata for 2 Pianos; Histoire du Soldât, I Stravinsky; Two Against Nature, Steely Dan (four Grammy awards, including Album of the Year 2001); Everything Must Go, Steely Dan, 2003. *Publications:* The Percussion of Carnival, for Modern Percussionist magazine, 1984; World Influences: Africa and South India, 1985; three articles on studio playing, 1985. *Honours:* Martha Baird Rockefeller Grant, 1980; four Grammy Awards, including for Paul Winters, Prayer for the Wild Things, 1994, Pete Seeger, Pete; NARAS Most Valuable Player Award, New York Studios, 1989; Meet the Composer Grant, 1989. *E-mail:* gorgot@earthlink.net.

GOTTLIEB, Jack S.; American composer; b. 12 Oct. 1930, New Rochelle, NY. *Education:* Queens Coll., Brandeis Univ., Univ. of Illinois, Berkshire Music Center with Aaron Copland, Boris Blacher, also studied with Karol Rathaus, Irving Fine. *Career:* Asst to Leonard Bernstein, New York Philharmonic 1958–66; Music Dir, Temple Israel, St Louis 1970–73; composer-in-residence, Hebrew Union Coll. 1973, Prof. at its New York School of Sacred Music 1975; Publications Dir, Amberson Enterprises 1977; consultant for the Bernstein Estate and Ed., Prelude, Fugue & Riffs, the Bernstein Newsletter; fmr Pres., American Soc. for Jewish Music; mem. ASCAP. *Compositions include:* orchestral works: Articles of Faith for orchestra and memorable voices 1965, Psalmistry 1979, Scenes from the Song of Songs (cantata) 1997; chamber works: String Quartet 1954, Twilight Crane for woodwind quintet and narrator 1961, revised 2000, Sessionals for brass quintet 1998; piano and organ: Piano Sonata 1960, The Silent Flickers for piano four hands 1968, revised 1996, A Rag, A Bone and A Hank of Hair 2000, Gershwin Medley: 3 by 2 for piano four-hands 2000; choral: Quodlibet: Kids' Calls for chorus and piano 1957, Presidential Suite (seven pieces for a capella chorus) 1989, Your Hand, O God, Has Guided 1999, Grant Us Peace (anthem) 2000; song cycles: Yes is a pleasant country (song cycle on poems of E. E. Cummings) 1998, Songs of Godlove (50 solos and duets) 2004; state works: Tea Party (one-act opera) 1955, The Song of Songs which is Solomon's opera 1976, The Movie Opera: a Music Drama for Torch Singer and a Chorus of People in her Life; songs for worship and concert and cabaret songs. *Recordings:* Downtown Blues for Uptown Halls (with The Ariel Ensemble), Evening, Morn and Noon – The Sacred Music of Jack Gottlieb (with six New York area cantors, reader, choir, organ and instrumental ensemble) 1991, Presidential Suite (with the Gregg Smith Singers) 1994, Presidential Suite (with the Carolina Chamber Choir, conducted by Timothy Koch) 2000, V'nislach and Mi sheshikein, After the Flood 2002, Hatsi Kaddish in Jewish Composers in America (Zamir Chorale of Boston Recordings, conducted by Joshua Jacobson) 2002, Mama's Cooking (song by Don Alan Croll). *Publications:* Leonard Bernstein, Young People's Concerts (ed.) 1992, Funny, It Doesn't Sound Jewish: How Yiddish Songs and Synagogue Melodies Influenced Tin Pan Alley, Broadway and Hollywood 2004; numerous writings on Bernstein and other musical topics. *Honours:* awards from Brown and Ohio Univs; Nat. Federation of Music Clubs and NEA awards; Center for Jewish Creativity and Culture Ahad Ha'am Award 1993; hon. mem. American Conference of Cantors (Reform) 2003. *Address:* c/o ASCAP, ASCAP Building, 1 Lincoln Plaza, New York, NY 10023, USA. *E-mail:* Theophi@ix.Netcom.com. *Website:* www.jackgottlieb.com.

GOTTLIEB, Jay (Mitchell); Pianist and Composer; b. 23 Oct. 1954, New York, USA. *Education:* BA, Hunter College, 1970; MA, Harvard University, 1972; Chatham Square Music School, New York; Conservatoire Americaïn de Fontainebleau, France with Nadia Boulanger; Festivals of Tanglewood and Darmstadt with Messiaen, Loriod, Ligeti, Kontarsky. *Career:* Recitals in New York: Alice Tully Hall, Merkin Hall, Carnegie Recital Hall, Third Street Settlement, Cooper Union, Radios WQXR, WNYC, New York University, Theatre des Champs-Elysées, Centre Pompidou, Paris, Alte Oper, Frankfurt; Soloist with Boston Symphony, Orchestra Della Radiotelevisione in Italy, Nouvel Orchestre Philharmonique, Paris, L'Orchestre Philharmonique d'Europe, Paris, L'Orchestre du Rhin, Geneva and radio and television in New York, Boston, Washington, Paris, Switzerland, Frankfurt, Cologne, Rome; Festivals of Berlin, Rome, Milan, Venice, Paris, Almeida, Aldeburgh, Autumn in Warsaw, Musica in Strasburg, Avignon, Toulouse, Frankfurt, Amsterdam; International Piano Festival of La Roque d'Anthéron, France. *Compositions:* Synchronisms for two percussionists and tape; Sonata for violin and piano; Improvisations for piano and percussion; Essay for orchestra; Soundtrack for film, La Discrète. *Recordings:* Trois Contes de L'Honorable Fleur of Maurice Ohana; Lys de Madrigaux; Piano and Percussion-Jay and Gordon Gottlieb; Appello of Barbara Kolb; Harawi of Messiaen; Figure of Michèle Reverdy; La Discrète, soundtrack; Arcane of Allain Gaussin; Concord Sonata of Ives; Piano Works of John Adams; Piano Sonata of Solbiati; Piano Works of John Cage; Recital, 2003, for Signature series Radio-France; Jazz Connotation of Bruno Mantovani;Le Piano du XXe siècle, 1998. *Honours:* Recording of the Month, Le Monde de la Musique, 1998, 1999 and 2000; Diapason d'or, 2001. *Address:* 29–31 Rue des Boulets, 75011 Paris, France. *Telephone:* (33) (1) 43 48 59 71. *Fax:* (33) (1) 43 48 58 30.

GOTTLIEB, Peter; Singer (Baritone); b. 18 Sept. 1930, Brno, Czechoslovakia. *Education:* Studied in Rio de Janeiro and in Florence with Raoul Frazzi. *Career:* Sang at first in Italy, Belgium and North America; Paris Opéra in 1962 premiere of L'Opéra d'Aran by Becaud and as Don Giovanni, Figaro, Papageno, Scarpia and Wozzeck, 1985; Glyndebourne Festival 1966–79 as Albert in Werther, Barber in Die schweigsame Frau, Mercurio in the first modern performance of Cavalli's Calisto, (1970) and Zastrow in the premiere of The Rising of the Moon by Nicholas Maw; Théâtre de la Monnaie Brussels 1983, in the premiere of La Passion de Gilles by Boesmans; Opéra du Rhin Strasbourg in 1984 premiere of H H Ulysses by Jean Prodromidès; Other roles include Iago, Don Carlos in La Forza del Destino and the Count in Capriccio; Professor, Paris Conservatoire from 1982. *Recordings include:* La Calisto (Decca); Opéra D'Aran (Pathe); La Passion de Gilles (Ricercare); H H Ulysses (Harmonia Mundi); La Cocarde de Mimi Pinson (Decca); La Traviata (Sofca). *Address:* 361 rue Lecourbe, 75015 Paris, France.

GÖTZ, Cornelia; Singer (soprano); b. 2 March 1965, Waiblingen, Germany. *Education:* Studied in Karlsruhe, Vienna and Munich. *Career:* First major role as Mozart's Zaide, at the Munich Staatsoper; Appearances as the Queen of Night in Die Zauberflöte throughout Germany and at the Wiener Festwochen; Nuremberg Opera 1992–94, as Mozart's Serpetta and Zerlina, Suppe's Galathée, and Rosina; Further roles include Mozart's Papagena, Blondchen and Constanze; Adele in Die Fledermaus and Olympia; First Flower Maiden in Parsifal at Covent Garden; Sang in Zimmermann's Die Weisse Rose at the Vienna Odeon, 1998; Concerts include Bach Passions, Messiah, Haydn Creation and Seasons, Mozart's C Minor Mass, and Carmina Burana; Schoenberg's Herzgewäcsche and Second String Quartet with Bavarian Radio; Season 1999–2000 as Constanze at Kassel and Frasquita in Carmen for the Deutsche Oper Berlin. *Current Management:* Athole Still International Management, Forresters Hall, 25–27 Westow Street, London, SE19 3RY, England. *Telephone:* (20) 8771-5271. *Fax:* (20) 8768-6600. *Website:* www.atholestill.com.

GÖTZ, Werner; Singer (Tenor); b. 7 Dec. 1934, Berlin, Germany. *Education:* Studied with Friedrich Wilcke and W Kelch in Berlin. *Career:* Debut: Oldenburg 1967, as Alvaro in La Forza del Destino; Sang in Düsseldorf, Karlsruhe, Munich, Stuttgart and Hamburg; Roles included Wagner's Erik, Lohengrin and Parsifal, Mozart's Tamino, Lionel in Martha by Flotow and parts in operas by Puccini, Janáček and Verdi; Further engagements in London, Zürich, Łódź, Barcelona, Amsterdam and Frankfurt; Munich Opera 1978, in the premiere of

Lear by Reimann; Karlsruhe Opera until 1984. *Recordings include:* Lear (Deutsche Grammophon); Melot in Tristan und Isolde; Eine Florentinische Tragödie by Zemlinsky (Fonit-Cetra). *Address:* c/o Bayerische Staatsoper, Postfach 745, 8000 Munich 1, Germany.

GÖTZEN, Guido; Singer (Bass); b. 1959, Düsseldorf, Germany. *Education:* Studied in Cologne with Joseph Metternich. *Career:* Sang first at the Cologne Opera Studio and at Berne, as Angelotti in Tosca, the Major Domo in Capriccio, Hobson in Peter Grimes, and Sarastro, 1988–89; Bayerische Staatsoper Munich, as the King in Aida, Colline, Masetto and roles in Palestrina, Meistersinger, Mathis der Maler, Parsifal, Orff's Trionfi, Dvořák's Dimitri and The Love for Three Oranges, 1989–94; Zürich Opera as Sparafucile in Rigoletto (under Nello Santi), Mozart's Commendatore and Sarastro, and the Bonze in Madama Butterfly, from 1994; Zürich Opera 2000 as Lamoral in Arabella and Schigolch in Lulu. *Recordings include:* Die Meistersinger, conducted by Sawallisch. *Honours:* Prizewinner at the Belvedere Competition, 1987. *Address:* c/o Opernhaus Zürich, Falkenstasse 1, 8008 Zürich, Switzerland.

GOULD, Clio; British violinist; b. 1968, England. *Education:* studied with Emanuel Hurwitz, Pauline Scott and Igor Ozim. *Career:* concerto debut at Royal Festival Hall, aged 17; recitalist and soloist at Bath, Cheltenham, Harrogate, Spitalfields (London) and Huddersfield festivals; Artistic Dir of the BT Scottish Ensemble –2004; currently principal violinist of the London Sinfonietta; concerto soloist with the Ulster Orchestra; Nat. Symphony Orchestra of Ireland and Royal Philharmonic (Barbican Hall, London); Proms debut 1999, with Inside Story by Piers Hellawell; Festival d'Automne, Paris, and chamber recitals in Japan; season 2000–01 with European tour of the Weill Concerto (London Sinfonietta) and concertos with the London Philharmonic Orchestra, Ulster Orchestra and Royal Scottish Nat. Orchestra; plays "Rutson" Stradivarius of 1694. *Recordings include:* Tears of the Angels, by John Tavener. *Honours:* Hon. RAM 1999. *Address:* c/o London Sinfonietta, Third Floor, Dominion House, 101 Southwark Street, London SE1 0JF, England. *Telephone:* (20) 7928-0828. *Fax:* (20) 7928-8557. *E-mail:* info@londonsinfonietta.org.uk. *Website:* www .londonsinfonietta.org.uk.

GOWLAND, David; British music coach; b. 1953. *Education:* Royal Coll. of Music and Nat. Opera Studio, London. *Career:* mem., Glyndebourne music staff 1987, as pianist, repetiteur and asst conductor in a wide repertory; Paris Opéra with La Clemenza di Tito and La Bohème, pianist in Porgy and Bess; Head of Music Staff at the Geneva Opera 1989–96, and appointments with Royal Danish Opera, Netherlands Opera, Covent Garden and Dublin Grand Opera; Festivals of Aix, Orange and Wexford; Weill's Threepenny Opera at RADA, London; concerts include Edinburgh and Aldeburgh Festivals, London Proms and BBC orchestras; season 1997–98 with The Ring in Australia, and Tristan, Idomeneo and Lohengrin in Copenhagen; Lucia di Lammermoor, Turandot and Porgy and Bess at Orange; La Traviata for the Opéra Bastille, Paris; Chief Coach of the Vilar Young Artists' Programme, Royal Opera House; visiting tutor, Nat. Opera Studio. *Honours:* Jani Strassi Award, Glyndebourne 1988. *Address:* c/o National Opera Studio, The Clore Building, 2 Chapel Yard, Wandsworth High Street, London, SW18 4HZ, England.

GRAEBNER, Eric Hans; Composer, Pianist, Lecturer and Conductor; b. 8 Jan. 1943, Berrington, England; one s. *Education:* MA, Cambridge University; PhD, York University; ARCO. *Career:* Lecturer in Music, University of Southampton, 1968–98; Visiting Fellow, Princeton, New Jersey, USA, 1973, 1981–82, 1983; Assistant Professor, William Paterson College, New Jersey, 1981–82; Director, Resurge Studio, 1998–; mem, EMAS (Sonic Arts Network), PRS; NMB (New Music Brighton). *Compositions:* Thalia, 1975; Between Words, 1976; String Quartet No. 1, 1979; String Quartet, No. 2, 1984; 4 Songs and an Aria, 1980; Aspects of 3 Tetrachords, 1973 Quintet, 1981; La mer retrouvée, 1985–86; 3rd Quartet, 1985; Dollbreaker, 1987; Trapeze Act, 1988; Berenice, 1990–91; Introduction and Passacaglia, 1993; Venus in Landscape, 1995; Resurge, 1997; Conversation with Clarinet, 1999; Morphologies, 2001; Wind Quintet, 2002; Naughty Plautus, 2002. *Recordings include:* Divertimento of the Statues, 1993; Resurge, 1997; Venus in Landscape; 1998; Fulminar, 1998. *Publications:* New Berlioz Edition, 1971–72. *Contributions:* Soundings; Perspectives of New Music; In Theory Only; Music Analysis. *Honours:* Fulbright-Hayes Fellowship, 1973; Dio Award, 1977; Fellow, Salzburg Seminar of American Studies, 1976. *Address:* Resurge Studio, 30 Dyke Road Drive, Brighton, East Sussex, BN1 6AJ, England.

GRAEME, Peter; Oboist; b. 17 April 1921, Petersfield, England; m. Inge Anderl, 14 June 1952, 1 s., 3 d. *Education:* Royal College of Music. *Career:* London Philharmonic Orchestra from 1938; Military service 1942–46, then freelance oboist; First Oboe in various orchestras including Kalmar Orchestra; Haydn Orchestra; Boyd Neel Orchestra; Philomusica; Goldsborough Orchestra; English Chamber Orchestra;

Melos Ensemble of London; Oboe Professor, Royal College of Music, 1949–91; Royal Northern College of Music, 1974–90; mem, Musicians Union. *Recordings:* Various with Kalmar Orchestra, Melos Ensemble of London, English Chamber Orchestra. *Honours:* Hon ARCM, 1959; FRCM, 1979; FRNCM, 1989. *Address:* 32 Bimport, Shaftesbury, Dorset SP7 8 AZ, England.

GRAF, Hans; Conductor; b. 15 Feb. 1949, Linz, Austria. *Education:* Studied at the Bruckner Conservatory of Linz and the Academy of Music at Graz; Further study with Franco Ferrara, Sergiu Celibidache and Arvid Yansons. *Career:* Director of the Iraqi National Symphony Orchestra, 1975; Vienna Staatsoper debut 1977, conducted new production of Petrushka, 1981; Munich and Vienna Festivals, 1980; In 1984 conducted Rigoletto at the Maggio Musicale Florence and appeared at the Prague Spring, Bregenz, Helsinki and Salzburg Festivals; Paris Opéra 1984, with Die Entführung and Il Barbiere di Siviglia; Music Director of the Mozarteum Orchestra of Salzburg, 1984; Guest appearances with the Vienna Symphony; Vienna, Leningrad, Dresden, Helsinki and Liverpool Philharmonic Orchestras; Leipzig Gewandhaus, RAI Symphony of Milan and the ORF (Austria) Symphony; Bournemouth Symphony Orchestra; Has led productions of Der Ring des Nibelungen and Fidelio at La Fenice, Venice; Così fan tutte at the Deutsche Oper Berlin; Otello at the Salzburger Kulturtage; Conducted Die Zauberflöte at the 1986 Orange Festival at Tokyo with the Vienna Staatsoper 1989 and the 1992 Savonlinna Festival; Production of Ariadne auf Naxos with John Cox for television, 1994; Conducted Wozzeck at Catania, 1996 and Figaro at Rome, 1998. *Recordings include:* Songs with Brigitte Fassbaender; Zemlinsky's Es war Einmal; Complete Symphonies of Mozart, with the Mozarteum Orchestra of Salzburg. *Honours:* First Prize, Karl Böhm Conductors Competition, Salzburg, 1979. *Address:* Unit 2, 39 Tadema Road, London SW10 0PY, England.

GRAF, Judith; Singer (Soprano); b. 1967, Switzerland. *Education:* Studied in Zürich, at Juilliard, New York and London. *Career:* Sang at Biel Opera from 1989 in Gianni Schicchi and as Donna Elvira, Monteverdi's Poppea, Anne Trulove, Pamina, Fiordiligi, Mozart's Vitellia, the Composer in Ariadne and Tchaikovsky's Tatiana; Pforzheim, 1991 as Marguerite in Faust; Landstheater Slazburg, 1993 in the premiere of Glaube, Liebe, Hoffnung by G Schedle; Biel 1995 as Sonja in Der Zarewitsch; Concert appearances throughout Switzerland. *Address:* Biel Opera, Burggasse 19, 2502 Biel, Switzerland.

GRAF, Maria; Singer (Mezzo-soprano); b. 1929, Germany. *Education:* Studied at the Vienna Academy with Anny Konetzni. *Career:* Sang in the chorus of the Vienna Staatsoper, 1950–55, solo debut at Innsbruck, 1955; Sang at Munster and Frankfurt, then Karlsruhe Opera, 1969–69; Guested at Bayreuth, 1955 (as Flosshilde and Rossweise) and Italy in operas by Wagner (Die Walküre at La Scala, 1963); Sang Helen in the German premiere of Tippett's King Priam, 1963; Other roles included Mozart's Marcellina, Herodias in Salome, Marie (Wozzeck) and Mistress Quickly (Falstaff); Teatro La Fenice, Venice, 1968, in the Ring.

GRAF, Peter-Lukas; Flautist and Conductor; b. 5 Jan. 1929, Zürich, Switzerland. *Education:* Studied at the Paris Conservatoire with Marcel Moyse (flute) and Eugene Bigot (conducting). *Career:* First flautist with the Winterthur Orchestra, 1951–57; Conductor at the Lucerne State Theatre 1961–66; Played in the Lucerne Festival Orchestra 1957–, and toured as soloist with the Edwin Fischer and Gunther Ramin; Performances with the English Chamber Orchestra, the Academy of St Martin in the Fields and the Lucerne Festival Strings; As Soloist and Conductor, tours of Europe, South America, Australia, Japan and Israel; Teacher at the Basle Conservatory 1973–. *Recordings include:* Spohr Concertante for violin, harp and orchestra; Bach A minor Triple Concerto and Saint-Saëns A minor Concerto (English Chamber Orchestra); Mozart Flute Concertos and Concerto K299 (Lausanne Chamber Orchestra); Swiss music with Orchestra della Radio Svizzera, and the Zürich Tonhalle. *Honours:* First prizes in flute and conducting, Paris Conservatoire, 1950, 1951; Winner, International ARD Competition, 1953; Bablock Prize, Harriet Cohen International Music Award, London, 1958.

GRAFFMAN, Gary; Pianist; b. 14 Oct. 1928, New York, USA; m. Naomi Helfman, 1952. *Education:* Curtis Institute of Music under Mme Isabelle Vengerova. *Career:* Debut: with Philadelphia Orchestra, 1947; Concert tours world-wide; Annual appearances with major orchestras, USA; Teacher, Curtis Institute, Manhattan School of Music, 1980–. *Recordings include:* Concertos of Tchaikovsky, Rachmaninov, Brahms, Beethoven, Chopin, Prokofiev; Also plays piano left hand repertory. *Publications:* I Really Should Be Practising, autobiography, 1981. *Honours:* Leventritt Award, 1949.

GRAHAM, Alasdair; Pianist and Professor; b. 19 April 1934, Glasgow, Scotland. *Education:* BMus, Edinburgh University; Performers Diploma, Vienna Hochschule für Musik; Royal Academy of Music with Peter Katin. *Career:* Debut: Bishopsgate Hall, 1958; Soloist with Scottish National Orchestra, London Philharmonic Orchestra, BBC Symphony Orchestra (Proms, 1963), Royal Liverpool Philharmonic, Hallé Orchestra, Sydney Symphony Orchestra, Melbourne Symphony Orchestra (Australian tour), 1967; Recitals, BBC television, the United Kingdom, Turkey, India; As Accompanist with Elisabeth Söderströ m, Josef Suk, John Shirley-Quirk; Professor, Royal College of Music, London; mem, Royal Society of Musicians of Great Britain. *Recordings:* Schubert: Sonata in B flat, 8 Ecossaises. *Honours:* Harriet Cohen Commonwealth Medal, 1963; Honorary RCM, 1973. *Address:* 184 Can Hall Road, London E11 3 NH, England.

GRAHAM, Colin; Stage Director, Librettist and Artistic Director; b. 22 Sept. 1931, Hove, Sussex, England. *Education:* New Covenant School of Ministry, St Louis, 1985–87, ordained Minister in 1988; Diploma, Royal Academy of Dramatic Art; Private study. *Career:* Debut: Playhouse Theatre, Nottingham, England; Artistic Director, Aldeburgh Festival, 1969–82, English Music Theatre, 1976–, Opera Theater of St Louis, 1982–; Director of Productions, English National Opera, Sadler's Wells Opera, 1976–82; Over 400 productions in opera, television and theatre, including 54 world premieres; staged the premiere of Corigliano's The Ghosts of Versailles at the Metropolitan, 1991, production of Britten's Death in Venice at Covent Garden, 1992, and Metropolitan Opera, 1993 and world premiere of Susa's The Dangerous Liaisons at San Francisco, 1994; The Barber of Seville at St Louis, 1996; staged premiere of Previn's A Streetcar Named Desire, San Francisco, 1998; staged plays, opera, television for Oled Vic Co, Royal Shakespeare Co, Bristol Old Vic, Nottingham Plyhouse, Oxford Playhouse, BBC TV, ITV, Belgian TV, Royal Opera Covent Garden, Glyndebourne Opera, Sadlers Wells Opera, English National Opera, Belgian National Opera La Monnaie; mem, Equity; Canadian Equity; American Guild of Musical Artists; Arts and Educational Council, 1993; Award of Personal Achievement in the Arts. *Publications:* Opera Libretti: The Golden Vanity by Britten, 1970, Penny for a Song by Bennett, 1970, King Arthur by Purcell, 1972, The Postman Always Rings Twice, by Paulus, 1983, Joruri by Miki, 1985, The Woodlanders by Paulus, 1985; The Tale of Genji by Miki, 1999; Silk by Previn, 1999; Anna Karenina by Carlson; Madame Mao by Sheng (libretto and world premiere productgion for Santa Fe Opera). *Contributions:* Opera Magazine; Musical Times; Opera News, 1992. *Honours:* Winston Churchill Fellowship, 1975; Prize for Opera Production for Orpheus, Germany, 1977; Honorary Doctor of Arts, Webster University, 1985 and University of Missouri, 1992; O.B.E., 2002. *Address:* PO Box 191910, St Louis, MO 63119, USA.

GRAHAM, Peter John; Arranger and Composer; b. 5 Dec. 1958, Bellshill, Scotland; m. Janey Buchan, 1 s., 1 d. *Education:* BMus, Edinburgh University, 1980; PGCE, Moray House College, 1981; MMus, Goldsmiths' College, 1994; PhD, University of Salford, 1999. *Career:* Arranger, Composer, New York, London, 1986–91; Lecturer, University of Salford, 1991–97; Senior Lecturer, 1997–2001; Reader in Composition, 2001–. *Compositions:* Numerous publications for brass and wind including: Dimensions, 1983; Montage, 1994; Harrison's Dream, 2000; Arrangements for BBC television and radio, commercial television and various recordings including Reflected in Brass, Evelyn Glennie meets the Black Dyke Band. *Honours:* Reflected in Brass nominated Best Classical Crossover Album, Grammy Awards, 1999; ABA/Ostwald Composition Prize, 2002. *Address:* c/o Gramercy Music, PO Box 41, Cheadle Hulme, Cheshire SK8 5HF, England.

GRAHAM, Susan; American singer (mezzo-soprano); b. 23 July 1960, Roswell, NM. *Education:* Manhattan School of Music, Texas Technical Univ. *Career:* sang Massenet's Chérubin while a student; engagements with St Louis Opera as Erika in Vanessa, Charlotte and at Seattle as Stephano in Roméo et Juliette; Season 1989–90 included Chicago Lyric Opera debut as Annius in La Clemenza di Tito, Sonia in Argento's Aspern Papers at Washington, Dorabella and the Composer at Santa Fe; Carnegie Hall debut in Des Knaben Wunderhorn and Bernstein concert in New York; Season 1990–91 as Octavian with San Francisco Symphony, Minerva in Monteverdi's Ulisse with San Francisco Opera, Berlioz's Beatrice at Lyon, Cherubino at Santa Fe; Mozart's C minor Mass under Edo de Waart and with Philadelphia Orchestra under Neville Marriner; Season 1991–92 at Metropolitan as Second Lady, Cherubino, and Tebaldo in Don Carlos; L'Opera de Nice as Cherubino and Les Nuits d'Été in Lyon; Beethoven's 9th in Spain conducted by Marriner; Salzburg Mozart Week, 1993, as Cecilio in Lucio Silla, Easter and Summer Festivals as Meg Page in Falstaff; Season 1993–94 as Massenet's Chérubin and Dorabella at Covent Garden, Ascanio in Les Troyens at the Met, Annius in Tito at San Francisco and 1994 Salzburg Festival; Octavian for Welsh National Opera, and Vienna State Opera and Marguerite in La Damnation de Faust for L'Opéra de Lyon; Season 1995 as Dorabella and as Arianna in the premiere of the opera by Goehr at Covent Garden; Season 1997 with Chérubin at Covent Garden and in Lucio Silla at Salzburg; Sang Octavian at Covent Garden, 2000; Created Sister Helen Prejean in Jack Heggie's Dead Man Walking, San Francisco, 2000; Season 2001 as Mignon at Toulouse and Dorabella at the New York Met. *Recordings include:* Falstaff conducted by Solti; La Damnation de Faust conducted by Kent Nagano; Béatrice et Bénédict conducted by John Nelson; Stravinsky's Pulcinella. *Current Management:* IMG Artists, Lovell House, 616 Chiswick High Road, London, W4 5RX, England. *Telephone:* (20) 8233-5800. *Fax:* (20) 8233-5801. *E-mail:* info@imgartists.com. *Website:* www.imgartists.com; www.susangraham .com.

GRAHAM-HALL, John; Singer (Tenor); b. 23 Nov. 1955, Middlesex, England. *Education:* Studied at King's College, Cambridge and Royal College of Music. *Career:* Debut: Opera North, as Ferrando in Così fan tutte, 1983; Has sung Albert Herring at Covent Garden and Glyndebourne, Pedrillo for Kent Opera, Cassio for Welsh National Opera and Don Ottavio for Opera Northern Ireland; Glyndebourne Touring Opera as Britten's Aschenbach, Lysander, Basilio and Ferrando; English National Opera debut as Cyril in Princess Ida, 1992, returning as Basilio, Tanzmeister in Ariadne and Schoolmaster in Cunning Little Vixen; Engagements at Lyon as Lensky and Frère Mass ée in Messiaen's St François d'Assise, Vancouver as Ferrando, Brussels and Lisbon as Cassio and Antwerp as Achilles in King Priam; Glyndebourne Festival as Kudrjas in Katya Kabanova and Flute in Midsummer Night's Dream; Scottish Opera as Eisenstein, and Schoolmaster in Cunning Little Vixen; Aix-en-Provence as Lysander and Bordeaux as Tanzmeister in Ariadne; Amsterdam as Basilio and Curzio; Conductors have included Haitink, Janowski, Tate, Rattle and Abbado; Concert career with all major British orchestras including Pulcinella with BBC Symphony, 1993; Further recent appearances include Moses and Aron in Amsterdam, La Belle Hélène with English National Opera, and Shapkin in House of the Dead in Nice; Season 1996 with Narciso in Il Turco in Italia at Garsington and in Moses and Aron at Salzburg; Basilio in Figaro for the Royal Opera, London; Recent engagements include Alwa, Herod for ENO, Tanzmeister for ROH, Mime for ENO; Further plans include Perela at Paris Bastille; Season 2000–01 in the premiere of The Silver Tassie, by Turnage, for ENO, and as Monostatos and Mime; Britten's Bob Boles at Amsterdam; Dancing Master in Ariadne at Covent Garden, 2002. *Recordings include:* Carmina Burana; L'Incoronazione di Poppea; A Midsummer Night's Dream; As Bob Boles in Peter Grimes. *Address:* c/o Musichall, Ivydene, Vicarage Way, Ringmer, East Sussex, BN8 5 LA, England.

GRAHN, Ulf (Ake Wilhelm); Composer; b. 17 Jan. 1942, Solna, Sweden; m. Barbro Dahlman, 15 Aug 1969, 1 s. *Education:* Degree in Violin Pedagogy, SMI, Stockholm, 1968; MM, Catholic University, Washington DC, USA, 1973; Business Administration, Development Studies, Uppsala University, Sweden, 1986. *Career:* Music Instructor, Stockholm and Lidingo Schools, 1964–72; Teaching Assistant, Instructor, Catholic University, Washington, 1972–76; Founder, Music Director, Contemporary Music Forum, 1973–85; Lecturer, Northern VA Community College, 1975–79; Lecturer, Associate Professor, George Washington University, 1983–87; Founder, Artistic Director, The Aurora Players, 1983–; Artistic and Managing Director, Lake Siljan Festival Sweden, 1988–90; Composer-in-Residence, Charles Ives Center, USA, 1988; Publisher and Owner, Edition NGLANI, 1985–; mem, STIM Sweden; Society of Swedish Composers. *Compositions:* Major orchestral works including Symphonies Nos 1 and 2; Concertos for piano, guitar and double bass; Chamber and Choral Music; Solo works for Guitar, Piano, Violin; Three Dances with Interludes, premiered in Stockholm, 1990; Blå Dunster, 1990, an instrumental opera premiered in Örebro, Sweden, 1991; As Time Passes By for orchestra, 1993; Aron's Interlude for 6 instruments, 1994; Summer '61 for ensemble, 1995; Morning Rush for orchestra, 1995; Cikadas for 4 instruments, 1996. *Recordings:* Cinq Preludes; Snapshots; Sonata for Piano with Flute and Percussion; In The Shade, Caprice; Sonata for Piano. *Contributions:* Many articles, and reviews in Europe; Tonfallet; Musik Revy and Ord och Ton. *Honours:* Stockholm International Organ Days, 1973; League International Society for Contemporary Music Piano Competition, 1976; First Prize in Music for, Toccata for Carillon, Dalarna Composition Contest, 1990. *Address:* PO Box 5684, Takoma Park, MD 20913-5684, USA.

GRANDISON, Mark; Composer; b. 9 Dec. 1965, Adelaide, South Australia. *Education:* BMus (Hons) 1987, MMus 1990, University of Adelaide; Study with Richard Meale, 1983–87. *Career:* Teacher and Acting Co-ordinator, Marryatville Special Interest Music Centre, Adelaide, 1992–93; Kambala School, Sydney, 1994–. *Compositions include:* Four Poems of Wilfrid Owen for contralto and ensemble, 1985; Contrasts for orchestra, 1987; Night Interiors for orchestra, 1988; Los Caprichos for chamber orchestra, 1989; Five Blake Songs for soprano and piano, 1990; Toccata for chamber ensemble, 1992; Three Dances for string orchestra, 1993; Surface Tension for string quartet, 1996; Kinetica for youth orchestra, 1997; Tarantella for Orchestra, 1998; Commissions from the Adelaide Chamber Orchestra, Vrizen and Australian Broadcasting Association. *Honours:* South Australia Young Composer's Award, 1993. *Address:* c/o APRA, 1A Eden Street, Crows Nest, NSW 2065, Australia.

GRANGE, Philip (Roy); Composer; b. 17 Nov. 1956, London, England; m. Elizabeth Caroline Hemming, 1986. 2 children. *Education:* York University, 1976–82; BA, 1979; Doctorate in Composition, 1984; Dartington Summer School of Music, Composition class with Peter Maxwell Davies, 1975–81. *Career:* Promenade Concert debut, 1983; Fellow in the Creative Arts, Trinity College, Cambridge, 1985–87; Northern Arts Fellow in Composition, Durham University, 1988–89; Appointed Lecturer in Composition, 1989–95, Reader in Composition, 1995–99, Professor of Composition, 1999–2000, Exeter University; Professor of Composition, Manchester University, 2001–; Performances of music at most major festivals in the United Kingdom, and in Europe, USA and the Far East. *Compositions:* Cimmerian Nocturne, 1979; Sextet, 1980; The Kingdom of Bones, 1983; La Ville Entière, 1984; Variations, 1986; Out in the Dark, 1986; In Memorian HK, 1986; The Dark Labyrinth, 1987; Concerto for Orchestra; Labyrinthine Images, 1988; In A Dark Time, 1989; Changing Landscapes, 1990; Focus and Fade, 1992; Lowry Dreamscape, 1992; Piano Polyptich, 1993; Bacchus Bagatelles, 1993; Des fins sont des commencements, 1994; Piano Trio: Homage to Chagall, 1995; A Puzzle of Shadows for soprano, violin and piano, 1997; Sky-Maze with Song Shards, 1999; Lament of the Bow, 2000. *Recordings:* La Ville Entière for clarinet and piano; Dark Labyrinths, recording of 6 pieces. *Current Management:* Maecenas Music, 5 Bushey Close, Old Barn Lane, Kenley, Surrey CR8 5AU, England. *Address:* Music Department, University of Manchester, Denmark Road, Manchester M15 6HY, England.

GRANT, Clifford (Scantlebury); Singer (Bass); b. 11 Sept. 1930, Randwick, New South Wales, Australia; m. (1) Jeanette Earle, 1 s., 2 d., (2) Ruth Anders, 1992. *Education:* Studied at Sydney Conservatorium with Isolde Hill; Melbourne with Annie Portnoj; London with Otakar Kraus. *Career:* Debut: New South Wales Opera Company, as Raimondo in Lucia di Lammermoor, 1952; Sang with Sadler's Wells/English National Opera from 1966, debut as Silva in Ernani; Leading roles in Oedipus Rex, The Mastersingers, Peter Grimes, The Magic Flute, Madama Butterfly, The Barber of Seville, The Ring of the Nibelung, Don Giovanni, The Coronation of Poppea, and Don Carlos; Sang in San Francisco, 1966–78; Glyndebourne Festival as Nettuno in Il Ritorno d'Ulisse, 1972; Further engagements with Covent Garden Opera, Welsh National Opera and in Europe; Sang in Sydney from 1976, as Nilakantha (Lakmé), 1986; Season 1990 as Marcel in Les Huguenots with Australian Opera; Returned to the United Kingdom, 1992 and sang Alvise in new production of La Gioconda, Opera North, 1993; Many concert appearances. *Recordings:* Don Giovanni; Rigoletto; Esclarmonde; L'Oracolo; Fafner in The Rhinegold and Hunding in The Valkryie, conducted by Reginald Goodall; Bartolo in Le nozze di Figaro; Il Corsaro; The Apostles by Elgar; Tosca; Les Huguenots. *Address:* c/o Australian Opera, Sydney Opera House, Sydney, NSW, Australia.

GRÄSBECK, Manfred; Violinist; b. 16 July 1955, Åbo, Finland; m. Maija Lehtonen, 14 May 1989, 1 s., 1 d. *Education:* Åbo Konservatorium, Åbo, Finland, 1962–79; Académie Internationale de Musique, Maurice Ravel, 1972–76; Académie Internationale d'été, Nice, France, 1974–77; Tjajkovskij-konservatoriet Kiev, Ukraina, 1978–81; Sibelius Academy, 1981–91; MMus, 1997, Postgraduate Studies, Sibelius-Akademin, Helsingfors, Finland. *Career:* Debut: Ludwig van Beethoven sonatas Nos 5, 7 and 9, Salle Gaveau, Paris, 1978; As soloist with orchestras: Århus, 1972; Copenhagen, 1972; Bordeaux, 1972; Toulouse, 1973, 1974; Västerås, 1977; Stockholm, 1983; Hamburger Symphoniker, 1983; Reykjavík, 1986; Volgograd, 1990; Beethoven Violin Concerto (with cadenzas by M. Gräsbeck), Vilnius and Kaunas, 1992; mem, Liszt Gesellschaft Ky, Helsinki; Attended Professor Jorma Panula Conducting Competition, Vaasa, Finland, November, 2003. *Compositions:* 7 symphonies; 6 violin concertos HRF op 23 and Integrity op 34; film music; and others. *Recordings:* Ellis B Kohs: Conductor, Passacaglia K 11 for organ and strings; Piano and organ, Kreisler with Love, vol. 1 and 2, with Maija Lehtonen; Paganini caprices op 1; K Aho violin concerto; L Bashmakov violin concerto No. 2. *Address:* Nallebackavägen 1B, 00700 Helsinki, Finland.

GRAUBART, Michael; Composer, Conductor and Lecturer; b. 26 Nov. 1930, Vienna, Austria; m. (1) Ellen Barbour, 1962, 1 s., 2 d., (2) Valerie Coumont, 1996. *Education:* BSc, Physics, Univ. of Manchester, England, 1952; Studied Composition privately with Matyas Seiber, 1953–57; Flute with Geoffrey Gilbert, 1953–56. *Career:* Conductor, Ars Nova Chamber Orchestra, 1960; Conductor, Hampstead Chamber Orchestra, 1962–66; Music Director, Focus Opera Group, 1967–71; Director of Music, Morley College, 1966–91; Adjunct Professor of Music, Syracuse University London Centre, 1989–91; Senior Lecturer, School of Academic Studies, Royal Northern College of Music, Manchester, 1991–96. *Compositions include:* Sonata for cello and piano; Sinfonia a 10 for 10 winds; Quintet for flute, clarinet, viola, cello and vibraphone; Canzonetta for triple chamber orchestra; Declensions for 10 instruments; To a Dead Lover for soprano and 7 instruments; Untergang for baritone, chorus and 11 instruments; Quasi una Sonata for piano; Three

Bagatelles for cello and piano; Sure I am only of uncertain things for a cappella chorus; Two songs for mezzo-soprano and piano; Concertino da Camera for viola and four woodwinds; Diptych (The Seed and the Harvest, Broken Mirror) for 4 winds; Scena and Capriccio for piano; Variants and Cadenzas for orchestra; Nightfall for chorus and piano; Elegy for orchestra; Speculum Noctuinum for 9 winds, cello and bass; Scena II and Finale for euphonium, 2 flutes, viola and cello, 1992 and 1995; Ricordanze for recorders and piano, 1995, 1997; String Quartet, 2000; Sonata for cello and piano; The Meridian Angel for counter tenors, 2 tenors and baritone; Scena III for solo cello; Editions: Music by Pergolesi, Dufay and Josquin. *Publications:* 4 articles on Leopold Spinner, including one for the revision of New Grove's Dictionary of Music; Numerous articles and reviews on Bach, Beethoven, Schubert, Echoenberg and Webern for Tempo and Musical Times. *Address:* 18 Laitwood Road, Balham, London SW12 9QL, England. *E-mail:* michael .graubart@btinternet.com.

GRAUNKE, Kurt; Violinist, Conductor and Composer; b. 30 Sept. 1915, Stettin, Germany. *Education:* Pupil in violin of Gustav Havemann, Berlin Hochschule für Musik; Received training in composition from Adolf Lessle and Hermann Grabner, in violin from Hanns Weiss and Hans Dunschede, and in conducting from Feliz Husadel; Completed violin studies with Wolfgang Schneiderhan. *Career:* Played violin in the Vienna Radio Orchestra; Founder-Conductor, Graunke Symphony Orchestra, Munich, 1945–. *Compositions:* 8 symphonies: 1969, 1972, 1975, 1981, 1982, 1983, 1985; Violin Concerto, 1959; Other orchestral works. *Recordings:* Numerous albums, film and television soundtracks. *Address:* c/o Symphonie Orchester Graunke, Schornstrasse 13, 8000 Munich 30, Germany.

GRAVES, Denyce; Singer (Mezzo-soprano); b. 1963, Washington DC, USA. *Education:* Studied at the Oberlin College and New England Conservatories. *Career:* Early roles included Maddalena at Washington and Giuletta in Les Contes d'Hoffmann at the Spoleto Festival; Further engagements as Dalila in Philadelphia and Montreal, Honegger's Antigone, the High Priestess in La Vestale at La Scala, Adalgisa in Zürich and Donizetti's Leonora (La Favorita) at Catania; Appearances as Carmen at San Francisco, Vienna, the Bergen Festival, Covent Garden, Berlin, Zürich, Houston, Los Angeles, Buenos Aires and Munich; Season 1995–96 as Carmen in Zürich and at the Met, Dalila in Washington, Carmen at San Francisco, 1998; Season 2000 as Carmen at Chicago, Amneris in Cincinnati, Dalila at the Met and Dulcinée in Don Quichotte for Washington Opera; The Nation's Favourite Prom at the London Proms, 2002; Concert repertory includes Messiah, the Verdi Requiem, Rossini's Stabat Mater, Ravel's Shéhérazade and Mahler's Kindertotenlieder. *Recordings include:* Gertrude in Hamlet by Ambroise Thomas; Emilia in Otello. *Honours:* Met Opera National Finalist; Grand Prix du Concours International du Chant de Paris; Marian Anderson Award. *Address:* c/o Opernhaus Zürich, Falkenstrasse 1, 8008 Zürich, Switzerland.

GRAVS, Leonard; Singer (Bass-baritone); b. 28 Jan. 1944, Maastricht, Netherlands. *Career:* Debut: Sang Sparafucile in Rigoletto at Maastricht, 1966; Sang with Netherlands Opera, Opéra de Wallonie at Liège, 1973–82; Hannover Opera, 1982–86; Saarbrucken, 1986–88; Geneva, 1988–94; Guest appearances at Marseille, Cologne, (Pallante in Agrippina), 1985 and Montreal; Other roles have included Puccini's Colline and Angelotti, Nourabad in Les Pêcheurs de perles and the Minister in Fidelio, Liège, 1996; Zuniga in Carmen, Verdi's Zaccaria, Grand Inquisitor and Ramphis; Escamillo and Kaspar; Season 1997–98 as Gessler in Guillaume Tell at Liège. *Address:* Opéra de Wallonie, 1 Rue des Dominicains, 4000 Liège, Belgium.

GRAY, George; Singer (Tenor); b. 26 May 1947, USA. *Career:* Sang Cavaradossi at Colorado Springs, 1984, Cairo and Radames with North Carolina Opera, 1986, 1988; New Jersey Festival, 1987, as Bacchus, Seattle, 1987, as Otello, Tristan at Columbus, Ohio; Season 1988 in Schoenberg's Gurrelieder at Frankfurt, and Pollione in Norma; Tristan at Nancy, 1990, with Aeneas at the opening of the Bastille Opéra, Paris; Sang Parsifal at Chicago, 1990, Siegfried at Zürich, 1988; Further appearances as Bacchus at Kassel, in Schreker's Schatzgräber at the Holland Festival and Meyerbeer's Vasco da Gama at the Berlin Staatsoper, 1992; Lohengrin at Leipzig; Season 1999–2000 at the San Francisco and Dallas Operas as Siegfried. *Address:* c/o Berlin Staatsoper, Unter den Linden 7, 1060 Berlin, Germany.

GRAY, James; Singer (countertenor), Keyboard player and Conductor; b. 1 Jan. 1956, London, England. *Education:* Royal Acad. of Music, London; private study with Maria Curcio, London; Acad. of Fine Arts, Prague; Centro Studio Musicali Rinascimento, Florence. *Career:* debut, Prague, 1976, Czech Philharmonic Society; Guest Dir of Prague Madrigalists, 1980–81 (Berlin television debut 1981); Repétiteur Nationaltheater, Mannheim, 1981–82; La Chaise-Dieu Festival, 1984 (French television); Domenico Scarlatti Tercentenary Celebrations, 1985 (Radio Madrid, Spanish television); many subsequent appearances

as singer, conductor and accompanist throughout mid and Eastern Europe. *Recordings:* Domenico Scarlatti Unpublished Cantatas, 1985; Monteverdi Lamento d'Arianna (awarded Grand Prix Academie du Disque Français), 1986; Benedetto Marcello Unpublished Vocal Works, 1990. *Address:* Via Romana 34, 50125 Florence, Italy. *E-mail:* horti_annalenae@tin.it.

GRAY, Linda Esther; Opera Singer (Soprano); b. 29 May 1948, Greenock, Scotland; m. Peter McCrorie, 1 d. *Education:* Royal Scottish Academy of Music and Drama, Cinzano Scholarship, 1969; Goldsmiths' School, 1970; James Caird School, 1971. *Career:* London Opera Centre, 1969–71; Glyndebourne Festival Opera, as Mimi and Mozart's Electra, 1972–75; Scottish Opera, 1974–79; Welsh Opera, 1980–; English National Opera, as Donna Anna, Wagner's Eva, Strauss's Ariadne and Verdi's Amelia, 1979–; American Debut, 1981; Royal Opera House, Sieglinde, 1982; Fidelio, 1983; Record of Tristan and Isolde, 1981; Principal Roles: Isolde, Sieglinde, Kundry (Wagner); Tosca (Puccini); Fidelio (Beethoven). *Honours:* Kathleen Ferrier Award, 1972; Christie Award, 1972. *Address:* 171 Queens Road, London SW19, England.

GREAGER, Richard; Singer (tenor); b. 5 Nov. 1946, Christchurch, New Zealand. *Education:* Studied in Australia. *Career:* Junior Principal at Covent Garden until 1975; Lyric Tenor at Scottish Opera from 1975, then sang widely in Germany, notably at Hanover, Dortmund, Wiesbaden, Karlsruhe and Bonn; Roles included Don Ottavio, Ferrando, Tamino, Rodolfo, the Duke of Mantua, Fenton and Ernesto; Australian Opera from 1980, as The Painter in Lulu, Edgardo (opposite Sutherland's Lucia), Peter Grimes, Lensky, Don José and Peter Quint (The Turn of the Screw); Guest appearances at the Grand Théâtre Geneva as Peter Quint, the Painter and the Negro in Lulu (Jeffrey Tate conducting) and Edgardo; Opéra de Lyon as Huon in Oberon; Season 1988–89 as Rodolfo at Melbourne and Covent Garden; Eisenstein in Die Fledermaus for Scottish Opera; Peter Quint in Schwetzingen and Cologne; Covent Garden 1991 as Arthur in the world premiere of Gawain by Harrison Birtwistle; Other roles include Tonio (La Fille du Régiment) and Werther; Season 1991–92 as Arbace in Idomeneo at Helsinki, Herod in Salome at Wellington and Mozart's Basilio with the Royal Opera in Japan; Sang Don José and Don Ottavio for Wellington City Opera, 1997; Torquemada in L'Heure Espagnole at Auckland, 1998; Captain in Wozzeck (Barrie Kosky's production), Sydney; Dr Caius in Falstaff for NBR New Zealand Opera, Roger in Love in the Age of Therapy for OzOpera, Melbourne and Sydney Festivals, 2001; Prince Shuisky in Boris Godunov for NBR New Zealand Opera; Herod in Salome for Opera Australia, 2003. *Recordings:* video: Gawain, Lucia di Lammermoor, La Traviata, Un Ballo in Maschera, Turn of the Screw, Dialogue of the Carmelites; also recorded Berlioz's Requiem and Schubert's 6 Masses. *Honours:* Winner, Sun Aria Competition, Australia. *Current Management:* Arts Management, Level 2, 420 Elizabeth Street, Surry Hills, NSW 2010, Australia.

GREEN, Anna, ARCM; Opera Singer; b. 27 Jan. 1933, Southampton, England; m. Howard Vanderburg 1965. *Education:* Royal Coll. of Music. *Career:* debut, Amelia in Verdi's Un Ballo in Maschera, Deutsche Oper am Rhein, Düsseldorf 1961; sang Aida, Tosca and Abigaille; later sang German roles, including Fidelio, Marschallin, Isolde, Brünnhilde and Elektra; appeared as Hecuba in King Priam at Royal Opera House, Covent Garden, London, Brünnhilde for ENO and WNO, Elektra for Vienna State Opera and in Karslruhe and Mannheim, Brünnhilde in Barcelona, Florence, Naples, Nice, Warsaw, Lisbon, Hamburg, Stuttgart and Cologne, Isolde in Berlin, Mannheim, Karlsruhe and Wiesbaden, Kostelnicka in Jenůfa in Stuttgart; also sang in Canada and USA, as Brünnhilde at founding of Pacific Northwest Wagner Festival and in subsequent four seasons; concert appearances include Stravinsky's Les Noces at Albert Hall, London, under Pierre Boulez, Schoenberg's Erwartung in Scotland, under Gari Bertini, Altenberg Lieder for RAI, Rome, Wagner concert with Los Angeles Philharmonic conducted by Zubin Mehta; mem. Genossenschaft Deutscher Bühnen. *Recordings:* Aus dem Essener Musikleben; Betulia Liberata KV 118 Mozart.

GREEN, Barry, BMus, MMus; American bassist, academic and writer; b. 10 April 1945, Newark, NJ; m. Mary Tarbell Green 1984; two s. one steps. *Education:* Indiana University School of Music, University of Cincinnati. *Career:* Principal Bassist, Nashville Symphony, 1965–66; Principal Bassist, Cincinnati Symphony, 1967–; Faculty, University of Cincinnati, 1967–; Cassals Festival Orchestra, 1979–87; International Workshops, 1982–86; mem, International Society of Bassists, Founder Director, Life Member; ASTA; Founder-Executive Director, International Society of Bassists. *Recordings:* (Solos) Baroque Bass; Romantic Music for Double Bass; New Music for Double Bass; Bass Evolution; Sound of Bass, Vol. 1 (Chamber Music Recordings) Heritage Chamber Quartet; Music Now; What of My Music Opus One. *Publications:* Fundamentals of Double Bass Playing; Advanced Techniques of Double Bass Playing, 1976; Inner Game of Music, 1986; contrib. to Suzuki

Journal; American Music Teacher; Instrumentalist; Bass World. *Address:* 3449 Lyleburn Place, Cincinnati, OH 45220, USA.

GREEN, Barton; Singer (Tenor); b. 1967, New Orleans, USA. *Education:* Studied at Washington and Yale Universities. *Career:* Sang Tamino at Tacoma Opera, 1986; Pinkerton for Sarasota Opera, 1994; Season 1995 with Alfredo for Pittsburgh Opera; Faust at Conneticut; Rossini's Almaviva for Da Capo Opera and Tonio in La Fille du régiment for Augusta Opera; Eugene Opera, 1996 as Rodolfo, and Gennaro in Lucrezia Borgia at Manhattan Opera; Giessen Opera, 1996 as Edgardo in Lucia di Lammermoor; Alfred in Die Fledermaus for Florida Grand Opera, 1998. *Honours:* Richard Tucker Award, 1994. *Address:* c/o Florida Grand Opera, 1200 Coral Way, Miami FL 33145, USA.

GREEN, Paul Jay; Clarinettist; b. 19 Dec. 1948, New York, USA; m. Lisa Dolinger Green, 19 December 1993. *Education:* BA, Yale College, 1970; MS, Performance, Juilliard School of Music, 1972; JD Brooklyn Law School, 1978; LLM, New York University School of Law, 1982; Studies with Leon Russianoff, Keith Wilson, Joseph Allard. *Career:* Debut: Young Concert Artists, Carnegie Recital Hall, 1966; Soloist: New York Philharmonic; Hartford Symphony Orchestra; New Haven Symphony Orchestra; Colorado Music Festival; Festival of Two Worlds in Spoleto, Italy; International Festival of Contemporary Music, Kraków, Poland; The Days of New Music Festival in Chisinau, Moldova; Chamber music performances with: Jacqueline Du Pré; Richard Goode; The Lark Quartet; The Borromeo Quartet; The Ying Quartet; The Alexander Quartet; The St Lawrence Quartet; The Miami String Quartet; The Eroica Trio; Founder and Artistic Director, Gold Coast Chamber Music Festival; Principal clarinettist of The New Haven Symphony Orchestra, 1989–90; Colorado Music Festival Orchestra; Symphony of the Americas; American Sinfonietta; Atlantic Classical Orchestra; Associate Professor of Music, Clarinet and Chamber Music, Conservatory of Music, Lynn University, Boca Roton, Florida, 1992–; Instructor of Music, Clarinet and Chamber Music, School of Music, Florida International University, Miami, Florida, 1996–. *Recordings:* Carnival of the Animals with Leonard Bernstein and the New York Philharmonic; Return to the Concert Stage, 1990; Quintet for Clarinet and Strings with the Miami String Quartet, 2001. *Current Management:* Marilyn Gilbert, Artists Management. *Address:* 717 Heron Drive, Delray Beach, FL 33444, USA.

GREENAN, Andrew, MA; singer (bass); b. 5 Feb. 1960, Birmingham, England; m. Susannah Davies 1989, two s. one d. *Education:* St Marys Coll., Liverpool, St Johns Coll., Cambridge, Royal Northern Coll. of Music with John Cameron. *Career:* debut, La Scala, Milan, 1983; Bayreuther Festspielchor, 1985–87; British Opera debut, Mozart's Bartolo Opera 80, 1989; Principal Bass, English National Opera, 1992–97; Roles include: King Henry, Sarastro, Rocco, Commendatore, Timur, Sparafucile, Swallow; Other engagements include: Bottom in Midsummer Night's Dream at Teatro Regio, Turin, 1995; Landgraf in Tannhäuser at Queen Elizabeth Hall; For Royal Opera Covent Garden: Swallow with Mackerras, Ataliba in Alzira with Elder, 1st Nazarene in Salome with Dohnányi, Pietro in Simon Boccanegra with Solti, Rocco for Welsh National Opera, Abimélech in Samson et Dalila for New Israeli Opera (1998), Swallow for Hamburg State Opera and Welsh National Opera; Recent concert work includes Verdi Requiem with Belgian National Orchestra and appearances with the English Chamber and BBC Symphony Orchestras. *Recordings:* The Nightingale by Stravinsky, with the Philharmonia and Robert Craft; Video recordings of Peter Grimes with ENO and Salome with the Royal Opera; Appears as Raymond/Larimondo in the film Lucia based on Donizetti's opera. *Current Management:* Robert Gilder & Co., Enterprise House, 59–65 Upper Ground, London, SE1 9PQ, England. *Telephone:* (20) 7928-9008. *Fax:* (20) 7928-9755. *E-mail:* rgilder@robert-gilder.com. *Address:* 3 Wheatsheaf Gardens, Lewes, East Sussex BN7 2UQ, England.

GREENAWALD, Sheri (Kay); Soprano; b. 12 Nov. 1947, Iowa City, Iowa, USA. *Education:* Studied with Charles Matheson at the University of Northern Iowa and with Hans Heinz, Daniel Ferro and Maria DeVarady in New York; Further studies with Audrey Langford in London. *Career:* Debut: Manhattan Theater Club 1974, in Les mamelles de Tirésias by Poulenc; Sang in the premieres of Bilby's Doll by Carlisle Floyd and Washington Square by Thomas Pastieri (Houston and Detroit, 1976); European debut with Netherlands Opera as Susanna in Le nozze di Figaro, 1980; Regular concert appearances with the St Louis and San Francisco Symphony Orchestras and the Rotterdam Philharmonic; Sang in the premiere of Bernstein's A Quiet Place, Houston 1983; Other roles include Violetta, Ellen Orford (Peter Grimes), Mozart's Despina and Zerlina, Sophie in Werther and Norina in Don Pasquale; Season 1991/92 at Chicago as Pauline in the US Stage premiere of Prokofiev's The Gambler and Mozart's Donna Anna, Fiordiligi at Seattle; Sang the Marschallin with Welsh National Opera, 1994; Susa's Transformations at St Louis, 1997; Los Angeles Opera debut 1998 as Catán's Florencia. *Address:* c/o Houston Grand Opera Association, 510 Preston Avenue, Houston, TX 77002, USA.

GREENBAUM, Stuart (Geoffrey Andrew); Composer; b. 25 Dec. 1966, Melbourne, Australia. *Education:* Studied at the University of Melbourne; BMus, hons, MMus, PhD (pending), Teachers include Brenton Broadstock and Barry Conyngham. *Career:* Debut: Upon the Dark Water (text by Ross Baglin), premiered at Sydney Opera House, 1990, by the Song Company; Works performed by groups including: The Modern Wind Quintet, I Cantori di New York, The Song Company, Melbourne Symphony, The Oxford University Philharmonia, The Arcadian Singers, Ormond College Choir, The Pacific Ocean Symphony Orchestra; mem, AMC; FAC; CPCF. *Compositions:* Ice Man, solo piano, 1993; The Killing Floors, orchestra, 1995; Four Minutes in a Nuclear Bunker, orchestra, 1995; Nelson, soprano, baritone, string quartet, 1997; The Foundling, choir, string quartet, vibraphone, 1997. *Recordings:* CDs: Upon the Dark Water, song company; Greenbaum, Hindson, Peterson, anthology; Music for Theatre, playbox; Portrait and Blues Hymn; Polar Wandering, Fairfield Days. *Honours:* ANA Composition Award, 1991; Dorian Le Galliene Composition Award, 1993. *Address:* 4/111 Rushall Crescent, North Fitzroy, Vic 3068, Australia.

GREENBERG, Sylvia; Singer (Soprano); b. 1951, Romania. *Education:* Studied at the Tel-Aviv Academy of Music and with Marc Belfort in Zürich. *Career:* Debut: Tel-Aviv concert, conducted by Zubin Mehta; Stage debut Zürich 1977, as the Queen of Night: later sang Zerbinetta, Olympia in Les Contes d'Hoffmann, and in operas by Monteverdi; Guest appearances in Hamburg, Berlin, Vienna, Munich and Cologne; Glyndebourne Festival 1978, Die Zauberflöte; US debut Chicago 1981, in Die Schöpfung, conducted by Solti; Bayreuth Festival 1983, as Waldvogel in Siegfried; Salzburg Festival 1984, premiere of Un Re in Ascolto by Berio; At La Scala in 1985 sang the Queen of Night; Aix-en-Provence as Ilia in Idomeneo, 1986; Sang in Doktor Faustus by Giacomo Manzoni at La Scala, 1989; Olga in Fedora at Bologna, 1996; Sang Donna Elvira for New Israeli Opera, 2000. *Recordings include:* Die Schöpfung; Te Deum by Bizet; Poulenc's Gloria; Carmina Burana. *Address:* c/o Teatro all Scala, Via Filodrammatici 2, 20121 Milan, Italy.

GREENFIELD, Edward (Harry); Music Critic; b. 30 July 1928. *Education:* Trinity Hall, University of Cambridge (MA). *Career:* Joined Staff of Manchester Guardian, 1953; Record Critic, 1955; Music Critic, 1964; Succeeded Sir Neville Cardus as Chief Music Critic, 1977 until 1993; Broadcaster on Music and Records for BBC radio, 1957–; Member, Critics Panel, Gramophone, 1960–; President, Federation of Recorded Music Societies, 1997–. *Publications:* Puccini: Keeper of the Seal, 1958; Monographs on Joan Sutherland, 1972, André Previn, 1973; With Robert Layton, Ivan March and initially Denis Stevens, Stereo Record Guide, 9 vols, 1960–74; Penguin Stereo Record Guide, 1st Edition, 1975, 4th edition 1984; Penguin Guide to Compact Discs, 1st edition, 1986, 11th edition, 1998. *Honours:* Goldener Verdienstzeichen, Salzburg, 1980; Honorary GSM, 1991; Gramophone Special Award, 1993; O.B.E., 1994. *Address:* 16 Folgate Street, London E1, England.

GREENHOUSE, Bernard; Cellist and Teacher; b. 3 Jan. 1916, Newark, New Jersey, USA; m. Aurora Greenhouse, 2 d. *Education:* Diploma, Juilliard Graduate School of Music, New York, 1938; Studied with William Berce, Felix Salmond, Emanuel Feuermann, Diran Alexanian, Pablo Casals. *Career:* Principal Cellist, CBS Symphony Orchestra, New York, 1938–42; Member, Dorian String Quartet, 1939–42; Solo Cellist, US Navy Symphony Orchestra; Member, Navy String Quartet, 1942–45; Annual recitals, Town Hall, New York, 1946–57; Member, Harpsichord Quartet, 1947–51; Bach Aria Group, 1948–76; Founder-member, Beaux Arts Trio, 1955–87; Guest artist, Juilliard, Guarneri and Cleveland String Quartets; Numerous appearances on major concert series and with festivals world-wide; Professor, Manhattan School of Music, New York, 1950–82; Juilliard School of Music, New York, 1951–61; Indiana University School of Music, Bloomington, summers 1956–65; State University of New York, Stony Brook, 1960–85; New England Conservatory of Music, Boston, 1986–92; Rutgers, the State University of New Jersey, 1987–92; Masterclasses around the globe; mem, Cello Society, president, 1955–59, 1987–92; Honorary Member, American String Teachers Association. *Recordings:* Numerous. *Honours:* Eva Jantzer Award, Indiana Univ., 1980; National Service Award, Chamber Music America, 1988; Distinguished Cellist Award, Manchester, UK, 1996; Many recording awards including Prix Mondial du Disque; Union de la Presse Musicale Belge; Gramophone Record of the Year; Stereo Review Record of the Year; 3 Grand Prix du Disques; American String Teachers Association Teacher of the Year Award, 1982; US Presidential Citation, 1982; US Presidential Medallion, 1985; Honorary Doctorate, State University of New York, Stony Brook, 1988; Hon. Faculty Mem., Central Conservatory, Beijing, China, 2003. *Address:* 12 East 86th Street, New York, NY 10028, USA.

GREENLAW, Kevin; Singer (Baritone); b. 1965, USA. *Education:* Interlocken Arts Academy; Eastman School of Music; Opera School of the Royal Scottish Academy. *Career:* Early appearances as Mozart's Guglielmo and Nardo, Schaunard in La Bohème, Britten's Tarquinius, and Papageno (at Aldeburgh); Concerts include Carmina Burana, Des

Knaben Wunderhorn by Mahler, Messiah and the Fauré Requiem; Paris Opéra Bastille in Manon, Parsifal, Don Carlos and War and Peace; Ned Keene in Peter Grimes at Montpellier 2001; Elsewhere in France as Belcore, Ramiro in L'Heure Espangole and Odoardo in Handel's Ariodante at the Paris Palais Garnier, 2001; Juan in Massenet's Don Quichotte and Morales in Carmen at the Bastille; Has sung at Dortmund Opera as Don Giovanni and Marcello; Festival engagements at Edinburgh (Fringe), Isle of Mann, Aldeburgh and Orange. *Address:* Chemnitzer Straße 30, D–44139, Dortmund, Germany. *Telephone:* 49 231 545 0083. *Fax:* 49 231 545 0083.

GREENWOOD, Andrew; Conductor; b. 1954, Todmorden, Yorkshire, England. *Education:* Studied at Clare College, Cambridge and at the London Opera Centre. *Career:* Opera For All, 1976; Member of the music staff of Covent Garden 1977–84, studying with Edward Downes and conducting the Dutch Radio and Television Orchestra; Principal Guest Chorus Master of the Philharmonia Chorus from 1981: concerts with Previn, Davis, Giulini, Sinopoli and Solti; Conducted Rossini's Petite Messe Solennelle at the Istanbul Festival 1985; Chorus master at Welsh National Opera from 1984, and has conducted performances of operas by Mozart, Bizet, Puccini, Verdi, Berlioz (The Trojans), Beethoven, Strauss and Smetana; Many concerts on BBC Radio 2 and 3, notably with the BBC National Orchestra of Wales; Debut with the Rotterdam Philharmonic 1990, Cologne Opera 1990, The Bartered Bride and Die Fledermaus; English National Opera 1990–92, The Magic Flute and Madama Butterfly; Conducted Manon Lescaut for the Chelsea Opera Group, 1992, Don Giovanni for ENO; The Pearl Fishers for English Touring Opera, 1996. *Current Management:* Athole Still International Management, Forresters Hall, 25–27 Westow Street, London, SE19 3RY, England. *Telephone:* (20) 8771-5271. *Fax:* (20) 8768-6600. *Website:* www.atholestill.com.

GREER, David (Clive); Professor of Music; b. 8 May 1937, London, England; m. 1. Patricia Regan, 25 Aug 1961, deceased 1999, two s., one d., m. 2. Harriet Matling, 18 Sept, 2002. *Education:* Dulwich College, 1952–55; Oxford Univ., 1957–60; BA, 1960; MA, 1964; D.Mus, Dublin, 1991. *Career:* Lecturer in Music, Birmingham Univ., 1963–72; Hamilton Harty Prof. of Music, Queen's Univ., Belfast, 1972–84; Professor of Music, Newcastle Univ., 1984–86; Prof. of Music, Durham Univ., 1986–2000; Emeritus Prof., 2000; Mellon Visiting Fellow, 1989, Mayers Visiting Fellow, 1991, at Huntington Library, California; Folger Visiting Fellow, Folger Shakespeare Library, Washington DC, 1994, 1998; Chair., Accreditation Panel, Hong Kong Baptist Univ., 1994. *Publications:* Editor with F W Sternfeld, English Madrigal Verse, 3rd edition, 1967; English Lute Songs, facsimile series, 1967–71; Hamilton Harty, His Life and Music, 1979; Songs from Manuscript Sources, 1979; Collected English Lutenist Partsongs (Musica Britannica, vols 53–4), 1987–89; A Numerous and Fashionable Audience: The Story of Elsie Swinton, 1997; John Dowland: Ayres for Four Voices (Musica Britannica, vol. 6), 2000; Musicology and Sister Disciplines, 2000; Editor, Journal (formerly Proceedings) of the Royal Musical Association, vols 103–115. *Contributions:* Music and Letters; Proceedings of the Royal Musical Association; Lute Society Journal; Musical Times; Shakespeare Quarterly; English Studies, Notes and Queries; Early Music; Music Review. *Honours:* FRSA 1986. *Address:* Department of Music, University of Durham, Palace Green, Durham DH 1 3RL, England. *E-mail:* d.c.greer@durham.ac.uk.

GREEVE, Gilbert-Jean de; Concert Pianist; b. 11 Nov. 1944, St Truiden, Belgium. *Education:* Studied Piano with Eugene Traey, Royal Conservatory of Antwerp, Belgium, 1958–69; Performing major, with First Prizes in Piano and Chamber Music and a Diplome superieur for Chamber music; Composition major, with First Prizes in Music Theory, Harmony, Analysis, Counterpoint and Fugue; 1970 Peabody Institute of Music, Baltimore, Maryland, USA; Private studies with Rudolph Serkin, Eugene Ormandy and Leonard Pearlmann; 1972, Franz Liszt Academy of Budapest, Hungary. *Career:* Active world-wide as pianist 1970–; Director of the State Music Academy of Antwerp and Professor of the Royal Conservatory of Antwerp, 1970–; Working in a permanent duo with the Belgian soprano Martine De Craene, 1988–, repertoire of more than 14 hours music from Baroque until today, including 3 books of melodies by Gabriel Fauré; Lieder cycles by composers from Hungary and Canada have been dedicated to and world-created by the Duo. Concerts and Masterclasses in 5 continents; Major foreign tours: Canada, Australia, New Zealand, Africa, Finland, Netherlands, Antilles, Greece. *Compositions:* Chamber Music, a Lieder cycle of 36 Lieder on poems by James Joyce. *Recordings:* Belgian Radio and Television; CBC Canada; Hungarian Radio Budapest. *Address:* Anselmostraat 38, 2018 Antwerpen, Belgium.

GREEVY, Bernadette; Singer (mezzo-soprano); b. 3 July 1940, Dublin, Ireland. *Career:* Concert appearances with many of the world's great orchestras and numerous recitals in all the major capitals of the world; Operatic repertoire includes Eboli, Charlotte, Dalila, Herodiade in the opera by Massenet and Gluck's Orfeo; Tour of China 1985, giving recitals and holding Masterclasses; Recital series at the National Concert Hall in Dublin and on RTE Radio and Televiion; Has sung Mahler's Rückert Lieder and the Choral Symphony with the Oslo Philharmonic; The Brahms Alto Rhapsody and Elgar's Sea Pictures in Ottawa; Recent concerts in Denmark, Italy, Spain, USA, France, Finland and Norway; Mahler series in London with the Royal Philharmonic under Charles Dutoit, 1989. *Recordings:* Handel Arias, Orlando, Ariodante; Brahms Lieder; Nuits d'Eté by Berlioz and songs by Duparc, with the Ulster Orchestra (Chandos); Bach Arias; Sea Pictures; Mahler's Lieder eines fahrenden Gesellen and Kindertotenlieder, with the RTE Orchestra. *Honours:* Harriet Cohen International Music Award; Order of Merit of the Order of Malta; Hon. DMus, National University of Ireland; DMus, Trinity College Dublin, 1988; Pro Ecclesia et Pontifice, 1988. *Address:* c/o Trinity College, University of Dublin, Dublin 2, Republic of Ireland.

GREGOR, Bohumil; Conductor; b. 14 July 1926, Prague, Czechoslovakia. *Education:* Studied with Alois Klima at the Prague Conservatory. *Career:* Worked at the Prague 5th May (Smetana) Theatre from 1947; Conducted at the Brno Opera 1949–51; Musical Director Ostrava Opera 1958–62; Performances of Janáček's Katya Kabanova and The Excursions of Mr Brouček and premieres of works by Pauer, Kaslik and Trojan; Conductor at the Prague National Theatre from 1962: led the company in the first British productions of Janáček's From the House of the Dead (Edinburgh 1964 and 1970); Royal Opera Stockholm 1966–69, Hamburg Staatsoper 1969–72: premiere of Kelemen's Belagerungzustand (after The Plague by Camus, 1970) and operas by Verdi, Smetana and Janáček; Performances of The Cunning Little Vixen in Vienna, Edinburgh, Brussels and Amsterdam; San Francisco Opera from 1969, Jenůfa, Otello and Salome; Conducted The Cunning Little Vixen at Zürich, 1989 and at the Bayreuth Youth Festival, 1990; New production of Dvořák's The Devil and Kate at Prague, 1990; Season 1993 with Katya Kabanova and a new production of The Bartered Bride; Principal Guest Conductor, National Theatre, Prague; Brandenburgers in Bohemia by Smetana, 1997; Premiere of Burian's Bubu from Montparnasse (composed 1927), 1999; Music Director, The Prague State Opera, 1999–. *Recordings:* Several sets of Czech opera: The Makropulos Case, The Cunning Little Vixen, Jenůfa and From the House of the Dead; Dvořák Symphonic Poems; Concert overtures; Slavonic rhapsodies. *Address:* Janackovo Nabrezi 7. 150 00 Prague 5, Czech Republic.

GREGOR, Joszef; Singer (Bass); b. 8 Aug. 1940, Rakosliget, Hungary. *Education:* Studied in Budapest with Endreh Poessler and sang in choir of Hungarian army. *Career:* Appearances at the Szeged Opera from 1964; Sang Sarastro at the Hungarian State Opera, Budapest, 1966; Played title role in Hungarian premiere of Attila, 1972 and appeared in operas by Goldmark, Rossini, Donizetti, Puccini and Bart ók (title role in Duke Bluebeard's Castle); Visited the Wiesbaden Festival 1970 and sang elsewhere in Germany as guest; Houston Grand Opera 1986 as Varlaam in Boris Godunov, Monte Carlo Opera 1988, in Cimarosa's Il Pittore Parigino; New York Met debut 1994, as a Priest in Lady Macbeth of the Mtsensk District; Sang the King in Aida at Szaged, 1997; Sang Dulcamara at the Erkel Theatre, Budapest, 1995; Sang Rossini's Bartolo at Antwerp, 1999, and in Jenůfa at Geneva, 2001; Many radio and television performances from 1975; Frequent concert engagements. *Recordings:* Goldmark's Die Königin von Saba; Haydn's L'Infedeltà delusa and La Fedeltà Premiata; Paisiello's Barbiere di Siviglia; Guntram (Strauss), Nerone (Boito) and Mosè in Egitto (Rossini); Don Pasquale, Gianni Schicchi and La Fiamma by Respighi; Duke Bluebeard's Castle; Liszt's Missa solemnis and Legend of St Elisabeth; Beethoven's Missa solemnis and 9th Symphony; Salieri's Falstaff; La Serva Padrona; Il Pittore Parigino; Andrea Chénier and Fedora; Der Geduldige Sokrates by Telemann (Hungaroton). *Address:* Hungarian State Opera House, Nepoztarsasag utja 22, 1061 Budapest, Hungary.

GREGSON, Edward; Composer and Conductor; b. 23 July 1945, Sunderland, England; m. Susan Carole Smith, 30 Sept 1967, 2 s. *Education:* Royal Academy of Music, 1963–67; LRAM, 1966; GRSM, 1967; BMus, University of London, 1977;. *Career:* Lecturer, 1976, Reader in Music, 1989, Professor of Music, 1996, Goldsmiths' College, University of London; Principal, Royal Northern College of Music, 1996–; Director: Associated Board of the Royal Schools of Music, Performing Right Society, Hallé Orchestra; Governor, Chetham's School of Music; As Composer commissioned by numerous orchestras, organisations, ensembles, the United Kingdom and abroad, 1970–, including English Chamber Orchestra, 1968, York Festival, 1976, Royal Shakespeare Company, 1988, 1990, Bournemouth Festival, 1991, Hallé Orchestra, 1999, also National Centre for Orchestral Studies, Wren Orchestra of London, BBC, Royal Liverpool Philharmonic, 1999; Extensive judging panel work includes BBC Young Musician of the Year and Royal Philharmonic Society, amongst others. *Compositions include:* Orchestral: Music for Chamber Orchestra, 1968; Horn Concerto, 1971; Tuba Concerto, 1976; Trombone Concerto, 1979; Metamorphoses, 1979; Contrasts, 1983, revised 2001; Trumpet Concerto, 1983; Celebration, 1991; Blazon, 1992; Clarinet Concerto, 1994; Concerto, piano and wind, 1995–97; And the Seven Trumpets, 1998; Violin Concerto, 2000; Choral, vocal: In the Beginning, 1966; 5 Songs of Innocence and Experience, 1979; Missa Brevis Pacem, 1988; Make a Joyful Noise, anthem, 1988; A Welcome Ode, 1997; The Dance, forever the Dance, 1999; Instrumental, chamber: Divertimento, 1967; 6 Little Piano Pieces, 1982; Piano Sonata in one movement, 1986; Alarum, 1993; Three Matisse Impressions, 1993; Romance for Recorder and string quartet, 1964, revised 2003; Brass Quintet, 1967; Equale Dances from brass quintet, 1983; Brass Band: Connotations, 1977; Dances and Arias, 1984; Of Men and Mountains, 1990; The Trumpets of the Angels, 2000; Symphonic Wind Band: Festivo, 1988; The Sword and the Crown, 1991; The Kings Go Forth, 1997; Educational music. Recordings: Most of these compositions have been commercially recorded: Blazon, Violin Concerto, Clarinet Concerto, Contrasts- a concerto for orchestra; Tuba Concerto; Clarinet Concerto; Brass and Wind music composed and conducted by the composer. Publications include: The Contemporary Repertoire of Brass Bands in the 20th Century, 1979. Honours: FRAM, 1990; FRNCM, 1999; FRCM, 2000 Hon. FLCM, 1997; FDCA, 1998; Hon. DMus from the Univ. of Sunderland, 1996; Fellow Dartington College of Arts, 1997; Hon. Fellow of Leeds College of Music, 1998; FRNCM 1999; FRCM 2000; Hon. Doctorate of Arts from Manchester Metropolitan Univ., 2003. Address: c/o The Royal Northern College of Music, 124 Oxford Road, Manchester M13 9RD, England.

GRELA-MOZEJKO, Piotr; Composer and Music Critic; b. 15 March 1961, Bytom, Poland; m. Kasia Zoledziowski 30 June 1990. Education: MA, University of Silesia, Katowice; Studied Composition with Dr Edward Boguslawski, Katowice, Dr Boguslaw Schaeffer, Kraków, Dr Alfred Fisher, University of Alberta. Career: Debut: The Silesian Tribune of Composers, 1982; 1st performance of work, 1977; Works performed at major festivals such as Warsaw Autumn Festival, Poznan Music Spring Festival, Gdansk Meetings of Young Composers; Founder, Fascinating Music Festival, Katowice, 1983–86; Co-Founder, J. S. Bach Festival, Kraków-Katowice, 1985; Took part in many exhibitions of musical scores, Institut Polonais, Paris, Royal Academy of Music, London, Warsaw, Salzburg, Katowice; Numerous interviews, Polish television and radio, also CBC; Polish television documentary on activities and the Fascinating Music Festival, 1992; Completed MMus Degree in Composition at the University of Alberta, Edmonton, 1992. Compositions: Archival radio recordings, Poland, Canada, USA: Ravenna, harpsichord; minimum-optimum-maximum, chamber ensemble; en attendant Bergson, string quartet; The Dreams of Odysseus, tape (performed in Warsaw, Poland, as part of the first exhibition of Polish artists in exile, Jestesmy); Epitaph for Jerzy, for tape included in A BEAMS Compilation; Xylotet Concerto, saxophone, orchestra; Horror Vacui, strings; Ordines, saxophone, organ, cello; Melodramas I–VI, solo instruments; Festivals: Canada, Pacific Market, Fringe, The Edmonton Music Festival, Warsaw. Address: No. 8 8807 101st Street, Edmonton, Alberta T6E 3Z9, Canada.

GRIBENSKI, Jean; Musicologist; b. 5 Aug. 1944, Castelmoron-sur-Lot, Lot-et-Garonne, France; m. Isabelle Serrand, 10 Sept 1980, 1 s., 3 d. Education: History, Musicology, Sorbonne, Paris, 1963–68; Studied Piano, Musical Theory and Harmony. Career: Teaching, History of Music, Sorbonne, Université Paris IV, 1970–2003, Université de Poitiers, 2003–; Editor-in-Chief, Revue de Musicologie, 1974–86; mem, Société française de musicologie, Board of Directors, 1974–, President, 1995–2001. Publications: Thèses de doctorat en langue française relative à la musique/French language dissertations in music, 1979; D'un opéra l'autre, 1996. Address: 23 avenue de Breteuil, 75007 Paris, France.

GRICE, Garry (Bruce); Opera Singer (Tenor); b. 25 Jan. 1942, Dayton, Ohio, USA; m. Patricia A Michael, 9 July 1983, 1 s., 2 d. Education: BA, History, University of Daytn, 1964; Musical studies with Hubert Kockritz, Cincinnati and Adelaide Saraceni, Milan. Career: Debut: National Opera, USA, 1970–71; 8 seasons in German and Swiss opera houses including: Debut, Stadttheater, St Gallen, Switzerland, 1974; Debut, Bavarian State Opera, 1974; Debut as Don José in Carmen, Florentine Opera, Milwaukee, 1980; Bacchus in Ariadne auf Naxos, Des Moines Metro Opera, 1980; Debut, New York City Opera, 1981; Bermuda Festival, 1981; Debut, Chicago as Don José in Carmen, 1983; Debut, Calgary Opera Association, 1985; Debut, Cairo, 1990; Has sung with conductors Kleiber, Prêtre, Guadagno, Keene and Rescigno; Has appeared in over 50 roles including Otello, Florestan, Bacchus, Canio, Max and Radames; Has sung throughout USA, also Canada, Bermuda and Europe mainly Germany, Austria, Switzerland; Faculty Voice and Opera, University of Notre Dame, 1991; Artistic Director, Indian Opera North since 1990; Performance: New Orleans Debut, Verdi Requiem, 1992. Recordings: Title role in Otello, Television Public Broadcasting, 1984; Turiddu in Cavalleria Rusticana, Canadian Public Radio, 1985. Publications: Translations into English of Otello, II Trovatore and Tales of Hoffmann. Current Management: Warden

Associated INc, 127 W 72nd Street, Suite 2-R, New York, NY 10023, USA.

GRIER, Francis; Organist, Pianist and Composer; b. 1955, England. Education: Chorister at St George's Chapel, Windsor Castle; Eton College; Organ Scholar at King's College, Cambridge; Piano Studies with Joseph Cooper, Fanny Waterman and Bernard Roberts; Organ with Gillian Weir. Career: Assistant Organist to Simon Preston, at Christ Church Cathedral, Oxford; Organist and Director of Music, 1981; Organ recitals throughout the United Kingdom; First Organ recital at the BBC Promenade Concerts, 1985; Sudied in India from 1985; Then worked with mentally handicapped in London and Bangladore; Resident in England from 1989; Works as psychodynamic counsellor; mem, FRCO. Compositions: Advent Responsories for King's College Chapel, 1990; Mass with motets for Westminster Abbey; Sequences of Readings and Music for Ascension, for the 550th anniversary of Eton College, 1990; The Cry of Mary, for BBC2, 1992; St Francis, opera, for Eton College and National Youth Music Theatre, 1993; Mass in Time of Persecution, for soloists, chorus and orchestra, including poems of Ratushinskaya, 1994; My Heart Dances, settings of Tagore, for soloists, chorus and orchestra, commissioned by 3 Choirs Festival, 1995. Recordings: Bach; Mendelssohn; Couperin, Franck; Messiaen: Messe de la Pentecôte and L'Ascension, all on the Rieger organ at Christ Church Cathedral. Address: 65 Tynemouth Road, London N15 4AU, England.

GRIEVES-SMITH, Jonathan Mark, BA; British conductor and artistic director; b. 14 Dec. 1962, Kendal, England; m. Sally; two s. one d. Education: Kingswood School, Bath and Univ. of Sussex. Career: Artistic Dir and Prin. Conductor, Melbourne Chorale; Artistic Admin., The Queensland Orchestra; Music Dir, Brighton Festival Chorus; Chorus Master, Huddersfield Choral Soc., Halle Choir, Reading Festival Chorus; guest conductor, Royal Philharmonic Orchestra, Royal Liverpool Philharmonic, London Mozart Players, Bournemouth Symphony Orchestra, New Zealand Symphony Orchestra, Melbourne Symphony Orchestra, Orchestre Nat. de Lille, Bochum Symphoniker, Europa Cantat in Denmark and Austria, Dartington Int. Summer School; Conductor Emer., Melbourne Chorale. Recordings: as chorus master for Bax/Handley, Beethoven/Menuhin, Walton/Previn, Tippett/Previn, Martin/Bamert, Lloyd/Lloyd, Patterson/Simon. Address: 14 Lambert Road, Toorak, Vic. 3142, Australia (home).

GRIFFEL, Kay; Singer (Soprano); b. 26 Dec. 1940, Eldora, Iowa, USA; m. Eckhard Sellheim. Education: Studied at Northwestern University, Illinois, in Berlin and with Lotte Lehmann at Santa Barbara. Career: Debut: Chicago 1960, as Mercédès in Carmen; Sang at the Deutsche Oper Berlin and in Bremen, Mainz, Karlsruhe, Hamburg and Düsseldorf; Salzburg 1973 in the premiere of De Temporum fine Comoedia by Orff; Glyndebourne Festival 1976–77, as Alice Ford in Falstaff; Tour of Japan with the Staatsoper Berlin 1977, as the Marschallin, Donna Elvira and Mozart's Countess; Lisbon 1978, Eva in Die Meistersinger; Metropolitan Opera from 1982, as Electra in Idomeneo, Rosalinde, Arabella, Tatiana and the Countess; Further appearances in Brussels, Moscow, Cologne and at the Orange Festival; Sang Eva in Die Meistersinger at Wellington, New Zealand, 1990. Recordings: Janáček Diary of One who Disappeared (Deutsche Grammophon); De Temporum fine Comoedia; Italian Arias. Honours: Doctorate of Fine Arts, Simpson College, Indianola, Iowa 1982. Current Management: Robert Lombardo, New York, USA; Stoll and Hilbert in Germany. Address: c/o Wellington City Opera (contracts), PO Box 6588, New Zealand.

GRIFFEY, Anthony Dean; American singer (tenor); b. 1968, North Carolina. Education: Metropolitan Young Artist Development Program. Career: debut, New York Met 1995, as First Knight in Parsifal; Appearances at the Met in Manon, Don Carlos, Aida, Billy Budd, Salome, Boris Godunov and The Queen of Spades; Further engagements as Peter Grimes and Sam Polk in Floyd's Susannah at the Met, Mitch in Previn's A Streetcar named Desire at San Francisco, and Mozart's Idomeneo for the Mainly Mozart Festival, New York; Season 2000–01 with Peter Grimes at Glyndebourne, Ferrando in Così fan tutte and Laca in Jenůfa at the Saito Kinen Festival, Japan, and The Dream of Gerontius with the New York Philharmonic; Other concerts include Britten's War Requiem, at Tanglewood. Recordings include: A Streetcar Named Desire. Current Management: Columbia Artists Management LLC, 165 W 57th Street, New York, NY 10019-2276, USA. Telephone: (212) 841-9500. Fax: (212) 841-9744. E-mail: info@cami.com. Website: www.anthonydeangriffey.com.

GRIFFIN, Judson; Violist and Violinist; b. 7 Sept. 1951, Lewes, Delaware, USA; m. Mara Paske, 7 May 1988. Education: DMA 1977, MM 1975, Juilliard School of Music; BM, Eastman School of Music, 1973. Career: Debut: Carnegie Recital Hall, New York City, January 1981; Violist, Rochester Philharmonic Orchestra, 1970–73; Freelance Violist, New York City, 1973–77; Assistant Professor, University of

North Carolina at Greensboro, 1977–79; Principal Viola, Aspen Chamber Symphony, 1977–80; Freelance Violinist and Violist, New York City, 1979–; Current activities, Violist of Smithson String Quartet and Smithsonian Chamber Players (Smithsonian Institution, Washington DC); Atlantis Ensemble (Europe); Violinist of Four Nations and Sonata a quattro (New York); Regular appearances with almost all period-instrument organisations in USA. *Recordings:* Chamber music on labels, Nonesuch, Harmonia Mundi (France, USA), L'Oiseau-Lyre, Reference, Harmonia Mundi (Germany), Columbia, CRI, CP2, Pro Arte, Newport; Many radio recordings. *Address:* 170 Claremont Avenue No. 7, New York, NY 10027, USA.

GRIFFITH, Lisa; Singer (Soprano); b. 1959, USA. *Education:* Studied at Indiana University and the Cincinnati Conservatory. *Career:* Debut: Seattle Opera, 1984; Sang at Wiesbaden Opera, 1984–89, Hanover, 1989–91, notably as Zerbinetta; Deutsche Oper am Rhein, Düsseldorf, from 1991, as Susanna in The Marriage of Figaro and Sophie in Rosenkavalier (1993); Other roles include Gilda and Pamina; Guest at the Munich Staatsoper, the Komische Oper Berlin and Staatsoper Stuttgart; Frequent concert appearances; Sang in premiere production of Beuys by Franz Hummel, Vienna, Berlin and Düsseldorf, 1998; Sang Irina in Three Sisters by Peter Eötvös at Dusseldorf, 1999, and Gounod's Juliette at Lubeck, 2000. *Address:* c/o Deutsche Oper am Rhein, Heinrich-Heine-Allee 16a, 40213 Düsseldorf, Germany.

GRIFFITH-SMITH, Bella; American singer and conductor; b. 1920. *Education:* studied with Howard Thain, Franco Iglesias, Dr Paul Csonka. *Career:* debut at the Civic Opera of the Palm Beaches; appeared with Louis Quilico, Metropolitan artist, Robert Merrill, Giuseppe Campora; television: Concert Version-Spanish Translation, Channel 2, Miami; Madama Butterfly; radio: La Traviata; leading roles in Madama Butterfly; La Bohème, Tosca, Cavalleria Rusticana, Pagliacci, Suor Angelica, Il Tabarro, Faust, Carmen (Micaela), Così fan tutte (Fiordiligi), Tales of Hoffmann (Antonia), Don Pasquale-Norina, L'Oca del Cairo (Celidora), La Traviata, Oratorio-Elijah, L'Enfant Prodigue, Messiah, Vivaldi's Gloria, Stabat Mater, Rossini; concerts: Salome, Otello, Turandot, with Alain Lombard/Greater Miami Philharmonic; guest soloist; Pres., Coral Gables Civic Opera and Orchestra, Inc. *Address:* 700 Santander Avenue, Coral Gables, FL 33134, USA.

GRIFFITHS, Graham (Charles Thomas); Conductor, Pianist and Lecturer; b. 13 May 1954, Tiverton, England; m. Miriam Regina Zillo, 18 Jan 1985, 2 s. *Education:* Bryanston School 1967–72; BMus (hons) Edinburgh University, 1976; PGCE (Cantab) Cambridge University, 1977. *Career:* Founder-Member, Edinburgh Experimental Arts Society, 1972–76; Founder-member, Grand Toxic Opera Company, Edinburgh, 1974–76; Member, Cambridge Contemporary Music Ensemble, 1976–78; Marketing/Education Officer, Scottish National Orchestra, 1978–81; Co-Administrator, International Musica Nova Festival, Glasgow, 1978–81; Arts Journalist, Scottish Television, 1981–86; Principal Conductor, Glasgow Chamber Orchestra, 1985–86; Lecturer in Twentieth Century Music, São Paulo State University, Brazil, 1987–89; Founder-Director, Jardim Musical Arts Centre, 1987–; Founder-Conductor, Ensemble Grupo Novo Horizonte, 1988–; Director of Education, Mozarteum Brasileiro, 1987–; Conductor, Choir of Cultura Inglesa, São Paulo, 1988–90; Choral Director, 1st National Festival of Brazilian Colonial Music (Juiz de Fora) 1990; Guest Conductor, Campos do Jordao Festival, 1990; Guest Conductor, Orquestra Sinfonica e Madrigal da Universidade Federal da Bahia, Salvador, 1990–; Director of Conducting Course, Festival Seminarios Internacionais Salvador, 1991; Lecture-Recital piano tours: 1990 Bridges Across Time, Brazil, Denmark, United Kingdom; 1991 New World Experience, Brazil, Denmark (25 concerts); Co-Founder-Director, Mostra de Musica Contemporanea, Ouro Preto, 1991; Regular broadcasts on Radio e Televisao Cultura, São Paulo, 1988–; Visiting Lecturer, Federal Universities of Rio de Janeiro, 1990, Bahia 1990/91, Uberlandia 1992; Guest Conductor, Camerata Antigua de Curitiba, 1993. *Compositions:* Sacred Choral Works include: Anglican Hymn Collection, 1988–; The Lords Prayer, 1990; Ta Voix, 1991; Cançao de Quatá for Trombone Quartet, 1993. *Current Management:* Jardim Musical, São Paulo. *Address:* Rua Angatuba 97, Pacaembu, 01247-000 São Paulo, SP, Brazil.

GRIFFITHS, Hilary; Conductor; b. 1950, Leamington Spa, England; m. Andrea Andonian, 28 June 1978, 2 s. *Education:* Studied at the Royal Academy of Music, London Opera Centre and in Siena and Milan. *Career:* Former principal staff conductor at the Cologne Opera, with appearances also in Dresden, Düsseldorf, Nuremberg and Basle; Former music director of Oberhausen Opera with further engagements in Oslo, Antwerp, Leeds (Opera North) and at the Edinburgh, Prague and Schwetzingen Festivals; Conductor at the State Opera Prague from 1992 (operas by Zemlinsky and Strauss), music director at Regensburg from 1993 and at the Eutin opera festival (Die Zauberflöte, Il Trovatore, Der Freischütz and Turandot); Season 1997 with Don Giovanni and Intermezzo at Regensburg, Die Zauberflöte and Aida in Cologne and Otello and Butterfly in Prague; Don Giovanni at the Perth Festival,

Australia and Der Prinz von Homburg to open the Wiesbaden May Festival; Concerts with the Rotterdam Philharmonic, the BBC National Orchestra of Wales, and the West German Radio Orchestra. *Recordings:* CD, Jommelli, Mass in D and Te Deum. *Publications:* World Premieres: Das Gauklermärchen and Lulu; German Premieres, A Christmas Carol and Simon Bolivar both by Thea Musgrave. *Contributions:* TV and Video: Il matrimonio segreto, from the Schwetzingen Festival, Lulu from Cologne. *Address:* Graf-Adolf-Strasse 28, 51065 Cologne, Germany.

GRIFFITHS, Howard (Laurence); Conductor; b. 24 Feb. 1950, Hastings, England; m. Semra Griffiths, 24 July 1971, 1 s., 1 d. *Education:* Viola with Cecil Aronowitz, Royal College of Music, London; ARCM; Conducting with Leon Barzin, Paris, Erich Schmid, Zürich. *Career:* Debut: Queen Elizabeth Hall, English Chamber Orchestra, 1989; Royal Festival Hall, Royal Philharmonic Orchestra, 1991; Principal Viola, Ankara State Opera until 1979; Member, Lucerne String Quartet; Principal Guest Conductor, Oxford Orchestra da Camera, 1994; Director and Principal Conductor, Zürich Chamber Orchestra, 1996–; Has conducted many prominent orchestras including Royal Philharmonic Orchestra, English Chamber Orchestra, Warsaw Philharmonic Orchestra, Basel Radio Symphony Orchestra, Istanbul State Symphony Orchestra, Northern Sinfonia of England, Stadtorchester Winterthur, Polish Chamber Orchestra, Tonhalle Orchestra Zürich, National Orchestra of Spain, London Mozart Players, Slovak Radio-Symphony Orchestra; Tchaikovsky SO of the Moscow Radio, Orchestre Nationale de Paris, Orchestre Philharmonique de Montpellier, Tapiola Sinfonietta; Repertory includes music by Henze (Requiem), Crumb, Kagel and Pärt; Artistic Director, Allensbach Chamber Music Festival, Germany, 1992–98; Artistic director since 2000 of the Orpheum Foundation for the Promotion of Young Soloists. *Recordings:* Over 60 CDs include 18th Century Swiss Composers Stalder and Reindl, English Chamber Orchestra; Instrumental Works of Othmar Schoeck, English Chamber Orchestra; Mozart Horn Concertos, Kalinski and Polish Chamber Orchestra; Works of Max Bruch, Royal Philharmonic Orchestra; 3 CDs of music by Turkish composers Saygun, Erkin, Rey, with Northern Sinfonia of England; Baroque Oboe Concertos and Mozart Sinfonia Concertante; Caspar Fritz Violin Concerto, English Chamber Orchestra; Ferdinand Ries Complete Symphonies 1–8 with Zürich Chamber Orchestra. *Current Management:* Konzertgesellschaft, Hochstrasse 51, Postfach, CH–4002 Basel, Switzerland.

GRIFFITHS, Paul Anthony, BA, MSc; British music critic and writer; b. 24 Nov. 1947, Bridgend, Glamorgan, Wales. *Education:* Lincoln Coll., Oxford. *Career:* music critic for various journals 1971–; Area Ed. 20th Century Music, New Grove Dictionary of Music and Musicians 1973–76; music critic, the Times 1982–92, New Yorker 1992–96, New York Times 1997–; compiled Mozart pasticcio The Jewel Box for Opera North 1991, Purcell pasticcio Aeneas in Hell 1995. *Publications:* A Concise History of Modern Music 1978, Boulez 1978, A Guide to Electronic Music 1979, Cage 1981, Peter Maxwell Davies 1982, The String Quartet 1983, György Ligeti 1983, Bartók 1984, Olivier Messiaen 1985, New Sounds, New Personalities: British Composers of the 1980s 1985, An Encyclopedia of 20th Century Music 1986, Myself and Marco Polo (novel) 1987, The Life of Sir Tristram (novel) 1991, The Jewel Box (opera libretto) 1991, Stravinsky 1992, Modern Music and After 1995, libretti for Tan Dun's opera, Marco Polo 1996, libretti for Elliott Carter's opera, What Next? 1999, The Sea on Fire 2004. *Address:* University of Rochester Press, 668 Mount Hope Avenue, Rochester, NY 14620-273, USA.

GRIFFITHS, Paul Wayne; Conductor; b. 1958, England. *Education:* Studied at Royal Northern College of Music and London Opera Centre. *Career:* Conducted The Judgement of Paris by John Woolrich in Royal Opera House Garden Venture Series, Orchestra of Royal Opera at Windsor Festival and Symphony Hall, Birmingham; Paris debut at Théâtre du Champs Elysées, with Orchestre du Conservatoire National; Further concerts with Royal Philharmonic, English Chamber Orchestra and Tokyo Philharmonic; Season 1992–93 with Il Trovatore for Scottish Opera, L'Elisir d'amore at Gothenburg, concert in Athens with Grace Bumbry and London with Josephine Bartsow and Montserrat Caballé; Covent Garden debut with Rigoletto (1994), returning for La Bohème and Turandot; Artistic Director and Accompanist of Luciano Pavarotti Masterclass; Recital Accompanist with Geraint Evans, José Carreras, Katia Ricciarelli, James King, Thomas Allen and Yevgeny Nesterenko; Staff Conductor, Royal Opera House, Covent Garden.

GRIGOREV, Alexei; Singer (tenor); b. 1968, Russia. *Education:* Sweelinck Conservatory; Netherlands International Opera Studio. *Career:* Appearances throughout Europe in Billy Budd, Antwerp; The Nose, Leipzig; Mozart's Mitridate at Lyon; Meistersinger, Parsifal and Figaro, Netherlands; Season 1998–99 in Moses und Aron, Die Zauberflote and La finta giardiniera, Darmstadt; Marzio, Mozart's Mitridate, Lyon, 1998; Season 1999–2000 at Châtelet, Paris, Amsterdam and Antwerp; Sang Innkeeper, Benvenuto Cellini, Festival Hall Concert, 1999; Season 2000–01: Le grand macabre, Antwerp; Boris Godounov,

Capriccio, DNO, Amsterdam; Don Pasquale, Luxembourg; Three Sisters by Eötvös; Bastien und Bastienne, Concertgebouw, Amsterdam; Season 2001–02: Le Coq d'or in Nantes; Three Sisters by Eötvös in Brussels, Lyon and Vienna; Pulcinella in Brussels and Amsterdam; Lucia di Lammermoor in Basel; Dido and Aeneas, Netherlands; Lustigen Weiber; Concert repertory includes Bach's St John and St Matthew Passions, Berlioz Messe solennelle and Mahler's Klagende Lied; Season 2001–02: Orff's Carmina Burana, Rossini's Stabat Mater, Debussy's L'invocation, Shostakovich's From Jewish Folk Poetry. *Current Management:* Athole Still International Management, Forresters Hall, 25–27 Westow Street, London, SE19 3RY, England. *Telephone:* (20) 8771-5271. *Fax:* (20) 8768-6600. *Website:* www.atholestill.com. *Address:* Sleewijkstraat 78, 1107 TW Amsterdam, Netherlands. *E-mail:* a .grigorev@freeler.nl.

GRIGORIAN, Gegam; Singer (Tenor); b. 29 Jan. 1951, Erevan, Armenia. *Education:* Studied at the Opera School of La Scala, Milan. *Career:* Debut: Lwów Opera, 1989, as Cavaradossi; Kirov Opera, St Petersburg, from 1990, notably as Vladimir in Prince Igor and Dimitri in Boris Godunov; Amsterdam from 1991, as Gennaro in Lucrezia Borgia, Andrea Chénier and Cilea's Maurizio; Pierre in War and Peace at the Opéra Bastille, Paris; Covent Garden debut, 1993, as Lensky; Season 1994–95, as Radames at Rome, Pollione in Norma at Genoa and Rimsky's Sadko in Paris; Sang Verdi's Riccardo at Santiago, Cavaradossi at Wiesbaden and Turiddu at Florence; Metropolitan Opera debut as Hermann in The Queen of Spades, 1995; Season 1998 as Riccardo at Monte Carlo, Vasily Golitsin in Khovanshchina at La Scala (Kirov Opera) and Alvaro in La Forza del Destino at St Petersburg (also televised); Sang Canio at Buenos Aires, 2000, Golitsin on tour with the Kirov to Covent Garden, and Pierre in War and Peace at La Scala. *Address:* Kirov Opera, 1 Theatre Square, St Petersburg, Russia.

GRIGORIU, Theodor; Composer; b. 25 July 1926, Galatzi, Romania; m. 28 Mar 1951. *Education:* Studied with Mihail Jora, Conservatory of Bucharest, Romania, and Aram Khachaturian, P I Tchaikovsky, Moscow, USSR; Faculty of Architecture, Bucharest. *Career:* Secretary-General, Union of Romanian Composers; Freelance Composer; His works performed world-wide. *Compositions:* Orchestral works include: Sinfonia Cantabile, Op 1, 1950, revised 1966; Variations Symphoniques sur une Chanson d'Anton Pann, (Six Tableaux d'Epoque), 1955; Concerto pour Double Orchestre de Chamber et Hautbois, 1957; Rêve Cosmique-poéme orchestral, 1959; Hommage à Enesco, 8(16) violons, 1960; Orchestral version of Sept Chansons (works Clement Marot), 1964; Tristia, in memoriam Ionel Perlea, Melodie Infinie, 1972; Suite Carpatine, string orchestra, 1980; Pastorale si Idylles de Transylvanie, 1984; Concerto pour violon et orchestre Byzance aprés Byzance, 1994; Chopin Orchestral, 25 Pieces pour un ballet imaginaire, 1995; Requiem for a Poetess, 1999; Aeterna verba im 2000 for mixed chorus and orchestra, 2000; Choral Music: Elegia Pontica, (vers d'Ovide), choir, baritone-bass, 1969; Canti per Europa (oratorio), mixed choir and orchestra, 1976; Les Vocalises de la Mer (choral symphony), mixed choir, organ and orchestra, 1984; Chamber music: Columna Modala (Cahiers I, II), investigations dans l'ethos roumain, piano, 1984; Quatuor à cordes A la recherche de l'echo, 1983; Film Music: Codine, 1963; La Foret des Pendus, 1965; Theatre music. *Recordings:* Various works, Electrocord. *Publications:* Muzica si Numbul Poeziei. *Address:* Str Pictor Rosenthal 2, Bucharest 71288, Romania.

GRIGSBY, Beverly; Composer; b. 11 Jan. 1928, Chicago, Illinois, USA. *Education:* Studied in California with Ernst Krenek and Ingolf Dahl and at Stanford University and the Royal College, London. *Career:* Teacher at California State University, Northridge, 1963–92. *Compositions include:* Stage works: Augustine The Saint, 1975, Moses, 1978, The Vision Of St Joan, 1987; Trio for violin, clarinet and piano, 1984; Wind Quintet, 1990; Keyboard Concerto, 1993; Concerto for orchestra, 1994; Computer music. *Address:* c/o ASCAP, ASCAP Building, 1 Lincoln Plaza, New York, NY 10023, USA.

GRILLO, Joann; Singer (Mezzo-Soprano); b. 14 May 1939, New York, USA; m. Richard Kness, 1 s. *Education:* BS, Hunter College, New York; Private study with Loretta Corelli, Franco Iglesias and Daniel Ferro. *Career:* Debut: New York City Opera 1962, as Gertrude in Louise; Metropolitan Opera, as Carmen, Meg Page in Falstaff, Preziosilla in La Forza del Destino, Santuzza, Laura in La Gioconda, Neocle in The Siege of Corinth and Suzuki (226 performances); Sang Massenet's Charlotte at Barcelona in 1963; Amneris at Frankfurt (1967); Carmen at the Vienna Staatsoper and in Paris (1978, 1981); Guest appearances in Essen, Hamburg, Zürich, Dallas, Philadelphia, Lisbon and Marseille; Other roles include Marguerite in The Damnation of Faust, Saint-Saëns's Dalila, Olga in Eugene Onegin, Fricka in The Ring and Verdi's Eboli, Ulrica and Azucena; Sang Amneris at Rio de Janeiro, 1988; Concert appearances as Jocasta in Oedipus Rex. *Current Management:* Eric Semon Associates, 111 W 57th Street, New York City, NY 10019, USA. *Address:* c/o Rio de Janeiro Opera, Teatro Municipal, Rio de Janeiro, Brazil.

GRIMAUD, Hélène; American (b. French) pianist; b. Aix en Provence, France. *Education:* studied in Marseille with Pierre Barbizet, Conservatoire Nat. Supérieur de Musique, Paris, studied with Jacques Rouvier, Gyorgy Sandor and Leon Fleischer. *Career:* Paris debut recital 1987; performances at MIDEM, Cannes, and at La Roque d'Anthéron Piano Festival 1987; has performed with orchestras worldwide, including Boston Symphony, Cleveland Orchestra, Los Angeles Philharmonic, New York Philharmonic, Philadelphia Orchestra, Montréal Symphony, London Symphony Orchestra, City of Birmingham Symphony Orchestra, London Philharmonic Orchestra, English Chamber Orchestra, Berlin Philharmonic, Bavarian Radio Symphony, Deutsches Symphonie-Orchester, Gewandhausorchester Leipzig, Tonhalle Zurich, Göteborg Symphony, Oslo Philharmonic, Tokyo NHK Symphony, St Petersburg Philharmonic, Concertgebouw Orchestra, Rotterdam Philharmonic, Orchestre Philharmonique de Radio France, Orchestre de Paris; recent performances include the première of a work for piano and orchestra by Arvo Pärt at the Tate Modern gallery, London, concerts in Amsterdam, London, Paris and Japan with the Czech Philharmonic and Ashkenazy, performances with the Philharmonia Orchestra under Christoph von Dohnányi, the Danish National Radio Symphony under Thomas Dausgaard, Detroit Symphony under Neeme Järvi and Netherlands Radio Philharmonic under Peter Eötvös; signed an exclusive contract with Deutsche Grammophon 2002; season 2003/04 appearances included performances with Orchester der Bayerische Staatsoper, San Francisco Symphony, Deutsches Symphonie Orchester Berlin, Tokyo Philharmonic, and tours with the Australian Youth Orchestra, the Chamber Orchestra of Europe and the Philharmonia Orchestra. *Recordings:* Rachmaninoff's Sonata No. 2 (Grand Prix du Disque 1986) 1985, Ravel Concerto in G and Rachmaninov Concerto No.2 with the Royal Philharmonic and Jesus Lopez-Cobos, Schumann Concerto and Strauss Burleske with David Zinman and the Deutsches Symphonie-Orchester Berlin, Brahms opus 116–119 1996, Gershwin Concerto in F and the Ravel Concerto in G with David Zinman and the Baltimore Symphony, Brahms Piano Concerto No.1 with Berlin Staatskapelle Orchester and Kurt Sanderling (Cannes Classical Recording of the Year 1999) 1997, Beethoven sonatas opus 109/110 and concerto No.4 with the New York Philharmonic under Kurt Masur 1999, Rachmaninov Etudes-Tableaux and concerto No.2 with the Philharmonia Orchestra and Vladimir Ashkenazy 2001, Credo 2002. *Honours:* Officier, Ordre des Arts et des Lettres 2002. *Current Management:* Jasper Parrott, HarrisonParrott Ltd, 12 Penzance Place, London, W11 4PA, England. *Telephone:* (20) 7229-9166. *Fax:* (20) 7221-5042. *E-mail:* jasper.parrott@ harrisonparrott.co.uk. *Website:* www.harrisonparrott.com; www .helenegrimaud.com.

GRIMM, Hans-Gunther; Singer (Baritone) and Professor; b. 1925, Germany. *Education:* Studied in East Berlin. *Career:* Sang at Berlin Staatsoper, 1950–52, Bremen, 1952–54, Mannheim, 1954–60; Engaged at Cologne, 1960–64, Theater am Gartnerplatz, Munich, 1964–66, Dortmund, 1966–70; Sang in Cologne, 1961, in German premiere of Nono's Intolleranza 60; Guest appearances as concert and opera singer, Frankfurt, Japan, North America, France and Barcelona; Roles included Mozart's Count, Don Giovanni, Guglielmo and Papageno, Malatesta, Marcello, Wolfram, Escamillo, Don Fernando in Fidelio and Carlos in Forza del Destino; Professor at Maastrich Conservatory, Netherlands, 1973–82. *Recordings include:* Undine by Lortzing; Eine Nacht in Venedig; Rossini's Petite Messe solennelle; Beethoven's Ninth.

GRIMSLEY, Greer; Singer (baritone); b. 1962, New Orleans, Louisiana, USA. *Career:* Sang Jochanaan in Salome with Scottish Opera, 1988; Saratoga Opera, 1988, as Alfonso in Così fan tutte and Wexford Festival in Der Templer und die Jüdin by Marschner; Tour of Australia, Canada and Europe in Peter Brook's La Tragédie de Carmen; Bregenz Festival, 1991, as Escamillo; Santa Fe in the US premiere of Henze's English Cat and appearances with the Lake George Festival as Pizarro and Don Giovanni; Italian debut, Bologna, 1995, as Escamillo; Metropolitan Opera, 1995–96, as Balstrode (Peter Grimes) and Jochanaan; Escamillo at Vancouver, 1996; Engaged as Donner and Gunther in The Ring, Seattle 2001. *Current Management:* Athole Still International Management, Forresters Hall, 25–27 Westow Street, London, SE19 3RY, England. *Telephone:* (20) 8771-5271. *Fax:* (20) 8768-6600. *Website:* www.atholestill.com.

GRINDENKO, Tatyana; Concert Violinist; b. 1946, Kharkiv, Ukraine. *Education:* Studied at: Central Music School, Kharkov; Moscow Conservatoire. *Career:* Debut: Kharkov, playing works by Bach, Wieniawski and Paganini, with orchestra, 1954, aged 8; Gave concerts throughout Russia and Europe as soloist and with major ensembles and in chamber concerts; Appeared with New York Philharmonic, London Symphony Orchestra, Leipzig Gewandhaus, Berlin Radio Symphony, Vienna Symphony, Chamber Orchestra of Europe; Conductors have included Mravinsky, Kondrashin, Kurt Masur and Nikolaus Harnoncourt; Formed with Alexei Lyubimov, Academy of Ancient Music, Moscow, 1982, the only ensemble in Russia performing on authentic instruments; Tours 1988–: USA, Germany, France, Italy, Netherlands, India, Austria, Belgium, Czechoslovakia, Hungary and Finland; Festival engagements: Namur, Schleswig-Holstein, Passau, Lockenhaus, Brno and Bratislava; London debut, playing the Roslavetz Violin Concerto with Royal Philharmonic under Ashkenazy, 1991. *Recordings:* Many for various companies. *Honours:* 1st Prize, World Youth Festival, Sofia, Bulgaria, 1968; Prizewinner, Tchaikovsky Competition, Moscow, 1970. *Address:* c/o Sonata, 11 Northpark Street, Glasgow, G20 7AA, Scotland.

GRINGOLTS, Ilya; Violinist; b. 1982, Russia. *Education:* Studied at the St Petersburg Special Music School with Tatiana Liberova and Jeanna Metallidi and at the Juilliard School New York with Itzhak Perlman and the late Dorothy Delay, from 1999. *Career:* Appearances with the St Petersburg Philharmonic Orchestra; Moscow Symphony and BBC Scottish Symphony Orchestras; Further engagements 1999–2000 with the National Symphony Orchestra, Washington, Melbourne Symphony Orchestra, Minnesota Orchestra, Royal Liverpool Philharmonic Orchestra and Tapiola Sinfonietta Finland; Recitals for the BBC 's Verbier Festival, The Louvre, Palais des Beaux Arts and Oleg Kagan Festival; Engaged for concerto tour of Italy with Moscow Soloists and Yuri Bashmet, 2000; Shostakovich's Concerto No.1 at the London Proms, 2002; Recent engagements include performances with the Chicago Symphony Orchestra under Daniel Barenboim, UBS Verbier Orchestra/ Kurt Masur and Mstislav Rostropovich, Israel Philharmonic with Zubin Mehta, the St Petersburg Philharmonic Orchestra and Yuri Temirkanov, Deutsche Symphonie Orchester Berlin, at the Proms with the BBC Philharmonic and Vassily Sinaisky, Rotterdam Philharmonic with Vladimir Jorowski, London Philharmonic, Atlanta Symphony, City of Birmingham Symphony, BBC Symphony, Warsaw Philharmonic, Swedish Chamber Orchestra, Minnesota Orchestra and New Zealand Symphony Orchestra. *Recordings:* Paganini Concerto no.1; Works by Ysaÿe, Ernst and Schnittke; Tchaikovsky and Shostakovich No. 1 concertos and Solo Bach for Deutsche Grammophon. *Honours:* Winner, 1998 International Violin Competition; Premio Paganini, and given special honours for being the youngest ever competitor to be placed in the final and the best interpreter of Paganini's Caprices; Has been selected as one of the twelve young artists on the BBC's New Generation Artists Scheme. *Address:* c/o Tom Carrig, Assistant, IMG Artists, Lovell House, 616 Chiswick High Road, London W4 5RX, England. *E-mail:* tcarrig@imgworld.com.

GRIST, Reri; Coloratura Soprano; b. 29 Feb. 1932, New York, USA. *Education:* Music and Art High School, New York; Queens College. *Career:* Debut: Consuelo, West Side Story, 1957; Appeared at: Metropolitan Opera, New York, 1966–77; Vienna State Opera Austria, 1963–88; Munich State Opera, Germany, 1965–83; San Francisco Opera Association, 1963–76, 1983, 1990; Royal Opera House, Covent Garden, London, 1962–1974; La Scala, Milan, 1963, 1977–78; Opernhaus Zürich, Switzerland, 1960–66; Netherlands Opera, Amsterdam, 1990–91; Chicago Lyric Opera, 1964; Deutsche Oper, Berlin; Washington Opera Society; European Debut, Cologne, Germany, 1960; New York City Opera, 1959; Santa Fe Opera, New Mexico, 1959; Festival Appearances include: Salzburg, Austria, 1964–77; Munich Festival, 1967–83; Vienna Festival, 1963–80; Holland Festival, 1963; Glyndebourne Festival, 1962; Spoleto Festival, Italy, 1961; The most important new productions were with the stage directors Guenther Rennert, Giorgio Strehler, Pierre Audi, Lofti Mansouri, Otto Schenk, Carl Ebert, Joshua Logan and Jerome Robbins; Repertoire: Mozart: Susanna, Queen of Night, Despina, Zerlina, Blondchen, Madame Herz; R Strauss: Zerbinetta, Sophie, Aminta, Italian Singer; Verdi: Gilda, Oscar, Nannetta; Donizetti: Adina, Norina, Marie; Rossini: Rosina, Fanny, Elvira; J Strauss: Adele; Offenbach: Olympia; Delibes: Lakmé; Poulenc: Constance; D Moore: Baby Doe; Britten: Titania; Morton Feldman: The Woman (Neither); Stravinsky: Le Rossignol; Concert appearances with NY Philharmonic, Wiener Philharmoniker, Boston Symphony, Munich Philharmonic, Die Reihe, etc and others with conductors: Bernstein, Ozawa, Boulez, Sawallisch, Paumgartner, Cerha, etc; Song recitals in Austria, France, Germany and USA; Pedalogical activities: Professor of Voice, IN Univ, Bloomington, IN, 1981–83, Hochschule für Musik, Munich, Germany, 1984–95; Steans Institute, Ravinia, IL, Song interpretation 1992–; Tanglewood Festival, London Opera Centre, Hochschule der Kuenste: Basel, Switzerland. *Recordings:* Marriage of Figaro, Don Giovanni, Die Entführung, Così fan tutte, The Impressario, Il Re Pastore; Ariadne auf Naxos; Ballo in Maschera, Rigoletto; Scarlatti's Endimione e Cintia; Le Rossignol. *Honours:* Bayerische Kammersaengerin. *Address:* c/o Columbia Artists Management, 165 West 57th Street, New York, NY 10019, USA.

GRITTON, Peter William, MA, LRAM; Composer, Arranger, Accompanist, Singer and Teacher; b. 7 Dec. 1963, Redhill, Surrey; m. Harriet; one s. one d. *Education:* chorister at Salisbury Cathedral; Reigate Grammar School; principal horn of the National Youth Orchestra; academic exhibitioner and choral scholar at Clare Coll., Cambridge. *Career:*

countertenor lay clerk at Christ Church Cathedral, Oxford 1985–87; has sung with The Sixteen, Hanover Band, I Fagiolini, Gabrieli Consort, The Light Blues, Tenebrae, Flash Harry, Cambridge Singers; accompanist to Ian Partridge, Henry Herford, Nicholas Clapton, Christopher Purves; Asst Dir of Music, St Paul's Boys School, London. *Compositions:* Run with Torches, Away in a Manger, Stille Nacht: Portraits of Peace, Love Songs, Mary Seacole. *Publications:* Follow that Star (Christmas Songs), With a little help from my friends (Beatles), Encores for Choirs (two vols), G & S for Choirs, Folksongs from around the world (India, Far East, Caribbean and Australia and the South Pacific); contrib. to The Faber Carol Book, Jazz Piano Time, Spooky Piano Time, Fingerprints, Here's a Howdy-do. *Address:* 89 Devonshire Road, London, SE23 3LX, England (home). *E-mail:* petergritton@tiscali.co.uk (office).

GRITTON, Susan; Singer (soprano); b. 31 Aug. 1965, Reigate, England. *Education:* Studied Botany at London and Oxford Universities, before a career in music. *Career:* Debut: Mozart Requiem, Wigmore Hall, 1994; Many engagements in such repertory as Mozart's C Minor Mass, Brahms Requiem, Handel's Theodora and Schubert's Der Hirt auf dem Felsen; Orchestras include the London Symphony Orchestra under Colin Davis, London Philharmonic Orchestra under Haitink, Hallé under Nagano, City of London Sinfonia under Hickox, Gothenburg Symphony under Järvi and the Orchestra of the Age of Enlightenment under Steuart Bedford; Opera roles include Mozart's Susanna and Zerlina at Glyndebourne, Marzelline for Rome Opera; Fulvia in Handel's Ezio at the Théâtre des Champs-Elysées; Tiny in Britten's Paul Bunyan for ROH, Atalanta in Xerxes and Xenia in Boris Godonov at English National Opera; Sister Constance in The Carmelites, 1999; Other ENO roles include Caroline in The Fairy Queen, Pamina, Monteverdi's Drusilla, Nannetta and Janáček's Vixen; Season 2001–02 with Euridice and Marenka for the Royal Opera, Handel's Cleopatra and Romilda (Xerxes) at Munich; Bach's St Matthew Passion at the London Proms, 2002. *Recordings include:* Messiah and Solomon; Haydn's Nelson's Mass and Vivaldi's Ottone in Villa; Miss Wordsworth in Albert Herring; Holst Songs; Handel; Vivaldi; Purcell; Handel's Theodora. *Honours:* Winner, Kathleen Ferrier Memorial Prize, 1994; Arts Foundation Fellowship, 1994. *Current Management:* Askonas Holt Ltd, Lonsdale Chambers, 27 Chancery Lane, London, WC2A 1PF, England. *Telephone:* (20) 7400-1700. *Fax:* (20) 7400-1799. *E-mail:* info@ askonasholt.co.uk. *Website:* www.askonasholt.co.uk.

GRIVNOV, Vsevolod; Singer (Tenor); b. 1968, Russia. *Education:* Studied at the Russian Chorus Academy and the Russian Music Academy. *Career:* Soloist with the New Opera company of the Moscow Municipal Theatre, from 1990; Roles have included Bayan in Ruslan and Lyudmilla, Lensky (Eugene Onegin) and Leicester in Maria Stuarda; Concerts with the Toscanini Orchestra, Italy, under Rudolf Barshai, with Beethoven's Missa solemnis and Bach's B minor Mass, 1991–92, Ghent 1992, as Don José in Peter Brook's Tragédie de Carmen; Fenton in Falstaff at Copenhagen, 1997; Engaged in Rachmaninov's Aleko at the 1999 London Proms. *Recordings include:* Filmed version of Eugene Onegin, 1993. *Current Management:* Askonas Holt Ltd, Lonsdale Chambers, 27 Chancery Lane, London, WC2A 1PF, England. *Telephone:* (20) 7400-1700. *Fax:* (20) 7400-1799. *E-mail:* info@ askonasholt.co.uk. *Website:* www.askonasholt.co.uk.

GROBEN, Françoise; cellist; b. 4 Dec. 1965, Luxembourg. *Education:* Köln Musikhochschule with Boris Perganenshikov, Amadeus (also William Pleeth, Daniel Shafran). *Career:* debut, Musikverein, Vienna, Festspielhaus, Salzburg; Major concert halls in Europe, Russia, Japan and Israel including Suntory Hall, Tokyo, St Petersburg Philharmonic Hall, Hamburg Musikhalle, Brussels Palais des Beaux Arts, Berlin Philharmonie; Soloist of St Petersburg Philharmonic Orchestra, Moscow Radio-TV Orchestra, Russian State Orchestra, NHK Orchestra, Tokyo; Jerusalem Philharmonic Orchestra, Conductor, Svetlanov, Kitajenko, Rostropovich; Bavarian Radio Sinfonia; Festivals: Berliner Festwochen, Schleswig-Holstein Festival, Radio France Montpellier, Kuhmo, St Petersburg Spring, Wallonie, MDR, Bratislava; Member of Zehetmair String Quartet. *Recordings:* many radio and television recordings, Busoni and Poulenc cello music; Zemlinsky Chamber Music. *Honours:* 2nd Prize (Silver Medal) International Tchaikovsky Competition, Moscow, 1990; Several special prizes. *Address:* Moltkestr 31, 50674 Cologne, Germany.

GROOP, Monica; Singer (Mezzo-soprano); b. 4 April 1958, Helsinki, Finland. *Education:* Studied at the Conservatory and Sibelius Academy in Helsinki; Masterclasses with Kim Borg, Hartmut Holl, Mitsuko Shirai and Erik Werba. *Career:* Has appeared with the Savonlinna Opera Festival from 1986 and the Finnish National Opera in Helsinki from 1987; Sang Dorabella in a production of Così fan tutte conducted by Salvatore Accardo at Naples, 1989; Concert performance of Così fan tutte in Rome, 1991; Concert engagements with leading Finnish and other Scandinvian orchestras under Erich Bergel, Jukka-Pekka Saraste, Leif Segerstam and Walter Weller; Tour of West Germany

1989 with the Drottningholm Baroque Orchestra in Bach's St John Passion (Bachwoche Ansbach Festival); Season 1989–90 with the Bach B minor Mass and St John Passion in Stockholm, Berlin and Edmonton, Canada; Mozart's Betulia Liberata with the Bachakademie in Stuttgart under Helmuth Rilling, 1991; Mahler/Schoenberg project with Philippe Herreweghe and the Ensemble Musique Oblique; Season 1991/92 with Cherubino at Aix-en-Provence, Wellgunde and the Walküre Waltraute at Covent Garden (debut), the Missa Solemnis at Aix, 1992; Tour of Così fan tutte with Sigiswald Kuijken to Spain, France and Portugal and appearances with the Drottningholm Theatre at the Barbican; Season 1993 with Cherubino at Toulouse, the Composer at the Paris Opéra Comique and Bach's St John Passion in Spain, Lucerne and Stockholm; Sang Mélisande for Netherlands Opera, 1996; Cherubino for the Royal Opera, 1998; Glyndebourne Festival 1999, as Sesto in La Clemenza di Tito; Sang in the premieres of works by Olli Kortekangas and Kalevi Aho at Savonlinna 2000; Dorabella at Tokyo, 2001; Wigmore Hall recital, 2002. *Recordings include:* Bach B minor Mass; Così fan tutte for television. *Current Management:* IMG Artists Europe (GM); Nordic Artists Management (Nordic Countries). *Address:* c/o IMG Artists Europe, Lovell House, 616 Chiswick High Road, London W4 5RX, England.

GROSCHEL, Werner; Singer (Bass); b. 18 Sept. 1940, Nuremberg, Germany. *Education:* Studied at the Richard Strauss Conservatory Munich with Marcel Cordes and Josef Metternich. *Career:* Debut: Flensburg 1967, as Fiesco in Simon Boccanegra; Member of the Zürich Opera from 1972, as Rocco, Mephistopheles, Falstaff (Nicolai) and Dikoy in Katya Kabanova; Mozart's Osmin, Don Giovanni and Sarastro; Verdi's King Philip, Silva (Ernani) and Zaccaria (Nabucco); Wagner's Daland, Landgrave, King Henry and Pogner; Sang in the 1975 premiere of Klebe's Ein Wahrer Held and the premiere of Kelterborn's Ein Engel kommt nach Babylon, 1977; Guest appearances elsewhere in Switzerland and in Germany; Sang Don Inigo in Ravel's L'Heure Espagnole at the Zürich Opera, 1996; Sang the Theatre Director in Lulu at Zurcih, 2000; Many concert engagements, notably in music by Bach and Monteverdi. *Recordings include:* Plutone in Monteverdi's Orfeo, L'Incoronazione di Poppea and Il Ritorno d'Ulisse. *Address:* c/o Opernhaus Zürich, Falkenstrasse 1, 8008 Zürich, Switzerland.

GROSGURIN, Daniel; Cellist; b. 13 July 1949, Geneva, Switzerland; m. Ferhan Güraydin, 21 June 1990. *Education:* Classical Baccalaureate, Geneva, 1967; Conservatoire Geneva, 1st Prize, 1968; Master of Music, Indiana University, 1972. *Career:* Debut: London, 1976; Lucerne Festival, 1975; Festival Strings, Lucerne, 1975–78; Regular appearances with Orchestre de la Suisse Romande, 1978–; Chamber music with several well-known artists including Martha Argerich; Professor, State Music College, Heidelberg, Mannheim, Germany, 1978–90; Tours with Stuttgart Philharmonic, 1987; Professor, Geneva Conservatory of Music, 1990; Salzburg Festival, 1990; London Festival Hall with LSCO, 1991; Tibor Varga Festival, 1991; Eastern Music Festival, USA, 1992–98; Founder of Les Solistes de Genève, 1995. *Recordings:* G. Cassadó: Pièces favorites, Le Violoncelle et l'Opéra. *Current Management:* Becker, Herdecke, Germany. *Address:* Unterer Rheinweg 46, 4057 Basel, Switzerland.

GROSS, Eric; Composer and Lecturer; b. 16 Sept. 1926, Vienna, Austria; m. Pamela Davies. *Education:* MA, MLitt, D.Mus, University of Aberdeen, Scotland; FTCL, LMusTCL, Trinity College of Music, London. *Career:* Freelance Pianist, Arranger, Conductor, Composer, 1941–58; Lecturer, New South Wales, Australia, 1959–60; Lecturer, Senior Lecturer, Associate Professor, Department of Music, Sydney University, New South Wales, 1960–91, retired 1991; Visiting Professor of Music, University of Guyana, Georgetown, 1989; Now Freelance Composer. *Compositions:* Symphonies Nos 1 and 2; Violin Concerto; Piano Concerto; Oboe Concerto; 2 Mandolin Concertos; The Amorous Judge, opera; Pacem in Terris, cantata; The Shepherd of Bethlehem, cantata; 5 Burns Songs, 6 Henry Lawson Settings. *Recordings:* Symphony No. 1, 1975; Quintet for alto saxophone and string quartet; Klavierstücke I, II, III, 1990; Concerto No. I for mandolin and chamber orchestra; Concerto No. II for mandolin and chamber orchestra; 6 Henry Lawson Settings and 5 Burns Songs. *Publications:* Background and Problems for an Historical and Critical Edition of the String Quartets of F X Dusek, 1972; Music Manuscripts in the Library of St Bonifaz, Munich–a Preliminary Catalogue, 1975. *Contributions:* The Contemporary Australian Composer and Society, 1971. *Current Management:* Inquiries to Australian Music Centre, Sydney, New South Wales. *Address:* 54/84 St George's Crescent, Drummoyne, NSW 2047, Australia. *E-mail:* egross@pacific.net.au.

GROSS, Ruth; Singer (Soprano); b. 1959, Kleve, Germany. *Education:* Studied Viola at Essen, Voice with Edda Moser, Cologne. *Career:* Debut: Regensburg, as Leonore in Fidelio, 1987; Sang at Ulm, 1988–89, notably in Golem by d'Albert and in operetta; Bayreuth Festival, 1989–90, as Ortlinde in Die Walküre; Sang Leonore at Basle, 1989; Has appeared at Staatsoper Stuttgart, 1989–, as Iphigénie (in Aulide), Arabella and Elsa

in production of Lohengrin conducted by Silvio Varviso; Season 1995–96 at Kaiserslantern as Wagner's Elisabeth and in the premiere of Gesualdo by Franz Hummel. *Address:* Staatsoper Stuttgart, Oberer Schlossgarten 6, 7000 Stuttgart, Germany.

GROSSNER, Sonja Elizabeth, MA; Violinist and Composer; b. 14 Dec. 1942, Maidenhead, England; one d. *Education:* Berkshire Junior Music School, Reading, Carl Maria von Weber Hochschule für Musik, Dresden, Germany, DeMontford Univ., Leicester, Birmingham Conservatoire. *Career:* violinist, State Theatre Orchestra, Freiberg Sachsen 1968–73; music teacher and violinist, Dresden 1974–84; teaching appointments, Leicestershire 1985–87; self-employed music teacher, Loughborough 1986–88; peripatetic violin and viola teacher, Derbyshire LEA 1988–91; instrumental teacher, Bedfordshire LEA 1991–92; violin and viola teacher, Nottingham LEA 1992–95; Northamptonshire Music Service 1996–97; private music teacher, PhD student 1997–; mem. Incorporated Soc. of Musicians, British Acad. of Composers and Songwriters, Central Composers' Alliance. *Compositions:* Sad Prelude and Carefree, for orchestra 1992, Summer Suite, for string orchestra 1993, Musical Moments, for five clarinets, Fantasy Fragments, for trumpet solo and electroacoustics 1996, Parody, for two pianos and percussion 1996, To each other strangers, for woodwind quintet, Elegy 2, for full orchestra, Dark Adagio, String Quartet No. 3 1999, Appassionato, for cello and piano, Destiny, for full orchestra. *Publications:* Sonata for viola and piano in one movement 1996, Four Kinds, for four clarinets 1997, I Am Nobody, four songs of poems by Emily Dickinson 1998. *Honours:* Birmingham Chamber Music Prize 1999, Almira String Quartet Prize 2002. *Address:* 85 Maple Road, London, W11 2JN, England. *Telephone:* (1509) 215960. *Fax:* (1509) 215960. *E-mail:* vontuba@onetel.net.uk.

GROVES, Glenys; Singer; b. 28 July 1949, Hillingdon, Middlesex. *Education:* Studied with Mavis Bennett, 1959–80, then Eduardo Asquez. *Career:* Debut: D'Oyly Carte Opera Company, 1968; Royal Opera House, Covent Garden, 1988; Regularly works with Ambrosian Singers, 1967–; West End Shows, The Great Waltz, Drury Lane, 1970; The Card, Tom Brown's School Days; Chichester Festival, 1983; Justinus, 1984; The Lily Maid; Wexford Festival, 1984, 1985, 1987; Royal Opera, Covent Garden, as Chief Hen, Cunning Little Vixen, Lady in Waiting, Les Huguenots; Solo Voice, Prince Igor; Newspaper Seller, Death in Venice; Modestina, Il Viaggio a Reims; Milliner, Der Rosenkavalier; Page, Lohengrin; Olga, Merry Widow; Ida, Die Fledermaus; BBC radio, roles in Gilbert and Sullivan; Operettas; Songs From The Shows, Friday Night is Music Night; Regular guest soloist with Black Dyke Band; Extensive concert and oratorio repertoire; Performs throughout the United Kingdom and Europe with The Garden Party; mem, The Friends of Robert Stolz. *Recordings:* Royal Opera, Cunning Little Vixen, Prince Igor; Vox Ottone, Trumpet and Soprano in Duet. *Current Management:* AHF Rigby. *Address:* Chapmans Barn, The Lee, Buckinghamshire HP16 9NA, England.

GROVES, Paul; Singer (Tenor); b. 24 Nov. 1964, Lake Charles, Los Angeles, USA; m. Charlotte Hellekant. *Education:* Louisiana State University; Juilliard Opera Center. *Career:* Debut: Steuermann in Der fliegende Holländer, Metropolitan Opera, 1992; Appearances in New York as Mozart's Ferrando and Verdi's Fenton, and roles in Ariadne, Death in Venice, Les Troyens, Parsifal, Die Zauberflöte and The Ghosts of Versailles; European debut as Belfiore in La Finta Giardiniera, for Welsh National Opera; Mozart's Don Ottavio at Salzburg, Idamante at Geneva and Tamino at Munich; Season 1995–96 with Tamino at La Scala, Tom Rakewell for WNO and New York recital debut at Alice Tully Hall; Season 1996–97 with Tom Rakewell at the Paris Châtelet, Nemorino, Flamand in Capriccio and Rossini's Almaviva at the Vienna Staatsoper; Recitals throughout the USA; Further roles include Nadir for Vancouver Opera, Lensky at St Louis and Arturo in I Puritani for Boston Lyric Opera; Sang Des Grieux in Manon at Berlin, 1998; Berlioz Faust at Salzburg, 1999; Season 2000–01 as Bellini's Arturo at Munich, Gluck's Pylades at Salzburg and Ferrando at the Met; Haydn's the Creation at the London Proms, 2002; Engaged as Tamino at Covent Garden, 2003. *Recordings include:* Rigoletto; Alceste; Parsifal and Idomeneo (DGG); Der fliegende Holländer (Sony); Manon Lescaut (Decca). *Address:* c/o Vienna Staatsoper, Opernring 2, A–1010 Vienna, Austria.

GRUBE, Michael; Violin-Virtuoso and Violin Professor; b. 12 May 1954, Uberlingen. *Education:* Privately with his violinist father, Professor Max-Ludwig Grube; Further violinistic studies with Henryk Szeryng and Ivan Galamin; Conservatory Diploma, 1975; Studies of Musicology and Composition (Professor Gunther Becker). *Career:* Debut: West Berlin, 1964; Concert Soloist in 110 countries of all continents, performances before His Majesty King Tupou IV of Tonga and Queen of Tonga; Concerts and Festival Performances in Vienna, Copenhagen, Prague, Warsaw, Leningrad, Moscow, New York, Washington DC, Jerusalem, Caracas, Buenos Aires, Canberra, Singapore, Osaka, Bangkok, Bogota, São Paulo, Delhi, Panama City, Madrid, Istanbul; Pro Musica International USA. *Compositions:* Souvenir de Senegal for

Solo Violin (Radio Dakar); Hommage a Colville Young an Olanchito (Landestonkunstler Festival 1986–87). *Recordings:* Garnet Records, Düsseldorf; Violin Concertos by Bruch, Mendelssohn, Mozart; Violin Music by Dvořák; Smetana, Suk, Handel, Paganini, Reger, Haas, also with Max Ludwig Grube (violin) and Helen Grube (Piano). *Current Management:* Konzertdirektion Olga Altmann. *Current Management:* Konzertdirektion Olga Altmann, Jaquingasse 37/55, 1030 Vienna, Austria.

GRUBER, Andrea; Singer (Soprano); b. 1965, New York, NY, USA. *Career:* Debut: Scottish Opera, 1990, as Leonore in Forza; Sang Third Norn in Götterdämmerung at the Metropolitan, 1990, followed by Elisabeth de Valois and Aida at the Met; Amelia (Ballo), Amelia (Simon Boccanegra); Opera debut as Leonora in Forza with Scottish Opera; Professional debut as Soprano Soloist in Verdi's Requiem with James Levine, Chicago Symphony, Ravinna Festival, 1989; Seattle Opera, 1992, as Aida, Cologne, 1993, as Amelia (Ballo in maschera); Further guest appearances in Toronto, at the Vienna Staatsoper and in Italy; Covent Garden debut 1996, Arabella; Sang Chrysothemis in Elektra at Seattle, 1996; Season 1998 as Amelia (Ballo in Maschera) at Monte Carlo; Elvira (Ernani) at Marseilles, 1999; Sang Odabella in Attila at Chicago, 2001. *Recordings:* Götterdämmerung. *Address:* c/o Metropolitan Opera, Lincoln Center, New York, NY 10023, USA.

GRUBER, Heinz Karl; composer; b. 3 Jan. 1943, Vienna, Austria. *Education:* Vienna Hochschule für Musik and with Gottfried von Einem. *Career:* Sang in Vienna Boys' Choir 1953–57; Double Bass player in ensemble Die Reihe from 1961; Principal Double Bass Tonkünstler Orchestra 1963–69; Co-Founder of MOB Art and Tone ART ensemble 1968–71; Has worked with Austrian Radio, Vienna, from 1969; conducted the premiere of his opera Gomorra at the Vienna Volksoper, 1993; Trumpet Concerto premiered at the 1999 London Proms. *Compositions:* 4 pieces for solo violin 1963; Manhattan Broadcasts 1962–64; 5 Kinderlieder for female voices 1965, revised 1980; The Expulsion from Paradise for speakers and 6 solo instruments 1966, revised 1979; 3 MOB Pieces for 7 instruments and percussion 1968, revised 1977; 6 Episodes from a Discontinued Chronicle for piano 1967; Frankenstein !! for baritone, chansonnier and orchestra 1976–77, ensemble version, 1979; Phantom-Bilder for small orchestra 1977; Violin Concerto 1977–78; Demilitarized Zones for brass band 1979; Charivari for orchestra 1981; Castles in the Air for piano 1981; Rough Music, concerto for percussion and orchestra 1982; Anagram for 6 cellos 1987; Nebelsteinmusik (2nd Violin Concerto) 1988; Cello Concerto 1989; Gomorra (opera), 1992; Gloria von Jaxtberg, music theatre, 1992–94; Trumpet Concerto, 1998; Television appearances include Nekrophilius the Pawnbroker in Bring Me the Head of Amadeus (for the Mozart Bicentenary, 1991). *Address:* c/o Boosey & Hawkes Ltd, 295 Regent Street, London W1, England.

GRUBEROVA, Edita; Singer (soprano); b. 23 Dec. 1946, Bratislava, Czechoslovakia. *Education:* Studied with Maria Medveckà in Prague and with Ruthilde Boesch in Vienna. *Career:* Debut: Bratislava 1968, as Rosina; Sang at the Vienna Staatsoper 1970, as the Queen of Night: sang Zerbinetta in Vienna 1976; Glyndebourne Festival 1973; Salzburg Festival from 1974, as the Queen of Night, conducted by Herbert von Karajan; Metropolitan Opera debut 1977, as the Queen of Night; Covent Garden 1984, as Giulietta in a new production of I Capuleti e i Montecchi by Bellini; Guest appearances at the Bregenz Festival and at La Scala, the Munich Staatsoper (Massenet's Manon) and the Hamburg Staatsoper; Other roles include Gilda, Lucia, Constanze and Violetta; Sang Lucia at La Scala, 1984, Chicago 1986 and Barcelona 1987; La Scala 1987, Donna Anna, Zürich Opera 1988, as Marie in La Fille du Régiment; Metropolitan Opera 1989, as Violetta; Sang Rossini's Rosina and Semiramide (concert) at Munich 1990; Barcelona 1990, as Ariadne; Vienna Staatsoper Oct 1990, as Elizabeth I in Donizetti's Roberto Devereux, Season 1992 as Lucia at Munich and Semiramide at Zürich; Linda di Chamounix, 1995; Anna Bolena at the 1997 Munich Festival; Season 1997–98 as Linda di Chamounix at Vienna and La Scala, Milan; Season 2000–01 as Anna Bolena at Zürich, Elvira in Puritani at the Vienna Staatsoper and Elizabeth I in Roberto Devereux in Hamburg (concert). *Recordings:* Video of Rigoletto, with Luciano Pavarotti; Lucia di Lammermoor; La Traviata; I Puritani; Roberto Devereux; Linda di Chamounix; La Fille du Régiment; Don Giovanni; Die Zauberflöte.

GRUBERT, Naum; Pianist; b. 1951, Riga, USSR. *Education:* Studied at the Riga Conservatory and with Professor Gutman in Moscow. *Career:* Performed first in Russia, Eastern Europe, Italy and Finland; Emigrated from USSR 1983 and has performed with the London Symphony, the Hague Philharmonic, Netherlands Philharmonic Orchestre de la Suisse Romande, Helsinki Philharmonic and orchestras in Germany and Spain; Conductors include Paavo Berglund, Sergiu Commisiona, Franz-Paul Decker, Valeri Gergiev, Hartmut Haenchen, Vernon Handley, Thomas Sanderling, Horst Stein and Christopher Seaman; Further engagements with the Rotterdam Philharmonic, the Tonkunstler Orchestra Vienna and the Scottish National Orchestra.

Honours: 2nd Prize, International Piano Competition, Montreal, 1977; Prizewinner at the 1978 Tchaikovsky Competition, Moscow. *Current Management:* Ingpen & Williams Ltd, 7 St George's Court, 131 Putney Bridge Road, London, SW15 2PA, England.

GRUDZEIŃ, Jacek; Polish composer; b. 7 Feb. 1961, Warsaw. *Education:* Akademii Muzycznej, Warsaw with Włodzimierz Kotoński (composition) and Szabolsca Esztényi (piano improvisation), studied composition at Darmstadt, Patras, Kazimierz and Dartington, studied in London with Paul Paterson and Giles Swayn, electronic studio work with Barry Anderson. *Compositions include:* Tristaniana 1984, Turdus musicus 1984, Dla Elizy czyli Straszny sen pewnego pianisty (For Elise, or The Terrible Dream of a Certain Pianist) 1985, Sonosfera 1985, Androvanda, gui 1986, Interludium 1986, Dźwięki nocy (Night Sounds) 1987, Lumen, chorus 1987, Hologram II 1988, Somnus 1988; Drzewa (Trees) 1992, Missa brevis 1992, Movement II 1992, Tritonos 1993, Wiatr od morza (Wind from the Sea) 1993, Pavana 1994, Hyacinth Girl 1995, One Jubilee Rag 1995, Gagliarda 1996, Nonstrom 1996, Saxophone Concerto 1996, Światła Pochylenie 1997, Pangea 1997. *Recordings include:* Vivienne Spiteri, Wiatr od morza. *Honours:* Konkursu Młodych Kompozytorów Polskich 1988, Ogólnopolskiego Konkursu Kompozytorskiego 1995. *E-mail:* Jacek.Grudzien@ddg.art.pl. *Website:* all.art.pl/ all.art.pl/on-line/Grudzien/Jacek.html.

GRUENBERG, Erich; Violinist; b. 12 Oct. 1924, Vienna, Austria. *Education:* Studied in Vienna and at the Jerusalem Conservatory. *Career:* Debut: Jerusalem 1938; Leader of the Palestine Broadcasting Corporation Orchestra 1938–45; Solo career from 1947; Leader of the Stockholm Philharmonic orchestra 1956–58, the London Symphony 1962–65, Royal Philharmonic 1972–76; Appearances as soloist throughout Europe, the USA and Canada, Australia, Netherlands, Germany, Switzerland and Scandinavia; Gave the first Russian performance of Britten's Concerto, in Moscow; Engagements with the Hungarian State Symphony Orchestra in Budapest and visits to the Far East; Associated with contemporary works by Goehr, Gerhard and David Morgan; Formerly leader of the London String Quartet and chamber music player with William Glock, Franz Reizenstein, Edmund Rubbra and William Pleeth; Professor at the Royal Academy of Music; Masterclasses and Competition Jury appearances around the world. *Recordings:* Beethoven's Concerto conducted by Horenstein and the complete Violin Sonatas with David Wilde; Works by Bach, Stravinsky, Messiaen (Quatuor pour la fin du Temps), Durkö, Parry and Vaughan Williams; Labels include EMI, Decca, Argo, Chandos, Hyperion, Hungaroton and Lyrita. *Honours:* Winner, Carl Flesch Competition, London, 1947. *Address:* c/o Intermusica, 16 Duncan Terrace, London N1 8BZ, England.

GRUENBERG, Joanna; Concert Pianist; b. 1957, Stockholm, Sweden. *Education:* Studied with Fanny Waterman, Louis Kentner and Peter Frankl; Guildhall School of Music with James Gibb. *Career:* Appearances at the Aldeburgh and Harrogate Festivals, at the Fairfields Hall, Croydon and for the City Music Society, London; Festival Hall debut 1978, with the Royal Philharmonic Orchestra; Recital tours with her father, Erich Gruenberg; Concerts with the GLC series at Ranger House and visits to Ireland and Spain; Played with the Bournemouth Symphony and Sinfonietta 1983–85; Barbican Centre with Tchaikovsky's 1st Concerto and the Grieg Concerto with the Royal Liverpool Philharmonic, 1984–85; Further engagements with the Hallé Orchestra (Mendelssohn's 1st Concerto, 1988) and the Philharmonia at the Barbican. *Recordings include:* Album for Unicorn. *Honours:* RAOS, Silver Medal 1980. *Address:* Intermusica Artists' Management, 16 Duncan Terrace, London N1 8BZ, England.

GRUESSER, Eva; Violinist; b. 1965, Black Forest, Germany. *Education:* Studied at: Freiburg Hochschule; Rubin Academy in Jerusalem; Juilliard School, USA. *Career:* Leader of Lark Quartet, USA; Recent concert tours to: Australia; Taiwan; Hong Kong; China; Germany; Netherlands; US appearances at: Lincoln Center, NY; Kennedy Center, Washington DC; Boston; Los Angeles; Philadelphia, St Louis; San Francisco; Repertoire includes quartets by Haydn, Mozart, Beethoven, Schubert, Dvořák, Brahms, Borodin, Bart ók, Debussy and Shostakovich. *Honours:* With Lark Quartet: Gold Medals at 1990 Naumberg and 1991 Shostakovich Competitions; Prizewinner: Premio Paulio Borciani, Reggio Emilia, 1990; Karl Klinger Competition, Munich, 1990; London International String Quartet, 1991; Melbourne Chamber Music, 1991. *Address:* c/o Sonata (Lark Quartet), 11 Northpark Street, Glasgow, G20 7AA, Scotland.

GRUFFYDD JONES, Angharad; Singer (Soprano); b. 1973, Wales. *Education:* Univ. of Cambridge; Royal College of Music, with Margaret Kingsley. *Career:* concert engagements with conductors Ivor Bolton, Richard Hickox, Roy Goodman and Roger Norrington; Mozart Exsultate Jubilate at Greenwich and York Minster, Messiah in Spain with Harry Christophers and the Monteverdi Vespers at Washington DC; song recitals in London (Purcell Room) and elsewhere; opera appearances in Orlando by Handel for the Cambridge Handel Opera Group, and

Fidalma in Muzio Scevola for the London Handel Festival, 2001; sings with chamber choirs The King's Consort, The Sixteen and the Monteverdi Choir; soloist in John Eliot Gardiner's Bach Cantata Pilgrimage, 2000. *Honours:* Prizewinner, Young Welsh Singer of the Year Competition, 2000. *Address:* c/o Royal College of Music, Prince Consort Road, London SW7, England.

GRUMBACH, Raimund; Singer (Baritone); b. 20 Jan. 1934, Eibelstadt, Würzburg, Germany. *Education:* Studied in Würzburg. *Career:* Sang at the Stadttheater Würzburg 1956–59; Nuremberg Opera 1959–62; Bayerische Staatsoper Munich from 1962, as Mozart's Sharples and Marcello; Wolfram in Tannhäuser; Guest appearances in Edinburgh (1965, with the Munich company), Paris, Vienna, Madrid and Tokio; Many concert appearances; Teacher at the Munich Hochschule from 1972. *Recordings:* Il Barbiere di Siviglia; Der Mond by Orff; Leoncavallo's La Bohème; Feuersnot by Strauss; Sutermeister's Romeo und Julia; Der Freischütz; Tristan und Isolde; Intermezzo. *Address:* c/o Staatliche Hochschule für Musik, Arcisstrasse 12, Munich 12, Germany.

GRUNDHEBER, Franz; singer (baritone); b. 27 Sept. 1937, Trier, Germany. *Education:* studied in Trier and Hamburg, Indiana University, USA, Music Academy of the West, San Diego. *Career:* has sung at the Hamburg Staatsoper from 1966, opening the 1997/98 season with a new production of Macbeth, playing the leading role and opening the 2000/01 season with a new production of Tosca, playing the role of Scarpia; Tours of the USA and many appearances in European opera houses; Vienna Staatsoper 1983, as Mandryka in Arabella; Salzburg Festival 1985, as Olivier in Capriccio; Other roles include Mozart's Masetto and Guglielmo, Faninal in Der Rosenkavalier, and Escamillo; Salzburg and Savonnlina Festivals 1989, as Orestes and Amonasro; Sang Barak in Die Frau ohne Schatten at the Holland Festival, 1990; Season 1992 as Germont at Barcelona; Wozzeck at the Châtelet, Paris, and Macbeth at Cologne; Sang Wozzeck at Chicago, 1994; Rigoletto at Covent Garden, 1997; Season 2000–01 as Wozzeck at the Vienna Staatsoper, Simon Boccanegra in Munich, Amfortas for the San Francisco Opera and Scarpia in Hamburg; Dr Schön in Lulu at Vienna, 2002; Contracted by Vienna State Opera until 2006; Has sung Rigoletto at the Metropolitan Opera in 1999, 2001 and 2004. *Recordings include:* Video of Elektra (as Orestes) conducted by Abbado, Don Giovanni; Video of Wozzeck conducted by Barenboim, 1997; Doktor Faust by Busoni; Die drei Pintos by Weber/Mahler. *Honours:* 'Kammersänger' from Hamburg State Opera, Vienna State Opera. *Address:* c/o Royal Opera House (Contracts), Covent Garden, London WC2E 9DD, England.

GRUNEWALD, Eugenie; Singer (Mezzo-soprano); b. 1962, USA. *Career:* Appearances as Amneris in Aida at Michigan, Orlando, Austin, Miami and for the San Francisco Opera (1997); European debut as Giovanna Seymour in Anna Bolena at Barcelona; Dido in Les Troyens at Toulouse and Athens, Tchaikovsky's Joan of Arc and Lyubov (Mazeppa) with the Opera Orchestra of New York; Azucena and Wagner's Venus with Austin Lyric Opera, the mezzo roles in Puccini's Trittico with Chicago Lyric Opera and Santuzza with Tulsa Opera; Fenena in Nabucco with Connecticut Opera, Preziosilla at Barcelona and the Nurse in Dukas' Ariane et Barbe-bleue at Hamburg (1997); Concerts with the New World Symphony under Michael Tilson Thomas, the Boston Philharmonic, Little Orchestra Society and the Pacific Symphony at the Aspen Festival. *Address:* c/o Austin Lyric Opera, PO Box 984, Austin, TX 78767, USA.

GRUSKIN, Shelley; Flautist and Recorder Player; b. 20 July 1936, New York, USA. *Education:* Studied at Eastman School, Rochester, graduated 1956. *Career:* Member, New York Pro Musica, 1961–74, playing recorder and other early wind instruments; Associated with such singers as Charles Bressler, Bethany Beardslee, Jan De Gaetani, Russel Oberlin; Premiere of liturgical drama The Play of Herod at the Cloisters, New York 1963; Tour of Europe, 1963, USSR 1964; Final performances with group in Marco da Gagliano's La Dafne, 1981; Formed Philidor Trio 1965, with soprano Elizabeth Humes and harpsichordist Edward Smith; Performances with group until 1980; Teacher of music history and early music performance practice at various institutions; Artist-in-Residence, College of St Scholastica, Duluth, Minnesota 1978–1998, faculty Emeritus 1998–; President of the American Recorder Society, 1980–88. *Recordings include:* Albums with New York Pro Musica and Philidor Trio. *Address:* College of St Scholastica, Duluth, Minnesota 55811, USA.

GRUZIN, Boris; Conductor; b. 1940, Tashkent, Russia. *Education:* Moscow Conservatoire. *Career:* Principal Conductor of the Novosibirsk and Odessa Opera and Ballet Theatres; Mariinsky Theatre, St Petersburg, from 1993; Professor at the St Petersburg Conservatoire 1986–; Repertoire includes Tchaikovsky's Mazeppa, Eugene Onegin, Swan Lake and Sleeping Beauty, Prince Igor, The Maid of Pskov by Rimsky-Korsakov and Giselle; Season 1999–2000 with War and Peace at St Petersburg and the Kirov Ballet at Covent Garden; other ballet

repertoire includes Romeo and Juliet and Le Corsaire; Symphonic Concerts in Moscow, Odessa, Kiev, Tomsk and abroad. *Honours:* Honoured Artist of the Russian Federation, 1992. *Address:* c/o Kirov Opera, Mariinsky Theatre, 1 Theatre Square, St Petersburg, Russia.

GUACCERO, Giovanni; Composer; b. 25 Sept. 1966, Rome, Italy. *Education:* Graduate, Conservatory of music of Rome, Santa Cecilia in composition, 1995, and in electronic music, 1997. *Career:* Debut: Rome, Folkstudio, 1991; Salmo Metropolitano, chorus and orchestra, Rome, Conservatorio, Santa Cecilia, 1995; Trane's Way, Rome, 1996; Theatre: Filottete, music for stage, Academie d'Arte Drammatica, Rome, 1991; Radio: Alquimia, 1998; mem, Nuova Consonanza. *Compositions:* Salmo Metropolitano, 1995; Infedelis Peregrinatio, 1996; Per Versi Diversi, 1997; Flute Dance, 1997; Il Canto dei Popoli, 1998. *Recordings:* Salmo Metropolitano, 1998; Flute Dance, 1999; Ascoltate e capire la luna, 1999. *Publications:* Dal Centro Del Corpo, 1999; Per Versi Diversi, 1999; Pincelada, 1999; Danza No. 2, 1999. *Contributions:* La Musica contemporanea è un genere musicale, NC News 2, 1999. *Honours:* Nuove Generazioni, project of Nuova Consonanza, 1997. *Current Management:* Alberto Giraldi. *Address:* Via Lidia 5, 00179 Rome, Italy.

GUARNERA, Piero; Singer (baritone); b. 1962, Rome, Italy. *Career:* Debut: Spoleto, 1987, as Belcore; Has sung at Spoleto as Malatesta, Enrico (Lucia di Lammermoor) and Ned in Treemonisha; Rome Opera debut, 1989, as Masetto, followed by Gluck's Oreste and Verdi's Ford; Other roles include Rossini's Figaro (at Naples), Mozart's Figaro (Florence), Fabrizio in Salieri's La locandiera at Lugo, Dandini in Malaga, Marcello on tour to Netherlands (1994), and Tarquinius in The Rape of Lucretia; La Scala Milan from 1990, in Idomeneo, Henze's Das verratene Meer and Arabella. *Current Management:* Athole Still International Management, Forresters Hall, 25–27 Westow Street, London, SE19 3RY, England. *Telephone:* (20) 8771-5271. *Fax:* (20) 8768-6600. *Website:* www.atholestill.com.

GUARRERA, Frank; Singer (Baritone); b. 3 Dec. 1923, Philadelphia, Pennsylvania, USA. *Education:* Studied with Richard Bonelli at the Curtis Institute, Philadelphia. *Career:* Debut: New York City Opera 1947, as Silvio in Pagliacci; Metropolitan Opera from 1948, as Escamillo, Amonasro, Don Alfonso, Eugene Onegin, Gianni Schicchi, Germont and Ford, 34 roles in 427 performances; La Scala Milan 1958, as Zurga in Les Pêcheurs de Perles; Other appearances in London, San Francisco, Paris, Chicago, and Los Angeles. *Recordings include:* Faust (Philips); Cavalleria Rusticana, Così fan tutte and Lucia di Lammermoor (CBS); Falstaff conducted by Toscanini (RCA). *Address:* 423 Second Avenue, Bellmawr, NJ 08031, USA.

GUBAIDULINA, Sofia Asgatovna; Russian (b. Tatar) composer; b. 24 Oct. 1931, Chistopol; d. of Asgat Gubaidulin and Fedossia Gubaidulina; m. Peter Meschaninov; one d. *Education:* Kazan and Moscow Conservatories, private studies with Nikolai Peiko, Vissarion Shebalin and Grigori Kogan. *Career:* first noticed abroad, Paris 1979; British debut playing Symphony in 12 Movements 1987; freelance composer in Moscow 1963–91, in Germany 1991–. *Compositions:* instrumental: Piano quintet 1957, Allegro rustico for flute and piano 1963, Five Etudes for harp, double bass and percussion 1965, Vivente non vivente for synthesizer 1970, Concordanza for chamber ensemble 1971, String Quartet No. 1 1971, Music for harpsichord and percussion 1971, Fairytale Poem 1971, Stufen (The Steps) 1971, Detto II for cello and ensemble 1972, Rumore e Silenzio for percussion and harpsichord 1974, Ten Preludes for solo cello 1974, Quattro for 2 trumpets and 2 trombones 1974, Concerto for bassoon and low strings 1975, Sonata for double bass and piano 1975, Light and Darkness for solo organ 1976, Dots, Lines and Zigzag for bass clarinet and piano 1976, Trio for 3 trumpets 1976, Concerto for orchestra and jazz band 1976, Duo-Sonata for 2 bassoons 1977, Quartet for 4 flutes 1977, Misterioso for 7 percussionists 1977, Te Salutant capriccio for large light orchestra 1978, Introitus concerto for piano and chamber orchestra 1978, Detto I sonata for organ and percussion 1978, De profundis for solo bayan 1978, Sounds of the Forest for flute and piano 1978, In Croce for cello and organ 1979, Jubilatio for 4 percussionists 1979, Offertorium concerto for violin and orchestra 1980, Garten von Freuden und Traurigkeiten for flute, harp and viola (speaker ad lib) 1980, Rejoice sonata for violin and cello 1981, Descensio for ensemble 1981, Seven Words for cello, bayan and strings 1982, In the Beginning there was Rhythm for 7 percussionists 1984, Et exspecto sonata for solo bayan 1985, Quasi Hoquetus for viola, bassoon, cello and piano 1985, Stimmen... vetummen..., symphony in 12 movements 1986, String Quartet No. 2 1987, String Quartet No. 3 1987, Answer without Question collage for 3 orchestras 1988, String Trio 1988, Pro et Contra for large orchestra 1989, Silenzio 5 pieces for bayan, violin and cello 1991, Even and Uneven for 7 percussionists 1991, Tatar dance for 2 double basses and bayan 1992, Dancer on a Tightrope for violin and piano 1993, Meditation on the Bach-Choral Vor deinen Thron tret ich hiermit for harpsichord, 2 violins, viola, cello and double bass 1993, String quartet No. 4 1993, Early in the Morning, Right Before Waking for 7 kotos 1993, The Festivities at Their Height for cello and orchestra

1993, Now Always Snow for chamber ensemble and chamber choir on poems of Gennady Aigi 1993, 2nd cello concerto 1994, In anticipation... for saxophone quartet and 6 percussion 1994, Zeitgestatten symphony in 4 movements 1994, Music for flute, strings and percussion 1994, Viola concerto 1996, Quaternion for 4 cellos 1996, Galgenlieder à 3 15 pieces for mezzo, double bass and percussion 1996, Galgenlieder à 5 1996, Ritorno perpetuo for harpsichord 1997, Canticle of the Sun for cello, chamber chorus and 2 percussionists 1997, Two Paths for 2 violas and orchestra 1998, Im Schatten des Baumes for koto, bass-koto, cheng and orchestra 1998; vocal: Phacelia vocal cycle for soprano and orchestra 1956, Night in Memphis cantata for mezzo-soprano, male chorus and chamber orchestra 1968, Rubaiyat 1969, Roses 5 romances for soprano and piano 1972, Counting Rhymes 5 children's songs 1973, Hour of the Soul for mezzo-soprano and large orchestra 1976, Perception for soprano, baritone and 7 string instruments 1981, Hommage à Marina Tsvetava suite in 5 movements for chorus a cappella 1984, Hommage à T. S. Eliot for soprano and octet 1987, Two Songs on German Folk Poetry for soprano, flute, harpsichord and cello 1988, Witty Waltzing in the style of Johann Strauss for soprano and octet 1987, for piano and string quartet 1989, Jauchzt vor Gott for chorus and organ 1989, Alleluja for chorus, boys soprano, organ and large orchestra 1990, Aus dem Stundenbuch for cello, orchestra, male chorus and female speaker 1991, Johannes Passion 2000. *Honours:* Royal Swedish Acad. of Music Polar Prize 2002. *Address:* Ziegeleiweg 12, 25482 Appen, Germany; 2d Pugachevskaya 8, Korp. 5, Apt. 130, 107061 Moscow, Russia.

GUBBAY, Raymond, CBE, FRSA; British music promoter; b. 2 April 1946, London; s. of David Gubbay and the late Ida Gubbay; m. Johanna Quirke 1972 (divorced 1988); two d. *Education:* Univ. Coll. School, Hampstead. *Career:* concert promoter 1966–; f. and Man. Dir Raymond Gubbay Ltd 1966–; presents regular series of concerts at major London and regional concert halls including Royal Albert Hall, Royal Festival Hall, Barbican Centre, Symphony Hall Birmingham, Bridgewater Hall Manchester, Royal Concert Hall Glasgow and in Ireland, Belgium and Scandinavia; has presented productions of: (operas and operettas) The Ratepayer's Iolanthe 1984, Turandot 1991–92, La Bohème (centenary production) 1996, Carmen 1997, Madam Butterfly 1998, 2000, 2003, The Pirates of Penzance 1998–99, 2000, Tosca 1999, Aida 2001; (ballets) Swan Lake 1997, 1999, 2002, 2004, Romeo and Juliet 1998, The Sleeping Beauty 2000, Cavallaria Rusticana and Pagliacci 2002, D'Oyly Carte Opera Co. Seasons 2000, 2001, 2002, 2003, Savoy Opera 2004. *Honours:* Hon. FRAM 1988, Hon. FTCL 2000. *Address:* Dickens House, 15 Tooks Court, London EC4A 1QH, England. *E-mail:* info@raymondgubbay.co.uk (office). *Website:* www.raymondgubbay.co.uk (office).

GUBRUD, Irene (Ann); Singer (Soprano); b. 4 Jan. 1947, Canby, Minnesota, USA. *Education:* Studied at St Olaf College, Northfield, Minnesota, and at Juilliard, New York. *Career:* Concert engagements with leading US orchestras; Tour of Germany with the Baltimore Symphony; Premiere of Star-Child by George Crumb with the New York Philharmonic conducted by Pierre Boulez, 1977; European engagements with the Stuttgart and Bavarian Radio Orchestras; Opera debut 1981, as Mimi with the Minnesota Opera, St Paul; Recitals at Lincoln and Kennedy Centers 1981; Appearances at the Aspen, Blossom and Meadowbrook Festivals; Teacher at Washington University, St Louis, 1976–81. *Honours:* First Prize, Concert Artists Guild competition 1970; Ford Foundation performance competition 1971; Rockefeller and Minna Kaufmann Ruud competitions, 1972; Winner, Naumburg International Voice Competition, 1980.

GUDBJORNSSON, Gunnar; Singer (Tenor); b. 1965, Reykjavík, Iceland. *Education:* Studied at New Music School, Reykjavík, with Hannelore Kuhse in Berlin, and with Nicolai Gedda in London. *Career:* Debut: Icelandic Opera, as Don Ottavio, 1988; Sang Clotarco in Haydn's Armida at Buxton Festival, 1988; Appearances with Opera North and Welsh National Opera; Opera galas at St David's Hall, Cardiff, and with Royal Philharmonic; Sang the Lawyer in Punch and Judy at Aldeburgh Festival and engaged with Wiesbaden Opera as Almaviva, Ottavio and Tamino; Concert repertoire includes St Matthew Passion (Queen's Hall, Edinburgh), Britten's Serenade, Die schöne Müllerin; Recitals at Covent Garden and Wigmore Hall, 1993; Further appearances at the BBC Proms (Les Noces, 1996), the Opéra Bastille, Bregenz Festival, Aix-en-Provence, Geneva and Lisbon; Wagner's Steersman at Lille, 1998; Season 2000–01 as Don Ottavio at the Deutsche Oper Berlin, Belmonte, and Fenton in Falstaff at the Berlin Staatsoper. *Recordings include:* Die schöne Müllerin; Albums in Mozart complete edition; Radio recordings for BBC, Radio France and Hessische with broadcasts in most of Europe. *Honours:* Gunnar Thoroddson Scholarship, 1987; Leoni Sonnering Prize, 1988. *Current Management:* Askonas Holt Ltd, Lonsdale Chambers, 27 Chancery Lane, London, WC2A 1PF, England. *Telephone:* (20) 7400-1700. *Fax:* (20) 7400-1799. *E-mail:* info@askonasholt.co.uk. *Website:* www.askonasholt.co.uk.

GUDMUNDSEN-HOLMGREEN, Pelle; Composer; b. 21 Nov. 1932, Copenhagen, Denmark; m. (1) Gunvor Kaarsberg, 21 Nov 1959, 1 s., 1 d., (2) Karin B. Lund, 29 Aug 1997. *Education:* Studied Theory and History of Music at The Royal Danish Conservatory of Music, 1953–58. *Career:* Teacher, Royal Danish Academy of Music in Århus, 1967–73; Works have been played at Scandinavian Music Days, international festivals, ISCM, on Danish Television and on Radio world-wide; Music for plays and films. *Compositions include:* Frère Jaques for orchestra, 1964; Recapitulations for small ensemble, 1965; Je ne me tairai jamais. Jamais, for voices and instruments, 1966; Piece by Piece for chamber orchestra, 1968; Tricolore IV for orchestra, 1969; Terrace in 5 Stages for woodwind quintet, 1970; Plateaux pour Deux for cello and percussion, 1970; Mirror II for orchestra, 1973; Songs Without for mezzo soprano and piano, 1976; Symphony, Antiphony for orchestra, 1977; Prelude to Your Silence, octet, 1978; Your Silence, septet and soprano, 1978; Mirror Pieces for clarinet trio, 1980; String Quartet V Step by Step, 1982; VI Parting, 1983; VII Parted, 1984; Triptycon, concerto for percussion, 1985; String Quartet VIII Ground, commissioned by the Kronos Quartet, 1986; Concord, Sinfonietta, 1987; Octopus for organ and 2 players, 1989; Trois Poèmes de Samuel Beckett for vocal group, 1989; Concerto Grosso for string quartet and symphonic ensemble, 1990; The Creation, the 6th day, for double choir and violin solo, 1991, For Piano, 1992; Turn for guitar, bass flute, harp and organ, 1993; Traffic, Sinfonietta, 1994; Double, for violin and piano, 1994; Album, for saxophone quartet, 1994; For Cello and orchestra, 1996; Blow on Odysseus for vocal soloists, chorus, brass instruments and percussion, 1998; Stepping Still, for string sextet, 1999; Still, Leben, for organ, 2000; Countermove I II III, for organ, 2000; In Triplum, for organ, 2000; Sound/Sight, for choir, 2001; For Violin and Orchestra, 2002; Two Madrigals for vocal ensemble, 2001; Three Stages for vocal ensemble, 2003. *Recordings:* Solo for electric guitar; Mirror Pieces; Symphony, Antiphony; Triptycon; Octopus; For cello and orchestra, Frère Jaques, Concerto Grosso; Music for voices and instruments, chamber music, organ music, all on he label dacapo. *Contributions:* Dansk Musiktidsskrift; Nutida Musik. *Honours:* Antiphony, Symphony was awarded the 1980 Music Prize of the Nordic Council. *Address:* Eggersvej 29, 2900 Hellerup, Denmark.

GUELFI, Giangiacomo; Singer (Baritone); b. 21 Dec. 1924, Rome, Italy. *Education:* studied in Florence and with Titta Ruffo. *Career:* Debut: Spoleto 1950, as Rigoletto; Sang at the Teatro Fenice Venice and in Catania; La Scala Milan from 1952; Chicago Lyric Opera from 1954; Appearances in Rome, Paris, Cairo, Naples, Berlin and Dallas; Covent Garden 1975, as Scarpia, Chénier; Verona Arena 1960, 1970, 1972; Rio de Janeiro 1964, as Macbeth and Scarpia; Lisbon 1965, as Guillaume Tell; Metropolitan Opera 1970, as Scarpia, and Jack Rance in La Fanciulla del West; Appeared at the Maggio Musicale, Florence, in revivals of L'Africaine by Meyerbeer, 1971, and Agnese di Hohenstaufen by Spontini; Sang in Giordano's La Cene delle Beffe at La Scala 1977. *Recordings include:* Tosca and Aida (Cetra); Cavalleria Rusticana (Deutsche Grammophon); Verdi's I Due Foscari, I Lombardi, Nabucco and Attila. *Address:* c/o Teatro alla Scala, Via Filodrammatici 2, 20120 Milan, Italy.

GUÉRINEL, Lucien; Composer; b. 16 Aug. 1930, Grasse, France; m. Marie-Claire, 22 Dec 1958, 1 s. *Education:* Studied piano with Yvonne Studer in Marseille; Studied harmony with Marcel Prévot in Marseille and André Jouve in Paris; Composition with Louis Saguer in Paris. *Career:* Mem, Sciences, Letters and Arts Academy of Marseille. *Compositions:* 7 Fragments d'Archiloque, for 12 voices; 4 poèmes d'E Montale, for 12 voices; 4 chants pour un visage, for 12 voices and four instruments; Canti Corali, Ungaretti, choir and orchestra; Les Sept Portes, choir, 16 strings and 2 percussionists; Prendre corps, string quartet with soprano and mezzo-soprano; Séquence, for reeds trio. *Recordings:* Strophe 21, 2nd string quartet; Ce chant de brume, for cello; 7 Fragments d'Archiloque; 4 poèmes d'E Montale; 4 chants pour un visage; Chants-Espaces, for 2 pianos; 8 préludes, for piano; Appels, for vibraphone; Cadence, for harpsichord; 6 Bagatelles, for wind quintet; Soleil ployé, for violin. *Publications:* Poetry: La parole échouée, 1969; La sentence nue, 1973; Acte de présence, 1997; Music published by several publishers. *Contributions:* Music critic for La Provence. *Honours:* Second Prize, Competition for string quartets, Philip Morris, Paris, 1983; Finalist, International Competition, Piano en Creuse, 1990, 1994. *Address:* 56 rue Paradis, F 13006 Marseille, France.

GUHL, Helmut; Singer (Baritone); b. 1945, Hamburg, Germany. *Education:* Studied in Hamburg. *Career:* Debut: Eutin Festival, 1973, as the Count in Lortzing's Wildschütz; Sang with Oldenburg Opera, 1974–78, notably as Sharpless, Papageno, Germont and Wolfram; Eutin Festival as Guglielmo, Rossini's Figaro and Belcore; Hanover Opera from 1978, as Don Giovanni, Orpheus, Rossini's Mosè (1991), and Beckmesser; Guest appearances at the Deutsche Oper am Rhein, Düsseldorf, and in Hamburg, Mannheim and Stuttgart. *Address:* c/o

Staatstheater Hanover, Opernhaus, Opernplatz 1, W-3000 Hanover 1, Germany.

GUIDARINI, Marco; Conductor; b. 1952, Genoa, Italy. *Education:* Studied conducting with Franco Ferrara, and at the Academy of Pescara. *Career:* Led regional orchestras in Italy, then assisted John Eliot Gardiner at the Lyon Opéra, making debut 1986 with Falstaff; Wexford Festival and London 1988–89, with the local premieres of Mercadante's Elisa e Claudio and Mozart's Mitridate; Season 1990–91 with Tosca at English National Opera, Figaro for Welsh National Opera, La Bohème for Scottish Opera and Manon Lescaut in Dublin; Vancouver and Sydney debuts with Don Pasquale and Tosca; Season 1993–94 with La Traviata at Stockholm, I Lombardi at Bologna and Il Barbiere di Siviglia at the Berlin Staatsoper; Season 1997 with Don Giovanni at Copenhagen, Rigoletto in Geneva, Barbiere at Los Angeles (US debut) and Don Carlos in Marseilles; Other repertory includes Così fan tutte (Australian Opera), Die Zauberflöte, Un Ballo in Maschera and Nabucco (Nice Opéra); Bellini's Capuleti at Reggio Emilia, 1998. *Address:* Allied Artists, 42 Montpelier Square, London SW7 1JZ, England.

GUILLAUME, Edith; opera and concert singer (lyric mezzo); b. 14 June 1943, Bergerac, France; m. Niels Hvass; two c. *Education:* Royal Danish College of Music, Copenhagen, private studies in Copenhagen and Paris. *Career:* opera debut as Thérèse, Dreaming of Therese, Jutland Opera; Sang with opera in Copenhagen, Århus, Hamburg, Mannheim, Geneva, Montpelier, Nancy, Metz, Lille, Liège, Le Havre; resident member, Royal Danish Opera, Copenhagen; roles with these companies include Bartók, Judith (Bluebeard's Castle); Bibalo, Julie (Miss Julie); Bizet, Carmen (Carmen); Campra, Clorinde (Tancrède); Davies, Miss Donnithorne's Maggott; Gluck, Orfeo; Gounod, Siebel (Faust); Mascagni, Santuzza (Cavalleria Rusticana); Massenet, Charlotte (Werther); Monteverdi, Ottavia and Poppea (L'Incoronazione di Poppea), Penelope (Ritorno d'Ulisse); Mozart, Cherubino (Le nozze di Figaro), Dorabella (Così fan tutte), Idamante (Idomeneo); Offenbach, La perichole (La Perichole); Penderecki, Jeanne (The Devils of Loudun); Poulenc (Voix Humaine); Ravel, Concepcion (L'Heure Espagnole); Rossini, Zaida (Turco in Italia), Angelina (Cenerentola); Strauss, Octavian (Der Rosenkavalier); Verdi, Maddalena (Rigoletto), Meg (Falstaff); Jutland Opera 1996, as Mozart's Marcellina; Sang in Die schweigsame Frau at Århus, 2000. *Recordings:* various Danish songs. *Honours:* Critics Prize of Honour, 1970; Tagea Brandt Memorial Fund, 1977. *Address:* Ellebakken 2, 2900 Hellerup, Copenhagen, Denmark.

GUILLOU, Jean; Organist, Composer and Pianist; b. 18 April 1930, Angers, France. *Education:* Paris Conservatoire from 1945 with Dupré, Durufle and Messiaen. *Career:* Professor, Instituto de Alta Cultura, Lisbon, 1953–57; recitalist in residence in West Berlin. 1958–62; Organist, St Eustache, Paris, 1963; Professor, International Masterclass, Zürich, 1970–. *Compositions:* Organ: Toccata, op 9, 1962; Sagas, op 20, 1968; Symphonie Initiatique, 1969; La Chapelle des Abimes, 1970; Scènes d'Enfants, op 28; Hyperion, op 45; Eloge, op 52; Alice au Pays de l'Orgue, 1995; Instants, op 57; Orchestra: Judith-Symphonie for mezzo and orchestra; Concerto Grosso, op 32; Concerto Héroïque; Concerto 2000, op 62; 5th Concerto (King Arthur); Missa Interrupa, op 51; Piano and organ: Colloques Nos 2, 4 and 5; Concertos for cello and organ, violin and organ; Peace, for 8 voices and organ, op 43; Aube, for 12 voices and organ, op 46; Andromeda, for soprano and organ, op 39; Fête, for clarinet and organ, op 55. *Recordings:* J. S. Bach, Complete Organ Works, Goldberg Variations, Musical Offering; Vivaldi, 5 Concertos; C. Franck, Complete Organ works; Mussorgsky, Pictures at an Exhibition; Stravinsky, Petrushka; Julius Reubke, piano and organ sonatas; Guillou Plays Guillou, 7 CDs, Philips. *Publications:* Author of the book about organ, history and design, L'Orgue, Souvenir et Avenir, Ed Buchet, Chastel. *Honours:* Gramophon Critics Prize, 1980; International Performer of the Year, USA, 1980; Prize of the Liszt Academy, Budapest, 1982; Diapason d'Or and Prix Choc of Le Monde, 1991. *Address:* 45 rue de l'Arbre Sec, 75001 Paris, France.

GULEGHINA, Maria; Singer (soprano); b. 9 Aug. 1959, Odessa, Russia. *Education:* Studied in Odessa. *Career:* Sang at the Minsk Opera from 1984 at first in small roles but after winning the Glinka Competition as Tatiana, Elisabeth de Valois, Aida and Rosina; La Scala, Milan, 1987, as Amelia (Ballo in maschera), Tosca, Lisa (Queen of Spades) and Elisabeth; Sang Tosca at Hamburg, 1990, and made Metropolitan Opera debut as Maddalena in Andrea Chénier; Further guest appearances at the Vienna Staatsoper (as Tosca), the Deutsche Oper Berlin, Bastille, Paris, Rome Opera (Macbeth), Florence Opera, Covent Garden, Chicago and San Francisco, sang Verdi's Elvira at London's Barbican Hall, 1994; Verdi's Odabella as Macerata and Abigaille at Verona Arena, 1996; Sang Tosca at the Metropolitan and Lady Macbeth at La Scala, 1997; Season 1998 as Manon Lescaut at La Scala and Abigaille at Verona; Sang Norma at Orange, 1999; Season 2000-01 as Abigaille at the Met, Lady Macbeth at the Vienna Staatsoper and Norma at Macerata; Verdi's Odabella at Covent

Garden, 2002; Engaged as Lady Macbeth at Covent Garden, 2002. *Current Management:* Askonas Holt Ltd, Lonsdale Chambers, 27 Chancery Lane, London, WC2A 1PF, England. *Telephone:* (20) 7400-1700. *Fax:* (20) 7400-1799. *E-mail:* info@askonasholt.co.uk. *Website:* www.askonasholt.co.uk.

GULIN, Angeles; Singer (Soprano); b. 18 1943, Ribadavia, Orense, Spain; m. Antonio Blancas-La Plaza. *Education:* Studied with her father. Montevideo, 1963 as the Queen of Night. *Career:* Debut: Montevideo; Appearances in Barcelona, London, San Francisco, Düsseldorf, Amsterdam, Naples, Turin, Monte Carlo and Mexico City; Festivals of Edinburgh, Aix-en-Provence, Rome, Florence and Verona; Hamburg Staatsoper 1973–77; Other roles include: Abigaille, Aida, Norma, Valentine in Les Huguenots, Donna Anna, Senta, Turandot and La Gioconda; Metropolitan Opera 1980, as Elena in I Vespri Siciliani; Trieste 1985, as Mélisande; Sang Fiorilla in Il Turco in Italia at Monte Carlo, 2000; Many concert appearances. *Recordings include:* Oberto, Il Corsaro and Stiffelio by Verdi, Fernand Cortez by Spontini; Andrea Chénier. *Honours:* Winner, Verdi Competition at Busseto, 1968; International Competition Madrid 1970. *Address:* c/o Hamburg Staatsoper, Grosse-Theaterstrasse 34, 2000, Hamburg, Germany.

GULKE, Peter; Conductor; b. 29 April 1934, Weimar, Germany. *Education:* Studied at the Franz Liszt Hochschule Weimar, the Friedrich Schiller University Jena and the Karl Marx University, Leipzig (PhD 1958). *Career:* Repetiteur at the Rudolstadt Theatre 1959; Music Director at Stendal 1964 and Potsdam 1966; Stralsund 1972–76; Kapellmeister at the Dresden Opera 1976; Musical Director at Weimar 1981; as Musicologist Technical University, Berlin 1984; Musical Director, Wuppertal Opera, 1986–96; Work as musicologist includes edition of Symphonic Fragments by Schubert, from sketches, broadcast at the Schubert Congress in Detroit, 1978; Lecturer at the Hochschule für Musik in Dresden; Conducted Poulenc's Dialogues des Carmélites at Wuppertal 1989, to commemorate the bicentenary of the French Revolution and numerous other operas including the Ring at Wuppertal, Graz, Kassel; Professor Staatliche Hochschule für Musik Freiburg, 1996–2000. *Recordings include:* Beethoven Piano Concerto of 1784 and Udo Zimmermann's Der Schuhu und der fliegende Prinzessin, works by Schreker, Ravel, Schoenberg, Berg, Webern, Baird; Symphonic Fragments by Schubert, Schumann. *Publications:* Bruckner, Brahms, Zwei Studien, 1989; Schubert und seine Zeit, 1991; Fluchtpunkt Musik, 1994; Triumph der neuen Tonkunst. Mozarts späte Sinfonien und ihr Umfeld, 1998. *Address:* Zum Rebberg 10, 79112 Freiburg.

GULLI, Franco; Concert Violinist; b. 1 Sept. 1926, Trieste, Italy; m. Enrica Cavallo. *Education:* Studied with father and at Trieste Conservatory; Accademia Chigiana, Siena. *Career:* Debut: 1932; World-wide appearances with leading orchestras, including Cleveland, Pittsburgh, Ottawa; Chamber music activity with wife and with Trio Italiano d'Archi; Former member, Pomeriggi Musical Orchestra of Milan and of I Virtuosi di Roma; Gave premieres of concertos by Malipiero and Viozzi and of Paganini's 5th Concerto (1959); Masterclasses, Accademia Chigiana, Siena, 1964–72; Professor of Music, Lucerne Conservatory, 1971–72; Professor of Music, Indiana University from 1972, Distinguished Professor of Music; mem, Accademia Nazionale Santa Cecilia, Rome. *Recordings include:* Duos with Bruno Giuranna; String Trios by Beethoven with the Italian Trio; Paganini's Concerto No. 5; Beethoven Sonatas, with Enrica Cavallo; Mendelssohn Sonata in F; Mozart Violin Concerti (complete). *Honours:* Premio dell'Accademia Chigiana, Siena. *Current Management:* Columbia Artists New York, 165 West 57th Street, NY 10019, USA.

GULYAS, Dénes; Singer (Tenor) and Producer; b. 31 March 1954, Budapest, Hungary. *Education:* Studied at the Liszt Academy and the Budapest Conservatory. *Career:* Debut: Budapest 1978, as Alfredo; Vienna Staatsoper debut 1978; Sang in the Verdi Requiem at Budapest and La Scala Milan 1981; US debut Philadelphia 1981; Royal Opera House Covent Garden 1984–85; Metropolitan Opera from 1985, as the Singer in Der Rosenkavalier, Romeo, Rodolfo, Massenet's Des Grieux and Andrei in Khovanshchina; Appearances in Belgium, France, Germany and Italy; Other roles include Don Ottavio, Ferrando, the Duke of Mantua, Almaviva and Ernani; Performances in La Bohème, Rigoletto, Massenet's Manon, Khovanshchina, Gounod's Romeo and Juliet; San Francisco, Così fan tutte, 1986; Florence–Elisir d'amore, Genoa; Staged and sang leading role in Roméo et Juliette at Budapest, 1988–89; Sang Faust with the Florentine Opera at Milwaukee, 1989 (recreated at Montreal); San Diego, 1990 as Tamino; Debut as Barcelona, 1989, as Lensky in Eugene Onegon; Sang Lensky at Tel-Aviv, 1992, Rodolfo 1993; Sang Vitek in The Makropulos Case at Toulouse, 1999. *Recordings:* Gianni Schicchi, Salieri's Falstaff, Hunyadi Laszlo by Erkel, Paisiello's Il Barbiere di Siviglia, Liszt's Hungarian Coronation Mass (Hungaroton); Pavarotti Competition, Philadelphia 1981. *Honours:* Winner, Pavarotti Competition, Philadelphia 1981. *Address:* c/o Hungarian State Opera House, Népoztársaság utja 22, 1061 Budapest, Hungary.

GULYAS, György; Conductor; b. 11 April 1916, Korostarca, Hungary; m. Eva Manya, 6 Nov 1958, 3 d. *Education:* Composition and Conducting, Academy of Music, Budapest, 1942. *Career:* Teacher, Music Teachers' Training College, Debrecen, 1942–46; Founder-Director, Music High School, Bekestarhos, also conductor, Tarhosi Korus, 1946–54; Director, Music High School, Debrecen, 1954–66; Debrecen Academy of Music, Budapest, 1966–76; Founder, Chief Conductor, Kodály Choir, Debrecen, 1955–83; Békéstarhosi Zenei Napok, music director 1976–. *Publications:* Author, Bekestarhos Zenei tanulsagai, 1968; Az enekkari intonacio kerdesei, 1972; Articles in various professional journals; Büneim... Büneim?, biography, 1988. *Address:* 8 Blaháné, Debrecen 4024, Hungary.

GUNDE, Peter; Conductor; b. 1942, Budapest, Hungary. *Education:* Studied Oboe at the Budapest Conservatory; Composition, Coducting, Franz Liszt Academy, Budapest; Seminars in Weimar and Petersburg with Arvid Jansons, 1965–75. *Career:* Oboist, National Orchestra, Budapest, 1961–63; Kapellmeister in Miskolc, Hungary, 1972–73; Opera Kapellmeister, Hungarian State Opera, 1973–75; Founder, Director, Corelli Chamber Orchestra, Budapest, 1975–77; Conductor, Artistic Director, Chorus and Orchestra, Kapisztran and Palestrina Choir, Budapest, 1973–77; Director of the Chamber Orchestra and Lecturer at the International Youth Festival, Bayreuth, 1975–77; Assistant to Peter Maag, Christoph von Dohnànyi, Herbert von Karajan, Salzburg Festival, 1977–78; Lecturer, University of Bielefeld and University of Osnabrück; Guest Conductor, Stavanger, Oslo and Hungary, 1981–83; Concerts with the Sudwesteutschen Kammerorchester in Pforzheim and Reutlingen; Concerts in Hungary and USA, 1984; Guest Conductor in Tokyo and Israel; Broadcasts with the Westdeutschen Rundfunk Cologne, 1985–89; Concert Tour with the Hungarian Virtuosi Orchestra, 1990–93, 1993–. *Address:* Heeperstrasse 52a, 33607 Bielefeld 1, Germany.

GUNN, Jacqueline; Stage Designer; b. 1959, Scotland. *Career:* Opera designs have included The Rake's Progress for Opera Integra, La Voix Humaine at the Bloomsbury Festival, La Pietra del Paragone at Wuppertal, Tannhäuser for New Sussex Opera, Henze's Labirinto at the Munich Biennale, Otello, L'Elisir d'amore and Trovatore for Lucerne Opera and Così fan tutte for English National Opera in 1994. *Address:* Phoenix Artists Management, 6 Windmill Street, London, W1B 1HF, England.

GUNN, Nathan; American singer (baritone); b. 1970. *Education:* Univ. of Illinois. *Career:* debut, New York Met 1995, as Morales in Carmen; appearances at the Metropolitan include Guglielmo, Paris in Roméo et Juliette, Strauss's Harlequin and Schaunard in La Bohème; European debut as Prince Andrei in Prokofiev's War and Peace at the Opéra Bastille, Paris: Season 2000–01 as Guglielmo at Glyndebourne, Mozart's Count in Brussels and Harlequin for the Royal Opera, Covent Garden; concerts with the Chicago Symphony and Cleveland Orchestras and recitals at the Wigmore Hall. *Recordings include:* American Anthems. *Current Management:* ICM New York, 40 W 57th Street, New York, NY 10019, USA. *Telephone:* (212) 556-5600. *Website:* www.icmtalent.com.

GUNS, Jan; Belgian bass clarinettist; b. 22 Nov. 1951, Antwerp, Belgium; one s. two d. *Education:* Royal Flemish Conservatorium, Antwerp, summer courses in Nice, France. *Career:* debut with Royal Flemish Opera, Antwerp, 1971; Assistant Professor of Clarinet, Royal Conservatorium, Gent, 1979; Played with Opera of Flanders, 1980; BRT Philharmonic Orchestra, 1983; Associate Professor, 1984, Professor of Bass Clarinet, 1991–, Royal Flemish Conservatorium, Antwerp; Bass Clarinet Player and Percussionist with Gemini Ensemble, 1990–: Professor of bass clarinet-basset horn at the Belgian Flanders Exchange Center in Osaka, Japan. *Recordings:* Introduction and Concertante for Bass Clarinet and Clarinet Choir, opus 58 (Norman Heim), with Walter Boeykens Clarinet Choir, 1986; Harry's Wonderland for Bass Clarinet and 2 Tapes (André Laporte), 1987; Mladi sextet (Leoš Janáček), with Walter Boeykens Ensemble, 1992; Spotlights on the Bass Clarinet, Concerto for Bass Clarinet and Concert Band (Jan Hadermann), with Concert Band of the Belgian Guides, conducted by N Nozy, 1993; With Gemini Ensemble, 1993; Sonata (Frits Celis); Van Heinde en Verre (Wilfried Westerlinck); Due Concertante (Ivana Loudova); Giuco per Due (Dietrich Erdmann); Exercises (Jean Segers); Tango (Frédéric Devreese); with Moscow Chamber Soloists, Trio Classicum and Gemini Ensemble, 2000; Elegie (Dirk Brossé); Zebus (Johan Favoreel); Divertimento (Alain Craens); Pierrot (Wilfried Westerlinck); Fantasy Quintet (York Bowen); Divertimento (Akira Yuyama); Duo-Sonata (Charles Camilleri); Experience (Alain Craens). *Address:* Hagelandstraat 48, 2660 Hoboken (Antwerp), Belgium. *Telephone:* (3) 288-9184. *E-mail:* guns.jan@pandora.be.

GUNSON, Ameral; Singer (Mezzo-soprano); b. 1960, England. *Career:* Many concerts and broadcasts in the United Kingdom and Europe; Frequent appearances at the Promenade Concerts London; Season 1985–86 with Walton's Gloria at the Last Night of the Proms and Hecuba and Anna in a concert performance of Les Troyens by Berlioz at Portsmouth, conducted by Roger Norrington; Sang Lady Toodle in a Frankfurt Opera production of The English Cat by Henze; L'Enfant et les Sortilèges in Rotterdam, conducted by Simon Rattle; Verdi's Aida in Glasgow and Requiem at the Albert Hall, conducted by David Willcocks; Elgar's Sea Pictures and Mozart's Mass in C Minor, conducted by Richard Hickox; Bach's Mass in B Minor and the Choral Symphony with the Bournemouth Symphony orchestra; Haydn Masses broadcast by Austrian television, with Roger Norrington; Tour of France with the Bach B Minor Mass; Many recitals with the pianist Paul Hamburger; Premiere recording of Britten's The Rescue for the BBC; Sang in the premiere of Goehr's Eve Dreams of Paradise, 1989 (Prom Concerts 1990), Season 1990–91 in Texeira's Mass, with The Sixteen, Berg's Altenberg Lieder with the Rotterdam Philharmonic, Hindemith's Requiem in Geneva and Mozart's Requiem conducted by Jane Glover; Covent Garden 1992 as a Young Nun in Prokofiev's The Fiery Angel. *Recordings include:* Maw's Scenes and Arias; Copland's In the Beginning, with the choir of King's College, Cambridge; Auntie in Peter Grimes, 1996; Old Nun in Hindemith's Sancta Susanna.

GUNSON, Emily Jill; Flautist and Musicologist; b. 28 Jan. 1956, Melbourne, Australia. *Education:* BMus, 1980, PhD, 2000, Univ. of Western Australia; postgraduate study with William Bennett, 1981–82; performance diplomas, LMusA, 1978, LRAM, LGSM, ARCM, 1980. *Career:* concerto debut, 1973; Principal Flute, West Australian Arts Orchestra, 1982–83; performances with West Australian and Sydney Symphony Orchestras; Artistic Dir, Leader, Australian chamber ensembles, Wendling Quartet, Cambini Quintet, Emanuel Ensemble, Music Autentica, performing on both modern and historical flutes; guest artist, Mozart Gesellschaft Kurpfalz; musicological research in field of 18th century flute history, performance and repertoire; international authority on Wendling family of musicians and singers in 18th century Mannheim and Munich. *Publications:* Johann Baptist Wendling (1723–1797): Life, Works, Artistry and Influence, Including a Thematic Catalogue of all his Compositions, 1999. *Contributions:* The Court of Carl Theodor: A Paradise for Flautists, in Quellen und Studien zur Geschichte der Mannheimer Hofkapelle, vol. eight, 2002; seven articles in New Grove Dictionary (second edn); RISM errata; 18th and 19th Century Flute Music (ed.). *Current Management:* Flutissimo, PO Clackline 6564, WA, Australia. *Telephone:* 0417 984887. *Address:* Emanuel Farm, Clackline 6564, WA, Australia (home). *Telephone:* (8) 9574-1591 (home).

GÜNTER, Horst; Voice Teacher, Professor of Voice and Singer (Baritone); b. 23 May 1913, Leipzig, Germany; m. 4 May 1938, 2 s., 2 d. *Education:* Choirboy, St Thomas, Leipzig; Musicology and Philosophy, Universities of Leipzig and Bologna; Voice, Leipzig Conservatory; Most influential teachers: Karl Straube, Fritz Polster, Emmi Leisner. *Career:* Debut: Matthäus-Passion, St Thomas, Leipzig, 1939; Count in Marriage of Figaro, Schwerin State Opera, 1941; Leading Lyric Baritone, Hamburg State Opera, 1950–68; Knappertsbusch and Böhm, Munich State Opera, 1958–63; Edinburgh Festival, 1952, 1956; Holland Festival, 1961; Guest Singer: Vienna State Opera, Frankfurt, with Solti; Ansbach Bach Festival, 1951–58; Numerous radio recordings; For television, 12 operas; First performance of Moses and Aaron in Hamburg, 1954; Teaching: Nordwest-deutsche Musikakademie, Detmold, 1959–65; Professor, 1963; Staatliche Musikhochschule, Freiburg, 1965–68; University of Southern California, Los Angeles, 1978–80; University of California, Los Angeles, 1981; Visiting Professor: Many US universities including Southern Methodist University, Dallas, North Texas State University, Denton, Oberlin Conservatory of Music, University of Minneapolis, University of Alaska; Musashino Academia Musicae, Tokyo, 1984, 1986, 1987, 1990, 1991, 1992; Frequent Judge, international voice competitions such as Munich, Budapest, Leipzig, 's-Hertogenbosch, Los Angeles, Dallas, Osaka; Founder of EVTA, European Voice Teacher Association, 1991; Voice Teacher at Studio Opera, Zürich, Switzerland, 2001–. *Recordings include:* Lohengrin, Schüchter; Moses und Aron, Rosbaud; Zillich, Così fan tutte, Jochum, Don Giovanni, Klemperer, Zauberflöte, Rother, La Traviata, Wagner, Die Fledermaus; Schüchter, Weihnachts Oratorium; Karl Richter, Matthäus Passion; Kurt Redel, Zar und Zimmermann; La Bohème, Erede; CD: Dokumente einer Sängerkarriere: 18 Operatic Arias; Hansel und Gretel; Lortzing, Zar und Zimmerman; Telemann: Matthaus Passion; Wagner Lohengrin. *Address:* Unterer Heimbach 5, 79280 Au bei Freiburg, Germany.

GUNTER, John; Stage Designer; b. 1938, England; m., 2 d. *Education:* Central School of Art and Design, London. *Career:* Head of Theatre Department at the Central School, then Head of Design at the National Theatre, London; Opera designs for the Glyndebourne Festival include Albert Herring, Simon Boccanegra, Porgy and Bess (British company premiere, 1986), La Traviata and Falstaff; Le nozze di Figaro 1994, revived 1997, Peter Grimes and Otello (also for Chicago Lyric Opera);

Further engagements with English National Opera, Welsh National Opera, Scottish Opera, Opera North and the Salzburg Festival; La Scala, Milan, and opera houses at Munich, Cologne, Hamburg, Buenos Aires, Sydney and Los Angeles; Original 1857 version of Simon Boccanegra for Covent Garden, 1997; Season 1996–97 with Samson et Dalila for Queensland Opera; Also, Ernani for National Reise Opera, Netherlands, and Der fliegende Holländer for Covent Garden; Revival of Albert Herring at Glyndebourne Festival, and tour with GTO, 2002 (from 1985 production at Glyndebourne); Anything Goes, musical, Drury Lane Theatre, London; Romeo and Juliette, opera for Los Angeles; Peter Grimes, opera for Salzburg (sets and costumes), 2003–(05). *Address:* c/o Richard Haigh, Performing Arts, 6 Windmill Street, London, W1T 2JB.

GUO, Wenjing; Chinese composer; b. 1 Feb. 1956, Chongqing; one d. *Education:* Central Conservatory of Music, Beijing. *Career:* violinist Dance and Choral Ensemble of Chongqing 1970–77; Dean and Prof., Composition Dept, Central Conservatory of Music, Beijing 1983–; works performed at major festivals in Europe; works performed by orchestras world-wide, including BBC Scottish Symphony Orchestra, China National Symphony Orchestra, Cincinnati Percussion Group, Göteborg Symphony Orchestra, Hong Kong Chinese Orchestra, Hong Kong Philharmonic Orchestra, HuaXia Chinese Ensemble, Lincoln Center Chamber Music Soc., London Sinfonietta, New York Music Consort, Nieuw Ensemble, Taiwan Symphony Orchestra; Visiting Scholar, Asian Cultural Council, USA; guest lecturer, Swedish Royal Inst. of Music, Univ. of Cincinnati, Manhattan School of Music; mem. Asscn of Chinese Musicians. *Film appearance:* Broked Silence. *Composition for film and television includes:* Hong fen 1994, Yangguang Canlan de Rizi 1994. *Compositions:* Ba 1982, The River of Sichuan 1981, Concerto 1986, Shu Dao Nan 1987, Shou Kong Shan 1991, Yun Nan 1993, The Wolfcub's Village (opera) 1993 (orchestral suite) 1994, Drama op. 23 1995, Inscriptions on Bone op. 24 1996, Concertino pour violoncelle et ensemble op. 26 1997, Echoes of Heaven and Earth op. 31 1998, The Night Banquet (opera) 1998, Journeys 2004. *Address:* c/o Central Conservatory of Music, 43 Baojia Street, Western District, Beijing 100031, People's Republic of China. *Telephone:* (10) 6641 2585. *Fax:* (10) 6641 3138. *E-mail:* imecwy@public.bta.net.cn. *Website:* www.ccom.edu .cn.

GURIAKOVA, Olga; Singer (Soprano); b. 1971, Novokuznetsk, Russia. *Education:* Graduated Moscow Conservatoire 1995. *Career:* Appearances at the Stanislavsky Musical Theatre, Moscow, from 1994; Kirov Opera, St Petersburg, from 1996, as Mimi, Natasha in War and Peace, Tatiana, Maria in Tchaikovsky's Mazeppa, Donna Anna, Desdemona and Elvira in Ernani; Further engagements as Gorislava in Ruslan and Lyudmilla and Militrissa in Rimsky-Korsakov's Tsar Saltan; Tours of Europe, Israel and the Far East with the Kirov; Tchaikovsky's Maria at the New York Met and Iolanta at Carnegie Hall, 1998; Season 1999–2000 with Maria and Donna Anna in St Petersburg and Natasha at the Opéra Bastille, Paris; Sang with the Kirov at Covent Garden, 2000. *Honours:* Winner 2nd Rimsky-Korsakov International Competition; Russian Golden Mask and Casta Diva Competition, 1996. *Address:* c/o Kirov Opera, Mariinsky Theatre, 1 Theatre Square, St Petersburg, Russia.

GUSCHLBAUER, Theodor; Conductor; b. 14 April 1939, Vienna, Austria. *Education:* Vienna Acad. of Music. *Career:* conducted the Vienna Baroque Ensemble 1961–69; Asst at the Vienna Volksoper 1964–66; Chief Conductor of the Salzburg Landestheater 1966–68, Lyon Opéra 1969–75; General Musik-Direktor, Linz-Bruckner Symphony Orchestra and the Landestheater Linz 1975–83; Chief Conductor, Strasbourg Philharmonic 1983–97, Rhineland-Palatinate Philharmonic 1997–; guest appearances at many festivals, including those at Salzburg, Aix-en-Provence, Prague, Bregenz, Flanders, Oxford, Lucerne, Montreux, Ascona, Maggio Musicale Fiorentino; regular guest conductor with the Vienna and Hamburg Operas, Geneva, Paris (Bastille), Munich, Cologne and Lisbon. *Recordings:* Symphonies by Mozart, Haydn, Schubert and Beethoven; Concertos by Strauss, Mozart, Haydn, Mendelssohn and Weber; Mozart's Divertimento K287, Cassation K99, Masses K194 and K220, Vesperae Solennes, Sinfonia Concertante K297b, Bassoon Concerto, Flute Concertos (Rampal), and Piano Concertos K271, K453 and K467 (Maria Joao Pires); K415; K488; Strauss Burleske, Horn Concerto No. 2 and Oboe Concerto; Beethoven's 6th Symphony and Schubert's Ninth, with the New Philharmonia; Bruckner 7, D'Indy, Hindemith, Grieg, Rachmaninov, Waldteufel, Dvořák, Scriabin. *Honours:* seven Grand Prix du Disque; Mozart Prize, Goethe Foundation, Basel, 1988; Légion d'Honneur, 1997.

GUSSMANN, Wolfgang; stage designer and costume designer; b. 1953, Germany. *Career:* collaborations from 1985 with Willy Decker at Cologne, including designs for La Finta Giardiniera, Billy Budd, Der fliegende Holländer, Eugene Onegin and Il Trittico; Capriccio at Florence, Bibalo's Macbeth (premiere) and Così fan tutte at Oslo; Partnership with Johannes Schaaf on Boris Godunov at Munich and

Die Entführung aus dem Serail at Hamburg; Season 1996–97 with Freischütz and Don Giovanni at Dresden, the premiere of Das Schloss by Reimann in Berlin, Die Frau ohne Schatten in Geneva and at the Paris Châtelet, Eugene Onegin at the Paris Opéra Bastille, Idomeneo in Munich and Tristan at Leipzig; Season 1997–98 with La Bohème at Cologne, Tosca at Stuttgart, Lulu at the Bastille, Katya Kabanova in Amsterdam, Lohengrin at Bayreuther Festspiele, Pelléas et Mélisande at Hamburg, Billy Budd and Lulu at the Vienna Staatsoper and The Ring in Brussels. Season 1998–99 with Der Rosenkavalier and The Ring in Dresden and Der fliegende Holländer at the Opéra National in Paris; Most recent projects include: Freischütz, Don Giovanni, Die Soldaten and Lear in Dresden; Billy Budd in Antwerp; Tosca in Stuttgart; Carmen in Amsterdam; Pelléas et Mélisande in Hamburg; Macbeth with Oper Leipzig; Merry Widow at the Hamburg Staatsoper. Further productions include: Boris Godunov in Amsterdam and Paris; Billy Budd and Lulu at the Vienna Staatsoper, Rheingold in Dresden, Arabella and Manon Lescaut in Munich, Jenůfa at the Komisches Oper, Berlin, and Katya Kabanova at the Hamburg Staatsoper. *Address:* c/o Haydn Rawstron Ltd, 36 Station Road, London SE20 7BQ, England.

GUSTAFSON, Nancy; Singer (Soprano); b. 27 June 1956, Evanston, Illinois, USA; m. Brian Dickie. *Education:* Studied in San Francisco on the Adler Fellowship Program. *Career:* San Francisco Opera debut as Freia in Das Rheingold: returned as Musetta in La Bohème and Antonia in Les Contes d'Hoffmann and Elettra in Idomeneo; Opera Colorado as Donna Elvira; Minnesota Opera as Leila in Les Pêcheurs de Perles; Canadian debut as Violetta for Edmonton Opera; Festival performances as Rosalinda in Sante Fe and Britten's Helena for Chataugua Opera; European debut as Rosalinde in Paris, season 1984–85; Glyndebourne debut as Donna Elvira, while tour to Hong Kong: Festival appearances as Katya Kabanova, in a new production of Janáček's opera, 1988, returned 1990; Chicago Lyric Opera debut as Marguerite in Faust; Covent Garden debut 1988, as Freia; Scottish Opera 1989, as Violetta; Metropolitan Opera debut 1989, as Musetta; Sang Freia in Rheingold at Munich, 1990; Seattle Opera 1989, as Elettra in Idomeneo, Antonia in Les Contes d'Hoffmann 1990; Sang Eva at La Scala and Amelia in a new production of Simon Boccanegra at Brussels 1990; Sang Lisa in The Queen of Spades at Glyndebourne 1992; Season 1991–92 as Violetta and Alice Ford at Toronto; Sang the Letter Scene from Eugene Onegin at the 1993 London Proms; Eva in a new production of Die Meistersinger at Covent Garden, 1993; Concert engagements in Mahler's 8th Symphony, with the San Francisco Symphony, and at the Carmel Bach Festival, California; Engaged as Floyd's Susannah, Houston, 1996; Returned to Covent Garden as Eva, 1997; Season 2000–01 as Laurie Moss in Copland's The Tender Land, at the Barbican, Ellen Orford in Los Angeles, and Mathilde in Guillaume Tell for the Vienna Staatsoper. *Address:* c/o Theateragentur Dr G. Hilbert, Maximillanstrasse 22, D–80539 München, Germany.

GUSTAVSSON, Jan; Trumpeter; b. 8 Dec. 1959, Vadstena, Sweden; m. Jessica Gustavsson, 13 July 1996, 1 s. *Education:* Studied at Gothenburg Music Conservatory; Trumpet Soloist. *Career:* Debut: Lisbon, Portugal, 1989; Principal Trumpet, Norrköping, 1982–92; Principal Trumpet, Royal Stockholm Philharmonic Orchestra, 1992–; Trumpet Soloist appearances in Sweden, Portugal, Austria and Switzerland. *Recordings:* Leopold Mozart, Giuseppe Tartini, Trumpet Concertos as Soloist with Winterthur Stadtorchester, conductor Franz Welser-Möst, 1989. *Honours:* 2nd Prize, Budapest International Trumpet Solo Competition, 1984. *Address:* Kungliga Filharmoniska Orkestern, Box 7083, 103 87 Stockholm, Sweden.

GUTIERREZ, Horacio; Pianist; b. 28 Aug. 1948, Havana, Cuba; m. Patricia Asher. *Education:* Juilliard School of Music, New York City, USA, 1967–70. *Career:* Debut: At age 11 with Havana Symphony Orchestra; Performed most major symphony orchestras as soloist in recitals throughout the world; Appearances on BBC television and also in France and USA; Tours in USA, Canada, Europe, South America, Israel, USSR, Japan. *Recordings:* Numerous including Rachmaninov Pian Concertos No. 2 and 3 with Lorin Maazel and Pittsburgh Symphony (nominated for a Grammy in 1992); Brahms Nos 1 and 2 and Tchaikovsky No. 1. *Honours:* Recipient, 2nd Prize, Tchaikovsky Competition, 1970; Avery Fisher Prize, 1982. *Current Management:* Cramer Marder Artists. *Address:* 3426 Springhill Road, Latayette, CA 94549 USA.

GUTMAN, Natalia; Cellist; b. 14 June 1942, Moscow, Russia. *Education:* Began cello studies aged 5 at Gnessin Music School, Moscow under R Saposhnikov, later at Moscow Conservatory with Rostropovich. *Career:* After winning awards at competitions in Moscow, Prague, Munich and Vienna she made many tours of Europe, American and Japan, appearing with the Vienna Philharmonic Orchestra, Orchestre National de France, Berlin Philharmonic Orchestra, the Philharmonia and the Concertgebouw Orchestra; Conductors include Abbado, Sawallisch, Muti, Rozhdestvensky, Stokowski, Svetlanov and Sinopoli; Tours of the USA with the Russian State Symphony Orchestra and of Russia with the BBC Symphony Orchestra and John Pritchard; Plays chamber music in Russia and Europe with Eliso Virsaladze and Oleg Kagan and chamber concerts with Sviatoslav Richter; Has performed works by various Russian composers including Gubaidulina, Denisov and Schnittke (Sonata and 1st Concerto dedicated to her); With Claudio Abbado founded Berlin Encounters, 1992. *Recordings include:* Both Shostakovich Concertos and Schnittke Concertos. *Address:* Edward-Schwid Stn 30 8 54 Munich, Germany.

GUTTLER, Ludwig; Trumpeter, Conductor and Professor; b. 13 June 1943, Sosa, Germany. *Education:* Degree in Architecture; Studied trumpet with Armin Mennel, Leipzig Hochschule für Musik, 1961–65. *Career:* Debut: Soloist with orchestra in 1958; Solo Trumpeter, Handel Festival Orchestra, Halle, 1965–, and Dresden Philharmonic, 1969–81; Founder, Director, Leipziger Bach-Collegium, 1976–, Blechbläserensemble Ludwig Guttler, 1978–; Virtuosi Saxoniae, 1985–; Solo tours throughout the world; Lecturer, 1972–80, Professor, 1980–, Head of Masterclasses in wind playing, 1982–, Dresden Hochschule für Musik; Guest Teacher at Weimar International Music Seminar, 1977–, also in Austria, Japan and the USA. *Recordings:* Over 21 albums. *Honours:* National Prize, German Democratic Republic, 1978; German Phonoakademie Recording Prize, 1983; Music Prize, City of Frankfurt, 1989. *Address:* c/o Gotthart Wilke, Edinger Konzer-und Kunstleragentur, Lindenstrasse 26, 8011 Zorneding, Germany.

GUTTMAN, Albert; Pianist; b. 12 Oct. 1937, Galati, Romania. *Education:* Conservatoire of Music, Bucharest; Graduate in Piano, Florica Musicescu; Studied Piano Accompaniment under Dagobert Buchholz; Graduate, Biennial Masterclasses, magna cum laude, Santa Cecilia Conservatoire, Rome with teacher Guido Agosti. *Career:* Professor of Piano, Chamber Music and Piano Accompaniment, Bucharest Conservatoire of Music, 1960–76; Official Assistant for Chamber Music, Santa Cecilia National Academy in Rome, 1972; Invited by Yehudi Menuhin to teach chamber music at International Menuhin Academy of Music, Gstaad, Switzerland, 1982–84; Taught summer courses in Italy and Switzerland between 1969 and 1983; Professor of Piano, Musikschule Saanenland, Gstaad and Professor of Piano Accompaniment, including permanent Masterclass for Graduate Pianists specializing in Piano Accompaniment, Musik Akademie der Stadt Basel, 1983–; World-wide tours and participant in numerous festivals; Recitals with Radu Aldulescu and Silvia Marcovici, and often performed with Yehudi Menuhin, Pierre Fournier, Ruggiero Ricci, Enrico Mainardi, Jean Pierre Rampal, Christian Ferras, Lola Bobesco, Pina Carmirelli, Ivry Gitlis, Raphael Sommer. *Recordings include:* Radio and Television recordings world-wide; Discopgraphy: Beethoven, Complete Edition Five Sonatas for Piano and Cello, Radu Aldulescu on cello; Schumann, Frauen Liebe und Leben; De Falla, Siete Canciones Populares Españolas, Elena Cernei, mezzo; Shostakovich Sonata Op 40 for Cello and Piano; Hindemith Sonata Op 11 No. 3 for Cello and Piano, Radu Aldulescu on Cello; Bach Sonata No. 4 for Violin and Piano BWV 1017; Beethoven Sonata Op 30 No. 3 for Piano and Violin, Lola Bobesco on Violin; Brahms Sonata No. 2 Op 100 in A major and No. 3 Op 108 in D minor for Piano and Violin, Angela Gavrila Dieterle on Violin; Beethoven Seven Variations in E flat WoO46 for Piano and Cello, Mirel Iancovici on Cello. *Honours:* The Hephzibah Menuhin International Prize for Pianists, 1981. *Address:* Chalet Bel Air, App 216, 3780 Gstaad, Switzerland.

GUY, Barry (John); Musician (Double Bass, Baroque Bass) and Composer; b. 22 April 1947, Lewisham, London, England. *Education:* AGSM. *Career:* Freelance Bassist; principal, City of London Sinfonia; Academy of Ancient Music, London Classical Players until 1995; Solo recitalist; Artistic Director, London Jazz Composers Orchestra; Barry Guy New Orchestra; Plays with improvisation groups, Parker/Guy/Lytton; Guy/Gustafsson/Strid, Cecil Taylor, Bill Dixon Quartet, Marilyn Crispell; Homburger-Guy Duo; mem, Musicians Union; PRS; MCPS'; BACS. *Compositions include:* Statements ll, 1972; String Quartet III, 1973; Anna, 1974; Play, 1976; EOS for double bass and orchestra, 1977; Details, 1978; Hold Hands and Sing, 1978; Waiata, 1980; Pfiff, 1981; Flagwalk, 1974; Voyages of the Moon, 1983; RondOH!, 1985; Circular for solo oboe, 1985; The Road to Ruin, 1986; Harmos, 1987; The Eye of Silence, 1988; UM 1788, 1989; Look Up!, 1990; Theoria, 1991; After the Rain, 1992; Bird Gong Game, 1992; Mobile Herbarium, 1992; Portraits, 1993; Witch Gong Game, 1993; Witch Gong Game ll, 1994; Un Coup Dés, 1994; Buzz, 1994; Celebration, 1995; Ceremony, 1995; Three Pieces for orchestra, 1995; Concerto for orchestra, Fallingwater, 1996; Double Trouble Two, 1996; Holyrood, 1998; Redshift, 1998, Bubblets, 1998, Remembered Earth, 1998; Octavia, 1999; Dakryon, 1999; Inscape (Tableaux), 2000; Nasca Lines, 2001; Switch, 2001; Inachis, 2002; Aglais, 2002; Anaklasis, 2002; Folio, 2002. *Recordings include:* Over 100 albums including: Ode, 1972; Endgame, 1979; Incision, 1981; Tracks, 1983; Zürich Concerts, 1988; Double Trouble, 1990; Elsie jo Live, 1992; Theoria, 1992; After the Rain, 1993; Fizzles, 1993; Portraits, 1994; Vade

Mecum, 1994; Imaginary Values, 1994; Witch Gong Game ll, 1994; Cascades, 1995; Obliquities, 1995; Iskra 1903, 1995; Three Pieces for orchestra, 1997; Sensology, 1997; Frogging, 1997; Natives and Aliens, 1997; Bingo, 1998, Double Trouble Two, 1998; At the Vortex, 1998; Ceremony, 1999; In Darkness Let Me Dwell, 2000; Melancholy, 2000; Nailed, 2000; Dividuality, 2001; Odyssey, 2002; Symmetries, 2002. *Honours:* Radcliffe Award 1st Prize, 1973; Royal Philharmonic Prize for Chamber Scale Composition, 1991; Joint Prizewinner, Hilliard Composition prize, 1994; Abendzeitung (Munich) Sterne des Jahres, 1999. *Address:* Griffinstown, Skeoughvosteen, Near Borris, County Kilkenny, Ireland.

GUY, (Ruth) Maureen; singer (mezzo-soprano); b. 10 July 1932, Penclawdd, Glamorgan, South Wales; m. John Mitchinson 1958. *Education:* Guildhall School of Music and Drama. *Career:* debut as Dryad in Ariadne auf Naxos, Sadler's Wells; Principal Mezzo-Soprano at Sadler's Wells, Royal Opera House Covent Garden and Frankfurt Opera; Recitals, oratorio and orchestral concerts world-wide; Tours of New Zealand, Australia and Europe; Performed in opera in New Zealand, Spain, Portugal, France and Budapest; Her roles included Delilah, Eboli, Amneris, Azucena, Fricka, Erda, Orpheus, Mrs Sedley and Adriano in Rienzi; Performed Oedipus Rex in Herodus Atticus in Athens, conducted by Stravinsky; Vocal Tutor at the Welsh College of Music and Drama. *Recordings:* Solti, Götterdämmerung; Leinsdorf, Die Walküre; Sadler's Wells, Rigoletto, as Maddalena. *Honours:* Glamorgan County Scholarship to Guildhall School. *Address:* The Verzons Granary, Munsley, Ledbury, Hertfordshire, England.

GUYER, Joyce; Singer (Soprano); b. 1961, USA. *Career:* Sang Mozart's Constanze at Washington, 1987; Chicago Opera, 1988, as Gluck's Euridice, Buxton Festival, 1989, as Livia in Cimarosa's L'Italiana in Londra; Metropolitan Opera, New York, from 1993, in Jenůfa, Ariadne auf Naxos, Parsifal and Idomeneo; Season 1991 at Montpellier and Nice, as Constanze and Donna Anna; Bayreuth Festival, 1995–96, in The Ring and Parsifal. *Recordings include:* Videos of Parsifal and Idomeneo. *Address:* c/o Metropolitan Opera, Lincoln Center, New York, NY 10023, USA.

GWYNNE, David; singer (bass); b. 1945, Pontnewydd, Cwmbran, Wales. *Education:* Guildhall School, London. *Career:* appearances with Welsh National Opera as Verdi's Zaccaria, and Grand Inquisitor, Wagner's Daland, Pimen in Boris Godunov, Mozart's Basileo and Rocco in Fidelio; Scottish Opera in The Trojans, Peter Grimes, Schnittke's Life with an Idiot, Katya Kabanova, Aida, Oedius Rex and Don Giovanni, as the Commendatore; Engagements with English National Opera in Henze's The Prince of Homburg and Gianni Schicchi; Opera North in Katya Kabanova, Attila, The Love for Three Oranges, Fidelio (Fernando) and Gloriana; Arkel in Pelléas et Mélisande, Ferrando in Il Trovatore and Hermit in Der Freischütz are other roles: Glyndebourne Festival 2000, as Antonio in Le nozze de Figaro.

GYLDENFELDT, Graciela Von; Singer (Soprano); b. 22 June 1958, Buenos Aires, Argentina. *Education:* Studied in Buenos Aires. *Career:* Debut: Sang Norina in Don Pasquale at Buenos Aires in 1979; Sang at Bern Opera from 1980, debut as Gilda, then as Zerlina, Martha, Pamina, Echo in Ariadne auf Naxos and Corilla in Donizetti's Convenzione Teatrali; Sang at Vienna Staatsoper, 1982–86, Salzburg Festival, 1984–86, as Frasquita and Tebaldo in productions of Carmen and Don Carlos conducted by Karajan; Sang at Enschede Netherlands from 1988 as Suor Angelica, Mimi and Donna Elvira; Member of Kiel Opera as Chrysothemis, Katya Kabanova and Ellen Orford, 1989–94; Sang the Princess in Zemlinsky's Es War Einmal in 1991, Marietta in Die Tote Stadt; Cincinnati, 1991 as Carmen; Appearances at Teatro Comunale, Florence, as Elena in Mefistofele and concert engagements in Beethoven's 9th and Janáček's Glagolitic Mass, Salud in La Vida Breve of Manuel de Falla at Dallas Opera, 1993; Teatro Col ón, Buenos Aires debut as Donna Elvira in Don Giovanni; Appearances throughout Germany as Amelia in Simon Boccanegra and Madama Butterfly; Sang Amelia at Freiburg, 1995; Sang Elena in Mefistofele at Buenos Aires, 1999. *Recordings:* CD, Mefistofele as Elena, with Samuel Ramey, 1990. *Honours:* Nomination for the Callas Award for her appearance as Salud in La Vida Breve at the Dallas Opera, 1993. *Address:* Muhliusstrasse 70, 24103, Kiel, Germany.

GYSELYNCK, Jean-Baptiste; Professor; b. 22 March 1946, Ghent, Belgium; m. Bruyneel Arlette, 1 June 1946, 1 s., 1 d. *Education:* Royal Atheneum of Ghent; Royal Music Conservatory of Ghent, 1962–66; Conservatory of Brussels, 1966–78. *Career:* Teacher of Counterpoint, Royal Flemish Music Conservatory of Antwerp, 1970; Professor of Harmony, Counterpoint and Composition at Lemmens Institute of Louvain, 1970–79; Professor Written Harmony 1970–, Professor of Harmony, Art Humanities Department, 1974–75, Royal Music Conservatory of Brussels. *Compositions include:* Recorded: Simfonia Da Camera, radio and television, 1975, Intermezzi for Wood Instruments, LP and radio, 1977, Trio for Strings, radio, 1979, Adagio En Allegro for

Alto Saxophone, radio, 1979, Adagio En Allegro for Alto Saxophone, Diptyque for Violin and Piano, radio, 1980, Diptyque for Violin and Piano, radio, 1982; Published: Intermezzi, Illuminatio, Diptyque, Music for 6 poems written by Johan Daisne. *Honours:* International Music

Competition Queen Elisabeth Laureat of Composition, 1980; Silver Prize of Her Majesty Queen Fabiola Composition Competition Sabam, 1980; 6 Poems of Johan Daisne given at the Albertine, Brussels, 1985. *Address:* Kortrijksesteenweg 934, 9000 Ghent, Belgium.

H

HAAN, Richard; singer (baritone); b. 1959, Kosice, Slovakia. *Career:* sang at Usti nad Labem and Olomouc, Slovak National Opera at Bratislava, 1990–93, Janáček Opera at Brno and National Theatre, Prague, as guest (Verdi's Amonasro and Renato, 1994–96); Edinburgh Festival, 1990, as Valentin in Faust, Salzburg, 1992, in Janáček's From the House of the Dead; US debut, 1996, at Virginia Opera, Norfolk, as Wagner's Dutchman; Sang Mathis in The Polish Jew by Karel Weis at the Prague State Opera, 2001; Other roles include Don Giovanni and Gershwin's Porgy; Numerous concert appearances. *Address:* c/o Virginia Opera, PO Box 2580, Norfolk, VA 23501, USA.

HAAS, Kenneth; Symphony Orchestra Executive; b. 8 July 1943, Washington DC, USA; m. (1) Barbara Dooneief, 14 Feb 1964, divorced 1990, 2 d., (2) Signe Johnson, 23 Mar 1990, 1 s. *Education:* BA, Columbia College, 1964. *Career:* Assistant to Managing Director, New York Philharmonic, 1966–70; Assistant General Manager, 1970–75, General Manager, 1976–87, Cleveland Orchestra; General Manager of Cincinnati Symphony Orchestra, 1975–76; Managing Director of Boston Symphony Orchestra, 1987–; Chairman of Orchestra Panel, National Endowment for The Arts, 1982–85; Co-Chairman of Music Overview Panel, National Endowment for The Arts, 1983–85; Chairman of Challenge Grant Panel, Ohio Arts Council, 1985–86; mem, American Symphony Orchestra League, Executive Committee, 1980–82, Board of Directors, 1993–94; Managers of Major Orchestras, US, Chairman, 1980–82. *Address:* Symphony Hall, 301 Massachusetts Avenue, Boston, MA 02115, USA.

HABBESTAD, Kjell (Helge); Teacher and Composer; b. 13 April 1955, Bomlo, Hordaland, Norway; m. Inger Elisabeth Brammer, 30 Dec 1976, 1 s., 2 d. *Education:* Studies of Church Music (organ), 1975–79; Studied Composition, Norwegian State Academy of Music, 1979–81. *Career:* Organist, Snaroya Church, Baerum 1977–81, Langhus Church, Ski 1986–87; Teacher of Harmony, Counterpoint, Composition, Bergen Conservatory of Music 1981–86, Ostlandets Conservatory of Music, Oslo, 1986–96; Norwegian State Academy of Music, 1996–. *Compositions:* 3 Cantica (Magnificat, Nunc Dimittis, Benedictus Dominus), 1978–83; Lament, soprano and orchestra, 1981; Mostraspelet, baritone solo, choir, orchestra and mediaeval instruments, 1983; Ave Maria, concerto for organ and string orchestra, 1984; Something New–Below Ground, concerto for tuba and brass band, 1985; Mostrasuite for baritone solo, unison choir and orchestra, 1986; Introduction and Passacaglia, over a theme by Fartein Valen, organ solo, 1987; Hammerklavier, piano solo, 1989; Orpheus, flute, piano and ballet dancer, 1993; One Night on Earth, oratorio, 1993; Hans Egedes Natt, opera, 1995; Ibsen Songs, song and piano, 1996; Liturgic dramas/church plays, choral works, chamber music, cantatas, organ chorals, motets. *Publications:* Cantate–Handbook of Norwegian Sacred Choral Works, 1989; Themes, Trends and Talents, 25 Years of Contemporary Norwegian Music, co-editor, 1992; Arrangements, Arenas and Actors in Contemporary Norwegian Music, editor and writer, 1992; Yearbook of Contemporary Norwegian Music, editor and writer, 1996 and 1997. *Address:* Wesselsvei 5, 1412 Sofiemyr, Norway.

HABEREDER, Agnes; Singer (Soprano); b. 1957, Kelheim, Germany. *Education:* Studied in Munich, Florence and Stuttgart. *Career:* Sang at Augsburg Mozart Festival, 1979 as Mozart's Donna Anna; Winner of Mozart Competition in Würzburg; Guest appearances at Florence and Paris as Wagner's Gutrune, 1981, Dresden as Marie in Wozzeck, 1984; Zürich Opera from 1984 as Strauss's Empress, Wagner's Senta, and Ursula in Hindemith's Mathis der Maler; Bayreuth Festival, 1983–86, in The Ring; Salzburg Festival, 1986, as Leonore in Fidelio; Other roles include Salome, Korngold's Marietta, and Cassandre in Les Troyens (Zürich, 1990); Other guest appearances at Vienna, Munich, Mannheim, RAI Turin; Concert performances all over the world; Teacher at Augsburg Music High School 1993–; Teacher at Munich Music High school, 1993–; mem, Bund Deutsche Gesangspädagogen; Muenchner Tonkuenstler EV. *Recordings:* Kantate, Von deutscher Seele, by Hans Pfitzner, Düsseldorfer Symphoniker, conductor Heinrich Hollreiser. *Address:* Kastanienweg 6, 89555 Steinheim, Germany.

HABERMANN, Michael (Robert); Pianist, Piano Instructor and Composer; b. 23 Feb. 1950, Paris, France. *Education:* AAS, Nassau Community College, Garden City, New York, 1976; BA 1978, MA 1979, Long Island University, Greenvale, New York; DMA, Peabody Conservatory, Baltimore, Maryland, 1985. *Career:* Debut: Carnegie Recital Hall, 1977; American Liszt Festival appearances in 1978, 1982, 1993; International Piano Festival, University of Maryland in 1979; Grand Piano Programme, National Public radio recital in 1981; McMaster University, Hamilton, Ontario, Canada, 1983; Rocky River Chamber Music Society, Ohio, 1984–2001; Lecturer, Elder Hostel Program, Peabody Conservatory, Baltimore, 1990–; International Concert Series,

Hempstead, New York, 1999; Performing Arts Center, Purchase, New York, 2000. *Recordings:* Sorabji: A Legend in His Own Time; Sorabji: Le Jardin Parfumé; Sorabji: Piano Music, vol. 3; Sorabji: The Legendary Works; Sorabji: Transcriptions and other works; Piano Music of Alexandre Rey Colaço Educo. *Publications:* Kaikhosru Shapurji Sorabji, The Piano Quarterly, 1983; The Exotic Piano Masterpieces of Sorabji, Soundpage and Score, Keyboard Magazine, 1986; A Style Analysis of The Nocturnes for Solo Piano by Kaikhosru Shapurji Sorabji with special emphasis on Le Jardin Parfumé, University Microfilms International; Author of Sorabji's Piano Music, in Sorabji: A Critical Celebration, 1993; Author, Essay for Remembering Horowitz: 125 Pianists recall a legend, 1993. *Address:* 4208 Harford Terrace, Baltimore, MD 21214, USA. *E-mail:* pf@michaelhabermann.com.

HACKER, Alan (Ray); Clarinettist, Conductor and Lecturer; b. 30 Sept. 1938, Dorking, Surrey; m. (1) Anna Maria Sroka, 1959, 2 d., (2) Karen Evans, 1977, divorced, 1 s., (3) Margaret Shelley Lee, 1995. *Education:* Royal Academy of Music; FRAM. *Career:* Joined London Philharmonic Orchestra, 1958; Professor, Royal Academy of Music, 1960–76; Co-Founder, Pierrot Players, 1965; Founded Matrix, 1971, Music Party for authentic performance of classical music, 1972, Classical Orchestra, 1977; Member, Fires of London, 1970–76; Guest Conductor, Orchestra La Fenice, Venice, 1981; Revived basset clarinet, restored original text to Mozart's concerto and quintet, 1967; Revived baroque clarinet, 1975; 1st modern authentic performances, 1977–, including: Mozart Symphonies 39, 40; Beethoven Symphonies 2, 3, 7, 9 and Egmont; Haydn Harmonie and Creation Masses, Symphony 104, Trumpet Concerto; Premieres, music by Birtwistle, Boulez, Feldman, Goehr, Maxwell Davies, Stockhausen, Blake, Mellers, Sciarrino; Conductor, 5 staged performances of Bach St John Passion, European Music Year, 1984; Directed Hallström's Den Bergtagna revival, Swedish National Opera (for Norrlands Operan), 1986–87, and 1st production of complete La Finta Giardiniera; Conducted Keiser's Claudius, Vadstena Academy, Sweden, 1989; Premiered Judith Weir's The Vanishing Bridegroom, Scottish Opera, 1990; Così fan tutte, La Finta Giardiniera, Opera North, 1990–91; Stuttgart Opera, 1990–96, Don Giovanni and Monteverdi's Ulisse; Così fan tutte, La Cenerentola, Barcelona, 1992, Giulio Cesare, Halle Handel Festival; La Clemenza di Tito, Vienna, 1994; Opéra de Paris Bastille, Magic Flute; Stuttgart Opera, Purcell's King Arthur, 1996–97; Handel's Xerxes, Cologne, 1996–97; Handel's Alcina at Stuttgart and Edinburgh, 1998; Sir Robert Mayer Lecturer, Leeds University, 1972–73; Senior Lecturer, Music, York University, 1976–85; Orchestral work with major orchestras world-wide; Handel's Saul, Berlin, 1999. *Recordings:* Many including Brahms Clarinet Sonatas, 1989; Mozart and Weber Quintets. *Publications:* Mozart Concerto and Quintet scores, 1972; Reconstructed Mozart Concerto, 1st edition, 1973; Schumann's Soirestücke, 1985. *Honours:* O.B.E., 1988; Patron, Artlink, 1993. *Address:* Hindlea, Broughton, Malton, North Yorkshire YO17 6QJ, England. *E-mail:* clarionet@hackers-at-hindlea.freeserve.co.uk.

HADARI, Omri; conductor; b. 10 Sept. 1941, Israel; m. Osnat Hadari 1965; one s. one d. *Education:* Tel-Aviv Music College; Guildhall School of Music and Drama, London. *Career:* Debut: London in 1974; Conductor, London Lyric Orchestra; Principal Guest Conductor, Adelaide Symphony Orchestra; Conducted Shostakovich's New Babylon in London in 1982, New York and Helsinki and at the Flanders Festival; Debut with Australian Opera in 1988 in La Bohème; Music Director and Principal Conductor, Cape Town Symphony Orchestra, South Africa, 1989–; Guest Conductor for Royal Philharmonic Orchestra, London Symphony Orchestra, City of Birmingham Symphony Orchestra, The Australian Opera, Sydney Symphony Orchestra, Melbourne Symphony Orchestra, South Australia Symphony Orchestra, Queensland Symphony Orchestra, Israel Chamber Orchestra, Jerusalem Symphony Orchestra, Beer-Sheva Sinfonietta, Het Brabant Symphony Orchestra, Dutch National Ballet, Victorian State Opera, Ulster Orchestra, National Symphony Orchestra of South Africa, Natal Philharmonic, Columbus Symphony Orchestra, Ohio, San Francisco Chamber Orchestra, Orchestra of Radio City New York, Lahti Symphony Orchestra, Avanti Orchestra, and Tasmania Symphony Orchestra; mem, Incorporated Society of Musicians. *Honours:* Winner, Dr Leo Kestenberg Prize, Israel, 1969; Conducting Prize, Guildhall School of Music, 1974; Capsalic Cup for Conducting, 1974; Fellow, Guildhall School of Music, 1983. *Current Management:* Tennant Artists, Unit 2, 39 Tadema Road, London, SW10 0PZ, England. *Telephone:* (20) 7376-3758. *Fax:* (20) 7351-0679. *E-mail:* info@tennantartists.demon.co.uk. *Address:* 7 Hurstwood Road, London NW11 0AS, England.

HADDOCK, Marcus; Singer (Tenor); b. 19 June 1957, Fort Worth, Texas, USA. *Education:* Vocal Studies, Baylor University, Waco, Texas, with Carol Blaickner-Mayo; Texas Tech University with John Gillas; Boston

341

University with Phyllis Curtin. *Career:* Roles include Count Almaviva in Il Barbiere di Siviglia, Ramiro in La Cenerentola, Lindoro in L'Italiana in Algeri, Tonio in La Fille du Régiment by Donizetti; International debut in Bordeaux as Ford in Salieri's Falstaff; Nemorino in L'Elisir d'amore; Festival appearances in Aachen, Karlsruhe and Bonn in La Bohème and Lucia di Lammermoor, La Traviata, Madama Butterfly, Werther and Les Contes d'Hoffmann; Debut with Opéra Paris de Bastille as Arbace in Idomeneo; 1992 debut with Teatro alla Scala as Matteo in Arabella with Wolfgang Sawallisch; 1994–95 season as Lenski in Eugene Onegin for Lausanne Opera, then Rodolfo in La Bohème in Geneva, Pinkerton in Madama Butterfly in Los Angeles and Don Carlo in Antwerp; Season 1995–96 included Ruggero in La Rondine, Roméo in Roméo et Juliette in Geneva and appearance in Gran Teatro la Fenice to sing Don Carlo in Warsaw; Season 1996–97 included appearance with Deutsche Oper Berlin as Faust, Tebaldo in I Capuleti e i Montecchi at Opera de Bastille and Lenski in debut with Nederlandse Opera in Amsterdam; Verdi Requiem with Orchestre de Paris; Season 2000–01 as Puccini's Ruggiero in Los Angeles, Julien in Louise in Toulouse, Pinkerton at the Teatro Col ón, Buenos Aires, and the Duke of Mantua for Dallas Opera; Sang Don José at Glyndebourne 2002. Concert repertoire includes Missa Solemnis and Janáček's Glagolitic Mass. *Recordings:* Orazi e Curiazi with London Philharmonic Orchestra; Il Guarany, with Oper der Stadt Bonn. *Address:* 1000 The Lane, Skaneateles, NY 13152, USA.

HADJINIKOS, George; Conductor, Concert Pianist, Lecturer and Teacher; b. 3 May 1923, Volos, Greece; m. Matina Crithary, deceased, 1 s. *Education:* Athens University; Diploma, Athens Conservatoire; Soloist and Conducting degrees with Distinction, Special Award of the Lilli Lehmann Golden Medal, Mozarteum at Salzburg; Postgraduate studies with Carl Orff, Munich, Ed Erdmann, Hamburg and G Chavchavadze, Paris. *Career:* Concert soloist, Conductor, Lecturer in Europe, USA, South Africa, India and Brazil; World premieres of works by Nikos Skalkottas; Soloist with many international orchestras including: BBC Orchestra with Antal Dorati, Hallé Orchestra with John Barbirolli, NDR with Herman Scherchen, Suisse Romande, Zürich and Copenhagen Radio; Conductor of many orchestras world-wide including: London Bach Festival Ensemble, RAI Milan Orchestra (Athens Festival opening concert), Rio de Janeiro Radio Orchestra, Sinfonie Orchester Berlin and numerous international youth orchestras; Concert tour of US universities; Prepared and Conducted 1st Greek performance of Brahms' German Requiem, 1992; Nexus Opera Workshop; Lectured, Wuerzburg European Council Symposium; Developed fresh approach, Logic and Foundations of Musical Interpretation presented at open seminars and articles; Musical Director of the Hortos International Seminars, where Greek musical youth meets musical youth from Europe, Russia, America and other countries, 1983–; Teacher, Royal Manchester and Royal Northern Colleges of Music, 1961–88. *Recordings:* Album with works by Bach, Bartók, Skalkottas, Konstantinidis and Poniridis; CD, Conducting Skalkottas Fairy Tale. *Publications:* Monographs on Skalkottas, 1981 and Mozart's Recitative, 1991; Co-editor, The Complete works by Nikos Skalkottas; Series of articles on Essence and Origins of Musical Interpretation; Centenary guide to the work and personality of Nikos Skalkottas (1904–2004). *Current Management:* PIA Agency. *Address:* Cultural Foundation, Amerikis 15, Athens 10672, Greece.

HADLEY, Jerry; Singer (Tenor); b. 16 June 1952, Peoria, Illinois, USA; m. Cheryll Drake Hadley. *Education:* Studied at University of Illinois and with Thomas LoMonaco. *Career:* Debut: Sarasota, FL in 1978 as Lionel in Martha; New York City Opera debut in 1979 as Arturo in Lucia di Lammermoor, returning as Werther, Tom Rakewell, Rodolfo, Pinkerton and Nadir; Vienna Staatsoper debut in 1982 as Nemorino in L'Elisir d'amore; Glyndebourne debut in 1984 as Idamante in Trevor Nunn's production of Idomeneo; Covent Garden in 1984 as Fenton in Falstaff; Metropolitan Opera debut in 1987 as Des Grieux in Manon; Guest engagements in Chicago, Hamburg, Berlin, Munich and Geneva; Other roles include Gounod's Faust, the Duke of Mantua and the tenor leads in Anna Bolena and Maria Stuarda; Hamburg in 1987 as Tamino and sang Edgardo at the Deutsche Oper Berlin and Washington, 1988–89; Candide in a concert performance of Bernstein's work in London in 1989; Sang Hoffmann in London in 1992; Sang Tom Rakewell at the 1994 Salzburg Festival; Created the title role in Myron Fink's The Conquistador, San Diego, 1997; Concert engagements with the Pittsburgh Symphony, Boston Symphony, Chicago Symphony, Philadelphia Orchestra, Vienna Philharmonic and Los Angeles Philharmonic; Recitals with pianist, Cheryll Drake Hadley; Sang Weill's Jimmy Mahoney at Salzburg, 1998; Created the title role in The Great Gatsby by John Harbison at the New York Met, 1999; Engaged as Idomeneo at Baden-Baden, 2000; Sang Steva in Jenůfa at Covent Garden, 2002. *Recordings include:* Schubert Mass in E flat; La Bohème; Beethoven's Choral Symphony; Requiems of Mozart and Verdi with the Robert Shaw Chorale; Britten's Serenade, Nocturne and Les Illuminations; Il Re

Pastore conducted by Neville Marriner. *Address:* c/o IMG Artists, Lovell House, 616 Chiswick High Road, London W4 5RX, England.

HAEBLER, Ingrid; Concert Pianist and Professor of Music; b. 20 June 1929, Vienna, Austria. *Education:* Studied at the Salzburg Mozarteum, the Vienna Academy and the Geneva Conservatory; Further study in Paris with Marguerite Long. *Career:* Debut: Salzburg in 1941; Many concert tours of Europe, Australia, USA, Canada, South Africa, South America and Japan; Festival appearances at Salzburg, Bath, Edinburgh, Wiesbaden, Amsterdam and Prague; Concerts with the Concertgebouw Orchestra, London Symphony, Royal Philharmonic, Vienna and Berlin Philharmonics, Boston Symphony, Lamoureux Orchestra, Stockholm and Warsaw Philharmonics, and London Mozart Players. *Recordings include:* Cycle of the Complete Piano Concertos of Mozart; Complete Sonatas of Mozart and Schubert; Beethoven's 2nd and 4th Concertos; Schumann Piano Concerto; Symphonic Variations by Franck; Works by J. C. Bach on the Fortepiano; Mozart and Beethoven Sonatas with Violinist Henryk Szeryng; 2 CDs included in the Philips Edition Great Pianists of the 20th Century. *Honours:* Winner, International Competition Munich and Schubert Competition Geneva, 1954; Beethoven Medal, Harriet Cohen Foundation, 1957; Grand Prix du Disque, Paris, 1958; Puthon Prize, Salzburg Festival; Mozart Medal, Vienna, 1971; Mozart Medal, Salzburg, 1979; Gold Medal of Honour by the Town of Vienna, 1986; Gold Medal 'Viotti d'Oro', Vercelli, Italy, 2000. *Address:* 5412 St Jakob am Thurn, Post Puch Bei Hallein, Land Salzburg, Austria.

HAEFLIGER, Ernst; Singer (tenor); b. 6 July 1919, Davos, Switzerland. *Education:* Studied in Zürich and with Fernando Carpi in Geneva; Further study with Julius Patzak in Vienna. *Career:* Debut: In 1942 as the Evangelist in Bach's St John Passion; Sang with Zürich Opera, 1943–52; Many concert appearances in Switzerland, Germany, Austria, France and Netherlands, notably in the St Matthew Passion and Lieder cycles by Schubert; Salzburg Festival in 1949 as Tiresias in the premiere of Antigonae by Orff, returning for Idomeneo and the Choral Symphony; Glyndebourne Festival, 1956–57 as Tamino in Die Zauberflöte and as Belmonte in Die Entführung; Guest appearances in Munich, Hamburg, Florence, Aix-en-Provence, Brussels and Berlin at the Deutsche Oper, 1952–74; Sang in the first performances of the oratorios Le Vin Herbé, Golgotha and in Terra Pax, by Frank Martin; Visited Moscow and Leningrad with the Munich Bach Choir in 1968; Professor at the Musikhochschule Munich from 1971; Sang the Shepherd in Tristan und Isolde at Munich, 1996; London Prom Concerts 2002, as the Speaker in Schoenberg's Gurrelieder. *Recordings:* St Matthew Passion; Missa Solemnis; Oedipus Rex; Pelléas et Mélisande; Die Entführung; Fidelio; Don Giovanni; Die Zauberflöte; Der fliegende Holländer; Brockes Passion by Handel; Die Israeliten in der Wüste by CPE Bach. *Publications:* Die Singstimme, 1984. *Current Management:* Ingpen & Williams Ltd, 7 St George's Court, 131 Putney Bridge Road, London, SW15 2PA, England.

HAEFLIGER, Michael, BMus, MBA; musician; b. 2 May 1961, West Berlin. *Education:* Juillard School of Music, St Gallen Univ., Harvard Business School. *Career:* Artistic and Exec. Dir, Davos Music Festival 1986–98, Lucerne Festival 1999–; mem. Int. Soc. of Performing Arts, Lions Club. *Honours:* World Economic Forum Global Leader for Tomorrow 2000, European Cultural Initiative Award 2003. *Address:* c/o Lucerne Festival, Hirschmattstr 13, 6002 Lucerne (office); Spissenstr 2, 6047 Kastanienbaum, Lucerne, Switzerland (home). *Telephone:* 412264400 (office). *Fax:* 412264460 (office). *Website:* www .lucernefestival.ch (office).

HAENCHEN, Hartmut; Conductor; b. 21 March 1943, Dresden, Germany. *Education:* Member of the Dresden Kreuzchor, 1953–60, under Rudolf Mauersberge and at the Dresden Musikhochschule, 1960–66. *Career:* Directed the Robert-Franz-Singakademie and the Halle Symphony, 1966–72; Music Director at the Zwickau Opera, 1972–73; Permanent Conductor of the Dresden Philharmonic, 1973–76, Philharmonic Chorus of Dresden, 1974–76 and 1985–1987 permanent guest conductor of the Staatsoper Dresden; Musical Director of the Schwerin Staatstheater and conductor of the Mecklenburg Staatskapelle, 1976–79; Professor of Conducting, Dresden Musikhochschule, 1980–86; Permanent Guest Conductor at Komische Oper Berlin and Berlin Staatsoper; Guest appearances in Europe, USA, Canada, Japan and China at leading opera houses in Europe, New York and at Kirishima Festival in Japan; From 1980 Artistic Director of the CPE Bach Chamber Orchestra, Berlin; From 1986 to 1999 Musical Director of the Netherlands Opera and 1986–2002 Chief Conductor of the Netherlands Philharmonic Orchestra and the Netherlands Chamber Orchestra; Conducted Bluebeard's Castle, La Damnation de Faust, Elektra, Salome, Rosenkavalier, Le nozze di Figaro, Entführung, Don Carlos, Tristan, Parsifal, Boris Godunov, Orphée et Eurydice; Conducted Gluck's Orfeo ed Euridice at Covent Garden in 1991 followed by Mozart's Mitridate; Die Frau ohne Schatten, Mitridate, La Damnation de Faust and Samson et Dalila at Amsterdam in 1992; Opened the 1994 season for Netherlands Opera with Lady Macbeth of the Mtsensk District; Elektra at Amsterdam, 1996, and Götterdämmerung 1998; After completion of his Ring for the Netherlands Opera in 1999, he changed from Musical Director to First Guest Conductor and conducted Alceste, Meistersinger, Capriccio, King Roger, Onegin, Lear, Lulu and Titus; Season 2002–03 with La Clemenza di Tito, Die Zauberflöte and Die Soldaten in Amsterdam and until 2005 the complete Ring cycle; From 2003, Intendant of the Dresdner Musik Festspiele. *Recordings:* Numerous including Gluck's Orfeo ed Euridice, earning the Preis der Deutschen Schallplatten and Gramophone Award Nomination. *Address:* Dresdner Musikfestspiele, Tiergartenstrasse 36, D 01219 Dresden, Germany.

HAENDEL, Ida; Concert Violinist; b. 15 Dec. 1923, Chelm, Poland. *Education:* Gold Medal at age 7, Warsaw Conservatorium; Private teachers, Carl Flesch and Georges Enesco. *Career:* Debut: British Queen's Hall London with Brahms Concerto under Henry Wood, 1937; Concerts for British and US Troops and in factories, World War ll; Then career developed to take in North and South America, Russia, Far East, Europe; Has played with conductors such as Beecham, Klemperer, Szell, Barenboim, Mata, Pritchard and Rattle; Has accompanied British orchestras on tours to China, Hong Kong and Australia; Performances with major orchestras world-wide include, Boston Symphony, New York Philharmonic, Berlin Philharmonic, City of Birmingham Symphony Orchestra, London Philharmonic, Philharmonia and Royal Philharmonic Orchestra; Major festival appearances including regular performances at BBC Promenade Concerts, London; Played the Britten Concerto at the 1994 Proms. *Recordings include:* Bach Solo Partitas, 1996. *Publications:* Woman with Violin, autobiography, 1970. *Honours:* Huberman Prize, 1935; Sibelius Medal, Sibelius Society of Finland, 1982; New Year's Honours List Awarded C.B.E. for Outstanding Services to Music, 1991. *Current Management:* Ernest Gilbert & Assocs, 109 Wheeler Avenue, Pleasantville, NY 10570, USA.

HAENEN, Tom; Singer (Bass); b. 1959, Amsterdam, Netherlands. *Education:* Studied at Amsterdam Conservatoire. *Career:* Debut: As Don Alfonso in Così fan tutte for Netherlands Opera; Appearances in the Netherlands and elsewhere as the General in Prokofiev's The Gambler, Arkel in Pelléas et Mélisande and Ferrando in Il Trovatore, Osmin in Die Entführung for Opera North and Leporello and Geronte in Manon Lescaut in Dublin; Further engagements as Sparafucile in Rigoletto at Barcelona, Don Cassandro in La Finta Semplice and Tom in Un Ballo in Maschera for Flanders Opera in 1992; Guest appearances at Spoleto, Israel and Las Palmas Festivals. *Honours:* Prizewinner at the International 's-Hertogenbosch and Rio de Janeiro Competitions.

HAFIDH, Munther Jamil; Iraqi musician (viola, cello); m. *Career:* viola player, Baghdad Symphony Orchestra 1959–. *Address:* Iraqi National Symphony Orchestra, Baghdad Convention Center, Green Zone, Baghdad, Iraq.

HAGEGARD, Erland; Baritone; b. 27 Feb. 1944, Brunskog, Sweden; m. Anne Terelius. *Education:* Studied in Sweden with Arne Sunnegaard, Erik Werba in Vienna and Gerald Moore in Vienna. *Career:* Debut: Vienna Volksoper in 1968 in Trois Opéras Minutes by Milhaud; Sang with Frankfurt Opera, 1971–74; Member of the Hamburg Staatsoper from 1974; Guest with the Vienna Staatsoper from 1976; Appearances at the Drottningholm Court Opera in Sweden; Danish television in Xerxes by Handel; Roles include Escamillo, Valentin, Don Giovanni, Eugene Onegin, Albert in Werther and Germont in La Traviata; Lieder singer in works by Schubert; Television appearances include Suppé's Boccaccio.

HAGEGARD, Håkan; Baritone; b. 25 Nov. 1945, Karlstad, Sweden; m. Barbara Bonney, dissolved, 2 c. *Education:* Music Academy of Stockholm; Student of Tito Gobbi, Rome, Gerald Moore, London, and Erik Werba, Vienna. *Career:* Debut: As Papageno in The Magic Flute, Royal Opera, Sweden, 1968; Metropolitan Opera debut in 1978 as Donizetti's Malatesta; Member of Royal Opera Stockholm; Appeared with major opera companies throughout Europe, in film of The Magic Flute in 1975 and at Glyndebourne from 1973 as the Count in Figaro and Capriccio and as Mozart's Guglielmo; Created role of Crispin in Tintomara, Royal Opera Stockholm in 1973; Covent Garden debut in 1987 as Wolfram in Tannhäuser, also at Chicago in 1988; Metropolitan Opera in 1988 as Guglielmo; Sang Eisenstein in Die Fledermaus at Chicago in 1989; Created Beaumarchais in The Ghosts of Versailles by Corigliano at the Metropolitan in 1991; Deutsche Oper Berlin in 1992 as Wolfram; Season 1996 at the Met as Prus in The Makropulos Case and in April Gala; The Officer in the US premiere of Lindberg's A Dream Play, Santa Fe, 1998; Sang Scarpia at Sydney, 2000; Recitalist. *Recordings include:* Die Zauberflöte under Armin Jordan; Don Giovanni, in title role, from Drottningholm. *Current Management:* Thea Dispeker. *Address:* c/o Thea Dispeker Artists' Management, 59 East 54th Street, New York, NY 10022, USA.

HAGEN, Christina; Singer (Mezzo-Soprano); b. 1956, Hamburg, Germany. *Education:* Studied singing with Naan Pold and Hilde Nadolowitsch; Concert Diploma, Exam as Private Music Instructor, Opera Diploma with Distinction, Hochschule für Musik und Darstellende Kunst, Hamburg; Masterclasses including with Sena Jurinac and at International Studio for Singing, Herbert von Karajan Stiftung, with Christa Ludwig. *Career:* Engaged at Staatstheater Oldenburg, 1983–84, then Deutsche Oper am Rhein, Düsseldorf-Duisburg, 1984–; Guest appearances in Germany at Berlin, Hamburg and Cologne, at Bolshoi Theatre in Moscow, Antwerp, Amsterdam and Staatsoper Berlin, National Theater Munich; Participant at Bayreuth Festival in 1989, 1990, 1991; Has sung Rosina in Barber of Seville, Micha in Samson by Handel, Judith in Bluebeard's Castle by Bartók and Jocasta in Oedipus Rex at Oldenburg, Olga in Eugene Onegin and Second Woman in Die Zauberflöte at Oldenburg and Düsseldorf, the Composer in Ariadne auf Naxos, Dorabella in Così fan tutte, Nicklausse in Tales of Hoffmann, Orlowsky in Die Fledermaus, Maddalena in Rigoletto, Fatima in Weber's Oberon, Sextus in Julius Caesar by Handel, Flosshilde, Erda and Fricka in Rheingold and in Walküre, Second Norn and Waltraute, Fenena in Nabucco, Britten's Lucretia, Olga in Das Schloss, Ottavia in Monteverdi's L'Incoronazione di Poppea, Eboli at Düsseldorf, Clytemnestra (Gluck) at Düsseldorf and Berlin, Fricka in Walküre at Munich, Santuzza in Cavalleria Rusticana at Eutiner Festival; Season 1995–96 at Düsseldorf as Wagner's Venus and Fricka; Many lieder recitals and concert appearances. *Honours:* Nominated Chamber Singer of Deutsche Oper am Rhein at Düsseldorf, 1992. *Address:* c/o Deutsche Oper am Rhein, Heinrich-Heine Allee 16, 40213 Düsseldorf, Germany.

HAGEN, Daron Aric, MMus; American composer and pianist; b. 4 Nov. 1961, Milwaukee. *Education:* Univ. of Wisconsin, Curtis Inst., Julliard School. *Career:* founding Dir, Perpetuum Mobile New Music Ensemble 1983–93; debut as concert pianist with Denver Chamber Orchestra 1986; composer-in-residence, Long Beach Symphony Orchestra 1994; composition teacher, Curtis Inst. 1996; Pres., Lotte Lehmann Foundation, New York 2004–; composer-in-residence, Princeton Univ. Atelier 2005. *Compositions include:* Prayer for Peace 1981, Echo's Songs 1983, Symphony No. 1 1985–88, Dear Youth 1991, Shining Brow (opera) 1990–92, Muldoon songs 1992, Vera of Las Vegas (cabaret opera) 1995, Symphony No. 3 1997, Chamber symphony 2003, The Antient Concert (opera) 2004. *Recordings include:* Vera of Las Vegas, Songs of Daron Hagen, Strings Attached (complete music for solo strings). *Honours:* Bearns Prize 1985, Barlow Int. Composition Prize for Chamber Music 1985, Friedheim Award 1994. *Address:* c/o Carl Fischer, Director of Concert Music, 65 Bleecker Street, New York, NY 10012, USA (office). *E-mail:* daron@daronhagen.com. *Website:* www.daronhagen.com.

HAGEN, Reinhard; Singer (Bass); b. 1966, Bremen, Germany. *Education:* Studied at Karlsruhe. *Career:* Sang at Kassel Opera, 1989–90, Dortmund, 1991–94, Deutsche Oper Berlin from 1993; Season 1991 as Sarastro at the Landestheater Salzburg and at Brussels; Salzburg Festival, 1993, as Plutone in Monteverdi's Orfeo; German premiere of Casken's The Golem, 1993; Season 1996 as Cadmus in Semele at Aix-en-Provence, Gounod's Frère Laurent at Geneva and Ferrando in Il Trovatore at Berlin; Sang Titurel in Parsifal at the Deutsche Oper, 1998; Season 2000–01 as Verdi's Banquo and Count Walter at the Deutsche Oper, King Henry in Lohengrin at San Diego, Sarastro in Barcelona, Rocco at Glyndebourne and bass solos in the St Matthew Passion for La Scala, Milan. *Recordings include:* Les Béatitudes, by Franck. *Address:* c/o Deutsche Oper Berlin, Richard Wagner Strasse 10, 1060 Berlin, Germany.

HAGEN-GROLL, Walter; Choral Conductor; b. 15 April 1927, Chemnitz, Germany. *Education:* Studied at the Stuttgart Musikhochschule, 1947–52. *Career:* Assistant Conductor at the Stuttgart Opera, 1952; Chorus Master at the Heidelberg Opera, 1957, and Deutsche Oper Berlin, 1961; Directed the chorus of the Berlin Philharmonic from 1961; Assisted Wilhelm Pitz at Bayreuth, 1960–62; Chorus Master at Salzburg Festival from 1965, Philharmonia Chorus, London, 1971–74; Chorus Master at the Vienna Staatsoper 1984, Vienna Singakademie 1987; Choral Director at the Salzburg Mozarteum from 1986.

HÄGER, Claus; Singer (Baritone); b. 1963, Wuppertal, Germany. *Education:* Studied in Cologne and Freiburg; Masterclasses with Dietrich Fischer-Dieskau. *Career:* Hamburg Staatsoper, 1991–92; Sang Papageno at the Berlin Staatsoper, 1994; Schwetzingen Festival, 1995; Other roles have included Mozart's Guglielmo, Silvio in Pagliacci, Puccini's Schaunard and Falke in La Bohème; Broadcast and concert engagements; Season 1998 as Marquis de Corcy in Le Postillon de Lonjumeau at the Berlin Staatsoper. *Honours:* Prizewinner, 1992 Oberdörfer Competition, Hamburg. *Address:* c/o Berlin Staatsoper, Unter den Linden 7, 1060 Berlin, Germany.

HAGER, Leopold; Conductor; b. 6 Oct. 1935, Salzburg, Austria; m. Gertrude Entleitner, 2 July 1960, 1 d. *Education:* Graduated in organ, piano, conducting, harpsichord, High School for Music (Mozarteum),

Salzburg. *Career:* Assistant Conductor, Staedtische Buhnen, Mainz, Germany, 1957–62; Principal Conductor: Landestheater, Linz, Austria, 1962–64; Opernhaus, Cologne, Germany, 1964–65; General Music Director: Staedtische Buhnen, Freiburg, Germany, 1965–69; Principal Conductor, Mozarteum Orchestra, Salzburg, 1969–81; Has conducted many performances of early operas by Mozart; Led the first modern performance of Mitridate, Salzburg, 1971; Symphony Orchestra, Radio Luxembourg, 1981–96; Guest Conductor: Vienna Opera; Munich Opera; Metropolitan Opera; Covent Garden; Teatro Col ón, Buenos Aires; Berlin and Vienna Philharmonics; Conducted Così fan tutte at the Metropolitan, 1991; Figaro, 1997. *Recordings:* Mozart Piano Concertos, with Karl Engel; Bastien und Bastienne, Lucio Silla, Il re Pastore, Ascanio in Alba, Mitridate Re di Ponto; CD of La Finta Semplice released 1990. *Honours:* Decorated, Ehrenkreuz 1 klasse für Kunst und Wissenschaft, Austria. *Address:* Morzgerstr 102, 5034 Salzburg, Austria.

HAGLEY, Alison; British singer (soprano); b. 9 May 1961, London, England. *Education:* Guildhall School of Music, National Opera Studio. *Career:* Sang in Handel's Rodelinda at the Aldeburgh Festival and Handel's Flavio with Musica nel Chiostro at the 1985 Batignano Festival in Italy; Camden Festival in 1986 in La Finta Giardiniera by Mozart; Sang Clorinda in Opera 80s 1987 production of La Cenerentola; Glyndebourne debut in 1988 as the Little Owl in L'Enfant et Les Sortilèges, returning in Jenůfa and as Susanna, Nannetta, Papagena and Zerlina; Glyndebourne Tour as Varvara in Katya Kabanova, Despina and Papagena; Covent Garden as a Flowermaiden in Parsifal and in Peter Grimes; English National Opera in 1991 as Lauretta in a new production of Gianni Schicchi and Gretel in Hansel and Gretel; Scottish Opera appearances as Musetta in La Bohème and Adele in Die Fledermaus; Sang Mélisande in 1992 with Boulez and Peter Stein, WNO; Sang Nannetta for ENO in 1992; Glyndebourne 1994, as Susanna; Covent Garden 1997, in Massenet's Chérubin; Bella in The Midsummer Marriage at Munich. 1998; Munich Opera Festival, 2000. *Honours:* FPC Opera Singer of the Year, National Opera Studio. *Current Management:* IMG Artists, Lovell House, 616 Chiswick High Road, London, W4 5RX, England. *Telephone:* (20) 8233-5800. *Fax:* (20) 8233-5801. *E-mail:* info@imgartists.com. *Website:* www.imgartists.com.

HAHN, Barbara; Singer (mezzo-soprano); b. 1965, Stuttgart, Germany. *Education:* Studied in Stuttgart and at Salzburg Mozarteum. *Career:* Sang at Bielefeld from 1987 as Dorabella, Cherubino and Orlofsky; Nicklausse in Les contes d'Hoffmann at Bregenz Festival, 1987; Appeared as Dorabella and Nicklausse at Hanover, 1988; Sang Grimgerde in Die Walküre at Bologna; Angelina, in La Cenerentola at Passau; Freiburg Opera, 1989–91, as Octavian, Idamantes, Hansel and Sonja in Der Zarewitsch; Concert performance of Schreker's Der ferne Klang in Berlin, 1990; Frankfurt Opera, 1992–, debut as Dorabella. *Recordings:* Der ferne Klang, conducted by Gerd Albrecht. *Current Management:* Athole Still International Management, Forresters Hall, 25–27 Westow Street, London, SE19 3RY, England. *Telephone:* (20) 8771-5271. *Fax:* (20) 8768-6600. *Website:* www.atholestill.com.

HAHN, Hilary; Violinist; b. 27 Nov. 1979, Lexington, Virginia, USA. *Education:* BMus, Curtis Institute of Music, Philadelphia. *Career:* Debut: Age 6 years, Baltimore, 1986; First Full Recital, Age 10 years, 1990; Major Orchestra Debut with Baltimore Symphony Orchestra, 1991; Utah and Florida Symphonies, 1992; Philadelphia Orchestra, 1993; New York Philharmonic Orchestra and Cleveland Orchestra, 1994; European concerto debut in Budapest, with Budapest Festival Orchestra, and European Recital debut at Festival de Sully et d'Orleans, France, 1994; German debut at 15 Playing Beethoven Violin Concerto with Bavarian Radio Symphony Orchestra and Lorin Maazel, Munich, 1995; Carnegie Hall debut at 16 with Philadelphia Orchestra and Christoph Eschenbach, 1996; Concerto Debuts in Berlin, Frankfurt, Hannover and Rotterdam, 1996; Recital debuts in Kennedy Center (DC), Alice Tully Hall, New York, Munich, Rotterdam and Paris, 1997; Concerto debuts in London, Glasgow, Birmingham, Zürich and Vienna with Bavarian Radio Symphony, and in Paris with French Radio Symphony Orchestra, 1998; As Chamber Musician Appears Regularly at Marlboro Music Festival, Skaneateles Festival and with the Chamber Music Society of Lincoln Center, New York. *Recordings include:* Solo Sonatas and Partitas of J. S. Bach; Concertos of Beethoven, Bernstein (Serenade), Samuel Barber, Edgar Meyer, Brahms and Stravinsky. *Honours:* Avery Fisher Career Grant, 1995. *Current Management:* IMG Artists. *Address:* c/o IMG Artists, 450 West 45th Street, New York, NY 10036, USA.

HAIDER, Friedrich; Pianist and Conductor; b. 1961, Austria. *Education:* Acad. of Music, Vienna; Mozarteum,Salzburg. *Career:* Theatrical debut: Klagenfurt, with Johann Stzrauss: Wiener Blut, 1984; Engagements from 1989 with Der fliegende Holländer at Barcelona, La Bohème in Stockholm, Figaro at Aix, Salome in Lisbon and Die Entführung at Bonn; Chief Conductor of the Opéra du Rhin, Strasbourg, 1991–95, with Il Trovatore, Rigoletto, La Traviata and Madama Butterfly; Debut,

Vienna Staatsoper in Die Fledermaus, 2003–04; Chief Conductor, City of Oviedo Orchestra, Spain, 2004–(2007); Guest appearances at Nice, with Faust and Tristan und Isolde, Barcelona (Lohengrin, Beatrice di Tenda), Lisbon (Norma, I Puritani), Hamburg (Don Giovanni) and Cologne (I Capuleti e I Montecchi); Concerts in Tokyo, Amsterdam, Munich, Milan and Budapest; Recital accompanist to Renata Scotto, Charlotte Margiono, Vesselina Kasarova and Rainer Trost. *Recordings include:* Roberto Devereux; Die schöne Müllerin, with Rainer Trost (Nightingale); Strauss Orchestral Lieder; Die Fledermaus; Richard Strauss: Eine Alpensinfonie, Ein Heldenleben, Till Eulenspiegel and world premiere recording of the integral Orchestral Songs; Brahms Serenade, op. 11. *Address:* c/o Theateragentur Dr G. Hilbert, Maximilianstrasse 22, 80539 Munich, Germany.

HAIGH, Andrew (Wilfred); Pianist; b. 26 April 1954, Lagos, Nigeria. *Education:* Student, 1969–74; Associate, Royal College of Music, London, 1975; Studied with Cyril Smith, Phyllis Sellick, Albert Ferber, 1974; Licenciate, Royal Academy of Music, 1975. *Career:* Debut: London Philharmonic Orchestra, Royal Festival Hall, 1965; Wigmore Hall, 1971; Soloist with all major British orchestras including: London Symphony; London Philharmonic; Philharmonia; Royal Philharmonic; BBC Philharmonic Orchestra; Soloist, Herbert von Karajan Festival, Berlin, 1970; Recitals in Europe; Head of Piano, Kent Centre for Young Instrumentalists; Examiner, Trinity College of Music, and Adjudicator; mem, Incorporated Society of Musicians. *Honours:* Gold Medallist, 1969; Winner, BBC Mozart Competition, 1969; Winner, Royal Overseas Competition; National Piano Competition; Hopkinson Silver Medal, 1973; Dannreuther Concerto Prize, Royal College of Music. *Address:* 15 Dornden Drive, Langton Green, Tunbridge Wells, Kent TN 3 0AA, England.

HAILSTORK, Adolphus Cunningham, MMus, PhD; American composer; b. 17 April 1941, Rochester, NY. *Education:* Howard Univ., Washington DC, Manhattan School, Michigan State Univ., with Nadia Boulanger in France. *Career:* teacher, Michigan State Univ. 1969–91, Youngstown State Univ. 1971–76, Norfolk Virginia State Coll. 1977–. *Compositions include:* The Race For Space, theatre piece, 1963; Phaedra, tone poem, 1966; Horn Sonata, 1966; Statement, Variation And Fugue for Orchestra, 1966; Sextet for Strings, 1971; Violin Sonata, 1972; Bagatelles for Brass Quintet, 1973; Pulse for Percussion Ensemble, 1974; Bellevue and Celebration, both for Orchestra, 1974; Concerto for Violin, Horn and Orchestra, 1975; Spiritual for Brass Octet, 1975; American Landscape, Nos 1, 3 and 4 for Orchestra, 1977–84; American Landscape for Violin and Cello, 1978; Piano Sonata, 1981; Sport of Strings, 1981; Piano Concerto, 1992; Symphony No. 2, 1996; Trumpet Sonata, 1996; Let the Heavens be Glad, for chorus, 1996; Unaccompanied choral music, and with brass and percussion accompaniment. *Honours:* Ernest Bloch Award, 1971; Commissions from the Edward Tarr Brass Ensemble and the Virginia Symphony. *Address:* 521 Berrypick Lane, Virginia Beach, VA 23462-1927, USA.

HAÏM, Emmanuelle; Conductor, Harpsichordist and Pianist; b. 1967, Paris, France. *Education:* harpsichord with Kenneth Gilbert and Christophe Rousset; coach and assistant to William Christie, Simon Rattle (Les Boréades by Rameau, Salzburg, 1999), Mark Minkowski and Christophe Rousset. *Career:* founded Paris-based early music group, Le Concert d Astrée, 2000; conducted Rodelinda for the Glyndebourne Tour, 2001; Season 2002–03 with Handel's Agrippina in Chicago and Poro at the Edinburgh Festival; guest conductor with Les Muses Galantes and the Orchestra of the Age of Enlightenment; appearances at the Beaune and Poitiers Festivals, recitals with Natalie Dessay, Sandrine Piau and Patricia Petibon; engaged for Theodora with GTO for 2003, and Rodelinda at the 2004 Festival; conducted Monteverdi's Orfeo at the London Barbican, 2003 and engaged for European and US tours, 2004–05; Handel's Tamerlano for Opéra Lille, 2004–05. *Recordings include:* Handel Arcadian Duets and Cantata Aci Galatea e Polifemo; Purcell's Dido and Aeneas, with Ian Bostridge and Susan Graham. *Current Management:* Askonas Holt Ltd, Lonsdale Chambers, 27 Chancery Lane, London, WC2F 1PF, England.

HAIMOVITZ, Matt; cellist; b. 3 Dec. 1970, Tel-Aviv, Israel. *Education:* Juilliard School, New York, Collegiate School, New York, Princeton University and Harvard University, studied cello with Gabor Rejto and Leonard Rose, music analysis with Carl Schahter. *Career:* appeared with Israel Philharmonic Orchestra under Mehta at Mann Auditorium, Tel-Aviv, broadcast on Israel national television, 1985; London debut with English Chamber Orchestra under Barenboim at the Barbican, 1985; Appearances with many conductors and orchestras and regular recitals throughout USA and Europe since 1985; Debut with Philharmonia Orchestra and Giuseppe Sinopoli at Royal Festival Hall in London, 1987; Debut with Chicago Symphony Orchestra under James Levine at Ravinia Festival, 1988; First tour to Japan in 1988, to Europe in 1989, and to Australia with Sydney and Melbourne Symphony Orchestras in 1991; Live concert appearance, The Performing Arts Pay Tribute to Public Television, PBS television, 1988; Documentary on early life, CBS television, 1989; First American recital tour in 1990; Debut with Berlin Philharmonic under James Levine in Berlin, 1990; Lucerne Festival debut with solo recital programme in 1990; Recital debuts with solo cello repertoire at Montreux Festival, Washington DC, New York and Paris in 1991; debut with Dallas Symphony in 1992. *Recordings include:* Lalo and Saint-Saëns Concerti with Chicago Symphony under Levine, 1989; Solo Cello in works by Reger, Britten, Crumb and Ligeti, 1991. *Honours:* Avery Fisher Career Grant Award 1985. *Current Management:* TransArt UK Ltd, Cedar House, 10 Rutland Street, Filey, North Yorkshire Y014 9JB, England.

HAITINK, Bernard John Herman; Conductor; b. 4 March 1929, Amsterdam, Netherlands. *Education:* Studied Conducting with Felix Hupke, Amsterdam Conservatory. *Career:* Debut: Holland, 1956; First conducted Concertgebouw, 1956; US debut 1958 with Los Angeles Philharmonic; Appointed, with Jochum, Concertgebouw's Permanent Conductor, 1961 and became Chief Conductor, 1964–88; Principal Conductor, London Philharmonic, 1967–79; Music Director, Glyndebourne Opera, 1978–88, with debut in 1972; Music Director, Royal Opera House, 1988–2002; Led new productions of The Ring (1989–91, 1994–95), Prince Igor (1990) and Katya Kabanova (1994); President, London Philharmonic, 1990–; Music Director of the European Union Youth Orchestra, 1994–99; Principal Guest Conductor, Boston Symphony Orchestra, 1995–; Chief Conductor of the Sächsische Staatskapelle Dresden, 2002–; Guest Conductor for many major international orchestras; Season 1998–99 leading the Royal Opera in The Ring at the Albert Hall and the Verdi Requiem at the Festival Hall, London; Mahler's 7th and 3rd Symphonies at the 1999 London Proms (European Union Youth Orchestra and CBSO); Die Meistersinger at Covent Garden and the Albert Hall, 2000; Tristan und Isolde, 2001–02; Conducted the London Symphony Orchestra at the London Proms, 2002. *Recordings include:* With London Philharmonic: Shostakovich, Liszt, Elgar, Holst and Vaughan Williams; With Concertgebouw: Complete symphonies of Mahler, Bruckner and Beethoven; With Vienna Philharmonic: Brahms and Bruckner; Opera includes: Don Giovanni, Così fan tutte and Figaro with Glyndebourne and the London Philharmonic Orchestra; The Ring Cycle with Bayerische Rundfunk; Peter Grimes with Royal Opera House. *Honours:* Recipient of many awards in recognition of his services to music including: Honorary KBE in 1977 and Honorary Doctorate of Music by University of Oxford, 1988; Erasmus Prize in Netherlands, 1991; House Order of Orange-Nassau from the Queen of the Netherlands, 1998; Conductor Laureate of the Concertgebouw, 1999; Companion of Honour, 2002. *Current Management:* Askonas Holt Ltd, Lonsdale Chambers, 27 Chancery Lane, London, WC2A 1PF, England. *Telephone:* (20) 7400-1700. *Fax:* (20) 7400-1799. *E-mail:* info@askonasholt.co.uk. *Website:* www.askonasholt .co.uk.

HAJDU, Andre; Composer; b. 5 March 1932, Budapest, Hungary. *Education:* Studied with Kodály and Kosa in Budapest, 1947–56 and with Milhaud and Messiaen in Paris. *Career:* Teacher at Tel-Aviv Academy of Music, 1967–70; Teacher, Bar Ilan University, 1970–. *Compositions:* Plasmas, 1957 for piano; Petit enfer for orchestra, 1959; Journey Around My Piano, 1963; 2 piano concertos, 1968, 1990; Ludus Paschalis for soloists, chorus and 9 instruments, 1970; Mishnayoth for voice, choir, orchestra and piano, 1972–73 Terouath Melech for clarinet and strings, 1974; The Unbearable Intensity of Youth for orchestra, 1976; Bashful Serenades, clarinet and orchestra, 1978; On Light and Depth for chamber orchestra, 1983; The Story of Jonas, opera for children, 1985–86; Dreams of Spain, cantata for orchestra and choir; Symphonie concertante for 6 soloists and strings, 1994; Ecclesiaste for narrator, solo cello and cello ensemble, 1994; Continuum, for piano and 15 instruments, 1995; Merry Feet, nursery songs, 1998. *Publications:* Milky Way, 4 vols piano pedagogic, 1975; The Art of Piano Playing, piano pedagogic, 1987. *Honours:* Israel prize for composition, 1997. *Address:* c/o ACUM Ltd, PO Box 14220, Acum House, Rothschild Blvd 118, Tel-Aviv 61140, Israel.

HAJOSSYOVA, Magdalena; Singer (Soprano); b. 25 July 1946, Bratislava, Czechoslovakia. *Education:* Studied at the Bratislava Music Academy. *Career:* Debut: Slovak National Theatre Bratislava, 1971, as Marenka in The Bartered Bride; Sang at the National Theatre Prague and elsewhere in Czechoslovakia; Berlin Staatsoper from 1975, as Mozart's Pamina, Fiordilgi, Contessa, Donna Anna, Handel's Alcina, Wagner's Eva, Elsa, Strauss's Arabella, Marschallin, Capriccio, Dvořák's Rusalka; Has also sung in the operas of Jan Cikker; Guest appearances as opera and concert singer in England, Belgium, Spain, Netherlands, Greece, Italy, France, USA, Japan, Russia, Austria, Iran and German Capitals. *Recordings include:* The Cunning Little Vixen, Don Giovanni and Mahler's 4th Symphony; Erindo by Sigismund Kusser; Beethoven's 9th Symphony; Mozart's Requiem; Dvořák's Requiem, Stabat Mater; Britten: Illuminations; Janáček: Missa Glagolitica; Dvořák: Dimitri; Mahler's 2nd Symphony; Schumann: Paradies und der Peri; Gounod: Margarethe in Faust; Wagner: Wesendonk-

Lieder; Strauss: Brentano-Lieder, 4 Letzte Lieder; Bruckner: Te Deum, and F minor Mass; Schubert: G major Mass and Stabat Mater; H Wolf, Italienisches Liederbuch; Mahler G and Alma: Lieder; Brahms, Lieder. *Current Management:* Deutsche Staatsoper Berlin, Unter den Linden 7, Germany. *Address:* Kopenicker Str 104, Berlin 19179, Germany.

HAKOLA, Riikka; Singer (Soprano); b. 1962, Finland. *Education:* Studied at the Sibelius Academy, Helsinki, in Italy and Berlin, New York and London. *Career:* Sang in the 1989 premiere of The Knife by Paavo Heininen, at the Savonlinna Festival; National Opera, Helsinki, 1990, as Lucia di Lammermoor; Guested in London in Haydn's opera Orfeo; Sang Marzelline in Fidelio at Savonlinna, 1992, and other roles have included Rosina, Gilda, Susanna, the Queen of Night and Violetta; Debut at the Bolshoi in Moscow, 1995; Frequent concert engagements in Finland and abroad; Turku 1996, as Zetulbe in Crusell's The Little Slave Girl. Has sung several world premieres by Finnish contemporary composers at Savonlinna Opera Festivals including the title role in Frieda by Tikka and Hilda in Alexis Kivi by Rautavaara; Sang Jenny in Weill's Mahagonny and First Nymph in Linkola's Angelika in recordings for Finnish television. *Address:* c/o Finnish National Opera, Bulevardi 23–27, 00180 Helsinki 18, Finland.

HALA, Tomás; Conductor and Composer; b. 6 Sept. 1963, Prague, Czechoslovakia. *Education:* Prague Conservatory, Piano, Composition, 1978–84; Prague Academy of Music, Piano, Conducting, 1984–90. *Career:* Conductor of Opera House, Ceskè Budejovice, 1990–91; Conductor, Prague National Theatre Opera, from 1991, Mozart: Don Giovanni (Assistant to Charles Mackerras), Die Zauberflöte, Le nozze di Figaro; Verdi: La Forza del Destino; mem, Czech Musical Fund. *Compositions:* Chamber Opera: Vejstupny Syn (Disobedient s.); Composition with Baritone Solo–Rough Sea; Variations for Cello; Piano Concerto. *Recordings:* Chamber Opera, Vejstupny Syn, Czech radio and television, 1985. *Publications:* Score of Opera Vejstupny syn, 1986. *Address:* Zavadilova 13, 160 00 Prague 6, Czech Republic.

HALBREICH, Harry (Leopold); Musicologist; b. 9 Feb. 1931, Berlin, Germany; m. Helène Chait, 11 April 1961, separated, 1 s., 2 d. *Education:* Geneva Conservatory, 1949–52; Studies with Arthur Honegger at Ecole Normale de Musique, Paris, 1952–54, and at Paris Conservatoire, 1955–58. *Career:* Teacher of Musical Analysis at Royal Conservatory, Mons, Belgium, 1970–; General Musical Adviser to the Brussels Philharmonic Society with about 180 concerts annually; Numerous lectures and seminars in Italy including Turin, Cagliari and Venice, in Spain at Madrid and Granada, in Japan at the Akiyoshidai Festival of Contemporary Music, and elswhere; Artistic Board (programme adviser), at the Venice Biennale for Contemporary Music; International jury member for International Record Critics Award, High Fidelity, New York, Academie Charles-Cros, Paris, Prix Cecilia, Brussels, and for several composition competitions at Parma, Turin and Cagliari; Regular Producer of radio programmes for RTB, Brussels and RSR in Geneva. *Publications include:* Edgard Varèse, in French, 1970; Olivier Messiaen, in French, 1980, revised edition, 1996; Claude Debussy, in French, 1980; Arthur Honegger, Un Musicien dans la Cité des Hommes, 1992; L'Oeuvre d'Arthur Honegger, 1993; Arthur Honegger, in the series, Les Grands Suisses, 1995; Founding Member and Co-Editor of the music magazine, Crescendo, Brussels; Large participation to the Fayard Music Guides, Paris: Piano Music, 1987, Chamber Music, 1989 and Choral Music, 1993, also several titles in the series, L'Avant-Scène Opéra, including Moses und Aron. *Contributions:* Harmonie, Paris, 1965–84; Le Monde de la Musique, Paris, 1982–89; Encyclopaedia Universalis; Crescendo. *Address:* Avenue Brugmann 513, 1180 Brussels, Belgium.

HALE, Robert; Singer (bass-baritone); b. 22 Aug. 1943, Kerrville, TX, USA; m. Inga Nielsen. *Education:* New England Conservatory of Music with Gladys Miller, Boston Univ. with Ludwig Bergman; Oklahoma Univ.; with Boris Goldovsky in New York. *Career:* debut with New York City Opera 1967; Metropolitan debut in the title role in Der Fliegende Holländer 1990, returning there as Wotan in Die Walküre 1993, 1996, Pizzaro in Fidelio 1993, Orest in Elektra 1994; performances as Wotan in Richard Wagner's Der Ring des Nibelungen include Vienna, La Scala, Paris, Berlin, Munich, Hamburg, Cologne, Tokyo, Sydney, San Francisco, Washington, DC and New York; other roles include Pizzaro in Fidelio, Salzburg Festival 1990, Barak in Die Frau ohne Schatten at the Easter and Summer Festival (televised) 1992, the title role in Béla Bartók's Bluebeard's Castle at the Summer Festival 1995, Handel's Saul at the Ludwigsburg Festival 2000–01; sings regularly with Vienna State Opera, Royal Opera Covent Garden, La Scala Milan, Paris, Munich State Opera, Deutsche Oper Berlin, Hamburg State Opera; guest appearances include performances with the orchestras of Boston, Philadelphia, Cleveland, Chicago, San Francisco, New York, Houston, Dallas, Los Angeles, Washington, DC, Toronto and Montréal, the Berliner Philharmonie, Musikverein Vienna, the Royal Albert Hall and the Barbican Centre in London, Concertgebouw Amsterdam; festival engagements include Ravinia, Tanglewood, Cincinnati and Wolftrap in the USA, and Salzburg, Munich, Bregenz, Bergen, Lausanne, Orange, Bordeaux, Ravenna and Athens in Europe. *Recordings include:* Der Fliegende Holländer, Das Rheingold, Die Walküre, The Messiah, Siegfried, Verdi Requiem, Das Paradies und die Peri, Song of Love (with Inga Nielsen) 1997, Salome 1999. *Video recordings include:* Die Frau ohne Schatten, Der Fliegende Holländer, Der Ring des Nibelungen. *Honours:* Singer of the Year, Nat. Asscn of Teachers of Singing. *Current Management:* Dr Germinal Hilbert Theateragentur, Maximillianstrasse 22, 80539 Munich, Germany.

HALE, Una; Singer (Soprano); b. 1922, Adelaide, South Australia; m. Martin Carr, 1960. *Education:* Studied in Adelaide and at Royal College of Music, London. *Career:* Sang with Carl Rosa Opera Company in many roles, notably as Marguerite in Faust; Royal Opera House, Covent Garden from 1953, as Micaela, Mimi, Musetta, Mozart's Countess, Eva, Ellen Orford, Liu (Turandot), Freia, Marschallin and Walton's Cressida; Sang with Sadler's Wells from 1964, Tosca, Ellen Orford, tour of Australia with the Elizabethan Opera Company, 1962, Théâtre de la Monnaie, Brussels, 1963; Further appearances at Aldeburgh Festival and Gulbenkian Festival in Portugal; Further study with Tiana Lemnitz in Berlin and Hilde Konetzni in Vienna; Sang Ariadne, Donna Anna and Alice Ford on tour in Australia. *Address:* Madron, Ostlings Lane, Bathford, Bath, Avon BA 1 7RW, England.

HALEM, Victor Von; Singer (Bass); b. 26 March 1940, Berlin, Germany. *Education:* Studied at the Musikhochschule Munich with Else Domberger. *Career:* Has sung at the Deutsche Oper Berlin, 1966–; Guest appearances in Hamburg, Munich, Stuttgart, Cologne, Rome, Geneva, Montreal, Athens and London; Roles include: Wagner's Daland, Pogner, King Henry, Fafner, Fasolt and Hans Sachs, Verdi's Padre Guardiano, The Grand Inquisitor, Mozart's Sarastro and Osmin, Puccini's Colline; Mephistopheles at Strasbourg, St Bris in Les Huguenots at Berlin and at the Spoleto Festival in Parsifal as Gurnemanz; Sang King Heinrich in Lohengrin at Nice, and in Meistersinger as Hans Sachs at Spoleto, Charleston; La Scala debut 1994, Walküre, Hunding; Dallas Opera debut 1994 in Der fliegende Holländer; San Francisco 1994, Tannhäuser, Landgraf; Season 1995–96 as the Commendatore at San Francisco and Ramphis at Verona; Many concert appearances. *Address:* c/o Deutsche Oper Berlin, Richard Wagnerstrasse 10, 10585 Berlin, Germany.

HALEVI, Hadar; Singer (Mezzo-soprano); b. 1966, Israel. *Career:* Appearances in Israel and throughout Europe in concerts and opera; Repertory includes Carmen, Bizet, Werther, Massenet, Il Barbiere, Rossini, Mozart operas, Ravel; Contestant at the 1995 Cardiff Singer of the World Competition. *Address:* 10 rue St Bernard, Toulouse, 31000 France.

HALFFTER, Cristobal; composer and conductor; b. 24 March 1930, Madrid, Spain; m. Maria Manuela Caro; two s. one d. *Education:* Madrid Conservatory with Del Campo, private studies with Alexander Tansman. *Career:* Studied harmony and composition with Conrado del Campo and at the Real Conservatorio de Musica in Madrid, graduated in 1951; 1961–1966 teacher of composition and musical forms at the Real Conservatorio de Musica in Madrid and director of this institute 1964–66; scholarships for the USA (Ford Foundation) and Berlin (DAAD); 1970–1978 Lecturer at the University of Navarra; Lecturer at the Internationale Ferienkurse für Neue Musik at Darmstadt; 1976–1978 president of the Spanish section of the ISCM; 1979: Artistic Director, Studio for electronic music at the Heinrich Strobel-Stiftung in Freiburg, 1980; Member, European Academy of Science, Arts and Humanities, Paris; 1981: was awarded the Gold Medal for Fine Arts by King Juan Carlos of Spain, 1983; Member, Royal Academy of the Fine Arts San Fernando, Madrid; Since 1989 Principal Guest Conductor of the National Orchestra, Madrid, since 1970 conductor of the chief orchestras in Europe and America; lives in Madrid; mem, Real Academia De Bellas Artes, Spain; Akademie Der Künste, Berlin; Kungl Musikaliska Akademien, Sweden, Stockholm. *Compositions:* Stage: Ballet Saeta 1955; Orchestral: Piano Concerto 1955; 5 Microformas 1960; Rhapsodia espanola de Albeniz for piano and orchestra 1960; Sinfonia for 3 instrumental groups 1963; Secuencias 1964; Lineas y Puntos for 20 winds and tape 1967; Anillos 1968; Fibonaciana for flute and strings 1970; Plaint for the Victims of Violence 1971; Requiem por la libertad imaginada 1971; Pinturas negras 1972; Processional 1974; Tiempo para espacios for harpsichord and strings 1974; Cello Concerto 1975; Elegias a la muerte de tres poetas espanoles, 1975; Officium defunctorum 1979; Violin Concerto; Tiento 1980; Handel Fantasia 1981; Sinfonia Ricercata 1982; Versus 1983; Parafrasis 1984; 2nd Cello Concerto 1985; Double Concerto for violin, viola and orchestra 1984; Tiento del Primer tono y Batalla Imperial 1986; Concerto for Cello and Orchestra, No. 2 (first performed by Rostropovich), 1986; Dortmund Variations 1987; Piano Concerto 1988; Preludio and Nemesis 1989; Concerto for saxophone quartet and orchestra 1989; Violin Concerto No. 2, 1991; Daliniana for chamber orchestra, 1994; Odradek, Homage à F. Kafka, for orchestra, 1996; Vocal: Regina Coeli 1951; Misa Ducal 1956;

In exspectatione resurrectionis Domini 1962; Brecht-Lieder 1967; Symposium 1968; Yes Speak Out 1968; Noche pasiva del sentido 1971; Gaudium et Spes for 32 voices and tapes 1972; Oracion a Platero 1975; Officium Defunctorum 1978; Noche Pasiva del Sentido 1979; Leyendo a Jorge Guillen 1982; Dona Nobis Pacem 1984; Tres Poemes de la Lirica Espanola 1984–86; Dos Motetes para Caro a Cappella, 1988; Muerte, Mudanza y Locura, for tape and voices, 1989 (text by Cervantes); La del alba seria, after Cervantes, for solo voices, chorus and orchestra, 1997; Opera, Don Quijote, premiered at Madrid, Teatro Real, 2000; Chamber: 2 String Quartets 1955, 1970; Solo Violin Sonata 1959; Codex for guitar 1963; Antiphonismoi for 7 players 1967; Noche activa del espiritu 1973; Mizar for 2 flutes and electronic ensemble 1980; String Sextet, 1994; Piano Music. *Recordings:* For Soprano, Baritone and Orchestra: 2nd Cello Concerto Rostropovich and Orchestra National De France, Erato. *Address:* Bola 2, Madrid 28013, Spain.

HALFVARSON, Eric; Singer (Bass); b. 1953, Texas, USA. *Education:* Studied at Houston Opera Studio. *Career:* Sang at Houston from 1977, notably as Sarastro, 1980; Carnegie Hall, New York, in Hamlet by Ambroise Thomas, 1981; San Francisco, 1982–, notably as Hagen in The Ring, 1990; Spoleto 1983, in European premiere of Barber's Antony and Cleopatra; Further appearances at Chicago, Toronto, Miami, St Louis (US premiere of ll Viaggio as Reims, 1986) and Dallas (premiere of The Aspern Papers by Dominick Argento, 1988); Sang Raimondo in Lucia di Lammermoor at Washington, 1989, Wagner's King Henry at Dallas and the Landgrave in Tannhäuser at Montpellier, 1991; Engagements at Santa Fe as Baron Ochs, 1989, 1992, and Morosus in Die schweigsame Frau, 1991; Other roles include Ramphis (Dallas 1991), Banquo, Rocco, Sparafucile (New York Met, 1995), the Commendatore in Don Giovanni, Puccini's Colline, Alvise in La Gioconda and Gremin in Eugene Onegin; Sang the King in Schreker's Der Schatzgräber at the 1992 Holland Festival; Pogner in Die Meistersinger at the 1996 Bayreuth Festival; Hagen at Buenos Aires, 1998; Season 2000–01 as Fafner and Hunding at the Met, Sarastro and the Grand Inquisitor at the Vienna Staatsoper; Claggart at Covent Garden and King Henry in Lohengrin at Bayreuth; Sang Sparafucile in Rigoletto at Covent Garden, Doctor in Wozzeck, 2002. *Recordings include:* Enobarbus in Antony and Cleopatra. *Address:* c/o Santa Fe Opera, PO Box 2408, Santa Fe, NM 87504, USA.

HALGRIMSON, Amanda; Singer (Soprano); b. 28 Nov. 1956, Fargo, North Dakota, USA. *Education:* Studied at Northern Illinois University. *Career:* Appearances at opera houses in 32 American States, notably as Fiordiligi, Norina, Clarice in ll Mondo della Luna and Rosalinde; Sang with Texas Opera on tour, 1987–88, as Lucia di Lammermoor; European debut 1988, as the Queen of Night with Netherlands Opera; Further engagements in Vienna (Volksoper and Staatsoper), St Gallen and Düsseldorf; Concert performances include Mozart's Schauspieldirektor and Salieri's Prima la musica, poi le parole with Houston Symphony; Sang the Queen of Night in a new production of Die Zauberflöte at the Deutsche Oper Berlin, 1991; Member of the ensemble of the Deutsche Oper Berlin, 1992–93; Sang Beethoven's Missa Solemnis with the Boston Symphony Orchestra under Roger Norrington, 1993; Sang Beethoven's 9th Symphony at the reopening of the Liederhalle in Stuttgart under G Gelmetti, 1993; Schumann's Faust/Gretchen with the Minnesota Orchestra as well as Beethoven's Missa Solemnis with the Boston Symphony Orchestra at the Tanglewood Festival; Sang Donna Anna with the Birmingham Symphony Orchestra under Simon Rattle, 1993; Concerts of Mozart's Requiem in London, Berlin and Paris with the Chamber Orchestra of Europe, 1993; Queen of Night at the Grand Théâtre de Genève, 1994; Sang the Trovatore Leonora and Donna Anna at the Deutsche Oper Berlin, 1996; Other roles include Strauss's Empress (Berlin, 1998) and Aithra in Die Aegyptische Helena; Season 2000 as Trovatore Leonora at Bonn and the Empress in Die Frau ohne Schatten at Essen; mem, Deutsche Oper, Berlin, 1992–2001. *Honours:* Prizewinner at Voci Verdiana (Bussetto) Competition, 1985 and the Metropolitan Auditions, 1987. *Address:* Sybelstr. 67, 10629 Berlin, Germany.

HALIM, Mohammed; Indonesian composer; b. 1963, Bukittinggi, Sumatra. *Education:* Acad. for Indonesian Performing Arts, Padangpanjang, and in Surakarta. *Career:* collaboration with dance ensemble, Gumarang Sakti 1990–; concert tours to Europe, America and Asia 1994; teacher of composition, Acad. for Indonesian Performing Arts (Sekolah Tinggi Seni Indonesia), Padangpanjang. *Compositions include:* Amai-Amai 1992, Awuak Tongtong 1993. *Address:* Sekolah Tinggi Seni Indonesia, Padangpanjang, West Sumatra, Indonesia (office). *E-mail:* mitramus@indo.net.id (office).

HALL, Aled; Singer (Tenor); b. 1970, Pencader, Wales. *Education:* Studied in Aberystwyth and London, National Opera Studio. *Career:* Sang as boy soprano then at Wexford Festival, 1995–96 in Pacini's Saffo and Meyerbeer's L'Etoile du Nord; Appearances in Falstaff and Le Pescatrici for Garsington Opera; Carmen and Poppea for Welsh National Opera and as Monostatos for Scottish Opera; Butterfly and Tosca for Raymond Gubay productions; Concerts include Janáček's

Diary at Wexford; Messiah at the Festival Hall and Mozart's Requiem. *Honours:* Joseph Maas prize at the Royal Academy. *Address:* c/o Harlequin Agency Ltd, 203 Fidles Road, Cardiff CF4 5NA, Wales.

HALL, Janice; Singer (Soprano); b. 28 Sept. 1953, San Francisco, USA. *Education:* Studied in Boston with Grace Hunter. *Career:* Sang in Cavalli's Egisto for the Wolf Trap Opera Company, 1977; New York City Opera 1978–81, as Ann in Die Lustigen Weiber von Windsor and Mozart's Servillia; European debut with the Hamburg Opera, 1982; Further appearances in Tel-Aviv, Venice and Drottningholm; Salzburg Festival 1985, as Fortuna in the premiere of Henze's version of Il Ritorno d'Ulisse; Cologne 1985, as Poppea in Handel's Agrippina; Has returned to the USA to sing at Houston, Washington DC, Santa Fe (Cavalli's Calisto 1989); Sang La Cambiale di Matrimonio at the 1989 Schwetzingen Festival and Micaela at the 1995 Eutin Festival; Other roles include Verdi's Oscar, Gilda and Violetta, Rosina, Pamina and Lauretta.

HALL, John; Singer (Bass); b. 1956, Brecon, Wales; m. Julie Crocker, 1 s., 2 d. *Education:* Studied at the Birmingham School of Music and at the Royal College of Music with Frederick Sharp. *Career:* Sang Rossini's Basilio and Mozart's Bartolo for Opera 80; Appearances with the English Bach Festival at Covent Garden and the Athens Festival; Glyndebourne Festival from 1981; Glyndebourne Touring Opera as Masetto in Don Giovanni (Hong Kong 1986), Mozart's Figaro and Quince in A Midsummer Night's Dream; Théâtre du Châtelet, Paris, 1985, in The Golden Cockerel; Opera North, 1986, in The Trojans and Madama Butterfly, and returned in Carmen, Tosca, Nielsen's Maskarade and Don Giovanni (as Leporello); Kent Opera, 1989, in The Return of Ulysses; Almeida Festival, 1989, in the premiere of Golem by John Casken; Glyndebourne Touring Opera, 1989–90, as Basilio and Rocco in Fidelio; Covent Garden, 1991, in Boris Godunov, as Mitiukha; English National Opera, 1992, in Return of Ulysses, as Time, Antinous; Throughout France in Midsummer Night's Dream, 1993–94; Premiere of Gruber's Gloria at Huddersfield Contemporary Music Festival, 1994; Midsummer Night's Dream at Torino and Ravenna, 1995; Sang Mozart's Antonio for GTO at Glyndebourne, 1996; Concert repertory includes Vaughan Williams's Serenade to Music (Last Night of the Proms, 1987), Messiah and Elijah. *Recordings:* Title role in Casken's Golem. *Address:* Ivydene, Vicarage Way, Ringmer. East Sussex BN8 5 LA, England.

HALL, Peter (John); Singer (Tenor); b. 7 April 1940, Surbiton, England. *Education:* BA 1964, MA 1968, King's College, Cambridge; Choral Scholarship, Private vocal study with Arthur Reckless, John Carol Case. *Career:* Lay-Vicar, Chichester Cathedral, 1965–66; Vicar-Choral, St Paul's Cathedral, London, 1972–2001; Member, various professional choral groups including John Alldis Choir, Schütz Choir of London, London Sinfonietta Voices; Sang Ugo and Il Prete in La Vera Storia (Berio), Florence 1986, un Prete and Reduce in Outis (Berio) at La Scala, Milan, 1996 and Dr Chebutykhin in Three Sisters (Eötvös) in Lyon, 1998 at the composers' personal request; mem. Incorporated Society of Musicians. *Recordings:* Carmina Burana (Orff), with Hallé Orchestra; Transit (Ferneyhough), with London Sinfonietta; At the Boar's Head (Holst), with Royal Liverpool Philharmonic Orchestra; Christmas Vespers (Monteverdi) with Denis Stevens; Prometeo (Nono) with the Ensemble Modern, Frankfurt and The Flood (Stravinsky) with the London Sinfonietta. *Honours:* Choral Scholarship, Cambridge. *Address:* 51 Treachers Close, Chesham, Bucks HP5 2HD, England.

HALL, Sir Peter Reginald Frederick, Kt, CBE, MA; British theatre director and film director; b. 22 Nov. 1930, Bury St Edmunds, Suffolk; s. of late Reginald Hall and Grace Hall; m. 1st Leslie Caron 1956 (divorced 1965); one s. one d.; m. 2nd Jacqueline Taylor 1965 (divorced 1981); one s. one d.; m. 3rd Maria Ewing 1982 (divorced 1989); one d.; m. 4th Nicola Frei 1990; one d. *Education:* Perse School and St Catharine's Coll., Cambridge. *Career:* produced and acted in over 20 plays at Cambridge; first professional production The Letter, Windsor 1953; produced in repertory at Windsor, Worthing and Oxford Playhouse; two Shakespearean productions for Arts Council; Artistic Dir Elizabethan Theatre Co. 1953; Asst Dir London Arts Theatre 1954, Dir 1955–57; formed own producing co., Int. Playwright's Theatre 1957; Man. Dir Royal Shakespeare Co., Stratford-upon-Avon and Aldwych Theatre, London 1960–68 (resgnd), Assoc. Dir–1973; mem. Arts Council 1969–73; Co-Dir, Nat. Theatre (now Royal Nat. Theatre) with Lord Olivier April-Nov. 1973, Dir 1973–88; f. Peter Hall Co. 1988; Artistic Dir Glyndebourne 1984–90; Artistic Dir The Old Vic 1997; Wortham Chair in Performing Arts, Houston Univ., Tex. 1999; Chancellor Kingston Univ. 2000–; Dir Kingston Theatre 2003–; Assoc. Prof. of Drama, Warwick Univ. 1964–67; mem. Bd Playhouse Theatre 1990–91; acted in The Pedestrian (film) 1973. *Productions:* Blood Wedding, The Immoralist, The Lesson, South, Mourning Becomes Electra, Waiting for Godot, Burnt Flowerbed, Waltz of the Toreadors, Camino Real, Gigi, Wrong Side of the Park, Love's Labours Lost, Cymbeline, Twelfth Night, A Midsummer Night's Dream, Coriolanus, Two Gentlemen of Verona, Troilus and Cressida,

Ondine, Romeo and Juliet, The Wars of the Roses (London Theatre Critics' Award for Best Dir 1963), Becket, The Collection, Cat on a Hot Tin Roof, The Rope Dancers (on Broadway), The Moon and Sixpence (opera, Sadler's Wells), Henry VI (parts 1, 2 and 3), Richard III, Richard II, Henry IV (parts 1 and 2), Henry V, Eh?, The Homecoming (London Theatre Critics' Award for Best Dir 1966, Antoinette Perry Award for Best Dir 1966), Moses and Aaron (opera, Covent Garden), Hamlet (London Theatre Critics' Award for Best Dir 1965), The Government Inspector, The Magic Flute (opera), Staircase, Work is a Four Letter Word (film) 1968, Macbeth, Midsummer Night's Dream (film) 1969, Three into Two Won't Go (film) 1969, A Delicate Balance, Dutch Uncle, Landscape and Silence, Perfect Friday (film) 1971, The Battle of Shrivings, La Calisto (opera, Glyndebourne Festival) 1970, The Knot Garden (opera, Covent Garden) 1970, Eugene Onegin (opera, Covent Garden) 1971, Old Times 1971, Tristan and Isolde (opera, Covent Garden) 1971, All Over 1972, Il Ritorno d'Ulisse (opera, Glyndebourne Festival) 1972, Alte Zeiten (Burgtheater, Vienna) 1972, Via Galactica (musical, Broadway) 1972, The Homecoming (film) 1973, Marriage of Figaro (opera, Glyndebourne) 1973, The Tempest 1973, Landscape (film) 1974, Akenfield (film) 1974, Happy Days 1974, John Gabriel Borkman 1974, No Man's Land 1975, Judgement 1975, Hamlet 1975, Tamburlaine the Great 1976, Don Giovanni (opera, Glyndebourne Festival) 1977, Volpone (Nat. Theatre) 1977, Bedroom Farce (Nat. Theatre) 1977, The Country Wife (Nat. Theatre) 1977, The Cherry Orchard (Nat. Theatre) 1978, Macbeth (Nat. Theatre) 1978, Betrayal (Nat. Theatre) 1978, Così Fan Tutte (opera, Glyndebourne) 1978, Fidelio (opera, Glyndebourne) 1979, Amadeus (Nat. Theatre) 1979, Betrayal (New York) 1980, Othello (Nat. Theatre) 1980, Amadeus (New York) (Tony Award for Best Dir 1981) 1980, Family Voices (Nat. Theatre) 1981, The Oresteia (Nat. Theatre) 1981, A Midsummer Night's Dream (opera, Glyndebourne) 1981, The Importance of Being Earnest (Nat. Theatre) 1982, Other Places (Nat. Theatre) 1982, The Ring (operas, Bayreuth Festival) 1983, Jean Seberg (musical, Nat. Theatre) 1983, L'Incoronazione di Poppea (opera, Glyndebourne) 1984, Animal Farm (Nat. Theatre) 1984, Coriolanus (Nat. Theatre) 1984, Yonadab (Nat. Theatre) 1985, Carmen (opera, Glyndebourne) 1985, (Metropolitan Opera) 1986, Albert Herring (opera, Glyndebourne) 1985, The Petition (New York and Nat. Theatre) 1986, Simon Boccanegra (opera, Glyndebourne) 1986, Salome (opera, Los Angeles) 1986, Coming in to Land (Nat. Theatre) 1986, Antony and Cleopatra (Nat. Theatre) 1987, Entertaining Strangers (Nat. Theatre) 1987, La Traviata (Glyndebourne) 1987, Falstaff (Glyndebourne) 1988, Salome (Covent Garden) 1988, Cymbeline (Nat. Theatre) 1988, The Winter's Tale (Nat. Theatre) 1988, The Tempest 1988, Orpheus Descending 1988, Salome (opera, Chicago) 1988, Albert Herring 1989, Merchant of Venice 1989, She's Been Away (TV) 1989, New Year (opera, Houston and Glyndebourne) 1989, The Wild Duck 1990, Born Again (musical) 1990, The Homecoming 1990, Orpheus Descending (film) 1990, Twelfth Night 1991, The Rose Tattoo 1991, Tartuffe 1991, The Camomile Lawn (TV) 1991, The Magic Flute 1992, Four Baboons Adoring the Sun (New York) 1992, Siena Red 1992, All's Well That Ends Well (RSC) 1992, The Gift of the Gorgon (RSC) 1992, The Magic Flute (LA) 1993, Separate Tables 1993, Lysistrata 1993, She Stoops to Conquer 1993, Piaf (musical) 1993, An Absolute Turkey (Le Dindon) 1994, On Approval 1994, Hamlet 1994, Jacob (TV) 1994, Never Talk to Strangers (film) 1995, Julius Caesar (RSC) 1995, The Master Builder 1995, The Final Passage (TV) 1996, Mind Millie for Me 1996, The Oedipus Plays (Nat. Theatre at Epidaurus and Nat. Theatre) 1996, A School for Wives 1995, A Streetcar Named Desire 1997, The Seagull 1997, Waste 1997, Waiting for Godot 1997, 1998, King Lear 1997, The Misanthrope 1998, Major Barbara 1998, Simon Boccanegra (Glyndebourne) 1998, Filumena 1998, Amadeus 1998, Kafka's Dick 1998, Measure for Measure (LA) 1999, A Midsummer Night's Dream (LA) 1999, Lenny (Queens Theatre) 1999, Amadeus (LA, NY) 1999, Cuckoos 2000, Tantalus (Denver, Colo) 2000, Japes 2000, Romeo and Juliet (LA) 2001, Japes 2001, Troilus and Cressida (NY) 2001, Tantalus 2001, A Midsummer Night's Dream (Glyndebourne) 2001, Otello (Glyndebourne) 2001, Japes (Theatre Royal) 2001, The Royal Family (Theatre Royal) 2001, Lady Windermere's Fan (Theatre Royal) 2002, The Bacchai (Olivier Theatre) 2002, Design for Living (Theatre Royal, Bath) 2003, Betrayal (Theatre Royal, Bath) 2003, The Fight for Barbara (Theatre Royal, Bath) 2003, As You Like It (Theatre Royal, Bath) 2003, Cuckoos (Theatre Royal, Bath) 2003, The Marriage of Figaro (Lyric Opera of Chicago) 2003, Happy Days (Arts Theatre, London) 2003, Man and Superman (Theatre Royal, Bath) 2004, Galileo's Daughter (Theatre Royal, Bath) 2004. *Publications:* The Wars of the Roses 1970, Shakespeare's three Henry VI plays and Richard III (adapted with John Barton), John Gabriel Borkman (English version with Inga-Stina Ewbank) 1975, Peter Hall's Diaries: The Story of a Dramatic Battle 1983, Animal Farm: a stage adaptation 1986, The Wild Duck 1990, Making an Exhibition of Myself (auto biog.) 1993, An Absolute Turkey (new trans. of Feydeau's Le Dindon, with Nicki Frei) 1994, The Master Builder (with Inga-Stina Ewbank) 1995, Mind Millie for Me (new trans. of Feydeau's Occupe-toi d'Amélie, with

Nicki Frei), The Necessary Theatre 1999, Exposed by the Mask 2000, Shakespeare's Advice to the Players 2003. *Honours:* Hon. Fellow St Catharine's Coll. Cambridge 1964; Chevalier, Ordre des Arts et des Lettres 1965; Dr hc (York) 1966, (Reading) 1973, (Liverpool) 1974, (Leicester) 1977, (Essex) 1993, (Cambridge) 2003; Hon. DSocSc (Birmingham) 1989; Hamburg Univ. Shakespeare Prize 1967, Evening Standard Special Award 1979, Evening Standard Award for Outstanding Achievement in Opera 1981, Evening Standard Best Dir Award for The Oresteia 1981, Evening Standard Best Dir Award for Antony and Cleopatra 1987, South Bank Show Lifetime Achievement Award 1998, Olivier Special Award for Lifetime Achievement 1999, New York Shakespeare Soc. Medal 2003. *Address:* 48 Lamont Road, London, SW10 0HX, England. *E-mail:* phpetard@aol.com (office).

HALL, Vicki; Singer (Soprano); b. 13 Nov. 1943, Jefferson, Texas, USA. *Education:* Studied in New York and with Josef Metternich in Cologne. *Career:* Sang at New York City Opera, 1970–; Made guest appearances in Vienna (Volksoper), Munich (Theater am Gärtnerplatz), Cologne, Wuppertal and Bregenz; Roles have included Mozart's Susanna and Blondchen, Carolina in Matrimonio Segreto, Frau Fluth in Die Lustige Weiber von Windsor, Olympia, Strauss's Sophie, Adele in Fledermaus, Gretel, and Janáček's Vixen; Many concert appearances.

HALLGRIMSSON, Haflidi; Composer and Cellist; b. 18 Sept. 1941, Akureyri, Iceland; m. 1975; three s. *Education:* The Music School, Reykjavík, Iceland; Academia Sancta Cecilia, Rome; Royal Acad. of Music, London; private studies in composition with Alan Bush and Peter Maxwell Davies. *Career:* mem., Haydn String Trio, 1967–70; English Chamber Orchestra, 1971–76; Principal Cellist, Scottish Chamber Orchestra, 1977–83; Mondrian Trio, 1984–88; many recitals, appeared as soloist with Symphony Orchestras and performed on BBC Radio 3; mem., Society of Promotion for New Music, Society of Scottish Composers, Performing Right Society. *Compositions:* Poemi; Verse I; Five Pieces for Piano; Seven Folksongs from Iceland; Scenes from Poland; Words in Winter, 1987; Ríma, 1994; Herma, 1995; Still-Life, 1995; Crucifixion, 1997; Mini-Stories, 1997; Ombra, 1999, Passia, 2000. *Recordings:* Strond; Poemi; Vers I; Daydreams in Numbers; Tristia; Jacob's Ladder; String Quartet No. 1; String Quartet No. 2; solitaire; Offerto; Seven Epigrams; Intarsia. *Honours:* Suggia Prize for Cello playing, 1967; Viotti Prize, Italy, 1975; Nordic Council Prize, 1986. *Address:* 5 Merchiston Bank Gardens, Edinburgh, EH10 5EB, Scotland.

HALLIN, Margareta; Singer (Soprano) and Composer; b. 22 Feb. 1931, Karlskoga, Sweden. *Education:* Studied at the Royal Stockholm Conservatory with Ragnar Hulten. *Career:* Sang at the Royal Opera, Stockholm, 1954–84, in the premieres of Blomdahl's Aniara 1959 and Drommen om Therese 1964 and Tintomora 1973, by Werle; Also heard as Constanze, Blondchen, Lucia di Lammermoor, Gilda and Leonora in Il Trovatore; Sang Anne Trulove in the Swedish premiere of The Rake's Progress, 1961; Glyndebourne Festival 1957, 1960, as the Queen of Night; Covent Garden 1960, with the Stockholm Company in Alcina by Handel; Drottningholm Court Opera from 1962, notably in the Abbé Vogler's Gustaf Adolf och Ebba Brahe, 1973; Appearances in Florence, Edinburgh, Hamburg, Zürich, Rome and Munich; Later in career sang Elsa, Elisabeth de Valois, Mathilde in Guillaume Tell, the heroines in Les Contes d'Hoffmann, Violetta, Donna Anna, Senta, Butterfly and the Marschallin; Sang Cherubini's Médée, 1984; Drottningholm 1991, as Clytemnestra in Electra by Haeffner. *Compositions include:* Miss Julie, opera after Strindberg. *Honours:* Swedish Court Singer 1966; Order Litteris et artibus, 1976. *Address:* c/o Kungliga Teatera, PO Box 16094, 10322 Stockholm, Sweden.

HALLSTEIN, Ingeborg; Singer (Soprano); b. 23 May 1937, Munich, Germany. *Education:* Studied with her mother. *Career:* Debut: Stadt Theater Passau 1956, as Musetta in La Bohème; Sang at Basle 1958–59; Munich from 1959; Salzburg Festival from 1960, as Rosina in La Finta Semplice and in the premiere of The Bassarids by Henze (1966); Theater an der Wien 1962, as the Queen of Night in Die Zauberflöte, conducted by Karajan; Sang in the first performance of Henze's Cantata Being Beauteous, Berlin, 1964; Guest appearances in Hamburg, Stuttgart, Dresden, Karlsruhe, Kassel, Venice, Paris, Montreal, Ottawa, Stockholm and Amsterdam, Royal Opera House Covent Garden, as the Queen of Night; Other roles include Mozart's Constanze, Fiordiligi and Susanna; Sophie in Der Rosenkavalier and Zerbinetta; Norina (Don Pasquale) and Aennchen in Der Freischütz; Professor at the Würzburg Musikhochschule from 1981. *Recordings:* Die Frau ohne Schatten (Deutsche Grammophon); Marzelline in Fidelio, conducted by Klemperer; Operettas by Lortzing and Benatzky. *Address:* c/o Hochschule für Musik, Holfstallstrasse 6–8, 8700 Würzburg, Germany.

HALMEN, Petre; stage designer, costume designer and stage director; b. 14 Nov. 1943, Talmaciu, Romania. *Education:* studied in Berlin. *Career:* worked at Kiel and Düsseldorf, then collaborated with director Jean-Pierre Ponnelle at Zürich from 1975 in cycles of operas by Monteverdi and Mozart; Munich 1978–, with premieres of Reimann's Lear and Troades, 1986, Das Liebesverbot by Wagner and Berg's Lulu, 1985; Designs for Aida at Berlin; Chicago and Covent Garden 1982–84; Parsifal at San Francisco 1988 and 2 Ring Cycles; Designed and Directed Lohengrin at Düsseldorf 1987, Paer's Achille at Bologna 1988, La Straniera at Spoleto Festival, Charleston, 1989, and Nabucco for Munich Festival, 1990; Designs for Parsifal seen at Mainz 1991, Mozart's Lucio Silla at Vienna Staatsoper; Directed The Golden Cockerel at Duisburg, 1991, La Clemenza di Tito at Toulouse, 1992; Directed and designed Turandot at Deutsche Oper am Rhein, Düsseldorf, 1993; Directed and designed: Aida at Staatsoper Berlin, 1995, Turandot at Opéra de Nice, France, 1995, Don Giovanni at Staatsoper Hamburg, 1996, Rosenkavalier at Staatstheater Darmstadt, 1997, Orfeo by Gluck at Opernhaus Halle, 1997, Ariadne auf Naxos at Toulouse, France, 1998, Idomeneo at Salzburg Festspielhaus, 1998 and Ezio by Handel at Festspiele Halle, 1998. *Address:* Tengstrasse 26, 80798 Munich, Germany.

HALMRAST, Tor; Composer; b. 26 April 1951, Sarpsborg, Norway. *Education:* MSc, Engineering (Acoustics), 1976; BMus, University of Trondheim, 1978; Private studies in Composition, State Scholarship, Sweelinck Conservatory, Amsterdam, 1988. *Career:* Composer-in-Residence, Music Conservatory, Tromsoe, 1988–90; Festival Composer, Northern Norwegian Festival, 1990; In charge of acoustic design of several buildings for music, concerts and theatre, and studios; mem, Vice-Chairman, Society of Norwegian Composers. *Compositions:* Works for symphony orchestra, chamber works, solo works, music for television, films and records and sound installation, including the prize-winning music for the Norwegian Pavillion at the World's Fair, Expo92 in Seville, Spain, and for ice/music sculpture for the Olympics in Lillehammer, 1994; Alfa and Romeo, radiopera for Norwegian Radio, 1997. *Recordings:* Hemera 2901; Music for EXPO92 and other electro-acoustic works: Aquaduct, Icille, Oppbrudd, Varang, Motgift; Alfa and Romeo (Radiopera). *Publications:* Several papers on room acoustics. *Address:* Spaangberg v 28a, 0853 Oslo, Norway.

HALSEY, Simon Patrick, MA; Conductor; b. 8 March 1958, Kingston, Surrey, England; m. Lucy Lunt 1986. *Education:* King's Coll., Cambridge, Royal Coll. of Music. *Career:* Conductor, Scottish Opera-Go-Round 1980, 1981; Dir of Music, Univ. of Warwick 1980–88; Chorus Dir, City of Birmingham Symphony Orchestra 1982–; Assoc. Dir, Philharmonia Chorus 1986–97; Music Dir, Birmingham Opera Company 1987–2000; Wagner's Ring 1990–91; Britten's Church Parables in London and elsewhere 1997; Dir, Acad. of Ancient Music Chorus 1988–92; Dir, Salisbury Festival 1989–93; Chorus Dir, Flanders Opera, Antwerp 1991–95; Consultant Ed., Faber Music Ltd 1996–; Artistic Dir, BBC National Chorus of Wales 1995–2000; Guest Conductor, Chicago Symphony Chorus 1993–94; Principal Guest Conductor, Netherlands Radio Choir 1995–2002; Chief Conductor 2002–; Principal Guest Conductor, Sydney Philharmonic Choirs 1997–; Chief Conductor, European Voices 2000–; Principal Conductor, Berlin Radio Choir 2001–. *Recordings include:* Rossini's Petite Messe Solennelle, Bruckner's Mass in E Minor 1990. *Publications:* Ed., Choral Music, Faber Music. *Honours:* Gramophone Record of the Year 1989, Deutsche Schallplatten Prize 1993; Hon. doctorate, Univ. of Central England 2000. *Current Management:* Hazard Chase Ltd, Norman House, Cambridge Place, Cambridge, CB2 1NS, England. *Telephone:* (1223) 312400. *Fax:* (1223) 460827. *Website:* www.hazardchase.co.uk.

HALSTEAD, Anthony (George); Conductor, Horn Player, Harpsichordist and Composer; b. 18 June 1945, Manchester, England; m. (1) Lucy Mabey, 20 Sept 1969, 2 s., (2) Ellen O'Dell, 6 Sept 1985, 1 d. *Education:* Chetham's School, 1956–62; Royal Manchester College of Music, 1962–66; Private study with Dr Horace Fitzpatrick, 1966 and 1978, Myron Bloom 1979–80, George Malcolm, 1979, Sir Charles Mackerras and Michael Rose. *Career:* Bournemouth Symphony Orchestra, 1966; BBC Scottish Symphony Orchestra, 1966–70; London Symphony Orchestra, 1970–73; English Chamber Orchestra, 1972–86; Professor, Guildhall School of Music, 1971–; mem, Musicians Union; British Horn Society; International Horn Society; ISM. *Compositions:* Divertimento Serioso, 1973; Prologue and Passus, 1976; Serenade for oboe and strings, 1978; Concertino Elegiaco, 1983; Suite for solo horn or trumpet. *Recordings:* Weber-Horn Concertino, World Premiere Recording on Original Instruments, 1986; Mozart Horn Concertos, 1987; L'Oiseau-Lyre, 1993; Haydn Horn Concertos, 1989; Britten-Serenade, 1989; 12 Harpsichord and 14 Fortepiano Concertos by J C Bach, a further 16 CDs of JS Bach's complete orchestral works. *Honours:* FRMCM, 1975; FGSM, 1979. *Current Management:* Patrick Garvey Management, Top Floor, 59 Lansdowne Place, Hove, East Sussex BN3 1 FL, England.

HALTON, Richard; Singer (Baritone); b. 1963, Devon, England. *Education:* Studied at the University of Kent and the Guildhall School of Music with Johanna Peters. *Career:* Has sung with most leading British opera companies including: Capriccio and Romeo and Juliette with the Royal Opera, Novice's Friend (Billy Budd) and Harry Easter (Street Scene) with English National Opera, Schaunard with Glyndebourne Touring Opera, Ravenal in Showboat at the London Palladium and on 2 national tours with Opera North/RSC, Glyndebourne Festival Opera, 1989, Opera 80, as Danilo in The Merry Widow; Other operatic appearances include: Capriccio at Covent Garden, 1991, in Billy Budd (ENO) and La Bohème (GTO); Holofernes in the world premiere of Ian McQueen's Line of Terror at the Almeida Festival, Harlequin (Ariadne auf Naxos) and Perrucchetto (La Fedeltà Premiata) for Garsington Opera; Repertoire also includes Mozart's Count in Figaro, Tarquinius in The Rape of Lucretia; Street Scene, by Kurt Weill, ENO, 1992; Italian Girl in Algiers by Rossini, Buxton Festival, 1992; Dancairo, Carmen, Dorset Opera, 1992; Janko in Petrified by Juraj Beneš for Mecklenburg Opera, 1992–93; Papageno, The Magic Flute, Scottish Opera, 1993; Sang Sid in Albert Herring at Garsington, 1996; Concert engagements include: A Child of Our Time, St John Passion and Messiah with the City of London Sinfonia conducted by Richard Hickox and Carmina Burana in Perugia and the Royal Albert Hall; Recital works includes Schumann's Dichterliebe with Stephen Barlow at St John's Smith Square; Further engagements include Jason in Gavin Bryars' Medea (Glasgow and BBC Radio 3), Valentin in Faust and Dandini in La Cenerentola. *Honours:* Walter Hyde Memorial Prize; Schubert Prize; Lawrence Classical Singing Bursary. *Address:* c/o Garsington Opera, Garsington, Oxfordshire OX44 9 DH, England.

HALTON, Rosalind; Harpsichordist and Musicologist; b. 4 Oct. 1951, Dunedin, New Zealand; m. David Halton 1979. *Education:* New Zealand Junior Scholarship, BA, Otago Univ. 1969–72; Commonwealth Scholarship to Oxford Univ. 1973–80, DPhil, St Hilda's Coll.; harpsichord study with Colin Tilney. *Career:* research and editing of Classical Symphonies (Beck-Holzbauer) and Cantatas of Alessandro Scarlatti; concerts of 17th and 18th century chamber music using period instruments; solo performances on harpsichord and pianos of 18th and early 19th centuries; Lecturer, Performance 1986–90, Senior Lecturer 1990–99, Univ. of New England, Armidale, Australia; Senior Lecturer in Performance and Musicology, Univ. of Newcastle, NSW 1999–; founder mem. of Chacona, baroque chamber ensemble; mem. Musicology Society of Australia. *Recordings:* The French Harpsichord: Music by F. and L. Couperin 1996, Olimpia and other cantatas by Alessandro Scarlatti 2001. *Publications:* Olimpia, A Scarlatti Cantata 1996, Toccata 1998, Clori mia, Clori bella 1998. *Contributions:* various reviews, Music and Letters. *Honours:* Soundscapes Award 1997. *Address:* c/o The Conservatorium, University of Newcastle, Auckland St, NSW 2300, Australia; 26 Rhondda Road, Teralba, NSW 2294, Australia. *E-mail:* R.Halton@newcastle.edu.au.

HAMARI, Julia; Singer (Mezzo-soprano); b. 21 Nov. 1942, Budapest, Hungary. *Education:* Studied piano at first, then singing with Fatima Martin and at the Music Academy Budapest. *Career:* Debut: Vienna 1966, in the St Matthew Passion, conducted by Karl Richter; Rome 1966, in the Brahms Alto Rhapsody, conducted by Vittorio Gui; Concert appearances with Karajan, Kubelik, Solti, Böhm, Boulez and Celibidache, most often heard in works by Mahler, Monteverdi, Handel, Bach, Beethoven, Mozart and Verdi; Stage debut Salzburg, 1967; Stuttgart 1968, as Carmen; US debut with Chicago Symphony Orchestra, 1972; Sang Celia in Haydn's La Fedeltà Premiata at Glyndebourne, 1979; Metropolitan Opera from 1984, as Rosina and Despina; Stuttgart and Philadelphia 1984, as Sinaide in Mosè and as Cenerentola in the opera by Rossini; Sang Vivaldi's Griselda at Ludwigshaven, 1989; Romeo in I Capuleti by Bellini at Budapest, 1992; Professor at the Stuttgart Musikhochschule, from 1993. *Recordings:* St Matthew Passion; Oberon, Il Matrimonio Segreto, Giulio Cesare, Beethoven Mass in C, Mozart Requiem; Ernani; Tito Manlio by Vivaldi; Cavalleria Rusticana, I Puritani; Bach B minor Mass; Pergolesi Stabat Mater; Hänsel und Gretel, Die Meistersinger, Eugene Onegin. *Address:* c/o Staatstheater Stuttgart, Oberer Schlossgarten 6, 7000 Stuttgart 1, Germany.

HAMBLETON, Tristan; Singer (Boy Soprano); b. 1988, London. *Career:* St Paul's Cathedral Choir, from 1996; Appearances as the youth in Mendelssohn's Elijah under Andrew Davis in Rome and with Richard Hickox; Engagements at English National Opera Studio and in Britten's War Requiem and Mahler's Third Symphony at the Royal Festival Hall; Handel's L'Allegro, il Penseroso ed il Moderato with Les Arts Florissants; Sang Amor in Gluck's Orfeo ed Euridice at Covent Garden, 2001. *Address:* c/o Dean and Chapter, St Paul's Cathedral, London, EC 1, England.

HAMBLIN, Pamela; Singer (Soprano); b. 14 June 1954, Cookeville, Tennessee, USA. *Education:* Studied at North Texas State University and Salzburg Mozarteum. *Career:* Debut: Karlsruhe, as Euridice in Orphée aux Enfers by Offenbach, 1980; Has sung at Karlsruhe in such roles as Handel's Florinda (Rodrigo), Almirena (Rinaldo) and Romilda (Serse); Micaela, Mozart's Susanna, Pamina, Constanze and Sandrina; Verdi's Gilda and Oscar, Constance in Cherubini's Les Deux Journées, Strauss's Sophie and Aminta (Die schweigsame Frau) and Titania in A Midsummer Night's Dream; Guest appearances at Dresden, Stuttgart, Zürich, Essen, Heidelberg, Strasbourg, Madrid, Barcelona and Athens.

Recordings include: Rodrigo. *Address:* Schillerstr. 15, 76275 Ettlingen, Germany.

HAMBRAEUS, Bengt; Composer, Organist and Musicologist; b. 29 Jan. 1928, Stockholm, Sweden. *Education:* Studied organ with Alf Linder, 1944–48; Uppsala University, PhD, 1956; Summer Courses at Darmstadt 1951–55, with Krenek, Messiaen and Fortner; Worked for Swedish Broadcasting Corporation from 1957, Director of Chamber Music 1965–68, Production Director 1968–72; Composed at Electronic Studios of Cologne, Munich, Montreal and Milan; Professor at McGill University, Montreal from 1972, Professor Emeritus, 1995–. *Compositions:* Chamber Operas Experiment X, 1971; Se Människan, 1972; Sagan, 1979; L'oui-dire, 1986; Concerto for organ and harpsichord, 1951; Antiphones en rondes for soprano and 24 instruments, 1953; Crystal Sequence for soprano choir and ensemble, 1954; Rota for 3 orchestras and tape, 1956–62; Transfiguration for orchestra, 1962–63; Constellations I–V, 1958–83; Segnali for 7 instruments, 1960; Mikrogram for ensemble, 1961; Interferences for organ, 1962; Klassiskt spel, electronic ballet, 1965; Fresque Sonore for soprano and ensemble, 1967; Rencontres for orchestra, 1971; Pianissimo in due tempi for 20 string instruments, 1972; Ricercare for organ, 1974; Advent for organ 10 brass instruments and percussion, 1975; Ricordanza for orchestra, 1976; Continuo for organ and orchestra, 1975; Livre d'orgue, 1980–81; Symphonia Sacra for 5 soloists, choir, wind instruments and percussion, 1985–86; Apocalypsis cum figuris for bass solo, choir and organ, 1987; Five Psalms for choir, 1987; Litanies for orchestra, 1988–89; Nocturnals for chamber orchestra, 1989; Piano Concerto, 1992; St Michael's Liturgy, 1992; Missa pro Organo, 1992; Organum Sancti Jacobi, 1993; Meteoros, 1993; Songs of the Mountain, The Moon and Television, 1993; Eco dalla montagna lontana, 1993; Triptyque pour orgue avec MIDI, 1994; Due Rapsodie, 1994; Concentio, 1995; Quatre tableaux, 1995; Horn Concerto, 1995–96; Archipel for 15 soloists, 1997; FM 643765 for organ, 1997. *Publications:* Codex Carminum Gallicorum, 1961; Om Notskifter (On Notation) 1970; Numerous articles and essays published since 1948. *Address:* RR1, Apple Hill, Ontario K0C 1B0, Canada.

HAMEENNIEMI, Eero (Olavi); Composer; b. 29 April 1951, Valkeakoski, Finland; m. Leena Peltola, 7 Oct 1977, (divorced Oct 1989), 1 d. *Education:* Diploma, Sibelius Academy, 1977; State Higher School of Music, Kraków, 1979; Eastman School of Music, Rochester, New York, USA, 1980–81. *Career:* Commissions for the Finnish Radio Symphony Orchestra, Swedish RSO, Helsinki Festival, Finnish National Ballet; Works performed by (the above) and Scottish National Orchestra, Malmö Symphony Orchestra, Gothenburg Symphony Orchestra; Senior Lecturer, Sibelius Academy, 1982–. *Compositions:* Symphony, 1982–83, 1984; Dialogue for Piano and Orchestra, 1987; Sonata for Clarinet and Piano; Loviisa, a ballet in two acts, premiere 19 Mar 1987, Finnish National Ballet; Second Symphony, 1988; 2 String Quartets, 1989, 1994; Leonardo, ballet in 2 acts; The Bird and the Wind for strings, soprano and two Indian classical dancers (choreography by Shobana Jeyasingh), 1994; The Dances of the Wind for strings, 1994; Valkalam for 2 viols and harpsichord, 1996; Chamber Concerto, 1997. *Recordings:* Duo l, for flute and cello; Pianosonata, 1979; Sonata for clarinet and piano, 1987. *Publications:* ABO–johdatus uuden musiikin teoriaan, Sibelius Academy Publications, 1982 (An Introduction to the Theory of Contemporary Music); Tekopalmun alla (Under an Artificial Palm Tree), essays on the interaction of cultures. *Honours:* Nattuvanar for male voice choir won the UNESCO Rostrum of Composers in 1994. *Address:* Lapilantie 8B7, 04200 Kerava, Finland.

HAMELIN, Marc-Andre; Concert Pianist; b. 1961, Verdun, Canada; m. Judy Karin Applebaum. *Education:* Studied, Vincent d'Indy School of Music and Temple University, Philadelphia. *Career:* Recitals in Montreal, Toronto, New York and Philadelphia; Concerto appearances in Toronto, Quebec, Ottawa, Albany, Detroit, Indianapolis, Minneapolis, New York (Manhattan Philharmonic and Riverside Symphony) and Philadelphia; Toured with the Montreal Symphony to Spain, Portugal and Germany, 1987; Duo partnership with cellist Sophie Rolland from 1988; Beethoven cycles in New York, Washington, Montreal and London (Wigmore Hall, Mar 1991); Soloist, Turangalîla Symphony with the Philadelphia Orchestra and Andrew Davis, 1996–97. *Recordings include:* Works by Leopold Godowsky (CBS Enterprises); William Bolcom Twelve New Etudes, Stefan Wolpe Battle Piece and Ives Concord Sonata (New World Records); Sorabji Sonata No. 1, Rzewski The People Will Never Be Defeated (Altarus). *Honours:* 1st Prize, Carnegie Hall International American Music Competition, 1985; Virginia P Moore Prize, Canada, 1989. *Address:* c/o GIA, 28 Old Devonshire Road, London SW12 9RB, England.

HAMILTON, David; Singer (Tenor); b. 1960, USA. *Career:* Appearances with opera companies at Philadelphia, San Diego, Tulsa, Sarasota, Hawaii, New York (City Opera), Milwaukee and St Louis; Metropolitan Opera debut, season 1986–87; Season 1991–92, as Tamino for Opéra de Nice, Lensky with Manitoba Opera, and Pinkerton with Chattanooga Opera; Season 1992–93, as Tamino with Vancouver Opera, Peter Quint in Turn of the Screw for Edmonton Opera and Lensky with Scottish Opera; Concert repertoire includes Messiah, Rinaldo by Brahms, Mozart's Requiem, Dvořák's Stabat Mater, the Berlioz Roméo et Juliette and Schumann's Scenes from Faust; Soloist with Israel Philharmonic, Baltimore Symphony, Mostly Mozart Festival Orchestra and Indianapolis Symphony under Raymond Leppard; As recitalist gave premiere of Hugo Weisgall's cycle Lyric Interval; Sang Belmonte in Die Entführung with the Metropolitan Opera. *Honours:* Winner, Paris International Voice Competition, 1984. *Address:* c/o Metropolitan Opera House, Lincoln Centre, New York, NY 10023, USA.

HAMILTON, David (Peter); Music Critic and Writer on Music; b. 18 Jan. 1935, New York, USA. *Education:* Princeton University; AB 1956, MFA in Music History, 1960. *Career:* Music and Record Librarian, Princeton University, 1961–65; Assistant Music Editor 1965–68, Music Editor 1968–74, W W Norton & Company, New York; Music Critic, The Nation, 1968–; Music Correspondent, Financial Times, London, 1969–74; Associate Editor, Musical Newsletter, 1971–77. *Publications:* The Listener's Guide to Great Instrumentalists, 1981; The Music Game: An Autobiography, 1986; Editor, Metropolitan Opera Encyclopedia: A Guide to the World of Opera, 1987. *Contributions:* Many articles and reviews in periodicals. *Address:* c/o The Nation, 72 Fifth Avenue, New York, NY 10011, USA.

HAMILTON, Ronald; Singer (Tenor); b. 1947, Hamilton, Ohio, USA. *Career:* Sang in opera at Ulm, 1975–77, Düsseldorf, 1977–85; Guest appearances throughout Germany, and in Stockholm, Geneva and Paris; Metropolitan Opera, 1988, as Alwa in Lulu, and Salzburg Festival, 1990, as Krenek's Orpheus; Paris Opéra Bastille, 1992, in Messiaen's St François d'Assise; Brussels, 1993, in From the House of the Dead, and the premiere of Reigen by Boesmans; Trieste and Montpellier, 1996, as Tristan; Other roles include Florestan, Wagner's Lohengrin and Walther, Strauss's Emperor and Bacchus, and Enée in Les Troyens; Sang Tannhäuser at Palermo, 1998; Season 2000–01 as Tristan at Hamburg and Wagner's Erik in Trieste. *Address:* Teatro Massimo, Via R Wagner 2, 90139 Palermo, Sicily, Italy.

HAMMES, Lieselotte; Singer (Soprano) and Professor; b. 1932, Siegburg, Germany. *Education:* Studied in Cologne. *Career:* Debut: Cologne, as Amor in Orfeo ed Euridice, 1957; Guest appearances at Stuttgart, Hamburg, Berlin (Deutsche Oper), Naples, Rome, Lisbon and Paris (1971); Glyndebourne Festival 1965, as Sophie in Der Rosenkavalier; Sang at Cologne until 1975 as Mozart's Pamina, Susanna and Papagena, Marzelline, Mimi, Manon Lescaut, Nedda, Marenka in The Bartered Bride and Anne Trulove in The Rake's Progress; Teacher at Bonn then Siegburg from 1973; Professor at Cologne Musikhochschule, 1985–. *Address:* Staatliche Hochschule für Musik, Dagobertstrasse 38, 5000 Cologne 1, Germany.

HAMMOND-STROUD, Derek, OBE; British concert and opera singer (baritone); b. 10 Jan. 1926, London, England. *Education:* studied with Elena Gerhardt, Gerhard Hüsch, Trinity College of Music, London. *Career:* debut in London 1955, in the British Premiere of Haydn's Orfeo et Euridice; Guest Artist with numerous opera companies; Principal Baritone, English National Opera, 1961–71, as Rossini's Bartolo, Verdi's Melitone and Rigoletto, Wagner's Alberich and Beckmesser; Royal Opera, Covent Garden, 1971–89; Glyndebourne, 1973–86; Broadcasts on BBC and European radio; Opera and Recital appearances: Netherlands; Denmark; Iceland; Germany; Austria; Spain; USA; Opera appearances: Metropolitan Opera, New York, 1977–89; Teatro Colón, Buenos Aires, 1981; National Theatre, Munich, 1983; Other roles included: Publio, in La Clemenza di Tito; Don Magnifico; Roles in the British premieres of La Pietra del Paragone, Der Besuch der Alten Dame, and Faninal in Der Rosenkavalier; mem, Incorporated Society of Musicians. *Recordings:* many recordings for various companies including the ENO Ring of the Nibelung and Der Rosenkavalier. *Honours:* Honorary Member, Royal Academy of Music; Honorary Fellow, Trinity College of Music, London; Sir Charles Santley Memorial Award by Worshipful Company of Musicians. *Address:* 18 Sutton Road, Muswell Hill, London N10 1HE, England.

HAMON, Deryck; Singer (Bass); b. 1965, Guernsey. *Education:* Royal Northern College of Music. *Career:* Concert performances throughout the United Kingdom of Messiah, Elijah, Samson, Haydn's Nelson Mass, Five Elizabethan Songs by Vaughan Williams and the Mozart and Fauré Requiems; Member of the D'Oyly Carte Opera, notably as The Mikado; Rossini's Basilio and Escamillo for Travelling Opera, Dikoy in Katya Kabanova at the Opera Theatre, Dublin, and Banquo in Macbeth for City of Birmingham Touring Opera; Other roles include Mozart's Sarastro, Commendatore and Alfonso, Rossini's Bartolo, Puccini's Angelotti (Tosca) and Colline (La Bohème). *Address:* Karen Durant Management, 298 Nelson Road, Whitton, Twickenham TW2 7BW, England.

HAMPE, Christiane; Singer (Soprano); b. 1948, Heidelberg, Germany. *Education:* Studied in Heidelberg and in Munich with Annelies Kupper.

Career: Sang at the Hagen Opera, 1971–73, Basle, 1974–76, Wuppertal, 1976–78, and Karlsruhe, 1979–80; Bregenz Festival, 1974, as Clarice in Haydn's Il mondo della luna, Vienna Staatsoper as Susanna and further guest appearances in Hamburg, throughout Europe and in the USA; Professor at the Karlsruhe Musikhochschule from 1988. *Recordings* include: Lortzing's Undine (Capriccio). *Address:* c/o Musikhochschule, Wolfortsuieies Strasse 7, 76131 Karlsruhe, Germany.

HAMPE, Michael; Actor and Director in International Opera Houses and Theatres; b. 3 June 1935, Heidelberg, Germany. *Education:* Study of Music (cello), Syracuse University, USA; Study of Literature, Musicology and Philosophy at Munich and Vienna Universities; PhD. *Career:* Vice-Director, Schauspielhaus, Zürich, 1965–70; Intendant, National Theatre, Mannheim, 1972–75; Member of Salzburg Festival Board of Directors, 1985–89; Intendant, Cologne Opera, 1975–95; Director of Opera: La Scala Milan, Covent Garden London (Andrea Chénier 1984, Il Barbiere di Siviglia 1985, Cenerentola, 1990), Paris Opéra, Salzburg and Edinburgh Festivals, Munich, Stockholm, Cologne, Geneva, Sydney, San Francisco, Buenos Aires, Tokyo and Zürich Operas, German, Austrian and Swedish television; Director of Drama: Munich, Bavarian State Theatre, Zürich Schauspielhaus, Schwetzingen Festival (double-bill of Rossini seen at Cologne, Schwetzingen and the Paris Opéra-Comique); Premiere of Farinelli, oder die Macht des Gesangs, by Matthus, Karlsruhe, 1998; Teaching: Professor at State Music Academy, Cologne and Cologne University, Kunitachi College of Music, Tokyo; University of California, Los Angeles; Consulting: Consultant for Theatre Building; Vice President, Deutsche Bühnentechnische Gesellschaft, Jury Opéra Bastille, Paris; Actor and Director in German Theatres; About 160 productions in opera, plays and television; Intendant, Dresden Music Festival, 1993–; mem, Board Member, Europäische Musiktheater Akademie, Vienna. *Publications:* 20 Jahre Kölner Oper, 1995; Reden und Afsätze, 2000. *Honours:* Grosses Bundesverdienstkreuz, Bundesrepublik Deutschland; Commendatore della Republica Italiana, Italy; Goldenes Ehrenzeichen Salzburg, Austria. *Address:* Dresdner Musikfestspiele, Tiergartenstrasse 36, D 01219 Dresden, Germany.

HAMPSON, Thomas; Singer (Baritone); b. 28 June 1955, Elkhart, Indiana, USA. *Education:* BA, Government, Eastern Washington University, Cheney; BFA, Voice with Marietta Coyle, Fort Wright College; Studied with Gwendolyn Koldowsky and Martial Singher, Music Academy of the West, summers 1978–79, with Elisabeth Schwarzkopf (Merola), and Horst Günther, 1980. *Career:* Debut: Hansel and Gretel, 1974; Sang first Marcello in La Bohème, 1981; Düsseldorf Ensemble, 1981–84; Guglielmo in Così fan tutte, St Louis Opera, sang title role in Henze's Der Prinz von Homburg, Darmstadt, 1982; Debuts, Cologne, Hamburg, Munich, Santa Fe, 1982–84; Recital debut, Wigmore Hall, 1984; Ponnelle's Don Giovanni, Zürich Opera, 1987; Edinburgh Festival, Schumann's Dichterliebe and German songs to Robert Burns texts, 1993; North American tour which featured solo recital debuts in St Paul, Ann Arbor, Omaha, Kansas City and Toronto, 1993; Solo Recital, Barber and Mahler songs, Salzburg Festival, 1994; Leading role of Vicomte de Valmont in world premiere of Conrad Susa/Philip Littell opera, The Dangerous Liaisons, San Francisco Opera, 1994; Sang first Das Lied von der Erde at Carnegie Hall under James Levine, 1995; Debut in San Francisco as Hamlet, 1996; Marquis de Posa in Verdi's Don Carlos, Châtelet Paris and Covent Garden, London, 1996; Riccardo in Bellini's I Puritani (Met, New York) and title role in Eugene Onegin (Vienna Staatsoper), 1997; Sang in Schubert's Alfonso und Estrella, Vienna Festival, 1997; Sang William Tell in Vienna, 1998; Sang Busoni's Dr Faust in Salzburg, 1999 and Bernstein's Wonderful Town at the 1999 London Proms; Busoni's Faust at the 1999 Salzburg Festival; Amfortas is Parsifal at Covent Garden, 2001; Lieder by Mahler at the 2002 Salzburg Festival; mem, Honorary Member, Academy of Music, London. *Recordings:* La Bohème, Mahler songs, with Bernstein; Des Knaben Wunderhorn solo album; Hamlet; Mahler songs with Geoffrey Parsons, critical edition; Voices from the Heart, 1996; I Hear America Singing, 1997; Schubert's Winterreise; Video, I Hear America Singing, 1997 and Great Performances, telecast. *Publications:* Co-editor, Mahler songs critical edition, 1993. *Honours:* Cannes Classical Award, Male Singer of Year, 1994; Toblacher Komitte Award (Mahler songs), 1994; Echo Preis, 1994; Six Grammy Nominations; Citation of Merit for Lifetime Contribution to Music and Education, National Arts Club of America; Honorary Doctorate, Whitworth College; Artist of the Year, EMI. *Current Management:* IMG Artists. *Address:* c/o IMG Artists, Lovell House, 616 Chiswick High Road, London W4 5RX, England.

HAMVASI, Sylvia; Singer (Soprano); b. 1972, Budapest, Hungary. *Education:* Franz Liszt Academy and Leo Weiner Conservatory, Budapest. *Career:* Roles with Budapest Youth Opera have included Mozart's Blonde and Mme Herz, Serpina in La Serva Padrona and Olympia; Concert tour with the Youth Opera Studio to Kuwait; Repertory includes Bach's St John Passion, Christmas Oratorio and

Masses, Mozart, Liszt and Kodály Masses, Carmina Burana and Handel's Messiah, Dixit Dominus and Solomon. *Recordings include:* Album with the Hungarian Radio Youth Orchestra, conducted by Tamas Vasary. *Honours:* European Mozart Foundation Award, at the 1996 Hommage á Lucia Popp Competition, Bratislava. *Current Management:* Ingpen & Williams Ltd, 7 St George's Court, 131 Putney Bridge Road, London, SW15 2PA, England.

HAN, Derek; Concert Pianist; b. 1951, USA. *Education:* Juilliard School, New York. *Career:* Many appearances in USA and Europe from 1976 notably with the Moscow Philharmonic, Berlin Symphony, Sinfonia Varsovia (conducted by Yehudi Menuhin), Frankfurt State Orchestra, Moscow State Symphony Orchestra and London Philharmonic; Season 2000–01 on tour with the Warsaw Philharmonic in the Far East, Netherlands tour with the Budapest Symphony and concerts in Berlin and New York; Tour of the United Kingdom with the Bolshoi Symphony and South America with Residentie Orchestra, the Hague; Further concerts with the Philharmonie der Nationen. *Recordings include:* Complete Concertos of Haydn, Mozart, Beethoven and Mendlessohn; Tchaikovsky and Shostakovich Concertos; Complete Mozart Violin and Piano sonatas, with Joseph Silverstein. *Honours:* Winner, 1977 Athens International Piano Competition. *Address:* c/o IMG Artists, Lovell House, 616 Chiswick High Road, London W4 5RX, England.

HANAK, Bohus; Singer (Bass-Baritone); b. 8 Jan. 1925, Banovce, Czechoslovakia. *Education:* Studied in Bratislava. *Career:* Sang at Bratislava from 1950 and made guest appearances with the company at Prague, Sofia and Wiesbaden; Engaged at Linz, 1958–60 and at Stadttheater Basle, 1968–88; Further performances at the Komische Opera Berlin, Bolshoi Moscow, Leningrad, State Operas of Dresden and Munich, Naples, Geneva, Innsbruck, Berne and Paris at Théâtre des Champs Elysées; Roles have included Mozart's Figaro and Don Giovanni, Pizarro, Rigoletto, Renato, Amonasro, Count Luna, Macbeth, Simon Boccanegra, Wolfram, Telramund, the Dutchman, Alberich, Prince Igor, Eugene Onegin, Scarpia, Cardillac, Nabucco and Mandryka. *Address:* c/o Theater Basel, Theaterstrasse 7, 4010 Basel, Switzerland.

HANANI, Yehuda; Cellist; b. 19 Dec. 1943, Jerusalem, Israel; m. Hannah Glatstein, 21 Mar 1971, 1 s. *Education:* Rubin Academy of Music, Israel; Juilliard School, USA. *Career:* Guest Performer with Chicago Symphony, Philadelphia Orchestra, Baltimore Symphony, St Paul Chamber Orchestra, Berlin Radio Symphony, Israel Philharmonic, BBC National Orchestra of Wales, etc; Aspen Music Festival; Chautauqua; Marlboro; Artistic Director, Chamber Music Series, Miami Center for the Fine Arts; Cello Faculty, The Peabody Conservatory and Cincinnati College-Conservatory. *Recordings:* Miaskovsky Cello Sonatas; Alkan Cello Sonata; Vivaldi Cello Sonatas; Aleksander Obradovic Cello Concerto; Leo Ornstein Sonata; Samuel Barber Sonata; Lukas Foss Capriccio. *Honours:* Nomination for Grand Prix du Disque; Recipient of 3 Martha Baird Rockefeller Grants for Music; America Israel Cultural Foundation Award.

HANCOCK, Gareth, ARAM; British pianist and conductor; b. 1960, England. *Education:* Clare Coll., Cambridge, Royal Acad., London. *Career:* engagements as repetiteur at English National Opera, playing harpsichord in The Barber of Seville; conducted Rigoletto for English Touring Opera 1996, and Misper for Glyndebourne Education 1997; repetiteur and assistant at Glyndebourne from 1995, including Chief Coach for Jonathan Dove's Flight 1999; teacher at the Royal Academy; Lieder recital accompanist in Britain, France, Germany and USA. *Recordings include:* The Barber of Seville, ENO. *Address:* c/o Royal Academy of Music, Marylebone Road, London, NW1 5HT, England.

HANCOCK, John; Singer (baritone); b. 1968, New York, NY, USA; m. Jane Gilbert. *Education:* Studied at the Juilliard Opera Center, New York. *Career:* Sang Oreste in Iphigénie en Tauride at Strasbourg, 1993, Rossini's Dandini in Kansas City and Raimbaud for the Spoleto Festival, USA; La Haine in Lully's Armide in Paris and Antwerp, Marcello in La Bohème at Glyndebourne and with the Canadian Opera Company, 1995, Rossini's Barber for the New Israeli Opera and Valentin in Philadelphia; Other roles include Silvio in Pagliacci, Malatesta and Tarquinius; Sang Lord Henry Wootton in the premiere of Lowell Liebermann's The Picture of Dorian Gray, Monaco, 1996; Belcore for Florida Grand Opera, 1998; Concert repertoire includes Mahler's Kindertotenlieder at Alice Tully Hall and Des Knaben Wunderhorn. *Current Management:* Athole Still International Management, Forresters Hall, 25–27 Westow Street, London, SE19 3RY, England. *Telephone:* (20) 8771-5271. *Fax:* (20) 8768-6600. *Website:* www.atholestill.com.

HANCOCK, Paul; Composer; b. 6 May 1952, Plymouth, Devon, England; m. Joan Baigent, 11 Oct 1986, sep, 3 step-s., 1 step-d. *Education:* MA, BMus, Trinity Hall, Cambirdge, 1971–76. *Career:* Composing and Private Music Teaching in Plymouth 1976–79, York 1979–83, Oxford 1983–85, Cambridge 1985–87; First London Recital at BMIC, Jan 1986;

mem, Composers Guild of Great Britain. *Compositions:* Main Compositions: 24 Preludes, piano solo, 1979–81; String Quartet, 1982; Who? Songs for children, 1981; With The Mermaids, wind quartet, 1983; The Gift Of A Lamb, children's opera, 1985; Maen Tans-Boskednan, piano solo, 1984; Silent Love, song cycle, 1985; Zennor, clarinet and viola, 1986; Little Gidding Variations, orchestra, 1985–86; Viola Concerto, 1986; The Mermaid of Zennor, opera, 1986–88;... O Very Most The Hidden Love..., song cycle, 1986; The Voice of the Hidden Waterfall, ensemble, 1987; Nocturne for Ragnhild, soprano and piano duet, 1988; Dancing On A Point Of Light, ensemble, 1988; Round 12 O'Clock Rock, baritone and piano; Sea Change, percussion ensemble, 1989; Vespers of St Mary Magdalene, soprano and organ, 1990, piano sonatas 1, 2 and 3, 1990–91; Ogo Pour, percussion solo, 1991; Matrice, piano duet, 1991; The Ring of Fire, piano solo, 1992; Journey Out of Essex, baritone and ensemble, 1993. *Recordings:* Two cassettes of piano music. *Address:* Brunnion Farmhouse, Lelant Downs, Hayle, Cornwall TR27 6 NT, England.

HANCORN, John; singer (baritone); b. 1954, Inverness, Scotland. *Education:* Trinity Coll. of Music, National Opera Studio; further studies with Hans Hotter in Munich and London. *Career:* debut, Edinburgh 1981, as Masetto in Don Giovanni; Aldeburgh from 1981 in Albert Herring, The Rape of Lucretia and Eugene Onegin; Glyndebourne Touring Opera from 1983 in The Love of Three Oranges, Kent Opera as Masetto in Don Giovanni and Fidelio; Debut at Covent Garden as Hermann in Les Contes d'Hoffmann; Tour of Italy 1986 with Monteverdi's L'Orfeo conducted by Roger Norrington; Concert performance of Charpentier's Médée with the Orchestra of the Age of Enlightenment, 1987; Season 1989–90 with Welsh National Opera as Kilian in Der Freischütz, Hector in King Priam with Musica nel Chiostro in Batignano, Italy, Handel's Israel in Egypt with the Royal Choral Society, 1990; Concert repertory also includes the Brahms Requiem; Appearances with the Royal Philharmonic Orchestra, Scottish Chamber Orchestra, Bournemouth Sinfonietta and at the festivals of Camden, Greenwich, Brighton, Aldeburgh, Flanders and Frankfurt; Sang in Weber's Oberon at the Edinburgh and Tanglewood Festivals and at the Alte Oper, Frankfurt, conducted by Ozawa; Season 1992–94 worked with Welsh National Opera and English National Opera in many major roles; Sang Jove in Semele by John Eccles, for Mayfield Chamber Opera, 1996; The Devil in Ordo Virtutum by Hildegard of Bingen for Vox Animae at the 1996 York Early Music Festival. *Recordings:* with Consort of Musicke and Anthony Rooley, 1994. *Current Management:* Robert Gilder & Co., Enterprise House, 59–65 Upper Ground, London, SE1 9PQ, England. *Telephone:* (20) 7928-9008. *Fax:* (20) 7928-9755. *E-mail:* rgilder@robert-gilder.com.

HAND, Richard; British classical guitarist; b. 27 Nov. 1960, Marsden, Yorkshire, England. *Education:* RAM. *Career:* concerts in Wigmore Hall, St John's Smith Square, Purcell Room, Barbican and BBC Proms at Royal Albert Hall; mem. of Hand-Dupré duo, tours to USA, Norway, Poland, Turkey, Azerbaijan, Hong Kong; with Pro Arte Trio to Sweden; with Lightfingered Gentry (flute and guitar) to Germany, Egypt, Dubai, Brunei, Malaysia; with English Guitar Quartet to Israel; with Tetra Guitar Quartet to Saudi Arabia and India; mem. elected Associate of RAM. *Recordings:* Carey Blyton: Complete Guitar Music, Hand-Dupré Duo, Scenes from Childhood)with Pro Arte Trio), Summer Waves (with English Guitar Quartet); world premières of works by Edward Cowie, Malcolm Williamson, Peter Dickinson, David Bedford, Tim Souster. *Honours:* Open Scholarship RAM 1979, Julian Bream prize RAM 1981, String Players prize RAM 1981, John Munday prize RAM 1981. *Address:* 61 Balcome Street, Marylebone, London, NW1 6HD, England (home). *Telephone:* (20) 7724-3806 (office). *E-mail:* info@richardhand.net (home). *Website:* www.richardhand.net (office).

HANDLEY, Vernon George, CBE, BA, FRCM; British conductor; b. 11 Nov. 1930, Enfield; s. of Vernon Douglas and Claudia Lillian Handley; m. 1st Barbara Black 1954 (divorced); one d. one s. (deceased); m. 2nd Victoria Parry-Jones (divorced); one s. one d.; m. 3rd Catherine Newby 1987; one s. *Education:* Enfield School, Balliol Coll., Oxford, Guildhall School of Music. *Career:* Conductor, Oxford Univ. Musical Club and Union 1953–54, Oxford Univ. Dramatic Soc. 1953–54, Tonbridge Philharmonic Soc. 1958–61, Hatfield School of Music and Drama 1959–61, Proteus Choir 1962–81; Musical Dir and Conductor, Guildford Corpn and Conductor, Guildford Philharmonic Orchestra and Choir 1962–83; Assoc. Conductor, London Philharmonic Orchestra 1983–86 (Guest Conductor 1961–83); Prof. for Orchestra and Conducting, Royal Coll. of Music 1966–72, for Choral Class 1969–72; Prin. Conductor, Ulster Orchestra 1985–89, Malmö Symphony Orchestra 1985–89; Prin. Guest Conductor Royal Liverpool Philharmonic Orchestra 1989–95 (Conductor Laureate 1995–), Melbourne Symphony Orchestra 1992–95; Chief Conductor W Australian Symphony Orchestra 1993–; Assoc. Conductor Royal Philharmonic Orchestra 1994– (Guest Conductor 1961–94); Bournemouth Symphony Orchestra, BBC Welsh Orchestra, BBC Northern Symphony (now BBC Philharmonic) Orchestra, Ulster

Orchestra, BBC Scottish Symphony Orchestra, New Philharmonia (now Philharmonia) Orchestra; conducted London Symphony Orchestra in int. series, London 1971; Fellow Goldsmiths' Coll., London 1987; tours of Germany 1966, 1980, S Africa 1974, Holland 1980, Sweden 1980, 1981, Germany, Sweden, Holland and France 1982–83, Australia 1986, Japan 1988, Australia 1989, 1991, 1992. *Recordings include:* Elgar Violin Concerto (Kennedy), Wand of Youth and 2nd Symphony (London Philharmonic), Vaughan Williams 5th Symphony and Flos Campi (Liverpool Philharmonic), Bridge the Sea and Britten Sea Interludes (Ulster Orchestra), Bax Enchanted Summer, Walsingham and Fatherland (Royal Philharmonic), Delius Florida Suite, North Country Sketches, Violin Concerto, Suite and Legende (Ralph Holmes), Dvořák Overtures and Scherzo Capriccioso, Finzi Cello Concerto (Rafael Wallfisch), Moeran Symphony, Simpson 2nd, 4th, 6th, 7th, 9th and 10th Symphonies, all Vaughan Williams Symphonies, Elgar Dream of Gerontius. *Honours:* Hon. RCM 1970; Hon. mem. Royal Philharmonic Soc. 1989; Hon. DUniv (Surrey) 1980; Hon. DMus (Liverpool) 1992; Hon. DLitt (Bradford) 1998; Arnold Bax Memorial Medal for Conducting 1962; Conductor of the Year, British Composer's Guild 1974; Hi-Fi News Audio Award 1982; Gramophone Record of the Year 1986, 1989; British Phonographic Industry Award 1988. *Address:* Cwm Cottage, Bettws, Abergavenny, Monmouthshire, NP7 7LG, Wales; Hen Gerrig, Pen-y-Fan, nr Monmouth (Gwent), Wales. *Telephone:* (1873) 890135.

HANDT, Herbert; Tenor, Conductor and Musicologist; b. 26 May 1926, Philadelphia, Pennsylvania, USA. *Education:* Juilliard School New York; Vienna Academy. *Career:* Debut: Vienna Staatsoper, 1949; Sang in the premieres of Venere Prigioniera by Malipiero (Florence 1957) and Maria Golovin by Menotti (Brussels 1958); Appeared in the Italian and French premieres of works by Henze, Berg, Busoni and Britten; Debut as Conductor, Rome, 1960; Founded own opera group and gave revivals of works by Boccherini, Rossini and Geminiani; Also heard in Haydn's Orfeo ed Euridice (L'Anima del Filosofo); Settled in Lucca, Italy and founded the Associazione Musicale Lucchese and the Lucca Chamber Orchestra. *Recordings:* Maria Golovin (RCA); Don Giovanni, Haydn's Orfeo, Idomeneo (Nixa); Giuseppe, Figlio di Giacobbe by Luigi Rossi; Rossini's Otello; Temistocle by JC Bach; Sesto in Giulio Cesare by Handel (Vox). *Publications include:* Performing editions of early Italian vocal music.

HANKEY, Tom; Violinist; b. 1975, England. *Education:* Royal College of Music, London. *Career:* Co-founded Tavec String Quartet at RCM, 1999; Coached by Simon Rowland-Jones and the Chillingirian Quartet; Performances at St Martin-in-the-Fields, Serpentine Gallery (BBC Proms) and National Gallery, London; Music Society concerts throughout Britain; Festival Engagements at Lower Wye Valley Chamber Music Festival, 2000–2001; Workshops and concerts in educational establishments; Concert at National Gallery, September 2001, with Octet by Schubert and Strauss's Till Eulenspiegel; Member and leader of the Piros Ensemble, 2000. *Honours:* Winner, Helen Just String Quartet Prize; Rio Tinto Ensemble Prize and NET4 music Prize. *Address:* c/o Royal College of Music, Prince Consort Road, London, SW7 2 BS, England.

HANLEY, Regina; Singer (Soprano); b. 1970, Dublin. *Education:* Dublin College of Music; Royal Northern College of Music. *Career:* Appearances with Glyndebourne Festival Opera as Micaela, Jenůfa, Katya Kabanova, Nedda and Tatiana; Season 1998–99, as Janáček's Emilia Marty for Scottish Opera, Go Round and Donna Anna for the Perth Festival; Concerts include Beethoven's Mass in C, Messiah, Verdi Requiem, Vivaldi's Gloria, Mozart Mass in C Minor, Strauss's Four Last Songs and Rossini's Stabat Mater. *Address:* Music International, 13 Ardilaun Road, London N5 2QR, England.

HANLON, Kevin (Francis); Composer; b. 1 Jan. 1953, South Bend, Indiana, USA. *Education:* Studied at Indiana University, the Eastman School of Music and the University of Texas, DMA 1983; Further study with Mario Davidovsky at the Berkshire Music Center. *Career:* Taught at the University of Kentucky, 1982–83; Composition and electronic music faculty at the University of Arizona, Tucson; Director of the Arizona Contemporary Music Ensemble; Appearances as Singer and Conductor. *Compositions include:* Through to the End of the Tunnel for low voice and tape delay 1976, revised 1980; Second Childhood for soprano and ensemble, 1976; Cumulus numbus for orchestra, 1977; Variations for alto saxophone and tape delay, 1977; Toccata for piano, 1980; String Trio, 1981; An die ferne Geliebte for low voice and piano, 1980; Lullaby for my Sorrows for chamber orchestra, 1982; Ostinato Suite for harpsichord, 1982; Centered for chamber ensemble and tape, 1983; A E Housman Song Cycle for low voice and chamber ensemble, 1982; Choral Introits for chorus and ensemble, 1982; Trumpet Sonata, 1983; Sratae for orchestra, 1983; Relentless Time for small orchestra, 1984; Kaleidoscopic Image for orchestra, 1986; On an Expanding Universe, 1986; Chronological Variations for strings, 1987; The Lark of Avignon for wind ensemble and piano, 1993; Clairon for orchestra,

1997. *Honours:* Joseph H Bearns Prize, 1978; Koussevitzky Prize, 1981. *Address:* c/o ASCAP, ASCAP Building, 1 Lincoln Plaza, NY 10023, USA.

HANLY, Brian (Vaughan); Concert Violinist and Music Professor; b. 3 Sept. 1940, Perth, Australia; m. Jeri Ryan Hanly, 25 Aug 1968, 2 s. *Education:* Performers Diploma 1960, Teachers Diploma 1961, Australian Music Examinations Board. *Career:* Violinist, Arts Trio, in residence at University of Wyoming and University of Houston, Texas, USA; Numerous tours with Western Arts Trio, Europe, USA, Mexico, also concerts throughout South America and Australia; Soloist with orchestras throughout Australia, Mexico, USA, with particular success with Beethoven and Prokofiev Concertos. *Recordings:* 1st recording of Claude Debussy's recently discovered piano trio; 7 albums with Western Arts Trio. *Honours:* Winner, Australian Broadcasting Commission Concerto Competition. *Address:* Music Department, University of Wyoming, Laramie, WY 82071, USA.

HANNAH, Ron; Composer and Teacher; b. 14 Dec. 1945, Moose Jaw, Saskatchewan, Canada. *Education:* BSc, Chemistry, 1969, BMus, Theory, Composition, 1973, MMus, Composition, 1975, EdDip, 1980, University of Alberta, Edmonton; Student of Violet Archer, Manus Sasonkin, Malcolm Forsyth. *Career:* Member, Da Camera Singers, 1973–; Instructor, Department of Extension, University of Alberta, 1975–76; Instructor, Harmony, Ear Training, Red Deer College, 1977–78; Music Instructor, Edmonton Public Schools, 1980–; Founder, Owner, Composer Publications, Edmonton, 1989; Commissions include 1 from Edmonton Symphony Orchestra and 2 from Canadian Broadcasting Corporation; Founding Editor, The Alberta New Music Review, magazine of Edmonton Composers' Concert Society; mem, Co-founder and Co-ordinator, Edmonton New Music Festival. *Compositions include:* From Song of Solomon, SATB, piano, 1972; An Immorality, SATB, piano, 1972; The Dinner Party, song cycle, soprano, clarinet, piano, 1973; String Quartet No. 1, 1973; Sonata for violoncello and piano, 1973; Three African Songs, tenor, piano, 1974; The Shrine of Kotje, chorus and orchestra, 1975; Variations on a Theme of Violet Archer, piano, 1975; Concert Piece, flute, piano, 1975; Visions of Nothingness, piano sonata in 2 movements, 1975; Sonata for French horn and piano, 1976; Prelude and Meditation on Coventry Cathedral, trumpet, organ, 1978; Five Preludes, organ, 1978; Songs of Myself, song cycle, soprano, violin, piano, French horn, 1979; The Lonely Princess, flute, guitar, 1981; Suite for Elan, piano, 1982; Piano Trio No. 1, 1982; Four Canons for three Voices, mixed chorus, piano, 1983; Mademoiselle Fifi, chamber opera, 1983; Three Songs on Poems of Robert Graves, voice, electronic tape, 1984; Fantasia on Ein Feste Burg, organ, 1984; Hypatia, a play with songs, 1984; Three Romantic Madrigals, 1985; Concerto for piano and tape, 1986; Morning's Minion: 4 songs after G M Hopkins, soprano, piano, 1987; Alleluia, SATB, 1989; Credo, mezzo-soprano, viola, piano, 1990; Divertimento for strings, 1991; Pastoral Suite for solo guitar, 1992–93; Suite of Orchestral Dances, 1992; Toccatissimo! for 2 pianos and 2 percussionists, 1993–94. *Recordings:* 5 Preludes for organ; Concert pieces for flute and piano; Meditation for cello and piano. *Address:* 11627 46th Avenue, Edmonton, Alberta T6H 0A6, Canada.

HANNAN, Eilene; Singer (Soprano); b. 4 Nov. 1946, Melbourne, Australia. *Education:* Studied in Australia and London. *Career:* Debut: Australian Opera 1971, as Barbarina in Le nozze di Figaro; Sang Natasha in Prokofiev's War and Peace at the opening of the Sydney Opera House, 1973; Other Australian roles have been Janáček's Vixen, Santuzza, Mozart's Zerlina and Cherubino and Leila in Les pêcheurs de Perles, Glyndebourne and Wexford 1977, as the Vixen and as Salomé in Herodiade by Massenet; English National Opera from 1978, as Janáček's Mila (Osud) and Katya Kabanova, the Duchess of Parma in Busoni's Doctor Faust, Mozart's Pamina and Susanna, Mélisande, Poppea (Monteverdi) and Natasha; Covent Garden debut 1978, in the British premiere of The King Goes Forth to France, by Sallinen; Sang in Britten's The Turn of the Screw at Brisbane in 1988; Season 1992, as Jenůfa at Sydney, Pat Nixon for the State Opera of South Australia and at Düsseldorf; Sang Katya Kabanova at Sydney, 1995; Emma in the premiere of Summer of the Seventeenth Doll, at Sydney, 1999. *Current Management:* Ingpen & Williams Ltd, 7 St George's Court, 131 Putney Bridge Road, London, SW15 2PA, England.

HANNAN, Michael (Francis); Composer, Writer, Educator and Keyboard Performer; b. 19 Nov. 1949, Newcastle, New South Wales, Australia. *Education:* BA 1972, PhD 1979, University of Sydney; Graduate Diploma of Musical Composition, University of Sydney, 1982. *Career:* Teacher, University of New South Wales 1975–76, University of Sydney 1977–83; Lecturer in Composition, Queensland Conservatorium of Music, 1985–86; Head of Music, Northern Rivers College of Advanced Education, 1986–; Research, Post-doctoral Scholar, University of California, Los Angeles, 1983–84; Research Affiliate, University of Sydney, 1985–. *Compositions:* Voices in the Sky for piano, 1980; Rajas for solo cello, 1982; Zen Variations for piano, 1982; Island Song for recorders, percussion and organ, 1983; In the Utter Darkness, for solo flute, 1983; Callisto for piano, 1986. *Recordings:* The Piano Music of Peter Sculthorpe, Move Records, 1982. *Publications:* Peter Sculthorpe: His Music and Ideas, 1929–79, 1982. *Contributions:* Various publications. *Address:* c/o School of the Arts, Northern Rivers College of Advanced Education, Lismore, NSW 2480, Australia.

HANNAY, Roger (Durham); Composer, Conductor and Teacher; b. 22 Sept. 1930, Plattsburg, New York, USA; m. Janet Roberts, 1 d. *Education:* BMus, Syracuse University, 1948–52; MMus, Boston University, 1952–53; PhD, Eastman School of Music, 1954–56; Berkshire Music School, 1959; Princeton Seminar for Advanced Studies, 1960; Bennington Composers Conference, 1964–65. *Career:* Debut: Music in Our Time, New York City, 1964; Teacher on the faculties of SUNY, Hamilton College, University of Wyoming, Concordia College; Teacher, University of North Carolina, where founded and directed Electronic Studio and the New Music Ensemble, 1967–82; Conducted the North Carolina Symphony Orchestra in his Symphony No. 4, American Classic, 1983, Greensboro Symphony Orchestra premiere of his orchestral suite, The Age of Innocence, 1985, Peter Fuchs Conductor; Winston-Salem Symphony Orchestra premiere of Symphony No. 6, 1990; Residencies, Charles Ives Center for American Music, MacDowell Colony, Yaddo, Ives Center for American Music. *Compositions include:* 7 symphonies, 1953–96, 5 chamber operas, 4 string quartets; Sphinx, trumpet and tape; Pied Piper, clarinet and tape; Clarinet Voltaire, saxophone, percussion and speaker; The Journey of Edith Wharton, opera in 2 acts for 5 voices and chamber orchestra, 1982; Rhapsody, flute and piano; Sic Transit Spiritus, 1984; Souvenir and Souvenir ll, 1984 and 1986; Ye Musick for the Globe Theatre, 1985; The Nightingale and the Rose, chamber opera after Wilde, 1986; Prologue to Chaucer's Canterbury Tales, commissioned. *Recordings:* Symphony for Band; Architecture in Sound, 1997. *Publications:* Transcribed and edited, Sonate for viola and piano by Mrs H H Beach, 1984; My Book of Life, collection of autobiographical essays, 1997. *Address:* 609 Morgan Creek Road, Chapel Hill, NC 27514, USA.

HANNIKAINEN, Ann-Elise; Composer and Pianist; b. 14 Jan. 1946, Hangö, Finland. *Education:* Academia Moderna de Música, Peru; Sibelius Acad., Finland; studies with composer, Ernesto Halffter, Spain. *Career:* debut, as composer, orchestral piece, Anerfálicas, Valencia, Spain, 1973; Tournée as pianist, Andalucia, 1975; performance, world premiere, Piano Concerto, Helsinki, 1976; Anerfálicas, Teatro Real, Madrid, Spain, 1977; Finnish and Spanish radio broadcasts; piano recitals; Festival Kuhmoinen, Andalucia, Madrid and others; mem., Société des Auteurs, Compositeurs et Editeurs de Musique (Paris), Society of Finnish Composers. *Compositions include:* Anerfálicas, orchestral, 1973; Pensamientos for piano, 1974; Toccata Fantasia for piano, 1975; Concerto for piano and orchestra, in memoriam Manuel de Falla's 100th Anniversary, 1976; Cosmos for orchestra, 1977; Trio, Sextetto, 1979; Chachara for flute and piano, 1980; Solemne for solo piano, 1982; Zafra for violin and piano, 1986. *Publications:* Pensamientos, 1974; Toccato Fantasia; Chachara; some works included in Centre de Documentation de la Musique Contemporaire, Paris, France. *Honours:* First Prize, Second Contest for Young Composers, JJMM Barcelona, 1980. *Address:* Kokonniementie 14B 3, 17800 Kuhmoinen, Finland.

HANNULA, Kaisa; Singer (Soprano); b. 1959, Finland. *Education:* Studied at the Sibelius Academy, Helsinki, and in London and Vienna. *Career:* Sang at first in concert and appeared at the 1989 Savonlinna Festival, in the premiere of The Knife by Paavo Heininen; Savonlinna, 1991, as Marenka in The Bartered Bride and Helsinki, 1992, in Pohjalaisia by Madetoja; Other roles include Marguerite and Violetta; Sang Schoenberg's Erwartung at Savonlinna, 1995; Princess in the premiere of Erik Bergman's The Singing Tree, Helsinki, 1995; Season 2000–01 as Papageno at Savonlinna and Wagner's Gunther in Bonn. *Address:* c/o Finnish National Opera, Bulevardi 23–27, SF 00180 Helsinki 18, Finland.

HANNULA, Tenno; Singer (Baritone); b. 1950, Vehmaa, Finland. *Education:* Studied in Finland with P Salomaa, in Rome with Luigi Ricci and at Musikhochschule Vienna. *Career:* Sang Escamillo and Posa in Don Carlos at Kaiserslautern, 1976; Nationaltheater Mannheim from 1977, as Wolfram, Enrico, Counts Luna and Almaviva, Eugene Onegin, Marcello, Rossini's Figaro and Lortzing's Tsar; Sang Almaviva at Ludwigsburg 1980–81, Savonlinna Festival 1981–89, as Papageno and in the 1984 premiere of Sallinen's The King Goes Forth to France; Stuttgart Staatsoper 1982–, notably in the 1984 premiere of Akhnaten by Philip Glass; Guest appearances at Hamburg, Hanover, Karlsruhe, Aachen, Vienna, Moscow, Leningrad and Munich; Finnish National Opera, Helsinki, as Rigoletto, Deutsche Oper Berlin as Thoas in Iphigénie en Aulide; Sang Blancsac in La Scala di Seta at Stuttgart Staatsoper, 1991; Forester in The Cunning Little Vixen at Karlsruhe, 1996, and Dunois in The Maid of Orleans, 1998. *Recordings include:* Akhnaten. *Address:* c/o Stuttgart Staatsoper, Oberer Schlossgarten 6, 7000 Stuttgart, Germany.

HANSELL, Kathleen (Amy Kuzmick); Musicologist and Music Editor; b. 21 Sept. 1941, Bridgeport, Connecticut, USA; 1 s., 1 d. *Education:* BA, Wellesley College, Massachusetts, 1963; MMus, University of Illinois at Urbana, 1969; PhD, University of California at Berkeley, 1980; Studied piano organ and harpsichord with private teachers. *Career:* Instructor in Music History, by correspondence, University of Illinois, 1967–68; Organist, Lutheran Church of the Good Shepherd, Sacramento, California, 1969–71; Gloria Dei Lutheran Church, Iowa City, 1973–74; Instructor in Musicology, Harpsichord, and Organ, Grinnell College, Iowa, 1975–76; Instructor in Music History, Cornell College, Mt Vernon, Iowa, 1979; Archivist, Swedish Music History Archive, Stockholm, Sweden, 1982–88; In-house Editor for critical editions, G Ricordi and Co, Milan, Italy, 1988–92; Music Editor, University of Chicago Press, Chicago Illinois, 1992–; Managing Editor, The Works of Giuseppe Verdi, 1992–; mem, American and Italian Musicology Societies; Society of Dance History Scholars. *Publications:* Editor, Mozart: Lucio Silla for Neue Mozart Ausgabe, 1986; Franz Berwald Complete Works, Vol. 14, Duos (Bärenreiter), 1987, Hindemith, Organ Concerto, 1962 for Hindemith-Ausgabe in preparation; Il balletto e l'opera italiana, in Storia dell'opera italiana (Turin), 1988; Editor, Rossini: Zelmira, for Tutte le opere di Gioachino Rossini; Editor, Verdi: Stiffelio for The Works of Giuseppe Verdi; Compositional Techniques in Stiffelio: Reading the Autograph sources in Verdi's Middle Period: Source Studies, Analysis and Performance Practice, 1997; Galetano Gioia, il ballo teatrale e l'opera del primo Ottocento in Creature di Prometeo: Il ballo teatrale dal divertimento al dramma, 1996; Gluck's Orpheus och Euridice in Stockholm: Performance practices on the way from Orpheo to Orphée in Gustavian Opera: An Interdisciplinary Reader in Swedish Opera Dance and Theatre, 1771–1809, 1991. *Contributions:* Numerous professional magazines and publications including Grove's Dictionary, 6th edition; The New Grove Dictionary of Opera. *Address:* 4940 S East End Avenue, Chicago, IL 60615, USA.

HANSFORD, Andrew, BMus, MA, ARCM, ARCO, LRSM, LGSM, LTCL, FLCM; British pianist and chamber musician; b. 25 May 1973, Taplow, Berkshire, England. *Education:* Univ. of Surrey, Guildford, Univ. of Bristol and Univ. of Wales, Cardiff. *Career:* freelance performer and tutor, notably pianist, Royal Ballet School, London 1996–97; piano tutor, Cheltenham Coll. and Cirencester Sixth Form Coll. 1998–; piano accompanist and tutor, Morley Coll., London 1998; Lecturer in Music on the panel at the Univ. of Bath in Swindon 2001–; CT ABRSM mentor (Oxford centre), Associated Bd of the Royal Schools of Music 2000–; specialist keyboard examiner for graded and diploma examinations of the Guildhall School of Music, London 1999–; examiner in music, for the Univ. of London Examinations Board and Assessment Council (ULEAC) 1999–, for Oxford & Cambridge Examinations and Assessment Council (OCR) 2001–, and for the Independent Contemporary Music Awards 1998–; adjudicator for competitive music festivals 2000–; accompanist for recitals and concerts, including the Cirencester Choral Soc. (Cirencester Parish Church 1999, Cheltenham Town Hall 2000), Bath Philharmonia (Bath Assembly Rooms 2001), conservatoire auditions and diplomas, examinations and festivals, including the 1995 Eisteddfod of Wales; church organist (at Sacred Hearts Catholic Church, Charlton Kings, Cheltenham c. 1989–95 and St Peter's Catholic Church, Cirencester 2001–); tenor in the Surrey Univ. Chamber Choir 1991–94, the Bristol Univ. Singers 1994–95; mem. Royal Coll. of Organists, RSA. *Honours:* Int. Hedy King Robinson Grade 8 Theory of Music Prize from the Associated Bd of the Royal Schools of Music 1999, Hon. FRSA 1999, Hon. FMusICMA 2000. *Address:* 62 Roberts Close, Stratton, Cirencester, Gloucestershire GL7 2RP, England. *E-mail:* andhmusic@yahoo.co.uk.

HANSLIP, Chloë; Concert Violinist; b. 1987, Guildford, England. *Education:* studied with Natasha Boyarskaya, 1991–; masterclasses in Vienna with Zakhar Bron, 1993–; further studies in Cologne and Madrid. *Career:* played child violinist in 1996 film, Onegin (Devil's Trill Sonata); recitals in Europe, Scandinavia and the USA; TV appearances at Europe, Russia and Israel; Bruch First Concerto at the Barbican, London, 2002; Sarasate's Carmen Fantasy at the 2002 London Proms; Wigmore Hall concert and concertos with the London Mozart Players. *Recordings include:* Paganini and Bloch (with John Williams) 2002. *Honours:* First Prize, Junior International Competition; Novosibirsk, 1997; Scholarship with Sibelius Foundation, 2001. *Current Management:* Hazard Chase, Norman House, Cambridge Place, Cambridge CB2 1NS, England. *Telephone:* (1223) 312400. *Fax:* (1223) 460827. *Website:* www.hazardchase.co.uk.

HANSMANN, Christine; Singer (Mezzo-soprano); b. 1964, Thuringia, Germany. *Education:* Studied in Leipzig. *Career:* Sang at Weimar Opera from 1989; Guest appearances at Leipzig, Kassel and elsewhere in Germany, as Mozart's Dorabella and Cherubino, Fricka, Ottavia in Poppea, the Composer in Ariadne auf Naxos and Hansel; Leipzig Opera from 1993 in Le Grand Macabre by Ligeti, Satyricon by Maderna and Schoenberg's Moses und Aron; Other roles include Wagner's Kundry and Brangaene; Concerts with the Leipzig Gewandhaus Orchestra, including US debut at New York in the Wesendonck Lieder. *Address:* c/o Leipzig Opera, Augustusplatz 12, 7010 Leipzig, Germany.

HANSON, Robert (Frederic); Composer, Musicologist and Teacher; b. 24 Oct. 1948, Birmingham, England; m. (1) Anthea Judith Carter, 11 July 1970, 1 d., (2) Rosalind Thurston, 1 Nov 1980, 2 s. *Education:* ARCO, 1967, BA, 1970, PhD, 1976, Southampton University. *Career:* Founder, Conductor, Southampton University Chamber Orchestra, 1970–72; Analytical research into the music of Webern, 1970–73; Freelance Teacher and Composer, 1973–74; Lecturer in Music, Dartington College of Arts, 1974–91; Degree Course Leader, 1983–91; Acting Head of Music, 1990–91; Director of Studies, Morley College, 1991–; mem, Society for the Promotion of New Music; Performing Right Society. *Compositions:* Metaphysical Verses for soprano and orchestra, 1980; Changes for string orchestra, 1982; Chamber Concerto, 1986; Song Cycles: Auguries of Innocence, 1988; Clarinet Concerto, 1991; Thanksgiving Music, 1994; String Quartet, 1997; Exequiae Muniae, 1999. *Contributions:* Tempo; Lutoslawski's Mi-Parti; Music Analysis; Webern's Chromatic Organisation. *Address:* Morley College, 61 Westminster Bridge Road, London, England.

HARA, Kazuko; Composer; b. 10 Feb. 1935, Tokyo, Japan. *Education:* Studied in Japan, with Dutilleux in Paris and with Tcherepinn, 1962; Singing at Venice Conservatory, 1963, Gregorian Chant in Tokyo. *Career:* Her operas have been successfully performed in Tokyo. *Compositions include:* Operas, The Casebook of Sherlock Holmes, the Confession, 1981; On the Merry Night, 1984; A Selection for Chieko, 1985; Sute-Hime: The Woman who Bit off a Man's Tongue, 1986; A Love Suicide at Sonezaki, 1987; Beyond Brain Death, 1988; Yosakoi-bushi: Junshin and Omma, 1990; Princess Iwanaga, 1990; Pedtro Kibe: recanted not, 1992; Nasuno-Yoichi, 1992; Tonnerre's miraculous tree, 1993; The Life of the Virgin Mary, oratorio, 1993; Lord Sansho, opera, 1995; Princess Nukata, opera, 1996; Crime and Punishment, opera after Dostoyevsky, 1998.

HARADA, Sadao; Japanese cellist; b. 4 Jan. 1944, Tokyo. *Education:* Juilliard School. *Career:* cellist of the Tokyo Quartet, 1969–1999; regular concerts in the USA and abroad; First cycle of the complete quartets of Beethoven at the Yale at Norfolk Chamber Music Festival, 1986; Repeated cycles at the 92nd Street Y (NY), Ravinia and Israel Festivals and Yale and Princeton Universities; Season 1990–91 at Alice Tully Hall, the Metropolitan Museum of Art, New York and in Boston, Washington DC, Los Angeles, Cleveland, Detroit, Chicago, Miami, Seattle, San Francisco, Toronto; Tour of South America, two tours of Europe including Paris, Amsterdam, Bonn, Milan, Munich, Dublin, London, Berlin; Quartet-in-Residence at Yale University, the University of Cincinnati College-Conservatory of Music. *Recordings:* Schubert's Major Quartets; Mozart Flute Quartets with James Galway and Clarinet Quintet with Richard Stoltzman; Quartets by Bartók, Brahms, Debussy, Haydn, Mozart and Ravel; Beethoven Middle Period Quartets (RCA). *Honours:* Grand Prix du Disque du Montreux; Best Chamber Music Recording of the Year from Stereo Review and the Gramophone; Four Grammy Nominations. *Current Management:* Kajimoto Concert Management, 8-6-25 Ginza, Chuo-ku, Tokyo, 104-0061, Japan.

HARBISON, John (Harris); Composer and Conductor; b. 20 Dec. 1938, Orange, New Jersey, USA. *Education:* Pupil of Walter Piston, Harvard College, BA 1960, Boris Blacher, Berlin Hochschule für Musik 1961, and Roger Sessions and Earl Kim, Princeton University, MFA 1983; Studied conducting with Eleazer de Carvalho, Berkshire Music Center, Tanglewood, Massachusetts and with Dean Dixon, Salzburg. *Career:* Teacher, Massachusetts Institute of Technology, 1969–82; Conductor, Cantata Singers and Ensemble, 1969–73, 1980–82; Composer-in-Residence, Reed College, 1968–69, Pittsburgh Symphony Orchestra 1982–84, Berkshire Music Center, 1984; New Music Adviser 1985–86, Composer-in-Residence 1986–88, Los Angeles Philharmonic Orchestra. *Compositions:* Operas: The Winter's Tale, 1974; Full Moon in March, 1977; The Great Gatsby, 1999. Ballets: Ulysses' Bow, 1984; Ulysses Raft, 1983; Orchestral: Sinfonia for violin and double orchestra, 1963; Confinement for chamber ensemble, 1965; Elegiac Songs for mezzosoprano and chamber orchestra, 1973; Descant-Nocturne, 1976; Diotima, 1976; Piano Concerto, 1978; Snow Country for oboe and strings, 1979; Violin Concerto, 1980; Symphony No. 1, 1981; Deep Potomac Bells for 250 tubas, 1983; Remembering Gatsby, 1986; Viola Concerto, 1989; Symphony No. 2, 1987; Oboe Concerto, 1991; Symphony No. 3, 1991; 14 Fabled Folksongs for violin and marimba, 1992; Suite for cello, 1993; Flute Concerto, 1993; Cello Concerto, 1993; The Most Often Used Chords, for orchestra, 1993; Emerson, for double chorus, 1995; Four Psalms for vocal soloists, chorus and orchestra, 1999; Chamber: Serenade for 6 instruments, 1968; Piano Trio, 1969; Bermuda Triangle for amplified cello, tenor saxophone and electric organ, 1970; Die Kurze for 5 instruments, 1970; Woodwind Quintet, 1979; Organum for Paul Fromm for chamber group, 1981; Piano Quintet, 1981; Exequien for Carlo Simmons for 7 instruments, 1982; Overture, Michael Kohlhass for

brass ensemble, 1982; Variations for clarinet, violin and piano, 1982; String Quartet No. 1, 1985, No. 2, 1987, No. 3, 1993; Choral Pieces; Songs. *Recordings:* Several compositions recorded. *Honours:* Guggenheim Fellowship, 1978; Pulitzer Prize in Music, 1986; Many commissions including opera The Great Gatsby, for performance at the Metropolitan on January 1 2000. *Address:* 4037 Highway 19, De Forest, WI 53532, USA.

HARBOTTLE, Guy; Singer (Baritone); b. 1960, England. *Education:* Royal College of Music, London. *Career:* Appearances with Kent Opera, Wexford Festival, European Chamber Orchestra and Travelling Opera as Bizet's Escamillo and Zurga, Germont, Amonasro, Gianni Schicchi, Marcello and Belcore; Further engagements with British Youth Opera, Pavilion Opera, at Gothenburg and the Edinburgh Festival; Sang Fritz in the British premiere of Korngold's Die tote Stadt (concert) at the Queen Elizabeth Hall, 1996; Orestes in the British premiere of Oresteia by Xenakis for the English Bach Festival, Linbury Studio, Covent Garden, 2000; Britten roles include Balstrode, Sid (Albert Herring) and Tarquinius in The Rape of Lucretia. *Address:* c/o English Bach Festival, 15 South Eaton Place, London SW1W 9ER, England.

HARDENBERGER, Hakan; Trumpeter; b. 27 Oct. 1961, Malmö, Sweden. *Education:* Trumpet with Bo Nilsson in Malmö aged 8; Royal College of Music, Malmö; Paris Conservatoire with Pierre Thibaud. *Career:* Prizewinner at competitions in Paris, Munich, Toulon and Geneva; Extensive tours of Europe and North and South America; British debut Aug 1984, playing the Howarth Trumpet Concerto at Crystal Palace; Tour of Germany 1984 with the Dresdner Baroque Soloists; 1985 Bournemouth Sinfonietta with Andrew Parrott playing Hummel and Bach; Harrogate and Warwick Festivals 1985, and South American tour with the Munich Bach Collegium; London Promenade Concert debut 1986, with the premiere of Array by Gordon Crosse conducted by James Loughran; May 1987 premiere of Harrison Birtwistle's Endless Parade with the Collegium Musicum Zürich conducted by Paul Sacher; Aug 1987 premiere of John McCabe's Rainforest II at the Harrogate Festival; Concerts with the Scottish National Orchestra and Neeme Jarvi and the Northern Sinfonia with George Malcolm; Other conductors with whom he has worked include Peter Eövtös, Charles Mackerras, John Pritchard, Seiji Ozawa and Rostropovich; Edinburgh Festival debut 1989, playing the Haydn Concerto with Esa-Pekka Salonen conducting the Swedish Radio Symphony; Premiered Henze's Concerto 1992 (Japan); Season 1993–94 with South America tour, appearances at Salzburg and the London Proms, tour of Europe with the London Sinfonietta; Played Michael Haydn's Concerto at St John's, London, 1997; Premiere of Gruber's Concerto at the 1999 London Proms. *Recordings:* Concertos by Haydn, Hummel, Hertel, Stamitz and Telemann with the Academy of St Martin in the Fields under Neville Marriner (Philips); Birtwistle Endless Parade, Concertos by Davies and Watkins; Mysteries of the Macabre, Baroque Trumpet Recital, At the Beach. *Honours:* RPO Charles Heidseele Music Award for best instrumentalist in 1988, 1989. *Current Management:* Svensk Konsertdirektion AB, Henrik F Lodding, Box 5076, 402 22 Göteborg, Sweden.

HARDING, Daniel; British conductor; b. 31 Aug. 1975, Oxford, England; m. Beatrice; one d. *Education:* Univ. of Cambridge. *Career:* season 1993–94 conducted The Miraculous Mandarin Suite with the City of Birmingham Symphony, followed by Schnittke's Viola Concerto with Yuri Bashmet; other CBSO repertory includes Das Lied von der Erde, The Rite of Spring and Stockhausen's Gruppen; season 1994–95 with the Rotterdam Philharmonic, London Symphony, Scottish Chamber Orchestra and BBC Philharmonic Orchestra; tour of the UK 1995 with the Birmingham Contemporary Music Group in The Soldier's Tale; further engagements with the Netherlands Wind Ensemble and the Jeunesse Musicales World Orchestra; London Proms debut 1996 (as youngest ever conductor), Principal Conductor of the Trondheim Symphony Orchestra 1997, Principal Guest of the Norköpping Symphony Orchestra; conducted Don Giovanni at Aix and Jenúfa for WNO 1998; Guest Conductor, Santa Cecilia Orchestra of Rome, Royal Stockholm Philharmonic, Frankfurt Radio Symphony Orchestra and the Residentie Orchestra of the Hague 1997–98; season 1998–99 conducted the London Philharmonic and Leipzig Gewandhaus Orchestras; Music Dir Deutsche Kammerphilharmonie, Bremen six years; further engagements include returns to the City of Birmingham and London Symphony Orchestras, Berlin Philharmonic and the Frankfurt and Swedish Radio Orchestras; debut at the Royal Opera House with Turn of the Screw 2001; season 2001–02 with San Francisco Symphony Orchestra, Philadelphia Orchestra, Los Angeles Philharmonic Orchestra, London Symphony Orchestra, Gewandhaus Orchestra, Dresden Staatskapelle and Concertgebouw Orchestra; Wozzeck at Aix 2003; cofounder and Music Dir, Mahler Chamber Orchestra; Principal Guest Conductor LSO 2004, 2006–07. *Recordings:* works by Lutoslawski with soprano Solveig Kringelborn and the Norwegian Chamber Orchestra, works by Britten with Ian Bostridge and the Britten Sinfonia 1998.

Honours: Choc de L'Année 1998, Le Monde de la Musique 1998. *Current Management:* Askonas Holt Ltd, Lonsdale Chambers, 27 Chancery Lane, London, WC2A 1PF, England. *Telephone:* (20) 7400-1700. *Fax:* (20) 7400-1799. *E-mail:* info@askonasholt.co.uk. *Website:* www .askonasholt.co.uk.

HARDY, Janet; Singer (Dramatic Soprano); b. 1940, Atlanta, Georgia, USA. *Education:* Studied at the Mississippi Southern and Louisiana Colleges; BM in Music Education, Louisiana College; Further study with Dorothy Hulse, Dominique Modesti, Gladys Kuchta and Hilde Zadek. *Career:* Has sung in Gelsenkirchen, Kassel and Augsburg as Elektra, Ortrud, Leonore in Fidelio, the Kostelnicka in Jenůfa, Kundry, Isolde, Senta and Turandot; Guest appearances in Frankfurt, Salzburg, Copenhagen, the Berlin Staatsoper, Trieste, Leipzig, Berne, Mannheim, Toulon and Düsseldorf; Season 1988–89 with the title role in new productions of Mona Lisa by Schillings in Augsburg and Elektra in Innsbruck; Sang Elektra at the Vienna Staatsoper, June 1991; Brünnhilde in Die Walküre at Liège, the Dyer's Wife in Die Frau ohne Schatten at Augsburg, Nov 1991; Sang Elektra with Welsh National Opera, 1992; Sang with the Augsburg Opera until end of season 2000–01. *Address:* Music International, 13 Ardilaun Road, London N5 2QR, England.

HARDY, Rosemary; Singer (Soprano); b. 1949, England. *Education:* Studied at the Royal College of Music and at the Franz Liszt Academy, Budapest. *Career:* Performances with Roger Norrington, Michel Corboz and John Eliot Gardiner in The Baroque repertoire; Solo cantatas with the Drottningholm Baroque Ensemble, Sweden, at the Berlin Staatsoper and the Wigmore Hall; Sang in Jonathan Miller's production of Orfeo by Monteverdi; Modern repertoire includes Webern's music for voice at the Venice Biennale 1983 and the Cheltenham Festival; Webern recital at the Vienna Konzerthaus 1983; Schoenberg's 2nd Quartet (Arditti) for the Maggio Musicale, in Geneva and in London (BBC); Premieres of Jonathan Harvey's Passion and Resurrection and Song Offerings; Tours of France with Ensemble Intercontemporain, performing Boulez, Ravel, Varèse and Kurtag (Scenes from a Novel); has also given Kurtag's Sayings of R V Troussova; Appearances at the Glyndebourne Festival in Knussen's Where the Wild Things Are and Higgelty Piggelty Pop; Concert showings with the Hallé, City of Birmingham, San Diego, Danish Radio, BBC Symphony and London Symphony Orchestras; Has sung in Henze's The English Cat for the BBC and in Frankfurt and Italy; Concert with the Schoenberg Ensemble and the Nieuw Ensemble at the Holland Festival; Pierrot Lunaire in Milan, 1991; Tour with Capricorn on the Contemporary Music Network; Has also sung in Schubert Masses with the London Philharmonic, Mozart and Handel concert for the Cambridge Festival and concerts at the Aldeburgh Festival; Knussen's Where the Wild Things Are and Higglety Piggelty Pop at the London Proms, 2002. *Recordings:* Cavalli's Ercole Amante (Erato); Monteverdi's Combattimento, Il Ballo delle Ingrate and Scherzi Musicale. *Honours:* Artijus Prize, Hungary, 1983. *Address:* Phoenix Artists Management, 6 Windmill Street, London W1P 1HF, England.

HARE, Ian Christopher, MA, MusB, FRCO, ADCM, ARCM; musician; b. 26 Dec. 1949, Kingston upon Hull, England; m. (divorced 2002); two d. *Education:* Hymers Coll., Hull, King's Coll., Cambridge, Royal Coll. of Music. *Career:* Lecturer in Music, subsequently Organist, Lancaster Univ.; Organist and Master of Choristers Cartmel Priory 1981–89; suborganist Carlisle Cathedral 1989–95; founded and Musical Dir Lancaster Singers 1975–89; currently Dir of Music Crosthwaite Church; directs the Keswick and Wigton Choral Socs; Chorus Master Cumbria Rural Singers; Associated Bd examiner; adjudicator for organ competitions; performed in Britain and abroad, including France, Germany, USA as organ recitalist and accompanist; played at many of the major London venues, including the Proms; mem. Incorporated Soc. of Musicians, Royal Coll. of Organists, Incorporated Asscn of Organists. *Compositions:* Thou, O God Art Praised in Sion, anthem 1973, Beethoven's Hymn to Joy, organ arrangement 1974, A Child is Born, anthem 1987, Three Dances for Organ, Except the Lord build the house, anthem for SATB and Organ. *Recordings:* Handel's Messiah, Bach Cantata 147 and motets, Britten's Missa Brevis, St Nicholas, Once in Royal David's City, Hymns for all Seasons, King's Coll. Choir Cambridge 1968–72; In Pastures Green (The Organ of Crosthwaite Church Keswick). *Current Management:* J. Audrey Ellison, International Artists' Management, 135 Stevenage Road, Fulham, London, SW6 6PB, England. *Telephone:* (20) 7381-9751 (office). *Fax:* (20) 7381-2406 (office). *E-mail:* Audrey-Ellison@Intel.freeserve.co.uk (office). *Address:* The Porch, Skiddaw Lodge, Crosthwaite Road, Keswick, Cumbria, CA12 5QA, England (home). *Telephone:* (1768) 773342. *Fax:* (1768) 773342. *E-mail:* ian.hare@btopenworld.com.

HAREWOOD, 7th Earl of, cr. 1812; **George Henry Hubert Lascelles,** KBE; Musical Administrator; b. 7 Feb. 1923, London, England; m. (1) Maria Donata Stein, 1949, divorced 1967, (2) Patricia Tuckwell, 1967, 4 s. *Education:* King's College, Cambridge University. *Career:* Board

Directors, 1951–53, 1969–72, Administrative Executive, 1953–60, Royal Opera House, Covent Garden, London; Chairman, British Council Music Advisory Committee, 1956–66; Director General, 1958–74, Chairman, 1988–90, Leeds Musical Festival; Artistic Director, Edinburgh International Festival, 1961–65; Arts Council Music Panel, 1966–72; Artistic Adviser, New Philharmonic Orchestra, 1966–76; General Advisory Council, BBC, 1969–77; Managing Director, Sadler's Wells Opera, 1972; Managing Director, 1974–85, Chairman, 1986–95, English National Opera; Governor of BBC, 1985–87; President, British Board of Film Classification, 1985–96; Artistic Director, Adelaide Festival, 1988; Artistic Adviser, Buxton Festival, 1993–98. *Publications:* Editor, Opera, 1950–53; Editor and compiler, Kobbé's Complete Opera Book, 1954, 1973, 1987, 1989, 1997; Autobiography, The Tongs and The Bones, 1982; Kobbé's Illustrated Opera Books, 1989. *Address:* Harewood House, Leeds, LS17 9LG, England.

HARGAN, Alison; Singer (Soprano); b. 1943, Yorkshire, England. *Education:* Studied piano and singing at the Royal Northern College of Music. *Career:* Debut: With Welsh National Opera, as Pamina in Die Zauberflöte; Concert performances of music by Strauss and Mahler, Four Last Songs and Resurrection Symphony, and Verdi (Requiem); Appearances include Tippett's A Child of our Time with Neville Marriner, the Fauré Requiem with the Royal Philharmonic Orchestra and Bach's B Minor Mass in Lisbon; Britten's War Requiem with the Boston Symphony Orchestra and Mahler's 8th Symphony at La Fenice, Venice, conducted by Eliahu Inbal; Has also worked with Andrew Davis, Eugen Jochum, Erich Leinsdorf, Leppard, Ozawa, Pritchard, Colin Davis, Lorin Maazel, Simon Rattle, Richard Hickox and Rozhdestvensky; Orchestras include the Vienna Philharmonic, Munich Philharmonic and Los Angeles Philharmonic, as well as leading orchestras in the United Kingdom. *Address:* c/o City of Birmingham SO, CBSO Centre, Berkeley Street, Birmingham, B1 2LF, England.

HARGITAI, Geza; Violinist; b. 1940, Hungary. *Education:* Studied at the Franz Liszt Academy, Budapest. *Career:* Second Violinist of the Bartók Quartet from 1985; Performances in nearly every European country and tours of Australia, Canada, Japan, New Zealand and the USA; Festival appearances at Adelaide, Ascona, Aix, Venice, Dubrovnik, Edinburgh, Helsinki, Lucerne, Menton, Prague, Vienna, Spoleto and Schwetzingen; Tour of the United Kingdom 1986 including concerts at Cheltenham, Dartington, Philharmonic Hall Liverpool, RNCM Manchester and the Wigmore Hall; Tours of the United Kingdom 1988 and 1990, featuring visits to the Sheldonian Theatre, Oxford, Wigmore Hall, Harewood House and Birmingham; Repertoire includes standard classics and Hungarian works by Bartók, Durko, Bozay, Kadosa, Soproni, Farkas, Szabo and Lang. *Recordings include:* Complete quartets of Mozart, Beethoven and Brahms; Major works of Haydn and Schubert (Hungarton); Complete quartets of Bartók (Erato). *Current Management:* Ingpen & Williams Ltd, 7 St George's Court, 131 Putney Bridge Road, London, SW15 2PA, England.

HARGREAVES, Glenville; Singer (Baritone); b. 26 July 1950, Bradford, England. *Education:* Studied at St John's College, York, Royal Northern College of Music and London Opera Centre. *Career:* Debut: Title role in Il Barbiere di Siviglia, 1981; Covent Garden debut, 1982, in Les Contes d'Hoffmann; English National Opera from 1982, notably in Magic Flute, War and Peace, Salome; Modern repertory includes The Old Man, in Purgatory by Gordon Crosse; Walworth in Wat Tyler by Alan Bush; Longinus in The Catiline Conspiracy by Iain Hamilton (creation); Ullmann's Emperor of Atlantis; Mittenhofer in Henze's Elegy for Young Lovers (Queen Elizabeth Hall, London); Sir Charles Keighley in John Metcalf's Tornrak (creation, 1990); Appeared with Opera North as The Dark Fiddler in A Village Romeo and Juliet, Kothner in Meistersinger and roles in Tosca and The Bartered Bride; Welsh National Opera debut as Marcello in La Bohème; Has sung Rossini's Figaro in Netherlands and Belgium, and Falstaff with City of Birmingham Touring Opera; Season 1992 with Don Magnifico for Pimlico Opera and the Guardian in Elektra and title role in Don Pasquale for Welsh National Opera; Ankarstroem in Un Ballo in Maschera, WNO, 1993, also Don Alfonso for English Touring Opera; Other roles include Zurga (Les Pêcheurs de Perles), Nick Shadow, Germont, Don Giovanni, Mandryka, Paolo (Simon Boccanegra), Tonio, Scarpia, Demetrius (A Midsummer Night's Dream), Mozart's Count; Concert repertory includes Elijah, Judas Maccabaeus, The Kingdom, Messiah, Bruch's Odysseus, Puccini's Messa di Gloria, Sea Drift by Delius, Lieder eines fahrenden Gesellen by Mahler; Has sung with Hallé Choir, National Orchestra of Spain, Royal Choral Society and Royal Philharmonic Orchestra; Also sings in Bach's Passions and Carmina Burana; Appearances at Garsington Opera: Musiklehrer in Ariadne, 1993 and Count in Capriccio, 1994; Rigoletto for English Touring Opera, 1996 (Germont 1997); Season 1998 with Baldassare in L'Arlesiana for Opera Holland Park and Krusina in The Bartered Bride for Opera North; Season 2000 at Garsington Opera in Schumann's Genoveva and at Bad Wildbad Festival as Astarotte in Rossini's Armida. *Recordings:* Old Man, in Purgatory. *Address:* c/o

Musichall Ltd, Vicarage Way, Ringmer, East Sussex, BN8 5 LA, England.

HARJANNE, Jouko; Finnish trumpeter; *Artistic Director, Lieksa Brass Week;* b. 21 June 1962, Rauma. *Education:* Tampere Conservatory with Raimo Sarmas, studied with Henri Adelbrecht and Timofey Dokshitser. *Career:* concerto debut with Finnish Radio Symphony Orchestra 1978; co-principal trumpeter, Tampere Philhamonic Orchestra 1978–84; principal trumpet, Finnish Radio Symphony Orchestra 1984–; chamber musician with many ensembles, including Finnish Brass Ensemble, Brasstime Quartet and Protoventus Ensemble; Prof., Sibelius Acad., Helsinki 1989–; Artistic Dir, Lieksa Brass Week 1996–; has given first performances of concertos by Segerstam 1984, Gruner 1987, 1992, Linkola 1988, 1993, Wessman 1991, Bashmakov 1992, European première of Schedrin's Concerto 1995. *Recordings include:* concertos by Haydn, Hummel, Shostakovich, Jolivet, Goedicke, Harut'unyan, Vasilenko, Tamberg and Zimmermann, and works by Finnish composers. *Honours:* second prize Prague Spring Int. Competition 1987, Lieksa Brass Week Brass Player of the Year Award 1989, first place Int. Trumpet Guild Ellsworth Smith Trumpet Competition 1990. *Address:* c/o Lieksa Brass Week, Koski-Jaakonkatu 4, 81700 Lieksa, Finland (office). *Telephone:* 13 689 4147. *Fax:* 13 689 4915 (office). *E-mail:* brass .week@lieksa.fi (office). *Website:* www.joukoharjanne.com.

HARLE, John (Crofton); Saxophonist, Composer, Arranger and Conductor; b. 20 Sept. 1956, England; m. 1985, Julia Jane Eisner, 2 s. *Education:* Royal College of Music, Foundation School; ARCM, Hons 1978; Private study in Paris, 1981–82; FGSM 1990. *Career:* Leader of Myrha Saxophone Quartet, 1977–82; Formed duo with Pianist John Lenehan, 1979; Saxophone soloist, 1980–, with major international orchestras including, London Symphony Orchestra, English Chamber Orchestra; Basel Chamber Orchestra; San Diego Symphony Orchestra; Principal Saxophone, London Sinfonietta, 1987–; Professor of Saxophone, GSMD, 1988–; Formed Berliner Band, 1983, John Harle Band, 1988; Premiered Birtwistle's Panic at the Last Night of the London Proms, 1995; Opera Angel Magick premiered at the 1998 London Proms; World premiere of The Little Death Machine at the London Prom, 2002. *Compositions:* Several Ensembles, 1983–, including London Brass and London Symphony Orchestra; Opera, Angel Magick, London Proms, 1998; Frequent composer and soloist on television and feature films; Regular broadcaster on BBC radio; Featured in One Man and his Sax, BBC2, 1988. *Recordings:* Has made many recordings; Major works written for him by Dominic Muldowney, Ned Rorem, Richard Rodney Bennett, Luciano Berio, Michael Nyman, Gavin Bryars, Mike Westbrook and Stanley Myers. *Publications:* John Harle's Saxophone Album, 1986. *Honours:* Dannreuther Concerto Prize, Royal College of Music, 1980; GLAA Young Musician, 1979, 1980. *Website:* www.johnharle.com.

HARNONCOURT, Nikolaus; Austrian cellist and conductor; b. 6 Dec. 1929, Berlin, Germany; s. of Eberhard and Ladislaja Harnoncourt (née Meran); m. Alice Hoffelner 1953; three s. one d. *Education:* Matura Gymnasium, Graz, Acad. of Music, Vienna. *Career:* cellist mem. of Vienna Symphony Orchestra 1952–69; solo concerts on viola da gamba; international debuts 1966; Prof., Mozarteum and Inst. of Musicology, Univ. of Salzburg 1972–; Founder-mem. of Concentus Musicus, Ensemble for Ancient Music 1954; Conductor, Zürich Opera and Amsterdam Concertgebouw Orkest; conducted Schubert's Alfonso, Vienna Festival 1997, La Perichole, Zürich 1998, Die Fledermaus, Vienna 2001; engaged for Le nozze di Figaro at Salzburg 2005; has given numerous concerts in Europe, Australia and the USA. *Recordings include:* many works with Concentus Musicus, notably Handel's Messiah, Bach's Brandenburg Concertos and Cantatas, operas by Monteverdi and Rameau (Castor et Pollux), Bach's B Minor Mass, Don Giovanni 1990, Die Schöpfung with Vienna Symphony Orchestra, Idomeneo with Zurich Opera, Telemann Tafelmusik. *Publications:* Musik als Klangrede, Wege zu einem neuen Musikverständnis 1982, Der musikalische Dialog 1983. *Honours:* Hon. DMus (Univ. of Edin.) 1987; shared Erasmus Prize 1980; H. G. Nägeli Medal, Zürich 1983; numerous awards for recordings. *Address:* 38 Piaristengasse, 1080 Vienna, Austria.

HARNOY, Ofra; Cellist; b. 31 Jan. 1965, Hadera, Israel. *Education:* Studied with father, Vladimir Orloff, William Pleeth; Masterclasses with Mstislav Rostropovich, Pierre Fournier, Jacqueline du Pré. *Career:* Debut: Aged 10, as Soloist with Boyd Neel and his Orchestra; Soloist with numerous major orchestras, and solo recitals, USA, Canada, Japan, France, Austria, Hong Kong, Italy, Turkey, Germany, England, Israel, Australia, Netherlands, Belgium, Spain, Luxembourg, Venezuela; Featured in over 500 nationally televised solo-concerts or documentaries in Canada, England, Japan, Australia, Netherlands, Belgium, Italy, France; Radio broadcasts throughout the world; Regular Soloist, world premiere of Jacques Offenbach Cello Concerto, North American premiere, Arthur Bliss Cello Concerto. *Recordings:* 38 solo albums RCA Victor; London; Pro Arte, including Vivaldi Cello Concertos. *Honours:* 1st Prize, Montreal Symphony Competition,

1978; Canadian Music Competition Winner, 1979; Concert Artists Guild Award, New York, 1982; Grand Prix du Disque, 1988; Juno Award (as Best Classical Soloist, Canada), 1988, 1989, 1990, 1992; Order of Canada, 1995. *Address:* Suite 1000, 121 Richmond Street West, Toronto, Ontario M5H 2K1, Canada.

HARPER, Edward (James); Composer and Teacher; b. 17 March 1941, Taunton, Somerset, England; m. Dorothy Shanks, 22 Oct 1984, (died 2000) 1 s., 1 d m. Louise Paterson 2003. *Education:* Studied music at Christ Church, Oxford, 1959–63, composition with Gordon Jacob at Royal College of Music; Further study with Franco Donatoni in Milan, 1968. *Career:* Lecturer, 1964–, Reader, Faculty of Music, Edinburgh Univ.; Dir of New Music Group of Scotland, 1973–91. *Compositions include:* Piano Concerto, 1969; Sonata for chamber orchestra, 1971; Bartók Games for orchestra, 1972; Quintet for piano, flute, clarinet, violin and cello, 1974; Ricercari in Memoriam Luigi Dallapiccola for 11 instruments, 1975; Fanny Robin, chamber opera, 1975; Fantasia 1 for chamber orchestra, 1976; Fantasia II for 11 strings, 1976; Fantasia III for brass quintet, 1977; Fern Hill for chamber orchestra, 1977; Poems, to text by e e cummings for soprano and orchestra, 1977; Chester Mass for chorus and orchestra, 1979; Symphony, 1979; Clarinet Concerto, 1982; Intrada after Monteverdi for chamber orchestra, 1982; Hedda Gabler, full length opera, 1985; Mass, Qui Creavit Coelum, 1986; In Memoriam Kenneth Leighton for cello and piano, 1989; Homage to Thomas Hardy for baritone and orchestra, 1990; The Lamb for soprano, chorus and orchestra, 1990; Lights Out, 4 poems by Edward Thomas for soprano, recorder, cello, harpsichord, 1993; The Spire, chamber opera, 1996; Trio for clarinet, cello and piano, 1997; Souvenir for 2 pianos and percussion, 1998; Etude for orchestra, 1999; Lochinvar, opera for schools, 2000; Elegy for horn and orchestra, 2002; Music for King Arthur, for primary school choirs, brass and percussion, 2002; The Voice of a City, for primary school choirs, adult community choir, chamber orchestra and organ, 2003. *Recordings:* Bartók Games; Fanny Robin; Fantasia III; Ricercari; Qui Creavit Coelum; The Universe; Lights Out; Clarinet Concerto, 2001. *Address:* 7 Morningside Park, Edinburgh EH10 5HD, Scotland.

HARPER, Heather; Singer (Soprano); b. 8 May 1930, Belfast, Northern Ireland; m. (2) Eduardo J Benarroch, 1973. *Education:* Trinity College of Music, London. *Career:* Debut: Eurydice, in first London performance of Haydn's Orfeo (concert), 1995; Created Soprano Role in Britten's War Requiem, Coventry Cathedral, 1962; Toured USA with BBC Symphony Orchestra, 1965, USSR 1967; Soloist, Opening Concerts, Maltings, Snape, 1967, Queen Elizabeth Hall, principal Soloist, BBC Symphony Orchestra on 1982 tour of Hong Kong and Australia; Principal Soloist, Royal Opera House, La Scala, Milan, 1976, Japan and Korea, 1979, USA Visit 1984; Professor and Consultant, Royal College of Music, London, 1985–; Director of Singing Studies, Britten-Pears School, Snape, 1986–; First Visiting Lecturer in Residence, Royal Scottish Academy, Glasgow, 1987–; Concerts in Asia, Middle East, Australia, European Music Festivals, South America; Principal Roles at Covent Garden, Bayreuth Festivals, La Scala (Milan), Teatro Col ón (Buenos Aires), Edinburgh Festival, Glyndebourne, Sadler's Wells, Metropolitan Opera House (New York), San Francisco, Frankfurt, Deutsche Oper (Berlin), Japan (with Royal Opera House Covent Garden Co), Netherlands Opera House, New York City Opera; Renowned performances of Arabella, Ariadne, Chrysothemis, Empress, Marschallin; Television roles include Ellen Orford; Mrs Coyle (Owen Wingrave); Ilia; Donna Elvira; La Traviata, La Bohème; Principal Soloist, Promenade Concerts, 25 consecutive years; Sang in the first performance of Britten's War Requiem 1962 and Tippett's 3rd Symphony 1972; Last solo appearance in the Four Last Songs of Strauss, Belfast March 1989; Nadia in The Ice Break at the 1990 Promenade Concerts. *Recordings include:* Les Illuminations (Britten); Symphony No. 8 (Mahler); Don Giovanni (Mozart); Requiem (Verdi) and Missa Solemnis (Beethoven); Seven Early Songs (Berg); Marriage of Figaro; Peter Grimes; Strauss's Four Last Songs (First British soprano recording). *Honours:* C.B.E.; Honorary Fellow, Trinity College of Music; Honorary Member, RAM; Hon D.Mus, Queen's University; Edison Award, 1971; Grammy Award, 1979; Grand Prix Du Disque, 1979; Grammy Award (Best Solo Recording), 1984.

HARPER, John Martin, MA, PhD; *Director-General, Royal School of Church Music;* b. 11 July 1947; m. Sally Harper. *Education:* King's Coll. School, Cambridge, Clifton Coll., Bristol, Selwyn Coll., Cambridge, Birmingham Univ. *Career:* music tutor West Bromwich Arts Centre 1970–71; Dir Edington Festival 1971–78; Dir of Music St Chad's Cathedral, Birmingham 1972–78; Lecturer in Music Birmingham Univ. 1974–75, 1976–81; Asst Dir of Music King Edward's School, Birmingham 1975–76; Fellow, organist, Informator Choristarum and tutor in music, Magdalen Coll.; Univ. Lecturer, Oxford 1981–90, Univ. Coll. of North Wales, Univ. of Wales, Bangor; Prof. of Music 1991–98; RSCM Resident Prof. in Christian Music and Liturgy 1998–; Leverhulme Fellow 1997–98; Dir of Centre for Advanced Welsh Music Studies 1994–;

Ed. Welsh Music History 1996–; mem. Plainsong and Medieval Music Soc. (chair. 1998–), Guild of Church Musicians, Cathedral Organists Asscn (sec. 1998–), Cathedral Music Working Party, Early English Organ Project (trustee 1999–), Panel of Monastic Musicians (adviser 1976–), General Synod Liturgical Commission (consultant 2001–). *Compositions:* Choral Compositions 1974–ed Orlando Gibbons; Consort Music 82; The Forms and Orders of Western Liturgy 1991; ed Hymns for Prayer and Praise 1996; ed RSCM Music for Common Worship Series 2000. *Recordings:* The English Anthem (five vols), Magdalen Coll. Choir (Benemerenti Papal Award 1978). *Publications:* New Grove Dictionary of Music and Musicians 1980, Frescobaldi Studies 1987, Die Musik in Geschichte und Gegenwart 1994, Blackwell History of Music in Britain Vol. 2 1995, articles and reviews in music journals and papers. *Honours:* Hon. Fellow Guild of Church Musicians 1996. *Address:* Royal School of Church Music, Cleveland Lodge, Westhumble, Dorking, Surrey RH5 6BW, England (office). *Telephone:* (1306) 872800 (office). *Fax:* (1306) 887260 (office). *E-mail:* enquiries@rscm.com (office). *Website:* www.rscm .com (office).

HARPER, Thomas; Singer (Tenor); b. 1950, Oklahoma, USA. *Education:* Studied in Los Angeles, Kansas City, Paris and Italy. *Career:* Sang in opera at Coburg, 1982–85, Kaiserslautern, 1985–87, in buffo and character roles; Stadttheater Hagen, 1987–, as the Duke of Mantua, Radames, Almaviva, Don Ottavio, Alwa in Lulu and Daniel in Belshazar by David Kirchner; Sang Fritz in Der Ferne Klang by Schreker, 1989; Seattle Opera, 1991 and 1995, as Mime in Der Ring des Nibelungen; Dortmund Opera, 1991–92, as Mime and in premiere of Sekunden und Jahre des Caspar Hauser, by Reinhard Febel; Sang Mime in Siegfried at Turin, 1998; Season 2000–01 as Mime for Dallas and Geneva Operas. *Recordings include:* Der Ferne Klang (Marco Polo). *Address:* c/o Seattle Opera Association, PO Box 9248, Seattle, WA 98109, USA.

HARRELL, Lynn; cellist; b. 30 Jan. 1944, New York, NY, USA; m. Linda Blandford 1976; one s. one d. *Education:* studied with Lev Aronson in Dallas, Leonard Rose at the Juilliard School and Orlando Cole at the Curtis Institute; masterclasses with Gregor Piatigorsky, Casals. *Career:* debut with Dallas Symphony Orchestra, 1957; Solo Principal Cellist with Cleveland Orchestra, conductor George Szell, 1963–71; Numerous appearances with major orchestras in USA, Europe and Japan and world-wide recitals, 1971–; Piatigorsky Chair of Cello at University of Southern California, Los Angeles, 1986–92; International Chair of Cello Studies, Royal Academy of Music, London, 1986–92; Artistic Director of Los Angeles Philharmonic Institute, 1988–91; Music Adviser, San Diego Symphony, 1988 and 1989; Principal, Royal Academy of Music, 1993–95. *Recordings:* Dvořák Concerto with Ashkenazy, Cleveland; Lalo, Chailly, RSO; Shostakovich No. 1 and Bloch Schelomo, Haitink, Concertgebouw; Schumann Concerto, Marriner, Cleveland; Brahms and Beethoven Sonatas, Ashkenazy; Beethoven Trios, Ashkenazy, Perlman; Solo Bach Suites. *Honours:* Merriweather Post Contest, 1960; Piatigorsky Award, 1962; 1st Winner, with Murray Perahia, Avery Fisher Prize, 1974. *Current Management:* IMG Artists, Lovell House, 616 Chiswick High Road, London W4 5RX, England.

HARRHY, Eiddwen; Singer (Soprano); b. 14 April 1949, Trowbridge, Wiltshire, England; m. Gregory Strange, 22 Jan 1988, 1 d. *Education:* Studied at the Royal Manchester College of Music and in London and Paris. *Career:* Debut: Royal Opera House, Ring Cycle, 1974; English National Opera 1975, Marriage of Figaro, Magic Flute, Carmen, Le Comte Ory; Appeared with all the major British orchestras and opera companies; Sang in Europe (Paris, Amsterdam, Berlin, Barcelona and many other venues), USA, Hong Kong, Sydney and Wellington; Vocal Tutor at Welsh College of Music and Drama, 1996–2001; Professor at Royal College of Music, London, 2001–; mem, Musicians Benevolent Fund. *Recordings:* Handel's Alcina and Amadigi, Beethoven's 9th Symphony, Fairy Queen for major record companies. *Honours:* Miriam Licette, 1972; Imperial League of Opera, RMCM, 1972. *Current Management:* Phoenix Artists Management, 6 Windmill Street, London W1P 1HF, England.

HARRIES, Kathryn; Singer (Soprano); b. 15 Feb. 1951, Hampton Court, Middlesex, England. *Education:* Studied at the Royal Academy of Music with Constance Shacklock. *Career:* Presented BBC television series Music Time; Festival Hall, London, debut 1977: concert repertoire ranges from Monteverdi to the 20th Century; Operatic debut with the Welsh National Opera 1982, as Leonore: returned as Sieglinde and Gutrune (also at Covent Garden, 1986), Adalgisa, and the Composer in Ariadne auf Naxos; English National Opera as Eva, Female Chorus in The Rape of Lucretia, Irene (Rienzi) and Donna Anna in The Stone Guest by Dargomyzhsky; Appearances with Scottish Opera as Leonore, the title role in the premiere of Hedda Gabler by Edward Harper, and Senta; Metropolitan Opera 1986, as Kundry in Parsifal: returned 1989, as Gutrune in a new production of Götterdämmerung; Sang Dido in the first complete performance of Les Troyens in France, Lyon 1987, Senta for Paris Opéra, Sieglinde in Nice and Paris and Leonore in Buenos Aires; Covent Garden debut 1989, in the British premiere of Un Re in

Ascolto by Berio; returned 1991 as Gutrune in a new production of Götterdämmerung; Dido in Les Troyens for Scottish Opera, 1990, also at Covent Garden; season 1990–91 with Katya Kabanova at ENO, Bartók's Judith for Scottish Opera, Dukas' Ariane, Netherlands Opera, Massenet's Cléopâtre in St Etienne and Giulietta in Les Contes d'Hoffmann at the Châtelet in Paris; Season 1992 with the Berlioz Dido in Brussels and Carmen at Orange; Sang Brangaene for Scottish Opera, 1994 and 1998; Kundry in Parsifal at the Opéra Bastille, Paris, 1997; Engaged for the Kostelnicka in Jenůfa at Chicago 2000; Season 2000–01 in the premieres of Rêves d'un Marco Polo by Claude Vivier, at Amsterdam, and David Sawyer's From Morning to Midnight, for ENO. *Current Management:* Ingpen & Williams Ltd, 7 St George's Court, 131 Putney Bridge Road, London, SW15 2PA, England.

HARRIS, Donald, BMus, MMus; American composer and musicologist; b. 7 April 1931, St Paul, MN; m. Marilyn Hackett 1983; two s. (from previous marriage). *Education:* University of Michigan; studied with Paul Wilkinson, St Paul, Minnesota, Ross Lee Finney, University of Michigan, Nadia Boulanger, Max Deutsch and André Jolivet in Paris, France. *Career:* Administrator, New England Conservatory, 1968–77; Dean, Hartt School of Music, University of Hartford, 1980–88; Dean, College of Fine Arts, The Ohio State University, 1988–97; Incidental Music, Poet with the Blue Guitar, Connecticut Public Radio, 1979; Incidental Music, Fires, Connecticut Public Radio, 1983. *Compositions include:* Piano Sonata; Violin Fantasy; Symphony in Two Movements; On Variations; For the Night to Wear; Balladen; Little Mermaid, opera; Two String Quartets; Ludus I; Ludus II; Of Hartford in a Purple Light (Wallace Stevens); Les Mains (Marguerite Yourcenar). *Publications:* Co-Editor, Correspondence between Alban Berg and Arnold Schoenberg, New York. *Contributions:* Journal of the Arnold Schoenberg Institute; Perspective of New Music; Newsletter, International Alban Berg Society; Music Journal; Alban Berg Studien, Universal Edition. *Address:* 5257 Courtney Place, Columbus, OH 43235-3474, USA.

HARRIS, Ellen, BA, PhD; American musicologist; b. 4 Dec. 1945, Paterson, NJ. *Education:* Brown Univ., Univ. of Chicago, with Edward Lowinsky and Howard M. Brown. *Career:* Columbia Univ. 1977–80; Univ. of Chicago from 1980, Prof. 1988; Massachusetts Inst. of Technology 1989–; active as singer in the Baroque repertory; musical consultant, Santa Fe Opera 2001; Renee Fleming 2003; Fellow, American Acad. of Arts and Sciences 1998; mem., Inst. for Advanced Study 2004. *Publications:* Handel and the Pastoral Tradition 1980, Henry Purcell's Dido and Aeneas 1987, Handel as Orpheus: Voice and Desire in the Chamber Cantatas 2001; editions: Purcell, Dido and Aeneas 1987, The Librettos of Handel's Operas (ed.) 1989, G. F. Handel, Alto Cantatas 2001; articles: The Italian in Handel 1980, Handel's London Cantatas 1984, Shakespeare in Music 1985, Handel's Ghost: The Composer's Posthumous Reputation in the Eighteenth Century 1992, Harmonic Patterns in Handel's Operas 1994, Integrity and Improvisation in the Music of Handel 1990, Why Study the Arts – Along with Science and Math 1992, King Arthur's Journey into the Eighteenth Century 1995, Twentieth Century Farinelli 1997, Metastasio and Sonata Form 1999, Jaames Hunter, Handel's Friend 2000. *Honours:* ACLS Fellowship 1980–81, NEH Fellowship 1988–89, Bunting Inst. Fellowship 1995–96, American Musicological Soc. Otto Kinkeldey Award 2002. *Address:* c/o Music Department, Massachusetts Institute of Technology, Boston MS, USA. *E-mail:* eharris@mit.edu (office).

HARRIS, Hilda; Singer (Mezzo-soprano); b. 1930, Warrenton, North Carolina, USA. *Education:* Studied at North Carolina State University and in New York. *Career:* Sang in musicals on Broadway; Made opera debut at St Gallen, Switzerland, 1971, as Carmen; Returned to New York, 1973, as Nicklausse in Les Contes d'Hoffmann at City Opera and in Virgil Thomson's Four Saints in Three Acts (as St Theresa) at the Metropolitan; Further roles at the Met have included the Child in L'Enfant et les Sortilèges, Cherubino, Hansel, Stephano in Roméo et Juliette and parts in Lulu; Sang Nicklausse at Seattle, 1990, Cherubino at the 1990 Spoleto Festival; Frequent concert appearances. *Address:* c/o Metropolitan Opera, Lincoln Center, New York, NY 10023, USA.

HARRIS, John; Singer (Dramatic Tenor); b. 5 Dec. 1944, England. *Education:* Studied at the Birmingham Conservatoire. *Career:* Appearances with the Royal Opera House, Covent Garden, Welsh National Opera, English National Opera, Scottish Opera and Opera North, Glyndebourne, The Old Vic; Performances in New York, Tokyo, Tel Aviv, Milan, Paris, Munich, Dortmund, Dublin; Concert work includes Messiah and Verdi's Requiem at the Royal Albert Hall; Roles have included: Mime, Wagner's Ring Cycle; Don José, Carmen; Peter Grimes; Lensky, Eugene Onegin; Skuratov, From the House of the Dead; Tichon in Katya Kabanova; Bardolfo, Falstaff; Goro, Madama Butterfly; Laca in Jenůfa; Vitek, Makropoulos Case; Don José, Carmen; Monostatos, The Magic Flute; Florestan, Fidelio; Melot, Tristan und Isolde; The Ringmaster, The Bartered Bride; Sang with Welsh National Opera in the premiere of Metcalf's Tornrak, 1990; Mime in Siegfried at Covent Garden and for WNO; Red Whiskers in Billy Budd, 1998; Television performances for BBC, Channel 4, HTV, RTE; BBC Radio 3. *Recordings include:* Opera recordings for EMI, Decca and Suprafon (Czech Republic). *Address:* 41 Queen's Road, Penarth, Vale of Glamorgan CF64 1 DL, Wales. *Telephone:* (0)29 20 700823.

HARRIS, Matthew; Composer; b. 18 Feb. 1956, North Tarrytown, New York, USA; m. 4 Dec 1988. *Education:* New England Conservatory, with Donald Martino, 1974–75; Fontainbleau School, with Nadia Boulanger, France, 1976; BM, 1978, MM, 1979, DMA, 1982, Juilliard School of Music; Harvard Graduate School, 1985–86. *Career:* Major performances: New York New Music Ensemble, 1983; Houston Symphony, 1986; Minnesota Orchestra, 1987; League/ISCM, New York, 1987; Florida Symphony Orchestra, 1988; Alea III, Boston, 1988; Assistant Professor, Fordham University, 1982–84; Instructor, Kingsborough College, City University of New York, 1985; Music Editor, Carl Fischer Inc, 1987–; mem, Broadcast Music Inc; Composers Forum; American Music Center; Board Member, League-International Society for Contemporary Music. *Compositions:* Music After Rimbaud; Songs of the Night, soprano, orchestra; Ancient Greek Melodies, orchestra; As You Choose, monodrama; Starry Night, piano trio; Invitation of the Waltz, string quartet; string Quartet No. 7. *Recordings:* Music After Rimbaud, Opus One Commissions: Casa Verde Trio, 1984; Haydn-Mozart Orchestra, 1985; Scott Stevens: Leigh Howard Stevens, marimbist, 1986; Minnesota Composers Forum: Omega String Quartet, 1988; The Schubert Club; Anthony Ross, cellist, 1988. *Address:* American Composers Edition, 170 W 74th Street, New York, NY 10023, USA.

HARRIS, Paul, ARAM, GRSM, ARCM, LRAM; British composer, teacher, performer and examiner and adjudicator; b. London, England. *Education:* Haberdashers' Aske's School, Royal Acad. of Music, London Univ. *Career:* mem. Incorporated Soc. of Musicians, Royal Soc. of Musicians. *Compositions:* five Buckingham Concertos, Arrows of Desire (ballet), The Meal (children's opera), the Improve your Sight Reading, Improve your Scales, Improve your Practice series. *Publications:* The Music Teachers' Companion 2000, Clarinet Basics; contrib. to Libretto (ABRSM), ICA Magazine, The Strad, BBC Music Magazine, ISM Journal, Clarinet and Saxophone Soc. Magazine, Beckus (Malcolm Arnold Soc.). *Address:* 15 Mallard Drive, Buckingham, MK18 1GJ, England (home). *Telephone:* (1280) 813144 (home).

HARRIS, Ross; Composer; b. 1 Aug. 1945, Amberley, New Zealand. *Education:* University of Canterbury, and with Douglas Lilburn at Victoria University, Wellington. *Career:* Associate Professor at Victoria University from 1989; Freelance composer, notably with electronic resources. *Compositions include:* Trio for flute, viola and harp, 1973; To a Child, for tape, 1973; Shadow Music, 1977; Skymning, 1978; Echo, 1979; The Hills of Time, for orchestra, 1980; Incantation, soprano and tape, 1981; Life in Peace, for choir and synthesizer, 1983; Waituki, opera, 1984; Evocation, for flute, cello and synthesizer, 1985; Flüchtig, flute and tape, 1986; Kaiku, 1987; Dreams, Yellow Lions, for baritone and chamber ensemble, 1987; Mosaic (Water), 1990; Tanz der Schwäne, chamber opera, 1989; Wind Quintet, 1989; Harmonicity, 1991; Horn Call on Makara Cliff, horn and tape, 1991; 2 string quartets, 1991, 1998; 2 Chamber Concertos, 1994, 1996; Piano Trio, 1995; Sinfonietta for strings, 1996; Inharmonicity, piano and tape, 1998. *Address:* c/o Music Faculty, Victoria University, Wellington, New Zealand.

HARRISON, Jonty; Composer and Lecturer; b. 27 April 1952, Scunthorpe, England; m. Alison Warne 1985. *Education:* BA, DPhil, University of York, 1970–76; British Youth Symphony Orchestra, National Youth Orchestra of Great Britain; Studied composition with Bernard Rands. *Career:* National Theatre, London; Visiting Composer, University of East Anglia Recording and Electronic Music Studio, 1978; Visiting Lecturer, City University, London, 1978–80; Reader in Composition and Electro-acoustic Music, Director of Electro-acoustic Music Studio, The University of Birmingham, 1980–; Hungarian Radio, 1982; IRCAM, 1985; Groupe de Recherches Musicales, Paris, 1986, 1993; Groupe de Musique Expérimentale de Bourges, 1987, 1995. *Compositions:* Q, 1976; Lunga, 1977; Pair/Impair, 1978; SQ, 1979; Rosaces 3, 1980; EQ, 1980; Monodies, 1981; Rosaces 4, 1982; Klang, 1982; Sons transmutants/sans transmutant, 1983; Hammer and Tongs, 1984; Paroles hérétiques, 1986; Tremulous Couplings, 1986; Farben, 1987; Aria, 1988; Concerto Caldo, 1991;... et ainsi de suite..., 1992; Ottone, 1992; Hot Air, 1995; Unsound Objects, 1995; Sorties, 1995; Hot Air, 1996; Surface Tension, 1996; Splintering, 1997; Abstracts, 1998. *Recordings:* Sons transmutants/sans transmutant (Fine Arts Brass Ensemble); Ottone (Fine Arts Brass Ensemble); Klang; EQ (Daniel Kientzy);...et ainsi de suite... EQ (Stephen Cottrell); Pair/Impair; Aria; Unsound Objects; Streams, 1999. *Publications:* Q; Sons transmutants/sans transmutant; Hammer and Tongs; Concerto Caldo; Rosaces 4; Paroles hérétiques; Paroles plus hérétiques; Tremulous Couplings; EQ; Ottone, all 1996. *Contributions:* Electro-Acoustic Music; Music and Letters; The Musical Times; Lien (Musiques et Recherches-Belgium); Upbeat to the Tate 88–Liverpool (Programme Book); The Journal of

Electro-acoustic Music; Organised Sound. *Address:* 9 Prospect Road, Moseley, Birmingham B13 9TB, England.

HARRISON, Sally; singer (soprano); b. 1965, England. *Education:* Univ. of Oxford and Royal Northern College of Music; further study with Ava June. *Career:* sang Manon and Gilda with Royal Northern College of Music, 1987–88; Season 1988–89 as Musetta in Singapore, Handel's Morgana at Royal Northern College of Music and Amour in Rameau's Pygmalion for the English Bach Festival at Queen Elizabeth Hall; Season 1989–90 with Scottish Opera as Polly in The Threepenny Opera, Minette in Henze's English Cat at Guttersloh and Berlin, repeated at Montepulciano Festival and for BBC, and Messiah with Bournemouth Sinfonietta; English National Opera debut, 1991, as Barbarina in Le nozze di Figaro; Sang Handel's Galatea with the English Bach Festival at Queen Elizabeth Hall, 1992; Despina, at the 1992 Buxton Festival; Other concert repertoire includes Elgar's The Kingdom, Henze's Being Beauteous (Barbican Hall debut, 1990) and works with the Hague Philharmonic and Ensemble Modern of Frankfurt; Sang Gilda at Bristol, 1994; Pamina, for English National Opera, 1996; Television appearance in The English Cat, for German television; Season 1998 with Lucia for Stowe Opera and Musetta in Hong Kong. *Honours:* Peter Moores Foundation Scholarship. *Current Management:* Robert Gilder & Co., Enterprise House, 59–65 Upper Ground, London, SE1 9PQ, England. *Telephone:* (20) 7928-9008. *Fax:* (20) 7928-9755. *E-mail:* rgilder@robert-gilder.com.

HART-DAVIS, Michael; Singer (tenor); b. 1968, Worcester, England. *Career:* Glyndebourne Festival from 1995, as Atallo in Rossini's Ermione, Messenger in Theodora, Lamplighter in Manon Lescaut, and Thomas in The Last Supper by Birtwistle, 2001; Glyndebourne Tour as Mozart's Don Curzio, Janek in The Makropulos Case and Rossini's Comte Ory; Further appearances as Don Curzio for Netherlands Opera, Agenor in Il Re Pastore for Opera North and Rossini's Almaviva for English National Opera and Mid-Wales Opera; Chelsea Opera Group as Innkeeper in Benvenuto Cellini and Pallas in Cherevichki by Tchaikovsky; Concerts include Messiah at the Albert Hall under David Willcocks, and engagements at Verbier, Geneva, Lyon and Annecy; Season 2001–2002 as Ramiro in La Cenerentola for Opera Zürich. *Current Management:* Musicmakers International Artists Representation, Tailor House, 63–65 High Street, Whitwell, Hertfordshire SG4 8AH, England. *Telephone:* (1438) 871708. *Fax:* (1438) 871777. *E-mail:* musicmakers@compuserve.com. *Website:* www.operauk.com. *Address:* c/o Glyndebourne Festival Opera, Lewes, Sussex BN8 5UU, England. *Telephone:* 01273 812321. *Fax:* 01273 812783.

HARTELIUS, Malin; Singer (Soprano); b. 1961, Vaxjo, Sweden. *Education:* Studied at the Vienna Conservatory with Margaret Bence. *Career:* Debut: Vienna (Raimund-Theater) as Christel in Der Vogelhändler, 1986; Sang at Baden and St Gallen, then Ludwigsburg Festival, 1990, as Blondchen; Vienna Staatsoper from 1990, notably as Esmerelda in The Bartered Bride; Member of the Zürich Opera, 1991–92, as Papagena, Sophie and Adele; Salzburg Festival, 1992, as Barbarina in Le nozze di Figaro; Many appearances in operetta and on the concert platform; Salzburg Festival 1993 as Nausikaa in Dallapiccola's Ulisse; Zürich from 1994 as Pamina, Rossini's Elvira and Cimarosa's Elisette; Salzburg 1998 as Mozart's Blondchen; Season 2000 as Schubert's Estrella at Zürich, Dirce in Cherubini's Médée at Salzburg and Marzelline in Munich. *Address:* c/o Zürich Opera, Falkenstrasse 1, 8008 Zürich, Switzerland.

HARTEROS, Anja; Singer (Soprano); b. 1972, Germany. *Education:* Studied at Cologne and Perugia. *Career:* Debut: 1996; Appearances in Germany and throughout Europe as Mozart's Countess and Fiordiligi; Mimi in La Bohème; Season 1999–2000: Cardiff Singer of the World Winner's Concert at the Barbican Hall, London and Fiordiligi in Così fan tutte for Bonn Opera; Engaged as Fiordiligi for the 2001 Edinburgh Festival; Sang Agathe and Mimi, Munich and Vienna State Operas, 1999; Season 2000–01 as Fiordiligi at Frankfurt and Lyon, Mozart's Countess at Munich and Mimi for the Deutsche Oper Berlin. *Honours:* Winner, Cardiff Singer of the World Competition, 1999. *Address:* c/o Bonn Opera, Am Boeselagerhof 1, 53111 Bonn, Germany.

HARTH, Sidney; Violinist, Conductor and Professor; b. 5 Oct. 1929, Cleveland, Ohion, USA; m. Teresa Testa Harth. *Education:* Cleveland Institute of Music, MB, 1947; Pupil of Joseph Fuchs and Georges Enesco. *Career:* Debut, Carnegie Hall, New York, 1949; Concertmaster and Assistant Conductor, Louisville Orchestra, 1953–58; Faculty Member, University of Louisville; Concertmaster, Chicago Symphony Orchestra, 1959–62; Faculty Member, De Paul University; Concertmaster, Casals Festival Orchestra, San Juan, 1959–65, 1972; Professor of Music and Chairman of the Music Department, Carnegie-Mellon University, Pittsburgh, 1963–73; Concertmaster and Associate Conductor, Los Angeles Philharmonic Orchestra, 1973–79; Music Director, Puerto Rico Symphony Orchestra, 1977–79; Interim Conductor, New York Philharmonic Orchestra, 1980; Orchestral Director, Mannes

College of Music, New York, 1981–; Professor of Violin at SUNY, Stony Brook. *Address:* c/o Mannes College of Music, 150 West 85th Street, New York, NY 10024, USA.

HARTKE, Stephen (Paul); Composer; b. 6 July 1952, New Jersey, USA; m. Lisa Stidham, 12 Sept 1981, 1 s. *Education:* BA, magna cum laude, Yale University, 1973; MA, University of Pennsylvania, 1976; PhD, University of California, Santa Barbara, 1982; Composition study with James Drew, George Rochberg and Edward Applebaum. *Career:* Fulbright Professor of Composition, University of São Paulo, Brazil, 1984–85; Professor of Composition, University of Southern California, 1987–; Composer-in-Residence, Los Angeles Chamber Orchestra, 1988–92; mem, American Music Center. *Compositions:* Alvorada; Iglesia Abandonada; The King of The Sun; Maltese Cat Blues; Oh Them Rats is Mean in My Kitchen; Pacific Rim; Sonata Variations; Songs for an Uncertain Age; Caoine; Night Rubrics; Post-Modern Homages; Symphony No. 2; Four Madrigals on Old Portuguese Texts; Wir Küssen Ihnen Tausendmal die Hände; Violin Concerto; Wulfstan at The Millennium, 1995; The Ascent of the Equestrian in a Balloon, 1995; Sons of Noah, 1996; The Horse with the Lavender Eye, 1997; Piano Sonata, 1998; The Rose of the Winds, 1998. *Recordings:* Caoine; Iglesia Abandonada; Oh Them Rats is Mean in My Kitchen; Wir Küssen Ihnen Tausendmal die Hände; The King of The Sun; Sonata-Variations; Night Rubrics; Concerto for violin and orchestra; Symphony No. 2; The Ascent of the Equestrian in a Balloon. *Contributions:* Caderno de Musica, 1985; Minnesota Composers Forum Newsletter, 1988. *Honours:* Rome Prize, 1992; Academy Award, American Academy of Arts and Letters, 1993; Chamber Music Society of Lincoln Center Stoeger Award, 1997; Guggenheim Fellowship, 1997–98. *Address:* School of Music, University of Southern California, Los Angeles, CA 90089, USA.

HARTLIEP, Nikki; Singer (Soprano); b. 22 Sept. 1955, Naha, Okinawa, Japan. *Education:* Studied at San Francisco Conservatory. *Career:* Debut: Western Opera, San Francisco, 1982; Appearances at Chicago Opera, 1987–88, as Ellen Orford in Peter Grimes (Tatiana in Eugene Onegin, 1990); Madama Butterfly at San Francisco Opera and elsewhere, from 1989 (Dublin, 1990); Other roles include Micaela, Antonia in Les contes d'Hoffmann, Alice Ford (Long Beach Opera, 1994) and Mimi; Numerous concert engagements. *Address:* c/o Long Beach Opera, 6372 Pacific Coast Highway, Long Beach, CA 90803, USA.

HARTMAN, Vernon; Singer (Baritone); b. 12 July 1952, Dallas, Texas, USA. *Education:* Studied at West Texas State University and in Philadelphia. *Career:* Debut: Philadelphia, as Masetto, 1977; Sang with New York City Opera from 1977 and made guest appearances at Cincinnati, San Antonio and Seattle; Spoleto Festival, 1977–78, as Guglielmo; Cincinnati 1990, as Enrico in Lucia di Lammermoor; Metropolitan Opera, 1983–, as Rossini's Figaro, Count Almaviva, Schaunard and Guglielmo; Other roles have included Rigoletto, Malatesta, Silvio, Marcello, Frank in Die Tote Stadt and Falke in Fledermaus; Sang Almaviva and Marcello at Milwaukee, 1991. *Address:* c/o Metropolitan Opera, Lincoln Center, New York, NY 10023, USA.

HARTMANN, Rudolf A.; Singer (baritone); b. 19 Jan. 1937, Bad Windsheim, Germany. *Education:* Munich Musikhochschule. *Career:* Sang at first as a bass, at Augsburg, then at Nuremberg in the baritone repertory; Member of the Zürich Opera from 1972, as Fluth in Die Lustige Weiber von Windsor, Faninal, Sharpless, Schaunard, Frank in Die Fledermaus (season 1996–97) and in the Swiss premiere of Jakob Lenz by Wolfgang Rihm; Guest engagements as Beckmesser at the Vienna and Hamburg State Operas and the Dresden Semperoper; Concert and recital engagements at Bayreuth, Florence, Salzburg, Munich and Vienna; Teacher of Voice at Zürich Conservatory and Musikhochschule. *Recordings:* Radio and CD recordings as Papageno, in the Solti Meistersinger, and the Eighth Book of Madrigals by Monteverdi, under Nikolaus Harnoncourt. *Address:* c/o Opernhaus Zürich, Falkenstrasse 1, 8008, Switzerland.

HARTMANN, Will; Singer (Tenor); b. 1968, Siegen, Germany. *Education:* Graduated Musikhochschule, Cologne, 1993. *Career:* Opera Studio, Cologne, 1991–93; Roles at Cologne Opera, 1993–96, included Papageno, Guglielmo, Schaunard, Morales (Carmen) and Harlequin in Ariadne auf Naxos; Hannover State Opera from 1996 as Dandini in Cenerentola, Monteverdi's Orfeo, Marcello and Rossini's Figaro; Further appearances at Munich, Bonn, Leipzig, Rome and Orange; Royal Opera debut 1998 as Da-ud in Die Aegyptische Helena (Concert); Title role in Birtwistle's Gawain, 2000; Concerts with Sinopoli, Janowski, and Christian Thielemann; Season 2002 engaged as Stewa in Jenůfa and Tom Rakewell in The Rake's Progress in Hannover; Macduff in Macbeth at Covent Garden; Season 2003 engaged as Tamino in Die Zauberflöte at Covent Garden and Pelléas in Pelléas et Mélisande in Hannover. *Honours:* Winner, Alexander Girandi Competition, Coburg, and International Wagner Singing Competition, Strasbourg. *Address:* c/o Theateragentur Dr G. Hilbert, Maximilianstrasse 22, Munich, Germany.

HARVEY, Jonathan (Dean); Composer and Professor of Music; b. 3 May 1939, Sutton Coldfield, England; m. Rosaleen Marie Barry, 1960, 1 s., 1 d. *Education:* St Michael's College, Tenbury; Repton; MA, D.Mus, St John's College, Cambridge; PhD, Glasgow University. *Career:* Lecturer, Southampton University, 1964–77; Harkness Fellow, Princeton University, 1969–70; Reader 1977–80, Professor of Music 1980–95, Sussex University; Professor of Music, Stanford University, 1995–2000; Visiting Professor, Imperial College, London, 1999; Works performed at many festivals and international centres; 23 Works heard as Musica 2002 Strasbourg; mem, Academia Europaea, 1989; Fellow, Royal College of Music, 1994. *Compositions include:* Persephone Dream for orchestra, 1972; Inner Light (trilogy) for performers and tape, 1973–77; Smiling Immortal for chamber orchestra, 1977; Passion and resurrection, church opera, 1981; Gong-Ring for ensemble with electronics, 1984; Madonna of Winter and Spring for orchestra, 1986; Lightness and Weight for tuba and orchestra, 1986; 3 String Quartets, 1977, 1988, 1995; One Evening for voices, instruments and electronics, 1994; Lotuses for flute quartet; Inquest of Love opera, 1992; Advaya, for cello and electronics, 1994; Percussion Concerto, 1997; Wheel of Emptiness, for ensemble, 1997; Death of Light/Light of Death for 5 players, 1998; Calling Across Time for chamber orchestra, 1998; Tranquil Abiding for orchestra, 1998; Hidden Voice (1) and (2) for ensemble, 1999; White as Jasmine for soprano and orchestra, 1999; Sweet/winterhart for solo violin and SATB choir, 2001; The Summer Cloud's Awakening, for SATB choir, solo flute and cello, and electronics, 2001; Magnificat and Nunc Dimittis for double choir and large ensemble, 1978–2002; Songs of Li Po, for mezzo, strings, two percussion and harpsichord, 2002; Chu, for soprano, clarinet and cello, 2002; Numerous choral and church pieces including Missa Brevis, 1995; How Could the Soul Not Take Flight, 1996; Ashes Dance Back, 1997; Mothers Shall Not Cry, 2000; Bird Concerto with Pianosong, 2001. *Recordings:* Bhakti NMCD001, Mortuos Plango, Vivos Voco, Song Offerings, Valley of Aosta; Cello Concerto; From Silence; String Quartets; Madonna of Winter and Spring, Percussion concerto, 2000; Wheel of Emptiness; Death of Light/Light of Death. *Publications:* The Music of Stockhausen, 1975; In Quest of Spirit, 1999; Music and Inspiration, 1999; Numerous Articles. *Honours:* Hon Doctor of Music, Southampton, 1991, Bristol, 1994; The Britten Award for Composition, 1993. *Current Management:* Patrick Garvey. *Address:* 35 Houndean Rise, Lewes, East Sussex BN7 1EQ, England.

HARVEY, Keith; Cellist; b. 1950, England. *Education:* Studied with Douglas Cameron at Royal Academy of Music and with Gregor Piatigorsky in Los Angeles. *Career:* Formerly youngest ever principal cellist of London Philharmonic Orchestra, then principal of English Chamber Orchestra; Plays cello by Montagnana of 1733, formerly belonging to Bernard Romberg; Founder member of Gabrieli Ensemble, with chamber music performances in the United Kingdom and abroad; Co-founded the Gabrieli Quartet, 1967, and toured with them to Europe, North America, Far East and Australia; Festival engagements in the United Kingdom, including Aldeburgh, City of London and Cheltenham; Concerts every season in London, participation in Barbican Centre's Mostly Mozart Festival; Resident Artist at University of Essex, 1971–; Has co-premiered by William Alwyn, Britten, Alan Bush, Daniel Jones and Gordon Crosse, 2nd Quartets of Nicholas Maw and Panufnik (1983, 1980) and 3rd Quartet of John McCabe (1979); British premiere of the Piano Quintet by Sibelius, 1990. *Recordings include:* 50 CDs including early pieces by Britten, Dohnányi's Piano Quintet with Wolfgang Manz, Walton's Quartets and the Sibelius Quartet and Quintet, with Anthony Goldstone. *Honours:* Emmy Award for solo playing in films.

HARVEY, Peter; Singer (Baritone); b. 1958, England. *Education:* Choral Scholar at Magdalen College Oxford, Guildhall School of Music. *Career:* Concert appearances with the St James Baroque Players in Telemann's St Matthew Passion at Aldeburgh and London; Visit to Lisbon with The Sixteen; Concerts of Monteverdi and Purcell in Poland and the Flanders Festival with London Baroque; Sang with Joshua Rifkin and the Bach Ensemble at St James Piccadilly, 1990; Engagements with La Chapelle Royale and Collegium Vocale in Belgium, France and Spain; Bach Cantatas for French television and tour of Messiah with Le Concert Spirituel; Other repertoire includes the War Requiem, Elijah and the Five Mystical Songs of Vaughan Williams; St John in The Cry of the Ikon by John Tavener (also televised); Bach's St John Passion (Westminster Abbey) and Christmas Oratorio; Schubert's E flat Mass; Visited Brazil 1989 with The Sixteen for Messiah; Belgium 1991 in Teixeira's Te Deum, conducted by Harry Christophers; Sang with Les Talens Lyriques at Versailles Baroque Days in Mondonville's Les Fêtes de Paphos, 1996. *Recordings:* Dido and Aeneas; Sacred music by CPE Bach with La Chapelle Royale (Virgin Classics); Gilles Requiem with Le Concert Spirituel. *Honours:* Walther Gruner International Lieder Competition, 2nd Prizewinner; Nonie Morton Award (leading to Wigmore Hall debut). *E-mail:* enquire@peterharvey.info.

HARVEY, Richard (Allen); Composer and Performer; b. 25 Sept. 1953, London, England. *Education:* Associate, Royal College of Music, 1971.

Career: Debut: Conductor, London Symphony Orchestra, Barbican Centre, 1985; Recorder/Woodwind Player; Conductor and Composer; Founder, London Vivaldi Orchestra; Guest Conductor, Royal Philharmonic and London Symphony Orchestras; Toured with guitarist John Williams, 1984–; Conductor and Performer with English Chamber Orchestra, Barbican Centre, London, 1987. *Compositions:* Concerto Antico for guitar and orchestra; Reflections on A Changing Landscape, viola concerto; Plague and the Moonflower, eco-oratorio; A Time of Miracles, children's opera; Compositions for films and television include Game, Set and Match, G.B.H, Jake's Progress and Defence of the Realm. *Recordings:* Italian Recorder Concertos; The Genteel Companion; Brass at La Sauve-Majeure; Four Concertos for Violins and Recorder; GBH soundtrack; Jake's Progress soundtrack. *Current Management:* Ian Amos, Tyringham House, Spring House, Brightlingsea, Essex, CO7 0PJ, England.

HARWOOD, Richard; English cellist; b. 8 Aug. 1979, Portsmouth. *Education:* Royal Northern Coll. of Music, Manchester with Prof. Ralph Kirshbaum; cello with Joan Dickson, Steven Doane, David Waterman, Heinrich Schiff; piano with Diana Bell and Joyce Rathbone. *Career:* debut, Kabalevsky op49 in G minor at Adrian Boult Hall, Birmingham 1990; Purcell Room debut with Julius Drake 1999; performed concerti in Royal Albert Hall, Queen Elizabeth Hall, St John's Smith Square and St George's Brandon Hill; collaborated with conductors, including David Parry, En Shao, and Yehudi Menuhin; soloist with numerous orchestras, including Bournemouth Symphony Orchestra and Philharmonia; toured New Zealand with Elgar Concerto 1993; recital performances include Schoenbrunn Palace Theatre, Vienna 1997, Wigmore Hall Recital debut 1998, Purcell Room debut 1999. *Recordings:* Elgar Concerto (BBC Radio 3) 1993, Tchaikovsky's Variations on a Rococo Theme (BBC Radio 3). *Honours:* Audi Junior Musician (youngest ever winner) 1992, Pierre Fournier Award for cellists 2004, numerous scholarships. *Current Management:* Hazard Chase, Norman House, Cambridge Place, Cambridge CB2 1NS, England. *Telephone:* (1223) 312400. *Fax:* (1223) 460827. *Website:* www.hazardchase.co.uk. *Address:* c/o 77 Highfield Avenue, Waterlooville, Hampshire PO7 7QP, England. *E-mail:* office@richardharwood.com. *Website:* www.richardharwood .com.

HASELBÖCK, Martin; Organist and Conductor; b. 23 Nov. 1954, Vienna, Austria. *Education:* Studied at the Musikhochschule, Vienna, and with Jean Langlais and Daniel Roth in Paris. *Career:* Debut: Konzerthaus, Vienna, 1973; Organist at Augustinekurche, Vienna, 1976; Vienna Hofkapelle, 1977; Solo appearances with leading orchestras in Berlin, Vienna and elsewhere in Europe; Premieres of organ concertos by Ernst Krenek Cristobàl Halffter and William Albright; Professor of Organ at the Lubeck Musikhochschule, 1986–2003; Vienna Music Univ., 2003–; Founded the Wiener Akademie 1985, giving many performances of Baroque and early Classical music; Guest Conductor with the Vienna Symphony, Philadelphia, Los Angeles, Pittsburgh Orchestra and many other orchestras; Opera engagements in Prague (Mozart Festival) and Zürich. *Recordings include:* Works by Haydn, Mozart, Bach, Biber and Telemann, with the Wiener Akademie; Complete organ works of Bach, Schoenberg and Liszt. *Honours:* Winner, Vienna-Melk International Organ Competition, 1992; Deutscher Schallplattenpreis, Ehrenkreuz für Wissenschaft und Kunst, Vienna, 1997; Hon. doctorate, Luther College, Iowa, USA, 2003. *Address:* c/o Universität für Musik, 1030 Vienna, Germany. *E-mail:* haselboeck@ chello.at.

HASHIMOTO, Eiji; Harpsichordist; b. 7 Aug. 1931, Tokyo, Japan; m. Ruth Anne Laves, 8 June 1963, 1 s., 2 d. *Education:* BM in Organ, 1954, Graduate Diploma in Organ, 1955, Tokyo University of Fine Arts; MA in Composition, University of Chicago, 1959; MM, Harpsichord, Yale University School of Music, 1962. *Career:* Harpsichord Instructor at Toho Gakuen School of Music, Tokyo, 1966; Assistant Prof. of Harpsichord and Artist-in-Residence, 1968–72, Assoc. Prof. of Harpsichord and Artist in Residence, 1972–77, Prof. of Harpsichord and Artist in Residence, 1977–2001, Prof. Emeritus of Harpsichord, 2001–, Univ. of Cincinnati College Conservatory of Music; Concerts: recitals and or solo appearances in Australia, Austria, Belgium, Brazil, Canada, Chile, China, England, Finland, France, Germany, Netherlands, Iran, Italy, Japan, Luxembourg, Mexico, New Zealand, Philippines, Spain, Switzerland, USA and Venezuela. *Recordings:* 18 recordings (including 8 CDs) of solo, solo with orchestra, conducting and ensemble performances. *Publications:* Editions: D Scarlatti, 100 Sonatas, in 3 vols, 1975 and 1988; C P E Bach, Sonatas in 3 vols, 1984, 1988; J B Loeillet, Pièces pour Clavecin, 1985; D Scarlatti, 90 Sonatas in 3 vols, 1999–. *Honours:* Prize of Excellence, Japanese Ministry of Cultural Affairs, 1978, 1982; Rockefeller Foundation Bellagio Residency Grant, 1998; Distinguished Research Professorship, Univ. of Cincinnati, 1998. *Address:* 4579 English Creek Drive, Cincinnati, OH 45245, USA. *E-mail:* eiji .hashimoto@uc.edu. *Website:* www.eijihashimoto.com.

HASKIN, Howard; Singer (Tenor); b. 1958, Kansas City, USA. *Education:* Studied at Bloomington, Illinois, and Zürich. *Career:* Sang Monostatos in Die Zauberflöte at Orange, 1981; Wexford Festival, 1982, in Griselidis by Massenet, and Opera North, 1983, as Ramphis in Aida; Kent Opera from 1984, as Paris in King Priam, Don José and Peter Grimes; Buxton Festival, 1984, as Jason in Cherubini's Médée; Amsterdam, 1989, as Dimitri in Boris Godunov and 1992 in the premiere of Schnittke's Life with an Idiot; Glyndebourne, 1990–91, as Monostatos, and Covent Garden, 1992, as Robbin in Porgy and Bess. *Address:* c/o Netherlands Opera, Waterloopleein 22, 1011 Amsterdam, Netherlands.

HASSON, Maurice; Concert Violinist; b. 6 July 1934, Berck-Plage, France. *Education:* Studied at Paris Conservatoire and with Henryk Szeryng. *Career:* Played the Mendelssohn Concerto in Paris, aged 16; Resident in London, 1973–; Has appeared with orchestras and given recitals in Europe, Israel, USA, South America, Australia, New Zealand and Hong Kong; Conductors have included Masur, Mata, Rattle and Alexander Gibson, Colin Davis, Rafael Fruebeck De Burgos; US debut with Cleveland Orchestra under Lorin Maazel, 1978; Guest concerts with European broadcasting stations; Prof., Royal Acad. of Music, 1986; Plays the Benvenuti violin by Stradivarius, 1727. *Recordings include:* Paganini Concerto No. 1, Prokofiev No. 2, Brahms and Bruch; Bach Double Concerto, with Szeryng and the Academy of St Martin in the Fields; Brilliant showpieces for the Violin, Virtuoso Violin and Concerto by Gonzalo Castellanos Yumar; French Sonatas (Franck–Debussy–Fauré) with Christian Ivaldi; Violin Favourites (with Ian Brown). *Honours:* Grand Prix and Prix d'Honneur at Paris Conservatoire; Hon. mem., Royal Acad. of Music; La Orden Andrés Bello (highest order of artistic distinction). *Address:* 18 West Heath Court, North End Road, London NW11 7RE, England. *Telephone:* (20) 458 3647. *Fax:* (20) 8455-8317.

HASTINGS, Baird; Musician, Writer and Educator; b. 14 May 1919, New York City, USA; m. Louise (Lily) Laurent, 22 Dec 1945, deceased 7 Mar 1997. *Education:* AB, Harvard College, 1939; Diploma, Paris Conservatory, 1946; Diploma, Tanglewood, 1957; Diploma, Mozarteum, Salzburg, 1961; MA, Queens College, 1966; PhD, Sussex College, 1976. *Career:* Conductor, Mozart Chamber Players, 1957–60; Conductor, Mozart Festival Orchestra, 1960–; Music Adviser, Eglevsky Ballet, 1961–78; Lecturer in Music, Conductor of Band and Orchestra, Trinity College, 1965–70; Administrator, Juilliard School of Music, New York City, 1972–85; Music Adviser, School of American Ballet, New York City, 1973–85; Music Director, Westport Point, Massachusetts, Summer Episcopal Church, 1974–92; Guest Conductor, American Symphony; Consultant, Royal Academy of Music, London; Panelist, Hofstra Mozart Conference, New York; mem, The Bohemians; Musicians Union; American Musicological Society. *Compositions:* Arranger of Music by Mozart, Wagner, Thomson and others including re-orchestration Act IV, La Vie Parisienne, Offenbach, 1984. *Recordings:* Music for Strings; Mozart Concerto No. 27 for piano and orchestra, with Beveridge Webster; Michael Haydn Symphony; Other Mozart works. *Publications include:* Berard, 1950; Sonata Form in Classic Orchestra, 1966; Treasury of Librettos, 1969; Don Quixote by Minkus, 1975; Choreographers and Composers, 1983; Mozart Research Guide, 1989. *Contributions:* American Record Guide; Carnegie Hall programmes; Alice Tully Hall programmes; Prose of Distinction to Ballet Review; Juilliard Journal; Guide to Thamos by Mozart, Conductor's Journal. *Honours:* Fulbright Fellowship, 1949–50, Tanglewood, 1957. *Address:* 33 Greenwich Avenue, New York, NY 10014, USA.

HATRIK, Juraj; Composer; b. 1 May 1941, Orkucany, Presov, Czechoslovakia; m. 17 April 1965, 2 s. *Education:* Academy of Music and Dramatic Arts, Bratislava. *Career:* Debut: Sinfonietta, 1963; Musical Education, Aesthetics and Psychology of Music, Academy of Music; Professor of Composition, Academy of Music and Dramatic Arts, Bratislava, 1997–; mem, Slovak Roma Club. *Compositions include:* Double Portrait for Orchestra, 1971; Da Capo al Fine for Orchestra, 1976; Diary of Tanja Savitchova for brass quintet and Soprano, 1976, television version 1983; Happy Prince, opera after Oscar Wilde, 1978; Sans Souci, 1st symphony, 1979; Vox Memoriae, cycle for 4 instruments, 1983; Canzona for organ, alto and viola, [after John Roberts], after R Tagore, 1984; Submerged Music for soprano and strings, 1985; Moment Music avec J. S. Bach for soprano and chamber group, 1985; Victor, 2nd symphony, 1988; Compositions for children, choirs and 4 monologues for accordion; Adam's Children, chamber opera after Slovak national proverbs and bywords, 1991; Diptych for violin, cello and piano, 1989; The Lost Children for string quartet with basso solo after Gregory Orr, 1993; The Brave Tin Soldier, musical by Hans Andersen, 1994; An die Musik, sonata-depêche for Schubert for clarinet, violin, cello and piano, 1995–96; Requiem for Iris, for actress and chamber ensemble, 1998; Skatingring 1951, 1998; Liebe, Sinn und Not, sonata for contrabasso and piano (in memoriam R M Rilke), 1999; Litany of While (after Arthur Lundkvist, symphonic poem for large orchestra), 2001; Ecce quod

Natura, phantasy for piano and orchestra, 2002; Eeee quod Natura..., concerto for piano and orchestra, 2002. *Publications:* Jewel of Music: Pedagogical texts about music, 1997. *Contributions:* Slovak Music; Musical Life. *Honours:* Premio di città Castelfidardo (Composition for Accordion Solo), 1993. *Current Management:* Academy of Music and Dramatic Arts, Bratislava, music analysis and composition. *Address:* Dubnická 2, 85102 Bratislava, Slovakia. *E-mail:* hatrik@vsmw.sk.

HATTORI, Joji; Concert Violinist and Conductor; b. 1969, Japan. *Education:* Studied in Vienna with Rainer Küchl; Further lessons with Lord Menuhin and Vladimir Spivakov. *Career:* Concert engagements throughout Europe; British debut with the Royal Philharmonic Orchestra; Concerts with Yehudi Menuhin at the Festival Hall and with Vienna Chamber Orchestra at the Vienna Konzerthaus; Appearances with the English Chamber Orchestra, the BBC National Orchestra of Wales and the Scottish Chamber Orchestra, London Mozart Players, Israel and Zürich Chamber Orchestras, Orchestre de la Suisse Romande, Munich Radio Symphony and most major Japanese orchestras including New Japan Philharmonic under Seiji Ozawa; Wigmore Hall, London, debut 1996, with pianist Bruno Canino; Plays a Guarneri del Gesu violin (Hämmerle 1733); Music Director of Tokyo Ensemble; Visiting Professor at Royal Academy of Music, London; Associate Conductor of Vienna Chamber Orchestra; Artistic Director of the Genius of the Violin Festival and the Menuhin International Violin Competition. *Recordings:* Bach Violin Concertos with the Scottish Chamber Orchestra, 1997; Kreisler with Joseph Seiger, 1998; Mozart Violin Concertos with London Mozart Players, 2001. *Honours:* Hon. RAM; Winner of a Carnegie Hall conducting debut and Lincoln Maazel Fellowship at the Maazel-Vilar Conducting Competition, 2002; Winner, Young Musician of the Year in Japan, 1992; Menuhin International Violin Competition, Folkestone, 1989. *Address:* 72 Leopold Road, London SW19 7JQ, England. *E-mail:* hatoff@attglobal.net. *Website:* www.jojihattori.com.

HATZIANO, Markella; Singer (Mezzo-soprano); b. 1960, Athens, Greece. *Education:* Studied with Gogo Georgilopoulu at the Athens National Conservatory and Tito Gobbi in Rome. *Career:* Sang Eboli in Don Carlos with the National Opera of Greece and made her US debut, as Azucena at Boston, in 1987; Returned to Boston as Suzuki, Amneris, Neris in Cherubini's Médée and in Verdi's Requiem; French repertory includes Carmen (Mexico 1992, under Enrique Batiz), Massenet's Charlotte (Malaga, 1993) and Marguerite in La Damnation de Faust (Trieste, 1993); Sang Dido in Les Troyens with the London Symphony Orchestra at the Barbican Hall, under Colin Davis, 1993; Further appearances as Judith in Bluebeard's Castle at the Salzburg Festival, Dido at La Scala, 1996, Amneris at Florence, under Zubin Mehta; Sang Dalila and Amneris at Covent Garden, 1996; Concert repertory includes Mahler's Das Lied von der Erde, Kindertotenlieder and 2nd and 3rd Symphonies; Season 1996–97 concerts with the New York Philharmonic, Chicago Symphony Orchestra, Los Angeles Philharmonic and the Orchestre de la Suisse Romande; Debut with the London Symphony in Schoenberg's Erwartung, 1997; Season 2000–01 with Giovanna Seymour in Anna Bolena at Athens and the Verdi Requiem for the Granada Festival. *Recordings include:* Verdi Requiem, with the London Symphony Orchestra under Richard Hickox. *Honours:* Winner, Tito Gobbi International Competition, 1983; American-Israel Competition, 1987. *Address:* c/o Steven Larson, PO Box 575, Creighton, Nebraska 68729, USA.

HAUBOLD, Ingrid; Singer (Soprano); b. 1943, Berlin, Germany; m. Heikki Toivannen. *Education:* Studied in Detmold and at the Munich Musikhochschule with Annelies Kupper. *Career:* Sang at the Munich Theater am Gärtnerplatz, 1965–66; Detmold Landestheater 1970–72, Bielefeld 1972, Lubeck from 1979; Guest engagements at Hanover (from 1981) and Karlsruhe (1981–84); Sang Isolde at Madrid 1986, Turin and Berlin 1988, Lucerne Festival 1989, Kassel 1992; Has also appeared at the Teatro Massimo Palermo, Teatro Comunale Bologna, the Vienna Staatsoper, Schwetzingen Festival (Ariadne, 1989) and the Metropolitan Opera, 1990–91; Other roles include Senta (Savonlinna Festival 1990), Pamina, Wagner's Elsa, Elisabeth, Brünnhilde (Wiesbaden, 1996), Gutrune, Eva, Freia, Sieglinde, Irene (Rienzi) and Ada (Die Feen); Leonore, Strauss's Chrysothemis and Marschallin, Janáček's Jenůfa and Katya Kabanova; Many concert appearances. *Address:* c/o Deutsche Oper Berlin, Richard Wagnerstrasse 10, Berlin, Germany.

HAUDEBOURG, Brigitte; French harpsichordist, pianofortist and teacher; b. 5 Dec. 1942, Paris; m. Paul Cousseran; one s. one d. *Education:* studied piano with Marguérite Long and Jean Doyen, masterclass with R. Veyron-Lacroix. *Career:* debut in Paris; Many television and radio appearances in France, USA, Canada, Europe, Russia, Tunisia, Hong Kong, Bangkok, Tahiti; Artistic Director of a French baroque festival in Tarentaise. *Recordings:* 70 Albums and CDs, including, Daquin, Dandrieu, 2 albums of suites; Devienne, for flute and harpsichord; Chevalier de St Georges, for violin and harpsichord; Jean Pierre Baur, for harp and harpsichord; W F Bach, 2 albums, No. 1, 3, 4,

5; CDs include, Louis Couperin, for harpsichord; Josse Boutmy for harpsichord, world premiere; Padre Antonio Soler; J Schobert for pianoforte; J A Benda for pianoforte; E N Mehul for pianoforte; J G Eckardt for pianoforte; L Kozeluh for pianoforte; Boutmy for harpsichord. *Publications include:* 2nd book of Josse Boutmy, (harpsichord). *Address:* 10 Avenue F. Roosevelt, 92150 Suresnes, France.

HAUG, Halvor; Composer; b. 20 Feb. 1952, Trondheim, Norway. *Education:* Degree, School Music Teacher, Conservatory of Music, Veitvet, Oslo, 1970–73, Sibelius Academy, Helsinki, 1973–74; Studies with Kolbjörn Ofstad, Oslo, 1974–75, London, 1978. *Career:* Performances in Norway and abroad with major musicians and orchestras; numerous radio and television performances in Norway and overseas; mem, Society of Norwegian Composers. *Compositions include:* Orchestra: 3 Symphonies, 1981–82, 1984, 1991–93; Symphonic Picture, 1976; Silence for Strings, 1977; Poema Patetica and Poema Sonora, 1980; Song of the Pines, 1987; Insignia, 1993; Glem aldri henne, song cycle for mezzo-soprano and orchestra, 1997; Il Preludio dell'Ignoto, 2000; Chamber: Brass Quintet, 1981; 2 String Quartets, 1985, 1996; Piano Trio, 1995. *Recordings include:* Symphony No. 1; Silence for Strings; Sinfonietta with the London Symphony Orchestra and Dreier; Symphonic Picture and Poema Patetica, with the London Philharmonic Orchestra and Dreier; Symphony No. 2, with Norwegian Youth Symphony Orchestra and Andersen; Symphony No. 3; Insignia; Song of the Pines; Silence for Strings, with Norrköping Symphony Orchestra, English Chamber Orchestra and Ruud. *Current Management:* Warner Chappell Music Norway A/S. *Address:* c/o PO Box 4523 Torshov, 0404 Oslo, Norway.

HAUNSTEIN, Rolf; Singer (Baritone); b. 18 Jan. 1943, Dresden, Germany. *Education:* Studied with Johannes Kemter in Dresden and Kurt Rehm in Berlin. *Career:* Sang in Bautzen, Freiberg and Cottbus, before engagement at the Dresden Staatsoper, 1971; Roles have included Germont, Posa, Ford, Scarpia, Beckmesser, Rigoletto, Pizarro, Klingsor, Telramund, Onegin and Wagner's Dutchman; Guest engagements at Leipzig, the Komische Oper Berlin, Kiel, Wiesbaden and Strasbourg; Member of the Zürich Opera from 1991; Season 1996–97, Telramund, the Minister in Fidelio and Dikoj in Katya Kabanova; Sang Kdenatý in The Makropulos Case, Toulouse, 1998; Sang the Animal Trainer and Athlete in Lulu at Zürich, 2000; Conductors have included Harnoncourt, Dohnànyi, Masur and Suitner and opera producers such as Ruth Berghaus, Robert Wilson, Joachim Herz and Harry Kupfer, 1976. *Address:* c/o Opernhaus Zürich, Falkenstrasse 1, 8008 Zürich, Switzerland.

HAUPTMANN, Cornelius; Singer (Bass); b. 1951, Stuttgart, Germany. *Education:* Graduated Stuttgart Musikhochschule 1982; Berne Conservatoire with Jakob St ämpfli; Further study with Dietrich Fischer-Dieskau in Berlin and masterclasses in Salzburg with Eric Tappy and Elisabeth Schwarzkopf. *Career:* Sang at Stuttgart from 1981, notably as Masetto; Heidelberg Opera 1985–87, as King Philip in Don Carlos and Osmin; Stadttheater Karlsruhe from 1987, as Sparafucile (Rigoletto), Plutone (Orfeo), Sarastro and Mozart's Figaro; Festival appearances at Lucerne, Salzburg, Singapore, Sapporo, Schwetzingen (1983 premiere of Henze's The English Cat) and Ludwigsburg (recital 1991); Further engagements in Munich, Paris, Berlin, Leipzig, Orleans, London, Lyon and Amsterdam (Publio and Sarastro in concert performances of La Clemenza di Tito and Die Zauberflöte, 1990); Sang Sarastro at Ludwigsburg, 1992; Conductors include John Eliot Gardiner, Hogwood, Janowski, Tilson Thomas, Masur, Barenboim, Maazel, Lothar Zagrosek, Roger Norrington, Neville Marriner, Pierre Boulez, Philippe Herreweghe; Concert performances include the St Matthew Passion (Gardiner) and Mozart's Requiem (Bernstein) in 1988; Frequent Lieder recitals, and other concerts under Nikolaus Harnoncourt, Trevor Pinnock, Helmut Rilling and Gary Bertini; Sang Rocco in a concert performance of Fidelio at Lyon, 1996; Gave masterclasses in Wales, Japan and England (Britten-Pears School of Advanced Music Studies, Aldeburgh). *Recordings:* Bach St John and St Matthew Passion, Mozart C minor Mass, Idomeneo, La Clemenza di Tito, and Die Entführung, with Gardiner and Mozart Requiem and C minor Mass (Bernstein) for Deutsche Grammophon; Beethoven: Missa Solemnis (Herreweghe); Schoenberg's Jakobsleiter (Inbal); Haydn Stabat Mater, with Pinnock (DG) and Die Zauberflöte with Norrington; Enescu Oedipe with Foster (EMI); Akhnaten by Philip Glass (CBS); Lieder by Loewe, Mozart, Schubert, Mendelssohn, Monteverdi; Schütz with Frieder Bernius. *Current Management:* IMG Artists, 54 avenue Marceau, 75008 Paris, France. *Address:* Waldburgstr 121, 70563 Stuttgart, Germany.

HAUSCHILD, Wolf-Dieter; Conductor; b. 6 Sept. 1937, Greiz, Germany. *Education:* Studied at Franz Liszt Musikhochschule, Weimar, with Ottmar Gerster and Hermann Abendroth; Further study with Hermann Scherchen and Sergiu Celibidache. *Career:* Conductor of the Deutsche National Theater Weiners and from 1963 Chief Conductor of the Kleist Theatre at Frankfurt Oder (also of Frankfurt Philharmonic); Chorus Master for RDA Radio, 1971–74, joint conductor of Berlin Radio

Symphony Orchestra, 1974–78; Chief Conductor of the Symphony Orchestra of Radio Leipzig, 1978–85; Professor of Conducting at the Musikhochschule of Berlin and Leipzig from 1981; Guest Conductor of Berlin Symphony Orchestra; Chief Conductor of Stuttgart Philharmonic Orchestra, 1985–91; Professor of Conducting at Karlsruhe Musikhochschule, 1988; Artistic Director and Chief Conductor at Essen Opera, 1991–98 (1806 Version of Fidelio, 1998); Guest appearances at Berlin Staatsoper and Komische Oper and the Semper-Oper Dresden; Conducted a new production of Tristan und Isolde at Essen, 1992. *Address:* c/o Theater und Philharmonie, Rolandstrasse 10, 45128 Essen, Germany.

HAUSER, Alexis; Music Director; b. 1947, Vienna, Austria. *Education:* Student at the Conservatory and the Academy of Music and Performing Arts in Vienna; Graduated summa cum laude in the masterclass of Professor Hans Swarowsky; Also studied with Franco Ferrara in Italy and Herbert von Karajan, Salzburg, Mozarteum. *Career:* Debut: With Vienna Symphony, 1973; Several concerts and broadcasts with Vienna Symphony; Invitations to conduct many other European orchestras including the Berlin RIAS Symphony, Belgrade Philharmonic and the Vienna Chamber Orchestra; Invited by Seiji Ozawa to spend summer of 1974 in Tanglewood; USA Debut with New York City Opera, 1975; Conducted Atlanta Symphony with Itzhak Perlman as soloist, 1975; Subsequently conducted with Symphonies of San Francisco, Minnesota, Seattle, Kansas City (with Maureen Forrester as soloist) and the Rochester Philharmonic; Music Director, Orchestra London Canada, 1981–; Led orchestra on its first European tour to the Festival Internationale dell Aquila in Italy; Directed Conductors' Seminar at the Royal Conservatory of Music in Toronto; Conducted the Toronto, Winnipeg and Kansas City Symphonies; Appeared at Chicago's Grant Park Festival. *Honours:* Winner of several conducting awards in Austria including 1st International Hans Swarowsky Conducting Competition in Vienna; Awarded Koussevitzky Conducting Prize at Tanglewood, 1974; In 1984 Orchestra London Canada received the Award of Merit presented by the Canadian Performing Right Organization.

HAUTZIG, Walter; Concert Pianist; b. 28 Sept. 1921, Vienna, Austria; m. Esther Rudomin, 10 Sept 1950, 1 s., 1 d. *Education:* State Academy of Vienna; Jerusalem Conservatory; Curtis Institute, Philadelphia; Principal Teacher, Mieczyslaw Munz; Private Study with Artur Schnabel. *Career:* Debut: Town Hall, New York, 31 Oct 1943; Recitals and Orchestral Appearances in over 50 Countries; Soloist with Berlin Philharmonic, Orchestra National Belgique, Oslo, Stockholm, Copenhagen, Helsinki, Zürich, New York, Baltimore, St Louis, Buffalo, Vancouver, Honolulu, Tokyo, Sydney, Melbourne, Auckland, Wellington, Mexico, Bogota, Jerusalem and Tel-Aviv; Played for BBC, Australian, New Zealand, Japanese, USA and Canadian Radio; Professor of Piano, Peabody Conservatory of the Johns Hopkins University, Baltimore, USA, 1960–87. *Recordings:* Numerous for labels, including Americus, Connoisseur Society, RCA, Vox Records. *Publications:* Playing Around–A Pianist Remembers, 1996. *Contributions:* Musical America; American Record Guide.

HAVERINEN, Margareta; Singer (soprano); b. 1951, Finland. *Education:* Studied with Pierre Bernac in Paris, Anita Välkki in Helsinki, Gladys Kuchta in Düsseldorf and Vera Rozsa in London. *Career:* After winning the 1978 Geneva International Competition sang in opera at Helsinki and Oslo as Gilda, Violetta, Tosca and Donna Anna; Welsh National Opera, 1988, and Dublin, 1992, as Tosca; London, 1992, in the British premiere of Sibelius's opera The Maiden in the Tower; Savonlinna Festival, 1994, as Judith in Bluebeard's Castle; Many concerts and Lieder recitals in Europe and the USA (Carnegie Hall, New York, and the Westminster Artsong Festival in Princeton). *Address:* c/o Dublin Grand Opera Society, John Player Theatre, 276–288 Circular Road, Dublin 8, Republic of Ireland.

HAVLAK, Lubomir; Violinist; b. 27 Feb. 1958, Prague, Czechoslovakia; m. Jarmila Havlakova, 26 Aug 1983, 1 s., 1 d. *Education:* Conservatoire in Prague; Academy of Music in Prague; Masterclasses: Nathan Milstein in Zürich; Masterclasses with leading ensembles: Tel-Aviv, Amadeus, Guarneri, Juilliard and Alban Berg Quartets. *Career:* Debut: Prague Spring Festival, 1980; Member, (Martinů) Quartet; Leader of Havlak and Martinů Quartet: Prague Spring Festival; UNESCO Hall in Paris, Kuhmo Festival (Finland), Wigmore Hall, London, Bath Festival, Brighton Festival; Festivals in Dartington, in Evian (France), Arjeplog (Sweden), Bratislava (Slovakia), Orlando Festival (Netherlands), Frankfurter Sonoptikum; Film: Meeting with Segerstam; Concerts in Europe, USA and Japan; Television, radio. *Recordings:* Leader of Martinů Quartet; Martinů Quartets (Naxos): Debussy, Martinů (Panton); Early Czech Composers–Krommer, Richter, Dvořák, Smetana-String Quartets; Antonin Wranitsky–Concertante Quartets; Janáček, String Quartets; Honegger. *Honours:* With Havlak Quartet: Prague Spring Competition, 2nd Prize, 1979; Evian: Contemporary Music, 1st Prize, 1978; Portsmouth, 2nd Prize, 1982; München, 2nd Prize, 1982; Florence, 2nd Prize, 1984. *Address:* Pod Vlastnim Krovem 27, 182 00

Prague 8, Czech Republic. *Telephone:* +42 (286) 884294; +42 (606) 888373. *E-mail:* lubomir.havlak@volny.cz. *Website:* www .musikerportrait.com/martinu-quartet.

HAVLIK, Jiri; Horn Player; b. 20 July 1956, Tabor, Czecholovakia; m. Helena Havlikova, 18 Mar 1978, 2 d. *Education:* French Horn, Composition, Conservatoire, Prague, 1971–77; Composition, 1977–78, Horn, 1978–81, Academy of the Musical Arts. *Career:* Member, Czech Philharmonic, 1979–, Horn Trio Prague, 1985–; Chamber and Solo Performances in Czech Republic, Switzerland, Netherlands, Japan, Canada; Founder, Horn Music Agency, Prague, 1991. *Compositions:* Concerto for Horn and Orchestra, 1976; The Cycle of the Piano Compositions, 1978; Three Fugues for Three Horns and Piano, 1997. *Recordings:* Czech Philharmonic Horn Section, 1989; Old Czech Concertos for 2 and 3 Horns, 1992. *Honours:* 2nd Prize, Concertino Prague International Competition, 1970; Special Prize, Czech Ministry of Culture, 1978; 3rd Prize, Prague Spring International Competition, 1978. *Current Management:* Pragoart Prague. *Address:* Na Spravedlnosti 1152, 27101 Nove Straseci, Czech Republic.

HAWKES, Tom; Stage Director; b. 21 June 1938, England. *Education:* Trained at the Royal Academy of Music. *Career:* Resident Staff Producer at Sadler's Wells 1965–69; For English National Opera has produced Un Ballo in Maschera, Madama Butterfly, La Vie Parisienne, La Gazza Ladra and Die Fledermaus; English Bach Festivals (seen at Covent Garden and in France, Greece, Italy and Spain) include Rameau's Castor et Pollux and Platée, Handel's Teseo and Gluck's Alceste and Orphée et Eurydice; Dido and Aeneas in London and at the Athens Festival; Artistic Director for Phoenix Opera and Director of Productions for the Handel Opera Society; La Finta Giardiniera for the English Music Theatre; Wat Tyler by Alan Bush, Hansel and Gretel and operettas at the Sadler's Wells Theatre; Season 1990–91 with The Maid of Orleans for Northern Opera, La Bohème in Hong Kong, Mitridate in Monte Carlo and Handel's Riccardo Primo at the Royal Opera House and in Limasol for the English Bach Festival; Has also conducted in Dublin, Nottingham, Oxford, Belgium and Guelph and St Louis, USA; Season 1993/94 with Rigoletto and Die Fledermaus at Singapore, L'Orfeo, for EBF at Royal Opera House, Covent Garden, and in Spain; Director of Productions for the Singapore Lyric Theatre and for Crystal Clear Productions. *Address:* c/o Music International, 13 Ardilaun Road, London N5 2QR, England.

HAWKINS, Brian; Viola Player and Teacher; b. 13 Oct. 1936, York, England; m. Mavis Spreadborough, 30 Dec 1960, 1 s., 1 d. *Education:* National Youth Orchestra, 1951–54; Royal College of Music, 1954–60. *Career:* Chamber Music, Edinburgh Quartet; Martin Quartet; Vesuvius Ensemble; Nash Ensemble; London Oboe Quartet; Gagliano String Trio; Member, English Chamber Orchestra, Academy of St Martin-in-the-Fields, London Sinfonietta, London Virtuosi; Professor, Viola and Chamber Music, Royal College of Music, 1967–; String Faculty Adviser, Royal College of Music, 1989; Head of String Faculty, Royal College of Music, 1992; mem, Royal Society of Musicians; European String Teachers' Association; Incorporated Society of Musicians. *Recordings:* With the Nash Ensemble, London Virtuosi, London Oboe Quartet and Gagliano Trio. *Honours:* Silver Medal, Worshipful Company of Musicians, 1960; Fellowship of The Royal College of Music, 1991. *Address:* The Old Vicarage, 129 Arthur Road, London, SW19 7DR, England.

HAWKINS, John; Composer and Pianist; b. 26 July 1944, Montreal, Canada. *Education:* Studied under Istvan Anhalt and received Master's degree in Composition, McGill University. *Career:* Joined Faculty of Music, University of Toronto, teaches theory and composition, 1970–; Remained active as pianist and performed frequently in the concerts of Societe de Musique Contemporaine du Quebec as well as Toronto's New Music Concerts, of which he is a member of Board of Directors; Conductor, Pierre Boulez' conducting seminar, Switzerland 1969. *Compositions:* Composed over 70 new works which include pieces for harpsichord and organ; Music for an Imaginary Musical, for chamber ensemble, 1994; Night Song for baritone, marimba and string quartet, 1995; If There Are Any Heavens for soprano and chamber ensemble, 1996. *Honours:* Won several major awards including first John Adaskin Memorial Fund Award, 1968 and BMI Student Composers' Award, 1969. *Address:* c/o SOCAN, 41 Valleybrook Drive, Don Mills, Ontario M3B 2S6, Canada.

HAWKINS, Osie; Singer (Baritone); b. 16 Aug. 1913, Phoenix City, Alabama, USA. *Education:* Studied in Atlanta and with Friedrich Schorr in New York; Sang at the Metropolitan Opera from 1942, as Wagner's Telramund, Kurwenal, Bitterolf, Wotan, Amfortas, Donner and Gunther; Zuniga in Carmen and Monterone in Rigoletto; Also sang with Central City Opera, Colorado and the Cincinnati Summer Opera; Many concert appearances; Executive Stage Manager at the Metropolitan 1963–78; 926 performances with the Metropolitan Opera, played 54 roles in 39 different operas in German, Italian, French and English; *Honours:* Awarded Metropolitan Opera National Council Verdi Memorial Award of Achievement, 1978; Inducted into Philadelphia Academy of Vocal Arts Hall of Fame, 1987. *Address:* c/o Metropolitan Opera, Lincoln Center, New York, NY 10023, USA.

HAWKSLEY, Deborah; Singer (mezzo-soprano); b. Singapore. *Education:* Royal Northern Coll.; Guildhall School of Music. *Career:* appearances in Death in Venice, with GTO; as Third Lady, Mozart; Prince Orlofsky, Composer, Ariadne auf Naxos for ENO; Dorabella for Opera Theatre, Dublin; Cenerentola for European Chamber Opera; Baba the Turk, in The Rake's Progress, Aldeburgh Festival; Carmen for First Act Opera, 1998–99; Season 1999, as Prince Orlofsky on tour to the USA, Armelinde in Massenet's Cendrillon for Central Festival Opera and Rossini's Petite Messe for Northern Sinfonia; gala concerts for City of London Sinfonia in the UK and Germany. *Current Management:* Music International, 13 Ardilaun Road, London, N5 2QR, England. .

HAWLATA, Franz; Singer (Bass); b. 26 Dec. 1963, Eichstatt, Germany. *Education:* Munich Musikhochschule, with Ernst Haefliger, Hans Hotter and Erik Werba. *Career:* Debut: Gärtnerplatztheater, Munich, 1986; Engagements at the Komische Oper Berlin and in Munich, with guest appearances as Altoum in Busoni's Turandot in Dortmund; Baron Ochs in Der Rosenkavalier at Würzburg, for Welsh National Opera, New York Metropolitan (1995) and the Paris Opéra Bastille (1998); Peneios in Strauss's Daphne at Hamburg, Wozzeck at Bad Urach, Rocco in Beethoven's Leonore, on tour with John Eliot Gardiner, Leporello at Covent Garden and Osmin in Die Entführung at Salzburg (1996); Vienna State Opera 1994–95 as Nicolai's Falstaff, Kaspar, Don Pasquale, Sarastro and Baron Ochs; The Monk in Don Carlos at the Opéra Bastille, 1998, and Kecal in The Bartered Bride for the Royal Opera; Ochs at Covent Garden, 2000; Season 2001 as the Dutchman in Chicago and Wotan in Meiningen. *Recordings include:* Mephisto in Spohr's Faust, from the Bad Urach Festival. *Honours:* Prizewinner, 1987 Belvedere International Singing Competition, Vienna. *Address:* c/o IMG Artists, Lovell House, 616 Chiswick High Road, London W4 5RX, England.

HAYASHI, Yasuko; Singer (Soprano); b. 19 July 1948, Kanagawa, Japan; m. Giannicola Piglucci. *Education:* Studied in Tokyo with Shibata and Rucci; Studied with Lia Gurani and Campogalliani in Milan. *Career:* Debut: La Scala 1972, as Madama Butterfly; Appearances in Florence, Rome, London, Venice, Turin, Barcelona, Chicago and Aix-en-Provence; Other roles include Donna Anna, Fiordiligi, Carolina in Il Matrimonio Segreto, Luisa Miller, Anne Trulove and Liu, in Turandot; Turin 1976, in Bianca e Fernando by Bellini; Sang Donna Anna at reopening of Stuttgart Staatsoper, 1984; Genoa 1985, in a revival of Il Diluvio Universale by Donizetti; Season 1987–88 as Butterfly at Verona and Leonora in La Forza del Destino in Tokyo; Appearances on television and in concert. *Recordings:* I Lituani by Ponchielli; Rachel in La Juive; Requiem by Bottesini, Fonit-Cetra; Video of Madama Butterfly from La Scala. *Address:* c/o Staatsoper Berlin, Unter den linden 7, 1060 Berlin, Germany.

HAYES, Jamie; Stage Director; b. 1959, England. *Career:* Productions of The Gondoliers, The Magic Flute and Midsummer Night's Dream at Freemason's Hall; Aida, Opera Northern Ireland; Il Barbiere di Siviglia and La Cenerentola for Garsington Opera, Thieving Magpie, Figaro, Così fan tutte and Albert Herring for British Youth Opera at Sadler's Wells and Edinburgh; Former Director of productions for Clonter Opera For All, with La Traviata, La Bohème and Carmen; Buxton Festival with L'Italiana in Algeri, Le Huron and L'Italiana in Londra; Wexford Festival with Zaza and Le Rencontre Imprévue; Other productions include Alcina for Royal Northern College of Music and The Pearl Fishers for Victorian State Theatre, Robinson Crusoe, British Youth Opera, The Bear, RSAMD; Appointed Director of Productions, British Youth Opera, in 1996; La Bohème, for BYO, 1998. *Address:* Park House, 33 Brackley Road, Towcester, Northamptonshire NN12 6 DH, England.

HAYES, Malcolm (Lionel Fitzroy); Music Journalist, Writer and Composer; b. 22 Aug. 1951, Overton, Marlborough, Wiltshire, England. *Education:* St Andrews University; BMus Honours, Edinburgh University, 1974. *Career:* Music Critic, The Times, 1985–86; Music Critic, The Sunday Telegraph, 1986–89; Music Critic, The Daily Telegraph, 1989–95; Frequent broadcasts (talks) for BBC Radio 3, 1985–, and Radio 4, 1986–; Music performed at Bath Festival, 1985, ICA, London, 1985, BBC, London, 1986, Viitasaari Festival, Finland, 1987; Edinburgh Contemporary Arts Trust, 2002. *Publications:* New Music 88 (co-editor), 1988; Anton von Webern, 1995; Selected Letters of William Walton, 2002. *Contributions:* Numerous articles for Tempo, 1982–92; The Listener, 1985–89; Musical Times, 1985–86; International Opera Guide, 1987; New Music 87, 1987; Opera Now, 1991–1996; BBC Music Magazine, 1995–; Classic FM Magazine, 1995–. *Honours:* Tovey Prize for Composition, Edinburgh University, 1974. *Address:* Sunday Telegraph, 1 Canada Square, Canary Wharf, London E14 5DT, England.

HAYES, Quentin; Singer (Baritone); b. 27 Nov. 1958, Southend, England. *Education:* Studied at Dartington College, the Guildhall School with Arthur Reckless and Rudolph Pernay, and at the National Opera Studio. *Career:* Created Eddy in Mark-Anthony Turnage's Greek, Munich, 1988, repeated it at Edinburgh and the London Coliseum; Rossini's Figaro with Glyndebourne Touring Opera, Verdi's Ford for CBTO, Morales in Carmen for Welsh National Opera, and Angelotti for Scottish Opera; Ford, Papageno and Marcel Proust in Schnittke's Life with an Idiot for English National Opera, 1995; Nachtigal in Die Meistersinger for Royal Opera House Covent Garden; Concerts include Les Troyens at the Amsterdam Concertgebouw, Elijah in Wells Cathedral, L'Enfance du Christ in Spain and music by Purcell with Collegium Vocale; Season 1997 with The Dream of Gerontius at Bath, Handel's Semele at the Berlin Staatsoper, Britten's Church Parables for CBTO and Henze's Elegy for Young Lovers with the London Sinfonietta; Frère Léon in Messiaen's St François d'Assise for Concertgebouw, Amsterdam; Season 2003 at Covent Garden as Yamadori in Butterfly and the Herald in Lohengrin. *Recordings include:* Pepusch Death of Dido for the BBC; Greek; Britten, Rejoice in the Lamb; Where the Wild Things Are, Knussen; Donald in Billy Budd with Hickox and the London Symphony Orchestra. *Honours:* Winner VARA Dutch Radio Prize at the Belvedere Singing Competition, Vienna, 1992; Winner Vara Dutch Radio Prize and Belvedere Singing Competition, 1993. *Address:* c/o Royal Opera House (contracts), Covent Garden, London, WC2, England.

HAYMON, Cynthia; Singer (Soprano); b. 6 Sept. 1958, Jacksonville, Florida, USA; m. Barrington Coleman. *Education:* Graduate, Northwestern University. *Career:* Debut: Santa Fe Opera, as Diana in Orpheus in the Underworld, 1985; Sang Xanthe in US premiere of Die Liebe der Danaë, Santa Fe, 1985; Has sung Micaela for Seattle Opera and Liu in Boston; Created Harriet, A Woman Called Moses, Virginia, 1985; European debut, 1986, as Gershwin's Bess at Glyndebourne; With Covent Garden has sung Liu on tour to Far East and Mimi in London; State Operas, Hamburg, Munich, as Liu, Theatre de la Monnaie, Brussels, as Gluck's Amor; Israel Philharmonic as Micaela, conducted by Zubin Mehta; Season 1988–89 with Eurydice at Glyndebourne, Mimi for Baltimore Opera, Marguerite with Opera Grand Rapids; Season 1989–90 included Susanna for Seattle Opera, Canadian Opera debut as Micaela; Coretta King opposite Simon Estes, West End; 1990–91 highlights: Lauretta in Gianni Schicchi at Seattle, Liu in Miami, and Mozart's Pamina at Bastille Opéra, Paris; 1991–92 highlights: San Francisco Opera debut as Micaela in Carmen, premiere of Rorem's Swords and Plowshares with Boston Symphony, Pamina at Opéra Bastille, Liu at Royal Opera House, Covent Garden, Gershwin in concert at Teatro La Fenice, Venice, recital at Northwestern University, Carmina Burana with Detroit Symphony Orchestra, Mendelssohn's Symphony No. 2 for RAI, Rome, Gershwin and Tippett concert with London Symphony Orchestra, Gala concert, Glyndebourne Festival, 1992–93 highlights: Bess in Porgy and Bess, Royal Opera House, Pamina at Opéra Bastille, Micaela in Birmingham and Dortmund, Marguerite at Deutsche Oper Berlin, Mimi at Santa Fe Opera; Sang Musetta at Amsterdam, 1996; Liu in Turandot at Dallas, 1997; Sang Gluck's Euridice at Leipzig, 2000; Concert engagements in Brahms Requiem conducted by Kurt Masur, Rossini's Stabat Mater (London debut) with London Symphony Orchestra conducted by Michael Tilson Thomas; Other conductors: Seiji Ozawa, Bernard Haitink, Isaiah Jackson. *Recordings include:* Tippett's A Child of Our Time, London Symphony Orchestra, Richard Hickox, conductor; Bess in Porgy and Bess, Glyndebourne Festival Opera, Simon Rattle, conductor. *Honours:* Grammy Award, 1990. *Address:* c/o Columbia Artists Management Inc, 165 West 57th Street, New York, NY 10019, USA.

HAYS, Sorrel Doris, MMus; American composer, keyboard player and multimedia artist; b. 6 Aug. 1941, Memphis, TN. *Education:* Hochschule für Musik, Munich, Germany, University of Wisconsin, studied with Hilda Somer, Paul Badura-Skoda, Harold Cadek, Hedwig Bilgram. *Career:* in 80s added film and video to media art; Commissions from West German Broadcasting Cologne; Film, music video production shown at Museum of Modern Art, New York and Stedelijk Museum, Amsterdam; Commissions from Westdeutscher Rundfunk, Cologne, 1988; Echo, Whatchasay Wie Bitte, 1989; The Hub, Megopolis Atlanta and Sound Shadows, commissioned as opening work for Whitney Museum Acoustica Festival, April 1990; Bits, NY City premiere, 1993, Merkin Hall; Performances of Opera, The Glass Woman, NYC, Interart Theater, 1993; Premiere, The Clearing Way, Chattanooga Symphony, 1992; Queen Bee-ing, The Bee Opera, comic opera commissioned by Cary Trust , premiered by Medicine Show Theater, New York City, 2003; mem, ASCAP; Frau und Musik. *Compositions:* Southern Voices for Orchestra and Soprano, 1982, 21 minutes; Celebration of No, tape, Soprano, Violin, Piano, Cello, 1983; Sunday Nights, Piano, 1979; HUSH, Soprano, 2 Percussion, 1986; The Clearing Way, for full orchestra, contralto, SATB chorus; 3 act opera, 11 soloists and chorus, The Glass Woman, 1993; Dream in Her Mind, opera, Commission/premiere West Deutsche Rundfunk, 1995; Mapping Venus, 2 act opera, 1998; The Bee Opera, 2003. *Recordings:* Dreaming the World. *Publications:* Tuning for string quartet; Southern Voices for Orchestra. *Honours:* Opera America, production award for opera, The Glass Woman, 1989 and National Endowment for the Arts, 1992; New York Foundation on the Arts, Fellowship on Music Composition, 1998. *Address:* 697 West End Avenue, PHB, New York, NY 10025, USA.

HAYWARD, Marie (Pauline); Opera Singer (Soprano) and Teacher; b. 1940, England; m. Michael Segal, deceased, 1 s. *Education:* Royal Academy of Music; London Opera Centre; Tito Gobbi, Italy; MA; ARAM; LRAM; RAMDipl. *Career:* Debut: Royal Opera House; Numerous worldwide appearances, including Royal Albert Hall, Festival Hall, Musikverein, Vienna, London Coliseum, Kiel Opera House, Germany; Also Ring Cycle at Lubeck, Mannheim and Kiel; Also Isolde; Engaged by Klaus Tennstedt as Dramatic Soprano, Kiel, for roles including Desdemona, Mozart's First Lady, Donna Anna (Don Giovanni); Verdi and Wagner roles; Major roles include: Abigail, Northern Ireland Opera, Brünnhilde for English National Opera, Elvira and Fiordiligi at Glyndebourne; Miss Jessel in Turn of the Screw at Geneva and Sadler's Wells, English Opera; Oratorio performances in England and Europe; BBC broadcasts, Melodies for You, Friday Night is Music Night; Workshops and Masterclasses at Milan and Heidelberg Universities; mem, ISM. *Recordings:* Serenade to Music; Pilgrim's Progress; Adrian Boult, Ave Maria. *Honours:* ARAM, 1993; 2nd Prize, 's-Hertogenbosch International Competition; Medal of Distinction, Geneva.

HAYWARD, Robert; Singer (Bass-baritone); b. Nov. 1956, Surrey, England. *Education:* Studied at the Guildhall School of Music and the National Opera Studio. *Career:* Sang Falstaff and Mozart's Figaro while at college; Glyndebourne Touring Opera, 1986, as Don Giovanni; Has sung Figaro, Don Giovanni, Marcello, Count and Sharpless for Welsh National Opera; Theseus and Haushofmeister (Capriccio) for Glyndebourne Festival; English National Opera appearances as Tomsky in The Queen of Spades, Escamillo (1995) and Jochanaan (1996); US debut as Figaro for Houston Grand Opera, 1988; German debut, 1990, as Don Giovanni for the Bayerische Staatsoper on tour to Teatro Liceo Barcelona; For Opera North Guglielmo, Figaro, Count, Escamillo, Don Giovanni, Malatesta, Marcello, Robert in Iolanta, Debussy's Golaud; For Royal Opera House, Spirit Messenger (Frau); For Glyndebourne Tour Count and Onegin; Sang Germont for GTO at Glyndebourne, 1996; Sang Iago in Otello for ENO, 1998; Concert engagements include Messiah with the Royal Liverpool Philharmonic, Hallé and London Philharmonic Orchestras; The Mask of Time, Elijah, Beethoven's Ninth and the Brahms Requiem with the Hallé; Das klagende Lied and Gurrelieder with the English Northern Philharmonia; The Dream of Gerontius with the Scottish National Orchestra; Haydn's Creation with the Bournemouth Sinfonietta and the Philharmonia conducted by Claus Peter Flor; Mozart Requiem with Georg Solti; New Israeli Opera as: Malastesta, Guglielmo; Season 2000–01 as Escamillo for WNO, Golo in Pelléas for ENO and Jochanaan in Salome at Glasgow. *Recordings:* Beethoven's 9th Symphony; Das klagende Lied. *Current Management:* Ingpen & Williams Ltd, 7 St George's Court, 131 Putney Bridge Road, London, SW15 2PA, England.

HAYWOOD, Lorna; Singer (Soprano); b. 29 Jan. 1939, Birmingham, England; m. Paul Crook. *Education:* Royal College of Music, with Mary Parsons and Gordon Cinton; Juilliard School with Sergius Kagen and Beverly Johnson. *Career:* Debut: Juilliard 1964, as Katya Kabanova; Covent Garden debut 1966, in Die Zauberflöte: sang Jenůfa in 1972; English National Opera from 1970, notably Janáček's The Makropulos Case and Katya Kabanova; Appearances with Welsh National Opera and at the Glyndebourne Festival; Guest engagements in Prague, Brussels, New York, Chicago, Dallas, Washington and Seattle: roles include Marenka in The Bartered Bride, Mimi, Micaela in Carmen, Sieglinde, Elizabeth Zimmer in Elegy for Young Lovers, Mozart's Countess, Madama Butterfly, Ariadne, the Marschallin and Lady Billows in Albert Herring (Los Angeles, 1992); Masterclass for Ohio Light Opera, 1996. *Address:* c/o English National Opera, St Martin's Lane, London, WC2, England.

HAZELL, Andrea; Singer (Mezzo-soprano); b. 1965, Southampton, England. *Education:* Studied at Royal Academy of Music. *Career:* Many appearances throughout the United Kingdom in oratorio; Sang Second Witch in Dido and Aeneas for Amersham Festival, Offenbach's Perichole in Reading and Dorabella at the 1990 Cheltenham Festival; Sang in Carmen at Earl's Court, 1989, and on tour to Japan; Royal Opera, Covent Garden, 1990–, in Les Huguenots and Die Frau ohne Schatten and as Tefka in Jenůfa, 1993; Other roles include Marcellina in Le nozze di Figaro. *Address:* c/o Royal Opera House (Contracts), Covent Garden, London WC2E 9 DD, England.

HAZELL, Richard; Singer; b. 1940, Staffordshire, England. *Education:* Royal College of Music. *Career:* Debut: Film, Phantom of the Opera, 1961; Theatre and television work until 1973; Appearances with Royal Opera, Covent Garden, in Manon, Carmen, The Merry Widow, Andrea Chénier, La Rondine, Der Rosenkavalier, La Bohème and Paul Bunyan; Servant in La Traviata, 2001; Orge in the British premiere of Henze's

Policino; International tours with the D'Oyly Carte Opera Company; Former chairman of the Amici di Verdi and founder member of the Royal Opera House Education advisory council. *Address:* c/o Royal Opera House (contracts), Covent Garden, London, WC2, England. *Telephone:* (20) 7240 1200. *Fax:* (20) 72129502.

HAZUCHOVA, Nina; Singer (Mezzo-soprano); b. 24 May 1926, Czechoslovakia. *Education:* Conservatory, Bratislava. *Career:* Appeared with Slovak National Theatre; Roles included: Carmen, Amneris in Aida; Azucena in ll Trovatore; Eboli in Don Carlos; Maddalena in Rigoletto; Suzuki in Madama Butterfly; Rosina, in The Barber of Seville; Marina in Boris Godunov; Cherubino in The Marriage of Figaro; Nancy in Martha; Isabella in The Italian Girl in Algiers; Catherine in The Taming of the Shrew; Appeared as a Concert Singer performing with the best Czech orchestras; Has toured many countries including USSR, Germany, Austria, Belgium, Italy, Yugoslavia, Arabia, China, Mongolia; Vocal-Teacher, Academy of Music Arts (Vysoka skola muzickych umeni) Bratislava; mem, Slovak Music Foundation, Bratislava. *Recordings:* Has made numerous records. *Honours:* Meritorious Artist, 1968. *Address:* c/o Bratislava Academy of Music Arts, Vocal Faculty, Jiráskova 3, 81301 Bratislava, Slovakia.

HEADLEY, Erin; lirone player and viola da gamba player; b. 1948, Texas, USA. *Career:* Member of Tragicomedia, three musicians performing in the Renaissance and Baroque repertory; Concerts in the United Kingdom and at leading European early music festivals; Gave Stefano Landi's La Morte d'Orfeo at the 1987 Flanders Festival; Francesca Caccini's La liberazione di Ruggiero dall'isola d'Alcina at the 1989 Swedish Baroque Festival, Malmö. *Recordings include:* Proensa (troubadour songs), My Mind to me a Kingdom is (Elizabethan ballads, with David Cordier); A Musicall Dreame (duets from Robert Jones's 1609 collection); Biber's Mystery Sonatas; Concert programmes include The Lyre of Timotheus (incidental music by Handel, Bach, Vivaldi and Abel); Orpheus I Am (music based on the Orpheus myth by Landi, Monteverdi, Lawes and Johnson); Il Basso Virtuoso (songs by Landi, Monteverdi, Strozzi, Huygens and Purcell, with Harry van der Kamp); Three Singing Ladies of Rome; Monteverdi Madrigals from Book VIII and L'Orfeo; Early Opera: Peri's Euridice, Landi's La Morte d'Orfeo and Rossi's Orfeo. *Address:* c/o 14 Nightingale Lane, London N8 7QU, England.

HEALEY, Derek; Composer; b. 2 May 1936, England. *Education:* Studied organ with Harol Darke and composition with Herbert Howells at Durham University; Further study at the Royal College of Music and with Petrassi and Celibidache in Italy. *Career:* Tutor: University of Victoria, BC, Australia, 1969–71, College of Arts, University of Guelph, 1972–78; Professor of Composition and Theory, University of Oregon, 1979, returning to the United Kingdom in 1988. *Compositions include:* Opera Seabird Island, 1977, and children's opera, Mr Punch, 1969; Ballets Il Carcerato 1965 and The Three Thieves, 1967; Orchestral: The Willow Pattern Plate, 1957; Concerto for organ, strings and timpani, 1960; Butterflies for mezzo and chamber orchestra, 1970; Arctic Images, 1971; Tribulation, 1977; Music for a Small Planet, 1984; Mountain Music, 1985; Gabriola (A West Coast Canadian Set), 1988; Salal (An Idyll), 1990; Triptych, 1996; Chamber: String Quartet, 1961; Cello sonata, 1961; Mobile for flute and ensemble, 1963; Laudes for flute and ensemble, 1966; Maschere for violin and piano, 1967; Wood II for soprano and string quartet, 1982; English Dances for percussion sextet, 1987; Piano music including Lieber Robert, 1974; Organ music and songs; 3 organ sonatas, 1961, 1992, 1996. *Address:* 29 Stafford Road, Ruislip Gardens, Middlesex HA4 6PB, England.

HEARTZ, Daniel (Leonard); Educator; b. 5 Oct. 1928, Exeter, New Hampshire, USA. *Education:* AB, University of NH, 1950; MA, 1951; PhD, 1957, Harvard University. *Career:* Assistant Professor, Music, University of Chicago, 1957–60; Assistant Professor, 1960–64, Associate Professor, 1964–66, Professor, 1966–, Chairman, 1968–72, Music, University of CA, Berkeley; mem, American Musicological Society, Vice President, 1974–76; IMS; RMA; Societe Française de Musicologie; Gesellschaft für Musikforschung. *Publications:* Pierre Attaingnant, Royal Printer of Music, 1969; Edition of Mozart's Idomeneo, Neue Mozart Ausgabe, 1972; Mozart's Operas, 1990; Haydn, Mozart and The Viennese School 1740–1780, 1995; Music in European Capitals: The Galant Style 1720–1780, 2003. *Contributions:* Professional Journals including The Beggar's Opera and opéra-comique en vaudevilles, 1999. *Honours:* Dent Medal, RMA, 1970; Kinkeldey Prize, American Musicological Society, 1970; Guggenheim Fellowship, 1967–68, 1978–79; Elected Fellow of American Academy of Arts and Sciences, 1988. *Address:* 1098 Keith Avenue, Berkeley, CA 94708, USA.

HEASTON, Nicole; Singer (Soprano); b. 1965, Ohio, USA. *Education:* University of Akron, Ohio; Cincinnati Conservatory. *Career:* Debut: Houston Grand Opera as Gounod's Juliette; As Pamina, Washington Opera; Anne Trulove, The Rake's Progress, on her European debut at Montpellier, 1997; Concerts with Marc Minkowski at Halle, Brussels and Barcelona, 1995; Created Jacqueline Onassis in Michael Dougherty's Jackie O at Houston; Concert repertory includes works by Handel and Bach. *Recordings:* Une Bergère in Gluck's Armide. *Honours:* William Matheus Sullivan Foundation award, 1998. *Address:* c/o Music International, 13 Ardilaun Road, London N5 2QR, England.

HEATER, Claude; Singer (Tenor); b. 1930, Oakland, California, USA. *Education:* Studied in Los Angeles; Further study in Europe with Mario del Monaco and Max Lorenz. *Career:* Sang at first as baritone, on radio and tv and in Broadway Musicals; Bayerische Staatsoper 1964, in König Hirsch by Henze; Sang Wagner roles in Amsterdam, Brussels, Hamburg, Berlin and Milan; Bayreuth Festival 1966, as Siegmund and Melot; Other roles included Turiddu, Otello, Florestan and Samson; Guest appearances in South America; Sang Tristan at Spoleto, 1968 and appeared at Dresden, 1968, Barcelona, Bordeaux and Geneva, 1968–69; Budapest and Venice, 1970. *Recordings:* As Melot in Tristan und Isolde, conducted by Karl Böhm (Deutsche Grammophon).

HEBERT, Bliss; Stage Director; b. 30 Nov. 1930, Faust, New York, USA. *Education:* Piano, Syracuse University, with Robert Goldsand, Simone Barrere, Lelia Gousseau. *Career:* Debut at Stage Director, Santa Fe, 1957; General Manager, Washington Opera Society, 1960–63; Stage Director, New York City Opera, 1963–75, Metropolitan Opera, New York City, 1973–75 (debut with Les Contest d'Hoffmann); Guest Director, Juilliard School, 1975–76; Director of Opera Companies of San Francisco, 1963; Washington 1959; Houston, 1964; Fort Worth, 1966; Caramoor Festival, Katonah, New York, 1966; Seattle Opera, 1967; Cincinnati, 1968; La Gune Festival, 1968–; Portland, Oregon, 1969; Vancouver, 1969; San Diego, 1970; New Orleans, 1970; Toronto, 1972; Baltimore, 1972; Tulsa, 1975; Miami, Florida, 1975; Charlotte, North Carolina, 1975; Dallas, 1977; Shreveport, Los Angeles, 1977; Chicago, 1983; Montreal, 1984; Boston, 1984; Cleveland, 1988; Opera Northern Ireland, 1988; Virginia Opera, 1991; Opera Mexico City, 1993; Austin Opera, 1993; Florentine Opera, Milwaukee, 1994; Don Giovanni, 1996; Roméo et Juliette at San Diego, 1998. *Address:* c/o Florentine Opera Company, 735 North Water Street, Suite 1315, Milwaukee, WI 53202, USA.

HEBERT, Pamela; Singer (Soprano); b. 31 Aug. 1946, Los Angeles, California, USA. *Education:* Studied at the Juilliard School with Maria Callas, Tito Capobianco, Margaret Hoswell and Boris Goldovsky. *Career:* Debut: New York City Opera 1972, as Donn Anna; Appearances in New York as Mimi, title role in L'Incoronazione di Poppea, Vespina in Haydn's L'Infedeltà delusa and the Composer in Ariadne auf Naxos; Frequent concert engagements. *Address:* c/o New York City Opera, Lincoln Center, New York, NY 10023, USA.

HECHT, Joshua; Singer (Baritone); b. 1928, New York City, USA. *Education:* Studied with Lili Wexberg and Eva Hecht in New York and with Walter Tassoni in Rome. *Career:* Debut: Baltimore 1953, as Des Grieux in Manon; Sang in Boston, Chicago, Miami, Pittsburgh, San Francisco, Seattle and New Orleans; Metropolitan Opera from 1964; Further appearances at the New York City Opera and in Graz, Johannesburg, Barcelona, Bucharest, Dublin and Vancouver; Roles include the Wanderer in Siegfried, Amfortas, Rigoletto, Iago, Scarpia and the title role in Einstein by Dessau (Gelsenkirchen 1980); Sang Prospero in Martin's Der Sturm (The Tempest), Bremen, 1992; Australian Opera at Sydney (1994) as Schigolch in Lulu.

HECKMANN, Harald; Musicologist; b. 6 Dec. 1924, Dortmund, Germany; m. Elisabeth Dohrn, 25 August 1953, 1 s. *Education:* Gymnasium, Dortmund, 1934–43; Musicology, Freiburg/Breisgau, 1944–52; Assistant to Wilibald Gurlitt, Freiburg/Breisgau, 1952–54. *Career:* Teacher of Church Music History, College of Music, Freiburg/Breisgau, 1950–54; Director, German History of Music Archives, Kassel, 1955–71; Director, German Broadcasting Archives, Frankfurt am Main, 1971–91; mem, Honorary President, International Association of Music Libraries; President, International Inventory of Musical Sources; Board Member, Robert-Schumann Society; Co-President, International Repertoire of Music Iconography; History of Music Commission, FRG; President, International Schubert Society; Rotary. *Publications:* Deutsches Musikgeschichtlichs Archiv, Katalog der Filmsammlung, 1955–72; W A Mozart, Thamos, Koenig in Aegypten, Choere und Zwischenaktmusiken, 1956; W A Mozart, Musik zu Pantomimen und Balletten, 1963; Ch W Gluck, La Rencontre imprévue, Editor and Critic, 1964; Elektronische Datenverarbeitung in der Musikwissenschaft, 1967; Das Tenorlied, 3 vols, co-editor, 1979–86; Musikalische Ikonographie, co-editor, 1994; Various essays on musicology including La sventurata musica, 1996. *Address:* Im Vogelshaag 3, D65779 Ruppertshain/Ts, Germany.

HEDGES, Anthony (John); Reader in Composition and Composer; b. 5 March 1931, Bicester, England; m. Delia Joy Marsden, 1957, 2 s., 2 d. *Education:* Keble College, Oxford, MA, BMus, LRAM. *Career:* Teacher, Lecturer, Royal Scottish Academy of Music, 1957–63; Lecturer in Music, University of Hull, 1963, Senior Lecturer 1968; Reader in Composition, 1978–95; Founder-conductor, The Humberside Sinfonia, 1978–81;

Chairman, Composers' Guild of Great Britain, 1972, Joint Chairman 1973; Executive Committee of Composers' Guild 1969–73, 1977–81, 1982–87; Council Member, Composers' Guild. *Compositions include:* Orchestral: Comedy Overture, 1962; Sinfonia Semplice, 1963; Expressions, 1964; Concertante Music, 1965; Variations on a theme of Rameau, 1969; An Ayrshire Serenade, 1969; Celebrations, 1973; Symphony, 1972–73; Sinfonia Concertante, 1980; Scenes from the Humber, 1981; Showpiece, 1985; Symphony No. 2, 1997; Divertimento for String Orchestra, 1997; Choral: Gloria, unaccompanied, 1965; Epithalamium for chorus and orchestra, to text by Spenser, 1969; Bridge for the Living, for chorus and orchestra, to text by Philip Larkin, 1976; I Sing The Birth, for chorus and chamber orchestra, 1985; I'll Make Me a World, chorus and orchestra, 1990; Symphony No. 2, 1997; Chamber: Five preludes for piano, 1959; Sonatinas for flute, viola, bassoon, trumpet and trombone, 1982; Flute Trios, 1985, 1989; Piano Quartet, 1992; Many anthems, partsongs, albums of music for children; Music for television, film and stage. *Recordings:* Scenes from the Humber; Kingston Sketches; Bridge for the Living; Four Breton Sketches; Four Miniature Dances; Overture: Heigham Sound; Cantilena; Divertimento for string orchestra; An Ayrshire Serenade; Fiddlers Green; A Cleveland Overture; Piano Sonata; Various solo and chamber works. *Publications:* Basic Tonal Harmony, 1987, Comprehensive Archive in Hull Central Music Library. *Contributions:* regular contributor to The Guardian, The Scotsman, The Glasgow Herald, The Musical Times, 1957–63; The Yorkshire Post, 1963–73. *Honours:* Honorary D.Mus, University of Hull, 1997. *Address:* 76 Walkergate, Beverly, East Yorkshire HU17 9ER, England. *E-mail:* ahedges@westfieldmusic.karoo.co.uk. *Website:* westfieldmusic@karoo.net.

HEDWALL, Lennart; Composer, Conductor and Musicologist; b. 16 Sept. 1932, Gothenburg, Sweden; m. Ingegerd Henrietta Bergman, 13 April 1957, 4 s. *Education:* Royal College of Music, Stockholm, 1951–59; Composing and Conducting at Darmstadt, Vienna, Hilversum and Paris. *Career:* Debut: As composer, 1950; As professional conductor, Messiah, 1954; Conductor: Riksteatern, 1958–60, Great Theatre Gothenburg, 1962–65, Drottningholmteatern, 1966–70, Royal Theatre, 1967–68, Örebro Orchestra Society, 1968–74; Teacher, Dramatic School in Gothenburg, 1963–67, State Opera School, 1968–70, 1974–80, 1985–97; Director of Swedish National Music Museum, 1981–83; Member of the Royal Swedish Academy of Music and the Accademia Filarmonica of Bologna. *Compositions:* 2 Operas: Herr Sleeman Kommer and America, America; The Dress of Birgitta, church opera; Symphony 1 (retrospettiva) and 2 (elegiaca); Sagan, symphonic phantasy; Legend and Pezzo pastorale for orchestra; Jul igen, a Christmas Rhapsody; Several works for String Orchestra; Concertos for Flute, Oboe, Violoncello; Chamber Music: 3 String Quartets and 2 String Trios and others; Organ and Piano works; Several Song Cycles; Choir pieces and cantatas; Stage and television works; Many editions of old Swedish music. *Recordings:* As conductor with Orebro Chamber Orchestra, Värmland Sinfonietta, Musica Vitae and Östersunds Serenade Ensemble; As accompanist, several song recitals; Also others as Organist and Pianist. *Publications:* Hugo Alfvén, monography, 1973; Operettas and Musicals, 1976; The Swedish Symphony, 1983; Wilhelm Peterson-Berger, a biography in pictures, 1983; The Concert Life in Åbo 1872–76, 1989; Hugo Alfvén, a biography in pictures, 1990; The Musical Life in the Manors of Vermland 1770–1830, 1992; Form Structures in Roman's Sinfonias, 1995; A Survey of The Music in Vermland, 1995; Swedish Music History, 1996; The Composer Erik Gustav Geijer, 2001; Oscar Byström, a biography, 2003. *Contributions:* Dagen Nyheter, 1957–78; Musikrevy and others. *Address:* Mårdvägen 37, 16756 Bromma, Sweden.

HEELEY, Desmond; Stage Designer; b. 1 June 1931, West Bromwich, England. *Education:* Trained at the Shakespeare Memorial Theatre, Stratford, 1947–52. *Career:* Debut: La Traviata for Sadler's Wells, 1960; Productions for Glyndebourne (I Puritani, 1960) and English National Opera (Maria Stuarda, 1973); Work for the Metropolitan Opera includes Norma 1970, Pelléas et Mélisande 1972, Don Pasquale 1978 and Manon Lescaut 1980; Chicago designs for La Traviata seen at Detroit and Seattle, 1996. *Address:* c/o Lyric Opera of Chicago, 20 North Wacker Drive, Chicago, IL 60606, USA.

HEGAARD, Lars; Composer; b. 13 March 1950, Svendborg, Denmark; m. Susanne Taub, 10 Oct 1984, 4 s. *Education:* Diploma in Guitar, 1973; BA, Music, 1975; Examination of Teaching, 1977; Diploma in Composition, 1980. *Career:* Has played at all major festivals in Denmark and Scandinavia including on Radio; Has several commissions through The Danish Arts Foundation and 3 year Stipendium, 1983. *Compositions include:* Orchestra: Symphony Nos 1 and 2, Letter To My Son; Chamber Orchestra: Decet, Intersections; The Rolling Force, cello concerto; The Seasons According to I Ching; Triptych with Objects; Chamber Works: Five Fragments for String Quartet; The Four Winds, clarinet, cello, piano; Music For Chameleons, wind quintet; Configurations, alto flute, guitar; Six Studies for Two Guitars, Song-lines, guitar trio; 13 short pieces for flute, viola, harp; Dreamtracks, flute, clarinet, horn, percussion, guitar, cello; Four Square Dances for Saxophone Quartet; Partials' Play, flute, guitar, cello; Inside for bass clarinet, percussion and electronics; Beings for flute, clarinet, vibraphone, piano, guitar, violin, cello; Rituals for solo guitar, flute, clarinet, percussion, piano, violin, cello; Solo works: Variations, guitar; The Conditions of a Solitary Bird, guitar; Canto, cello; The Great Beam..., piano; Worldes Bliss, organ; Labyrinthus, electric guitar; Chains, organ; Vocal: Hymns, baryton, sinfonietta; Haiku, soprano, violin, piano; Far Calls, Coming Far, mezzo soprano, electric guitar, percussion, Text: James Joyce; The Dimension of Stillness, soprano, flute, guitar, cello, Text: Ezra Pound; Orchestra: Symphony No. 3; Chamber Orchestra: Twine for 9 instruments; Chamber works: Four visions for string quartet; Invocations for organ and 2 saxophones; Short Cuts for oboe, clarinet, saxophone and bassoon; Singing Sculpture for recorder, violin, cello and guitar; Ambient Voices for violin, clarinet, cello and piano; Octagora Room for guitar and string quartet; Vocal: Night Flower; Four Poems by Sylvia Plath for mezzo-soprano, percussion, piano, viola, double-bass; Nogle Lykkelige Sekunder: 4 Poems by Poul Borum for organ and basso. *Recordings include:* The Great Beam of the Milky Way, piano; 5 Fragments for string quartet; Decet for wind and string quintet; Partials Play for flute, guitar, cello; Four Square Dances for saxophone quartet; Triptych with objects; 13 Short Pieces; Twine; The Four Winds; Ambient Voices. *Contributions:* Interviews in Dansk Musiktidskrift. *Current Management:* Publishers: The Society for Publication of Danish Music, Gråbrodrestraede 18,1, 1156 Copenhagen, Denmark. *Address:* c/o Danish Composers' Society, Gråbrodre Torv 16, 1154 Copenhagen K, Denmark.

HEGARTY, Mary; Singer (soprano); b. 1960, Cork, Republic of Ireland. *Education:* Cork School of Music, at Aldeburgh and the National Opera Studio in London; further study with Josephine Veasey. *Career:* Has sung for Radio Telefis Eireann in Britten's Quatres chansons Françaises and the Brahms Requiem; Bach's Christmas Oratorio with Harry Christophers; Recitals in Ireland, the USA and at the Aix-en-Provence Festival (Une Heure avec Mary Hegarty); Covent Garden debut as a Flowermaiden in Parsifal, followed by Pousette in Manon; English National Opera as Nannetta and Naiad (Ariadne); Appearances with Opera Factory in La Calisto; With Opera North as Leonora in the British premiere of Nielsen's Maskarade (1989) in Ariane et Barbe-Bleue, the Mozart pasticcio The Jewel Box (1991) and as Frasquita; Buxton Festival 1991, in Mozart's Il Sogno di Scipione; Requiem for RTE; Princess Laula in Chabrier's Etoile, (Opera North); Papagena in Magic Flute (ENO); Eurydice in Orpheus in The Underworld, (D'Oyly Carte); Adele in Die Fledermaus, (Dublin Grand Opera Society); Eurydice in Orpheus in the Underworld; Cherubino in The Marriage of Figaro, Elisa in Mozart's Il Re Pastore, The Italian Soprano in Strauss's Capriccio and Gloria in world premiere of Gloria-A Pigtale, Nerina in La Fedeltà Premiata, Tanterabogus in The Fairy Queen; 1996–97 with the English National Opera included Norina in Don Pasquale, Blonde in Die Entführung aus dem Serail and Elvira in L'Italiana in Algeri; Fiorilla in Il Turco In Italia for Garsington in 1996; Susanna in The Marriage of Figaro at Grange Park, 1998; Season 2000 as Jessie in the premiere of Turnage's The Silver Tassie, for ENO, Puccini's Lisette and Donizetti's Adina for Opera North. *Recordings:* Debut solo album, A Voice is Calling; Title role in Gilbert and Sullivan's Patience; Eurydice in Offenbach's Orpheus in the Underworld; Mendelssohn Lobgesang with Naxos. *Honours:* Winner, Golden Voice of Ireland, 1984; Bursary for study at Aldeburgh; Irish Life, Sunday Independent Classical Music Award, 1988; Allied Irish Bank, RTE National Entertainments Award for Classical Section, 1987.

HEGEDUS, Olga; Cellist; b. 18 Oct. 1920, London, England. *Education:* London Violoncello School; Private Study, Pierre Fournier. *Career:* Debut: Recital, Wigmore Hall, London; Solo recitals; Many BBC and television appearances with trios, chamber ensembles and others; Member, Davey String Quartet; mem, Incorporated Society of Musicians; Musicians Union. *Recordings:* Art of Fugue, Bach, and Musical Offering, with Tilford Festival Ensemble; The Curlew, Warlock, with Haffner Ensemble; Vivaldi Motets with Teresa Berganza and English Chamber Orchestra; Dvořák Serenade, with English Chamber Orchestra Wind Ensemble; Schubert Quintet in C, with Gabrieli Quartet. *Contributions:* A Pictorial Review, English Chamber Orchestra, 1983. *Address:* 8 Kensington Place, London W8 7PT, England.

HEGGEN, Almar; Singer (bass); b. 25 May 1933, Valldal, Norway. *Education:* studied at Oslo Conservatory, with Paul Lohmann in Wiesbaden and with Clemens Kaiser-Breme in Essen. *Career:* debut, Oslo, 1957, as Masetto in Don Giovanni; sang in Wuppertal, Berlin, Frieburg, Wiesbaden, Nuremburg, Munich; guest performances in Sweden, Yugoslavia and others; Nuremburg 1969, in premiere of The Dream of Liu-Tung by Isang Yun; roles include: Rocco (also filmed), King Philip, Padre Guardiano, Sarastro, Don Alfonso, Tiresias (in Oedipus Rex), Daland, Pogner, Fafner, Hagen, Baron Ochs, Ptolomeo,

in Giulio Cesare; Wagner: Landgraf, King Henry, Marke, Hunding; Verdi: Zacharias, Ramphis; Mozart: Osmin; Rossini, Don Basilio; Smetana, Kezal; many oratorios including: Creation and Seasons of Haydn, Verdi's Requiem, Mozart's Requiem; teacher of singing; mem., Norsk Operasangerforbund, Norsk Musikerforening; Norsk Tonekunstnersamfunn, Kunsterforeningen. *Address:* Hareveien 40A, 1413 Tårnasen, Norway.

HEICHELE, Hildegard; Singer (soprano); b. Sept. 1947, Obernburg am Main, Germany; m. Ulrich Schwalb. *Education:* Studied at the Munich Musichochschule. *Career:* Debut: Klagenfurt, as Jennie in Aufstieg und fall der Stadt Mahagonny; Munich Staatsoper from 1971, notably as Mozart's Zerlina, Despina, Susanna and Ilia; Appearances in Vienna, Cologne (as Gretel), Karlsruhe (as Adina), Berlin, Zürich and Barcelona; Covent Garden 1977, 1983, as Adele in Die Fledermaus; Frankfurt 1981, in the Symphony of a Thousand, by Mahler; Monte Carlo 1982, Brussels 1984, as Susanna; Bayreuth Festival 1984, as the Woodbird in Siegfried; Sang at Kassel and Hanover 1988, as Elsa and Elisabeth; Concert engagements in Vienna, Graz and Venice (1985). *Recordings include:* Mahler's 8th Symphony; Egisto by Cavalli; Bach Magnificat, Handel Dettinger Te Deum; Video of Die Fledermaus (Covent Garden 1983).

HEIDEMANN, Stefan; Singer (Baritone); b. 1961, Germany. *Education:* Studied in Hanover and with Joseph Greindl. *Career:* Sang at Nuremberg Opera, 1988–91, Düsseldorf from 1991; Komische Oper Berlin, 1993, as Guglielmo, Ford in Falstaff, 1996; Season 1995–96 at Düsseldorf as Wagner's Wolfram, Falke in Die Fledermaus, and in the premiere of Gervaise Macquart by Klebe; Other roles include Lortzing's Tsar Peter, Mozart's Count, Nicolai's Herr Fluth, and Marcello in La Bohème; Guest engagements in concert and opera throughout Germany; Sang in the premiere production of Beuys by Franz Hummel, Düsseldorf and Vienna, 1998. *Address:* Deutsche Oper am Rhein, Heinrich-Heine Alle 16a, 40213 Düsseldorf, Germany.

HEIDSIECK, Eric; Pianist; b. 21 Aug. 1936, Reims, France. *Education:* Studied at the Ecole Normale de Musique, Paris and with Marcel Ciampi at the Paris Conservatoire; Private study with Alfred Cortot and Wilhelm Kempff. *Career:* Many appearances in London, France and elsewhere from 1955; Mozart's last twelve concertos in Paris, 1964, and the Beethoven Sonatas (1969, 1979); Frequent chamber music engagements, notably with Paul Tortelier; Repertory also includes the Suites of Handel; Professor at the Lyon Conservatoire, 1980–98. *Recordings include:* Le Tombeau de Couperin, by Ravel; Concertos by Mozart and Beethoven's Sonatas. *Publications include:* Cadenzas to Mozart's Piano Concertos. *Honours:* Premier Prix, Paris Conservatoire, 1954. *Address:* c/o Conservatoire National Supérieur de Lyon, 3 Rue de Angile, 69005 Lyon, France.

HEIFETZ, Daniel (Alan); Violinist and Teacher; b. 20 Nov. 1948, Kansas City, Missouri, USA. *Education:* Pupil of Theodore Norman; Studied with Sascha Jacobson, Israel Baker, and Heimann Weinstine, Los Angeles Conservatory, 1962–65, and with Efrem Zimbalist, Ivan Galamian, and Jascha Brodsky, Curtis Institute of Music, Philadelphia, 1966–71. *Career:* Debut as soloist in the Tchaikovsky Violin Concerto with the National Symphony Orchestra of Washington DC, on tour in New York; Thereafter regular tours of North America and the world; Appointed to the faculty of the Peabody Conservatory of Music, Baltimore, 1980. *Recordings:* For Leonarda. *Honours:* 1st prize, Merriweather-Post Competition, Washington DC, 1969; 4th prize, Tchaikovsky Competition, Moscow, 1978. *Address:* c/o Shaw Concerts Inc, ASCAP Building, 1900 Broadway, New York, NY 10023, USA.

HEIFETZ, Robin (Julian); Composer; b. 1 Aug. 1951, Los Angeles, California, USA. *Education:* Studied at UCLA with Paul Chihara and Roy Travis; University of Illinois with Salvatore Martirano and Ben Johnston, DMA 1978. *Career:* Composer-in-Residence at Shiftelsen Electronic Studio, Stockholm, 1978–79; Worked at various music departments in Canada and the USA; Director of the Centre for Experimental Music at the Hebrew University of Jerusalem, 1980. *Compositions include:* 2 Pieces for Piano 1972; Leviathan for piano 1975; Chirp for euphonium and piano 1976; Susurrus for computer and tape 1978; Child of the Water for piano 1978; For Anders Lundberg Mardrom 29 30 10 for tape 1979; A Clear and Present Danger for tape 1980; Spectre for tape 1980; Wanderer for synthesizer 1980; The Unforgiving Minute for 9 instruments 1981; In the Last, Frightened Moment for tape 1980; The Vengeance for Synthesizer 1980; The Arc of Crisis for tape 1982; A Bird in Hand is Safer than one Overheard for 2 or more performers 1983; At Daggers Drawn for tape 1983. *Honours:* Awards at the Concours International de Musique Electro-Acoustique, Bourges, France, 1979, 1981; International Computer Music Competition at Boston, 1983. *Address:* c/o ASCAP, ASCAP Building, 1 Lincoln Plaza, New York, NY 10023, USA.

HEILGENDORFF, Simone; Violist and Musicologist; b. 4 April 1961, Opladen, Germany. *Education:* Graduated. Final Artistic Examination (Viola Performance), Staatliche Hochschule fuer Musik im Rheinland,

Cologne, Germany, 1987; Magister Artium (Musicology), Albert-Ludwigs-University in Freiburg, Germany, 1989; Master of Music (Viola Performance), University of Michigan, USA, 1991; PhD (Musicology), Humboldt Universität zu Berlin, 1999. *Career:* Violist and founding member of the Kairos Quartet; Former member of symphonic orchestras: Junge Deutsche Philharmonie, , Serenata Basel (chamber orchestra); Work in Progress; Performances: Contemporary Music: Ensemble Modern (ISCM-Ens); Aventure Freiburg, Contemporary Ensemble (Aspen Music Festival 1991); Early Music: Ensemble für Alte Musik, Dresden; Concerto Köln; Faculty, Universität der Künste, Berlin; Member of the Kairos Quartet specializing in contemporary music in Berlin. *Recordings:* Numerous CD productions. *Publications:* Various musicological publications; Experimentelle Juszenierung Von Sprache und Musik, Vergleichende Analysen zu Dieter Schnebel und John Cage, Freiburg, Germany 2002. *Address:* Jagowstr 16, 10555 Berlin, Germany.

HEILMANN, Uwe; Singer (tenor); b. 7 Sept. 1960, Darmstadt, German; m. Tomoko Nakamura. *Education:* Studied in Detmold with Helmut Kretschmar. *Career:* Sang at Detmold from 1981 as Tamino, Don Ottavio and the Italian Singer in Rosenkavalier; Stuttgart Staatsoper from 1985, notably as Tamino, Belmonte, Don Ottavio, Cassio in Otello and Max in Der Freischütz; Munich Staatsoper as Don Ottavio, Vienna as Tamino; Sang Pylades in Iphigénie en Tauride at the Deutsche Oper Berlin; Appearances at the Salzburg and Ludwigsburg Festivals, 1988–89, including Max; Concert engagements and Lieder recitals, notably in works by Schubert and Wolf; Sang Cassio in Metropolitan Opera Gala, 1991; Season 1993–94 as Belmonte at La Scala and Steuermann at the Met. *Recordings include:* Tamino in Die Zauberflöte, conducted by Solti; Belmonte in Die Entführung conducted by Hogwood; Die schöne Mullerin, with James Levine; Haydn's Orfeo ed Euridice, with Cecilia Bartoli (L'Oiseau Lyre, 1997). *Current Management:* Askonas Holt Ltd, Lonsdale Chambers, 27 Chancery Lane, London, WC2A 1PF, England. *Telephone:* (20) 7400-1700. *Fax:* (20) 7400-1799. *E-mail:* info@askonasholt.co.uk. *Website:* www.askonasholt.co.uk.

HEIMANN, Robert; Singer (Baritone); b. 1958, Boston, USA. *Education:* Studied at Stanford University and in New York. *Career:* Sang in musicals on Broadway from 1981; Concert appearances at Carnegie Hall, including Linda di Chamounix, 1993; European debut, Belfast Opera, 1991, as Mozart's Figaro; Leipzig Opera from 1991, as Rossini's Figaro, Guglielmo, Papageno, Count Luna in Il Trovatore, and Leporello; Guest engagements in Brussels, 1992, Israel and Brunswick (as Silvio in Pagliacci). *Address:* c/o Leipzig Opera, Augustusplatz 12, 7010 Leipzig, Germany.

HEININEN, Paavo; Composer; b. 18 Jan. 1938, Järvenpää, Finland. *Education:* Studied Theory and Composition, Sibelius Academy, Helsinki, Finland, College of Music, Cologne, Germany and at Juilliard School of Music, New York, USA, 1956–62; Training as Pianist, Conductor and Musicologist. *Career:* Teacher of Theory and Composition, Turku Institute of Music, Turku, Finland, and at Sibelius Academy, Helsinki, 1966–. *Compositions include:* Orchestral Works: Symphony No. 1, 1958, revised 1960, Piano Sonata, Symphony No. 3, 1969, revised 1977, Dia, 1979; Works for Solo Instrument and Orchestra: Concerto for Piano and Orchestra No. 3, 1981; Cello Concerto, 1985; Violin Concerto, 1993; Lightings, 1998; Muraski in Casa Ando, 1998; Chamber Music: Jeu l and ll, 1980; Works for Solo Instrument: Gymel for Bassoon and Tape, 1978; What an Evening, What a Lightning for ensemble, 1999; Bluekeys for piano, 1999; Vocal and Choral Works: The Silken Drum, opera, 1980–83, Floral View with Maidens Singing, folk melody, 1980–83, Dicta, computer music, 1980–83; Another Heaven, Blooming Earth for male chorus, 1999. *Recordings include:* Adagio with Royal Philharmonic Orchestra under Walter Süsskind; Da Camera Magna; Sonatine, 1957; Sonatina Della Primavera; The Autumns, Finnish Radio Chamber Choir under Harald Andersén; Maiandros, tape composition; Discantus I; Touching; Concerto III with Paavo Heininen on Piano, the Sibelius Symphony Orchestra under Ulf Söderblom. *Address:* TEOSTO, Lauttassarentie 1, 00200 Helsinki 20, Finland.

HEINIÖ, Mikko; Composer and Professor of Musicology; b. 18 May 1948, Tampere, Finland; m. Riitta Pylvänäinen, 2 April 1977, one s., one d. *Education:* MA, 1972, PhD, 1984, University of Helsinki; Hochschule der Kunste, West Berlin, 1975–77; Diploma in Composition, Sibelius Academy, 1977. *Career:* Composer, 1972–; Teacher, University of Helsinki, 1977–85; Professor, Musicology, University of Turku, 1985–; President, Finnish Composers' Society, 1992–; Board Member, Copyright Organisation TEOSTO, 1984–. *Compositions include:* Orchestral: 6 piano concertos; Concerto for French horn and orchestra; Concerto for Orchestra; Possible Worlds, Symphony No. 1; Dall'ombra all'ombra; Trias; Symphony No. 2 (Songs of Night and Love); On the Rocks for orchestra, 1998; Minne, for sting orchestra, 1996; Envelope for Haydn's Trumpet Concerto, 2002; Chamber music: Duo for Violin and Piano; Brass Mass; Piano Trio; In G, violoncello and piano; Wintertime, harp

and marimba/vibraphone; Piano Quintet; Relay for cello and violin, 1998; Vocal: Landet som icke är, children's choir and piano; Vuelo de alambre, soprano and orchestra; The Shadow of the Future, soprano and brass instruments; La, piano and 4 voices; Wind Pictures, choir and orchestra; Hermes, piano, soprano, string orchestra and dance theatre, 1994; Treno della notte, clarinet, violin, cello and piano, 2000; Works for the stage: The Knight and the Dragon, church opera, 2000; Khora, Piano, 5 percussionists and dance theatre, 2001. *Recordings include:* Notturno di fiordo for flute and harp; Champignons à l'hermeneutique; Genom kvällen; Vuelo de alambre; Possible Worlds; Wind Pictures; Duo for Violin and Piano; Piano Quintet; Hermes; Piano Trio; In G; Wintertime; The Knight and the Dragon; Sextet. *Publications:* Contemporary Finnish Composers and their background, 1981; Contemporary Finnish Music, 1982; The Idea of Innovation and Tradition, 1984; The Reception of New Classicism in Finnish Music, 1985; The Twelve Tone Age in Finnish Music, 1986; Postmodern Features in New Finnish Music, 1988; Contextualisation in the research of art music, 1992; Finnish Composers (co-author), 1994; Finnish Music History 4: Music of Our Time, 1995; From Tones to Words, 1997; The Reception of New Finnish Operas 1975–1985, 1999. *Address:* Mustainveljestenkuja 2a, 20700 Turku Finland. *E-mail:* mikko.heinio@composers.fi.

HEINRICH, Siegfried; Conductor and Künstlerischer Direktor für Oper und Festspielkonzerte Bad Hersfeld; b. 10 Jan. 1935, Dresden, Germany. *Education:* Studied in Dresden and Frankfurt am Main, 1954–61. *Career:* Debut: Sänger im Dresdner Kreuzchor, 1948; Conductor, Frankfurt Chamber Orchestra, 1957; Since 1961, Artistic Director, Hersfeld Festival Operas and Concerts; Lecturer, Music Academy of Kassel; Künstlerischer Leiter des J. S. Bach-Institutes und Bachchores Frankfurt (M), 2000; Conductor, Radio Symphony Orchestras, Prague, Frankfurt am Main, Hanover, Luxemburg, ORTF, France, Budapest, Warsaw, Katowice, Kraków, Venice, Stuttgart; Concert Tours throughout Europe; New Interpretations of Bach's The Art of the Fugue, Beethoven's opera Fidelio with parts of Leonore I, Handel's Messiah, Monteverdi's Marian Vespers, Orfeo, Poppea, Il ritorno d'Ulisse. *Recordings:* Bach, Beethoven, Bizet, Brahms, Britten, Bruckner, Carissimi, Dvořák, Honegger, Liszt, Mahler, Mozart, Monteverdi, Ockeghem, Spohr, Telemann, Weber. *Publications:* Prospectuses and press reviews from Jubilate Schallplatten; Bärenreiter, Koch International. *Honours:* Bundesverdienstmedaille, 1976; Goethe-Medaille, 1983; Bundesverdienstkreuz, 1988. *Current Management:* Rainer Zagovec, Rathausstr 42, 65428 Rüsselsheim. *Address:* Arbeitkreis Für Musik e V, Nachtigallenstr 7, 36251 Bad Hersfeld, Germany.

HEISSER, Jean-François; pianist; b. 7 Dec. 1950, St Etienne, France. *Education:* Paris Conservatoire with Vlado Perlemuter. *Career:* many appearances in Europe and North America from 1975; Recital engagements from 1976 (Lincoln Center, New York) with violinist Regis Pasquier; Soloist with the Nouvel Orchestre Philharmonique de Radio-France, 1976–85; Professor at the Paris Conservatoire from 1986 and Director of the Maurice Ravel Summer Academy 1993–; Repertory includes Beethoven, Schubert, Dukas, Berio and Schoenberg. *Recordings include:* Albeniz, Granados, Turina, Falla, and Martinů's Double Concerto, with Georges Pludermarker. *Honours:* Premier Prix, Paris Conservatoire, 1973; Winner, International Competition at Jaén, Spain, 1974. *Address:* c/o Paris Conservatoire, 14 rue de Madrid, 75008 Paris, France.

HEJA, Domonkos; Conductor; b. 20 Dec. 1974, Budapest. *Education:* Piano, violin, trumpet, percussion at Bart ók Conservatory, 1997; Conducting degree, Ferenc Liszt Music Academy, 1998. *Career:* Debut: Budapest, 1993; Founder and Music Director, Danubia Youth Symphony Orchestra, 1993–; Conductor, Hungarian National Philharmonics; Budapest Philharmonic; Budapest Symphony; Franz Liszt Chamber Orchestra; Kosice Philharmonic. *Recordings:* M Haydn St Theresienmesse Hungaroton. *Honours:* First prize, National Percussion Competition, 1990; First prize, 9th International Conductors Competition, Budapest, 1998; Caripodis Prize, Mitropoulos Competition, Athens. *Current Management:* Budapest Artists Management. *Address:* 1118 Budapest, Somloi ut 39, Hungary.

HELD, Alan; Singer (bass-baritone); b. 1959, Washburn, Illinois, USA. *Education:* Studied at Millikin and Wichita State Universities. *Career:* Appearances with the Met Opera New York, in Billy Budd, Boris Godunov, Rigoletto, Tannhäuser and Tosca, from 1989; European debut at the Spoleto Festival, as the Villains in Les Contes d'Hoffman, 1989; Frankfurt Opera, as Šiškov in From the House of the Dead, the Rheingold Wotan and Leporello, from 1993; Royal Opera Covent Garden, as Gunther in Götterdämmerung, Borromeo in Palestrina and Orestes in Elektra, from 1996; Season 1997–98 with San Francisco Opera as Orestes and in Wagner's Ring, Gunther at Munich, London and Birmingham and Kurwenal for Chicago Lyric Opera; Further appearances with Washington Opera (ten roles), Seattle Opera and the Théâtre de la Monnaie, Brussels; Season 2001 Bass soloist, Beethoven's 9th with Simon Rattle and the Vienna Philharmonic; Chicago

Symphony, Houston Symphony, Pittsburgh Symphony, Metropolitan Opera Orchestra; Leporello in Don Giovanni at Covent Garden, 2002; Sang Wotan at the 2002 Bayreuth Festival. *Honours:* Richard Tucker Music Foundation Career Grants; Winner Birgit Nilsson Competition. *Current Management:* Askonas Holt Ltd, Lonsdale Chambers, 27 Chancery Lane, London, WC2A 1PF, England. *Telephone:* (20) 7400-1700. *Fax:* (20) 7400-1799. *E-mail:* info@askonasholt.co.uk. *Website:* www.askonasholt.co.uk.

HELESFAY, Andrea; Violinist; b. 18 Nov. 1948, Budapest, Hungary. *Education:* Béla Bart ók Conservatoire, 1968–73; Franz Liszt University of Music; Study with Vilmoš Tatrai, Andras Mihály. *Career:* Debut: Aged 11, Budapest; Member, Hungarian Chamber Orchestra, Budapest Chamber Ensemble, often as Soloist; Zürich Chamber Orchestra, Tonhalle Orchestra, Zürich, 1973–; Many appearances as soloist in Germany, Switzerland; frequent appearances on radio and television; Founder, Trio Turicum; mem, Various professional organisations. *Honours:* Award Winner, International Mozart Violin Competition, Salzburg. *Address:* Hadlaubstrasse 148, CH 8006 Zürich, Switzerland.

HELEY, John; Cellist; b. 1948, London. *Education:* Studied at the Guildhall School of Music with William Pleeth. *Career:* Sub-Principal Cellist of the Royal Philharmonic Orchestra, 1970–80; Freelance career from 1981 with chamber recitals London Sinfonietta and other ensembles; Associate Principal Cellist of the Academy of St Martin-in-the-Fields from 1986 including solo appearances; Principal cello of Orchestra of St John's, Smith Square,1977–. *Address:* c/o Academy of St Martin in the Fields, Raine House, Raine Street, London, E1W 3RJ, England.

HELFRICH, Paul M.; Composer; b. 5 May 1955, Philadelphia, USA. *Education:* BMus, Pennsylvania State University, 1978; MMus, Composition, Temple University, 1980; DMA, Composition, Temple University, 1986, studied with Clifford Taylor and Maurice Wright. *Career:* Owner, Nu Trax Recording Studio, Upper Darby, PA, 1981–; Senior Project Manager, 1987–91, Assistant Director, Exhibit Development, 1991–, Franklin Institute Science Museum, PA. *Compositions include:* Sine Nomine for brass chorale, 1974; Metamorphosis 1 for string orchestra, 1976; Theme and Five Variations for string orchestra and percussion, 1977; Five Short pieces for piano, 1977; Sonata Allegro in G for symphonic wind ensemble, 1978; Winds from a longer Distance, for tape and seven dancers, 1989; Song for healing, tape and solo dancer, 1990; The Robot Game Show, for tape, 1990; Movie soundtracks: Spirits in the Valley II, 1991, The Alchemist's Cookbook, 1991. *Address:* 130 Cunningham Avenue, Upper Darby, PA 19082, USA.

HELIN, Jacquelyn; Concert Pianist; b. 24 Sept. 1951, Chicago, Illinois, USA. *Education:* BM, University of Oregon, 1973; Graduate Studies, Yale University School of Music, 1973–74; MA, Stanford University, 1976; DMA, University of Texas, 1982. *Career:* Performances at Wigmore Hall, London, The Chagall Museum, Nice, American Embassy, Paris, Merkin Hall and Town Hall, New York, Dumbarton, Oaks, The Corcoran Gallery, Hirshhorn Museum, Washington DC and The Brooklyn College Conservatory of Music; The Dame Myra Hess Series; The Beethoven Discovery Series, The Aspen Music Festival; Featured Artist, PBS television programme honouring Virgil Thomson's 90th birthday; Premiered Joan Tower's Piano Concerto with Hudson Valley Philharmonic, 1986; Numerous radio appearances; WFMT Chicago, WNCN New York, WGMS Washington and throughout USA on National Public Radio. *Recordings:* For Musical Heritage, Virgil Thomson Ballet and Film Scores for Piano.

HELLAWELL, Piers; Composer and University Lecturer; b. 14 July 1956, Chinley, Derbyshire, England. *Education:* New College, Oxford, 1975–78; BA (Hons 1st Class), 1978; MA, 1984. *Career:* Composer-in-Residence, 1981–85, Lecturer in Music, 1986–, Queens University of Belfast; Northern Ireland Co-ordinator, European Music Year, 1985; Regular broadcasts, BBC, Radio 3. *Compositions:* Xenophon, commissioned, performed Belfast, elsewhere, Radio 3, by Ulster Orchestra, 1985; How Should I Your True Love Know, 1st performed by The Fires of London, Queen Elizabeth Hall, Peter Maxwell Davies conducting, 1986; Sound Carvings From Rano Raraku, commission (ACNI), 1st performed Northern Ireland tour and BBC, Martin Feinstein Quartet, 1988; Das Leonora Notenbuch, commissioned North West Arts, 1st performed Buxton Festival by William Howard, 1989, 1st broadcast BBC Radio 3, 1990; The Erratic Aviator's Dance, commissioned, performed at the Dance Place, Washington DC and elsewhere by Alvin Mayes Dance and Collaborations Ensemble, 1989; Memorial Cairns, commission, premiere, Ulster Orchestra, 1992, BBC Radio 3, 1993; River and Shadow, commission, premiere, Hilliard Ensemble, Antwerp, 1993, CBC Radio Canada, 1994; Victory Boogie-Woogie, commission, premiere, Riga Piano Duo, Riga, 1993; High Citadels, commission, premiere, Jorg Vögel, Meerbusch Kunst Expo (Germany), 1994; Truth or Consequences, BBC broadcast, 1994; Camera Obscura, commission, premiere,

Philip Mead, Rainbow Over Bath, 1994; Sound Carvings from the Ice Wall, BBC commission, premiered by Psappha, Manchester, 1995, BBC, 1995; Takla Makan, commission, premiere, Evelyn Glennie at Cheltenham Festival, 1995, BBC, 1995; Do Not Disturb, youth chorus, 1996; Let's Dance, for percussion, 1996; Sound Carvings from the Water's Edge, for 11 strings, 1996; The Building of Goves for piano quartet, 1998. *Current Management:* Maecenas Music, London. *Address:* Department of Music, Queens University of Belfast, Belfast BT7 1NN, Northern Ireland.

HELLEKANT, Charlotte; Singer (Mezzo-soprano); b. 15 Jan. 1962, Hogalid, Sweden. *Education:* Eastman School of Music, with Jean DeGaetani, at the Curtis Institute. *Career:* Opera engagements include Cherubino for Portland and Washington Operas, Dorabella for the Canadian Opera Company, Charlotte and the Composer in Ariadne for Glimmerglass Opera and Musetta in Leoncavallo's Bohème at St Louis; Season 1995–96 as Bart ók's Judith with the Orchestre de Paris, Charlotte at Washington, the Page in Salome for the Metropolitan Opera (debut role) and Ino in Semele at Aix-en-Provence; Contemporary roles include Lotte in Bose's Werther at Santa Fe, Erika in Barber's Vanessa, Cherubino in Corigliano's Ghosts of Versailles, at Chicago, the leading role in Bergman's The Singing Tree, for Finnish National Opera and Nastassja in Krasa's Verlobung in Traum; Concerts include Marguerite in La Damnation de Faust (Stockholm Philharmonic Orchestra), Mahler's 2nd Symphony (San Francisco Symphony Orchestra), Les Nuits d'Eté (Cleveland) Mahler's Rückert Lieder and Das Lied von der Erde (Netherlands Radio Philharmonic Orchestra); Berlioz L'Enfance du Christ with John Nelson and Mozart's Requiem under Neeme Järvi; Berio's Epiphanies with the composer conducting, Des Knaben Wunderhorn with the Swedish Radio Symphony Orchestra and Le Martyre de Saint Sebastien; Season 1997 as Cherubino at the Opéra Bastille, Salzburg debut as Amando in Ligeti's Le Grand Macabre, and Charlotte for New Israeli Opera; Season 1999–2000 as the Berlioz Marguerite at Salzburg, Nicklausse in Hoffmann at Antwerp and Varvara in Katya Kabanova at Amsterdam. *Recordings include:* Krasa's Verlobung in Traum; Mahler's 2nd Symphony; Ligeti's Le Grand Macabre. *Address:* c/o IMG Artists, Lovell House, 616 Chiswick High Road, London W4 5RX, England.

HELLELAND, Arild; Singer (Tenor); b. 29 Nov. 1949, Norway. *Education:* Studied in Oslo, Bergen and Gothenburg. *Career:* Concert appearances throughout Scandinavia; Norwegian State Opera at Oslo from 1989, as Janek in The Makropulos Case, Eisenstein in Die Fledermaus, and Mime in Wagner's Ring (also at Helsinki, 1996); Deutsche Oper Berlin, 1994–95, as Shuisky in Boris Godunov, Monostatos in Die Zauberflöte; Royal Opera, Stockholm, in A Dreamplay by Lidholm; Sellem in The Rake's Progress on Swedish television; Edinburgh, and other Festival engagements; Sang Mime in Siegfried at Helsinki, 1998. *Address:* c/o Finnish National Opera, PO Box 176, Helsingkatu 58, 00251 Helsinki, Finland.

HELLER, Richard (Rainer); Composer; b. 19 April 1954, Vienna, Austria; m. Shihomi Inoue, 26 Aug 1980. *Education:* Diploma in Composition, 1979; Final Examination in Composition for Audio-Visual Media, 1978, Final Examination for Cultural Management, 1979, Hochschule für Musik und Darstellende Kunst, Vienna. *Career:* Numerous performances of own works in Argentina, Austria, Belgium, Bulgaria, Czechoslovakia, Denmark, Egypt, France, Germany, Greece, Hungary, Italy, Japan, Kazakhstan, Netherlands, Romania, Russia, Switzerland, Spain, Saudi Arabia, South Africa, Turkey, Uruguay, Yugoslavia; Teaching Composition and Music Theory, Music Academy, Augsburg, Germany, 1979–. *Compositions include:* Concerto for violin; Concerto for 2 pianos and orchestra; Sinfonietta for wind orchestra; Concerto for bass clarinet; Concerto for marimba; Concertino for orchestra; Concerto per fiati; Toccata for wind orchestra; Novelette, piano trio; 3 moments musicaux, guitar quartet; string quartet; Cellophonie, 8 violoncellos; Statement, string trio; Elegy on texts out of Duineser Elegien by R M Rilke; Ballade, piano 4 hands; Various pieces for chamber ensembles; Songs; Solo pieces for piano, organ, bass clarinet; Numerous commissions. *Recordings:* Augsburger Gitarrenquartett; Organ-piano; MC, live documentations; Numerous radio recordings. *Address:* Reichenberger Strasse 24, 86161 Augsburg, Germany.

HELLERMANN, William, MA, DMA; composer; b. 15 July 1939, Wisconsin, USA; m. 1985; one s. one d. *Education:* Columbia University School of Arts; private study with Stefan Wolpe. *Career:* mem. BMI; ACA. *Compositions:* Time and Again, for orchestra, 1967; Anyway..., for orchestra, 1976; But the Moon..., for guitar and orchestra, 1975; Tremble, for solo guitar; Squeek for desk chair, 1978; Post/Pone for guitar and 5 instruments, 1990; Hoist by Your Own Ritard, 1993. *Recordings:* Ariel, for electronic tape, 1967; At Sea; Ek-Stasis I; Passages 13–The Fire. *Publications:* Articles published; Beyond Categories, 1981; Experimental Music, 1985; Scores: Row Music, Tip of the Iceberg, Time and Again for symphony orchestra; Long Island

Sound; Distances/Embraces; Circle Music 2 and 3; Passages 13–The Fire; To the Last Drop; Ek-Stasis I. *Honours:* Prix de Rome, American Academy, 1972; NEA Fellowship, 1976–79; Composer in Residence, Center for Culture and Performing Arts, State University of New York at Buffalo. *Address:* PO Box 31, Philmont, NY 12565, USA.

HELLMANN, Claudia; Singer (Mezzo-soprano); b. 1931, Berlin, Germany. *Education:* Studied in Berlin. *Career:* Debut: Oper, Munster, 1958–60; Stuttgart Staatsoper, 1960–66, Nuremberg, 1966–75; Appearances at Bayreuth Festival, 1958–61, as Wellgunde and a Flower Maiden; La Scala Milan, 1963, as Flosshilde; Sang in concert at the Salzburg Festival, 1961–85; Hamburg Staatsoper from 1960, Théâtre de la Monnaie Brussels, 1963–67; Other roles have included Marcellina, Magdalena in Die Meistersinger, Mistress Quickly, Fidalma in Matrimonio Segreto and Frau von Hufnagel in Henze's Der Junge Lord; Many concert and oratorio appearances. *Recordings:* Ismene in Orff's Antigonae, Bruckner's F minor Mass; Die Walküre; Bach's Easter Oratorio; Bach Church Cantatas. *Address:* c/o Stuttgart Staatsoper, Oberer Schlossgaten 6, 7000 Stuttgart, Germany.

HELLWIG, Klaus; Pianist and Educator; b. 3 Aug. 1941, Essen, Germany; m. Mi-Joo Lee. *Education:* Folkwang Hochschule Essen with Detlek Kraus, in Paris with Pierre Sancan; summer courses with Guido Agosti and Wilhelm Kempff. *Career:* concerts throughout Europe, USA and Canada, Far and Middle East, all German radio stations, BBC London, NHK Tokyo; Prof., Univ. of the Arts, Berlin. *Recordings:* FX Mozart Concerti in C and E Flat, Cologne Radio Orchestra, conductor Roland Bader (Schwann); Haydn Concerto in D, Mozart Concerto KV 537; Bach Inventions; recordings of 20 other works; Carl Reinecke: The Four Piano Concerti. *Honours:* Prize at the Concours Internationale M. Long–J. Thibaud, Paris, 1965; First Prize, Concorso Internazionale G. B. Viotti, Vercelli, Italy, 1966. *Address:* Mommsenstr 58, 10629 Berlin, Germany. *E-mail:* hellwig.lee@t-online.de.

HELM, E(rnest) Eugene; Musicologist and Professor; b. 23 Jan. 1928, New Orleans, Louisiana, USA. *Education:* Southeastern Louisiana College, BME, 1950; Louisiana State University, MME, 1955; North Texas State University, PhD, 1958. *Career:* Faculty Member, Louisiana College 1953–55, Wayne (Neb) State College 1958–59, University of Iowa 1960–68; Associate Professor 1968–69, Professor 1969–, of Music, Chairman, Musicology Division 1971–87, University of Maryland; Co-ordinating Editor, Carl Philipp Emanuel Bach Edition, 1982–89. *Publications:* Music at the Court of Frederick the Great, 1960; With A Luper, Words and Music, 1971, 2nd edition 1982; A Thematic Catalogue of the Works of Carl Philipp Emanuel Bach, 1987; The Cannon and the Curricula, 1994. *Contributions:* Articles in numerous periodicals and other publications. *Address:* c/o Department of Music, University of Maryland, College Park, MD 20742, USA.

HELM, Hans; Singer (Baritone); b. 12 April 1934, Passau, Germany. *Education:* Studied with Else Zeidler and Franz Reuter-Wolf in Munich, Emmi Muller in Krefeld. *Career:* Debut: Graz 1957, in Boris Godunov; Sang in Vienna, Cologne, Frankfurt, Munich, Düsseldorf and Hanover; Salzburg Festival 1973, in the premiere of De Temporum fine Comoedia by Orff; Glyndebourne Festival 1976, as the Count in Le nozze di Figaro (also at Covent Garden, 1976 and 1991); Vienna Staatsoper, 1987 and 1990, as Agamemnon in Iphigénie en Aulide, and in Die Soldaten; Munich 1989, as Faninal in Der Rosenkavalier; Sang The Forester in The Cunning Little Vixen at the Vienna Volksoper, 1992; Season 1995–96 as Donner in Das Rheingold at Vienna and Strauss's Faninal in Munich; Many concert appearances. *Recordings:* Otello (EMI); De Temporum fine Comoedia and Die Frau ohne Schatten (Deutsche Grammophon). *Address:* c/o Staatsoper, Opernring 2, 1010 Vienna, Austria.

HELM, Karl; Singer (Bass); b. 3 Oct. 1938, Passau, Germany. *Education:* Studied with Else Zeidler in Dresden and with Franz Reuter-Wolf in Munich. *Career:* Debut: Berne 1968, as Don Alfonso in Così fan tutte; Member of the Bayerische Staatsoper, Munich; Guest appearances in Geneva, Paris, Düsseldorf, Hamburg and Stuttgart; Other roles include Arkel in Pelléas et Mélisande, Rocco, King Philip, Zaccaria, Varlaam, Fasolt, Falstaff in Die Lustigen Weiber von Windsor, Dulcamara, and Melitone in La Forza del Destino; Berlin Staatsoper 1987, in La Cenerentola; Munich 1990, as First Nazarene in Salome; Sang Swallow in Peter Grimes at Munich, 1991; Many concert appearances. *Recordings include:* Die Feen by Wagner. *Address:* Bayerische Staatsoper, Postfach 745, 8000 Munich 1, Germany.

HELMS, Dietrich, MA, DPhil; Musicologist; b. 23 July 1963, Westfalan, Germany. *Education:* Westfälische Wilhelms, Universität Münster, Germany, St Peter's Coll., Oxford. *Career:* editorial work for the Hallesche Händel-Ausgabe 1996–7; lecturer at the Institut für Musik und Didaktik at Dortmund Univ. 1997–; lectureships at the Univs of Münster, Hamburg and Bremen; mem. Gesellschaft für Musikforschung, Royal Musical Asscn, Arbeitskreis Studium Populäres Musik, Arbeitskreis musikpädagogische Forschung. *Publications:*

Heinrich VIII und die Musik: Überlieferung, musikalische Bildung des Adels und Kompositionstechniken eines Königs 1998, Beiträge zur Popularmusikforschung (ed.), Samples: Notizen, Projekte und Kurzbeiträge zur Popularmusikforschung (ed.); contrib. to Die Musikforschung, Beiträge zur Popularmusikforschung, Hamburger Jahrbuch für Musikwissenschaft. *Address:* Institut für Musik und ihre Didaktik, Universität Dortmund, 44221 Dortmund, Germany (office). *Telephone:* (231) 755-2975 (office). *Fax:* (231) 755-6236 (office). *E-mail:* Dietrich.Helms@Uni-Dortmund.de (office).

HELMS, Joachim; Singer (Tenor); b. 24 June 1943, Rostock, Germany. *Education:* Studied at the Franz Liszt Musikhochschule Weimar and in Dresden. *Career:* Debut: Erfurt, 1974, as Ernesto in Don Pasquale; Sang at Erfurt, 1974–83, as Mozart's Ferrando and Tamino, the Duke of Mantua, Nemorino, Don Carlos, Max in Der Freischütz and Sergei in Katerina Izmailova; Dresden Staatsoper from 1984, as Rodolfo, Alfredo and Don Ottavio; Guest appearances in the former Soviet Union, Poland, Bulgaria, Austria and Switzerland; Sang Ernesto at Leipzig, 1989; Many concert appearances and broadcasting engagements. *Address:* c/o Staatsoper, 8012 Dresden, Germany.

HELPS, Robert; Composer, Pianist and Professor; b. 23 Sept. 1928, New Jersey, USA. *Education:* Juilliard Preparatory Department and Institute of Musical Arts, 1936–43; Private study with Abby Whiteside, piano; and Roger Sessions, composition, 1943–60. *Career:* Debut: Recital, New York, 1990; Active piano and chamber music performances including many premieres with leading contemporary music groups in New York, Boston, Chicago, San Francisco, Los Angeles; Tours with Bethany Beardslee, Soprano, Rudolf Kolisch, Isidore Cohen, Jorja Freezanis, Violin. *Compositions:* Symphony, Two Piano Concertos, various chamber music and songs; Many solo piano pieces, voice and orchestra. *Recordings include:* Nocturne, 3 Hommages; Hommage a Faure; 3 Hommages, Nocturne for string quartet. *Publications include:* Nocturne, 1975; Valse Mirage, 1978; Eventually the Carousel Begins, 1991; The Running Sun, 1976; Symphony No. 1; Piano Concerto No. 1. *Address:* 4202 E Fowler Avenue, USF 30838, Tampa, FL 33620-9951, USA.

HELTAY, Laszlo (Istvan); British (b. Hungarian) Conductor; b. 5 Jan. 1930, Budapest, Hungary. *Education:* MA, Franz Liszt Academy of Music, Budapest, with Kodály and Bardos; BLitt, Merton Coll., Oxford. *Career:* Director of Music, Merton Coll., Oxford, 1960–64; Founded the Kodaly Choir, and Schola Cantorum of Oxford (subsequently Collegium Musicum Oxoniense), 1960 and gave premiere of Kodaly's The Music Makers, 1964; Associate Conductor, New Zealand Broadcasting Corporation Symphony Orchestra 1964–65; Musical Dir, New Zealand Opera Company, 1964–66; Conductor, Phoenix Opera Company, London, 1967–69, 1973; Conductor, Collegium Musicum of London, 1970–89; Dir of Music, Gardner Centre, Sussex Univ. 1968–78; Founder and Music Dir Brighton Festival Chorus 1967–94, Conductor Emeritus 1994–; Music Dir, Chorus of the Academy of St Martin in the Fields, 1975–99; Dir of Royal Choral Society, 1985–94; Dir, Coro de Radio-Television Española, Madrid 1997–2000; concerts with Norddeutscher Rundfunk Chor; the Philharmonia, the Royal Philharmonic, London Philharmonic and Dallas Symphony Orchestras; masterclasses for young choral conductors in Europe and USA. *Recordings:* Choral works of Kodály, Respighi, Rossini and Haydn (Stabat Mater and Salve Regina) on Argo and Decca Labels; Paco Peña, Misa Flamenca for Virgin; recordings for CBS and Nimbus; Chorus Director for film 'Amadeus'. *Honours:* International Kodály Medal, 1982; Hon. DMus Univ. of Sussex, 1995; Hon. Fellow of Merton Coll., Oxford, 1997. *Address:* Can Lleuger, Apto 43 08318 Canyamars Spain.

HEMM, Manfred; Singer (Baritone); b. 1961, Mödling, Austria; m. Amanda Roocroft, 1995. *Education:* Studied at the Vienna Conservatory with Waldemar Kmentt. *Career:* Debut: Klagenfurt 1984, as Mozart's Figaro; Sang at Augsburg 1984–86, Graz, 1986–88, notably as Papageno, Leporello and Polyphemus in Acis and Galatea; Vienna Staatsoper from 1988 (title role in the premiere of Von Einem's Tuliphant, 1990); Guest appearances as Bayreuth, Basel, Berne, Zürich, Salzburg (Figaro, 1989–91) and Orange; Sang Figaro at the Deutsche Oper Berlin, 1990, Aix-en-Provence Festival, 1991; Metropolitan Opera debut 1991, as Papageno; Salzburg Festival, 1992, as the One Eyed Brother in Die Frau ohne Schatten; Philadelphia 1995, as Giorgio in I Puritani; Sang Kuno in Der Freischütz in concert with the Royal Opera, 1998; Sang Amfortas for Scottish Opera and Mozart's Figaro in Munich 2000; Frequent Lieder recitals and concert appearances. *Recordings include:* Video of Die Zauberflote, from the Met. *Address:* c/o Metropolitan Opera, Lincoln Center, New York, NY 10023, USA.

HEMSLEY, Thomas, CBE, FGSM; British opera and concert singer, producer and educator; b. 12 April 1927, Coalville, Leicestershire, England; m. Gwenllian James 1960; three s. *Education:* Brasenose College, Oxford, private music studies. *Career:* opera debut, Mermaid Theatre, London, 1951; St Paul's Cathedral, London, 1950–51; Stadttheater, Aachen, 1953–56; Deutsche Oper am Rhein, 1957–63; Opernhaus Zürich, Switzerland, 1963–67; Performed at Glyndebourne, 1953–83, as Hercule (Alceste), Masetto (Don Giovanni), Sprecher (Zauberflöte), Minister (Fidelio), Dr Reischmann (Elegy for Young Lovers), Musiklehrer (Ariadne), Aeneas (Dido), Arbace (Idomeneo); Edinburgh and Bayreuth Festivals, (1968–70, as Beckmesser), Covent Garden, Scottish Opera, Welsh Opera, English National Opera, English Opera Group, Kent Opera (Falstaff, 1980); Created Demetrius in A Midsummer Night's Dream (Aldeburgh 1960), Mangus in The Knot Garden at Covent Garden, 1970, and Caesar in Iain Hamilton's Catiline Conspiracy, 1974; Produced The Return of Ulysses for Kent Opera, 1989; Soloist with many major orchestras; Frequent broadcast on radio and television; Repertoire includes more than 150 Operatic Roles; Masterclasses, BBC television, Danish television, Music colleges in the United Kingdom, Denmark, Sweden, Norway; Visiting Professor, Royal College of Music, London and Royal Northern College of Music; Guest Professor, Royal Danish Academy of Music; Director of Opera, Dartington International Music Summer School; mem, Equity; ISM; Garrick Club; Member, Royal Philharmonic Society; Fellow Royal Society of Arts. *Recordings:* Operas: Dido and Aeneas; The Fairy Queen; Saul; Xerxes; Alcina; Alceste; Midsummer Night's Dream; Savitri; The Knot Garden; Meistersinger; The Olympians; The Wandering Scholar. Cantatas: Bach; Handel; Schütz; Songs: Schubert; Schumann; Wolf; Berkeley; Fauré, Duparc, Roussel; Choral: Delius Requiem. *Publications include:* Singing and Imagination 1998. *Honours:* Honorary RAM, 1974; Hon FTCL, 1988. *Address:* 10 Denewood Road, London N6 4AJ, England.

HENCK, Herbert; Pianist and Writer on Music; b. 28 July 1948, Treysa, Hesse, Germany. *Education:* Studied in Mannheim and Stuttgart, and at the Hochschule für Musik, Cologne, with Aloys Kontarsky. *Career:* Many appearances in Germany and elsewhere in 20th Century repertory, notably with music by Cage, Stockhausen, Boulez and Schoenberg; leader of courses at Darmstadt, Cologne and other avant-garde centres. *Recordings include:* Boulez Sonatas; Music of Changes, Cheap Imitation and Music for Piano, 1–84, by John Cage; Stockhausen's Klavierstücke I–IX; Les Heures persanes, by Koechlin; Music by Schoenberg and Charles Ives. *Publications include:* Neuland, Ansätze zur Musik der Gegenwart, 1980–85; Experimentelle Pianistik, 1994. *Address:* c/o Hochschule für Musik, Dagoherstrasse 38, 50688 Cologne, Germany.

HENDERSON, Gavin Douglas, CBE; British *Principal, Trinity College of Music*; b. 3 Feb. 1948, Brighton, England; m. Mary Jane Walsh, 1992, 2 s. *Education:* Brighton Coll. of Art, Kingston Art Coll., Slade School of Fine Art, Univ. Coll. London. *Career:* debut as soloist, Wigmore Hall 1972; performer, BBC radio and television, festivals including City of London, Brighton, Artistic Dir, Brighton, York, Portsmouth, Crawley, Bracknell (jazz, folk and early music), Bournemouth festivals; Chief Exec., the New Philharmonia and Philharmonia Orchestra 1975–79; Chair., Music Panel, Arts Council of England; Vice-Pres., British Arts Festivals Asscn; Vice-Pres., European Festivals Asscn; Principal, Trinity Coll. of Music, London; Artistic Dir, Dartington Int. Summer School 1985–; Chair., Nat. Foundation for Youth Music 1998–; mem. RSA, ISM, Musicians' Union, Worshipful Co. of Musicians, RSM. *Publications:* Picasso and the Theatre 1982, Festivals UK Arts Council 1986, National Arts and Media Strategy (Festivals Section) 1991; contrib. to Musical Times, Classical Music, Tempo, The Listener. *Honours:* Hon. MA (Sussex); Hon. Fellow, Sussex Univ., Univ. of Brighton. *Address:* Trinity College of Music, Mandeville Place, London, W1M 6AQ, England.

HENDERSON, Katherine; Singer (Mezzo-soprano); b. 1970, Cape Town, South Africa. *Education:* University of Cape Town; National Opera Studio, 1998. *Career:* Debut: Beethoven's Choral Fantasia, Cape Town Symphony Orchestra, 1994; Sang title role in Peter Brook's La Tragédie de Carmen, Cape Town; Concert for Nelson Mandela, 1996; Appearances at Cape Town as Lola in Cavalleria Rusticana and as Maddalena in Rigoletto; Carmen for Castleward Opera, Belfast; Bess in Porgy and Bess Suite, Peterborough; Mercédès in Carmen for Opera North and Mozart's Requiem at Basingstoke; Season 1999 at Mercedes, at Leeds; The Kingdom by Elgar, Isle of Wight; Further concerts. *Honours:* Winner, Wendy Fine Opera Prize Competition, 1994. *Address:* Music International, 13 Ardilaun Road, London N5 2QR, England.

HENDERSON, Moya; Composer; b. 2 Aug. 1941, Quirindi, New South Wales, Australia. *Education:* Studied at the University of Queensland and with Maurice Kagel in Cologne. *Compositions include:* Sacred Site for Organ and Tape, 1983; The Dreaming for Strings, 1985; Celebration 40,000, piano concerto, 1987; Currawong: A Symphony Of Bird Sounds, 1988; Waking Up The Flies, piano trio, 1990; Wild card for Soprano, Cello and Piano, 1991; Anzac Fanfare for soprano and orchestra, 1995; Lindy, opera, 1997; In Paradisum for chorus, 1997; I Walked into my Mother, music drama for radio, 1998; Music theatre pieces, chamber

and vocal music. *Address:* c/o 1A Eden Street, PO Box 567, Crows Nest, NSW 2065, Australia.

HENDL, Walter; Conductor, Pianist and Composer; b. 12 Jan. 1917, West New York, New Jersey, USA; m. Barbara Helsley, 1 d. by previous marriage. *Education:* Studied piano with Clarence Adler; Piano scholarship student of David Saperton and conducting scholarship student of Fritz Reiner, Curtis Institute of Music, Philadelphia; Conducting student of Serge Koussevitzky, Berkshire Music Center, Tanglewood, Massachusetts, summers 1941–42. *Career:* Assistant Conductor, New York Philharmonic Orchestra, 1945–49; Music Director, Dallas Symphony Orchestra, 1953–72; Associate Conductor, Chicago Symphony Orchestra, 1958–64; Music Director, Ravinia Festival, 1959–63; Director, Eastman School of Music, Rochester, New York, 1964–72; Music Director, Erie (Pennsylvania) Philharmonic Orchestra, 1976–. *Recordings:* Several. *Address:* c/o Erie Philharmonic Orchestra, 409 G Daniel Baldwin Building, Erie, PA 16501, USA.

HENDRICKS, Barbara; Singer (Soprano); b. 20 Nov. 1948, Stephens, Arkansas, USA. *Education:* Juilliard School of Music with Jennie Tourel. *Career:* Debut: Mini-Met, New York, 1973 in Four Saints in Three Acts; Glyndebourne 1974, in La Calisto; San Francisco, 1976, as Monteverdi's Poppea; Berlin Deutsche Oper, 1978, as Susanna in Le nozze di Figaro; Orange Festival, 1980, as Gilda; Paris Opéra, 1982, as Gounod's Juliette; Los Angeles and Covent Garden, 1982, as Nannetta in a new production of Falstaff conducted by Giulini; Metropolitan Opera debut 1986, as Sophie in Der Rosenkavalier (returned 1987, as Susanna); Song recitals in the USA, Europe and Russia with Dimitri Alexeev, Daniel Barenboim, Michel Béroff and Radu Lupu as accompanists; Concert appearances with Barenboim, Bernstein, Dorati, Giulini, Karajan, Maazel, Mehta and Solti; Tours of Japan with Karajan, Bernstein and the Vienna State Opera; Festival engagements at Aix, Edinburgh, Montreux, Orange, Prague, Salzburg and Vienna; Debut at La Scala 1987, Susanna; Sang at the opening concert of the Opéra Bastille Paris, 1989; Norina in Don Pasquale at Lyon, 1989 (also at Venice 1990); Debut as Manon at Parma, 1991; Sang Micaela at Orange, 1992; Mahler's 4th Symphony at Ludwigsburg Festival, 2000; Engaged for premiere of Angels in America, by Peter Eötvös, Paris Châtelet, 2004. *Recordings include:* Mahler 2nd Symphony and Mozart Masses (Deutsche Grammophon); Haydn Nelson Mass (EMI); Handel's Solomon, Les Pêcheurs de Perles (Philips); La Bohème, Don Pasquale and Le Roi d'Ys (Erato); Orphée et Eurydice and Hänsel und Gretel (EMI). *Honours:* Commandeur des Arts et des Lettres, 1986; Goodwill Ambassador of the High Commissioner for Refugees at the United Nations, 1987. *Current Management:* Ingpen & Williams Ltd, 7 St George's Court, 131 Putney Bridge Road, London, SW15 2PA, England.

HENDRICKS, Marijke; Singer (Mezzo-soprano); b. 18 April 1956, Schinveld, Netherlands. *Education:* Studied in Maastricht and Cologne. *Career:* Sang at the Cologne Opera 1981–85, notably as Nancy in Martha, Cherubino, Hansel, Meg Page and Olga in Eugene Onegin; Sang the Marchesa in Musgrave's The Voice of Ariadne at the 1982 Edinburgh Festival; Guest appearances at Geneva 1985, as Cherubino, Salzburg, 1986 as Second Lady in Die Zauberflöte and Innsbruck, 1986 in the title role of Cesti's Orontea; Bordeaux and Lyon 1987, as Ramiro in La Finta Giardiniera; Amsterdam 1987, in a concert performance of Tancredi, as Isaura; Visits to the Orange Festival and to Israel with the company of Cologne Opera, 1984; Antwerp 1988, as Dulcinée in Massenet's Don Quichotte; Maastricht 1989 in La Belle Hélène; Television appearances in Austria and Switzerland. *Address:* Oper der Stadt Köln, Offenbachplatz, 5000 Cologne, Germany.

HENDRICKS, Scott; Singer (Baritone); b. 1970, San Antonio, Texas. *Education:* University of Arkansas. *Career:* Season 1997–98 as Mozart's Count, and in Billy Budd and Carmen, at Houston; Season 1998–99 as Dmitry in the premiere of Todd Machover's Resurrection and as Sharpless in Butterfly; other roles include Ford in Falstaff, Gianni Schicchi, Papageno and Don Giovanni; Season 1999–2000 as Dandini in La Cenerentola at Santa Barbara, Rossini's Figaro at Kansas City and Messiah in New York; Complete Songs of Franz Schubert Recital Series, with John Wustmann; Season 2000–01 as Eugene Onegin for Utah Opera, Wagner's Donner, Posa in Don Carlos and Malatesta in Don Pasquale, for Cologne Opera; Ford at Santa Fe, Marcello in San Diego and Don Giovanni for Arizona Opera, 2001. *Address:* c/o IMG Artists, Lovell House, 616 Chiswick High Rd, London W4 5RX, England.

HENDRIKX, Louis; Singer (Bass); b. 13 March 1927, Antwerp, Belgium. *Education:* Studied at the Antwerp Conservatory and with Willem Ravelli. *Career:* Debut: Antwerp 1963, as Samuel in Un Ballo in Maschera; Sang in Antwerp and Kassel; Further appearances in Hannover, Cologne; Dortmund; Munich; Hamburg, Nuremberg, Lyon, Bordeaux, Toulouse, Venice, Palermo, Milan, Monte Carlo, Stockholm, Glasgow and London (Gurnemanz at Covent Garden); Promenade Concerts 1972; Théâtre de la Monnaie and Rome Opera 1973, as Boris Godunov and as King Mark in Tristan und Isolde; Also Salzburg, Fafner in Rheingold and Pogner in Meistersinger for the Easter Festivals. *Recordings include:* Gessler in Guillaume Tell (EMI); Rheingold with Herbert von Karajan. *Address:* c/o Théâtre de la Monnaie, 4 Léopoldstrasse, 1000 Brussels, Belgium.

HENKEL, Kathy, BA, BM, MA; American composer, writer and lecturer; b. 20 Nov. 1942, Los Angeles, CA; d. of Norman Nicholas Henkel and Lila Rhea Lee; m. Michael E. Manes (divorced). *Education:* Univ. of California at Los Angeles, California State Univ. at Northridge. *Career:* music reviewer, Los Angeles Times 1979; programme annotator, education co-ordinator, Chamber Music/LA Festival 1987–95; programme annotator, Los Angeles Chamber Orchestra 1988–98; liner notes writer, Pro Piano Records 1993–2003; owner, Sign of the Silver Birch Music 2003–; works premiered and performed at Gubbio Music Festival, Italy, Montevarchi Festival, Italy, Alaska Women Festival, Fairbanks, Dana Festival, Ohio, Toronto Guitar Society, live broadcasts on KFAC, Los Angeles, London, England, Greenwich Village, New York; mem. Chamber Music America, Phi Beta Women's Professional Arts Fraternity, Nat. Acad. of Recording Arts and Sciences. *Compositions:* Pioneer Song Cycle 1968, Trumpet Sonata 1979, Lost Calendar Pages 1984, Moorland Sketches 1985, Piano Sonata 1986, Bass Clarinet Sonata 1987, River Sky for Solo Guitar 1988, Book of Hours for Solo Harp 1990, Sonata for Flute and Piano 1992, Alaskan Fantasy and Fanfare 1993, Sea Songs 1997, Suite Spice for clarinet, bassoon and piano 2001, Gotta Minute Suite 2003. *Publications:* contrib. to Performing Arts Magazine. *Address:* 2367 Creston Drive, Los Angeles, CA 90068-2201, USA (office).

HENN, Brigitte; Singer (Soprano); b. 21 Oct. 1939, Freudenthal, Czechoslovakia; m. Raymond Henn. *Education:* Studied in Frankfurt, in Wiesbaden with Helena Braun and in Basle. *Career:* Sang at the Basle Opera, 1968–75, Deutsche Oper Berlin, 1976–80; Guest appearances at Basle from 1982, and in Düsseldorf, Frankfurt, Zürich and Hanover; Roles have included Mozart's Countess, Donna Anna and Fiordiligi, Agathe, Euridice, Marenka in The Bartered Bride, Wagner's Senta, Elsa and Sieglinde, Elisabeth de Valois, Alice Ford and Amelia in Un Ballo in Maschera; Operetta engagements in works by Lehar and Zeller; Many concert appearances.

HENRY, Antoni Garfield; Singer (Tenor); b. 1970, England. *Education:* Studies with Ludmilla Andrew and Nicholas Powell. *Career:* Debut: Luigi in Il Tabarro for Broomhill Opera; Appearances as Don José for Opera North, 1999; Rodolfo for European Chamber Opera and at Holland Park, 1998–99; The Duke of Mantua for English Touring Opera; Canio in Pagliacci for Central Festival Opera; Alfred in Die Fledermaus and Pinkerton for European Chamber Opera; Carmen Jones, Old Vic and West Side Story for Pimlico Opera. *Address:* c/o Music International, 13 Ardilaun Road, London N5 2QR, England.

HENRY, Claire; Singer (Mezzo-soprano); b. 1970, England. *Education:* Studied at Trinity College, London and with Ryland Davies. *Career:* Appearances as Mozart's Sesto, Bloomsburg Theatre; Cherubino for Clonter Opera; Périchole for Dorset Opera; Kate Pinkerton, English National Opera; In Die Meistersinger, Covent Garden; Concerts include Elgar's The Kingdom; Messiah and works by Haydn, Mendelssohn, Bach, Mozart and Vivaldi; Season 1999: With Herr Mozart and Doctor Strauss for the Covent Garden Festival. *Honours:* First Prize, English Song Competition, TCM. *Address:* Music International, 13 Ardilaun Road, London N5 2QR, England.

HENRY, Didier; Singer (Baritone); b. 24 May 1953, Paris, France. *Education:* Studied at the Paris Conservatoire and the studio of the Grand Opéra. *Career:* Sang at St Etienne, 1988, in a revival of Massenet's Amadis; Aix-en-Provence, 1989, in The Love for Three Oranges and in Belfast as Valentin the same year; Season 1990 as Marc-Antoine in Massenet's Cléopâtre at St Etienne, followed by Blondel in Grétry's Richard Coeur de Lion; Has sung in Moscow in Pelléas et Mélisande, in Marseille as Pietro in La Muette de Portici by Auber and at the Paris Théâtre du Châtelet in L'Enfant et les Sortilèges; Other roles include Gluck's Orestes (La Scala, 1991), Puccini's Lescaut, Pelléas and Hamlet; Marquis de la Force in Poulenc's Carmelites at the 1999 London Proms; Sang Gluck's Oreste at Marseille, 2000. *Recordings include:* Pelléas et Mélisande, The Love for Three Oranges and Massenet's Amadis and Cléopâtre, Mélodies de Ravel, Massenet, Poulenc and Saint-Saëns. *Address:* BP 27, 28290 Arrou, France.

HENSCHEL, Dieter; Singer (Baritone); b. 1967, Berlin, Germany. *Education:* Studied in Munich and Berlin. *Career:* Sang in Opera at Munich from 1990; Concert appearances in Festivals at Stuttgart, Urach and Feldkirch (Schubertiade); Kiel Opera, 1993–96, as Mozart's Papageno and Count, Rossini's Figaro, Valentin in Faust, Pelléas, Henze's Prince of Homburg, and Monteverdi's Orfeo; Engagements with leading orchestras in Germany, Netherlands and Austria; Season 1998 in the title role of Nixon in China, with the London Symphony Orchestra, at the London Barbican and Tuzenbach in the premiere of Trois Soeurs by Peter Eötvös, at Lyon; Season 2000–01 as Olivier in

Capriccio at Amsterdam and as the Barber in Die schweigsame Frau at the Opéra Bastille; Concert repertory includes Messiah, Gounod's St Cecilia Mass and Carmina Burana. *Address:* c/o IMG Artists, Lovell House, 616 Chiswick High Road, London W4 5RX, England.

HENSCHEL, Jane; Singer (mezzo-soprano); b. 1952, Wisconsin, USA. *Education:* Univ. of Southern California. *Career:* sang in the ensembles of the opera houses in Aachen, Wuppertal, Dortmund and Düsseldorf; extensive repertoire from Baroque through Modern with emphasis on Verdi, Strauss and Wagner; Debut at Covent Garden: the Nurse in Strauss's Die Frau ohne Schatten, which she has also sung in Amsterdam, Los Angeles, Paris Berlin, Munich, Vienna and the Metropolitan Opera New York; Sang Ortrud in Lohengrin in Berlin, Düsseldorf, Cologne, Munich; Clytemnestra in Elektra, London, San Francisco, Tokyo, Berlin, Munich; Cassandra in Les Troyens with the London Symphony Orchestra and at La Scala (Sir Colin Davis); Mistress Quickly in Falstaff in Munich and Vienna; Various roles in Wagner's Ring in London, Düsseldorf and Vienna; Brangäne in Tristan und Isolde in Los Angeles and Paris Festivals include: Salzburg, Tanglewood, Orange, Edinburgh, Matsumoto; Orchestra concerts: Berlin Philharmonic, London Symphony, BBC Orchestra, Radio France, Sydney Symphony, Melbourne Symphony, New Japan Symphony, Swedish Radio Orchestra, Munich Opera Orchestra, Philadelphia Orchestra, Boston Orchestra. *Recordings:* Albeniz: Merlin and Clifford; Britten: The Turn of the Screw; Krasa: Die Verlobung im Traum; Mahler: Symphonies 2 and 8; Stravinsky: The Rake's Progress. *Current Management:* Askonas Holt, 27 Chancery Lane, London, WC2A 1PF, England. *Website:* www.askonasholt.co.uk.

HENZE, Hans Werner; German composer and conductor; b. 1 July 1926, Gütersloh; s. of Franz Henze and Margarete Geldmacher. *Education:* Staatsmusikschule, Braunschweig, Kirchenmusikalisches Institut, Heidelberg. *Career:* musical collaborator Deutsches Theater in Konstanz 1948; Artistic Dir and Conductor Ballet of the Hessian State Theatre in Wiesbaden 1950; living in Italy as an ind. artist since 1953; Prof. of Composition, Mozarteum, Salzburg 1962–67; Prof. of Composition, Hochschule für Musik, Cologne 1980–91; Artistic Dir Accad. Filarmonica Romana 1982–91; Prof. of Composition RAM, London 1987–91; founder and Artistic Dir Munich Biennale for Contemporary Music Theatre 1988–; composer-in-residence Berlin Philharmonic Orchestra 1990; 'Voices' series of concerts to celebrate 75th birthday, London 2001; mem. Akad. der Künste, Berlin 1960–68, Bayerische Akad. der Schönen Künste, Munich, Akad. der Künste, Hamburg. *Compositions include:* opera and music theatre: Das Wundertheater 1948, Boulevard Solitude 1951, Ein Landarzt 1951, Das Ende einer Welt 1953, König Hirsch (revised as Il Re Cervo) 1953, Der Prinz von Homburg 1958, Elegy for Young Lovers 1959, Der Junge Lord 1964, Die Bassariden 1964, Das Ende einer Welt 1964, Ein Landarzt 1964, Der langwierige Weg in die Wohnung des Natascha Ungeheuer 1971, La Cubana 1973, We Come to the River 1974, Don Chischiotte della Mancia 1976, Pollicino (for children) 1979, The English Cat 1980, Il ritorno d'Ulisse in Patria 1981, Das verratene Meer 1986, Il re Teodoro in Venezia 1991, Venus and Adonis 1993, L'Upapa–oder der Triumph der Sohnesliebe 2003; ballet: Jack Pudding 1949, Ballet-Variationen 1949, Das Vokaltuch der Kammersängerin Rosa Silber 1950, Die Schlafende Prinzessin 1951, Labyrinth 1951, Der Idiot 1952, Maratona 1956, Undine 1956, Des Kaisers Nachtigall 1959, Tancredi 1964, Orpheus 1978, Le disperazioni del Signor Pulcinella 1992, Le fils de l'air 1995, Labyrinth 1996, Tanzstunden, Ballet Triptych 1997; oratorio: Novae de Infinito Laudes 1962, The Raft of the Medusa 1968; cantata: Being Beauteous 1963, Ariosi 1963, Cantata della Fiaba Estrema 1963, Moralities 1967; vocal music: Whispers from Heavenly Death 1948, Der Vorwurf 1948, Apollo and Hyacinth 1949, 5 Neapolitan Songs 1956, Nachtstücke and Arien 1957, Kammermusik 1958, Novae de Infinito Laudes 1962, Ariosi 1963, Being Beateous 1963, Lieder von einer Insel 1964, Musen Siziliens 1966, Versuch über Schweine 1968, Das Floss der Medusa 1968, El Cimarrón 1969, Voices 1973, Jephte 1976, El Rey de Harlem 1979, Canzoni for Orpheus 1980, Paraphrasen über Dostoiewsky 1990, Richard Wagnersche Klavierlieder 1998, Six Songs from the Arabic 1998; orchestral: Sinfonie 1947, three concertos for violin 1947, 1971, 1997, two concertos for piano 1950, 1967, Symphonic Variation 1950, Ode to the West Wind 1953, Quattro Poemi 1955, Concerto per il Marigny 1956, Jeux des Tritons 1957, Quattro Fantasie 1958, Sonata for Strings 1958, 3 Dithyrambs 1958, Antifone 1960, Los Caprichos 1963, Double Bass Concerto 1966, Telemanniana 1967, Compases para preguntas ensimisadas 1970, Heliogabalus Imperator 1971, Tristan 1973, Ragtimes and Habaneras 1975, In Memoriam: Amicizia 1976, Aria de la Folía española 1977, Il Vitalino raddoppiato 1977, Barcarola 1979, Apollo Trionfante 1979, Le Miracle de la Rose 1981, Canzona 1982, I Sentimenti di Carl P. E. Bach 1982, Sonata for 6 1984, Guitar Concerto 1986, Sieben liebeslieder 1986, Allegro brillante 1989, Requiem 1990, Quintetto 1990, Fünf Nachtstücke 1990, Trumpet Concerto 1992, Sieben Boleros 1998, Trio in drei Sätzen 1998, Fraternité 1999, Tempest 2000, Scorribanda Sinfonica 2001, L'heure bleue 2001,

Scornbanda 2001, 10th Symphony 2002. *Publications:* Das Ende einer Welt 1953, Undine, Tagebuch eines Balletts 1959, Essays 1964, El Cimarrón: ein Werkstattbericht 1971, Musik und Politik 1976, Die Englische Katze—Ein Arbeitsbuch 1978–82 1983, Reiselieder mit böhmischen Quinten 1996, Komponieren in der Schule 1998, Bohemian Fifths: An Autobiography (trans. by Stewart Spencer) 1998, Briefe Einer Freundschaft (with Ingeborg Bachmann) 2004. *Honours:* Hon. FRNCM 1998; Hon. DMus (Edin.) 1971; Robert Schumann Prize 1951, North-Rhine-Westphalia Art Prize 1957, Prix d'Italia 1954, Sibelius Gold Medal, Harriet Cohen Awards, London 1956, Music Critics Prize, Buenos Aires 1958, Kunstpreis, Berlin, Niedersächsischer Kunstpreis 1962, Ludwig-Spohr-Preis 1976, Heidelberg-Bach-Preis 1983, Siemens-Preis 1990, Apollo d'Oro, Bilbao 1990, Preis des Internationales Theaterinstituts 1991, Grosses Bundesverdienst-kreuz 1991, Kultureller Ehrenpreis, Munich 1996, Hans-von-Bülow Medal of the Berlin Philharmonic Orchestra 1997, Bayerischer Maximiliansorden für Wissenschaft und Kunst 1998, Praemium imperiale, Tokyo 2000, Best Living Composer, Cannes Classical Award 2001, German Dance Prize 2001. *Address:* c/o Künstler Sekretariat Christa Pfeffer, Schongauer Str. 22, 81377 Munich, Germany (office); c/o Chester Music, 8–9 Frith Street, London, W1D 3JB, England. *Telephone:* (20) 7432-4238 (London) (office); (89) 718041 (Munich). *Fax:* (20) 7287-6329 (London) (office). *E-mail:* com@schott-musik.de (office); wiebke.busch@musicsales.co.uk. *Website:* www.hanswernerhenze.de (home).

HEPPNER, Ben; Singer (tenor); b. 14 Jan. 1956, Murrayville, British Columbia, Canada. *Education:* Bachelor of Music Degree, University of British Columbia, 1979; LLD, 1997. *Career:* Many oratorio and concert performances in Canada; Opera Bacchus in Ariadne auf Naxos; Canadian Opera Company as Zinovy in Lady Macbeth of Mtsensk; American debut in Tannhäuser at the Chicago Lyric Opera, 1988; Has sung the Prince in Rusalka with the Philadelphia Opera Company, Seattle Opera (1990) and at the Vienna State Opera (1991); European debut at the Royal Opera Stockholm 1989, as Lohengrin; Sang Walther von Stolzing on his La Scala and Covent Garden debuts (1990) and in Seattle; San Francisco Opera debut 1989, as Lohengrin; Season 1991–92 with Janáček's Laca at Brussels, the Emperor in Die Frau ohne Schatten at Amsterdam and the premiere of William Bolcom's McTeague in Chicago; Season 1992 with Dvořák's Dimitrij at Munich, Mozart's Titus at Salzburg; Sang Lohengrin at Seattle, 1994; Walther at the Met, New York, 1995; Debut as Tristan at Seattle 1998 and under Abbado at Salzburg, 1999; Sang Aeneas in Les Troyens with the London Symphony Orchestra at the Barbican Hall, 2000; Schoenberg's Gurrelieder at the London Proms, 2002; Engaged as Otello at the Vienna Staatsoper, 2003. *Recordings:* Fidelio, conducted by Colin Davis, 1996; Two of Die Meistersinger, conducted by Wolfgang Sawallisch and by Solti (1997); Rusalka, conducted by Charles Mackerras, 1998; Les Troyens, conducted by Sir Colin Davis, 2001. *Honours:* Birgit Nilsson Prize, 1988; Singer of the Year, ECHO Deutscher Schallplattenpreis, 1993; Juno Award: Best Classical Album: Vocal or Choral Performance, 1996; Artist of the Year, Seattle Opera, 1996; Grammy Award, Best Opera Recording, 1998; Officer of the Order of Canada, 2002; Best Opera Recording and Best Classical Album, Grammy Awards, 2002. *Current Management:* Columbia Artists Management, 165 West 57th Street, New York, NY 10019, USA. *Address:* Administrative Office, 35 Kearney Drive, Toronto, ON M9W 5J5, Canada (office). *Telephone:* (416) 743-2761 (office). *E-mail:* eldonmcbride@sympatico.ca (office). *Website:* www .benheppner.com (office).

HERBERT, Trevor, *PhD, CertEd, ARCM, LGSM*; Musician and Musicologist; b. 18 Oct. 1945, Cwmparc, Wales; pnr Helen Grace Barlow. *Education:* Tonypandy Grammar School, St Luke's Coll., Exeter, Royal Coll. of Music, Open Univ. *Career:* trombone player (modern and period instruments), BBC Symphony Orchestra, Royal Philharmonic Orchestra, WNO, Musica Reservata, Taverner Players, Wallace Collection 1969–76; Music Department, Open Univ. 1976–, Prof. of Music 1998–; freelance performer, writer, composer and broadcaster; mem. Royal Musical Asscn, American Musicological Soc., Historic Brass Soc., Galpin Soc.. *Compositions:* several TV scores, including Wales! Wales? (BBC 1993) and Under Milk Wood (Syriol/BBC 1992). *Recordings:* with major orchestras, Taverner Players, Musica Reservata. *Publications:* Cambridge Companion to Brass (ed with J. Wallace), The British Brass Band: A Musical and Social History, An introduction to the Cultural Study of Music (ed with M. Clayton and R. Middleton; contrib. to New Grove Dictionary of Music and Musicians, New Dictionary of National Biography, The Encyclopaedia of Popular Music of the World. *Honours:* Foundation scholar, Royal Coll. of Music 1967, Martin Scholarship 1968, Christopher Monk Award (Historic Brass Soc.) 2002.

HERBIG, Gunther; Conductor; b. 30 Nov. 1931, Usti-nad-Labem, Czechoslovakia. *Education:* Studied with Hermann Abendroth at the Franz Liszt Academy, Weimar, and with Hermann Scherchen; Further study with Herbert von Karajan. *Career:* Held posts in Erfurt, Weimar, Potsdam and East Berlin; General Music Director, Dresden Philhar-

monic Orchestra, 1972–77; London debut with the New Philharmonia Orchestra, 1973; Music Director, Berlin Symphony Orchestra, 1977–83; Guest Conductor, Dallas Symphony Orchestra, 1979–81; Principal Guest Conductor, BBC Philharmonic Orchestra, 1982–86; Music Director, Detroit Symphony, 1984–90; Debut with London Symphony Orchestra, 1986; Orchestre de Paris, 1986; Appearances with the New York Philharmonic, Boston Symphony, Philadelphia Orchestra and Los Angeles Philharmonic from 1984; Music Director, Toronto Symphony, 1989–94; Toured Europe, 1989 with the Detroit Symphony Orchestra and Gidon Kremer as soloist; Chief Conductor of the Saarbrücken Radio Orchestra, Germany, 2001–. *Recordings include:* Haydn's London Symphonies; Reger's Piano Concerto; Beethoven's ballet Die Geschöpfe des Prometheus; Brahms 4 Symphonies and Nielsen's 5th; 104 works recorded. *Current Management:* Terry Harrison Artists Management, The Orchard, Market Street, Charlbury, Oxfordshire OX7 3PJ, England. *Telephone:* (1608) 810330. *Fax:* (1608) 811331. *E-mail:* artists@terryharrison.force9.co.uk.

HERCHERT, Jörg; Composer; b. 20 Sept. 1943, Dresden, Germany. *Education:* Studied at the Dresden and East Berlin Conservatories, 1962–69, and with Paul Dessau at the Berlin Academy, 1970–74. *Career:* Freelance composer from 1975; Professor of Composition at the Dresden Conservatory 1992–. *Compositions:* Ode an eine Nachigall, for soprano and oboe, 1972; Komposition, for soprano, baritone and 12 instruments, 1975; Seligpreisungen I–VIII for organ 1974–85; Flute Concerto, 1976; Sextet, 1978; Das geistliche Jahr, cantata cycle, 1978–96 (9 works for soloists, chorus and ensemble with percussion); Horn Concerto, 1980; Octet, 1984; 2 String Quartets, 1981, 1986; Nonet, 1990; Nachtwache, opera, 1993; Abraum, opera, 1997; Namen Gottes I–XXI, for organ, 1990–97. *Address:* c/o Hochschule für Musik (Carl Maria von Weber), Blochmannstrasse 2–4, 01001 Dresden, Germany.

HERFORD, (Richard) Henry, MA, ARNCM, GRNCM; singer (baritone); b. 24 Feb. 1947, Edinburgh, Scotland; m. Lindsay John 1982; two s. one d. *Education:* King's College, Cambridge, Royal Northern College of Music. *Career:* Glyndebourne Chorus, 1977–78; Forester in Janáček's Cunning Little Vixen; Roles with Royal Opera House, Covent Garden, Scottish Opera, Handel Opera, Chelsea Opera Group, Batignano, Nancy, English Bach Festival; Frequent concerts with leading orchestras in the United Kingdom, Europe and North and South America; Appearances with many ensembles and on radio and television (Maxwell Davies: The Lighthouse, BBC 2); Numerous recitals; Visiting Professor at Royal Northern College of Music, Royal College of Music, Birmingham Conservatoire. *Recordings:* Recital of American Songs; High Priest in Rameau's Castor and Pollux; Handel's Messiah, excerpts with Scottish Chamber Orchestra and George Malcolm; Dickinson, A Dylan Thomas Song Cycle; Handel's Dixit Dominus and Israel in Egypt with King's College Cambridge Choir; Joubert, The Instant Moment with English String Orchestra; Vaughan Williams's Five Tudor Portraits, Five Mystical Songs; Britten's A Midsummer Night's Dream; Charles Ives: Songs, 2 vols; Songs with Instruments with Ensemble Modern; Maxwell Davies, Resurrection; Bridge, The Christmas Rose; Michael Berkeley, Père du doux repos; George Lloyd, Iernin; Stravinsky, Pulcinella; Edward Gregson, Missa Brevis Pacem; Bliss, Complete Songs; John Manduell: Songs of the Renaissance. *Honours:* Curtis Gold Medal (RNCM); Benson & Hedges Gold Award (Suape); First prize, American Music Competition (New York); British Retailers Record of the Year. *Address:* Pencots, Northmoor, Oxford OX29 5AX, England.

HERINCX, Raimund; Singer (Bass-Baritone); b. 23 Aug. 1927, London, England. *Education:* Studied with Van Dyck in Belgium and with Valli in Milan. *Career:* Concerts in Belgium and France, 1950; Stage debut Welsh National Opera 1950, as Mozart's Figaro; Sang Mephistopheles in Faust 1956; Sadler's Wells Opera from 1956, as Count Almaviva, Rigoletto, Germont, Pizarro, Nick Shadow, Creon in Oedipus Rex, and in the premiere of Our Man in Havana by Malcolm Williamson, 1963; Sang in the 1964 British premiere of The Makropulos Case; Philharmonic Hall New York 1966, in A Mass of Life by Delius; Boston Opera 1967; BBC, 1967, in L'Erismena by Cavalli; Covent Garden from 1968, as King Fisher in The Midsummer Marriage and in the premieres of The Knot Garden, 1970, and Taverner, 1972; Other Covent Garden roles include Escamillo, Macbeth and Alfio; Salzburg Easter Festival 1973–74, as Pogner in Die Meistersinger and Fafner in Siegfried, conducted by Karajan; English National Opera 1974–76, in the British stage premiere of The Bassarids by Henze and as Wotan and Hagen in The Ring; Seattle Opera 1977–81; Metropolitan Opera debut 1977, as Matthisen in Le Prophète; San Francisco 1983 in The Midsummer Marriage; Les Contes d'Hoffmann for Opera North 1983; Sang in the US premiere of Taverner at Boston, 1986; Sang Dalua in Boughton's The Immortal Hour, Glastonbury, 1996; Has reviewed opera for Music and Musicians magazine. *Recordings include:* Dido and Aeneas (Decca); Les Contes d'Hoffmann (Electrola); Hansel and Gretel, Koanga, A Village Romeo and Juliet, I Capuleti e i Montecchi, The Pilgrim's Progress,

Aronte in Armide by Gluck, Oedipus Rex; The Midsummer Marriage (Philips); Das Liebesverbot by Wagner. *Address:* c/o English National Opera, St Martin's Lane, London WC2N 4ES, England.

HERING, Karl-Josef; Singer (Tenor); b. 14 Feb. 1929, Westonnen, Germany. *Education:* Studied with Fred Husler, Max Lorenz and Franz Volker. *Career:* Debut: Hanover 1958, as Max in Der Freischütz; Engagements at the Deutsche Oper Berlin and in Cologne, Karlsruhe, Stuttgart, Vienna and Hamburg; Royal Opera House Covent Garden, as Siegfried in Der Ring des Nibelungen, 1966; Further appearances in Trieste, Toronto, Barcelona, Marseille and Buenos Aires; Other roles include Florestan, Canio, Aegisthus, Hermann in The Queen of Spades and Erik in Der fliegende Holländer; Many concert performances. *Address:* c/o Deutsche Oper Berlin, Richard Wagnerstrasse 10, 1000 Berlin, Germany.

HERMAN, Silvia; Singer (Soprano); b. 1954, Vienna, Austria. *Education:* Studied in Vienna with Anton Dermota: worked at the Opera Studio of the Vienna Staatsoper, 1976–79. *Career:* Appearances in Vienna 1979–82, Hamburg 1983–85; Guest engagements in Stuttgart, Geneva, Barcelona, Madrid and Cologne, 1989–90; Salzburg Festival, 1978–81; Bayreuth Festival 1978 as a Flowermaiden, 1985–88 as Wellgunde and Waltraute in Die Walküre; Bruckner Festival in Linz, 1982–88, and elsewhere, in Lieder recitals and concert showings. *Recordings:* Das Rheingold and Die Walküre, conducted by Haitink; Schumann's Das Paradies und der Peri. *Address:* Oper der Stadt Koln, Offenbachplatz, 5000 Cologne, Germany.

HERMAN, Vasile; Composer; b. 10 June 1929, Satu Mare, Romania; m. Titina Herman, 2 c. *Education:* Diploma of Composition, 1957, Doctor of Musicology, 1974, High School; Diploma of Teacher of Music, 1954. *Career:* Television and radio appearances; mem. Composers' Union of Romania. *Compositions:* Double Concerto; Poliphony; Concert of Strings; Chamber works: Melopee, Variante, Epsodi, 5 Symphonies, Concerto for Strings and Percussion; Paos, 1993; Sysma, 1993; Refractus for violin and percussion, 1993; Fonologhion for oboe, harp, string and percussion, 1993; Gelou Quidam Blacus, 1996; Paos, 1996; Hora Lunga for clarinet piano and percussion, 1997; Variazioni for oboe, piano and percussion, 1998; Monocantata for tenor solo, clarinet solo and percussion, 1998; Akes Samenos for flute solo. *Recordings:* Cantilations; Rimes Nostalgique; Variante. *Publications:* Form and Style in Contemporary Romanian Music 1977; contrib. to Muzica, Steaua, Tribuna, Utunk (Romania). *Honours:* Prize, Composers' Union, Romania; Prize, Romanian Academy. *Address:* Str Octavian Goga No. 33 Apt 4, 3400 Cluj-Napoca, Romania.

HERMAN, Witold Walenty, MA, DPhilMus; Polish cellist and professor of music; b. 14 Feb. 1932, Toruń; m. Catherine Bromboszcz 1970; one s. one d. *Education:* Szymanowski Conservatory, Torun, Academy of Music, Kraków, Ecole Normale de Musique, Paris, France, World University, Tucson, AZ, USA. *Career:* debut with State Philharmonie, Kraków, May 1954; Cello concerts with orchestras and cello recitals in Poland and other European countries; Professor, Music Academy, Kraków; Visiting Professor of the Franz Liszt Musik Akademie in Weimar, 1972; Jury of the International Pablo Casals Cello Competition in Budapest, 1968. *Recordings:* For radio and television in Poland and the rest of Europe including Radio Luxembourg; As a solo cellist with major symphony orchestras. *Publications:* Notes for Cello, edited in Poland, Polish Music Edition. *Address:* Academy of Music, ul Starowislna 3, Kraków, Poland; ul Friedleina 49 m 5, 30-009 Kraków, Poland.

HERMANN, Roland; Singer (Baritone); b. 17 Sept. 1936, Bochum, Germany. *Education:* Vocal studies with Paul Lohmann, Margarethe von Winterfeldt and Falmino Contini. *Career:* Debut: Trier 1967 as Count Almaviva; Member of the Zürich Opera from 1968; Guest appearances in Munich, Paris, Berlin and Cologne; Buenos Aires 1974, as Jochanaan in Salome and Wolfram in Tannhäuser; US debut 1983, with the New York Philharmonic; La Scala Milan debut 1986, with Claudio Abbado; Roles include Don Giovanni, Amfortas, Germont, Gunther in Götterdämmerung and the title roles in Karl V by Krenek and Doktor Faust by Busoni; Apollo (L'Orfeo), Cinna (Lucio Silla), Morald (Die Feen), Forester (The Cunning Little Vixen); Mauregato (Alfonso und Estrella); Beckmesser, Achille (Penthesilea); Vendramin (Massimila Doni), Orff's Prometheus; Took part in the European stage premiere of Die Jakobsleiter by Schoenberg (Hamburg 1983) and the world premiere of Kelterborn's Der Kirschgarten (Zürich 1984); Sang in the premiere of Krenek's Oratorio Symeon der Stylites at the 1988 Salzburg Festival, conducted by Lothar Zagrosek; BBC London 1989, in the title role of Der Prinz von Homburg by Henze; sang the Forester in The Cunning Little Vixen at Zürich 1989, The Master in the premiere of York Höllier's Der Meister und Margarita (Paris 1989) and Gunther at a concert performance of Götterdämmerung at the Holland Festival; Sang Busoni's Doktor Faust at Leipzig, 1991; Season 1992 as Nekrotzar in Le Grand Macabre at Zürich, followed by the Count in Capriccio; Sang Paolo in Simon Boccanegra at Zürich, 1996; Gurlitt's Wozzeck at

Florence, 1998; Many Lieder recitals and concert appearances. *Recordings include:* Penthesilea by Schoeck (BASF); Prometheus and Trionfi by Orff, Die Meistersinger, CPE Bach's Magnificat (Deutsche Grammophon); Moses and Aron by Schoenberg (CBS); Zemlinsky's Der Kreidekreis; Mathis der Maler by Hindemith; Peer Gynt by Werner Egk; Der Vampyr by Marschner; Schumann's Genoveva. *Current Management:* Ingpen & Williams Ltd, 7 St George's Court, 131 Putney Bridge Road, London, SW15 2PA, England.

HERMANOVA, Vera; Organist; b. 9 Sept. 1951, Brno, Czechoslovakia; m. Zdenek Spatka, 8 July 1977. *Education:* Conservatoire in Brno, 1967–73; Master's degree, Janáček Academy of Performing Arts in Brno, 1973–77; Postgraduate study at the Janáček Acdemy, 1978–81; Conservatoire National de Saint-Maur, Paris (with Professor Gaston Litaize), 1980–81; Postgraduate study of musical science, Doctor's degree, Masaryk University in Brno Faculty of Philosophy, 1991–97. *Career:* Special attention to French and Czech organ music of all periods; Master course with prominent European organists (Gaston Litaize, Piet Kee, Lionel Rogg); Radio and television recordings in Czech Republic, Denmark, Germany, Austria, Slovenia; Organ recitals in a number of European culture centres including Prague, Paris, Vienna, Linz, Berlin, Munich, Hamburg, Dresden, Copenhagen, Oslo, Ljubljana, Haarlem, Utrecht, and in festivals at home and abroad (the United Kingdom, Germany, Denmark, Netherlands, Austria); mem, Association Jehan Alain, Romainmôtier, Switzerland. *Recordings:* French Organ Works (Messiaen, Dupré, Alain); Les Grandes Orgues de Notre Dame de Chartres (French Organ Music); Musica Nova Bohemica (Eben, Kohoutek); Musik der Gegenwart (Bodorová); Czech Organ Music of the 18th Century; Czech Organ Music of the 20th Century; F. X. Brixi (1732–1771) Organ Concertos (with authentic period instruments), 1999. *Honours:* Finalist, International Organ Competition, Bologna, 1975; Premier Prix à l'Unanamité, Saint-Maur, 1981; Czech Music Fund Prize for CD recordings, Prague, 1992. *Address:* Udolní 13, 602 00 Brno, Czech Republic.

HERNANDEZ, Cesar; Singer (Tenor); b. 13 Oct. 1960, Puerto Rico. *Career:* Debut: New Jersey, 1989, as Rodolfo in La Bohème; Spoleto Festival, 1991, in Menotti's Goya; Appearances in opera houses at Trieste, Catania and Genoa; Season 1995 as Pinkerton at Hamburg, Alfredo at Vienna and Cavaradossi at Helsinki; Further engagements as the Duke of Mantua at Tel-Aviv and for Miami Opera, Edgardo in Lucia di Lammermoor and San Diego as Cavaradossi (1996); Sang Paco in La Vida Breve at Brussels, 1998; Season 2000 as Pinkerton at the Deutsche Oper Berlin, Cavaradossi in Brussels, Faust at the Salzburg Landestheater and Falla's Paco in Venice; Concerts include the Verdi Requiem. *Address:* c/o Théâtre Royale de la Monnaie, 4 Leopoldstrasse, 1000 Brussels, Belgium.

HERNANDEZ-IZNAGA, Jorge; Violist; b. 1950, Havana, Cuba; m. Lozano Carola, 1972, 1 s., 1 d. *Education:* National School of Art, Havana, 1964–72; Conservatory Tchaikovsky, Moscow, 1976–79, 1981–83. *Career:* Debut: Havana, 1972; Professor, Viola, Conservatory Roldan, Havana, 1972–76, Superior Institute of Arts, Havana, 1983–92; Principal Viola, National Symphonic Orchestra of Cuba; Founder, The Havana String Quartet; Television and radio appearances in Cuba, 1972–92, Moscow, 1977, 1979, Hungary, 1979, Argentina, 1987, 1988, Uruguay, 1988, Korea, 1988, Bulgaria, 1990, Mexico, 1990, Spain, 1992–97; Co-Principal, Orchestra of Cordova, Spain; mem, Writers and Artists Union of Cuba; Individual Member, Chamber Music of America. *Recordings:* Havana String Quartet, L Brouwer's Quartets and M Ravel-H Villa Lobos No. 1. *Honours:* Prize, Interpretive Mastery, Chamber Music Festival of Havana, 1987. *Current Management:* KH Productions SL. *Address:* Basilica No. 18, Madrid 28020, Spain.

HERNANDEZ-LARGUIA, Cristian; Choir Conductor; b. 6 Oct. 1921, Buenos Aires, Argentina; m. Eugenia Barbarich 1953. *Education:* Studied with T. Fuchs, E. Leuchter, R. Shaw, N. Greenberg and G. Graetzer. *Career:* Debut: Madrigal Group, Asoc Ros de Cultura Inglesa 1941; Conductor, Coro Estable de Rosario, since 1946; Founder and Conductor, Pro Musica de Rosario, 1962; Appearances in concert tours to North, Central and South America and Europe, 1967–92, Hunter College, NY, Coolidge Auditorium, Washington DC and St Martin in the Fields, London; Professor of Choir Conducting, Musical Morphology and Acoustics, University of Litoral, University Rosario. *Recordings:* 35 titles. *Publications:* Performances: Mass in B Minor, Bach's first version with Argentine cast, 1985; St John Passion, Bach, 1977; First Argentine performance of complete and original version Messiah, 1973, Brocke's Passion, 1980, Handel. *Honours:* Numerous personal and joint awards (with Pro Musica and CER) as well as National Culture Glory, 1984, Illustrious citizen, 1985, Concorso Internazionale Guido D'Arezzo, Italy, 1967–81. *Address:* San Luis 860, 4J 2000 Rosario, Argentina.

HERNON, Paul; Director and Designer; b. 1947, Northumberland, England. *Career:* Co-founded the London Music Theatre Group, 1982, and directed the British stage premieres of Martin's Le Vin Herbé and

Vivaldi's Juditha Triumphans at the Camden Festival, London; British premieres of Salieri's Prima la Musica and Ward's The Crucible; Directed a tercentenary production of Handel's Acis and Galatea for the English Bach Festival in Reggio Emilia, Seville and Madrid; In Northern Ireland has directed Don Giovanni, Così fan tutte, Le nozze di Figaro, Die Zauberflöte and Der Schauspieldirektor and works by Haydn, Donizetti, Puccini and Purcell; Has designed productions of Hansel and Gretel at Sadler's Wells, La Favorita in Dublin, Offenbach operas in Belfast and Crispino e la Comare at the Camden Festival; Designed the Yuri Lyubomov productions of Jenůfa (first in Zürich, 1986) and Das Rheingold at Covent Garden, 1986, 1988; Eugene Onegin for Bonn, 1987, and Tannhäuser for Stuttgart, 1988. *Address:* Music International, 13 Ardilaun Road, London N5 2QR, England.

HERR, Karlheinz; Singer (Bass); b. 27 Dec. 1933, Zellhausen, Germany. *Education:* Studied with Paul Lohmann in Frankfurt. *Career:* Sang first in opera at Mainz 1959, then appeared at Darmstadt, 1960–63, Mannheim from 1963 until 1988; Among his best roles have been Klingsor, Osmin, Mozart's Bartolo, Leporello, Rocco, Daland, and Varlaam in Boris Godunov; Guest appearances at the Paris Opéra, 1974, Bayreuth Festival, 1974, and in The Ring at Warsaw, 1988–90; Concert engagements in Haydn's Seasons and Creation, Messiah, Rossini's Stabat Mater and the Verdi and Fauré Requiems. *Address:* c/o Nationaltheater Mannheim, Am Goetheplatz, W-6800 Mannheim, Germany.

HERREWEGHE, Phillippe; Conductor and Choral Director; b. 2 May 1947, Ghent, Belgium. *Education:* Studied piano at Ghent Conservatory; Studied medicine and psychiatry, graduated 1975. *Career:* Founder, Collegium Vocale of Ghent, 1975; Founder, La Chapelle Royale, 1977; Orchestre des Champs Elysées, 1991; Ensemble Vocal Européen; Performances include: St Matthew's Passion, Bach, with La Chapelle Royale; C Minor Mass and Requiem, Mozart; Elias, Paulus, A Midsummer Night's Dream, Mendelssohn; Missa Solemnis, Beethoven; German Requiem, Brahms; Les Nuits d'Eté, L'Enfance du Christ, Berlioz; Guest conductor with many orchestras including: Concertgebouw Orchestra, Rotterdam Philharmonic Berlin Philharmonic, Leipzig and Vienna Philharmonic; Artistic Director, Saintes Festival, 1982–; Cultural Ambassador for Flanders, 1993–; Musical Director, Royal Flanders Philharmonic Orchestra, 1998. *Recordings:* Over 60 with the above ensembles including music by Rameau, Lalande and Lully. *Honours:* Officier des Arts et Lettres, Doctor Honoris Causa, Leuven University, 1997–. *Address:* c/o Stephane Maciejewski, 10 rue Coquillere, 75001 Paris, France.

HERRMANN, Anita; Singer (Mezzo-soprano); b. 1947, Karlsruhe, Germany. *Education:* Studied in Strasbourg and with Joseph Metternich in Cologne. *Career:* Sang with the Bonn Opera, 1971–79, Karlsruhe, 1980–86, with further engagements at the Staatsoper Stuttgart, the Berlin Deutsche Oper and the Vienna Volksoper; Bregenz Festival, 1987–90, in Contes d'Hoffmann and Fliegender Holländer; Roles have included Mozart's Marcellina, Ino in Semele, Mistress Quickly in Falstaff, Lubasha in Sadko, Carolina in Elegy for Young Lovers and Mirza in Judith by Matthus (Berne, 1992); Sang Strauss's Annina at Deutsche Oper, Berlin, 1993. *Address:* c/o Stadttheater Bern, Nägelistrasse 1, 3011 Bern, Switzerland.

HERRMANN, Karl Ernst; stage director and stage designer; b. 1936, Neukirch, Upper Lusatia, Germany. *Education:* Hochschule für Bildende Kunst, Berlin. *Career:* designed for theatre at Ulm from 1961 and associated with Peter Stein at Bremen and Berlin, 1969–78; Designed Das Rheingold and Die Walküre at the Paris Opéra, 1976; Théâtre de la Monnaie, Brussels, from 1978, with a cycle of seven operas by Mozart, La Traviata and Orfeo ed Euridice; Eugene Onegin at Hamburg, 1979; Die Zauberflöte at the Salzburg Landestheater, to inaugurate the Mozart Bicentenary, 1991; Die Entführung at the Vienna Staatsoper, 1991; Brussels productions of La Clemenza di Tito and La finta Giardiniera seen at Salzburg Festival, 1992; Designed sets for the Peter Stein production of Pelléas et Mélisande at Welsh National Opera, 1992. *Address:* Théâtre Royale de la Monnaie, 4 Leopoldstrasse, 1000 Brussels, Belgium.

HERSANT, Philippe; Composer; b. 21 June 1948, Rome. *Education:* Studied at the Paris Conservatoire, with André Jolivet, in Madrid (1970–72) and at the Villa Médici, Rome, 1978–80. *Career:* Producer, Radio France, 1973–; Composer-in-Residence with the Orchestre National de Lyon, 1998–2000. *Compositions include:* Les Visites Espacées, chamber opera, 1982; Stances, for orchestra, 1992; Aztlan, for orchestra, 1983; String Quartet no. 1, 1985; Missa Brevis, 1986; Nachtgesang, for clarinet, violin, cello and piano, 1988; String Quartet No.2, 1988; 2 Cello Concertos, 1989, 1997; Sextet, 1994; Le Chateau des Carpathes, opera, 1991; Landschaft mit Afgonauten, cantata, 1994; L'Infinito, for 12 voices, 1994; 5 Pièces, for orchestra, 1997; Piano Trio, 1998; Paysage avec ruines, for mezzo and orchestra, 1999. *Honours:* Prix Arthur Honegger, 1994; Prix Maurice Ravel, 1995; Grand Prix de la

Musique Symphonique, 1998. *Address:* c/o Orchestre National de Lyon, 82 Rue de Bonnel, 69431 Lyon Cédex, France.

HERZ, Joachim; professor and director of production; b. 15 June 1924, Dresden, Germany; m. Charlotte Kitze 1954, one s. *Education:* Colls of Music, Leipzig and Dresden, Humboldt Univ., Berlin. *Career:* debut, Dresden Nat. Opera in Die Bremer Stadtmusikanten 1950; Producer, Dresden Touring Opera 1951–53, Berlin Komische Oper 1956, Cologne 1957; Dir, Leipzig Opera 1976; Man. Dir, Berlin Komische Oper 1981, Dresden Nat. Opera 1981–; Chief, Music Theatre Dept, Coll. of Music, Dresden 1991; Music Coach, Dresden 1946–49; teaching asst, Dresden Drama Studio 1949–51, teacher 1951–53; teacher, Berlin 1953–56, Cologne 1957; Lecturer, Berlin Univ. 1956; Prof., Leipzig Univ. 1976–; Visiting Lecturer, Univs of Munich, Salzburg, Eichstatt, Paris VIII, London, California, Göttingen, Lisbon, Heidelberg. Cincinnati, British Columbia, New York City, Banff Centre; guest producer, Buenos Aires, London, Cardiff, Moscow, Stockholm, Belgrade, Bern, Munich, Glasgow, Essen, Hamburg, Frankfurt, Vienna, Vancouver, Zürich, Salzburg, Helsinki, Vienna, Bamberg, Stockholm, Tartu, Tokyo and the music colleges Tkyo, Osaka, Tallinn, Wagner Societies New York, Nagoya, Tokyo and London; Consulting producer at Taipei; radio producer; produced Lohengrin at Vienna 1975, Così fan tutte, Helsinki 1989, The Love for Three Oranges at Dresden Music Festival; Dir of Productions at the Dresden National Opera 1981–1991; tours with Salzburg Così fan tutte to Japan and with Leipzig Xerxes through 13 countries; Ring des Nibelungen, Leipzig, 1973–1976; War and Peace, Leipzig; Flying Dutchman Bolshoi Moscow; Salome, ENO; Opeing Leipzig New Opera House, Meistersingr 1960; guest lecturer, Europe and the former Soviet Union; staged Peter Grimes for Scottish Opera 1994; hon. bd mem., Music Theatre Cttee; hon. mem., Bolshoi Theatre; mem. Acad. of Arts, Berlin. *Film:* The Flying Dutchman. *Television:* Xerxes, Copenhagen; BBC4 Butterfly, Nose, Salome, Mahagonny, BumBum. *Recordings:* Freischütz (with Carlos Kleiber), Zauberflöte (with Colin Davis), Meistersinger (with Dresden Semperoper), Freischütz, Rosenkavalier. *Publications:* Musiktheater (with others), Joachim Herz–Regisseur im Musiktheater, Oper als idee und Interpretation, Joachim Herz über Musiktheater, Gesammelte Schriften; contrib. to magazines, newspapers, programmes, congresses. *Honours:* Grand prix du disque, Freischütz; Best production of the year, Salome, London- Orpheus Magazin, West Berlin; 4 times National Prize. *Address:* Seestr. 8, 01067 Dresden, Germany.

HESS, Andrea; Cellist; b. 7 May 1954, London, England; m. John Leonard, 20 Jan 1985. *Education:* Recital Diploma, Royal Academy of Music, 1974; Nordwestdeutschemusikakademie, Detmold, Germany. *Career:* Debut: Wigmore Hall, London, 1979; Numerous performances as a soloist throughout United Kingdom, Europe, Canada and the Far East; Performed as a member of several chamber ensembles notably the Kreisler Trio of Germany and the Raphael Ensemble; Appeared on stage as solo cellist in National Theatre production of The Elephant Man, 1980–81; Solo Cellist for Royal Shakespeare Company, 1982–87; Appearances in drama productions for BBC and major independent television companies; Several broadcasts for BBC Radio 3; Composer and Onstage Solo Cellist in the National Theatre and West End for Arthur Miller's Broken Glass, 1994–95; Currently a member of the Swartzentruber piano trio. *Recordings:* Volker David Kirchner Trio, Wergo; Chopin cello works and Chamber Music with the Kreisler Trio, Pantheon; Hyperion recordings of both Brahms sextets, Dvořák, Quintet and Sextet, Korngold Sextet and Schoenberg's Verklärte Nacht, Martinů and Schulhoff Sextets, Arensky Quartet, and Tchaikovsky's Souvenir de Florence Sextet, Strauss Sextet from Capriccio, Bruckner Quintet, Schubert String Trio and Double Cello Quintet and both Brahms Quintets and the Mendelssohn Quintets and Frank Bridge Quintet and Sextet with the Raphael Ensemble. *Honours:* Associate of the Royal Academy of Music, 1997. *Address:* 10 Belsize Park, London NW3 4ES, England.

HESSE, Ruth; Singer (Mezzo-soprano); b. 18 Sept. 1936, Wuppertal, Germany. *Education:* Studied with Peter Offermans in Wuppertal and with Hildegard Scharf in Hamburg. *Career:* Sang in Lubeck from 1958; Hamburg Staatsoper from 1960; Operas by Wagner, Verdi and Strauss at the Deutsche Oper Berlin from 1962; Bayreuth Festival as Mary, Magdalene and Ortrud; Berlin, 1965, in the premiere of Der junge Lord by Henze; Vienna Staatsoper, 1966, Ortrud, Brangaene and Eboli; Paris Opéra, 1966, 1972, as Kundry and as The Nurse in Die Frau ohne Schatten; Salzburg Festival, 1974–75, as The Nurse; Sang Clytemnestra in Elektra at the Deutsche Oper Berlin, 1988; Concert and oratorio appearances. *Recordings:* Die Meistersinger; Die Frau ohne Schatten; Der junge Lord; Fricka in Der Ring des Nibelungen; Violanta by Korngold. *Address:* c/o Deutsche Oper Berlin, Richard Wagnerstrasse 10, 1000 Berlin, Germany.

HESSE, Ursula; Singer (Mezzo-soprano); b. 1970, Cologne, Germany. *Education:* Studied at the Berlin Musikhochschule with Ingrid Figur and Gundula Hintz-Lukas; Masterclasses with Hilde Rössl-Majdan and

Brigitte Fassbaender; Lieder study with Aribert Reimann. *Career:* Komische Oper Berlin, in the song cycle Love, Life and Death by Siegfried Matthus, 1995; Toured Brussels, London, Dresden and Copenhagen in Mozart concert arias for the ballet Un Moto di Gioa, 1995; Concerts at the Berlin Festival with the Berlin Singakademie and with the New Bach Collegium in Brussels and Amsterdam; Season 1996–97 as Carmen at Lubeck and in Die Zauberflöte at Brussels; Alcina, Handel, Amsterdam. *Recordings include:* Webern Lieder, with Aribert Reimann. *Honours:* Prizewinner, Paula-Saloman-Lindberg Lieder Competition, 1993; Deutscher Musikweitbewer, 1995. *Address:* c/o Netherlands Opera, Waterlooplein 22 1011 PG, Amsterdam, Netherlands.

HETHERINGTON, Hugh; Singer (Tenor); b. 1958, England. *Education:* Studied at the Guildhall School of Music, at St John's College, Cambridge, and with Frederick Cox in Manchester; Further studies with Audrey Langford. *Career:* With Glyndebourne Festival and Touring Companies has sung Dr Caius (Falstaff), Truffaldino (Love of Three Oranges), Where the Wild Things Are and Idomeneo; Appearances with Scottish Opera as Dema in Cavalli's L'Egisto, Pang in Turandot, The Devil in The Soldier's Tale, Basilio in Le nozze di Figaro and roles in Iolanthe, Lulu, La Vie Parisienne and Eugene Onegin; With English National Opera as Piet in Ligeti's Le Grand Macabre and in The Return of Ulysses and L'Orfeo (1992); Covent Garden from 1985 in King Priam and Samson et Dalila; Further engagements with University Opera, New Sussex Opera, Opera Factory, Zürich and London Sinfoniettas, the Singers' Company, Channel 4 television and the Endymion Ensemble double bill of Monteverdi and Michael Nyman (1987); New York debut, 1989, in HMS Pinafore with New Sadler's Wells Opera at the City Center Theater; Concerts with the City of Birmingham Symphony and the Matrix Ensemble.

HEUCKE, Stefan; Composer; b. 24 May 1959, Gaildorf, Germany. *Education:* Studied Piano with Professor Renate Werner, Stuttgart, 1978–82; Piano with Professor A von Arnim, Composition with Professor G Schafer, Musikhochschule, Dortmund, 1982–86. *Career:* Debut: Premiere of Vier Orchesterstücke, op 5, performed by Saarland State Orchestra, Saarbrucken, 1985; Dozent (University Lecturer) in Theory of Music, Musikhochschule, Dortmund, 1989–; Production and editing live for WDR, SDR and Saarlandischer Rundfunk broadcasting stations; Numerous performances in Germany, Russia, Netherlands, France and Chile; mem, GEMA; Interessenverband deutscher Komponisten. *Compositions:* Self-published: Vier Orchesterstücke, op 5, 1983; Variations on a theme of Webern for orchestra, op 10, 1988; Piano trio, op 11, 1989; Symphony No. 1, op 12, 1990; Symphony No. 2, op 19, 1993; The Selfish Giant for narrator and orchestra, op 20, 1994; Sonata for bass clarinet and piano op 23, 1995; Quintet for violin, viola, violoncello, double bass and piano op 25, 1995; The Happy Prince, 21 Easy Piano Pieces op 28. *Recordings:* CD, Abendgebete, op 14, with Berthold Schmid, tenor, and Sinfonietta Tubingen. *Honours:* Prize, Forum of Young German Composers Competition, 1985; Grant, City of Dortmund, 1990. *Address:* Markt 10a, 59174 Kamen, Germany.

HEWITT, Angela; Pianist; b. 26 July 1958, Ottawa, Canada. *Education:* Began studies with parents aged 3; Royal Conservatory of Music, Toronto, 1964–73; BMus, University of Ottawa, 1973–77. *Career:* Debut: First recital aged 9, Toronto; Appeared around the world as soloist with orchestra (Canada, USA, the United Kingdom, Japan, Australia) and in recitals (in China, Mexico and throughout Europe); New York debut, Alice Tully Hall, 1984; Wigmore Hall debut in 1985; Proms debut in 1990. *Recordings:* First Bach recording in 1986; Cycle of Bach on CD: Inventions, 1994, French Suites, 1995, Partitas, 1997; Granados' Spanish Dances; Bach, Well-Tempered Klavier Book I, 1998, Book II, 1999. *Honours:* International Bach Piano Competition, 1985; Prizewinner in Washington DC (Bach, 1975; Leipzig, 1976; Zwickau, 1977; Cleveland, 1979; Milan, 1980; First Prize in Viotti Competition, Italy, 1978; First Prize in Toronto International Bach Piano Competition, 1985; Honorary Doctorate, University of Ottawa, 1995; Key to the City of Ottawa, 1997. *Current Management:* Cramer/Marder Artists. *Address:* 3436 Springhill Road, Lafayette, CA 94549, USA.

HEYER, John (Hajdu); Musicologist and Conductor; b. (John H. Hajdu), 4 Jan. 1945, Altoona, PA, USA; m. Sandra Lee Heyer 1973; two s. *Education:* BMus, Composition, DePauw Univ., 1966; MA, PhD, Musicology, Univ. of Colorado, 1971–73; studied with Nadia Boulanger, 1967–70. *Career:* teacher, Univ. of Colorado 1971–73; teacher, 1973–87, Chair., Music Department, 1980, Univ. of California, Santa Cruz; Lecturer, Programme Annotator, Carmel Bach Festival, 1979–; Dean, Coll. of Fine Arts, Indiana Univ. of Pennsylvania, Indiana, PA, 1987–; mem. of International Committee preparing the New Collected Works of Jean-Baptiste Lully for publication; Pres., Rocky Ridge Music Center Foundation, 1989–; Dean, Coll. of Arts and Communication, Univ. of Wisconsin, Whitewater, 1997–. *Recordings:* Conducted J. Gilles, Messe des Morts, Musical Heritage Society, 1981. *Publications:* Critical Edition: Jean Gilles, Messe des Morts, 1983; Lully and the Music of

the French Baroque, 1989; Critical edition: J.-B. Lully, Notus in Judaea, 1996; Lully Studies, 2000. *Contributions:* Notes; The New Grove. *Address:* College of Arts and Communication, University of Wisconsin Whitewater, Whitewater, WI 53190, USA.

HEYNIS, Aafje; Singer (Contralto); b. 2 May 1924, Krommenie, Netherlands. *Education:* Studied with Aaltje Noordewier-Reddingius, Laurens Bogtman and Bodi Rapp; Further study with Roy Henderson in England. *Career:* Sang at first in oratorio and other sacred music; Amsterdam, 1956, in Der Wildschütz by Lortzing; Concertgebouw Amsterdam from 1958, in the Alto Rhapsody, Mahler, Bach (St Matthew Passion, B Minor Mass), Monteverdi, Schubert, Handel, Beethoven and Frank Martin; Retired 1984. *Recordings:* Orfeo ed Euridice by Gluck; Madrigals by Monteverdi; Music by Bach. *Honours:* Harriet Cohen Medal, 1961. *Address:* c/o Concertgebouworkest, Jacob Obredhstrasse 51, 1017 Amsterdam, Netherlands.

HÅGGANDER, Mari Anne; Singer (Soprano); b. 23 Oct. 1951, Trokorna, Sweden. *Education:* Opera School, Gothenburg. *Career:* Debut: As Micaela in Carmen, Ponelle production, Royal Opera, Stockholm; Has sung Cherubino, Elisabetta in Don Carlo at Savonlinna in Finland, Pamina and the Countess in Figaro at Bonn and Buxton Festival, Eva in Meistersinger at Bayreuth in 1981, Mimi at Stockholm and Hamburg, Eva at the Metropolitan in 1985, and Elsa in Lohengrin at San Francisco; Guest appearances include Berlin, Munich, Paris, Brussels, Vienna, New York, Seattle and Toronto; Other roles include Butterfly, Amelia in Un Ballo in Maschera and Simon Boccanegra, Marschallin, Tatiana in Eugene Onegin, Lisa in The Queen of Spades, Sieglinde, Arabella, and Donna Anna. *Recordings:* Das Rheingold with Levine; Peer Gynt with Blomstedt; Several lieder and sacred music recordings. *Honours:* Court Singer to His Majesty the King of Sweden. *Current Management:* Ulf Tornqvist. *Address:* c/o Artistsekretariat Ulf Tornqvist, Sankt Eriksgatan 100 2 tr, 113 31 Stockholm, Sweden.

HICKEY, Angela; Singer (mezzo-soprano); b. 1949, England. *Education:* Guildhall School of Music. *Career:* Appearances with Royal Opera House, English National Opera, Scottish Opera, Opera North, Glyndebourne, City of Birmingham Touring Opera, Opera Northern Ireland, Monte Carlo Opera, Teatro Carlo Felice, Genoa; Roles include: Verdi's Preziosilla, Mistress Quickly and Azucena; Kabanicha in Katya Kabanova; Jocasta in Oedipus Rex; Carmen; Hélène in War and Peace with ENO; Annina in Der Rosenkavalier with Monte Carlo Opera; Mrs Sedley in Peter Grimes; Madame Larina in Eugene Onegin; Marcellina in Figaro with Opera Northern Ireland, 1991, Glyndebourne, 1992, Opera North, 1996; Mother Goose at Glyndebourne, 1994; Sang Mrs Sedley at Genoa, 1998; Mrs Trapes in Beggar's Opera in Caen and Rouen, 1999; Concerts include: Stabat Mater, Rossini; Requiem, Verdi; The Dream of Gerontius and Sea Pictures, Elgar; Ninth Symphony and Missa Solemnis, Beethoven; 2nd Symphony, Mahler; Nuits d'Eté; Appearances throughout Spain, France, Germany, Italy, Brazil, Czech Republic and Denmark. *Recordings include:* Hippolyte et Aricie, Rameau; Street Scene, Weill; Arianna, Alexander Goehr; Sea Pictures, Elgar. *Current Management:* Athole Still International Management, Forresters Hall, 25–27 Westow Street, London, SE19 3RY, England. *Telephone:* (20) 8771-5271. *Fax:* (20) 8768-6600. *Website:* www .atholestill.com.

HICKOX, Richard Sidney; Conductor and Music Director; b. 5 March 1948, Stokenchurch, Buckinghamshire, England; m. Frances Ina Sheldon-Williams, 1976, 1 s. *Education:* Royal Academy of Music (LRAM); Organ Scholar, Queens' College, Cambridge (MA). *Career:* Debut: As Professional Conductor, St John's Smith Square, 1971; Prom debut, 1973; Artistic Director, Woburn Festival, 1967–, St Endellion, 1974–, Christ Church Spitalfields Festival, 1974–, Truro Festival, 1981–, Summer Music Festival, 1989; Appeared at other festivals including Flanders, Edinburgh, Bath and Cheltenham; Conductor, Music Director, City of London Sinfonia and Richard Hickox Singers, 1971–, London Symphony Chorus, 1976–, Bradford Festival Choral Society, 1978–; Principal Guest Conductor, Dutch Radio Operator, 1980–85; Artistic Director, Northern Sinfonia, 1982–; Associate Conductor, San Diego Symphony Orchestra, 1983–84; Regularly conducts London Symphony Orchestra, RPO, Bournemouth Symphony Orchestra and Sinfonietta, Royal Liverpool Philharmonic Orchestra, BBC Symphony, Concert, Scottish and Welsh Orchestras, BBC Singers, Hallé Orchestra, Århus and Odense Orchestras; Conducted ENO, 1979; Opera North, 1982, 1986, Scottish Opera, 1985, 1987; Royal Opera, 1985, Los Angeles Opera, 1986; Conducted Rimsky's Mozart and Salieri at the Festival Hall, 1990, A Midsummer Night's Dream at Sadler's Wells; Season 1992/93 with Rossini Birthday Gala at the Barbican Hall and Giulio Cesare at Schwetzingen; Conducted the City of London Sinfonia at the 1993 Prom Concerts (Strauss's Oboe Concerto, Saxton's Viola Concerto and Mendelssohm's 4th Symphony); Conducted Rusalka at Rome, 1994; New production of Fidelio for English National Opera, 1996; Ariadne auf Naxos for Australian Opera, 1997; Mozart's Jupiter Symphony and Haydn's Nelson Mass with the Collegium Musicum

Choir and Orchestra London Proms, 1999; Conducted BBC National Orchestra of Wales at the London Proms, 2002. *Recordings include:* Belshazzar's Feast, with David Wilson-Johnson; Britten's Frank Bridge Variations; Elgar's Cello Concerto and Bloch's Schelomo (Steven Isserlis); Moeran's Sinfonietta and Serenade in G; Finzi Dies Natalis and Clarinet Concerto (Martyn Hill, Michael Collins); Rossini Stabat Mater (Field, D Jones, A Davies, Earle); L'Incoronazione di Poppea (Auger, Jones); Alcina (Auger); A Midsummer Night's Dream; Vivaldi's Ottone in Villa; The Pilgrim's Progress and Billy Budd. *Address:* 35 Ellington Street, London N7, England.

HIDALGO, Manuel; Composer; b. 4 Feb. 1956, Antequera, Andalusia, Spain. *Education:* Studied at the Zürich Conservatory, 1976–78, with Hans Ulrich Lehmann, and in Hanover and Stuttgart with Helmut Lachenmann, 1979–84. *Career:* Freelance composer from 1982, with performances at Donaueschingen, Stuttgart, Saarbrücken and elsewhere. *Compositions include:* Hacia, string quartet, 1980; Harto, for orchestra, 1982; Al componer, for viola, cello, double bass and orchestra, 1986; Alegrias piano concerto, 1987; Gloria, for six voices and orchestra, 1989; Trio esperando, 1989; Fisica, for orchestra, 1991; Vomitorio, Stage, 1991; Desastres de la guerra, after Goya, for narrator and 19 instruments, 1996; Des Kaisers neues Kleid, after Andersen, 1996; String Quartet No. 2, 1996; Musik nach Gedichten, for soprano, alto and orchestra, 1996; Dali, opera, 1999. *Address:* c/o Saarländisches Staatstheater, Schillerplatz, 66111 Saarbrücken, Germany.

HIDAS, Frigyes; Composer; b. 25 May 1928, Budapest, Hungary; m. Erzsebet Zombori, 5 July 1966, 1 d. *Education:* Degree in Composing, Academy of Music, Budapest, 1946–51. *Career:* Music Director, Budapest National Theatre, 1951–66; Music Director, Budapest Operetta Theatre, 1974–79; Freelance Composer. *Compositions include:* Cedar, ballet in 2 acts, 1975; Three Movements for orchestra, 1987; The Undanced, ballet, 1989; Chamber music: Three Sketches, 1982; Divertimento, 1982; Hungarian Folksongs, 1985; Pian-Org, 1985; Musique pour six, 1985; Alteba Trio, 1986; String Quartets Nos 1, 2, 3; Brass chamber music: Trio, 1980; Six Etudes, 1980; Play, 1981; Three Little Scherzos, 1982; Movement, 1982; Septet, 1982; Training Patterns, 1982; 5 x 5, 1983; Trumpet Fantasy, 1983; Little Suite, 1983; Academic Quintet, 1983; Musik für Bläser, 1983; Four-in-Hand, 1985; Sextets Nos 1 and 5 for bass trombone and wind quintet; Tuba Quartet, 1990; Saxophone Quartet, 1990; Works for concert band: Ballet Music, 1980; Merry Music, 1980; Concertino, 1981; Suite, 1981; Fantasy and Fugue, 1984; Folksong Suites Nos 1 and 2, 1985; Circus Suite, 1985; Festive Music, 1985; 17 concertos including: Ballad, 1982; Rhapsody, 1982; Flute Concerto No. 2, 1983; Trumpet Concerto No. 2, 1983; Baroque Concerto, 1984; Széchenyi Concerto, 1984; Quintetto concertante, 1985; Requiem for symphonic band, 4 soloists and mixed choir, 1996; Save the Sea, symphonia for symphonic band, 1997; Concerto for symphonic band, 1998; Saxophonia in E flat for alto saxophone, symphonic band and symphonic orchestra, 1998; Sax-Fantasy for symphonic band, 1998; Concerto for saxophone quartet and symphonic band, 1998; Birthday Concerto for trombone, symphonic band and symphonic orchestra, 1998; History of Vriezenveen, concerto for symphonic band, 1998; Swiss Rhapsody for symphonic band, 1998; Oboe Concerto No. 2, for oboe and wind ensemble, 1999; Missouri Overture for symphonic band, 1999; Oratorios; Music for films, television and theatre. *Recordings:* Wind Concerto No. 2; Flute Concerto No. 2; Toccata, Movement No. 3 of Organ Sonata; Violin Concertino; Oboe Concerto; Rhapsody for Brass Trombone; Training Patterns, excerpts; Four-in-Hand. *Honours:* Erkel Prize, 1958, 1982; Merited Artist of the Hungarian Republic, 1987; Bartók Pásztory Prize, 1993. *Address:* Attila ut 133, 1012 Budapest, Hungary.

HIDJOV, Plamen; Singer (Bass); b. 20 March 1953, Sofia, Bulgaria. *Education:* Studied in Sofia, and in Rome with Boris Christoff. *Career:* National Opera, Sofia, 1981–88, Kaiserslautern from 1994; Prokofiev's Napoleon in War and Peace, Theatre Champs-Elysées, Paris, Teatro Massimo, Palermo, 1986; Wexford Festival and Queen Elizabeth Hall, London, 1988, in Mercadante's Elisa e Claudio; Scottish Opera, 1989, and Madrid, 1991, as Leporello; Other roles include Rossini's Bartolo, Basilio, Don Magnifico, Donizetti's Dulcamara, Don Pasquale, Raimondo, Verdi's Philip II, Procida, Attila and Mussorgsky's Boris Godunov, Pimen, Dosifey and Varlaam; Wagner's Daland, King Marke and Wotan, Baron Kelbar in Verdi's Un Giorno di Regno, Kaiserslautern, 1996; Glinka's Ivan Susanin at Kaiserslautern, 1997; Concerts include Bach's B minor Mass, Messiah, and Mozart's Coronation Mass; Beethoven's 9th Symphony at Paris and Medellin, Colombia, 1987; Liszt Festival Tour, Oratorio Christus, 1990; Verdi's Requiem in Granada, 1993. *Address:* c/o Pfalztheater Kaiserslautern, 6750 Kaiserslautern, Germany.

HIELSCHER, Ulrich; Singer (Bass); b. 29 April 1943, Schwarzengrund, Germany. *Education:* Studied in Düsseldorf and with Paul Lohmann in Wiesbaden. *Career:* Sang at Essen from 1967, member of the Cologne Opera from 1974; Guest appearances at Hamburg, Hanover, Wuppertal, Frankfurt, Düsseldorf, Stuttgart and the Vienna Staatsoper, Ghent Opera, 1984–85, and further appearances as concert singer in Netherlands, Belgium, France, Switzerland and Colombia; Further guest appearances, Stadtstheater Schwerin, Staatsoper Berlin, Staatsoper Dresden, Theatre in Kiel and Freiburg; Opera roles have included Mozart's Osmin, Figaro, Leporello, Alfonso, Sarastro and Speaker, Verdi's Falstaff and Padre Guardiano, Kecal in The Bartered Bride, Mephistopheles in Faust, Plunket in Martha; Wagner's Daland, Hagen and Gurnemanz, Baron Ochs, the Doktor in Wozzeck, Don Pasquale, Rodrigo in Lulu, Rocco in Fidelio, Pogner in Die Meistersinger and Massenet's Don Quichotte; Season 1994–95 at Schwerin as Don Quichotte and Pogner; Season 2000–01 at Cologne in Werther, Billy Budd, Falstaff, Carmen and The Love for Three Orange; Concert showings in works by Bach, Handel, Haydn, Mozart, Beethoven and Bruckner; Lied repertoire includes Schubert, Schumann, Beethoven, Richard Strauss, Wolf, Brahms, P Cornelius, Dvořák, F Martin, C Loewe, Paul Gräner, Hans Pfitzner, Moussorgsky, Mendelssohn and Robert Franz. *Recordings include:* Messa di Gloria by Puccini. *Address:* Oper der Stadt Köln, Offenbachplatz, 50667 Cologne, Germany.

HIERHOLZER, Babette; Pianist; b. 27 March 1957, Freiburg, Breisgau; m. D. Michael Simpler, 31 Aug 1990. *Education:* Studied with Elisabeth Dounias-Sindermann, Berlin, 1964–73; With Herbert Stessin, pre-college of Juilliard School of Music, New York, 1973–74; With Lili Kraus, Texas Christian University, Fort Worth, 1973–74; With Wolfgang Saschowa, Berlin, 1974–76; With Maria Tipo, Florence, Italy, 1975; With Paul Badura-Skoda, Folkwang-Hochschule Essen (Künstlerische Reifeprüfung Diploma, 1981), and Vienna, 1976; With Bruno Leonardo Gelber, Buenos Aires, Argentina, 1979. *Career:* Debut: With orchestra at age 11 at Philharmonic Hall, Berlin; Regular appearances with orchestra and solo recitals in Berlin, Hamburg, Bonn, Frankfurt, Munich, Salzburg, Lausanne, Torino, Bordeaux, Caracas, Santiago, New York, Chicago, St Louis, Pittsburgh, Washington DC; Numerous engagements with the Berlin Philharmonic Orchestra with conductors: Colin Davis, Klaus Tennstedt, Leopold Hager, Semyon Bychkov, Lothar Zagrosek, Gerd Albrecht, Sixten Ehrling, Paavo Berglund; USA debut with Pittsburgh Symphony Orchestra, 1984; Recital-debut at Carnegie Hall, New York, 1991; Canadian debut with Saskatoon Symphony Orchestra, 1994; Several Performances of the Clara Schumann Piano Concerto (on the occasion of the 100th anniversary of Clara Schumann's death) in Berlin, Winnipeg, Ottawa, Festivals at Merida and Maracaibo, Venezuela; Solo recitals with an original recital programme of Clara Schumann at Schumann Houses at Bonn and Zwickau. *Recordings:* CDs: Music by Couperin, Debussy, Schumann, Mozart, Schubert, Scarlatti Piano Sonatas Vols. 1, 2 and 3; Played Soundtrack and Double for Clara Wieck (played by Natassja Kinski) in the Schumann Movie: Spring Symphony (by Peter Schamoni); CD Kinderszenen (Scenes of Childhood), 1999. *Current Management:* Konzert-Direktion Hans Adler, Berlin, Germany; Del Rosenfield Associates Inc. USA. *Address:* 46 Aspinwall Road, Red Hook, New York 12571, USA.

HIESTERMANN, Horst; Singer (Tenor); b. 14 Aug. 1934, Ballenstadt, Harz, Germany. *Career:* Stadtheater Brandenburg from 1957, debut as Pedrillo in Die Entführung; Sang in Leipzig, Weimar, Berlin and Dresden; Deutsche Oper am Rhein Dusseldorf, 1976–84; Salzburg Festival from 1978 as Monostatos, as the Dancing Master in Ariadne auf Naxos, and as Robespierre in Dantons Tod, 1983; Dallas Opera, 1982, as Loge in Das Rheingold; Tokyo, 1983, as Mime in Siegfried; Other appearances in Geneva, Rouen, Amsterdam, Houston and New York (Metropolitan Opera); Barcelona, 1984, as Aegisthus in Elektra; Member of the Zürich Opera from 1984; Deutsche Oper Berlin, 1984, in the premiere of Reimann's Gespenstersonate; Vienna Staatsoper, 1987, as Herod in Salome; Sang Mime in a new production of The Ring at the Metropolitan, 1988–90; Shuisky in Boris Godunov at Barcelona, 1990; Herod in Berlin; Sang Aegisthus at Athens, 1992; Other roles include the Captain in Wozzeck (Catania, 1998) and David in Die Meistersinger. *Recordings:* Wozzeck; The Duenna by Prokofiev; Puntila by Dessau; Carmina Burana; Trionfi by Orff; Die Zauberflöte; Karl V by Krenek; Die Meistersinger conducted by Karajan. *Publications:* E: Mime bist du so witzig?, 2000. *Address:* c/o Deutsche Oper Berlin, Richard Wagnerstrasse 10, D-1000 Berlin, Germany.

HIETIKKO, Jaakko; Singer (Bass); b. 16 May 1950, Kurikka, Finland. *Education:* Studied at the Helsinki Sibelius Academy. *Career:* Sang in the chorus of the Finnish National Opera from 1975 and was appointed as a soloist in 1980; Has appeared in most of the classical bass roles; Has specialised in such modern repertory as The Red Line by Sallinen (premiere, 1978), Vincent by Rautavaara (premiere, 1990); Sang in the premiere of The Book of Jonah by Olli Kortekanges, Helsinki, 1995 and The Last Temptations by Kokkonen; Many appearances at the Savonlinna Festival and as a concert singer. *Address:* c/o Finnish National Opera, PO Box 176, 00251 Helsinki Finland.

HIGBEE, Dale Strohe, AB, PhD; American music director and musician (flute, recorder); *Music Director, Carolina Baroque;* b. 14 June 1925, Proctor, VT; one d. *Education:* Harvard Univ., Univ. of Texas at Austin;

studied flute with Georges Laurent, Arthur Lora, Marcel Moyse, recorder with Carl Dolmetsch. *Career:* freelance flautist 1942–77, recorder player 1956–; clinical psychologist, South Carolina State Hospital, Columbia 1954–55, VA Medical Center, Salisbury, NC 1955–87; book and record review editor, The American Recorder 1967–89; Music Dir and recorder soloist, Carolina Baroque 1988–; mem. American Bach Soc., American Handel Soc., American Musical Instrument Soc. (bd of dirs 1972–74, 1985–88), American Musicological Society, American Recorder Soc. (bd of dirs 1963–65), Dolmetsch Foundation (gov. 1963–), Early Music America, Galpin Soc., Mozart Soc. of America, Music Library Asscn, Royal Musical Asscn, Soc. for Eighteenth-Century Music. *Recordings with Carolina Baroque:* The Great Mr Handel, Three Baroque Titans and a Minor Master, Handel and his Contemporaries, Music of the French Court and Chapel, Solo, Double and Triple Concertos of Bach and Telemann, Bach and Handel: Baroque Prometheans, Songs and Sonatas of Handel, Bach and his Peers, Cantatas and Concertos of Bach, Bach and Handel: Baroque Masters, Viva Voce! Two Mini Operas by Handel, Bach: Music to Challenge the Intellect and Touch the Heart, Arias, Duets and Ballet Music from Handel Operas, Sacred and Secular Cantatas of J. S. Bach, Bach Arias, Duets and Chamber Music. *Publications include:* A Survey of Musical Instrument Collections in the United States and Canada (with William Lichtenwanger, Cynthia Adams Hoover and Phillip T. Young) 1974; numerous articles and book, record and music reviews in American Recorder, Consort, Continuo: The Magazine of Old Music, Early Music, Galpin Society Journal, Journal of the American Musical Instrument Society, MLA Notes, Music & Letters, Music Journal, National Flute Association Newsletter, Newsletter of the American Musical Instrument Society, Southeastern Historical Society Newletter, Woodwind World. *Honours:* Combat Infantry Badge, Purple Heart. Pfc., 314th Infantry Regiment, 79th Division, 1943–45. *Address:* c/o Carolina Baroque, 412 South Ellis Street, Salisbury, NC 28144-4820, USA (office). *Telephone:* (704) 633-9311 (office). *E-mail:* info@carolinabaroque .org (office). *Website:* www.carolinabaroque.org (office).

HIGDON, Jennifer, BM, PhD; American composer; b. 31 Dec. 1962, Brooklyn, NY. *Education:* Bowling Green State Univ., Univ. of Pennsylvania. *Career:* composer-in-residence, American Composers' Forum Continental Harmony Project 2000, Nat. Youth Orchestra Festival 2002, Bravo! Vail Valley Music Festival 2002, 2003, Tanglewood Festival of Contemporary Music 2002, Bard Conductor's Inst. 2003, Cabrillo Festival of Contemporary Music 2004, Composers' Conference at Bennington Coll. 2004, Philadelphia Singers; featured composer, Tanglewood Festival of Contemporary Music 2003; mem. composition faculty, Curtis Inst. of Music. *Compositions include:* Shine 1995, Blue Cathedral 1999, Wind Shear 2000, City Scape 2002, Concerto for Orchestra 2002, Machine 2002, Piano Trio (Ithaca Coll. Heckscher Prize 2003), Dooryard Bloom 2004, Logo 2004. *Recordings include:* Blue Cathedral (with Atlanta Symphony Orchestra), City Scape and Concerto for Orchestra (with Atlanta Symphony Orchestra). *Honours:* winner ASCAP Foundation Commission Project 1995, Pennsylvania Council on the Arts Fellowship 1996, 2000, American Acad. of Arts and Letters Charles Ives Fellowship 1997, Guggenheim Fellowship 1997, Pennsylvania Council on the Arts Artist's Fellowship 2000. *Address:* c/o Cheryl Lawson (Artist Representative), Lawdon Press, 1008 Spruce Street, Suite 3F, Philadelphia, PA 19107, USA (office). *Telephone:* (215) 592-1847 (office). *Fax:* (215) 592-1095 (office). *E-mail:* lawdonpress@aol .com (office). *Website:* jenniferhigdon.com.

HIGGINBOTTOM, Edward, BMus, MA, PhD, FRCO; British university lecturer; *Director of Music, New College, Oxford;* b. 16 Nov. 1946, Kendal, Cumbria, England; m. Caroline M. F. Barrowcliff 1971; three s. four d. *Education:* Corpus Christi College, Cambridge. *Career:* Research Fellow, Corpus Christi College, Cambridge 1973–76; Dir of Music and Fellow of New College, Oxford 1976–. *Recordings:* over 80 recordings. *Publications:* various edns of music, contribs to Grove 6 and 7, Musical Times, Organists Review, Music and Letters. *Honours:* Hon. Fellowship, Royal School of Church Music 2002, Guild of Church Musicians 2003; Royal College of Organists Harding and Read Prizes; Commdr, Ordre des Arts et des Lettres. *Address:* New College, Oxford, England.

HILEY, David; University Professor; b. 5 Sept. 1947, Littleborough, England; m. Ann Fahrni, 28 Feb 1975, 2 d. *Education:* BA (Oxon), 1973; PhD, London, 1981. *Career:* Assistant Music Master, Eton College, 1968–73; Lecturer, Royal Holloway College, London, 1976–86; Professor, Regensburg University, Germany, 1986–; mem, Plainsong and Mediaeval Music Society; Gesellschaft für Musikforschung. *Publications:* New Oxford History of Music II (co-editor), 1990; Western Plainchant: A Handbook, 1993; Die Offizien des Mittelalters (co-editor), 1999; Das Repertoire der normanno-sizilischen Tropare I: Die Sequenzen, 2001. *Address:* Sonnenstrasse 10, 93152 Nittendorf, Germany. *E-mail:* david.hiley@psk.uni-regensberg.de.

HILL, David Neil, MA; British master of music and organist; b. 13 May 1957, Carlisle; s. of Brian and Jean Hill; m. 1st Hilary Llystn Jones 1979; one s. one d.; m. 2nd Alice Mary Wills 1994; one d., one s. *Education:* Chetham's School of Music, Manchester; St John's Coll., Cambridge. *Career:* Conductor, Alexandra Choir, London, 1979–80, Musical Dir, 1980–87; Sub-Organist, Durham Cathedral, 1980–82; Organist, Master of Music, Westminster Cathedral, 1982–88; Organist, Dir of Music, Winchester Cathedral, 1988–2002; Artistic Dir, Philharmonia Chorus, 1990–98; Musical Dir, Waynflete Singers, 1988–2002; Musical Dir, The Bach Choir, 1998–; Dir of Music, St John's College, Cambridge, 2003–; frequently directs choral workshops and summer schools, in UK, USA and Australia; regularly conducts the BBC Singers; Chief Conductor, Southern Sinfonia. *Recordings:* three albums of Choral Works by Stanford (with Westminster Cathedral Choir) 1997–98. *Publications:* Giving Voice (co-author) 1995; contrib. several articles on choir training. *Honours:* Hon. DMus (Southampton); Gramophone Award, 1985; Grammy Award, 1997. *Address:* St John's College, Cambridge, CB2 1TP, England. *Telephone:* (1223) 338683 (office). *E-mail:* dnh21@cam.ac.uk (office).

HILL, George R.; Musicologist and Music Bibliographer; b. 12 July 1943, Denver, Colorado, USA. *Education:* AB, Music, with Department Honours, Stanford University, 1965; AM, Library Science, University of Chicago, 1966; PhD, Historical Musicology, New York University, 1975. *Career:* Librarian, Music Division, New York Public Library, 1966–70; Assistant Music Librarian, New York University, 1971–72; Fine Arts Librarian, University of California, Irvine, 1972–73; Associate Professor of Music, Baruch College, City University of New York, 1973–. *Publications:* A Thematic Locator for Mozart's Works as Listed in Kochel's Chronologisch-Thematisches Verzeichnis - 6th Edition (principal author), 1970; A Preliminary Checklist of Research on the Classic Symphony and Concerto to the Time of Beethoven (excluding Haydn and Mozart), 1970; A Thematic Catalogue of the Instrumental Music of Florian Leopold Gassmann, 1976; Florian Leopold Gassmann, Seven Symphonies, 1981; Joseph Haydn Werke, Floetenuhrstuecke, 1984; A Handbook of Basic Tonal Practice, 1985. *Contributions:* Articles and Reviews to various professional journals, including The New Grove Dictionary of Music and Musicians. *Address:* 84 Highgate Terrace, Bergenfield, NJ 07621-3922, USA.

HILL, Jackson; Composer and University Professor of Music; b. 23 May 1941, Birmingham, Alabama, USA; m. Martha Gibbs 1966, 1 s. *Education:* AB, 1963, MA, 1966, PhD, Musicology, 1970, University of North Carolina; Composition with Iain Hamilton, 1964–66, and Roger Hannay, 1967–68. *Career:* Assistant/Associate Professor of Music, 1968–80, Head of Department of Music, 1980–90, Associate Dean of Faculty, 1990–95, Presidential Professor, 1996–, Bucknell University, Lewisburg, Pennsylvania; Conductor, Bucknell Symphony Orchestra, 1969–79; Member, Research Unit, Manchester College, Oxford, England, 1975; Choral Conductor Assistant, Exeter College, Oxford; Hays/Fulbright Fellow, Japan, 1977; Visiting Fellow, Clare Hall, Cambridge, England, 1982–83. *Compositions:* More than 100 works including: Serenade, 1970; Three Mysteries, 1973; Paganini Set, 1973; Missa Brevis, 1974; English Mass, 1975; By the Waters of Babylon, sonata, 1976; Whispers of the Dead, 1976; Streams of Love, 1979; Enigma Elegy, 1987; Symphony No. 1, 1990; Symphony No. 2, 1993; Symphony No. 3, 1997. *Recordings:* Sonata: By the Waters of Babylon; Ecce vidimus eum; Rhapsody, 1995; Tholos, 1998; Tango, 1998. *Publications:* The Music of Kees van Baaren, 1970; The Harold E Cook Collection of Musical Instruments; numerous articles on music and mysticism, Japanese music and Buddhist liturgical music. *Contributions:* Ethnomusicology; Studia Mystica; Notes. *Address:* Bucknell University, Lewisburg, PA 17837, USA.

HILL, Jenny; opera and concert singer (soprano); b. 20 June 1944, London, England; m. (divorced); two d. *Education:* National School of Opera, London Opera Centre. *Career:* debut, Sandman, Hansel and Gretel, Sadler's Wells Opera Company (now known as ENO); English Opera Group with Benjamin Britten performing in London, Russia and Canada; created role of Pretty Polly in Punch and Judy premiere, Aldeburgh and Edinburgh Festivals, 1968, and Mrs Green in Birtwistle's Down by the Greenwood Side, premiere at the London and Brighton Festivals, 1969; repertory operas performed include Traviata, Lucia, La Sonnambula, Rigoletto, Marriage of Figaro, Magic Flute, A Midsummer Night's Dream; concert appearances include A Mother Goose Primer, with the Pierrot Players, and Petrassi's Magnificat, with Giulini, both British premieres at the Royal Festival Hall, 1972; City of London Opening Concert, Bach's B minor Mass with Giulini at St Paul's Cathedral; opening concert, English Bach Festival, Blenheim Palace; performances on radio and television as well as numerous song recitals of classical and avant-garde music; teaching singing from home as well as performing; mem., Equity, Incorporated Society of Musicians, Asscn of Singing Teachers. *Recordings include:* The Rape of Lucretia, as Lucia; Schumann's Faust; Bach's St John Passion. *Honours:* Leverhulme Scholarship, 1960–63; Gulbenkian Fellowship for Most Outstanding

Young Performer, 1969–72. *Address:* 5 Oaklands Grove, London, W12 0JD, England.

HILL, Martyn; Singer (Tenor); b. 14 Sept. 1944, Rochester, Kent, England; m. Marleen De Maesschalck, 1974, 3 s., 1 d. *Education:* Royal College of Music; ARCM; Vocal Studies with Audrey Langford. *Career:* Established a reputation as one of the most distinguished international tenors of his generation; He is known throughout the world as a concert and oratorio soloist and recitalist; Repertoire includes Elgar's Dream of Gerontius, Berlioz's Damnation of Faust, Brucker's Te Deum, Verdi's Requiem and Mahler's Das Lied von der Erde; Performs regularly the works of Benjamin Britten; Glyndebourne 1985 and 1988, as Idomeneo and Belmonte; Recently sang War Requiem with the Sydney Symphony and Edo de Waart, Spring Symphony with the Hallé Orchestra and Kent Nagano, and Serenade with the Czech Philharmonic and Christopher Seaman; Evangelist in Bach's St John Passion, Festival Hall, 1997; Sang Eumete in Monteverdi's Ulisse at Florence, 1999. *Recordings include:* Britten's Serenade with the RPO and Vladimir Ashkenazy; Herbert Howells's Missa Sabrinensis with the London Symphony Orchestra and Rozhdestvensky for Chandos and Bach's St Matthew Passion with the choir of King's College, Cambridge for Columns Classics. *Address:* Owen/White Management, 14 Nightingale Lane, London N8 7QU, England.

HILL, Peter; Pianist and University Lecturer; b. 14 June 1948, Lyndhurst, England; m. Charlotte Huggins, 21 April 1981, 2 d. *Education:* MA, Oxford University; Royal College of Music. *Career:* Debut: Wigmore Hall, London, 1974; Regular broadcasts, BBC; International festival appearances include: Harrogate, Bath, English Bach, Dublin, Stuttgart; Founder Member, Ensemble Dreamtiger; Professor, University of Sheffield. *Recordings:* Complete Piano Music of Havergal Brian; Dreamtiger; East-West Encounters; Nigel Osborne: Remembering Esenin; Piano Works by Nigel Osborne, Douglas Young, Howard Skempton; Messiaen: The Complete Piano Music; Beethoven: Diabelli Variations; The Complete Piano Works of Schoenberg, Berg and Webern; Stravinsky: Music for Four Hands; Stravinsky: Solo Piano Music. *Publications:* The Messiaen Companion (editor); Stravinsky: The Rite of Spring. *Contributions:* Tempo. *Honours:* Chappell Gold Medal, Royal College of Music, 1971; 1st Prize, Darmstadt Ferienkurs, 1974. *Address:* c/o Department of Music, University of Sheffield, Sheffield S10 2 TN, England.

HILL, Robert (Stephen); Harpsichordist, Fortepianist and Musicologist; b. 6 Nov. 1953, Philippines. *Education:* Solo Diploma, Amsterdam Conservatory, 1974; Licentiate, Trinity College of Music, London, 1974; MA, 1982, PhD, 1987, Harvard University, USA. *Career:* Tours with Musica Antiqua Köln; Radio and television broadcasts for West German, British, Dutch, Belgian and French networks, and National Public Radio and CBC, USA. *Recordings:* J. S. Bach. Sonatas for Violin and Harpsichord with Reinhard Goebel; J. S. Bach, Art of Fugue, early version; Solo Harpsichord. *Contributions:* Early Music; Bach Jahrbuch. *Honours:* Erwin Bodky Award, 1982; Solo Recitalist Award, National Endowment for the Arts, 1983; Noah Greenberg Award, American Musicological Society, 1988. *Current Management:* Andreas Braun, Cologne, Germany. *Address:* Staatliche Hochschule für Musik Freiburg, Freiburg, Germany.

HILL SMITH, Marilyn; Singer (Soprano); b. 9 Feb. 1952, Carshalton, Surrey, England. *Education:* Guildhall School of Music. *Career:* Toured in: USA; Canada; Australia; New Zealand; Appearances at: Sydney Opera House; Hollywood Bowl; English National Opera from 1978 as: Adele, in Fledermaus, Susanna, in Le nozze di Figaro, Olympia in Les Contes d'Hoffmann, Zerbinetta and Mozart's Despina, Papagena and Blonde; Covent Garden debut, 1981 in Peter Grimes; New Sadler's Wells Opera in works by Lehàr, Kalman and Sullivan; Principal roles with Canadian Opera, Welsh National, Scottish Opera and Lyric Opera, Singapore; Other engagements include, Camden Festival, English Bach Festival, London Promenade Concerts; Regular concerts and broadcasts; Foreign appearances in Hong Kong, Coburg, Versailles, Granada, Siena, Cologne, Athens, Rome, Madrid, Seville, Oman, Zimbabwe and Cannes; Singing teacher and adjudicator; Rosalinde in Die Fledermaus at Nottingham, 2001. *Recordings:* Several works for Chandos, That's Entertainment, Opera Rara, including A Hundred Years of Italian Opera, and award winning operetta series. *Address:* c/o Music International, 13 Ardilaun Road, Highbury, London, N5 2QR, England.

HILLEBRAND, Nikolaus; Singer (Bass); b. 1948, Oberschlesien, Germany. *Education:* Studied with Rolf Dieter Knoll in Cologne and Hanno Blaschke in Munich. *Career:* Debut: Lubeck, 1972; Israel, 1972, as Mosè in the opera by Rossini; Salzburg Easter Festival, 1974, in Die Meistersinger; Vienna Staatsoper, 1974; Bayreuth Festival, 1974–75, in Parsifal and Die Meistersinger; Further engagements in Munich (Lohengrin), Karlsruhe, London, Paris, Rome and Brussels; Taormina Festival 1991, as Telramund; Many concert appearances, notably in music by Bach; Conductors include Abbado, Böhm, Kleiber, Karajan

and Muti. *Recordings include:* Stefano Colonna in Rienzi; St John Passion by Bach; Egisto by Cavalli; Romeo und Julia by Sutermeister; Reger's Requiem. *Current Management:* Ingpen & Williams Ltd, 7 St George's Court, 131 Putney Bridge Road, London, SW15 2PA, England.

HILLEBRANDT, Oskar; Singer (Baritone); b. 15 March 1943, Schopfheim, Baden, Germany. *Education:* Studied at Cologne Musikhochschule with Josef Metternich. *Career:* Sang at the Stuttgart Staatsoper from 1969; Appearances at Saarbrucken, Kiel and Brunswick from 1971; Member of the Dortmund Opera from 1985; Guest appearances at Hamburg, Munich, Düsseldorf, Mannheim and Zürich; La Scala Milan as Telramund and the Teatro Zarzuela Madrid as Achillas in Giulio Cesare by Handel; Seattle Opera as Alberich in the Ring; Further engagements in Antwerp, Copenhagen and at the Santander Festival, Marseilles and Turin, 1986, as Kaspar and Donner; British debut, 1989, as Mandryka at the Glyndebourne Festival; Other roles include Pizarro, Scarpia, Count Luna, Amonasro, Simon Boccanegra and Jochanaan in Salome, Wagner's Dutchman, Amfortas and Klingsor; Sang Alberich at Santiago, 1996; Season 1995–96 as Wotan at Dortmund, Pizarro at Rome and Alberich in Oslo; Sang Alberich and Gunther in Götterdämmerung at Buenos Aires, 1998; Sang Alberich in Siegfried, and Falstaff at the Komische Oper Berlin, 2000; Concert showings in Paris, London, New York, Barcelona and Rome. *Address:* Opernhaus, Kuhstrasse 12, 4600 Dortmund, Germany.

HILLEBRECHT, Hildegard; Singer (Soprano); b. 26 Nov. 1927, Hanover, Germany. *Education:* Studied with Margarethe von Winterfeld, Franziska Martianssen Lohmann and Paul Lohmann. *Career:* Debut: Freiburg, 1951, as Leonora in Il Trovatore; Sang at Zürich, 1952–54, notably in the premiere of the revised version of Hindemith's Cardillac (1952); Düsseldorf, 1954–59, Cologne, 1956–61; Sang Maria in Strauss's Friedenstag at Munich, 1961; Many appearances at the State Operas of Vienna, Hamburg and Munich; Salzburg Festival, 1946, 1964, as Ilia, Chrysothemis and Ariadne; Deutsche Oper Berlin, 1968, in the premiere of Ulisse by Dallapiccola; Covent Garden, 1967, as the Empress in Die Frau ohne Schatten; Metropolitan Opera, 1968–69; Sang with the Zürich Opera from 1972; Appearances in Rio de Janeiro, Paris, Rome, San Francisco, Edinburgh, Copenhagen, Barcelona, Dresden, Brussels and Prague; Repertoire includes works by Wagner, Puccini (Tosca), Verdi and Strauss, Elena in I Vespri Siciliani, Elisabeth de Valois, Desdemona, Sieglinde, Jenůfa and Ursula in Mathis der Maler. *Recordings:* Excerpts from Don Giovanni and Tannhäuser; Cavalleria Rusticana; Der Rosenkavalier; Ariadne auf Naxos; Don Giovanni; Duchess of Parma in Doktor Faust by Busoni; Die Zauberflöte.

HILLER, Wilfried; Composer; b. 15 March 1941, Weissenhorn, Swabia, Germany. *Education:* Studied with Günther Bialas at the Munich Musikhochschule (1963–68), with Boulez and Stockhausen at Darmstadt (1963) and with Carl Orff, from 1968. *Career:* Founded concert series Musik Unserver Zeit, 1968; Editor at Bavarian Radio, from 1971; Composition Department of the Richard Strauss Conservatory, Munich, from 1993. *Compositions include:* Katalog I–V for percussion, 1967–74; An diesem heutigen Tage, theatre, 1973; Schumamit, from the Song of Songs, for soloists, choruses and orchestra, 1977–93; Niobe, theatre, 1977; Der Josa mit der Zauberfiedel, for speaker, violin and chamber orchestra, 1985; Chagall-Zyklug, for clarinet and chamber orchestra, 1993; Peter Pan, theatre, 1997; Der Schimmel-reiter, stage, 1997; Der Geigenseppel, melodrama for marionettes, 1999; Aias, after Sophocles and Ovid, for mezzo, baritone, speaker and orchestra, 2000; Oswald von Wolkenstein, opera, 2001. *Honours:* Richard Strauss Prize, Munich, 1968; Schwabinger Arts Prize, 1978. *Address:* c/o Schott & Co Ltd, 48 Great Marlborough Street, London WC1, England.

HILLIER, Paul (Douglas); Singer, Conductor and Writer; b. 9 Feb. 1949, Dorchester, England; m. Lena-Liis Kiesel, 19 Mar 1977, 2 d. *Education:* AGSM, 1970; Guildhall School of Music. *Career:* Debut: Purcell Room, London, 1974; Vicar-Choral, St Paul's Cathedral, 1973–74; Director, Hilliard Ensemble, 1974–90; Early Music Masterclasses, York, London, Vancouver, Canada; Visiting Lecturer, University of California, Santa Cruz, 1980–81; Television debut, Music in Time, 1983; Copland Fellow, Amherst College, MA, 1984; Director, Theatre of Voices, 1989–; Professor of Music, University of California, Davis, 1990–96; Director, Early Music Institute, Indiana University School of Music, 1996–. *Recordings:* Many for various labels. *Publications:* 300 Years of English Partsongs, 1983; Romantic English Partsongs, 1986; The Catch Book, 1987; Arvo Pärt, 1997. *Honours:* Edison Klassik, 1986. *Address:* School of Music, Indiana University, Bloomington, IN 47405, USA.

HILLMAN, David; Singer (Tenor); b. 1936, England. *Education:* Studied at the National School of Opera. *Career:* Sang at Sadler's Wells, London, from 1962 as Tamino, Ferrando, Hoffmann, Rodolfo and Essex in Gloriana; Sang also in the premieres of Benjamin's Tartuffe, 1964, Bennett's The Mines of Sulphur, 1965, Williamson's The Violins of St Jacques, 1966, and Musgrave's Mary Queen of Scots (Edinburgh, 1977);

English premiere of Nielsen's Saul and David, 1977, as David, and in Szymanowski's King Roger with the New Opera Company, 1975; Guest appearances as Macduff at Covent Garden, at Stuttgart, Bonn, with Netherlands Opera (as Tom Rakewell, 1972), Santa Fe (Oliver's Duchess of Malfi, 1978) and at Glyndebourne (Elemer in Arabella, 1985); Also appeared in operettas by Gilbert and Sullivan.

HILTON, Janet Lesley, ARMCM; clarinettist; b. 1 Jan. 1945, Liverpool, England; m. David Richardson 1968, two s. (one deceased) one d. *Education:* Royal Manchester Coll. of Music, Vienna Konservatorium. *Career:* soloist with BBC Philharmonic, concert tours with Margaret Price; Festival appearances include Bath, Cheltenham, Aldeburgh, Henry Wood Proms, 1979; Edinburgh; BBC 2 television with Lindsay Quartet; Principal Clarinettist, Welsh National Opera, 1970–73; Scottish Chamber Orchestra, 1973–80; Kent Opera, 1984; Teacher, Royal Scottish Academy of Music and Drama, 1974–80; Royal Northern College of Music, 1982–86; Head of Woodwind, Birmingham Conservatoire, 1992; Principal Clarinet of Manchester Camerata and Director of Camerata Wind Soloists; Professor, University of Central England, Birmingham; Head of Woodwind, Royal College of Music, 1998–. *Recordings include:* Weber clarinet concertos with CBSO; Chamber Music of Brahms and Weber; Concertos of Malcolm Arnold, Nielsen, Copland, Stanford, Alun Hoddinott, Edward Harper, John McCabe, Elizabeth Maconchy with the BBC Scottish Symphony Orchestra. *Honours:* Boise Foundation Scholarship; Prize, National Federation of Music Societies. *Current Management:* Robert Gilder & Co., Enterprise House, 59–65 Upper Ground, London, SE1 9PQ, England. *Telephone:* (20) 7928-9008. *Fax:* (20) 7928-9755. *E-mail:* rgilder@robert-gilder.com. *Address:* 56B Belsize Park Gardens, London, NW3 4ND, England.

HIMMELBEBER, Liat; Singer (Mezzo-soprano); b. 27 April 1956, Stuttgart, Germany. *Education:* Studied in Berlin, and in Hamburg with Judith Beckmann; Masterclasses with Aribert Reimann and Dietrich Fischer-Dieskau. *Career:* Sang at the Eutin Festival, 1982–83, Oldenburg, 1984–85, and from 1985 as member of the Theater am Gärtnerplatz, Munich; Among her best roles have been Rosina, Mozart's Dorabella and Cherubino, and Hansel; Guest with the Hamburg Staatsoper and appearances with the Augsburg Opera from 1992; Concerts include premieres of works by Reimann, Von Bose and Manfred Trojahn; Sang also in the Munich 1987 premiere of Miss Julie by A Bibalo. *Address:* c/o St ätdische Buhnen Augsburg, Kasernstrasse 4–6, Pf 111949, 86159 Augsburg, Germany.

HIND, Rolf; Pianist, Composer; b. 1964, England. *Education:* Studied at Royal College of Music with John Constable and Kendall Taylor; Los Angeles with Johanna Harris-Heggie. *Career:* Has premiered works by Ligeti, Kurtag, Berio, Ruders, McMillan, Holt, Unsuk Chin and many others; played in festivals and major venues throughout Europe and Australasia under conductors including Sir Simon Rattle, Oliver Knussen, Vladimir Ashkenazy and Franz Welser-Most. *Compositions:* composed works for piano and for ensemble, BBC Radio and WDR; chamber collaborations with cellist Frances-Marie Uitti and David Alberman. *Recordings include:* solo works by of Messiaen and John Adams. *Address:* c/o Clarion/Seven Muses, 47 Whitehall Park, London N19 3TW, England.

HIND O'MALLEY, Pamela, ARCM; fmr composer, cellist and pianist; b. 27 Feb. 1923, London, England; m. Raymond O'Malley (died 1996); two s. one d. *Education:* studied cello with Ivor James, Piet Lentz and Pablo Casals, piano with Dorothea Aspinall and Imogen Holst, composition with Herbert Howells. *Career:* debut at Wigmore Hall, 1963; Cello Soloist and Ensemble Player; As One Pair of Hands, gave recitals for solo cello and solo piano in programmes that always include one contemporary work; Solo recitals playing Cello and Piano from 1967; Wigmore Hall 1969 and 1970; fmr Teacher of Cello and Piano, Cambridge; Part time Cello Teacher, Kings College School; Part time Ensemble Coach, Cambridge University Music Society. *Compositions:* Keyboard Music, Songs, Duo for Violin and Cello, Trio for Flute, Viola and Cello; Suite for String Orchestra. *Publications:* Cycle of Four Rounds for Four Violins; Arrangements of two Fauré songs for either Viola or Cello with Piano; contrib. to Royal College of Music Magazine; Casals as Teacher (Royal College of Music Magazine, 1950); Casals and Intonation (ESTA News and Views, 1981, and re-printed in the STRAD, 1983). *Address:* c/o 94 Fernside Road, London, SW12 8LJ, England.

HINDS, Esther; Singer (Soprano); b. 3 Jan. 1943, Barbados, West Indies. *Education:* Studied with Clyde Burrows in New York, and at Hartt College, Hartford, with Helen Hubbard. *Career:* Debut: New York City Opera, 1970, as First Lady in Die Zauberflöte; Has sung in New York as Donna Elvira, Madama Butterfly and Gershwin's Bess (on Broadway); Engagements at opera houses in Houston, Cincinnati and San Diego; Other roles include Liu (Turandot) and Micaela; Spoleto Festival, 1983, as Cleopatra in Antony and Cleopatra by Samuel Barber; Many concert performances. *Address:* c/o New York City Opera, Lincoln Center, New York, NY 10023, USA.

HINDS, Geoffrey (William John); Composer and Piano Teacher; b. 2 April 1950, Auckland, New Zealand. *Education:* BA, Auckland, 1974; MPhil (Mus) Auckland, 1976; BDiv, Melbourne College of Divinity, 1980; LRSM (Piano Teachers), 1983. *Compositions:* Held in New Zealand Music Archive Canterbury University - Sonata for viola and pianoforte, 1975; Suite for string quintet, 1975; String Quartet, 1976; Cantata Upon This Rock, 1982; Held in Music Library, Radio New Zealand, Wellington Motet for the Lord has Purposed, 1980–81; Overture into a Broad Place, 1981; String Quartet, 1981; Symphonic Moments of Our Time, 1982; And His Name Shall Be Called, 1981; Through The Grapevine, 1982; Anthems written for St Barnabas Choir; Song Cycle, Water Water Everywhere, 1985; Song Cycle, Pieces of Peace, 1986; Colyton Overture, 1986–87, written for Manawatu Youth Orchestra; String Quartet 1983–84; Song cycle, Innocence and Experience, 1987; Blowing in the Wind for wind quintet, 1987; Song Cycle, Nine Mystical Songs, 1988–89; Godzone Re-evaluated for Youth Orchestra, 1989; Great Outdoors Suite for piano, 1989; String Quartet, 1989; Symphony, St Barnabas Ballads (Tenor and piano); Creation Cantata; The Good Life (Musical), 1990; Piano Sonata; Two Edged Sword (Song Cycle for soprano and piano); Sonata for trombone, organ, 1991–; Flights of Fancy, for clarinet and string quartet; Gardens (SATB); Suite for viola; Our Good Keen Men (Song cycle for tenor and piano), 1992; A Tree For All Seasons (soprano, cello and piano); City of… (Song cycle for tenor, piano), 1993; String Quartet No. 2, 1995; The Mind, canticle (soprano, piano), 1995; Reflections, 1995; From the Rising of the Sun, 1996; Solitude: A Pilgrim's Progress; Creation in Reverse, 1997; Spiritual, suite for guitar, 1997; From Dawn to Dusk, wind quintet; 1997; Piano Suite, 1997; At Akito for SATB, 3 trombones and timpani, 1997; Tension for alto, tenor and pianoforte, 1997; The Cave for SATB, 1998; Rhapsody in White for clarinet, trombone, pianoforte, 1998; On Watching the Sailboats for tenor and pianoforte, words by J G Brown, 1998; String Quartet No. 6 (…of Ages), 1998; Bully Boys for tenor solo, men's chorus, 3 trombones and percussion, 1999. *Address:* 72 Valley Road, Mount Eden, Auckland 1003, New Zealand.

HINTERMEIER, Margareta; Singer (Mezzo-soprano); b. 11 Sept. 1954, St Polten, Austria. *Education:* Studied in Vienna with Hilde Konetzi. *Career:* Has sung at the Vienna Staatsoper from 1982 as Dorabella, Cherubino, Octavian, the Composer in Ariadne auf Naxos and Federica (Luisa Miller); Tour of Japan with the Staatsoper Company as Cherubino; Guest appearances at Geneva, Lisbon (as Orlofsky), Liège (Idamante in Idomeneo) and Dresden; Salzburg Festival, 1978–83, as Idamante; Concert appearances include Beethoven's Ninth at the 1989 Vienna Festival and Wagner's Wesendonck Lieder; Schubert Festival Hohenems, Carinthia Summer and Flanders Festivals; Further concert engagements in Istanbul, Nice and Bologna; Sang in Mahler's 3rd Symphony with the Vienna Symphony Orchestra at the Festival Hall, London, 1993; Season 1994–95 as Clairon in Capriccio, the Composer in Ariadne, Wagner's Magdalena and Federica in Luisa Miller at the Vienna Staatsoper. *Recordings include:* Maidservant in video of Elektra, conducted by Abbado; Die Walküre; Beethoven's Ninth. *Address:* c/o Staatsoper, Opernring 2, 1010 Vienna, Austria.

HIRAI, Motoki, BPhil, MA; Japanese pianist and composer; b. Tokyo. *Education:* Keio Univ., Tokyo, RAM, City Univ. and Guildhall School of Music and Drama, London. *Career:* Japanese govt artistic emissary on tours of Sri Lanka 1994, Portugal 1996, Malaysia 1997; resident in UK from 1996; numerous concerts and broadcasts throughout the UK; concert tour of Europe and Japan 2005; solo recital, St John's, Smith Square, London 2005. *Compositions include:* Valse Pathétique 1993, Hommage à Chopin 1999. *Honours:* Sir Jack and Lady Lyons Performance Award. *E-mail:* info@motokihirai.com. *Website:* www.motokihirai.com.

HIROKAMI, Jun'ichi; Conductor; b. 5 May 1958, Tokyo, Japan. *Education:* Studies, Tokyo Music University. *Career:* Debut: Israel Philharmonic Orchestra, 1988, London Debut, London Symphony Orchestra, 1989; Assistant Conductor, Nagoya Philharmonic Orchestra, 1983; International career from 1984; Conducted the NHK Symphony Orchestra, 1985, Orchestre National de France, 1986; Royal Philharmonic Orchestra, 1990; Further engagements with the Stockholm Philharmonic, Norrkoeping Symphony Orchestra (Principal Conductor from 1991), Malmö and Gothenburg Symphony Orchestras and radio orchestras in Netherlands and Italy; Operatic debut (July 1989), Un Ballo in Maschera followed by Rigoletto and La Forza del Destino, all with the Australian Opera; International concert activities spread to other countries: Spanish National Orchestra, Berlin Radio Symphony, Royal Concertgebouw Amsterdam, Montreal Symphony and with many European Orchestras; Conducted all major Japanese orchestras and appointed Principal Guest Conductor of the Japanese Philharmonic Orchestra, 1995. *Recordings:* Debut with the London Symphony Orchestra (BMG) and subsequent recordings with BIS Records of Sweden and Fun House Records, Japan, mainly made with his own Norrkoping Symphony Orchestra. *Honours:* Winner, 1st International

Kondrashin Conducting Competition, Amsterdam, 1984. *Current Management:* Hazard Chase, Norman House, Cambridge Place, Cambridge CB2 1NS, England. *Telephone:* (1223) 312400. *Fax:* (1223) 460827. *Website:* www.hazardchase.co.uk.

HIRSCH, Michael; Musician and Composer; b. 1958, Munich, Germany. *Career:* Composer, 1976–; Member of several groups for contemporary music; Collaboration with Dieter Schnebel, Josef Anton Hledl, Helmut Lachenmann; Performances and broadcasts for European radio and television; Actor, Stage Director, several European theatres and festivals; Translates works from music to speech, theatre to music; Work performed at several international festivals including Donaueschingen Festival, Klangaktionen, Musica Viva, in Munich; Witten Festival for new chamber music, Grenzenlos; Berlin in Moscow, 1996; XIII Cigle de m úsica del segle XX, Barcelona; Dresden Festival for Contemporary Music; Music Biennale, Berlin. *Compositions include:* Il Viaggio, music theatre, 1982–83; Memoiren 1. Buch, string quartet, 1983–85; Memoiren 3. Buch, concert for 6 instruments, 1986–91; Beschreibung eines Kampfes, music theatre, 1986–92; Hirngespinste, nocturnal scene for 2 players and accordion, 1996; Odradek, novel for chamber ensemble, 1994–97; Passagen/Szenen, for flute, clarinet, piano and string trio, 1997; Le carnet d'esquisse, for chamber ensemble, 1997–98; Das stille Zimmer, opera, 1998–99. *Address:* Gleditschstr 38, 10781 Berlin, Germany.

HIRSCH, Peter; Conductor; b. 1956, Cologne, Germany. *Education:* Studied at the Hochschule, Cologne. *Career:* Assistant to Michael Gielen at the Frankfurt Opera, 1979; First Conductor at Frankfurt Opera, 1983–87; Debut at La Scala with Prometeo by Luigi Nono; World premiere of Stephen Climax by Hans Zender, 1986; Guest conductor at many German theatres as well as Welsh National Opera, English National Opera, Netherlands Opera; Chief Conductor of Jeune Philharmonie de Belgique, 1993–95; Regular Guest amongst others at Staatsoper unter den Linden, Berlin, Deutsches Symphonie-Orchester Berlin, Berliner Sinfonie-Orchester, Residentie Orkest Den Haag, Orchestre National de Belgique, Bournemouth Symphony, Radio Orchestras of WDR Cologne and MDR Leipzig, ensemble recherche, at Bologna Festival, Berliner Festwochen and Munich Biennale. Many world premieres of works by Nono, Lachenmann, Zender, Knaifel and others. *Recordings:* CD recordings of Mahler 5th Symphony, Nono, Brahms, Schoenberg. *Address:* Weinbergstr. 26, 14548 Caputh, Germany.

HIRSCH, Rebecca; British violinist. *Education:* Royal Coll. of Music, London with Jaroslav Vanecek. *Career:* debut with the London Sinfonietta at the Barbican, playing Strauss' Bougeois Gentilhomme; has appeared as soloist with numerous orchestras in the UK and elsewhere in Europe, including Ålborg Symphony Orchestra, Bournemouth Symphony Orchestra, BBC Concert Orchestra, BBC Philharmonic, BBC Scottish Orchestras, Danish National Radio Symphony Orchestra, London Sinfonietta, Philharmonia, Ulster Orchestra. *Honours:* English Speaking Union scholarship 1984. *Address:* c/o London Sinfonietta, Third Floor, Dominion House, 101 Southwark Street, London, SE1 0JF, England.

HIRST, Grayson; Singer (Tenor); b. 27 Dec. 1939, Ojai, California, USA. *Education:* Studied at the Music Academy of the West with Martial Singher and at the Juilliard School with Jennie Tourel. *Career:* Debut: Sang Cavalli's Ormindo with the Opera Society of Washington, 1969; Sang Tonio in La fille du régiment at Carnegie Hall, 1970; New York City Opera debut, 1970, in Britten's The Turn of the Screw; Kennedy Center, Washington, in the premiere of Ginastera's Beatrix Cenci; Other premieres include works by Robert Aitken, Ned Rorem, Robert Starer, Virgil Thomson (Lord Byron) and Jack Beeson; Sang Tonio in Pagliacci at Carnegie Hall, New York, 1990; Further appearances in France, Brazil, England and Switzerland; Other roles include Don José, Pelléas, Faust and Mozart's Tamino, Ferrando and Belmonte. *Recordings include:* Schubert's Die schöne Müllerin.

HIRST, Linda; Singer (Mezzo-soprano); b. 1950, Yorkshire, England. *Education:* Flute and singing at the Guildhall School of Music, London. *Career:* Joined Swingle Singers and often appeared with Cathy Berberian; Concerts with the London Sinfonietta with Berio, Ligeti and Henze conducting their works; Premiere performances of Muldowney's Duration of Exile, Osborne's Alba, Simon Holt's Canciones and Judith Weir's The Consolations of Scholarship; Performances of Schoenberg's Pierrot Lunaire in Paris and Florence and for Channel 4 television; Glyndebourne Festival debut, 1985, Knussen's Where the Wild Things Are; 1986 world premiere of Osborne's The Electrification of the Soviet Union; Appearances at Bath and Almeida Festivals; Frankfurt Opera, Henze's Elegy for Young Lovers; Arts Council Network Tour with the London Sinfonietta; Also performs earlier music such as Incoronazione di Poppea in Spitalfields for Opera London; Sang in the premiere of Vic Hoyland's La Madre (written for her), London,

1990. *Recordings:* Songs Cathy Sang; Ottavia in L'Incoronazione di Poppea. *Fax:* (20) 7680-0665.

HIRSTI, Marianne; Singer (Soprano); b. 1958, Oslo, Norway. *Education:* Studied in Oslo and Lubeck. *Career:* Sang at Kiel, 1980–81; Staatsoper Hamburg, 1981–85; Cologne, 1985–87; Staatsoper Stuttgart from 1987; San Meroe in Reinhard Keiser's Die grossmütige Tomyris at Ludwigshafen, followed by Constanza in Bononcini's Griselda and Blondchen in Die Entführung; Cologne Opera as Maire in Zar und Zimmermann; Ludwigsburg Festival as Susanna in Le nozze di Figaro; Théâtre de la Monnaie, Brussels, as Berta in Il Barbiere di Siviglia, 1992; Other roles have included Despina, Marzelline, Gretel, Sophie in Werther and Tytania in A Midsummer Night's Dream; Many Lieder recitals and concert appearances, including Wigmore Hall, London, 1988. *Recordings include:* Beethoven Missa Solemnis; Die Grossmütige Tomyris; Der Zwerg by Zemlinsky; Blondchen in Die Entführung, conducted by Hogwood. *Address:* c/o Staatsoper Stuttgart, Oberer Schlossgarten 6, 7000 Stuttgart, Germany.

HIRTE, Klaus; Singer (Baritone); b. 28 Dec. 1937, Berlin, Germany. *Education:* Studied at the Stuttgart Musikhochschule with Hans Hager. *Career:* Sang at the Stuttgart Staatsoper from 1964; Bayreuth Festival, 1973–75, as Beckmesser in Die Meistersinger; Salzburg Festival as Antonio in Le nozze di Figaro; Ludwigsburg Festival, 1972, as Papageno; Further appearances in Nuremberg, Munich, Düsseldorf, Mannheim, Venice, Chicago and San Antonio; Other roles include Don Pasquale and Dulcamara by Donizetti; Wagner's Kurwenal and Klingsor and parts in operas by Strauss, Gluck, Mascagni and Weber; Sang Oberon in the premiere of Der Park by Hans Gefors, Wiesbaden, 1992; Stuttgart Staatsoper 1993, in Don Quichotte by Hans Zender; Sang the Impresario in Donizetti's Convenienze Teatrali at Stuttgart, 2001. *Recordings include:* Tannhäuser; Die Meistersinger; Le Cadi Dupé by Gluck; Der Schauspieldirektor; Cavalleria Rusticana; Intermezzo; Die schweigsame Frau. *Address:* c/o Staatstheater Stuttgart, Oberer Schlossgarten 6, 7000 Stuttgart 1, Germany.

HIRVONEN, Anssi; Singer (Tenor); b. 1948, Finland. *Education:* Qualified as Cantor-organist, 1976, Singing Teacher and leaving certificate from the General Department, 1978, Singing Diploma, 1986, Sibelius Academy, Helsinki; Studied at the Conservatoire of Tampere, Helsinki; Private studies with Jolanda di Maria Petris; Further studies in Berlin and Vienna. *Career:* Appearances as Oratorio and Concert Soloist in Finland, Sweden, Germany, Hungary, USA, Estonia, Russia, Latvia and the Faroe Islands; Opera Debut at Tampere Opera, 1975; Solo engagements at the Heidelberg Opera, 1979–80, the Savonlinna Opera Festival 1978–, the Finnish National Opera 1980–, and provincial operas in Finland; Sang in the world premieres of Ilkka Kuusisto's The War of the Light, 1982, Rautavaara's Thomas, 1986 and his Vincent, 1990, Atso Almila's 30 Silver Coins 1988; Guest Soloist at the operas of Stockholm and Tallinn; Numerous television and radio appearances and recordings; Professor and Lecturer of Singing, Sibelius Academy; Guest Soloist, Finnish National Opera; Sang Don Ottavio in Don Giovanni for St Michael Opera, 1999. *Recordings include:* Contemporary Finnish Choir Music; Sacred Songs of C Franck, T Kuusisto, Y Karanko, E Linnala, A Maasalo and L Madetoja; Christmas Songs of O Kotilainen, A Maasalo, S Palmgren and S Ranta; Musica Humana, Sacred Songs of P Kostiainen and J Sibelius; Rautavaara's Vincent, 1986 and Thomas, 1990; Jean Sibelius: The Tempest op 19, 1992. *Honours:* Director Musices, 1998. *Address:* Satamasaarentie 7, 00980, Finland.

HIRZEL, Franziska; Singer (Soprano); b. 28 Nov. 1952, Zürich, Switzerland. *Education:* Studied in Basel, Fribourg, Frankfurt am Main and Zürich. *Career:* Sang at Darmstadt Opera from 1980, notably in the 1983 premiere of Klebe's Die Fastnachtsbeichte and as Mozart's Blondchen, Donna Elvira, Fiordiligi and Pamina, Micaela, Martha, Euridice, Gilda, Musetta and Gretel; Concert repertoire has included sacred works by Bach, Beethoven, Mozart, Haydn and Schoenberg; Many Lieder recitals and broadcasting engagements; Guest appearances at concert halls and opera houses throughout Germany; Sang Marie in Gurlitt's Wozzeck at Turin, 2000. *Address:* Staatstheater, Postfach 111432, 6100 Darmstadt, Germany.

HITCHCOCK, Hugh Wiley, BA, MMus, PhD; American musicologist and writer; b. 28 Sept. 1923, Detroit, MI. *Education:* Dartmouth Coll., Univ. of Michigan. *Career:* faculty mem., Univ. of Michigan 1947–61; Prof. of Music, Hunter Coll., CUNY 1961–71; Ed., Prentice-Hall History of Music Series 1965–, Earlier American Music 1972–98, Recent Researches in American Music 1976–94; mem. of exec. cttee and area ed. for the Americas, The New Grove Dictionary of Music and Musicians 1980; co-ed., The New Grove Dictionary of American Music 1986; Prof. of Music, Brooklyn Coll., CUNY 1971–80, Distinguished Prof. of Music 1980–93; Founder-Dir, Inst. for Studies in American Music, Brooklyn Coll. 1971–93; J. Paul Getty Center for Art History and the Humanities scholar 1985–86; mem. American Musicological Soc. (pres. 1991–92, hon. mem. 1994–), Charles Ives Soc. (pres. 1973–93), Music Library Asscn (pres. 1966–68). *Publications:* Music in the United States: A Historical Introduction 1969, Charles Ives Centennial Festival-Conference 1974, Ives 1977, An Ives Celebration: Papers and Panels of the Charles Ives Centennial Festival-Conference (ed. with Vivian Perlis) 1977, The Phonograph and Our Musical Life 1980, The Music of Ainsworth's Psalter 1612 (with L. Inserra) 1981, The Works of Marc-Antoine Charpentier: Catalogue Raisonné 1982, Ives: A Survey of the Music 1983, Marc-Antoine Charpentier 1990; contrib. to scholarly books and professional journals. *Honours:* Fulbright Sr Research Fellowships 1954–55, 1968–69, Guggenheim Fellowship 1968–69, Nat. Endowment for the Humanities grant 1982–83; Soc. for American Music lifetime achievement award 2003; Chevalier, Ordre des Arts et des Lettres 1995. *Address:* 1192 Park Avenue, No. 10-E, New York, NY 10128, USA.

HJORTSO, Merete; Singer (Soprano); b. 1944, Denmark. *Education:* Studied in Copenhagen and Vienna. *Career:* Debut: Royal Opera Copenhagen, 1971 in Kagel's Halleluja; Sang frequently with the Jutland Opera at Århus, notably in the 1983 premiere of Det guddommelige Tivoli by Norgaard; Major roles have included Marguerite in Faust, Susanna and Cherubino in Le nozze di Figaro, Zdenka, Micaela, Massenet's Thaïs and Leonora in Nielsen's Maskarade; Guest engagements in Strasbourg, Brussels and elsewhere; Frequent concert appearances. *Recordings:* Nielsen's Maskarade. *Address:* c/o Den Jyske Opera, Thomas Jensens Alle, DK 8000 Århus, Denmark.

HO, Allan (Benedict); Musicologist; b. 30 March 1955, Honolulu, Hawaii, USA. *Education:* BA, Music History, 1978, MA, Musicology, 1980, University of Hawaii; PhD, Musicology, University of Kentucky, 1985. *Career:* Discovered a copy of the lost full score of Wilhelm Stenhammar's First Piano Concerto, the manuscript of which was believed destroyed during WWII, and which was the most widely performed Swedish composition at the turn of the century; mem, American Musicological Society; Pi Kappa Lambda. *Publications:* A Biographical Dictionary of Russian/Soviet Composers, 1989; Music for Piano and Orchestra: The Recorded Repertory; Critical editions of the 2-piano score and full score of Wilhelm Stenhammar's First Piano Concerto; Shostakovich Reconsidered, 1998. *Contributions:* Journal of the American Liszt Society; Notes; The New Grove Dictionary of American Music; New Grove Dictionary of Opera; New Grove Dictionary of Women Composers; New Grove Dictionary, new version. *Address:* Box 1771, Music Department, Southern Illinois University, Edwardsville, IL 62026, USA.

HOARE, Peter; Singer (Tenor); b. 1965, Bradford, England. *Education:* Huddersfield School of Music. *Career:* Appearances with Welsh National Opera from 1992, as Jacquino, Mozart's Tito, Arbace and Basilio, and the Shepherd in Tristan und Isolde; Nemorino for Mid Wales Opera and Sellem in The Rake's Progress at Lausanne; Bardolfo in Falstaff at Covent Garden, 1999; Concerts include the Mozart and Berlioz Requiems, Messiah with George Malcolm, Bach's Christmas Oratorio, Britten's Serenade and the Verdi Requiem; Season 1999 with Vitek in The Makropulos Case at Aix-en-Provence. *Address:* c/o Harlequin Agency Ltd, 203 Fidlas Road, Cardiff CF4 5NA, Wales.

HOBKIRK, Christopher; Singer (Tenor); b. 1965, Henley-on-Thames, England. *Education:* Studied at the Royal Scottish Academy and at Royal College of Music with Neil Mackie. *Career:* Concert engagements in Finland and Norway with Britten's St Nicolas and Bach's St John Passion; Bach's Magnificat with the Las Palmas Philharmonic, the B minor Mass at Edinburgh and Telemann's Luke Passion at St John's Smith Square; Created Eochd in Edward McGuire's opera The Loving of Etain, 1990, at Glasgow; Season 1991 with Britten's Serenade at Palma, Bach's St Matthew Passion at Darmstadt and Bergen, Mozart's Requiem with the Manchester Camerata and the B minor Mass conducted by William Boughton; Sang Misael in The Burning Fiery Furnace for St James's Opera, 1991.

HOBSON, Ian, BA, MA, DMus; pianist and conductor; b. 1953, Wolverhampton, England; m.; four s. one d. *Education:* Magdalene College, Cambridge, Yale University. *Career:* Finalist in 1978 Baltimore Symphony Conducting Competition; Silver Medals at Artur Rubinstein and Vienna-Beethoven Competitions; 1st Prize, Leeds International Piano Competition, 1981; Soloist with Royal Philharmonic Orchestra, Philharmonia and Scottish National Orchestra; USA with Orchestras of Chicago, Philadelphia, Pittsburgh, St Louis, Baltimore, Indianapolis and Houston; Complete cycles of Beethoven's Sonatas; Founded Sinfonia da Camera, 1984; The Age of Anxiety for Bernstein's 70th birthday, 1988; As conductor led Mozart's Concertos from the keyboard with English National Orchestra on its Far Eastern tour; Illinois Opera Theatre in Così fan tutte and Die Fledermaus; 1988–89 season engagements with San Diego Chamber Orchestra and in Israel; Professor, University of Illinois, 1983–. *Recordings:* Chopin/Godowsky Etudes and the complete piano sonatas of Hummel; Strauss's Burlesque and the Paregon on the Symphonia Domestica, with the Philharmonia;

Concertos by Françaix, Saint-Saëns and Milhaud, with the Sinfonia da Camera; 24 Chopin Etudes, Rachmaninov Transcriptions and Mozart's Concertos Nos 23 and 24. *Fax:* (20) 8287-9428.

HOCH, Beverly; American singer (soprano); b. 1956, Kansas City, Kansas. *Education:* studied in New York. *Career:* Concert performances from 1980, notably at Carnegie Hall, New York, and the Kennedy Center, Washington; European concerts in Madrid, Gothenburg and Brussels; Opera appearances at Spoleto, the Wexford Festival (Philine in Mignon), and Santa Fe; Her best known role is Mozart's Queen of Night, which she sang at the 1991 Glyndebourne Festival. *Recordings include:* Die Zauberflöte.

HOCH, Francesco; Composer and Professor of Music; b. 14 Feb. 1943, Lugano, Switzerland; m. 1 May 1971, 2 s. *Education:* G Verdi Conservatory, Milan; Composition, Padua, Darmstadt. *Career:* Professor of Music, Lugano; Assistant, Composition Course, Chigiana Academy, Siena Italy, 1974; Invited, International Laboratory, Venice Biennial, 1975; Founder Oggimusica Association of Contemporary Music, 1977; Regular radio broadcasts of compositions, Europe, Israel, Canada, USA, Australia, Japan, Russia, Latin America; Television recordings. *Compositions:* 63 published works including: Dune, 3 instruments, 2 percussion, 2 voices, 1972; L'Oggetto Disincantato, 13 instruments, 1974; Trittico, clarinet, viola; Leonardo e/und Gantenbein, opera-ballet, 1980–82; Ostinato variabile, I, bass clarinet, 1981, II, bass clarinet, piano, III, 2 guitars, IV, piano, violin, 1982; Sans, oboe, orchestra, 1985; Un Mattino, 2 flutes, 1986; Der Tod ohne des Mädchen, string quartet, 1990; Memorie da Requiem, choir, orchestra, 1989–91; Postludio degli Spettatori, choir, 1991; Péché d'outre-tombe, for clarinet and string quartet, 1993; La Passerelle des Fous, opera, for 3 sopranos, 5 actors and 8 instruments, 1994–95; Canti e danze dai nuovi gironi for 13 instruments, 1995; Der hoffnungsvolle Jean und der Moloch for narrator and chorus, 1995; Suite Palomar for 5 instruments, 1995–97; L'isola dell'amore for 3 voices and mandolin orchestra, 1997–98; The Magic Ring opera, for 6 voices, 3 e-guitars, 3 percussions, electronic tape and video scenes, 1995–2000; Su Gentile Invito for violin and cello, 2000; Es ist Zeit for flute, 2000; Doppio Concerto for cello, piano and orchestra, 2001–02; Duo dal doppio for cello and piano, 2002; Ave lucanum for choir, 2003. *Recordings include:* Chamber and orchestral works, CD; Il Mattino Dopo, CD, 2000; Memorie da Requiem, CD Doron, 2002; Fantasia da L'isola dell'amore, Cd Altrisuoni, 2003; The Magic Ring, opera, CD, MGB, CH, 2004; Video Recordings include: Trasparenza per nuovi elementi, Video TSI, CH, 1977; Leonardo e/und Gantenbein, opera, video TSI, CH, 1985; F.Hoch- Ritratto and Suite Palomar PARS MEDIA, Munich, 2001. *Publications:* Enc Musica UTET (Torino); Enc Grove; Francesco Hoch, Swiss Composer, by Pro Helvetia, 1994; Donazione opere, Zentralbibliothek, Zurich, 2001; F.Hoch: Influssi sulla mia musica in Entre Denge et Denzy, P Sacher Stiftung, Basel; Carlo Piccardi: La sfida musicale di F.Hoch in CdT, CH, 15/04/2002' Paolo Petazzi: Magie de la Bourse in Dissonanz, CH, 2003; Paolo Repetto: Utopie und Erinnerung in Dissonanz, CH, 2003; Carlo Piccardi: Il futuro nel passato (F.Hoch) in bloc notes 48, 2003. *Address:* Campo dei Fiori 9, 6942 Savosa, Switzerland.

HOCHMANN, Klaus; German composer; b. 29 Dec. 1932, Angerbürg, Ostpreuáen, Poland. *Education:* Composition and Conducting at Stuttgart and Salzburg. *Career:* Piano Teacher, Music School of Herrenberg; mem., Society for Promotion of Radio Symphony Orchestra Stuttgart, Leoš Janáček Society Bern. *Compositions include:* Der Findling, opera, 1970; Midsummer Night, 5 choirs ac, 1963; Requiem für einen Unbekannten, 3 songs for bass and organ, 1965; Concertino I for percussion, 1969; Concertino III for percussion solo and tutti, 1974; Bilder des Todes for recorder and percussion, 1991; one to four for string quartet, 1991; Mary, poem with music, text by Dorothea Spears, 1992. *Recordings:* Requiem für einen Unbekannten, 1968; Tenebrae factae sunt for mixed choir ac, 4 speaker, percussion, 1992; In Memoriam, song cycle for baritone and piano, 1980; Und suche Gott, for mixed choir ac and speaker, 1991; Mein Bruder Tod for mixed choir a cappella, after Agnes Miegel, 1985; Intrada for organ, 1993; Selbst die Steine umarmen wir; Strophen for 5 solo voices a cappella, after Nelly Sachs, 1994. *Honours:* Composition Prizes, Kassel, 1965, Bern, 1975, Bonn, 1984; Promotion Prizes, 1971, 1977. *Address:* Beethovenstrasse 62, 71083 Herrenberg, Germany.

HOCKNEY, David, CH, RA; British artist and stage designer; b. 9 July 1937, Bradford; s. of the late Kenneth Hockney and Laura Hockney. *Education:* Bradford Coll. of Art and Royal Coll. of Art. *Career:* taught at Maidstone Coll. of Art 1962, Univ. of Iowa 1964, Univ. of Colo 1965, Univ. of Calif. (Los Angeles) 1966, Hon. Chair. of Drawing 1980, (Berkeley) 1967; has travelled extensively in Europe and USA; Assoc. mem. Royal Acad. 1985. *Film:* A Bigger Splash (autobiog. documentary) 1974. *Exhibitions:* first one-man Exhbn, Kasmin Gallery, London 1963; subsequent one-man exhbns at Museum of Modern Art, New York 1964, 1968, Laundau-Alan Gallery, New York 1964, 1967, Kasmin Gallery 1965, 1966, 1968, 1969, 1970, 1972, Stedeljik Museum, Amsterdam

1966, Palais des Beaux-Arts, Brussels 1966, Studio Marconi and Galleria dell'Ariete, Milan 1966, Galerie Mikro, Berlin 1968, Whitworth Art Gallery, Manchester 1969, André Emmerich Gallery, New York 1972–96, Gallery Springer, Berlin 1970, Kestner-Ges., Hanover 1970, Whitechapel Gallery (retrospective exhbn), London 1970, Kunsthalle, Bielefeld 1971, Musée des Arts Décoratifs, Louvre, Paris 1974, Galerie Claude Bernard, Paris 1975, Nicholas Wilder, Los Angeles 1976, Galerie Neundorf, Hamburg 1977, Warehouse Gallery 1979, Knoedler Gallery 1979, 1981, 1982, 1983, 1984, 1986, Tate Gallery (retrospective Exhbn) 1980, 1986, 1988, 1992, Hayward Gallery (photographs) 1983, 1985, Museo Tamayo, Mexico City 1984, LA County Museum of Art (retrospective) 1988, 1996, The Metropolitan Museum of Art (retrospective) NY 1988, Knoedler Gallery, London 1988, LA Louver Gallery, Calif. 1986, 1989–, Venice 1982, 1983, 1985, 1986, 1988, Nishimura Gallery, Tokyo, Japan 1986, 1989, 1990, 1994, Royal Acad. of Arts, London 1995, Hamburger Kunsthalle 1995, Manchester City Art Galleries (retrospective exhbn) 1996, Nat. Museum of American Art, Washington, DC 1997, 1998, Museum Ludwig, Cologne 1997, Museum of Fine Arts, Boston 1998, Centre Georges Pompidou, Paris 1999, Musée Picasso, Paris 1999, Annely Juda Fine Art 2003, Nat. Portrait Gallery 2003; group exhbns include ICA, Second and Third Paris Biennales of Young Artists, Musée d'Art Moderne 1961, 1963, Third Inst. Biennale of Prints, Nat. Museum of Art, Tokyo 1962, London Group Jubilee Exhbn 1914–1964, Tate Gallery 1964, Painting and Sculpture of a Decade, Gulbenkian Foundation, Op and Pop, Stockholm and London 1965, Fifth Int. Exhbn of Graphic Art, Ljubljana 1965, First Int. Print Biennale, Cracow 1966, São Paulo Biennale 1967, Venice Biennale 1968, Pop Art Redefined, Hayward Gallery, London 1969, 150 Years of Photography, Nat. Gallery, Wash., DC 1989–90; touring show of prints and drawings Munich, Madrid, Lisbon, Tehran 1977, Saltaire, Yorks, New York, LA 1994, Royal Acad. (drawings) 1995–96. *Stage design:* set: Ubu Roi, Royal Court Theatre, London 1966, Rake's Progress, Glyndebourne 1975, Die Zauberflöte, Glyndebourne 1978, La Scala 1979, Nightingale, Covent Garden 1983, Varii Capricci, Metropolitan Opera House, New York 1983, Tristan and Isolde, LA Music Centre Opera, LA 1987, Turandot, Lyric Opera 1992–, San Francisco 1993, Die Frau Ohne Schatten, Covent Garden, London 1992, LA Music Centre Opera 1993; costume and set: Les Mamelles de Teresias, Metropolitan Opera House, New York 1980, L'Enfant et les sortilèges, Metropolitan Opera House, New York 1980, Parade, Metropolitan Opera House, New York 1980, Oedipus Rex, Metropolitan Opera House, New York 1981, Le Sacre du Printemps, Metropolitan Opera House, New York 1981, Le Rossignol, Metropolitan Opera House, New York 1981. *Publications:* Hockney by Hockney 1976, David Hockney, Travel with Pen, Pencil and Ink 1978 (autobiog.), Paper Pools 1980, Photographs 1982, China Diary (with Stephen Spender), 1982, Hockney Paints the Stage 1983, David Hockney: Cameraworks 1984, Hockney on Photography: Conversations with Paul Joyce 1988, David Hockney: A Retrospective 1988, Hockney's Alphabet (ed. by Stephen Spender) 1991, That's the Way I See It 1993 (autobiog.), Off the Wall: Hockney Posters 1994, David Hockney's Dog Days 1998, Hockney on Art: Photography, Painting and Perspective 1999, Hockney on "Art": Conversation with Paul Joyce 2000, Secret Knowledge: Rediscovering the Lost Techniques of the Old Masters 2001, Hockney's Pictures 2004; illustrated Six Fairy Tales of the Brothers Grimm 1969, The Blue Guitar 1977, Hockney's Alphabet 1991. *Honours:* Hon. PhD (Aberdeen) 1988, (Royal Coll. of Art) 1992: Hon. DLitt (Oxford) 1995; Guinness Award 1961, Graphic Prize, Paris Biennale 1963, First Prize 8th Int. Exhbn of Drawings and Engravings, Lugano 1964, prize at 6th Int. Exhbn of Graphic Art, Ljubljana 1965, Cracow 1st Int. Print Biennale 1966, First Prize 6th John Moores Exhbn 1967, Hamburg Foundation Shakespeare Prize 1983, Praemium Imperiale, Japan Art Asscn 1989, Fifth Annual Gov.'s Award for Visual Arts in Calif. 1994. *Address:* c/o 7508 Santa Monica Boulevard, Los Angeles, CA 90046-6407, USA.

HODDINOTT, Alun; Composer; b. 11 Aug. 1929, Bargoed, South Wales; m. Beti Rhiannon Huws, 1953, one s. *Education:* University College, Cardiff. *Career:* Lecturer, Cardiff College of Music and Drama, 1951–59; Lecturer, 1959–65, Reader, 1965–67, Professor, Music, 1967–87, University College, Cardiff; Artistic Director, Cardiff Festival of 20th Century Music, 1966–89. *Compositions include:* 12 piano sonatas, 1959–93; Welsh Dances; Investiture Dances; Black Bart; Dives and Lazarus, 1965; Variants, 1966; Fioriture, 1968; Sonatas, harp, clarinet, horn; The Tree of Life, 1971; Ritornelli; The Beach at Falesa, opera, 1974; 2 sonatas, cello, piano, 1977; The Magician, opera; Ancestor Worship; 5 Landscapes, song cycles; A Contemplation Upon Flowers, songs, soprano, orchestra; What the Old Man Does Is Always Right, opera; Sonatina, guitar; Sonatina, 2 pianos; The Rajah's Diamond, opera; The Trumpet Major, 3-act opera; Nocturnes and Cadenzas, solo flute; Doubles, oboe, harpsichord, strings; 5 Studies, orchestra; 4 Scenes from The Trumpet Major, orchestra; Quodlibet, orchestra, 1982, brass quintet, 1983; Masks, oboe, bassoon, piano, 1983; Lady and Unicorn, cantata; Piano Trio No. 2; Bagatelles, oboe, harp; String Quartet No. 2,

1984, No. 3, 1988; Scenes and Interludes, trumpet, harpsichord, strings; Bells of Paradise, cantata, 1984; Scena, string orchestra; Sonata, 2 pianos; The Silver Hound, song cycle; Fanfare with variants for brass band; Sonata, 4 clarinets, 1985; Triple Concerto, Divisions for horn, harpsichord, strings; Concerto, orchestra, 1986; Concerto, clarinet and orchestra; Welsh Dances, brass band; The Legend of St Julian, 1987; Lines from Marlowe's Dr Faustus, mixed voices, brass, percussion; Noctus Equi, cello, orchestra, 1989; Songs of Exile, tenor, orchestra; Star Children, orchestra; Symphony for organ and orchestra; Advent Carol, SATB, organ; Emynan Pantycelyn, baritone solo, chorus, orchestra, 1990; Novelette, flute, oboe, piano; Sonata, flute, piano, 1991; Sonata No. 5, violin, piano, 1992; Chorales Variants and Fanfare, organ, brass, 1992; Symphony No. 8, brass, percussion, 1992, No. 9, A Vision of Eternity, brass, orchestra, 1993; Gloria, chorus, organ; 3 Motets, chorus, organ; Wind Quintet, 1993; Concerto No. 2, violin and orchestra; Concerto for trumpet and orchestra; Sonata for oboe and harp, 1995; Mass, baritone, chorus and ensemble; Sonata No. 3 for cello and piano; String Quartet No. 4; Piano Trio No. 3; Sonata No. 2 for clarinet and piano, 1996; Tower, opera in 3 acts, 1999; Symphony No. 10, 1999; Doubles, Oboe Quintet, 2000; Horn Trio, 2001; String Quartet No. 5, 2001. *Recordings include:* Symphony No. 6 and Star Children, BBC WSO; Passagio, Otaka; Piano Sonatas 1–10, Martin Jones; Noctis Equi; 3 Advent Carols, St John's College Choir; Viola Concertino, Nocturnes and Cadenzas, Sinfonia Fidei; Symphonies 2, 3, and 5; Concerto No. 2 for Clarinet and Orchestra; Folk song suite; Concerto for Orchestra, RLPO; Song Cycles, Welsh Folksongs, Jeremy Huw Williams. *Publications:* Sonata No. 6 for viola and piano; Tempi, Sonata for harp, 1997; Dragon Fire, concertante for timpani, percussion and orchestra, 1998; Tower, opera in 3 acts, 1999; Symphony No. 10, 1999; Concerto for Percussion and brass, 2000; La Serenissima, 2000; Piano Sonata No. 13, 2001; Bagatelles for 11 instruments; Concerto for Euphonium and Orchestra; Lizard, concerto for Orchestra; Sonata for Euphonium and Piano. *Honours:* Walford Davis Prize, 1954; Bax Medal, 1957; Fellow: University College, Cardiff, 1981; Welsh College of Music and Drama, 1991; Honorary D.Mus (Sheffield), 1993; C.B.E.; Hopkins Medal, St David's Society, New York; Glyndwr Medal; Honorary RAM; Fellow RNCM. *Current Management:* Oriana Publications. *Address:* Tan-y-Rhiw, 64 Gowerton Road, Three Crosses, Swansea SA 4 3PX, Wales.

HODGES, Nicolas; Composer and Pianist; b. 4 June 1970, London, England. *Education:* Studied composition at Dartington and Winchester with Morto Feldman and Michael Finnissy; Piano with Robert Bottone and privately with Susan Bradshaw; Music at Cambridge University. *Career:* As pianist, premieres including music by Finnissy, Weir, Skempton, Toovey, Powell, Holloway, Bill Hopkins, some as part of the Bach project, broadcast on Radio 3. *Compositions:* Piano Studies, solo piano, 1988–92; Small Shadows, 1990; Twothreefourfive, violin and piano, 1991–92; Do I detect a silver thread between you and this young lady, solo viola, 1993; Concertino, 1993; Scripture for soprano, oboe d'amore and 2 percussion, 1994. *Recordings:* Bach Project released on CD. *Contributions:* Various articles and reviews to Tempo, Musical Times, including The Music of Bill Hopkins, 1993, The Music of Luigi Nono 1950–58 - Analytical investigations. *Address:* Flat 3, 68 Norwood Road, Herne Hill, London SE24 9BB, England.

HODGSON, Julia; Viol Player; b. 1960, England. *Career:* Member of Fretwork, first London concert at the Wigmore Hall, London, July 1986; Appearances in the Renaissance and Baroque repertoire in Sweden, France, Belgium, Netherlands, Germany, Austria, Switzerland and Italy; Radio broadcasts in Sweden, Netherlands, Germany and Austria; Televised concert on ZDF, Mainz; Tour of Soviet Union, Sept 1989, and Japan, June 1991; Festival engagements in the United Kingdom; Repertory includes In Nomines and Fantasias by Tallis, Parsons and Byrd; Dance music by Holborne and Dowland (including Lachrimae); Six-part consorts by Gibbons and William Lawes; Songs and instrumental works by Purcell; Collaborations with vocal group Red Byrd in verse anthems by Byrd and Tomkins, London Cries by Gibbons and Dering, Resurrection Story and Seven Last Words by Schütz; Gave George Benjamin's Upon Silence at the Queen Elizabeth Hall, Oct 1990; Wigmore Hall concerts, 1990–91, with music by Lawes, Purcell, Locke, Dowland and Byrd. *Recordings:* Heart's Ease (late Tudor and early Stuart); Armada (Courts of Philip II and Elizabeth I); Night's Black Bird (Dowland and Byrd); Cries and Fancies (Fantasias, In Nomines and The Cries of London by Gibbons); Go Nightly Care (consort songs, dances and In Nomines by Byrd and Dowland). *Address:* c/o Fretwork, 16 Teddington Park Road, Teddington, Middlesex, TW11 8 ND, England.

HODKINSON, Juliana; Composer; b. 17 March 1971, Exeter, England. *Education:* King's College, Cambridge, 1990–93; MA Double Honours, Music and Philosophy, University of Cambridge, 1993; Diploma in German; Private studies under Hans Abrahamsen and Per Nørgård; MA, Japanese Studies, Sheffield University, 1997. *Career:* Debut: 1st professional performance of composition Recalling Voices of the Child, Capricorn ensemble, ICA, London, 3 Mar 1994; Works performed at

ICA, London, Den Anden Opera, Copenhagen, Nordic Music Days, 1998, Stockholm, Musikhalle, Hamburg, Paul Gerhardt Kirche and Neuköllner Saalbau, Berlin, Tokyo University of Fine Arts, La Machine à Eau, Mons, Belgium; Works performed by Capricorn (London), Athelas Sinfonietta (Copenhagen), Sonanza (Stockholm), Orchestre Royal de Chambre de Mons (Belgium), Contemporary Alpha (Tokyo), Matthias Arter (Zürich), Prisma (Berlin), Ensemble 2000 (Denmark), Danish Radio Concert Orchestra; mem, Dansk Komponist Forening; Koda-NCB, Denmark. *Compositions:* In Slow Movement, 1994; Water Like a Stone, 1996; Machine à Eau, 1998; Music for Gilles Requiem, 1999. *Contributions:* Dansk Musik Tidsskrift, 1994, 1997; Japanese Society Proceedings, 1996. *Honours:* Danish Arts Council Grants, 1994, 1998, 1999; Daiwa Foundation, Scholarship, 1995–97; Pépinières Européens Jeunes Artistes residency, 1997–98; Kongegaarden Centre for Music and Visual Arts, residency, 1999. *Address:* Kongegaarden, Algade 25, 4220 Korsír, Denmark.

HOEL, Lena; Singer (Soprano); b. 1957, Sweden. *Education:* Studied at the Stockholm Music High School. *Career:* Sang at the Stockholm Royal Opera, from 1984 as Gilda, Sophi in Der Rosenkavalier and in the premieres of Backanterna by Daniel Börtz, 1991; Festival of Drottningholm from 1989; In Soliman II by JM Kraus and Isme in Elektra by JC Haeffner; Mozart: Pamina/Magic Flute, Fiordiligi/Così fan tutte; Puccini: Mimi/La Bohème; Bizet: Carmen; Janáček: The Cunning Little Vixen; Lidholm: A Dreamplay/Indra's d.; Sandströ m: Staden/Cecilia; Other roles in Aniara by Blomdahl; Sang Dorinda in Handel's Orlando at Stockholm, 2000; Recitals and chamber music as well as oratorios. *Recordings:* Sandström/The High Mass; Blomdahl/Aniara; Börtz/The Bacchantes. *Honours:* The Jenny Lind Scholarship, until 1983. *Current Management:* The Royal Opera, Stockholm. *Address:* Kungliga Operan, PO Box 16094, 10322 Stockholm, Sweden.

HOELSCHER, Ulf; Violinist; b. 17 Jan. 1942, Kitzingen, Germany. *Education:* Privately with father and Bruno Masurat; Studied with Max Rostal in Cologne; Studied 3 years in USA with Josef Gingold, Indiana University, and with Ivan Galamian, Curtis Institute, Philadelphia, USA. *Career:* Member, International Geiger Elite; Violin Concertos of Kirchner with Berlin Philharmonic, 1984; Franz Hummel's Violin Concerto, Baden-Baden, 1987; Performed Double Concerto by Aribert Reimann, with Wolfgang Reimann, Hannover, 1989; Performances and recordings from a wide repertoire featuring Frankel, Tchaikovsky, Schumann, Mendelssohn, Richard Strauss, Brahms and Beethoven, and the chamber music of Bart ók, César Franck, and Szymanowski. *Recordings:* Hummel's Violin Concerto, with USSR State Symphony Orchestra. *Current Management:* Astrid Schoerke. *Address:* c/o Monckebergallee 41, 30453 Hannover, Germany.

HOENE, Barbara; Singer (Soprano); b. 4 Feb. 1944, Cottbus, Germany. *Education:* Studied at the Leipzig Musikhochschule and with Johannes Kempter. *Career:* Debut: Dessau, 1966 as Laura in Der Bettelstudent; Sang at Halle/Saale, 1968–73; With the Dresden Opera roles have included Mozart's Fiordiligi and Pamina, Sophie in Der Rosenkavalier, Carolina in Il Matrimonio segreto, Orff's Die Kluge and Verdi's Nannetta; Many further roles in operas by Handel; Guest appearances in Berlin, St Petersburg, Italy, France and Japan; Season 1994–95 as Marcellina in Le nozze di Figaro; Sang in the premiere of Reimann's Melusine; Sang in the premiere of Celan by Peter Ruzicka at Dresden, 2001; Lieder recitals and oratorios by Bach and Handel. *Address:* c/o Staatsoper Dresden, Theaterplatz 2, 01067 Dresden, Germany.

HOEPRICH, Thomas (Eric); Clarinettist; b. 5 Sept. 1955, Baltimore, Maryland, USA. *Education:* AB cum laude, Harvard University, 1976; Solo Diploma, Royal Conservatory of Music, Netherlands, 1982. *Career:* Principal Clarinet, Orchestra of the 18th Century, 1983–; Founding Member of Amadeus Winds, Stadler Trio (basset horns), Nachtmusik and Trio d'Amsterdam; Regular appearances with London Classical Players, Tafelmusik and The Orchestra of the Handel and Haydn Society; Professor, Royal Conservatory of Music, Netherlands. *Recordings:* Mozart Clarinet Concerto and Quintet with Orchestra of the 18th Century, Philips; Other recordings as soloist: Taverner Players, EMI; Musica Antiqua Cologne, DGG-Archiv; Other recordings for Decca, Harmonia Mundi, Accent, Erato and SONY Classical. *Contributions:* Early Music; Tibia; Galpin Society Journal; NOTES. *Honours:* Mozart Clarinet Concerto and Quintet recording named one of the best 15 CDs of 1988, Le Monde de la Musique. *Address:* Bredeweg 39-2, 1098 BN Amsterdam, Netherlands.

HOFFMAN, Gary; Concert Cellist; b. 1956, Vancouver, Canada. *Education:* Indiana University School of Music. *Career:* Faculty member at Bloomington, Indiana, 1980s; Soloist with major orchestras in Chicago, London, San Francisco and Montreal; English Moscow and Los Angeles Chamber Orchestras, Orchestre National de France, Suisse Romande and Rotterdam Philharmonic; Conductors include Previn, Dutoit, Andrew Davis, Kent Nagano and James Levine; Festival engagements at Ravinia, Aspen, Marlboro, Bath, Helsinki, New York (Mostly Mozart)

and Verbier; Chamber Music with the Emerson, Tokyo, Brentano and Ysaye String Quartets; Artist Member of the Lincoln Center Chamber Music Society, New York. *Recordings:* Albums for BMG, Song, EMI and Chant du Monde labels. *Honours:* Winner, Rostropovich International Competition, Paris, 1986. *Address:* c/o Musicaglotz, 11, rue le Verrier, 75006 Paris, France.

HOFFMAN, Grace; Singer (Mezzo-soprano); b. 14 Nov. 1926, Cleveland, Ohio, USA. *Education:* Studied with Friedrich Schorr in New York, Mario Basiola in Milan, and with Maria Wetzelsberger in Stuttgart. *Career:* Debut: With the US Touring Company as Lola, 1951; Sang at Florence from 1951; Zürich, 1952, as Azucena; Wurttemberg Staatsoper Stuttgart from 1955; La Scala Milan, 1955, as Fricka in Die Walküre; Bayreuth Festival, 1957–70, as Brangaene, Fricka and Waltraute; Metropolitan Opera, 1958, Brangaene; Covent Garden debut, 1959, as Eboli in Don Carlos; Florence, 1961, as Ortrud in Lohengrin; Carnegie Hall, New York, 1964, as Elisabetta in Donizetti's Maria Stuarda; Appearances in Paris, Vienna, Munich and Düsseldorf; Teacher of singing at the Stuttgart Musikhochschule from 1978; Sang Mary in Der fliegende Holländer at Stuttgart, 1989; Other roles include Mother Wesener in Die Soldaten by Zimmermann (Strasbourg, 1988). *Recordings:* Das Lied von der Erde; Salome; Der Barbier von Bagdad; Tristan und Isolde. *Address:* c/o Staatstheater Stuttgart, Oberer Schlossgarten 6, 7000 Stuttgart 1, Germany.

HOFFMAN, Irwin; Symphony Conductor and Violinist; b. 26 Nov. 1924, New York City, USA; m. Esther Glazer Hoffman, 3 s, 1 d. *Education:* Juilliard School of Music. *Career:* Conductor of Vancouver Symphony, BC, Canada, 1952–64; Associate Conductor and Acting Music Director, Chicago Symphony, IL, USA, 1964–70; Music Director of The Florida Orchestra, 1968–87; Chief permanent conductor of Belgian Radio and Television Symphony, 1972, 1976; Guest Conductor for various leading orchestras in Europe, North America, Israel and South America. *Recordings:* Several. *Address:* c/o Everett Wright, 3876 Oak Grove Drive, Sarasota, Florida, USA.

HOFFMAN, Joel (Harvey); Composer, Pianist and Teacher; b. 27 Sept. 1953, Vancouver, British Columbia, Canada; m. 30 Dec 1988. *Education:* BM, University of Wales, Cardiff, Wales, 1974; MM, 1976, DMA, 1978, Juilliard School, New York, USA. *Career:* Graduate Teaching Assistant, Juilliard School, New York, 1976–78; Professor of Composition, College-Conservatory of Music, University of Cincinnati, Ohio, 1978–; Commissions: Cincinnati Symphony Orchestra, 1993; Shanghai String Quartet, 1993; National Chamber Orchestra, 1993; Golub-Kaplan-Carr Trio, 1991; Artistic Director, Music Ninety-eight, Music Ninety-nine and Music 2000 Festivals. *Compositions:* Variations for violin, cello and harp, 1975; Music from Chartres for 10 brass instruments, 1978; September Music for double bass and harp, 1980; Chamber Symphony, 1980 Sonata for harp. 1982; 5 Pieces for two pianos, 1883; Double Concerto, 1984; Violin Concerto, 1986; Fantasia Fiorentina, for violin and piano, 1988; Hands Down, for piano, 1986; Crossing Points for string orchestra, 1990; Partenze, for solo violin, 1990; Each for Himself, for piano solo, 1991; Cubist Blues for violin, cello and piano, 1991; Music in Blue and Green, for orchestra, 1992; Metasmo for percussion trio, 1992; Self-Portrait with Mozart, violin, piano and orchestra, 1994; Music for Chamber Orchestra, 1994; ChiaSsO for orchestra, 1995; L'Immensitá dell'Attimo, song cycle for mezzo and piano, 1995; The Music Within the Words, 1996; Portogruaro Sextet, 1996; Millennium Dances, for orchestra, 1997; Self-Portrait with Gebirtig for cello and orchestra, 1998; Kraków Variations for viola sola, 1999; Reyzele: A portrait for chamber ensemble, 1999. *Recordings:* Duo for viola and piano, 1991; Partenze, 1992; Music for Two Oboes, 1995; Tum-Balalayke, 1996; Fantasy Pieces, 1999. *Honours:* National Endowment for the Arts Commissions, 1985, 1991; BMI Award, 1972; Bearns Prize, Columbia University, 1978; American Academy Institute of Arts and Letters, 1987. *Address:* College-Conservatory of Music, University of Cincinnati, Cincinnati, OH 45221, USA.

HOFFMAN, Stanley; Violinist and Violist; b. 8 Dec. 1929, Baltimore, Maryland, USA. *Education:* Private study with Arthur Grumaux, Belgium; BSc, Juilliard School of Music; Study with Mischa Mischakoff, Raphael Bronstein and Oscar Shumsky. *Career:* Debut: Carnegie Recital hall, New York City; Regular Member, New York Philharmonic Orchestra under Leonard Bernstein, 1961–64; Jerusalem Radio Symphony Orchestra, Israel, 1981–83; Bohemians, New York; Local 802 Association Federation of Musicians. *Recordings:* Vocal Chamber Music, Vol. I with Susan Reid-Parsons as soprano, 1971, Vol. II with Elinor Amlen and Rose Macdonald, sopranos, 1973; Taping session for Radio Kol Israel, 1984, 1986; Solo violin sonatas, Béla Bartók, Honegger, Hindemith, Ralph Shapey, Paul Ben-Haim, Bach C Major, Roger Sessions. *Address:* Poste-Restante, Tel-Aviv, Israel.

HOFFMANN, Anke; Singer (Soprano); b. 19 Sept. 1969, Siegen, Germany. *Education:* Musikhochschule Cologne, from 1989. *Career:* Deutsche Oper am Rhein, Düsseldorf, from 1990 as Gounod's Juliette,

Papagena in Die Zauberflöte, Nicolai's Anne, Frasquita in Carmen and Olympia in Les contes d'Hoffmann; Wiesbaden, 1992, in the premiere of Der Park by Hans Gefors; Further guest engagements in Mainz, as Zerbinetta and in Henze's Der junge Lord at Saarbrucken, as Zerlina, and at Bremerhaven, as Gilda; Other roles include Mozart's Blondchen and Queen of Night, Nannetta, Adele, and Philene in Mignon; Bonn Opera from 1993; Sang Aennchen in Der Freischütz at Eutin, 2000; Concerts include Bach's Passions, Handel's Messiah and Joshua, Mozart's Requiem and Mendelssohn's Elijah. *Honours:* Medal Winner in competitions at Berlin and Salzburg (1990, 1993). *Address:* c/o Oper der Stadt Bonn, Am Boeselagerhof 1, Pf 2440, 53111 Bonn, Germany.

HOFFMANN, Horst; Singer (Tenor); b. 13 June 1935, Oppeln, Germany. *Education:* Studied with Thilde Amelung in Hildesheim and Otto Kohler in Hanover. *Career:* Debut: Hanover, 1961, in Zar und Zimmermann; Has sung at the Stuttgart and Munich State Operas and the Deutsche Oper am Rhein, Düsseldorf; Komische Oper Berlin and the Opéra du Rhin, Strasbourg; Bayreuth Festival, 1967–68; Further appearances in Cologne, Lisbon, Zürich, Vienna (Volksoper) and Sydney, 1984 (Lohengrin and Siegmund, 1987 and 1989); Teatro Regio, Turin, 1987, as Don Ottavio; Otello, Sydney and Melbourne, 1988, and in Sydney, 1992; From the House of the Dead, Cologne, Germany, 1992; Sang Florestan at Sydney, 1992; Tristan and Isolde, Sydney and Melbourne, 1993, and Essen, Germany, 1993; Die Meistersinger, Sydney, 1993; Roles include Tamino, Belmonte, Nemorino, Edgardo, Pinkerton, Alfredo in La Traviata and Alfred in Die Fledermaus; Sang Otello at Sydney, Lohengrin at Dresden, Walküre at Düsseldorf and Tristan at Trieste, 1996; Season 1997–98 Tannhäuser at Sydney and Melbourne, Bacchus in Ariadne and Samson at Sydney, and Erik in The Flying Dutchman in Melbourne; Season 1999–2000 Florestan in Fidelio in Capetown, Andres in Wozzeck and Aegisthus in Elektra in Sydney and Tristan in Sydney and Melbourne; Season 2003: Gurrelieder in Perth; Messiah in Tampa, 2004. *Recordings include:* Bruckner Te Deum and CD Great Opera Heroes, 1996. *Current Management:* Jenifer Eddy Artists' Management, Melbourne. *Address:* 2504 Gulf Blvd #506, Indian Rocks Beach Fl 33785 USA.

HOFFMANN, Richard; Composer and Musicologist; b. 20 April 1925, Vienna, Austria. *Education:* Studied at the University of New Zealand and the University of California at Los Angeles; Composition studies with Arnold Schoenberg. *Career:* Secretary and assistant to Schoenberg, 1948–51; Teacher of University of California at Los Angeles, 1951–52; Oberlin College from 1954; Visiting Professor at the University of California, Berkeley, 1965–66; Co-editor of the complete works of Schoenberg, 1961, edited the score of Von Heute auf Morgen. *Compositions include:* Prelude and Double Fugue for strings, 1944; Piano Sonata, 1946; Violin Concerto, 1948; 4 String Quartets, 1947, 1950, 1974, 1977; 3 Songs, 1948; Duo for violin and cello, 1949; 3 Songs, 1950; Piano Quartet, 1950; Fantasy and Fugue for organ, 1951; Piano Sonatina, 1952; Piano Concerto, 1954; Cello Concerto, 1956–59; String Trio, 1963; Memento Mori for male voices and orchestra, 1966–69; Music for strings, 1971; Decadanse for 10 players, 1972; Changes for 2 chimes, 4 performers, 1974; Souffler for orchestra, 1976; In memorium patris for computer-generated tape, 1976; Intavolatura for strings and percussion, 1980. *Honours:* Guggenheim Fellowships, 1970, 1977. *Address:* c/o ASCAP, ASCAP Building, 1 Lincoln Plaza, New York, NY 10023, USA.

HOFFMANN-ERBRECHT, Lothar; Professor; b. 2 March 1925, Strehlen Schlesien, Germany; m. Margarete Fischer, 2 d. *Education:* Graduate, Academy of Music, Weimar, 1949; PhD, University of Jena, 1951; Habilitation, Department of Musicology, University of Frankfurt, 1961. *Career:* Professor of Musicology, University and Academy of Music of Frankfurt am Main, University of Technology of Darmstadt; mem, Society for Music Research; International Musicological Society. *Publications include:* Deutsche und italienische Klaviermusik zur Bachzeit, 1954; Thomas Stoltzer, Leben und Schaffen, 1964; Thomas Stoltzer, Ausgewaehlte Werke II–III; Heinrich Finck, Ausgewaehlte Werke, I–II; Beethoven Klaviersonaten (with Claudio Arrau); Henricus Finck-musicus excellentissimus, 1445–1527, 1982; Musikgeschichte Schlesiens, 1986; Jüdische Musiker aus Breslau, 1996; Schlesisches Musiklexikon, 2001. *Contributions:* Various professional journals. *Honours:* Bundesverdienstkreuz, 1997. *Address:* 9 Amselweg, 63225 Langen, Germany.

HOFMAN, Srdjan; Composer; b. 4 Oct. 1944, Glina, Serbia. *Education:* Studied at the Belgrade Academy, 1963–72. *Career:* Assistant 1974, and Professor, 1986–, at the Belgrade Academy of Music; Electronic Music Festivals at Bourges and Helsinki; Further performances at ISCM Festivals in Essen and Stockholm. *Compositions include:* Symphony in Two Movements, 1969; Concerto Dinamico, 1971; Konzertanttne epizode, for violin and orchestra, 1972; The Legal Code of Succession; for clarinet and 2 string sextets, 1974; Cantus de Morte, for speaker, mezzo and orchestra, 1978; Who Am I? fairy tale, for actors, mezzo, female chorus ensemble and tape, 1986; Rebus I and II for electronics,

1988–89; Replika for violin and piano, 1990; Koncertantna muzika for piano, 13 strings and electronics 1993; Duel, for piano and live electronics, 1996. *Honours:* First prize, Belgrade International Composers' Forum, 1994, 1995. *Address:* c/o Union of Bulgarian Composers, Iv Vazov 2, 1000 Sofia, Bulgaria.

HOFMANN, Manfred; Singer (Bass); b. 10 Oct. 1940, Kahl am Main, Germany. *Education:* Studied at the Frankfurt Musikhochschule. *Career:* Sang at Saarbrucken, 1970–71, Lucerne, 1972–74, Mainz Opera, 1974–77, St Gallen, 1977–80, and Berne, 1980–84; Member of the Graz Opera from 1985, notably in the 1987 premiere of Der Rattenfänger by Friedrich Cerha; Major roles have included Mozart's Bartolo, Alfonso and Sarastro, Rocco in Fidelio, Donizetti's Raimondo and Dulcamara, Rossini's Bartolo, Alidoro in La Cenerentola and Geronimo in Il Turco in Italia; Waldner in Arabella, the Grand Inquisitor in Don Carlo and Wagner's Landgrave; Many buffo and character roles. *Address:* c/o Graz Opera, Kaiser Josef Platz 10, 8010 Graz, Austria.

HOFMANN, Peter; Singer (Tenor); b. 12 Aug. 1944, Marienbad, Germany; m. Deborah Sasson, 1983, divorced 1990. *Education:* Karlsruhe Hochschule. *Career:* Debut: Lubeck, 1972, as Tamino in Die Zauberflöte; Early engagements at Wuppertal and Stuttgart; Bayreuth Festival from 1976, as Siegmund, Lohengrin and Parsifal; Vienna State Opera, 1976; as Loge, then Siegmund and Lohengrin; Covent Garden debut, 1976, as Siegmund; Returned to London as Max in a new production of Der Freischütz and as Alfred in Die Fledermaus; Metropolitan Opera debut, 1980, as Lohengrin; Returned to New York as Parsifal, Siegmund and Walther; Sang Tristan at Bayreuth in 1986, and Siegmund in Harry Kupfer's new production of The Ring, 1988; Tour of Germany 2000, in Advent and Christmas songs; Guest appearances in Moscow, Lisbon, San Francisco, Los Angeles, Munich and Chicago. *Recordings:* Parsifal; Die Zauberflöte; Die Walküre; Tristan und Isolde; Lohengrin; Orfeo ed Euridice. *Address:* PO Box 100262, Bayreuther Festspiele, 8580 Bayreuth 1, Germany.

HOFMANN, Rosmarie; Singer (Soprano); b. 1 July 1937, Lucerne, Switzerland. *Career:* Concerts, throughout Europe, overseas; Appeared, many regular international festivals; Many recent world premieres, including works composed for her; Extensive repertoire includes: J. S. Bach: Johannes, Matthäus and Markus Passions, Mass in B minor, Mass No. 2 A major, Weihnachts-Oratorium, Magnificat plus Einlagesätze, 6 solo soprano and some 60 other cantatas; Beethoven: 9th Symphony, Christus am Oelberge, Missa solemnis, Mass C major, lieder; Brahms: Ein Deutsches Requiem, lieder, duets, quartets; Bruckner: Requiem D minor, Te Deum, Grosse Messe No. 3 F minor, Grosse Messe D minor; Carissimi: Historia de Jephther; Charpentier: Te Deum, Messe de Minuit; Durufle: Requiem; Dvořák: Te Deum, Stabat Mater, Mass in D, Zigeunerlieder; Fauré: Requiem; Handel: Israel in Egypt, Dettinger and Utrechter Te Deums, Brockes and St John Passions, Messias, Joshua, Saul, Jephtha, Judas Maccabaeus, Das Alexanderfest, Belshazzar, Psalms 96, 109, 112, 51, German arias, duets, cantatas Cäcilien Ode, Ode for Queen Anne, Salve Regina; J Haydn: L'incontro improvviso (1st soprano), L'anima del Filosofo (Genio, Euridice), Die Schöpfung, Die Jahreszeiten, Die sieben Wörte des Erlösers am Kreuz, Stabat Mater, 6 Grosse Messen, many other Masses; Honegger: Le Roi David, Jeanne d'Arc au bûcher, La Vierge, La danse des morts; Frank Martin: In Terra Pax, Golgotha; Mendelssohn: Paulus, Elias, 2nd Symphony Lobgesang, Hochzeit des Camacho (main role), lieder, duets; Monteverdi: Vespreae della Maria Vergine, Magnificat, Psalm 111, solo motet, duets; Mozart: Solo motet Exsultate jubilate, oratorio La Betulia liberata, Die Schuldigkeit des ersten Gebots, cantatas, funeral music, Requiem, Regina Coeli KV 108, KV 127, many small works, C minor Mass, Davidde penitente, many masses, lieder; Pergolesi: Stabat Mater, Salve Regina, Psalm 112; Poulenc: Gloria, Stabat Mater; Schubert: Magnificat, Salve Regina, Masses Der Hirt auf dem Felsen, Auf dem Strom; Saint-Saëns: Christmas Oratorio, Requiem Mass, oratorio Le Déluge; Schütz: Die Weihnachts-Historie, Die Auferstehungs-Historie, sacred concertos and duets; Telemann: Matthaus-Passion 1746, Lukas-Passion 1744, Magnificat, Grosse Kantate, many solo cantatas; Vivaldi: Gloria, Magnificat, Psalm Laudate pueri, cantatas, solo motets. *Recordings:* Phyllis und Thirsis, C P E Bach; Canzonette amorose, Rossi; Stabat Mater, Dvořák; Sacred music, J and M Haydn; Bach cantatas; Mozart motets, Scholar Cantorum Basiliensis Orchestra, conductor Peter Sigrist; Quiteria (main role), Die Hochzeit des Camacho, 1993; Many more. *Address:* Mozartstrasse 46, 6006 Lucerne, Switzerland.

HOFMEYR, Hendrik (Pienaar); Composer; b. 20 Nov. 1957, Cape Town, South Africa. *Education:* Univ. of Cape Town, 1976–1981; Studied at the Conservatoires of Florence and Bologna, 1982–91. *Career:* Freelance Composer in South Africa and elsewhere, from 1986; Lecturer, Univ. of Stellenbosch, 1992–; Senior Lecturer, Univ. of Cape Town, 1998–2000; Assoc. Prof., Univ. of Cape Town, 2001–. *Compositions include:* The Fall of the House of Usher, opera, 1987 (premiered at Pretoria, 1988); Vala, ballet after William Blake, 1998; Missa Sancti Ignatii de Loyala, for soprano, chorus and orchestra 1989; The Land of Heart's Desire, opera after W.B. Yeats, 1990; Alice, ballet 1991; Cadenza for cello, 1994; Lumukanola, opera 1995; Raptus for violin and orchestra, 1996; Alleenstryd, for medium voice and piano, 1997; String Quartet, 1998; Flute Concerto, 1999; Piano Concerto, 1999; Of Darkness and the Heart for soprano and orchestra, 2000; Concerto for violin and flute, 2001; Die Laaste Aand, opera, 2002; Sinfonia africana, 2003; Die Stil Avontuur for soprano and piano, 2003. *Honours:* Winner, Queen of Belgium Composition Competition, 1997; winner of the Dimitri Mitropoulos Competition, Greece. *Address:* SA College of Music, UCT Private Bag, Rondebosch, 7700 South Africa. *E-mail:* mushhh@protem.uct.ac.za.

HOGLUND, Paul; Singer (Bass-baritone); b. 1927, Alno, Sweden. *Education:* Studied in Stockholm and Essen. *Career:* Debut: As Rossini's Bartolo, Royal Opera, Stockholm, 1948; Sang as Leporello, Stora Theater, 1955–60; Sparafucile in Rigoletto and the villains in Les Contes d'Hoffmann; Sang Mozart's Masetto and Figaro, Don Pasquale, Leporello, the Sacristan in Tosca, Schigolch in the local premiere of Berg's Lulu at the Royal Opera Stockholm, 1960–83; Premiere of Berwald's Queen of Golconda, 1968; Many buffo and character roles in other operas. *Address:* Kungliga Teatern, PO Box 16094, 10322 Stockholm, Sweden.

HÖGMAN, Christina; Singer (Soprano); b. 18 Feb. 1956, Danderyd, Sweden; m. Nils-Erik Sparf, 17 May 1991, 2 s. *Education:* Musicology, History of Art, University of Uppsala, Sweden, 1974–78; Royal Music Academy, Stockholm, 1978–83; State Opera School, Stockholm, 1984–86; Masterclasses: Elisabeth Schwarzkopf, Nicolai Gedda, Geoffrey Parsons, Vera Rozsa. *Career:* Debut: Drottningholm Court Theatre, 1985; Hamburg State Opera, Germany, 1986–88; Guest Contracts, 1988–97; Basel Opera, Innsbruck Opera, Opéra du Rhin, Strasbourg, Monte Carlo Opera, Montpellier Opera, Royal Opera in Stockholm; Major Roles: Donna Elvira, Countess Almaviva, Cherubino, Annio, Erste Dame (Mozart; Soloist with Academy of Ancient Music, Mozart Tour, Japan, 1991); Folkoperan Stockholm 1992, 1996 as Elisabeth de Valois and Donna Elvira; Sang title role in premiere of Marie Antoinette by Daniel Börtz, Stockholm, 1998. *Recordings:* Donna Elvira in Don Giovanni; Vitige in Flavio (Handel); Telemacho in Il Ritorno d'Ulisse in Patria and Valelto in L'Incoronazione di Poppea (Monteverdi); English Lute Songs with Jakob Lindberg; Lieder by Clara Schumann; Les Illuminations by Britten; 2nd String Quartet by Schoenberg; Matthew Passion and John Passion (Bach); Neun Deutsche Arien (Handel). *Current Management:* Kristina Hennel-Lee, Scherzo Stockholm Management. *Address:* c/o Scherzo Stockholm Management, Högbergsgatan 66A, 11854 Stockholm, Sweden.

HOGWOOD, Christopher (Jarvis Haley); Harpsichordist, Conductor, Musicologist and Author; b. 10 Sept. 1941, Nottingham, England. *Education:* Cambridge University; Charles University, Prague; MA; FRSA. *Career:* Founder Member of Early Music Consort of London, 1967–76; Founder and Director of The Academy of Ancient Music, 1973–; Faculty, Cambridge University, 1975–; Artistic Director, Handel and Haydn Society, Boston, USA, 1986–2000; Honorary Professor of Music at Keele University, 1986–89; Director of Music, 1987–92, Principal Guest Conductor, St Paul Chamber Orchestra, Minnesota, USA, 1992–98; International Professor of Early Music Performance at Royal Academy of Music, London, 1992–; Visiting Professor, Department of Music, King's College London, 1992–96; Artistic Director, Summer Mozart Festival National Symphony Orchestra, USA, 1993–; Associate Director, Beethoven Academie, Antwerp, 1998–; Conducted Haydn's Orfeo ed Euridice at Covent Garden, 2001; Conductor Laureate, Handel and Haydn Society, 2001–; Principal Guest Conductor, Kammerorchester Basel, 2000–; Principal Guest Conductor, Orquesta Ciudad de Granada, 2001–2004; Principal Guest Conductor, Orchestra Sinfonica di Milano Giuseppe Verdi, 2003–; Beethoven Academie, Antwerp, 1998–2002. *Recordings include:* Many recordings of Baroque and classical music including: 9 vols of Symphonies by Haydn, Complete Mozart Piano Concertos, with Robert Levin, La Clemenza di Tito, Pergolesi Stabat Mater, Handel's Orlando, Haydn's Orfeo ed Euridice and Purcell's Dido and Aeneas (The Academy of Ancient Music). *Publications:* Music at Court, 1977; The Trio Sonata, 1979; Haydn's Visits To England, 1980; Co-author, Music in Eighteenth-Century England, 1983; Handel, 1984; Editor, Holmes' Life of Mozart, 1991; Many editions of musical scores. *Contributions:* New Grove Dictionary of Music and Musicians; Editor, The Keyboard in Baroque Europe, 2003. *Honours:* Walter Willson Cobbett Medal, 1986; C.B.E., 1989; Honorary Fellow, Jesus College, Cambridge, 1989; Freeman, Worshipful Company of Musicians, 1989; Honorary Fellow, Pembroke College, Cambridge, 1992; Incorporated Society of Musicians Distinguished Musician Award, 1997. *Address:* 10 Brookside, Cambridge CB2 1JE, England.

HOHEISEL, Tobias; Stage Designer; b. 1956, Frankfurt, Germany. *Education:* Studied in Berlin. *Career:* Collaborations with director Nikolaus Lehnoff include Janáček Trilogy (Katya, Jenůfa and Makropulos Case) at Glyndebourne and Pfitzner's Palestrina at Covent Garden (season 1996–97, also seen at the Metropolitan, New York); Debut as set and costume designer with Salome at Rio de Janeiro; Britten's Death in Venice for the Glyndebourne Tour, La Bohème, and the Tales of Hoffmann for English National Opera (1997–98); Further engagements at Berlin (Deutsche and Staats-Oper), Vienna, La Scala Milan, San Francisco, Chicago, Amsterdam, Antwerp, Zürich and Cologne; Lohengrin at Théâtre de la Monnaie Brussels, for Anja Silja's debut as producer; Season 1997 with Der Freischütz in Berlin, Ariadne at Brussels, Macbeth in Hamburg and Don Carlos at the Opéra Bastille, Paris; Designs for Henze's Boulevard Solitude at Covent Garden, 2001. *Address:* c/o English National Opera, St Martin's Lane, London WC2N 4ES, England.

HÖHN, Carola; Singer (Soprano); b. 3 March 1961, Erfurt, Germany. *Education:* Studied at the Franz Liszt Musikhochschule, Weimar. *Career:* Sang at Eisenach, 1984–87, Altenburg, 1987–88; Berlin Staatsoper from 1988, notably as Marie Antionette in the 1989 premiere of Graf Mirabeau by Siegfried Matthus; Other roles have included Antonia, Mozart's Fiordiligi and Pamina, Gretel, Marie in Zar and Zimmermann and Sophie in Der Rosenkavalier; Agathe, Eva, the Countess in Capriccio and Albertine in Die Brautwahl by Busoni; Concert repertoire includes Carmina Burana by Orff; Guest engagements elsewhere in Germany and broadcasting commitments; Pamina in Die Zauberflöte at Bordeaux, 1992; Season 2000–01 in Berlin as Eva and Donna Elvira. *Address:* Deutsche Staatsoper Berlin, Unter den Linden 7, 1086 Berlin, Germany.

HOIBY, Lee; Composer and Pianist; b. 17 Feb. 1926, Madison, Wisconsin, USA. *Education:* BA, University of Wisconsin, 1947; MA, Mills College, 1952; Diploma, Curtis Institute, 1952; Private study with Egon Petri and Gunnar Johansen. *Career:* Debut: As Pianist at Alice Tully Hall, New York City, 1978; Commissions from Ford Foundation, Curtis Institute, St Paul Opera, Des Moines Metro Opera, USIA, Dorian Wind Quintet, G Schirmer, Library of Congress; mem, Yale Univ. American Society of Composers, Authors and Publishers. *Compositions:* Operas: The Scarf, 1954, A Month in the Country, 1964, Summer and Smoke, 1971, Something New for the Zoo, 1980, The Tempest, 1986, This is the Rill Speaking, 1993; Romeo and Juliet, 2003; What is this Light?, melodrama, 1995; Sonata for Violin and Piano; Serenade for Violin and Orchestra; The Italian Lesson, musical monologue; Galilo Galilei, oratorio; For You O Democracy; A Hymn of the Nativity, Cantatas; The Tides of Sleep, symphonic song; Various solo piano works, songs and choral pieces; St Mary Magdalene, 1995. *Recordings:* After Eden, ballet; Piano Concerto; Choral Music of Lee Hoiby. *Honours:* Fulbright Fellow, 1952; Arts and Letters Award, 1957; Guggenheim Fellow, 1958; Honorary Member, American Guild of Organists; Honorary DFA, Simpson College, 1983. *Address:* 800 Rock Valley, Long Eddy, NY 12760, USA. *E-mail:* aquarius@catskill.net.

HOJSGAARD, Erik; Composer; b. 3 Oct. 1954, Århus, Denmark. *Education:* Studied Composition with Per Norgård, Royal Academy of Music, Århus, 1978; Student of Composition, Cantiere Internazionale d'Arte, 1976; Royal Academy of Music, Copenhagen, 1982–84. *Career:* Manager, Århus Young Composers' Society, 1974–76; Member of Organising Committee, Young Nordic Music Festival, 1974–81; Music Committee, Århus Regional Council, 1977–78; Music Copyist, 1977–82; Professor (ear training), Royal Academy of Music, Copenhagen, 1982–; Member of Governing Body, Society for the Publication of Danish Music, 1982–92; His works performed at various music festivals in the Nordic countries, also at International Society for Contemporary Music festivals (1980, 1983). *Compositions:* Orchestral: Untitled symphony, 1974; Cello Concerto, 1975; Refleksion, 1977; Scherzo e notturno, 1982; Piano Concerto, 1984–85; Four Sketches, 1990; Nocturne, 1994; Fragment, 1995; Symphony, 2000; Symphony, 2003; Chamber music: Dialogues, 1972; Solprismer, 1974; The Sunflower, 1978; Intrada, 1981; Fantasy Pieces, 1982–84; Watercolours, 1983; Intermezzi, 1983; Carillon, 1986; Two Mobiles, 1990; Paysage blême, 1991; Paysage triste, 1994; Equali, 1996; Four Small Pieces, 1996; Paysage, 1997; Solo instruments: Cendrée, 1976; Sonata in C major, 1980; C'est la mer mêlée au soleil, 1981; Corellage, 1992; Epreuve, 1993; Violin Sonata, 1997; Etude, 1999; Three small pieces, 2000; Solo voice with instruments: Landet som icke är, 1974; Tuan's Songs, 1976; Variations: 6 Songs of Autumn, 1976; Vise, ballad, 1977; Täglich kommt die gelbe Sonne, 1977; Joyous, 1979; Fragments, 1979; The Lost Forest, 1980; Summer Songs, 1981; The Rose, 1981; Two Songs, 1985; Le città continue, 1986; Two songs for mixed choir, 1985–86; Don Juan kommt aus dem Krieg, opera, 1991. *Recordings:* Numerous. *Honours:* Carl Nielsen Prize 1993. *Address:* Esbern Snaresvej 16, 4180 Soro, Denmark. *E-mail:* erik@hojs.dk. *Website:* www.hojs.dk.

HOKANSON, Leonard (Ray); Concert Pianist and Professor of Piano; b. 13 Aug. 1931, Vinalhaven, Maine, USA; m. Rona Wolk, 17 April 1976. *Education:* BA, Clark College, 1952; MA, Bennington College, 1954; Studied piano with Hedwig Rosenthal, 1947–48, Artur Schnabel, 1948–51, Karl Ulrich Schnabel, 1951–53 and Claude Frank, 1952–55. *Career:* Debut: Philadelphia Orchestra. 1949; Played at festivals of Aldeburgh, Berlin, Lucerne, Prague, Salzburg, and Vienna; Played with Philadelphia Orchestra, Halle Orchestra, Vienna Symphony, Berlin Philharmonic, Bavarian Radio Symphony Orchestra and Rotterdam Philharmonic; Radio and television appearances throughout Europe; Extensive touring in North and South America, Europe, Russia and Southeast Asia; Recognised also as a chamber music player and song accompanist; Professor of Piano, University of Frankfurt School of Music, 1976–86 and Indiana University School of Music, 1986–; Guest Professor, Tokyo College of Music. *Recordings:* Solo, chamber music and song recital recordings. *Publications:* Beethoven Piano Sonatas Op 49/1 and 2 Fingerings and Notes on Interpretation, 1986. *Address:* 839 Sheridan Road, Bloomington, IN 47401, USA.

HOLDEN, Amanda (Juliet); Musician, Translator, Writer and Librettist; b. 1948, London. *Education:* Oxford University 1966–69; Guildhall School 1969–71; American University, Washington DC 1979–81. *Career:* Freelance accompanist and Teacher at Guildhall School, 1973–86; Freelance Translator and Writer; Opera translations include Haydn's Armida, Handel's Ariodante and Alcina, Rameau's Les Boréades; Cimarosa's L'Italiana in Londra; Verdi's Rigoletto, Un Ballo in Maschera, Aida and Falstaff; Wagner's Lohengrin, Mozart's La finta giardiniera, Il re pastore, Idomeneo, Die Entführung, Le nozze di Figaro, Don Giovanni and La clemenza di Tito; Rossini's L'Occasione fa il ladro and The Barber of Seville; Puccini's La Bohème, Tosca, Madama Butterfly and Il Trittico; Donizetti's L'Elisir d'amore and Mary Stuart; Gounod's Faust; Bizet's The Pearl Fishers and Carmen; Massenet's Werther; Rachmaninov's Francesca da Rimini; General Editor, The Viking Opera Guide, 1993, The Penguin Opera Guide, 1995, The New Penguin Opera Guide, 2001; Libretto for The Silver Tassie by Mark Anthony Turnage, English National Opera, 2000. *Recordings include:* Translations of: The Barber of Seville; Don Giovanni; A Masked Ball; Falstaff (for Chandos Opera in English Series). *Contributions:* The Mozart Compendium, 1990. *Honours:* Olivier Award for Outstanding Achievement in Opera, 2001. *Address:* 107 Sotheby Road, London N5, England.

HOLDORF, Udo; Singer (Tenor); b. 10 July 1946, Bonn, Germany. *Education:* Studied in Cologne with Josef Metternich, and in Düsseldorf. *Career:* Debut: Würzburg, 1971, as Otello; Deutsche Oper am Rhein, Düsseldorf, from 1973 as Edgardo in Lucia di Lammermoor, Puccini's Calaf and Luigi (Il Tabarro), Strauss's Herod and Matteo, the Captain in Wozzeck and Janáček's Boris, Albert Gregor and Mr Brouček; Guest appearances in Frankfurt, Stockholm, Paris and Lisbon; Sang in the 1985 Duisburg premiere of Goehr's Behold the Sun and at Bayreuth, 1981–88, in Die Meistersinger; US engagements in New York, Atlanta and Los Angeles; Season 1995–96 in Athens as Berg's Captain and at Amsterdam in The Nose by Shostakovich; Sang Jack in Weill's Mahagonny at Salzburg, 1998; Season 2000–01 as Vitek in The Makropulos Case at Dusseldorf and Aegithus in Elektra at Essen; Many concert engagements. *Recordings include:* Der Silbersee by Weill. *Address:* c/o Netherlands Opera, Waterlooplein 22, 1011 PG Amsterdam, Netherlands.

HOLECEK, Heinz; Singer (Baritone); b. 13 April 1938, Vienna, Austria. *Education:* Studied in Vienna with Elisabeth Höngen. *Career:* Debut: Vienna Volksoper, 1960 as Papageno; Sang at the Vienna Staatsoper from 1962, debut there as Papageno; Other roles have included Mozart's Leporello and Guglielmo, Rossini's Figaro; Gianni Schicchi; Frosch in Die Fledermaus at Turin, 1993; Salzburg Festival, 1981 in the premiere of Baal by Cerha; Concert appearances in music by Haydn, Mozart and Beethoven; Cabaret engagements in Moscow and Montreal and throughout Europe; Television appearances in Austria. *Recordings:* Der Rosenkavalier; Salome; Die Fledermaus; Land des Lächelns. *Address:* c/o Staatsoper, Opernring 2, 1070 Vienna, Austria.

HOLECEK, Sebastian; Singer (Baritone); b. 1965, Vienna, Austria. *Education:* Studied in Vienna. *Career:* Vienna Volksoper, 1987–90, notably in Die Weise von Liebe und Tod by Matthus; Theater am Gärtnerplatz, Munich, 1990–92; Monte Carlo, 1991, as Papageno; The Speaker in Die Zauberflöte at Ludwigsburg, 1993; Further appearances in Paris, Santiago and Turin; Vienna Volks and Staatsoper, from 1992; Other roles include Mozart's Masetto and Figaro; Schaunard in La Bohème; Sang Papageno at St Margareth, 1999. *Recordings:* Irrelohe by Schreker. *Address:* c/o Staatsoper, Opernring 2, 1010 Vienna, Austria.

HOLEK, Vlastimil; Violinist; b. 1950, Czechoslovakia. *Education:* Studied at the Prague Conservatory. *Career:* Founder member of the Prazak String Quartet, 1972; Tour of Finland, 1973, followed by appearances at competitions in Prague and Evian; Concerts in

Salzburg, Munich, Paris, Rome, Berlin, Cologne and Amsterdam; Tour of the United Kingdom, 1985, including Wigmore Hall debut; Tours of Japan, the USA, Australia and New Zealand; Tour of the United Kingdom, 1988, and concert at the Huddersfield Contemporary Music Festival, 1989; Recitals for the BBC, Radio France, Dutch Radio, the WDR in Cologne and Radio Prague; Appearances with the Smetana and LaSalle Quartets in Mendelssohn's Octet. *Honours:* 1st Prize, Chamber Music Competition of the Prague Conservatory, 1974; Grand Prix, International String Quartet Competition, Evian Music Festival, 1978; 1st Prize, National Competition of String Quartets in Czechoslovakia, 1978; Winner, String Quartet Competition of the Prague Spring Festival, 1978. *Current Management:* Ingpen & Williams Ltd, 7 St George's Court, 131 Putney Bridge Road, London, SW15 2PA, England.

HOLICKOVA, Elena; Singer (Soprano); b. 1950, Czechoslovakia. *Education:* Conservatory of Music, Bratislava; Academy of Music and Drama, Bratislava. *Career:* Slovak National Theatre; Musetta in La Bohème, Lisa in The Queen of Spades, Rusalka in Rusalka, Jenůfa, Julietta, Adriana in Adriana Lecouvreur, Marina in Dimitriy; Verdi's Gilda; Feodor in Mussorgsky's Boris Godunov; Small Shepherd in Suchon's The Whirlpool; Nuri in The Lowlands; Queen in Dance over the Crying; Swallow in The Happy Prince; A Servant in Elektra; Marenka in The Bartered Bride; Orphan in The Siege of Bystrica; Amelia Grimaldi in Simon Boccanegra, 1984–85. *Recordings:* Songs by Mikulus Schneider-Trnavsky; Cycles by Alexander Moyzes; Glimpse into the Unknown; Mutations by Ilja Zeljenka, 1980; Ode to Joy, 1983; Submerged Music. *Honours:* Slovak Music Fund Prize, 1984. *Address:* c/o Slovak National Theatre, Gorkého 2, 815 06 Bratislava, Slovakia.

HÖLL, Hartmut; Pianist; b. 24 Nov. 1952, Heilbronn, Germany. *Education:* Studied in Milan, Stuttgart and Munich. *Career:* Many recitals from 1972 in Europe, Japan and the Americas with Mitsuko Shirai and other leading singers; Accompanist for Dietrich Fischer-Dieskau, 1982–93; Further engagements with violist Tabea Zimmermann and other instrumentalists. *Recordings include:* Many Lieder albums with Mitsuko Shirai and Beethoven songs with Fischer-Dieskau; Sonatas by Brahms and Shostakovich with Tabea Zimmermann. *Honours:* Joint winner, Hugo Wolf Competition, Vienna, Robert Schumann Competition at Zwickau (1974) and prizes at Athens and 's-Hertogenbosch, Netherlands, 1976. *Address:* c/o Karlsruhe Staatlich, Hochschule fur Musik, Postfach 6040, 76040 Karlsruhe, Germany.

HOLL, Robert; Singer (Bass-baritone); b. 10 March 1947, Rotterdam, Netherlands. *Education:* Studied with Jan Veth and David Hollestelle. *Career:* Sang with the Bayerische Staatsoper Munich from 1973; Has concentrated on concert career from 1975; Appearances at the Vienna, Holland and Salzburg Festivals, the Schubertiade at Hohenems; Salzburg Mozartwochen, 1981–83, as the Priest in Thamos, König in Ägypten, as the Voice of Neptune in Idomeneo and Cassandro in La Finta Giardiniera; Many engagements as a singer of Lieder, in music by Schubert, Brahms and Wolf; Concert appearances with Bernstein, Giulini, Harnoncourt, Jochum, Karajan, Sawallisch, Stein and De Waart; Promenade Concerts, London, 1987, in the Choral Symphony; Judge, Walter Gruener International Lieder Competition, London, 1989; Sang in Schubert's Fierrabras at the Theater an der Wien, Vienna, 1988; Season 1992 at Zürich, as Assur in Semiramide and La Roche in Capriccio; Sang Hans Sachs at the Bayreuth Festival 1996–2002; Vienna Festival, 1997, Schubert's Des Teufels Lustschloss; Season 2000–01 as Hans Sachs at Bayreuth, Mozart's Commendatore and Wagner's Daland at the Berlin Staatsoper; Future engagements include the part of Gurnemanz (Parsifal) at the Weiner Staatsoper and Bayreuth Festival, 2004. *Recordings include:* Mozart's Requiem; Mozart and Salieri by Rimsky-Korsakov; Lieder by Pfitzner; Requiems by Bellini and Donizetti; Mozart's Zaide and La Finta Semplice; St Matthew Passion by Bach; Die Schöpfung; Utrecht Te Deum by Handel; Mozart's Mass in C Minor; Bach Mass in B Minor; Wagner's Die Meistersinger von Nuremberg (Sachs); Wagner's Der Fliegende Holländer (Daland). *Honours:* Winner, Munich International Competition, 1972. *Current Management:* Ingpen & Williams Ltd, 7 St George's Court, 131 Putney Bridge Road, London, SW15 2PA, England.

HOLLAND, Ashley; Singer (Baritone); b. 1969, England. *Career:* Many concert and opera engagements throughout the United Kingdom; Opera repertory includes Handel's Giulio Cesare and Walton's The Bear; Also sings Mahler's Rückert Lieder; Contestant at the 1995 Cardiff Singer of the World Competition; Season 1998 in Mozart's Grabmusik for the Classical Opera Company and Cecil in Mary Stuart for ENO. *Address:* c/o IMG Artists, Lovell House, 616 Chiswick High Road, London, W4 5RX, England.

HOLLAND, Mark; singer (baritone); b. 19 Sept. 1960, Salford, England. *Education:* Royal Northern College of Music with John Cameron, and with Roberto Benaglio in Italy. *Career:* joined Welsh National Opera in 1984 and has appeared as Rossini's Figaro, Mozart's Count, Eugene Onegin, Schaunard in La Bohème, Don Carlo in Ernani and Enrico in

Lucia di Lammermoor; Sonora in La Fanciulla del West, 1991; Festival engagements include Piccinni's La Buona Figliola at Buxton; Season 1989–90 as Falke in Fledermaus for Opera Northern Ireland and Masetto for Dublin Grand Opera; Season 1990–91 as Ford in Falstaff at the Théâtre des Champs Elysées, tour to Japan with La Bohème and Carmina Burana with the Royal Philharmonic; Sang Puccini's Marcello and Mozart's Allazim (Zaïde) with the City of Birmingham Touring Opera, 1991–92; Bregenz Festival, 1992, as Morales in Carmen; Minister in Fidelio at Bregenz, 1995; Sang Andrei in Three Sisters by Peter Eötvös at Hamburg, 2000. *Current Management:* Robert Gilder & Co., Enterprise House, 59–65 Upper Ground, London, SE1 9PQ, England. *Telephone:* (20) 7928-9008. *Fax:* (20) 7928-9755. *E-mail:* rgilder@robert-gilder.com.

HOLLANDER, Julia; Stage Director; b. 1965, Bristol, England. *Education:* St Catherine's College, Cambridge, and also in Paris. *Career:* Opera productions have included Orfeo ed Euridice for The Cambridge Arts Theatre, Les Mamelles de Tiresias at The Edinburgh Festival, Giovanna d'Arco at the Bloomsbury Theatre in London, Samson and Delilah for Northern Opera in Newcastle, The Rake's Progress for Aldeburgh, Acis and Galatea for Gregynog and Manchester Festivals, Turn of The Screw at the Britten Theatre in London, La Bohème for Mid Wales Opera, La Wally at the Bloomsbury Theatre and Love of Three Oranges in London; Staff Producer at ENO, 1988–91, working on numerous productions and reviving Xerxes, Lear and Macbeth in London and abroad; Solo production debut for ENO with Fennimore and Gerda, 1990, returning for the premiere of John Buller's Bakxai, 1992 and Eugene Onegin in 1994; Directed Margareta Hallin's Miss Julie for Operate at Hammersmith, 1996. *Current Management:* Ingpen & Williams Ltd, 7 St George's Court, 131 Putney Bridge Road, London, SW15 2PA, England.

HOLLANDER, Lorin D.; Pianist; b. 19 July 1944, New York, NY, USA. *Education:* Studied with Eduard Steuermann at the Juilliard School and with Leon Fleisher and Max Rudolf. *Career:* Debut: Carnegie Hall, 1955; Has performed with leading orchestras in the USA including the New York Philharmonic, Philadelphia Orchestra, Washington National and Chicago Symphony Orchestra; European engagements with the Warsaw Philharmonic, Orchestre de la Suisse Romande, London Philharmonic and Concertgebouw; Has performed in prisons, hospitals and other institutions; Series of programmes on television; Adviser to the Office of the Gifted and Talented for the US Government; Lecturer on psychological aspects of musical performance.

HÖLLE, Matthias; Singer (Bass); b. 8 July 1951, Rottweil am Nekkar, Germany. *Education:* Studied in Stuttgart with Georg Jelden and in Cologne with Josef Metternich. *Career:* Sang first in concerts and oratorios; Sang in opera at Cologne from 1976; Ludwigsburg Festival, 1978, as the Commendatore in Don Giovanni; Has appeared at the Bayreuth Festival from 1981 as the Nightwatchman, Titurel, Fasolt and Hunding (1988 in Der Ring des Nibelungen, conducted by Daniel Barenboim); King Marke in Tristan und Isolde at Bologna (1983), Florence (1989) and Cologne (1990); Sang in the premiere of Stockhausen's Donnerstag (1981) and created Lucifer in Stockhausen's Samstag aus Licht at the Palazzo dello Sport with the company of La Scala Milan, 1984; Guest appearances in Hanover, Geneva, Tel-Aviv and New York (Fidelio at the Metropolitan, 1986); Season 1989 as Don Fernando in Fidelio at Brussels, Daland in Stuttgart and the Commendatore at Parma; Sang Hunding in Bonn and the Bayreuth Festival, 1992; Fafner in The Ring at Covent Garden, 1996; Hermit in Der Freischütz at Rome, 1998; Season 2000–01 as Pogner and Gurnemanz at Bayreuth, Speaker in Die Zauberflöte at Barcelona and Fasolt at Toulouse; Television appearances in Die Schöpfung and Beethoven's Christus am Olberge. *Recordings include:* Don Giovanni; Haydn's Seven Last Words on the Cross; Handel's Saul; Lieder by Schumann; Fourth Shepherd in Daphne, conducted by Haitink; Samstag aus Licht by Stockhausen; Gurnemanz in Parsifal, conducted by Barenboim. *Address:* Vischerweg 11, 7290 Freudenstadt, Germany.

HÖLLER, York (Georg); Composer; b. 11 Jan. 1944, Leverkusen, Germany. *Education:* Studied at the Cologne Musikhochschule, 1963–70, with B A Zimmermann and Herbert Eimert; Ferienkurse Darmstadt, 1965, with Boulez; Worked at the Electronic Music Studios, Cologne, with Stockhausen. *Career:* Freelance composer from 1965; First orchestral work, Topic, performed at Darmstadt, 1970; Invited by Boulez to work at the studios of IRCAM, 1978; Piano Concerto given French premiere by Daniel Barenboim, Paris, 1988; Der Meister und Margarita last new production at the Paris Opéra, Salle Garnier, before the opening of the Opéra de la Bastille; Professor for analysis and music theory at the College Musikhochschule, 1975–89; Director of the Electronic Studio at WDR Cologne, 1990–. *Compositions:* 5 Pieces, piano, 1964; Diaphonie, 2 pianos, 1965; Topic, orchestra, 1967; Sonate Informelle, 1968; Cello Sonata, 1969; Epitaph, violin, piano, 1969; Piano Concerto, 1970, No. 2, 1983–84; Chroma, orchestra, 1972–74; Horizont, electronics, 1972; Tangent, electronics, 1973; Klanggitter, electronics,

1976; Antiphon for string quartet, 1977; Arcus, orchestra, 1978; Moments Musicaux, flute, piano, 1979; Umbra, orchestra, 1979–80; Mythos, orchestra, 1979–80; Résonance, orchestra, tape, 1981–82; Schwarze Halbinselu, orchestra, tape, 1982; Traumspiel, soprano, orchestra, tape, 1983; Magische Klanggestalt, orchestra, 1984; Improvisation sur le nom de Pierre Boulez, 1985; Der Meister und Margarita, opera, 1985–89; Piano Sonata No. 2, Hommage à Franz Liszt, 1987; Fanal, trumpet, orchestra, 1990; Pensée, piano, orchestra, electronics, 1991; Aùna, large orchestra, 1992; Caligùla, opera after A Camus, 1992; String quartet No. 2, 1997; Aufbruch for orchestra, 1999. *Recordings:* Schwarze Halbinselu; Résonance; Arcùs. *Publications:* Composition of the Gestalt on the making of an organism, 1984; B A Zimmermann Moine et Dionysos, 1985; Auf der süche nach den Klang von Morgan, 1990. *Honours:* Chevalier, Ordre des Arts et des Lettres, Paris; Rolf-Liebermann Preis für Opera Komponisten. *Address:* c/o Boosey & Hawkes Ltd, 295 Regent Street, London W1R 8JH, England.

HOLLEY, William; Singer (tenor); b. 4 Dec. 1930, Bristol, Florida, USA. *Education:* Studied in Florida. *Career:* Debut: As Gounod's Faust, Salzburg Landestheater, 1961; Sang as Gelsenkirchen Opera, 1962–65; Deutsche Oper Berlin, 1971–79; Bavarian State Opera, 1971–76; Stuttgart, 1973–82; Deutsche Oper am Rhein, Düsseldorf, 1966–84; Guest appearances in San Francisco, Don Ottavio, 1968; Vienna, Copenhagen, Barcelona and Houston; Salzburg Festival, 1969–71 in Cavalieri's La Rappresentatione di Anima e di Corpo; Other roles have included Mozart's Tamino, Ferrando and Belmonte, Verdi's Duke of Mantua and Alfredo, Hoffman, Froh in Das Rheingold, Puccini's Cavaradossi and Calaf, Andrea Chénier, Don José, Lensky and Laca in Jenůfa; Des Grieux in Manon Lescaut, Don Carlos and Verdi's Riccardo. *Address:* c/o Deutsche Oper am Rhein, Heinrich Heine Alle 16a, 40213 Düsseldorf, Germany.

HOLLIDAY, Melanie; Singer (Soprano); b. 12 Aug. 1951, Houston, Texas, USA. *Education:* Studied at Indiana University School and at the Graz Academy of Music. *Career:* Sang at Hamburg and Klagenfurt from 1973; Basle Opera as Zerbinetta in Ariadne auf Naxos; Vienna Volksoper from 1976, as Olympia in Les Contes d'Hoffmann, Frau Fluth, Constanze, Philine in Mignon, Adele (Die Fledermaus), Valencienne (Die Lustige Witwe) and in Die Schöne Galatea by Suppé; Tours of Japan with the Volksoper, 1979, 1982, 1985; Guest appearances in Germany, Italy, Netherlands, Spain and Switzerland; Vienna Staatsoper; Houston Opera, 1983; Operetta tour of West Germany with René Kollo, 1984; Theater am Gärtnerplatz, Munich, 1986, as Musetta in La Bohème; Turin and Berlin 1994, 1996, Adele and Valencienne. *Recordings include:* Die Fledermaus; Film of L'Elisir d'amore. *Address:* c/o Volksoper, Währingerstrasse 78, 1090 Vienna, Austria.

HOLLIER, Donald Russell; Composer and Conductor; b. 7 May 1934, Sydney, Australia. *Education:* Studied at the NSW State Conservatorium, the RAM in London and the University of London (D Mus, 1974). *Career:* Head of Academic Studies at the Canberra School of Music, 1967–84; Musical Director of the Canberra Choral Society and Canberra Opera; Australian premieres of works by Vaughan Williams, Walton, Britten and Poulenc. *Compositions include:* Operas, The Heiress (1975, staged Melbourne 1988); The Beggar's Bloody Opera, 1991; For the Term of his Natural Life, 1993; Myra Breckinridge; The Revelation of St John the Divine, oratorio, 1974; 7 Psalms and Lamentations of David, 1979; 7 New Psalms, 1986; 9 Concertos, 1966–89; All Between the Earth and Sphere, for orchestra, 1991; Variations on a theme of Debussy for trumpet and piano, 1998; Many songs and piano pieces. *Honours:* Churchill Fellowship, 1973. *Address:* c/o Australian Music Centre Ltd, 1st Floor, Argyle Stores, 18 Argyle Street, The Rocks, Sydney, Australia.

HOLLIGER, Heinz; Oboist, Composer and Conductor; b. 21 May 1939, Langenthal, Switzerland. *Education:* Berne, Paris and Basle under Emile Cassagnaud (oboe) and Pierre Boulez (composition). *Career:* Professor of oboe, Freiburg Music Academy, 1965–; Has appeared at all the major European music festivals and in Japan, USA, Australia, Israel; British premiere of Scardanelli Cycle at the Queen Elizabeth Hall, 1988; Has recorded over 200 works, mainly for two labels; Berio, Krenek, Henze, Stockhausen and Penderecki have written works for him; Played in the British premiere of Gemeux by Takemitsu, Edinburgh, 1989; Premiered Henze's Doppio Concerto, 1966, Eucalypts I and II by Takemitsu, 1970–71, Ferneyhough's Coloratura and Ligeti's Double Concerto, 1972, Lutoslawski's Double Concerto, 1980, and Carter's Oboe Concerto, 1988; Conducted the Chamber Orchestra of Europe in Beethoven's 7th Symphony and Schnittke's 3rd Violin Concerto, London, 1992; Conducted the London Sinfonietta in his own music at the Queen Elizabeth Hall, London, 1997; Composer-in-Residence at the Lucerne Festival, 1998. *Compositions include:* Der magische Tanzer; Trio; Siebengesang; Wind Quintet; Dona nobis pacem; Pneuma; Psalm; Cardiophonie; Kreis; String Quartet; Atembogen; Die Jahreszeiten; Come and Go; Not I; Trema; Turm-Mask, Tonscherben, Scardanelli-Cycle; 2 Liszt Transcriptions; Gesänge der Frühe; What Where, Opera, Schneewittchen, premiered at Zürich, 1998. *Honours:*

Recipient of several international prizes. *Current Management:* Ingpen & Williams Ltd, 7 St George's Court, 131 Putney Bridge Road, London, SW15 2PA, England.

HOLLIGER, Ursula; Harpist; b. 8 June 1937, Basle, Switzerland; m. Heinz Holliger. *Education:* Studied in Basle and at the Brussels Conservatoire. *Career:* World-wide appearances with leading orchestras, including the Philharmonics of Berlin, Vienna and Los Angeles, the Orchestre de Paris, English Chamber Orchestra, Orchestra of South German Radio and the Schweizerisches Festspielorchester Luzern; Conductors have included Pierre Boulez, Michael Gielen, Simon Rattle, André Previn and Neville Marriner; Composers who have written for her and her husband include Edison Denisov, Henze (Doppio Concerto, 1966), André Jolivet, Ernst Krenek, György Ligeti (Double Concerto, 1972), Witold Lutoslawski (Double Concerto, 1977); Several works written for her by her husband; Professor at the Basle Music Academy. *Recordings include:* Spohr Concertos for Harp and Concertos for Violin and Harp. *Current Management:* Ingpen & Williams Ltd, 7 St George's Court, 131 Putney Bridge Road, London, SW15 2PA, England.

HOLLOP, Markus; Singer (Bass); b. 1968, Berlin, Germany. *Education:* Studied at the Munich Musikhochschule. *Career:* Major roles with the opera studio of the Bayerische Staatsoper, from 1991; Sarastro in Die Zauberflöte and Rossini's Basilio in Gorlitz; Ulm Opera as the King in The Love for Three Oranges, Offenbach's Crespel at Wiesbaden and engagements with the Bayerische Staatsoper, from 1993; Further appearances in Schumann's Genoveva (Zürich), Hamlet and Wozzeck (Geneva) and Salome (Paris Châtelet, under Semyon Bychkov, 1997); Concerts include Weill's Ozeanflug in Munich and Solo Voice in Schoenberg's Moses und Aron with the Philharmonia Orchestra under Christoph von Dohnányi at the Festival Hall, London, 1996. *Honours:* Winner, Carl Maria von Weber Competition, Munich, 1993. *Address:* c/o Bayerische Staatsoper, Max-Joseph Platz, Pf 100148, 8000 Munich 1, Germany.

HOLLOWAY, David; Singer (Concert Baritone) and Teacher; b. 12 Nov. 1942, Grandview, Missouri, USA; m. Deborah Seabury, 25 May 1975, 4 s., 1 d. *Education:* Bachelor's Degree, Master's Degree in Voice, University of Kansas, 1967; Studied with Luigi Ricci in Rome, 1972–81; Voice training with Richard Torigi in New York; French repertoire with Janine Reiss and Jacqueline Richard; German repertoire with Frank Eggermann. *Career:* Debut: With Kansas City Lyric Opera, 1968; Sang with Deutsche Oper am Rhein, 1981–91, Metropolitan Opera, 1974–87, New York City Opera, 1972–80, Glyndebourne Opera Festival, 1985, 1987, Chicago Lyric Opera, Dallas Opera, Houston Opera, National Opera Center, Ottawa, Canada, Santa Fe Opera, Central City Opera Festival, San Francisco, Cincinnati Opera; Voice/Opera Faculty, North Park University and Music Institute of Chicago. *Recordings:* Escamillo in Carmen with Glyndebourne Festival Opera; The Face on the Barroom Floor by Mollicone; Songs by Frederick Rzewski; Songs by Karl and Vally Weigl. *Honours:* Winner, San Francisco Opera audition, 1968; Martha Baird Rockefeller Docent, 1970; HiFidelity/Musical America Award, Tanglewood Festival, 1971; National Opera Institute Grantee, 1973–74. *Address:* 936 Sunset Road, Winnetka, IL 60093, USA.

HOLLOWAY, John; Violinist; b. 19 July 1948, Neath, Wales. *Education:* Studied with Yfrah Neaman at the Guildhall School, London; Further study with William Pleeth, Sándor Végh and Sigiswald Kuijken. *Career:* Leader of Kent Opera Orchestra, 1972–79, Taverner Players (1977–91) and London Classical Players, 1978–92; Founded L'Ecole d'Orphée 1975, with many performances of Baroque music in London and elsewhere; Professor of the GSM, London, and guest professor at the Schola Cantorum, Basle, and Indiana University. *Recordings include:* Chamber Music by Handel, with L'Ecole d'Orphée; Biber's Mystery Sonatas, Buxtehude Chamber Music, with Jaap ter Linden and Lars Ulrik Mortensen. *Honours:* Gramophone Award, 1991. *Address:* Guildhall School of Music and Drama, Silk Street, Barbican, London EC 2Y 8DT, England.

HOLLOWAY, Robin Greville, PhD, DMus; British composer, writer and academic; *Professor of Musical Composition*; b. 19 Oct. 1943, Leamington Spa; s. of Robert Charles Holloway and Pamela Mary Holloway (née Jacob). *Education:* St Paul's Cathedral Choir School, King's Coll. School, Wimbledon, King's Coll., Cambridge and New Coll., Oxford. *Career:* Lecturer in Music, Univ. of Cambridge 1975–, Reader in Musical Composition 1999–, Prof. 2001–; Fellow of Gonville and Caius Coll., Cambridge 1969–. *Compositions include:* Garden Music opus 1 1962, First Concerto for Orchestra 1969, Scenes from Schumann opus 13 1970, Evening with Angels opus 17 1972, Domination of Black opus 23 1973, Clarissa (opera) opus 30 1976, Second Concerto for Orchestra opus 40 1979, Brand (dramatic ballad) opus 48 1981, Women in War opus 51 1982, Seascape and Harvest opus 55 1983, Viola Concerto opus 56 1984, Peer Gynt 1985, Hymn to the Senses for chorus 1990, Serenade for strings 1990, Double Concerto opus 68, The Spacious Firmament for

chorus and orchestra opus 69, Violin Concerto opus 70 1990, Boys and Girls Come Out To Play (opera) 1991, Winter Music for sextet 1993, Frost at Midnight opus 78, Third Concerto for Orchestra opus 80 1994, Clarinet Concerto opus 82 1996, Peer Gynt opus 84 1984–97, Scenes from Antwerp opus 85 1997, Gilded Goldberg for two pianos 1999, Symphony 1999, Missa Caiensis 2001, Cello Sonata 2001, Spring Music opus 96 2002. *Recordings:* Sea Surface Full of Clouds chamber cantata, Romanza for violin and small orchestra opus 31, 2nd Concerto for Orchestra opus 40, Horn Concerto Opus 43, Violin Concerto opus 70, Third Concerto for orchestra, Fantasy Pieces opus 16, Serenade in DC opus 41, Gilded Goldberg opus 86, Missa Caiensis, Organ Fantasy, Woefully Arrayed. *Publications:* Wagner and Debussy 1978, On Music: Essays and Diversions 1963–2003 2004; numerous articles and reviews. *Address:* Gonville and Caius College, Cambridge, CB2 1TA, England. *Telephone:* (1223) 335424. *E-mail:* rgh1000@cam.ac.uk (home).

HOLLOWAY, Stephen; Singer (bass); b. 1951, England. *Education:* studied at the Guildhall School and with Vera Rozsa; Christ's Coll., Cambridge. *Career:* appearances with Scottish Opera as Don Fernando in Fidelio, Private Willis in Iolanthe, Doctor Grenvil in La Traviata and Thanatos/The Oracle in Alceste; Sparafucile and Mozart's Bartolo for European Chamber Opera; The Speaker in The Magic Flute under Jane Glover at the Covent Garden Festival; Chub in Tchaikovsky's Cherevichki and The Chamberlain in Stravinsky's Nightingale for Chelsea Opera Group. *Current Management:* Musikmakers. *Address:* Little Easthall, St Paul's Walden, Hertfordshire SG4 8DH, England.

HOLLREISER, Heinrich; Conductor; b. 24 June 1913, Munich, Germany. *Education:* Akademie der Tonkunst Munich. *Career:* Conducted at opera houses in Wiesbaden, Mannheim, Darmstadt and Duisburg; Munich Opera from 1942, notably with operas by Strauss, then Musical Director in Düsseldorf; Hamburg Opera, 1947, with the local premiere of Peter Grimes by Britten; Vienna Staatsoper from 1952; Principal Conductor at the Deutsche Oper Berlin, 1981–64; Blacher's Zweihundertausend Thaler, 1969; Modern repertory includes operas by Bartók, Hindemith and Berg; Bayreuth Festival, 1973–75, Tannhäuser and Die Meistersinger; Wagner's Ring at the Vienna Staatsoper, 1976; Guest Conductor with the Cleveland Orchestra, 1978. *Recordings include:* Mozart Piano Concertos; Tchaikovsky and Mendelssohn Violin Concertos; Bartók Cantata Profana and Concerto for Orchestra; Symphonies by Schubert, Brahms, Dvořák, Tchaikovsky, Bruckner, Stravinsky, Apollo, Pulcinella and Jeu de Cartes. *Address:* c/o PO Box 100262, Bayreuther Festspiele, 8580 Bayreuth 1, Germany.

HOLLWEG, Werner; Singer (Tenor); b. 13 Sept. 1936, Solingen, Germany; m. Constance Daucha, 2 c. *Education:* Studied in Detmold, Munich and Legano. *Career:* Debut: Vienna Kammeroper, 1962; Bonn, 1963–67; Gelsenkirchen, 1967–68; Maggio Musicale, Florence, 1969, as Belmonte in Die Entführung; Guest appearances in Hamburg, Munich, Berlin, Rome, Paris, New York and Los Angeles; Salzburg Festival as Mozart's Tamino, Ottavio, Ferrando and Belmonte; Osaka, Japan, 1970, in Beethoven's 9th Symphony; Covent Garden debut, 1976, as Mozart's Titus; Paris Opéra, 1986, as Jason in Cherubini's Médée; Promenade Concerts, London, 1989, in Psalmus Hungaricus by Kodály; Created Matthew Levi in Höller's Der Meister und Margarita, Paris, 1989; Sang the High Priest in Idomeneo at Salzburg, 1990; Acted in Henze's Il Re Cervo at Wuppertal, 1996; Wuppertal 1993, as Vova in Schnittke's Life with an Idiot; Berne 1996, as Prospero in the premiere of The Tempest by Daniel Schnyder. *Recordings:* Haydn, Die Jahreszeiten; Mozart, Le nozze di Figaro; Mahler, Das klagende Lied; Mozart, La Finta Giardiniera and Zaide; Lehar, Die lustige Witwe; Mozart, Mitridate and Idomeneo; Monteverdi, Il Combattimento; Ballads by Schubert, Schumann and Loewe. *Current Management:* Ingpen & Williams Ltd, 7 St George's Court, 131 Putney Bridge Road, London, SW15 2PA, England.

HOLM, Mogens (Winkel); Composer; b. Oct. 1936, Copenhagen, Denmark. *Education:* Studied Oboe and Composition, Royal Danish Academy of Music, Copenhagen. *Career:* Oboe player in various Copenhagen orchestras including the Danish Radio Light Orchestra, 1964–65; Choreographer to his own ballet scores, 1975–. *Compositions include:* Opera: Aslak, 1961; Sonata for Four Opera Singers, 1967–68; Ballet: Tropisms, 1963; Chronicle, 1968; Galgarien, 1970; Report, 1972; Tarantel, 1975; Eurydice Hesitates, 1977; Whitethroat under an Artificial Firmament, 1979–80; To Bluebeard, 1982; Orchestra: Kammerkoncertante, 1959; Concerto piccolo, 1961; Cumulus, 1965; Ricercare, 1966; The Glass Forest, 1974; Aiolos, symphony in 1 movement, 1972–77; Cries, 1983–84; Chamber Music: Abracadabra, 1960; Tropismer, 1960; Sonata, 1965; Transitions, 1972; Seven Letters to Silence, 1976; Adieu, 1982; Note-book, 1983; Vocal: October Morning, 1964; Transitions, 1971; Nightmare, 1973; For Children, 1984. *Recordings:* Has made numerous recordings. *Address:* KODA, Rosenvaengets Hovedvej 14, 2100 Copenhagen, Denmark.

HOLM, Peder; Composer and Educator; b. 30 Sept. 1926, Copenhagen, Denmark. *Education:* Graduate in Violin and Theory, Royal Danish Conservatorium, 1947; Teacher's Examination in Piano and Violin. *Career:* Director, Western Jutland Conservatorium; Director, West Jutland Symphony Orchestrs; mem, Programme Committee, Danish Radio, 1963–67; Music Committee, State Cultural Foundation, 1965–68. *Compositions include:* Pezzo Concertante for orchestra, 1964; VYL for orchestra, 1967; Khebeb for 2 pianos and orchestra, 1968; 2 pieces for wind quintet, 1968; Music for brass band, 1969; Ole Wivel, children's song for children's choir, 1970; Concertino for clarinet and chamber orchestra, 1970; Legend, Erik Knudsen, for children's choir, 1971; Ene Mene, Inscription, Mobile, September Evening, Regards to Borge, 5 choral songs for mixed choir; Pikkutikka for children's choir and orchestra, 1973; *Arrangements:* Works by Schumann, Grieg, Couperin and Mozart; Pieces for the Musica Ensemble Series; Works for solo voice, orchestra, symphonic works, concertos and chamber music; The Wandering Prince and the Poor Maiden, drama, 1984; Ode for the Year, 1988; Voices of Funen for mixed chorus and ensemble, 1995. *Publications include:* The String Method; Wind Method; Violin 1 and 2 (editor); All part of Wilhelm Hansen's MUSICA-Methods series. *Address:* c/o KODA, Maltegardsvej 24, 2820 Gentofte, Denmark.

HOLM, Renate; Singer (Soprano); b. 10 Aug. 1931, Berlin, Germany. *Education:* Studied with Marie Ivogun in Vienna. *Career:* Sang in films and entertainment programmes from 1953; Vienna Volksoper from 1957, debut as Gretchen in Der Wildschütz by Lortzing; Appearances at the Vienna Staatsoper, Bolshoi Theatre, Moscow, Covent Garden, London, and the Teatro Colón, Buenos Aires in the soubrette repertory, including Despina, Norina, Sophie, Zerlina and Marzelline; Salzburg Festival from 1961, as Blondchen in Die Entführung, Papagena and Musetta, 1975. *Recordings:* Die Fledermaus, Der Vogelhändler, Das Land des Lächelns; Die Zauberflöte; Die Entführung. *Address:* c/o Staatsoper, 1010 Vienna, Austria.

HOLMAN, Peter; Harpsichordist and Chamber Organist; b. 19 Oct. 1946, London, England. *Education:* King's College, London with Thurston Dart; D Mus (London), 1995. *Career:* As student, directed the pioneering early music group Ars Nova; Founded, The Parley of Instruments, with Roy Goodman, 1979, The Parley now recognised as one of the leading exponents of Renaissance and Baroque string consort music; Musical Director and co-founder, 1985, Opera Restor'd which specialises in authentic productions of eighteenth century English operas and masques; Past Professor, Royal Academy of Music in London for 10 years and has taught at many conservatories, universities and summer schools in England and abroad; Artistic Director of the annual Suffolk Village Festival; Joint Artistic Director, with Paul O'Dette, of the 1995 Boston Early Music Festival; Presently, Reader in Historical Musicology at the University of Leeds; Regular Broadcaster on BBC Radio 3; He spends much of his time in writing and research; Special interests in the early history of the violin family, in European instrumental ensemble music of the Renaissance and Baroque and in English seventeenth and eighteenth century music; Edition of Arne's Artaxerxes performed London, 1995; Directed Opera Restor'd in Lampe's The Dragon of Wantley, 1996, and double bill of Scarlatti's La Dirindina and Haydn's La Canterina, 1998. *Publications:* Many editions of early music; Four and Twenty Fiddlers; The Violin at the English Court 1540–1690, 1993; Ed, Section: Commonwealth and Restoration in The Early Baroque Era, C A Price in the Man and Music (Music and Society in the USA) series (London), 1993; Paper on Monteverdi's string writing in the Nov 1993 issue of Early Music; Henry Purcell, A General Survey of Purcell's Music, 1st edition, 1994; Dowland, Lachrimae, 1999. *Contributions:* Various articles and reviews to a range of newspapers and journals. *Honours:* Hon ARAM, 1979. *Address:* 119 Maldon Road, Colchester, Essex CO3 3AX, England.

HOLMES, Eugene; Singer (Baritone); b. 7 March 1932, Brownsville, Tennessee, USA; m. Katja L Holmes. *Education:* BS, Music Education, Indiana University, Bloomington; Special award, Performer's Certificate; Studied with W D Walton in St Louis, Frank St Leger at the Indiana University in Bloomington, and with Dorothy Ziegler in Miami. *Career:* Debut: Goldovsky Opera, New York, 1963, in The Crucible by Ward; Kammersänger, Deutsche Oper am Rhein, Düsseldorf; Sang in San Diego, San Francisco, Seattle and New York (City Opera, 1971, in the premiere of The Most Important Man by Menotti); Washington, 1970, in the US premiere of Koanga by Delius; Düsseldorf, 1983, as Don Carlos in La Forza del Destino, Nabucco, and Enrico in Lucia di Lammermoor; Munich, 1983, in a concert performance of Porgy and Bess; Other roles include Amonasro, Macbeth, Iago, Rigoletto, Boccanegra, Jochanaan and parts in operas by Mozart, Wagner and Puccini; Verdi's La Traviata, Germont, Puccini's La Bohème, Marcello, Madama Butterfly, Sharpless, Manon Lescaut, Verdi's Il Trovatore, Count di Luna; Performed with the Deutsche Oper am Rhein in the USSR, Magic Flute; Concert tours in Japan and Israel; Sang the Minister in Fidelio at Dusseldorf, 1999. *Recordings include:* Porgy and Bess; Koanga.

Address: c/o Deutsche Oper am Rhein, Heinrich Heine Allee 16, 4000 Düsseldorf, Germany.

HOLOMAN, D(allas) Kern; Musicologist, Conductor and Music Educator; b. 8 Sept. 1947, Raleigh, North Carolina, USA; m. Elizabeth R Holoman, 1 s., 1 d. *Education:* Studied bassoon and conducting, North Caroline School of the Arts; Accademia Musicale Chigiana, Siena, Italy, 1967, 1968; BA, Duke University, 1969; MFA, 1971, PhD, 1974, Princeton University. *Career:* Founding Director, Early Music Ensemble, 1973–77, 1979, Conductor, Symphony Orchestra, 1978–, Chairman, Music Department, 1980–88, University of California at Davis; Founding Co-Editor, 19th Century Music Journal, 1977; General Editor, Recent Researches in the Music of the Nineteenth and Early Twentieth Centuries, 1989; Guest Lecturer, various professional organisations; mem, American Musicological Society; Music Library Association; Association National Hector Berlioz. *Publications:* The Creative Process in the Autograph Musical Documents of Hector Berlioz, c. 1818–1840, 1980; Musicology in the 1980s (edited with C Palisca), 1982; Dr Holoman's Handy Guide to Concert-Going, 1983; Catalogue of the Works of Hector Berlioz, 1987; Writing About Music: A Style-Sheet from the Editors of the 19th Century Music, 1988; Berlioz, 1989; Berlioz's Roméo et Juliette, New Berlioz Edition (editor). *Contributions:* Numerous articles and reviews to journals and other publications. *Address:* c/o Department of Music, University of California at Davis, Davis, CA 95616, USA.

HOLSZKY, Adriana; Composer; b. 30 June 1953, Bucharest, Romania. *Education:* Studied at the Bucharest Conservatory with Milko Kelemen, in Germany and with Franco Donatoni in Italy. *Career:* Teacher at the Stuttgart Hochschule, 1980–89. *Compositions include:* Space for 4 Orchestras, 1980; Erewhon for 14 Instruments, 1984; Bremer Freiheit, opera, 1987; Lichtflug for Violin, Flute and Orchestra, 1990; Gemalde Eines Erschlagenen for 74 Voices, 1993; The Rise of the Titanic, music theatre, 1998; Other vocal and chamber music. *Honours:* Prizewinner in competitions in Rome, Paris, Mannheim and Heidelberg.

HOLT, Olivier; Conductor; b. 1960, Paris, France. *Education:* Vienna Hochschule für Musik. *Career:* Assistant at Opéra de Nancy and Opéra de Paris; Conducted performances at the Paris Châtelet, Opéra-Comique and at Marseille Opéra; Music Director of the Orchestre Symphonique d'Europe, 1987–91, with tours to Vienna, Salzburg and Madrid; Guest with the Orchestre National de Lille, Marseille Philharmonique and Colonne Concerts; Season 1999/2000 with the Orchestre de Picardie (Haydn/Bach/Webern) and at Lille (Franck/Liszt/Saint-Saëns); Conductor at the Conservatoire de Rouen, 1997–; Season 2001 with concerts in Miami and throughout France. *Recordings include:* Albums with Nathalie Dessay, Françoise Pollet and Isabelle Vernet; Stabat Mater by Gouvy. *Address:* c/o Musicaglotz, 11 rue le Verrier, 75006, France.

HOLT, Simon; Composer; b. 21 Feb. 1958, Bolton, Lancashire, England. *Education:* Bolton College of Art, 1976–77; Composition, Piano and Harpsichord at Royal Northern College of Music, 1978–82. *Career:* Featured composer at Bath Festival, 1985; Commissions from London Sinfonietta: Kites, Ballad of the Black Sorrow and Nash Ensemble: Shadow Realm, Era Madrugada, Canciones, Sparrow Night, All Fall Down, and Proms for 1987 and 1992; Also featured at Music in London Now Festival in Japan, 1986; Featured at Huddersfield Festival, 1998. *Compositions include:* Lunas Zauberschein for mezzo and bass flute, 1979; Palace at 4am; Mirrormaze; Maiastra; Burlesca Oscura; Tauromaquia; Syrensong; Capriccio Spettrale; String Quartet: Danger of The Disappearance of Things, 1989; Lilith; Walking With the River's Roar; Icarus Lamentations; A Knot of Time; Minotaur Games; A Book of Colours; Daedalus Remembers for Cheltenham Festival, 1995; The Nightingale's to Blame, for Opera North, 1998; eco-pavan, for ensemble, 1998; Sunrise's Yellow Noise for soprano and orchestra, 1999; Boots of Lead (texts by Emily Dickinson) for alto voice and orchestra, 2002. *Recordings:* CD, Era Madrugada, Canciones, Shadow Realm, Sparrow Night with Nash Ensemble. *Honours:* Fellow of RNCM, 1993. *Address:* c/o Chester Music Ltd, 8/9 Frith Street, London W1V 5TZ, England.

HOLTEN, Bo; Composer and Choral Director; b. 22 Oct. 1948, Rudkobing, Denmark. *Career:* conducts vocal group, Ars Nova, performances of rare works; music critic and ed., Dansk Musiktidsskrift; pioneer, many unusual concerts combining classical music/jazz; led the BBC Singers at the 1999 London Proms in Brumel's Mass Et ecce terra motus. *Compositions include:* works for symphony orchestras with/without chorus, works for large/small chamber ensembles; vocal and instrumental music; choral works with/without instruments; The Bond (opera) 1978–79; tape, film scores; symphonic works include: Mahler-Impromptu 1972–73, Caccia 1979, Symphony 1982, Tertia Die 1985, Imperia for soprano, bass, double chorus and orchestra 1997.

HOLTENAU, Rudolf; Singer (Baritone); b. 1937, Salzburg, Austria. *Education:* Studied in Linz and in Vienna with Alfred Jerger. *Career:* Sang in concert, 1959–61; Opera engagements at Klagenfurt, 1961–62,

Regensburg, 1962–65, Bielefeld, 1965–67, Essen, 1967–75; Further appearances at Cologne, 1972–73, Vienna Staatsoper, 1973–75, Graz, 1977–79; Guest throughout the 1970s at Stockholm, Lyon, Brussels, Barcelona, Monte Carlo, Lisbon, Marseille and Bologna; Performances of Der Ring des Nibelungen at Seattle, 1978–79; Sang such roles as Wagner's Dutchman, Sachs, Wotan, Gunther, Kurwenal and Amfortas, Strauss's Mandryka and Verdi's Amonasro at Hamburg, Berlin (Deutsche Oper), Buenos Aires, Venice, San Francisco and Rio de Janeiro; Sang at Cape Town, 1982, 1985. *Recordings:* Ballads by Carle Loewe.

HOLTHAM, Ian; Concert Pianist and Educationalist; b. 1 Feb. 1955, Melbourne, Victoria, Australia. *Education:* BA, PhD, DipEd, Melbourne University; BMus, Durham University; Studied with Peter Feuchtwanger, Geza Anda and Geoffrey Parsons. *Career:* Debut: Purcell Room and Wigmore Hall, both 1977; Appearances in the United Kingdom, Switzerland, France, Austria, Italy, Thailand, Hong Kong and Australia; Concerto soloist and recitalist; Numerous radio and television appearances including frequently for Australian Broadcasting Corporation; Head of Keyboard and Practical Studies at the Faculty of Music, University of Melbourne. *Recordings:* Chopin: 24 Etudes, Op 10 and Op 25; Godowsky: Selection of transcriptions of Chopin Etudes; Imo pectore-music by Beethoven, Schubert, Schumann and Rachmaninov; Acts of Homage–Music by Brahms and Schubert. *Publications:* The Essentials of Piano Technique, 1992; Various articles in the Oxford Companion to Australian Music. *Current Management:* Alan Watkinson Management. *Address:* Heavitree, PO Box 412, Canterbury, Victoria 3126, Australia.

HOLTMANN, Heidrun; Pianist; b. 18 Oct. 1961, Munster, Westphalia, Germany. *Education:* Study with Eleonore Jäger, Münster, 1966–70; Professor Renate Kretschmar-Fischer, Musikhochschule Detmold/Westphalia, 1970–83; Nikata Magaloff, Geneva, Switzerland, 1978; Vladimir Ashkenazy, Lucerne, Switzerland, 1981. *Career:* Concerts in England, France, Germany, Israel, Italy, Japan, Yugoslavia, North Africa, Austria, Poland, Hungary, Switzerland, USA; Concerts at Festivals in Bordeaux, France; Brescia and Bergamo, Italy; Salzburg; Lockenhaus, Austria; Lucerne, Switzerland; Berlin, West Germany; Concerts with Detroit Symphony Orchestra (Ivan Fischer), Royal Philharmonic Orchestra, London (Antal Dorati), Mozarteum Orchestra/Salzburg, Tonhalle Orchestra/Zürich (Gerd Albrecht, Ferdinand Leitner, David Zinman), ARD/NDR-ZDF, West Germany; DRS-TV, Zürich, Switzerland; RTV Skopje, Yugoslavia; Television recordings at ARD and ZDF, West Germany; Radio Recordings several times with all Radio stations in West Germany. *Recordings:* Gidon Kremer Chamber Music Festival, 1983; Anneliese Rothenberger Presents, 1984; Bach, Goldberg Variations, 1986; Schumann, Carnaval and Kreisleriana, 1987. *Current Management:* Konzertagentur Fahrenholtz, Oberweg 51, 6000 Frankfurt/Main 1. *Address:* Büsingstrasse 1, 1000 Berlin 41, Germany.

HOLTON, Ruth; Singer (Soprano); b. 1961, England. *Education:* Choral exhibitioner at Clare College, Cambridge; Further study with Elizabeth Lane, Nancy Long and Julie Kennard. *Career:* Appearances from 1985 in Baroque music at Bruges, Turku (Finland), Berlin, Amsterdam, Rome, Vienna, Paris; Recitals in Cambridge, Oxford, London, Glasgow and at the Three Choirs Festival in Gloucester; Fauré's Requiem at the Théâtre du Châtelet, Paris, and Ilia in Idomeneo, 1991; Radio broadcasts, BBC Recital, Radio 3, 1992, 1994, 1995, 1996, 1997; WDR Recital, 1992; World-wide broadcast of Bach's St John Passion with choir of St Thomas', Leipzig, 1997; Concert work with Fretwork, Orchestra of the Age of Enlightenment, Ton Koopman, John Eliot Gardiner, Gustav Leonhardt, Taverner Consort. *Recordings:* Bach's St John Passion and Cantatas, Jephtha by Handel and Carissimi, Dido and Aeneas, Handel's Messiah, Mozart's Salzburg Masses, works by Schütz and Buxtehude; Angel in Schütz's Christmas Story with the King's Consort; Grand Pianola Music by John Adams, also music by Steve Reich. *Address:* 27 Casewick Road, London SE27 0TB, England.

HOLZAPFEL, Marcela; Singer (Soprano); b. 1960, Chile. *Education:* Studied in Chile. *Career:* Sang at Santiago Opera, 1985–88, as Clorinda in La Cenerentola, Mozart's Constanze, Strauss's Zerbinetta and Verdi's Nannetta; Rio de Janeiro, 1988, as Zerbinetta; Stuttgart Staatsoper from 1990, as Sophie in Werther, Antonoe in Henze's Bassarids, Puccini's Musetta and Oscar in Un Ballo in Maschera; Berlin Staatsoper, 1991, as Constanze in Die Entführung; Santiago from 1992, notably as Gilda and as Micaela in Carmen; Many concert engagements. *Address:* c/o Opera del Teatro Municipal, San Antonio 149, Santiago Central, Chile.

HOLZMAIR, Wolfgang; Singer (Baritone); b. 24 April 1952, Vöcklabruck, Austria. *Education:* Studied in Vienna. *Career:* Appearances in opera and concert halls throughout Germany, Austria and Switzerland; British Lieder recitals from 1990, including Schubert's Schwanengesang, with Imogen Cooper at the Wigmore Hall, 1993; Engagements

with Berne Opera from 1985, including Rossini's Figaro, Valentin and Papageno, 1985–86, Gluck's Orpheus and Eugene Onegin, 1991; Season 1987–88 in Udo Zimmermann's Die Weisse Rose at the Vienna Konzerthaus, as Ireo in Cesti's Semiramide at Innsbruck and as Serezha in The Electrification of the Soviet Union by Nigel Osborne at Wuppertal; Season 1989–90 as Peri's Orfeo at Wuppertal, in Die Weisse Rose at Innsbruck and as Pelléas at Essen; Premiered Berio's orchestration of Mahler Lieder, 1992; Covent Garden debut, 1993, as Papageno; Season 1995–96 as Papageno at La Scala and Creonte in Haydn's Orfeo at Vienna; Wigmore Hall, recital, 1997; Schubert Lieder recitals, 1998. *Recordings:* Lieder albums. *Address:* c/o AMI Ltd, 22 Tower Street, Covent Garden, London WC2H 9 NS, England.

HOMOKI, Andreas; Director; b. 16 Feb. 1960, Marl, Germany. *Education:* Studied at Bremen Hochschule and Academy of Fine Arts in Berlin. *Career:* Assistant at Deutsche Oper Berlin, Theater des Westens and Komische Oper, Berlin; Assistant to Harry Kupfer at Salzburg Festival, Stuttgart State Opera and Cologne Opera, 1986–87; From 1987, has assisted Michael Hampe, Willy Decker and Harry Kupfer, at Cologne Opera; Assistant to Michael Hampe at Salzburg Festival; Opera productions have included: Mozart's Bastien und Bastienne in Oslo; Le nozze di Figaro for Kammeroper Herdecke, 1988; Fidelio and Jakob Lenz by Wolfgang Rihm for the Cologne Music Academy, 1989–90; Directed the Michael Hampe Australian Opera production of Die Meistersinger, 1990, for New Zealand International Festival of the Arts; Il Trovatore for Wellington City Opera, 1991; Instructor of Drama at Opera Department, Cologne Music Academy, 1988–93; Since 1993, Freelance Director; Opera productions have included: L'Enfant et les Sortilèges, 1992 for Cologne Music Academy; Die Frau ohne Schatten, Geneva Grand Opera, 1992; Cav and Pag in State Theatre, Mainz, 1993; Madama Butterfly, Essen, 1993; Das Schloss by Reimann, Hannover, 1994; Frau ohne Schatten, Paris, 1994; Wildschütz, Cologne, 1994; Rigoletto, Hamburg, 1994; Tristan und Isolde, Wiesbaden, 1994; Idomeneo at the Nationaltheater, Munich, 1996; Arabella, 2001, Manon Lescaut, 2002, Nationaltheater Munich; Falstaff 1996, The love of three Oranges 1998, The Merry Widow 2000, The Bartered Bride 2002, Eine Florentinische Trgoedie/ Der Zwerg by Zemlinsky 2002, The Gypsy Princess 2003, Komische Oper Berlin. *Honours:* French Theatre Critics Award for Best Opera, 1994. *Address:* c/o Komische Oper Berlin, Behrenstr. 55–57, D-10117 Berlin Germany. *E-mail:* a.homoki@komische-oper-berlin.de.

HONECK, Manfred; Conductor; b. 1963, Vienna, Austria. *Career:* Assistant Conductor to Claudio Abbado in the Gustav Mahler Youth Orchestra, from 1987; Principal Conductor of the Jeunesse Orchestra, Vienna, and regular concerts with the NDR Orchestra Hanover and the Radio Symphony Orchestras of Berlin, Leipzig, Munich, Frankfurt, Cologne, Saarbrucken and Stuttgart; Kapellmeister at the Zürich Opera from 1991; Opera productions include Die Fledermaus, Figaro and Il Barbiere di Siviglia at the Vienna Volksoper, 1989–90; Giordano's Fedora and Andrea Chénier, Massenet's Hérodiade at Zürich; Così fan tutte at Hamburg, 1993; The premiere of Herbert Willi's opera Schlafes Bruder, 1996; Ballet includes Pulcinella at the Vienna Staatsoper, 1990; Debut with the Vienna Philharmonic Orchestra and Houston Symphony, 1994; Season 1995 with the Chicago Symphony Orchestra and the BBC Symphony at the Festival Hall, London; Season 1996–97 with the Dresden Staatsapelle, Oslo Philharmonic, Danish Radio Symphony and Royal Danish Orchestras; Music Director of Norwegian Opera from 1997; Further concerts with the BBC Symphony Orchestra, 1997–98; Conducted them in Strauss family concert at the 1999 London Proms. *Honours:* European Prize for Conducting, 1993. *Address:* c/o IMG Artists, Lovell House, 616 Chiswick High Road, London W4 5RX, England.

HONG, Hei-Kyung; Singer (soprano); b. 1958, Seoul, Republic of Korea. *Education:* Juilliard School, New York. *Career:* debut, Houston, 1983, as Gilda in Rigoletto; Sang Musetta at Chicago, 1983, and at the Metropolitan Opera from 1985 (debut as Servilia in La Clemenza di Tito), followed by Mimi, Despina, Susanna, Lauretta (Gianni Schicchi), Ilia and Pamina; Toronto, 1992, as Gounod's Juliette; Other roles include Leila (Les Pêcheurs de Perles), Manon, Butterfly, Bellini's Giulietta and Woglinde in Das Rheingold; Sang Zerlina at Dallas, 1996. *Recordings include:* Rheingold and Götterdämmerung. *Address:* c/o Metropolitan Opera, Lincoln Center, New York, NY 10023, USA.

HÖNIGSBERG, David; Composer, Conductor and Pianist; b. 28 Oct. 1959, Johannesburg, South Africa; 1 d. *Education:* BMus, RAND, Hochschule für Musik und Darstellende Kunst, Vienna, Austria, 1987; (Roman Haubenstock-Ramati), 1988–89. *Career:* Debut: Market Theatre, Johannesburg, 1980; Assistant Conductor, Imilonji Kantu Choir Soweto, 1989 Frankfurt Choir Festival; Concerto for Evi and orchestra, Johannesburg; Tomas and the Rainbow Dragon, Zürich; Piano concerto, St Cecilia Players, Zürich; mem, Schweizersche Tonkunstler Verein; SUISA; SMPV; SME. *Compositions:* 8 canzoni for cello and piano; Stefan Thut, cello; D Honigsberg, piano; Tomas and the Rainbow Dragon

(Tudor). *Publications:* Music critic The Star Tonight, 1988–93. *Honours:* Samro Overseas Scholarship, 1988; First Prize, Total Composition, 1987. *Address:* Marktgasse 3, 8180 Bulach, Switzerland.

HONNA, Tetsuji; Conductor; b. 19 Jan. 1957, Koriyama, Japan. *Education:* Tokyo University of Fine Arts and Music; Studied Conducting under Michiyoshi Inoue; Studied at the Concertgebouw, Amsterdam. *Career:* Debut: Tokyo, Japan Philharmonic Orchestra, 1986; Hungarian State Symphony Orchestra, Corinthian Summer, 1994; Netherlands Philharmonic Orchestra, Holland Music Session, 1997; Salzburg, Mozarteum Orchestra, 1998; Philharmonia Orchestra, 1997; Many recordings for NHK FM with Tokyo Philharmonic Orchestra; Permanent Conductor of the Orchestra Osaka Symphoniker, 1994–; Guest Permanent Conductor of the Nagoya Philharmonic Orchestra, 1998–; Conductor of the Shirakawa Symphonia, 2000–. *Recordings:* Akutagawa Works with Japan Philharmonic Orchestra; Dvořák and Schumann with New Japan Philharmonic Orchestra. *Address:* c/o Dr Raab und Dr Bohm GmBH, Plankengasse 7, 1010 Vienna, Austria.

HOOKS, Bridgett; Singer (Soprano); b. 1967, New York, USA. *Education:* Studied at the Manhattan School of Music and the Curtis Institute, Philadelphia. *Career:* Sang at the Ghent Opera from 1990 as Mozart's Countess, and Madame Cortese in Rossini's Viaggio a Reims; Philadelphia Opera, 1990–92, in Argento's Postcard from Morocco, Copland's The Tender Land and Don Giovanni, as Donna Anna; Concerts include Alice Tully Hall, New York (1994), Aspen Festival (Verdi Requiem), Spoleto Festival (1995), and Mahler's 8th Symphony (Cologne, 1995); Further repertory includes Spirituals (at the Vatican), Beethoven's Ninth and Shostakovich's 14th Symphonies, and Poulenc's Stabat Mater; Many lieder recitals. *Address:* c/o Opera Company of Philadelphia, 510 Walnut Street, Suite 1600, Philadelphia, PA 19106, USA.

HOOPER, Adrian John; Australian conductor and mandolinist; b. 6 May 1953, Sydney, NSW; m. Barbara Michele Jackson 1975; two s. one d. *Education:* New South Wales Conservatorium of Music. *Career:* founder and conductor of Australia's foremost mandolin orchestra, The Sydney Mandolins; regular player with the Australian Opera and Ballet Orchestra which accompanies the Australian Opera, and performed in such works as Otello and The Merry Widow; Worked with Sydney Symphony Orchestra in such works as Agon by Stravinsky; Regularly takes part in radio and concert performances as a Mandolin Soloist and Conductor for the Australian Broadcasting Commission; Soloist, Australian Chamber Orchestra; Mandolin Teacher, New South Wales State Conservatorium of Music, 1983; Teacher in Performance, Sydney University, 1996–. *Recordings:* over 80 recordings of music by Australian composers. *Publications:* Published and edited a number of Ancient Mandolin works; Editing all Mandolin Concertos. *Address:* 24 Kitchener Street, Oatley, NSW 2223, Australia. *E-mail:* mail@sydneymandolins.com.

HOOVER, Katherine, BM, MM; American composer and flautist; b. 2 Dec. 1937, Elkins, WV. *Education:* Eastmann School and the Manhattan School of Music. *Career:* Lecturer at the Manhattan School and Juilliard; organizer, Women's Interart Center music festivals, New York 1978–81. *Compositions include:* Homage to Bartók, for wind quintet 1975, Trio, for clarinet, violin and piano 1978, Piano Book 1977–82, From the Testament of François Villon, for baritone, bassoon and string quartet 1982, Lyric Trio, for flute, cello and piano 1983, Clarinet Concert 1987, Wind Quintet 1987, Eleni: a Greek Tragedy, for orchestra 1987, Double Concerto for 2 violins and strings 1989, Da pacem, piano quintet 1989, Night Skies, for orchestra 1992, Dances and Variations for flute and harp 1996, Bounce, for orchestra 1997, Kyrie, for 12 flutes 1998, The Heart Speaks, 7 songs for soprano and piano 1998, String quartet 1998, Trio for 3 flutes 1999, Suite for flute, guitar and bassoon 2000. *Honours:* Acad. of Arts and Letters Award in Composition 1994. *Address:* c/o Papagena Press, PO Box 20484, Park West Station, New York, NY 10025, USA (office). *Telephone:* (212) 749-3012. *Fax:* (212) 316-2235. *E-mail:* info@papagenapress.com. *Website:* www.papagenapress.com.

HOPE, Daniel; Concert Violinist; b. 1974, South Africa. *Education:* Menuhin School of Music and with Felix Andrievsky at the Royal Coll. of Music, junior department. *Career:* played duos with double-bassist Garry Karr, 1983, Bartók duos with Yehudi Menuhin for German television, 1984; International debut with the Jyväskylä Symphony Orchestra of Finland, playing the Mendelssohn Concerto; Brighton Festival in Bach's Fifth Brandenburg Concerto, recitals at the Purcell Room, London, the Bach Violin Concertos with the Milton Keynes Chamber Orchestra and concert with the Hallé Orchestra under Menuhin; Vivaldi's Four Seasons with the Aachen City Orchestra, Prokofiev's First Concerto in Finland and London, and the Beethoven Concerto on tour in Europe; Appearances at the Schleswig-Holstein Festival, Germany. *Honours:* Winner: Hugh Bean Violin Competition, 1986; Peter Morrison Concerto Competition, 1989. *Address:* Matthias Vogt Artists' Management, 211 Gough Street, Suites 112–113, San Francisco, CA 94102, USA. *Telephone:* (415) 788-8073. *E-mail:* matthias.vogt@usa.net. *Website:* www.matthiasvogt.com; www.danielhope.com.

HOPFERWEISER, Josef; Singer (Tenor); b. 25 May 1938, Graz, Austria. *Education:* Musikhochschule Graz. *Career:* Frequent appearances at the Vienna Volksoper, notably in Notre Dame by Schmidt; State Operas of Hamburg, Munich and Stuttgart; Further engagements in Nancy, Frankfurt, Graz, Milan, Rome and San Francisco; Sang in the premiere of Troades by Aribert Reimann, Munich, 1986; Sang Froh in Das Rheingold at Munich, 1987, Alwa in Lulu at Madrid, 1988; Vienna Staatsoper, 1990, as Walther in Die Meistersinger; Herod in Salome, 1994; Many concert appearances. *Recordings include:* Alwa in Berg's Lulu, conducted by Christoph von Dohnányi.

HOPKINS, Antony; Composer and Author; b. 21 March 1921, London, England; m. Alison Purves, 1947 (deceased 1991). *Education:* Royal College of Music with Cyril Smith. *Career:* Lecturer, Royal College of Music, 15 years; Director, Intimate Opera Company, 1952–64; Series of radio broadcasts, Talking About Music, 1954–90. *Compositions include:* Operas: Lady Rohesia; Three's Company; Hands Across the Sky; Dr Musikus; Ten o'clock Call; The Man from Tuscany; Ballets: Etude; Café des Sports; 3 Piano Sonatas; Numerous scores of incidental music including: Oedipus; The Love of Four Colonels; Cast a Dark Shadow; Pickwick Papers; Billy Budd; Decameron Nights. *Publications include:* Understanding Music, 1979; The Nine Symphonies of Beethoven, 1980; The Concertgoer's Companion, 2 vols, 1984, 1986; The Seven Concertos of Beethoven, 1996, and numerous other titles. *Honours:* Gold Medal, Royal College of Music, 1943; Italia Prize for Radio Programme, 1951, 1957; Medal, City of Tokyo for Services to Music, 1973; C.B.E., 1976. *Address:* Woodyard, Ashridge, Berkhamsted, Hertfordshire HP4 1PS, England.

HOPKINS, John (Raymond); Conductor and Director; b. 19 July 1927, Preston, England; m. (1) Ann Rosemary Blamey, deceased, 5 d., (2) Geraldene Catherine Scott, 1 July 1987. *Education:* Cello student, Associate Fellow, Royal Manchester College of Music. *Career:* Assistant Conductor, BBC Glasgow, 1949–52; Conductor, BBC Northern Orchestra, 1952–57; National Orchestra, New Zealand; Musical Director, New Zealand Opera Company, 1957–63; Director of Music, ABC, 1963–73; Dean, School of Music, Victoria College of Arts, Melbourne, Australia, 1973–86; Principal Conductor, Auckland Philharmonic Orchestra, 1983–; Director of New South Wales State Conservatorium of Music, 1986–93; Artistic Adviser, Sydney Symphony Orchestra, 1986–88; Education Consultant, Sydney Symphony Orchestra. *Recordings:* Various with Melbourne, New Zealand and Moscow Symphony Orchestras. *Honours:* O.B.E., 1970; Queen's Silver Jubilee Medal, 1977; Title of Professor, Sydney University, 1991. *Address:* 1290 Mountain Lagoon Road, Bilpin, NSW 2758, Australia.

HOPKINS, Sarah; Composer and Performer; b. 1958, Lower Hutt, New Zealand. *Education:* New South Wales Conservatorium of Music High School; Victorian College of the Arts Music School. *Career:* Toured extensively throughout Australia, the United Kingdom, Europe and the USA; Musician in Residence, GIAE, Gippsland, Victoria, Australia, 1978; Musician in Residence, CIT, Caulfield, Victoria, 1979; Composer in Residence, Arts Victoria Music '81, 1981; Musician in Residence, 1981, Guest Artist in Residence, 1983, Brown's Mart Community Art Project; Let's Make Music, Northern Territory, 1982; New Music ACTION Residency, Victorian College of the Arts, Melbourne, 1982; Composer-Performer in Residence, Darwin Theatre Group, 1984; Artist in Schools, 1985, 1986; Composer-Performer, Sky Song Project, Brown's Mart, Darwin, and major tour, 1987 and 1988; Performer in Residence, The Exploration San Francisco, 1988; Composer in Residence, Northern Territory Arts Council, Darwin, 1989. *Compositions:* Ensemble works: Cello Timbre, 1976; Seasons II, 1978; Cellovoice, 1982; Whirlies, 1983; Sunrise/Sunset, 1983; Interweave, 1984; Deep Whirly Duo, 1984; Aura Swirl, 1986; Eclipse, 1986; Bougainvillea Bells, 1986; Cello Chi, 1986; Flight of the Wild Goose, 1987; Ring, 1987; Songs of the Wind, 1989; Circle Bell Mantra, 1989; Spiral Bells, 1989; Soul Song, 1989; Transformation, 1989; Heart Songs, 1989. *Recordings:* Soundworks 1: Collaborative Works; Soundworks 2: Solo and Duo Works; Soundworks 3: Whirliworks Performance; Interweave; Soundworks Performance.

HOPKINS, Tim; Stage Director and Performer; b. 1963, London, England. *Education:* Graduated from Queen's College, Cambridge in 1986. *Career:* Productions at Musica nel Chiostro, Battignano, 1989–91; Peter Grimes for Dublin Grand Opera, 1990; The Gondoliers for New Doyle Carte in 1991, Falstaff for English Touring Opera in 1992, Mario and the Magician for Almeida Opera, 1992, Così fan tutte for Welsh National Opera, 1992; Zampa at the 1993 Wexford Festival; Staged the premiere of Judith Weir's Blond Eckbert for English National Opera in 1994 and Berio's Vera Storia at the Festival Hall; Yeomen of the Guard for Welsh National Opera in 1995 (also seen at Covent Garden and in the USA), Così fan tutte, also for Welsh National Opera and Rimsky's Golden Cockerel for Rome Opera; Iphigénie en Aulide for Opera North,

1996; Season 1997–98 with Il Trovatore at Graz Oper, Maria Stuarda at Basel Opera and at the Royal Opera with a new production of The Golden Cockerel; Season 1999–2000, Radamisto for Opera North, Aronne for Almeida Opera and Eugen Onegin for Basel Opera; Season 2001–02, Forest Murmurs for Opera North, Kantan/Damask Drum by Goehr for Almeida Opera; Only the Names Have Been Changed for the Munich Festival; Mare Nostrum for Theatre Basel; The Rake's Progress, in Hanover. *Honours:* NESTA Fellowship, 2002. *Address:* c/o T.J.H., 26A Cole Street, London SE1 4YH, England. *E-mail:* thopkins@ divcon.co.uk.

HORACEK, Jaroslav; Singer (Bass) and Teacher; b. 29 April 1924, Dehylov, Czechoslovakia. *Education:* Studied with Rudol Va šek, Karel Kugler and Peter Burja in Ostrava, Apollo Granforte in Prague. *Career:* Debut: Opava, 1945, as Kecal in The Bartered Bride; Sang in Ostrava, 1951–53, then at the National Theatre, Prague; Sang in the standard bass repertory, and in operas by Smetana, Janáček and Dvořák; Took part in the 1959 premiere of Mirandolina by Martinů; Guest appearances in Warsaw, Sofia, Amsterdam, Boston, Edinburgh (1964, with the Prague Company), Naples, Barcelona and Boston; Sang Debussy's Arkel at Prague, 1986; Don Giovanni at the bicentenary performance of the opera, 1987; Many concert appearances; Producer of Czech operas at La Scala Milan; Teacher at the Prague Conservatory. *Address:* c/o National Theatre, PO Box 865, 112 30 Prague 1, Czech Republic.

HORAK, Josef; Bass Clarinettist and Music Educator; b. 24 March 1931, Znojmo, Czechoslovakia. *Education:* State High School of Musical and Dramatic Arts. *Career:* Clarinettist, Czech Radio Symphony Orchestra and State Philharmonic, Brno; Concert Soloist; Professor, State Music High School, Prague; Chamber Music Lecturer, Biberach, West Germany; Member, chamber music ensemble Due Boemi di Praga, with Emma Kovarnova, Prague, 1963–; Concerts in Europe, USA, Asia and Africa; Television programmes in Czechoslovakia, Germany and Romania; Radio programmes, many European countries and USA; Discovered the bass clarinet as a solo instrument, giving the first bass clarinet recital in the world (1955); Chamber soloist of the Czech Philharmonic Orchestra; mem, Union of Czech Interpreters; Honorary member, Jeunesses Musicales de Suisse. *Recordings:* Due Boemi di Praga; At the New Ways; Bass Clarinet, the New Solo Instrument; The Paganini of the Bass Clarinet; The Singing Bass Clarinet; CD: Horák-New Age of Bass Clarinet, Horák and his Bass Clarinet-New Sound, The Singing Bass Clarinet; Also about 85 single recordings on various records. *Honours:* Gold Medal, 1958; Prize, L Janáček Competition, 1959; Hi-Fi Festival, Paris, 1965; Pick of the Year, London, 1974; Clarinet Super Record, Tokyo, 1986. *Address:* Bubenska 39, 170 21 Prague 7, Czech Republic.

HORIGOME, Yuzuko; Violinist; b. 1960, Tokyo, Japan. *Education:* Studied at Toho Gakuen School of Music, Tokyo, with Toshiya Eto; Graduated, 1980. *Career:* Won Queen Elisabeth of the Belgians International Competition, 1980; London debut, 1983, concerts with London Symphony Orchestra under Claudio Abbado and André Previn; US debut, 1982, at Tanglewood, with Boston Symphony; Later appearances in Pittsburgh, Chicago, Los Angeles and Montreal; 1988/89 season included concerts in Europe and Japan with the Salzburg Camerata, Royal Liverpool Philharmonic and Scottish National Orchestras, and at the Prague Spring Festival; USA tour with the Chamber Music Players of Marlboro, 1995; Featured in film Testimony, on the life of Shostakovich. *Recordings:* Bach Concerti with the English Chamber Orchestra with A Litton; Bach's Solo Violin Sonatas; Sibelius and Mendelssohn Concertos with the Concertgebouw Orchestra and Ivan Fischer, music by Bruch (Tring, 1996); Mozart Concerti, Camerata Academic Salzburg with Sándor Végh; Takemitsu by Denon, 1999; Beethoven, Kakadu Variations with Rudolph Serkin and Peter Willey. *Current Management:* Cadenza Conzert, Salzburg; Kajimoto Management, Tokyo, Japan. *Address:* 26A Avenue Emile Van Becelaere, Box 90, 1170 Brussels, Belgium.

HORN, Heiner; Singer (Bass-baritone); b. 20 June 1918, Darmstadt, Germany. *Education:* Studied in Darmstadt and Berlin. *Career:* Sang at first in Darmstadt, then at the Cologne Opera; Sang Jochanaan, Kaspar in Der Freischütz and Wozzeck at the Paris Opéra, Amsterdam, Brussels, Luxembourg, Zürich, Bern, Venice, Bologna, Trieste, Lisbon, Barcelona; Der fliegende Holländer; Bett in Zar und Zimmermann, Plunkett in Martha and Kothner in Die Meistersinger; Other roles: Pizarro, Mephisto (Gounod, Berlioz), Ramphis, Sarastro, Nick Shadow, Dapertutto, King Henry, Gunther, Klingsor, Fasolt, Fafner, Daland, Zar Saltan, Varlaam, Tomsky, Scarpia, Alfio, Escamillo, Basilio, Father Guardian, Inquisitor, and many more; 15 years in WDR Opera and about 20 Germany opera houses; Sang in the 1965 premiere of Die Soldaten by Zimmermann; Concert appearances, and guest engagements elsewhere in Germany; Retired 1985. *Recordings:* Sparafucile in Rigoletto; Die Soldaten. *Address:* c/o Staatstheater Darmstadt, PO Box 111432, D–64229 Darmstadt, Germany.

HORN, Volker; Tenor; b. 1945, Klagenfurt, Germany. *Education:* Studied at the Vienna Musikhochschule. *Career:* Sang as boy soprano in the Bayreuth production of Tannhäuser directed by Wieland Wagner, 1954–55; Has sung at the Deutsche Oper Berlin from 1976; Guest appearances in Lyon, Karlsruhe, Munich and Strasbourg as Max in Der Freischütz and Loge in Das Rheingold, and at Bayreuth and Salzburg Easter Festivals in 1980; Deutsche Oper Berlin in 1987 as Galba in Die Toten Augen by d'Albert; Sang Hans Kraft in Der Kobold by Siegfried Wagner, Rudolstadt, 1992; Other roles include Tamino, Florestan, Lohengrin and Tristan; Sang in premiere of Gesualdo by F Hummel at Kaiserslautern, 1996; Season 2000–01 as Malcolm in Macbeth and Hervey in Anna Bolena at the Deutsche Oper; Concert and oratorio appearances in Germany, Austria and Switzerland. *Recordings:* Die Zauberflöte; Nabucco. *Address:* c/o Deutsche Oper Berlin, Richard Wagnerstrasse 10, 1000 Berlin, Germany.

HORNE, David; Concert Pianist and Composer; b. 12 Dec. 1970, Tillicoultry, Stirling, Scotland. *Education:* Studied at St Mary's Music School in Edinburgh, the Curtis Institute, Philadelphia and Harvard University. *Career:* Soloist with BBC Philharmonic and Symphony, Welsh and Scottish Orchestras, CBSO, the Scottish National and London Sinfonietta; Festival engagements at Edinburgh, Aldeburgh, Almeida and London; BBC Promenade Concert debut in 1990 with Prokofiev's Third Concerto; Other repertory includes Ravel G major, Gershwin Concerto, Brahms Concerto in D minor, Beethoven 1st Concerto and Choral Fantasia, Iain Hamilton 2nd Concerto (world premiere), Mozart K271, Frank Symphonic Variations, and Tchaikovsky 1st Concerto. *Compositions:* String Quartet, 1988; Splintered Unisons for clarinet, violin, cello and piano, 1988; Towards Dharma for 6 instruments, 1989; Light Emerging for symphony orchestra, 1989; Out of the Air, 1990; Contraries and Progressions for ensemble, 1991; Northscape for chamber orchestra, 1992; Piano Concerto, 1992; Pensive, for mezzo, voices and chamber orchestra, 1998; Spike, for ensemble, 1998; Broken Instruments, 1999; Zip, for cello and piano, 1999; Vocal music: Jason Field (ENO Opera Studio), Travellers, cantata The Lie; Opera, Friend of the People (Scottish Opera, 1999). *Honours:* 1st Prize, National Mozart Competition, 1987; 1st Place for Piano, BBC Young Musician of The Year, 1988; Winner, Huddersfield Contemporary Music Festival Composers Competition, 1988. *Address:* c/o Boosey and Hawkes, 295 Regent Street, London W1R 8JH, England.

HORNE, Marilyn; Singer (Mezzo-soprano); b. 16 Jan. 1934, Bradford, Pennsylvania, USA; Divorced, 1 d. *Education:* University of Southern California under William Vennard. *Career:* Debut: Gelsenkirchen, 1957; San Francisco Opera in 1960 as Berg's Marie; Performed with several German Opera Companies in Europe in 1956 then appeared at Covent Garden, the Chicago Lyric Opera, La Scala Milan, and Metropolitan Opera; Repertoire includes Eboli, Marie in Wozzeck, Adalgisa in Norma, Jane Seymour in Anna Bolena, Amneris, Carmen, Rosina, Fides in La Prophète, Mignon, Isabella in L'Italiana in Algeri, Romeo, Tancredi, Orlando in Orlando Furioso, and Dalila; Returned to Covent Garden in 1989 as Isabella; Other Rossini roles include Malcolm in La Donna del Lago at Covent Garden in 1985, Falliero and Andromache in Ermoine at Pesaro in 1986 and 1987 and Calbo in Maometto II at San Francisco in 1988; Sang Rosina at the Metropolitan in 1989, Vivaldi's Orlando at San Francisco and Gluck's Orpheus at Santa Fe in 1990; Season 1992 in a Rossini 200th birthday gala at Fisher Hall, NY and as Isabella at San Francisco; Last appearance in Rossini as Isabella in L'Italiana in Algeri at Covent Garden in 1993; Retirement galas in New York and San Francisco, 1998. *Recordings include:* Semiramide; Orfeo ed Euridice; Anna Bolena; Don Giovanni; Il Trovatore; Le Prophète; Mignon; Tancredi; Il Barbiere du Siviglia; Suor Angelica; Carmen; Norma; Falstaff; Orlando Furioso; La Navarraise; L'Italiana in Algeri; La Damnation de Faust. *Honours:* 5 Honorary Doctorates. *Address:* c/o Columbia Artists Management Inc, 165 West 57th Street, New York, NY 10019, USA.

HORNIK, Gottfried; Baritone; b. 5 Aug. 1940, Vienna, Austria. *Education:* Studied in Vienna. *Career:* Sang at Klagenfurt as Papageno and as Silvio in Pagliacci; Graz Opera as Mozart's Figaro, Don Giovanni and Alberich; Deutsche Oper Berlin and San Francisco as Beckmesser in Die Meistersinger; Salzburg Easter Festival as Kurwenal in Tristan und Isolde, under Karajan; Sang Alberich and other Wagner roles at the Vienna Staatsoper; Sang at Leipzig Opera as the Villains in Les Contes d'Hoffmann, Cologne Opera in 1983 as Klingsor in Parsifal, Covent Garden in 1987 as Faninal in Der Rosenkavalier, Deutsche Oper Berlin in 1988 as Alberich in The Ring and sang Wozzeck at the Metropolitan in 1990; Sang Orestes in Elektra at Athens in 1992; Vienna Staatsoper 1995, in the premiere of Schnittke's Gesualdo; Emperor in Turandot, 2001. *Recordings:* Die Zauberflöte, Tosca, and Die Meistersinger conducted by Karajan; Der Wildschütz by Lortzing.

HOROVITZ, Joseph; Composer; b. 26 May 1926, Vienna, Austria. *Education:* New College Oxford; Royal College of Music, London; Nadia Boulanger, Paris. *Career:* Music Director, Bristol Old Vic, 1949–51;

Conductor, Festival Gardens Orchestra, London, 1951; Co-conductor, Ballets Russes English Season, 1952; Associate Director, Intimate Opera Company, 1952–63; Assistant Conductor, Glyndebourne Opera, 1956; Professor of Composition, Royal College of Music, 1961–; mem, Council of Composers' Guild, 1970; Board of Performing Right Society, 1971–96; Fellow, Royal College of Music, 1981; President, CIAM of the International Federation of Societies of Authors and Composers, 1981–89. *Compositions:* 16 Ballets, including Alice in Wonderland, Les femmes d'Alger, Concerto for Dancers; Two one-act Operas, The Dumb Wife and Gentleman's Island; Orchestral: Concertos for violin, trumpet, jazz-harpsichord, 2 for clarinet, tuba, oboe, percussion; Horizon Overture; Jubilee Serenade; Sinfonietta; Fantasia on a Theme of Couperin; Toy Symphony for 17 instruments and piano quintet, 1977; Choral: Samson, oratorio; Captain Noah and his Floating Zoo; Summer Sunday; Endymion; Brass Band Music includes a Euphonium Concerto, Ballet for Band and Concertino Classico; For Wind Band, Ad Astra, Windharp, Dance Suite, Bacchus on Blue Ridge, Theme and Co-Operation, 1994; Chamber, 5 String Quartets, 1946–69, Oboe Sonatina; Oboe Quartet, Clarinet sonatina; Two pieces for Hoffnung Concerts, Metamorphoses on a Bed-Time Theme and Horroratorio; Numerous scores for theatre productions, films and television series. *Honours:* Gold Order of Merit, City of Vienna, 1996; Nino Rota Prize, Italy, 2002. *Address:* Royal College of Music, Prince Consort Road, London SW7 2 BS, England.

HORSLEY, Colin; Pianist and Professor; b. 23 April 1920, Wanganui, New Zealand. *Education:* Royal College of Music. *Career:* Debut: At Invitation of Sir John Barbirolli at Hallé Concerts, Manchester, 1943; Soloist with all leading orchestras of Great Britain, the Royal Philharmonic Society, 1953, 1959, Promenade Concerts; Toured Belgium, Netherlands, Spain, France, Scandinavia, Malta, Sri Lanka, Malaysia, Australia and New Zealand; Festival appearances include Aix-en-Provence, International Contemporary Music Festival, Palermo, British Music Festivals in Belgium, Netherlands and Finland; Broadcasts frequently. *Recordings:* EMI Meridian; Symposium Records; CDs of John Ireland Piano Concerto and Mozart Quintet for Piano and Wind. *Honours:* O.B.E., 1963; FRCM, 1973; Hon RAM. *Address:* Belmont, Dreemskerry, Maughold, Isle of Man.

HORTON, Peter Bernard, MA, DPhil, DipLib; British music librarian; b. 19 June 1953, Ashford, England; m. Elaine Horton; two s. one d. *Education:* Sir Roger Manwood's Grammar School, Sandwich and Magdalen Coll., Oxford. *Career:* Asst Reference Librarian, Royal Coll. of Music 1984–95; Reference Librarian and Research Co-ordinator, Royal Coll. of Music 1995–; mem. Royal Musical Asscn, Hymn Soc., Church Music Soc. *Publications:* Samuel Sebastian Wesley: Anthems 1 1990, Anthems 2 1992, Samuel Sebastian Wesley: A Life 2004. *Address:* 13 Spencer Gardens, London, SE9 6LX England (home); Royal College of Music, Prince Consort Road, London, SW7 2BS England (office). *Telephone:* (20) 7591-4324 (office); (20) 8850-3791 (home). *Fax:* (20) 7589-7740 (office). *E-mail:* phorton@rcm.ac.uk (office); PBHSpencerGdns@aol.com (home).

HORVAT, Milan; Conductor; b. 28 July 1919, Pakrac, Yugoslavia. *Education:* Studied at the Zagreb Music Academy, 1939–46. *Career:* Began as pianist and choral conductor; Conductor of the Zagreb Philharmonic, 1946–53 and 1958–59; Chief Conductor of the Radio Telefis Eireann Symphony, 1953–58; Principal Conductor of the Zagreb Opera, 1958–65 with many premieres of Yugoslav music; Guest Conductor with many major orchestras in Europe and the USA; Musical Director of the Dubrovnik Festival, 1965; Principal Conductor of the Austrian Radio Symphony, 1969–75; Professor of Conducting at the Graz Academy, 1975; Conductor of the Zagreb Symphony Orchestra, 1975–. *Recordings:* Haydn Harpsichord Concertos, with Robert Veryon-Lacroix; Mozart Violin and Piano Concertos, with Jean Fournier and Jörg Demus; Hindemith Mathis der Maler Symphony; Shostakovich Symphonies Nos 1 and 9, and 1st Piano Concerto with the Zagreb Philharmonic; Beethoven Violin Concerto, with Igor Ozim. *Address:* c/o Zagreb Philharmonic Orchestra, Trjanska 66, 4100 Zagreb, Croatia.

HORVATH, László; Clarinettist; b. 14 July 1945, Koszeg, Hungary; Divorced, 1 s., 1 d. *Education:* Music Gymnasium, Gyor, 1960–64; Studied with Professor György Balassa, 1964–69, MMus with distinction, 1969, Liszt Ference Academy of Music, Budapest; Bursary student, Conservatoire de Musique, Paris, 1969–70; Studied with Professor Ulysse Delecluse. *Career:* Debut: Competition in Budapest in 1965; Clarinettist, 1965–68, Soloist and Leading Clarinettist, 1968–, Hungarian State Symphony Orchestra, Budapest; Professor at Conservatory of Music Debrecen, 1974–79, and at Béla Bart ók Conservatory of Music, Budapest, 1980–; Toured as soloist, Buffet-Crampon Company, Japan, 1981, 1986; Many solo recitals world-wide and appearances as clarinet duo with Klara Kormendi, and chamber music with Philharmonic Wind Quintet in Europe, USA, Canada, Australia and Japan, 1983–; Recitals at Claude Champagne Hall, Montreal, 1991 and 1993; Radio broadcasts in Budapest, Paris, London and Tokyo and television appearances in

Hungary; Masterclasses at Montreal, 1991, 1993 and Jury Member for International Competition for Musical Performers, Geneva, 1990. *Recordings:* Works by Leo Weiner, 1970, Attila Bozay, 1976, 1979, Carl and Johann Stamitz, 1979, Johann Molter, 1979, 1991, Mozart, 1981; 20th Century Clarinet Music, 1991; Clarinetto all'Ungherse, 1992. *Current Management:* Interkoncert, Vorosmarty ter 1 m, 1368 Budapest, Hungary. *Address:* 6 Jászai Mari Tér V-44, 1137 Budapest, Hungary.

HORWOOD, Michael Stephen; American/Canadian composer; b. 24 May 1947, Buffalo, New York, USA; m. Celia M. Roberts 1974, 2 s. *Education:* BA, Music, 1969, MA, Composition, 1971, State University of New York, Buffalo. *Career:* Debut: Performance of his works at Baird Hall, SUNY, Buffalo in 1966; Professor of Music and Humanities at Humber College of Applied Arts and Technology, Ontario, Canada, 1972–2003; Featured Composer, Saskatoon Symphony, Saskatchewan, Canada, 1991–92; Featured Composer, Composers and Orchestras – What's the Score? conference, Kitchener, Ontario, 1995; Retrospective concerts of his works: Buffalo, NY, 1966, Toronto, Ontario, 1982, 1990; Adjudicator: SOCAN Young Composers Competition, 1987, Alliance for Canadian New Music Projects Awards, 1989, Ontario Arts Council Music Commissioning Program, 1993; Contemporary Canadian Music Workshop for Emerging Composers Competition, 1997. *Compositions include:* Durations for 1–4 Keyboards, 1965; Piece Percussionique No. 1 for 6 percussionists and piano, 1965, revised 1979; Women Of Trachis, incidental music for chamber orchestra, 1966; Piece Percussionique No. 3 for 3 percussionists, 1966; Piece Percussionique No. 4 for 4 percussionists, 1967, revised 1981; Concerto for double bass and string orchestra, 1967, revised, 2002; Double Quintet for 2 wind quintets, 1968; Asteroids for brass quartet, 1969; 8 Microduets, 1969–83; Piece Percussionique No. 5 for 2 percussionists and Tape, 1970; Sextet for chamber ensemble, 1971; Little Bow Piece for percussion octet, 1972; 5, 3, 4 for jazz orchestra and percussion ensemble, 1973; Facets for augmented chamber group, 1974; Talos IV for solo accordion, 1975; Interphase for chamber sextet, 1975; Andromeda for wind ensemble, 1976, revised 1980; Bipolarity for accordion and string trio, 1979; Birds for piccolo, piano and optional visual program, 1979; Io for double bass and violin, 1979; Splinters for chamber sextet, 1981; Residue for tuba and vibraphone, 1981; Three Cadenzas for guitar and harpsichord, 1981; Exit To Your Left for wind quintet, 1982; String Quartet No. 1, 1982; Sonata for cello and piano, 1983; Brass-Fast for brass quintet, 1984; Symphony No. 1, 1984; Three Landscapes for solo piano, 1984; Suite for accordion and percussion, 1985; Amusement Park Suite, for orchestra, 1986; Nervous Disorder, chamber trio, 1988; Broken Chords for solo piano, 1990; National Park Suite for orchestra, 1991; Psalm 121 for SSA choir, 1991; Symphony No. 2, Visions of a Wounded Earth, for chorus and orchestra, 1995; Do You Live For Weekends? for chamber orchestra, 1996; Symphony No. 3, Andromeda, for tenor saxophone and orchestra, 1996; Intravariations for piano and orchestra, 1997; Quartzite Dialogues for narrator and wind quintet, 1999; T + I = Ewigkeit, for solo piano, 2000; Three Interludes for orchestra, 2000. *Recordings:* Overture for piano player and 2 assistants; Piece Percussionique No. 5, 1982; Birds, 1982; Dynamite, 1983; Six Pieces for piano; Broken Chords, 1998; Tantrum IV, 2000; Fugue for Sam, 2000; Motility, 2000; Brass Fast, 2001; Asteroids, 2001; Birds, 2001; Horizontal Tango, 2002. *Publications:* Birds, 1982; Brass-Fast, 1992; Music as History, The Representation of the Individual in Western Music (co-author), 1996; That Pioneering Spirit (co-ed.), 1998. *Honours:* Three times recipient Composer Residency Program, SOCAN Foundation, 1997, 1998, 1999. *Address:* POB 69, Cowley, Alberta, T0K 0P0, Canada (home). *E-mail:* Michael@HorwoodComposer.com (home). *Website:* www .HorwoodComposer.com (home).

HORYSA, Inghild; Singer (Mezzo-soprano); b. 2 Jan. 1944, Bielitz, Germany. *Education:* Studied with Helena Braun in Munich. *Career:* Debut: Munich Staatsoper in 1966 in Hansel and Gretel; Munich in 1969 in the premiere of The Play of Love and Death by Cikker; Sang at Nuremberg, the Vienna Volksoper, Düsseldorf, Frankfurt, Mannheim, Hamburg and Stuttgart; Other roles include Dorabella, Amneris, Eboli, Venus, Brangaene, Marina in Boris Godunov, Orsini in Lucrezia Borgia, Fricka in Walküre, Clytemnestra in Elektra, Baba the Turk in The Rake's Progress and Octavian; Frequent concert appearances. *Address:* c/o Nuremberg Opera House, Nuremberg, Germany.

HOSE, Anthony (Paul); Musician and Conductor; b. 24 May 1944, London, England; m. Moira Griffiths, 8 July 1977, 2 d. *Education:* Junior Exhibitioner, 1955–62, Student, 1962–66, Royal College of Music, London; ARCM. *Career:* Glyndebourne Festival, 1966–68; Bremen Opera, Federal Republic of Germany, 1968–69; Welsh National Opera, 1969–83; Music Director, Buxton Festival, 1979–87; Artistic Director, Welsh Chamber Orchestra, 1986–; Artistic Director, Beaumaris Festival, 1986–; Realisation of Cavalli's Giasone; Artistic Director, Buxton Festival, 1988–91; Professor, Royal College of Music, 1991–; Professor, Royal Academy of Music, 1992–98; Artistic Director,

Rhyl Easter Festival, 1994–95; Artistic Director, Llandudno October Festival, 1994–2000; Artistic Director, Mount Dora Spring Festival, Florida, 1998–; Orchestra Conductor, Stetson University, Florida, 2000–. *Publications:* English translation: Grétry: Le Huron; Elektra (Strauss); Ariodante (Handel); Don Quixote (Conti). *Current Management:* Michael Brewer, 8 Edward Court, 317 Hagley Road, Birmingham B16 9LQ, England. *Address:* 6 Lôn-y-Celyn, Cardiff CF14 7BW, Wales. *Telephone:* (1386) 8228963. *Fax:* (1386) 8228948. *E-mail:* ahose@stetson .edu.

HOSEK, Jiri; Czech violoncellist; b. 20 Aug. 1955, Prague; m. Marie Kaplanova 1977; two d. *Education:* Prague Conservatory, Academy of Music, Prague, Conservatory National, Paris, and courses at Nice and Szombately. *Career:* debut in Tchaikovsky's Rococco Variations, 1974; Tours to Russia, Germany, France, Italy and Poland; Many television and radio appearances including Anton Kraft Concertos. *Recordings:* Elgar Concerto, 1985; Anton Kraft Concertos; Radio recordings of Vivaldi Concerto, D Popper Konzertstücke, Dvořák's Rondo, Tchaikovsky's Rococco Variations, Prokofiev Symphony Concerto and Elgar Concerto. *Address:* Sudomerska 29, 13000 Prague 3, Czech Republic.

HOSIER, John; College Principal; b. 18 Nov. 1928, England. *Education:* MA, St John's College, Cambridge, 1954. *Career:* Lecturer in Ankara, Turkey, 1951–53; Music Producer, BBC Radio for Schools, 1953–59 then seconded to ABC, Sydney to advise on educational music programmes, 1959–60; Music Producer and subsequently Senior and Executive Producer for BBC television, pioneering the first regular music broadcasts to schools, 1960–73; ILEA Staff Inspector for Music, Director of Centre for Young Musicians, 1973–76; Principal at Guildhall School of Music and Drama, 1978–88; Director, Hong Kong Academy for Performing Arts, 1989–93; mem, Founder Member, Vice Chairman, United Kingdom Council for Music Education and Training, 1975–81; Gulbenkian Enquiry into Training Musicians, 1978; Trustee, Hirnichsen Foundation, 1981–88; Music Panel, British Council, 1984–88; GLAA, 1984–86; Vice Chairman, Kent Opera, 1985–88; Council of Management, Royal Philharmonic Society, 1982–89; Governing Body, Chetham's School; Governing Body, NYO FRSA, 1976; Hong Kong Council for the Performing Arts; General Committee, Hong Kong Philharmonic Orchestra. *Compositions:* Music for Cambridge revivals of Parnassus, 1949 and Humourous Lovers, 1951; Something's Burning, Mermaid, 1974; Many radio and television productions. *Publications:* The Orchestra, 1961, revised edition, 1977; Various books, songs and arrangements for children. *Contributions:* Professional journals. *Honours:* FGSM, 1978; Honorary RAM, 1980; FRCM, 1989; C.B.E., 1984; FRNCM, 1985; Honorary D.Mus, The City University, 1986; Honorary FTCL, 1986. *Address:* c/o Chetham's School of Music, Long Millgate, Manchester, M3 1 SB, England.

HOSKINS, Donald, BMus, MA, PhD; British pianist and conductor; b. 9 June 1932, Abertillery, Wales; m. Dinah Patricia Stanton 1972. *Education:* Abertillery Grammar School, Univ. of Wales, Cardiff. *Career:* Nat. Service 1954–56; directed choral groups, gave lectures and piano recitals, performed on television; teacher, Tudor Grange Grammar School, Solihull 1956–60; presented piano recitals; adjudicated at school festivals; founded local arts orchestra; performed as soloist with the Birmingham Philharmonic Orchestra 1956–60; guest conductor, Birmingham Philharmonic Orchestra on a visit to Wales 1962; Dir of Music, Hayes Grammar School, Middlesex 1960–64; founded and conducted local chamber orchestras and ensembles; solo recital, Paris; Lecturer, Eastbourne Coll. of Education, East Sussex 1964–67; soloist Hillingdon Festival 1964; Sr Lecturer, Dept of Education, Barking Regional Coll. of Technology 1967; song recital accompanist, Purcell Room, South Bank 1972; Head of NE London Polytechnic Music Centre 1978; established annual two-day Univ. of East London concert band festival 1980; guest conductor London Mozart Players 1983; piano recital, Athens 1984; founder and Dir Aminta Chamber Orchestra (of London) 1985; soloist with combined Desford Dowty, Fodens and Coventry brass bands 1989; soloist at inaugural concert, Zweibrucken, Germany 1994; presented concert band performances, Witten, Germany 1995, Univ. of Kaiserslautern 1997, Royal Star and Garter Home, Richmond 1998–2002; Visiting Prof., Univ. of Provo, Salt Lake City 1994, Music Conservatorium, Univ. of Cincinnati, USA 1994; guest conductor, Royal Philharmonic Concert Orchestra 1995, 1996, BBC Concert Orchestra 1997, 1998, London Philharmonic Choir 1999; conducted concerts at the QEH, London 2000, 2002; Pres., Redbridge Music Soc.; consultant and Dir of Concerts, Univ. of E London 1996; presented the 26th annual concert band performance at Univ. of E London, the 21st annual concert of the Aminta Chamber Orchestra in Church of St Martin-in-the-Fields, London 2005; children's concerts and open-air symphony concerts; guest conductor, 'Cantus Firmus' Chamber Orchestra, Bulgarian Cultural Centre, Moscow 2004. *Honours:* Hon. DMus (Barbican Theatre, London) 2003. *Address:* 'Aminta', 12 Hurst Park, Midhurst, West Sussex GU29 0BP, England (home).

HOSOKAWA, Toshio; Composer and Pianist; b. 23 Oct. 1955, Hiroshima, Japan. *Education:* Berlin with Isang Yun and in Frieburg with Klaus Huber and Brian Ferneyhough. *Career:* Composer in residence at festivals in Geneva, London, Darmstadt, Seattle and Warsaw. *Compositions:* Manifestation for violin and piano, 1981; In Tal der Zeit for string quartet and piano, 1986; Ferne Landschaft I for orchestra, 1987; Flute concerto, 1988; Ave Maria, 1991; Hiroshima Requiem for voices and orchestra, 1988–92; Fragmente for wind quintet, 1989; Landscape for string quartet, 1992; Landscape II for harp and string quartet, 1993; Landscape III for orchestra, 1993; Super flumina Babylonis for soloists and orchestra, 1995; String Trio, 1996; Cello Concerto, 1997; Seascapes-Night for chorus and ensemble, 1997; Voyage I–III for ensemble, 1997; Cloudscapes-Moon Night for sho and accordion, 1998; Memory of the Sea, Hiroshima Symphony, 1998; Seascapes-Oita for orchestra, 1998; Piano Concerto 'Ans Meer', 1999; Silent Flowers for string quartet, 1999; Voiceless Voice in Hiroshima for chorus and orchestra, 2000. *Honours:* Berlin Philharmonic Centenary Prize, 1982. *Address:* c/o Documentation Centre for Modern Japanese music, 8-14 Azabudai I-chome, Minato-ku, Tokyo 106, Japan.

HOSSFELD, Christiane; Singer (Soprano); b. 2 March 1961, Schwerin, Germany. *Education:* Studied at the Hanns-Eisler Musikhochschule, Berlin, 1977–83. *Career:* Sang at Halberstadt from 1983, Dresden Staatsoper from 1986, notably as Zerbinetta, Gilda, Nannetta (Falstaff), Gretel, and Olympia in Les contes d'Hoffmann; Premiere of Meyer's Der goldene Topf, 1989, and Zemlinsky's Der Zwerg, 1993; Guest engagements at the Berlin Staatsoper and elsewhere; Bayreuth Festival, 1989–95, in Parsifal and Tannhäuser; Sang Zerlina and Papagena at Dresden, 2000; Many radio and television engagements. *Recordings include:* Die Lockende Flamme by Künneke. *Address:* Staatsoper Dresden, Theaterplatz 2, 01067 Dresden, Germany.

HOTEEV, Andrei; Pianist; b. 2 Dec. 1946, St Petersburg, Russia. *Education:* St Petersburg Conservatoire; Moscow Conservatoire under Lev Naumov. *Career:* Debut: Moscow, 1983, Rotterdam, 1990; Recitals: Shostakovich in Concertgebouw, Amsterdam, 1990; Prokofiev in Musikhalle, Hamburg, 1991; Hommage a Schnittke, Hamburg, 1992; Manuscript Version of Mussorgsky's Pictures at an Exhibition, 1st British Performance in Purcell Room, London, 1993; VARA Television Holland, Television St Petersburg, 1995; Interpreter, Manuscript, Tchaikovsky's 3rd Piano Concerto; Recital in Moscow, 1996, of the original versions of Tchaikovsky's 4 Piano Concertos. *Recordings:* Tchaikovsky Piano Concerto No. 3; All the Works of Tchaikovsky for Piano and Orchestra; Mussorgsky Pictures at an Exhibition–manuscript version; Boris Godunov Suite. *Contributions:* Fono Forum, 1998; Klassik Heute, 1998; Frankfurter Allgemein, 1999; Fanfare, 1999. *Current Management:* Colombia Artists, Luzern. Address Kapuzinerweg 7, 6006 Luzern, Switzerland.

HOU, Runyu; Orchestral Conductor; b. 6 Jan. 1945, Kunming, China; m. Su Jia Hou 1971, 1 s., 1 d. *Education:* Musical study at Middle School of Shanghai Conservatory and conducting at Shanghai Conservatory; Further study at Musikhochschule, Cologne, Germany and at the Mozarteum, Salzburg, Austria, 1981–85. *Career:* Debut: Kunming in 1954; Orchestral Conductor, 1977, Vice Music Director, 1986, Shanghai Symphony Orchestra; Guest Conductor for Rheinische Philharmonic, 1985, China Broadcasting Symphony Orchestra, 1988, China Central Philharmonic, 1988, and Hong Kong Philharmonic, 1988; Principal Conductor for Shanghai Symphony Orchestra, 1990, with debut at Carnegie Hall in New York in 1990 for the 100 years celebration of Carnegie Hall; mem, Chinese Musicians Association. *Honours:* Honorary Member, Richard Wagner-Verband, Cologne. *Current Management:* Konzertdirektion Drissen, International Artists' Management, Postfach 1666, 6500 Mainz, Germany. *Address:* 105 Hunan Road, Shanghai, People's Republic of China.

HOUGH, Stephen; Pianist; b. 22 Nov. 1961, Heswall, Cheshire, England. *Career:* Performances with many leading orchestras including: Chicago, Detroit, Toronto, Philadelphia and Baltimore Symphonies, Cleveland, New York and Los Angeles Philharmonics, Montreal, NHK Japan, Czech Philharmonic, all major British orchestras including London Symphony, Philharmonia, Royal and London Philharmonics, BBC Symphony, English Chamber; Numerous radio broadcasts, the United Kingdom and USA; Recitals and orchestral appearances throughout the United Kingdom, USA, Canada, Germany, France, Scandinavia, Switzerland, Spain, Italy, Netherlands, Australia and Far East; London Proms debut, 1985 and appeared annually until 2003; Appeared annually, Ravinia Festival, 1984–90, Blossom Festival, Mostly Mozart Festival, 1988, 1989, and 1996, Hollywood Bowl, annually, Edinburgh Festival; Mendelssohn Anniversary concerts at the 1997 Salzburg Festival; Mozart's Concerto No. 23 in A major at the London Proms, 2002. *Recordings:* 2 Hummel Piano concertos; 2 Mozart piano concertos; Music by Liszt and Schumann; Piano Albums 1 and 2; Brahms 1st and 2nd Piano Concertos; Britten Piano Music; Scharwenka and Sauer piano concertos; Solo piano music, Franck, York Bowen, Hummel,

Mompou; Complete Mendelssohn music for piano and orchestra with the CBSO (1997); New York Variations, 1998; Schubert Piano Sonatas, 1999; The New Piano Album, 1999; Clarinet trios of Brahms and Frühling, 1999; Liszt: Sonata and other works, 2000; Brahms F Minor Sonata and Ballades, 2001; Saint-Saens Complete Music for piano and orchestra; English Piano Album. *Publications:* Various vols of transcriptions and other works, Josef Weinberger Ltd, 1999–2001. *Honours:* Dayas Gold Medal, Royal Northern College of Music; Winner, Naumburg International Piano Competition; Best Concerto Record Award, Gramophone magazine, 1987, 1996, 1998; Fellow, Royal Northern College of Music, 1993; Gramophone Record of the Year, 1996; Deutsche Schallplatteupreis; Diapason d'Or; MacArthur Fellowship, 2001; Gramophone Record of the Year, 2002; mem. RAM 2002. *Current Management:* Harrison/Parrott Ltd, 12 Penzance Place, London, W11 4PA, England. *Telephone:* (20) 7229 9166. *Fax:* (20) 7221 5042. *E-mail:* shough@compuserve.com. *Website:* www.stephenhough.com.

HOVLAND, Egil; Composer and Organist; b. 18 Oct. 1924, Mysen, Norway. *Education:* Studied at Oslo Conservatory, 1946–49, with Holmboe in Copenhagen, Copland at Tanglewood and Dallapiccola in Florence. *Career:* Music critic and organist in Fredrikstad. *Compositions:* Church opera the Well, 1982; Ballets Dona Nobis Pacem, 1982; Den Heliga Dansen, 1982; Veni Creator Spiritus, 1984; Danses de la Mort, 1983; 3 Symphonies, 1953, 1955, 1970; Concertino for 3 trumpets and strings, 1955; Music for 10 instruments, 1957; Suite for flute and strings, 1959; Missa Vigilate, 1967; Mass to the Risen Christ, 1968; All Saints' Mass, 1970; The Most Beautiful Rose, after Hans Christian Andersen, 1972; Trombone Concerto, 1972; Missa Verbi, 1973; Violin Concerto, 1974; Piano Concerto, 1977; Tombeau de Bach for Orchestra, 1978; Pilgrim's Mass, 1982; Concerto for piccolo and strings, 1986; Chamber music including Piano Trio, 1965, 2 Wind Quintets, 1965, 1980, and String Quartet, 1981; Opera Captive and Free, 1993; Oboe Concerto, 1996; Viola Concerto, 1997. *Recordings include:* Works for Choir; Concertos: Trombone, Violin and Piccolo; Chamber works; (all for Norwegian Aurora). *Honours:* Knight of the Royal Order of St Olav, 1983. *Address:* c/o Labråten 14 C, 1614 Fredrikstad, Norway.

HOWARD, Ann; Opera Singer (Mezzo-soprano); b. 22 July 1936, Norwood, London, England; m. Keith Giles; one d. *Education:* Studied with Topliss Green and Rodolfo Lhombino; Special Grant, Royal Opera House Covent Garden, to study with Modesti, Paris, France. *Career:* Debut: As Czipra in Gypsy Baron at Sadler's Wells Opera, 1964; In various shows, chorus, Royal Opera House, Covent Garden; Principal, Sadler's Wells; Freelance appearances with English National Opera, National Opera, Scottish Opera, Welsh National Opera, Royal Opera House, Santa Fe Festival Opera, Canadian Opera Company, Metropolitan Opera New York, New York City Opera, Baltimore Opera, New Orleans Opera, Fort Worth Opera, Vienna State Opera, Performing Arts Center, New York State University; Many leading roles including Carmen, Amneris, Fricka, Brangaene, Dalila, Azucena, Cassandra, Grande Duchess, Hélène, Gingerbread Witch; Appearances in Mexico, Italy, Chile, Belgium, Portugal, France, Canada and USA; Regular broadcasts BBC, radio and television, Scottish Television; Marzellina, Marriage of Figaro, 1989; Step-mother, Into the Woods, Sondheim, 1990; Auntie, Peter Grimes; Prince Orlofsky, Die Fledermaus, ENO, 1992; Sang the Hostess in Boris Godunov for Opera North, 1992; Strauss Concerts at the 1993 London Proms; New York debut 1995, as Auntie; 2nd Official, The Doctor of Myddfai, Peter Maxwell Davies world premiere, Welsh National Opera, 1996; Emma Jones, Street Scene (Weill); Further roles include: Auntie in Peter Grimes, WNO, 1998–99; Performances in Aix-en-Provence Festival, and performances with Nederlands Opera. *Recordings:* Has made many recordings including the Witch in Hansel and Gretel; Old Lady in Candide, Scottish Opera. *Current Management:* Stafford Law Associates, Surrey. *Address:* 6 Barham Close, Weybridge, Surrey KT 13 9 PR, England.

HOWARD, Brian (Robert); Composer and Conductor; b. 3 Jan. 1951, Sydney, New South Wales, Australia. *Education:* BMus (Hons), University of Sydney, 1972; D.Mus, University of Melbourne, 1985; Composition studies with Peter Sculthorpe, Bernard Rands, Richard Meale and Maxwell Davies; Conducting with Neville Marriner and Michael Gielen, 1974–76. *Career:* Resident, Royal Danish Ballet 1980–81, State Opera of South Australia, 1989; Musical Director, Western Australia Ballet, 1983–85; Dean, WA Conservatory, 1992–95; Commissions from Festivals of Sydney and Perth, and from Opera Factory Zürich (1991), among others. *Compositions include:* A Fringe of Leaves, for chorus and orchestra, 1982; Metamorphosis, opera for 6 voices and chamber ensemble, 1983; The Rainbow Serpent, for ensemble, 1984; Fly Away Peter, for wind quintet, 1984; Sun and Steel, for string orchestra, 1986; The Celestial Mirror, for orchestra, 1987; Whitsunday, opera for 10 voices and chamber ensemble, 1988; Wildbird Dreaming for orchestra, 1988; The Enchanted Rainforest, musical, 1989; Masquerade, ballet, 1994; Wide Sargasso Sea, opera, 1996.

Recordings include: Sun and Steel, Chandos. *Address:* c/o APRA, 1A Eden Street, Crows Nest, NSW 2065, Australia.

HOWARD, Jason; Singer (baritone); b. 1960, Merthyr Tydfil, Wales. *Education:* Studied at Trinity College of Music and with Norman Bailey at the Royal College of Music (performances of the Ballad Singer in Paul Bunyan, 1988). *Career:* Gained early experience as Alfio, Blow's Adonis, Zurga, Don Giovanni and Sharpless; With Scottish Opera has sung Guglielmo, Don Giovanni, Germont and Figaro; Further engagements as Ned Keene for English National Opera, Billy Budd and Ezio in Attila for Opera North, and Ramiro in L'Heure Espagnole for Scottish Opera; Concert appearances in Carmina Burana, L'Enfance du Christ, Messiah, Fauré's Requiem, The Kingdom, Elijah and Haydn's Lord Nelson Mass; Other engagements include Rossini's Figaro and Eugene Onegin for Seattle Opera, 1992–93; Television showings in Scotland and Wales; Sang Marcello at Covent Garden, 1996; Germont at Cincinnati, 1998; Sang Puccini's Sharpless for Scottish Opera, 2000. *Recordings include:* Student Prince; Song of Norway; A Little Night Music. *Honours:* Ricordi Prize, Rowland Jones Award and Singing Faculty Award, TCM. *Current Management:* Askonas Holt Ltd, Lonsdale Chambers, 27 Chancery Lane, London, WC2A 1PF, England. *Telephone:* (20) 7400-1700. *Fax:* (20) 7400-1799. *E-mail:* info@askonasholt.co.uk. *Website:* www.askonasholt.co.uk.

HOWARD, Jeffrey John; Vocal Coach, Organist, Pianist, Conductor and Arranger; b. 19 March 1969, Cardiff, Wales; Rachael Jones 1992; two s. *Education:* piano studies, Welsh College of Music and Drama, 1983; BMus, Cardiff University, 1987; Advanced Organ studies, Royal Academy of Music, London, 1990. *Career:* accompanist to many male voice and mixed choirs; solo organist and pianist in recital and concert; appeared as accompanist on several recordings and television and radio work; foreign tours; Voice Coach at Welsh College of Music and Drama; has worked extensively with the Swansea Bach Choir, BBC Welsh Chorus, South Glamorgan Youth Choir and early music performances including the Orchestra of the Age of Enlightenment; performer on the Live Music Now scheme; Guest Artist-in-Residence at First United Methodist Church, Lubbock, Texas, USA, 1996–97; Visiting Professor of Organ, Texas Tech University, 1996–97; Repetiteur at WNO, 1999–; arranger for BBC's Songs of Praise; Repetiteur work on opera and music theatre; Royal Albert Hall solo debut in Shostakovich's 2nd Piano concerto, 2002. *Recordings:* several Christian recordings with Cambrensis (South Wales Baptist Choir) including Hymns, 1995; recording as Organist with Cor Meibion de Cymru, 1995; Bryn Terfel, organist with male voice choir and orchestra of the WNO; arranger for solo vocal albums with Royal Philharmonic Orchestra, 2000 and Budapest Symphony Orchestra, 2002. *Publications:* Kevin Mayhew–Welsh Folk Song Arrangements for flute and harp. *Honours:* Glynne Jones Prize for Organ, 1990; Michael Head Accompaniment Prize, 1991; Prizewinner, San Antonio Organ Competition, 1997. *Address:* 9 Clos Alyn, Pontprennau, Cardiff, CF23 8LB, Wales.

HOWARD, John (Stuart); Composer, Lecturer, Writer and Conductor; b. 22 Dec. 1950, Glasgow, Scotland; m. Ellen Jane Howard, 15 April 1974, 1 s., 1 d. *Education:* Ilford County High School; Junior Exhibitioner, Royal College of Music, 1965–69; BA, 1st Class Honours, University of Durham, 1969–72; PhD in Composition awarded, 1979. *Career:* School teaching, various posts; Senior Lecturer and Principal Lecturer, Kingston Polytechnic/University, 1979–92; Associate Professor and Head of Music, Nanyang Technological University, Singapore, 1993–; Honorary Senior Research Fellow, Kingston University, 1993–95; mem, PRS; ISME. *Compositions:* Dunstable Cantus for Piano, 1974; The Two Regions for Brass Band, 1976; Bubbles for Ever? for Flute, Clarinet, Violin and Cello, 1981; Games/End Game for Chinese Orchestra, 1983; Sonata for Brass Quintet, 1983; Fantasia and Dance, for Chinese Orchestra, 1985. *Publications:* Learning to Compose, Cambridge, 1990; Performing and Responding, Cambridge, 1995. *Contributions:* Various; Schools Council Magazine; Pears Encyclopedia; Music File, four articles, 1991–93; IJME, Reviewer; Proceedings of British-Swedish Ethnomusicology Conference, 1991. *Address:* Division of Music, National Institute of Education, Nanyang Technological University, 469 Bukit Timah Road, Singapore 259756.

HOWARD, Leslie (John); Pianist and Composer; b. 29 April 1948, Melbourne, Australia. *Education:* AMusA, 1962; LMus, 1966; BA, 1969; MA, Monash University, 1973 Piano Studies with June McLean, Donald Britton and Michael Brimer (Australia), Guido Agosti (Italy) and Noretta Conci (London). *Career:* Debut: Melbourne 1967; Staff, Monash University, 1970–73; Guildhall School of Music and Drama, London, 1987–92; Concertos with various orchestras in Australia, England, Europe, America, South America, Asia; Regular broadcasts as Pianist, Chamber Musician and Musicologist for BBC, ABC, RAI, and various American networks; Telecasts in the Americas, Australia and Southeast Asia; Council, Royal Philharmonic Society; Trustee, Geoffrey Parsons and Erich Vietheer Memorial Trusts; President, Liszt Society; Grainger Society; Prokofiev Foundation. *Compositions:* Fruits of the Earth, ballet;

Hreidar the Fool, opera; Prague Spring, opera; Sonatas for violin, clarinet, percussion, double bass horn, cello and piano; Piano Solo; Canzona for brass ensemble; Missi Sancti Petri, 1993; Songs; Motets; Trios, String Quartets. *Recordings:* Complete keyboard works of Grainger; Works by Franck, Rachmaninov, Glazunov, Rubinstein, Granados, Mozart, Beethoven, Tchaikovsky, Stravinsky;96 CDs of the works and transcriptions of Liszt. *Publications:* Edition of complete works of Liszt for cello and piano, 1992, and Piano Trio, 1993 and Violin and Piano 2003; A Liszt Catalogue, with Michael Short, 1993; Volumes of piano and Choral Music and Songs, 1999–. *Contributions:* Liszt Society Journal, on Liszt; Music and Musicians, on Grainger; Musical Opinion, on Liszt; Viking Opera Guide, on Liszt and Rachmaninov; Dubal's Hovowitz Symposium. *Honours:* Diploma d'Onore, Siena, 1972, Naples, 1976; Ferenc Liszt Medal of Honour, 1986; Liszt Grand Prix du Disque, Liszt Academy Budapest, 5 times; Ferenc Liszt Medal of Honour, Hungarian Republic, 1989; Member of the Order of Australia, 1999. *Current Management:* Michael Brownlee Walker, BW Associates. *Address:* 128 Norbury Crescent, Norbury, London SW16 4JZ, England.

HOWARD, Patricia; Writer; b. 18 Oct. 1937, Birmingham, England; m. David Louis Howard, 29 July 1960, 2 d. *Education:* BA, 1959, MA, 1963, Lady Margaret Hall, Oxford University; PhD, University of Surrey, 1974. *Career:* Lecturer, Tutor, Music, Open University, 1976–; Many broadcasts both on network and for Open University; mem, Royal Musical Association. *Publications:* Gluck and the Birth of Modern Opera, 1963; The Operas of Benjamin Britten: An Introduction, 1969; Haydn in London, 1980; Mozart's Marriage of Figaro, 1980; C W Gluck: Orfeo, 1981; Haydn's String Quartets, 1984; Beethoven's Eroica Symphony, 1984; Benjamin Britten: The Turn of The Screw, 1985; Christoph Willibald Gluck: A Guide to Research, 1987; Music in Vienna, 1790–1800, 1988; Beethoven's Fidelio, 1988; Music and the Enlightenment, 1992; Gluck: An eighteenth century portrait, 1995; Gluck's Orpheus Operas, 1997; From Composition to Performance: The String Family, 1998; The Solo Voice: Evidence for a Historical Investigation, 1998; In Defence of Modern Music and its Celebrated Performers, translation and critical edition of Vincenzo Manfredini, Difesa della musica moderna (1788), 2002; An introduction to gender studies: Mozart's operas and sonatas, 2002; Beethoven's Eighth Symphony; reception studies, 2002; The Turn of the Screw: analysis and interpretation, 2002. *Contributions:* Musical Times; Music and Letters; The Consort; The Listener; The Gramophone; Opera; ENO and Friends; Acta musicologica; Eighteenth-Century Fiction; Il Saggiatore musicale; Notes; Cambridge Opera Journal; The Opera Journal; Programme books for Covent Garden Opera, Glyndebourne Opera and The Barbican Centre. *Honours:* Susette Taylor Travelling Fellowship, 1971; Leverhulme Research Award, 1976; British Academy Research Award, 1988. *Address:* Stepping Stones, Gomshall, Surrey GU5 9 NZ, England.

HOWARD, Yvonne; Singer (mezzo-soprano); b. 1950, Staffordshire, England. *Education:* Studied at the Royal Northern College of Music. *Career:* Operatic appearances as Mozart's Marcellina with Glyndebourne Touring Opera, Cenerentola for English Touring Opera and Suzuki for Birmingham Music Theatre; Sang Fricka and Waltraute in The Ring of the Nibelungen, City of Birmingham Touring Opera; Season 1990–91 sang Mercedes at Covent Garden, and Meg Page in Falstaff for ENO; Sang Amastris in Xerxes, Meg Page and Maddalena in Rigoletto for ENO in 1992; Glyndebourne 1994, as Mrs Sedley in Peter Grimes; Royal Opera 1998, as Marcellina; Sang Meg Page for Opera North and in Rinaldo at Garsington, 2000; Concert engagements include Mozart's Requiem under Menuhin at Gstaad, Messiah with the Tokyo Philharmonic, Vivaldi's Gloria with the English Chamber Orchestra, Messiah with the Hallé Orchestra and Liverpool Philharmonic, De Falla's Three Cornered Hat at Festival Hall and with Ulster Orchestra; Song recitals include Wigmore Hall debut in 1989. *Honours:* Curtis Gold Medal, RNCM.

HOWARTH, Elgar; Conductor, Composer and Trumpeter; b. 4 Nov. 1935, Cannock, Staffordshire, England; m. Bridget Neary, 1 s., 1 d. *Education:* BMus, Manchester University; ARMCM, 1956, FRMCM, 1970, Royal Manchester College of Music. *Career:* Played in the orchestra of the Royal Opera House, Covent Garden, 1958–63; Royal Philharmonic Orchestra, 1963–69; Member, London Sinfonietta, 1968–71; Philip Jones Brass Ensemble, 1965–76; Freelance Conductor, 1970–; Conducted the premieres of Ligeti's Le Grand Macabre (Stockholm 1978) and Birtwistle's The Mask of Orpheus (London Coliseum 1986); Musical Adviser, Grimethorpe Colliery Brass Band, 1972–; Principal Guest Conductor, Opera North, 1985–88; Conducted the BBC Symphony Orchestra at the 1989 Promenade Concerts, in a programme of Bart ók, Birtwistle and Stravinsky; Conducted Le Grand Macabre at the Festival Hall, 1989; British professional premiere of Nielsen's Maskarade for Opera North, 1990; Premiere of Birtwistle's Gawain at Covent Garden, 1991; Premiere of Birtwistle's The Second Mrs Kong at Glyndebourne, 1994; Conducted Zimmermann's Die Soldaten for English National Opera, 1996; British premiere of Strauss's Die Aegyptische Helena at

Garsington, 1997; Die Liebe der Danaë 1999; British premiere production of Birtwistle's The Last Supper, 2000, Glyndebourne. *Recordings:* Maxwell Davies's Trumpet Concerto and Birtwistle's Endless Parade, 1991; Gawain, 1998. *Publications:* Various compositions for brass instruments and an arrangement of Mussorgsky's Pictures at an Exhibition for Brass Band. *Honours:* Doctor's degree, University of Central England, 1993; Fellow of the Royal Northern College of Music, 1994. *Current Management:* Allied Artists, 42 Montpelier Square, London, England. *Address:* 27 Cromwell Avenue, London N6, England.

HOWARTH, Judith; Singer (soprano); b. 11 Sept. 1962, Ipswich, Suffolk; m., 1 d. *Education:* Studied at the Royal Scottish Academy and at the Opera School; Further studies with Patricia Macmahon. *Career:* Debut: Mozart arias with the English Chamber Orchestra, 1984; Student roles included Donna Anna, Countess Almaviva, Pamina, Fiordiligi and Mimi; Covent Garden debut in 1985 as First Maid in Zemlinsky's Der Zwerg; Salzburg and Aix debuts in 1991 in Der Schauspieldirektor and as Susanna; US debut in Seattle in 1989 in a concert with Domingo and further collaborations with Domingo in Brussels and Amsterdam, televised; Promenade Concerts in 1991 in Dvořák's The Spectre's Bride; Appearances in Tony Palmer's films of Handel and Puccini and concerts in 1992 with Domingo at Hong Kong, Adelaide and Auckland; Sang Morgana in a new production of Handel's Alcina, at Covent Garden 1992–93, Beethoven's 9th at 1993 London Proms and Gilda in Rigoletto at Covent Garden; Has sung for Royal Opera, Opera North, Scottish Opera, with BBC Symphony and London Philharmonic Orchestras, City of Birmingham Symphony, and Huddersfield Choral Society among others; Other roles include Siebel, Barbarina (televised), Iris in Semele, Adele, Norina, the Woodbird in Siegfried and Marguerite de Valois; Sang Sophia in Philidor's Tom Jones at Drottningholm, 1995; Engaged as Donizetti's Marie, Geneva, 1998; Sang in Il Guarany by Gomes for Chelsea Open Group, 1998; Season 2000 as Mme. Mao in Nixon in China and Rossini's Fiorilla for ENO; Season 2003 as Violetta in Minneapolis and Christine (Intermezzo) at Santa Fe. *Recordings include:* Menotti's The Boy Who Grew Too Fast; Madama Butterfly under Sinopoli; Caractacus, 1992; Elgar's Light of Life, 1993. *Honours:* Lieder Prize, Governor's Recital Prize and the Margaret Dick Award at Royal Scottish Academy; John Noble Prize, 1984; Kathleen Ferrier Prize, 1985; Heinz Bursary for Young Singers at Covent Garden, 1985–87. *Current Management:* Askonas Holt Ltd, Lonsdale Chambers, 27 Chancery Lane, London, WC2A 1PF, England. *Telephone:* (20) 7400-1700. *Fax:* (20) 7400-1799. *E-mail:* info@askonasholt.co.uk. *Website:* www .askonasholt.co.uk.

HOWELL, Gwynne Richard, CBE, BSc, DipTP, MRTPI; British singer (bass); b. 13 June 1938, Gorseinon, Wales; m. Mary Edwina Morris 1968; two s. *Education:* Univ. of Wales, Manchester Univ., Manchester Royal College of Music with Gwilym Jones, studied with Otakar Kraus. *Career:* principal bass at Sadler's Wells, singing roles including Monterone and the Commendatore; Sang at Glyndebourne and Covent Garden in debut as First Nazarene in Salome, 1969–70; Metropolitan House debut in 1985 as Lodovico in Otello and Pogner in Die Meistersinger; Sang Gurnemanz in a new production of Parsifal at London Coliseum in 1986; Sang the Parson and the Badger in a new production of The Cunning Little Vixen in 1990 and sang the Fliedermonolog at the Reginald Goodall Memorial Concert in London, 1991; Sang at London Coliseum in 1992 as King Philip in a new production of Don Carlos, Daland at Covent Garden and Mozart's Bartolo on tour with the company to Japan; Sang Dikoy in Katya Kabanova at Covent Garden, 1997; Seneca in Poppea for WNO; Arkel in Pelléas et Mélisande at Glyndebourne and the London Proms, 1999; Sang in Martinů's Greek Passion, Covent Garden, 2000; Premiere of Turnage's The Silver Tassie for ENO and the Commendatore at Glyndebourne, 2000; Repertory includes Verdi and Mozart Requiems, and Missa Solemnis; Sings in Europe and USA and records for BBC and major recording companies; Other roles include the King in Aida, Mephisto in Damnation of Faust, High Priest in Nabucco, Hobson in Peter Grimes, and Sparafucile in Rigoletto. *Address:* 197 Fox Lane, London N13 4BB, England.

HOWELLS, Anne Elizabeth; Singer (mezzo-soprano); b. 12 Jan. 1941, Southport, Lancashire, England; m. 1st Ryland Davies; m. 2nd Stafford Dean; one s. one d. m. 3rd Peter R. Fyson. *Education:* Royal Northern Coll. of Music, Manchester with Frederik Cox; later study with Vera Rozsa. *Career:* debut, Manchester Coll. in 1963 in the British premiere of Gluck's Paride ed Helena; sang at Covent Garden from 1967 in roles including Rosina, Siebel in Faust, Ascanio in Benvenuto Cellini and Mélisande; sang Ophelia in the London premiere of Searle's Hamlet and Lena in the world premiere of Bennett's Victory; Glyndebourne Festival from 1967 as Erisbe in L'Ormindo, Dorabella, Minerva in Il Ritorno d'Ulisse, the Composer in Ariadne auf Naxos and as Cathleen in the 1970 premiere of The Rising of The Moon, by Maw; US debut in 1972 as Dorabella at Chicago; appearances with Scottish Opera, at the

Metropolitan Opera and with the Covent Garden Company at La Scala in 1976; Geneva Opera in 1987 as Régine in the premiere of La Fôret by Liebermann, Chicago Lyric Opera in 1989 as Orlofsky in Die Fledermaus and sang Magdalene in Die Meistersinger at Covent Garden in 1990; sang Adelaide in Arabella and Meg Page in Falstaff at the 1990 Glyndebourne Festival; Covent Garden in 1992 as Giulietta in Les Contes d'Hoffmann; Season 1992 with Despina at Covent Garden, and Weill's Begbick at Geneva; Prince Orlofsky in Die Fledermaus for Scottish Opera, 1997; Geneva 1998, as Prokofiev's Duenna; sang Mozart's Marcellina at Barcelona and Santa Fe, 2000. *Recordings include:* L'Ormindo; Der Rosenkavalier; Les Troyens.

HOWIE, Alan Crawford, MMus, PhD; Lecturer; b. 6 Nov. 1942, Stornoway, Scotland; m.; three c. *Education:* Coatbridge High School, Scotland, Royal Scottish Acad. of Music and Drama (junior student), Univ. of Edinburgh, Acad. of Music, Vienna, Univ. of Manchester. *Career:* Lecturer in Music at the Univ. of Manchester, especially on the 19th century and research in the music of Schubert and Bruckner; papers at international 19th-century music conferences, early 1980's–; Assoc. Ed., Bruckner Journal 1997–; Ed. of the Schubertian 2002–; mem. Royal Musical Asscn, Incorporated Soc. of Musicians, Internationales Franz Schubert Institut. *Publications:* Perspectrives on Anton Bruckner (ed. with Paul Hawkshaw and Timothy Jackson) 2001, Anton Bruckner: A Documentary Biography (two vols) 2002; contrib. to Music and Letters, Music Quarterly. *Address:* Department of Music, University of Manchester, Manchester, M13 9PL, England (office). *Telephone:* (161) 2754991 (office). *Fax:* (161) 2754994 (office). *E-mail:* crawford.howie@man.ac.uk (office).

HOWLETT, Neil (Baillie); Singer (Baritone); b. 24 July 1934, Mitcham, Surrey, England; m. Elizabeth Robson, 2 d. *Education:* MA (Cantab); St Paul's Cathedral Choir School; King's College, Cambridge; Hochschule für Musik, Stuttgart. *Career:* Debut: In the world premiere of Britten's Curlew River at Aldeburgh in 1964; Major roles with Sadler's Wells, English Opera Group, Royal Opera House, Covent Garden, Hamburg, Bremen, Nantes, Bordeaux, Toulouse, Nice, and Marseille; Principal Baritone for English National Opera, London; Has sung most major baritone roles; Sang title roles in the premieres of Blake's Toussaint and Crosse's The Story of Vasco; Appearances at most major festivals; Sang Hector in King Priam with the Royal Opera at Athens in 1985 and Amfortas in Buenos Aires in 1986; Sang Scarpia in Tosca with English National Opera, 1987–90; Holland Festival in 1990 as Ruprecht in Prokofiev's The Fiery Angel; Faninal in Der Rosenkavalier at Catania, 1992; Wotan in Das Rheingold and Die Walküre at Leicester, 1998–99; Other roles include Golaud in Pelléas, King Fisher in The Midsummer Marriage and Wagner's Dutchman; Recitalist, teacher and regular broadcaster; Professor at Guildhall School of Music. *Honours:* Kathleen Ferrier Memorial Prize. *Current Management:* Ingpen & Williams Ltd, 7 St George's Court, 131 Putney Bridge Road, London, SW15 2PA, England. *Address:* c/o English National Opera, London Coliseum, St Martin's Lane, London, WC2N 4ES, England.

HOYLAND, Vic, DPhil; British composer; b. 11 Dec. 1945, Wombwell, Yorkshire, England. *Education:* University of Hull, York University with Robert Sherlaw Johnson and Bernard Rands. *Career:* Hayward Fellow in Music, University of Birmingham, 1980–83; Visiting Lecturer at York University, 1984 and Lecturer 1985–93, Senior Lecturer, 1993–98, Reader in Composition, 1998–, the Barber Institute for Fine Arts, University of Birmingham; Founder Member and Co-Director of the Northern Music Theatre; Compositions have been featured at the Aldeburgh, Bath, Holland and California Contemporary Music Festivals; Survey of works at the 1985 Musica Concert Series in London; Commissions from the Northern Music Theatre, the Essex Youth Orchestra, New MacNaghten Concerts, Musica, the Barber Institute, BBC Promenade series, BCMG, Southbank Summerscope, Huddersfield Festival, Almeida Festival, York and Cheltenham Festivals. *Compositions include:* Em for 24 voices, 1970; Jeux-Theme for mezzo and ensemble, 1972; Esem for double-bass and ensemble, 1975; Xingu, music theatre, 1979; Reel for double-reed instruments, 1980; Michelagniolo for male voices and large ensemble, 1980; Quartet Movement, 1982; Head And Two Tails, 3 pieces for voice(s) and ensemble, 1984; String Quartet, 1985; Seneca/Medea for voices and ensemble, 1985; In Transit for orchestra, 1987; Work-Out for trombone, 1987; Work-Out for marimba, 1988; Trio, 1990; The Other Side Of The Air for Rolf Hind, piano solo, 1991; In Memoriam P.P.P., 1992; Piano Quintet, 1992; Concerto for pianoforte ensemble, 1993; String Quartet No. 3, Bagatelles, 1994; Vixen, large scale work for full orchestra, 1997; QIBTI, full orchestra, 2002; Phoenix, full orchestra, 2003. *Address:* c/o University of York Music Press Ltd, Department of Music, University of York, Heslington, York YO1 5DD, England.

HOYLE, Ted; Cellist; b. 17 Aug. 1942, Huntsville, Alabama, USA. *Education:* BMus, Eastman School of Music; MMus, Yale University; DMA, Manhattan School of Music, 1981; Studied with André Navarra, Ecole Normale de Musique, Paris, France. *Career:* Cellist, Kohon

Quartet; Professor of Music, Kean University, New Jersey; Cellist, Performing Arts Trio, New Jersey; Co-Director, Hear America First, Manhattan concert series, 1978–81; mem, Violoncello Society; American String Teachers' Association. *Compositions:* Edited works by Bach, Schumann, Scriabin for Belwin Mills. *Recordings:* A number with the Kohon Quartet including: String quartets by Walter Piston, Peter Mennin, Charles Ives, William Schuman, Aaron Copland, Julia Smith, Roger Sessions and Penderecki; Quartet of Joseph Fennimore; Quintet of Robert Baksa; Trio Sonatas of J. S. Bach, G F Handel, G Telemann. *Address:* 276 Riverside Drive, New York, NY 10025, USA.

HRUBA-FREIBERGER, Venceslava; Singer (soprano); b. 28 Sept. 1945, Dublocive, Czechoslovakia. *Education:* studied in Prague. *Career:* debut, Prague National Theatre, 1969, in Wranitsky's Oberon; sang at Pilzen Opera, 1970–72, Leipzig Opera, 1972–88; roles have included Verdi's Gilda, Mozart's Constanze and Queen of Night, Lucia di Lammermoor, Janáček's Vixen, Violetta, and Glinka's Lyudmila; Guest appearances at the Aix Festival, 1982, Nice and Prague; Staatsoper Berlin from 1987; Concerts in Austria, Spain, England, Poland and Japan. *Recordings include:* Bach's The Choice of Hercules; C. P. Bach's Magnificat, Handel's L'Allegro ed il Pensieroso and Mozart's Apollo et Hyacinthus. *Address:* c/o Staatsoper Berlin, Unter den Linden 7, 1060 Berlin, Germany.

HSU, John T.; Professor of Music and Performer on Cello, Viola da gamba, and Baryton; b. 21 April 1931, Swatow, China; m. Martha Russell, 31 July 1968. *Education:* BMus 1953, MMus 1955, New England Conservatory of Music. *Career:* Teacher, 1955–; Fellow, Cornell Society for the Humanities, 1971–72; Instructor, 1955–58; Professorial Staff, 1958–76; Chairman, Department of Music, 1966–71; Artist-Faculty, Aston Magna Foundation, 1973–90; Old Dominion Professor of Music and Humanities, Cornell University, Ithaca, New York, 1976–; Barytonist, Haydn Baryton Trio, 1982–; Artist-in-Residence, University of California, Davis, 1983; Regents Lecturer in Music, University of California, Santa Cruz, 1985; Viola da gamba Recitalist, including radio broadcast, in North America and Europe; Director, Aston Magna Performance Practice Institute, 1986–90; Artistic Director, Aston Magna Foundation for Music and the Humanities, 1987–90; Music Director and Conductor, Apollo Ensemble, 1991–; John Hsu in a course in French Baroqua Viol Playing, presented by The Viola da gamba Society of America. *Recordings include:* Pièces de Viole, by Louis de Caix d'Hervelois and Antoine Forqueray, Belgium, 1966; 3 Gamba Sonatas, by J. S. Bach, Germany, 1971; First complete recording of the 5 suites for viola da gamba by Antoine Forqueray, 1972; Pièces de viole by Maria Marais, 1973–76; Pièces de viole, by Charles Dollé and Jacques Morel, 1978; 2 vols of Baryton Trios by Joseph Haydn, London, 1988–89; Apollo Ensemble and John Hsu, Conductor; 3 vols of Symphonies by Joseph Haydn, USA, 1993–99; Baryton Trios by Haydn, 1996; Apollo Ensemble and John Hsu, conductor, Symphonies by Joseph Haydn. *Publications:* Editor, The Instrumental Works, by Marin Marais (1656–1728), Vol. I, 1980, Vol. II, 1987, Vol. III, 1995, Vol. IV, 1998, Vol. V, 2000, Vol. VI, 2001, Vol. VII, 2002; A Handbook of French Baroque Viol Technique, 1981. *Contributions:* Early Music, 1978. *Honours:* Doctor of Music, New England Conservatory of Music, 1971; Doctor of Arts, Ramapo College of New Jersey, 1986; Chevalier de l'Ordre des Arts et des Lettres, France, 2000. *Address:* 402 Hanshaw Road, Ithaca, NY 14850, USA.

HSU, Ya-Ming, DipMus, MA, DMus; Taiwanese composer; b. 5 Feb. 1963; m. Wen-Chi Lin 1994; one s. one d. *Education:* National Taipei Teachers' College, Tunghi University, Boston University, USA. *Career:* debut aged 17, received First Prize in Taiwan Composition Competition, Taiwan Educational Ministry; Lecturer, Chinese Culture University; Head of Chinese Music Talent Development Association; mem, ASCAP; Asian Composer League; National Association of Composers, USA. *Compositions:* Two Romantic Suites, Arts Trio commission, 1994; The Joyful News from Heaven, 1995; Bright be the Place of Thy Soul, 1997; Wind-Color, China Found Music Ensemble commission, 1998; A Tone Poem for Baritone, Chorus and String Quartet, Chinese Choral Society of Rochester commission, 1998; Four Choral Music, 1998; Snowing in June, 1999; Taiwan Mass, Taipei Philharmonic Chorus commission, 2000; Elegy, Arts Trio Taipei commission, 2000; Elegy for cello and piano, 2003; Twelve preludes for piano, 2003. *Recordings:* Snowing in June, Taipei Philharmonic Chamber Choir, 1999. *Publications:* Four Choral Music, 1998. *Honours:* Several Prizes, Taiwan Educational Ministry, Provincial Music Association, Chung Hwa Rotary Educational Association, National Taipei Teachers' College, Taipei International Community Cultural Association; Best Composition, The Golden Melody Award, 2000. *Address:* 2F, Nr 10 51st Alleyway, 102 Lane, Shei-fu Road, Tamshui, Taipei County, Taiwan. *Telephone:* (2) 26263274. *Fax:* (2) 26215713. *E-mail:* taiwanmass@yahoo.com.

HUA, Lin; Composer and Professor; b. 8 Aug. 1942, Shanghai, China. *Education:* Shanghai Conservatory of Music, piano and composition with Sang Tong, Wang Jianzhong and Chen Mingzhi. *Career:* composer for Shanghai Wind Band 1967–76, Shanghai Opera and Ballet House 1976–79; Assoc. Prof., Counterpoint, Fugue, Shanghai Conservatory of Music 1979–; consultant, Shanghai Philharmonic Asscn 1982–. *Compositions include:* Bright Mountain Flowers In Full Bloom, ballet, 1976; Fantasy for piano and accordion, 1978; Love of The Great Wall for piano and accordion, 1978; Farewell Refrains At Yang Gate Pass for piano quartet, 1978; Beauty of Peking Opera for string quartet, 1979; Album of Woodcuts for piano quintet, 1979; Amid Flowers Beside a River Under the Spring Moon for 4 harps, 1979; Flower and Song, concertino for soprano and orchestra, 1980; Suite Tragedy for chamber symphony, 1988; 24 Preludes and fugues on reading Sikong Tu's Shipin (Personalities of Poetry in Tang Dynasty), 1990; Album of World Folk Songs for piano, 1991; stage, film and television music. *Publications:* Guide the Teaching of Polyphony by Using Creative Psychology 1980, Stravinsky Techniques in Polyphonic Writing 1987, The Sense of Ugliness and its Application in Western Music 1988, Abstraction of Art and Abstractionism 1989, Course of Polyphone 1994, The Pilgrimage to Music 1995, Talk on Music 1998, 101 World Folk Songs 1998. *Address:* 20 Fenyang Road, Shanghai, People's Republic of China.

HUANG, An-Lun, MMus; Composer; b. 15 March 1949, Canton, China; m. Ruili Ouyang 1974, one s. *Education:* Conservatory of Music, Beijing, Trinity Coll., London, Yale Univ. *Career:* Composer-in-Residence, Central Opera House of China, Beijing 1976–; freelance composer 1980–; major stage, film, television and radio appearances; mem. Canadian Chinese Music Soc. of Ontario (pres. 1987–). *Compositions:* two grand operas, six grand opera scores, one musical, three ballets, four film scores and over 20 orchestral works, two oratorios as well as chamber, electronic, incidental, choral and vocal music. *Recordings include:* Piano Concerto in G, 1988; Selections from the ballet, Dream Of Dunhuang for orchestra, 1990; Poem For Dance for piano solo, 1992; Chinese Rhapsody No. 2 for piano solo, 1992; The Special Orchestra Album, 1997. *Publications:* numerous music scores. *Honours:* Dream of Dunhuang selected one of the Masterpieces of Chinese Music in the 20th Century 1993. *Address:* 15 Carlton Road, Markham, ON L3R 1Z3, Canada.

HUANG, Zhun; Composer; b. 25 June 1926, Huang Yan County, Zhe Jang Province, China. *Education:* Studied with composer Xian Xinghai and others. *Career:* Singer, mezzo-soprano, 1941–42; Composer, Peking Film Studio, 1949–51; Composer and music director at Shanghai Film Studio, 1951–87; mem, Standing Committee of Chinese Musicians Association; Vice-Chairman of China Film Music Society; Committee of Shanghai Artists Association; Standing Committee of Chinese Music Copyright Society. *Compositions:* Over 40 film scores which include Old Man and Nymph, 1956; Red Women Soldiers, 1960; Sisters on Stage, 1964; Horsekeeper, 1982; Numerous television music and songs. *Publications:* Selected songs of Huang Zhun; Life and Melodies; Music and My Life. *Honours:* The theme song for Red Women Soldiers, chosen as one of the 20th century masterpieces of Chinese Music, 1989; Winner, 50th anniversary of Chinese television and films music prize, 1999. *Address:* Apmt 9C, 34 Fu Xing Xi Lu, Shanghai 200031, People's Republic of China.

HUANGLONG, Pan; Composer; b. 9 Sept. 1945, Puli, Taiwan. *Education:* National Taiwan University, 1967–71; Studies with Ulrich Lehmann in Zürich, 1974–76, and Helmut Lachenmann in Hanover, 1976–78; Berlin Hochschule der Kunste with Isang Yun, 1978–80. *Career:* Professor at National Institute of Arts in Taipei, 1981–; Founded Modern Music Centre, 1984; Co-founded Taiwan branch of ISCM, 1989. *Compositions:* Night-Mooring near a Maple Bridge, for orchestra, 1974; Bird's Eye View for marimba and vibraphone, 1977; Metempsychose for 5 solo strings and orchestra, 1977; String Quartet, 1977; Paradise for orchestra 1978; Enlightenment for ensemble, 1979; Clarinet Quartet, 1980; 2nd String Quartet, 1981; Series: Expelling Yearnings, 1975–76; Elements of Change, 1979–86; Kaleidoscope, 1986–95; Formosa Land-scape, 1987–95; Labyrinth Promenade, 1988–98; Ying-Yong, 1992–95; Cello Concerto, 1997; Concerto for cello and 3 instruments, 1997; Totem and Taboo for 6 percussion, 1997; East and West, for ensemble, 1998; Solo I for harpsichord, 1998. *Address:* c/o CHA, 2nd Floor, No. 7 Ching Dao East Road, Taipei, Taiwan.

HUBER, Klaus; Composer; b. 30 Nov. 1924, Berne, Switzerland. *Education:* Studied at the Zürich Conservatory 1947–49 with Stefi Geyer and Willy Burkhard; Further study with Boris Blacher in Berlin. *Career:* Taught violin at the Zürich Conservatory from 1950; Lucerne Conservatory 1960–63; Basle Music Academy from 1961. *Compositions:* Orchestral: Invention und Choral, 1956; Litania instrumentalis, 1957; Terzen-Studie, 1958; Alveare vernat, 1967; James Joyce Chamber Music, 1967; Tenebrae, 1967; Tempora for violin and orchestra, 1970; Turna, 1974; Zwischenspiel, 1986; Lamentationes, 1994; Choral: Quem terra, 1955; Das Te Deum Laudamus Deutsch, 1956; Antiphonische Kantate, 1956; Soliloquia, 1959–64; Cuius legibus rotantur poli, 1960; Musik zu eines Johannes-der-Taufer Gottesdienst, 1965; Kleine Deutsche Messe, 1969;... inwendig voller figur... after the Apocalypse

and Durer, 1971; Hiob xix, 1971; Vocal: Abendkantate, 1952; Kleine Tauf Kantate für Christof, 1952; 6 Kleine Vokalisen, 1955; Der Abend ist mein Buch, 1955; Oratorio Mechtildis, 1957; Des Engls Anredung an der Seele, 1957; Auf die ruhige Nacht-Zeit, 1958; Askese, 1966; Psalm of Christ, 1967; Grabschrift, 1967; Der Mensch, 1968; Traumgesicht, 1968;... ausgespant..., 1972; Jot oder Wann kommt der Herr zuruck, opera, 1973; Im Pardies, opera pieces, 1975; A Prayer on a Prayer for women's voices and ensemble, 1996; Umkehr–im Licht Sein for mezzo, chorus and ensemble, 1997; Instrumental: Ciacona for organ, 1954; Concerto per la camerata, 1955; In Memoriam Willy Burkhard for organ, 1955; Partita, 1955; Noctes intelligibis lucis for oboe and harpsichord, 1961; Moteti-Cantiones for string quartet, 1963; 6 Miniaturen, 1963; In te Domine spervai for organ, 1964; Sabeth, 1967; Ascensus for flute, cello and piano, 1969; 3 kleine Meditationen for string trio and harp, 1969; Ein Hauch von Unzeit I–III, 1972; Chamber Concerto for piano and ensemble, 1994; Ecce homines for string quintet, 1998; L'ombre de notre âge for ensemble, 1999. *Honours:* First Prize at the 1959 ISCM Competition, Rome (for Die Engels Anredung an die Seele); Arnold Bax Society Medal, 1962; Beethoven Prize of Bonn, 1970 (for Tenebrae). *Address:* c/o SUISA, Bellariastrasse 82, CH–8038 Zürich, Switzerland.

HUBER, Nicolaus A.; Composer; b. 15 Dec. 1939, Passau, Germany. *Education:* Studied in Munich with Gunter Bialas, at Darmstadt with Stockhausen and in Venice with Luigi Nono. *Career:* Professor at the Folkwanghochschule, Essen, from 1974. *Compositions include:* Spär-enmusik, for orchestra, 1981; 6 Bagatellen, for 10 instruments and tape, 1981; Nocturnes, for orchestra, 1984; La force du vestige, for ensemble, 1985; Vier Stücke, for orchestra and tape, 1986; Doubles, mit einem beweglichkmen ton, for string quartet, 1987; Clash Music, for cymbals, 1988; Tote Metren, for baritone and ensemble, 1989; Off enes Fragment, for soprano and ensemble, 1991; First Play Mozart, for flute, 1993; En face d'en face, for orchestra and tape, 1994; Disappearances, for piano, 1995; Sein als Einspruch, for 8 solo voices, 1997;... in die Stille, for cello, 1998; Covered with Music, for soprano and ensemble, 1998; Ach, des Erhabene... beträubte Fragmente, for double chorus, 1999; Mixed Media works, including Eröffnung und Zertrümmerung, for ensemble and tape, 1992. *Address:* c/o German Music Information Centre, Weber Strasse, 59, 53113 Bonn, Germany.

HUBERMAN, Lina; Violinist; b. 1955, Moscow, Russia. *Education:* Studied at Moscow Conservatoire with Yanketevich. *Career:* Member of the Prokofiev Quartet, founded at the Moscow Festival of World Youth and the International Quartet Competition at Budapest; Many concerts in the former Soviet Union and on tour to Czechoslovakia, Germany, Australia, the USA, Canada, Spain, Japan and Italy; Repertoire includes works by Haydn, Mozart, Beethoven, Schubert, Debussy, Ravel, Tchaikovsky, Bart ók and Shostakovich. *Current Management:* Sonata, Glasgow, Scotland. *Address:* c/o Prokofiev Quartet, 11 North-gate Street, Glasgow G20 7AA, Scotland.

HUDECEK, Vaclav; Violinist; b. 7 June 1952, Rozmital, Czechoslovakia; m. Eva Trejtnarova, 8 Feb 1977. *Education:* Academy of Music Prague and private lessons for 4 years with David Oistrakh in Moscow. *Career:* Debut: With Royal Philharmonic Orchestra in London, 1967; Concert tours in Europe, Japan and USA since London debut, and tours in Europe, USA, Japan and Australia; Soloist with Czech Philharmonic Orchestra, 1983; mem, Central Committee, Union of Czech Composers and Concert Artists; Association of Czech Musicians. *Recordings:* Most of the world violin repertoire. *Honours:* Artist of Merit of Czechoslovakia, 1980; Record of the Year in 1992 for Vivaldi's Four Seasons and Best Selling Record of Czechoslovakia. *Current Management:* Dr Raab-Dr Böhm Künstleragentur, Plankengasse 7, 1010 Vienna, Austria. *Address:* Londynskà 83, 120 00 Prague 2, Czech Republic.

HUDSON, Benjamin; Violinist; b. 14 June 1950, Decatur, Illinois, USA. *Education:* Studied in New York. *Career:* Co-founded the Schoenberg String Quartet in 1977 becoming Columbia String Quartet in 1978; Has performed many modern works including the premieres of Charles Wuorinen's Archangel in 1978 with trombonist, David Taylor, and 2nd String Quartet in 1980, Berg's Lyric Suite in its version with soprano, Bethany Beardslee, New York, 1979, and Roussakis' Ephemeris in 1979; Further premieres include quartets by Morton Feldman in 1980, Wayne Peterson in 1984 and Larry Bell in 1985. *Recordings include:* String Quartet No. 3 by Lukas Foss and Ned Rorem's Mourning Song with baritone, William Parker. *Honours:* National Endowment of The Arts Grants, 1979–81.

HUDSON, John; Singer (Tenor); b. 1967, Barnsley, Yorkshire, England. *Education:* Studied at the Guildhall School with Laura Sarti; Further study with Josephine Veasey. *Career:* Debut: English National Opera, as Verdi's Macduff, 1993; Seasom 1993–94 with ENO as Rodolfo, Nadir in The Pearl Fishers and Don Ottavio; Alfredo in La Traviata for Welsh National Opera and for Auckland Opera, New Zealand; Concerts include Beethoven's Ninth at the Barbican and in Paris, Messiah in

Ottawa with Trevor Pinnock and Mozart's Requiem with the English Chamber Orchestra; 50th Anniversary Concert with ENO and television appearance with Lesley Garrett in Viva la Diva, on BBC 2; Season 1996–97 as Alfredo and Nadir with ENO; Season 1998 as Des Grieux in Manon and Robert Dudley in Mary Stuart, for ENO. *Current Management:* Ingpen & Williams Ltd, 7 St George's Court, 131 Putney Bridge Road, London, SW15 2PA, England.

HUDSON, Paul; Singer (Bass); b. 24 June 1946, Barnsley, England. *Education:* Studied at the Royal College of Music and the London Opera Centre. *Career:* Debut: Sadler's Wells Opera, 1969, in the premiere of Williamson's Lucky Peter's Journey; Many appearances with English National Opera and the Welsh National Opera, in works by Puccini, Britten and Wagner; Opera North, 1979, in Der fliegende Holländer and Peter Grimes; Guest appearances elsewhere in Baroque and contemporary music; Frequent concert engagements; Season 1998 as Rocco in Fidelio for English Touring Opera and Cacique in Il Guarany by Gomes for Chelsea Opera. *Recordings include:* Music by Stravinsky and La fanciulla del West; Laertes in Hamlet by Thomas; Scenes from Gilbert and Sullivan. *Address:* c/o Alexander Management, 38 Lytton Grove, Putney, London SW15 2HB, England.

HUDSON, Richard; Stage Designer; b. 1954, Rhodesia (now Zimbabwe). *Education:* Wimbledon School of Art. *Career:* Designs for English National Opera include The Force of Destiny and The Marriage of Figaro; Premieres of Judith Weir's A Night at the Chinese Opera (Kent Opera) and The Vanishing Bridegroom (Scottish Opera); Glyndebourne debut 1992, The Queen of Spades, followed by Eugene Onegin, the British stage premiere of Rossini's Ermione, and Manon Lescaut (1997); Die Meistersinger von Nurnberg at Covent Garden, 1993; Further engagements with I Puritani at La Fenice, Venice, The Rake's Progress for the Lyric Opera Chicago, Lucia di Lammermoor at Zürich and Munich, Rossini's L'Inganno felice at the Pesaro Festival; Samson et Dalila at the Metropolitan Opera, New York; The Rake's Progress at the Saito Kinen Festival, Japan; Ernani and Guillaume Tell at the Vienna Staatsoper, season 1997–98; Other designs for Manon (Opera North), Mary Stuart (Scottish Opera) Les Contes d'Hoffmann (Staatsoper, Vienna); Così fan tutte, (Glyndebourne), 1998; Season 2001–02 with Carlisle Floyd's Of Mice and Men at Bregenz, Houston and Washington; The Cunning Little Vixen for Opera North; Les Vêpres Siciliennes and Khovanschina in Paris; Tamerlano and Idomeneo in Florence; Benvenuto Cellini in Zürich; Peter Grimes in Amsterdam; Fellow, Royal Society of Arts; Royal Designer for Industry; British Scenography Commissioner to the Organisation Internationale des Scenographes, Techniciens et Architects de Théâtre (OISTAT). *Honours:* Laurence Olivier Award, 1988; Tony Award, 1998; Gold Medal for set design, Prague Quadreniale, 2003. *Address:* Judy Daish Associates, 2 St Charles Place, London W10 6EG, England.

HUEBER, Kurt (Anton); Composer and University Lecturer; b. 9 July 1928, Salzburg, Austria. *Education:* Diploma, Piano and Conducting, Musik Hochschule Mozarteum, Salzburg, 1948. *Career:* Section Leader, Konservatorium der Stadt Wien; Works performed in concerts and on radio; Teacher, Musical Acoustics, Hochschule für Musik, Vienna, 1980–93. *Compositions:* Scenic Music for Stage, Linz, 1958–60; Schwarz auf Weiss, 1st opera composed for Austrian television, 1968; Symchromie I, 1970; Symchromie II, 1972; Formant spectrale for string orchestra, 1974; Sonata for viola solo; Sonata for trumpet and piano; Opera, The Canterville Ghost (O Wilde), 1990–91; Dankos Herz, string quartet, 1992–93; Völuspa, 3 mythological scenes for violin and string orchestra; Maskenspiel de Genien (F v Herzmanovsky-Orlando), opera op 50, 1995–98. *Recordings:* Glockenspektren for pipe-bells and piano; Iris for piano and percussion; Horn und Tuba, Requiem for 4 Wagner-Tubas and Contrabass Tuba, 1977; Osiris Hymnus; Schein und Sein; 22 songs for Baritone and Piano; CD: Musik for Violoncello and Piano, 1994; CD: Trondheim Bläserquintett Hören über Grenzen, Wind Quintet op 10, 1995; CD: Neue Orgelmusik aus Skandanavien und Mitteleuropa, 1 Fantasie für Orgel op 1, 1996; CD: Vienna Classic and Modern, Völuspa Violinkonzert op 39, 1997; CD: Neue Musik Österreich 2 Ekmelische Musik (Balance) string quartet Dankos Herz op 37, 1998. *Publications:* Pseudoharmonische Partialtonreihen, ihre ekmelischen Intervallstrukturen, ein neuer Klangraum der Musiktheorie, Mikrotöne I; Mathematisch-physikalische Grundlagen einer ekmelischen Intervallehre, Mikrotone II, 1988; Ekmelische Harmonik, Mikrotone III, 1990; Nachbildung des Glockenklanges mit Hilfe von Röhrenglocken und Klavierklängen, Acustica vol. 26, 1972; Instrumentenbau Musik International, 1975; Various other professional publications. *Address:* 3712 Grübern 34, Nö, Austria.

HUFFSTODT, Karen; Singer (soprano); b. 31 Dec. 1954, Peru, Illinois, USA. *Education:* Studied at the Illinois Wesleyan and Northwestern Universities. *Career:* Sang with the New York City Opera from 1982 as Lehar's Merry Widow, Micaela, Violetta and Donna Anna; Santa Fe Opera in 1984 as the Soldier's Wife in the US premiere of Henze's We Come to The River, returning in 1989 as L'Ensoleillad in Massenet's

Chérubin; Other engagements with Chicago Opera as Magda in La Rondine and Fiordiligi, Illinois Opera in title role in Mary, Queen of Scots by Thea Musgrave, Washington Opera in the premiere of Menotti's Goya in 1986, Cologne Opera as Constanze, Agrippina, Donna Anna and Mozart's Countess, and Metropolitan Opera as Violetta and Rosalinda in season 1989–90; Other roles include Musetta at Los Angeles and Hamburg, Thais at Paris Opéra, Nancy and Toulouse, Amalia in I Masnadieri by Verdi for Australian Opera, Salome at Lyon, Agathe and Arabella at Catania, and Odabella in Attila for Opera North in 1990 and Covent Garden in 1991; Season 1992 as Tosca at Antwerp, Turandot at Lyon, and Chrysothemis at the Opéra Bastille Paris; Opened season at La Scala in 1993 as Spontini's Vestale; Sang Strauss's Ariadne at the Opéra Comique, Salome at the Bastille Opéra and Alice Ford at Antwerp in 1994; Season 1996–97 as Sieglinde at Covent Garden and Salome at San Francisco; Season 1998 as Elisabeth at Palermo, Isolde at Monte Carlo and Katerina Izmailova at Florence; Season 1999–2000 as Katerina Izmailova at Dresden, the Walküre Brünnhilde for Geneva Opera and Kundry in Washington. *Recordings include:* Salomé in a French language version of Strauss's opera. *Current Management:* Athole Still International Management, Forresters Hall, 25–27 Westow Street, London, SE19 3RY, England. *Telephone:* (20) 8771-5271. *Fax:* (20) 8768-6600. *Website:* www .atholestill.com.

HUFSCHMIDT, Wolfgang; Composer; b. 15 March 1934, Mülheim, Germany. *Education:* Studied church music and composition at Essen, 1954–58. *Career:* Church organist at Essen, 1954–68; Lecturer in composition, 1971–88, Folkwang Hochschule; Rektor, 1988–96. *Compositions include:* Mass, for soprano and chorus, 1961; Easter Story, 1964; Meissner Te Deum, 1968; Verwandlungen, for string quartet, 1969; Stephanus, mixed media, 1972; Solo, for violin, 1972; Agende for 4 choruses and ensemble, 1973; Trio, I–IV, 1970–95; We Shall Overcome for speaker, low voice, chorus and 9 instruments, 1984; Lieder ohne Worte, 24 Klavierstücke, with tape, 1986; Double Woodwind quintet 1989; an E for low voice and piano, 1995. *Honours:* Ruhr Prize, Mülheim, 1973. *Address:* c/o German Music Information Centre, Weber Strasse, 59, 53113 Bonn, Germany.

HUGGETT, Monica; Violinist; b. 16 May 1953, London, England. *Education:* Studied at the Royal Academy of Music with Manoug Parikian; Early performance practice with Sigiswald Kuijken, Gustav Leonhardt and Ton Koopman. *Career:* Co-founded the Amsterdam Baroque Orchestra with Koopman, 1980, and was its leader until 1987; Many performances on authentic gut-string violins with such ensembles as the Hanover Band, Academy of Ancient Music, Raglan Baroque Players and Hausmusik; World-wide tours as soloist, director and chamber musician in a repertoire extending from the late Renaissance to the Romantic with performances and recordings of Mozart, Beethoven, Schubert, Mendelssohn and the concertos of Vivaldi and Bach; Played the Beethoven Concerto with the Orchestra of the Age of Enlightenment under Ivan Fischer at the Queen Elizabeth Hall, April 1991; The Mendelssohn Concerto under Charles Mackerras, 1992; Professor of Baroque and Classical Violin at the Hochschule für Kunste in Bremen and Artistic Director of the Portland Baroque Orchestra, USA; Founded The Greate Consort, 1995. *Recordings include:* Symphonies by Beethoven with the Hanover Band (as director); Vivaldi La Stravaganza and Schubert Octet with the Academy of Ancient Music; Vivaldi La Cetra and Schubert Trout Quintet with the Raglan Baroque Players and Hausmusik; Rameau Pièces de Clavécin en Concerts and Corelli Violin Sonatas Op 5 with Trio Sonnerie and Vivaldi Four Seasons, Mozart Violin Concertos; Bach Violin Concertos with the Amsterdam Baroque Orchestra; Beethoven Concerto and Mendelssohn Concerto with the Orchestra of the Age of Enlightenment. *Address:* c/o Francesca McManus, 71 Priory Road, Kew Gardens, Surrey TW9 3 DH, England.

HUGH, Tim; Concert Cellist; b. 1965, England. *Education:* Studied at Yale and with William Pleeth and Jacqueline Du Pré. *Career:* Former solo cellist with the BBC Symphony Orchestra and joint principal with the London Symphony Orchestra; Many concerts with the Liverpool Philharmonic Orchestra, the Royal and BBC Philharmonics, Bournemouth Symphony Orchestra and Sinfonietta, and London Mozart Players; Appearances at the Leipzig Gewandhaus, La Scala Milan and Amsterdam Concertgebouw; Solo cello suites by Bach and Britten at 1994 Glasgow Mayfest, tour of the United Kingdom with the Polish State Philharmonic and engagements at Aldeburgh and the London Proms; Chamber music by Fauré and others with Domus and the Solomon Trio. *Recordings include:* Britten's Suites; Sonatas by Beethoven and Grieg with Yonty Solomon; CP Bach and Boccherini Concertos. *Honours:* Prizewinner at 1990 Tchaikovsky International Competition, Moscow. *Telephone:* (20) 7602-1416. *Fax:* (20) 7371-2726. *E-mail:* lisapeacock@aol.com.

HUGHES, Martin (Glyn); Pianist; b. 23 March 1950, Hemel Hempstead, England; 1 s., 1 d. *Education:* Salisbury Cathedral Choir School,

1960–63; Music Scholar, Bryanston School, 1963–66; Paris Conservatoire, France, 1966–67; Private study with Yvonne Lefebure, 1967–70; Moscow Conservatory, Russia, 1970–71. *Career:* Debut: Wigmore Hall, London, England, 1972; Proms, 1972; French radio and television, 1972; Cheltenham Festival, 1973; Making a Name, BBC television, 1974; Tour of USSR, 1974; RPO and London Symphony Orchestra debuts, 1975; Chichester and Llandaff Festivals, 1975; Recital and Concerto debut, Queen Elizabeth Hall, 1977; Tours and radio recitals, Portugal and Germany, 1977; Beethoven Sonata Cycle, 1979; regular Radio 3 broadcasts, solo appearances including: Royal Festival Hall, European tours, 1980–; Founder, 1984, Artistic Director of Music, Fens Festival and summer school, 1984, 1986; Fengate Music trust; Director, Annual Summer School, Val de Saire, France, 1988, 1989; Bath Festival, 1983, 1985, 1986; Member, Kreutzer Piano trio, 1985; Tours of USA, Israel, 1987–88; Study with Wilhelm Kempff, 1980; Professor, Hochschule für der Kunste, Berlin, Germany, 1991–; Tour of Japan, 1993; Guest teacher, Academy of Music, Bucharest, 1993, 1994, 1995. *Publications:* Russian School of Piano Playing, translation and editing, 1976. *Contributions:* Chapter in Performing Beethoven, 1994. *Honours:* Bronze Medal, Marguerite Long Competition, 1969; British Council Scholar, 1970–71; Arts Council of Great Britain Award, 1975; Honorary MMus, University of Surrey, 1991. *Address:* Leibnizstrasse 58, 10629 Berlin, Germany.

HUGHES, Owain Arwel, OBE; Conductor; b. 21 March 1942, Cardiff, Wales; m. Jean Bowen Lewis 1966; one s. one d. *Education:* Univ. Coll., Cardiff, Royal Coll. of Music with Adrian Boult and Harvey Philips, 1964–66, and with Kempe in London and Haitink in Amsterdam. *Career:* professional career from 1968; Music Dir, Royal National Eisteddfod of Wales, 1977, and Huddersfield Choral Society, 1980–86; Assoc. Conductor for BBC National Orchestra of Wales, 1980–, and Philharmonia Orchestra; Guest Conductor with WNO and ENO and with the BBC National Orchestra of Wales, and Hallé Orchestras (Mahler's Resurrection Symphony and Tippett's 4th Symphony in Manchester); concerts in the UK and abroad including Shostakovich's 10th and Leningrad Symphonies, the Verdi Requiem and Elgar's Violin Concerto with Itzhak Perlman; founded and became Artistic Dir of the Welsh Proms, 1986; series of programmes for BBC television, featuring settings of the Requiem Mass, 1987; Rossini's Stabat Mater in television for Holy Week, 1988; Mahler's 8th Symphony on Channel 4 television, 1990, and at the Royal Albert Hall, 2001; choral concert in Harrow School Speech Hall, 1999. *Recordings include:* Music by Paul Patterson with London Philharmonic, and by Delius and 2nd Symphony by Vaughan Williams; works with Hallé Orchestra and Huddersfield Choral Society. *Honours:* Hon. DMus, Univ. of Wales and from Council for National Academic Awards in London; Fellowship, Univ. Coll., Cardiff and from Polytechnic of Wales; Hon. Bard of Royal National Eisteddfod of Wales. *Current Management:* Hazard Chase, Norman House, Cambridge Place, Cambridge CB2 1NS, England. *Telephone:* (1223) 312400. *Fax:* (1223) 460827. *Website:* www.hazardchase.co.uk.

HULA, Pavel; Violinist; b. 23 Jan. 1952, Prague, Czechoslovakia; m. Helena Sirlova, 29 June 1976, one d. *Education:* Violin, 1970–74, and Chamber Music, 1980–82, Academy of Music Arts, Prague. *Career:* Debut: Prague Festival, Spring 1976; First Violin, Kocian Quartet, 1975–, with performances at over 2,500 concerts in 30 countries; Appearances on radio and television; Wigmore Hall debut, 1992; Artistic Director of Praga Camerata (String Orchestra) 2001–;. *Recordings:* Virtuoso Violin Duets; Mozart's String Quartets; Dvořák's String Quartets; Haydn: Quartets; Hindemith's String Quartets. *Honours:* 1st Prize, Kocian Violin Competition, 1963, 1964; 2nd Prize, Concertino Praga, Radio Competition, 1969; Prize, Society of Chamber Music of Czech Philharmonic, 1981; Grand Prix du Disque de l'Académie Charles Cross, Paris, 1997. *Address:* Secská 1875/11, 100 00 Prague 10, Czech Republic.

HULL, Eric; Conductor; b. 1967. *Education:* Vienna Hochschle für Musik. *Career:* Assistant at La Scala, Toronto Symphony, Florence and Salzburg Festivals; Opera and concerts with the Berlin Radio, Teatro San Carlo, Naples (Fioravanti's Le Cantatrici Villane), Teatro La Fenice, Genoa and Treviso; La Scala Milan from 1988, with the premiere of Donatoni's Il Vello Dissotto, La Clemenza di Tito, Iphigénie en Tauride and Pergolesi's Lo Frate 'nnamorato; Edition of Salieri's L'Europa Riconosciuta for La Scala; Belcanto Gala in Moscow, and engagements with the Milan Symphony and Monte Carlo Philharmonique; Modern premiere of Piccinni's L'Americano at Martina Franca, 1996. *Recordings include:* L'Americano Incivilito. *Address:* c/o Teatro alla Scala, Via Filodrammatici 2, 12112 Milan, Italy.

HULMANOVA, Stefania; Singer (Soprano); b. 20 Jan. 1920, Dolné Dubové, Czechoslovakia; m. Cyril Hulman, 23 Feb 1943, 2 s. *Education:* State Conservatory, Bratislava. *Career:* Debut: Sang Rusalka in Dvořák's Rusalka, State Theatre, Kosice, 1948; Soloist, Opera of the State Theatre, Kosice, 1948–51; Soloist, Opera of the Slovak National Theatre, Bratislava, 1952–79; Core repertoire: Julia in Jakobin by A

Dvořák, Marenka in The Bartered Bride, Vendulka in The Kiss by Smetana, Halka in Halka by Moniuszko, Santuzza in Cavalleria Rusticana by Mascagni, Countess in The Marriage of Figaro, Aida, Nella in Gianni Schicchi; Soloist, Opera of the Slovak National Theatre, Bratislava, 1952; Numerous other roles performed include Leonora in Trovatore, Elisabeth de Valois in Don Carlos, Desdemona in Otello, all by Verdi; Tosca; Guest Performances include The Whirlpool by Suchon at Dresden; Tosca, Moscow; Svätopluk, Perugia, Italy; Concert, Peking, China; Concert, Hanoi, Viet Nam; The Whirlpool, Budapest, Hungary; mem, Honorary Member, Opera of the Slovak National Theatre. *Address:* Ostravska 7, 811 04 Bratislava, Slovakia.

HUMBLET, Ans; Singer (Soprano); b. 17 Sept. 1957, Maastricht, Netherlands. *Education:* Studied with Elisabeth Ksoll and at Amsterdam. *Career:* Appearances with Netherlands Opera from 1983 and Wuppertal Opera, 1986–90 in such roles as the Queen of Night, Blondchen, Marie in Zar und Zimmermann, Woglinde, Despina and Musetta; Sang Kunigunde in the German premiere of Bernstein's Candide at Wuppertal in 1990; Enschede Holland in 1990 as Ninetta in Mozart's La Finta Giardiniera; Guest appearances at Düsseldorf and Aachen as the Queen of Night, and at Mönchengladbach as Frasquita in Carmen; Concert engagements in Beethoven's 9th, Mendelssohn's St Paul, Bruckner's Te Deum, Carmina Burana and Masses by Haydn and Mozart; Broadcasts in Netherlands, Germany and Belgium; Engaged at Maastricht from 1990. *Address:* De Nederlandse Opera, Waterlooplein 22, 1011 PG Amsterdam, Netherlands.

HUMPERT, Hans Ulrich; Composer; b. 9 Oct. 1940, Paderborn, Germany. *Education:* Studied at the Cologne Musikhochschule, with Petzold and Eimert; Darmstadt Courses, 1964, 1965, with Pierre Boulez and György Ligeti. *Career:* Co-founder, with Wolfgang Rihm and York Höller, of Gruppe 8, 1969; Performances of electronic music as percussionist and synthesizer, Professor of electronic composition at Cologne, 1972–; Commission for the KunstklangRaum, Gelsenkirchen, 1997. *Compositions include:* Clarinet Concerto, 1969, rev. 1980; Waves and Forms, 1971; Synesis, 1971; Das Ohr auf der Strasse, 1972; Electronic Maniac, 1973; Assonanzen, 1977; Approcia Petraca, 1985; Die Ehe der Andromache, 1991; Construction in MicroPolyGons 1994; Candide, radio play, 1995; KunstklangRaum 1997; Die Bandbrücke spricht, 1997; Strophen, flugelhn, 1998. *Address:* Elektronische Musik Studio, Musikhochschule Köln, Dagobnerstrasse 38, 50608 Cologne, Germany.

HUNKA, Pavlo; singer (bass); b. 7 April 1959, England. *Education:* Royal Northern College of Music with Joseph Ward. *Career:* has performed in concerts throughout the United Kingdom as soloist and conductor; Royal Albert Hall in London, 1988 in a concert celebrating 1000 years of Christianity in the Ukraine; Opera debut as Melisso in a 1989 production of Handel's Alcina at the RNCM; Has also sung Theseus in A Midsummer Night's Dream and Philip II in Don Carlos with the RNCM; Professional opera debut as Basilio in Il Barbiere di Siviglia with Welsh National Opera, 1990; Recent engagements as Rangoni in Boris Godunov for Basle Opera and Dulcamara in L'Elisir d'amore; Other roles include Colline in La Bohème and Prince Gremin in Eugene Onegin; Now on contract to Basel Stadttheater, Switzerland; Salzburg 1994–95, in Boris Godunov and Elektra, Bregenz Festival, 1995 as Pizarro; Bonn 1995–96, as Leporello and Tomsky in The Queen of Spades; Basle Opera 1996, as Rigoletto; Season 2000–01 as Verdi's Renato at Bregenz, Telramund in Munich, Wozzeck for Dallas Opera and Creon in Oedipus Rex at Naples; Weber's Euryanthe at the London Proms, 2002. *Honours:* Diploma with Distinction in Performance, RNCM, 1990; Ricordi Opera Prize; Peter Moores Foundation and Wolfson Foundation Scholarships. *Current Management:* Artists Management Zurich, Rütistrasse 52, 8044 Zürich-Gockhausen, Switzerland. *Telephone:* (1) 821 89 57. *Fax:* (1) 821 01 27. *Website:* www.artistsman.com.

HUNT, Alexandra, BA, BS; American opera and concert singer (soprano), librettist and libretto translator; b. 1940. *Education:* Vassar College, Juilliard School of Music, Sorbonne University, Paris, France. *Career:* debut as Marie in La Scala's first production of Wozzeck in German, 1971, conducted by Claudio Abbado; Sang title role of Lulu at Metropolitan Opera and Katya Kabanova sung in Czech, Janáček Festival, Brno; Jenůfa at Lincoln Center, NY; Soprano Soloist in Penderecki Passion According to St Luke, Philadelphia Orchestra; Amelia in Ballo in Maschera, Providence, RI, and Bucharest; Title role of Tosca in Bulgaria, Romania and Czechoslovakia; Sang Marie in Wozzeck at Hamburg Staatsoper; Lady Macbeth in Macbeth at Florentine Opera and Kentucky Opera; Soprano Soloist in Mahler's Fourth Symphony, Bogota Filarmonica; In Beethoven's Ninth Symphony, Omaha and Des Moines Symphonies; many other roles. *Recordings:* Songs of John Alden Carpenter, Charles T. Griffes and Edward MacDowell. *Publications:* New English Translation of Mozart's Don Giovanni and Così fan tutte. *Address:* 170 West 74th Street, Apt 1106, New York, NY 10023, USA.

HUNT, Fionnuala; Concert Violinist; b. 1960, Belfast, Northern Ireland. *Education:* Studied at Ulster College of Music, Royal College of Music and The Vienna Hochschule für Musik with Wolfgang Schneiderhan. *Career:* Leader and Soloist with the Vienna Chamber; Former member of the Bavarian State Opera Orchestra in Munich; Co-Leader of the RTE Symphony Orchestra in Dublin; Guest Leader of the Ulster Orchestra; Duo recitals with pianist sister, Una Hunt, performing throughout: Ireland; Austria; Germany; Czechoslovakia; Italy; The United Kingdom; Member of the Dublin Piano Trio; Solo appearances with: The National Symphony Orchestra of Ireland; The RTE Concert Orchestra; The Ulster Orchestra; Played Lutoslawski's Partita at the Maltings Concert Hall, Snape; Artistic Director and Leader of the Irish Chamber Orchestra. *Address:* c/o Owen and White Management, 14 Nightingale Lane, London, N8 7QU, England.

HUNT, Gordon; Oboist; b. 1950, London, England. *Education:* Studied with Terence MacDonagh at the Royal College of Music. *Career:* Principal Oboist with the Philharmonia Orchestra, formerly principal with the BBC National Orchestra of Wales and London Philharmonic Orchestra; Guest Oboist with the Berlin Philharmonic Orchestra and solo and chamber music appearances throughout Europe, USA and the Far East and in New Zealand; Played Bach's Double Concerto on 1994 world tour with Pinchas Zukerman and the ECO, 1994; Music Director of The Swedish Chamber Winds, 1991–97; Consultant Professor at the Royal Academy of Music; Principal Oboist with London Chamber Orchestra; Conducts and directs many orchestras and ensembles; Gives masterclasses in 4 continents. *Recordings include:* Works by Mozart, Malcolm Arnold, Vivaldi, Strauss and Haydn with English CO, London Philharmonic and Berlin Radio Orchestra; Recordings with London Chamber Orchestra. *Address:* c/o Royal Academy of Music, Marylebone Road, London, W1, England.

HUNT, Lorraine; Singer (Mezzo-soprano); b. 1 March 1954, San Francisco, USA. *Education:* Studied in San Francisco and began career as a violist. *Career:* Concert appearances include Krasa's Chamber Symphony with the Boston Symphony Orchestra, tour of Australia with the Australian CO, Dido and Aeneas with the Philharmonia Baroque, San Francisco, and L'Enfance du Christ under Roger Norrington, at the Paris Théâtre des Champs Elysées; Further concerts with the San Francisco, Houston, Boston and St Louis Symphonies; Mark Morris Dance Group, as singer, at the Adelaide, Edinburgh and Brooklyn Academy Festivals; Early opera appearances as Sextus in Giulio Cesare, Mozart's Donna Elvira, Octavia in Poppea and Handel's Serse, all directed by Peter Sellars; Season 1995–96 with Haydn's Scena di Berenice at Tanglewood, Charpentier's Médée with Les Arts Florissants in Europe and New York; Handel's Ariodante at the Göttingen Festival and Xerxes at the Los Angeles Music Center; Season 1996 with Irene in Handel's Theodora at Glyndebourne, the Berlioz Nuits d'Ete under Nicholas McGeegan, recitals with Dawn Upshaw in New York and tour of Europe with the Australian CO; Season 1996–97 with Sesto in Handel's Giulio Cesare and the title role in Carmen at the Paris Opéra Bastille, Massenet's Charlotte with the Opéra de Lyon; Further opera enagements in Vienna, Brussels, Lausanne, Aix, Amsterdam, Tokyo and Boston; Sang Handel's Serse with New York City Opera, 1997; Monteverdi's Ottavia at San Francisco, 1998; Sang Myrtle in the premiere of Harbison's The Great Gatsby, NY Met 1999; Premiere of El Niño by John Adams at the Paris Châtelet, 2000. *Recordings include:* Britten's Phaedra and Charpentier's Médée (Erato); Handel's Susanna, Theodora, Clori, Tirsi e Fileno, and Messiah, Purcell's Fairy Queen, Monteverdi's Ulisse (Harmonia Mundi); Videos of Peter Sellars productions of Don Giovanni (as Donna Elvira), Giulio Cesare (Sesto) and Theodora (Glyndebourne 1996). *Address:* c/o IMG Artists, 420 West 45th Street, New York, NY 10036-3503, USA.

HUNT, Michael; Stage Director; b. 1957, London, England. *Education:* Studied at Liverpool University. *Career:* Debut: Gounod's Mireille for Liverpool Grand Opera; Artistic Director of the Cheltenham Arts Centre from 1980, staging a number of plays and Così fan tutte; Directed the British premiere of Berwald's Queen of Golconda at Nottingham and The Rake's Progress at Cambridge; Staff Director at English National Opera, directing Aida and Orpheus in the Underworld, also Madama Butterfly for the Education Unit; Oedipus Rex for Opera North; Rossini's Tancredi at Las Palmas; Der Freischütz in an outdoor touring production; Oedipus Rex and Iolanthe for Scottish Opera; La Traviata for Dublin; Figaro for British Youth Opera; World Premieres of Giles Swayne's Le nozze di Cherubino and Harmonies of Hell; Artistic Director, Bloomsbury Festival; Director of Performing Arts, Riverside Studios in London; Teacher at The Royal Academy, Birmingham School of Music and various Drama Schools; In 1996 directed Puccini's La Bohème at the Royal Albert Hall. *Address:* Performing Arts, 6 Windmill Street, London W1P 1HF, England.

HUNZIKER, Bernhard; Singer (Tenor); b. 27 Aug. 1957, Thun, Switzerland. *Education:* Studied with Paul Lohmann in Wiesbaden, in Zürich with Irwin Gage, Munich with Ernst Haefliger and with Heather Harper and Peter Pears at Aldeburgh. *Career:* Zürich Opera Studio, 1987–88, Augsburg Opera, Athens Megaron, Lucerne, St Gall, including solo appearances; Has worked with conductors including: Jesus Lopes-Cobos, Marc Soustrot, K A Rickenbacher, Helmut Rilling, Yehudi Menuhin; Concert engagements in Switzerland, Austria, Italy, Germany and France, and several performances at the Israel Festival, Lucerne Festival, Opera Festival, Bad Hersfeld, Germany and Aldeburgh Festival; Repertory includes works from Monteverdi, Bach, Mozart, Schubert to Britten, masses and oratorios; President, European Voice Teachers Association, Swiss Section, 2001–. *Recordings include:* Musikalische Exequien by Schütz; CD, Swiss Lieder by Schoeck, Huber and others, 2001; Lieder Quartets by Swiss composers, Zürich Vocal Quartet; St John Passion, J. S. Bach. *Honours:* Promotion Prize, Migros Company, Zürich, 1983; Kiefer-Hablitzel-Prize, 1985; Prize, Swiss Musicians Association, 1987. *Address:* c/o Kirchgasse 15, 8001 Zürich, Switzerland. *E-mail:* hunziker.bretscher@bluewin.ch.

HURD, Michael John; Composer and Author; b. 19 Dec. 1928, Gloucester, England. *Education:* Pembroke Coll., Oxford. *Career:* Prof. of Theory, Royal Marines School of Music 1953–59; freelance composer and author 1959–. *Compositions include:* opera: Widow of Ephesus, 1971; The Aspern Papers, 1993; The Night of the Wedding, 1998; choral: Missa Brevis, 1966; Music's Praise, 1968; This Day to Man, 1974; Shepherd's Calendar, 1975; The Phoenix and the Turtle, 1975; Genesis, 1987; Night Songs of Edward Thomas, 1990; Five Spiritual Songs, 1996; Five Songs of Praise, 1999; orchestral: Sinfonia concertante, 1968; Dance Diversions, 1972; Concerto da Camera, 1987; Overture to Unwritten Comedy, 1987; chamber music: Flute Sonatina, 1964; Violin Sonata, 1987; various other works. *Publications include:* Immortal Hour: Life and Times of Rutland Boughton, 1962; Outline History of European Music, 1968; Ordeal of Ivor Gurney, 1978; Vincent Novello and Company, 1981; Rutland Boughton and the Glastonbury Festivals, 1993. *Contributions:* New Grove Dictionary of Music and Musicians; New Oxford Companion to Music; Athlone History of British Music; Musik in Geschichte und Gegenwart. *Address:* 4 Church Street, West Liss, Hampshire GU33 6JX, England.

HUREL, Philippe; Composer; b. 24 July 1955, Domfront, France. *Education:* Studied with Betsy Jolas at the Paris Conservatoire, Computer Science with Tristan Murail, 1984; Research at IRCAM, electronic music studios (Paris), 1985–90. *Compositions include:* Eolia, for flute, 1982; Trames, for strings, 1982; Memento pour Marc, for orchestra, 1983; Diamants imaginaire, diamant lunaire, for ensemble and electronics, 1986; Pour l'image, for 14 instruments, 1987; Fragment de lune, 1987; Mémoire vive, for orchestra, 1989; Remanences, for 14 instruments, 1992; La celebration des invisibles, shadow theatre, 1992; Leçon des choses, 1993; Pour Luigi, for ensemble, 1994, Kits, for 6 percussion instruments and double bass, 1996;......a mèsure, for flute and ensemble, 1997. *Honours:* Siemens Prize, Munich, 1995. *Address:* Centre de Musique Contemporaine, Cité de la Musique, 16 Place de la Fontaine, 75019 Paris, France.

HURFORD, Peter; Organist; b. 22 Nov. 1930, Minehead, England; m. Patricia Matthews, 6 Aug 1955, 2 s., 1 d. *Education:* Blundell's School 1944–8; Royal College of Music, 1948–49; ARCM; Organ Scholar, Jesus College, Cambridge, 1949–53; MA, Music and Law; BMus; FRCO; Commissioned Royal Signals, 1954–56. *Career:* Debut: Royal Festival Hall, London, 1956; Master of the Music, St Albans Cathedral, 1958–78; Concert tours of Europe, America, Canada, Australasia and Japan, 1958–98; Bach Organ Music Cycle 50th Edinburgh International Festival, 1997; Founder, St Albans International Organ Festival, 1963, Artistic Director, 1963–78, Honorary President, 1978–; Visiting Professor, Universities of Cincinnati, 1967–68 and Western Ontario, 1976–77; Visiting Artist in Residence, Sydney Opera House, 1980–82; Betts Fellow, University of Oxford, 1992–93; Radio and television appearances; Radio includes complete organ works of Bach in 34 programmes, 1980–82; Council, 1964–2003, President, 1980–82, Royal College of Organists; Member, Incorporated Society of Musicians; President, Incorporated Association of Organists, 1995–97. *Recordings include:* Complete Organ Works of J. S. Bach, F Couperin, Handel and Hindemith. *Publications:* Making Music on the Organ, 1988; Articles in Musical Times. *Honours:* FRSCM, 1977; Gramophone Award, 1979; D.Mus, Baldwin-Wallace College, Ohio, 1981; Honorary Member, RAM, 1982; O.B.E., 1984; FRCM, 1987; D.Mus, Bristol University, 1992. *Address:* Broom House, St Bernard's Road, St Albans, Hertfordshire AL 3 5 RA, England.

HURLEY, Laurel; Soprano; b. 14 Feb. 1927, Allentown, PA, USA. *Education:* Studied with her mother. *Career:* Debut: Sang in the Student Prince at New York in 1943; New York City Opera debut as Zerlina in 1952; Sang at the Metropolitan Opera from 1955 as Oscar, Musetta, Mimi, Adele, Susanna, Olympia, Papagena, Zerlina and Perichole; Also sang in I Capuleti e i Montecchi by Bellini; Many concert appearances in North America. *Address:* c/o Metropolitan Opera, Lincoln Center, New York, NY 10023, USA.

HURNÍK, Ilja; Composer, Pianist and Writer; b. 25 Nov. 1922, Ostrava, Czechoslovakia; m. Jana Hurnikova, 26 Mar 1966, 1 s. *Education:* Academy of Musical Arts, Prague. *Career:* Debut: As Composer, Piano Piece, 1933; As Pianist, Concert, Prague, 1942; Professor, Prague Conservatorium; As Pianist gave concerts in Europe and USA, including piano duo with wife Jana; Regular guest appearances on radio and television as composer, pianist and music commentator. *Compositions:* Lady Killers, opera; Diogenes, opera; Ezop, cantata; Sonata da camera; Variations on a theme of Pergolesi; Missa Venea Crucis, 1991; Sinfonietta, 1995. *Recordings:* Compositions: Oboe Concerto; Sulamith; Esercizi for wind quartet; Maryka, cantata; Musica da camera for strings; Ezop; As Pianist: Debussy, Preludes, Images, Estampes, Arabesques. *Publications:* Beletrie: Trumpeter of Jericho, 1965; The Geese of the Capitol, 1969; En Route with the Aviator; 2 radio plays. *Address:* Narodni tr 35, 11000 Prague, Czech Republic.

HURSHELL, Edmund; Singer (Bass-baritone); b. 1921, USA. *Education:* Studied in the USA and Germany. *Career:* Engaged at the Stadtische Oper Berlin, 1952–53, Kiel 1953–55, Vienna Staatsoper 1955–60, as Amonasro, Scarpia, Alfio, Pizarro Hans Sachs, Orestes and Mandryka; Théâtre de la Monnaie Brussels, 1961, as the villains in Les Contes d'Hoffmann, Bologna and Amsterdam 1963, as Wolfram and Wotan; Sang Handel's Giulio Cesare at Barcelona 1964, the Dutchman and the Wanderer at Buenos Aires and Lille, 1965; Further engagements at Nuremberg, Rome, Tel-Aviv, Athens and Philadelphia; Metropolitan Opera 1967, as Kurwenal in Tristan; Appearances at Graz 1967–69; Other roles included Kaspar, the Grand Inquisitor and Falstaff. *Address:* c/o Vereinigte Buhnen, Kaiser Josef Platz 10, 8010 Graz, Austria.

HURST, George; Conductor; b. 20 May 1926, Edinburgh, Scotland. *Education:* Various preparatory and public schools in England and Canada; Royal Conservatory, Toronto. *Career:* Assistant Conductor, Opera, Royal Conservatory of Music, Toronto, 1946; Lecturer, Harmony and Counterpoint, Composition etc, Peabody Conservatory of Music, Baltimore, USA, 1947; Conductor, York Pennsylvania Symphony Orchestra, 1950–55, concurrently of Peabody Conservatory Orchestra, 1952–55; Assistant Conductor, London Philharmonic Orchestra 1955–57 with tour of Russia, 1956; Associate Conductor, BBC Northern Symphony Orchestra, 1957; Principal Conductor, BBC Northern Symphony Orchestra (previously BBC Northern Orchestra), 1958–68; Artistic Adviser, Western Orchestral Society, 1968–73; Staff Conductor, Western Orchestral Society (Bournemouth Symphony Orchestra and Bournemouth Sinfonietta), 1973–; Principal Guest Conductor, BBC Scottish Symphony Orchestra, 1986–89; Principal Conductor, National Symphony Orchestra of Ireland, 1990–93; Frequent Guest Conductor, Europe, Israel, Canada, 1956–. *Address:* 21 Oslo Court, London NW8, England.

HURST, John; Singer (Tenor); b. 1958, Norfolk, West Virginia, USA. *Education:* Studied in the USA, in Vienna and at the Salzburg Mozarteum. *Career:* Sang at the Vienna Volksoper from 1987, notably as Mozart's Idomeneo, Max in Der Freischütz, Erik in Der fliegende Holländer and Lenski in Eugene Onegin (1990); Alwa in Berg's Lulu; Guest appearances at the Schwetzingen Festival, Hamburg Staatsoper, Cologne (as Eisenstein in Die Fledermaus), Strasbourg and Tokyo. *Honours:* Winner, 1982 Belvedere Competition, Vienna. *Address:* c/o Vienna Volksoper, Währingerstrasse 78, 1090 Vienna, Austria.

HURWITZ, Emanuel; Violinist; b. 7 May 1919, London, England. *Education:* Royal Academy of Music and with Bronislav Huberman. *Career:* Led the Hurwitz String Quartet, 1946–51, and the Goldsborough (later English Chamber) Orchestra, 1946–68; Leader of the Melos Ensemble, 1956–72, and the New Philharmonia Orchestra, 1969–71; Leader of the Aeolian Quartet from 1970; Visiting Professor, Michigan University, Music Department, East Lansing, Michigan, USA, 1995–; mem, FRAM, 1963; FRSAMD, 1994; President, Incorporated Society of Musicians, 1995–96; FRSA, 1980. *Recordings include:* Brandenburg Concertos; Handel's Concerti Grossi with the English Chamber Orchestra; Schubert's Octet and Trout Quintet, Mozart and Brahms Clarinet Quintets with the Melos Ensemble; Complete Haydn Quartets edited by H C Robbins Landon; Ravel, Debussy and Late Beethoven Quartets. *Honours:* Gold Medal, Worshipful Company of Musicians, 1967; C.B.E., 1978. *Address:* 25 Dollis Avenue, London N3 1DA, England.

HUS, Walter; Composer and Pianist; b. 2 July 1959, Mol, Belgium. *Education:* Diploma supérieur, Brussels Royal Conservatory, 1984. *Career:* Recitals as classical pianist since early childhood, Italy, Germany, Poland; Performances as improviser/interpreter of own compositions, 1982–; Concerts throughout Europe with group Maximalist, own compositions, 1984–; Member, Belgisch Pianokwartet, Simpletones, etc; Various radio and television appearances; Video film with Marie André and Walter Verdin; Composer, several works for ballet, full-sized opera. *Compositions include:* 8 etudes on improvisa-

tion, piano solo; Music for fashion show, Yamamoto, Brussels; Muurwerk, music for choreography, Roxane Huilmand; Die Nacht, opera, 2 acts, libretto by Wolfgang Klob (unfinished); Compositie, video film by Marie André about W Hus; Hus/Verdin, video tape by Walter Verdin; Liefde, composition for 4 pianists at 2 pianos; La Theorie, idem, both written for Belgisch Pianokwartet; Nox aeterna for piano, 1994; Kopnaad, incidental music, 1995. *Recordings:* 8 etudes on improvisation, 1984; Maximalist, 1985; Muurwerk, 1986; Die Nacht, radio recording, 1987. *Honours:* 1st Prize, Piano 1981, Harmony 1981, Practical Harmony 1983, Brussels Royal Conservatory. *Current Management:* Lucifer Productions.

HUSA, Karel; Composer, Conductor and Professor Emeritus; b. 7 Aug. 1921, Prague, Czechoslovakia; m. Simone Perault, 2 Feb 1952, 4 d. *Education:* Conservatory of Music, 1941–45; Academy of Music, 1945–47; Ecole Normale de Musique de Paris with Arthur Honegger, 1946–48; Conservatoire de Musique de Paris, 1948–49; Private study with Nadia Boulanger (composition), Andre Cluytens, (conducting). *Career:* Assistant Professor, 1954, Associate Professor, 1957, Full Professor, 1961, Kappa Alpha Professorship, 1972, Emeritus Professor, 1992, teaching composition, theory, conducting and orchestration, Cornell University; Conductor, Cornell University Orchestra, 1956–75, Ithaca Chamber Orchestra, 1955–61; Guest Conductor with national orchestras throughout Europe, USA, Hong Kong, Puerto Rico, Asia and Japan; mem, Belgian Royal Academy of Arts and Sciences; American Academy of Arts and Literature. *Compositions include:* Symphony No. 1, for orchestra, 1953; String Quartet No. 3, 1968; Music for Prague, 1968; Apotheosis of this Earth, 1972; An American Te Deum, for baritone chorus and orchestra, 1977; Fanfare for brass and timpani, 1980; Pastoral for string orchestra, 1980; Three Dance Sketches, 1980; Intradas and Interludes, 1980; The Trojan Women, ballet 1981; Concertino for piano, 1983; Concerto for orchestra, 1984; Symphonic Suite, 1986; Concerto for organ, 1987; Concerto for trumpet, 1987; Frammenti for organ, 1987; Concerto for violoncello, 1988; String Quartet No. 4, 1990; Concerto for violin, 1993; Les couleurs fauves, for orchestra or winds, 1994; 5 Poems, woodwind quintet, 1994; Les couleurs fauves, 1995; Celebración, for orchestra, 1995. *Recordings include:* Conducted recordings with Cento Soli Orchestra in Paris (Bartók and Brahms), Stockholm and Prague Symphonies (Husa); Orchestre des Solistes (Husa Fantasies); CD Discs; Music for Prague, 1968; String Quartets Nos 2 and 3 and Evocations of Slovakia; Symphony No. 1 Serenade, Mosaiques, Landscapes; Apotheosis of this Earth, Monodrama; Concerto for Percussion; Karel Husa: I. String Quartet, Variations; Five Poems; Karel Husa: Sonatina, Suite, Sonatina for Violin and Piano; Overture for Orchestra; Sinfonietta for Orchestra. *Publications include:* Variations for Piano Quartet, 1984; Sudler Award, for Concerto for Winds, 1985; Concerto for Orchestra, 1986; Concerto for Violoncello, 1989, among others. *Honours:* Pulitzer Prize, for String Quartet No. 3, 1969; Grawemeyer Award, for Violoncello Concerto, 1993; Czech Gold Medal, President Havel, 1st Order, 1995; Honorary Medal of the City of Prague, 1998. *Current Management:* G. Schirmer, 20th Floor, 257 Park Avenue South, New York, NY 10010, USA. *Address:* 1 Belwood Lane, Ithaca, NY 14850, USA.

HUSS, Hugo (Jan); Symphony Orchestra Conductor; b. 26 Jan. 1934, Timisoara, Romania; m. Mirella Regis, 1 Aug 1970, 1 d. *Education:* Diplomat in Arts, speciality Symphony Orchestra Conducting, Bucharest Conservatory of Music, 1958; Master of Business Administration, Roosevelt University of Chicago, 1977. *Career:* Debut: Concert, Romanian Athenaeum, Bucharest; Television appearance, performance of Tosca with Placido Domingo; Radio broadcasts with La Crosse Symphony, Wisconsin; Radio Louisville with Louisville Symphony, Kentucky; Radio Birmingham with Alabama Symphony; Guest Conductor, Cape Town Symphony, South Africa; Tbilisi, Russia; Kraków, Poland; Brno, Czechoslovakia; Sarajevo, Yugoslavia; Veracruz, Mexico; Grand Rapids, Michigan and Huntsville, Alabama, USA; Music Director and Conductor of Arad Symphony, Romania; Principal Guest Conductor of Gunthe Symphony, Munich, Germany; Titular Director and Principal Conductor of Guadalajara Symphony, Mexico; Music Director of the La Crosse Symphony, Wisconsin, USA; Guest Conducting engagements around the world; Opened the Constantin Silvestri International Festival with a concert in Târgu-Mures, Romania, 1997. *Address:* N1972 Hickory Lane, La Crosse, WI 54601, USA. *E-mail:* hugo@hugohuss.com.

HUSSON, Suzanne; Pianist; b. 4 April 1943, Buenos Aires, Argentina. *Education:* Began musical studies at age 5 with Mrs E Westerkamp; Later attended Conservatoire M de Falla, Buenos Aires; Conservatory of Geneva (Prof Hilbrandt); Staatliche Hochschule für Musik, Köln (Prof B Seidhofer); Special Courses given by Arturo Benedetti Michelangeli (Italy and Switzerland). *Career:* Debut: 1st Public Recital at age 8, Buenos Aires; Various international performances in recitals and as soloist with conductors such as Marc Andreae, W Sawallisch, C Dutoit, and Orchestra Philarmonique de Lyon, Stuttgart Philharmonic,

Orchestra de la Radio Suisse Italienne and Orchestra of Swiss Romande; Television and radio appearances in Germany and Switzerland; Radio appearances in Argentina, Poland and France. *Recordings:* Stravinsky, Les Noces, directed by Charles Dutoit, Erato Label, 1973; R Vuataz, Concert for Piano and Orchestra, Opus 112, Orchestra of Swiss Romande, directed by Wolfgang Sawallisch, CBS Label, 1981; Scarlatti-Ginastera-Debussy-Ravel, Fono Label, 1987; Latin American Classics, Guatemala, Manuel Martinez-Sobral piano music, Vols 3 and 5, 1999, 2003. *Current Management:* Wismer-Casetti, Rue Merle-d'Aubigné 26, 1207 Geneva, Switzerland. *Address:* 24 rue de la Dôle, 1203 Geneva, Switzerland (office). *Telephone:* (22) 345-3470 (office). *E-mail:* shusson@ bluemail.ch (office). *Website:* www.musicedition.ch/interpret (office).

HUSZAR, Lajos; composer; b. 26 Sept. 1948, Szeged, Hungary. *Education:* Secondary Music School, Szeged, with Istvan Vantus, 1963–67; Academy of Music, Budapest, with Endre Szervanszky and Zsolt Durko, 1967–73; Academy of St Cecilia, Rome, Italy, with Goffredo Petrassi, 1975. *Career:* mem. Association of Hungarian Composers; Hungarian Society of Music. *Compositions include:* Csomorkány for 10 players, 1973; Musica concertante for 13 players, 1975; 69th Psalm for tenor and piano, 1976; 5 Pieces for piano, 1977; 2 Songs to poems by Endre Ady for bass and piano, 1977–83; Scherzo and Adagio for chamber orchestra, 1979; Sonata for harpsichord, 1979–85; Brass Quintet, 1980; 3 Songs to poems by Else Lasker-Schüler for soprano and viola, 1981–89; Serenata Concertante for flute and string orchestra; Songs of Solitude for soprano and percussion, 1983; Notturno for piano, 1984; Concerto Rustico for chamber orchestra, 1985; Chamber Concerto for cello and 17 strings, 1987; Libera me for organ, 1993; The Silence, opera in 2 acts, 1994–98; Trittico estivo for oboe and piano, 1998; Icons to the memory of János Pilinszky for soprano and chamber orchestra, 2000–01; Pedagogic pieces for choirs. *Recordings:* Musica concertante; Ave Maria and Dies Sanctificatus, female choirs; Chamber Concerto; 69th Psalm; Brass Quintet; Songs of Solitude. *Honours:* Erkel Prize, 1994. *Address:* Postás u. 12, 6729 Szeged, Hungary. *E-mail:* husarla@hotmail.com.

HUTCHESON, Jere (Trent); Composer and Professor of Music; b. 16 Sept. 1938, Marietta, Georgia, USA; m. (1) Virginia Bagby, 1 d., (2) Mary Ellen Gayley Cleland, 21 June 1982, 1 s., 1 d. *Education:* BMus, Stetson University; MMus, Louisiana State University; PhD, Michigan State University; Berkshire Music Center. *Compositions include:* Passacaglia for band; 3 Things for Dr Seuss; Shadows of Floating Life; Wonder Music I, II, III, IV, V; Sensations; Transitions; Construction Set; Colossus; 3 Pictures of Satan; Electrons; Fantaisie-Impromptu; Nocturnes of the Inferno; Passing, Passing, Passing; Patterns; Cosmic Suite; Earth Gods Symphony; Chromophonic Images for symphonic band; Will-O-The-Wisps for solo violin; The Song Book for tenor and flute; Duo Sonata for clarinet and percussion; Concerto for piano and wind orchestra; Metaphors for orchestra; Interplay for alto saxophone and mallet percussion; Ritual and Dance for female chorus; Five French Portraits for wind orchestra; Duo Concertante in memoria di Margot Evans for violin and piano; Concerto for violin and small orchestra; Long Live the Composer, chamber opera; Dance of Time Symphony, 1995; Caricatures for wind symphony, 1997; Portfolio for cello and chamber ensemble, 1997; More Caricatures for wind symphony, 1999; Glosses, Annotations and an Exegesis for cello and piano (also violin and piano), 1999; Mrs Dalloway's Party for mezzo-soprano and piano, 1999; Caricatures III for wind symphony, 2000; Three Notions for saxophone quartet, 2000; Three Visions for full orchestra, 2001; Quirky Etudes for piano; Sonata for Piano; Concerto for solo percussion and wind symphony; Divertimento for flute solo, winds and percussion; Three Pieces for Tuba and Piano, Gradus ad Parnassum – Caricature IV for wind symphony; Petals Over Time for mezzo-soprano and piano; Variations and Excursions for string trio; Concerto for saxophone and wind symphony, Histwhist for mixed chorus and arranged for children's chorus SA, Lament for mixed chorus and arranged for women's chorus SSA. *Recordings:* Deja View contains Caricatures for wind symphony, 1997; DuoDenum (saxophone and percussion). *Publications:* Musical Form and Analysis, text, 1995. *Address:* 6064 Abbott Road, East Lansing, MI 48823, USA.

HUTCHINSON, Nigel; Concert Pianist; b. 1963, England. *Education:* University of Glasgow, Guildhall School with Craig Sheppard and Juilliard with Earl Wild. *Career:* Debut: Wigmore Hall, 1988; Concerts in France, Germany, Italy, Czechoslovakia and elsewhere in Europe; Concerto debut with the London Mozart Players under Jane Glover; Festival engagements at Harrogate and Glasgow, and recitals at the Salle Pleyel Paris, Barbican Centre and Festival Hall, London and Symphony Hall Birmingham; Broadcasts for BBC and Italian Radio; Purcell Room recital 1993, with Schubert (D664), Liszt and Debussy. *Recordings:* Rachmaninov music for six hands, with John Ogdon and Brenda Lucas, and Carnival of the Animals with the London Symphony Orchestra under Barry Wordsworth.

HUTCHINSON, Stuart; Conductor and Concert Accompanist; b. 3 March 1956, London, England. *Education:* Royal Academy of Music,

London; Cambridge University; BMus (Honours), 1977; LRAM, 1979; ARAM, 1997; Studied with Bernstein and Pritchard. *Career:* Opera, Ballet and Music-Theatre Conductor: Productions for English National Opera, Scottish Opera, Theater des Westens Berlin, New Sadler's Wells Opera Company, Sadler's Wells Theatre/ROH, London International Opera Festival, Royal Academy of Music; Conductor, Scottish Ballet, 1991; Chorus Master, Dublin Grand Opera and Wexford Festival Opera; Music Staff, English National Opera, Opera North; Director of Music, Organist, University of London Chaplaincy, 1976–89; Music Director, Northcott Theatre, Exeter, 1982–84; Music Director, Artistic Director, Morley Opera, London, 1986–90; Music Director, Jonathan Miller's Company/Old Vic Theatre, 1988–89; World premiere, Alice in Wonderland (Carl Davis), Lyric Theatre, Hammersmith, 1986; British premiere, Postcard From Morocco, (Dominick Argento) LIOF, 1988; World premiere, Tables Meet, (Stephen Oliver), Royal Festival Hall, 1990; Also productions for the Royal Shakespeare Company, (London), On Your Toes, with Makarova, West End, 1984; mem. Performing Right Society; Musicians Union. *Compositions:* Incidental theatre music including King Lear (Miller/Old Vic); Frequent arranger and orchestrator. *Recordings:* National Philharmonic Orchestra with James Galway; Philharmonia Orchestra with Michie Nakamaru; Several recordings for BBC Radio 3 and 4; Many for BBC Radio Drama; BBC and Independent Television. *Publications:* Prepared/Edited the 1995 (Opera North) Version of William Walton's Troilus and Cressida. *Contributions:* Opera magazine (Troilus and Cressida: Forty Years On), 1995. *Current Management:* Music International, 13 Ardilaun Road, London N5 2QR, England. *Address:* Suite 390, 37 Store Street, Bloomsbury, London WC1E 7QF, England.

HUTTENLOCHER, Philippe; Singer (Baritone); b. 29 Nov. 1942, Neuchatel, Switzerland. *Education:* Studied with Julette Bise in Fribourg. *Career:* Sang with the Ensemble Vocal de Lausanne and with the Choeurs de la Foundation Gulbenkian, Lisbon; Festival appearances in Montreux, Lausanne, Strasbourg and Ansbach in the Baroque repertory; Tour of Japan 1974; Zürich Opera 1975, as the title role in Monteverdi's Orfeo, produced by Jean-Pierre Ponnelle; London Bach Festival, 1978; Guest appearances in Vienna, Berlin, Hamburg, Milan and Edinburgh; Genoa 1987, in Dido and Aeneas and Les Malheurs d'Orphée by Milhaud. *Recordings include:* Bach Cantatas and operas by Monteverdi including Il Ritorno d'Ulisse and L'Orfeo (video); St Matthew Passion; Le Devin du Village by Rousseau; Die Jahreszeiten by Haydn, Bach B Minor Mass; Les Indes Galantes by Rameau, Così fan tutte, Il Maestro di Capella, Pénélope, St John Pasion, Handel Dettingen Te Deum and works by Carissimi, MA Charpentier and Gabrieli.

HUYBRECHTS, Francois; Conductor; b. 15 June 1946, Antwerp, Belgium. *Education:* Studied Cello and Clarinet at the Antwerp Conservatory; Conducting studies with Daniel Sternefeld, Bruno Maderna and Hans Swarowsky. *Career:* Debut: As Cellist, 1960; Conducting, 1963 The Fairy Queen by Purcell, Royal Flemish Opera; Conducted the Netherlands Chamber Opera, 1966–67; Concerts at the Salzburg Mozarteum 1967; Assisted Bernstein at the New York Philharmonic and conducted the Los Angeles Philharmonic and the Berlin Philharmonic; Musical Director of the Wichita Symphony 1972–79, San Antonio Symphony 1979–80. *Recordings include:* Janáček's Taras Bulba and Lachian Dances (London Philharmonic); Nielsen's 3rd Symphony (London Symphony Orchestra/Decca). *Honours:* Winner, Dimitri Mitropoulos Competition, New York, 1968; Prizewinner, Herbert von Karajan Foundation Competition, 1969. *Address:* c/o Polygram Classics, PO Box 1420, 1 Sussex Place, Hammersmith, London W6 9XS, England.

HVOROSTOVSKY, Dmitri; Singer (Baritone); b. 16 Oct. 1962, Krasnoyarsk, Siberia, Russia. *Education:* Studied at the Krasnoyarsk High School of Arts with Jekatherina Yofel, 1982–86. *Career:* Soloist with the Krasnoyarsk Opera, 1986–; Appeared on BBC television as winner of the Cardiff Singer of the World Competition, 1989; Sang songs by Tchaikovsky and Rachmaninov at the Wigmore Hall, Dec 1989; Recitals at New York Alice Tully and at Washington Kennedy Center, Mar 1990; Opera engagements include Yeletsky in The Queen of Spades at Nice 1989 (western operatic debut), Eugene Onegin in Venice, 1991; I Puritani at Covent Garden, 1992; Sang Onegin at the Paris Châtelet, 1992, Germont at the Chicago Lyric Opera, season 1993–94; Promenade Concert debut 1993, Mussorgsky's Songs and Dances of Death; Concert showings in Boston, Paris, Moscow and St Petersburg; Recital of Russian songs at the Barbican Hall, London, 1997; Sang with the Royal Opera in Verdi's Masnadieri, 1998; Yeletsky in The Queen of Spades at the Met, 1999; Rigoletto at the Novaya Opera, Moscow, 2000; Season 2002–03 as Francesco in I Masnadieri at Covent Garden, Don Giovanni at the Met and Verdi's Renato for Chicago Lyric Opera; Engaged as Verdi's Miller at Covent Garden, 2004. *Recordings include:* Arias by Tchaikovsky and Verdi with the Rotterdam Philharmonic conducted by Valery Gergiev; Arias from Cavalleria Rusticana, Eugene Onegin and

Don Carlos (Philips Classics). *Honours:* First Prize, USSR National Competition, 1987; Toulouse Singing Competition, 1988; BBC Cardiff Singer of the World Competition, 1989. *Current Management:* Askonas Holt Ltd, Lonsdale Chambers, 27 Chancery Lane, London, WC2A 1PF, England. *Telephone:* (20) 7400-1700. *Fax:* (20) 7400-1799. *E-mail:* info@ askonasholt.co.uk. *Website:* www.askonasholt.co.uk.

HWANG, Der-Shin; Singer (Mezzo-soprano) and Teacher; b. 8 Feb. 1958, Taiwan. *Education:* BA in piano/voice, Taiwan University; Master of Fine Arts in Singing, University of California, Los Angeles; Associate of RCM honours in performing singing, Royal College of Music, London. *Career:* Debut: Suzuki, Holland Park; Serenade to Music with Hanley/ RPO in Festival Hall and with Charles Groves/Philharmonia in the Barbican, 1989; Anitra in Peer Gynt with Neeme Järvi/Gothenburg Symphony Orchestra, Barbican, 1992–93; Haydn and Handel solo contatas with Tallis Chamber Orchestra, 1993; Mozart arias in Sandwich Festival, 1993; Christmass Magnificat with English Baroque Orchestra in Queen Elizabeth Hall, 1993; Judas Maccabaeus in Handel's Canon Park Church with London Mozart Players, 1994; Many other oratorio concerts with the choral societies in the United Kingdom including works such as Elgar's The Music Makers, Rossini's Stabat Mater, Petite Messe Solennelle, Mozart's C Minor Mass. Opera: Suzuki with many companies including Singapore Lyric Theatre, Crystal Clear and in Festival Mozart at Roubaix, France; Other operatic roles including Prince Orlofsky, Siebel, Despina, Cherubino, Baba the Turk, Olga; Worked with companies such as Clonter Opera for All, City of Birmingham Touring Opera, Opera Factory and English National Opera; Solo Recitals. *Current Management:* Dal Segno Management. *Address:* Flat 2, 19 Woodstock Road, London NW11 8ES, England.

HYDE, Miriam Beatrice; Composer and Pianist; b. 15 Jan. 1913, Adelaide, South Australia; m. Marcus Bruce Edwards, 26 Dec 1939, deceased, 1 s., 1 d. *Education:* AMUA, Elder Conservatorium, Adelaide University, 1928; LAB, 1928; MusBac, 1931; Elder Scholarship, Royal College of Music, London, 1931; ARCM, Piano and Composition, 1935; LRAM, 1935. *Career:* Debut: Small public concert, South Australia, 1924; Performed own 2 concertos with major London orchestras including London Philharmonic Orchestra, London Symphony Orchestra and BBC; Performances with Australian orchestras under eminent conductors including Malcolm Sargent, Constant Lambert, Bernard Heinze, Geoffrey Simon; mem, Patron of Eisteddfods of Blue Mountains and Inner West, NSW; ABC presented a concert of her music on her 90th birthday, 2003. *Recordings:* 2 self-composed concertos with West Australia Symphony Orchestra; CDs: Anthology of Chamber Music; Clarinet Sonata; Village Fair; Happy Occasion Overture; Piano solos including Sonata in G minor; Both Piano Concertos and Village Fair in new Eloquence CD, 2000. *Publications:* Autobiography, Complete Accord, 1991; Fantasy Trio, 1999; Viola Sonata, 1999; Piano Sonata, 2000; Clarinet Sonata, 2000. *Honours:* Hon. Fellow of Institute of Music Teachers, 2001; OBE, 1981; AO, 1991; Hon. DLitt (Macquarie), 1981; Int. Woman of the Year for Service to Music, Cambridge Biog. Centre, 1998; Long Term Contribution to the Advancement of Australian Music Award, Australian Music Centre, 2002; Distinguished Alumni Award, S Australia Univ., 2004. *Address:* 12 Kelso St, Burwood Heights, NSW 2136, Australia.

HYDE-SMITH, Christopher; Flautist and Teacher; b. 11 March 1935, Cairo, Egypt; 1 s., 1 d. *Education:* Royal College of Music, London. *Career:* Debut: Royal Festival Hall, 1962; Member, Camden Wind Quintet, London Mozart Players; Many flute and piano and/or harpsichord concerts with Jane Dodd; Appearances in Netherlands, Switzerland, Italy, France, Germany, Spain, Portugal, Scandinavia, Russia, North and South America; Professor, Royal College of Music; Dedicatee of works by Alwyn, Dodgson, Horovitz, Mathias and Rawsthorne; Judge at Leeds, Mozart and Tunbridge Wells Competitions; mem, Haydn Mozart Society; Chairman, British Flute Society. *Recordings:* Numerous recordings. *Current Management:* Lotte Nicholls, 16 Upper Wimpole Street, London WC1, England. *Address:* 94 Dorien Road, London SW20 8EJ, England.

HYKES, David (Bond); Composer; b. 2 March 1953, Taos, New Mexico, USA. *Education:* Studied Classical Azerbaijani and Armenian Music with Zevulon Avshalomov, 1975–77; North Indian Raga Singing with S Dhar from 1982. *Career:* Founded the Harmonic Choir, 1975; Resident at the Cathedral of St John the Divine, New York from 1979; Tours of the USA and Europe from 1980. *Compositions:* Harmonic Tissues for electronics, 1971; Shadow Frequencies for piano and electronics, 1975; Looking for Gold/Life in the Sun for children's voices and ensemble,

1975; Well-struck Strings for dulcimer, 1975–83; Special Delivery/ Rainbow Voice for low voice, 1975–84; Test Studies for Harmonica Orchestra for ensemble, 1975–85; Hearing Solar Winds for voices, 1977–83; Outside of Being There for voices, 1981; Turkestan for synthesizer, 1979; Current Circulation for voices, 1984; Subject to Change for low voice and drones, 1983; Desert Hymns, 1984. *Honours:* Grants from the National Endowment for the Arts, 1978, 1983, The Rockefeller Foundation 1980–83, and UNESCO, 1983. *Address:* c/o ASCAP, ASCAP Building, 1 Lincoln Plaza, NY 10023, USA.

HYNES, Rachel; Singer (Soprano); b. 1965, South Wales. *Education:* Leeds University and Royal Scottish Academy of Music. *Career:* Appearances from 1997 with Scottish Opera in Rigoletto, The Queen of Spades, Aida and Macbeth (also at Vienna Festival); Company Principal from 2000, with Freia in Das Rheingold, Helmwige in Die Walküre and Third Norn in Götterdämmerung (2000–03); Further engagements as Inès in Il Trovatore, Giannetta (L'Elisir d'amore) and Mozart's Fiordiligi; Essential Scottish Opera tours, 2001–2002; Sang Anna Kennedy in Donizetti's Maria Stuarda (concert) at the 2002 Edinburgh Festival; Season 2002–2003 with Gluck's Euridice and Third Lady in The Magic Flute. *Honours:* Hobart Trust Award. *Address:* c/o Scottish Opera, 39 Elmbank Crescent, Glasgow, G2 4PT, Scotland.

HYNNINEN, Jorma; Opera Singer (Baritone); b. 3 April 1941, Leppä-virta, Finland; m. Reetta Salo, 6 Aug 1961, 1 s., 2 d. *Education:* Sibelius Academy, Helsinki, 1969. *Career:* Debut: As Silvio in Pagliacci, Finnish National Opera, 1969, as Tonio in Pagliacci; Staatsoper Vienna, 1977; La Scala, Milan, 1977; Paris Opéra, 1978; Bavarian State Opera, Munich, 1979; Metropolitan Opera, New York, 1984 as Posa; San Francisco Opera, 1988; Lyric Opera of Chicago, 1989; Deutsche Oper Berlin, 1991 as Hindemith's Mathis der Maler; Lieder recitals, New York, London, Europe and Beijing; Soloist with Vienna Symphony, Boston Symphony and Israel Philharmonic; Sang Amfortas in Parsifal at Antwerp, 1996; Savonlinna Festival 1998, as Wagner's Wolfram; Premieres include: The Red Line and The King Goes Forth to France by Sallinen (1978, 1984), Thomas, and Vincent by Rautavaara (1985, 1990) and Sallinen's Kullervo (1992); Season 2000 at Helsinki as Simon Boccanegra, Papageno, and Gloucester in the premiere of Lear by Aulis Sallinen; Engaged as Tsar Nicholas in the premiere of Rautavaara's Rasputin, Helsinki 2003. *Recordings:* Le nozze di Figaro with Riccardo Muti; Orestes in Elektra with Seiji Ozawa; Brahms' Requiem and Mahler's Eighth with Klaus Tennstedt; Winterreise, Die schöne Müllerin, Dichterliebe; Songs of Sibelius; Die schöne Magelone; Lieder eines Fahrenden Gesellen; Evergreen Love Songs. *Honours:* Professor of Arts, Finland, 1990. *Current Management:* Allied Artists, London Opera et Concert Paris. *Address:* Ruskokuja 3 B, 01620 Vantaa, Finland.

HYPOLITE, Andée-Louise; Singer (Mezzo-soprano); b. 1975, London, England. *Education:* Royal Scottish Academy, with Patricia McMahon, and National Opera Studio, London. *Career:* Early roles include Clarice in Rossini's La Pietra del Paragone, Mrs Herring, and Bizet's Mercedes; Other roles include Dorabella, and Mrs Grose, in The Turn of the Screw; Concerts include Ravel's Chansons madècasses, Elgar's Sea Pictures, Vier ernste Gesänge by Brahms and Berio's Folk Songs; Sang Mahler's Rückert Lieder for Scottish Ballet. *Address:* c/o National Opera Studio, Morley College, 61 Westminster Bridge Road, London, SE1 7XT, England.

HYTNER, Nicholas; Opera Producer; b. 7 May 1956, Manchester, England. *Education:* Trinity Hall, Cambridge, graduated 1977. *Career:* Debut: Dreigroschenoper at Cambridge; The Turn of the Screw for Kent Opera, 1979; Tippett's King Priam in season 1984–85; Wagner's Rienzi for English National Opera, 1983; Xerxes, 1985; Handel's Giulio Cesare for the Paris Opéra, 1987; Covent Garden debut 1987, with the British premiere of Sallinen's The King Goes Forth to France; The Knot Garden, 1988; The Magic Flute for English National Opera and Netherlands Opera; Debut with Geneva Opera 1989, Le nozze di Figaro; Glyndebourne debut 1991, La Clemenza di Tito; La Forza del Destino, for ENO, 1992; Staged The Cunning Little Vixen at the Théâtre du Châtelet, Paris, 1996; Film work includes The Crucible, 1997; Staging of Handel's Giulio Cesare for the Paris Palais Garnier, 1987 (revised 2002); Director of the National Theatre, London, 2002–. *Recordings include:* videos of Xerxes and King Priam. *Current Management:* Askonas Holt Ltd, Lonsdale Chambers, 27 Chancery Lane, London, WC2A 1PF, England. *Telephone:* (20) 7400-1700. *Fax:* (20) 7400-1799. *E-mail:* info@askonasholt.co.uk. *Website:* www.askonasholt.co.uk.

I

IANNACCONE, Anthony; Composer, Conductor and Teacher; b. 14 Oct. 1943, New York, USA; m. Judith Trostle, 1 s., 1 d. *Education:* BMus, MMus, Manhattan School of Music; PhD, Eastman School of Music. *Career:* Conducted Orchestras, Choruses, Wind Ensembles and Chamber Groups throughout the USA including: Lincoln Center, New York; Many University appearances as Guest Conductor and Composer; Teacher, Manhattan School of Music, 1967–68; Composition Professor, 1971, Director of Collegium Musicum, 1973; Record Debut as Conductor of Cornell Wind Ensemble, 1983. *Compositions include:* 3 Symphonies, 1965, 1966, 1992; Approximately 40 published works, 14 commercially recorded for orchestra, chorus, wind ensemble and chamber ensembles; Octet, 1985; Chautauqua Psalms, 1987; Concertante for clarinet and orchestra, 1994; Crossings for orchestra, 1996; Piano Quintet, 1995; 2 string quartets, 1965, 1997; West End Express for orchestra, 1997. *Recordings include:* Partita, for piano, 1967; Rituals for violin and piano, 1973; Aria Concertante for cello and piano, 1976; Walt Whitman Song, for chorus, soloists and winds, 1981; No. 2 Terpsichore, 1981; Images of Song and Dance, No. 1 Orpheus, 1982; Divertimento, for orchestra, 1983; Two Piano Inventions, 1985; Night Rivers, Symphony No. 3, 1992; Sea Drift, 1993; String Quartet No. 3, 1999; Waiting for Sunrise, 2002. *Address:* PO Box 981272, Ypsilanti, MI 48198, USA.

ICHIHARA, Taro; Singer (Tenor); b. 2 Jan. 1950, Yamagata, Japan. *Education:* Studied at the Juilliard School, New York, and in Italy. *Career:* Debut: Tokyo, 1980, as Gounod's Faust; Sang at the Teatro San Carlos, Lisbon, from 1982, notably as Calaf; Paris Opéra from 1983, as Verdi's Macduff, Don Carlos, Riccardo and Duke of Mantua; Salzburg Festival, 1984–85, as Malcolm in Macbeth; Further engagements at Nice, Turin, Naples, Buenos Aires (Verdi Requiem), Orange Festival (Ismaele in Nabucco) and Tokyo; Metropolitan Opera, New York, 1986–89, as the Italian Singer in Der Rosenkavalier and the Duke of Mantua; La Scala, 1989, as Gabriele Adorno; Cologne Opera, 1992; Other roles include Alfredo, Enzo in La Gioconda and Edgardo. *Address:* c/o Kajimoto Management Ltd, Kahoku Building, 8-6-25 Ginza, Chuo-Ku, Tokyo 104–0061,.

ICONOMOU, Panajotis; Singer (Bass); b. 1971, Munich, Germany. *Education:* Guildhall School of Music from 1995; National Opera Studio in London. *Career:* Concert choir of the Tolzer Knabenchor, 1982–86, with the tours of Europe and solos under leading conductors; Bass with the Tolzer concert choir, 1988–92, with Mozart's Vespers at Versailles; Bach's Christmas Oratorio at the First Israel Bach Festival, under Peter Schreier; Further concerts at Munich, Hamburg, Milan and Vienna; Season 1997–98 with Bach and Telemann cantatas at the York Early Music Festival; Beethoven's Missa Solemnis at the Barbican; Christmas Oratorio in Munich; Mozart Sarastro at Holland Park and Osmin at Saar; Season 1999–2000 with Sparafucile for Welsh National Opera and Masetto for Scottish Opera. *Address:* c/o Welsh National Opera, John Street, Cardiff, CF1 ASP,.

IDANE, Yasuhiko; Singer (Tenor); b. 1962, Japan. *Career:* Frequent appearances in the Far East and Europe, in operas by Puccini (Il Tabarro), Leoncavallo (La Bohème) and Mascagni (Cavalleria Rusticana); Also songs by Japanese composers, including Kobayashi; Contestant at the 1995 Cardiff Singer of the World Competition. *Address:* 6-23-3 Akatsuka, Itabashi-ku, Tokyo,.

IGOSHINA, Valentina; Concert Pianist; b. 1972, Bryansk, Russia. *Education:* Moscow Conservatory Central Music School, 1990. *Career:* recitals and concerts throughout Russia and Western Europe 1993–, with repertory including Bach, Chopin, Brahms and Schumann; performed Rachmaninov Preludes in Tony Palmer's film biography, The Harvest, and appeared as Delfina Potocka in The Mystery of Chopin; Season 2000–01 with Hallé Orchestra and BBC Scottish Symphony Orchestra; London debut, 2002, at South Bank Harrods International Piano Series concert; Season 2002–03 with Hallé Orchestra concerts, debut with London Philharmonic and tours of Channel Islands and Yugoslavia. *Honours:* winner, Arthur Rubinstein International Piano Competition, 1993; Rachmaninov International Competition, Moscow, 1997. *Current Management:* Ingpen & Williams Ltd, 7 St George's Court, 131 Putney Bridge Road, London, SW15 2PA, England.

IHLE, Andrea; Singer (Soprano); b. 17 April 1953, Dresden, Germany. *Education:* Studied at Musikhochschule Dresden. *Career:* Debut: Dresden Staatsoper, 1976, as Giannetta in L'Elisir d'amore; Appearances in Dresden have included Aennchen and Marianne, in the productions of Freischütz and Rosenkavalier which opened the rebuilt Semperoper, 1985; Other roles in Dresden and elsewhere in Germany, have included Mozart's Papagena and Despina, Euridice, Gretel, Sophie (Der Rosenkavalier), Carolina (Il Matrimonio Segreto) and Marie in La

Fille du Régiment; Concert and oratorio engagements; Season 1999–2000 at Dresden in Lady Macbeth of the Mtsensk District and Der Rosenkavalier. *Recordings:* Freischütz and Rosenkavalier; Bach's Christmas Oratorio; Missa Brevis by Carl Friedrich Fasch. *Address:* Semper Oper Dresden, 8012 Dresden,.

IHLOFF, Jutta-Renate; Singer (Soprano); b. 1 Nov. 1944, Winteberg, Germany. *Education:* Studied with Marja Stein in Hamburg and with Giorgio Favaretto in Rome and Siena. *Career:* Debut: Staatsoper Hamburg 1973, as Zerlina in Don Giovanni; Has sung in Munich, Berlin, Vienna and Salzburg; Frequent guest appearances elsewhere in Europe; Other roles include Mozart's Despina, Susanna, Blondchen and Pamina; Marzelline in Fidelio; Monteverdi's Poppea; Sophie and Zdenka; Mimi, Marie in Die Soldaten by Zimmermann, Adele in Die Fledermaus and Nannetta in Falstaff. *Recordings:* Serpetta in La Finta Giardiniera by Mozart.

IKAIA-PURDY, Keith; Singer (Tenor); b. 1956, Hawaii, USA. *Education:* Studied with Tito Gobbi, and with Carlo Bergonzi in Busetto. *Career:* Sang in opera throughout the USA from 1983, notably as Turiddu, the Duke of Mantua, Riccardo (Ballo in maschera), Cavaradossi, and Don José; Florestan in the original version of Fidelio at Berkeley, 1987; European debut at Bussetto, 1988, as Corado in Il Corsaro; Guested at Wiesbaden, 1989, as Alfredo, returning as Tebalo in Bellini's Capuleti; Vienna Staatsoper, 1993, Alfredo; Season 2000–01 as Arnold in Guillaume Tell, Ismaele, Macduff, Don Carlos and Hoffmann at the Vienna Staatsoper; Gaston in Jérusalem at Dresden (concert); Concert repertory includes Schubert's Die schöne Müllerin. *Address:* c/o Staatsoper, Opernring 2, 1010 Vienna,.

IKEDA, Kikuei; Violinist; b. 31 Aug. 1947, Yokosuka, Japan; Studied at the Juilliard School with Dorothy DeLay and members of the Juilliard Quartet. *Career:* Second violin, Tokyo Quartet from 1974; Regular concerts in the USA and abroad; First cycle of the complete quartets of Beethoven at the Yale at Norfolk Chamber Music Festival, 1986; Repeated cycles at the 92nd Street Y New York, Ravinia and Israel Festivals, Yale, Princeton Universities; Season 1990–91 at Alice Tully Hall, the Metropolitan Museum of Art, New York, Boston, Washington DC, Los Angeles, Cleveland, Detroit, Chicago, Miami, Seattle, San Francisco, Toronto; Tour of South America, two tours of Europe including Paris, Amsterdam, Bonn, Milan, Munich, Dublin, London, Berlin; Quartet-in-residence at Yale University and at the University of Cincinnati College-Conservatory of Music. *Recordings:* Schubert's Major Quartets; Mozart Flute Quartets with James Galway and Clarinet Quintet with Richard Stoltzman; Quartets by Bartók, Brahms, Debussy, Haydn, Mozart and Ravel; Beethoven Middle Period Quartets. *Honours:* Grand Prix du Disque du Montreux; Best Chamber Music Recording of the Year from Stereo Review and the Gramophone; Four Grammy nominations. Address; Intermusica Artists' Management, 16 Duncan Terrace, London N1 8BZ, England.

IKONOMOU, Katharine; Singer (Soprano); b. 1957, Tashikent, Usbekistan, Russia. *Education:* Studied in Tashkent and at the Cologne Musikhochschule with Joseph Metternich. *Career:* Debut: Würzburg, 1984, as Salome; After further study in Italy sang Salome at Zürich, 1986, and Jenůfa at the 1988 Spoleto Festival (Chrysothemis, 1990); Sang Beethoven's Leonore at Trieste, 1990, and Fevronia in Rimsky's Invisible City of Kitezh (Florence, 1990); Rome, 1991, as Ariadne, Amelia in Ballo in Maschera at Genoa and Wagner's Senta at Catania, 1992. *Recordings include:* Songs by Russian composers. *Address:* c/o Theater Massimo Bellini, Via Perrotta 12, 95131 Catania,.

ILLES, Eva; Singer (Soprano); b. 1939, Hungary. *Education:* Studied in Hungary. *Career:* Sang at the Regensburg Opera, 1967–69, Freiburg, 1969–71, Zürich, 1971–75, and Hanover, 1974–81; Guested at Covent Garden as Senta, 1972, at Barcelona and the Vienna Staatsoper; Other roles included Wagner's Elsa and Elisabeth, Ariadne, Amelia Grimaldi, Maddalena (Andrea Chénier), the Forza Leonora, and Turandot. *Address:* c/o Staatstheater Hanover, Opernhaus, Opernplatz 1, W-3000 Hanover 1,.

ILOSVALVY, Robert; Singer (Tenor); b. 18 June 1927, Hodmezovasarhely, Hungary. *Education:* Studied with Andor Lendvai at the Budapest Academy. *Career:* Soloist with the Artistic Ensemble of the People's Army from 1949; Budapest Opera from 1954, debut in the title role of Erkel's Hunyadi Laszlo; Sang widely in eastern Europe; San Francisco Opera 1964–68, New York Metropolitan Opera 1966; Member of Cologne Opera from 1966; Covent Garden, 1968, as Des Grieux in Manon Lescaut; Concerts with the Berlin Philharmonic and the Orchestra of the Accademia di Santa Cecilia; Career centred on the Budapest Opera from 1981; Theatre de la Monnaie Brussels 1985, as Walther in Die Meistersinger; Sang Walther von Stolzing at the 1986

Maggio Musicale, Florence; Other roles included Rodolfo, Tamino, Dick Johnson, Don José, Alfredo, Manrico and the Duke of Mantua. *Recordings:* Madama Butterfly and Manon Lescaut, Hungaroton; Roberto Devereux, with Beverly Sills; Requiem by Dvořák, conducted by Kertesz. *Address:* c/o Hungarian State Opera House, Nepoztarsasag utja 22, 1061 Budapest,.

IMAI, Nobuko; Violist and Professor of Music; b. 18 March 1943, Tokyo, Japan; m. Aart van Bochove, 1981, 1 s., 1 d. *Education:* Toho School of Music, Tokyo; Juilliard School of Music, New York; Yale University, USA. *Career:* Member of Vermeer Quartet, 1974–79; Professor, Musikhochschule, Detmold, Germany, 1985–; Soloist with the London Symphony Orchestra, Royal Philharmonic, Chicago Symphony, Berlin Philharmonic, Concertgebouw Orchestra, Montreal Symphony, Boston Symphony, Vienna Symphony, Orchestre de Paris, Stockholm Philharmonic; Festivals include: Marlboro, Casals, South Bank, London, Bath, Cheltenham and Aldeburgh, BBC London Proms, International Viola Congress, Houston, Lockenhaus; Performed world premiere of Takemitsu Viola Concerto entitled A String Around Autumn; Conceived Viola Festivals for Casals Hall, Tokyo, Wigmore Hall, London, Columbia University, New York on Birth Centenary of Hindemith, 1995. *Recordings include:* Tippett Triple Concerto; Berlioz: Harold in Italy; Walton and Schnittke Concertos. *Honours:* 1st Prize, Munich International Viola Competition; 2nd Prize, Geneva International Viola Competition; Education Ministry's Award for Services to Music, 1993; Arvon Art Award, 1993; Mainichi Arts Award, 1995; Suntory Prize, Tokyo, 1996. *Current Management:* Irene Witmer Personal Management, Leidsegracht 42, 1016 CM, Amsterdam, Netherlands.

IMBRIE, Andrew W.; Composer and Professor; b. 6 April 1921, New York, USA; m. Barbara Cushing, 31 Jan 1953, 2 s., 1 deceased. *Education:* Studied Piano with Leo Ornstein and Robert Casadesus; Composition with Roger Sessions. *Career:* Professor, University of California, Berkeley, 1949–91; Vising Professor at various universities and institutions; mem, American Academy of Arts and Letters; American Academy of Arts and Sciences; Phi Beta Kappa; Board of Directors, Koussevitzky Foundation. *Compositions include:* Orchestral: Violin Concerto, 1954; Three Symphonies, 1965, 1970; Cello Concerto, 1972; 3 Piano Concertos, 1973, 1974, 1992; Flute Concerto, 1977; Chamber: 5 String Quartets, 1942–87; 2 Piano Trios, 1946, 1989; Impromptu, for violin and pianoforte, 1960; To A Traveler for clarinet, violin and piano, 1971; Pilgrimage for flute, clarinet, violin, cello, piano and percussion, 1983; Dream Sequence for flute, oboe, clarinet, violin, viola, cello, piano and percussion, 1986; Spring Fever, for flute, oboe, clarinet, 2 violins, viola, violoncello, contrabass; pianoforte, percussion, 1996; Chicago Bells, for violin and piano, 1997; Piano Quartet, 1998; From Time to Time for flute, oboe, clarinet, bassoon, percussion, 2 violins, viola and 2 cellos, premiered at Chamber Music Society of Minnesota, 2001; Vocal: Operas; Christmas in Peebles Town (wincor), 1960; Angle of Repose, (Stegner-Hall), 1976, commissioned by San Francisco Opera; Requiem for Soprano, Chorus and Orchestra, 1984; 5 Roethke Songs for soprano and piano, 1990; Adam, cantata for Mixed Chorus, Soprano Solo, Chamber Orchestra, 1994; Songs of Then and Now for girls chorus, soprano, alto, flute, clarinet, violin, piano and percussion, 1998. *Recordings:* Pilgrimage; Collage Ensemble, Gunther Schuller; Trio No. 2, Francesco Trio; Quartet No. 4, Emerson Quartet; Quartets No. 4 and No. 5, Pro Arte Quartet; Impromptu for violin and pianoforte; Parnassus Ensemble: Dream Sequence, Five Roethke Songs, Three Piece Suite, Campion Songs, To a Traveler, Symphony No. 3, London Symphony; Serenade; Piano Sonata; Requiem and 3rd Piano Concerto. *Publications:* Extra Measures and Metrical Ambiguity in Beethoven, 1973. *Honours:* Guggenheim Fellowship, 1953–54, 1959–60; Naumberg Award, 1960; Holder, Jerry and Evelyn Hemmings Chambers Chair in Music, University of California, Berkeley, 1989–91; Various grants and commissions. *Address:* 2625 Rose Street, Berkeley, CA 94708, USA.

IMDAHL, Heinz; Singer (Baritone); b. 9 Aug. 1924, Düsseldorf, Germany. *Education:* Studied with Berthold Putz in Krefeld and at the Cologne Musikhochschule. *Career:* Debut: Detmold 1948, as Morales in Carmen; Sang in Bremen, Berlin and Düsseldorf, the became a member of the Bayerische Staatsoper Munich; Guest appearances in Florence 1953, Rio de Janeiro, Turin 1972 and Oslo 1973; Repertoire included leading roles in operas by Wagner, Verdi, Strauss and Verdi. *Recordings:* Das Liebesverbot by Wagner.

IMMELMAN, Niel; Pianist; b. 13 Aug. 1944, Bloemfontein, South Africa. *Education:* Royal College of Music with Cyril Smith, 1964–69; Studied privately with Maria Curcio, 1970–77. *Career:* Debut: Rachmaninov, London Philharmonic Orchestra, 1969; Has given concerts at the Royal Festival Hall, London, and Amsterdam Concertgebouw with major orchestras and leading conductors; Concert tours of all continents; Teaching positions: Professor of Piano at Royal College of Music, 1980–; Masterclasses at Chopin Academy (Warsaw), Hong Kong Academy for Performing Arts, Moscow Conservatoire, Sibelius Academy (Helsinki),

Toronto Royal Conservatory and the Universities of Berlin and Vienna; mem, Royal Society of Musicians of Great Britain; European Piano Teachers' Association. *Recordings include:* Complete Piano music of Suk; Works by Beethoven, Schubert, Schumann, Dale and Bloch; Featured in Classic CD Magazine's Pick of the Year. *Contributions:* International Piano Quarterly; Musicus and The Independent. *Honours:* Chappell Gold Medal, 1969; Fellow of the Royal College of Music, 2000. *Address:* 41 Ashen Grove, London, SW19 8B1,. *Telephone:* (20) 8947-7201. *Fax:* (20) 8946-8846. *E-mail:* immelman@lineone.net.

INBAL, Eliahu; British/Israeli conductor; b. 16 Feb. 1936, Jerusalem; s. of Jehuda Joseph Inbal and Leah Museri Inbal; m. Helga Fritzsche 1968; three s. *Education:* Acad. of Music, Jerusalem, Conservatoire Nat. Supérieur, Paris. *Career:* from 1963 guest conductor with numerous orchestras including Milan, Rome, Berlin, Munich, Hamburg, Stockholm, Copenhagen, Vienna, Budapest, Amsterdam, London, Paris, Tel Aviv, New York, Chicago, Toronto and Tokyo; Chief Conductor, Radio Symphony Orchestra, Frankfurt 1974–90, Hon. Conductor 1995–, Teatro La Fenice 1984–87; Hon. Conductor, Nat. Symphony Orchestra, RAI Torino 1996–; Chief Conductor Berlin Symphony Orchestra 2001–; has made numerous recordings, particularly of Mahler, Bruckner, Berlioz and Shostakovich. *Honours:* First Prize, Int. Conductors' Competition 'G. Cantelli' 1963; Officier des Arts des Lettres 1995; Goldenes Ehrenzeichen, Vienna 2001. *Address:* Hessischer Rundfunk, Bertramstrasse 8, 6000 Frankfurt, Germany. *Telephone:* (611) 1552371.

INCIHARA, Taro; Singer (Tenor); b. 2 Jan. 1950, Yamagata, Japan. *Education:* Studied in Japan and at the Juilliard School, New York. *Career:* Debut: Tokyo, 1980, as Gounod's Faust; European debut, 1982, as Calaf at the Teatro San Carlo, Naples; Paris Opéra from 1983 as Macduff, Riccardo, Don Carlos and the Duke of Mantua; Guest appearances at Nice, Turin, Naples, Santiago and Buenos Aires, Verdi's Requiem, 1987; Macerata Festival, 1987, Orange, 1989, as Isamaele in Nabucco; Metropolitan Opera, 1987–89, as the Italian Singer and the Duke of Mantua; Further European engagements at Turin and Genoa; Sang Riccardo in Un Ballo in Maschera for Opera Pacific at Costa Mesa, California, 1991; Other roles include Gabriele Adorno, La Scala, 1989; Verdi's Rodolfo and Alfredo, Enzo in La Gioconda and Edgardo in Lucia di Lammermoor. *Address:* c/o Opera Pacific, 3187 Red Hill Avenue, Suite 230, Costa Mesa, CA 92626, USA.

INCONTRERA, Roxana; Singer (Soprano); b. 1966, Ploiesti, Romania. *Education:* Studied in Bucharest. *Career:* Sang at the Rudolstadt Opera, then at the Dresden Staatsoper (Queen of Night, Magic Flute, 1989); Guest appearances at Barcelona, in La Cenerentola, 1992, Salle Pleyel (Paris), Berlin, Essen, Düsseldorf, Hannover, Chemnitz, Leipzig, Halle; Other roles include Rossini's Rosina, Mozart's Sandrina (La finta giardiniera) and Constanze, Violetta, Zerbinetta, Fiakermilli (Arabella), Italian Singer (Capriccio), Olympia and Oscar; Sang Elvira in L'Italiana in Algeri at Dresden, 1998; Sang the Queen of Night and Verdi's Oscar at Dresden, 2000; Frequent concert engagements. *Address:* c/o Staatsoper Dresden, Theaterplatz 2, 01067 Dresden,.

INGLE, William; Singer (Tenor); b. 17 Dec. 1934, Texhoma, Texas, USA. *Education:* Studied at the Academy of Vocal Arts in Philadelphia with Dorothy di Scala; With Sidney Dietsch in New York and Luigi Ricci in Rome. *Career:* Debut: Flensburg 1965, as Tamino; Sang at the Linz Opera, Düsseldorf, Kassel, Frankfurt, Graz, Leipzig, Montreal, Hanover, Wellington and Vienna; Other roles include Ernesto, Don Ottavio, Manrico, Lohengrin, Parsifal, Walther, Canio, Erik, Radames, Ferrando, Rodolfo, Almaviva, Flamand in Capriccio, the Duke of Mantua and Alfredo; Sang at Linz, 1976, in the premiere of Der Aufstand by Nikolaus Eder; Masaniello in La Muette de Portici by Auber, 1989; Television appearances as Herod, (Salome), in Canada and Tom Rakewell, (The Rake's Progress), in Austria.

INGOLFSSON, Atli; Composer; b. 21 Aug. 1962, Keflavik, Iceland; m. Thuridur Jonsdottir, 18 Aug 1990. *Education:* Diploma in Classical Guitar, 1983, BM, Theory and Composition, 1984, Reykjavík School of Music; BA, Philosophy, University of Iceland, 1986; Study with D Anzaghi, Milan Conservatory, 1985–88; Private study with G Grisey and Auditor at CNSMP, Paris, 1988–90. *Career:* Performances at Young Nordic music festivals, other Nordic music festivals and various occasions in Iceland, 1981–; His Due Bagattelle for Clarinet premiered in Milan, 1986 and widely performed; Various performances in Europe, 1990–, including Montreuil, May 1991, Varèse, July 1991; Amsterdam, Sept 1991, Milan, Nov and Dec 1991; Commissioned by IRCAM, Paris, to write for computer piano and ensemble, 1993. *Compositions:* Recorded on CD, Due Bagettelle for Clarinet; Et Toi Pale Soleil, for 4 voices and instruments; A Verso for piano, and O Versa for piano and 12 instruments, OPNA for bass clarinet and marimba; Le Pas Les Pentes for 8 instruments. *Address:* Borgarvegur 28, 260 Njardvik,.

INGRAM, Jaime (Ricardo Jean); Concert Pianist and Diplomat; b. 13 Feb. 1928, Panama City, Panama; m. Nelly Hirsch, 29 Jan 1950, 2 s., 1 d. *Education:* Piano Diploma, Juilliard Institute of Music, New York,

USA, 1949, studied with Olga Samarof and Joseph Bloch; Piano Diploma, Conservatoire Nationale de Paris, France, 1950, studied with Yves Nat; Additional studies with Alberto Sciarretti, Panama, and Bruno Seidlhofer, Vienna. *Career:* Professor of Piano, National Conservatory of Music, Panama, 1952–56; Escuela Paulista de Musica, São Paulo, Brazil, 1958–60; Escuela Profesional, Panama, 1962–64; Conservatorio Jaime Ingram, 1964–69, University of Panama, 1972–74; Director of Culture, 1969–73; General Director of Culture, 1974–78, Panamanian Ambassador to Spain, 1978–82; Panamanian Ambassador to the Holy Sea, 1982–; Concert tours as soloist and piano duo with Nelly Hirsch; South and Central America, Cuba, Spain, Italy, Federal Republic of Germany; Bulgaria, Poland, Zürich and Geneva, Switzerland, London, England, Amsterdam, Netherlands, USSR, Israel. *Publications:* Hector Villa Lobos; Muzio Clementi, the Father of the Pianoforte, Antonio de Cabezon, Tientos y Diferencias; Orientacion Musical 1974, Historia, Compositores y Repertorio del Piano 1978.

INOUE, Michiyoshi; Conductor; b. 23 Dec. 1946, Tokyo, Japan. *Education:* Studies, Toho Gakuen Academy of Music with Professor Saitoh. *Career:* Associate Conductor of the Tokyo Metropolitan Symphony Orchestra, 1970; Conducted at La Scala, 1971; Conducted Orchestras in Paris, Vienna, Geneva, Berlin, Brussels, Hamburg, Munich, Stuttgart, Madrid, Naples, Turin, Florence, Lisbon, London, Helsinki, Leipzig, Copenhagen; Tours of Israel, Eastern Europe, Russia; Conducted the East Berlin Orchestra on tour to Japan; Concerts in Australia, New Zealand and with the Washington National Symphony in the USA; Conducted Opera in Vienna and at Cluj, Romania; Music Director, New Japan Philharmonic Orchestra, 1983–88; Music Director of the Kyoto Symphony Orchestra, 1990. *Recordings include:* Mahler's 6th, 5th and 4th Symphonies with the Royal Philharmonic; Albums with the Netherlands Chamber Orchestra (Nippon Columbia). *Honours:* First Prize, Guido Cantelli Competition, Milan, 1971. *Current Management:* Kajimoto International, Tokyo, Japan. *Address:* 3–7–16–103, Uehara, Shibuyaku, Tokyo,. *E-mail:* maestro@sc4.so-net.ne.jp.

IOACHIMESCU, Calin; Composer; b. 29 March 1949, Bucharest, Romania; m. Anca Vartolomei-Ioachimescu, 1 s., 1 d. *Education:* Graduate, Bucharest Music College, 1968; Graduate, 1st Place, Bucharest High School, Academy of Music, Composition with Stefan Niculescu, 1975; Computer music courses, IRCAM, Paris, 1985; International New Music Holiday Courses, Darmstadt, 1980, 1984. *Career:* Debut: In concert, Bucharest Radio Symphonic Orchestra, 1978; Symphonic, chamber and electronic works played throughout Romania and over the world; Compositions broadcast: Bucharest, France and Brussels; Sound Engineer, Romanian Broadcasting; Head, Computer Music Studio, Bucharest. *Compositions include:* Magic Spell for female voices, strings and percussion, 1974; String Quartet No. 1, 1974; Tempo 80, 1979; Oratio ll, 1981; Hierophonies, 1984; String Quartet No. 2, 1984; Spectral Music for saxophones and tape, 1985; Concerto for trombone, double bass and orchestra, 1986; Celliphonia for cello and tape, 1988; Palindrom/7, 1992; Concerto for saxophones and orchestra, commissioned by the Ministry of Culture, France, 1994; Les Eclats de l'Abîme for double bass, saxophone and tape, Radio France, 1995; Heptagrama for saxophones and tape, Ministry of Culture, France, 1998; Concerto for violin, cello and orchestra, 2002; Film music. *Recordings:* Various labels. *Publications:* Oratio ll, Paris; Bucharest: Tempo 80; String Quartet No. 2; Celliphonia. *Address:* Str Ardeleni 28, Sect 2, 72164-Bucharest,. *Telephone:* 216104425. *E-mail:* ucmr@itcnet.ro.

IONESCO-VOVU, Constantin; Pianist and Professor; b. 27 May 1932, Floresti, Romania; m. Margareta Gabriel, 7 Sept 1961, deceased 1983. *Education:* Bucharest Superior Music Conservatory Hochschule, (Univ. of Music), 1955. *Career:* Concerts as Soloist with Symphony Orchestras, Piano Recitals and Chamber Music in Romania, France, Germany, Poland, Russia, Norway, Sweden, Denmark, Netherlands, Hungary, Czechoslovakia, Switzerland, Austria, Portugal, USA, Korea, Japan, Warsaw Autumn Festival, Evian Festival; Professor, (concert class, piano) Head of Piano Section, University of Music, Bucharest; Visiting Professor Nagoya, Japan and Keimyung Univ., Taega, Korea; Masterclasses in Romania, Germany, Netherlands, USA, Korea, Japan; Member of International Juries for Piano Competitions in Romania, , France, Germany, Italy, Portugal mem. Pres. of European Piano Teachers Association, Romania. *Recordings:* Radio recordings and albums in Romania, Germany, the Netherlands, Austria. *Publications:* Aurèle Stroë, concert music for piano, percussion and brass, 1968; C Silvestri Piano Works, Vol. I, 1973, Vol. II 1979; Romanian Piano Music, 1989; Dinu Lipatti Fantaisie, 1999; Essays about technique, aesthetics, and style of musical interpretation in musical periodicals. *Address:* Str Vasile Lascar 35, 020492 Bucharest, . *Fax:* +4021 211–3095. *E-mail:* cionvovu@hotmail.com.

IONITZA, Alexandru; Singer (Tenor); b. 1953, Romania. *Education:* Studied Voice with Constantin Stroescu of the Bucharest Conservatory of Music. *Career:* Sang in opera at Bucharest and Munster, then the Deutsche Oper am Rhein, Düsseldorf, from 1984 (Rodolfo in La Bohème, 1993); Bregenz Festival, 1987–88, as Hoffmann; Cologne Opera, 1991, as Alfredo and Nemorino; Further engagements as Mozart's Belmonte at the Vienna Volksoper, at San Diego, the Theater am Gärtnerplatz, Munich, and Stuttgart; Many concert appearances. *Recordings include:* Elemer in Arabella; Oedipus Rex by Stravinsky; Beppo in Pagliacci; Alzira by Verdi; Narraboth in Salome. *Address:* c/o Deutsche Oper am Rhein, Heinrich-Heine Alle 16a, 40213 Düsseldorf,.

IRANYI, Gabriel; Composer, Pianist and Lecturer; b. 6 June 1946, Cluj, Romania; m. Elena Nistor, 20 Aug 1969, 1 s. *Education:* Special School of Music, Cluj, 1955–65; George Dima High School of Music, Cluj, Composition and Musicology Department, Student of Prof D Sigismund Todutza. *Career:* Teaching Assistant, George Enesco High School of Music, Jassy, Romania, 1971–76; Lecturer, Cfar Saba Conservatoire, 1982–86; Since 1988 Professor of the Leo–Borchara–Musikschule in Berlin. *Compositions:* Segments, De Profundis; Bird of Wonder; Until the Day Breaks; Portraits of JS Bach; For solo piano; Laudae for 2 pianos; Song of Degrees for Chamber Ensemble; Altermances for percussion; Alef for soprano voice, clarinet, cello and piano; Realm for solo cello and electric amplification; Solstice for violin, cello and clarinet; Electric Amplication; Shir Hamaalot for organ; Tempora for string quartet, Meditation and Prayer, for violin and 15 strings; Laudae, for 2 pianos, or with chamber orchestra. *Address:* Gierkeplatz 10, Berlin 10585,.

IRELAND, Helen Dorcas, BMus, MMus; British musician; b. 2 Nov. 1952; m. Gregory Rose; one s. *Education:* Purcell School London, Univ. of Birmingham, Royal Northern Coll. of Music, Peabody Conservatory, Baltimore, USA. *Career:* accompanist and ensemble player 1976–84; Theatre Musical Dir in many English repertory theatres and the Royal Nat. Theatre; extensive work in Germany; education work in drama schools and summer schools; private coaching, on staff of Guildhall School of Music and Drama 1984–; mem. Musicians' Union, Incorporated Soc. of Musicians. *Address:* 57 Whitehorse Road, Stepney, London, E1 0ND, England (home). *Telephone:* (20) 7790-5883 (home). *Fax:* (20) 7265-9170 (home). *E-mail:* gregory-rose@tisl.co.uk (home).

IRELAND, (William) Patrick, ARCM, MMus; viola player; b. 20 Nov. 1923, Helston, Cornwall, England; m. Peggy Gray; four c. *Education:* Wellington College, Worcester College, Oxford, Hull University. *Career:* Viola, Allegri String Quartet, 1953–77, 1988; has taken part in the premieres of quartets by Martin Dalby, 1972, Nicola LeFanu, Peter Sculthorpe, Elizabeth Maconchy, Robert Sherlaw-Johnson and Sebastian Forbes; Two Clarinet Quintets by Jennifer Fowler and Nicola LeFanu, 1971; 4 Quartets by Barry Guy, Jonathan Harvey, Alison Bauld, Edward Cowie, 1973; Complete Beethoven Quartets at the 1974 Cheltenham Festival; Taught and coached chamber music at the Menuhin School of Music in the 1960s; Assistant Head of Strings at Royal Northern College of Music, 1977–80. *Recordings:* With Allegri String Quartet; Bach Brandenburg Concertos with Menuhin and Bath Festival Orchestra; 2 CDs with Lindsay Quartet, as 2nd viola: Dvořák and Mozart Quintets. *Honours:* Doctor of Music, honoris causa, Southampton University. *Address:* Hillgrove House, Dunkerton, Bath, Somerset BA2 8AS, England.

IRMAN, Regina; Composer; b. 22 March 1957, Winterthur, Switzerland. *Education:* Studied guitar and percussion at Winterthur Conservatory. *Compositions include:* In Darkness Let me Dwell for mezzo and ensemble, 1982; Speclum for 4 clarinets and 2 percussion, 1984; Ein vatter ländischer Liederbogen, based on texts by Adolf Wölfli, for mezzo and partly prepared grand piano, 1985–86; Zahlen for prepared piano, 1986; Ein Trauermarsch, based on texts by Adolf Wölfli, for percussion trio and speaker, 1987; Passacaglia for clarinet 1990; Requiem, based on a text by Anna Achmatova, for 25 female and 3 male voices, 1991–93; Drei Tänze, based on a text by Anna Achmatova, for soprano, female speaker/piano, clarinet and accordion, 1996–97. *Recordings:* Portrait, 2001. *Address:* c/o SUISA, Bellariastrasse 82, 8038 Zürich,.

IROSCH, Mirjana; Singer (Soprano); b. 24 Oct. 1939, Zagreb, Yugoslavia. *Education:* Studied at the Zagreb Conservatory with Fritz Lunzer. *Career:* Debut: Linz 1962, as Mercedes in Carmen; Sang for many years at the Vienna Volksoper: Took part in the 1968 premiere of the revised version of Der Zerrissene by Von Einem; Tour of Japan 1982; Guest appearances in Graz, Frankfurt, Basle, Brussels and Munich; Other roles include Micaela, Marenka in The Bartered Bride, Fiordiligi, Donna Elvira, Judith in Duke Bluebeard's Castle, Concepcion in L'Heure Espagnole, Rosina and Rosalinde. *Recordings:* Die Lustige Witwe. *Address:* Volksoper, Wahringerstrasse 78, 1090 Vienna, Austria.

IRVINE, Robert; Cellist; b. 11 May 1963, Glasgow, Scotland. *Education:* Royal College of Music, London; Studied with Christopher Bunting, Amaryllis Fleming. *Career:* Member, Brindisi String Quartet, 1984–; Philharmonia Orchestra, 1986–; Appeared on Channel 4 television, and BBC television and radio; Principal Cello, London Soloists Chamber Orchestra, Britten-Pears Orchestra, 1985–86; mem, Musicians Union.

Recordings: Britten 2nd Quartet; Berg Op 3 Quartet. *Honours:* Foundation Scholar, Royal College of Music; Ivor James Cello Prize; Stern Award for Diploma Recital; Dip.RCM; ARCM. *Address:* 8 Berwyn Road, London SE24 9 BD,.

IRWIN, Jane; Singer (Mezzo-soprano); b. 1968, England. *Education:* Lancaster University and Royal Northern College of Music. *Career:* Early appearances in Mahler's 3rd Symphony, under Kent Nagano, and Des Knaben Wunderhorn; Tchaikovsky's Maid of Orleans at the RNCM, 1994; Recitals at the Paris Châtelet, Bienne, Poland, Japan and Geneva; Elgar's Sea Pictures in Scotland, Beethoven's Ninth and Missa Solemnis at the Edinburgh Festival, 1996–97; Rossini's Stabat Mater under Semyon Bychkov, Penderecki's Te Deum with the composer and The Dream of Gerontius conducted by David Willcocks; Covent Garden 1995–96, in Götterdämmerung and Die Walküre; Season 1997 in Die Zauberflöte and Ariadne auf Naxos at Aix, concert tour with the English Concert to Italy and Vienna and Hallé Orchestra concert. *Honours:* Decca Kathleen Ferrier Prize, 1991; Frederic Cox Award, 1992; Winner, 1993 Singers' Competition at the Geneva International Competition; Richard Tauber Prize, 1995. *Current Management:* Ingpen & Williams Ltd, 7 St George's Court, 131 Putney Bridge Road, London, SW15 2PA, England.

ISAACS, Mark; Australian composer and pianist; b. 22 June 1958, London, England. *Education:* BMus, New South Wales Conservatorium of Music, 1976; MMus, Eastman School of Music, 1986; study with Peter Sculthorpe, Josef Tal and Samuel Adler, among others. *Career:* mem., Mark Isaacs Jazz Trio; commissions from Musica Viva, Australia Ensemble, Sydney String Quartet and Seymour Group, among others; conductor and producer of various projects; toured Russia, 1994, 1995, 1996; established GraceMusic record label, 1997. *Compositions include:* Three Excursions for woodwind, 1971; Reverie for piano and orchestra, 1972; Reflections for piano and orchestra, 1973; Three to Go for big band, 1974; Interlude for flute and piano, 1975; Ballade for big band, 1976; D'Urbeville House for big band, 1976; Mad Jean: A Musical, 1977; Ode to Peace for big band, 1977; Footsteps for big band, 1977; Sad Girl for big band, 1977; Lamente for oboe and piano, 1978; Fantasy for violin and piano, 1979; Four Lyric Pieces for string trio, 1980; Liturgy for string orchestra, 1980; Ha Laitsun for two pianos, 1981; Quintet for Brass, 1981; Moving Pictures for piano and orchestra, 1982; Four Glimpses for orchestra, 1982; Diversion for six players, 1983; I Am for mixed chorus a cappella, 1984; Three Scherzi for winds and cello, 1984; String Quartet, 1984; So It Does for six players, 1985; Ballade for Orchestra, 1985; Three Songs for soprano and piano, 1985; Character References for violin and piano, 1985; Memoirs for percussion and piano, 1986; Preludes for piano, 1986; Visitation for solo piano, 1986; Four Comments for winds, 1986; Cantilena for bass clarinet and piano, 1987; Piece for flute and strings, 1987; Elegy for cello and piano, 1987; Variations for flute, clarinet and cello, 1988; Debekuth for violin and orchestra, 1988; Burlesque Miniatures for String Quartet, 1988; Drums of Thunder, 1988; Purple Prayer for jazz quartet and strings, 1989; Beach Dreaming (one-act opera for young people), 1990; Litany for piano and orchestra, 1991; Threnody for violin and cello, 1992; Lyric Caprice for cello and piano, 1993; Songs of the Universal for viola, cello, clarinet and piano, 1994; Scherzo for small orchestra, 1995; Voices The Passion of St Jeanne, 1996; The Burning Thread for mixed chorus a cappella, 1997; Scherzo for wind quintet, 1998; Three Excursions for concert band and strings, 1999; Chaconne/Salsa for cor anglais and orchestra, 2001; Three Days of Rain, 2001; Kensington Rags, 2002; Ave Maria for cello and piano, 2003; Canticle for trumpet and orchestra, 2003; various television and film themes. *Recordings:* Originals, 1981; Preludes, 1987; Encounters, 1990; For Sure, 1993; The Elements (four vols, Earth, Air, Water and Fire), 1996; Elders Suite (with Kenny Wheeler), 1997; On Reflection, 1998; Closer, 2000. *Honours:* 3rd Prize, 1st Tokyo International Competition for Chamber Music Composition, 1996; Fellowship Australia Council for the Arts, 1996–98; Commendation, Albert H Maggs Composition Prize, University of Melbourne, 1997; Membership: APRA. *E-mail:* gracemusic@bigpond.com. *Website:* www.listen.to/gracemusic.

ISAKADZE, Liana; Violinist and Conductor; b. 2 Aug. 1946, Tbilisi, Georgian Republic. *Education:* Tbilisi School for Most Educated Children, 1953–63; Tchaikovski Conservatory, Moscow, 1963–70. *Career:* Debut: International Festival Congregation, Moscow, 1956; Concerts all over the world; Russian television; Georgian television; Germany ZDF television film, Portrait Liana Ysakadze; Art Director and Conductor, Georgia State Chamber Orchestra, 1980–; mem, Leader of David Oistrakh School, Lenting bei Ingolstadt, Germany; Opened D Oistrakh Akademie Ingolstadt, 1993. *Compositions:* Many arranged for string orchestra; Sextets of Brahms, Tchaikovsky, Boccherini, Gershwin, Haydn, Bernstein, Dvořák, Mendelssohn and others. *Recordings:* Over 100 recordings and CDs including Firma Melodia, Firma Orfeusm Munich; Radio BR; MDR; Moscow radio. *Honours:* Folk Artist of USSR, 1988; Georgia State Prizes, 1982; Rustaveli prize, Taliashvili prize;

First prizes at International violin competitions; Tchaikovsky, 1970; Paris, 1965; Sibelius, 1970. *Address:* Siegrune Str 1, 60639 Munich,.

ISAKOVIC, Smiljka; Harpsichordist and Pianist; b. 23 March 1953, Belgrade, Yugoslavia. *Education:* Music secondary school, with honours, Belgrade 1965–69; American Community Schools, Athens, National Honour Society, 1969–71; Graduated, Belgrade Music Academy, 1974; Master's degree, Faculty of Music, Belgrade, 1979; Postgraduate piano studies, Tchaikovsky Conservatory, Moscow, USSR, 1978–79; Graduate, harpsichord, Royal Conservatory of Music, Madrid, Spain, 1984. *Career:* Debut: Belgrade, 1972; Performances throughout the former Yugoslavia, including festivals at Dubrovnik, Ljubljana, Ohrid, Belgrade, East and West Europe, the United Kingdom, USSR, USA, Cuba, Columbia; Masterclasses, harpsichord, international Centre des Jeunesses Musicales, Groznjan, Yugoslavia; Lectures, harpsichord; Music reviews, Evening News and Student newspapers, and Radio Belgrade; President, Association of Serbian Musicians. *Recordings:* Lady Plays–Keyboards, 1998; Radio and television appearances, Yugoslavia, Spain, Columbia. *Honours:* First Lady of the Harpsichord; Masaryk's Prize, artistic activities, Masaryk Academy of Arts, Prague, 1997; Title Queen of the Harpsichord, 1997. *Current Management:* Direccion artisitca Daniel, Los Madrazo, 16, 28014 Madrid, Spain. *Address:* Admirala Geprata 10, 11000 Belgrade, Serbia and Montenegro.

ISEPP, Martin Johannes Sebastian, ARCM; Pianist, Harpsichordist and Conductor; b. 30 Sept. 1930, Vienna, Austria; m. Rose Henrietta Harris 1966; two s. *Education:* Lincoln Coll., Oxford; private study with Prof. Leonie Gombrich, Oxford. *Career:* English Opera Group 1950s; music staff, Glyndebourne Festival Opera 1957, Chief Coach 1973, Head of Music Staff 1978–93; Head of Opera Training, Juilliard School of Music, New York, USA 1973–77; Head of Music Studies, National Opera Studio, London 1978–95; Head of Acad. of Singing, Banff Centre School of Fine Arts, Banff, AB, Canada 1981–93; accompanist to leading singers including Ilse Wolf, Janet Baker, John Shirley-Quirk, Elisabeth Schwarzkopf, Elisabeth Söderström, Jessye Norman, Anne Howells, Sheila Armstrong and Hugues Cuenod; conductor, Le nozze di Figaro 1984, Don Giovanni 1986, Glyndebourne Touring Company, Entführung, Washington Opera 1986–87 season; Music Dir for The Actor in Opera courses, William Walton Foundation on Ischia 1992–96; Asst Conductor, Metropolitan Opera, New York 1996–; various opera productions annually, at Fondation, Royaumont, Centre de la Voix 1998–. *Recordings:* as accompanist and continuo player. *Honours:* Carroll Donner Stuchell Medal for Accompanying, Harriet Cohen International Musical Foundation 1965, Hon. DFA, Wake Forest Univ. of North Carolina, USA 2002. *Address:* 37A Steeles Road, London, NW3 4RG, England. *E-mail:* miseppmusic@yahoo.co.uk.

ISHII, Kan; Composer; b. 30 March 1921, Tokyo, Japan. *Education:* Studied at the Mmasashino School of Music, 1939–43 and with Carl Orff in Munich, 1952–54. *Career:* Taught at the Toho Gakuen School of Music, 1954–56, the Aichi Prefectural Arts University at Nagoya, 1966–86, and 1939–43 and with Carl Orff in Munich, 1952–54. *Compositions:* The Mermaid and the Red Candle, 1 act opera, 1961; Princess Kaguya, 1 act opera, 1963; En no Gyoja, 3 act opera, 1965; Kesa and Morito, 3 act opera, 1968; Women are Wonderful, comic opera in 1 act, 1978; Kantomi, 3 act opera, 1981; Blue Lion, operetta, 1989.

ISHIKAWA, Shizuka; Violinist; b. 2 Oct. 1954, Tokyo, Japan; m. Jiri Schultz, 26 May 1978. *Education:* Diploma, Prague Music Academy, 1978; Studied with Professor Shin-ichi Suzuki and Saburo Sumi. *Career:* Performances at The Prague Spring Festival; Belgrade Music Festival; Warsaw Autumn Festival; Hungarian Music Week; Helsinki Music Festival; Czechoslovak Music Festival in Japan; Performances in Tokyo, Copenhagen, Prague, Vienna, Brussels, Bonn; Numerous Radio and Television broadcasts; Soloist with many major orchestras. *Recordings:* Concertos by Bartók, Bruch, Mozart, Myslivecek and Paganini. *Honours:* 2nd Prize, Wieniawski International Violin Competition, 1972; Silver Medal, Queen Elisabeth in Brussels, 1976; 3rd Prize, International Violin Competition of F Kreisler, 1979. *Current Management:* Konzerburo Andreas Braun, Koln 41, Lindenthal; Japan Arts Corp, Tokyo, Japan.

ISOKOSKI, Soile; Singer (Soprano); b. 14 Feb. 1957, Posio, Finland. *Education:* Studied at the Sibelius Academy, Kuopio and with Dorothy Irving in Sweden. *Career:* Debut: Formerly church organist, then gave concert debut as singer at Helsinki, 1986; Appearances at concert halls in Europe, Japan, USA; Performances at Milan, La Scala, Paris, Bastille, London, Covent Garden; State Operas in Hamburg, Berlin, Munich, Vienna; Salzburger Festspiele, Savonlinna Opera Festival; Season 1993 with Salzburg Festival debut, as First Lady in Die Zauberflöte, and Mozart's Countess at Hamburg; Covent Garden debut 1997 as Fiordiligi in Così fan tutte; Strauss's Four Last Songs with the Bavarian State Orchestra under Zubin Mehta at the 1999 Prom concerts, London; Season 2000–01 as Amelia Grimaldi at Helsinki,

Wagner's Eva at Covent Garden, Liu in Turandot and Desdemona at the Vienna Staatsoper; Engaged for New York Met debut as the Countess in Figaro, 2002; Mahler's Symphony of a Thousand at the London Proms, 2002. *Recordings:* Schumann, Frauenliebe und Leben, Liederkreis; Sibelius, Luonnotar, conducted by Neeme Järvi; Zemlinsky, Der Zwerg, conducted by James Conlon; Mozart, Donna Elvira in Don Giovanni conducted by Claudio Abbado; Beethoven, Fidelio conducted by Barenboim. *Honours:* Winner, Lappeenranta Singing Competition, 1987; 2nd prize, Cardiff Singer of the World Competition, 1987; Winner, Elly Ameling and Tokyo International Competitions. *Current Management:* Allegro Artist Management. *Address:* Tapiolan Keskustorni, 02100 Espoo,.

ISOMURA, Kazuhide; Violinist; b. 27 Dec. 1945, Tokyohashi, Japan. *Education:* Studied at the Juilliard School with members of the Juilliard Quartet. *Career:* Violist of the Tokyo Quartet from 1969; Regular concerts in the USA and abroad; First cycle of the complete quartets of Beethoven at the Yale at Norfolk Chamber Music Festival, 1986; Repeated cycles at the 92nd Street Y, NY, Ravinia and Israel Festivals, Yale, Princeton Universities; Season 1990–91 at Alice Tully Hall, Metropolitan Museum of Art, NY, Boston, Washington DC, Los Angeles, Cleveland, Detroit, Chicago, Miami, Seattle, San Francisco, Toronto; Tour of South America and two tours of Europe including Paris, Amsterdam, Bonn, Milan, Munich, Dublin, London, Berlin; Quartet-in-residence at Yale University; The University of Cincinnati College-Conservatory of Music. *Recordings:* Schubert's major Quartets; Mozart Flute Quartets with James Galway and Clarinet Quintet with Richard Stoltzman; Quartets by Bartók, Brahms, Debussy, Haydn, Mozart and Ravel; Beethoven Middle Period Quartets. *Honours:* Grand Prix du Disque du Montreux; Best Chamber Music Recording of the Year from Stero Review and the Gramophone; Four Grammy nominations. *Address:* Intermusica Artists' Management, 16 Duncan Terrace, London N1 8BZ,.

ISRAEL, Robert; Violist, Teacher and Composer; b. 12 June 1918, Berlin, Germany; m. Tamar Amrami, 20 Dec 1951, 1 s., 1 d. *Education:* Studied violin with Rudolph Bergmann, Viola with Oedeon Partos; Theory, Harmony Counterpoint Composition with Yitshak Edel, Rosowsky and Mordecai Seter; Teaching Diploma, 1942; Viola Diploma, Rubin Academy, Jerusalem and Tel-Aviv. *Career:* Debut: Elegie for Viola with string orchestra by Mordecal Seter, 1969; Violist and Tubist, Opera Orchestra, Tel-Aviv; Violin Teacher at various Kibbuzim, 1946–48; Teacher of Violin and Viola and Theory at Conservatory Hadera, 1952–; Member, Bass, Rinat Choir, 1957–58; Principal Violist, Haifa Symphony Orchestra, 1962–83; Performed with many chamber music groups. *Compositions include:* Five verses from Song of Songs for 2 voice choir, 1955; 6 pieces for violin and piano, 1988; Arrangement of Rosamunde, the Trout, Marche militaire (Schubert), 3 violins or 2 violins and viola, 1989; 14 songs, arrangement for popular orchestra, 1990; Saraband, Bourrée, Polonais (J. S. Bach) Sonatine (Beethoven), arranged for two violas or viola and violoncello, 1993; Diatonic, 3 octave scales with special fingering for violin, 1997, the same for viola, 2000; Music for 4 violas; Accompaniment parts for Mazas op.36 Etudes. *Address:* Ytsiat-Europa st 11, Beth Eliezer PO Box 10772, Hadera 38484,.

ISSERLIS, Steven; Cellist; b. 19 Dec. 1958, London, England. *Education:* International Cello Centre, 1969–76; Oberlin College, Ohio, 1976–78. *Career:* Debut: Wigmore Hall, London, 1977; Concerto, recital and chamber music appearances world-wide; Artistic Adviser to Cricklade Music Festival, Wiltshire; Played the Elgar Concerto with the Philharmonia, London, 1997; Chamber music by Mendelssohn at the 1997 Salzburg Festival; Chamber music by Brahms at the 2000 Salzburg Festival; Further engagements include concerts with Vladimir Ashkenazy and the Czech Philharmonic; The Wiener Symphoniker and again with Ashkenazy and Philadelphia; Season 2001 with chamber concerts in Berlin and Vienna; mem, Liszt Society, London; Dvořák Society; Honorary member, Royal Academy of Music. *Compositions:* Various arrangements for cello including Beethoven's Mandolin Variations. *Recordings include:* Britten Cello Symphony with City of London Sinfonia; Elgar Concerto, Bloch Schelomo with London Symphony Orchestra, Hickox; Tchaikovsky: Rococo Variations with Chamber Orchestra of Europe, Gardiner; Boccherini Concertos and Sonatas; John Tavener: The Protecting Veil with London Symphony Orchestra, Rozhdestvensky; Saint-Saëns: Concerto No. 1, Sonata No. 1, The Swan with London Symphony Orchestra, Tilson Thomas, CD and video; Tavener, Eternal Memory, Bloch, From Jewish Life with Moscow Virtuosi, Spivakov; Mendelssohn: Cello works with Melvyn Tan; Fauré: Cello works with Pascal Devoyon; Brahms and Frühling Clarinet Trios with Michael Collins and Stephen Hough; Don Quixote, conducted by Lorin Maazel, 2001. *Publications:* Why Beethoven Threw the Stew, 2001. *Honours:* C.B.E., 1998. *Current Management:* Harrison/Parrott Ltd, 12 Penzance Place, London, W11 4PA, England. *Telephone:* (20) 7229 9166. *Fax:* (20) 7221 5042. *Website:* www.harrisonparrott.com.

ITAMI, Naomi; Singer (Soprano); b. 1961, USA. *Education:* Guildhall School, London; Manhattan School, New York; Columbia University, New York. *Career:* Debut: As Zerlina in Don Giovanni under Charles Mackerras, Estates Theatre, Prague, 1991; Engagements at the Bach Festival, California; Tours of the USA and Far East with the Gregg Smith Singers; Covent Garden Young Artists' Recital series; Mozart's Blondchen with Scottish Opera; Lincoln Center Out-of-Doors Festival, New York; Divas' Tour of Europe; Despina at the Ludlow Festival, England; Susanna for Neath Opera, Wales and the European Centre of Vocal Arts, Belgium; Snape Maltings with the Borodin String Quartet; Buxton Festival; Maria, West Side Story, Dublin; Lady Thiang, The King and I, Broadway tour. *Recordings:* Four Lehar Operettas under Richard Bonynge. Honours; Maggie Teyte Prize, 1991; Prix de Maurice Ravel, France, 1991. *Address:* Music International, 13 Ardilaun Road, London N5 2QR,.

ITIN, Ilya; Concert Pianist; b. 1970, Russia. *Education:* Studied with Natalia Litvinova at the Sverdlovsk Music School for Gifted Children; Tchaikovsky State Conservatoire, Moscow; New York with Yin Cheng Zong, from 1990. *Career:* Appearances with leading orchestras including the Cleveland under Dohnányi, and National Symphony under Skrowaczewski, from 1991; Recitals at Washington Kennedy Center and Lincoln Center, New York; Further concerts with European orchestras; Season 1997–98 debut at the London Proms with the BBC Philharmonic under Sinaisky, engagements associated with the Leeds Piano Competition, and European tour with the City of Birmingham Symphony under Simon Rattle. *Honours:* First Prize and Chopin Prize in the Ninth Robert Casadesus Competition, Cleveland; First Prize and Contemporary Music Prize in the Leeds International Piano Competition, 1996. *Address:* c/o BBC Philharmonic Orchestra, New Broadcasting House, Oxford Road, Manchester, M60 1 SJ,.

IVALDI, Jean-Marc; Singer (Baritone); b. 6 May 1953, Toulon, France. *Education:* Studied in Paris at the Conservatoire National and The School of the Grand Opera. *Career:* Debut: Paris Opéra in 1983 as Yamadori in Butterfly; Sang Rossini's Figaro at Liège, 1983, and appeared at Bordeaux, Toulouse, Nancy, Metz, Dijon, and Tours; As Bretigny in Manon and Ramiro in L'Heure Espagnole at Paris; Philadelphia in 1986 as Morales in Carmen, and Heidenheim 1989 as Escamillo; Other roles include Alfonso in La Favorite, Belcore, Albert in Werther, Ourrias in Mireille, Manuel in La Vida Breve, Germont, Paquiro in Goyescas, Frederic in Lakmé and Jarno in Mignon; Sang Valentin in Faust at St Etienne in 1990; Concert engagements include Carmina Burana at St Etienne and Joseph in L'Enfance du Christ at Nancy; Sang Escamillo at St Etienne, 1995. *Recordings:* La Favorite; Sonora in La Fanciulla del West, conducted by Leonard Slatkin. *Address:* Saison Lyrique de Saint Etienne, 8 Place de l'Hotel de Ville, 42000 St Etienne,.

IVAN, Monica; Singer (Soprano); b. 1940, Stockholm, Sweden. *Education:* Studied in Stockholm, and in Siena with Luigi Ricci. *Career:* Debut: Stora Theater, Gothenburg, 1964, as the Queen of Night; Sang at the Hanover Opera, 1966–68, Zürich, 1968–69, Gothenburg from 1970; Sang the Queen of Night at the 1974 Savonlinna Festival; Guest appearances in Moscow and elsewhere in Russia from 1976, as Violetta, Gilda and Marguerite in Faust; Other roles have included Santuzza, Butterfly, the Trovatore Leonora and Amelia (Un Ballo in Maschera). *Address:* c/o Göteborgs Opera, C Nilssons Gatan, 41104 Göteborg,.

IVANOV, Emil; Singer (Tenor); b. 1960, Rome, Italy. *Education:* Studied in Sofia, Bulgaria. *Career:* Sang first at the National Opera, Sofia, then appeared as Don Carlos at Essen, 1987; St Gallen, 1988–89, as Ernani and Pollione in Norma; Macerata Festival as Manrico; Guest engagements as Cavaradossi and Radames at Frankfurt, Zamoro in Verdi's Alzira at Fidenza, as the Prince in Rusalka at Houston and Don José at the Bregenz Festival, 1991; Vienna Staatsoper, 1992, as Dvořák's Dimitri, Radames and in Carmen; Il Tabarro at Volksoper; Attila at Nice; Cavaradossi in Tosca at Metropolitan New York, 1993–94; 1994–95 Season: Carmen, La Traviata, Hérodiade, Madama Butterfly at Vienna-Staatsoper; Alfredo, Pinkerton, Don José, Carmen at Cologne, Il Tabarro at Birmingham and Don José at Pretoria; I Lombardi at St Gallen; Otello at Varna; Season 1999–2000 as Smetana's Dalibor at Cagliari, Alim in Le Roi de Lahore by Massenet at Bordeaux, Radames in Karlsruhe and Henri in Les Vêpres Siciliennes at St Gallen; Covent Garden debut 2002, as Carlo in I Masnadieri. *Address:* Karl Schweighoferg 8/1/1, 1070 Vienna,.

IVASHKIN, Alexander (Vasilevich); Cellist, Conductor, Writer and Critic; b. 17 Aug. 1948, Blagoveshchensk, Russia; m. Natalia Mikhailovna Pavlutskaya, 30 July 1969. *Education:* BMus, Performance and Musicology, Gnessin Special Music School, 1966; MMus, Russian Academy of Music, Moscow, 1971; PhD, Russian Art History Institute, 1978; Higher Doctorate, 1993. *Career:* Solo Cellist, Bolshoi Theatre Orchestra, Moscow, Russia, 1971–91; Member, Board of Directors, Bolshoi Opera Company, 1987–91; Solo recitals and appearances with orchestras, chamber music concerts, recording in over 30 countries in Europe, Russia, USA, Australia, Japan and New Zealand; Artistic Director, Bolshoi Soloists, 1978–91; Professor of Cello, University of Canterbury, New Zealand, 1991–99; Artistic Director, Adam International Cello Festival/Competition, 1995–; Professor of Music, Director, Centre for Russian Music, University of London, 1999–. *Recordings include:* Shostakovich, Cello Concertos Nos 1 and 2, 1998; Schnittke, Complete Cello Music, 1998–2002; Schumann, Gretchaninov, Cello Concertos, 1999–2000; Prokofiev, Complete Cello Music, 1996–2002; Tcherepnin, Complete Cello Music, 2000; Roslavets, Complete Cello Music, 2001; Rachmaninov, Complete Cello Music, 2003; Kancheli: Cello Concertos, 2002–04. *Publications:* Krzysztof Penderecki, 1983; Charles Ives and the 20th Century Music, 1991; Conversation with A Schnittke, 1994; Alfred Schnittke, 1996; Rostrospective (on M Rostropovich), 1997; A Schnittke Reader, 2002. *Current Management:* Columbia Artists, 28 Cheverton Road, London, N19. *Current Management:* (Netherlands only): Ivy Artists, Postbus 592, 1200 AN Hilversum, Netherlands. *Address:* c/o Music Department, Goldsmiths College, University of London, London SE14 6NW, England. *Telephone:* (20) 7919-7646. *Fax:* (20) 7919-7247. *E-mail:* a.ivashkin@gold.ac.uk.

IWAKI, Hiroyuki; Conductor; b. 6 Sept. 1932, Tokyo, Japan. *Education:* Studied percussion at the Tokyo Music Academy and conducting with Akeo Watanabe. *Career:* Assistant Conductor of the NHK, Japanese Broadcasting Symphony Orchestra, 1954; Conducted many premieres between 1957 and 1960; Conducted the Philharmonic Choir of Tokyo and was Musical Director of the Fujiwara Opera Company, 1965–67; Guest conductor of orchestras in Hamburg, Vienna and Berlin, 1966–69; Musical Director of the NHK Symphony from 1969, the Melbourne Symphony Orchestra from 1974; Director of the Orchestra-Ensemble Kanazawa, 1988; Conducted the first performances of works by Dallapiccola, (Concerto per la notte di natale de l'anno, 1956); Takemitsu: Marginilia, 1976, Dreamtime, 1982, A Way to Love, 1982 and Star-Isle, 1982; Isang Yun, (Symphony No. 4, 1986). *Recordings include:* Beethoven's 9th Symphony, with the NHK Orchestra; Bartók Concerto for Orchestra (Melbourne Symphony); Hungarian Rhapsodies by Liszt (Vienna State Opera Orchestra); Messiaen Couleurs de la cité céleste, Oiseaux Exotiques, Reveil des Oiseaux and Sept Hai-Kai (Decca); Dutch music with the Hague Philharmonic. *Address:* c/o Melbourne Symphony, PO Box 443, East Caulfield, Vic 3145,.

IWASAKI, Ko; Cellist; b. 16 Aug. 1944, Tokyo, Japan; m. Yurie Ishio, 21 Dec 1979, 2 s. *Education:* Toho Conservatoire; Juilliard School of Music, USA, 1964–66; Studied with: Leonard Rose, Harvey Shapiro, 1964–66; Pablo Casals, Puerto Rico, 1966. *Career:* Debut: Recital at Carnegie Recital Hall, New York, 1966; Recital at Wigmore Hall, London, England, 1968; Performed with: London Symphony, 1972; Participant, Summer Festivals: Marlboro; Portland, Oregon; Kuhmo, Finland; Lockenhaus, Austria; Performances in USA, Europe, Russia and the Orient; Director, Moonbeach Music Camp, Okinawa, Japan, 1979–; Director, Cello Masterclass, Southern Methodist University, USA. *Recordings:* Ko Iwasaki Plays Schubert Arpeggione Sonata; Beethoven Sonatas; Shostakovich Sonata; Japanese Contemporary Works for Cello; Ko Iwasaki and Staffan Scheja Play Sonatas by Rachmaninov and Grieg; Iwasaki, Requibros; 19 Short Pieces, Compact Disc; Beethoven: 2 Trios; Dvořák, Tchaikovsky with Polish National Radio Symphony; Haydn Cello Concerto No. 1 and No. 2, with Polish Chamber Orchestra. *Honours:* 3rd Prizes: Vienna International Cello Competition, 1967; Munich International Competition, 1967; Budapest International Cello Competition, 1968, Tchaikovsky International Competition; 2nd Prize, Cadao International Cello Competition. *Address:* 5732 Still Forest Drive, Dallas, TX 75252, USA.

IZQUIERDO, Juan Pablo; Musician and Conductor; b. 21 July 1935, Santiago, Chile; m. Trinidad Jimenez, 15 Dec 1973, 1 s., 1 d. *Education:* Graduate in Musical Composition, University of Chile, 1957; Conducting studies with Professor Hermann Scherchen, in Gravesano, Switzerland, 1958–61. *Career:* Debut: With National Symphony of Chile, Sept 1961; Director of Music Department, Catholic University of Santiago; Principal Conductor, Gulbenkian Orchestra, Lisbon, Philharmonic Orchestra of Chile, National Symphony of Chile; Guest conducting, Berlin, Frankfurt, Hamburg, Vienna, Paris, Madrid, Jerusalem, Munich, elsewhere; Director of Orchestral Studies at Carnegie-Mellon University, Pittsburgh, USA; Music Director, National Symphony of Chile. *Recordings:* Bach: The Art of Fugue; Mozart: Requiem; Beethoven Symphonies; Brahms German Requiem; Mahler Symphonies: Britten: War Requiem; Stravinsky: Rite of Spring, and Firebird; Schoenberg: Transfigured Night; Messiaen: Turangalîla Symphony; Varèse: Amériques; Xenakis, Kagel, Scelsi, other contemporary composers. *Honours:* Critics Award, Santiago, 1963, 1999; 1st Prize, Dimitri Mitropoulos Competition, New York, 1966. *Current Management:* Conciertos Gama, Buenos Aires; MUSIESPANA, Madrid. *Address:* 1022 Murray Hill Avenue, Pittsburgh, PA 15217, USA.

IZZO D'AMICO, Fiamma; Singer (Soprano); b. 1964, Rome, Italy. *Education:* Studied at Santa Cecilia Conservatory, Rome, 1981–84. *Career:* Debut: Sang Mimi in La Bohème at the Teatro Regio, Turin, 1984; Sang Violetta at Treviso 1985, was discovered by Herbert von Karajan, Sang Elisabeth de Valois at the 1986 Salzburg Festival followed by Micaela in Carmen; US debut Philadelphia 1986 in La Bohème, with Luciano Pavarotti, celebrated his 15th anniversary with him at Modena, 1986; Bologna 1986 in La Traviata, conducted by Riccardo Chailly; Season 1987–88 with appearances in Bohème at Vienna, Metropolitan, New York; Manon in Genoa, Tosca and the Verdi Requiem at Salzburg; Further engagements at the Paris Opéra, London, Chicago, Monte Carlo, Monaco and Hamburg. *Address:* Metropolitan Opera, Lincoln Center, NY 10023, USA.

J

JABLONSKI, Krzysztof; Polish pianist; b. 2 March 1965, Wrocław. *Education:* Karol Szymanowski Academy of Music in Katowice, 1986 with Professor Andrzej Jasinki. *Career:* numerous concert engagements in Poland and abroad, including Austria, Belgium, Bulgaria, Canada, Czechoslovakia, Denmark, Germany, Finland, the United Kingdom, Netherlands, Israel, Italy, Japan, Norway, Soviet Union, Spain and USA. Many recordings for radio and television in Poland and abroad. *Recordings:* Chopin: 24 Preludes Op 28; Haydn: Sonata in C Minor No. 33, Beethoven: Sonata in C Minor Op 13, Pathetique; Mozart: Piano Concerto in F Major K 459, Orchester der Ludwigsburger Festspiele, W Goennenwein, Bayer Records; Chopin: 24 Preludes Op 28, Polonaise in A flat Major, Op 43, Heroique, Study in G flat Major Op 10-5 Black Keys, Study in C Minor Op 10-12, Revolutionary, Yamaha Piano Player; Chopin: Sonata in B Minor Op 58, Barcarolle in F sharp Major Op 60, Polonaises in A flat Major Op 53, Heroique in G Minor in B flat Major, in A flat Major, Nocturnes, in B flat Major Op 9-3 in F sharp Major Op 15,2; More recently: Mussorgsky: Piano solo, Pictures at an Exhibition; Schumann: Kinderszenen Op. 15; Debussy: Children's Corner, Kos Records, Kos CD 10 CD, 1993. *Address:* Ul Kwiska 43-9, 54-210 Wrocław, Poland.

JABLONSKI, Peter; Concert Pianist; b. 1971, Lyckeby, Sweden. *Education:* Studied at the Malmö Music College and the Royal College of Music, London. *Career:* Started as a percussionist; Performed Jazz with Thad Jones and Buddy Rich at Village Vanguard, New York, 1980; Has appeared with such orchestras as the Royal and Moscow Philharmonics, Philharmonia, Philadelphia, Cleveland and the Los Angeles and Japan Philharmonics in Berlin and Milan; Annual concert tours to Japan and Far East and America since 1992; Visits to Australia and New Zealand; Recent and future engagements include Deutsche Symphonie Orchestra, Philharmonia, Royal Stockholm Philharmonic, Swedish Radio, Hong Kong Philharmonic, Orchestre National de France and Czech Philharmonic under Ashkenazy; World premiere of Kilar's Piano Concerto, 1997. *Recordings include:* Concertos by Gershwin, Rachmaninov, Lutoslawski and Tchaikovsky; Chopin Waltzes and solo music by Liszt; Grieg recital, 1997. *Honours:* Edison Award, 1993; Årets Svensk I Varlden, 1996; Orpheus Award at Warsaw Autumn Festival, 1998. *Current Management:* Harrison/Parrott Ltd, 12 Penzance Place, London, W11 4PA, England. *Telephone:* (20) 7229 9166. *Fax:* (20) 7221 5042. *Website:* www.harrisonparrott.com.

JACKIW, Stefan; Concert Violinist; b. 1985, USA. *Education:* Studies with Zinaida Gilels, and with Michéle Auclair at the New England Conservatory. *Career:* Season 1997 with the Wieniawski Second Concerto at the Boston Pops, and with the Minnesota Orchestra and Pittsburgh Symphony; Further engagements with the Boston Symphony Orchestra's Youth Concert, conducted by Keith Lockhart; European debut with the Philharmonia, London, in Mendelssohn's Concerto, conducted by Benjamin Zander, April. 2000; Season 2000–01 with the Strasbourg Philharmonic conducted by Yoel Levi. *Address:* c/o IMG Artists, Lovell House, 616 Chiswick High Road, London W4 5RX, England.

JACKMAN, Jeremy S., BMus; Conductor, Composer and Arranger; b. 22 April 1952, London, England; m. Angela; one s. one d. *Education:* Junior Exhibitioner Royal Coll. of Music, Hull Univ. *Career:* mem. of King's Singers 1980–90; chorus master, Belfast Philharmonic choir 1991–97, London Philharmonic Choir 1992–94; founded OSJ Voices in 1994 for the Orchestra of St John's Smith Square; Dir of Music, English Baroque Choir 2000–; mem. Asscn of British Choral Dirs, Incorporated Soc. of Musicians. *Compositions:* 22 compositions, arrangements and editions for Harmonia; Veni Emanuel, Who Shall Hold the Heart of Man?, Music of the World. *Recordings:* many recordings for The King's Singers. *Publications:* contrib. to Meistersinger, Church Music Quarterly. *Address:* Palace Music, 64 Park Avenue N, London, N8 7RT, England (office). *Telephone:* (20) 8341-3408 (office). *Fax:* (20) 8341-3408 (office). *E-mail:* jeremy@jackman.primex.co.uk (office).

JACKSON, Garfield; Violist; b. 1955, England. *Career:* Founder-member and Violist of the Endellion Quartet, from 1979; Many concerts in Munich, Frankfurt, Amsterdam, Paris, Salzburg and Rome; South Bank Haydn Festival 1990 and Quartet Plus series 1994; Wigmore Hall Beethoven series 1991; Quartet in Residence at the University of Cambridge from 1992; Residency at MIT, USA, 1995. *Recordings include:* Works by Haydn, Barber, Bartók, Dvořák, Smetana and Walton (Virgin Classics). *Current Management:* Hazard Chase Ltd, Norman House, Cambridge Place, Cambridge, CB2 1NS, England. *Telephone:* (1223) 312400. *Fax:* (1223) 460827. *Website:* www .hazardchase.co.uk.

JACKSON, Isaiah; Conductor; b. 22 Jan. 1945, Virginia, USA; m. Helen Tuntland, 6 Aug 1977, 1 s., 2 d. *Education:* MS, Juilliard School of Music, 1969; DMA, 1973. *Career:* Assistant Director, American Symphony, 1970–71; Associate Conductor, Rochester Philharmonic, 1973–87; Music Director, Royal Ballet, Covent Garden, 1987–90; Music Director, Dayton Philharmonic, 1987–95; Principal Guest Conductor, Queensland Symphony, 1993–; Music Director, Youngstown Symphony, 1996–; Guest conducting, New York Philharmonic, Cleveland Orchestra, Boston Pops, San Francisco Symphony, Orchestre de la Suisse Romande, BBC Concert Orchestra, Berlin Symphony, Royal Liverpool Philharmonic, Houston Symphony. *Recordings:* String orchestra compositions of Herrmann, Waxman, Rozsa, Berlin Symphony; Dance music of William Grant Still, Berlin Symphony; Gospel at the Symphony, Louisville Orchestra; Harp concerti of Ginastera and Mathias, English Chamber Orchestra. *Honours:* 1st Governor's Award for Arts, Virginia, 1979; Signet Society Medal for the Arts, Harvard University, 1991. *Address:* c/o United Arts, 3906 Sunbeam Drive, Los Angeles, CA 90065, USA.

JACKSON, Laurence; Concert Violinist; b. 1967, Lancashire, England. *Education:* Studied at Chetham's School of Music and at the Royal Academy with Maurice Hasson and Anne-Sophie Mutter. *Career:* Concerto repertoire includes works by Bruch, Mendelssohn, Vaughan Williams and Tchaikovsky; Aldeburgh Festival, 1988, in the Concerto Grosso by Schnittke; Soloist at the Casals Festival Hall, 1990, in The Four Seasons; Recitals at the Fairfields Halls, Queens Hall, Edinburgh, Brangwyn Hall and Turner Sims Hall; Member of Britten-Pears Ensemble tour of USA, 1991; As member of Borante Piano Trio has performed from 1982 at the Purcell Room and Wigmore Hall, in Dublin and Paris, and at the 1989 Festival Wiener Klassik (Beethoven's Triple Concerto); Season 1990 at the Bath and Perth Festivals, tour of Scandinavia, Russia and the Baltic States and master classes with Andras Schiff at Prussia Cove, Cornwall; Duo partnership with pianist Scott Mitchell; Solo concert tour of Chile, Colombia and Venezuela, 1991; Concerto and recital performances in Spain, 1992. *Recordings:* Solo recording with the ensemble Laureate, 1991. *Honours:* David Martin Concerto Prize, 1987, and Principal's Prize, 1988; The Royal English Heritage Award, 1983, 1985, 1986; 1st Prize at Vina del Mar, Chile, 1990; 3rd Prize, First Pablo Sarasate International Violin Competition, 1991. *Current Management:* Scott Mitchell Management, 26 Childebert Road, London SW17 8EX, England. *Address:* 23 Fulwell Park Avenue, Twickenham, Middlesex TW2 5HF, England.

JACKSON, Sir Nicholas Fane St George (Bart), Kt, LRAM, ARCM; organist, harpsichordist and composer; b. 4 Sept. 1934, London, England; m. Nadia Michard 1971; one s. *Education:* Radley College, Wadham College, Oxford, Royal Academy of Music with C. H. Trevor, George Malcolm, Gustav Leonhardt. *Career:* debut Wigmore Hall, 1964; Organist at St James's, London, 1971–74; St Lawrence Jewry next Guildhall, 1974–77; Organist and Master of the Choristers of St David's Cathedral, 1977–84; Organ recital at Royal Festival Hall, 1984; Director of Concertante of London, 1987–; Masterclasses at Segovia, Spain, 1989; Director of Festival Bach, Santes Creus, Spain; Tour of Croatia, 2002; Solo performances at South Bank, London and at Nôtre Dame Paris, Teatro Real Madrid and New York; World premiere of his opera The Reluctant Highwayman at Broomhill, 1995; mem. Master of the Worshipful Company of Drapers, 1994–95; Liveryman of the Worshipful Company of Musicans. *Compositions:* Mass for a Saint's Day; 4 Images for Organ; 20th Century Merbecke; Divertissement for Organ; Anthems and Choral Settings; Mass for Organ, 1984; Opera: The Reluctant Highwayman, 1992; Organ Sonata, 1995. *Recordings include:* The Organ of St David's Cathedral; Bach's Christmas Organ Music for Trumpet and Organ; 2 albums with Maurice Murphy; Complete Organ Works of Richard Arnell; Bach's 2 and 3 Part Inventions; François Couperin; Harpsichord Concertos; Mass for a Saint's Day; Own Organ Works and Works for Trumpet and Organ, played at Chartres Cathedral, 2000; Spanish Organ Music, Segovia Cathedral priory, 2001; Scarlatti CD. *Publication:* 'Recollections' of Sir T. G. Jackson RA (ed. and arranger). *Honours:* Honorary Fellowship, Hertford College, Oxford, 1995. *Address:* 42a Hereford Road, London, W2 5AJ, England.

JACKSON, Richard; Singer (baritone); b. 1960, Cornwall, England. *Education:* studied with Pierre Bernac and Audrey Langford. *Career:* widely known as a concert singer, in song and oratorio; founder mem., Songmakers' Almanac, with appearances in the USA, at the Saintes Festival, Three Choirs Festival and the Wigmore and Queen Elizabeth Halls; solo recital with songs by Poulenc at the Wigmore Hall, 1989; concerts with David Willcocks, Neville Marriner, Bertini, Rostropovich, Mackerras and Gardiner; has sung Bach and Handel in Spain and Portugal; Monteverdi's Vespers in Venice; The Starlight Express by

Elgar; opera engagements at the Glyndebourne and Aldeburgh Festivals and with Kent Opera, New Sadler's Wells Opera and with the Handel Opera Society; sang Aeneas to the Dido of Janet Baker; Almeida Festival, London, 1987–88, in the British premiere of Jakob Lenz by Wolfgang Rihm and the world premiere of The Undivine Comedy by Michael Finnissy. *Current Management:* Caroline Phillips Management, The Old Brushworks, Pickwick Road, Corsham, Wiltshire, SN13 9BX, England. *Telephone:* (1249) 716716. *Fax:* (1249) 716717. *E-mail:* cphillips@caroline-phillips.co.uk. *Website:* www .caroline-phillips.co.uk/jackson.

JACOBS, René, BPhil; Belgian conductor and singer (countertenor); b. 30 Oct. 1946, Ghent; m. Suzy Depporter. *Education:* Univ. of Ghent, studied singing with Louis Devos in Brussels, Lucie Frateur in The Hague. *Career:* recitals in Europe, Canada, USA, Mexico and the Philippines; performances with madrigal ensembles and with such early music groups as the Leonhardt Consort, Il Complesso Barocco, La Petite Bande and groups led by Alan Curtis and Nikolaus Harnoncourt; sings Baroque music and directs his own ensemble, Collegium Vocale; best known in operas by Monteverdi, Cesti, Handel, Gluck and Cavalli; sacred music by Charpentier and Couperin; teacher of performing practice in Baroque singing, Schola Cantorum, Basle; appointments at the Int. Summer School for Early Music, Innsbruck, and the Aston Magna Acad. for Baroque Music, USA; conducted Cavalli's Giasone in his own edition at the Innsbruck Festival 1988; Flavio 1989; L'Incoronazione de Poppea with the ensemble I Febi Armonici 1989; conducted Graun's Cleopatra e Cesare at the Baroque Festival, Versailles 1992; Conti's Don Chisciotte at the Innsbruck Festival of Early Music 1992; led Poppea at the Teatro Colón, Buenos Aires 1996; Monteverdi's Orfeo at the Barbican Theatre, London 1998; Artistic Dir, Innsbruck Festival. *Recordings:* Cesti's L'Orontea, from the 1982 Holland Festival; Arias by Monteverdi and Benedetto Ferrari; Motets by Charpentier; Bach's St Matthew Passion; Handel's Admeto and Partenope; Lully's Bourgeois Gentilhomme; Gluck's Orfeo ed Euridice and Echo et Narcisse; Giasone and La Calisto by Cavalli; Handel's Alessandro and Tamerlano; Charpentier's David et Jonathas; Handel's Giulio Cesare; Così fan tutte; DVD Monteverdi, Poppea. *Address:* c/o Innsbrucker Festwochen der alten Musik GmbH, Burggraben 3, 1. Stock, 6020 Innsbruck, Austria; Langenakkerlaan 34, 9130 Lochristi, Belgium.

JACOBSON, Bernard (Isaac); Writer on Music; b. 2 March 1936, London, England; m. (1) Bonnie Brodsky, 11 Aug 1968, dissolved 1982, 1 s., 1 d., (2) Dr Laura Dale Belcove, 3 Jan 1983. *Education:* City of London School, 1947–54; Corpus Christi College, Oxford as Open Scholar, 1956–60; Classical Honour Moderations, 1958; Lit Hum BA 1960; MA 1962. *Career:* Music Critic, Chicago Daily News, 1967–73; Director, Southern Arts Association, Winchester, England, 1973–76; Deputy Director of Publications, 1979–81, Director of Promotion, Boosey and Hawkes Music Publishers Ltd, London, 1982–84; Manager, Publications and Educational Programmes, 1984–88, Programme Annotater and Musicologist, 1988–91, Philadelphia Orchestra; Artistic Director, Residentie Orkest, Hague Philharmonic, 1992–94; Independent Associate, Joy Mebus Artists' Management, 1993–94; Artistic Adviser, North Netherlands Orchestra, 1994–. *Compositions:* Libretto, 16 poems, for Death of a Young Man, song cycle by Wilfred Josephs commissioned and performed by 1971 Harrogate Festival; Poems for Songs and other works by Richard Wernick. *Recordings:* Schoenberg Ode to Napoleon, 1968; Stravinsky, The Flood, 1995. *Publications include:* The Music of Johannes Brahms, USA and London, 1977; Conductors on Conducting, USA and London, 1979; A Polish Renaissance, in press; Many translations including Holofernes, Judith and Die Weise von Liebe und Tod des Cornets Christoph Rilke, all by Siegried Matthus, for Schott. *Contributions:* Dictionary of 20th Century Music, 1974; The New Grove, 1980. *Address:* Buys Ballotstraat 89, 2563 ZK Den Haag, Netherlands.

JACOBSON, Julian; Pianist; b. 1947, Scotland. *Education:* Studied piano with Lamar Crowson and Louis Kentner; Composition with Arthur Benjamin and Humphrey Searle; Graduate, Royal College of Music and Oxford University. *Career:* Debut: London, Purcell Room, 1974; Appearances in over 30 countries including concerto engagements with London Symphony, BBC Symphony, City of Birmingham Orchestra, English Chamber Orchestra, London Mozart Players, Bournemouth Sinfonietta; Chamber music recitals with: Nigel Kennedy, Lydia Mordkovitch, Zara Nelsova, Steven Isserlis, Colin Carr, Christian Lindberg, Ivry Gitlis, Brodsky and Arditti Quartets; Artistic Director, Paxos Festival, Greece; Teacher and Performer, Dartington International Summer School; Head of Keyboard Studies, Welsh College of Music and Drama, 1992–96; Solo recitals include five cycles of the complete Beethoven Sonatas; Concerts; Masterclasses in France, Germany, Malta, Hungary and China, 1994–95; Conductor, European Union Chamber Orchestra, 1999; Secretary, Beethoven Piano Society of Europe. *Compositions:* Songs; Piano Works; Chamber Music; 6 Film Scores. *Recordings include:* Albums on various labels; CD recordings of

Complete piano sonatas of Weber. *Address:* 34 St Margaret's Road, London SE4 1YU, England.

JACOBSSON, John-Eric; Singer (Tenor); b. 6 Oct. 1931, Hogran, Sweden. *Education:* Studied in Stockholm with Toivo Ek, Arne Sunnegaard and Sonny Peterson. *Career:* Debut: Royal Opera, Stockholm, 1964, as Turiddu in Cavalleria Rusticana; Sang at Stockholm in the premiere of Kalifens Son by Eiyser (1976) and as Alwa in the local premiere of Berg's Lulu; Other roles include Pedrillo in Die Entführung, Jacquino in Fidelio, Cavaradossi, Albert Herring, Eisenstein in Die Fledermaus and Ismaele in Nabucco, Števa in Jenůfa and title role in Xerxes and more than 100 different roles; Guest appearances in Oslo, Copenhagen, Hamburg, Munich, Edinburgh, Moscow, Hong Kong and at the Drottningholm Festival; Many concert appearances. *Address:* c/o Kungliga Teatern, PO Box 16094, 10322 Stockholm, Sweden.

JAFFE, Monte; Singer (Baritone); b. 5 June 1940, USA. *Education:* Studied at the Curtis Institute and with Giorgio Tozzi. *Career:* Appearances with Krefeld Opera as Wotan, Kaspar (Der Freischütz), Dr Schön (Lulu), Reimann's Lear, the Dutchman, and in Cerhaa's Baal and the premiere of Judith by Matthus. Further engagements at the Metropolitan in Death of Venice, Lear with English National Opera, the Hoffmann villains for Israel Opera and Bluebeard (Bartók) for Scottish Opera; Returned to English National Opera for the title role in the premiere of Timon of Athens by Stephen Oliver, 1991, and has also sung at Karlsruhe (Graf Mirabeau by Matthus), Berne (Nekrotaz in Le Grand Macabre), Tel-Aviv (Mephistopheles in Faust), Bonn (Gianni Schicchi), 1993, Turin (Walküre Wotan), Antwerp (Klingsor) and Bielefeld (Barak in Die Frau ohne Schatten); Other roles include Scarpia, Konchak (Prince Igor), Zaccaria (Nabucco) and Old Sam in Bernstein's A Quiet Place; Sang the Rheingold Wotan at Braunschweig and Osmin for New York City Opera, 1999; Nekrotzar in Ligeti's Le Grand Macabre for Flemish Opera, 2001. *Current Management:* Ingpen & Williams Ltd, 7 St George's Court, 131 Putney Bridge Road, London, SW15 2PA, England.

JAFFE, Stephen; Composer; b. 30 Dec. 1954, Washington DC, USA; m. Mindy Oshrain, 29 May 1988, 2 d. *Education:* AM, AB summa cum laude, University of Pennsylvania, with George Crumb, George Rochberg and Richard Wernick, 1973–78; Also at University of Massachusetts and Conservatoire de Musique, Geneva. *Career:* Director, Encounters with the Music of Our Time, Duke University, 1981–; Performances with San Francisco, New Jersey, New Hampshire Symphonies, Rome Radio Orchestra, New York New Music Ensemble, Spectrum concerts, Berlin, Aurora and Ciompi Quartets. *Compositions:* First Quartet, 1991; Double Sonata, two pianos, 1989; Four Songs with Ensemble, for mezzo soprano and ensemble, 1988; Four Images, 1983–87; The Rhythm of the Running Plough, 1988; Triptych, for piano and wind quintet, 1993; Pedal Point, baritone, low strings, harp and timpani, 1992; Pedal Point, baritone and consort of low instruments, 1994. *Recordings:* First Quartet; Centering for two violins; Three Figures and a Ground; The Rhythm of the Running Plough; Double Sonata; Four Songs with Ensemble; Fort Juniper Songs. *Publications:* First Quartet, 1991; Double Sonata, 1992; Three Figures and a Grand, 1993; Four Images for Orchestra, 1988. *Contributions:* Contemporary Music Review; Conversation between JS and SJ on the New Tonality, article, 1992. *Honours:* American Academy of Arts and Letters Prize, 1993; Brandeis University Creative Arts Citation, 1989. *Current Management:* Theodore Presser Co, Bryn Mawr, PA 19010, USA. *Address:* Box 90656, Durham, NC 27708, USA.

JAFFEE, Kay; Musician and Musicologist; b. 31 Dec. 1937, Michigan, USA; m. Michael Jaffee, 24 July 1961. *Education:* BA, University of Michigan, 1959; MA, New York University, 1965; PhD, New York University, 2001. *Career:* Debut: Carnegie Recital Hall, 1966; Founding Member and Associate Director, The Waverly Consort, 1964–; Performer on Renaissance wind and keyboard instruments, harps, psalteries and percussion; Annual tours of North America since 1967; Also tours to the United Kingdom and Latin America; Festival appearances include: Casals Festival, 1981 and 1983, Madeira Bach Festival, 1981, Hong Kong Festival, 1988 and Caramoor Festival; Television appearances in USA; mem, American Musicological Society; Society for 17th Century Music; Renaissance Society of America. *Recordings:* 13 with the Waverly Consort. *Publications:* Articles and reviews to the Journal of Musicology, The American Recorder and The Brass Quarterly. *Current Management:* Musicians Corporate Management Ltd, PO Box 589, Millbrook, NY 12545, USA. *Address:* PO Box 386, Patterson, NY 12563, USA.

JÄGGI, Andreas; Singer (Tenor); b. 30 March 1952, Basle, Switzerland. *Education:* Studied with Maria Stader in Zürich. *Career:* Singer and Designer with the Companie Alain Germain in Europe and the USA, from 1976; Sang at Kiel Opera from 1985, Paris from 1987 (Weill's Mahagonny at the Opéra Bastille, 1995); Guest appearances at Covent Garden, Cologne (from 1988), Paris Opéra-Comique (Handel's Theodora) and Strasbourg (Narraboth in Salome, 1994); Other roles include Mozart's Pedrillo, Wagner's David, Andreas in Wozzeck and Flute in A Midsummer Night's Dream; Further engagements at the Athens, Orange and Granada Festivals; Sang Sylvester in Turnage's The Silver Tassie at Dublin, 2001. *Address:* c/o Opéra de la Bastille, 120 Rue de Lyon, 75012 Paris, France.

JAHN, Gertrude; Singer (Mezzo-soprano); b. 13 Aug. 1940, Zagreb, Croatia. *Education:* Studied at the Vienna Music Academy with Elisabeth Rado and Lily Kolar; Further study with Erik Werba and Josef Witt. *Career:* Debut: Basle, 1963, as Gluck's Orpheus; Appearances at the State Operas of Vienna, Hamburg, Munich and Stuttgart; Glyndebourne, 1968, as Olga in Eugene Onegin; Salzburg Festivals from 1967, as Feodor in Boris Godunov, Mozart's Ascanio, Margret in Wozzeck and Countess Laura in the premiere of Penderecki's Die schwarze Maske, 1986; Munich and Madrid, 1988, as Adelaide in Arabella and the Countess Geschwitz in Lulu; Further engagements in Düsseldorf, Salzburg, Moscow, Trieste and Montreal; Other roles include Carmen, Giulietta in Les Contes d'Hoffmann, Octavian, Eboli, Preziosilla (La Forza del Destino), Fatima in Oberon and Magdalene in Die Meistersinger; Frequent concert appearances. *Recordings include:* Masses by Haydn and Schubert; Missa Choralis by Liszt; Wozzeck.

JAHNS, Annette; Singer (Mezzo-soprano); b. 1958, Dresden, Germany. *Education:* Studied at the Dresden Musikhochschule and with Judith Beckmann in Hamburg and Ute Niss in Berlin. *Career:* Sang with the Dresden Opera, 1982–99, as Mozart's Ramiro (Finta giardiniera), Dorabella and Cherubino, Nicklausse, Mistress Quickly, and Maddalena in Rigoletto; Carmen, Orpheus, Hansel and Olga; Has also performed in the Brecht/Weill Sieben Todsunden; Season 2000–01 as Sarah in Thomas Chatterton by Matthias Pintscher at the Vienna Volksoper and in the premiere of Celan by Peter Ruzicka. *Honours:* Berlin Reviewers' Award, 1987; Dresden Art Award, 1995. *Current Management:* Agentur Arias, Via Roma 15, 03912 Meran.Laubegaster Strasse 5, 01326 Dresden, Germany.

JAHREN, Helen Mai Aase, MFA; Swedish oboist; b. 2 May 1959, Malmö. *Education:* Malmö College of Music, Staatliche Hochschule für Musik, Freiburg, Konservatorium für Musik, Berne. *Career:* debut solo appearance with orchestra, age 17; Tours, France, Italy, Spain, Germany, Switzerland, Poland, Denmark, Norway, Finland, Iceland, Japan, 1980–; Belgian tour with Orchestre National de Belgique, 1982; Vienna debut, Grosses Konzerthaus, 1983; Toured Colombia, Ecuador, Peru, Argentina, Uruguay, Brazil, Venezuela, Costa Rica, Mexico, 1984; Debut with Stockholm Philharmonic Orchestra, 1987; Invited to Louisville Symphony Orchestra's 50th Anniversary, USA, 1987; Pan Music Festival, Seoul, 1988; Gala Opening Concert, with Hong Kong Philharmonic Orchestra, World Music Days, Hong Kong, 1988; Debut with Swedish Radio Orchestra, 1988; Many television and radio appearances world-wide; Artist Portrait by Swedish Television, 1991–93; Teaching: Malmö College of Music, 1984–87; Ingesund College of Music, 1991–93; Stockholm Royal College of Music, 1993–95; Masterclasses; Initiator and Artistic Director of Båstad Chamber Music Festival; Many pieces dedicated to her by composrers such as Erik Bergman, Poul Ruders, Daniel Börtz, Jouni Kaipainen, Per-Henrik Nordgren, Sven-David Sandström and many others. *Recordings include:* Swedish music for oboe and organ with Hans-Ola Ericsson, 1986; Schnittke Double Concerto for oboe and harp, with Stockholm Chamber Orchestra, 1987; J H Roman, Oboe Concerto, 1988; L-E Larsson, Oboe Concertino, 1990; J Kaipainen, Oboe Concerto, 1995; Mozart, Oboe Concerto in C major, J C Bach: Oboe Concertos, Ferlendis: Oboe Concerto, 2000; Börtz: Oboe Concerto, Kithairon for Oboe Solo, Ekström: Oboe Concerto, The Accelerating Ice-cube, Gamstorp: Oboe Concerto, Pulse II for oboe solo, 2000. *Address:* Nybrogatan 81, 11441 Stockholm, Sweden.

JAKSIC, Djura; Conductor and Writer on Music; b. 30 April 1924, Karlovac, Yugoslavia; m. Slobondanka Ilic, 21 July 1962, 2 s. *Education:* School of Music, Belgrade, 1939–45; Music Science, Charles University, Prague and Prague Conservatoire, 1945–48; Diploma, Academic Musician-Conductor, Academy of Music, Zagreb, 1948–50. *Career:* Debut: Symphonic concert, Radio Belgrade Symphony, 1950; Conductor, Radio Symnphony, Radio Chamber and Radio Studio Orchestras, 1950–53; Associate Conductor, Belgrade Philharmonic Orchestra, 1953–66; Art Director, Principal Conductor, Chamber Orchestra Pro Musica, 1967–; Art Director, National Opera/Ballet, Belgrade, 1977–80; Concerts and tours in Yugoslavia, Austria, Belgium, Bulgaria, Czechoslovakia, Denmark, France, the United Kingdom, Hungary, Italy, Netherlands, Norway, Romania, Spain, Switzerland, Turkey and USSR; Autobiography broadcast on Belgrade Radio and Television, 1987, 1988. *Recordings:* Vivaldi, The Seasons, and J Slavenski, Suite of Dances, both with Chamber Orchestra Pro Musica; Pro Musica Plays Vivaldi, 1991; Over 300 radio recordings. *Publications:* On the Symphony Orchestra, 1954; State of Music in Serbia, 1969; Two Symphonies of Amando Ivancic; Revisions, editions and orchestrations of Yugoslav composers from the 15th to 19th century; Essays on Vivaldi, Telemann, Britten's War Requiem, Berg's Wozzeck, Finnish music, Bulgarian music; G B Shaw on Music: Selection of music criticisms, Serbocroat translation, selection and comment, 1989; Over 200 other articles. *Contributions:* Editor in chief, Pro Musica magazine, 1964–90; Yugoslav Music Encyclopaedia, 1958–. *Address:* Pozeska 92, 11031 Belgrade, Serbia and Montenegro.

JAMES, Buddug Verona; Singer (mezzo-soprano); b. 1963, Cardigan, Wales. *Education:* Guildhall School of Music and Drama; Nat. Opera Studio. *Career:* 50 operatic roles include Gluck's Orfeo in America and Canada; Dardano in Handel's Amadigi in New York and Europe; Cherubino in Mozart's Marriage of Figaro in Tokyo and Toronto; Has worked with Netherlands Opera, Cleveland Opera (USA), Glyndebourne; Almedia Opera; Opera Theatre Co.; Opera Northern Ireland; Opera North; Opera Atelier; Opera Circus; English Pocket Opera; Opera 80; Operavox Cartoons, Siobhan Davies Dance Co.; Music Theatre Wales and Mid Wales Opera; Premieres in operas by Gerald Barry, Jonathan Dove, Deirdre Gribbin, Wolfgang Rihm and John Woolrich; Concert repertoire includes Mozart's Ch'io mi scordi di te with BBC Welsh Symphony Orchestra and Jane Glover; Matthaus Passion with Paul Steinitz; Johannes Passion with Thomas Dausgaard; Theodora with Paul McCreesh; Bach Cantatas with John Georgiadis; Elijah with Owain Arwel Hughes. *Recordings include:* Thomas Chilcot Songs; Arias by Handel and Gluck; The James Sisters Sing Gospel. *Website:* www.buddug.co.uk.

JAMES, Carolyn; Singer (Soprano); b. 1963, USA. *Education:* Studied at Arizona State University and the Juilliard School. *Career:* Sang Mozart's Countess at Miami and the New York Metropolitan (1991–92); Vienna Volksoper, 1990, as Donna Anna, Fiordiligi at Cologne, 1993; Vienna Staatsoper, 1993–94, Metropolitan, 1995, as Ellen Orford in Peter Grimes; Verdi's Elisabeth de Valois at Seattle and Elettra in Idomeneo at the Paris Opéra Bastille, 1996; Other roles include Berlioz's Beatrice and Purcell's Dido; Concerts include the Mozart and Verdi Requiems, Messiah, Elijah, and Mahler's 8th Symphony. *Address:* c/o Metropolitan Opera, Lincoln Center, New York, NY 10023, USA.

JAMES, David; Singer (countertenor); b. 1949, England. *Education:* Magdalen College, Oxford. *Career:* From 1978 has sung with the Hilliard Ensemble and other early music groups; Tours of Russia and Mexico, Schütz's Psalms of David and Cesti's Orontea in Innsbruck and at the Holland Festival; Handel's Orlando in Spain and Portugal with the Amsterdam Baroque Orchestra; Messiah in Finland and with The Sixteen (tours include visit to Utrecht 1990); Concerts with the Collegium Vocale Gent and La Chapelle Royale; Bach's St John Passion in London and Salzburg, the B minor Mass at Bruges and Cantatas in Finland (1991); Promenade Concerts 1990, in the cantata Herz und Mund und Tat und Leben; Contemporary Music Network tour with the Hilliard Ensemble in Pärt's St John Passion; Has sung at the Aldeburgh Festival, for Handel Opera in London, English National Opera and at Covent Garden; Frantz in the premiere of Dr Ox's Experiment, by Bryars, ENO, 1998; Gen. Dir, New Sussex Opera, mid-scale touring opera with emphasis on new or lesser known works. *Recordings:* Orlando; Messiah; Pärt St John Passion (ECM) Bach St John Passion. *Honours:* Winner, 's-Hertogenbosch Competition, Netherlands, 1978. *Current Management:* Hazard Chase Ltd, Norman House, Cambridge Place, Cambridge, CB2 1NS, England. *Telephone:* (1223) 312400. *Fax:* (1223) 460827. *Website:* www.hazardchase.co.uk; www.newsussexopera .com (office).

JAMES, Eirian; Singer (Mezzo-Soprano); b. 1952, Cardigan, Wales. *Education:* Royal College of Music with Ruth Packer. *Career:* Debut: Kent Opera, 1977, as Olga in Eugene Onegin, returned as Cherubino, Poppea, Rosina, and Meg Page in Falstaff; English National Opera in The Makropulos Case, War and Peace, Rigoletto and Rusalka; Buxton Festival in Handel's Ariodante; Lyon Opéra as Fatima (Oberon) and Rossini's Isolier; Genera Opera as Hansel; Houston Opera as Siebel in Faust and Sesto in Handel's Giulio Cesare; Aix-en-Provence as Dorabella (Così fan tutte); Covent Garden debut 1987 as Annina in Der Rosenkavalier, returned as Smeton in Anna Bolena, 1988 and Nancy in Albert Herring, 1989; Sang Dorabella at Aix-en-Provence, 1989, second Lady in Die Zauberflöte at the 1990 Prom Concerts; Ascanio in Benvenuto Cellini for Netherlands Opera, Cherubino at Houston; Concert Appearances at the BBC Promenades, Aldeburgh Festival, the Barbican and with the BBC National Orchestra of Wales; repertoire includes the Lieder eines fahrenden Gesellen (Lyon), Beethoven's Mass in C (London), Mozart's C Minor Mass (Edinburgh and Paris); Haydn's Harmoniemesse; Mendelssohn's Elijah; Gluck's La Corona (City of London Festival); Hermia, Midsummer Night's Dream, Aix-en-Provence, 1991; Orlofsky, Fledermaus, 1991, English National Opera; Rosina (Barber of Seville), 1992; Scottish Opera, Sextus (Julius Caesar), 1992; Sang Cyrus in Handel's Belshazzar at the 1996 Göttingen Festival; Sang Falsirena inMazzochi's La Catena d'Adone at Innsbruck and Britten's Hermia at Rome, 1999. *Recordings include:* Zerlina in Don Giovanni, conducted by John Eliot Gardiner, (Deutsche Grammophon); Sextus (Julius Caesar by Handel) conducted by Jean-Claude Malgoire. *Current Management:* IMG Artists Europe. *Address:* c/o Music International, 13 Ardilaun Road, London, N5 2QR, England.

JAMES, Ifor; Horn Player and Conductor; b. 30 Aug. 1931, Carlisle, England; m. Helen Hames. *Education:* Royal Academy of Music. *Career:* Radio and television performances in the United Kingdom and abroad; Orchestral concerts; Chamber music recitals; Premieres of concertos by Alun Huddinott and Peter Racine Fricker; Teacher at the RNCM, 1972–83; Professor at the Freiburg Musikhochschule, 1983. *Recordings:* Brahms Trio op 40: Mozart Quintet K407 and Sinfonia Concertante K297b; Solo recital records; Philip Jones Brass Ensemble records; Brandenburg Concerto No. 1; Concertos by Haydn, Strauss and Mozart. *Publications:* Practice Method, 1976. *Contributions:* Various journals. *Address:* c/o Musikhochschule Freiburg, Schwarzwaldstrasse 141, D–79102 Freiburg im Breisgau, Germany.

JAMES, Kevin G. G.; Canadian modern and baroque violist, violinist, researcher and writer; b. 30 July 1961, Toronto. *Education:* summer sessions University of Toronto, Carleton University, University of Ottawa, Oberlin College, McGill University. *Career:* freelance orchestral and chamber player, recitalist; Staff writer, Encyclopedia of Music in Canada, 1989–92; Occasional Contributor on Canadian topics to The Strad, Early Music, Musick, Performing Arts in Canada, Continuo, Newsletter of the American Musical Instrument Society, Canadian Viola Society Newsletter. Premieres: Jan Jarvlepp, Encounter, 1991; Alyssa Ryvers, Two Songs for Viola and Voice, 1990, and Synergy for nine violas, 1994; Gilles Leclerc, Suite for Viola and Organ, 1997; Michael Spassov, Fantasy for Solo Viola, 1997; Brian Pantekoek, The Letter, for viola and percussion, 1998; Deirdre Piper, Fantasy for Solo Viola, 1999; Eldon Rathburn, Soliloquy for Solo Viola, 1999; Andrew Ager, Garden Shadows, for viola and chamber choir, 2000; Jan Jarvlepp, Street Scene, for viola and electric guitar, 2000; Peter Amsel, Poème pour Alto, for solo viola, 2000; Jan Jarvlepp, Suite for Viola and Strings , 2001; Peter Willsha, Intermezzo for Viola and Strings, 2002; mem, Association of Canadian Orchestras, 1985–; Canadian Viola Society, 1991–. *Recordings:* John Playford, The English Dancing Master, 1983; Jan Jarvlepp, Encounter, 1994, and Trio No. 2, 2000; The Mystical Music of Andalucia, with Barbara Solís, piano, 2003; Chamber and recital performances for Radio-Canada. *Address:* 505-455 Lisgar Street, Ottawa, ON K1R 5G9, Canada. *E-mail:* kggjames@canada.com.

JAMES, Peter Haydn, BMus, PhD, CertEd; Music Editor; b. 17 Oct. 1940, Melbourne, Australia; m. A. Heather; one s. one d. *Education:* Univ. of Wales, Cardiff, Bristol Univ. *Career:* Lecturer then Dir of Studies, Birmingham School of Music (now Birmingham Conservatoire) 1970–83; Vice-Principal, Royal Acad. of Music 1983–95; series ed., Cathedral Press Ltd 1997–; part-time lecturer, Open Univ. 1973–81; Vicar choral, Lichfield Cathedral 1969–74; Chorus master, City of Birmingham Symphony Orchestra Chorus 1974–76; mem. Royal Musical Asscn. *Recordings:* Chorus master for City of Birmingham Symphony Orchestra Chorus recordings 1975–77. *Publications:* over 40 editions of early sacred music; contrib. to Music & Letters 1983, Annual Byrd Newsletter 1999, 2000, Johnson Society 1981. *Honours:* FBSM 1984, Hon. RAM 1984, Hon. RCM 1985. *Address:* Series Editor, Cathedral Press Ltd, Alltycham House Pontardawe, Swansea, SA8 4JT, Wales (office). *Telephone:* (1792) 865197 (office). *E-mail:* james@cathpress.fsnet.co.uk (office).

JANACEK, Bedrich; Organist; b. 18 May 1920, Prague, Czechoslovakia; m. Elisabet Wentz, 1 Jan 1951, 1 s. *Education:* Soloist in Organ, 1942, Masterclass in Organ, 1945–46, Diploma, 1946, State Conservatory of Music, Prague; Choir Master Degree, Royal High Music School, Stockholm, Sweden, 1961. *Career:* Organist, various concerts in Europe and USA, including Royal Festival Hall, London, England, 1942–; Soloist with orchestras; Teacher of Organ, State Conservatory of Music, Prague, 1946–48; Parish Musician, Cathedral Parish, Lund, Sweden, 1965–85. *Compositions:* Organ compositions; Choral works including 2 cantatas with orchestra; Works for brass and organ. *Recordings:* Various. *Honours:* City of Lund Cultural Prize, 1980, 1988; Commander of Merit, Ordo Militaris et Hospitalaris Sancti Lasari Hierosolymitani, 1992; Litteris et Artibus, Sweden, 1993. *Address:* Kyrkogatan 17, 222 22 Lund, Sweden. *Telephone:* 046 129602. *E-mail:* janacek.wentz@swipnet .se.

JANARCEKOVA, Viera; Composer; b. 23 Sept. 1944, Svit, Czechoslovakia. *Education:* Studied at the Bratislava Conservatory and the Prague Academy. *Career:* Keyboard performer and composer in Germany from 1981. *Compositions include:* Radio drama Biomasse, 1984; 4 string quartets, 1983–89; Pausenfabrik for 2 clarinets and ensemble, 1987; Beschattungtheater for 4 cellos, 1990; Piano concerto, 1991; Vocal music including Donna Laura for mezzo and 15 instruments, 1989; Der

Gehemnisvolle Nachen for mezzo cello, 1989. *Address:* c/o OSA. Cs armady 20, 160-56 Prague 6, Bubenec, Czech Republic.

JANDER, Owen (Hughes); Musicologist and Music Educator; b. 4 June 1930, Mount Kisco, New York, USA. *Education:* BA, University of Virginia, 1951; MA, 1952, PhD, 1962, Harvard University. *Career:* Faculty Member, 1960–1992, Chairman, 3 terms, Department of Music, Wellesley College; Founder Collegium Musicum, originated and oversaw project to build the Fisk Organ, Wellesley College; Editor, The Wellesley Edition and The Wellesley Edition Cantata Index Series, 1962–74; mem, American Musicological Society. *Publications:* Charles Brenton Fisk, Organ Builder (co-editor), 1986; Orpheus Revisited (Andante of Beethoven's 4th Piano Concerto), 1996. *Contributions:* Articles on 17th century Italian music and on Beethoven to various journals; 78 articles, The New Grove Dictionary of Music and Musicians, 1980. *Honours:* Guggenheim Fellowship, 1966–67; National Endowment for the Humanities Fellowship for Senior Scholars, 1985; Catherine Mills Davies Professorship in Music History, Wellesley College. *Address:* 72 Denton Road, Wellesley, MA 02181, USA.

JANES, Fiona; Singer (Mezzo-soprano); b. 1961, Sydney, NSW, Australia. *Education:* Studied at the New South Wales Conservatory and in Munich with Sena Jurinac. *Career:* Member of the Australian Opera 1988–91, notably as Mozart's Annio, Cherubino, Dorabella and Zerlina; Siebel in Faust for Victoria State Opera and Rosina for the Lyric Opera of Queensland; Buxton Festival 1992 as Nero in Handel's Agrippina and sang Rosina with English National Opera; Season 1993–94 at the Edinburgh Festival, as Sesto in La Clemenza di Tito for the Glyndebourne Tour, and Australian Opera as Cenerentola; Season 1995–96 at the Semperoper Dresden, Mozart's Idamantes with the Flanders Philharmonic Orchestra and Rossini's Isabella in Australia under Richard Bonynge; Sang Lucia di Lammermoor at Auckland, 1998; Concerts include Mozart's Requiem, Beethoven's Missa Solemnis (under Walter Weller), and Ninth Symphony under Charles Mackerras; Berlioz Faust with the Scottish National Orchestra. *Address:* c/o Arien Arts & Music B.V.B.A de Boeystraat 6, B–2018 Antwerp, Belgium.

JANEVA-IVELIC, Veneta; Singer (Soprano); b. 1950, Bulgaria. *Education:* Studied at Sofia Conservatory. *Career:* Sang at the Sofia Opera from 1973, National Opera Zagreb, from 1980; Guest appearances in Salzburg (with Zagreb company as Norma, 1985), Berlin Staatsoper, Paris Opéra (Abigaille in Nabucco), Luxembourg and Karlsruhe; Other roles have included Maddalena (Andrea Chénier), the Forza and Trovatore Leonoras, Violetta, Desdemona, Lady Macbeth, Butterfly and Elvira in I Puritani. *Honours:* Prizewinner, Rio International Competition, 1980. *Address:* Slovensko Narodno Gledaslisce, Zupancicava 1, 61000 Ljubljana, Serbia.

JANICKE, Heike; Violinist; b. 20 Dec. 1962, Dresden. *Education:* Diploma of Violin, Musikhochschule, Dresden, 1987; Soloist Degree, Musikhochschule Freiburg, 1990. *Career:* Violin Soloist with Philharmonic Dresden, Berliner Sinfonie Orchestra, Rundfumksinfonie Orchestra Berlin, Radio Sinfonieorchestra Stuttgart, Gewandhaus Orchestra, Leipzig, Odense Sinfonie Orchestra, Bucharest Philharmonic; Solo and Chamber Music Concerts throughout Europe, Middle East, Japan, Middle and South America; Television and radio productions; Member of Berlin Philharmonic Orchestra, 1991–93; Member, London Symphony Orchestra, 1993–; Concertmaster of Dresden Philharmonic Orchestra, 1995–. *Honours:* Scholarship, Mendelssohn, 1988; International Violin Competitions, Music Competition, Geneva, 1985; Fritz Kreisler, France, 1987; Georg Kulenkampff, Cologne, 1988; Carl Nielsen, Odense, 1988; Zino Francescatti, Marseille, 1989. *Address:* c/o London Symphony Orchestra, Silk Street, Barbican Centre, London, England.

JANIS, Byron; Pianist; b. 24 March 1924, McKeesport, Pennsylvania, USA; m. (1) June Dickson-Wright, 1 s., (2) Maria Veronica Cooper. *Education:* Studied with Josef and Rosina Lhevinne in New York and with Adele Marcus and Horowitz. *Career:* Debut: With Pittsburgh Symphony Orchestra, 1944, in Rachmaninov's 2nd Concerto; Carnegie Hall debut, 1948; European debut with Concertgebouw Orchestra, 1952; Toured Russian, 1960, 1962, appearing with Moscow Philharmonic Orchestra; Further engagements with Boston Symphony, Philadelphia Orchestra and Indianapolis Symphony; Liszt concerts in Boston and New York, 1962; Repertoire also includes Chopin, Prokofiev and Gottschalk; Career interrupted by illness in 1960s but resumed in 1972; White House concert, 1985; Discovered manuscripts of two Chopin waltzes in France, 1967. *Recordings include:* Concertos by Liszt and Rachmaninov. *Honours:* Harriet Cohen Award; First American to receive Grand Prix du Disque; Chevalier of the Order des Arts et Lettres, 1965; Ambassador for the Arts of the National Arthritis Foundation, 1985.

JANK, Helena; Concert Harpsichordist; b. 1955, Salvador, Bahia, Brazil; m. Eduardo Ostergren, 11 July 1992, 1 d. *Education:* Studied at Staatliche Hochschule für Musik, Germany. *Career:* Debut: Munich,

1967; Professor at Campinas State University, Brazil; Harpsichordist with Münchener Bach-Orchester; Performances as soloist and in chamber music ensembles in Germany, USA and Brazil; mem, International Bach Society. *Recordings:* Helena Jank Plays Bach, Scarlatti, Ligeti; The Finest Baroque Sonatas, Erich; Mozart Sonatas; J. S. Bach Goldberg Variations: A Guide for the Complete Person. *Publications:* Goldberg Variations. *Honours:* Academic Recognition for Excellence in Teaching. *Address:* Rua Alvaro Muller 150, Ap 32, 13023 180 Campinas, São Paulo, Brazil.

JANKOVIC, Eleonora; Singer (Mezzo-soprano); b. 18 Feb. 1941, Trieste, Italy. *Education:* Studied in Trieste and Milan. *Career:* Member of the Opera at Zagreb, then made Italian debut at Trieste, 1972, in Smareglia's Nozze Istriane; Appearances at La Scala from 1974, Bologna, 1975, Florence, 1976, Teatro Lirico Milan, 1975, in the premiere of Al gran sole carico d'Amore by Luigi Nono; Guest engagements at Turin, Venice, Naples and Catania; Verona Arena, 1975–78, 1983, 1987; Rio de Janeiro and Buenos Aires, 1982–83; Sang Enrichetta in I Puritani at Rome, 1990, and appeared in Luisa Miller at Trieste, 1990; Sang in Wolf-Ferrari's I Quattro Rusteghi, for Geneva Opera, 1992; Has also sung the Countess in The Queen of Spades, Ulrica, Amneris, Leonora in La Favorita, Carmen, Charlotte, Marina in Boris Godunov and Mother Goose in The Rake's Progress; Many concert appearances. *Address:* Teatro dell'Opera di Roma, Piazza B Gigli 8, 00184 Rome, Italy.

JANOVICKY, Karel; Composer, Pianist and Broadcaster; b. 18 Feb. 1930, Plzeň, Czechoslovakia; m. Sylva Simsova, 22 May 1950, 1 s., 1 d. *Education:* Realne Gymnasium; Surrey College of Music, England; Private Studies with Jan Sedivka (chamber music) and Matyas Seiber (composition). *Career:* Debut: Wigmore Hall, London, 1956; Many scores in MS; Recent performances at British Music Information Centre. *Compositions include:* Sonata for Bass Clarinet and Piano, Three Cambridge Songs; Clarinet Quartet, 2000; Harp Sonata, 2000; In Praise of Rossini, for flute and piano, 2001. *Recordings include:* Song Cycle Passages of Flight; Terzina for Violin and Piano, 1988. *Publications include:* Saxophone Quartet, 1996; Sonata for Alto Saxophone and Piano, 1999. *Contributions:* New Edition of Leoš Janáček: A Biography by Jaroslav Vogel, for Orbis Publishing, London, 1981; Introducing Mr Brouček, English National Opera, 1978; Jaroslav Seifert's Nobel Prize, The Listener, 1984. *Honours:* First Prize, Shakespeare Competition, Bournemouth Symphony Orchestra, 1957 for Variations on a Theme of Robert Johnson Op 17; Sonata for 2 Violins and Piano on SPNM Recommended List, London. *Address:* 18 Muswell Avenue, London N10 2EG, England.

JANOWITZ, Gundula; singer (soprano); b. 2 Aug. 1937, Berlin, Germany; m.; one d. *Education:* Academy of Music and Performing Arts, Graz. *Career:* debut with Vienna State Opera; Sang with Deutsche Oper Berlin, 1966; Metropolitan Opera, New York, 1967, as Sieglinde in Die Walküre, conducted by Karajan; Salzburg Festival, 1968–81, as Mozart's Donna Anna, Fiordiligi and Countess, Strauss's Marschallin and Ariadne; Teatro Colón, Buenos Aires, 1970, Munich State Opera, 1971, Grand Opera, Paris, 1973, Covent Garden Opera, 1976, La Scala, 1978; Concerts in major cities throughout the world; Appearances at Bayreuth, Aix-en-Provence, Glyndebourne (as Ilia in Idomeneo, 1964), Spoleto, Munich Festival, Salzburg Festival 1968–81, as Mozart's Countess, Donna Anna and Fiordiligi; Strauss's Marschallin and Ariadne; Member, Vienna State Opera and Deutsche Oper Berlin; Among her roles were Mozart's Pamina, Wagner's Eva and Elisabeth, Strauss's Empress, and Arabella and Puccini's Mimi; Returned to Covent Garden, 1987, as Ariadne; Opera Director at Graz, 1990–91; Recent concert engagements in Four Last Songs by Stauss; Schubert Bicentenary concert at St John's, London, 1997.

JANOWSKI, Marek; Conductor; b. 18 Feb. 1939, Warsaw, Poland. *Education:* Studied at Cologne Musikhochschule and in Siena. *Career:* Assistant Conductor in Aachen, Cologne and Düsseldorf opera houses; London debut, 1969, leading the Cologne Opera in the British premiere of Henze's Der junge Lord; Musical Director, Freiburg and Dortmund Operas, 1973–79; Guest Conductor at opera houses in Hamburg, Paris, Munich and Berlin; American opera debut, San Francisco, 1983; Metropolitan Opera, 1984, Strauss's Arabella; Artistic Adviser and Conductor, Royal Liverpool Philharmonic Orchestra, 1983–86; Chief Conductor of the Nouvel Philharmonique de Radio France and the Gurzenich Orchester, Cologne; Conducted the company of the Cologne Opera in Fidelio at Hong Kong, 1989; Die Meistersinger at the Théâtre du Châtelet, Paris, 1990; Conducted Elektra at Orange, 1991; Guest Conductor to Pittsburgh Symphony Orchestra, 2005–. *Recordings:* Opera sets including Ring, with the Dresden Staatskapelle, Weber's Euryanthe, Strauss's Die schweigsame Frau and Penderecki's The Devils of Loudun; Weber's Oberon, 1997. *Address:* IMG Artists (Europe), Lovell House, 616 Chiswick High Road, London W4 5RX, England.

JANSEN, Rudolf; Pianist; b. 19 Jan. 1940, Arnhem, Netherlands; m. (1) Margreet Honig, 2 c., (2) Christa Pfeiler, 2 c. *Education:* Amsterdam Conservatory, Studied piano with Nelly Wagenaar, organ with his father, Simon C Jansen and harpsichord with Gustav Leonhardt. *Career:* Soloist; Accompanist for numerous leading singers and other artists throughout the world including: Elly Ameling, Robert Holl, Han de Vries, Andreas Schmidt, Olaf Bär, Barbara Bonney, Tom Krause and Hans-Peter Blochwitz; Conducts master classes for singers and accompanists in Europe, North America and the Orient; Gave a master class at the Juilliard School, New York, 1996; Teaches at the Amsterdam Conservatory. *Recordings:* More than 100 recordings as Lieder Accompanist or Chamber Music Player. *Honours:* Prix d'Excellence for organ, 1964; Toonkunst Jubileum Prize, 1965; Prix d'Excellence for piano, 1966; Zilveren Vriendenkrans, Friends of Amsterdam Concertgebouw, 1966. *Address:* Schepenenlaan 2, 1181 BB Amstelveen, Netherlands.

JANSONS, Maris; Latvian conductor; *Chief Conductor, Royal Concertgebouw Orchestra;* b. 14 Jan. 1943, Riga; s. of Arvid Jansons and Erhaida Jansons; m. Irina Jansons 1967; one d. *Education:* studied with father, Leningrad Conservatory with N. Rabinovich, Vienna Conservatory with Hans Swarovsky and Salzburg under von Karajan. *Career:* Prin. Guest Conductor Leningrad (now St Petersburg) Philharmonic Orchestra; Chief Conductor Oslo Philharmonic 1979–2002; Guest Conductor Welsh Symphony Orchestra 1985–88; Salzburg debut with the Vienna Philharmonic 1994; Prin. Guest Conductor London Philharmonic Orchestra –1997; Music Dir Pittsburgh Symphony Orchestra 1995; Chief Conductor 1997–2002; Musical Dir Bavarian Radio Symphony Orchestra 2002–; conducted the London Symphony Orchestra at the London Proms 2002; Prof. of Conducting, St Petersburg Conservatory 1995–; has appeared all over world, with Baltimore Symphony Orchestra, Berlin Philharmonic, Boston Symphony Orchestra, Chicago Symphony Orchestra, Cleveland Orchestra, London Philharmonia Orchestra, New York Philharmonic, Philadelphia Orchestra; Chief Conductor Royal Concertgebouw Orchestra 2004–. *Honours:* winner Herbert von Karajan Competition 1971, Anders Jahre Cultural Prize (Norway), RSFSR People's Artist 1986, Royal Philharmonic Soc. best conductor 2004; Commdr with Star Royal Norwegian Order of Merit. *Current Management:* IMG Artists Europe, Media House, 616 Chiswick High Road, London, W4 5RX, England. *Address:* c/o Royal Concertgebouw Orchestra, Jacob Obrechtstraat 51, 1071 KJ Amsterdam, Netherlands.

JANULAKO, Vassilio; Singer (Baritone); b. 14 Sept. 1933, Athens, Greece. *Education:* Studied at the Athens Conservatory. *Career:* Debut: Athens, 1961, as the High Priest in Alceste; Engagements at opera houses in Stuttgart, Berlin, Düsseldorf, Hamburg, Munich, Vienna, Frankfurt, Nuremberg, Zürich, Toulouse and San Francisco; Roles include Pizarro, the Dutchman, Telramund, Amfortas, Don Giovanni, Mozart's Count, Gerard, Scarpia, Escamillo, Mandryka, Milhaud's Christopher Columbus and parts in operas by Verdi; Cologne, 1986, as Pandolfe in Cendrillon by Massenet; Spoleto and Philadelphia, 1988, in Jenůfa and Rusalka; Sang Paolo in Simon Boccanegra at Cologne, 1990. *Address:* c/o Oper der Stadt Köln, Offenbachplatz, 5000 Cologne, Germany.

JAPE, Mijndert; Dutch lutenist, classical guitarist, writer and music historian; b. 11 July 1932, Geleen, Limburg; m. Marie-Hélène Habets 1960 (died 1987). *Education:* Muzieklyceum Heerlen, Conservatory of Maastricht, Schola Cantorum, Paris, Royal Conservatory of the Hague; studied with Hans-Lutz Niessen, Ida Presti, Alexandre Lagoya, Toyohiki Satoh, Eugen Dombois, Thomas Binkley, Anthony Bailes. *Career:* soloist, accompanist on lute instruments, baroque operas, vocal groups, Belgium, Netherlands, France; Director, Delitiae Musicae, specialising in 1550–1650 music and poetry concerts, Netherlands, Belgium, France; Plays 1820 Moitessier guitar and 8 lute instruments; Guest Lecturer; Teacher of Lute and Guitar, 1955–92, Musical director, 1986–92, Sittard Musical School, 1955–92; Teaching Lute and Guitar, Music Academy, Maasmechelen and Tongeren, Belgium. *Recordings:* 4 (solo, ensemble), Belgium, Netherlands. *Publications:* Fernando Sor–Opera Omnia for the Guitar; On Lute Tuition, 1987; Classical Guitar Music in Print, bibliography, 12 vols (with Marie-Hélène Habets), vols 5, 8 and 9, 1980–1989; Louys de Moy–le Petit Boucquet, 1990; Elementa Pro Arte, lute tutor, in progress; The 'Wilhelmus van Nassouwe', Dutch National Anthem, development and relationship to the lute music, 1994. *Address:* PO Box 81, 6190 Beek, Limburg, Netherlands.

JAR, Valentin; Singer (Tenor); b. 1950, Bucharest, Romania. *Education:* Bucharest and Hague Conservatories. *Career:* Sang at Gelsenkirchen Opera, 1981–82; Frankfurt, 1984–93; Roles have included Mozart's Monostatos and Pedrillo, Verdi's Macduff and Cassio, Apollo in Monteverdi's Orfeo, Mime in Siegfried and Janáček's Mr Brouček, Vitek and Luka for Opéra du Rhin Strasbourg; Iro in Monteverdi's Ulisse at Antwerp, Avignon and Lausanne; Strauss's Valzacchi at Toulouse; Weill's Fatty, Wexford; Season 1998–99 with Monostatos at

Liège; Iro for Opera North and Lisbon. *Address:* Music International, 13 Ardilaun Road, London N5 2QR, England.

JARMAN, Douglas; Lecturer and Writer; b. 21 Nov. 1942, Dewsbury, Yorkshire, England; m. Angela Elizabeth Brown, 26 Sept 1970, 2 d. *Education:* BA Honours, Music, Hull University, 1964; PhD, Durham University, 1968; Research Fellow, Liverpool University, 1968–70. *Career:* Lecturer in Music, University of Leeds, 1970–71; Lecturer, 1974–86, Principal Lecturer, 1986, Academic Studies, Royal Northern College of Music, Manchester; mem, Artistic Director, Young Musicians' Chamber Music Festival; Chairman Psappha; Advisory Board, Music Analysis. *Recordings:* Talk, Lulu; The Historical Background, recording of The Complete Lulu. *Publications:* The Music of Alban Berg, 1979, 1983; Kurt Weill, 1982; Wozzeck, 1989; The Berg Companion, 1989; Alban Berg, Lulu, 1991; Expressionism Reassessed, 1993; Alban Berg: Violin Concerto, critical edition, 1998; Hans Werner Henze at the RNCM, vols 1–3, 1999; The Twentieth Century String Quartet, 2002. *Contributions:* Perspectives of New Music; Musical Quarterly; Musical Times; Music Review; Journal of Royal Musical Association; Newsletter of International Alban Berg Society; Alban Berg Studien, vol. 2. *Honours:* Honorary Fellow, Royal Northern College of Music, 1986; Honorary Professor of Music, University of Manchester, 2002. *Address:* 1 Birch Villas, Birchcliffe Road, Hebden Bridge HX7 8DA, England.

JARRETT, Keith; American pianist and composer; b. 8 May 1945, Allentown, PA. *Education:* Berklee School of Music. *Career:* gave first solo concert aged 7, followed by professional appearances; two-hour solo concert of own compositions 1962; led own trio in Boston; worked with Roland Kirk, Tony Scott and others in New York; joined Art Blakey 1965; toured Europe with Charles Lloyd 1966, with Miles Davis 1970–71; soloist and leader of own groups 1969–; Guggenheim Fellowship 1972. *Recordings include:* albums Bach's Well-Tempered Klavier, Personal Mountains 1974, Luminessence 1974, Mysteries 1975, Changeless 1987, Nude Ants, The Cure 1990, Bye Bye Black 1991, At the Dear Head Inn 1992, Bridge of Light 1993, At the Blue Note 1994, La Scala 1995, Tokyo '96 1998, The Melody at Night With You 1999, Whisper Not 2000, Inside Out 2001, Always Let Me Go 2002, Selected Recordings 2002. *Honours:* Prix du Prés. de la République 1991, Royal Swedish Acad. of Music Polar Prize 2003; Officier, Ordre des Arts et des Lettres. *Current Management:* Vincent Ryan, 135 W 16th Street, New York, NY 10011, USA.

JÄRVI, Neeme; symphony and opera conductor; b. 7 June 1937, Tallinn, Estonia; m. 1961; two s. one d. *Education:* Tallinn Music School, Leningrad State Conservatory with Nicolai Rabinovich and Yevgeni Mravinski. *Career:* Music Director, Estonian State Symphony Orchestra, 1960–80; Music Director, Principal Conductor, Theatre Estonia, Tallinn, 1964–77; Guest Conductor with Leningrad Philharmonic, Moscow Philharmonic, USSR Radio Philharmonic Moscow, USSR State Symphony Orchestra, USSR and abroad; New York Philharmonic, Philadelphia, Boston, Chicago and Los Angeles Philharmonic Orchestras; San Francisco, Washington, Toronto, Cincinnati, Atlanta, Montreal and Ottawa, 1980–; Metropolitan Opera, Eugene Onegin, 1979, 1984; Samson and Delilah, 1982; New production of Mussorgsky's Khovanshchina, 1985/1986 season; Music Director, Principal Conductor, Göteborg Symphony, 1982–; Musical Director, Principal Conductor, Scottish National Orchestra, 1984–88; Music Director, Detroit Symphony Orchestra, 1989–; Guest Conductor, Paris, Cologne Radio, Amsterdam Concertgebouw, Bavarian Radio, Berlin Philharmonic, Hamburg Radio, Bamberg Symphony; Scandinavian orchestras; Led the BBC Symphony Orchestra at the 1999 London Proms: Nielsen's Aladdin Suite and premiere of Gruber's Trumpet Concerto. *Recordings:* Complete symphonies by Berwald, Niels Gade, Prokofiev, Tubin, Dvořák, Brahms, Rimsky-Korsakov, Stravinsky, Tchaikovsky, Shostakovich, Glazunov, Scriabin and Rachmaninov; Rachmaninov's Aleko and Zandonai's Francesca da Rimini, 1997. *Honours:* 1st Prize, Conductor Competition, Academy di Santa Cecilia, Rome; Toblach Prize, 1993, for best Mahler Symphony, new recording (Mahler 3 with Royal Scottish National). *Address:* Göteborgs Konserthus, Stenhammarsgatan 1, 41256 Gothenburg, Sweden.

JÄRVI, Paavo; Conductor; b. 1962, Tallinn, Estonia. *Education:* Studied in Tallinn, at the Juilliard School, with Bernstein in Los Angeles and Max Rudolf at the Curtis Institute. *Career:* Has conducted most of the major orchestras, notably as Principal Guest Conductor of the Royal Stockholm Philharmonic and the City of Birmingham Symphony Orchestras; Further engagements with the Philharmonia, Orchestra of the Age of Enlightenment, London, Munich, Czech, Israel, St Petersburg, BBC and Berlin Philharmonic Orchestras, Orchestre Nat. de France, Accademia Nazionale di Santa Cecilia, RAI Turin, Maggio Musicale Fiorentino, Orchestra Filarmonica della Scala, NHK, Boston, Vienna, London an Sydney Symphony Orchestras; Music Director of the Cincinnati Symphony Orchestra, 2001–; Artistic Dir, Die Deutsche Kammerphilharmonie Bremen, 2004–. *Recordings:* Sibelius album with the Royal Stockholm Philharmonic Orchestra, Sibelius Kullervo, 1997;

Britten and Shostakovich with the CBSO, Sibelius Cantatas, The Maiden inthe Tower and 2 CDs by Arvo Pärt, with the Estonian Nat. Symphony Orchestra; albums of music by Berlioz, Sibelius, Tubin, Stravinsky and Prokofiev (Romeo and Juliet), with the Cincinnati Symphony Orchestra. *Current Management:* Harrison Parrott Ltd, 12 Penzance Place, London, W11 4PA, England. *Telephone:* (20) 7229-9166. *Fax:* (20) 7221-5042. *E-mail:* nicole.rochman@harrisonparrott.co.uk. *Website:* www.harrisonparrott.com.

JARVLEPP, Jan Eric; composer, teacher and cellist; b. 3 Jan. 1953, Ottawa, ON, Canada. *Education:* BMus, University of Ottawa, 1976; MMus, McGill University, Montreal, Canada, 1978; PhD, University of CA, San Diego, USA, 1981. *Career:* CBC Chamber Music Broadcasts; Member, Ottawa Symphony Orchestra, 1981–; Nepean Symphony Orchestra, 1981–91; Electronic compositions performed on several different Canadian and US University campuses and Radio stations; Music Director of Espace Musique Concert Society, 1993–99; mem, SOCAN; Canadian Music Centre. *Compositions:* Lento, 1975; Ice, 1976; Aurora Borealis, 1976; Buoyancy, 1977; Flotation, 1978; Transparency and Density, 1978; Trumpet Piece, 1979; Cello Concerto, 1980; Time Zones, 1981; Night Music, 1982; Harpsichord Piece, 1984; Evening Music for Carillon, 1984; Cadenza for Solo Cello, 1985; Guitar Piece, 1985; Morning Music for Carillon, 1986; Afternoon Music for Carillon, 1986; Sunrise, 1987; Sunset, 1987; Trio, 1987; Liquid Crystals, 1988; Camerata Music, 1989; Dream, 1990; Life in The Fast Lane, 1990; Encounter, 1991; Underwater, 1992; Music from Mars, 1993; Moonscape, 1993; Robot Dance, 1994; Pierrot Solaire, 1994; Garbage Concerto, 1995; Tarantella, 1996; Bassoon Quartet, 1996; Saxophone Quartet, 1996; Trio No. 2, 1997; Earth Song, 1998; Five-Way Crossover, 1998; Overture, 1999; Dilemma, 1999; Concerto 2000, 2000; Quintet 2000, 2000; Street Scene, 2000; Quintet 2001, 2001; Suite for Viola and Strings, 2001; Shinkausen, 2001; Quintet 2002, 2003; Cornet, 2002; The Lord's Prayer, 2002. *Recordings:* Chronogrammes; Soundtracks of The Imagination; Flights of Fancy; Garbage Concerto. *Publications:* Compositional Aspects of Berio's Tempi Concertati, Interface, vol. II, No. 4, 1982; Pitch and Texture Analysis of Ligeti's Lux Aeterna, ex tempore, Vol. 2-1, 1982; Alchemy in the Nineties, 1997. *Address:* PO Box 2684, Station D, Ottawa, ON K1P 5W7, Canada. *E-mail:* jarvlepp@magma.ca. *Website:* www.janjarvlepp.com.

JASINKA-JEDROSZ, Elzbieta; Musicologist; b. 11 Jan. 1949, Katowice, Poland; m. Janusz Jedrosz, 25 July 1970, 1 s. *Education:* Musicological studies, Warsaw University, 1968–73. *Career:* Engaged in bibliographic documentation of Polish musical works and in other tasks at Archive of 20th Century Polish Composers, Polish Composers Archive, Warsaw University Library Music Collection, 1973–; mem, Polish Composers Union; Karol Szymanowski Music Association, Zakopane; Polish Librarians Association; Association of Polish Musicians. *Publications:* Expositions: Music and Polish Musicians in French 1925–1950, 1977; Karol Szymanowski 1882–1937, 1983; Karol Szymanowski: Writer-Poet-Thinker, 1997; Collection of the 20th Century Polish Composers' Archives, 1999; Other publications: The Manuscripts of Karol Szymanowski's Musical Works, catalogue, 1983; Co-author, Karol Szymanowski in the Polish Collections, guide-book, 1989; The Manuscripts of the Young Poland's Composers, catalogue, 1997. *Contributions:* Muzyka, 1981; Ruch Muzyczny, 1980, 1981, 1983, 1988–90, 1998–99; Pagine 1989; Przeglad Biblioteczny, 1989. *Honours:* Honours for popularisation of Karol Szymanowski's compositions, 1998. *Address:* u. Janinówka 11 m 122, 03562 Warsaw, Poland.

JEDLICKA, Dalibor; Singer (Bass-baritone); b. 23 May 1929, Svoyanov, Czechoslovakia. *Education:* Studied in Ostrava with Rudolf Vasek. *Career:* Debut: Opava, 1953, as Mumlala in The Two Widows by Smetana; Sang at the National Theatre, Prague, 1957–77, also guest appearances with the company in Brno, Amsterdam, Zürich and Edinburgh (1970 in the British premiere of The Excursions of Mr Brouček by Janáček); Engagements at Belgrade, Zagreb, Warsaw, Venice and Bologna; Repertoire included buffo roles and German, French and Czech operas; Mozart's Figaro and Papageno, Don Pasquale and Kaspar in Der Freischütz; Opéra Comique, Paris, 1988, in From the House of the Dead. *Recordings include:* Janáček's Katya Kabanova, The Cunning Little Vixen and From the House of the Dead, conducted by Charles Mackerras; Pauer's Suzanna Vojirva and Don Giovanni; Another recording of Cunning Little Vixen.

JEDLICKA, Rudolf; Singer (Baritone); b. 22 Jan. 1920, Skalice, Czechoslovakia. *Education:* Studied with Tino Pattieri, Pavel Ludikar and Fernando Carpi in Vienna and Prague. *Career:* Debut: Dresden Staatsoper, 1944, as Marcel in La Bohème; Sang in Prague from 1945; Produced opera at Usti nad Labem, 1946–49; Guest with the Staatsoper Berlin from 1958; Appearances at the Vienna Staatsoper and in Russia, German and Polish opera houses as Mozart's Figaro and Don Giovanni, Posa in Don Carlos and Rossini's Figaro; Sang with the Prague National Opera at the Edinburgh Festival, 1964, 1970, in the British premieres of Janáček's From the House of the Dead and The Excursions of Mr

Brouček; Professor at the Prague Conservatory, 1973–75; Director of the National Theatre, Prague, 1989; Sang Grigoris in Martinů's Greek Passion at Wiesbaden, 1990. *Recordings:* Jenůfa. *Address:* National Theatre, PO Box 865, 112 30 Prague 1, Czech Republic.

JEFFERS, Gweneth-Ann; Singer (Soprano); b. 1975, England. *Education:* University of Exeter; Goldsmiths College and Guildhall School, London; Royal Opera Vilar Young Artist Programme, from 2001. *Career:* Appearances with major London orchestras; Concert repertoire includes Schubert, Schumann, Ravel, Barber, Messiaen (Harawi at the Cheltenham Festival, 2000) and Cage; Verdi Requiem at Truro Cathedral, Brahms Requiem and Strauss's Vier Letzte Lieder in Canterbury Cathedral; Season 2000–2001 as Massenet's Navarraise at the Guildhall, Strauss's Ariadne with the Orchestre de Picardie and the original version of Berg's Lyric Suite with the Endellion Quartet at Aldeburgh. *Honours:* represented England at 2001 Cardiff Singer of the World Competition. *Current Management:* Askonas Holt Ltd, Lonsdale Chambers, 27 Chancery Lane, London, WC2A 1PF, England. *Telephone:* (20) 7400-1700. *Fax:* (20) 7400-1799. *E-mail:* info@askonasholt.co.uk. *Website:* www.askonasholt.co.uk.

JEFFERS, Ronald Harrison; Composer and Conductor; b. 25 March 1942, Springfield, Illinois, USA. *Education:* Studied composition with Ross Lee Finney at University of Michigan; University of California at San Diego, 1970–72, with Pauline Oliveros, Kenneth Gaburo and Robert Erickson; Choral conducting at Occidental College, Los Angeles, 1968–72. *Career:* Director of choral activities at Stony Brook, New York, and at Oregon State University; Tours of Europe, 1978 and 1982. *Compositions include:* Missa concrete for 3 choruses, 1969, revised, 1973; In Memoriam for chamber ensemble, 1973; Time Passes for mezzo, tape and ensemble, 1974–81; Transitory for chorus and tape, 1980; Arise My Love for 12 voices, chimes and gongs, 1981; Crabs for tape, 1981; This We Know, for chorus, 1987; Songs of the Sea, 1991; Salut au Monde! for chamber ensemble, 1993. *Address:* c/o ASCAP, ASCAP Building, 1 Lincoln Plaza, New York, NY 10023, USA.

JEFFERSON, Alan (Rigby); Author; b. 20 March 1921, Ashtead, Surrey, England; m. Antonia Dora Raeburn, 24 Sept 1976, 2 s.; 3 s., 1 d. from previous marriages. *Education:* Old Vic Theatre School, 1947–48. *Career:* Theatre Stage Manager/Director; Administrator, London Symphony Orchestra, 1968–69; Manager, BBC Concert Orchestra, 1969–73; Visiting Professor in Vocal Interpretation, Guildhall School of Music and Drama, London, 1968–74; Editor, The Monthly Guide to Recorded Music, 1980–82; mem, Royal Society of Musicians of Great Britain. *Publications:* The Operas of Richard Strauss in Great Britain 1910–1963, 1964; The Lieder of Richard Strauss, 1971; Delius (Master Musicians), 1972; The Life of Richard Strauss, 1973; Inside the Orchestra, 1974; Strauss (Music Masters), 1975; The Glory of Opera, 1976, Norwegian version, 1980, 2nd edition, 1983; Discography of Richard Strauss's Operas, 1977; Strauss (Short Biographies), 1978; Sir Thomas Beecham, 1979; The Complete Gilbert and Sullivan Opera Guide, 1984; Der Rosenkavalier, 1986; Lotte Lehmann, A Centenary Biography, 1988, German language edition, 1991; Elisabeth Schwarzkopf (biography) and German edition, 1996. *Contributions:* Blätter Internationale Richard Strauss Gesellschaft, Vienna; Classical Express.

JEFFERY, Darren; Singer (bass-baritone); b. 1976, England. *Education:* Royal Northern Coll. of Music; Vilar Young Artists Programme, Covent Garden 2001. *Career:* sang Falstaff and Der Sprecher (Die Zauberflote) with Royal Northern Coll. of Music; sang Antinöus in Monteverdi's Il ritorno d'Ulisse at the Creakes Festival and Solino in Gli Equivoci for the Batignano Festival, Italy; Glyndebourne Festival 2001, covering Don Fernando in Fidelio and Matthew in The Last Supper; sang Masetto in Don Giovanni at Covent Garden 2002; other roles with the Royal Opera, Covent Garden are Rambaldo, Mandarin (Turandot) 2002, Monterone (Rigoletto) 2002, Tutor (Elektra), Baron Douphol (La Traviata) 2002, Masetto (Don Giovanni) 2003, Bonzo (Madama Butterfly) 2003, Der Sprecher (Die Zauberflote) 2003, Gravedigger (Hamlet) 2003, Bartender (Sophie's Choice, world premiere) 2003; roles elsewhere include Cadmus in Handel's Semele, Donner in The Rheingold (ENO), Figaro in Le Nozze di Figaro (Savoy Opera Theatre). *Current Management:* Harlequin Agency Ltd, 203 Fidlas Road, Llanishen, Cardiff CF14 5NA, Wales. *Telephone:* (29) 2075-0821. *Fax:* (29) 2075-5971. *E-mail:* info@harlequin-agency.co.uk. *Website:* www.harlequin-agency.co.uk.

JEFFERY, Peter; Professor of Music; b. 19 Oct. 1953, New York, NY, USA; m. Margot Fassler, 1983, 2 s. *Education:* MFA, 1977, PhD, 1980, Princeton University. *Career:* Hill Monastic Manuscript Library, 1980–82; Mellon Faculty Fellow, Harvard University, 1982–83; University of Delaware, 1984–92; Boston College, 1992–93; Princeton University, 1993–; mem, American Musicological Society; Medieval Academy of America; North American Academy of Liturgy; Societas Liturgica. *Publications:* A Bibliography for Medieval and Renaissance Musical Manuscript Research, 1980; Re-Envisioning Past Musical Cultures. *Contributions:* Journal of the American Musicological Society;

Studia Liturgica; Archiv für Liturgiewissenschaft; Created Gregorian Chant website. *Honours:* Alfred Einstein Award, 1985; National Endowment for the Humanities Grant, 1986–88; John D MacArthur Fellowship, 1987–82. *Address:* Music Department, Princeton University, NJ 08544, USA.

JEFFES, Peter; Singer (Tenor); b. 1951, London, England. *Education:* Royal College of Music, London; Rome with Paolo Silveri. *Career:* Italian debut in Rome Opera in Spontini's Agnese di Hohenstaufen; Paris Opéra in Doktor Faust; With English Bach Festival at Covent Garden in Rameau's Castor et Pollux; Nero in L'Incoronazione di Poppea for Swiss television; European engagements as Lohengrin, Tamino and Lensky; Sang Mozart in Rimsky's Mozart and Salieri at Barcelona in 1987; Festival appearances at Aix-en-Provence, Orange, Monte Carlo, Athens and in the USA; Engagement with British companies in Roméo et Juliette, Les Contes d'Hoffmann, Die Zauberflöte, The Rake's Progress and A Midsummer Night's Dream; Opera North in the British premiere of Strauss's Daphne, 1987; Season 1988–89 in The Love for Three Oranges for Opera North; Since 1988, repertoire, roles in Cavalleria Rusticana, Pagliacci, Idomeneo, Faust, Werther, Salome, Fliegende Holländer, Macbeth, Attila and Eisenstein in Die Fledermaus; Now sings extensively in Europe and regularly in Israel; The Prince in the Love for Three Oranges, 1992; Sang Wagner's Rienzi for Chelsea Opera Group (concert) and the High Priest in Idomeneo at Lyon, 1999. *Address:* c/o Music International, 13 Ardilaun Road, Highbury, London N5 2QR, England.

JEFFREYS, Celia; Singer (Soprano); b. 20 Jan. 1948, Southampton, England. *Education:* Studied music at the Royal College of Music, ARCM. *Career:* Debut: Welsh National Opera, 1970, as Adele in Die Fledermaus; Sang at various regional opera houses in the United Kingdom; Appeared on BBC and Southern Television, United Kingdom; Sang at: Kassel and Darmstadt, Germany, Theater am Gärtnerplatz, Munich from 1976, Stadttheater Basel, 1978–81; From 1981–88 appeared as guest artist in: Bern, Berlin Koblenz, Salzburg, Theater an der Wien, Schlosspiele Heidelberg, Festspiele, Bregenz; From 1988–91 engagements in Linz, Austria; Appearing regularly in Salzburg and Linz, 1997–; Opera roles include Donna Elvira, in Don Giovanni; Mimi, in La Bohème, the Marschallin in Rosenkavalier; Agathe in Der Freischütz; Nedda, in Pagliacci; Leonore, in Fidelio; Operetta roles include: Hanna Glawari, in The Merry Widow and Rosalinde in Die Fledermaus; Teacher, Bayerische Theaterakademie, Munich. *Recordings:* Student Prince; Brahms, German Requiem. *Current Management:* ASM, Obergütschrain 3, CH 6003 Lucerne, Switzerland. *Address:* Grasmeierstrasse 12 B, 80805 Munich, Germany.

JEFFRIES, James Huw; Singer (countertenor); b. 1970, Canterbury, England. *Education:* Magdalen College, Oxford; Royal College of Music; Britten-Pears School; Further studies with Valerie Masterson, Jennifer Smith, Geoffrey Mitchell, Nicholas Powell. *Career:* Debut: Handel's Israel in Egypt, St John's, Smith Square, London; Concerts in oratorio and concert repertoire throughout the United Kingdom at Barbican Hall, South Bank Centre, Snape Maltings and most major cathedrals; Also performances in Canada, France, Greece, Netherlands, Ireland; Opera performances include Gluck's Orfeo at Riverside Studios, London; Rinaldo at Bloomsbury Theatre, London; Andronico in Tamerlano at Aldeburgh Festival; Nero in L'Incoronazione di Poppea, Cavalli Baroque Ensemble, Cambridge; Spirit in Dido and Aeneas at Sadler's Wells, London; Caspar in world premiere of Alexander Knaifel's Alice in Wonderland for Netherlands Opera; Season 1999–2000 included Oberon in A Midsummer Night's Dream at Landestheater Magdeburg; Concerts in Canada and the Netherlands, with Northern Chamber Orchestra, at Brighton Festival and throughout the United Kingdom; Season 2001–02 with Nireno in Giulio Cesare for Royal Danish Opera; Concerts in Germany, Netherlands, Republic of Ireland and the United Kingdom; during 2002/2003 member of the Südostbayerisches Städtetheater. *Current Management:* Connaught Artists Management Ltd, 2 Molasses Row, Plantation Wharf, London, SW11 3UX, England. *Telephone:* (20) 7738 0017. *Fax:* (20) 7738 0909. *E-mail:* classicalmusic@connaughtartists.com. *Website:* www.connaughtartists.com.

JEHLICKOVA, Zora; Singer (Soprano); b. 10 April 1950, Brno, Czechoslovakia. *Education:* Studied at the Prague Conservatory. *Career:* Sang at the Prague National Theatre from 1974, notably as Natasha in War and Peace, Marenka in The Bartered Bride, Rusalka, Pamina, Donna Elvira, Tatiana in Eugene Onegin, and Mimi; Title role in Dvořák's Armida, 1987; Smetana Theatre, Prague, 1992, as the Princess in Der Zwerg by Zemlinsky; Guest appearances in Dresden, the Komische Oper, Berlin, La Scala, Milan, and the Nationaltheater Mannheim; Many concert appearances. *Address:* c/o National Theatre Prague, PO Box 865, 11230 Prague 1, Czech Republic.

JELEZNOV, Irina; pianist; b. 4 Oct. 1958, Astrakhan, Russia; m. 1980; one s. *Education:* Tchaikovsky Conservatoire, Moscow. *Career:* debut in

Tashkent Conservatoire Hall 1984; annual recitals and orchestra performances, Tashkent 1984–93; appearances in Moscow at The Maly Hall, Moscow Conservatoire 1986, 1987, Rachmaninov Hall and Shuvalova's Home 1991; piano duo festivals at Sverdlovsk 1989, Leningrad 1990, Nizny Novgorod 1991, Novosibirsk 1992; int. piano duo competitions in Belgrade, Yugoslavia 1989, Caltanissetta, Italy 1990, Hartford, CT 1990, Miami, FL 1991; television and radio appearances; Docent, Chair of Chamber Music, Tashkent Conservatoire; mem. Int. Piano Duo Asscn, Tokyo, Japan. *Address:* Prospekt Kosmonavtov d 12-106, 700015 Tashkent, Uzbekistan.

JELEZNOV, Maxim; Duo Pianist; b. 19 May 1958, Moscow, Russia; m. 29 Aug 1980, 1 s. *Education:* Piano Faculty, 1981, Postgraduate course as Piano Duo, 1987, Tchaikovsky Conservatoire, Moscow. *Career:* Debut: Tashkent Conservatoire Hall, 1984; Performances: Tashkent, yearly 1984–93; Maly Hall, Moscow Conservatoire, 1986, 1987; Sverdlovsk Piano Duo Festival, 1989; Belgrade, Yugoslavia, 1989; International Piano Duo Festival Leningrad, 1990; Hartford, USA, 1990; Caltanissetta, Italy, 1990; Rachmaninov Hall, Moscow, 1991; Shuvalova's Home, Moscow, 1991; Nizny Novgorod Piano Duo Festival, 1991; International Piano Duo Festival, Ekaterinburg, 1991–93; Piano Duo Festival, The Masters of Piano Duo, Novosibirsk, 1992; Television and radio appearances. *Address:* Prospekt Kosmonavtov d 12-106, 700015 Tashkent, Uzbekistan.

JELINEK, Ladislav; Concert Pianist; b. 21 Feb. 1947, Brno, Czechoslovakia; m. 2 s. *Education:* State Conservatory in Brno, 1958–62; Janáček University of Musical Arts, Brno, majoring in solo piano under Professor Frantisek Schäfer. *Career:* Debut: Besedni Dum, Brno, 1966; Appearances as soloist with orchestra, solo pianist and chamber musician in Czechoslovakia and majority of Eastern European countries; Radio and television appearances in Eastern Europe, 1968–81; Numerous appearances (including radio and television appearances) in nearly all European countries, America and Japan, 1981–; University Teacher at the Frankfurter Hochschule für Musik and Darstellende Kunst, 1984–; mem, Artistic Advisory Board, Janáček University of Musical Arts, Brno. *Recordings include:* Beethoven, Brahms, Chopin, Dvořák, Haydn, Janáček, Liszt, Liszt-Wagner, Mozart, Jan Novák, V. Novák, Prokofiev, Rachmaninov, Smetana and others. *Honours:* Piano competitions: Academy of Music, Czechoslovakia, 1961; Hradec Kralove, 1963. *Address:* Lerchenweg 2, 61350 Bad Homburg, Germany. *E-mail:* contact@classicalpiano.de. *Website:* www.classicalpiano.de.

JENISOVA, Eva; Singer (Soprano); b. 1963, Presov, Czecholovakia. *Education:* Studied at the Bratislava Conservatory. *Career:* Soloist with the National Theatre Bratislava from 1986; Further appearances (from 1988) with the Deutsche Oper Berlin, Bolshoi Moscow, Budapest State Opera, National Theatre Prague and the Israel and Edinburgh Festivals; Vienna Staatsoper from 1990, as Marguerite in Faust, Donna Elvira, Katya Kabanova and Rusalka; Elvira under Harnoncourt at Amsterdam, Pamina and Violetta at Trieste, and Janáček's Vixen at the Paris Châtelet; Covent Garden debut 1997, as Katya Kabanova; Season 1997–98 as the Duchess of Parma in Busoni's Faust at Lyon, the Vixen in Madrid and Paris, and Mozart's Vitellia at Nancy; Concerts include Mareiken in Martinů's Legends of Mary, with the Vienna Symphony Orchestra, the Missa Solemnis at Madrid, the German Requiem in Bologna, Carmina Burana in Munich, and Dvořák's Stabat Mater at Salzburg; Mahler's Second Symphony in Graz, and Rusalka at the Salle Pleyel, Paris; Teatro Regio Turin 1997, as Mélisande. *Address:* c/o 13 Ardilaun Road, London N5 2QR, England.

JENKINS, Carol; Violinist; b. 1965, Toronto, Canada. *Education:* Studied at University of Toronto with Rodney Friend and Victor Danchenki. *Career:* Associate Leader, Denver Symphony Orchestra and other orchestras; Second Violinist, Da Vinci Quartet from 1988, founded in 1980 under the sponsorship of the Fine Arts Quartet; Many concerts in USA and elsewhere in a repertoire including works by Mozart, Beethoven, Brahms, Dvořák, Shostakovich and Bart ók. *Honours:* (With the Da Vinci Quartet), Awards and Grants from the NEA, the Western States Arts Foundation and the Colorado Council for the Humanities; Artist in Residence, University of Colorado. *Current Management:* Sonata, Glasgow, Scotland. *Address:* c/o Da Vinci Quartet, 11 Northpark Street, Glasgow G20 7AA, Scotland.

JENKINS, Graeme James Ewers; Conductor; b. 1958, England; m. Joanna, 2 d. *Education:* Studied at Dulwich College and Cambridge University; Royal College of Music with Norman Del Mar and David Willcocks; Adrian Boult Conducting Scholar. *Career:* Debut: Conducted Albert Herring and the Turn of the Screw at college; The Beggar's Opera, Die Entführung and Le nozze di Figaro for Kent Opera; Andrea Chénier, Brighton Festival; Cesti's La Dori (Spitalfields); Il Trovatore, Le nozze di Figaro and Così fan tutte with Scottish Opera; Così fan tutte with English National Opera (ENO debut), 1988; European debut, 1987, Hansel and Gretel and Ravel double bill with Geneva Opera; Simon Boccanegra, Netherlands Opera, 1989; As Music Director of Glynde-

bourne Touring Opera, 1986–91, has conducted A Midsummer Night's Dream, Albert Herring, Simon Boccanegra and Così fan tutte; La Traviata and Death in Venice (on BBC television), 1989; Glyndebourne Festival debut, 1987, with Carmen and Capriccio; Returned for Ravel double bill and Falstaff; Arabella, 1989; Oedipus Rex and Petrushka with Scottish Opera, 1989; Further engagements include Carmen and La Rondine with Canadian Opera in Toronto, La Bohème with Australian Opera, 1990; Concert appearances with the Hallé Orchestra, BBC Scottish, BBC Philharmonic, BBC Symphony, Royal Philharmonic, Kraków Radio Symphony and Scottish Chamber Orchestras; Fidelio (Glyndebourne Tour); Iphigénie en Tauride (Netherlands Opera); La Bohème (Australian Opera), 1990; Idomeneo (Glyndebourne Festival), 1991; Appearance at Hong Kong Festival, 1991; Conducted the world premiere of Stephen Oliver's Timon of Athens, London Coliseum, 1991; Residente Orkest The Hague, Netherlands Chamber Orchestra, 1991; Così fan tutte, US Opera debut, Dallas; Elektra, Dallas Opera, 1994; Death in Venice at the 1992 Glyndebourne Festival, Cologne Opera, 1996, Handel's Serse; Meistersinger, Australian Opera, 1993; Music Director, Dallas Opera, 1994; Chief Director, Cologne Opera, 1997–2002; Season 1997–98, numerous opera performances including Billy Budd, Katya Kabanova (with David Alden), Dallas; Macbeth (with Robert Carsen), Cologne; Appearances with Finnish Radio Symphony Orchestra; Debut with Utah and Dallas Symphony Orchestras; Work as orchestral conductor with major orchestras in the United Kingdom and with broadcasts on radio; Conducted London Philharmonic Orchestra at Royal Festival Hall, 1998; Artistic Director, Arundel Festival, 1992–1998; Has strong reputation in Netherlands and has worked with many other leading European orchestras; Season 1998–99 with a new production of Parsifal in Cologne and the Ring Cycle in Dallas; Since 1999 Clemenza di Tito for Glyndebourne Festival; Makropolos Case and Love of three Oranges for Cologne Opera; Wozzeck, Simon Boccanegra and Acis and Galatea in Dallas; Cunning Little Vixen for Deutsche Oper Berlin, 2001; Ballo in Maschera, 2002; Paris concert debut 2001; Orchestra Philharmonique de Radio France; Houston Symphony Debut, 2001; Perth and Melbourne Symphony Debuts 2002. *Current Management:* Askonas Holt Ltd, Lonsdale Chambers, 27 Chancery Lane, London, WC2A 1PF, England. *Telephone:* (20) 7400-1700. *Fax:* (20) 7400-1799. *E-mail:* info@askonasholt.co.uk. *Website:* www.askonasholt.co.uk.

JENKINS, Karl William Pamp, OBE, FRAM, ARAM; Welsh composer, pianist and oboist; b. 17 Feb. 1944, Penclawdd. *Education:* Gowerton Grammar School, Univ. of Wales, Cardiff and RAM. *Career:* initially resident jazz oboist at Ronnie Scott's; co-founder, Nucleus, then played in Soft Machine; currently composer and conductor; Pres., Friends of the Nat. Youth Orchestra of Wales, Penclawdd Brass Band; patron, Nat. Youth Choir of Great Britain; Fellow, Royal Welsh Coll. of Music and Drama, Trinity Coll., Carmarthen, and Swansea Inst.. *Compositions include:* Palladio 1992–95, Adiemus I: Songs of Sanctuary 1994, Adiemus II: Cantata Mundi 1996, Eloise 1997, Adiemus III: Dances of Time 1998, The Armed Man: A Mass for Peace 1999, Y Celtiaid (film score) (BAFTA Cymru Award for Best Original Music Soundtrack) 2000, Dying to Dance (TV score) 2001, Over the Stone 2002, Pwy Ysgrifennodd Y Testament Newydd? (film score) (BAFTA Cymru Award for Best Original Music Soundtrack) 2003, In These Stones Horizons Sing 2003, Quirk 2005, River Queen (film score) 2005. *Recordings include:* Adiemus (Songs of the Sanctuary), Palladio (with Smith Quartet and London Philharmonic Orchestra), Imagined Oceans, The Armed Man: A Mass for Peace (with Nat. Youth Choir of Great Britain and London Philharmonic Orchestra). *Honours:* first prize Montreal Jazz Festival (with Nucleus), two D&AD awards for best advertising music, Classic FM Red F Award for outstanding service to classical music. *Address:* Karl Jenkins Music Ltd, 46 Poland Street, London, W1F 7NA, England (office). *Telephone:* (20) 7434-2225. *Fax:* (20) 7494-4998. *E-mail:* info@karljenkins.com. *Website:* www.karljenkins.com.

JENKINS, Neil, MA; British opera and concert singer (tenor); b. 9 April 1945, Sussex, England; m. Penelope Anne 1982; four s. one d. *Education:* King's College Cambridge, Royal College of Music. *Career:* debut in Purcell Room, London, Song Recital with Roger Vignoles, 1967; Guest Soloist, Israel Chamber Orchestra, 1968–69; London Bach Society, 1971, 1973; Member of Deller Consort, 1967–76; Appearances at festivals in Israel, Paris, London and Spain; Performances with Welsh National Opera, Scottish Opera, Opera North, Glyndebourne, Edinburgh and Frankfurt, Kent Opera; New productions of Le nozze di Figaro and the Ravel double bill in Geneva; Wexford 1989 in Prokofiev's The Duenna; Sang in Bernstein's Candide, 1989; Also heard in oratorio and concert, in the orchestral version of Tippett's The Heart's Assurance at Canterbury, 1990; Debut at the ENO in Monteverdi's Orfeo and Il Ritorno d'Ulisse, 1992; Sang the Marquis in Lulu at the 1996 Glyndebourne Festival; Isaiah in Weill's Propheten at the 1998 London Proms; Sang Vitek in The Makropulos Case at Academy of Music, NY, 2001; mem, Warden of the PCS, Incorporated Society of Musicians, 1998–99. *Compositions include:* Christmas Carols for unaccompanied

SATB singers in Christmas is Coming, 1993. *Recordings include:* Bernstein Candide; White House Cantata, Bernstein; King Priam; Mozart, Le nozze di Figaro; Henze Kammermusik, 1958; Britten, Serenade for tenor, horn and strings, with Oriol Ensemble. *Publications:* Editor, The Carol Singer's Handbook, 1993; Editor, Bach: St Matthew Passion; St John Passion, 1998; Christmas Oratorio, 1999; Sing Solo Sacred. *Address:* 10 Hartington Villas, Hove, Sussex BN3 6HF, England. *E-mail:* neil@neiljenkins.com. *Website:* www.neiljenkins.com.

JENKINS, Speight; Administrator; b. 31 Jan. 1937, Dallas, Texas, USA. *Education:* Studied at the University of Texas and Columbia University Law School, graduating in 1961. *Career:* Editor, Opera News, 1967–73; Music Critic for the New York Post, 1973–81; Host for the Live from the Met broadcasts, 1981–83; General Director of Seattle Opera, 1983–; Has presided over such productions as The Ring Cycle, 1986–87, 1991, 1995, War and Peace, Die Meistersinger, and Werther in the version for baritone, 1989, the US premiere of Gluck's Orphée et Eurydice; Les Dialogues des Carmelites, 1990, Glass Artist Dale Chihuly's scenic debut in Pelléas et Mélisande, 1993, Norma, 1994; Der Rosenkavalier, 1997; Tristan und Isolde, 1998. *Honours:* Honorary Doctorates: Seattle University, 1992; University of Puget Sound, 1992. *Address:* Seattle Opera Association, PO Box 9248, Seattle, WA 98109, USA.

JENKINS, Terry; Operatic Tenor; b. 9 Oct. 1941, Hertford, England; m. Pamela Ann Jenkins 1965, 1 s., 1 d. *Education:* BSc (Eng), University College London, 1964; Guildhall School of Music, 1964–66; London Opera Centre, 1967–68. *Career:* Debut: Opera for All, 1966–67, Nemorino (L'Elisir d'amore); Basilic Opera, 1968–71; Glyndebourne Touring Opera, 1969–71; Malcolm (Macbeth), M Triquet (Eugene Onegin), Schmidt (Werther), Scarramuccio (Ariadne auf Naxos); Glyndebourne Festival Opera, 1971, Major Domo (Queen of Spades), Officer (Ariadne auf Naxos); Glyndebourne Festival Opera, 1972, Scarramuccio; Sadler's Wells Opera, 1972–74; English National Opera, 1974–, roles include Basilio (Marriage of Figaro), Pedrillo (Entführung), Remendado (Carmen), Goro (Madama Butterfly), Gaston (La Traviata), Vanya (Katya Kabanova), Spoletta (Tosca), Schmidt (Werther), Fenney (Mines of Sulphur), Tchekalinsky (Queen of Spades), Loge (Rheingold), Borsa (Rigoletto), Duke (Patience), Orpheus (Orpheus in the Underworld); Various roles, Pacific Overtures, Hauk Sendorf (Makropulos Case), Schoolmaster (Cunning Little Vixen), Dr Caius (Falstaff); English National Opera tour, USA, 1984; New Opera Company, 1976, 1979, 1980; Royal Opera, Covent Garden, 1976, 1977, 1981; English Bach Festival, 1983, Versailles and Sadler's Wells; City of London Festival, 1978; Barbican Hall, 1984–88; Seattle Opera, 1983, Loge-Rheingold; Vienna Festival with English National Opera, 1985; Chelsea Opera Group, 1986; Boston Concert Opera, USA, 1986, Guillot-Manon; Aix-en-Provence Festival, 1991, 1992, Snout, A Midsummer Night's Dream, Britten; Sang Dr Caius at Garsington. 1998. *Recordings:* Justice Shallow in Sir John in Love, Vaughan Williams; Borsa in Rigoletto; Pacific Overtures, Street Scene; Several video recordings. *Contributions:* Musicians' Handbook. *Current Management:* Music International, Ardilaun Road, London N7, England. *Address:* 9 West End Avenue, Pinner, Middlesex, England.

JENNINGS, Diane; Singer (Soprano); b. 1959, California, USA. *Education:* Studied at the San Diego Opera School. *Career:* Sang small roles in opera at San Diego, then studied further in Munich, 1984–86; Sang at the Landestheater Salzburg 1986–87, as Marzelline in Fidelio, Susanna, Pamina and Marenka in The Bartered Bride; Aachen opera, 1988–91, as Mimi; Mainz, 1990, as Donna Anna, Concert engagements in Vienna, Graz, Munich and Verona. *Recordings include:* Suor Angelica and Brixi's Missa pastoralis. *Address:* c/o Stadtheater Aachen, Theaterplatz, W-5100 Aachen, Germany.

JENSEN, Julian; Singer (Tenor); b. 1968, Fowey, Cornwall. *Education:* Royal Academy of Music, London. *Career:* Principal with D'Oyly Carte Opera, 1992; Opera roles include: Mozart's Tamino, Basilo and Ferrando, Theatre Kernow, 1999; Verdi's Alfredo, Holland Park, 1999; Duke in Rigoletto; Wexford Festival, 1998, in Pavel Haas's Sarlatan and Zandonai's I Cavalieri di Ekebu; Laerte in Mignon, University College Opera; Bardolph in Falstaff, Palace Opera; Concerts include: Puccini's Messa di Gloria; Haydn's Creation; Pärt's St John Passion. *Address:* Music International, 13 Ardilaun Road, London N5 2QR, England.

JENSON, Dylana (Ruth Lockington); Violinist; b. 14 May 1961, Los Angeles, California, USA. *Education:* Began violin training with mother; Pupil of Manuel Compinsky, Jascha Heifetz and Josef Gingold; Masterclasses with Nathan Milstein in Zürich, 1973–76. *Career:* First public appearance as soloist in the Bach A Minor Concerto at age 7; Professional debut as soloist in the Mendelssohn Concerto with the New York Philharmonic Orchestra, 1973; European debut as soloist with the Zürich Tonhalle Orchestra, 1974; Thereafter regular tours world-wide as a soloist with leading orchestras, as a recitalist, and as a chamber music player. *Recordings:* Several. *Honours:* 2nd Prize in Tchaikovsky

International Competition in Moscow, 1978. *Address:* c/o Konzertdirektion Jurgen Erlebach, Beim Schlump, 2000 Hamburg 13, Germany.

JEPPSSON, Kerstin (Maria); Composer; b. 29 Oct. 1948, Nyköping, Sweden. *Education:* BA, Musicology, Pedagogy, Social University of Stockholm, 1977; Studies, 1968–73, Music Teacher's Diploma, 1973, Stockholm Conservatory of Music; Composition with Maurice Karkoff, Stockholm, 1968–73, with Krzysztof Meyer and Krzysztof Penderecki, Kraków Conservatory of Music, Poland, 1974, 1977; Composition with Melvin Powell, 1978–79, MFA, 1979, California Institute of the Arts. *Compositions include:* Orchestral, chamber, solo instrumental, piano, vocal and choral works and songs, including: 3 Sentenzi for orchestra, 1970; Tre visor, choral, 1972; Blomstret i Saron, choral, 1972; Tre ryska poem for soprano and clarinet, 1973; 5 Japanese Images, choral, 1973; Hindemith in memoriam for clarinet and piano, 1974; Crisis for string orchestra and percussion, 1976–77; Vocazione, guitar solo, 1982; Prometheus for percussion, 1983; Tendenze for strings and piano, 1986; Kvinnosånger (female songs), published. *Recordings:* Various pieces. *Address:* Föreningen Svenska Tonsättare, Sandhamnsgatan 79, Box 27 327, 1002 54 Stockholm, Sweden.

JEPSON, Kristine; Singer (mezzo-soprano); b. 1965, USA. *Education:* Indiana University. *Career:* Season 1997–98 as Stephano in Roméo et Juliette at the Metropolitan, Hansel with the Canadian Opera Company and Schoolboy in Berg's Lulu at San Francisco; Other roles include Bartók's Judith (Vancouver Opera), Strauss's Composer for Santa Fe Opera, Rosina with New York City Opera, and Cherubino at the Met; Season 1999–2000 as Mozart's Annio in Dallas and Dorabella with Florida Grand Opera; Season 2000–2001 as Octavian and Cherubino at the Met, Sister Helen in the premiere of Jake Heggie's Dead Man Walking, at San Francisco, and Siebel in Faust at the Paris Opéra; Octavian at the Monnaie, Brussels, Mozart's Sesto for Netherlands Opera and Nicklausse in Paris; Concerts include Falla's El Amor Brujo at Alice Tully Hall and Bernstein's Jeremiah Symphony with the American SO. *Current Management:* Askonas Holt Ltd, Lonsdale Chambers, 27 Chancery Lane, London, WC2A 1PF, England. *Telephone:* (20) 7400-1700. *Fax:* (20) 7400-1799. *E-mail:* info@askonasholt.co.uk. *Website:* www.askonasholt.co.uk.

JERSILD, Jörgen; Composer; b. 1913, Copenhagen, Denmark. *Education:* Studied Composition and Music Theory with Poul Schierbeck and Piano with Alexander Stoffregen; Studied under Albert Roussel, Paris, France; Further studies in USA and Italy; MA, University of Copenhagen, 1940. *Career:* Danish Radio Music Department, 1939; Professor of Theory, Royal Academy of Music, Copenhagen, 1943–75. *Compositions:* Orchestral: Pastorale, 1946; Little Suite, 1950; The Birthday Concert, 1945; Harp Concerto, 1972; Ballet, Kings Theatre, 1954; Capricious Lucinda; Chamber Music; Music Making in the Forest, 1947; Fantasia e Canto Affetuoso, 1969; String Quartet, 1980; Für Gefühlvolle Spieler for Two Harps, 1982; Solo Instruments: Trois Pieces en Concert, for Piano, 1945; Pezzo Elegiaco, for Harp, 1968; Fantasia, for Harp, 1977; Fantasia, for Piano, 1987; 15 Piano Pieces for Julie, 1985; Jeu Polyrythmique for Piano, 1990; Lille Storstrom Suite for ensemble, 1995; Fantasia per Organo, 1985; Vocal Music: 3 Songs, 1944; 3 Danish Madrigals, 1958; 3 Danish Love Songs; 3 Romantiske Korsange, 1984; 3 Latin Madrigals, 1987; Il Cantico delle Creature, 1992; Music for Children: Quaretti Piccolo, 1950; Duo Concertante, 1956, 30 Polyrythmic Etudes, 1975. *Publications:* Laerebog i Rytmelaesning, 2nd edition, 1961; Laerbog i Melodilaesning, 2nd edition, 1963; Ear Training I–II, 1966; Elementary Rhythm Exercises; Advanced Rhythmic Studies, 1975; Romantic Harmony, 1970; Analytical Harmony I–II, 1989. *Honours:* several hon. appointments. *Address:* Söllerödvej 38, 2840 Holte, Denmark.

JERUSALEM, Siegfried; Singer (Tenor); b. 17 April 1940, Oberhausen, Germany. *Education:* Studied violin, piano and bassoon in Essen; Voice with Hertha Kalcher in Stuttgart. *Career:* Played bassoon in various orchestras and made debut as singer at Stuttgart in 1975; Appeared widely in Germany as Lohengrin; Bayreuth Festival from 1977, as Parsifal, Lohengrin, Walther, Siegmund and Siegfried (1988); Deutsche Oper Berlin, 1977–80, as Mozart's Tamino and Idomeneo, Weber's Max, Tchaikovsky's Lensky and Beethoven's Florestan; Metropolitan debut, 1980, as Lohengrin; Guest appearances in Munich, Milan, Hamburg, San Francisco and Geneva; In 1986 sang Parsifal at the London Coliseum and Erik in Der fliegende Holländer at Covent Garden; Sang Loge and Siegfried in The Ring at the Metropolitan, 1990 (also televised); Siegfried at the 1990 Bayreuth Festival; Season 1992 with Parsifal at the Met and Siegfried at Bayreuth; Sang Tristan in a new production at Bayreuth, 1993, returned 1996; Season 1998 as Tristan at Munich and the Götterdämmerung Siegfried with the Royal Opera at Birmingham; Featured Artist (People No. 182), Opera Magazine, Aug 1992, pp 904–909; Sang Tristan at Madrid, 2000; Season 2001 debut with Herod in Salome; Season 2002 sang the whole Ring of the Nibelung at Vienna State Opera (Loge, Siegmund, Siegfried); Aegisthus in Elektra at Covent Garden, 2003;Professor for vocal musik and the artistic. direktor of the new university of Music Nürnberg/Augsburg, 2001. *Recordings:* Martha, Les Contes d'Hoffmann, Violanta, Leonore, Die Zauberflöte, Die Walküre, Tannhäuser; Videos of Parsifal and Die Meistersinger from Bayreuth, The Ring from the Metropolitan, Der Ring des Nibelungen, conducted by Haitink. *Address:* c/o Theateragentur Dr G Hilbert, Maximilianstr 22, 80538 München, Germany.

JEURISSEN, Herman G. A.; Horn Player and Arranger; b. 27 Dec. 1952, Wijchen, Netherlands. *Education:* Soloist Diploma, Brabants Conservatorium, Tilburg, 1976. *Career:* co-first horn, Utrecht Symphony Orchestra, 1975–78; solo horn, The Hague Philharmonic Orchestra, 1978–; solo and concerto, radio and television appearances with orchestras in Netherlands, Austria, Germany, France and USA. *Recordings:* Mozart's Complete Horn Concertos; Complete Horn Music, by Leopold Mozart; Chamber Music, Franz and Richard Strauss; compositions for horn and organ; compositions for brass and carillon. *Publications:* Reconstruction and completion of Mozart's unfinished Horn Concertos K370b and K371, K 494A; compositions and arrangements for horns; Mozart and the Horn, 1978; Basic Principles of Horn Playing (three vols), 1997. *Contributions:* Mens en Melodie; Praeludium; Horn Call Brass Bulletin; Historic Brass Society Journal. *Honours:* Prix d'excellence, 1978; Silver Laurel of the Concertgebouw Friends, 1979. *Address:* Jacob Mosselstraat 58, 2595 RJ The Hague, Netherlands.

JEWELL, Ian; Violinist; b. 1950, England. *Education:* Studied at the Royal College of Music with Cecil Aronowitz and in Italy with Bruno Giuranna. *Career:* Solo performances of the Walton and Rubbra Concertos, Harold in Italy by Berlioz and the Mozart Concertante; Philharmonic at the Royal Academy of Music and Head of Strings, Purcell School; Co-founder, Gabrieli Quartet, 1967, and toured with them to Europe, North America, the Far East and Australia; Festival engagements in the United Kingdom, including the Aldeburgh, City of London and Cheltenham; Concerts every season in London in the Barbican's Mostly Mozart Festival; Resident Artist, University of Essex, from 1971; Co-premiered works by William Alwyn, Britten, Alan Bush, Daniel Jones and Gordon Crosse, 2 Quartets of Nicholas Maw and Panufnik, 1980, 1983, and the 3rd Quartet of John MacCabe, 1979; British premiere of the Piano Quintet by Sibelius, 1990. *Recordings include:* 50 CDs, including early pieces by Britten, Dohnányi's Piano Quintet with Wolfgang Manz, Walton's Quartets and the Sibelius Quartet and Quintet, with Anthony Goldstone.

JIRIKOVSKY, Petr; Pianist; b. 24 June 1971, Prague, Czechoslovakia. *Education:* Conservatory in Prague (Emil Leichner); Academy of Performing Arts in Prague (Ivan Klansky); Conservatoire De Paris (Solo Piano–Theodor Paraschivesco, Chamber Music–Itamar Golan); Hochschule für Musik in Vienna (Chamber Music–Michael Schnitzler); Masterclasses and private lessons–Eugen Indjic. *Career:* Concerts all round the Czech Republic, Europe, Japan; Prague-Rudolfinum, Munich-Gasteig, Paris, London, Warsaw, Kyoto Concert Hall; Prague Spring Festival, Orlando Festival, Ohrid Summer Festival Member, Academia Trio; More than 40 recordings for Czech Radio. *Recordings:* B Smetana, CD, Czech Dances, 1994; B Smetana, CD, My Country (Piano Four Hands), 1995; B Smetana, Polkas (complete), 1997; A Dvořák, CD, Piano Trios (Academia Trio), 1997; Dvořák, Brahms, CD, Gypsy Songs (with Bernarda Fink–Mezzo Soprano), 1997; B Martinů, CD, Concerto Grosso for 2 Pianos and Chamber Orchestra (with Josef Hala, Prague Chamber Orchestra), 1997; B Smetana, CD, Works for 2 and 4 pianos (Live recording from Prague Spring Festival with other young Czech pianists, 1998; Beethoven, CD, Geister Trio, Shostakovich Trio No. 2, Academia Trio, 1999. *Honours:* 1st Prize, Beethoven Piano Competition, Czech Republic, 1986; 1st Prize, Chopin Competition, 1987; 3rd Prize, Smetana Piano Competition, 1988; 1st Prize, North London Festival, 1992; 1st Prize, Heerlen (Netherlands), with Academia Trio, 1995. *Address:* Grafická 44, 15000 Prague 5, Czech Republic.

JO, Sumi; Singer (soprano); b. 22 Nov. 1962, Seoul, Republic of Korea. *Education:* Studied in Seoul and at the Accademia di Santa Cecilia, Rome, 1983–86. *Career:* Debut: Teatro Verdi, Trieste, 1986, as Gilda; Sang at Lyon, Nice and Marseille, 1987–88; Appeared in Jomelli's Fetonte at La Scala, 1988; Discovered by Karajan and sang Barbarina at the 1988 Salzburg Festival; Oscar in Un Ballo in Maschera, 1989–90, conducted by Solti; Guest appearances at Munich from 1988, Vienna from 1989, and Paris; La Scala Milan in Ravel's L'Enfant et les Sortilèges, conducted by Lorin Maazel, and as Zerlina in Auber's Fra Diavolo, 1992; Metropolitan Opera as Gilda, 1988 and 1990; Royal Opera, Covent Garden, as Olympia in Tales of Hoffmann and as Elvira in I Puritani in 1991 and 1991; Chicago Lyric Opera as Queen of Night in 1990 and as Queen of Night with Danish Philharmonic conducted by Zubin Mehta in 1991; Season 1992 as Matilde in Rossini's Elisabetta at Naples, Olympia at Covent Garden (followed by Adina); Sang Zerbinetta at Lisbon, 1996; Season 1997–98 with L'Enfant et les Sortilèges at Boston, Zerbinetta at Lisbon and Turin, and in Mozart's Lucio Silla at Mozart Festival, New York. *Recordings:* Arias; Adèle in Le Comte Ory;

Un Ballo in Maschera; Queen of Night in Die Zauberflöte, conducted by Armin Jordan and by Solti; Fiorilla in Rossini's Il Turco in Italia, conducted by Neville Marriner; Soprano soloist in Mahler Symphony No. 8, conducted by Sinopoli; Soprano soloist in Rossini's Messa di Gloria, conducted by Neville Marriner; Angèle d'Olivarès in Auber's Le Domino Noir, conducted by Richard Bonynge. *Current Management:* Columbia Artists Management, 165 West 57th Street, New York, NY 10019, USA.

JOACHIM, Otto; Composer, Violist, Violinist and Gambist; b. 13 Oct. 1919, Düsseldorf, Germany; Separated, 1 s. *Education:* Concordia School, Düsseldorf; Buths-Neitzel Conservatory, Düsseldorf; Rheinische Musikschule, Cologne. *Career:* CBC Soloist, Montreal String Quartet, L'Ensemble des Instruments Anciens de Montreal, Canada; 1st Violist, Montreal Symphony. *Compositions include:* Nonet, 1960; Psalm for Choir, 1960; Concertante No. 2 for string quartet and string orchestra, 1961; Fantasia for organ, 1961; 12 Twelve-tone Pieces for Children, 1961; Contrastes for orchestra, 1967; Kinderspiel for violin, cello, piano and speaker, 1969; 5,9 for 4-channel tape, 1971; Night Music for alto flute and guitar, 1978; 4 Intermezzi for flute and guitar, 1978; Requiem for violin or viola or cello, 1969; Paean for violoncello solo, 1989; Stacheldraht, melodrame, 1993; Metamorphoses for orchestra, 1995; String Quartet, 1997. *Address:* 7910 Wavell Road, Côte St-Luc, Montreal, Quebec Province H4W 1L7, Canada.

JOBIN, André; Singer (Tenor); b. 20 Jan. 1933, Quebec, Canada. *Education:* Studied as an actor in Paris and worked with Jean-Louis Barrault. *Career:* Sang at first as a baritone in Parisian musicals; Operatic roles as tenor from 1962, notably Pélleas at Marseilles, Nice, Paris, Madrid and San Francisco, 1965; Glyndebourne Festival, 1976, New York City Opera from 1970; Other roles have been Romeo, Don José, Massenet's Des Grieux, Rodrigo and John the Baptist, Julien (Louise) and Hoffmann; Many appearances at Quebec, Lyon, Brussels, Berlin and Madrid; Liège Opera, 1982–87, as Rodrigo in Le Cid, John the Baptist (Hérodiade) and Des Grieux; Cologne Opera, 1987, as Werther; Engaged in musical and operettas in Chicago, London and Detroit; Sang in Bernstein's Candide at Turin 1997. *Recordings:* Several albums.

JOCHUM, Veronica; Pianist; b. 6 Dec. 1932, Berlin, Germany; m. Wilhelm Viggo von Moltke, 15 Nov 1961. *Education:* MA, 1955, Concert Diploma, 1957, Staatliche Musikhochschule, Munich, Germany; Private study with Edwin Fischer, Josef Benvenuti, 1958–59 and Rudolf Serkin, 1959–61. *Career:* Debut: Germany, 1954; Numerous appearances as soloist with orchestras in Europe North and South America, 1961–; Appeared with Boston Symphony, London Symphony Orchestra, London Philharmonic Orchestra, Berlin, Hamburg and Munich Philharmonics, Vienna Symphony and Concertgebouw Orchestra among others; Radio and television appearances; Recitals in over 50 countries in Europe, North and South America, Africa and Asia; Featured in a German film, Self-Attempt, on a novel by Christa Wolf. *Recordings:* Various labels. *Honours:* Cross of Order of Merit by German President (Bundesverdienstkreuz), 1994; Bunting Fellowship, Harvard-Radliff, 1996. *Address:* New England Conservatory of Music, 290 Huntington Avenue, Boston, MA 02115, USA.

JOEL, Emmanuel; Conductor; b. 1958, Paris, France. *Education:* Studied with at the Paris Conservatoire. *Career:* Early engagements with Opéra de Lyon and at the Aix-en-Provence Festival; Paris Opéra debut with Offenbach's Les Brigands, 1993; Semele and Les Pêcheurs de Perles in Melbourne and regular appearances with the Opéra de Nantes; Boildieu's La Dame Blanche at the Wexford Festival and Don Quichotte for English National Opera, 1996; La Belle Hélène for Scottish Opera, Carmen and Werther in Israel; Season 1996–97 with Chausson's Le Roi Arthus in Montpellier, Samson et Dalila in Sydney and Israel, Butterfly in Rouen, La Bohème for ENO and Eugene Onegin in Toulouse. *Address:* c/o Allied Artists, 42 Montpelier Square, London SW7 1JZ, England.

JOËL, Nicolas; Stage Director; b. 1945, Paris. *Career:* Opéra du Rhin, Strasbourg, from 1973, with Der Ring des Nibelungen, 1979; Stagings of Samson et Dalila at Chicago and San Francisco, Aida in Vienna, Lohengrin at Copenhagen and Eugene Onegin in Amsterdam; Rigoletto and La Traviata for Zürich Opera, Parsifal in San Francisco and Roméo et Juliette at Covent Garden, London; Artistic Director of Théâtre du Capitole, Toulouse from 1990: Falstaff, Elektra, Die Walküre and Il Trovatore; Further engagements for La Scala, Milan (Manon and La Rondine), New York Metropolitan (Andrea Chénier and Lucia di Lammermoor); Other stagings include Boris Godunov, Cav and Pag double bill and Salome (at Essen). *Address:* c/o Théâtre du Capitole, Place du Capitole, 31000 Toulouse, France.

JOERES, Dirk; Conductor and Pianist; b. 13 Aug. 1947, Bonn, Germany. *Education:* studied piano, conducting and composition, Berlin, Cologne, London and Paris. *Career:* Engagements with renowned orchestras; Repeat appearances at festivals in Berlin, London, Prague, Klavierfestival Ruhr and Schleswig-Holstein; Artistic Director, Westdeutsche Sinfonia, 1987; Recordings and television productions; World-wide orchestral tours; Guest conductor, London Royal Philharmonic. *Recordings:* Solo recording, Brahms and his Friends; Two Brahms Serenades, with Westdeutsche Sinfonia; Associate Conductor, Royal Philharmonic Orchestra. *Honours:* First prize, International piano competition, Vercello, 1972; Critic's Choice, two Brahms Serenades, Gramaphone Magazine, London; 100 Top CDs, BBC Music Magazine. *Address:* Humboldtstr 17, 51379 Leverkusen, Germany.

JOHANNESEN, Grant; Concert Pianist; b. 30 July 1921, Salt Lake City, Utah, USA; m. Zara Nelsova, 1963–73. *Education:* Studied with Robert Casadesus at Princeton University and with Egon Petri at Cornell University. *Career:* Debut: Times Hall, New York, 1944; First international tour, 1949; Tour of Europe with New York Philharmonic and Mitropoulos, 1956–57; Tour of USSR and Europe with Cleveland Orchestra and George Szell, 1968; Solo tours of the USSR, 1962, 1970; Appearances at all major music festivals; Aspen Festival for 6 seasons; On faculty of Aspen Music School, 1960–66; Music Director of the Cleveland Institute of Music, 1974–84. *Recordings:* Fauré's complete piano music; Works by Dukas, Roussel and De Séverac; Sonatas for cello and piano with Zara Nelsova.

JOHANNSEN, Kay; Organist and Church Musician; b. 1 Oct. 1961, Giengen, Germany; m. Andrea Ermer, 29 April 1987, one s., one d. *Education:* Studies at Freiburg in organ and conducting; Organ studies at NEC, Boston, with William Porter. *Career:* Concerts in major German cities and in foreign countries, broadcast concerts with almost all German stations, several concerts with orchestras such as the Nurnberg Symphonic, Radio Symphony Orchestra Prague, Radio Symphony Orchestra Hannover, Staatsphilharmonic Rheinland-Pfalz, Philharmonic Orchestra Gelsenkirchen, Berlin Philharmonic Orchestra and Stuttgart Philharmonic Orchestra; Guest Teacher, Freiburg Conservatory, 1992–93; Teacher, Karlsruhe Conservatory, 1994–2000; Organist of the Siftskirche Stuttgart, 1994–; Masterclasses in Frankfurt, Sofia, Kiev and Seoul. *Recordings:* CDs: Bach, Reger, Fortig, 1990; Christian Hommel, Bach, Mozart, Huber, ars musici; 1993; French organ music from the 19th century, 1993; Brahms, Complete Organ Works, 1996; Bach, Trio Sonatas, 1997; Bach Masterworks of Weimar, 1998; Bach III. Part of Clavierübung, 1999; Bach, the Young Bach–a Virtuoso, 1999; Bach, Neumeister–Chorales, 1999; Bach, Sonatas for violin and harpsichord, 2003. *Honours:* Various prizes in music competitions; German National Foundation Scholarship. *Address:* c/o Evang Bezirkskantorat, Altes Schloss, Schillerplatz 6, 70173 Stuttgart, Germany.

JOHANNSSON, Kristjan; Singer (Tenor); b. 1950, Akureyi Du, Iceland. *Education:* Studied at Nicolini Conservatory, Piacenza and with Campogalliani and Tagliavini. *Career:* Debut: National Theatre of Iceland, Reykjavík, as Rodolfo in 1961; Sang Pinkerton in a production of Madama Butterfly, by Ken Russell, at Spoleto, 1983; Engagements as guest artist at the Chicago Lyric Opera in Faust, 1991, Metropolitan New York, Vienna, Staatsoper and La Scala Milan; Roles have included Radames, Alvaro in La Forza del Destino, Cavaradossi and Dick Johnson; Sang Turiddu in Cavalleria Rusticana at Naples and Florence, season 1990–91; Calaf at the Verona Arena, 1991; Sang Manrico in the opening production at the New Teatro, Carol Felice, Genoa, 1991; Andrea Chénier at Florence, Calaf at Chicago, Cavaradossi at Rome and Manrico at Turin, 1992; Calaf at Torre del Lago, 1996; Dick Johnson at Zürich, 1998; Season 2000 as Otello at Budapest and Enzo in La Gioconda at the Deutsche Oper Berlin.

JOHANOS, Donald; Conductor; b. 10 Feb. 1928, Cedar Rapids, Iowa, USA; m. (1) Thelma Trimble, 27 Aug 1950, 2 s., 3 d., (2) Corinne Rutledge, 28 Sept 1985. *Career:* BMus, 1950, MMus, 1952; Eastman School of Music, Rochester, New York; Advanced conducting studies with Eugene Ormandy, George Szell, Thomas Beecham, Eduard van Beinum, Herbert von Karajan, Otto Klemperer, 1955–58.; Teacher, Pennsylvania State University, 1953–55; Music Director, Altoona (Pennsylvania) Symphony Orchestra, 1953–56; Johnstown (Pennsylvania) Symphony Orchestra, 1955–56; Associate Conductor, 1957–61, Resident Conductor, 1961–62, Music Director, 1962–70, Dallas Symphony Orchestra; Teacher, Southern Methodist University, 1958–62; Hockady School, 1962–65; Associate Conductor and Director, Pittsburgh Symphony Orchestra, 1970–80; Music Director, Honolulu Symphony Orchestra, 1979–; Artistic Director, Hawaii Opera Theater, 1979–83; Guest conducting engagements with various orchestras at home and abroad. *Recordings:* For various labels. *Address:* c/o Honolulu Symphony Orchestra, 1441 Kapiolani Boulevard, Suite 1515, Honolulu, HI 96814, USA.

JOHANSSON, Eva; Singer (Soprano); b. 25 Feb. 1958, Copenhagen, Denmark. *Education:* Studied at the Copenhagen Conservatory, 1977–81; Opera School of the Royal Opera, Copenhagen, 1981–84; New York, with Oren Brown. *Career:* Sang at the Royal Opera, Copenhagen, 1982–88, as the Countess in Figaro (debut), Tatiana,

Pamina, Marie in Wozzeck and Chrysothemis (Elektra); Guest appearances in Oslo as Marie and Donna Anna (1985, 1987); Marie at the Paris Opéra, 1986; Sang in productions of Der Ring des Nibelungen at Berlin and Bayreuth, 1988, as Gutrune and as Freia and Gerhilde; Sang Freia in a concert performance of Das Rheingold at Paris, 1988, conducted by Daniel Baremboim; Vienna Staatsoper, 1989, as Fiordiligi; Tel-Aviv, 1990, as Donna Anna in Don Giovanni, conducted by Claudio Abbado; Since 1990: Elsa in Lohengrin at Bayreuth; Guest appearances in Barcelona, Munich, Dresden, Japan, Paris, Seville, Nice, Madrid, Stuttgart, Cologne and Hamburg; Debut as Donna Anna, at Covent Garden, 1992; Sang Elsa at the Accademia di Santa Cecilia, Rome, 1996; Chrysothemis in Elektra at Århus, 1998; Season 2000–01 at the Deutsche Oper Berlin as Sieglinde, Elsa, Tatiana, Eva, Liu, Senta, and Elisabeth in Tannhäuser. *Recordings:* Das Rheingold conducted by Bernard Haitink; Es War Einmal, by Zemlinsky. *Address:* Bühnenagentur Marianne Bottger, Dahlmannstrasse 9, 1000 Berlin 12, Germany.

JOHNS, William; Singer (Tenor); b. 2 Oct. 1936, Tulsa, Oklahoma, USA. *Education:* Studied in New York. *Career:* Debut: Lake George, 1967, as Rodolfo in La Bohème; Sang with the Bremen Opera as the Prince in The Love of Three Oranges and the Duke of Mantua; Welsh National Opera, 1970–72, as Radames and Calaf; Further appearances in Cologne, Düsseldorf, Dallas, Hamburg, Bregenz, Houston, Vienna, Aix-en-Provence, Rome and New York (Metropolitan Opera); Covent Garden debut, 1987, as Bacchus in Ariadne auf Naxos; Philadelphia Opera, 1988, as Florestan in Fidelio; Holland Festival, 1989, as Siegfried in a concert performance of Götterdämmerung; Other roles include Wagner's Lohengrin, Tannhäuser, Siegmund and Tristan, Huon (Oberon), the Emperor in Die Frau ohne Schatten, Jason in Medea in Corinto by Mayr, Hoffmann and Verdi's Otello; Sang Tristan at San Francisco, 1991. *Address:* c/o San Francisco Opera, War Memorial Opera House, San Francisco, CA 94102, USA.

JOHNSON, Camellia; Singer (Soprano); b. 1960, Delaware, USA. *Education:* Studied at Daytona Beach, Florida, and the Manhattan School of Music, New York. *Career:* Debut: Strawberry Woman, in Porgy and Bess at the Metropolitan, 1985; Sang in Porgy and Bess at Glyndebourne, 1986, and Helsinki, 1989, 1992; Season 1992–93, in Don Carlos at San Francisco and as Aida at Michigan; Beethoven's Ninth in Indianapolis and Montreal; Verdi's Requiem with the Saint Louis Symphony and the Long Island Philharmonic; Metropolitan Opera as Serena in Porgy and Bess, High Priestess in Aida and Madelon in Andrea Chénier; Mozart's Solemn Vespers and Requiem with the Cincinnati Symphony; Other repertoire includes the Four Last Songs of Strauss, Les Nuits d'Eté, Schubert's Rosamunde, Rossini's Stabat Mater and Beethoven's Missa Solemnis. *Recordings:* Porgy and Bess. *Address:* c/o Metropolitan Opera, Lincoln Center, New York, NY 10023, USA.

JOHNSON, David Cale; Singer (Bass); b. 1950, Texas, USA. *Education:* New York; San Francisco, El Paso. *Career:* Opera engagements in Paris, Athens, Vienna, Geneva, Leipzig, São Paulo, Bogotá, Rio de Janeiro, Caracas, San Francisco also cover at the Metropolitan Opera; Concert soloist, New York Philharmonic, Honolulu, New Jersey, São Paulo Symphonies; Flensburg Opera, 1986–87; Hannover, 1987–91, notably König Heinrich in Lohengrin, Zaccaria in Nabucco, Colline in La Bohème and Don Pasquale; Mozart's Osmin and Sarastro at Lucerne in 1991, Bartered Bride (Kezal) in Basel and roles at the Vienna State and Volks Operas from 1991, including Fidelio (Rocco), Jerusalem (Roger), Prophète (Mathison), Zauberflöte (Sarastro), Aida (Il Re), Nabucco (Zaccaria). *Address:* c/o Vienna Staatsoper, Opernring 2, 1010 Vienna, Austria.

JOHNSON, David (Carl); Composer and Flautist; b. 30 Jan. 1940, Batavia, New York, USA. *Education:* Studied composition with Donald Keats and David Epstein at Antioch College; Leon Kirchner at Harvard University and Nadia Boulanger in Paris, 1964–65; Further study in Cologne. *Career:* Teacher at the Rheinische Musikschule Cologne, 1966–67; Worked with Stockhausen in the creation of Hymnen at the studios of West German Radio; Member of the Stockhausen ensemble at the Osaka World Fair, 1970; Co-founded Feedback Studio at Cologne, 1970; Director of the electronic music studio at the Basle Music Academy, 1975. *Compositions:* Five movements for flute, 1962; Bells for flute, guitar and cello, 1964; Thesis for string quartet, 1964; 3 Pieces for string quartet, 1964; 3 Pieces for string quartet, 1966; Tonantiton for tape, 1968; Process of Music for tape and instruments, 1970; Sound-environment pieces Music Makers, Gyromes mit und für Elise, Cybernet, Gehlhaar, Organica I'IV and Klangkoffer, 1969–74; Proganica for speaker and 2 electric organs, 1973; Audioliven for flute and electronics, 1976; In Memoriam Uschi for tape and 3 instruments, 1977; Jadermann incidental music to play by Hoffmansthal, 1980; Bach: Encounter of the Third Kind, stage piece, 1981; Calls in Search, for tape, 1981. *Address:* c/o ASCAP, ASCAP Building, 1 Lincoln Plaza, New York, NY 10023, USA.

JOHNSON, David (Charles); Composer, Musical Historian, Writer and Music Publisher; b. 27 Oct. 1942, Edinburgh, Scotland; 1 s. *Education:* MA, Aberdeen; BA, PhD, Cambridge. *Career:* Organised recitals for Edinburgh Festival, 1975, 1985, 1986, 1988; Cellist, McGibbon Ensemble, 1980–96; Tutor, Musical History, Edinburgh University, 1988–94; Founded self-publishing company,David Johnson Music Edns, 1990; mem, PRS; MCPS. *Compositions:* 5 Operas; Church Music; Piobaireached for Solo Recorder; God, Man and The Animals (recorded by Alison Wells, soprano, and instrumental ensemble, 2001, Metier, England); Piano Trio; Sonata for Cello and Piano; Trio for Recorders (published by Forsyth); Seven MacDiarmid Songs for Soprano, Trumpet, Piano; 12 Preludes and Fugues for Piano (recorded by Ian Hobson, 1998, Zephyr, USA); 3 Suites for solo cello; Other songs, chamber and orchestral music. *Publications:* Music and Society in Lowland Scotland, 1972, 2nd Edn, 2003; Editor, Ten Georgian Glees for Four Voices, 1981; Scottish Fiddle Music in the 18th Century, 1984, 2nd Edn, 1997; The Scots Cello Book, 1990; Stepping Northward, 1990; Scots on the Fiddle, 1991; Chamber Music of 18th Century Scotland, 2000; The Art of Robert Burns (CD), recorded by The Musicians of Edinburgh, 2003. *Contributions:* The New Grove Dictionary of Music and Musicians, 1981, 2001; Writes regularly for Early Music Today. *Address:* 8 Shandon Crescent, Edinburgh EH11 1QE, Scotland.

JOHNSON, Douglas; Singer (Tenor); b. 1958, CA, USA. *Education:* Studied at the University of Los Angeles. *Career:* Appearances in Les Dialogues des Carmelites, La Fille du Régiment and La Clemenza di Tito while a student; Sang at Aachen, 1984–87, notably as Don Ottavio, Handel's Serse, Jacquino, Count Almaviva, Rinuccio in Gianni Schicchi, Belmonte and the Steuermann; Hanover, 1988–89, Frankfurt am Mainz, from 1989 notably as Tamino, 1991; Salzburg Festival, 1987, 1991 in Moses und Aron and as Arbace in Idomeneo; Guest appearances at Hamburg, Chateauneuf in Zar und Zimmermann, Deutsche Oper Berlin, Nicolai's Fenton, Vienna Staatsoper, Tamino, Cologne, Nemorino, 1987 and Ludwigshafen, Gualterio in Vivaldi's Griselda, 1989; Sang Rossini's Almaviva at Seattle, 1992. *Recordings include:* L'Oca del Cairo by Mozart.

JOHNSON, Emma, MBE; Clarinettist and Conductor; b. 20 May 1966, Barnet, Hertfordshire, England. *Education:* Pembroke College, Cambridge University; Studied with John Brightwell, Sidney Fell. *Career:* Debut: Barbican, London, 1985; Appearances with ECO, London Symphony Orchestra, Ulster Orchestra, Royal Liverpool Philharmonic Orchestra, Hallé Orchestra, City of London Sinfonia and Royal Philharmonic Orchestra; Debut in Vienna at the Musikverein, 1985; French Debut, with Polish Chamber Orchestra, 1986; Performances in Netherlands, Finland and Monte Carlo; Television and radio appearances in United Kingdom; Japanese debut, Tokyo, 1990; New York debut, 1992; Schumann Weekend concerts at Blackheath, 1997; Visiting Professor, Royal College of Music, 1997–; Conducting debut with London Mozart Players, 2001. *Recordings:* Mozart Clarinet Concerto, 1984; Crusell Clarinet Concerto No. 2, 1985; Bottesini Duo for Clarinet and Double Bass with Tom Martin, 1986; Weber Clarinet Concerto No. 1, 1987; Recital Disc La Clarinette Française with Gordon Back, 1988; The Romantic Clarinet (concertos by Weber, Spohr and Crusell); Finzi and Stanford Concertos with Royal Philharmonic Orchestra, 1992; Recital of Encores, 1992; Michael Berkeley Concerto, 1993; British Recital Disc, 1994; Encores II, 1994; Malcolm Arnold, Complete Clarinet Works, 1995; Mozart and Weber Clarinet Quintets, 2000. *Honours:* BBC TV Young Musician of the Year, 1984; Bronze Award European Young Musician of the Year Competition, Geneva, 1984; Voted Young Professional All Music Musician, Wavendon All Music Awards, 1986; Honorary Fellow Pembroke College, Cambridge, 1999. *Current Management:* Hazard Chase, Norman House, Cambridge Place, Cambridge CB2 1NS, England. *Telephone:* (1223) 312400. *Fax:* (1223) 460827. *Website:* www.hazardchase.co.uk. *Address:* Christa Phelps, 6 Malvern Road, London, E8 3LT, England. *Website:* www.emmajohnson.co.uk.

JOHNSON, Graham (Rhodes); Pianist and Concert Accompanist; b. 10 July 1950, Rhodesia. *Education:* Royal Academy of Music, London; FRAM, 1984; FGSM, Guildhall School, 1988. *Career:* Debut: Wigmore Hall, 1972; Accompanist to Brigitte Fassbaender, Elisabeth Schwarzkopf, Jessye Norman, Victoria de los Angeles (US tour, 1977), Janet Baker, Peter Pears, Felicity Lott, Margaret Price (US tour, 1985), Peter Schreier, John Shirley Quirk, Tom Krause, Christine Schäfer, Ian Bostridge, Matthias Goerne; Work with contemporaries led to formation of The Songmakers' Almanac (Artistic Director); Has devised and accompanied more than 150 London recitals for this group since Oct 1976; Tours of USA with Sarah Walker, Richard Jackson and of Australia and New Zealand with The Songmakers' Almanac, 1981; Writer and Presenter, major BBC Radio 3 series on Poulenc songs, and BBC television series on Schubert songs; Lecturer, song courses, Savonlinna (Finland), USA and at Pears-Britten School, Snape; Artistic Adviser and Accompanist, Alte Oper Festival, Frankfurt, 1981–82; Appearances at Salzburg, Hohenems and Munich Festivals. *Recordings:*

Recitals for several labels, including recitals with Felicity Lott and Ann Murray; Complete cycle of Schubert Lieder; Has recorded with Elly Ameling, Peter Schreier, Arleen Auger, Thomas Hampson, Margaret Price and Lucia Popp; Complete cycle of Schumann Lieder and Major French Song Series. *Publications:* The Spanish Song Companion, 1992; A French Song Companion, 2000. *Contributions:* The Britten Companion (editor Christopher Palmer), 1984; Gerald Moore, The Unashamed Accompanist, revised edition, 1984; Reviews to the Times Literary supplement. *Honours:* O.B.E., 1994; Gramophone Awards, 1989, 1997, 1998; Royal Philharmonic Society Award: Instrumentalist of the Year, 1999. *Current Management:* Askonas Holt Ltd, Lonsdale Chambers, 27 Chancery Lane, London, WC2A 1PF, England. *Telephone:* (20) 7400-1700. *Fax:* (20) 7400-1799. *E-mail:* info@askonasholt.co.uk. *Website:* www.askonasholt.co.uk. *Address:* 83 Fordwych Road, London, NW2 3TL, England.

JOHNSON, Marc; Cellist; b. 1945, USA. *Education:* Studied at the Eastman School of Music and Indiana University. *Career:* Played with the Rochester Philharmonic while a student; Solo appearances in Rochester and with the Denver Philharmonic; Recital and chamber concerts in Washington DC, St Louis and Baltimore; Founder member of the Vermeer Quartet at the Marlboro Festival, 1970; Performances in all major US centres, Europe, Israel and Australia; Festival engagements at Tanglewood, Aspen, Spoleto, Edinburgh, Mostly Mozart (New York), Aldeburgh, South Bank, Santa Fe, Chamber Music West, and the Casals Festival; Resident quartet for Chamber Music Chicago; Annual master classes at the Royal Northern College of Music, Manchester; Member of the Resident Artists' Faculty of Northern Illinois University. *Recordings:* Quartets by Beethoven, Dvořák, Verdi and Schubert; Brahms Clarinet Quintet with Karl Leister. *Honours:* Denver Symphony and Washington International Competitions; Received title of Kämmersängen during the 1960s. *Address:* Allied Artists, 42 Montpelier Square, London SW7 1JZ, England.

JOHNSON, Mary Jane; Singer (Soprano); b. 22 March 1950, Pampa, Texas, USA. *Education:* Studied at West Texas University, and elsewhere in USA. *Career:* Debut: New York Lyric Opera as Agathe in Der Freischütz, 1981; Philadelphia and Santa Fe, 1982, as Musetta and Rosalinde; Sang at the San Francisco Opera from 1983, as Freia in Das Rheingold, Jenifer in the US premiere of The Midsummer Marriage, 1983, Marguerite, and the Empress in Die Frau ohne Schatten, Washington Opera from 1984, Boston and Cincinnati from 1986; European engagements with Opera North at Leeds, Torre del Lago (Puccini Festival), Bologna, Geneva and the Baths of Caraccala at Rome (Minnie in La Fanciulla del West); Sang Salome at Santiago, 1990, Desdemona at Pittsburgh and Minnie at the 1991 Santa Fe Festival; Helen of Troy in Mefistofele at Chicago, 1991; La Scala and Opéra Bastille, Paris, 1992, in the title role of Lady Macbeth of Mtsensk; Teatro Municipal Santiago as Senta in Der fliegende Holländer, 1992; Other roles include Mozart's Countess, Leonore, Alice in Falstaff, Tosca, Giulietta, the Duchess of Parma in Busoni's Faust, and Mrs Jessel in The Turn of the Screw; Sang Janáček's Emilia Marty at Vancouver, 1996, and Salome there in 1998; Sang Elektra at Santa Fe, 2000. *Address:* c/o Santa Fe Opera, PO Box 2408, Santa Fe, NM 87504, USA.

JOHNSON, Nancy; Singer (Soprano); b. 1954, California, USA. *Education:* Studied at California State University, Hayward. *Career:* Sang at the Landestheater Detmold, 1980–81, Wiesbaden, 1981–82, Mannheim, 1982–87; Engaged at the Stuttgart Staatsoper from 1987 and has made guest appearances at Düsseldorf, the Vienna Staatsoper, San Francisco (Eva in Die Meistersinger, 1988); Other roles have included Manon Lescaut, and the Empress in Die Frau ohne Schatten (Mannheim, 1984). *Address:* c/o Stuttgart Staatsoper, Oberer Schlossgarten 6, 7000 Stuttgart, Germany.

JOHNSON, Robert; Singer (Tenor); b. 10 Dec. 1940, Moline, Illinois, USA. *Education:* Studied at Northwestern University in Evanston and at New York. *Career:* Debut: New York City Opera, 1971, as Count Almaviva; Sang in New York, Chicago, Baltimore, Houston, New Orleans and Washington as Mozart's Ferrando, Belmonte and Tamino; Ernesto, Beppo in Donizetti's Rita, Alfredo, Fenton in Falstaff, Hoffmann, Rodolfo, Sali in A Village Romeo and Juliet, and Tom Rakewell; Frequent concert appearances. *Address:* c/o New York City Opera, Lincoln Center, New York, NY 10023, USA.

JOHNSON, Russell; American theatre designer and acoustician; *Chairman, Artec Consultants Inc.;* b. 1923, Briar Creek, PA. *Education:* Carnegie-Mellon Univ., Yale Univ. School of Architecture. *Career:* began career in research and consulting on the design, theatre planning, and acoustics of buildings for the performing arts 1946–; first professional projects under leadership of Prof. E. C. Cole 1946–50; Assoc. Bolt, Beranek and Newman (BBN), Cambridge, MA 1954–70; Founder and Prin. Consultant Theatre Planning and Consulting Div.; Founder Russell Johnson Assocs (renamed Artec Consultants) 1970, Chair. and Prin. Consultant, Artec Consultants Inc. 1970–; Fellow

Acoustical Soc. of America, US Inst. for Theatre Tech. (USITT). *Designs include:* Culture and Congress Centre (Lucerne, Switzerland), Morton H. Meyerson Symphony Centre (Dallas), Sibelius Concert Hall (Lahti, Finland), Symphony Hall (Birmingham, UK), NJ Performing Arts Centre (Newark), Kravis Centre for the Performing Arts (W Palm Beach, FL), Derngate Centre (Northampton, UK), Kimmel Centre for the Performing Arts (Philadelphia), Pikes Peak Centre (Colorado Springs), Calgary Centre for the Performing Arts (Alberta), George Weston Recital Hall (Toronto, Ont.), Morsani Hall (Tampa Bay, FL), Performing Arts Centre (Tampa, FL), Royal Concert Hall (Nottingham, UK), Armenian Theatre, Centre-in-the-Square (Kitchener, Ont.), Crouse-Hinds Concert Theatre (Syracuse, NY), Hamilton Place (Ont.), Prudential Hall Opera House (Newark, NJ), Chan Shun Concert Hall (Vancouver BC), Toronto Centre for the Arts (Ont.), Concert Hall (Budapest, Hungary), Rose Hall for Jazz at Lincoln Centre (NY), Concert Hall and Opera House (Miami FL), Concert Hall and Opera House (Singapore), Concert Hall (Orange County, CA). *Honours:* USITT Award 1996, Wallace Clement Sabine Medal, Acoustical Soc. of America (ASA) 1997, Int. Citation of Merit, Int. Soc. of Performing Arts (ISPA) 1998. *Address:* Artec Consultants Inc., 114 West 26th Street, New York, NY 10001, USA (office). *Telephone:* (212) 242-0120 (office). *Fax:* (212) 645-8635 (office).

JOHNSON, Tom; Composer; b. 18 Nov. 1939, Greeley, Colorado, USA. *Education:* BA, 1961, MMus, 1967, Yale University; Private study with Morton Feldman. *Career:* Music Critic, Village Voice, New York, 1971–82; Freelance Composer, 1982–. *Compositions include:* Spaces, 1969; An Hour for Piano, 1971; The Four Note Opera, 1972; Septapede, 1973; Verses for alto flute, horn and harp, 1974; The Masque of Clouds, opera, 1975; Verses for viola, 1976; Trinity for SATB, 1978; Dragons in A, 1979; Movements for wind quintet, 1980; Harpiano, 1982; Predictables, 1984; Voicings for 4 pianos, 1984; Tango, 1984; Choral Catalogue, 1985; Pascal's Triangle, 1987; Riemannoper, 1988; Una Opera Italiana, 1991; Trigonometry, for 4 baritones and 4 percussion, 1995; Formulas, for string quartet, 1995. *Publications:* Imaginary Music, 1974; Private Pieces, 1976; Symmetries, 1981; Rational Melodies, 1982. *Address:* c/o ASCAP, ASCAP Building, 1 Lincoln Plaza, New York, NY 10023, USA.

JOHNSSON, Bengt (Gustaf); Professor, Pianist and Organist; b. 17 July 1921, Copenhagen, Denmark; m. Esther Paustian, 1 d. *Education:* MA, Musicology, University of Copenhagen, 1947; Studies with Georg Vasarhelyl and Walter Gieseking; Degree as Organist and Church Musician, Royal Academy of Music, Copenhagen, 1945. *Career:* Debut: Copenhagen, 1944; Concert tours, broadcasts, Scandinavia, German Federal Republic, Switzerland, France, Netherlands; Recitals in many European countries; US tour, 1964; Organist, Danish Broadcasting, 1949–70; Teacher, Royal Academy, Copenhagen, 1958–61; Professor, Royal Academy of Music, Århus, Jutland; Numerous master classes; Studied at Vatican Library, Rome, 1977, Benedictine Monastery, Montserrat, Spain, 1978, 1980–83; Spanish Cultural Department invitation to study in libraries in Barcelona and Montserrat, 1979, 1983. *Recordings include:* N W Gade Piano Music; Rissager, Complete Piano Works; Chamber Music of Beethoven, Brahms, Busoni; Roman Organ and Harpsichord Music from the 17th Century, 1982; Rued Langgaard: Piano Music, 1985; Catalan Organ Music, 1988. *Publications include:* History of the Danish School of Music until 1739, 1973; Roman Organ Music for the 17th Century; Roman Harpsichord Music from the 17th Century; Piano Music of Manuel Blasco de Nebra, 1984; 23 Piano Sonatas for Josep Galles, 1984; Editor: Heptachordum Danicum 1646 (translation, historical comments, source studies), 1977; Hans Mikkelsen Ravn: The Vatican Manuscript, 1981; Selected Sonatas of D Scarlatti including 1st edition of 4 new editions, 1985; Selected Piano Music of N W Gade, 1986; Catalan Organ Music of the 18th Century, 1986; Scarlatti Vol. II, 1988, vol. III, 1992; Niels W Gade: Klavierwerke, 1989; Piano Music for Franz Liszt, 1989; Selected Piano Works of Rued Langgaard, 1994. *Honours:* Bronze Medal Winner, Piano Music of Manuel Blasco de Nebra, International Book Messe, Leipzig, 1986. *Address:* Porsevænget 18, Kongens Lyngby, 2800 Copenhagen, Denmark.

JOHNSSON, Catrin; Singer (Mezzo-soprano); b. 1973, Sweden. *Education:* Royal University College of Music, Stockholm; Royal Academy of Music with Anne Howells. *Career:* Appearances for Diva Opera in Die Zauberflöte, La Traviata and The Tales of Hoffmann, as Nicklausse (2001); Idelberto in Handel's Lotario, Adalberto in Ottone, Purcell's Dido and Third Boy in Die Zauberflöte; Recitals at Aix-en-Provence and concerts in New Zealand, 1999; Bach's Magnificat in Vienna (2000) and St Matthew Passion for the London Handel Festival, 2001. *Honours:* Christine Nilsson Prize, Royal Academy of Music, Stockholm, 1997; Elena Gerhardt Lieder Prize, RAM, London. *Address:* c/o Royal College of Music, Prince Consort Road, London SW7, England.

JOHNSTON, Ben(jamin) Burwell; Composer and Teacher; b. 15 March 1926, Macon, Georgia, USA. *Education:* AB, College of William and Mary, 1949; MM, Cincinnati Conservatory of Music, 1950; MA, Mills College, 1953. *Career:* Faculty member, University of Illinois, 1951–83. *Compositions:* Concerto for brass, 1951; St Joan, ballet, 1955; Passacaglia and Epilogue for orchestra, 1955–60; Septet for wind quintet, cello and bass, 1956–58; Gambit, ballet, 1959; Knocking Piece for 2 percussionists and piano, 1962; Gertrude, or Would She Be Pleased to Receive It?, opera, 1965; Quintet for groups, 1966; Carmilla, opera, 1970; Trio for clarinet, violin and cello, 1982; The Demon Lover's Doubles for trumpet and microtonal piano, 1985; Symphony, 1988; 10 string quartets, 1959–96; Piano pieces; Choruses; Songs; Sleep and Waking for percussion ensemble, 1994; Quietness, for speaking bass and string quartet, 1996. *Honours:* Guggenheim Fellowship, 1959–60. *Address:* 120 Charlotte Street, Rockymount, NC 27804–3706, USA. *E-mail:* benbetjo@aol.com.

JOHNSTONE, Harry (Diack); University Lecturer (retired); b. 29 April 1935, Vancouver, Canada; m. Jill Margaret Saunders, 5 Aug 1960, deceased 8 April 1989, 1 s., 1 d. *Education:* Royal College of Music, London, 1954–57; Balliol College, Oxford, 1957–63; MA, DPhil (Oxon), 1968; BMus (TCD); FRCO; FTCL; ARCM. *Career:* Assistant Organist, New College, Oxford, 1960–61; Assistant Lecturer, Music, University of Reading, 1963; Lecturer, 1965, Senior Lecturer, 1970, Tutorial Fellow, Music, Emeritus Fellow, St Anne's College, Oxford; Lecturer, Music, St John's, 1980–2000; Visiting Professor, Music, Memorial University, St John's, Newfoundland, 1983; Reader in Music, University of Oxford, 1998–2000; General Editor, Musica Britannica, 2002–; mem, Elected Fellow of the Society of Antiquaries, London, 1998. *Publications:* Editor and part Author of the Blackwell History of Music in Britain IV; The Eighteenth Century, 1990; Editor, Maurice Greene: Cambridge Ode and Anthem, Musica Britannica 58, 1991, Phoebe Greene: a Pastoral Opera, Musica Britannica 82, 2004; Numerous editions of 18th century music, mainly English; Articles and Reviews in The Journal of the Royal Musical Asscn, Notes, RMA Research Chronicle, The Musical Times, Music and Letters, Proceedings of the Royal Musical Association, Early Music, Early Music History, The New Grove; The New DNB. *Address:* St Anne's College, University of Oxford, Oxford OX2 6HS, England.

JOLAS, Betsy; Composer and Professor of Composition and Advanced Analysis; b. 5 Aug. 1926, Paris, France; m. Gabriel Illouz, 27 Aug 1949, 2 s., 1 d. *Education:* French Baccalaureate; Studied composition with Paul Boepple, piano with Helen Schnabel and organ with Carl Weinrich and graduated from Bennington College, USA, 1940–46; Studied with Darius Milhaud, Simone Ple-Caussade and Olivier Messiaen at Paris Conservatory, 1946. *Career:* Replaced Olivier Messiaen at his course at Paris Conservatory, 1971–74, Appointed to Faculty, 1975; Also taught at: Tanglewood, Yale, Harvard, Darius Milhaud Chair at Mills College, Berkeley, Univ. of Southern California, San Diego Univ., Univ. of Michigan, USA. *Compositions include:* 9 Episodes for Solo Instruments, 1964–90; Motet II for Chorus and Ensemble, 1965; Quatuor II, 1964; Points d'aube, 1968; Quatuor III, 1973; Le Pavillon au bord de la Rivière for Chamber Opera, 1975; 4 Duos for Alto and Piano, 1979; Liring Ballade, baritone and orchestra, 1980; Points d'or, saxophone and ensemble, 1982; Trio for Piano, Violin and Violoncello; Schliemann, opera in 3 acts, 1988; Quatuor IV, 1989; Trio Les Heures for String Trio, 1990; Frauenleben for Viola and Orchestra, 1991; Perriault le Deluné for 12 Voices, 1993; Quatuor V, 1994; Sigrancia Ballade, 1995; Petite symphonie concertante, violin and orchestra, 1996; Lumor 7 Lieder, 1996; Für Celia Affettuoso for six voices; Trio sopra: et sola facta, for clarinet, violin and piano, 1998. *Recordings include:* Stances; Points d'Aube: D'un opéra de voyage. *Publications:* Molto espressivo – collection of writings on music ed by Alban Ramaut, 1999; D'un Opéra de voyage – collection of interviews ed by Bruno Serrou, 2000. *Current Management:* Leduc, Salabert, Billaudot Publishers. *Address:* 12 Rue Meynadier, 75019 Paris, France. *E-mail:* betsyjolas@noos.fr. *Website:* www.betsyjolas.com.

JOLL, Philip; Singer (Baritone); b. 14 March 1954, Merthyr Tydfil, Wales. *Education:* Studied at the Royal Northern College of Music with Nicholas Powell and Frederick Cox; Further study at the National Opera Studio in London. *Career:* Sang with English National Opera from 1979, as Donner and The Dutchman; Welsh National opera as Wotan (also with the company at Covent Garden, 1986), Kurwenal, Amfortas, Chorebus in The Trojans, The Forester (Cunning Little Vixen), Onegin, Orestes, Don Fernando in Fidelio, Jochanaan in Salome and Barak in Die Frau ohne Schatten; Covent Garden debut, 1982, in Salome, returning in Der Freischütz, Das Rheingold and Die Frau ohne Schatten; German debut, Frankfurt, 1983, as Amfortas, returning for The Dutchman; Guest appearances in Düsseldorf, 1985–86, Berlin and Wiesbaden (with the Welsh National Company in The Midsummer Marriage, 1986); Metropolitan Opera debut, 1988, as Donner in Das Rheingold; Australian debut as Jochanaan, for the Lyric Opera of Queensland, 1988; Bregenz Festival, 1989, in Der fliegende Holländer; Lyric Opera of Queensland, 1989–90, as Jochanaan in Salome and Marcello; Sang Orestes in Elektra and Rigoletto for Welsh National Opera, 1992–97; Season 2000 as Gurlitt's Wozzeck at Turin, Wotan for

Seattle Opera and Britten's Balstrode at Amsterdam; Engaged as Wotan in The Ring, Seattle 2000–01. *Recordings include:* The Greek Passion by Martinů; Amfortas in Parsifal; Kurwenal in Tristan und Isolde, conducted by Reginald Goodall. *Address:* c/o IMG Artists, Lovell House, 616 Chiswick High Road, London W4 5RX, England.

JOLLY, James; British writer; *Editor, Gramophone. Education:* Univ. of Bristol, Univ. of Reading. *Career:* producer, Record Review (BBC Radio 3); Asst Ed., Gramophone –1989, Ed. 1990–. *Publications as editor:* The Greatest Classical Recordings of All Time 1995, The Gramophone Opera 75: The 75 Best Opera Recordings of All Time 1997, The Gramophone Opera Good CD Guide 1998, The Gramophone Classical 2001 Good CD Guide (co-ed.) 2002. *Address:* Gramophone, Haymarket Magazines Ltd, PO Box 568, Haywards Heath, Sussex RH16 3XQ, England (office). *Website:* www.gramophone.co.uk.

JOLY, Simon; Conductor and Repetiteur; b. 14 Oct. 1952, Exmouth, Devon, England. *Education:* Organ Scholar, Corpus Christi Coll., Cambridge, 1971–74; BA, MA; ARCO. *Career:* music staff, Welsh National Opera, 1974–78; Assoc. Chorus Master, ENO, 1978–80; Asst, then Principal Conductor BBC Singers, 1980–95; conducted opera at ENO, BBC, Wexford Festival, Dublin, Berlin; conducted the Dutch, Irish, Finnish and French Radio Choirs; concerts with the BBC Singers include the Proms; many festivals including Warsaw, 2001; numerous programmes and concerts emphasising 20th Century music; Orchestral work includes concerts and BBC programmes with the BBC Symphony, Philharmonic and Concert Orchestras, National Orchestra of Wales, London Sinfonietta and Endymian Ensemble. *Recordings include:* Choral Works of Peter Maxwell Davies, Granville Bantock. *Address:* 49b Disraeli Road, Putney, London, SW15 2DR, England. *Telephone:* 020 8785 9617. *Fax:* 020 8785 2568. *E-mail:* simonjoly@toadflax1.demon.co.uk.

JONAS, Hilda Klestadt; harpsichordist, pianist and teacher of harpsichord and piano; b. 21 Jan. 1913, Düsseldorf, Germany; m. Gerald Jonas 1938; two d. *Education:* Hochschule für Musik, Cologne, Gumpert Conservatory, studies with Michael Wittels in Cologne, Rudolf Serkin in Switzerland and Wanda Landowska in Paris, France. *Career:* concert soloist and recitalist world-wide, with recitals in France, Germany, Spain, Italy, Austria, Belgium, Australia, New Zealand, Hawaii, USA, at colls, univs, museums and art centres, including Harvard, Carnegie-Mellon, Cincinnati Taft Museum, Haifa Music Museum, Milano Centro Culturale San Fedele, Empire Saal of Schloss Esterházy, Eisenstadt, Brussel's Musée Instrumental, Castello Buonconsiglio, Trento, Palais Wittgenstein, Düsseldorf, Stanford Univ., California, Palace of the Legion of Honour San Francisco, San Francisco State Univ., Goethe Inst., California West Coast, from Olympia Evergreen State Coll. to Santa Barbara, Westmont, Ventura, Monterey Peninsula Colls, Sacramento Crocker Art Museum, Ojai Valley Art Center and other cultural centres in Marin County and San Francisco; soloist with major symphony orchestras, including Cleveland, Cincinnati; regular series and May festivals under Max Rudolf and Josef Krips, Honolulu, Oxford, Jerusalem, Strasbourg and elsewhere; owner of private piano studio, Honolulu 1938–42, and Cincinnati 1942–75; founder 1965, Dir 1965–75, Harpsichord Festival Put-in-Bay, OH; mem. Hadassah, Brandeis Univ. *Recordings include:* Listen Rebecca, The Harpsichord Sounds, for children of all ages; Johann Kuhnau: Six Biblical Sonatas, with text based on authentic edition; Hilda Plays Bach: Italian Concerto, Chromatic Fantasia and Fugue, Partita 1, Capriccio on the Departure of his Beloved Brother, and others; Johann Sebastian Bach: Goldberg Variations. *Publications:* contrib. to various music magazines. *Address:* 50 Chumasero Drive 1-L, San Francisco, CA 94132, USA. *Website:* www.hildajonas.com.

JONAS, Sir Peter, Kt, BA, LRAM, FRCM, FRNCM, FRSA; *General and Artistic Director, Bavarian State Opera*; b. 14 Oct. 1946, London, England. *Education:* Univ. of Sussex, Northern Coll. of Music, Royal Coll. of Music, London, Eastman School of Music, Univ. of Rochester, USA. *Career:* Asst to Music Dir, Chicago Symphony Orchestra 1974–76, Artistic Administrator 1976–85; Dir of Artistic Administration, Orchestral Asscn, Chicago 1977–85; Gen. Dir, ENO 1985–93; Gen. and Artistic Dir (Staatsintendant), Bavarian State Opera, Munich 1993–; Bd of Management, National Opera Studio 1985–93; mem. of council, Royal Coll. of Music 1988–95, London Lighthouse 1990–93; mem., Deutsche Opernkonferenz 1993–, Chair. 2001–; mem., Deutsche Buhnverein 1994–; mem. Bd of Governors, Bavarian Radio and Television Corporation 1998; Visiting Lecturer, Univ. of St Gallen, Switzerland 2003–, Univ. of Zürich 2004–; mem., Athenaeum; mem. advisory bd, Hypovereinsbank, Munich 1994–. *Honours:* Hon. DMus, Univ. of Sussex 1994, City of Munich Prize for Culture 2003. *Address:* c/o Bayerische Staatsoper, Nationaltheater, Max-Joseph-Platz 2, 80539 Munich, Germany.

JONES, Bryn Terfel (see Terfel Jones, Bryn)

JONES, Della; Singer (Mezzo-soprano); b. 13 April 1946, Neath, Wales. *Education:* Royal College of Music, London, and Centre Lyrique Music School, Geneva. *Career:* Sang first at Grand Théâtre, Geneva; Member of English National Opera, 1977–82, in La Gazza Ladra, Il Barbiere di Siviglia, La Cenerentola, Le Comte Ory, Figaro, Giulio Cesare, Orfeo, Carmen, L'Incoronazione di Poppea and La Forza del Destino; Appearances with Welsh National Opera in Les Troyens, Salome, Barbiere di Siviglia and Tristan und Isolde; Scottish Opera in L'Egisto, Hansel and Gretel and Don Giovanni; Opera North as Rosina and in La Cenerentola, Le Comte Ory, Die Meistersinger, Oedipus Rex and Salome; Other engagements with English Music Theatre (world premiere of Tom Jones by Stephen Oliver and The Threepenny Opera), Dublin Opera and Handel Opera Society; Baba the Turk in The Rake's Progress in Geneva and Venice; Ruggiero in Alcina for Los Angeles Opera; Sang Cecilio in Lucio Silla, also La Finta Giardiniera for Mostly Mozart Festival, New York; Other festivals in London (English Bach), Cheltenham, Aldeburgh, Chester, Salisbury, Athens, Orange, throughout France, Switzerland and Edinburgh; Sang Preziosilla in Forza del Destino for Scottish Opera, 1990; Ruggiero in Alcina at Geneva and Théâtre du Châtelet, Paris; Mrs Noye in Noyes Fludde at 1990 Promenade Concerts, Hermia in Midsummer Night's Dream at Sadler's Wells, many other Prom appearances including Last Night, 1993; Marchesa Melibea at Covent Garden, 1992 (Il Viaggio a Reims); Sang Gluck's Armide at the Baroque Festival Versailles, 1992 and Clytemnestra in Iphigénie en Aulide for Opera North, 1996; Welsh National Opera, 1994, as Ariodante; Sang Rossini's Isabella for English National Opera, 1997; Aunt Hermance in the premiere of Dr Ox's Experiment, ENO, 1998; Sang Mozart's Marcellina at the Opéra Bastille, Paris, 2002; Concerts and recitals in USSR, USA, Europe and Japan. *Recordings include:* Haydn L'Incontro Improvviso and Il Ritorno di Tobia, conductor Dorati; Alcina, conductor Hickox; Marcellina in Figaro and Elvira in Don Giovanni, conductor Arnold Östmann; Donizetti L'Assedio di Calais; L'Incoronazione di Poppea; Rossini Stabat Mater and Arias, Bliss Pastoral, conductor Hickox; Recital of French Songs with Malcolm Martineau; The Bear by Walton; Dido in Dido and Aeneas; Video of ENO production of Giulio Cesare.

JONES, Gareth; Conductor; b. 1960, Port Talbot, Wales. *Education:* Studied at the Royal Northern College of Music with Gunther Herbig. *Career:* Assistant Conductor with Opera North; Associate with D'Oyly Carte Opera, from 1988; Welsh National Opera, 1990–98, with Nabucco, The Barber of Seville, Ernani, Faust, Fidelio and Un Ballo in Maschera; The Carmelites, 1999; Founder of the Cardiff Bay Chamber Orchestra, 1996, and concerts with the Scottish Chamber Orchestra at Edinburgh including Handel's L'Allegro and Purcell's Dido; Australian Chamber Orchestra at the Adelaide Festival; Season 1998–99 with the Royal Liverpool Philharmonic. *Address:* c/o Harlequin Agency Ltd, 203 Fidles Road, Cardiff CF4 5NA, Wales.

JONES, Gordon; Singer (Bass-baritone); b. 1960, Northampton, England. *Education:* Studied at York University; Choral Scholarship to York Minster. *Career:* Concert engagements include visits to the Lincoln Center in New York, the Royal Palace in The Hague, Hallé Orchestra, Martin's Le Vin Herbé at the Siena Festival and The Fairy Queen on tour in Italy; Performances of Berio's Sinfonia conducted by the composer, Simon Rattle and Esa-Pekka Salonen; Bach's St John and St Matthew Passions with the Choir of King's College, Cambridge; Sang in Arvo Pärt's St John Passion at the 1986 Almeida Festival and on tour of the United Kingdom, 1988; Further engagements in Bristol and Aberdeen and at the Malvern and Aix-en-Provence Festivals; Bach's St John Passion with The Sixteen on tour in Spain. *Recordings:* Vièrne's Les Angelus; Lully's Idylle pour la Paix, BBC; Schütz Schwanengesang and Bach Motets with the Hilliard Ensemble; Pärt St John Passion.

JONES, Gwyn Hughes; Singer (Tenor); b. 1968, Llanbedrgoch, Wales. *Education:* Studied at the Guildhall and National Opera Studio, London. *Career:* Engagements with Welsh National Opera as Ismaele in Nabucco, 1995; The Duke of Mantua, Don Ottavio, Rodolfo in La Bohème; Rinuccio in Gianni Schicchi for English National Opera; Season 1999–2000 with Fenton in Falstaff at Brussels and Chicago, Ismaele for San Francisco Opera; concerts include Mozart's C Minor Mass with the London Symphony Orchestra; Verdi Requiem; Mendelssohn's Elijah; West Coast of USA tour with Orchestra of Royal Opera House, 1999; Sang Elektra at the Deutsche Oper Berlin, 1999. *Honours:* Winner, Neue Stimmen Competition, Gutersloh, 1995. *Address:* Harlequin Agency Ltd, 203 Fidlas Road, Cardiff CF14 5NA, Wales.

JONES, Dame Gwyneth, DBE; Singer (soprano); b. 7 Nov. 1936, Pontenywynydd, Wales; m. Till Haberfeld, 1 d. *Education:* Royal College of Music, London; Accademia Chigiana, Siena; Zürich International Opera Centre. *Career:* With Zürich Opera House, 1962–63; Royal Opera House, Covent Garden, 1963–; Vienna State Opera House, 1966–; Bavarian State Opera, 1967–; Guest performances, numerous opera houses world-wide including La Scala Milan, Rome Opera, Berlin State Opera, Munich State Opera, Hamburg, Paris, Metropolitan Opera (New

York), San Francisco, Los Angeles, Zürich, Geneva, Dallas, Barcelona, Chicago, Teatro Col ón (Buenos Aires), Tokyo, Bayreuth Festival (debut 1966), Salzburg Festival, Arena di Verona, Edinburgh Festival, Welsh National Opera; Known for many opera roles including: Brünnhilde, Ring des Nibelungen; Marschallin, Rosenkavalier; Leonora, Il Trovatore; Desdemona, Otello; Aida and Turandot (Covent Garden 1990); Leonore, Fidelio (Beethoven); Senta, The Flying Dutchman; Medea; Elisabeth, Don Carlos; Madama Butterfly; Tosca; Donna Anna, Don Giovanni; Salome; Kundry, Parsifal; Helena, Ägyptische Helena; Dyer's Wife, Frau ohne Schatten (San Francisco 1989); Elektra (Geneva 1990); Elisabeth/Venus, Tannhäuser; Sang Brünnhilde at San Francisco, 1990, Covent Garden, 1990–91; Sang the Dyer's Wife at Covent Garden, 1992, Los Angeles, 1993; Wagner's Liebestod at the 1993 Prom Concerts, London; Sang Ortrud in Lohengrin at Covent Garden, 1997; Begbick in Mahagonny at Salzburg, 1998; Debut as Producer, Weimar National Theatre, Der Fleigender Hallander, Richard Wagner. *Recordings:* Various labels and television films, including: Fidelio; Aida; Flying Dutchman; Beethoven 9th Symphony; Tannhäuser; Poppea (Monteverdi); Rosenkavalier; Die Walküre, Siegfried and Götterdämmerung, in the 1976 Bayreuth Ring, released on DVD, 2002; Die Lustige Witwe; Turandot. *Honours:* Dr hc, University of Wales; Bundes Verdienstkreuz 1 Klasse; Honorary Member, Vienna State Opera; Commdr, Ordre des Arts et des Lettres 1992; Verdienst-kreuz; 1st Klasse Austria Shakespeare Prize Hamburg, 2001; Premio Puccini Award; Golden Medal of Honour, Vienna. 1991. *Address:* PO Box 2000, 8700 Kusnacht, Switzerland. *E-mail:* damegwyneth@bluewin.ch.

JONES, Ieuan; Harpist; b. 1955, Wales. *Education:* Royal College of Music, with Marisa Robles. *Career:* Appearances, the United Kingdom, Dutch and Italian television; Soloist, London Rodrigo Festival, 1986; Soloist, Mozart Concerto for Flute and Harp, Bournemouth Sinfonietta, 1986; Invited performer, World Harp Congress, Vienna, 1987; Recitals, Spain, North America; Featured, premiere of Alan Hoddinott's Tarantella for Harp and Orchestra, St David's Day Concert, Cardiff, 1988; Mozart and Daniel Jones Concertos, Flute and Harp, Swansea, Aberystwyth, 1988; Replaced Marisa Robles, Mozart Flute and Harp Concerto, Debussy's Danses Sacrées et Profanes, Margam Festival, Swansea, 1988; USA Miami recital, North Wales tour; Promotional video, Welsh Development Board, 1990; Brussels, Mozart Concert Recordings release, 1990; Premiere, Rodrigo Concierto, Wales, 1991; Guest soloist of Enrique Batiz and the State Orchestra of Mexico, 1992; Soloist, Rodrigo Homage Concert, Seville EXPO celebrations, 1992; Welsh premiere of Sonata for Harp by William Mathias (dedicated to Ieuan Jones), at 1993 Machynlleth Festival. *Recordings:* The Uncommon Harp, selection of light classics and ballads, 1987; 2 Sides of Ieuan Jones, 1988;... In The French Style, 1990; Mozart in Paris, 1990; All Through The Night, with Huw Rhys-Evans (tenor). *Honours:* All major prizes including Tagore Gold Medal and 1st-time award from HM the Queen Mother, Royal College of Music; All honours including overall Gold Medal, Royal Overseas League Music Competition; Joint winner, Israel International Harp Contest. *Current Management:* Neil Chaffey Concert Promotions, 8 Laxton Gardens, Baldock, Hertfordshire SG7 5DA, England.

JONES, Isola; Musician and Singer (Mezzo-soprano); b. 27 Dec. 1949, Chicago, Illinois, USA; m. Russell Thomas Cormier, 31 Mar 1984. *Education:* BA, Musical Education, Northwestern University, 1971. *Career:* Debut: Olga in Eugene Onegin, Metropolitan Opera, 15 Oct 1977; Live From the Met television series; Maddalena in Rigoletto, 1977, 1981; Lola in Cavalleria Rusticana, 1978; Girl in Mahagonny, 1979; Madrigal in Manon Lescaut, 1980; Recital with Placido Domingo, 1982; The Met Centennial Gala, 1983; Preziosilla in La Forza del Destino, 1984; Smaragdi in Francesca da Rimini; Spoleto Festival, 1989, as Giulietta in Les Contes d'Hoffmann. *Recordings:* Porgy and Bess, with Cleveland Orchestra conducted by Lorin Maazel; Flying Dutchman, with Chicago Symphony conducted by Georg Solti; Les Noces, with Chicago Symphony conducted by James Levine; Cavalleria Rusticana, with New Philharmonic Orchestra conducted by James Levine. *Honours:* Merit Award, Northwestern University, 1984. *Current Management:* Robert Lombardo Associates.

JONES, J. Barrie, MA, MusB, PhD, ARCO, ARCM; Emeritus University Lecturer; b. 23 April 1946, Manchester, England. *Education:* Downing Coll., Cambridge. *Career:* research asst in music, Open Univ. 1972–75, research fellow 1975–83, lecturer 1983–2003; mem. Royal Musical Asscn, Downing Coll. Asscn. *Publications:* Gabriel Fauré: A Life in Letters, Sixty Years of Friendship: The Correspondence of Saint-Saëns and Fauré (trans.); contrib. to Open Univ. teaching units on 19th-century music (especially keyboard), articles for The Music Review. *Honours:* Limpus Prize, ARCO 1965. *Address:* 46 Western Drive, Hanslope, Milton Keynes, England (home). *Telephone:* (1908) 510424 (home).

JONES, Jonathan Hellyer, MA, FRCO, ARCM; Teacher and Performer; b. 1 June 1951, Warwickshire, England. *Education:* Oakham School,

Rutland, Royal Coll. of Music, St John's Coll., Cambridge. *Career:* taught at Perse School, Cambridge 1974–82, Anglia Polytechnic Univ. 1979–, Cambridge Univ. 1995–, Guildhall School of Music and Drama 1979, St John's Coll. School, Cambridge 1974–80; Fellow, Hughes Hall, Cambridge 2000–02; Fellow, Precentor and Organist, Magdalene Coll., Cambridge 2002–. *Recordings:* The Muse Delight'd 1981, The Organ in the Age of Reason 1983, Principia Musica 1988, Rare Baroque Flute Concertos 1991, Brandenburg Concertos 1998. *Honours:* Brian Runnett Prize (organ playing Cambridge Univ.) 1973, John Stewart of Rannoch Scholarship in Sacred Music (Cambridge Univ.) 1972. *Current Management:* Neil Chaffey Concert Promotions, 9 Munts Meadow, Weston, Herts SG4 7AE, England. *Telephone:* (1462) 790919 (office). *Fax:* (1462) 790920 (office).

JONES, Karen; Concert Flautist; b. 8 July 1965, Hampton, Middlesex, England. *Education:* Studied at the Guildhall School, in Vienna with Wolfgang Schulz and in New York. *Career:* Played the Ibert Concerto with the London Symphony Orchestra, 1985; Concerto performances with Neville Marriner at the Queen Elizabeth Hall, Andrew Litton at the Festival Hall and George Malcolm at the Snape Concert Hall; Further engagements with the Ulster Orchestra, the Philharmonia, the Wren Orchestra and London Musici; Solo recitals at the Purcell Room and Wigmore Hall; Member of the Pears-Britten Ensemble with performances in the United Kingdom and the USA; Guest Principal with the Australian Chamber Orchestra at the 1992 Promenade Concerts. *Recordings include:* Arnold's Concerto No. 1 and Panufnik's Hommage à Chopin; Malcolm Arnold Flute Concerto No. 2; The Flute Album–Karen Jones. *Honours:* Winner, Woodwind Section, BBC television Young Musician of the Year, 1982; Gold Medal of The Shell, London Symphony Orchestra Scholarship, 1985. *Current Management:* Owen/White Management. *Address:* c/o Owen/White Management, 14 Nightingale Lane, London N8 7QU, England.

JONES, Leah-Marian; Singer (Mezzo-soprano); b. 1964, Wales. *Education:* Studied at the Royal Northern College of Music and the National Opera Studio. *Career:* Appearances with the Royal Opera at Covent Garden as Mercédès (Carmen), Zulma (L'Italiana in Algeri), Flosshilde (Rheingold), Second Lady (Die Zauberflöte), Emilia (Otello), Rosette (Manon), Flora (La Traviata), Annina (Der Rosenkavalier), Dorotea (Stiffelio), Elena (Aroldo), Flosshilde (Götterdämmerung); Season 1995/96 with Welsh National Opera as Lola in Cavalleria Rusticana; Other roles include Maddalena, Carmen, Siebel, Isolier (Comte Ory) Adalgisa (Norma); Season 1996 with Royal Opera as Fenena (Nabucco) and Dorabella and Carmen for English National Opera; Sang Laura in Luisa Miller for the Royal Opera at Edinburgh, 1998; Season 2000–01 as Tisbe in La Cenerentola and Emilia in Otello, at Covent Garden; Flowermaiden in Parsifal at Covent Garden, 2002. *Recordings:* Solo CD: Intermezzo. *Address:* Harlequin Agency 203 Fidlas Road, Cardiff, CF4 5NA, Wales.

JONES, Martin; Concert Pianist; b. 4 Feb. 1940, England. *Education:* Studied in London. *Career:* Debut: Played at the Queen Elizabeth Hall, London, and Carnegie Hall, 1968; Regular appearances with major British orchestras at the Festival Hall, the Barbican and other venues; Tour of Canada with the BBC National Orchestra of Wales and recitals in Florida, Tennessee and California; Broadcasts in Britain, Ireland and the USA; Pianist-in-Residence at University College, Cardiff, 1971–88; Brahms recital at the Wigmore Hall, 1993; Repertoire includes many standard concertos and also those by Busoni, Benjamin, Barber, Mathias, McCabe, Lambert and Scharwenka; Played Grainger's Bridal Lullaby and Mock Morris on the soundtrack of the film Howard's End. *Recordings:* Extensively for Nimbus Records. *Address:* c/o Owen/White Management, 14 Nightingale Lane, London N8 7QU, England.

JONES, Maureen; Pianist; b. 1940, Australia. *Education:* Studied at the New South Wales Conservatorium, Sydney. *Career:* Formed Trio with Breton Langbein and Barry Tuckwell and gave the premiere of the Horn Trio by Don Banks at the 1962 Edinburgh Festival; Regular tours of Australia and Europe, including recent appearances in Dublin, Siena, Innsbruck, Paris, Sydney and Melbourne; Duo recitals with Barry Tuckwell; Concert debut playing Beethoven's 1st Concerto with the Sydney Symphony; Appearances at the Edinburgh Festival include concerts with the Berlin Philharmonic. *Address:* c/o Barry Tuckwell, Northern Sinfonia, Sinfonia Centre, 41 Jesmond Vale, Newcastle, NE1 1PG, England.

JONES, Nerys; Singer (Mezzo-Soprano); b. 1965, Wales. *Education:* Studied at the Royal Scottish Academy, RSAMD, and at the Guildhall School; Further study with David Pollard. *Career:* Debut: Karolka in Jenůfa for Scottish Opera; Appearances with Scottish Opera as Marzelline in Fidelio and Welsh National as Norina in Don Pasquale; English National Opera debut as Melissa in Ken Russell's production of Princess Ida, 1992; Further roles with ENO (Principal from 1994) include Cherubino, Despina, Zerlina, Proserpina (Orfeo), Mercédès (Carmen), Rosette (Manon), Flora (Traviata), Hansel, Flower Maiden

(Parsifal), Sister Mathilde (Dialogues des Carmélites); Sang in the premiere of Blond Eckbert by Judith Weir, 1994; Cherubino at Grange Park Opera, and Kitchen Boy in Rusalka for ENO, 1998; Sang Rosina for Grange Park Opera, 1999; Sang Lisette in Haydn's Il mondo della luna, Garsington Opera, 2000; Dorabella in Così fan tutte, Grange Park Opera, 2001; Other roles include Flight (Jonathan Dove) for Reims Opera, 2001 and Antwerp, 2002; Many concert engagements. *Recordings:* CD Blond Eckbert. *Honours:* Peter Morrison Prize at the Royal Scottish Academy; John Noble Bursary. *Current Management:* Musichall. *Address:* Musichall, Vicarage Way, Ringmer, East Sussex, BN8 5 LA, England.

JONES, Paul Carey; Singer (Baritone); b. 1965, Cardiff, Wales. *Education:* Queen's College Oxford; Royal Academy of Music, with Mark Wildman and Julius Drake. *Career:* Appearances as Mozart's Figaro, Marcello and Schaunard in La Bohème, Enby in Purcell's The Indian Queen and Ariodates in Handel's Xerxes; Eleven baritone roles in Stephen Oliver's A Man of Feeling; Concerts recitals and broadcasts throughout the United Kingdom; Season 2001–2002 with Purcell's The Fairy Queen at the Linbury Theatre, Covent Garden, National Eisteddfod in Wales and St David's Hall, Cardiff. *Honours:* Hubert Kiver Prize, Royal Academy. *Address:* c/o English Bach Festival, Linbury Theatre, Royal Opera House, London WC2, England.

JONES, Richard; Producer; b. 7 June 1953, Lambeth, London, England. *Education:* Studied at the Universities of Hull and London. *Career:* Debut: A Water Bird Talk by Dominick Argento for Scottish Opera, 1982; Has directed for theatre and for the following opera companies: Musica nel Chiostro, Battingano (Mozart's Apollo et Hyacinthus 1984); Salieri's La Grotta di Trofonio and Paisiello's Il re Teodoro in Venezia, 1985; Opera Northern Ireland (Don Pasquale, 1985); Wexford Festival (Mignon 1986); Cambridge University Opera (The Magic Flute, 1986); Opera 80 (The Rake's Progress, 1986, Rigoletto, 1987); Opera North (Manon, 1987, Carmen and The Love for Three Oranges, 1987); Scottish Opera-Go-Round (Macbeth and Die Entführung, 1987); Scottish Opera (Das Rheingold, 1989); Kent Opera (Le Comte Ory and A Night at the Chinese Opera, 1988); The Love for Three Oranges and David Blake's The Plumber's Gift, world premiere, for English National Opera, 1989; Bregenz Festival, Austria (Mazeppa, 1991); Netherlands Opera (The Flying Dutchman, 1993); Bavarian State Opera (Julius Caesar), 1994; Royal Opera House (Das Rheingold and Die Walküre, 1994, Siegfried and Götterdämmerung, 1995); Netherlands Opera (Mazeppa, 1991); English National Opera (Die Fledermaus, 1991); Scottish Opera (Die Walküre, 1991); The Midsummer Marriage at Munich, 1998; Production of the Trojans for ENO, 2003; Engaged for Les Troyens at ENO, 2003. *Honours:* Laurence Olivier Award as Best Newcomer in Theatre in 1988; Best Director at the 1990 Evening Standard Drama awards. *Address:* c/o Royal Opera House (contracts), Covent Garden, London, WC2, England.

JONES, Roland Leo, BMus; American violinist, violist and music teacher; b. 16 Dec. 1932, Ann Arbor, MI. *Education:* University of Michigan, Columbia University, National Orchestra Association Training Orchestra, Interlochen Music Camp, Meadowmount Music School and Tanglewood Music School. *Career:* soloist with Ann Arbor Civic Symphony, 1951, 1953; Violinist, Denver Symphony Orchestra, 1960–75; Jackson Hole, Wyoming Fine Arts Festival, 1964–65; Tours throughout USA and Canada; Founder, 1st Violinist, Highland Chamber Players, 1978–79; 1st Violinist, Highland String Quartet, 1979–2002; Tour with Denver Chamber Orchestra and San Francisco Opera, Western Opera Theater, 1987; Joined Musica Sacra Chamber Orchestra, Denver, Colorado, 2000; Toured Austria, Hungary and Italy, 2000. *Compositions:* New Cadenzas for all the Mozart Violin Concertos, 1991. *Recordings:* With orchestra, Milena by Alberto Ginastera and Concertos No. 2 of Chopin. *Publications:* New Cadenzas for all the Mozart Violin Concertos, 1992, 2003. *Address:* 3004 S Kearney, Denver, CO 80222, USA.

JONES, Samuel; Composer, Conductor and Educator; b. 2 June 1935, Inverness, Mississippi, USA; m. (1) 2 d., (2) Kristin Barbara Schutte, 22 Dec 1975. *Education:* BA, Millsaps College, 1957; MA, PhD, Eastman School of Music, University of Rochester, 1958–60. *Career:* Director of Instrumental Music, Alma College, Michigan, 1960–62; Music Director, Saginaw Symphony, 1962–65; Conductor, Rochester Philharmonic, 1965–73; Founding Dean, Shepherd School of Music, 1973–79; Professor of Conducting and Composition, Rice University, 1973–97; Composer in Residence, Seattle Symphony Orchestra, 1997–; Guest Conductor, Buffalo Philharmonic Symphonies of Detroit, Pittsburgh, Houston, Prague and Iceland. *Compositions:* In Retrospect; Symphony No. 1 (recorded); Elegy for String Orchestra (recorded); Overture for a City; Let Us Now Praise Famous Men (recorded); Spaces; Contours of Time; Fanfare and Celebration; A Christmas Memory; A Symphonic Requiem; Variations on a Theme of Howard Hanson; The Trumpet of the Swan; Listen Now, My Children (recorded); Two Movements for Harpsichord; Canticles of Time, Symphony No. 2; Symphony No. 3 (Palo Duro Canyon), 1992; The Seas of God, 1992; The Temptation of Jesus

(oratorio), 1995; Janus, 1998; Roundings, 1999; Aurum Aurorae, 2001; Eudora's Fable (The Shoe Bird), 2002. *Recordings:* Symphony No. 3 recorded by Amarillo Symphony; Let Us Now Praise Famous Men and Elegy recorded by Houston Symphony; Roundings recorded by Amarillo Symphony (with Cello Sonata); Piano Sonata recorded by John Perry; Two Movements for Hapsichord recorded by Barbara Harbach. *Current Management:* Carl Fischer Inc. *Address:* 35247 34th Avenue S, Auburn, WA 98001, USA.

JONES, Warren; Vocal Coach and Accompanist; b. 11 Dec. 1951, Washington, District of Columbia, USA. *Education:* BM, New England Conservatory of Music, 1973; MM, San Francisco Conservatory of Music, 1977. *Career:* Accompanist to Luciano Pavarotti, Marilyn Horne, Frederica von Stade, Judith Blegen, Håkan Hagegård, Elisabeth Söderströ m, Martti Talvela, Carol Vaness, Lynn Harrell, Thomas Allen, Roberta Peters, Robert Alexander and Samuel Ramey; Appearances at Tanglewood, Ravinia, Caramoor and Salzburg Festivals; Assistant Conductor, Metropolitan Opera, San Francisco Opera; Classes at Harvard, San Francisco Conservatory of Music, Hartt School of Music, California State University; mem, Lifetime Member, Pi Kappa Lambda. *Address:* 711 West End Avenue, Apartment 6JN, New York, NY 10025, USA.

JOOS, Martina; Recorder Player; b. 15 Feb. 1972, Glarus, Switzerland. *Education:* Studied at the Hochschule für Musik und Theater in Zürich, Switzerland, with Kees Boeke and Matthias Weilenmann. *Career:* Member of 'Trio O'Henry' together with Claudia Gerauer and Barbara Nägele; Appearances (among others) at Bludenzer Tage für Zeitgemässe Musik, Austria, 1997; Festival of Ancient Music, Stary Sacz, Poland, 2000; Festival Musica Nova, Sofia, Bulgaria, 2001; Festival Bohemia-Saxony, Czech Republic, 2001; Cycle of premieres with works of Swiss composers, Zürich, 2000–01; Radio appearances (live recordings): St Peter's Church, Zürich, 1996; Great Hall of the HFMT, Zürich; Radio features: Austrian Radio ORF 1, 1998; Swiss Radio DRS 2, 2000; Bulgarian radio and television, Sofia, 2001; Premieres: Kees Boeke's The Unfolding, 1997; Martin Derungs's A Set of Pieces, 2000; Thomas Müller's Erste Etappe in Richtung farbiger Eindrücke, 2000; Giorgio Tedde's Medio Aevo, 2000; Andreas Nick's Trio pour flûtes à bec, 2000. *Address:* Hanfrose 19, CH 8055 Zürich, Switzerland.

JORDAN, Armin (Georg); Conductor; b. 9 April 1932, Lucerne, Switzerland; m. Kate Herkner, 1 s., 1 d. *Education:* University of Fribourg; Conservatoire de Lausanne (degrees in piano teaching and conducting). *Career:* Debut: Bienne Opera, 1957; Chief Conductor in Biene, 1961–63; First Conductor, Zürich Opera, 1963–71; Music Director, Basle Opera from 1971; Music Director, Orchestre de Chambre de Lausanne, 1973–85; Music Director, Orchestre de la Suisse Romande from 1985; Principal Guest Conductor, Ensemble Orchestral de Paris from 1986; Conducted Massenet's Manon at the Geneva Opera, 1989; Numerous appearances on television and radio in various countries; International career from 1963; Guest conductor at the Lyon, Vienna, Munich, Hamburg, Geneva, Brussels and Seattle Operas; Paris, Orchestre National de France and Nouvel Orchestre Philharmonique; Season 1991/92 with Die Fledermaus at Geneva and Don Giovanni at Aix-en-Provence; Led Parsifal at the Opéra Bastille, Paris, 1997; Tristan and Isolde at Seattle, 1998; Siegfried at Geneva, 2001; Engaged for the Ring at Seattle, 2001. *Recordings:* Actor and Conductor in Syberberg's film of Parsifal; Orchestral works by Dukas, Mozart, Dvořák, Ravel, Chausson, Schubert, Chopin and Franck; Mozart Violin Concertos, with Franco Gulli. *Honours:* Grand Prix, Académie Charles Cros, 1985; Cecilia Award, Belgium, 1985; Académie du Disque Lyrique, Paris, 1987; Prix de la Critique Internationale, 1987; Prix Académie du Disque Françcais, 1988. *Address:* Bunishoferstrasse 234, 8706 Feldmeilen (ZH), Switzerland.

JORDAN, Irene; Singer (Soprano); b. 25 April 1919, Birmingham, Alabama, USA. *Education:* Studied at Judson College, Alabama, and with Clyrie Mundy in New York. *Career:* Sang first as mezzo-soprano (Mallika in Lakmé at the Metropolitan, 1946), and after further study sang Donna Anna and Micaela at the Chicago Lyric Theatre, 1954; Appeared at the New York City Opera and the Metropolitan (the Queen of Night) in 1957; Elsewhere in America she sang Verdi's Aida and Lady Macbeth, Madama Butterfly, Weber's Euryanthe, Mozart's Vitellia (La Clemenza di Tito) and Leonore in Fidelio. *Recordings include:* Stravinsky's Pulcinella, conducted by the composer, and songs by Schoenberg.

JORDAN, Philippe (Dominique); Conductor; b. 18 Oct. 1974, Zürich, Switzerland. *Education:* Piano lessons from age 6 years; Singing lessons from age 8 years; Violin lessons from age 11 years; Piano and composition studies, with Boris Mersson, Karl Engel and Hans Ulrich Lehmann, Konservatorium, Zürich. *Career:* Debut: Assistant of Jeffrey Tate at the Théâtre du Châtelet in Paris and Festival of Aix-en-Provence; Theatre in Ulm; Opera Ireland, Dublin; Aalto-Theater Essen, Théâtre de la Monnie, Brussels; Kapellmeister and Assistant to Daniel

Barenboim, Staatsoper Unter den Linden in Berlin, opening with D. Milhaud's Christophe Colomb with Peter Greenaway, Teatro dell'Opera in Rome, Grand Théâtre Genève, Wiener Staatsoper, Théâtre du Châtelet Paris, Semperoper Dresden, Opéra National de Lyon, Festival d'Aix-en Provence, Salzburger Festspiele; Houston Grand Opera; Glyndebourne Festival; ROH; Metropolitan Opera NY; Metropolitan Opera; Royal Opera House Covent Garden; Opera Bastille; Berlin Philharmonic Orchestra; Philharmonic Orchestra; Orchestre Philharmonique de Radio France; Chamber Orchestra of Europe; From Season 2001–02 youngest General Music Director of Europe at the Opera of Graz. *Current Management:* IMG Artists, Paris. *Address:* Grieskai 2, 8020 Graz, Austria.

JORDIS, Eelco van; Singer (Bass); b. 11 May 1943, Graz, Austria. *Education:* Studied in Graz, Zürich and Milan, 1960–67. *Career:* Debut: Graz, 1967, as the Monk in Don Carlos; Sang at Regensburg Opera, 1969–72, Saarbrucken and Kassel, 1972–79; Bielefeld Opera from 1979, notably as Mephisto in Faust by Spohr, 1993; Further engagements throughout Germany and in Milan, Brussels and Zagreb; Other roles include Mozart's Alfonso, Don Giovanni and Sarastro, Verdi's King Philip and Ramphis, Scarpia in Tosca, Boris Godunov, Prince Igor, Daland and Wagner's Landgrave; Guest appearances in Russia and North America; Dresden Semperoper, 1999–2001, Gianni Schichi, Music master in Ariadne; opera Leibzig, 1998, Gustav in Abraum, Herchet; Opera Hamburg, 1984–1991, Ferrando in Trovatore, Grand-inquisitore in Don Carlo; Munich National Opera, 1984–1988, Monterone in Rigoletto; Felsensteinoper in Dessau, 1997–2002, Die Kluge (Orff), Don Alfonso in Cosi fan tutte, Reich in Lustige Weiber. *Recordings:* Ludwig Spohr, Faust, Mephistofeles, CPO; Catott-Romanzia MArio Ruffini, E.Pentirario- Editoria Ellectronica; Charles Gounod, Margarethe. *Address:* Eelco von Jordis, D-33613 Bielefeld, Bremerstrasse 28 Germany. *Telephone:* 521 130730.

JORGENSEN, Jerilyn; Violinist; b. 1960, New York, USA. *Education:* Studied at the Juilliard School with Joseph Fuchs. *Career:* Soloist with several orchestras in the Brahms and Tchaikovsky Concertos; Further study with members of the Juilliard Quartet and Co-founded the Da Vinci Quartet, 1980, under the sponsorship of the Fine Arts Quartet; Many concerts in the USA and elsewhere in the repertoire including works by Mozart, Beethoven, Brahms, Dvořák, Shostakovich and Bartók. *Honours:* With the Da Vinci Quartet: Awards and grants from the NEA, the Western States Arts Foundation and the Colorado Council for the Humanities; Artist in Residence at the University of Colorado. *Address:* 11 Northpark Street, Glasgow G20 7AA, Scotland.

JOSEFOWICZ, Leila; Concert Violinist; b. 1978, USA. *Career:* Engagements with the Chicago Symphony Orchestra (Tchaikovsky Concerto, Philadelphia Orchestra under Sawallisch, Los Angeles Philharmonic and London Philharmonic with Franz Welser-Möst; Carnegie Hall debut with the Academy of St Martin in the Fields under Neville Marriner, 1994; Returned to New York, with the Boston Symphony and Seiji Ozawa, 1996; Season 1996–97 with the Bamberg Symphony, the Rotterdam Philharmonic under Gergiev, the Danish Radio Symphony Orchestra, Monte Carlo Orchestra, Dallas Symphony Orchestra; Tour of USA with Neville Marriner and Mendelssohn's Concerto at the London Proms, 1997; 1997–98 Season with Sydney Symphony Orchestra, Swedish RSO, tour of Germany with Neville Marriner and ASMF, Orchestre National de France/Dutoit, Budapest Festival Orchestra, Finnish RSO; 2003–04 season: Soloist at Last Night of the Proms, London 2003; Concerts with the Oslo Philharmonic for Norwegian premiere of Knussen Violin Concerto, 2004. *Recordings include:* Tchaikovsky and Sibelius Concertos with the Academy of St Martin in the Fields; Bartók's Solo Sonata and pieces by Pagnanini, Ysaÿe, Kriesler and Ernst; Bohemian Rhapsodies with Marriner/ASMF. *Honours:* Cover Feature, BBC Music Magazine, 1997. *Address:* Harrison Parrott Ltd, 12 Penzance Place, London W11 4PA, England.

JOSELSON, Rachel; Singer (Mezzo-soprano); b. 16 Sept. 1955, Englewood, New Jersey, USA. *Education:* Studied at Florida State and Indiana Universities, 1971–70; Further study with Mario del Monaco at Treviso. *Career:* Sang at Darmstadt Opera, 1982–84, Hamburg from 1984; Roles have included Mozart's Idamante, Cherubino and Dorabella, Gluck's Orpheus, and Siebel in Faust; Soprano roles include Mimi, Micaela, Eva in Die Meistersinger, Elisabeth de Valois and Gounod's Mireille; Debussy's Mélisande at Essen, 1990; Guest appearances at Berlin, Brussels, Barcelona and Atlanta; Frequent concert appearances. *Address:* Essen Opera, Rolandstrasse 10, 4300 Essen 1, Germany.

JOSEPH, David (Robin); Composer; b. 27 Jan. 1954, Melbourne, Victoria, Australia. *Education:* BMus (Hons), University of Melbourne, 1979. *Career:* Adelaide Chamber Orchestra, 1986–87; Tutor, University of Melbourne, 1993–95; Commissions from Kammermusiker Zürich, Adelaide CO, Queensland Ballet and others. *Compositions include:* Images for orchestra, 1983; The Dream, for orchestra, 1986; Clarinet

Concerto, 1987; Horn Concerto, 1988; 2 String Trios, 1988, 1990; Symphony, 1989; The Haunting for orchestra, 1990; Chamber Concerto for strings, 1992; Dialogues for violin and strings, 1992; Pelléas and Mélisande, ballet, 1994; The Memory, for orchestra, 1994; From Endymion for 2 sopranos, alto, tenor, baritone, and bass, 1995. *Honours:* Alex Burnard Scholarship, 1980; AC International and AC Composers Fellowships, 1982, 1992. *Address:* c/o APRA, 1A Eden Street, Crows Nest, NSW 2065, Australia.

JOSEPHSON, Kim Alan; Singer (Baritone); b. 1954, Akron, Ohio, USA. *Career:* Debut: Sang in Strauss's Salome at Houston, 1977; Spoleto Festival, USA, 1991, in Menotti's Maria Golovin and Sarasota Festival, 1992, as Simon Boccanegra (both versions); Vancouver Opera as Rigoletto; Metropolitan Opera, New York, from 1991, as Sonora in La Fanciulla del West, Enrico in Lucia di Lammermoor, Germont in Traviata, Sharpless in Madama Butterfly, Silvio in Pagliacci, Count in Capriccio, the title role in Rigoletto and Marcello in La Bohème; Vienna Staatsoper debut, 1994, as Marcello in La Bohème followed by roles as Count di Luna in Il Trovatore, Germont in Traviata, Enrico in Lucia and Belcore in L'Elisir d'amore; Chicago debut as Marcello in La Bohème and in 1999 sang Eddie Carbone in the world premiere of A View from the Bridge by Bolcom; Many concert performances. *Honours:* Winner of many awards and competitions including Richard Tucker Foundation Grant; William Sullivan/George London Award; Puccini Foundation Award; Baltimore Opera Competition. *Address:* c/o Metropolitan Opera, Lincoln Center, New York, NY 10023, USA.

JOSHUA, Rosemary; Singer (Soprano); b. 16 Oct. 1964, Cardiff, Wales. *Education:* Studied in London at the Royal College of Music; Masterclasses with Thomas Allen, Graziella Sciutti and Claudio Desderi. *Career:* Debut at the Aix-en-Provence festival as Angelica in Orlando; Engagements with Opera Northern Ireland as Pamina, and at the 1992 Buxton Festival as Blondchen in Die Entführung; English National Opera as Adele in Die Fledermaus, Yum-Yum in The Mikado, Princess Ida, Norina, Sophie in Der Rosenkavalier and Susanna; Covent Garden Festival, 1993, as Pamina; Royal Opera debut, 1994, as Pousette in Manon; Angelica in Orlando at Aix-en-Provence Festival, Poppea in Agrippina and Susanna, Cologne Opera, 1994; Sang Sophie with ENO, 1997; Season 1999 as Handel's Semele for ENO and in Fauré's Requiem at the London Proms; Sang Poppea in Agrippina at Brussels, Sophie at the Deutsche Oper, Berlin; the title role of La Calisto at the Deutsche Staatsoper, Berlin, and in Brussels; Juliette in Romeo and Juliette and Ginevra in Ariodante in San Diego; The title role in The Cunning Little Vixen at the Flanders Opera and at the Theatre des Champs Elysées in Le nozze di Figaro, the Glyndebourne Festival as Cleopatra in Giulio Cesare and to the Royal Opera House as Oscar in Un ballo in Maschera.Anne Trulove at Glyndebourne and Handel's Cleopatra for Florida Opera, 2000; Janáček's Vixen for Netherlands Opera, 2001 and at La Scala; Mahler's Symphony of a Thousand at the London Proms, 2002; Season 2002–03 in Die Fledermaus at the Met and in Handel's Saul and Der Rosenkavalier at Munich; Recent concert appearances include Bach's B Minor Mass with the London Philharmonic Orchestra under MArk Elder at the Royal Festival Hall, Beethoven's Symphony no. 9 with Sir Simon Rattle and the Orchestra of the Age of Enlightenment, Jephtha with René Jacobs and the Orchestra of the Age of Enlightenment in London, Brussels and New York, Mahler's Symphony no. 8 with Sir Simon Rattle and the National Youth Orchestra of Great Britain at the BBC Proms, Handel's Messiah with Daniel Harding and the Deutsche Kammerphilharmonie Bremen, Bach Cantatas with Nikolaus Harnoncourt and the Concentus Musicus Wien and Bach's B Minor Mass with Sir Roger Norrington and the Orchestra of the Age of Enlightenment.. *Recordings:* 'Orlando' with Les Arts Florissants and William Christie for Erato; 'Venus and Adonis' and 'Dido and Aeneas' with René Jacobs for Harmonia Mundi; Sophie in Der Rosenkavalier for Chandos; the Sandman in 'Hansel und Gretel' for Teldec. *Honours:* Royal Philharmonic Award in debut category; Nominated for a Laurence Olivier Award in the category for Outstanding Achievement in Opera. *Address:* Askonas Holt Limited, Lonsdale Chambers, 27 Chancery Lane, London WC2A 1PF England. *Telephone:* 20 7400 1700. *Fax:* 20 7400 1799. *E-mail:* info@askonasholt.co.uk. *Website:* www .askonasholt.co.uk.

JOSIPOVIC, Ivo; Composer and Lawyer; b. 28 Aug. 1957, Zagreb, Croatia. *Education:* PhD, Law, University of Zagreb; Graduate, Music Academy, Zagreb. *Career:* Debut: 2 children's songs, 1978; Compositions performed in nearly all European countries, USA, Canada and Japan (EBU concert transmitted over 30 stations world-wide); Recordings for several radio and television stations; Performances at several European music festivals; Director of Music, Zagreb Biennale, 1981–; Docent, Music Academy, University of Zagreb, 1992–. *Compositions include:* Variations for piano; Play of the Golden Pearls for piano; Enypion for harp solo; Quartetto rusticano for string quartet; Per fiati for wind quintet; Passacaglia for string orchestra; Samba da camera for 13 strings; Dyptich for large orchestra; Epicurus' Garden for symphony orchestra; Man and Death for soloists, choir and orchestra; Pro musica for accordenon orchestra; The Most Beautiful Flower for voice and instrumental ensemble; Mrmesh for Mr Penderecki for folk orchestra; Thousands of Lotuses for choir and instrumental ensemble; Jubilus for piano solo; Elegaic Song for violin and piano; Dreams for voice and string orchestra. *Recordings:* Several compositions on CDs. *Address:* Palmoticeva 26, 10000 Zagreb, Croatia.

JOUBERT, John Pierre Herman, FRAM; Composer and University Lecturer; b. 20 March 1927, Cape Town, South Africa; m. Florence Mary Litherland 1951, one s. one d. *Education:* Diocesan Coll., Cape Town, Royal Acad. of Music, London. *Career:* Lecturer in Music, Univ. of Hull, England 1950–62; Lecturer (later Reader) in Music, Univ. of Birmingham 1962–86; mem. British Acad. of Composers and Songwriters, British Music Soc.. *Compositions:* four String Quartets, 1950, 1977, 1987, 1988; Concertos, for violin, 1954, piano, 1957, bassoon, 1973; 2 Symphonies, 1955, 1969; two Sonatas for piano, 1957, 1972; Pro Pace Motets for unaccompanied choir, 1959; String Trio, 1960; Octet, 1961; Silas Marner, opera, 1961; Under Western Eyes, Opera, 1969; six Poems of Emily Brontë for soprano and piano, 1969; Déploration for orchestra, 1978; The Turning Wheel for soprano and piano, 1979; Herefordshire Canticles for choir and orchestra, 1979; Gong-Tormented Sea for choir and orchestra, 1981; Temps Perdu for orchestra, 1984; Rorate Coeli for unaccompanied choir, 1985; Piano Trio, 1987; Wings of Faith, orarorio, 2000. *Recordings:* Temps Perdu, Sinfonietta, The Instant Moment. *Honours:* Royal Philharmonic Soc. Prize, 1949; Hon. DMus, Univ. of Durham 1991. *Address:* 63 School Road, Moseley, Birmingham, B13 9TF, England.

JUDD, James; Conductor; b. 30 Oct. 1949, Hertford, England. *Education:* Trinity College of Music, London. *Career:* Assistant Conductor, Cleveland Orchestra, 1973–75; Associate Conductor, European Community Youth Orchestra, 1978–; Founder/Director, Chamber Orchestra of Europe; Music Director, Florida Philharmonic Orchestra; Artistic Director, European Communities Youth Orchestra, 1990; Artistic Director of Greater Miami Opera, 1993–; Guest Conductor with the Vienna and Prague Symphonies, Berlin Philharmonic, Orchestre National de France, Zürich Tonhalle and Suisse Romande Orchestra; Conducted La Cenerentola at Glyndebourne, 1985; Traviata, Il Trovatore, Il Barbiere di Siviglia, Rigoletto and Figaro for English National Opera; US Opera debut, 1988, with Don Giovanni in Miami; Season 1992/93 included tours with the Hallé and English Chamber Orchestras, London Symphony Orchestra, Royal Philharmonic and the Chamber Orchestra of Europe and Salzburg Festival; Conducted the Michael Nyman Band and the Philharmonia in the premiere of Nyman's Concerto for Saxophone and Orchestra, 1997. *Recordings:* With Chamber Orchestra of Europe; With English Chamber Orchestra; With Philharmonia Orchestra. *Current Management:* London Artists. *Address:* c/o Michael Emmerson, London Artists, 10 Guild Street, Stratford-upon-Avon, Warwickshire, CV 37 6RE, England.

JUDD, Wilfred; Opera Director; b. 1952, Hertford, Hertfordshire, England. *Education:* Studied at Oxford and London Opera Centre. *Career:* Began as freelance director, 1979; Has been producer with Royal Opera, 1984–, for which has staged Die Zauberflöte, Tosca, and La Fanciulla del West; Notable recent production Finnissy's Thérèse Raquin for The Garden Venture; Artistic Director, Royal Opera House Garden Venture, 1988–93; wrote and directed The Inner Ear, a concert drama premiered by Florida Philharmonic Orchestra, 2002; Director of Productions, Opera 80, 1988–91. *Address:* 15 Cornwall Road, Twickenham, Middlesex, TW1 3LS England.

JUDGE, Ian; Stage Director; b. 21 July 1946, Southport, England. *Education:* Guildhall School of Music and Drama, London. *Career:* Joined the RSC in 1975, productions there include: The Wizard of Oz, The Comedy of Errors, Love's Labours Lost, The Relapse, Twelfth Night, A Christmas Carol, Troilus and Cressida and The Merry Wives of Windsor; Opera productions include: Faust, The Merry Widow, Cavalleria Rusticana, Pagliacci, Don Quixote La Belle Vivette and Mephistopheles for the ENO: Macbeth, Tosca, Acis and Galatea, Boris Godunov, Attila for Opera North; The Flying Dutchman (Royal Opera House); He has staged operas regularly in Europe, Australia and the USA; Macbeth (Cologne), Faust (Sydney), Les Contes d'Hoffmann (Houston), Tosca and Madama Butterfly (Los Angeles), Simon Boccanegra (Washington); Directed the original 1857 version of Verdi's Simon Boccanegra at Covent Garden, 1997; Staged Falstaff for the BBC Proms, 1998; Mephistopheles by Boito for ENO, 1999; Falstaff for Théâtre du Châtelet, Paris, 2001; La Bohème for Kirov Opera, St Petersburg, 2001; Ernani for National Reisoper, Netherlands, 2002. His credits include many plays and musicals, A Little Night Music (Piccadilly Theatre), Show Boat (London Palladium) and West Side Story in Australia. *Current Management:* Simpson Fox Association. *Address:* 52 Shaftesbury Avenue, London W1V 7DE, England.

JUDSON, Colin; Singer (Tenor); b. 1968, England. *Education:* Graduated Guildhall School of Music, 1992. *Career:* Engagements with touring opera companies, British Youth Opera, De Vlaamse Opera, Antwerp and at the Covent Garden Festival; Roles have included Remendado (Carmen), Isaac in La Gazza Ladra, Rossini's Almaviva, Purcell's Aeneas and Mozart's Monostatos, Tamino and Ferrando; Season 1996 with Werther for English Touring Opera, season 1997 as Coryphée in Le Comte Ory at Glyndebourne and in the Verdi Requiem at Hereford; Haydn's Nelson Mass for the Brighton Festival; Concerts include Schumann's Dichterliebe, Bach's Christmas Oratorio, The Dream of Gerontius, Puccini's Messa di Gloria and Stravinsky's Pulcinella. *Address:* C&M Craig Services Ltd, 3 Kersley Street, London SW11 4 PR, England.

JUNE, Ava; Singer (Soprano); b. 23 July 1934, London, England. *Education:* Studied with Kate Opperman, Clive Carey and Joan Cross in London. *Career:* Joined Sadler's Wells Chorus, 1953; Sang solo roles from 1957, Leila in The Pearl Fishers, 1959; Covent Garden debut, 1958, as the Heavenly Voice in Don Carlos; Sang Mrs Schomberg in the 1970 premiere of Victory by Richard Rodney Bennett; Appearances with the Welsh National Opera, Phoenix Opera, Scottish Opera and in Sofia, Vienna, Düsseldorf, Paris, Zagreb and Johannesburg; English National Opera, 1973, as Sieglinde in The Ring, conducted by Reginald Goodall; US debut, San Francisco, 1974, as Ellen Orford; Sang Countess Vrouskaya in the premiere of Iain Hamilton's Anna Karenina, English National Opera, 1981; Other roles have included Countess Almaviva, Pamina, Agathe, Musetta, Butterfly, Violetta, Eva, the Marschallin, Elizabeth in Gloriana and in Maria Stuarda, Donna Anna, Marzelline, Micaela, Norina, Marguerite, Tosca, Aida and Santuzza; Teacher of Singing. *Recordings include:* Mrs Grosse in The Turn of the Screw; The Ring of the Nibelung, from the London Coliseum. *Address:* c/o English National Opera, St Martin's Lane, London WC2N 4ES, England.

JUNG, Doris; Singer (Dramatic Soprano); b. 5 Jan. 1924, Centralia, Illinois, USA; m. Felix Popper, 3 Nov 1951, 1 s. *Education:* University of Illinois; Mannes College of Music; Vienna Academy of Performing Arts; Student of Julius Cohen, Emma Zador, Luise Helletsgruber and Winifred Cecil. *Career:* Debut: As Vitellia in Clemenza di Tito, Zürich Opera, Switzerland, 1955; Appearances with Hamburg State Opera, Munich State Opera, Vienna State Opera, Royal Opera Copenhagen, Royal Opera Stockholm, Marseille and Strasbourg, Naples Opera Company, Catania Opera Company, Italy, New York City Opera, Metropolitan Opera, and in Minneapolis, Minnesota, Portland, Oregon, Washington DC, and Aspen, Colorado; Soloist, Wagner concert conducted by Leopold Stokowski, 1971; Soloist, Syracuse Symphony, New York, 1981; Voice Teacher, New York City, 1970–. *Address:* 40 W 84th Street, New York, NY 10024, USA.

JUNG, Manfred; Singer (Tenor); b. 9 July 1940, Oberhausen, Germany. *Education:* Studied in Essen with Hilde Wesselmann. *Career:* Bayreuth Youth Festival, 1967, as Arindal in Die Feen by Wagner; Sang in the Bayreuth Festival Chorus, 1970–73; Sang in Dortmund and Kaiserslautern from 1971; Member of the Deutsche Oper am Rhein Düsseldorf from 1977; Bayreuth Festival from 1977, as Tristan, Parsifal and Siegfried (production of Der Ring des Nibelungen, 1983, by John Bury and Peter Hall); Sang in Wagner operas at the Salzburg Easter Festival, under Karajan (Tristan and Parsifal, 1980); Metropolitan Opera debut, 1981; Guest appearances in Zürich, Chicago, Toronto, Vienna; Hamburg, Munich, Barcelona, Cologne, Frankfurt, Lisbon, Rome and Montreal; Other roles include Walther, Florestan, Loge and Siegmund; Sang Herod in Salome at Munich, 1990, Aegisthus in Elektra at the Spoleto Festival; Season 1991/92 as Herod at Barcelona and Valzacchi in Rosenkavalier at Catania; Season 1997–98 as Mime in The Ring, at Kassel. *Recordings include:* Siegfried in The Ring from Bayreuth. *Address:* c/o Hilbert Agentur, Maximilianstr 22, 8000 Munich 22, Germany.

JUNGHÄNEL, Konrad; Lutenist and Musical Director; b. 1953, Germany. *Career:* Appearances as soloist and member of early music ensembles throughout Europe, in the USA, Japan, South America and Africa; Collaborations with René Jacobs as soloist and continuo player in opera performances from the Baroque era and concerts with La Petite Bande, Musica Antiqua Köln, Les Arts Florissants and Tafelmusik; Founded Cantus Cölln 1987, with festival performances at Berne, Stuttgart, Utrecht, Innsbruck and Breslau; Conducted Francesco Cavalli's La Calisto in Cologne and Domenico Mazocchi's La Catena d'Adone in Innsbruck and Antwerp and a scenic production of Monteverdi's Madgrigals throughout Europe; Directed the production of Heinrich Schütz's Was liegt die Stadt so wüste at the Theater Basel, 2000 and at the Sächsischen Staaatsoper Dresden, 2004–(06), Henry Purcell's Evening Hymn, Staatsoper Hannover, 2004 and Rameau's Les Paladins, Basel, 2004; conducted staged production of Bach cantatas at the Hamburg Opera, 2000; Directed Handel's Israel in Egypt at Basle, 2002; Handel's Semele and Monteverdi's L'Incoronazione di poppea, 2003; Repertory centres on Italian and German Renaissance and

Baroque music. Recordings include Lute solos by Silvius Leopold Weiss; Schein's Diletti Pastorali; Rosenmuller's Vespro della beata Vergine; J. S. Bach: Lute Works; J. S. Bach: Motets; H Schütz: Psalmen Davids; Monteverdi: Vespro della beata Vergine. *Honours:* German Critics' Prize, for Weiss lute solos; Numerous Diapason d'Or Awards, 1991–98; Grand Prix du Disque, Académie Charles Cros, 1993; Editors Choice, Gramophone, 1999; Diapason d'Or and Lux du Monde de la Musique for CD Artus tragicus, 2000; Gramophone Award, Cecilia Award, Preis der deutschen Schallplattenkritik (CD, Monteverdi: Selva morale e spirituale), 2002. *Address:* Mittelstrasse 6a, 50321 Brühl, Germany.

JUON, Julia; Singer (mezzo-soprano); b. 28 Nov. 1943, St Gallen, Switzerland. *Education:* Zürich Conservatory. *Career:* sang in opera at St Gallen, 1975–80, Karlsruhe, 1980–83, and Kassel from 1984, notably as Ortrud and as Tina in the European premiere of The Aspern Papers by Dominick Argento; guest appearances as Fricks at Amsterdam and at the Hamburg Staatsoper as the Nurse in Die Frau ohne Schatten, 1989; other roles include Waltraute, Carmen, Agrippina, Donizetti's Leonora, Verdi's Ulrica, Eboli, Amneris and Azucena, Wagner's Kundry, Venus and Brangaene; modern repertoire includes Bartók's Judith, the Priestess in Schoeck's Penthesilea and Catherine in Jeanne d'Arc au Bûcher by Honegger; sang Kabanicha in Katya Kabanova at Basel in 1991 and Kundry at Essen in 1992; Countess Geschwitz in Lulu at Opéra Bastille, Paris, 1998; sang Waltraute and Azucena for Bonn Opera, 2000; Brangaene at Hamburg and Antwerp, 2000–01; concert engagements in Switzerland and Germany, at the Bregenz Festival and in Vienna. *Address:* Staatstheater, Friedrichplatz 15, 34117 Kassel, Germany.

JURINAC, Sena; Singer (soprano); b. 24 Oct. 1921, Travnik, Yugoslavia; m. Dr Josef Lederle. *Education:* Studied with Maria Kostrencic. *Career:* First appearance as Mimi, Zagreb, 1942; Member, Vienna State Opera Company, 1944–83 (last performance as the Marschallin); Now works as voice teacher; Sang at Salzburg Festival from 1947, as Dorabella, Cherubino, Amor in Orpheus, Marzelline in Fidelio, Octavian, the Composer in Ariadne, Mozart's Countess and Elisabeth in Don Carlo; Glyndebourne Festival, 1949–56, as Dorabella, Fiordiligi, Ilia, Cherubino, Donna Elvira, Donna Anna and Leonora in La Forza del Destino; Also sang Strauss's Octavian and Tatiana in Eugene Onegin; Sang in Der Rosenkavalier, Tosca, Iphigénie en Tauride; Numerous tours and recordings. *Honours:* Austrian State Kammersängerin, 1951; Ehrenkreuz dienste um die Republik Österreich, 1967; Ehrenring der Wiener Staatsoper, 1968; Ehrenmitglied der Wiener Staatsoper, 1971. *Address:* c/o State Opera House, Vienna 1, Austria.

JUROWSKI, Vladimir; Russian conductor; *Music Director, Glyndebourne Festival Opera;* b. 1972, Moscow. *Education:* Music Acad., Berlin and Dresden, Germany. *Career:* chief conductor, Sibelius Orchestra, Berlin 1993–96; founder and conductor, United Berlin ensemble, performing modern music; int. debut conducting May Night by Rimsky-Korsakov, Wexford Festival 1995; fmr prin. guest conductor, Orchestra Sinfonica Verdi, Milan; prin. guest conductor Teatro Comunale, Bologna 2001; Music Dir Glyndebourne Festival Opera 2001–; chief prin. guest conductor London Philharmonic Orchestra 2004; has conducted in major venues world-wide, including Metropolitan Opera (New York), Opera Bastille (Paris), Komische Oper (Berlin), Teatro Comunale (Bologna), Teatro Real (Madrid), Royal Opera House (London), Welsh Nat. Opera (Cardiff), ENO (London), Edin. Festival. *Recordings include:* Werther by Massenet. *Current Management:* Stage Door, Via Marconi 71, 40122 Bologna, Italy. *Telephone:* (051) 19984750. *Fax:* (051) 19984779. *E-mail:* info@stagedoor.it. *Website:* www .stagedoor.it.

K

KAASCH, Donald; singer (tenor); b. 19 Dec. 1968, Denver, Colorado, USA. *Education:* Colorado and Northwestern Universities. *Career:* Sang at the Chicago Lyric Opera, 1985–88; European engagements at Florence in 1989 in Idomeneo and at Geneva; Metropolitan Opera in 1989 in the character roles in Les Contes d'Hoffmann and returned for Jacquino in Fidelio and Mozart's Titus; Opéra Bastille in 1991 as Idamante in Idomeneo, Salzburg, 1992 as Argirio in Rossini's Tancredi; Other roles include Mozart's Tamino, Ferrando and Don Ottavio, Count Almaviva, the Prince in Lulu, Rinuccio and Argento's The Voyage of Edgar Allan Poe; Frequent concert performances including Leukippos in Strauss's Daphne at Antwerp, 1998; Sang the Priest in Stravinsky's Persephone at the Festival Hall, London, 1997; Royal Opera debut 1998, in The Golden Cockerel; Sang Gluck's Admète at Amsterdam 1999; Season 2000–01 as Britten's Male Chorus at Lausanne and Mozart's Mitridate in Sydney; Season 2002–03 in Thais at Chicago and in Der fliegende Holländer at Los Angeles. *Address:* c/o IMG Artists, Lovell House, 616 Chiswick High Road, London W4 5RX, England.

KABAIVANSKA, Raina; Singer (Soprano); b. 15 Dec. 1934, Burgas, Bulgaria. *Education:* Studied in Bulgaria and in Italy with Zita Fumagalli. *Career:* Debut: Sofia, 1957, as Titania in Eugene Onegin; Italian debut, 1959, as Nedda; La Scala, 1961, in Beatrice di Tenda by Bellini, with Sutherland; Covent Garden, 1962–64, as Desdemona and Liu; Metropolitan Opera from 1962, Nedda, Mimi, Elisabeth de Valois, Alice Ford, Lisa in The Queen of Spades, and Butterfly; Guest appearances at the Hamburg Staatsoper from 1971; Genoa and Trieste, 1973, as Tosca and Gioconda, Turin, 1973–74, Elena in I Vespri Siciliani and Francesca da Rimini; Paris Opéra debut, 1975, as Leonora in La Forza del Destino; Further engagements in Dallas, Chicago, New Orleans, San Francisco, Buenos Aires and Vienna; Verona Arena, 1978–82, Butterfly and Mimi; Sang Adriana Lecouvreur at Rome, 1989; Returned 1990, as Butterfly and Hanna Glawari in The Merry Widow; Sang the Trovatore Leonora at Parma, 1990; Season 1991/92 as Leonora at the restored Carlo Felice Theatre, Genoa, and Hanna Glawari at Rome; The Governess in The Turn of the Screw at Bologna, 1997; Sang Janáček's Emilia Marty at Naples, 1999; La Voix Humaine by Poulenc at Palermo and Bologna, 2000. *Recordings include:* Il Trovatore, Francesca da Rimini, Madama Butterfly, Fausta by Donizetti; Wagner's Rienzi; Video of Tosca. *Address:* c/o Teatro Comunale, Largo Respighi 1, 40126 Bologna, Italy.

KACZANOWSKI, Andrzej; Double Bass Player; b. 22 April 1955, Białystok, Poland; m. 14 Dec 1974, 2 s., 1 d. *Education:* Chopin Academy of Music, Warsaw, diploma with Honour, 1980, MA, Double Bass Player. *Career:* Debut: Dragonetti Concerto with Bilalystok Philharmonic Orchestra, 1975; Regular appearances as soloist or chamber player with famous orchestras; Warsaw Chamber Orchestra, 1978–84; Salle Pleyel, under K Teutsch, 1980; Chamber Filharmonic, Karol Teutsch conducting, 1980–84; Santa Cecilia, under J Kasprzyk, 1981; Carnegie Hall, under K Teutsch, 1982; Polish Chamber Orchestra with Jerzy Maksymiuk, 1984–85; Camerata Vistula Chamber soloist, 1986; Teatro alla Scala under Delmann; Barbican Centre under Maksymiuk; Teatro alla Scala under Abbado; Akademie der Künste, Berlin, 1992; Warsaw Autumn, Warsaw, 1992; Teacher, Josef Elsner First Music School in Warsaw, 1991–; Played in Spain and Germany in 1994. *Recordings:* Polish Chamber Orchestra, Warsaw; Chamber Philharmonic Orchestra, Bach Keyboard Concerts, 1980; Lutoslawski, Prokofiev and Gorecki, 1990; Schubert's Quintet, op 114, Trout; Dvořák, op 77 for Polish Radio SA. *Honours:* Festivals: Lille 1979, Bordeaux 1980, Bergen, Tivoli, 1981, Cheltenham, 1982, Brighton 1984, Glasgow 1988, Warsaw Autumn, 1985, 1986, 1988 and 1989. *Address:* Pradzynskistr 20a 109, 05-200 Wotomin, Poland.

KAEGI, Dieter; Stage Director; b. 1950, Zürich, Switzerland. *Education:* Musicology and German Literature at Zürich and Paris. *Career:* Assistant Director at English National Opera, 1980; Director of Productions at Aix-en-Provence Festival, 1989; Artistic Director, Opera Ireland; Der Rosenkavalier and Der Freischütz for Seattle Opera; Stagings of Tristan und Isolde at Monte Carlo, Idomeneo and Figaro at Copenhagen, Roméo et Juliette in Geneva and Anna Bolena by Donizetti at Metz; Bartók's Bluebeard's Castle at Strasbourg; Fidelio in Liège and Lady Macbeth of Mtsensk for Opera Ireland; Season 2001–2002 with Der Freischütz at Ulm, Don Carlos in Ireland and Die Entführung in Nancy. *Current Management:* Athole Still International Management, Forresters Hall, 25–27 Westow Street, London, SE19 3RY, England. *Telephone:* (20) 8771-5271. *Fax:* (20) 8768-6600. *Website:* www.atholestill.com.

KAGEL, Mauricio; Argentine composer; b. 21 Dec. 1931, Buenos Aires. *Education:* Univ. of Buenos Aires. *Career:* Artistic Dir Agrupación Nueva Música 1949; co-founder, Cinemathèque Argentine 1950; Dir and Conductor, Teatro Colón, Buenos Aires 1955; emigrated to Germany 1957; f. Kölner Ensemble für Neue Musik, Cologne 1959; Slee Prof. of Composition, State Univ. of New York 1964–65; Visiting Lecturer, Berlin Acad. of Film and TV 1967; Dir Scandinavian Courses for New Music, Gothenburg 1968–69; Dir Courses for New Music, Cologne 1969–75; Prof. of New Music and Theater, Cologne Conservatory 1974–97. *Compositions include:* Música para la Torre 1953, String Sextet 1953, Sur Scène 1959, Journal de théâtre 1960, Le Bruit 1960, Heterophonie 1959, Metapiece 1961, Antithese 1962, Die Frauen 1962, Diaphonie 1962, Phonophonie 1963, Mirum 1965, Match 1965, Tremens 1963, Camera Obscura 1965, Die Himmelsmechanik 1965, Musik für Renaissanceinstrumente 1965, String Quartet 1965, Variaktionen 1967, Kommentar Extempore 1967, Montage 1967, Phantasie 1967, Hallelujah 1968, Der Schall 1968, Acustica 1968, Unter Strom 1969, Ludwig Van 1969, Staatstheater (ballet) 1969, Tactil 1970, Klangwehr 1970, Zwei-Mann-Orchester 1971, Programm, Gasprache mit Kammermusik 1972, Exotica 1972, Variationen ohne Fuge 1973, 1898 1973, Kantrimusik 1975, Mare Nostrum 1975, Bestiarium 1975, Die Umkehrung Amerikas 1976, Variete 1977, An Tasten 1977, Die Erschöpfung der Welt (opera) 1979, Aus Deutschland 1981, Fragen 1982, Nach einer Lektüre von Orwell 1984, La trahison orale 1984, Two Ballads of Guillaume de Machaut 1984, Sankt Bach Passion 1985, Piano Trio 1985, Old/New 1986, A Letter 1986, Quodlibet 1988, Tantz-Schul (ballet) 1988, Osten 1989, Fragende Ode 1989, Nah und Fern 1993, Playback Play 1997, Entführung aus dem Konzertsaal 2000. *Television includes:* Sur Scène 1963, Match 1966, Duo 1968, Tactil 1971, Pas de Cinq 1964, Blue's Blue 1980, Dressur 1985, Repertoire 1989, Die Erschöpfung der Welt 2000. *Honours:* Koussevitzky Prize 1966, Karl Sczuka Prize for play Ein Aufnahmezustand 1969, Scotoni Prize for film Hallelujah, City of Zürich 1969. *Current Management:* c/o Universal Edition, Bösendorferstrasse 12, Postfach 3, 1015 Vienna, Austria.

KAHANE, Jeffrey Alan, BMus; Pianist and Conductor; b. 12 Sept. 1956, Los Angeles, CA, USA; m. Martha Philips 1979, 1 s. *Education:* San Francisco Conservatory of Music. *Career:* Debut as pianist: San Francisco, California, 1973; Soloist, New York and Los Angeles Philharmonics, Pittsburgh, San Francisco and Atlanta Symphonies; Appearances with Cleveland Orchestra, New York, Los Angeles, Rotterdam and Israel Philharmonics, Boston, Chicago, Pittsburgh, San Francisco, Atlanta Symphonies; Soloist in Bernstein's Age of Anxiety at the 1991 Promenade Concerts, London; Music Dir, Santa Rosa Symphony, Los Angeles Chamber Orchestra, Green Music Festival; mem, Piano Faculty, New England Conservatory of Music, Boston. *Recordings:* Works of Gershwin and Bernstein with Yo-Yo Ma; Paul Schoenfield's Four Parables; Strauss' Burleske with the Cincinnati Symphony; Brandenburg Concerti (on harpsichord) with the Oregon Bach Festival Orchestra; Schubert's complete works for violin and piano with Joseph Swensen; Bach's Sinfonias and Partita No. 4 in D Major; Bernstein's Age of Anxiety. *Honours:* Grand Prize, Arthur Rubinstein International Piano Competition, Tel-Aviv, Israel, 1983; 4th Prize, Van Cliburn International Piano Competition, 1981. *Current Management:* IMG Artists, 825 Seventh Avenue, 8th floor, New York, NY 10019, USA. *Telephone:* (212) 774-6774 (office). *Fax:* (212) 246-1596 (office). *E-mail:* akatin@imgworld.com.

KAHLER, Lia; Singer (Mezzo-soprano); b. 1952, USA. *Education:* Studied in Los Angeles, New York and Milan. *Career:* Sang at the Holland Festival, 1982, Detmold, 1983–85, notably as Eboli and Brangaene; Sang at Gelsenkirchen 1985–89, as Laura in La Gioconda, Monteverdi's Ottavia, the Witch and Mother in Hansel und Gretel, and in the premiere of Deinen Kopf, Holofernes by Blumenthaler, 1989; Other roles at Gelsenkirchen and elsewhere in Germany have included Ortrud, Maddalena, Marina in Boris Godunov, Dalila and Baba the Turk in The Rake's Progress; Many concert appearances. *Address:* Musiktheater im Revier, Kennedyplatz, 4650 Gelsenkirchen, Germany.

KAHMANN, Sieglinde; Singer (Soprano); b. 28 Nov. 1937, Dresden, Germany; m. Sigurdur Bjornsson. *Education:* Studied in Stuttgart. *Career:* Debut: Stuttgart Staatsoper 1959, as Aennchen in Der Freischütz; Engaged at the Theater am Gärtnerplatz, Munich, and sang at Hamburg, Vienna, Stuttgart, Leipzig, Karlsruhe and Kassel; Roles have included Mozart's Pamina, Donna Elvira, Countess and Cherubino, Lortzing's Gretchen and Mair, Martha and Musetta; Guest appearances at Lisbon, Strasbourg, Bucharest, Salzburg and Edinburgh, as Micaela, Lisa (Queen of Spades), Marenka (Bartered Bride) and Adele in Fledermaus. *Address:* c/o Stuttgart Staatsoper, Oberer Schlossgarten 6, 7000 Stuttgart, Germany.

KAIN, Timothy, DipMus; Australian classical guitarist; b. 25 Jan. 1951, Braidwood, NSW. *Education:* Canberra School of Music, Royal Northern College of Music, Manchester, and in Alicante, Spain. *Career:* debut,

Purcell Room, 1982; Played all over the world for 20 years; Major tours of the United Kingdom and Australia with John Williams in 1992 and 1996, also Australia in 1996; Leader of Guitar Trek, a quartet playing a family of different sized guitars; Head of the Guitar Department at Canberra School of Music, Australian National University, 1982–; mem, Australian Music Centre. *Compositions:* has commissioned close to 30 new works for guitar, solo, chamber and concerto from Australian composers. *Recordings:* The Mantis and The Moon with John Wiliams; Guitar Trek, music for a guitar family; Guitar Trek II, the family continues; For Flute and Guitar; Music of the Americas with flautist Virginia Taylor. *Publications:* Three Preludes by Richard Vella is the first of a series, published 1998; Black Wattle Caprices, by Ross Edwards, 1999. *Honours:* First prize, Int GTR Competition, Spain, 1977; RNCM Bach Prize, 1979. *Address:* 84 Dryandra Street, O'Connor, ACT 2602, Australia.

KAIPAINEN, Jouni (Ilari); Composer; b. 24 Nov. 1956, Helsinki, Finland; m. Sari-Anne Liljendahl, 9 Sept 1977, 1 s. *Education:* Sibelius Academy of Helsinki, 1975–81. *Career:* Freelance Composer, 1981–. *Compositions:* The Miracle of Konstanz, television opera, 1985–87; Symphony, Opus 20, 1980–85; String Quartets, I 1973; II, 1974; III, 1984; IV, 1994; Ladders To Fire (A Concerto for 2 pianos), 1979; Trios, I, 1983; II, 1986; III, 1987; Cinq poemes de René Char, Opus 12a, for soprano and orchestra, 1978–80. Chamber Music; Vocal Music; Incidental Music; Vernal Concerto for saxophone quartet and orchestra, 1996; Piano Concerto, 1997; Viola Concerto, 1997; Sestetto for ensemble, 1997. *Contributions:* Numerous essays and articles in Finnish magazines, including Finnish Music Quarterly; Ammatti: säveltäjä (Profession: Composer), ed. by R. Nieminen and P. Hako, 1981. *Honours:* UNESCO International Rostrum, The Chosen Work of the Year Prize, 1981; Spurs of Criticism (The most eminent debut of the year) by The Union of Finnish Critics, 1982. *Address:* Martinkyläntie 64, G 35 01660 Vantaa, Finland.

KAISER, Barbara; Conductor; b. 1 June 1947, Bremen, Germany. *Education:* Abitur; Studied in Schulmusik, Violin and Singing, Hochschule für Musik, Freiburg/Breisgau, 1967–73; Studies in Conducting, Hochschule der Künste, Berlin, 1979–85. *Career:* Debut: Guest Conductor, Philharmonisches Staatsorchester, Bremen, 1986; Founding Member, Musikfrauen Berlin, 1978; Manager, several projects with contemporary music of women composers; Manager of series of concerts with contemporary music at Hochschule der Künste Berlin, 1984–96; Neue Musik Berlin in cooperation, 1986; Lecturer at Hochschule der Künste Berlin, 1986–96; Guest Conductor, Philharmonisches Staatsorchester Bremen, Filharmonia Pomorska, Poland and Orchester der Stadt Heidelberg; mem, International Arbeitskreis Frau und Musik; Kulturinstitut Komponistinnen gestern-heute, Heidleberg. *Recordings:* Instrumental and Vocal, Musik von Komponistinnen, 1985; Komponistinnen in Berlin, 1987. *Contributions:* Some interviews on radio, magazines and journals. *Address:* Gneisenaustrasse 94, 10961 Berlin, Germany.

KAKUSKA, Thomas; Violist; b. 25 Aug. 1940, Austria. *Education:* Studied in Vienna, with Edith Steinbauer and Franz Samohyl. *Career:* mem., Wiener Solisten, 1963–67; first violinist, European String Quartet, 1967–81; first leader, Vienna Tonkuenstler Orchestra, 1971–81; mem., Vienna String Trio; Violist of the Alban Berg Quartet, 1981–; Many concert engagements including complete cycle of the Beethoven Quartets in 15 European cities, 1987–88, 1988–89 seasons; Bartók/Mozart cycle in London, Vienna, Paris, Frankfurt, Munich, Geneva, Turin, 1990–91; Annual concert series at the Vienna Konzerthaus and festival engagements world-wide; Associate Artist at the South Bank Centre, London; US appearances San Francisco and New York (Carnegie Hall); also performed as viola soloist: standard repertoire plus world premieres of Lucca Lombardi Viola Concerto, with Koelner Philharmonie; Joji Yuasa and Makoto Moroi at Saitama Arts Theatre; Prof., Univ. for Music, Vienna, 1971–; Guest Prof. for Chamber Music, Hochschule für Musik in Cologne, Germany, 1993–. *Recordings include:* Complete quartets of Beethoven, Brahms, Berg, and Bartók; Late quartets of Mozart and Schubert; Ravel, Debussy and Schumann Quintet; Live recordings from Carnegie Hall (Mozart, Schumann); Konzerthaus in Vienna (Brahms); Opéra-Comique Paris (Brahms); South Bank concerts for the Schubert bicentenary, 1997. *Honours:* Grand Prix du Disque; Deutsche Scallplatenpreis; Edison Prize; Japan grand Prix; Gramophone Magaxine Award. *Current Management:* Intermusica Artists Management, 16 Duncan Terrace, London N1 8BZ, England.

KALABIS, Viktor; Composer; b. 27 Feb. 1923, Cerveny Kostelec, Czechoslovakia; m. Zuzana Ruzickova, 8 Dec 1952. *Education:* Composition, Prague Conservatory and Academy of Arts and Music, 1945–48; Philosophy and Musical Science, Charles University, Prague. *Career:* Editor, Musical Producer, Czech Radio, 1953–72; Full-time Composer, 1972–; mem, Czech Musical Society. *Compositions include:* Orchestral works: 5 symphonies, 1957, 1961, 1971, 1972, 1976; Concerto for large orchestra, 1966; 9 instrumental concertos; 4 compositions for chamber orchestra; Chamber works include: 2 nonets; Spring Whistles, octet for wind, 1979; 2 wind quintets; 7 string quartets; Sonatas for violin and harpsichord, violoncello and piano, clarinet and piano, trombone and piano, violin and piano, 1967–82; 7 string quartets, 1949–93; Solo works include: 3 piano sonatas; 3 pieces for flute; Reminiscences for Guitar, 1979; Four Enigmas for Graham, piano solo, 1989; Several choral works; Five romantic love songs for higher voice and strings, 1977; Two Worlds (Alice in Wonderland), ballet, 1980; Incantations for 13 wind instruments, 1988; Carousel of Life songs for bass and piano, 1989; Strange Pipers for ensemble, 1990; Ludus per 4, for piano quartet, 1996. *Recordings:* Diptych for strings, CD; Chant du Monde. *Honours:* Musical Critics Portrait Prize, 1967; State Prize, 1969; Artist of Merit, 1983; President, Bohuslav Martinů Foundation, 1991; Parent's Choice Award, USA, 1993. *Address:* Slezska 107, 13000 Prague 3, Czech Republic.

KALE, Stuart; Singer (tenor); b. 27 Oct. 1944, Neath, Glamorgan, Wales. *Education:* Studied at the Guildhall School of Music and Drama and at the London Opera Centre. *Career:* Debut: With Welsh National Opera in 1971, as the Prince in the first production by a British company of Berg's Lulu; Sang with English National Opera notably as Don Ottavio and in Jonathan Miller's production of The Mikado; Sang Wagner's Siegfried at Bucharest in 1983 and appeared in the local premiere of Prokofiev's The Fiery Angel for South Australian Opera in 1988; Covent Garden debut 1988, in Manon, returning in 1989 as Bob Boles in Peter Grimes; has sung the Captain in Wozzeck at Strasbourg, 1987, Reggio Emilia, 1989 and Toronto 1990; In 1989 sang in L'incoronazione di Poppea at the Théâtre du Châtelet, Paris, the Drum Major in Wozzeck at Turin and Zinovy Ismailov in Lady Macbeth of the Mstensk District at Nancy, France; Sang Don Eusebio in Rossini's L'Occasione fa il ladro at the 1992 Schwetzingen festival; Sang Shuisky at Montpellier, 1996; Gafforio in Paisiello's Il Re Teodoro in Venezia at Padua, 1998; Season 1999–2000 as Diomedes in Penthesilea by Schoeck, at Lucerne, and the Captain in Wozzeck at La Scala. *Recordings:* Video of Idomeneo (title role) from Drottningholm. *Current Management:* Athole Still International Management, Forresters Hall, 25–27 Westow Street, London, SE19 3RY, England. *Telephone:* (20) 8771-5271. *Fax:* (20) 8768-6600. *Website:* www.atholestill.com.

KALES, Elisabeth; Singer (Soprano); b. 1952, Graz, Austria. *Education:* Studied at the Graz Conservatory. *Career:* Sang at the Graz Opera, 1975–79, Vienna Volksoper from 1979; Sang Papagena in Die Zauberflöte at Salzburg, 1980 and 1986; Bregenz Festival, 1984, as Christel in Zeller's Der Vogelhändler; Other roles have included Millöcker's Laura, and the Fox in The Cunning Little Vixen; Director of the Baden Opera from 1996; Further guest engagements at the Vienna Staatsoper. *Address:* c/o Stadttheater, Theaterplatz 7, 2500 Baden bei Wien, Austria.

KALICHSTEIN, Joseph; Pianist; b. 15 Jan. 1946, Tel-Aviv, Israel. *Education:* Juilliard School with Eduard Steuermann and Ilona Kabos. *Career:* Debut: New York Recital, 1967; Appeared with the New York Philharmonic in a televised performance of Beethoven's 4th Piano Concerto, 1968; European debut with Previn and the London Symphony, 1970; Appearances with Atlanta, Baltimore, Barcelona, Boston, Chicago, Cincinnati, Detroit, Indianapolis, London, National, NHK (Tokyo), Pittsburgh, San Francisco, San Diego, Saint Louis, Seattle, Utah and Vienna symphony orchestras; the Berlin, Helsinki, Israel, London, Los Angeles, Monte Carlo, New York, Oslo, Rotterdam and Stockholm philharmonic orchestras; the Cleveland, Hallé and Minnesota orchestras; and the English, Scottish, Franz Liszt and Saint Paul chamber orchestras; Tours to Australia, Japan and South America; Performances in Piano Trio with Jaime Laredo and Sharon Robinson, 1976–; Brahms series with the Guarneri Quartet in New York, 1983. *Honours:* Young Concert Artist Award, 1967; Winner, Leventritt Competition, 1969. *Current Management:* Harrison/Parrott Ltd, 12 Penzance Place, London, W11 4PA, England. *Telephone:* (20) 7229 9166. *Fax:* (20) 7221 5042. *E-mail:* nicole.rochman@harrisonparrott.co.uk. *Website:* www.harrisonparrott.com.

KALININA, Galina; Singer (Soprano); b. 1951, Russia. *Education:* Studied in Moscow. *Career:* Member of the Bolshoi Opera, Moscow from 1977, notably as Donna Anna, Verdi's Trovatore Leonora, Elisabetta, Desdemona and Amelia (Ballo in Maschera); Tchaikovsky's Tatiana and Lisa and Madama Butterfly; Guest appearances in the West from 1982, notably as Tosca at Stuttgart 1988, and with Scottish Opera, Yaroslavna in Prince Igor at Wiesbaden and Zemfira in a concert performance of Rachmaninov's Aleko at Rome; Season 1987–88, as Tatiana at Buenos Aires, Butterfly in Oslo and Yaroslavna at Verona; Covent Garden 1991, as Tosca; Aida at Buenos Aires, 1996; Turandot at Toronto, 1997; Season 2000 as Lady Macbeth for Oslo Opera and Abigaille at St Margareth. *Recordings:* Fevronia in The Legend of the Invisible City of Kitezh by Rimsky Korsakov.

KALISH, Gilbert; Pianist and Teacher; b. 2 July 1935, New York, USA. *Education:* BA, Columbia Coll., 1956; Columbia University Graduate School of Arts and Sciences, 1956–58; Pupil of Isabelle Vengerova, Leonard Schure and Julius Herford. *Career:* New York Recital debut, 1962; European debut, London, 1962; Subsequent tours of the US, Europe and Australia; Pianist with the Contemporary Chamber Ensemble and the Boston Symphony Chamber Players; Regular accompanist to Jan DeGaetani until 1989; Artist-in-Residence, Rutgers, The State University of New Jersey, 1965–67, Swarthmore College, 1966–72; Head of Keyboard Activities, Chairman of Faculty, 1985–, Tanglewood Music Center, Tanglewood, Massachusetts; Faculty Member, Head of Performance Faculty, State University of New York at Stony Brook, 1970–. *Recordings:* as a soloist chamber player, and accompanist. *Honours:* Paul Fromm Award, University of Chicago for Distinguished Service to the music of our time, 1995. *Address:* c/o Music Department, State University of New York, Stony Brook, NY 11794, USA.

KALJUSTE, Tonu; Choral Director and Conductor; b. 1953, Tallinn, Estonia. *Education:* Studied at the Tallinn and Leningrad Conservatories. *Career:* Lecturer at the Tallinn Conservatory, 1978–81; Conducted works by Mozart, Britten and Weber with Estonian Opera; Founded the Estonian Philharmonic Chamber Choir, 1981; Artistic Director of choral festivals Tallinn '88 and Tallinn '91; Founded the Tallinn Chamber Choir, 1992; Founded the Tallinn Chamber Orchestra, 1993; Principal Conductor of the Swedish Radio Choir, from 1994; Guest conductor with choir and orchestras in Europe, Australia and North America; Has featured contemporary Estonian composers and concert series of Bach and other Baroque composers; Principal Conductor of the Netherlands Chamber Choir, 1998–; Concurrently Principal Conductor of the Estonian Philharmonic Chamber Choir and the Tallinn Chamber Orchestra. *Recordings:* Forgotten Peoples by Veljo Tormis, 1992; Te Deum by Arvo Pärte, 1993; Vespers Op 37 by Sergei Rachmaninov, 1995; Requiem by Alfred Schnittke and Miserere by Henryk Gorecki, 1995; Crystallisatio by Erkki-Sven Tüür, 1996; Casting a Spell by Veljo Tormis, 1996; Arvo Pärt's Litany, 1997, Beatus, 1997, Kanon Pokajanen, 1998; Psalms of Repentance by Alfred Schnittke, 1999. *Honours:* Nomination at 1995 Grammy Awards, for Best Choral Performance; The State Award of the Republic of Estonia, 1997; The Best Musician of Estonia, 1998; The ABC Music Award to Tonu Kaljuste and The Swedish Radio Choir for the year 1998. *Address:* Uus Str 22-5, Tallinn 10111, Estonia.

KALLISCH, Cornelia; Singer (Mezzo-soprano); b. 1955, Marbach am Neckar, Germany. *Education:* Studied in Stuttgart and Munich with Josef Metternich in Cologne. *Career:* Sang at first as Lieder recitalist, then sang in opera at Gelsenkirchen and elsewhere from 1984; Roles have included Orpheus, Octavian, the Composer in Ariadne auf Naxos, Monteverdi's Nero, Sesto in La Clemenza di Tito, (Ludwigsburg 1983–84), and Dorabella; Sang Cornelia in a concert performance of Tito at the Grosses Festspielhaus Salzburg, 1991; Arsace in Semiramide and Clairon in Capriccio at Zürich, 1992; Lieder recitals and concerts at Berlin, Vienna, Stuttgart and Frankfurt and in France and Italy; Performances of Wagner's Brangaene in concert with the Pittsburgh Symphony Orchestra and Kundry at Brussels, 1998; Bartók's Judith at Zürich, 1996; Season 1999–2000 as Paulina in the premiere of Wintermärchen by Boesmans at Brussels, and as soloist in the premiere of St Luke Passion by Rihm, at Stuttgart. *Recordings include:* Le Roi David by Honegger; Bach's Christmas Oratorio; Mozart's Requiem; Die Meistersinger by Wagner; F Schmidt, Das Buch mit sieben Siegeln; Klavierlieder by O Schoek; C Franck's Les Béatitudes. *Address:* Kunstler Sekretanat am Gasteig, Rosenheimer strasse 52, 81669 Munich, Germany.

KALMAR, Magda; Singer (Soprano); b. 4 March 1944, Budapest, Hungary. *Education:* Department of Singing, Béla Bartók Conservatory, Budapest. *Career:* Budapest State Opera, 1969–; Frequent performer in Hungary's concert halls and on Hungarian radio and television; Guest Performer at numerous operas including Austria, Belgium, Cuba, Czechoslovakia, Teatro la Fenice, Italy, Berlin, Leningrad, Stockholm and Paris; Roles include Mozart's Blondchen, Despina and Cherubino, Verdi's Oscar, Adele in Die Fledermaus, Don Pasquale and Norina by Donizetti, Adina in L'Elisir d'amore, Mozart's Pamina, Rossini's Rosina, Alban Berg's Lulu, Sophie in Der Rosenkavalier and Gilda in Rigoletto; Sang at Budapest 1987, in the premiere of Szokolay's Ecce Homo. *Recordings:* Has made numerous recordings including Haydn's Il Ritorno di Tobia, Rossini's Mosè in Egitto and Dittersdorf's oratorio Esther; Motets. *Honours:* Grand Prix du Disque, 1975, 1977; 1st Prize, International Rostrum for Young Performing Artists, Bratislava, 1972; Scholarship, Budapest State Opera, 1967. *Address:* c/o Hungarian State Opera House, Népöztarsasag utja 22, 1061 Budapest, Hungary.

KALT, Frederic; Singer (Tenor); b. 1963, Utah, USA. *Education:* Studied in Anchorage, Alaska. *Career:* Debut: New York City Opera, 1987, as

Faust in Mefistofele; Puerto Rico, 1987, as Don José; Sang in Europe from 1991, notably Bacchus at Karlsruhe; Des Grieux in Manon Lescaut at La Scala and Otello at Cologne, 1996; Vienna Staatsoper from 1992, as Calaf, Cavaradossi and Verdi's Manrico; Other roles include Samson, Paolo in Francesca da Rimini (Bregenz, 1995), Pinkerton and Erik in Der fliegende Holländer (Los Angeles, 1995); Apollo in Daphne by Strauss at Santa Fe, 1996; Concerts include Verdi Requiem at Carnegie Hall. *Address:* c/o Santa Fe Opera, PO Box 2408, Santa Fe, NM 87504, USA.

KALUDOV, Kaludy; Singer (Tenor); b. 1953, Varna, Bulgaria. *Education:* Studied at Sofia Conservatory with Jablenska, graduating in 1976. *Career:* Member of the Sofia Opera from 1978; Guest engagements in Europe and North America, including Dimitri in Boris Godunov at Houston and Chicago, conducted by Abbado; Sang Faust in Mefistofele at Lisbon 1990, Alvaro in La Forza del Destino at Poznan, 1991; Riccardo (Ballo in Maschera) at Genoa 1991, Puccini's Des Grieux at Trieste and Radames at Tel-Aviv, 1992; Manrico in Trovatore at Salzburg 1992, Deutsche Oper Berlin 1992 and 1993, Wiener Staatsoper, 1994; Puccini's Des Grieux at La Scala, Milan, 1992 and at Palermo, 1993; Foresto in Attila at Wiener Staatsoper, 1984 and at La Scala 1991 (conducted by Riccardo Muti) and RAI Video; Singer in Rosenkavalier at Wiener Staatsoper, 1990 and at Deutsche Oper Berlin 1993, Staatsoper Berlin, 1992; Don Carlo at Bayerische Staatsoper, Munich 1993, National Opera, Sofia 1988, Madrid 1986; Requiem, G Verdi at London 1983 at Houston 1992, Tel-Aviv with Israel Philharmonic Orchestra conducted by Zubin Mehta; Radames in Aida at Staatsoper Berlin 1993, Finland 1994 and Philadelphia, 1996; Sang Alvaro at Savonlinna, 1998. *Recordings:* Golitsin in Khovanschchina and Vladimir in Prince Igor, with forces of the Sofia Opera conducted by Emil Tchakarov; Janáček's Glagolitic Mass with Charles Dutoit, Montreal, Decca, 1991; Rachmaninov's The Bells with Charles Dutoit, Philadelphia, Decca, 1992; Puccini's Des Grieux (Manon Lescaut) with BRT Philharmonic Orchestra, Brussels (conducted by Alexander Rahbari), Naxos, 1992. *Address:* Sreniawitow 7 m 59, 03-188 Warsaw, Poland.

KALUZA, Stefania; Singer (Mezzo-soprano); b. 1950, Katowice, Poland. *Education:* Studies in Wroclaw and Vienna with Hans Hotter and Anton Dermota. *Career:* Debut: Opera, Wroclaw; Sang in Warsaw and Poznan; Also at the Landestheater Salzburg from 1984, and made guest appearances at the Vienna Staatsoper, Bregenz Festival and Brussels (in The Cunning Little Vixen); Versailles Festival, 1989, as Bersi in Andrea Chénier, Düsseldorf 1989, as Amneris; Appearances with the Zürich Opera from 1988, as Marcellina in Figaro, Martha in Mefistofele, Pamela in Fra Diavalo and Larina in Eugene Onegin, 1991; Sang Preziosilla at Zürich, 1992; Other roles include Dorabella, Frau Fluth, Ulrica and Rosina; Concert engagements in Poland, Hungary, Italy and Russia; Sang Amneris at San Diego, 1996; Season 1999–2000 at Zürich as Wagner's Venus, Enrichetta in I Puritani and Verdi's Maddalena. *Recordings include:* Frau Litumlei in Zemlinsky's Kleider Machen Leute. *Honours:* Winner, Belvedere International Competition, Vienna, 1983. *Address:* c/o Opernhaus Zürich, Falkenstrasse 1, 8008 Zürich, Switzerland.

KAMBASKOVIC, Rastislav, MA; professor of theory and music analysis; b. 20 June 1939, Prokuplje, Yugoslavia; m. (divorced); one s. one d. *Education:* Acad. of Music, Belgrade; diplomas in theory of music, composition. *Career:* debut, Serious Variation for Violins, Belgrade, 1965; Ed., Ed.-in-Chief, Chamber and Vocal, Symphonic Music, 1964–88; Chief Admin., Belgrade Radio-Television Symphony Orchestra, 1970–76; Prof. of Theory and Music Analysis, Theory Dept, Faculty of Music, Belgrade, 1988–, Head, Theory Dept, 1992–. *Compositions:* Solo Instrumental Music: Violin and Piano Sonata in G, 1964; Sonata for Two Violins, 1975; Six Piano Preludes, 1991; Chamber Music: Serious Variations for Flute and String Orchestra, 1966; Wood Wind Quintet, 1967; Piano Trio, 1975; Kumb Brass Wind Quintet, 1980; Pester Sketches for 14 Flutes, 1988; Four Harp Sonata, 1991; Jefimia Lamentoso for Cello and String Orchestra, 1993. *Publications:* Interaction—Diatonic and Chromatic in Prokofiev's Symphonies, 1992. *Honours:* Belgrade Music Festival Award, 1974; Serbian Asscn of Composers Awards, 1974, 1975, 1982, 1983; Belgrade Radio-Television Award, 1982. *Address:* 109 Nova 22, 11060 Belgrade, Serbia and Montenegro.

KAMENIKOVA, Valentina (Jurijevna); Pianist; b. 20 Dec. 1930, Odessa, Russia; m. Jaroslav Kamenik, 1954, 2 s. *Education:* Odessa Music High School; Prague Academy of Arts. *Career:* Prague Spring Festival; Salzburg Festival; Concerts in West Berlin, London, Madrid, Vienna, Palma de Mallorca; Chopin Festival in Polensa; Concert Tour, Europe; Professor, Prague Academy of Arts; mem, Jury Member, International Piano Competitions. *Recordings:* Tchaikovsky, Great Sonata and Dumka; Rachmaninov, Piano Concerto No. 1; Rhapsody on Paganini Theme; Chopin, Ballades; Mazurkas; Beethoven, Piano Sonatas No. 4 and No. 32; Tchaikovsky, Piano Concerto No. 1; Mozart, Sonatas No. 11 and 12; Haydn, 4 Piano Concertos; Liszt, Sonata in B Minor; Mephisto Waltz; Brahms, Sonata No. 1; Rhapsodies; Liszt, Piano

Concertos No. 1 and 2; Prokofiev, Sonatas No. 1 and 3. *Honours:* Prize Supraphon for Recording of Tchaikovsky Piano Concerto No. 1, 1973; Wiener Flotenuhr, Preis der Mozartgeminde, Wien. *Address:* Cechovo nam 9, 101 00 Prague, Czech Republic.

KAMINKOVSKY, Rimma; Violinist; b. 1940, Russia. *Education:* Studied in Odessa and Warsaw, at Tel-Aviv from 1969 and in the USA with Samuel Ashkenazi. *Career:* Teacher at the Rubin Academy of Music in Jerusalem, former co-leader of the Jerusalem Symphony Orchestra; Member of the Israel Philharmonic, with appearances as soloist; Co-Founder, Jerusalem String Trio, 1977, performing in Israel and Europe from 1981; Repertoire includes String Trios by Beethoven, Dohnányi, Mozart, Reger, Schubert and Taneyev, Piano Quartets by Beethoven, Brahms, Dvořák, Mozart and Schumann; Concerts with Radu Lupu and Daniel Adni.

KAMINSKY, Laura; Composer; b. 28 Sept. 1956, New York, USA. *Education:* Studied at Oberlin College and City College of New York. *Career:* Co-founder in 1980 of the ensemble, Musicians' Accord; Artistic Director of New York Town Hall, 1988–92. *Compositions include:* String Quartet, 1977; Duo for Flute and Percussion, 1982; Steepletop Dances for Oboe and Percussion, 1984; Proverbs Of Hell for Soprano, Marimba and Piano, 1989; Triftmusik for Piano, 1991; Whitman Songs for Baritone and Piano, 1992. *Address:* c/o ASCAP, ASCAP Building, 1 Lincoln Plaza, New York, NY 10023, USA.

KAMMERLOHER, Katharina; Singer (Mezzo-Soprano); b. 16 Nov. 1968, Munich. *Education:* Studied with Mechthild Böhme in Detmold; since 1998 with Vera Rozsa in London. *Career:* Member of the Staatsoper, Berlin from 1993, as Rosina, Costanza in Haydn's L'isola disabitata, Suzuki, as Meg Page under Claudio Abaddo, Mélisande under Michael Gielen, Octavian under Philippe Jordan. Under Daniel Barenboim she sang Magdalene, Wellgunde, Zerlina and Dorabelle in the Doris Dörrie-Production of Così fan tutte; Salzburg debut, Lulu, 1995; Schwetzingen Festival 1997, Anna in Cavalli's Didone, 1997; Concerts include Ravel's Shéhérazade, Kantscheli's Lamento (with Gidon Kremer, violin) and Beethoven's Ninth Symphony with Daniel Barenboim, Bach Cantatas under René Jacobs, Elijah with Wolfgang Sawallisch, Berlioz's Romeo with Luisi, Orchesterlieder by Schönberg in Munich and Vienna 2001 and Le Visage Nuptial by Boulez (Proms, London and Edinburgh 2001) both with Boulez; Tour of Japan with the Berlin State 2002; Second Lady in Magic Flute and Mozart Requiem at Salzburg, 2002; Anita in West Side Story with Kent Nagano, March 2003; Debut as Komponist in Ariadne auf Naxos with Fabia Luisi in Berlin, June 2003. *Recordings include:* Elektra (Teldec); Haydn's L'isola disabitata; Bach Cantatas (Harmonia Mundi); DVD of Così fan tutte (Barenboim/ Dörrie); DVD of Otello (Barenboim/ Flimm). *Address:* c/o Deutsche Staatsoper Berlin, Unter den Linden 9–11, 10117 Berlin, Germany.

KAMMINGA, Martin; Organist; b. 23 Dec. 1933, Muiden, Netherlands; m. Renske van der Hauw, 27 August 1957, 2 s., 1 d. *Education:* Organ with Piet Kee, Choral Conducting with Frans Moonen, Orchestral Conducting with Anton Kersjes, Amsterdam Conservatory. *Career:* Organist, live and on radio, in major churches and cathedrals in Netherlands and France; Conductor, Royal Christian Choral Society, Amsterdam, 1967; Conductor, numerous major works for large orchestra, choir and soloists, Concertgebouw Amsterdam; Director, Hilversum Conservatory of Music, 1979–98; Chair and jury member, organ and choral conducting examinations, Conservatorium van Amsterdam, 1999–; mem, Royal Netherlands Society of Organists. *Honours:* Conductor of the Year, City of Amsterdam, 1981; Choir of the Year, City of Amsterdam, 1983; Ridder in de Orde van Oranje Nassau, on the 40th anniversary as a musician, Concertgebouw Amsterdam, 1999. *Address:* Prinses Beatrixlaan 12, 1381 AH Weesp, Netherlands.

KAMNITZER, Peter; Violist and College Professor; b. 27 Nov. 1922, Berlin, Germany. *Education:* Studied at the Juilliard and Manhattan Schools, New York. *Career:* Co-founded the La Salle String Quartet at the Juilliard School, 1949; Many concerts featuring modern composers and the quartets of Beethoven; European debut 1954; Composers who have written for the ensemble include, Hans Erich Apostel, Earle Brown, Henri Pousseur, Mauricio Kagel, György Ligeti, Penderecki and Witold Lutoslawski; Quartet-in-Residence, Colorado College 1949–53, the Quartet-in-Residence and Professor, Cincinnati College-Conservatory of Music; Quartet disbanded 1988. *Recordings include:* Works by Berg, Schoenberg, Webern and Zemlinsky; Beethoven's Late Quartets. *Address:* c/o Cincinnati College-Conservatory of Music, Cincinnati, OH 45221, USA.

KAMP, Harry van der; Singer (Bass); b. 1947, Kampen, Netherlands. *Education:* Studied with Alfred Deller, Pierre Bernac, Max von Egmond and Herman Woltman. *Career:* Appearances in solo recitals and in oratorios; Conductors include Nikolaus Harnoncourt, Gustav Leonhardt and Ton Koopman; Leading parts in operas by Monteverdi, Handel, Mozart, Pergolesi and Rossini in Milan, Venice and elsewhere

in Europe; Engagements at the Berlin, Carinthian, Flanders, Spoleto and Holland Festivals; Founder and Director of the Dutch vocal ensemble Gesualdo Consort Amsterdam; Member and Artistic Adviser of Netherlands Chamber Choir; Guest Teacher at the Early Music Academy in Bremen and Antwerp; Sang in the Towards Bach concert series on London's South Bank, Aug 1989; Sang in Cesti's L'Orontea at the 1990 Innsbruck Festival of Ancient Music; Season 1999–2000 as Valeso in Handel's Theodora at Göttingen, and in the premiere of Rêves d'un Marco Polo by Claude Vivier, at Amsterdam. *Recordings include:* Le Testament de François Villon, by Ezra Pound. *Honours:* Edison Prize, for Ezra Pound Recording. *Address:* c/o De Netherlandse Opera, Waterlooplein 22, 1011 PG Amsterdam, Netherlands.

KAMPE, Anja; Soprano; b. 1968, Germany. *Career:* Many appearances in opera throughout Germany and elsewhere in Europe, notably in Rossini's Il Turco in Italia and as Fiordiligi in Così fan tutte; Also sings songs by Bizet and Wolf (Spanisches Liederbuch); Contestant in the 1995 Cardiff Singer of the World Competition. *Address:* c/o Via Alfieri No. 9, Cento (Fe) 44042, Italy.

KAMPEN, Bernhardt Anthony van; viol player, violone player and double bassist; b. 4 March 1943, Bushey, Hertfordshire, England; m. Julia Henriette Bockhacker 1991; one d. *Education:* Hornsey College of Art, Guildhall School of Music. *Career:* Art Editor, Aldus Books, 1964–66; Founder Member, New BBC Orchestra (later Academy of the BBC), 1966; Principal Bass, New BBC Orchestra, 1967–68; Studied with Josef Racz, solo-contrabassist in Dublina nd Bournemouth, 1966–67; Studied with Prof. František Pošta, solo-contrabassist at the Czech Philharmonic Orchestra, 1969; Freelance in London with London Symphony Orchestra, Royal Philharmonic Orchestra, and others; BBC Symphony Orchestra, 1972–78; Studied the Viol with Alison Crum and Mark Caudle, 1983–85; Freelance Musician and Artist, Composer and Conductor, viols, violone, and Baroque and Classical double-bass with various early music groups; Teacher; Pianist; Harpsichordist. *Recordings:* With BBC Symphony Orchestra, Academy of Ancient Music, London Classical Players, City of London Sinfonia, Hanover Band, London Sinfonietta and many others; Founder and Director, 'Harmonie Universelle'. *Address:* Harmonie Universelle, Heinrich-Krapoth-Str 4, 51647 Gummersbach/Hülsenbusch, Germany. *Telephone:* (2261) 28067. *Fax:* (2261) 28067.

KAMU, Okko; Conductor; b. 7 March 1946, Helsinki, Finland. *Education:* Violin studies with Väinö Arjava from 1949 and with Professor Onni Suhonen at the Sibelius Academy, Helsinki, 1952–67. *Career:* Leader of the Suhonen Quartet, 1964; Leader of the Finnish National Opera Orchestra, 1966–69; Conducted Britten's The Turn of the Screw in Helsinki, 1968; Guest Conductor, Swedish Royal Opera, 1969; Chief Conductor, Finnish Radio Symphony Orchestra, 1971–77; Music Director, Oslo Philharmonic, 1975–79; Music Director, Helsinki Philharmonic, 1981–88; Principal Conductor, Dutch Radio Symphony, 1983–86; Principal Guest Conductor, City of Birmingham Symphony Orchestra, 1985–88; Principal Conductor, Sjaelland Symphony Orchestra (Copenhagen Philharmonic), 1988–89; Guest engagements with the Berlin Philharmonic, Suisse Romande Orchestra, Vienna Symphony Orchestra and orchestras in the USA, Far East, Australia, South America and Europe; Conducted the premieres of Sallinen's operas The Red Line and The King Goes Forth to France; Metropolitan Opera, 1983, US premiere of The Red Line; Covent Garden, 1987, in the British premiere of The King Goes Forth to France; Principal Conductor of the Helsingborg Symphony Orchestra, 1991–2000; Music Director of the Finnish National Opera, 1996–2000; Principal Guest Conductor, Singapore Symphony Orchestra, 1995–2001 and principal Guest Conductor of Lausanne Chamber Orchestra, 1999–2002. *Recordings:* About 70 recordings for various labels; Sallinen's Shadows, Cello Concerto and 5th Symphony. *Honours:* Winner, 1st Herbert von Karajan Conductors' Competition, Berlin, 1969; Member of the Royal Swedish Academy of Music. *Address:* Villa Arcadia, C/Mozart 7, Rancho Domingo, 29639 Benalmadena Pueblo, Spain.

KANAWA, Dame Kiri (see Te Kanawa, Dame Kiri)

KANCHELI, Giya (Georgy); Georgian composer; b. 10 Aug. 1935, Tbilisi; s. of Alexander Kancheli and Agnessa Kancheli; m. Valentina Djikia; one s. one d. *Education:* Tbilisi State Conservatory with I. Tuskia. *Career:* Prof. Tbilisi Conservatory 1970–90; Music Dir Rustaveli Drama Theatre 1971–; First Sec. Georgian Composers' Union 1984–89; Composer in Residence, Berlin (German Academic Exchange Service) 1991–92; Composer in Residence, Royal Flemish Philharmonic Orchestra, Antwerp 1995–96. *Compositions include:* symphonies: First 1967, Second 1970, Third 1973, Fourth (in Memoriam Michelangelo) 1975, Fifth 1977, Sixth (In Memory of Parents) 1980, Seventh (Epilogue) 1986; other symphonic works: Mourned by the Wind for orchestra and viola 1989, Lament (in memory of Luigi Nono), for violin, soprano and orchestra 1995; opera: Music for the Living 1984; chamber works: Life Without Christmas 1989–90 (cycle of four works for chamber ensembles), Magnum Ignotum, for wind ensemble and tape 1994, Exil, for soprano, small ensemble and tape 1994; music to plays by Shakespeare, including King Lear, Richard III and other productions of Rustaveli Drama Theatre, incidental music. *Honours:* USSR State Prize 1976, USSR People's Artist 1988, State Prize of Georgia 1982, Nika Prize for film music 1987, Triumph Prize Moscow 1998. *Address:* Tovstonogov str. 6, 380064 Tbilisi, Georgia; Consience Straat 14, 2018 Antwerp, Belgium. *Telephone:* (3) 295-03-39 (Tbilisi); (3) 230-85-53 (Antwerp).

KANG, Dong-Suk; Violinist; b. 28 April 1954, Seoul, Republic of Korea; m. Martine Schittenhelm 1983, 1 s., 1 d. *Education:* Juilliard School, 1967–71; The Curtis Institute of Music, Diploma, 1975. *Career:* Solo appearances with orchestras of Philadelphia, Cleveland, St Louis, San Francisco, National Symphony, Montreal, Stuttgart Philharmonic, Munich Philharmonic, Orchestre national de France, Royal Philharmonic, Philharmonia, BBC Orchestras, Birmingham, Hallé, Scottish National, Bournemouth, Northern Sinfonia, London Mozart Players; Promenade Concerts London 1987 (Glazunov Concerto), 1990 (Sibelius) and 1991 (Tchaikovsky); Season 1992–93 included tour to Japan and concerts throughout England. *Recordings:* Sibelius Violin Concerto with Orchestre National de Belgique, G Octors Conducting; J Fontyn Violin Concerto (DG); Franck and Lekeu Violin Sonatas with Pascal Devoyon Piano, (RGIP); Nielsen Violin Concerto, Göteborg Orchestra, M W Chung Conducting, (BIS), 1987; Elgar Concerto (Polish National Radio Symphony/Leaper). *Honours:* San Francisco Symphony Foundation Competition, 1971; Merriweather Post Competition, 1971; Carl Flesch Competition, 1974; Montreal Competition, 1975; Queen Elizabeth Competition, 1976. *Address:* 23 rue Daumesnil, 9430 Vincennes, France.

KANG, Philip; singer (bass); b. 10 April 1948, Seoul, Republic of Korea. *Education:* studied in Seoul and Berlin. *Career:* sang small roles at the Deutsche Oper Berlin from 1976; engagements at Wuppertal, Kiel and Nuremberg, Nationaltheater Mannheim from 1986; roles have included Sarastro, Rocco, Kaspar, Verdi's Sparafucile, Ramphis, Philip II, Ferrando and Padre Guardiano, Wagner's Daland, Pogner, Mark, King Henry and Gurnemanz; Sang in Italy from 1982, Rodolfo in Sonnambula at Toulouse 1983, Lisbon 1984, as Attila, Sarastro at the Théâtre des Champs Elysées, 1987; American engagements at New York and Philadelphia, European at Madrid, Rome, Frankfurt (as Rocco) and Cologne, as Rossini's Basilio; Théâtre de la Monnaie Brussels as Pimen in Boris Godunov and as Antonios in Stephen Climax by Hans Zender, 1990; Bayreuth Festival 1987–92, as Fafner, Hagen and Hunding; Season 1999–2000 as Verdi's King Philip at the Komische Oper, Berlin, and as Fafner and Hunding at Bayreuth. *Honours:* Mario del Monaco Competition winner 1979. *Address:* c/o Théâtre Royale de la Monnaie, 4 Leopoldstrasse, 1000 Brussels, Belgium.

KANGA, Skaila; Harpist; b. 8 Jan. 1946, Bombay, India; Divorced, 2 s., 2 d. *Education:* Royal Academy of Music, Junior Exhibitioner, 1959–64; Full-time Student, 1964–66; Studied Piano with Professor Vivian Langrish and Harp with Professor Tina Bonifacio. *Career:* BBC Concert Orchestra and Freelance with regional and major London orchestras; Solo career includes concertos and broadcasts as well as numerous commercial recordings with such artists as Sutherland, Domingo, Pavarotti, Kiri te Kanawa and composers John Williams, Richard Rodney Bennett, Michel Legrand; Performed the Ravel Introduction and Allegro at the Proms, 4th time, 1994; Michael Tippett's 90th Birthday Celebrations, Barbican Hall, 1994; Fauré and the French Connection, festival in Manchester, 1995; Head of Harp, Royal Academy of Music; mem, PRS; BASCA; MCPS. *Compositions include:* Les saisons de la harpe, for solo harp; British Folk Songs Vol. I for flute and harp; Miniatures Bks I and II, harp duets for flute and harp; American Sketches for clarinet (or flute) and harp; Cadenzas for Mozart Concerto for flute and harp; all published by Alaw at www.alawmusic.ndo.co.uk. *Recordings include:* 3 Chamber works of Arnold Bax for Hyperion the Elegiac Trio, The Harp Quintet and the Nonet; French Chamber Music with Academy of St Martins; 2 Solo Albums with Tommy Reilly; Mozart Flute and Harp Concerto, City of London Sinfonia; Bax Chamber Music, Nash Ensemble. *Honours:* LRAM, 1966; ARAM, 1990; FRAM, 1994. *Address:* c/o Head of Harp, Royal Academy of Music, Marylebone Road, London NE1 5HT, England.

KANI, Wasfi, OBE, BMus; British violinist and conductor and opera director; *Chief Executive, Grange Park Opera;* b. 1956, London. *Education:* Univ. of Oxford. *Career:* played violin in Nat. Youth Orchestra; fmr programmer and designer financial computer systems, London; studied conducting with Sian Edwards 1980s; est. computer consultancy 1986–93; f. Pimlico Opera (touring co.) 1989, productions staged in banks, hosps, country houses, prisons (performance of Sweeney Todd was inspiration for BBC TV film Tomorrow La Scala 1991); Chief Exec. Garsington Opera 1992–97; cr. Grange Park rural opera festival, Hants. 1997, Chief Exec. 1997–, performances of Rinaldo, Eugene Onegin, I Capuletti e I Montecchi 2001, The Mikado, Iolanthe 2003. *Address:* General Administration, Grange Park Opera, 5

Chancery Lane, London, EC4A 1BU, England (office). *Telephone:* (20) 7320-5588 (office). *Fax:* (20) 7320-5429 (office).

KANKA, Michal; Cellist; b. 23 May 1960, Prague, Czechoslovakia; m. 1982, 2 d. *Education:* Prague Conservatory and Academy of Performing Arts, University of Southern California. *Career:* Debut: Dvořák Concerto with Czech Philharmonic Orchestra, 1983; Regular appearances with Czech Orchestras, 1982–; Foreign tours to Europe, America, Japan and Australasia, 1982–; Member of the Prazak Quartet, 1986–; Berlin debut with RIAS, 1987; Regular concerts in Salzburg, Munich, London, Amsterdam, Milan, Tokyo and Sydney; Official soloist, Prague radio orchestra, 2003–. *Recordings:* Chopin, Sonata; Stravinsky's Italian Suite, 1984; Schubert's Sonata in C, 1989; Franck, Sonata, 1989; Mozart's Concertone with S Accardo, 1990; Martinů, 3 Sonatas, 1991; Beethoven, Mozart and Janáček works with Prazak Quartet, 1989–91; Vivaldi, 7 Cello Concertos, 1993; Complete works for cello and orchestra by B Martinů, 2 CDs, 1995; Boccherini, 7 Sonatas, 1998; Myslivecek, 6 Sonatas, world premiere recording, 1999; Rubinstein: Complete set for cello/piano; Haydn Cello Concertos. *Honours:* Laureate, Tchaikovsky Competition in Moscow, 1982; 1st Prize, Prague Spring Competition, 1983; Winner, Cello International Competition, ARD Munich, 1986; Soloist of the State Philharmony Brno, 1995; Diapason D'or, Chock de la Musique, Télérama, 1995. *Address:* Peckova 17, Karlin, 18600 Prague 8, Czech Republic.

KANN, Hans; Austrian pianist, composer and professor of piano; b. 14 Feb. 1927, Vienna; m. Kue Hee Ha 1953; one s. one d. *Education:* Vienna Music Academy, studied piano with Bloch, Göllner, Wührer, Schulhof, composition with Lechthaler, Polnauer. *Career:* debut in Brahmssaal, Vienna, 1946; Concerts in whole of Europe, Russia, Asia, China (3 concert tours), South America and USA, 1946–; Professor at Ueno University of Arts, 1955–58; big concerts in Japan, 1955–58, 1960, 1972, 1974, 1976, 1980–86; Professor at the Hochschule für Musik, 1977–95. *Compositions:* Sonatina for piano; Abschnitt; 10 Stücke ohne Bassschlüssel; Fingerübungen; Concertino; Chamber Music; Music for Television; Experimental Music. *Publications include:* Sonatina; Abschnitt 37; Tägliche Fingerübungen für Pianisten; Models; 4 Stücke für Blockflöte und Klavier; Piano enso oboegaki, 1987; Pianists Memories; contrib. to Österreichische Musikzeitung; Gendai Ongaku (Tokyo). *Address:* Sonnenfelsgasse 11/14, Vienna 1010, Austria.

KANNEN, Günter von; Singer (Bass-Baritone); b. 22 March 1940, Rheydt, Germany. *Education:* Studied Philology and History and then Voice and Music with Paul Lohmann and Franziska Martienssen. *Career:* Sang first at the Pfalztheater Kaiserslautern; subsequently member of the troupe in Bonn and Karlsruhe, and from 1979–90 Principal Bass at the Zürich Opera; since 1992, at the Staatsoper in Berlin; Guest appearances in Cologne, Hamburg, Deutsche Oper Berlin, Washington DC, Vienna, Brussels, Dresden, Amsterdam, Paris Châtelet, with NHK Symphony Tokyo (Pizarro under Ferdinand Leitner), Israel Philharmonic (Doktor in Wozzeck under Daniel Barenboim), Chicago Symphony Orchestra (Klingsor in Parsifal); Sang at the Festivals of Santa Fe, Salzburg, Drottningholm, Schwetzingen, Aix-en-Provance, Lucerne; From 1988–92, Alberich in the Bayreuth Festival's Ring cycle, conducted by Daniel Barenboim and produced by Harry Kupfer; Sang also Klingsor at Bayreuth, (conductor James Levine); Alberich at both Berlin Opera Houses and at Hamburg State Opera; Alberich in the Bayreuth Millennium Cycle 2000, conductor Giuseppe Sinopoli, producer Jürgen Flimm; Other important roles are Hans Sachs (Meistersinger); Ochs Von Lerchenau (Rosenkavalier), La Roche (Capriccio); Cardillac; Sang Alberich in Harry Kupfer's production of The Ring at the Berlin Staatsoper, 1996; Sang Morosus in Die schweigsame Frau by Strauss, Dresden, 1998; Season 2000–01 as the Doctor in Wozzeck at La Scala and Falstaff in Dresden, Alberich at Bayreuth and the Berlin Staatsoper. *Recordings include:* Lebendig Begraben by Schoeck (Atlantis); Bartolo in Nozze di Figaro (Barenboim); Klingsor in Parsifal (Barenboim/Berlin Philharmonic); Osmin in Entführung aus dem Serail; Tiresias in Oedipus Rex by Stravinsky (Neeme Järvi); Manasse in Brautwahl by Busoni (Barenboim); Commendatore in Gazzaniga's Don Giovanni; Alberich in the Bayreuth Ring (Barenboim); Doktor in Wozzeck and Pizarro in Fidelio (Colin Davis); Capriccio/La Roche, conductor Georges Prêtre. *Current Management:* Balmer & Dixon Management AG, Kreuzstrasse 82, 8032 Zürich, Switzerland. *Telephone:* (43) 244-8644. *Fax:* (43) 244-8649. *Website:* www.badix.ch.

KANTA, Ludovit; cellist; b. 9 July 1957, Bratislava, Czechoslovakia; m. 1977; two s. one d. *Education:* Bratislava Conservatorium with G. Vecerny, Academy of Music, Prague with A. Vectomov. *Career:* debut in Strauss' Don Quixote, with Slovak Philharmonic, International Music Festival, Bratislava, Oct 1982; 1st Solo Cello, Slovak Philharmonic, Bratislava, 1983; Concert tours and international festivals as Soloist with Slovak Philharmonic, Bulgaria, 1984, USSR and Poland, 1985, Japan, 1987, Spain, 1988; Other foreign tours, Germany, 1980, 1983, 1986, Italy, 1981, Bulgaria, 1983, 1985, Yugoslavia, 1985, Romania,

1985, 1987, Sweden, 1985; Solo Cellist, Orchestra Ensemble, Kanazawa, Japan, 1990–; Associate Professor, Aichi Prefectural University of Arts, Nagoya, 1995–. *Recordings:* Dvořák-Cello Concerto, Haydn-Concerto in D Major, with Large Orchestra of Bratislava Radio, conducted by Kurt Hortnagel and Ondrej Lenárd; Igor Dibak-premiere recording of Cello Concerto, with Slovak Philharmonic, conductor Bystrik Rezucha; Haydn-Boccherini Concertos, Capella Istropolitana, conductor Peter Breiner; Cello Recital, 1997; Ludovit Kanta Cello Recital, with Heller on piano; Kodaly: Cello Solo Sonata op. 8; Dvořák: Concerto h-mol op.104 with Orchestra Ensemble Kanazawa, conductor Jan Latham. *Honours:* 1st Prize, Beethoven Competition, OPAVA, 1977; 2nd Prize, Prague Spring International Competition, 1980; Concert Imagine; Concert Service Company. *Address:* Midorigaoka 1-2, 929-03 Tsubata-machi, Ishikawa, Japan.

KAPELLMANN, Franz-Josef; Singer (baritone); b. 23 Sept. 1945, Cologne, Germany. *Education:* studied in Cologne. *Career:* sang at the Deutsche Oper Berlin, 1973–75, Dortmund from 1975, notably as Verdi's Luna, Posa, Germont, Iago and Amonasro, Scarpia, Gianni Schicchi, Wolfram, Beckmesser and Kurwenal; Alberich in a new production of Das Rheingold, 1990; Guest appearances at Düsseldorf, Wiesbaden, Karlsruhe, Klagenfurt, Lubeck and Paris (Alberich in Götterdämmerung); Other roles have included Riccardo in Puritani, Guglielmo, Papageno, Toby in The Red Line by Sallinen, Escamillo (at Regensburg), Mozart's Figaro (Gelsenkirchen) and Don Fernando in Fidelio (Granada Festival); Gala concert at the Alte Oper Frankfurt, 1989; Sang Alberich in Siegfried at Brussels, 1991, Beckmesser at Trieste, 1992; Pizarro in a concert of Fidelio, Edinburgh, 1996; Season 1998 at La Scala, Milan and Catania as Weber's Kaspar and Pizarro in Fidelio; Season 2000–01 as Alberich for Bonn Opera, Pizarro at La Scala and Kaspar in Der Freischütz at the Staatsoper Berlin. *Recordings:* Handel's L'Allegro, il Penseroso ed il Moderato. *Current Management:* Theateragentur Dr Germinal Hilbert, Maximilianstrasse 22, 80539 Munich, Germany. *Telephone:* (89) 290 747-0. *Fax:* (89) 290 747-90. *Website:* www.hilbert.de.

KAPLAN, Abraham; Conductor; b. 5 May 1931, Tel-Aviv, Israel. *Education:* Studied at the Israel Academy in Jerusalem and at the Juilliard School, 1954–57; Conducting studies with William Steinberg and Frederick Prausnitz, composition with Darius Milhaud. *Career:* Directed the Kol Israel Chorus, 1953–54 and 1958–59; Conductor of the Haifa Oratorio Society, 1958–59; Founded the Camerata Singers, USA, 1960; Director of Choral Music at Juilliard, 1961–77 and the Symphonic Choral Society of New York, 1968–77; Founded the Camerata Symphony Orchestra 1968 and appeared as Guest Conductor with leading orchestras in the US and Israel; Teacher at the Berkshire Music Center and at Union Theological Seminary New York, 1961–73; Director of Choral Studies at Chautauqua, New York, 1976; Professor of Music at University of Washington, Seattle, 1977; Many choral engagements and recordings with the New York Philharmonic. *Address:* University of Washington, Department of Music, Washington State, USA.

KAPLAN, Lewis; Concert Violinist; b. 10 Nov. 1933, Passaic, New Jersey, USA; m. Adria Goodkin, 6 Aug 1961, 1 s., 1 d. *Education:* Bachelor's degree, 1958, Master's degree, 1960, Juilliard School. *Career:* Debut: Town Hall, New York, 1961; Solo concerts, USA, Europe and Far East, 1953–; Violinist-Founder, Aeolian Chamber Players, 1961–; Violin and Chamber Music Faculties, the Juilliard School, 1964–; Artistic Director and Co-Founder, Bowdoin Summer Music Festival, 1964–; Violin Faculty, Summer Academy Mozarteum, Salzburg, Austria, 1987; Violin Faculty, Mannes College of Music, 1987–; Numerous conducting appearances in USA and Europe. *Recordings:* Numerous. *Publications:* Caprice Variations for Unaccompanied Violin by George Rochberg (editor), 1973. *Address:* 173 Riverside Drive, New York, NY 10024, USA.

KAPLAN, Mark; Violinist; b. 30 Dec. 1953, Boston, Massachusetts, USA. *Education:* Studied with Dorothy DeLay at Juilliard School, New York; Fritz Kreisler Memorial Award. *Career:* US engagements from 1973, after gaining the Award of Special Distinction in the Leventritt Competition; Performances with the Cleveland, Philadelphia, Los Angeles, Pittsburgh and Baltimore Orchestras; Summer Festivals of Aspen, Blossom, Ambler, Grant Park and Santa Fe; European career from 1980; Concerts with the Berlin Philharmonic and Klaus Tennstedt; Engagements in England and Israel with Rudolf Barshai, and thereafter with all major European Orchestras gave the American premiere of Marc Neikrug's Violin Concerto with the Hallé Orchestra; BBC Promenade Concerts and Concerts with the Royal Philharmonic in London and Italy; Associations with the Conductors Marek Janowski, Michael Gielen and Charles Dutoit; Piano Recitals in Europe and America; Recitals with the Golub/Kaplan/Carr Trio playing each season in the USA and Europe; In 1994–95 the Trio toured Italy and the United Kingdom appearing at St John's Smith Square. *Recordings:* Paganini and Wieniawski concertos repertoire; Mendelsohn, Brahms and Schubert Piano Trios; Sarasate Solo Violin Works. *Current Management:*

Askonas Holt Ltd, Lonsdale Chambers, 27 Chancery Lane, London, WC2A 1PF, England. *Telephone:* (20) 7400-1700. *Fax:* (20) 7400-1799. *E-mail:* info@askonasholt.co.uk. *Website:* www.askonasholt.co.uk.

KARAI, József; Composer, Pianist and Conductor; b. 8 Nov. 1927, Budapest, Hungary; m. Katalin Kertész. *Education:* Studied composition and 3 years conducting training, Academy of Music, Budapest, 1947–54. *Career:* Debut: 1950; mem, Association of Hungarian Composers; Hungarian Art Foundation; Hungarian Kodály Society. *Compositions:* About 300 works for chorus based on 20th Century Hungarian Poets' poems and poems of Goethe, Shelley, C Sandburg, Christina Rossetti, Petrarca, Edward Lear, Rilke, Trakl, J R Jimenez, Th Storm, Christian Morgenstern, G Carducci; Works for wind instruments, strings, piano, organ and orchestra; 89 works published by Edition Musica and 80 by other publishers. *Recordings:* 176 Works. *Publications:* Children and Female Choruses, 1970; Mixed Choruses, 1977; Twelve Spirituals, 1978; Easy Children's Choruses, 1978; Tenders of The Fire, 14 mixed choruses, 1968–69; Selected Female Choruses, Zenon, Tokyo, 1992; Hungarian Christmas Songs, suite, 1993; Missa Brevis, 1999. *Honours:* Erkel Prize, 1972; SZOT Prize, 1980. *Address:* 1151 Budapest, Gyöztes u 19, Hungary.

KARAS, Joza; Violinist and Musicologist; b. 3 May 1926, Warsaw, Poland (Czech Nationality); m. Anne Killackey, 14 Feb 1976, 5 s., 1 d. *Education:* Academic Gymnasium, Prague, 1945; State Conservatory of Music, Prague, 1949; Hartt College of Music, University of Hartford, USA, 1957. *Career:* Violin Soloist, Recitalist, USA and Canada; Founder, Karas String Quartet; mem, Czechoslovak Society of Arts and Sciences in America. *Compositions:* Violin Method. *Recordings:* Hans Krása's Brundibár, 1993. *Publications:* Music in Terezín 1941–1945, 1985. *Contributions:* STTH; Jewish Digest; Journal of Synagogue Music; Review of the Society for the History of the Czechoslovak Jews; Theatrical Performances during the Holocaust. *Address:* 212 Duncaster Road, Bloomfield, CT 06002, USA.

KARASEV, Grigory; Singer (Bass); b. 1960, Russia. *Career:* Concert and opera performances throughout Russia: appearances at the Kirov Opera, St Petersburg, from 1987 as Ferrando in Il Trovatore, Mozart's Antonio (Figaro), Raimondo in Lucia di Lammermoor and Rossini's Don Basilio; Other roles include Don Pasquale, Orlik in Mazeppa, Nikitich in Boris Godunov and Storm Wind in Rimsky-Korsakov's Kashchei the Immortal; Guest appearances with New Israel Opera and La Fenice, Venice; Sang with the Kirov Opera in Summer Season at Covent Garden, 2000. *Address:* c/o Kirov Opera, Mariinsky Square, St Petersburg, Russia.

KARASIK, Gita; Concert Pianist; b. 14 Dec. 1952, San Francisco, California, USA; m. Lee Caplin, 25 June 1975. *Education:* Private study with Mme, Rosina Lhevinne, Juilliard; Karl Ulrich Schnabel; Lev Schorr; San Francisco Conservatory of Music. *Career:* Debut: San Francisco/SF Symphony, 1958; NYC/Carnegie Hall, 1969; First American Pianist to make official concert tour of People's Republic of China; Guest Soloist, National Television Debut, The Bell Telephone Hour, NBC, 1963; Guest Soloist, San Francisco Symphony, 1958, 1969, 1972, 1974; Los Angeles Philharmonic, 1971; St Louis Symphony, 1974–75; Boston Pops Orchestra with Arthur Fiedler, 1975; Indianapolis Symphony, 1972, 1976; Atlanta Symphony, 1972; Singapore Symphony, 1980–81; Hong Kong Philharmonic, 1980–82; Tours of Latin America, Far East, Europe, USA; Film Scores, Andy Warhol: Made in China, 1986; The Serpent and the Rainbow, 1988; To Die For, 1989; Son of Darkness, 1992. *Compositions:* Concerto for Gita Karasik No. 2 by Andrew Imbrie, as first prize Ford Foundation Artists Award, World Premiere with Indianapolis Symphony for Bicentennial, 1976. *Address:* 8332 Melrose Avenue, Hollywood, CA 90069, USA.

KARAYANIS, Plato; Opera Administrator; b. 26 Dec. 1928, Pittsburgh, USA. *Education:* Voice at Carnegie Mellon University, and at Curtis Institute; Administration and Stage Technology at the Hamburg Opera. *Career:* Six years as a leading baritone in major European houses; Director of Rehearsal Department, San Francisco Opera; Assistant Stage Director and Administrator for Metropolitan Opera National Company, 1965–67; Executive Vice President of Affiliate Artists Incorporated until 1977; General Director, the Dallas Opera, 1977–; President of Board of Directors, OPERA America, 1993–97; General Director, Dallas Opera 1977–2000, presiding over a complete Ring cycle and the world premiere of Argento's The Aspern Papers in 1988; US Premieres of operatic works by Vivaldi and Falla, and institutional stabilization of this major American opera company; Under his direction the company has committed to innovative productions of traditional repertoire, regular inclusion of major 20th century opera and new American works; Artistic Consultant, Palm Beach Opera, 2002–. *Honours:* Award for Excellence in the Creative Arts, Dallas Historical Society, 1993; TACA Award for Excellence in the Performing Arts, 1998; New rehearsal production centre for the Dallas Opera was named The Dorothy and Plato Karayanis Rehearsal Center. *Address:* 3327 Prescott

Avenue, Dallas, TX 75219, USA. *Fax:* (214) 521–7084. *E-mail:* skarayan@swbell.net.

KARCHIN, Louis; Composer; b. 8 Sept. 1951, Pennsylvania, USA; m. Julie Sirota, 7 June 1987, 2 d. *Education:* BMus, Eastman School of Music, 1973; PhD, Harvard University, 1978. *Compositions:* Capriccio for Violin and Seven Instruments, 1979; Duo for Violin and Cello, 1981; Viola Variations, 1982; Songs of John Keats, 1984; Songs of Distance and Light, 1988; Sonata for Cello and Piano, 1989; String Quartet, 1990; Galactic Folds for Chamber Ensemble, 1992; String Quartet No. 2, 1994; Sonata da Camera for violin and piano, 1995; Rustic Dances, 1995; Rhapsody for orchestra, 1996; Cascades, 1997; American Visions: Two Songs on Poems of Yevgeny Yevtushenko, 1998; Romulus, an Opera in One Act, 1990; Quartet for Percussion, 2000; Deux Poemes de Mallarmé, 2001; Songs- Meditation, Interlude, Echoes, Memory, Carmen de Boheme, To the Sun, 2001–03; Voyages, for alto saxophone and piano, 2001; Orpheus a Masque for baritone, chamber ensemble and dancers, 2003. *Recordings:* Duo for Violin and Cello; Songs of John Keats; Capriccio for Violin and Seven Instruments; Galactic Folds, Songs of Distance and Light, American Visions, String Quartet #2, Rustic Dances, Sonata da Camera. *Honours:* Hinrichsen Award, American Academy of Arts and Letters, 1985; Koussevitzky-Tanglewood Award, 1971; Commission from Fromm Foundation at Harvard, 1994; Commission from Serge Koussevitzky Music Foundation, 1998; Hecksher Foundation Prize, 1999; Goddard Lieberson Award, American Academy of Arts and Letters, 2001; Barlow Endowment Commission, 2001;. *Current Management:* Howard Stokar Management, New York. *Address:* 24 Waverly Place, Rm 268, New York, NY 10003, USA.

KARCZYKOWSKI, Ryszard; Singer (Tenor); b. 6 April 1942, Tczew, Poland. *Education:* Studied in Gdansk with Halina Mickiewiczowna. *Career:* Sang in Gdansk and Stettin, then at the Landestheater Dessau (debut as Beppe in Pagliacci 1969); Other roles included Tamino, Ferrando, Fenton and Rodolfo; Sang in Leipzig from 1974, then in Berlin, Dresden (Tamino and Lensky), Moscow, Zürich, Vienna, New York, Rome, Prague and Aix-en-Provence; Covent Garden debut 1977, as Alfred in Die Fledermaus, returned as the Duke of Mantua, Ferrando and Alwa in the first local production of Berg's Lulu, 1981; Sang in the 1981 stage premiere of Prokofiev's Maddalena (Graz) and the same year sang in Haydn's Orlando Paladino, at the Vienna Festival; Other roles include Ernesto, Nemorino, Rinuccio, Lionel (Martha), Jenik (Bartered Bride), Belmonte, Macduff and Elemer in Arabella; Further appearances in Boston (Duke of Mantua, 1981), Washington, Leningrad, Los Angeles, Zagreb and Lisbon; Sang in Rigoletto with the company of the Deutsche Oper Berlin at the Wiesbaden Festival, 1989; Star Guest at the Vienna Opernball, 1998. *Recordings include:* Szymanowski's 3rd Symphony, The Bells by Rachmaninov, Shostakovich 13th Symphony; Die Lustige Witwe and Die Fledermaus; Arias and Duets From Celebrated Operas, 1991; Laudate Dominum Omnes Gentes, 1992; A. Schoenberg–Von Heute auf Morgen, 1997; A. Berg–Lulu, 1998; F. Lehar–Gold and Silver, 1999. *Address:* Niederraeder Landstr. 6a, 60598 Frankfurt, Germany.

KARIS, Aleck; Pianist; b. 21 Jan. 1945, Washington DC, USA. *Education:* BM, Manhattan School 1976, with Charles Wuorinen; Juilliard School with Beveridge Webster; Private study with Artur Balsam and William Daghlian. *Career:* Latin American debut 1981 at São Paulo; New York debut 1984, playing Chopin, Schumann, Stravinsky and Elliott Carter; Has premiered works by Mario Davidovsky, Milton Babbitt and Morton Subotnick; Member of Speculum Musicae from 1983 and has performed with the Contemporary Chamber Ensemble, New York, St Luke's Chamber Ensemble and the Group Contemporary Music; Associate in Music Performances at Columbia University from 1983. *Honours:* Prizewinner, Rockefeller Foundation International Competition, 1978; fromm Foundation Grant, 1983. *Address:* Music Department, Columbia University, City University of New York, USA.

KARKOFF, Maurice (Ingvar); Composer; b. 17 March 1927, Stockholm, Sweden; 2 s., 1 d. *Education:* Music Theory with Karl Birger Blomdahl, 1944–46; Studied Composition with Lars-Erik Larsson, Royal Conservatory of Music, Stockholm, 1948–53; Piano, 1945–46; Counterpoint, 1949–53; Conducting, 1950–52; Teacher's Degree, 1951; Additional composition studies with Erland von Koch, Hans Holewa, Wladimir Vogel, André Jolivet. *Career:* Debut: Duo for Clarinet and Bassoon, Fylkingen, 1951; Assistant Music Critic, Stockholmstidningen, 1962–66; Teacher, Stockholm Municipal Institute of Music, 1965–96; mem, Royal Swedish Academy of Music; Swedish Society of Composers. *Compositions include:* Lyric Suite for Chamber Orchestra; Nine Aphoristic Variants; 12 Symphonies and 5 Small Symphonies; 14 Solo Concertos; Dolorous Symphony for String Orchestra No. 9; Symphonic Reflections; Voices from the Past for Soprano and Strings; Quartet; 2 Tenor Horns and Trombone; Characters for Flute, Oboe, Clarinet, Bassoon, French Horn, Trombone, Euphonium, percussions; 4 Momenti for Violin and Piano; Aspects for Guitar; Spring in Hanger; Poem for Flute (or Alto Flute); Ballata, intermezzo e leggenda per Pianoforte; 15

Album leaves for piano; Glühende Rätsel, Fünf Lieder, Middle Voice and Piano; Early Summer, Songs for Middle Voice and Pianoforte: Scenes in the Desert, for low voice and pianoforte; When The Day Waned for High Voice and Pianoforte; 2 Fantasies for left hand; Kleine Music, English Horn; Chamber opera, The Frontier Kibbutz op 115. *Recordings include:* Six Chinese Impressions; 7 Pezzi per Grande Orchestra; Swedish Radio Symphony Orchestra; Vision Swedish Radio Orchestra, Serious Songs with Filharmonic Orchestra Kemstin Merzer; Symphony No. 4; Glühende Rätsel, soprano and piano; Dolorous Symphony (ninth) for strings; Symphony No. 11 (Symphony of Life); 9 Chinese Songs, soprano, piano;Oriental Pictures for piano, (composer plays); Ernst und Spass for Saxophone Quartet; Sonatin for Alto Saxophone and Piano, new CD. *Address:* Tackjärnsvägen 18, 16868 Bromma, Sweden.

KARKOSCHKA, Erhard; Composer and Composition Teacher; b. 6 March 1923, Mor Ostrava, Czechoslovakia; m. Rothraut Leiter, 27 July 1950, 3 s., 1 d. *Education:* DPhil. *Career:* Conductor, University Hohenheim, 1948–68; Professor, Musikhochschule Stuttgart, 1958–1996; Executive Board, Institut für Neue Musik und Musikerziehung, Darmstadt, 1964–72; President, IGNM, Section West Germany, 1974–80; Member of Academy of Free Art, Mannheim, 1980–; Lectures world-wide. *Compositions:* About 100 including music for orchestra, chamber music, chorus scenic works, opera, electronic music, organ music and multimedia projects; Chamber Opera, Orpheus oder Hadeshöhe, 1990; Paul Celan Variations I–V, 1996–98. *Recordings:* Ad Hoc 1; Bläsergedichte (Wind Poems) for woodwind quintet, 1988; Desideratio Dei for Organ, 1963; Quattrologe for string quartet, 1966; Antimony for wind quintet, 1968; Dialog for Bassoon and Electronics, 1982; Doch Fülle Zwei und Werde Vier, 1982; Entfalten for 4 soloists and big orchestra, 1983. *Publications:* Das Schriftbild Der Neuen Musik, 1965; Notation in New Music, 1972, Japanese translation 1977, Chinese translation, 1996; Analyse Neuer Musik, 1976; Hörerziehung Mit Neuer Musik, Ear Education With New Music, 1981. *Contributions:* Melos; Musik und Bildung; Musica; Musik und Kirche; Die Musikforschung. *Address:* Nellingerstrasse 45, 70619 Stuttgart, Germany. *Telephone:* 0771 445433. *Fax:* 0771 4403476. *E-mail:* karkoschkaerhard@aol.com.

KARLINS, M(artin) William, BM, MM, PhD; American composer and educator; *Harry N. and Ruth F. Wyatt Prof. of Music Theory and Composition Emeritus, Northwestern Univ., Evanston;* b. 25 Feb. 1932, New York, NY; m. Mickey Cutler 1952; one s. one d. *Education:* Manhattan School of Music, Univ. of Iowa. *Career:* Asst Prof. of Music, Western Illinois Univ. 1965–67, Assoc. Prof. 1967–73, Dir Contemporary Music Ensemble 1967–81; Prof. of Theory and Composition 1973–98, Harry N. and Ruth F. Wyatt Prof. of Music Theory and Composition 1998–2003, Emeritus 2003–, Northwestern Univ., Evanston, Illinois; music performed worldwide 1959–; guest, visiting composer in USA, England, France, Germany, Netherlands, Italy and Hungary; guest composer in Vienna, Austria, Bulgaria; composer, co-ordinator, Stefan Wolpe Festival, Northwestern Univ. 2001. *Compositions include:* Concert Music No. 1, orchestra, II, chorus and orchestra III, woodwinds, brass, piano, percussion, IV and V, orchestra, Symphony No. 1 for orchestra; Chamber music includes, Infinity, oboe d'amore, clarinet, viola, female voice; 2 woodwind quintets; 3 saxophone quartets; Quintet, alto saxophone and string quartet; Catena I for clarinet and little orchestra, II for soprano, saxophone and brass quintet and III concerto for horn and orchestra; Various choral works a cappella; 3 piano sonatas; Solo piece with passacaglia, clarinet; Reflux, concerto for amplified double bass, solo wind ensemble, piano percussion; Concerto for alto saxophone and orchestra; Chameleon, harpsichord; Drei kleiner Cembalostücke, 1994; Impromptu, alto saxophone and organ; Suite of Preludes for piano, 1988; Saxtuper, saxophone, tuba and percussion; Introduction and Passacaglia, 2 saxophones and piano; Looking out My Window, treble chorus and viola; Quartet For Strings with soprano in the last movement, 1959–60; Nostalgie for ensemble of 12 saxophones, 1991; Elegy for orchestra, 1992; Nightlight; Quartet for Saxophones No. 3, 1992–93; Lamentations-In Memoriam, 3 flutes (piccolos), 3 trumpets, 3 trombones, tuba, harp, percussion, organ and narrator; Under and Over, for flute (alto flute) and contrabass, version for violin and contrabass, 2003; Graphic Mobile, for any 3 or multiples of 3 instruments (with or without dancers); Kindred Spirits for mandolin, guitar and harp, 1998; Humble Harvest for solo piano, 2000; Just a Line from Chameleon for two clarinets, 2001; Improvisations on Lines Where Beauty Lingers for solo bass clarinet, 2002. *Recordings of compositions:* Klecka Plays Broege and Karlins, Nostalgie: A Retrospective of Saxophone Music by M. William Karlins, Salvatore Spina Piano Music by Karlins, Lombardo and Stout. *Address:* School of Music, Northwestern University, Evanston, IL 60208, USA. *E-mail:* m-karlins@northwestern.edu.

KARLSEN, Turid; Singer (Soprano); b. 1961, Oslo, Norway. *Education:* Studied at the Maastricht Conservatory, Netherlands. *Career:* Prizewinner at the 1984 Francisco Vinas Competition, Barcelona and sang at the Weikersheim Festival in 1985 as Romilda in Xerxes and Gluck's

Euridice; Karlsruhe Opera from 1986 in Wiener Blut and as Donna Elvira, which she has also sung in Stuttgart, Wiesbaden and Düsseldorf; Sang in the premiere of Graf Mirabeau by Matthus at Stuttgart in 1989; Guest at Dresden in 1989 as Isotta in Schweigsame Frau and Luxembourg in 1991 as Butterfly; Other roles include Mozart's Countess and Pamina, Mimi, Natasha in War and Peace and Violetta; Concert engagements include Bach's St Matthew Passion at Bogota. *Address:* c/o Badisches Staatstheater, Baumeisterstrasse 11, Pf 1449, W-7500 Karlsruhe, Germany.

KARLSON, Erik (Mikael); Composer; b. 10 Dec. 1967, Nynäshamn, Sweden. *Education:* Studied composition and computer music with Tamas Ungvary, Anders Blomquist and others. *Career:* Composer at EMS, Stockholm, Swedish Broadcasting Corporation, Danish Institute for Electro-acoustic Music, Århus, also in Berlin and France; Appearances at festivals and concerts for electro-acoustic music in Europe and elsewhere and many international radio appearances. *Compositions:* Threads and Cords, 1990; Anchorings, Arrows, 1992; La Disparition de L'Azur, 1993; Interiors and Interplays, 1994; Épitaphe pour Iqbal Masih, 1995, all recorded. *Publications:* Author, Circle Almost Closing, and Fylkingen–60 Years of Experimental Art, 1994. *Contributions:* Various articles on contemporary music in Nutida Musik. *Address:* Junkergatan 16/ll, 126 53 Hägersten, Sweden.

KARLSSON, Lars Olof; Composer; b. 24 Jan. 1953, Jomala, Åland, Finland; m. Helena Hartikainen, 31 Dec 1994, 1 s., 1 d. *Education:* Studies at the Sibelius Academy, 1972–82; Cantor Organist, 1976; Higher Degree in Piano, 1979; Composition Studies at the Hochschule der Künste, West Berlin, 1982–83; Diploma in Composition, 1983. *Career:* Lecturer at the Sibelius Academy, 1983–; Co-founder of the Åland Culture Festival, 1983; mem, Society of Finnish Composers; Board Member, Scandinavian Guitar Festival, 1986–. *Compositions:* Five Aphorisms for Piano, 1973; Med Havet, song cycle for Baritone and Piano, 1976; Canto Drammatico, for Solo Violin, 1980; Concerto for Violin and Orchestra, 1993; Suite for Helena, for Wind Quintet, 1994; Toccata, Variations and Fugue on the Chorale Den Blomstertid Nu Kommer, for Organ, 1994; Ludus Latrunculorum, Oratorio, 1996; String Quartet, 1997; Two Love Scenes and a Daydream, for Voice, Soprano Saxophone and Big Band, 1997. *Recordings:* Arioso; Canto Drammatico; Composition for Organ; Passacaglia et Fuga B-A-C-H. *Contributions:* Critic for Hufvudstadsbladet, 1982–89; The Isle Is Full Of Noises, Nordic Sounds No. 3, 1996. *Honours:* 3-year grant from the Svenska Kulturfonden, 1986; 5-year State artists grant, 1995. *Address:* Landgränden 3 C 39, 02700 Helsingfors, Finland.

KARMINSKI, Mark; Composer; b. 30 Jan. 1930, Kharkiv, Ukraine; m. Irini Smichcovitch, 30 Aug 1955, 1 s. *Education:* Department of Philology and Literature, Kharkov State University; Composition, Kharkov State Conservatory. *Career:* 1st orchestral works and instrumental music performed in USSR cities; Opera Bukovinians premiered at Kharkov Opera House, 1957, Moscow, 1960; Other opera stagings: Ten days that shook the world, Donetsk, 1970, Prague National Theatre, 1972, Lvov, 1977, 1984; Irkutsk story, Kiev, Kharkov, Chelabinsk, Saratov, 1977–78; Only one day, Odessa, Lvov, 1987; Musical Robin Hood, Moscow, 1968, then 25 cities, USSR; Author, Philharmonic Concertos (radio, television). *Compositions include:* 4 operas; Rembrandt, ballet; Symphony; Oratorio; 5 Suites for string orchestra including Baroque faces and Play music in ancient style; 6 partitas for piano; Concertina for violin and piano, for flute and piano; Instrumental pieces; Vocal and choral works; Music for over 100 plays. *Recordings include:* The soldier forgot nothing, television film; Robin Hood; Songs from Robin Hood; O K Musketry, disco musical; Merri pencil, children's songs; M Karminsky's 9 songs; Symphony with Gorky Symphony Orchestra, conductor I Husman. *Publications:* Collected songs, 1970–85; Ten days that shook the world, 1973; Robin Hood songs, 1981; Irkutsk story, 1985; Choral music books, 15 choruses a cappella, 1988; Music for children, piano pieces, 1990; Kharkov Selected Works, 1995; 27 Pieces in Three-Part Rhythm, music for piano, 1996–. *Address:* Klotchkovskaja str 150a, ap 40, Kharkiv 310145, Ukraine.

KARNEUS, Katarina; Singer (Mezzo-Soprano); b. 1965, Stockholm, Sweden. *Education:* Trinity College of Music, London; National Opera Studio. *Career:* Varied concert repertoire including Beethoven's Ninth with Frans Brüggen and the Hallé Orchestra, Mozart's C Minor Mass in the Salzburg Festival with Roger Norrington, Les Nuits d'Eté and a Sylvester Concert with the Filharmonisch Orkest and Grant Llewellyn, Rossini-Mozart programme with Nicholas McGegan and the Hanover Band, Pergolesi Stabat Mater with the Netherlands Chamber Orchestra and Hartmut Haenchen and a concert at Buckingham Palace with Franz Welser-Möst; Prom debut with Rafael Frühbeck de Burgos and Edinburgh Festival debut with Charles Mackerras; Appearances at the Albert Hall with David Willcocks and at the Royal Festival Hall with the Bach Choir; Broadcast of Lieder eines fahrenden Gesellen with Grant Llewellyn and the Ulster Orchestra; Two concerts with Scottish Chamber Orchestra; South Bank debut in Purcell Room with a

programme of Spanish and Scandinavian songs; Wigmore Hall recital as part of the Voices series; For Welsh National Opera: Angelina in La Cenerentola, Cherubino in Le nozze di Figaro and Rosina in Il Barbiere di Siviglia; Sesto in La Clemenza di Tito, Mercédès in Carmen for ENO and Opéra de Paris; Rosina and the title role in Carmen for Opéra Comique, Paris; The Page in Salome for Lyric Opera of Chicago; Tamiri in Il Re Pastore for Netherlands Opera; Further engagements include Sesto in La Clemenza di Tito for WNO; Debut with Glyndebourne Festival Opera as Dorabella; Cherubino at La Monnaie; Varvara in Katya Kabanova for Metropolitan Opera; Returned to the Bastille in 1999 to sing Dorabella, to the Opéra-Comique for Carmen and as Annio in La Clemenza di Tito at the Bayerische Staatsoper; Returned to WNO as Octavian in Der Rosenkavalier in 2000; Season 2000–01 as Gluck's Orpheus for WNO, as Dorabella at Munich and engaged as Olga in Eugene Onegin, New York Met; Also engaged to sing La Belle Hélène, Châtelet, Paris, 2001, Annio in La Clemenza di Tito at Covent Garden, 2002, and Adalgisa in Norma at Houston Grand Opera 2003. *Recordings:* R. Strauss, Mahler, Marx, Lieder. *Honours:* Christine Nilsson Award, 1994; Winner, Cardiff Singer of the World Competition, 1995. *Address:* Ingpen & Williams Ltd, 7 St George's Court, 131 Putney Bridge Road, London, SW15 2PA, England.

KAROLYI, Sandor; Professor; b. 24 Sept. 1931, Budapest, Hungary; m. 1st Suzanne Godefroid, 3 July 1954, 2 s., 1 d; 2nd Regina Bauer, 1 July 1998, one s. *Education:* Virtuosity Diploma, Franz Liszt Music Academy, Budapest, 1948; Virtuosity Diploma with distinction, Music Conservatory of Brussels, 1954; Teachers include Ede Zathureczky, Leo Weiner, Antal Molnar, André Gertler. *Career:* Debut: Franz Liszt Academy, 1941; Violin solo, Opera House in Frankfurt, 1956; Professor, Musikhochschule, Frankfurt am Main and at the Akademie Tonkunst Darmstadt; Concerts for the BBC and broadcasting companies in Europe; Television appearances in Germany, Japan, Philippines and Australia; mem, Deutsche Bachsolisten. *Recordings:* Paul Hindemith: 4 Violin Sonatas with Werner Hoppstock, piano, and Károlyi String Quartet recorded Quartets Nos 2 and 6 plus the Clarinet-Quartet of Paul Hindemith; Max Reger: Violin Sonatas A and C major with Suzanne Godefroid, piano; Prelude and Fugas for violin solo; Giuseppe Tartini Devil's Trill. *Publications:* Gustav Mahler Orchestra studies for the 10 symphonies, 1989. *Honours:* Diploma Contests in Geneva, 1947, Budapest, 1948, London, 1953; Contemporary Contest, Darmstadt, 1952; Vieuxtemps Prize, Belgium, 1959; Medaille Eugene Ysaye, Brussels, 1967. *Address:* Dehnhardtstrasse 30, 60433 Frankfurt am Main, Germany. *E-mail:* sandor.karolyi@t-online.de.

KARPATI, Janos; Musicologist, Professor and Librarian; b. 11 July 1932, Budapest, Hungary. *Education:* PhD, Eotvos Lorand University, Budapest; Diploma, Faculty of Musicology, Ferenc Liszt Academy, Budapest; DSc, Musicology, Hungarian Academy of Sciences. *Career:* Folk Music Research in Morocco, 1957–58; Recording production, Hungaroton, 1959–61; Head Librarian and Lecturer, Ferenc Liszt Academy of Music, Budapest, 1961–; Professor, 1983–; Folk Music Research in Japan, 1988. *Recordings:* Kagura: Japanese Shinto Ritual Music. *Publications:* D Scarlatti, 1959; A Schoenberg, 1963; Muzsikalo zenetortenet, vols II, IV, 1965, 1983; Bartók String Quartets, 1975; Bartók kamarezeneje, 1976; Kelet zeneje, Music of the East, 1981; Bartók's Chamber Music, 1994. *Address:* Mester u 77, 1095 Budapest IX, Hungary.

KARR, Gary; Double Bass Player; b. 20 Nov. 1941, Los Angeles, California, USA. *Education:* Studied with Herman Reinshagen, Warren Benfield and Stuart Sankey. *Career:* Debut: New York 1962 in concert with Leonard Bernstein, ad at New York Town Hall; European tour 1964, playing at Wigmore Hall London; Founded the International Institute for the String Bass, 1967; Teaching appointments at Juilliard School, Yale School of Music, Indiana University, New England Conservatory and Hartt School of Music, Hartford (1976); Formed duo with keyboard player Harmon Lewis in 1972, tours of Europe, the Far East, USA and Canada; Appearances as Soloist with the Chicago Symphony, New York Philharmonic, English Chamber Orchestra, London Symphony and Toronto Symphony; Composers who have written for him include Vittorio Giannini, Henze, Wilfred Josephs, Lalo Schifrin, John Downey and Gunther Schuller; Debut tour of Australia 1987–88; Television appearances include series Gary Karr and Friends on CBC in Canada and Bass is Beautiful for Channel 4, England; Further television engagements in France, Belgium, Japan, Norway, Switzerland and USA; Karr Doublebass Foundation Inc formed 1983 to provide valuable instruments for talented players. *Recordings:* Transcriptions of Paganini's Moses Fantasy and Dvořák Cello Concerto; Concerto by Lalo Schifrin. *Address:* Kaye Artists Management, 7 Chertsey Road, Woking, Surrey GU21 5 AB, England.

KARR-BERTOLI, Julius; Conductor; b. 11 June 1920, Munich, Germany; m. Charlotte Langesee, 1 d. *Education:* Graduate in Conducting, Piano, Violin, Horn, Academy of Music, Munich, 1939. *Career:* First Conducted aged 18 at the Bavarian State Theatre

(Prinzregententheater) Grieg's Peer Gynt; Conductor, Dortmund Opera, 1942–45; Freelance, Bavarian Radio, Assistant to Eugen Jochum, 1945–60; Professor, Richard Strauss Conservatory, Munich, 1972–85; Concerts and music festivals in about 50 countries on 4 continents with some of the world's leading orchestras including the Philharmonic Orchestras of Munich, Berlin, Beijing (Peking), Bucharest, Riga, Sofia, St Petersburg; Numerous concert-tours in Russia and the former USSR initiated by D. Shostakovich, who named the maestro 'his authentic interpreter'; Anniversary of 60 years at the conductors desk, 1999; 80 years, June 2000 with festive concerts in Weimar and Munich; First concerts in Mexico City and Xalapa with first performance of works by Liszt and Dvořák, 2001; Principal concert for the Fesaam Music Festival with works by black composers, e.g. William Grant Still and Powell Nash, and new concerts in Mexico, Belarus and Germany; 82nd Birthday concerts in Ecuador, 2002. *Recordings:* Music of Pergolesi and Romanian Composers; Music of G B Pergolesi with the Suk Chamber Orchestra and Joseph Suk as violin soloist; Symphonies of L van Beethoven and C Franck; Symphonies Nos 3, 4 and 7 by Dvořák; Principal Guest Conductor Suk Chamber Orchestra, Prague. *Current Management:* AIM, Artists International Management, PO Box 2146, Morristown, NJ 07961, USA; International Concert Management, ICM Artists and Tours, 23 Farmleigh Ave, Stillorgan, Co Dublin, Ireland. *Address:* Sommerstrasse 9, 81543 Munich, Germany.

KARSKI, Dominik, MMus; Australian composer; b. 24 June 1972, Szczebrzeszyn, Poland. *Education:* West Australian Conservatorium of Music, 1996; Queensmald Conservatorium, Brisbane, 1999. *Career:* Freelance composer; Instrumental works from solo to orchestra commissioned and performed in Australia, N America, Asia and Europe; Radio broadcasts in Australia and Europe;. *Compositions:* Instrumental works from solo to orchestra include: Les Eruptions du Rêve, performed by Le Nouvel Ensemble Moderne, Forum 2000, Telstra Adelaide Festival; Glimmer, performed at Gaudeamus Music Week, 2002; Streams of Consciousness, performed by Ensemble Offspring, European tour, 2003; Inner Stream II, performed at Gaudeamus Music Week, 2003; Streams Within, Libra Ensemble commission performed Melbourne, 2003. *Recordings:* Floating on the River of Time, West Australian Symphony Orchestra 20th Century Ensemble; Les Eruptions du Rêve, Le Nouvel Ensemble Moderne. *Publications:* all most important scores are distributed by the Australian Music Centre. *Honours:* ABC Young Composers' Award, 1998; Ian Potter Music Commissions, Melbourne, 1999; Le Nouvel Ensemble Moderne, Forum 2000; First Prize, Panufnik Int. Young Composers Competition, Kraków, 2001; Hon. mention, Gaudeamus Music Week, Amsterdam, 2002; Albert H. Maggs Composition Award, 2003. *Address:* 2 Everett Lane, Currambine, WA 6028, Australia. *Telephone:* (8) 9304-2271 (office). *E-mail:* dominikk@echidna.id.au (office). *Website:* www.amcoz .com.au/comp/k/dkarski.htm (office).

KARTTUNEN, Aussi (Ville); Cellist; b. 30 Sept. 1960, Helsinki, Finland; m. Muriel Von Braun, 16 Aug 1985, 1 d. *Education:* Sibelius Academy, Helsinki; Teachers Vili Pullinen, Erkki Rautio, Private studies in London with William Pleeth; Jacqueline du Pré; In Netherlands with Tibor de Machula. *Career:* Soloist with all major Scandanavian Orchestras; Los Angeles Philharmonia, Philharmonia Orchestra, BBC Symphony, BBC Scottish, Orchestre de Paris, Dutch Radio Orchestra, London Sinfonietta, Ensemble Modern among others; Appearances in major festivals including: Edinburgh, Lockenhaus, Salzburg, Berlin, Vienna, Venice, Strasbourg, Montpellier, Helsinki; Artistic Director, Avanti! Chamber Orchestra, 1994–98; Artistic Director; Helsinki Biennale, 1995. Recordings include complete Beethoven works for cello; 20th Century Solo Cello; Concertos by Zimmermann, Hindemith, Lindberg and Saariaho with London Sinfonietta, the Los Angeles Philharmonia and Avanti!. *Honours:* First prize in Young Concert Artist Competition, Tunbridge Wells, England, 1981. First Prize and Gold Medal at the Festival Des Jeunes Solistes, in Bordeaux, 1982.

KASAROVA, Vesselina; Singer (Mezzo-Soprano); b. 1963, Stara Zagora, Bulgaria. *Education:* Studied at the Sofia Conservatory. *Career:* Appearances at the Sofia National Opera as Fenena, Rosina, Preziosilla and Dorabella; Member of the Zürich Opera, 1988–91 as Annio in Clemenza di Tito, Stephano in Roméo et Juliette, and Anna in Les Troyens; Salzburg Festival 1991–92 as Annio and Rossini's Tancredi; Further appearances as Rosina at the Vienna Staatsoper in 1991 and the Geneva Opera, and as Pippo in La Gazza Ladra at Barcelona in 1992; Season 1996 with Mozart's Zerlina at the Salzburg Festival and Idamante at Florence; Season 1998 as Cenerentola at Pesaro and Charlotte in a concert performance of Werther at the Deutsche Oper Berlin; Octavian at New York Met, 2000; Season 2000–01 as Mozart's Idamante at Salzburg and Sesto at Covent Garden (returned, 2002); Giovanna Seymour in Anna Bolena at Zürich and Rosina for Chicago Lyric Opera; Concert repertory includes Mozart's Requiem in Milan, and Agnese in Bellini's Beatrice di Tenda in Vienna. *Recordings include:*

Romeo in Bellini's I Capuleti, 1998. *Address:* c/o Staatsoper, Opernring 2, 1010 Vienna, Austria.

KASHKASHIAN, Kim; Violist and Teacher; b. 31 Aug. 1952, Detroit, Michigan, USA. *Education:* Studied with Walter Trampler, 1969–79 and Karen Tuttle, 1970–75, Peabody Conservatory of Music, Baltimore. *Career:* Various engagements as a soloist with leading orchestras in North America and Europe; Recitals; Chamber music appearances notably with the Tokyo and Guarneri Quartets and the Beaux Arts Trio; Faculty Member, New School of Music, Philadelphia, 1981–86, Mannes College of Music, New York, 1983–86, Indiana University School of Music, Bloomington, 1985–87; Staatliche Hochschule für Musik, Freiburg, 1989–; Has prepared transcriptions and has commissioned various works for viola including music by Betsy Jolas, Schnittke and Sofia Gubaidulina. *Recordings:* As a soloist and chamber music artist, notably two unpublished sonatas by Hindemith. *Address:* Hartliebstr 2, 8000 Munchen 19, Germany.

KASPRZYK, Jacek; Conductor; b. 10 Aug. 1952, Biala, Poland. *Education:* Studied at Warsaw Conservatory. *Career:* Debut: Warsaw Opera, 1975; Principal Conductor and Music Director of the Polish National Radio Symphony until leaving for England 1982; Guest Conductor with Berlin Philharmonic, Orchestre National de France, the Stockholm and Oslo Philharmonic Orchestras, the Bavarian Radio Symphony and the Rotterdam Philharmonic; 1982 debuts with the Philharmonia and Detroit Opera and the San Diego Symphony; British orchestras include the Hallé, Northern Sinfonia, Scottish National Orchestra and regional BBC Orchestras; London Prom Concert Debut 1984, with the BBC National Orchestra of Wales; Return visits to Frankfurt, Vienna, Hamburg and Scandinavia and to the Cincinnati and San Diego Orchestras; Guest at Lyon Opéra for A Midsummer Night's Dream, at Bordeaux for Eugene Onegin and at the Stockholm Royal Opera for Die Zauberflöte; Season 1988–89 Fledermaus for Scottish Opera and Der fliegende Holländer for Opera North; English National Opera debut 1992, The Barber of Seville. *Recordings:* Numerous. *Address:* c/o The Music/Partnership, 41 Aldebert Terrace, London, SW8 1BH, England.

KASRASHVILI, Makvala; Singer (Soprano); b. 13 March 1942, Kutaisi, Georgia, Russia. *Education:* Studied with Mme Davidova in Tbilisi. *Career:* Debut: Bolshoi Theatre Moscow 1968, as Countess Almaviva; Member of the Bolshoi ensemble, with guest appearances in Warsaw, Sofia and Brno; Savonlinna Festival Finland 1983, as Elisabeth de Valois; Covent Garden debut 1984, as Donna Anna; Many appearances in operas by Tchaikovsky, Verdi and Puccini; Verona Arena 1985, as Aida; Wiesbaden Festival 1987, as Tosca; Sang Voislava in Rimsky's Mlada at the Bolshoi, 1988 (also at Pittsburgh 1989); Sang in Mlada at the Barbican Hall, 1989 (first British performance). *Recordings include:* Francesca da Rimini by Rachmaninov (Melodyia). *Honours:* Prizewinner, Sofia International Competition, 1968; Winner, Montreal Competition, 1973. *Address:* c/o Bolshoi Theatre, Pr Marxa 8/2, 103009 Moscow, Russia.

KASSEL, Wolfgang; Singer (Tenor); b. 1930, Germany. *Career:* Sang at the Flensburg Opera, 1954–57; Engagements at Mainz, 1957–58, Wuppertal 1958–60, Krefeld 1960–66, Bielefeld 1967–74; Sang at Nuremberg, 1974–80 and made guest appearances at Munich 1973–76; Appeared as Tannhäuser at Covent Garden, 1973, Siegmund at Rouen, 1975; Other roles have included Lohengrin, Walther, Siegfried, Florestan, Max, Herod in Salome and Bacchus (Ariadne auf Naxos); Further engagements at Toulouse, Oslo, Würzburg and elsewhere in Europe. *Address:* c/o St ädtische Buhnen, Richard Wagnerplatz 2–10, 8500 Nuremberg, Germany.

KASTON, Motti; Singer (Baritone); b. 1965, Tel-Aviv, Israel. *Education:* Studied at the Tel-Aviv Conservatory and the Mannes College of Music, New York. *Career:* Sang Schaunard in La Bohème at Tel-Aviv, 1987; Germont and other roles at the Metropolitan, New York; Philadelphia, 1991, as Malatesta in Don Pasquale: Staatsoper Stuttgart from 1991, as Sharpless in Madama Butterfly, Dandini in La Cenerentola, Wolfram in Tannhäuser and Rossini's Figaro; Opéra-Comique, Paris, 1991, as Alphonse in La Favorite; Tel-Aviv, 1994, as Valentin in Faust and Stuttgart, 1996, as Roderick in La Chute de la Maison Usher, by Debussy; Season 1998 as Dandini in La Cenerentola at Tel-Aviv. *Address:* c/o New Israeli Opera, 28 Leonardo da Vinci St, PO Box 3321, Tel-Aviv 61332, Israel.

KASTU, Matti; Tenor; b. 3 Feb. 1943, Turku, Finland. *Education:* School of Royal Opera, Stockholm. *Career:* Principal Tenor at Stockholm Opera from 1973 with debut as Laca in Jenůfa at Edinburgh in 1974; Roles include Rodolfo in La Bohème, Bacchus in Ariadne auf Naxos, Walter in Die Meistersinger, Parsifal, and Florestan in Fidelio; Guest appearances in Vienna, San Francisco, Munich, Düsseldorf, Frankfurt and Berlin; Tour of USA in 1979 appearing in Detroit, Washington and New York; Welsh National Opera in 1981 as the Emperor in Die Frau ohne Schatten, Milan in 1983 in Mahler's Das klagende Lied; Created the

Guide in Sallinen's The King Goes Forth to France, Savonlinna, 1984; Sang at Edinburgh Festival in 1990 as Tristan in a concert performance of Wagner's opera with the Jutland Opera; Sang Tristan at Århus in 1992. *Recordings include:* Menelaos in Aegyptische Helena. *Address:* c/o Den jske Opera, Thomas Jensens Allee, 8000 Århus, Denmark.

KASZA, Katalin; Singer (Soprano); b. 1942, Szeged, Hungary. *Education:* Graduate, Ferenc Liszt Academy, Budapest, 1967. *Career:* Debut: Abigail in Nabucco, Budapest State Opera, 1967; Judith in film of Duke Bluebeard's Castle and guest performer as Judith in the Edinburgh Festval, 1973 and at many other international venues; Brünnhilde in Wagner's Ring at Covent Garden Opera House, London, 1974–76, and at Geneva and several German cities, 1977–78; US debut in Duke Bluebeard's Castle, Los Angeles, CA, 1980; Sang Eudossia in Respighi's La Fiamma at Erkel Theatre, Budapest, 1989; Other roles include: Octavia in L'Incoronazione di Poppea, Leonore in Fidelio, Lady Macbeth, Title roles of Salome and Elektra, Senta in Der fliegende Holländer, Ortrud in Lohengrin, Fricka in Rheingold, Isolde in Tristan und Isolde and Kundry in Parsifal. *Recordings:* Radio and television film recording of Fidelio, 1969; As Judith in Duke Bluebeard's Castle, 1970, in television film and the same role for the complete Bartók edition; Kundry in Parsifal, 1983. *Honours:* The Best Dramatic Performer's Diploma, Sofia International Singing Concours, 1968; Liszt Prize 1, 1974; Béla Bart ók–Ditta Pasztory Prize, 1992. *Address:* c/o Hungarian State Opera House, Andrássy ut 22, 1061 Budapest, Hungary.

KATIMS, Milton; Conductor and Violist; b. 24 June 1909, New York, NY, USA; m. Virginia Peterson, 7 Nov 1940, 1 s., 1 d. *Education:* BA, Columbia University; Private violin study from age 8; Conducting at National Orchestral Association with Leon Barzin, 1931–35. *Career:* Debut: NBC Symphony, 1947; Solo Violist and Assistant Conductor, WOR, Mutual Broadcasting Company, 1935–43; Faculty, Juilliard, 1946–54; NBC New York, First Desk Violist with Toscanini, Staff Conductor, 1943–54; Principal Guest Conductor with NBC Symphony, 1947–54 (52 broadcasts); Music Director, Seattle Symphony, 1954–76; Guest Conductor of orchestras on five continents; Solo viola appearances, chamber music with Budapest String Quartet, New York Piano Quartet, Pablo Casals and Isaac Stern; Artistic Director, University of Houston School of Music, 1976–84; mem, American Viola Society; American String Teachers Association. *Compositions:* Editions for Viola for International Music Company include 6 Solo Suites of Bach, 3 Gamba Sonatas of Bach, 2 Brahms Sonatas, Schubert Arpeggione Sonata and 25 other compositions. *Recordings:* Numerous as Conductor and Violist including: Bach Solo Viola Suites, Bach Gamba Sonatas, with Milton Katims and colleagues. *Publications:* Co-authored with his wife Virginia Peterson, cellist, The Pleasure Was Ours (Personal Encounters with the Greats, the NearGreats, and Ingrates), 2002; Contributions to: Various journals. *Honours:* Hon. doctorates (Seattle, Whitworth College, Cornish College of Arts, Columbia Univ. Medal of Excellence, 1954; Lifetime Achievement Award, Academy of Music Northwest, 1999; American Viola Soc. Career Achievement Award, 2002; Ditson and ASCAP awards for championing American composers. *Address:* Fairway Estates, 8001 Sand Point Way NE, Seattle, WA 98115, USA. *E-mail:* milvir@aol.com.

KATIN, Peter; Concert Pianist; b. 14 Nov. 1930, London, England; m. Eva Zweig 1954, divorced, 2 s. *Education:* Westminster Abbey Choir; Royal Academy of Music. *Career:* Debut: Wigmore Hall, 1948; International concert career involving appearances in major concert halls and collaboration with the best known orchestras and conductors; Teaching achievements include professorships at Royal Academy of Music, University of Western Ontario, Royal College of Music. *Recordings:* Approximately 35 recordings for several major companies; Complete sets include Grieg's Lyric Pieces, Mozart's Sonatas, Chopin's complete Polonaises and Waltzes, Chopin's Nocturnes and Impromptus, Rachmaninov's Preludes. *Publications:* Autobiography, 2000; Various contributions notably to Classical music (United Kingdom) and Clavier (USA). *Honours:* ARCM, 1952; FRAM, 1960; Chopin Arts Award, 1977; HonD.Mus, 1994. *Current Management:* TransArt (UK) Ltd, Cedar House, 10 Rutland Street, Filey, YO14 9JB, North Yorkshire, England. *Telephone:* (1723) 515819. *Fax:* (1723) 514678. *E-mail:* transartuk@transartuk.com. *Website:* www.transartuk.com.

KATS-CHERNIN, Elena; Composer and Lecturer; b. 4 Nov. 1957, Tashkent, Uzbekistan (Resident in Australia from 1975). *Education:* Diploma of the State Conservatorium of Music, New South Wales, 1979; Hanover Musikhochschule 1980–84, with Helmut Lachenmann. *Career:* Composer of incidental music for dance theatre in Germany, 1985–93; Lecturer, New South Wales Conservatory, 1995; Commissions from ZKM Karlsruhe (1993), Munchener Biennale (1994) and Sydney Alpha Ensemble (1995), among others; Sehrayahn Resident, Ministry for the Arts Lower Saxony, 1984–85; Iphis premiered by Music Theatre Sydney, 3 Dec 1997. *Compositions include:* Piano Concerto, 1979; Bienie for orchestra, 1979; In Tension, for 6 instruments, 1982; Reductions, for 2 pianos, 1983; Duo I for violin and piano, 1984; Stairs,

for orchestra, 1984; Transfer, for orchestra, 1990; Tast-en, for piano, 1991; Totschki: Dots, for oboe and clarinet, 1992; Clocks, for 20 musicians and tape, 1993; Retonica for orchestra, 1993; Clip for percussion, 1994; Concertino for violin and 11 players, 1994; Coco's Last Collection, dance theatre, for 2 pianos, 1994; Cadences, Deviations and Scarlatti for 14 instruments, 1995; Wild Rice for cello, 1996; The Schubert Blues for piano, 1996; Charleston Noir for double bass quartet, 1996; Purple Prelude for six instruments, 1996; Russian Rad for ensemble, 1996; Zoom and Zip for string orchestra, 1997; Iphis, opera after Ovid's Metamorphoses, 1997; Champagne in a Teapot for horn and 13 instruments, 1997; Matricide, the musical, 1998; Umcha for percussion ensemble, 1998; Sonata Lost and Found for piano, 1998; Stur in Dur for piano, 1999; Portrait CD, Clocks, 1997. *Honours:* Sounds Australian, 1996. *Address:* c/o Boosey & Hawkes, 295 Regent Street, London W1R 8JH, England.

KATZ, Arnold; conductor; b. 18 Sept. 1924, Baku, Azerbaijan. *Education:* Central Music School, Moscow State Conservatoire; studied conducting at the Leningrad State Conservatoire. *Career:* conducting career in Russia from 1956; f. USSR Philharmonic of Novosibirsk and brought the orchestra on tour of England 1988; German tour 1989; guest appearances with the Stockholm Philharmonic, BBC Nat. Orchestra of Wales, Tivoli Orchestra (Copenhagen), Residentie Orchestra (Netherlands) and RT Luxembourg season 1990–91. *Recordings include:* music by Shostakovich and Siberian composers with the USSR Philharmonic of Novosibirsk; Russian music with the Leningrad Philharmonic. *Address:* c/o Residentie Orkest, PO Box 11543, 2502 AM, The Hague, Netherlands.

KATZ, Martin; Pianist and University Professor; b. 27 Nov. 1945, Los Angeles, California, USA. *Education:* Studied at the University of Southern California at Los Angeles, accompaniment with Gwendolyn Koldovsky. *Career:* Pianist for the US Army chorus in Washington, 1966–69; Accompanist to such leading singers as José Carreras, Kiri Te Kanawa, Teresa Berganza, Katia Ricciarelli and Nicolai Gedda; Concert tours of North and South America, Australia, Europe and Asia, notably with Marilyn Horne; Editions of Rossini operas performed by Houston Grand Opera and at the Rossini Festival, New York, 1982–83; Edition of Handel's Rinaldo performed at the Ottawa Festival 1982, Metropolitan Opera 1984; Associate Professor at Westminster Choir College, 1976; Professor at the University of Michigan, 1983. *Address:* Music Department, University of Michigan, Ann Arbor, MI 48109, USA.

KATZ, Paul; Cellist; b. 1941, USA. *Career:* Member of the Cleveland Quartet, 1969–94; Regular tours of the USA, Canada, Europe, Japan, Russia, South America, Australia, New Zealand and the Middle East; On Faculty of the Eastman School, Rochester and in residence at the Aspen Music Festival, co-founding the Center for Advanced Quartet Studies; Tour of the Soviet Union and five European countries, 1988; Season 1988–89 with appearances at the Metropolitan Museum and Alice Tully Hall, New York; Concerts in Paris, London, Bonn, Prague, Lisbon and Brussels; Festivals of Salzburg, Edinburgh and Lucerne; Many complete Beethoven cycles and annual appearances at Lincoln Center's Mostly Mozart Festival; In addistion to standard repertory, has commissioned works by John Harbison, Sergei Slonimsky, Samuel Adler, George Perle, Christopher Rouse, Toru Takemitsu, Stephen Paulus, Libby Larsen, John Corigliano and Oswaldo Golyov. *Recordings:* Repertoire from Mozart to Ravel; Collaborations with Alfred Brendel (Schubert Trout Quintet), Pinchas Zukerman and Bernard Greenhouse (Brahms Sextets), Emanuel Ax, Yo-Yo Ma and Richard Stoltzman; Complete Beethoven Quartets, 1982. *Publications:* Interpretation problems of the Beethoven Quartets, RCA, 1982. *Current Management:* ICM Artists, New York. *Address:* Eastman School of Music, 26 Gibbs Street, Rochester, NY 14604, USA.

KATZ, Shelley; Concert Pianist, Composer, Conductor and Accompanist; b. 1960, Montreal, Canada. *Education:* Studied at the Montreal Conservatoire and the Juilliard School in New York, BMus (Hon), 1982; MMus, 1983; PhD 1997. *Career:* Solo repetiteur at the Deutsche Oper am Rhein from 1987, Studienleiter in Koblenz from 1989, Kappelmeister and Assistant to the General Music Director at Mainz Opera; Accompanist to such singers as Nicolai Gedda, Gwyneth Jones and Jochen Kowalski; Musician-in-Residence, International Study Centre, Queen's University. *Compositions:* Drei Jüdische Lieder, 1988; Eyshes Chayil, 1998; Kaddish, 2000. *Recordings:* Songs by Canadian Composers with D. Gilchrist; Solo Piano Works by Canadian Composers; Of Fire and Dew, 21 Baritone Songs by John Jeffreys with J Veira; Lieder: Mozart Beethoven Schumann with J Kowalski. *Publications include:* A Description of Research into Electronically Generated Expressivity, with F Rumsey, 1994. *Address:* International Study centre, Queen's University, Herstmonceux Castle, Hailsham, East Sussex BN27 1 RP, England.

KATZER, Georg; Composer; b. 10 Jan. 1935, Habelschwerdt, Germany; m. Angelika Szostak, 13 May 1975, 3 s. *Education:* Hochschule für

Musik, Berlin; AMU, Prague; Akademie der Kunste, Germany. *Career:* Freelance Composer, 1960; Professor of Composition, Academy of Fine Arts, Berlin. *Compositions:* Mainly published; Chamber music; More than 10 symphonic works; Solo concertos (with orchestra), for flute, oboe, piano, cello, harp and cello; Electro-acoustic works; Multi-media works; 2 ballets; 3 operas; Offene Landschaft for orchestra; Landschaft mit steigender Flut for orchestra. *Recordings:* Sound House, after F Bacon's The New Atlantis, for 3 orchestras, organ and tape; Kommen und Gehen, woodwind quintet and piano; Aide-Memoirem, tape composition; Harpsichord Concerto; Konzert für Orchester No. 1; Baukasten for orchestra; Empfindsame Musik; Streichermusik 1. *Address:* Weserstrasse 5, 15738 Zeuthen, Germany.

KAUFMAN, Frederick; Composer; b. 24 March 1936, Brooklyn, New York, USA. *Education:* Studied Composition with Vittorio Giannini at the Manhattan School, MMus, 1960; Juilliard School with Vencent Persichetti. *Career:* Played trumpet in the New York City Ballet Orchestra and for various New York bands; Composer-in-Residence at the University of Wisconsin, 1969; Director of Music for the city of Haifa, Israel, 1971–72; Music performed by major Israeli orchestras and dance companies; Chairman of the Music Department at Eastern Montane College, 1977–82; Professor of Composition at the Philadelphia College of the Performing Arts, 1982. *Compositions:* A Children's Opera, 1967; The Nothing Ballet, 1975; 3 Symphonies, 1966, 1971, 1978; Concerto for violin and strings, 1967; Interiors for violin and piano, 1970; Violin Sonata, 1970; And the World Goes On for percussion and ensemble, 1971; 3 Cantatas for chorus and organ, 1975; Triple Concerto, 1975; 5 Moods for oboe, 1975; Percussion Trio, 1977; Echoes for chorus, clarinet and percussion, 1978; 5 Fragrances for clarinet, harp and percussion, 1980; When the Twain Meet for orchestra, 1981; Metamorphosis for piano, 1981; Southeast Fantasy for wind ensemble, 1982; Mobile for string quartet, 1982; Stars and Distances, spoken sounds and chorus, 1981; Meditation for a Lonely Flute, 1983; Kiddish Concerto for cello and strings, 1984; A/V Slide Show for trombone, 1984; Masada for chorus, clarinet and percussion, 1985. *Publications include:* The African Roots of Jazz, 1979.

KAUFMANN, Jonas; German singer (tenor); b. 1969, Munich. *Education:* Munich Hochschule für Musik; masterclasses with Hans Hotter and James King. *Career:* sang with Saarbrucken Opera 1994–96; Salzburg Festival debut in Busoni's Dr Faust 1999; engagements from 1999, including Stuttgart, Chicago, Milan and Salzburg; season 2002 appearances included Flamand in Capriccio at Turin, Don Ottavio in Don Giovanni at Munich, Fierrabras at Zürich Oper; season 2003 appearances included Alfredo Germont in La Traviata at Chicago Opera, Rinaldo in Armida at Zürich Oper, Faust in La Damnation de Faust at Geneva, Belmonte in Die Entfuhrung aus dem Serail at Salzburg Festival, Tannhauser, Die Zauberflote and Die Entfuhrung aus dem Serail at Zürich Oper, and a recital at the Wigmore Hall, London; season 2004 includes Max in Der Freischutz at Berlin, Fidelio at Zürich Oper, Cassio in Otello at Paris, Die Schopfung at Naples, and a recital in Brussels; other roles include Mozart's Ferrando, Belmonte, Tamino, Titus, Jacquino in Fidelio, Rossini's Almaviva, Alfredo in Otello. *Recordings:* Carl Loewe's The Three Wishes. *Honours:* prizewinner, Meistersinger Competition, Nuremberg 1993. *Current Management:* IMG Artists, Lovell House, 616 Chiswick High Road, London, W4 5RX, England. *Telephone:* (20) 8233-5800. *Fax:* (20) 8233-5801. *E-mail:* sthomson@imgworld.com. *Website:* www.imgartists.com.

KAUFMANN, Julie; Singer (Soprano); b. 25 May 1955, Iowa, USA. *Education:* Studied at Iowa University, at the Zürich Opera Studio and at the Musikhochschule in Hamburg. *Career:* Sang at Hagen, then at Frankfurt as Oscar in Un Ballo in Maschera, Blondchen, and Norina; Appearances in Hamburg, Bonn, Stuttgart, Berlin, Salzburg and Düsseldorf; Bayerische Staatsoper Munich, 1983, as Despina, Sophie and Zdenka; Aminta in Schweigsame Frau; Covent Garden debut, 1984, as Zerlina in Don Giovanni; Gave the premiere of Udo Zimmermann's Gib Licht meiner Augen, 1986; Sang at the Salzburg and Wiesbaden Festivals, 1987, as Blondchen and Despina; Aminta in Die schweigsame Frau at the Munich Opera, 1988 (tour of Japan, 1988 and at La Scala, Milan), Woglinde in the Ring, 1989 (also televised and available on video); Ludwigsburg Festival, 1989, as Susanna, and Carmina Burana at the 1990 Munich Festival; Sang Zdenka in Arabella at La Scala, 1992; Woglinde in Wagner's Ring at Paris Châtelet, 1994; World premiere of Manfred Trojahn's Frammenti di Michelangelo, 1995; Sang Pamina, 1996, Susanna, 1997 and Musetta, 1998 at the Opera Cologne; Sang Atalanta in Handel's Serse at the 1996 Munich Festival; Maria in the premiere of Trojahn's Was ihr Wollt (Twelfth Night), Munich 1998; Dalinda in Ariodante, Munich, 2000; Sang St Matthew Passion with Chicago Symphony, 1997; Brahms Requiem with NHK Orchestra, Tokyo, 1997; Mahler's 8th Symphony, San Francisco, 1998; Recital Tours and radio broadcasts Wolf's Italienisches Liederbuch in Italy, USA, France and Germany; Hindemith's Marienleben in Germany; Professorship in Voice at the Universität der Künste, Berlin, 1999;

Hindemith's Sancta Susanna, Cologne, 2001; Season 2000–01 at the Munich Staatsoper as Ginevra in Ariodante, and Despina; World premiere, Manfred Trojahn's 'Tritticino', Cologne, 2003; NATS, (USA); Paul Hindemith Gesellschaft, Berlin; Hans Pfitzner Gesellschaft. *Recordings:* Despina in Così fan tutte; Amor in Orfeo ed Euridice; Walther in La Wally; Woglinde in Das Rheingold, conducted by Haitink; Echo in Ariadne and Naxos, Schumann's Mignon Requiem and Mendelssohn's Lobgesang; Rezia in Pilgrims from Mecca; Nannetta in Falstaff, with Colin Davis; Solo Recital CD with Schoenberg, Debussy, Strauss, 1993, with Irwin Gage; Brahms Duette and Lieder with Marilyn Schmiege and Donald Sulzen; Beethoven Welsh, Scottish, Irish Songs with Neues Münchener Klavietrio; Hans Pfitzner Lieder with Donald Sulzen, 1999; Carl Loewe Lieder und Balladen with Cord Garben, 1999. *Honours:* Bayrischer Kammersängerin, 1991; Bayerischer Verdienstorden, 2000. *Address:* c/o Impresariat Sonia Simmenauer, Barnstrasse 12, 20146 Hamburg, Germany.

KAUPOVA, Helena; Singer (Soprano); b. 1965, Czechoslovakia. *Education:* Studied at the Brno Conservatory; Bratislava Academy. *Career:* Slovak National Theatre, Bratislava, 1990, as Pamina and Micaela; National Theatre, Prague, 1992; As Mozart's Donna Anna; Donna Elvira; Pamina and Countess; Mimi, Jenůfa, Nedda and Tatiana; Guest appearances as Mimi at Toronto; Countess, Vancouver; Jenůfa in Santiago; Smetana's Marenka at Monte Carlo; Edinburgh Festival, 1993 as Janáček's Sarka and Krasava in Libuše, 1998. *Recordings:* Libuše and highlights from Don Giovanni and Die Zauberflöte. *Address:* Music International, 13 Ardilaun Road, London N5 2QR, England.

KAVAFIAN, Ani; Violinist and Teacher; b. 10 May 1948, Istanbul, Turkey. *Education:* Pupil of Ara Zerounian, 1957–62, and Mischa Mischakoff, 1962–66, Detroit; Studied with Ivan Galamian and Felix Galimir, Juilliard School of Music, New York, MA, 1972. *Career:* Debut: Carnegie Recital Hall, New York, 1969; European debut, Salle Gaveau, Paris, 1973; Soloist with many major orchestras; Recitalist; Duo recitals with sister, Ida Kavafian; Artist-Member, Chamber Music Society of Lincoln Center, New York, 1980–; Teacher, Mannes College of Music, New York, 1982–, Manhattan School of Music, New York 1983, Queens College of the City University of New York, 1983–. *Recordings:* Discs as a recitalist and chamber music artist. *Honours:* Avery Fisher Prize, 1976. *Address:* c/o Konzert-direktion H. Adler, Beaux Arts Trio, Auguste-Viktoria-Strasse 64, D–14199 Berlin, Germany.

KAVAFIAN, Ida; Violinist; b. 29 Oct. 1952, Istanbul, Turkey. *Education:* Studied with Ara Zerounian and Mischa Mischakoff, Detroit and with Oscar Shumsky and Ivan Galamian, Juilliard School, New York, MA, 1975. *Career:* Founding Member of the chamber group Tashi, 1973; New York recital debut, 1978; European debut, London, 1982; Appearances in duo recitals with sister, Ani Kavafian; Violinist of the Beaux Arts Trio, appointed 1992. *Recordings:* Discs as a chamber music artist; RCA and Nonesuch. *Honours:* Winner, Vienna da Motta International Violin Competition, Lisbon, 1973; Silver Medal, International Violin Competition of Indianapolis, 1982; Avery Fisher Career Grant, 1988; Artistic Director of 2 Festivals, Music from Angel Fire, N M and Bravo! Colorado, Vail; Artist Member of Chamber Music Society of Lincoln Center. *Current Management:* Harry Bell. *Address:* c/o Beall Management, PO Box 30, Teneafly, NJ 07670, USA.

KAVAKOS, Leonidas; Violinist; b. 1967, Athens, Greece. *Education:* Studied at the Greek Conservatory with Stelios Kafantaris; Further studies with Joseph Gingold at the University of Indiana. *Career:* Debut: Athens Festival, 1984; Cannes Festival, 1985; US debut with the Santa Barbara Symphony, 1986; Athens Festival 1988, conducted by Rostropovich, leading to concerts with the National Symphony Orchestra in Washington DC; Concerts at the Helsinki Festival and with the Swedish Radio Symphony conducted by Esa-Pekka Salonen; European tour with the Helsinki Philharmonic conducted by Okku Kamu, 1989; Further appearances in Italy, Spain, France, Cyprus, Turkey, Hungary and Japan; Television and radio recordings in Greece, France, Germany, Spain and England; Dvořák's Concerto at the 1999 London Proms; London Proms, 2002. *Honours:* Winner, 1985 Sibelius Violin Competition, Indianapolis; 1986 International Competition; 1988 Winner, Naumburg Competition, New York; Winner 1988 Paganini Competition, Genoa. *Current Management:* Ingpen & Williams Ltd, 7 St George's Court, 131 Putney Bridge Road, London, SW15 2PA, England.

KAVRAKOS, Dimitri; Singer (Bass); b. 26 Feb. 1946, Athens, Greece. *Education:* Athens Conservatory of Music. *Career:* Debut: Athens Opera 1970, as Zaccaria in Nabucco; Athens Opera until 1978; US debut at Carnegie Hall, in Refice's Cecilia; Metropolitan Opera debut 1979, as the Grand Inquisitor in Don Carlos, returned to New York as Silva (Ernani), Walter (Luisa Miller), Ferrando (Il Trovatore), Capulet (Roméo et Juliette) and in I Vespri Siciliani; Chicago Lyric Opera in Aida, Lakmé, Les Contes d'Hoffmann and Fidelio; San Francisco Opera in La Gioconda; Guest engagements at La Scala, Paris Opéra, Aix-en-Provence, Spoleto, Lyon and Avignon; British debut Glyndebourne

1982, as the Commendatore in Don Giovanni; London debut at the Barbican Hall in Cherubini's Medée; Covent Garden debut 1984, as Pimen in Boris Godunov, returned in new productions of La Donna del Lago (Douglas 1985), Le nozze di Figaro (Bartolo) and Anna Bolena (Enrico VIII 1988); Rome Opera 1989, as Silva in Ernani, Bellini's Giorgio in Florence; Sang Fiesco in Simon Boccanegra at Cologne, 1990 and Prince Gremin in Eugene Onegin in Chicago; Maggio Musicale Florence, 1990 as Ernesto in Donizetti's Parisina; Season 1992–93 as Timur in Turandot at Chicago, Rossini's Mosè with the Israel Philharmonic, Banquo at Cologne and the Commendatore at Aix-en-Provence; Don Giovanni (Commendatore) and Le nozze di Figaro (Bartolo, Salzburg); I Puritani, Bregenz, 1985; Il Barbiere di Siviglia, Florence, 1994; Paris Opéra: Don Carlos and Puritani, 1987; Lucia, 1995; Lucrezia Borgia, Teatro San Carlo Naples, 1992; La Vestale, La Scala, 1993; Sang Banquo at Florence, 1995; La Scala 1997, in Lucia di Lammermoor; Season 1998–99 at Paris Opéra with Lucia di Lammermoor and I Capuleti e i Montecchi; Sang Arkel in Pelléas at Toronto, 2000. Recordings include: Don Giovanni; La Vestale, La Scala, 1993; Rigoletto, La Scala, 1994; Ravenna, Norma, 1994. Address: c/o Patricia Greenan, 19B Belsize Park, London NW3 4DU, England.

KAWAHARA, Yoko; Singer (Soprano); b. 3 Sept. 1939, Tokyo, Japan. Education: Studied with Toishiko Toda in Tokyo and with Ellen Bosenius at the Cologne Musikhochschule. Career: Debut: Niki Kai Opera Tokyo 1958, as Fiordligi; Sang in Bonn as Pamina, 1969; Bayreuth Festival 1972–77, as the Woodbird in Siegfried; Member of the Cologne Opera from 1975; Guest appearances in Frankfurt, Hamburg and Tokyo; Staatsoper Hamburg 1986, in La Clemenza di Tito; Other roles include Euridice, Sophie in Der Rosenkavalier, Desdemona, Freia and Liu; Many concert appearances. Recordings include: Reger's Requiem (Schwann). Address: c/o Oper der Stadt Köln, Offenbachplatz, 5000 Cologne, Germany.

KAWALLA, Szymon (Piotr); Conductor and Composer; b. 2 June 1949, Kraków, Poland; m. Hanna Kiepuszewska, 28 April 1973, 1 d. Education: Studies as Solo Concert Violinist 1972, as Conductor 1973, as Composer 1974, Chopin Academy of Music, Warsaw. Career: Debut: Philharmonic, Kraków, 1964; Conductor, Philharmonic Poherien, 1974–78; Conductor-Director, Torun Chamber Orchestra, 1978–80; Conductor-Director, Philharmonic and Opera Zielona Gora, 1980–86; Symphonic Orchestra and Chorus, RTV Kraków, 1985–; Concerts in Austria, Bulgaria, Canada, Cuba, England, Germany, Netherlands, France, Italy, Poland, Romania, Spain, Czechoslovakia, Russia, Vatican; Radio, television and films; Professor, Chopin Academy of Music, Warsaw. Compositions: Divertimento, Capriccio for violin solo, Oratorio, Pater Kolbe, Cantata, Wit Stwosz, Stabat Mater, Quartet for Strings. Address: Lazurowa 6/100, 01-315 Warsaw, Poland.

KAWASAKI, Masaru; University Professor and Composer; b. 19 April 1924, Tokyo, Japan; m. Taeko Koide, 11 June 1953, 2 s. Education: Diploma 1947, Postgraduate Diploma 1949, Tokyo Academy of Music. Career: 1st performance of Compos at Festliche Musiktage Uster, Switzerland, 1971, 1974, 1977, 1981; Director, International Youth Musicale, Shizuoka, Japan, 1979, 1982 and 1985; mem, International Society Contemporary Music; Japanese Society Rights Authors and Composers; National Band Association. Compositions: March Ray of Hope, 1963; March Forward for Peace, 1966; Essay on a Day for flute and piano, 1969; March Progress and Harmony, 1969; Warabe-Uta for symphony band, 1970; Prayer Music Number 1, Dirge, commissioned by Hiroshima City, 1975; Poem for symphony band, 1976; Prayer Music Number 2, Elegy, 1977; Romantic Episode, 1979; Romance for trumpet and symphony band, 1982; March Dedicated to Cupid, 1983; In the Depth of Night for flute and cello, 1993. Publications: Instrumentation and Arrangement for Wind Ensemble, 1972; New Band Method, 1979. Contributions: Band Journal, Tokyo. Honours: Composition Prize, Ministry of Education and President of NHK, 1956; Creative Artists Fellow, UNESCO, 1966–67. Address: 4-2-38 Hamatake, Chigasaki-shi, 2530021, Japan.

KAY, Donald (Henry); Composer; b. 25 Jan. 1933, Smithton, Tasmania. Education: BMus, University of Melbourne, 1955; Study with Malcolm Williamson, 1959–64. Career: Faculty member, Tasmanian Conservatorium, 1967–; Commissions from APRA, Lyrian String Quartet, Tasmanian Symphony Chamber Players, and others. Compositions include: Dance Movement for small orchestra, 1968; Four Australian Folk Songs, for women's or young voices, 1971; The Quest, for string quartet, 1971; There is an Island, for children's choir and orchestra, 1977; The Golden Crane, opera for children and adults, 1984; Dance Cameos, for mandolin, wind quintet, 1986; Hastings Triptych, for flute and piano, 1986; Northward the Strait, for chorus, soprano, baritone and wind band, 1988; Tasmania Symphony: The Legend of Moinee, for cello and orchestra, 1988; Dance Concertante for string orchestra, 1989; Haiku, for women's voices, piano and string quartet, 1990; Night Spaces, for flute, string trio and piano, 1990; Piano Concerto, 1992; Moonlight Ridge for string quintet or string orchestra, 1994; AEstiver-

nal for mandolin, wind quintet or orchestra, 1994; River Views for trombone and string orchestra, 1995; The Edge of Remoteness for piano trio, 1996; Symphony–The South Land, 1997; Sonata for cello and piano, 1999; Sonata for piano, 1998; Different Worlds, for piano, 1999; Bird chants, for piano, 1999; Blue sky through still trees, for flute and piano, 1999; String Quartet No, 5, a trgaic life, 2002; The death of Ben Hall, for SATB chorus and concert band, 2002. Recordings: Tasmania Symphony–The Legend of Moinee. Honours: Sounds Australian Awards, 1989, 1990; Member of the General Division of the Order of Australia, 1991. Address: 4 Utiekah Drive, Taroona, Tasmania 7053, Australia.

KAY, Serena; Singer (Mezzo-soprano); b. 1973, England. Education: London University, Royal College of Music- Opera School, currently studies with Paul Farrington. Career: Opera roles include Hermia (Midsummer Night's Dream), English Touring Opera; Second Lady (Magic Flute), Opera North; Cenerentola, Mid Wales Opera; Rosina (Il Barbiere), Clonter Opera; Guido (Flavio), London Handel Society; Dorabella (Cosi fan tutte), Mananan Opera; concerts include Messiah (Handel), Huddersfield Choral Society; Les Nuits d'ete (Berlioz), Oxford Sinfonia; Lieder eines fahrenden gesellen (Mahler); Barber of Seville highlights (with Gerald Finlay). Address: c/o Ingpen and Williams Ltd, St George's Court, 131 Putney Bridge Road, London, SW15 2PA England.

KAZARAS, Peter; Singer (Tenor); b. 1956, New York, USA. Career: Debut: New York in 1981 in a concert performance of Khovanshchina; Houston in 1983 as Francois in the premiere of Bernstein's A Quiet Place; Santa Fe and Seattle in 1985 in Henze's English Cat and as Steva in Jenůfa; Returned to Seattle as Wagner's Froh and Erik, Hoffmann, Lensky and Pierre in War and Peace; New York City Opera debut in 1988 as Quint in The Turn of The Screw; Sang with Metropolitan Opera from 1990 as Narraboth in Salome, Shuisky in Boris Godunov and Almaviva in the premiere of Corigliano's The Ghosts of Versailles; Other modern repertory includes Udo Zimmermann's Die Weisse Rose, at Omaha in 1986, Pelegrin in the premiere of Tippett's New Year, at Houston in 1989, and Busoni's Die Brautwahl at Berlin Staatsoper in 1991; Sang Boris in the New Zealand premiere of Katya Kabanova, 1996; Captain Vere in Billy Budd at Dallas, 1997. Address: c/o Metropolitan Opera, Lincoln Center, New York, NY 10023, USA.

KAZARNOVSKAYA, Lyuba; Singer (Soprano); b. 1960, Moscow, Russia. Education: Studied at the Moscow Conservatory 1976–81, with Irina Arkhipova and Elena Shumilova. Career: Debut: La Scala Milan 1989 in Verdi's Requiem under R. Muti; Has sung at the Bolshoi, Moscow, as Nedda, Mimi and Lida in La Battaglia di Legnano; Tour of Italy with the Maily Theatre, Leningrad, 1984; Kirov Theatre, Leningrad from 1986 as Leonora (La Forza del Destino and Trovatore), Marina, Violetta, Marguerite, Donna Anna and Tchaikovsky's Iolanta; Paris Opéra and Covent Garden 1987, as Tatiana with the Kirov Company; Salzburg Festival 1989, in the Verdi Requiem, conducted by Karajan; Zürich Opera 1989–90, as Amelia Boccanegra and the Trovatore Leonora; Cologne Opera 1989–90, as Manon Lescaut and Amelia; Covent Garden 1990, as Desdemona; Metropolitan Opera: Tatjana in Eugene Onegin under Levine, Desdemona in Otello, Nedda in Pagliacci, 1991–95; Debut in Strauss' Salome, 1995; New productions of Clemenza di Tito and Il Trovatore at San Francisco Opera and at Lyric Chicago, Tosca in Houston, Berlin and Vienna; Recitals at the major music festivals; Sang Pauline in Prokofiev's The Gambler at La Scala and in Paris, 1996–97; Aithra in Strauss' Aegyptische Helena under Thielemann with the Royal Opera at the Festival Hall, 1998; First time ever singing 2 Manons in one evening; Massenet and Puccini premiere at the Bolshoi Theatre, Moscow and afterwards at opera festivals in Italy, Sweden, Germany and USA; 2000: Personal television music show 'Glimpse of Love'; Concert and oratorio appearances, song recitals with works by Brahms, Wolf, de Falla, Dvořák and Rachmaninov; mem, Russian Opera Forum; President, Ljuba Kararnovskaya Foundation. Recordings include: Shostakovich's 12th Symphony; Prokofiev's The Gambler; Tchaikovsky's The Complete Songs Op 103, 5 CDs; Videos: The Great Singers of Russia 1901–99; Gypsy Love. Honours: The Voice of the Year, Russia, 2001. Current Management: IMG. Address: Arbat 35, Moscow 121002, Russia. E-mail: kazarnovskaya@888.ru.

KEATING, Roderic Maurice, MA, MMus, DMus; opera and concert singer (tenor); b. 14 Dec. 1941, Maidenhead, Berkshire, England; m. Martha Kathryn Post 1968, one d. Education: Gonville and Caius Coll., Cambridge, Yale Univ., USA, Univ. of Texas, USA. Career: debut, Houston Grand Opera, Tales of Hoffmann, 1970; Glyndebourne Touring and Festival Opera, 1971–73; Theater an der Wien, Freddy, My Fair Lady, 1971; Permanent contracts in: Lübeck, 1972–74, Saarbrücken, 1974–80, Wuppertal, 1980–86, Bonn, 1986–89, Stuttgart, 1989–; Over 80 roles as lyric and character tenor; Guest throughout Germany; Guest appearances: Tbilisi, Russia, 1976, Interlaken Festspiel, 1975, Wiesbaden, 1977, Paris Opéra, 1981, London Coliseum, 1982, Warsaw, 1983, Cologne, 1985, Salzburg Festival, 1986, Covent Garden, 1988, Moscow, 1989, Vienna and Schwetzingen Festivals, 1990; Edinburgh Festival,

2001; Sang Tiresias in Henze's The Bassarids at Stuttgart, 1989; Der Rosenkavalier, Théâtre Châtelet, Paris, 1993 and Bologna, 1995; Weill's Seven Deadly Sins, Tel-Aviv, 1997; Sang the Doctor in Three Sisters by Eötvös at Freiburg, 2000; Concerts and radio recordings for BBC, Bavarian Radio, and SWF, WDR, SDR in Germany; Oratorio and church concerts in: Italy, France, Spain, Belgium, Netherlands, Germany. *Publications:* The Songs of Frank Bridge 1970. *Contributions:* Musical Times, Musical Opinion. *Current Management:* Allied Artists, 42 Montpelier Square, London, SW7 1JZ, England. *Address:* Lehenbühlstrasse 36, 71272 Renningen, Germany. *Telephone:* 7159 18156. *Fax:* 7159 18156. *E-mail:* Roderickeating@aol.com.

KEATS, Donald (Howard); Composer and Professor; b. 27 May 1929, New York, NY, USA; m. Eleanor Steinholz, 13 Dec 1953, 2 s., 2 d. *Education:* BMus primi honoris, Yale University School of Music, 1949; MA, Columbia University, 1952; Staatliche Hochschule für Musik, Hamburg, 1954–56; PhD, University of Minnesota. *Career:* Professor of Music, Antioch College, Ohio; Visiting Professor of Music, University of Washington, Seattle; Lawrence C Phipps Professor in the Humanities, University of Denver, 1982–85; Professor of Music, 1975–99, Professor Emeritus, 1999–, University of Denver, Colorado; Composer, Pianist, at concerts devoted solely to his music in USA, England and Israel. *Compositions include:* Symphonies No. 1 and No. 2 (An Elegiac Symphony); String Quartets No. 1, No. 2 and No. 3 (2001); Piano Sonata; The Hollow Men (T. S. Eliot), for chorus and instruments; Anyone Lived in a Pretty How Town (Cummings), for a cappella chorus; The Naming of Cats (T. S. Eliot), for chorus and piano; Tierras del Alma (Poemas de amor), song cycle for soprano, flute and guitar; Theme and Variations for Piano; Concerto for Piano and Orchestra; Diptych for cello and piano; Polarities for violin and piano; A Love Triptych (W B Yeats), song cycle; Musica Instrumentalis for 9 instruments; Elegy for full or chamber orchestra; Branchings for orchestra; Revisitations for violin, cello and piano. *Recordings:* String Quartet No. 2 (CD 1999); Piano Sonata, 1999. *Publications:* Many of above compositions published by Boosey and Harber. *Honours:* Fulbright Scholar, 1954–56; Guggenheim Fellowships, 1964–65, 1972–73; ASCAP Awards Annually since 1964. *Address:* 12854 West Buckhorn Road, Littleton, CO 80127, USA. *Telephone:* 303 948 3033. *E-mail:* dkeats@du.edu.

KEBERLE, David (Scott); Composer, Clarinettist and College Professor; b. 6 June 1952, Wausau, Wisconsin, USA. *Education:* BM, Composition, with distinction, Indiana University, 1975; BM, Education, with distinction, Indiana University, 1975; MMus, Composition, New England Conservatory of Music, Boston, 1977; Accademia di S Cecilia, Rome, 1980; Studied composition with Bernhard Heiden and Donald Martino, clarinet with Earl Bates, Joe Allard and W O Smith. *Career:* Instructor of Music, University of Wisconsin, Baraboo, 1977–81; Co-Founder of Electravox Ensemble, Rome, 1983; Instructor of Music, Loyola University, Chicago, Rome Centre, 1984–88; As Clarinet Soloist, performed in Brazil, Uruguay, Argentina, France, Italy, Israel, Austria and USA; Performed on National Italian Radio, 1987, 1988; Instructor of Music, St Mary's College, Rome Program, 1991–; mem, American Music Center, New York. *Compositions:* Incantation for clarinet and live electronics, 1986; Galoppando Attraverso il Vuoto for solo clarinet 1986; Concerto for Trumpet and Chamber Ensemble, 1980; Murmurs for solo flute, published by EDI-PAN Rome, 1989. *Recordings:* ElectraVox Ensemble Incantation for Clarinet and Live Electronics 1986, EDI-PAN Rome; Musicisti Contemporanei Clarinet and Piano EDI-PAN, 1989. *Honours:* Fulbirght Scholarship in Composition, 1979. *Address:* Via del Pellegrino 75, Int 18, 00186 Rome, Italy.

KECHABIAN, Rafael; Violinist, Concert Performer and Professor of Violin; b. 14 Feb. 1949, Yerevan, Armenia; m. Irene Kechabian, 25 Mar 1978, 2 s. *Education:* Special Musical School and Musical Secondary School, Sukhumi, 1957; State Yerevan Conservatory, Armenia, 1969; Postgraduate Course, State Yerevan Conservatory, Armenia, 1989–92; Diploma Violinist, Concert Performer, Professor of Violin and Chamber Music. *Career:* Professor of Violin, Yerevan Music School, Armenia, 1970–83; Concertino, National Symphony Orchestra, Nicaragua, 1983–87; Professor of Violin, National Conservatory, Nicaragua, 1983–87; Soloist, State Chamber Ensemble of Armenia, 1987–93; Professor of Chamber Music, State Yerevan Conservatory, Armenia, 1987–93; Principal of the second violins, Symphony Orchestra of the Murcian Region, Spain, 1993–94; Professor of Violin, Musical Academy, Murcia, Spain, 1995; Violin Maker, Murcia, Spain, 1995. *Recordings:* Violinist, over 30 titles including: first recording of classical music in history of Nicaragua with National Symphony Orchestra, Miami, USA, 1984; Violinist, joint recordings with Orchestra Moscow Virtuosos of Spivakov, Moscow, 1983. *Honours:* Diploma, Ministry of Culture of the Republic of Nicaragua, 1987. *Address:* c/o Mariano Aroca, 7–4 1zq, 30011 Murcia, Spain.

KEE, Piet; Organist and Composer; b. 30 Aug. 1927, Zaandam, Netherlands; 2 c. *Education:* Studied with father, Cor Kee; Organ with Anthon van der Horst, Final Certificate cum laude and Prix d'excellence, 1948,

Conservatoire of Amsterdam. *Career:* Debut: Zaandam, 1941; Organist of Schnitger organ, St Laurens Church, Alkmaar, 1952–87; Municipal Organist, St Bavo Church, Haarlem, 1956–89; Professor of Organ, Conservatoire of the Society Muzieklyceum, Sweelinck Conservatoire, Amsterdam, until 1987; Professor, International Summer Academy, Haarlem; Many concert tours world-wide; Television films of compositions Confrontation and Integration. *Compositions:* Two Songs (text Edgard Lemaire) for mezzo soprano and string quartet; Variations on a Carol, 1954; Triptych on Psalm 86, 1960; Two Organ Works, 1962; Four Manual Pieces, 1966; Music and Space for 2 Organs and 5 Brasswinds, 1969; Intrada for 2 Organs; Chamber Music; Valerius Gedenck-Clanck, 1976; Confrontation for 3 street organs and church organ, 1979; Integration for mixed choir, flageolet, mechanical birds, barrel organs and church organ, 1980; Frans Hals Suite for Carillon, 1990; Flight for flute solo, 1992; Bios for organ, 1994; Network for 2 organs, electronic keyboard, alto saxophone and descant recorder, 1996; Op-streek, for violin and piano, 1997; The World (text Henry Vaughan) for mixed choir and continuo instrument, 1999; Winds, for reed winds quintet, 2000; The Organ, homage to Pieter Saenredam, for organ, 2000; Heaven for mixed choir, 2001; Festival Spirit for five organs (commissioned by the International Organ Festival of St. Albans), 2001; Bios II for Organ, percussion and one violin, 2002; Heaven (text George Herbert) echo-fantasy for mixed choir and two solo sopranos; Festival Spirit for grand organ and 4 box organs; Bios II for organ, keyboard percussion, one violin and more percussion. *Recordings include:* Baroque music, romantic and modern music; New series of CDs including Bach organ works (4 vols); Franck organworks (San Sebastian); Piet Kee at Weingarten; Piet Kee at the Concertgebouw; Piet Kee plays Sweelinck and Buxtehude; Piet Kee plays Bruhns; Piet Kee plays Hindemith and Reger. *Publications:* The Secrets of Bach's Passacaglia, Musik und Kirche, 1982; Astronomy in Buxtehude's Passacaglia, The Diapason, Ars Organi, Het Orgel, 1984; Numbers and Symbolism in the Passacaglia and Ciacona, Het Orgel, 1986; Musik und Kirche, 1987; Loosemore Papers. *Honours:* Hon. FRCO. *Address:* Nieuwe Gracht 41, 2011 ND Haarlem, Netherlands.

KEEFFE, Bernard; Conductor and Broadcaster; b. 1 April 1925, London, England; m. Denise Walker, 10 Sept 1954, 1 s., 1 d. *Education:* BA Honours, Clare College, Cambridge, 1951; Private studies: Cello with Di Marco, Voice with Roy Henderson and Lucie Manen, Conducting with Berthold Goldschmidt. *Career:* Appearances as solo baritone in opera, concerts, musical plays (London, Edinburgh Festival); Producer and Conductor, 1955–60, Head of Radio Opera, 1959, BBC Music Department; Controller of Opera Planning, Royal Opera House, London, 1960–62; Conductor, BBC Scottish Orchestra, 1962–64; Many appearances on BBC television as Commentator and Conductor; Concerts and broadcasts with major orchestras; Chief Conductor, Bournemouth Municipal Choir, 1972–81; Professor, Trinity College of Music, 1966–89; Many engagements as international jurist for various competitions including Italia Prize for Broadcasting, Anvers, Liège, Sofia, London; mem, Former Warden, Solo Performers Section, Incorporated Society of Musicians; Chairman, Anglo-Austrian Music Society. *Recordings:* L'Oiseau-Lyre, as conductor with Melos Ensemble and Janet Baker; Music of Ravel and Delage. *Publications:* English National Opera Guide to Tosca; Harrap Dictionary of Music and Musicians (editor); Authorised translations: Janáček, Diary of One Who Disappeared; Petrassi, Death in the Air. *Contributions:* BBC Music Magazine, World Service; Hi-Fi News; Music Teacher; Classical Music Fortnightly. *Honours:* Honorary Fellow, Trinity College, London, 1968. *Address:* 153 Honor Oak Road, London SE23 3 RN, England.

KEEGAN, Liane; Singer (contralto); b. 1963, Australia. *Education:* Melba Conservatorium, Melbourne; National Opera Studio, London, Graz Summer School. *Career:* Appearances as Suzuki in Butterfly for Opera North (1996) Barbara in Korngold's Violanta at the 1997 London Proms and Waltraute in Act III of Die Walküre at the 1997 Edinburgh Festival; Other roles include Fricka, Dalila, Ulrica, Mistress Quickly, Dorabella and Rosina; Azucena for the State Opera of South Australia, 1999; Recitals throughout the United Kingdom and in France and Austria; Concerts include Mahler's Lieder eines fahrenden Gesellen, Das Lied von der Erde, Symphonies 2 and 3; Elijah, The Dream of Gerontius, Verdi Requiem, the Wesendonck lieder and Elgar's Sea Pictures; Schubert documentary on German television, 1995; Sang Erda, First Norn and Waltraute in Der Ring des Nibelungen for the State Opera of South Australia, 1998; Season 2002 Ulrica for Opera Australia (Un Ballo in Maschera), Gaea for Vara Radio Amsterdam Concertgebouw (Daphne); Season 2003, First Norn in The Ring, Offred's Mother in The Handmaid's Tale for ENO; Season 2004, Erda, 1st Norn and Waltraute in the Ring at Adelaide, Australia. *Current Management:* Arts Management. *E-mail:* enquiries@artsmanagement.com.au.

KEEN, Catherine; Singer (Mezzo-soprano); b. 1970, California, USA. *Education:* Adler Fellow, San Francisco Opera. *Career:* Appearances as Dalila at the Deutsche Oper Berlin and with Netherlands Opera as

Federica in Luisa Miller, Verdi's Emilia and Suzuki in Butterfly; Wagner's Flosshilde, 1999–2000; San Francisco Opera as Britten's Hermia, Magdelene, Venus in Tannhäuser, Fricka and Offenbach's Giulietta; Verdi's Amneris and Fenena at the 1998 Verona Arena and Brangaene in Tristan with the Cincinnati Symphony Orchestra; Season 1999–2000 with Waltraute and Fricka at Catania, Amneris in Houston and Kundry and Handel's Cornelia in Giulio Cesare at Washington; Concerts include Das Lied von der Erde in Paris, Mahler 8 at the Edinburgh Festival, Beethoven 9 and Schubert's Rosamunde. *Address:* c/o IMG Artists, Lovell House, 616 Chiswick High Road, London W4 5RX, England.

KEENLYSIDE, Raymond; Musician and Violinist; b. 9 May 1928, Southsea, Hampshire, England; m. Cynthia J Page, 2 s., 1 d. *Education:* Trinity College of Music, London. *Career:* Principal of Chamber Orchestras including: Boyd Neel; Philomusica; English Chamber Orchestra; Academy of St Martin-in-the-Fields; member of London Harpsichord Ensemble, 1959–62; David Martin String Quartet; Aeolian String Quartet, 1962–81; Professor of Violin, Royal College of Music; Senior Tutor, Royal College of Music Junior Department; Numerous radio appearances; Series on BBC television of late Beethoven String Quartets; Other television appearances. *Recordings:* Complete Haydn String Quartets, re-issued, 1997; Works by Schubert, Mozart, Elgar, Vaughan Williams, Ravel, Debussy, all with the Aeolian Quartet; Others with other groups. *Contributions:* Daily Telegraph Magazine. *Honours:* LTCL (TTD); Honorary MA, Newcastle University, 1970; Honorary FTCL, 1983; Honorary FRCM. *Address:* Bailiwick, Upper Woodford, Salisbury, Wiltshire SP4 6PF, England.

KEENLYSIDE, Simon; Singer (baritone); b. 3 Aug. 1959, London, England. *Education:* studied at the Royal Northern Coll. of Music. *Career:* gave concert performances, then engaged with Scottish Opera as Papageno and Billy Budd; Season 1994–95 as Mozart's Count and Guglielmo at Covent Garden, Hamlet in the opera by Thomas at Geneva; sang Guglielmo at the reopened Palais Garnier, Paris, 1996, and Thomas's Hamlet in Geneva; also sings lieder by Schubert; concerts include Britten's War Requiem at the Festival Hall (CBSO, 1997); Marcello and Figaro at the Vienna State Opera, 1999; sang Monteverdi's Orfeo with Concerto Vocale under René Jacobs, Barbican Theatre, 1998; sang Papageno at the New York Met, 2001; Season 2000–01 as Pelléas in Geneva, Marcello at the Met, Guglielmo at Salzburg and Billy Budd; Wagner's Wolfram in Munich and Belcore (L'Elisir d'amore) at La Scala. *Honours:* winner, Richard Tauber Competition, 1986. *Current Management:* Askonas Holt Ltd, Lonsdale Chambers, 27 Chancery Lane, London, WC2A 1PF, England. *Telephone:* (20) 7400-1700. *Fax:* (20) 7400-1799. *E-mail:* info@askonasholt.co.uk. *Website:* www.askonasholt .co.uk.

KEHL, Sigrid; singer (soprano, mezzo-soprano); b. 23 Nov. 1932, Berlin, Germany. *Education:* studied in Erfurt, Berlin Musikhochschule and with Dagmar Freiwald-Lange. *Career:* debut at Berlin Staatsoper 1956, in Prince Igor; Member of the Leipzig Opera from 1957, notably as Brünnhilde in Der Ring des Nibelungen, 1974; Engagements at the Berlin Staatsoper from 1971, Vienna Staatsoper from 1975; Further appearances at the Komische Oper Berlin and in Prague, Bucharest, Rome, Bologna, Geneva, Warsaw and Basle; Lausanne Festival 1983, as Isolde.

KEINONEN, Heiki; Singer (Baritone); b. 1951, Finland. *Education:* Studied in Helsinki. *Career:* Sang in concert from 1976, and at the Savonlinna Festival; Finnish National Opera at Helsinki from 1981, notably as Germont in La Traviata, 1993, and the premiere of Insect Life by Kalevi Aho, 1996; Vasa Opera, 1994, in the premiere of Miss Julie by Ilkka Kuusisto; Sang Pontto in the premiere of The Key, by Aho at Helsinki, 1995; Title role in Sweeney Todd, 1998. *Recordings include:* Kung Karls Jakt by Pacius. *Address:* c/o Finnish National Opera, PO Box 176, Helsingkatu 58, 00251 Helsinki, Finland.

KEITH, Gillian; Singer (Soprano); b. 1971, Canada. *Education:* McGill University, Montreal; Royal Academy, London, with Ian Partridge. *Career:* Concert repertoire includes Les Illuminations by Britten, Finzi's Dies Natalis, Strauss's Ophelia Lieder, Schubert's Mignon Lieder and Debussy's Quatre chansons de jeunesse; Soloist in Bach Cantatas on tour with John Eliot Gardiner, 2000, including Falsche Welt, dir trau ich nicht; Appearances in Brussels, New York, Edinburgh, London and Winchester; Season 2001 with Josabeth in Athalia for the London Handel Festival, Messiah and Israel in Egypt on tour to Austria, Germany and Turkey; Song recitals at Covent Garden, St George's Bristol and Tel-Aviv; Wigmore Hall debut June 2001; Handel's Israel in Egypt at the London Proms, 2002; Other repertory includes Purcell's Fairy Queen. *Recordings include:* Purcell's The Tempest, Hasse's Il Cantico de' tre fanciulli. *Honours:* Winner, Lieder, Early Music and French Song prizes, RAM. *Address:* Royal Academy of Music, Marylebone Road, London WC1, England.

KEKULA, Josef; violinist; b. 1952, Czechoslovakia. *Education:* studied with Václav Snítil and members of Smetana Quartet, Kostecky and Kohout. *Career:* co-founder and 2nd Violinist, Stamic Quartet of Prague, 1977; Performances at Prague Young Artists and Bratislava Music Festivals; Tours to: Spain, Austria, France, Switzerland, Germany, Eastern Europe; USA tour, 1980; Debut concerts in the United Kingdom at London and Birmingham, 1983; British tours, 1985, 1987, 1988 at Warwick Arts Festival, 20 concerts in 1989; Season 1991–92: Channel Islands, Netherlands, Finland, Austria, France, Edinburgh Festival, Debut tours of Canada, Japan and Indonesia; In 1994 visited Korea and Japan; In 1995 visited USA. *Recordings:* Shostakovich No. 13; Schnittke No. 4 Panton; Mozart K589 and K370, Lyrinx; Dvořák; Martinů; Janáček complete quartets, Cadenza; Complete Dvořák String Quartets; Complete Martinů String Quartets; 1 CD, Clarinet Quintets by Mozart and Krommer. *Publications:* Complete Works of Smetana and Janáček String Quartet. *Honours:* with members of Stamic Quartet: Winner, International Festival of Young Soloists, Bordeaux, 1977, Winner, EBU International String Quartet Competition, 1986, Academie Charles Cros Grand Prix du Disque, 1989 for Dvořák Quartets, 1991 for Martinů Quartets; Diapason d'Or, 1994 for Dvořák Quintets. *Current Management:* Robert Gilder & Co., Enterprise House, 59–65 Upper Ground, London, SE1 9PQ, England. *Telephone:* (20) 7928-9008. *Fax:* (20) 7928-9755. *E-mail:* rgilder@robert-gilder.com.

KELANI, Reem Yousef; Palestinian singer and musicologist; b. 7 Aug. 1963, Manchester, England. *Education:* Kuwait Univ. *Career:* initially singer of jazz, subsequently Arab music; based in London 1989–, as performer and researcher of Palestinian music; research into traditional music from interviews in Palestine and in Lebanese refugee camps; featured vocalist, Gilad Atzmon and The Orient House Ensemble 2002–03; performed at Vossa Jazz Festival, Norway 2003. *Recordings:* Exile (BBC Jazz Award for Best CD) 2003. *Address:* The Miktab, PO Box 31652, London, W11 2YF, England (office). *Telephone:* (7092) 811747 (office). *E-mail:* reem@reemkelani.com. *Website:* www.reemkelani.com.

KELEMEN, Barnabas; Violinist; b. 12 June 1978, Budapest, Hungary. *Education:* Franz Liszt Academy, Budapest. *Career:* Appeared at Brabant Festival, Netherlands, and Cambridge Festival, England, 1992; Performances in Italy, 1995, Spain, 1996, on 3SAT television, Saarbrücken, Germany, 1997, and at Wigmore Hall, London, 1998. *Recordings:* F Liszt: Works for Violin and Piano, with Sergely Bogányi. *Honours:* 2nd Prize, Szigeti Competition, Budapest, 1997; 1st Prize, Mozart Competition, Salzburg, 1999. *Current Management:* Clemens Concerts Ltd, Attila út 61, 1013 Budapest, Hungary. *Address:* Széchenyi-emlek út 23, 1121 Budapest, Hungary.

KELEMEN, Milko; Composer; b. 30 March 1924, Slatina, Croatia. *Education:* Studies, Zagreb Academy of Music and with Messiaen and Aubin, Paris; Further study with Wolfgang Fortner, Freiburg, also Siemens Electronic Music Studio, Munich. *Career:* Taught Composition, Zagreb Conservatory, 1955–58, 1960–65; Founder, Zagreb Biennial Festival, President, 1961; Taught, Schumann Conservatory, Düsseldorf, 1972; Professor of Composition, Hochschule für Musik, Stuttgart, 1973; Professor of Composition, Hochschule Hans Eisler, Berlin, 1999. *Compositions include:* The Abandoned, ballet, 1964; O Primavera, tenor, strings, 1965; Words, cantata, 1966; Composé, 2 pianos, orchestra, 1967; Changeant, cello, orchestra, 1968; Motion, string quartet, 1969; The Siege, opera after Camus, 1970; Floreal, orchestra, 1970; Varia Melodia, string quartet, 1972; Gasho, 4 choir groups, 1974; Seven Agonies, mezzo, 1975; Mageia, orchestra, 1978; Apocalypse, ballet opera, 1979; Grand Jeu Classique, violin, orchestra, 1982; Love Song, strings, 1984; Dramatico, cello, orchestra, 1985; Fantasmus, viola, orchestra, 1986; Archetypon, orchestra, 1986; Landscapes, mezzo, string quartet, 1986; Memories, string trio, 1987; Sonnets, string quartet, 1987; Nonet, 1988; Requiem, speaker, ensemble, 1994; Salut au Monde, oratorio, soloists, 2 choruses, orchestra, projections, light actions, text Walt Whitman, 1995; Concerto for Oboe, English Horn, Oboe D'Amore and chamber orchestra; Good Bye My Fancy for violin and piano; Fantastic Animals for chorus, 1996; For Anton (Bruckner) for orchestra, 1996; Delicate Clusters for orchestra, 1999; Concerto 2000 for 5 singers and orchestra, 1999; Horn and Strings, 1999; Glissade, concerto for clarinet and orchestra, 2001; Tromberia, concerto for trumpet and orchestra, 2001; Aural, trio for violin, cello and piano, 2002; Orion, Venus, Andromeda, chorus for children; Inferno di Dante for bass solo; Intonazioni Poetiche for chamber orchestra; Pas de Deux, duo for violin and cello; Incanto for solo violin. *Recordings:* Various labels. *Publications:* Klanglabyrinthe, 1981, French, 1985, Croatian, 1994; Poruka Pateru Kolbu (Croatian), 1995, Message to Father Kolb (English), 1995; Klangwelten (German), 1995; Schreiben an Strawinsky (German). *Address:* Bergstrasse 62/II, 70186 Stuttgart, Germany.

KELÉN, Peter; Singer (Tenor); b. 27 July 1950, Budapest, Hungary. *Career:* Sang at the National Opera, Budapest, from 1974, notably as Werther, Edgardo in Lucia di Lammermoor, Alfredo, Don Carlos, the Duke of Mantua, Don Ottavio and Don José; Guest appearances at La

Scala, Milan, as Fenton in Falstaff, 1983, Ernesto in Don Pasquale at the Vienna Staatsoper, Des Grieux in Rio de Janeiro and Riccardo at Milwaukee, 1990; Earl's Court, London, 1991, as Cavaradossi in Tosca; Budapest, 1995, in the premiere of Karl and Anna by Balassa. *Address:* Hungarian National Opera, Nepoztasarag utja 22, 1061 Budapest, Hungary.

KELESSIDI, Elena; Singer (Soprano); b. 1970, Kazakhstan. *Education:* Alma-Ata Conservatory. *Career:* Season 1991 at the Alma-Ata Opera as Bizet's Leila, Zerlina in Auber's Fra Diavalo, Wolf-Ferrari's Serafina and Amor in Orfeo ed Euridice; Mozart's Mme Herz and Constanze at the Athens State Opera, 1992; Donna Anna for Latvian Opera, under Gustav Kuhn; Royal Opera, Covent Garden from 1996, as Voice from Heaven in Don Carlos, Violetta and Handel's Cleopatra (1997). Season 1998–99 as Violetta for the Bavarian State Opera; Sang the Queen of Shemakha in The Golden Cockerel with the Royal Opera at Sadler's Wells (1991) and Giulietta in I Capuleti e i Montecchi at Covent Garden, 2001; Further engagements as Violetta in Monte Carlo and Hamburg, Tatiana (Eugene Onegin) at Montpellier and Gilda in Rio; Season 2001–2002 as Mimi at the Opéra Bastille and the New York Met, Susanna for Dallas Opera and Liu in Turandot for Netherlands Opera. *Address:* c/o Royal Opera (Contracts) Covent Garden, London WC2, England.

KELLER, András; violinist; b. 1960, Hungary. *Education:* Franz Liszt Acad., Budapest and with Sandor Devich, György Kurtág and András Mihaly. *Career:* member of the Keller String Quartet from 1986, debut concert at Budapest March 1987; Played Beethoven's Grosse Fuge and Schubert's Death and the Maiden Quartet at Interforum 87; Series of concerts in Budapest with Zoltan Kocsis and Deszö Ranki (Piano) and Kalman Berkes (Clarinet); Further appearances in Nuremberg, at the Chamber Music Festival La Baule and tours of Bulgaria, Austria, Switzerland, Italy (Ateforum 88 Ferrara), Belgium and Ireland; Concerts for Hungarian Radio and Television. *Recordings:* albums for Hungaroton (from 1989). *Honours:* 2nd Prize, Evian International String Quartet Competition, May 1988. *Address:* Vitorla U.3, 1031 Budapest, Hungary.

KELLER, Heinrich; flautist and composer; b. 14 Nov. 1940, Winterthur, Switzerland; m. 1968; three s. *Education:* Conservatory, Zürich. *Career:* debut, 1965; Philharmony, Bremen, 1965–66; Orchestra of St Gallen, 1967–72; Musikkollegium Winterthur, solo Flautist, 1972–; mem, Schweizerischer Tonkunstlerverein; Musikkollegium Winterthur, solo Flautist, 1972–1990; Musikhochschule Winterthur, Professor of Flute, 1972–2003. *Compositions:* Aleph, 1966; Blaserquintett, 1972; Puzzle, 1973; Streichquartett, 1973–74; Reduktion, 1974; Refrains, 1975; Ritual, 1979; Rencontre, flute and harpsichord, 1985; Verlorene Spur for piano, 1986; Rand for flute solo, 2002. *Recordings:* Flotenmusik aus Frankreich und Italien; Schubert, ihr Blumlein; Baroque and Rokoko, Flute music; 'Wie Risse im Schatten' by Mathias Steinauer; Sonata for Flute by Philipp Jarnach. *Honours:* Prize for composing String Quartet, Tonhalle, Zürich, 1974; Carl-Heinrich-Ernst Prize, 1998; Cultural Award of the City of Winterthur, 2000. *Address:* Grüzenstrasse 14, 8400 Winterthur, Switzerland.

KELLER, Helen; Singer (Soprano); b. 5 March 1945, Horgen, Zürich, Switzerland. *Education:* Studied in Zürich and with Agnes Giebel in Cologne. *Career:* Concert performances in Switzerland and elsewhere from 1971 with a repertoire including Rossini's Stabat Mater, L'Enfance du Christ, Schöpfung and Jahreszeiten, Elijah and St Paul, works by Bach and Handel and Honegger's Roi David; Appearances at Amsterdam, Antwerp, Paris, Milan, Annsbach, Karlsruhe and the USA in Britten, Brahms, Schubert, Monteverdi, Pergolesi, Vivaldi and Schumann; Stage engagements as Salome in San Giovanni Battista by Stradella at St Gallen and in Le Convenzione Teatrali by Donizetti at Zürich. *Recordings:* Messiah, Schubert's Mass in G and San Giovanni Battista. *Address:* c/o Peter Keller, Opernhaus Zürich, Falkenstrasse 1, 8008 Zürich, Switzerland.

KELLER, Peter; Singer (Tenor); b. 16 March 1945, Thurgau, Switzerland; m. Helen Keller. *Education:* Studied in Zürich, with Ernst Haefliger in Berlin and Agnes Giebel in Cologne. *Career:* Has sung at the Zürich Opera from 1973, notably in the Monteverdi series and as Pedrillo, Monostatos, Jacquino, Wagner's David and Steuermann, Valzacchi in Rosenkavalier and M Triquet in Eugene Onegin (1991); Guest engagements at Munich, Hamburg, Düsseldorf (Edgar in Reimann's Lear), Milan, Edinburgh, Berlin and Vienna; Concert singer in Europe and on tour with Helen Keller in the USA; Sang in Puccini's Trittico at Zürich, 1996; Season 2000–01 at Zürich in Lulu, Carmen, The Queen of Spades and Die Zauberflöte (Priest). *Recordings include:* Die Zauberflöte, Il Ritorno d'Ulisse and Monteverdi's Orfeo; Diary of One who Disappeared by Janáček; Handel's Israel in Egypt and Mendelssohn's Christus; Zemlinsky's Kleider Machen Leute. *Address:* c/o Peter Keller, Opernhaus Zürich, Falkenstrasse 1, 8008 Zürich, Switzerland.

KELLER, Verena; Singer (Mezzo-soprano); b. 8 Sept. 1942, Schwerin, Germany. *Education:* Studied in Vienna with Hans Hotter and in Berlin; Lieder with Erik Werba. *Career:* Engaged at Hanover 1963–66, Bonn 1979–88, Mainz 1983–86; Guest appearances at Cologne, Geneva, Naples, Herrenhausen and Göttingen; Roles have included Mozart's Ramiro, Carmen, Santuzza, Ortrud, Brangaene, Kundry, Venus, Fricka; Verdi's Amneris, Azucena and Ulrica, Strauss's Clytemnestra and Herodias, Janáček's Kabanicha and the Witch in Hansel and Gretel; Concert engagements in Baroque music throughout Germany and in Paris, Rome, Los Angles and Vancouver. *Recordings include:* Dvořák's Mass in D. *Address:* Staatstheater, Gutenbergplatz 7, 6500 Mainz, Germany.

KELLERMAN, Julia Eleanor Margaret, BA; Music Books Editor; b. 10 March 1937, London, England; m., one s. *Education:* Bristol Univ., Birkbeck Coll., London Univ. *Career:* House Ed. Master Musicians Series, J. M. Dent & Sons Ltd 1972–1994; freelance Ed., Oxford Univ. Press 1994–99; Man., Music & Letters Trust 1996–; mem. Royal Musical Asscn. *Address:* 87 Hampstead Way, London, NW11 7LG, England (home). *Telephone:* (20) 8458-6113 (home). *E-mail:* jkellerman@compuserve.com (home).

KELLOGG, Cal (Stewart); Conductor and Composer; b. 26 July 1947, Long Beach, California, USA. *Education:* Conservatorio di Musica Santa Cecilia, Rome, Diplomas in Bassoon, Composition and Conducting. *Career:* Debut: Symphonic: Monte Carlo, 1975; Opera: Rome Opera, 1976; As Bassoonist, Toured with Renato Fasano's Piccola Teatro Musicale di Roma, 1967–72; Soloist with RAI Orchestra of Rome, 1972; Conductor of Symphonic Concerts with Baltimore Symphony, New World Symphony, Monte Carlo, Accademia Nazionale di Santa Cecilia, Maggio Fiorentino, La Fenice, San Carlo, RAI Orchestras of Rome, Torino and Naples, Antwerp Philharmonic, Spoleto Festival Orchestra, Orchestra of Illinois, Seattle Symphony, Israel Sinfonietta of Beersheva; Director of Opera at Rome Opera, Teatro Communale di Firenze, San Francisco Opera, San Carlo, Teatro Regio di Parma, NYC Opera, Santa Fe, Washington Opera, St Louis, Houston Grand Opera, Canadian Opera Company, Opera Montreal, Seattle Opera, Edinburgh Opera Festival, Israel Festival, Spoleto Festival, Chautauqua Festival PBS television live from Lincoln Center, New York City Opera production of Menotti's The Saint of Bleecker Street; Radio broadcasts of Tosca, 1978, Houston Grand Opera, Ballo in Maschera, 1981, Canadian Opera Company, Il Trovatore, 1984 and Macbeth, 1986; Conducted Andrea Chénier at Philadelphia, 1997. *Compositions:* Sullivan Ballou's Letter to his Wife for Bass Baritone and Orchestra, a setting of a Civil War letter, 1990. *Recordings:* Thomas Pasatieri: Three Sisters, opera in 2 acts, 1986. *Address:* c/o Opera Company of Philadelphia, 510 Walnut Street, Suite 1600, Philadelphia, PA 19106, USA.

KELLY, Bryan; Composer, Pianist and Conductor; b. 3 Jan. 1934, Oxford, England. *Education:* Royal College of Music 1951–55, with Gordon Jacob and Herbert Howells; Paris with Boulanger. *Career:* Has taught at the Royal Scottish Academy of Music; Professor of Composition, Royal College of Music, 1962–84; Resident at Castiglione del Lago, Italy, 1984–. *Compositions:* Orchestral: The Tempest Suite, for strings, 1964; Cookham Concertino, 1969; Divertimento for brass band, 1969; Oboe Concerto, 1972; Edinburgh Dances for Brass Band, 1973; Guitar Concerto, 1978; Andalucia and Concertante Music or Brass, 1976, 1979; 2 Symphonies, 1983, 1986; Vocal: Tenebrare Nocturnes for tenor, chorus and orchestra, 1965; Magnificat and Nunc Dimittis for chorus and organ, 1965; The Shield of Achilles for tenor and orchestra, 1966; Sleep little Baby, carol, 1968; Stabat Mater, 1970; At the Round Earth's Imagin'd Corners for tenor, chorus and strings, 1972; Abingdon Carols, 1973; Let There Be Light for soprano, narrator, chorus and orchestra, 1973; Latin Magnificat, 1979; Te Deum and Jubilate for chorus and organ, 1979; Dover Beach for chorus, 1995; Piano Sonata, 1971; Prelude and fugue for organ, 1960; Pastorale and Paen for organ, 1973; Chamber music; Children's Pieces: Herod to your Worst, nativity opera, 1968; On Christmas Eve, suite of carols, 1968; The Spider Monkey Uncle King, opera pantomime, 1971. *Recordings:* The Choral Music of Bryan Kelly, Abbey Records. *Address:* c/o British Music Information Centre, 11 Stratford Place, London, W1, England.

KELLY, Declan; Singer (Tenor); b. 1965, Ireland. *Education:* Studied singing, Royal Irish Academy of Music; Singing, National Opera Studio, London. *Career:* Debut: Mozart's The Magic Flute, Opéra du Rhin, A Midsummer Night's Dream, 1998; Member, National Chamber Chior, Dublin; Member, St Patrick's Cathedral Choir, Dublin; Tamino, Mid Wales Opera; Wexford Festival Opera; Holland Park Opera; European Chamber Opera; Opera Theatre Company, Dublin; Ferrando, Young Dublin Opera; Camille, Clonter Opera; Borsa, Pimlico Opera and Holland Park Opera; Frederic, Carl Rosa Productions, and both La Chericia and the Villager, Wexford Arithmetic/Teapot/Frog in L'Enfant et les Sortilèges, National Concert Hall, Dublin; Spirit, and understudy of Pylade, English Bach Festival, Covent Garden and Athens; Regular soloist, National Symphony and RTE Concert Orchestra; Concerts, television and radio; Solo recitals in Ireland, the United Kingdom and USA; Charity concerts for Irish Youth Fund, New Jersey, 1991; Mozart Requiem, Ulster Orchestra, 1998–99, performances in Belfast, Wexford and at the NCH, Dublin; Festival Company Tenor, Buxton Festival, 1998; Tamino, Mid-Wales Opera on tour; Messiah, Fairfield Halls, London Mozart Players; Mozart Requiem with Vladimir Spivakov and Moscow Virtuosi, Madrid; Rossini Petite Messe Solennelle, Gower Chorale; Carmina Burana, Hastings; The Creation, Dublin; Scaramuc-cio, Opéra National du Rhin; Almaviva, The Barber of Seville, Mid-Wales Opera. *Recordings:* Te Deum with Myung-Whun Chung and L'Accademia di Santa Cecilia. *Current Management:* Helen Sykes Artists Management. *Address:* c/o Helen Sykes Artists Management, 100 Felsham Road, Putney, London SW15 1DQ, England.

KELLY, Frances; Harpist; b. 1955, England. *Career:* Regular perfor-mances with the New London Consort in medieval and renaissance music; Has toured in Europe and the Far East; Early Music Network tours in the United Kingdom 1986 and 1988; Freelance engagements with the Consort of Musicke, and the Gabrieli Consort and Players Recitals with soprano Evelyn Tubb; On modern harp was member of the Ondine Ensemble, giving performances in the United Kingdom and the USA; Partnership with the flautist Ingrid Culliford from 1977; BBC Recital with tenor Ian Partridge; Concerto soloist in the premieres of Edward Cowie's Concerto in Newcastle and London and for Tyne Tees Television; Season 1988 included Debussy and Ravel with the Lindsay Quartet, chamber music by Bruch for the BBC and concerts in London, Denmark, Bruges and Utrecht as continuo player with the Consort of Musicke; South Bank Summer Music Festival with the New London Consort; Played in Oswald von Wolkenstein concert, 1997. *Recordings include:* Debussy's Trio Sonata with the Athena Ensemble; Britten's A Ceremony of Carols with the Choir of Christ Church Cathedral, Oxford; Mozart's Concerto K299 with the Academy of Ancient Music; Solo, Harp collection, (Amon Ra). *Address:* South Bank Centre, Press Office, London SE1, England.

KELLY, Janis; Singer (Soprano); b. 1955, Glasgow, Scotland. *Education:* Studied at Royal Scottish Academy of Music, the Royal College of Music and in Paris. *Career:* Represented Britain at the UNESCO Young Musicians' Rostrum at Bratislava, 1981; Operatic roles include Serpetta in La Finta Giardiniera (Glyndebourne, 1991); Flora in The Knot Garden and Mozart's Despina, Zerlina and Susanna, 1991, for Opera Factory; English National Opera as Amor (L'Incoronazione di Poppea), Flora (The Turn of the Screw), Kitty (Anna Karenina by Iain Hamilton), Barbarina, Bekhetaten in Akhnaten, Woman/Fury in The Mask of Orpheus, Papagena, Yum-Yum, and Rose in Street Scene; Magnolia in Show Boat for Opera North; Concert appearances in the USA, Canada, Paris and Czechoslovakia; Season 1992 as Ottavia in The Coronation of Poppea, and Countess in Marriage of Figaro for Opera Factory, Governess in Turn of the Screw, Bath City Opera, Tatyana in Eugene Onegin for Kentish Opera; In 1995 sang the Countess in Figaro ENO, Amaranta in La fedeltà Premiata (Garsington), and Fairy in Purcell's Fairy Queen, for ENO; Dorabella at Garsington and Romilda in Xerxes and the Countess in Figaro for ENO, 1997; Rosalinda in Die Fledermaus for Scottish Opera and Opera Ireland, 1998; Violetta in La Traviata with Opera North, 1998; Wigmore Hall Soiree Fauré, 1999; King Arthur in Concert in Portugal and St John Passion in Madrid; La Rondine with Opera North, 1999; Mrs Nixon in Nixon in China with ENO; The Cunning Little Vixen with Opera North, 2001; Directed Così fan tutte, Grange Park, 2001; Marschallin in Der Rosenkavalier with Opera North, 2002; Despina in Così fan tutte with ENO, 2002; Miss Jessel, Grange Park; Elettra in Mozart's Idomeneo with Opera North, 2003; Directed Iolanthe, Grange Park. *Recordings:* Magnolia, Showboat; Rose, Street Scene; Mozart, Gluck, Puccini, Massenet Arias on Inspector Morse soundtrack albums. *Honours:* Anna Instone Award, Royal College of Music; Countess of Munster, Caird and Royal Society of Arts Scholarships. *Current Management:* Musichall, Vicarage Way, Ringmer, BN8 5 LA. *Address:* 159 Purves Road, London NW10 5TH, England.

KELLY, Paul Austin; Singer (Tenor); b. 1964, USA. *Career:* Debut: New York City Opera, as Tamino in Mozart's Die Zauberflöte; Roles in Rossini's Barbiere di Siviglia at Royal Opera, Rome Opera, Pesaro and New York Metropolitan Opera in 2000; In Zelmira at Pesaro, Opéra de Lyon and Paris; In Ermione at Glyndebourne; In Comte Ory at Canadian Opera and Glimmerglass; Cenerentola at Die Vlaamse Opera and Philadelphia; Turco in Italia at La Scala; Donizetti roles include Tonio at La Scala, Rome Opera, Opéra de Monte Carlo, Ernesto at Bologna and Austin Lyric Opera; Mozart roles include Tamino at La Scala, City Opera and Opera Pacific; Belmonte at Catania and Hawaii Opera; Don Ottavio at Dublin, Santiago and New York City Opera; Alessandro in Il Re Pastore at Opéra de Nice and Mostly Mozart Festival; Season 1999–2000 with Don Ottavio at New Israeli Opera; Ferrando at Glyndebourne; Bach B Minor Mass in Paris; Other repertory includes roles in Bellini's La Sonnambula, Donizetti's

Lucrezia Borgia, Offenbach's La Belle Hélène, and Rossini's Pietra del Paragone and Otello; Concerts include Rossini's Stabat Mater in Paris and Wexford, Mozart Requiem in Rome and Lisbon, Messiah, St Matthew Passion, Magnificat and Missa Solemnis. *Recordings include:* Three Rossini Tenors; Zoraide di Granata; La Romanzesco; Rossini Cantatas; Der Stein der Weise; The Holy Sonnets of John Donne by Britten. *Current Management:* Herbert Barrett Management. *Address:* c/o Herbert Barrett Management, 1776 Broadway, New York, NY 10019, USA.

KELM, Linda; Singer (soprano); b. 11 Dec. 1944, Utah, USA. *Education:* studied with Jennie Tourel at the Aspen School of Music and in New York. *Career:* debut, Seattle 1977, as Helmwige and Third Norn in the Ring; sang Turandot with Wilmington, 1979, followed by performances at Seattle, New York City Opera 1983, Chicago, San Francisco and Amsterdam; sang Salome at St Louis and Princess in Rusalka at Carnegie Hall; Perugia 1983, as Dirce in Cherubini's Demofoonte; Seattle Opera, 1985; as Brünnhilde; further guest appearances include Helmwige in the Ring.

KELTERBORN, Rudolf; Composer, Conductor and Professor; b. 3 Sept. 1931, Basel, Switzerland; m. Erika Kelterborn Salathe, 6 July 1957, 1 s., 1 d. *Education:* Diplomas in Theory and Conducting, Music Academy, Basel, 1953; Studied composition with Blacher and Fortner, Salzburg and Detmold, and conducting with Markevitch. *Career:* Teacher, Conductor, Basel, 1956–60; Professor of Composition: NW German Music Academy, Detmold, 1960–68, HS Zürich, 1968–75; Editor of Swiss Music Review, 1968–75; Head of Music Department, Swiss Radio, 1975–80; Professor of Composition, HS Karlsruhe, 1980–83; Director of Music Academy, Basel, 1983–94. *Compositions include:* Four Sympho-nies and five Operas Kaiser Jovian, 1967; Ein Engel Kommt nach Babylon, 1977; Der Kirschgarten, 1984; Ophelia, 1984; Julia, 1990; A ballet; Various works for Orchestra; Namenlos for ensemble and electronics, 1996; Herbstmusik, 7 pieces for orchestra, 2002; 4 Move-ments for Classical Orchestra, 1996; Concertos for various solo instruments; Chamber music including 6 string quartets, 1954–2001; Cantatas; Piano and organ works. *Recordings:* Several under various labels. *Publications:* Komponist, Musikdenker, Vermittler (various authors), Zürich, Bern, 1993. *Address:* Delsbergerallee 61, CH-4053 Basel, Switzerland.

KEMENY, Alexander; Violinist; b. 22 April 1943, Solna, Sweden; Divorced, 1 d. *Education:* Bratislava Conservatory, Czechoslovakia, 1960–66; Music Academy in Prague with Professor A Plocek, 1966–70. *Career:* Debut: 1970; Concertmaster, Innsbruck Symphonic Orchestra, 1973–75; Violinist, Prague Symphonic Orchestra, also Norrkoping Symphony Orchestra, Sweden; Freelance Concert Violinist, 1978–; Soloist with orchestra playing works by Myslivecek, Mozart, Beethoven, Brixi, Mendelssohn, Wieniawski, Eklund, and chamber music player of both classical and modern music, concerts in Czechoslovakia, Sweden, Denmark and Poland; Performed in Piano Trio and in Duo with guitarist Vladimir Vectomov; Radio performances, Czechoslovakia, Sweden and Austria; Performed at Bornholm Music Festival, Denmark, 1987. *Recordings:* Paganini, Giuliani, and Kowalski, Radio Prague and Bratislava; Smetana, Johansson and Telemann, Radio Sweden; Suk, Smetana, Foerster, and Suchoň, Radio Austria.

KEMMER, Mariette; Singer (Soprano); b. 1960, Luxembourg. *Education:* Studied at the Luxembourg Conservatoire and at the Rheinland National College of Music in Düsseldorf. *Career:* Sang at the Théâtre de la Monnaie, Brussels, as Mélisande, Sophie, Pamina, Micaela and Mozart's Countess; Guest appearances at the Vienna Staatsoper, Munich, Berlin, Hamburg, Frankfurt, Dresden, Stuttgart, Zürich, Geneva, Basle, Berne, Lausanne, Verona, Dublin, Karlsruhe, Man-nheim, Nürnberg, Strasbourg, Marseille, Nancy, Montpellier, Nantes, Avignon, Metz and Liège; Has appeared at the festivals of Aix-en-Provence, Wexford and Bregenz; Other roles include Mozart's Ilia, Fiordiligi and Donna Elvira, Marguerite, Antonia, Tatiana and the Countess in Capriccio; Has appeared in concert, with major orchestras in Vienna, Paris Prague, Zürich, Brussels, Luxembourg, Monte-Carlo, Antwerp, Liège, Bregenz, Bonn, Nürnberg, Bamberg, Stuttgart, Heidelberg, Metz, Nancy, Nantes, Montpellier and the festival at Round Top, Texas. *Address:* Music International, 13 Ardilaun Road, London N5 2QR, England.

KEMP, Nicola-Jane; Singer (Coloratura Soprano); b. 1965, England. *Education:* Chetham's School of Music; Girton College, Cambridge; Royal College of Music; RSAMD, Glasgow; Further study with Margaret Hyde. *Career:* Appearances with British Youth Opera; Music Theatre Wales; London Opera Players; Central Festival Opera; Music Theatre Kernow; Aix-en-Province Festival; Covent Garden; Roles have included Verdi's Oscar; Mozart's Constanze and Queen of Night; Birtwistle's Pretty Polly in Punch and Judy; Season 1998, Covent Garden Festival; Jauchzet Gott (Bach) at the Purcell Room; Barbican with the London Soloists CO and at Crans Montana Festival; Season 1999 with Strauss's

Zerbinetta, St John's Smith Square, and the Académie Européenne de Musique at Aix-en-Provence; A Mind of Winter (Benjamin) with Orchestre de Rouen, 2001; Lakmé (Belcanto Opera), 2001; Queen of Night and Papagena at Covent Garden, 2002; Jubilee Concert at Chatsworth House, 2002; UK Tour with Vienna Galan, 2002–03; Concerts throughout the United Kingdom. *Address:* Music International, 13 Ardilaun Road, London N5 2QR, England.

KEMPF, Frederick; Concert Pianist; b. 14 Oct. 1977, England. *Education:* Studied at the Royal Academy of Music, with Ronald Smith; Further study with Christopher Elton. *Career:* Debut: Mozart's Concerto K414, with the Royal Philharmonic, 1985; Concerto engagements with the Royal Liverpool Philharmonic Orchestra, London Mozart Players, European Community CO, Netherlands Radio Symphony Orchestra, BBC National Orchestra of Wales and the Hallé Orchestra; Conductors have included Libor Pešek, Ashkenazy, Taddaki Otaka and Feodor Gluschenko; Solo recitals at the Chichester, Canterbury, Bath, Guidlford and Exeter Fetsivals; Season 1996 with debut appearance at Berlin (Deutsches Symphonie Orchester), Munich and Prague recitals, and debut with the Philharmonia Orchestra; Season 1996–97 with tour of Japan, recitals in Washington and New York and concerts with American orchestras; Season 2001–02 with San Francisco Symphony Orchestra, Rotterdam Philharmonic Orchestra; Tours to Italy, France, Russia, Japan and Germany. *Recordings include:* Schumann and Rachmaninov recitals (BIS); Beethoven Sonatas Op. 109 and Op. 110 (BIS) and Chopin. *Honours:* Joint winner, National Mozart Competition, 1987; Winner, BBC Young Musician of the Year, 1992. *Address:* c/o Grant Rogers Musical Artists Management, 8 Wren Crescent, Bushey Heath, Hertfordshire, WD23 1AN, England.

KEMPSTER, David; Singer (Baritone); b. 1969, Wales; m. Charlotte Kinder, one s. *Education:* Royal Northern College of Music. *Career:* Engagements with English National Opera in Tosca, House of the Dead, 1997–98; Otello, La Traviata, Carmen, Salome and Dialogue of the Carmelites, 1998–99; Lescaut in Manon Lescaut; Schaunard in La Bohème, Toddy Foran in the world premiere of the Silver Tassie, Chouen Lai in the London premiere of Nixon in China, 1999–2000; Di luna in Il Trovatore, Poacher in A Cunning Little Vixen, 2000–01; Marcello in La Bohème, Pilate in St John Passion and Renato in Ballo in Maschera, 2001–02; Roles for Glyndebourne: Escamillo in Carmen, Germont in La Traviata; for Welsh National Opera: Belcore in L'Elisir d'Amore, Marcello in La Bohème; Other roles include Rigoletto, Barber's Figaro, Don Giovanni, and Mozart's Count Almaviva; Concert repertoire includes Handel's Messiah, Saul and Judas Maccabaeus, Elgar's The Dream of Gerontius, Fauré's Requiem, Mendelssohn's Elijah, Orff's Carmina Burana, Mozart's Requiem, Puccini's Messa di Gloria, Vaughan Williams' A Sea Symphony and Walton's Belshazar's Feast. *Address:* Harlequin Agency Ltd, 203 Fidlas Road, Cardiff CF4 5NA, Wales.

KENDALL, Christopher (Wolff); Conductor, Lutenist and Artistic Director; b. 9 Sept. 1949, Zanesville, Ohio, USA. *Education:* BA, Antioch College, 1972; MM, Conducting, University of Cincinnati Conservatory, 1974; Dalcroze School of Music, NY, 1969–70. *Career:* Director of 20th Century Consort in residence at the Smithsonian Institution, Washington, 1976–, Associate Conductor of the Seattle Symphony, 1987–; Founder and Lutenist of Folger Consort, Ensemble-in-Residence at Folger Shakespeare Library in Washington DC 1977–; Artistic Director of Millennium Inc, 1980–; Guest Conductor: Seattle Symphony, Chamber Music Society of Lincoln Center, Eastman Musica Nova, Da Capo Chamber Players, Washington Sinfonia. *Recordings:* 20th Century Consort Vols I and II, Smithsonian Collection; Into Eclipse (Stephen Albert) 20th Century Consort, Nonesuch; Shakespeare's Music, Folger Consort, Delos; A Distant Mirror, Carmina Burana, Folger Consort, Delos. *Honours:* Gold Award, Houston Film Festival for Millennium: 10 Centuries of Music 1986; Emmy Award for 20th Century Consort PBS Programme on Aaron Copland 1984.

KENDALL, William; Singer (Tenor); b. 1960, London, England. *Education:* King's School, Canterbury; Choral Scholar, Cambridge University; Further study with Robert Tear and Peter Pears. *Career:* Concert appearances under such conductors as Hogwood, Harnoncourt, Gardiner, Mackerras and Boulez; Works by Tippett and Tavener conducted by the composers; Sang in the world premiere of Penderecki's Polish Requiem; Tour of Germany, 1989 with the Monteverdi Choir and Orchestra in the Missa Solemnis and Beethoven's Mass in C; Further appearances in season 1990–91 as the Evangelist in the St John Passion, in The Dream of Gerontius and Britten's Serenade in Australia; Mozart Requiems in Oxford and Cambridge and Bach's B Minor Mass with The Sixteen at St John's Smith Square; London Promanade concert appearances and showings at the Holland Festival, Festival Berlin, 1987, and the 1989 Salzburg Festival. *Recordings:* Beethoven Missa Solemnis and Mass in C; Bach and Schütz with the Stuttgart Kammerchor; Sacred music by Haydn.

KENGEN, Knud-Erik; Organist, Pianist and Composer; b. 17 July 1947, Copenhagen, Denmark; m. Gerlinde Maria Pagel, 6 Dec 1969, 1 s., 1 d. *Education:* Studies in Musicology, University of Copenhagen, 1972–76; Final Diploma, Royal Danish Academy of Music, 1974; Studied under Professor Aksel Andersen; Consultations in Composition with Leif Kayser. *Career:* Assistant Organist, Dome of Copenhagen, 1974; Organist, Gladsaxe Church, Copenhagen, 1979–; Performances: Concert Organist at numerous concerts, mainly in Denmark but also in Germany, England and Sweden; also played as Soloist at first performance of Musica Autumnalis by Axel Borup Jorgensen in The Danish Broadcasting Corporation; as Pianist, Rehearser and Chorus Master; Accompanist at Lieder-Recitals. *Compositions:* Organ and Choir-Music in style somewhat indebted to modern French church-music since Langlais, Duruflé and early Messiaen; For Organ: Toccata, Opus 5; Choral Preludes, Opus 14 and 26, 7 Chorales for the Concert, Op 43, 1993; Rhapsody, Surrexit Dominus, Opus 22; Organ Fantasy, Victimae Paschali, Opus 24; Missa Fons Bonitatis, Opus 26; Proprium for Hallo-Mass, Opus 28; Choral Fantasy, Veni Creator Spiritus, Opus 40; For Choir: Psalm 12, Opus 21; Cantatas with Instruments, Opus 35; Stabat Mater, 1992; Psalm 23, 1999. *Publications:* Contributed to the lexical part of the History of Music in Denmark, 1978. *Address:* Tranegardsvej 69, 1 TV, DK 2900 Hellerup, Denmark.

KENNEDY, (Nigel Paul), ARCM; British violinist; b. 28 Dec. 1956, Brighton, England; s. of John Kennedy and Scylla Stoner; m. Agnieska; one s. *Education:* Yehudi Menuhin School, Juilliard School of Performing Arts, New York. *Career:* debut playing Mendelssohn's Violin Concerto at the Royal Festival Hall with the London Philharmonic Orchestra under Riccardo Muti 1977; subsequently chosen by the BBC as the subject of a five-year documentary on the devt of a soloist; other important debuts include with the Berlin Philharmonic 1980, New York 1987; has made appearances at all the leading UK festivals and in Europe at Stresa, Lucerne, Gstaad, Berlin and Lockenhaus; tours to Australia, Austria, Canada, Denmark, Germany, Hong Kong, India, Ireland, Italy, Japan, Republic of Korea, New Zealand, Norway, Poland, Spain, Switzerland, Turkey and the USA; has given concerts in the field of jazz with Stephane Grappelli, including at the Edinburgh Festival and Carnegie Hall; runs his own jazz group; five-year sabbatical 1992–97; Artistic Dir, Polish Chamber Orchestra 2002–; Sr Vice-Pres. Aston Villa Football Club 1990–. *Television:* Coming Along Nicely (BBC documentary on his early career) 1973–78. *Recordings include:* Strad Jazz 1984, Elgar Sonata with Peter Pettinger 1985, Elgar's Violin Concerto with the London Philharmonic and Vernon Handley (Gramophone magazine Record of the Year, BPI Award for Best Classical Album of the Year) 1985, Vivaldi's Four Seasons, Bartók Solo Sonata and Mainly Black (arrangement of Ellington's Black Brown and Beige Suite), Sibelius Violin Concerto with the City of Birmingham Symphony Orchestra conducted by Sir Simon Rattle, Walton's Violin Concerto with the Royal Philharmonic Orchestra and André Previn, Bruch and Mendelssohn concertos with the English Chamber Orchestra conducted by Jeffrey Tate, Kafka (Kennedy's compositions), Tchaikovsky's Chausson Poème with the London Philharmonic Orchestra 1988, Brahms Violin Concerto with the London Philharmonic under Klaus Tennstedt 1991, Beethoven Violin Concerto with the NDR-Sinfonieorchester and Klaus Tennstedt 1992, chamber works by Debussy and Ravel, Berg's Violin Concerto, Vaughan Williams' The Lark Ascending with Sir Simon Rattle and the CBSO, works by Fritz Kreisler 1998, The Kennedy Experience, chamber works by Bach, Ravel and Kodaly (with Lynn Harrell) 1999, Classic Kennedy with the English Chamber Orchestra 1999, Bach's Concerto for Two Violins in D Minor, Concerto for Oboe and Violin in D Minor and the A Minor and E Major violin concertos the Berlin Philharmonic 2000. *Publication:* Always Playing 1991. *Honours:* Hon. DLitt (Bath) 1991; Golden Rose of Montreux 1990, Variety Club Showbusiness Personality of the Year 1991, BRIT Award for Outstanding Contribution to British Music 2000, Male Artist of the Year 2001. *Current Management:* Askonas Holt Ltd, Lonsdale Chambers, 27 Chancery Lane, London, WC2A 1PF, England. *Telephone:* (20) 7400-1700. *Fax:* (20) 7400-1799. *E-mail:* info@askonasholt.co.uk. *Website:* www.askonasholt.co.uk. *Address:* c/o John Stanley, Kennedy, 90–96 Brewery Road, London, N7 9NT, England.

KENNEDY, Andrew; Singer (Tenor); b. 1977, England. *Education:* Choral Scholar at King's College, Cambridge; Royal College of Music, with Neil Mackie. *Career:* Concerts include Cavalli's Messa Concertata with The Parley of Instruments, Messiah in Romsey Abbey, Haydn's Harmoniemesse in Canterbury Cathedral and Beethoven's 9th with the Hanover Band; Evangelist in Bach's St John and St Matthew Passions and Schubert's E flat Mass with the Brandenburg Consort; Modern repertory includes Britten's Nocturne and Serenade (King's College Chapel, St John's Smith Square) and Dies Natalis by Finzi. Principal conductor of The Allegri Singers; Stage appearances in Janácek's Diary of One who Disappeared, Haydn's Die Feuerbrunst, The Rake's Progress and Holst's Savitri; Title role in Hugh the Drover by Vaughan Williams and tour of the United Kingdom as Mozart's Ferrando; Sang

Ugone in Flavio for the London Handel Festival, 2001. *Address:* c/o Royal College of Music, Prince Consort Road, London SW7, England.

KENNEDY, (George) Michael Sinclair, CBE, MA, CRNCM, FIJ; British journalist and music critic; b. 19 Feb. 1926, Chorlton-cum-Hardy, Manchester; s. of Hew G. and Marian F. Kennedy; m. 1st Eslyn Durdle 1947 (died 1999); m. 2nd Joyce Bourne 2002. *Education:* Berkhamsted School. *Career:* staff music critic, The Daily Telegraph 1941–50, northern music critic 1950–60, Northern Ed. 1960–86, jt chief music critic 1986–89; music critic, The Sunday Telegraph 1989–; Gov. Royal Northern Coll. of Music. *Publications:* The Hallé Tradition: A Century of Music 1960, The Works of Ralph Vaughan Williams 1964, Portrait of Elgar 1968, Elgar: Orchestral Music 1969, Portrait of Manchester 1970, History of the Royal Manchester College of Music 1971, Barbirolli: Conductor Laureate 1971, Mahler 1974, The Autobiography of Charles Hallé, with Correspondence and Diaries (ed.) 1976, Richard Strauss 1976, Britten 1980, Concise Oxford Dictionary of Music (ed.) 1980, The Hallé 1858–1983 1983, Strauss: Tone Poems 1984, Oxford Dictionary of Music (ed.) 1985, Adrian Boult 1987, Portrait of Walton 1989, Music Enriches All: The First 21 Years of the Royal Northern College of Music, Manchester 1994, Richard Strauss: Man, Musician, Enigma 1999, The Life of Elgar 2004, Buxton: an English Festival 2004; contrib. to newspapers and magazines, including Gramophone, Listener, Musical Times, Music and Letters; BBC. *Honours:* Hon. mem. Royal Manchester Coll. of Music 1971; Hon. MA (Manchester) 1975, Hon. MusD (Manchester) 2003. *Address:* The Bungalow, 62 Edilom Road, Manchester, M8 4HZ, England. *Telephone:* (161) 740-4528 (home). *Fax:* (161) 720-7171 (home). *E-mail:* majkennedy@bungalow62.fsnet.co.uk.

KENNEDY, Nicki; Singer (Soprano); b. 1968, England. *Education:* Bristol University; Royal Scottish Academy of Music and Drama; Royal College of Music. *Career:* Appearances with European Chamber Orchestra; Philharmonia; Les Musiciens du Louvre; Glasgow Philharmonia; London Festival Orchestra; London Handel Festival; Concertgebow Amsterdam, Snape Maltings; Glasgow Royal Concert Hall; Glasgow International Early Music Festival; Three Choirs Festival; Aix-en-Provence Festival; Appearances throughout Europe; Japan, Egypt, Dubai; 11 operatic roles; Broadcast with Camerata Hispanica; La Serenissima; Les Musiciens du Louvre; Founder, Cromata, specialising in 17th century Italian music. *Recordings:* Vivaldi Cantatas; Spanish Lute Songs; Les Musiciens du Louvre; The Musicians of the Globe; Modo Antiquo; Charivari Agreable. *Current Management:* Helen Sykes Artists Management, 100 Felsham Road, Putney, London SW15 1DQ, England.

KENNEDY, Roderick; Singer (Bass Baritone); b. 7 May 1951, Birmingham, England. *Education:* Studied at Guildhall School and with Otakar Kraus. *Career:* Debut: Covent Garden, 1975; Over 30 roles with the Royal Opera; Created Lt of Police in The Ice Break by Tippett, 1977; Appeared with Royal Opera on visits to La Scala, 1976, Korea and Japan in 1979 and 1986; Sang The Doctor in Wozzeck at Edinburgh and San Francisco, 1980–81, with further engagements at opera houses throughout Europe; Glyndebourne debut, 1981 as Don Fernando in Fidelio, followed by Alidoro, Rocco, Seneca in Poppea, and Britten's Theseus; Further festival appearances at Aldeburgh, Aix-en-Provence, Montpellier, Starasbourg and Florence; Regular performances with English National, Welsh National and Scottish Operas; Repertoire includes: The Coloratura Works of Handel and Rossini; Roles include: Don Alfonso, King Philip, Pogner, Bottom as well as many 20th century works; Regular Promenade and Concert appearances in the United Kingdom and abroad; Has worked with such conductors as Muti, Kleiber, Colin Davis, Ozawa, Harnoncourt, Solti, Haitink, Mehta, Prêtre and Mackerras; Sang Britten's Bottom for ENO, 1996; Director of the Winter Gardens, Charitable Trust, Bournemouth, England; General Director of Kent Opera, 1998–; Sang the Animal Trainer and Athlete in Lulu at Palermo, 2001. *Recordings include:* Messiah; La Traviata; Hérodiade; La Forza del Destino; Maria Padilla; Die Sieben Todessunden; Offenbach's Robinson Crusoe, The Immortal Hour and Le Comte Ory; Television films of Lucrezia Borgia, Giulio Cesare, Idomeneo, L'Egisto, Hérodiade, L'Incoronazione di Poppea, La Cenerentola and A Midsummer Night's Dream; The Complete Vocal and Piano Works of Lord Berners (One of Gramophone Magazine's Records of the Year, 1998); Berg's Lulu, 2001. *Current Management:* Music International. *Address:* The White House, Witchampton, Dorset BH21 5AU, England.

KENNER, Kevin; Concert Pianist; b. 19 May 1963, California, USA. *Education:* Peabody Conservatory, Baltimore; Hochschule für Musik in Hannover; Studied with Leon Fleisher. *Career:* Has appeared in Europe, North and Central America, the Orient and former Soviet Union, since 1989 performing with St Paul Chamber Orchestra, Rochester Philharmonic and ensembles in San Diego, San Francisco, Kansas City and Baltimore; Recitals at the Salle Pleyel in Paris, the Châtelet, Queen Elizabeth Hall London (International Piano Series) and at the Kennedy Center, Washington DC; Broadcasts in Japan, Australia, Poland,

Germany and Costa Rica. *Honours:* Winner: Gina Bachauer Competition, Utah, 1988; Van Cliburn Competition, Fort Worth, 1989; International Tchaikovsky Competition, Moscow, 1989; International Terence Judd Award, Manchester, 1990; International Chopin Piano Competition, 1990. *Current Management:* Connaught Artists Management Ltd, 2 Molasses Row, Plantation Wharf, London, SW11 3UX, England. *Telephone:* (20) 7738 0017. *Fax:* (20) 7738 0909. *E-mail:* classicalmusic@connaughtartists.com. *Website:* www.connaughtartists.com. *Address:* c/o Joan Parry, 14 Nursery Road, Sunbury-on-Thames, Middlesex TW16 6LB, England.

KENNY, Courtney (Arthur Lloyd); Pianist, Repetiteur and Accompanist; b. 8 Nov. 1933, Dublin, Republic of Ireland; m. Caroline Anne Florence Arthur 1972, 1 s. *Education:* Wellington College, Berkshire, 1947–51; Royal College of Music, London, 1951–54. *Career:* Musical Director, Bristol Old Vic, 1954–57; Solo Pianist, Royal Ballet, 1957; Member, Glyndebourne Festival Opera Music Staff; Founder, Western Opera, Ireland, 1963; Wexford Festival Opera Staff, 1963–96; Head of Music Staff, 1974; Senior Repetiteur, 1982; New Sadler's Wells Opera Head of Music Staff, 1983–89; Associate Music Director, Ohio Light Opera, 1983; Member of various ensembles including, Bureau Piano Trio, Barbican Ensemble, Peter Lloyd Baroque Trio; Faculty, Blossom Festival School of Cleveland Orchestra and Kent State University, 1972–80; Many concert appearances as soloist and accompanist in Europe, USA, Middle East; Conducting Debut, John Curry Theatre of Skating, then Ohio Light Opera, New Sadler's Wells Opera; Cabaret–Songs at the Piano; Appearances in USA, Canada, Middle East, England, Scotland and Ireland; mem, Incorporated Society of Musicians. *Recordings:* With Glyndebourne Festival Opera; Recitals with Ian Wallace. *Contributions:* Opera. *Address:* Russets, Straight Mite, Etchingham, East Sussex, TN19 7BA, England. *Telephone:* (1580) 819125. *E-mail:* ccfkenny@aol.com.

KENNY, Jonathan (Peter); Singer (Countertenor); b. 1960, England. *Education:* Studied at Exeter University and the Guildhall School. *Career:* Appearances with English National Opera, Opera Theatre Company, Dublin, Opera Factory Zürich, Musica nel Chiostro and at Karlsruhe; Roles have included Bertarido in Rodelinda, Arsamenes in Xerxes, Guido in Flavio, Medoro in Orlando and Britten's Oberon; Other engagements as Andronico in Tamerlano for Glimmerglass Opera, (US debut 1995), Amadigi at Prague and Monteverdi's Ottone at the Brooklyn Academy; Royal Opera debut as Nireno in Giulio Cesare, 1997; Season 1998–99 as Handel's Amadigi at Lisbon, Hamor in Jephtha with the Netherlands Bach Society and Arsamenes in Handel's Serse with the Gabrieli Consort in France; Other roles include Gluck's Orfeo; Concerts throughout Europe including St Matthew Passion, in Jonathan Miller's dramatisation and Handel's Theodora in Berlin. *Recordings include:* Albums with John Eliot Gardiner (Philips) and Andrew Parrott (Sony). *Address:* c/o Musichall Ltd, Vicarage Way, Ringmer, East Sussex, BN8 5 LA, England.

KENNY, Yvonne, AM, BSc; Singer (soprano); b. 25 Nov. 1950, Sydney, Australia. *Education:* Sydney Univ., Sydney Conservatory of Music, Opera School of La Scala Milan. *Career:* debut, London 1975 as Donizetti's Rosamunda d'Inghilterra (concert performance); Covent Garden 1976, in the world premiere of Henze's We Come to the River; Later appeared as Mozart's Susanna, Ilia (Idomeneo) and Pamina, Verdi's Oscar, Bizet's Micaela and Handel's Semele 1988, Liu in Turandot; English National Opera debut 1977, as Sophie, in Der Rosenkavalier, returned as Romilda in Handel's Xerxes and (also on USSR Tour) Semele at La Fenice, Venice; Guest appearances at La Scala, Paris, Lyon, Vienna, Cologne, Hamburg, Sydney and Munich; Festivals of Salzburg, Aix, Strasbourg, Edinburgh and Glyndebourne (Ilia 1985); Sang Alcina in a new production of Handel's opera at Covent Garden, 1992–93; Deborah in Handel's oratorio in the 1993 Proms; Strauss, Capriccio, at Berlin Staatsoper in 1993; Sang in Purcell's Fairy Queen at the London Coliseum 1995 (also televised); Concert engagements under Pritchard, Colin Davis, Leppard, Harnoncourt, Solti, Abbado, Mackerras and Tennstedt; Featured artist (People, No. 185) Opera Magazine, Dec 1992; Debut as the Marschallin 1997, English National Opera; Sang in a revival of Cavalli's La Didone at the 1997 Schwetzingen Festival; Season 1998 with Fiordiligi for Opera Australia and as Purcell's Titania for ENO; Season 2000–01 as the Countess in Capriccio and Kallmán's Czardasfürstin, at Sydney. *Recordings:* Britten folk songs, Etcetera; Barbarina in Figaro, Solti; Constanze in Die Entführung and Aspasia in Mitridate with Harnoncourt; Donizetti's Ugo Conte di Parigi and Il Castello di Kenilworth; Bach's Cantata Der zufriedengestellte Aeolus, Telefunken; Elgar's The Kingdom; Mozart's Requiem; Sings Aspasia in Unitel film of Mitridate directed by Jean-Pierre Ponnelle; Vaughan Williams, Sea Symphony; Mendelssohn's Elijah; Stravinsky, Pulcinella; Mozart's Coronation Mass. *Address:* 46 Muswell Avenue, Muswell Hill, London, N10 2EL, England.

KENT, Christopher; Musicologist, Organist and Teacher; b. 12 Aug. 1949, London, England; m. Angela Thomas, 21 July 1973 (deceased).

Education: BMus, University of Manchester; MMus, PhD, King's College, London; FRCO; ARMCM. *Career:* Assistant Music Master, City of London School for Girls, 1975–80; Senior Lecturer in Music, 1980–2002, Hon. Fellow, 2002–, University of Reading; Editorial Board, Elgar Complete Edition, 1979–; mem, Fellow of the Society of Antiquaries of London (FSA); Athenaeum Club. *Recordings include:* Pachelbel's Hexachordum Apollinis and organ music by John Blow. *Publications:* Co-Editor, 5 vols of Elgar Complete Edition: Symphony No. 1, 1981; The Dream of Gerontius, 1982; The Apostles, 1983; The Kingdom, 1984; Music for Organ, 1987; The Music of Edward Elgar: A Guide to Research, 1993. *Contributions:* Musical Times; The Listener, Journal of British Institute of Organ Studies; The Organ Year Book; Music and Letters, Journal of the Royal College of Organists; Proceedings of the Royal Music Association. *Address:* The Laurels, Tytherton Lucas, Wiltshire SN15 3RJ, England.

KENYON, Nicholas; Writer and Administrator; b. 23 Feb. 1951, Altrincham, Cheshire, England; m. Marie-Ghislaine Latham-Koenig. *Education:* BA, Modern History, Balliol College, Oxford. *Career:* Music critic, The New Yorker, 1979–82; Music critic, The Times, 1982–85; Music Editor, The Listener, 1982–87; Music critic, The Observer, 1986–92; Editor, Early Music, 1983–1992; Programme Adviser, Mozart Now Festival at South Bank, London, 1991; Controller, BBC Radio 3, 1992–98; Director, BBC Proms, 1996–; Controller, Millennium Programmes, 1998–2000; Controller, BBC Proms, Live Events and Television Classical Music, 2000–. *Publications include:* the BBC Symphony Orchestra 1930–80; Simon Rattle, The Making of a Conductor, revised edition: Simon Rattle, From Birmingham to Berlin, 2001; Authenticity and Early Music, Editor; Co-Editor, Viking Opera Guide, 1993; Editor, Musical Lives, 2002; Editor, The BBC Proms Pocket Guide to Great Symphonies, 2003; Editor, The BBC Proms Pocket Guide to Great Concertos, 2003. *Honours:* C.B.E., 2001. *Address:* BBC, Broadcasting House, London W1A 1AA, England.

KERMAN, Joseph Wilfred, BA, PhD; American musicologist, writer, critic and editor; b. 3 April 1924, London, England; m. Vivian Shaviro 1945; two s. one d. *Education:* New York Univ., Princeton Univ. *Career:* Dir of Graduate Studies, Westminster Choir Coll., Princeton 1949–51; Asst Prof. 1951–56, Assoc. Prof. 1956–60, Prof. of Music 1960–71, 1974–94, Chair., Dept of Music 1960–63, 1991–93, Univ. of California at Berkeley; Heather Prof. of Music, Univ. of Oxford 1971–74; Fellow, Wadham Coll., Oxford 1972–74; founder/Co-Ed., 19th Century Music 1977–89; Ed. California Studies in 19th Century Music 1980–; Charles Eliot Norton Prof. of Poetry, Harvard Univ. 1997–98; Fellow, American Acad. of Arts and Sciences 1973, American Philosophical Soc. 2001. *Publications:* Opera as Drama 1956, The Elizabethan Madrigal: A Comparative Study 1962, Beethoven Quartets 1967, A History of Art and Music (with Horst W. Janson and Dora Jane Janson) 1968, Listen (with Vivian Kerman) 1972, Beethoven Studies (ed. with Alan Tyson) 1973, The Masses and Motets of William Byrd 1981, The New Grove Beethoven (with Alan Tyson) 1983, Contemplating Music: Challenges to Musicology 1985, Music at the Turn of the Century (ed.) 1990, Write All These Down: Essays on Music 1994, Concerto Conversations 1999, The Art of Fugue: Bach Fugues for Keyboard 1715–1750 2005; contrib. to scholarly journals, including New York Review of Books. *Honours:* Guggenheim Fellowship 1960, Fulbright Fellowship 1966; National Inst. and American Acad. of Arts and Letters Award 1956, Hon. Fellow, Royal Acad. of Music, London 1972, hon. mem. American Musicological Soc. 1995. *Address:* Music Department, University of California, Berkeley, CA 94720 (office); 107 Southampton Avenue, Berkeley, CA 94707, USA (home).

KERN, Patricia; Singer (Mezzo-soprano); b. 14 July 1927, Swansea, Wales. *Education:* Guildhall School, London, with Parry Jones (1949–52). *Career:* Sang with Opera for All 1952–55; Sadler's Wells/ English National Opera from 1959, debut in Rusalka; appearances as Rossini's Isolier, Rosina, Cinderella and Isabella; Mozart's Cherubino, Monteverdi's Messenger; Sang in the 1966 premiere of Malcolm Williamson's Violins of St Jacques; Covent Garden debut 1967, as Zerlina in Don Giovanni; returned as Cherubino and as Mrs Herring (1989); US debut 1969, Washington Opera; Scottish Opera in A Midsummer Night's Dream, L'Incoronazione di Poppea, Cenerentola and The Rape of Lucretia; Premiere of Iain Hamilton's Catiline Conspiracy, 1974; Foreign engagements include Cherubino at the New York City Center and Dallas Civic Opera; Rossini's Cenerentola in Stratford Ontario and Isolier in Washington; Isabella in Spoleto; Monteverdi's Ottone at Drottningholm; Concerts in Paris, Turin and Hong Kong; Chicago Lyric Opera, 1987, as Marcellina in Le nozze di Figaro, Repeated for Vancouver Opera, 1992. *Recordings:* Stravinsky, Cantata; Berlioz, Roméo et Juliette conducted by Colin Davis; Anna Bolena, Manon and Les Contes d'Hoffmann with Beverly Sills; Monteverdi Madrigals conducted by Raymond Leppard; Video of L'Incoronazione di Poppea, Glyndebourne, 1984. *Address:* c/o Music International, 13 Ardilaun Road, Highbury, London N5 2QR, England.

KERR, Virginia; singer (soprano); b. 1964, Ireland. *Education:* Royal Irish Academy and the Guildhall School, London. *Career:* appearances with Dublin Grand Opera as Leila, Liu (Turandot), Musetta, Micaela and Elvira in L'Italiana in Algeri (1996); Other roles include Fiordiligi for City of Birmingham Touring Opera, Anita in Krenek's Jonny Spielt Auf (at Leipzig), Mozart's Countess (Malta), and Grete in Schreker's Der ferne Klang (Opera North); Appearances with Scottish Opera as Jenůfa, Salome, Julia in Dvořák's Jacobin and the soprano lead in Judith Weir's The Vanishing Bridegroom; Ariadne for Castleward Opera, Tchaikovsky's Enchantress for New Sussex Opera and Donna Elvira at Leipzig (season 1996–97); Ortlinde in Die Walküre and Jenifer in The Midsummer Marriage at Covent Garden; Concerts include Stravinsky's Pulcinella, Schreker's Von Ewigen Leben (BBC Philharmonic Orchestra), Missa solemnis and Verdi Requiem (Mississippi Symphony Orchestra) and Carmina Burana at the Festival Hall; Beethoven's Ninth and Mahler's 2nd Symphony in Mexico. *Current Management:* Robert Gilder & Co., Enterprise House, 59–65 Upper Ground, London, SE1 9PQ, England. *Telephone:* (20) 7928-9008. *Fax:* (20) 7928-9755. *E-mail:* rgilder@robert-gilder.com.

KERRY, Gordon, BA; Australian composer, writer and critic; b. 21 Jan. 1961, Melbourne, Vic.. *Education:* University of Melbourne, studied with Barry Conyngham. *Career:* freelance composer; music critic for the Sydney Morning Herald 1996–; commissions from Musica Viva, ABC, Adelaide Chamber Orchestra and others. *Compositions include:* Winter Through Glass, for piano, 1980; Canticles for Evening Prayer, for choir, 1983; Siderius Nuncius for Organ, 1985; Obsessions, for mezzo and piano, 1985; Phaselus, for ensemble, 1986; Ongaku, for mandolin, 1987; Paradi, for viola and piano, 1988; Cantata for chorus and chamber orchestra, 1989; Cipangu for choir and orchestra, 1990; Torquing Points, for string quartet, 1991; Viola Concerto, 1992; Medea, chamber opera in 3 scenes, 1992; Quadrivial Pursuits, for clarinet, piano, viola and cello, 1993; No Orphean Lute, piano trio, 1994; Harmonie for wind quintet, 1996; Concerto for cello, percussion and strings, 1996; Variations for orchestra, 1996; Breathtaking for soprano and ensemble, 1999; Such Sweet Thunder for orchestra, 1999. *Honours:* Sounds Australian Award 1990. *Address:* c/o APRA Ltd, 1A Eden Street, Crows Nest, NSW 2065, Australia.

KERSJES, Anton (Frans Jan); Conductor; b. 17 Aug. 1923, Arnhem, Netherlands; m. Margaretha van de Groenekan, 8 Aug 1946. *Career:* 1st Violinist, Arnhem Symphony Orchestra, 1941; Choir Conductor, 1945–46 and 1949; Co-founder, Kunstamaand Chamber Orchestra, 1953; Conductor, Netherlands Ballet Sonia Gaskell, 1953–61; 1st Conductor 1953–83, Principal Guest Conductor 1983–, Amsterdam Philharmonic Orchestra; Conductor, Netherlands Opera Company, 1955–60; Conductor, Amsterdam Ballet, 1960–62; Conductor of all Dutch symphony orchestras including Concertgebouw Orchestra, Orchestra Radio Hilversum; Guest Conductor, Netherlands Opera Company; Permanent Guest Conductor, Netherlands Philharmonic Orchestra, Amsterdam; Leader of conductors' class, Amsterdam Muziekleceum, Sweelinck Conservatory, 1969–79; Leader conductors' and opera class, Deputy Director, Maastricht Conservatory; Tours in Europe, Scandinavia, the United Kingdom and USSR; Conductor of over 125 concerts, 5 operas on television. *Recordings:* For EMI and HMV. *Honours:* Decorated Officer, Order of Orange Nassau; Silver Medal, City of Amsterdam; Silver Medal, Concertgebouw. *Address:* 6 Honthorst Straat, 1071 Amsterdam, Netherlands.

KERTESI, Ingrid; Soprano; b. 1961, Budapest, Hungary. *Education:* Studied at the Franz Liszt Academy in Budapest and in Bayreuth. *Career:* Debut: Budapest in 1985 as Oscar in Un Ballo in Maschera; Sang Olympia at the Vienna Volksoper in 1987, Sophie in Budapest and Frasquita in Carmen at the 1991 Bregenz Festival; Other roles include Blondchen, Despina, Susanna and Mozart's Zerlina, Donizetti's Norina, Lucia and Adina, Amina in La Sonnambula, Gilda, Nannetta and Aennchen in Der Freischütz; Sang Adina at Budapest, 1996; Concert repertoire includes works by Handel, Haydn, Mozart, Bach and Vivaldi. *Address:* c/o Bregenz Festival, Postfach 311, 6901 Bregenz, Austria.

KERTESZ, Otto; Cellist; b. 1960, Hungary. *Education:* Studied at the Franz Liszt Academy, Budapest and with Sandor Devich, György Kurtàg and András Mihaly. *Career:* Member of the Keller String Quartet from 1986, debut concert at Budapest March 1987; Played Beethoven's Grosse Fuge and Schubert's Death and the Maiden Quartet at Interforum 87; Series of concerts in Budapest with Zoltán Kocsis and Deszö Ranki (piano) and Kalman Berkes (clarinet); Further appearances in Nuremberg, at the Chamber Music Festival La Baule and tours of Bulgaria, Austria, Switzerland, Italy (Ateforum 88 Ferrara), Belgium and Ireland; Concerts for Hungarian Radio and Television. *Recordings:* Albums for Hungaroton (from 1989). *Honours:* 2nd Prize Evian International String Quartet Competitin, May 1988. *Address:* c/o SullivSweet, 28 Albion Street, London, W2 2AX, England.

KESTEREN, John Van; Singer (Tenor); b. 4 May 1921, The Hague, Netherlands. *Education:* Studied in The Hague with Lothar Wallerstein and with Nadia Boulanger in Paris; Further study with Vera Schwarz in Salzburg. *Career:* Debut: Scheveningen 1947, as the Italian Singer in Der Rosenkavalier; Sang operetta in Netherlands, on Dutch Radio and in Utrecht; Sang at the Komische Oper Berlin from 1951, St ädtische Oper Berlin from 1953; Salzburg Festival from 1957, as Basilio in Le nozze di Figaro and in concert; Guest appearances in Vienna (from 1954), Düsseldorf, Munich, Stuttgart, Frankfurt, Ghent, Milan, the Drottningholm Festival (Stockholm), New York City Opera, Boston, Cincinnati, Dallas and Buenos Aires; Many concert appearances. *Recordings:* Belmonte in Die Entführung; Le Postillon de Lonjumeau by Adam; Pfitzner's Palestrina, Ariadne auf Naxos, Die Kluge by Orff; Leonore by Paer; Carmina Burana.

KESZEI, János; Timpanist and Percussionist; b. 1 June 1936, Hungary; two s., one d. *Education:* Music High School, Budapest, Hungary; Béla Bart ók Conservatorium and Franz Liszt Academy of Music, Budapest, Hungary. *Career:* Debut: Principal Percussionist, RESO, Dublin, 1957; Principal Timpanist, RESO, Dublin, 1964; Principal Timpanist, Ulster Orchestra, 1966; Principal Timpanist, City of Birmingham Symphony Orchestra, 1969; Principal Timpanist, P Boulez, BBC Symphony Orchestra, 1972–78; Freelance, 1978–, with: ECO; RPO; LMP; CLS; English Symphonia; OAE; GTO; Solo Timpanist, Rotterdam Philharmonic, 1984–87; Toured and recorded ROH; Contributed to more than 320 films, records and CD's, lectures, master classes in the United Kingdom and abroad; Involved in early and baroque, Hanover Band, King's Consort and OAE in Glyndebourne summer seasons, Salzburg, New York, Paris, Vienna, Berlin; Professor of Timpani, Royal College of Music, 1973–; mem, Royal Society of Musicians of Great Britain. *Address:* 17 Grove Gardens, Tring, Herts HP23 5PX, England. *Telephone:* (1442) 828150. *Fax:* (1442) 828150.

KETILSSON, Jon; Singer (tenor); b. 1970, Reykjavík, Iceland. *Education:* Studied in Vienna. *Career:* Debut: Offenbach's Barbe-bleue at Schönbrunn; Sang Alfredo and Florestan at Prague State Opera, Max in Der Freischütz, Cavaradossi, Wagner's Erik and Candide at Dortmund; Strauss's Bacchus at Lausanne and Enée in Les Troyens at Lisbon; Cologne Opera as Tamino, Cavaradossi, Macduff, Don José, and Herr M. in Hindemith's Neues vom Tage; Other roles include Hoffmann, Pinkerton, Rodolfo and Sergei in Lady Macbeth of Mtsensk; Season 2001–2002 as Don José at Brussels and Geneva, Max in Lausanne and Enée at the Salzburg Festival; Concerts include Beethoven's Ninth, Carmina Burana, Messiah and Dvořák's Requiem. *Current Management:* Athole Still International Management, Forresters Hall, 25–27 Westow Street, London, SE19 3RY, England. *Telephone:* (20) 8771-5271. *Fax:* (20) 8768-6600. *Website:* www.atholestill.com.

KETTING, Otto; Composer; b. 3 Sept. 1935, Amsterdam, Netherlands. *Education:* Studied at the Hague Conservatory, 1952–58. *Career:* Trumpeter in The Hague Philharmonic Orchestra 1965–60; Teacher of composition, Rotterdam Conservatory 1967–71 and at the Royal Conservatory in The Hague 1971–74; Artistic Adviser to the Utrecht Symphony Orchestra 1983; Opera Ithaka was premiered at the opening of the Muziektheater Amsterdam, 1989. *Compositions include:* Operas: Dummies 1974 and O, Thou Rhinoceros 1977; Ballets The Last Message 1962; Interieur 1963; Barriers 1963; The Golden Key 1964; Choreostruction 1963; Theatre Pice 1973; Concerto for solo organ 1953; Sinfonietta 1954; Sonata for brass quartet 1955; Piano Sonatia 195; Passcagalia for orchestra 1957; Serenade for cello and piano 1957; Concertino 1958; Symphony 1959; Concertino for jazz quintet and orchestra 1960; Variations for wind, harp and percussion 1960; Series of works entitled Collage; Minimal Music for 29 toy instruments 1970; In Memoriam Igor Stravinsky for orchestra 1971; Time Machine for wind and percussion 1972; For Moonlight Nights for flute and 26 players 1973; Adagio for chamber orchestra 1977; Symphony for saxophones and orchestra 1978; Opera Ithaka 1986; Symphony No. 3, 1990; Medusa for saxophone and orchestra, 1992; Summer Moon for soprano and ensemble, 1992; Come, Over the Sea, for orchestra, 1994; Cheops for horn and orchestra, 1995. *Honours:* Guadeamus Prize 1958; Warsaw Autumn Festival Award 1963. *Address:* c/o BUMA/STERMA huis, Postbus 725, 1180 AS Amstelveen, Netherlands.

KEYES, John; Singer (Tenor); b. 1964, Illinois, USA. *Education:* Studied in Chicago. *Career:* Based with the Chicago Lyric Opera until 1991; Season 1991–92 with Siegmund in Die Walküre for Scottish Opera, Radames at Mexico City and Parsifal in Robert Wilson's production of Wagner's opera for Houston Grand Opera; Concert performances of Otello (as Roderigo) in Chicago an New York under Solti, 1991; Season 1992–93 as Siegmund at Hamburg and Nantes, Erik in Fliegende Holländer at Toulouse and Parsifal at Antwerp and Hamburg; Other roles include Walther von der Vogelweide and Eisenstein (Houston), Samson, Don Carlos, Don José and Dick Johnson; Sang Lohengrin in a new production of Wagner's opera for English National Opera, 1993; Season 1996–98 with Parsifal at Munich; Jean in Massenet's Hérodiade

at San Francisco and Turiddu and Canio for Israel Opera; Florestan at Buenos Aires and Siegmund in Amsterdam; Sang Parsifal in Munich, Lohengrin in San Diego and Strauss's Emperor at the Deutsche Oper, Berlin. *Recordings include:* Otello. *Honours:* Winner, 1990, San Antonio Competition; Ruth Richards Grant in 1990 Richard Tucker Competition; Concert repertoire includes Beethoven's Ninth. *Address:* c/o Tivoli Arists Management, 3 Vesterbrogade, DK–1630 Copenhagen, Denmark.

KEYLIN, Misha; Violinist; b. 5 March 1970, St Petersburg, Russia. *Education:* The Juilliard School. *Career:* Debut: Carnegie Hall in New York (aged 11), 1981; Performed both in recital and as soloist in major concert halls in over 30 countries. *Recordings:* The complete cycle of the Henri Vieuxtemps Violin Concertos. *Honours:* Winner of Hannover, Paganini, Sarasate and Sigall International Violin Competitions. *Current Management:* IMG Artists, Paris. *Address:* PO Box 230705, New York, NY 10023, USA.

KEYTE, Christopher (Charles); Singer (Bass-Baritone); b. 11 Sept. 1935, Shorne, Kent, England; m. June Matthews. *Education:* Choral Scholar, King's College, Cambridge. *Career:* Oratorio, opera, concert and recital appearances; Founder Member, Purcell Consort of Voices, 1963–75; Opera with The Fires of London; Professor of Singing, Royal Academy of Music, 1982–87; Royal Opera House, Covent Garden, 1989–. *Recordings:* Monteverdi Songs, Sacred Concertos; Purcell Anthems, Indian Queen; Haydn and Schubert Masses; Vaughan Williams Serenade to Music and Pilgrim's Progress; Songs by Quilter, Gurney and Glazunov; Mass of the Sea by Paul Patterson; The Lighthouse by Peter Maxwell Davies. *Honours:* Honorary RAM, 1983. *Address:* 20 Brycedale Crescent, Southgate, London N14 7EY, England.

KHACHATRYAN, Sergei; Concert Violinist; b. 1985, Yerevam, Armenia. *Education:* Taunus Music School, Eschborn, Germany; Wurzburg and Karlsruhe Music Academies; Masterclasses in Keshet Eilon, Israel, under Shlomo Mintz. *Career:* Participation in music competitions in Rome, Kracow, Germany and Spain, from 1995; Appearances with symphony and chamber orchestras throughout Europe, including Bruch Concerto with English CO at Fairfields Hall, Croydon, 2001; Concerts throughout Finland, notably with the Sibelius Concerto, and in Israel, Ecuador, Brazil and Armenia; Season 2001–2002 with Music at Oxford recital, concerts with Bournemouth SO, Royal Philharmonic, Frankfurt Radio SO and Bochum Symphony. *Recordings include:* Recital for EMI. *Honours:* Winner, Louis Spohr Competition, Freiburg, and International Team Sibelius Competition, Helsinki. *Current Management:* Askonas Holt Ltd, Lonsdale Chambers, 27 Chancery Lane, London, WC2A 1PF, England. *Telephone:* (20) 7400-1700. *Fax:* (20) 7400-1799. *E-mail:* info@askonasholt.co.uk. *Website:* www.askonasholt.co.uk.

KHADEM-MISSAGH, Bijan; Violinist, Conductor and Composer; b. 26 Oct. 1948, Tehran, Iran. *Education:* Univ. of Vienna, Austria; diploma, Acad. of Music, Vienna, 1971. *Career:* debut, as soloist with orchestra aged 13; concert tours, including radio and television appearances and festivals throughout Europe, Asia, Latin America and Australia; founder, Eurasia Quartet 1969–75; founder, The Dawnbreakers, Austrian Baha'i singing group 1970; founder, conductor and soloist, Tonkuenstler Chamber Orchestra, Vienna 1977–; Artistic Dir, Allegro Vivo, International Chamber Music Festival, Austria 1979–, Midsummer Music Festival, Sweden 1981–90, Badener Beethoventage 1980–86; Prof., J. M. Hauer Konservatory, Wiener Neustadt 1988; masterclasses for violin; Pres., Globart, 1997–; Musical Dir, Music Forum Landegg, Switzerland 1991–2000. *Compositions:* instrumental and vocal works. *Recordings:* works by Beethoven, Schubert, Schoenberg, Weigl, Mendelssohn, Vitali, Paganini, Debussy, Szymanowski, Bach, Tchaikovsky, Haydn, Handel, Dvořák, Respighi, Bartók, Strauss, Kreisler; albums: Dawnbreakers 1976, The Child 1979, To A Friend 1982, Vision 1986, Call of the Beloved, Phoenix, Glad Tidings, Wie Sterne. *Publications:* Lieder–Book of Songs 1976, Das Musische als Lebensweise, Ein Credo 1998. *Honours:* Austrian Cross for Arts and Sciences. *Address:* Allegro Vivo. International Chamber Music Festival Austria, Wiener Strasse 16, A-3580 Horn, Austria. *Telephone:* +43 2982–4319. *E-mail:* office@allegro-vivo.at. *Website:* www.allegro-vivo.at.

KHALEMSKAIA, Marianna; Singer (Soprano); b. 1960, St Petersburg, Russia. *Education:* Studied at St Petersburg State Conservatory and with soloists of the Mariinsky Theatre. *Career:* Concerts from 1992, including Mozart's Requiem and Kurt Weill songs; Opera debut in V Plesak's opera Tale of a Dead Princess, 1996; Paris Opéra-Comique as Elisetta in Il Matrimonio Segreto; Seasons 1996–98 as Annina in A Night in Venice, Rosina in Mozart's La Finta Semplice and Musetta in La Bohème. *Honours:* Prizewinner at Barcelona and Toulouse competitions. *Address:* Harlequin Agency Ltd, 203 Fidles Road, Cardiff CF14 5NA, Wales.

KHAN, Ustad Bismillah; Indian musician; b. 21 March 1916, Bihar. *Career:* Hindustani shehnai player; performed All India Music Conf., Calcutta 1937; has performed in Europe, USA, Africa, USSR, Japan,

Iran, Iraq, Afghanistan; features on over 50 albums. *Recordings include:* on T Series: Bismillah Khan Vols 1–15, Shaan-E-Shenai, Shenai Samraat; on Navras: Live In London 1985 Vols 1 and 2, Live at the Queen Elizabeth Hall, Uphaar, Shenai, The Eternal Spirit 1993; on EMI India: An Exposition of Ragas, From Benaras- The Seat of Shenai, Fifty Golden Years, The Magnificence Of Shenai, Shaadi Ki Shenaiyan, Shenai Recital, The Enchanter, Majestic Ragas; on Music Today: Romantic Raga Vol. 2, Megh Malhar Vol. 4, Basant Bahar Vol. 1, Raga, Maestros Choice. *Honours:* Bharath Rathna (India's highest civilian honour), Padma Vibhushan, Tansen Award Dr hc Benares Hindu Univ. Sangeet Natak Academi Award. *Address:* c/o Navras Records, 22 Sherwood Road, London, NW4 1AD, England. *Telephone:* (20) 8203-2553. *E-mail:* music@navrasrecords.com. *Website:* www .navrasrecords.com.

KHANZADIAN, Vahan (Avedis); Operatic Tenor; b. 23 Jan. 1939, Syracuse, New York, USA. *Education:* BEd, University of Buffalo, 1961; Curtis Institute of Music, 1963. *Career:* Debut: San Francisco Spring Opera as Ruggero in Puccini's La Rondine, 1968; Many roles in numerous productions including: Wozzeck, Fra Diavolo, Madama Butterfly, Lucia di Lammermoor; Appearances with major opera companies throughout USA and Canada including: NY City Center, Baltimore, Houston, Memphis, New Orleans, St Paul, Providence, Birmingham, Kentucky, Kansas City, Dayton, Toledo, Portland, Honolulu, Montreal, Edmonton, Vancouver; Guest soloist with major orchestras including: Boston, Chicago, Philadelphia, Baltimore, Boston Pops; Numerous recital tours; Masterclasses; Television and radio broadcasts; Tenor soloist in world premiere of Menotti's Lanscapes and Remembrances at Milwaukee, 1976; European debuts: Cavaradossi in Tosca at Aachen, 1992, Title role in Don Carlo at Basel, 1992, Metropolitan Opera debut as Riccardo in Ballo in Maschera, 1993, Lyric Opera, Chicago debut as Riccardo, 1993; Bavarian State Opera, Munich as Calaf in Turandot, 1995; Cincinnati Opera, USA as Radames in Aida, 1995. *Recordings:* Broadway cast recording of Follies, 1998. *Address:* Hunter Highlands, PO Box 741, Hunter, NY 12442, USA. *E-mail:* vahan@optonline.net.

KHARITONOV, Dimitri; Singer (baritone); b. 18 Oct. 1958, Kuibyshev, Russia. *Education:* Rimsky-Korsakov College of Music, Leningrad from 1976; Vocal studies, piano, with honours, Nezhdanova State Conservatory, Odessa, 1978–84. *Career:* Recital Singer, Odessa Philharmonic Society; Principal Baritone, Odessa State Opera, 1984; Sang 55 times at the Bolshoi Opera, Kremlin Hall, roles included: Prince Yeletsky, Queen of Spades, Duke Robert, Iolanta (Tchaikovsky), Duenna (Prokofiev); Also sang in Moussorgsky's Khovanshchina and Boris Godunov, Rimsky-Korsakov's Tzar Saltan, Germont (La Traviata) and Conte di Luna, Il Trovatore (Verdi), Figaro, Il Barbiere di Siviglia (Rossini), Silvio in Pagliacci; Sang in main opera houses and concert halls, Moscow, Leningrad, Kiev, Minsk; Appeared regularly on Russian television, settled in England, 1989; British debut as Jokanaan in Salome, Edinburgh Festival, 1989, returning for Tchaikovsky's Cantata Moskow; Season 1989–90 as Germont in Liège, Opera de Wallonie; In America sang at the Chicago Lyric Opera with Placido Domingo in La Fanciulla del West (Puccini) amongst others; In 1992 gave recital in Brussels at the Palais des Beaux Arts; In 1994 sang title role of Nabucco at Genoe; Also sang Oslo and Lillehammer in Rachmaninov lieder recitals; Sang in Buenos Aires at the Teatro Colón Sharpless in Madama Butterfly; In 1993 was Prince Yeletsky (The Queen of Spades) in the Glyndebourne Festival Opera and gave 3 recitals at the Risor Festival in Norway. *Recordings include:* Shostakovich's romances on Pushkin's poems with the City of Birmingham Symphony Orchestra; Tchaikovsky's Ode to Joy; Eugene Onegin; Khovanshchina; Prince Yeletsky in Queen of Spades, Glyndebourne production video. *Honours:* Winner All-Ukranian Lysenko Competition for Opera Singers, Kiel, 1983, Odessa, 1984; All-USSR M. I. Glinka Competition with special prize for best interpretation of Rimsky-Korsakov works, 1984; Grand Prix, Verviers International Opera Competition, Belgium, 1987; Gold Medal, Bastianini International Competition, Siena, 1988; Voci Verdiane Competition, Brusseto, 1988; Carlo Alberto Cappelli Competition, Arena di Verona, for International Competition Winners. *Current Management:* Allied Artists, 42 Montpelier Square, London SW7 4JZ, England.

KHARITONOVA, Yelena; Violinist; b. 1960, Moscow, Russia. *Education:* Studied at the Moscow Conservatoire with Andrei Shislov. *Career:* Co-Founder, Glazunov Quartet, 1985; Many concerts in the former Soviet Union and recent appearances in Greece, Poland, Belgium, Germany and Italy; Works by Beethoven and Schumann at the Beethoven Haus in Bonn; Further engagements in Canada and Netherlands; Teacher at the Moscow State Conservatoire and resident at the Tchaikovsky Conservatoire; Repertoire includes works by Borodin, Shostakovich and Tchaikovsky, in addition to the standard works. *Recordings include:* CDs of the six quartets of Glazunov. *Honours:* Prizewinner of the Borodin Quartet and Shostakovich Chamber Music Competitions with

the Glazunov Quartet. *Address:* c/o Sonata (Glazunov Quartet), 11 Northgate Street, Glasgow G20 7AA, England.

KHERSONSKAJA, Natalya (Mikhailovna); Musicologist, Pianist and Organist; b. 1 Nov. 1961, Poltava, Ukraine; m. Sergei Zagny, 26 July 1986, 1 s. *Education:* Piano and Musicology at Poltava Music College, 1981; Preparatory Section of Philosophical Faculty of Moscow State M Lomonosov University, 1982–83; Studied organ with Professor L I Roizman at Moscow State Conservatory, 1984–89; Musicologist, 1990 and Postgraduate, 1993, Moscow State Conservatory. *Career:* Editor of the chief edition of Ostankino, Television-Radio company musical broadcasting, Moscow, 1990–; Chief Scientific Collaborator of Database Section (electronic musical encyclopaedia) of the Computer Centre of Moscow State Conservatory, 1995–. *Recordings include:* Many broadcasts as author and interviewer including cycles, Music of 20th Century including Webern, Berg, Schoenberg, Scriabin, Mosolov and Boulez, Sviatoslav Richter plays Franz Schubert, Rondo; Masters of Antique Music including English virginalists and S Scheidt and Schütz; 9 Hours of French Music from Perotin to Messiaen. *Publications include:* Author of musicologic works including separate studies of the music of Samuel Scheidt (first in Russia) entitled, Word and Number as a Structural Idea of Organ Composition of S Scheidt, 1987, Tabulatura Nova of S Scheidt, new concept, 1990, Word For Windows As Possible Cover for Database, 1995. *Address:* Ul Vagonoremontnaja 5 korpus 1, kv 23, Moscow 127411, Russia.

KHOLMINOV, Alexander; Composer; b. 8 Sept. 1925, Moscow, Russia. *Education:* Studied with Golubev at the Moscow conservatory, graduated 1950. *Career:* Stage works have been widely performed in Moscow and Elsewhere in Russia. *Compositions:* Operas An Optimistic Tragedy Frunze, 1965; Anna Snegina, Gorky, 1967; The Overcoat, after Gogol, 1975; The Carriage, after Gogol, Moscow, 1975; Chapayev, Moscow Radio, 1977; The Twelfth Series, Moscow, 1977; The Wedding, after Chekhov, Moscow, 1984; Vanka, Monodrama after Chekhov, Moscow, 1984; The Brothers Karamazov, after Dostoyevsky, Moscow, 1985; Hot Snow, 1985; The Fruits of Enlightenment, after Tolstoy, 1990; 5 Symphonies, 1973, 1975, 1977, 1990, 1995; Viola Concerto, 1989; 3 string quartets, 1980, 1985, 1994; 24 Preludes for piano, 1994. *Honours:* USSR State Prize, 1978; People's Artist of the URSSR, 1984. *Address:* c/o RAO, Bolchaia Bronnai 6a, Moscow 103670, Russia.

KHOMA, Natalia; Cellist; b. 5 Dec. 1963, Lviv, Ukraine; m. Suren Bagratuni, 5 July 1986, 1 d. *Education:* BM, Lviv Music School; MM, DMA, Tchaikovsky Moscow Conservatory; Diploma, Boston University. *Career:* Debut: Soloist with Lviv Philharmonia Orchestra, 1975; Performances and Recitals at: Weill Recital Hall, Carnegie Hall, New York, Merkin Hall, New York, Jordan Hall, Boston, Rachmaninov Hall, Moscow, Moscow Conservatory Small Hall, Academy of Music Big Hall, Oslo, Norway, Palais des Beaux Arts, Brussels, Belgium, Schauspielhaus, Berlin, Germany, Grand Hall of Academy of Music, Budapest; Performed Throughout the Soviet Union, East Europe, Spain, Germany, Belgium, Italy, Norway, Canada, USA. *Recordings:* Numerous. *Honours:* 1st Prize, All Ukrainian Competition, 1981; Max Reger Special Prize, 1985; 2nd Prize, Markneukirchen International Competition, Germany, 1987; 1st Prize, Belgrade International Competition, 1990; 4th Prize, Tchaikovsky Competition, Moscow, 1990. *Address:* c/o Tchaikovsky Moscow Conservatory, Ul Gertzena 13, 103009 Moscow, Russia.

KHRENNIKOV, Tikhon (Nikolayevich); Composer; b. 10 June 1913, Elets, Liptsk Region, Russia; m. Klara Arnoldovna Vax 1936, 1 d. *Education:* Gnesin School and College, Moscow, 1929–32; Moscow Conservatoire, 1932–36. *Career:* Director of Music, Central Theatre of Soviet Army, 1941–54; General Secretary 1957–; First Secretary of the composers' Union of the USSR, 1948–91; Deputy to USSR Supreme Soviet, 1962–91; Committee Member, USSR Parliamentary Group; Member, Central Auditing Commission, CPSU, 1961–91; Chairman, Soviet-Italian Parliamentary Group, USSR Supreme Soviet, 1970–91; Chairman of organizing committees of international music festivals in the USSR, 1981, 1984, 1988; Member of Santa Cecilia Academy, 1983; Tibara Academy, 1985; Prize of UNESCO International Music Council (IMC), 1977; Chairman of Tchaikovsky Contest Organising Committee. *Compositions include:* Three Piano Concertos, 1933, 1971, 1983; 5 Pieces for Piano, 1933; First Symphony, 1935; 3 Pieces for Piano, 1935; Suite for Orchestra from Music for Much Ado About Nothing, 1936; In the Storm (Opera), 1939; Second Symphony 1940–43; Incidental Music for Play, Long Ago, 1942; Frol Skobeyev (Opera), 1950; Mother (Opera) 1956; Concerto for Violin and Orchestra, 1959; A Hundred Devils and One Girl (Operetta), 1961; Concerto for Cello and Orchestra, 1964; White Nights (Operetta), 1967; Boy Giant (opera for children), 1969; Our Courtyard (ballet for children), 1970; Concerto No. 2 for Violin and Orchestra, 1975; Much Ado About Nothing, ballet, 1976; Much Ado About Hearts (Chamber Opera), 1976; Third Symphony 1976; The Hussar's Ballard (Ballet), 1979–80; Three Pieces, for violin and piano, 1980; Dorotea–comic opera, 1983; Golden Calf–comic opera, 1985;

String Quartet, 1987; The Naked King, comic opera, 1987; Second concerto for cello and orchestra, 1990; Sonata for cello and piano, 1990; Piano Concerto No. 4, 1991; Three Sonnets of Shakespeare for voice and piano, 1991; Six Choruses based on text by Nekrasov, 1992; Fourth Concerto for piano and chamber orchestra, 1992; Napoleon Bonaparte, ballet, 1995; Five Romances based on text by Bunin, 1996; The Captain's Daughter, ballet after Pushkin, 1999; Clever Things, musical play after the play by Marshak, 2001. *Publications:* Sovetskij Kompozitor; Several Recorded Works. *Address:* Plotnikov Lane 10, Appt. 19, 121002 Moscow, Russia.

KIBERG, Tina; Singer (Soprano); b. 30 Dec. 1958, Copenhagen, Denmark. *Education:* Studied in Copenhagen. *Career:* Debut: Royal Opera Copenhagen, 1983, as Leonora in Nielsen's Maskarade; Sang Elsa in Lohengrin at Copenhagen, 1984, the Marschallin 1988, Mozart's Countess and Purcell's Dido, 1990, Hélène in Les Vepres Siciliennes, 1991; Guest appearances at Geneva and Frankfurt, 1988, as Agathe and the Countess, at Århus as Mimi, Vienna Staatsoper 1990, as Elsa and Opéra Bastille Paris, 1991 as Lisa in The Queen of Spades; Lieder recitals in England, Germany and Italy from 1984; Sang Strauss's Ariadne at Copenhagen and Elisabeth in Tannhäuser at Bayreuth, 1992; Sang Wagner's Eva with the Royal Danish Opera, 1996; Other roles in opera have included Donna Elvira, Pamina, Desdemona, and Tatiana in Eugene Onegin; Sang Chrysothemis in Elektra at Catania, 1998; Concert repertoire includes Schmidt's Das buch mit Sieben Siegeln (Copenhagen), Beethoven's Mass in C (Lausanne), Haydn's Lord Nelson Mass (Vienna) and Elijah in Berlin; Tour of Moscow, Dresden, Berlin and London with Missa Solemnis conducted by Antal Dorati; Season 1999–2000 as Salome and Lisa in The Queen of Spades at Copenhagen, Sieglinde for Geneva Opera and Chrysothemis in Elektra for New Israeli Opera at Savonlinna. *Recordings include:* Lulu by Kuhlau. *Address:* c/o Det Kongelie Teater, Box 2185, DK 1017 Copenhagen, Denmark.

KIEMER, Hans; Singer (Bass-Baritone); b. 9 Feb. 1932, Munich, Germany. *Education:* Studied in Munich. *Career:* Engaged at Innsbruck, 1968–70, Augsburg, 1970–76, Wiesbaden, 1976–79; Appearances at Karlsruhe from 1979, notably at the Dutchman and Wagner's Kurwenal, Wotan and Amfortas, Verdi's Falstaff and Amonasro, in the 1986 premiere of Kunaud's Der Meister und Margarita and as Waldner in Arabella, 1989; Guest engagements at Amsterdam, Barcelona, Brussels, (the Wanderer in Siegfried, 1981), Bordeaux (as Jochanaan), Trieste (Pizarro), Vienna, Lisbon and Warsaw (Wanderer, 1989); Other roles include Strauss's Mandryka and Barak, Borromeo in Palestrina, Baron Ochs, Don Alfonso and Scarpia; Noted interpreter of the Ballades of Carl Loewe; Sang Mefistofele at Innsbruck, 1990. *Address:* Rebisches Staatstheater, Baumeisterstrasse 11, 7500 Karlsruhe, Germany.

KIERNAN, Patrick; Violinist; b. 1962, England. *Career:* Debut: Wigmore Hall, 1984 with Peter Pears; Co-Founder, Brindisi String Quartet, Aldeburgh, 1984; Concerts in a wide repertory throughout the United Kingdom and in France, Germany, Spain, Italy and Switzerland; Festival engagements at Aldeburgh (residency, 1990), Arundel, Bath, Brighton, Huddersfield, Norwich, Warwick and Prague Spring Festival; First London performance of Colin Matthews' 2nd Quartet, 1990, premiere of David Matthews' 6th Quartet, 1991; Quartet by Mark Anthony Turnage, 1992; World premiere of Colin Matthews' 3rd Quartet, Aldeburgh, 1994; Many BBC recitals and resident artist with the University of Ulster. *Recordings include:* Quartets by Britten, Bridge and Imogen Holst; Works by Pierné, Lekeu, Schoenberg, Berg and Webern. *Honours:* Prizewinner, Third Banff International String Quartet Competition in Canada, 1989, with Brindisi Quartet. *Address:* c/o Owen/White Management, 14 Nightingale Lane, London N8 7QU, England.

KIKUCHI, Yoshinori; Conductor; b. 16 Sept. 1938, Yawatahama, Japan. *Education:* Studied at Tokyo National University of Fine Arts and Music. *Career:* Chief Assistant at the Nikikai Opera, Tokyo, 1961–64; Studied further with Kasei Yamada in Japan, with Peter Maag at the Accademia Chigiana at Siena and with Franco Ferrara in Rome; Engagements at Palermo (Teatro Lirico and Teatro Massimo), 1973–77; Hessisches Staatstheater Wiesbaden, 1978–84; Guest Conductor in Japan, Italy, Germany, France, Spain and Belgium; La Scala, Milan, 1985–86; Verona Arena, 1987. *Address:* c/o Theateragentur Luisa Petrov, Glauburgstrasse 95, 60318 Frankfurt am Main, Germany.

KILAR, Wojciech; Polish composer; b. 17 July 1932, Lvov; m. Barbara Pomianowska. *Education:* State Higher School of Music, Katowice, (student of B. Woytowicz) Nadia Boulanger School. *Career:* mem. Cttee Int. Festival of Contemporary Music Warszawska Jesień 1975, Polish Composers Union 1953–; mem. Polish Acad. of Arts and Sciences 1998–. *Works include:* Mała uwertura 1955, I Symfonia 1955, II Symfonia 1956, Oda Bela Bartok im Memoriam 1957, Riff 62 1962, Générique 1963, Diphthongs 1964, Springfield Sonnet 1963, Solenne 1967, Upstairs Downstairs 1971, Przygrywka i Kolęda 1972, Krzesany 1974, Bogur-

odzica 1975, Kościelec 1909 1976, Siwa mgła 1979, Exodus 1981, Victoria 1983, Angelus 1984, Orawa 1986, Prelude for Strings 1988, Dracula 1991, Piano Concerto 1997, Missa pro pace 2000; music for about 30 plays and 150 films including Illumination 1973, The Promised Land 1974, Death and the Maiden 1994, Portrait of a Lady 1997, The Ninth Gate 1999, The Pianist 2002. *Honours:* Dr hc (Opole Univ.) 1999; numerous awards in Poland and abroad. *Address:* ul. Kościuszki 165, 40-524 Katowice, Poland. *Telephone:* (32) 2514965.

KILDEA, Paul Francis, BMus, MMus, DPhil; Conductor; b. 10 Feb. 1968, Canberra, Australia. *Education:* Univ. of Melbourne, Univ. of Oxford. *Career:* Conductor on Young Artist Programme, Opera Australia 1996; Conductor of The Cunning Little Vixen, Opera Australia 1997; Asst to Simone Young 1999–2002; Conductor, Opera Australia, on The Barber of Seville 1998, La Bohème 2001, The Turn of the Screw 2002; Head of Music, Aldeburgh Productions 1999–2003; Artistic Dir, Wigmore Hall, London 2003–. *Publications:* Selling Britten: Music and the Market Place 2002, Britten on Music 2003; contrib. to The Cambridge Companion to Britten 1999, many journals and newspapers. *Address:* Arts Management, Level 2, 420 Elizabeth Street, Surry Hills, NSW 2010, Australia (office). *Telephone:* (61 2) 9310-2466 (office). *Fax:* (61 2) 9310-5334 (office). *E-mail:* virginia@artsmanagement.com.au (office).

KILDUFF, Barbara (Jane); Opera Singer (Soprano); b. 31 May 1959, Huntington, New York, USA. *Education:* BM, State University College, New York at Fredonia, 1981; MM, University of Connecticut, Storrs, 1983; MM, Vale University, 1984. *Career:* Debut: Washington Opera, Blonde; Performances include: Sang Blonde with Metropolitan Opera, conductor James Levine, 1990; With Baltimore Symphony, David Zinman, July 1990; With Zürich Opera, April–May 1990, Barenreiter–Carlos Kalmar; Sang Zerbinetta in Munich 1987 and 1988; Conductors Bender, Sawallisch, Köhler in Vienna, 1987, 1991; Conductor Theodor Guschlbauer, Metropolitan Opera, 1987; James Levine, Hamburg, 1988; Julius Rudel, Basel, 1988; Vancouver, January 1989 (Martin André); In Vienna, April 1991 with Horst Stein; Olympia, Bregenz, Summer 1987 and 1988; Marc Soustrot, in Geneva, June 1990; Sang Adele at Metropolitan Opera, 1987, 1988, 1990, 1991; Julius Rudel; Cleopatra, Metropolitan, October 1988; Trevor Pinnock; Sophie in Der Rosenkavalier, Munich October 1989, 1990, 1991; Director: Brigitte Fassbaender, Heinrich Hollreiser; Metropolitan Opera, March 1991, Jiri Kout; Queen of Night, Oviedo, Spain, September 1991; Many concert appearances and television and radio performances; Season 1993 as the Countess in Capriccio at Vienna; Appears as Papagena in Met video of Die Zauberflöte; Sang Mozart's Blondchen at Bonn, 2000. *Address:* c/o CAMI, Crittenden Division, 165 West 57 Street, New York, NY 10019, USA.

KILLEBREW, Gwendolyn; Singer (Mezzo-Soprano); b. 26 Aug. 1939, Philadelphia, USA. *Education:* Templeton University; Juilliard School; Metropolitan Opera Studio. *Career:* Debut: Metropolitan Opera 1967, in Die Walküre; 1968–69 sang Carmen in Munich and at the New York City Opera; 1970 Copenhagen, Geneva and Prague in Handel's Tamerlano; 1972–73 Salzburg Festival, as Amneris and in the premiere of Orff's De Temporum fine Comedia; 1973 Washington Opera as Baba the Turk (The Rake's Progress) and San Francesco as Marina (Boris Godunov); Deutsche Oper am Rhein, Düsseldorf, from 1976, as Gluck's Orfeo, Verdi's Preziosilla and Azucena and Rossini's Isabella; Bayreuth debut 1978, as Waltraute in Götterdämmerung; Zürich 1981, as Mistress Quickly in Falstaff; Sang Frau Leimgruber in Klebe's Der Jüngste Tag, Duisburg, 1989; Season 1991–92 as the Nurse in Rimsky's Golden Cockerel and Strauss's Herodias at Duisburg; Also sings in concert. *Recordings:* Tamerlano; Orlando Paladino by Haydn; Edgar (Puccini), Schvanda the Bagpiper; De Temporum fine Comedia (Orff); Mahler's 3rd Symphony. *Honours:* Outstanding Musician, Temple University, 1971. *Current Management:* Ingpen & Williams Ltd, 7 St George's Court, 131 Putney Bridge Road, London, SW15 2PA, England.

KILLMAYER, Wilhelm; Composer; b. 21 Aug. 1927, Alunich, Germany. *Education:* Studied with Carl Orff, among others. *Career:* Ballet conductor at the Bavarian State Opera, 1961–64; Professor at the Munich Hochschule für Musik, 1973–91. *Compositions:* Operas La tragedie di Orfeo, 1961; Yolimba, 1963, 1970; Un lecon de francais, 1964; Der Weisse Hut, 1967; Ballets Encores, 1969; Paradies, 1974; 2 string quartets, 1969, 1975; 3 symphonies, 1968, 1969, 1973; Encore for orchestra, 1970; Kammermusik 1–3, 1970–73; The Broken Farewell for trumpet and chamber orchestra, 1977; Brahms-bildnis, piano trio, 1977; French songbook for soprano, baritone and ensemble, 1980; Im Freien, symphonic poem, 1980; Sostenuto for cello and strings, 1984; 4 songs in 4 European languages, 1993; Die Schönheit des Morgens for viola and piano, 1994; 8 Poesies for soprano and ensemble, 1995; La joie de vivre for small orchestra, 1996; Neue Heine-Lieder for tenor and piano, 1999; Pindar Odes for mixed chorus and organ, 1999. *Address:* c/o GEMA, Rosenheimer Str 11, 81667 Munchen, Germany.

KIM, Ettore; Singer (baritone); b. 14 Nov. 1965, Republic of Korea. *Education:* Studied in South Korea and Italy. *Career:* Debut: Theatro Delle Erbe, Milan, in Salieri's Arlecchinata, 1990; Sang in Henze's We Come to the River at La Scala and in the premiere of Ferroro's La Figlia del Mago at the Teatro San Carlo, 1992; Concert performances of Otello, as Iago, at Bordeaux, 1992; Engaged as Germont at Covent Garden, 1993, Chorebus in concerts of Les Troyens with the London Symphony Orchestra and on stage at La Scala, 1993–94, Belcore at Strasbourg, Antonio in Linda di Chamounix at Stockholm and Riccardo in Puritani for Bavarian Radio; Other roles include Scarpia, and Gerard in Andrea Chénier; Sang Camoëns in Donizetti's Don Sébastien at Aachen, 1998. *Recordings include:* Linda di Chamounix and I Puritani, both with Edita Gruberova. *Honours:* Gold Medal, International Giuseppe Verdi Competition at Bussetto, 1989. *Current Management:* Athole Still International Management, Forresters Hall, 25–27 Westow Street, London, SE19 3RY, England. *Telephone:* (20) 8771-5271. *Fax:* (20) 8768-6600. *Website:* www.atholestill.com.

KIM, Hae-Jung; Concert Pianist; b. 18 May 1965, New York, USA. *Education:* BM and MM, Juilliard School of Music; Peabody Conservatory; Moscow Conservatory. *Career:* Debut: Vienna Tonkunstler Orchestra, Vienna, 1985; Pittsburgh Symphony, St Louis; Royal Philharmonic, London Philharmonic, Moscow State Symphony, Barcelona Philharmonic, NHK Symphony, Lausanne Chamber, English Chamber, Monte Carlo Philharmonic. *Recordings:* Rachmaninov concertos no. 2 and 3; Prokofiev Concerto no. 1 and Tchaikovsky Concerto no.1, St Petersburg Symphony; Rachmaninov no. 4 and Rhapsody. *Honours:* 1st prize, Köln International Competition, 1998; D'Angelo Young Artist Competition; Medal award from Korean Government. *Current Management:* IMG Artists Management. *Address:* 3 Lincoln Center, NY 10023, USA.

KIM, Michael (Injae); Professor of Piano and Concert Pianist; b. 13 Feb. 1968, Quebec, Canada. *Education:* BMus, University of Calgary; MM, DMA, Juilliard School New York. *Career:* Debut: Calgary Philharmonic Orchestra, Canada, 15 years old; Performances with major orchestras of Canada and US, including Boston, Milwaukee, Cincinnati, Oklahoma City, Toronto, Vancouver, National Arts Centre, Calgary, Edmonton, Regina, Saskatoon, Winnipeg, London, toured Scotland with the Royal Scottish National Orchestra; Appearances in Glasgow, Edinburgh, Dundee, Aberdeen (1994); BBC Scottish Symphony, Glasgow (1992); Recitals throughout Canada and US, including appearances in virtually every series in Canada; Recital tour, Scotland, 1994; Recitals broadcast regularly by CBC, BBC, National Public Radio; As Chamber Musician, appeared throughout Canada and US with sister violinist Helen Hwaya Kim (The Kim Duo), including appearances at Carnegie Hall, New York, 1992. *Recordings:* Chamber Works of Saint-Saëns; Ballades of Chopin and Grieg; Works of Stravinsky, Rachmaninov, Mussorgsky. *Honours:* Laureate of 1992 Scottish (Glasgow), 1993 Leeds, 1993 Ivo Pogorelich (Pasadena, California) International Piano Competitions; Grand Prize-winner, 1988 Canadian Music Competitions (Montreal, Quebec) and 1989 Canadian Broadcasting Corporation Competition for Young Performers, Toronto. *Address:* c/o Conservatory of Music, Lawrence University, 420 East College Avenue, Appleton, WI 54911, USA.

KIM, Re Yang; Singer (mezzo-soprano); b. 1953, Republic of Korea. *Education:* Studied in Seoul, Vienna and Augsburg. *Career:* Sang at the Berne Opera, 1977–78, Karlsruhe Staatstheater from 1978; Deutsche Oper am Rhein, Düsseldorf, 1982–87; Sang the Nurse in Die Frau ohne Schatten at Bonn, 1992, and Ulrica in Un Ballo in Maschera at Cologne, 1993; Other roles include Azucena in Il Trovatore, Eboli in Don Carlos, Carmen, Brangaene in Tristan und Isolde, Ortrud in Lohengrin and Herodias in Salome. *Address:* c/o Oper der Stadt Bonn, Am Boeselagerhof 1, Pf. 2440, 53111 Bonn, Germany.

KIM, Sun-Joo, BMus; Conductor and Educator; b. 5 Oct. 1929, Sun Cheh Pyung an Buk-Do, Korea; m. Hye Sook Lee, 5 May 1955, 1 c. *Education:* Kyung Hee Univ. *Career:* Principal Associate Conductor, Korean Broadcasting Symphony, Seoul, 1963–; Instructor, Yung-Hee University, Seoul, 1965; Principal Associate Conductor, Seoul Philharmonic, 1965–69; Principal Conductor, National Symphony Korea, 1969–70; Professor, Kyung Hee University; Conductor, Korean Symphony Orchestra, Seoul; mem, Board of Executives, 1975–82, Korean Musicians Union. *Address:* Kyung-Hee University, School of Music, Whoe Ki Dong, Seoul, Republic of Korea.

KIM, Young-Mi, BA, MA; opera and concert singer (soprano); b. 6 Nov. 1954, Seoul, Republic of Korea; m. Sung-Ha Kim 1984. *Education:* Seoul Art School, Conservatory of Santa Cecilia, Rome, Academy of Santa Cecilia, Rome. *Career:* debut at Alice Tully Hall, New York Lincoln Center, 1980; Appearances with New York City Opera, Los Angeles Music Center Opera, Houston Grand Opera, Opera Company of Philadelphia, Opéra de Paris, Bastille Orchestra, National Symphony, Seattle Symphony, San Diego Symphony, Minnesota Orchestra, Colorado Symphony. *Recordings:* Sung-Eum Gramophone. *Honours:* Verona

International Contest, 1977; Giacomo Contest, 1979; Maria Callas International Voice Competition, 1980; Luciano Pavarotti International Voice Competition, 1981. *Current Management:* Athole Still International Management, Forresters Hall, 25–27 Westow Street, London, SE19 3RY, England. *Telephone:* (20) 8771-5271. *Fax:* (20) 8768-6600. *Website:* www.atholestill.com.

KIM, Young-Uck; Concert Violinist; b. 1 Sept. 1947, Seoul, Republic of Korea. *Education:* Studied with Ivan Galamian at the Curtis Institute, Philadelphia from 1958. *Career:* Debut: Philadelphia Orchestra conducted by Ormandy, 1963; Tours of South America and Europe: appearances with the Berlin Philharmonic, Concertgebouw Orchestra, Vienna Philharmonic and London Symphony; Season 1987–88 in USA with the St Paul Chamber Orchestra, St Louis Symphony, Cleveland Orchestra, Pittsburgh Symphony and the New York Philharmonic; Concerts in Sweden, Italy and the United Kingdom; Season 1988–89, with the Hallé Orchestra and BBC National Orchestra of Wales; Tours to Eire, Sweden, Norway and Germany; USA recitals with Peter Serkin playing Beethoven sonatas; Piano Trio recitals with Emanuel Ax and Yo-Yo Ma: 1989 concerts in Switzerland, Germany and Italy; Concerto repertoire includes works by Bach, Berg, Mozart, Prokofiev, Sibelius, Stravinsky and Vivaldi; Concerts and Recitals American and Europe: New York Philharmonic, Los Angeles Philharmonic, London Symphony Orchestra, Hong Kong Philharmonic, Rotterdam Philharmonic; Tours, America and Far East; Season 1992 with World and European Premieres of newly commissioned concerto by Gunther Schuller (New York and Rotterdam). *Recordings include:* 5 Mozart Concertos with the London Philharmonic under Christoph Eschenbach; Ax/Kim/Ma Trio recording of Dvořák Trios (Sony Classical-Record of the Year Award, 1988); Mozart Piano Quartets with Previn, Heichiro and Gary Hoffman. *Current Management:* Gottschalk, Impresario A/S, Tollbugaten 3, 0152 Oslo, Norway.

KIMBELL, David Rodney Bertram, MA, DPhil, LRAM; Academic; b. 26 June 1939, Gillingham, Kent; m.; one s. two d. *Education:* Worcester Coll., Oxford. *Career:* Lecturer, Edinburgh Univ. 1965–78; Prof. of Music, St Andrews Univ. 1979–1987, Edinburgh Univ. 1987–2001. *Publications:* Verdi in the Age of Italian Romanticism 1981, Italian Opera 1991, Vincenzo Bellini: Norma 1998; contrib. to Hallische Händel-Ausgabe, New Oxford History of Music, Cambridge History of Italian Literature, Viking Opera Guide. *Address:* 3 Bellevue Crescent, Edinburgh, EH3 6ND, Scotland (home). *E-mail:* d.kimbell@virgin.net (home).

KIMBROUGH, Steven; Singer (Baritone); b. 17 Dec. 1936, Athens, Alabama, USA. *Education:* Studied at Birmingham Southern College, Duke University, Princeton Theological seminary; Further study in Italy. *Career:* Debut: Mantua, 1968, as Marcel in La Bohème; Appearances in Mannheim, Frankfurt, London, San Francisco, New York and Philadelphia; Member of the Bonn Opera, 1971–; Sang in the premiere of Christophorus by Schreker, Freiburg, 1978; Essen 1989 as Mirabeau by Siegfried Matthus; Concert tours of the USA, Germany, Italy and Austria; Guest appearances at the opera houses of Vancouver, Cincinnati, Rio de Janeiro, Barcelona; Repertoire includes roles in operettas and musicals; German premiere Op 2 Zemlinsky, 1994; mem, American Guild of Musical Artists; Actors Equity. *Recordings include:* Lieder by Korngold, Zemlinsky, Weill, Kienzl, Schreker, Schoenberg for EMI and Koch. *Address:* 128 Bridge Avenue, Bay Head, NJ 08742, USA.

KIMM, Fiona; Singer (mezzo-soprano); b. 24 May 1952, Ipswich, Suffolk, England. *Education:* Studied at the Royal College of Music, London. *Career:* Has sung at the Glyndebourne Festival in Die Zauberflöte, The Love for Three Oranges, Titus and L'Enfant et les Sortilèges; Appearances with Opera North as Hansel, Mercédès, Rosalind in The Mines of Sulphur, Hermia (A Midsummer Night's Dream) and Baba the Turk; Sang in the premiere of Edward Cowie's Kate Kelly's Road Show, Chester, 1983; With English National Opera has sung Orlofsky, Lola and Fyodor (Boris Godunov), and in Orpheus in the Underworld and Rusalka; Covent Garden debut in Boris Godunov; Berlioz Festival at Lyon in Dido and Aeneas; Sang in the premiere of Greek by Mark Anthony Turnage (Munich 1988) and again at the Edinburgh Festival; Scottish Opera in Lulu, Die Zauberflöte, Eugene Onegin and Das Rheingold; Bath Festival in El Rey de Harlem by Henze, with Ensemble Modern; Sang Smeraldina in The Love for Three Oranges, ENO 1989, Siebel in Faust, 1990; Opera North/RSC at Stratford as Julie in Showboat; Glyndebourne Festival 1990, as Third Lady in Die Zauberflöte; Michael Berkeley, Baa Baa Black Sheep, world premiere, 1993; Concert performances with the London Symphony, English Chamber Orchestra, City of Birmingham Symphony and London Sinfonietta; Conductors include Abbado, Haitink, Elder, Hickox, Andrew Davis, and Roger Norrington; Sang in Param Vir's Snatched by the Gods, for Almeida Opera, 1996; Mistress Quickly for Garsington Opera and Rosa Mamai in Cilea's L'Arlesiana for Opera Holland Park, 1998; Mrs Sedley in Peter Grimes for Frankfurt Opera; Markolfa in Simon Holt's The Nightingale's to Blame and in L'Enfant et les Sortilèges for Opera North and Larina in Onegin for Glyndedbourne Touring Opera; Television appearances in The Gondoliers, L'Enfance du Christ and Man and Music series on Channel 4. *Current Management:* Connaught Artists Management Ltd, 2 Molasses Row, Plantation Wharf, London, SW11 3UX, England. *Telephone:* (20) 7738 0017. *Fax:* (20) 7738 0909. *E-mail:* classicalmusic@connaughtartists.com. *Website:* www.connaughtartists .com.

KINCSES, Veronica; Singer (Soprano); b. 1954, Hungary. *Education:* Studied at the Budapest Academy and the Accademia di Santa Cecilia Rome. *Career:* Member of the Hungarian State Opera from 1973: roles include Susanna, Fiordiligi, Sulamith in Die Königin von Saba by Goldmark, Euridice, Mimi and Madama Butterfly; Teatro Liceo Barcelona and Montreal, 1986, as Donna Elvira and as Suor Angelica; 3 Concerts in Chicago, 1981; Budapest 1986, as Eva in Die Meistersinger; Frequent concert appearances; Has appeared in several Hungarian television programmes; Guest performer in Austria, Belgium, Czechoslovakia, Germany, France, Netherlands, Italy and Russia; Teatro Col ón, Buenos Aires, Caracas, 1987; Deutsche Oper West-Berlin, 1985, 1986; Sang Madama Butterfly at Chicago, 1989; Professor of singing at Science Universty of Pecs, Hungary. *Recordings:* Die Königin von Saba, Haydn's Der Apotheker and La Fedeltà Premiata; Songs by Bellini; Liszt's Hungarian Coronation Mass; Madama Butterfly; Orfeo ed Euridice; La Bohème. *Honours:* Winner, Dvořák International Singing Concours, Prague, 1971; Prix de l'Academie du Disque, Paris, 4 times; Kossuth Prize, Hungarian People's Republic. *Address:* Hungarian State Opera House, Andrassy UT 22, 1061 Budapest, Hungary.

KING, Andrew (Graham), BA, PGCE, ARCM; Singer (tenor) and Musical Director; b. 8 May 1953, Bury St Edmunds, England. *Education:* St John's Coll., Durham, Dunelm, King's Coll., Cambridge, vocal studies with Graham Watts, Ivor Davies, David Johnston, Eric Vietheer, Iris dell' Acqua. *Career:* Durham Cathedral Choir 1972–75; King's College Choir 1975–76; debut, Wigmore Hall, 1977; Proms, Baroque Cantatas, BBC Singers, 1978; Lay Clerk, Guildford Cathedral, 1976–77; BBC Singers, 1977–80; Sang with many emerging early music groups, including Tallis Scholars, Clerkes of Oxenford, The Sixteen, Medieval Ensemble of London, Landini Consort, Gothic Voices, Taverner Consort, King's Consort, New London Consort: Member of Consort of Musicke since 1978; Also performs with Ex Cathedra and Pro Cantione Antiqua; Performed contemporary works with the song group English Echoes and Singcircle; Noted as an Interpreter of Renaissance and Baroque Music and is in particular demand as Evangelist in the Bach Passions; Performances throughout Europe, also USA, Canada, Middle East, Japan and Australia; Festival appearances include Bruges, Edinburgh, Prague, Salzburg, Utrecht, York and many appearances at the Proms; Performances of early operas and masques in Austria, Belgium, UK, Germany, Netherlands, Italy, Norway, Spain and Sweden; Elected as a professional tenor of the Noblemen and Gentlemen's Catch Club, 2001; Has given a number of world premieres, most notably Leaving by Mark-Anthony Turnage with CBSO; Teacher, Birmingham Conservatoire; Masterclasses: England, Israel, Italy, Poland and Sweden; Musical Director, The Renaissance Ensemble, formed in 1997. *Recordings:* Over 80 including Monteverdi Vespers (New London Consort also Taverner Consort), Apollo and other roles in Monteverdi's Orfeo (NLC/Decca), many Monteverdi Madrigal recordings (Consort of Musicke/Decca/ Harmonia Mundi/Musica Oscura/Virgin Classics), Handel's Esther (Academy of Ancient Music/Decca), Purcell's Ode on St Cecilia's Day (Taverner Consort/EMI), Purcell Late Songs (Mantle of Orpheus-Consort of Musicke/Musica Oscura); Bach's Christmas Oratorio (New London Consort/Decca); live recording of Mendelssohn's version of Bach's St Matthew Passion, with Choir and Orchestra of Swiss Italian Radio TV; Many other recordings of Medieval and Renaissance Music; Frequent radio broadcasts BBC Radio 3 and WDR; Video of Monteverdi Madrigals Banquet of the Senses with Consort of Musicke; Several television appearances including Proms and a series of Music in Venice with King's Consort (Channel 4). *Honours:* Choral Scholarship, Durham Cathedral, 1972–75. *Current Management:* Concert Directory International, Lyndhurst, Ben Rhydding, Ilkley, Yorkshire, LS29 8QR, England. *Address:* 49 Dalmeny Avenue, London SW16 4RS, England.

KING, James; Singer (Tenor); b. 22 May 1925, Dodge City, Kansas, USA. *Education:* Studied at Louisina University, University of Kansas City and with Martial Singher in New York. *Career:* Debut: San Francisco 1961, as Don José; Moved to Europe 1961 and sang Cavaradossi in Florence; Deutsche Oper Berlin from 1962; Salzburg Festival 1962–64, as Achilles in Iphigénie en Aulide and Aegisthus in Elektra; Vienna Staatsoper from 1963, debut as Bacchus in Ariadne auf Naxos; Bayreuth Festival 1965, as Siegmund; Covent Garden 1967, as the Emperor in Die Frau ohne Schatten, returned 1985, as Bacchus; Metropolitan Opera from 1966, Florestan, the Emperor, Siegmund, Walther and Don José; La Scala 1983, in Cherubini's Anacréon; Sang Jove in Il Ritorno d'Ulisse (arranged Henze) at Salzburg 1985 (also

televised); Returned to Salzburg 1989, as Aegisthus in Elektra; Sang the Drum Major in Wozzeck at the Metropolitan 1990; Lohengrin at Nice; Holland Festival 1990, as the Emperor in Die Frau ohne Schatten; Sang Aegisthus at the Met, 1992; Other roles include Parsifal, Otello (San Francisco 1974); Pfitzner's Palestrina, Manrico and Calaf. *Recordings:* Die Frau ohne Schatten, Daphne, Die Meistersinger, Lohengrin, Parsifal; Salomé, Fidelio; Die Walküre; Mathis der Maler by Hindemith and Ariadne auf Naxos; Samson et Dalila; Video of Elektra conducted by Abbado. *Address:* c/o Metropolitan Opera, Lincoln Center, NY 10023, USA.

KING, Mary; Singer (Mezzo-soprano); b. 16 June 1952, Tonbridge Wells, England. *Education:* BA, English, Birmingham University; PGCE, St Anne's College, Oxford; Postgraduate Diploma, Guildhall School of Music. *Career:* Sang in opera at Glyndebourne, 1980, US debut, 1985, Covent Garden, 1990; Regular appearances with major British orchestras; Spanish tour with BBC Symphony Orchestra, 1991; Proms, 1991; New music a speciality with many first performances including: The Undivine Comedy by Finnissy in Paris and London, Valis, by Machover in Paris, Boston, and Tokyo; Teacher, Guildhall School of Music, London, 1990–; Artistic Director of Live Culture, a youth group of English National Opera, Baylis Programme; Formed Green Light Music Theatre, 1990; Has sung Marcellina and Baba the Turk at Glyndebourne, The Cockerel in The Cunning Little Vixen at Covent Garden; Sang Florence Pike in Albert Herring at Garsington, 1996 and Meg Page in Falstaff, 1998; Knussen's Where the Wild Things Are and Higglety, Pigglety, Pop! at the London Proms, 2002; mem, Equity; Association of Teachers of Singing. *Recordings:* Where the Wild Things Are, by Knussen; The Cunning Little Vixen; Britten's Praise We Great Men; Machover's Valis; Birtwistle's Meridian; Stilgoe's Brilliant the Dinosaur. *Current Management:* Mary Craig. *Address:* 34a Garthone Road, Honor Oak, London SE23 1EW, England.

KING, Robert (John Stephen); Conductor, Harpsichordist and Editor; b. 27 June 1960, Wombourne, England. *Education:* MA, St John's College, Cambridge. *Career:* Director, The King's Consort, 1980–; Guest Conductor: Netherlands Chamber Orchestra, Orquesta Sinfonica Euskadi, Atlanta Symphony Orchestra, Minnesota Symphony, National Symphony Orchestra of Washington, Houston Symphony Orchestra, English Chamber Orchestra, Madrid Symphony Orchestra, Granada Symphony Orchestra, Seville Symphony Orchestra, Royal Orchestra of Galicia, Norrköping Symphony Orchestra; Israel Camerata, Euskadi Symphony Orchestra, Swiss Radio Choir, Netherlands Chamber Choir, Danish Radio Choir, Filharmonisch Orkest van Vlaanderen; Conducted The Coronation of King George II at the London Proms, 2002; Editor; Artistic Director, Nordic Baroque Festival, 2002–; Artistic Director, ION Festival Nürnberg, 2003–. *Recordings:* 80 CDs with The King's Consort. *Publications:* Henry Purcell, 1994. *Address:* 34 St Mary's Grove, London W4 3 LN, England.

KING, Terry B.; Cellist, Conductor and Teacher; b. 20 Aug. 1947, Santa Monica, California, USA; m. Leslie Morgan 1976. *Education:* BM, Mt St Mary's College, Los Angeles, 1970; Postgraduate, Claremont Graduate School, 1974; University of Northern Iowa, 1989–91; Assistant Professor, University of Northern Iowa, 1990–. *Career:* Debut: Carnegie Recital Hall, New York, 1975; Assistant to Piatigorsky, University of Southern California, 1971–72; Instructor, San Francisco Conservatory, 1972; Lecturer, California University, Fullerton, 1972–75; Artist-in-Residence, Grinnell College, 1975–; Vienna Chamber Orchestra, 1978; St Paul Sunday Morning, 1984–87; Voice of America, America in Concert, Music from the Frick Museum, New York, Austrian Radio, NPR, PBS, several documentaries; Piatigorsky, McPhee, Harrison. *Compositions:* Arrangements, Trio music by Anderson, Enesco, de Falla, Fauré, Glinka; Voice and Instruments, Mozart, Bachelet, Godard; Cello Ensembles, Sibelius, Prokofiev, Shostakovich. *Recordings:* 17 recordings, Cello Music by Cowell, Barber, Cooper, Harris; Concertos by Harrison, Reale, Beethoven, Haydn; Trios with Mirecourt Trio, Beethoven to present day composers.

KING, Thea; Clarinettist and Professor of Clarinet; b. 26 Dec. 1925, Hitchin, Hertfordshire, England; m. Frederick Thurston (deceased). *Education:* ARCM, 1944, 1947, Royal College of Music, London. *Career:* Frequent appearances as soloist, broadcaster, recitalist and principal clarinet with English Chamber Orchestra; Member of Melos Ensemble of London and Robles Ensemble; Purcell Room recital 1997 (Finzi, Brahms and Stravinsky). *Recordings include:* Mozart, Brahms, Spohr, Finzi, Bruch, Mendelssohn, Stanford and Crusell; 20th Century Music. *Publications:* Editor and Arranger of Clarinet Solos; Chester Woodwind Series; Arrangements of J. S. Bach Duets for 2 Clarinets, Schumann for The Clarinet, 1991, and Mendelssohn for The Clarinet, 1993; The Romantic Clarinet, Mendelssohn, 1994 and Tchaikovsky, 1995. *Honours:* FRCM, 1975; O.B.E., 1985; FGSM, 1992. *Address:* 16 Milverton Road, London NW6 7AS, England.

KINGDOM, Elizabeth; Singer (Soprano); b. 1932, USA. *Career:* Sang in opera at Bielefeld, 1958–63, notably in the 1962 German premiere of Scarlatti's Griselda, Nuremberg, 1962–68, (Hostess in the 1980 premiere of Zemlinsky's Der Traumgörge); Guest appearances at Cologne 1964, Oslo 1970, Graz 1982, and London 1988; Other roles have included Mozart's Donna Anna and Fiordiligi, Verdi's Elisabetta, Forza Leonora and Aida, Elisabeth in Tannhäuser, Giulietta and Myrtocle in Die Toten Augen by d'Albert. *Recordings include:* Don Giovanni. *Address:* St ädtische Buhnen, Richard-Wagnerplatz 2–10, 8500 Nuremberg, Germany.

KINGSLEY, Colin; Lecturer and Pianist; b. 15 April 1925, London, England; m. 16 April 1955, 2 s., 2 d. *Education:* King's Scholar, Westminster School, 1938–43; BMus, Gonville and Caius College, Cambridge, 1946; D.Mus, Edinburgh, 1968; RCM, 1943–44, 1946–47; Leverhulme Scholar, ARCM, 1945. *Career:* Debut: 1947; Freelance Keyboard Playing, Broadcasting, 1948–; Solo Pianist, Royal Ballet, 1957–59; Several performances of contemporary music in the USA, Japan, Poland, France and the United Kingdom; Member of Macnaghten Committee, 1957–63; Associated Board Examiner, 1959–93; Pianist, University College of Wales, Aberystwyth, 1963–64; Principal Radio: Concertos, 1955–; University of Edinburgh Lecturer, 1964; Senior Lecturer, 1968, retired 1992; Series, Piano Music of P R Fricker, 1974 followed by premiere of his Anniversary for Piano, Cheltenham International Festival, 1978; Series, The English Musical Renaissance, Piano Music, 1977; mem, Incorporated Society of Musicians. *Recordings:* Lyrita, Sonatas for Piano by John White; Various BBC Recordings for broadcasting purposes. *Address:* 236 Milton Road East, Edinburgh EH15 2PF, Scotland.

KINGSLEY, Margaret, ARCM, FRCM, LRAM; Singer (soprano, mezzo-soprano); b. 20 Feb. 1939, Poole, Cornwall, England; m. W. A. Newcombe. *Education:* Royal Coll. of Music. *Career:* debut, With Opera for All; Glyndebourne debut 1966, in Die Zauberflöte; appearances with Covent Garden Opera, ENO, Scottish Opera, Opera North, State Operas of Hamburg, Munich, Stuttgart and Vienna, Stockholm Royal Opera, Paris Opéra, Naples, Miami, Washington; roles include Wagner's Gutrune, Beethoven's Leonore, Waltraute, Eboli, Elvira, Verdi's Amelia and Lady Macbeth, Mozart's Fiordiligi, Donna Anna and Electra, Cassandre in Les Troyens, Reiza in Oberon, Gluck's Euridice, Brünnhilde, title role in Ariadne auf Naxos, Azucena; ENO 1983–84, as Amneris, Marina (Boris Godunov), Akhrosimova (War and Peace) and Mrs Grose (The Turn of the Screw); concert appearances with leading British orchestras and on television; Prof. of Singing, Royal Coll. of Music; teacher at Centre de Formation Lyrique at the Opéra Bastille; giving masterclasses and teaching in Europe. *Address:* Montagu House, 8 White Court, Kings Ride, Alfriston, East Sussex BN26 5XP, England.

KIRBY, James (Nicholas Joseph); Pianist; b. 15 April 1965, Hull, England. *Education:* Royal Academy of Music; Moscow Tchaikovsky Conservatoire. *Career:* Debut: Wigmore Hall, London, 1991; As Recitalist, Chamber Musician and Concerto Soloist, performances throughout the United Kingdom including Wigmore Hall, South Bank Centre, Royal Albert Hall, London, and Europe; Performed with English Chamber Orchestra, Scottish Chamber Orchestra and Moscow Symphony Orchestra; Member, Barbican Piano Trio, performing on four continents. *Recordings:* Lalo: Complete piano trios, and Trios by Rachmaninov, Tchaikovsky and Schnittke with Barbican Piano Trio; Appassionato, pieces for violin and piano with Lydia Mordkovitch. *Honours:* Semi-finals, International Tchaikovsky Competition, 1990; 1st Prize, Città di Marsala International Competition, Sicily, 1992; Associate, Royal Academy of Music, 1997; Hon. Prof. of the Rachmaninov Institute, Tambov, Russia. *Address:* 3 Campbell Road, Bow, London E3 4 DS, England.

KIRCHHOF, Lutz; Lutenist; b. 15 May 1953, Frankfurt-on-Main, Germany. *Education:* Studied with Lother Fuchs; Musicology at Frankfurt University, with research on John Dowland and Sylvius Leopold Weiss. *Career:* Appearances throughout Germany and Europe from 1964; Studio der Frühen Musik, Frankfurt, 1973–80; Founded own Ensemble, 1976, for performances of early music; Repertoire from Renaissance to Contemporary music; Recitals with Max von Egmond (bass) and Derek Lee Ragin (Countertenor); Festival of Lute Music, Frankfurt, from 1988, as Founder and Director: later International Festival of Lute Music; Founded Research Society 1990, to assemble lute manuscript music from 16th–17th centuries. *Honours:* Winner, Jugend Musiziert Competition, 1972. *Address:* c/o Hochschule für Musik (Frankfurt am Main) Eschersheiner, Landstrasse 29–39, 60322 Frankfurt, Germany.

KIRCHNER, Leon; Composer, Pianist and Conductor; b. 24 Jan. 1919, Brooklyn, New York, USA. *Education:* Studies with Schoenberg at University of California, Berkeley (BA 1940) and in New York with Sessions; Further study at Berkeley (MA). *Career:* Lecturer at Berkeley from 1949; Lecturer, then Professor at the University of Southern California, 1950–54; Luther Brusie Marchant Professor at Mills College in Oakland, 1954–61; Appointed to Harvard Faculty, 1961, Walter Bigelow Rosen Professor of Music from 1966; Director of the Harvard Chamber Players, 1973; Director of the Harvard Chamber Orchestra and Friends, 1975; Pianist and Conductor of his own music and the Viennese Classics; Composer-in-Residence and Performer at the Santa Fe Chamber Music Festival, 1983; Tanglewood Music Center, 1985; Soloist and Conductor, Boston Symphony, New York Philharmonic, Philadelphia Orchestra, S F Symphony, St Paul Chamber Orchestra, Sudwest Funk Baden Baden, Tonhalle Zürich, London Sinfonietta, Buffalo Philharmonic; mem, National Institute of Arts and Letters; American Academy of Arts and Sciences. *Compositions:* Opera, Lily 1973–76; Orchestral, Sinfonia 1951; 2 Piano Concertos 1953, 1963; Toccata for strings, wind and percussion; Concerto for violin, cello, 10 wind instruments and percussion 1960; Music for Orchestra, 1969; Music for Flute and Orchestra; Music for Cello and Orchestra, 1992; Vocal, Words from Wordsworth for chorus, 1968; The Twilight Stood, song cycle after Emily Dickinson, 1983; Of Things Exactly As They Are, for soprano, baritone, chorus and orchestra, 1997; Instrumental, Duo for violin and piano, 1947; Piano Sonata, 1948; Little Suite for piano, 1949; 3 String Quartets, 1949, 1958, 1966; Sonata Concertante for violin and piano, 1952; Trio for violin, cello and piano, 1954; A Moment for Roger for piano; Five Pieces for piano, 1987; Interlude for piano, 1989; For Solo Violin II, 1987; For Solo Violin II, 1988; Triptych, Violin, Cello, 1988; Piano Trio, 1993; Five Pieces for piano; Music for Twelve, 1985. *Honours:* George Ladd Paris Prize, University of California; Two Awards from New York Music Critics' Circle (First two string quartets); Naumburg Award for 1st Piano Concerto; Pulitzer Prize for 3rd String Quartet; Commissions from the Ford Foundation and the New York Philharmonic. *Address:* c/o ASCAP, ASCAP Building, 1 Lincoln Plaza, NY 10023, USA.

KIRCHNER, Volker David; Composer; b. 25 June 1942, Mainz, Germany. *Education:* studied with Gunther Kehr and Gunter Raphael, Peter Cornelius Conservatory, Mainz, 1956–59; Cologne Musikhochschule, 1959–63, with B. A. Zimmermann; Detmold 1964–65, with Tibor Varga. *Career:* violinist with the Kehr String Trio 1964–67, Frankfurt Radio Symphony Orchestra 1966–88; freelance composer 1989–. *Compositions include:* Music theatre: Riten für kleines klangtheater, 1971; Die Traung, 1975; Die funf Minuten des Isaak Babel, 1980; Belshazar, 1986; Das Kalte Herz 'Ein Deutsches Märchen', 1988; Erinys Threnos, 1990; Inferno d'amore 'Shakespearion I', 1995; Other works include Fragmante for orchestra, 1961–67; Chorale Variations for 15 solo strings, 1968, rev. 1990; Nachtmusik for ensemble, 1970; Nachtstück for viola and orchestra, 1980; Piano Trio, 1980; Bildnisse I–III for orchestra, 1981–1991; 2 Symphonies, 1980, 1992; String Quartet, 1982; Violin Concerto, 1982; Mysterion, for ensemble, 1985; Piano Sonata, 1986. Requiem, 1988; Saitenspiel for violin and viola, 1993; Missa Moguntina, 1993; Hortus Magicus for orchestra, 1994; Horn concerto, 1996; Ahasver, Scenic Oratorio, 2000. *Current Management:* Schott & Co Ltd, Promotion Department, 48 Great Marlborough Street, London, W1 F7BB, England.

KIRCHSCHLAGER, Angelika; Singer (Mezzo-soprano); b. 1965, Salzburg, Austria. *Education:* Studied at the Salzburg Mozarteum and with Walter Berry in Vienna. *Career:* Season 1991 in Martinů's Julietta at Salzburg and Mozart's Requiem at Moscow; Opera performances at Graz from 1992, notably as Octavian in Der Rosenkavalier and Rossini's Rosina; Vienna from 1993, as Zerlina in Don Giovanni and in Massenet's Chérubin; Ravenna Festival, 1996, as Dorabella; Guest engagements at Frankfurt and the Berlin Staatsoper; Lieder recitals in London, 1998, and elsewhere; Metropolitan Opera debut, 1997, as Annio in La Clemenza di Tito; Cherubino at San Francisco, 1997; Engaged season 2000–01 at the Opéra Bastille as Nicklausse and Octavian; Many lieder recitals. *Address:* c/o San Francisco Opera (contracts), War Memorial Opera House, Van Ness Avenue, San Francisco, CA 94102, USA.

KIRCHSTEIN, Leonore; Singer (Soprano); b. 29 March 1933, Stettin, Germany. *Education:* Studied at the Robert Schumann Conservatory, Düsseldorf, with Franziska Martiensen-Lohman. *Career:* Sang first with the St ädtische Opera Berlin, from 1958; Kiel 1960–63, Augsburg 1963–65, Cologne 1965–68; Has sung with the Bayerische Staatsoper Munich from 1968; Salzburg Festival 1961 and 1970, Edinburgh Festival 1965 and 1971; Montreux Festival, 1965; Guest appearances in Hamburg, Stuttgart, Zürich and Vienna; Concert tours of USA, Argentina, England, Italy and Turkey. *Recordings include:* Die Zauberflöte and Cardillac; Bach Cantatas; Beethoven's Missa solemnis.

KIRK, Vernon; Singer (Tenor); b. 1966, England. *Education:* Royal Academy of Music and Actors Centre, London; Britten-Pears School, Aldeburgh. *Career:* Concerts include tour of Germany and Netherlands in Monteverdi's Christmas Vespers with the Academy of Ancient Music; Bach St Matthew Passion with the London Baroque Soloists, St John Passion in Norway; Messiah and The Creation under David Willcocks; Berlioz L'Enfance du Christ and Brahms Lieder at the London Proms;

Schumann's Manfred at the Festival Hall, Die schöne Müllerin at St Martin in the Fields; Lutoslawski Paroles Tissées at the Barbican Hall; Opera roles include Mozart's Tamino, Ferrando and Don Ottavio, Donizetti's Ernesto and Nemorino; Lensky, and Gonslave in L'Heure Espagnole (season 1996–97). *Address:* C&M Craig Services Ltd, 3 Kersley Street, London SW11 4 PR, England.

KIRKBRIDE, Simon; British singer (baritone); b. 1970, Northamptonshire, England. *Education:* Peterborough Cathedral, Guildhall School and Royal College, London. *Career:* debut, Jankel in Arabella at Glyndebourne, 1996; Appearances as Publio in La Clemenza di Tito for Welsh National Opera, Masetto, and Morales in Carmen for Scottish Opera; Mozart's Figaro and Thaddeus in Birtwistle's The Last Supper (2001) at Glyndebourne; Concerts include the Requiems of Brahms, Mozart, Fauré and Duruflé, The Dream of Gerontius, Mozart's C Minor Mass, Bach's Passions and B Minor Mass, Belshazzar's Feast and Mendelssohn's Elijah; Soloist with the Britten Sinfonia, London and Calgary Philharmonics, London Handel Orchestra, Florilleguim, Montreal SO, London Baroque and London Mozart Players. *Address:* c/o Den Norske Opera, Storgaten 23, 0028 Oslo, Norway.

KIRKBY, Emma; Singer (Soprano); b. 26 Feb. 1949, Camberley, Surrey, England. *Education:* Studied Classics at Oxford; Vocal studies with Jessica Cash. *Career:* Debut: London Concert, 1974; Many concert appearances with the Consort of Musicke directed by Anthony Rooley, Andrew Parrott's Taverner Players and the Academy of Ancient Music with Christopher Hogwood, the Jaye Consort of Viols and other London groups; From 1980, tours and concerts with London Baroque; Tour of USA, 1978; Tours to Middle East with Anthony Rooley, 1980–83; Appearances with Andrew Parrott at the Promenade Concerts in Monteverdi's Vespers and the Bach B Minor Mass; Festival appearances include: Bruges, Utrecht, Luzern, Mosel, and Rheingau, Passau, Schleswig-Holstein, Saintes, Beaune, Ottawa, Elora, Tanglewood, Mostly Mozart (New York) and many others; Sang Dorinda in Handel's Orlando, 1989; Television appearances in Messiah and the Central television series Man and his Music; Repertoire ranges from early renaissance Haydn, Mozart and Lieder, and songs of Amy Beach; London Prom Concerts 1993, in Charpentier's Messe pour les Trépassés and Monteverdi Madrigals Book VI; Sang in Behind the Masque, a Purcell Celebration, at the London Barbican, 1996; Tours to USA,Canada, Japan, South America with above mentioned ensembles and Freiburger Barockorchester, Academy of Ancient Music and the Orchestra of the Age of Enlightenment. *Recordings:* Several hundred, including: Monteverdi's Orfeo and German arias by Handel: Handel and Italian cantatas, Mozart Motets; Dido and Aeneas; Venus and Adonis by Blow and Locke's Cupid and Death with the Consort of Musicke; Arne Cantatas (The Parley of Instruments); Bach Cantatas including 84, 199, 202, 210, 211 and 212 (Academy of Ancient Music); Handel Aci, Galatea e Polifemo (London Baroque) and Athalia; Monteverdi Sacred Vocal Music; Pergolesi Stabat Mater; Songs by Maurice Greene, Arie Antiche; Songs by Arne and Handel; Handel and Vivaldi opera arias; Christmas with Emma Kirkby and the Westminster Abbey Choir, 1999; Bach Sacred Vocal Music; Handel Motets with London Baroque and with Freiburger Barockorchester; Handel Gloria; "Classical Kirkby"; "Chanson d'Amour", Songs by Amy Beach. *Honours:* Artist of the Year, Classic FM, 1999; OBE, 2000; Hon. Doctorates at the uUniversities of Salford, Bath, Sheffield; Hon. Fellowships at Somerville College, Oxford, Guildhall School of Music, Royal Academy of Music, Royal College of Music. *Address:* c/o Consort of Musicke, 13 Pages Lane, London N10 1PU, England. *E-mail:* consort@musicke.net.

KIRKENDALE, Ursula; Music Historian; b. 6 Sept. 1932, Dortmund, Germany; m. Warren Kirkendale, 16 June 1959, 3 d. *Education:* Dr phil, Bonn, 1961. *Career:* Taught at University of Southern California, University of California, Duke University, Columbia University, USA, as Visiting Professor. *Publications:* Antonio Caldara: Sein Leben und seine venezianisch-römischen Oratorien, 1966. *Contributions:* Acta Musicologica; Journal American Musicological Society; Chigiana; Music and Letters; Studi musicali; Dizionario Biografico degli Italiani. *Honours:* fellow, Deutscher Akademischer Austauschdienst; American Council of Learned Societies; Alfred Einstein Award; Deems Taylor Award; Elected Wirkendes Mitglied der Gesellschaft zur Herausgabe von Denkmälen der Tonkunst in Österreich; Festschrift: Musicologia Humana (with bibliography), 1994. *Address:* Via dei Riari 86, 00165 Rome, Italy.

KIRKENDALE, Warren; Music Historian; b. 14 Aug. 1932, Toronto, Canada; m. Ursula Schöttler, 1959, 3 d. *Education:* BA, University of Toronto, 1955; PhD, University of Vienna, Austria, 1961. *Career:* Assistant Professor, University of Southern California, 1963–67; Associate Professor, Duke University, 1967–75; Professor, 1975–82; Professor Ordinarius, University Regensburg, Germany, 1983–92; Visiting Professor, Harvard University for Italian Renaissance Studies in Florence; mem. Italian and American Musicological Societies. *Publications:* Fuge und Fugato in der Kammermusik des Rokoko und

der Klassik, 1967, English, 1979; L'Aria di Fiorenza, 1972; Madrigali a diversi Linguaggi, 1975; The Court Musicians in Florence during the Principate of the Medici, 1993; Emilio dei Cavalieri, 2001. *Contributions:* Journal of American Musicological Society; Acta Musicologica; Musical Quarterly; Mozart-Jahrbuch; Quadrivium; Dizionario Biografico degli Italiani; Volkswagen-Stiftung; Rivista italiana di musicologica; Studi musicali. *Honours:* Fellow, Deutscher Akademischer Austauschdienst; NEH; American Council of Learned Societies; Volkswagen-Stiftung; Elected Wirkendes Mitglied der Gesellschaft zur Herausgabe von Denkmälern der Tonkunst in Österreich; Doctor honoris causa, University of Pavia, 1986; Accademico Filarmonico honoris causa, Bologna, 1987; Medal, Collège de France, 1994; Festschrift: Musicologia Humana (with bibliography), 1994. *Address:* Via dei Riari 86, 00165 Rome, Italy.

KIRSHBAUM, Ralph; Cellist; b. 4 March 1946, Denton, Texas, USA. *Education:* Studied with his father Joseph Kirshbaum, with Lev Aronson in Dallas and with Aldo Parisot at Yale University. *Career:* Debut: With the Dallas Symphony, 1959; From 1970 has performed with most leading orchestras including those in: London, Berlin, Amsterdam and Paris; USA engagements with many American orchestras including the Boston Symphony, Chicago Symphony and the Los Angeles Philharmonic; Tours of Germany, Hungary, Switzerland, Israel, Scandinavia, New Zealand, Australia and Japan; Debut with the Orchestre de Paris in 1990; Festival appearances include: Edinburgh, London's South Bank and the Mostly Mozart Festival in NY; Promenade Concerts in London include premiere of Tippett's Triple Concerto in 1980; Premiered the Cello Concerto by Peter Maxwell Davies with Cleveland Orchestra under Christoph von Dohnànyi in 1989; Has appeared with many renowned conductors including: Georg Solti, Yuri Temirkanov, Simon Rattle, André Previn and Colin Davis; Founder and Artistic Director of the RNCM Manchester International Cello Festival; Fellow and Tutor at The RNCM; Regular concerts with violinist György Pauk and pianist Peter Frankl; Frequent guest of the violinist and conductor Pinchas Zukerman, playing Brahms' Double Concerto in London, Edinburgh, Tokyo and Chicago; Played the Schumann Concerto at St John's, London, 1997; Elgar's Concerto with the BBC Philharmonic Orchestra at the 1999 London Proms. *Recordings include:* Barber Concerto; Elgar Concerto; Tippett Triple Concerto; Bach Suites; Haydn Concertos. *Honours:* Winner, International Tchaikovsky Competition in Moscow, 1970. *Current Management:* Ingpen & Williams Ltd, 7 St George's Court, 131 Putney Bridge Road, London, SW15 2PA, England.

KISER, Wieslaw (Maria); Conductor, Critic and Composer; b. 20 July 1937, Poznań, Poland. *Education:* High School of Music, Poznan. *Career:* Debut: As composer, Poznan, 1965; As Conductor, Poznan, 1963; Over 750 concerts in Poland, Bulgaria, Finland, France, Germany, USSR and Czechoslovakia; Artistic Manager, The Boys Choir of Gniezno, Poland, 1989; Music Lecturer and Promotor of Music Life, 1990–; The Thrushes; Television and Radio broadcasts in Poland, Finland, France, USSR and Germany; Several concerts in Belgium as Conductor of The Starlings (Men's Choir). *Compositions:* From the Years 1989–1990; Scherzo for the violin and string orchestra; Aria to J. S. Bach's chorale for the violin and string orchestra; Trio for the viola, violoncello and contrabass; Impromptu for the viola, violoncello and contrabass; Six Children compositions for the piano Sonata for the piano; Over 70 choral compositions; Sonatina for string quartet, 1995; 12 Preludes for piano, 1996–98; 30 one choirs song, 1995–98. *Recordings:* Radio and television Poland, Finland, USSR, Germany and France. *Publications:* Organisation and Education of Children's Choirs, 1971; Aerials of Poznan, 1975; The Selected Problems of Music History, 1969; Watchword, The Music, in Encykloeadia Wielkopolska, The Great Poland Encyclopaedie; Watchword, The Music, in Dzieje Poznania, The Aets of Poznan, 1989–90; Mr Jerzy Kurczewski: The Man and the Artist, 1994; The Poznan Inhabitants on the records, 1994. *Current Management:* The Artistic Manager of the Men's Choir, The Starlings, Gniezno, Poland. *Address:* u Szelagowska 12, 61-626 Poznań, Poland.

KISSIN, Evgeny Igorevich; Russian pianist; b. 10 Oct. 1971, Moscow. *Education:* Moscow Gnessin Music School, studied piano with Anna Kantor. *Career:* debut playing Mozart's D-minor concerto aged 10; appeared with Moscow Philharmonic, playing Chopin concertos 1984; tour of Japan with the Moscow Virtuosi; debut in Western Europe with the Berlin Radio orchestra 1987; British debut at the Lichfield Festival with the BBC Philharmonic 1987; London Symphony Orchestra concert 1988; concerts with the Royal Philharmonic and Yuri Temirkanov 1990; promenade concert debut with the BBC Symphony, playing Tchaikovsky's First Concerto 1990; US debut with the New York Philharmonic 1990, subsequent US tour included Tanglewood, Carnegie Hall 1991; Grammy Award ceremony and performances with the Chicago Symphony and Philadelphia Orchestra 1991–92; performed with the Boston Symphony, London recital debut and concert with the Philharmonia, and Prokofiev Concertos with the Berlin Philharmonic 1992–93; played

Chopin and Schumann at the Royal Festival Hall, London 1997; first pianist to perform a recital at the London Proms 1997; Chopin's First Concerto at the London Proms with the Bavarian State Orchestra 1999; first concerto soloist to play in the Proms Opening concert 2000; 10th anniversary tour of recitals in the USA, including Carnegie Hall 2000–01; appearances with the Warsaw Philharmonic, Philharmonia Orchestra, Bavarian Staatskapelle, Chicago Symphony, Boston Symphony, Metropolitan Opera, Bayerische Rundfunk, and the Leipzig Gewandhaus 1999–2001; Brahms' Concerto No. 2 in B flat major at the London Proms 2002. *Recordings include:* Rachmaninov 2nd Concerto and Etudes Tableaux with the London Symphony conducted by Gergiev, Rachmaninov Concerto No. 3, Chopin Vols I and II live recital from Carnegie Hall, Prokofiev Piano Concertos 1 and 3 with Berlin Philharmonic conducted by Claudio Abbado, Haydn and Schubert Sonatas 1995, Beethoven: Moonlight Sonata, Franck: Prelude, Choral et Fugue, Brahms: Paganini Variations 1998, Chopin: 4 Ballades, Berceuse op 57, Barcarolle op 60, Scherzo No. 4 op 54 1999, Chopin recital including 24 Preludes Op. 28, Sonata No, 2 and Polonaise in A-flat, Brahms 2003. *Honours:* Hon. DMus (Manhattan School of Music) 2001; Diapafon d'Or (France), Grand Prix Nobel Academie de Disque (France), Edison Klassiek Award (Netherlands) 1990, Chigiana Acad. Musician of the Year (Sienna) 1991, Musical America's Instrumentalist of the Year 1995, Triumph Award for outstanding contribution to Russia's culture 1997, Echo Award (Germany) 2002, Shostakovich Award (Moscow) 2003. *Current Management:* Askonas Holt Ltd, Lonsdale Chambers, 27 Chancery Lane, London, WC2A 1PF, England. *Telephone:* (20) 7400-1700. *Fax:* (20) 7400-1799. *E-mail:* info@askonasholt.co.uk. *Website:* www.askonasholt.co.uk.

KIT, Mikhail; Singer (bass); b. 1950, Russia. *Education:* Studied at the Odessa Conservatoire. *Career:* Sang first with the Perm Opera, then joined the Kirov Opera, 1966, singing Pimen, Boris, Prince Igor, Dosifei, Ivan Susanin, Gremin, Basilio, Leporello, Mephistopheles, Iago and Sarastro; Visited Edinburgh and the Metropolitan with the Kirov, 1991–92, Japan, 1993; Sang Dosifei in Khovanshchina with the Kirov Opera at Tel-Aviv, 1996; Engaged as Gremin at the Opéra Bastille, Paris, 1997; Season 1998 in Mazeppa with the Kirov Opera at the Metropolitan, as Mussorgsky's Dosifey at La Scala. *Recordings include:* The Fiery Angel and the title role in Prince Igor; Shostakovich songs with Larissa Gergieva for the BBC. *Current Management:* Askonas Holt Ltd, Lonsdale Chambers, 27 Chancery Lane, London, WC2A 1PF, England. *Telephone:* (20) 7400-1700. *Fax:* (20) 7400-1799. *E-mail:* info@askonasholt.co.uk. *Website:* www.askonasholt.co.uk.

KITCHEN, Linda; Singer (Soprano); b. 1960, Morecambe, Lancashire, England. *Education:* Studied at Royal Northern College of Music with Nicholas Powell; National Opera Studio, 1983; Later study with David Keren. *Career:* Sang Blonde in Mozart's Die Entführung 1983 and Monteverdi's Amor at the 1984 Glyndebourne Festival; Later sang Flora in The Knot Garden at Covent Garden and Barbarina in The Marriage of Figaro at the London Coliseum; Other roles include Mozart's Susanna, Papagena and Zerlina; Concert repertory includes Rossini's Stabat Mater, Mozart's Requiem, Poulenc's Gloria and Schoenberg's Pierrot Lunaire; In 1988 sang Iris in Handel's Semele, at Covent Garden; Later Studied with David Ceren and Audrey Langford; Sang Oscar in Ballo in Maschera, Flora in The Knot Garden, Sophie in Werther, Jemmy in Guillaume Tell; In Dublin, Pamina, Magic Flute; Opera North, Cherubino, Zerlina, Serpetta in Finta Gardiniera and Magnolia in Showboat; Other Roles include Adele; Sang Eurydice in a new production of Orpheus in the Underworld for Opera North, 1992, followed by Susanna in The Marriage of Figaro; Season 1997–98 with Despina and Martinů's Julietta for Opera North and Drusilla in Poppea for Welsh National Opera; Season 1998 as Xenia in Boris Gounov at Brighton and Celia in Mozart's Lucio Silla for Garsington Opera. *Recordings:* A Serenade to Music. *Honours:* Heinz Bursary. *Current Management:* Askonas Holt Ltd, Lonsdale Chambers, 27 Chancery Lane, London, WC2A 1PF, England. *Telephone:* (20) 7400-1700. *Fax:* (20) 7400-1799. *E-mail:* info@askonasholt.co.uk. *Website:* www.askonasholt.co.uk. *Address:* c/o Musichall Ltd, Vicarage Way, Ringmer, East Sussex, BN8 5LA, England.

KITCHINER, John; Singer (Tenor); b. 2 Dec. 1933, England. *Education:* Studied at the London Opera Centre with Joan Cross. *Career:* Debut: Glyndebourne 1965, as Count Almaviva; Appearances with English National Opera, Scottish Opera and Welsh National Opera; Roles include Guglielmo, Don Alfonso, Don Giovanni, Renato in Un Ballo in Maschera, Count di Luna, Figaro and Bartolo in Il Barbiere di Siviglia, Robert in Le Comte Ory, Marcello, Escamillo, and Count Eberbach in Der Wildschütz by Lortzing; Also sang in the British stage premieres of Prokofiev's War and Peace and The Bassarids by Henze, at the London Coliseum, 1972, 1974; Frequent concert engagements. *Address:* c/o English National Opera, London Coliseum, St Martin's Lane, London WC2N 4ES, England.

KITSENKO, Dmitry; Composer; b. 24 July 1950, Belay Tserkov, Kiev province, Moldovia. *Education:* Kishinyov Institute of Arts; Bucharest Music Academy. *Career:* Lecturer at Kishinyov Institute, 1977–82; Musicescu Academy, 1990–. *Compositions include:* concertos for Bayan (1977), Oboe (1977), Organ (1982), Trombone (1990, 1991) and Cello (1992); 4 Symphonies (1986, 1992, 1995, 1998); The Seasons for children's chorus and orchestra, 1980; Stabat Mater, for mezzo and chamber orchestra, 1989; Mariengebet, for women's chorus, 1989; Tinitatea Iupului for contralto and chamber orchestra, 1995; Ave Maria for soprano, clarinet and organ, 1993; Alleluja for soprano and trumpet, 1999; 2 string quartets, 1975, 1983; In Memoriam Oscar for 13 solo strings, 1988; Pastoral Games for ensemble, 1988; The Field for brass quintet, 1991; Transfiguration for ensemble, 1991; Exodus for ensemble, 1994; Kyrie, 1997; Concerto for 'Ars poetica' ensemble, 1999; Exodus 2 for ensemble, 1999; Strikhira for 4 cellos, 1999; keyboard and incidental music. *Address:* c/o Conservatorium de Muzic, Str. Stirbei Voda 33, 70732 Bucharest, Romania.

KITTS, Christopher (Martin); Conductor, Violinist and Educator; b. 7 April 1943, London, England; m. 16 Dec 1982. *Education:* Trinity College of Music, London, 1968; Conducting Studies with Dr Boyd Neel, Toronto, 1964–67, Dr Hans Lert, Virginia, 1966; Violin Studies with Bernard Robbins, New York Philharmonic, Clifford Evans, Toronto. *Career:* Conductor, Royal Conservatory Orchestra, Toronto, 1967, 1968, 1969; Conductor, Scarborough College Choir and Band, 1970; Concertmaster, North York Symphony Orchestra, 1971, 1972; Freelance Violinist, Toronto, 1972–85; Conducted Tours in England, France, West Germany, Netherlands, with Birchmount Park Collegiate, 1980, 1983, 1987, 1991; Adjudicator, Toronto International Music Festival, 1986, 1987; Music Director and Conductor, Scarborough Philharmonic Orchestra, 1985–93; Guest Conductor, Brampton Symphony, Mississauga Symphony, Scarborough Philharmonic, 1994–95. *Address:* 3663 Danforth Avenue, Scarborough, Ontario M1N 2GZ, Canada.

KLAES, Armin; Conductor; b. 17 Sept. 1958, Koblenz, Germany; m. Monika Hachmoller, 16 Mar 1982, 1 s. 1 d. *Education:* Conducting, Reinhard Peters at the Folkwang-Musikhochschulen Essen; Music pedagody and composition, Musikhochschule, Cologne; Musicology, University of Cologne; Chamber Music with Gunter Kehr. *Career:* Debut: Bedford Springs Festival for the Performing Arts, Pennsylvania, USA; Guest conductor with several orchestras since 1978; Founder and regular leader, Kolner Konzertgemeinschaft, 1978–85; Music Director, Mannesmann-Sinfonieorchester Duisburg, 1985–92; Founder and conductor of the Amadeus Kammerorchester, 1991; Since 1992, Artist leader of the Musikgemeinschaft Marl, symphonic orchestra and oratorio chorus. *Recordings:* Bach, Concert for organ with H Schauerte, Le Carnaval des Animaux. *Honours:* Folkwang–Forderpries, 1987. *Address:* Corneliusstrasse 167, 47918n Tonisvorst, Germany.

KLANSKA, Vladimira; Horn Player; b. 9 Sept. 1947, Ceské Budejovice, Czechoslovakia; m. Ivan Klansky, 1973–84, 2 s. *Education:* Conservatory of Music, Prague, 1965–69; Academy of Music, Prague, 1969–73; Masterclasses with Herrmann Baumann, 1976. *Career:* Debut: Mozart II, Rudolfinum Hall, Prague, 1966; Co-Principal, Prague Symphony Orchestra, 1968–74; Concert Tours Throughout Europe in Duo Recitals with Pianist Ivan Klansky, Mozarteum Salzburg, 1972, Concertgebouw, Amsterdam, 1974; Member, Prague Wind Quintet, 1980; Member, Czech Nonet, 1982; Artistic Leader, PWQ and CN, 1991–, Concert Tours with Both Ensembles in Europe, USA and Japan, including Festivals in Salzburg, Edinburgh, Stresa, Sorrento; Radio Recordings in Prague, Stockholm, Brussels, Bremen, Genève, Montreux; President, Stich Punto Horn Society, 1989–. *Recordings:* CDs, both solo and chamber music. *Honours:* Prizewinner, International ARD Music Competition, Munich, 1973; Juror, International Horn Competitions. *Address:* Stronjnicka 9, 17000 Prague 7, Czech Republic.

KLAPER, Michael; German musicologist; b. 25 Dec. 1970, Bietigheium-Bissingen. *Career:* wiss. Assistent (Mittelalter), Univ. Erlangen-Nürnberg; mem. Royal Musical Asscn. *Publications:* Die Musikgeschichte der Abtei Reichenau im 10. und 11. Jahrhundert: ein Versuch, 'Die musikalische Überlieferung aus dem Kloster Reichenau im 11. Jahrhundert und die kompositorische Tätigkeit des Abtes Bern (1008–1048)' in Pass & Rausch, Beiträge zur Musik, Musiktheorie und Liturgie der Abtei Reichenau. *Address:* Institut für Musikwissenschaft, Bismarckstr 1, 91054 Erlangen (office); Hartmannstr 105, 91052 Erlangen, Germany (home). *Telephone:* 9131 8522906 (office); 913132084 (home). *Fax:* 9131 8522403 (office).

KLAS, Eri; conductor; b. 7 June 1939, Tallinn, Estonia. *Education:* Tallinn Conservatoire with Gustav Ernesaks. *Career:* debut, conducted West Side Story at the Estonian Opera House, 1964; Instrumentalist with the Symphony Orchestra of Estonian Radio from 1964; Studied further at the Leningrad Conservatoire with Nikolai Rabinovich, then at the Bolshoi School, Moscow, Boris Khaikin, 1969–72; Conducted at the Bolshoi from 1972; Musical Director of Tallinn Opera 1975; Founded the Estonian Chamber Orchestra 1977; Guest engagements at the Paris Opéra and in Japan; Conductor of the Royal Opera Stockholm, 1985; Conducted Don Giovanni at Stockholm 1988, Eugene Oengin for the Finnish National Opera at Helsinki and Essen, 1989; Music Director, Royal Opera, Stockholm, 1985–89; Chief Conductor, Århus Symphony Orchestra, Denmark since 1990; Since 1990 frequent guest conductor of major Symphony Orchestras in USA; Los Angeles, Cleveland, Detroit, Baltimore, Dallas and others; Guest conductor at Hamburg Opera, premiere of Schnittke ballet Peer Gynt, 1989; Debuts with the Los Angeles Philharmonic and the Baltimore Symphony, 1992; Conducted Porgy and Bess at the 1992 Savonlinna Festival; Don Carlos at Helsinki, 1996. *Recordings:* Recordings for BISA record label includes works by Alfred Schnittke, with the 3rd Symphony, Stockholm Philharmonic and the 4 Violin Concertos, Malmö Symphony. *Honours:* Order of WASA, Swedish Royal Medal; Order of Finnish Lion, 1992. *Current Management:* c/o Konserbolaget AB, Kungsgaten 32, 111 35 Stockholm, Sweden. *Address:* Nurme 54, 0016 Tallinn, Estonia.

KLATZOW, Peter; Composer; b. 14 July 1945, Springs, South Africa. *Education:* Studied in Johannesburg, with Bernard Stevens at the RCM, London, and with Nadia Boulanger in Paris. *Career:* Rhodescan Broadcasting Corporation, producer; Cape Town University from 1973 (Associate Professor 1979); Founder of UCT Contemporary Music Society, 1974. *Compositions include:* Piano Sonata, 1969; In Memoriam, for soprano and strings, 1970; Interactions I for piano, percussion and ensemble, 1971; Symphony 'Phoenix', 1972; The Temptations of St Anthony for cello and orchestra, 1972; Time Structure I, for piano (1973), II for tape and orchestra, 1974; Still Life with Moonbeams for orchestra, 1975; Gardens of Memories and Discoveries for soprano and tape, 1975; 2 string quartets (1977, 1997); Concertos for Organ (1986), Marimba (1985) Clarinet (1989), and Piano with 8 instruments (1995); Hamlet, ballet, 1992; A Mass for Africa, 1994; Prayers and Dances from Africa, for chorus and brass quintet, 1996. *Publications include:* Composers in South Africa Today, editor, 1987. *Address:* c/o New Music SA, PO Box 7004, Grahamstown North 6148, South Africa.

KLEBE, Giselher; Composer; b. 28 June 1925, Mannheim, Germany; m. Lore Schiller 1946, 2 d. *Education:* Berlin Conservatoire; Studied, Boris Blacher. *Career:* Composer in Berlin until 1957; Professor, Composition and Theory of Music, Hochschule für Musik Detmold, 1957–98; Member, Academy of Fine Arts, Berlin 1964 and Hamburg 1963, Bavarian Academy of Fine Arts, 1978; mem, President Dramatiker Union, Berlin, 1986–; President of Academy of Fine Arts, Berlin, 1986–89. *Compositions:* Principal Works include: Oratorio: Weinacht-soratorium, 1989; Operas: Die Räuber (Schiller) 1957; Die tödlichen Wünsche (Balzac) 1959; Die Ermordung Caesars (Shakespeare) 1959; Alkmene (Kleist) 1961; Figaro lässt sich scheiden (Oedoen von Horvath), 1963; Jakobowsky und der Oberst (Werfel), 1965; Das Märchen von der Schönen Lilie (Goethe), 1969; Ein Wahrer Held (Synge/Boell), 1975; Rendezvous (Sostschenko) 1977; Der Juengste Tag (Oedoen von Horvath), 1980; Die Fastnachtsbeichte (Zuckmayer), 1983; Gervaise Macquart; (Emile Zola), 1995; Ballets: Signale, 1955; Mena-gerie, 1958; Das Testament, 1971; Orchestral Works: Die Zwitscher-maschine 1950; Deux Nocturnes 1952; 6 Sinfonien, 1952, 1953, 1967, 1971, 1977, 1996; Clarinet Concerto, 1984; Harp Concerto, 1988; cello Concerto, 1990; Fantasie für Sonie for orchestra, 1997; Adagio und Fuge (with theme from Wagner's Walküre), 1962; Five Lieder, 1962; Vier Vocalisen für Frauenchor, a Cappella 1963; La Tomba di Igor Strawinsky (oboe and chamber orchestra), 1979; Konzert for organ and orchestra, 1980; Church Music; Missa, 1964; Stabat Mater, 1964; Messe (Gebet einer armen Seele), 1966; Chamber Music: 3 String Quartets, 1949, 1963, 1981; 2 Solo Violin Sonatas, 1952, 1955; 2 Sonatas for Violin and Piano, 1953, 1974; Piano Trio Elegia Appasionata, 1955; Chamber Music: Soirée für Posaune und Kammerensemble, 1987; Many other musical works. *Address:* Bruchstrasse 16, 34694 Detmold 1, Germany.

KLEE, Bernhard; Conductor; b. 19 April 1936, Schleiz, Germany. *Education:* Studied piano, composition and conducting at the Cologne Conservatoire; Assistant to Otto Ackermann and Wolfgang Sawallisch at the Cologne opera house. *Career:* Debut: Cologne 1960, Die Zauberflöte; Early appointments in Salzburg, Oberhausen and Han-over; Music Director in Lubeck 1966–73; British debut with the Hamburg Opera at the 1969 Edinburgh Festival, Der fliegende Holländer; Chief Conductor of the North German Radio in Hanover 1976–79; General Music Director in Düsseldorf from 1977; Chief Guest Conductor of the BBC Philharmonic Orchestra 1985–89; Conducted the orchestra at the 1989 Promenade Concerts, with Berg's Three Pieces from Wozzeck and Mahler's 6th Symphony; Has conducted all the major German and London orchestras, the English Chamber Orchestra, Stockholm and Rotterdam Philharmonics, Zürich Tonhalle, RAI Rome, Vienna Symphony, and NHK Tokyo; US debut 1974, with the New York Philharmonic: has since conducted in San Francisco, Chicago, Detroit and Washington; Regular guest conductor at opera houses in

Hamburg, Munich, Berlin, Covent Garden and Geneva; Festival engagements at Edinburgh, Salzburg, Netherlands, Hong Kong and Dubrovnik; Promenade Concerts, London 1991, Mozart's Clarinet Concerto and Bruckner's 9th Symphony (BBC Philharmonic). *Record-ings:* extensive catalogue with Polydor and EMI. *Current Management:* Ingpen & Williams Ltd, 7 St George's Court, 131 Putney Bridge Road, London, SW15 2PA, England.

KLEIBERG, Ståle; Composer and Associate Professor; b. 8 March 1958, Stavanger, Norway; m. Ásta Ovregaard, 25 June 1982, 1 d. *Education:* Degree in Musicology, University of Oslo; Diploma in Composing, State Academy of Music, Oslo. *Career:* Associate Professor, University of Trondheim; mem, Norwegian Society of Composers. *Compositions:* 32 Opuses since 1981, many of which have been commissioned by leading orchestras and ensembles; Compositions include large works for full orchestra and church music as well as chamber works for various ensembles and solo works; Main Works: String Quartet, 1985; Stilla for orchestra and soprano/tenor, 1986; Two Poems by Montale, 1986; The Bell Reef, Symphony No. 1, 1991; The Rose Window, 1992; Dopo for cello and strings, 1993; Chamber Symphony, Symphony No. 2, 1996; Sonanza e Cadenza, 1998; Concerto for double bass and orchestra, 1999. *Recordings:* Sonetto di Tasso, 1992; Chamber Music, 1997; Dopo, 1998; The Rose Window, 1999 Publications: Form in Impressionism, 1985; The Music of Hans Abrahamsen, 1986; CPE Bach and The Individual Expression, 1989; Sturm und Drang as Style and Period Designation in Music History, 1991; Grieg's Slåtter, Op. 72: Change of Musical Style or New Concept of Nationality, Journal of the Royal Musical Association, 1996; A National Music by French Means, 1999; Following Grieg, 1999. *Address:* Stokkanhaugen 201, 7048 Trondheim, Norway.

KLEIN, Judith; Composer; b. 14 April 1943, Chicago, USA. *Education:* BA at Berkeley, CA, 1967; Basle Conservatory; MA, New York University, 1987; Teachers included Charles Dodge and Ruth Anderson. *Career:* Director, computer music studios and Instructor, Computer Music Composition, New York University; Consultant for Electro-Acoustic Music at the New York Public Library for the Performing Arts; Guest Lecturer at Cincinnati College Conservatory, Studio for Electro-nic Music, Basle; Guest Composer at the Brooklyn College Center for Computer Music; Founder Electro-Acoustic Music Archives at New York Library for the Performing Arts; Guest and Artist-in-Residence at Dartmouth College and Studio for Electronic Music, Basle; Guest Composer at Computer Music Centre at Columbia University 2000–. *Compositions include:* Little Piece, 1979; Dead End, 1979; Dream/Song, 1980; Journeys, art installation collaboration, 1982; The Mines of Falum, Part 1, 1983; God Bites, 1983; The Tell-Tale Heart, film music, after Edgar Allan Poe, 1983; From the Journals of Felix Bosonnet, 1987; 88" for Nick, 1992; Elements 1 and 2, sound installation, 1993; The Wolves of Bays Mountain, 1998; Music for radio plays and theatre productions include Family Play, 1981; Unheile Dreifaltigkeit, 1983; Sound installations in collaboration with visual artists include Jour-neys, 1982 and Elements 1.2, 1984. *Honours:* Honours at Bourges Electro-Acoustic Music Competition, 1988, for Journals; Finalist, 16th Electro-Acoustic Music Competition, Bourges, 1998. *Address:* c/o ASCAP, ASCAP Building, One Lincoln Place, New York, NY 10023, ; 130 West 17th Street, New York NY 10011 USA. *E-mail:* jakmail@earthlink.net.

KLEIN, Kenneth; Music Director and Conductor; b. 5 Sept. 1939, Los Angeles, California, USA. *Education:* Graduated Magna cum Laude, University of Southern California; Stanford University. *Career:* Debut: Europe, 1970; Paris, 1974; Moscow, 1974; Vienna, 1975; Conductor, Stuttgart Ballet in Stuttgart and then the Metropolitan Opera in all major cities of the USA; Toured USSR, Romania and Sweden, 1971, 1972; Invited by Pablo Casals to conduct 4 concerts in Puerto Rico, 1974; Conducted Suisse Romande Orchestra, Lamoureux Orchestra, Paris, France, Vienna Symphony, Montreux Festival; Debut with American Symphony Orchestra at Carnegie Hall, New York; Bruckner Orchestra, Austria, 1978; Debut at Rome Festival, 1979; Debut with Philharmonia Orchestra, Royal Albert Hall, London, England, 1979; Florida Philhar-monic, Miami, Florida, USA, 1980–81; Edmonton Symphony; Louisville Orchestra; North Carolina Symphony; Kansas City Philharmonic; San Francisco Chamber Orchestra; Music Director, conducting over 60 concerts per season, Guadalajara, Mexico; Music Director, New York Virtuosi, South Dakota Symphony and the Waterville Valley Festival; Has made numerous guest appearances world-wide.

KLEIN, Lothar; Composer and Professor of Composition; b. 27 Jan. 1932, Hanover, Germany. *Education:* PhD, Degree in Musicology and Composition, University of Minnesota, 1961. *Career:* As an under-graduate wrote music for many theatre and film productions; Professor of Composition, University of Toronto; Chairman, Graduate Studies in Music; Guest Lectures for 150th anniversary of Hochschule für Musik, Berlin, American Society for Aesthetics and Fulbright Commission. *Compositions include:* Stage Works: Canadiana 1980; Last Love

1950–56; Orpheus 1976; The Prodigal Son 1966; Orchestral: Appassionata for Orchestra 1958; The Bluebird 1952; Charivari: Music for an Imaginary Comedy 1966; Epitaphs for Orchestra 1963; Fanfares for Orchestra 1978; Musique a Go-Go 1966; Orchestral Suite from The Masque of Orianna, 1971; Presto for Orchestra, 1958; Rondo Giocoso for Orchestra 1964; Symmetries for Orchestra 1958; Symphonic Etudes (Symphony No. 3) 1972; Symphony No. 1, 1955; No. 2, 1966; Band: Divertimento for Band, 1953; Eroica: Variations on A Promethean Theme 1970; Gloria for Band 1961; Small Orchestra: Janizary Music 1970; Sinfonia Concertante 1956; String Orchestra: Passacaglia of The Zodiac 1971; Soloists with Orchestra: Boccherini Collage for Cello and Orchestra 1978; Concerto for Winds, Timpani and Strings, 1956; Design for Percussion and Orchestra 1970; Ecologues for Horn and Strings, 1954; Invention, Blues and Chase, 1975; Musica Antiqua, 1975; Music for Violin and Orchestra, 1972; Paganini Collage for Violin and Orchestra, 1967; Scenes for Timpani and Strings, 1979; Slices of Time, 1973; Le Tresor des Dieux, 1969; Trio Concertante, 1961; Voices with Orchestra: Dorick Musick, 1973; Herbstlieder, 1962; The Masque of Orianna, 1973; Meditations on The Passyoun, 1961; The Philosopher in The Kitchen, 1974; Voices of Earth; Chorus: 8 Madrigals 1957; An Exaltation, 1960; Good Night, 1970; A Little Book of Hours, 1962; 3 Ancient Folksongs, 1959; 3 Chinese Laments, 1968; 3 Pastoral Songs, 1963; 3 Reflections, 1976; Travellers, 1981; 2 Christmas Madrigals, 1961; numerous works for Solo Voices; Solo Voice with Instrumental Ensemble; Instrumental Ensemble, Instrumental Solos; Piano Works; Concerti Sacro for viola and orchestra, 1980; Symphonic Partita, 1985; Centre-Stage for wind ensemble, 1991; Trocadero for winds and piano, 1994; Hachcava-Memorial Meditations for bass, voice, harps, 3 percussion, 1979; The Jabberwock in Ogden Nash's Dining Room, 1992; Birds, Bells and Bees: An Emily Dickinson Quilt for soprano, alto and pianist, 1986; String Quartet No. 2 on poems of Wallace Stevens, 1991; Danceries for large orchestra, 1995; Market Cries for mixed chorus, 1998; Symphonia Harmoniae Celestium Revelationem for soprano, viola, harps and percussion, 1998. *Address:* PROCAN, 41 Valleybrook Drive, Don Mill, Ontario M3B 2S6, Canada.

KLEINDIENST, Stella; singer (soprano); b. 1957, Germany; m. Johannes Schaaf. *Education:* Studied at the Cologne Opera Studio. *Career:* Sang at the Bremen Opera, 1981–88, Deutsche Oper Berlin, 1988–89 and the Vienna Staatsoper from 1990; Sang in Musgrave's Voice of Ariadne at the 1981 Edinburgh Festival and in Zemlinsky's Der Kreidekreis at Amsterdam in 1986; Covent Garden in 1987 and 1989 as Cherubino in a production of Figaro by her husband; Further guest appearances at Stuttgart as Ariadne and at Geneva and Antwerp; Other roles include Mila in Janáček's Osud, Anne Trulove, Belinda in Dido and Aeneas and Weber's Agathe; Sang Boulotte in Offenbach's Barbe-bleue at Stuttgart, 1996; Marzelline in Fidelio, 1998.

KLEMENS, Adam; Composer and Conductor; b. 14 Jan. 1967, Prague, Czechoslovakia. *Education:* Composition, 1989, Conducting, 1994, Conservatoire, Prague; Composition, Academy of Performing Arts, Prague, 1994. *Career:* Debut: Composer, Sinfonia Lacrimosa, Piano Concerto, 1989; Conductor, Prague Conservatoire Symphony Orchestra, 1994; Conductor, Amy, with Lynn Barber (US Percussionist); With George Crumb, Night of the Four Moons, 1994; Suk Chamber Orchestra, 1997; Bambini di Praga, 1997; Teacher, Musical Theory, Prague Conservatoire, 1996–; mem. Association of Musical Artists; Jeunesses Musicales of the Czech Republic. *Compositions:* Clarinet Sonata, 1987; Sinfonia Lacrimosa, 1989; Perspectives for Oboe Solo, 1992; Music for Four Players, 1993; Piano concerto, 1994; Windy Music for Wind Orchestra, 1995; Fantasy for Wind Quintet and Harp, 1997; Composer of Film and Theatre Music. *Honours:* 1st Prize, Composers Competition, Generace, 1989, 1990; 3rd Prize, Composers Competition, Czech Ministry of Culture, 1990. *Address:* Chudenicka 1080/12, 02 10200 Prague 10, Czech Republic.

KLIMOV, Valery (Alexandrovich); Violinist; b. 16 Oct. 1931, Kiev, USSR. *Education:* Studied with Mordkovich in Odessa, then joined David Oistrakh at the Moscow Conservatory, graduated 1959. *Career:* Prizewinner at competitions in Paris and Prague 1956; Soloist with Moscow Philharmonic 1957; Gold Medal Tchaikovsky Competition Moscow 1958; British debut with BBC Symphony Orchestra at the Royal Festival Hall 1967; Regular visits to America, Canada, Australia, Italy, Germany, Switzerland, Sweden; Appearances with such conductors as Ormandy, Svetlanov, Rozdestvensky, Temirkanov and Arvid Yansons; Other than the standard repertoire, plays music by Prokofiev, Khachaturian, Hindemith and Schnittke; Head of violin studies at the Moscow Conservatory 1975–. *Recordings include:* CD of the Khachaturian Concerto (Olympia). *Honours:* National Artist of the RSFSR 1972.

KLINKOVA, Zhivka; Composer; b. 30 July 1924, Samokov, Bulgaria. *Education:* Studied at the Sofia Academy and with Wagner-Régeny and Blacher in Berlin, 1960–68. *Career:* Performances of her stage works in Germany and elsewhere. *Compositions include:* Ballets and musicals: Kaliakra, 1966, Vietnamese Poem, 1972, Isle Of Dreams, 1978, Cyril

And Methodius, 1981, Vassil Levski, 1992; Symphony, 1974; Piano Concerto, 1992; Olympic Endeavour, opera-ballet, 1995; Sofia, opera, 1996; Chamber and keyboard music. *Address:* c/o Musicautor, 63 Tzar Assen Street, 1463 Sofia, Bulgaria.

KLINT, Jorgen; Singer (Bass-baritone); b. 6 April 1931, Elmelund, Denmark. *Education:* Studied at the Odense Conservatory, 1971–73. *Career:* Debut: Jutland Opera, 1975, as Luther in Les Contes d'Hoffmann; Sang at the Royal Opera Copenhagen, from 1975 including Boris in Lady Macbeth, 1991, Faninal in Der Rosenkavalier, 1994; Sang Alberich in The Ring at Århus, 1983–87; Other Wagner roles include Daland, the Dutchman and Titurel; Sang in The Ring for Jutland Opera, 1994–96; Other roles include Gremin, Sarastro, Pizarro, Rocco and Banquo; Nielsen's Samuel in Saul and David. *Recordings:* Nielsen's Maskarade; Saul and David. *Address:* Den Jyske Opera, Thomas Jensens Alle, DK 8000 Århus, Denmark.

KLOBUCAR, Berislav; Conductor; b. 28 Aug. 1924, Zagreb, Yugoslavia. *Education:* Studied in Salzburg with Lovro von Matacic and Clemens Krauss. *Career:* Assistant at Zagreb Opera 1943–51; Conducted the Vienna Staatsoper from 1953; General Director Graz Opera, 1960–71; Bayreuth Festival, 1968–69, Die Meistersinger and Lohengrin; Metropolitan Opera, 1968, Der fliegende Holländer, Die Walküre and Lohengrin; Music Director, Royal Opera Stockholm, 1972–81; Principal Conductor, Nice Opera, 1983–; Conducted L'amore dei tre re at Palermo, 1989; Many appearances as guest conductor with leading orchestras. *Address:* Orchestre Philharmonique de Nice, Opéra de Nice, rue Saint-François de Paule, 06300 Nice, France.

KLOS, Wolfgang; Austrian violist and viola professor; b. 15 July 1953, Vienna; m. Olga Sommer 1982. *Education:* Univ. of Vienna, Musikhochschule, Vienna, masterclasses with M. Rostal, U. Koch, B. Giuranna. *Career:* leader, Viola Sections, Tonhalle Orchestra, Zürich, Switzerland 1977–81, Vienna Symphony Orchestra 1981–89; teacher, viola, chamber music and orchestra, Vorarlberg State Conservatory of Music, Feldkirch, Austria 1977–89; Prof., viola and chamber music and masterclasses, Vienna Musikhochschule 1988–91, Head of String Dept 1991–2002; Vice-Pres., Universität für Musik und Darstellende Kunst (University of Music and Performing Arts), Vienna 2002–; masterclasses, various locations world-wide; soloist world-wide 1975–; mem. Vienna String Trio, numerous concerts, radio, television recordings world-wide. *Recordings include:* gradually recording entire string trio repertory; numerous recordings with various orchestras and chamber music groups. *Honours:* Das Große Ehrenzeichen für Verdienste um die Republik Österreich (Austria) 2003. *Address:* c/o Universität für Musik und Darstellende Kunst, Anton-von-Webern-Platz 1, 1030 Vienna, Austria. *Website:* www.mdw.ac.at.

KLOSINSKA, Izabella; Singer (Soprano); b. 1959, Poland. *Education:* Studied at the Warsaw Academy. *Career:* Appearances with Warsaw National Opera as Roxana in King Roger, Micaela, Pamina, Mozart's Countess, and Mimi; Season 1989 in Moniuszko's Haunted Castle at Vienna and Cassandra in Les Troyens at Amsterdam; Season 1993–94 as Roxana at Cincinnati and Buffalo, New York; Mozart Gala at Vienna; Carnegie Hall and Cologne concerts, 1995; Lieder recitals and further concerts at many venues; Sang in Penderecki's Polish Requiem at the Viva il Canto Festival, Cieszyn, 1997. *Address:* c/o National Theatre, Plac Teatrainy 1, 00-950 Warsaw, Poland.

KLOUBOVA, Zdena; Singer (Soprano); b. 1963, Czechoslovakia. *Education:* Studied at the Prague Academy and at Zwickau. *Career:* Sang at the Smetana Theatre, Prague, from 1992, National Theatre from 1993; Roles have included Mozart's Blondchen, Susanna, Servilia, Queen of Night and Despina, Verdi's Gilda; Strauss's Zerbinetta and Sophie and the title role in The Cunning Little Vixen; Guest appearances in Denmark, Russia, Israel and Japan; Many concert appearances, in repertory from Baroque to contemporary. *Recordings include:* Carmina Burana; Schnittke's Requiem; Bach Mass in B minor; Kitchen Boy in Rusalka, conducted by Charles Mackerras, 1998. *Address:* Prague National Theatre, PO Box 865, 11230 Prague 1, Czech Republic.

KLUSAK, Jan-Filip; Composer; b. 18 April 1934, Prague, Czechoslovakia; m. Milena Kaizrova, 29 Mar 1979, 1 s. *Education:* Academy of Music, Dramatic Arts, Prague; Studied composition with Jaroslav Ridky and Pavel Borkovec, 1953–57. *Compositions include:* Published: Four Small Vocal Exercises, 1–11, for flute, 1965; Rondo for piano, 1967; Published and Recorded: Proverbs for Deep Voice and Wind Instruments, 1959; Pictures for 12 wind instruments, 1960; 1st Invention for chamber orchestra, 1961; 2nd String Quartet, 1961–62; Variation on a Theme by Gustav Mahler for orchestra, 1960–62; Sonata for violin and wind instruments, 1965–66; 6th Invention for Nonet, 1969; Invenzionetta per Flauto Solo, 1971; Monody in Memoriam Igor Stravinsky, 1972; 7th Invention for orchestra, 1973; 3rd String Quartet, 1975; Variations for two harps, 1982; Fantasia on Adam Michna of Otradovice for brass quintet and harp, 1983; Six Small Preludes for orchestra, Vor deinen Thron Tret ich Hiermit, 1984; What You Want, opera in 2 acts,

1984–85; The King with the Golden Mask, ballet, 1990; Hero and Leandros, ballet, 1988; Dämmerklarheit, Songs on Friedrich Rückert, 1988; 4th String Quartet; Mozart-Sickness, Fancy for chamber orchestra, 1991; Concerto for oboe and small orchestra, 1991; Tetragrammaton sive Nomina Eius for orchestra, 1992; Die Kunst des guten Zusammennspiels for wind, 1992; 5th string quartet, 1994; Ein Bericht für eine Akademie, opera in 1 act, 1993–97; It is a Paradise to Look At, symphonic poem, 1999; Bertram and Mescalinda, opera pasticcio in 1 act, 2002; GaDe, Fancy for violin, 2002; 6th String Quartet, 2003; Axiws temporum for orchestra, 2003. *Address:* Blanicka 26, 120-00 Prague 2, Czech Republic.

KLUSON, Jospef; Violist; b. 1953, Czechoslovakia. *Education:* Studied at the Prague Conservatory and Academy of Fine Arts. *Career:* Founder member of the Prazak-Quartet, 1972; Tours throughout Europe, America, Japan, Australia and New Zealand; Tours in the United Kingdom 1982, 1985, 1988, 1989, 1993 (Wigmore Hall, Queen Elizabeth Hall, Huddersfield Contemporary Music Festival); Recitals for BBC, Dutch Radio, Czech Radio, Radio France; Teaching: master classes at Orlando Festival, Mozart European Foundation, Antwerp, Bremen. *Honours:* First Prize in the Czech National String Quartet Competition, 1978; Grand Prix in Evian, 1978; Grand Prix at Prague Spring Competition, 1979. *Current Management:* Ingpen & Williams Ltd, 7 St George's Court, 131 Putney Bridge Road, London, SW15 2PA, England.

KMENTT, Waldemar; Singer (Tenor); b. 2 Feb. 1929, Vienna, Austria. *Education:* Studied at the Vienna Musikhochschule with Adolf Vogel, Elisabeth Rado and Hans Duhan. *Career:* Debut: Vienna 1950, in the Choral Symphony, conducted by Karl Böhm; Toured Europe with Viennese student group, appearing in Die Fledermaus and Le nozze di Figaro; Vienna Volksoper from 1951, debut as the Prince in The Love for Three Oranges: later roles in Vienna have included Belmonte, Don Ottavio, Ferrando, Idomeneo, Walther, Bacchus and the Emperor in Die Frau ohne Schatten; Sang Jacquino in Fidelio at the opening of the rebuilt Vienna Staatsoper, 1955; Salzburg Festival from 1955, in the premiere of Irische Legende by Egk and as Idamante (Idomeneo), Gabriel in Le Mystère de la Nativité by Martin, Ferrando and Tamino; Bayreuth Festival 1968–70, as Walther von Stolzing; Further engagements in Milan, Düsseldorf, Paris, Amsterdam, Munich and Stuttgart, and at the Drottningholm and Edinburgh Festivals; Sang Baron Zeta in Die lustige Witwe for Opéra National de Paris, 1997; Many concert appearances, notably in Das Lied von der Erde by Mahler. *Recordings:* Salome, Tiefland, Lulu, Bastien et Bastienne, Così fan tutte (Philips); Beethoven's Missa solemnis (Electrola); Die Fledermaus, Das Rheingold, Arabella, Tristan und Isolde (Decca); Video of Turandot from the Vienna Staatsoper, 1983. *Address:* c/o Staatsoper, Opernring 2, 1010 Vienna, Austria.

KNAIFEL, Alexander; Composer; b. 28 Nov. 1943, Tashkent, Russia; m. Tatiana Melentieva, 31 Dec 1965, 1 d. *Education:* The Secondary Music School at the Leningrad Conservatoire, 1950–61; Moscow Conservatoire, 1961–63; Leningrad Conservatoire, 1963–67. *Career:* Freelance composer; mem. Composers Union, 1968–; Cinematographers Union, 1987–. *Compositions:* Ostinati, 1964; Angel, 1964; The Coming City of the Seeking After, 1964; Disarmament, 1966; 150 000 000, 1966; Monodia, 1968; Argumentum de jure, 1969;A Prima Vista, 1972; Joan, 1970–78; Status nascendi, 1975; Ainana, 1978; Rafferty, 1980; Solaris, 1980; A Chance Occurrence, 1982; Pagan Fate, 1982; Nika, 1983–84; Counteraction, 1984; God, 1985; Agnus Dei, 1985; Wings of a Serf, 1986; Madness, 1987; Litania, 1988; Through the Rainbow of Involuntary Tears, 1987–88; Shramy marsha (Scars of march), 1988; Voznoshenije (The Holy Oblation), 1991; Svete Tikhiy (O Gladsome Light), 1991;; Once Again on the Hypothesis, 1992; Scalae Iacobis, 1992;; Maranatha, 1993; Butterfly, 1993; In Air Clear and Unseen, 1994; Prayers to the Holy Spirit, 1994–95; Psalm 51(50), 1995; Amicta sole, 1995; The Beatitudes, 1996; Bliss, 1997; Lux aeterna, 1997; This Child, 1997; Tabernacle, 1998; With the White on the White, 1998; Snowflake on a Spiderthread, 1998; Daylight, 1999; Small Blue Feathers, 2001; Morning Prayers, 2001; Entrance, 2001; Fairy-Tale of a Fisherman and a Fish, 2002; Alice in Wonderland, 1994–2002; Avowal of Love, 2003; Nativity, 2003; Lukomoriye, 2003; Music for 40 films. *Recordings:* The Canterville Ghost, BBC, 1980; Lamento (Le Chant du Monde, 1991); Monodia (Le Chant du Monde, 1990); Vera (Faith), BBC, 1993; A Silly Horse (Melodia, 1988); Passacaglia, Megadisc, 1996; Shramy marsha (Scars of March), (Megadisc) 1996; Postludia, (Megadisc) 1996; Svete Tikhiy, 2002; In Air Clear and Unseen, ECM, 2002; O Heavenly King, (Megadisc) 1996; Chapter Eight, (Teldec) 1997; Comforter, 1998; Lux Aeterna (ECM), 2000. *Publications:* Diada (two pieces), 1975; Classical Suite, 1976; Five Poems by Mikhail Lermontov, 1978; Musique militaire, 1974; The Canterville Ghost, 1977; Passacaglia, 1990; Lamento, 1979, 1992, 1997; The Petrograd Sparrows, 1981; A Silly Horse, 1985; Medea, 1989; Vera (Faith), 1990; Da (Yes), 1991; O Comforter, 1997; Bliss, 1997. *Honours:* DAAD Honoured grant-aided

composer, Berlin, 1993; Honoured Art Worker of Russia, 1996. *Address:* Skobelevski prospekt 5, apt130, Sankt-Petersburg 194214, Russia.

KNAPP, Peter; Opera Singer (Baritone) and Director; b. 4 Aug. 1947, St Albans, England; m. Mary Anne Tennyson, 2 June 1984, 1 s. *Education:* St Albans School; St John's College, Cambridge. *Career:* Debut: Glyndebourne Touring Company; Kent Opera: Monteverdi's Orfeo (televised on BBC); Eugene Onegin; Don Giovanni; La Traviata; English National Opera: Don Giovanni; La Traviata; English National Opera: Don Giovanni; The Marriage of Figaro; Abroad: Sofia, Zürich, Frankfurt, Venice, Florence; Tour of Australia; Regular Broadcasts; 1978 began directing own opera company–La Périchole filmed for BBC television; 1988/89 2 week season at Sadler's Wells Theatre, London, 1989; sang Mozart's Figaro, 1989, Zelta in The Merry Widow for Scottish Opera, sang Wolfram in Tannhäuser for New Sussex Opera, 1990; Made version of Carmen for Travelling Opera, 1992. *Recordings:* Monteverdi Vespers; De Falla Master Peter's Puppet Show. *Publications:* Translations of Così fan tutte, The Marriage of Figaro, La Périochole, Orpheus in the Underworld, La Bohème, The Barber of Seville. *Honours:* First Benson and Hedges Gold Award, 1977. *Address:* Kaye Artists Management, Barratt House, 7 Chertsey Road, Woking GV21 5 AB, England.

KNEZKOVA-HUSSEY, Ludmila; Concert Pianist, Composer, Choral Conductor, Chamber Performer and Clinician; b. 22 April 1956, Mukacevo, Ukraine; m. Bernard Hussey, 17 Nov 1990, 1 d. *Education:* Doctorate in Music, Lvov Central Music School; Moscow Music School; Tchaikovsky Conservatory, Moscow; Academy of Music, Prague; Studies: France, 1986 and 1987; Germany, 1989 and 1990; Banff Centre School of Fine Arts, Canada, 1992. *Career:* Many recitals and concert engagements with leading orchestras in USA, Canada, Germany, Italy, Russia, Czech Republic, Slovakia, Austria, Hungary, Poland, Ukraine, Switzerland; Television and radio appearances in Canada, USA, Czech Republic, Russia, Latvia, Austria, Germany, Italy, Ukraine; In 1993 established the Ludmilla Knezkova-Hussey International Piano Competition which attracts many gifted and talented students from all over the world and is held every two years. *Recordings include:* Original compositions: Symphonic Fantasy for orchestra, 1985; Sonata for piano and flute, 1986; Compositions for a chorus, 1986; Symphonic Ballad for orchestra, 1988; Fantaisie for piano and orchestra, 1991; Moods of Mustique, 2000; If This Be Love, for piano, soprano and violin, 2000; St Andrews Anthology for piano, soprano and orchestra, 2001; CDs, Canada, 1994, 2000; Many recordings in Europe. *Address:* 155 Allison Crescent, Bathurst, NB E2A 3B4, Canada.

KNIAZEV, Alexander A.; Russian cellist; b. 21 April 1961, s. of Alexandre S. Schwarzmann and Ludmila P. Kniazeva; m. (deceased). *Education:* Moscow State Conservatory, Nyzhny-Novgorod State Conservatory. *Career:* Prof. Moscow State Conservatory 1995; masterclasses in France, Spain, Republic of Korea, Philippines; concerts 1978–, in Russia, UK, France, Germany, Italy, Spain, Belgium, Austria, USA, S Africa, S America, Republic of Korea, Japan and elsewhere; performed with partners V. Afanasyev, S. Milstein, E. Leonskaya, B. Engerer, Kun Woo Oark, V. Spivakov, V. Tretyakov, M. Brunello, Yu. Bashmet, Yu. Milkis. *Honours:* First Prize Nat. Competition, Vilnius, Lithuania 1977, Third Prize G. Cassado Int. Competition, Florence, Italy 1979, First Prize Int. Chamber Music Competition, Trapani, Italy 1987, Second Prize Tchaikovsky Int. Competition, Moscow, Russia 1990, First Prize Unisa Int. Competition, Pretoria, S Africa. *Address:* Skornyzhny per. 1, apt 58, Moscow 107078, Russia (home).

KNIE, Roberta; Singer (Soprano); b. 13 May 1938, Cordell, Oklahoma, USA. *Education:* Studied at Oklahoma University with Elisabeth Parham, Judy Bounds-Coleman and Eva Turner. *Career:* Debut: Hagen (Germany) 1964, as Elisabeth in Tannhäuser; Sang at Freiburg, 1966–69; Graz Opera, 1969, as Salome, Tosca and Leonore; Zürich and Nice, 1972–73, as Brünnhilde; Metropolitan Opera from 1975; Guest appearances in Kassel, Mannheim, Montreal, Buenos Aires, Brussels, Barcelona, Hamburg, Berlin, Munich and Stuttgart; Other roles include Isolde, Senta, Elsa, Sieglinde, Donna Anna, Elektra, the Marschallin, Lisa in The Queen of Spades, Electra in Idomeneo and both Leonoras of Verdi. *Recordings include:* Isolde in Tristan und Isolde.

KNIGHT, Daniel, BFA; British singer (bass, bass-baritone), voice teacher and artistic and musical director; b. (Nicolino Giacalone), 28 Nov. 1956, Montréal, Canada. *Education:* Marianopolis Coll., McGill Univ., Conservatoire de Musique, Québec, Concordia Univ.; studied singing with Benjamin Luxon, Vera Rozsa, James Bowman, Rita Streich, Max van Egmond, Daniel Ferro and Emma Kirkby. *Career:* Dir, Dido and Aeneas, Waltham Abbey 1995; singing, St John's Smith Square, London 1997; BBC radio debut, Glenn Gould, Bach; private singing teacher, masterclasses in Canada, USA, Ireland, England 1974–; singing, modern world premiere singing title role of full staged complete performance of Purcell's Dioclesian, Dartington and Croatia with Paul Goodwin conducting 1995, 19th- and 20th-Century Austrian Lieder to mark Austria's Thousand Years 1996; Artistic Dir, founding mem.,

Handel Opera Company 1995; recital and voice masterclass, Houston, TX 1999; Musical Dir, Artistic Dir and Chair. of Handel Opera Company Ltd. *Recordings:* Music of the Second Generation 1995, Dioclesian by H. Purcell 1995, Baroque Opera Arias for Bass 1997. *Publications:* A Scarlatti Cantatas and Serenatas 1997, articles on singing in NODA London News. *Address:* Flat 3, Regina House, 65 Wimpole Street, London, W1G 8AN, England (home). *Telephone:* (20) 7487 2892. *E-mail:* danielknight@angelsong.co.uk. *Website:* www.danielknight.net.

KNIGHT, Gillian, LRAM, BA; Singer (mezzo-soprano); b. 1 Nov. 1939, Redditch, Worcestershire, England. *Education:* Royal Academy of Music, London, Open University. *Career:* D'Oyly Carte Opera, 1959–64, sang in contralto roles as Katisha (Mikado), Ruth (Pirates of Penzance), and Lady Jane (Patience); Sadler's Wells/English National Opera as Suzuki in Butterfly, Ragone (Comte Ory), Juno (Semele) and Carmen; Covent Garden from 1970, in the premiere of Maxwell Davies' Taverner, 1972, Der Ring des Nibelungen, Rigoletto, Eugene Onegin and Semele, 1988; Paris Opéra debut, 1978, in Die Zauberflöte; US debut, 1979, as Olga in Eugene Onegin at Tanglewood: Tours of USA singing Gilbert and Sullivan; Season 1986/87 Gertrude in Hamlet for Pittsburgh Opera; Nurse in Die Frau ohne Schatten for Welsh National Opera, 1989; Sang the Forester's Wife in The Cunning Little Vixen at Covent Garden; France: Rouen, Lile, Nantes, Avignon, Tours, Paris, Toulouse (Carmen, Don Quixote, Werther); Germany; Frankfurt, Ulrica in Ballo in Maschera; Spain: Carmen with Domingo in Valencia and Zaragoza; Switzerland: Rigoletto, Geneva; Sang Marguérite in La Dame Blanche at the 1990 Wexford Festival; Sang the title role in the British premiere of Gerhard's The Duenna, Opera North, 1992; Third Maid in Elektra at the First Night of the 1993 London Proms; Sang Annina in La Traviata at Covent Garden, 1996; Roméo et Juliette, 2000; Concert engagements with conductors such as Bertini, Boulez, Colin Davis, Charles Groves and Solti. *Recordings:* Six Gilbert and Sullivan roles; Messiah, Damnation of Faust and Mozart Masses with Colin Davis; Schoenberg's Moses und Aron with Boulez; Suor Angelica, Il Tabarro and Madama Butterfly with Maazel; La Forza del Destino with Levine. *Address:* c/o Royal Opera House (Contracts), Covent Garden, London WC2E 9DD, England.

KNIGHT, Katherine; Cellist; b. 1960, USA. *Education:* Johns Hopkins University; New England Conservatory. *Career:* Co-Founder, Da Vinci Quartet, 1980, under the sponsorship of the Fine Arts Quartet; Many concerts in the USA and elsewhere in a repertoire including works by Mozart, Beethoven, Brahms, Dvořák, Shostakovich and Bartók. *Honours:* With the Da Vinci Quartet: Grants from the NEA, Western States Arts Foundation and Colorado Council for the Humanities; Artist-in-Residence, University of Colorado. *Current Management:* Sonata, Glasgow, Scotland. *Address:* c/o Da Vinci Quartet, 11 Northpark Street, Glasgow G20 7AA, Scotland.

KNIGHT, Mark Anthony; British professor of violin and viola; b. 24 April 1941, Worcestershire, England; m. Patricia Noall 1965; one s. one d. *Education:* Guildhall School of Music and Drama, London, Tanglewood International Summer School, Massachusetts, USA. *Career:* debut in Brighton, 1962; freelance violinist, 1965–69, including London Philharmonic Orchestra; Leader, New Cantata Orchestra of London, 1966–69; Senior String Tutor, Wells Cathedral School, Wells, Somerset, 1975–88; Professor of Violin, Viola and Chamber Music, Guildhall School of Music and Drama, London, 1976–; several radio and television broadcasts. *Compositions:* Cadenzas: for Mozart's Violin Concertos No. 1 in B flat, K207, and No. 2 in D, K211; for Karl Stamitz's Viola Concerto in D; for Hoffmeister's Viola Concerto in D; for Haydn's Cello Concerto in C; for Mozart's Horn Concerto in E flat K495 for both valve and natural horn; Transcriptions for viola of Haydn's Cello Concerto in C with cadenzas; Geoffrey Burgon's Six Studies for solo cello. *Recordings:* A Boy Is Born, as Conductor of Wells Cathedral School Chamber Orchestra, 1977. *Publications:* Editor: Violin Sonatas Op 5 by Archangelo Corelli, 1991; 42 Violin Studies by Rodolphe Kreutzer, 1992. *Current Management:* Strings Attached Ltd, Great Skewes Cottage, St Wenn, Bodmin, Cornwall PL30 5PS, England.

KNIPLOVA, Nadezda; Singer (Soprano); b. 18 April 1932, Ostrava, Czechoslovakia. *Education:* Studied at the Prague Conservatory with Jarmila Vavrdova and at the Academy of Musical Arts with K Ungrova and Zdenek Otava. *Career:* Sang at Usti nad Labem 1956–59 and the Janáček Opera Brno (1959–64), notably as Renata in The Fiery Angel, Katerina in The Greek Passion and Katerina Izmailova; Principal of The Prague National Theatre from 1965: roles included the Kostelnicka in Jenůfa, Brünnhilde, Leonore, Milada (Dalibor), Libuše, Emilia Marty, Isolde, Tosca, Aida and Senta; Guest appearances in Salzburg (Brünnhilde, 1967), Barcelona (as Isolde), Turin (in Götterdämmerung) Berlin, Hamburg, New York and San Francisco (Die Walküre); Sang with the Berlin Staatsoper on tour in Japan; Janáček's Glagolitic Mass at the 1971 Salzburg Festival. *Recordings:* Jenůfa, Libuše, Dalibor, Orfeo ed Euridice; Katya Kabanova; Der Ring des Nibelungen. *Honours:* Prizewinner at competitions in Geneva (1958), Vienna (1959) and Toulouse (1959); Czech Artist of Merit, 1970. *Address:* National Theatre, PO Box 865, 11230 Prague 1, Czech Republic.

KNITTEL, Krzysztof; Composer; b. 1 May 1947, Warsaw, Poland. *Education:* Warsaw Academy of Music, 1966–77, with Tadeusz Baird. *Career:* Experimental Studio of Polish Radio, 1973–; co-founder of various electro-acoustic and improvised music groups in Poland; Director of Warsaw Autumn Festival, 1995–98; President of Union of Polish Composers, 1999. *Compositions include:* String Quartet, 1976; Women's Voice, ballet, 1980; Low Sounds nos 1–5, 1979–91; Norcet 1 and 2, for tape, 1980; Black Water, White Water, Old Stream for instruments and tape, 1983; String quartet, with tape and percussion, 1985; 14 Variations on 14 Words by John Cage, 1986–92; Three songs Without Words, for soprano and tape, 1987; Nibiru, for strings and harpsichord, 1987; Histoire I–III, 1988–90; Borders of Nothing, computers, 1990; Instant reactions, for ensemble and computer, 1992; Satan in Goray, ballet, 1993; Legs, sound installation, 1993; Sonata da Camera 1–3, 1994–95; Radio Sculpture, 1994; Der Erwählte, ballet after Thoman Mann, 1995. *Honours:* Solidarity Prize, 1985. *Address:* c/o Polish Cultural Institute, 23 Portland Place, London WIN 4 HQ, England.

KNIZIA, Martin; Organist and Harpsichordist; b. 1960, England. *Education:* Organ with David Titterington and Martin Haselböck; Harpsichord and conducting at Lübeck and the Royal Academy, London. *Career:* Organ and harpsichord soloist, and continuo playing, with London Sinfonia, London Mozart Players and other orchestras; Founder of the Sweelink Ensemble, performing at St Martin-in-the-Fields, St James's Church, Brompton Oratory, and for the London Bach Festival; Assistant Director for the English Bach Festival, Lully/Molière Bourgeois Gentilhomme, Linbury Theatre Covent Garden, 2001; Teacher of figured bass and baroque organ improvisation, Royal Academy. *Publications include:* Editions of organ works by Orlando Gibbons (Universal). *Honours:* Foundation Fellowship, RAM. *Address:* c/o English Bach Festival, 15 South Eaton Place, London, SW1W 9ER, England.

KNOBEL, Marita; Singer (Mezzo-soprano); b. 1947, Johannesburg, South Africa. *Education:* Studied in Pretoria and at the London Opera Centre. *Career:* Sanga at the Cologne Opera 1973–85, notably as Auntie in Peter Grimes, Magdalene in Meistersinger and Mother Goose in The Rake's Progress; Guest appearances in Düsseldorf, Dresden, Basle, Barcelona and Edinburgh; Sang at the Munich Staatsoper 1990–91 and at the Vienna Staatsoper from 1992, in such roles as Suzuki, Fidalma (Matrimonio Segreto) and the Witch in Hansel and Gretel. *Address:* c/o Staatsoper, Opernring 2, 1010 Vienna, Austria.

KNODT, Erich; Singer (bass); b. 1945, Germany. *Education:* Studied in Koblenz. *Career:* Sang at the Stadttheater Koblenz, 1970–72; Wuppertal, 1972–76, Mannheim, 1976–87; Guest appearances at Düsseldorf, Hamburg, Stuttgrt, Brussels, 1989, Paris, Barcelona, Strasbourg and Madrid; Bregenz and Aix-en-Provence Festivals, 1985, 1989, as Sarastro; Wagner repertoire includes King Mark, Lisbon 1985, King Henry in Lohengrin, 1986, Hunding, Lisbon, 1989, Pogner and Hagen; also sang Mozart's Commendatore, Rocco, King Philip, Boris Godunov, Banquo and Ramphis (Bordeaux 1989); Sang Peneois in a concert performance of Daphne at Rome, 1991; Sarastro at Bordeaux, Pogner at Trieste and Roldano in Franchetti's Christoforo Colombo at the Montpellier Festival, 1992; Sang King Mark in Tristan und Isolde at Trieste, 1996. Many further concert engagements. *Address:* Nationaltheater, Am Goethplatz, 6800 Mannheim, Germany.

KNOX, Garth (Alexander); Violist; b. 8 Oct. 1956, Dublin, Ireland. *Education:* ARCM, Royal College of Music, London, 1974–77; Studies with Frederick Riddle; Masterclasses with Paul Doktor and Peter Schidloff. *Career:* Member of English Chamber Orchestra, 1979–81, and of London Sinfonietta; Dedicatee and 1st performance of Henze's Viola Sonata, Witten, 1981; 1st performance of James Dillon's Timelag Zero, Brighton, 1981; Guest Principal Viola, Opera La Fenice, Venice, 1981–83; Performances of Harold in Italy and Jonathon Lloyd's Viola Concerto with Danish Radio Symphony Orchestra, Copenhagen, 1982; Member of Pierre Boulez's Ensemble Intercontemporain, Paris, 1983–90; Concertos-Luciano Berio and Marc-Andre Dalbavie conducted by Pierre Boulez in Bordeaux, Lisbon, Paris and New York; Concerto by Karl-Amadeus Hartmann, Théâtre du Rond-Point, Paris, 1987; Tour of USSR with Jan Latham Koenig playing Shostakovich Viola Sonata, 1987; 1st performance of Donatoni's La Souris sans Sourire with Quator Ensemble Intercontemporain, Paris, 1989; Joined the Arditti String Quartet, 1990, premiering quartets by Ferneyhough (No. 4), Goehr (No. 4), Xenakis' Tetora and Feldman's Quintet; 1st Performance of Ligeti's Loop, for solo viola, 1991; Left Arditti Quartet in 1998 to concentrate on solo career. *Recordings:* Henze's Viola Sonata, Ricordi, 1981; Schoenberg's Verklärte Nacht, supervised by Boulez, CBS; Embellie, for solo viola by Iannis Xenakis; Bruno Maderna, Viola; Solo CD for Naïve/Montaigue. *Address:* 3 rue Saigne, 93100 Montreuil, France.

KNUSSEN, (Stuart) Oliver, CBE; composer and conductor; b. 12 June 1952, Glasgow, Scotland; m. Susan Freedman 1972; one d. *Education:* Purcell School of Music; composition with John Lambert. *Career:* debut conducting Symphony No. 1, London Symphony Orchestra, 1968; Study with Günther Schuller, USA, 1970–73; Koussevitzky Centennial Commission, 1974; Composer-in-Residence, Aspen Festival 1976, Arnolfini Gallery 1978; Instructor in composition, Royal College of Music Junior Department, 1977–82; BBC commission, Proms (Symphony No. 3), 1979; Guest teacher, Berkshire Music Center, Tanglewood, USA, 1981; Co-ordinator of Contemporary music activities, Tanglewood, 1986–90; Associate Guest Conductor, BBC Symphony Orchestra, 1989–; Frequent guest conductor, London Sinfonietta, Phiharmonia Orchestra, numerous other ensembles, the United Kingdom and abroad, 1981–; Co-artistic director, Aldeburgh Festival, 1983–; Conducted Birtwistle's Punch and Judy for Netherlands Opera, 1993; London Proms 1999 with the BBC Symphony Orchestra (Horn Concerto) and London Sinfonietta (L. Andriessen's Trilogy of the Last Day); Conducted Where the Wild Thins Are and Higglety, Pigglety, Pop! at the London Proms, 2002; mem, Executive committee, Society for Promotion of New Music, 1978–85; Leopold Stowkowski Society; International Alban Berg Society, New York. *Compositions:* Symphony No. 1, 1966–67, No. 2, 1970–71, No. 3, 1973–79; Where the Wild Things Are, opera (Maurice Sendak), 1979–83; Numerous orchestral, chamber, vocal works, including Concerto for Orchestra 1968–70, 1974; Cantata for oboe and string trio 1977; Ocean de la Tenre for soprano and chamber ensemble 1972–73, 1976; Autumnal for violin and piano 1976–77; Four Late Poems and an Epigram of Rainer Maria Rilke for soprano 1988; Piano Variations 1989; Secret Song for solo violin 1990; Whitman Settings for soprano and orchestra, 1992; Horn Concerto, 1994; Organa for chamber orchestra, 1994; Prayer Bell Sketch for piano, 1997; Violin Concerto, 2002. *Recordings:* Contract with DGG from 1995 for 20th Century repertory and his own works. *Contributions:* Tempo, The Listener. *Honours:* Winner, 1st Park Lane Group composer award, 1982. *Current Management:* Harrison/Parrott Ltd, 12 Penzance Place, London, W11 4PA, England. *Telephone:* (20) 7229 9166. *Fax:* (20) 7221 5042. *Website:* www.harrisonparrott.com.

KNUTSON, David; Singer (Tenor); b. 19 March 1946, Wisconsin, USA. *Education:* Studied in Wisconsin. *Career:* Has sung in West Germany from 1971; Sang lyric roles at the Deutsche Oper Berlin from 1972; Guest appearances in Hamburg; Munich 1978, in the premiere of Lear by Reimann; Berlin 1975 and 1980, in the local premieres of La Calisto by Cavalli and Hippolyte et Aricie by Rameau; Spoleto Festival 1986, as the Witch in Hansel and Gretel; Sang Bishop Abdisu in Pfitzner's Palestrina, Berlin, 1996. *Recordings include:* Lear (Deutsche Grammophon). *Address:* c/o Deutsche Oper Berlin, Richard Wagner Strasse 10, 1000 Berlin, Germany.

KOBA, Jadviga; Singer (Soprano); b. 1948, Västerås, Sweden. *Education:* Studied in Stockholm. *Career:* Debut: Vadstena, 1970, in Falken by Mazzocchi; Sang at Oslo Opera, 1972–74, Värmlandsoperan in Sweden, 1975–79; Norrlandsoperan, 1975, as Zulma in L'Italiana in Algeri; Royal Opera, Stockholm, from 1979, as Micaela, Nedda in Pagliacci, Mimi, Tatiana, Tosca, Elisabeth in Tannhäuser and Monteverdi's Octavia; Other roles include Mozart's Bastien and Cherubino, and Mrs Grose in The Turn of the Screw; Season 1984–85 at Wisby in Petrus de Dacia by Mehler; Frequent concert appearances. *Address:* c/o Royal Opera, PO Box 16094, 10322 Stockholm, Sweden.

KOBAYASHI, Junko; Concert Pianist; b. Sept. 1960, Kobe, Japan. *Education:* Osaka College of Music; Essen Musik Hochschule, Germany; Studied with Maria Curcio and Louis Kentner. *Career:* Debut: Royal Festival Hall, London, 1988; The Purcell Room Recitals, 1983–93; St John's, Smith Square concerts 1995–2001; Appearances in England, Germany, France, Denmark, Bulgaria, Poland, Thailand, Canada, USA, Venezuela, Zambia and Japan; Played with orchestras such as the London Philharmonic Orchestra, the Osaka Philharmonic Orchestra, the New Philharmonic Orchestra, The Academy of St Nicholas, Polish Baltic Symphony Orchestra; Broadcasts on BBC Radio 3, WKAR Televion, USA, ZDF Television, Germany; mem, Founder-Chairman, Takemitsu Society, 1997–. *Contributions:* Essays to Kansai Music newspaper; Monthly music column for Pelican Club Europe. *Address:* 26 Sandown Road, West Malling, Kent ME19 6NS, England.

KOBAYASHI, Ken-Ichiro; Conductor; b. 9 April 1940, Fukushima, Japan. *Education:* University of Fine Arts and Music at Tokyo, 1960–64, notably with Akeo Watanabe. *Career:* Debut: Tokyo Symphony Orchestra, 1972; Music Director of the Metropolitan Symphony Orchestra, Tokyo, then Symphony Orchestra of Kyoto (1985–90); Principal Guest with the Tokyo Symphony and Professor at the Tokyo College of Music; Many appearances with European orchestras, notably the Amsterdam Philharmonic and other Dutch ensembles; Succeeded Janos Ferencsik as Permanent Conductor of the Hungarian National Philharmonic Orchestra, 1987. *Honours:* Prizewinner, International Competition Min-On, Tokyo, 1970; Budapest International Competi-

tion, 1974. *Address:* c/o Hungarian Philharmonic Orchestra, Vorosmarty ter. 1 1051 Budapest, Hungary.

KOBAYASHI, Marie; Singer (Mezzo-soprano); b. 31 Aug. 1955, Kamakura, Japan. *Education:* Arts and Music National University, Tokyo; National Conservatory of Music, Paris. *Career:* Debut: With 2E2M, International Contemporary Music Festival, Strasbourg, 1983; *Appearances:* C R Alsina's Prima Sinfonia, Radio France concert with National Orchestra of France, 1985; Satie's La Mort de Socrate, Radio France concert with Nouvel Orchestre Philharmonique, 1989; Smeton in Donizetti's Anna Bolena, Nimes, 1989; Birtwistle's Meridian with Pierre Boulez, Châtelet Theatre, 1990; J Fontyn's Roses des Sable, Radio Brussels (RTBF), 1991; Has sung in many concerts of oratorios by Bach, Handel, Rossini, Mozart, others. *Recordings:* Les Madrigaux of G Arrgo, 1990; Motets of Vivaldi, 1990; Mozart's Requiem, 1991. *Address:* 49 rue Riquet, Apt 2, 75019 Paris, France.

KOBEKIN, Vladimir; Composer; b. 22 July 1947, Sverdlovsk, Russia. *Education:* Studied with Sergei Slonimsky at the Leningrad Conservatory, graduating in 1971. *Career:* Teacher, Urals Conservatory, 1971–80. *Compositions include:* Swan Song, chamber opera after Chekhov, Moscow, 1980; Dairy of a Madman, mono-opera, Moscow 1980; The Boots, chamber opera, 1981; Pugachyov, musical tragedy, Leningrad, 1983; The Prophet, a Pushkin Triptych, Sverdlovsk 1984; Play about Maximilian, Eleanor and Ivan, Moscow, 1989; The Jester and the King, chamber opera, 1991; The Happy Prince, chamber opera after Wilde, 1991; A Tale of Witchcraft, opera, 1992; N.F.B., after The Idiot by Dostoyevsky, 1995; The Young David, opera, 1997; Moses, monodrama, 1999; Instrumental, choral and chamber music including Cello Concerto, 1997; Fantasia for piano and orchestra, 1999; The Seventh of September: Demons, symphonic poem, 1999. *Honours:* USSR State Prize, 1987, Honoured Artist of the RSFSR. *Address:* c/o RAO, Bolchaia Bronnai 6-a, Moscow 103670, Russia.

KOBEL, Benedikt; Singer (Tenor); b. 1960, Vienna, Austria. *Education:* Studied at the Vienna Musikhochschule and the Studio of the Staatsoper. *Career:* Sang in concert performances of Gurlitt's Wozzeck and Reimann's Gespenstersonate, Vienna 1985; Appearances throughout Austria and the Theater am Gärtnerplatz, Munich, in operettas by Lehar, Zeller, Oscar Straus and Johann Strauss; Vienna Volksoper 1991–92, as Don Ottavio, Camille in Dantons Tod, Tamino, Belmonte, Ferrando, Almaviva and Rinuccio; Vienna Staatsoper 1992, as Cassio in Otello and Narraboth, Flamand (Capriccio), Steuermann (Flying Dutchman). *Address:* c/o Volksoper, Wahringerstrasse 78, 1090 Vienna, Austria.

KOBILZA, Siegfried; Austrian classical guitarist; b. 24 Aug. 1954, Villach, Carinthia; m. Vera Kobilza-Schweder 1983. *Education:* Musisch-Padagogisches Realgymnasium, Hermagor, Academy of Music, Vienna, studied with Karl Scheit. *Career:* first concert tour, Austrian cities including Vienna, 1979; Recitals in main Austrian venues including Wiener Musikverein, Wiener Konzerthaus, Grosses Festspielhaus Salzburg, Mozarteum Salzburg, Brucknerhaus Linz; Soloist with orchestras including Vienna Symphony, Mozarteumorchester Salzburg, Vienna Chamber Orchestra; Television and radio recordings; Teaching master classes, various European countries and China; Debuts in London, Paris, New York, 1982; Concert tours, Germany, Switzerland, the United Kingdom, France, Netherlands, Iceland, Yugoslavia, Hungary, USA, USSR, Czechoslovakia, Turkey, Tunisia, China. *Address:* Servitengasse 7/16, 1090 Vienna, Austria.

KOBLER, Linda; Harpsichordist; b. 1952, New York City, USA; m. Albert Glinsky 10 June 1979. *Education:* BM, Peabody Conservatory of Music; MM, Juilliard School, 1977. *Career:* Debut: Carnegie Recital Hall, 1984; Concerto Soloist with: Zürich Chamber Orchestra, New York Chamber Orchestra, Broadway Bach Ensemble, American Baroque Ensemble, Bach Gesellschaft, Seabrook Chamber Players, Cathedral Orchestra, New York Chamber Symphony, Toronto Symphony; Former Member, Ensemble Tafelmusik Quartet; performances in New York, Ohio, New Jersey, California, Washington DC, South Carolina, Louisiana, including Philips Collection, Cleveland Institute, University of California, Carnegie Recital Hall, Merkin Concert Hall, Spoleto Festival, Town Hall, New York City, Metropolitan Museum of Art, Indianapolis, Early Music Festival, Smithsonian Institute; Performances in Switzerland and Germany; Radio appearances in USA; World premiere of works by Zwillich and Persichetti; Faculty, Juilliard School, 1989–96; Harpsichord coach to film star Gwyneth Paltrow, 1994; Commentator, National Public Radio programme, Performance Today, 1997. *Recordings:* Musical Heritage Society; Works of Christophe Moyreau and Pancrace Royer; Classic Masters; Works of Frescobaldi, Strozzi. *Contributions:* Encyclopaedia of the Keyboard. *Address:* 4201 Sassafras Street, Erie, PA 16508, USA.

KOC, Jozik; Singer (Baritone); b. 1968, Oxford, England. *Education:* Studied at York University and the Guildhall School, London. *Career:* Concerts and recitals throughout the United Kingdom, 1991–92, leading to Wigmore Hall debut 1993; Opera debut as Fiorello in Il Barbiere di Siviglia, and Guide in Death in Venice, for Glyndebourne Touring Opera; Spirit in Monteverdi's Orfeo for English National Opera, Purcell's Aeneas for Opera Factory and Prince Lindoro in Haydn's Pescatrici (Garsington Festival Opera, 1997); Other roles include Mozart's Don Giovanni, Count and Guglielmo, Sancho in Massenet's Don Quichotte, and Schaunard (La Bohème); Concert repertoire includes Bach's B minor Mass, Messiah, Rossini's Petite Messe and the Fauré Requiem; Appearances with the London and Royal Philharmonics, and the English Chamber Orchestra. *Recordings include:* Baroque Anthems. *Address:* Music International, 13 Ardilaun Road, London N5 2QR, England.

KOCH, Sophie; Singer (Mezzo-soprano); b. 19 Feb. 1969, Versailles, France. *Education:* Paris Conservatoire, with Jane Berbié. *Career:* Appearances throughout France, notably in Marseille, Strasbourg, and Théâtre du Châtelet, Paris; Season 1998–99 as Rossini's Rosina and Mozart's Dorabella with the Royal Opera in London; Zerlina at the Schwetzingen Festival, in Monteverdi's Orfeo at the Vienna Festival, the Prince in Massenet's Cendrillon at Geneva, and Mercédès (Carmen) at the Opéra Bastille, Paris; Composer in Ariadne auf Naxos at Dresden and Zerlina in Munich, Season 1999–2000 with Cherubino and Octavian at the Vienna Staatsoper and the Composer at La Scala; other roles include Sextus in La Clemenza di Tito, Silla in Pfitzner's Palestrina and Cenerentola, all with the Royal Opera at Covent Garden, 2000–01; Mozart's Cherubino in Brussels and Paris, and on tour with the Bavarian State Opera to Japan; Engagements until 2005 include Siebel and the Composer at Covent Garden, and Octavian on tour with the Vienna State to Israel; Concerts include Beethoven's Missa Solemnis and Elgar's Sea Pictures. *Address:* c/o MusicaGlotz, 11, rue le Verrier, 75006 Paris, France.

KOCMIEROSKI, Matthew; Percussionist, Conductor, Historian and Educator; b. 18 Aug. 1953, Roslyn, New York, USA; m. Elaine S Schmidt, 28 Dec 1974. *Education:* Nassau Community College, 1971–74; Mannes College of Music, 1974–77. *Career:* Marimba concertos performed with: Atlantic Wind Symphony, New York, Broadway Chamber Symphony, Thalia Chamber Symphony, Seattle, Philharmonia Northwest, Midsummer Musical Retreat Festival Orchestra and The Bainbridge Orchestra; Numerous concerto and recital appearances in the Pacific North West; Chamber music performances include: New Music America, Seattle Chamber Music Festival, Bergen International Festival, Goodwill Arts Festival, Seattle Spring Festival of Contemporary Music; Aeolian Chamber Players, Seattle Chamber Players; Freelance performances with Martha Graham Dance Company, Seattle Symphony, Seattle Opera, Bolshoi Ballet, Joffrey Ballet, Northwest Chamber Orchestra; Instructor of Percussion and Music History, Classical New Music Programme, Cornish College of The Arts, Seattle; Member, New Performance Group, 1981–96; Artistic Director, New Performance Group, Seattle, beginning with the 1984–85 season; Principal Percussionist, Pacific Northwest Ballet Orchestra; Founding Member, Pacific Rims Percussion Quartet, 1995–. *Recordings:* Paul Dresher's Night Songs, 1984; Atlas Eclipticalis, John Cage conducting, 1986. *Address:* 12724 19th Avenue NE, Seattle, WA 98125, USA.

KOCSAR, Miklós; Composer; b. 21 Dec. 1933, Debrecen, Hungary. *Education:* Studied with Farkas at the Budapest Academy of Music, 1954–59. *Career:* Teacher, Béla Bart ók Conservatory, Budapest, 1972–; Deputy Head of Music, Hungarian Radio, 1983–. *Compositions:* Horn concerto, 1957; Capriccio for orchestra, 1961; Solitary song for soprano and chamber ensemble, 1969; Variations for orchestra, 1977; Capricorn concerto for flute and chamber orchestra, 1978; Metamophoses for orchestra, 1979; Sequenze for strings, 1980; Elegia for bassoon and chamber ensemble, 1985; Formazioni for orchestra, 1986; Visions of the Night, oratorio for mezzo-soprano solo, mixed choir and orchestra, 1987; Concerto for violoncello and orchestra, 1994; Choral music including I will invoke you, Demon, 1985; Missa in A for equal voices, 1991; Chamber: Wind Quintet, 1959; Brass Trio, 1959; Variziioni for woodwind quintet, 1968; Sestetto d'ottoni, 1972; 7 Variations for viola, 1983; Wind Quintet, No. 3, 1984; Quintetto d'ottoni, 1986; Rhapsody for Trombone, piano and percussion, 1989; Trio for strings, 1990; Music for 4 Trombones and Percussion, 1991; Songs and piano pieces; The Fire of St Anthony for orchestra, 1992; Salve Regina for voices and orchestra, 1995; Notturno for piano, 1996; Magnificat, 1996; Missa Seconde, 1997. *Honours:* Erkel Prize, 1973, 1980; Merited Artist of the Hungarian People's Republic, 1987; Merited Artist of the Hungarian People's Republic, 1987; Bart ók-Pasztory Award, 1992. *Address:* Artisjus, PO Box 593, 1538 Budapest, Hungary.

KOCSIS, Zoltán; Pianist, Composer and Conductor; b. 30 May 1952, Budapest, Hungary; m. Erika Toth, 1998. *Education:* Béla Bart ók Conservatory, Budapest, 1964–68; Ferenc Liszt Academy of Music, Budapest, 1968–73. *Career:* Debut: 1970; US debut 1971, London and Salzburg, 1972; Often heard in Bach and Bart ók; in 1988 he played Bart ók's 2nd Piano Concerto at the Royal Festival Hall, London; Co-founder

and Artistic Director of Budapest Festival Orchestra, 1983–96; Music Director of the Hungarian National Philharmonic Orchestra. *Compositions:* Premiere, String Ensemble; 33 December, Chamber Ensemble; The Last But One Encounter, for piano or harpsichord; Transcriptions and arrangements for piano and two pianos. *Recordings:* For numerous labels, including all Bach's concertos, Bartók's Concertos Nos 1 and 2. *Contributions:* Mozgó Világ (Budapest) Music Section, 1982–83; Holmi (Budapest), 1989–. *Honours:* Liszt Prize, 1973; Kossuth Prize, 1978; Merited Artist, 1984. *Current Management:* IMG Artists, London. *Address:* Riugló u. 60/A, Budapest 1116, Hungary.

KODALLI, Yelda; Opera Singer (Soprano); b. 20 Oct. 1968, Turkey; m. *Education:* Hacettepe University, Ankara State Conservatory, 1990; Instructed by Professor Mustafa Yurdakul. *Career:* Debut: ORF Austrian television, 1991; Vienna State Opera, 1992; Zauberflöte, Reykjavík, 1991; Performed in Vienna at Staatsoper and at Volksoper, Mannheim, Essen, Düsseldorf; Opéra Bastille, Paris; Munich Staatsoper; Strasbourg Festival; Schönbrunn Festival; La Scala; Hamburg and Wiener Staatsoper; Lyric Opera of Chicago; In Vienna in Hansel and Gretel, Arabella, Capriccio, Zauberflöte and Siegfried; New production of Zauberflöte, Teatro Regio, Turin, 1994; Lucia di Lammermoor, Teatro Carlo Felice, Genoa; Sang in Japan, Tel-Aviv and Haifa; Opened La Zarzuela Theatre of Madrid in Stravinsky's Le Rossignol, 1995; Sang Gilda in Rigoletto in Japan, RAI orchestra of Turin; Sang in concerts in Ankara and Istanbul, Zürich and Basel; On tour with the Orchestra della Toscana; Performed Luciano Berio's Outis, La Scala; I Puritani, Tenerife; Christmas Concert, ABAO, Bilbao; Zauberflöte, Vienna. *Recordings:* CD, Constanze in Mozart's Die Entführung aus dem Serail with the Scottish Chamber Orchestra conducted by Charles Mackerras; Film: Mozart in Turkey at the Topkapi Palace in Istanbul, directed by Elijah Moshinsky. *Publications:* Musica Viva, Lucia, Franca Cella, 1994. *Contributions:* La Stampa, 1994; Opera International Herald Tribune, 1996; Readers Sun Times, 1996; L'Opera TAA The Best Vocal of the Year, 1996. *Current Management:* Europe: Mario Dradi; America: Herbert Breslin. *Address:* Wiedner Gurtel No. 48, 3-15 1040 Vienna, Austria.

KODOMA, Momo; Concert Pianist; b. 1972, Japan. *Career:* Concerts with Seiji Ozawa with the new Japanese Philharmonic, and with Boston Symphony Orchestra, 2000; Further concerts with Kent Nagano, Eliaha Inbal, Bernard Klee, Gerard Schwarz and Charles Dutoit, re-engaged for season 2000; Orchestras include Berlin Radio, Bayerische Rundfunk, Strasbourg Philharmonic and the Hallé; All major Japanese orchestras; Wigmore Hall recital debut, 1999, with Chopin, Ravel and Messiaen; Festival engagements at Davos, 1999–2000, Berlin and Lucerne; Mostly Mozart and Marlboro, USA and Enescu Festivals; Further recitals at the Paris Châtelet and Tonhalle, Zürich; Repertory includes Messiaen's Vingt regards sur l'enfant Jésus. *Address:* c/o Kathryn Naish, IMG Artists, Lovell House, 616 Chiswick High Road, London W4 5RX, England.

KOEHNE, Graeme (John); Composer and University Lecturer; b. 1956, Adelaide, South Australia. *Education:* BMus, 1st class honours, MMus, University of Adelaide; Studied composition with Richard Meale, Tristam Cary and Bernard Rands; Composition under Virgil Thomson and Louis Andriessen, School of Music, Yale University, USA. *Career:* Appointed Tutor in Piano and Composition, University of New England, Armidale, New South Wales, 1978; Collaborated with choreographer Graeme Murphy and Sydney Dance Orchestra; Commissions, Australian Bicentenary, West Australian Ballet Company, Queensland Ballet Company, Australian Chamber Orchestra, Seymour Group (Sydney), Australian Ballet; Lecturer in Composition, University of Adelaide. *Compositions:* Orchestral: The Iridian Plateau, 1979; First Blue Hours, 1979; Toccata, 1981; Fanfare, 1981; Rain Forest, 1981; riverrun.., 1982; Once Around the Sun, 1988; Unchained Melody, 1991; Powerhouse, 1993; Elevator Music, 1997; Ballet Suite from The Selfish Giant, 1985; Capriccio for Piano and Strings, 1987; Ensemble: Sextet, 1975; Cantilene, 1978; Crystal Islands, 1982; Divertissement Trois Pièces Bourgeoises, string quartet, 1983; Ricecare and Burletta, string trio, 1984; Miniature, 1985; String Quartet No. 2; Shaker Dances, 1995; Voice and ensemble: Cancion, text F Garcia Lorca, 1975; Fourth Sonnet, text S Mallarmé, Suite, 1984; Nearly Beloved, 1986; Nocturnes, 1987; Keyboard Music: Piano Sonata, 1976; Harmonies in Silver and Blue, piano, 1977; Twilight Rain, piano, 1979; Gothic Toccata, 1984 (aka Toccata Aurora). *Address:* c/o Boosey & Hawkes (Australia) Pty Ltd, Unit 12/6 (PO Box 188), Artarmon, NSW 2064, Australia.

KOERPPEN, Alfred; Composer; b. 16 Dec. 1926, Wiesbaden, Germany. *Education:* Education. Studied with Kurt Thomas in Frankfurt. *Career:* Professor, Staatliche Hochschule für Musik und Theater, Hanover, 1964–91. *Compositions include:* Virgilius der Magier von Rome, opera, 1951; Der Turmbauzu Babel, oratorio, 1951; Das Feuer des Prometheus, oratorio, 1956; 17 Choralfantasien und Partiten, for organ, 1948–90; Wassermarken for soprano, tenor and string quartet, 1961; Joseph und seine Brüder, for female chorus and speakers, 1967; Arachne, ballet,

1968; Parabel vom Dornbusch, for mixed chorus and ensemble, 1969; Das Stadtwappen for solo voices, chorus and orchestra, 1973; Konzert im Dreieck, 1974; Donum Kinguarum, for 3 solo voices and chours, 1976; Ein Abenteuer auf dem Friedhof, chamber opera, 1980; Symphony, 1985; ECHO for solo voices and three chourses, 1985; Trio in zwei Sätzen for violin, cello and piano, 1986; Jona for chorus and organ, 1995; Abgesang for violin and orchestra 1995; Concerto for bass tuba and orchestra, 1998. *Honours:* Low Saxony Prize for culture, 1983. *Address:* German Music Information Centre, Weberstrasse 59, 53113 Bonn, Germany.

KOETSIER, Jan; Composer and Conductor; b. 14 Aug. 1911, Amsterdam, Netherlands; m. Margarete Trampe. *Education:* Academy of Music, Berlin. *Career:* Debut: As Composer and Conductor, Concertgebouw, Amsterdam, 1937; Second Conductor, Concertgebouw Orchestra, 1942–48; Conductor, Residentieorkest, The Hague, 1949–50; Conductor, Bavarian Radio Symphony Orchestra, Munich, 1950–66; Professor, Musikhochschule, Munich, 1966–76. *Compositions include:* 3 Symphonies; Orchestral Works; The Man Lot, cantata for Soli, Men's Choir and Orchestra; Concert Rondo for piano and strings, 1991; Opera, Frans Hal; Chamber Music; Various Solo Concertos with Orchestra; Piano Music; Lieder. *Recordings:* Petite Suite; Brass Quintet; Partita for English Horn and Organ; Concerto for Trumpet, Trombone and Orchestra; Brass Symphony; Die Abreise by D'Albert, reissued 1998. *Current Management:* Donemus, Paulus Potterstraat 14, Amsterdam, Netherlands. *Address:* Florianhaus, Unterkagn, 84431 Heldenstein, Germany.

KOFRON, Petr; Composer; b. 15 Aug. 1955, Prague, Czechoslovakia. *Education:* Janacek Academy Brno, 1974–79. *Career:* Founder and Director, Agon Orchestra, 1983–; Co-founder, Czech Society for New Music; Editor, Konzerva/Na Hudbu, music journal, 1989–. *Compositions include:* In Memoira I.O Dunayevsky, for speaker and brass quintet, 1975; Farewell Waltz, for orchestra, 1977; The Bow, for orchestra, 1979–81; String Quartet, 1982; For Soprano and Orchestra, after Georg Trakl, 1982; E.S.T. concerto for piano and ensemble, 1988; Liber LXXII, for 2 orchestras and tape, 1988; Alpha and Centaur, for violin and ensemble, 1989; Spira, for clarinet and ensemble, 1990; Enhexe, ensemble, 1991; The Golden Fern, opera, 1991; The Fire is Mine, for ensemble and electronics, 1993; Abram for 8 instruments, 1994; Tworl, string quartet, 1994; Big Dipper, for ensemble, 1996. *Publications include:* Graphic Scores and Concepts, 1996. *Address:* c/o Music Information Centre, Besedne 3, 11800 Prague 1, Czech Republic.

KOGAN, Lev, MA; composer and pianist; b. 6 March 1927, Baku, USSR; m. Ethel Kovensky 1969; two d. *Education:* Aram Khatchaturian diploma in piano composition. *Career:* Conservatory Teacher of Music Composition, Theory of Music, Moscow State Conservatory 1946–52; mem. League of Composers of the USSR and Israel. *Compositions:* 160 works; four ballets performed in the USSR; six musicals; 54 compositions for theatre; music for cinema and television; Jewish songs. *Recordings include:* Hassidic Music; 11 albums; six song collection albums 1958–99; ballet score 1960. *Honours:* Honoured Musician of the USSR; Recipient of the Prize of the Jewish Song Festival; Israel Acum Prize. *Address:* 55/9 Rubinstein Street, Jaffa D, Tel-Aviv, Jaffa 68212, Israel.

KOGAN, Semjon; Conductor; b. 24 April 1928, Bobruisk, Ukraine. *Education:* Studied violin and conducting at the St Petersburg Conservatoire. *Career:* Founded the State Symphony Orchestra at Omsk; Artistic Director, Rostov State Symphony Orchestra, 1976, participating in the 1990 Tchaikovsky International Competition, Moscow; Guest appearances with the USSR State Symphony, Moscow Philharmonic, Moscow Radio and St Petersburg Philharmonic Orchestras and invitations to conduct in Poland, Czechoslovakia and Germany; Repertoire includes Stravinsky and Shostakovich in addition to the standard repertoire; Has given the premieres of works by Denisov, Shchedrin and Khrennikov; Professor, Rostov on Don Conservatoire; Founded Rostov Conservatoire Orchestra, 1993. *Recordings:* With the Rostov Symphony Orchestra. *Current Management:* Sonata, Glasgow, Scotland. *Address:* 11 Northpark Street. Glasgow G20 7AA, Scotland.

KOHN, Karl-Christian; Singer (Bass); b. 21 May 1928, Losheim, Saarbrucken, Germany. *Education:* Studied with Irene Eden at the Musikhochschule Saarbrucken. *Career:* Sang at the Deutsche Oper am Rhein, Düsseldorf, 1954–57; St ädtische Oper Berlin, 1956–58; Sang the title role in Le nozze di Figaro, at the reopening of the Cuvillies-Theater Munich, 1958; Member of the Bayerische Staatsoper Munich from 1958, notably in the 1963 premiere of Die Verlobung in San Domingo by Egk; Schwetzingen Festival, 1961, in the premiere of Elegie für junge Liebende by Henze; Guest appearances in Hamburg, Vienna, Berlin and elsewhere in Europe; Other roles included Mozart's Osmin, Sarastro and Commendatore. *Recordings:* Der Freischütz, Don Giovanni, Oedipus der Tyrann by Orff; Arabella, Doktor Faust, Don Giovanni, Wozzeck, Cardillac by Hindemith (Deutsche Grammophon); Bach's

Christmas Oratorio. *Address:* c/o Bayerische Staatsoper, Postfach 745, 8000 Munich 1, Germany.

KOHN, Karl George; Pianist, Conductor and Composer; b. 1 Aug. 1926, Vienna, Austria; m. Margaret Case Sherman, 23 June 1950, 2 d. *Education:* Certificate, New York College of Music, 1944; BA, 1950, MA, 1955, Harvard University; Studied piano with Werschinger, conducting with Prüwer and composition with Piston, Ballantine, Fine and Thompson. *Career:* Instructor in Music, 1950–54, Assistant Professor, 1954–59, Associate Professor, 1959–65, Professor, 1965–85, William M Keck Distinguished Service Professor, 1985–95 now Professor Emeritus, Pomona College, Claremont, California; Teaching Fellow, Harvard University, 1954–55; Teacher, Berkshire Music Center, Tanglewood, summers 1954, 1955, 1957; Appearances as Pianist and Conductor. *Compositions include:* Orchestral: Sinfonia concertante for Piano and Orchestra, 1951; Castles and Kings, suite, 1958; Concerto mutabile for Piano and Orchestra, 1962; Episodes for Piano and Orchestra, 1966; Interlude ll for Piano and String Orchestra, 1969; Centone for Orchestra, 1973; The Prophet Bird l, 1976; Time Irretrievable, 1983; Lions on a Banner, Seven Sufi Texts for Soprano Solo, Chorus and Orchestra, 1988; Ode for String Orchestra, 1991; Concert Music for String Orchestra, 1993; End Piece for Chamber Ensemble, 1993; Ternaries for Flute and Piano, 1993; Middle Piece for Chamber Ensemble, 1994; Chamber Music: Encounters I–VI for various instrumental combinations; Choral Works, Songs, Piano pieces and Organ music; Reconnaissance for large chamber ensemble, 1995; Memory and Hope: Essay for Orchestra, 1996; Sax for 4, for saxophone quartet, 1996; More Reflections for clarinet and piano, 1997; Tripartita for vihuela and guitar, 1998; Number Play for two pianos, 1999; Trio, 2K for violin, cello and piano, 1999; Again, Again, for two pianos, 2000; Prelude for organ, 2000; Night Music for six guitars, 2000; Violaria for viola and piano, 2000; Night Music 2 for six guitars, 2000; After 09/11/01 for piano; November Piece for piano, 2001; Return – Symphonic Essay, transcribed for 2 pianos, 2001; Grand Fantasy for organ, 2002; Fourth Rhapsody for piano, 2003; Three Proverbs for chorus of mixed voices, a cappella, 2003; Sonata for cello and piano, 2003. *Publications:* End Piece, 1994; Ternaries, 1995; Set of Three, 1996; Reconnaissance, 1997. *Address:* 674 West 10th Street, Claremont, CA 91711, USA. *E-mail:* Kkohn@pomona.edu.

KOHONEN, Jyrrki; Singer (bass); b. 1965, Finland. *Education:* Sibelius Academy, Helsinki, with Tom Krause, Opera Studio of Zürich Opera. *Career:* Appearances with Finnish National Opera from 1994, as Mozart's Bartolo, Colline in La Bohème and Fafner in The Ring; Savonlinna Festival 1994, as Gremin and Banquo; Darmstadt Opera as Mozart's Osmin, Lord Plunkett in Martha, Raimondo, Sarastro and the Landgrave in Tannhäuser; Engagements at Cagliari in Wagner's Die Feen and at Bayreuth in Die Meistersinger; Season 2000–2001 in Beethoven's 9th and Mahler's 8th Symphonies under Riccardo Chailly, Rocco in Fidelio at Pisa and Truffaldino in Ariadne auf Naxos under Simon Rattle; Bayreuth 2001, in Lohengrin. *Current Management:* Athole Still International Management, Forresters Hall, 25–27 Westow Street, London, SE19 3RY, England. *Telephone:* (20) 8771-5271. *Fax:* (20) 8768-6600. *Website:* www.atholestill.com.

KOHOUTEK, Ctirad; Composer and Theorist; b. 18 March 1929, Zábřeh na Moravě, Czechoslovakia; m. Jarmila Chlebníčková, 8 July 1953, 1 s., 2 d. *Education:* Composition, Brno Conservatory, 1948–49; Janáček Academy of Music Arts, 1949–53; PhD, Palacký University, Olomouc, 1973; CSc, Masaryk University, Brno, 1980. *Career:* Debut: First performance of symphonic poem Mnichov (Munich), 1953; Junior, Composition, 1953–59, Fellow, Composition, 1959–65, Senior Lecturer, Composition, Theory of Composition, 1965–80, Janáček Academy of Music Arts, Brno; Professor of Composition, Academy of Music Arts, Prague, 1980–90; Artistic Director, Czech Philharmonic, Prague, 1980–87; Full-time Composer, occasional Theorist and Pedagogue; mem., Asscn of Music Artists and Scientists, Prague; Club of Moravian Composers, Brno, 1992–. *Compositions include:* String Quartet, 1959; Concertino, violoncello, chamber orchestra, 1964; Rapsodia eroica, organ, 1965; Inventions, piano, 1965; Miniatures, 4 French horns, 1965; Memento, concerto for percussion and wind instruments, 1966; Teatro del mondo, large orchestra (Janáček Prize, Brno, 1975), 1969; Panteon, orchestra (Janàček Prize, Brno, 1975), 1970; Festive Prologue, large symphony orchestra, 1971; Celebration of Light, large orchestra, 1975; Symphonic Actualities, orchestra, 1976–78; Tissues of Time, bass clarinet, piano, 1977; Minutes of Spring, wind quintet, 1980; Omaggio a vita, orchestra, 1989; About Cockerel and Little Hen, children's opera, 1989; Motifs of Summer, violin, violoncello, piano, 1990; Funs and Smiles, oboe, clarinet, bassoon, 1991; Winter Silences, brass, percussion, 1993; The Little Peach, mixed choir, piano, percussion, to text by Josef Kainar (1st Prize Jihlava, 1994), 1993; Autumn Songs, 2nd string quartet, 1995; The Water Metamorphoses, 4 flutes, 1996; L'unica speranza (The Only Hope), orchestra, 1997; Opposite Poles, 2 trumpets, 1998–99; The Magic of Wood, violin, piano, 1999–2000; Numerous pieces for choirs. *Publications include:* Modern Trends in Music Composition, 1965; Project Music Composition, 1969; Musical Styles from the Composer's Viewpoint, 1976; Music Composition, 1989. *Honours:* Music Critics' Prize for Memento, Paris, 1967. *Address:* Helfertova 40, 613 00 Brno, Czech Republic. *Telephone:* (545) 573021. *E-mail:* c.kohoutek@tiscali.cz. *Website:* www.musica.cz/comp/kohoutek.htm.

KOITO, Kei; Concert Organist, Composer and Professor; b. 4 Jan. 1950, Kyoto, Japan. *Education:* Studied organ, philosophy, musical aesthetics and psychology at Tokyo School of Fine Arts; Studied organ with Pierre Segond at the Geneva Conservatory, Analysis, orchestration and composition with Eric Gaudibert; Associated with electro-acoustic studios; Private study of organ with L F Tagliavani, Xavier Darasse and Reinhard Goebel. *Career:* Debut: Solo recitalist at Victoria Hall, Geneva, Maurice Ravel Auditorium, Lyons; Soloist with symphonic and chamber orchestras, regularly performing at festivals and on radio and television; Since 1978 has performed over 80 new works for organ, premiering a large number written especially for her; Professor of Organ at the Conservatoire in Lausanne; Adjudicator, guest lecturer and masterclasses in USA, Europe and Asia. *Compositions include:* Les Tours Du Silence for Narrator and Chamber Ensemble; Labryrinthe Dynamique for Brass Ensemble; Orestes-Stasimon for Choir; Esquisse Alpha for 2 Pianos; Wenn Aus Der Ferne for Organ; Splendid Rotation for 2 Amplified Harpsichords; In Step for String Quartet; Poème Pulvérisé for Voice and Percussion; Meta-Matic No. 22 for Tape. *Recordings:* 6 Trio Sonatas, 5 Concertos, Canonic Variations of JS Bach; Sonatas of CPE Bach and contemporary organ music. *Current Management:* Europe General: Camille Kiesgen, Bureau International de Concerts et de Conférences, Faubourg Saint-Honoré 252, 75008 Paris, France. *Address:* c/o Conservatoire de Musique de Lausanne, 6 rue du Midi, CH–1002 Lausanne, Switzerland.

KOIZUMI, Kazuhiro; Conductor and Music Director; b. 16 Oct. 1949, Japan; m. Masami. *Education:* University of The Arts, Tokyo; Hochschule für Musik, Berlin; Worked with Seiji Ozawa for 2 years. *Career:* Assistant Conductor, Japan Philharmonic, 1970–72; Music Director, New Japan Philharmonic, 1975–80, Winnipeg Symphony Orchestra, 1983–; Chief Conductor, Tokyo Metropolitan Orchestra, 1984–; Guest Conductor, Berlin Philharmonic, Chicago Symphony, National Orchestra of France, Royal Philharmonic, Vienna Philharmonic, Toronto Symphony, Tokyo Metropolitan, Kyoto Symphony, Nagoyo Symphony, Montreal Symphony, RAI in Naples and Munich Philharmonic; Adviser, Manitoba Conservatory of Music and Arts. *Recordings:* Lalo Concerto Russe/Concerto in F with Radio France, Decca label; Tchaikovsky, Kodály, Dvořák with WSO. *Honours:* First Prize, 2nd International Conductors Competition (MIN-ONO, 1970); First Prize, von Karajan Competition, 1972; Grand Prix du Disque. *Current Management:* Columbia Artists Management Inc. *Address:* c/o Columbia Artists Management Inc, New York, USA.

KOK, Nicholas; Conductor; b. 1962, England. *Education:* Organ Scholar at New College, Oxford; Royal College of Music as Repetiteur. *Career:* Music Staff of English National Opera from 1989–93; Music Adviser to Contemporary Opera Studio; Has conducted for English National Opera, The Return of Ulysses, The Marriage of Figaro, Così fan tutte and King Priam; The Fairy Queen, (Purcell) and Così fan tutte in 1995 and Orfeo in 1996; For English National Opera Bayliss Programmes he conducted Arion and the Dolphin, a new commission by Alec Roth; For Almeida Opera, Mario and The Magician by Stephen Oliver and A Family Affair, a new commission by Julian Grant; He has conducted Cosi fan tutte, The Coronation of Poppea, Reimann's The Ghost Sonata, Xenakis's The Bacchae and Nigel Osborne's Sarajevo for Opera Factory, London; For Opera Factory Zürich, Marschner's Der Vampyr in his own version for chamber orchestra and Cavalli's La Calisto; Further engagements with Opera Factory London include Dido and Aeneas and Britten's Curlew River; Other operatic engagements have included Don Giovanni for English Touring Opera, The Barber of Seville for Dublin Grand Opera, Gerald Barry's The Intelligence Park for the Almeida Festival/Opera Factory and Trois Operas Minutes by Milhaud and The Judgement of Paris by Eccles for Trinity College of Music; Has also worked with Scottish Opera, Philharmonia, Ulster Orchestra, London Sinfonietta; Scottish Chamber Orchestra; Royal Scottish National Orchestra; Bournemouth Sinfonietta; Endymion Ensemble; Almeida Ensemble; Cambridge University Chamber Orchestra; London Pro Arte Orchestra and the Philippines Philharmonic Orchestra; A number of Choral Societies; BBC engagements include The Soldier's Tale, The Carnival of the Animals, Reginald Smith Brindle's Journey Towards Infinity, Mondrial by Erollyn Wallen and several television and radio plays; The Marriage of Figaro for English National Opera, 1997. *Honours:* Countess of Munster Award and Lofthouse Memorial Prize. *Address:* Allied Artists, 42 Montpelier Square, London SW7 1JZ, England.

KOKKOS, Yannis; stage director and stage designer; b. 1944, Athens, Greece. *Education:* National Theatre of Strasbourg. *Career:* has created designs for sets and costumes for productions of Macbeth, Lohengrin and Reimann's Lear at Paris Opéra Garnier, Pelléas et Mélisande at La Scala and the Vienna Staatsoper, Don Carlos at Bologna and Elektra at Geneva and San Francisco; Directed the Oresteia by Xenakis in Sicily; Directed and designed Boris Godunov in Bologna and Opéra Bastille, Paris, Ariane et Barbe Bleue in Geneva, La Damnation de Faust at the Théâtre du Châtelet, Paris, Nancy Opéra with Death in Venice, Festival d'Orange with Carmen, Tosca and Don Giovanni, Welsh National Opera and Scottish Opera with Tristan und Isolde, 1993, and Opera de Bordeaux with Salome; Pelléas et Mélisande and Tristan seen at Covent Garden, 1993; Norma, Opéra Bastille, Paris, 1996; Alceste, Scottish Opera, 1996; Tristes Tropiques by Aperghis, world premiere with Opéra Strasbourg, 1996; Elektra, Opéra de Lyon, 1997; Clemenza di Tito, Welsh National Opera, 1997; Hänsel and Gretel, Châtelet, Paris, 1997; Queen of Spades for Scottish Opera and Götterdämmerung at the Teatro Alla Scala, Milan, 1998; Outis, Luciano Berio, Châtelet, Paris, 1999; Pelléas et Mélisande in Bordeaux, 2000; Fliegende Holländer in Bologna, 2000; L'Orestie, Epidaure, 2001; Iphigénie en Avlide, La Scala, Milan, 2002; Phaedra, Dido and Aeneas, Opéra de Nancy, 2003; Les Troyens, Châtelet, Paris, 2003. *Publications:* Yannis Kokkos, Le Hèron et le Scénographe, 1989. *Honours:* Commandeur des Arts et Lettres, France; Medaille d'or, Quadriennale of Prague, 1987; Laurence Olivier Award, 1997. *Address:* 7 rue Bourdaloue, 75009 Paris, France.

KOLB, Barbara; Composer; b. 10 Feb. 1939, Hartford, Connecticut, USA. *Education:* Studied at the Hartt College of Music, MM 1964 and with Lukas Foss and Gunther Schuller at the Berkshire Music Center. *Career:* Played clarinet in the Hartford Symphony Orchestra 1960–66; Composer-in-Residence at the Marlboro Music Festival, 1973, and at the American Academy in Rome, 1975; Taught theory and composition at Brooklyn College and Temple University; Artistic Director of Music New to New York at the Third Street Music School Settlement, 1979. *Compositions:* Rebuttal for 2 clarinets 1964; Chanson bas for voice, harp and percussion 1965; Three Place Settings for narrator and ensemble, 1968; Trobar clus for 13 instruments 1970; Soundings for 11 instruments and tape 1972 (version for orchestra 1975 and 1977); Frailities for tenor, tape and orchestra, 1971; Spring, River, Flowers, Moon, Night for 2 pianos and tape, 1975; Appello for piano 1976; Musique pour un vernissage for ensemble 1977 (concert version 1979); Songs before an Adieu for flute, guitar and voice 1979; Chromatic Fantasy for narrator and ensemble 1979; 3 Lullabies for guitar 1980; Related Characters for viola and piano 1980; Related Characters for viola and piano 1980; The Point that Divides the Wind for organ and 4 percussionists 1981; Cantico, film score 1982; Millefoglie for ensemble and computer-generated sound, 1985; Time... and Again for oboe, string quartet and tape, 1985; Umbrian Colours for violin and guitar 1986; Yet that things go Round for Chamber Orchestra, 1986–88; Molto Allegra for guitar 1988; The Enchanted Loom for orchestra 1988–89; Extremes for flute and cello, 1989; Voyants for piano and chamber orchestra, 1991; Clouds for organ and piano, recorded tape, 1992; All in Good Time for orchestra, 1993; In Memory of David Huntley, string quartet, 1994; New York Moonglow for ensemble, 1995; Sidebars for bassoon and piano, 1996. *Honours:* Rome Prize 1969–71; Fulbright Scholarship 1966–67; MacDowell Colony and Guggenheim Fellowships; Grants from the Ford Foundation and the National Endowment for the Arts (1972–79). *Address:* Boosey & Hawkes Ltd (promotion), 295 Regent Street, London W1R 8JH, England.

KOLLO, René; Opera Singer (Tenor); b. 20 Nov. 1937, Berlin, Germany; m. (1) Dorthe Larsen, 1967 (2) Beatrice Bouquet, 1982, 1d. *Career:* Began with Staatstheater, Brunswick, 1965; First Tenor, Deutsche Oper am Rhein, 1967–71; Guest appearances with numerous leading opera companies, and at annual Bayreuth Wagner Festival, from 1969; Performances include: The Flying Dutchman, 1969, 1970, Lohengrin, 1971, Die Meistersinger von Nurnberg, 1973, 1974, Parsifal, 1975, Siegfried, 1976, 1977; Tristan (Zürich), 1980, (Bayreuth 1981); Covent Garden debut 1976, as Siegmund in Die Walküre; Metropolitan Opera debut, 1976, Lohengrin; Sang Otello at Frankfurt, 1988; Returned to Covent Garden 1989, as Siegmund in a new production of Die Walküre conducted by Bernard Haitink; Young Siegfried 1990; Sang Tannhäuser at Hamburg 1990, and as Walther in Die Meistersinger; Season 1991–92 as Peter Grimes at Munich, Tannhäuser at the Deutsche Oper Berlin and in Barcelona; Sang Tannhäuser at the Deutsche Oper, Berlin, 1995; Season 2000–01 as Tristan at the Deutsche Oper Berlin and as Offenbach's Jupiter at Trier. *Recordings include:* Tannhäuser from Munich, directed by David Alden (DVD). *Address:* Opéra et Concert, 1 rue Volney, F–75002 Paris, France.

KOLLY, Karl-Andreas; Pianist; b. 26 May 1965, Switzerland. *Education:* Music Academy, Zürich, 1988; Studied with Karl Engel and Mieczyslaw Horszowski. *Career:* Debut: Grieg Piano Concerto at Zürich, 1982; Concerto as soloist and chamber musician all over Europe, USA, Japan and Australia; Several radio and television programmes in Switzerland, Germany, Spain and Czech Republic, 1991; Professor, Hochschule für

Musik, Zürich, 1991–. *Recordings:* CDs of Schumann piano works including Symphonic Etudes; Brahms, the Piano Trios, with Trio Novanta; The Piano Concertos of Skriabin, Glazunov, d'Albert, Wellesz, Schmidt; Liszt/Bach: The Complete Piano Transcription. *Honours:* First Prize, Jecklin Competition, 1975; University Competition of Zürich, 1988; Young Musicians Competition, Union of Swiss Banks, 1990; Tschumi prize for best soloist diploma of the year, 1991; Prix Maurice Sandoz, 1990. *Address:* Rosenrain 12, 8400 Winterthur, Switzerland. *Telephone:* 522133220. *Fax:* 522133220.

KOLOMYJEC, Joanne; Singer (soprano); b. 1955, Canada. *Career:* appearances in concert and opera throughout Canada, the USA and England 1983–; opera roles include the Countess and Susanna in Le Nozze di Figaro, Donna Elvira and Donna Anna in Don Giovanni, Fiordiligi in Cosi fan Tutti, Tatiana in Eugene Onegin, the title roles in Tosca and Jenůfa, Marguerite in Faust, Magda Sorel in The Consul, Violetta in La Traviata, Mimi in La Bohème, Agathe in Der Freischutz, Micaela in Carmen, Madame Lidoine and Blanche in Les Dialogues des Carmelites, Lia in L'Enfant Prodigue, Rosalinda in Die Fledermaus and Anna Glawari in The Merry Widow; concert engagements with Toronto Symphony and Calgary Philharmonic Orchestra; repertoire includes the Mozart and Verdi Requiems, Messiah, Rossini's Stabat Mater, Bruckner's Te Deum, Beethoven's Ninth and Shostakovich's 14th Symphony; sang David Del Tredici's Alice for the National Ballet of Canada at the London Coliseum, 1987, followed by Zemlinsky's Lyric Symphony. *Recordings include:* None But the Lonely Heart (with Janina Fialkowska), Song to the Moon (with Mario Bernardi and the Calgary Philharmonic Orchestra), A Night in Vienna, Raffi Armenian. *Current Management:* Dean Artists Management, 204 St George Street, Toronto, ON M5R 2N5, Canada.

KOLTAI, Ralph, CBE; Stage Designer; b. 31 July 1924, Germany. *Education:* Studied in Berlin and London School of Arts and Crafts (now Central St Martin's College of Art and Design). *Career:* Angélique, London Opera Club, 1950; Tannhäuser at Royal Opera House, 1955; Volpone at New Opera Company SW, 1961; Murder in the Cathedral, Sadler's Wells, 1962; Otello and Volo di Notte for Scottish Opera, 1963; Attila for Sadler's Wells, 1963; The Rise and Fall of the City of Mahagonny, 1963; Don Giovanni for Scottish Opera, 1964; Boris Godunov for Scottish Opera, 1965; From the House of the Dead, Sadler's Wells, 1965; The Rake's Progress for Scottish Opera, 1967 and 1971; The Valkyrie, Coliseum ENO, 1970; Elegy for Young Lovers, Scottish Opera, 1970; Twilight of the Gods, ENO Coliseum, 1971; Lulu for National Welsh Opera, 1971; Rheingold and Duke Bluebeard's Castle, ENO Coliseum, 1972; Taverner, Royal Opera House, 1972; Tristan and Isolde for Scottish Opera, 1973; Lulu, Kassel, 1973; Siegfried, ENO Coliseum, 1973; Tannhäuser at Sydney Opera House, 1973; Wozzek, Netherlands Opera, 1973; Ring Cycle, touring version, ENO, 1974; Fidelio, Bavarian State Opera, 1974; Don Giovanni, 1975; Midsummer Marriage, Welsh National Opera, 1976; The Ice Break, Royal Opera House, 1977; Threepenny Opera, Aalborg, Denmark, 1979; Anna Karenina, ENO Coliseum, 1981; Die Soldaten at Opéra Lyon, 1983; Italian Girl in Algiers, 1984 and Tannhäuser, 1986 at Grand Théâtre de Geneva, 1986; (also directed) The Flying Dutchman 1987 and La Traviata, 1990 at Hong Kong Arts Festival; Pacific Overtures, ENO Coliseum, 1987; The Makropulos Case, De Norske Opera, Oslo, 1992; La Traviata, Kungliga Operan, Stockholm, 1993; Otello for Opera Essen, 1994; Madama Butterfly in Tokyo, 1995; Carmen at the Albert Hall, London, and Nabucco at the Amphitheatre Orange, 1997; Dalibor for Scottish Opera, 1998; Simon Boccanegra, Welsh National Opera and Strasbourg, 1998–99; Don Giovanni, Kirov Opera, Mariinski Theatre, 1999; Genoveva, Opera North, 2000; Fellow, Hong Kong Academy of Performing Arts; The London Institute; The Bruford College of Art; The Royal Society of Art. *Publications:* Ralph Koltai–Designer for the Stage, 1997. *Current Management:* London Management, 2–4 Noel Street, London W1V 3RD, England.

KOMLOS, Péter; Violinist; b. 25 Oct. 1935, Budapest, Hungary; m. (1) Edit Fehér, 2 s., (2) Zsuzsa Arki, 1 s. *Education:* Budapest Music Academy. *Career:* Founded Komlos String Quartet, 1957; 1st Violinist, Budapest Opera Orchestra, 1960; Leader, Bart ók String Quartet, 1963; Extensive tours to Russia, Scandinavia, Italy, Austria, Germany and Czechoslovakia, 1958–64, USA, Canada, New Zealand and Australia, 1970 including Days of Human Rights Concert, UN HQ New York, Japan, Spain and Portugal, 1971, Far East, USA and Europe, 1973; Performed at many festivals including: Ascona, Edinburgh, Adelaide, Spoleto, Menton, Schwetzingen, Lucerne, Aix-en-Provence. *Recordings:* Beethoven's String Quartets, Budapest; Bartók's String Quartets, Paris. *Honours:* 1st Prize, International String Quartet Competition, Liège, 1964; Liszt Prize, 1965; Gramophone Record Prize, Germany, 1969; Kossuth Prizes, 1970, 1997; Eminent Artist Title, 1980; UNESCO Music Council Plaque, 1981. *Address:* Törökvész ut 94, Budapest 1025, Hungary.

KOMLOSI, Ildiko; Singer (Mezzo-soprano); b. 1959, Békésszentandra's, Hungary. *Education:* Studied at Szeged Music Academy with Valeria Berdal and at Franz Liszt Academy, Budapest with András Miko; Guildhall School with Vera Rozsa and the Studio of La Scala with Giulietta Simionato. *Career:* Concert appearances have included the Verdi Requiem in Philadelphia, conducted by Lorin Maazel; Concerts with the BBC Symphony, the Royal Philharmonic with Antal Dorati and the Hungarian Radio and State Television Company; Engagements with the Hungarian State Opera Company, Budapest and the State Operas of Berlin, Vienna, La Scala and in America, San Francisco, Portland, Houston, Columbus, Ohio; Roles include Carmen, Sextus, Leonora in Favorita, Laura, Octavian, Giovanna Seymour (Anna Bolena) and Purcell's Dido; Sang Judit in a concert performance of Duke Bluebeard's Castle with the BBC Philharmonic conducted by András Ligeti, Feb 1991, and at the 1992 Prom Concerts London; Giovanna Seymour at Santiago; Sang Octavian at Palermo, 1998.

KOMLOSSY, Erzsebet; Singer (Contralto); b. 9 July 1933, Salgotarjan, Hungary. *Education:* Studied at the Bart ók Conservatory in Budapest. *Career:* Member, Hungarian State Opera Budapest; Guest appearances in Moscow, London, Cologne, Edinburgh and elsewhere in Europe; Roles include Azucena (Covent Garden, 1970), Amneris, Ulrica, Preziosilla, Eboli, Carmen, Dalila and parts in operas by Kodály, Szokolay and Erkel. *Recordings:* Aida, Madama Butterfly, Bank Ban by Erkel, The Spinning Room by Kodály and Blood Wedding by Szokolay (Hungaroton); Hungarian Coronation Mass by Liszt (Deutsche Grammophon); Háry János by Kodály (Decca). *Address:* c/o Hungarian State Opera House, Népöztársasáy utja 22, 1061 Budapest, Hungary.

KOMOROUS, Rudolf; composer and bassoonist; b. 8 Dec. 1931, Prague, Czechoslovakia. *Education:* Conservatory of Music; Academy of Musical Arts, Prague with Pavel Borkovec. *Career:* teacher, Central Conservatory of Peking, China, 1959–61; co-founder, Musica Viva Pragensis, Czechoslovakia; Emigrated to Canada 1969; Associate Professor of Composition and Theory, University of Victoria, 1971–. *Compositions:* Published by Universal Edition, Vienna and some of them have been issued on Supraphon Records; Mignon for string quartet, 1965; Gone for tape, 1969; Bare and Dainty for Orchestra, 1970; Lady Whiterose, Chamber opera, 1971; Anatomy of melancholy for tape, 1974; 4 Sinfonies, 1988, 1990, 1995, 1997; No, no, Miya, chamber opera, 1988; Hermione Dreaming for ensemble, 1992; The Seven Sides of Maxines' Silver Die for ensemble, 1998. *Honours:* First Prize, Concours International d'Exécution Musicale, Geneva, 1957.

KONG, Joanne; Pianist and Harpsichordist; b. 2 March 1957, Suffern, New York, USA; m. Paul Hanson 1981. *Education:* BMus, Piano and Harpsichord Performance, University of Southern California, 1979; MMus, Piano Performance, 1981, DMA, 1986, University of Oregon. *Career:* Critically acclaimed as Solo and Chamber Pianist and Harpsichordist; Special expertise in music of J. S. Bach, including performances of Goldberg Variations and complete Well-Tempered Klavier; Artist Faculty, University of Richmond, Virginia. *Honours:* Ruth Lorraine Close Fellowship Winner, Harpsichord, 1979, Piano, 1980, 1981; Laureate, Beethoven Foundation Fellowship Auditions, 1981; Fellowships to Bach Aria Festival and Institute, SUNY Stony Brook, 1982, 1984; 4th Place, J. S. Bach International Piano Competition, 1983. *Address:* 1211 Claremont Avenue, Richmond, Virginia 23227-4008, USA.

KONGSTED, Ole (Dan); Musicologist and Composer; b. 22 Sept. 1943, Copenhagen, Denmark; m. Ida Wieth-Knudsen, 25 Nov 1967, 1 s., 2 d. *Education:* Musicology, University of Copenhagen. *Career:* Jazz Musician; Holder of Scholarship, Danish State, 1976–80; Freelance Collaborator, Danish Radio, 1976–; Conductor, Choir of the Jeunesses Musicales, 1978–86; Assistant Director, Musikhistorisk Museum and Carl Claudius Samling, Copenhagen, 1980; Choirmaster, Church of the Sacred Heart, Copenhagen, 1983–; Composer; Founder, Leader, Capella Hafniensis, 1990–; Holder of Scholarship, Danish State/Royal Library, 1994–. *Compositions:* 27 opus numbers including: Opus 2, Puer natus est nobis for choir, soloists and organ; Opus 3a, Kyrie fons bonitatis for choir a cappella. *Recordings:* With Choir of the Jeunesses Musicales; With Ben Webster and Arnved Meyer Band, and Capella Hafniensis. *Publications:* E turri tibiis canere–Traek af taarnblaesningens historie, in Festskrift Johannes Simons (editor), 1974; Census as Source Material for the History of Music, 1976; Nils Schioerring: Musikkens Historie i Danmark (editor), 1977–78; Music in Denmark at the Time of Christian IV, 1988; Heinrich Schütz und die Musik in Dänemark zur Zeit Christians IV (co-editor), 1989; Kronborg-Motetterne Tilegnet Frederik II og Dronning Sophie 1582, 1990; Kronborg-Brunnen und Kronborg-Motetten, Ein Notenfund des späten 16 Jahrhunderts aus Flensburg und seine Vorgeschichte, 1991; Royal Danish Water Music 1582, 1994; Gregorius Trehou in the Vatican Library, 1998. *Honours:* Organist and Kantor Otto Koebkes Mindelegat, 1992. *Address:* The Royal Library, PO Box 2149, 1016 Copenhagen K, Denmark.

KÖNIG, Klaus; Singer (Tenor); b. 26 May 1936, Beuthen, Germany. *Education:* Studied with Johannes Kemter in Dresden. *Career:* Sang in Cottbus in 1970; Dessau from 1973, as Max, Don Carlos, and Erik in Der fliegende Holländer; Sang at Leipzig 1978–82, Staatsoper Dresden from 1982; Guest appearances in Karlsruhe 1983–85 (Tristan and Tannhäuser), at La Scala and Covent Garden in 1984 (as Tannhäuser) and the Théâtre de la Monnaie Brussels 1985, as Tristan; Sang Max in Der Freischütz, at the opening of the restored Semper Opera House, Dresden (1985); Guest appearances in Paris, Parma, Strasbourg, Madrid, Venice and Barcelona; Other roles include Lensky, Florestan, Radames, Don José, Alvaro in La Forza del Destino, Lohengrin, Walther, Parsifal and Bacchus; Lisbon 1986, as Florestan; Sang Tannhäuser at Cologne and London 1987; Munich Opera 1988, as Menelaos in Die Aegyptische Helena by Strauss; Buenos Aires and Vienna Staatsoper 1988, as Florestan and Bacchus; Sang the Mayor in Friedenstag by Strauss, Dresden, 1998; Many engagements in concerts and oratorios. *Recordings:* Tannhäuser (EMI); Der Rosenkavalier (Denon); Choral Symphony (Philips). *Address:* c/o Allied Artists Agency, 42 Montpelier Square, London SW7 1JZ, England.

KONSTANTINOV, Julian; Singer (bass); b. 1966, Sofia, Bulgaria. *Education:* Sofia Academy, 1987–93. *Career:* Sang in The Rake's Progress and Il Barbiere di Siviglia while a student and represented Bulgaria at the 1992 Cardiff Singer of the World Competition; Appearances with the Sofia National Opera in Lucia di Lammermoor, Aida, Rigoletto, Luisa Miller and Turandot (as Timur); Season 1998 with the Royal Opera at Savonlinna and elsewhere as Massimiliano in Verdi's Masnadieri; Further engagements include Fiesco in Simon Boccanegra with the Berlin Philharmonic and Salzburg Festival conducted by Claudio Abbado, Padre Guardino in La Forza del Destino at the Savonlinna Festival and Cardinal Brogni in La Juive at the New Israeli Opera, 1999–2000. *Current Management:* Askonas Holt Ltd, Lonsdale Chambers, 27 Chancery Lane, London, WC2A 1PF, England. *Telephone:* (20) 7400-1700. *Fax:* (20) 7400-1799. *E-mail:* info@askonasholt.co.uk. *Website:* www.askonasholt.co.uk.

KONSULOV, Ivan; Singer (Baritone); b. 29 May 1946, Varna, Bulgaria. *Education:* Studied with Jossifov in Sofia and with Aldo Protti in Italy. *Career:* Debut: Opera National Russe (Bulgaria) 1972; Sang in Berne from 1977, as Simon Boccanegra, Marcello (La Bohème), Scarpia, Don Giovanni, Mandryka, Tonio, Pizarro, Don Carlos (La Forza del Destino), Alfio and Iago; Bologna 1980, Zurga in Les pêcheurs de Perles; Philadelphia Opera 1982, Marcello: Bratislava 1984, as Eugene Onegin; Stuttgart and Berlin 1985, Don Giovanni; At the Monte Carlo opera in 1986 sang Gryaznoy in The Tsar's Bride by Rimsky-Korsakov; Engagements at Graz, Barcelona, Madrid and Karlsruhe; Sang Amfortas in Parsifal at Berne, 1989; Season 1992 as the Major-domo in Zemlinsky's Der Zwerg at Trieste. *Recordings include:* La Bohème-Marcello Opus-Bratislava Stereo with P Dvorsky and television film 1980; The Queen of Spades (Tomsky), Musik Mundial-Sofia with International Stars, 1988; Don Carlo-Posa, Balkanton, Sofia, 1988; Opera Recital Arias Balkanton, 1988. *Address:* c/o Stadttheater Bern, Nägeligasse 1, 3011 Bern, Switzerland.

KONT, Paul; Composer; b. 19 Aug. 1920, Vienna, Austria; 1 s. *Education:* Conductor's Diploma, 1947, Composer's Diploma, 1948, Vienna University of Music. *Career:* Professor of Composition, 1969–86, Emeritus, 1986–, Vienna Academy of Music. *Compositions:* Commissioned operas: Lysistrate (for Komische Oper Berlin), 1957; Peter und Susanne (for Austrian Television), 1959; For the Time Being (for Austrian Television), 1965; Celestina (for Stadt-Buhnen, Cologne), 1966; Plutos (for Austrian Government), 1976; Traumleben, musical, 1958; Ballets: Italia Passata; Die Traurigen Jäger; Amores; Il Ballo del Mondo; Monoballette, ballet film; Vom Manne und vom Weibe, oratorio; 4 Symphonies, 1979, 1981, 1981, 1983; Concertos; Chamber music; Lieder; Piano Sonatas; Roma, ballet, 1984; Lebenslauf, ballet, 1987; 3 Kleine Klavierkonzerte, 1989; Cronica Hungarica for orchestra, 1992; Sequenzen, 1994; Oesterreich for clarinet and piano trio, 1997. *Publications:* Antianiorganikum. *Address:* 47 Geusaugasse, Vienna 1030, Austria.

KONTARSKY, Alfons; Pianist; b. 9 Oct. 1932, Iserlohn, Germany. *Education:* Studied in Cologne with Else Schmidt-Gohr and Maurits Frank; Further study in Hamburg with Eduard Erdmann, 1955–57. *Career:* Many appearances with his brother in modern music programmes from 1955, including works by Earle Brown, Kagel, Stockhausen, Pousseur, Berio and Bussotti; Seminar at Darmstadt, 1962–69; Teacher at the Musikhochschule from 1969; Professor, Salzburg Mozarteum, 1983–; Formed Piano Trio with Saschko Gawriloff and Klaus Storck, 1971. *Recordings include:* Bartók's Sonata for two Pianos and Percussion. *Publications:* Pro Musica Nova: Studien zum Spielen neuer Musik für Klavier, 1973. *Honours:* First prize for Piano Duo at the 1955 Munich Radio International Festival. *Address:* Stacthiche Hochschule für Musik Rheinland, Degobertstrasse 38, 5000 Köln 1, Germany.

KONTARSKY, Alois; Pianist; b. 14 May 1931, Iserlohn, Germany. *Education:* Studied in Cologne with Else Schmitz-Gohr and Maurits Frank; Further study in Hamburg with Eduard Erdmann. *Career:* International performances with his brother from 1955 in modern repertoire: Michael Gielen, de Grandis, Henri Pousseur, Berio and Zimmermann; Gave premiere of Stockhausen's Klavierstücke I–XI, Darmstadt 1966; Concerts with the Stockhausen ensemble and duo with the cellist Siegfried Palm; Masterclass at the Cologne Musikhochschule from 1969; Premieres of music by Kagel, Stockhausen (Mantra), Berio and Bussotti. *Recordings include:* Bartók's Sonata for Two Pianos and Percussion; Klavierstücke I–XI by Stockhausen. *Honours:* First prize for Piano Duo at the Munich Radio International Festival, 1955. *Address:* Staatliche Hochschule für Musik Rheinland, Degobertstrasse 38, 5000 Köln 1, Germany.

KONTARSKY, Bernhard; Conductor; b. 1940, Germany. *Education:* Musikhochschule, Cologne. *Career:* Engagements at Bonn Opera and throughout Europe: Berg's Lulu for Flanders Opera and Wozzeck at the Deutsche Oper am Rhein; Adriana Hölszky's Die Wände and Henze's Boulevard Solitude for Frankfurt Opera; Henze's Der Prinz von Homburg at Antwerp and Schoenberg's Moses und Aron for the Deutsche Oper, Berlin; Productions for the Staatstheater Stuttgart include Zender's Don Quixote, Intolleranza by Nono, Bluebeard's Castle, and Zimmermann's Die Soldaten; Boulevard Solitude at Covent Garden, London, 2001; Professor at Academy of Frankfurt, 1981–. *Honours:* Mendelssohn Award, Cologne; International Disc Award of the German Press, 1992. *Address:* Staatstheater Stuttgart, Obererschlossgarten 6, 70173 Stuttgart, Germany.

KOOPMAN, Ton; Conductor, Organist and Harpsichordist; b. 2 Oct. 1944, Zwolle, Netherlands; m. Tini Mathot. *Education:* BMus, University of Amsterdam; Solo Degree Organ, 1969; Solo degree harpsichord, 1970. *Career:* Founder, Music ensemble Musica da Camera, 1966; Music Antiqua Amsterdam, 1970; Numerous concerts and recordings; Founder, Amsterdam Baroque Orchestra, 1979; Amsterdam Baroque Choir, 1992; Appearances on radio and television the world over; Solo tours to USA and Japan, and yearly with Amsterdam Baroque Orchestra and choir, to Europe, USA and Japan; Frequently invited as guest conductor, and forms duo with wife; Professor of Harpsichord, Royal Conservatory, The Hague; Season 1997 included Schubert Bicentenary concert in Amsterdam and Bach's B Minor Mass in London; created own music label, Antoine Marchand, a sub-label of Challenge Classics 2003. *Compositions:* Reconstruction: J. S. Bach's St Mark Passion, 1999, performed at the BBC London Prom concerts, 2000; Permanent guest-conductor at the Lausanne Chamber Orchestra. *Recordings:* over 250 records as a soloist, of which 70 with the Amsterdam Baroque Orchestra including Buxtehude Cantatas 1997, Complete Bach Organ Works 2000, Complete Bach Cantatas 2004. *Honours:* Toonkunst Award, 1974; Johan Wagenaar Award, 1978; Edison Awards for Recordings; 3M Award for contribution to Ancient Music, 1989; Crystal Award, Osaka Symphony Hall Japan, 1992; Prix de l'Academie du Disque Lyrique, 1994; Premio Internationale Del Disco Antonio Vivaldi, Venice, 1995; Deutsche Schallplattenpreis Echo Klassik, 1997; Honorary Doctorate at Urecht University, 2000. *Address:* Amsterdam Baroque Orchestra, Meerweg 23, 1405 BC Bussum, Netherlands.

KOPCAK, Sergei; Singer (Bass); b. 23 April 1948, Dacov, Carpathia. *Education:* Studied in Leipzig, Vienna and Milan. *Career:* Slovak National Opera at Bratislava, from 1974 in the Slav, French and German repertory; Metropolitan Opera, New York from 1983, as Ivan Khovansky, Wurm in Luisa Miller and Sparafucile in Rigoletto; The Commendatore, and Pimen in Boris Godunov; Salzburg Festival, 1986–87 in Moses und Aron; Edinburgh Festival, 1989 as Konchak in Prince Igor and Marseille, 1994, as Boito's Mephistopheles; Shostakovich's Boris at Florence, Maggio Musicale, 1998. *Recordings:* Janáček's Glagolitic Mass. *Address:* c/o Teatro Comunale, Via Solferino 15, 50123 Florence, Italy.

KOPP, Miroslav; Singer (tenor); b. 23 Feb. 1955, Plzeň, Czechoslovakia. *Education:* studied at the Prague Conservatory. *Career:* Prague National Theatre from 1981 as Alfredo, Ernesto, Don Pasquale, Pelléas, 1986 and the Prince in Rusalka, 1991; Vienna Staatsoper, 1986, in The Bartered Bride and Paris Opéra Comique in From the House of the Dead, 1988, (also at the Salzburg Festival); Geneva, 1992 as Boris in Katya Kabanova and Florence, 1993 as Števa in Jenůfa; Basle Opera as Don Carlos; Other roles include Wenzel in The Bartered Bride and Vitek in Smetana's Dalibor. *Recordings:* Dvořák's The Cunning Peasant; Smetana's Dalibor and Martinů's Ariane; Tikhon in Katya Kabanova, under Charles Mackerras. *Address:* Prague National Theatre, PO Box 865, 11230 Prague 1, Czech Republic.

KOPPEL, Lone; Soprano; b. 20 May 1938, Copenhagen, Denmark. *Education:* Studied at the Royal Danish Academy of Music. *Career:* Debut: Copenhagen in 1962 as Musetta; Sang at Kiel Opera, 1964–65, and Royal Opera Copenhagen, 1962–95; Guest appearances at Sydney, 1973–78, and Århus from 1972 as Leonore in Fidelio and the Trovatore Leonora; Sang Salome at Bonn and Oslo, 1973–74, and Lady Macbeth in Macbeth at Stockholm in 1981; Copenhagen as Judith in Bluebeard's Castle and Shostakovich's Katerina Izmailova; Other roles included Mikal in Saul and David, Wagner's Elisabeth, Kundry, Ortrud and Senta, Elektra, Jenůfa, Eboli, Donna Anna and Donna Elvira, Sang Mme de Croissy in Poulenc's Carmélites at Copenhagen, 1997; Season 2002: The Old Countess in The Queen of Spades and Herodias in Salome. *Address:* c/o Det Kongelige Teater, Box 2185, 1017 Copenhagen, Denmark.

KOPTAGEL, Yuksel; Pianist and Composer; b. 27 Oct. 1931, Istanbul, Turkey; m. Danyal Kerven, 30 Dec 1964. *Education:* Private studies with composer Djemal Rechid; Graduated, Real conservatorio de Music, Madrid, 1955; Diplome Superieur, Schola Cantorum, Ecole Superieure de Musique, Paris, 1958; Certificates on Composition and Spanish Music Interpretation, Santiago, 1959. *Career:* Debut: First public concert, Istanbul, aged 5; Concerts in Europe (Spain, France, Italy, Switzerland, Czechoslovakia, Germany) USA, India, Pakistan, Russia; Compositions published by Max Eschig, Paris and Bote and Bock, Berlin; International concert career with European Orchestras, 1953–; Member of Jury, Schola Cantorum, Paris; Participant, numerous music festivals. *Address:* Caddebostan Plajyolu 21/32, 81060 Istanbul, Turkey.

KOPYTMAN, Mark; Composer and Pianist; b. 6 Dec. 1929, Kamenetz-Podolski, USSR; m. Miriam Kopytman, 5 July 1955, 2 d. *Education:* MD, Tchernovitz, USSR, 1952; MMus, Lvow Academy of Music, USSR, 1955; PhD, Moscow Conservatory, USSR, 1958. *Career:* Senior Teacher, Theory and Composition, USSR State Academies of Music, 1955–72; Chairman of Theory and Composition Department, 1974–76, 1979–82, 1985–, Professor, 1976–, Rubin Academy of Music, Jerusalem, Israel; Deputy Head of Rubin Academy of Music and Dance, Jerusalem, Israel, 1985–; Guest Professor, Hebrew University Musicological Department, Jerusalem, 1979–; Guest Professor of Composition, University of Pennsylvania, USA, 1985 and 1989; Composer in Residence, Canberra School of Music, Australia, 1985; Music Director, the Doron Ensemble for the Performance of 20th Century music, 1990–93; Music Adviser, International Festival in St Petersburg, 1991–; Chairman, International Composers Contest in Moldova, 1992; Composer in Residence, Israel Camerata (Jerusalem), 1992–; Chairman, International Symposium, The Art of Composition, Jerusalem, 1998. *Compositions:* Case Mare (Opera), 1966; Songs of Kodr (oratorio), 1966; String Quartet III, 1969; Voices, 1974–75; October Sun, 1974; Monodrama (Ballet), 1975; Concerto for Orchestra, 1976; About an Old Tune, 1977; Rotations, 1979; Cantus II, 1980; Memory, 1981; Kaddish, 1982; Susskind von Trimberg (Opera), 1982–83; Cantus III, 1984; Life of the World to Come, 1985; Variable Structures, 1985–86; Letters of Creation, 1986; Dedication, 1986; Letters of Creation for voice and strings, 1987; Circles for voice, clarinet, cello and piano, 1987; Ornaments for harpsichord and orchestra, 1987; Scattered Rhymes for choir and orchestra, 1988; Eight Pages from the Book of Questions for voice solo, 1988; A Poem for the Numbers for the Dead for baritone and chamber ensemble, 1988; Love Remembered for choir and orchestra, 1989; To Go Away for mezzo-soprano and five instruments, 1989; Cantus V, 1990; Alliterations for piano, 1993; Tenero for cello solo, 1994; Strain, for string quartet, 1995; Beyond for chamber orchestra, 1997; Fermane for voice and three clarinets; String Quartet No. 4, 1997. *Recordings:* Six Moldavian Dances for Orchestra; String Quartet No. 2; About an Old Tune; October Sun; For Harp; Memory; Rotations; Cantus II; Lamentation; Cantus V; Strain, Beyond, Music for strings. *Publications:* Choral Composition, 1971. *Address:* 4 Tchernichovsky Str, Jerusalem 92581, Israel.

KORD, Kazimierz; Conductor; b. 18 Nov. 1930, Pogorze, Poland. *Education:* Studied piano at the Leningrad Conservatory, composition and conducting at the Kraków Academy. *Career:* Conducted at the Warsaw Opera, 1960–62; Artistic Director, Kraków Opera, 1962–68 (staged own productions of opera); Music Director, Polish National Orchestra, 1968–73; Metropolitan Opera, 1972, The Queen of Spades: returned for Così fan tutte, Boris Godunov and Aida; San Francisco, 1973, Boris Godunov and Rigoletto; Other opera engagements in London (Eugene Onegin 1976), Amsterdam and Copenhagen; Took the Toronto Symphony Orchestra on its first European tour, 1974: has also conducted the Detroit, Chicago and Cleveland Symphony Orchestras; Artistic Director, Warsaw Philharmonic from 1977; Chief Conductor of the South West German Radio in Baden-Baden, 1980; Principal Conductor of the Cincinnati Symphony, 1980–82; Pacific Symphony Orchestra, Irvine, CA, 1989–91; Has conducted orchestras in Moscow, Leningrad, New York, London, Stockholm, Rotterdam, Pittsburgh, Vienna and Tokyo; Conducted Otello at San Francisco, 1989. *Current Management:* Ingpen & Williams Ltd, 7 St George's Court, 131 Putney Bridge Road, London, SW15 2PA, England.

KORDES, Heidrun; Singer (Soprano); b. 1960, Germany. *Education:* Freiburg Musikhochschule. *Career:* Debut: Gelsenkirchen Opera;

Engagement at the Hessichen Staatstheater, Wiesbaden, from 1986; Roles have included Mozart's Pamina and Susanna, Nedda in Pagliacci, Gilda in Rigoletto and parts in operas by Handel; Guest engagements at Leipzig, Dresden, Mannheim, Frankfurt and the Deutsche Oper am Rhein, Düsseldorf; Frequent concert appearances. *Recordings include:* Oreste and Xerxes by Handel; Albums of Lieder. *Address:* c/o Allied Artists, 42 Montpelier Square, London SW7 1JZ, England.

KOREVAAR, David; Pianist and Composer; b. 25 July 1962, Madison, Winsconsin, USA; m., 1 s., 1 d. *Education:* BMus, 1982, MMus, 1983, DMA, in progress, expected 2000, The Juilliard School. *Career:* Debut: Town Hall, New York, 1985; Recitals throughout USA, Japan; Chamber music appearances in USA, Japan, Australia, Europe; Founding member, Hexagon, piano and Wind Ensemble; Prometheus Piano Quartet; mem, Chamber Music America; College Music Society; American Liszt Society. *Compositions:* Piano concerto; 2 piano sonatas; Major works for piano trio; Violin and piano; string trio; Clarinet and piano. *Recordings:* Bach, Well-Tempered Klavier, Musicians showcase; Brahms, Later piano music; Liszt, Orchestral music transcribed for piano; Dohnànyi Etudes; Ruralia Hungarica. *Honours:* Top prize, William Kapell International competition, 1988; Peabody Mason music foundation award, 1985; French music award from Robert Casadesus international competition, 1989. *Current Management:* Jecklin Associates. *Address:* 3 Sasqua Pond Road, Norwalk, CT 06855, USA.

KORF, Anthony; Composer and Conductor; b. 14 Dec. 1951, New York City, USA. *Education:* BA, MA, Manhattan School of Music. *Career:* Artistic Director, Conductor, Parnassus, 1975–; Guest Conductor, Group for Contemporary Music; League ISCM; Co-Founder, Artistic Director, The Riverside Symphony; Commissioned by San Francisco Symphony, American Composers Orchester and others. *Compositions:* Symphony No. 2; Symphony in the Twilight; Oriole; A Farewell; Cantata; Double Take; Brass Quintet; Symphonia; Requiem, 3 Movements for Clarinet Solo. *Recordings:* A Farewell; Symphony No. 2; Conductor: Stefan Wolpe (Koch International); Andrew Imbrie (New World); Babbitt; Davidovsky; Korf; Lundborg; Olan. *Publications:* Stefan Wolpe Chamber Piece No. 2, Editor. *Honours:* Koussevitsky Commission, 1992; American Academy of Arts and Letters Lieberson Fellowship, 1988. *Address:* 258 Riverside Drive, New York, NY 10025, USA.

KORHONEN, Ritva-Liisa; Singer (Soprano); b. 1959, Finland. *Education:* Studied in Helsinki and Zürich. *Career:* Debut: Helsinki in 1984 as Gilda; After further study at the Sibelius Academy sang Musetta and Adina in Helsinki, Fiordiligi at Tampere, Traviata at Oulu and Adele in Die Fledermaus at Lahti; Further appearances at the Savonlinna Festival and in concert; Sang Pamina at Helsinki, 1998. *Address:* c/o Finnish National Opera, Bulevardi 23–27, 00180 Helsinki 18, Finland.

KORN, Artur; Singer (Bass); b. 4 Dec. 1937, Wuppertal, Germany; m. Sabine Hass. *Education:* Studied in Cologne, Munich and Vienna with Clemens Glettenberg and Schuch-Tovini. *Career:* Debut: Cologne Opera Studio 1963, in Un Ballo in Maschera; Sang in Graz 1965–68, Vienna Volksoper and Staatsoper from 1968; Glyndebourne Festival 1980–84, as Baron Ochs, Bartolo in Le nozze di Figaro and Waldner in Arabella; Metropolitan Opera from 1984, as Osmin, Bartolo and Ochs; Engagements in Chicago (debut 1984), San Francisco, Detroit, London and Toronto and in Germany, Italy, South Africa and Switzerland; Salzburg Festival 1987, in Schoenberg's Moses and Aron; Sarastro in Magic Flute, Buenos Aires; Ochs in Rosenkavalier, Santiago de Chile; Met Tour, Japan, 1988; State Opera Munich Tour, Japan, 1988; Vienna Festival State Opera Vienna with Harnoncourt (Osmin-Entführung), 1988; Sang 1991/92 as Hagen at Brussels and Mozart's Bartolo at the Salzburg Festival; Often heard in oratorios and Lieder. *Recordings include:* Alfonso und Estrella by Schubert; Le nozze di Figaro with Haitink; Vespro della Beata Vergine with Harnoncourt; Video. *Recordings:* Ariadne auf Naxos (Met/Levine); Arabella (Strauss) Glyndebourne/Haitink; Le nozze de Figaro; Die Entführung, Vienna State Opera/Harnoncourt. *Address:* c/o Staatsoper, Opernring 2, 1010 Vienna, Austria.

KORONDI, Anna; Singer (soprano); b. 1967, Budapest, Hungary. *Education:* studied in Budapest, Bartók Conservatory and Vienna. *Career:* concerts from 1991, notably at the Styriarte and Prague Spring Festivals; Komische Oper Berlin 1993–1997, as Mozart's Susanna and Zerlina, Lauretta in Gianni Schicchi; Sophie in Werther and Nannetta in Falstaff; concerts include Bach's Christmas Oratorio, Vienna 1994, Mendelssohn's St Paul, Carmina Burana, and appearances at the Leipzig Gewandhaus 1996; mem. of the Komische Oper Berlin 1993–97, Bonn Opera 1997–99; world premiere of opera Bernarda Albas Haus by Aribet Reiman, Bayerische Staatsoper 2000; Adele in Die Fledermaus, Salzburg Festival 2001; sang Lied at the Kissinger Sommer; has worked with orchestras across Europe, under Hans Neuenfels, Marc Minkowski, Howard Arman, Frans Brügen, Adam Fischer, Nikolaus Harnoncourt and Helmuth Rilling; Repertoire from baroque to modern, including Lieder; Season 2002–2003 included Mendelssohn's Athalia, Mozart's Requiem, Bach Cantatas and Brahms's Requiem; Season 2003–2004 included debut as Sophie in Der Rosenkavalier and Parsifal under Pierre Boulez. *Recordings:* Mendelssohn's Athalia (Cappricio). *Honours:* Prizewinner, Schubert and Pavarotti International Competitions 1991, won ARD Competition, Munich 1993. *Current Management:* Boris Orlob Management, Jägerstrasse 70, 10117 Berlin, Germany. *Telephone:* 49 (30) 20450839. *Fax:* 49 (30) 20450849. *E-mail:* info@orlob .net. *Website:* www.orlob.net.

KOROVINA, Tatiana; Singer (Soprano); b. 1967, Kursk, Russia. *Education:* Studied at the Tchaikovsky Conservatory, Moscow. *Career:* Sang the Queen of Night in Die Zauberflöte at Staatsoper Vienna, 1990; Concert arias and Exultate Jubilate by Mozart, La Scala, Milan, Prague and Tokyo Suntory Hall, 1990–91; Komische Oper Berlin as Princess in The Legend of Tsar Saltan by Rimsky-Korsakov, 1994–2002; Blondchen in Die Entführung aus dem Serail, 1995; Adele in Fledermaus, 1996; Ninetta Prokofiev's Love for Three Oranges, 1998; Scolatella in Henze's König Hirsch, 1998; Zerbinetta in R Strauss's Ariadne auf Naxos, 1999; Sang at Rossini Festival in Wildbad with Cerere in Le Nozze di Teti e di Peleo, 1994; Aldimira in Sigismondo, 1995; Zenobia in Aureliano in Palmira, 1996; Argene in Un vero omaggio, 1997; Sang in Rossini's Stabat Mater at Philharmonic Berlin, 1996; Gabrielle and Eve in Die Schöpfung in Closter Chorin, 1998. *Recordings:* Abramo ed Isaaco by Mysliveček; Boccherini, Stabat Mater; Mozart's Concert Arias and Exultate jubilate; Rossini's Sigismondo; Aureliano in Palmira; Le nozze di Teti e di Peleo. *Address:* Komische Oper Berlin, Behrenstrasse 55–57, 10177 Berlin, Germany. *E-mail:* st_home@t-online.de. *Website:* st_home .bei.t-online.de/Korovina_Tatjana.htm.

KORSAKOVA, Natasha; Concert Violinist; b. 29 Jan. 1973, Moscow, Russia. *Education:* Studied at Central Music School, Moscow. *Career:* Debut: Concerts with Moscow Chamber Orchestra at the Conservatoire; Has given concerts in Bulgaria, Germany, Greece, Yugoslavia, China, Italy, Belgium and Japan, 1989–; Played at the Panatei Festival, Italy, 1991, and the Bruch Second Concerto with the Russian State Symphony Orchestra, October 1991; Repertoire also includes works by Vivaldi, Bach, Mendelssohn, Mozart, Tchaikovsky and Lalo; Chamber recitals in Japan, 1991 with her mother Iolanthe Miroshnikova as accompanist in works by Brahms, Saint-Saëns, Beethoven and Prokofiev; Based in Germany since 1993. *Honours:* awards at Wieniawski and Lipinski Competitions, Poland, 1988; Young Violinists International Competition, Kloster Schontal, Germany, 1989. *Current Management:* Sonata, Glasgow, Scotland. *Address:* 11 Northpark Street, Glasgow G20 7AA, Scotland.

KORTE, Karl Richard; American composer; b. 23 June 1928, Ossining, NY. *Education:* Juilliard School with Peter Mennin, Vincent Persichetti, Otto Luening, Goeffredo Petrassi and Aaron Copland. *Career:* teacher, Arizona State Univ. 1963–64, State Univ. of New York at Binghamton 1964–70; Prof. of Composition, Univ. of Texas at Austin 1971–96, Emeritus Prof. of Music 1996–; Visiting Prof., Williams Coll. 1996–99. *Compositions:* music in many categories, including chamber music, symphonic music, choral and piano; orchestral: Concertino on a Choral Theme, 1955; For a Young Audience, 1959; 2 Symphonies, 1961, 1968; Southwest, dance overture, 1963; Concerto for piano and winds, 1976; chamber: 2 string quartets, 1948, 1965; Quintet for oboe and strings, 1960; Matrix, 1968; Facets, 1969; Remembrances for flute and tape, 1971; Symmetrics, 1973; Piano Trio, 1977; Concertino for bass trombone, wind and percussion; The Whistling Wind for mezzo and tape, 1982; Double Concerto for flute, double bass and tape, 1983; Texarkana for band, 1991; Band music and works for chorus including Mass for Youth, 1963; Aspects of Love, 1968; Pale is this Good Prince, oratorio, 1973, Of Time and Seasons, 1975. *Honours:* two Guggenheim Fellowships, Fulbright Fellowships to Italy, 1953, to New Zealand, 1985; Gold Medal, Queen Elizabeth Int., 1969. *Address:* 545 Stage Road, Kuskirk, NY 12028, USA. *E-mail:* kkorte@aol.com. *Website:* www .kkorte.com.

KORTEKANGAS, Jaakko; Singer (baritone); b. 1961, Finland. *Education:* Sibelius Academy, Helsinki, and in Zürich. *Career:* sang at the Freiburg Opera from 1989, notably as Posa in Don Carlos, Belcore, Rossini's Figaro, Billy Budd and Wolfram in Tannhäuser; Guest at Berne in 1992 in Shostakovich's Lady Macbeth and as concert singer in Europe and North America including New York in 1990; Guest at Zürich as Barber of Seville, 1993, also at the Finnish National Opera, and Savonlinna Opera Festival; The Captain in The Death of Klinghoffer by John Adams, 2001. *Recordings:* opera: Madetoja; Pohjalaisia, Finlandia; television opera: Rantavaara; Tietäjien lahja; solo: Me kiitämme sinua; Sibelius, Cantata for the Conferment Ceremony; Nuori Psyyke (Songs of Erkki Melartin). *Honours:* First Prize, 1989 Lappeenranta competition. *Address:* Leirikaari 2 C, 02600 Espoo, Finland.

KORTEKANGAS, Olli; Composer; b. 16 May 1955, Turku, Finland. *Education:* Studied Composition and Music Theory, Sibelius Academy,

1974–81, West Berlin, 1981–82. *Career:* Composer; Journalist; Choral Conductor, Pedagogue (Sibelius Academy, National Theatre Academy); mem, Founding Member, Korvat auki Society (society for promotion or new music), Board Member of Society of Finnish Composers, Finnish Composers' Copyright Bureau TEOSTO. *Compositions include:* Television opera Grand Hotel, 1984–85; Orchestral: Okologie1-Vorspiel, 1983; Okologie, 2; Konzert, 1986–87; Alba, 1988; Amores, 1989; Organ concerto, 1997; Ark, 1998; Instrumental Threnody, 1977; Sonata per organo, 1979, Emotion, 1988; Imaggio a M C Escher, 1990, Iscrizione, 1990, Choral MAA, 1984–85, Verbum, 1987, A, 1987–88, Movement Echoing, 1997, Electronic Memoria, 1988–89. *Recordings:* Has made several recordings of his work (on Finlandia and Ondine labels). *Honours:* Salzburg Opera Prize, 1989; Gianfranco Zaffrani Prize, 1989. *Address:* Ruohoahdenkatu 20, 00180 Helsinki, Finland.

KOS, Bozidar; Composer; b. 3 May 1934, Novo Mesto, Slovenia; m. Milana Karlovac 1963; one d. *Education:* BMus, 1974, BMus, composition, 1975, MMus, 1980, Univ. of Adelaide; PhD, Univ. of Sydney, 1998. *Career:* teacher, cello, music theory, State Music School, Novo Mesto, 1943–54; Lecturer in Music, Torrens Coll. of Advanced Education, Adelaide, South Australia, 1975; Tutor in Composition, Electronic Music, 1976–77, Fellow in Composition, 1978–83, Univ. of Adelaide; Lecturer in Composition, 1984–91, Senior Lecturer in Composition, 1992–, Chair. Composition Division, 1994–2002, Sydney Conservatorium of Music, Univ. of Sydney, NSW. *Compositions:* Orchestral: Axis 5-1-5, 1973; Mediations, 1974; Metamorphosis, 1978; Sinfonietta, 1983; Violin Concerto, 1986; Guitar Concerto, 1992; Crosswinds for jazz trumpet, alto saxophone and orchestra, 1993; Aurora Australis, 1997; Viola Concerto, 2000; Ensemble works: Integration, 1972; Chamber Piece, 1973; Little Fantasy, 1978; Quartet, 1980; String Quartet, 1982; Three Movements, 1982; Catena 1, 1985, Quasar, 1987; Catena 2, 1989; Ludus ex Nominum, 1989; Bravisssimo, 1991; solo works: Reflections, piano solo, 1976; Piano Sonata, 1981; Kolo, piano solo, 1984; Evocations for solo cello, 1994; Evocations 2 for solo guitar, 1999; instrumental works with synthesiser, computer or tape: Modulations, 1974; Dialogue 1, tape, 1976; Spectrum, 1988. *Recordings:* Quasar for percussion quartet, on Synergy Percussion; Piano Sonata, on The Hands The Dream, Tall Poppies; Violin Concerto, on Forbidden Colours; Violin Concerto, on Crosswinds; Guitar Concerto on Bozidar Kos Skladatelj-Composr; Evocations for solo cello, on Australian Cello, Tall Poppies; Catena 2, on Samsara/Australia Ensemble, Vox Australis. *Honours:* Albert H. Mapps Composition Award 1983, Best Australian Orchestral Work, Nat. Music Critics' Awards 1991. *Address:* 62 Grand Boulevard, Blackwood Park, SA 2006, Australia. *E-mail:* bozidar.kos@bigpond.com.

KOSMO, Ingeborg; Singer (Mezzo-soprano); b. 1967, Denmark. *Career:* Frequent concert and opera engagements throughout Scandinavia and Europe; Repertory includes L'Enfant Prodigue by Debussy, the Composer in Ariadne auf Naxos, with songs by Schubert, Strauss and Stravinsky; Contestant at the 1995 Cardiff Singer of the World Competition. *Address:* Schweigaardsgate 69, 0560 Oslo, Norway.

KOSTAS, Rudolf; Singer (Baritone); b. 1950, Vienna, Austria. *Education:* Studied in Vienna, with Waldemar Kmentt. *Career:* Sang at the Vienna Kammeroper and Staatsoper from 1975; Salzburg Festival, 1981 in the premiere of Cerha's Baal; Stadttheater Freiburg, 1984–89; Season 1995–96 at Schwerin as Hans Sachs in Die Meistersinger and Westmoreland in Sly by Wolf-Ferrari; Other roles include Wagner's Amfortas and Wolfram; Mozart's Don Giovanni and Count; Berg's Wozzeck; Verdi's Luna; Rigoletto and Iago; Mozart's Figaro; Further appearances in Tel-Aviv, Munich and throughout Germany; Many concerts and Lieder recitals. *Address:* c/o Staatstheater Schwerin, Alter Garten, 19055 Schwerin, Germany.

KOSTLINGER, Josef; Singer (Tenor); b. 24 Oct. 1946, Braunau am Inn, Austria. *Education:* Studied at Salzburg and Stockholm. *Career:* Sang in the 1973 Stockholm premiere of Tintomora by Werle; Tamino in the Ingmar Bergman version of Die Zauberflöte; Salzburg Landestheater from 1974, in the premieres of König Ubu by F Hummel, 1994; Roles have included Mozart's Ferrando, Tamino and Belmonte; Ernesto in Don Pasquale; Many concert appearances. *Recordings:* Magic Flute. *Address:* c/o Landestheater, Schwarstrasse 22, 5020 Salzburg, Austria.

KOSZEWSKI, Andrzej; Composer and Musicologist; b. 26 July 1922, Poznań, Poland; m. Krystyna Jankowska, 9 Sept 1959, 1 d. *Education:* Studies in Musicology, Poznan University with Adolf Chybinski; Diploma, 1950; Studies in Composition with Theory of Music, State Higher Schools in Poznan with Stefan B Poradowski, Diploma, 1948 and 1953; With Tadeusz Szeligowski, Warsaw, Diploma, 1958. *Career:* Teacher of Composition and Theory of Music as Professor of Academy of Music, Poznan; Choral works are performed at numerous international festivals and competitions, mainly in Europe, America and Asia; mem, Polish Composer's Union; F Chopin Society; Polish Author's Society. *Compositions include:* Concerto Grosso, 1947; Suita Kaszubska (Kashubian Suite), 1952; Trzy Kotysanki (Three Cradle Songs), 1952–69;

Allegro Symfoniczne, 1953; Sinfonietta, 1956; Sonata Breve, 1954; Muzyka Fa-Re-Mi-Do-Si, 1960; Tryptyk Wielkopolski (Great Poland Triptych), 1963; La espero (The Hope), 1963; Nicolao Copernico dedicatum, 1966; Gry (Games), 1968; Makowe ziarenka (Poppy Seeds). 1969; Przystroje (Ornamentations), 1970; Ba-No-Sche-Ro, 1971–72; Da fischiare, 1973; Canzone e danza, 1974; Trzy koledy (Three Christmas Carols), 1975; Prologus, 1975; 3 Sonatinas, 1978; Ad musicam, 1979; Campana (The Bell), 1980; Angelus Domini, 1981; Three Euphonic Chorales, 1982; Suita Lubuska (Lubusz Suite), 1983; Zaklecia (Incantations), 1983; Strofy trubadura, 1985; Tre pezzi, 1986; Trois chaconnes, 1986; Enigma 575, 1986; Krople teczy (Drops of a Rainbow) 1988; Wi-La-Wi, 1988–94; Serioso-Giocoso, 1989; Miserere, 1989; 3 Tance polskie (3 Polish Dances), 1989; Canti sacri, 1990; Tristis est anima mea, 1992; Ave Maria, 1992; Trittico di Messa, 1992; Carmina Sacrata, 1992–94; Et lux perpetua, 1992–96; Epitaphium, 1994; Iubilatio, 1994; Non sum dignus, 1996; From Dream and From Legend, 1997; Missa Gaude Mater, 1998. *Recordings:* 60 various titles. *Publications:* Author of many publications dealing with Chopinology and Musical Education including Melodics of Chopin's Walzes, 1953; Materials for Piano Improvisation Training, 1968. *Honours:* Many awards and prizes. *Address:* ul Poznanska 37 m 9, 60-850 Poznań, Poland.

KOSZUT, Urszula; Singer (Soprano); b. 13 Dec. 1940, Psycszyna, Poland; m. Gerhard Geist. *Education:* Studied with Maria Eichler-Cholewa in Katowice and with Bogdan Ruskiewicz in Warsaw. *Career:* Debut: Stuttgart in 1967 as Lucia di Lammermoor; Guest appearances in Germany, Warsaw, Geneva, Zürich, Lisbon, Chicago and Toronto; Roles include Regina in Mathis der Maler, Norma, Gounod's Juliette, Mozart's Donna Anna and Fiordiligi and parts in operas by Strauss, Verdi and Puccini; Concert engagements in works by Beethoven, Bach, Brahms, Handel, Haydn, Mozart and Mahler; Glyndebourne in 1970 as the Queen of Night; Member of the Vienna Staatsoper from 1971; Hamburg Staatsoper in the premieres of Ein Stern geht auf aus Jakob by Burkhard, Staatstheater by Kagel and Under Milkwood by Steffens; Further engagements at Cologne and Stuttgart. *Recordings:* Beethoven's 9th Symphony, conducted by Kempe; Roles in Don Giovanni, Mathis der Maler, Sutermeister's Romeo and Juliet and Paer's Leonora; Countess de la Roche in Zimmermann's Die Soldaten. *Address:* Lilienstrasse 26, 6670 St Ingbert, Germany.

KOTCHERGA, Anatoly; Singer (Bass); b. 1947, Ukraine, USSR. *Education:* Studied conducting at the Vinitza Conservatory, then singing at the Tchaikovsky Conservatory, Kiev; Further study with Marguerita Corosio and Giulio Cassaletta, 1975–76. *Career:* Leading soloist at the Kiev Opera from 1972, notably as Basilio, Mephistopheles, Pimen and Arkel; Guest appearances at La Scala Milan, and in Canada, Spain, France, Bulgaria, Czechoslovakia, Germany and Australia; Has sung Boris Godunov with the company of Warsaw Opera (also televised, 1986); Vienna Staatsoper 1988–91, as Shaklovity in Khovanshchina and in Don Carlos; Theater an der Wien, Vienna, as the Commendatore in Don Giovanni (1990); Season 1992 as Boris and The Sergeant in Lady Macbeth of the Mtsensk District at the Opéra Bastille, Paris and La Scala Milan; Concert appearances include Rimsky's Mozart and Salieri at the Vienna Konzerthaus and a recital of Russian songs in Lyons; Sang Boris Godunov at Montpellier, 1996; Pimen in Boris at Toulouse, 1998. *Recordings:* Khovanshchina by Mussorgsky, conducted by Abbado. *Honours:* Winner, Glinka Competition 1971 (Prize from the Ukrainian Ministry of Culture); Prizewinner at international competitions in Berlin 1973 and Moscow (Tchaikovsky Competition) 1974. *Address:* c/o Schaddeck Gasse 5/H, Anately, 1060 Vienna, Austria.

KOTCHINIAN, Arutjun; Singer (Bass); b. 1965, Armenia. *Education:* Tchaikovsky Conservatory, Moscow, with Yevgeny Nesterenko, and with Helmuth Rilling. *Career:* Principal of the Deutsche Oper Berlin from 1996, as Wurm in Luisa Miller, Zaccaria in Nabucco, Gounod's Mephistopheles and Henry VIII in Anna Bolena; Guest artist in Munich, Dresden, Barcelona and Bregenz as Don Giovanni, Leporello, Banquo, Sparafucile, Philip II and the Grand Inquisitor; Season 2001–2002 as Lodovico in Otello at Covent Garden, Verdi Requiem in Berlin, Zaccaria at Bilbao and Fiesco in Simon Boccanegra at San Diego. *Honours:* Winner, ARD Competition; Munich, 1996. *Address:* Deutsche Oper, Bismarckstrasse 35, 10627 Berlin, Germany.

KOTIK, Petr; Composer, Conductor and Flautist; b. 27 Jan. 1942, Prague, Czechoslovakia; m. 30 Sept 1966, 2 s. *Education:* Flute, State Conservatory, Prague, 1956–62; Flute, Music Academy, Prague, 1962–63, 1966–69; Composition, Flute, Music Academy, Vienna, 1963–66. *Career:* In 1964 performed with John Cage and Merce Cunningham Dance Company in Vienna, Prague and Warsaw; Founder of SEM Ensemble, group dedicated to performance of post-Cagean music including Kotik's compositions, 1970; Since 1972 SEM Ensemble performs yearly concerts, USA and Europe; In 1992 founded Orchestra of the SEM Ensemble, recording CD of works by Cage; Conducted the SEM Orchestra, to critical acclaim, in major concerts at Carnegie Hall, 1992, Schausspielhaus Berlin, Alice Tully Hall at Lincoln Center,

Prague Spring Festival and Oji Hall, Tokyo; Performed and conducted at 400 Years of Music in Prague, 1994; Conducted Manhattan Book of the Dead, opera by David First, New York, 1995; Premiered works by Myers, Michell, Lewis and Smith in New York, 1995; Many performances in Europe and the USA with the SEM Ensemble. *Compositions include:* Music for Three, 1964; Kontrabandt, live electronic music, WDR Cologne commission, 1967; There is Singularly Nothing, text Gertrude Stein, 1971–73; John Mary, text Gertrude Stein, 1973; Many Many Women, text Gertrude Stein, 1975–78; Explorations in the Geometry of Thinking, text R Buckminster Fuller, 1978–80; Solos and Instrumental Harmonies, 1981–83; Wilsie Bridge, WDR Cologne commission, 1986–87; Letters to Olga, text Václav Havel, 1989–91; Quiescent Form for orchestra, 1994–95. *Recordings include:* 1st record: There is Singularly Nothing Nos 1 and 11, 1975; Entire Music by Marcel Duchamp, 1976; With John Cage, 1991; Petr Kotik: SEM Ensemble. *Address:* SEM Ensemble, 25 Columbia Place, Brooklyn, NY 11201, USA.

KOTILAINEN, Juha; Singer (Baritone); b. 1954, Finland. *Education:* Studied at the Kuopio Academy and the Sibelius Academy in Helsinki. *Career:* Sang at first in concert, then made opera debut at Helsinki in 1986 as Dandini in La Cenerentola; Has made many appearances as Mozart's Figaro and sang in the premieres of Rautavaara's Vincent at Helsinki in 1990 and Sallinen's Kullervo at Los Angeles in 1992; Engaged at the Aalto Theatre in Essen where roles have included Besenbinder in Humperdinck's Hansel and Gretel, Krushina in Smetana's The Bartered Bride and Pantalon in Prokofiev's The Love for Three Oranges; Recently he has appeared in title roles of Tchaikovsky's Eugene Onegin, Bartók's Duke Bluebeard's Castle and Guglielmo in Così fan tutte; Has also performed in Paul Dessau's opera Die Verurteilung des Lukullus and appeared as Paolo in Verdi's Simon Boccanegra; Title role of Mozart's Don Giovanni at the Aalto Theatre in 1995; Sang the Priest in Dallapiccola's Prigioniero, for Tampere Open, 1996; Season 2000–01 with Puccini's Sharpless and Marcello at Helskinki and Leontes in the premiere of Boesmans's Wintermärchen, at Brussels and the Paris Châtelet; Repertoire also includes solo songs and bass and baritone parts in great church music works; Has appeared in Bach's St Matthew Passion and the B minor Mass; Has given recitals in Finland, Scandinavia, Germany, Greece and Russia. *Recordings:* Numerous for various labels. *Address:* c/o Fazer Artists' Management Inc., Nervanderink, 5 E Y6, 00100 Helsinki, Finland.

KOTKOVA, Hana; Violinist; b. 3 May 1967, Olomouc, Czechoslovakia. *Education:* Conservatory Ostrava; Music Academy, Prague; International Menuhin Music Academy, Gstaad; Masterclasses with W Marschner, J Gingold, P Amoyal. *Career:* Debut: Opava with Opava Chamber Orchestra, 1977; Recitals and solos with orchestras in Czech Republic, Switzerland, Sweden, Italy and France, 1985–; Plays with Camerata Lysy, Yehudi Menuhin and A Lysy in Europe and USA, 1990–93; Chamber Music with N Magaloff, Jeremy Menuhin, P Coker; Recital in Prague, Rudolfinum (Dvořáks Hall) for Y Menuhin's 80, 1996; Duo with English Pianist S Mulligan, 1996–. *Recordings:* 1 CD with Enescu and Janáček, Sonatas; 1 CD with Martinů, 3 Sonatas. *Honours:* Laureat of Kocian's International Competition, 1977; 1st Prize, Beethoven International Competition, 1985; Winner, Prague Spring Competition, 1997; The Gideon Klein Foundation Prize, 1997; City of Prague Prize, 1997. *Current Management:* Prague Autumn, Prague. *Address:* Case di Sopra, 6935 Bosco Luganese, Switzerland.

KOTONSKI, Wlodzimierz; Composer; b. 23 Aug. 1925, Warsaw, Poland; m. Jadwiga Chlebowska, 1951, 1 s. *Education:* MMus, Warsaw State Highter School of Music. *Career:* With Experimental Music Studio of Westdeutscher Rundfunk, Cologne, Federal Republic of Germany, 1966–67; Professor of Composition, Head of Electronic Music Studio, Academy of Music, Warsaw, Poland, 1967–; Chief Music Director, Polish Radio and Television, 1974–76; Lecturer on Composition, USA, 1978; 1983–89, President of the ISCM Polish Section. *Compositions include:* Orchestral and chamber music, electronic and tape music and instrumental theatre; Guitar Concerto, 1994; Winter Journey for ensemble, 1995; Symphony, 1995; Speculum vitae, for orchestra and tape, 1996; Violin Concerto, 1996; Mijikayo, for Japanese instruments, 1996. *Publications:* Goralski and Zbojnicki, 1958; Percussion Instruments in the Modern Orchestra, 1967; Muzyka elektroniczna, 1989. *Address:* Academy of Music, Okolnik 2, Warsaw 00-368, Poland.

KOTOSKI, Dawn; Singer (Soprano); b. 1967, Maryland, USA. *Education:* Studied in New York. *Career:* Sang in the YCA concert series in Washington and New York, 1990–91; Further concerts at Carnegie Hall, Avery Fisher Hall, with the Atlanta, Baltimore and Chicago Symphony Orchestras and at the Metropolitan Opera; Sang Mozart's Susanna with the Canadian Opera Company at Calgary, in Handel's Partenope at Omaha and as Massenet's Sophie at St Louis; European engagements as Pamina, Oscar and Musetta at the Vienna Staatsoper, Susanna at Munich, Gilda in Strasbourg and Oscar at the Opéra Bastille, Paris; Gilda, Adele in Die Fledermaus, Sophie and Musetta, Zürich Opera season 1996–97; Engaged as Jemmy in a new production of Guillaume

Tell in Vienna and as Zdenka in Arabella at Santa Fe; Concert repertory includes Die Schöpfung, by Haydn. *Recordings include:* Handel's Acis and Galtaea, and Giustino; Lisa in La Sonnambula, with Edita Gruberova. *Address:* c/o Opernhaus Zürich, Falkenstrasse 1, 8008 Zürich, Switzerland.

KOUBA, Maria; Singer (Soprano); b. 1924, Altenmarkt, Austria. *Education:* Studied at the Graz Conservatory. *Career:* Debut: Graz, 1957, as Salome; Sang at Graz, 1957–61, Frankfurt from 1961: roles included Madama Butterfly, Salome, both Leonoras of Verdi, Alice Ford, Jenůfa, Senta, Eva, Tosca and Octavian; Guest appearances in Paris, 1962, London 1963 as Salome; Metropolitan Opera 1964–65; Brussels, Vancouver, Santa Fe, Naples, Vienna, Hamburg and Berlin; Other roles include Donna Anna, Liu, and Marenka in The Bartered Bride.

KOUKL, George; Pianist and Composer; b. 23 March 1953, Origlio, Switzerland. *Education:* Milan Conservatory; Diploma, Zürich Conservatory; Masterclasses. *Career:* Debut: 1972; Radio recordings for BBC London, NRK Oslo, Radio Vienna, SR6 Zürich, SSR Lausanne; Television appearances for Swiss television; Concerts in Europe, USA, Japan, South America; Festivals; Masterclasses; mem. Schweizerischer Tonkunstlerverein; Mensa Music, USA. *Compositions:* Pandora's Box; Te Deum; Quartet for wind instruments; Sonata for clarinet and piano; Ideograms, 1991, Radio Lugano. *Recordings:* Various. *Honours:* Alienor Award, Washington, 1986. *Current Management:* Music Play Management, 6947 Vaglio, Switzerland. *Address:* Casa La Campagnola, 6945 Origlio, Switzerland.

KOUKOS, Periklis; Composer and Opera Director; b. 3 Jan. 1960, Athens, Greece. *Education:* Studied Composition with Yannis Papaionnou and Dimitris Dragatakis in Athens, with Hans Werner Henze and Paul Patterson in London. *Career:* Composer; Professor of Piano, Advanced Theory and Composition at the National and the Athens Conservatories, 1990–; Artistic Director, Greek National Opera, 1997–99; Artistic Director and Supervisor of Millennium Advent, Acropolis, 1999–2000; President of the Hellenic Festival SA, 2000–. *Compositions include:* Merlin the Magician, children's opera, 1987–89; Conroy's Other Selves, opera in 1 act, Athens, 1990; The Manuscript of Manuel Salinas, opera in 3 acts; A Midsummer Night's Dream, opera-ballet, 1982. *Address:* c/o Hellenic Festival SA, Hadjichristou 23 and Mauriyanni S, 11742 Athens, Greece.

KOUNADIS, Arghyris; Composer; b. 14 Feb. 1924, Constantinople, Turkey. *Education:* Studied Piano at Athens Conservatory and with Yanni Papaionnou at the Hellenic Conservatory; Further studies with Wolfgang Fortner in Freiburg. *Career:* Director of Musica Viva concerts at Freiburg from 1963, Professor at Hochschule für Musik, 1972. *Compositions include:* Operas: The Return (performed Athens, 1991); Der Gumminsarg, Bonn, 1968; Die verhexten Notenstander, Freiburg, 1971; Tirésias, Heidelberg, 1975; Der Ausbruch, Bayreuth, 1975; Die Bassgeige, Freiburg, 1979; Lysistrate, Lubeck, 1983; Der Sandmann, Hamburg, 1987. *Address:* c/o Staatliche Hochschule für Musik, Freiburg im Breisgau, Schwarzwaldstrasse 141, 7800 Freiburg im Breisgau, Germany.

KOUT, Jiri; Conductor; b. 26 Dec. 1937, Novedvory, Czechoslovakia. *Education:* Studied conducting and organ at the Prague Conservatory; Further studies at the National Academy of Music in Prague. *Career:* Resident Conductor, Pilsener Opera and Symphony Orchestra; Principal Conductor of the National Opera in Prague, also appearing with the Prague Symphony Orchestra and the National Radio Orchestra; Principal conductor, Deutsche Oper am Rhein, Düsseldorf, 1978–84; Conducted Der Rosenkavalier at Munich 1985, leading to engagements in Stuttgart, Berlin and Vienna; Debut with the Berlin Philharmonic 1987; Regular appearances in Saarbrucken (The Ring) also Venice, Naples, Florence, Cincinnati and Birmingham; Conducted Katya Kabanova in Paris and Los Angeles, 1988; Lady Macbeth at the Deutsche Oper Berlin (Principal Resident Conductor from 1990), followed by Tristan und Isolde and Mathis der Maler; Bluebeard's Castle at the Vienna Staatsoper; Returned to Los Angeles with Boris Godunov and Parsifal; Metropolitan Opera debut 1991 (Der Rosenkavalier); Season 1992 with Tannhäuser at the Deutsche Oper Berlin and The Makropulos Case at Los Angeles; Covent Garden debut 1993, Jenůfa; Wagner's Ring at the Deutsche Oper, 1997; Elektra at San Francisco, 1997–98; Der Rosenkavalier at the Met, 2000. *Honours:* Winner of conducting competitions at Besancon and Brussels, 1965, 1969. *Current Management:* Athole Still International Management, Forresters Hall, 25–27 Westow Street, London, SE19 3RY, England. *Telephone:* (20) 8771-5271. *Fax:* (20) 8768-6600. *Website:* www .atholestill.com.

KOVACEVICH, Stephen; Pianist and Conductor; b. 17 Oct. 1940, Los Angeles, California, USA. *Education:* Studied under Lev Shor and Dame Myra Hess. *Career:* Debut: London debut, 1961; Appeared at international music festivals in Edinburgh, Bath, Harrogate, Berlin, San Sebastian and Salzburg; Soloist, Henry Wood Promenade Concerts

for 14 seasons; Frequent tours in Europe and America; Played Beethoven's Sonatas Op 30 Nos 1 and 2, Op 96 with Kyung Wha Chung, Barbican Centre, 1991; In the United Kingdom has conducted the City of Birmingham Symphony, BBC Philharmonic, Bournemouth Symphony and the Royal Liverpool Philharmonic Orchestras, Chamber Orchestra of Europe and National Youth Chamber Orchestra (at the 1993 Proms); Conducting abroad in Copenhagen and Lisbon, the Los Angeles Philharmonic at the Hollywood Bowl Festival, 1990; Also works at the Aspen Music Festival each summer, as Pianist and Conductor of the Festival Orchestra and the Student Orchestra; Played Mozart's Concerto K503 and Dvořák's Piano Quintet at the Festival Hall, London, 1997. *Recordings:* Numerous including CDs of the Grieg and Schumann Concertos (BBC Symphony under C Davis), Mozart Concerto K467 and K503 (London Symphony), Brahms Rhapsodies, Waltzes and Six Piano Pieces, Op 118, Schubert Sonata D960, Brahms Piano Concertos Nos 1 and 2 (W Sawallisch); Recording complete Beethoven Sonatas; Complete Beethoven 32 Sonatas (EMI Box set), 2003. *Publications:* Schubert Anthology. *Honours:* Winner, Kimber Award, California, 1959; Mozart Prize, London, 1962; Edison Award for recording of Bart ók's 2nd Piano Concerto; Gramophone Award for recording of Brahms Piano Concerto No. 1, 1993; Diapason d'Or for Brahms Piano Concerto No. 2. *Current Management:* Van Walsum Management. *Address:* c/o Van Walsum Management, 4 Addison Bridge Place, London W14 8XP, England.

KOVACIC, Ernst; Violinist and Conductor; b. 12 April 1943, Kapfenberg, Styria, Austria; m. Anna Maria Schuster 1968, 4 s. *Education:* Studied violin, composition and organ, Academy of Music, Vienna. *Career:* Concerts throughout Europe and the USA, Australia, Near, Middle and Far East including performances with London Symphony Orchestra, RPO, Philharmonia, Hallé, London Sinfonietta, London Mozart Players, Scottish Chamber Orchestra, all BBC Orchestras, all German Radio Orchestras, Detroit, Vienna, Prague Symphony, Rotterdam Philharmonic, Budapest Symphony; Teacher, University of Music, Vienna, 1975–; Artistic Director of the Vienna Chamber Orchestra, 1996–98; British premiere of Janáček's Concerto, Liverpool, 1989; Plays British works by Nigel Osborne and Robin Holloway and gave the Concerto by Thomas Wilson at the 1993 London Proms; Henze's Arioso at the Royal Festival Hall with BBC Symphony Orchestra under Oliver Knussen. *Recordings:* All pieces for violin and orchestra by Mozart with Scottish Chamber Orchestra; Sir Michael Tippett's Triple Concerto with BBC Philharmonic; Bernard Stevens' Violin Concerto with BBC Philharmonic under Edward Downes; Robin Hollway's Concerto (Music Retailers Asscn Best Concerto Recording of the Year); H.K.Gruber's Nebelsteinmusik with the Camerata Academica Salzburg and Franz Welser-Möst; other 20th century works include compositions by Krenek, Schwertsik, Eder, Erod, Gruber, Lampersberg. *Honours:* International Competition Prizes: Geneva 1970, Barcelona 1971, Munich ARD, 1972. *Current Management:* Clarion/Seven Muses, 47 Whitehall Park, London, N19 3TW, England.

KOVACK, Eszter; Singer (Soprano); b. 18 May 1939, Tiszanana, Hungary. *Education:* Studied at the Franz Liszt Academy, Budapest. *Career:* Debut: Budapest National Opera, 1965, as Mercédès in Carmen; Sang in the dramatic repertory throughout Hungary, and as a guest in Prague, Warsaw, Moscow, Berlin and Washington; Metropolitan Opera, New York, 1982–84, notably as Brünnhilde in Die Walküre; Other roles include Leonore in Fidelio; Wagner's Elisabeth, Elsa, Eva and Sieglinde; Frequent concert appearances. *Address:* c/o National Opera, Nepoztarasag utja 22, 1061 Budapest, Hungary.

KOVACS, Dénes; Violinist; b. 18 April 1930, Vac, Hungary; m., 1 s., 1 d. *Education:* Budapest Academy of Music under Ede Zathureczky. *Career:* 1st Violinist, Budapest State Opera, 1951–60; Leading Violin Professor, Budapest Music Academy, 1957–; Director, Budapest Music Academy, 1967–; Rector, Ferenc Liszt Academy of Music, 1971–80; Dean of String Department, 1980–; Concert tours all over Europe, USA, USSR, Iran, India, China and Japan; Member of Jury in International Competitions: Tchaikovsky, Moscow; Long-Thibaud, Paris; Jean Sibelius, Helsinki; Joseph Joachim, Vienna; Wieniawski, Warsaw; Tokyo. *Honours:* Kossuth prize, 1963; Awarded Eminent Artist Title, 1970; Golden Medal of labour, 1974. *Address:* Music Academy, Liszt Ferenc ter 8, 1061 Budapest VI, Hungary.

KOVACS, Janos; Conductor; b. 1951, Budapest, Hungary. *Education:* Study under Professor Andràs Korodi, Ferenc Liszt Academy of Music, Budapest, 1971. *Career:* Coach, Conductor, Budapest State Opera; Musical Assistant, Bayreuth Festival, 1978, 1979; Frequent Conductor of top Hungarian Symphony Orchestras; Has conducted several guest performances given by the Budapest State Opera at the Dresden Festival and in the Berlin State Opera House; Two guest performances with Hungarian State Symphony Orchestra and festive concert series marking opening of Berlin's reconstructed Neues Konzerthaus, 1984; Conductor of several performances at Vienna Chamber Opera, 1984; Suisse Romande Orchestra, Geneva, Switzerland, 1985. *Honours:* Liszt

Prize, 1985; Conducted Le nozze di Figaro at Budapest, 1998. *Address:* Hungarian State Opera, Nepotarsasag utja 22, 1061 Budapest, Hungary.

KOVACZ, Peter; Singer (Baritone); b. 1952, Budapest, Hungary. *Education:* Studied in Budapest, Dortmund and Munich. *Career:* Sang in opera at Munich and Pforzheim, followed by Gelsenkirchen and Dortmund; Appearances throughout Germany in operas by Mozart, Verdi and Wagner, notably as Gunther in Götterdämmerung, 1994, Dortmund. *Honours:* Treviso Singers Competition, 1978, winner for performances as Silvio in Pagliacci. *Address:* Dortmund Opera, Kuhstrasse 12, 4600 Dortmund, Germany.

KOVATS, Kolos; Singer (Bass); b. 1948, Hungary. *Education:* Ferenc Liszt Academy of Music, Budapest. *Career:* Budapest State Opera. Has made numerous appearances including operas The Magic Flute, Eugene Onegin, Boris Godunov, Don Carlos, La Forza del Destino, Ernani, Simon Boccanegra, Norma and title role in Rossini's Moses, in concert halls and opera houses around the world; Title role in Bart ók's Duke Bluebeard's Castle; Sang Zaccaria in Nabucco at Brussels, 1987; Bluebeard at Turin, 1989; Sang Catalani's La Wally at the 1990 Bregenz Festival; Other roles include Verdi's Philip, Banquo, Sparalucile, Fiesco, Padre Guardiano, Pagno (Lombardi), Fernando, Silva and Ramphis; Also Mozart's Sarastro and Commendatore, Mephistopheles, Creon, Oroveso, Pimen, Gremin and Henry VIII in Anna Bolena; Sang Bluebeard at the Théâtre du Châtelet, Paris, 1996; Has appeared in television and films; Oratorios. *Recordings include:* Has made numerous records: Medea, Ernani, Don Carlos, Lombardi, Macbeth, Liszt's St Elizabeth, Masses by Mozart and Schubert, Guillaume Tell; Video of Bluebeard's Castle, conducted by Solti. *Honours:* 1st Prize, Erkel International Voice Contest, 1973; 1st Prize, Rio de Janeiro International Vocal Competition, 1973; 2nd Prize, Moscow Tchaikovsky International Vocal Concours, 1974; Recipient, Liszt Prize; Kossuth Prize, 1992. *Address:* c/o Hungarian State Opera House, Andrássy u 22, 1061 Budapest, Hungary.

KOWALKE, Kim H.; Professor of Music, Musicologist and Foundation President; b. 25 June 1948, Monticello, Minnesota, USA; m. Elizabeth Keagy, 19 Aug 1978, 1 s. *Education:* BA, cum laude with special departmental honours in Music, Macalester College, 1970; MA, 1972, MPhil, 1974, PhD, 1977, Yale University. *Career:* Assistant Professor of Music, 1977–82, Associate Professor, 1982–86, Occidental College, Los Angeles, CA; Professor of Music and Musicology, Eastman School of Music, University of Rochester, NY, 1986–; President of Kurt Weill Foundation for Music Inc; Member of Editorial Board, Kurt Weill Edition, 1992–. *Publications:* Kurt Weill in Europe, 1979; Accounting for Success: Misunderstanding Die Dreigroschenoper, 1990; Editor: A New Orpheus: Essays on Kurt Weill, 1986, A Stranger Here Myself: Kurt Weill Studien, 1993; Speak Low: The Letters of Kurt Weill and Lotte Lenya, 1995, published in German , 1999. *Honours:* 5–time winner ASCAP-Deems Taylor Award for Excellence in Writing About Music; Friedley Award from the Theatre Library Association; 2–time winner of Irving Lowens Prize, Sonneck Society for American Music, for best article on American Music; Goergen Award for Distinguished Achievment and Artistryin undergraduate education, University of Rochester. *Address:* 888 Quaker Road, Scottsville, NY 14546-9757, USA. *E-mail:* kkwk@mail.rochester.edu.

KOWALSKI, David (Leon); Composer; b. 29 March 1956, New Haven, Connecticut, USA; m. Michelle Disco, 2 Sept 1983, deceased 29 April 1994. *Education:* BA, University of Pennsylvania, 1978; MM, Composition, New England Conservatory of Music, 1981; PhD, Composition, Princeton University, 1985; Private studies with Donald Martino, Arthur Berger, Milton Babbitt. *Career:* Freelance Composer, 1978–. *Compositions include:* Quintus Obscurus, bass flute, viola, celeste and 2 percussion, 1977; Metamorphosis, jazz trio and orchestra, 1978; Dichotomies, solo viola, 1979, revised 1983; Come Sopra, oboe and cello, 1979; Les Voyageurs, horn and 3 celli, 1979, revised 1991; Quintetino, string quartet and piano, 1980; Concertino, flute/piccolo, clarinet, horn, violin, cello, bass, harp, piano and 2 percussion, 1980; Double Helix, orchestra, 1980, revised 1991; Alle Tode, soprano and piano, 1981; String Quartet No. 2, 1982; Chamber Concerto, 1982, revised 1984; Toccata, organ, 1982; Circonspection, soprano and clarinet, 1983; Four Frames, percussion quartet, 1983; Clarinet Quartet, clarinet, violin, cello and piano, 1983; Variations, wind quartet, 1983, revised 1991; Premonitions, piano solo, 1983; Skid Row, computer-generated tape, 1983; Masques, oboe, 1984; Echoes, soprano and computer-generated tape, 1984; Windhover, soprano and piano, 1985; Masques II, solo flute, 1986; Masques III, solo clarinet, 1987; Two Sonnets for soprano and piano, 1988; A Memory of Evening, mezzo and piano, 1989. *Recordings:* Double Helix performed by Silesian Philharmonic, with Joel Suben conducting, CD, 1995. *Address:* 32 Academy St, PO Box 501, Kingston, NJ 08528, USA.

KOWALSKI, Jochen; Singer (Counter-tenor); b. 30 Jan. 1954, Wachow, Brandeburg, Germany. *Education:* Studied at the Berlin Musikhochschule with Heinz Reeh; Further study with Marianne Fischer-Kupfer. *Career:* Sang at the Handel Festival Halle 1982, in the pasticcio Muzio Scevola; Has appeared with the Komische Oper Berlin from 1983, debut as Feodor in Boris Godunov; Guest appearances at the State Operas of Munich and Hamburg; Paris Opéra 1987 as Ptolomeo in Giulio Cesare; Vienna Staatsoper 1987 as Orlofsky in Die Fledermaus; Vienna Volksoper in Giustinio by Handel; Has also sung in Düsseldorf, 1989, Amsterdam and Minneapolis; Sang Gluck's Orpheus with the Komische Oper at Covent Garden 1989, returned as Orlofsky 1990, in performances which also featured Joan Sutherland's retirement; Other roles include Daniel in Handel's Belshazzar, and Annio in La Clemenza di Tito; Sang Farnace in Mozart's Mitridate, Covent Garden 1991, Amsterdam 1992; Ottone in L'Incoronazione di Poppea at the 1993 Salzburg Festival; Sang Britten's Oberon at the Met, 1996–97 and at the Vienna Volksoper, 1998. *Recordings include:* Baroque Arias by Prussian composers; Handel and Mozart Arias; Gluck's Orfeo and Euridice; Symphoniae Sacrae by Schütz (Capriccio). *Address:* Komische Oper, Behrenstrasse 55/57, 1080 Berlin, Germany.

KOX, Hans; Composer; b. 19 May 1930, Arnhem, Netherlands. *Education:* Studied at Utrecht Conservatory and with Henk Badings, 1951–55. *Career:* Director of Doetinchem Music School, 1957–71; Teacher at Utrecht Conservatory, 1971–. *Compositions include:* Over 200 symphonic, operatic and chamber music works including: Dorian Gray, opera, 1974, Lord Rochester, opera, 1978, 3 Symphonies, 1959, 1966 and 1985, Le Songe du Vergier for Cello and Orchestra, 1986, Magnificat I and II for Vocal Ensemble, 1989–90, Das Grune Gesicht, opera, 1981–91, Sonate for Violoncello and Piano, revised 1991, Face to Face, concerto for Altosaxophone and Strings, 1992, Cyclophony XIV, The Birds of Aengus for Violin and Harp, 1992, Oratorium Sjoah, 1993, Violin Concerto No. 3, 1993, Orkester Suite Aus der Oper Das Grune Gesicht, 1994, Ballet Suite for Orchestra, revised 1994, Das Credo Quia Absurdum for Soprano Solo, Bass Solo, Choir and Orchestra, 1995. *Recordings:* 3 CDs: L'Allegria, Oratorium Sjoah and Chamber music 'Through a Glass, Darkly'. *Honours:* Visser Neerlandia Prize for Symphony No. 1, 1959; Prix Italia for In Those Days, 1970; 1st Prize, Rostrum of Composers for L'Allegria, 1974. *Address:* c/o Hans Kox Foundation, Vier Heemskinderenstraat 42 hs, 1055 LL Amsterdam, Netherlands.

KOZAR, John; Concert Pianist and Conductor; b. 12 June 1946, Indiana, USA. *Education:* Academy of Music, Zagreb, Croatia; BMus, MMus, Indiana University, USA. *Career:* Debut: New York, 1978; British Concerto Debut, 1981; Teacher: University of Kansas, Indiana University, New England College, State University of New York, Ball State University; Recitals: New York City, London, Chicago, Munich, Vienna, Zagreb, Hong Kong, Johannesburg, Paris, Vancouver, Sydney; Concertos: Australia, London Philharmonic, Brooklyn Philharmonic; Television: Public Broadcasting Systems, Hong Kong Television, Scottish Television, SABC, CBC, Vancouver; Radio: Numerous radio performances, Nationally and Internationally; Conducting: Music Director, Kentish Opera Group, England; Music Director, Opera Program, State University of New York, Potsdam; Program Director, The Beethoven Foundation, Indiana; Freelance, Conductor, Opera, Ballet; Founded Piano Productions, 1989; Music Director and Conductor of Grand Piano Orchestra, including three tours of China. *Recordings:* Various albums. *Publications:* Annotated Bibliography of American Composer Emerson Whithorne, in progress. *Contributions:* Articles in professional journals. *Current Management:* Piano Productions Inc, 2063 Lombard Street, Philadelphia, PA 19146, USA.

KOŽELUHOVA, Jitka; Composer, Pianist and Singer; b. 19 Nov. 1966, Prague, Czechoslovakia; m. Marcus Gerhardts 1996; one s. *Education:* Conservatory of Prague; Music Faculty of the Acad. of Performimg Arts in Prague. *Compositions:* Sonatine for pianoforte, 1986; Touzeni (Longing) cycle of songs for soprano and pianoforte, 1987; Obrazy (Images), string quartet, 1990–91; Six Songs On The Texts Of The Poems Of Emily Dickinson, cycle for soprano and pianoforte, 1991–92; Three Sentences About The Story Of Christmas, quartet for oboe, clarinet, bassoon and pianoforte, 1992–93; further compositions: Pierres (Stones) (cycle of women's choirs), 1992; Aus Der Tiefe (de Profundis) for mixed choir with soprano solo, 2 narrators and organ, 1994; Secret Dolour, Fantasy on themes from Schubert's Rondo Op 84, for 4 piano hands, 1994; The Inner Voice, viola solo and symphony orchestra, 1994–95; All You Are Thirsty, Come To The Waters, small cantata for alto and baritone solo, English horn, piano and percussions, 1995; For Angels, for 2 flutes, 2 clarinets, string quartet and piano, 1996; Yet, Still, the Hallelujah is Sounding, for piano and cello, 1998. *Address:* Na Roktyce 30, 18000 Prague 8, Czech Republic.

KOŽENÁ, Magdalena; Czech singer (mezzo-soprano); b. 26 May 1973, Brno. *Education:* Conservatoire, Brno, Acad. of Music and Dramatic Art, Bratislava. *Career:* guest singer, Janáček Opera, Brno 1991–; debut as soloist, Vienna Volksoper 1996–97; recent appearances include Bach's B Minor Mass at the QEH, London 2000, Salzburg Festival debut as Zerlina in Don Giovanni 2002, charity concerts following floods in Czech Repub. 2002, Idamante in Idomeneo at Glyndebourne 2003; regular appearances for Czech radio and television; tours in Europe, USA, Japan, Venezuela, Taiwan, Hong Kong, Republic of Korea, Canada; roles include Dorabella in Così fan tutte, Isabella in Italiana in Algeri (Rossini), Venus in Dardanus (Rameau), Mercedes in Carmen, Annius in La Clemenza di Tito, Paris in Paride ed Elena, lead in Orfeo ed Eurydice (both Gluck), lead in Hermia (Britten), Poppea in L'Incoronazione di Poppea (Monteverdi), Mélisande (Debussy). *Honours:* First Place in Int. Scheider Competition 1992, First Place in Int. Mozart Competition, Salzburg 1995, George Solti Prize (France), Echo Preis (Germany) 2000, Golden CD for Bach's Airs 2000, Gramophone Awards (London) 2001, 2004. *Current Management:* Agency Symfonieta, Beethovenova 4, 602 00 Brno, Czech Republic. *Telephone:* (5) 42215726 (office). *Address:* Národní divadlo, Dvořákova 11, 600 00 Brno, Czech Republic (home). *E-mail:* obchodni.ndb@seznam. *Website:* www .ndbrno.cz.

KOZMA, Lajos; Singer (Tenor); b. 1938, Lepesny, Hungary. *Education:* Franz Liszt Academy Budapest; Further study at the Accademia di Santa Cecilia Rome with Giorgio Favaretto and Franco Capuana. *Career:* First success as Debussy's Pelléas, Budapest, 1962; Appearances from 1964 in Florence, Venice, Rome, Milan, London, Philadelphia, New York and Copenhagen; Amsterdam 1982, as Monteverdi's Orfeo; Teatro San Carlo Naples in Rossellini's La Reine Morte; Further engagements in Paris, Brussels, Aix-en-Provence and Strasbourg; Many concerts in oratorio and Lieder. *Recordings include:* Lucia di Lammermoor; Monteverdi Orfeo; Orlando Furioso by Vivaldi. *Address:* c/o Hungarian State Opera House, Népóztársaság utja 22, 1961 Budapest, Hungary.

KRAEMER, Nicholas; Conductor and Harpsichordist; b. 7 March 1945, Edinburgh, Scotland; m. Elizabeth Andreson; three s. (one deceased) two d. *Career:* Harpsichordist with Acad. of St Martin-in-the-Fields and English Baroque Soloists; founded Raglan Baroque Players, 1978, concerts, numerous radio and television broadcasts; first Musical Dir, Opera 80 (now English Touring Opera); conducted Mozart at Glyndebourne, 1980–83, ENO, 1992, Handel and Monteverdi operas, Paris, Lisbon, Amsterdam, Geneva, Marseille; Assoc. Conductor, BBC Scottish Symphony Orchestra, 1983–85; concerts with Polish Chamber Orchestra, Israel Chamber Orchestra, and Frysk Orkest, Netherlands; Artistic Dir, Irish Chamber Orchestra, 1986–92; Handel in Dublin concerts, 1988–89; concerts with Australian Chamber Orchestra, 1991, with Orchestra of the Age of Enlightenment in Mozart in London, 1991; Principal Guest Conductor, Manchester Camerata, 1992–; debuts, ENO, with Magic Flute, 1992, Marseille Opera, with Poppea, 1993; Artistic Dir, London Bach Orchestra; Season 1994–95 included visits to Munster Philharmonic and National Arts Centre Orchestra, Ottawa; with Scottish Chamber Orchestra: Purcell's Fairy Queen, Edinburgh and Glasgow, and two concerts, Orkney Festival; appeared with London Classical Players, Salzburg and Vienna, 1995; Season 1995–96 included concerts with Orchestra of Age of Enlightenment (Purcell series), CBSO and Northern Sinfonia (Purcell's Fairy Queen); Handel's Rodelinda for recording, dir, Jonathan Miller; Handel's Messiah with Scottish Chamber Orchestra; led the Raglan Baroque Players in Rodelinda for Broomhill Opera, 1996; Handel's Tolomeo in 1998; mem., Royal Society of Musicians. *Recordings:* Vivaldi Violin Concertos Op 9 with Monica Huggett, Op 8 including The Four Seasons with Raglan Baroque Players; complete harpsichord concertos of Bach; complete cello concertos of Vivaldi with Raphael Wallfisch; Locatelli Op 1, Op 3, with Raglan Baroque Players; Vivaldi Wind Concertos, La Stravaganza Op 4 with City of London Sinfonia. *Current Management:* Caroline Phillips Management, The Old Brushworks, Pickwick Road, Corsham, Wiltshire, SN13 9BX, England. *Telephone:* (1249) 716716. *Fax:* (1249) 716717. *E-mail:* cphillips@caroline-phillips.co.uk. *Website:* www .caroline-phillips.co.uk/kraemer.

KRAFT, Jean; Singer (mezzo-soprano); b. 9 Jan. 1940, Menasha, Wisconsin, USA. *Education:* Studied with Giannini Gregory at the Curtis Institute, Theodore Harrison in Chicago, William Ernst Vedal in Munich and Povla Frijsch in New York. *Career:* Debut: New York City Opera 1960, in Six Characters in Search of an Author by Weisgall; Sang in Houston, Boston, New Orleans, Philadelphia, Santa Fe, Chicago and Dallas; Metropolitan Opera from 1970, as Flora in La Traviata, Emilia (Otello) 1987, Herodias, Ulrica and Suzuki; Maggio Musicale Florence 1988, as Mrs Sedley in Peter Grimes. *Recordings include:* Andrea Chénier and Cavalleria Rusticana (RCA). *Address:* Metropolitan Opera, Lincoln Center, New York, NY 10023, USA.

KRAFT, Leo (Abraham); Composer and Teacher; b. 24 July 1922, New York, NY, USA; m. Amy Lager, 16 May 1945, 2 s. *Education:* Pupil in composition of Karol Rathaus, Queens College of the City University of New York, BA, 1945, Randall Thompson, Princeton University, MFA,

1947, and Nadia Boulanger, Paris, 1954–55. *Career:* Faculty Member, Queens College, 1947–. *Compositions:* Orchestral: Concerto for Flute, Clarinet, Trumpet and Strings, 1951; Variations, 1958; 3 Pieces, 1963; Concerto for Cello, Wind Quintet, and Percussion, 1968; Concerto for 12 Instruments, 1966–72; Music, 1975; Concerto for Piano and 14 Instruments, 1978; Chamber Symphony, 1980; Symphony in One Movement, 1985; Ricercare for Strings, 1985; Concerto for Oboe and Strings, 1986; Clarinet Concerto, 1986; Chamber Symphony No. 2, 1996; Chamber: 2 string quartets, 1951, 1959; Sextet, 1952; Partita for Wind Quintet, 1964; Trios and Interludes for Flute, Viola and Piano, 1965; Dialogues for Flute and Tape, 1968; Line Drawings for Flute and Percussion, 1972; Diaphonies for Oboe and Piano, 1975; Dialectica for Flute, Clarinet, Violin, Cello, and Tape, 1976; Conductus Novus for 4 Trombones, 1979; Episodes for Clarinet and Percussion, 1979; Interplay for Trumpet and Percussion, 1983; Strata for 8 Instruments, 1979–84; Washington Square, for 12 players, 1990; 5 Short Pieces for woodwind quintet; Piano pieces; Vocal works including The Vision of Isaiah, for chorus and orchestra, 1998. *Publications:* With S Berkowitz and G Fontrier, A New Approach to Ear Training, 1967; Gradus: An Integrated Approach to Harmony, Counterpoint, and Analysis, 1976, 2nd edition, 1987. *Address:* 9 Dunster Road, Great Neck, NY 11021, USA.

KRAFT, William; Composer; b. 6 Sept. 1923, Chicago, Illinois, USA; m. 2 s., 1 d. *Education:* Bachelor's Degree, cum laude, 1951; Master's Degree, 1954; Columbia University; Studied under Jack Beeson, Henry Brant, Henry Cowell, Paul Henry Lang, Otto Luening, Vladimir Ussachevsky. *Career:* Organised and directed Los Angeles Percussion Ensemble; as percussion soloist performed American premiere of Stockhausen's Zyklus and Boulez's Le Marteau sans Maitre; also recorded Histoire du Soldât under Stravinsky's direction; Conductor of contemporary and other music; Assistant Conductor of Los Angeles Philharmonic, 3 years; served as Musical Director and Chief Adviser, Young Musicians Foundation Debut Orchestra, Los Angeles; appeared frequently at Monday Evening Concerts; Visiting Professor in Composition, USC; Guest Lecturer in Composition, California Institute of Arts, Faculty of Banff Center for Performing Arts; similar residences at University of Western Ontario, Royal Northern College of Music, Manchester, England among others; frequent lecturer at festivals and concert series including Percussive Arts Society International Conference, California State University, Sacramento Festival of New American Music, Res Musica Baltimore concert series; given numerous seminars and master classes at universities and music festivals; Composer-in-Residence, Los Angeles Philharmonic; Founder/Director, Los Angeles Philharmonic New Music group, 1981–85; Composer-in-Residence, Cheltenham International Music Festival, Cheltenham, England, 1986; Visiting Professor in Composition, UCLA, 1988–89. *Compositions include:* Dialogues and Entertainments for soprano solo and wind ensemble, 1980; Double Play for violin, piano and chamber orchestra, 1982; Gallery 83, 1983; Timpani Concerto, 1983; Contextures II: The Final Beast, 1984; Interplay, 1984; Weavings for string quartet, 1984; Gallery 4-5, 1985; Quintessence, 1985; Mélange, 1986; Of Ceremonies, Pageants and Celebrations, 1986; Quartet for the Love of Time, 1987; Interplay, 1984; Episodes, 1987; Horn Concerto, 1988; Kennedy Portrait, 1988; Vintage Rennaissance, for orchestra, 1989; Songs of Flowers, Bells and Death, 1991; Concerto for percussion and chamber ensemble, 1993; Music for String Quartet and Percussion, 1993; Symphony of Sorrows, 1995; Encounters IX, for English horn and percussion, 1999. *Recordings:* Many of his compositions recorded. *Address:* 1437 Crest Drive, Altadena, CA 91001, USA.

KRAINEV, Vladimir (Vsevolodovitch); Pianist; b. 1 April 1944, Krasnoyarsk, Siberia, Russia; m. Tatiana Tarasova, 2 Mar 1979. *Education:* Kharkov Music School, Ukraine; Central Music School, Moscow; Class of Heinrich Neuhaus, Moscow Tchaikovsky Conservatoire. *Career:* Debut: Haydn Concerto in D Major and Beethoven Concerto No. 1 in C Major with Kharkov Philharmonic Orchestra, at age 8; Soloist with world-famous orchestras: London Philharmonic Orchestra, London Symphony Orchestra, London Royal Philharmonic Orchestra, Royal Liverpool Philharmonic Orchestra, BBC Philharmonic, Washington National Symphony, Minneapolis Symphony, Los Angeles Philharmonic, Bavarian Broadcasting Symphony Orchestra, Leipziger Gewandhausorchester, Dresden Philharmonic Orchestra, Sächsische Staatskapelle Dresden, Berlin Symphony Orchestra, Berlin Philharmonic Orchestra, Frankfurt Radio Symphony Orchestra, Tonhalle Orchester Zürich, Berner Symphonie Orchester, NHK Symphony Orchestra, Tokyo Philharmonic Orchestra, all major Russian orchestras; Played with great conductors including Pierre Boulez, Bernard Haitink, Kurt Masur, Carlo Maria Giulini, Yevgeny Svetlanov, Gennadi Rohzdestvensky, Yuri Temirkanov, Dmitri Kitaenko, Antal Dorati, Kurt Sanderling, Alexander Dimitriev, Michael Schonwandt; Founder, Chairman, Vladimir Krainev International Young Pianists Competition, Kharkov, and International Vladimir Krainev Charity Fund; Founder, Artistic Director, concert programme Vladimir Krainev, his Friends and Pupils, Moscow Tchaikovsky Conservatoire Large Hall;

Professor, Musik Hochschule, Hanover, Germany; Jury Member, international piano competitions, Leeds, Tokyo, Bolzano, Moscow, Clara Haskil, Seoul. *Recordings:* Prokofiev's 5 Piano Concertos with Frankfurt Radio Symphony Orchestra, conductor Dmitri Kitaenko; Mozart's 27 Piano Concertos with Lithuanian Chamber Orchestra, conductor Saulus Sondezkis; Anthology of Russian Piano Concertos, Shchedrin, Eshpaï, Schnittke. *Current Management:* Agence Artistique Catherine Petit, 26 rue de la Libération, 92210 Saint-Cloud, France. *Address:* Hochschule für Musik und Theater, Emmichplatz 1, Hanover, Germany.

KRAJNY, Boris; Pianist; b. 28 Nov. 1945, Kromeriz, Czechoslovakia. *Education:* Conservatory Kromeriz, 1959–63; Academy of Prague, 1963–69. *Career:* Soloist, Prague Chamber Orchestra, 1972–80 and with Czech Philharmonic, 1982–. *Recordings:* Bach's Complete Organ Works, and Busoni's Complete Organ Works, and works by Beethoven, Chopin, Ravel, Debussy, Prokofiev, Bartók, Honegger, Roussel, Poulenc, Martinů. *Honours:* 1st Prize, Piano Competition, Senigallia, 1976; Grand Prix du Disque Charles Gros Paris, 1982. *Address:* Czech Philharmony, Dum umelcu, 11000 Prague, Czech Republic.

KRÄMER, Gunter; Stage Director; b. 2 Dec. 1940, Neustadt an der Weinstrasse, Germany. *Education:* Studied at Heidelberg and Freiburg Universities. *Career:* Debut: First opera production, Krenek's Karl V at Darmstadt, 1979; Head of Drama at Bremen and produced Nono's Intelleranza 60 at Hamburg Staatsoper, 1985; Deutsche Oper am Rhein, Düsseldorf, 1986–87, with Die Tote Stadt and Schreker's Die Gezeichneten; Productions at Deutsche Oper Berlin have included The Makropulos Case (seen at Los Angeles, 1992); Die Entführung and Die Zauberflöte, 1991; Intendant of the Theatre Company of Cologne, 1990, producing Weill's Die Dreigroschenoper with it at the Spoleto Festival, 1991; Les Contes d'Hoffmann at Cologne, 1998. *Address:* c/o Opera Köln, Offenbachplatz, 50667 Köln, Germany.

KRÄMER, Toni; Singer (Tenor); b. 14 Sept. 1935, Malsch, Germany. *Education:* Studied at the Karlsruhe Musikhochschule. *Career:* Debut: Stuttgart 1965, in Les Contes d'Hoffmann; Sang in Stuttgart as Pinkerton and Alvaro, and other roles in operas by Puccini and Verdi; Sang Florestan and Erik in Klagenfurt, Parsifal and Lohengrin in Saarbrucken; Stuttgart Staatsoper as Walther in Die Meistersinger, Siegfried, and König Hirsch in the opera by Henze; Munich Staatsoper as Dimitri in Boris Godunov; Bayreuth Festival 1985–86, as Siegfried in Der Ring des Nibelungen; Deutsche Oper Berlin 1987, as Siegfried and Froh in the Ring; Metropolitan 1988, as Siegfried in Götterdämmerung; sang Aegisthus in Elektra at Stuttgart, 1989; Stuttgart Staatsoper 1992, as Bacchus in Ariadne auf Naxos. *Recordings include:* Lohengrin; Video of Der Freischütz. *Address:* c/o Staatstheater Stuttgart, Oberer Schlossgarten 6, 7000 Stuttgart 1, Germany.

KRANTJA, Mustafa; Composer, Publicist and Conductor; b. 10 April 1921, Kavaje, Albania; m., 3 s. *Education:* Piacenza Conservatory, 1933–40; The Conducting and Composition, The Academy of Music, Prague, 1947–50. *Career:* Debut: Primary conductor, opera house, Tirana; Opera House, Tirana; Bolshoi Theatre, Moscow; Barbiere di Siviglia, Bucharest, 1959–60; The Bartered Bride, Brno, 1960; The Prague Spring Festival, 1950, 1952, 1960; Symphonic concerts, USSR, Romania; mem, Alexander Moislu Foundation; Albanian Association. *Compositions:* Suite for chamber orchestra played in Prague, 1952; Instrumental pieces, songs. *Recordings:* Mozart, flute, harp and orchestra concerto; Mrika, first Albanian opera; Schubert, Symphony no. 8; About 20 major works. *Publications:* Krantja, Ave Musicus, 1998; About 300 symposium research studies, published in Albanian, Italian, Russian and English. *Contributions:* Review, On The Musical Language of the Czech Composer, Janáček. *Honours:* People's Artist, 1985; People's Republic Award, 1956; Dvořák Medal, 1975. *Address:* Pr KongresiLushnjesi, p 41 Sh 3 ap 27, Tirana, Albania.

KRANZLE, Johannes Martin; Singer (baritone); b. 1962, Augsburg, Germany. *Education:* Studied at the Frankfurt Musikhochschule. *Career:* Sang in opera at Dortmund, from 1987; Hanover Staatstheater from 1991, notably as Papageno, Guglielmo, Rossini's Figaro and Dandini, 1996; Sang in the premiere of Draussen vor der Tur by F X Thoma, 1994; Guest appearances at the State Operas of Hamburg and Munich, in Henze's Junge Lord, 1994; In Leipzig, as Eisenstein, 1995; Festival engagements at Spoleto and Schleswig Holstein; Season 1998 as Lescaut in Henze's Boulevard Solitude, Frankfurt. *Honours:* Prizewinner at Vercelli, Paris, Perpignan and Rio de Janeiro Competitions.

KRAPP, Edgar; Organist, Harpsichordist and University Professor; b. 3 June 1947, Bamberg, Germany; m. Dr Maria-Christine Behrens, 22 July 1978, 2 s. *Education:* Regensburg Cathedral Church Choir, 1956–64; Studied Organ, College of Music, Munich, 1966–71; Pupil of Marie Claire Alain, Paris, 1971–72. *Career:* Concerts in Europe, North and South America, Japan; Radio and television programmes in Germany and Japan; Succeeded Helmut Walcha as Professor of Organ

at the Hochschule für Musik, Frankfurt, 1974; Visiting Professor at the Salzburg Mozarteum, 1982–91; Professor of Organ, Hochschule für Musik, Munich, 1993–; Concerts with conductors such as Rafael Kubelik, Colin Davis, Horst Stein, Christoph Eschenbach; Member of Jury of International Organ Competitions at Berlin, Munich, Nuremberg, Linz, Tokyo, Chartres; Member, Bayerische Akademie der Schönen Künste; Member, Board of Directors, Neue Bachgesellschaft, Leipzig; Artistic Director, Organ Series at New Concert Hall Bamberg. *Recordings:* Handel: all organ and harpsichord works; Organ recordings in Haarlem (St Bavo Church), Berlin (St Hedwig's Cathedral), Passau Cathedral, historical instruments in Germany (Brandenburg Cathedral and Benediktbeuern, Ottobeuren Basilica). *Honours:* 1st Prize, ARD Competition, Munich 1971; Mendelssohn Prize, Berlin, 1971; German Recording Prizes for Organ, 1981; Harpsichord, 1983; Grand Prix du Disque, 1983; Frankfurt Music Prize, 1983. *Address:* Hauptstrasse 15, 82054 Sauerlach-Altkirchen, Germany. *E-mail:* Ekrapp@t-online.de. *Website:* www.edgar-krapp.de.

KRASSMANN, Jurgen; Singer (Baritone); b. 6 April 1933, Gorlitz, Germany. *Education:* Studied at the Dresden Musikhochschule and with Rudolf Bockelmann. *Career:* Sang with the Dresden Staatsoper, 1956–64, and appeared there and elsewhere in Germany, notably at Halle in operas by Handel, in roles of Cleontes in Alessandro, Gernando in Faramondo, as Scipio, Phoenix in Deidamia, Garibaldo in Rodelinda and Ottone in Agrippina; Sang in Ariodante at Wiesbaden in 1972 and Floridante at Linz in 1987; Further appearances in Leipzig and elsewhere in Germany as Pizarro, the Dutchman, Rigoletto, Macbeth, Scarpia and Nick Shadow in The Rake's Progress. *Address:* c/o Landestheater, Promenade 39, 4010 Linz, Austria.

KRAŠTEVA, Neva; composer and organist; b. 2 Aug. 1946, Sofia, Bulgaria. *Education:* Moscow Conservatory and in Prague and Zürich. *Career:* Lecturer, Sofia State Acad. 1974–; founder of Bulgaria's first organ school. *Compositions include:* Mythological Songs for Soprano and Ensemble 1976, The Old Icon for Low Voice and Organ 1987, Apokriff, cantata 1989, Quantus Tremor, cantata, for mezzo, trumpet, organ and cello 1989, Missa Angelus for female chorus 1991, Oboe Sonatina 1991, Reflections, for low voice and piano 1994, Obretenov's Requiem for contralto, chorus and organ 1995. *Address:* c/o Sofia State Academy, Sofia 1505, Bulgaria.

KRAUKLIS, Georgij; Musicologist; b. 12 May 1922, Moscow, Russia; m. Irina Shklaeva, 4 Aug 1946, 1 d. *Education:* Musical College, Conservatory of Moscow, 1946–48; Theoretical Studies, Composition Faculty, 1948–53, Postgraduate course in Musical History, 1953–56, Conservatory of Moscow. *Career:* Consultant to Moscow Philharmonic, 1952–60; Teacher, Choral College, Moscow, 1955–62; Teacher, 1956–67, Docent, 1967–80, Dean, 1978–89, Professor, 1980–, Conservatory of Moscow; Director of Stage, France's Violinists, Sarla, France, 1982; mem, Associate Editor, JALS, USA, 1987–92. *Publications:* Piano Sonatas of Schubert, 1963; Operatic overtures of R Wagner, 1964; Symphonic Poems of R Strauss, 1970; Symphonic Poems of F Liszt, 1974; Conceptions of Orchestral Program Music in The Age of Romanticism, 1999. *Contributions:* Bayreuth Music Festival after 116 years, in Musical Academy, 1993. *Honours:* Prize for article, Ministry of Culture, 1979; Honorary Title of Merited Man (representative) of Russian Art, 1994. *Address:* Kostiakova Street 6/5, Ap 81, 125422 Moscow, Russia.

KRAUS, Michael; Singer (Baritone); b. 17 Jan. 1957, Vienna, Austria. *Education:* Studied in Vienna with Otto Edelmann and Josef Greindl. *Career:* After winning various competitions, including the Hugo Wolf in Vienna, sang at Aachen Opera, 1981–84, Ulm, 1984–87, Vienna Volksoper, 1988–91, notably as Papageno; US debut in 1991 at San Francisco Opera; Guest appearances in France, Hungary, Netherlands, Greece and Israel, as Mozart's Leporello, Guglielmo and Count, Puccini's Marcello and Lescaut, Janáček's Forester, Monteverdi's Ottone and the Count in Lortzing's Wildschütz. *Recordings include:* Die Zauberflöte; Jonny Spielt auf by Krenek; Der Rosenkavalier; Turandot by Busoni; Krasa's Verlobung im Traum. *Address:* c/o Volksoper, Wahringerstrasse 78, 1090 Vienna, Austria.

KRAUSE, Tom; Singer (Baritone); b. 5 July 1934, Helsinki, Finland. *Education:* Studied in Hamburg and Vienna and in Berlin with Margot Skoda, Serjo Nazor and Rudolf Bautz. *Career:* Debut: As Lieder singer in Helsinki, 1957; Stage debut at the Städtische Oper Berlin as Escamillo, 1959; Appearances in Milan, Vienna, Paris, Brussels, Bordeaux, Buenos Aires, Cologne, Munich and Toulouse; Bayreuth 1962, as the Herald in Lohengrin; Glyndebourne and London 1963, as the Count in Capriccio and in Britten's War Requiem; Hamburg Staatsoper from 1962, notably in the premieres of Der Goldene Bock by Krenek, 1964, and Searle's Hamlet, 1967; Metropolitan Opera from 1967, Count Almaviva, Malatesta, Escamillo and Guglielmo; Grand Théâtre Geneva 1983, as Golaud in Pelléas et Mélisande; In Chicago with Lyric Opera, San Francisco Opera and Houston Operas; Other roles include Don

Giovanni, Renato, Kurwenal, Amonasro, Germont, Pizarro, Amfortas and Mefistopheles; Sang at the 1985 Savonlinna Festival as King Philip in Don Carlo; Active career as Lieder recital singer and Oratorio Singer; Kammersänger in Hamburg; Salzburg Festival 1992, as Frère Bernard in St François d'Assise by Messiaen; Sang the Music Master in Strauss's Ariadne, Fort Lauderdale, 1996; Frère Bernard in St François d'Assise at Salzburg, 1998. *Recordings:* Tristan und Isolde, Le nozze di Figaro, Così fan tutte, Fidelio, Andrea Chénier, La Bohème, Don Pasquale, Turandot, Elektra, Salome, Un Ballo in Maschera and Otello; Carmen; Lohengrin; Oedipus Rex; Euryanthe. *Honours:* Deutsche Schallplatten Prize; Edison Prize; English Gramophone Prize for Sibelius Songs, 1986. *Address:* c/o Finnish National Opera, Bulevardi 23–27, 00180 Helsinki 18, Finland.

KRAUZE, Zygmunt; Composer and Pianist; b. 19 Sept. 1938, Warsaw, Poland. *Education:* Studied with Kazimierz Sikorski and Maria Wilkomirska at the Warsaw Conservatory, MA, 1964; Further study with Nadia Boulanger in Paris, 1966–67. *Career:* Soloist in recitals of new music in Europe and the USA; Founded the Warsaw Music Workshop, 1967: group consisting of clarinet, trombone, cello and piano, for which 100 composers have written works; Taught piano at Cleveland State University, 1970–71; Lectures at the International Course for New Music at Darmstadt, in Stockholm, Basle and at US Universities; President of the Polish Section of ISCM from 1980; Resident in Paris from 1982; Has worked for IRCAM (Electronic Music Centre) with Boulez; President of the International Society for Contemporary Music, 1987. *Compositions:* Malay Pantuns for 3 Flutes and Female Voice, 1964; Triptych for Piano, 1964; Esquisse for Piano, 1967; Polychromy, for Clarinet, Trombone, Piano and Cello, 1968; Quatuor pour la Naissance, for Clarinet, Violin, Cello and Piano, 1985; Voices for 15 Instruments, 1968–72; Piece for Orchestra No. 1 and 2, 1969–70; 3 String Quartets, 1960, 1969, 1982; Fallingwater for Piano, 1971; Folk Music for Orchestra, 1972; Aus aller Welt Stammende for 10 Strings, 1973; Automatophone for 14 Plucked Instruments and 7 Mechanical Instruments, 1974; Fete Galante et Pastorale, 1975; Piano Concerto No. 1, 1974–76; Suite de danses et de chansons for Harpsichord and Orchestra, 1977; The Star, Chamber Opera, 1980; Violin Concerto, 1980; Tableva Vivant for Chamber Orchestra, 1982; Piece for Orchestra No. 3, 1982; Arabesque for Piano and Chamber Orchestra, 1983; Double Concerto for Violin, Piano and Orchestra, 1985; Symphonie Parisienne, 1986; Nightmare Tango for Piano, 1987; From Keyboard to Score for Piano, 1987; Sigfried und Zygmunt for Piano and Cello, 1988; Piano Quintet, 1993; Terra Incognita for piano and 10 strings, 1994; Pastorale for wind quintet, 1995; Rapsod, for strings, 1995; Piano Concerto No. 2, 1996; Trois Chansons for 16-voice chorus, 1997. *Honours:* Chevalier dans l'ordre des Arts et des Lettres, 1984. *Address:* c/o Society of Authors ZAiKS, 2 Hipoteczna Street, 00 092 Warsaw, Poland. *Telephone:* (4822) 828 17 05. *Fax:* (4822) 828 13 47. *E-mail:* sekretariat@zaiks.org.pl. *Website:* www.zaiks.org.pl.

KRAVITZ, Ellen King, BA, MM, PhD; American musicologist and academic; b. 25 May 1929, Fords, NJ; m. Hilard L. Kravitz 1972; two d. three step-s. *Education:* Georgian Court College, Lakewood, NJ, University of Southern California. *Career:* Full Professor of Music History, California State University, Los Angeles, 1967; researcher in musicology and related arts; Director, Exhibition of Schoenberg's art and music during Schoenberg Centennial Celebration, University of Southern California, 1974; founder, Friends of Music, 1976, Gala; Chair, 1978–1982; participant in Faculty Vocal Extravaganza, California State University, Los Angeles, 1981, 1983, 1985, 1987, 1989, 1991, 1993, 1995, 1997; mem, Pacific Southwest Chapter, American Musicological Society. *Publications:* A Correlation of Concepts Found in German Expressionist Art, Music and Literature, 1970; Editor, Journal of the Arnold Schoenberg Institute, Vol. I, No. 3, Vol. II, No. 3; Catalogue of Schoenberg's Paintings, Drawings and Sketches, 1978; Music in Our Culture, 1996; 3 CDs Edition, 1997; contrib. to Arnold Schoenberg as Artist: Another Look, paper for Musicology Meeting, 1995. *Address:* 526 N Foothill Road, Beverly Hills, CA 90210, USA.

KREBBERS, Herman (Albertus); Violinist; b. 18 June 1923, Hengelo, Netherlands; m. A Torlau, 1 s., 1 d. *Education:* Studied at the Amsterdam Musiklyceum with Oscar Back. *Career:* Debut: Gave first concert in 1932; Soloist with the Concertgebouw Orchestra, 1945; Leader of the Gelderland Orchestra, then the Hague Residentie Orchestra, 1950–62; Leader of the Concertgebouw Orchestra 1962–79; Many tours of Europe and the USA as Soloist; Founded the Guarneri Trio, 1963, and played in Violin Duo with Theo Olof; Teacher at the Amsterdam Musiklyceum. *Recordings:* Bach and Badings Concertos for Two Violins, with Theo Olof and the Hague Philharmonic; Beethoven Concerto with the Hague Philharmonic; Brahms and Bruch Concertos with the Brabant Orchestra; Paganini 1st Concerto with the Vienna Symphony; Haydn Concertos with the Amsterdam Chamber Orchestra. *Honours:* Prix d'Excellence, Amsterdam Musiklyceum, 1940; Knight, Oranje Nassau Order; Many prizes from International Competitions.

Address: c/o Concertgebouworkest, Jacob Obrechtstraat 51, 1071 KJ Amsterdam, Netherlands.

KREBS, Helmut; Singer (Tenor); b. 8 Oct. 1913, Dortmund, Germany. *Education:* Berlin Musikhochschule, 1934–37. *Career:* Began as concert singer; Stage debut, 1937 at the Volksoper, Berlin; Returned to Berlin, 1947; Salzburg Festival, 1949, in the premiere of Orff's Antigonae; Ernesto in Don Pasquale, 1952; Guest appearances in Milan, London, Vienna, Munich, Netherlands and Belgium; Glyndebourne, 1953 as Mozart's Belmonte and Idamantes; Hamburg Radio, 1954 as Aron in the first performance of Schoenberg's Moses und Aron; Berlin, 1956 and 1965, in premieres of Henze's König Hirsch and Der junge Lord; Also heard as the Evangelist in the Passions of Bach; Professor at the Frankfurt Musikhochschule from 1966; Sang at the Deutsche Oper Berlin, 1988 in From the House of the Dead. *Compositions:* Orchestral, Operatic, Chamber, Choral and Vocal works published. *Recordings:* Monteverdi, Orfeo; Henze, Der junge Lord; Bach, Christmas Oratorio; Verdi, Requiem; Stravinsky, Oedipus Rex; Strauss, Ariadne auf Naxos; Schoenberg, Moses und Aron; Wagner, Der fliegende Holländer. *Honours:* Berliner Künstpreis, 1952; Berliner Kammersänger, 1963. *Address:* 11 Im Dol, 14195 Berlin, Germany.

KREIZBERG, Yakov; Russian conductor; b. 24 Oct. 1959, St Petersburg; brother of Semyon Bychkov. *Education:* studied with Ilya Musin in St Petersburg, conducting fellowships at Tanglewood and the Los Angeles Philharmonic Inst. *Career:* emigrated to the USA 1976; Music Dir Mannes Coll. Orchestra, New York 1985–88; Music Dir Krefeld Opera and Lower Rhine Symphony 1988–94; led Così fan tutte and Don Giovanni with Canadian Opera 1991–92, Der Rosenkavalier for ENO 1994; Music Dir Komische Oper Berlin 1994–2001; Principal Conductor Bournemouth Symphony Orchestra 1995–2000; Don Giovanni for Chicago Lyric Opera 1996; opera in Berlin includes The Queen of Spades, Goldschmidt's Der gewaltige Hahnrei, Fidelio, Lucia di Lammermoor, Henze's König Hirsch and Die Zauberflöte 1999; Music Dir and Artistic Adviser Jeunesses Musicales (World Youth Orchestra); further engagements with the Chicago Symphony, Los Angeles Philharmonic Orchestra, San Francisco Symphony Orchestra, Detroit Symphony Orchestra, Berlin Philharmonic, Royal Concertgebouw, Leipzig Gewandhaus, Philharmonia, New York Philharmonic, Philadelphia Orchestra, Boston Symphony, Munich Philharmonic; conducted Jenůfa at Glyndebourne 1992, Don Giovanni 1995, Katya Kabanova 1998; Chief Conductor and Artistic Adviser Netherlands Philharmonic and Netherlands Chamber Orchestras 2003–; Principal Guest Conductor Vienna Symphony Orchestra 2003–(08). *Current Management:* Harrison/Parrott Ltd, 12 Penzance Place, London, W11 4PA, England. *Telephone:* (20) 7229-9166. *Fax:* (20) 7221-5042. *Website:* www .harrisonparrott.com.

KREJCI, Jiri; Oboist; b. 11 Dec. 1935, Dolni Hbity, Czechoslovakia; 2 s., 1 d. *Education:* Military Music School, Kosice; Conservatory of Music, Prague. *Career:* Debut: Soloist, Haydn Concerto, Radio Symphony Orchestra, Prague, 1960; Solo Oboist of the Theatre Orchestra, Vinohrady, Prague, 1953–56; Karlin, Prague, 1957–59; Principal Oboe, Radio Symphony Orchestra, Prague, 1959–64; Solo Oboist, Prague Chamber Orchestra without Chef, 1965–77; Artistic Leader, Collegium Musicum Pragense, 1965–90; Member, Czech Nonet, 1977–; Member, Prague Wind Quintet, 1982–93; Live Recordings for the BBC in London. *Honours:* Prize, Composers Society, 1984; Honorary Award, Ministryof Culture, Czech Republic. *Address:* Ceskolipska 400/20, 1900 Prague 9, Czech Republic.

KREK, Uros; Composer; b. 21 May 1922, Ljubljana, Slovenia; m. Lilijana Pauer 1960. *Education:* Classical Coll., Ljubljana; Music High School, Ljubljana. *Career:* debut, first performance of compositions, Ljubljana 1945; performances of compositions on concert stages, radio and television, film, theatre, records and editions. *Compositions:* Concerto for violin and orchestra; Sinfonietta, Concerto for French horn and orchestra; Concerto for piccolo and orchestra; Rhapsodic Dance for orchestra; Sonata for 2 violins; Five Songs for voice and piano; Movements Concertants, Inventions ferales for violin and strings; Symphony for Strings; Duo for violin and violoncello; La Journée d'un Bouffon for brass quintet; Trio for violin, viola and violoncello; String Quartet; Sur un Melodie for piano; Sonatina for clarinet; Songs for Eva; Concert Diptych for violoncello and orchestra; Sonata for violoncello and piano; 3 Impromptus for violin solo; Sextet for 2 violins, 2 violas and 2 violoncellos; Espressivo and Appassionato for flute and piano; Songs on Folk Tradition for voice and piano; Canticum Resianum, 1988; Vigoroso for violin and piano, 1991; Cantus gratias agentis for soprano, trumpet and organ, 1994; Reflections, 2nd sonata for violin and piano, 1994; Capriccio notturno for violin and harp, 1996; Contrabasso concertante for contrabass and chamber orchestra, 1998 Chamber music, choir music, film and stage music. *Recordings:* numerous recordings of his compositions for radio and television. *Honours:* Preseren Prize, 1952, 1992. *Address:* SI 4248 Lesce, Na Vrtaci 5, Slovenia.

KREMER, Gidon; Violinist and Director; b. 27 Feb. 1947, Riga, Latvia. *Education:* Studied at the Moscow Conservatory with David Oistrakh. *Career:* Many performances as Concert Soloist in Europe, USA and elsewhere in the standard repertoire and in modern works: often heard in Schnittke, and in May 1986 performed Bernstein's Serenade, London; Duo recitals with the pianist Martha Argerich: sonatas by Franck, Schumann and Bart ók, London, 1988; Television appearances include Berg Concerto, with the Bavarian Radio Symphony under Colin Davis; Premieres include Schnittke's First Concerto Grosso (1977), Violin Concerto No. 4 (1984) and Trio (1985); BBC Promenade Concerts, London, 1991, with Gubaidulina's Offertorium, conducted by Simon Rattle; Schubert Contemporary Celebration concert at the Barbican Hall, London, 1997; Premiered Reimann's Concerto at Chicago, 1997; Vivaldi's Four Season at the 1999 London Proms. *Recordings include:* Concertos by Mendelssohn, with Martha Argerich, 1989; Gubaidulina's Offertorium, with the Boston Symphony under Charles Dutoit, Mozart Trio K498 and Duos K423 and K424; Schumann Sonatas, with Argerich. *Honours:* First Prize of the Latvian Republic, 1963; Winner, Tchaikovsky International Competition, Moscow, 1970. *Address:* c/o Mona Fossen, Theresien Strasse 45, 50931 Cologne, Germany.

KRENZ, Jan; Conductor and Composer; b. 14 July 1926, Wloclawek, Poland; m. Alina Krenz, 1 s. *Education:* Warsaw and Łódź. *Career:* Conductor, Łódź Philharmonic Orchestra, 1945; Conductor, Poznan Philharmonic Orchestra, 1948–49; Director and First Conductor, Polish Radio Symphony Orchestra, Katowice, 1953–67; British debut 1961; Conducted Polish Music at the 1967 Cheltenham Festival; Artistic Director, First Conductor, Grand Opera House, Warsaw, 1967–73; General Director, Music, Bonn Orchestra, 1978–82; Tours in Hungary, Romania, Czechoslovakia, France, USSR, Germany, Italy, the United Kingdom, USA, Japan, Australia. *Compositions include:* Symphony; 2 String Quartets; Noctures for Orchestra; Rozmowa dwoch miast; Rhapsody for Strings, Xylophone, Tam-Tam, Timpani and Celesta, 1952; Concertino for Piano and Small Symphony Orchestra, 1952; Orchestral transcriptions of Microcosmos (B Bartók, 1958); Mythes (Szymanowski), 1964. *Recordings:* Paderewski's Piano Concerto; Lutoslawski's 1st Symphony and Wieniawski Violin Concertos; Brahms, Mendelssohn and Tchaikovsky Violin Concertos; Chopin Piano Concertos. *Address:* Al 1 Armii Wojaska Polskiego 16/38, 00-582 Warsaw, Poland.

KRETH, Wolfgang; Lutenist; b. 29 May 1946, Cologne, Germany. *Education:* Studied Music, 1967–75 at: Musikhochschule, Köln; Musikhochschule, Düsseldorf; Musikhochschule, Frankfurt; Musikhochschule, Aachen; Musiklehrer-Examen; Staatl Diplom for Lute, summa cum laude. *Career:* Several Concerts in Europe (Schwetzinger Festspiele, Musica Bayreuth, Dubrovnik-Festival, Wiener Festwochen, Brühler Barock-Fest; Radio appearances, interviews; mem, Lute Society of England; Lute Society of America; Society Nova Giulianiad, Freiburg; Member of EGTA. *Recordings:* Lute Music of Anthony Holborne and Nicolas Vallet; Lute Concerto of Antonio Vivaldi. *Contributions:* Several articles in Gitarre und Laute, Köln. *Address:* Theophanoplatz Nr 8, 5 Köln 51, Germany.

KRETSCHMAR, Helmut; Singer (Tenor); b. 3 Feb. 1928, Kleve, Germany; m. Renate Fischer. *Education:* Studied in Frankfurt with Kurt Thomas and Hans Emge. *Career:* Sang first in concerts and oratorios from 1953; At Hamburg in 1954 sang in the first performance (concert) of Schoenberg's Moses und Aron; Sacred music by Bach at the Berliner Festwochen and the Bach Festivals at Luneberg and Heidelberg, 1960–62; Further appearances at the Handel Festival at Göttingen and in Düsseldorf, Japan, Korea, Paris, Madrid, Bombay, London and Ceylon; Lieder recitals with Renate Fischer, Piano; Repertoire includes sacred music by Handel, Haydn and Mendelssohn; Songs by Wolf, Debussy, Schubert and Schumann; Professor at the Detmold Musikhochschule from 1963. *Recordings include:* Fidelio; Moses und Aron, conducted by Hans Rosbaud; St Matthew Passion, Christmas Oratorio and B Minor Mass by Bach; Beethoven's Missa solemnis; Schubert's Mass in A flat; Die Jahreszeiten by Haydn. *Honours:* First Prize, German Music High Schools, 1953; Kunstpreis of Nordrhein-Westfalen, 1958.

KREUTER, Melanie; Singer (Soprano); b. 24 Feb. 1963, Braunschweig, Germany. *Education:* Studied in Hanover and with Ileana Cotrubas. *Career:* Sang at Stuttgart Opera, 1989–91, as Mozart's Susanna, Zerlina and Papagena; Aennchen in Der Freischütz and Lucilla in La Scala di Seta; Komische Oper Berlin from 1989, with guest appearances at Wiesbaden and Hannover; Dortmund Opera from 1992, as Mozart's Susanna, Pamina and Despina; Sophie in Der Rosenkavalier; Sang in local premieres of Argento's The Voyage of Edgar Allan Poe and Casken's The Golem; Many concert and Lieder programmes. *Address:* Dortmund Opera, Kuhstrasse 12, 4600 Dortmund, Germany.

KRIKORIAN, Mari; Opera Singer (Soprano); b. 25 May 1946, Varna, Bulgaria. *Education:* Secondary School of Music, Varna, 1964; Grad-

uated, 1971, Master's Class, 1972, Bulgarian State Conservatoire, Sofia; Specialisation course with James King, Vienna, 1977. *Career:* Debut: As Adalgisa in Norma, Varna National Opera, 1976; 1st Soprano, Varna National Opera, in La Bohème, Simon Boccanegra, Fliegende Holländer, Otello, Don Carlo and Tosca; 1st Soprano, Sofia National Opera, 1983–; Permanent Repertoire includes Norman, Attila, Aida, Il Trovatore, La Forza de Destino, Don Carlos, Otello, La Bohème, Madama Butterfly, Tosca, Liu, Senta, Adriana Lecouvreur, Tatiana in Eugene Onegin, Lisa in Queen of Spades, Yaroslavna in Prince Igor, Verdi's Requiem, Donizetti's Requiem, Bruckner's Requiem, Brahms Deutsches Requiem, Liszt's Christus Oratorio, Rossini's Stabat Mater, Pergolesi's Stabat Mater; Foreign tours, Prague, Budapest, Russia, Armenia, Germany, Italy, France, Spain, Austria, Greece, Egypt, Cyprus, India, Mexico; Film portrait for Bulgarian Television, 1989; Un Ballo in Maschera, 1993; Foreign Tours: Los Angeles (USA) concerts, 1993. *Recordings:* Opera recital, airs from Bellini, Verdi and Puccini, with Sofia Opera Orchestra, conductor Ivan Marinov, State Recording Company Balkanton, 1984; Attila, by Verdi, with Sofia Philharmonic Orchestra, conductor Vladimir Ghiaurov, and with Nicola Guzelev; Chants Liturgiques Armeniens CD EDITION JADE, Paris, France, 1992; Live and studio recordings for Bulgarian radio and television. *Honours:* 1st Prize, Opera Belcanto Competition, Ostende, Belgium, 1980; Honoured Artist of Bulgaria, 1984. *Current Management:* SOFIACONCERT, Bulgaria. *Address:* Druzba 2 bl 213 A, Ap 11, Sofia 1582, Bulgaria.

KRILOVICI, Marina; Singer (Soprano); b. 11 June 1942, Bucharest, Romania. *Education:* Studied with Mdme Vrabiescu-Varianu in Bucharest and with Matia Caniglia and Luigi Ricci in Rome. *Career:* Debut: National Opera Bucharest, 1966, as Donna Anna; Sang major roles in the Italian repertory with the Bucharest Opera, Covent Garden debut, 1971, as Aida; Chicago Lyric Opera, 1972, as Mimi; Further appearances in Vienna, Berlin, Munich, Montreal, Lisbon, San Francisco and Strasbourg; Hamburg Staatsoper, 1968–76; Sang Adriana Lecouvreur at Athens, 1998. *Recordings include:* Cavelleria Rusticana; Donizetti's Il Duca d'Alba.

KRINGELBORN, Solveig; Singer (Soprano); b. 4 June 1963, Lillestrom, Norway. *Education:* Studied at Stockholm Royal Academy. *Career:* Appearances at the Royal Swedish Opera as Susanna and Papagena, Oslo Opera, 1990–91 as Mimi, Jenůfa and Micaela, with further engagements at the Bolshoi, Moscow, Vienna Staatsoper, Strasbourg, Los Angeles as Mozart's Countess in 1993, Brussels in the premiere of Boesmans' Reigen, Salzburg as Fiordiligi in 1993, Bastille as Antonia in 1993, Geneva as Ilia in 1994 and Mozart's Countess in Salzburg in 1995; Other roles include Musetta, Marguerite, Pamina, Nedda, Serpina in La Serva Padrona, and Drusilla in Poppea; BBC Promenade Concerts in 1991, with the premiere of Lutoslawski's Chantefleurs et Chantefables, conducted by the composer, also televised; Wigmore Hall recital debut in 1992; Other concert repertoire includes Haydn's Jahreszeiten in Paris, Nielsen's 3rd Symphony in London under Simon Rattle, Mahler's 2nd Symphony with the Israel Philharmonic and Cleveland Orchestra, and in Los Angeles in 1993; Sang Mozart's Countess at the 1995 Salzburg Festival and for the San Francisco Opera, 1997–98; Fiordiligi at the 1996 Glyndebourne Festival; Marenka in The Bartered Bride at Glyndebourne and Marie in Wozzeck at the Zürich Opera, 1999; Covent Garden debut as Wagner's Senta, 2000; Engaged as Donna Elvira in Don Giovanni on tour with the Isaeli Philharmonic, and at Bastille Opéra Paris and the Met in New York, 2000. *Recordings include:* Grieg Songs conducted by Rozhdestvensky, a Grieg Solo Song and Tavener Choral Music conducted by David Hill. *Address:* c/o IMG Artists, Lovell House, 616 Chiswick High Road, London W2 5RX, England.

KRISCAK, Manuela; Singer (Soprano); b. 1965, Trieste, Italy. *Education:* Studied at the G Tartini Conservatoire, Trieste. *Career:* Debut: Musetta in La Bohème at the Teatro Nuovo, Spoleto, 1990; Appearances as Tisbe in Cenerentola at Spoleto and Rome, Bianca in La Rondine and Zerlina at Catania; Gianetta in L'Elisir d'amore for French television, Un Plaisir in Gluck's Armide at La Scala (1996); Sang Kristina in The Makropulos Case at Glyndebourne (1995–97) and at Strasbourg and Lisbon; Season 1997–98 as Papagena (Die Zauberflöte) and in Paisiello's Il Barbiere di Siviglia at Trieste. *Address:* Teatro Comunale, G Verdi di Trieste, Rive Novembre 1, 34121 Trieste, Italy.

KRIVINE, Emmanuel; Conductor and Violinist; b. 7 May 1947, Grenoble, France. *Education:* Studied Conducting with Karl Böhm and at the Conservatoire de Paris; Studied Violin with Henryk Szeryng and Yehudi Menuhin. *Career:* Laureate of Violin competitions during 1960s; Conductor in Belgium from 1964; First Guest Conductor of the New Philharmonic Orchestra in Paris, 1976; Musical Director of the Lorraine Philharmonic Orchestra at Metz, 1981–83; Teacher at Lyon Conservatoire, 1979–81; Chief Guest Conductor, 1983–85, Musical Director, 1987–2000, Orchestre National de Lyon; Conducted the premiere of Michel Legrand's Concertoratorio 89, for the bicentenary of the French Revolution; Has conducted most of the major orchestras of the world, including Berlin Philharmonic, Boston Symphony, Concertgebouw, London Symphony, Cleveland Symphony, Philadelphia, Chamber Orchestra of Europe. *Recordings include:* Numerous recordings with London Symphony, Philharmonia, Bamberg Symphony, Orchestre de Lyon, Chamber Orchestra of Europe and others. *Honours:* Prizewinner at violin competitions in Brussels, 1965 and 1968, London, Naples and Bratislava. *Current Management:* Askonas Holt Ltd, Lonsdale Chambers, 27 Chancery Lane, London, WC2A 1PF, England. *Telephone:* (20) 7400-1700. *Fax:* (20) 7400-1799. *E-mail:* info@askonasholt.co.uk. *Website:* www.askonasholt.co.uk. *Address:* 2 rue Hotel de Ville, 1800 Vevey, Switzerland.

KROLL, Mark; Harpsichordist and Professor of Music; b. 13 Sept. 1946, Brooklyn, New York, USA; m. Carol Lieberman, 9 July 1975, 1 s. *Education:* BA, 1968, Graduate School, Musicology, 1968–69, Brooklyn College, City University of New York; MMus, Harpsichord, Yale University School of Music, 1971. *Career:* Debut: Carnegie Hall, New York City, 1975; Performance in solo recitals, chamber music ensembles and as concerto soloist throughout Europe, South America, USA and Canada; Radio and Television appearances; Numerous television shows for Public broadcasting System and BBC; Professor of Harpsichord and Theory and Chair of the Department of Historical Performance, Boston University; Conductor, Orchestral works of Rameau, CPE Bach, Vivaldi; Artist-in-Residence, Lafayette College, Conductor and Artistic Director, Opera New England; Visiting Professor: Würzburg Conservatory, Zagreb Music Academy and Belgrade Music Academy; Visiting Professor at the Academies of Music at Warsaw, Cracow and Athens. *Recordings include:* J. S. Bach, complete sonatas for violin and harpsichord; Handel and Scarlatti, harpsichord works; G F Handel, complete works for recorder and harpsichord; Vivaldi's The Seasons, with Boston Symphony Orchestra; Solo Harpsichord works of J. S. Bach; Harpsichord works of JNP Royer; Franz Schubert, 3 Sonatinas for violin and fortepiano; M de Falla, El Retablo de Maese Pedro, with Montreal Symphony; Contemporary American Harpsichord Music; H. von Biber Sonatas of 1681. *Publications:* French Harpsichord Music, 1994; 17th Century Keyboard Music, 1997; Beethoven Violin Sonatas, 2002; Hummel Transcriptions, 2001, 2002; Hummel's Piano Method, 2003; Early Music America Magazine, 2001, 2002. *Contributions:* Numerous articles for Bostonia magazine. *Honours:* Grants from: NEA, 1984; CIES, 1989; Whiting Foundation, 1993; DAAD, 1996; IREX, 1996; NEH, 2002; Copland Fund, 2001,2002; DAAD, 2002. *Address:* Boston University School of Music, 855 Commonwealth Avenue, Boston, MA 02215, USA.

KROLOPP, Wojciech (Aleksander); Musician, Manager and Journalist; b. 12 April 1945, Poznań, Poland. *Education:* Academy of Music Poznan, 1973–77; Pedagogy, 1968–70. *Career:* Debut: Soloist Soprano, 1957; Soloist Baritone, 1964; Soloist from 1957 (soprano, bass from 1964); Teacher and Conductor, Polish Choir School, Poznan, 1968–; Managing Director, 1969–, Poznan Boys' Choir, and Director of International Boys' Choir Festival, Poznan, 1980–; 3000 concerts with the Poznan Boys' Choir, 400 conducted concerts in 24 countries; Solo parts in major vocal-instrumental works and songs; Camerata, chamber orchestra, 1980–83; Premiere of Mozart opera, Bastien und Bastienne at the Great Theatre in Poznan also in Taiwan and Hong Kong; By end of 1990 nominated as manager and artistic director of the Polish Nightingales. *Recordings:* Mozart's Coronation Mass and Szymanowski's Stabat Mater, 1991. *Publications include:* The Poznan Choir School, monography, 1989. *Current Management:* Polish Artists' Agency, Warsaw and Penta Promotions, Netherlands. *Address:* Torenstraat 13, 9160 Lokeren, Belgium.

KROSNICK, Aaron (Burton); Violinist, Performer-in-Residence and Artist-in-Residence; b. 28 June 1937, New Haven, Connecticut, USA; m. Mary Lou Wesley, 25 Aug 1961, 1 s. *Education:* BA, magna cum laude, Yale College, 1959; MS, Juilliard School of Music, 1961; Fulbright Scholar, Royal Conservatory of Music, Brussels, Belgium, 1961–62; Major teachers, Howard Boatwright, Joseph Fuchs, Ivan Galamian, Arthur Grumiaux. *Career:* Concertmaster (and soloist with orchestras), Springfield, Ohio, Symphony Orchestra, 1962–67; Jacksonville Symphony Orchestra, 1969–80; Sewanee Festival Orchestra, 1969–82; Florida Bicentennial Chamber Orchestra, 1976; Faculty Positions, Wittenberg University, 1962–67; Jacksonville University, 1967–; Summers, Syracuse University, Kneisel Hall Summer School of Ensemble Playing, Sewanee Summer Music Centre, Soloist with extensive concerto repertoire; Appearances with Rome Festival Orchestra, Florida Symphony Chamber Orchestra, Jacksonville University Orchestra and many others; Summers of 1985, 86, Concertmaster and featured Artist, Rome Festival in Italy. *Recordings:* Music of Frederick Delius, Musical Heritage Society. *Honours:* Semi-finalist, Paganini International Competition, Genoa, 1970. *Address:* 13734 Bermuda Cay Court, Jacksonville, FL 32225-5426, USA. *E-mail:* abkmlk@hotmail.com.

KROSNICK, Joel; Cellist; b. 3 April 1941, New Haven, Connecticut, USA. *Education:* Studied with William d'Amato, Luigi Silva and Claus Adam; Further study at Columbia University. *Career:* Co-founded and directed the Group for Contemporary Music at Columbia University, 1962; Professor at University of Iowa, 1963–66; Cellist in Uniersity String Quartet; Professor at University of Massachusetts, 1966–70; Performed with New York Chamber Soloists and made solo tours to Belgrade, Hamburg, Berlin, London and Amsterdam; New York solo debut, 1970; Has given first performances of works by Babbitt, Subotnick and Ligeti; Taught at California Institute of Arts, 1970–74; Cellist with the Juilliard Quartet from 1974; World-wide tours in the standard repertoire and contemporary works; Performances in London, 1990 (works by Mozart). *Recordings include:* Albums with the Juilliard Quartet; Carter's Cello Sonata. *Address:* c/o Library of Congress, Washington DC, USA.

KROSS, Siegfried; Professor of Musicology; b. 24 Aug. 1930, Wuppertal, Germany; m. Dorothee Brand, 23 Mar 1962, 2 s. *Education:* Studied musicology, German literature, psychology, and experimental physics at Universities of Bonn and Freiburg, Br Gurlitt; DPhil, 1956; Habilitation, 1966. *Career:* Scholar, Deutsche Forschungsgemeinschaft, Vienna, 1959; Assistant, Beethoven Archives, Bonn; Assistant Professor, 1970, Professor, Dean, Faculty of Humanities, 1988, University of Bonn; Vice-President, Landes-Musikrat; mem, American Musicological Society; Gesellschaft für Musikforschung. *Publications:* Die Chorwerke von J Brahms, 1957, 2nd edition, 1963; Das Instrumentalkonzert bei G Ph Telemann, 1969; Dokumentation zur Geschichte des Deutschen Liedes Seit, 1973; Geschichte des Deutschen Liedes, 1989; Briefe Robert und Clara Schumanns, 1978, 2nd edition, 1982; Brahms-Bibliographie, 1983; Johannes Brahms, 2 vols, 1997. *Contributions:* Die Musikforschung, 19th Century Music, 1982; American Choral Review 25, 1983; Brahms, 1983–87; Festschrift: Beitrage zur Geschichle des Konzerts, 1990. *Address:* Musikwissenschaftliches Seminar der Universitat Bonn, Adenauer Allee 4–6, 53113 Bonn, Germany.

KRUGER, Anna; Violist; b. 1965, USA. *Education:* Studies at Manhattan School of Music and at Indiana University with James Buswell. *Career:* Former principal of New Jersey Symphony; Co-Founder, Lark String Quartet, New York; Recent concert tours to Australia, Taiwan, Hong Kong, China, Germany and Netherlands; US appearances at the Lincoln Center, New York, Kennedy Center, Washington DC and in Boston, Los Angeles, Philadelphia, St Louis and San Francisco; Repertoire includes quartets by Haydn, Mozart, Beethoven, Schubert, Dvořák, Brahms, Borodin, Bart ók, Debussy and Shostakovich; Concerts at the Wigmore Hall, London, 1994. *Honours:* With Lark Quartet: Gold Medals at 1990 Naumberg and 1991 Shostakovich Competitions; Prizewinner at 1991 London International String Quartet, 1991 Melbourne Chamber Music, 1990 Premio Paulio Borciani, Reggio Emilia and 1990 Karl Klinger Competition, Munich. *Current Management:* Sonata, Glasgow, Scotland. *Address:* c/o Lark Quartet, 11 Northpark Street, Glasgow G20 7AA, Scotland.

KRUGLOV, Jurij; Singer (Bass); b. 1960, Sevastopol, Ukraine. *Education:* Studied at Tchaikovsky Academy, Kiev. *Career:* Appearances at the Sevtchenko Opera Theatre, Kiev; National Theatre, Prague and Estates Theatre, 1989, notably as Masetto and the Commendatore in Don Giovanni, conducted by Charles Mackerras; Guest appearances at Odessa, St Petersburg and Ostrava; Festivals of Savonlinna, Wexford and Macerata; Concerts in France, Germany, Russia, the Czech Republic and Slovakia. *Address:* Music Intenational, 13 Ardilaun Road, London N5 2QR, England.

KRUMM, Philip Edwin; Composer; b. 7 April 1941, Baltimore, Maryland, USA. *Education:* Studied orchestration and composition with Raymond Moses (student of Casals), 1957–59, with Frank Sturchio (student of Puccini), St Mary's University, with Ross Lee Finney, University of Michigan, 1962–64 and Karlheinz Stockhausen, University of California, Davis, 1966. *Career:* Produced early concert series of major modern works at McNay Art Institute, San Antonio, 1960–61; Performer and Composer at Once Festivals, Ann Arbor, MI, 1962–64; Music Hour, television with Jerry Hunt, 1964; Sampler, television programme with Robert Wilson, 1964 and others. *Compositions:* Paragenesis for 2 Violins and Piano, 1959; Axis; Mumma Mix; Soundtrack score for short film, Angel Of God; Music for Clocks, 1962, Once Festival Chamber Orchestra; Concerto for Saxophone, Phil Rehfeldt, 1964, Bass Clarinet Concerto Performer, Martin Walker, 1972, by Scott Vance and Redlands Ensemble, 1978 and 1986; Farewell To LA, electronic theatre piece, 1975; Sound Machine ('66), 1979; Secret Pleasures, dance suite, 1988–89; No Time At All, electronic-instrumental set, 1989; Short pieces for electronics and instruments: Into The Pines, The Gabrieli Thing; Banshee Fantasia, commissioned by Bay Area Pianists for 100th Anniversary of Henry Cowell's Birth; World Premiere by Blue Gene Tyranny, 3 Day Festival, University of California at Berkeley, 1997. *Recordings:* Sound Machine, by Dallas Chamber Ensemble, Jerry Hunt, 1966; Concerto for bass clarinet, with Scott Vance and Redlands Ensemble, 1996; Music for Clocks (1962) on Music from the Once Festival 1961–1966, 2003; Formations (1962), performed by Blue Gene Tyranny, 2004; Axis and Other Works, 2004. *Publications:* Music Without Notes, 1962. *Address:* 103 Erskine Place, San Antonio, TX 78201-2638, USA. *Telephone:* (210) 733-1008 (home).

KRUMMACHER, Friedhelm (Gustav-Adolf); Professor; b. 22 Jan. 1936, Berlin, Germany; m. Aina Maria Landfeldt, 12 June 1964, 1 s., 1 d. *Education:* Abitur, 1954; Musicology, Philosophy, Germanistics studies, Berlin, Marburg and Uppsala, Sweden; Music Teachers Certificate, 1957; DrPhil, Free University of Berlin, 1964; Habilitation, University of Erlangen-Nurnberg, 1972; DPhil, Uppsala, 2002. *Career:* Assistant, 1965, Private Docent, 1973, Erlangen-Nurnberg University; Professor, Musikhochschule Detmold, 1975; Professor, Christian Albrechts University, Kiel, 1976–; Professor, Director, Musicological Institute, University of Kiel, in charge of Brahms Gesamtausgabe; Leipziger Mendelssohnausgabe; mem, Vetenskapssocietet Lund, Sweden, 1975; Jungius-Gesellschaft der Wissenschaften, Hamburg, 1990; Norwegian Academy, 1994; Royal Swedish Academy of Music, 1996;. *Publications:* Die Uberlieferung…, 1965; Mendelssohn der Komponist, 1978; Die Choralbearbeitung…, 1978; Mahlers III Symphonie, 1991; Bach's Jahrgang der Choralkanten, 1995; Musik im Norden, 1996; Bachs Weg in der Arbeit am Werk, 2001; Das Streichquartett, Vol.I, 2001, Vol. II, 2003; Festschrift: Rezeption als Innovation, 2001; Editor, Kieler Schriften zur Musikwissenschaft, Vols 22–49, 1978–2002;; On Mendelssohn's Oratorios, in The Mendelssohn Companion, 2001. *Contributions:* About 145 in Archiv für Musikwissenschaft, Die Musikforschung, Kongressberichte, Festschriften. *Address:* Wippen 1, 24107 Kiel 1, Germany.

KRUSE, Heinz; Singer (Tenor); b. 1940, Schleswig, Germany. *Education:* Studied at the Hamburg Musikhochschule. *Career:* Sang at the Stuttgart Opera, 1966–68, Hamburg from 1970 in such character roles as Pedrillo and David; Guest appearances in Paris, Toulouse and Bayreuth; Heroic tenor roles from 1987 with Florestan at Mainz, Parsifal at Brunswick, Tristan at Kiel and in concert in London in 1993, and in Hamburg, 1995 and in New York's Carnegie Hall, Siegfried at Hamburg in 1993 and in 1994 in Paris and the Edinburgh Festival; Further engagements as the Emperor in Die Frau ohne Schatten, and Albi in Schreker's Schatzgräber, Hamburg in 1989; Sang Florestan in a concert Fidelio at Edinburgh, 1996; Siegfried in Götterdämmerung for Netherlands Opera, 1998. *Recordings include:* Monostatos in Die Zauberflöte. *Address:* c/o Staatsoper Hamburg, Grosse Theaterstrasse 34, Pf 302448, W-2000 Hamburg 36, Germany.

KRUSE, Tone; Singer (Contralto); b. 1958, Oslo, Norway. *Education:* Studied at the Oslo Music High School. *Career:* Sang at the Oslo Opera, 1982–85, then at Cologne Opera; Roles have included Gluck's Orpheus, Magdalene in Die Meistersinger, Margaret in Wozzeck, Suzuki in Madama Butterfly, Zulma in L'Italiana in Algeri, Mother Goose in The Rake's Progress; Sang Erda in Das Rheingold, 1996; Sang Erda in The Ring at Norwich, on tour with the Norwegian National Opera, 1998; Frequent guest appearances in opera and concert throughout Germany. *Recordings:* The Maiden in the Tower, Sibelius. *Address:* c/o Norwegian National Opera, PO Box 8800 Youngstorget, N–0028 Oslo, Norway.

KRUTIKOV, Mikhail; Singer (bass); b. 23 Aug. 1958, Moscow, Russia. *Education:* Moscow State Conservatory and the Opera Studio of Bolshoi Opera, 1982–85; further studies with Evgeni Nesterenko. *Career:* Appearances with Bolshoi Opera, 1985–, as Boris Godunov, Pimen, Mephistopheles, Basilio, Mendoza in Prokofiev's The Duenna and Dunua in The Maid of Orleans by Tchaikovsky; Sang in La Straniera and La cena delle Beffe at Wexford Festival, and with the Bolshoi Company on tour to England, 1990; Season 1991–92 as the Inquisitor in Prokofiev's The Fiery Angel at the Prom Concerts, London, The Love for Three Oranges at Florence, the Commendatore in Dargomizshky's Stone Guest at Salzburg and as King Philip in Don Carlos at the Deutsche Oper Berlin; Concert engagements at Queen Elizabeth Hall, London, Shostakovich's 14th Symphony in Vancouver and Lausanne, the Verdi Requiem and Tchaikovsky's Moscow Cantata at the Salle Pleyel, Prokofiev's Ivan the Terrible in Rome and Elijah at Düsseldorf. *Recordings include:* Holofernes in Serov's Judith, Saison Russe; The Gamblers by Shostakovich. *Current Management:* Athole Still International Management, Forresters Hall, 25–27 Westow Street, London, SE19 3RY, England. *Telephone:* (20) 8771-5271. *Fax:* (20) 8768-6600. *Website:* www.atholestill.com.

KRYSA, Oleh; Violinist; b. 1 June 1942, Lublin, Poland; m. Tatiana Tchekina 1966, 3 s. *Education:* Lviv Musical School, Ukraine; Moscow Conservatory with David Oistrakh. *Career:* Debut: Lviv, Ukraine, 1958; Professor of Violin, Kiev Conservatory, Moscow Conservatory, Manhattan School of Music; Eastman School of Music; Solo Recital Tours in USSR, Europe, North America, Far East, Australia, New Zealand; First Violin, Beethoven String Quartet, Moscow; Soloist with Symphony Orchestras of Moscow, Leningrad, Kiev, Berlin, Leipzig, Dresden, Stuttgart, Warsaw, Prague, Budapest, Bucharest, Belgrade, Torino, London, Stockholm, Bergen, New York, Chicago, Washington, Well-

ington, Cape Town. *Recordings:* Mozart Concertos Nos 3 and 5; Bruch Scottish Fantasy; Viotti No. 22; Tchaikovsky; Wieniawski No. 1; Schnittke No's 3 and 4; Shostakovich No. 1; Prokofiev No. 1; Works for Violin and Piano by Beethoven, Brahms, Paganini, Wieniawski, Ravel, Debussy, Poulenc, Franck, Dvořák, Elgar, Delius, Walton, Szymanowski, Prokofiev, Bartók, Schulhoff, Berio, Schnittke; String quartets by Beethoven, Brahms, Arensky; Shostakovich, Berg, Schnittke, String Sextet, Souvenirs de Florence, by Tchaikovsky; Beethoven Violin Concerto; Tchaikovsky Piano Trio. *Honours:* Wieniawski Competition 2nd Prize, 1962; Paganini Competition 1st Prize, 1963; Tchaikovsky Competition 3rd Prize, 1966; Montreal Competition 2nd Prize, 1969; Outstanding Artist of Ukrainian Republic, 1970. *Current Management:* Connaught Artists Management Ltd, 2 Molasses Row, Plantation Wharf, London, SW11 3UX, England. *Telephone:* (20) 7738 0017. *Fax:* (20) 7738 0909. *E-mail:* classicalmusic@ connaughtartists.com. *Website:* www.connaughtartists.com. *Address:* 265 Westminster Road, Rochester, NY 14607, USA.

KRZANOWSKA, Grazyna; Composer; b. 1 March 1952, Legnica, Poland. *Education:* Studied in Wroclaw. *Career:* Teacher at the Bielsko-Biala Music School. *Compositions include:* Melodies, cantata, 1975; Passacaglia for Orchestra, 1976; Drumroll Symphony, 1978; Bonfires for 2 Voices and Chamber Ensemble, 1979; String Quartet No. 2, 1980; The Little Choral Symphony, 1985; Silver Line for 15 Strings, 1991. *Honours:* Prizewinner at the 1988 Karol Szymanowski Competition. *Address:* c/o Society of Authors ZAiKS, 2 Hipoteczna Street, 00 092 Warsaw, Poland. *Telephone:* (4822) 828 17 05. *Fax:* (4822) 828 13 47. *E-mail:* sekretariat@zaiks.org.pl. *Website:* www.zaiks.org.pl.

KUBIAK, Teresa; Soprano; b. 26 Dec. 1937, Łódź, Poland. *Education:* Studied at the Łódź Music Academy with Olga Olgina; BA 1960; MA 1965. *Career:* Debut: Music Festival in Łódź, Amelia in Amelia al Ballo; Grand Opera Theatre Łódź as Michaela in Carmen, 1967; Appeared in the 1969 world premiere of The Story of St John and Herod by Twardowski; Other roles at Łódź, Aida, Tosca, Lohengrin, 1970; US debut at Carnegie Hall in 1970 as Shulamith in Goldmark's Die Königin von Saba; Glyndebourne Festival in 1971 as Lisa in The Queen of Spades and Juno in La Calisto by Cavalli-Leppard; Covent Garden in 1972 as Madama Butterfly and Metropolitan Opera from 1973 as Lisa, Jenůfa, Giorgietta in Il Tabarro, Tosca, Elsa in Lohengrin, Eva in Meistersinger and Elisabeth in Tannhäuser; Appearances in San Francisco, Chicago, Houston, Seattle, Miami, Leipzig, Prague, Warsaw, Venice, Barcelona, Madrid, Lisbon, Munich, Vienna, Paris Opéra, Rome, Canada, Bulgaria, United Arab Emirates, China, Philippines, Soviet Union (Georgia); other roles include Ariadne, Euryanthe, Halka, Senta, Tatiana, Chrysothemis in Elektra, Leonore in Fidelio and Ellen Orford; many recitals and orchestra appearances; Professor of Music/ Voice, Indiana University School of Music, Bloomington, Indiana, 1990–; judging national and international vocal competitions. *Recordings include:* Operatic Arias–Muza; 14 Symphonies-Shostakovich; Glagolitic Mass; La Calisto; Eugene Onegin; Euryanthe Elektra, Strauss; Fidelio, Beethoven;. *Honours:* National Opera Competition, Katowice, Poland, 1960; International Music Competition, Toulouse, France, 1963; International Music Competition, Munich, Germany, 1965; Cross of Knight, Polish Government, 1975. *Address:* 2912 Dale Court, Bloomington, IN 47401, USA.

KUBICKA, Vitazoslav; Composer, Broadcasting Editor Music and Dramaturg; b. 11 Oct. 1953, Bratislava, Czechoslovakia; m. Gabriela Jurolekova 1988 one s. one d. *Education:* composition, Univ. of Music, Bratislava. *Career:* debut, Rostrum of Composers, UNESCO, Paris 1982; mem. Union of Slovak Composers. *Compositions include:* orchestral: Dramatic Overture for Large Orchestra 1980, Concerto for Piano and Orchestra 1984, Maturing, Overture for Orchestra 1984, Fantasy for Violoncello and Large Orchestra 1985; chamber opuses: Fantasy for Flute and Piano 1979, Quintet for Clarinet, Violin, Viola, Violoncello and Piano 1982, Winter, Sonata for Piano 1986; choral: Fugue for Children's Choir 1982; electro-acoustic: Dedicated to Mussorgsky 1981, Satyr and Nymph 1985; for children and youth: Five Stories for Piano 1982, 1985, Harpsichord Concerto 1986, Bass Clarinet Concerto 1989, Autumn Music for violin and strings 1990, Hedge By the Danube for accordion 1990, Way, electro-acoustic 1991, 30 Biblical Songs and Choirs 1990–2003, Gospel according to St Luke, opera to the Biblical text 2000, Born Again, opera to the Biblical text 2003, Danube Requiem for soprano, bass, mixed choir, 3 trombone, timpani 2004; incidental music for radio (130 pieces), television (20 pieces), film (12 pieces), theatre and video. *Honours:* Jan Levoslav Bella Prize, Slovak Music Fund Bratislava 1988, Prix Critique Radiomagazin Bratislava 1989. *Address:* Drotarska 9, 81102 Bratislava, Slovakia.

KUBIK, Ladislav; Composer; b. 26 Aug. 1946, Prague, Czechoslovakia; m. Natalie Bartosevicova, 7 Nov 1974, 1 s., 1 d. *Education:* Composition, 1970, Theory of Music, 1972, PhD, 1981, Prague Academy of Music. *Career:* Music Director, Czechoslovak Radio Prague, 1979–83; General Secretary, Union of Czech Composers and Concert Artists, 1983–.

Compositions: Symphonic Works: Symphony, 1970; Drammatic Toc-cata, 1972; Concerto for Piano and Orchestra, 1974; Hommage a Majakowski, 1976; Concerto for Violin and Orchestra, 1980; Choral Works: Songs of Hope, 1982; Chamber-Cantat: Lament of a Warrior's Wife, 1974; Radio Opera: Solaris, 1975; Ballet: Song of Man, 1984; Vocal Symphony Works: February, 1973; Wolkeriana, 1982; To the Earth of Future, 1985; Songs with Orchestra: Words; Chamber Music: 2 String Quartets, 1981, 1986; Trio Concertante, 1983; Duo Concertante; Concerto Grosso, 1987; Divertimento for 8 wind, 1988; Symphony No. 2, 1993; Harpsichord Concerto, 1995; The River in Spring for mezzo and percussion, 1997; In Night for baritone and ensemble, 1997; Piano Concerto, 1999; Sinfonietta, 1999. *Recordings:* 15 titles and numerous recordings in Czechoslovak and foreign radio broadcasts. *Current Management:* Charles University, Prague. *Address:* Na Brezince 6, 150 00 Prague 5, Czech Republic.

KUBIK, Reinhold; Musicologist; b. 22 March 1942, Vienna, Austria; 1 s., 1 d. *Education:* Abitur, Humanistic College, Vienna II, 1960; PhD, University Erlangen-Nuremberg, Germany, 1980; Studied Piano, Composition, Conducting wth Hans Swarowsky, Hochschule für Musik, Vienna. *Career:* Conductor, Deutsche Oper am Rhein, Düsseldorf/ Duisburg and many European cities including Lille, Barcelona, Ljubljana, 1966–74; Pianist; Composer; Choirmaster; Lecturer, 1980; Proprietor, Hänssler Musik Verlag, Kirchheim, Germany, 1980–90; Visiting Professor, Yale University, USA, 1987; Production Manager, Universal Edition, Vienna, 1992–97; Chief Editor of Gustav Mahler Gesamtausgabe and of Wiener Urtext Edition; Teacher of period acting techniques in Vienna, London, Karlsruhe and Michaelstein; Editor of all Bach Cantatas for J.E Gardiner's project Bach Cantata Pilgrimage; Vice Pres., Int. Gustav Mahler Soc., Vienna. *Publications:* Handel's Rinaldo, 1980; About 120 editions including 80 cantatas by J. S. Bach (Hänssler), EdM 96, 106 and 110, Schubert, Lazarus (Neue Schubert Ausgabe II/ 10); Handel, Arianna in Creta; Mahler, 5th Symphonie and Das Klagende Lied (3 movement version). *Contributions:* Festschrift Arnold Feil, 1985; KB Stuttgart, 1985; Festschrift Martin Ruhnke, 1986; Veröffentlichungen der International, Handel-Akademie Karlsruhe, vols 2, 3 4 and 7; Handel-Symposium Halle, 1989. *Address:* Liechten-stein Strasse 39/6, 1090 Vienna, Austria. *E-mail:* reinhold.kubik@chello .at.

KUBO, Yoko; Composer, Pianist and College Lecturer; b. 5 Dec. 1956, Nishinomiya, Japan. *Education:* BA, 1979, MA, 1981, Osaka College of Music; Diplome d'Etudes Approfondies, University of Paris, France, 1985. *Career:* Debut: 1979; Many concerts of her compositions, Japan and France, 1979–; Lecturer, Osaka College of Music, 1981–; Associate, Instittut Recherche Coordination Acoustique/Musique, Paris, France, 1984–. *Compositions:* La Sensation de Vingtième Siecle, 12 Percussio-nists, 1977; Collage, Orchestra, 1978; Objet, 2 Pianos and Percussions, 1979; Play, Violin, Violoncello, Piano, 1979; Crossword, Piano, 1980; Mon parc, String Orchestra, 1980; Quatuor à Cordes No. 2, 1980; Concerto pour Violon No. 1, 1981; Puzzle, 3 Marimbas, 1981; On the Tree, Soprano, 8 Voices, Piano, 1981; Chikya ni hajimete yuki ga futta hi no koto, Soprano, 8 Voices, Piano, 1981; Quatuor à Cordes No. 3, 1981; Concerto pour Orgue, 4 Cuivres et Percussions, 1981; Livre Illustré des chats, String Orchestra, 1982;... SONG..., 5 Voices and Piano, 1982; Quatuor à Cordes No. 4, 1982; Paysage, Flute, Percussion, Piano, 1983; Quatuor pour Flute, Hautbois, Violon et Violoncelle, 1983; Quintette pour Piano No. 1, 1983; Marche du roi (extract from Le Roi Nu), String Orchestra, 1984; Espace, 11 Players, 1985; Vision, Piano, 1987; Concerto pour 7 Interprètes, 1987. *Address:* No. 9-25 2-chome, Nigawa-cho Nishinomiya-shi, Hyogo-ken, Japan.

KUCERA, Vaclav; Composer and Musicologist; b. 29 April 1929, Prague, Czechoslovakia; m. Maria Jerieová, 11 Aug 1951, 2 s. *Education:* PhD, Charles University, Prague; Tchaikovsky Conservatory in Moscow: Composition with Vissarion Shebalin, Musicology with L Mazel, V Zuckerman, N Tumanina, graduated with ballet Brigands Fire and a dissertation on Janáček, 1956. *Career:* Music Department of Radio Prague, 1956–59; Cabinet for New Music Studies, 1959–62; Institute of Musicology, 1962–69; General Secretary, Union of Czech Composers and Concert Artists, 1969–83; Teacher of Composition, 1972–, Profes-sor, 1988–, at Music Faculty of Academy for Performing Arts in Prague mem. Union of Czech Composers and Concert Artists, 1957–1969; ISCM, member of Executive Committee, 1978–1982; President of the International Prague Spring Festival, 1992–1998; European Associa-tion of Conservatoires, Academies de Musique et Musikhochschulen, 1992–1998; Member of Supervisor Board for Society for Performance and Mechanical Rights of Composers, Authors and Publishers, 1994–. *Compositions:* About 100 include: Dramas for 9 Instruments, 1961; Symphony for large Orchestra, 1962; Protests, 1963; Blue Planet, male chorus on M. Červanka, 1964; The Pied Piper, 1964; Hic Sunt Homines, a cycle for Piano quartet, 1965; Genesis, 1965; Spectra, for dulcimer, 1965; Diptychon, 1966; Duodrama, 1967; "To be", 1968; Panta rhei, 1969; Invariant, 1969; Tableau, 1970; Scenario, 1970; Argot, 1970;

Diario, 1971; Taboo a Due Boemi, 1972; Salut, 1975; Orbis Pictus, 1975; Amoroso, 1975; Consciousness of Continuities, 1976; Aphorisms, 1978; Horizons, 1978; Epigrams, 1978; Catharsis, 1979; SCience Fiction, 1980; Rosen für Rosa, 1980; Aquarelles, 1981; Capriccios, 1983; Cardiograms, 1983; Bird, 1983; Nouvelles, 1984; Ballad and Romance, 1984; Eruptions, 1984;Gogh's Self Portrtait, 1985; Bitter and Other Songs, 1985; A Serious Hour, 1986; Prague Ritornelles, 1986; Duettinos, 1988;Consonanza, 1990; Celebrations of Phantasy, 1991; Oraculum, 1992; Tuning, 1994; Concierto Imaginativo, 1994; Guitariana, 1996; Invocation of Joy, 1996; Criterion for orchestra, 1997; Intimate Conversations, 1998; Mimesis, for dulcimer and harp, 1998; Metathesis, 1998; Satiricon De Creatione, 1999; Mysterious Players, 2000; Pax imago vitae, 2000; Cryptoblues, 2000; Two Sonnets on Shakespeare, 2000; When We Two Parted, 2001;Drei Frauenchöre mit Epitaf auf Gedichte von R.M.Rilke, 2002; Cum Grano Lorca, 2001; Saxonata, 2002; Esta noche, 2002; Imagination, 2003; Electro-acoustic compositions: Kinetic Ballet, 1968; Kinechromia, 1969; Lidice, 1972; Spartacus, 1976. *Publications:* M P Mussorgsky–Music of Life, 1959; Talent, Mastery, World Outlook, 1962; New Trends in Soviet Music, 1967; Musicological studies, Radio and television lectures. *Honours:* Prize of Queen Marie-José, Geneva, 1970; Prix d'Italia, Rome, 1972; Prize of Czech Radio Prague, 1977; Prize of Czech Trade Unions, Prague, 1977; Prize of Union of Czech Composers and Concert Artists, Prague, 1983; Trentino International Prize, 1994; Prize of Canary Islands, 2002. *Address:* Jizni II, 778, 141 00 Prague 4, Czech Republic. *Telephone:* 272766326. *Fax:* 272766326. *E-mail:* vac.kuc@tiscali.cz.

KUDELA, Irene; pianist; b. 1965, France. *Education:* studied in Prague and at Paris Conservatoire. *Career:* vocal coach at Glyndebourne Festival from 1997 (The Makropulos Case 2001); other engagements at Philadelphia, New York, Rome, Washington, Helsinki, Budapest, Orange, Salzburg and Paris (Châtelet and Opéra Bastille); Assistant to Mstislav Rostropovich 1985–88, in Europe and USA; Associate Chorus Master at Opéra National de Paris 1999; Season 2001–02 with Dialogues des Carmélites at Gothenberg. *Recordings:* Albums for Erato, Hungaroton and Teldec. *Address:* c/o Göteborgs Operan, Christina Nilssons Gata, 411 04 Göteborg, Sweden.

KUDRIASCHOV, Vladimir; Singer (Tenor); b. 1947, Russia. *Education:* Studied at the Gnessin Conservatory, Moscow. *Career:* Sang at the Stanislavsky Theatre in Moscow, 1971–83, then at the Bolshoi Theatre; Roles have included Sobinin in Glinka's Life for the Tsar, Shuisky in Boris Godunov, Count Almaviva, Rodolfo and Sergei in Lady Macbeth of Mtsensk; Guest at Edinburgh in 1991 as Diak in Christmas Eve by Rimsky-Korsakov. *Address:* c/o Bolshoi Theatre, 103009 Moscow, Russia.

KUDRIAVCHENKO, Katerina; Singer (soprano); b. 2 March 1958, Karpnsk, Sverdlovskaya, Russia; m. Paolo Kudriavchenko. *Education:* Graduated, Tchaikovsky Conservatoire, Moscow, 1985. *Career:* Member of Bolshoi Opera, 1986–, as Iolanta, Tatiana, Agnes Sorell in The Maid of Orleans, Marfa in The Tsar's Bride, Gilda, Antonida in A Life for the Tsar, Lisa in The Queen of Spades, Prokofiev's The Duenna, Rachma-ninov's Francesca, Violetta, Mimi, Liu and Oxsana in Rimsky's Christmas Eve; Western debut as Iolanta at La Scala, 1989; Season 1990–91 with Bolshoi Opera on tour to Spain, Italy, USA (Metropolitan), Japan and Glasgow, Scotland; Freelance Artist debut as Tatiana for New Israel Opera Company at Tel-Aviv, 1992; Season 1992–93 as Mimi with Scottish Opera, Liu and Titania at the Bolshoi; Sang Butterfly at Bologna, 1996. *Honours:* Gold Medallist, Madama Butterfly Competi-tion, Miami, 1990. *Current Management:* Athole Still International Management, Forresters Hall, 25–27 Westow Street, London, SE19 3RY, England. *Telephone:* (20) 8771-5271. *Fax:* (20) 8768-6600. *Website:* www.atholestill.com.

KUDRIAVCHENKO, Paolo; Singer (tenor); b. 12 Aug. 1952, Odessa, Crimea, Russia; m. Katerina Kudriavchenko. *Education:* Studied at Tchaikovsky Conservatory, Odessa. *Career:* Sang first with Odessa Opera, then Kiev Opera; Bolshoi Opera, Moscow, 1984–, in Rimsky's Invisible City of Kitezh and as Canio, Turiddu, Dimitri in Boris Godunov, Don José and Jéromir in Mlada; Sang Sobinin in A Life for the Tsar with the Bolshoi Company at La Scala and made US debut, 1989, as Manrico for Greater Miami Opera (repeated for Omaha Opera, 1991), as Turiddu and Dimitri; Season 1991–92 as Turiddu at Munich Staatsoper and as Ernani for Welsh National Opera, followed by Manrico for Scottish Opera, Ishmaele in Nabucco at Bregenz Festival, 1993, and Canio at Rouen; season 1993–94 as Calaf and Radames at the Bolshoi; Many concert appearances. *Current Management:* Athole Still International Management, Forresters Hall, 25–27 Westow Street, London, SE19 3RY, England. *Telephone:* (20) 8771-5271. *Fax:* (20) 8768-6600. *Website:* www.atholestill.com.

KUEBLER, David; Singer (Tenor); b. 23 July 1947, Detroit, Michigan, USA. *Education:* Studied with Thomas Peck in Chicago and Audrey Field in London. *Career:* Sang in the chorus of the Chicago Opera; Solo career with the Santa Fe Opera from 1972; European debut Berne Opera 1974, as Tamino; Sang Mozart and bel canto roles with Cologne Opera; Glyndebourne Festival, 1976, as Ferrando in Così fan tutte; Metropolitan Opera from 1979; Bayreuth Festival, 1980–82, as the Steersman in Der fliegende Holländer; Santa Fe Opera, 1984, in We Come to the River by Henze; Other roles include Don Ottavio, Rodolfo, Pinkerton, Lionel (Martha), Jacquino in Fidelio, Paolino in Il Matrimonio Segreto and Gianneto in La Gazza Ladra; Donizetti's Ernesto and Nemorino; Glyndebourne, 1987–90, Strauss's Flamand and Matteo; Schwetzingen Festival, 1988, as Rossini's Almaviva, (1989 in La Cambiale di Matrimonio); sang Don Ottavio in Rome and Madrid, 1989; Schwetzingen 1990 as Doric in Rossini's La Scala di Seta; Sang in The Spectre's Bride by Dvořák at the 1991 Promenade Concerts, London; Sang the Berlioz Faust at Wellington and Bregenz, 1992; Rome Opera, 1997 in I Vespri Siciliani; Salzburg Festival 1998, as Boris in Katya Kabanova and for Netherlands Opera, 2000. *Recordings include:* Mitridate re di Ponto by Mozart; Fidelio; Videos of La Scala di Seta and Idomeneo, as Idamante. *Current Management:* Balmer & Dixon Management AG, Kreuzstrasse 82, 8032 Zürich, Switzerland. *Telephone:* (43) 244-8644. *Fax:* (43) 244-8649. *Website:* www.badix.ch.

KUENTZ, Paul; Conductor; b. 4 May 1930, Mulhouse, France; m. Monique Frasca-Colombier, 1956. *Education:* Studied at the Paris Conservatoire, 1947–50, with Noel Gallon, Georges Hugon and Eugene Bigot. *Career:* Founded the Paul Kuentz Chamber Orchestra, 1951: many tours of Europe and the USA, including the orchestral works of Bach at Saint-Severin and concert at Carnegie Hall, 1968; Frequent performances of French music, including premieres of works by P M Dubois, J Casterede and J Charpentier; Founded Paul Kuentz Chorus, 1972. *Recordings include:* Bach's Orchestral Suites, Mass in B Minor and Musikalisches Opfer; Vivaldi's Four Seasons, and other concertos; Flute Concertos by Haydn, Blavet, Mozart, Leclair and Pergolesi; Music by Delalande, Mouret, Gabrieli and Gluck; Mozart's Concerto K299, Requiem, Bastien und Bastienne and Church Sonatas; Harp concertos by Handel, Albrechtsberger, Boieldieu, Wagenseil and Dittersdorf; Haydn Symphonies Nos 85 and 101.

KUERTI, Anton (Emil); Pianist and Composer; b. Vienna, 1938; m. Kristine Bogyo, 13 Sept 1973, 2 s. *Education:* BM, Cleveland Institute of Music; Diploma, Curtis Institute, 1959; PhD (Hon), York University, 1985, Laurentian University, 1985, Memorial University, 1999, Dalhousie University, 2001. *Career:* Soloist, New York Philharmonic, Cleveland Orchestra, Detroit Symphony, Philadelphia Orchestra, Buffalo Philharmonic, San Francisco Symphony, Denver Symphony, 41 appearances with Toronto Symphony, National Arts Centre Orchestra (Ottawa), Dresden Staatskapelle, Leipzig Gewandhaus, London Symphony; Tours world-wide including Soviet Union, Far East, Australia, Latin America; Numerous television appearances, radio broadcasts; Founder, Festival of Sound, Parry Sound, Ontario; mem, Amnesty International. *Compositions:* Linden Suite for Piano, 1970; String Quartet, 1972; Violin Sonata and Symphony Epomeo, 1975; Piano Man Suite and Piano Concerto, 1985; Clarinet Trio, 1989; Concertino, Jupiter Concerto, 1996. *Recordings:* Recordings include complete cycle of Beethoven Sonatas and Concerti; Brahms and Schumann Concerti; Complete Schubert Sonatas. *Honours:* Leventritt Award, 1957; Honorary Doctorate, Cleveland Institute of Music, 1996; Toronto Arts Award, 1997; Officer, Order of Canada. *Current Management:* Concertmasters Incorporated, 22 Linden Street, Toronto, M4Y 1V6. *Address:* 20 Linden Street, Toronto, Ontario M4Y 1V6, Canada.

KUHN, Alfred; Singer (Bass); b. 2 Nov. 1938, Ober-Roden, Germany. *Education:* Studied at the Frankfurt Musikhochschule. *Career:* Debut: Trulove in The Rake's Progress, Darmstadt, 1963; Guest appearances throughout Germany, notably as Wagner's Daland and Landgrave; Rocco in Fidelio; Mozart's Osmin and Sarastro; King Philip in Don Carlos; Donizetti's Dulcamara; Kaspar in Der Freischütz; Düsseldorf, 1986, in the premiere of Belshazzar by Kirchner; Mozart's Antonio at the 1991 Salzburg Festival; La Scala, 1992 as Waldner in Arabella; Sang Varlaam in Boris Godunov at Munich, 1995. *Address:* c/o Bayerische Staatsoper, Max-Josephplatz, 80539 Munich, Germany.

KUHN, Gustav; Conductor and Stage Director; b. 28 Aug. 1947, Salzburg, Germany; m. Andrea, 6 Jan 1971, 1 s., 1 d. *Education:* Studies, Academies of Salzburg and Vienna, Universities of Salzburg and Vienna; PhD, 1970. *Career:* Debut: Ankara 1970, Fidelio; Conducting: Vienna State Opera, 1977 (debut there with Elektra), Munich National Theatre, 1978, Covent Garden, London, 1981 Don Giovanni, Glyndebourne (1980, Entführung), Munich Opera Festival, Salzburg Festival, 1980, USA Chicago, 1981, Grand Opera, Paris, 1982, Scala Milan, 1984, Arena of Verona, 1985, Rossini Opera Festival, Pesaro, 1987 (Ermione), Salzburg Festival, 1989, Japan, Tokyo, 1991, Salzburg Festival, 1992; Verona 1992, Don Carlos; Stagings of Parsifal in Naples, Capriccio in Parma and Der fliegende Holländer at Trieste; Founder, Institut für aleatorische Musik, Salzburg, 1974; Concerts of Contemporary Music in Collaboration with Josef Anton Riedl, 1983–85; Conducted Orfeo ed

Euridice at Naples, 1998. *Publications:* Aus Liebe zur Musik, 1993. *Address:* Hans Adler, Auguste Viktoria Strabe 64, 14199 Berlin, Germany.

KUHN, Pamela; Singer (Soprano); b. 1960, Oregon, USA. *Education:* Bachelor of Music, University of Oregon; Master of Music, University of Southern California with Gwendolyn Koldofsky and Margaret Schaper. *Career:* Debut: London, Wigmore Hall with Graham Johnson, 1984; Recitals at the Purcell Room with Stephen Wilder, Stephen Coombs and Geoffrey Parsons; Isle of Man Festival with Roger Steptoe; Oratorio includes Rossini Petite Messe Solennelle at Queen Elizabeth Hall, Verdi Requiem at Fairfield Halls, Dartington (Diego Masson), Oregon Bach Festival (Helmut Rilling), Penderecki Polish Requiem at Oregon Bach Festival (Penderecki), Brahms Requiem at the Royal Festival Hall and in the USA, Beethoven Missa Solemnis in Lugano, Switzerland, Janáček Glagolitic Mass at Salisbury Cathedral; Opera: Ariadne at Dartington, Aida with Florentine Opera in Milwaukee, Rezia with Scottish Opera at La Fenice, Venice, Soloist in Oberon conducted by Seiji Ozawa at Tanglewood, Edinburgh Festival and Frankfurt Alte Oper, High Priestess with Scottish Opera; Other roles include Micaela, Tosca, Amelia and Sieglinde; Further concert repertory includes operatic evenings with City of Birmingham Symphony Orchestra, Southampton Symphony and Ernest Read Symphony at the Barbican, Shostakovich Symphony 14 with Mark Wigglesworth at St John's Smith Square and Four Last Songs in Nottingham. *Address:* Lombardo Associates, 61 West 62nd, Suite 6F, New York, NY 10023, USA.

KUIJKEN, Barthold; Flautist, Recorder Player and Conductor; b. 8 March 1949, Dilbeek, Brussels, Belgium. *Education:* Conservatoires of Bruges, Brussels and the Hague, with Frans Vester and Frans Brueggen; self-taught on the Baroque flute. *Career:* Concerts in Europe, North and South America, Japan, Australia, New Zealand, Korea and Israel with his brothers, Lucy van Dael, René Jacobs, Frans Brueggen, Gustav Leonhardt, Bob van Asperen, Luc Devos, Ewald Demeyere. the Parnassus Ensemble, La Petite Bande and the Collegium Aureum; Teacher of Baroque flute at the Hague and Brussels Conservatories; Repertoire includes music by Couperin, Telemann, Handel, Haydn, Bach, Mozart, Schubert and Debussy; Took part in the Towards Bach concert series on the South Bank, London, August 1989. *Recordings:* Solos by J. S. and C. P. E. Bach, Boismortier, Debussy, Fischer, Hotteterre, Telemann, Vivaldi, Weiss; Duos by Boismortier, Hotteterre and W.F. Bach; Suites by Couperin, Hotteterre and Montéclair; Sonatas by Albinoni, J. S. and C. P. E, Bach, Benda, Blavet, Boismortier, Corelli, Friedrich der Grosse, Geminiani, C.H. and J.G. Graun, Guignon, Händel, Kirnberger, Leclair, Locatelli, Müthel, Platti, Quantz, Telemann, Veracini, Vivaldi; A recital of 19th century works for flute and fortepiano (Hummel, F.X. Mozart, Mendelssohn, Schubert); Chamber music by J. S., C. P. E. and J. C. Bach, Boismortier, Couperin, Debussy, Devienne, Dornel, Galuppi, Geminiani, Händel, Haydn, Hotteterre, Janitsch, Mozart, Rameau, Telemann; Concertos by J. S. Bach, Haydn, Mozart, Richter, J. and C. Stamitz, Telemann, and Vivaldi; As a condcutor: Mozart's Gran Partita and a program of suites concertantes from the German baroque (J. L. and J. S. Bach, Teleman, Handel). *Publications:* J. S. Bach's flute compositions (editor). *Address:* Zwartschaapstraat 38, 1755 Gooik, Belgium. *Website:* bartholdkuijken .be.

KUIJKEN, Sigiswald; Violinist and Conductor; b. 16 Feb. 1944, near Brussels, Belgium. *Education:* Studied at Bruges Conservatory from 1952; Conservatoire Royale Brussels from 1960 under M Raskin. *Career:* Began to re-establish old technique of violin playing, resting the instrument on the shoulder not under the chin, in 1969, adopted by many players in early 1970s; Played in the Alarius Ensemble (with Wieland Kuijken, Robert Kohnen and Janine Rubinlicht), 1964–72, performances throughout Europe and USA; Founder of the Baroque orchestra, La Petite Bande in 1972; Tours of Europe, Australia, South America, China and Japan with La Petite Bande and in chamber music and solo programmes; Founder, Kuijken String Quartet (with François Fernandez, Marleen Thiers and Wieland Kuijken), specialising in quartets and quintets (with Ryo Terakado, 1st violin) of the Classical period, 1986–; Occasional conductor of modern symphonic orchestras such as Royal Philharmonic Orchestra of Flanders, Cappella Colonienses (WDR Köln), Orchestre Nat. de Bordeaux & Aquitaine, in Romantic programmes (Beethoven, Schumann, Brahsm, Mendelssohn), 1998–; Teacher of Baroque violin, Koninklijk Conservatorium, The Hague, 1971–96; Koninklijk Muziekconservatorium, Brussels, 1993–; Guest teacher at many institutions, including Royal College of Music, London, Salamanca Univ. and Accademia Chigiana, Siena. *Recordings include:* Many with La Petite Bande including: Music by Lully, Muffat, Gluck, Haydn's Creation and Symphonies, Mozart's Requiem and Davidde Penitente, Così fan tutte, 1992 and Brandenburg Concertos, 1994; Bach Sonatas with Gustav Leonhardt; 20 Haydn Symphonies; Mozart Concert Arias; German Chamber Music; Don Giovanni, 1997; Le nozze di Figaro, 1998; Schütz, 1999. *Honours:* Deutsche Schallplattenpreis several times; Grand Prix du Disque, France several times; Deutsche Handel Preis, 1994; Choc de l'année for recording Debussy chamber music, 2000. *Address:* La Petite Bande, Geert Robberechts, Vital Decosterstraat 72, 3000 Leuven, Belgium.

KUIJKEN, Wieland; viola da gamba player, cellist and conductor; b. 31 Aug. 1938, Dilbeek, Brussels, Belgium. *Education:* Bruges Conservatory, Brussels Conservatoire Royale. *Career:* played with the Alarius Ensemble, 1959–72; Played in the avant-garde group Musiques Nouvelles from 1962; Kuijken Early Music Group from 1972; Teacher at the Conservatories of Antwerp, Brussels and the Hague; Masterclasses in the United Kingdom, Innsbruck and the USA; Festival appearances at Flanders, Saintes and the English Bach Festival; Tour of New Zealand and Australia with Gustav Leonhardt, 1979; Cellist with the Kuijken String Quartet from 1986: London debut 1990; Collaborations with his brothers, Frans Brueggen, Alfred Deller and René Jacobs; Repertoire includes music by French, English, Italian and German composers; Performed in the Towards Bach concert series on the South Bank, London, August 1989. *Recordings include:* Leclair Flute Sonatas, Marais Pièces de Viole du Cinquieme Livre and German Chamber Music. *Current Management:* Allied Artists Agency, 42 Montpeiler Square, London, SW7 1JZ, England.

KUJAWINSKA, Krystyna; Singer (Soprano); b. 4 April 1938, Kalisz, Poland. *Education:* Studied at the Poznán Academy, 1962–67. *Career:* Debut: Bytom in 1967 as Arabella; Sang at the Poznán Opera from 1970 notably as Elisabeth de Valois, Aida, Desdemona, Micaela, Butterfly, Gioconda and Santuzza; Later roles have included Tosca, the Forza Leonora and Turandot; Guest appearances in France as Electra (Idomeneo), Hamburg as Aida, Parma as Halka, Dresden in Verdi Requiem and Leonora (La Forza del Destino), in Netherlands as Tosca and Santuzza and in Germany and Belgium as Abigaile in Nabucco; Has also appeared at the National Theatre Warsaw as Fidelio, Aida and the Trovatore Leonora. *Address:* c/o Poznán Grand Theatre, Fredry 9, 60-987 Poznán, Poland.

KULENTY, Hanna, BMus; Polish composer; b. 18 March 1961, Białystok; one d. *Education:* Acad. of Music, Warsaw and Conservatory, The Hague, studied under Włodzimierz, Kotoński and Louis Andriessen. *Career:* guest performer, Deutscher Akademischer Austauschdienst in Berliner Künstler Programm 1990–91; performances of works by many orchestras in countries including the Netherlands, Latvia, UK, Denmark, Germany. *Works include:* Ad Unum 1985, Symphony No. 1 1986, Perpetuus 1989, Trigon 1989, Concerto for piano and chamber orchestra 1990, Air 1991, A Cradle Song 1993, A Sixth Circle 1995, Drive Blues 2000, Asjaawaa 2001, Hoffmanniana 2003; works for solo instruments and Chamber Orchestras. *Recordings include:* 12½ Musis Sacrum, Chronicles from Warsaw Autumn Festivals, Hanna Kulenty: Ad Unum, Sesto, Arci, Piano Concerto No. 1, Violin Concerto No. 1, Arcs and Circles: Portrait of Hanna Kulenty. *Honours:* Stanisław Wyspiański Award 1987, first prize Composers' Competition, Polish Composers' Union 1986, 1987, first prize Int. Rostrum of Composers 2003, other awards in music competitions. *Address:* c/o Jana Pawła II 69/52, 00-170 Warsaw, Poland.

KULESHA, Gary (Alan); Composer, Conductor and Pianist; b. 22 Aug. 1954, Toronto, Canada; m. Larysa Kuzmenko, 30 Dec 1983. *Education:* Associate in Piano, 1973, Associate in Composition, 1978, Royal Conservatory of Music, Toronto; Private Studies with John McCabe, London, England and John Corigliano, New York, USA; L Mus, 1976, Fellow 1978, Trinity College, London, England. *Career:* Composer-in-Residence, Kitchener-Waterloo Symphony, 1989–92; Composer-in-Residence, Candia Opera Company, 1993–95; Composer Adviser, Toronto Symphony Orchestra, 1995–, guest conducting throughout Canada; Principal Conductor, Festival Theatre, Stratford Festival, Canada; Artistic Director and Principal Conductor, Canadian Contemporary Music Workshops and the Composers Orchestra; Works performed throughout North America, Europe, Iceland, Australia and Latin America. *Compositions:* Essay for Orchestra; Second Essay for Orchestra; Chamber Concertos 1–5; Duo for Bass Clarinet and Piano; Second Sonata for Piano; Lifesongs for Alto and String Orchestra, text by composer; Nocturne for Chamber Orchestra; Angels for Marimba and Tape, recorded, 1986; Scores for several Shakespearean plays including All's Well That End's Well, Nimrod, Sydney, Australia 1986 and Henry VIII, Stratford 1986; Shama Songs, 1991; Concerto for Recorder, 1990; 3 Essays for Orchestra, 2nd and 3rd Pico Sonata; Concerto for Viola, 1992; Opera Red Emma, 1995; Symphony, 1998; Partita for piano and strings, 1999; Violin Concerto, 1999. *Recordings:* Recorder Concerto, Michela Petri and ECO conducted by Kamn; Political Implications, Indiana Clarinet Quartet. *Address:* 54 Springbrook Gardens, Toronto, Ontario M8Z 3C1, Canada.

KULHAN, Jaroslav; Czech cellist; b. 7 Dec. 1950, Ceske Budejovice; m. Stepanka Kazilova 1978; one s. two d. *Education:* Prague Conservatory; Acad. of Music and Arts, Prague. *Career:* mem., Panocha Quartet 1968–;

teacher, Prague Conservatory 1990–. *Recordings:* Haydn Op 51, Op 33, Op 55, Op 76; Smetana Quartets 1 and 2; Dvořák's Chamber Music, Martinů's Quartets; Janáček Quartets No. 1, Schubert Op 29, 125, 161. *Honours:* Grand Prix Academy Charles Cros (Martinů's Quartet Nos 4, 6), 1983; Midem Cannes Classical Awards, 1994. *Address:* Prague Conservatory, Na Rejdisti 1, 11000 Prague, Czech Republic.

KULINSKY, Bohumil; Conductor; b. 5 May 1959, Prague, Czechoslovakia. *Education:* Prague Conservatory, 1978–81; Prague Music Academy, 1981–84; Music Academy of Janáček-Brno, 1984–86. *Career:* Conductor, Czechoslovak Children's Choir Bambini di Praga, 1976–; Concert tours: France; Italy; Democratic Republic of Germany, Federal Republic of Germany, Mongolia, Finland; the United Kingdom; Japan; Appeared on radio and television; Conductor, Prague Symphony Orchestra, appearing at Concerts and Festivals, 1984; Conductor, Czech Chamber Philharmonic Orchestra; Concert Tours: Spain and Germany. *Recordings:* CBS, Sony, Polydor, King Record Japan, Supraphon, Panton; Recordings with Prague Symphony Orchestra. *Address:* Anenska 2, 11000 Prague 1, Czech Republic.

KULJERIC, Igor; Composer; b. 1 Feb. 1938, Sibenik, Croatia. *Education:* Studied at Zagreb Academy of Music, graduated 1965 and the Electronic Music Studios in Milan. *Career:* Has conducted various orchestras in Zagreb and elsewhere in Croatia; Art Director, Opera Zagreb and Dubrovnik Festival; Art Director, competition for young conductors, L Matacic, Zagreb; Has conducted various orchestras in Croatia, Europe and the USA; Employs electronic and other advanced techniques in his music. *Compositions include:* The Ballads of Petrica Kerempuh, 1973; Ballets and Incidental Music; Opera: The Power of Virtue, Zagreb, 1977 and Rikard, 2 Acts, after Shakespeare, 1987; Ballad of Petrica Kerempuh, vocal-instrumental, 1973; Canconiere, 1983; Ballet: Ricki Levy, 1991; Croatian Glagolic Requiem, 1996; Chamber music. *Address:* Jagiceva 23, 10000 Zagreb, Croatia.

KULJUNTAUSTA, Petri; Composer and Musician; b. 28 Feb. 1961, Tampere, Finland. *Education:* MA, University of Jyväskylä, Finland; Studies in Philosophy, Aesthetics and Pedagogy. *Career:* Electronic compositions and performances as improvisor, 1980s; Music for Petri Kuljuntausta Project, 1989–94; Played with Petri Kuljuntausta Ensemble, string quartet, piano, synthesiser, saxophone, guitar and percussion, 1993–94; Sound/media works and installations in galleries, museums and halls, 1993–; Founder and Chairman, Charm of Sound, 1995–; Member of the Muu, 1995–; Co-Director, Charm of Sound concert series, 1997–; Editor, Charmed Sounds radio programme, Finnish Radio, 1997–; Curator, Sound Box webcast project, Museum of Contemporary Art, Finland, 1998–; mem, DEGEM; WFAE. *Compositions:* Various works for improvisers, 1980s; Chamber Music: Kuun arvet, 1988; Chain, 1994; Ancient Dream, 1994; Pro, 1994; Time, 1994; Enigma, 1994; Big Band: Storm..., 1993; Sound/Media installations: Soundscapes I, 1994; Birdscape Music, 1997; Free Zone, 1998; Transitions, 1998; Formation, 2002; Mixer, 2002; Electronic Film Soundtracks: Texas Scramble, 1995; The Blow, 1997; Days, 2002; Electronic Music: Lux in tenebris, 1995; The Good and Evil, 1995; Flow, 1996; La Mer, 1996; Momentum, 1998; Idea of Proof, 1999; The Waiting Room, 1999; Hysteria, 1999; Aurora Borealis 1, 2002; Four Notes, 2002; Departs/Arrivals, 2002; VROOM! 2000–2002; Canvas, 2002. *Recordings:* Numerous for various labels throughout Europe and the USA. *Publications:* Several contributions to journals, newspapers and books; On/Off, 2002. *Honours:* Farao Horn Competition Prize, 1995; Luigi Russolo Competition finalist, 1996; Finnish Cultural Foundation, 1998; State's Art Grant, 2000. *Address:* c/o Charm of Sound, PO Box 353, 00131 Helsinki, Finland. *E-mail:* petriear@nic.fi. *Website:* www.nic.fi/~petriear.

KULKA, Janos; Conductor; b. 11 Dec. 1929, Budapest, Hungary. *Education:* Studied at the Franz Liszt Academy, Budapest, with Janos Ferencsik and Laszlo Somogyi. *Career:* Repetiteur and Chorus Master at the Budapest Opera from 1950; Conducted Opera in Budapest from 1953 until the 1956 Revolution; Conducted at the Bavarian State Opera, 1957–59, Wurttemberg State Opera, Stuttgart, 1959–61; Principal Conductor of the Hamburg State Opera, 1961–64, Music Director at the Wuppertal Opera, 1964–75; Chief Conductor at Stuttgart from 1976, Nordwestdeutsche Philharmonie, 1976–87; Has worked with leading opera houses in Cologne, Geneva, Paris, Munich, Vienna, Barcelona, Copenhagen, Boston and Buenos Aires; Conducted the premieres of Blacher's Yvonne, Prinzessin von Burgund, 1973, Klebe's Jacobovsky und der Oberst, 1982, and Boehmer's Doktor Faustus, 1985; Has also led operas by Gluck, Mozart, Verdi, Wagner, Schoenberg, Janáček, Dallapiccola and Penderecki; Conducted The Queen of Spades at Berne, 1996. *Recordings include:* Chopin's 2nd Piano Concerto with Tamas Vasary and the Berlin Philharmonic; Opera recital albums with Grace Bumbry, Thomas Tipton, Walter Berry, Sandor Konya, Brigitte Fassbaender and Teresa Stratas; Il Trovatore; Die Abreise by d'Albert with Peter Schreier and Hermann Prey (CPO). *Address:* c/o Staatstheater Stuttgart, Oberer Schlossgarten 6, 70103 Stuttgart, Germany.

KULKA, Konstanty (Andrzej); Violinist; b. 5 March 1947, Gdańsk, Poland; m. 2 c. *Education:* Higher State School of Music, Gdansk. *Career:* Participant in 2 music competitions: Paganini Competition, Genoa, 1964, Diploma and Special Prize, Music Competition, Munich, 1966 (1st Prize); Since 1967 has given concerts all over the world and has participated in many international festivals including Lucerne, Prague, Bordeaux, Berlin, Granada, Barcelona; Premiered Concerto by Zygmunt Krauze, 1980; Many recordings, both gramophone and radio/television. *Honours:* Prize, Minister of Culture and Art, 1969, 1973; Prize, Minister of Foreign Affairs, 1977; Prize, President of Radio and Television Committee, 1978; Prize Winner, 33rd Grand Prix du Disque International Sound Festival, Paris, 1980; Gold Cross of Merit.

KUN, Hu; Concert Violinist; b. 1963, China. *Education:* Studied at Szechuan and Peking Central Conservatories and at Menuhin International School. *Career:* Debut: Played with Helsinki Radio Symphony and Helsinki Philharmonic Orchestras, 1979; London debut, 1985, followed by concerts with London Symphony Orchestra and the Philharmonic at the Barbican; Further concerts as Wigmore Hall and on tour to Canada, Japan, Singapore, Hong Kong, Brazil, Australia and Europe; Engagements at Concertgebouw Amsterdam and Zürich Tonhalle; Vienna and Berlin debuts, 1987, with the Beethoven and Sibelius Concertos. *Recordings include:* Prokofiev First Concerto with the English String Orchestra and the Sibelius and Khachaturian Concertos, both conducted by Yehudi Menuhin. *Honours:* Winner, City of Paris Menuhin Competition, 1984, Francescatti Competition, 1987, and Lipizer Competition, Italy, 1988.

KUNDE, Gregory; Singer (Tenor); b. 1954, Kankakee, Illinois, USA. *Education:* Studied at Illinois State University and the Opera School of Chicago Lyric Opera. *Career:* Sang at Chicago from 1979, Washington Opera, 1983, Dallas, 1986, Seattle, 1987; Metropolitan Opera debut, 1987, as Des Grieux in Manon; European engagements at Nice, Théâtre des Champs Elysées, Paris, 1989, and Geneva, in Guillaume Tell; Montpellier, 1990; as Raoul in Les Huguenots; Detroit, 1989, as Gounod's Roméo; Other roles have included Mozart's Belmonte and Tamino, Ernesto, Alfredo, Montreal 1987, Berlin 1991, San Francisco 1993, Carnegie Hall 1995; sang Arturo in Bellini's Puritani; Other roles include Edgardo in Lucia, Tormo 1993, Leicester in Maria Stuarda, Bologna 1994; Ernesto in Don Pasquale, La Scala 1994, Don Ottavio in Don Giovanni, Geneva 1992, La Scala 1993; Rodrigo in Donna del Lago, La Scala 1993, Rinaldo in Armida, Pesaro 1993; Tonio in Fille du Régiment and Nadir in Les Pêcheurs de Perles; Montpellier and Chicago, 1989, as Des Grieux, and Laertes in Hamlet by Thomas; Sang Lindoro in L'Italiana in Algeri at Berlin, 1992, Idreno in Semiramide at the 1992 Pesaro Festival; Danish Knight in Gluck's Armide to open the 1996–97 season at La Scala. *Recordings:* Bianca e Fernando; Semiramide; Armide; Hamlet. *Address:* c/o Robert Lombardo Associates, 61 West 62nd Street, Suite 6F, NY, NY 10023, USA.

KUNDLAK, Josef; Singer (Tenor); b. 1956, Bratislava, Czechoslovakia. *Education:* Studied in Bratislava and the European Opera Centre in Belgium. *Career:* Sang with Bratislava State Opera, 1983–, in works by Janáček and Smetana, in addition to standard repertory; Sang Nemorino in L'Elisir d'amore at Teatro Comunale, Bologna, 1987; Ferrando in Così fan tutte at La Scala Milan, 1989, returning in Die Meistersinger in 1990; Sang at Donizetti Festival at Bergamo in 1991 in Elisabetta al Castello di Kenilworth; Further engagements at Teatro San Carlo, Naples and Bayerische Staatsoper, Munich; Appeared as Belmonte in a new production of Die Entführung at Deutsche Oper Berlin in 1991; Sang Rossini's Almaviva at Genoa in 1992. *Recordings include:* Kudryash in Katya Kabanova, under Charles Mackerras (Supraphon, 1997). *Honours:* Winner, Luciano Pavarotti Competition in Philadelphia, 1985. *Address:* c/e Deutsche Oper Berlin, Richard Wagnerstrasse 10, 1000 Berlin, Germany.

KUNKEL, Renata; Composer; b. 1 Sept. 1954, Gdańsk, Poland. *Education:* Studied at the Warsaw Academy of Music. *Career:* Lecturer at the Warsaw Academy; Performances of her music in Europe, the USA and Central America. *Compositions include:* 3 String Quartets, 1979–91; Symphony, 1983; Inner Landscapes for Chamber Orchestra, 1984; Where Worlds Are Naught for String Orchestra, 1987; In A Lit-Up Streak Of Sounds for Ensemble, 1989; The Stream for Orchestra, 1990; Andos for Violin, 1990; Vocal music. *Honours:* Prizewinner at the First Lutoslawski International Composers' Competition, 1990. *Address:* c/o Society of Authors ZAiKS, 2 Hipoteczna Street, 00 092 Warsaw, Poland. *Telephone:* (4822) 828 17 05. *Fax:* (4822) 828 13 47. *E-mail:* sekretariat@zaiks.org.pl. *Website:* www.zaiks.org.pl.

KUNTZSCH, Matthias; symphony and opera conductor and professor; b. 22 Sept. 1935, Karlsruhe, Germany; m. Sylvia Anderson 1966; one s. one d. *Education:* Hochschule für Musik und Theatre, Hannover, Mozarteum, Salzburg with Lovro von Matacic, Hermann Scherchen, Herbert von Karajan, Zermatt with Pablo Casals, Karl Engel. *Career:* debut conducting Don Pasquale, State Theatre, Braunschweig, 1960; Con-ductor, Jeunesse Musicale Orchestra, Braunschweig, 1957; Musical Assistant, Hannover Opera, 1958; Kapellmeister, Opera Braunschweig, 1959; Assistant to Wolfgang and Wieland Wagner, Bayreuth Festival, 1959–64; Principal Conductor, Bonn Opera, 1962–64, Mannheim Opera, 1964–66, Hamburg State Opera, 1966–69, Staatskapellmeister, Munich State Opera, 1969–73; Generalmusikdirektor, Lübeck Opera and Symphony, 1973–77; Generalmusikdirektor and Operndirektor, Saarbrücken State Opera and Symphony, 1977–85; Conductor, International Youth Festival Orchestra, Bayreuth, 1981–86; Principal Guest Conductor and Artistic Adviser, Basque National Symphony, San Sebastian, Spain, 1986–89; Music Dir, Bay Area Summer Opera Theatre Inst. (BASOTI) 1992–; conducted world premieres of operas, Humphrey Searle's Hamlet, Hamburg, 1968 and Gian Carlo Menotti's Help Help the Globolinks, Hamburg, 1968; Günther Bialas's Aucassin et Nicolette, Munich, 1969; Detlev Mueller-Siemens's Genoveva, Germany TV ZDF; Guest Conductor with Utah Opera and Symphony, Colorado Symphony and Vancouver Opera. *Recordings:* With soloists Ruggiero Ricci, Eugene List and others; Conrad Susa's The Blue House with the Colorado Symphony, 2002. *Address:* 123 Nantucket Cove, San Rafael, CA 94901, USA. *E-mail:* operaprof@aol.com.

KUNZEL, Erich; Conductor; b. 21 March 1935, New York, USA. *Education:* Studied at Dartmouth College, AB, 1957 and at Harvard and Brown Universities, AM, 1960. *Career:* Assistant to Pierre Monteux, 1963–64; Teacher and Director of Choral Music, Brown University, 1958–65; Conducted the Rhode Island Philharmonic, 1960–65; Assistant to Max Rudolf at the Cincinnati Symphony, 1965, Associate Conductor, 1967, Resident Conductor, 1969–74; Led Pergolesi's La Serva Padrona at Santa Fe, 1957, and the US premiere of The Nose by Shostakovich, 1965; Conducted the Cincinnati Opera, 1966; New Haven Symphony Orchestra, 1974–; Founded the Cincinnati Pops Orchestra, 1977 and toured with it to the Far East, 1990; Has also conducted orchestras in Chicago, Boston, Los Angeles, San Francisco, Montreal, Ottawa and Detroit; Music Director of the Indianapolis Symphony Orchestra; Jazz collaborations with Dave Brubeck, Ella Fitzgerald, Duke Ellington, Benny Goodman, George Shearing and Gerry Mulligan. *Recordings include:* Albums with the Dave Brubeck Trio and the Cincinnati Symphony; Carnaval Roman overture by Berlioz and Pictures at an Exhibition. *Address:* c/o Cincinnati Symphony Orchestra, 1241 Elm Street, Cincinnati, OH 45210, USA.

KUPFER, Harry; Opera Producer; b. 12 Aug. 1935, Berlin, Germany. *Career:* Worked at theatres in Halle, Stralsund and Karl-Marx-Stadt (now Chemnitz); Director, Deutsches Nationaltheater, Weimar, 1963–72; Chief Producer of Staatsoper Dresden, 1972–81; Chief Producer, Komische Oper Berlin from 1981 and Director from 1994; Has produced for Bayreuth: Der fliegende Holländer, 1978, Der Ring des Nibelungen, 1988; Opera Productions for Welsh National Opera at Cardiff, Covent Garden London, Staatsoper and Volksoper Vienna, Amsterdam, San Francisco, Paris, Hamburg, Cologne, Stuttgart and Frankfurt; Important productions include: Orfeo ed Euridice by Gluck, Mozart Cycle, La Damnation de Faust, Pelléas et Mélisande, Moses und Aron, Lear by A Reimann, premiere production of Die schwarze Maske by Penderecki (Salzburg, 1991), Die Soldaten by B A Zimmermann; Shortened version of The Invisible City of Kitezh by Rimsky-Korsakov at the 1995 Bregenz Festival; Has staged Wagner's Parsifal and the Ring, Berlin Staatsoper, 1995–96; Boris Godunov at the Vienna Volksoper, 1998.

KUROSAKI, Hiro; Violinist; b. 1949, Tokyo, Japan. *Education:* Studied at the Vienna Musikhochschule. *Career:* Solo engagements with the Royal Philharmonic, Dresden Staatskapelle, Salzburg Mozarteum and Vienna Symphony Orchestras; Leader of Les Arts Florissants, under William Christie, and has also played in Baroque and early music ensembles with the Clemencic Consort of Vienna and London Baroque; Teacher at the University of Vienna and the Salzburg Mozarteum. *Recordings include:* Mozart's violin sonatas, with Linda Nicholson. *Honours:* Prizewinner at the Wieniawski and Kreisler Competitions, 1977 and 1979. *Address:* c/o Les Arts Florissants, 10 Rue de Florence, 75008 Paris, France.

KURTAG, György; Composer; b. 19 Feb. 1926, Lugos, Romania. *Education:* Budapest Music Academy and in Paris. *Career:* Retired Professor of Chamber Music, Music Academy of Budapest. *Compositions:* Concerto for Viola, 1954; String Quartet, 1959; Quintet for Wind Instruments, 1959; Eight Pieces for Piano, 1960; Signs for Solo Viola, 1961; Eight Duets for Violin and Cimbalom, 1961; The Sayings of Peter Bornemissza, for Soprano and Piano, 1968; In Memory of a Winter Sunset, Four Fragments for Soprano, Cimbalom and Violin, 1969; Four Capriccios for Soprano and Chamber Ensemble, 1970; Splinters Solo for Cimbalom, 1974; Four Pilinszky Songs, SK Rememberence Noise, Hommage a Mihály András, Twelve Microludes for String Quartet, Herdecker Eurythmie, Guitar Pieces, Omaggio a Luigi Nono, Messages of the Late Miss R V Troussova, Songs of Despondency and Grief, Scenes from a Novel, Attila Jozsef Fragments, Seven Lieder, Eight Tandori

Choruses; Kafka Fragments for Soprano and Violin, 1985; Quasi una Fantasia for Piano and Chamber Ensemble; Three Old Inscriptions for Soprano and Piano, 1986; Requiem po drugu for Soprano and Piano, 1987; Introduction, Kyrie A, Hommage à Stockhausen, Trumpet, Double-Bass, Piano, 1992; In Memoriam Thomas Blum, Piano, Celesta, Double-Bass, 1992; Hommage à John Cage, Trumpet, Double-Bass, 1992; Hommage à Tristan, Trumpet, Double-Bass, Piano, Celesta, 1992; Les Adieux in Janáček's Manier, Piano Solo, 1992; Antiphone in F Sharp, Trombone, Double-Bass, Piano, Celesta, 1992; Kyrie, b, Double-Bass, Piano, 1992; Curriculum vitae, Op 32, 2 Pianos, 2 Basset Horns, 1992; Samuel Beckett: What is the Word, Op 30b; Op 27 No. 2, Double Concerto; Stele, Op 33; Grabstein für Stephan, Op 15c; Messages for orchestra, 1991–96; Lettre a Peter Eötvös, Lagebericht, Aus der Ferne; Epilog to Requiem der Versöhnung, 1. Inscription on a Grave in Cornwall, 2. Flowers We Are, to Zoltan Kocsis; New Messages, 1998; 3 Pezzi for clarinet and cimbalom, 1996; Scenes for Flute, 1999; Peter Esterházy for piano and celesta, 1999; Zweigespräch for string quartet and live electronics, 1999. *Address:* 2621 Veröce, Lihegoutca 3, Hungary.

KURTAKOV, Krassimir; Singer (Bass-baritone); b. 1953, Sofia, Bulgaria. *Education:* Studied in Sofia. *Career:* Sang at the Bulgarian National Opera from 1979; Guest tour of Russia, Cuba, France and Austria, 1980–82; Vienna Kammeroper, 1987–88, as Nicolai's Falstaff and Don Alfonso; Bremerhaven, 1988–90 and Gelsenkirchen Opera, from 1990, including Denisov's L'ecume des jours, 1992; Vienna Staatsoper and elsewhere as Rocco in Fidelio, Mozart's Bartolo, Verdi's Fiesco, King Philip and Ramphis; Colline in La Bohème; Boris, Varlaam and Pimen, in Boris Godunov; Bonn Opera, 1992 in Jakob Lenz by Rihm. *Address:* c/o Bonn Opera, Am Boeselagerhof 1, 5311 Bonn, Germany.

KURTZ, Eugene (Allen); Composer; b. 27 Dec. 1923, Atlanta, Georgia, USA. *Education:* BA, Music, University of Rochester, 1947; MA, Music, Eastman School of Music, 1949; Study with Arthur Honegger and Darius Milhaud, Ecole Normale de Musique, Paris, France, 1949–51; Study with Max Deutsch, Paris, 1953–57. *Career:* Guest Professor of Composition, University of Michigan, 1967–68, 1970–71, 1973–74, 1980–81, 1988; Eastman School of Music, 1975; University of Illinois, 1976; University of Texas, 1977–78, 1985–86; Hartt School of Music, 1989; Consultant, Editions Jobert, Paris, 1972–. *Compositions:* The Solitary Walker, 1964; Conversations for 12 Players, 1966; Ca... Diagramme Pour Orchestre, 1972; The Last Contrabass in Las Vegas, 1974; Mécanique, 1975; Logo, 1979; Five-Sixteen, piano, 1982; World Enough and Time, 1982–; String Trio, Time and Again, 1984–85; From Time to Time, violin and piano, 1986–87; The Broken World, for string quartet, 1993–94; Shadows on the Wind, for 17 players, 1995–96; Icare, for solo flute, 1997. Also film scores and incidental music for radio, theatre and television. *Address:* 6 rue Boulitte, 75014 Paris, France.

KURZ, Ivan; Composer; b. 29 Nov. 1947, Prague, Czechoslovakia; m. Zdenka Sklenávová, 21 May 1951, 2 s., 1 d. *Education:* Studied music theory privately with Karel Risinger, 1964–66, composition study with Emil Hlobil, 1966–71 and postgraduate study with Vaclav Dobias, 1973–76, Academy of Arts and Music, Prague. *Career:* Dramaturgist for Prague television, 1972–74; Teacher of Music Theory at Academy of Music, 1976–. *Compositions include: Orchestral:* Concertino for Piano, Flute, Percussion and Strings, 1974, Slanting Plane, symphonic picture, 1979, Allegory, 1982, Symphony No. 3, 1986; The Confession, concerto for bassoon and symphonic orchestra, 1991; *Chamber:* Sonata for Piano, 1976, Circle Of Notes for String Quartet, 1979, The Touch for Piano Trio, 1982, Litanie for Organ and Percussion, 1984, Expectation for French Horn and Piano, 1985; *Vocal:* For Your Little Mozart, suite for Contralto and Piano, 1975, Got Mint?, vocal and acting etudes for Children's choir, 1982; *Instructive works:* Fiddlers Are Coming for Children's Recitation and Singing, 1980; Reverie, electronic music, 1982, Toward You I Come, symphonic picture, 1989, Evening Meeting, opera, 1989–90. *Address:* Drtinova 26, 150 00 Prague 5, Czech Republic.

KUSCHE, Benno; Singer (Bass-Baritone); b. 30 Jan. 1916, Freiburg, Germany. *Education:* Studied in Karlsruhe and with Fritz Harlan in Freiburg. *Career:* Debut: Koblenz in 1938 as Renato; Sang in Augsburg, 1939–42; Member of the Bayerische Staatsoper Munich from 1946, and Deutsche Oper an Rhein Düsseldorf from 1958; Sang at Salzburg Festival in 1949 in the premiere of Antigonae by Orff, Covent Garden in 1952 as Beckmesser, and in 1953 as La Roche in the first British performance of Capriccio, Glyndebourne Festival in 1954, 1963–64 as Leporello, La Roche and Don Fernando in Fidelio, Komische Oper Berlin in 1958 as Papageno in Die Zauberflöte and Metropolitan Opera, 1971–72 as Beckmesser; Guest appearances in Philadelphia, Amsterdam, Buenos Aires, Zürich, Florence and Bregenz. *Recordings:* Die Meistersinger; Die Kluge and Der Mond by Orff; La Bohème; Lulu. *Address:* c/o Bayerische Staatsoper, Postfach 745, 8000 Munich 1, Germany.

KUSIEWICZ, Piotr; Pianist and Singer; b. 30 June 1953, Gdańsk, Poland. *Education:* Pianist Diploma with Professor Zbigniew Sliwinski, 1977; Singer Diploma with Distinction, with Professor Jerzy Szymanski, 1980; Academy of Music, Gdansk. *Career:* Singer, Kraków State Opera, 1981–, Teatr STU, 1983–, Warsaw Opera House, 1984–, Wroclaw State Opera, 1986–; Guest performances in operas in West Germany, Switzerland, Austria, Netherlands, Luxembourg and Italy; Cooperation with Philharmonic Societies, chamber ensembles and member of vocal ensemble of ancient music, Bornus Consort; As pianist, performances with leading Polish singers as accompanist in Poland and abroad, and accompanist in Geneva International Singer Competition, 1978; As singer and pianist, at Festival of Contemporary Music, Warsaw Autumn, 1981, 1983, 1984, 1987, Krzysztof Penderecki's Festival in Lusawice, Poland on invitation from the composer, 1983, and recordings for Polish Radio; Vocal teacher at Academy of Music in Gdansk, 1986. *Recordings:* GF Handel's Sosarme, Opera Seria in 3 Acts. *Publications:* Co-author, Gdansk Composers, 1980. *Address:* ul Michala Glinki 4–9, 80-271 Gdańsk, Poland.

KUSNJER, Ivan; Singer (Baritone); b. 10 Nov. 1951, Rokytancy, Czechoslovakia. *Career:* Sang in operas at Ostrava and Brno from 1977; National Theatre Prague from 1982; Roles have included Mozart's Count, Verdi's Macbeth and Rigoletto, Marcello, Bohus in Dvořák's Jacobin, 1995, and Constantin in Martinů's Greek Passion; Vienna Staatsoper as Germont in La Traviata; Further guest appearances in Paris, Janáček's From the House of the Dead; Berlin, Brussels and Milan; Concerts include Carmina Burana; Zemlinsky's Lyric Symphony and the Spectre's Bride by Dvořák; Season 1998 as Tausendmark in Smetana's Brandenburgers in Bohemia at Prague and Premoyl in Libuše at the Edinburgh Festival. *Recordings:* Dimitri by Dvořák, Smetana's Dalibor and Janáček's Osud. *Address:* c/o National Theatre, PO Box 865, 11230 Prague 1, Czech Republic.

KÜTHEN, Hans-Werner, MA, PhD; German musicologist; b. 26 Aug. 1938, Cologne; m. Annette Magdalena Leinen; one s. *Education:* Bonn University; Bologna. *Career:* Editor, Beethoven Archives; mem. Gesellschaft für Musikforschung; Patron of the Verein Beethoven-Haus Bonn; VG Musikedition. *Publications:* On Beethoven: Essay, Kammermusik mit Bläsern, 1969; Article Beethoven Herder, Das Grosse Lexikon der Musik, 1978; Complete edition: Ouverturen und Wellingtons Sieg, 1974; Critical Report, separately, 1991; Klavierkonzerte I, 1984; Klavierkonzerte II (nos 4 and 5), with Critical Report separately; Klavierkonzerte Nos 1–3 (Bärenreiter Studienpartituren), 1987, Nos 4 and 5 Henle Studien-Editionen, 1998; same in practical edition for 2 pianos, 1988–99. *Contributions:* International professional publications including: Beethoven Yearbooks, congress reports, scholarly periodicals; International Congress of the Gesellschaft für Musikforschung, Freiburg i.Br, 1993: Gradus ad partituram; Erscheinungsbild und Funktionen der Solostimme in Beethovens Klavierkonzerten, Congress Report, 1999; Ein unbekanntes Notierungsblatt Beethovens aus der Entstehungszeit der Mondscheinsonate, Prague, 1996; Rediscovery and reconstruction of an authentic version of Beethoven's Fourth Piano Concerto for pianoforte and 5 strings, see Beethoven Journal Vol. 13 No. 1, San José, 1998; On Viadana: Article V in Herder-Lex, 1982, id in Lexikon für Theologie und Kirche, Herder, 2000; Co-Editor, Beethoven im Herzen Europas. Leben und Nachleben in den Böhmischen Ländern, 2000. *Address:* Am Hofgarten 7, 53113 Bonn, Germany.

KUTTENBAUM, Annette; Singer (Mezzo-soprano); b. 15 July 1957, Germany. *Career:* Debut: Opernhaus, Zürich, 1981; Sang at Hannover from 1983 and throughout Germany as guest, notably in The Ring and Parsifal at Bayreuth, 1988–92; Dorabella at Nuremberg; Adriano in Rienzi at Berlin and Brangäne in Tristan und Isolde at Weimar, 1996; Octavian in Der Rosenkavalier at Bologna, 1995; Further appearances as Hansel at Amsterdam and Fricka in Walküre at Trieste, 1998; Ortrud in Lohengrin, Braugüne in Tristan, Fricka in Walküre and Kundry in Parsifal, all at Weimar; Concert engagements in Vienna and elsewhere. *Recordings:* Video and CD of Das Rheingold and Götterdämmerung. *Address:* Deutches Nationaltheater Weimar, Theaterplatz 2, 99423 Weimar, Germany.

KUUSISTO, Ilkka Taneli; Composer; b. 26 April 1933, Helsinki, Finland; m. Marja-Lisa Hanninen, 26 Nov 1972, 2 s., 2 d. *Education:* Diploma, Precentor-Organist, 1954, Music Teacher, 1958; Studied Composition with Aarre Merikanto and Nils-Eric Fougstedt, Sibelius Academy; Studies, School of Sacred Music and Union Theological Seminary, New York under Seth Bingham, 1958–59, Studied in Germany, 1960 and Vienna, 1961. *Career:* Debut: Conductor, 1955, Composer, 1956; Assistant Head of Music Section, Finnish Broadcasting Corporation; Choral Director, Finnish National Opera; Artistic Director, Fazer Music Corporation, 1982–84; General Director, Finnish National Opera, 1984–92; President, Finnish Copyright Association, 1990–94; Musical Director, Helsinki City Theatre; Conductor, Radio Symphony Chorus; mem, Composers of Finland; Finnish Light and Film

Music Composers. *Compositions:* Operas: The Moomin Opera, 1974; The Rib of a Man, 1978; The War for the Light, 1981; Jaeger Stahl, 1982; Pierrot or the Secrets of the Night, 1991; Mail Maiden, 1992; Miss Julia, 1994; The Daughters of the Fatherland, 1998; Gabriel Come Back, 1998; Aino Kallas, 2000; Kings Ring, 2001; The Shortage, 2002; Ballets: Snow Queen, 1978; Robin Hood, 1986. *Recordings:* Christmas Carols from Finland with Soile Isokoski (soprano). *Honours:* World Council of Churches Scholarship, 1958; Scholarship, Finnish State, 1968; Pro Finlandia Medal, 1990; Professor honoris causa, 1992. *Current Management:* Tactus. *Address:* Apollonkatu 7, 00100, Helsinki, Finland. *E-mail:* tactus.oy@koluonbus.fi.

KUUSISTO, Pekka; Concert Violinist; b. 1976, Espoo, Finland. *Education:* East Helsinki Music Institute with Geza Szilvay; Sibelius Academy, with Tuomas Haapanaen, from 1985; Indiana University School of Music, Bloomington, with Miriam Fried and Paul Bliss; Steans Institute for Young Artists at the Ravinia Festival, 1995. *Career:* Many concerts with leading Finnish orchestras, including the Finnish Radio Orchestra and the Helsinki Philharmonic Orchestra; Tour of Japan, season 1996–97; Festival engagements at Helsinki, Turku, Ravinia and Schleswig-Holstein; Concertos with the Stockholm Sinfonietta and Okku Kamu, Orchestra of St John's Smith Square with John Lubbock, BBC Scottish Symphony Orchestra under Osmo Vänskä and the Malmö Symphony Orchestra under Paavo Berglund; Season 1998–99 Australian Tour; Season 1999–2000 tours to the USA and Japan with the Lahti Symphony and Osmo Vänskä, a tour to South America with Ashkenazy and the Czech Philharmonic and a tour to Germany with the Sibelius Academy and Lief Segerstam; Season 2002–03 Henze's Violin Concerto Number 3 with Orchestra della Toscana, the Beethoven concerto with Beethoven Academie Antwerp, visits to Malaysian Philharmonic, Singapore Symphony, Deutsche Kammerphilharmonie and Australian Chamber Orchestras. *Recordings include:* Sibelius Concerto, with the Helsinki Philharmonic Orchestra under Segerstram; Recital CD, Strings Attached, 1997; Vivaldi's Four Seasons with the virtuosi di Kuhmo; Bach Violin Concertos with Tapiola Sinfonietta and Jaako Kuusisto; A disc of Olli Mustonen's works conducted by the composer; Folk Trip, a recording of Finnish Folk Music with the Luomu Players. *Honours:* Winner, International Jean Sibelius Violin Competition, Helsinki, and the Kuopio Violin Competition, 1995. *Current Management:* Harrison/Parrott Ltd, 12 Penzance Place, London, W11 4PA, England. *Telephone:* (20) 7229 9166. *Fax:* (20) 7221 5042. *Website:* www .harrisonparrott.com.

KUZMENKO, Vladimir; Tenor; b. 1960, Kiev, Ukraine, Russia. *Education:* Studied in Kiev. *Career:* From 1988 has sung with the National Opera Company of Kiev as Lensky, Rodolfo, Don José, Faust, Dimitri and Count Almaviva; Guest appearances in France, Finland, Austria, Switzerland and Spain; Warsaw Opera in season 1994–95; British debut with the Kiev Opera as Alfredo in La Traviata, on tour in 1995; Hermann in The Queen of Spades for Scottish Opera, 1998. *Address:* c/o Sonata Ltd, 11 Northgate Street, Glasgow G20 7AA, Scotland.

KUZNETSOV, Fyodor; Singer (Bass); b. 1960, Sverdlovsk, Ekaterinburg, Russia. *Career:* Many appearances in concerts throughout Russia: Repertoire includes Mahler No.8, Beethoven No.9 and Shostakovich no.14 symphonies, Rossini's Stabat Mater, Bruckner's Missa Solemnis and Handel's Hercules and Samson; Engagements with the Kirov Opera, St Petersburg, from 1994 as Verdi's Philip II, Ferrando, Grand Inquisitor and Sparafucile; Mozart's Figaro and Commendatore, Boris, Pimen and Varlaam in Boris Godunov, Dosifei in Khovanshchina, Prince Gremin and Rimsky-Korsakov's Tsar Saltan; Sang Nikolai Bolkonsky in War and Peace with the Kirov at Covent Garden, 2000; Other roles include Khan Konchak in Prince Igor, Maliuta in The Tsar's Bride and Salieri in Rimsky-Korsakov's Mozart and Salieri; Mussorgsky's Boris Godunov at the London Proms, 2002. *Honours:* Winner, All-Russia Competition, 1987; Laureate Prize of the Mayor of St Petersburg, 1994. *Address:* c/o Kirov Opera, Mariinsky Theatre, Theatre Square, St Petersburg, Russia.

KUZUMI, Karina; Violinist; b. 29 April 1973, Tokyo, Japan. *Education:* Study, Toho Gakuen, Tokyo, 1992; Graduated, Pre-College, University of Music and Arts, Tokyo, 1992; Study, Escuela Superior de Musica Reina Sofia, Madrid, 1993; Study, Musikhochschule, Lübeck, 1995; Hochschule für Musik, Cologne, 1998. *Career:* Debut: Tokyo City Philharmonic Orchestra, Tokyo, 1986; Concert, Nara, 1992; NHK-FM, Japan, 1992; Radio II Classica, Spain, 1994; Recitals at Auditorio Nacional, Madrid and Tokyo, 1994, Burgos, Melilla, Malaga, Valencia and Santander, 1995; Concert at Tokyo, Gronau and Rheine, 1997; Tour of Japan, 1998; La Radio Suisse Romande, 1998; Recital at Tokyo Opera City Recital Hall, 1999; Concert at Alte Oper in Frankfurt, 1999; Concerts with Budapest Symphony Orchestra, Klassiche Philharmonie Bonn, 1999–2000; Leader (Concertmaster) of the Stuttgart Philharmonic in Germany, 2001–. *Honours:* 1st Prize, All-Japan Student Music Competition, 1988; Scholarship, Foundation Isaac Albeniz, 1994; Scholarship, Culture Department, Japan, 1997; 3rd Prize, 33rd Szigeti

International Competition, 1997; 3rd Prize, 5th Brahms International Competition, 1998. *Address:* Sanda-cho 4-33-8, Hachioji, 193-0832 Tokyo, Japan; Sodener Str. 31, 70372 Stuttgart, Germany. *E-mail:* kkuzumi@gmx.de.

KVAPIL, Jan; Violinist; b. 1943, Czechoslovakia. *Education:* Studied at Prague Academy of Arts. *Career:* Member of the Talich String Quartet from 1962; Tours to most European countries and to Egypt, Iraq, North America, Japan and Indonesia; Member, Talich Quartet, 1962–94; Radio Symphony Orchestra, Prague, 1994–97; Czech Philharmonic Orchestra, 1997. Trio Mysterium Musicum Prague (sacred music) with Talich Quartet annual visits to France from 1976 and tours of the United Kingdom, 1990–91 with concerts at Wigmore Hall, appearances at the Bath and Bournemouth Festivals, Queen Elizabeth Hall and on BBC 2's Late Show, with Janáček's 2nd Quartet; Played Beethoven's Quartet Op 74, the Brahms A minor, Smetana D minor and works by Mozart, in England, 1991; Festival appearances in Vienna, Besançon, Lucerne, Helsinki, Amsterdam, Prague and Salzburg; Repertoire also includes works by Debussy, Bartók (complete quartets recorded), Shostakovich, Ravel and Dvořák. *Recordings include:* Complete Quartets of Beethoven and Mozart. *Honours:* Grand Prix Charles Cros; Diapason d'Or; Grand Prix de l'akademie du Disque Francais; Award Supraphon. *Address:* Mazursuá 526, 18100 Prague 8-Troja , Czech Republic. *Telephone:* 322 555353.

KVAPIL, Radoslav; Pianist; b. 15 March 1934, Brno, Czechoslovakia; m. Eva Kvapilova-Maslanova, 11 June 1960, 1 s. *Education:* Gymnasium Brno, 1944–52; Janáček Academy of Music, Brno, 1952–57; Aspiranteur, Janáček Academy with Prof L Kundera, 1960–63. *Career:* Debut: Recital, Brno, 1954; Numerous concerts in more than 20 countries including Europe, USA, Canada and Japan, 1956–; Appearances on numerous radio stations including BBC and Radio France; Professor, Conservatory Prague, 1963–73; Chairman, EPTA Czech Republic; Chairman, The South Bohemis Festival Society; Chairman, AMAT Czech Republic; Chairman, Menuhin Live Music Now Czech Republic, 1992; Chairman, Dvořák Society, Prague. *Recordings:* All piano works by A Dvořák, 1967–69, All works J H Vorisek, 1975, Concerto A Reicha, A Dvořák; All piano works of L Janáček, 1969; All polkas of B Smetana, 1969; BIS B Martinů Studies and Polkas, Sonata, 1982; Piano works of Moussorgsky, Calliope: Works of Smetana, and Janáček; Hindemith, Janáček, with Wallace Collection; All piano, violin and violoncello works of L Janáček; 2CD with works of B Martinů/first and last period; Anthology of Czech piano music: Till end of 1995 released 8 vols containing works of Dvořák, Smetana, Martinů/Paris period/Vorišek, Fibich, Janáček and Suk, Project will continue; Dvořák: Cypresses, Biblical songs with P Langridge; Radio recording BBC includes Dvořák piano concerto, Martinů Concertos No. 3, 4, Divertimento, Debussy Phantasie for piano and orchestra. *Contributions:* Musical Review Prague. *Honours:* International Competition, Radio CSSR, 1st prize, 1968; Janáček medal of Ministry culture CSSR, 1978; Honorary Vice President, Dvořák Society of Great Britain; Prize for Czech music, Prague, 1990; CD of the month, Reporter, Paris, 1994–97. *Current Management:* Margaret Murphy, 28 Windsor Road, Wanstead, London E11 3QU, England. *Address:* Hradecka 5, 13000 Prague 3, Czech Republic.

KVARAN, Gunnar; Cellist; b. 1960, Reykjavík, Iceland. *Education:* Studied at the Reykjavík College of Music, at the Copenhagen Conservatory and in Basle and Paris. *Career:* Solo concerts, recitals and chamber music throughout Scandinavia, France, Germany, Netherlands and North America; Appearances with the Icelandic Symphony, the Tivoli Orchestra and the Jutland Philharmonic; Professor at the Reykjavík College of Music and member of the Reykjavík Piano Trio. *Address:* c/o World-wide Artists, 6 Petersfield Crescent, Coulsdon, Surrey CR5 2JQ, England.

KVECH, Otomar; Composer; b. 25 May 1950, Prague, Czechoslovakia; m. Miluska Wagnerova, 30 Mar 1972, (died 2000), 2 d, m. Dr. Jane Smékalová, 1 Aug, 2003. *Education:* Composition, Organ, Music Conservatory, Prague, 1965–69; Composition with Professor Pauer, Academy of Music Arts, Prague, 1974–77. *Career:* Debut: Symphony for Organ and Orchestra, Dvořák's Hall, Prague; Pianist, National Theatre, Prague, 1974–77; Music Producer, 1977–80, Dramaturgist, Editor, 1988–, Radio Prague; Secretary, Organisation of Czech Composers and Concert Artists, 1980–90; Professor, 1990–, Chief of the Composing Section, 1998–, Music Conservatory, Prague; Professor, Academt of Arts, Prague, 2002–. *Compositions include:* 5 symphonies: Organ, 1974, E Flat Major, 1982, D Major, 1984, E Minor with String Quartet, 1987, Four saisons for Organ and Orchestra, 2001; 6 String Quartets, 1972, 1973, 1974, 1979, 1985, Four saisons 2000, 2001; 3 Violin Sonatas, 1974, 1978, 1982; The World Carnival, 1983; Cello Sonata, 1985; 2 Sonatas for Organ, 1986; RUR, 1986; Capriccio, concerto, piano trio, orchestra, 1986; Piano Quintet, 1990; Requiem, 1991; 3 songs for voice and organ, 1993–97; Oboe Sonata, 1995; Serenata notturna, 1996; Nokturnalie, 1997; Missa con viola obligata, 1998; Sextet for string quartet, oboe and harp, 1999; Recitatives and arias for corno inglese and orchestra, 2004; Methamoforsis for violin solo and strings, 2004;. *Recordings:* Piano Trio; The Waltz Across the Room; Symphonies 1, 2; RUR; String Quartet No. 5; For Radio Prague: Symphony in E Minor, World Carnival, The Honour to Bach, Capriccio, String Quartets 2, 3, 4; Sonatas for Violin 1, 2, 3, Viola Sonata, Cello Sonata, Wind Quintet; Many works recorded in England, Germany, France. *Publications:* When the Path Disappeared, song cycle; Three Moments for Accordion; Piano Trio; Prague Panorama; Six Preludes for Flute Solo; String Quartet No. 5; Symphony, E Flat Major. *Contributions:* Hudebni Rozhledy, Prague; Opus Musicum, Brno. *Address:* Korunni 67, 13000 Prague 3, Czech Republic. *E-mail:* otomar.kvech@rozhals.cz.

KWELLA, Patrizia; Singer (Soprano); b. 26 April 1953, Mansfield, England. *Education:* Royal College of Music, London. *Career:* Promenade Concert debut in 1979 with John Eliot Gardiner; Concerts and festivals include Ansbach, Bergen, Innsbruck, Aldeburgh, Bologna, Warsaw, Bath, City of London, Edinburgh and Salzburg; Conductors include Richard Hickox, Peter Maag, Christopher Hogwood and Trevor Pinnock; US debut in 1983 with the San Diego Symphony; Further concerts with the San Francisco, Houston and Washington Symphony Orchestras; Sang in many of the Bach, Handel and Scarlatti tercentenary concerts of 1985; Premiere of Night's Mask by Colin Matthews at the 1985 Aldeburgh Festival; Sang Handel's Alcina at the 1985 Spitalfields and Cheltenham Festivals; Repertoire includes Haydn, Mozart, Brahms, Mahler, Stravinsky and Britten. *Recordings:* Handel's L'Allegro, Alcina, Alceste, Resurrezione and Esther; Monteverdi's Orfeo and Il Combattimento; Bach's B minor Mass, Magnificat and St John Passion; Mozart's Coronation Mass, Missa Solemnis and Regina Coeli; Television includes many Man and Music appearances for Channel 4. *Address:* c/o Music and Musicians Artists' Management, 54 Regent's Park Road, London NW1 7SX, England.

KWIECIEN, Martin; Polish singer (baritone); b. 1965, Kraków. *Career:* debut, Kraków Opera 1993 as Purcell's Aeneas; appearances as Mozart's Figaro in Luxembourg and Poznan and Papageno at Warsaw; Sang in premiere of Zemlinsky's König Kandaules at Hamburg, 1996; Metropolitan Young Artists Program from 1998; appearing in Katya Kabanova, Rigoletto, Giulio Cesare and I'Italiana in Algeri; Season 2000–01 as Mozart's Count at Glyndebourne, Marcello at Antwerp and Donizetti's Enrico in Buenos Aires. *Honours:* Winner, Breslau International Competition, 1994; Hans Gabor/Belvedere Competition, Vienna, 1996; Mozart Interpretation Prize, Francisco Viñas Competition, Barcelona, 1998; Represented Poland at 1999 Cardiff Singer of the World Competition.

KWON, Hellen; Singer (Soprano); b. 11 Jan. 1961, Seoul, Korea. *Education:* Studied in Cologne. *Career:* Debut: Wiesbaden in 1984 as the Queen of Night; Has sung at Mannheim, 1985–, Paris Opéra, 1986 in Die Zauberflöte, and Hamburg, 1987; Created the role of Alexis de Lechebot in Liebermann's La Forêt in Geneva, 1987; Sang at Bayreuth Festival in 1988 as a Flower Maiden, Glyndebourne Festival in 1990 as the Queen of Night followed by performances at Bonn and Vienna in 1991; Sang Susanna at Hamburg in 1990, Wellgunde in a concert performance of Götterdämmerung at Rome in 1991 and Blondchen in Die Entführung at Salzburg Festival in 1991; Other roles include Strauss's Sophie and Zerbinetta, Rosina, Norina and Musetta; Sang Susanna at the 1992 Israel Festival, Adele in Die Fledermaus at Hamburg, 1996; Constanze in Die Entführung at the Vienna Kammeroper, 1998; Concert tours of USA, France, Italy, Belgium and the Netherlands notably in the B minor Mass and St Matthew Passion of Bach. *Recordings include:* Nightingale in Die Vögel by Braunfels, 1997. *Address:* c/o Hamburgische Staatsoper, Grosse Theaterstrasse 34, 2000 Hamburg 36, Germany.

KYHLE, Magnus; Singer (Tenor); b. 1959, Sweden. *Education:* Studied at Stockholm College of Music and the State Opera School in Stockholm. *Career:* Debut: Vadstena Academy in 1983; Engaged at the Royal Opera, Stockholm, 1986–89, Stadttheater Darmstadt, 1989–90 and Landestheater Salzburg, 1990–92; Roles include Mozart's Don Ottavio, Tamino, Monostatos and Ferrando, Pelléas, and Paris in La Belle Hélène; Guest appearances at Tenerife and Tokyo; Season 1990–92 as Tamino and Don Ottavio with the Royal Opera Stockholm, Tamino at Salzburg Landestheater and Ferrando at Semperoper Dresden; Season 1992–93 as Beppe in a new production of Pagliacci at Stockholm, and in

a new production of Traviata; Stockholm production of The Phantom of the Opera, 1994–. *Address:* IM Audio and Music HB, Åsögatan 67Vl, 11829 Stockholm, Sweden.

KYLLONEN, Timo-Juhani; Finnish composer, accordion player and conductor; b. 1 Dec. 1955, Saloinen. *Education:* Tchaikovsky Conservatoire and Gnesin Music Institute, Moscow. *Career:* debut concert of his works at the Tchaikovsky Conservatory, Moscow, April 1986; biographical programmes, Finnish Television, 1982, 1988; Several concerts and radio and television programmes in Finland, Sweden, USSR, Peru, Ecuador and Norway; Composer-portrait on Netherlands Radio, 1990, also on Argentinian, Brazilian, Cuban, Israeli and Peruvian radio; mem, Finnish Composer's Union. *Compositions include:* Symphony No. 1, op 8, 1985–86; Symphony No. 2 op 29, 1991–95; Suite for String Orchestra op 27, 1991; Awakening op 23b for string orchestra; Two Kalevala Songs for chorus and piano, 1996. *Recordings include:* Compositions by Timo-Juhani Kyllonen, Finlandia Records; Elegia quasi una sonata, op 15, 1987; Trio No. 1, op 9, 1986; Triology for 2 pianos, op 4, 1984; String Quartet No. 1 op 3, 1984, Ondine Records; Ciclo para coro mixto op 5. *Honours:* Pro Musica Award, 1988; Espoo City Arts prize, 1989; Three year Stipendum, Finnish Ministry of Education, 1991–93; 3 different television programmes (personal portraits) on Finnish television. *Current Management:* Finnish Music Information Centre, Lauttasaarentie 1, 00200 Helsinki, Finland. *Address:* Joupinmäki 3C49, 02760 Espoo, Finland.

KYNASTON, Nicolas; Concert Organist; b. 10 Dec. 1941, Morebath, Devon, England. *Education:* Accademia Musicale Chigiana, Siena, 1957; Conservatorio Santa Cecilia, Rome, 1958; Royal College of Music, 1960. *Career:* Debut: Royal Festival Hall, 1966; Organist, Westminster Cathedral, 1961–71; Organist of the Athens Megaron Concert Hall, 1995–; Travels widely giving regular recitals throughout the United Kingdom, most European countries and to many exotic places including Barbados, Nassau, Ankara, Istanbul, Tokyo, Hong-Kong, Bangkok, Seoul-Korea and the famous Bamboo Organ of Las Pinas, Philippines and tours of North America; Varied and extensive solo repertoire; Broadcasts regularly on BBC Radio and Television and Foreign Networks (particularly West Germany); Teaches Cambridge University; Masterclasses in USA, Hong-Kong, Norway, Singapore and Germany; Chairman, National Organ Teacher's Encouragement Scheme, 1993–96; mem, Association of Independent Organ Advisors. *Recordings:* Numerous commercial recordings for British, French and German companies; 5 nominated Critics Choice; 2 Popular records Great Organ works at Royal Albert Hall earning EMI Sales Award; Bach from Clifton Cathedral nominated Best Solo Instrumental Record of the Year; Received Deutscher Schallplatten preis for Vierne's 6th Symphony (German recording); CD on IMP Masters of Bach Organ Work, 1994; Liszt Organ Works, re-issued, 2001. *Publications include:* Transcriptions for organ of works by Liszt and Mendelssohn. *Address:* 28 High Park Road, Kew Gardens, Richmond-upon-Thames, Surrey TW9 4BH, England.

KYR, Robert (Harry); Composer and Teacher; b. 20 April 1952, Cleveland, Ohio, USA. *Education:* BA, Yale University, 1974; Royal College of Music, London, 1974–76; MA, University of Pennsylvania, 1978; PhD, Harvard University, 1989. *Career:* Composer-in-Residence, New England Philharmonic, 1985–89; Resident Composer of Extension Works, Composers and Performers Consortium, Boston, MA, 1985–; Teacher of Composition and Theory at Harvard University (teaching fellow), 1985–89, Longy School of Music (Director of Compositional Studies), 1986–, Hartt School of Music (visiting lecturer), Fall 1988. *Compositions include:* Commissions: Maelstrom (The Fires Of London), 1981, The Greater Changing, Symphony No. 2 (Mystic Valley Orchestra, Boston), 1986, A Signal In The Land (Johnson City Symphony Orchestra, TN), 1987, The Fifth Season, Symphony No. 3 (Friends Of Music at Yale, Yale Symphony), 1988, Book Of The Hours, Symphony No. 1 (New England Philharmonic), 1988, Toward Eternity (Radcliffe Choral Society, Harvard University), 1988, Symphony No. 4 (New England Philharmonic), 1989, Symphony No. 5 (Pro Arte Orchestra, Boston), 1990; There Is A River for Soprano, Women's Chorus and Orchestra, 1985; Images From Stillness for String Trio, 1986; Images of Reminiscence for Piano, 1987; One for Solo Clarinet. *Publications:* Complete Works published. *Address:* 16 Forest Street No. 41, Cambridge, MA 02140, USA.

L

LA BARBARA, Joan Lotz; composer, singer and writer; b. 8 June 1947, Philadelphia, Pennsylvania, USA; m. Morton Subotnick 1979; one s. *Education:* Syracuse University School of Music, 1965–68; Berkshire Music Center, Tanglewood, summers, 1967–68; BS, New York University, 1968–1970. *Career:* Debut: With Steve Reich and Musicians, Town Hall, New York, 1971; With Steve Reich, 1971–74, Philip Glass, 1973–76, John Cage, premiering Solo for Voice 45 with Atlas Eclipticlis, Winter Music with Orchestra of the Hague, 1976; In Avignon premiere, Einstein on the Beach, 1976; Premiered Subotnick's Double Life of Amphibians, Los Angeles Olympics Arts Festival, 1984; Own work, Houston and San Francisco Symphonies, 1982, Los Angeles Philharmonic, 1983, New York Philharmonic, 1984; Premiered: Subotnick's chamber opera Jacob's Room, American Music Theater Festival and MANCA Festival, Nice, 1993–94, quartet of operas Now Eleanor's Idea (R Ashley), Brooklyn Academy of Music and Avignon Festival, 1994; Balseros (Ashley) for Miami Grand Opera, 1997; Dust (Ashley) Yokohama, Japan, 1998; Celestial Excursions (Ashley), Berliner Fest Spiele, 2003; Messa di Voce (own interactive media work), with Jaap Blonk, Golan Levin and Zachary Lieberman, Ars Electronica, Linz, Austria, 2003; Vocal soloist on soundscore by John Frizzell for the film, I Still Know What You Did Last Summer, 1998; Filmscore for Immersion, 1998; Many commissions; Newborn vocals for film Alien Resurrection, 1997; Series Director and Performer, When Morty Met John…, a three-year series focussing on the New York School of Composers (John Cage, Morton Feldman, Earle Brown, Christian Wolff) at Carnegie Hall, 2001–03; Artistic Dir and Host, Insights, a series of encounters with distinguished composers, for The American Music Center, 2003–; Curator, EMF@Chelsea Art Museum, 2003; mem. ASCAP; The American Music Center; SAG; AFTRA; AEA. *Compositions:* Most recent: To hear the wind roar, choral, 1989–91; In the Dreamtime, (self portrait, sound painting), 1989; L'albero dalle foglie azzurre, solo oboe with tape, 1989; Awakenings, chamber ensemble, 1991; Klangbild Köln, 1991; 73 Poems to poems by Kenneth Goldsmith, 1994; Calligraphy II/Shadows, voice, dizi, erhu, yangqi, Chinese percussion, 1995; In the shadow and act of the haunting place, voice, chamber ensemble, 1995; Film: Angel Voice, for Date with an Angel, 1987; Score for Anima, 1991; A Trail of Indeterminate Light, for solo cello, 1991; de profundis: out of the depths, a sign; 1996; A Different Train, 1996; Snowbird's Dance, Into the Light, for voice, flute and string quartet, 2000; Dragons on the Wall, Tianji for voices, instruments and tape collage, 2001. *Recordings include:* The Art of Joan La Barbara; Sound Paintings; Joan La Barbara Singing through John Cage; Three Voices for Joan La Barbara (Morton Feldman); Jacob's Room (M Subotnick); 73 Poems, CD and CD with book, 1994; Awakenings; L'albero dalle Foglie azzurre; Only: Works for Voice and Instruments (Feldman), 1996; ShamanSong, 1998; Voice is the Original Instrument, 2003. *Exhibition:* 73 Poems, a collaborative work with text artist Kenneth Goldsmith, included in The American Century Part II: Soundworks, The Whitney Museum of American Art. *Publications:* Contributions to Grove's Dictionary; Contemporary Music Journal, Los Angeles Times, Musical America/High Fidelity magazine, Schwann/Opus. *Honours:* DAAD Artist-in-Residency, Berlin; 7 Nat. Endowment for the Arts Fellowships; ISCM Int. Jury Award; Akustische Int. Competition Award; ASCAP awards. *Address:* 25 Minetta Lane (4B), New York, NY 10012-1253, USA. *Website:* www.joanlabarbara.com.

LA GRANGE, Henry-Louis de; Writer on Music; b. 26 May 1924, Paris, France. *Education:* Studied letters at Aix-en-Provence and the Sorbonne, Paris; Yale University School of Music, 1946–47; Yvonne Lefébure (piano) and Nadia Boulanger, (Harmony, counterpoint, analysis), 1947–53. *Career:* Music Critic for French and American publications; Guest Lecturer at Columbia, Stanford and Indiana Universities, 1974–81, Geneva, 1982, Leipzig, Juilliard, University of California at Los Angeles, 1985, Budapest, 1987, Hamburg, 1988, Oslo, 1993, also Paris Conservatory, Kyoto, Hong-Kong, Wellington, Sydney, Canberra, Melbourne, Boulder, San Francisco, 1998; Taught a DEA Seminar at the Ecole Normale Supérieure, Paris; Founded the Bibliothèque Musicale Gustav Mahler, Paris, 1986. *Publications include:* Gustav Mahler: Chronique d'une Vie, 3 vols, 1979–84; Vienne, Une Histoire musicale, 2 vols, 1990–91; Mahler, Vol. I, England and USA, 1973–74. Vols II and III, England and USA, 1995–2000. *Honours:* Chevalier de la Légion d'honneur; Commandeur, Ordre du Mérite national; Title of Professor granted by Austrian Government. *Address:* c/o Médiathèque Musicale Mahler, 11 bis, rue de Vézelay, 75008 Paris, France.

LA MONTAINE, John; Composer; b. 17 March 1920, Chicago, Illinois, USA. *Education:* Studied with Bernard Rogers and Howard Hanson at the Eastman School, with Wagenaar at Juilliard School and with Nadia Boulanger at the American Conservatory, Fontainebleau. *Career:* Pianist with the NBC Symphony conducted by Toscanini, 1950–54; Composer in Residence at American Academy, Rome, 1962; Visiting Professor at the Eastman School, 1964–65; Nixon Chair at Whittier College, California, 1977; President of Fredonia Press. *Compositions include:* Songs of the Rose of Sharon, for soprano and orchestra, 1947; Wonder Tidings for SATB, harp and percussion, 1957; Piano Concerto No.1, 1958; Fragments from the Song of Songs, for soprano and orchestra, 1959; A Trilogy of Medieval Christmas Operas, Novellis, Novellis, The Shephardes Playe and Erode the Greate, 1961–9; Overture: From Sea to Shining Sea (commissioned for the Inauguration of President Kennedy, 1961); Birds of Paradise for piano and orchestra, 1964; Sacred Service, 1964–8; Wilderness Journal, after Thoreau, for bass-baritone, organ and orchestra (commissioned for the opening of the Kennedy Center and the dedication of the Filene Great Organ), 1971; The Nine Lessons of Christmas for SATB, harp and percussion, 1975; Be Glad Then America, a Bicentennial opera (commissioned by Penn State University), 1976; The Lessons of Advent, 1983; Piano Concertos 2, 3, and 4, 1987–9; Arrangement of Bach's Well-Tempered Klavier for Electronic Keyboard, 1991–2; In Praise of Britain's Queen and Elgar's Enigma, a complete solution of Elgar's Enigma, SATB and two orchestras, 1991; Piccolo Sonata, 1993; Passacaglia and Fugue for orchestra, an adaptation of Paul J Siffler's Recitative Passacaglia and Fugue, 2000. *Recordings include:* Piano Concerto No. 1 and No. 4; Piano Sonata; Birds of Paradise; Songs of The Rose of Sharon; Flute Concerto; Wilderness Journal; Incantation for Jazz Band; Conversations for Violin and Piano; Six Shakespeare Sonnets; The Nine Lessons of Christmas; The Well-Tuned Keyboard, 2 CDs, after Bach. *Publications:* Many works published. *Honours:* Guggenheim Fellowships; Pulitzer Prize for Piano Concerto, 1959; American Academy of Arts and Letters Award, 1962. *Address:* 3947 Fredonia Drive, Hollywood, CA 90068, USA.

LA PIERRE, John; Singer (Tenor); b. 1961, USA. *Education:* Purchase, New York; St Louis Conservatoire. *Career:* Appearances in opera at Atlanta; St Louis; Omaha; Nevada; Mobile; Cologne Opera as Mozart's Tamino; Ferrando; Ottavio; Belmonte; Belfiore; Glyndebourne as Idamante in Idomeneo; Opéra Comique in La Cambiale di Matrimonio and Il Signor Bruschino by Rossini; Netherlands Opera as Andres in Wozzeck and in Die Meistersinger; Concerts include Bach's B Minor Mass, Washington; Mozart's Requiem, St Louis Symphony Orchestra; Messiah, St Matthew Passion; Haydn's Seasons, Cologne. *Honours:* Finalist, Met Opera National Auditions, 1985. *Address:* Music International, 13 Ardilaun Road, London N5 2QR, England.

LA RUE, (Adrian) Jan Pieters, MFA, PhD; academic; b. 31 July 1918, Kisaran, Sumatra; m. 1st Helen Robison 1946 (died 1998); two d.; m. 2nd Marian Green 2000. *Education:* Harvard Univ., Princeton Univ. *Career:* Instructor to Associate Professor and Chairman of Music Department, Wellesley College, 1942–43, 1946–57; Profesor of Music, Graduate School of Arts and Science, New York University, 1957–88; Chairman, 1970–71, Executive Dean, 1963–64; Professor Emeritus, 1988; Visiting Professor, 1947; University of Michigan, 1963; Bar Ilan, Israel, 1980, Tokyo, 1988, Indiana, 1990, Queens, Canada, 1995; Research Professor, Austria, 1954–56; 1st Lieutenant, Transportation Corps, Okinawa Campaign, 16 months in Pacific Theatre, 1943–46; Music Curriculum Project, 1966–67; Councillor, Smithsonian Institute, 1967–73; Musicologist-in-Residence, Kennedy Centre, Washington, 1975; Fellow, American Acad. of Arts and Sciences, 2003. *Compositions:* Concertino, clarinet and orchestra, 1941; Trio, strings, 1942. *Publications:* Guidelines for Style Analysis, 1970 (Sp ed 1988), 2nd ed, 1992; Methods and Models for Musical Style Analysis, with Ohmiya, Makoto, 1988; A Catalogue of 18th Century Symphonies, 1988; Bifocal Tonality in Haydn's Symphonies, 1992. *Contributions:* Die Musik in Geschichte und Gegenwart, 1968; Grove's Dictionary, 6th ed, 1980; Articles in numerous journals and Festschriften, including Festschriften Davison, 1957; Albrecht, 1962; Voetterle, 1968; Geiringer, 1970; Larsen, 1972; Johnson, 1990; Southern, 1992; Ratner, 1992; Editor: Festschriften Reese, 1966; Deutsch, 1968. *Honours:* Ford Foundation Fellow, 1954; Guggenheim Fellow, 1964–65; ACLS Fellow, 1964–65; NEH Research Grant, 1980–84; LaRue Festschrift Studies in Musical Sources and Style (ed Wolf and Roesner), 1990. *Address:* Woods End Road, New Canaan, CT 06840, USA.

LA SCOLA, Vincenzo; Singer (Tenor); b. 1958, Palermo, Italy. *Education:* Studied with Carlo Bergonzi. *Career:* Debut: Parma in 1983 as Ernesto in Don Pasquale; Sang in Genoa and Liège, 1984, as Nemorino in Brussels and Rinuccio in Gianni Schicchi and Tonio in La Fille du Régiment in Paris, 1987–88; La Scala debut in 1988 as Nemorino returning 1991–92 as Alfredo and Edgardo in Lucia di Lammeroor; Other roles include Elvino in La Sonnambula at Venice in 1989, Orombello in Beatrice di Tenda, Mascagni's Amico Fritz, the Duke of Mantua, and Florindo in Mascagni's Le Maschere; Sang Donizetti's

Roberto Devereux at Bologna and Edgardo at La Scala in 1992, and Rodolfo in La Bohème at the Verona Arena in 1992; Sang Edgardo in Lucia di Lammermoor at Florence, 1996; Cavaradossi at the Verona Arena, 1998; Season 2000–01 as Nemorino in Chicago, Werther in Palermo and Verdi's Jacopo Foscari at Naples; Gabriele Adorno in Munich, Ernani for the Vienna Staatsoper and the Verdi Requiem in Florence. *Recordings include:* Rossini's Petite Messe Solennelle; Beatrice di Tenda; Rigoletto under Muti; Le Maschere. *Address:* c/o Teatro alla Scala, Via Filodrammatici 2, 20121 Milan, Italy.

LAADE, Wolfgang; Ethnomusicologist; b. 13 Jan. 1925, Zeitz, Germany; m. Dagmar Diedrich, 15 Aug 1962. *Education:* Musikhochschule Leipzig, 1943; Staatliche Musikhochschule Berlin, 1949–54; PhD, Freie Universität, Berlin, 1954–60. *Career:* Research Fellow, Australian Institute of Aboriginal Studies, 1963–67; Research Fellow, Deutsche Forschungsgemeinschaft, 1968–70; Lecturer in Ethnomusicology, University of Heidelberg, 1969–71; Professor of Ethnomusicology, University of Zürich, Switzerland, 1971–90; Guest lectures at German, Austrian, American and Canadian Universities; Guest professorships: Helsinki, Stockholm, Innsbruck, Moscow; Field research in Lapland, Corsica, Tunisia, Australia, Torres Strait, New Guinea, New Britain, India, Sri Lanka, Taiwan, Zimbabwe. *Recordings:* 17 titles. *Publications:* Books: Die Struktur der korsischen Lamento-Melodik, 1962; Die Situation von Musikleben und Musikforschung in den Laendern Afrikas und Asiens und die neuen Aufgaben der Musikenthnologie, 1969; Neue Musik in Afrika, Asien und Ozeanien; Diskographie und historisch-stilistischer Ueberblick, 1971; Gegenwartsfragen der Musik in Afrika und Asien; eine grundlegende Bibliographie, 1971; Oral traditions and written documents on the history and ethnography of the Northern Torres Strait Islands, Vol. 1, 1971; Klangdokumente historischer Tasteninstrumente, Orgeln, Kiel-und Hammerklaviere eine Diskographie, 1972; Das Geisterkanu; Suedseemaerchen aus der Torres-Strasse, 1974; Musik der Goetter, Geister und Menschen; die Musik in der mythischen, fabulierenden und historischen Ueberlieferung der Voelker Afrikas, Nordasiens, Amerikas und Ozeaniens, 1975; Musikwissenschaft zwischen gestern und morgen; Das korsische Volkslied; ethnographische und historische Fragen, Gattungen und Stil, 3 vols, 1981–87; Musik und Musiker in Maerchen, Sagen und Anekdoten der Voelker Europas, Vol. 1: Mitteleuropa, 1988; Music and Culture in South-East New Britain, 1998; Compact Discs accompanied by books: The Confucius Temple Ceremony, Taiwan, 1991; Taiwan: Music of the Aboriginal Tribes, 1991; Zimbabwe: The Ndebele People, 1991; Papua New Guinea: The Coast of the Western Province, 1993; Music and Culture in Southeast New Britain, 2001. *Address:* Holzmoosrütistrasse 11, 8820 Wädenswil, Switzerland.

LAAKMAN, Willem; Singer (Bass-baritone); b. 7 Oct. 1940, Aachen, Germany. *Education:* Studied in Maastricht and Cologne. *Career:* Debut: Lord Tristan in Martha, Amsterdam, 1969; Sang in Netherlands until 1975; Then Krefeld and from 1984 at Coburg; Roles have included Boris Godunov, 1987; Don Giovanni, Macbeth and Papageno; Altenburg from 1992 as Amonasro and Jochanaan in Salome; Dessau Opera from 1995; Other roles elsewhere in Germany have been Strauss's Faninal and Dandini in La Cenerentola; Concerts include Beethoven's Ninth. *Address:* c/o Landestheater Dessau, Fritz-Hesse Platz 1, 4500 Dessau, Germany.

LABELLE, Dominique; Singer (soprano); b. 1960, Montréal, Canada. *Education:* Boston Univ. and with Phyllis Curtin. *Career:* concert appearances with Symphony Orchestras of Dallas, Montreal and Boston; Messiah with Pittsburgh Symphony, Mahler's 2nd Symphony in St Louis and Vaughan Williams's Antarctica Symphony at Indianapolis; other repertory includes the Verdi Quattro Pezzi Sacri, the Requiems of Mozart and Frank Martin, Mahler's Fourth, Les Nuits d'Eté and Mozart's Exsultate Jubilate; opera engagements as Donna Anna in the Peter Sellars production of Don Giovanni, Elizabeth Zimmer in Elegy for Young Lovers, Mimi for Glimmerglass Opera, New York, the Countess and Susanna in Le nozze di Figaro at Vancouver 1992; Giulietta in I Capuleti e i Montecchi with Toledo Opera; sang Handel's Rodelinda at Göttingen, Sigismondo in Arminio and Arianna in Vivaldi's Giustino at Solothurn 2000. *Recordings include:* Elektra, with Boston Symphony; Don Giovanni, on video; Masha and Chloe in The Queen of Spades, conducted by Ozawa. *Honours:* Winner, Metropolitan Opera National Council Auditions 1989. *Current Management:* IMG Artists Paris, 54 Avenue Marceau, 75008, Paris, France.

LABÈQUE, Katia; French pianist; b. 3 March 1950, Bayonne; fmr partner John McLaughlin. *Education:* Paris Conservatoire. *Career:* performs world-wide with sister Marielle Labèque; performs works by Mozart, Gershwin, Bernstein, Berio, Boulez, Miles Davis, Chick Corea, Schubert, etc.; appearances with the Cleveland Orchestra, Concertgebouw Orchestra, New York Philharmonic, Vienna Philharmonic and London Symphony Orchestra; festival performances at Hollywood Bowl, Salzburg, Tanglewood, Edinburgh and Berlin; jazz collaborations with guitarist John McLaughlin. *Recordings:* Gershwin's Rhapsody in Blue

and Concerto in F, recitals of Brahms, Liszt, Debussy, Ravel and Stravinsky, Rossini's Petite Messe (with the choir of King's College Cambridge), Bartók's Concerto for 2 Pianos and Orchestra, Symphonic Dances from West Side Story, España, Encores, Love of Colours, Visions de l'Amen (jtly), Little Girl Blue. *Current Management:* TransArt (UK) Ltd, Cedar House, 10 Rutland Street, Filey, YO14 9JB, North Yorkshire, England. *Telephone:* (1723) 515819. *Fax:* (1723) 514678. *E-mail:* transartuk@transartuk.com. *Website:* www.transartuk.com.

LABÈQUE, Marielle; French pianist; b. 6 March 1952, Bayonne; pnr Semyon Bychkov. *Education:* Paris Conservatoire. *Career:* performs world-wide with sister Katia Labèque; performs works by Mozart, Gershwin, Bernstein, Berio, Boulez, Miles Davis, Chick Corea, Schubert, etc.; appearances with the Cleveland Orchestra, Concertgebouw Orchestra, New York Philharmonic, Vienna Philharmonic and London Symphony Orchestra; festival performances at Hollywood Bowl, Salzburg, Tanglewood, Edinburgh and Berlin; jazz collaborations with guitarist John McLaughlin. *Recordings:* Mozart's Concertos K242 and K365 (with the Berlin Philharmonic), Carnival of the Animals (with the Israel Philharmonic), Poulenc's Concerto for Two Pianos, recitals of Liszt, Debussy, Brahms and Stravinsky, Dvořák Slavonic Dances, Concertos for two pianos by Bruch and Mendelssohn, Visions de l'Amen (jtly). *Current Management:* TransArt (UK) Ltd, Cedar House, 10 Rutland Street, Filey, YO14 9JB, North Yorkshire, England. *Telephone:* (1723) 515819. *Fax:* (1723) 514678. *E-mail:* transartuk@transartuk.com. *Website:* www.transartuk.com.

LABUDA, Izabela; Singer (Soprano); b. 1961, Poland. *Career:* Sang Adina in L'Elisir d'amore and other roles in Poland from 1982; Moved to Germany in 1990 singing at the Essen Opera as Frau Fluth, Janáček's Vixen, and Hanna Glawari in Die Lustige Witwe; Guest at Mannheim Opera, the Vienna Volksoper and the State Opera of Vienna as First Lady in Die Zauberflöte, 1992; Antonia in Hoffmann at Cologne, 1998; Other repertory includes Lucille in Dantons Tod at Volksoper. *Address:* c/o Staatsoper, Opernring 2, 1010 Vienna, Austria.

LACHENMANN, Helmut; Composer; b. 27 Nov. 1935, Stuttgart, Germany. *Education:* Studied at Stuttgart with Jurgen Uhde (piano) and Johann Nepomuk David (composition); Venice with Luigi Nono. *Career:* Teacher of music theory at Stuttgart Hochschule für Musik, 1966–70, Ludwigsburg Hochschule, 1970–76, Hanover Hochschule für Musik, 1976–81 and Musikhochschule Stuttgart, 1981–99; Masterclasses in composition at Basle Music Academy; Instructor at the Ferienkurse in Darmstadt, 1978, 1982, 1998, Cursos Latinamericanos de Musica Contemporanea in Brazil, 1978, and Dominican Republic in 1980; Composition seminars in Blonay 1988, Oslo and Paris, 1989, St Petersburg, 1992, Barcelona and Chicago, 1997, Viitasaari adn Akiyoshidai, 1998; Member of Akademie der Künste, Berlin, Akademie der Schönen Künste, Munich, Freie Akademie der Künste, Hamburg, Leipzig, Mannheim and Academie voor Wetenschapen, Letteren in Schone Kunsten van Belgie, Brussels. *Compositions include:* Souvenir for 41 Instruments, 1959; String Trio, 1966; Les Consolations I and II for voices and percussion, 1967–68, Les Consolations, 1977–78; TemA for flute, voice and cello, 1968; Air for percussion and orchestra, 1968–69; Pression for cello, 1969; Dal Niente for clarinet, 1970; Klaangschattenn mein Seitenspiel, for 48 strings and 3 pianos, 1972; Kontrakaadenz for large orchestra, 1971; Faassade, for large orchestra, 1973; Accanto for clarinet and orchestra, 1975; Tanzsuite mit Deutschlandlied for string quartet and orchestra, 1979–80; Harmonica for tuba and orchestra, 1981–83; Mouvement - vor der Erstarrung, for ensemble, 1983–84; Ausklang for piano and orchestra, 1984–85; Allegro Sostenuto for clarinet, cello and piano, 1986–88; Two string quartets, Gran Torso, 1972, Reigen seligen Geister, 1989; Zwei Gefühlen, Musik mit Leonardo for ensemble, 1992; Das Mädchen mit den Schwefelhölzern, opera, 1990–96; Serynade for piano, 1998; Nun for flute, trombone and orchestra, 1999. *Honours:* Cultural Prize of Music, City of Munich, 1965; Composition Prize, City of Stuttgart, 1968; Bach Prize, Hamburg, 1972; Siemens Prize, 1997. *Address:* c/o Breitkopf and Hartel, Walkmuhlstr 52, 65195 Wiesbaden, Germany.

LACHMANN, Elisabeth; Singer (Soprano); b. 20 April 1940, Vienna, Austria. *Education:* Studied in Vienna. *Career:* Debut: Berne in 1961 as Despina, and Cagliari in Wiener Blut; Sang at Karlsruhe, 1962–64 as Micaela, Marenka, Cherubino and Regina in Mathis der Maler, and Graz, 1964–68 as Pamina, Susanna, Frau Fluth and Zdenka in Arabella; Engaged at Dortmund from 1968 as Mimi, Sophie, Sieglinde, Desdemona, Donna Anna, the Trovatore Leonora, Wagner's Elisabeth, Venus and Brünnhilde, Tosca, Amelia in Un Ballo in Maschera, Aida, Senta, Ariadne, Abigaille, Marschallin, Leonore (Fidelio) and Elektra, (R Strauss); These and other roles in guest appearances at Vienna State Opera, Hamburg, Stuttgart, Frankfurt, Cologne, Zürich and Antwerp; Concert and opera tours to the Netherlands, France, Far East, Africa, South America and Switzerland; Professor at Detmold Musikhochschule, 1984–. *Honours:* Kammersängerin, 1994. *Address:* Heiligenpesch 18A, 41069 Mönchengladbach, Germany.

LACKNER, Christopher; Singer (Baritone); b. 1950, New Zealand. *Education:* London Opera Centre, and with Otakar Kraus. *Career:* Chorus member of Opera North, then principal roles with Kent Opera, Pavilion Opera and Opera 80; Appearances with the Royal Opera from 1990, in Turandot, Die Zauberflöte (Man in Armour), Les Huguenots, Die Frau ohne Schatten, Rigoletto, Paul Bunyan, Der Freischütz (Kilian), Palestrina, La Bohème (as Benoit), Andrea Chenier and Otello (Herald 2001). *Honours:* Winner, Mobil Song Contest, 1974; Prize of Friends of English National Opera. *Address:* c/o Royal Opera House (contracts), Covent Garden, London, WC2, England.

LADERMAN, Ezra; Composer; b. 29 June 1924, Brooklyn, New York, USA. *Education:* Studied with Stefan Wolpe, 1946–49; Studied with Miriam Godeon, BA, 1949, Brooklyn College; Columbia University with Douglas Moore and Otto Luening, 1950–52. *Career:* Teacher, Sarah Lawrence College, 1960–61; State University of New York at Binghamton, 1971–82; Director of the Music program, National Endowment for the Arts, 1979–82; Dean, School of Music, 1989–95, Professor of Music, 1995–, Yale University; mem, ASCAP; ACO; AAAL. *Compositions:* 150 works include: Dramatic: Jacob and the Indians, opera, 1954; Goodbye to the Clowns, opera, 1956; The Hunting of the Snark, opera-cantata, 1958; Sarah, television opera, 1959; Ballets Dance Quartet, Esther, Song of Songs, Solos and Chorale, 1965; Shadows Among Us, opera, 1967; The Black Fox, 1968; Galileo Galilei, opera, 1978; Film and television scores; Orchestral: Piano Concerto, 1939; Leipzig Symphony, 1945; Piano Concerto, 1957; Flute Concerto, 1968; Viola Concerto, 1975; Violin Concerto, 1978; Piano Concerto No. 1, 1978; Concerto for string quartet and orchestra, 1981; Cello Concerto, 1984; Vocal: oratorios The Eagle Stirred, 1961, A Mass for Cain, 1983; Columbus, cantata, 1975; Chamber: Wind Octet, 1957; Clarinet Sonata, 1958; Double Helix for flute, oboe and string quartet, 1968; Partita for violin, 1982; Double String Quartet, 1983; 8 Symphonies, 1963–93; 11 String Quartets, 1959–85, 1997, 2000 (2); Marilyn, opera, 1993; Fantasia for cello, 1997; Cello Ensemble Trilogy, Albo, 1997, Parisot, 1997, Simoes, 1999; Scenes From an Imagined Life I and II, 1997, 1999; Yisrael for orchestra, 1998; Brotherly Love, oratorio, 1999. *Recordings:* Piano Quintet; Quartet No. 6; Concerto for Double Orchestra; Pentimento; Quartet No. 7; June 29th; Chamber Music of Ezra Laderman, vols 1–4, Albany Records. *Honours:* Oscar for film music, The Eleanor Roosevelt Story, 1965. *Address:* 311 Greene Street, New Haven, CT 06051, USA.

LAFFAGE, Jean-Pierre; Singer (Baritone); b. 26 June 1926, Paris, France. *Education:* Studied at the Dijon and Paris Conservatories. *Career:* Debut: Paris Opéra 1957, as Valentin in Faust; Sang at the Paris Opéra until 1972 and the Opéra-Comique until 1980; Guest appearances throughout France and Italy; Among his best roles were Don Alvar in Les Indes Galantes, Mozart's Figaro, Escamillo, Sharpless, the Villains in Les Contes d'Hoffmann, Ourrais in Mireille, Scarpia, Ford, Amonasro and Oreste in Iphigénie en Aulide; Professor at the Paris Conservatoire, 1977–87. *Address:* c/o Conservatoire National, 14 Rue de Madrid, 75008 Paris, France.

LAFITTE, Florence; Piano Duettist; b. 10 July 1961, France. *Education:* Conservatoire National Superieur de Musique, Lyon, France; Liszt Academy, Budapest, Hungary; Manhattan School of Music, New York, USA. *Career:* Numerous concert appearances in France, Germany, Hungary, USA and Sweden; Tours of Australia, New Caledonia, Indonesia, Brazil, Argentina and Chile. Radio and television appearances at home and abroad. *Recordings:* Concerto for 2 pianos and orchestra by Poulenc, Orchestre Symphonique Francais, Conductor Laurent Petitgirard, VMG; 2 Piano Recital, Mozart, Liszt, Mendelssohn. *Honours:* International Music Video Competition, Fuji television Network, Tokyo, 1987; Honorary Award, Murray Dranoff's Two Piano Competition, Miami, 1990. *Current Management:* Liliane Weinstadt. *Address:* 69 1180 Brussels, Belgium.

LAFITTE, Isabelle; Piano Duettist; b. 10 July 1961, France. *Education:* Conservatoire National Superieur de Musique, Lyon, France; Liszt Academy, Budapest, Hungary; Manhattan School of Music, New York, USA. *Career:* Numerous concerts at home and abroad including Germany, Hungary, USA, Sweden; Tours of Australia, New Caledonia, Indonesia, Brazil, Argentina and Chile; Several Radio and Television appearances. *Recordings:* Concerto for Two Pianos and Orchestra by Poulenc, Orchestre Symphonique Francais, Conductor Laurent Petitgirard; Two Piano Recital, Mozart, Liszt, Mendelssohn. *Honours:* International Music Video Competition, Fuji television Network, Tokyo, 1987; Honorary Award, Murray Dranoff's Two Piano Competition, Miami, 1990. *Current Management:* Liliane Weinstadt. *Address:* Rue Langeveld 69, 1180 Brussels, Belgium.

LAFONT, Jean-Philippe; Singer (Bass-Baritone); b. 4 Feb. 1951, Toulouse, France. *Education:* Studied in Toulouse with Denise Dupleix and in Paris with Gabriel Bacquier. *Career:* Debut: Toulouse in 1974 as Papageno; Sang at Paris Opéra in 1977 as Nick Shadow in The Rake's Progress, Albi from 1977 as Mozart's Guglielmo and in Grétry's Les Femmes Vengées and Tom Jones, and Paris from 1978 in operas by Gounod, Offenbach, Gluck and Cherubini; Sang in Berlin in the European premiere of Debussy's La Chute de la Maison Usher, at Lyon in 1980 as Choroebus in the French premiere of Les Troyens, and at Aix-en-Provence in 1982 as Boréas in the stage premiere of Rameau's Les Boréades; Guest appearances in Strasbourg, Geneva, Lille, Hamburg, Hanover and Nimes; New York debut in 1983 as Fieramosca in Benvenuto Cellini at Carnegie Hall; Perugia in 1983 in Salieri's Les Danaides, Paris Opéra in 1983 as Rossini's Moise, Brussels and Barcelona in 1984 as Mozart's Count, Rome in 1985 in Cherubini's Demophoon, Aix in 1986 as Leporello in Don Giovanni and sang Amonasro at Bonn in 1989, Debussy's Golaud at Marseilles in 1990, and Alcide in Lully's Alceste at the Théâtre des Champs Elysées, 1991–92; Rigoletto for New Israeli Opera, 1997; Season 1998 with Amfortas at Brussels and Falstaff at the London Prom concerts; Season 2000–01 as Gerard in Nice, Macbeth at Montpellier and Scarpia for Chicago Lyric Opera; Other roles include Thaos in Iphigénie en Tauride and Astor in Cheubini's Démophon. *Recordings include:* Les Boréades; Gounod's Messe Solennelle; La Belle Hélène; Le Postillon de Lonjumeau by Adam; Verdi's Falstaff, conducted by John Eliot Gardiner, 2001. *Address:* c/o Opéra de Marseilles, 2 Rue Molière, 13231 Marseille Cédex 01, France.

LAGRANGE, Michele; Singer (Soprano); b. 29 May 1947, Conches, Saone-et-Loire, France. *Education:* Studied in Pasis. *Career:* Engaged at Lyon Opéra from 1978; Sang at Paris Opéra, 1984–85 in Jerusalem by Verdi and as Alice in Robert le Diable by Meyerbeer; Opéra Comique, 1987 as Donna Anna at the Teato Colon in Buenos Aires, 1982 as Teresa in Benvenuto Cellini at the Aix-en-Provence Festival, 1989 as Fata Morgana in The Love for Three Oranges; Sang Marguerite in Faust at Avignon and St Etienne, season 1990–91; Montpellier Festival in 1991 in Bizet's Ivan IV, concert performance; Sang Fiorella in Offenbach's Les Brigands at Amsterdam and Isabella in Franchetti's Christoforo Colombo at Montpellier in 1992; Other roles include Musette and Elisabeth de Valois. *Recordings include:* Poulenc Salve Regina and Stabat Mater; Guercoeur by Magnard; The Love for Three Oranges. *Address:* c/o Saison Lyrique de St Etienne, 8 Place de L'Hotel de Ville, 4200 St Etienne, France.

LAGZDINA, Vineta; Composer and Performer; b. 11 Nov. 1945, Oldenberg, Germany; 1 d. *Education:* BMus, University of Adelaide, 1976; Instrumental Teachers' Certificate, 1979; Computer music studies, Adelaide University Conservatorium, 1980–81. *Career:* Sound works included in exhibitions in Australia, New Zealand and Japan; Film music includes electronic, computer generated and instrumental, 1978–; Video art music; Grants for experimental music and movement performances, 1981–82; Composer's grant for radio, 1983; Curated Audio-Eyes, exhibition, 1983; Lecturer, Sydney College of The Arts, Music Across the Arts, 1984–; ABC Radio, 1987; The White Bird Music Theatre, 1987; Shock Of The New, video soundtrack, 1987; Speaking Out, film soundtrack, 1987. *Compositions:* Obstruction, computer sound tape for dance, 1981; Noh-Work, a quadrophonic Percussion Tape, 1982; The Black Snake, tape piece for voice and electronics, 1983; Double-Dream, Triple fate, video soundtracks, 1984–85; Media Massage, spoken song, 1986. *Publications:* 22 Contemporary Australian Composers. *Contributions:* Article in Art Network, 1983 and in New Music Australia 4, 1985. *Address:* Flat 11, 26 Pearson Street, Balmain East 2041, Australia.

LAHO, Marc; Belgian singer (tenor); b. 1964, Seraing. *Education:* studied at Liège with Gabriel Bacquier and Luigi Alva. *Career:* appearances at Rennes as Mylio in Le Roi d'Ys, at Marseilles in Thais, I Puritani, L'Africaine, Die Meistersinger and Montségur by Landowski, 1993; Zürich 1994–95 in La Périchole by Offenbach and at Strasbourg as Alfredo in La Traviata; Further appearances in Italy and the USA, Orlando, Florida; Dijon Opera as Don Ottavio, Des Grieux in Manon Lescaut and Paris in La Belle Hélène; Sang Rossini's Comte Ory at Glyndebourne, 1998; Sang Laërte in Hamlet by Thomas in Toulouse and Donizett's Tonio at St Gallen, 2000. *Honours:* Prizewinner, Pavarotti Competition, Philadelphia, 1992. *Address:* c/o Opera Municipal de Marseille, 2 rue Molière, 13001 Marseille, France.

LAKATOS, Roby; Hungarian violinist; b. 1965. *Education:* Béla Bartók Conservatory, Budapest. *Career:* resident with his ensemble at Restaurant Les Ateliers de La Grande Ile, Brussels 1986–1996; performances at the Schleswig-Holstein, Ludwigsburg and Helsinki festivals, at the Académies Musicales de Saintes in New York Central Park, and with the Orchestre Nat. de Radio France and Dresden Philharmonic 1996–; 'homecoming' concerts, Thalia Theatre, Budapest 1999; Autumn Strings Music Festival in Prague 2003; concerts with The Lakatos Sextet in the cultural programme of Ireland's presidency of EU 2004. *Compositions include:* On the Waves of the Balaton. *Recordings:* In Gypsy Style 1991, König der Zigeunergeiger 1998, Lakatos Gold 1998–99, Lakatos Best 1998–99, Lakatos: Live from Budapest 1999, With Musical Friends 2001, Kinoshita Meets Lakatos 2002, As Time Goes By (film score from

Le Grand Blonde) 2002, The Legend of the Toad 2004. *Honours:* first prize Béla Bartók Conservatory 1984. *Telephone:* 475-76-55-96 (Belgium) (office). *Fax:* (3) 449-02-94 (Belgium) (office). *E-mail:* lakatos@pandora.be (office). *Website:* www.robylakatos.com.

LAKES, Gary; Singer (Tenor); b. 26 Sept. 1950, Dallas, Texas, USA. *Education:* Vocal studies with William Eddy at Seattle Opera. *Career:* Debut: Seattle in 1981 as Froh in Das Rheingold; Sang at Mexico City in 1983 as Florestan in Fidelio and Charlotte Opera in 1984 as Samson in Samson et Dalila; Metropolitan Opera debut in 1986 as the High Priest in Idomeneo, returning as Tannhäuser and as Siegmund in a new production of Die Walküre; Sang the Emperor in Die Frau ohne Schatten at the Metropolitan in 1989, Radames at New Orleans, Erik in Der fliegende Holländer at the Metropolitan in 1990 followed by Siegmund in New York (also televised) and San Francisco; Sang in Das Lied Von der Erde at the 1991 Promenade Concerts, London; Season 1991–92 as Lohengrin at Buenos Aires and Erik at the Metropolitan; Sang the Berlioz Faust at the Festival Hall, London, 1994; Florestan at the Lincoln Center Festival, 1996. *Recordings include:* Die Walküre conducted by James Levine. *Address:* c/o Metropolitan Opera, Lincoln Center, New York, NY 10023, USA.

LAKI, Krisztina; Singer (Soprano); b. 14 Sept. 1944, Budapest, Hungary. *Education:* Studied at Budapest Conservatory. *Career:* Debut: Berne, 1976 as Gilda in Rigoletto; Sang with the Deutsche Oper am Rhein, Düsseldorf, in Cologne, and at Bregenz and Edinburgh Festivals; Glyndebourne, 1979–80 as Aminta in Die schweigsame Frau and Sophie in Der Rosenkavalier; Salzburg in 1980 as Lucille in Von Einem's Dantons Tod; Tour of Germany in 1984 notably in cantatas by Bach; Paris Opéra in 1984 as Sophie; Other roles include Zdenka in Arabella, Mozart's Queen of Night, Zerlina and Susanna, Carolina in Il Matrimonio Segreto and Nannetta in Falstaff; Sang Marzelline in Fidelio at Hamburg in 1988 and Zdenka at Barcelona in 1989; Sang Marzelline with the company of the Cologne Opera at Hong Hong; Also widely heard in oratorio. *Recordings:* St Matthew Passion by Bach; Handel's Partenope; Masses by Haydn; Dantons Tod; Concert Arias by Mozart; Bach's Christmas Oratorio; Mozart's C minor Mass; Paisiello's Il Barbiere di Siviglia; Mozart's Schauspieldirektor and Myslivecek's Il Bellerofonte. *Address:* Oper der Stadt Köln, Offenbachplatz, 5000 Cologne, Germany.

LALANDI-EMERY, Lina (Madeleine), OBE; British festival director; b. Athens, Greece; m. Ralph Emery. *Education:* Athens Conservatory, studied privately in England. *Career:* int. career as harpsichordist, London, Paris, Geneva, Athens; radio and television broadcasts; founder and Dir, English Bach Festival Trust 1962, specialising in baroque opera, Purcell, Handel, Rameau, Gluck; Handel's Oreste and Oresteia by Xenakis at Covent Garden (Linbury Theatre) 2000; Purcell's Fairy Queen 2001; Gluck, Telemann, Hellenic Festival, Athens and Sadler's Wells, London 2003. *Honours:* Officier, Ordre des Arts et des Lettres 1979, Gold Cross of the Phoenix (Greece). *Address:* 15 South Eaton Place, London, SW1W 9ER, England.

LALE, Peter; Violist; b. 1960, England. *Career:* Founder Member of the Britten Quartet with debut concert at Wigmore Hall in 1987; Quartet in Residence at the Dartington Summer School in 1987 with quartets by Schnittke; Season 1988–89 includes BBC Lunchtime Series at St John's Smith Square, concerts with the Hermann Prey Schubertiade and collaborations with the Alban Berg Quartet in the Beethoven Plus Series; Season 1989–90 includes debut tours of Netherlands, Germany, Spain, Austria and Finland, festival appearances at Brighton, City of London, Greenwich, Canterbury, Harrogate, Chester, Spitalfields and Aldeburgh; Formerly resident quartet at Liverpool University; Teaching role at Lake District Summer Music, 1989 and Universities of Bristol and Hong Kong in 1990. *Recordings:* Beethoven Op 130 and Schnittke Quartet No. 3; Vaughan Williams On Wenlock Edge and Ravel Quartet; Britten, Prokofiev, Tippett, Elgar and Walton Quartets. *Current Management:* Ingpen & Williams Ltd, 7 St George's Court, 131 Putney Bridge Road, London, SW15 2PA, England.

LALLOUETTE, Olivier; Singer (Baritone); b. 1960, Paris, France. *Career:* Appearances with Glyndebourne Festival and Tour, as Dancaïre in Carmen, and Mozart's Guglielmo; Don Giovanni at Rennes, Count Almaviva for Flanders Opera, Simone in La finta Semplice at Versailles and Papageno for Opéra d'Avignon; Geneva Opera as Puccini's Sharpless, La Monnaie Brussels as Giove in Cavalli's La Calisto and Berlin Staatsoper as Passagallo in L'Opera seria, by Gassmann; Further Baroque opera roles with René Jacobs, William Christie, Christophe Rousset and Phillipe Hereweghe; Season 2000–01 as Tusenach in Three sisters by Peter Eövös, at Hamburg, Edinburgh and Vienna; Concerts with Pierre Boulez, Webern Cantata, and Kent Nagano, Carter's opera What Next?; Season 2001–2002 with Massenet's Lescaut at Lyon, Don Giovanni in Avignon, Guglielmo at Liège and Merlin in Chausson's Le Roi Arthus at La Monnaie, Brussels. *Recordings:* Giulio Cesare; Il Ritorno d'Ulisse; Handel's Scipione and Riccardo Primo, Les Fêtes de

Paphos by Mondonville; Carmen. *Address:* c/o Musicaglotz, 11, rue le Verrier, 75006 Paris, France.

LALOR, Stephen; Composer and Musical Director; b. 11 Jan. 1962, Sydney, New South Wales, Australia. *Education:* MMus, University of New South Wales, 1988; Tchaikovsky Conservatory, Moscow, 1984–85 and 1988–89. *Career:* Freelance Composer and Music Education Writer; Director and Arranger for the Sydney Domra Ensemble, 1978–85; Commissions from Macquarie University (1994), among others. *Compositions include:* Alice: A Musical for Children, 1986; Prelude and Dance for violin and piano, 1988; Six Angels, song cycle for baritone and piano; Three Pieces for piano, 1989; Three Pieces for solo violin, 1989; Damascus, opera, 1990; At the Edhe, for orchestra, 1991; String Quartet, 1991; Maroubra Song Cycle, for soprano, 1991; Capricornia, for string orchestra, 1993; Way Home for soprano or treble, narrator and tape, 1994. *Honours:* USSR Government Ukrainian Society Scholarship, 1988. *Address:* c/o APRA, 1A Eden Street, Crows Nest, NSW 2065, Australia.

LAMA, Lina; Concert Violist and Professor of Viola; b. 20 April 1932, Faenza, Italy. *Education:* Diplomas in Violin and Viola, Piano and Composition. *Career:* Debut: Teatro S Carlo, Naples; Professor at Conservatorio di Musica S Cecilia, Rome, 1959; Appearances on BBC and Italian television and radio; Concerts in Germany, Belgium, Italy, Israel, Hungary, Greece, Finland, France, North and South America, Africa, Asia and Japan; Concerts throughout Europe under Italian and foreign Maestri; Sonata per La Gran Viola by Paganini performed at Teatro San Carlo, Naples; Teacher of Viola at Conservatoire of S Cecilia, Roma Festival; International specialisation courses at Festival of Jywaskyla, Finland, Città di Castello, Lanciano, and Mezzolombardo, Italy; Jury Member for international viola competitions: Budapest, 1979, N Paganini, Genova, 1988 and for national viola competition at Vittaorio Veneto, 1986. *Honours:* Concert Prizes in Italy; Accademico of Accademia di S Cecilia, Roma; Cavaliere al Merito della Repubblica Italiana. *Address:* Via Ugo de Carolis 31, 00136 Rome, Italy.

LAMARCHINA, Robert; Cellist and Conductor; b. 3 Sept. 1928, New York City, USA. *Education:* Paris Conservatoire; Curtis Institute with Piatigorsky and Feuermann. *Career:* Debut: With St Louis Symphony under Vladimir Golschmann; Played in NBC Symphony Orchestra under Toscanini, 1944; Conductor and Musical Director with Young Musicians Foundation, Los Angeles, 1952–53; Solo Cellist with Chicago Symphony under Fritz Reiner in 1960; Conducted at Metropolitan Opera, La Traviata at Spoleto and Menotti's The Medium at the New York City Opera; Artistic and Musical Director with Honolulu Symphony Society and Hawaii Opera Theatre, 1967–79; Conductor of numerous symphony orchestras and opera companies including New York Philharmonic, St Louis Symphony, Chicago Symphony, Radio Italiana, Zürich Symphony, Vancouver Opera Association and Fujiwara Opera Institute.

LAMB, Anthony (Stuart); Clarinettist; b. 4 Jan. 1947, Woodford, England; m. Philippa Carpenter-Jacobs, 1 s., 2 d. *Education:* Royal College of Music; ARCM. *Career:* Debut: With Chamber Ensemble Capricorn at Wigmore Hall in London, 1974; Principal Clarinet with Royal Ballet Orchestra, 1969–71; Founder member of Capricorn (violin, clarinet, cello and piano), 1973 with many concerts and broadcasts; Co-Principal with English National Opera Orchestra, 1976–; Several BBC broadcasts; Freelance Clarinettist with most major British orchestras; mem, Musicians Union. *Recordings:* With Capricorn: Rimsky-Korsakov's Quintet in B flat for Piano and Wind, Glinka's Grand Sextet in E flat for Piano and Strings, 1985. *Address:* 22 Munster Road, Teddington, Middlesex TW11 9LL, England.

LAMBERTI, Giorgio; Singer (Tenor); b. 9 July 1938, Adria, Rovigo, Italy. *Education:* Studied in Mantua. *Career:* Debut: Rome in 1964 as Arrigo in I Vespri Siciliani; US debut at Chicago in 1965 as Radames; Rome in 1965 in the premiere of Wallenstein by Zafred; Metropolitan Opera from 1974 as Enzo, Cavaradossi, Radames and Turiddu; Engagements in Paris, Brussels, Budapest, Baltimore, Amsterdam, Helsinki, Florence and Venice; Covent Garden debut, Don Carlos in 1979; Other roles include Pollione, Don José, Jason in Médée, Verdi's Ernani, Alvaro, Manrico and Riccardo, Wagner's Tannhäuser and Lohengrin, Edgardo in Lucia di Lammermoor; Sang Radames at Berlin and Luxor in 1987 and Caracalla Festival, Rome, 1989; Andrea Chénier at Stuttgart in 1988 and appeared as Stiffelio in the first Covent Garden production of Verdi's opera in 1993. *Recordings include:* Ernani; I Lombardi; Il Corsaro; Gemma di Vergy by Donizetti; Bellini's Zaira. *Address:* c/o Stuttgart Staatsoper, Oberer Schlossgarten 6, D–70173 Stuttgart, Germany.

LAMBERTINI, Marta; Composer; b. 13 Nov. 1937, San Isidri, Buenos Aires, Argentina. *Education:* Studied at the Catholic University in Argentina and in Buenos Aires. *Compositions include:* Chamber operas: Alice in Wonderland in 1989 and, Oh, Eternidad… Ossia SMR Bach, 1990; Concertino Serenata in 1981 and Galileo Descubre Las Cuatro

Lunas De Jupiter, 1985 for orchestra; Instrumental pieces include Assorted Kochels, 1991 and vocal music, Escena De La Falsa Tortuga, 1993; Reunión for string quartet and piano, 1994; La Ribera for speaker and string quartet, 1996; Pathfinder, string trio, 1997. *Address:* c/o Lavalle 1547, Apartado Postal Number 11, Sucursal 44-B, 1048 Buenos Aires, Argentina.

LAMBRO, Phillip; Composer, Conductor and Pianist; b. 2 Sept. 1935, Wellesley, MA, USA. *Education:* studied Music in Boston, later in Miami, FL; Music Acad. of the West, CA, 1955; teachers include Donald Pond and György Sandor. *Career:* debut, Pianists' Fair, Symphony Hall, Boston, 1952; composed and conducted music for several motion pictures including documentaries; major performances in Israel, Europe and the Orient; compositions performed by Leopold Stokowski, Philippe Entremont, the Philadelphia Orchestra, the Rochester Philharmonic, Baltimore, Indianapolis, Miami, Denver, Oklahoma and New Orleans Symphonies. *Compositions include:* Miraflores for string orchestra; Dance Barbaro for percussion; Two Pictures for solo percussionist and orchestra; Four Songs for soprano and orchestra; Toccata for piano; Toccata for guitar; Parallelograms for flute quartet and jazz ensemble; Music for wind, brass and percussion; Obelisk for oboist and percussionist; Structures for string orchestra; Fanfare and Tower Music for brass quintet; Night Pieces for piano; Biospheres for 6 percussionists; Trumpet Voluntary; Eight Little Trigrams for Piano. *Address:* 1801 Century Park E, Suite 2400, Los Angeles, CA 90067-2326, USA.

LAMOREAUX, Rosa (Lea); Musician and Singer (Soprano); b. 19 Oct. 1955, Farmington, New Mexico, USA; m. James L McHugh, 8 Sept 1991. *Education:* Bachelor of Music, University of Redlands, 1977; ARCM, Royal College of Music, London, England, 1979; Master of Music, University of Redlands, California, 1980. *Career:* Debut: Kennedy Center; Numerous performances at Kennedy Center, Mozart-Requiem, Exultate Jubilate, Bach-B-minor Mass and Magnificat, Coffee Cantata and Peasant Cantata both staged; Carmel Bach Festival in California: Mozart, Bastien Bastienne, Handel, Xerxes, role of Romilda, Bach, B minor Mass, Haydn, Paukenmasse, Lord Nelson Mass, St John Passion, Lieder Recitals; Bach, St Matthew Passion; St Theresa Mass, Pergolesi, La Serva Padrona, Purcell, Dido and Aeneas (the role of Belinda); Bethlehem Bach Festival: B minor Mass, St John Passion and Coffee Cantata, Atlanta Symphony with Robert Shaw, B minor Mass, La demoiselle Elue by Debussy, Cincinnati May Festival; Mozart C minor Mass, Rheingau Music Festival, Germany. *Recordings:* Four Centuries of Song; Spain in the New World; Masters in this Hall; Luminous Spirit, Hildegard von Bingen, chants; I Love Lucette, 15th and 16th century French Theatre music; Berlioz's Messe Solennelle; Gentle Annie, Stephen Foster and Charles Ives; Bach Mass in B minor. *Address:* 4112 Fessenden Street NW, Washington, DC 20016, USA.

LANCE, Albert; Singer (Tenor); b. 12 July 1925, Menindie, Australia. *Education:* Studied in Australia and sang minor roles and in operetta. *Career:* Sang Cavaradossi in Sydney in 1952, Offenbach's Hoffmann in 1954 and in Paris from 1956 at Paris Opéra and Opéra-Comique in operas by Puccini, Gounod and Cherubini; Covent Garden debut in 1958 as the Duke of Mantua opposite Joan Sutherland; Bolshoi Theatre Moscow, 1965–66; Guest appearances in Bordeaux, Lyon, Los Angeles, San Francisco, Vienna, Leningrad, Kiev and Buenos Aires; London Coliseum in 1969 in the first British performance of Roussel's Padmâvati; Teacher at Nice Conservatory from 1974. *Recordings include:* Werther; Madama Butterfly; Tosca.

LANCELOT, James, MA, MusB, FRCO (CHM), ARCM; Master of Chorister and Organist; b. 2 Dec. 1952; m.; two d. *Education:* St Paul's Cathedral School, Ardingly Coll., Royal Coll. of Music, King's Coll., Cambridge. *Career:* sub-organist, Winchester Cathedral 1975–85; Master of the Choristers and Organist, Durham Cathedral 1985–; conductor, Durham Univ. Choral Soc. 1987–; Lay Canon, Durham Cathedral 2002–; mem. Royal Coll. of Organists Council (1988–2000, 2001–), Cathedrals Liturgy Group, Cathedral Organists' Assscn (pres. 2001–03). *Recordings:* numerous with King's Coll. Choir, Winchester Cathedral Choir, Durham Cathedral Choir; solo including Complete Organ Works of Hubert Parry. *Publications:* Durham Cathedral Organs (with Richard Hird); contrib. to The Sense of the Sacramental. *Honours:* Turpin Prize (FRCO) 1969, Stuart Prize RCM 1971, Hon. FGCM. *Address:* 6 The College, Durham, DH1 3EQ, England (home). *Telephone:* (191) 3864766 (office). *Website:* www.durhamcathedral.co.uk (office).

LANDER, Thomas; Singer (Baritone); b. 1961, Sweden. *Education:* Studied at Stockholm College of Music and the State Opera School. *Career:* Sang with Norrlandsoperan, 1982–83; Engaged at Hamburg Staatsoper, 1986–87, and Vienna Volksoper, 1987–89 as Mozart's Count and Guglielmo; Guest appearances at Aix-en-Provence, Opéra de Lyon and in Italy, Iceland and Israel; Engaged at Hanover, 1990–; Other roles include Mozart's Don Giovanni and Papageno, Malatesta, and Harlequin in Ariadne auf Naxos; Sang Christus in Bach's St John Passion at

Lucerne Easter Festival in 1993. *Address:* Nordic Artists Management, Sveavagen 76, 11359 Stockholm, Sweden.

LANDON, Howard Chandler Robbins, BMus; musicologist; b. 6 March 1926, Boston, Massachusetts, USA; m. Else Radant. *Education:* Boston University. *Career:* Resident in Europe from 1947; Talks on BBC radio and television, 1954–; Guest Teacher, British and American Universities, 1969–; Honorary Professorial Fellow, University College Cardiff, 1972; John Bird Professor of Music, Cardiff; Producer of numerous recordings for the Haydn Society, Vox, Library of recorded Masterpieces; President, International Joseph Haydn Stiftung, Eisenstadt. *Publications:* The Symphonies of Joseph Haydn, 1955; Collected Correspondence and London Notebooks of Haydn, 1959; Essays on Viennese Classical Style, 1970; Beethoven, 1970; Haydn: Chronicle and Works, 5 vols, 1976–80; Mozart as a Mason, 1983; Edition of Handel's Roman Vespers, 1983; Joseph Haydn, single vol. reduction of Chronicle and Works, 1988; 1791: Mozart's Last Year; Mozart: The Golden Years 1781–1791, 1989; Five Centuries of Music in Venice (with John Julius Norwich), 1991; Vivaldi, 1993; The Mozart Essays, 1995; Horns in High C (memoirs), 1999; Editor of all Haydn's Symphonies, numerous String Quartets and Operas. *Honours:* Hon. DMus (Boston University) 1969, (Queen's College, Belfast) 1974. *Address:* Château de Foncoussières, 81800 Rabastens (Tarn), France.

LANDOWSKI, Marcel François Paul; composer; b. 18 Feb. 1915, Pont l'Abbe, France; m. Jacqueline Potier 1941; two s. one d. *Education:* Lycee Janson-de-Sailly, Conservatoire Nationale de Musique de Paris. *Career:* Director, Conservatoire Boulogne-sur-Seine, 1960–65; Director of Music, Comédie Française, Paris, 1962–66; Inspector-General, Musical Studies, 1964, Director of Music Service, Ministry of Cultural Affairs, 1966–70, Music, Lyric and Dance, 1970–74; Founder, Orchestre de Paris, 1967, Honorary President, 1975–; Inspector-General de l'Instruction Publique, 1974–; mem. Institute of France, Academy des Beaux-Arts, 1975. *Compositions:* Operas Rabelais, 1953, La vieille maison, 1983, Montségur, 1985, P'tit Pierre, 1988; Numerous orchestral and choral compositions; Film music and music for Cyrano de Bergerac at Comédie Française; Opera, Galina, premiered at Lyon, 1996. *Honours:* Officer, Légion d'Honneur; Commander des Arts et des Lettres; Croix de Guerre. *Address:* 10 rue Max-Blondat, 92100 Boulogne-sur-Seine, France.

LANDSMAN, Vladimir; Violinist; b. 1941, Dushambe, Russia. *Education:* Moscow School of Music; Doctorate, Moscow State Conservatory. *Career:* Soloist, Moscow Philharmonic Society; Toured Soviet Union; Hollywood Bowl, Los Angeles; Concert tours throughout the world; Guest soloist; Bolshoi Hall, Moscow Conservatory; Artistic Director, Seasons Orchestra, Moscow, 1994–95; Teacher, Music Faculty, Université de Montréal; Associate Professor; Teacher, academies all over the world; Teacher, Orford Arts Centre, Quebec; Masterclasses; Served on examination juries. *Recordings:* Over 10 works. *Honours:* Third prize, Jaques Thibaud International Violin Competition, Paris, 1963; First prize, Montreal International Competition, 1966. *Address:* 4039 Grand Blvd, Montreal H4B 2X4, Canada.

LANE, Gloria; Singer (Mezzo-Soprano and Soprano); b. 6 June 1930, Trenton, New Jersey, USA; m. Samuel Krachmalnick. *Education:* Studied with Elisabeth Westmoreland in Philadelphia. *Career:* Debut: Philadelphia in 1950 in the premiere of Menotti's The Consul; Broadway in 1954 in the premiere of Menotti's The Saint of Bleecker Street; British debut in 1958 as Baba the Turk in The Rake's Progress, returning in 1972 as Dorabella in Così fan tutte, Strauss's Ariadne and Lady Macbeth; Covent Garden debut in 1960 as Carmen and sang at Florence in 1966 as Federica in Verdi's Luisa Miller; Guest appearances in Vienna, Paris, Venice, Rome, Palermo, Boston, Chicago and San Francisco; New York City Opera, 1971 as Santuzza in Cavalleria Rusticana. *Recordings:* The Consul; Rossini's Mosè in Egitto; The Saint of Bleecker Street. *Address:* c/o New York City Opera, Lincoln Center, New York, NY 10023, USA.

LANE, Jennifer (Ruth); Singer (Mezzo-soprano); b. 25 Nov. 1954, Berwyn, Illinois, USA; m. James H Carr, 21 Nov 1987. *Education:* BMus, Chicago Musical College, Roosevelt University, 1977; MA in Performance, City University of New York, 1980. *Career:* Debut: Elsbeth in Strauss's Feuersnot, Santa Fe Opera in 1988; Performances with Santa Fe Opera, New York City Opera, Opera Monte Carlo, L'Opéra Français de New York, Opera Omaha, US stage premiere of Handel's Partenope, Milwaukee's Skylight Opera, Opera Ensemble of New York; Prior to operatic career, toured North and South America with the Waverly Consort; Also tours of the Far East with the Gregg Smith Singers; Many concert performances including appearances with the Atlanta Symphony under Robert Shaw, San Francisco Symphony, The National Symphony, St Louis Symphony, and Harrisburg Symphony in Mahler's 2nd and 3rd Symphonies; Many radio broadcasts including Mahler's 3rd Symphony, personal interviews and Radio Canada recital with countertenor, Alan Fast; Sang Alessandro in

Handel's Tolomeo at Halle, 1996; Handel's Serse with New York City Opera, 1997. *Recordings include:* JS Bach's St John Passion, Smithsonian Collection of Recordings; Handel's Theodora with Nicholas McGegan conducting; Bach's Solo Cantata for Alto; John Adams, Grand Pianola Music with composer conducting. *Current Management:* Byers, Schwalbe and Associates Inc, 584 Broadway, Suite 1105, New York, NY 10012, USA. *Address:* 514 West 110th Street, Apt 92, New York, NY 10025, USA.

LANE, Piers; Concert Pianist; b. 1958, London, England. *Education:* Studied with Nancy Weir at the Queensland Conservatorium, Bela Siki in Seattle and Kendall Taylor and Yonty Solomon at the Royal College of Music. *Career:* Debut: Broadcast recital for ABC, aged 12; Solo and concert appearances in the USA, France, Germany, Spain, Hungary, Italy, India, the United Kingdom, Australia, Greece, Middle East and New Zealand; Tour of 4 Latin American countries in 1989; Season 1990–91 with visits to Cyprus and Morocco, concerts in the United Kingdom, 2 visits to Australia and engagements in France and South America, and played Bliss Piano Concerto at the 1991 Promenade Concerts; Has played with such orchestras as the Philharmonia, Royal Philharmonic, BBC Philharmonic, Hallé, City of London Sinfonia and the London Festival Orchestra; Frequent recitals on the BBC and chamber concerts with Kathron Sturrock, the New Budapest Quartet, Alexander Baillie and Julian Lloyd Webber; Many recitals at Wigmore Hall; Contemporary repertory includes Dave Heath's Piano Concerto; Professor of Piano at the Royal Academy of Music; mem, European Piano Teachers Association; The Liszt Society; The Beethoven Pianoforte Society of Europe. *Recordings:* Music by Shostakovich, Prokofiev, Schnittke and Rachmaninov with Alexander Baillie; Moskowski and Paderewski Concertos, the Complete Etudes by Scriabin, and Brahms Piano Quintet; Recitals with violinist, Tasmin Little; Mussorgsky's Pictures at an Exhibition, Stravinsky's Petroushka and Balakirev's Islamey. *Honours:* Royal Overseas League Outstanding Musician of The Year, 1982. *Current Management:* Patrick Garvey Management. *Address:* 51 Portland Road, Hove, East Sussex BN3 5DQ, England.

LANG, Aidan; Stage Director; b. 1959, England. *Education:* Studied English and Drama at Birmingham University. *Career:* Glyndebourne from 1984, becoming Director of Productions for the Tour in 1991; Principal Associate Director for the Festival; Productions with GTO have included La Bohème (1991, debut), Matthus's Song of Love and Death and Il Barbiere di Siviglia; Premiere of Hamilton's Lancelot at the Arundel Festival, Tamerlano at Göttingen, Carmen for Canadian Opera and La Traviata, Die Zauberflöte (Barcelona), 1990–97; Artistic Director of Opera Zuid, Netherlands, with productions of Werther, Ariadne, The Cunning Little Vixen and Don Giovanni; Further engagements include Le Comte Ory for Welsh National Opera, Hansel and Gretel in Belfast; Così fan tutte at Cologne, and Tosca at Nice; Die Entführung for Istanbul Festival; Il Ritorno d'Ulisse, Lisbon; Mozart's La Finta Semplice at Buxton, 1998, and Lucio Silla at Garsington; Season 1999 Magic Fountain by Delius (Scottish Opera) and Don Giovanni (Brazil); Season 2000 Fierrebras (Buxton) and Cav and Pag (São Páolo); Recent productions of La Sonnambula (São Páolo), A new Ring Cycle (Manaus) and Semele (Buxton); Artistic Director of Buxton Festival, 2000–. *Address:* c/o Musichall, Vicarage Way, Ringmer, East Sussex BN8 5 LA, England. *Website:* www.musichall.uh.com.

LANG, David; Composer; b. 8 Jan. 1957, Los Angeles, CA, USA. *Education:* Stanford Univ. and the Univ. of Iowa; Doctorate from Yale School of Music, 1989; teachers include Jacob Druckman, Hans Werner Henze, Martin Brenick and Henri Lazarof. *Career:* freelance composer from 1983; founded the Bang On A Can Festival, New York City. *Compositions:* Orchestral: Eating Living Monkeys, 1985, revised 1987, International Business Machine, 1990, Bonehead, 1990; Stage: Judith and Holofernes, Puppet Opera, 1989, premiered at the 1990 Munich Biennale; Modern Painters, 1994, premiered in 1995 by Santa Fe Opera; The Difficult of Crossing a Field, opera, 1999; Chamber and ensemble: Hammer Amour, 1979, revised 1989, Frag, 1985, Spud, 1986, Are You Experienced?, 1987–88, Burn Notice, 1988, Dance/Drop, 1988–89; Solo and Duo: Illumination Rounds for violin and piano, 1982, While Nailing At Random for piano, 1983, Orpheus Over And Under for 2 pianos, 1989, Vent for flute and piano, 1990, The Anvil Chorus for percussion solo, 1990, Bitter Herb for cello and piano, 1990, My Evil Twin, 1992, Face So Pale, 1992, Cheating, Lying, Stealing, 1993, Music For Gracious Living, 1993, Slow Movement, 1993; Follow, for ensemble, 1996; Hell, for narrator and ensemble, 1997; Trample Young Lions, 1997; The Passing Measures for bass clarinet, female voices and orchestra, 1998; By Fire, commissioned by the BBC Singers; Other commissions from City of Munich, Boston Symphony Orchestra, American Composers Orchestra, Cleveland Orchestra, Santa Fe Opera and Saint Paul Chamber Orchestra.

LANG, Edith; Singer (Soprano); b. 28 April 1927, Chicago, USA. *Education:* Studied in Chicago and Italy. *Career:* Sang in Italy from 1954 with debut as Madama Butterfly, and Hamburg from 1955 as Verdi's Aida, Amelia, Elisabeth de Valois, Leonora and Abigaille, Beethoven's Leonore and Mozart's Donna Anna; Guest appearances in London, Vienna, Milan and Paris; San Francisco in 1959 as the Empress in the US premiere of Die Frau ohne Schatten; Also heard as concert singer; Taught at Lubeck Musikhochschule from 1973. *Address:* Schleswig-Holsteinische Musikakademie, Jerusalemberg 4, Lubeck, Germany.

LANG, Istvan; Composer; b. 1 March 1933, Budapest, Hungary; m. Csilla Fülöp, 28 Dec 1966, 1 s. *Education:* Academy of Music, Budapest. *Career:* Freelance Composer, 1958–66; Musical Adviser, State Puppet Theatre, 1966–84; Professor of Chamber Music, Academy of Music, Budapest, 1973–; Secretary General, Association of Hungarian Musicians, 1978–90; Member, Ex Committee of International Society for Contemporary Music, 1984–87; Member, Ex Committee of International Music Council, 1989–93; mem, Hungarian Composers' Union. *Compositions:* Dream about the Theatre, Rounded up television operas; In memorian NN; Symphonies Nos 2, 3, 4, 5, 6 and 7; Violin Concerto; Double Concerto for clarinet and harp; Concerto Bucolico; Pezzo Lirico; Rhymes; Constellations; Affetti, Intarsia around a Bartók theme; Music 2-3-4; Sempre in tensione; Solo pieces for various instruments; String Quartets Nos 2 and 3; Wind Quintets Nos 1, 2 and 3; Sonata for violin and piano, 1990; Cimbiosis, 1991; Sonata for cello and piano, 1992–93; Off and On for harp and live electronics; Budapest Liaz Terenc Square, Vibrating Object on Parabola Line; Knotes on the Line, chamber music, 1993; Viviofa, chamber music, 1995; The Coward Opera in 1 act, 1998; Night-fall for trumpet and life electronic, electronic music; Meeting a Young Man, electroacustic radioplay; Concertino for soprano and live electro-acoustic, 1999; No Man is an Island (John Donne), Chamber Cantata No. 3. *Recordings:* Several. *Honours:* Erkel Prize, 1968, 1975; Merit Artist, 1985; Bart ók Pásztori Prize, 1994. *Address:* Frankel Leo Ut 24, H 1027 Budapest, Hungary.

LANG, Klaus; Composer and Organist; b. 26 April 1971, Graz, Austria. *Education:* Studied, University of Music, Graz, with H M Pressl and B Fürrer; Composition and Music Theory, with Y Pagh-Paan in Bremen; Organ with O Bruckner at University of Graz. *Career:* Performances at Steirischer Herbst, 1994–98, Metopher, Stuttgart, 1997, Wien modern, 1998, 1999, Eclat Stuttgart, 1999, Kryptonale '99, Berlin, Lörgange 2000, Vienna. *Compositions:* Der Weg des Prizen; Cetus candidus; Die Ewigheitisteine Badehütte mit... cimeinte der Rock wäre aus... Die 3 Spiegel der schönen Karin; Das kaum wahruehmreheib Dostojkis. *Recordings:* Klaus Lang Trauermusiken Laubert, 1995; Amras Quartett; Dir Uberwinterungder der Mollusken Kurien, 1999; Klangforum Wien. *Publications:* Book, Auf Wehlklanswellen durch der Töne Meer, 1999; Contributions to New Grove Dictionary. *Honours:* Musikförderungspreis der Stadt Graz, 1992; Würdigungspreis des Bundesministeriums, 1993; Preis der Kompositionswettbewerbes der Musikpratokolls in steirischentterbst, 1993; Kompanistesseminer des Klompforum, 1998. *Address:* Zeitvertrieb Wien Berlin, Zollergasse 5/13, 1070 Vienna, Austria.

LANG, Petra; Singer (Mezzo-soprano); b. 29 Nov. 1962, Frankfurt, Germany. *Education:* Studied in Darmstadt and Mainz. *Career:* Studio, Bavarian State Opera, Munich from 1989; Sang at Basle Opera from 1990, Karlsruhe, Nürnberg, 1991, Dortmund (Cherubino, Dorabella, Rosina, Suzuki, Octavian, Waltraute, Fricka), 1992–95; Brunswick (Brangäne, Judith in Bleubeard's Castle, Marie in Wozzeck), 1995–97; Salzburg Festival, as Virtu in Monteverdi's Poppea, Bregenz, 1993, as Fenena in Nabucco, 1994; La Scala, 1995, in Die Zauberflöte; Lieder recitals throughout Germany, Schubertiade Hohenems, Théâtre du Châtelet, Paris, Carnegie Hall, Edinburgh Festival, Brussels, Gent; Sang Waltraute in Götterdämmerung at Covent Garden and Berlin DO; Brangäne in Tristan und Isolde, London, Amsterdam, Dresden, Gent, Turin, Paris, Vienna and Carnegie Hall (US debut); Kundry at the BBC Proms, in Dresden, Tokyo, Gent; Venus in Rome, Baltimore, Berlin DO; Ortrud at Edinburgh Festival, 2003; Ariadne at Covent Garden; Concert performances as Judith in Bluebeard's Castle in Philadelphia, New York, Brussels, London, Modena, Ferrara; Cassandre in Les Troyens in London, Birmingham, Edinburgh Festival, Amsterdam, Leipzig, Mannheim. *Recordings include:* Cherubino; Bach Cantatas; Cassandre – LSO Live (2 Grammy Awards, 2 BRIT Awards, Preis der Deutschen Schallplatten Kritik, Orphée d'Or de l' Acad. du disque lyrique); Mahler No. 2; Mahler No. 3; Rossini: Stabat Mater; Beethoven IX; Bruckner: Te Deum. *Current Management:* Balmer & Dixon Management AG, Kreuzstrasse 82, 8032 Zürich, Switzerland. *Telephone:* (43) 244-8644. *Fax:* (43) 244-8649. *Website:* www.badix.ch.

LANG, Rosemarie; Singer (Mezzo-soprano); b. 1955, Grünstädtel, Schwarzenberg, Germany. *Education:* Studied in Leipzig. *Career:* Sang in opera at Altenburg, then Leipzig; Guest engagements at Dresden as Venus by Wagner, 1988; Berlin Staatsoper as Gluck's Clytemnestra and Wagner's Brangäne, and in premiere of Graf Mirabeau by Siegfried Matthus, 1989 (also televised), and as Azucena by Verdi, 1989; Other roles include Mozart's Dorabella, Cherubino and

Sextus, Bellini's Romeo, Rossini's Cenerentola and Rosina, Strauss's Octavian and Composer in Ariadne; Sang Countess Geschwitz in Lulu, 1997; Many concert appearances. *Recordings include:* Mendelssohn's St Paul; Larina in Eugene Onegin; Schoenberg's Gurre-Lieder; Mozart's Masses; Songs by Schumann and Brahms; Pfitzner's Palestrina as Silla; 8th Symphony by Mahler under Abbado; Rheingold and Walküre (Fricka) by Wagner; Götterdämmerung by Wagner under Barenboim; Guest appearances in Oslo. *Address:* c/o Staatsoper Berlin, Unter den Linden 7, 10117 Berlin, Germany.

LANG LANG; Chinese pianist; b. 1982, Shenyang. *Education:* Shenyang Conservatory of Music, Central Music Conservatory, Beijing, Curtis Inst., Philadelphia, USA. *Career:* played the complete Chopin Etudes, Beijing Concert Hall 1995; performed as one of the soloists at the inaugural concert of the China National Symphony 1996; US debut with the Baltimore Symphony Orchestra 1998; last-minute substitution at the Ravinia Festival Gala of the Century, playing the Tchaikovsky Concerto with the Chicago Symphony Orchestra 1999; Carnegie Hall debut playing the Grieg Concerto with the Baltimore Symphony under Yuri Temirkanov, April 2001; joined the Philadelphia Orchestra and Wolfgang Sawallisch for the orchestra's 100th anniversary tour, including a performance in the Great Hall of the People, Beijing, June 2001; BBC Proms debut, playing Rachmaninov's Third Concerto, Aug. 2001; 2001/02 season included recital debuts at London's Wigmore Hall, Washington's Kennedy Center and the Paris Louvre, tour of Europe with the NDR Symphony Orchestra of Hamburg, and performance with the NHK Symphony Orchestra under Charles Dutoit; performed in five concerts at the Ravinia Festival 2002; season 2002/03 included performances with the New York Philharmonic and Lorin Maazel in New York and a tour of Asia, concerts with the Cleveland Orchestra at Severance Hall, a tour of the Midwest with Franz Welser-Möst, appearances with the Los Angeles Philharmonic, the San Francisco Symphony, the Pittsburgh Symphony, the Philadelphia Orchestra; in 2003 he toured China in with concerts and recitals, and festival appearances included the opening concert of the BBC Proms, London, Mostly Mozart, Aspen, Tanglewood, Ravinia, Saratoga, Blossom, Verbier, Schleswig-Holstein and the Ruhr Piano Festival; Carnegie Hall recital debut Nov. 2003; orchestral appearances with the Philadelphia, Los Angeles Philharmonic, London Philharmonic, Orchestre de Paris, Israel Philharmonic, Staatskapelle Berlin, Berliner Philharmoniker. *Recordings:* Peter Tchaikovsky Piano Concerto No. 1 and Mendelssohn Piano Concerto No. 1, with Chicago Symphony Orchestra under Daniel Barenboim, Haydn, Rachmaninov, Brahms, recorded Live at Seiji Ozawa Hall, Tanglewood 2001, Rachmaninov Piano Concerto No. 3 and Scriabin Etudes, with St Petersburg Philharmonic under Yuri Temirkanov 2003, Lang Lang live at Carnegie Hall 2004. *Honours:* first prize in the Shenyang Piano Competition 1987, first prize in the Fifth Xing Hai Cup Piano Competition, Beijing, first prize and outstanding artistic performance in the Fourth International Young Pianists Competition, Germany, first prize at the Second Tchaikovsky International Young Musicians' Competition, Japan 1995, Leonard Bernstein Award 2002. *Address:* c/o Telarc Records, 23307 Commerce Park Road, Cleveland, OH 44122, USA (office). *Website:* www.LangLang.com (office).

LANGAN, Kevin; Singer (Bass); b. 1 April 1955, New York, USA; m. Sally Wolf, 16 July 1983. *Education:* New England Conservatory of Music, 1973–75; Indiana University, 1975–80; BM, MM in Voice; Vocal Instruction with Margaret Harshaw. *Career:* Debut: New Jersey State Opera in 1979 in Don Carlos; Principal Bass with San Francisco Opera, 1980–; Appeared with New York City Opera, Houston Grand Opera, Philadelphia Opera, Canadian Opera, Miami, Detroit and Dallas Opera, Geneva, Lyon, Winnipeg and St Louis Opera, Colorado, Santa Fe, Edmonton, Vancouver, Seattle, Tulsa, Pittsburgh, San Diego and Washington DC Opera; Appeared with Chicago Lyric and Metropolitan Opera and sang Astofolo in Vivaldi's Orlando Furioso at San Franciscio in 1989, and Colline at San Diego in 1990; Season 1992 as Donizetti's Raimondo at Seattle followed by Rossini's Basilio, and Leporello at the 1992 Santa Fe Festival; Appears on 1993 video of San Francisco Opera production of Turandot in role of Timur; Appeared as Leporello in 1996 Santa Fe festival production of Don Giovanni; Sparafucile in 1997 as San Francisco Opera's Rigoletto; Timur in Turandot in 1998 with Dallas Opera and Flanders Opera, Antwerp; Season 2000–01 as Sobackini in The Tsar's Bride by Rimsky, at San Franscisco, Pimen in Seattle and Sarastro in San Diego. *Recordings:* Nozze di Figaro with Nicklaus Harnoncourt, conductor, 1994. *Honours:* Finalist, National Metropolitan Opera, 1980; 2nd Place, San Francisco Opera Auditions, 1980; Richard Tucker Foundation Award for Advanced Studies, 1984. *Current Management:* Elizabeth Crittenden. *Address:* Columbia Artists Management Inc, c/o Crittenden Division, 165 West 57th Street, New York, NY 10019, USA.

LANGDON, Sophie (Catherine); Concert Violinist and Professor of Violin; b. 26 Aug. 1958, Hemel Hempstead, Hertfordshire, England.

Education: Royal Academy of Music; Juilliard School, New York, USA; Curtis Institute, Philadelphia, USA; Guildhall School of Music and Drama. *Career:* Debut: As Soloist, 1981 Spitalfields Festival, London in Kurt Weill's Violin Concerto; Violinist of Trio Zingara, 1980–83, winning Munich International Competition, 1981; Recitals, Concertos, Leading, Directing and Chamber Music Performances and Broadcasts in England at Festivals and all London's major venues and throughout Europe and North America; Teacher, Guildhall School of Music and Drama 1981–86, Central Ostrabothnian Conservatoire, Finland 1986–87, Trinity College of Music 1987–, Menuhin School 1991–92, Chetham's School, Manchester 1988–90, Royal Academy of Music 1990–, Professor of Violin at TCM and RAM; Concerto performances and recordings with the Royal Philharmonic Orchestra, Philharmonia, BBC Symphony Orchestra, BBC National Orchestra of Wales, BBC Scottish Symphony Orchestra, BBC Philharmonic and Berlin Radio Orchestra; Chamber music performances and recordings with, Lontano, Jeux, Aquarius, Music Projects, Langdon Chamber Players and London Sinfonietta; Leader and Director of London Chamber Symphony, Ambache Chamber Orchestra and Academy of London; Guest Leader of City of London Sinfonia, London Mozart Players and Orchestra of St John's Smith Square. *Recordings:* Dame Ethel Smyth Double Concerto for violin and horn on Chandos label; Mozart Chamber Music with Ambache Chamber Ensemble on Pickwick label. *Honours:* Associate of the Royal Academy of Music, 1993. *Address:* 84 North Grove, London N15 5QP, England.

LANGER, Elena; Composer; b. 1974, Moscow, Russia. *Education:* Gnessin Music School, Moscow, 1989; Moscow Conservatoire; 1993-98, with Yuri Vorontsov; Royal College of Music, London, from 1998 with Julian Anderson; PhD studies at the Royal Academy, with Simon Bainbridge, from 2001. *Career:* Commissions from Moscow Variety Theatre and Almeida Theatre (first Jerwood Composer in Association). *Compositions:* The Crying, for four clarinets, 1994; Transformations for violin and piano, 1998; Reflection for piano, 1999; Ariadne for voice and ensemble, 2002; Music Theatre commission from the Almeida 2003. *Recordings:* Transformations, and Reflection, 1999. *Address:* c/o Julian Anderson, Royal College of Music, Prince Consort Road, London, SW7 2 BS, England.

LANGFORD, Roger; Singer (Baritone); b. 1965, England. *Education:* Studied at the Royal College of Music and Royal Academy of Music. *Career:* Soloist with Yorkshire Bach Choir in the St John Passion, Christmas Oratorio, Bach B minor Mass and Monteverdi Vespers; Concerts in France and Germany including Purcell's Aeneas for Cologne Radio; Music theatre includes Eight Songs For A Mad King by Maxwell Davies, Master Peter's Puppet Show and Monteverdi's Combattimento; Visits to Europe with Nigel Rogers's group, Chiaroscuro, performing English and Italian Baroque music; Sang Elijah at Lincoln Cathedral and The Apostles by Elgar at St Albans Abbey; Season 1989–90 as Papageno for British Youth Opera and in Trouble in Tahiti at Edinburgh Festival; Sang title role of Nicolson's Cat Man's Tale at BOC Covent Garden Festival, 1998.

LANGHURST, Rebecca; Singer (soprano); b. 1965, USA. *Education:* Yale Opera Program, Princeton. *Career:* Roles at Yale included Olympia in Les Contes d'Hoffmann, Zdenka in Arabella and Mozart's Despina; Professional debut as Pamina, for Minnesota Opera, followed by appearances in Ariadne auf Naxos at St Louis and Il Trittico for Spoleto Festival, USA; Corinna in Il Viaggio a Reims and Verdi's Nannetta for Wolf Trap Opera; Hero in Béatrice et Bénedict at Alice Tully Hall, New York, and Rossini's Elvria at Kansas City; Other roles include Alexandra in Blitzstein's Regina and Angel More in Thomson's The Mother of us All, for New York City Opera; Staatstheater Mannheim, from 2000, as Mozart's Ilia and Sandrina, Gretel, and Helena in A Midsummer Night's Dream. *Current Management:* Athole Still International Management, Forresters Hall, 25–27 Westow Street, London, SE19 3RY, England. *Telephone:* (20) 8771-5271. *Fax:* (20) 8768-6600. *Website:* www.atholestill.com.

LANGMAN, Krzysztof (Maria); Flautist; b. 22 July 1948, Kraków, Poland. *Education:* Academy of Music Kraków, 1970–74; Study under S Gazzeloni at Santa Cecilia Academy of Music, Rome, 1976–77. *Career:* Principal Flautist at State Opera House and Philharmonic Society, Wroclaw; Principal Solo Flute with Baltic Philharmonic Orchestra, Gdansk, 1974–; Assistant Professor of Flute, Academy of Music, Gdansk; Co-operates with Ensemble MW 2 Vanguard Group; Concerts in various countries including Austria, Germany, Greece, Norway, Sweden, Denmark, Netherlands, Belgium, the United Kingdom, Italy, Mexico, Spain, Luxemburg, Switzerland and France. *Recordings:* Numerous for Polish radio and television. *Current Management:* Polish Artists Agency, Warsaw, Poland. *Address:* ul Pawla Gdanca 4a-42, 80-336 Gdańsk, Poland.

LANGRÉE, Louis; Conductor; b. 1961, Mulhouse, France. *Career:* Music Director of the Orchestre de Picardie, 1993–98; Director of Opéra

National de Lyon; Music Director of Glyndebourne Touring Opera, with Don Giovanni 1993, La Bohème 1995, Così fan tutte 1998, Pelléas et Mélisande 1999; Carmen and Fidelio, 2000–01; Appearances with Netherlands Radio Philharmonic, Monte Carlo Orchestra, Orchestre de Paris, and Orchestre de la Suisse Romande; Netherlands Opera, Opéra National de Paris, Geneva Opera, and festivals at Drottningholm, Orange, Spoleto and New York (Mostly Mozart); London Proms debut 2000, with the Orchestra of the Age of Enlightenment, in Haydn's 44th Symphony and Beethoven's 8th; Season 2001–2002 with Manon Lescaut in Geneva, Fidelio and Figaro at Glyndebourne (2001), Hamlet for the Royal Opera and Idomeneo at Glyndebourne (2002). *Recordings include:* Berlioz songs, with Veronique Gens; Mozart Arias with Natalie Dessay and the OAE. *Address:* 42, rue Piere Nicole, F-75005 Paris, France.

LANGRIDGE, Philip (Gordon); Singer (Tenor); b. 16 Dec. 1939, Hawkhurst, Kent, England; m. (1) 1 s., 2 d., (2) Ann Murray, 1981, 1 s. *Education:* ARAM, Royal Academy of Music, 1977. *Career:* Debut: Glyndebourne Festival in 1964; Sang at BBC Promenade Concerts, 1970–, Edinburgh Festival, 1970–, Netherlands Opera, Scottish Opera, Handel Opera and major opera houses in the United Kingdom and abroad; Concerts with major international orchestras and conductors including Boston with Previn, Chicago with Solti and Abbado, Los Angeles with Christopher Hogwood, Sydney with Mackerras, Vienna Philharmonic with Previn, Orchestre de Paris with Barenboim and Mehta and with all major British orchestras; Many first performances with some dedicated to or written for him; Has sung in Osud, Turn of the Screw, Mask of Orpheus, Don Giovanni, Fidelio, Idomeneo, The Rake's Progress, Wozzeck, Castor and Pollux, Rigoletto, Poppea, Lucio Silla, Rossini's Otello, La Donna del Lago, and Così fan tutte. Sang in the television production of Tippett's The Midsummer Marriage in 1989, in Mozart's Idomeneo in a new production at Covent Garden in 1989, Berlioz' Benedict for ENO in 1990, Idomeneo at the 1990 Salzburg Festival, Pelegrin in Tippett's New Year at Glyndebourne, Mozart's Titus at Glyndebourne and the Promenade Concerts in 1991; Season 1992–93 included Aschenbach in a new production of Death in Venice at Covent Garden and Nero in Poppea at Salzburg Festival; Sang in Stravinsky's Pulcinella at 1993 London Proms; Jupiter in Semele at Covent Garden, 1996; Captain Vere in Billy Budd at the Met, 1997; Mark in The Midsummer Marriage at Munich, 1998; Title role in Pfitzner's Palestrina, Covent Garden, 2001; Schoenberg's Gurrelieder at the London Proms, 2002; mem, Music Panel, Arts Council of Great Britain. *Recordings:* Over 50 records, including Moses und Aron. *Address:* c/o Allied Artists Agency, 42 Montpelier Square, London SW7 1JZ, England.

LANKESTER, Michael; Conductor, Musical Director and Professor of Conducting; b. 12 Nov. 1944, London, England. *Education:* Royal College of Music; ARCM; GRSM. *Career:* Musical Director, National Theatre, 1969–75, composing and conducting numerous items to accompany productions; Conductor, Surrey Philharmonic Orchestra, 1972–, and English Chamber Orchestra; Founder of Contrapuncti; Radio and television broadcasts for BBC and Collaborator with Young Vic Theatre in various productions; Conductor, Cheltenham Festival, Sadler's Wells Theatre and at opening of Royal Northern College of Music, 1973; Made orchestral suite of Britten's The Prince of the Pagodas, and conducted it at the 1979 Promenade Concerts; mem, Noise Abatement Society. *Recordings include:* Gordon Crosse, Purgatory, Ariadne. *Honours:* Watney/Sargent Conducting Scholarship, 1967.

LANSKY, Paul; Composer; b. 18 June 1944, New York, USA. *Education:* Studied with George Perle and Hugo Weisgall at Queen's College, New York, BA 1966; Princeton University with Milton Babbitt and Earl Kim, PhD 1969. *Career:* Teacher, Princeton University from 1969; Associate Editor of Perspectives of New Music, 1972. *Compositions:* Modal Fantasy for piano, 1969; String Quartet, 1972–77; Mild Und Leise for tape, 1974; Crossworks for piano and ensemble, 1975; Artifice, on Ferdinand's Reflections, for tape, 1976; Folk Images for tape, 1981; As If for string trio and Electronics, 1982; Folk Images and As It Grew Dark for tape, 1980–83; Electro-acoustic: Night Traffic, 1990; Now and Then, 1991; Word Color, 1992; Memory Pages, 1993; Thinking Back, 1996; For the Moment, 1997; Shadows, 1998. *Publications include:* Affine Music, dissertation, 1969. *Honours:* League of Composers ISCM electronic music award, 1975; Koussevitzky Foundation Award, 1981. *Address:* c/o ASCAP, ASCAP Building, 1 Lincoln Plaza, New York, NY 10023, USA.

LANTOS, Istvan; Pianist; b. 1949, Budapest, Hungary. *Education:* Studied piano under Mme Erzsebet Tusa, Budapest Bela Bartók Conservatory; Ferenc Liszt Academy of Music; Graduate with Distinction, Liszt Academy of Music. *Career:* Played solo part in Messiaen's Turangalîla Symphonie, Bayreuth International Youth Festival, 1970, Hitzacker Festival, Germany, and Bratislava International Rostrum of Young Artists; Numerous appearances in Hungarian concert halls and world-wide; Guest performances in eastern Europe and Cuba, Austria, the United Kingdom, Canada, Germany, Netherlands, Ireland, Italy and Switzerland; Has twice toured and held masterclasses in Japan;

Soloist with Hungarian State Symphony Orchestra during USA tour; Has toured every 2nd year the major cities in Germany with Hungarian State Symphony Orchestra, 1972–; Also renowned organist; Assistant Professor, Budapest Liszt Academy of Music, 1974–.

LANZA, Alcides Emigdio; Canadian composer, pianist, conductor and university professor; b. 2 June 1929, Rosario, Argentina; 2 s., 2 d. *Education:* Centro Latino Americano de Altos Estudios Musicales Instituto Di Tella, Buenos Aires; Postgraduate Courses, Electronic Music, Columbia University, New York, USA; Studied Composition with Julián Bautista and Alberto Ginastera, Piano with Ruwin Erlich, Conducting with Roberto Kinsky; Further Instruction Courses with various noted artists. *Career:* Concert Tours of Europe, North and South America; Artistic Staff, Teatro Colón, Buenos Aires, 1959–65; Pianist, Lecturer and Conductor, Composers/Performers Group, touring Europe; Composer and Teacher, Columbia-Princeton Electronic Music Centre; Dir Emeritus of Electronic Music Studio and Prof. of Composition, McGill University, Montreal, Quebec, Canada, 1971–; Artistic Dir, Group GEMS (Group of the Electronic Music Studio). *Compositions include:* Módulos II, 1982; Módulos III, 1983; Sensors III, for organ and two percussionists, 1982; Eidesis VI, for string orchestra with piano, 1983; Interferences III, for chamber ensemble and electronic sounds, 1983; Acúfenos V, for trumpet, piano and electronic-computer tape, 1980; Ekphonesis VI, actress-singer tape, 1988;... there is a way to sing it... (solo tape), 1988; un mundo imaginario, choir and computer tape, 1989; Vôo, for voice, electro-acoustic music and digital signal processing, 1992; Ontem for voices, tabla, tape and digital signal processing, 1999; aXents, for chamber orchestra and tape, 2003. *Honours:* Hon. Diploma (High Distinction) awarded by OAS and Int. Centre for Music Education, 1996; Victor Martin Lynch-Staunton Award, for exceptional talent and achievements as a composer, 2003. *Current Management:* Shelan Concerts. *Address:* 6351 Trans Island Avenue, Montreal, QC H3W 3B7, Canada. *Telephone:* (514)7337216. *E-mail:* alcides@music .mcgill.ca. *Website:* www.music.mcgill.ca/~alcides.

LAPERRIERE, Gaétan; Singer (Baritone); b. 1959, Montreal, Canada. *Education:* Studied with Robert Savoie. *Career:* Sang in opera at Montreal from 1981, Canadian Opera at Toronto from 1986 as Gounod's Mercutio, Donizetti's Enrico, Mozart's Count (1991) and Raimbaud in Le Comte Ory (1994); US appearances at Washington as Bizet's Zurga, Miami as Hamlet, and Houston (Marcello, 1991); San Francisco and New York City, 1991, as Germont; Toronto, 1993, as Ford in Falstaff, and Montreal, 1995, as de Siriex in Fedora; Mercutio at Dallas and Escamillo in Carmen at Metz, 1996; Sang Debussy's Golo at Bologna and Rigoletto for the New York City Opera, 2000; Many concert performances. *Address:* c/o Opéra de Montreal, 260 de Maisonneuve Boulevard West, Montreal, Quebec H2X 1Y9, Canada.

LAPINSKAS, Darius; Composer and Conductor; b. 9 March 1934, Kaunas, Lithuania; m. Laima Rastenis, 28 Nov 1970, 1 s. *Education:* South Boston High School; BA, Composition, Conducting, New England Conservatory, Boston, 1953–57; Akademie fuer Musik und Darstellende Kunst, Vienna, 1957–58; Musik Hochschule, Stuttgart, 1958–60. *Career:* Musikdirektor, Tuebingen Landestheatre, 1960–65; Kapelmeister, Staatsoper Stuttgart, 1961–65; Schiedsgericht, Composer-Conductor, Mainz television; Guest Conductor with Stuttgart Symphony Orchestra, Stuttgart Philharmonic, South German Radio Orchestra; Mannheim Opera Orchestra; National Symphony Orchestra of Bogotà, and Symphony Orchestra of Antioquia; Artistic Director of New Opera Company of Chicago. *Compositions:* Operas: Lokys, Maras, Amadar, Dux Magnus, Rex Amos; Ballet: Laima; Concerto for piano, strings and percussion; Concerto for violin and orchestra; Haiku, song cycle; Balyvera, song cycle for mezzo-soprano and orchestra; Les Sept Solitudes, aria for mezzo-soprano and orchestra; Ainiu Dainos, song cycle for voice and chamber orchestra. *Recordings:* Les Sept Solitudes; Ainiu Dainos; Mergaites Dalia. *Honours:* BML Prize for Composition, Boston, 1955; Wurttemberg Prize for Composition, 1961; Illinois Arts Council Grant for Composition, 1985, 1986. *Address:* 9368 South Longwood Drive, Chicago, IL 60620, USA.

LAPLANTE, Bruno; Singer; b. 1 Aug. 1938, Beauharnois, Quebec, Canada; 2 s. *Education:* 1st Prize in Vocal Art, Conservatoire de Musique du Québec, Montreal. *Career:* Debut: Cimarosa's The Secret Marriage in Germany; Under scholarships from Canada Arts Council, The Government of Quebec, private foundations and from Goethe Institute in Munich; Worked first in Germany, in Paris under the direction of Pierre Bernac and in Montreal with Lina Narducci; Numerous radio and television appearances including Susanna's Secret, Gounod's Romeo and Juliette, and Lehar's Merry Widow; Engagements with major Canadian Symphony Orchestras; Les Noces and Carmina Burana with Grands Ballets Canadiens; 30 concerts in Canada for Les Jeunesse Musicales du Canada; A film dealing with his career in the series, Les Nouveaux Interprètes; Stage appearances include Carmen, Il Trittico, Manon, Don Giovanni and many others; Regular tours throughout Europe for concerts and festivals including

Festival du Marais, Paris, 1979 and 2 recitals at Festival International de Musique et d'Art Lyrique, Aix-en-Provence; mem, Union des Artistes de Montreal. *Recordings include:* Integrale des 15 Mélodies de Duparc; Mélodies de Lalo et de Bizet; Mélodies de Berlioz; Works by Offenbach, Jules Massenet, Reynaldo Hahn, Charles Gounod, and César Franck among others. *Honours:* Concours International de Genève, 1966, de Barcelona, 1966, de Montreal, 1967; Grand Prix du Disque, 1977.

LAPORTE, André; Composer; b. 12 July 1931, Oplinter, Belgium. *Education:* Studied at Catholic University of Louvain; Organ with Flor Peeters and counterpoint with Marinus de Jong, 1956–58. *Career:* Producer for Belgian Radio, 1963; Brussels Conservatory from 1968; Artistic Director of Belgian Radio Philharmonic Orchestra, 1989–96. *Compositions:* Piano Sonata, 1954; Psalm for 6 voices and brass, 1956; Jubilus for 12 brass instruments and 3 percussionists, 1966; Story for string trio and harpsichord, 1967; Ascension for piano, 1967; De Profundis for mixed choir, 1968; Le Morte Chitarre for tenor, flute and 14 strings, 1969; Night Music for orchestra, 1970; La Vita Non E Sogno for vocalists, chorus and orchestra, 1972; Peripetie for brass sextet; Chamber Music for soprano and ensemble, 1975; Transit for 48 strings, 1978; Das Schloss, opera in 3 acts after Kafka, 1986; Fantasia-Rondino for violin and orchestra, 1988; The Magpie On The Gallows, 1989. *Honours:* Lemmens-Tinel Award, 1958; Koopal Award from the Belgian Ministry of Culture, 1971 and 1976; Prix Italia, 1976. *Address:* c/o SABAM, Rue d'Arlon 75–77, 1040 Brussels, Belgium.

LAPPALAINEN, Kimmo; Singer (Tenor); b. 1944, Helsinki, Finland. *Education:* Sibelius Academy, 1966–68; Vocal studies with Fred Hustler in Lugano and Luigi Rici in Rome, 1969–70. *Career:* Finnish National Opera, Helsinki, 1968–72 and Stuttgart Opera from 1972; Sang at Glyndebourne Festival, 1972–74 as Pedrillo in Die Entführung and Idamantes in Idomeneo; Many performances at the Savonlinna Festival in Finland; Sang at Stuttgart in 1983 as Britten's Albert Herring; Also heard in concert. *Address:* c/o Finnish National Opera, Bailevardi 23–27, 00180 Helsinki 18, Finland.

LAPTEV, Yuri; Singer (Baritone) and Stage Director; b. 1955, Russia. *Education:* Graduated St Petersburg Conservatoire 1986. *Career:* Stage director at Kirov Opera, St Petersburg, from 1988; Head of Planning, 1991–; Director of the Welcome Back St Petersburg Gala at the Royal Opera House, 1992; Co-productions with the Kirov of Otello, Boris Godunov, The Fiery Angel, Le nozze di Figaro and War and Peace, Opera roles include Mozart's Almaviva, Valentin in Faust, Mathias in The Fiery Angel and Don Carlos in Prokofiev's Betrothal in a Monastery; Sang Captain Jacqueau in War and Peace with the Kirov at Covent Garden, 2000. *Recordings include:* at Covent Garden, 2000. *Recordings include:* The Maid of Pskov, The Fiery Angel, War and Peace, Khovanshchina. *Address:* c/o Kirov Opera, Mariinsky Theatre, Theatre Square, St Petersburg, Russia.

LARA, Christian; Singer (Tenor); b. 15 Aug. 1946, Merignac, France. *Education:* Studied in Bordeaux. *Career:* Sang at Lille Opéra, 1976–79 and studied further with Michel Sénéchal in Paris; Sang Juan in Don Quichotte at Venice in 1982, Rodolfo at Nantes, Cavaradossi at Avignon, Faust at Ghent and Antwerp; Theater des Westens, Berlin in 1987 as Sou-Chong in Das Land des Lächelns; Sang Faust at Cologne in 1989 and appeared in La Rondine at Tours in 1991; Concert repertoire includes Mendelssohn's 2nd Symphony; Sang Faust at Vienna in 1991, Ismaele in Nabucco at Karlsruhe, Samson at Besançon, Ruggero in La Rondine at Tours, Cavaradossi in Tosca at Angers, Don José in Carmen at Bregenz and Liège, and Florestan in Fidelio at Tours, all in 1991; In 1992 sang Oedipe Roi by Paul Bastide at Strasbourg, Andrei Khovansky at Strasbourg, Ismaele at Karlsruhe, Florestan at Angers, Don José at the Festival of Bregenz, Jean in Hérodiade at Liège, and in Vestale at Nantes; In 1993 sang Luigi in Il Tabarro at Tours, Jean at Toulon and in 1994 sang Des Grieux in Manon and Don José at Bordeaux. *Address:* 11 Rue Jean Jaurès, 33127 Martignas-sur-Jalle, France.

LAREDO, Jaime; Violinist; b. 7 June 1941, Cochabamba, Bolivia; m. Sharon Robinson. *Education:* studied violin with Antonio de Grassi and Frank Hauser in San Francisco, Josef Gingold and George Szell in Cleveland, and Ivan Galamian at the Curtis Institute, Philadelphia. *Career:* orchestral debut San Francisco 1952; won Queen Elisabeth of the Belgians Competition 1959 and subsequently appeared with most major orchestras in Europe and America; New York debut Carnegie Hall 1960; London debut Albert Hall 1961; frequent visitor to summer festivals at Spoleto, Tanglewood, Hollywood Bowl, Ravinia, Marlboro and Edinburgh; repertoire ranges from Baroque to contemporary works; gave the premiere of Ned Rorem's Concerto; Dir, soloist, works with St Pauls and Scottish Chamber Orchestras; Dir Chamber Music at the 92nd Street NY series in New York; Piano Trio concerts from 1977 with Joseph Kalichstein and Sharon Robinson. *Recordings:* Trios by Mendelsshn, Brahms and Beethoven for Vox Cum Laude and Pickwick International; Brahms Piano Quartets with Emanuel Ax, Isaac Stern, Yo-Yo Ma. *Honours:* New York City Handel Medallion, 1960; Stadium in

La Paz named after him; Bolivian stamps with his portrait issued in his honour, enscribed with the notes A, D and C (la-re-do). *Current Management:* Askonas Holt Ltd, Lonsdale Chambers, 27 Chancery Lane, London, WC2A 1PF, England. *Telephone:* (20) 7400-1700. *Fax:* (20) 7400-1799. *E-mail:* info@askonasholt.co.uk. *Website:* www .askonasholt.co.uk.

LAREDO, Ruth, BMus; concert pianist; b. 20 Nov. 1937, Detroit, MI, USA; m. 1960 (divorced 1974), one d. *Education:* Curtis Inst. of Music, under Rudolf Serkin. *Career:* debut, Carnegie Hall with New York Orchestra American Symphony under Leopold Stowkowski; Appeared at Carnegie Hall, the Kennedy Center, Library of Congress and the White House with orchestras the New York Philharmonic, Philadelpha and Cleveland Orchestras, Boston Symphony, St Louis Symphony, Detroit Symphony, National Symphony, the orchestras of Baltimore, Indianapolis, Houston, Buffalo and American Symphony; Participated in The Music from Marlboro Concerts from their inception 1965–; Performed at the Spoleto Festival USA 1983, 1985; Frequent Guest Artist with ensembles, The Tokyo and Shanghai Quartets; Tours with flautist Paula Robison. *Recordings:* Complete Works of Rachmaninov; Complete sonatas of Scriabin and works of Barber. *Contributions:* Columnist, Keyboard Classics Magazine; Editor, C F Peters Publishing Company. *Current Management:* Gurtman & Murtha Associates, 450 Seventh Avenue, Suite 603, New York, NY 10123, USA.

LARGE, Brian; Musicologist, Pianist, Writer and Television Producer; b. 1937, London, England. *Education:* Studied at Royal Academy of Music and London University. *Career:* Producer of opera on BBC television with many other opera television engagements in Europe and the USA. *Recordings:* Many operas on video, including La Cenerentola from the Houston Opera. *Publications:* Books on Smetana, Martinů and Czech Opera; Wrote entry on Martinů in The New Grove Dictionary of Music and Musicians, 1980.

LARIN, Sergei; Singer (Tenor); b. 1956, Daugavpils, Latvia. *Education:* Studied at the Vilnius Conservatory. *Career:* Early roles included Alfredo, Hermann and Vladimir in Prince Igor; Sang at Bratislava Opera from 1989 and guested at Dresden same year in Wagner-Régeny's Prometheus; Further appearances in Paris, at Monte Carlo as Don José and the Vienna Staatsoper as Lensky; Frankfurt 1993, as Sergei in Lady Macbeth of the Mtsensk District, La Scala 1993 as Don Carlo; Many appearances with the Kirov Opera, St Petersburg; Season 1996 with Loris in Fedora at La Scala and Don José at the Verona Arena; Sang Dick Johnson at Florence, Lensky at Turin and Don Carlos at the Salzburg Festival, 1998; Season 2000 as Don Carlos in Munich, Don José at the Vienna Staatsoper and Paolo in Francesca da Rimini at Buenos Aires; Engaged as Rienzi at the Vienna Staatsoper, 2003. *Address:* c/o Teatro alla Scala, Via Filodrammatici 2, 2 Milan 1021, Italy.

LARMORE, Jennifer; Singer (Mezzo-Soprano); b. 21 June 1958, Atlanta, Georgia, USA. *Career:* Debut: Sang Sesto in La Clemenza di Tito at Nice, 1986; Many performances in Europe and USA with a repertoire including operas by Mozart, Rossini, Debussy, Handel and Ravel; La Scala debut as Isolier in Le Comte Ory; From 1990 has sung Rossini's Rosina in Paris, Amsterdam, London and Rome, L'Enfant et les Sortilèges at La Scala, Giulio Cesare in Paris, Zerlina in Bonn, Rossini's Isabella and Isolier, in Turin and Milan; Season 1992–93 as Rosina in Bilbao and Berlin, Monteverdi's Ottavia in Bologna and Antwerp, Bellini's Romeo at Geneva and Carnegie Hall, Cenerentola in Florence and Dorabella at Salzburg Festival; Wigmore Hall recital, Mar 1993, with arias by Handel and Massenet and French and Spanish songs; Metropolitan debut as Rosina, Feb 1995; Concerts of Mahler Rückertlieder with R Muti and Vienna Philharmonic, April 1995; At Bastille Opéra, Paris, as Romeo in I Capuletti and Angelina in La Cenerentola; Season 1996 with Rossini's Isabella at Los Angeles; Season 1998 with Rossini's Isabella at the Paris Palais Garnier, and Offenbach's Giulietta at the Met; Season 2000–01 as Rossini's Cenerentola and Isabella at the Met; London Proms, 2002; Sang Rossini's Elisabetta at Banqueting House, London, 2002; Charlotte in Bilbao, 2002–03. *Recordings include:* L'Incoronazione di Poppea; Mozart's C minor Mass; Giulio Cesare; Il Barbiere di Siviglia; Hansel und Gretel; La Cenerentola; Alice in Lucia di Lammermoor; Marianna in Il Signor Bruschino; Arsace in Semiramide; Rossini Songs, Duets and Quartets; Solo CD of Handel and Mozart; Carmen; L'Italiana in Algeri; Solo CD of Travesti arias for Mezzo-Soprano. *Honours:* Winner, Richard Tucker Award, presentation and Gala at Lincoln Center, Oct 1994. *Current Management:* Caroline Woodfield and David Foster, ICM, USA; IMG and Tom Graham, London. *Address:* c/o IMG Artists, Lovell House, 616 Chiswick High Road, London W4 5RX, England.

LARNER, Gerald; Music Critic; b. 9 March 1936, Leeds, England; m. Celia Ruth Mary White, 2 d. *Education:* BA, New College, Oxford. *Career:* Assistant Lecturer, Manchester University, 1960–62; Member of the Guardian staff from 1962; Chief Northern music critic from 1965;

Translated Wolf's Der Corregidor into English; Wrote libretto for John McCabe's The Lion, The Witch and The Wardrobe, 1971; Artistic Director, Bowden Festival, 1980–84; mem, Critics Circle. *Contributions:* Musical Times; The Listener. *Address:* 11 Higher Downs, Altrincham, Cheshire WA14 2QL, England.

LARROCHA, Alicia de; Pianist; b. 23 May 1923, Barcelona, Spain; m. Juan Torra, 1 s., 1 d. *Education:* Studied with Frank Marshall in Barcelona. *Career:* Performed in public from age 4; Concerto debut in 1934 with the Madrid Philharmonic; British debut in 1953 at Wigmore Hall; US debut in 1955 with the Los Angeles Philharmonic; Formed duo with cellist, Gaspar Cassado in 1956; Solo recitals and concerts with major orchestras in Europe, USA, Canada, Central and South America, South Africa, New Zealand, Australia and Japan; Director, Marshall Academy Barcelona from 1959; Recent British appearances with the City of Birmingham Symphony, Philharmonia and the London Symphony Orchestra; Played Falla's Nights in The Gardens of Spain at the 1986 Promenade Concerts also televised; Barbican Hall recital in 1989; Edinburgh Festival, 1995; Ravel's Concerto in G at the Barbican, 1997. *Recordings:* Works by Granados, Falla, Albeniz, Mozart and Romantic composers. *Honours:* Paderewski Memorial Medal, London, 1961; Decorated Spanish Orders of Civil Merit, 1962 and Isabella la Católica, 1972; Medalla d'oro of City of Barcelona, 1982; Gold Medal of Spanish National Assembly, 1982; Principe de Asturias Prize, 1994; Edison Award, 1968, 1978; Grammy Awards for recordings of Iberia by Albeniz, 1974 and 1989, Ravel Concertos 1975 and Granados Goyescas, 1991; Deutsche Schallplatten Prize, 1979; Grand Prix du Disque, 1991; Musician of the Year, USA, 1978. *Current Management:* Herbert H Breslin Inc. *Address:* c/o Herbert H Breslin Inc, 119 West 57th Street 1505, New York, NY 10019, USA.

LARSEN, Libby (Brown); Composer; b. 24 Dec. 1950, Wilmington, Delaware, USA. *Education:* Studied at the University of Minnesota with Dominick Argento. *Career:* Co-founded Minnesota (American) Composers Forum, 1973; Resident Composer with the Minnesota Orchestra, 1983–87 and Artistic Director of the Hot Notes series, 1993; Many commissions from leading orchestras and organizations; Has appeared widely as speaker and teacher. *Compositions include:* Operas: Frankenstein, The Modern Prometheus, music drama, 1990; A Wrinkle In Time, 1992; Mrs Dalloway, 1993; Symphony, Water Music, 1985; Piano Concerto, Since Armstrong, 1990; Ghosts Of An Old Ceremony for orchestra, 1991; Sonnets from the Portuguese for soprano and chamber orchestra, 1989; String Quartet: Schoenberg, Schenker and Schillinger, 1991; The Atmosphere As A Fluid System for flute, strings and percussion, 1992; Mary Cassatt form Mezzo, trombone and orchestra, 1994; Eric Hermannson's Soul, opera, 1997; String Symphony, 1998; Songs of Light and Love for soprano and chamber orchestra, 1998; Solo Symphony, 1999. *Recordings:* Missa Gaia, 1994; Dancing Solo, 1997; Water Music, London Symphony Orchestra, 1997. *Honours:* Grammy Award, 1994. *Address:* c/o ASCAP, ASCAP Building, 1 Lincoln Plaza, New York, Ny 10023, USA.

LARSON, Lisa; Singer (Soprano); b. 1964, Sweden. *Education:* Vocal studies in Zürich, after a career as flautist. *Career:* Major roles at the Zürich Opera studio followed by Barbarina in Figaro at the Opera in season, 1996–97; Schubert operas at Potsdam, Barbarina at Lausanne, Amor in Gluck's Orfeo at the Cologne Philharmonic and Papagena under Muti at the opening of the season at La Scala; Komische Oper Berlin, as Barbarina and Papagena, 1996; Adele at Ludwigsburg and Frasquita and Tebaldo at Hamburg; Oscar in Un Ballo in Maschera at Basle, 1997; Concerts include Stockholm Festival appearances with Gösta Winbergh and Messiah in Vienna and at the Vatican. *Recordings include:* Schubert operas; Orff's Trionfi, under Franz Welser-Möst; Schumann's Manfred, under Mario Vanzago; Royal Festival Concert, Stockholm, with Gösta Winbergh. *Address:* c/o Opernhaus Zürich, Falkenstrasse 1, 8008 Zürich, Switzerland.

LARSON, Sophia; Singer (Soprano); b. 1954, Linz, Austria; m. Hans Sisa. *Education:* Salzburg Mozarteum with Seywald-Baumgartner; Further study with Ettore Campogalliani. *Career:* Sang at St Gallen from 1976 as Verdi's Amelia Boccanegra, Mozart's Ilia, and Silvia in Mascagni's Zanetto; Sang at Ulm, 1979–80 as Fiordiligi, the Marschallin, Beethoven's Leonore and Katya Kabanova; Bremen, 1980–83, and guest at Hamburg, Stuttgart, Trieste and Rome; Sang at Bologna in 1985 as the Duchess of Parma in Busoni's Doktor Faust, and Turin in 1986 as Puccini's Turandot and in Ghedini's Maria d'Alessandria; Further appearances in South America, Berlin, Berne, Wiesbaden and Bratislava; Bayreuth Festival, 1984–85 as Gutrune in The Ring, and Festival of Verona in 1986 as Minnie in La Fanciulla del West; Studio recordings for French and Italian Radio; Sang Venus in Tannhäuser at Bayreuth Festival in 1987, Gutrune in The Ring at Staatsoper Munich in 1987, Tosca at Turin in 1987, Isolde at Toronto in 1987, War Requiem at Carnegie Hall in 1988, Fedra by Pizzetti at Palermo in 1988, Renata in The Fiery Angel at Grand Théâtre Genève in 1988, Turandot at Zürich in 1988, Senta at Nice and San Francisco in 1988, Sieglinde in

Die Walküre at Bayreuth Festival in 1989, Renata at Amsterdam in 1989, Lyrische Symphonie by Zemlinsky at Amsterdam in 1989, Brünnhilde at Linz Brucknerfestival in 1989, Fidelio at Catania in 1989 and Turandot and Tosca at Turin and Zürich in 1990; British debut as Turandot at the London Coliseum, 1995; Sang Leonore in Fidelio at Toronto, 1998. *Address:* c/o Opernhaus Zürich, Falkenstrasse 1, 8008 Zürich, Switzerland.

LARSSON, Anders; Swedish singer (baritone); b. 1965. *Education:* Royal Univ. Coll. of Music, Stockholm. *Career:* many appearances in Europe and North America, as Eugene Onegin at Spoleto, Debussy's Pelléas at Brussels, Mozart's Guglielmo and Rossini's don Alvaro at Gothenburg, Papageno for Värmlane Opera, Sweden, and Creon in Haydn's Orfeo at Enschede; Strauss's Harlekin for the Minnesota Symphony Orchestra, Marcello and the Count in Capriccio at Copenhagen; concerts include the Brahms Requiem and Mahler's Des Knaben Wunderhorn; Season 2001–02 with Count Almariva at Glyndebourne, Silvio in Pagliacci at Brussels and Eugene Onegin in Malmö. *Honours:* Christina and Birgit Nilsson Awards. *Current Management:* Ann Braathen Artist Management AB, Folskolegatan 5, 117 35 Stockholm, Sweden. *Telephone:* 8 556 908 50. *Fax:* 8 556 908 51. *E-mail:* info@braathenmanagement.com. *Website:* www.braathenmanagement.com.

LARSSON, Charlotte; Singer (Soprano); b. 1966, Sweden. *Education:* Studied at the State Opera School in Stockholm from 1989. *Career:* Debut: Norrlandsoperan as Signe in Stenhammar's Gillet pa Solhaug; Concert appearances including opening of Århus Festival, 1991; Sang at Karlstad Opera Festival in 1992 and as Liu in Turandot for Stockholm Folkoperan in 1993; Other roles include Mozart's Pamina and Sandrina, Rosalinda and Dvořák's Rusalka; Engaged at Stockholm Royal Opera, 1994. *Address:* Nordic Artists Management, Sveavagen 76, 11359 Stockholm, Sweden.

LASCARRO, Juanita; Singer (soprano); b. 1971, Bogota, Colombia. *Education:* Studied in Bogota and at the Cologne Musikhochschule, notably with Hartmut Holl and Mitsuko Shirai. *Career:* Has sung at the Leipzig Opera and at Cologne Opera as Papagena and in Peter Grimes; Markgräflichen Theater Bayreuth in JC Bach's Amadis des Gaules; Appearances at the Teatro Colón Bogotá as Adina, Susanna and Micaela; British opera debut as Daphne at Garsington, 1995; Season 1996–97 with Netherlands Opera as Euridice in L'Orfeo, Frasquita and First Flower Maiden at the Opéra Bastille and Mahler's 4th Symphony in Germany; Sang Euridice at the Barbican Theatre, 1998; Season 2000 Handel's Cantata Galatea e Polifemo at Beaune and Cavalli's Dido for Lausanne Opera; Other appearances as Mozart's Susanna, (Opéra Bastille and Deutsche Oper Berlin); Janáček's Vixen for WNO, Mélisande at La Monnaie, Brussels, Cavalli's Dido at Lausanne and Montpellier; Weill's Der Kuhhandel with the BBc at the Barbicam; Season 2002–03 with Emma in Schubert's Fierrabras, Manon and Pamina for Oper Frankfurt; Leoncavallo's Mimi in Vienna. *Honours:* Winner of the Leipzig Opera, Mendelssohn and Munchner Konzertgesellschaft Competitions (1992–93). *Current Management:* Harrison/Parrott Ltd, 12 Penzance Place, London, W11 4PA, England. *Telephone:* (20) 7229 9166. *Fax:* (20) 7221 5042. *Website:* www.harrisonparrott.com.

LASKE, Otto, BMus, MMus, PhD, EdD; composer, poet and musicologist; b. 23 April 1936, Olesnica, Oels, Silesia, Poland. *Education:* Akademie für Tonkunst, Darmstadt, New England Conservatory of Music, Boston, USA, Goethe University, Frankfurt am Main, Germany, Harvard University, USA, Institute of Sonology, Utrecht, Netherlands. *Career:* debut, Composers' Forum, New York 1969; freelance composer; Prof. of Music; Artistic Dir, Newcomp Inc 1981–91. *Compositions:* 65 works for instrumental, vocal and electro-acoustic music including: Kyrie Eleison, a cappella, 1969, Distances and Proximities for tape, 1973, Perturbations for chamber orchestra, 1979, Terpsichore for tape, 1980, Soliloquy for double bBass, 1984, Furies And Voices, 1989, Treelink for tape, 1992. *Publications:* Music, Memory and Thought 1977, Understanding Music with Al (co-ed.) 1992. *Address:* 83 Appleton Street, Arlington, MA 02174, USA.

LASSEN, Morten Ernst; Singer (Baritone); b. 1969, Denmark. *Education:* Diploma, Royal Danish Academy of Music, with Professor Kirsten Buhl-Miller, 1996. *Career:* Debut: Papageno with The Young Operacompagnie, 1993; Sang Bach's B minor Mass, St John and St Matthew Passions, as Jesus and the bass arias; Fauré's Requiem, Handel's Messiah, Mahler's Des Knaben Wunderhorn; Concerts with MDR-Sinfonieorchester, Berliner Symfoniker, Deutsches Symfonie Orchester Berlin, Danish Radio Orchestras; Several radio and television productions; Appearances in festivals of modern music, including Davos Musikfestival with works by Kurt Weill and Ernst Krenek; Season 1996–97, Sang Masetto at Confidencen in Stockholm, and sang at Tiroler Landestheater at Innsbruck as Dandini in Cenerentola and in Willi's Schlafes Bruder; Season 1999–2000 at Deutsche Oper Berlin, Papageno in Die Zauberflöte, Sharpless in Madama Butterfly, Schaunard in La Bohème, Masetto in Don Giovanni, Dancairo in Carmen and

Bill in Mahagonny; Concert engagements include appearances with the Danish symphony orchestras and bass part in B minor Mass with Danish Radio Symfony Orchestra conducted by Herbert Blomstedt; Several recitals in Denmark and abroad. *Honours:* Carl Nielsen Travel Scholarship, 1996; EBU Competition Winner, 1997; Prize Winner, VII International Hugo Wolf Lieder Competition, Stuttgart; Aksel Schiotz Prize, 1997. *Current Management:* IMG Artists. *Address:* c/o IMG Artists, Lovell House, 616 Chiswick High Road, London W4 5RX, England.

LASSMANN, Peep; Pianist; b. 19 March 1948, Tartu, Estonia; m. Anne Lassmann, 5 Nov 1982, 1 s. *Education:* Tallinn Conservatory, 1966–71; Pianist Diploma, Moscow Conservatory, postgraduate studies, 1971–73. *Career:* Teacher, 1973; Associate Professor, 1985; Head of Piano Department, 1987; Professor and Prorector, 1991; Rector of Tallinn Conservatory, 1992 (since 1993 Estonian Academy of Music); Many Concert Tours in 23 Countries; Recent Recitals, Complete Piano Works of Messiaen; mem, Estonian Piano Teachers Association (President); Music Council of Estonia, (President). *Recordings:* E Tubin Concertino for piano and orchestra, A Rubinstein Sextet for piano and wind instruments; Many recordings in Estonian, Swedish and Moscow Radios. *Contributions:* Numerous articles in various Estonian newspapers and magazines. *Honours:* Various Prizes and Diplomas from The Competitions of Pianists of USSR; The Musician of the Year 1989 of the Estonian Radio Merited Artist of Estonia, 1987. *Address:* Trummi 23–26, Tallinn 200026, Estonia.

LASZLO, Magda; Singer (Soprano); b. 1919, Hungary. *Education:* Studied at Franz Liszt Academy, Budapest with Irene Stoasser and Ferenc Szekelyhedi. *Career:* Debut: Budapest in 1943 as Elisabeth in Tannhäuser and Amelia in Simon Boccanegra; Resident in Rome from 1946; Sang in the radio and stage premieres of Dallapiccola's Il Prigioniero in 1949 and 1950; Sang further in modern works by Ghedini, Casella, Lualdi and Malipiero; Guest appearances in Austria, Germany, France, Netherlands and Switzerland; Covent Garden in 1954 as Cressida in the premiere of Walton's Troilus and Cressida; Glyndebourne, 1953–54, 1962–63 as Mozart's Cherubino, Gluck's Alceste and as Monteverdi's Poppea; Other roles were Marie in Wozzeck, Wagner's Isolde and Senta, Strauss's Daphne, Busoni's Turandot, Alfano's Sakuntala, Prokofiev's Renata, Handel's Agrippina, Roxana in King Roger, Gluck's Elena and Bellini's Norma. *Recordings:* Bach Cantatas and St Matthew Passion; L'Incoronazione di Poppea.

LATARCHE, Vanessa Jayne, FTCL, LRAM, ARCM; British pianist and teacher; b. 3 April 1959, Isleworth, Middlesex, England. *Education:* Royal College of Music, studied with Kendall Taylor. *Career:* broadcasts for Radio 3, BBC television and Cable television in USA; Piano Teacher at Purcell School and Royal College of Music, Junior Department; Performed at Harrogate International Festival, Battle Festival, various music clubs and concert halls throughout the United Kingdom including Fairfield Halls, Croydon, Purcell Room and Queen Elizabeth Hall and Wigmore Hall, London; Recital and concerto appearances; Director of Latarche Trio. *Address:* 10 Ravenswood Gardens, Isleworth, Middlesex TW7 4JG, England.

LATCHEM, Malcolm; Violinist; b. 28 Jan. 1931, Salisbury, England; m. 24 June 1964, 1 s., 3 d. *Education:* Royal College of Music, 1947–49, 1951–53; ARCM Performers. *Career:* Philharmonia Orchestra, 1960–65; Sub-Leader, London Philharmonic Orchestra, 1965–69; Dartington String Quartet, 1969–80; Founder Member, 1959, Academy of St Martin-in-the-Fields. *Recordings:* Chamber music with Academy of St Martin-in-the-Fields Chamber Ensemble; Handel Trio Sonatas; Mozart's Divertimenti; Spohr's Double Quartets; Other chamber music. *Honours:* Honorary MMus, Bristol University, 1980. *Address:* Station House, Staverton, Totnes, Devon TQ9 6 AG, England. *Telephone:* (1803) 762670.

LATEINER, Jacob; Pianist; b. 31 May 1928, Havana, Cuba. *Education:* Studied in Havana with Jascha Fischermann, 1934–40 and Curtis Institute from 1940 with Isabelle Vengerova; Studied chamber music with Piatigorsky and Primrose. *Career:* Debut: With the Philadelphia Orchestra under Ormandy in 1945; Tanglewood Festival with Koussevitsky in 1947; New York recital debut in 1948; Tours of Europe, USA and Australia from 1954; Premiered the Concerto by Elliott Carter in 1967 and the Third Sonata of Roger Sessions in 1968; Taught at Mannes College, 1963–70, and Juilliard School, NY, from 1966. *Recordings:* Works by Beethoven and other 19th Century repertory; Contemporary American works. *Address:* Juilliard School of Music, Piano Faculty, Lincoln Plaza, New York, NY 10023, USA.

LATHAM, Alison Mary, BMus; Editor and Writer; b. (Alison Mary Goodall), 13 July 1948, Southsea, England; m. Richard Latham; three s. *Education:* The Maynard School, Exeter, Birmingham Univ. *Career:* Senior Copy Ed., The New Grove Dictionary of Music and Musicians 1971–77; Asst Ed., The Grove Concise Dictionary of Music 1986–88; Co-Ed., The Musical Times 1977–88; Publications Ed., Royal Opera House,

Convent Garden 1989–2000; Ed., Edinburgh Festival programmes 2003–; mem. Royal Soc. of Arts, Royal Musical Asscn, Soc. of Authors, Critics Circle. *Publications:* The Cambridge Music Guide (with Stanley Sadie) 1985, The Oxford Companion to Music (ed. with Roger Parker) 2001, Sing Ariel: Essays and Thoughts for Alexander Goehr's Seventieth Birthday (ed.) 2003, various dictionaries, CD booklets, programmes. *Current Management:* c/o Joanna Harris, Oxford University Press, Walton Street, Oxford, OX2 6DP, England. *Telephone:* (1865) 556767 (office). *Fax:* (1865) 354635 (office). *E-mail:* joanna.harris@oup .com (office). *Website:* www.oup.com (office).

LATHAM, Catherine; Oboe d'amore player; b. 1965, England. *Education:* Guildhall School of Music, London,. *Career:* concerts with the European Baroque Orchestra, 1985–86, under Ton Koopman, William Christie and Roger Norrington: Regular appearances with the London Handel Orchestra (Flavio and Muzio Scevola, 2001); The King's Consort, and the Orchestra of the Age of Enlightenment; Concerto performances in Edinburgh, Dublin, Utrecht and the Wigmore Hall, London; Tour of Europe in John Eliot Gardiner's Bach Cantata Pilgrimage, 2000; Handel's Amadigi with The New Chamber Opera at New College, Oxford, 2001. *Recordings include:* Bach Brandenburg Concertos, Concertos for 2 oboes by Vivaldi and Albinoni. *Address:* c/o The King's Consort, 34 St Mary's Grove, London W4 3LN, England.

LATHAM-KOENIG, Jan; Conductor and Pianist; b. 15 Dec. 1953, London, England. *Education:* Studied at the Royal College of Music with Norman del Mar, Kendall Taylor and Lamar Crowson. *Career:* Regular appearances as conductor with Royal Philharmonic, Philarmonia, London Philharmonic, BBC Symphony, BBC Philharmonic Orchestra and BBC National Orchestra of Wales; Guest Conductor of the Los Angeles Philharmonic and St Paul Chamber Orchestras, the Danish and Swedish Radio Orchestras, Stockholm Philharmonic, Maggio Musicale Orchestras, RAI, Italy, Zürich Tonhalle and the Gulbenkian Orchestra in Lisbon; Founded the Koenig Ensemble in 1976; Concert Pianist until 1981; Opera engagements include Giulio Cesare with Royal Swedish Opera in 1985, La Vestale at Genoa in 1984, From the House of the Dead at Venice, 1985–86, Tosca for English National Opera in 1987, The Cunning Little Vixen at Vienna Volksoper in 1992; Festival appearances with La Straniera at Wexford, 1987, Manon and Macbeth at Macerata, 1987–88, world premiere of L'Ispirazione by Bussotti at Maggio Musicale in 1988, and Catalani's Dejanice at Lucca; Has conducted Szymanowski's King Roger for Danish Radio and a cycle of Weill operas and cantatas for West German Radio; Rome Opera in 1988 with the premiere of Bussotti's Fedra returning with Donizetti's Poliuto to open the 1988–89 season; Debut at Vienna Staatsoper in 1988 in Macbeth; Conducted Leoncavallo's La Bohème at Venice in 1990 and Weill's Mahagonny at the 1990 Maggio Musicale Florence; Permanent Guest Conductor at Vienna State Opera from 1991; Conducted Aida at Covent Garden, 1996; Danish premiere of Poulenc's Carmélites, 1997 and at the London Prom concerts, 1999; Jenůfa at Santiago, 1998. *Recordings include:* Weill's Mahagonny with Anja Silja; Der Zar Lässt sich Photographieren; Walton Concertos with London Philharmonic Orchestra. *Current Management:* Askonas Holt Ltd, Lonsdale Chambers, 27 Chancery Lane, London, WC2A 1PF, England. *Telephone:* (20) 7400-1700. *Fax:* (20) 7400-1799. *E-mail:* info@ askonasholt.co.uk. *Website:* www.askonasholt.co.uk.

LATRY, Olivier; French organist; b. 22 Feb. 1962, Boulogne-sur-Mer; m. Marie-Therese; three c. *Education:* Saint Maur-des-Fossés Conservatoire with Gaston Litaize, Paris Conservatoire with Jean-Claude Raynaud. *Career:* organiste titulaire, Meaux Cathedral 1981–85; organiste titulaire du grand orgue, Cathédrale Notre-Dame de Paris 1985–; teacher of organ, Conservatoire at St Maur-des-Fossés 1990–95; Organ Prof., Paris Conservatoire 1995–; recitals in Europe, Russia, N and S America, Japan and Australia, concentrating on 17th- to 20th-century French organ music; renowned for improvisation. *Recordings include:* music of J S Bach, the complete organ works of Maurice Duruflé, Louis Vierne's Symphonies 2 and 3, Widor's Symphonies 5 and 6, Boëllmann's Suite Gothique, works by Litaize, the complete organ works of Olivier Messiaen, transcriptions for the organ ('Midnight at Notre-Dame'). *Honours:* Prix de la Fondation Cino et Simone del Duca 2000. *Address:* c/o Cathédrale Notre-Dame de Paris, Ile de la Cité 6, Place du Parvis, 75004 Paris, France (office).

LAUBENTHAL, Horst; Singer (Tenor); b. 8 March 1939, Duderstadt, Germany; m. Marga Schiml. *Education:* Studied in Munich with Rudolf Laubenthal. *Career:* Debut: Würzburg, 1967, as Mozart's Don Ottavio; Staatsoper Stuttgart from 1968, in operas by Wagner, Mozart and Beethoven; Guest appearances in Vienna, Hamburg and Barcelona; Bayreuth Festival, 1970, as the Steersman in Der fliegende Holländer; Deutsche Oper Berlin, as Lensky in Eugene Onegin and Pfitzner's Palestrina; Glyndebourne, 1972, as Belmonte in Die Entführung; Paris Opéra, 1977; Turin, 1985, as Tamino in Die Zauberflöte (returned 1987, as Don Ottavio); Often heard as the Evangelist in the Passions of Bach. *Recordings:* Tannhäuser, Fidelio, Die Meistersinger; Wozzeck and Lulu;

Bach Cantatas and Christmas Oratorio; Trionfi by Orff; Konrgold's Violanta; Schubert's Lazarus.

LAUBER, Anne (Marianne); Composer and Conductor; b. 28 July 1943, Zürich, Switzerland. *Education:* Studied at the Lausanne Conservatory and the University of Montreal, 1973–77, with André Prevost. *Career:* Teacher at French-language universities in Canada and president of the Canadian Music Centre from 1987; Commissions from leading orchestras and soloists. *Compositions include:* Au-Dela Du Mur Du Son, symphonic tale, 1983; Concertos for string quartet, 1983, Violin, 1986, and Piano, 1988; Le Songe for flute and string quartet, 1985; Jesus Christus, oratorio, 1986; Piano Quintet, 1989; Requiem, 1989; Canadian Overture, for strings, 1989; Other vocal music. *Address:* c/o Canadian Music Centre, 20 St Joseph Street, Toronto, Ontario M4Y 1J9, Canada.

LAUFER, Beatrice; Composer; b. 27 April 1923, New York City, USA. *Education:* Studied at Juilliard School from 1944 with Roger Sessions, Marion Bauer and Vittorio Giannini. *Career:* Performances of her music in Germany, Stockholm, China and USA. *Compositions include:* 2 Symphonies, 1944 and 1961; Opera Ile, after O'Neill's Long Voyage Home, premiered at Stockholm in 1958, revived at Yale School of Music under Phylis Curtin in 1977 and at Shanghai in 1988; Violin Concerto; Concerto for flute, oboe trumpet and strings, 1962; Lyric for string trio, 1966; The Great God Brown, ballet, 1966; My Brother's Keeper, biblical opera, 1968; Adam's Rib for soloists, chorus and orchestra; Concertante for violin, viola and orchestra, 1986; Choral music. *Address:* c/o ASCAP, ASCAP Building, 1 Lincoln Plaza, New York, NY 10023, USA.

LAUGHLIN, Roy; conductor and pianist; b. 1954, Belfast, Northern Ireland. *Education:* Edinburgh and Durham Univs. *Career:* conducted Haydn's L'Infedeltà Delusa at Durham; Head of Music with Opera North, conducting The Magic Flute, Orpheus in The Underworld, La Cenerentola and Der Freischütz; Twice Chorus Master at Wexford Festival and conducted Die Schöpfung in 1989; Assistant Conductor of Halifax Choral Society; Recent engagements with Opera North include Fidelio, The Pearl Fishers, Peter Grimes and the British premiere production of Verdi's Jérusalem in 1990, also La Traviata, Attila and Faust; Season 1992–93 with Falstaff for English Touring Opera and Cimarosa's Secret Marriage for the Cheltenham and Buxton Festivals; Led British Youth Opera in La Bohème, 1998. *Current Management:* Robert Gilder & Co., Enterprise House, 59–65 Upper Ground, London, SE1 9PQ, England. *Telephone:* (20) 7928-9008. *Fax:* (20) 7928-9755. *E-mail:* rgilder@robert-gilder.com.

LAUKKA, Raimo; Singer (Baritone); b. 1954, Finland. *Education:* Studied in Helsinki. *Career:* Sang with Finnish National Opera from 1989, as Mozart's Figaro, Count, Don Giovanni, Guglielmo and Papageno; Posa in Don Carlos, 1995–96, Germont, Eugene Onegin, Gounod's Valentin in Faust, Donner in Das Rheingold (1996), Escamillo and Marcello; Tampere, 1996, in the title role of Dallapiccola's Il Prigioniero; Savonlinna Festival, 1996, as Wolfram in Tannhäuser and Carlo in La Forza del Destino, 1998; Concert tours include USA, 1988, with Neeme Järvi; London Proms, 2002. *Recordings include:* Kullervo by Sibelius. *Address:* c/o Finnish National Opera, PO Box 176, Helsingkatu 58, 00251 Helsinki, Finland.

LAUKVIK, Jon; Organist, Harpsichordist and Composer; b. 16 Dec. 1952, Oslo, Norway. *Education:* Studied Organ, Church Music and Piano, Conservatory of Oslo, 1972–74; Organ with Professor M Schneider, Harpsichord with Professor H Ruf, Musikhochschule, Cologne, 1974–80; Organ studies with M C Alain, Paris, 1975–77. *Career:* Debut: Oslo, 1973; Recitals in Western and Eastern Europe, Israel, Japan, Korea and USA; Recordings for several European radio stations; Masterclasses; Jury Member, international competitions. *Compositions:* Via Crucis; Triptychon; Suite for organ; Anrufung for 2 organs, tape and brass; Euphonie I for organ and 5 percussionists; Euphonie III for cello and organ; Contre-danse for orchestra. *Recordings:* Neresheim Monastery (works by J. S. and C P E Bach, Raison, Kittel). *Publications:* Orgelschule zur historischen Aufführungspraxis, 1990, English Version, Historical Performance Practice in Organ Playing, 1996; G F Handel: Organ Concertos op 7 and Nos 13–16 (with W Jacob), 1990; Orgel und Orgelmusik in der Romantik, 2000. *Honours:* 1st Prize and Bach Prize, International Organ Week, Nuremberg, 1977. *Address:* Alte Weinsteige 20, LD-70180 Stuttgart, Germany.

LAURENCE, Elizabeth; English/French singer (mezzo-soprano); b. (Elizabeth Scott), 22 Nov. 1949, Harrogate, Yorkshire, England. *Education:* Princess Helena Coll., Herts, Colchester School of Art and Trinity Coll. of Music, London. *Career:* Vienna in Le Marteau sans Maître under Boulez 1983; further concerts with Barenboim, Casadesus, Downes, Myrat, Jordan and Zender; recording for French television, L'Heure Espagnole by Ravel 1985–86; sang at Madrid Opera as Jocasta in Oedipus Rex 1986, also in Buffalo, USA with M. Valdes 1991, Paris Opéra as Erda in Siegfried and as Cherubino in Le nozze di Figaro, returning for the 1989 world premiere of Der Meister und Margarita by Höller; sang in the world premiere of The Electrification of the Soviet Union by Nigel Osborne, Glyndebourne Festival 1987; tour of Italy and Germany with Ensemble Intercontemporain 1987, in Le Marteau sans maître and Matchavarian ballet music, Pierrot Lunaire, Proms 1987; sang in the premiere of Boulez's revised version of Le Visage Nuptial, La Scala, Milan 1988; sang Fricka in Das Rheingold at Salle Pleyel, Paris 1988, and Schoenberg's Op 22 songs and Mahler's 3rd Symphony in Turin under Lothar Zagrosek and Rudolf Barshai; Covent Garden debut in the British premiere of Berio's Un Re in Ascolto 1989, La Bastille Opéra, Paris 1991; appeared as Judith in a BBC TV production of Bartók's Bluebeard's Castle 1989; contemporary recital of Berio, Bartók, Britten, Reger and Schoenberg at Festival of Montreux; Gurrelieder at Leeds Town Hall 1989; sang Erda in Rheingold at Bonn Opera 1990, Ligeti's Requiem in Belgium and Germany 1991; sang and recorded Le Rossignol, Stravinsky, for the Proms with Boulez; sang Lady de Hautdesert in the premiere of Birtwistle's Gawain at Covent Garden 1991; season 1991–92 as Ravel's Concepcion at Turin and the Duchess of Alba in the premiere of Osborne's Terrible Mouth at the Almeida Theatre; Verdi Requiem, London 1992; season 1993, Die Wuste bat zwolf Ding, Zender, Berlin Opera (concert), Folksongs by Berio, Ulisse by Dallapiccola, Salzburg Festival; season 1994, The Page in Salome, Opéra de Marseille, toured Germany in Pulcinella by Stravinsky, Orchestre de Paris; season 1996, toured France in Pelléas et Mélisande by Debussy, Flora in La Traviata, Marseille Opera, Salzburg Festival with Ravel's Trois Poèmes de S. Mallarmé, L'Enfance du Christ by Berlioz in Malaga, Spain; French premiere of Gurlitt's Wozzeck in Rouen and Caen Opéras; Schoenberg recital, Academia S. Caecilia, Rome; Japanese premiere of Bluebeard's Castle by Bartók in Tokyo conducted by Peter Eötvös; debut at Théâtre Champs Elysées, Paris, with Les Nuits d'été by Berlioz; Stabat Mater by Rossini in Imola; season 1997, Drei Lieder by Stockhausen at Concertgebouw, Amsterdam; Sechs Gesänge by Zemlinsky with Vienna Philharmonic; Second Symphony by L. Bernstein; Das Lied von der Erde Kindertotenlieder; concert of symphonic music 1998, Die Mutter in Lulu, Paris Bastille Opéra; La madre in Nono's Al gran sole carico d'amore, Hamburg Staatsoper; Ommou in Hölszky's Die Wände, Frankfurt Staatsoper; debut as Mère Marie in Les Dialogues des Carmelites at La Scala, Milan; Leucade: L. Martin Toulouse/Nice; premiered Bluebeard's Castle in Tbilisi, Georgia; also Phaedra: Britten; sang Rückert Lieder and Act 3 of Die Walküre in BBC Proms, London 2000; Rihm: Die Eröberung von Mexico under M. Stentz at Frankfurt Staatsoper 2001–02; Geneviève in Pelléas et Mélisande, De Vlaamse Opera, Antwerp 2001; Gertrude in A. Thomas' Hamlet for Chelsea Opera Group; Bluebeard's Castle for Graz Opera 2001; regular recitals in Europe; season 2002, Erwartung SWF Saarbrücken; Rihm's Dies; Henze's The Bassarids, Amsterdam; Henze's We Come to the River, Hamburg Staatsoper; Monleone's Cavelleria Rusticana, Schmidt's Mascagni and Notre Dame at Festival Montpellier; Frau ohne Schatten, Der Rosenkavalier and Lulu at Opéra Bastille; concert of Berio in Milan; recital of Schoenberg with Jay Gottlieb; Falstaff with NSO, UK 2004; has given masterclasses in France and the UK. *Television:* numerous TV recordings, including educational programmes on 20th century music, P. Boulez, D. Masson. *Recordings include:* Le Marteau sans Maître, Le Visage Nuptial, Bartók's Bluebeard's Castle, Gurlitt's Wozzeck, L'Heure Espagnole, Stravinsky's Le Rossignol. *Honours:* Diapason d'or, Prix d'Italia 1988, Grand Prix du Syndicat de la Presse 1997–98. *Current Management:* Robert Gilder & Co., Enterprise House, 59–65 Upper Ground, London, SE1 9PQ, England. *Telephone:* (20) 7928-9008. *Fax:* (20) 7928-9755. *E-mail:* rgilder@robert-gilder.com. *Address:* 123 rue de Grenelle, 75007 Paris, France (home). *Telephone:* 1 47 05 01 27 (home). *Fax:* 1 47 05 57 93 (home). *E-mail:* elizabethlaurence@yahoo.co.uk (home).

LAURENS, Guillemette; Singer (Mezzo-soprano); b. 1950, Fontainebleau, France. *Education:* Studied at the Toulouse Conservatoire and the Paris Opéra Studio. *Career:* Debut: Paris Salle Favart as Anne Trulove in The Rake's Progress; Has performed throughout Europe, the USA and South America; Sang Cybele in Lully's Atys at the Paris Opéra with Les Arts Florissants; Repertoire includes German Lieder, French and Italian Baroque chamber music, Pierrot Lunaire by Schoenberg, La Clemenza di Tito, Giulio Cesare, and I Puritani (Paris Opéra); Appeared with Capriccio Stravagante in America in 1989; Engagements with the Ensemble Sequentia in 12th Century Liturgical Drama; Sang at the Festival of Aix-en-Provence in Iphigénie en Aulide, with John Eliot Gardiner, and Towards Bach concert series on London's South Bank in 1989; Monteverdi's Penelope at the 1998 Vienna Festival. *Recordings:* Monteverdi's Vespers with Philippe Herreweghe; Atys and Il Ballo dell'Ingrate, conducted by William Christie; Bach's B minor Mass with Gustav Leonhardt; Charpentier's Le Malade Imaginaire under Marc Minkowski; Diana in Iphigénie en Aulide under John Eliot Gardiner. *Address:* Opéra et Concert, 1 Rue Volney, F–75002, Paris, France.

LAURIE, Alison Margaret, MA, BMus, PhD, ARCM; Music Librarian and Musicologist; b. 5 Jan. 1935, Glossop, England. *Education:* Beacon School, Bridge of Allan, Stirlingshire, Glasgow Univ., Univ. of Cambridge. *Career:* Senior Asst Librarian, Glasgow Univ. Library 1961–63;

Music Librarian, Reading Univ. Library 1963–99; mem. Purcell Soc. Cttee (sec. 1983–88, chair. 1989–), Royal Musical Asscn. *Publications:* Purcell: Dioclesian 1961, Dido and Aeneas (with Thurston Dart) 1961, King Arthur 1971, Secular Songs for Solo Voice 1985, The Indian Queen 1994, The Gresham Autograph (facsimile edition introduction with Robert Thompson) 1995, Dramatic Music, Part 1; contrib. to Musik in Geschichte und Gegenwart 1973, New Grove Dictionary of Music and Musicians 1980, Music and Bibliography: Essays in Honour of Alec Hyatt King (ed. O. W. Neighbour) 1980, Source Material and the Interpretation of Music: a Memorial Volume to Thurston Dart (ed. Ian Bent) 1981, Music in Britain: The Seventeenth Century (ed. Ian Spink) 1992, Henry Purcell, Dido and Aeneas: an Opera (ed. Curtis Price) 1986, Purcell Studies 1995, periodicals Brio, Fontes Artis Musicae, Irish Musical Studies, Musical Times, Proceedings of the Royal Musical Association. *Address:* 123 Nightingale Road, Woodley, Reading, RG5 3LZ, England (home). *Telephone:* (118) 9696313 (home).

LAVENDER, Justin; Singer (tenor); b. 4 June 1951, Bedford, England. *Career:* Debut: Sang Nadir in Les Pêcheurs de perles at Sydney Opera House, 1982; Has sung Medoro in Haydn's Orlando Paladino at St Gallen, Tamino at Vienna Staatsoper, Pilade (Rossini's Ermione) at Madrid, Le Comte Ory at La Scala, Don Ottavio for Rome Opera and Arnold (Guillaume Tell) and Almaviva at Covent Garden; Appearances in premieres of Il Ritorno di Casanova by Arrigo at the Grand Théâtre Geneva and La Noche Triste by Prodomidès at Théâtre des Champs Elysées, Paris; Further engagements as Fernande in La Favorite at Vichy, Almaviva at Pittsburgh (US debut), Belmonte in Vienna and Berlin, Ferrando (Così fan tutte) at Essen, Lindoro at Buxton Festival and Neocles in Le Siège de Corinthe by Rossini at Madrid and the Festival Hall, London; Season 1993 in Il Pirata at Lausanne, Marzio in Mitridate and Arone in Mosè in Egitto at Covent Garden; Sang Don José in Raymond Gubay's Carmen, Albert Hall, 1997; Gluck's Admeto at Drottningholm, 1998; Concert repertoire includes Bartók's Cantata Profana with Georg Solti, Schubert's Mass in E flat with Giulini and Berlin Philharmonic, Schnittke's Faust Cantata under Claudio Abbado and Oedipus Rex conducted by Bernard Haitink; Mahler's 8th Symphony at the Royal Albert Hall, 2001; Season 2000 as the Duke of Mantua for Florida Opera, the Berlioz Faust in Helsinki and Count Hugo in Spohr's Faust at Cologne; Other conductors have included John Lubbock (Dream of Gerontius), John Pritchard, Menuhin, Alberto Zedda and Leonard Slatkin;. *Contributions:* The Singer, Rhinegold Publications. *Current Management:* Athole Still International Management, Forresters Hall, 25–27 Westow Street, London, SE19 3RY, England. *Telephone:* (20) 8771-5271. *Fax:* (20) 8768-6600. *Website:* www.atholestill.com.

LAVIRGEN, Pedro; Singer (Tenor); b. 31 July 1930, Bujalance, Andalusia, Spain. *Education:* Studied with Miguel Barrosa in Madrid. *Career:* Debut: Mexico City in 1964 as Radames; European debut at the Teatro del Liceo, Barcelona as Don José; Sang at Metropolitan in 1969 as Cavaradossi in Tosca, Verona Arena in 1974 and 1976 as Radames, Covent Garden in 1975 and 1978 as Don José and Pollione in Norma, La Scala Milan in 1975 as Don José repeating the role at the 1978 Edinburgh Festival; Other appearances in Hamburg, Munich, Prague, Budapest and Madrid. *Recordings include:* Il Retablo de Maese Pedro by De Falla.

LAVISTA, Mario; Composer; b. 3 April 1943, Mexico City. *Education:* Studied composition with Carlos Chávez, musical analysis with Rodolfo Halffter, National Conservatory of Mexico, 1963–67; Studied in Paris with Jean Etienne Marie, in Cologne with K Stockhausen and Henry Pousseaur, 1967–70. *Career:* Professor of Theory and Composition, National Conservatory of Mexico, 1970–; Founder of group, Quanta, 1970–73; Editor of Pauta, Journal of Music, 1982–; mem, International Society of Contemporary Music; Mexican Editions of Music; National College of Mexico; Mexican Academy of Arts. *Compositions include:* Canto Del Alba in C for flute; Nocturno in G for flute; Lamento for bass flute; Ofrenda for alto recorder; Dusk for contrabass; Cante for 2 guitars; Marsias for oboe and crystal cups; Ficciones for orchestra; Simurg for piano; Lacrymosa for orchestra; Missa ad Consolationis Dominam Nostram for choir a capella; Clepsidra for orchestra; Reflections Of The Night for string quartet; Hacia El Comienzo for mezzo-soprano and orchestra, poems by Octavio Paz; Ciucani in B flat for flute and clarinet; Madrigal in B flat for clarinet; Three Nocturnes for mezzo-soprano and orchestra, poems by Alvaro Mutis; Aura, one-act opera based on Aura, a short story by Carlos Fuentes; Music for My Neighbor for string quartet; Danza isorrítmica for four percussionists; Lacrymosa for orchestra, 1994. *Address:* Pirineos 455, Lomas de Chapultepec, 11000, México, DF, Mexico.

LAWLESS, Stephen; Stage Director; b. 1958, England. *Career:* Director of Productions for Glyndebourne Touring Opera, 1986–91; Death in Venice televised and staged at the 1992 Festival; Directed The Pearl Fishers for Scottish Opera, Falstaff at Glyndebourne and Rameau's Les Boréades at the Royal Academy, 1985; Kirov Opera debut with Boris Godunov, 1990, also directed the above at the Vienna Staatsoper and La Fenice Venice, 1994; Figaro and Rosenkavalier for Canadian Opera, Ariadne and Ballo in Maschera in Los Angeles, Capriccio in San Francicso and Così fan tutte in Chicago; Hamlet by Thomas at the Vienna Volksoper and a Baroque double bill at Innsbruck: Venus and Adonis, with Dido and Aeneas; Season 1996–97 with Wozzeck in Braunschweig, Carmen for New Israeli Opera, Il Trovatore in Los Angeles, The Rake's Progress in Pisa and Mozart's Finta Semplice at Potsdam; Has also directed opera in Seoul and Hong Kong; L'Elisir d'amore at Madrid, 1998. *Current Management:* Askonas Holt Ltd, Lonsdale Chambers, 27 Chancery Lane, London, WC2A 1PF, England. *Telephone:* (20) 7400-1700. *Fax:* (20) 7400-1799. *E-mail:* info@askonasholt.co.uk. *Website:* www.askonasholt.co.uk.

LAWLOR, Thomas; Singer (Bass-Baritone); b. 1938, Dublin, Ireland. *Education:* BA, National University of Ireland; Dublin College of Music; Guildhall School of Music. *Career:* Sang with D'Oyly Carte Company, 1963–71 with tours of North America; Glyndebourne, 1971–, in Eugene Onegin, Ariadne, Così fan tutte, Die Entführung, La Bohème, Le nozze di Figaro, Capriccio, Intermezzo, and The Cunning Little Vixen; Engagements with Opera North in A Village Romeo and Juliet, Tosca, Der Rosenkavalier, Der Freischütz, A Midsummer Night's Dream, Manon Lescaut, the premiere of Rebecca by Wilfred Josephs in 1983, Werther, La Cenerentola, Beatrice and Benedict, Jonny Spielt Auf, Die Meistersinger, The Golden Cockerel and Intermezzo; Further appearances with Kent Opera, English Music Theatre, New Sadler's Wells Opera and Opera Northern Ireland, Royal Opera, Dublin Grand Opera; Sang in Rising of The Moon at Wexford Festival in 1990 and Prokofiev's The Duenna; Regular broadcaster on Radio Telefis Eireann and on BBC radio and television; mem, Faculty Member of Summer Conservatory of Music, Bay View, MI, USA. *Address:* Music International, 13 Ardilaun Road, Highbury. London N5 2QR, England.

LAWRENCE, Amy; Singer (soprano); b. 1962, Philadelphia, USA. *Education:* Florida State University, New England Conservatory and Zürich Opera, 1992. *Career:* Sang in La Forza del Destino and Albert Herring at Zürich, Der Schauspieldirektor by Mozart at Basle; Kiel Opera from 1994, as Dianora in Mona Lisa by Schillings, Adele (Fledermaus), Constanze, Susanna, and Speranza in L'Orfeo in Monteverdi's Orfeo; Concerts include Messiah, Die Schöpfung, and Mozart's C minor Mass; Carmina Burana and Barber's Knoxville Summer of 1915 with the Louisiana Philharmonic Orchestra; Season 1997 with the Mozart's Queen of Night for the Norwegian Opera, Oslo, and at Oper Frankfurt in 1998; Constanze with Opera Memphis, 1999; In concert with Brahms Requiem in Basel and Zürich and Bernstein's Symphony No. 3, Kaddish, with London Philharmonic Orchestra. *Recordings:* Beethoven Volkslieder, Weltliche Vokalwerke; Mona Lisa, opera by Max Schillings. *Honours:* National Finalist, Metropolitan Opera Competition; Semi-finalist, Belvedere Opera Competition, New York. *Current Management:* Athole Still International Management, Forresters Hall, 25–27 Westow Street, London, SE19 3RY, England. *Telephone:* (20) 8771-5271. *Fax:* (20) 8768-6600. *Website:* www.atholestill.com.

LAWRENCE, Helen (Ruth), LRAM ARAM; Opera Singer (Mezzo-Soprano); b. 22 July 1942, London, England; m. Abraham Marcus, 1969, two c. *Education:* Royal Academy of Music, London,. *Career:* Guest Artist: Covent Garden, English National Opera, Handel Opera, Chelsea Opera, Phoenix Opera, Germany, Far East; concerts and recitals: UK music clubs and choral socs, Wigmore Hall, South Bank, Barbican, and in Germany, Italy, Netherlands, Israel; Songmakers' Almanac, SPNM, Lontano, Hallé Orchestra; Roles as Soprano include: Donna Anna, Constanze, Fiordiligi, Médée (Cherubini), Lucrezia Borgia, Lady Macbeth, Violetta, Leonora, Amelia, Abigaille, Tosca, Santuzza, Carmen; Mezzo-Soprano roles since 1989: Carmen, Fidalma, Marcellina, Azucena and Mistress Quickly; Artistic Director and Administrator, New Shakespeare Company's Opera season, Regent's Park Open Air Theatre, 1983; London Masterclasses, 1989–92; Chair., Hampstead & Highgate Festival; mem Equity; Incorporated Society of Musicians. *Recordings include:* BBC radio: Title roles Giordano's Fedora; Berthold Goldschmidt's Beatrice Cenci; recent discs: Amme Meme in Goldschmidt's Der Gewaltige Hahnrei, Berlin, 1992; Ornamente by A Krein, 1997; Portrait of an Artist, 1999. *Publications:* Life of Mozart, translation from Italian, Great Men Series for Children, A History of the Camden Festival, 2004. *Address:* 38 Glenilla Road, London, NW3 4AN, England. *E-mail:* helen@helenlawrence.co.uk.

LAWRENCE-KING, Andrew; Baroque Harpist and Director; b. 1959, Guernsey, Channel Islands. *Career:* Founder-Member and Director of The Harp Consort, Soloist and Director, appearances with Hilliard Ensemble, Hesperion XX, The King's Singers, Jordi Savall, Paul Hiller. Concerts in Europe, Scandanavia, USA, Canada, Japan, Australia, New Zealand, South America, Russia; Directed Monteverdi's Ulisse at 1992 Swedish Baroque Festival, Malmö; Handel's Almira at Bremen Goethetheatre in 1994, Purcell's Dido and Aeneas in Helsinki in 1995;

Ribayaz's Luz y Norte at Sydeny Opera House, Madrid National Auditorium, Berlin & Warsaw Philharmonics, Wigmore Hall, London (1997–1999); Florentine 1589 Intermedi, 2000; Peri's Euridice in Los Angeles, 2000; Padilla's Missa Mexicana at La Scala, Milan 2001 and Queen Elizabeth Hall, London, 2001; Solo recital to open 1992 Utrecht Festival, three concerts within 1995 Boston Early Music Festival, solo tours of USA and Japan; Season 2002–03 on tour in England, Scotalnd, Ireland, Spain and Portugal with Torrejon's la Purpura de la Rosa. *Recordings:* Over 100 titles on Hyperion, EMI, TelDec, Deutsche Harmonia Mundi, Harmonia Mundi USA and others include: The Harp of Luduvico & The Secret of the Semitones (solo harp music), Luz y Norte (Spanish 17th century dances with guitar band), Almira (Handel's first opera), La Purpura de la Rosa (first New World opera), The Italian Concerto (concerto soloist abd director, Bach, Handel, Vivaldi), Carolan's Harp (baroque Irish), Missa Mexicana (17th century polyphony and dances from Puebla Cathedral), The Play of Daniel and Miracles (medival); Concert programmes include: Luz y Norte (with Spanish dance), Missa Mexicana (vocal and instrumetal ensemble), Miracles (medival lyrics), His Majesty's Harper (solo recital) as well as orchestral repertoire and operas from medival to 21st century. *Publications:* Der Harpfenschlaeger (Historical harp technique); Luz y Norte (Spanish harp music); Article in Companion to Medieval and Renaissance Music, Dent 1992. *Honours:* First Winner of the International Award from Cambridge Early Music Society, 1992. Winner Gramophone Award, 1992; Winner German Phonographic Scoiety, Best Early Music CD, Echo Prize, 1998. *Current Management:* Helen Coombs. *Address:* 9 Cliff Street, St Peter Port, Guernsey, GY1 1LH, Channel Islands. *Telephone:* 01481 713037. *Fax:* 01481 700502. *E-mail:* TheHarpConsort@compuserve.com. *Website:* www.TheHarpConsort.com.

LAWSON, Colin (James); Clarinettist, Musicologist and Broadcaster; b. 24 July 1949, Saltburn-by-the-Sea, England; m. Hilary Birch, 16 April 1982, 1 s. *Education:* ARCM, 1967; Keble College, Oxford; BA (Oxon), 1971; MA (Oxon), 1975; MA, Birmingham University, 1972; PhD, Aberdeen University, 1976; D.Mus, London University, 2000. *Career:* Lecturer in Music at University of Aberdeen, 1973–77; Lecturer, Senior Lecturer and Reader in Music, 1978–97, Sheffield University; Guest Principal Clarinet, Orchestra of the Age of Enlightenment, 1987–; Professor of Classical Studies and Early Clarinet, Guildhall School of Music, London, 1988–91; Principal Clarinet with Hanover Band, 1987–, London Classical Players, 1989–92 and English Concert, 1991–; Visiting Lecturer, RNCM and RAM, 1992; Chair of Performance Studies, Goldsmiths College, 1998–2001; Pro Vice-Chancellor/Dean, Thames Valley University, 2001–; Current specialisation in historical performance; Member of contemporary ensemble, Lysis; Solo, chamber and orchestral appearances throughout the United Kingdom, Europe and USA; Performed Mozart Concerto on a specially designed basset clarinet. *Recordings:* With Academy of Ancient Music, Albion Ensemble, Classical Winds, CM90, Cristofori, English Concert, The Parley of Instruments, La Petite Bande, L'Ecole d'Orphée and The King's Consort; Concertos by Mahon, Hook, Weber, Spohr. *Publications:* The Chalumeau in Eighteenth-Century Music, 1981; Editor, The Cambridge Companion to the Clarinet, 1995; Mozart Clarinet Concerto, 1996; Brahms Clarinet Quintet, 1998; Co-author, The Historical Performance of Music: An Introduction, 1999; The Early Clarinet: A Practical Guide, 2000; Editor, The Cambridge Companion to the Orchestra, 2003. *Contributions:* Beethoven and the development of wind instruments, in Beethoven and the Performer, 1994; Performing through history, in Musical Performance; a guide to Understanding, 2002. *Address:* Thames Valley University, St Mary's Road, Ealing, London, W5 5RF.

LAWTON, Jeffrey; Singer (Tenor); b. 1941, Oldham, Lancashire, England. *Education:* Studied with Patrick McGuigan. *Career:* With Welsh National Opera has sung Tikhon in Katya Kabanova, also televised, various roles in The Greek Passion by Martinů, Florestan, Huon in Oberon, in Janáček's From The House of the Dead and Jenůfa as Laca, Otello, Aeneas in The Trojans and Don José; Sang Siegfried in a new production of The Ring also seen at Covent Garden in 1986, and the Emperor in Die Frau ohne Schatten; Other operatic appearances for Opera North as Erik and Florestan, in Paris, Brussels and Nancy (Otello), and as Siegmund at Cologne; Concert engagements include the Choral Symphony with the Royal Liverpool Philharmonic, Das Lied von der Erde with the BBC Symphony at the Brighton Festival and in Paris, and Mahler's 8th Symphony in Turin; Sang Siegfried in Götterdämmerung in Cologne, Edmund in Lear for English National Opera, Edinburgh Festival in 1990 in Martinů's Greek Passion, Laca in Jenůfa for Welsh National Opera and Tristan, 1992–93, Shuisky in Boris for Opera North, 1993–94, Laca for New Israeli Opera and Tristan for Scottish National Opera; Sang Herod in the final scene from Salome at Promenade Concerts in 1993; Sang Pedro in the premiere of Macmillan's Inès de Castro, Edinburgh, 1996; Wagner concert with the Philharmonia, London, 1997; Tristan for Welsh National Opera and at Buenos Aires, 1999–2000. *Recordings include:* The Greek Passion. *Current*

Management: Music International. *Address:* Music International, 13 Ardilaun Road, Highbury, London, England.

LAYTON, Richard; Violinist; b. 1940, Redditch, Worcestershire, England; m.; four c. *Education:* studied in London. *Career:* freelance musician, then co-leader of the Bournemouth Symphony Orchestra from 1964; leader of the Bournemouth Sinfonietta, 1969; soloist in concertos by Bach, Haydn, Mozart, Prokofiev and in the Brandenburg Concertos; leader of the Silvestri String Quartet, with concerts at Dartington and at Bath Festival; sub-leader of the London Philharmonic Orchestra, 1973, including appearances with the Glyndebourne Festival; guest leader with the BBC National Orchestra of Wales, ENO Orchestra, the Park Lane Players and the Philharmonia; Assoc. Leader of the Royal Philharmonic Orchestra, 1983–98; moved to France 2003. *Address:* Tessé, La Forêt de Tessé, Charente 16240, France. *E-mail:* richard.layton@wanadoo.fr.

LAYTON, Robert; Critic, Producer and Writer on Music; b. 2 May 1930, London, England; m. Ingrid Nina Thompson. *Education:* Worcester College, Oxford, 1949–53; Universities of Uppsala and Stockholm, 1953–55; Studied composition with Edmund Rubbra and history of music with Egon Wellesz; Further studies with Professor Carl-Allan Moberg. *Career:* Swedish Film Industry, 1954–55; Teacher in London, 1956–59; BBC Music Division, 1959–90 (music presentation, 1959, music talks, 1960); General Editor, BBC Music Guides, 1973–; Producer of BBC Lunchtime Concerts at St John's Smith Square, 1984–88. *Publications:* Franz Berwald, 1959; Jean Sibelius, 1965; Sibelius and His World, 1970; Dvořák Symphonies and Concertos, 1977; Sibelius, 1981; Companion to The Concerto, 1988; Responsible for Scandinavian music in The New Grove Dictionary of Music and Musicians, 1980; Translated Erik Tawaststjerna's Sibelius, Vol. I, 1976, Vol. II, 1986, Vol. III, 1997; Editor, Companion to The Symphony, 1993; Grieg–A Short Life, 1997. *Contributions:* The Symphony, 1966; The Gramophone; The Listener; The Times; Professional journals in the United Kingdom and Sweden. *Honours:* Finnish State Literary Prize, 1985; Sibelius Medal, 1987; Knight of the Order of The White Rose of Finland, 1988; Knight of the Order of the Polar Star, Sweden, 2001. *Address:* 112 Goldhurst Terrace, London NW6 3HR, England.

LAYTON, Stephen; Choral Director and Organist; b. 1962, England. *Education:* Chorister at Winchester Cathedral; Music Scholar at Eton College, Organ Scholar at King's College, Cambridge. *Career:* Appearances with King's College Chapel Choir in Europe, USA and Japan; Conducted Messiah and Gluck's Orfeo at Cambridge; Founder and Director of chamber choir Polyphony, making London Proms debut 1995, with Pärt's Passio and Dido and Aeneas; Musical Director of the Holst Singers; Organist and Director of the Choir at Temple Church, London, from 1996; Engagements with the Philharmonic Chorus, London Philharmonic Choir and BBC Symphony Orchestra Chorus; Tour of Brazil with Polyphony and Bournemouth Sinfonietta, 1995; Bach's Christmas Oratorio and Messiah with the Brandenburg Concert in London, 1996; Further concerts in Estonia, Hong Kong, France, Spain and Copenhagen; Directed Poulenc's Figure Humaine at the 1999 London Proms; Conducted the BBC Singers at the London Proms Chamber Music, 2002. *Recordings include:* Macmillan's Seven Last Words from the Cross (BMG Catalyst); Folksongs by Holst and Vaughan Williams (Hyperion). *Current Management:* Hazard Chase, Norman House, Cambridge Place, Cambridge CB2 1NS, England. *Telephone:* (1223) 312400. *Fax:* (1223) 460827. *Website:* www.hazardchase.co.uk.

LAZAR, Hans Jurgen; Singer (tenor); b. 1958, Bad Salzuflen Germany. *Education:* Studied in Detmold with Sandor Konya. *Career:* Debut: Detmold 1982, as Mozart's Pedrillo; Sang at the Hagen Opera 1985–87, Essen 1988–91, notably as Wagner's David, Janáček's Fox, Alfred in Fledermaus and Nicolai's Fenton; Frankfurt Opera 1988–91, notably as Britten's Flute; Sang Mime at Trieste and Monteverdi's Arnalta in Frankfurt, 2000–01; Many concert appearances, including Mozart masses, and Janáček's Diary of One Who Disappeared.

LAZAREV, Alexander; conductor; b. 5 July 1945, Moscow, Russia. *Education:* Moscow and Leningrad Conservatories. *Career:* Has conducted at the Bolshoi Theatre Moscow from 1973, Chief Conductor and Artistic Director, 1987–95; Founded the Ensemble of Soloists of the Bolshoi Theatre, 1978, for the promotion of contemporary music; Regular guest conductor of the St Petersburg Philharmonic and the Russian State Symphony Orchestra; Guest appearances with the Berlin Philharmonic, Bavarian Radio Symphony, Munich, Rotterdam and Netherlands Radio Philharmonics, the Orchestre National de France, the Orchestra of the Accademia di Santa Cecilia, Rome, Royal Concertgebouw, Orchestra Filarmonica della Scala, Oslo Philharmonic, Swedish Radio Symphony, Danish National Radio Symphony, NHK Symphony, Clevelenad Orchestra, Montreal Symphony, Théâtre Royal de la Monnaie, Arena di Verona, Opéra Bastille, Bavarian State Opera; British debut, 1987, with the Royal Liverpool Philharmonic; Later engagements with the City of Birmingham Symphony, London

Philharmonic, the Royal Scottish National, Philharmonia and the BBC Symphony Orchestras; Edinburgh Festival, 1987, with the Orchestra of the Bolshoi Theatre; Led the Bolshoi Company in Glasgow with Rimsky-Korsakov's Mlada and Tchaikovsky's Maid of Orleans, 1990; Edinburgh Festival, 1990, 1991; Prokofiev's The Duenna; Conducted the BBC Symphony Orchestra in Henze's Tristan and 7th Symphony at the Barbican Hall, 1991; Promenade Concerts, 1991, 1992, 1993, 1994, 1995; Principal Guest Conductor of BBC Symphony Orchestra, 1992–95; Led the Bolshoi Company on tour to La Scala, Milan, 1989, and the Metropolitan, New York, 1991; Led Schnittke's adaptation of The Queen of Spades at Bonn, 1996; Principal Conductor, The Scottish National Orchestra, 1997–; Season 1998–99 conducted Kashchey The Immortal at the London Philharmonic's Rimsky-Korsakov Festival and conducted the St Petersburg Philharmonic in a double bill of Rachmaninov operas in Vienna. *Recordings:* Various recordings on Melodiya, Virgin Classics, Erato, Hyperion, BIS and Sony Classical. *Honours:* 1st Prize, Young Conductors' Competition, Moscow, 1971; Winner, Herbert von Karajan Competition, Berlin, 1972. *Current Management:* Tennant Artists, Unit 2, 39 Tadema Road, London, SW10 0PZ, England. *Telephone:* (20) 7376-3758. *Fax:* (20) 7351-0679. *E-mail:* info@tennantartists.demon.co.uk.

LAZARIDIS, Stefanos; Stage Designer; b. 28 July 1942, Ethiopia. *Education:* Studied in Geneva, 1960–62 and at Central School of Speech and Drama, London. *Career:* Designed Le nozze di Figaro at Covent Garden in 1972 followed by Idomeneo and Werther, 1978–79; Collaborated with John Copley at English National Opera with Die Entführung in 1971 and Il Trovatore in 1972; Further designs for ENO have included Katya Kabanova, Dalibor, Euryanthe, Aida, Der fliegende Holländer, Rusalka, Madama Butterfly, Hansel and Gretel and The Mikado; Collaborations with Yuri Lyubimov for Tristan und Isolde at Bologna in 1983, Rigoletto at Florence in 1984 and Fidelio at Stuttgart in 1985; British stage premieres of Janáček's Osud in 1984 and Busoni's Doktor Faust in 1986; Designed Tosca at Florence and English National Opera, with Jonathan Miller, in 1986, Nabucco for Opera North and Oedipus Rex and Bluebeard's Castle for Scottish Opera in 1990; Der fliegende Holländer with David Pountney at Bregenz Festival in 1989, Carmen at Earl's Court in London, 1989, and on tour to Japan and Australia; La Fanciulla del West at La Scala in 1991; Pag and Cav at the Berlin Staatsoper, 1996; La Fanciulla del West at Zürich, 1998; Lohengrin at the Bayreuth Festival, 1999. *Honours:* Associate Artist at English National Opera; Diploma of Honour, International Exhibition of Stage Design, Prague Quadrennial, 1999. *Current Management:* Athole Still International Management, Forresters Hall, 25–27 Westow Street, London, SE19 3RY, England. *Telephone:* (20) 8771-5271. *Fax:* (20) 8768-6600. *Website:* www.atholestill.com.

LAZARO, Francisco; Singer (Tenor); b. 13 March 1932, Barcelona, Spain. *Education:* Liceo Conservatory, Barcelona. *Career:* Debut: Barcelona in 1962 as Gaspare in Donizetti's La Favorita; Sang in Macbeth and Der Rosenkavalier at the 1964 Salzburg Festival, under Karajan; Guest appearances in Berlin, Düsseldorf and Frankfurt, San Francisco in 1965, and Barcelona in 1967 as Calaf in Turandot; Frequent performances at the Munich Staatsoper from 1970; Sang at Hamburg in 1984 as Otello; Other roles include Verdi's Manrico and Radames, Des Grieux in Manon Lescaut, Rodolfo and Don José.

LAZAROF, Henri; Composer; b. 12 April 1932, Sofia, Bulgaria. *Education:* Studied with Paul Ben-Haim in Jerusalem; Santa Cecilia Academy in Rome with Petrassi, 1955–57; Brandeis University with Harold Shapero, 1957–59. *Career:* Teacher at University of California, Los Angeles, 1962–; Artist in Residence at University of West Berlin, 1970–71. *Compositions include:* Piano Concerto, 1957; Violin Concerto, 1962; Concerto for piano and 20 instruments, 1963; Odes for orchestra, 1963; Double Concerto for violin, viola and chamber orchestra, 1964; Structures Sonores for orchestra, 1966; Mutazione for orchestra, 1967; Cello Concerto, 1968; Events, ballet, 1973; Concertazioni for orchestra, 1973; Spectrum for trumpet, orchestra and tape, 1975; Chamber Symphony, 1977; Mirrors, Mirrors, ballet, 1980; Sinfonietta, 1981; Clarinet Concerto, 1990; Symphony No. 2, 1991, No. 3 (Choral), 1994, No. 4 (Choral), 1995; Oboe Concerto, 1997; Viola Rhapsody, 1997; String Quintet, 1997; Chronicles, string trio, 1997; 3 String Quartets, 1956–80; String Trio, 1957; Wind trio, 1981. *Address:* c/o ASCAP, ASCAP Building, 1 Lincoln Plaza, New York, NY 10023, USA.

LAZARTE, Julio (Ricardo); Pianist and Conductor; b. 12 July 1956, Tucuman, Argentina. *Education:* Medico Degree, National University of Tucuman; Piano and Professor of Piano from School of Musical Arts, National University of Tucuman; Dalcroze Certificate, Carnegie Mellon University, Pittsburgh. *Career:* Debut: Pianist, Integral version of sonatas and interludes by John Cage, US Embassy, Argentina, 1985; Conductor, Complete version of church sonatas by Mozart, Santisimo Rosario Basilica, Tucuman, 1990; As pianist has performed complete cycles of works for keyboard or chamber music with piano, by Pachelbel, Zipoli, Marcello, Handel, Haydn, Clementi, Mozart, Brahms, Weber,

Debussy, Ravel, Satie, Cage, Ginastera and pioneers of Argentinian and Latin American keyboard music; Tours of USA, Spain, Netherlands and Argentina; As conductor founded and is artistic music director for Camerata Lazarte Chamber Orchestra performing widely; Has taught in many academic and cultural institutions. *Publications:* Author, Lazarte Methodology. *Current Management:* CESI. *Address:* c/o CESI, Marcos Paz 250, Tucuman, 250, Argentina.

LE, Tuan Hung; Composer, Performer and Musicologist; b. 15 Oct. 1960, Viet Nam. *Education:* Graduate Diploma, Information Services, Royal Melbourne Institute of Technology, 1992; Bachelor of Music, University of Melbourne, 1996; Doctor of Philosophy, Musicology, Monash University. *Career:* Freelance Composer, Performer and Musicologist, 1987–; Program Manager, Music, Australia Asia Foundation, 1994–; Program Dir (Music), Australia Asia Foundation, 2000–; mem. Australian Music Centre; Victorian Folklife Association. *Compositions:* Reflections, 1990; Spring, 1991; Prayer for Land, 1991; Longing for Wind, 1996; Calm Water, 1996; Water Ways, 1997; Scent of Memories, 1998; Lotus Pond, 1998; Scent of Time, 2000; Echoes of an Old Festive Song, 2003. *Recordings:* Quivering String, 1992; Musical Transfigurations, 1993; Landscapes of Time, 1996; Echoes of Ancestral Voices, 1997; Scent of Time, 2003. *Publications:* Dan Tranh Music of Vietnam: Traditions and Innovations, 1998; Numerous articles in magazines, reviews and journals. *Honours:* Overseas Fellowship, Australian Academy of Humanities, 1993. *Address:* PO Box 387, Springvale, Vic. 3171, Australia.

LE BRIS, Michele; Singer (Soprano); b. 1938, France. *Education:* Studied at Conservatoire National, Paris. *Career:* Debut: Paris Opéra as Marguerite, 1961; Many appearances at such French opera centres as Marseilles, Nantes, Vichy, Strasbourg, Toulouse and Rouen; Strasbourg in 1965 in local premiere of Mozart's La Finta Giardiniera, Amelia in Un Ballo in Maschera, Tokyo, 1972; Sang Halévy's Rachel in London, 1973 and at Barcelona in 1974; Sang at Barcelona in 1976 as Thais; Other roles have included Rossini's Mathilde, Verdi's Desdemona and Trovatore Leonora, Manon Lescaut, Tosca, Mimi, Minnie and Musetta, Massenet's Salome and Sapho, Regina in Mathis der Maler, Mozart's Countess and Donna, Lisa in The Queen of Spades and Janáček's Jenůfa. *Recordings include:* Highlights from Un Ballo in Maschera and Il Trovatore. *Address:* c/o Theatre National de L'Opéra de Paris, 8 Rue Scribe, 75008 Paris, France.

LE BROCQ, Mark; Singer (tenor); b. 1966, England. *Education:* Studied at St Catharine's College, Cambridge, Royal Academy and National Opera Studio. *Career:* Principal with English National Opera; Appearances at the Covent Garden and Aix-en-Provence Festivals; Roles include Don Ottavio, Cavalli's Egisto, Paolino in Il Matrimonio Segreto, Berlioz's Benedict, Spirit/Autumn in The Fairy Queen and Odoardo in Ariodante; Concerts in the USA, throughout Europe and in the Middle East with Les Arts Florissants, The Gabrieli Consort and others; Sang in The Prince of Homburg and Don Quixote for English National Opera, 1996; Cassio in a new production of Otello, 1998. *Current Management:* Hazard Chase, Norman House, Cambridge Place, Cambridge CB2 1NS, England. *Telephone:* (1223) 312400. *Fax:* (1223) 460827. *Website:* www.hazardchase.co.uk.

LE DIZES, Maryvonne; Violinist and Professor; b. 25 June 1940, Quimper, France; m. 23 May 1964, 3 s., 1 d. *Education:* 1st Prize, Violin, National Conservatory of Music, Paris, 1957; 1st Prize, Chamber Music, National Conservatory of Music, Paris, 1958. *Career:* Debut: Violin Concert; Soloist with Ensemble Intercontemporain, 1978–; Professor at Conservatory of Music, Boulogne Billancourt, France, 1977–. *Recordings:* Works by Berio, Messiaen, Xenakis, Machover, Carter, Brahms. *Honours:* Prize, International Thibaud Competition, Paris, 1961; 1st Prize, N Paganini Competition, Genoa, 1962, and International American Music Competition, NY, 1983; SACEM Paris, 1987. *Address:* CIUP, Maison IAA, 5 Boulevard Jourdan, 75690 Paris Cédex 14, France.

LE FLEMING, Anthony Ralph, BA; British composer, organist and conductor; b. 16 March 1941, Wiltshire, England; m.; three c. *Education:* Salisbury Cathedral School and Queens' Coll., Cambridge. *Career:* organist Bedford School 1965–68; Dir of Music, Abingdon School 1968–73; Musician Advising Birmingham LEA 1973–81, Devon County Music Adviser 1981–93; freelance composer, organist, conductor 1993–; mem. Incorporated Soc. of Musicians. *Compositions:* works for choir and orchestra, choir unaccompanied and with organ, songs with instrumental or piano accompaniment, instrumental pieces, arrangements in various styles. *Recordings:* Some Shadows of Eternity. *Honours:* first prize English Poetry and Song Soc.. *Address:* 64 Park Hall Road, West Dulwich, London, SE21 8BW, England (home). *Telephone:* (20) 8761-4397 (home). *E-mail:* a.lefleming@btinternet (home). *Website:* www.impulse-music.co.uk/lefleming.htm (office).

LE PAGE, David; Violinist; b. 1965, England. *Career:* Co-founder and Second Violinist of the Kreutzer Quartet from 1988; South Bank debut in 1989 followed by Amsterdam Concertgebouw and recital at Palazzo

Labia in Venice; 1991 Recital at Lancaster House for Queen Elizabeth; Established repertoire and new compositions with improvisations in The Chamber, featuring live film projection and static coloured images within a darkened set. *Honours:* With Kreutzer Quartet: Winner of 1991 Royal Overseas League Competition. *Address:* Manygate Management, Kreutzer Quartet, 13 Cotswold Mews, 30 Battersea Square, London SW11 3 RA, England.

LE ROUX, Francois; Singer (Baritone); b. 30 Oct. 1955, Rennes, France. *Education:* Studied with Francois Loup and at Paris Opéra Studio with Vera Rozsa and Elisabeth Grummer. *Career:* Sang at the Opéra de Lyon, 1980–85 as Mozart's Don Giovanni, Papageno, Guglielmo and Count; From 1985 appeared as Debussy's Pelléas at the Paris Opéra, La Scala, Milan, 1986, Vienna Staatsoper, 1988, Barcelona, Helsinki, 1989, Cologne, 1992, Covent Garden, 1994; Glyndebourne Festival debut in 1987 as Ramiro in L'Heure Espagnole; Hamburg in 1987 as Marcello in La Bohème; Sang Lescaut in a new production of Manon at Covent Garden, 1988, returning as Papageno in 1989; Appeared as Hidraot in Armide at Amsterdam in 1988 and Orestes in Iphigénie at Frankfurt, Ulisse in Il Ritorno at Lausanne, 1989; Also sings Valentin in Faust and has sung Don Giovanni at Paris Opéra and in Zürich under Nikolaus Harnoncourt; Created the title role in the world premiere of Birtwistle's Gawain at Covent Garden, 1991; Season 1992 as Maletesta in Don Pasquale at Covent Garden and the title role in Henze's Der Prinz von Homburg at Munich; sang Pelléas at Covent Garden, 1994; Sang Stravinsky's Nick Shadow at Madrid, 1996; Season 1998 with Golaud in Pelléas at the Paris Opéra-Comique and Monteverdi's Orpheus at the Vienna Festival; Sang Monsieur de in Madame de by Damase at Geneva, 2001. *Recordings include:* Pelléas et Mélisande, under Claudio Abbado. *Honours:* Prizewinner at International Maria Casals Competition, Barcelona and the International Competition at Rio de Janeiro. *Address:* c/o Matthias Vogt Management, 1714 Stockton Street, Suite 300, San Francisco, CA 94133-2930, USA.

LE ROUX, Maurice; Conductor and Composer; b. 6 Feb. 1923, Paris, France. *Education:* Studied at the Paris Conservatoire, 1944–52, with Messiaen and Fourestier, composition with René Leibowitz and conducting with Dmitri Mitropoulos. *Career:* Worked on musique concrète project with French Radio, 1951; Music Director of the Orchestre National, 1960–68; Artistic Adviser at the Paris Opéra, 1969–73; Inspector General of Music for the Ministry of Culture, 1973–88; Conductor of leading orchestras in guest engagements in France and abroad; Repertoire has included the Monteverdi Vespers and music by Berg, Schoenberg and Xenakis; Music programme Arcana for French television from 1968; Film scores for Truffaut, Godard and others. *Recordings include:* Messiaen Turangalila Symphonie. *Publications:* Introduction a la Musique Contemporaine, 1947; Claudio Monteverdi, 1951; La Musique, 1979; Mussorgsky, Boris Godunov, 1980.

LE SAGE, Sally; Singer (Soprano) and Professor of Singing; b. 1937, Farnborough, England. *Education:* Studied at the Royal College of Music and with Pierre Bernac on a scholarship in Paris. *Career:* Sang with Deller Consort, 1964–67; Concert appearances throughout the United Kingdom, Europe and USA which included the Vienna, Aix, Ghent and Three Choirs Festivals; Many BBC concerts and recitals; Other concert repertoire included L'Enfant et Les Sortilèges in Leeds with Simon Rattle, Haydn Nelson Mass at Carnegie Hall, NY, USA, Beethoven's 9th for Dutch television in Amsterdam, Mozart's C minor Mass at Royal Festival Hall with Charles Groves, A Child of Our Time in Stockholm under Michael Tippett, Messiah with the Hallé in Manchester, and Mahler's 8th Symphony at the Albert Hall in London; Opera appearances with Scottish Opera as The Woodbird in Siegfried, Covent Garden and Glyndebourne, Teofane in Handel's Ottone at Sadler's Wells Theatre and Ann Trulove in The Rake's Progress at Cambridge Arts Theatre. *Recordings:* Various. *Honours:* 1st Prize Vocal Concours, 's-Hertogenbosch, Netherlands, 1967. *Address:* 13 Observatory Road, East Sheen, London SW14 7QB, England.

LE TEXIER, Vincent; Singer (Bass-baritone); b. 1957, France. *Education:* Studied privately at the Grenoble Conservatory and at the studio of the Paris Opéra. *Career:* Appearances at the Paris Opéra in Orphée aux Enfers and with the Opéra-Comique in From the House of the Dead; Sang Golaud in Pelléas et Mélisande and appeared at the 1989 Aix Festival, in The Love for Three Oranges; Lyon, as Schaunard in La Bohème, the four devils in Les Contes d'Hoffmann, the King in Debussy's Rodrigue et Chimène (word creation); In Bordeaux, as Leporello in Don Giovanni, Escamillo in Carmen, the Count in Le nozze di Figaro, Frère Laurent in Roméo et Juliette by Berlioz; In Rouen, as Basilio in Il Barbiere di Siviglia, Kaspar in Freischütz (French version by Berlioz), the Count in Capriccio, the Speaker in Zauberflöte, Mephisto in Faust, Sade in Teresa by Marius Constant, Wozzeck in Wozzeck by Gurlitt (French version); Appearances at the Paris Opéra in Madama Butterfly, and in Pelléas et Mélisande; Golaud in Impressions de Pelléas, by Peter Brook and Marius Constant, in Paris

and on tour around Europe, 1991–92; Created the role of Ethnologist in Georges Aperghis's Tristes Tropiques, Strasbourg, 1996; Season 2000–01 as the Berlioz Mephisto at Naples (concert), Eumée in Fauré's Pénélope at Lausanne and Golo for Leipzig Opera. *Recordings include:* The Love for Three Oranges; Alcyone by Marais; Salome, Strauss; Psalm 129, Guy Ropartz; Messa di Gloria, Donizetti; Platée by Rameau; L'Enfant et les Sortiléges by Ravel; Mélodies by Duparc, Ropartz and Fauré. *Honours:* Grand Critics' Prize, 1997. *Address:* 30 rue Darceau, 93100 Montreuil, France.

LEA, Yvonne; Singer (Contralto); b. 1960, Cheshire, England. *Education:* Studied at Royal Northern College of Music with Frederick Cox and at the National Opera Studio, London. *Career:* Appearances with Glyndebourne Festival in Die Zauberflöte, Hippolyta in A Midsummer Night's Dream, Rosina in Il Barbiere di Siviglia and Linette in The Love for Three Oranges; Royal Opera House, Covent Garden, in Der Rosenkavalier and Third Lady in Die Zauberflöte; Sang Suzuki with Welsh National Opera and appeared at Batignano and Spitalfields Festivals in Cesti's La Dori; Recent engagements in Graham Vick's version of The Ring for the City of Birmingham Touring Opera, as Hippolyta at the 1991–92 Aix Festivals and Grimgerde in Die Walküre for Scottish Opera; Tour of France with A Midsummer Night's Dream, 1994; Sang Mother Goose in The Rake's Progress for Welsh National Opera, 1996; Concert repertoire includes Messiah, Elgar's Sea Pictures, Elijah and Beethoven's Mass in C. *Recordings include:* Williamson's Six English Lyrics.

LEA-COX, Graham Russell; Conductor; b. 15 Feb. 1957, Bulawayo, Rhodesia. *Education:* London Univ.; Royal Coll. of Music, London; MA, Magdalen Coll., Oxford; ARCM, ARCO (CHM), MTC, 1975–81. *Career:* debut, Carnegie Hall, New York, 1983; Artistic Dir, Texas Boys' Choir, USA, 1983–85; freelance conductor, performer, 1985–; tours of USA, Canada, Japan, Hong Kong; conducting and solo and chamber recitals in Europe, Scandinavia, Africa; Artistic Dir, English Performing Arts Ensemble, 1988–; Conductor and Artistic Dir, Elizabethan Singers of London, 1987–97; Conductor, Hanover Band; regular tours of Europe and Scandinavia; Artistic Dir and Conductor of Festivals including the South Bank, London. *Compositions:* choral and instrumental music, incidental music for stage, and recordings of poetical/literary compilations. *Recordings:* film and television music; chamber music and song from The Court of Queen Victoria; Warchild Festival Highlights, Festival Hall, London; William Boyce Critical Editions and recording series, conducting the Hanover Band, New College Choir, Oxford, Soloists and others, 1998–; Secular Masque; Cantata: David's Lament on the Death of Saul and Jonathan; Odes to St Cecilia; The Symphony in Britain, Volume 1: Early British Symphonies, 2001; operas and songs. *Publications include:* Gluck: The Swedish Opera Mss, Kungliga Teatra 1770–1815 (research for publication); William Boyce Masterworks (critical edn); British Symphonies of the 18th and 19th Centuries (critical edn). *Website:* www.grahamlea-cox.com.

LEACH, Mary (Jane); Composer and Performer; b. 12 June 1949, St Johnsbury, Vermont, USA. *Education:* BA, Theatre, Music, University of Vermont; Postgraduate, Composition, with Mark Zuckerman, Columbia University. *Career:* Appeared: Experimental Intermedia Foundation (New York), 1982, 1984, 1987, 1992; Relache (Philadelphia), 1984, 1987; Music Gallery (Toronto), Metronome (Barcelona), Newband (New York), 1985; Roulette, New York, 1985, 1995; Charles Ives Center (Connecticut), Logos (Gent, Belgium), 1986, 1987; BACA Downtown (Brooklyn), New Music America (Philadelphia), Palais des Beaux Art (Brussels), Sankt Peter (Cologne), Apollohuis (Eindhoven, Netherlands), 1987; Clock Tower (New York), 1988; Real Ways (Hartford, Connecticut), Franzenzeichen Festival (Cologne), Ton Gegen Ton (Vienna), New Music America (New York), 1989; Kunsthalle Bremen, Romanische Summer Festival (Cologne), Music Today (Tokyo), 1990; Experimentelle Music (Munich), 1991; Sound Symposium (Newfoundland), Ijsbreker (Amsterdam), Corn Palace (Minneapolis), 1992; Bang on a Can Festival (New York), 1992, 1993; Interpretations Series (New York), Walker Art Center, 1993; Subtropics Festival (Miami), 1994; Radio: John Schaeffer's New Sounds, 3 MBS Australia, Radio Bremen, WDR-Köln, Earworks; CBC, 1992; Radio Cultura (São Paulo), Radio 2 (Brussels), 1994; First Art, 1995; For television: WDR Köln. *Compositions:* Note Passing Note, 1981; Solar Spots, 1983; 4BC, Held Held, 1984; 8x4, 1985; Bare Bones, Bruckstück, Pipe Dreams, Sephardic Fragments, 1989; The Upper Room, 1990; Kirchtraum, 1991; Feu de Joie, 1992; Ariadne's Lament, He Got Dictators, Xantippe's Rebuke, 1993; Corrina Ocarina, 1994; Tricky Pan, Windjammer, 1995; Song of Sorrows, 1995; Call of the Dance, 1997; O Magna Vasti Creta, 1997. *Recordings:* MJL 2, 1986; Celestial Fires, 1993; Aerial No. 6; Ariadne's Lament, 1998. *Address:* 90 LaSalle Street #13H, New York, NY 10027, USA.

LEADBETTER, Martin (John); Composer; b. 6 April 1945, London, England; m. Ivy G, 7 June 1969, 2 s. *Education:* Associate and Licentiate Trinity College of Music, London; BA (Hons); Dip Mus (Open) Studied with Dr Alan Bush, 1982–88. *Career:* Television film, Anglia television, BBC 3 Music Weekly and BBC 4 Womans Hour; mem, Performing Right Society. *Compositions include:* 2 Symphonies, 3 String Quartets, An English Requiem, Violin Concerto, 1972; Songs, Instrumental and Choral Works; Marche Tragique for orchestra, 1991; Laudate Dominium, 1992, Tombeau Fontainebleau, France, 1993; I Hear America Singing, 1994; Clarinet Concerto, 1999; Some 150 Works to Date. *Publications include:* Soliloquy; Little Prelude and Fugue. *Honours:* Commissioned By Radio Victory to Compose String Trio. *Address:* Ivy Lodge, 2 Priory Lane, Little Wymondley, Hertfordshire SG4 7 HE, England. *E-mail:* leadzart@btopenworld.com.

LEAH, Philip; British Music Educator; b. 23 Oct. 1948, Dulwich, London; divorced, 2 s. *Education:* Northern School of Music, Manchester, 1968–71; Awarded GNSM, 1971; Studies in flute, piano and composition. *Career:* Peripatetic Music Teacher, Glamorgan, 1972–73; Peripatetic Music Teacher, City of Birmingham, 1973–90; Lecturer, North Worcestershire College of Education, 1977–80, University of Wolverhampton, 1982–90; Founder and Musical Director, West Birmingham Schools Wind Band, 1985–90, Halesowen Symphony Orchestra, 1986–89; Examiner, Guildhall School of Music and Drama, 1988–; Flute Tutor, University of Wales, Aberystwyth, 2000–;; mem, Royal Society of Musicians of Great Britain; Incorporated Society of Musicians, Spnm, Musicians' Union. *Compositions:* Concertino for bass tuba and orchestra; Sinfonia for flute and strings; Acme, a suite for chamber orchestra; Sinfonia for chambaer orchestra; Elegy for string sextet. Prelude and Scherzo for string quartet; Three Penny Bit for wind; Wind quintet; Fanfare (1969); Fanfare for a Golden Jubilee; Conversations for flute and piano; Fanfare for a Golden Jubilee; Chorale Prelude on Austria for organ; Wedding Suite for organ; In Annum for tenor solo, SATB choir and string quartet; Winter for SATB choir and string quartet; Song: Meditation for soprano and piano; Psychological Songs for bass voice and piano; Various arrangements for woodwind instruments. *Honours:* First prize, Horatio Albert Lumb Composition Competition, 1992. *Address:* 62 Y Lanfa, Trefechan, Aberystwyth, Ceredigion SY23 1AS, Wales. *E-mail:* philleah@aol.com.

LEAPER, Adrian; Conductor; b. 1953, England. *Education:* Studied at the Royal Academy of Music and with George Hurst. *Career:* Assistant Conductor at the Halle Orchestra in season 1986–87 and has subsequently worked with all leading British orchestras, and the Vienna, Prague and Moscow Symphonies, and the Belgium National Orchestra; Music Director of the Orquesta Filarmonica de Gran Canaria from 1994. *Recordings include:* Albums of Sibelius, Elgar, Holst, Havergal Brian, Tchaikovsky and Nielsen. *Current Management:* Hazard Chase, Norman House, Cambridge Place, Cambridge CB2 1NS, England. *Telephone:* (1223) 312400. *Fax:* (1223) 460827. *Website:* www.hazardchase.co.uk.

LEAR, Evelyn; Singer (Soprano); b. 8 Jan. 1926, Brooklyn, New York, USA; m. (1) 1 s., 1 d., (2) Thomas Stewart. *Education:* New York University; Hunter College; Juilliard Opera Workshop; Fulbright Scholar to Germany, 1955. *Career:* British debut in Four Last Songs with London Symphony Orchestra, 1957; Stage debut as the Composer in Ariadne auf Naxos, Berlin, 1959; Deutsche Oper Berlin, 1961, creating title role in Klebe's Alkmene; Jeanne in premiere of Egk's Die Verlobung in San Domingo, Munich, 1963; Covent Garden debut, 1965, as Donna Elvira; Lulu in Berg's opera at Vienna Opera House, 1962, and Sadler's Wells Theatre, 1966; Metropolitan Opera debut in premiere of Levy's Mourning Becomes Electra, 1967; La Scala debut, 1971, in Wozzeck; Performed regularly with leading opera companies and orchestras in Europe and USA; Guested with Berlin Opera and Vienna State Opera; Soloist with leading US orchestras including New York Philharmonic and Los Angeles Philharmonics, Philadelphia Orchestra, and Chicago, Boston and San Francisco Symphonies; Many recitals and orchestral concerts and operatic performances with Thomas Stewart; Major roles include Marie in Wozzeck, Marschallin in Der Rosenkavalier, Countess in Figaro, Fiordiligi in Così fan tutte, Desdemona, Mimi, Dido in The Trojans, Donna Elvira in Don Giovanni, Marina in Boris Godunov, Tatiana in Eugene Onegin, Lavinia in Mourning Becomes Electra, and title role in Lulu; Appeared in film Buffalo Bill, 1976; Sang in premieres of The Seagull by Pasatieri, 1974, Robert Ward's Minutes to Midnight, 1980, and Kelterborn's Der Kirschgarten, Zürich, 1984; The Met, 1985, as the Marschallin; Countess Geschwitz in Lulu at Florence, 1985, Chicago, 1987, and San Francisco, 1989; Miss Dilly in Bernstein's On the Town at the Barbican Hall, London, 1992; Mme. Armfelt in A Little Night Music at Houston, 1999. *Recordings include:* Wozzeck; Lulu; The Flying Dutchman; Magic Flute excerpts; Boris Godunov; Eugene Onegin; Der Rosenkavalier; Bach's St John Passion; Pergolesi's Stabat Mater; Children's Songs from Around the World; Songs of the Sea; Song recitals include: Vivaldi, Fauré, Strauss, Bizet, Debussy, Wolf, Chausson, Sondheim, Copland, Ives and Porter; Evelyn Lear and Thomas Stewart sing Strauss and Wagner; Evelyn Lear: A celebration of 20th Century Song; Evelyn Lear: Songs my Mother

Taught Us; Russian Art Songs: Tchaikovsky to Rachmaninov; Evelyn Lear Sings Songs by Richard Strauss; 2nd String Quartet by Schoenberg (Philips). *Honours:* Concert Artists' Guild Award, 1955; Kammersängerin Award by Berlin Senate, 1963. *Address:* 15101 Rosecroft Road, Rockville, MD 20853, USA.

LEATHERBY, Carol Ann; Singer (Mezzo-contralto) and Director of Victoriana (Victorian Musical Entertainment); b. 1948, Barking, London, England. *Education:* Morley College with Ilse Wolf, 1968–69; Guildhall School of Music and Drama, 1969–71; Vienna with Eugenie Ludwig, 1981–82; Private study in London with Lyndon Van der Pump, 1972–. *Career:* Debut: Purcell Room, London, 1973; Welsh National Opera, 1973–75; Covent Garden Opera, 1975–78; Glyndebourne Festival Opera, 1979–80; New Opera, 1981; Music in Camera, Southern Television, 1980; Delius Talk on Radio London, 1980; Broadcasts for BBC, London and Cardiff; Recitals at Purcell Room, Wigmore Hall; Concerts at Festival Hall and Queen Elizabeth Hall; Memorial concert for Princess Grace of Monaco at Queen Elizabeth Hall, 1983; Specialist in the songs of Frederick Delius; Athens Festival, 1985; Alte Oper, Frankfurt, 1985, 1986; Purcell Room concerts as member of Quintessence founded in 1984, presenting Victorian and Edwardian entertainment in costume and performing music by Gershwin and Cole Porter, 1984, 1985 and 1986; The Vampyr, soap opera for BBC 2 television, music by Heinrich Marschner, 1992; Street Singer (Dance to the Music of Time) BBC television, 1998. *Recordings:* Czech songs by Foerster, Smetana and Dvořák, 1983; Songs of Praise, BBC television; Sita-Mother Earth-Holst recorded at St John's Smith Square in conjunction with the Holst Society. *Current Management:* Pat Nash, Nash International, 135 Epping New Road, Buckhurst Hill, Essex IG9 5TZ. *Address:* 278 Monega Road, Manor Park, London E12 6TS, England.

LEBARON, Alice Anne; Composer and Professor of Music; b. 30 May 1953, Baton Rouge, LA, USA; m. Edward J. Eadon 1982; one d. *Education:* BA, music, Univ. of Alabama, 1974; MA, music, State Univ. of New York, Stony Brook, 1978; Darmstadt, 1980; Köln Musikhochschule, 1980–81; National Classical Music Institute, Korea, 1983; DMA, Columbia Univ., 1989. *Career:* Composer-in-Residence (Meet The Composer New Residencies), Washington, DC, 1993–96; Asst Prof. of Music Composition and Theory, Univ. of Pittsburgh, 1997–2001; Prof. of Music, Calif. Inst. of the Arts 2001–. *Compositions:* The E and O Line; Croak (The Last Frog), chamber opera; orchestral: Strange Attractors; Southern Ephemera, 1994; Lasting Impressions, 1995; Mambo, 1995; American Icons, 1996, Traces of Mississippi 2000; chamber music: Pope Joan, Sauger, Inner Voice, Telluris Theoria Sacra, The Sea and the Honeycomb, Noh Reflections, Metamorphosis, Rite of the Black Sea, Planxty Bowerbird, I Am An American... My Government Will Reward You, Lamentation-Invocation, Concerto for Active Frogs, Dish, Waltz for Quintet, Three Motion Atmospheres, Southern Ephemera, Devil in the Belfry, Light Breaks Where No Sun Shines, Story of My Angel, Sachamama 1995, Croak 1997, Solar Music 1997, Sukey 1998; choral: Nightmare 1999. *Recordings include:* Rana, Ritual and Revelations; The Music of Anne LeBaron, 1992; Phantom Orchestra: The Anne LeBaron Quintet, 1992; The Musical Railism of Anne LeBaron, 1995. *Address:* c/o Cal Arts, 24700 McBean Parkway, Valencia, CA 91355, USA.

LEBHERZ, Louis; Singer (Bass); b. 14 April 1948, Bethesda, Maryland, USA. *Education:* Studied at Indiana University. *Career:* Debut: Memphis Opera, as Padre Guardiano in La Forza del Destino, 1974; Many appearances at opera houses in North and South America (Caracas, 1981); European engagements at Frankfurt, 1981, Karlsruhe, 1984–85, Berne, 1985–86, Geneva, 1988; Sang Melothal in Guillaume Tell at Covent Garden and the Grand Inquisitor in Don Carlos at Los Angeles, 1990; Appeared in Massenet's La Navarraise with Long Beach Opera, 1990, as Basilio, the Commendatore in Don Giovanni at Los Angeles Music Center, 1991; Sang Rocco at New Orleans, 1992; Grech in Fedora at Los Angeles, 1997; Other roles include Sarastro, King Mark, Fasolt, Baldassare in La Favorita, Verdi's Zaccaria, Nabucco and Fiesco, Colline, and Don Diego in L'Africaine. *Recordings include:* Verdi's Aroldo; Jone by Petrella.

LEBIC, Lojze; Composer, Conductor and Professor of Music Theory; b. 23 Aug. 1934, Prevalje, Slovenia; m. Jelena Ukmar 1961, one d. *Education:* Diploma in Archaeology, University of Ljubljana, 1957; Academy of Music, Ljubljana, 1972; studies in Darmstadt. *Career:* Conductor, RTV Ljubljana 1962–72; appeared at Musica Antiqua Europae Orientalis Festival, Bydgozscz, Poland, 1968; Festival van Vlaanderen, 1968; Ohrid Festival, 1968; Jihlava Festival, Czechoslovakia, 1969; Zagreb Biennale, 1969; Dubrovnik Festival, 1969; ISCM Festivals, Brussels, 1981, Zürich, 1991 and Bucharest, 1999; Prof., Univ. of Ljubljana, 1985–. *Compositions include:* Orchestral works: Voices; Korant; Ouverture; Tangram; Cantico I; Nicina, Qeensland Music; Solo instruments with orchestra: Sentences; Symphony with organ, 1993; Voice with orchestra: Myth and Apocrypha, November Song, Burnt Grass; Music About Time, 1996; Chamber Music: Kons a, Kons b; Expressions,

String Quartet, Quartet for percussion; Illud tempus; Invisibilia, April vignettes, Chalumeau I–III, Meditation for two; Epicedion; From nearby and far away; Rubato per viola; A taste of time fleeting away; Rej; Impromptus I–IV; Vocal Instrumental: Ajdna for choirs, recorders and percussion instruments; Fauvel 86-vocal instrumental scene; In the Silent Rustle of Time; Eulogy to the World. *Recordings:* various as conductor and composer. *Publications:* The Basis of Music Art, book, 1982; Sound and Silence, Compositional Synthesis of the Eighties, Music Biennale Zagreb, 1985. *Address:* Bratov Ucakar 134, 1000 Ljubljana, Slovenia. *Website:* www2.arnes.si/~hlebic.

LEBRECHT, Norman; British writer; b. 11 July 1948, London, England; m. Elbie Spivack 1977; three d. *Education:* Bar Ilan Univ., Israel. *Career:* radio and television producer 1969–78; writer 1978–; Asst Ed., Evening Standard, London 2002–; mem. Soc. of Authors. *Publications:* Discord 1982, Hush! Handel's in a Passion 1985, The Book of Musical Anecdotes 1985, Mahler Remembered 1987, The Book of Musical Days 1987, The Maestro Myth 1991, Music in London 1991, The Companion to Twentieth-Century Music 1992, When the Music Stops 1996, Who Killed Classical Music? 1997, Covent Garden: Dispatches from the English Culture War, 1945–2000 2000, The Song of Names (Whitbread First Novel Award) 2002. *Current Management:* Curtis Brown Ltd, Haymarket House, 28–29 Haymarket, London, SW1Y 4SP, England. *Telephone:* (20) 7393-4400. *Fax:* (20) 7393-4401. *E-mail:* info@curtisbrown.co.uk. *Website:* www.curtisbrown.co.uk. *Address:* 3 Bolton Road, London, NW8 0RJ, England.

LECHNER, Gabriela; Singer (Soprano); b. 8 March 1961, Austria. *Education:* Studied at the Hochschule für Musik und Darstellende Kunst in Vienna. *Career:* Sang Sulamith in The Queen of Sheba with the Graz Opera, appeared later in Don Giovanni, Mefistofele (Margarita and Elena), La Forza del Destino, Otello, Don Carlos, Trovatore, Elektra and Cavalleria Rusticana; Amelia in Un Ballo in Maschera at the Vienna Staatsoper (with Pavarotti) followed by such operas as Simon Boccanegra, Trovatore, Otello, Zauberflöte, Rusalka, Elektra, Der Rosenkavalier, Capriccio, Contes d'Hoffmann and Die Walküre (in Vienna); Engagements with the Zürich Opera as Elsa in Lohengrin, Der fliegender Holländer (Senta), the Marschallin in Der Rosenkavalier, Capriccio (Gräfin), both Verdi Leonoras, Chrysothemis in Elektra, Elisabetta (Don Carlos) Tosca, the Empress (Die Frau ohne Schatten), Ariadne, Falstaff (Alice Ford), Aida, Amelia in Ballo, Giulietta in Contes d'Hoffmann, Andrea Chénier, (Maddalena); Guest appearances at Madrid, Barcelona, Berlin, Paris, Frankfurt, Hamburg, Cologne, Amsterdam, Munich, Prague, Florence, Rome, Edinburgh and Glasgow; Conductors have included Abbado, Bernstein, Mehta, Maazel, Barenboim, Dohnányi and Sinopoli; Other roles include Valentine (Huguenots), Elettra (Idomeneo), Alceste in Amsterdam, Vitellia (Titus) in Barcelona, Regan (Lear) in Germany) Carlotta in Die Gezeichneten by Schreker (at Zürich and Paris); Guest professor for vocal technique and interpretation at the University of Music in Vienna, 2001–. *Recordings include:* Un Ballo in Maschera–Amelia with Pavarotti/Abbado. *Honours:* Several major competition awards. *Address:* c/o Theaterplatz 2, 2500 Baden/Vienna, Austria.

LEDGER, Sir Philip Stevens, Kt, CBE, MA, DMus, LLD, FRCM, FRNCM, FRCO; British musician; b. 12 Dec. 1937, Bexhill-on-Sea, Sussex; s. of the late Walter Stephen Ledger and Winifred Kathleen Ledger (née Stevens); m. Mary Erryl Wells 1963; one s. one d. *Education:* Bexhill Grammar School, King's Coll. Cambridge. *Career:* Master of the Music, Chelmsford Cathedral 1962–65; Dir of Music, Univ. of East Anglia 1965–73, Dean of School of Fine Arts and Music 1968–71; an Artistic Dir Aldeburgh Festival of Music and Arts 1968–89, Vice-Pres. 1989–; Conductor, Cambridge Univ. Musical Soc. 1973–82; Dir of Music and Organist, King's Coll. Cambridge 1974–82; Prin. Royal Scottish Acad. of Music and Drama 1982–2001; John Stewart of Rannoch Scholar in Sacred Music; Pres. Royal Coll. of Organists 1992–94; Pres. Inc. Soc. of Musicians 1994–95; Chair. Cttee of Prins of Conservatoires 1994–98. *Publications:* (Ed.) Anthems for Choirs 2 and 3 1973, Oxford Book of English Madrigals 1978, edns of Byrd, Handel and Purcell and carol arrangements. *Honours:* Hon. Prof. Univ. of Glasgow 1993–98; Hon. mem. RAM, Guildhall School of Music; numerous hon. degrees; Silver Medal of Worshipful Company of Musicians. *Address:* 2 Lancaster Drive, Upper Rissington, Cheltenham, Glos., GL54 2QZ, England (home).

LEE, Chan-Hae, BM, MM; Composer; b. 8 Oct. 1945, Seoul, Republic of Korea. *Education:* Yonsei Univ., Catholic Univ. of America, Washington, DC. *Career:* Lecturer, Prof., Yonsei Univ. 1977–; Visiting Prof. Wayne State Univ. 1984, Oakland Univ. 1985; Research Assoc. Nationale conservatoire de Paris, France 1994; Pres., The Korean Society of 21st Century Music 1998–; Pres. Korean Women's Society of Composition 2001–; mem. bd Korean Music Society 1996–; Gen. Sec. Asian Composers' League 1999–, Vice-Pres. (Korea) 2000–; mem. Int. Soc. of Contemporary Music 1990–. *Major compositions:* Hyesang and Chosaeng for voices and ensemble 1980–91, Galpiri for clarinet 1982,

The Pilgrim's Progress for chamber ensemble 1990, Glorification for three percussion instruments 1990, The Martyr for string orchestra 1993, From the Point, From the Line for violin solo 1997, Transfiguration for string quartet 1998, Fire Flame for violin and orchestra 1999, Tabernacle for four percussion 1999, Musical He 1999, Be a Light in the Eastern Land for orchestra 2000, Soricil for taeguem solo 2000, To The Hwangseung for pansori and chamber ensemble 2001. *Major recordings:* Galpiri 1985, From the Point, From the Line 1998, Musical He 1999, Fire Flame 2000, Soricil 2000. *Publications:* Music Theory 1978, 16C Counterpoint 1985, Contemporary Music I and II 1991, New Approach to Sightsinging and Ear Training I and II 1995, Introduction to Contemporary Music 1998. *Honours:* Korean Nat. Composition Prize 1999. *Address:* Itaewondong Chongwha Apt 2-603, Yongsanku, Seoul, Republic of Korea. *Telephone:* (2) 2123-3080. *Fax:* (2) 313-2821. *E-mail:* chhlee@yonsei.ac.kr.

LEE, Dennis (Ean Hooi); Pianist; b. 2 Dec. 1946, Penang, Malaysia; m. Chee-Hung Toh, 16 Aug 1990. *Education:* BMus, London University; MMus, with Angus Morrison, Royal College of Music, London, 1964–68; Studied with Josef Dichler, Vienna Hochschule, 1968–69; Studied with Ilonka Deckers in Milan. *Career:* Debut: Purcell Room, London, and Kennedy Center, Washington DC; Concerts (recitals, chamber music and orchestral appearances), television and radio recordings, the United Kingdom, Europe, USA, Canada, South America, Hong-Kong, Japan, China, South-East Asia, Australia, New Zealand; Radio broadcasts include live transmissions for BBC Radio 3; Festivals include Adelaide, Montreux, Spoleto, Cheltenham, Brighton, Lincoln, Newbury, Warwick, Mananan, Arundel; Orchestral appearances include BBC Regional, Hallé, Wiener Symphoniker, London Mozart Players, RAI Milan, Polish and Slovak Chamber Orchestras, Warsaw Philharmonic Orchestra, Shanghai Symphony, Singapore Symphony, Malaysian Philharmonic; Adjudicator at festivals and competitions; Examiner for the Associated Board of the Royal Schools of Music, 1977–. *Recordings:* Szymanowski Piano Pieces; Ravel Duets with Philippe Entremont. *Honours:* Prizes: BBC Competition, 1971; Casagrande, Italy, 1975, 1977; Sydney, 1977; Busoni, Italy, 1978. *Address:* Flat 5, 12 St Quintin Avenue, London, W10 6NU, England. *E-mail:* dleepiano@aol.com.

LEE, Douglas (Allen); Professor of Musicology; b. 3 Nov. 1932, Carmel, Indiana, USA; m. Beverly Haskell, 2 Sept 1961. *Education:* BMus, DePauw University, 1954; MMus 1958, Rackham Fellow, 1961–63, PhD 1968, University of Michigan; National Endowment for the Humanities Seminar in Editing Early Music, 1985; Piano Studies with Theodore Lettvin and György Sandor. *Career:* Instructor, Mount Union College, Alliance, Ohio, 1959–61; Professor, Music, Wichita State University, Kansas, 1964–86; Professor, Musicology, Vanderbilt University, Nashville, Tennessee, 1986–98, Professor Emeritus, 1998–; Faculty, Mount Union College, University of Michigan, International Music Camp-Interlochen, Wichita State University, Vanderbilt University; Editor, American Music Teacher, 1968–70; Sonneck Society Newsletter, 1988–90. *Publications:* The Works of Christoph Nichelmann, 1971; Christoph Nichelmann-Two Concertos, 1977; Six Sonatas of Franz Benda, with Embellishments, 1981; Franz Benda–A Thematic Catalogue, 1984; Chapters in Great Lives in Music–Renaissance to 1800, 1989; 2 chapters in Great Events in History, Arts and Culture, 1993; C P E Bach: Six Keyboard Concertos (Collected Works); A Musician at Court: An Autobiography of Franz Benda, 1998; Masterworks of Twentieth Century Music, 2002; 2 essays in a reference encyclopedia on The Fifties in america, 2 volumes, 2005. *Contributions:* 23 articles, New Grove Dictionary of Music and Musicians. *Address:* Vanderbilt Unviersity, Blair School of Music, 2400 Blakemore Avenue, Nashville, TN 37212, USA.

LEE, Lynda; Singer (Soprano); b. 1969, Ireland. *Education:* Studied at the Dublin College of Music. *Career:* Opera engagements with Opera Northern Ireland, Wexford Festival, Musica nel Chiostro and at the Covent Garden Festival as Irene in Tamerlano; Karlsruhe Handelfestspiel, Halle Handelfestspiele; Théâtre de Caen; Expo 98 Lisbon; Covent Garden Festival; On Contract with Opera Leipzig until 2001; Concerts with the Ulster Orchestra, at the Glasgow Mayfest, Bath Festival and in Jonathan Miller's production of the St Matthew Passion; RTE Symphony Orchestra; RIAS Kammerchor, Berlin; Represented Ireland at the 1993 Cardiff Singer of the World Competition; Sang Handel's Agrippina and Zenobia in Radamisto at Halle, 2000–01. *Recordings include:* Bach's, St Matthew Passion, Wallace's Maritana. *Current Management:* Neill Thornborrow at Heissler Remy. *Address:* Drakestrasse 2, 40545 Düsseldorf, Germany.

LEE, Mi-Joo; Pianist; b. 7 July 1959, Seoul, Republic of Korea; m. Klaus Hellwig. *Education:* Folkwanghochschule, Essen; Hochschule der Künste, Berlin; New England Conservatory, Boston; Mozarteum, Salzburg. *Career:* stage appearances with orchestra and solo recitals at Berlin Philharmonic Hall, Schauspielhaus, Munich, Dresden, Paris, Milan, Brussels, Tokyo, Seoul, various European countries and many German cities; television and radio appearances on WDR, NDR, RIAS

Berlin, Deutschlandfunk, Deutschland Radio Berlin, Radio France, BRT Brussels, Czechoslovak broadcast, Korean broadcast, Deutsche-Welle, Südwestfunk 3. *Recordings:* C. Saint-Saëns op 72, 52, 111; Humoresken (Schumann, Reger, Dohnany, Rachmaninov); M. Ravel Concerto G-Major; R. and C. Schumann Op 105, 121, Op 22; Beethoven Op 13, Chopin, Liszt and six Paganini Études; R. Schumann Op 3, 10, 14. *Address:* Mommsenstr 58, 10629 Berlin, Germany.

LEE, Michelle; Flautist; b. 31 May 1952, London, England; one d. *Education:* Bartók Conservatory, Budapest, Hungary, 1970–71; Royal College of Music, London, 1971–75; Robert Schumann Institute, Düsseldorf, Germany, 1975–76, 1977–78; Franz Liszt Academy, Budapest, Hungary, 1978–80; ARCM, Flute, Recorder and Piano; Examiner of Music for Trinity College, London; MA in Education and Professional Development. *Career:* Regular solo performances world-wide; Soloist for BBC Radio 3 and given many first performances including the World Premiere of György Kurtág's Seven Bagatelles, Op 14b, 1982 at her Wigmore Hall debut recital; First broadcast performance of Fauré's Morceau de Concours for Flute and Piano on BBC Radio 3, 1985; First British broadcast of György Kurtág's Seven Bagatelles, Op 14B on BBC Radio 3, 1987; First British broadcast of László Sáry's Pezzo Concerto on BBC Radio 3, 1988; Francisco Estévez, Roland Freisitzer, Philip Grange, Raimund Jülich, György Kurtág and Geoffrey Winters have written specially for her; founded the Charles Cros Festival of Music Fabrezan, France, 2003; mem British Flute Society; FRSA. *Compositions:* Scarlet Runner, for Flute, Percussion, Prerecorded Tape and 5 Synthesizers. *Recordings:* Soloist, Record of Contemporary Music with Live Electronics (Germany); Morton Feldman Flute Concerto with Moscow Philharmonic Orchestra, 1992; Günther Becker–Drei Inventionen, 1999. *Contributions:* Editor, Trinity College London Woodwind World Flute Albums 4 and 5. *Address:* 4 rue des Tonneliers, 11200 Fabrezan, France.

LEE, Ming Cho; Stage Designer; b. 3 Oct. 1930, Shanghai, China. *Education:* Occidental College and University of California at Los Angeles. *Career:* Theatre and ballet designs in New York, 1955–59; Peabody Arts Theater, Baltimore, 1959–63, with designs for Il Turco in Italia, Mahagonny, Werther, Hamlet and Les Pêcheurs de Perles; Designed Tristan und Isolde for Baltimore Civic Opera and Butterfly for the Opera Company of Boston, 1962; Resident Designer at San Francisco Opera from 1961, Juilliard School, New York, 1964–70; Metropolitan Opera, 1965–, with Figaro, Boris Godunov, Lohengrin and Khovanshchina (1985); Premiere of Ginastera's Bomarzo for the Opera Society of Washington, 1967, Giulio Cesare and Lucia di Lammermoor for Hamburg Staatsoper, 1969, 1971; Teacher of set design at Yale Drama School from 1968. *Address:* c/o Metropolitan Opera, Lincoln Center, New York, NY 10023, USA.

LEE, Noël; American Composer and Concert Pianist; b. 25 Dec. 1924, Nanking, China. *Education:* BA cum laude, Harvard University, Cambridge, Massachusetts, USA, 1948; Artist's Diploma, New England Conservatory of Music, Boston, 1948. *Career:* Numerous concert tours and appearances in North and South America, Europe, Australia; Engagements on every European State Radio; Vast solo, concerto and chamber repertoire. *Compositions include:* Caprices on the name Schoenberg, piano and orchestra; 8 études, piano; Dialogues, violin and piano; Convergences, flute and harpsichord; Chroniques, piano; Errances, band; 5 songs on Lorca, soprano, flute, guitar; Songs of Calamus, voice, clarinet, cello, percussion; Triptyque, violin, piano and orchestra; Dance Fantasy, orchestra; 5 Preludes prolonged, piano; Partita, quintet piano and winds; Le tombeau d'Aaron Copland, sextet; Azurs, voice and piano 4 hands, plus 13 other song cycles; Variations antiques, flute and piano; 3 Fantasy pieces, flute and guitar. *Recordings include:* 198 solo, piano 4-hand, chamber, and vocal works of Schubert, 19th–century French composers, Debussy, Ravel, Stravinsky, Bartók, Copland, Ives, Carter and other American composers. *Publications:* Critical edition of Debussy's Two Piano works, 1989, and Four-Hand Works, 2001. *Honours:* Commdr des Arts et Lettres, 1998; Grand Prix for Music, City of Paris, 1999. *Address:* 4 Villa Laugier, 75017 Paris, France. *E-mail:* noel.lee@wanadoo.fr.

LEE, Sung-Sook; Singer (soprano); b. 1948, Korea. *Education:* Studied in Korea and at the Juilliard School, New York. *Career:* Debut: Premiere of Menotti's Tamu Tamu, Chicago, 1973; Sang at Spoleto Festival and San Francisco, 1974; La Scala and Covent Garden 1975; Frankfurt Opera 1976–77; Seattle Opera and Miami from 1978; New York City Opera 1975–76; Concert appearances with the Buffalo Philharmonic, Seattle, Dallas and Pittsburgh Symphonies; Repertoire has included music by Puccini and Rossini (Stabat Mater). *Address:* c/o New York City Opera, Lincoln Center, New York, NY 10023, USA.

LEE, Young-Ja; Composer; b. 4 June 1936, Wonju, Korea. *Education:* Studied in Seoul, at the Paris and Brussels Conservatoires and the Manhattan School of Music. *Career:* Performances of her work in Europe, Korea and Central America. *Compositions include:* Suite for

orchestra, 1971; Movement symphonique for orchestra, 1972; Piano concerto, 1973; Piano sonata, 1985; Three Love Songs for soprano and harp, 1991; Gae-chun for orchestra, 1991; Quintet for flute, harp and string trio, 1992. *Address:* c/o KOMCA, 2,3/F Samjeon Building, 236-3 Nonhyeon-dong, Kangnam-gu, Seoul, Korea.

LEECH, Richard; Singer (Tenor); b. 1956, Binghamton, California, USA. *Career:* Sang first as baritone, then sang Offenbach's Hoffmann while a student; Many concert and opera appearances from 1980, notably at Cincinnati, Pittsburgh, Baltimore, Houston and Chicago; European debut at the Deutsche Oper Berlin, 1987, as Raoul in Les Huguenots; Chicago Lyric Opera, 1987, and La Scala, 1991, as Rodolfo; Has sung Gounod's Faust at San Diego, 1988, and at the Orange Festival and Metropolitan Opera, 1990; Pinkerton in Washington DC and Florence and La Scala (debut 1990), 1987 and 1989; Donizetti's Edgardo and Nemorino at the Deutsche Oper Berlin, 1988–89, and the Duke of Mantua at the New York City Opera (1988) and Metropolitan Opera, 1990; Season 1991/92 as Raoul in a new production of Les Huguenots at Covent Garden (debut), Pinkerton at Chicago and the Duke of Mantua at the Met; Rodolfo at the Met, 1994; Sang Faust at the Met, 1997; Season 1998 with Gounod's Roméo at San Diego, Werther for Nether-lands Opera, 1999; Season 2000–01 as Boito's Faust and Don José at the Met, Rodolfo in Luisa Miller for Palm Beach Opera and Verdi's Riccardo on debut at the Vienna Staatsoper; Concert engagements include Beethoven's Ninth and Verdi Requiem. *Recordings:* Les Huguenots; Fledermaus; Salome; Faust; Rosenkavalier. *Address:* c/o Metropolitan Opera, Lincoln Center, New York, NY 10023, USA.

LEEDY, Douglas; Composer, Conductor and Educator; b. 3 March 1938, Portland, Oregon, USA. *Education:* BA, Pomona College, 1959; MA, University of California, Berkeley, 1962; Karnatic vocal music with K V Narayanaswamy. *Career:* French horn, Oakland Symphony Orchestra, San Francisco Opera, Ballet Orchestras, Cabrillo Festival Orchestra, 1969–65; Music faculty, University of California, Los Angeles, 1967–70; Reed College, 1973–78; Professor of Electronic Music, Centro Simon Bolivar, Caracas, Venezuela, 1972; Musical Director, Portland Baroque Orchestra, 1984–85; Complete performances of Handel's Jephtha and Theodora, Portland Handel Festival, 1985; mem, Music Library Association; International Heinrich Schütz Society. *Compositions:* Usable Music I for Very Small Instruments with Holes, 1968; The Twenty-Fourth Psalm for chorus and orchestra, 1971; Fantasy on Wie schön leuchtet der Morgenstern for organ and voice; Canti/Music for contrabass and chamber ensemble; Music for Meantone Organ; Hymns from the Rig Veda for chorus and Javanese or American gamelan; Pastorale (Horace) for chorus and just-tuned piano, 4-hands, 1993; This is a Great Country, or What?, multimedia, 1995; 7 symphonies, No. 7 'Selene', 1997; 2 string quartets, 1975, 1995; No More Beethoven! for voices and electric guitar, 1997. *Recordings:* Entropical Paradise: 6 Sonic Environments, Seraphim. *Publications:* Harpsichord Book III (just tuning); Chansons from Petrucci in Original Notation, 1983. *Contributions:* Interval; The Courant; MLA Notes; The New Grove Dictionary of American Music. *Address:* c/o ASCAP, ASCAP Building, One Lincoln Plaza, New York, NY 10023, USA.

LEEF, Yinam (Arie); Composer; b. 21 Dec. 1953, Jerusalem, Israel; m. Tanya Fonarev, 23 Nov 1978, 1 s., 1 d. *Education:* BMus, Artist Diploma, Rubin Academy of Music, Jerusalem; MA, PhD, University of Pennsylvania; Composition Fellow, Tanglewood, 1982. *Career:* Visiting Lecturer, Swarthmore College, USA, 1982–84; Philadelphia College of the Performing Arts, 1984; Teaching, University of Pennsylvania, 1984–85; Lecturer, Senior Lecturer, Jerusalem Rubin Academy of Music and Dance, 1985–; Commissions including Fromm Music Foundation at Harvard, Swarthmore Music and Dance Festival, Concerto Soloists Chamber Orchestra of Philadelphia, Penn Contemporary Players, Jerusalem Symphony Orchestra, Israel Sinfonietta Be'er Sheva, Jerusalem Dance Workshop, Rinat Choir; Recent commissions include the Haifa Symphony Orchestra, Philadelphia Chamber Music Society, The Verdehr Trio, The Mannheim Series for Contemporary Music; mem, ACUM; League of Composers in Israel. *Compositions:* Gilgulim, woodwind trio, 1976, for string trio, 1980; Three Pieces, piano; Fireflies, soprano, flute, harpsichord, 1977; String Quartet No. 1, 1978; KO, solo oboe, 1978; Ha'Bor, 1978; Laments, chamber orchestra, 1979; Flowers, Insects and a Very Thin Line, flute, oboe, piano trio, 1979; Canaanit Fantasy, piano, 1981; The Invisible Carmel, soprano and 5 players, 1982; Violin concerto, 1983; Octet, 1984; A Place of Fire, mezzo and 11 players, 1985; Fanfares and Whispers, trumpet and string orchestra, 1986; Sounds, Shadows for choir, 1987; How Far East, How Further West?, piano, 1988; Trio for oboe, violin, horn, 1988; Scherzos and Serenades, orchestra, 1989; Elegy, harpsichord, 1990; Tribute, orchestra, 1991; Elegy for string quartet, 1991; Symphony No. 1, 1992; Sea Songs, equal voice choir, 1993; Cantilena, guitar, 1993; Threads of Time and Distance, alto, oboe and string orchestra, 1995; Visions of Stone City, Symphony No. 2, orchestra, 1995; Yizkor, flute, 1995; Said His Lover, alto and clarinet, 1996; Night Light orchestra, 1996; Triptych for clarinet, string trio and piano, 1997; T'filah for three violins, 1997; Viola Concerto, 1998; Thre Lyrical Songs for tenor and string trio, 1999; Bagatelles for flute and piano, 2000; String Quartet No. 2, 2001; most works published by the Israel Music Institute, Tel-Aviv, and by Theodore Presser Co in the USA. *Recordings include:* Symphony No. 1, Jerusalem Symphony Orchestra; Violin Concerto, Jerusalem Symphony Orchestra; Yizkor for flute, Noam Buchman, flute; T'filah for Three Violins, 2001; Numerous for Israel Broadcasting Authority. *Honours:* ACUM Prize, 1992; Israel Prime Minister Prize, 1993. *Current Management:* Israel Music Institute, Tel-Aviv. *Address:* 1 Ramban Street 10, Jerusalem 92422, Israel.

LEEK, Stephen; Composer and Conductor; b. 8 Oct. 1959, Sydney, New South Wales, Australia. *Education:* Study with Larry Sitsky, 1979–83; BA (Music), Canberra School of Music, 1983; ABC Young Composers Workshop, 1985. *Career:* Tasmanian Dance Company, 1982–85; Director, Arts Now; Artistic Director, Conductor, The Australian Voices; Commissions from Seymour Group, Chamber Made Opera, Brisbane Biennial Festival, Opera Queensland, The Australian Voices, Gondwana Voices, Centenary of Federation Ceremony, among others; Residencies with St Peters Lutheran College, 1988, 1989, 1996, and Tasmanian Dance Theatre, 1993; Part-time Lecturer, Composition and Improvisation, Queensland Conservatorium. *Compositions include:* At Times... Stillness, for organ, 1985; Thought, for female chorus, flute and piano, 1988; Once on a Mountain, and Songs of Space, Sea and Sky, for choir, 1988–89; Killcallow Catch, music theatre, 1990; Stroke, music theatre in 1 act, 1990; Voyage, for chorus, 1990; Five Songs, for female chorus, 1990; Five Song of the Sun, for orchestra, 1991; As You Like It, for piano, 1992; Great Southern Spirits, for chorus, and vocal soloists, 1993; Island Songs, for chorus, female soloists and piano, 1994; Ancient Cries, 1999; Seeking True South, opera, 2001. *Recordings include:* Sea Children, The Australian Voices; One World, Chanticleer. *Honours:* Sounds Australian Awards, 1991; Churchill Fellowship, 1997. *Address:* PO Box 839, Indooroopilly, Qld 4068, Australia. *E-mail:* artsnow@thehub.com.au. *Website:* www.the australianvoices.com.au.

LEES, Benjamin; Composer; b. 8 Jan. 1924, Harbin, China. *Education:* University of Southern California with Halsey Stevens, Ingolf Dahl; With George Antheil and in Europe. *Career:* Teacher, Peabody Conservatory, 1962–64, 1966–68; Queens College, New York, 1964–66; Manhattan School, 1972–74; Juilliard, 1976–77; Commissions, Tokyo String Quartet, Dallas, Delaware, Wichita and Pittsburgh Symphonies, Philadelphia and Louisville Orchestras, Chamber Music America, Cypress String Quartet, Seattle Symphony Orchestra, Detroit Symphony Orchestra, Orchestre Philharmonique de Monte Carlo, Ford Foundation. *Compositions:* 5 Piano Sonatas; 4 String Quartets; 5 Symphonies; 3 Violin Sonatas; Sonata, 2 pianos, 1951; Profile, orchestra, 1952; Declamations, strings, piano, 1953; 5 Symphonies; 3 Violin Sonatas; Concertos: Piano, 1955, 1966, Violin, 1958, Orchestra, 1959, Oboe, 1963, String Quartet, Orchestra, 1965, Chamber Orchestra, 1966, Woodwind Quintet, Orchestra, 1976, Brass, Orchestra, 1983, French Horn, Orchestra, 1992; The Oracle, music drama, 1955; Divertimento burlesca, orchestra, 1957; Concertante breve, 1959; Visions of Poets, cantata after Whitman, 1962; Spectrum, orchestra, 1964; The Gilded Cage, opera, 1964; Silhouettes, wind, percussion, 1967; Medea of Corinth, vocalists, wind quintet, timpani, 1970; Odyssey 1, piano trio, 1971, 2, solo piano, 1980; The Trumpet of the Swan, narrator, piano, 1972; Collage, string quartet, woodwind quintet, percussion, 1973; Etudes, piano, orchestra, 1974; Variations, piano, orchestra, 1976; Passacaglia, orchestra, 1976; Fanfare for a Centennial, 1976; Scarlatti Portfolio, ballet, 1979; Mobiles, orchestra, 1979; Double Concerto, piano, cello, 1982; Fantasy Variations, piano, 1984; Portrait of Rodin, orchestra, 1984; Mirrors, piano solo, 1992–94; Borealis, orchestra, 1993; Echoes of Normandy, tenor, orchestra, 1994; Celebration, orchestra, 1996; Constellations, orchestra, 1997; Piano Trio No. 2, Silent Voices, 1998; Trio for piano, violin and cello (Silent Voices), 1998; Intermezzo, string orchestra, 1998; Concerto for percussion and orchestra, 1999; Night Spectres, unaccompanied cello, 1999; 5 string quartets; Mirrors for piano (complete version), 2002; Tableau for two pianos, 2003; Tapestry for flute, clarinet, cello, piano, 2003; The Nervous Family for SSA chorus and 1 bassoon, 2003. *Recordings:* Symphonies 2, 3, Concerto for orchestra, Louisville Orchestra; Concerto for string quartet and orchestra, Royal Philharmonic; Violin Concerto, American Symphony; 4th Piano; 4th Piano Sonata, Gary Graffman; Complete Violin Works, Ellen Orner violin, Joel Wizansky piano; Concerto for french horn and orchestra, 1997; Symphony No. 4, Memorial Candles, 1998; Symphony Nos 2,3 and 5, Staatsphilharmonie Rheinland-Pfalz, 2001; Piano Concerto No.2, Albany Symphony Orchestra, withIan Hobson, piano, 2002; Piano Trio No.2 Silent Voices, 2002; Piano Concerto No.1, Nat. Orchestral Asscn, with Joseph Bloch, piano, 2003; Passacaglia for orchestra, Oregon Symphony, 2003. *Honours:* Guggenheim Fellow, 1954, 1966; Fulbright Fellow, 1956–57; Sir Arnold Bax Medal, 1958; Lancaster Symphony Orchestra Composer Award, 1985. *Address:* 2451-A Birdie Way, Palm Springs, CA 92264, USA.

LEFANU, Nicola (Frances); Composer and Professor of Music; b. 28 April 1947, Wickham Bishops, Essex, England. *Education:* MA (Oxon). *Career:* Broadcasts and performances in the United Kingdom, America, Europe and Australia; Professor of Music at University of York. *Compositions:* Over 50 vocal, choral, solo, chamber, orchestral, theatre and ballet works including: Variations for oboe quartet, The Same Day Dawns for soprano and chamber ensemble, Columbia Falls for orchestra, But Stars Remaining for soprano; Variations for piano and orchestra, 1982; Alto Saxophone Concerto, 1989; Concerto for Clarinet and Strings, 1997; Duo Concertante for violin, viola and orchestra, 1999; 2 string quartets, 1988, 1997; Sextet: A Wild Garden, 1997; Operas: Dawnpath, 1977, The Story of Mary O'Neill, radio opera for 17 voices, 1989; The Green Children, 1990; Blood Wedding, 1992; The Wildman, opera, 1995. *Honours:* Cobbett Chamber Music Prize, 1968; 1st Prize, BBC Composition Competition, 1971; Mendelssohn Scholarship, 1972; Gulbenkian Dance award, 1972; Harkness Fellowship, 1973; Honorary Fellow, St Hilda's College, Oxford, 1993; Honorary D.Mus, Durham, 1995; FRCM, 1995; Hon. FTCL. *Current Management:* Novello (Music Sales); Maecenas. *Address:* 5 Holly Terrace, York YO10 4 DS, England.

LEFEBVRE, Claude; Composer; b. 11 Nov. 1931, Ardres, Calais, France; m. Ingeborg Giese, 1 May 1965, 2 d. *Education:* Studied composition with Darius Milhaud, Paris Conservatory, 1959–60; Composition with Pierre Boulez, Musikakademie, Basel, Switzerland, 1961–62. *Career:* Teacher, Analysis and Composition, Conservatory, Metz, France, 1966–96; Founder, Artistic Director, Centre européen pour la recherche musicale, and International Meeting of Contemporary Music, Metz, 1972–92; Lecturer, Contemporary Music, University of Metz, 1976; Founder and Artistic Director, electro-acoustic studio, Lorraine, 1978; Founder and Artistic Director, Music Centre, Rendez-vous musique nouvelle, Forbach, France, 1996. *Compositions include:* Suite, for baritone and ensemble, 1960; D'un arbre de nuit, for flute, cello and piano, 1971; Etwas weiter, for 24 musicians, 1972; Verzweigungen, for organ, 1976; Dérives nocturnes, for choir, 4 horns and organ, 1978; Mémoires souterraines, for flute, clarinet and amplified cello, 1980; Océan de Terre, after a poem by Apollinaire, for soprano, flute, clarinet, trumpet, cello and magnetic band, 1981; Lorraine, for horn and magnetic band, 1983; Oregon, own poem, for soprano and quintet, 1984; Mosella, after a poem by d'Ausone, for organ, 2 trumpets and magnetic band, 1984; Savoure, on a text by Nathalie Méfano, for solo bass, 1984; La Chute, own poem, for bass, piano and magnetic band, 1987; Vallée, Homage to Maurice Ravel, for solo horn, 1987; Virage, on a poem by the composer, 12 mixed voices, 1987; Sur le lac... la main, for children's choir, 1991; L'Insoumise, 2 trumpets, piano and string orchestra, 1991; D'un arbre-océan, for piano, 1992; X..., for baritone and 12 instrumentalists, 1994; Vertigo for soprano and string sextet, 1994; Mort, for baritone, piano and 3 brass instruments, 1996; L'homme et la mer, for organ, 1997; Musique pour René Char, for horn and cello, 1998. *Honours:* Grand Prix, SACEM, for chamber music, 1980; Officier des Arts et Lettres, Cultural Ministry, Paris, 1985. *Address:* 9 rue Claude Debussy, 57130 Jouy-aux-Arches, France.

LEFEBVRE, Pierre; Tenor; b. 1959, Drummondville, Quebec, Canada. *Education:* Studied in Montreal and Italy. *Career:* Sang at first in such roles as Edgardo and Rodolfo; Guest appearances in Lucca, Rome and Montreal; La Scala Milan in Fidelio, Traviata and Don Carlos; Frankfurt Opera Franchetti's Cristoforo Colombo; Further Giovanna d'Arco at Bologna, and in Don Zauberflöte at Turin; Sang in Les Contes de Hoffmann at the Met, 1998. *Recordings include:* Video of Giovanna d'Arco (Teldec). *Address:* c/o Teatro alla Scala, Via Filodrammatici 2, 20121 Milan, Italy.

LEFKOWITZ, Mischa; Concert Violinist; b. 17 March 1954, Riga, Latvia; m. Irini Lefkowitz, 15 June 1980. *Education:* Special School of Music, Riga; Moscow Conservatory of Music; Wayne State University, Detroit, USA; Mozarteum Academy, Salzburg. *Career:* Debut: New York, 1984; Paris, 1985; Radio Show, KPFK; Radio appearances, KPFC, Los Angeles, KCRW, Los Angeles; Television appearances on CBS; Orchestral appearances with major orchestras and recitals; mem, Chamber Music America; College Music Society. *Compositions:* (Recorded) Mozart Concerto A Major; Giardini Concerto A Major; Bloch Concerto; Works by Sarasate, Prokofiev. *Recordings:* Laurel and Sequence Records; Recorded with London Philharmonic and English Chamber Orchestras. *Contributions:* New York Times; Boston Globe; LA Times. *Honours:* City of Paris Prize, 1985; Carnegie Hall American Music Prize, 1983. *Current Management:* ICA Management. *Address:* 3435 Bonnie Hill Drive, Los Angeles, CA 90068, USA.

LEFTERESCU, Petre; Violinist and Professor; b. 1 May 1936, Bistrita, Romania; m. Ogneanca Tomici, 27 Sept 1958. *Education:* Bucharest Music Academy, 1953–58 with I. Geanta; Postgraduate courses, Moscow Conservatory, USSR, at D Oistrakh Violin Chair, 1967; Doctor in Musicology, Bucharest, National University of Music, 1999. *Career:* Solo concerts and chamber music, tours as violinist, Romania, 1958–; Violin professor, Cluj Music Academy, 1958–69; Professor of Chamber Music,

Bucharest Academy of Music, 1960–; 1st violin, Forum String Quartet, 1985–; Rector of the National University of Music, Bucharest, 1992–96 and 1996–2000; Vicepresident Association Europeanne des Conservatoires, AEC, Paris, 1992–2000; Concert Tours in Germany, Spain, Hungary, China, Singapore. *Recordings:* Romanian and universal music. *Contributions:* Muzica Contemporanul. *Current Management:* ARIA, Romanian Artists' Management Company. *Address:* Calea Victoriei Nr 83, et IX, ap 37, Bucharest 70176, Romania. *Telephone:* 0040 21 6503739.

LEGA, Luigi; Singer (Tenor); b. 7 April 1940, Bordighera, Italy. *Education:* Studied in Rome, Basle and Mannheim. *Career:* Debut: Overhausen, as Pinkerton, 1961; Many appearancea at such German opera centres as Munich, Hamburg, Stuttgart, Mannheim, Berlin (Deutsche Oper) and Wuppertal; Further engagements at Amsterdam, Palermo, Barcelona, Rio de Janeiro, Trieste and Vienna as Verdi's Radames, Duke of Mantua, Alvaro, Alfredo, Don Carlos, Manrico and Riccardo; Also a noted interpreter of Don José, Edgardo, Florestan, Andrea Chénier, Turiddu, Rodolfo, Cavaradossi and Des Grieux in Manon Lescaut; Teacher of singing in Wuppertal. *Address:* c/o Wuppertal Buhnen, Spinnstrasse 4, 5600 Wuppertal, Germany.

LEGANY, Denes; Composer, Pianist, Conductor and Professor; b. 14 May 1965, Budapest, Hungary; m. Eva Toth 1990; three s. one d. *Education:* BM, Bartók Conservatory of Music; MM, DMA, Liszt Acad. of Music; MD, General Education Management, Budapest Univ. *Career:* Prof., Budapest Univ. School of Music, 1987–94; Prof., Vice-Pres., Budapest Conservatory of Music, 1993–98; specialist, Hungarian Music Council, 1997–; Dir, László Lajtha School of Music and Arts, 1998–99; Artistic and Educational Adviser, Hungarian Music Council, 1999–; Liason Officer, Hungarian Music Information Centre, 1999–; Visiting Prof., several colls and univs; recitals in three continents; lectures on television and radio. *Recordings:* Hommage à Bartók, 1995; works recorded by Hungarian and foreign record companies; Werner Brüggemann series. *Publications:* Easy Piano Pieces for children; Festival Music, for band; Trios for French horn; Suite for trumpet; Trombone Quartets; Saxophone Quartet; Air, for saxophone and piano; Flute Duos; Three Children's Choruses; Fragments, for saxophone solo; Developing Contemporary Art Pedagogical Concepts, 1993. *Address:* Apahida Utca 11, 1112 Budapest, Hungary.

LEGANY, Dezsö; Musicologist; b. 19 Jan. 1916, Szombathely, Hungary; m. Erzsébet Hegyi, 23 Sept 1961, 2 s. *Education:* LLD, University of Pécs; Composition, Liszt Academy of Music, Budapest; D.MusSc, Hungarian Academy of Sciences, Budapest. *Career:* Professor, Liszt Academy of Music, Budapest, 1951–58; Professor, Bartók Conservatory of Music, Budapest, 1958–73; Head of Hungarian Music Department, Institute for Musicology, Hungarian Academy of Sciences, 1973–83. *Publications:* Henry Purcell, 1959, 2nd Edition, 1981; A Chronicle of Hungarian Music: A Thousand Years of Music History in Documents, 1962; Works of F Erkel, 1975; Liszt in Hungary 1869–1873, 1976; Letters of Z Kodály, 1982; Liszt and His Country, 1869–1873, 1983, 2nd edition, 1997; F Liszt Unbekannte Presse und Briefe aus Wien 1822–1886, 1984; Liszt in Hungary 1874–86, 1986; Liszt and His Country, 1874–1886, 1992; Letters of Z Kodály, Vol. II, 2000. *Contributions:* New Grove Dictionary; New Grove Dictionary of Opera; Sohlmans Musiklexikon; The Concise Oxford Dictionary of Opera; Zenei Lexikon; Studia Musicologica; Magyar Zene; The New Hungarian Quarterly; Bulletin of the International Kodály Society. *Address:* Apahida u 11, 1112 Budapest, Hungary.

LEGGATE, Robin; Singer (Tenor); b. 18 April 1946, West Kirby, Cheshire, England. *Education:* Studied at Queen's College, Oxford (1964–67) and the Royal Northern College of Music. *Career:* Royal Opera House, Covent Garden from 1977–2003, as Cassio in Otello (conducted by Zubin Mehta, Christoph von Dohnányi and Colin Davis); Elemer (Arabella), Narraboth (Salome), the Painter in Lulu and Tamino in a new production of Die Zauberflöte, 1979; Has also sung in Prince Igor and Il Trovatore at Covent Garden; Appearances with the Netherlands Opera and at the Hamburg Staatsoper from 1978; South Australian Opera, 1982, as Ferrando in Così fan tutte; Théâtre du Châtelet, Paris, as Tamino, 1983; Other Mozart roles include Belmonte and Don Ottavio, which he has sung with most of the regional British companies; Recent engagements in Le nozze di Figaro in Madrid, Weber's Oberon with Scottish Opera, Eisenstein in a new production of Die Fledermaus for Scottish Opera, and the premiere of André Laporte's Das Schloss, in Brussels; Has sung at the Festival Hall from 1976 (debut with the London Symphony in Pulcinella); In 1981 sang in Mendelssohn's Elijah at Florence and appeared in Mozart's C minor Mass with the London Philharmonic, conducted by Solti; Sang in the stage premiere of Gerhard's Duenna, Madrid, 1992; Sang in world premiere of Life with an Idiot by Schnittke at Netherlands Opera, 1992; Opéra Bastille (St François d'Assise) and at Salzburg Festival (Salome), 1993; Sang in first production of Stiffelio (Verdi) at Royal Opera House, 1993; Cassio at Covent Garden, 1994; The Scribe (Khovanshchina) at La

Monnaie, Brussels; Don Basilio in Figaro for the Royal Opera, 1998; Sang Dr. Caius in Falstaff which opened the new Royal Opera House and Pollux in Die Liebe der Danaë at Garsington, 1999; Panait in The Greek Passion by Martinů at Covent Garden, 2000 and Peter Quint with Chicago Opera Theater, 2003. *Recordings include:* La Fanciulla del West from Covent Garden; Haydn's Armida; The Light of Life by Elgar. *Address:* 26 Baronsmere Road, London, N2 9QU.

LEGGE, Anthony; Pianist and Chief Coach; b. 1958, England. *Education:* Guildhall School London; Oxford University; London Opera Centre: Piano accompaniment with Geoffrey Parsons and Paul Hamburger. *Career:* Coach at Glyndebourne from 1993, with Béatrice et Bénédict, Eugene Onegin (1996) and Rodelinda, 1998; Song recitals with Janet Baker, Thomas Allen, Alan Opie and Robert Tear; Assistant at Bayreuth for Die Meistersinger and Barenboim-Kupfer Ring cycle; Head of music at English National Opera and engagements with other British opera companies. *Recordings include:* Recital albums with Linda Finnie. *Publications:* The Art of Auditioning (Rhinegold). *Address:* c/o English National Opera, St Martin's Lane, London, WC2, England.

LEHANE, Maureen; concert and opera singer (mezzo-soprano); b. 19 Sept. 1932, London, England; m. Peter Wishart 1966 (died 1984). *Education:* Guildhall School of Music and Drama; studied with Hermann Weissenborn in Berlin, John and Aida Dickens. *Career:* has sung numerous leading roles, (Operas including Arianna and Faramondo) with Handel Opera Societies of England and America, in London and in Carnegie Hall, New York, also in Poland, Sweden and Germany, gave a numer of Masterclasses on the interpretation of Handel's vocal music (notably at 's-Hertogenbosch Festival, Netherlands, 1972, 1973); Debut at Glyndebourne, 1967, as Melide in Cavalli's L'Ormindo; Festival appearances include Stravinsky Festival, Cologne; City of London; Aldeburgh; Cheltenham; Three Choirs; Bath; Oxford Bach; Göttingen Handel Festival; Toured North America, 3 month tour of Australia, 2 month tour of Far East and Middle East, 1971; Sang in Netherlands and for Belgium television; Visits to Berlin, Lisbon, Poland and Rome, 1979–80; Warsaw, 1981; Title role of Handel's Ariodante, Sadler's Wells, 1974; Wishart's Clytemnestra, London, 1974; Purcell's Dido and Aeneas, Netherlands Opera, 1976; Started an annual music festival dedicated to the memory of Peter Wishart, 1986–; Great Elm Music Festival (Jackdaws, Great Elm, devoted to music education); Jury, International Singing Competitions', 's-Hertogenbosch Festival, Netherlands, 1982–, and Llangollen International Eisteddfod from 1991. *Recordings include:* Bach, Haydn, Mozart, Handel. *Publications:* Songs of Purcell (ed. with Peter Wishart). *Honours:* Arts Council Award to study in Berlin.

LEHMANN, Charlotte; Singer (Soprano) and Professor; b. 16 Jan. 1938, Zweibrücken, Germany; m. Ernst Huber-Contwig, 21 June 1965, 1 s. *Education:* Academy of Music and University of Saarland, Saarbrücken, with Sibylle Ursula Fuchs, then private study with Paul Lohmann, Wiesbaden. *Career:* Sang at concerts in Europe and America; Broadcasts, all German radio stations, France Musique, Schweizerischer Rundfunk, RTB Brussels, NL Hilversum, Turkish Radio, others; Television performances on ARD and ZDF; Started teaching at Hanover Music Academy, 1972; Appointed to Chair of Voice, Würzburg Academy of Music, 1988–; Has taught winners of international prizes, including Lioba Braun, Thomas Quasthoff and Maria Kowollik; Has led international master classes in Brazil, Chile, England, Bulgaria, Japan and Luxembourg; Has regularly given courses at the Haus Marteau music centre, Lichtenberg-Bayreuth; Editor, Bach and Mozart arias for all voice parts, for publishers Bärenreiter-Verlag; International jury service; Lectures; President, Bundesverband Deutscher Gesangspädagogen. *Recordings:* Works of Bach, Mozart, Schumann, Wolf, Fauré, Debussy, Hindemith, Schoenberg, other composers. *Honours:* Prizewinner, L'Amour du Chant International Competition and UFAM, Paris; German Record Critics Prize for Debussy and Schoenberg recording, 1982. *Address:* Bundesverband Deutscher Gesangspädagogen, Gellerstrasse 55, 30175 Hannover, Germany.

LEHMANN, Hans Ulrich; Composer and Professor; b. 4 May 1937, Biel, Switzerland; m. Ursula Lehmann. *Education:* BA, 1956; Universities of Berne, Zürich and Basle, 1956–67; Diplomas: Violoncello, 1960, Music Theory, 1962; Masterclasses in Composition with Boulez and Stockhausen, 1960–63. *Career:* Lecturer, Zürich University, 1969–90; Professor, Theory, Composition, 1972–98, Director, 1976–98, Musikhochschule, Zürich; President, SUISA (Swiss Authors Association), 1991–; mem, Numerous professional organisations. *Compositions include:* Quanti, 1962; Mosaik, 1964; Noten, 1964–66; Spiele, 1965; Rondo, 1967; Instants, 1968; Konzert, 1969; Régions III, 1970; discantus I and II, 1970; Sonata da chiesa, 1971; Tractus, 1971; zu streichen, 1974; zu blasen, 1975; Tantris, 1976–77; Motetus Paraburi, 1977–78; Kammermusik I, 1978–79; Kammermusik II, 1979; Duette, 1980; Lege mich wie ein Siegel auf dein Herz, 1980–83; Canticum I and II, 1981; Stroking, 1982; Mirlitonnades, 1983; battuto a tre–tratto, 1983;

Mon amour, 1983; Triplum, 1984; ludes, 1985; Alleluja, 1985; In Memoriam Nicolai de Flue, 1986–87; Fragmente, 1986–87; Streichquartett, 1987–88; Osculetur me, 1988–89; de profundis, 1988–89; Esercizi, 1989; Wandloser Raum, 1989; ad missam Prolationum, 1989–90; etwas Klang von meiner Oberfläche, 1989–90; Nocturnes, 1990–91; Ut signaculum, 1991–92; El mar, 1993; Prélude à une étendue, 1993–94; Battements, 1994–95; Book of Songs, 1999; Twi-Light, for soprano and ensemble, 1999; Vagues, 1999–2000; Inquiétudes, 2000; Instantanés, 2000; Ritenuto, 2000; Notturo, 2001; Dédales, 2001–02; Der Rat der Rose, 2002; Annäherungen an HH, 2002–03; Trajets, 2003; Viola in all moods and senses, 2003; Um-risse, 2003. *Contributions:* Professional journals. *Honours:* Composers Prize, Swiss Musicians Association, 1988; Music Prize, City of Zürich, 1993. *Address:* Haldenstrasse 35, 8615 Wermatswil, Switzerland.

LEHMANN, Wilfred; Composer, Violinist and Conductor; b. 1929, Melbourne, Victoria, Australia. *Education:* Studied in Australia and London; Violinist with the Birmingham Orchestra, 1958–60; Conductor, Tokyo Philharmonic Orchestra, 1960–70; Assistant Conductor Queensland Symphony Orchestra, 1972; Nashville Symphony, and Chamber Orchestra, 1976–79; Conductor ABC Sinfonia, Australia, 1982; Member of Sydney String Quartet; Commisions include: Song of Mululu, 1977; Two String Quartets (2nd 1988); Bacchanals, for orchestra, 1988; Concerto for two pianos and percussion, 1991. *Recordings include:* Bacchanals, and 2nd String Quartet. *Honours:* First Prize, Carl Flesch International Violin Competition (London), 1958; Fellowship in Composition, Tennessee Arts Commission, 1979. *Address:* c/o APRA, 1A Eden Street, Crows Nest, NSW 2065, Australia.

LEHNHOFF, Nikolaus; opera producer and stage designer; b. 20 May 1939, Hanover, Germany. *Career:* trained as asst stage dir, Deutsche Oper Berlin and at Bayreuth and the Metropolitan Operas 1963–71; Staged Die Frau ohne Schatten at the Paris Opéra, 1971; Director of several opera productions in Germany and Switzerland; San Francisco, 1985, Der Ring des Nibelungen; Produced Katya Kabanova at Glyndebourne and Der fliegende Holländer at Santa Fe, both in 1988; Returned to Glyndebourne, 1989, Jenůfa; Idomeneo at the Salzburg Festival, 1990; Munich Opera, 1990, Der fliegende Holländer; Elektra at Leipzig, 1991; Season 1991/92 with Lohengrin at Frankfurt and Henze's Der Prinz von Homburg at the Munich Festival; Produced The Makropulos Case by Janáček at Glyndebourne, 1995; Pfitzner's Palestrina at Covent Garden, 1997; Tosca for Netherlands Opera, 1998; Bartered Bride at Glyndebourne, 1999; Henze's Boulevard Solitude at Covent Garden, 2001; Tristan und Isolde at Glyndebourne 2003. *Address:* c/o Glyndebourne Festival Opera, Lewes, Sussex BN8 5UU, England.

LEHR, Edit; Singer (Soprano); b. 1954, Budapest, Hungary. *Education:* Studied at the Budapest School of Music and at the Cologne Musikhochschule. *Career:* Sang at Wuppertal Opera, 1980–82, the Freiburg Opera 1982–86, then at Gelsenkirchen; Guest appearances in Heidelberg, Vienna, Basel and Budapest; Among her best roles are Gilda, Violetta, Musetta, Donna Anna, Lauretta, Rosina, Fiordiligi, Susanna, Gretel, the Princess in Der Zwerg by Zemlinsky; Frequent concert appearances throughout Europe. *Address:* c/o Musiktheater im Revier, Kennedyplatz, Pf 101854, 45881 Gelsenkirchen, Germany.

LEHRBAUMER, Robert; Pianist, Conductor and Organist; b. 20 July 1960, Vienna, Austria. *Education:* Studied Piano, Organ, Conducting, Composition, Vienna School of Music and Dramatic Art; Diplomas with highest distinction, Organ, Piano, 1987, 1988. *Career:* Played with Vienna Philharmonic Orchestra, Vienna Symphonic Orchestra, Austrian Broadcasting Corporation Orchestra and other major orchestras; Conductors: Claudio Abbado, Yehudi Menuhin, André Previn, Sándor Végh; Appeared with Wolfgang Schneiderhan, Anton Dermota, Walter Berry, Philippe Entremont; Concerts in most European countries, Korea, Japan, Thailand, Indonesia, Malaysia, Mexico, Argentina, USA (including Schubert Festival, Washington, and Carnegie Recital Hall, New York, Kenya, Uganda); International festivals, Vienna, Salzburg, Lucerne, Nurnberg, Prague Spring Festival, Bruckner Festival, Linz Festival and Cervantino, Mexico; Many radio and television performances; Teaching, summer academies, Austria and abroad; World premieres of new works; Specialist, Schubert piano works, Haydn, Mozart, Beethoven piano concertos, A Berg, F Schmidt, E Schulhoff, K Szymanowski. *Recordings:* Baroque, Romantic and contemporary piano music (Liszt, Schumann, Tchaikovsky, Brahms, Schubert, Complete Piano Works by Gottfried von Einem, Albinoni, Pachelbel, Muffat, Kerll). *Current Management:* Freunde der Claviermusik. *Address:* Freunde der Claviermusik, Penknergasse 21, 3150 Wilhelmsburg, Austria.

LEHRMAN, Leonard (Jordan); Conductor, Composer, Pianist and Organist, Accompanist, Translator, Editor and Director; b. 20 Aug. 1949, Kansas, USA; m. 1st Karen S Campbell, 31 July 1978, divorced 1986; 2nd Helene R Williams (Spierman), 14 July 2002. *Education:*

Private study with Elie Siegmeister, 1960–69; Fontainebleau Conservatoire, 1969; BA, Harvard College, 1971; Ecole Normale de Musique, Paris, 1971–72; Salzburg Mozarteum, 1972; Opera conducting, Indiana University, 1975–76; MFA, 1975, DMA, Composition, 1977, Cornell University; MS-LS, Long Island University, 1995. *Career:* Debut: As Pianist, Carnegie Recital Hall, 1979; As Conductor, Bremerhaven and Berlin, 1981, 1983; Assistant Chorus Master and Assistant Conductor, Metropolitan Opera, 1977–78; Assistant Conductor, Heidelberg Festival, 1979, Augsburg Städtische Bühne, 1980, and Basler Theater, 1980–81; Conductor, Schauspielhaus Wien, 1981; Kapellmeister, Stadttheater Bremerhaven, 1981–83; Chief Coach, Conductor, Theater des Westens, 1983–84; Founder, Jewish Music Theatre of Berlin, 1983, Laureate Conductor, 1986–; President, Long Island Composers Alliance, 1991–98, Archivist Emeritus, 1999–; Founder, Dir, Long Island Composers Archive, Long Island Univ., 1994–; Librarian, Oyster Bay-East Norwich Public LIbrary, 1995–; Ed., The Marc Blitzstein Songbook, Vols 1–3, 1999–2003; Dir Oceanside Chorale, 2003–; Minister of Music, Christ Church Babylon, 2003–; Has appeared on ZDF, WTIU and WCIC television and various other television and radio stations including WQXR, WGBH, WBUR, WFMT, KPFA, WHRB (Chief Producer, 1968–70), and WBAI (Producer, 1989–91). *Compositions:* 165, including Flute Concerto; Violin Concerto; 6 musicals: Comic Tragedy of San Po Jo, Growing Up Woman, Let's Change the Woild!, E.G.: A Musical Portrait of Emma Goldman, Superspy!: The S-e-c-r-e-t Musical, The Booby Trap or Off Our Chests; 10 operas: Idiots First (completion of work begun by Marc Blitzstein), Karla, Suppose a Wedding (all part of Tales of Malamud), Sima, Hannah, The Family Man, The Birthday of the Bank, New World: An Oopera About What Columbus Did to the "Indians", Sacco and Vanzetti (completion of work begun by Marc Blitzstein), The Wooing. *Address:* 33 Court Street, Valley Stream, NY 11580, USA. *Telephone:* (516) 256-4209 (after 10am). *Fax:* (516) 256-4210. *E-mail:* elehrman@liu.edu. *Website:* ljlehrman.artists-in-residence.com.

LEIB, Gunther; Singer (Baritone) and Professor; b. 12 April 1927, Gotha, Thuringen, Germany. *Education:* After violin studies entered vocal class at the Weimar Conservatory. *Career:* First violin in Landeskapelle at Gotha from 1949; Stage debut at Kothen, 1952, as Bartolo in Il Barbiere di Siviglia., Sang at Kothen, Meinigen and Nordhausen; Stadttheater Halle, 1956–57; Staatsoper Dresden from 1957, Berlin from 1961; Sang Christus in Bach's St John Passion in Italy, 1957, conducted by Franz Konwitschny; Annual appearances at the Handel Festivals, Halle; Salzburg Easter Festival, 1974–75, as Beckmesser in Die Meistersinger, conducted by Karajan (also at the Met, 1976); Guest engagements at the Paris Opéra, Moscow Bolshoi, Hamburg Staatsoper, National Operas of Warsaw, Prague and Budapest, Sofia, Stockholm and Helsinki; Other roles were Guglielmo, Raimondo, Papageno, Don Pasquale and Germont; Professor at the Carl Maria von Weber Hochschule, Dresden, 1964–76; Professor at the Musikhochschule Berlin. *Recordings:* Così fan tutte; Die Zauberflöte; Ein Deutsches Requiem; Lucia di Lammermoor; Don Pasquale; La Traviata; St Matthew Passion; Der Dorfjahrmarkt by Benda; La Bohème; Einstein by Dessau. *Address:* Hochschule für Musik Hanns Eisler, Otto-Grotewohlstrase 19, 1008 Berlin, Germany.

LEIDLAND, Hilde; Singer (Soprano); b. 1957, Lillestrom, Norway. *Education:* Studied in Oslo, Stockholm and Rome. *Career:* Royal Opera, Stockholm, from 1986, as Mozart's Susanna and Papagena, Gilda in Rigoletto, 1988, and in Monteverdi's Poppea; Other roles in Stockholm include Olympia, Sophie in Rosenkavalier, Zerbinetta, Queen of Night, Constanze, Zerlina and Oscar in Ballo in Maschera; Hanover, 1984, as Mozart's Blondchen; Bayreuth Festival, 1985–92, as the Woodbird, Flower Maiden and Woglinde; Guested at Nice several times, as Oscar in Un Ballo in Maschera and Marcelline in Fidelio; Other guest appearances in Paris, Brussels, Berlin, Stuttgart, Düsseldorf, Wiesbaden, Salzburg and Oslo; Sang Fortuna in Carmina Burana for the Royal Opera, Stockholm, 1998; Regular concert engagements. *Recordings include:* Barbarina in Figaro and Flower Maiden; Parsifal with Barenboim and the Berlin Philharmonic; The Ring and Parsifal from Bayreuth; A live recording made at the Théâtre de la Monnaie of Pascal Dusapin's Opera Medea. *Address:* Royal Opera, PO Box 16094, 10322 Stockholm. Sweden.

LEIFERKUS, Sergey Petrovich; Russian singer (baritone); b. 4 April 1946, Leningrad. *Education:* Leningrad Conservatory with Barsov and Shaposhnikov. *Career:* stage debut in Leningrad Theatre of Musical Comedy 1972; soloist Maly Theatre of Opera and Ballet 1972–78, sang in Eugene Onegin, Iolanta, Il Barbiere di Siviglia and Don Giovanni; Kirov (now Mariinsky) Theatre of Opera and Ballet 1977–85, sang Prince Andrei in War and Peace by Prokofiev; Wexford Festival 1982–86, in Grisélidis and Le Jongleur de Notre Dame by Massenet, Hans Heiling by Marschner and Königskinder by Humperdinck; Scottish Opera from 1985, as Don Giovanni, Germont and Eugene Onegin 1988; Covent Garden 1987, as Eugene Onegin and Tomsky in

The Queen of Spades, with the Kirov Company; ENO 1987, as Zurga in Les Pêcheurs de Perles; US debut 1987, in Symphony No. 13 by Shostakovich, with the Boston Symphony; Wigmore Hall debut recital, sang Luna in a new production of Il Trovatore at Covent Garden and appeared in a concert performance of Giovanna d'Arco at the Festival Hall 1989; concert performance of Mlada by Rimsky-Korsakov, Barbican Hall; US opera debut at San Francisco, as Telramund in Lohengrin, and the title role in Prince Igor at Covent Garden 1989–90; sang Rangoni in Boris Godunov at the Kirov Theatre, St Petersburg 1990; Luna at the Teatro Colón, Buenos Aires, Mazeppa at the Bregenz Festival and Netherlands Opera, Amsterdam, Ruprecht in Prokofiev's Fiery Angel at the BBC Promenade Concerts, London; Tomsky in The Queen of Spades in Boston and New York with the Boston Symphony; Onegin in Montreal, Ruprecht in St Petersburg, Tomsky at Glyndebourne and Vienna State Opera, Rangoni at San Francisco, Iago at Covent Garden and at the Metropolitan 1992; sang Carlo in La Forza del Destino for VARA Radio at the Amsterdam Concertgebouw, Shostakovich 13th Symphony with the New York Philharmonic, Scarpia, Amonasro, Escamillo and Luna 1993; debut at La Scala in The Fiery Angel, further performances as Iago at the Metropolitan, New York, Scarpia at Opéra Bastille, Paris, sang Mephistopheles in La Damnation de Faust with Ozawa and the Berlin Philharmonic in Berlin, the title role in Nabucco at the Bregenz Festival, sang Ruprecht in San Francisco and gave recitals across America, Escamillo at the Teatro Colón, Buenos Aires and Prokofiev's Ivan the Terrible at La Scala 1994; sang Iago at Covent Garden, Mazeppa at Netherlands Opera, Amsterdam, Shostakovich 13th Symphony in Leipzig with the Gewandhaus Orchestra, Gryaznoy in The Tsar's Bride for Opera Orchestra of New York in Carnegie Hall, Escamillo in a gala performance of Carmen in Stuttgart, Iago at the Vienna State Opera, recitals at Cologne and Graz, Amonasro at the Berlin State Opera under Mehta, Scarpia at the Ravinia Festival 1995; Boccanegra in the original version of Verdi's opera and Telramund in Lohengrin at Covent Garden 1997; Klingsor in Parsifal with the Royal Opera, RFH 1998; Klingsor at the Royal Albert Hall (concert), Simon Boccanegra at Melbourne and Prince Igor in Houston 2000–01; season 2001–02 in Pique Dame in Los Angeles and Washington, DC, Simon Boccanegra in Dallas, Aida in Berlin, Lohengrin in Munich, Tosca in London and Munich, solo recitals in Paris and London; season 2002–03 in Otello in Japan (tour), London and San Francisco, Pique Dame in Munich, Fidelio in Dallas, Tosca in Munich, Shostakovich Symphony No. 13 in Prague and Lohengrin in London. *Current Management:* Askonas Holt, Lonsdale Chambers, 27 Chancery Lane, London, WC2A 1PF, England.

LEIGH, David (Anthony); Harpsichordist and Fortepianist; b. 3 April 1953, London, England. *Education:* BA, Reading University, 1975; Guildhall School of Music. *Career:* Debut: Wigmore Hall, 1975; Recitals all over the United Kingdom, Canada, USA, Netherlands, Belgium, Austria; Lectures in USA and Austria; Masterclasses in USA and the United Kingdom; Radio broadcasts in the United Kingdom, Canada and USA; Known for knowledge of early keyboard instruments and their restoration. *Recordings include:* Harpsichords Historic and Unique, 3 vols, in preparation. *Publications:* Book on early pianos in preparation; Encyclopaedia articles on harpsichord and clavichord. *Contributions:* Antique Collector, on square pianos. *Address:* Greystones, The Slade, Charlbury, Oxford OX7 3 SJ, England.

LEISNER, David, BA; American classical guitarist, composer and teacher; b. 22 Dec. 1953, Los Angeles, CA. *Education:* Wesleyan University and studied with John Duarte, David Starobin, Richard Winslow, Virgil Thomson and David Del Tredici. *Career:* teacher of guitar at Amherst College, 1976–78; New England Conservatory from 1980; Manhattan School of Music from 1993; New York debut at Merkin Hall, 1979; Solo and Chamber Music Recitals in USA, Canada and Europe; Concerto Soloist with L'Orchestre de la Suisse Romande, Australian Chamber Orchestra, New York Chamber Ensemble and others; Compositions performed by the Fresno Philharmonic, Sanford Sylvan, Eugenia Zukerman, The Saturday Brass Quintet and the Los Angeles Guitar Quartet. *Compositions include:* Embrace of Peace, orchestra, 1991; Dances in the Madhouse, violin (or flute) and guitar, 1982; Orchestrated, 1989; Battlefield Requiem, percussion quartet and solo cello; Ad Majoren Dei Gloriam, brass quintet, 1992; Confiding, for voice and piano, voice and guitar, 1985–86; Candles in Mecca, piano trio, 1988. *Address:* c/o ASCAP, ASCAP Building, One Lincoln Plaxa, New York, NY 10023, USA.

LEIXNER, Vladimir; Cellist; b. 1953, Czechoslovakia. *Education:* Studied in Prague with members of the Smetana Quartet. *Career:* Cellist in various Czech ensembles from 1970; Co-Founder and Cellist of the Stamic Quartet, Prague, 1977; Performances at the Prague Young Artists and the Bratislava Music Festivals; Tours to Spain, Austria, France, Switzerland, Germany and Eastern Europe; Tour of the USA in 1980 with debut concerts in the United Kingdom at London and Birmingham in 1983; Further British tours in 1985 and 1988 (Warwick

Arts Festival) and 20 concerts in 1989; Gave the premiere of Helmut Eder's 3rd Quartet in 1986; Season 1991–92 with visit to the Channel Islands with Festival of Czech Music, to Netherlands, Finland, Austria and France, Edinburgh Festival and debut tours of Canada, Japan and Indonesia. *Recordings:* Shostakovich No. 13; Schnittke No. 4; Mozart's K589 and K370; Dvořák, Martinů and Janáček's Quartets. *Honours:* With Stamic Quartet: Prizewinner, International Festival of Young Soloists, Bordeaux, 1977, Winner ORF Austria International String Quartet Competition, 1986, followed by live broadcast from Salzburg Mozarteum, Academie Charles Cros Grand Prix du Disque, 1991 for Dvořák Quartets.

LEJET, Edith; Composer and Professor; b. 19 July 1941, Paris, France. *Education:* Conservatoire National Superieur de Musique de Paris. *Compositions:* Monodrame, pour violon et orchestre, 1969; Journal D'Anne Frank, oratorio, 1970; Quatuor De saxophones, 1974; Harmonie Du Soir, 1977; Espaces Nocturnes, 1976; Gemeaux, 1978 and Balance, 1982, for guitar; Triptyque for organ, 1979; Volubilis for Violoncello, 1981; Aube Marine, 1982; L'Homme Qui Avait Perdu Sa Voix, Théâtre Musical, 1984; Ressac, 1986; Les Rois Mages, oratorio, 1989; Améthyste for 12 strings, 1990; Trois Eaux-Fortes, for piano, 1992; Trois Chants pour un Noël, for children's chorus, 1994; Océan Pathétique, for 5 different instruments, 1994; Almost a Song for guitar and viola, 1995; Missa Brevis for choir and organ, 1996; Des Fleurs en Forme de Diamants, for guitar and 7 instruments, 1997; Psaume De Joie, mixed chorus, 1998; Parcours En Duo, Baritone Saxophone and Percussion, 2001; Diptyque pour orgue et cordes, 2003. *Publications:* Pedagogic Books: La Precision Rythmique Dans la Musique 3 vols. *Honours:* Numerous 1st Prizes at Paris Conservatory, Vocation Foundation, 1967; Grand Prix de Rome, 1968; Prix Florence Gould, 1970; Prix Herve Dugardin, 1974; Grand Prix de la Musique de Chambre de la SACEM, 1979; Prix Nadia et Lili Boulanger, 2003. *Address:* 11–13 rue Cino Del Duca, 75017 Paris, France. *E-mail:* e.lejet@free.fr. *Website:* www.edith-lejet.com.

LEKA, Dhora; Composer; b. 23 Feb. 1923, Korca, Albania. *Education:* Institute for Women Nena Mbretereshe; Graduated, Conservatory Tchaikovsky, Moscow, 1953. *Career:* Teacher, Korca, 1942–43; Various political activities; Began composing, 1942; Maestro at Lyceum Jordan Misja, Tirana; Secretary General, Artists' League, 1954; Many years of imprisonment; Director, Cultural Foundation Dhora Leka; mem, Society of Women Composers. *Compositions include:* The Clarion Call; Youth; From the Heart of the Youth; Revenge; Those Striped Mountain Peaks that Thunder; Overture on two folk motifs, for symphonic orchestra, 1952; Cantate in four parts, Albania my Homeland to lyrics of Andrea Varti, 1953; Spring Songs, 1957; Opera in Three Acts, Stormy Autumn, 1966–67; Opera song, Zonja Curre, 1971; Three sketches for string orchestra, 1995; Ode for soloist and string orchestra, for 85th birthday of Mother Teresa, 1995; Dance on folk motifs for symphonic orchestra, 1996; In memorium, for string orchestra for Lithuanian violinist Grazhina Fiulipajtes-Lubockij, 1997. *Publications:* Songs in the Storm; My Mother. *Honours:* People's Artist, 1992; Great Master of Labour, 1998. *Address:* RR Durresit, P 240, Sh 8, Ap 66, Tirana, Albania.

LEMALU, Jonathan; Singer (bass-baritone); b. 1978, New Zealand. *Education:* Royal Coll. of Music, London. *Career:* concert appearances include the Serenade to Music at the London Proms, Stravinsky's Pulcinella and Symphony no. 14 by Shostakovich with the English CO at the Barbican; season 2001 in Les Troyens at Edinburgh and Messiah in Vienna; festival engagements at King's Lynn, Rávinia (Chicago SO) and Tanglewood (Boston SO) 2002; sang in Falla's Master Peter's Puppet Show at the 2002 London Proms, and as Talbot in Donizetti's Maria Stuarda at the Edinburgh Festival; season 2002–03 as Rossini's Basilio for ENO, Leporello at Sydney, in La Damnation de Faust under Colin Davis and as Neptune in Idomeneo at Glyndebourne; recitals include Schubert's Schwanengesang (Wigmore Hall) and Winterreise (Edinburgh) 2002; Zorastro in Handel's Orlando at Covent Garden 2003. *Current Management:* Askonas Holt, Lonsdale Chambers, 27 Chancery Lane, London, WC2A 1PF, England. *Telephone:* (20) 7400-1700. *Fax:* (20) 7400-1799. *E-mail:* info@askonasholt.co.uk. *Website:* www.askonasholt.co.uk; www.jonathanlemalu.com.

LEMANN, Jean (Juan); Composer, Pianist and Professor of Composition; b. 7 Aug. 1928, Vendôme, France; m. Maria Luisa Herreros, 28 Sep 1957, 2 d. *Education:* BA, Mathematics, 1948; Architecture, Catholic University of Chile, 1948–50; Piano studies, 1942–54, Postgraduate, 1955–59, University of Chile, National Conservatory of Music; Composition at University of Chile, Catholic University of Chile, privately; Visiting Fulbright Scholar, Juilliard School of Music, NY, 1970–71. *Career:* Professor of Piano, Music Theory, Choral Conductor, Experimental School of Arts, 1957–61; Professor of Piano, Composition, 1961–91, Vice-Dean, 1981–82, Faculty of Arts, University of Chile; Adviser, cultural and artistic institutions; Pianist, Lecturer, Adjudicator, Composer and Professor of Composition at Faculty of Arts,

University of Chile. *Compositions include:* Orchestral, chamber, choral, mime, theatre, ballet, and film music including Leyenda Del Mar; Sonata Para Arpa; El Cuerpo La Sangre; Variaciones Para Piano; Puentes (words, P Neruda); Eolica Para Cello Solo; Akustika for Recorder; Obertura de Concierto for orchestra, 1986; Maestranza de Noche for alto, violin, clarinet, cello and piano, 1987; Fantasia Concertante, piano and orchestra, 1988; Rapsodia for guitar, 1996; Viola da Gamba and Piano, 1992, Barrio Sin Luz for soprano voice and piano, 1992. *Address:* Laura de Noves 460, Las Condes, Santiago, Chile.

LEMELIN, Stéphane; Pianist; b. 2 April 1960, Rimouski, Quebec, Canada. *Education:* BM 1982, MM 1983, Peabody Conservatory, USA; Doctor of Musical Arts, Yale University, 1990. *Career:* Performs as soloist and chamber musician across Canada, the USA, Europe and Asia; Frequent CBC and NPR broadcasts; Piano Faculty, Yale University, USA, 1986–90 and University of Alberta, Canada, 1990–2001; Professor of Music, University of Ottawa, 2001–; Visiting Professor, Université de Montréal, 2001–. *Recordings:* Works by Schubert, Schumann, Fauré, Saint-Saëns, Roussel, Poulenc, Debussy, Samazeuilh, Ropartz, and others; Complete Nocturnes by Fauré. *Honours:* Prizewinner, Casadesus International Competition, 1983. *Current Management:* Colwell Arts Management. *Address:* RR #1, New Hamburg, Ontario, N0B 2G0, Canada.

LEMMING, Christopher; Singer (Tenor); b. 1965, Camberley, Surrey. *Education:* Guildhall School, London. *Career:* Appearances with Glyndebourne Festival as Dancing Master in Manon Lescaut, Servant in Capriccio, and Bartholomew in Birtwistle's The Last Supper (2001); Glyndebourne Tour as Lechmere in Britten's Owen Wingrave and Mozart's Titus and Belmonte; Further engagements as Don Ottavio at Cologne and Verona, as Ferrando and Rossini's Almaviva for Opera Holland Park and Molqui in The Death of Klinghoffer by John Adams, for Finnish National Opera (2001); Concerts with the King's Consort, BBC Singers, Royal Liverpool PO, Monteverdi Choir and London PO under Riccardo Muti. *Address:* c/o Glyndebourne Festival Opera, Lewes, Sussex BN8 5UU, England. *Telephone:* 01273 812321. *Fax:* 01273 812 783.

LEMPER, Ute; German singer and dancer and actress; b. 4 July 1963, Münster; one s. one d. *Education:* Dance Acad., Cologne, Max Reinhardt Seminar on Dramatic Art, Vienna. *Career:* leading role in Viennese production of Cats 1983; appeared in Peter Pan, Berlin, Cabaret, Düsseldorf and Paris (recipient of Molière Award 1987), Chicago (Laurence Olivier Award) 1997–99 (London and New York), Life's a Swindle tour 1999, Punishing Kiss tour 2000; Die sieben Todsünden (Weill) at Covent Garden Festival, London 2000; collaborations with Michael Nyman include Six Celan Songs 1990, Songbook 1992. *Recordings include:* Ute Lemper Sings Kurt Weill 1988, (Vol. 2) 1993, Threepenny Opera 1988, Mahagonny Songspiel 1989, Illusions 1992, Espace Indécent 1993, City of Strangers 1995, Berlin Cabaret Songs 1996, All that Jazz/The Best of Ute Lemper 1998, Punishing Kiss 2000. *Television appearances include:* L'Affaire Dreyfus (Arte), Tales from the Crypt (HBO), Illusions (Granada) and The Look of Love (Gillian Lynn). *Film appearances include:* L'Autrichienne 1989, Moscou Parade 1992, Coupable d'Innocence 1993, Prêt à Porter 1995, Bogus 1996, Combat de Fauves, A River Made to Drown In, Appetite 1997. *Honours:* French Culture Prize 1993. *Address:* c/o Oliver Gluzman, 40 rue de la Folie Régnault, 75011 Paris, France. *Telephone:* 1-44-93-02-02. *Fax:* 1-44-93-04-40. *E-mail:* info@visiteursdusoir.com (office). *Website:* www .visiteursdusoir.com (office).

LENDVAY, Kamilló; Composer and Professor and Head of Music Theory Department; b. 28 Dec. 1928, Budapest, Hungary; m. 6 June 1972, 1 d. *Education:* Ferenc Liszt Academy of Music, Budapest, 1959. *Career:* Musical Leader, State Puppet Theatre, 1960–66; Musical Director, Artistic Ensemble, Hungarian People's Army, 1966–68; Conductor and Artistic Director, Operetta Theatre, Budapest; Musical Lector, Hungarian Radio, 1962–; Composer; Professor and Head of Music Theory Department, Ferenc Liszt Academy of Music, Budapest, 1973–; President, Artisjus, Bureau for Protecting Protecting Authors' Rights; President, Association of the Hungarian Composers. *Compositions include:* Orogenesis, oratorio, 1969–70; Requiem; Cantatas: Cart-Drive into the Night, 1970; Scenes from Thomas Mann's Joseph and His Brothers, 1978–81; Orchestral works: Mauthausen, symphonic poem, 1958; Four Invocations, 1966; Expressions for 11 strings, for chamber orchestra, 1974; The Harmony of Silence, 1980; Chaconne for Orchestra, 1988; Rhapsody for orchestra, 1997; Concertos: Concertino, 1959; Violin Concerto No. 1, 1961–62; Pezzo Concerto, 1975; Violin Concerto No. 2, 1986; Concerto semplice, 1986; Trumpet Concerto, 1990; Concerto for violin, harpsichord and strings, 1991; Concerto for Piano, 2000; Chamber music; Solo pieces; Several works for wind orchestra and choir; Music for films and stage; Stabat Mater. *Recordings:* Numerous. *Honours:* Erkel Musical Prize, 1962, 1964, 1978; Trieste Competition, 1975; Title of Merited Artist, 1981; Grand Prix Inernational du Disque Lyrique for opera The Respectable Street-Walker, 1983; Kossuth Prize,

1988; Bart ók-Pasztory Prize, 1989. *Address:* 1137 Szt Istvan Park 23, Budapest, Hungary.

LENHART, Renate; Singer (Soprano); b. 1942, Austria. *Education:* Studied at the Vienna Conservatory. *Career:* Concert tour of South America, 1966–67; Subsequent engagement at Zürich Opera: roles there included Micaela, Marzelline in Fidelio, Mozart's Pamina and Zerlina, Constanza in Henze's Il Re Cervo, Julia Farnese in Ginaster's Bomarzo, Miranda in The Tempest by Frank Martin and Lisa in The Queen of Spades; Further roles at Zürich and as guest in Munich, Paris, Amsterdam and Vienna have included Alice Ford, Lyudmila, Glauce in Médée, Sophie, and Frau Fluth in Die Lustigen Weiber von Windsor; Appearances in Monteverdi's Poppea and Ulisse at Bregenz and in the Jean-Pierre Ponnelle cycle at Zürich; Most frequently heard as Pamina, also sang First Lady in the Ponnelle production of Die Zauberflöte. *Address:* c/o Opernhaus Zürich, Flakenstrasse 1, 8008 Zürich, Switzerland.

LENTZ, Daniel (Kirkland); Composer; b. 10 March 1942, Latrobe, Pennsylvania, USA; m. Marlene Helen Wasco, 24 Aug 1964, 1 d. *Education:* BS, Music, St Vincent College, 1962; MFA, Ohio University, 1965; Brandeis University, 1965–67; Tanglewood, summer, 1966; Musicology, Stockholm University, Sweden, 1967–68. *Career:* Founder, Director of ensembles, California Time Machine, 1969–73; The San Andreas Fault, 1974 and 1976, The Daniel Lentz Ensemble, 1978–80, Lentz, 1983–85 and Daniel Lentz and Group, 1986–; 10 European tours and major/premiere performances: Gaudeamus Foundation, 1972, New Music America Festivals in 1983 and 1986, LA Olympic Arts Festival, 1984, Wild Turkeys at Carnegie Hall, 1986, The Crack In The Bell, LAPhil New Music Group, 1986. *Compositions include:* Canon And Fugle, 1971; Loverise, 1971; King Speech Song, 1972; Song(s) Of The Sirens, 1973; Missa Umbrarum, 1973; O-Ke-Wa, 1974; Sun Tropes, 1975; Requiem Songs, 1976; Three Pretty Madrigals, 1976; Composition In Contrary And Parallel Motion, 1977; Elysian Nymph, 1978; Wolf Is Dead, 1979, 1982; Uitoto, 1980; Music By Candlelight, 1980; Dancing On The Sun, 1980; Point Conception, 1981; Adieu, 1983; On The Leopold Altar, 1983; Lascaux, 1984; Is It Love, 1984; Bacchus, 1985; Topanga Tango, 1985; Time's Trick, 1985; Wild Turkeys, 1985; The Crack In The Bell, 1986; Apache Wine, for chamber orchestra, 1989; Apologetica for soprano, mezzo chorus and ensemble, 1996; Ze ghosts, for ensemble, 1997. *Recordings:* Several including, Dinner Music, a set of 10 pieces each based on a particular dish at a particular Parisian restaurant, 1999; Self Portrait, 1999. *Address:* Box 311, US Route 30, Latrobe, PA 15650, USA.

LEON, Tania (Justina); Composer; b. 14 May 1943, Havana, Cuba. *Education:* Studied in Havana and at New York University. *Career:* Resident in USA from 1967 and creative association with the Dance Theatre of Harlem; Teacher at Brooklyn College, 1985–; Vice Chair, Board of Directors, 1994, Artistic Adviser, New Residencies Program, 1994, Meet the Composer; Professor, Brooklyn College Conservatory of Music, 1994; Visiting Lecturer, Harvard University, 1994; Revson Composer Fellow, New York Philharmonic, 1993–; Visiting Professor, Yale University, 1993; Artistic Adviser, Latin American Project, American Composers Orchestra, 1992; Numerous conducting engagements include: Savannah Symphony Orchestra, Georgia, 1996; Charlotte Symphony Orchestram North Carolina, 1996; Associate Conductor for The Voyage, Metropolitan Opera, 1996; Residencies include: Composer, Scripps College, Claremont, California, 1996. *Compositions include:* Ballets The Beloved (1972) and Bele (1981); Opera Scourge of Hyacinths, 1994; Kabiosile, piano concerto, 1988; Carabali (1991) and Indigena for orchestra; Son sonore for flute and guitar (1992) and other chamber music; Instrumental and vocal music, including Batey for vocal soloists and 2 percussion, 1989. *Address:* c/o ASCAP, ASCAP Building, 1 Lincoln Plaza, New York, NY 10023, USA.

LEONARD, Lysiane; Singer (Soprano); b. 1957, Belgium. *Education:* Studied with Jules Bastin in Brussels, at the Juilliard School and with Hans Hotter in Munich. *Career:* Has sung at the Liège Opera from 1982, notably as Fenena in Nabucco, Elvira (Rossini) Norina, Siebel (Faust), Frasquita (Carmen) and Liu; Guest appearances at Rouen in Les Indes Galantes, the Paris Opéra-Comique in La Belle Hélène and at Montpellier in Schumann's Faust (1985) concert repertory also includes Les Nuits d'été by Berlioz (Aix, 1983); Further concerts in music bv Vivaldi, Bach, Handel, Haydn and Telemann. *Address:* c/o Opera Royale de Wallonie, 1 Rue des Dominicains, 4000 Liège, Belgium.

LEONARD, Sarah (Jane); Singer (Soprano); b. 10 April 1953, Winchester, England; m. Michael Parkinson, 5 April 1975, divorced, 1 s., 1 d. *Education:* Music Department, Winchester School of Art, 1969–71; GGSM Diploma, Guildhall School of Music and Drama, London, 1971–76. *Career:* Member, BBC Singers, 1976–81; Member, London Sinfonietta Voices; High Soprano; Broadcasts with BBC Singers, Endymion Ensemble and London Sinfonietta; Television appearances, Video Alice, Channel 4 television, and The Middle of the Road Hour,

Channel 4 television; Sang the Mad Boy in Goehr's Sonata about Jerusalem, Aldeburgh Festival, 1990; Sings with Michael Nyman Band; Guest appearances with Hilliard Ensemble; Sang at La Scala, Milan, 1989 and 1992; International Soloist in 20th century repertoire; Sang in the premiere of Lachenmann's Das Mädchen, Hamburg, 1997; Sang Queen Elizabeth in the premiere of Harle's Angel Magick, London Proms, 1998; mem, Incorporated Society of Musicians. *Recordings include:* Drusilla in L'Incoronazione di Poppea; Miserere by Arvo Pärt with Hilliard Ensemble; My Heart is Like a Singing Bird, English Song Company. *Honours:* Susan Longfield Award, Guildhall School of Music and Drama, 1976; Winner, Young Artists and 20th Century Music, Park Lane Group, 1984. *Current Management:* Allied Artists. *Address:* 42 Montpelier Square, London SW7 1JZ, England.

LEONHARDT, Gustav; Harpsichordist, Organist and Conductor; b. 30 May 1928, Graveland, Netherlands. *Education:* Schola Cantorum Basle, 1947–50, with Eduard Muller. *Career:* Debut: Vienna in 1950 with Bach's The Art of Fugue on the harpsichord; Professor of Harpsichord at Vienna Academy of Music, 1952–55; Teacher at Amsterdam Conservatory from 1954; Organist at Waalse Kerk, Amsterdam until 1981, since then organist at Nieuwe Kerk, Amsterdam; Founded Leonhardt Consort in 1955; Played the organ and harpsichord and acted the part of JS Bach in a 1967 film, The Chronicle of Anna Magdalena Bach; Visiting Professor at Harvard University, 1969–70; Work as conductor includes Monteverdi's L'Incoronazione di Poppea, Amsterdam in 1972; Extensive tours of USA and Europe as harpsichordist, notably in the works of Bach, Frescobaldi, Sweelinck, Froberger and Louis Couperin; Music by Bach and Böhm at the 1999 London Bach Festival. *Recordings:* About 150 including Bach's Goldberg Variations, as harpsichordist. *Publications:* Editions of The Art of Fugue, 1952 and keyboard music by Sweelinck for the Dutch Critical Edition. *Honours:* Erasmus Prize, 1980; Honorary Doctorates, 1982, 1983 and 1991. *Address:* c/o Allied Artists, 42 Montpelier Square, London, SW7 1JZ, England.

LEOSON, Markus; Swedish percussionist, timpanist and cimbalom player; b. 16 Aug. 1970, Linköping. *Education:* Royal Conservatory of Music, Stockholm. *Career:* debut in Stockholm Concert Hall, April 1995; Live radio concert, Stockholm and Reykjavík, Iceland, 1995; Artist in Residence, Swedish Radio, 1996–97, also solo concerts, Norrtelje Festival, Stockholm, Linköping with wind orchestra; Soloist with Tampere Philharmonic Orchestra; Portrait in television programme NIKE, Copenhagen; Solo concert, Gothenburg; Solo, Stockholm, 1997, also soloist with Swedish Radio Symphony Orchestra, Kalmar; Cimbalom Player and Solo Timpanist with Royal Opera orchestra, Stockholm; 1998 engagements with Gothenburg Symphony Orchestra, Helsingborg Symphony Orchestra, St Petersburg, Braunschweig; Concerts in Cologne, Ludwigshafen, 1999; Engaged to play with Norrköping Symphony Orchestra, Malmö Symphony Orchestra and a debut recital with the Philharmonie in Berlin, 2000. *Recordings:* Markus Leoson, Percussion; Numerous for Swedish Radio P2; Chamber music with Ann Sofie von Otter; Percussion and flute. *Honours:* 1st Prize of the Soloist Prize, Sweden, 1995; 2nd Prize, Nordic Soloist Competition, 1995; 2nd Prize, ARD, Munich, 1997; 1st Prize, EBU IFYP Competition, Bratislava, 1997. *Current Management:* H. F. Artists Management, Nibblev 25, 17736 Järfälla, Sweden.

LEPPARD, Raymond John, CBE; Conductor, Harpsichordist and Composer; b. 11 Aug. 1927, London, England. *Education:* Trinity College, Cambridge. *Career:* Fellow, Trinity College, University Lecturer in Music, 1958–68; Honorary Keeper of the Music, Fitzwilliam Museum, Cambridge, 1963; Conductor, Covent Garden (debut 1959, Handel's Solomon), Sadler's Wells, Glyndebourne, (debut 1964, L'Incoronazione di Poppea); Various overseas orchestras; Principal Conductor, BBC Northern Symphony Orchestra, 1972–80; Principal Guest Conductor, St Louis Symphony Orchestra, 1984–; Music Director, Indianapolis Symphony Orchestra, 1987–2001; London Proms, 1993, with Tchaikovsky's Second Symphony and Ravel's Shéhérazade; Handel's Orlando at the Royal Opera, Stockholm, 2000. *Publications:* Realisations of Monteverdi: Il Ballo delle Ingrate, 1958; L'Incoronazione di Poppea, 1962; L'Orfeo, 1965; Il Ritorno d'Ulisse, 1972; Realisations of Francesco Cavalli: Messa Concertata, 1966; L'Ormindo, 1967; La Calisto, 1969; Magnificat, 1970; L'Egisto, 1974; L'Orione, 1983; Realisation of Rameau's Dardanus, 1980; British Academy Italian Lecture, 1969 (Proceedings, Royal Musical Association); Raymond Leppard on Music, 1993. *Honours:* Commendatore al Merito della Republica Italiana, 1974. *Current Management:* Clarion/Seven Muses, 47 Whitehall Park, London, N19 3TW, England. *Website:* www.c7m.co .uk.

LERDAHL, Fred; Composer and Music Theorist; b. 10 March 1943, Madison, Wisconsin, USA; m. 29 Nov 1980, 3 d. *Education:* BMus, Lawrence University, 1965; MFA, Princeton University, 1967. *Career:* Professor of Music at University of California at Berkeley, 1969–71, Harvard University, 1971–79, Columbia University, 1979–85, and University of Michigan, 1985–91; Fritz Reiner Professor at Columbia University, 1991; Residency at IRCAM, 1981 and at American Academy in Rome, 1987; Works commissioned by the Fromm Music Foundation, the Koussevitzky Music Foundation, the Juilliard Quartet, the Pro Arte Quartet and the Spoleto Festival. *Compositions:* String trio, 1966; Wake for soprano and chamber ensemble, 1968; Chords for orchestra, 1974–83; Eros for mezzo-soprano and chamber ensemble, 1975; First String Quartet, 1978; Waltzes for chamber ensemble, 1981; Second String Quartet, 1982; Beyond The Realm of Bird for soprano and chamber orchestra, 1984; Fantasy Etudes for chamber ensemble, 1985; Cross-Currents for orchestra, 1987; Waves for chamber orchestra, 1988; Quiet Music, for orchestra, 1994. *Recordings:* Fantasy Etudes; First String Quartet; Second String Quartet; Eros; String Trio. *Publications:* Co-Author, A Generative Theory of Tonal Music, 1983. *Current Management:* Musical Associates of America. *Address:* c/o MAA, 224 King Street, Eaglewood, NJ 01631, USA.

LERNER, Mimi; Singer (Mezzo-soprano); b. 1954, Poland. *Education:* Studied at Queen's College, New York and Carnegie-Mellon University. *Career:* Debut: New York City Opera as Sextus in La Clemenza di Tito, 1979; Sang at various American opera houses and at Glyndebourne in 1984 as Marcellina in Le nozze di Figaro; La Scala in 1985 as Alcina, Théâtre Châtelet, Paris, in 1986 as Isabella in L'Italiana in Algeri, and at Amsterdam in 1987 as Eboli in Don Carlos; Sang with New Orleans Opera Association, 1989–90, as Amneris and Adalgisa; Sang Ruggiero in Alcina at Vancouver in 1990, Rosina at Pittsburgh and Despina at Toronto in 1991; Santa Fe Festival in 1991 as Carlotta in Die schweigsame Frau; Sang Marcellina in Figaro at Orchestra Hall, Chicago, 1992; Other roles include Smeton in Anna Bolena, Suzuki, Siebel and Cenerentola; Mistress Quickly in Falstaff at Glimmerglass, 1998. *Recordings include:* Second Lady in a video of Die Zauberflöte, from the Metropolitan. *Address:* c/o New Orleans Opera Association, 333 St Charles Avenue, Suite 907, New Orleans, LA 70130, USA.

LESCOVAR, Monika; Cellist; b. 15 March 1981, Kreutztal, Germany. *Education:* Third year pupil, Funktional Musical Pedagogie School, Zagreb; Student, Musikhochschule Lubeck. *Career:* Debut: Second International Tchaikovsky Competition For Young Musicians, Dendai, 1995; Overseas Concert for Children Competition, Japan; Solo performances, Hungarian State Symphony Orchestra, The Eurovision Festival, Budapest, 1993; Philharmonia Hungarica, The UNICEF Concert, 1994; Moscow Philharmonic, Zagreb, 1994; Sendai Philharmonic, Sendai, 1995; Slovenian Philharmonic, Slovenia, 1996; Symphony Orchestra of Sevilla, 1997; Zagreb Philharmonic, the Zagreb soloists, the Croatian Chamber Orchestra, the Dubrovnik Orchestra, Litvania Chamber Orchestra; Recitals all over the world. *Recordings:* Two albums. *Honours:* First prize, Second International Tchaikovsky for Young Musicians Competition, Sendai, 1995; Second prize, Janigro Competition, Zagreb, 1996; Third prize, 6th Rostropovich Competition, Paris, 1997. *Address:* Oboj 20 1, HR 1000 Zagreb, Croatia.

LESSER, Laurence; Cellist; b. 28 Oct. 1938, Los Angeles, California, USA; m. Masuko Ushioda, 23 Dec 1971, 1 s., 1 d. *Education:* BA, Harvard University, 1961; Fulbright Scholar, Cologne, with Gaspar Cassadò; Studied with Gregor Piatigorsky in Los Angeles. *Career:* Concert performances in USA, Europe, Japan and South America; Appearances with Boston Symphony, Los Angeles Philharmonic, London Philharmonic and other major orchestras; Assistant to Piatigorsky, University of Southern California, Los Angeles; Teacher at Peabody Institute, Baltimore; Visiting Professor at Toho School of Music, Tokyo; Teacher, appointed President, 1983, New England Conservatory, Boston, Massachusetts, retired 1996; Full-time Cello and Chamber Music Faculty, NEC. *Recordings:* Schoenberg/Monn Concerto; Lazarof Concerto; Chamber Music in Heifetz-Piatigorsky Series. *Address:* New England Conservatory, 290 Huntington Avenue, Boston, MA 02115, USA.

LESSING, Kolja; Violinist, Pianist and Composer; b. 15 Oct. 1961, Karlsruhe, Germany. *Education:* Violin lessons, 1964–, piano, 1966–, with mother; Violin studies, Hansheinz Schneeberger masterclasses, Diploma with Distinction, 1982, Basel, Switzerland, 1978–; Piano studies with Peter Efler, Diploma, 1983, Basel, 1979–83. *Career:* Debut: Violin recital at Ettlingen Castle in 1981; Piano, Lausanne in 1982; Concerts throughout Europe; Solo violin recitals and chamber music concerts; Orchestral concerts with Dresdner Philharmonic, Nationaltheaterorchester Mannheim, Radio Sinfonieorchester Basel and others; Several premieres and numerous recitals, violin solo and piano solo with thematic programmes; Founder Member with Rainer Klaas and Bernhard Schwarz, Trio Alkan, 1988–; Professor, Musikhochschule Würzburg, 1989–. *Compositions:* Mostly recorded, German and Swiss Radio Stations; Various works for solo violin, solo clarinet, 2 clarinets and violin, 1978–. *Recordings include:* Works by Franz Berwald, Walther Geiser, Karl Michael Komma, Isang Yun; Numerous radio recordings, some first recordings, extensive repertoire in Germany, Switzerland and Sweden; Playback recording of Fauré's 2nd Sonata for Violin and Piano, 1989.

LESTER, Richard; Cellist; b. 1959, England. *Education:* Studies at the Royal College of Music with Ameryllis Fleming. *Career:* Member of Domus from 1979; Performances in a portable white geodesic dome on informal locations in Europe and Australia; Public workshops, discussion groups and open rehearsals in a wide repertoire; Frequent performances in London at the Wigmore Hall and on the South Bank, throughout the United Kingdom and on Radio 3; Festival engagements at Bath, Cheltenham, Salisbury, Sheffield and the City of London; Tours of South America, Canada, Spain, Italy, Germany, Ireland and Norway; 1991 tours of the Netherlands and New Zealand; Solo concerts and recitals throughout the United Kingdom and tours of Europe, Japan and the Middle East; Concerto performances with the Chamber Orchestra of Europe at Carnegie Hall and in Berlin and Vienna; Salzburg Camerata Academica in Austria, Germany and Italy under Sándor Végh; Cellist with Florestan Trio; Principal Cello, Chamber Orchestra of Europe and Orchestra of the Age of Enlightenment; Member of Hausmusik; Formerly member of Domus; Performs mostly as chamber musician at major festivals and concert venues throughout the world. *Recordings include:* Piano Quartets by Fauré, Dvořák, Brahms, Mozart and Mendelssohn; Schubert's Trout Quintet and Adagio and Rondo Concertante with pianist, Chi-Chi Nwanoku; Works by Martinů, Suk, Kodály and Dohnányi; Complete cello repertoire of Mendelssohn; Boccherini Cello Sonatas; Schumann Trios with the Florestan Trio. *Honours:* Deutsche Schallplattenpreis, 1986 and Gramophone Magazine Award for Best Chamber Music Record of 1986 for Fauré Piano Quartets; Prizewinner at International Scheveninges Cello Competition, 1987; Gramophone Award for Schumann Trios recording, 1999. *Current Management:* Sulivan Sweetland. *Address:* 5 Reynolds Close, London NW11 7EA, England.

LETHIEC, Michel; clarinettist; b. 11 Dec. 1946, Poitiers, France. *Education:* studied in Bordeaux and at the Paris Conservatoire. *Career:* concerto engagements with the Monte Carlo Philharmonic, Radio France Philharmonic, Ensemble Orchestre de Paris and the Lausanne Chamber Orchestra; British appearances with the English Chamber Orchestra, Academy of St Martin in the Fields and the Scottish Ensemble; Recitals and chamber concerts with Leonard Rose, Aurèle Nicolet, Karl Engel, Joseph Suk, Elly Ameling, Philippe Entremont and the Talich, Vermeer, Takacs and Sibelius Quartets; Has premiered works by Ballif, Boucourechliev, Marco, Corigliano and Scolari; Festival engagements include Edinburgh and the Eastern Music Festival, USA; Concert repertoire includes music by Copland, Crusell, Hindemith, Krommer, Mercadante, Mozart, Pleyel, Spohr, Stamitz and Weber; Boulez Domaines and Busoni Concertino; Double Concertos by Bruch with viola, Strauss with bassoon, Danzi with flute and Devienne with clarinet; With string quartets plays works by Mozart, Brahms, Weber, Reger, Reicha, Hindemith, Birtwistle, Yun and Bloch; Director of the Pau Casals Festival in Prades. *Honours:* Interpretation Prize at the International Competition in Belgrade; Grand Prix du Disque, 1978 for Asceses by Jolivet; Chevalier de L'Ordre National du Merite, Professeur an Conservatoire de Paris. *Address:* Les Templiers, 06790 Aspremont, France.

LETNANOVA, Elena; Concert Pianist, Author and Music Critic; b. 23 Oct. 1942, Bratislava, Slovakia; m. Andrej Mraz 1966 (divorced); one d. *Education:* Faculty of Architecture, Slovak Technical Univ.; VSMU, Music Faculty, Bratislava; postgraduate, PWSM, Acad. of Chopin, Warsaw, Poland, 1968; PhD, Faculty of Philosophy, Comenius Univ., Bratislava, 1979; postgraduate courses in Aesthetics, Comenius Univ., 1983. *Career:* debut, solo pianist with Slovak Philharmonic Orchestra, 1969, recital, Carnegie Hall, New York, 1992; taught at univs of Comenius, Dayton, VSMU and STU, Academia Istropolitana; performed at festivals in Rome, Vienna, San Franciscso, Katowice, Ghent, Munich, Prague, Bratislava and recitals in Madrid, Zaragosa, Zagreb, London, Zürich, Baden, Bordeaux, Bologna, Ljubljana, Warsaw, Bruges, New York, Dallas, Denver, Dayton, Washington DC, Fairfax, Berkeley, Rochester, Cortland, Oxford and other cities in Canada, Israel, Netherlands, Croatia, Belgium, Slovakia, Austria, Italy; Dir, Festival of Flemish Music, Bratislava, 2000. *Recordings:* 30 recordings from Slovak radio, TV, Bratislava and Supraphon Prague: Scarlatti, Liszt, Chopin, Scriabin, Tchaikovsky, Szymanowski, F. Nietzsche to Bartók and J. Cage; Piano Concertos by J. S. Bach, J. Haydn, F. Chopin, H. Górecki, B. Buckinx, J. Hatrik, J. Farkas; 2 CDs with F. Nietzsche Music, Antwerp, 1997, and UNESCO Burgenland, Austria, 2000; performed in three television films (Three Women Artists, 1969, Jan Zelibsky, 1972, Paper's Heads (directed by Hanak), 1996). *Publications:* Books: The Piano Interpretation in 17th, 18th, 19th Centuries, 1991; The Presence of the Past, 1996; Translations: Fundamentals of Musical Thinking by J. Kresanek, Belgium; A.Soljenitsyn's The Message from Exile, 1979; Scenario: Kandinsky-Mussorgsky: Pictures at an Exhibition, multimedia event premiered in Kennedy Union Boll Theatre, Dayton, Ohio, 1990; more than 66 articles in journals in Northfield, Illinois, USA, London, Ghent, Delft, Moscow, Prague, Bratislava. *Honours:* Winner, Special Prize, Chopin Competition, Czech Repub.. *Address:* Mudronova

95, 81104 Bratislava, Slovakia. *Telephone:* (2) 6280-4323. *E-mail:* letnanova@ba.telecom.sk. *Website:* elenaletnanova.slke.org.

LEUCHTMANN, Horst; Musicologist; b. 26 April 1927, Brunswick, Germany; m. Brita-Angela von Wentzel, 28 Nov 1952, 1 s., 2 d. *Education:* PhD, State Music School, Brunswick, University of Munich, 1957; Honorary Professor, Musikhochschule Munich, 1986. *Career:* Editor, Musikhistorische Kommission, Bayerische Akademie der Wissenschaften; Lecturer, University of Munich and Musikhochschule Munich; Ordentliches Mitglied der Bayerischen Akademie der Schönen Kunst, 1989. *Publications:* Editor, Complete Works of Orlando di Lasso; Editor, Musik in Bayern; Books; Editions; Dictionaries; Translations. *Address:* Markgrafenstrasse 50, 81827 Munich 82, Germany.

LEVAILLANT, Denis; Pianist, Composer and Musical Director; b. 3 Aug. 1952, Paris, France; m. Christine Rigaud, 21 Oct 1972, 1 s., 1 d. *Education:* MPhil, 1973; Piano studies since age of 5 years and composition studies since age of 12 years at Nancy, France; Advanced study at Paris, France. *Career:* Debut: As pianist in concert in 1969; First composition record ed, Radio France, 1975; Many occupations as producer and artistic director; mem, SACEM; SACD; SPEDIDAM; ADAMI. *Compositions:* 60 including Le Baigneur, opéra-bouffe, 1976; Douze Mouvements for piano, 1980; Piano Transit, for piano and tape, 1983; Les Pierres Noires, for chamber choir, 1984; OPA MIA, opera, 1987–89; Les Couleurs de la Parole, for orchestra, 1990–91; Tombeau de Gesualdo, for chamber choir, 1994–95; Echo de Narcisse, concerto for piano and orchestra, 1995–96; Le Clair l'Obscur, string quartet #2, 1996–97. *Recordings:* 12 CDs. *Publications:* L'Improvisation Musicale, 1981; Le Piano, 1986. *Contributions:* Le Monde de la Musique, 1981–1983. *Honours:* Villa Medicis, 1983; Prix Italia, 1988. *Current Management:* Bleu 17. *Address:* Bleu 17, 21 Paris-Forêt, 77760 Achères La Forêt, France.

LEVI, Yoel; American Conductor; b. 16 Aug. 1950, Stomar, Romania; m. Jacqueline Levi, 3 s. *Education:* MA, Violin and Percussion, University of Tel-Aviv, Israel, 1975; Graduate degree, Jerusalem Academy of Music, 1976; Diploma, Guildhall School of Music and Drama, London, 1978; Studied with Mendi Rodao, Franco Ferrara, Siena, and Kirill Kondrashin, Hilversum; Accademia di Santa Cecilia, Rome. *Career:* Percussionist, Israel Philharmonic Orchestra, 1975; Conducting Assistant, 1978–80; Resident Conductor, 1980–84, Cleveland Orchestra, USA; Music Director and Conductor, Atlanta Symphony Orchestra, 1988–; Guest Conductor with major North American and European orchestras; Season 1997 with the Yomiuri Nippon Symphony Orchestra, Tokyo and KBS Symphony, Korea; La Fanciulla del West at Florence; Director of the Israel Festival, 1997, 1998. *Honours:* 1st Prize, Conductors' International Competition, Besançon, France, 1978. *Address:* c/o Atlanta Symphony Orchestra, 1280 Peachtree Street NE, Atlanta, GA 30306, USA.

LEVI MINZI, Carlo; Pianist; b. 10 Dec. 1954, Milan, Italy. *Education:* Giuseppe Verdi Conservatory, Milan; Piano Diploma, 1974; Piano Certificate, Tchaikovsky Conservatory, Moscow, 1975 and from Curtis Institute of Music, Philadelphia, 1978. *Career:* Recitals and appearances with various orchestras in Europe and USA, 1972–; Television and radio appearances on national stations in Italy, Switzerland, France, Spain, Austria, Germany, Poland, Bulgaria, USA and Mexico; mem, Vice President, Classical Frontiers, NY, USA. *Compositions:* Completion Of Schubert's F Sharp Minor Sonata, 1983, with Quirino Principe; First Performance, Town Hall, NY, 1984; First Radio Recording, WDR, Koln, 1985. *Recordings:* Several. *Contributions:* Various journals.

LEVIN, Robert D.; Pianist, Musicologist and Theorist; b. 13 Oct. 1947, Brooklyn, New York, USA; m. (1) Christine Noël Whittlesey, 18 May 1974, divorced 1991, (2) Ya-Fei Chuang, 30 July 1995. *Education:* AB magna cum laude with highest honours, Music, Harvard University, 1968; Private studies with Nadia Boulanger, 1960–64; Conducting with Hans Swarowsky, 1966. *Career:* Solo and chamber appearances throughout Europe, USA, Australia and Japan, 1970–; Pianist, New York Philomusica, 1971–; Head Theory Department, Curtis Institute of Music, Philadelphia, USA, 1968–73; Professor of music, School of the Arts, SUNY Purchase, 1972–86; Professor of Piano, Staatliche Hochschule für Musik, Freiburg, Germany, 1986–93; Professor of Music, Harvard University, 1993–; President, International Johann Sebastian Bach Competition, Leipzig; American Academy of Arts and Sciences. *Compositions:* Mozart Completions: Requiem, Concerto for piano, violin, orchestra in D; Quintet for clarinet and strings in B flat; Symphonie concertante for flute, oboe, horn, bassoon and orchestra in E flat; Larghetto and Allegro in E flat for 2 pianos; Oboe concerto in F; Horn Concertos in E flat and in D, published and recorded; Sonata Movement in G; Cadenzas to Beethoven Violin Concerto; Hoffmeister Viola Concerto; Mozart Concertos for violin, flute, oboe, horn; Stamitz Viola Concerto (all published). *Recordings:* Mozart Sonatas for piano 4 hands, with Malcolm Bilson; Music for 2 pianos, with Malcolm Bilson;

Brahms and Hindemith, Complete Viola/Piano Sonatas, with Kim Kashkashian; Complete Beethoven Piano Concertos with ORR and John Eliot Gardiner; Mozart Concertos, with AAM and Christopher Hogwood; Haydn 4 Piano Trios; Schubert, Sonatas; Schubert 4-hand works with Malcolm Bilson; Complete Bach harpsichord concertos, English Suites, The Well-Tempered Clavier. *Publications:* Who Wrote the Mozart Four Wind Concertante?, 1988; Sightsinging and Ear Training Through Literature (with Louis Martin), 1988; Other texts in harmony and counterpoint published privately. *Contributions:* Mozart-Jahrbuch; Early Music; Various musicological congress reports; Performance Practice, The New Grove; The Mozart Compendium; Eighteenth Century Keyboard Music; The Cambridge Companion to Music. *Address:* Music Department, Harvard University, Cambridge, MA 02138, USA.

LEVIN, Walter; Violinist and College Professor; b. 6 Dec. 1924, Berlin, Germany. *Education:* Studied at the Juilliard School with Ivan Galamian. *Career:* Co-founded the La Salle String Quartet at the Juilliard School, 1949, with many concerts featuring modern composers and the quartets of Beethoven, and with European debut in 1954; Composers who have written for the ensemble include Hans Erich Apostel, Earle Brown, Henri Pousseur, Mauricio Kagel, György Ligeti, Penderecki and Witold Lutoslawski; Quartet in Residence at Colorado College, 1949–53, then at the Cincinnati College, Conservatory of Music (also Professor there); Quartet disbanded in 1988; Jury Member, International String Quartet Competition, London, 2000. *Recordings include:* Works by Berg, Schoenberg, Webern and Zemlinsky; Beethoven's Late Quartets.

LEVINE, Gilbert; Conductor; b. 22 Jan. 1948, New York, NY, USA. *Education:* Reed College, 1965–67; Juilliard School of Music, 1967–68; Studied music history with Arthur Mendel and Louis Lockwood; Conducting with Jacques-Louis Monod; Music Theory with Milton Babbitt and J K Randall; AB, Princeton University, 1971; MA, Music Theory, Yale University, 1972; Conducting with Franco Ferrara, Siena. *Career:* Debut: Nouvel Orchestre Philharmonique de Radio France, Paris, 1973; Guest Conductor with various major North American and European Orchestras including: North German Radio Symphony Orchestra, Hamburg, 1977; Royal Philharmonic Orchestra, London, 1978; (West) Berlin Radio Symphony Orchestra, 1980; Minnesota Orchestra, 1984; Toronto Symphony; New York Philharmonic Orchestra; Dresden State Orchestra; San Francisco Symphony; Philadelphia Orchestra; Baltimore Symphony; Bayerische Staatsorchester; St Paul Chamber Orchestra; L'Orchestre de la Bastille; Montreal Symphony; London Philharmonic; Music Director, Karkow Philharmonic Orchestra, 1987–; TV concerts with Kraków Philharmonic Orchestra, Royal Philharmonic Orchestra, London Philharmonic, Philharmonia Orchestra, Dresden Staatskapelle, Pittsburgh Symphony Orchestra; Artistic Dir and Conductor, Philharmonica Orchestra Creation Series, 2000; Artistic Dir and Conductor, Papal Concerts, RAI Roma, 1988, Royal Philharmonic, 1994, Philharmonia Orchesra, 2000, Pittsburgh Symphony Orchestra, 2004; Dresden Staatskapelle, 2002, Montreal Symphony, 2002, London Philharmonic, 2003. *Recordings:* with RSO Berlin, English Chamber Orchestra, Kraków Philharmonic, Royal Philharmonic, London Philharmonic. *Honours:* Pontifical Kt Commdr, Equestrian Order of St Gregory the Great. *Address:* 1 Gracie Terrace, Apt 2F, New York, NY 10028-7956, USA. *E-mail:* mozart492g@cs.com.

LEVINE, James; American musician, conductor and pianist; *Artistic Director, Metropolitan Opera;* b. 23 June 1943, Cincinnati, OH; s. of Lawrence M. Levine and Helen Levine (née Goldstein). *Education:* Walnut Hills High School, Cincinnati, The Juilliard School, New York. *Career:* Asst Conductor, Cleveland Orchestra 1964–70; Prin. Conductor, Metropolitan Opera, New York 1973–, Music Dir 1976–, Artistic Dir 1986–; Music Dir Ravinia Festival 1973–93, Cincinnati May Festival 1974–78; Chief Conductor, Munich Philharmonic 1999–2004; Music Dir UBS Verbier Festival Youth Orchestra 2000–; Music Dir Boston Symphony Orchestra 2004–; regular appearances as conductor and pianist in Europe and the USA with orchestras including Vienna Philharmonic, Berlin Philharmonic, Chicago Symphony, Philadelphia Orchestra, Philharmonia, Dresden Staatskapelle, Boston Symphony, New York Philharmonic, Israel Philharmonic, Salzburg and Bayreuth Festivals; conducted Metropolitan Opera premieres of I Vespri Siciliani, Stiffelio, I Lombardi (Verdi), The Rise and Fall of the City of Mahagonny (Weill), Lulu (Berg), Porgy and Bess (Gershwin), Oedipus Rex (Stravinsky), Idomeneo, La Clemenza di Tito (Mozart), Erwartung, Moses und Aron (Schönberg), La Cenerentola (Rossini), Benvenuto Cellini (Berlioz), The Ghosts of Versailles (Corigliano) (world premiere), The Great Gatsby (Harbison) (world premiere); conductor Salzburg Festival premieres of Offenbach's Les contes d'Hoffmann 1980 and Schönberg's Moses und Aron 1987; conducted Munich Philharmonic Orchestra at the London Proms 2002, Benvenuto Cellini at the Met 2003. *Recordings:* over 100 albums of symphonic works, chamber music, lieder and song recitals, solo piano music and 36 complete operas.

Honours: Dr hc (Univ. of Cincinnati, New England Conservatory, Northwestern Univ., State Univ. of New York, The Juilliard School); Grammy Awards for recordings of Orff's Carmina Burana, Mahler's Symphony No. 7, Brahms' A German Requiem, Verdi's La Traviata, Wagner's Das Rheingold, Die Walküre, Götterdämmerung, Strauss' Ariadne auf Naxos; Cultural Award of New York City 1980, Smetana Medal 1987, Musical America's Musician of the Year Award, Gold Medal, Nat. Inst. of Social Sciences 1996, Nat. Medal of Arts 1997, Anton Seidl Award 1997, Lotus Award 1997, Kennedy Center Honors 2002, World Econs Forum Crystal Award 2003. *Address:* Metropolitan Opera, Lincoln Center, New York, NY 10023, USA. *Website:* www.metopera.org (office); www.bso.org (office); www.verbierorchestra.com (office).

LEVINSKY, Ilya; Singer (Tenor); b. 1965, Baku, Russia. *Education:* Studied at the Baku Academy of Music, until 1989. *Career:* Soloist with the Baku Opera, from 1987; Israel Philharmonic summer opera, from 1991; Member of the Komische Oper Berlin with leading roles in Falstaff, La Traviata, Don Giovanni, Così fan tutte and Die Zauberflöte, until 1998; Season 1996–97 as Dimitri in Boris Gudunov with the Frankfurt Opera, in The Nose by Shostakovich for Netherlands Opera and as Sinodal in Rubinstein's The Demon at the Bregenz Festival; Further engagements include Tamino in Die Zauberflöte at Salzburg Festival, Komische Oper and Frankfurt Opera; Lensky in Eugene Onegin at the Tivoli Festival and Števa in Jenůfa at the Salzburg Festival, 2001. *Recordings include:* Lady Macbeth of Mtsensk and Shostakovich Japanese Songs, Rachmaninov Aleko and Francesca da Rimini; Tchaikovsky Songs; Kalman's Die Herzogin von Chicago, under Richard Bonynge. *Current Management:* Askonas Holt Ltd, Lonsdale Chambers, 27 Chancery Lane, London, WC2A 1PF, England. *Telephone:* (20) 7400-1700. *Fax:* (20) 7400-1799. *E-mail:* info@askonasholt.co.uk. *Website:* www.askonasholt.co.uk.

LEVY, Edward (Irving); Composer; b. 2 May 1929, Brooklyn, New York, USA. *Education:* BA, City College New York, 1957; Princeton University with Milton Babbitt; EdD, Columbia University Teachers College, 1967; Further study with Ralf Shapey and Stefan Wolpe. *Career:* Teacher at CW Post College, Long Island University, 1961–67; Professor of Music at Yeshiva University, 1967. *Compositions include:* Duo for violin and cello, 1950; 2 Songs for mezzo and piano, 1951; Clarinet Sonata, 1956; String Trio, 1959; Trio for clarinet, violin and piano, 1961; Images for soprano and piano, 1961; Quintet for flute and ensemble, 1967; Variations On A Theme by Brahms for flute, clarinet and horn, 1979; Concatenations for 2 flutes, clarinet and cello, 1980; Movement for brass quintet, 1980; Works for chorus and for chamber orchestra. *Address:* c/o ASCAP, ASCAP Building, 1 Lincoln Plaza, New York, NY 10023, USA.

LEVY, Marvin (David); Composer; b. 2 Aug. 1932, Passaic, New Jersey, USA. *Education:* BA, New York University, 1954; MA, Columbia University, 1956. *Career:* Archivist, American Opera Society, 1952–58; Music Critic for a number of leading publications including Opera News, Musical America, American Record Guide, New York Herald Tribune and Composer; mem. ASCAP. *Compositions include:* Opera: The Tower, 1956, Escorial, 1958, Sobata Electra, 1957, Mourning Becomes Electra, 1967; Vocal: Echoes, 1956, For The Time Being, 1959, One Person, 1962, Sacred Service For The Sabbath Eve: Shir Shel Moshe, 1964, Masada, 1973, In Memoriam WH Auden, 1984; Orchestra: Caramoor Festival Overture, 1958, Symphony, 1960, Kyros, 1961, Piano Concerto, 1970, Trialogus, 1972, Canto De Los Maranos, 1977, Pascua Florida, 1988; Instrumental: String Quartet, 1955, Rhapsody, 1956, Chassidic Suite, 1956, Arrows Of Time, 1988; The Grand Balcony, musical, 1978–92; The Zachary Star, musical, 1996. *Honours:* 2 Prix de Rome Scholarships, 1962, 1965; 2 Guggenheim Fellowships, 1960, 1964; Grants include Ford Foundation, 1965, Damrosch, 1961, National Endowment for The Arts, 1974, 1978; Recipient, Scroll, City of New York. *Current Management:* Sheldon Softer Management. *Address:* c/o Sheldon Softer Management, 130 West 56, New York City, NY 10019, USA.

LEWIN, David (Benjamin); Composer and Theorist; b. 2 July 1933, New York, USA. *Education:* Studied with Edouard Steuermann, 1945–50; MFA, Princeton University, 1958, with Milton Babbitt, Roger Sessions and Earl Kim. *Career:* Junior Fellowship at Harvard, 1958–61; Computer music at the Bell Laboratories, Murray Hill, New Jersey; Teacher at the University of California at Berkeley, 1961–67, Stony Brook, New York, 1967–80, Yale University, 1979–85 and Professor at Harvard University, 1985–. *Compositions include:* Viola Sonata, 1958; Essay On A Subject By Webern for chamber orchestra, 1958; Classical Variations On A Theme by Schoenberg for cello and piano, 1960; Fantasia for organ, 1962; Fantasy-Adagio for violin and orchestra, 1963–66; Quarter Piece for string quartet, 1969; Woodwind Trio, 1969; Computer Music, 1971; Fanfare, 1980, for piano, 1982; Generalized Musical Intervals and Transformations, 1987. *Publications include:* Studies of Parsifal, Moses und Aron and Rameau's Traité de l'Harmonie, Some Notes on Pierrot Lunaire, 1997. *Contributions:* Journal of Music

Theory; Perspectives of New Music. *Address:* Harvard University, Music Building, Harvard, Cambridge, MA 02138, USA.

LEWIS, Brenda; Singer (Soprano); b. 2 March 1921, Harrisburg, Pennsylvania, USA. *Education:* Studied in Philadelphia. *Career:* Sang in The Bartered Bride with the Philadelphia Opera Company; Sang with New York City Opera, 1943–67 with debut as Santuzza in Cavalleria Rusticana, in San Francisco in 1950 as Salome, at Metropolitan Opera from 1952 as Musetta in La Bohème, Marina in Boris Godunov, Barber's Vanessa and Rosalinde in Die Fledermaus, and at Chicago in 1965 as Marie in Wozzeck; Guest appearances in South America. *Address:* c/o New York City Opera, Lincoln Center, New York, NY 10023, USA.

LEWIS, Daniel; Conductor; b. 10 May 1925, Flagstaff, Arizona, USA. *Education:* Studied composition with Nino Marcelli in San Diego, 1939–41; BM, San Diego State College, 1949; Further study with Eugen Jochum in Munich, 1960. *Career:* Leader of the Honolulu Symphony during war service; Assistant Conductor with San Diego Symphony, 1954–56; Leader and Associate Conductor, 1956–59; Music Director of the Pasadena Symphony, 1972–83 notably in neglected 18th century and American music; Guest Conductor with the Los Angeles Philharmonic, Oakland Symphony, Atlanta Symphony, Minnesota Orchestra, Utah Symphony, Seattle Symphony, Los Angeles Chamber Orchestra and the Louisville Orchestra; Chairman of the Conducting Studies Department at the University of Southern California. *Address:* Music Department, UCLA, Los Angeles, California, USA.

LEWIS, Jeffrey; Composer; b. 28 Nov. 1942, Port Talbot, South Wales; 1 s., 1 d. *Education:* BMus 1st class honours, 1965, MMus, 1967, University College, Cardiff; PhD, University of Wales, 1977; ARCM Organ Performers; Studied composition with Boguslaw Schaffer, Kraków, Poland, with Don Banks, London, with Stockhausen and Ligeti, Darmstadt, Germany, 1967–68. *Career:* Pianist, Paris Chamber Ensemble, 1967–68; Lecturer in 20th Century Composition Techniques and Experimental Music, City of Leeds College of Music, England, 1969–72; Lecturer, Department of Music, University College of North Wales, Bangor, 1973–; Lecturer, 1973–87, Senior Lecturer, 1987–93, Department of Music, University College of North Wales, Bangor. *Compositions:* Orchestral: Praeludium; Piano Concerto; Mutations I; Antiphony; Fanfares with Variations; Aurora; Memoria; Limina Lucis; Instrumental: Mutations II; Esultante; Momentum for organ; Threnody for piano; Trilogy for piano; Tableau for Piano; Fantasy for piano; Two Cadenzas for Piano; Night Fantasy for piano duet; Chamber: Epitaph for Abelard and Heloise; Antiphon; Litania; Stratos; Ritornel; Mobile II; Time-Passage; Wind Quintet: Sonante; Piano Trio; Cantus; Teneritas; Dead Leaves; Choral: Carmen Paschale; Pro Pace; Hymnus Ante Somnum; Westminster Mass; Lux Perpetua; Sequentia de Sancto Michaele; Recordatis. *Recordings:* Commercial CD (Sea of Glass, Lontano Records Ltd); Dreams, Dances and Lullabies for harp; Jeffrey Lewis: Threnody; Cantus; Teneritas; Sonante; Trilogy (ASC CS CD43). *Publications:* Novello; Roberton; Curiad; Article: The Current State of British Cathedral Music, Choir and Organ, 1993. *Address:* Crafnant, Park Crescent, Llanfairfechan, Gwynedd LL33 0AU, Wales. *Telephone:* (1248) 680776.

LEWIS, Keith; Singer (Tenor); b. 6 Oct. 1950, Methven, New Zealand. *Education:* Studied in New Zealand and in London from 1976. *Career:* Sang in premiere of Tavener's Thérèse at Covent Garden returning as Rossini's Almaviva and as Bellini's Tebaldo and Tamino in Magic Flute; Appearances world-wide in such operas as Don Giovanni, Armide, La Clemenza di Tito, Eugene Onegin, as Mozart's Ferrando, Belmonte, and Monteverdi's Giove; Concert engagements in Damnation of Faust, Haydn's Creation, Schumann's Paradies und der Peri, The Dream of Gerontius, Bach B minor Mass, and Beethoven's 9th with such conductors as Solti, Giulini and Abbado; Further appearances include Mendelssohn's Elijah with Colin Davis, Verdi's Requiem, Mozart's Requiem and Bach Mass in B minor; Sang in the opening concert of the 1991 Promenade Concerts, in Idomeneo at Glyndebourne in 1991, in Britten's Serenade in London, and Haydn's Creation under Sinopoli; Sang Alwa in Berg's Lulu at the Berlin Staatsoper, 1997; Gregor in The Makropulos Case at Toulouse, 1998; Season 2000–01 as Bizet's Zurga and Verdi's Paolo in Sydney and Posa (Don Carlos) at Melbourne. *Recordings include:* Rossini's Tancredi, Otello and Moses; Gluck's Alceste; Don Giovanni conducted by Haitink; Messiah under Solti; Masses by Haydn under Marriner; Paradies und der Peri under Albrecht; Berlioz Lelio, Te Deum and Requiem under Inbal; Berlioz Requiem under Bertini; Mozart Requiem; Beethoven's 9th, Wand and Giulini; Salome under Mehta. *Current Management:* IMG Artists Europe. *Address:* c/o IMG Artists Europe, Lovell House, 616 Chiswick High Road, London W4 5RX, England.

LEWIS, Michael; Singer (Baritone); b. 1948, Adelaide, South Australia. *Education:* Studied in Adelaide and at the London Opera Centre. *Career:* Sang first at Wexford Festival, then with Glyndebourne Festival and Touring Operas, Welsh National and Scottish Operas, Frankfurt Opera and companies in Australia; Resident principal with Opera North and Australian Opera; Season 1992–93 as Verdi's Luna, Amonasro, Rigoletto and Renato in Australia, Rigoletto at La Fenice Venice, Rossini's Figaro for English National Opera; Performances of L'Africaine and Tiefland in Berlin, I Masnadieri and Macbeth in Australia (1998) and Bizet's Zurga in San Diego; Other roles include Mozart's Guglielmo, Alfonso, the Count and Papageno, Malatesta, Lescaut in Manon, Riccardo in I Puritani, Marcello, and Don Carlo in La Forza del Destino; Concert repertoire includes Carmina Burana, Belshazzar's Feast and Elijah. *Address:* c/o State Opera of South Australia, PO Box 211, Marleston BC, SA 5033, Australia.

LEWIS, Oliver; Violinist; b. 12 May 1966, London, England. *Education:* Purcell School of Music, London; Konservatorium für Musik, Bern, Switzerland; Studied with Carl Pini, David Takeno, Sándor Végh, Aaron Rosand, Igor Ozim, Wen Xun Chen. *Career:* Debut: British Concerto debut with National Children's Orchestra of Great Britain, age 12; Solo concert tours, England, France, Spain, Portugal, Switzerland, Germany, Austria, Netherlands, Georgia; Broadcasts world-wide, including German television and radio, Swiss Radio, BBC Radio 3, Classic FM Radio; Swiss Concerto debut with Bern Symphony Orchestra, Casino Berne, 1990; Became Concertmaster and Soloist, Heidelberg Chamber Orchestra, 1991; Gives masterclasses at Dartington International Summer School; Concert performances with the Royal Philharmonic Orchestra, 1999; Leader of Ceruti Ensemble of London. *Recordings:* CDs including world premiere recordings of rare English music; English Romanticism, music by Ferguson, Goossens and Ireland; English Romanticism II, music by Elgar and Goossens; Recorded all the solo violin music of Ennio Morricone for the film The Inverse Cannon, 1999; Malcolm Arnold String Quartets, 2001. *Current Management:* Sessions International (UK). *Address:* 8 Colmans Wharf, 45 Morris Road, London E14 6 PA, England. *E-mail:* sessions.international@ virgin.net.

LEWIS, Richard, FRSA, BEd, MA; Singer (tenor), Senior Educationalist, Counsellor and Therapist; b. Trowbridge, Wiltshire, England. *Education:* Metropolitan Univ. of London; Trinity Coll. of Music with John Carol Case, GTCL, FTCL, LTCL, ATCL; Guildhall School of Music and Drama with Ellis Keeler; privately with Ilse Wolf. *Career:* debut, Wigmore Hall, as tenor soloist with Praetorius Consort; sang with BBC Singers and other leading choirs; much work as an oratorio singer; Gentleman in Ordinary of Her Majesty's Chapel Royal, St James's Palace, 1976–2002; soloist with Opera for All and in world premieres in St Paul's Cathedral and South Bank; mem., Royal Soc. of Musicians, Equity; accred mem., British Asscn of Counsellors and Psychotherapists. *Recordings:* numerous as chorister; Music for the Christening of Prince William; Britten's Journey of the Magi (with James Bowman and Graham Trew); Royal Composers with Her Majesty's Chapel Royal Choir, St James's Palace. *Honours:* Queen's Silver Jubilee Medal; Queen's Golden Jubilee Medal; MVO, 2002; Oriana Madrigal Society Prize; Joseph Maas Prize for Tenors; Beryl Searle Scholarship; Vaughan Williams Scholarship; Mitchell City of London Scholarship; Alfred and Catherine Howard Scholarship; Corporation of London Scholarship; Max Hecht Scholarship. *Address:* Melin-y-Grogue, Llanfair Waterdine, Knighton, Powys LD7 1TU, Wales. .

LEWIS, William; Singer (Tenor); b. 23 Nov. 1935, Tulsa, Oklahoma, USA. *Education:* Studied at Fort Worth and New York. *Career:* Debut: Fort Worth in 1953 in Gianni Schicchi; Early appearances in Cincinnati, San Francisco and Dallas; New York City Opera in 1957 in Die Fledermaus, Metropolitan Opera from 1958 in Salome, Elektra, Boris Godunov, Jenůfa, The Queen of Spades, La Bohème and Francesca da Rimini; Sang Aeneas in the 1983 New York production of Les Troyens and at Spoleto in 1959 in the premiere of Barber's A Hand of Bridge; Sang at San Francisco, 1984–85 as Loge in The Ring, Wexford Festival and La Scala, 1986–87 in Humperdinck's Königskinder and the title role in the premiere of Testi's Riccardo III; Spoleto Festival in 1989 as Aegisthus in Elektra; Sang Arbace in Idomeneo at San Francisco in 1989 and in the premiere of Blimunda by Azio Corghi at the Teatro Lirico Milan in 1990; Other roles include Pollione in Norma, the Emperor in Die Frau ohne Schatten, Don José, Offenbach's Hoffmann, Radames, Gabriele Adorno in Simon Boccanegra and Strauss's Guntram; Sang Pollux in Die Liebe der Danaë at Avery Fisher Hall, NY, 2000 (concert). *Recordings include:* Adolar in Euryanthe. *Address:* c/o San Francisco Opera, War Memorial Opera House, San Francisco, CA 94102, USA.

LEWKOVITCH, Bernhard; Composer and Organist; b. 28 May 1927, Denmark. *Education:* Graduate in Music Theory, 1948, Organ, 1949, Royal Danish Conservatry of Music; Composition teachers were Poul Schierbeck and Jorgen Jersild; Studied in France. *Career:* Organist, 1947–63, Cantor, 1953–63, Sankt Ansgar Catholic Church, Copenhagen; Organist and Cantor, Church of Holy Sacrament, Copenhagen, 1973–; Founder and Leader of Schola Gregoriana Men's Choir, Schola Cantorum Mixed Choir, both now under the name Schola Cantorum.

Compositions include: Vocal music and instrumental music for orchestra, ensemble, piano and organ including: Mass for 2 corui and mixed choir, Songs of Solomon for tenor and clarinet, horn and bass trombone, Deprecations for tenor, horn and bass trombone, Preacher and Singer for tenor and piano; Six Partitas for 5 brass instruments, vols I–II; Improperia Per Voce (Good Friday); 3 Tasso Madrigali for mixed choir; Responsoria for mixed choir (Good Friday); Helligandskoraler (Holy Ghost Chorales) for 4 brass players, 1980; Il Cantico delle Creature for 8 male voices; Alle meine Kinder, 48 motets, 1996; 5 English Madrigals for tenor, clarinet, horn and bassoon, 1997; Orgelchoräle: Notizen zu den Lübecher-Dialoguen; Ten Songs for baritone and piano. *Honours:* Carl Nielsen Prize, 1997. *Current Management:* Engstrí m & Sídring Musikforlag, Borgergade 17, 1300 Copenhagen K, Denmark. *Address:* Bredgade 69, 1260 K Copenhagen, Denmark.

LI, Hong-Shen; Singer (tenor); b. 1960, Beijing, China. *Education:* Studied at the Central Conservatory of Beijing and the Juilliard School with Ellen Faull. *Career:* Joined the San Francisco Opera Merola Program, 1987, performing Rinuccio in Gianni Schicchi and Lindoro in L'Italiana in Algeri; Further appearances as the Duke of Mantua, Aufidio in Mozart's Lucio Silla, the Italian Singer, Alfredo, Tebaldo, Pirro in Ermione and Leukippos in Daphne with the San Francisco Opera; Other roles include Rossini's Count Almaviva, Steuermann in Fliegende Holländer (debut with the Metropolitan Opera), Nadir, Macduff, Nemorino and Idreno in Semiramide; Season 2000–01 as Zerlina at the Met, Handel's Cleopatra for Washington Opera and Manon for Dallas Opera; Concert repertoire includes the Verdi Requiem and Mozart's Requiem, Beethoven's 9th Symphony and Rossini's Stabat Mater. *Honours:* Highest Fellowship Scholarship at Central Conservatory of Beijing; Winner, 1991 Metropolitan Opera Competition Nationals; George London Award; Adler Fellow with the San Francisco Opera, 1989–91. *Address:* c/o San Francisco Opera, War Memorial House, Van Ness Avenue, San Francisco, CA, USA.

LI, Ming Qiang; Professor of Piano; b. 1936, Shanghai, China; m. Li Ben Wang, one d. *Education:* studied piano with Alfred Wittenberg and with Prof. Tatiana Petrovna Kravchenko, St Petersburg Conservatory of Music. *Career:* numerous concerts world-wide, performing with many major orchestras; lectures and masterclasses world-wide, including Carnegie Mellon Univ., Rutgers Univ., Univ. of California at Santa Barbara, Univ. of Illinois, Oberlin Coll. Conservatory of Music, Cincinnati Coll. Conservatory of Music, Yale Univ., School of Music, Acad. of Music in Bucharest and National Taiwan Normal Univ.; Vice-Pres., Shanghai Conservatory of Music 1984–89; Artist-in-Residence, Dept of Music and Fine Arts, Hong Kong Baptist Univ. 1993–97; piano masterclasses at other Hong Kong univs; judge in numerous international piano competitions, including International Chopin Piano Competition, Arthur Rubinstein International Piano Master Competition, Van Cliburn International Piano Competition, Sydney International Piano Competition, Montréal International Music Competition and Tchaikovsky Piano Competitions; life mem. American Liszt Soc.. *Recordings:* repertoire of works by Bach, Beethoven, Brahms, Chopin, Handel, Liszt, Mozart, Rachmaninov and Schubert; piano music by Chinese composers He Luting, Ding Shande, Wan Jianzhong and Zhe Jainer. *Honours:* Third Prize, Third International Smetana Piano Competition, Prague Spring Festival 1957; First Prize, First George Enescu International Piano Competition, Bucharest 1958; Fourth Prize, Sixth International Chopin Piano Competition, Warsaw 1960. *Address:* 11B Mansion Building, 846 King's Road, Quarry Bay, Hong Kong.

LI, Yundi; Chinese pianist; b. 1982, Chongqing; s. of Li Chuan. *Education:* Sichuan Music Acad. with Dan Zhao Yi, Shenzhen School of Arts, studied with Arie Vardi in Hanover, Germany. *Career:* originally learned to play accordion, started piano lesson aged seven; concert performances in the USA, Europe and Asia 2004, including New York recital debut, Metropolitan Museum. *Recordings include:* Chopin Recital 2002, Liszt Piano Sonata in B minor 2003, Liszt Klaviersonate h-moll 2003, Chopin Scherzi Impromptus 2004, Love Moods 2004, Chopin 4 Scherzi 3 Impromptus 2004. *Honours:* prize winner, Stravinsky Int. Youth Piano Competition 1995, South Missouri Int. Youth Piano Competition, USA 1998, Liszt Int. Piano Competition, Netherlands 1999, China Int. Piano Competition 1999; first prize at the Chopin Int. Piano Competition, Warsaw, Poland 2000. *Current Management:* Askonas Holt Ltd, Lonsdale Chambers, 27 Chancery Lane, London, WC2A 1PF, England. *Telephone:* (20) 7400-1700. *Fax:* (20) 7400-1799. *E-mail:* info@askonasholt.co.uk. *Website:* www.askonasholt .co.uk. *Address:* c/o Deutsche Grammophon GmbH, Alte Rabenstrasse 2, 20148 Hamburg, Germany. *Website:* www.deutschegrammophon.com.

LIANG, Ning; Singer (mezzo-soprano); b. 1957, Peking, China. *Education:* Studied in Gwangdong and Peking; Further studies at Juilliard School and American Opera Center in New York. *Career:* Debut: Central Conservatory Peking, 1983; Sang at Peking and Shanghai as Carmen and Rosina, Cenerentola at the 1987 Aspen Festival; Philadel-

phia and Helsinki, 1988 as Dorabella and Carmen; Studied further at the Juilliard School, 1986–89; Sang Cherubino in London and Hamburg, 1989–91; La Scala, Milan 1990, as Suzuki in Butterfly; Sang Rosina at Toronto and at the Vienna Festiva, 1992; Concert engagements include Beethoven's Ninth in Lisbon and Bellini's Il Pirata in New York; Opera engagements include, Ottavia in L'Incoronazione di Poppea (Marseille and Amsterdam), Stephano in Roméo et Juliette (Hamburg), Octavian (Deutsche Oper Berlin and Hamburg) and Sesto in La Clemenza di Tito (Stuttgart). *Recordings include:* Carmen and Le nozze di Figaro. *Honours:* Numerous Prizes in American Competitions: Metropolitan Opera National Council Competition, Rosa Ponselle International Vocal Competition, Loren L Zachery Competition and the Luciano Pavarotti Competition. *Address:* c/o Hamburgisches Staatsoper, Grosses-Theaterstrasse 34, 2000 Hamburg 36, Germany.

LIAO, Chang-Yong; Singer (baritone); b. 1969, China. *Career:* Many engagements in the Far and East and Europe, notably in operas by Mozart (Le nozze di Figaro) and Massenet, with chansons by Duparc, Debussy and Ravel; Contestant at the 1995 Cardiff Singer of the World Competition. *Address:* c/o Mr Wu Xun, Bureau of External Relations, Ministry of Culture, 2 Shatan Beijie, Beijing 100722, People's Republic of China.

LICARET, Nicolae; Pianist, Organist and Harpsichordist; b. 24 Sept. 1943, Bucharest; m., 1 s. *Education:* Music School George Enescu, Bucharest; Music Academy, Bucharest. *Career:* Debut: Dalles Hall, Bucharest, 1959; Piano Teacher, Bucharest Hight Music School, 1966–68; Soloist, Bucharest George Enescu Philharmonic Orchestra, 1968–; mem, UNESCO; Union of Romanian Musicians. *Recordings:* Bach's Sonatas; Concertino Ensemble; George Enescu's Pieces; Italian Music; L Alexandra Symphony; Pan Flute and Organ; Phonogram; Handel Organ Concertos; Mozart Piano Quartets; Aurel Stroe Orestia I; Ave Maria; Rameau Harpsichord Pieces; Nicolae Licaret piano, organ, harpsichord; Brahms Piano Quartets; Enescu cello and piano sonatas. *Current Management:* Artexim, Romania. *Address:* Bucharest Philharmonic Orchestra, str Franklin 1, 79741 Bucharest, Romania.

LICHTENSTEIN, Romelia; Singer (Soprano); b. 1965, Sofia, Bulgaria. *Education:* Studied in Leipzig. *Career:* Debut: Chemnitz, 1988, as Rossini's Rosina; Appearances at Chemnitz Opera as Pamina, Lortzing's Marie and the soprano roles in Les Contes d'Hoffmann; Leipzig Opera from 1992, notably as Mimi and Fiordiligi; Handel Festival at Halle, 1996, as Elisa in Tolomeo; Cleofide in Handel's Poro, 1998; Guest appearances as concert singer throughout Germany. *Honours:* Winner at Gera, 1990, and Barcelona International Competitions. *Address:* c/o Opernhaus Halle, Universitätsring 24, 4020 Halle an der Salle, Germany.

LICITRA, Salvatore; Singer (Tenor); b. 1967, Berne, Switzerland. *Education:* Accademia Verdiana Parma, and with Carlo Bergonzi. *Career:* Sang Riccardo (Ballo in Maschera) at Parma and Verona Arena, 1998; La Scala Milan 1999-2000, as Alvaro (Forza del Destino) and Manrico in Il Trovatore; Season 2001–2002 as Alvaro, Pinkerton and Manrico at Verona, and as Manrico at the Vienna Staatsoper; Further appearances at Zürich, Rome, Turin and Torre del lago; New York Met debut 2002, as Cavaradossi. *Address:* c/o Metropolitan Opera, Lincoln Center, New York, NY 10023, USA.

LIDDELL, Nona (Patricia); Musician; b. 9 June 1927, London, England; m. Ivor McMahon, 15 July 1950, deceased, 1 d. *Education:* Royal Academy of Music. *Career:* Leader, English String Quartet, 1957–73; Leader, Richards Piano Quintet, 1964–79; Leader, London Sinfonietta, 1970–94; Currently, Schiller Trio, London Piano Quartet; Professor, Trinity College of Music; Professor of Violin, Royal Academy of Music, 1978–94; mem, Incorporated Society of Musicians. *Recordings:* Violin Concerto, Kurt Weill; Phantasie by Schoenberg with John Constable; Gemini by Roberto Gerhard with John Constable; Chamber Music by Martinů, Chausson, Herbert Howells; Brahms' Horn Trio and Berkeley Horn Trio with Schiller Trio; Stravinsky's Soldier's Tale; Chamber Music by Schoenberg; Chamber Music by Cyril Scott; Chamber music by Alan Bush. *Honours:* M.B.E.; Fellow of The Royal Academy of Music. *Address:* 28B Ravenscroft Park, Barnet, Hertfordshire EN5 4 NH, England.

LIDL, Vaclav; Composer; b. 5 Nov. 1922, Brno, Czechoslovakia; m. Eva Hromadkova, 1 s. *Education:* Graduate Business Academy; Brno Conservatoire. *Career:* Writer of many musical scores for films and television; mem, Association of Musicians and Musicologists. *Compositions include:* Divertimento for flute, clarinet and bassoon; 3rd string quartet; Dandelions, for flute, soprano and harp; 1st Symphony for grand orchestra; Cantus Variabilis for violin, clarinet and piano; Hic Homo Sum, Cantata for mixed choir, tenor, piano and percussion; Our Little Drummer, Cantata for child's voice and grand orchestra; 2nd Symphony for chamber orchestra; 3rd Symphony for grand orchestra; Many compositions for various types of choirs; Ballade on a June Morning (Lidice 1942), for grand orchestra; Concerto for trumpet and orchestra. *Current Management:* Music Information Centre, Besedni 3, 118 00 Prague 1, Czech Republic. *Address:* Soukenicka 14, 110 00 Prague 1, Czech Republic.

LIDTH DE JEUDE, Philip; Singer (baritone, tenor); b. 17 June 1952, Voorburg, Netherlands. *Education:* Studied at the Curtis Institute and Manhattan School. *Career:* Sang at Pennsylvania Opera from 1974, Chicago from 1979; Guest appearances elsewhere in USA as Marcello, Enrico (Lucia di Lammermoor), Germont and Gerard in Andrea Chénier; Studied further at Zürich and sang as tenor from 1988, notably at Krefeld Opera as Don José, Riccardo, Radames, Florestan, Bacchus, Peter Grimes and Dimitri in Boris Godunov; Engagements throughout Germany, including Otello at Detmold, 1996; Sang Samson in Netherlands, 1995. *Honours:* Prizewinner at 1981 Geneva Competition. *Address:* c/o Landestheater Detmold, Theaterplatz 1, 4930 Detmold, Germany.

LIE, Tom Erik; Singer (baritone); b. 1965, Olso, Norway. *Education:* Olso Conservatory, and Oslo Studio, with Ingrid Bjoner; Further study with Theo Adam, Berlin. *Career:* Sang at Gelsenkirchen Opera, as Malatesta, Silvio, and Wagner's Wolfram; Further appearances throughout Germany, and for Norwegian State Opera, as Silvio; Leipzig Opera as Morales in Carmen, Frère Leon in Messiaen's St François, Guglielmo, Papageno, Siegfried in Schumann's Genoveva, and Wolfram; Concerts throughout Norway, and in Germany, the Czech Republic and Spain (National SO); Season 2001–2002 as Donizetti's Belcore in Norway and Robert Storch in Strauss's Intermezzo for Garsington Opera (British debut); Deutsche Oper Berlin from 2002. *Current Management:* Athole Still International Management, Forresters Hall, 25–27 Westow Street, London, SE19 3RY, England. *Telephone:* (20) 8771-5271. *Fax:* (20) 8768-6600. *Website:* www.atholestill.com.

LIEBERMAN, Carol; Musician, Violinist and Baroque Violinist; b. 18 Aug. 1943, New York, NY, USA; m. Mark Kroll, 9 July 1975, 1 s. *Education:* BA, City College of New York, 1965; MMus, 1967, DMA, 1974, Yale University School of Music; Violin studies with Raphael Bronstein and Broadus Erle. *Career:* Debut: Carnegie Recital Hall, New York, 1975; Faculty, Boston University School of Music, 1979–; Concertmaster, Masterworks Chorale Orchestra, 1980–; Concerts throughout USA and in Rome, Italy, Antwerp, Caracas, Lisbon and Canada; Broadcasts for WGBH Radio-TV and WBUR Radio, Boston, including 6 part simulcast series for Maine Public Television; Radio and Television Programmes for Canadian Broadcasting Corporation; Former Member, Israel Philharmonic Orchestra and Toronto Symphony; Assistant Professor, College of Holy Cross, 1985–88; Associate Professor, 1989–; Co-Director, Holy Cross Chamber Players, 1985–; Broadcasts for Radio National de Espana, Madrid, 1985; Soloist with Connecticut Early Music Festival, 1985–; mem, Co-Director, Holy Cross Chamber Players; Violinist with Early Music Ensemble of Boston; Violinist of Lieberman/Kroll Duo. *Recordings:* CDs: Schubert Sonatinas for Violin and Fortepiano; Dohnányi Sonata for Violin, Piano and Second Piano Quintet; Numerous recordings for various labels. *Address:* Department of Music, College of the Holy Cross, PO Box 151A, Worcester, MA 01610, USA.

LIEBERMAN, Janis Joy; French Hornist; b. 23 Aug. 1950. *Education:* Studied with W. Erol Gomürgen, Ankara, Turkey; BMus, Boston University School of the Arts, principal tutor, Harry Shapiro, 1972; Further studies, American University, Washington DC, with Ted Thayer; MA, San Francisco State University. *Career:* Debut: Soloist, Mozart Concerto No. 2 and No. 4; Schumann Konzertstück for 4 horns and orchestra, San Francisco Concerto Orchestra; Israel Sinfonietta Orchestra, 1975–79, 1993–95, Principal Horn, 1977–79; Jerusalem Symphony, 1975–79; Israel Symphony, 1994–95; Ensemble EnCor, chamber music trio, 2000–; mem, International Horn Society. *Recordings:* With the Israel Sinfonietta and the Women's Philharmonic. *Honours:* Israel America Cultural Foundation Grant, 1977. *Address:* 2001 Santa Clara Street, Richmond, CA 94804, USA.

LIEBERMANN, Lowell; Composer, Conductor and Pianist; b. 22 Feb. 1961, New York, USA. *Education:* BM, 1982, MM, 1984, DMA, 1987, The Juilliard School, New York; Composition with David Diamond and Vincent Persichetti; Conducting with Laszlo Halasz; Piano with Jacob Lateiner. *Career:* Debut: Carnegie Recital Hall, New York City, 1978; Composer-in-Residence, Dallas Symphony Orchestra, 1999–; mem, Director of Yaddo Colony; ASCAP; NARAS. *Compositions:* Symphony Op 9; Piano Concerto Op 11; 2 Piano Sonatas Op 1, 10 and 82; Sechs Gesänge Nach Gedichten von Nelly Sachs for soprano and orchestra Op 18; Sonata for viola and piano Op 13; Missa Brevis for chorus and organ; Song Cycles; Chamber Music; Sonata for flute and piano Op 24; Quintet for piano, clarinet and string trio Op 26; Domain of Arnheim Op 33; Quintet for piano and strings Op 34; Nocturnes Op 20, 31, 35; Gargoyles Op 29; Piano Concerto No. 2 Op 36, 1992; Concerto for flute and orchestra Op 39, 1992; Songs and Piano Pieces; The Picture of Dorian Gray, opera, Op 45, 1995; Sonata for violin and piano Op 46, 1994;

Album for the Young for piano Op 43, 1994; Revelry for orchestra, Op 47, 1995; Longfellow Songs Op 57; Loss of Breath Op 58; Flute and Harp Concerto Op 48; Concerto for trumpet and orchestra Op 64, 1999; Nocturne No. 7 Op 65 for piano, 1999; Album Leaf Op 66 for cello and piano; Symphony No. 2, Op 67, 1999; Three Impromptus Op 68 for piano, 2000; Nocturne Fantasy Op 69 for two guitars, 2000; Dorian Gray: A Symphonic Portrait Op 70, suite from opera, 2000; Pegasus Op 71 for narrator and orchestra, 2000; Rhapsody on a Theme by Paganini Op 72 for piano and orchestra, 2001; The Next Time Op 73 for baritone and piano, 2001; Concerto for violin and orchestra Op 74, 2001. *Recordings:* Piano Music of Lowell Liebermann, Koch International; James Galway plays Lowell Liebermann, BMG, 1998; Symphony No. 2 (Dallas Symphony Orchestra), 2000; Many recordings on various labels. *Honours:* Grammy Nomination for Best Contemporary Classical Composition, 1998; Grand Prize, Van Cliburn International Piano Competition Inaugural Composers' Invitational Competition. *Address:* 820 West End Avenue Apt #10B, New York, NY 10025, USA. *E-mail:* lowell@lowellliebermann.com.

LIEBERSON, Peter; composer; b. 25 Oct. 1946, New York, USA; m. Ellen Kennedy; three d. *Education:* New York University, Columbia University, Brandeis University; composition with Milton Babbitt, Charles Wuorinen, Donald Martino and Martin Boykan. *Career:* mem. BMI. *Compositions include:* Opera, Ashoka's Dream, 1997; Worlds Turning, 1991; Drala; Lalita; Ziji; Raising The Gaze; Variations for violin and piano; Piano Fantasy; Flute Variations; Concerto for 4 groups of instruments; 2 piano concertos, 1983, 1999; Viola Concerto, 1994; Fire, for orchestra, 1995; Horn Concerto, 1999; Cello Concerto, 2000; String Quartet, 1994. *Recordings:* Piano Concerto; Bagatelles; Lalita; Raising The Gaze; Piano Fantasy; Concerto for 4 groups of instruments. *Honours:* Charles Ives Fellowship; National Endowment for The Arts; American Academy of Arts and Letters; Brandeis University Creative Arts Award. *Address:* 47 Anchor Drive, Halifax, Nova Scotia B3N 3E4, Canada.

LIEBL, Karl; Singer (Tenor); b. 16 June 1915, Schiltberg, Germany. *Education:* Studied with Paul Bender in Munich and with Albert Meyer in Augsburg. *Career:* Debut: Regensburg in 1950; Sang in Wiesbaden from 1951, Cologne Opera, 1955–59 notably as Huon in Oberon, and Vienna Staatsoper, 1956–59; Sang the Cardinal in Mathis der Maler under Hindemith; Sang at Metropolitan Opera, 1959–68, as Wagner's Lohengrin, Tristan, Loge, Walther, Siegfried, Siegmund and Parsifal; Guest appearances in Munich, Hamburg, Chicago, Baltimore, Brussels, Zürich, Venice and Madrid; Teacher at University of Mainz from 1967. *Recordings:* Der fliegende Holländer; Die Zauberflöte; Lohengrin; Die Meistersinger; Oberon. *Address:* c/o Staatliche Hochschule für Musik, Bingerstrasse 26, 6500 Mainz, Germany.

LIEBOLD, Angela; Singer; b. 15 Aug. 1958, Dresden, Germany. *Education:* Studied at Dresden Musikhochschule. *Career:* Appearances at the Dresden Opera from 1985 in the title role of the premiere of Weise Von Liebe und Tod Des Cornets Christopher Rilke by Siegfried Matthus; Lieder recitals in Russia, Hungary, France and Germany; Engagements in opera elsewhere in Germany; Teacher of Singing at the Dresden Musikhochschule from 1983. *Honours:* Prize Winner at the Walter Gruner Lieder Competition, Bach International, Maria Callas Competition, Athens, and Robert Schumann Competition. *Address:* c/o Semper Oper, 8012 Dresden, Germany.

LIELMANE, Rasma; Concert Violinist; b. 1958, Latvia, Russia. *Education:* Studied with David Oistrakh at the Moscow Conservatoire. *Career:* Appearances with the leading orchestras of Europe and North America; Collaborations with the Munich Philharmonic, Berlin Symphony and the Dresden Philharmonic; Appearances in London, Hamburg, Toronto, Montreal, Nice and Milan. *Honours:* First Prize, International Violin Competition, Sofia; Prizewinner at the Vianna de Motta Competition in Portugal, Nicola Paganini in Italy, and Maria Canals Competition in Montreal; Tibor Varga Prize in Switzerland.

LIFCHITZ, Max; Composer, Conductor and Pianist; b. 11 Nov. 1948, Mexico City, Mexico. *Education:* Studied at the Juilliard School of Music, New York, and Harvard University, Cambridge, Massachusetts, also Berkshire Music Center. *Career:* Debut: Mexico City, 1955; Pianist, Juilliard Ensemble; Lecturer, National Music Camp, Michigan; Faculty, Manhattan School of Music; Assistant Professor in Music, Columbia University; Executive Director, Conductor, North South Consonance Inc; Associate Professor in Music, State University of New York; Chair, Music Department, 1995–98, Chair, Latin American Studies Department, 1996–99, State University of New York at Albany. *Compositions include:* Intervencion for violin and orchestra; Night Voices #13 for cello and orchestra; Kaddish, choir and chamber ensemble, Tiempos; Tientos, Accordion. *Recordings:* Affinities, Piano Solo; Transformation, Cello; Yellow Ribbons No. 2; Canto de Paz; Yellow Ribbons No. 21; Consorte; Winter Counterpoint, flute, oboe, bassoon, viola; Exceptional String Quartet; 5 Albums of American Piano Music; Of Bondage and Freedom.

Publications: String Quartets and Piano Sonatas by Carlos Chávez for G Schirmer. *Honours:* 1st Prize, Gaudeamus Competition, 1976. *Current Management:* North/South Concerts. *Address:* North/South Concerts, PO Box 5108, Albany, NY 12205-0108, USA.

LIFSCHITZ, Constantin; Concert Pianist; b. 1977, Ukraine. *Education:* Gnessin School Moscow, from 1982; Studying with international piano teachers at International Piano Foundation, Lago di Como. *Career:* Concerts in the West from 1990; Collaboration with violinist Vladimir Spivakov, including tour of Japan with the Moscow Virtuosi; Further concerts with the Monte Carlo Philharmonic, Moscow Philharmonic in Munich, Moscow State Symphony Orchestra (concerto debut) and the St Petersburg Philharmonic on tour to Europe, with Yuri Temirkanov, 1997; Chamber music with Lynn Harrell, Gidon Kremer and Mischa Maisky; Contracted to appear at Shostakovich Festival in Tokyo, performing Shostakovich Piano Concerto No. 1, and also for a recital tour of Japan including a performance with the Tokyo Symphony Orchestra; Debut with Chicago Symphony Orchestra, 1999. *Recordings include:* Recitals. *Honours:* Russian Cultural Foundation New Name Scholarship, 1990; Winner, German Echo Classic Record Prize, 1995. *Address:* c/o Chicago Symphony Orchestra (Contracts), Symphony Hall, Chicago, IL, USA.

LIGENDZA, Catarina; Singer (Soprano); b. 18 Oct. 1937, Stockholm, Sweden; m. Peter Ligendza. *Education:* Studied in Vienna and Wuerzburg with Henriette Klink, Stuttgart with Trudi Eipperle and Saarbrücken with Josef Greindl. *Career:* Debut: Linz in 1963 as Mozart's Countess; Sang in Brunswick and Saabrücken, 1966–69 as Verdi's Elisabeth de Valois and Desdemona and Strauss' Arabella; Sang at Hamburg Staatsoper from 1967, Deutsche Oper Berlin; Staatsoper Stuttgart from 1970, and Staatsoper Vienna from 1971 with Wagner's Ring, Isolde with Carlos Kleiber, Lisa in The Queen of Spades, and Elsa in Lohengrin with Placido Domingo; Sang at Staatsoper München in Fliegende Holländer, Lohengrin from 1978 and Götterdämmerung; Sang Arabella at La Scala in 1970 and at Salzburg Easter Festival under Karajan; Metropolitan Opera debut in 1971 as Beethoven's Leonore; Bayreuth Festival, 1971–77 as Brünnhilde and Isolde, 1986–87 as Elsa in Lohengrin and Isolde; Covent Garden debut in 1972 as Senta in Der fliegende Holländer; Sang in Wagner's Ring with Deutsche Oper Berlin in 1987 in Japan; Retired from the stage in 1988; Television productions and opera films: Der fliegende Holländer, Lohengrin as Elsa, Freischütz as Agathe, and Elektra as Chrysothemis, with conductors Sawallisch, Russell Davies and Karl Böhm. *Recordings:* Third Norn in Götterdämmerung; Arias by Handel; Eva in Meistersinger von Nürnberg; Lars Erik Larsson, Förkläddgud; Three Songs, Rangström; Tristan und Isolde, conducted by Carlos Kleiber.

LIGETI, András; Conductor; b. 1953, Hungary. *Education:* Franz Liszt Academy, Budapest, violin diploma, 1976; Conducting with András Korodi. *Career:* Orchestra Leader, Hungarian State Opera House, 1976–80; Regular concerts as solo violinist in Europe and Canada; Associate Conductor, with György Lehel, of the Budapest Symphony Orchestra, 1985, with tours of the United Kingdom, Europe and America; Regular conductor at the Budapest Opera; British debut in 1989 with the BBC Symphony Orchestra, returning to conduct the BBC Scottish Symphony Orchestra and BBC Philharmonic in 1991, with Bart ók's Duke Bluebeard's Castle, Weber's 2nd Piano Concerto and Mahler's 5th Symphony. *Address:* c/o Music Partnership Ltd, 41 Aldebert Terrace, London SW8 1BH, England.

LIGETI, György Sandor; composer; b. 28 May 1923, Romania; m. Vera Spitz 1957; one s. *Education:* Budapest Academy of Music with Ferenc Farkas and Sándor Veress. *Career:* taught at Budapest Academy of Music, 1950–56; left Hungary in 1956; guest Professor at Stockholm Academy of Music, 1961–71; composer-in-residence at Stanford University, California in 1972; worked in electronic studios, Cologne, Germany; active in music composition at Cologne, Vienna, Stockholm and Darmstadt; Professor of Composition, Hamburg Music Academy, 1973–89; Festival of Music, including Le Grand Macabre on London's South Bank, 1989; concert series Clocks and Clouds, London, 1997; mem. Swedish Royal Academy of Music, Academy of Arts Berlin, Free Academy of Arts, Hamburg, Bavarian Academy of Fine Arts, Munich, American Academy and Institute of Arts and Letters. *Compositions include:* Artikulation, tape piece, 1958; Atmosphères for orchestra, 1960; Poème Symphonique for 100 metronomes, 1962; Requiem for soprano, mezzo-soprano, 2 choirs and orchestra, 1963–65; Concerto for cello and orchestra, 1966; Ten Pieces for wind quintet, 1968; string quartet No. 2, 1968; Melodien for orchestra, 1971; Clocks and Clouds for 12 female voices and orchestra, 1973; Monument, Selbstportrait, Movement for 2 pianos, 1976; Le Grand Macabre, opera, 1977, revised 1996; 3 Phantasies After Hölderin, 1982; 6 Etudes for piano, 1985; Nonsense Madrigals for 6 voices, 1988; Violin Concerto, 1989–93; L'escalier du diable for piano, 1993; Viola Sonata, 1994. *Recordings:* complete works recorded from 1996. *Honours:* Dr hc (Hamburg Univ.) 1988; Prix Ravel 1984, Prix Honegger 1985, Grawemeyer Award 1986,

Prix Prince Pierre de Monaco 1988, Royal Swedish Academy of Music Polar Music Prize 2004; Orden pour le mérite, Bonn 1975, Commandeur, Ordre National des Arts et des Lettres 1988. *Address:* Mövenstrasse 3, 2000 Hamburg 60, Germany.

LIGI, Josella; Singer (Soprano); b. 10 Jan. 1948, Imperia, Italy. *Education:* Studied in Milan. *Career:* Debut: La Scala, 1972, as a Priestess in Aida; Sang in Milan and appeared as guest in Turin, Valencia and Toulouse, 1974, as Mimi, Desdemona and Aida; Verona Arena, 1983, and Ravenna Festival, 1984, as Amelia in Un Ballo in Maschera; La Scala and Wexford Festival, 1985, in Rossi's Orfeo and as Catalani's Wally; Turin, 1986, as Alice Ford; US debut, 1988, as the Trovatore Leonora for Newark Opera; Concerts include Debussy's Le Martyre de St Sebastian, Salzburg Festival, 1986. *Recordings include:* Sesto in Handel's Giulio Cesare. *Address:* c/o Teatro Regio, Piazza Costello 215, 10124 Turin, Italy.

LIIMOLA, Heikki Sakari; Choir Conductor and Teacher; b. 24 March 1958, Tampere, Finland; m. Katri Liimola, 30 July 1983, 3 d. *Education:* MMus, Sibelius Academy, Finland, 1988; Choral Conducting; Studied trumpet, voice, orchestra conducting, with Professor Jorma Panula; Mastercourses and private studies in choir conducting, with Professor Eric Erikson. *Career:* Assistant Conductor and Singer, Finnish Radio Chamber Choir, 1982–87; Conductor, Chorus Cantorum Finlandie; Conductor EOL Chamber Choir, Helsinki; Conductor, Savonlinna Opera Festival Chorus; and others; Teacher of Choir Conducting, Voice Teacher, many courses in Finland and abroad; Conductor, Tampere Philharmonic Choir; Conductor, Harju Chamber Choir; Conductor, Tampere Opera Choir; Conductor, Chamber Choir of Silbelius-Academy; Artistic Director, Tampere International Choir Festival; mem, International Federation of Church Music. *Recordings:* Harju Youth Choir, Christmas Music, 1980; EOL Chamber Choir, Sacred and Profane, 1990; Male Choir of Finnish Church Musicians, 1990; Jaakko Ryhanen and Opera Festival Chorus, 1993; Savonlinna Opera Festival Chorus and Helsinki Philharmonic Orchestra, 1995; Tampere Philharmonic Choir and Tampere Philharmonic Orchestra, 1998, 2000; Harju Chamber Choir, Church Music, 2001. *Publications:* Article in Companion ot Singing. *Honours:* Conductor of the Year, 1998. *Address:* Tohlopinkatu 46G 29, 33310 Tampere, Finland.

LIKA, Peter; Singer (Bass-baritone); b. 1949, Germany. *Education:* Studied in Munich. *Career:* Sang with the Augsburg Opera 1972–81 and later joined the Bavarian Chamber Opera for performances of Baroque opera; a noted interpreter of sacred music by Bach and Mozart, appearing in Cologne (1989), Berlin and the Ludwigsburg Festival; Tour of Japan 1987, with Haydn's Die Jahreszeiten; Brussels 1991, in Mozart's Requiem. *Recordings include:* Count Heribert in Die Verschworenen by Schubert (Opus III).

LIKIN, Jurij; Oboist; b. 11 Nov. 1967, Minsk, Belarus; m. Anna Jermolowitch, 7 Mar 1987, 1 d. *Education:* Studies with Professor Boris Nitchkov, Music Lyceum, Belarusian State Music Academy, Minsk; 1 year stage in Paris, Class of Maurice Bourgue, Prague Mozart Academy, 1994. *Career:* Debut: Age 16, Stage of Belarusian Philharmonic, Minsk; Ekaterinburg, Moscow, Minsk, Kaliningrad, Prague, Berlin, Brunswick, 1991–94; Trieste, 1993; Stresa, Italy, 1994; Paris Théâtre des Champs-Elysées, 1994; Marseille, 1995; Les Grands Heures de Saint-Emilion, France, 1995; Principal Oboist of State Symphony Orchestra of Belarusian Philharmonic, 1990–94; Soloist of Prague Symphony Orchestra, Prague Chamber Philharmonic and Member of Prague Wind Quintet, 1994–. *Recordings:* (CDs): B Martinů; A Reicha; E Bozza; Max Stern; F Poulenc Sonata, Sextet. *Honours:* 1st Prizes in National Competitions of USSR, 1986, 1987. *Address:* Trytova 1120, 19800 Prague 9, Czech Republic.

LILL, John Richard, CBE, FRCM, FLCM, FTCM; British pianist; b. 17 March 1944, London; s. of George Lill and the late Margery (née Young) Lill. *Education:* Leyton County High School and Royal Coll. of Music. *Career:* London debut at Royal Festival Hall 1963; plays regularly in European capitals, the USA and the Far East, as recitalist and as soloist with most prin. orchestras; recognized as leading interpreter of Beethoven; Prof., Royal Coll. of Music. *Recordings include:* complete Beethoven piano sonatas, concertos and bagatelles, complete piano works of Rachmaninov (with BBC Nat. Orchestra of Wales/Otaka), Brahms piano concertos, Tchaikovsky Piano Concerto No. 1 (with London Symphony Orchestra), complete Prokofiev sonatas 1991. *Honours:* Hon. DSc (Univ. of Aston), Hon. DMus (Exeter Univ.);Hon. FTCL, FLCM; first prize Royal Overseas League Competition 1963, first prize Int. Tchaikovsky Competition, Moscow 1970, Dinu Lipatti Medal, Chappel Gold Medal. *Current Management:* Askonas Holt Ltd, Lonsdale Chambers, 27 Chancery Lane, London, WC2A 1PF, England. *Telephone:* (20) 7400-1700. *Fax:* (20) 7400-1799. *E-mail:* info@askonasholt.co .uk. *Website:* www.askonasholt.co.uk.

LILOVA, Margarita; Singer (Mezzo-soprano); b. 26 July 1935, Tscherwen, Bulgaria. *Education:* Studied in Sofia with Maria Zibulka and

Michail Jankov. *Career:* Debut: Varna Opera in 1959 as Maddalena in Rigoletto; Sang in Varna as the Countess in The Queen of Spades and Azucena; Covent Garden and Vienna Staatsoper debuts in 1962 and 1963 as Amneris; Guest appearances at the Paris Opéra, Komische Oper Berlin and the Teatro Col ón, Buenos Aires, also at Los Angeles, Berlin, Montreal and Moscow; Member of the Vienna Staatsoper from 1963 including a tour of Japan in 1986, as Marcellina in Le nozze di Figaro and Annina in Der Rosenkavalier; Sang at Salzburg Festival, 1965–67 as the Hostess in Boris Godunov under von Karajan, La Scala Milan in 1973 as Ulrica in Un Ballo in Maschera returning in 1988 as Mary in Der fliegende Holländer; Many concert appearances and song recitals; Professor, Hochschule für Musik und Dorstellende Kunst, Wien, 1993. *Recordings:* Les Contes d'Hoffmann; Boris Godunov; Der Rosenkavalier; Bruckner Te Deum and Mass No. 2; Verdi Messa da Requiem; Video, Maidservant in Elektra conducted by Abbado. *Honours:* Kammersängerin, 1984, Staatsoper Wien. *Address:* c/o Staatsoper, Opernring 2, 1010 Vienna, Austria.

LILTVED, Oystein; Singer (Bass); b. 20 Jan. 1934, Arendal, Norway; m. Virginia Oosthuizen. *Education:* Studied with Maria Hittorf in Vienna, Luciano Donaggio in Trieste and Frederick Dalberg in Kapstad, South Africa. *Career:* Debut: Basle in 1959 as Konshak in Prince Igor; Many appearances at the opera houses of Oslo, Stockholm, Düsseldorf, Kassel and Barcelona; Sang in South Africa at Cape Town and at Johannesburg; Sang at Seattle Opera as Hagen in Götterdämmerung; Other roles have been Wagner's Daland, Landgrave and Fafner, Verdi's King Philip and Fiesco, Mozart's Osmin and Sarastro, Mephistopheles, Varlaam in Boris Godunov, Oroveso, Rocco, Raimondo in Lucia di Lammermoor and Swallow in Peter Grimes; Many appearances in concerts and oratorios.

LIM, Liza; Composer and Lecturer; b. 30 Aug. 1966, Perth, Western Australia. *Education:* BA, Victoria College of the Arts, 1986; Study with Ton de Leeuw, 1987; MMus, University of Melbourne, 1993. *Career:* Lecturer in Composition, University of Melbourne, 1991; Commissions from Duo Contemporain, The Seymour Group; Intercontemporain (Paris), ABC/BBC, Ensemble Modern (1995) and others. *Compositions include:* Blaze for mezzo and ensemble, 1986; Pompes Funebres for string quartet, 1987; Koan, for alto saxophone and percussion, 1987; Tarocchi, for 3 guitars, double bass and percussion, 1988; Voodoo Child for soprano and ensemble, 1989; Constellations, for violin and string orchestra, 1989; Garden of Earthly Desire, for ensemble, 1989; Diabolical Birds, for ensemble, 1990; Amulet, for viola, 1992; Hell, for string quartet, 1992; The Oresteia, opera for 6 voices, 11 instruments and 1 dancer, 1993; Koto, for ensemble, 1993; Lin Shang Yin for coloratura soprano and 15 instruments, 1993; Cathedral, for orchestra, 1994; Sri Vidya for chorus and orchestra, 1994–95; Street of Crocodiles for ensemble, 1995; Gothic, for 8 strings, 1996; The Alchemical Wedding, for orchestra, 1996; The Cauldron: Fusion of the 5 Elements, for 6 voices and instruments, 1996; The Heart's Ear for flute, clarinet and string quartet, 1997. *Honours:* Sounds Australian Award, 1990. *Address:* c/o APRA, 1A Eden Street, Crows Nest, NSW 2065, Australia.

LIM, Soon-Lee; Violist and Conductor; b. 3 Aug. 1957, Singapore; m. 23 June 1983. *Education:* Licentiate, Royal Schools of Music (Violin and Viola); BM with distinction, Eastman School of Music, University of Rochester. *Career:* Debut: Paganini, Grand Viola Sonata, Kilburn Hall, Eastman School of Music; Sub-Principal, Singapore Symphony Orchestra; Assistant Conductor, Singapore Youth Orchestra, 1991–97; Conducted Singapore Symphony Orchestra for the opening and closing ceremonies of the 17th South East Asia Games, 1993; Conducted the Singapore Symphony Orchestra for the World Trade Organisation First Ministerial Conference's Farewell Concert for 4,000 delegates, 1996; Conducted the Asian Youth Orchestra for the National Day Celebration, 1997; Music Director, Resident Conductor, National University of Singapore Symphony Orchestra; mem, American Conductors' Guild; American Viola Society; American String Teachers' Association. *Honours:* 1st Prize, Viola/Cello Open, Singapore National Music Competition, 1981; Jean Frederic Petrenoud Prize with Certificate of Distinction in Orchestra Conducting, 4th Vienna International Music Competition, 1995. *Address:* 58 Toh Tuck Crescent, Singapore 596959.

LIMA, Luis; Singer (Tenor); b. 12 Sept. 1948, Cordoba, Argentina. *Education:* Studied voice with Carlos Guicchandut in Buenos Aires and with Gina Cigna in Italy. *Career:* Debut: Lisbon in 1974 as Turiddu in Cavalleria Rusticana; Guest appearances in Mainz, Munich, Stuttgart and Hamburg; Sang at La Scala Milan in 1977 as Edgardo in Lucia di Lammermoor; Further appearances in Strasbourg and Spain as Rodolfo, Cavaradossi, and Faust in Mefistofele; US debut in 1976 in a concert performance of Donizetti's Gemma di Vergy at Carnegie Hall; Metropolitan Opera debut in 1978 as Alfredo in La Traviata; Sung at New York City Opera in 1979 in La Bohème and Rigoletto, Salzburg Festival in 1984 as Verdi's Macduff, Maggio Musicale Florence, 1985–86 as Don Carlos and as Riccardo in Un Ballo in Maschera, and Covent Garden in 1985 as Nemorino and Don Carlos, returning to London in 1988 as Edgardo; Salzburg Easter Festival in 1988 as Cavaradossi, and

sang Faust at the opening of the season at the Teatro Col ón Buenos Aires in 1990; Sang Don José in a new production of Carmen at Covent Garden in 1991 and Verdi's Don Carlos at San Francisco in 1992; Madrid in 1992 as Don José and New York Metropolitan in 1994 as Cilea's Maurizio; Season 1996 with Rodolfo at Covent Garden; Don Carlos at the New York Met, 1997; Season 2000–01 as Rodolfo at the Met, Turiddu for the Vienna Staatsoper, Don José at Zürich and Don Carlos in Madrid. *Recordings include:* Gemma di Vergy; Le Roi de Lahore; Video of Don Carlos and of Carmen, both from Covent Garden. *Address:* c/o Stafford Law Associates, 6 Barham Close, Weybridge, Surrey KT 13 9 PR, England.

LIMA, Paulo (Costa); Composer and Professor of Music; b. 26 Sept. 1954, Salvador, Bahia, Brazil; m. Ana Margarida Cerqueira Lima e Lima, 2 s. *Education:* Music School, UFBa, 1969–76; BM, Composition, 1978, MS, 1978, University of Illinois, Urbana, USA; PhD, UFBA, 1998. *Career:* Professor of Music at Universidade Federal da Bahia, 1979; Head of Music Department, UFBa, 1986–88; Director of Music School, UFBa, 1988–92; Participation as composer at many national and international events; Festivals: Campos de Jordao, São Paulo, UFRJ; Director of Music School, Universidade Federal da Bahia, 1988–92; International events at Dresden and Urbana; Assistant President, Universidade Federal da Bahia, 1996–98. *Compositions:* Bundle for Solo Flute, 1977, FCEBa, 1981; Ubaba, O Que Diria Bach, 1983, Funarte for Chamber Orchestra; Atôtô-Balzare, UFBA for Percussion and Piano; Cuncti-Serenata, 1983, Funarte UFBA for Piano Solo; Fantasia, 1984, Funarte UFBA for Piano Solo; Pega Essa Nega e Chera, for piano solo, 1993; Corrente de Xango, for cello, 1995; Ponteio, for piano solo, 1995; Atoto do L'homme armè, for chamber orchestra, 1996; Ibejis, for flute and clarinet, 1996; Frevo, for piano solo, 1997. *Recordings:* Compositores Da Bahia, 5, 7 and 8; Outros Ritmos, 1997; Impressionem, 1997. *Publications:* Editor of Art, Music Periodical, 1981–91. *Contributions:* Musical and academic journals. *Honours:* Composition Prize, Max Feffer, São Paulo 1995; Fellowship in Composition, Vitae Foundation, 1995; Copene Prize, 1996. *Address:* R Sabino Silva 304, ap 401, Chame 40155-250, Salvador, Brazil.

LIN, Chiu-Ling; Pianist; b. 13 May 1948, China. *Education:* Licentiate with distinction, Royal School of Music, Singapore, 1964; BMus, New England Conservatory, 1969; MMus, 1972, D.Mus, 1998, Indiana University. *Career:* Debut: Carnegie Recital, 1979; Solo recitals in China, Hong Kong, Singapore, Malaysia, Peru, Argentina, Brazil, England, and Chicago, Minneapolis, Seattle, Atlanta, New York; Soloist with Singapore Orchestra, Des Moines Symphony, Atlanta Symphony, Chicago Civic Orchestra; Artist-in-Residence, Indiana University at South Bend, 1975–76; Professor of Piano, Drake University, Des Moines, 1976–. *Recordings:* Kamran Ince's Cross Scintillation, with Sylvia Wang. *Publications:* Around the World on 88 Keys. *Address:* Music Department, Drake University, 2507 University Avenue, Des Moines, IA 50311, USA.

LIN, Cho-Liang; Violinist; b. 21 Jan. 1960, Taiwan. *Education:* Studied violin from age 5; Sydney Conservatoire, 1972–75; Juilliard School, 1975–78, with Dorothy DeLay. *Career:* Debut: Played with the Philadelphia Orchestra under Ormandy and with the London Symphony Orchestra under Previn, 1976; Many performances with leading orchestras in Europe and America; Season 1993–94 with concerts in the United Kingdom, North America, Finland, Germany, Belgium, France and Far East; United Kingdom, Netherlands, France, Finland and Spain, 1995; Tchaikovsky's Concerto at the 1999 London Proms; Plays a 1707 Stradivarius once owned by Samuel Dushkin. *Recordings:* Mendelssohn Concerto with the Philharmonia Orchestra conducted by Michael Tilson Thomas; Mozart's 5 Concerti with the English Chamber Orchestra under Raymond Leppard; Concertos by Sibelius and Nielsen conducted by Esa-Pekka Salonen; Bruch Violin Concerto and Scottish Fantasy with Chicago Symphony conducted by Leonard Slatkin; Stravinsky, Prokofiev 1 and 2 violin concertos with Los Angeles Philharmonic conducted by Esa-Pekka Salonen. *Address:* c/o IMG Artists, Lovell House, 616 Chiswick High Road, London, England.

LINCÉ, Janet Isabel, GGSM; British conductor; b. 4 Feb. 1951, London. *Education:* Guildhall School of Music and Drama. *Career:* guest Chorus Master, BBC Symphony Chorus, London Symphony Chorus, Philharmonia Chorus; Chorus Master, Newbury Spring Festival Chorus; Musical Dir, Royal Lemington Spa Bach Choir; Musical Dir, Reading Festival Chorus; Musical Dir, Choros; performances in Germany and four tours of New Zealand. *Recording:* album: He came all so stille 2004. *Address:* 6 Mill Lane, Upper Heyford, Oxfordshire OX25 5LH, England. *Telephone:* (1869) 232618. *Fax:* (1869) 232618. *E-mail:* info@choros.org.

LINCOLN, Christopher; Singer (Tenor); b. 1965, Canberra, Australia. *Education:* Studied with Dame Joan Hammonds. *Career:* Appearances throughout Australia as Tamino, Nadir, Fenton, Rossini's Almaviva, Ferrando (Opera Queensland) and Alfredo (in Perth); Donizetti's Edgardo and Gounod's Faust in Auckland; Cologne Opera from 1990, as Mozart's Pedrillo and Tamino; Rodolfo in Luisa Miller in Sofia and Dessau, Alwa in Lulu and Andrès in Wozzeck (1999) at San Francisco; Števa in Jenůfa for Welsh National Opera; Concerts include Handel's Saul, Samson and Solomon, Haydn's Creation and Seasons and the Verdi Requiem; Solos in music by Bach; Recital at Teatre del Liceu, Barcelona, 1999. *Address:* c/o Harlequin Agency Ltd, 203 Fidlas Road, Cardiff CF4 5NA, Wales.

LIND, Eva; Singer (Soprano); b. 14 June 1965, Innsbruck, Austria. *Education:* Studied in Vienna. *Career:* Debut: Landestheater Innsbruck, 1983, as a Flowermaiden in Parsifal; Sang Lucia di Lammermoor at Basle, 1985 and the Queen of Night at Vienna and Paris, 1987; Salzburg Festival 1986 and 1987, as the Italian Singer in Capriccio; Vienna Staatsoper from 1986, as Lucia (Lucia di Lammermoor) and Sophie in Werther; Stuttgart Staatsoper as Adele in Die Fledermaus; British debut as Nannetta in Falstaff, Glyndebourne, 1988; Gounod's Juliette at Zürich, 1990, followed by Sophie in Der Rosenkavalier at Vienna, Brussels and Berne Opera; Concerts with Francisco Araiza at the Teatro Col ón, Buenos Aires, 1990; Sang Mozart's Blonde at Catania, 1996; Season 2000–01 as Gounod's Juliette at Karlsruhe and the Primadonna in Donizetti's La Convenienze Teatrali at Stuttgart. *Recordings:* Die Fledermaus, conducted by Placido Domingo; Naiad in Ariadne auf Naxos, with the Leipzig Gewandhaus Orchestra conducted by Kurt Masur; Coloratura arias, including Elisabeth ou La Fille proscrit by Donizetti; Papagena in Die Zauberflöte, conducted by Marriner; Olympia in Tales of Hoffmann, with Jeffrey Tate; Opera duets with Francisco Araiza; Aennchen in Der Freischütz, conductor, Colin Davis.

LINDBERG, Christian; Swedish trombonist; b. 15 Feb. 1958, Danderyd, Stockholm; m.; four c. *Education:* studies in Stockholm, London, Los Angeles. *Career:* mem., Royal Stockholm Opera Orchestra 1977–78; Prof., Swedish Royal Acad. 1996–; gives over 100 concerts a year as trombone soloist with world's major symphony orchestras; solo programmes, including music theatre; appearances with Per Lundberg, piano, and with Hakan Hardenberger, trumpet; repertoire includes contemporary music, baroque music played on original instruments, classical and romantic music; works composed for him include concertos by Schnittke, Xenakis, Takemitsu and Arvo Pärt; played at several British festivals and Pitea Festival, North Sweden 1993; season 1993–94 with concerts in Germany, Switzerland, Iceland, Denmark, Sweden, Israel; tours to USA and with Scottish Chamber Orchestra; Schnittke's Dialogue with Nash Ensemble, London; performances with Prague Symphony Orchestra, Czech Republic, and Gothenburg Symphony Orchestra, Sweden; Carnegie Hall debut with Zwilich Trombone Concerto and world premiere of Trombone Concerto by Toru Takemitsu with St Paul Chamber Orchestra, USA; several German festivals and Japan tour 1994; 1994–95 season included performances of Trombone Concerto by Iannis Xenakis, new works by Kalevi Aho and Arvo Pärt, also tours to Australia, France, Japan; season 1998–99 participated at the Israel, Rheingau, Cadaquez and Stavanger Festivals and at the Chamber Unlimited Festival, Stockholm; played with the Singapore Symphony Orchestra and in Brussels and Helsinki; season 1999–2000 with concerts at the Gran Canaria Festival with the Norwegian Chamber Orchestra; premiere of new opera production by Luciano Berio at the Salzburg Festival; premiere of Trombone Concerto by Berio with the Tonnhalle Orchestra in Zürich, Australian premiere with the Sydney Symphony Orchestra; masterclasses; designs instruments and mouthpieces for CONN Instrument Co.; Prince Consort Prof., Royal Coll. of Music, London. *Recordings include:* British Trombone Concerti, American Concerti, Italian repertoire for Trombones, Voice and Chamber Organ, Gemeaux by Takemitsu, Frank Martin's Ballade with Concertgebouw Orchestra and Riccardo Chailly. *Current Management:* Svensk Konsertdirektion, PO Box 5076, 402 22 Goteborg, Sweden.

LINDBERG, Magnus; Composer and Pianist; b. 27 June 1958, Helsinki, Finland. *Education:* Studied at the Sibelius Academy, Helsinki; Further studies with Globokar in Paris, Donatoni in Siene and Ferneyhough at Darmstadt. *Compositions include:* Three Pieces for horn and string trio; Arabesques for wind quintet; Quintet for piano and wind; De Tartuffe je Croi for string quartet and piano; Drama for orchestra; Sculpture II for orchestra; Linea d'Ombra for flute and ensemble; Action Situation Signification for horn or clarinets and ensemble (1982); Ritratto for orchestra; Zona for ensemble; Metal Work for accordion and percussion; Kraft for orchestra (1985); UR for 5 players and live electronics; Twine for piano; Trios Sculptures for orchestra; Tape: Etwas Zarter; Ohne Audruck; Faust; Ensemble triptych Kinetics, Marea and Joy (1988–90); (orrente II, 1991); Aura, 1994; Arena, 1995; Cello Concerto, 1999; Grand Duo for orchestra, 2000. *Honours:* Prix Italia for Faust; Nordic Music Prize for Kraft. *Address:* c/o Boosey and Hawkes Ltd, 295 Regent Street, London W1R 8JH, England.

LINDE, Hans-Martin; Recorder Player, Flautist and Conductor; b. 24 May 1930, Werne, Germany; m. Gudrun Olshausen, 1 s., 2 d. *Education:* Staatliche Hochschule für Musik, Freiburg, 1947–51, with Konrad Lechner (conducting) and Gustav Scheck (flute). *Career:* Solo flautist of the Cappella Coloniensis of West German Radio, Cologne; Concert tours in Europe, USA, South America, Middle and Far East from 1955; Teacher of Baroque Flute, Recorder and Conducting from 1957; Conductor of Vocal Ensemble, 1965–; Conductor of Chamber Orchestra, 1970–, of the Schola Cantorum Basiliensis, Basle; Co-Editor, Zeitschrift für Spielmusik, 1966–; Concert associations with August Wenzinger and Frans Brueggen; Conducted with Basler-Linde Concert in Keiser's Tomyris and Vivaldi's La Griselda at Ludwigshafen, 1988, 1989. *Recordings include:* Flute Concertos by Leclair, Stamitz, Dittersdorf and Mozart; Recorder Concertos by Sammartini and Vivaldi; English Consort Music and Chamber Music by Bach, Handel, Haydn with the Linde-Consort; Conductor of the Linde-Consort and the Cappella Coloniensis; Guest Conductor of several orchestras and choirs in different European countries and in the USA; Recordings as a conductor include: Bach; Masses, Brandenburg Concertos, Orchestral Suites; Schütz: Exequien; Handel: Water-Music, Music for the Royal Fireworks, Concerti grossi op 6, Keiser's Der Grossmutige Tomyris. *Publications:* Kleine Anleitung zum Verrzieren alter Musik, 1958; Handbuch des Blockflötenspiels, 1962.

LINDÉN, Magnus; Singer (Baritone); b. 1 Nov. 1954, Sweden. *Education:* Studied in Stockholm with Erik Saedén and in London with Vera Rozsa. *Career:* Royal Opera, Stockholm, from 1980, notably as Papageno and Guglielmo and in the 1994 premiere of Sctschedrin's Lolita; Drottningholm Festival, 1987, as Don Giovanni, and 1991 as Egisth in Haeffner's Electra; Other roles include Tolomeo in Handel's Giulio Cesare, Zuniga in Carmen and Jovanni in the 1991 premiere of Don Juan Freestyle by Hillerud-Wannefors; Many concert appearances. *Recordings include:* Così fan tutte, from Drottningholm. *Address:* Royal Opera, PO Box 16094, 10322 Stockholm, Sweden.

LINDENSTRAND, Sylvia; Singer (Mezzo-Soprano); b. 24 June 1942, Stockholm, Sweden. *Education:* Studied at the Opera School of the Royal Opera, Stockholm. *Career:* Debut: Stockholm 1962, as Olga in Eugene Onegin; Has sung at the Royal Opera, Stockholm as Dorabella, Cherubino, Marina in Boris Godunov, Octavian, Brangäne, Fricka in the Ring and Cenerentola; Sang Tchaikovsky's Maid of Orleans, 1986 and sang in Singoalla by Gunnar de Frumerie 1988; Guest appearances at Bayreuth, 1964, Copenhagen and the Moscow Bolshoi; Glyndebourne 1975 and 1979, as Dorabella and Amaranta in La Fedeltà Premiata; Aix-en-Provence, 1976, Zerlina in Don Giovanni; Sang Idamante in Idomeneo at Drottningholm; Royal Opera Stockholm, 1991 as Dionysus in the premiere of Backanterna by Daniel Börtz (production by Ingmar Bergman); Many concert engagements. *Recordings include:* Songs by Liszt. *Honours:* Swedish Court Singer, 1982. *Address:* c/o Kungliga Teatern, PO Box 16094, 102 51 Stockholm, Sweden.

LINDHOLM, Berit Maria; Opera Singer (soprano); b. (Berit Maria Jonsson), 18 Oct. 1934, Stockholm, Sweden; m. Hans Lindholm, 2 d. *Education:* Stockholm Opera School. *Career:* debut, Countess in Le nozze di Figaro, Stockholm, 1963; Performances all over the world including, New York Met, Carnegie Hall, San Francisco, Chicago, London, Paris, Hamburg, Berlin, Munich, Moscow, Naples, Madrid, Geneva, Zürich, Düsseldorf, Vienna, Barcelona, Bayreuth; Repertoire included: Isolde, Brünnhilde, Kundry, Tosca, Salome, Elektra, Turandot, Fidelio, Dyer's Wife in Die Frau ohne Schatten; Sang in the premiere of Backanterna by Daniel Börtz, Stockholm 1991; Teaches singing; mem, Swedish Royal Academy of Music. *Recordings include:* Les Troyens; Die Walküre; Songs by Swedish Composers. *Honours:* Opera Singer by Appointment of the King of Sweden; Litteris et Artibus, 1988. *Address:* Artistsekretariat Ulf Törnqvist, Sankt Eriksqatan 100, 11331 Stockholm, Sweden.

LINDNER, Brigitte; Singer (Soprano); b. 1959, Munich, Germany. *Education:* Studied in Munich. *Career:* Debut: Gärtnerplatz-Theater Munich as a Boy in Die Zauberflöte; Sang Gretel in Humperdinck's opera (also televised) and in Mozart's Bastien and Bastienne; Adult debut at the Ludwigsburg Festival 1980, as Barbarina in Le nozze di Figaro; Bayreuth Festival 1985, as the Shepherd boy in Tannhäuser; Sang Despina in Così fan tutte for Kiel Opera, 1990; Other roles include Papagena and parts in operettas by Lehar and Johann Strauss; Concert appearances in oratorios by Bach, Haydn and Mozart. *Recordings:* Hansel and Gretel, Die Zauberflöte.

LINDSEY, John Russell; Professor of Violin and Violinist; b. 26 Aug. 1947, Chicago, IL, USA; Divorced. 2 s., 1 d. *Career:* Former Concertmaster, Dallas Chamber Players, the Lexington Philharmonic Orchestra, The Warren (Ohio) Chamber Orchestra, The Castle Farm Summer Festival Orchestra (Michigan), the Champlain Valley Symphony Orchestra; Chair. of Strings, Baylor University; The Governor's School of North Carolina; University of Kentucky; Teacher of Strings, Dallas, Texas, Public Schools; Performed and taught violin in the Stage de Musique, Marcillat-en-Combraille, France, 1988, the Incontri di Canna International Chamber Music Festival in southern Italy, 2000 and

Ameropa 2004 in Prague; Concertmaster, Orchestra of Northern New York and Hanover, New Hampshire Chamber Orchestra; Violinist, Ruggieri Chamber Soloists; First Violinist, Aurora Quintet; Prof. of Music and a mem. of the Potsdam Piano Quartet, Crane School of Music, 1981–; Mem., violin faculties, Ithaca Summer Chamber Music Institute, the Adult Chamber Music Conference at Interlochen, Michigan and the Manitou Music Festival in Glen Arbor, Michigan; Solo recitals at the Carnegie Recital Hall, Museum of the City of New York, St Joseph's Church, Bruno Walter Auditorium, Lincoln Center, New York City; Also in Boston, Montreal, Atlanta, and Chicago; mem, Triple Nine Society; Chamber Music America; American String Teachers' Asscn. *Honours:* Mozart Award, 1972; Winner, City of Dayton's Second Annual Allegro Residency for the Arts, 1989; President's Award for Excellence in Teaching (Teacher of the Year Award), Potsdam College, State University of New York, 1993; State Univ. of New York Chancellor's Award for Excellence in Teaching, 2003. *Address:* Crane School of Music, SUNY Potsdam, Potsdam, NY 13676, USA.

LINDSKOG, Par; Singer (Tenor); b. 1962, Kungelv, Sweden. *Education:* Vocal studies at Gothenburg, from 1981. *Career:* Secondary roles at the Opera Studio and Theatre in Gothenburg; Berlin Staatsoper as Max in Der Freischütz, Narraboth (Salome), Števa (Jenůfa) and the Steersman in Der fliegende Holländer, from 1987; Further engagements in Lisbon, Salzburg, Dresden and Leipzig; Season 1995/96 as Young Man in Moses und Aron under Pierre Boulez at Amsterdam and Salzburg, and under Christoph von Dohnányi with the Philharmonia Orchestra at the Festival Hall, London; Further roles include Tamino, Don Ottavio and Barinkay in Der Zigeunerbaron, Vienna, 1996. *Honours:* Bayreuth Scholarship, 1993. *Address:* c/o Deutsche Staatsoper Berlin, Unter den Linden 7, 1060 Berlin, Germany.

LINDSLEY, Celina; Singer (Soprano); b. 1953, USA. *Education:* Studied at the Eastman School of Music. *Career:* Sang at Bielefeld, Kassel and Nuremberg; New York City Opera, 1977, as the Queen of Night; Düsseldorf Opera from 1978, with Autonoe in The Bassarids, 1991; Vienna Staatsoper and Covent Garden, 1985, as Zerbinetta and in Zemlinsky's Der Zwerg; Duisburg, 1985, in the premiere of Goehr's Behold the Sun; Komische Oper Berlin, 1991, as Donna Anna and Essen, 1994, as Violetta; Sang Marie in Gurlitt's Wozzeck at Florence, 1998; Many concerts and Lieder recitals. *Recordings include:* Zemlinsky's Der Kreidekreis and Busoni's Turandot. *Address:* c/o Teatro Comunale, Via Solferino 15, 50123 Florence, Italy.

LINGE, Ruth; Opera Singer (Lyrical Soprano); b. 13 Oct. 1927, Porsgrunn, Norway; m. Tormod Linge. *Education:* Private, Oslo, Stockholm, Vienna. *Career:* Debut: As Norina in Don Pasquale, Oslo, 1951; Norsk Operaselskap, 1951–58; Member, Den Norske Opera, 1958–; Main roles include Zerlina, Donna Elvira, Donna Anna, Cherubino, Papagena, Adina, Gilda, Rosina, Musetta, Olympia; Appearances in television opera productions, radio concerts; Secretary, Board Society of Norwegian Opera Singers; Society of Norwegian Musica Artists.

LINJAMA, Jouko; Composer; b. 1934, Finland. *Education:* Sibelius Academy; Musicology and Literature, Helsinki University; Further studies in Composition, Cologne, 1962–64; Staatliche Hochschule für Musik; Kölner Kurse für Neue Musik. *Career:* Organist, St Henrik's Catholic Church, Helsinki, 1958–60; Cantor-Organist, Parish of Tuusula, 1964–97. *Compositions include:* Opera: Finnish Taper, 1998–99 Orchestra: 2 Symphonies from oratorio Homage to Aleksis Kivi, 1972; La Migration d'Oiseaux Sauvages, 1977; Choral Works: How It Is, oratorio, 1968; Homage to Aleksis Kivi, symphonic oratorio, 1970, 1974, 1976; Missa De Angelis, 1969; La Sapienza, oratorio da camera, 1980; Mailman Algusta ia Loomisesta, oratorio, 1983; Requiem, 1998; Chamber Music: String Quartet No. 1, 1978; No. 2, 1979; Concerto for organ, marimba, vibraphone, 2 Wind Quartets, 1981; Concerto for horn and organ, 2001; Quartetto for cornetto, corno and organo, 2002; Duo for piano and organ, 2002; Trio for clarinet, horn and organ, 2003Works for organ: Sonatina supra B-A-C-H, 1968; Magnificat for organ, 1970; Partitasonata Veni Creator Spiritus, 1969; Missa Cum Jubilo for organ, 1977; Organum supra B-A-C-H, 1982; Toccata in D, 1985; Reflections, duet for organ, 1991; Three Liturgical Stained-Glass Paintings, 1993; Cappella Choral Works: Partita per coro, 1979; On The Road to Splendour, 1980; Kalevala Suite, 1981; Toward the Future and Hope, 1984; Has composed numerous solo songs. *Recordings:* Numerous recordings of his work. *Publications:* When My Father Composed the Olympic Hymn, Gummeus, 2002. *Address:* Teosto, Lauttasaarentie 1, 00200 Helsinki 20, Finland.

LINKE, Fritz; Singer (Bass); b. 15 May 1923, Claussnitz, Germany. *Career:* Sang in Chemnitz from 1950; Dresden Staatsoper, 1951–56; Staatsoper Stuttgart, 1956–86; Guest appearances in Hamburg, Munich, Paris, Barcelona, Venice, Rome, Bologna, Mannheim, Cologne, Zürich and Karlsruhe; Bayreuth Festival, 1963–70; Roles include Mozart's Osmin and Sarastro, Verdi's Padre Guardiano and King

Philip, Wagner's Daland, Fafner, Hunding and Landgrave, Beethoven's Rocco and Baron Ochs in Der Rosenkavalier. *Address:* c/o Staatstheater Stuttgart, Oberer Schlossgarten 6, 7000 Stuttgart 1, Germany.

LINN, Robert; Composer; b. 11 Aug. 1925, San Francisco, California, USA. *Education:* Studied with Darius Milhaud at Mills College; MM, 1950, University of California at Los Angeles, with Roger Sessions, Bernard Stevens and Ingolf Dahl. *Career:* Faculty member at University of California at Los Angeles, 1958; Chairman of the department of music theory and composition, 1973–. *Compositions:* Clarinet Sonata, 1949; String Quartet, 1951; Four Pieces for concert band, 1954; 2 Piano Sonatas, 1955, 1964; Symphony, 1956; Concerto Grosso, 1961; Brass Quintet, 1963; Woodwind Quintet, 1963; Hexameron for piano and orchestra, 1963; Elevations for wind, 1964; Concertino for violin and wind octet, 1968; Sinfonia for strings, 1967, revised, 1972; Pied Piper of Hamelin, oratorio, 1968; Fantasia for cello and strings, 1976; Twelve, 1977; Concerto for flute and winds, 1980; Partita for winds, 1980; Concertino for woodwind quintet and strings, 1982; Concerto for piano and wind, 1984; Vocal music, including Songs of William Blake for chorus, 1981. *Honours:* Commissions and grants from the American Guild of Organists, the Louisville Orchestra and the Huntington Hartford Foundation. *Address:* c/o ASCAP, ASCAP Building, 1 Lincoln Plaza, New York, NY 10023, USA.

LINNENBANK, René; Singer (Bass); b. 1961, Abcoude, Netherlands. *Education:* Maastricht and Sweelinck Conservatories; Guildhall School, London. *Career:* Debut: Osmin in Die Entführung for Scottish Opera Go Round, 1992; Appearances with Opera-SKON, Netherlands, as Mozart's Sarastro, and Cols (Bastien und Basitienne); Bagheera the Panther in Berkeley's Baa-Baa-Black-Sheep for Opera North; Other roles include Mozart's Figaro, Harasta in The Cunning Little Vixen. Nicolai's Falstaff, and King Tartaglia in Jonathan Dove's The Little Green Bird; Concerts and recitals throughout Europe with such conductors as William Christie, Paul Daniel and Mstislav Rostropovich; Sang Un Turk in the Lully/Molière Bourgeois Gentilhomme, Linbury Theatre, 2001; Season 2001–2002 in Orfeo by Monteverdi at La Monnaie, Brussels, under René Jacobs. *Address:* c/o English Bach Festival, 15 South Eaton Place, London, SW1W 9ER, England.

LINOS, Glenys; Singer (Mezzo-soprano); b. 29 Sept. 1941, Cairo, Egypt. *Education:* Athens Conservatory; London Opera Centre. *Career:* Sang in Mainz, Ulm and Wiesbaden from 1970; Guest appearances in most major German opera houses; Bayreuth and Salzburg Festivals; Toulouse, 1983, as Carmen; Festival Hall, London, 1983, in the Verdi Requiem; Ghent, 1984, as Santuzza in Cavalleria Rusticana; Zürich, 1984–85, as Pensithelia in the opera by Schoeck; Paris Opéra-Comique, 1985, in The Stone Guest by Dargomyzhsky; Lausanne and La Scala Milan, 1986, as the Sorceress in Dido and Aeneas and Geneviève in Pelléas et Mélisande; Rome Opera, 1986, as Ermengarda in Agnese di Hohenstaufen by Spontini; Sang Clairon in Capriccio at Bologna, 1987; Auntie in Peter Grimes at the Zürich Opera, 1989; Clytemnestra in Elektra at the Teatro Nuovo, Spoleto, 1990; Television appearances include Adriano in Rienzi, Wiesbaden Opera. *Recordings include:* Monteverdi's Orfeo. *Address:* c/o Opernhaus Zürich, Falkenstrasse 1, 8008 Zürich, Switzerland.

LIPKIN, Malcolm (Leyland); Composer and Lecturer; b. 2 May 1932, Liverpool, England; m. Judith Frankel, 5 Aug 1968, 1 s. *Education:* Liverpool College, 1944–48; Royal College of Music, London, 1949–53; Privately with Mátyás Seiber, 1954–57; D.Mus, London, 1972; ARCM; LRAM. *Career:* Debut: Gaudeamus Foundation, Netherlands, 1951; Numerous broadcast and public performances of own compositions of orchestral, choral, vocal, chamber and instrumental music in many countries, 1951–. *Compositions:* Sinfonia di Roma, Symphony No. 1; The Pursuit, Symphony No. 2; Sun, Symphony No. 3; Two Violin Concertos, Piano Concerto, Flute Concerto; Oboe Concerto; Psalm 96 for chorus and orchestra; Four Departures for soprano and violin; Five Shelley Songs; Clifford's Tower for instrumental ensemble; String Trio; Harp Trio; Five Piano sonatas; Violin sonata; Wind Quintet; Metamorphosis for harpsichord; Naboth's Vineyard for recorders, cello and harpsichord; Interplay; Pastorales for horn and strings; Piano Trio; Prelude and Dance for cello and piano; Nocturnes 1–5 for piano, 1987–2001; Bartók Variations for string quartet; Dance Fantasy for solo violin; Five Bagatelles for oboe and piano, 1993; Duo for violin and cello, 1994; Second Violin Sonata, 1997; Pierrot Dances for viola and piano, 1998; From Across La Manche for string orchestra, 1998; Sixth Piano Sonata (Fantasy Sonata), 2002. *Recordings:* Clifford's Tower; Pastorale, string trio recorded by Nash Ensemble, 1986; Piano Trio recorded by English Piano Trio, 1992. *Contributions:* Musical Times; Musical Opinion; Classical Music. *Address:* Penlan, Crowborough Hill, Crowborough, Sussex, TN 6 2EA, England. *Website:* www.malcolmlipkin.co.uk.

LIPKIN, Seymour; Pianist and Conductor; b. 14 May 1927, Detroit, Michigan, USA. *Education:* Studied at the Curtis Institute, 1938–47, with David Sapert, Rudolf Serkin and Horsowski; Conducting studies with Koussevitsky at the Berkshire Music Center and as apprentice to George Szell at the Cleveland Orchestra, 1947–48. *Career:* Debut: Conducted the Cleveland Little Symphony, 1948; Soloist with the New York Philharmonic, 1949; Concerts with leading American orchestras; Teacher of conducting at the Berkshire Music Center, 1951–54; Conducted the New York City Opera, 1958, New York Philharmonic, 1959, Long Island Symphony, 1963–79; Joffrey Ballet, 1966–79; Teacher of piano at the Curtis Institute from 1969, Manhattan School from 1972; Resumed solo piano career in New York, 1981. *Honours:* Winner, Rachmaninov Piano Competition, 1948. *Address:* c/o Manhattan School for Music, 120 Claremont Avenue, New York, NY 10027, USA.

LIPMAN, Michael; Cellist and Educator; b. 15 March 1954, Meriden, Connecticut, USA; m. Shirli Nikolsburg, 1999. *Education:* Paul Olefsky, Hartt College of Music; Ronald Leonard and Paul Katz, Eastman School of Music; Leonard Rose, Blossom Music Festival; BMus, 1976, MMus in Performance and Literature, 1978, Eastman School of Music. *Career:* Debut: Recital, Pittsburgh, 1985; Soloist, Aspen Philharmonia Orchestra, 1977; Cello, Rochester Philharmonic, 1977–78; Principal Cello, Aspen Chamber Symphony, 1978–80; Associate Principal Cello, New Haven Symphony, 1978–79; Cello, Pittsburgh Symphony, 1979–; Soloist, Pittsburgh Symphony, 1985, 1993; Recitals and chamber music concerts throughout USA; Participant, Aspen Music Festival, New York String Seminar, Cleveland Chamber Seminar, Grand Teton Music Festival; Cellist and Founding Member, The California University of Pennsylvania String Quartet, 1986; Full-length radio broadcast of Pittsburgh debut recital, WQED, 1986; Solo and chamber music performances in Beijing, China, and Moscow, Russia, 1987, 1989; Faculty, Duquesne University School of Music, 1994–1996; Founding Member, The Dalihapa Ensemble, 1995–; Performing with the Pittsburgh Chamber Music Project. *Recordings:* With Pittsburgh Chamber Music Project, 2002. *Honours:* 1st Prize, Aspen Concerto Competition, 1977; Passamaneck Award, Pittsburgh (Pennsylvania) Y Music Society, 1985. *Address:* 4011 Boulevard Drive, Pittsburgh, PA 15217, USA. *Telephone:* 412 421 8852. *Fax:* 412 421 8852. *E-mail:* niklip@aol.com.

LIPOVETSKY, Leonidas; Concert Pianist, Lecturer and Educator; b. 2 May 1937, Montevideo, Uruguay; m. Astrid Eir Jonsson, 14 April 1973, 1 s., 2 d. *Education:* Juilliard School of Music, NYC, USA; Studied Piano with Wilhelm Kolischer, The Kolischer Conservatory, Montevideo, Uruguay and with Rosina Lhevinne and Martin Canin. *Career:* Debut: National Symphony, Montevideo, Uruguay, 1959; NYC, 1967; Recital, NYC, 1964; South American premiere of Britten's Piano Concerto in D at Montevideo, 1959; Concert tours in the United Kingdom, Europe, Russia, Scandinavia, USA, Canada, Central and South America; Soloist on tour with Czech Philharmonic, Leoš Janáček in Spain and Czechoslovakia and with English Chamber Orchestra in USA National Symphony Orchestra, Mexico; National Orchestra Association, NYC, USA; Juilliard Orchestra, NYC, USA; Winnipeg Symphony, Canada; Royal Liverpool Philharmonic; Seville Philharmonic, Spain; National Symphony of Iceland, Reykjavík; Chicago Chamber Orchestra, Chicago; Cedar Rapids Symphony, Iowa; National symphony of Columbia, Bogota, South America; Ossodre, Montevideo, Uruguay, South America; Mexico National Conservatory, Mexico; Broadcasts include BBC, London; Television appearances and Special Guest Artist, UN General Assembly; Lectures at Trinity College of Music and Dartington College, United Kingdom and at the Juilliard School of Music, New York City, USA; Moscow Conservatory, Moscow, Russia. *Current Management:* Project Music and The Arts, 1802 Atapha Nene, Tallahassee, FL 32301, USA. *Address:* 1802 Atapha Nene, Tallahassee, FL 32301, USA.

LIPOVSEK, Marjana; Singer (mezzo-soprano); b. 3 Dec. 1946, Ljubljana, Slovenia. *Education:* Studied in Ljubljana and at the Music Academy in Graz. *Career:* Started in Vienna, then Hamburg, then Munich; Has sung in Munich, Marie (Wozzek), La Forza del Destino; Nurse (Frau ohne Schatten); Kundry (Parsifal); Has sung at the Bavarian State Opera, Munich, from 1983, notably as Konchakovna in Prince Igor and Fricka in Der Ring des Nibelungen; Bregenz Festival from 1988, as Dalila and Carmen (1991); Appearances at the Vienna Staatsoper and in Berlin, Stuttgart, Frankfurt, Hamburg, Madrid and Milan, and in the USA with Chicago and San Francisco Opera; Covent Garden debut, 1990, as Clytemnestra in Elektra, conducted by Georg Solti; Other roles include Ulrica, Orfeo, Octavian, Dorabella, Mistress Quickly, Azucena, Amneris, Brangaena, Marfa in Khovanshchina; Concert engagements with Abbado, Horst Stein, Harnoncourt, Helmuth Rilling, Colin Davis, Sinopoli, Maazel, Sawallisch and Haitink; Beethoven's Missa Solemnis under Michael Gielen (also televised); London debut, 1988, in Das Lied von der Erde with the London Symphony; Salzburg Festival recitals from 1985; Other recitals at the Schleswig-Holstein and Hohenems Festivals, in Brussels, Amsterdam, Vienna and Germany and at the Wigmore Hall, London (1990); Season 1990/91 US concert debut with the New York Philharmonic conducted by Ozawa and the Boston Symphony Orchestra; Sang the Nurse in Die Frau ohne Schatten at the

1992 Salzburg Festival; Sang Clytemnestra at the 1996 Florence Maggio Musicale; Brangaene at the 1998 Munich Festival; Season 2000–01 as Clytemnestra and Mistress Quickly at Munich, Brangaene for the Salzburg Festival. *Recordings include:* Bach's Passions; Orfeo by Gluck and Messiah; Beethoven's 9th Symphony; Fricka in Das Rheingold and Die Walküre; Orlofsky in Die Fledermaus; The Witch in Hansel and Gretel under Jeffrey Tate; Clytemnestra in Elektra under Sawallisch; DVD of Tristan und Isolde, Munich, 1998. *Honours:* Grand Prix du Disque for recording of Martin's Cornet. *Current Management:* Askonas Holt Ltd, Lonsdale Chambers, 27 Chancery Lane, London, WC2A 1PF, England. *Telephone:* (20) 7400-1700. *Fax:* (20) 7400-1799. *E-mail:* info@askonasholt.co.uk. *Website:* www.askonasholt.co.uk.

LIPP, Wilma; Singer (Soprano); b. 26 April 1925, Vienna, Austria. *Education:* Studied in Vienna and with Toti dal Monte in Milan. *Career:* Debut: Vienna, 1943, as Rosina in Il Barbiere di Siviglia; Member of the Vienna Staatsoper from 1945, notably as Mozart's Queen of Night; Salzburg Festival from 1948, as Mozart's Servilia, Blondchen, Donna Elvira and Queen of Night; Covent Garden, 1951, as Gilda in Rigoletto; La Scala Milan, 1950, and Glyndebourne, 1957, as Constanze in Die Entführung; US debut at San Francisco, 1962, as Nannetta in Falstaff; Guest appearances in London, Hamburg, Munich, Berlin and Paris; Returned to Salzburg, 1983–84, as the Duenna in Der Rosenkavalier (also at Turin, 1986). *Recordings:* Brahms Ein Deutsches Requiem; Die Zauberflöte; Die Entführung; Fra Diavolo; Die Fledermaus; Fidelio; Der Rosenkavalier. *Address:* c/o Staatsoper, Opernring 2, 1010 Vienna, Austria.

LIPPERT, Herbert; Singer (Tenor); b. 1963, Germany. *Career:* Sang at the Lubeck Opera 1987–91, in such roles as Pedrillo and Albert Herring; Bregenz Festival 1989, as Ferrando in Così fan tutte, followed by Tamino in Vienna, Munich and Cologne; Salzburg Festival from 1990, in Fidelio, Die Zauberflöte and Die Frau ohne Schatten; Naples and Aix Festival 1992 as Wagner's Steersman and as Don Ottavio; Further engagements at the Stuttgart and Leipzig Operas; Sang Wagner's David at Covent Garden, 1997; Sang Ferrando at Buenos Aires, 1999; Concert repertory includes Bach's St Matthew Passion. *Recordings include:* Don Ottavio in Don Giovanni under Solti. *Address:* c/o Salzburg Festival (Opera). PO Box 140, 5010 Salzburg, Austria.

LIPTAK, David; Composer, Pianist and Teacher; b. 18 Dec. 1949, Pittsburgh, Pennsylvania, USA; m. Catherine Tait, 1 d. *Education:* Duquesne University, 1967–71; BM, Eastman School of Music, 1973–76; MM, DMA, Composition. *Career:* Composition and Theory Faculties, Michigan State University, 1976–80; University of Illinois, 1980–87; Eastman School of Music, 1986–, including Chairman of Composition Department, 1993–. *Compositions:* Duo, 1979, 1992; Seven Songs, 1984; Arcs, 1986; Loner, 1989; Trio, 1990; Shadower, 1991; Rhapsodies, 1992; Ancient Songs, 1992. *Recordings:* Seven Songs, 1984; Illusions, 1989. *Publications:* Compositions. *Address:* Composition Department, Eastman School of Music, 26 Gibbs Street, Rochester, NY 14064, USA.

LIPTON, Daniel B.; Conductor and Artistic Director; b. 1950, Paris, France; m. Olga Lucia Gaviria 1983. *Education:* High School of Music and Art, Manhattan School of Music, Juilliard School, Mannes Coll., Ecole Normale Supérieure, Accademia Chigiana. *Career:* conductor, Settimane Senese, American Ballet Theater, Denver Symphony, Holland Festival (Concertgebouw), Teatro Comunale Bologna, Maggio Musicale Fiorentino (Florence), Zürich Opera, Liceo Barcelona, Madrid Opera, Teatro La Fenice (Venice), Châtelet (Paris), Sadler's Wells (London), Houston Grand Opera, Utah Opera, San Antonio Festival, Hamburg Staatsoper, throughout North and South America, Paris Opéra Orchestra and Bayerische Staatsoper (Munich); Artistic Dir, Colombia Symphony Orchestra and Opera de Colombia, Bogotà 1975–83, Opera Hamilton, ON, Canada 1986–, San Antonio Festival, San Antonio, TX 1987–; conducted world premiere of Gian Carlo Menotti's The Wedding; season 2003 conducted Rigoletto in Montreal, Die Zauberflote in Avenches, Carmina Burana in Mallorca; season 2004 conducted Rigoletto in Oviedo, Macbeth in Seville, Otello in Hamilton. *Recordings:* Tosca, Puccini; Recital of Montserrat Caballé and José Carreras at Gran Teatre del Liceo in Barcelona; on video: Donizetti, Don Pasquale; Giordano, Andrea Chénier; Leoncavallo, Pagliacci; Mascagni, Cavalleria Rusticana; Mozart, Nozze di Figaro; Ponchielli, Gioconda; Puccini, La Bohème, Tosca, Turandot; Verdi, Aida, Ballo, Forza, Rigoletto, Trovatore. *Current Management:* Harwood Management Group Inc., 509 W 110 Street, New York, NY 10025, USA. *Telephone:* (212) 864-0773. *Fax:* (212) 663-1129. *E-mail:* jim@harwood-management.com. *Website:* www.harwood-management.com.

LIPTON, Martha; Singer (Mezzo-soprano); b. 6 April 1916, New York, USA. *Education:* Studied at the Juilliard School, New York. *Career:* Debut: New Opera Company, New York, 1941, as Pauline in The Queen of Spades; New York City Opera, 1944, in Martha; Metropolitan Opera from 1944, as Siebel in Faust, Verdi's Emilia, Amneris and Maddalena, Bizet's Mercedes and Humperdinck's Hansel; 298 performances in 36 parts, Rio de Janeiro, 1950; Carnegie Hall, 1952, in a concert performance of Wolf's Der Corregidor; Chicago, 1956, as Herodias in Salome; Other roles include Verdi's Meg Page and Ulrica, Mozart's Cherubino and Strauss's Octavian; Also heard as Lieder singer and in oratorio. *Recordings:* Mother Goose in The Rake's Progress; Orlofsky in Die Fledermaus; Handel's Messiah. *Address:* c/o Metropolitan Opera, Lincoln Center, New York, NY 10023, USA.

LISICHENKO, Yuri; Russian pianist and academic; b. 1 Feb. 1954, Lvov; m. Irina Plotnikova 1974; one s. one d. *Education:* Lvov Special Music School, Moscow Conservatory. *Career:* debut with Philharmonic Orchestra, Hall of Lvov Philharmonia; Professor, Moscow Conservatory; Performed: The Great Hall, 1973, 1975, The Small Hall, 1988, 1989, Moscow Conservatory; Milan, Turin, Verona, Italy, 1991; Basel, Switzerland, with violinist Tatiana Grindenko, 1991; Many television and radio appearances including television film Avantgarde in Music (Company of Musical Programmes), 1989; mem, Union of Musicians, Moscow. *Recordings:* Chopin Sonata, Anton Rubinstein Sonata, Schumann; Melody; Baroque music with Chamber Orchestra under Tatiana Grindenki, 1990; Ondine, Finland. *Honours:* 3rd Prize, Marguerite Long and Jacques Thibaud Competition, Paris, 1975; Honorary Diploma, Tchaikovsky Competitions, 1978. *Address:* Teply Satn styr 25 K1, Apt 244, Moscow 117133, Russia.

LISOWSKA, Hanna; Singer (Soprano); b. 15 Sept. 1939, Warsaw, Poland. *Education:* Studied at Warsaw University and Music High School. *Career:* Debut: Teatr Wielki, Warsaw, as Tatiana in Eugene Onegin, 1967; Fidelio as Leonore at Staatsoper Berlin, Deutsche Oper Berlin, Deutsche Oper Düsseldorf, Staatsoper Hamburg, Munich, Stuttgart, Bonn, Zürich, Rome, Wiesbaden, Madrid, Frankfurt am Main, Tokyo, Hanover; Wagnerian repertoire includes Isolde at Leipzig, Senta, Sieglinde, Brünnhilde, Gutrune in Götterdämmerung, Eva in Meistersinger, Elisabeth and Venus from Tannhäuser, all at international venues; Gutrune in Covent Garden; Gutrune und Sieglinde in Metropolitan Opera, New York; German repertoire includes Marschallin, Chrysothemis, Eglantine, Martha; Italian repertoire includes Elisabeth in Don Carlos, Tosca, Minnie, Tatiana, Lisa; Sang Aida and Lady Macbeth and Turandot in Warsaw. *Address:* Teatr Narodowy, Plac Teatralmy, 00-950 Warsaw, Poland.

LISSITSIAN, Rouben; Singer (Tenor); b. 9 May 1945, Moscow, Russia. *Education:* Central Music School, Moscow, 1953–60; Russian Music Academy, Moscow, 1965–69. *Career:* Debut: Great Hall of Conservatory, Moscow, 1965; Soloist-Vocalist, Cellist, Flautist, Madrigal Ensemble, 1965–69; Part of Evangelist in Mattauspassion by Bach, Great Hall of Philharmonic, St Petersburg, 1973; Samson in Oratorio Samson by Handel, Great Hall of Conservatory, Moscow, 1974; War Requiem by Britten, Wrozlaw-Festival, 1974; Ninth Symphony by Beethoven, Paris Congres de Palais, 1974; Rubajat by Gubaidulina with Schoenberg Ensemble in Amsterdam, 1996; Tours of Germany, Israel, France, Finland, Netherlands, Hungary, USA, Canada, Poland; President, German-Russian Cultural and Educational Academy; Art Director, Russian Dramatic Theatre, Cologne. *Recordings:* P Cornelius, Weihnachtslieder; R Schumann, Lieder; W A Mozart, Requiem; J Brahms, Walzer; S Gubaidulina, Perception; Pärt, Stabat Mater. *Honours:* 1st Prize, Gold Medal, International R Schumann Competition, Germany, 1969. *Address:* Ossendorfer Weg 37, 50827 Cologne, Germany.

LISTER, Marquita; Singer (Soprano); b. 1961, Washington DC, USA. *Education:* New England Conservatory of Music; Oklahoma City University. *Career:* Appearances with Houston Opera as Fiordiligi, Micaela, Vitellia and Gershwin's Bess; Further engagements at San Francisco as Vitellia, 1993, and Aida, 1997, Portland Opera (Verdi's Alice and Elisabetta), Teatro Bellas Artes, Michagan Opera Theater (Aida), Utah and Pittsburgh Operas (Aida) and Baltimore (Liu in Turandot); European appearances at Verona (Nedda and Musetta), Staatstheater Stuttgart (Liu and Mimi), London, Milan, Paris, Berlin and the 1997 Bregenz Festival (all as Bess); Concerts with the Boston Pops, Leipzig Radio Orchestra, Bilbao Orkestra Sinfonika and the Academy of St Martin in the Fields; Gala Concert at Houston Grand Opera with Placido Domingo; Gala Concert, Johnstown Symphony Orchestra with Justino Diaz; Gershwin's Bess at Bregenz, 1998. *Recordings include:* Excerpts from Porgy and Bess, and Gershwin's Blue Monday (Cincinnati Pops). *Honours:* Female Artist of the Year, Pittsburgh Opera. *Address:* c/o John J Miller Artist Management, 801 West 181st Street #20, New York, NY 10033, USA.

LISTOVA, Irene; Violinist; b. 1960, Moscow, Russia. *Education:* Studied at the Moscow Conservatoire with Leonid Kogan. *Career:* Member of the Prokofiev Quartet (founded at the Moscow Festival of World Youth and the International Quartet Competition at Budapest); Many concerts in the former Soviet Union and on tour to Czechoslovakia, Germany, Austria, USA, Canada, Spain, Japan and Italy; Repertoire includes works by Haydn, Mozart, Beethoven, Schubert, Debussy, Ravel, Tchaikovsky, Bart ók and Shostakovich. *Current Management:* Sonata,

Glasgow, Scotland. *Address:* 11 Northpark Street, Glasgow G20 7AA, Scotland.

LITSCHAUER, Walburga; Musicologist; b. 15 Oct. 1954, Klagenfurt, Austria. *Education:* Klagenfurt High School; Musicology, Philosophy and Theatre Sciences, University of Vienna; Piano studies, Vienna Conservatory, completed 1979; PhD, thesis The Italian Song in Vienna from 1750 to 1820, University of Vienna, 1980. *Career:* Member of Editorial Board, Director of Vienna Office, Neue Schubert Ausgabe, compendium of all Schubert's compositions; Has edited vols of Schubert's piano music; Director of the Austrian Society of Music, 1998–; mem, Board Member, several national and international Schubert societies. *Publications:* About 100 publications; Neue Dokumente zum Schubert-Kreis, vol. 1, 1986, vol. 2, 1993; Schubert und das Tanzvergnügen, with Walter Deutsch, 1997; About 70 publications on Schubert, Bruckner and music history. *Contributions:* Reclams Musikfuehrer, 1991; Anton Bruckner-Handbuch, 1996; Schubert-Handbuch and Schubert-Lexikon, 1997; Oesterreichisches Musiklexikon, 2001. *Honours:* Franz Schubert Grand Prix, for special achievements in Schubert research. *Address:* Neue Schubert-Ausgabe, Österreichische Akademie der Wissenschaften, Dr Ignaz Seipel-Platz 2, 1010 Vienna, Austria.

LITTLE, Tasmin; Violinist; b. 13 May 1965, London; m. Michael Hatch 1993. *Education:* Yehudi Menuhin School, The Guildhall School of Music and with Lorand Fenyves in Canada. *Career:* Many solo engagements with leading orchestras, including appearances with the Leipzig Gewandhaus, the Berlin Symphony Orchestra, the Royal Philharmonic, Philharmonia, BBC Symphony, Royal Danish and Royal Liverpool Philharmonic; Conductors include Kurt Masur, Vladimir Ashkenazy, Leonard Slatkin, Charles Groves, Vernon Handley, James Loughran, Edward Downes, Sian Edwards, Yehudi Menuhin, Yan Pascal Tortelier, Richard Hickox and Andrew Davis; Performances in Germany from 1986, including the Delius Concerto and the Concerto by Dvořák; British engagements at the South Bank Centre, Barbican and Harewood House and the Henley, Chester, Chichester, Cambridge and Salisbury Festivals; Three Choirs Festival 1989, Returned 1993 with the Elgar Concerto; Concerto and recital performances in France, Germany, Denmark, Canada, China, Oman, Zimbabwe, Hong Kong and India; BBC Symphony debut 1990, returning to premiere the concerto by Robert Saxton at the Leeds Festival; French debut 1990 with the Haydn C major and Bach A minor concertos; Promenade Concerts 1990 in the London premiere of the concerto by Janáček conducted by Charles Mackerras; Season 1990–91 included debut with the London Symphony and Bournemouth Symphony Orchestras and a return to the Promenade Concerts, with the Dvořák Concerto; Walton Concerto at the 1993 Proms; US debut 1997 with Cleveland Orchestra and New York Philharmonic Orchestra; Television documentary on Delius, 1997; Concerts in Vienna and London with Simon Rattle performing the Ligeti Concerto. *Recordings include:* Bruch and Dvořák Concertos with the Liverpool Philharmonic; Sonatas by George Lloyd, with Martin Roscoe; Delius Violin and Double Concertos with Rafael Wallfisch and Charles Mackerras; Brahms and Sibelius Concertos; Vaughan Williams's The Lark Ascending conducted by Andrew Davis; Finzi Concerto; Elgar and Bax Second Sonata. *Honours:* Finalist, 1982 BBC Young Musician of the Year; Gold Medal, Guildhall School of Music, 1986; Cosmopolitan Magazine's Woman of Tomorrow in the Arts; FGSM, 1998; Hon. DMus, Leicester, 2002; Hon. DLitt, Bradford, 1996. *Current Management:* Askonas Holt Ltd, Lonsdale Chambers, 27 Chancery Lane, London, WC2A 1PF, England. *Telephone:* (20) 7400-1700. *Fax:* (20) 7400-1799. *E-mail:* info@askonasholt.co.uk. *Website:* www.askonasholt.co.uk; www.floatingearth.demon.co.uk/tasmin/tlhome.html.

LITTLE, Vera; Singer (Contralto); b. 10 Dec. 1928, Memphis, Tennesee, USA; m. Professor S Augustithis. *Education:* Studied in Paris, Rome, Copenhagen and Germany. *Career:* Debut: New York City Opera 1950, as Preziosilla in La Forza del Destino; Guest appearances in Israel, Germany and Italy; Deutsche Oper Berlin 1958–85, notably as Carmen and as Melanto in Dallapiccola's Ulisse and in the 1965 premiere of Henze's Der Junge Lord; Vatican Concert 1959, in a Bach Cantata for the Pope; Salzburg Festival 1966 as Beroe, in the premiere of The Bassarids by Henze. *Recordings:* Gaea in Daphne by Strauss and Begonia in Der Junge Lord.

LITTON, Andrew; Conductor; b. 16 May 1959, New York City, USA. *Education:* Juilliard School of Music. *Career:* Assistant Conductor at La Scala, Milan after Graduation; Has conducted Oslo Philharmonic, Swedish Radio Orchestra; Stockholm Philharmonic; Goteberg Symphony Orchestra, Berlin Radio Symphony Orchestra, WDR Koln, Chicago Symphony, Pittsburgh Symphony, Los Angeles Philharmonic, Philadelphia Orchestra, Utah, Washington National Symphony Orchestra; Appointed Principal Guest Conductor, 1986 and Principal Conductor and Artistic Adviser from 1988 of Bournemouth Symphony Orchestra; Metropolitan Opera debut in 1989 with Eugene Onegin; Conducted

Bournemouth Symphony in Bernstein's Age of Anxiety and Sibelius's Second Symphony at 1991 Promenade Concerts, London; Covent Garden debut in 1992 with the house premiere of Porgy and Bess; London Proms in 1993 with Walton's Violin Concerto and Tchaikovsky's Fourth Symphony; Music Director and Conductor of Dallas Symphony, 1994–; Led Porgy and Bess at the 1997 Bregenz Festival. *Recordings include:* Over 30 including: Elgar Enigma Variations, Mahler Symphony No. 1 and Das Lied von der Erde, Tchaikovsky's Symphonies Nos 1–5, Shostakovich's Symphony No. 10, Rachmaninov Symphonies Nos 1, 2 and 3. *Honours:* Winner, Rupert Foundation International Conductors' Competition, 1982; Winner, Bruno Walter Conducting Scholarship, Juilliard School. *Current Management:* IMG Artists. *Address:* c/o IMG Artists, Lovell House, 616 Chiswick High Road, London W4 5RX, England.

LITZ, Gisela; Singer (Soprano); b. 14 Dec. 1922, Hamburg, Germany. *Education:* Studied in Hamburg. *Career:* After singing in Wiesbaden joined the Hamburg State Opera: visited Edinburgh with the company, 1952; Sang in the 1954 stage premiere of Martinů's The Marriage; Bayreuth Festival, 1953–54; Often heard in operetta and in Bach's cantatas; Guest engagements in Buenos Aires, Rome, Lisbon, Munich and Brussels; Professor at Hamburg Musikhochschule from 1969. *Recordings:* Lortzing's Der Waffenschmied and Die Opernprobe; Nicolai's Die Lustige Weiber von Windsor; Le nozze di Figaro; Hansel and Gretel; Scenes from operettas. *Address:* Hochschule für Musik und Darstellende Kunst, Harvestehuderweg 12, 2000 Hamburg 13, Germany.

LIU, Zhuang; Composer; b. 24 Oct. 1932, Shanghai, China. *Education:* Shanghai Conservatory. *Career:* Teacher at the Peking Central Conservatory and composer with the Central Philharmonic Society; Collaborated with others in the 'Yellow River' piano concerto, 1971. *Compositions include:* Violin concerto, 1963; Plum Blossom Triptych for orchestra, 1979; Moon Night by the Spring River, woodwind quintet, 1978; Three Trios for flute, cello and harp, 1987; Impressions of Tashgul-Kan for orchestra, 1987. *Address:* c/o Music Copyright Society of China, 85 Dongsi Nan Jajie, Beijing 100703, People's Republic of China.

LIUBAVIN, Leonid; Singer (Tenor); b. 1970, Krasnodar, Russia. *Education:* State Tchershakov Theatre and St Petersburg Conservatoire. *Career:* Appearances with the Kirov Opera, St Petersburg, from 1996 as Narraboth in Salome, Tamino, the Prince in The Love for Three Oranges, Antonio in Prokofiev's Betrothal in a Monastery and the Simpleton in Boris Godunov; Further engagements as Iskra in Tchaikovsky's Mazeppa, the Fisherman in Stravinsky's Nightingale and Erik in Der fliegende Holländer; Zinovy in Lady Macbeth of Mtsensk and Tchekalinsky in The Queen of Spades; Sang the Master of Ceremonies in War and Peace with the Kirov Opera at Covent Garden, 2000. *Address:* c/o Kirov Opera, Mariinsky Theatre, Theatre Square, St Petersburg, Russia.

LIVELY, David; Pianist; b. 27 June 1953, Ironton, Ohio, USA. *Education:* Ecole Normale de Musique de Paris Licence de Concert, 1970; Studied Privately with Wilhelm Kempff, Claudio Arrau. *Career:* Debut: St Louis Symphony Orchestra, 1968; Soloist with: Cleveland Symphony Orchestra; Baltimore Symphony Orchestra; Kennedy Center, Washington, DC; English Chamber Orchestra; Royal Philharmonic Orchestra; Vienna Symphony Orchestra; Bavarian Radio Orchestra; Berlin Symphony Orchestra; Orchestre National de France; Orchestre National de Monte Carlo; La Scala; Orchestre de la Suisse Romande; Director, St Lizier Festival, France; Guest Professor, University for Music and Performing Arts, Vienna. *Contributions:* Analyse Musicale Masterclasses: Royal Scottish Academy, Glasgow, Hochschule, Vienna. *Honours:* Prizewinner, Queen Elisabeth Competition, Brussels 1972; Tchaikovsky, Moscow 1974, Geneva 1971, Marguérite Long 1971; Dino Ciani Award, La Scala, 1977. *Current Management:* Liliane Weinstadt Artists Management, 59 avenue de Busleyden, 1020 Brussels, Belgium. *Telephone:* (2) 263-65-65 (office). *Fax:* (2) 263-65-66 (office). *E-mail:* info@concerts-weinstadt.com. *Website:* www.concerts-weinstadt.com.

LIVENGOOD, Victoria; Singer (Mezzo-soprano); b. 1961, USA. *Education:* BM, University of North Carolina at Chapel Hill, 1983; MM, Honours, Opera, Boston Conservatory, 1985. *Career:* Sang Gertrude in Hamlet for Miami Opera (1987) followed by Beauty in Beauty and the Beast by Oliver at St Louis; New York Academy of Music 1988, as Juno in Platée; Charlotte in Werther, Seattle Opera, 1989; Meg Page in Falstaff, Calgary Opera, 1991; European debut 1991, as Mozart's Idamante at Nice; Guest appearances as Dorabella for Hawaii Opera (1990) and Carmen at Cologne (1992); Metropolitan Opera debut 1991, as Laura in Luisa Miller; Isolier in Le Comte Ory, Spoleto Festival, Charleston, 1993; Maddalena in Rigoletto, Cologne and Edmonton, 1994; Lola, Cavalleria Rusticana, Metropolitan Opera, 1994; Girl in Mahagonny for Met Opera, 1995; Carmen, Edmonton Opera, 1995; Dalila, Baltimore Opera, 1995; Giulietta in Tales of

Hoffmann, Santiago, Chile, 1995; Preziosilla in La Forza del Destino for Met Opera, 1996; Isabella in The Voyage and Maddalena in Rigoletto, for Met Opera, 1996; Hippolyta in A Midsummer Night's Dream, 1996; Waltraute in Die Walküre, 1997; Giulietta in Les Contes d'Hoffmann, 1998; Sonyetka, Lady Macbeth of Mtsensk; Recitalist, Kennedy Center, 1986; Carnegie Hall debut, 1986; Recitalist, Smithsonian Institute, Washington DC, 1986; New York City recital debut, 1987; Soloist with symphonies of Atlanta, Cologne, San Diego, Baltimore, Minnesota and Washington; Cincinnati May Festival, and Lincoln Center Chamber Music Society, 1996; Season 1998–99 Verdi's Requiem Soloist, Carnegie Hall; Sang at the Spoleto Festival and at L'Opéra de Montréal Gala; Sang Marina in Boris Godunov for Washington Opera and Maddalena in Rigoletto at the Met, 2000; Sonyetka, Lady Macbeth of Mtsensk, Met Opera, 2000 as well as Myrtle Wilson in The Great Gatsby; Baba in The Rake's Progress for Vancouver, 2000; Dalila for Cleveland Opera, 2000; Meg Page in Falstaff for San Franscio Opera debut, 2001; Ttitle role in the world premiere of La Señorita Cristina by Luis de Pablo in Madrid, 2001; Baba in The Rake's Progress in Buenos Aires, 2002; Madame Flora in The Medium for Spoleto Festival, Italy, 2002; Azucena in Il Trovatore for Portland Opera, 2002; 2002 Met Opera roles include title role of Carmen, Hippolyta in A Midsummer Night's Dream as well as Helene in War and Peace. *Recordings include:* Puck in Oberon; The Secretary in The Consul; Akrosimova in War and Peace; Abbie in Desire Under The Elms; Soloist on Aid's Requiem; Memento Mori as well as Piercing Eyes; Haydn Canzonettas; Also solo CD: The Secret of Christmas and on Holy Ground.. *Address:* c/o Tony Russo, ICM Artists Ltd, 40 W 57th Street, New York, NY 10019, USA. *Telephone:* 212 556 5775. *Website:* www.victorialivengood.com.

LIVINGSTONE, Laureen, DipMusEd, RSAMD; singer (soprano) and teacher; b. 3 Feb. 1946, Dumbarton, Scotland; 1 s., 1 d. *Education:* Royal Scottish Acad. of Music, London Opera Centre. *Career:* wide variety of operatic, concert and television appearances in the United Kingdom and abroad; BBC Proms; recitals including Wigmore Hall and 1st BBC Lunchtime recital in 1976; Guest appearances with London Symphony Orchestra, Hallé, English Sinfonia, Northern Sinfonia, Scottish National and Scottish Chamber Orchestras; Operatic roles include: Zerlina, Pamina, Gretel, Lucia in Rape of Lucretia with Scottish Opera, Susanna, Sophie and Vrenchen in A Village Romeo and Juliet with Opera North, Gilda in Rigoletto and Sophie in Der Rosenkavalier for English National Opera, 1988; Major roles with the New Sadler's Wells Opera, Handel Opera and others; Engagements abroad include Woglinde at Teatro di San Carlo, Naples, 1980 and Gilda for Royal Flemish Opera in Antwerp, 1985; Professor of Singing at Trinity College of Music, London. *Recordings:* several recital programmes for BBC; Countess Maritza; Gianetta in The Gondoliers, 1st colour production for BBC television; Ninetta in L'Amour des Trois Oranges, BBC television, 1980; Elsie in The Yeomen of the Guard, Channel 5 video; Amore in Il Ritorno d'Ulisse in Patria, Glyndebourne, video 1973. *Honours:* Caird Scholarship, 1967; Winner, Peter Stuyvesant Scholarship, 1969. *Address:* 12 Pymmes Brook Drive, New Barnet, Hertfordshire EN4 9RU, England.

LLEWELLYN, Grant; Conductor; b. 29 Dec. 1960, Tenby, Wales; m. Charlotte Imogen Rose, 7 April 1984. *Education:* Cheetham's School of Music, Manchester, 1972–79; Gonville and Caius College, Cambridge, 1980–83; Royal College of Music, London; Tanglewood Music Center, 1986. *Career:* Has conducted City of Birmingham Symphony Orchestra, English Chamber Orchestra, Scottish National Orchestra, Royal Liverpool Philharmonic Orchestra, Northern Sinfonia, Scottish Chamber Orchestra, City of London Sinfonia and BBC Symphony, Philharmonic and Welsh Orchestras; Took Stockholm Sinfonietta on British tour, 1986 and conducted at Spoleto, Charleston and Jeunesse Musicale World Orchestra at Berlin Festival; London Proms debut 1993, with the BBC National Orchestra of Wales in Mendelssohn's Violin Concerto and Beethoven's Seventh Symphony; Conducted BBC National Orchestra of Wales Opera Gala, 1996; American premiere of Goehr's Arianna at St Louis, 1998. *Honours:* Royal College of Music Tagore Gold Medal, 1984; Tanglewood Conducting Fellowship and English-Speaking Union Scholar, 1985; Leeds Conductors' Competition, 1986 (first prize). *Current Management:* Hazard Chase, Norman House, Cambridge Place, Cambridge CB2 1NS, England. *Telephone:* (1223) 312400. *Fax:* (1223) 460827. *Website:* www.hazardchase.co.uk. *Address:* Bassett Cottage, 43 Main Road, Long Hanborough, Oxfordshire, England.

LLEWELLYN, William Benjamin James, MBE; British composer and conductor; b. 6 May 1925, Farnworth, Widnes, Lancashire; m. Mildred Llewellyn; two s. one d. *Education:* Rydal School, Colwyn Bay, Emanuel Coll., Cambridge and Royal Acad. of Music; studied composition under William Alwyn and Eric Thiman. *Career:* Asst Music Master, Charterhouse 1950; f. the Linden Singers; Dir of Music, later Second Master, Charterhouse 1965–87; Music Adviser, Nat. Federation of Women's Insts for six years; Pres., Incorporated Soc. of Musicians 1984; Festival Conductor, Leith Music Festival 14 years, Petersfield Festival six years;

conductor, Bridgewater Choral Soc.; mem. jury, Great Grimsby Int. Singing Competition 1992, Chair. of Cttee of Adjudicators 1995; adjudicated regularly at competitions and festivals, including Hong Kong; Chair., Royal School of Church Music in Devon 10 years. *Compositions:* compiled and edited the Novello Book of Carols, Sing With All My Soul (52 Worship Songs for choirs) Royal School of Church Music followed by Worship in Song 1997, Lincolnshire Voices for the Grimsby Philharmonic Choir's 140th anniversary, Flying Colours for the Farnham Festival 1987, On Earth in Concert Sing a requiem, Cross and Grave and Glory a passion sequence, The Figure on the Shore 2002. *Address:* Forecourt, Queen's Square, Cloyton, Devon EX24 6JX, England (home). *Telephone:* (1297) 552414 (home). *Fax:* (1297) 552414 (home). *E-mail:* wllewellyn@freeuk.com (home).

LLOYD, Anthony (Stuart); Singer (Bass-baritone); b. 1970, Cardiff, Wales. *Education:* Welsh College of Music and Drama. *Career:* Don Magnifico in Cenerentola at Ischia, 1993; Welsh National Opera as Mozart's Bartolo; Rossini's Basilio, the Commendatore and High Priest in Nabucco; Freiburg Opera from 1997, as Leporello, Lodovico in Otello; Concerts include Les Troyens under Colin Davis, London and Michel Plasson, Toulouse; Eremit in Der Freischütz for Chelsea Opera; Season 1998–99 as Mephistopheles in Faust and Selim in Il Turco in Italia. *Honours:* Geraint Evans Memorial Prize, Pontypridd. *Address:* Harlequin Agency Ltd, 203 Fidlas Road, Cardiff CF4 5NA.

LLOYD, David; Singer (Tenor); b. 29 Feb. 1920, Minneapolis, Minnesota, USA. *Education:* Minneapolis College of Music; Curtis Institute, Philadelphia; Berkshire Music Center. *Career:* After 1947 debut sang with New York City Opera, then with New England Opera Company; Athens Festival, 1955; Glyndebourne, 1957, as Tamino in Die Zauberflöte and Bacchus in Ariadne auf Naxos; Other roles were Mozart's Belmonte and Idomeneo, Flamand in Capriccio, Rodolfo, Jacquino and Gonsalve in L'Heure Espagnole; Also heard in concert and oratorio; Artistic Director, Hunter College, New York; Director of the Lake George Opera Festival, USA, 1974.

LLOYD, David (Bellamy); Piano Accompanist; b. 22 Nov. 1937, Stockport, Cheshire, England. *Education:* ARMCM (Performance and Teaching). *Career:* Debut: Recital with Heddle Nash, Wigmore Hall, 1956; Accompanist to Jan Peerce, Festival Hall, London and tour of France, Germany, Switzerland, Austria and Netherlands; Television appearances with Jack Brymer, Adele Leigh and Charlotte Rimmer; Former accompanist to Jack Brymer, Leon Goossens and Elizabeth Harwood in recitals and broadcasts, Singapore, Hong Kong, India, New Zealand, Spain, Canada and USA; Senior Lecturer, Royal Northern College of Music and Professional Accompanist, 1967–93; Examiner, Associated Board of Royal Schools of Music, 1969–2002. *Compositions:* Schubert Arpeggione Sonata, arranged by David Lloyd, published. *Recordings:* Brahms Clarinet Sonata Op 120/1, Weber Duo Concertante; Brahms Clarinet Sonata Op 120/2; Schubert Arpeggione Sonata arranged for Clarinet; Schumann Phantasiestücke Op 73; Hurlstone Four Characteristic Pieces; Art of Leon Goossens. *Honours:* Hilary Haworth Prize, RMCM, 1958; *Membership:* Incorporated Society of Musicians. *Address:* 32 Clarence Court, Bare Lane, Morecambe, Lancashire, LA 4 6 DL, England.

LLOYD, Jonathan; Composer; b. 30 Sept. 1948, London, England. *Education:* Composition lessons from Emile Spira; Studied at Royal College of Music, London, with Edwin Roxburgh and John Lambert; Worked with Tristram Cary at Electronic Music Studio. *Career:* Twentieth Century Ensemble, 1968; Awarded Mendelssohn Scholarship and lived in Paris, 1969–70; Occasional work as performer, busker, street musician, 1974–77; Composer-in-Residence, Dartington College Theatre Department, 1978–79. *Compositions include:* Orchestral: Cantique, 1968, 5 Symphonies, 1983–89, Rhapsody for Cello and Orchestra, 1982, Viola Concerto, 1979–80, Everything Returns for Soprano and Orchestra, 1977–78, Mass for 6 Solo Voices, 1983, Missa Brevis, 1984, Toward the Whitening Dawn for Chorus and Chamber Orchestra, 1980, Revelation for 8 Voices, 1990, Marching to a Different Song for Soprano and Chamber Orchestra, 1991, Ballad for The Evening of a Man for Mixed Quartet, 1992; Dramatic: The Adjudicator, community opera, 1985, Music for Alfred Hitchcock's Blackmail, 1993; Edition of the Beggar's Opera, 1999; Tolerance for Orchestra, 1994, People Your Dreams for Voice and Ensemble, 1994, Blessed Days of Blue for Solo Flute and Strings, 1995, Violin Concerto, 1995; Piano Concerto, 1995; And Beyond for chorus and ensemble, 1996; A Dream of a Pass, 1997; Shadows of Our Future Selves for ensemble, 1998. *Recordings:* Mass; Second Symphony, 1992; Largo. *Address:* c/o Boosey and Hawkes Ltd, 295 Regent Street, London W1R 8JH, England.

LLOYD, Phyllida, BA; British theatre director and film director; b. 17 June 1957, Bristol; d. of Patrick and Margaret (née Douglas-Pennent) Lloyd. *Education:* Lawnside School (Great Malvern) and Univ. of Birmingham. *Career:* fmr Floor Asst BBC TV; Assoc. Dir Manchester Royal Exchange. *Theatre includes:* Six Degrees of Separation (Royal Court) 1992, Hysteria (Royal Court) 1993, Pericles 1993, The Threepenny Opera 1994, The Way of the World 1995, Dona Rosita (Almeida) 1997, The Prime of Miss Jean Brodie (Royal Nat. Theatre) 1998, Mamma Mia! (London and elsewhere) 1999–, Boston Marriage (Donmar) 2001. *Opera includes:* Gloriana 1993, La Bohème (Opera North at Sheffield Lyceum) 1993, Medea (Opera North) 1996, Carmen 1998, Dialogues of the Carmelites (ENO) 1999, Macbeth (Paris Opera) 1999, Verdi Requiem (English Nat. Opera) 2000, The Handmaid's Tale (Copenhagen) 2000, Fidelio (Glyndebourne) (Royal Philharmonic Soc. opera award) 2001, The Valkyrie (Glastonbury Festival) 2004, Siegfried (ENO) 2004. *Television film:* Gloriana (BBC2) (Emmy Award 2000) 1999. *Current Management:* Annette Stone Associates, Second Floor, 22 Great Marlborough Street, London, W1F 7HU, England. *Telephone:* (20) 7734-0626. *Fax:* (20) 7734-2346.

LLOYD, Robert Andrew; Opera Singer (bass); b. 2 March 1940, Southend-on-Sea, Essex, England; m. 1964, 1 s., 3 d. *Education:* BA, Modern History, Keble College, Oxford, 1962; Private Study with Otakar Kraus, London Opera Centre, 1968–69. *Career:* Debut: Fernando in Beethoven's Leonore, Collegiate Theatre, London, 1969; English National Opera, 1969–72; Covent Garden, 1972–83; Freelance in all major opera houses, 1983–; Met debut, 1988; Principal roles, Boris Godunov; Philip II; Sarastro, Gurnemanz, Fiesco; Mephistopheles, Osmin, altogether 120 roles; Appearances with most leading orchestras; Film: Parsifal, Director, Hans Jurgen Syberberg; Video: Notably Don Carlos, Coronation of Poppea, and Tales of Hoffmann, Boris Godunov and Fidelio; First British Bass to sing Boris Godunov at Kirov Opera, 1990 (also televised); Vienna Staatsoper, 1990, as King Henry in Lohengrin; At Covent Garden sang Georgio Walton, Arkel and Commendatore, 1993; Sang in Britten's version of The Beggar's Opera at the 1993 Aldeburgh Festival; Season 1997 with Chérubin and Lohengrin at Covent Garden, Die Zauberflöte and Pélleas et Mélisande at Salzburg; Sang Gurnemanz for Netherlands Opera, 1997; Charles V in Don Carlos and Bartolo in Nozze di Figaro at Salzburg, sang in Aida, Mephistopheles and Rigoletto at the Metropolitan Opera in New York, 1998; Frère Laurent in Roméo et Juliette at Covent Garden, 2000; mem, Garrick Club, London. *Recordings:* Over 60 recordings with all the major companies, Parsifal, Entführung, Barbiere di Siviglia, Nozze di Figaro, Messiah, Mozart Requiem, Il Trovatore, Macbeth, Rigoletto; Romeo and Juliette and Damnation de Faust in Denon's Berlioz Cycle, Elgar's Apostles. *Contributions:* to magazines and BBC radio and television. *Honours:* Grammy (Mozart Requiem); Grammy Nomination (Figaro); Prix Italia; R P Society Award for BBC 's Bluebeard's Castle, 1989; C.B.E., 1991; Elected Honorary Fellow, Keble College, Oxford; Foreign Artist of the Year, Theatro Colon, 1997; Charles Sautley Prize, Worshipful Company of Musicians, 1998; Chaliapin Commemerative Medal, St Petersburg, 1998; Elected Honorary Member of Royal Academy of Music, 1999; Visiting Professor, Royal College of Music. *Current Management:* Askonas Holt Ltd, Lonsdale Chambers, 27 Chancery Lane, London, WC2A 1PF, England. *Telephone:* (20) 7400-1700. *Fax:* (20) 7400-1799. *E-mail:* info@askonasholt.co.uk. *Website:* www.askonasholt.co.uk.

LLOYD-DAVIES, Mary; Singer (Soprano); b. 1965, Llanuwchllyn, Wales. *Education:* Studied at the Royal College of Music and in Paris with Pierre Bernac. *Career:* Appearances with Welsh National Opera at Elektra, Turandot, Tosca and Leonore in Fidelio; Isolde, Ortrud and Mrs Grose in The Turn of the Screw for English National Opera; Elisabeth in Tannhäuser and Wagner's Senta for Chelsea Opera Group; Concerts in Germany, South America, USA and Canada; Beethoven's Ninth in Lisbon and Ravel's Schéhérazade in Toulouse; Season 1998–99 with Amelia in Un Ballo in Maschera and Isolde for Welsh national Opera. *Address:* Harlequin Agency Ltd, 203 Fidlas Road, Cardiff CF4 5NA, Wales.

LLOYD DAVIS, John; Stage Director, Stage Designer and Lighting Designer; b. 1960, England. *Education:* BA, Philosophy and European Literature Bristol University. *Career:* Staff director, English National Opera, (20 productions, directed 5 revivals) 1984–89; Since 1988 freelance work includes Don Giovanni, Die Zauberflöte, Rigoletto, Death In Venice, Das Schloss, Fall of the House of Usher, Weisse Rose, all in Vienna; Madama Butterfly (Dublin, Ludwigshafen, Royal Danish Opera); Un Ballo in Maschera (Klagenfurt), and other productions throughout Europe and Scandinavia; Also active in theatre in Austria and Germany; Director of Productions for New Sussex Opera; Translations include The Enchantress (Tchaikovsky), and Bluebeard's Castle (Bartók) for English National Opera, Scottish Opera and the BBC. *Publications:* Works on Michael Tippett. *Honours:* Josef Kainz Medal for work at Vienna Volkstheater, 1999. *Current Management:* Athole Still International Management, Forresters Hall, 25–27 Westow Street, London, SE19 3RY, England. *Telephone:* (20) 8771-5271. *Fax:* (20) 8768-6600. *Website:* www.atholestill.com.

LLOYD-HOWELLS, David; Composer; b. 11 Jan. 1942, Cardiff, Wales. *Education:* Ealing Music Centre, London, 1960–64; Trinity College of

Music, 1967; Pontypridd Technical College 1972–73; South Gwent College 1974; BMus, Honours, Wales, 1977–80; FTCL, FLCM, Diplomas, 1979–80; MMus, Distinction, University of London, 1981–83; York University, 1984–85. *Career:* Tutor in Music, Gwent, 1971–77; Adult Education, 1980–83; Community Musician, 1984; Freelance Composer, Conductor, Artistic Director, Adjudicator; Works mainly with electronic-live media; Music Theatre, Modern Dance Groups, Cedar Dance Theatre Company, London, 1983; D.L.H. Productions, music for film, video and self-therapy, 1990; Artistic Director Sonicity 2000, archive of scores, sonic art works, recordings, essays, poems letters at the National Library of Wales, 1993; Guild for the Promotion of Welsh Music Composers database, Arts Council of Wales. *Compositions include:* Bleak Sleaze; Dark Clowns; Nightcity Pulses; Canticles of Goth; Druidika; The Wrath Conference: (Black Rain, Red Grass, Blue Snow, Green Sand); Digital Weave; Life Music; Surfing the Strobe; Sounds from the Noisebath; Dark Clowns; MEC; Legacy of the Icon Slave; The Insects Convention; Fractosonic Graffiti; NOK; Requiem I-Spy; Youthworks; Rites of War; Mind Songs; Piani Melismata; Freakspeak; Edge of Shadows; Molecular Analysis; Ungrateful Utterance; Everything but Silence; Shadowself Connection; Miscreant Hues 9sound opera in seven cadenzas). *Recordings:* Piano Sonata 2, 1978. *Publications:* Soundgazing: A personal view about the future of music. *Address:* 26, Bevelin Hall, Saundersfoot, Pembrokeshire SA 69 9PG.

LLOYD-JONES, David (Mathias); Conductor; b. 19 Nov. 1934, London, England; m. Anne Carolyn Whitehead, 1964, 2 s., 1 d. *Education:* Magdalen College, Oxford. *Career:* Chorus Master, New Opera Co, 1961–64; Conducted at Bath Festival, 1966, City of London Festival, 1966, Wexford Festival, 1967–70, Edinburgh International Festival, 1989, Scottish Opera, 1968, Welsh National Opera, 1968, Royal Opera, Covent Garden, 1971; Assistant Music Director at Sadler's Wells, Opera Co (now English National Opera), 1969–78; Artistic Director, Opera North, 1978–90; Conductor for television operas (Eugene Onegin, The Flying Dutchman, Hansel and Gretel); Conducted concerts and operas throughout Central Europe and in Scandinavia, Russia, Poland, Bulgaria, Israel, Australia and North and South America; Appearances with most British Symphony Orchestras; mem, Council of The Royal Philharmonic Society. *Recordings:* Many recent commercial recordings of British and Russian Music including first recordings of works by Constant Lambert and a Bax symphony cycle. *Publications:* Boris Godunov, translation; Vocal Score, Eugene Onegin; Translation, Vocal Score, Boris Godunov–Critical Edition of Original Full Score; General Editor of William Walton Edition for which he has edited several volumes; numerous contributions to publications including Grove's Dictionary of Music and Musicians, Musik in Geschichte und Gegenwart, Music and Letters, The Listener. *Honours:* Honorary D.Mus, University of Leeds, 1986. *Address:* 94 Whitelands House, Cheltenham Terrace, London SW3 4 RA, England.

LLOYD ROBERTS, Carys; Singer (Soprano); b. 1969, Wales. *Education:* Studied at the Welsh College of Music and Drama. *Career:* Engagements with the Welsh National Opera, Musica nel Chiostro and City of Birmingham Touring Opera as Papagena, First Lady, Barbarina and Hansel; Purcell's King Arthur with Les Arts Florissants at Covent Garden and The Fairy Queen with the Northern Sinfonia; Concerts include the Jonathan Miller production of the St Matthew Passion and appearances at Llandaff Cathedral and St Martin-in-the-Fields, London; Sang Lensky for Grange Park Opera, 2000.

LLOYD-ROBERTS, Jeffrey; Singer (Tenor); b. 1968, Wales. *Education:* Studied at the Royal Northern College of Music with Barbara Robotham and at Lancaster University. *Career:* Appearances with Welsh National Opera in The Makropulos Case, as Nemorino with English Touring Opera in Le Roi malgré Lui for Chelsea Opera and in Aroldo at the Buxton Festival; Season 1995 as Lindoro in La fedeltà premiata for Garsington Opera and concerts of Korngold's Ring of Polycrates, the B Minor Mass, the Verdi Requiem, Mahler's 8th Symphony and The Dream of Gerontius. *Address:* c/o Musichall Ltd, Vicarage Way, Ringmer, East Sussex, BN8 5 LA, England.

LLOYD WEBBER, Baron (Life Peer), cr. 1997, of Sydmonton in the County of Hampshire; **Andrew Lloyd Webber,** FRCM; British composer; *Chairman, The Really Useful Group Ltd*; b. 22 March 1948, s. of the late William Southcombe Lloyd Webber,CBE, DMUS, FRCM, FRCO and Jean Hermione Johnstone; brother of Julian Lloyd Webber; m. 1st Sarah Jane Tudor (née Hugill) 1971 (divorced 1983); one s. one d.; m. 2nd Sarah Brightman 1984 (divorced 1990); m. 3rd Madeleine Astrid Gurdon 1991; two s. one d. *Education:* Westminster School, Magdalen Coll. Oxford, Royal Coll. of Music. *Career:* Chair. The Really Useful Group Ltd. *Works:* (musicals): Joseph and the Amazing Technicolor Dreamcoat (lyrics by Tim Rice) 1968 (revised 1973, 1991), Jesus Christ Superstar (lyrics by Tim Rice) 1970 (revised 1996), Jeeves (lyrics by Alan Ayckbourn) 1975 (revised as By Jeeves 1996), Evita (lyrics by Tim Rice) 1976 (stage version 1978), Tell Me on a Sunday (lyrics by Don Black) 1980, revised 2003, Cats (based on T. S. Eliot's Old Possum's

Book of Practical Cats) (Tony Awards for Best Score and Best Musical 1983) 1981, Song and Dance (lyrics by Don Black) 1982, Starlight Express (lyrics by Richard Stilgoe) 1984, The Phantom of the Opera (Tony Award for Best Musical 1988) (lyrics by Richard Stilgoe and Charles Hart) 1986, Aspects of Love (lyrics by Don Black and Charles Hart) 1989, Sunset Boulevard (Tony Awards for Best Score and Best Musical 1995) (lyrics by Christopher Hampton and Don Black) 1993, Whistle Down the Wind (lyrics by Jim Steinman) 1996, The Beautiful Game (with lyrics by Ben Elton) 2000; (other compositions): Variations (based on A minor Caprice No. 24 by Paganini) 1977 (symphonic version 1986), Requiem Mass 1985, Amigos Para Siempre (official theme for 1992 Olympic Games); (film scores): Gumshoe 1971, The Odessa File 1974. *Producer:* Joseph and the Amazing Technicolor Dreamcoat 1973, 1974, 1978, 1980, 1991, Jeeves Takes Charge 1975, Cats 1981, Song & Dance 1982, Daisy Pulls it Off 1983, The Hired Man 1984, Starlight Express 1984, On Your Toes 1984, The Phantom of the Opera 1986, Café Puccini 1986, The Resistible Rise of Arturo Ui 1987, Lend Me a Tenor 1988, Aspects of Love 1989, Shirley Valentine (Broadway) 1989, La Bête 1992, Sunset Boulevard 1993, By Jeeves 1996, Whistle Down the Wind 1996, 1998, Jesus Christ Superstar 1996, 1998, The Beautiful Game 2000, Bombay Dreams 2002, Tell Me On A Sunday, 2003, Woman in White 2004, and others. *Art Collection:* Pre-Raphaelite and other masters – The Andrew Lloyd Webber Collection, Royal Acad., London, 2003. *Films:* The Phantom of the Opera (Dir Joel Schumacher) 2004/05. *Publications:* Evita (with Tim Rice) 1978, Cats: the book of the musical 1981, Joseph and the Amazing Technicolor Dreamcoat (with Tim Rice) 1982, The Complete Phantom of the Opera 1987, The Complete Aspects of Love 1989, Sunset Boulevard: from movie to musical 1993; food critic Daily Telegraph 1996–. *Honours:* awards include seven Tony Awards, four Drama Desk Awards, six Laurence Olivier Awards, Triple Play Awards, 1996, ASCAP 1988, Praemium Imperiale Award 1995, three Grammy Awards, Golden Globe Award, Golden Globe, Academy Award 1996, Richard Rodgers Award 1996, London Critics' Circle Best Musical 2000. *Address:* The Really Useful Group Ltd, 22 Tower Street, London, WC2H 9TW, England. *Telephone:* (20) 7240-0880 (office). *Fax:* (20) 7240-1204 (office). *Website:* www.reallyuseful.com (office).

LLOYD WEBBER, Julian, FRCM; British cellist; b. 14 April 1951, London; s. of the late William Southcombe Lloyd WebberCBE, DMUS, FRCM, FRCO and of Jean Hermione Johnstone; brother of Lord Lloyd Webber; m. 1st Celia M. Ballantyne 1974 (divorced 1989); m. 2nd Zohra Mahmoud Ghazi 1989 (divorced 1999); one s.; m. 3rd Kheira Bourahla 2001. *Education:* Univ. Coll. School and Royal Coll. of Music. *Career:* debut at Queen Elizabeth Hall 1972; debut with Berlin Philharmonic Orchestra 1984; appears at major int. concert halls and has undertaken concert tours throughout Europe, N and S America, S Africa, Australasia, Singapore, Japan, China, Hong Kong and Korea; numerous television appearances and broadcasts in UK, Netherlands, Africa, Germany, Scandinavia, France, Belgium, Spain, Australasia and USA. *Recordings:* world premieres of Britten's 3rd Suite for Solo Cello, Bridge's Oration, Rodrigo's Cello Concerto (Spanish Ministry of Culture Award for world premiere recording 1982), Holst's Invocation, Gavin Bryar's Cello Concerto, Michael Nyman's Cello and Saxophone Concerto, Sullivan's Cello Concerto, Vaughan Williams' Fantasia on Sussex Folk Tunes, Andrew Lloyd Webber's Variations (Gold disc 1978), Elgar's Cello Concerto (British Phonographic Industry Award for Best Classical Recording 1986), Dvořák Concerto, Saint-Saëns Concerto, Lalo Concerto, Walton Concerto, Britten Cello Symphony; Philip Glass Cello Concerto. *Publications:* Classical Cello 1980, Romantic Cello 1981, French Cello 1981, Frank Bridge, Six Pieces 1982, Young Cellist's Repertoire (three vols) 1984, Holst's Invocation 1984, Travels with my Cello 1984, Song of the Birds 1985, Recital Repertoire for Cellists (four vols) 1986, Short Sharp Shocks 1990, The Great Cello Solos 1992, The Essential Cello 1997, Cello Moods 1999, String Quartets, 2003; Made in England 2003. Contributions to: The Times, The Sunday Times, The Daily Telegraph, USA Today. *Honours:* Suggia Gift 1968, Seymour Whinyates Award 1971, Percy Buck Award 1972, Brit Award for Elgar Cello Concerto recording 1987, Crystal Award, World Economic Forum (Switzerland) 1998, Hon. doctorate, Univ. of Hull. *Current Management:* IMG Artists Europe, Lovell House, 616 Chiswick High Road, London, W4 5RX, England. *Telephone:* (20) 8233-5800. *Fax:* (20) 8233-5801. *E-mail:* vcorley-smith@imgworld.com (office). *Website:* www.julianlloydwebber.com (office).

LOBANOV, Vassily; Composer and Pianist; b. 2 Jan. 1947, Moscow, USSR. *Education:* Studied at the Tchaikovsky Conservatoire, Moscow, 1963–69, with Leo Naumov, Sergei Balasanyan and Alfred Schnittke. *Career:* Has accompanied Natalia Gutman and Oleg Kagan individually and as member of trio; Interpreter of modern works at festivals in Moscow, Witten, Vienna and Kuhmo, Finland; Premiered his Second Piano Sonata at the Moscow Autumn Festival, 1980; Has partnered Sviatoslav Richter in duets; December Nights concert in the Pushkin Museum Moscow, 1981; Soloist with the Moscow Philharmonic from 1982; Professor of Piano, Cologne Hochschule, 1997–. *Compositions* *include:* Oratorio Lieutenant Schmidt, 1979; Opera Antigone, 1985–88; Orchestra: Symphony for chamber orchestra, 1977; Piano Concerto 1981; Cello Concerto, 1985; Sinfonietta, 1986; Concerto for viola and strings, 1989; Piano Concerto No. 2, 1993; Double concerto for violin and clarinet, 1995; Trumpet Concerto; 1998; Viola Concerto No. 2, 1998; Chamber: 5 string quartets, 1966, 1968, 1978, 1987, 1988; Twelve Preludes for piano, 1965; Partita for piano, 1967; 2 Cello Sonatas, 1971, 1989; 2 piano sonatas, 1973, 1980; 3 Suites for piano; Seven Pieces for cello and piano, 1978; Variations for two trumpets, 1979; Seven Slow Pieces for piano, 1978–80; Flute Sonata, 1983; Clarinet Sonata, 1985; Fantasia for solo cello, 1987; Violin Sonata, 1989; Viola Sonata, 1990; Piano Quintet, 1991; Piano Quartet, 1996; String Trio, 1996; Clarinet Quintet, 1999; Vocal: Three Haikus for low voice and piano, 1963; Three Romances (bass), 1965; Five Romances, 1971; Four Poems to texts by Alexei Parin (bass), 1984; Eight Poems (soprano), 1984; Stravinsky's Italian Suite adapted for cello and chamber orchestra, 1985. *Address:* c/o Boosey & Hawkes Ltd, 295 Regent Street, London W1R 8JH, England.

LOCKHART, Beatriz; Composer; b. 17 Jan. 1944, Montevideo, Uruguay. *Education:* Studied at the Montevideo Conservatory and in Buenos Aires. *Career:* Teacher at the Caracas Conservatory (1974–88), University of Montevideo, and elsewhere. *Compositions include:* Ecos for orchestra; Concerto Grosso; Masia muju for flute and orchestra (1987); Theme and variations for piano; Ejercio I for tape and other electronic music; Vision de los vencidos for voice and orchestra, 1990; Homenaje a Astor Piazzola for piano, 1994; Concertino for double bass and orchestra, 1999. *Address:* c/o AGADU, Calle canelones 1122, Montevideo, Uruguay.

LOCKHART, James, BMus, ARCM, FRCM, FRCO (CHM); conductor and accompanist; b. 16 Oct. 1930, Edinburgh, Scotland; m. Sheila Grogan 1954, two s. one d. *Education:* Edinburgh Univ., Royal College of Music, London. *Career:* debut, Yorkshire Symphony Orchestra, 1954; Assistant Conductor, Yorkshire Symphony Orchestra; Repetiteur, St ädtische Bühnen Münster, 1955–56; Bayerische Staatsoper München, 1956–57; Director, Opera Workshop, University of Texas, 1957–59; Repetiteur, Glyndebourne Opera, 1957–59; ROH Covent Garden, 1959–60; Assistant Conductor, BBC Scottish Symphony, 1960–61; Conductor, Sadler's Wells Opera, 1960–62; Conductor at ROH Covent Garden, 1962–68; Professor, Royal College of Music, 1962–72; Music Director, Welsh National Opera, 1968–73; General Music Director, Staatstheater Kassel, 1972–80; Rheinische Philharmonie and Koblenz Stadttheater, 1981–91; Director of Opera, RCM London, 1986–92; Director of Opera, London Royal Schools Vocal Faculty, 1992–96; Opera Consultant, Royal Academy and Royal College of Music, London, 1996–98; Guest Professor of Conducting, 1998–2001, Professor Emeritus, 2001–, Tokyo National University of Fine Arts and Music (Tokyo Geidai); Conducted at the Welsh National Opera 50th Anniversary Gala, 1996; mem, ISM. *Recordings include:* Walton: The Bear; Dittersdorf: Doktor and Apotheker; Brahms, Schumann, French and Spanish Songs with Margaret Price; Le Flem, and Schmitt with the Rheinische Philharmonie; Royal Philharmonic Orchestra: Beethoven Symphonies 2 and 8, Mozart Symphonies, 36 and 39; Puccini Arias with Shinobu Sato (Soprano) and the Philharmonia Promenade Orchestra; Aria/Mieko Sato (Soprano) and the Philharmonia Orchestra. *Honours:* Solti Scholarship for Most Promising Young British Musician, 1964; Hon. RAM 1993. *Current Management:* Robert Gilder & Co., Enterprise House, 59–65 Upper Ground, London, SE1 9PQ, England. *Telephone:* (20) 7928-9008. *Fax:* (20) 7928-9755. *E-mail:* rgilder@robert-gilder.com. *Address:* 105 Woodcock Hill, Harrow, Middlesex HA3 0JJ, England. *Telephone:* (20) 8907-2112. *E-mail:* Lockgrog@aol.com.

LOCKLEY, Michael Allen; Singer (Tenor); b. 7 March 1960, Sodus, New York, USA; m. Jennifer Bates, 11 Nov 1989, 1 s. *Education:* BS, Geneseo College; MM, Binghamton University; Resident Artist, Tri-Cities Opera and European Mozart Academies. *Career:* Debut: Tri-Cities Opera, 1983; Performances with New York City Opera, Baltimore Opera, Tulsa Opera, Ash Lawn-Highland Opera Festival and Maggio Musicale, Florence; Has sung Rodolfo in La Bohème, Alfredo in La Traviata, Ferrando in Così fan tutte, Tamino in Die Zauberflöte, Romeo in Roméo et Juliette, and Don José in Carmen; mem, AGMA; Association of Film, Television and Radio Artists. *Recordings:* Arabesque, Greenhays Rivertown. *Honours:* Richard F Gold Grant, Ezio Pinza Council for American Singers. *Current Management:* William R Hendrickson Artists Management. *Address:* 47 Penny Lane, Ithaca, NY 14850, USA.

LOCKWOOD, Annea (Ferguson); Composer, Performer and University Lecturer; b. 29 July 1939, Christchurch, New Zealand. *Education:* BMus, University of Canterbury, New Zealand, 1961; Royal College of Music, London, 1961–63, LRAM, ARCM Piano Performance; Musikhochschule Cologne, 1963–64; Institute for Sound and Vibration Research, psychoacoustical research, postgraduate, Southampton University, England, 1971–73. *Career:* Major performances of own compositions: Cheltenham Festival, United Kingdom, 1965, 1969; Commonwealth Festival, United Kingdom, 1965; Parie Biennale,

1965; Fylkingen Festival, Stockholm, 1970; Queen Elizabeth Hall, London, 1971; Lincoln Center Plaza, New York, 1974; New Music America Festivals, 1979, 1982, 1986; Autunno Musicale a Como, Italy, 1979; Sydney Biennale, 1982; Westdeutscher Rundfunk, Meet the USA Festival, 1982; Asia Pacific Festival, 1984; Westdeutscher Rundfunk, Ives & Co, 1988; New York-Cologne Festival, 1989; New York: Alice Tully Hall, 1992, The Kitchen, 1997, Engine 27, 2000, Hudson River Museum, 2003, Bang on a Can Marathon, 2003; Los Angeles County Museum of Modern Art, 1995; Summergarden Museum of Modern Art, 1997; Whitney Museum of American Art, 2000; Mystic und Maschine festival, Münster, 2000; De Ijsbreker, New Music, New Zealand, Amsterdam, 2001; Other Minds 8 Festival, San Francisco, 2002; mem, BMI Inc; American Music Center. *Compositions include:* Red Mesa, 1989; Thousand Year Dreaming, 1991; Shapeshifter, 1995; Ear-Walking Woman, 1997; Duende, 1998; Floating World, 1999; Piano Transplants; Immersion; Vortex; Ceci n'est pas un piano; A Sound Map of the Danube River. *Recordings:* Glass Concert; World Rhythms; Tiger Balm; A Sound Map of the Hudson River; Thousand Year Dreaming; Red Mesa; Delta Run; Duende; The Angle of Repose; Night and Fog; I Give You Back; Nautilus; Ear-Walking Woman; Monkey Trips. *Publications:* Malaman; Spirit Catchers; Humming; Delta Run; Sound Map of the Hudson River; Glass Concert, World Rhythms, Tiger Balm, Malolo, A Sound Map of the Hudson River; Red Mesa, 1993; I Give You Back, 1995. *Honours:* National Endowment for the Arts Composition Fellow, USA, 1979; CAPS Composition Fellowship, USA, 1979; Arts Council of Great Britain, 1972; Gulbenkian Foundation Grants, 1972; Dr hc Fine Arts, Clark Univ., Worcester (USA), 1999. *Address:* Baron de Hirsch Road, Crompond, NY 10517, USA.

LOEBEL, David; Conductor; b. 7 March 1950, Cleveland, Ohio, USA; m. Jane Cawthorn 1977. *Education:* BS 1972, MMus 1974, Northwestern University. *Career:* Assistant Conductor, Syracuse Symphony Orchestra, 1974–76; Music Director, Binghamton Symphony Orchestra, 1977–82; Music Adviser, Anchorage Symphony Orchestra, 1983–86; Assistant, 1982–86, Associate Conductor, 1986–90, Cincinnati Symphony Orchestra; Associate Conductor, 1990–94, Associate Principal Conductor, St Louis Symphony Orchestra, 1994–2000; Conductor-in-Residence, New World Symphony, 1997–99; Music Director, Memphis Symphony Orchestra, 1999–. *Honours:* 3rd Prize, 1976, Co-winner, 1978, Baltimore Symphony Orchestra Young Conductors' Competition; ASCAP Award, Adventuresome Programming, 1981, 2001, 2002; Seaver NEA Conductors Award, 1992; Northwestern Univ. Alumni Merit Award, 2000. *Address:* c/o Memphis Symphony Orchestra, 3100 Walnut Grove, Suite 501, Memphis, TN 38111, USA. *E-mail:* musdir@ memphissymphony.org.

LOEVAAS-GERBER, Kari; Singer (Soprano); b. 13 May 1939, Oslo, Norway; m. Manfred Gerber, 1968, 1 d. *Education:* Conservatory Oslo; Musikakademie Wien; Studies with Erna Westenberger, Frankfurt. *Career:* Debut: Nuri, Oslo, 1959; Opera Houses in Dortmund and Mainz; Festivals at Salzburg, Vienna, Lucerne, Bergen, Ludwigsburg, Schwetzingen, Athens, Flanders; Television includes Fischer und seine Fru/ Schoeck, 1981 and Peer Gynt, W Egk, 1983; All major radio stations in Germany, Austria, Norway, Switzerland, France and Italy. *Recordings include:* Debut record: Lieder (Grieg, Mussorgsky, Sibelius) with Erik Werba; Petite Messe Solennelle, Rossini; Die Feen, Wagner; War Requiem, Britten; more than 30 records. *Honours:* Deutsche Grammophon Sonderpreis, Vienna, 1960. *Current Management:* Sudwestdeutsche Konzertdirektion Russ, Stuttgart. *Address:* Gugerhalde 10, 8207 Schaffhausen, Switzerland.

LOGIE, Nicholas; Violist and Orchestra Manager; b. 12 May 1950, Hemel Hempstead, Hertfordshire, England; m. Marina Orlov, 4 Sept 1972, 2 s. *Education:* Yehudi Menuhin School, 1963–67; Royal College of Music, London; Northwest Deutsche Musikakademie, Detmold, Germany; Santa Cecilia, Rome, Italy. *Career:* Debut: Wigmore Hall, London, 1984; Member of Vienna Symphony Orchestra. 1973–78; Chilingirian String Quartet, 1978–81; Orchestra Manager, Glyndebourne Touring Opera, 1990; Baroque Viola, London Baroque, 1985–; Senior Lecturer, Director of Early Music, Royal Northern College of Music. *Recordings:* Schubert Cello Quintet; 6 Mozart Quartets with Chilingirian Quartet. *Contributions:* 5 Sketches for Solo Viola by Elizabeth Maconchy; Newsletter No. 24, The Viola Society, March 1985. *Address:* Lott's End, Highgate, Forest Row, Sussex RH18 5 BE, England.

LOH, Lisa; Pianist; b. 6 Jan. 1967, Hong Kong. *Education:* Diploma, Management Studies; Associate, Licentiate, Guildhall School of Music and Drama; Licentiate, Royal Academy of Music; Associate, Royal College of Music. *Career:* Debut: Purcell Room, South Bank, London, 1993; Appearances in Concerts and Recitals, Fairfield Halls, South Bank and Barbican Centre; Broadcasts on ITV, RTHK Radio Hong Kong; Fellow, Guild of Musicians and Singers. *Honours:* Several Prizes, British Competitions. *Address:* 301 Cromwell Tower, Barbican, London EC 2Y 8 NB, England.

LOJARRO, Daniela; Italian/Swiss Singer (soprano); b. 24 June 1964, Rivoli, Turin, Italy. *Education:* studied with Carlo Bergonzi, among others. *Career:* debut, sang Gilda at Bussetto; Performances at major opera houses in Naples, Parma, Trieste, Bari, Covent Garden London, Zürich, Monte Carlo, Turin, Pretoria, Palm Beach, Liège and Opera Ireland; also Rossini Opera Festival, Pesaro and Martina Franca Festival; Repertoire includes main roles in Bellini's La Sonnambula, Bizet's Les Pêcheurs de perles, Delibes' Lakmé, Donizetti's Don Pasquale, l'Elisir d'amore, Lucia di Lammermoor, La Fille du Regiment, Handel's Alcina, Leoncavallo's Pagliacci, Mozart's Don Giovanni, Rossini's Barbiere di Siviglia, La Donna del Lago, Salieri's La Secchia rapita, Verdi's Rigoletto, Falstaff, Un Ballo in maschera, La Traviata; Worked with conductors including Allemandi, Brüggen, Carignani, Kuhn, Oestman, Oren, Paternostro, Rizzi, Viotti and Zedda; Concert and oratorio repertoire includes Bach's Cantata Jauchzet Gott, Corghi/Rossini's Dodo Suite, Mozart's Concert Arias, Pergolesi's Stabat Mater. *Recordings include:* Ermione by Rossini, Nina by Paisiello, Crispino e la Comare by Ricci. *Television:* appeared in Ermione, La Sonnambula and Lakmé. *Film:* sang Lucia and Gilda on soundtrack of Zeffirelli's Toscanini. *Honours:* Winner, Giuseppe Verdi Competition, Parma. *Address:* Gladbachstrasse 48, 8044 Zürich, Switzerland (home). *Telephone:* (1) 3620134 (home). *E-mail:* daniela.lojarro@bluewin.ch.

LOMBARD, Alain; Conductor; b. 4 Oct. 1940, Paris, France. *Education:* Studied at the Paris Conservatoire with Line Talleul (Violin) and Gaston Poulet (Conducting). *Career:* Debut: Salle Gaveau, Pais, aged 11 with the Pasdeloup Orchestra; Assistant, the Principal Conductor with Lyon Opéra, 1961–65; American Opera Society, 1963, with Massenet's Hérodiade; Conducted New York Philharmonic and at Salzburg Festival, 1966; Musical Director, Miami Opera, Florida, 1966–74; Metropolitan Opera, 1967, Gounod's Faust; Director of the Strasbourg Philharmonic, 1972–83; Opéra du Rhin, 1974–80; Guest conductor with Schveningen Festival, Netherlands, Hamburg Opera, L'Orchestre de Paris and other leading orchestras; Conducted Die Zauberflöte at Bordeaux, 1992; Conducted Falstaff at Catania, 1996 and Les Contes d'Hoffmann, 1998. *Recordings include:* Mozart's Così fan tutte, with Strasbourg Ensemble; Berlioz Symphonie Fantastique, Harold in Italy and Roméo et Juliette; Verdi Requiem; Prokofiev Violin Concertos (Amoyal) and Ballet Suites; Bartók Concerto for Orchestra and Miraculous Mandarin; Ravel Piano Concerto, Queffelec, and Daphnis et Chloe No. 2; Gounod Roméo et Juliette. *Honours:* Gold Medal, Dimitri Mitropoulos Competition, 1966.

LOMBARDO, Bernard; Singer (Tenor); b. 15 Nov. 1960, Marseille, France. *Education:* Studied in Marseille and Treviso. Career: Sang widely in France including Bruno in I Puritani at the Paris Opéra-Comique, 1987; Tour of Australia 1988–89, notably as Turiddu at Sydney and Melbourne; St Gallen in 1988 as Edgardo and Opéra Bastille in France in 1990 as Cassio in Otello; La Scala Milan debut in 1991, as Floreski in Cherubini's Lodoiska; Season 1992 as Hoffmann at Kaiserslautern and Roland in Esclarmonde at St Etienne; Other roles include Jacopo in I Due Foscari, Tybalt in Roméo et Juliette at Zürich, Ismaele in Nabucco and Gabriele Adorno at Geneva. *Recordings include:* Lodoiska and Lucia di Lammermoor. *Address:* c/o Teatro alla Scala, Via Filodrammatici 2, 20121 Milan, Italy.

LOMON, Ruth; Composer; b. 7 Nov. 1930, Montreal, Canada; m. Earle Lomon, 4 Aug 1951, 1 s., 2 d. *Education:* McGill University; New England Conservatory. *Career:* Debut: Piano, Montreal, Canada; 2 Piano team with Iris Graffman Wenglin with appearances on radio and television, performing and lecturing on works by women composers, playing contemporary and classical repertoire, 1973–83; Composer/Resident Scholar, Women's Studies Research Center, Brandeis University, Waltham, Massachusetts, 1998–. *Compositions include:* Published: Esquisses for piano solo; Seven Portals of Vision for organ, 5 Songs on poems by William Blake for contralto and violin, Dust Devils for harp, Janus for string quartet, Diptych for woodwind quintet, Metamorphoses for cello and piano, Songs for a Requiem for soprano, piano or woodwinds, Equinox for brass quartet, Celebrations for 2 harps, bassoon concerto, Dialogue for harpsichord and vibraphone, Requiem Mass for full chorus and brass accompaniment; Butterfly Effect for string quartet, 1990, Terra Incognita for orchestra, 1993, and Shadowing for piano quartet, 1993; Oddyssey, trumpet concerto, 1997; Nocturnal Songs for mezzo and harp, 1997; 2 piano quartets, 1993, 1995; Songs of Remembrance, 60-song cycle on poems of the Holocaust for soprano, tenor, mezzo, bass, oboe, English horn and piano, 1996; Odyssey, trumpet concerto, 1997. *Recordings include:* Five Ceremonial Masks for Piano; Soundings and Triptych for two pianos, 1992; Terra Incognita with Warsaw Philharmonic Orchestra under Jerzy Swoboda, 1993; Bassoon Concerto in 3 movements, with bassoonist Grertzer under Gerard Schwarz with Prague Radio Symphony Orchestra; Songs of Remembrance. *Address:* 2A Forest Street, Cambridge, MA 02140, USA.

LONDON, Edwin; Composer; b. 16 March 1929, Philadelphia, Pennsylvania, USA. *Education:* Studied at Oberlin College Conservatory and the University of Iowa, PhD, 1961; With Gunter Schullar at Manhattan School of Music and with Milhaud and Dallapiccola; Conducting studies with Izler Solomon. *Career:* Teacher at Smith College, Northampton, 1960–68; University of Illinois, 1973–83; Chairman of the Music Department at Cleveland State University, 1978–; Founder and leader of the Cleveland Chamber Orchestra. *Compositions:* Santa Claus, Mime Opera, 1960; 3 Settings of Psalm 23 for Choruses, 1961; Woodwind Quintet, 1958; Sonatina for Viola and Piano, 1962; Brass Quintet, 1965; Portraits of Three Ladies, Theatre Piece, 1967; Four Proverbs, 1968; The Iron Hand, Otarorio, 1975; The Death of Lincoln, Opera, 1976; Psalms of These Days, 1976–80; Metaphysical Vegas, Musical 1981; Bottom Line, for tuba and chamber orchestra, 1997. *Honours:* Guggenheim Foundation Grant; NEA Grants; Hamburg Opera Contemporary Festival Grant. *Address:* c/o ASCAP, ASCAP Building, 1 Lincoln Plaza, New York, NY 10023, USA.

LONGHI, Daniela; Soprano; b. 1956, Italy. *Education:* Studied in Verona and Mantua. *Career:* Sang at the Verona Arena from 1981, as the Priestess in Aida and Liu in Turandot; Guest appearances at Turin as Micaela and at Liège as Violetta and Thais; Sang at and Parma as Leonore in the French version of Il Trovatore, 1990; Marseille and Madrid, 1990–91 as Anna Bolena, Montpellier in 1991 as Elizabeth 1 in Roberto Devereux by Donizetti; Other roles include Manon and Mimi; Sang Violetta at Detroit, 1998. *Address:* c/o Opéra de Montpellier, 11 Boulevard Victor Hugo, 34000 Montpellier, France.

LONSDALE, Michael (James); Composer; b. 11 Oct. 1961, Newcastle, New South Wales, Australia. *Education:* New South Wales Conservatory, 1985–87; Study with Nigel Butterley 1984–85 and Bozidar Kos, 1986–88. *Career:* Faculty Member, Barker College, Hornsby; Commissions from David Forrest (1986) and Warringah Council, 1989–91. *Compositions include:* Calm Obstables, Mouna, and Pais, all for piano, 1985–86; Celeritas for string trio, piano and wind trio, 1985; Fulgur Arbor for tenor trombone, 1986; I See Past the River... for chorus and orchestra, 1988; Lung Gompa for piano, 1993; It Stirs Beneath, for chorus, 1994; Time is the Loser, for string quartet, 1994; Viper for contra bassoon, 1995. *Honours:* ABC/Department of Education Young Composer of the Year Award, 1979. *Address:* c/o APRA, Locked Bag 3665, St Leonards, NSW 2065, Australia.

LOOSLI, Arthur; Concert Singer (Baritone); b. 23 Feb. 1926, La Chaux d'Abel, Berner, Jura, Switzerland; m. Theresia Rothlisberger, 2 s. *Education:* Conservatoire of Berne with Felix Loeffel; Studies with Mariano Stabile, Venice, and Arne Sunnergard, Stockholm, Sweden. *Career:* Debut: Berne, 1958; Performances in Switzerland, Belgium, Sweden, Netherlands, Germany and Italy; Guest Artist at Stadttheater, Berne; mem, Othmar Schoeck Association; Swiss Music Teachers Association. *Recordings:* Elegie, Lieder (Othmar Schoeck); Winterreise (Schubert); Schwanengesang (Schubert); Johannes–Passion (Bach). *Publications:* Illustrations of Franz Hohler's Tschipo and Der Granitblock im Kino. *Honours:* Recipient, 1st Prize, International Singers Competition, Bass Baritone, 's-Hertogenbosch, Netherlands, 1959; Further professional activities. *Address:* Gurtenweg 31A, 3074 Muri, Switzerland.

LOOTENS, Lena (Helena-Alice); Singer (Soprano); b. 14 April 1959, Genk, Belgium; 1 d. *Education:* Royal Atheneum of Maasmechelen; Conservatories of Brussels and Gent; Private studies with Vera Rozsa, London; Margreet Honig, Amsterdam; Kristina Deutekom, Amsterdam. *Career:* Appearances with numerous orchestras; Concert tours to Belgium, Netherlands, Germany, England, Switzerland, Israel and Poland; Appearances on Radio and Television includes, BRT, BBC, WDR, NDR, SDR; Opera engagements in Innsbruck, Monte Carlo, Antwerp, Montpellier, Liège and Versailles, Sang Fulvia in Handel's Ezio at Halle, 1998. *Recordings:* L'Infedelà Delusa; Concert Arias; Flavio by Handel, Deutsche Schallplattenpreis; L'Incoronazione di Poppea by Monteverdi; Die Israeliten in der Wüste, C P E Bach; Requiem/Mozart; La Guiditta/Almeida; Die Heirat Widerwillen/Humperdinck; CD: Mahler's 4th Symphony. *Honours:* 1st Prize Singing, National Competition for the Youth of Belgium; Alex Devries Scholarship, Roeping Foundation. *Current Management:* Internationaal Concertbureau Arien. *Address:* Platte-Lostr 341, B03010 Kessel-Lo, Belgium.

LOPARDO, Frank; Singer (Tenor); b. 23 Dec. 1957, New York, USA. *Education:* Studied in New York. *Career:* Debut: St Louis, 1984, as Tamino; Season 1985–86 at Dallas and Naples, Don Ottavio at Aix and La Scala, Milan; Sang Fenton in Falstaff at Amsterdam 1986, Ferrando at Glyndebourne, 1987; Vienna Staatsoper from 1987, notably as Belfiore in Il Viaggio a Reims, conducted by Abbado; Sang Elvino in La Sonnambula and Rossini's Almviva at Chicago, 1989; Sang Lindoro in L'Italiana in Algeri, Covent Garden, 1989; Season 1991 as Elvino and Ferrando at Florence, Don Ottavio at San Francisco; Sang Rossini's Lindoro at San Francisco, 1992; Alfredo at Covent Garden, 1995; Lensky in Paris, 1996; Season 2000–01 as the Duke of Mantua at Los Angeles, Nemorino in Chicago and Rodolfo for the New York Met. *Recordings* *include:* Mozart's Requiem and Don Giovanni; Don Pasquale; Così fan tutte; L'Italiana in Algeri; Falstaff. *Address:* Metropolitan Opera, Lincoln Center, New York, NY 10023, USA.

LOPEZ-COBOS, Jesus; Conductor and Editor; b. 25 Feb. 1940, Toro, Spain; m. Alicia Lopez-Cobos 1987, 3 s. *Education:* PhD in Philosophy, 1964; Diploma in Composition, Madrid Conservatory, 1966; Diploma in Conducting, Vienna Academy, Austria, 1969. *Career:* Debut: Concert, Prague, 1969; Opera, La Fenice, Venice; Debuts at: Deutsche Oper in 1970 with La Bohème and San Francisco, USA in 1972 with Lucia di Lammermoor; Conducted Carmen at Covent Garden, 1975, Adriana Lecouvreur at the Metropolitan, 1978, Der Ring with Deutsche Oper Berlin on tour to Japan, 1987; Principal Guest Conductor with London Philharmonic, 1982–86; Principal Conductor and Artistic Director of Spanish National Orchestra, 1984–89; Music Director of Cincinnati Orchestra, 1986–, and Lausanne Chamber Orchestra, 1990–; Concerts with many leading orchestras in the United Kingdom, USA, Germany, Amsterdam, Vienna, Switzerland, Norway and Israel. Opera productions at Royal Opera House, Covent Garden, and La Scala; Conducted La Serva Padrona at Lausanne, 1996; Editions include: Lucia di Lammermoor. *Recordings include:* Franck's Symphony in D minor, Ravel's Bolero and Bruckner's Symphonies Nos 4, 6 and 7 with Cincinnati Orchestra; Donizetti Lucia di Lammermoor, Rossini's Otello, Recitals and opera with José Carreras and Liszt Dante Symphony, Falla, Three-Cornered Hat, Chabrier España. *Honours:* 1st Prize, Besançon International Conductors Competition, 1969; Prince of Asturias Award, from the Spanish Government, 1981; First Class Cross of Merit of Germany, 1989. *Current Management:* Terry Harrison Artists Management, The Orchard, Market Street, Charlbury, Oxfordshire OX7 3PJ, England. *Telephone:* (1608) 810330. *Fax:* (1608) 811331. *E-mail:* artists@terryharrison.force9.co.uk.

LOPEZ-YANEZ, Jorge; singer (tenor); b. 1963, Mexico. *Education:* studied in Mexico City and California. *Career:* debut, Long Beach Opera in 1986 as Rossillon in Die Lustige Witwe; European debut at Hanover in 1988 as the Duke of Mantua; Düsseldorf and Stuttgart, 1988–89 as Ramiro in La Cenerentola; Further engagements as Fenton at Los Angeles and Bordeaux, Oronte in Alcina at the Paris Châtelet, Rossini's Almaviva at Munich, Donizetti's Tonio at Zürich and Alfredo in La Traviata at the Vienna Staatsoper, 1992; Glyndebourne debut in 1995 as Pyrrhus in the British stage premiere of Rossini's Ermione; Sang Nemorino at Santiago and Ernesto at Turin, 1998; Sang Ramiro in Cenerentola at Monte Carlo, 2000; Alfredo for Australian Opera, 2001. *Current Management:* Robert Gilder & Co., Enterprise House, 59–65 Upper Ground, London, SE1 9PQ, England. *Telephone:* (20) 7928-9008. *Fax:* (20) 7928-9755. *E-mail:* rgilder@robert-gilder.com.

LORAND, Colette; Singer (Soprano); b. 7 Jan. 1923, Zürich, Switzerland. *Education:* Musikhochschule Hanover; Zürich with Frau Hirzel. *Career:* Debut: Basle 1946, as Marguerite in Faust; Frankfurt Opera 1951–56, notably as the Queen of Night; Hamburg Opera from 1955, often in operas by Henze, Penderecki and Orff; Edinburgh Festival 1955; Lisbon 1961, as Constanze in Die Entführung; Deutsche Oper Berlin 1972, in the premiere of Fortner's Elisabeth Tudor; Created roles in Orff's De Temporum fine Comoedia, Salzburg Festival, 1973, and Reimann's Lear, Munich 1978 (as Regan, repeated at the Paris Opéra, 1982). *Recordings:* Lear and De Temporum fine Comoedia; Orff's Prometheus. *Address:* c/o Bayerische Staatsoper, Postfach 745, 8000 Munich, Germany.

LORANGE, Nicole; Singer (Soprano); b. 28 Nov. 1942, Montreal, Canada. *Education:* Studied with Pierrette Alarie and at the Vienna Music Academy with Erik Werba. *Career:* Sang at first in concert and made stage debut at the Linz Landestheater in 1969 as Desdemona; Further appearances with the Canadian Opera Company as Musetta in 1972, and Opéra Montreal as Tosca in 1980; Metropolitan Opera, 1982–84 as Butterfly, Adriana Lecouvreur and Francesca da Rimini; Other roles include Donna Elvira and Offenbach's Giulietta; Many concert appearances. *Address:* c/o L'Opéra de Montréal, 260 de Maisonneuve Boulevard West Montreal, Province Québec H2H 1Y9, Canada.

LORD, Bernadette; Singer (Soprano); b. 1965, Derby, England. *Education:* Studied at the Guildhall School and with Suzanne Danco in Florence; Further study at the European Arts Centre, 1988. *Career:* Joined Opera Wallonie, Liège, and sang Helena in Schubert's Der Häusliche Krieg in Belgium, Netherlands and Paris; Glyndebourne and Covent Garden debuts as Cis in Albert Herring; Other roles include Despina for British Youth Opera at the Cheltenham Festival, Miss Wordsworth in Albert Herring, Lucia in The Rape of Lucretia, Gretel for Opera East, Susanna and Barbarina in Le nozze di Figaro; Sang Jano in Jenůfa at Covent Garden, 1993. *Address:* c/o Opéra Royal de Wallonie, 1 rue des Dominicains, B–4000 Liege, Belgium.

LORENTZEN, Bent; Composer; b. 11 Feb. 1935, Stenvad, Denmark; m. Edith Kaerulf Moeller 1958; one s. three d. *Education:* Royal Acad. of Music, Copenhagen, 1960. *Career:* performances throughout Europe of

works including Euridice, Die Music kommt mit äusserst bekannt vor!, Eine Wundersame Liebesgeschichte, Stalten Mette, Toto, Fackeltanz, Samba, Pianoconcerto Nordic Music Days, Saxophone Concerto, two choral songs to Enzensberger, 1991, Bill and Julia (opera), The Magic Brilliant, (The Danish National Opera), 1993; The Scatterbrain, Royal Theatre, 1995; Pergolesi's Home Service. *Compositions include:* Purgatorio, choral; Granite; Quartz; Syncretism; Wunderblumen; Flamma; Zauberspiegel; Farbentiegel; Blütenweiss; Colori; Concerto for oboe; Cello Concerto; Hunting Concerto; Double Concerto; Samba; Paradiesvogel; Graffiti; Purgatorio; 3 Madrigals; 5 Motets; Genesis; Stabat Mater; Canon I–V for 2 accordions; New Choral Dramatics; Ammen Dammen Des; Round; 5 easy Piano Pieces, Flood of Paradise; Olof Palme for mixed choir; Comics; 3 Latin Suites; Venezia; Tordenskiold; Der Steppenwolf, opera, 2000. *Recordings include:* The Bottomless Pit; Visions; Cloud-Drift; Mambo, Intersection, Puncti, Triplex, Groppo, Nimbus, Cruor, Goldranken; Abgrund; Die Musik kommt mir äusserst bekannt vor!; Syncretism; A Wonderous Love Story; Sol; Luna; Mars, for organ, 1985; Mercurius; Jupiter; Venus; Saturnus; Umbra, Paesaggio, Dunkelblau, Round, Cyclus I–IV; Piano and oboe concertos; Regenbogen; Comics; Lines; Tears; Orfeo Suite; Intrada; Alpha and Omega; Pergolesi's Home Service, theatre, 1998. *Publications:* Ej Sikkelej, 1967; Recorder System, 1962–64; Musikens AHC, 1969; Mer om Musiken, 1972; Introduction to Electronic Music, 1969. *Current Management:* Edition Wilhelm Hansen, Bornholmsgade 1, 1266 Copenhagen K, Denmark. *Address:* Sotoften 37, 2820 Genofte, Denmark.

LORENZ, Andrew (Bela); Violinist; b. 17 Oct. 1951, Melbourne, Victoria, Australia; m. Wendy Joy Lorenz, 1 s. *Education:* DSCM Performers Diploma and Teachers Diploma, Sydney Conservatory of Music, 1970. *Career:* Recitals; Concerto, radio and television performances; Deputy Leader, Melbourne Elizabethen Trust Orchestra, 1972; Led for D'Oyly Carte Opera Company, Sadler's Wells, England, 1973–74; Leader, New England Ensemble (resident piano quartet) and Lecturer, Music Department, University of New England, Armidale, New South Wales, Australia, 1975–82; Founding Member and Leader, New England Sinfonia; World tours with New England Ensemble; Associate Concertmaster, Adelaide Symphony Orchestra, 1983–86; Leader, Australian Piano Trio, 1983–87; Senior Lecturer in Strings, University of Southern Queensland, Toowoomba, Queensland; Leader, Darling Downs Ensemble; Director, McGregor Chamber Music School. *Recordings:* Works by Beethoven, Turina, Margaret Sutherland, Mozart, Fauré, John McCabe, Mendelssohn, Goossens; Mary Mageau; Sundry chamber works and Concerto Soloist with many of Australia's leading orchestras and Slovak Radio Symphony; Australian premieres of Benjamin, McCabe and Myslivecek Concertos. *Honours:* Winner, Victorian ABC Concerto Competition, 1972. *Address:* 21 Merlin Court, M/S 852 Toowoomba Mail Servce, Queensland 4352, Australia.

LORENZ, Gerlinde; Singer (Soprano); b. 1939, Chemnitz, Germany. *Education:* Studied at the Vienna Music Academy. *Career:* Sang at the Vienna Volksoper from 1967, Staatsoper from 1972; Cologne Opera, 1971–86, with debut as Mimi; Bielefeld, 1985, as Lola in Schreker's Irrelohe and Oldenburg, 1992, as Ortrud in Lohengrin; Other engagements at Zürich, the Munich Staatsoper, Deutsche Oper Berlin and Frankfurt; Further roles include Mozart's Donna Elvira and Donna Anna, Wagner's Elsa, Eva and Sieglinde, Strauss's Elektra and Elisabeth de Valois; Concerts in Vienna, Salzburg, Paris and elsewhere. *Address:* c/o Oldenburgische Staatstheater, Theaterwall 18, 2900 Oldenburg, Germany.

LORENZ, Ricardo, MM, PhD; Venezuelan composer; b. 24 May 1961, Maracaibo. *Education:* Olivares Conservatory, Landaeta Conservatory, Indiana Univ. and Univ. of Chicago. *Career:* Acting Dir, Indiana Univ. Latin American Music Center 1987–92, Visiting Assoc. Dir 2003–04; composer-in-residence, Chicago Symphony Orchestra 1998–2002, Billings Symphony Orchestra, Montana 1998–99. *Compositions include:* Sinfonietta concertante 1987, Concerto for Orchestra 1993, En Tren Vá Changó 2001. *Recordings:* Pataruco: Concerto for Venezuelan Maracas and Orchestra, Está Lloviendo Afuera y No Hay Agua. *Publications:* Scores and Readings at Indiana University Latin American Music Center 1995. *Address:* Latin American Music Center, School of Music, Indiana University, Bloomington, IN 47405, USA (office). *Telephone:* (812) 855-2991 (office). *Fax:* (812) 855-4936 (office). *E-mail:* rieloren@ indiana.edu (office). *Website:* www.music.indiana.edu (office).

LORENZ, Siegfried; Singer (Baritone); b. 30 Aug. 1945, Berlin, Germany. *Education:* Studied in Berlin. *Career:* Debut: Komische Oper Berlin, 1969, in The Love for Three Oranges; Sang at the Komische Oper and Staatsoper Berlin, notably as Guglielmo, Wolfram, Mozart's Count, Germont, and Posa in Don Carlos; Agamemnon in Gluck's Iphigenia in Aulis, 1987; Soloist at the Leipzig Gewandhaus from 1974, in concert music by Bach, Brahms and Schubert; International appearances in Lieder recitals. *Recordings include:* Winterreise, Die schöne Müllerin and the Brahms Requiem. *Address:* c/o Gewandhausorchester, Augustusplatz 8, 04109 Leipzig, Germany.

LORIMER, Heather; Singer (Soprano); b. 1961, Wallasey, Cheshire; m. Gerard Quinn. *Education:* Studied at the Royal Northern College of Music, Manchester with Frederick Cox and now with Iris Dell'Acqua. *Career:* Scottish Opera Go Round, Mimi in La Bohème, 1987; Glyndebourne Festival and Touring Opera, Constanze, Die Entführung aus dem Serail, 1988; Countess, Le nozze di Figaro, 1989; Opera 80, Tatiana in Eugene Onegin in 1989 and Hanna Glawari in The Merry Widow, 1990; Travelling Opera, Mimi; Countess; Donna Elvira; Don Giovanni; Fiordiligi in Così fan tutte; Violetta in La Traviata and Micaela in Carmen; English Touring Opera, Mimi, 1994; Education tours for Glyndebourne, Opera 80 and English National Opera's Lillian Bayliss Programme; Other roles performed include: Giorgetta, Il Tabarro; Liu, Turandot; Norina, Don Pasquale; Rosina, Il Barbiere di Siviglia; Rosalinde, Die Fledermaus; Rosario, Goyescas; Dirce, Medea; Leila, The Pearl Fishers and in 1993 she created the title role in Michael Finnissy's Thérèse Raquin, for the Royal Opera's Garden Venture; Concert repertoire includes, Verdi Requiem; Rossini Stabat Mater; Dvořák Requiem; Elijah; Carmina Burana; Brahms Requiem; Fauré Requiem; Sea Symphony and The Kingdom. *Honours:* International Opera and Bel Canto Duet Competition, Antwerp, Gerard Quinn; Scottish Opera John Noble Competition. *Address:* 92 Sturla Road, Chatham, Kent ME4 5QH, England.

LORIOD, Yvonne; Pianist; b. 20 Jan. 1924, Houilles, Seine-et-Oise, France; m. Olivier Messiaen, deceased 1992. *Education:* National Conservatory of Music, Paris. *Career:* Solo Recitals in most European countries, North and South America, and Japan with leading orchestras; 1st Performaces in Paris of 21 Concerti by Mozart and Concerti by Bart ók and Schoenberg and many works by Jolivet; all Messiaen works with piano including Visions de l'Amen, 1943, Turangalila Symphonie 1948, Catalogue d'Oiseaux 1958, Des Canyons aux Etoiles 1974; Professor of Piano, Paris Conservatoire of Music; Masterclasses at summer schools, Darmstadt and Bayreuth, France and USA. *Recordings:* Numerous works issued. *Honours:* Officer, Legion of Honour; Grand Prix du Disque.

LORTIÉ, Louis; Concert Pianist; b. 27 April 1959, Quebec, Canada. *Education:* Studied in Quebec with Yvonne Hubert. *Career:* Debut: 1972, Montreal Symphony Orchestra,; World-wide appearances from 1978, with concerts throughout Canada and tours to Europe, USA and Far East; Founded the Lortié-Berick-Lysy Trio, 1995; Engagements as soloist and conductor with Orchestra di Padova e del Veneto; Prokofiev's 1st Concerto at the London Prom Concerts, 2001Ravel's concerto for the Left Hand at the London Proms, 2002. *Address:* c/o Cramer/Marder Artists, 3436 Springhill Road, Lafayette, CA 94549, USA.

LOSKUTOVA, Irina; Singer (Soprano); b. 1965, Salavat, Bashkiria, Russia. *Education:* Graduated State Mussorgsky Conservatoire of Sverdlovsk, 1989. *Career:* Appearances with Mussorgsky Opera and Ballet Theatre, St Petersburg, from 1989; Kirov Opera, Mariinsky Theatre, from 1995, as Tatiana, Yaroslavna in Prince Igor, Mimi, Elisabeth de Valois, Madama Butterfly and Paulina in The Gambler by Prokofiev; Tours of Europe and North America with the Mussorgsky and the Kirov Opera companies; Further roles include Tchaikovsky's Iolanta and Maria (Mazeppa) and Katerina Izmailova: Sang Lyubka in Semyon Kotko by Prokofiev with the Kirov at Covent Garden, 2000 (British premiere). *Recordings include:* Mazeppa. *Honours:* Prizewinner, 1989 Mussorgsky Vocal Competition. *Address:* c/o Kirov Opera, Mariinsky Theatre, Theatre Square, St Petersburg, Russia.

LOTHIAN, Helen; Singer (mezzo-soprano); b. 1968, Scotland. *Education:* Studied at the Royal Scottish Academy and the Guildhall School; Further study with Patricia Hay in Scotland. *Career:* Concert appearances throughout the United Kingdom in music by Verdi, Bruckner, Beethoven, Mozart and Haydn; Recitals at the Covent Garden Festival, Clonter Opera Farm and elsewhere; Sang the Lady Artist in Berg's Lulu with the BBC Symphony Orchestra, 1995; Opera engagements include Christoph Rilke's Song of Love and Death by Matthus, for Glyndebourne Touring Opera; Dorabella, Carmen and Cherubino for British Youth Opera, Dardane in Haydn's L'Incontro Improvviso at Garsington and Mozart's Third Lady at the Covent Garden Festival; Romeo in Bellini's I Capuleti e i Montecchi for Castleward Opera, 1995; Royal Opera and Scottish Opera debuts as Flora in La Traviata, 1996. *Current Management:* Askonas Holt Ltd, Lonsdale Chambers, 27 Chancery Lane, London, WC2A 1PF, England. *Telephone:* (20) 7400-1700. *Fax:* (20) 7400-1799. *E-mail:* info@askonasholt.co.uk. *Website:* www.askonasholt.co.uk.

LOTT, Dame Felicity Ann Emwhyla, DBE, BA, LRAM, FRAM; British singer (soprano); b. 8 May 1947, Cheltenham; d. of John A. Lott and Whyla Lott (née Williams); m. 1st Robin Golding 1973 (divorced); m. 2nd Gabriel Woolf 1984; one d. *Education:* Pate's Grammar School for Girls, Cheltenham, Royal Holloway Coll., Univ. of London and Royal Acad. of Music. *Career:* debut with ENO as Pamina in Die Zauberflöte 1975; prin. roles at Glyndebourne, Covent Garden, ENO, WNO, New York Metropolitan Opera, Vienna, La Scala, Paris Opéra, Brussels, Hamburg, Munich, Chicago, San Francisco, Dresden; wide recital repertoire; roles include Countess in Le Nozze di Figaro, Ellen Orford in Peter Grimes, Fiordiligi in Così fan tutte, Elvira in Don Giovanni, Xiphares in Mitridate, the Marschallin in Der Rosenkavalier, Countess in Capriccio; founder mem. Songmakers' Almanac; mem. Equity, Incorporated Soc. of Musicians. *Honours:* Hon. Fellow Royal Holloway Coll.; Officier des Arts et des Lettres 2000, Chevalier Légion d'honneur 2001; Dr hc (Sussex) 1990; Hon. DLitt (Loughborough) 1996; Hon. DMus (London) 1997, (Royal Scottish Acad. of Music and Drama) 1998, (Oxford) 2001; Kammersängerin, Bayerische Staatsoper, Munich 2003. *Current Management:* Askonas Holt Ltd, Lonsdale Chambers, 27 Chancery Lane, London, WC2A 1PF, England. *Telephone:* (20) 7400-1700. *Fax:* (20) 7400-0799. *E-mail:* info@askonasholt.co.uk (office). *Website:* www.askonasholt.co.uk (office); www.felicitylott.de.

LOTT, Maria-Elisabeth; Concert Violinist; b. 1987, Germany. *Education:* Studies with Josef Rissin at Karlsruhe, 1991–. *Career:* Concert engagements throughout Europe and the USA, including British debut performances Feb 2000 with the Bournemouth Symphony Orchestra and Royal Liverpool Philharmonic Orchestra, playing Paganini's First concerto; Further appearances with the Minnesota Orchestra and Malaysia Philharmonic in Kuala Lumpur; Season 2000–01 with the London Philharmonic, Ensemble Orchestral de Paris, the Ulster Orchestra and NDR Hanover Orchestra. *Recordings include:* Album of Mozart, played on violin used by the composer in 1760's. *Address:* IMG Artists, Lovell House, 616 Chiswick High Rd, London W4 5RX, England.

LOTTI, Antonio; Singer (Tenor); b. 1957, Lucca, Italy. *Education:* Studied at São Paulo, Brazil. *Career:* Debut: São Paulo, 1982, as Cavaradossi; Sang in opera throughout South America, Europe from 1987; Verdi's Stiffelio in Amsterdam, Oslo and Copenhagen as Cavaradossi; Paolo in Francesca da Rimini at Bologna, Don Carlos at Catania; Bonn Opera from 1994, as Pery in Il Guaramento by Gomes, Turiddu in Cavalleria Rusticana, and Hoffmann; Other roles include Rodolfo in Luisa Miller. *Address:* c/o Oper der Stadt Bonn, Am Boeselagerlof 1, 53111 Bonn, Germany.

LOU, Qian-Gui; Singer (tenor); b. 1923, China. *Career:* Sang roles in opera including Pinkerton in Madama Butterfly, 1958, Lensky in Eugene Onegin, 1962; Soloist, concerts in USSR, Poland, Romania, Czechoslovakia, North Korea, 1953–54; Solo recitals, Beijing, Shanghai, elsewhere in China, 1978–97, and at Redlands Summer Music Festival, USA, 1990; Appearances on Central television programmes, MTV; Documentary films for stage performances; Artistic Director, Central Opera House of China, also Savonlinna Opera Festival, Finland (1988); Professor of Voice, Central Conservatory of Music, Beijing; Member, Jury for National Vocal Competition, China. *Recordings:* Album released in Moscow, 1954; Album released in Beijing, 1956; Album released in Beijing, 1980; Album released in Guangzhou, 1983; The Treasurable Version of 100 Anthologies of Vocal Music performed by famous Chinese Musicians, 1998. *Address:* Twuan Jie Hu Bei Li 6-2-302, Beijing 100026, People's Republic of China. *Telephone:* 85988808.

LOUGHRAN, James; Conductor; b. 30 June 1931, Glasgow, Scotland; m. (1) Nancy Coggon, 20 Sept 1961, (2) Ludmila Navratil, 15 April 1985, 2 s. *Career:* Debut: Royal Festival Hall, London, 1961; Associate Conductor, Bournemouth Symphony Orchestra, 1962–65; Principal Conductor, BBC Scottish Symphony Orchestra, 1965–71; Principal Conductor and Musical Adviser, Hallé Orchestra, 1971–83; Principal Conductor, Bamberg S.O, 1979–83; Guest Conductor of Principal Orchestras in Europe, America, Australasia and Japan; Tours with Munich Philharmonic, BBC Symphony, Stockholm, London and Japan Philharmonic and Scottish Chamber Orchestras; Permanent Guest Conductor, Japan Philharmonic Symphony Orchestra, 1993; Principal Conductor 1996–2003, Aarnus Symphony Orchestra, Denmark. *Recordings include:* Symphonies by Beethoven, Brahms and Elgar, as well as works by Mozart, Berlioz, Schubert, Dvořák, Rachmaninov, Havergal Brian, Walton, Holst and McCabe. *Honours:* Philharmonia Orchestra Conducting, First Prize, 1961; FRNCM, 1976; FRSAMD, 1983; Freeman, City of London, 1991; Liveryman, Musicians' Company, 1992; Hon D.Mus, Sheffield, 1983; Gold Disc, EMI, 1983. *Current Management:* Caecilia, 29 Rue de la Coulouvrenieae, CH-1204 Geneva. *Address:* R & B Agentur, Plankengasse 7, A–1010 Wien, Austria; 34 Cleveden Drive, Glasgow, G12 0RX, Scotland.

LOUIE, Alexina (Alexi); Composer and Pianist; b. 30 July 1949, Vancouver, British Columbia, Canada. *Education:* Studied at the University of British Columbia and at San Diego with Pauline Oliveros. *Career:* Teacher in Pasadena and Los Angeles, 1974–80; Commissions from leading Canadian orchestras; Teacher in Canada from 1980. *Compositions include:* Journal, music theatre, 1980; Music for a Thousand Autumns for orchestra, 1983; The Eternal Earth (1986) and The Ringing Earth (1986) for orchestra; Piano concerto, 1984; Thunder Gate for violin and orchestra, 1991; Piano quintet Music from Night's

Edge (1988) and other chamber music; Love Songs for a Small Planet, for soprano, chamber choir and ensemble (1989) and other vocal music. *Address:* c/o 41 Valleybrook Drive, Don Mills, Ontario M3B 2S6, Canada.

LOUKIANETS, Viktoria; Ukrainian singer (soprano); b. 1965, Kiev, Russia. *Education:* Kiev Music School and Kiev Conservatoire. *Career:* soloist with Ukrainian Opera, Kiev 1989; guest appearances in France, Portugal, Czech Republic, Italy and Switzerland; prinicipal with the Vienna Staatsoper, singing Adina (L'Elisir d'amore), Elvira (L'Italiana in Algeri), Rosina, the Queen of Night and Olympia (Contes d'Hoffman); other roles include Oscar in Ballo in Maschera, Donna Anna, Wagner's Woglinde; appearances include Violetta at the Salzburg Festival, New York Met debut 1996, Opéra Bastille, Paris 1998, La Scala Milan debut as the Queen of Night 1995, Gilda in Rigoletto at Covent Garden, London 1996–97, Berthe in Le Prophète at the Vienna Staatsoper 1998, Violetta at Covent Garden and the Vienna Volksoper 2000–01. *Honours:* Mozart Bicentennial Competition winner, Italy 1991, Maria Callas Competition winner, Athens 1991. *Current Management:* Askonas Holt Ltd, Lonsdale Chambers, 27 Chancery Lane, London, WC2A 1PF, England. *Telephone:* (20) 7400-1700. *Fax:* (20) 7400-1799. *E-mail:* info@askonasholt.co.uk. *Website:* www.askonasholt.co.uk.

LOUP, François; singer (bass); b. 4 March 1940, Estavayer-le-lac, Switzerland. *Education:* studied piano organ, composition and singing at Fribourg. *Career:* sang at the Geneva Opera 1964–66, notably in the premiere of Monsieur de Pourceaugnac by Martin; Directed various vocal ensembles for which he harmonised motets, madrigals and Swiss folk songs; Soloist with the Ensemble Vocal de Lausanne, under Michel Corboz; Many performances of Baroque music, notably with the Societa Cameristica di Lugano and with the Opéra de Lyon, in Orfeo by Monteverdi; Oratorio performances in many European countries; Sang in Bizet's Docteur Miracle at the 1975 Spoleto Festival; Sang Bartolo in Le nozze di Figaro at Houston 1988, repeated at Glyndebourne 1989, later at the Albert Hall, London; San Diego and the Opéra de Lyon 1989, as Don Pasquale and as Balducci in Benvenuto Cellini; Season 1992 with Mozart's Bartolo at San Diego, Don Pasquale at Vancouver and the Sacristan in Tosca at San Francisco; Sang in La Bohème at the Met, 1994; Bailiff in Werther at Tel-Aviv, 1996; Debut as Don Pasquale and sang Rossini's Bartolo at Teatro Colón Buenos Aires, 1997; Sang Don Alfonso in Rio de Janeiro and in Florida, 2000; Other roles include Leporello, Figaro, Dulcamara, Masetto, Arkel, Pimen, Frère Laurent in Roméo et Juliette and Sarastro; Dedicatee of several contemporary compositions, and teacher of singing; Pupils include François Le Roux. *Current Management:* Trawick Artists Management, 1926 Broadway, New York, NY 10023, USA.

LOVE, Shirley; Singer (Mezzo-soprano); b. 6 Jan. 1940, Detroit, Michigan, USA. *Education:* Studies with Avery Crew in Detroit and Margaret Harshaw in New York; Continued study with Armen Bayajean in New York City. *Career:* Debut: Metropolitan Opera in 1963 in Die Zauberflöte; Remained in New York for 20 seasons, as Carmen, Dalila, Verdi's Maddalena, Amneris and Emilia, Rossini's Angelina and Rosina, Siebel in Faust, Pauline in The Queen of Spades and in operas by Ravel, Menotti and Bernstein; Guest appearances in Cincinnati, Chicago, Miami and Philadelphia; Sang at Baltimore in 1962, in the premiere of Kagen's Hamlet; Concert appearances in Amsterdam, Bologna and Florence; 3 recital tours of South Africa; Three television performances in the Live from the Met series, Otello, Il Barbiere di Seviglia, Der Rosenkavalier; Recent opera performances include: Albert Herring, Cleveland Opera; Cavalleria Rusticana, Milwaukee Florentine Opera; Festival appearances include: Mostly Mozart, New York; Basically Bach, New York; Saratoga festival (Philadelphia Orchestra); Blossom Festival, Cleveland; Madeira Bach Festival, Portugal. *Recordings:* Diary of One Who Vanished, Janáček; The Rake's Progress, Stravinsky. *Honours:* Arts Achievement Award, Wayne State University, 1990; Honorary Doctorate of Music, University of West Virginia, 1999; Listed in several Who's Who publications. *Address:* c/o Metropolitan Opera, Lincoln Center, New York, NY 10023, USA.

LOVEDAY, Alan (Raymond); Violinist; b. 29 Feb. 1928, England; m. Ruth Stanfield, 1952, 1 s., 1 d. *Education:* Private study; Royal College of Music, prizewinner. *Career:* Debut: Childhood debut, age 4; Debut in England, 1946; Numerous concerts, broadcasts, television appearances, the United Kingdom and abroad; Played with all leading conductors and orchestras; Ranges from Bach, on un-modernised violin, to contemporary music; Professor, Royal College of Music, 1955–72; Soloist, Academy of St Martin-in-the-Fields. *Address:* c/o Academy of St Martin-in-the-Fields, Raine House, Waine Street, Wapping, London E1 9RG, England.

LOWENTHAL, Jerome; Concert Pianist; b. 11 Feb. 1932, Philadelphia, Pennsylvania, USA; m. Ronit Amir, 7 July 1959, 2 d. *Education:* BA, University of Pennsylvania, 1953; MS, Juilliard School of Music, 1956; Premier License de Concert, Ecole Normale de Musique; Piano studies,

Olga Samaroff, William Kapell, Eduard Steuermann, Alfred Cortot. *Career:* Debut: Philadelphia Orchestra, 1945; Appearances with orchestras of: New York, Philadelphia, Boston, Cleveland, Israel Philharmonic, Stockholm, Chicago, Los Angeles, Detroit, Pittsburgh; Conductors: Monteux, Stokowski, Bernstein, Ormandy, Giulini, Tennstedt, Mehta, Ozawa, Barenboim, Comissiona; Tours of Southeast Asia, New Zealand, Latin America, Western Europe, USSR, Poland, Romania; Piano Faculty, Juilliard School, 1990–. *Recordings:* Rorem Concerto No. 3, Louisville-Mester; Tchaikovsky Concerti 1, 2 and 3, London Symphony Orchestra Comissiona; Liszt Opera Paraphrases; Gershwin Concerto in F and Rhapsody in Blue, Utah Symphony Orchestra; Sinding, Sonata and short pieces for solo piano; Liszt Concerto No. 1, No. 3, Totentanz, Malediction: Vancouver Symphony, Commissiona. *Honours:* Laureat, Darmstadt Competition 1957; Busoni Competition 1957; Reine Elizabeth 1960. *Current Management:* Herbert Barrett. *Address:* 865 West End Avenue, Apt 11A, NY 10025, USA.

LOY, Christof; Stage Director; b. 1950, Essen, Germany. *Education:* Folkwang Hochschule, Essen. *Career:* Staged Falstaff at Maastricht, Die Entführung at Freiburg and La Damnation de Faust at Bremen; Mozart's La finta giardiniera at Mannheim, Le nozze di Figaro in Brussels and Idomeneo at Bonn; Manon, Lucia di Lammermoor, Orfeo and Don Carlos for the Deutsche Oper an Rhein, Dusseldorf; Don Giovanni at Graz, Alcina for Hamburg Opera and Carmen in Cologne; Season 2002 with Gluck's Iphigénie en Aulide at Glyndebourne and Ariadne auf Naxos at Covent Garden, London; Further productions include Der Rosekavalier and Eugene Onegin for the Théâtre de la Monnaie, Brussels, and The Queen of Spades at Bremen. *Address:* c/o Royal Opera House (contracts), Covent Garden, London, WC2, England.

LU, Jia; Conductor; b. 1964, Shanghai, China. *Career:* Chief Conductor of the National Youth Orchestra of China, 1987; Further engagements with the Leipzig Gewandhaus, Berlin Symphony nd NDR Hamburg Symphony Orchestras; Chief Conductor and Music Director of the Trieste Opera, 1991–95; Principal Conductor of the Orchestra della Toscana, Principal Conductor of Opera of Genova, Carlo Felice, Florence, appearances with the Santa Cecilia Orchestra, Rome, and at the Bologna Opera; Season 1995–96 included debuts with the Bamberg and Chicago Symphonies, English Chamber Orchestra, Deutsch Oper Berlin, Orchestre National de Lyon and Chamber Orchestra of Europe; Season 1996–97 with the Oslo and St Petersburg Philharmonic Orchestras; Artistic Adviser and Principal Conductor of Norrkoping Symphony Orchestra; Performed with the Stockholm Philharmonic, Hong Kong Philharmonic, Bournemouth Symphony Orchestra, Halle Orchestra and the Malaysian Philharmonic in Kuala Lumpur. *Honours:* Winner, National Chinese Conducting Competition, 1986; First Prize, Pedrotti Competition in Trento, 1990. *Current Management:* IMG Artists, Lovell House, 616 Chiswick High Road, London W4 5RX, England.

LU, Yen; Composer; b. 20 Nov. 1930, Nanking, China. *Education:* Department of Music, Taiwan National Normal University; Mannes College of Music, New York; Department of Music, University of Philadelphia, Pennsylvania, USA. *Career:* Musical World of Lu Yen, concert of his music, National Concert Hall, Taipei, 1995; Festival des Compositeurs Taïwanais, Paris, 1996; Composer, Soochow University, Taipei, Taiwan; mem, American Society of Composers, Authors and Publishers. *Compositions:* Fantasy for Orchestra I, Song of the Sea, 1987; Music for Fifteen Strings, 1987; Song, for solo violoncello, 1997. *Recordings:* Piece for Four Hands, played by Rolf-Peter Wille and Lina Yeh, 1988. *Publications:* Piece for Seven Players, 1973; Concert Piece I, Long T'ao Sha, 1976. *Honours:* Taiwan National Jing Din Prize for Recordings, 1988; Taiwan National Prize for Arts, 1992, 1998. *Address:* Department of Music, Soochow University, Shih Lin, Taipei, Taiwan.

LUBAVIN, Leonid; Singer (Tenor); b. 1962, Krasnodar, Russia. *Education:* State Academy of Theatre, Music and Cinema, Leningrad, 1980–85; State Rimsky-Korsakov Conservatory of St Petersburg, 1989–94. *Career:* Debut: Narraboth in Salome at the Mariinsky Theatre, 1995; Principal Soloist of the Mariinsky Theatre (Kirov Opera), 1995–; Appearances as Faust, Lohengrin, Tamino, Lensky, Fenton and Hermann in The Queen of Spades; Almaviva in Il Barbiere di Siviglia; Tours with the Kirov to Japan, France, Italy and Germany; Iskra in Mazeppa and Yurodivity in Boris Godunov, New York Met, and tour of Latin America, 1998; With New Israel Opera, Tel-Aviv in Falstaff by Verdi as Fenton, 1998; Performed Das Lied von der Erde by Mahler, Mikkeli Festival, Finland, 1997; Other roles include Benvenuto Cellini by Berlioz at the St Petersburg Opera with the Mariinsky Orchestra, and with the Rotterdam Philharmonic, 1999. *Address:* 12 Krasnoarmeiskaya 23-8, St Petersburg 198103, Russia.

LUBBOCK, John; Conductor; b. 18 March 1945, Hertfordshire, England. *Education:* Chorister at St George's Chapel, Windsor then Royal Academy of Music; Conducting studies with Sergiu Celibidache. *Career:* Founder, Camden Chamber Orchestra, 1967 becoming in 1972 the

Orchestra of St John's Smith Square; Frequent concerts at St John's Church in Westminster and on tour in the United Kingdom, Europe, USA and Canada; Guest Conductor with City of Birmingham Symphony, London Philharmonic, BBC Scottish Symphony, Bournemouth Symphony and Sinfonietta, London Mozart Players, Irish Chamber Orchestra, Stuttgart Symphony Orchestra and Netherlands Chamber Orchestra; Works regularly with the Ulster Orchestra and as Principal Conductor with Belfast Philharmonic Society and the Oxford University Orchestra; Worked with the Hallé Orchestra in 1992 and again in 1995; Conducted Berio's Sinfonia at Barbican Hall, 1985 and the premiere of Meirion Bowen's orchestration of Tippett's The Heart's Assurance; Schumann's Requiem and Dvořák's Symphonic Variations at St John's, 1997; Conducted Orchestra of St John's at the London Proms, 2002. *Recordings include:* Arnold Guitar Concerto and Rodrigo Concierto de Aranjuez; Haydn Symphonies Nos 44 and 49; Mendelssohn Symphonies Nos 3 and 4; Schubert Symphony No. 5; Stravinsky Apollo and Orpheus; Tchaikovsky Serenade; Vivaldi Concerti op 10, all with the Orchestra of St John's Smith Square. *Current Management:* Owen-White Management. *Address:* c/o Owen-White Management, 14 Nightingale Lane, London N8 7QU, England.

LUBIN, Steven; Pianist and Musicologist; b. 22 Feb. 1942, New York, USA; m. Wendy Lubin 2 June 1974; two s. *Education:* AB, Harvard Coll.; MS, Juilliard School of Music; PhD, New York Univ.; piano studies with Lisa Grad, Nadia Reisenberg, Seymour Lipkin, Rosina Lhevinne and Beveridge Webster. *Career:* debut, Carnegie Recital Hall, New York, 1977; soloist, Mostly Mozart Festival, Summerfare and other festivals; concert tours in North America and Europe, 1977–; soloist and Conductor of continuing series, the Metropolitan Museum, New York; filmed as soloist in Mozart and Beethoven works for British television documentary, in London and Vienna, 1986; repeated appearances at Mostly Mozart Festival, Lincoln Center, New York, Metropolitan Museum series, Alice Tully Hall, Y series, Kennedy Center, Ravinia Festival; Dir of the Mozartean Players, a chamber group performing on 18th century period instruments; faculty appointments have included Juilliard, Vassar, Cornell; concerto performances with Los Angeles and St Paul Chamber Orchestras, National Symphony, Odessa Philharmonic, Mozarteum Orchestra, Wiener Akademie, as well as the Acad. of Ancient Music. *Recordings:* ongoing cycle of Mozart piano concertos as soloist and conductor; cycle of Beethoven piano concertos, soloist with Christopher Hogwood and the Acad. of Ancient Music, 1987; also works of Mozart, Beethoven, Schubert and Brahms; Schubert's Piano Trios and Trout Quintet; albums of solo and duo sonatas by Mozart; 6 Trios by Haydn with the Mozartean Players. *Current Management:* Hunstein Artist Services, 65 W 90th Street, Suite 13F, New York, NY, USA. *Telephone:* (212) 724-2693. *Address:* Conservatory of Music, School of the Arts, SUNY, Purchase, NY 10577, USA.

LUBLIN, Eliane; Singer (Soprano); b. 10 April 1938, Paris, France. *Education:* Studied in Paris then at the Verdi Conservatory in Paris. *Career:* Debut: Aix-en-Provence as Debussy's Mélisande; Paris Opéra-Comique; Monte Carlo Opéra in Menotti's The Medium; Paris Opéra from 1969 in Les Dialogues des Carmélites, as Massenet's Manon, Marguerite in Faust, Ellen Orford in Peter Grimes and in the 1981 French premiere of Ligeti's Le Grande Macabre. *Recordings include:* Sapho by Gounod. *Address:* c/o Théâtre National de L'Opéra de Paris, 8 Rue Scribe, F75009 Paris, France.

LUBOTSKY, Mark; Violinist; b. 18 May 1931, Leningrad, Russia. *Education:* Moscow Conservatory from 1953, with A Yampolsky and D Oistrakh. *Career:* Debut: Bolshoi Hall of Moscow Conservatory, 1950, Tchaikovsky Concerto; Solo recitals and concerts with major orchestras in the United Kingdom, Scandinavia, Germany, Netherlands, Italy, USA, Australia, Japan and Israel; Many television and radio performances; Teacher, Gnessin Institute, Moscow, 1967–76; Professor, Sweelinck Conservatory, Amsterdam, 1976–; Professor, Hochschule für Musik, Hamburg, 1986–; British debut, 1970, Britten's Concerto at the Promenade Concerts. *Recordings:* Concertos from the Baroque by Mozart, Britten, Schnittke, Tubin; Solo Sonatas by Bach; Sonatas by Brahms, Mozart, Shostakovich, Schnittke. *Honours:* Mozart International Competition, Salzburg, 1956; Tchaikovsky International Copetition, Moscow, 1958. *Current Management:* Encore Concerts Ltd. *Address:* Caversham Grange, The Warren, Mapledurham, Berkshire RG4 7TQ, England.

LUCA, Sergiu; Violinist and Teacher; b. 4 April 1943, Bucharest, Romania. *Education:* Studied at the Bucharest Conservatory 1948–50, with Max Rostal in London and at the Berne Conservatory; Curtis Institute with Galamian. *Career:* Debut: With the Philadelphia Orchestra conducted by Eugene Ormany, playing the Sibelius Concerto, 1965; Founder and Director, Chamber Music Northwest Festival in Portland, 1971–80; Professor of violin at the University of Illinois 1980–83; Starling Professor of Classical Violin and Violinist-in-Residence at the Shepherd School of Music, Houston, 1983–; Music Director of the Texas Chamber Orchestra, 1983–88; Founder and

General Director of Da Camera, in Houston, Texas, an Arts Organisation producing approximately 50 concerts a year of small ensemble repertoir, from Renaissance to Jazz, 1988–; Solo performances in the USA, Europe, and Japan; Recitals of the unaccompanied works of Bach with authentic instrument and bow; Mozart sonatas with Malcolm Bilson. *Recordings:* Bach sonatas and partitas for unaccompanied violin; Bartók works for violin and piano. *Honours:* Finalist, 1965 Leventritt Competition; Winner, 1965 Philadelphia Orchestra Youth Auditions. *Address:* Shepherd School of Music, Rice University, Houston, Texas, USA.

LUCAS OGDON, Brenda; Pianist and Teacher; b. 23 Nov. 1935, Cheshire, England; m. John Ogdon (deceased); one s. one d. *Education:* Convent of the Nativity, Romiley, Cheshire, Royal Northern Coll. of Music, Manchester, Mozarteum, Salzburg. *Career:* solo career, including debut in Grieg; Piano Concerto with Liverpool Philharmonic Orchestra 1956; duo piano career with John Ogdon; appearances in the 1960s included Edinburgh Festival 1962, 1963, 23rd Cheltenham Festival, Aldeburgh Festival, Sintra Festival, the Royal Concert at Royal Festival Hall with Andre Previn and Houston Symphony Orchestra 1969; Hong Kong, solo appearances 1969; mem. Incorporated Soc. of Musicians. *Recordings:* Bartók: Sonata for 2 Pianos 1968, Mendelssohn: Concerto for 2 Pianos 1970, Rachmaninov: Suites Nos 1 and 2 1975, Saint-Saëns: Carnival of the Animals 1972, Schoenberg: Chamber Symphony 1974, Liszt: Concerto Pathétique, works by Schumann 1972, Brahms: Hungarian Dances, Arensky: Waltz, Bach, Milhaud, Stravinsky, Dvořák 1989. *Publications:* 'Virtuoso' The Story of John Ogdon. *Honours:* Gold Medal of Associated Board 1949, Harriet Cohen Silver medal Royal Northern Coll. of Music 1956, ARMCM Teacher's Distinction, ARMCM Performers. *Current Management:* J. Audrey Ellison, 135 Stevenage Road, London, SW6 6PB, England. *Telephone:* (20) 7381-9751 (office). *Fax:* (20) 7381-2406 (office). *E-mail:* Audrey@Ellison-Intl.Freeserve.co.uk (office).

LUCHETTI, Veriano; Singer (Tenor); b. 12 March 1939, Viterbo, Italy; m. Mietta Sighele. *Education:* Studied with Enrico Piazza and in Milan and Rome. *Career:* Debut: Wexford festival 1965, as Alfredo in La Traviata; Spoleto 1967, as Loris in Fedora and in Donizetti's Il Furioso all'isola di San Domingo; Guest appearances in Palermo, Parma, Venice, Vienna, Munich, Paris, Mexico City, Dallas and Houston; Maggio Musicale Florence 1971, 1974, in L'Africaine and Agnes von Hohenstaufen by Spontini; La Scala 1975, in Verdi's Attila; Covent Garden 1973–76, as Rodolfo, Pinkerton and Gabriele Adorno in Simon Boccanegra; Aix-en-Provence 1976, as Jason in Cherubini's Médée, Verona 1984, in Verdi's I Lombardi; Vienna Staatsoper 1988, as Foresto in Attila; Sang Radames at Turin 1990, Don José at the Verona Arena; Also heard in concert, Verdi's Requiem at Covent Garden, 1976. *Recordings:* Médée, Hungaroton; Nabucco and Verdi Requiem; Piccinni's La Cecchina; Griselda by Scarlatti; 2 further recordings of the Verdi Requiem.

LUCIER, Alvin; Composer; b. 14 May 1931, Nashua, New Hampshire, USA; m. Wendy Wallbank Stokes, 27 Aug 1979, 1 d. *Education:* The Portsmouth Abbey School; BA, Yale University, 1954; MFA, Brandeis University, 1960; Fulbright Scholarship, Rome, 1960–62. *Career:* Choral Director, Brandeis University, 1962–70; Professor of Music, Wesleyan University, 1970–, Chair of Department, 1979–84; Co-Founder, Sonic Arts Union, 1966–77; Music Director, Viola Farber Dance Company, 1972–77. *Compositions:* Action Music for Piano, 1962, BMI Canada; Music for Solo Performer, 1965 for enormously amplified brain waves and percussion; Vespers, 1967; Chambers, 1968; I Am Sitting in a Room, 1970; Still and Moving Lines of Silence in Families of Hyperbolas, 1972–; Bird and Person Dyning, 1975; Music in A Long Thin Wire 1977; Crossings, 1982–84; Seesaw, 1984; Sound on Paper, 1985; Fideliotrio for viola, cello and piano, 1987; Navigations for string quartet, 1992; Small Waves for piano, trombone and string quartet, 1997; Cassiopeia for orchestra, 1998; Diamonds, for 1, 2 or 3 orchestras, 1999; Electro-acoustic works, including Amplifier and Reflector, 1991; Sound Installations, Empty Vessels, Resonant Objects and Sound on Glass, 1997. *Recordings include:* Bird and Person Dyning; The Duke of York, Cramps Records, Italy. *Publications:* Chambers in collaboration with Douglas Simon, 1980. *Contributions:* Professional publications. *Address:* Music Department, Wesleyan University, Middletown, CT 06457, USA.

LUCIUK, Juliusz (Mieczyslaw); Composer; b. 1 Jan. 1927, Brzeznica, Poland; m. Domicela Dabrowska, 10 Nov 1956, 2 d. *Education:* Academy of Music, Kraków; Studied with Nadia Boulanger and Max Deutsch in Paris, 1958–59. *Career:* Debut: 3 songs performed, 1954; Various works recorded by Polish Radio, BBC, Sender freies Berlin, ORTF France, Italian Palermo, Netherlands Radio. *Compositions:* Numerous including: 3 Passion Songs for soprano and organ; Image, Preludes and Tripticum Paschale for organ; Sonata for bassoon and piano; Variations for cello and piano; Monologues and Dialogues for soprano recorders; Ballets: Niobe; Death of Euridice; Medea; L'Amour d'Orphée, opera-ballet; Demiurgos, chamber opera; Works for solo voice and chamber ensemble: Floral dream; Le Souffle du Vent; Portraits Lyriques; Works for solo voice and chamber orchestra: Tool of the Light; Poéme de Loire; Wings and Hands; Oratorios: St Francis of Assisi; Gesang am Brunnen; Sanctus Adalbertus flos purpureus; Adalbertus Oratorio, 1997; Christus Pantocrator; Polish Litany, The Polish Mass for mezzo-soprano, mixed choir and wind orchestra; Choral works include: 4 Antiphonae and vespera in Assumptione Beatae Mariae Virginis for men's choir; The Mass for men's choir and organ; The Mass, Hymnus de Caritate and Magnificat for mixed choir; Apocalypsis for 4 soloists and mixed choir; Adalbertus Oratorio, 1997; Orchestral Works: Four Symphonic Sketches; Symphonic Allegro; Composition for Four Orchestral Ensembles; Speranza Sinfonica; Lamentazioni in memoriam Grazyna Bacewicz; Warsaw Legend (Quasi Cradle Song); Osiers, 5 pieces for string chamber orchestra; Concertino for piano and small symphony orchestra; Concerto for double bass and symphony orchestra; Hommage for strings, 1993. *Address:* Os Kolorowe 6 m 10, 31-938 Kraków, Poland.

LUCKE, Hannfried; Organist; b. 27 Feb. 1964, Freiburg, Germany. *Education:* Hochschule für Musik, Freiburg; Mozarteum Salzburg and Conservatoire de Musique, Geneva. *Career:* International concert organist with concert performances and broadcasting recordings in numerous countries in Europe, USA, Canada, Japan, Hong Kong and Australia; Professor, University Mozarteum Salzburg, 2000. *Recordings:* Major organ works of JS Bach; Organ works of the romantic period of instruments in Europe, USA and Japan. *Honours:* Prize of honour, Austrian Minister for Cultural Affairs; Premier Prix at Conservatoire de musique, Geneva. *Address:* Meierhofstrasse 44, FL-9495 Triesen, Principality of Liechtenstein.

LUCKY, Stepán; Composer; b. 20 Jan. 1919, Zilina, Czechoslovakia. *Education:* Prague Conservatory, 1936–39; Studied with Ridky, 1945–47; Musicology at Prague University, 1945–48; PhD. *Career:* Member of Czech resistance; Committee member of Pritomnost Association for Contemporary Music, 1946–48; Music Critic for Prague papers; Head of Music for Czech television, 1954–58; Taught at Prague Academy, 1956–61; PhD, Charles University Prague, 1990. *Compositions:* Divertimento for 3 Trombones and Strings, 1946; Cello Concerto, 1946; Piano Concerto, 1947; Opera Midnight Surprise, 1959; Violin Concerto, 1965; Octet for strings, 1970; Double Concerto for violin, piano and orchestra, 1971; Nenia for violin, cello and orchestra (dedicated to the victims of the Second World War), 1974; Concerto for orchestra, 1976; Fantasia Concertante for bass clarinet, piano and orchestra, 1983; Wind Quintet, 1985; Sonatina for 2 guitars, 1986; Much film music, 1950–88; Chamber and Instrumental music. *Honours:* State Order for Outstanding Accomplishment, 1969; Artist of Merit, 1972. *Address:* Lomena 24, 162 00 Prague 6, Czech Republic.

LUDWIG, Christa; Singer (mezzo-soprano); b. 16 March 1924, Berlin, Germany; m. (1) Walter Berry, (2) Paul-Emile Deiber 1972, 1 s. *Education:* German Abitur, 1944; Studies with mother, Eugenie Besalla, singing. *Career:* Debut: Frankfurt, Germany, 1946; After Frankfurt, Darmstadt, Hanover; Vienna Staatsoper, 1955–94; All important Opera Houses, London Covent Garden, Amneris and Carmen; Scala, Milan; Tokyo; Chicago; San Francisco; Berlin; Munich; Some opera and concerts, television, films, concerts all over the world; Salzburg Festival from 1954, debut as Cherubino, sang Mistress Quickly in Falstaff 1981; Metropolitan Opera 1959–90, as the Dyer's Wife in Die Frau ohne Schatten, Cherubino, Dido in Les Troyens, Fricka and Waltraute in the Ring, Ortrud, Kundry, Charlotte, Clytemnestra and Marschallin; Sang in concert performances of Bernstein's Candide at the Barbican, 1989, Clytemnestra in Vienna, Berlin, New York, Paris and Innsbruck 1990; Other roles included Eboli, Leonore, Dalila, Lady Macbeth, Marie in Wozzeck and Ottavia in L'Incoronazione di Poppea; Gave Lieder recital at the Wigmore Hall, London, 1991, Von Einem, Wolf, Strauss and Schubert; Farewell recitals in London and the USA, 1993; Retired after singing Clytemnestra in Vienna, 1994. *Recordings:* with Böhm: Così fan tutte, Marriage of Figaro, Missa Solemnis; with Karajan: Götterdämmerung, Tristan and Isolde, Verdi's Requiem, Das Lied von der Erde; Rosenkavalier-Octavian; with Bernstein: Rosenkavalier–Marschallin, Das Lied von der Erde, Brahms–Recital; With Giulini: Verdi's Requiem; With Klemperer: Wesendonck Lieder, Das Lied von der Erde; Farewell to Salzburg, recital 1993. *Publications:* Paul Lorenz; Christa Ludwig, Walter Berry; Eine Kunstler Biographie. *Honours:* 1st prize Radio Frankfurt, 1948, 1962; Kammersängerin Staatsoper Wien, 1962; Osterreich Grosses Verdienstkreuz 1 Classe für Kunst and Wissenschaft, 1980; Ehrenmitglied Staatsoper Wien and Goldenen Ehrenring Ehrenmitglied Konzerthaus Wien-Silberne Rose der Wiener Philharmoniker, 1980; Wolf, Mozart, Mahler Medals; Grammy Awards and many other different prizes; Chevalier Legion D'Honneur, France, 1989; Commandeur de L'Ordre des Arts Et des Lettres, France, 1989; Medaille Ville de Paris and Shibuya-Preis, Japan, 1993; Echo Deutscher Schallplattenpreis and Berliner Bär and Karajan-Preis, 1994; Musician of Year, Musical America, 1994; Professor E H Stadt Berlin and

Ehrenmitglied Wiener Philharmoniker, 1995. *Address:* La Guestière, 1458 Ter, Chemin des Colles, 06740 Chateauneuf de Grasse, France.

LUFF, Enid; Composer; b. 21 Feb. 1935, Ebbw Vale, Glamorgan, Wales; m. Alan Luff, 30 June 1956, 3 s., 1 d. *Education:* MA (Cantab), 1957; LRAM, Piano Teacher's Diploma, 1965; BMus, Honours, 1971, MMus, 1974, University of Wales; Advanced Composition with Elisabeth Lutyens and Franco Donatoni. *Career:* Composer, 1971–; Runs Primavera self-publishing company with Julia Usher, 1980–; mem, British Academy of Composers and Songwriters; PRS; MCPS; Women in Music; Cyfansoddwyr Cymru/Composers of Wales. *Compositions:* Four piano pieces, Tapestries for chamber group; Symphony No. 1; Mathematical Dream, solo harp; Wind Quintet: The Coastal Road; Sheila NaGig, for soprano and pianoforte; Dream Time for Bells for chamber group; Sky Whispering for solo piano; Sonata: Storm Tide for piano; Come the Morning, for chamber ensemble; Peregrinus, Trilogy for organ, 1991; Listening for the Roar of the Sun, for oboe, speaker, dance and slide projection, 1992; Symphony 2, 1994; The Glass Wall for solo cello, dancers and electronic tape, 1996. *Recordings:* Hierusalem, for chamber ensemble, 2000; Heaven's Bird for chamber ensemble, 2002;Several works recorded on BBC Recordings and Danish Radio Recordings. *Address:* 12 Heol Tyn y Cae, Cardiff, CF14 6DJ, Wales. *E-mail:* enidluff@globalnet.co.uk.

LUGANSKY, Nikolai L.; Russian pianist; b. 26 April 1972, Moscow; s. of Lev Borisovich Lugansky and Anna Nikolayevna Luganskaya; m. Lada Borisovna Luganskaya; one s. one d. *Education:* Moscow State Conservatory. *Career:* wide repertoire comprises over 40 piano concertos and music from Bach to modern composers; ensemblist and interpreter of chamber music; performances in Russia and abroad in Australia, Austria, Belgium, Brazil, Canada, England, France, Germany Italy, Japan and elsewhere, including at the Royal Festival Hall and Wigmore Hall in London, the Gaveau and Louvre in Paris, Conservatoria Verdi in Milan, Gasteig in Munich, Concertgebouw in Amsterdam, Alte Oper in Frankfurt. *Recordings include:* some 25 albums. *Honours:* first prize All-Union students' competition Tbilisi Georgia 1988, silver medal Bach Int. Competition, Leipzig, Germany 1988, second prize Rachmaninov Competition, Moscow 1990, first prize Tchaikovsky Int. Competition, Moscow 1994, Terence Judd award for the most promising pianist of a generation 1995. *Address:* Kosygina str. 2, apt 2, Moscow 119334, Russia (home). *Telephone:* (095) 137-18-36 (home).

LUITZ, Josef; cellist; b. 2 Aug. 1934, Vienna, Austria; m. Sonja Edelgard Mayerhofer 1962; one s. one d. *Education:* School for Musical Instrument Makers, Vienna, Konservatorium, Vienna with W. Kleinecke; masterclass with N. Hubner in Santiago de Compostella. *Career:* debut at Musikverein, Vienna, 1957; first Cellist, Tonkuenstler Orchestra, 1957–61; Solo Cellist, 1962–; Member, Haydn Quartet, 1965–72, Ensemble Kontrapunkta, 1968–75; Philharmonia Quintet, 1971–77; Professor, Cello, Konservatorium, Vienna, 1972–; Chairman, Tonkuenstler Chamber Orchestra, 1978–; Concordia Trio, 1979–; Chairman, International Chamber Music Festival, Austria, 1978–. *Recordings:* Chamber Music Series for Musical Heritage Society Inc, New York; Spohr Octet with Vienna Octet; With Tonkuenstler Chamber Orchestra; many Radio Productions as Soloist. *Honours:* Professor, Austrian Government, 1985.

LUKACS, Ervin; Conductor; b. 1928, Budapest, Hungary. *Education:* Bela Bart ók Conservatory, 1950–51; Conductor's Diploma, Ferenc Liszt Academy of Music, 1956. *Career:* Conductor, Hungarian People's Army Artistic Ensemble, 1954–56; Principal Conductor, Miskolc Opera House and Miskolc Symphony Orchestra, 1956–57; Professor, Department of Conducting, Liszt Academy of Music, Budapest, 1956–59; Conductor, Budapest State Opera, 1957–; Masterclass held by Franco Ferrara in Venice and Accademia di Santa Cecilia, Rome, Italy, 1961, 1962; As conductor has made several extensive tours with Hungarian State Symphony Orchestra. *Honours:* 2st Prize, Santa Cecilia International Concours for Conductors, 1962; Liszt Prize; Merited Artist of the Hungarian People's Republic. *Address:* c/o Hungarian State Opera, Budapest, Hungary.

LUKAS, Laslo; Singer (Baritone); b. 1964, Budapest, Hungary. *Education:* Franz Liszt Music Academy, Budapest. *Career:* Sang with the Budapest State Opera four seasons, then with the Prague State Opera; Trier Opera from 1991, including Tcherikov in the first production this century of Zemlinsky's first opera, Sarema; Guest appearances in Germany and elsewhere as Rigoletto, Scarpia, Jochanaan in Salome, Macbeth, Posa, Count Luna, Kaspar, Cardillac, and the Man in Hindemith's Mörder, Hoffnung der Frauen; Simone in Zemlinsky's Florentinische Tragödie, at the Prague State Opera. *Recordings include:* Sarema (Koch International). *Address:* c/o Theater der Stadt Trier, Am Augustinerhof, 5500 Trier, Germany.

LUKAS, Zdenek; Composer; b. 21 Aug. 1928, Prague, Czechoslovakia. *Education:* Tutorials led by Miloslav Kabelac, 1961–70. *Career:* Worked for Czech Radio 1953–65; Choral conductor in Plzeň 1955–65; Teacher,

Prague Conservatoire' Choirmaster, Czechoslovak State Song and Dance Ensemble; Freelance Composer from 1965. *Compositions include:* Radio Opera Long Live the Dead Man 1968; Home Carnival, one-act opera 1968; Orchestral: Piano Concerto 1955; Violin Concerto 1956; Cello Concerto 1957; 6 Symphonies 1960–91; Concerto Grosso for string quartet and orchestra 1964; Symphonietta solemnis 1965; Sonata concertata for piano, winds and percussion 1966; Concerto for violin, viola and orchestra 1969; Variations for piano and orchestra 1970; Postludium for strings 1970; Concertos for Bassoon (1976), Clarinet (1976), Harpsichord (1980), Violin (1980), Flute (1981), Viola (1983), Piano (1984), Cello (1986), Horn (1989); Piano concerto No. 3, 1993; Opera, Revenge for Revenge, 1986; Choral music includes Adam a Eva, oratorio 1969; The Spring is Coming, cycle for male choir and solo violin, 1975; The Message of Music, four-voice girls' choir with piano accompaniment, 1982; Chamber: 3 String Quartets 1960, 1965, 1973; Partita semplice for 4 violins and piano 1964; Wind Quintet 1969; Saxophone Quartet 1970; Electronic work You do not Kill 1971; Trio for Violin, Violoncello and Piano, Op 106, 1974; Prague Pastorale for Organ Solo, Op 158, 1981; Rondo for Bassoon and Piano, Op 168, 1981; 3 Duets for 2 Violins Op 188, 1984; Duo di basso, violoncello and double-bass, op 210, 1987; 4th String Quartet Op 213, 1987. *Address:* Murmanska 13, 100 00 Prague 10, Czech Republic.

LUKE, Ray; Composer and Conductor; b. 30 May 1926, Fort Worth, Texas, USA. *Education:* Studied at Texas Christian University and at the Eastman School of Music, Rochester with Bernard Rogers. *Career:* Taught at the East Texas State College 1951–62; Oklahoma City University from 1962; Associate Conductor, Oklahoma City Symphony 1969–73; Principal Guest Conductor 1974–78. *Compositions:* Opera Medea 1979; Ballet Tapestry 1975; 4 Symphonies 1959–70; Bassoon Concerto, 1965; 2 Suites for Orchestra 1958, 1967; Symphonic Dialogues for violin, oboe and orchestra 1965; String Quartet 1966; Piano Concerto 1970; Septet 1979; Operas Drowne's Wooden Image (1994) and Mrs Bullfrog (1994). *Honours:* Grand Prix Gold Medal Queen Elisabeth of the Belgians Competition, for Piano Concerto, 1970. *Address:* c/o ASCAP, ASCAP Building, 1 Lincoln Plaza, NY 10023, USA.

LUKHANIN, Viacheslav; Singer (Bass); b. 1960, Maimi-Sai, Russia. *Education:* Graduated Frunze Conservatoire, Kirgizia, 1985. *Career:* Sang at opera houses in Frunze, Novosibirsk and St Petersburg, 1985–94; Mariinsky Theatre, St Petersburg, from 1994 as Mozart's Figario, Verdi's Grand Inquisitor and King of Egypt, Storm Wind in Kshchei the Immortal by Rimsky-Korsakov and the Priest in Katerina Izmailova; European tours with the Mussorgsky Opera and Kirov Opera companies, St Petersburg; Sang in the British premiere of Prokofiev's Semyon Kotko, with the Kirov at Covent Garden, 2000; other roles include Angelotti in Tosca and the Bonze in Madama Butterfly. *Honours:* Prizewinner, Glinka National vocal and Chaliapin International Competitions, 1987–89. *Address:* c/o Kirov Opera Mariinsky Theatre, Theatre Square, St Petersburg, Russia.

LUKOMSKA, Halina; Singer (Soprano); b. 29 May 1929, Suchedniow, Poland. *Education:* State Opera High School, Poznan, 1951–54; Warsaw State Music High School; Further study with Toti dal Monte in Venice. *Career:* Wide appearances as concert singer from 1960, notably in works by Webern, Serocki, Boulez, (Pli selon Pli), Maderna, Schoenberg, Nono and Lutoslawski; Festival engagements at Edinburgh, Perugia, Vienna, Toulouse, and Warsaw; Holland Festival 1967, in Monteverdi's Orfeo; North American tour with Cleveland Orchestra 1973. *Recordings:* Works by Berg (Altenberglieder) and Webern; Pli Selon Pli; Confitebor Domine by JC Bach; Boris Godunov. *Honours:* Winner, 's-Hertogenbosch Competition, 1956.

LUMSDAINE, David; Composer; b. 31 Oct. 1931, Sydney, New South Wales, Australia; m. Nicola LeFanu, 1 s., 2 d. *Education:* NSW Conservatorium of Music; Sydney University; Studied with Matyas Seiber, Royal Academy of Music, London; D.Mus, 1981. *Career:* Composer; Teacher of Composition and Music Editor, London, England; Lecturer in Music, Durham University, 1970–; Founder, Electronic Music Studio, Durham; Lecturer, King's College, London, 1981–93. *Compositions include:* Orchestral: Episodes, 1969, Looking Glass Music, 1970, Sunflower for chamber orchestra, 1975, Shoalhaven, 1982, Mandela V for symphony orchestra, 1988; Vocal: The Ballad of Perse O'Reilly for tenor, male chorus and 2 pianos, 1953–81, Annotations of Auschwitz for soprano and ensemble, 1964, 1970, Aria for Edward Eyre for soprano and double bass soloists, chamber ensemble, narrators, tape and electronics, 1972, Tides for narrator, 12 voices and percussion, Caliban Impromptu for piano trio, tape and electronica, 1972, Empty Sky, Mootwingee for ensemble, 1986, Round Dance for sitar, table, flute, cello and keyboard, 1989; Piano Works: Canberra, piano solo, 1980, Wild Ride to Heaven, with Nicola LeFanu, for electronics, 1980; Garden of Earthly Delights, 1992; Kalí Dances for ensemble, 1994. *Current Management:* Sounds Australian, PO Box N690, Grosvenor Place, Sydney, NSW 2000, Australia; University of York Music Press, YO10 5 DD. *Address:* 5 Holly Terrace, York YO1 4 DS, England.

LUMSDEN, Sir David James, Kt, MA, MusB, DPhil; academic; b. 19 March 1928, Newcastle upon Tyne, England; m. Sheila Gladys Daniels 1951; two s. two d. *Education:* Selwyn Coll., Cambridge. *Career:* organist at New Coll., Oxford; Rector, Chori, Southwell Minster; founder and conductor of Nottingham Bach Soc.; Dir of Music, Keele Univ.; Visiting Prof. at Yale Univ.; Principal, Royal Scottish Acad. of Music and Drama 1978–82 and Royal Acad. of Music 1982–93; Hugh Porter Lecturer at Union Theologial Seminary, NY 1967; mem. Incorporated Soc. of Musicians (pres. 1984–85), Royal Coll. of Organists (pres. 1986–88), Incorporated Asscn of Organists (pres. 1966–68), Church Music Soc. (hon. ed. 1970–73), National Youth Orchestra of Great Britain (chair. 1985–94), Early Music Soc. (chair. 1985–89), Scottish Opera (mem. of bd 1977–83), ENO (mem. of bd 1983–88). *Publications:* An Anthology of English Lute Music 1954, Thomas Robinson's Schoole Musike 1603 1971; contrib. to The Listener, The Score, Music and Letters, Galpin Society Journal, La Luth et sa Musique, La musique de la Renaissance. *Honours:* Hon. DLitt 1990; Hon. Fellow, Selwyn Coll., Cambridge 1986, Kings Coll., London 1991, New Coll., Oxford 1996. *Address:* 26 Wyke Mark, Dean Lane, Winchester, Hampshire SO22 5DJ, England.

LUMSDEN, Ronald; Pianist; b. 28 May 1938, Dundee, England; m. (1) Annon Lee Silver, deceased, 1 s., (2) Alison Paice Hill, 1975, 1 s., 1 d. *Education:* Harris Academy, Dundee; Royal College of Music, London; ARCM; LRAM. *Career:* Pianist in Residence, University of Southampton, 1965–68; Henry Wood Promenade Concerts, 1973, 1974; Soloist in Arts Council Contemporary Music Network, 1974–76; Visiting Piano teacher, 1976–; Honorary Director of School of Music, 1984–, Reading University; Frequent broadcasts and recitals in United Kingdom; mem, Executive Committee, Society for Promotion of New Music, 1975–78; Incorporated Society of Music; European Piano Teachers Association. *Recordings:* Messiaen's Canteyodjaya for Gaudeamus Foundation; Open University's Modern Music. *Contributions:* Bartók, in Makers of Modern Culture, 1981. *Honours:* 1st Prize Winner, International Competiton for Interpreters of Contemporary Music, Utrecht, 1968. *Address:* 50 Grosvenor Road, Caversham, Reading, Berkshire, RG4 0EN, England.

LUND, Tamara; Singer (Soprano); b. 1941, Finland. *Career:* Sang with Finnish National Opera from 1967, notably in the 1968 local premiere of Berg's Lulu, title role; Member of the Teater am Gärtnerplatz Munich from 1973, with tours to Berlin, Komische Oper and Theater des Westerns; The Theater an der Wien, Vienna; Engaged at the Zürich Opera, 1979–83; Helsinki 1973, as Daphne in the premiere of Apollo and Marsyas by Rautavaara; Other roles have included Carmen, Musetta, Janáček's Vixen and Jenny in Aufsteig und Fall der Stadt Mahagonny; Sang Juno in the incidental music to The Tempest by Sibelius, Savonlinna 1986; Many appearances in operetta.

LUNDBERG, Gunnar; Singer (Baritone); b. 1958, Sweden. *Education:* Studied at the State Opera School Stockholm and in Salzburg. *Career:* Debut: Vadstena Accademy, 1984; Member of the Royal Opera Stockholm from 1988, notably as the Herald in Lohengrin, Escamillo, Valentin, Mozart's Count and Figaro, Don Giovanni and Rossini's Figaro; Season 1991 as Barelli in the European premiere of The Aspern Papers by Argento; Engaged for seasons 1992–94 as Silvio in Pagliacci and Marcello in La Bohème; Sang in Carmina Burana at the Stockholm Royal Opera, 1998; Concert repertoire includes Ein Deutsches Requiem, the Bach Passions and B Minor Mass; St John Passion at the 1993 Lucerne Easter Festival.

LUNDBERG, Mark; Singer (Tenor); b. 1953, USA. *Education:* Studied with Margaret Harshaw and in New York. *Career:* Santa Fe, 1988, in the American premieres of Die schwarze Maske by Penderecki and Strauss's Friedenstag; Florestan with Cleveland Opera; Nice Opéra as Bacchus in Ariadne auf Naxos, Dortmund, 1995, as Siegmund and Siegfried; Deutsche Oper Berlin, 1995, as Siegmund; Concerts include Das Lied von der Erde, by Mahler. *Honours:* James McCracken Award. *Address:* c/o Deutsche Oper Berlin, Richard Wagnerstrasse 10, 10585 Berlin, Germany.

LUNDBORG, Charles (Erik); Composer; b. 31 Jan. 1948, Helena, Montana, USA; m. Zinta Bibelnieks, 14 Nov 1981. *Education:* BM, New England Conservatory of Music, Boston; MA, 1974, DMA, 1985, Columbia University. *Career:* Performances and Commissions by Houston Symphony Orchestra, American Composers Orchestra, Ursula Oppens, Piano, Speculum Musicae, Group for Contemporary Music, Parnassus, New Music Consort, Pittsburgh, New Music Ensemble, Light Fantastic Players, Composers Ensemble, Light Fantastic Players, Composers Ensemble, New Jersey Percussion Ensemble, many others; mem, BMI; American Composers Alliance, Board Member, 1980–82; Board, ISCM, League of Composers, 1975–78. *Compositions:* Passacaglia, Two Symphonies, from Music Forever, No. 2 Piano Concerto; Soundsoup; Solotremolos. *Recordings:* Passacaglia from Music Forever No. 2; Soundsoup. *Contributions:* Milton Babbitt, String Quartet No. 3,

Contemporary Music Newsletter, 1974. *Honours:* Guggenheim, 1976–77; NEA Fellowships, 1975, 1981, 1983. *Address:* 2465 Palisade Ave, 8F, Riverdale, NY 10463, USA.

LUNDGREN, Stefan; Swedish lutenist and composer; b. 5 May 1949, Hogsby; m. Henrike Brose 1985. *Education:* Music School, Oskarshann, Sweden, Lund University, Schola Cantonum Basiliensis, Basel. *Career:* teacher, performer, composer and publisher; Ed., Lute Music 1979–; Dir, annual lute course, Ried im Zillertal, Austria 1983–; teacher of summer courses, Svenska Gitarr och lutasallskapets 1985. *Compositions:* Sonatas 1–3 for solo lute 1981–84, Sonata No. 4 for solo lute 1986. *Publications:* New School for the Renaissance Lute 1985, 50 English Duets (publisher, four vols), Charles Mouton, Suite in G Minor, J. A. Losy Two Suites, Little Book for Lute 1: Renaissance Lute, Little Book for Lute 2: Baroque Lute, J. S. Bach Complete Works for Lute. *Address:* c/o Lundgren Edition, Postfach 40 11 32, 80711 München, Germany. *Website:* www.luteonline.de.

LUNDSTEN, Ralph; Swedish composer, film-maker and artist; b. 6 Oct. 1936, Ersnäs. *Career:* owner, Andromeda picture and electronic music studio 1959–worked, Opera House in Stockholm and Oslo, Modern Museum and Nat. Museum in Stockholm, Louvre and Biennale in Paris, Triennale in Milan, Museum of Contemporary Crafts in New York; has made 12 short films; Cultural Ambassador for Luleå 1999, London Diplomatic Acad. 2000. *Art Exhibitions include:* portrait exhibition at Music Museum, Stockholm 1991–92, 2000. *Compositions include:* Nordic Nature Symphonies: No. 1 The Water Sprite, No. 2 Johannes and the Lady of the Woods, No. 3 A Midwinter Saga, No. 4 A Summer Saga, No. 5 Bewitched, No. 6 Landscape of Dreams, No. 7 The Seasons; Erik XIV (ballet), Gustav III (ballet), Cosmic Love, Ourfather, Nightmare, Horrorscope, Shangri-La, Universe, Discophrenia, Alpha Ralpha Boulevard, Paradise Symphony, The New Age, Pop Age, Music for Relaxation and Meditation, Cosmic Phantazy, The Dream Master, The Gate of Time, The Ages of Man, Sea Symphony, Mindscape Music, Nordic Light, The Symphony of Joy, The Symphony of Light, The Symphony of Love, In Time and Space, Andromedian Tales, Happy Earthday, Inspiration, At the Fountain of Youth, A Vagabond of the Soul. *Honours:* Grand Prix Biennale, Paris 1967, Swedish Film Inst. Prize 1964–67, Schwingungen Preis, Germany 1997, Schwingungen Preis 1999. *Address:* Frankenburgs väg 1, 132 42 Saltsjö-Boo, Sweden. *E-mail:* ralph.lundsten@andromeda.se. *Website:* www.andromeda.se.

LUNELL, Hans; Composer and Computer Scientist; b. 12 April 1944, Skellefteå, Sweden. *Education:* Fil kand, Uppsala University, 1967; Fil dr (PhD), Linköping University, 1983; Musicology, Uppsala University; Music Theory and Composition, Royal College of Music, Stockholm; Piano study with Greta Erikson. *Career:* Assistant Professor, Linköping University, 1971–83; Associate Professor, KTH, Stockholm, 1983–86; Director of Institute for Electro-Acoustic Music in Sweden, 1989–93; mem, Society of Swedish Composers; International Confederation for Electro-Acoustic Music; STIM. *Compositions:* Intensità for piano trio, 1981–82; La notte in Sicilia for soprano, bass clarinet and vibraphone, 1984; Affinities I for piano solo, 1985. *Contributions:* Numerous articles, many to Nutida Musik. *Address:* Teknikvägen 105, 175 75 Järfälla, Sweden.

LUNETTA, Stanley; Composer; b. 5 June 1937, Sacramento, California, USA. *Education:* BA Sacramento State College; MA University of CA at Davis, with Jerome Rosen and Larry Austin; Further study with John Cage, David Tudor and Karlheinz Stockhausen. *Career:* Founded New Music Ensemble, 1963; Editor of Source: Music of the Avant Garde 1971–77; Percussionist and teacher in Sacramento. *Compositions:* Many Things for Orchestra 1966; Piano Music 1966; A Piece for Bandoneon and Strings 1966; Free Music 1967; Ta Ta for chorus and mailing tubes 1967; The Wringer, mixed media 1967; Funkart 1967; Twowomanshow, theatre piece 1968; Spider Song with Lartry Austin, 1968; Mr Machine for flute and tape 1969; A Day in the Life of the Mooscak Machines 1972; The Unseen Force theatre piece with dancers 1978; From 1970 much music from a series of self-playing electronic sound sculptures, e.g. Mooscak Machine, Sound Hat and Cosmic Cube. *Address:* c/o ASCAP, ASCAP Building, 1 Lincoln Plaza, NY 10023, USA.

LUNN, Joanna; Singer (Soprano); b. 1973, England. *Education:* Royal College of Music, and with Denise Mulholland. *Career:* Engagements with the English Baroque soloists under John Eliot Gardiner, including Bach Cantata Pilgrimage (2000), Gluck and Verdi at the Châtelet, Paris, and Handel's Israel in Egypt at Salzburg and Vienna (2001); Bach's B minor Mass with the New London Consort in New Zealand and Spain; Tour of Japan with the Musicians of the Globe; Debut with English National Opera in The Coronation of Poppea, 2000; St Matthew Passion with the London Handel Festival, 2001; Other appearances with The King's Consort and the Gabrieli Consort. *Honours:* Tagore Gold Medal, RCM. *Address:* c/o Royal College of Music, Prince Consort Road, London SW7, England.

LUPERI, Mario; Singer (Bass); b. 1954, Sardinia, Italy. *Education:* Studied in Calgliari, Verona and Siena. *Career:* Debut: Perugia 1979, in Olympie by Spontini and in Cherubini's Requiem; Palermo and Florence 1981, as Publio in La Clemenza di Tito and as Thoas in Iphigénie en Tauride; La Scala from 1982, as the Emperor in The Nightingale, Simone in Gianni Schicchi and Pluto in the Monteverdi Orfeo; Macerata Festival 1984–86, as Colline and Timur, Salzburg Easter Festival 1986, as the Grand Inquisitor; Sang Ramphis in Aida at the Munich Staatsoper 1986, Luxor 1987; Season 1986–87 as Verdi's Pistol at Brussels, Oroe in Semiramide and Oroveso in Norma at Naples; North American debut 1988, as Timur at Pittsburgh; Sang Colline at Genoa, 1990, Giorgio in I Puritani in Marseilles, 1991; Mozart's Bartolo in Venice 1991 and in Fra Diavolo at La Scala, 1992; Sang Charon in Monteverdi's Orfeo at Milan, 1998; Season 2000 as the Cardinal in La Juive for New Israeli Opera, Mozart's Commendatore at La Coruña and Pistol in Falstaff in La Monnaie, Brussels; Many concert appearances; including the Commendatore in Don Giovanni at the Festival Hall, London, 1996. *Address:* c/o Teatro alla Scala, Via Filiodrammatici 2, 20121 Milan, Italy.

LUPTACIK, Jozef; Musician (clarinet); b. 10 Jan. 1947, Vysoka pri Morave, Czechoslovakia; m. Eva 1972; one s. one d. *Education:* Musical Conservatory, Bratislava, 1962–69; Academy of Music, Bratislava, 1969–73; summer courses with Professor V. Riha, Prague, 1970–71. *Career:* debut, A. Copland, Concerto, Music Festival, Bratislava, 1973; E. Suchon, Concertino (first performance), with Czech Philharmonic, Prague, 1978; Mozart, Weber, Krommer, Concertos with Slovak Philharmonic; mem, Slovak Philharmonic Orchestra, first clarinet Bratislava; Associate Professor, Academy of Music, Bratislava. *Recordings:* E. Suchon, Concertino; Weber/Mozart, Quintets (B Major, A Major); Weber, Concerto in F Minor, E Major; Brahms/Beethoven, Trio; J. Brahms, Sonatas in E Major, F Minor; Mozart, Clarinet Concerto; J. Hummel, Clarinet Quartet. *Honours:* fourth Prize, Belgrade, 1971; member of international juries, international clarinet competitions. *Address:* Hlavna 36, 900 66 Vysoka pri Morave, Slovakia.

LUPU, Radu; pianist; b. 30 Nov. 1945, Galati, Romania. *Education:* Moscow Conservatoire. *Career:* Leading Interpreter for German classical composers; Frequently appears with all major British orchestras; Toured Europe with London Symphony Orchestra; American debut, 1972; Gave world premiere of André Tchaikovsky's Piano Concerto, London, 1975; Brahms D Minor Concerto with the Berlin Philharmonic at the 1996 London Proms. *Recordings:* For Decca including complete Beethoven cycle with Israel Philharmonic and Zubin Mehta, 1979; Mozart sonatas for violin and piano, with Szymon Goldberg; Brahms Piano Concerto No. 1 with Edo de Waart and the London Philharmonic Orchestra; Mozart Piano Concerto K467 with Uri Segal and the English Chamber Orchestra; Various Beethoven and Schubert sonatas; Mozart and Beethoven wind quintets in E Flat, Mozart Concerto for 2 pianos, concerto for 3 pianos transcribed for 2 pianos, with Murray Perahia and the English Chamber Orchestra; Schubert Fantasia in F Minor and Mozart in D for 2 pianos, with Murray Perahia; Schubert Leider with Barbara Hendricks; Schubert Duets with Daniel Barenboim. *Honours:* First Prize, Van Cliburn Competition, 1966; Enescu International Competition, Bucharest. 1967; Leeds International Competition, 1969; Edison Award, 1995; Grammy Award, 1995. *Current Management:* Terry Harrison Artists Management, The Orchard, Market Street, Charlbury, Oxfordshire OX7 3PJ, England. *Telephone:* (1608) 810330. *Fax:* (1608) 811331. *E-mail:* artists@terryharrison.force9.co.uk.

LUTHER, Mark; Singer (tenor); b. 14 Nov. 1961, Bristol, England. *Education:* Studied at the National Opera Studio, and at the Guildhall School with Noelle Barker. *Career:* Debut: St John's Smith Square, 1989, in Elijah; Concert appearances include Opera Gala Evening at Covent Garden, Vivaldi's Gloria with the Northern Symphonia and showings at the Purcell Room and the Queen Elizabeth Hall; Opera engagements include touring performances with British Youth Opera as Rodolfo; Other roles include: Idomeneo, Don Ottavio and Remendado (Carmen); Macduff and Arturo in Lucia di Lammermoor for Welsh National Opera, Don José at Rotterdam and the Verdi Requiem in Netherlands; Don Ottavio in Schönbrunn Vienna; Sang Lensky for Opera North at Norwich, 1998; Sang Tamino at Wellington, 1999. *Current Management:* Athole Still International Management, Forresters Hall, 25–27 Westow Street, London, SE19 3RY, England. *Telephone:* (20) 8771-5271. *Fax:* (20) 8768-6600. *Website:* www .atholestill.com.

LUTSIUK, Viktor; Singer (Tenor); b. 1965, Ivanitchi, Ukraine. *Education:* Kolliarevsky conservatoire, Kharkov. *Career:* Sang at the Dnypropetrov Opera until 1996; Mariinsky Theatre, St Petersburg, from 1996 as Lohengrin, Parsifal, Don Carlos, Lensky in Eugene Onegin, Herman (Queen of Spades), Vladimir in Prince Igor and Dmitiri in Boris Godunov; Andrei in Mazeppa at La Scala (1999), Parsifal at the Royal Albert Hall and Lohengrin in Baden-Baden; Sang the title role in the

British premiere of Prokofiev's Semyon Kotko, with the Kirov Opera at Covent Garden, 2000; Sofia Gubaidulina St John Passion at the London Proms, 2002; Other roles include Alfredo, Radamès, the Duke of Mantua, Don José, Pinkerton, and Andrei in Khovanshchina. *Recordings include:* Mazeppa and Boris Godunov. *Address:* c/o Kirov Opera Mariinsky Theatre, Theatre Square, St Petersburg, Russia.

LUTZE, Gert; Singer (Tenor); b. 30 Sept. 1917, Leipzig, Germany. *Education:* Sang in the choir of St Thomas's Leipzig from 1928. *Career:* Bach's St Matthew Passion conducted by Gunter Ramin; Many appearances as concert and oratorio singer; Opera roles included Puccini's Pinkerton and Rodolfo, Mozart's Ferrando and Rimsky-Korsakov's Sadko; Engagements as Bach singer in Schaffhausen, Zürich, Basle, Berne, Helsinki, Paris, Brussels and Luxembourg; Sang in Prague and China 1955; St Matthew Passion in Bologna and Florence 1957; Further concerts with Karl Richter as conductor.

LUXON, Benjamin Matthew, CBE, FGSM; British singer (baritone); b. 24 March 1937, Redruth, Cornwall; s. of Maxwell Luxon and Lucille Grigg; m. Sheila Amit 1969; two s. one d. *Education:* Truro School, Westminster Training Coll., Guildhall School of Music and Drama. *Career:* always a freelance artist; sang with English Opera Group 1963–70; has sung with Royal Opera House, Covent Garden and Glyndebourne Festival Opera 1971–96, Boston Symphony Orchestra 1975–96, Netherlands Opera 1976–96, Frankfurt Opera House 1977–96, Paris Opéra 1980, La Scala, Milan 1986; roles include Monteverdi's Ulisse, Janáček's Forester, Mozart's Don Giovanni and Papageno, Tchaikovsky's Onegin, Verdi's Posa and Falstaff, Wagner's Wolfram, Alban Berg's Wozzeck, Count Almaviva and Sherasmin in Oberon; performs as recitalist with piano accompanist David Willison; folk-singing partnership with Bill Grofut 1976–96; has recorded for all major record cos; retd from professional singing due to severe hearing loss 1996; vocal coach at Tanglewood, USA 1996. *Recordings include:* Mahler's 8th Symphony, Schubert's Song Cycles. *Honours:* Hon. mem. RAM; Bard of Cornish Gorseth; Hon. DMus (Exeter), (RSA of Music and Drama) 1996, (Canterbury Christ Church Coll.) 1997. *Address:* The Mazet, Relubbus Lane, St Hilary, Penzance, Cornwall, TR20 9DS, England.

LVOV, Boris; Concert Pianist; b. 1928, Moscow, Russia. *Education:* Studied at the Central School of Music and at the Moscow Conservatoire. *Career:* Debut: First public concert aged nine years; performed at the Moscow Conservatoire in 1946; Many concerts in the former Soviet Union, Eastern Europe and China from 1948; Appearances with David Oistrakh, Rostropovich, Kondrashin and Emil Gilels; Former Professor of Piano, Moscow Conservatoire, then emigrated to Israel and is Professor at the Rubin Academy of Music in Jerusalem; Recent concert tours to Europe, Japan, Scandinavia and USA, both in recital and concert; Repertoire includes music by Haydn, Mozart, Schumann, Liszt, Prokofiev, Bartók and Stravinsky. *Honours:* Winner, Beethoven Cometition for performance of the Hammerklavier Sonata. *Address:* 11 Northpark Street, Glasgow G20 7AA, Scotland.

LYMPANY, Dame Moura, DBE, FRAM, FRCM; Concert Pianist; b. 18 Aug. 1916, Saltash, Cornwall, England. *Career:* debut performance at Harrogate, 1929; Mendelssohn's First Concerto; played in USA, Canada, South America, Australia, New Zealand, India and most European countries including Russia; often heard in music by Khachaturian, Rachmaninov, Ireland, Delius, Rawsthorne, Cyril Scott and Chopin; played Mendelssohn at the 1991 Promenade Concerts, London. *Recordings:* numerous on major labels. *Publications:* Moura: Her Autobiography. *Address:* Chateau Perigord 2, Apt 81, Monte Carlo, Monaco.

LYONS, Graham John, AGSM; Composer, Music Publisher and Instrument Manufacturer; b. 17 July 1936, London, England. *Education:* Univ. of Oxford, Guildhall School of Music and Drama. *Career:* played saxophone, clarinet and piano in jazz groups and dance bands 1954–58; freelance as a woodwind doubler in many styles and orchestras 1962–80; arranger for BBC light orchestras 1970–80; arranger and session musician for New Zealand TV 1980–81; started own music publishing co. 1983; launch of the Lyons C clarinet 1991; mem. Incorporated Soc. of Musicians, Musicians' Union, Nat. Secular Soc.. *Compositions:* Mixed Bag: series of woodwind ensembles, Take up the Flute, Take up the Clarinet, 60 vols of solo and ensemble compositions for woodwind, Sonata for Clarinet and Piano 1986. *Publications:* Educational compositions 1979. *Honours:* British Design Award for the Lyons C clarinet 1993. *Address:* 11 Tinley Garth, Kirkby Moorside, North Yorkshire, YO62 6AR, England (home). *Telephone:* (1751) 433379 (home). *Fax:* (1751) 430611 (home). *E-mail:* usefulmusic@aol.com (home). *Website:* www.firstclarinet.com (home).

LYSIGHT, Michel (Thierry); Composer, Conductor, Professor and Publisher; b. 14 Oct. 1958, Brussels, Belgium. *Education:* Musicology, Free University of Brussels, 1978; Academy of Schaerbeek; Conservatoire Royal de Musique, Mons; Conservatoire Royal de Musique, Brussels; Advanced Diplomas, Solfege 1980, Chamber Music 1988, Composition 1989, Conducting, 2002. *Career:* Professor, Academies of Schaerbeek, 1979–, Woluwe Saint-Pierre, 1981–90, Professor, 1989–90; Professor, Conservatoire Royal de Musique, Brussels, 1980–; Deputy Director, Academy of Brussels, 1990–94; Professor, Bikent University of Ankara, Turkey, 2000–01; Founder, Michel Lysight Ensemble for Contemporary Music, 1991; Founder, Ensemble Nouvelles Consonances, 1995; Founder, Fibonacci Publishing, 1999; Artistic Director, Kalidisc, 2000–. *Compositions include:* Chamber music, orchestral music, piano, percussion including, Prelude et Toccata, piano, 1982; Reflexion, clarinet or bassoon and piano; Soleil Bleu, 1 wind instrument and piano; Onirique, full orchestra, 1989; Trois Croquis, violin or flute or clarinet or cello or bassoon or saxophone and piano or string orchestra, 1990–93; Chronographie I for wind quintet; Quatrain, flute, oboe, clarinet, bassoon, 1990; Chronographie II for string orchestra, 1992–93; Chronographie III 2 instruments and piano, 1993; Trois Instantanés, 1994; Epode, 1997; Piano Concerto, 1995; Chronogrpahie IV for violin and piano, 1996; Hal pot rhythm for wind ensemble, 1999; Couleurs noires for 4 cellos, 1999; Chronographie V, piano, 2001; Anamnèse for choir and string orchestra, 2001; Élémentaires, 3 instruments, 2001; Enigma, 2 instruments and piano or harp, 2001; Alchemy, clarinet quartet or sax quartet, 2001; Random walk, brass quintent or clarinet and string quartet, 2002; Hexagramme, 6 instruments ad lib, 2002; Concerto, clarinet and orchestra, 2002; Trois points, horn, 2002; An awakening, string quartet, 2002; Perseides, recorder, 2002; This is not a bossa, piano, 2003; Initiation, flute and marimba, 2003. *Recordings:* XXth Century Belgian Works for Clarinet and Piano, Ronald Vanspaendonck, clarinet and Leonardo Anglani, piano; Sit Down and Listen, Mireille Gleizes, piano; Oréades; Discoveries; Belgian Sextets; Récital Joseph Grau; Labyrinthes; Serenata for 2000 (Serenata Forlana); XXth Century Belgian Works for Flute and Piano; Thrène, Chronographie IV (Stéphane De May, piano and Damien Paroen, violin); Masterpieces for Horn and Piano (Francis Orval, horn and Jean-Claude Vanden Eynden, piano); Couleurs XXème siècle for trumpet and organ; Soledad; I Musici Brucellensis; Ritual. *Publications:* La Transposition, 1982. *Honours:* Irène Fuérison Prize, Belgian Academy of Fine Arts, 1990; Silver Medal, Academy of Lutèce, Paris, 1992; Fuga, Belgian Composers Union, 1997. *Address:* 1 rue Vanderlinden, 1030 Brussels, Belgium. *E-mail:* lysight@fibonacci.be.

LYSY, Alberto; Violinist and Teacher; b. 11 Feb. 1935, Buenos Aires, Argentina; Divorced, 4 c. *Education:* Studied with Ljerko Spiller and Yehudi Menuhin. *Career:* Solo recitals and performances with orchestras in Europe, Asia, Israel, North and South America under Adrian Boult, Colin Davis, Pierre Boulez, Mstislav Rostropovich and others. Performed chamber music with Pablo Casals, Yehudi Menuhin, Benjamin Britten, Nadia Boulanger, Gaspar Cassadò and others; Musical Director, International Menuhin Music Academy and Camerata Lysy, Gstaad, Switzerland; Rencontres Musicales Internationales in Blonay, Switzerland and Festival International Lysy in Buenos Aires. *Honours:* Honorary Doctorate, University of Cordoba, Argentina. *Address:* IMMA, Centre d'Etudes, rte de Vevey 7, 1807 Blonay, Switzerland.

LYSY, Antonio; Cellist; b. 1963, Rome, Italy. *Education:* Studied with his father, the violinist Alberto Lysy; Menuhin School with Maurice Gendron and William Pleeth; Menuhin Academy with Radu Aldulescu; Royal Northern College of Music with Ralph Kirshbaum. *Career:* Concert engagements in Austria, Argentina, France, Germany, Israel, Italy and Spain; British venues include the Royal Festival Hall, Wigmore Hall, Queen Elizabeth Hall and St John's Smith Square; Chamber concerts with Radu Aldulescu, Gidon Kremer, Lamar Crowson and Yehudi and Jeremy Menuhin; Principal Cellist with the Chamber Orchestra of Europe and appearances with the Manchester-based Goldberg Ensemble; Camerata of Salzburg 1988, with Sándor Végh as conductor; Solo performances of Tchaikovsky's Rococo Variations in Buenos Aires and Italy; Further engagements with the Philharmonia Orchestra and at the Brighton Festival; Artistic Director of Chamber Music Festival in Tuscany, Incontri Musicali in Terra di Siena, from summer 1989. *Recordings:* Bloch's Prayer and Tchaikovsky's Souvenirs de Florence with the Camerata Lysy.

LYUBIMOV, Yuri (Petrovich); Stage Director; b. 30 Sept. 1917, Yaoslal, Russia. *Career:* Actor at the Moscow Arts Theatre and Vakhtangov Theatre; Artistic Director of the Taganka Theatre, Moscow, 1964–84; Opera productions have included The Queen of Spades at the Paris Opéra, Don Giovanni in Budapest, Khovanshchina at La Scala, Rigoletto in Florence and Tristan und Isolde at Bologna; Produced Mussorgsky's Salammbô in Paris and Naples, 1986; Royal Opera House, Covent Garden 1986 and 1988, with Jenůfa and Das Rheingold; Produced The Queen of Spades at Karlsruhe 1990, The Love for Three Oranges at the Bayerische Staatsoper, Munich, 1991; Staged The Queen of Spades, adapted by Alfred Schnittke, at Bonn, 1996. *Address:* c/o Bayerische Staatsoper, Postfach 100148, 8000 Munich 1, Germany.

M

MA, Yo-Yo, BA; American cellist; b. 7 Oct. 1955, Paris, France; of Chinese parentage; m. Jill A. Hornor 1978; one s. one d. *Education:* Harvard Univ. and cello studies with his father, with Leonard Rose and at Juilliard School of Music, New York. *Career:* first public recital at age of five; performed under many distinguished conductors with all the maj. orchestras of the world, including Berlin Philharmonic, Boston Symphony, Chicago Symphony, Israel Philharmonic, London Symphony and New York Philharmonic; regularly participates in festivals of Tanglewood, Ravinia, Blossom, Salzburg and Edinburgh; also appears in chamber music ensembles with artists such as Isaac Stern, Emanuel Ax, Leonard Rose, Pinchas Zukerman, Gidon Kremer and fmrly Yehudi Menuhin; premiered the Concerto by H. K. Gruber, Tanglewood 1989; recital tour with Emanuel Ax celebrating 20th anniversary of their partnership 1995–96; Bach's suites for solo cello at the Barbican Hall, London 1995; established The Silk Road Project to promote study of cultural, artistic and intellectual traditions of the route 2001; Smithsonian Folklife Festival 2002. *Recent recordings include:* John Williams Greatest Hits 1969–1999 1999, My First 79 Years 1999, Solo 1999, Brahms: Piano Concerto No.2, Cello Sonata Op.78 1999, Lulie the Iceberg 1999, Songs and Dances 1999, Franz Joseph Haydn 1999, Simply Baroque 1999, Crouching Tiger, Hidden Dragon (film soundtrack) 2000, Corigliano: Phantasmagoria 2000, Simply Baroque II 2000, Appalachian Journey 2000, Dvorak: Piano Quartet No. 2, Sonatina in G, Romantic Pieces 2000, Classic Yo-Yo 2001, Classical Hits 2001, Heartland: An Appalachian Anthology 2001, Naqoyqatsi (film soundtrack) 2002, Yo-Yo Ma Plays the Music of John Williams 2002, Silk Road Journeys—When Strangers Meet 2002, Obrigado Brazil 2003, Paris—La Belle Époque 2003. *Honours:* Dr hc (Northeastern) 1985 and from 11 other colls or univs, including Harvard, Yale, Tufts and Juilliard, Chinese Univ. of Hong Kong; Avery Fisher Prize 1978; Glenn Gould Prize 1999; 14 Grammy Awards including one for his recording of the six Bach Suites for Unaccompanied Cello 1984, two Emmy Awards, 19 Canadian Gemini Awards. *Current Management:* ICM Artists, 40 W 57th Street, New York, NY 10019, USA. *Website:* www.sonyclassical.com/artists/ma/.

MAASS-GEIGER, Joachim; Singer (Bass-baritone); b. 1957, Essen, Germany. *Education:* Studied in Lubeck and Hamburg. *Career:* Sang in opera at Kaiserslautern, 1981–85, Essen from 1986. Appearances at Eutin, Gelsenkirchen and elsewhere as Mozart's Figaro and Leporello, the Grand Inquisitor in Don Carlos, and Alberich in The Ring; Klingsor at Essen, 1993, Don Giovanni and the Doctor in Wozzeck at Saarbrücken and Gelsenkirchen, 1996; Other roles include Curio in Giulio Cesare, Golaud in Pelléas et Mélisande, and Kecal in The Bartered Bride. *Address:* Staatstheater, Schillerplatz, 66111 Saarbrucken, Germany.

MAAZEL, Lorin; American conductor and musician; b. 6 March 1930, Neuilly, France; m. Dietlinde Turban, 3 s., 4 d. *Education:* Music studies with Vladimir Bakaleinikoff; Philosophy major, University of Pittsburgh. *Career:* Composer, Conductor, American Symphony orchestras 1938–; European debut, 1953; Violin Recitalist; Conductor of operas including new productions, Metropolitan Opera, New York, Teatro alla Scala, Milan, Royal Opera House, London, Paris Opéra; Festivals include Bayreuth (The Ring), Salzburg, Edinburgh, Lucerne: Tours, South America, Australia, former USSR, Japan, China; Artistic Director, Deutsche Oper Berlin, 1965–71; Musical Director, Radio Symphony Orchestra, Berlin, 1965–75; Associate Principal Conductor, New Philharmonia Orchestra, London, 1970–72; Director, Cleveland Orchestra, 1972–82; Director, Vienna State Opera, 1982–84; Music Director, Pittsburgh Symphony Orchestra, 1988–96; Music Director, Bavarian Radio Symphony Orchestra, 1993; Since 1987 participation in over 25 benefit concerts, many for international relief organisations such as UNHCR, UNICEF, World Wildlife Fund; Ninth New Year's Day concert with the Vienna Philharmonic, 1996; Led the premiere of Panderecki's Seven Gates of Jerusalem, 1997; Verdi's Don Carlos at the 1998 Salzburg Festival; Mahler cycle with the Bavarian Radio Symphony Orchestra, 2002; Opera commission from Covent Garden, Orwell's 1984. *Recordings:* Over 350 including full cycles of Beethoven, Mahler, Rachmaninov, Sibelius, Tchaikovsky symphonic works; Puccini opera cycle; Music visualisation: Holst, Planets and Vivaidi, Four Seasons, Mozart, Don Giovanni, Bizet, Carmen. *Address:* c/o Z des Aubris, Tal 15 5th Floor, 80331 Munich, Germany.

MACAL, Zdenek; Conductor; b. 8 Jan. 1936, Brno, Czechoslovakia. *Education:* Brno Conservatory, 1951–56; Janáček Academy 1956–60. *Career:* Debut: Czech Philharmonic Orchestra 1966, at the Prague Spring Festival; British Debut, 1969, with the Bournemouth Symphony: US debut with the Chicago Symphony 1972; Conductor of the Moravian Symphony Orchestra at Olomouc, 1963–67; Tours to Hungary,

Bulgaria, West Germany, Austria and Switzerland; Music Director of the Cologne Radio Symphony Orchestra 1970–74; Chief Conductor of the Orchestra of Hanover Radio from 1980; Music Director, Milwaukee Symphony from 1986, Sydney Symphony, 1986–93; Conducted Prince Igor at the Grant Park Concerts, Chicago, 1990. *Recordings:* Dvořák's Cello and Piano Concertos; Brahms Alto Rhapsody, Soukupova; Mozart Piano Concertos K488 and K595; Schoeck's Penthesilea; CD of Dvořák's 9th Symphony and Symphonic Variations, Classic for Pleasure. *Honours:* Winner, International Conductors Competition at Bescançon, 1965; Mitropoulos Competition, NY, 1966. *Address:* c/o Concerto Winderstein GmbH, Leopoldstrasse 25, D–80802 München, Germany.

McALISTER, Barbara; singer (mezzo-soprano); b. 1944, Oklahoma, USA. *Education:* Oklahoma University and in Los Angeles. *Career:* sang at Koblenz Opera from 1976, in The Medium, as Stravinskys Mother Goose ad Vercli's Uirica; Sang at Passau 1980–81, Flensburg 1981–83 and Bremerhaven 1983–87; Roles have included Presiosilla, Carmen, Herodias, and Orlofsky; Guest at Monte Carlo 1987, as Meg Page; Concert repertoire includes Messiah, Beethoven's Ninth, the Kindenotenlieder and the Alto Rhapsody. *Address:* c/o Stadttheater Bremerhaven, Theodor-Heuss-Platz, Pf 120541 2850 Bremerhaven, Germany.

McANDREW, Fiona; singer (soprano); b. 1967, Ireland. *Education:* University of Western Australia and Guildhall School, London. *Career:* appearances with English Touring Opera; Opera Ireland; Castleward Opera; Covent Garden Festival; Opera Holland Park; Roles include: Poulenc's Blanche, Miss Wordsworth in Albert Herring, Pamina, Donna Elvira, Frasquita and Marie in La Fille du Regiment, Adina, Cilea's Vivetta, Woglinde; Concerts include Reich's Tehillim, Dresden, 1998; Bach's St Matthew Passion and Christmas Oratorio, National Concert Hall, Ireland; Debussy's Le Martyre at St John's Smith Square; 1999 season with La Fée in Cendrillon and Prima Donna in Convenienze Teatrali, Mayfair Festival; Isabella in L'Inganno Felice, Pesaro, Italy and Lady Harriet in Martha for Castleward Opera. *Address:* Music International, 13 Ardilaun Road, London N5 2QR, England.

MacANN, Rodney; singer (baritone); b. 1950, New Zealand. *Career:* European debut as The Speaker in The Magic Flute, with Welsh National Opera; Sang with New Zealand Opera before studying singing and theology in London; Appearances with Opera North as Don Alfonso, Sharpless and Jochanaan, and in La Cenerentola and Samson et Dalila; English National Opera as Tchaikovsky's Mazeppa, Ariodates in Xerxes by Handel, Don Alfonso, Klingsor in Parsifal; Scarpia and Escamillo; With the Royal Opera Covent Garden has sung in Andrea Chénier, King Priam, Les Contes d'Hoffmann and Tosca; Engagements in France, Norway and Italy, as Arthur in The Lighthouse by Peter Maxwell Davies; Adelaide Festival, South Australia as Ruprecht in The Fiery Angel; Sang Cuno in Der Freischütz at Covent Garden, 1989, the Music Master in Ariadne for ENO, 1990; Concerts with all the leading British orchestras and frequent performances of Christus in the Bach Passions; Further concerts in Bergen, Florence, NY, and Toulouse; Sang Mozart's Figaro at Wellington, New Zealand, 1995; Sang Sharpless in Butterfly at Wellington, 1999. *Recordings:* Video of Andrea Chénier, Covent Garden, 1984. *Address:* c/o Stafford Law Associates, 6 Barham Close, Weybridge, Surrey KT13 9PR, England.

McCABE, John, CBE, BMus, FRMCM, FLCM, FRCM; British pianist; b. 21 April 1939, Huyton, Lancashire, England. *Education:* Manchester University, Royal Manchester College of Music, Hochschule für Musik, Munich, Germany. *Career:* piano recitals, wide repertoire but specialising in contemporary music and Haydn; English premiere, Corigliano's Piano Concerto; Danish premiere, Delius Piano Concerto; Director, London College of Music, 1983–90; mem, British Academy of Composers and Songwriters. *Compositions:* Operas, ballets, symphonies, concertos, choral and keyboard works, television and film music; Works include, 5 Symphonies 1965, 1971, 1978, 1994, 1997, Chagall Windows (orchestra); Notturni ed Alba (soprano and orchestra); Cloudcatcher Fells (brass band); Concerto for Orchestra, US premiere, 1984; Rainforest 1, 1984; Fire at Durilgai (orchestra), premiered BBC Philharmonic Orchestra, Manchester, later performances Prague, London Promenade Concerts, 1989; Flute Concerto, 1990; Red Leaves for small orchestra, 1991; Tenebrae for piano, 1993; Edward II, full-length ballet, Stuttgart, 1995, British premiere, Birmingham Royal Ballet, 1997; Arthur, ballet in 2 parts (Arthur Pendragon and Le Morte d'Arthur) for Birminham Royal Ballet, 1998–2001; The Golden Valley, for orchestra, 2001; The Woman by the Sea, Piano Quintet, 2001. *Recordings:* Wide range from Scarlatti, Clementi, Haydn, Bax, Walton, Hindemith, Howells and Grieg to contemporary British, American, Australian composers, including own piano music and complete Haydn piano music (12 CDs); Wide range of own orchestral, chamber and piano music recorded including Edward II (ballet) complete. *Publications include:* Alan

Rawsthorne–Portrait of a Composer, 1999. *Honours:* Hon. RAM, FTCL. *Current Management:* Novello & Company, 8–9 Frith Street, London W1V 5TZ, England.

McCAFFERTY, Frances; singer (mezzo-contralto); b. 1965, Edinburgh, Scotland. *Education:* Royal Scottish Academy and Hans Hotter. *Career:* debut, sang in Il Barbiere di Siviglia and Manon Lescaut at Dublin; Appearances as Verdi's Mistress Quickly, with Opera North; Mozart's Third Lady; Ericlea in Monteverdi's Ulisse; Kabanicha in Katya Kabanova; Ulrica in Ballo in Maschera, Neath Opera; First Maid in Elektra, Covent Garden; Wexford Festival in Rimsky's May Night; Sang with ENO as Mistress Quickly; Dorset Opera as Naina in Ruslan and Lyudmila; 1999–2000 Season: Mozart's Marcellina for Opera Holland Park; La Cieca, La Gioconda, Dorset; Concerts with Scottish CO; BBC Scottish Symphony Orchestra; Ulster Orchestra. *Current Management:* Music International, 13 Ardilaun Road, London N5 2QR, England.

McCALDIN, Denis James, BMus, BSc, PhD; conductor, broadcaster and editor; b. 28 May 1933, Nottingham, England; m. Margaret Anne Smith; one d. one s. *Education:* Birmingham Univ., Nottingham Univ., Mozarteum, Salzburg, Austria. *Career:* Lecturer in Music, Liverpool Univ. 1966–71; Prof. of Performance in Music, Lancaster Univ. 1971–98; guest conductor Royal Liverpool Philharmonic Orchestra, Manchester Camerata, London Mozart Players, Royal Philharmonic Orchestra, Hallé Orchestra; Artistic Dir Lake District Summer Music 1999–; Dir Haydn Soc. of Great Britain 1979–; mem. Incorporated Soc. of Musicians, Royal Musical Asscn. *Compositions:* Fanfare for a Celebration 1993. *Recordings:* Schubert and Haydn: Church Music 1989, Haydn: Nelson Mass 1998. *Publications:* Stravinsky 1972, Berlioz: Te Deum (ed.) 1973, Mahler 1981, Haydn: Te Deum, Nelson Mass, Little Organ Mass (ed.) 1987–98, Haydn Mass in F 1993, editions of Haydn, Bach and Mozart 1998–; contribs to Beeethoven Companion, Music Review, Music Times, Music and Letters, Music in Education, Times Higher Education Supplement, Soundings. *Honours:* Freeman, City of Lancaster 1990. *Address:* Department of Music, University of Lancaster, Bailrigg, Lancaster, LA1 4YW (office); Heron House, Aldcliffe Mews, Lancaster, LA1 5BT, England (home). *Telephone:* (1524) 61553 (home). *Fax:* (1524) 61553 (home). *E-mail:* d.mccaldin@lancaster.ac.uk (office). *Website:* haydnsocietyofgb.netfirms.com (office).

McCALLA, Kathleen; singer (soprano); b. 1957, Iowa, USA. *Education:* Manhattan Institute and with Tito Gobbi and Mario del Monaco in Italy. *Career:* debut, Treviso 1981 in Le nozze di Figaro; Sang throughout Germany from 1983, notably as Traviata, and in the Mozart and Puccini repertory; Bonn Opera from 1992, as Desdemona, Suor Angelica and Leonore in Fidelio; Guest engagements as Alice in Falstaff, Abigaille in Nabucco at Naples and Turandot in Rome, 1996; Other roles include Mozart's Vitelia, Constanze, Countess and Fiordiligi. *Address:* c/o Bonn Opera, Am Boeselageshof 1, 5311 Bonn, Germany.

McCARTHY, Fionnuala; singer (soprano); b. 1963, Ireland. *Education:* studied in Johannesburg and at Detmold, Germany. *Career:* debut, Kaiserslautem 1987, as Mimi; Sang at the Mannheim Opera from 1988, debut as Wagner's Woglinde with further appearances as Lauretta, Euridice, Echo, Marzelline, Famine, Zerlina and Mozart's Countess; Sang Marguerite at Giessen (1990) and appeared with the Deutsche Oper am Rhein 1990–92; Sang Donna Elvira with Pimlico Opera at Tullnally, Ireland, 1996; Ighino in Pfitzner's Palestrina at the Deutsche Oper, Berlin, 1996, and Manon there 1998; Season 2000–01 as Sophie, Janáček's Vixen, Pamina and Alice Ford at the Deutsche Oper. *Address:* c/o Deutsche Oper am Rhein, Richard-Wagner-Strasse 10, 10585 Berlin, Germany.

McCARTHY, John, OBE; choral director and director of music; b. 1930, England. *Career:* Musical Director of the Ambrosian Singers and Ambrosian Opera Chorus and many other famous Choral Groups; Director of Music, Carmelite Priory; Former Chorus Master, Royal Opera House, Covent Garden; Professor, Royal College of Music; Choral Director to nearly all the greatest conductors in the world; Director of many hundreds of very successful recordings and broadcasts. On television has been Choral Director for many operas and music programmes; In London Theatre has been involved in a number of musicals and revivals and several Royal Command Performances; Shows include: Mame; The Great Waltz; Gone With The Wind, Showboat; The King and I; Beyond the Rainbow; Charlie Girl; Hans Anderson; 2 Ronnies; Barnham; I Love My Wife; Plumbers Progress; Phil the Fluter; Joan of Arc; Luther; Biograph Girl; Cats; Choral Director for hundreds of films including the Oscar winning Oliver, Tom Jones, Goodbye My Chips, Scrooge, Cromwell, Fiddler on the Roof, The Great Waltz, Man of la Mancia, Close Encounters, Chariots of Fire; Amadeus. *Recordings include:* Over 150 recordings of operas in French, German, Italian, Russian and English; Conductor of 3 award winning albums for European Grand Prix du Disques; Fauré Requiem, Lucia di Lammermoor; Beethoven's 9th Symphony; Vivaldi's Gloria. *Publications include:* Editor, series of Tudor and Renaissance Music. *Honours:*

National Academy of Performing Arts Awards. *Address:* c/o Ambrosian Singers, 4 Reynolds Road, Beaconsfield, Buckinghamshsire HP9 2NJ, England.

McCARTNEY, Sir (James) Paul, Kt, MBE, FRCM; British songwriter and performer; b. 18 June 1942, Liverpool; s. of James McCartney and Mary McCartney; m. 1st Linda Eastman 1969 (died 1998), one s. two d. one step-d.; m. 2nd Heather Mills 2002, one d. *Education:* Stockton Wood Road Primary School, Speke, Joseph Williams Primary School, Gateacre and Liverpool Inst. *Career:* plays guitar, piano and organ; taught himself to play trumpet at age of 13; wrote first song 1956, wrote numerous songs with John Lennon; joined pop group The Quarrymen 1956; appeared under various titles until formation of The Beatles 1960; appeared with The Beatles for performances in Hamburg 1960, 1961, 1962, The Cavern, Liverpool 1960, 1961; world-wide tours 1963–66; attended Transcendental Meditation Course at Maharishi's Acad., Rishikesh, India Feb. 1968; formed Apple Ltd, parent org. of The Beatles Group of Cos 1968; left The Beatles after collapse of Apple Corpn Ltd 1970; formed MPL Group of Cos 1970; first solo album McCartney 1970; formed own pop group Wings 1971–81, tours of Britain and Europe 1972–73, UK and Australia 1975, Europe and USA 1976, UK 1979, World Tour 1989–90; solo performance at Party at the Palace, Buckingham Palace 2002; Fellow British Acad. of Composers and Songwriters 2000. *Recordings:* albums: with The Beatles: Please Please Me 1963, A Hard Day's Night 1964, Beatles for Sale 1965, Help! 1965, Rubber Soul 1966, Revolver 1966, Sgt Pepper's Lonely Hearts Club Band 1967, Magical Mystery Tour 1967, The Beatles (White Album) 1968, Yellow Submarine 1969, Abbey Road 1969, Let It Be 1970, 1962–1966 (Red Album) 1973, 1967–1970 (Blue Album) 1973, Past Masters Vol. One 1988, Past Masters Vol. Two 1988, The Beatles Anthology: 1 1995, The Beatles Anthology: 2 1996, The Beatles Anthology: 3 1996, 1 2000; with Wings: Wild Life 1971, Red Rose Speedway 1973, Band On The Run 1973, Venus and Mars 1975, Wings at the Speed of Sound 1976, Wings Over America 1976, London Town 1978, Wings Greatest 1978, Back To The Egg 1979, Wingspan 2001; solo: McCartney 1970, Ram 1971, McCartney II 1980, Tug of War 1982, Pipes of Peace 1983, Give My Regards to Broad Street 1984, Press To Play 1986, All the Best! 1987, CHOBA B CCCP 1988, Flowers in the Dirt 1989, Tripping the Live Fantastic 1990, Unplugged: The Official Bootleg 1991, Paul McCartney's Liverpool Oratorio (with Carl Davis) 1991, Off The Ground 1993, Paul Is Live 1993, Flaming Pie 1997, Standing Stone (symphonic work) 1997, Run Devil Run 1999, Working Classical 1999, A Garland for Linda (with eight other composers for a capella choir) 2000, Driving Rain 2001, Back In The US: Live 2002, Back in the World 2003; film soundtracks: The Family Way 1966, James Paul McCartney 1973, Live and Let Die 1973, The Zoo Gang (TV series) 1973. *Radio:* (series) Routes of Rock (BBC) 1999. *Films:* A Hard Day's Night 1964, Help! 1965, Yellow Submarine (animated colour cartoon film) 1968, Let it Be 1970, Magical Mystery Tour (TV film) 1967, Wings Over the World (TV) 1979, Rockshow 1981, Give My Regards to Broad Street (wrote and directed) 1984, Rupert and the Frog Song (wrote and produced) (BAFTA Award Best Animated Film) 1985, Press to Play 1986, Get Back (concert film) 1991. *Publications:* Paintings 2000, The Beatles Anthology (with George Harrison and Ringo Starr) 2000, Sun Prints (with Linda McCartney) 2001, Many Years From Now (autobiog.) 2001, Blackbird Singing: Poems and Lyrics 1965–1999 2001. *Honours:* Hon. Fellow (Liverpool John Moores Univ.) 1998; Dr hc (Sussex) 1988; two Grammy Awards for Band on the Run (including Best Pop Vocal Performance) 1975, Ivor Novello Award for Best Selling British Record 1977–78 for single Mull of Kintyre, for Int. Hit of the Year 1982 for single Ebony and Ivory, for Outstanding Services to British Music 1989; Guinness Book of Records Triple Superlative Award (43 songs each selling more than 1m copies, holder of 60 gold discs, estimated sales of 100m albums and 100m singles) 1979; Lifetime Achievement Award 1990; Freeman of the City of Liverpool 1984; Lifetime Achievement Award People for the Ethical Treatment of Animals (with Linda McCartney) 1996, Polar Music Prize 1992. *Current Management:* MPL Communications Ltd, 1 Soho Square, London, W1V 6BQ, England. *Website:* www.paulmccartney.com.

McCARTY, Patricia, BMus, MMus; viola player, recitalist and chamber musician; b. 16 July 1954, Wichita, Kansas, USA; m. Ronald Wilkison 1982. *Education:* University of Michigan, University of Michigan. *Career:* debut, New York, 1978; Wigmore Hall, London, England, 1986; Beethovenhalle, Bonn, 1991; Japan Tour, 1993; Viola Soloist, Recitalist and Chamber Musician in performances throughout the USA, Europe and Japan; Appearances include Detroit, Houston, Brooklyn, Boston Pops, Beethovenhalle, Suisse Romande, Kyoto and Shinsei Nihon Tokyo orchestras; Recitals in New York, San Francisco, Detroit, Boston and London; Chamber Music performances at Marlboro, Aspen, Tanglewood, Hokkaido and Sarasota festivals; Faculty, Boston Conservatory, Longy School, Meadowmount School of Music. *Recordings:* Viola Works of Rebecca Clarke; Songs of Charles Martin Loeffler; Brahms Viola Quintets; Dvořák String Sextet; Keith Jarrett Concerto; Bach Suites; Schubert Arpeggione Sonata/Beethoven Notturno &

Romances; Brahms Sonatas/Schumann Marchenbilder. *Current Management:* c/o Anne Thomas, Ashmont Music, 25 Carruth Street, Boston, MA 02124, USA. *E-mail:* AshmontMus@aol.com.

McCAULEY, Barry; singer (tenor); b. 2 June 1950, Altoon, Pennsylvania, USA. *Education:* Eastern Kentucky University and Arizona State University. *Career:* debut, San Francisco Spring Opera 1977, as Don José; San Francisco Opera 1977, as Faust; Further appearances in Houston and San Diego; European debut Frankfurt 1979, as Edgardo in Lucia di Lammermoor; New York City Opera from 1980; Aix-en-Provence Festival, 1980 as Don Ottavio; Paris Opéra from 1982, Teatro Comunale Florence, 1983 (debut as Wilhelm Meister in Mignon); Théâtre de la Monnaie Brussels, 1984 and 1986, as Idamante and Belfiore in La Finta Giardiniera; Glyndebourne Festival, 1985–88, as Don José and Boris in Katya Kabanova; Metropolitan Opera debut 1985, as Jacquino; Vienna Staatsoper, 1984, Don Ottavio; Has sung Offenbach's Hoffmann at the Spoleto Festival, 1989 and Seattle and Geneva, 1990; Other roles include Alfredo at Seattle, 1988, Maurizio in Adriana Lecouvreur, Trieste, 1989, Belmonte, Gluck's Admete, Nemorino, Robert Dudley in Maria Stuarda, the Duke of Mantua, Fenton, Pinkerton, Gerald in Lakmé, Nadir, Lensky and Froh in Das Rheingold; Debut as Parsifal at Amsterdam, 1991. *Address:* Seattle Opera Association, PO Box 9248, Seattle, WA 98109, USA.

McCAULEY, John J., BS, BMus, MSc, MusEd; American pianist, conductor and teacher; b. 16 Nov. 1937, Des Moines, IA. *Education:* Univ. of Illinois at Urbana, Juilliard School of Music, piano with Claire Richards, Carlo Zecchi, Friederich Wuehrer, conducting with Jorge Mester and Jean Morel, piano with Josef Raieff and Beveridge Webster, Tanglewood, Aspen, Mozarteum Summer Acad., Salzburg, Austria, masterclasses in conducting with Herbert von Karajan. *Career:* piano solo debut, Carnegie Recital Hall, New York 1975; Columbia Artists Management Community Concerts recital accompanist throughout USA 1980–84; piano recitals, chamber music concerts throughout USA and Europe, including Lincoln Center and Juilliard 1978–91; New York Radio, The Listening Room with Robert Sherman (WQXR) 1983, 1990; pianist in New York performance of The Night of the Murdered Poets, for narrator and chamber ensemble, by Morris Cotel 1985; American Cathedral's Arts George V recital series in Paris 2002, 2003; 92nd Street Y Tisch Center for the Performing Arts, Meet the Virtuoso Series of chamber music performances, spring 2003; solo piano recital Nov. 2004; conductor, Bel Canto Opera, New York; east coast tours with Opera Northeast and Eastern Opera Theater 1978–85; Asst Conductor and musical coach, Des Moines Metro Opera 1984–94; Guest Conductor, Bronx Symphony Orchestra 1985, 1997; Asst Conductor, Arizona Opera at Tucson and Phoenix 1984; Music Dir, Nevada Opera Studio 1995; Assoc. Conductor, Brooklyn Philharmonic 1983; founder, Music Dir and Conductor, Chamber Orchestra of Science & Medicine (COSM), New York 2001–, with concerts at Rockefeller Univ., Music at St Paul's Series, Columbia Univ., Advent Lutheran Church, Good Shepherd Church at Lincoln Center; mem. piano faculty, Riverdale Country School and School of Music 1967–80; instructor, Lehman Coll., CUNY 1972–82; instructor in piano, vocal coaching, accompanist for student recitals and masterclasses, 92nd Street Y Music Dept 1997–; adjunct vocal coach, Manhattan School of Music 1997–. *Recording:* The Night of the Murdered Poets, for narrator and chamber ensemble, by Morris Cotel (pianist). *Publications:* contrib. reviews of new music in NOTES (journal of Music Library Asscn). *Honours:* scholarship, Univ. of Illinois, fellowships at Tanglewood, Aspen, graduate teaching fellowship, Juilliard.

McCAWLEY, Leon, FRSA; pianist; b. 12 July 1973, Culcheth, Warrington, England. *Education:* Chetham's School of Music, Curtis Institute of Music. *Career:* debut, London Philharmonic Orchestra, Bryden Thomson, Royal Festival Hall 1990; works with top orchestras including LPO, CBSO, BBC Nat. Orchestra of Wales, RPO, Philharmonia, BBC Symphony, Royal Scottish Nat., Vienna Symphony, Vienna Chamber, Dallas Symphony, Minnesota Orchestra; recital performances at Wigmore Hall, Queen Elizabeth Hall, Zürich Tonhalle, Vienna Musikverein, Berlin Philharmonie, Washington Kennedy Centre; performances at BBC Proms;. *Recordings include:* Schumann: Piano Music; Beethoven: Sonatas and Variations; Complete Piano Works of Samuel Barber; frequent broadcasts on BBC Radio 3;. *Honours:* BBC Young Musician of the Year, piano section, 1990; First prize, Beethoven Int. Piano Competition, Vienna, 1993; Second prize, Leeds Int. Piano Competition, 1993. *Current Management:* Clarion/Seven Muses, 47 Whitehall Park, London, N19 3TW, England. *Telephone:* (20) 7272 4413/5125. *Website:* www.leonmccawley.com.

McCOLL, William Duncan; clarinettist and basset hornist; b. 18 May 1933, Port Huron, MI, USA; m. Sue McColl; one s. *Education:* Oberlin Coll., Manhattan School of Music, State Acad. of Music and Representational Arts, Vienna. *Career:* solo clarinettist with US Seventh Army Symphony Orchestra 1957–58 and Philharmonia Hungarica, Vienna 1959; clarinettist, Festival Casals; solo clarinettist with Puerto Rico

Symphony Orchestra and clarinet instructor for Puerto Rico Conservatoire 1960–68; clarinettist, Soni Ventorum Wind Quartet 1963–; Prof., Univ. of Washington 1968–; bass clarinettist, Orquestra Filarmonica de las Americas, Mexico City, summer 1976–78. *Recordings:* Villa-Lobos, Trio for Bassoon, Clarinet, Oboe and quartet ditto with flute; Reicha Quintet in G major; Haydn Clock Organ pieces, arranged for wind quintet; Beethoven, Clock Organ pieces, arranged for wind quintet; Reicha Quintet in E minor; Danzi Quintet in F major; Poulenc Duo for Clarinet and Basson; Villa-Lobos Trio for Clarinet, Bassoon and Piano; Numerous other compositions and arrangements. *Address:* c/o School of Music, University of Washington, Seattle, WA 98195, USA.

McCORMACK, Elizabeth, BA; singer (mezzo-soprano); b. 1964, Fife, Scotland; m. Douglas Vipond 1990. *Education:* Glasgow University; Royal Scottish Academy with Duncan Robertson and London Opera Studio. *Career:* Edinburgh Festival debut 1986 with Alan Ramsay's The Gentle Shepherd; Concert performances include Handel's Messiah, Samson and Coronation Anthem; Mozart Requiem, Beethoven Missa Solemnis and CPE Bach Magnificat; Stravinsky's Pulcinella with the English Chamber Orchestra at the Barbican; Sang De Nebra's Requiem and Handel's Dixit Dominus with La Chappelle Royale and Philippe Herreweghe 1989; Haydn's Theresian Mass with the Orchestra of the Age of Enlightenment at the Queen Elizabeth Hall; Has also sung in Elgar's The MusicMakers, Vivaldi's Gloria and the Duruflé Requiem; English National Opera debut, 1989 in The Mikado; Scottish Opera 1990 in the premiere of Judith Weir's The Vanishing Bridegroom; Season 1994–95 as Cenerentola for Castleward Opera and Iolanthe for Scottish Opera; Season 1997 at the Opéra Bastille, Paris, in Parsifal and as Mozart's Annius. *Honours:* Scottish Opera John Noble Bursary, 1987; Decca-Kathleen Ferrier Prize, 1987; Isobel Baillie Performance Award, 1987; Scottish Opera John Noble Award, 1987; Royal Overseas League, 1987; English Speaking Union, 1988; Caird and Munster Scholarships, 1987–89. *Address:* c/o Scottish Opera, 32 Elmbank Crescent, Glasgow, G2 4PT, Scotland.

McCRAY, James; singer (tenor); b. 21 Feb. 1939, Warren, Ohio, USA. *Education:* studied with Raymond Buckingham. *Career:* debut, Stratford Festival, Canada, in Weill's Aufstieg und Fall der Stadt Mahagonny; Appearances in Seattle, Kansas City, Miami, San Francisco and the New York City Opera; Guest with Tel-Aviv Opera, Israel; Roles include Verdi's Ismaele, Radames and Manrico, Wagner's Siegmund and Siegfried, Don José, Samson, Ponchielli's Enzo and Puccini's Calaf, Dick Johnson and Cavaradossi; Sang Florestan at Montreal, 1999; Young Siegfried in the first modern Polish production of the Ring, Warsaw, 1989; Wuppertal 1989, as Tristan. *Address:* c/o Wuppertaler Bühnen, Spinnstrasse 4, 5600 Wuppertal, Germany.

McCREADY, Ivan; cellist; b. 1963, England. *Education:* Royal Academy of Music with Derek Simpson. *Career:* member of the Borante Piano Trio from 1982; Concerts at the Wigmore Hall and in Dublin and Paris; Beethoven's Triple Concerto at the Festival Wien Klassik, 1989; Season 1990 at the Perth and Bath Festivals and tour of Scandinavia, Russia and the Baltic States; Cellist of the Duke String Quartet from 1985; Performances in the Wigmore Hall, Purcell Room, Conway Hall and throughout England; Tours of Germany, Italy, Austria and the Baltic States; South Bank series 1991, with Mozart's early quartets; Soundtracks for Ingmar Bergman documentary The Magic Lantern, Channel 4 1988; Features for French television 1990–91, playing Mozart, Mendelssohn, Britten and Tippett; Brhams Clarinet Quintet for Dutch Radio with Janet Hilton; Live Music Now series with concerts for disadvantaged people; The Duke Quartet Invites. . . at the Derngate, Northampton 1991, with Duncan Prescott and Rohan O'Hara; Resident quartet of the Rydale Festival 1991; Residency at Trinity College, Oxford, tours to Scotland and Northern Ireland and concert at the Queen Elizabeth Hall 1991. *Recordings include:* Quartets by Tippett, Shostakovich and Britten (Third) for Factory Classics. *Honours:* Awards include the Harold Craxton at the RAM and the Leche Scholarship. *Address:* c/o Ingrassia, Duke Quartet, Via San Zanobi 7, 50018 Scandicci, Italy.

McCREDIE, Andrew Dalgarno, AM, MA, DPhil, FAHA; musicologist and dramaturg; b. 3 Sept. 1930; one d. *Education:* Sydney Grammar School, Sydney Conservatorium, Royal Acad. of Music, Univ. of Copenhagen. *Career:* mem. Musicological Soc. of Australia, Int. Musicological Soc. (cttee 1979–89), Royal Musical Asscn, American Musicological Soc., Societé International de Musicologie. *Compositions:* Three songs for tenor, french horn and piano 1954, Symphonic Study 1955, Violin Concerto 1957. *Honours:* British Council and Winston Churchill Awards (Copenhagen) 1955–56, Edward J. Dent Medal 1974. *Address:* Tintorettostrass II, 80638 Munich, Germany (office); 13/18 Lansell Road, Toorak, Vic. 3142, Australia (home). *Telephone:* (89) 1782325 (office); (3) 9826-6348 (home).

McCREESH, Paul D.; conductor; b. 24 May 1960, London, England; m. Susan Jones 1983. *Education:* University of Manchester. *Career:* debut,

St John Smith's Square, 1981; Director, Gabrieli Consort and Players, founded 1982; Frequent performances and recordings of Baroque and Renaissance in the United Kingdom and abroad; Directed Bach's St Matthew Passion at Barbican Hall, London, 2001. *Recordings include:* Lutheran Mass for Christmas Morning, with Motets by Praetorius; Reconstructions, Venetian Easter Mass and Venetian Vespers; Handel's Soloman and Messiah;Video, music for San Rocco. *Honours:* Gramophone Award, 1990 for A Venetian Coronation and 1993; ABC Record of the Year, 1991; Dutch Edison Award, 1991 and 1995; Grammy nomination, USA, 1994; Diapason D'Or, France, 1994, 1999; Echo Prize, Germany, 1995. *Current Management:* Intermusica Artists' Management Ltd, 16 Duncan Terrace, London, N1 8BZ, England.

McCULLOCH, Jenifer Susan, ARCM; opera singer (lyrico-spinto soprano) and voice teacher; b. 3 Aug. 1957, London, England. *Education:* Royal College of Music, National Opera Studio. *Career:* debut as Countess Almaviva in Mozart's Marriage of Figaro with English National Opera, 1986; Concerts at the major London venues and at festivals in Edinburgh, Cambridge, Henley and Manchester; Appeared in oratorio all over the United Kingdom and Europe; Has sung Brahms' Requiem with David Willcocks and Mendelssohn's Infelice with Solti; Recorded Mozart's Exultate Jubilate and Strauss's Four Last Songs for BBC; American debut in the Four Last Songs, with San Jose Symphony Orchestra; Verdi's Requiem at the Three Choirs Festival and Usher Hall, Edinburgh; Beethoven's Ninth under Laszlo Heltay at 1992 Kenwood Summer Season opening; Appearances in opera include Donna Anna in Don Giovanni for English National Opera; Glyndebourne Festival debut as Vitellia in La Clemenza di Tito, followed by Musetta in La Bohème and Donna Anna for the Touring Opera; Tosca in Dublin; Mozart's Marcellina in Hong Kong, Netherlands (Opera Zuid and Amsterdam), Lisbon, Paris, Ludwigsburg and London; Various television broadcasts including 2 episodes of Inspector Morse; Professor of Singing, Guildhall School of Music and Trinity College of Music, London; International Adjudicator and Course Director; mem, BVA. *Recordings:* Marriage of Figaro; A Victorian Christmas; Gilbert and Sullivan. *Current Management:* Robert Gilder & Co., Enterprise House, 59–65 Upper Ground, London, SE1 9PQ, England. *Telephone:* (20) 7928-9008. *Fax:* (20) 7928-9755. *E-mail:* rgilder@robert-gilder.com. *Address:* Flat One, 80 Sunnyhill Road, Streatham, London, SW16 2UL, England.

McDANIEL, Barry; singer (baritone); b. 18 Oct. 1930, Lyndon, Kansas, USA. *Education:* Juilliard School, New York; Stuttgart Musikhochschule with Alfred Paulus and Hermann Reutter. *Career:* debut sang in recital at Stuttgart in 1953; Mainz Opera, 1954–55; Stuttgart Opera, 1957–59; Karlsruhe, 1960–62; Deutsche Oper Berlin from 1962, notably in Baroque and contemporary works, also Mozart and Wagner; Sang in the premieres of Henze's Der junge Lord, 1965, and Reimann's Melusine, 1971; Salzburg Festival, 1968; Metropolitan Opera, 1972 as Debussy's Pelléas; Other roles include the Barber in Die schweigsame Frau and Olivier in Capriccio; Guest appearances in Schubert Lieder and as Christus in the St Matthew Passion. *Recordings:* Bach, Christmas Oratorio; Ariadne auf Naxos, Dido and Aeneas, La Finta Giardiniera and Der junge Lord, Deutsche Grammophon; Orff's Trionfi, BASF. *Address:* c/o Deutsche Oper Berlin, Richard Wagnerstrasse 10, 1000 Berlin, Germany.

MacDONALD, Hugh, MA, PhD, FRCM; academic; *Avis Blewett Professor of Music, Washington University, St Louis;* b. 31 Jan. 1940, Newbury, Berkshire, England; m. 1st Naomi Butterworth 1963; one s. three d.; m. 2nd Elizabeth Babb 1979; one s. *Education:* Pembroke College, Cambridge. *Career:* General Editor, Complete works of Berlioz, 1965; Lecturer, Cambridge University, 1966–71; Oxford University, 1971–80; Visiting Professor, Indiana University, 1979; Gardiner Professor of Music, Glasgow University, 1980–87; Avis Blewett Professor of Music, Washington University, St Louis, 1987–. *Publications:* Editor, New Berlioz Edition, 1967; Skryabin, 1978; Berlioz, 1982; Berlioz: Selected Letters, 1995; Berlioz's Orchestration Treatise, 2002. *Contributions:* The New Grove Dictionary of Music and Musicians; The New Grove Dictionary of Opera. *Honours:* Szymanowski Medal. *Address:* Department of Music, Washington University, Campus Box 1032, St Louis, MO 63130, USA.

McDONALD, John, BA, DMA; composer and pianist; b. 27 Oct. 1959, Norfolk, Virginia, USA; m.; two s. one d. *Education:* Yale University, Yale School of Music. *Career:* debut recital, Carnegie Hall, 1995; Associate Professor of Music, Tufts University, 1998–, Chair., Tufts Music Dept, 2000–03; Co-Director of Extension Works, Boston, 1990–2003; Artistic Ambassador, Cultural Specialist in Asia, 1994, 1995; Appearances on NPR, German radio; Premieres in Havana, Shanghai, St Petersburg; Commissions: Fleet Boston Celebrity Series, 1994, 2003; mem, Broadcast Music Inc. *Compositions:* More than 800 works including 20 piano albums, 9 piano sonatas; 2 piano concertos; 2 string quartets; 100 songs; Works for piccolo, flute, early instruments, chamber ensembles, wind ensemble and orchestra; 4 film scores; *Recordings:* Duetto for Piano; Sonatina for Soprano Sax and Piano; As

pianist, featured in recordings of music by Donal Fox, John Harbison, Gardner Read, Gunther Schuller, George Walker. *Publications:* Sonatina for Piccolo and Piano, 1997; 2 solo Piccolo albums, 1995 and 1998; Ricercata, for three bass viols, 1998. *Contributions:* Essays, One Composer's Manifesto in the Form of a Wish List; Musings and Minor Writings. *Honours:* First prize, Leo M Traynor Competition for New Viol Music, 1997; Mellon Fellowship, 1996; NEA Grant, 1995. *Address:* Music Department, Tufts University, 48 Professors Row, Medford, MA 02155, USA.

MacDONALD, Malcolm Calum; writer on music and journalist; b. 26 Feb. 1948, Nairn, Scotland. *Education:* Downing College, Cambridge. *Career:* freelance writer for musical journals; music copyist; editor; Managing Ed., Tempo Magazine; compiler, Gramophone Classical Catalogue. *Compositions:* Surface Measure and Before Urbino, two songs with orchestra; At the Firth of Lorne and other songs with piano; Piano Pieces; arrangements of various contemporary works. *Publications:* Havergal Brian, Perspective on the Music 1972, John Foulds: His Life in Music 1975, Schoenberg 1976; contrib. to The Listener, Musical Times, Tempo, Musical Events, Records and Recordings. *Address:* 95 King Henry's Road, Swiss Cottage, London NW3, England.

McDONALD, Margaret; singer (mezzo-soprano); b. 1964, Grimsby, England. *Education:* Royal Northern College of Music and in Milan. *Career:* early experience with Glyndebourne Festival and Touring Opera; Engagements with Opera North as Carmen, and in Mason's Playing Away, Oberon (1985), Rebecca by Josephs and Gianni Schicchi; Eboli in Don Carlos for Scottish Opera Go Round, Ascanio in Benvenuto Cellini and Bizet's Djamileh for Chelsea Opera Group; Further appearances with English National Opera, English Bach Festival and Buxton Festival; Concerts include the Three Choirs, Quimper, Spitalfields, Saintes and Dublin Contemporary Festivals; Extensive oratorio repertory at concert halls and cathedrals throughout the United Kingdom, including works by Henze and Boulez. *Recordings include:* Isoletta in Bellini's La Straniera, with the Northern Sinfonia; She-Ancient in Tippett's Midsummer Marriage (Nimbus). *Honours:* Curtis Gold Medal, RNCM. *Current Management:* Musicmakers International Artists Representation, Tailor House, 63–65 High Street, Whitwell, Hertfordshire SG4 8AH, England. *Telephone:* (1438) 871708. *Fax:* (1438) 871777. *E-mail:* musicmakers@compuserve.com. *Website:* www .operauk.com.

McDONALD, Lois; singer (soprano); b. 7 Feb. 1939, Larkspur, Alberta, Canada. *Education:* studied in Edmonton, Vancouver and Toronto and with Otakar Kraus in London. *Career:* debut, Toronto 1969 in Wolf-Ferrari's Il Segreto di Susanna; Sang in Ottawa and Toronto, then Flensburg, Germany; Sadler's Wells/English National Opera from 1970, notably as Handel's Semele and in the title role of Hamilton's Anna Karenina (1981); Other roles include Mozart's Countess, Constanze and Fiordiligi, Massenet's Manon and the Marschallin; Sang the Comtesse de Coigny in Andrea Chénier at Toronto, 1988; Teaching at University of Toronto (retired 2001); Freelance singing roles include Fedora, Opera in concert, Anna in Anna Karenina as guest of ENO; mem, National British Equity, ACTRA Canadian Society; Appeared in concert and freelance opera, including at the Miami Festival in Don Sanche, Lizst, with Opera Barrie as the Witch in Hansel and Gretel, The Old Maid in The Old Maid and the Thief; Having retired from the Univ. University of Toronto, she continues to teach privately and adjudicate music festivals; Many appearances for BBC Radio 2 and 3. *Recordings include:* Freia in The Ring (HMV) and Donizetti's Maria Padilla; Kurt Weill's Der Protagonist, Lizst's Don Sanche; Delius's Margot-la-rouge; Wagner's Rienzi. *Address:* c/o Canadian Opera Company, 227 Front Street E, Toronto, ON M5A 1EB, Canada.

McDONNELL, Thomas Anthony; singer (baritone); b. 27 April 1940, Melbourne, Australia; m. Mary Jennifer Smith. *Education:* Melba Conservatorium, Melbourne with Lennox Brewer. *Career:* debut, Belcore in L'Elisir d'amore at Brisbane, 1965; Sadler's Wells/English National Opera from 1967, as Mozart's Figaro, Verdi's Germont, Escamillo and in the first British stage performance of Prokofiev's War and Peace (1972) and Henze's The Bassarids (1974); Sang in War and Peace at the opening of the Sydney Opera House, 1973; Created roles in Crosse's The Story of Vasco, 1974, Henze's We Come to the River and Tippett's The Ice Break (both at Covent Garden); Iain Hamilton's The Royal Hunt of the Sun and Nicola LeFanu's Dawnpath (both 1977); London Collegiate Theatre 1977 in the British premiere of Nielsen's Saul and David; Well known as Mozart's Papageno and Tchaikovsky's Onegin; Sang Mozart's Commendatore with Opera Factory, Queen Elizabeth Hall, 1990 and Silva in Ernani for Chelsea Opera Group; Sang Lictor in The Coronation of Poppea for Opera Factory, 1992. *Recordings include:* Israel in Egypt; La Fanciulla del West; Tancredi; Donizetti rarities. *Honours:* Showcase Australia, 1965; Leverhulme Youth and Music Scholarship to Rome.

MacDOUGALL, Jamie; Scottish singer (tenor); b. 25 Jan. 1966, Glasgow. *Education:* Royal Scottish Acad. of Music, Guildhall School of Music, studied in Italy with Carlo Bergonzi. *Career:* appeared with Songmakers' Almanac 1988 at the Nottingham Festival, at the Buxton Festival and in London in Handel's Israel in Egypt and Mozart's C minor Mass; Season 1990–91 with Haydn's Creation in Aberdeen and at the Usher Hall, Edinburgh; Bach's Magnificat and Purcell's King Arthur at the Queen Elizabeth Hall; Mozart's C Minor Mass conducted by Frans Brueggen; Handel's Belshazzar; Orlando Paladino by Haydn at Garsington Manor; Bach's Magnificat and B Minor Mass in Belgium; Recital in the Szymanowski series at the Purcell Room; Operatic engagements include the Prologue and Quint in The Turn of the Screw and Gluck's Alceste with the English Bach Festival in Monte Carlo and at Covent Garden; Season 1996 with Septimus in Theodora at Glyndebourne, Fernando in Handel's Almira at Halle, Bach's Magnificat in Manchester and Mozart's Ottavio for GTO. *Recordings:* King Arthur conducted by Trevor Pinnock. *Honours:* Jean Highgate Scholarship and Lieder Prize at RSAM; Finalist in the Kathleen Ferrier Singing Competition, 1986.

McELROY, Sam; singer (baritone); b. 1974, Cork, Ireland. *Education:* Centre de Formation Lyrique, Paris. *Career:* appearances with Opéra National de Paris in Katya Kabanova, Un Maris a la Porte, and Parsifaland as Dandini in Cenerentola for English Touring Opera, Nick Shadow in The Rake's Progress, Lockit in The Beggar's Opera and Blazes in Peter Maxwell Davies' The Lighthouse for Opera Theatre Company, Dublin, Rigoletto at Dartington; Concerts include Messiah with the Irish Chamber Orchestra and in Düsseldorf; Season 1999–2000 with Mozart's Count in Dublin; His opera roles for Opera Ireland include Figaro in Il Barbiere di Siviglia, Sharpless in Madame Butterfly, Harry Heegan in Silver Tassie and Cappadocian in Salome;; For Scottish Opera Go Round he has performed Malattesta in Don Pasquale; Japanese debut at the Pacific Music Festival, 1997; He has sung Lescaut in Manon for Opera Monte Carlo. *Honours:* Winner, Lombard and Ulster Music Awards 1992. *Current Management:* Harlequin Agency Ltd, 203 Fidlas Road, Cardiff, CF4 5NA, Wales. *Telephone:* (29) 2075-0821. *Fax:* (29) 2075-5971. *E-mail:* sioned@harlequin-agency.co.uk.

McFADDEN, Claron; singer (soprano); b. 1961, Rochester, NY, USA. *Education:* Eastman School, Rochester. *Career:* has sung in concert, opera and oratorio from 1984; Opera debut 1985 in Hasse's L'Eroe Chinese conducted by Ton Koopman; Regular appearances with William Christie in Europe and North and South America, notably as Amour in Rameau's Anacréon at the Opéa Lyrique du Rhin; Netherlands Opera debut 1989, as Zerbinetta in Ariadne auf Naxos; Season 1991 included Mozart's Impresario at the Salzburg Festival and on South Bank, Acis and Galatea with the King's Consort and Rameau's Les Indes Galantes with Les Arts Florissants in Montpellier; Has also worked in concert with the Schoenberg Ensemble and composers Gunther Schuller, Louis Andriessen and Steve Reich; Carmina Burana conducted by Leopold Hager and L'Enfant et les Sortilèges under Sergiu Comissiona; Sang in Purcell's Fairy Queen with Les Arts Florissants at the Barbican Hall, 1992; King Arthur at Covent Garden, 1995; Sang in Bach's B Minor Mass at St John's London, 1997; Lulu at the 1996 Glyndebourne Festival and Controller in the premiere of Jonathan Dove's Flight, 1998; Tippett's The Mask of Time at the 1999 London Proms; Season 2000–01 as Britten's Tytania for Opera North, Musetta for Glyndebourne Touring Opera and Schoenberg's Pierrot Lunaire at the London Proms. *Recordings:* Acis and Galatea and Handel's Ottone with the King's Consort; Haydn's Orfeo with La Stagione Frankfurt; Vocal works by Glenn Gould (Sony Classical); Les Indes Galantes. *Honours:* Prize Winner at the 1988 International Competition, 's-Hertogenbosch. *Current Management:* Phoenix Artists, 6 Windmill Street, London W1P 1HF, England.

McFARLAND, Robert; singer (baritone); b. 1958, Canada. *Career:* Season 1987 as Donner in Das Rheingold at the Metropolitan and Amonasro at Miami and Houston; European debut Nice 1988, as Jack Rance (repeated for Opera North at Leeds, 1990); Further guest appearances at Miami (Luna in Trovatore), Lisbon (Iago, 1990), Toronto (Escamillo, 1990) and Monte Carlo (Nottingham in Roberto Devereux); Other roles include the villains in Les Contes d'Hoffmann; Renato at Antwerp, 1992 and Tonio (Miami, 1991). *Address:* c/o Greater Miami Opera, 1200 Coral Way, Miami, FL 33145, USA.

McGEGAN, Nicholas, BA, MA; conductor; b. 14 Jan. 1950, Sawbridgeworth, Hertfordshire, England. *Education:* Corpus Christi College, Cambridge, Magdalen College, Oxford. *Career:* Professor of Baroque Flute, 1973–79, Professor of Music History, 1975–79, Director of Early Music, 1976–80, Royal College of Music; Artist-in-Residence, Washington University, St Louis, Missouri, 1979–85; Music Director, Philarmonia Baroque Orchestra, San Francisco, 1985–; Music Director, Ojai Music Festival, Ojai, California, 1988; Baroque Artistic Consultant, Santa Fe Chamber Music Festival, 1990–92; Music Director, Gottingen Handel Festival, Gottingen, Germany, 1991–; Artistic Director and Founder, Arcadian Academy, San Francisco, 1992–; Principal Conductor, Drottningholm Court Theatre, Sweden, 1993–96; Principal Guest Conductor, Scottish Opera, 1993–98; (new production of Così fan tutte, 1998); Baroque Series Director, St Paul Chamber Orchestra, 1999–2003, Artistic Pnr, 2003–(06); Conducted Alcina at Göttingen, 2002; Music Dir, Irish Chamber Orchestra, 2002–; Artistic Dir, Killaloe Music Festival, 2003–; Artist-in-Residence, Milwaukee Symphony Orchestra, 2003–; Appearances as Guest Conductor include San Francisco Symphony, Los Angeles Philharmonic, City of Birmingham Symphony Orchestra, Hallé Orchestra, Sydney Symphony, Melbourne Symphony, Houston Symphony, National Symphony, Atlanta Symphoniy, Minnesota Orchestra, Orchestre de la Suisse Romand, St Louis Symphony, Detroit Symphony, Malaysian Philharmonic, Royal Concertgebouw Orchestra, Aspen Music Festival, Toronto Symphony; Philadelphia Orchestra, New York Philharmonic; mem, Advisory Boards, Maryland Handel Festival and London's Handel House. *Recordings:* (as a soloist) CPE Bach's Quartets (flute); JC Bach's Sonatas Op1 18 (flute) with Christopher Hogwood); JS Bach's Anna Magdelena Notebook (harpsichord); Music For Two Flutes By The Bach Family with Stephen Preston); Haydn's London Trios (flute), Piano Trios (piano and flute); Vivaldi's Concertos For Two Flutes; (as conductor) JS Bach's Cantatas and around 20 operas and oratorios by Handel, of which Susanna and Ariodante have both won Gramophone Awards, and works by Arne, Corelli, P Humfrey, Matteis, Monteverdi, Mozart, Purcell, Rameau (including 3 operas), A Scarlatti, Telemann, Uccellini, Vivaldi. *Publications:* Editions, Philidor's Tom Jones, 1978. *Contributions:* Articles include Handel, Musical Times, 1994; Handel as a practical opera composer, in the collected edition Die Gegenwart der musikalischen Vergangenheit: Meisterwerke der Musik in der Werkstatt des Dirigenten, 1999. *Honours:* 2 Diapason d'Or Awards for recordings with the Arcadian Academy; Handel Prize, Halle Handel Festival, Germany; Drottningholmsteaterns Vanners Hederstecken, honorary medal of the Friends of the Drottningholm Theatre. *Current Management:* Schwalbe and Partners, 170 East 61 Street #5N, New York, NY 10021, USA.

McGIBBON, Roisin; singer (soprano); b. 1960, Northern Ireland. *Education:* Guildhall School of Music with Margaret Lensky, and at the National Opera Studio. *Career:* represented Northern Ireland in the Cardiff Singer of the World Competition, 1985; Appearances for Radio Telfis Eireann include Lieder by Schumann and Liszt; Wexford Festival 1986, in Humperdinck's Königskinder and Rossini's Tancredi; Has also sung the Composer in Ariadne auf Naxos; Concert engagements in Messiah at Armagh, Britten's War Requiem in Belfast, Savitri by Holst at Aix and Elgar's Apostles in Nottingham. *Current Management:* Magenta Music International, 64 Highgate High Street, London N6 5HX, England.

McGILLOWAY, Emer; singer (mezzo-soprano); b. 1967, Northern Ireland. *Education:* Medecine in Belfast and Dublin, Guildhall School with Laura Sarti. *Career:* Maddalena in Linda di Chamounix, Juno in La Calisto, Der Trommler in Der Kaiser von Atlantis and Veruna in Dvořák's Cunning Peasant at the GSM; Further study at the National Opera Studio, 1997–98; Studying with Robert Dean; Opera North from 1998 as Olga in Eugene Onegin, Lady Essex in Gloriana, also televised, and Mozart's Cherubino; Season 1998–99 in Rusalka and as Hope in Gluck's Orfeo for English National Opera. *Honours:* Herbert Morris Griffen Opera Award; Ann Price Mezzo-soprano Award; Finalist Grimsby International Singing Competition. *Current Management:* Music International, 13 Ardilaun Road, London, N5 2QR, England.

McGREEVY, Geraldine, Dip RAM, ARAM; British singer (soprano); b. 1968. *Education:* Univ. of Birmingham; Royal Acad. of Music; National Opera Studio. *Career:* operatic roles include: Contessa Almaviva, Donna Anna, Vitellia, Rosalinde in Fledermaus, Micaela, First Lady and Miss Jessel (WNO); Ellen Orford (Oper Frankfurt); Alice Ford (Aix-en-Provence, 2001 and Paris, 2002); Ghita Der Zwerg, La Monnaie; Fiordiligi (RAM conducted by Sir Colin Davis, 1997 and Opera Zuid, 1999); Female Chorus in Rape of Lucretia (Edinburgh Festival); Alcina, Cleopatra in Giulio Cesare, Angelica in Orlando and Poppea in Agrippina (Early Opera Co); Galatea in Acis and Galatea; Laurette in Le Docteur Miracle; Donna Anna, First Lady, Mistress Page in Sir John in Love, Casilda in Gondoliers (British Youth Opera); concert repertoire includes: Schoenberg's Pierrot Lunaire; Villa Lobos' Bachianas Brasileiras No. 5; Berg's Orchestral Extracts from Wozzeck with Gennadi Rozhdestvensky; Britten's Les Illuminations; Strauss' Vier Letzte Lieder; Wigmore Hall debut, 1997, many appearances there since; Purcell Room debut, 1997; recitals at St John's Smith Square, Frankfurt Opera House, Klavier Festival Ruhr with Graham Johnson, Edinburgh Festival, and in Newcastle with Julius Drake; numerous broadcasts for the BBC and for European radio stations; recent concert engagements include: The English Concert with Trevor Pinnock, The Acad. of St Martin in the Fields with Sir Neville Marriner, the Moscow Tchaikovsky Symphony Orchestra in Zurich with Jane Glover, the London

Philharmonic Orchestra with Kurt Masur, the Sharoun Ensemble and Anne Manson in the Cologne Philharmonic and the Royal Liverpool Philharmonic Orchestra with Petr Altrichter and Libor Pesek. *Recordings:* Wolf Goethe Leider (with Graham Johnson); songs by Arthur Bliss (with the Nash Ensemble); contributions to Complete Schubert Edition; music by John Blow (with Red Byrd and the Parley of Instruments); Consort Songs by William Byrd (with Phantasm); Spanish Renaissance Music (with Music Antiqua of London). *Honours:* Worshipful Company of Musicians Silver Medal, 1995; RAM Shinn Fellowship, 1996; Kathleen Ferrier Award, 1996. *Current Management:* Askonas Holt Ltd, Lonsdale Chambers, 27 Chancery Lane, London, WC2A 1PF, England. *Telephone:* (20) 7400-1700. *Fax:* (20) 7400-1799. *E-mail:* info@ askonasholt.co.uk. *Website:* www.askonasholt.co.uk; www .geraldinemcgreevy.com (home).

MacGREGOR, Joanna Clare, BA, FRAM; British concert pianist; b. 16 July 1959, London; d. of Angela MacGregor and Alfred MacGregor; m. Richard Williams 1986; one d. (deceased). *Education:* South Hampstead High School for Girls, New Hall Coll. Cambridge, Royal Acad. of Music. *Career:* Young Concert Artists Trust concerts and recitals, UK 1985–88; performances of classical, jazz and contemporary music in over 40 countries; has performed with Rotterdam, Oslo and Netherlands Radio and Royal Philharmonic Orchestras, Sydney, Berlin, Chicago, BBC and London Symphony Orchestras, New York Philharmonic, Philharmonia, London Mozart Players, Royal Scottish, Royal Liverpool, English Chamber Orchestras; has worked with Sir Harrison Birtwistle, Pierre Boulez, John Adams, Lou Harrison and jazz artists Django Bates and Andy Sheppard; numerous radio and TV appearances including Last Night of the Proms 1997; established own record label Sound Circus 1998; Prof. of Music, Gresham Coll. 1998–; conducting debut on UK tour with Britten Sinfonia, Assoc. Artistic Dir 2002–; mem. Arts Council of England 1998–. *Recordings:* American Piano Classics, Britten Concerto, Satie, The Gershwin Songbook, and music by Bach, Nancarrow, Scarlatti, Bartók, Debussy, Ravel and Messaien; Memoirs of an Amnesiac (radio play). *Publications:* Music Tuition Book, Joanna MacGregor's Piano World (5 vols) 2001. *Honours:* Hon. Fellow Royal Acad. of Music, Trinity Coll. of Music, RSA; European Encouragement Prize for Music 1995, NFMS Sir Charles Grove Award 1998, South Bank Show Award for Classical Music 2000. *Current Management:* Ingpen and Williams, 26 Wadham Road, London, SW15 2LR, England. *Telephone:* (20) 8874-3222.

McGUIRE, Edward, ARCM, ARAM; composer; b. 15 Feb. 1948, Glasgow, Scotland. *Education:* Royal Academy of Music with James Iliff, State Academy of Music, Stockholm, Sweden with Ingvar Lidholm. *Career:* radio broadcasts on BBC Radio 3 include: Symphonic Poem, Calgacus, 1976, Symphonic Poem, Source, 1979; Euphoria performed by The Fires of London, 1980, Edinburgh International Festival; Debut at London Proms, 1982; BBC Radio 3 series features trilogy, Rebirth, Interregnum, Liberation, 1984; Wilde Festival commission (String Trio) for performance by The Nash Ensemble, 1986; Premiere of Guitar Concerto, 1988; Peter Pan for Scottish Ballet, 1989; mem, Whistlebinkies Folk Music Group, 1973–; Scottish Arts Council Music Committee, 1980–83; Chair, Musicians' Union, Glasgow Branch, 2001–. *Compositions:* A Glasgow Symphony, 1990; The Loving of Etain, 1990 for Paragon Opera; Trombone Concerto, 1991; Viola Concerto, 1998; Accordion Concerto, 1999; Violin Concerto, 2000. *Recordings:* music has featured on albums, including Paragon Premieres, 1993 and Scotland's Music, 1993; The Best of the BBC Orchestras, BBC Music Magazine. *Honours:* Hecht Prize, RAM, 1968; National Young Composers Competition, Liverpool University, 1969; Competition for Test Piece for Carl Flesch International Violin Competiton, 1978; Competition for a String Quartet for performance at SPNM 40th Anniversary Gala Concert, Barbican, 1983; Featured composer, Park Lane Group Purcell Room series, 1993; BBC Radio 3 Composers of The Week, 1995; Featured composer Bath International Guitar Festival, 1996 and International Viola Congress, 1998. *Current Management:* Scottish Music Information Centre, 1 Bowmont Gardens, Glasgow G12 9LR, Scotland. *Website:* www.smic.org .uk.

MACHL, Tadeusz; Composer, Organist and Professor; b. 22 Oct. 1922, Lwow, Poland; m. Irena Paszkiewicz-Machl; two c. *Education:* State College of Music, Kraków, 1949–52, under guidance Professor Malawski and Professor Rutkowski. *Career:* Works recorded in Poland, played through Poland and abroad; Professor, Prorector, 1969–72, Academy of Music, Kraków; Director of Chair of Composition, 1966–72; President of Disciplinary Committee of Pedagogical Staff, 1972–77; Leader of Amateur Choirs, 1960–1980; President, Union of Amateur Choirs and Orchestras, 1979–83; mem, Union of Polish Composers and Society of Authors ZAiKS, Warsaw. *Compositions:* For great symphony orchestra: 6 Symphonies: 1947, 1948, 1948, 1954, 1963, 1998; 7 Organ Concertos: 1950, 1952, 1953, 1957, 1979, 1983; Concerto for 3 organs, 1969; 9 Instrumental Concertos: Concerto for voice, 1958; Violin Concerto, 1960; Harpsichord Concerto, 1962; Piano Concerto, 1964; Arpa Concerto,

1965; Concerto for piano and harpsichord, 1966; Violoncello (or Viola) Concerto, 1967; Concerto for 2 pianos and organ, 1969; Concerto for bugle-horn, 1971; 4 Cantatas: Work Day, 1948; Cantata for Youth, 1954; Icar's Flight, 1968; Blue Cross, 1974; Rapsod, 1996; Transcriptions for organ compositions of J. S. Bach: Preludes and Fugues, 1956; Chaconne, 1973; Fantasy G, 1993; Poems: Jubilee Poem, 1979, My Town, 1992, Dirge, 1994; Lyric Suite, 1956; Requiem, 1980; Ouverture Silvery Wings, 1985; Symphonic Scherzo, 1986; Symphonic Poem, 1996; Chamber Music: 4 string quartets, 1950, 1957, 1961, 1972; Lyric Suite, 1955; Herbarium, 1980; Terrarium, 1982; Triptych–Heartiness Landscapes, 1993; Suite for stringed instruments, 1997; Composition for 20 Years of Pontificate of Jan Pawel II, 1998; In Memoriam St Kinga, 1998; Triptych in memoriam Amdrzej Hiolski for chamber orchestra, 2001; Rosary Poems for chamber orchestra, 2001; Organ Music: 5 Virtuoso etudes, 1950; Deux pieces pour grand orgue, 1964; Pièce in cinque movements, 1965; Mini Suita, 1967; Triptych, 1968; 10 Compositions pour orgue, 1970; Landscapes I, 1976, II, 1978, III, 1982; Great Fantasy with B-A-C-H Fugue, 1980; Rupicaprae, 1982; 15 Rosary Poems, 1983; Sonate for 3 orgue, 1984; Disonatio, 1989; Poem, 1992; Stained Glass Windows, 1993; 45 Preludes to Polish Church Songs, 1997; Epitafium dédie a Jean Langlais, 1999; Choruses; Songs; Piano Music; Music for cinema, theatre and ballet. *Honours:* Award: Special Mention for String Quartets in Liège, I, 1956, II, 1959; Golden Cross of Merit, 1965; Active Man of Culture, 1970; Bachelors and Officers, Polonia Restituta, 1972, 1988; Merit Teacher of Poland, 1989; 1st Degress Ministry of Culture and Art, 1971 and 1990. *Address:* ul Bol Chrobrego 29/27, 31-428 Kraków, Poland.

MACHOVER, Tod, MM; American composer and cellist; b. 24 Nov. 1953, New York; m. June Kinoshita. *Education:* Juilliard School of Music, Univ. of California at Santa Cruz, Columbia Univ. *Career:* Composer-in-Residence, Institut de Recherche et Coordination Acoustique/Musique, Paris 1978–79; Dir, Musical Research 1979–85; faculty mem., Assoc. Prof. of Music and Media, Dir of Experimental Media Facility, Media Laboratory, MIT 1985–, Co-Dir of research consortium 1994–; invented technology named hyperinstruments 1986, began instrument design for this technology 1991–; Brain Opera, first performance, Lincoln Center Festival 1996; tours with his repertoire in the USA, Europe and Asia; music performed by many prominent musicians, such as Yo-Yo Ma, and ensembles. *Compositions include:* Fusione Fugace, 1981–82; Electric Etudes, 1983; Hyperstring Trilogy, 1991–93; Bounce, 1992; Wake-up Music, 1995; Brain Opera, 1995–96; He's Our Dad, 1997; Hypermusic installations at Meteorite Museum, Essen, 1998; Resurrection, premiered at Houston, 1999. *Publications include:* Hyperinstruments: A Progress Report 1992; contrib. book chapters, articles in learned musical journals. *Honours:* Gaudeamus Prize, 1977; Grant, Gulbenkian Foundation, 1980; Grants from National Endowment for the Arts, 1981, 1983, 1985; Prix de la Creation, French Culture Ministry, 1984; Friedheim Award, Kennedy Centre, 1987; Grant, Aaron Copland Fund for music, 1994; Chevalier, Ordre des Arts et des Lettres, 1995. *Address:* MIT Media Laboratory, E15-444, 20 Ames Street, Cambridge, MA 02139, USA. *Website:* www.media.mit.edu/~tod.

MACIAS, Reinaldo; Singer (Tenor); b. 1 Sept. 1956, Cuba. *Education:* Studied in the USA and at the Geneva Conservatory. *Career:* Sang at first in concert, notably with Messiah, Haydn's Schöpfung and Jahreszeiten and the Requiems of Dvořák, Britten and Mozart; Verdi Requiem in Paris, 1989; Opera roles from 1989, with Almaviva in Vienna and Zürich, Don Ottavio and Ferrando in Netherlands, the Berlioz Iopas at Zürich and Gounod's Roméo in Liège (1993); Other roles include the Duke of Mantua, Tamino and Lindoro (all in Zürich, 1991–92). *Address:* c/o Opernhaus Zürich, Falkenstrasse 1, 8008 Zürich, Switzerland.

McINTOSH, Thomas Lee, FRSA, MSc; conductor; b. 3 Dec. 1938; m. Miranda Harrison Vincent 1982. *Education:* Juilliard School of Music. *Career:* conductor and Music Dir London City Chamber Orchestra 1973–; Artistic Dir E Anglian Summer Music Festival 1978–, Penang Malaysia Music Festival 1986–87, Opera Anglia 1989–, Artanglia Ltd 1988; principal guest conductor Canton Symphony Orchestra 1994–. *Publications:* Eighteenth-Century Symphonic Music (contributing ed.), arrangements for orchestra of Valentine Waltzed (George Antheil), Rag Suite (various composers), Flower Rag Suite (Scott Joplin). *Honours:* first prize Int. Kranichstein Competition, prize winner Busoni Competition, Bolanzo. *Address:* Stacey Sowman, The Old School, Bridge Street, Hadleigh, Suffolk IP7 6BY, England (office). *Telephone:* (1473) 822596 (office). *Fax:* (1473) 824175 (office). *E-mail:* Thomas.McIntosh@ minstrelmusic.co.uk (office). *Website:* www.minstrelmusic.co.uk/ thomasmcintosh.htm (office).

McINTYRE, Sir Donald Conroy, Kt; singer (baritone); b. 22 Oct. 1934, Auckland, New Zealand; m. Jill Redington 1961; two d. *Education:* Auckland Teachers Training College, Guildhall School of Music, London. *Career:* debut, Welsh National Opera, as Zachariah in Nabucco, 1959; Principal Bass, Sadler's Wells Opera, 1960–67, Royal Opera

House, Covent Garden, 1967–; Annual appearances at Bayreuth Festival, 1967–81 as Wotan in the Ring and frequent international guest appearances; Sang Amfortas at Bayreuth, 1987–88, Monterone in a new production of Rigoletto at Covent Garden, 1988, followed by Prospero in British premiere of Berio's Un Re in Ascolto, 1989, Wotan in Die Walküre for Australian Opera, 1989; debut as Balstrode in Peter Grimes at Covent Garden, 1989, Hans Sachs in New Zealand premiere of Die Meistersinger, Wellington, 1990; Telramund, Teatro San Carlos, Lisbon, 1990; Wagner's Hans Sachs at Covent Garden, 1993 and in Lady Macbeth of Mtensk at Munich, 1993; Sang Gurnemanz in Parsifal at Antwerp, 1996; Sang Prus in The Makropulos Case at Toulouse, 1998; Other roles include: The Wanderer in Der Ring, Barak in Die Frau ohne Schatten, Pizarro in Fidelio, Golaud in Pelléas et Mélisande, Kurwenal in Tristan und Isolde, Heyst in Victory, Jochanaan in Salome, Scarpia in Tosca, Nick Shadow in The Rake's Progress, Doctor Schön in Lulu; Sang King Mark in Tristan for Opera North, 2001. *Recordings:* Pelléas et Mélisande, Oedipus Rex, Il Trovatore; Video of Der Ring des Nibelungen, from Bayreuth (DVD), 2000. *Honours:* Fidelio Medal from the International Association of Opera Directors and Intendants for Oustanding Service to the Royal Opera House, 1967–89. *Address:* Foxhill Farm, Jackass Lane, Keston, Bromley, Kent, England.

McINTYRE, Joy; singer (soprano); b. 24 Sept. 1938, Kinsley, Kansas, USA. *Education:* New England Conservatory, Salzburg Mozarteum. *Career:* sang at the Saarbrucken Opera 1964–66, Dortmund 1966–74 and Munich Staatsoper 1976–81; Roles have included Suzuki, Brangaene, Leonore, Venus, Ortrud, the Dyer's Wife, Marie, Abigaille, Santuzza, Turandot, Judith in Bluebeard's Castle and Lady Macbeth; Guest appearances at the Vienna Staatsoper, Lyon, Strasbourg, Brussels, Hamburg and Glasgow (Scottish Opera). *Address:* c/o Bayerische Staatsoper, Max Joseph Platz, Pf 100148, 8000 Munich 1, Germany.

McKAY, Elizabeth Norman, BSc, LRAM, DPhil; musicologist and pianist; b. 21 Nov. 1931, London, England; m. Gilbert Watt McKay 1960; one s. two d. *Education:* Bristol University, Somerville College Oxford University. *Career:* chamber musician, accompanist, coach, theatre work; teacher; Lecturer in Musical History. *Publications include:* Schubert's Music for the Theatre, Proceedings of The Royal Musical Association, 1966–67; Schubert as a Composer of Operas, Schubert Studies, 1982; The Impact of The New Pianofortes: Mozart, Beethoven and Schubert, 1987; Franz Schubert's Music for the Theatre, 1991; Schuberts Klaviersonaten von 1815 bis 1825, in Franz Schubert Reliquie-Sonate, 1992; Franz Schubert: A Biography, 1996; Proceedings of the Oxford Schubert Bicentenary Symposium 1997, co-editor; Schubert's String and Piano Duos in context, Schubert Studies, 1998; Schubert and the professional musicians with whom he associated, Schubert und seine Freunde, 1999. *Contributions:* The New Grove Dictionary of Music; Pipers Enzyklopadie des Musik Theaters, 1994; Schubert Lexikon, 1997; The Music Review; The Musical Times; Österreichische Musikzeitschrift; Music and Letters; The Beethoven Newsletter; Schubert Lexicon. *Honours:* Honorary Member of the Board of International Franz Schubert Institute. *Address:* Gamrie, Swan Lane, Long Hanborough, Witney, Oxfordshire OX29 8BT, England.

McKAY, Marjory Grieve; singer (soprano); b. 23 June 1951, Edinburgh, Scotland; m. Frederick Charles McKay 1981. *Education:* Trinity Academy, Edinburgh, Royal Manchester College of Music, Royal Northern College of Music. *Career:* debut as Esmeralda, Scottish Opera, 1980; Scottish opera roles Esmeralda in Bartered Bride, Belleza in L'Egisto and Feklusa in Katya Kabanova; Scottish Opera Go Round, Violetta; Welsh National Opera Workshop, Violetta in La Traviata; Many concerts and recitals in Scotland and the north of England; Now living in Sydney, Australia; Debut in Australian Opera as Gerhilde in Die Walküre, 1985 and Xenia in Boris Godonuv, 1986; debut with Western Australian Opera as Madama Butterfly, 1987; Created the title role in Alan Holley's new opera, Dorothea; Les Huguenots Video (Joan Sutherland's Farewell), 1990. *Address:* 4 Pelican Street, Gladesville, Sydney, NSW 2111, Australia.

MACKAY, Penelope Judith; Singer (soprano); b. 6 April 1943, Bradford, Yorkshire, England. *Education:* secretarial coll., Lycée Français, London, Guildhall School of Music and Drama. *Career:* debut, Glyndebourne 1970; sang at Glyndebourne 1970–72, with English Opera Group 1973–75, English Music Theatre 1976–78, ENO 1980–83; freelance work in the UK, Europe and USA; over 20 leading roles; sang in premieres of Lutyens's Time Off 1971, Britten's Death in Venice 1973; British premieres of Hans Werner Henze's La Cubana in the title role 1978, Krenek's Jonny Spielt Auf (Anita) 1984, Ligeti, Le Grand Macabre (Miranda) 1982; Austrian premiere in modern times of Fux's Angelica, Vincitrice di Alcina (Angelica), Graz 1984, and British premiere in modern times of Handel's Rodrigo (Rodrigo) 1985; Prof. of Singing, Royal Acad. of Music, London and Guildhall School of Music and Drama, London; mem. Incorporated Soc. of Musicians, British Voice Asscn,

Asscn of Teachers of Singing. *Address:* 30 Fairfield Road, Saxmundham, Suffolk IP17 1BA, England.

MACKAY, Robert Andrew, BSc, MMus; British composer, actor, singer (baritone) and musician (flute, classical guitar, bass); b. 12 July 1973, London, England. *Education:* Keele Univ., Bangor Univ. *Career:* session musician in Wales 1997–2001; composer-in-residence, Radio Bratislava, Slovakia 1998–99; bass player, Gyroscope 1998; flute, guitar and bass player, Tystion 1998–2002; collaborator with Pwyll ap Siôn on commission for Nat. Youth Choir of Wales and Opera Heloise 1999; works performed in UK, France, USA and New Zealand; several television appearances and radio broadcasts; mem. PRS, PRC, Equity, Soc. for the Promotion of New Music, BMIC, SAN. *Theatre:* Only Just 1997. *Film appearances:* Merlin, A Beautiful Mistake. *Television appearances:* Idot (S4C), Garej (S4C), Lois (S4C), Sesiwn Hwyr (S4C). *Compositions include:* Tempestuous Relationships 1995, Environs 1996, Sea Pictures 1997, Voicewind 1998, Postcards from the Summer 1999, Peiriant Gorllewinol, Meddwi Dros Gymru (Radio Cymru Rap Award for Album of the Year 2000) 1999, Flute Melt 2000, Augustine's Message 2001, Need Without Reason 2001, Joyce's Vision 2002. *Honours:* Bourges Synthése Festival Prix Résidence, France 1997, Hungarian Radio Special Prize 1999. *Address:* 239 Earlsfield Road, Earlsfield, London, SW18 3DE, England.

McKELLAR FERGUSON, Kathleen; singer (mezzo-soprano); b. 1959, Stirling, Scotland. *Education:* Royal Scottish Academy, Royal College of Music; studied with Margaret Hyde. *Career:* South Bank debut 1987, with the London Bach Orchestra; Beethoven's Ninth at the Gstaad Festival, 1990 and with the Ulster Orchestra; Other repertoire includes Mozart's Requiem, the Brahms Alto Rhapsody, Mahler's 8th, Songs of the Auvergne and A Child of our Time; Season 1990–91 with Haydn's Nelson Mass and the English Chamber Orchestra, Messiah with the Liverpool Philharmonic; Also sings Elgar's Sea Pictures and Music Makers, St Matthew Passion (Fairfields Hall) and Elijah; Concerts with Yehudi Menuhin at Festival Halls; Opera repertoire includes Florence Pike in Albert Herring (Aldeburgh 1986), Maketaten in Aknaten by Philip Glass for ENO 1987, Mozart's Marcellina and Third Lady for Pavillion Opera, Cherubino, and Handel's Bradamante (Alcina) for Flanders Opera 1991, Second Lady (Magic Flute) at Théâtre Royale de la Monnaie, Brussels, 1993, Suzuki (Madama Butterfly) for Opera Forum in Nederlands, 1994–, and Bradamante (Alcina) with Nikolaus Harnoncourt at Zürich Opera; Second Lady at Festival of Aix en Provence. *Address:* c/o Zürich Opera, Falkenstrasse 1, 8008 Zürich, Switzerland.

McKERRACHER, Colin; singer (tenor); b. 1960, Falkirk, Scotland. *Education:* Royal Northern College of Music with Joseph Ward, studied with Nicolai Gedda. *Career:* has sung with Glyndebourne Touring Opera and the Festival in Simon Boccanegra and Capriccio, 1986–87; Appearances with Scottish Opera-Go-Round as Števa in Jenůfa, Beppe and Turiddu (Cav and Pag) and Don Carlos; Lensky in Eugene Onegin for Opera 80 followed by Monostatos in The Magic Flute and Ernesto in Don Pasquale; English National Opera and Covent Garden debuts season, 1990–91, as Ferrando and in Così fan tutte. *Honours:* Prizewinner, 1989 Rio de Janeiro International Singing Competition.

MacKERRAS, Sir (Alan) Charles MacLaurin, Kt; orchestra and opera conductor; b. 17 Nov. 1925, Schenectady, NY, USA; m. Helena Judith Wilkins 1947; two d. *Education:* Sydney Conservatorium of Music, Prague Academy of Music, Czech Republic. *Career:* debut in Die Fledermaus, Sadler's Wells Opera, 1948; Principal Oboist, Sydney Symphony Orchestra, 1943–46; Staff Conductor, Sadler's Wells Opera, 1949–53 (British premiere of Janáček's Katya Kabanova, 1951); Principal Conductor BBC Concert Orchestra, 1954–56; Principal Conductor, Hamburg State Opera, Germany, 1966–69; Musical Director English National Opera, 1970–77; Chief Guest Conductor, BBC Symphony Orchestra, 1976–79; Chief Conductor, Sydney Symphony Orchestra, Australian Broadcasting Corporation, 1982–85; Musical Director Welsh National Opera, 1987–92; Principal Guest Conductor: Royal Liverpool Philharmonic Orchestra, 1986–88; Scottish Chamber Orchestra, 1992–95; San Francisco Opera, 1993–96; Royal Philharmonic Orchestra, 1993–96; Conductor, Laureate Scottish Chamber Orchestra, 1995–; Conductor Emeritus, Welsh National Opera, 1993–; Principal Guest Conductor, Czech Philharmonic Orchestra since January 1997; Musical Director Orchestra of St Luke's, 1998; Conducted new production of Don Giovanni at Covent Garden, 2002; Conducted Haydn's The Creation at the London Proms, 2002; Concert performance of Donizetti's Maria Stuarda at the 2002 Edinburgh Festival; mem, Royal Philharmonic Society. *Recordings include:* Handel for DDG, Janáček, Mozart and Brahms, Beethoven and Schubert. *Publications:* Ballet arrangements: Sullivan's Pineapple Poll, Verdi's Lady and the Fool; Reconstruction of Sullivan's lost Cello Concerto;. *Contributions:* Opera magazine; Where we are Now (interview) 1990; Music and Musicians; Contributed four appendices to Charles Mackerras, a Musician's Musician, by Nancy Phelan, 1987. *Honours:*

Gramophone Record of the Year, 1977, 1980, 1999; Gramophone Best Opera Recording Award, 1983, 1984, 1994, 1999; Janáček Medal, 1978; Fellow, Royal College of Music, 1987; D.Mus (Hon), from Universities of: Hull, 1990, Nottingham 1991, Brno (Czech republic), 1994, York 1994, Griffith, Brisbane (Australia), 1994, Oxford, 1997, Prague Academy of Music, 1999, Napier, 2000; Medal of Merit, Czech Republic, 1996.

MACKIE, David, MA, BMus, DipMus Ed, RSAM, ARCM; Accompanist, Repetiteur and Conductor; b. 25 Nov. 1943, Greenock, Scotland. *Education:* Greenock Acad., Royal Scottish Acad. of Music, Glasgow Univ., Birmingham Univ. *Career:* Repetiteur, D'Oyly Carte Opera Co 1975–76; Chorus Master and Assoc. Conductor, D'Oyly Carte Opera Co 1976–82; freelance accompanist, repetiteur, conductor 1982–. *Publications:* Reconstruction (with Sir Charles Mackerras) of Sullivan's Cello Concerto. *Address:* 187A Worple Road, Raynes Park, London, SW20 8RE, England (home). *Telephone:* (20) 8946-7892 (home). *Fax:* (20) 8946-7892 (home).

MACKIE, Neil; Singer (Tenor); b. 11 Dec. 1946, Aberdeen, Scotland. *Career:* Debut: London with the English Chamber Orchestra under Raymond Leppard; European engagements at the Flanders and Savonlinna Festivals, Concertgebouw Orchestra, in Rome for RAI and in Scandinavia; Tours of Netherlands and Belgium with La Petite Bande conducted by Sigiswald Kuijken; Association with Peter Maxwell Davies includes premieres of The Martyrdom of St Magnus, 1977, The Lighthouse 1980 and Into the Labyrinth 1983; Sang Gomatz in Mozart's Zaide at Wexford, 1981; Premiered Henze's Three Poems of W H Auden at Aldeburgh, 1984; Appeared at Cheltenham and Aldeburgh Festivals; British engagements with the Hallé, Bournemouth Sinfonietta, BBC Symphony and Scottish Chamber Orchestras, and with the London Sinfonietta under Simon Rattle; June 1988, Into the Labyrinth at the Ojai Festival in America; 1988–89 tour of USA with the Scottish Chamber Orchestra and appearances with the Orchestre National de Paris; Professor of Singing, Royal College of Music, London, 1985; Head of Vocal Studies, Royal College of Music, 1993. *Recordings include:* Mozart's Requiem and Haydn's Die Schöpfung with La Petite Bande; Mozart Masses with the King's College Choir; Britten's Serenade, with premiere of Now Sleeps the Crimson Petal and unpublished songs. *Honours:* FRSAMD, 1992; Hon D Mus, Aberdeen, 1993; CStJ, 1996; C.B.E., 1996; FRCM, 1996; FRSE, 1999. *Address:* c/o Royal College of Music (vocal faculty), Prince Consort Road, London, SW7 2 BS.

MACKIE, William; Singer (Bass); b. 16 Aug. 1954, Ayr, Scotland. *Education:* Royal Scottish Academy, Glasgow. *Career:* Debut: Scottish Opera, 1980, as Antonio in Le nozze di Figaro; Welsh National Opera, 1982–83, in Cenerentola, A Midsummer Night's Dream and Butterfly; English National Opera, 1989, in Lear by Reimann; Season 1989–90 in Die Zauberflöte at Aix-en-Provence and Hansel and Gretel at Strasbourg; Pocket Opera Nuremberg, 1991, as Assur in Semiramide; Other roles include Rossini's Basilio, Fasolt in Das Rheingold and Lodovico in Otello. *Recordings include:* Parsifal. *Address:* c/o English National Opera, St Martin's Lane, London WC2N 4ES, England.

McKINNEY, Thomas; singer (baritone); b. 5 May 1946, Lufkin, TX, USA. *Education:* studied in Houston, Hollywood and New York. *Career:* debut, Houston 1971 as Tchelkalov in Boris Godunov; Sang in opera in Cincinnati, Houston, San Diego and San Francisco; European engagements at the Wexford Festival (Thaïs), the Vienna Volksoper and the Théâtre Royale de la Monnaie, Brussels; Other roles have included Pelléas, Guglielmo, Don Giovanni, Mozart's Count, Papageno, Rossini's Figaro, Eugene Onegin, Hamlet, Belcore, Massenet's Hérode and Athanael (Thais), Verdi's Posa and Ford and Peachum in The Beggar's Opera; San Diego, 1972 in the premiere of Medea by Alva Henderson; Frequent concert appearances. *Address:* c/o Volksoper, Wahringerstrasse 78, 1090 Vienna, Australia.

MacKINTOSH, Catherine; violinist; b. 1948, England. *Career:* debut concert at St John's Smith Square, London, 1984; Extensive tours and broadcasts in France, Belgium, Netherlands, Germany, Austria, Switzerland, Italy and Spain. Tours of the USA and Japan, 1991–92; British appearances include four Purcell concerts at the Wigmore Hall, 1987, later broadcast on Radio 3; Repertoire includes music on the La Folia theme by Vivaldi, Corelli, CPE Bach, Marais, A Scarlatti, Vitali and Geminiani; Instrumental works and songs by Purcell, music by Matthew Locke, John Blow and Fantasias and Airs by William Lawes; 17th Century virtuoso Italian music by Marini, Buonamente, Gabrieli, Fontana and Stradella; J. S. Bach and his forerunners, Biber, Scheidt, Schenk, Reincken and Buxtehude; frequent engagements with other ensembles; member of the Purcell Quartet. *Recordings:* six album set on the La Folia theme; Purcell sonatas by Vivaldi and Corelli.

McLACHLAN, Murray, FRSA; concert pianist; b. 6 Jan. 1965, Dundee, Scotland; m. 1st Mary Russell 1993; m. 2nd Kathryn Page 2001; three c. 2 step-c. *Education:* Chetham's School, Magdalene College, Cambridge with Peter Katin and Norma Fisher. *Career:* debut, Free Trade Hall, Hallé Proms, Manchester, 1983; Performed extensively throughout the United Kingdom as a recitalist and concerto soloist with Royal Philharmonic Orchestra, Scottish Chamber Orchestra, BBC Scottish Orchestra, Manchester Camerata; Toured Belorussia, 1991; Has performed complete cycle of 32 Beethoven sonatas from memory in Glasgow, Dundee and Aberdeen; Head of Keyboard, Chetham's School of Music, Manchester; Tutor, Royal Northern College of Music; Adjudicator, British Federation of Festivals; repertoire also includes complete works of Brahms. *Recordings include:* Complete sonatas of Prokofiev, Myaskovsky Beethoven and Kabalevsky and solo works of Khatchaturian; Piano concerto of Ronald Stevenson; Complete Piano Works of Camilleri; 6 Concertos of Alexander Tcherepnin; 24 Preludes and Fugues of Shchedrin. *Honours:* Piano Prize, Chetham's; Cambridge Instrumental Exhibition; Penguin Rosette Award, for CD of music from Scotland; Knight of the Order of St John of Jerusalem, 1997. *Address:* c/o Chetham's School of Music, Long Millgate, Manchester M3 1SB, England. *E-mail:* info@murraymclachlan.co.uk. *Website:* www .murraymclachlan.com.

McLAUGHLIN, Marie; singer (soprano); b. 2 Nov. 1954, Hamilton, Lanarkshire, Scotland. *Education:* London Opera Centre, National Opera Studio. *Career:* sang Susanna and Lauretta while a student; English National Opera from 1978, in The Consul, Dido and Aeneas, A Night in Venice and Rigoletto; Royal Opera Covent Garden from 1980 as Barbarina and Susanna in Le nozze di Figaro, Zerlina, Iris in Semele, Marzelline in Fidelio, Nannetta in Falstaff, Zdenka in Arabella and Tytania in A Midsummer Night's Dream; Glyndebourne Festivals as Micaela (Carmen) and Violetta, 1985, 1987, Salzburg Festival as Susanna, conducted by James Levine; Scottish Opera in Orfeo ed Euridice and Le Nozze di Figaro; Deutsche Oper Berlin as Susanna and Marzelline; Hamburg, Susanna, Marzelline; Chicago Lyric, Zerlina, Despina; Washington, Susanna; Met New York as Marzelline; La Scala, Milan, Adina; Paris Opéra in Roméo et Juliette; Sang Zdenka in Arabella at Covent Garden, 1990; Marzelline in Fidelio at the 1990 Salzburg Festival, Zerlina at the Vienna Festival; Geneva Opera 1992, as Despina, and Jenny in Mahagonny; Sang Jenny at the Opéra Bastille, Paris, 1995; Donna Elvira at Lausanne, 1996. Concert appearances in London, Edinburgh, New Work, Chicago, Berlin, Spain, France, Belgium and Germany; Conductors worked with include Maazel, Bernstein, Haitink, Barenboim, Davis, Leppard, Celibidache, Harnoncourt, Mehta and Levine; Season 1992–93, as Blanche in the Carmélites at Geneva, Susanna on tour with the Royal Opera to Japan, Ilia in Idomeneo at Barcelona and Ivy in On the Town at the Barbican Hall; Sang Anna Elisa in Lehar's Paganini at the Theater an der Wien, Vienna, 1998; Season 2000–01 as Katerina in Martinu's The Greek Passion at Covent Garden and Weill's Jenny in Geneva. *Recordings include:* Video of Covent Garden Fidelio (Virgin), Handel's L'Allegro, il Pensieroso ed Il Moderato; Die Zauberflöte and Dido and Aeneas; Così fan tutte (Levine), Mozart, Requiem (Bernstein), (Phonogram); Videos of Rigoletto, Carmen, Traviata, Mozart's C Minor Mass and Haydn's Mass in Time of War. *Current Management:* IMG Artists, Lovell House, 616 Chiswick High Road, London W4 5RX, England.

McLEAN, Barton Keith, BS, MM, DMus; composer; b. 8 April 1938, Poughkeepsie, NY, USA; m. Priscilla McLean 1967. *Education:* State University College, Potsdam, NY, Eastman School of Music, Indiana University. *Career:* teacher, State University College, Potsdam, 1960–66, Indiana University, South Bend, 1969–76, University of Texas, Austin, 1976–83; Teacher, iEar Studios, 1987–88, 1990–92, Director, iEar Studios, 1987–88, Rensselaer Polytechnic Institute. *Compositions include:* Dimensions I, violin, tape, 1973, II, piano, tape, 1974, III, saxophone, tape, 1978, IV, saxophone, tape, 1979, VIII, piano, tape, 1982; Metamorphosis, orchestra, 1975; Heavy Music, 4 crowbars, electronic, 1979; Ixtlan, 2 pianos, 1982; The Last Ten Minutes, computer generated, 1982; The Electric Sinfonia, 1982; String Quartet, from the Good Earth, 1985; In the Place of Tears, chamber ensemble, voice, 1985; In Wilderness is the Preservation of the World, environmental-electronic, 1986; Voices of the Wild–Primal Spirits, orchestra, 1987; Visions of a Summer Night, computer tape, 1989; Rainforest, 1989; Rainforest Images, computer tape, 1992; Rainforest Reflections, electronic processed soloist and orchestra, 1993; Rainforest Images I and II, video, 1993; Forgotten Shadows, computer tape, 1996; Jambori Rimba, 1996; Desert Spring, 1996; Dawn Chorus, 1996; Forgotten Shadows, 1996; The Ultimate Symphonius 2000, audience interactive sound installation, 1999; Journey on a Long String, for double bass and electronics, 2001; Into the Fire, for stereo sound featuring the voice of Athena Burke, 2003. *Recordings:* Visions of a Summer Night, 1992; Rainforest Images, 1993; Demons of the Night, Fireflies, Earth Music, 1994; The Electric Performer; The McLean Mix and the Golden Age of Electronic Music; Ritual of the Dawn, Forgotten shadows, Rainforest Reflections. *Address:* Coon Brook Road, Petersburgh, NY 12138, USA. *E-mail:* mclmix@aol.com. *Website:* members.aol.com/mclmix2/index .html.

McLEAN, Priscilla Taylor, BEd, BMusEd, MM; composer; b. 27 May 1942, Fitchburg, Massachusetts, USA; m. Barton Keith McLean 1967. *Education:* State College, Fitchburg, University of Lowell, Massachusetts, Indiana University. *Career:* concerts, The McLean Mix (husband-wife duo performing own electronic acoustic music), Netherlands, Belgium, Zagreb Muzicki Biennale, 1981; Amsterdam, Holland Radio, Oslo, Finland, Sweden, 1983; Australia, New Zealand, Hawaii, 1990; Tours, USA, 1981–95, yearly; Canada, 1986; Guest Composer, Kennedy Center for the Performing Arts, 1977; Gaudeamus Musiekweek, Netherlands, 1979; Guest Professor and Composer/Performer, University of Hawaii, 1985; Guest Soprano Soloist, Cleveland Chamber Orchestra (Wilderness), 1989; Guest composer/performer (residency), University of Sarawak, Malaysia, 1996; Tunugan Festival of Asian music, Philippines, 1997; mem, BMI; American Music Center; Seamus; SCI; The Electronic Music Foundation. *Compositions include:* Variations and Mozaics on a Theme of Stravinsky; Dance of Dawn; Invisible Chariots; The Inner Universe; Fantasies for Adults and Other Children; Beneath the Horizon I, III; Night Images; Messages; Fire and Ice; Elan!; 3 Pieces for In Wilderness is the Preservation of the World; In Celebration; Wilderness; A Magic Dwells, orchestra and tape, 1986; Voices of the Wild, Orchestra and Soloist, electronic music, 1988; The Dance of Shiva, electronic tape and Multiple Slides), 1990; Rainforest, coil with B McLean, 1990; Everything Awakening Alert and Joyful, full orchestra and narrator, 1991; In the Beginning, 1995; Rainforest Images, 1993; Desert Spring with Barton McLean, 1996; Jambori Rimba with Barton McLean, 1997; Desert Voices for midi violin, tape and electronics, 1998; The Ultimate Symphonius 2000, with Barton McLean, 1999; Angels of Delirium for electronic tape, 2001. *Recordings include:* Dance of Dawn 1975; Interplanes, 1978; Variations and Mozaics on a Theme of Stravinsky, 1979; Invisible Chariots, 1979; Electronic Music from the Outside In, 1980; Beneath the Horizon III and Salt Canyons, 1983; In Wilderness is the Preservation of the World, 1987; Rainforest Images II; The Electric Performer; Gods, Demons and the Earth; McLean Mix and the Golden Age of Electronic Music; Fantasies for Adults and Other children: The Vocal music of Priscilla McLean. *Address:* The McLean Mix/MLC Publications, 55 Coon Brook Road, Petersburgh, New York, NY 12138, USA.

MacLEAN, Susan; singer (mezzo-soprano); b. 1962, California, USA. *Education:* Minneapolis and Zürich Opera Studio. *Career:* sang at Bielefeld Opera from 1988, notably in Yerma by Villa Lobos and Der Sprung uber den Schatten by Krenek; Zürich, 1989, as Fenena in Nabucco; Wuppertal, 1991, in the premiere of Katharina Blum by Tilo Medek; Heidelberg Festival, 1994–95, as Mignon, by Thomas; Other roles include Carmen, Cenerentola, Strauss's Octavian and Composer, Selika in L'Africaine, and Honegger's Judith. *Recordings include:* Zulma in L'Italiana in Algeri. *Address:* c/o Theater der Stadt Heidelberg, Friedrichstrasse 5, 69117 Heidelberg, Germany.

McLEAN-MAIR, Kevin; British singer (tenor); b. 1969, St Albans. *Education:* Royal Academy of Music, Britten-Pears School, Aldeburgh; IVC masterclasses with Tom Krause. *Career:* performed throughout the United Kingdom, including Barbican Hall, St James', Piccadilly, St John's, Smith Square, BBC Friday Night is Music Night and many choral societies; Recitals in Lincoln, Bristol and Settle; International engagements in Canada, Germany, Netherlands (including Concertgebouw) and the USA; Opera includes Attendant Spirit, Comus, Benslow Music Trust; Lucano and Nutrice, L'Incoronazione di Poppea, The Cavalli Baroque Ensemble; Ferrando, Così fan tutte, Dartington Hall; Chinese Man, The Fairy Queen, English Bach Festival at the Linbury Studio Theatre, Covent Garden, 2001. *Recordings:* Dixit Dominus; The Songs of Ian Venables. *Honours:* Erna Spoorenberg Award for Oratorio, Netherlands, 1996. *Current Management:* Helen Sykes Artist's Management, 100 Felsham Road, Putney, London, SW15 1DQ, England.

McLEOD, John; composer, conductor and lecturer; b. 8 March 1934, Aberdeen, Scotland; m. Margaret Murray 1961; one s. one d. *Education:* Royal Academy of Music; composition with Lennox Berkeley, conducting with Adrian Boult. *Career:* Director of Music, Merchiston Castle School, Edinburgh, 1974–85; Visiting Lecturer, Royal Scottish Academy of Music and Drama, 1985–89; Visiting Lecturer in Composition and Contemporary Music at Napier University of Edinburgh, 1989–94; Visiting Composer, Lothian Specialist Music Scheme, 1986–92; Ida Carroll Research Fellow, Royal Northern College of Music, 1988–89; Guest Conductor for various Scottish orchestras including Royal Scottish National Orchestra; Director of postgraduate course in composing for film and television at Thames Valley University and London College of Music, 1991–97; Visiting Professor, Royal Academy of Music, 1993–97; Freelance Composer, Conductor and Lecturer, 1997–; Director of The Performing Right Society, 2000–; Director of the British Academy of Composers and Songwriters, 2001–; Member of the Council of the Society for the Promotion of New Music, 2000–. *Compositions include:* The Gokstad Ship for Orchestra, National Youth Orchestra of Scotland Commission, 1982; Stabat Mater for Soloists, Choir and

Orchestra, Edinburgh Royal Choral Union Commission, 1986; Percussion Concerto, Evelyn Glennie Soloist, National Youth Orchestra of Scotland Commission; The Song of Dionysius for Percussion and Piano, premiered at the 1989 London Proms with Evelyn Glennie and Philip Smith; Piano Concerto, 1988; A Dramatic Landscape, for clarinet and wind, 1990; The Chronicle of Saint Machar, for baritone, choruses, strings, percussion and organ, 1998; Song of the Concubine for soprano and ensemble, 1998; Film scores for many television and cinema films including, Another Time, Another Place; Works now performed and recorded by leading artists, orchestras and at major international festivals. *Address:* Hill House, 9 Redford Crescent, Colinton, Edinburgh EH13 0BS, Scotland.

McLEOD, Linda; singer (soprano); b. 29 Nov. 1952, Indiana, USA. *Education:* Guildhall School, London. *Career:* sang with Opera for All, London, from 1978; English National Opera, as Sonia in War and Peace, as Donna Elvira, and Rusalka and in the premiere of Harvey's Inquest of Love, 1993; Brünnhilde in The Ring with Birmingham Touring Opera; Elisabeth de Valois and Tippett's Andromache for Opera North; Donna Anna for Scottish Opera; Washington Opera, 1992 as Wagne's Santa. *Recordings:* Video of Rusalka; Giovanna in Verdi's Ernani. *Address:* c/o English National Opera, St Martin's Lane, London WC2N 4ES, England.

McMASTER, Brian John, LLB; arts administrator; b. 9 May 1943, Hitchin, England. *Education:* Wellington College, Bristol University. *Career:* International Artists Department, EMI, 1968–73; Controller, Opera Planning, English National Opera, 1973–76; General Administrator, Subsequently Managing Director. Welsh National Opera, Cardiff, Wales, 1976–91; Artistic Director, Vancouver Opera, British Columbia, Canada, 1983–89; Director, The Edinburgh International Festival, since 1991. *Address:* The Hub, Edinburgh's Festival Centre, Castlehill, Edinburgh EH1 2NE, Scotland. *Telephone:* (131) 473 2032. *Fax:* (131) 473 2002. *E-mail:* eif@eif.co.uk. *Website:* www.eif.co.uk.

McMASTER, Zandra; singer (mezzo-soprano); b. 1960, Ballymena, Northern Ireland. *Education:* Trinity College of Music, London Opera Centre. *Career:* debut, Purcell Room, London, 1983; Sang Mahler's 4th Symphony at Madrid 1984 and has been resident in Spain singing in concert with most leading Spanish Orchestras; Salzburg Mozarteum 1989–91, Concertgebouw Amsterdam 1990 and US debut 1991, in Bernstein's 1st Symphony at Colorado; Seville World 'Expo concert 1992 and Beethoven's Ninth in Berlin; Concerts in Portugal, Israel, Belgium, Poland, Norway, Canada, Ireland, Germany, Austria, Hungary, USA, Brazil, Greece and Finland. *Current Management:* Conciertos Augusto, 15 calle Viento, 28220 Madrid, Spain.

MacMILLAN, James Loy, CBE; composer, conductor and lecturer in music; b. 16 July 1959, Kilwinning, Ayrshire, Scotland. *Education:* Univs of Edinburgh and Durham. *Career:* formerly lecturer in the music departments of Edinburgh and Manchester Univs; Lecturer at the Royal Scottish Acad. of Music and Drama; performances of his music by the New Music Group of Scotland, Circle, Nomos, Lontano and the Scottish Chamber Orchestra; commissions from the Edinburgh Contemporary Arts Trust, The Traverse Theatre, Scottish Chamber Orchestra, the Paragon Ensemble, Cappela Nova and the Scottish Chamber Choir; Prom Commission, The Confession of Isobel Gowdie, BBC Scottish Symphony Orchestra; featured composer, 1990 Musica Nova Festival, Glasgow; Seven Last Words from the Cross premiered on BBC television, Easter, 1994; Composer and Conductor, BBC Philharmonic Orchestra, 2000–. *Compositions:* Study on Two Planes for cello and piano 1981; Three Dawn Rituals for ensemble 1983; Beatus Vir for chorus and organ 1983; The Road to Ardtalla for ensemble 1983; Songs of a Just War for soprano and ensemble 1984; Piano Sonata 1986; Two Visions of Hoy for oboe and ensemble 1986; The Keening for orchestra 1986; Festival Fanfares for brass band 1986; Litanies of Iron and Stone for ensemble with tape 1987; Untold for ensemble 1987; Visions of a November Spring for string quartet 1988; Busqueda for 8 actors, 3 sopranos, speaker and ensemble 1988; Into the Ferment for Orchestra 1988; Cantos Sagrados for chorus and organ 1989; The Exorcism of Rio Sumpul for Chamber Ensemble 1989; As Mothers See Us, for ensemble 1990; The Berserking, Piano Concerto, 1990; The Confession of Isobel Gowdie for orchestra 1990; Soweton Spring for wind band 1990; Catherine's Lullabies for chorus and ensemble 1990; Scots Song for Soprano and Ensemble 1991; Tuireadh for clarinet and string quartet 1991; Sinfonietta 1991; Tourist Variations, 1 act chamber opera 1992; Visitatio Sepulchri for 7 singers and chamber orchestra, 1993; Trumpet Concerto, 1993; Vs for orchestra, 1993; Seven Last Words from the Cross for choir and strings, 1994; Ines de Castro, opera, 1996; Clarinet Concerto, 1997; Gaudeamus in loci pace for organ, 1998; Quickening for soloists, chorus and orchestra, 1998; Triduum for London Symphony Orchestra, 1996–97; Cello Concerto, 1996; Symphony: Vigil; Raising Sparkes for soprano and chamber ensemble, 1997; 14 Little Pictures for piano trio, 1997; Why is this Night Different?, string quartet, 1997. *Recordings include:* Confession of Isobel Gowdie; Veni Veni Emmanuel;

Cello Concerto. *Honours:* Gramophone Award, 1993; Classic CD Award, 1993; Hon. DUniv Univ. of Paisley, 1995; Hon. DLitt, Univ. of Strathclyde, 1996; South Bank Show Award for Classical Music, 1997; Evening Standard Classical Music Award for Outstanding Artistic Achievement. *Current Management:* Boosey & Hawkes PLC, 295 Regent Street, London, W1B 2JH, England. *Website:* www.boosey.com. *Address:* c/o BBC Philharmonic, New Broadcasting House, Oxford Road, Manchester, M60 1SJ, England.

McNAIR, Sylvia; singer (soprano); b. 23 June 1956, Mansfield, Ohio, USA. *Education:* India University. *Career:* sang in Messiah at Indianapolis, 1980; Euroean debut in the premiere of Kelterborn's Ophelia, Schwetzingen, 1984; Concert appearances in Cleveland, Baltimore, San Francisco, Detroit, Montreal, Indianapolis, Atlanta, St Louis, Washington and Los Angeles; New York at the Carnegie, Avery Fisher and Alice Tully Halls; Season 1991–92 with the Chicago Symphony under Solti, Berlin Philharmonic under Haitink, City of Birmingham Symphony under Rattle, Concentus Musicus under Harnoncourt and London Philharmonic under Masur; Mozart's Ilia and Servilia with the Monteverdi Choir and Orchestra conducted by John Eliot Gardiner; US opera appearances as Pamina at Santa Fe, Ilia; Hero (Béatrice et Bénédict) and Morgana in Alcina at St Louis; Sang Ilia in Lyon and Strasbourg and Susana with Netherlands Opera; Pamina at the Deutsche Oper Berlin and the Vienna Staatsoper; Glyndebourne Festival 1989 as Anne Trulove; Covent Garden and Salzburg debuts as Ilia in Idomeneo; Season 1991–92 with Bastille Opéra (Paris) and Metropolitan Opera (as Marzelline in Fidelio) debuts; Covent Garden 1992, in Rossini's Il Viaggio a Reims; Sang Poppea at the 1993 Salzburg Festival and returned for Pamina in Die Zauberflöte, 1997; The Daughter in the US premiere of Lidholm's A Dream Play, Santa Fe, 1998; Sang Cleopatra in Handel's Giulio Cesare at the New York Met, 1999; Messiah at the 1999 Salzburg Festival. *Recordings:* Albums with Neville Marriner, Roger Norrington, John Eliot Gardiner, Colin Davis, Kurt Masur, James Levine and Bernard Haitink; Idomeneo with John Eliot Gardiner (Deutsche Grammophon). *Current Management:* Askonas Holt Ltd, Lonsdale Chambers, 27 Chancery Lane, London, WC2A 1PF, England. *Telephone:* (20) 7400-1700. *Fax:* (20) 7400-1799. *E-mail:* info@askonasholt.co.uk. *Website:* www.askonasholt.co.uk.

MacNEIL, Cornell; singer (baritone); b. 24 Sept. 1922, Minneapolis, Minnesota, USA. *Education:* Hartt School, Hartford with Friedrich Schorr, New York with Virgilio Lazzari and Dick Marzollo, Rome with Luigi Ricci. *Career:* debut, Philadelphia 1950, in the premiere of Menotti's The Consul; NYC Opera debut, 1953, as Germont; San Francisco 1955, as Escamillo; Chicago, 1957, in Manon Lescaut; Metropolitan Opera from 1959–87, as Verdi's Rigoletto, Amonasro, Nabucco, Iago and Luna, Puccini's Scarpia and Michele, and Barnaba in La Gioconda, 460 performances in 26 parts; La Scala Milan 1959, as Carlo in Ernani; Covent Garden debut 1964, as Verdi's Macbeth; Verona Arena 1971; Guest appearances in Caracas, Mexico City, Vienna, Buenos Aires, Barcelona, Rome and Naples. *Recordings:* Un Ballo in Maschera, Rigoletto, Aida, Cavalleria Rusticana, Luisa Miller, La Fanciulla del West, La Gioconda, La Traviata, Falstaff, Pagliacci. *Address:* c/o Metropolitan Opera, Lincoln Center, New York, NY 10023, USA.

MacNEIL, Walter; singer (tenor); b. 1957, New York, USA; s. of Cornell MacNeil. *Career:* sang at the San Francisco Opera from 1983, as Froh, Rodrigo in Otello and Alfredo; Sang Alfredo at New Orleans 1984, with his father as Germont père; Carnegie Hall 1985, in Semele, and Don Ottavio at Milwaukee 1986; Glyndebourne 1987–88 and Metropolitan 1989, as Alfredo; Sang Aubry in Der Vampyr by Marschner at the 1992 Wexford Festival; Other roles include Tamino (Connecticut Opera, 1991), Ruggiero in La Rondine and Nadir in Les pêcheurs de Perles (Honolulu 1987). *Address:* c/o Metropolitan Opera, Lincoln Center, New York, NY 10023, USA.

McPHEE, George, MBE, FRCO, BMus, FRCO, DipMusEd, FRSCM; organist and composer; b. 10 Nov. 1937, Glasgow, Scotland; m.; one s. two d. *Education:* Royal Scottish Acad. of Music and Drama, Edinburgh Univ., organ study with Herrick Bunney and Fernando Germani. *Career:* Asst Organist, St Giles Cathedral, Edinburgh 1959–63; Dir of Music, Paisley Abbey 1963–; conducted and played organ with all major Scottish orchestras; numerous recital tours of USA, Canada and Europe; mem. Incorporated Soc. of Musicians, Royal Coll. of Organists. *Compositions:* Magnificat and Nunc Dimittis (Paisley Service), Make we joy, Whence is that goodly fragrance, The New Oxford Song Book (editor), The Saltire Two-Part Song Book. *Honours:* Limpus Prize 1961, Hon. doctorate, Paisley Univ. 1997. *Address:* 17 Main Road, Castlehead, Paisley, PA2 6AJ, Scotland (home). *Telephone:* (141) 8893528 (home). *Fax:* (141) 8404906 (home). *E-mail:* profmcphee@aol.com (home).

McPHERSON, Gordon, DMus; Scottish composer and accordion player; b. 27 Aug. 1965, Dundee. *Education:* Univ. of York, Royal Northern Coll. of Music. *Career:* composition teacher, Univ. of Edinburgh; composer-in-residence, Royal Scottish Acad. of Music and Drama; Lecturer in 20th-Century Music and Analysis, Univ. of St Andrews; Head of Composition, Royal Scottish Acad. of Music and Drama 1999–. *Compositions include:* Oh, why should I cry upon my wedding day? 1985, String Quartet No. 2 'Dead Roses' 1990, Maps and Diagrams of our Pain 1990, Handguns: a Suite 1995, The Baby Bear's Bed 1998, String Quartet No. 3 'The Original Soundtrack' 1999, Upbeat Destroyer (guitar concerto), Born of Funk and the Fear of Failing (guitar concerto) 2000–01, The Waterworks (multi-media), Morning Drunk and Buzzard, The New Black 2005. *Recordings include:* Detours (two-vol. collection). *Honours:* Creative Scotland Award 2003. *Address:* Royal Scottish Academy of Music and Drama, 100 Renfrew Street, Glasgow, G2 3DB, Scotland (office). *E-mail:* g.mcpherson@rsamd.ac.uk (office). *Website:* www.rsamd.ac.uk (office).

McTIER, Duncan Paul, BSc, ARCM; double bass player and teacher; b. 21 Nov. 1954, Stourbridge, Worcestershire, England; m. Yuko Inoue 1984. *Education:* King Edward VI Grammar School, Stourbridge, Bristol University. *Career:* Member, BBC Symphony Orchestra, 1975–77; Principal Bass, Netherlands Chamber Orchestra, 1977–84; Senior Double Bass Tutor, Royal Northern College of Music, 1984–; Professor of Double Bass, Royal College of Music, 1987–91; Double Bass Consultant, Royal Scottish Academy of Music and Drama, 1991–; Solo appearances with Netherlands Chamber Orchestra, Concertgebouw Chamber Orchestra, Bournemouth Sinfonietta, Netherlands Philharmonic Orchestra, Orchestre Regional d'Auvergne, Barcelona Municipal Orchestra, Northern Sinfonia Orchestre de Chambre Detmold, Nippon Telemann Ensemble of Osaka, Lausanne Chamber Orchestra, BBC Concert Orchestra, Scottish Chamber Orchestra, Bournemouth Symphony Orchestra; World Premieres of Concertos written by Peter Maxwell Davies, John Casken and Derek Bourgeois; Recitals and master classes throughout Europe and Japan. *Recordings:* Bottesini Grand Duo for Philips; Various pieces with Paganini Ensemble for Denon; Dutch television recordings of Bottesini Grand Duo and 2nd Concerto; Dvořák String Quintet and Waltzes with Chilingirian Quartet (Chandos); Extensive radio recordings. *Honours:* 1st Prize Winner, Isle of Man International Double Bass Competition, 1982. *Current Management:* Music Productions 'J' House, 6 Studland Street, London W6 0JS, England.

MacURDY, John; singer (bass); b. 18 March 1929, Detroit, Michigan, USA; m. Justine May Votypka; one s. one d. *Education:* Wayne State University, Detroit; singing with Avery Crew, Detroit. *Career:* debut, New Orleans, 1952, in Samson et Dalila; Appearances in Baltimore, Houston, Philadelphia, San Francisco and Santa Fe; NYC Opera debut 1959, in Weill's Street Scene; Metropolitan Opera from 1962 as the Commendatore, Crespel in Les Contes d'Hoffmann and Rocco in Fidelio; Sang in the premieres of Antony and Cleopatra, 1966 and Mourning Becomes Elektra, 1967; 1st local Performance of Les Troyens, 1973; Paris Opéra 1973, as Arkel in Pelléas et Mélisande; La Scala Milan 1974, as Rocco in Fidelio; Salzburg Festival 1977–78, as the Commendatore in Don Giovanni; Milan 1984 as the Landgrave in Tannhäuser; Seattle Opera 1986, as Hagen and Hunding in the Ring; Metropolitan 1987, as Fasolt in Das Rheingold; Hunding at San Francisco 1990; Appearances at Aix and Orange Festivals, Hollywood Bowl, Miami Opera and Scottish Opera; Season 1992 in Billy Budd at the Met, as Trulove in The Rake's Progress at Aix-en-Provence, as Fiesco in Simon Boccanegra Montpellier, The Flying Dutchman in Buenos Aires as Daland and L'Africaine in Marseille; 1011 performances as Leading Bass; 1780 operatic performances; Sang Fafner in Das Rheingold at Marseille, 1996; Hunding at the Met, 1996; mem. Bohemian Club. *Recordings:* Don Giovanni; Béatrice et Bénédict; Otello; The Rev Hale in Ward's The Crucible. *Honours:* City of Detroit Medal, 1969; Rockefeller Foundation Grant, 1959; Presently only American to be listed in the Wagnerian Annals for singing all the Bass Roles in the Ring Cycle; Inducted into the Academy of Vocal Arts Hall of Fame; Arts Achievement Award, Wayne State Univ., 2003. *Address:* 73 Tall Oaks Court, Stamford, CT 06903, USA.

McVEAGH, Diana Mary, ARCM, GRSM; writer on music; b. 6 Sept. 1926, Ipoh, Malaya; m. Dr C. W. Morley 1950 (died 1994). *Education:* Malvern Girls' College, Royal College of Music. *Career:* Assistant Editor, Musical Times, 1965–67; Executive Committee of the New Grove, 1970–76; Contributor to The Times, 1947–69, also to Musical Times, The Listener, Records and Recordings; Executive Committee of the GKN English Song Award, 1982–89; mem, Royal Musical Association Council, 1961–76, Vice President, Elgar Society. *Publications:* Elgar (Dent) 1955; Contributor to New Grove Dictionary of Music (articles on Elgar and Finzi), 1980 and 2000 editions. Twentieth-Century English Masters (MacMillan) 1986. *Address:* Ladygrove, The Lee, Great Mssenden, Bucks HP16 9NA, England.

McVICAR, David; stage director; b. 1967, Glasgow, Scotland. *Education:* Royal Scottish Academy of Music and Drama. *Career:* main productions: The Magic Flute, Rigoleteto (Covent Garden); Billy Budd (Chicago Lyric

Opera); Agrippina, Don Giovanni (La Monnaie Brussels); Manon, Alcina, Tosca, The Rape of Lucretia (ENO); Hamlet, Sweeney Todd, Don Giovanni, Der Rosenkavalier (Opera North); Idomeneo, Der Rosenkavalier, Madama Butterfly (Scottish Opera); Macbeth (Kirov Opera St Petersburg); Tales of Hoffmann (Salzburg Festival). *Address:* Performing Arts, 6 Windmill Street, London W1P 1HF, England.

MADDALENA, James; Singer (Baritone); b. 1954, Lynn, Massachussetts, USA. *Education:* Studied at the New England Conservatory of Music. *Career:* Debut: Rogers and Hammerstein medley with the Boston Pops Orchestra, 1974; From 1974 has appeared in a complete cycle of Bach's cantatas at Emmanuel Church Boston, conducted by Craig Smith; Founder member of the Liederkreis Ensemble, Naumburg Awad, 1980; Association with director Peter Sellars from 1981 includes the title role in Don Giovanni and Leading roles in Handel's Orlando, American Repertory Theatre, 1982; Così fan tutte, Castle Hill Festival, 1984; Haydn's Armida, New Hampshire Symphony, 1983; Giulio Cesare and the Brecht/Weill Kleine Mahagonny, Pepsico Summerfare, 1985; Soloist in Messiah at Carnegie Hall 1984, with Banchetto Musicale; Sang the title role in the world premiere of Nixon in China by John Adams, Houston, 1987, repeated at Edinburgh 1988 and The Captain in the premiere of Adams's The Death of Klinghoffer, Brussels 1991, and at Lyon, Vienna and NY; Has appeared as Mozart's Count in the Sellars version of Le nozze di Figaro, seen at Purchase, NY and Papageno at Glyndebourne, 1990; Created Merlin in Tippett's New Year at Houston 1989 and in the British premiere at Glyndebourne; Season 1992 in Nixon in China at Adelaide and Frankfurt, Don Alfonso at Glyndebourne; Sang in Susa's Transformations at St Louis, 1997; Frédéric in Lakmé at New Orleans, 1997. Recordings. Brahms Liebeslieder Waltzes, with Liederkreis; Nixon in China and The Death of Klinghoffer. *Address:* c/o Houston Grand Opera Association, 510 Preston Avenue, Houston, TX 77002, USA.

MADDISON, Dorothy; Singer (Lyric Coloratura Soprano); b. 12 Jan. 1956, Fergus Falls, Minnesota, USA; m. 29 Dec 1979, Ian Maddison. *Education:* BMus, St Olaf College, Minnesota, 1977; Guildhall School of Music and Drama, London, England, 1977–79; Britten-Pears School, Aldeburgh; Private study with Audrey Langford and Andrew Feidld, Cantica Voice Studio, London. *Career:* Debut: Purcell Room, London, April 1986 with Graham Johnson, piano; Freelance concert and operatic singer; Operatic roles include The Queen of Night in The Magic Flute; Zaide; Madames Herz and Silberklang in The Impressario, Mozart; Norina in Don Pasquale; Adina in Elixir of Love; Rita by Donizetti; Tytania in Midsummer Night's Dream, Britten; Mable, Pirates of Penzance; Zerbinetta, Ariadne auf Naxos, Strauss; The Nightingale, Stravinsky; Oratorio repertoire: includes works by Bach, Handel, Haydn, Mozart, Mendelssohn, Orff; Recital Repertoire: Standard works by European composers, also songs from the American Midwest, a programme featuring works by Minnesota composers Argento, Dougherty, Franklin, Larsen, Paulus, first given in April 1988, Purcell Room, London with Robin Bowman, piano; Recent appearances with: English Bach Festival, New Sadler's Wells Opera Company, Opera Factory, London Opera Players; mem, Equity. *Honours:* Honours and Distinction, St Olaf College, Walter Hyde Memorial Prize, Guildhall School. *Address:* 95 Tanfield Avenue, London NW2 7 SB, England.

MADER-TODOROVA, Marina; Singer (Soprano); b. 20 Aug. 1948, Silistra, Bulgaria. *Education:* Studied in Varna, Sofia and Vienna. *Career:* Sang at first in opera at Varna then Mainz and Bremen, 1976–77 as Desdemona and Micaela; Gelsenkirchen 1977–80 as Elisabeth de Valois, Ariadne and Tosca; Further appearances at Dortmund, 1980–83, Hamburg, Stuttgart, Frankfurt and Basle; Engaged at the Deutsche Oper am Rhein, 1984–86, Graz, 1984–89, notably as Eva, Amelia in Ballo in Machera, Leonara in Il Trovatore, Agathe and Ariadne; Further appearances at the Deutsche Oper Berlin, Budapest, Mannheim, Palermo, Zürich, Copenahgen and Liège; Other roles have included Butterfly, Elisabeth in Tannhäuser, Elsa, Mozart's Fiordiligi and Countess, Mimi and Arabella; Many concert appearances. *Address:* Vereinigte Buhnen, Kaiser Josef Platz 10, 8010 Graz, Austria.

MADGE, Geoffrey (Douglas); Concert pianist and Professor; b. 3 Oct. 1941, Adelaide, Australia; m., one s., one d. *Education:* Elder Conservatorium University of Adelaide, Australia. *Career:* Debut: London, 1969; Toured Australia as a pianist in a piano trio, 1959–63; Professor of classical and contemporary piano repertoire, Royal Conservatorium of The Hague; International Society for Contemporary Music Festival, Athens, 1979, first performance of 32 Piano Pieces by Skalkottas; Annual Holland Festival, Utrecht, 1982, 2nd complete performance of Kaikhosru Sorabji's mammoth Opus Clavicembalisticum. *Compositions:* Viola Sonata, 1963; String Quartet, 1965; Violin Sonatina, 1966; Monkeys in a Cage, ballet, 1976, premiere Sydney Opera house, 1977; Etude for two pianists, 1977; Tendrils of the Rock 3 movements for piano, 1979; Piano concerto, 1979, premiere Amsterdam 1980. *Recordings:* First recording of Opus Clavicembalisticum by K. Sorabji, 1983; 1st complete anthology of F Busoni's music for solo piano,

1988 (Philips); 1st recording of Skalkottas 1st Piano Concerto, 1999 (BIS). *Honours:* Edison, Netherlands; Caecilia Prize, Belgium; Schallplatten Preis, Germany; Prix du Président de la République, France. *Address:* Van Beuningenstraat 77, 2582 KL Den Haag, Netherlands.

MADRA, Barbara; Singer (Soprano); b. 1958, Koszian, Poznan, Poland. *Education:* Studied in Poznan. *Career:* Sang at first with the Poznan Opera then from 1980 at the Brussels Opera, notably as Mimi, Violetta, Fiordiligi, Elisabeth de Valois, Mozart's Vitellia and Arminda, the Trovatore Leonora and Amelia Grimaldi; Guest appearances in Geneva, Lausanne, at the Holland Festival, Buenos Aires, Barcelona and Toulouse (Donna Elvira, 1990); Sang Tatiana at Zürich 1990 and at La Scala in Rimsky's Tale of Tsar Saltan, and as Eva in Die Meistersinger. *Address:* c/o Théâtre Royale, 4 Leopoldstrasse, 1000 Brussels, Belgium.

MADROSZKIEWICZ, Joanna (Dorota); Violinist; b. 22 March 1956, Szczecin, Poland; 1 s., 2 d. *Education:* Magister of Art; Akademia Muzyczna Gdansk; Hochschule für Musik, Vienna. *Career:* Engagements at Geneva, Prague, Lublin, Naples; Concerts with Vienna Symphony Orchestra, Polish National Philharmonie, London Mozart Players, Residentre Orkest, Austria Radio Orchestra, Deutsche Kammerakad; Numerous Recitals; Debut at Salzburg Festival as a violin soloist in Weill's Violin Concerto with Vienna Philharmonic Orchestra. *Recordings:* Schubert, Haydn, Beethoven, Wieniawski. *Honours:* Best Young Artist of Poland Award, 1977; Commander of the Order of Polonia Restituta, 1994. *Current Management:* Patricia Garrasi, RESIA, Milan. *Address:* Kielmansegg 26, 2340 Mödling, Austria.

MADZAR, Aleksandar; Concert Pianist; b. 1968, Belgrade, Yugoslavia. *Education:* Belgrade Academy of Music, with Eliso Virsaladze in Moscow, at the Strasbourg Conservatory and with Daniel Blumenthal in Brussels. *Career:* Frequent appearances from 1985 with leading orchestras in France, Germany, Italy, Spain, Scandinavia and the United Kingdom; Berlin Philharmonic debut 1990 and further engagements with the Chamber Orchestra of Europe, Royal Philharmonic, Leipzig Gewandhaus, Bremen Philharmonic Orchestra and Czech Philharmonic (1996); Further engagements include visits to the Scottish Chamber Orchestra and the Aldeburgh festival; Chamber Concerts in Munich and Italy; Recitals at Salzburg, Davos, Bad Kissingen and Ivo Pogorelich Festivals and at the Théâtre de la Ville in Paris; Chamber music collaborations in Boston, New York (Carnegie Hall), Milan, Amsterdam Concertgebouw, Vienna Musikverein, and South Africa. *Recordings include:* Prokoviev Violin Sonatas with Kyoko Takezawa; Chopin Concertos and solo works by Ravel; Two concertos by Erwin Schulhoff; Chabrier's music for two pianos. *Honours:* Prizewinner, 1996 Leeds International Piano Competition; Winner, Ferruccio Busoni Competition, 1989; Winner, Barenreiter Prize at the International Mozart Competition, Salzburg, 1985. *Current Management:* Harrison/Parrott Ltd, 12 Penzance Place, London, W11 4PA, England. *Telephone:* (20) 7229 9166. *Fax:* (20) 7221 5042. *Website:* www.harrisonparrott.com.

MAE, Vanessa (Vanessa Mae Nicholson); Concert Violinist; b. 27 Oct. 1978, Singapore. *Education:* Studied with Lin Yao Ji, Central Conservatoire, Beijing; Felix Andrievsky, Royal College of Music, London. *Career:* First National Tour of Britain 1990, featuring the Tchaikovsky Concerto; First International Tour with the London Mozart Players, 1990; Over 400 Live Performances in 35 countries; The Classical Tour, 1997, visiting Sheffield, Birmingham (Symphony Hall), Leicester, London (Barbican) and Manchester (Bridgewater Hall); Frequent Television Appearances and participant in 'crossover' concerts. *Recordings include:* Tchaikovsky and Beethoven Concertos, 1990; Compilation Albums, including arrangement of Bach Toccata and Fugue; The Classical Collection, Part 1, 2000. *Honours:* Winner, BAMBI Top International Classical Artist Award and ECHO Klassik Award for Bestselling Album of the Year, 1995. *Address:* c/o Trittico Ltd, 34 Philimore Walk, London W8 7 SA, England.

MAEGAARD, Jan (Carl Christian); Composer and Musicologist; b. 14 April 1926, Copenhagen, Denmark; m. Kirsten Offer Andersen, 14 Aug 1973, divorced, 2 d. *Education:* Royal Danish Conservatory; Dr phil, University of Copenhagen, 1972. *Career:* Freelance Musician, 1949–56; Music Critic, 1952–60; Teacher, Royal Danish Conservatory of Music, 1953–58; Teaching Assistant, 1959–61, Associate Professor, 1961–71, Professor, 1971–96, University of Copenhagen; Guest Professor, State University of New York at Stony Brook, USA, 1974; Professor of Music, University of California, Los Angeles, 1978–81; mem, Royal Danish Academy, 1986; Norwegian Academy of Science and Letters, 1988; International Musicological Society, 1982; The Sonning Foundation, 1989–96. *Compositions include:* Musica riservata No. 1, op 52, string quartet, 1970; Two choruses, op 57, Nos 2 and 3, 1971; Musica riservata No. 2, op 61, for oboe, clarinet, bassoon and saxophone, 1976; Pastorale, op 63, for 2 clarinets, 1976; Labirinto 1, op 77, viola solo, 1986; Orchestration of P Heise, Dyvekes Sange I–VII, op 78, for soprano and orchestra; Labirinto II, op 79, for guitar, 1987; Partita, op 89, for organ,

1991; Cello Concerto, op 98, 1993; Jeu Mosaique for harp and chamber orchestra, op 99, 1995; Elegia for viola and strings, op 108, 1999; Fantasia II for organ, op 109, 2003. *Recordings include:* Chamber Concerto no2, op 38; Octomeri, op 40, for violin and piano; Musica riservata No. 1 op 52; Trio Serenade, O alter Duft aus Märchenzeit, op 36, for Violin, Cello and Piano; Triptykon for Violin and String Orchestra, op 72; Cello Concerto, op 98; Jeu Mosaïque for Harp and Orchestra, op 99; Partita for Cello, op 103. *Publications:* Books: Musikalsk Modernisme, 1964; Studien zur Entwicklung des dodekaphonen Satzes bei Arnold Schönberg I–III, 1972; Schoenberg's Late Tonal works, in The Arnold Schoenberg Companion, 1998. *Contributions:* Numerous articles to magazines and journals including: The Nomenclature of Pitch-Class Sets, 1985; Die Komponisten der Wiener Schule und ihre Textdichter sowie das Komponisten-Dichter-Verhaltnis heute, 1988; Zur harmonischen Analyse der Musik des 19 Jahrhunderts, eine theoretische Erwägung, 1990; Kuhlau Kanons, 1996. *Address:* Duevej 14, Sixth Floor, 2000 Frederiksberg, Denmark.

MAFFEO, Gianni; Singer (Baritone); b. 30 March 1939, Vigevano, Milan, Italy. *Education:* Studied at the Liceo Musiale di Vercelli. *Career:* Debut: Sang Tonion in Pagliacci with the Associazione Lirico Compagnia, 1961; Many appearances at such opera centres as La Scala Milan, Genoa, Palermo, Turin and Verona, 1973; Sang Schaunard in the Zeffirelli/Karajan Bohème at La Scala, 1963; Guest engagements at Vienna, Prague, Rouen, Monte Carlo, Brno, Lisbon, Munich and the NYC Opera; Further appearances at Toulouse, Nice, Bordeaux and Frankfurt as Marcello, Sharpless, Germont, Count Luna and Rigoletto. *Recordings:* Madama Butterfly; La Bohème. *Address:* Teatro alla Scala, Via Filodrammatici 2, 20121 Milan, Italy.

MAGA, Othmar; Conductor; b. 30 June 1929, Brno, Czechoslovakia. *Education:* Studied at the Stuttgart Hochschule für Musik, 1948–52; Tubingen University, 1952–58; Accademia Chigiana at Siena with Paul van Kempen, 1954–55; Further studies with Sergiu Celibidache, 1960–62. *Career:* Conducted the Göttingen Symphony Orchestra, 1963–67, Nuremberg Symphony, 1968–70; General Music Director at Bochum, 1971–82; Artistic Director of the Odense Symphony Orchestra, Denmark, and Permanent Conductor of the Orchestra of the Pomeriggi Musicali de Milano, 1987–90; Also Professor at the Folkswangschule at Essen; Chief Conductor of the KBS-Symphony Orchestra in Seoul, Korea, 1992–96; Guest Conductor with leading orchestras in Europe, Japan and America. *Current Management:* Musicontact, Egbert Zinner, Hamburg; Svensk Konsertdirektion G. Lodding, Gotenburg; Conciertos Gama, Buenos Aires; Walter Beloch, Milano. *Address:* Merlos 19, 36323 Grebenau, Germany.

MAGEAU, Mary; Composer and Harpsichordist; b. 4 Sept. 1934, Milwaukee, Wisconsin, USA. *Education:* BMus, DePaul University, Chicago, 1963; MMus, University of Michigan, 1969. *Career:* Faculty Member, Queensland Conservatory, 1987–91; Queensland University of Technology, 1992–95; Founder Member of the Brisbane Baroque Trio. *Compositions include:* Concerto for harpsichord and strings, 1978; Australia's Animals, for piano, 1978; Concert Pieces for violin, cello and piano, 1984; Indian Summer, for youth orchestra, 1986; Concerto Grosso, 1987; Australis 1788, music drama, 1987; Triple Concerto, for violin, cello, piano and orchestra, 1990; Suite for Strings, 1991; An Early Autumn's Dreaming for orchestra, 1993; Dialogues, for clarinet, viola, cello and piano, 1994; The Furies, for piano and orchestra, 1995. *Honours:* 4th Alienor Harpsichord Composition Awards, 1994. *Address:* c/o APRA, 1A Eden Street, Crows Nest, NSW 2065, Australia.

MAGEE, Emily; Singer (Soprano); b. 1968 New York, USA. *Education:* University of Indiana, with Margaret Harshaw. *Career:* Debut: As Mozart's Fiordiligi, Chicago, 1994; As Fiordiligi, European debut, Paris Opéra, 1996; Sang Elsa, Berlin Staatsoper, 1996; Châtelet, Paris, and Bayreuth Festival, 1997 as Eva and Elsa; Further engagements at Portland and San Diego Operas, La Scala, Opéra Bastille, Vienna Staatsoper and Florence; Sang Liu in Turandot and Britten's Ellen Orford at the Chicago Lyric Opera, 1997; Other roles include Mozart's Countess, and Donna Elvira; Marguerite, Poppea, Agathe, Desdemona and Arabella; Covent Garden debut as Jenůfa, 2001. *Recordings:* Lohengrin and Die Meistersinger von Nürnberg under Barenboim. *Honours:* MacAllister Award and Richard F Gold Career Grant. *Address:* c/o Berlin Staatsoper, Unter den Linden 7, 1060 Berlin, Germany.

MAGEE, Gary; Singer (baritone); b. 1968, England. *Education:* Studied at the Guildhall School and the National Opera Studio. *Career:* Debut: Opera North as Schaunard in La Bohème, 1995; Appearances as Eugene Onegin for British Youth Opera, Papageno for Scottish Opera and Masetto for Mid-Wales Opera; Guglielmo for Central Festival Opera, Mozart's Figaro for Opera Omnibus and Schaunard at the Albert Hall, 1996; Almeida Festival apperances and concert with the London Symphony Orchestra in West Side Story; Season 1996–97 as Sharpless in Butterfly at Santiago, in Billy Budd at the Opéra Bastille, Paris,

Guglielmo for Opera North; Royal Opera debut as Silvio in Pagliacci, 1997–98; Rachmaninov's Spring at the 1999 London Prom concerts. *Honours:* Prizewinner, Kathleen Ferrier Awards, 1995. *Current Management:* Harrison/Parrott Ltd, 12 Penzance Place, London, W11 4PA, England. *Telephone:* (20) 7229 9166. *Fax:* (20) 7221 5042. *Website:* www.harrisonparrott.com.

MAGNUSON, Elizabeth; Singer (Soprano); b. 1968, Chicago, USA. *Education:* Studied in Chicago and with Lucille and Robert Evans in Salzburg. *Career:* Appearances with the Zürich Opera as the Queen of Night, Amanda in Ligeti's Le Grand Macabre, Genio in Haydn's Orfeo and Euridice and Marzelline in Fidelio, from 1992. Concert engagements in the Missa Solemnis, Carmina Burana, Henze's Being Beauteous and Bach's Christmas Oratorio; Concert tours to St Petersburg and South America, with further opera appearances at the Würzburg Festival, the Deutsche Oper Berlin (Queen of Night, 1996), and Zürich, Oberto in Alcina and Mozart's Constanze, season 1996–97; Conductors include Christoph Eschenbach, Rolf Beck, Jesus Lopez Cobos (Messiah in Lausanne) and Ingo Metzmacher (Strauss's Burger als Edelmann, in Stuttgart); Season 1999–2000 as Constanze in the Deutsche Oper Berlin, Marcelina in Pa êr's Leonora at Winterthur, and Woglinde for Zürich Opera. *Honours:* Winner, Chicago Belcanto Competition, 1991. *Address:* c/o Opernhaus Zürich, Falkenstrasse 1, 8008 Zürich, Switzerland.

MAGNUSSON, Lars; Opera Singer (tenor); b. 10 March 1955, Gothenburg, Sweden. *Education:* Studied at University of Gothenburg and the Opera School in Stockholm. *Career:* Principal tenor at the Royal Opera, Stockholm, from 1982; Roles have included, the Italian Tenor in Der Rosenkavalier, Lensky, the Duke of Mantua, Alfredo, David in Die Meistersinger and Rodolfo in La Bohème; Sang Pedrillo in a new production of Die Entführung at Covent Garden in 1987; Further performances in Monte Carlo, Nice, Strasbourg, Vienna, Staatsoper, and San Francisco, 1990; Metropolitan Opera debut 1990 as Pedrillo, returning as David, 1992; Royal Opera Stockholm, Gabriele in Verdi's Simon Boccanegra, 1991; Further engagements as David in Paris, Vienna and Marseilles, and the Steersman in Der fliegende Holländer in Geneva; Sang David in a new production of Die Meistersinger at the Metropolitan, 1993, also San Francisco; Season 1997–98 as the Swan in Carmina Burana at Stockholm, Royal Opera. *Current Management:* Athole Still International Management, Forresters Hall, 25–27 Westow Street, London, SE19 3RY, England. *Telephone:* (20) 8771-5271. *Fax:* (20) 8768-6600. *Website:* www.atholestill.com.

MAGOMEDOVA, Ludmilla; Singer (Soprano); b. 23 May 1961, Ukraine, Russia. *Education:* Studied in Moscow. *Career:* Made concert tour of Siberia, 1986–87, and made stage debut 1987, as the Trovatore Leonara at Kuibishev; Verdi birthday concert in Moscow (1988) and Staatsoper Berlin from 1989, as Tosca and Leonora; Sang Norma at Graz in 1989, Aida at the Split Festival 1990; Other roles include Violetta, Lisa in The Queen of Spades and Amelia (Un ballo in maschera); Turandot with the Latvian National Opera at the Albert Hall, 1998; Season 2000–01 as Lady Macbeth at the Macerata Festival and Abigaille at the Bolshoi, Moscow. *Address:* c/o Staatsoper Berlin, Unter den Linden 7, 1060 Berlin, Germany.

MAGUIRE, Hugh; Violinist and Conductor; b. 2 Aug. 1926, Dublin, Ireland. *Education:* College of Music, Dublin; Royal Academy of Music, London; Studies with George Enescu in Paris, 1949–50. *Career:* Debut: Dublin, 1938; London Debut, Wigmore Hall, 1947; Leader of the Bournemouth Municipal (Symphony) Orchestra, 1953–56, London Symphony Orchestra, 1956–62, BBC Symphony, 1962–67; Leader of the Allegri Quartet, 1968–76; Performances of contemporary British composers including Nicola LeFanu, Sebastian Forbes and Elizabeth Maconchy; Leader of the Melos Ensemble, 1977; Co-Leader of the Orchestra of The Royal Opera House, Covent Garden, 1983–91; Tours of British universities giving concerts and lectures under the auspices of the Radcliffe Trust; Professor at the Royal Academy of Music, London; Director of the Orchestra and Director of String Studies at the Britten-Pears School. *Recordings:* Works by Britten, Sherlaw Johnson, Maconchy, Forbes, Elgar, Alexander Goehr and Frank Bridge with the Allegri Quartet. *Honours:* FRAM, 1960; MMus, The University of Hull, 1975; DLitt, University of Ulster, 1986; D.Mus, The National University of Ireland, 1992. *Address:* Manor Farm, Benhall Green, Saxmundham IP17 1HN, England.

MAHLER, Hellgart; Composer and Music Teacher; b. 7 May 1931, Vienna, Austria; m. Robert Flitney (died 1995); three c. *Education:* Associate of the Royal College of Music, London. *Career:* Freelance composer; Music teacher, 1954–. *Compositions include:* Three Galactic Fragments, for piano, 1966, 1980; Mira Ceti for violin and orchestra, 1973; Albedo 0.43 for symphony orchestra, 1965, 1973; Glasscapes, 1976; Equations for trumpet and percussion, 1980; And the Desert Shall Blossom for small orchestra, 1980; The Icknield Quartett II for string quartet and flute, 1978; Zero-G for winds, brass, 6 percussion, harp, piano and violin, 1982; Skyscapes for Five Players, for percussion orchestra, piano and solo horn, 1989; Scherzo and Quatro for violin, 1989; Divertimento for guitar, 1989; How Beautiful Are Thy Dwelling Places, for flute; Quintet, 1991; Sonnets for strings, vol. 1, for cello, 1991; Isochasm, for violin, cello and piano, 1991; Sound Sculptures for clarinet, bass clarinet and bassoon, 1994; Commissions from Silver Harns, 1977, Geoffrey Tozer, 1988, Jan Sedivka, 1989, John Bussey (1994) and Gabriella Smart (1994–95), among others; Scherzos for the wholse piano, 1994, 1995; The Moon and the Lamp 2 for soprano and clarinet, 2000; In Hungarian Mode for Violin, Tubular Bells, Piano, 2003. *Publications:* Three Galactic Fragments, Photons, for solo piano, The 1991 Quintet; Sonnets for Strings, vol. 1; Scherzo and Quatro; Divertimenti, Five Caprices and Isochasms 91 all published by Quamby Books; Several articles published in The Stirng Teacher and a large contribution to Sitzky's book on the piano and its role. *Address:* 108 Stoney Rise road, Devonport, Tasmania 7310 Australia. *Telephone:* (03) 6423 2313.

MAIER, Franz-Josef; Violinist and Conductor; b. 27 April 1925, Memmingen, Germany. *Education:* Studied at the Augsburg Conservatory, at the Munich Academy of Music and the Music Gymnasium Frankfurt. *Career:* Debut: Violin recital at Munich, 1942; Soloist with the Reichs Symphony Orchestra on tour of Germany 1942; Studied further at Saarbrucken and after war service at the Hochschule für Musik, Cologne with Philip Jarnach; Played in Schaffer Quartet and the Schubert Trio; Lecturer at the Robert Schumann Conservatory, Düsseldorf, 1949–59; Professor and leader of the violin master classes at the Cologne Musikhochschule 1959; Performances of contemporary, Baroque and early classical music; Co-founded the Collegium Aureum 1964, becoming conductor and leader of the ensemble on violin; Concerts played on original instruments or copies; Leader of the Collegium Aureum Quartet 1970. *Recordings:* Suites from Campra's Les Fêtes Venetiennes and Lully's Amadis; Bach Suites, Brandenburg Concertos; Pergolesi La Serva Padrona; Mozart Serenades, Divertimenti, Piano Concertos and Symphonies, Coronation Mass, Requiem and Solemn Vespers; Beethoven 3rd Symphony, 4th Piano Concerto and Triple Concerto; Handel Concerti Grossi Op 3, Alexander's Feast, Water Music, Music for the Royal Fireworks and Organ Concertos, (Harmonia Mundi and BASF).

MAISENBERG, Oleg; Pianist; b. 29 April 1945, Odesa, Ukraine. *Education:* Special music college in Kishinev, Moldavia; Gnessin Institute of Art, Moscow, Russia. *Career:* Debut: Age 15 at Rachmaninov piano concerto Nr.1 with National Moldavia Orchestra; Since 70th regular sold in the year; orchestra and chamber concerts over the world, Moscow, Berlin, Prague, Paris, Milan, Amsterdam, Stockholm, London, Vienna, Madrid, Buenos Aires, San Francisco, Philadelphia, New York, Sydney, Tokyo, Hong Kong; Many television and radio productions; mem, Honorary member of Konzerthaus Gesellschaft Vienna. *Recordings:* Schubert; Schumann;Liszt; Scriabin; Berg; Stravinsky, piano, solo; R Strauss; Dvořák; Milhaud; Webern; Schoenberg; Bartók; Rachmaninov; Prokofiev, chamber music. *Honours:* Franz Schubert competition, Vienna, 1967; Music of XX Century, Vienna, 1967. *Current Management:* Agentur Dr Raab/Dr Böhm, Plankengasse 7, 1010 Vienna, Austria. *Address:* IN Der Gugl 7-9, 3400 Klosterneuburg, Austria.

MAISKY, Mischa; Concert Cellist; b. 10 Jan. 1948, Riga, Latvia; m. M Kay Lipman, 1 Jan 1983, 1 s. 1 d. *Education:* Moscow Conservatory; Studied with Mstislav Rostropovich; Masterclasses with Gregor Piatigorsky. *Career:* Debut: Leningrad Philharmonic Orchestra, 1965; Appearances at Carnegie Hall, Royal Festival Hall, Berlin Philharmonic Hall; Recitals with Martha Argerich, Radu Lupu, Boris Belkin, Malcolm Frager; Television and radio, Japan, the United Kingdom, Germany, Netherlands, France, Spain, Mexico, USA, Israel, USSR; Various films; Played the Walton concerto at the Festival Hall, London, 1993. Shostakovich 1st Concerto at the 1993 Proms. *Recordings:* Bach Sonatas, with Martha Argerich; Bach, 6 Cello Solo Suites; Schumann Cello Concerto with Vienna Philharmonic, Leonard Bernstein; Brahms Double Concerto with Gidon Kremer, Vienna Philharmonic, Leonard Bernstein; Haydn Concertos with the Chamber Orchestra of Europe. *Honours:* All Russian Cellists Competition, 1965; Tchaikovsky International Competition, Moscow, 1966; Gaspar Cassado International Competition, Florence, 1973; Grand Prix du Disque, Paris; Record Academy Prize, Tokyo, 1985 and 1989. *Current Management:* Intermusica Artists Management, London, England. *Address:* 138 Meerlaan, 1900 Overijse, Belgium.

MAISURADZE, Badry; Singer (tenor); b. 1967, Georgia, Russia. *Career:* frequent recitals, concerts and opera appearances throughout Europe and in Russia; contestant at the 1995 Cardiff Singer of the World Competition; repertory includes Donizetti's Il Duca d'Alba, Carmen, Tosca, Verdi's Il Corsaro and songs by Rachmaninov; sang Cavaradossi at Covent Garden, 2000. *Current Management:* Askonas Holt Ltd, Lonsdale Chambers, 27 Chancery Lane, London, WC2A 1PF, England.

Telephone: (20) 7400-1700. *Fax:* (20) 7400-1799. *E-mail:* info@askonasholt.co.uk. *Website:* www.askonasholt.co.uk.

MAIXNEROVA, Martina, MMus; Singapore pianist and professor of piano; b. 20 Sept. 1947, Prague, Czechoslovakia; m. Pavel Pranti 1972; two s. *Education:* Conservatory of Music, Prague, Academy of Musical Arts, Prague. *Career:* Professor of Piano in Singapore, 1980; Assistant Professor of Piano at the Academy of Musical Arts, Prague, 1975–80; Professor of Piano at the Music School for Especially Gifted Children in Prague, 1970–73; Adjudicator at the First Rolex Piano Competition in Singapore, 1987; Festival appearances in England, Germany, Czechoslovakia, Austria, Poland, USA and Korea; Solo appearances with orchestras including: Guest soloist with the Prague Chamber Orchestra without a Conductor, 1980; Guest soloist with the Singapore Symphony Orchestra, 1981, England, Sweden, Czechoslovakia and Japan; mem, ARS Cameralis Ensemble, 1976–80; Prague Baroque Ensemble, 1973–80. *Address:* 110 Wishart Road, 03-07 Pender Court, 0409 Singapore.

MAJOR, Dame Malvina Lorraine; Opera Singer (soprano); b. 28 Jan. 1943, Hamilton, New Zealand; m. Winston Fleming, 16 Jan 1965, deceased 1990, 1 s., 2 d. *Education:* Singing under Dame Sister Mary Leo, St Mary's Music School, Auckland, 1960–65 and Ruth Packer, Royal College of Music, London; London Opera Centre, United Kingdom, 1965–67. *Career:* Debut: Camden Town Festival, 1968 in Rossini's La Donna del Lago; Performances as: Pamina, Magic Flute, London Opera Centre, 1967; Matilda in Elisabetta Regina d'Inghilterra, Camden Town, 1968; Rosina, Barber of Seville, Salzburg (conductor, Claudio Abbado), 1968–69; Marguerite, Gounod's Faust, Neath and London, 1969; Bruckner's Te Deum, conductor Daniel Barenboim, 1968; Cio Cio San, Madama Butterfly; Widow, The Merry Widow; Gilda in Rigoletto; Tosca; Constanze in Die Entführung; Arminda in La Finta Giardiniera, Brussels, 1986; Donna Elvira, Don Giovanni, Brighton Festival, 1987; Donna Anna in Don Giovanni at Sydney, Australia, 1987; Operas include further productions of Rosalinda (Die Fledermaus) and Lucia di Lammermoor, Mimi in La Bohème and Constanze in New York and Australia; Sang Arminda at Lausanne, 1989, Constanze with the Lyric Opera of Queensland; Season 1992–93 with Lucia at Adelaide, Arminda at Salzburg, Violetta and Gilda at Wellington; Sang in Eugene Onegin and Don Giovanni with Wellington City Opera, 1997. *Recordings:* To The Glory of God, 1964; L'amico Fritz, opera (Caterina), 1969; Songs for All Seasons, Mahler Symphony No. 4, 1970; Scottish Soldiers Abroad, 1975; Alleluia, 1974; Operatic Arias, conductor John Matheson, 1987; La Finta Giardiniera, Brussels. *Contributions:* London Sunday Times (article by Desmond Shawe-Taylor). *Honours:* New Zealand Mobil Song Quest, 1963; Melbourne Sun Aria, Australia, 1964; Kathleen Ferrier Scholarship, London, 1966; O.B.E., 1985; D.B.E., 1991; Hon D Litt, 1993; Hon D Waik, 1993. *Address:* PO Box 4184, New Plymouth, New Zealand.

MAJOR, Margaret; Violist; b. 1932, Coventry, England. *Education:* Royal College of Music. *Career:* Debut: Wigmore Hall, London, 1955 with Gerald Moore; Principal Viola, Netherlands Chamber Orchestra, 1955–59; Oromonte Trio, 1958–65; Principal Viola, Philomusica of London, 1960–65; Viola, Aeolian String Quartet, 1965–81; Professor of Viola, Royal College of Music, London, 1969–97. *Recordings:* Complete String Quartets of Haydn; Late Beethoven Quartets; Ravel and Debussy Quartets; Complete Mozart Viola Quintets. *Honours:* Lionel Tertis Prize, 1951; International Music Association Concert Award, 1955; MA, University of Newcastle upon Tyne, 1970; FRCM, 1992. *Address:* White Barn, 97 North Bersted Street, Bognor Regis, West Sussex PO 22 9 AF, England.

MAKINO, Yutaka; Composer; b. 5 July 1930, Tokyo, Japan. *Education:* Studied with Koscak Yamada. *Career:* Freelance composer of operas and instrumental works. *Compositions:* Operas Ayame, Radio Opera, CBS, 1960; Mushrooms, comic opera, Tokyo, 1961; Benkei in the Boat, Tokyo, 1962; Hanjo, Tokyo, 1963; Snow-Woman, Yokohama, 1964; The Origin of the Deer Dance, Tokyo, 1967; The Millionaire Ayaginu, comic opera, Tokyo, 1979; The Tale of Ogetsu, 1990. *Honours:* Argentine Music Festival Prize, 1955; National Arts Festival Grant Prize, 1960; Spanish Radio Prize, 1962. *Address:* c/o JASRAC, Jasrac House 7-13, 1-Chome Nishishimbashi, Minato-ku, Tokyo 105, Japan.

MAKLAKIEWICZ, Tadeusz (Wojciech); Composer; b. 20 Oct. 1922, Mszczonow, Poland; m. Maria Pawluskiewicz 1952, 3 d. *Education:* Department of Law, Jagiellonian University, Kraków, 1949; State High School of Music, 1958. *Career:* Debut: Festival of Polish Music, Warsaw, 1951; Dean of Music Education Faculty, 1968–69; Deputy Rector, 1969–71, State High School of Music, Warsaw; Head of Music Education Department, 1973; Rector, 1975–78; President, Authors Agency Ltd, Warsaw, till 1985; Union of Polish Composers; President, Society of Authors ZAiKS, Warsaw, 1993–97; Vice-President, Polish Board of Société Européene de Culture, 1994–. *Compositions:* The Kurpie Suite, for Soprano and Mixed Choir a Cappella, 1957; Cantata: Peace;

Friendship; Work; Epitaphium for Symphony Orchestra, 1959; Rondo for Clarinet and Piano or Orchestra; Vienna, Vocalisation for Soprano and Orchestra, 1964; Polonais of the Tank Corps; The Clocks are Ringing; Songs for Children for Voice and Piano; Mazovian Dance for Piano, 1977; Hands Friendly With Hands, for Mixed Choir and Organ, 1977; Quintet for Flute, 2 Clarinets, Bassoon and Harp, 1977; Above Clouds, for Mixed Choir, 1978; March for Brass Band, 1979; Salvum Fac, for Mixed Choir, 1981; The Bible Triptych, for 2 Clarinets and Bassoon, 1982; Suite for Cello, 1983; The Gorals Mass, for Mixed Choir and Organ, 1983; Chryzea Phorminx Ode for 4 Trombones, 1984; Arch of Triumph, for Woodwind Quintet, 1984; Wistful Songs for Baritone and Piano, 1985; Love Letters, Variations for String Orchestra, 1985; Ave Maria, for 3 Violins, 1986; At Zelazowa Wola, 3 Stanzas for Baritone, Flute, Alto, Horn and Harp, 1986; Violin Concerto for Children, 1987; A Memory, for 3 Cellos, 1987; A Flag for Female Choir, 1988; Credo, Motet for Mixed Choir and Organ, 1992; Ave Maria in Honour of Notre Dame of Lourdes, for Soprano and Organ, 1993; Romantic Swans, for Soprano and Piano, 1994; Aria for Soprano and Orchestra, 1995. *Address:* Smolna 8/90, 00-375 Warsaw, Poland.

MAKRIS, Andreas; Composer; b. 7 March 1930, Salonika, Greece; m. Margaret Lubbe, 12 June 1959, 2 s. *Education:* Phillips University, Enid, Oklahoma, USA, 1950; Postgraduate studies, Kansas City Conservatory, Missouri, and Mannes College of Music, 1956; Aspen Music Festival; Fontainebleau School, France; Studied with Nadia Boulanger. *Career:* Compositions premiered and performed, USA, Canada, Europe, South America, Japan, USSR; Appeared twice with premieres, national television networks, USA, 1978, 1984; Composer-in-residence, National Symphony Orchestra, 1979–90; Adviser to Matislav Rostropovich for new music, 1979–90; His complete short works performed on Voice of America Radio, 1980, 1982. *Compositions include:* Scherzo for Violins, 1966; Concerto for Strings, 1966; Aegean Festival, 1967; Concertino for Trombone, 1970; Anamnesis, 1970; Viola Concerto, 1970; Efthymia, 1972; Five Miniatures, 1972; Mediterranean Holiday, 1974; Fantasy and Dance for saxophone, 1974; Sirens, 1976; Chromatokinesis, 1978; In Memory, 1979; Variations and Song for orchestra, 1979; Fanfare Alexander, 1980; 4th of July March, 1982; Life-Nature Symphonic Poem, 1983; Concerto Fantasia for Violin and Orchestra, 1983; Caprice Tonatonal, 1986; Intrigues for solo clarinet and wind ensemble, 1987; Concertante for Violin, Cello, French Horn, Clarinet, Percussion and Orchestra, 1988; Sonata for Cello and Piano, 1989; Symphony to Youth, 1989; Trilogy for Orchestra, 1990; Alleluia for mixed chorus and brass quintet, 1990; Concertino for organ, flute and string quartet, 1992; A Symphony for soprano and strings, 1992; Woodwind Quintet, 1993; Decalog–Ten Songs for Young Students, 1995; Antithesis for Orchestra, 1995; TFK Commemorative Fanfare for Strings and Snare Drum, 1995; Concerto for Violin and Strings, 1996; Introduction and Kalamatianos for Solo Trumpet, Strings, Snare and Bass Drum, 1997; Sonatina for Solo Violin, 1997; Sextet for Woodwind Quintet and Piano, 1999; Concertino for Flute or Violin and Piano, 1999; Serenade for Soprano and Violin, 2001; Voyage Caprice for Violin, 2003; Hellenic Odyssey for Orchestra, 2003; Various works for violin, string quartets, voice quintets, duets, arrangements of Paganini and Bach; Compositions for special anniversaries and festival openings. *Address:* 11204 Oak Leaf Drive, Silver Spring, MD 20901, USA.

MAKRIS, Cynthia; Singer (Soprano); b. 1956, Sterling, Colorado, USA. *Education:* Studied at the University of Colorado and Adams State College. *Career:* Sang Alice Ford, Donna Elvira and Tosca while a student; European debut at Graz as Violetta; Stadttheater Freiburg, 1980–82 as Constanze, Pamina, Violetta and Saffi in Zigeunerbaron; Sang at Bielefeld from 1982 as Donna Anna, Agathe, Marenka, Lucia di Lammermoor and Manon Lescaut and in revivals of Schreker's Irrelohe and Max Brand's Maschinist Hopkins; Member of the Dortmund Opera from 1986 as Desdemona, Leonora in Il Trovatore, Amelia in Un Ballo in Maschera, and Arabella; Other roles include Marietta in Die Tote Stadt at Düsseldorf and at Antwerp, 1995, Marie in Wozzeck at Karlsruhe, Mozart's Countess, Wagner's Eva and Freia and the Empress in Die Frau ohne Schatten; Has sung the title role in Salome, at Dortmund, Berlin Staatsoper and Deutsche Opér, Tokyo and Scottish Opera at Glasgow, 1990; Verdi's Lady Macbeth at Buenos Aires, 1998 and Norma at Philadelphia; Season 2000 as the Forza Leonora at Savonlinna, Leonora in Trovatore and Beethoven's Leonore in Helsinki; Salome at theWiesbaden festival, Marie in Wozzeck at Santiago and Zandonai's Francesca in Bueons Aires. *Address:* c/o Opernhaus, Kuhstrasse 12, 4600 Dortmund, Germany.

MAKSYMIUK, Jerzy; Conductor; b. 9 April 1936, Grodno, Poland. *Education:* Studied Violin, piano, conducting, composition, Warsaw Conservatory, Poland. *Career:* Conducted, Warsaw Grant Theatre where later founded Polish Chamber Orchestra; Principal Conductor, Polish National Radio Orchestra, 1975–77; Touring Eastern Europe and USA; United Kingdom debut with Polish Chamber Orchestra, 1977, since appearing in Western Europe, Scandinavia, Japan, Australia,

New Zealand, Salzburg and Edinburgh Festivals, festivals at Aix, Flanders, Granada, Lucerne, Vienna, BBC Promenade Concerts in London; Guest Conductor, Northern Sinfonia, Scottish Chamber Orchestra, BBC Philharmonic Orchestra, 1980–; Chief Conductor, BBC Scottish Symphony Orchestra, 1983–93; Premiered Birtwistle's Still Movement, 1984; Guest Conductor, London Symphony Orchestra, London Philharmonic Orchestra, Tokyo Metropolitan Orchestra, Indianapolis Symphony, Sydney Symphony; Conducted Don Giovanni for English National Opera, 1991 (debut), Die Fledermaus, 1993; Led Premiere of Macmillan's The Confession of Isobel Gowdie, Proms, 1990, and Robin Holloway's Violin Concerto, 1992; Season 1999–2000 with the Finnish Radio Symphony Orchestra, the Singapore Symphony Orchestra, Winterthur Symphony Orchestra and Prague Autumn Festival. *Recordings:* Haydn, Bach, Vivaldi, Tchaikovsky, Mendelssohn; Music for Pleasure; Schumann with London Philharmonic Orchestra and Devoyon; Shostakovich Piano Concerto with Dimitri Alexeev and the English Chamber Orchestra; Paderewski's 1st Symphony. *Honours:* Honorary DLitt, Strathclyde University, 1990; Gramophone Award for Contemporary Music, 1993; Honorary Title, Conductor Laureate, BBC Scottish Symphony. Current Management. IMG Artists. *Address:* c/o IMG Artists, Lovell House, 616 Chiswick High Road, London W4 5RX, England.

MALACHOVSKY, Martin; Opera Singer (Bass); b. 23 Jan. 1968, Bratislava, Czechoslovakia; m. Iveta Pasková, 1 d. *Education:* Academy of Arts, Bratislava, 1986–92; Hochschule für Musik und darstellende Kunst in Wien, Masterclasses–E Nesterenko, 1990; Conservatoire National Superieur de Paris (Prof Gottlieb), 1991. *Career:* Debut: Slovak National Theatre, 1991; J Massenet, Don Quixote; Rossini, Il Barbiere di Siviglia (Don Basilio); La Bohème (Colline), Slovak National Theatre, Bratislava; J Offenbach: Les Contes d'Hoffmann (Luther and Crespel), Opéra Comique, Paris, 1996; W A Mozart, Le nozze di Figaro, Bartolo, 1995; Mozart Festival, Madrid, 1992; May Festival, Wiesbaden, 1996; Gounod: Faust (Wagner), National Theatre Prague, 1996; Tour of Japan as Sagristano in Puccini's Tosca with Sherrill Milnes as Scarpia, Peter Dvorsky as Cavaradossi and Shinobu Satoh as Tosca, 1997; mem, Slovak Music Union. *Honours:* 3rd Place, International A Dvořák's Singing Competition in Carlsbad, 1988. *Address:* Interartists, Slovakia. *Address:* Gorkého 13, 811 01 Bratislava, Slovakia.

MALAGNINI, Mario; Singer (Tenor); b. 1959, Salo, Italy. *Education:* Studied at the Brescia Conservatory and the Giuseppe Verdi Conservatory, Milan with Piermirando Ferraro; Further study with Tito Gobbi and Giuseppe di Stefano. *Career:* Sang in Frankfurt and Milan, La Scala, 1985, as Radames, and in Il Corsaro; Returned to La Scala 1986–87, as Alfredo and Ismaele in Nabucco; Verona Arena from 1987, as Foresto in Attila, Pinkerton, Riccardo and Radames; Appeared as Don José at Glyndebourne 1987, and in a concert performance of La Battaglia di Legnano at Carnegie Hall, as Arrigo; Further engagements at Florence, as Pinkerton and Gabriele Adorno, Nîmes and Monte Carlo, Pollione in Norma, Vienna, Berlin, Houston, Budapest and Seoul; 1988; Teatro La Fenice Venice, 1990 as Rodolfo in Leoncavallo's Bohème; Sang Radames at Verona and Pinkerton for the Munich Staatsoper, 2000. *Recordings:* Emilia di Liverpool, with the Philharmonia Orchestra, Opera Rara; Norma conducted by Emil Tchakarov. *Honours:* Winner, Tito Gobbi Competition, 1983; Concorso Enrico Caruso and Belvedere Competition, Vienna, 1984. *Address:* c/o Arena di Verona, Piazza Bra 28, 37121 Verona, Italy.

MALANIUK, Ira; Singer (Mezzo-Soprano); b. 29 Jan. 1923, Stanislava, Poland. *Education:* Studied with Adam Didur in Lwow and with Anna Bahr-Mildenburg in Vienna; Salzburg Mozarteum. *Career:* Debut: Graz 1945; Sang in Zürich from 1947, notably in The Rake's Progress, 1951; Bayreuth Festival 1951–53, as Brangaene, Magdalena, Fricka and Waltraute, Munich Opera from 1952, as Orpheus, Lady Macbeth and Bart ók's Judith; Vienna Opera from 1956; Covent Garden 1953, as Adelaide in Arabella, with the Munich Company; Paris Opéra 1956, in Das Rheingold; Salzburg Festival from 1956, notably in the 1958 local premiere of Barber's Vanessa; Concert performances from 1966; Professor at the Graz Conservatory from 1971. *Recordings:* Die Meistersinger, Arabella, Aida, Così fan tutte, Le nozze di Figaro; Waltraute in Götterdämmerung, conducted by Clemens Krauss, Bayreuth 1953; Brangaene in Tristan und Isolde, under Karajan, Bayreuth, 1952.

MALAS, Spiro; Singer (Bass-baritone); b. 28 Jan. 1933, Baltimore, Maryland, USA; m. Marlene Kleinman. *Education:* Studied with E Nagy, Peabody Conservatory of Music, Baltimore; E Baklor and D Ferro, NY; Coached by I Chicagov. *Career:* Debut: Marco, Gianni Schicchi, Baltimore Civic Opera, 1959; NYC Opera debut, Spinellocchio in Gianni Schicchi, 1961; Toured Australia with Sutherland-Williamson International grand Opera Co 1965; Covent Garden debut, London as Sulpice in La fille du Régiment, 1966; Pluto in Haydn's Orfeo ed Euridice, Edinburgh Festival, 1967; Chicago Lyric Opera debut as Assur in Semiramide, 1971; Metropolitan Opera debut NY as Sulpice,

1983; Other roles have been the Sacristan in Tosca, Zuniga, Mozart's Bartolo and Frank in Die Fledermaus; Sang Frank Maurrant in the British premiere of Weill's Street Scene, Glasgow 1989; Don Isaac in Prokofiev's Duenna at the 1989 Wexford Festival; Vancouver 1990, as Baron Zeta in The Merry Widow; Many concert engagements; Teacher, Peabody Conservatory of Music. Recordings. For Decca-London. *Honours:* Winner, Metropolitan Opera Auditions, 1961. *Address:* c/o Columbia Artists Management Inc, 165 West 57th Street, NY 10019, USA.

MALAS-GODLOEWSKA, Ewa; Singer (Coloratura Soprano); b. 1955, Warsaw, Poland. *Education:* Studied in warsaw. *Career:* Sang at the Warsaw Opera from 1978 as Zerbinetta, the Queen of Night, Rosina, Norina, and Constanze in Die Entführung; Leading roles at the Vienna Volksoper, Paris Opéra-Comique, Nantes, Olympia, Basle, Berne, Wiesbaden and Dresden; Sang Celia in Mozart's Lucio Silla, at Nanterre and Brussels, 1986; Sang Madeleine in Le Postillon de Longjumeau at the Grand Theatre Geneva, 1990; Queen of Night in new productions of Die Zauberflöte at Houston and Paris, Opéra Bastille, 1991; Théâtre du Châtelet Paris in L'Enfant et les Sortilèges; Concert performances in the United Kingdom, Switzerland, Poland, Germany, Netherlands, Belgium, and France, Gstaad Festival, 1987 in Beethoven's Ninth, conducted by Yehudi Menuhin. *Honours:* Winner, Toulouse International Competition, 1978. *Address:* c/o Opera de la Bastille, 120 Rue de Lyon, 75012 Paris, France.

MALASPINE, Massimiliano; Singer (Bass); b. 17 May 1925, Fara Novarese, Italy. *Education:* Studied with Lina Pagliughi. *Career:* Appearances from 1959 at such Italian Opera centres as La Scala Milan, Teatro San Carlo Naples, Teatro Fenice Venice and the Teatro Regio Parma; Further engagements at Genoa, Turin, Brussels, Munich Staatsoper, Montreal, Toulouse, Frankfurt, Rio de Janeiro, Paris, Barcelona and Miami; Roles have included Colline in La Bohème, Oroveso in Norma; Ptolomey in Giulio Cesare; Sarastro and Verdi's Padre Guardiano; Banquo and Ramphis; Teacher of singing in Milan after retiring from stage. *Address:* c/o Teatro alla Scalla, Via Filodrammatici 2, 20121 Milan, Italy.

MALCOLM, Carlos Edmond; composer and pianist; b. 24 Nov. 1945, Havana City, Cuba; one s. one d. *Education:* Vedado Institute, Havana, Amadeo Roldan Conservatory, Superior Institute of Arts, Havana. *Career:* debut, National Theatre, Cuba, 1964; Composer and Pianist; National Modern Dance Ensemble, 1964–68; Cuban Institute of Radio, occasionally Cuban Institute of Film, 1968–70; Belongs to The Staff of Composers of The Ministry of Culture of Cuba, 1970–; Toured throughout Mexico, Jamaica, Ecuador, playing own works, teaching and lecutring; Works have been played in New Music Concerts, Warsaw Autumn, Berlin's Biennalle, Japan, Argentina, Hungary. *Compositions:* Quetzalcoat!, Song of the Feathered Serpent, for flute and piano; Beny More redivivo, for string quartet; Adagio for piano, 4 hands; El Remediano; Eclosion; Articulations for piano; 13 studies for piano; Songs set to texts by Caribbean Poets; Rumours, for violin, cello and piano; Meditation for piano, all composed between 1963–90; ACCORDES quartet played, Benny More redivivo; Played with flautist Robert Aitken, Quetzalcoat ! for flute and piano; Other compiositions for piano solo, at Toronto's Premier Grand Theater, Royal Conservatory of Music; Bayreuth Festival of Music; AMBER Trio, Israel, played piano trio, Rumours and first performance of Meditation for piano solo, Germany, 1990; University La Salle of Philadelphia. *Address:* ul Piekna 16, m2, 00-539 Warsaw, Poland.

MALEK, Viktor; Conductor; b. 20 Dec. 1922, Velká Polana, Czechoslovakia. *Education:* Conducting and Composition, Conservatoire of Music, Prague, 1946; Musical Sciences, Philosophical-Historical Faculty, Charles University, Prague. *Career:* Assistant Conductor, State Theatre, Ostrava, 1946–48; Conductor, Opera Ustí nad Labem, 1948–62; Opera Conductor, 1962–90, Chief Conductor, 1976–84, National Theatre, Bratislava; Conductor, Wien Volksoper, 1977–81; Teacher, Academy of Music, Bratislava, 1981–; Guest Conductor, Prague, Brno, Budapest, Temisoara, Kiev, Edinburgh, Bilbao, Oviedo and Valladolid; Conducted around 800 performances; Conducted first nights for 20 Czech and 12 Slovak operas, composers including Smetana, Dvořák, Janáček, Martinů, Cikker, Beneš, Verdi, Giordano, Mozart, Gounod, Bizet, Wagner, Borodin, Britten, Puccini, Berg; Recordings for radio and television: Così fan tutte, Ballo in Maschera, Benes' The Emperor's New Clothes, King Oedipus, Hatrik The Lucky Prince and others; Founder, Chamber Orchestra Camerata Slovaca, 1969 and Chamber Opera of Slovak National Theatre, 1973–; Chamber opera tours throughout Europe, especially Spain, Germany, Netherlands, Poland, Yugoslavia, Austria; Founder, Symphony Orchestra of the Academy of Music Bratislava, 1994; Conducted Britten's Albert Herring, Don Carlos, L'Elisir d'amore, Berg's Wozzeck, Beggar's Opera; mem, Slovak Music Association; Slovak Concert Artists' Association. *Recordings:* With chamber orchestra Camerata Slovaca, 1969–: Kusser Meier Erindo, opera; 2 profile records with singers; 3 profile records of Slovak

composers Bagin, Malovec and Meier; 300 recordings with instrumental and vocal soloists from Baroque to modern music; 2 CDs. *Honours:* Honoured Artist of Czechoslovakia, 1976. *Address:* Cs Parasutistov 31, 83103 Bratislava, Slovakia.

MALFITANO, Catherine; Singer (Soprano); b. 18 April 1948, New York, NY, USA. *Education:* High School of Music and Art; Manhattan School of Music; With violinist father and dancer/actress mother; Voice with Henry Lewis. *Career:* Debut: Nannetta in Falstaff, Central City Opera, 1972; With Minnesota Opera, 1973, New York City Opera, 1973–79, debut as Mimi/La Bohème; Netherlands Opera: Susanna in Figaro, 1974, Eurydice, 1975, Mimi, 1977; Tosca 1998; Salzburg Festival: Servilia in Tito, 1976, 1977, 1979, 3 Hoffmann roles, 1981, 1982, Salome, 1992, 1993, Elvira in Giovanni, 1994, 1995, 1996; Jenny in Mahagonny, 1998; Met debut as Gretel, 1979, returning for many other roles; Vienna Staatsoper: Violetta, 1982, Manon, 1984, Grete in Schreker's Der Ferne Klang, 1991, Salome and Butterfly, 1993; Wozzeck, 1997; Maggio Musicale Florence: Suor Angelica, 1983, Jenny in Weill's Mahagonny, 1990, Salome, 1994; Teatro Comunale, Florence: Antonia in Hoffmann, 1980–81, Mimi, 1983, Faust, 1985, Butterfly, 1988, Poppea, 1992; Munich: Berg's Lulu, 1985, Mimi, 1986, Daphne, 1988; Covent Garden: Susanna, Zerlina, 1976, Butterfly, 1988, Lina (Stiffelio), Tosca, Tatyana, 1993, Salome, 1995, 1997; Berlin Deutsche Oper: Butterfly, 1987, Amelia in Boccanegra, Mimi, Susanna, 1989, Salome, 1990; Berlin Staatsoper, Marie (Wozzeck), 1994, Leonore (Fidelio), 1995; Geneva: Fiorilla (Turco), 1985, Poppea, Manon, 1989, Leonore, 1994; La Scala: Daphne, 1988, Butterfly, 1990; Wozzeck, 1997; Lyric Opera, Chicago: Susanna, 1975, Violetta, 1985, Lulu, 1987, Barber's Cleopatra, 1991, Butterfly, 1991–92, Liu, 1992; McTeague/Bolcom, 1992; Makropulos Case, 1995–96; 3 Roles/Il Trittico, 1996; Salome, 1996; Butterfly 1997, 1998; Mahagonny, 1998; View from Bridge/Bolcom, 1999; Macbeth, 1999; World premiere roles created: Conrad Susa's Transformations, 1973, Bilby's Doll (Carlisle Floyd), 1976, Thomas Pasatieri's Washington Square, 1976, William Bolcom's McTeague, 1992; Engaged as the Kostelnička in Jenůfa for Houston Opera, 2004. *Recordings:* Rossini Stabat Mater, conductor Muti; Gounod Roméo et Juliette, conductor Plasson; Strauss's Salome, conductor Dohnányi; Music for Voice and Violin with Joseph Malfitano; Tosca–Zubin Mehta; Others; Videos include Tosca with Domingo; Stiffelio with Carreras and Salome. *Honours:* Emmy, Best Performance in Tosca film; Honorary Doctorate De Paul University, Chicago. *Current Management:* CAMI, 165 W 57th Street, New York, NY 10019, USA; Rita Schütz, Artists Management Zürich, Rütistrasse 52, 8044 Zürich-Gockhausen, Switzerland.

MALGOIRE, Jean-Claude; Conductor and Oboist; b. 25 Nov. 1940, Avignon, France. *Education:* Studied in Avignon and at the Paris Conservatory, prizes for oboe and chamber music, 1960. *Career:* 1966 founded La Grande Ecurie et la Chambre du Roy, for the performance of Baroque music; Founded Florilegium Musicum de Paris; Concerts of medieval and Renaissance Music; Handel's Rinaldo at the Festival Hall, London; Rameau's Hippolyte et Aricie for the English Bach Festival at Covent Garden; Campra's Tancrède for the Copenhagen Royal Opera and at the Aix-en-Provence Festival 1986; L'Incoronazione di Poppea at the Stockholm Opera; Rameau's Les Indes Galantes at the Versailles Opéra Royal; Conducted Cephale et Procris by Elisabeth Jacquet de la Guerre at St Etienne, 1989, Kreutzer's Paul et Virginie at Tourcoing; Season 1992 with Lully's Alceste at the Théâtre des Champs-Elysées, Paris, a Vivaldi pastiche, Montezuma, at Monte Carlo and Gnecco's Prova di un'opera seria at Montpellier; Conducted Salieri's Falstaff at Tourcoing, 1996; Polish premiere of Lully's Alceste with the Warsaw Chamber Orchestra, 1998. *Recordings:* Rinaldo; Handel's Xerxes; Hippolyte et Aricie and Les Indes Galantes; Tancrède; Cavalli's Ercole Amante; Handel Concerti Grossi Op 3 and 6, Water and Fireworks Music; Lully Alceste, Psyché and Le Bourgeois gentilhomme; Vivaldi Beatus Vir, Gloria and flute concertos; Charpentier Messe de Minuit; Renaissance music with the Florilegium Musicum de Paris. *Honours:* Prix Internationale de Geneve, Oboe, 1968. *Address:* La Grand Ecurie et la Chambre du Roy, 9 Place des Federées, 93160 Noisy le Grand, France.

MALIPIERO, Riccardo; Composer; b. 24 July 1914, Milan, Italy; m. Victoria Schneider, soprano, 21 Dec 1988. *Education:* Studied at the Milan Conservatory, 1930–1937 and with his uncle Gian Francesco Malipiero, at the Venice Conservatory 1937–39. *Career:* Began career as a pianist, interrupted by WWII; After WWII began as Composer and Music Critic; Organized the first International Congress of Dodecaphonic Music, Milan 1949; Lectured in USA 1954 and 1959; Masterclasses at the Di Tella Institute Buenos Aires, 1963 and the University of Maryland, 1969; Director of the Varese Liceo Musicale 1969–, 1984. *Compositions:* Operas Minnie la candida 1942; La Donna e Mobile 1954; Television opera Battono alla Porta 1962; L'Ultima Eva, 1995; Orchestral: Piano Concerto, 1937; 2 Cello Concertos, 1938 and 1959; Balletto 1939; Piccolo Concerto for piano and orchestra, 1945; Antico sole for soprano and orchestra 1947; Cantata sacra for soprano, chorus and orchestra 1947; 3 Symphonies 1949, 1956, 1959; Violin Concerto

1952; Studi 1953; Overture-Divertimento del Ritorno 1953; Concerto for piano and ensemble, 1955; Concerto Breve for ballerina and chamber orchestra 1956; Cantata di Natale for soprano, chorus and orchestra 1959; Concerto per Dimitri for piano and orchestra, 1961; Nykteghersia 1962; Cadencias 1964; Muttermusik 1966; Mirages 1966; Carnet de Notes 1967; Rapsodia for violin and orchestra 1967; Serenata per Alice Tully 1969; Monologo for male voice and strings 1969; Concerto for Piano Trio and orchestra 1976; 2 Piano Concertos 1974; Requiem 1975; Ombre 1986; Go Placidly for baritone and chamber orchestra 1975; Loneliness for soprano and orchestra 1987; Due Arie for soprano and orchestra, 1990; Lieder études for soprano and piano, 1991; Chamber: Musik 1 for cello and 9 instruments 1938; 3 String Quartets 1941, 1954, 1960; Violin Sonata 1956; Piano Quintet 1957; Musica da camera for wind quintet 1959; Oboe Sonata 1959; 6 Poesie di Dylan Thomas 1959 for soprano and 10 instruments; Mosaico for wind and string quartets, 1961; Preludio, Adagio e Finale for soprano, 5 percussionists and piano 1963; In Time of Daffodils, Cummings, for soprano, baritone and 7 instruments 1964; Nuclei for 2 pianos and percussion 1966; Cassazione for string sextet 1967; Piano Trio 1968; Ciaccona di Davide for viola and piano 1970; Giber Folia for clarinet and piano 1973; Memoria for flute and harpsichord 1973; Winter quintet for quintet 1976; Apresmiro for 11 instruments 1982; Voicequintet for soprano and string quartet 1988; Piano Music. *Address:* Via A Stradella 1, 20129, Milano, Italy.

MALIPONTE, Adriana; Singer (Soprano); b. 26 Dec. 1938, Brescia, Italy. *Education:* Conservatoire de Mulhouse with Suzanne Stappen Bergmann and with Carmen Melis in Milan; Protegée of Rosa Ponselle, Baltimore. *Career:* Debut: Paris Opéra as Micaela in Carmen, 1962–63; Gran Teatro Liceo, Barcelona with Massenet's Manon, 1964; Sang in San Carlo Naples, Lisbon, Milan, Marseille, Tokyo and in all major operas of the world; Has wide repertoire of some 60 roles; British debut, 1967, at Glyndebourne Festival in Elisir d'amore; La Scala debut in Manon with Pavarotti, Mar 1970, returning in I Masnadieri, 1978, and La Bohème, Elisir d'amore, Carmen, Turandot (Liu), Luisa Miller; Metropolitan Opera debut in La Bohème with Pavarotti, 1971; Japan, in La Bohème, (Mimi), Traviata and Carmen, 1975, returning in La Bohème, with Carlos Kleiber director, 1981; Pagliacci with Placido Domingo, Covent Garden, 1976; La Bohème and Traviata, Vienna Staatsoper and at Mozart Festival, director Karl Böhm, 1977; Iris at Newark Symphony Hall; La Traviata with Alfredo Kraus, Pretoria, 1983; Maria Stuarda, director Santi, and Guglielmo Tell, Zürich, 1986–87, 1990; Debut in Adriana Lecouvreur, Tenerife, 1989–90; Recent concerts in Taipei, also Carmen, Turandot and Liu, 1994; Gave recital at Salle Gaveau, Paris, 1994. *Recordings include:* Micaela in Carmen, with Bernstein, 1973; Le Villi (Puccini), RCA; Les Pêcheurs des Perles; Pagliacci with Placido Domingo, video. *Honours:* Winner, Génève International d'Execution Musicale, 1960; Prix Villabella, Grand Prix du Disque, 1965; Grammy, USA, 1973; Maschera d'Argento, Campione d'Italia, 1976; Premio Illica, 1983; Rosa d'Oro, 1984; Vittoria Alata, Brescia, 1985; Chevalier des Arts et des Lettres, Académie de France. *Address:* Via Macchi 75, Milan, Italy.

MALIS, David; Singer (Baritone); b. 1961, USA. *Career:* Many appearances in concert and opera in North America and Europe, from 1985; Season 1995 with performances in Athens, Buenos Aires from Pittsburgh; Metropolitan Opera in Peter Grimes and La Bohème; Sang Belcore at San Diego, 1996; Wolfram in Tannhäuser at Palermo, 1998. *Honours:* Winner, 1985 Cardiff Singer of the World Competition. *Address:* c/o Metropolitan Opera, Lincoln Center, New York, NY 10023, USA.

MÄLKKI, Susanna; Conductor; b. 1977, Finland. *Education:* Sibelius Academy, Helsinki, from 1995 with Eri Klas and Leif Segerstram (former studies as cellist, with Yo-Yo Ma, Steven Isserlis and Janos Starker). *Career:* Co-principal cellist with Gothenburg SO, Sweden, 1995–98; Conductor of the Finnish Radio SO, Gothenburg SO, Århus SO, Lahti SO, BBC Scottish SO, Tokyo SO and Tokyo PO; Powder her Face by Adès at 1999 Musica Nova Festival; Helsinki and Almeida Festival, London; Principal Guest of the Oslo SO and Co–Artistic Director of the Stavanger SO (19th and 20th Century repertory); Season 2002–03 with the Royal Flanders PO, Stockholm, PO, Northern Sinfonia, Swedish Radio SO and Oslo PO; US debut with Charlotte SO; Cello recitalist and chamber musician. *Current Management:* Harrison/Parrott Ltd, 12 Penzance Place, London, W11 4PA, England. *Telephone:* (20) 7229 9166. *Fax:* (20) 7221 5042. *Website:* www .harrisonparrott.com.

MALMBERG, Urban; Singer (Baritone); b. 29 March 1962, Stockholm, Sweden. *Education:* Sang in the Boy's Choir of the Stockholm Opera and appeared as First Boy in the 1974 Bergman film version of Die Zauberflöte; Studied in Stockholm with Helge Brilioth and Erik Saeden. *Career:* Sang at Stockholm in works by Peter Maxwell Davies and Janake Hillerud; Hamburg Staatsoper from 1983, as Malatesta, Don Pasquale, Masetto, Papageno, Schaunard in La Bohème, Harlequin in Ariadne and in Nono's Intolleranza and Die Gespenstersonate by

Reimann; Guest appearances in Düsseldorf, Las Palmas, London, Moscow, San Francisco and Tokyo; Other roles have included Guglielmo and Donner, Brussels and Bonn, 1990, Belcore, Marcello and Lescaut; Season 1992 with Malatesta at Vancouver and Frère Leon in Messiaen's St François d'Assise at the Salzburg Festival; Concert repertoire includes the St Matthew Passion, Beethoven's Ninth, Ein Deutsches Requiem and Peer Gynt; Sang title role in premiere of Matthias Pintscher's Thomas Chatterton, Dresden 1998. *Recordings:* Ariadne auf Naxos and Les Contes d'Hoffmann; The Count in Schreker's Der Schatzgräber, with Hamburg forces. *Address:* Hamburgische Staatsoper, Grosse-Theaterstrasse 34, 2000 Hamburg 36, Germany.

MALMBORG, Gunila; Singer (Soprano); b. 26 Feb. 1933, Lulea, Sweden; m. Lars af Malmborg. *Education:* Royal Stockholm Academy of Music. *Career:* Debut: Stockholm 1960, as Marzeline in Fidelio; Guest appearances in Copenhagen, Oslo, Monte Carlo, Cologne and Kiel; Munich 1968, as Salome and Aida; Glyndebourne 1965, as Lady Macbeth; Well known in Wagner roles and as Verdi's Abigaille and Amelia, Mozart's Donna Anna, Puccini's Tosca and Turandot and Offenbach's Giulietta; mem, Stockholm Opera from 1960. *Address:* c/o Kungliga Teatern, PO Box 16094, 10322 Stockholm, Sweden.

MALONE, Carol; Singer (Soprano); b. 16 July 1943, Grayson, Kentucky, USA. *Education:* Studied at the University of Indian at Bloomington, at the Hamburg Musikhochschule and with Joseph Metternich in Cologne. *Career:* Debut: Cologen 1966, as Aennchen in Der Freischütz; Many appearances at such German opera centres as the State Operas of Hamburg, Munich and Stuttgart, Deutsche Oper am Rhein Düsseldorf, Nationaltheater Mannheim and Frankfurt; Further engagements at Brussels, Vienna Volksoper, Salzburg, San Francisco, Amsterdam, Venice and the Edinburgh Festival; Sang with the Deutsche Oper Berlin in the premiere of Love's Labour Lost by Nabokov, Brussels, 1973 and as Zerlina in Don Giovanni, Berlin, 1988; Other roles have included Marzelline, Nannetta, Despina, Susanna, Blondchen, Sophie, Adele in Die Fledermaus and Adelaide in Blacher's Preussiches Märchen; Many concert appearances. *Recordings:* Trionfo d'Afrodite by Orff. *Address:* c/o Deutsche Oper Berlin, Richard Wagnerstrasse 10, 1000 Berlin, Germany.

MALSBURY, Angela (Mary); Clarinettist; b. 5 May 1945, Preston, Lancashire, England; m. David Pettit, 24 July 1965, 1 s. *Education:* Beauchamp School, Kibworth, Leicester, 1960–62; Associated Board Scholar, Royal College of Music, London, 1962–66; ARCM, Clarinet Teacher and Piano Teacher; LRAM, Clarinet Performer. *Career:* Debut: Concert debut, Royal Festival Hall, with London Mozart Players, 1976; Concerto Soloist with major orchestras world-wide; Clarinet Quintets including classical and contemporary repertoire; Member of De Saram Trio, Albion Ensembles and London Winds; Principal Clarinet of London Mozart Players; Clarinet Professor, Royal Academy of Music; mem, Musicians Union. *Recordings:* Richard Baker's Musical Menagerie, Cameristi of London. *Recordings:* Mozart Serenade for 13 Wind Instruments (Academy of St Martins, Albion and LMP); Mozart, Clarinet Quintet with the Coull String Quartet (LDR); Mozart, Clarinet Concerto, London Mozart Players and Jane Glover (ASV); Mississippi Five with Albion Quintet; A Trio of French Styles with De Saran Trio. *Honours:* Philip Cardew Memorial Prize, 1963; Marjorie Whyte Prize, 1964; Mozart Memorial Prize, 1974; Hon. RAM, 1991. *Current Management:* Stephanie Williams Artists. *Address:* 40 Greenford Avenue, Hanwell, London W7 3QP, England.

MALTA, Alexander; singer (bass); b. 28 Sept. 1942, Visp, Wallis Canton, Switzerland. *Education:* studied with Desider Kovacz in Zürich, Barra-Carracciolo in Milan and Enzo Mascherini in Florence. *Career:* debut at Stuttgart 1962, as the Monk in Don Carlos. US 1976, with the San Francisco Opera; Sang in Brunswick, Munich, Berlin, Vienna, Frankfurt, Geneva, Paris and Venice from 1966; Chicago Lyric Opera in Ariadne auf Naxos; Seattle Opera as Osmin in Die Entfuhrung; Brussels Opera from 1979, notably in Wozzeck, Lulu and Schubert's Fierrabras; Rome Opera as Orestes in Elektra; Maggio Musicale Florence as Wagner's Fasolt and Landgrave; La Scala Milan in Handel's Ariodante; Hamburg Opera as Golaud in Pelléas et Mélisande, Colline in La Bohème, Die Fledermaus, Munich State Opera, Hoffmann, Adriana Lecouvreur, Deutsche Oper Berlin as Nicolai's Falstaff, Gounod's Mefistophélès and Rocco in Fidelio; Salzburg Festival in Carmen and Don Giovanni, conducted by Karajan; Covent Garden 1985, in Tippett's King Priam, title role; Sang the Voice of Neptune in Idomeneo at the 1990 Salzburg Festival. *Recordings:* Lady Macbeth of the Mtsenk District; Carmen, Don Giovanni and the Bruckner Te Deum; Rigoletto; Zar und Zimmermann; Wozzeck.

MALTA, Alvaro; Singer (Bass); b. 19 May 1931, Lisbon, Portugal. *Education:* Studied in Lisbon. *Career:* Has sung at the Teatro San Carlos Lisbon, as Figaro, Papageno, Mephistophélès and Klingsor further appearances until 1984 as the Commendatore, Wurm in Luisa Miller, Ramphis and Trulove in The Rake's Progress; Guest engagements in Italy and France and at the Wexford Festival (1977–79) in Herodiade, Tiefland and L'Amore dei tre Re; Other roles have included Monterone, Colline and Des Grieux. *Address:* c/o Teatro São Carlos, Rua Serpa Pinto 9, 1200 Lisbon, Portugal.

MALTMAN, Christopher; Singer (baritone); b. 1970, England. *Education:* Studied at the Royal Academy of Music and with Sesto Bruscantini and Thomas Hampson. *Career:* Concert engagemnts include Haydn's St Nicholas Mass with the English Chamber Orchestra, Elgar's The Apostles, under Vernon Handley, the Fauré Requiem at the Albert Hall and the Vaughan Williams Serenade to Music with the CBSO; Recitals at the Châtelet, Paris, 1996, and the Wigmore Hall, 1997; Opera includes Silvio in Pagliacci and Billy Budd, for Welsh National Opera, 1997; Haydn's L'Isola Disabitata and Hasse's Solimano at the Berlin Staatsoper, Tarquinius in The Rape of Lucretia at Montpellier and Raimbaud in Le Comte Ory for Glyndebourne Touring Opera, season 1997–98; Fauré's Requiem at the 1999 London Prom concerts; Title role in Billy Budd for Welsh National Opera. *Recordings include:* Paris in Roméo et Juliette; Serenade to Music; Beethoven Folk Songs; Warlock Songs; Ireland Songs. *Honours:* Queen's Commendation for Excellence at the RAM. *Current Management:* Askonas Holt Ltd, Lonsdale Chambers, 27 Chancery Lane, London, WC2A 1PF, England. *Telephone:* (20) 7400-1700. *Fax:* (20) 7400-1799. *E-mail:* info@askonasholt.co .uk. *Website:* www.askonasholt.co.uk.

MAMLOK, Ursula; Composer; b. 1 Feb. 1928, Berlin, Germany. *Education:* Studied in Berlin and Ecuador, NY with Szell at Mannes College and Manhattan School of Music with Vittorio Viannini; Further study with Wolpe, Steuermann, Shapey and Sessions. *Career:* Teacher, NYU, 1967–76, Kingsborough Community College, 1972–75, Manhattan School, 1976–; Represented USA at the 1984 International Rostrum of Composers. *Compositions:* Concerto for strings, 1950; Grasshoppers: 6 Humoresques, 1957; Oboe Concerto, 1974; Concertino for wind quartet, 2 percussion and string orchestra, 1987; Constellations, for orchestra, 1993; Woodwind Quintet, 1956; 2 string quartets, 1962, 1997; Capriccios for oboe and piano, 1968; Variations and Interlude for percussion quartet 1971; Sextet 1978; String Quintet, 1981; From my Garden for violin or viola, 1983; Akarina for flute and ensemble, 1985; Bagatelles for clarinet, violin and cello, 1988; Rhapsody for clarinet, viola and piano, 1989; Stray Birds for soprano, flute and cello, 1963; Hiku settings for soprano and flute, 1967; Der Andreas Garten for mezzo, flutes and harp, 1987; Sunflowers for ensemble, 1990; Five Intermezzi for guitar, 1992; Piano music and pieces for tape. *Recordings:* Walter Hinrischen Award, American Academy and Institute of Arts and Letters, 1989. *Address:* c/o ASCAP, ASCAP Building, 1 Lincoln Plaza, NY 10023, USA.

MAMMOSER, Carmen; Singer (Mezzo-soprano); b. 1953, Stuttgart, Germany; m. Ulrich Walddörfer, one s. *Education:* Studied in Stuttgart with Hildegard Dietz and Konrad Richter. *Career:* Sang at Hagen Opera from 1980, Stuttgart Staatsoper from 1985; Roles have included Mozart's Cherubino and Annio, Offenbach's Nicklausse, Eboli in Don Carlos, Suzuki in Butterfly, Adalgisa in Norma, Emilia in Othello (with Plaido Domingo), Carmen; Premiere of Hans Zender's Don Quichote, 1993; Concert tour of South America with the Verdi Requiem; 1999 Concert tour of Australia with Wagner Wesendonck-Lieder; Other concert repertory includes the Passions of J S Bach, Bruch's Achilleus and Orchestral Songs by Manfred Trojahn. *Recording:* Rêve d'Amour, French Songs by Fauré and Duparc. *Address:* Staatsoper Stuttgart, Oberer Schlossgarten 6, 70173 Stuttgart, Germany.

MANAGER, Richetta; Singer (Soprano); b. 1952, USA. *Education:* Bachelor, Applied Voice, Washburn University of Topeka, Kansas. *Career:* Leading Artist with Gelsenkirchen Opera from 1982, appeared in the roles of Violetta in La Traviata, Amelia in Un Ballo in Maschera, Alice Ford in Falstaff, Elena in l Vespri Siciliani, Leonora in La Forza del Destino, Nella in Gianni Schicchi, Mimi in La Bohème, Leonore in Fidelio, Tosca, Elsa in Lohengrin, Venus and Elisabeth in Tannhäuser, Agathe in Der Freischütz, The Countess in Le nozze di Figaro, Donna Anna in Don Giovanni, First Lady in Die Zauberflöte, Cleopatra in Handels Giulio Cesare, and Title Role in Alcina, Giulietta in Les Contes d'Hoffmann, Marenka in The Bartered Bride, Rosalinde in Die Fledermaus, Saffi in Der Zigeunerbaron, The Duchess of Parma in Busoni's Dr Faustus, Ariadne, Arabella, the Countess in Capriccio, Denise in Tippett's The Knot Garden; Sang in the premiere of Tippett's New Year, Houston and Glyndebourne, 1989–90; Season 1996 as Elisabeth de Valois at Wuppertal and Isolde at Würzburg; Season 1999–2000 in Leonore at Eutin, and Salome and Alice Ford at Wuppertal; Performed at Numerous Festivals with Several Professional Orchestras. *Honours:* 1st Prize, Metropolitan Opera Guild Auditions; 1st Prize, Federated Music Clubs Competition; Gelsenkirchen's Alfred Weber Prize of Excellence. *Address:* Grenzstr 131, 45881 Gelsenkirchen, Germany.

MANASSEN, Alex (Jacques); Composer; b. 6 Sept. 1950, Tiel, Netherlands. *Education:* Studied composition at Sweelinck Conservatory, Amsterdam, with Ton de Leeuw, 1972–79. *Career:* Performances live, on radio and television in the Netherlands; Performances in Italy, France, England, Germany, Israel, Sweden, USA, Poland; Commissions for all important Dutch funds; Teacher of Contemporary and Electronic Music, Sweelinck Conservatory, Amsterdam, 1991; Co-founder, Composer, Manager, Delta Ensemble; Teacher of Music and Informatica, Utrecht Conservatory, 1990; Dean, Director, Teacher of Composition, Swolle Conservatory, 1991–. *Compositions:* Katarsis-Arsis for organ, 1973; Prelude, for strings and harpsichord, 1973/95; Mei, for flute and string quartet, 1974; Citius, Altius, Fortius, Variable instrumentation, 1979; Pandarus Sings, for mezzo soprano, flute, clarinet and piano, 1980; Pandarus Sings, Higher, for soprano, flute, clarinet and piano, 1980; De Waal, for 1 or more instruments, especially for beginners, 1980; Interlude 1, Sextet, for oboe, bassoon, french horn and string trio, 1980; Bass Clarinet Concerto, for bass clarinet and orchestra, 1982; Helix for marimba, 1983; Denkmal an der Grenze des Fruchtlandes, for soprano and chamber ensemble, 1983; Air for Orchestra, 1985; Air for electronic music, 1986; Air-Facilmente, clarinet, violin, cello and piano, 1986; Songs and Interludes, for soprano and chamber ensemble, 1979–88; A Call to La Source Possible, for soprano and chamber ensemble, 1988; Air Conditioned, computer controlled player piano, 1988; Lamento for a landscape, electronic music, 1988; Moordunkel, for soprano, accordion, bass clarinet and percussion, 1990; Two Ears to Hear Two Eyes to See, contralto, tenor and piano, 1990, and for soprano, clarinet and piano, arranged Paul van Ostaijen, 1993; Hallo, Hallo, computer controlled sound generating object on request of the Art Foundation Neerijnen; commissioned by the Amsterdam Fund for the Arts and the Province of Gelderland, 1991; Evening Beach Piano, 1991; Farewell to a Landscape, for high voice and clarinet, 1994; Lamento for the Hanze Towns, 1994; Requiem for a Landscape, based on The Tree Bible by William van Toorn, Gerrit Noordzij and others; Elegy in Memoriam Chris Walraven for 8 celli, 1996; Commissioned by the Fund for the Creation of Music. *Address:* Ankummerdijk 6, NL 7722, XJ Dalfsen, Netherlands.

MANCA DI NISSA, Bernadette; Singer (Mezzo-soprano); b. 27 Sept. 1954, Cagliari, Sardinia. *Education:* Studied at the Salzburg Mozarteum. *Career:* Debut: Pesaro Festival, 1982 as Isaura in Rossini's Tancredi; La Scala, 1983 and 1988, as Bradamante in Alcina and Libya in Jommelli's Fetonte; Gluck's Orpheus, 1989; Venice Teatro Fenice, 1991–92, as Farnace in Mitridate and Isabella in L'Italiana in Algeri; Palermo and Chicago, 1996, as Orpheus and the Princess in Suor Angelica by Puccini; Other roles include Otho in Handel's Agrippina; Tolomeo in Giulio Cesare and Meg Page in Falstaff; Sang Gluck's Orfeo at Naples, 1988; and La Scala, Milan, 1989; Covent Garden debut 1999 as Mistress Quickly in Falstaff. *Recordings:* Video of Tancredi. *Address:* c/o Teatro San Carlo, Via S Carlo, 80132 Naples, Italy.

MANCINELLI, Aldo; Concert Pianist and Professor of Music; b. 1929, Steubenville, Ohio, USA; m. (1) 1 s., 1 d., (2) Judith Elaine Young, 1 June 1971, 1 s., 1 d. *Education:* Graduated, 1952, Graduate Study, 1953, Oberlin Conservatory of Music; Graduated, Accademia Nazionale di Santa Cecilia, Rome, Italy, 1955; Studied with Claudio Arrau, Rudolf Firkusny and Carlo Zecchi. *Career:* Debut: Beethoven 1st Piano Concerto, with Wheeling (West Virginia) Symphony, 1941; Recitals throughout Europe, North Africa, Middle East, North America; Appeared as Soloist with major symphony orchestras throughout Europe and USA, including Cleveland Symphony, San Antonio Symphony, La Scala (Milan), Royal Liverpool Philharmonic, Santa Cecilia Orchestra (Rome), NDR Orchestra (Hamburg). *Recordings:* Piano Music of Charles Griffes, Musical Heritage Society; Beethoven's Concerto No. 5 (Emperor). *Recordings:* Many recordings for Radiotelevisione Italiana; French North Africa Radio, Tunis; Romanian Radio, Bucharest; Beethoven 4th Concerto with the Czech National Symphony Orchestra. *Contributions:* Charles Griffes, An American Enigma, in Clavier, 1985. *Honours:* 1st Prize Winner, Ferruccio Busoni, International Piano Competition, Bolzano, Italy, 1954; Laureate, Liverpool International Piano Concerto Competition, 1959; Laureate, Casella, International Piano Competition, Naples, 1953. *Address:* 341 Timber Place, Decatur, IL 62521, USA.

MANCINI, Caterina; Singer (Soprano); b. 1920, Italy. *Education:* Studied in Milan and elsewhere in Italy. *Career:* Many appearances from 1948 at such Italian opera centres as Bologna, Venice, Rome, Leonora in Il Trovatore; The Baths at Caracalla; La Scala Milan from 1951, debut as Donizetti's Lucrezia Borgia; Sang Agathe at Rome, 1952, and appeared at the Maggio Musicale Florence and the Verona Arena, 1956; Guest engagements in concert and opera elsewhere in Europe. *Recordings:* La Battaglia di Legnano, Ernani and Il Trovatore; Santuzza in Cavalleria Rusticana and Anaide in Rossini's Mosè in Egitto; Guillaume Tell; Attilia; Il Duca d'Alba by Donizetti. *Address:* c/o Teatro alla Scala, Via Filodrammatici 2, 20121 Milan, Italy.

MANDAC, Evelyn; Singer (Soprano); b. 16 Aug. 1945, Malaybalay, Mindanao, Philippines. *Education:* Oberlin College Conservatory; Juilliard School New York. *Career:* Debut: Mobile, Alabama, 1968 in Orff's Carmina Burana; Santa Fe 1968, in the US premiere of Henze's The Bassarids; Washing DC 1969, as Mimi in La Bohème; Toured with Juilliard Quartet, 1969, in Schoenberg's 2nd Quartet; Seattle Opera 1972, in the premiere of Pasatieri's The Black Widow; Sang in the US premiere of Berio's Passaggio; San Francisco 1972, as Inez in L'Africaine; Glyndebourne 1974–75, as Susanna and Despina; Houston Opera 1975, as Lauretta in Gianni Schicchi; Baltimore Opera 1976, in the premiere of Pasatieri's Inez de Castro; Lisa in The Queen of Spades for US television, 1977; Guest appearances in Toulouse, Turin, Rome, Salzburg Festival and Geneva. *Recordings:* Carmina Burana, conducted by Ozawa.

MANDANICI, Marcella; Composer; b. 15 April 1958, Genoa, Italy; m. Giuseppe Venturini, 22 Dec. 1978. *Education:* Piano diploma, Brescia, 1979; Harpsichord Diploma 1984, Composition Diploma 1986, Milan; Composition Diploma, Santa Cecilia Academy, Rome, 1988. *Career:* Autumn Musicale, Como, 1984; Aspekte, Salzburg, 1986; Nuove Musica Italiana, Rome, 1987–88; Settimana di Musica Contemporanea Desenzano, 1987–88; Musica Rave, Milano, 1985; Spazio Musica, Cagliari, 1988; Founded, Nuovi Spazi Sonori, Italian Association for Contemporary Music, Artistic Director, 1987–. *Compositions:* Author of many compositions for solo instruments, chamber ensemble and orchestra including: Invenzione a Cinque, for flute, clarinet, viola, cello and piano, 1982; Edipan Steps for piano, 1983; Rugginenti; Senza Testo, for voice, 1987. *Recordings:* Invenzione a Cinque; Senza Testo. *Honours:* Steirischer Herbst Selection, Graz, 1986; IGNM Selection, Koln, 1987; Antologia Radiotre Selection, Rome, 1988, with Double Path. *Address:* Via Vittorio Emanuele 11-60, 25122 Brescia, Italy.

MANDEL, Alan (Roger); Concert Pianist, Professor of Music and Artistic Director; b. 17 July 1935, New York, USA; m. Nancy Siegmeister, 1 June 1963, divorced 1989. *Education:* BS 1956, MS 1957, Juilliard School of Music; Diploma in Piano and composition, Akademie Mozarteum, Salzburg, Austria, 1962; Diploma, Accademia Monteverdi, Bolzano, Italy, 1963. *Career:* Debut: Town Hall, New York City, 1948; Over 305 International Concert Tours in 50 Countries; Noted for his repertoire of esoteric and seldom-played masterpieces; Professor of Music, The American University, Washington DC; Artistic Director, Washington Music Ensemble; Chairman of the Music Division, The American University, Washington DC, 1992. *Compositions:* Symphony, piano concerto, many piano compositions and songs. *Recordings include:* The Complete Piano Works of Charles Ives; Louis Moreau Gottschalk; Forty Works for the Piano; Anthology of American Piano Music 1790–1970; Three Sides of George Rochberg; Carnival Music; Elie Siegmeister; Sonata No. 4 for Violin and Piano; American Piano (CD); Rags and Riches, CD, Premiere Recordings Inc, New York, 1992. *Publications:* Charles Ives: Study No. 5 for Piano, edited by Alan Mandel with Preface Performance notes, Editorial notes and Analytical notes, 1988. *Current Management:* Guy Friedman, 37 Robins Crescent, New Rochelle, NY 10801, USA. *Address:* 3113 Northampton St NW, Washington DC 20015, USA.

MANDELBAUM, Joel; Composer; b. 12 Oct. 1932, NY, USA. *Education:* Studied with Walter Piston, Irving Fine, Harold Shapero and Bernhard Heiden; BA, Harvard, 1953; MFA, Brandeis University, 1957; PhD, Indiana University, 1961. *Career:* Teacher, Queen's College, NY, 1961, retired 1999; Director of the Aaron Copeland School of Music, 1981–84; Fellow, MacDowell Colony 1968; mem, American Festival of Microtonal Music; American Society for Jewish Music; Long Island Composers Alliance. *Compositions:* Operas: The Man in the Man-Made Moon 1955; The Four Chaplains, 1957; The Dybbuk, 1971; The Village, 1995; Orchestral: Concovation Overture, 1951; Piano Concerto, 1953; Sursum Corda, 1960; Sinfonia Concertante for oboe, horn, violin, cello and chamber orchestra, 1962; Memorial for string orchestra, 1965; Trumpet Concerto, 1970; Chamber: 2 wind quintets, 1957, 1991; 2 string quartets, 1959, 1979; Sonatas with piano for flute, 1951, recorder, 1972, second piano, 1980, oboe, 1981, clarinet, 1983, cello, 1986; Duo sonata for violin and cello, 1989; Works for special microtonal instruments, 1961, 1963, 1967, 1977, 1991; Choruses; 11 Song cycles; Musicals and incidental music. *Recordings include:* Three Song Cycles, Erika Sunnegärdh. *Address:* c/o ASCAP, ASCAP Building, 1 Lincoln Plaza, NY 10023, USA.

MANDUELL, Sir John, Kt; Composer and Music Director; b. 2 March 1928, Johannesburg, South Africa; m. Renna Kellaway, 1955, 3 s., 1 d. *Education:* Haileybury College; Jesus College, Cambridge, University of Strasbourg; Royal Academy of Music; FRAM 1964; FRNCM 1974; FRCM 1980; FRSAMD 1982; FWCMD 1991; Hon FTCL 1973; Hon GSM 1986. *Career:* BBC Music Producer, 1956–61; Governor, National Youth Orchestra, 1964–73 and 1978–; Chief Planner, The Music Programme, 1964–68; Director of Music, University of Lancaster, 1968–71; Associated Board of Royal Schools of Music, 1971–; Governor of Chetham's School, 1971–; Principal, Royal Northern College of Music, 1971–96; Honorary Lecturer in Music, University of Manchester, 1976–; Programme Director of Cheltenham Festival, 1969–95; Director, Young Concert Artists' Trust, 1983–, and Lake District Summer Music Festival, 1984–; President of European Association of Music Academies, 1988–; Opera Board, 1988–, and Board, 1989–, Royal Opera House; Board of Manchester Arts, 1991–; Engagements and tours as composer, conductor and lecturer in Canada, Europe, Hong Kong, South Africa and USA; Chairman of numerous committees; Chairman or member of many international musical competition juries; European Opera Centre opened with Tosca at Manchester, 1998; Mozart's Lucio Silla in London and elsewhere, 1999. *Compositions:* Overture, Sunderland Point, 1969; Diversions for Orchestra, 1970; String Quartet, 1976; Prayers from the Ark, 1981; Double Concerto, 1985; Vistas for Orchestra, 1997. *Contributions:* The Symphony, 1966. *Honours:* 1st Leslie Boosey Award, Royal Philharmonic Society and PRS, 1980; Chevalier de l'Ordre des Arts et de Lettres, France, 1990; Honorary DMus at Lancaster, 1990 and Manchester, 1992. *Address:* c/o Royal Northern College of Music, 124 Oxford Road, Manchester M13 9RD, England.

MANN, Robert; Violinist, Composer, Conductor and Teacher; b. 19 July 1920, Portland, Oregon, USA; m. Lucy Rowan. *Education:* Juilliard School of Music with Edouard Dethier, Adolfo Beti, Felix Salmond, Edgar Schenkman, Bernard Wagenar and Stefan Wolpe. *Career:* Debut: Violin recital NY 1941; Joined faculty of Juilliard School after wartime service; Founded Juilliard String Quartet 1948; Many concert engagements in Europe and USA; Established 1962 as Quartet-in-Residence under the Whittall Foundation at the Library of Congress, Washington, DC; Quartet-in-Residence at Michigan State University from 1977; First performances of Quartets by Carter, Kirchner, Schuman, Sessions, Piston, Babbitt, Copland and Foss; First US Quartet to visit USSR, 1961; Repertory of 600 wroks; Concertor of contemporary music; Has performed and lectured at the Aspen Music Festival; President of the Naumburg Foundation 1971; Chairman of Chamber Music panel 1980; Coach to Concord, Tokyo, LaSalle and Emerson String Quartets; Formed Duo with s. Nicholas Mann 1980; Visited London with the Juilliard Quartet, 1996 and 2000. *Recordings:* Complete Beethoven Quartets and Mozart's Quartets dedicated to Haydn; Contemporary works. *Address:* c/o Violin Faculty, Juilliard School of Music, Lincoln Plaza, NY 10023, USA.

MANN, Werner; Singer (Bass); b. 25 June 1935, Berlin, Germany. *Education:* Studied in Munich and Berne. *Career:* Sang at Aachen Opera, 1980–84; Trier, 1985–90; Pforzheim, from 1993; Roles have included Mozart's Osmin and Sarastro, Pizarro, Don Pasquale, Falstaff, Verdi's Attlia, King Philip and Padre Guardiano; Rossini's Basilio, Wagner's Daland and King Mark; Ochs in Der Rosenkavalier and Trulove in The Rake's Progress; Guest appearances in Geneva, Glasgow and Salzburg; Frequent concert engagements throughout Europe. *Recordings:* Schoenberg's Moses und Aron. *Address:* c/o Stadttheater Pforzheim, Am Weisenhausplatz 5, 3530 Pforzheim, Germany.

MANNING, Jane, OBE, FRCM, FRAM; Singer (Soprano) and Lecturer; b. 20 Sept. 1938, Norwich, England; m. Anthony Payne, 24 Sept 1966. *Education:* LRAM, 1958; GRSM, 1960; ARCM, 1962. *Career:* 20th century music specialist, more than 300 world premieres; Sings in leading concert halls and festivals world-wide; BBC broadcasts since 1965, and Promenade concerts; Wexford Festival Opera, 1976; New Opera Company, 1978; Scottish Opera, 1979; Brussels Opera, 1981; Garden Venture, 1991, 1993; Founder, Jane's Minstrels (ensemble), 1988, regular appearances in London and Europe, for BBC, also many CDs; Visiting Professor, Mills College, California, 1982–86; Visiting Lecturer, University of York, 1987; Visiting Professor, Royal College of Music, London, 1995–; Honorary Professor, University of Keele, 1996–2002; mem, Vice-President, Society for Promotion of New Music; Executive Committee, Musicians' Benevolent Fund; Chairman, Nettlefold Festival Trust; ISM; Equity. *Recordings include:* Complete song cycles of Messiaen; Schoenberg's Pierrot Lunaire, Moses und Aron; Ligeti Aventures Nouvelles Aventures; Complete vocal works of Erik Satie, 1994; Jane Manning, 1995. *Publications:* Book chapter in How the Voice Works, 1982; New Vocal Repertory–An Introduction, 1986, Vol. 1, reissued, 1994, Vol. 2, 1997. *Contributions:* A Messiaen Companion, 1995; Articles to Composer, Music and Musicians, The Independent. *Honours:* Special Award, Composers' Guild of Great Britain, 1973; DUniv, University of York, 1988; Hon. DMus (Keele), 2004. *Address:* 2 Wilton Square, London N1 3 DL, England.

MANNING, Peter; Violinist; b. 17 July 1956, Manchester, England. *Education:* Chathams School 1969–73; Royal Northern College of Music; Indiana University, USA 1973–81. *Career:* Debut: Concert at Wigmore Hall, 1987; Solo appearances with Philharmonia Orchestra, Hallé Orchestre, City of Birmingham Symphony; Co-leader, London Philharmonic Orchestra; Professor, Royal Northern College of Music; Quartet in Residence at the Dartington Summer School, with quartets by Schnittke; Season 1988–89 in the Genius of Prokofiev series at

Blackheath and BBC Lunchtime Series at St John's Smith Square; South Bank Concerto conducted by Neville Marriner concerts with the Hermann Prey Schubertiade and collaborations with the Alban Berg Quartet in the Beethoven Plus series; Tour of South America 1988, followed by Scandinavian debut; Season 1989–90 with debut tours of Netherlands, Germany, Spain, Austria and Finland; Tours from 1990 to the Far East, Malta, Sweden and Norway; Schoenberg-Handel Concerto with the Gothenburg Symphony; Festival appearances at Brighton, the City of London, Greenwich, Canterbury, Harrogate, Chester, Spitalfields and Aldeburgh; Collaborations with John Ogdon, Imogen Cooper, Thea King and Lynn Harrell; Formerly resident quartet at Liverpool University; Teaching role at Lake District Summer Music 1989; Universities of Bristol, Hong Kong 1990. *Recordings:* Beethoven Op 130 and Schnittke Quartet No. 3; Vaughan Williams On Wenlock Edge and Ravel Quartet; Britten, Prokofiev, Tippett, Elgar and Walton Quartets; Exclusive contract with EMI from 1990. *Current Management:* Ingpen & Williams Ltd, 7 St George's Court, 131 Putney Bridge Road, London, SW15 2PA, England.

MANNINO, Franco; Conductor, Composer and Pianist; b. 25 April 1924, Palermo, Italy. *Education:* Piano with R Silvestri, Composition with V Mortari, Academy of Santa Cecilia, Rome; Graduated in Piano, 1940, Composition, 1947. *Career:* Debut: As Composer, 1932; As Pianist, 1940; As Conductor, 1955; 1st American tour as Pianist, 1946, as Conductor with Maggio Musicale Fiorentino, 1957; Artistic Director, 1969, 1970, Artistic Adviser, 1974, Teatro San Carlo, Naples; Numerous Guest Conductor appearances including with Leningrad Orchestra, Orchestras of Peking and Shanghai; Major US Orchestras, etc; Many years as Principal Guest Conductor, Opera of Monte Carlo; Principal Conductor, Artistic Adviser, 1982–86, Principal Guest Conductor, 1986–89; National Arts Centre Orchestra, Ottawa; Numerous US tours; Toured Hong Kong and Japan with National Arts Centre Orchestra, 1985; His works performed by many leading orchestras. *Compositions:* 562 works including opera, ballet, oratorios, symphonies, chamber music, music for theatre; Operas Il ritratto di Dorian Grey, after Wilde, Catania, 1982, Il principe felice, after Wilde, La Scala, Milan, 1987, and Le notte bianche, after Dostoyevsky, Rome, 1989; Music for over 100 films by directors such as Huston, Visconti, Moguy; Composed Missa Solemnis Pro Jubileo Anno Domini 2000 for the Millennium. *Recordings:* Conductor of own works and works of Bach, Mendelssohn, Mozart, Liszt, Wagner, Schubert, Schumann, Puccini, Franck, Chopin, Verdi, Scarlatti; Artistic Director, Visconti Record Album, CBS-Sony. *Publications:* Essays about copyright, 1994 and 1995. *Honours:* Recipient of numerous awards and other honours including Culture Prize, 1996. *Address:* Via Citta di Castello 14, 00191 Rome, Italy.

MANNION, Rosa; Singer (Soprano); b. 29 Jan. 1962, Ormskirk, England. *Education:* Studied at the Royal Scottish Academy. *Career:* Debut: 1984 as Adina (L'Elisir d'amore) Scottish Opera; Glyndebourne Festival debut 1987, as Constanze; Has sung with Scottish Opera as Gilda, Adina, Pamina, Dorinda, Handel's Orlando, Sophie in Werther and Susanna, 1989; English National Opera from 1987 as Sophie in Der Rosenkavalier, Anna in the world premiere of Holloway's Clarissa, Cordelia in King Lear, Oscar, Atalanta, Xerxes and Nannetta; Has sung Magnolia in Show Boat with Opera North and Gilda (Rigoletto), Asteria (Tamburlaine) and Minka (La Roi Malgré Lui); Concert appearances with the Manchester Camerata, the Scottish Chamber and National Orchestras, the Hallé, the City of London Sinfonia, Les Arts Florissants, Rundfunk Symphony Orchestra, Berlin, and the London Mozart Players; ECO, BBC Philharmonic; Conductors include Raymond Leppard, Jeffrey Tate, Richard Hickox and Jane Glover, Philippe Herreweghe, Charles Mackerras, Yehudi Menuhin; Neeme Järvi at the Edinburgh Festival; Season 1992 as Atalanta at ENO, Dorabella under John Eliot Gardiner at Amsterdam and Lisbon, Gilda for Opera North; Royal Opera debut as Pamina, 1993; Aix-en-Provence debut 1993 as Dorinda (Orlando); American debut 1996 with Orlando in New York; Sang Maria in Schubert's Lazarus, RCM, London, 1997; Manon in a new production of Massenet's opera for ENO, 1998. *Recordings:* Mozart's Ascanio in Alba, with Musique en Sorbonne; Così fan tutte; Die Zauberflöte; Missa Solemnis; Orlando; Entführung. *Honours:* Winner, Scottish Opera International Singing Competition; John Scott Award, Scottish Opera. *Address:* c/o English National Opera, St Martin's Lane, London, WC2, England.

MANNOV, Johannes; Singer (Baritone); b. 1965, Copenhagen, Denmark. *Education:* Studied at the Conservatoires of Freiburg and Karlsruhe. *Career:* Sang with the boys' choir Kobenhauns-Drengekor before adult study; Has sung with the Kassel Opera from 1987 as Mozart's Papageno, Masetto and Figaro; Concert performances under such conductors as Helmuth Rilling, Luigi Nono, George Malcolm, Frans Brüggen, Leif Segerstram and Hans Martin Schneidt; Has performed Mozart's Requiem in Bremen, the Christmas Oratorio in Cologne and Frankfurt and an Italian tour with Bach's St John Passion, 1991–92; Britten's War Requiem in Frankfurt; Sang Mozart's Figaro for

Opera Northern Ireland 1991; Season 2000–01 as Christus in the St Matthew Passion, in Berlin, Siegfried in Schumann's Genoveva at Garsington and Papageno for San Diego Opera. *Recordings include:* Keresmin in Holger Danske by Kunzen, 1996. *Honours:* Prizewinner, 's-Hertogenbosch Competition, 1986; Helsinki Competition, 1989.

MANSON, Anne; Conductor; b. 1961, USA. *Education:* Studied at Harvard University, King's College London, the Royal College of Music with Norman del Mar and James Lockhart and the Royal Northern College of Music. *Career:* As Music Director of Mecklenburgh Opera conducted a wide range of 20th century and contemporary chamber operas; First woman to conduct Vienna Philharmonic Orchestra, in a rehearsal of Boris Godunov in 1997, also first woman to conduct at the Salzburg Festival in 1994; Conducted English Touring Opera in Don Pasquale and Don Giovanni; The Rise and Fall of the City of Mahagonny for Netherlands Touring Opera, 1996; Seven Deadly Sins at the Proms, 1997; Assistant to Claudio Abbado at 1992 Salzburg Festival in From the House of the Dead and in Boris Godunov at Vienna Staatsoper; Conducted at La Monnaie Brussels in 1993 in a triple bill of works by Monteverdi and Judith Weir; Conducted Boris Godunov with the Vienna Philharmonic and Sam Ramey in 1994; US debut at Washington Opera with Samuel Barber's Vanessa in 1995, returned with Dangerous Liaisons in 1998; Conducted Royal Scottish National Orchestra, BBC Scottish, Los Angeles Philharmonic, St Pauls Chamber Orchestra, Scharoun Ensemble; Regular Guest of Ensemble Intercontempoain and Iceland Symphony; Music Director, Kansas City Symphony, 1999–; Conducted Susannah, by Carlisle Floyd, Théâtre de Genève, 2000; Conducted Houston Symphony, 2001. *Recordings:* Tristan Keuris with Residentie Orchestra; Jon Leifs with Iceland Symphony Orchestra. *Honours:* Fellow in Conducting, Royal Northern College of Music; Marshall Scholarship; Prizes at the RCM and RNCM. *Current Management:* ICM Artists Ltd. *Address:* c/o Rachel Bowron, ICM Artists, 40 West 57th Street, New York, NY 10019, USA.

MANSOURI, Lotfollah (Lotfi); Opera Stage Director; b. 15 June 1929, Tehran, Iran; m. Marjorie Anne Thompson 1954, 1 d. *Career:* Assistant Professor, University of California, Los Angeles, USA, 1957–60; Dramatic Coach, Music Academy of the West, Santa Barbara, California, 1959; Resident Stage Director, Zürich Opera, Switzerland, 1960–65; Director of Dramatics: Zürich International Opera Studio, 1961–65, Centre Lyrique, Geneva, 1967–72; Chief State Director, Geneva Opera, 1965–75; Artistic Adviser, Tehran Opera, 1973–75; Opera Adviser, National Arts Centre, Ottawa, Canada, 1977; General Director, San Francisco Opera, 1988–99; Guest Director, various opera companies including New York Metropolitan, San Francisco Opera, La Scala, Verona, Vienna Staatsoper, Vienna Volksoper, Salzburg Festival, Covent Garden, Amsterdam Opera, Holland Festival, L'Opéra de Nice, Festival d'Orange, Australian Opera, Kirov Opera, Lyric Opera Chicago; Dallas Opera; With Surtitles TM initiated above-stage projection of simultaneous opera texts, 1983; Presided over the redevelopment of the War Memorial Open House, gala reopening, Sept 1997; mem, Board of Directors, Opera America, 1979–91, 1993–96; American Guild of Musical Artists; AFTRA; Canadian Actors' Equity Association. *Publications:* An Operatic Life (co-author), 1982. *Address:* War Memorial Opera House, 301 Van Ness Ave, San Francisco, CA 94102-4509, USA.

MANSUR, Cem; Conductor; b. 4 Sept. 1957, Istanbul, Turkey; m. Lale Mansur 1984. *Education:* BSc in Music, The City Univ., London, England 1981; studied advanced conducting at the Guildhall School in London and with Leonard Bernstein at the Los Angeles Philharmonic Institute 1982. *Career:* Conductor of the Istanbul State Opera 1981–89, also giving orchestral concerts; London debut 1985, with the English Chamber Orchestra; first performance of Elgar, The Spanish Lady, London 1986; further engagements with orchestras and opera companies in Sweden, Mexico, Spain, Germany, Netherlands, Italy, Romania, Russia, France, Israel and Czechoslovakia; regular appearances at Holland Park Opera and Mid Wales Opera; Kirov Opera at St Petersburg 1993 and 1994 for several operas; Principal Conductor of the City of Oxford Orchestra, 1989–96, including tours to Vienna, Zürich, Prague and Budapest; led Debussy's Le Martyre de Saint Sebastian at St John's Smith Square; further concerts with the Royal Philharmonic, Georges Enescu Philharmonic, City of London Sinfonia, BBC Concert Orchestra, Mexico City Orchestra, Helikon Opera, Moscow, London Mozart Players and the Hungarian State Orchestra 1989–96; Principal Conductor, Akbank Chamber Orchestra, Istanbul, Turkey 1998–; first performance since its creation of Offenbach's Whittington at the City of London Festival 2000; mem. Conductors' Guild (USA). *Recordings:* works by Turkish composers with the Hungarian State Orchestra. *Honours:* Ricordi Conducting Prize, Guildhall School 1981. *Address:* 31 Carlingford Road, London, NW3 1RY, England. *E-mail:* cemmansur@aol.com.

MANTEL, Gerhard (Friedrich); Concert Cellist; b. 31 Dec. 1930, Karlsruhe, Germany; m. Renate Mantel, 1 s. *Education:* Music

Academies in Mannheim and Paris; Musikhochschule Saarbrucken; Studied with August Eichhorn and Pierre Fournier. *Career:* Solo cellist, Bergen Symphony, Norway; WDR Orchestra, Cologne; World-wide recital tours, mainly with pianist Erika Friesar; Professor, Frankfurt Musikhochschule, 1973–; Assistant Director 1975–; mem, European String Teachers Association. *Recordings:* With Erika Friesar, Sonatas by Mendelssohn, Strauss, Grieg. *Publications:* Cello Technik 1973. *Honours:* Kulturpreis der Stadt Karlsruhe, 1955. *Address:* 6236 Eschborn 2, Felderbergstrasse 44, Germany.

MANTLE, Neil (Christopher); Conductor; b. 16 March 1951, Essex, England; m. Inga Wellesley, 17 Oct 1980, 1 s., 1 d. *Education:* Royal Academy of Music, London, 1969–70; Royal Scottish Academy of Music, 1970–73. *Career:* Conducting with Scottish Sinfonia, 1970–, Edinburgh Opera Company, 1975–81, Sinfonia Opera, 1983–84; Guest Conductor, Scottish National Orchestra, 1984; Guest Conductor, BBC Scottish Symphony Orchestra, 1986–; mem, Elgar Society. *Honours:* Hugh S Robertson Conducting Prize, Royal Scottish Academy of Music, 1973; 2nd prize, Leeds Conductors Competition, 1986. *Address:* c/o BBC Scottish SO, Broadcasting House, Queen Margaret Dr, Glasgow, G12 8DG, England.

MÄNTYNEN, Jaana; Singer (Soprano); b. 1964, Finland. *Education:* Studied at the Sibelius Academy, Helsinki. *Career:* Represented Finland at 1992 Cardiff Singer of the World Competition; Appearances at Helsinki in Die Zauberflöte, in the title role of Suor Angelica, Gabriel Come Back by Ilkka Kuusisto, The Telephone by Menotti, La Vida Breve, Eugene Onegin (as Tatiana) and The Maiden in the Tower by Sibelius; Savonlinna Festival, 1995, in the premiere of The Palace by Sallinen. *Honours:* Prizewinner at Timo Mustakallio and Lappeenranta Competitions, 1991–92. *Address:* c/o Finnish National Opera, PO Box 176, Helsinginkatu 58, 00251 Helsinki, Finland.

MANZ, André; Organist, Pianist, Harpsichordist and Teacher; b. 15 Dec. 1942, Chur, Switzerland; m. Irene Pomey. *Education:* Music Academy Zürich; Conservatory Winterhur; Hochschule für Musik, Cologne, Germany; Masters degree in Organ and Piano; Concert Diploma in Organ. *Career:* Debut: 1964; Organ recitals in Switzerland, Germany, Italy, Denmark, Japan, Poland, USA, Canada, Spain and Austria; Various radio series; Piano Duo with Irene Manz-Pomey; mem, Schweizer Tonkunstlerverein, STV; Schweizer Musikpadagogischer Verband, SMPV; President of Thurgau Organists Association; Rotary Club. *Compositions:* Play B-A-C-H for 6 organists and assistants, 1971. *Recordings include:* Swiss Baroque Soloists; Several organ solo recordings including the complete organ works by Franz Liszt; CDs: Variations on National Anthems, Battles and Thunderstorms for Organ, and Four Hands Organ-Playing Throughout Five Centuries; Festive organ music of the 19th and 20th century, 2003. *Contributions:* Various musical journals. *Honours:* Many musical prizes and scholarships; Annual Prize of Eastern Swiss Radio and Television Association, 1994; Annual Cultural Prize of Canton Thurgau Government, 1996. *Address:* Brunnenfeldstrasse 11, 8580 Amriswil, Switzerland.

MANZ, Wolfgang; Pianist; b. 6 Aug. 1960, Düsseldorf, Germany; m. Julia Goldstein, 2 Aug 1985, 2 s., 1 d. *Education:* Studied with Professor Drahomir Toman, Prague and Professor Karlheinz Kaemmerling at High School of Music, Hanover. *Career:* Performed at Promenade Concerts in London, England with the BBC Symphony Orchestra, 1984; Gilels Memorial Concert in Düsseldorf, 1986; Recital at Karajan Foundation in Paris, 1987 and Concert Tours, recitals, Broadcasts and Concerto performances all over Europe; Concert tours since 1988 in Japan; Teacher, Karlsruhe Music High School, 1994–98; mem, Chopin Society, Hanover; Mozart Society, Dortmund, 1989–. *Recordings:* Beethoven Triple Concerto with English Chamber Orchestra and Saraste, Dohnányi Piano Quintet op 1 with Gabrieli String Quartet; Chopin Studies; Russian Piano Music for 2 Pianos; Brahms Piano Concertos 1 and 2. *Honours:* First Prize, Mendelssohn Competition, Berlin, 1981; Second Prize, Queen Elisabeth Competition, Brussels, 1983; Second Prize, Leeds Piano Competition, 1981; Van Cliburn International Piano Competition, Texas, USA, Jury Discretionary Award, 1989. *Current Management:* J Hannemann, Haynstr 15, 20249 Hamburg, Germany. *Address:* Pasteurallee 55, 30655 Hanover, Germany.

MANZE, Andrew (Mark); Violinist and Conductor; b. 14 Jan. 1965, Beckenham, Kent. *Education:* Cambridge University (Classics), Royal Academy, London, and with Marie Leonhardt, Amsterdam. *Career:* Performances of 17th Century music with La Romanesca, 1987–88; Leader of Amsterdam Baroque Orchestra, under Tom Koopman, 1989–93; Conductor with La Stravaganza, Cologne, Orchestra of the Age of Enlightenment and Philharmonic Baroque Orchestra, San Francisco; Associate conductor, Academy of Ancient Music, 1996–; Concerto debut at the London Proms, 1998; Broadcast programmes with BBC Radio 3. *Recordings include:* 1681 Sonatas of Biber; Bach St Matthew Passion; Tartini solo violin works; Bach Violin Concertos and

Handel Concerto Grossi op. 6. *Honours:* Edison Award, 1998. *Address:* c/o Academy of Ancient Music, 10 Brookside, Cambridge, CB 2 1JE, England.

MANZINO, Leonardo; Pianist and Musicologist; b. 24 Feb. 1962, Montevideo, Uruguay. *Education:* Piano Diploma, Kolischer Conservatory, Montevideo, 1978; Licentiate in Musicology, University of Uruguay, 1986; Master of Music in Piano Performance, 1988, PhD Musicology-Latin American Music, The Catholic University of America, 1993. *Career:* Debut: Sala Martins Pena, Brasilia, 1983; International Summer Music Festivals of Brasilia, 1983–84; Uruguayan Music Students Association, 1983; Jeunesses Musicales of Uruguay Series, 1984–85; Argentine Music Foundation Series, 1986; Professor, School of Music, University of Uruguay, 1993; Director, Musicanga Classics, 1995. *Publications:* Composers of the Americas, vol. 20, editor, 1993; Uruguayan Music in the 1892 celebrations for the IV Centenary of the Encounter of Two Worlds, Latin American Music Review, 1993. *Honours:* Winner, Uruguayan Music Students' Piano Competition, 1983; Winner, Jeunesses Musicales of Uruguay Piano Competition, 1984. *Address:* Brito del Pino 1423, Montevideo 11600, Uruguay.

MANZONE, Jacques (Francis); Violinist and Professor of Music; b. 4 June 1944, Cannes, France. *Education:* Studied at Nice Conservatoire with Henri Mazioux; Paris Conservatoire with Roland Charmy and Jacques Fevrier; Further study with Eugène Bigot and Henryk Szeryng. *Career:* Soloist with the French Radio Orchestra and Société des Concerts du Conservatoire; Co-founded Ensemble Instrumental de France, Paris, 1966; Soloist with Orchestra of Paris, founded by Charles Munch, 1967; Professor, Nice Conservatoire, 1977; Soloist, Nice Philharmonic Orchestra; Professor of Chamber Music, Nice International Summer Academy; Musical Director, Chamber Orchestra of Nice, 1984; Plays a Maggini violin; Musical Director, Chamber Opera of France. *Recordings:* About 30 records as soloist or conductor. *Address:* 7 Avenue des Fleurs, 06000 Nice, France.

MANZONI, Giacomo; Composer and Teacher; b. 26 Sept. 1932, Milan, Italy; m. Eugenia Tretti, 1960, 1 s. *Education:* Liceo Musica Laudamo, Messina and Conservatorio Verdi, Milan (Composition); Foreign Languages, Università Bocconi, Milan; Piano Diploma, Milan. *Career:* Teacher of Composition, Conservatorio Verdi, Milan, 1962–64, 1968–69, 1974–91, Conservatorio Martini, Bologna, 1965–68, 1969–74, Masterclass, Composition, Scuola di Musica, Fiesole, 1988–, and Accademia Pescarese, 1992–97; Composer, international festivals include Amsterdam, Berlin, Osaka, Prague, Warsaw, Venice, Vienna, Salzburg; Master courses for composition held in San Marino, Santiago, Granada, Osaka, Buenos Aires, Vancouver, Tokyo, Beijing; mem, Accademia Santa Cecilia, Rome. *Compositions:* Operas: La Sentenza (Bergamo), 1960; Atomtod (Piccola Scala, Milan), 1965; Per Massimiliano Robespierre (Bologna), 1975; Doktor Faustus, by Thomas Mann (La Scala, Milan), 1989; Inferno di Dante, 1995; Moi, Antonin A, texts by A Artaud, for soprano, narrator and orchestra, 1997; Orchestral includes: 'Insiemi', 1967; Masse: omaggio a E Varèse, piano, orchestra, 1977; Modulor, 1979; Ode, 1982; Scene Sinfoniche per il Dr Faustus, 1984; Dedica, texts by B Maderna, bass, flute, orchestra, choir ad lib, 1985; Sembianti, 2003; Chorus, orchestra: 5 Vicariote, 1958; Ombre (to memory of Che Guevara), 1968; Parole da Beckett, 1971; Hölderlin (frammento), 1972; Il deserto cresce (Nietzsche), 1992; Trame D'Ombre for tenor, soprano, choir, and ensemble, 1998; Chamber includes: Musica notturna, 7 instruments, 1966; Quadruplum, 4 brass instruments, 1968; Spiel, 11 strings, 1969; String quartet, 1971; Percorso GG, clarinet, tape, 1979; D'improvviso, percussion, 1981; Klavieralbum 1956; Incontro, violin, string quartet, 1983; Opus 50 (Daunium), 11 instruments, 1984; 10 versi di E Dickinson, soprano, harp, strings, 1988; Quanto Oscura Selva Trovai (Dante) for trombone, chorus and live electronics, 1995; Oltre la Soglia, for soprano and string quartet. *Recordings:* Masse: omaggio a E Varèse; Parole da Beckett; Ode; Dedica; Quadruplum; Musica notturna; 10 Versi di E Dickinson; Scene Sinfoniche per il Dr Faustus; Musica per Pontormo, per quartetto d'archi; Other chamber music. *Publications:* Guida all'ascolto della musica sinfonica, 1967; A Schoenberg–L'uomo, l'opera, i testi musicali, 1975, 1997; Per M Robespierre–Testo e materiali per le scene musicali (with L Pestalozza and V Puecher), 1975; Scritti, 1991; Tradizione e Utopia, 1994; Translations: many works by T W Adorno and A Schoenberg. *Contributions:* Music critic, L'Unità, 1958–66; Many Italian and foreign periodicals. *Address:* Viale Papiniano 31, 20123 Milan, Italy.

MARAN, George; Singer (Tenor); b. 25 July 1926, Massachusetts, USA. *Education:* Studied at Harvard University and New York. *Career:* Sang in sacred music at the Salzburg Festival, 1951–66; European tour 1956 with the Salzburg Festival Company in Mozart's La Finta Semplice, directed by Bernhard Paumgartner; Sang at the Darmstadt Opera 1956–94, notably as Titus by Mozart, Death in Venice by Britten, 1983; Appearances at the Aldeburgh Festival, 1959–60, in The Rape of Lucretia and in the premiere of A Midsummer Night's Dream; Concert and oratorio engagements in Germany, England and Austria, all European Countries. *Recordings:* La Finta Semplice; Messiah, conducted by Adrian Boult, and Elijah under Josef Krips. *Address:* c/o Staatstheater, Postfach 111432, 64283 Darmstadt, Germany.

MARANGONI, Bruno; Singer (Bass); b. 13 April 1935, Rovigo, Italy. *Education:* Studied with Campogalliani and in Venice. *Career:* Debut: Venice 1960, as Anselmo in La Molinarelli by Piccinni; Many apearances at the Teatro Fenice Venice, Teatro San Carlo Naples, Teatro Massimo Palermo and in Turin, Triste and the Caracalla Baths, Rome; Verona Reana, 1973, 1978, 1983–84; Guest engagements at Aix-en-Provence, Lisbon, Barcelona and Chicago; Other roles have included Geronimo in Il Matrimonio Segreto, Mozart's Leporello, Osmin and Sarastro, Marcel in Les Huguenots, Bartolo in Paisiello's Il Barbiere di Siviglia, Uberto in Pergolesi's La Serva Padrona, Alvise in La Gioconda and Wagner's Daland, Pogner and Hunding; Television appearances in La Pietra del Paragone, as Asdrubal, L'Elisir d'amore, Don Carlos, Il Trovatore, Guillaume Tell and Aida. *Address:* c/o Arena di Verona, Piazza Bra 28, 37121 Verona, Italy.

MARC, Alessandra; American singer (soprano); b. 29 July 1957, Berlin, Germany. *Education:* studied in the USA. *Career:* Debut: Waterloo Festival 1983, as Mariana in Wagner's Das Liebesverbot; Sang Gluck's Iphigénie (en Aulide) 1984, Tosca at the Connecticut Opera 1987; Wexford Festival 1987, as Lisabetta in La cena delle beffe; Santa Fe 1988, as Maria in Strauss's Friedenstag, followed by Adriadne 1990; Chicago and San Francisco as Aida, which she also sang on her Metropolitan Opera debut; Other roles include the Empress in Die Frau ohne Schatten (Holland Festival, 1990), Sieglinde, and Silvana in La Fiamma by Respighi; Turandot at Philadelphia and Covent Garden (1994); Sang Turandot at the 1996 Macerata Festival and at Turin, 1998 and La Scala, 2001; Sang Königin der Erdgeister in Hans Heiling by Marschner at the Deutsche Oper, 2001; Concert repertoire includes the Verdi Requiem and Beethoven's Ninth; Also a noted recitalist (Wigmore Hall, London, 1990). *Recordings include:* Two versions of Elektra, as Chrysothemis under Barenboim, 1996, and the title role under Sinopoli, 1997. *Current Management:* IMG Artists, 616 Chiswick High Road, London W4 5RX, England.

MARCELLINO, Raffaele; Composer; b. 1964, Sydney, New South Wales, Australia. *Education:* BMus, New South Wales Conservatory, 1985; Dip Ed, Sydney College of Advanced Education, 1987. *Career:* Faculty Member, St Vincent's College, Potts Point, 1990–94; University of Tasmania, 1995; Resident Composer, Sydney Youth Orchestra, 1992; Director, Tasmanian Conservatorium, 1996–98; mem, Australian Music Centre (full representation). *Compositions:* Woodwind Quintet, 1983; Cathedrale for 7 brass instruments, 1984; Five Bells for string quartet and percussion, 1984; Five Bells for string quartet and percussion, 1984; Incunabula, for orchestra, 1985; Responsorio for chorus, 1987; Antipodes, for orchestra, 1987; Suite Etuis for orchestra, 1988; Whispers of Fauvel, for clarinet and percussion, 1988; The Remedy, 1 act opera, 1989; Nona for violin, 1991; Prester John, for ensemble, 1991; Don Juan, dance theatre, 1992; Corbaccio, for trombone and orchestra, 1993; Leviathan, for trombone, 1994; Fish Tale, song cycle, 1995; The Lottery in Babylon, chamber work, 1995; On the Passing of Time, triple concerto, 1996; Art of Resonance, tuba concerto, 1998; Maze, ensemble, 1998; Terror Australis, ensemble, 1998. *Recordings:* Don Juan, 1992; Whispers of Fauvel, 1999. *Publications:* Tubaphonics; Tall Poppies; The Crotchet Factory. *Honours:* Australian Composers National Opera Award, 1988; Paul Lowin Prize, Highly Commended, 1997. *Address:* 43 Carawa Street, Mornington, Tasmania, Australia.

MARCHADIER, Ludmila; Singer (Soprano); b. 1970, Paris. *Education:* Geneva Conservatoire and Royal Academy, London. *Career:* Appearances in Rigoletto at the Grand Théâtre, Geneva, and King Arthur at the Teatro Arriaga, Bilbao; Despina in Così fan tutte with Garden Opera and Adele in Die Fledermaus for European Chamber Opera; Sang in Purcell's Fairy Queen and the Lully/Molière Bourgeois Gentilhomme for the English Bach Festival at the Linbury Theatre, Covent Garden, 2001; Other roles include Niece in Peter Grimes; Member of chorus at Glyndebourne Festival Opera. *Address:* c/o English Bach Festival, 15 South Eaton Place, London, SW1W 9ER, England.

MARCHAND, Jacques; Composer; b. 1 Dec. 1948, Quebec, Canada. *Education:* BAC in Composition, McGill University, Montreal; BAC in Piano, Vincent D'Indy Music School, Montreal. *Career:* Nearer the Stars, Ballet for Violin Solo (Colorado Ballet Company), 1981; Founder, Orchestre Symphonique Regional d'Abitibi-Temiscamingue, 1986; mem, SOCAN; SODRAC; AOC. *Compositions:* Nearer the Stars, 1981; Suite Pour Orchestre, 1987; Fantaisie Pour Orchestre, 1989; Impromptu Pour Piano et Orchestre, 1993; Un Dimanche A Poznan (Poème Symphonique), 1993. *Recordings include:* Jacques Marchand Compositeur, 1988. *Honours:* Citoyen d'Honneur de la Societe Nationale des Quebecois, 1992; Hommage de la Chambre de Commerce de Rouyn-

Noranda, 1993. *Address:* 22, 8 Rue Rouyn-Noranda, Quebec J9X 2A4, Canada.

MARCHI, Claudia; Singer (Mezzo-soprano); b. 1967, Bologna, Italy. *Education:* Studied with Elvina Ramella. *Career:* Appearances at Savona from 1992 as Isabella (L'Italiana in Algeri), Verdi's Maddalena and as Sigismonda in the opera by Rossini, under Richard Bonynge, 1992; Australian tour, with Luciano Pavarotti in Verdi's Requiem, 1994; Season 1995 as Fenena in Nabucco and Azucena in Trovatore, at Marseilles; Season 1996–97 as Isabella in Genoa and Isaura in Rossini's Tancredi at the Zürich Opera; Further engagements as Rosina and in works by Jommelli, Bach, Mozart and Pergolesi. *Honours:* Prizewinner at the Verdi Competition in Parma and the Luciano Pavarotti International Voice Competition. *Address:* c/o Opernhaus Zürich, Falkenstrsse 1, 8008 Zürich, Switzerland.

MARCINGER, Ludovit; Pianist and Pedagogue; b. 21 Dec. 1932, Malacky, Czechoslovakia; m. Maria Marcingerova, 7 May 1977, 2 d. *Education:* State Conservatoire, Bratislava; Academy of Music and Drama, Bratislava; Ferencz Liszt Academy of Music, Budapest. *Career:* Debut: Recital, Dresden, 1958; Recitals: Prague, 1965; Havana, 1980; With Orchestra, Prague, 1964; J Cikker, Concertino for Piano and Orchestra; Carlsbad, 1966; Grieg, Concerto in A Minor, Bratislava, 1967; A Rubinstein, Concerto No. 5 in D Minor; Piano Accompaniment of the Vocalists: Peter Dvorsky, Tenor, Song Recitals, Oper der Stadt, Bonn, 1983; Grosser Musikvereinssaal, Vienna, Teatro alla Scala, Milano, Brucknerhaus Linz, Slovak National Theatre Bratislava, 1984; Deutsche Oper Berlin, Théâtre de L'Athénée Paris, 1986; Suntory Hall Tokyo, 1989; Peter Mikulas-Bass, Songs Recitals, Mexico City, Caracas, Managua, San Jose, 1992, Bratislava Music Festival, 1994, Prague, 1996; With Other Vocalists, Peking, 1987, Buenos Aires, 1996; mem, Slovak Music Union; Association of Concert Artists of Bratislava. *Recordings include:* A Dvorák, Biblical Songs, Op 99, Tchaikovsky, Songs-Peter Mikulas, Bass, 1990; R Schumann, Frauenliebe und Leben, A Dvorák, 4 Songs, Op 2 V narodnim tonu; F Schubert, Lieder, Peter Mikulas, Bass, 1997. *Honours:* Several Prizes in Music Competitions. *Address:* Vysoka skola muzickych umeni, Zochova 1, 81103 Bratislava, Slovakia.

MARCO-BUHRMESTER, Alexander; Singer (Baritone); b. 1963, Basle, Switzerland. *Education:* Studied in Basle and Berne. *Career:* Debut: Berne 1985, as Weber's Abu Hassan; Toured Switzerland as Dandini in La Cenerentola and sang at the Biel Opera 1986 as Marcello in La Bohème; Essen Opera 1989–92, Dortmund from 1992, notably in the premiere of Caspar Hauser by Reinhard Febel; Season 2000–01 in Moses und Aron at the Deutsche Oper Berlin and as Count Luna in Bielefeld. *Address:* c/o St ädtische Buhnen, Kuhstrasse 12, 4600 Dortmund, Germany.

MARCUSSEN, Kjell; Composer; b. 19 May 1952, Arendal, Norway. *Education:* Studied at the Agder Music Conservatorium; Diploma in Guitar and Composition, Guildhall School of Music, London with Robert Saxton. *Career:* Debut: Cardiff Festival of Music, 1982; mem, Norwegian Composers' Society. *Compositions:* Cantatas; Orchestral works; Guitar Concerto; Solo and Chamber works; Festival Overture for Symphonic Band, 1994. *Recordings include:* CD, Woodcut for Violin, Flute and Cello; CD, Festival Overture; CD, Tordenskjold Kantate. *Publications:* Guitar Sonata No. 1, 1988; Woodcut for Violin, Flute and Cello, 1988; Partita Jubilante for Brass, 1993; Early Part of Summer for Flute and Harp; Introduction and Allegro for Guitar Duo. *Honours:* Special Mention at 15th Concorso internazionale di composizione originale per banda Corciano, 1994. *Address:* Skoleveien 6, 1380 Heggedal, Norway.

MARESTIN, Valerie; Singer (Mezzo-soprano); b. 1962, Pau, France. *Education:* Studied in Lyon with Eric Tappy and in Paris. *Career:* Debut: Théâtre de Paris 1987, as La Belle Hélène; Guest appearances throughout France, including Carmen at Angers (1988); Sang Debussy's Geneviève at Moscow (1987) and Mistress Quickly at Limoges; Other roles include Maddalena, Rossweise, Marcellina in Figaro, Rossini's Isabella (at Rheims and Tours), Massenet's Dulcinée and Fenena in Nabucco; Bregenz Festival 1991, as Carmen; Frequent concert appearances. *Address:* c/o Bregenz Festival, Postfach 311, 6901 Bregenz, Austria.

MARGGRAF, Wolfgang; Musicologist; b. 2 Dec. 1933, Leipzig, Germany; m. Anne-Marie Lorz, 4 Jan 1975, 2 s. *Education:* Studied at Universities of Leipzig and Jena, 1952–57; PhD, Leipzig, 1964. *Career:* Professor, 1987; Rector, Musikhochschule Weimar, 1990–93; mem, The Liszt Society, Weimar, 1984–; Gesellschaft für Musikforschung, 1991–. *Publications:* Franz Schubert, 1967, 2nd edition, 1978; Giacomo Puccini, 1977; Franz Liszt, Schriften zur Tonkunst, 1980; Giuseppe Verdi, 1982; Franz Liszt in Weimar, 1985; Bach in Leipzig, 1985. *Address:* Barfuáerstrasse 12, Eisenach, Germany.

MARGIONO, Charlotte; Singer (Soprano); b. 24 March 1955, Amsterdam, Netherlands. *Education:* Studied at the studio of Netherlands

Opera. *Career:* Appearances with Netherlands Opera from 1983, as Kate Pinkerton, Fiordiligi, Pamina, Liu and Amelia Grimaldi; Komische Oper Berlin 1985 as Marenka in The Bartered Bride; Berne and the Aix Festival 1988, as Mozart's Countess and Vitellia; Fiordiligi in Così fan tutte at Amsterdam, 1990; repeated Vitellia at Salzburg 1991 and sang Pamina at Bordeaux, 1992; Strauss's Four Last Songs at the 1995 Prom Concerts, London; Beethoven concert with Roger Norrington at Bremen, 1995 (also televised); Season 1995–96, as Agathe at Florence and Desdemona in Amsterdam; Sang Leonore in Fidelio at Glybdebourne, 2001. *Recordings include:* Die Zauberflöte, as First Lady (Erato); Beethoven's Mass in C and Missa Solemnis (DGG); Ein Deutsches Requiem (Philips); Così fan tutte and La Finta giardiniera (Teldec); Countess in Le nozze di Figaro, conducted by Harnoncourt; Donna Elvira in Don Giovanni, under John Eliot Gardiner. *Address:* c/o De Nederlandse Opera, Waterlooplein 22, 1011 PG Amsterdam, Netherlands.

MARGISON, Richard (Charles); Operatic Tenor; b. 16 July 1953, Victoria, BC, Canada; m. Valerie Mary Kuinka, 12 Aug 1989. *Education:* University of Victoria, Victoria Conservatory of Music: AVCM; Banff School of Fine Arts; Voice Teacher: Selena James; Coaches Leopold Simoneau, Frances Adaskin. *Career:* Debut: The Bartered Bride with the Pacific Opera Company, Victoria BC; Has performed with many orchestras, including: Vancouver 1989, Toronto 1989, Montreal 1990, London Philharmonic 1991, Chicago 1991, Victoria 1991; Regular appearances with Opera Companies including: English National Opera, 1989 and 1991 as Verdi's Riccardo and as Vakula in Rimsky's Christmas Eve, Montreal Opera 1991, Canadian Opera Company, 1991, Santiago Opera (Teatro Municipal) 1991, Den Norske Opera (Norway) 1991, Calgary Opera 1991 as Nadir in Les Pêcheurs de Perles; Other roles include Mozart's Ferrando (Ottawa) and Tito, Pinkerton (Edmonton), Fenton in Falstaff, Faust (at Houston), Don Carlos (San Francisco, 1992), Nemorino, Edgardo, Alfredo, Rodolfo and Lensky; Season 1992/93 as Riccardo at Antwerp, Don José at Brussels, Don Carlos at Melbourne and Cavaradossi at Covent Garden; Many appearances on radio and television in opera, oratorio and concert; Cavaradossi in Tosca at the reopening of the San Francisco Opera, 1997 and at Amsterdam, 1998; Boito's Faust at the New York Met, 2000, and Manrico in Il Trovatore, 2000. *Recordings:* Beethoven 9th with London Philharmonic Orchestra, Yehudi Menuhin conducting, RPO Records 1991; Les Grand Duos D'Amour from French Operas: Quebec Symphony, Simon Streatfield conducting, 1988. *Contributions:* Richard Margison (People) Opera Magazine. pp. 1182–1188, Oct. 2001. *Current Management:* Columbia Artists: Zemsky Green Division, New York, USA. *Address:* 42 Aberdeen Avenue, Toronto, Ontario, M4X 1A2, Canada.

MARGITA, Stefan; Singer (Tenor); b. 3 Aug. 1956, Kosice, Czechoslovakia; Studied in Kosice and was member of the National Theatre Prague 1986–91, notably as Hoffmann; Guest appearances in Moscow, Genoa, Stuttgart, Paris and Budapest; Wexford Festival 1991, as Lucentio in The Taming of the Shrew by Goetz; Season 1991–92 as Don Ottavio at the Savonlinna Festival and Bellini's Tebaldo at Budapest; Sang Lensky at Trieste, 1996; and in Smetana's Libuše at Edinburgh, 1998; Season 2000–01 as Laca in Jenůfa at Glyndebourne, Lensky at Montpellier and Anatol in War and Peace for the Opéra Bastille, Paris. *Recordings include:* Bellerofonte by Myslivecek and Mahler's Das klagende Lied (Supraphon). *Address:* c/o National Theatre, PO Box 865, 11230 Prague 1, Czech Republic.

MARGOLINA, Yelena; Concert Pianist; b. 1964, Lviv, Ukraine, Russia. *Education:* Studied in Lvov and at the St Petersburg State Conservatoire. *Career:* Debut: Beethoven's Second Concerto, Lvov, 1974; Notable performances at Moscow, Kiev, Khabarovsk, Lvov and Dnepropetrovsk; Western debut playing Prokofiev's Third Concerto, Berlin Schauspielhaus, 1985; Concerts at the Prokofiev Centenary Festival in Scotland, 1991; Performs in chamber concerts and as solo recitalist in a repertoire including works by Haydn, Mozart, Liszt, Beethoven, Debussy and Shostakovich; Concerto repertoire includes: Beethoven 1–4, Schumann, Chopin, Tchaikovsky, Ravel and Prokofiev. *Honours:* Scottish International Piano Competition Winner, 1990; Casals Monferrato in Italy, 1990. *Address:* c/o Sonata, 11 Northpark Street, Glasgow G20 7AA, Scotland.

MARIANI, Lorenzo; Stage Director; b. 1950, New York, USA. *Education:* Studied at Harvard and the University of Florence, Italy. *Career:* Debut: Maggio Musicale Florence, 1982, Bluebeard's Castle; Directed L'Heure Espagnole at Florence, La Traviata, Luisa Miller and Offenbach's Barbe-Bleue, 1994 at Bologna; Montepulciano Festival with the Henze-Paisiello Don Chisciotte, Greek by Mark Anthony Turnage and Puccini's Edgar; Recent productions include La Forza del Destino at Florence, Massenet's Esclarmonde in Turin, I Quattro Rusteghi in Geneva, La Bohème in Chicago and Don Giovanni in Tel-Aviv; Revived Antoine Vitez's production of Pelléas et Mélisande for Covent Garden, 1993; Aida

at Florence, 1996. *Address:* c/o Teatro Comunale di Firenze, via Solferino 15, 50123 Florence, Italy.

MARIATEGUI, Suso; Singer (tenor); b. 1947, Las Palmas. *Education:* studied in Spain, Austria and Italy. *Career:* sang Tamino at the Salzburg Landestheater 1971; Wexford Festival 1973, in Donizetti's L'ajo nell'imbarazzo; Teatro Liceo, Barcelona 1987, in the local premiere of Mozart's Lucio Silla; guest engagements in Spain, Italy, Vienna and Tehran; Madrid concerts in Bach's St Matthew Passion and Haydn's Creation. *Recordings include:* L'ajo nell'imbarazzo.

MARIMPIETRI, Lydia; Singer (Soprano); b. 1932, Italy. *Education:* Studied in Italy. *Career:* Sang at La Scala Milan in 1959, at first as Nella in Gianni Schicchi, and as Micaela; Further appearances in Rome, Venice, Parma (Pamina, 1974) and Covent Garden (Nedda and Nannetta, 1973–75); Glyndebourne Festival 1962–65, as Drusilla in Poppea and Susanna; Other roles have included Mimi (at the Vienna Staatsoper), Marguerite, Manon, Bizet's Leila, Donna Elvira, Butterfly (Dallas, 1966) and Rossini's Elvira; Sang Mimi at Rome, 1976. *Recordings include:* L'Incoronazione di Poppea (EMI). *Address:* c/o Teatro dell'Opera di Roma, Piazza B Gigli 8, 00184 Rome, Italy.

MARIN, Carlos; Singer (baritone); b. 1965, Germany. *Education:* Madrid Conservatoire, and with Montserrat Caballé and Jaime Aragall. *Career:* Appearances at Teatro de la Zarzuela Madrid, as Rossini's Figaro, Sulpice in La Fille du Régiment and Marcello in La Bohème; Sang Marcello at Bologna, 1999, and Taddeo in L'Italiana in Algeri at Garsington (British debut); Other roles include Donizetti's Belcore and Alfonso, Riccardo in I Puritani, Valentin (Faust), Dandini, Guglielmo, and Ford in Falstaff; Concerts include Halfter's Siete Cantos de Espana and Ostasio in Francesca da Rimini, in Amsterdam; Season 2001–02 as Sharpless at Montpellier, Posa in Don Carlos and Enrico in Lucia di Lammermoor for Minnesota Opera and in Parma, Silvio in Pagliacci at Oviedo; Season 2002–03 as Marcello in La Bohème and Don Giglio in La Capricciosa Coretta with Opéra de Lausanne; as Don Giglio also in Bordeaux, Madrid and Konzerthaus Vienna. *Honours:* Winner, Francisco Alonso and Julian Gayarre Competitions. *Current Management:* Athole Still International Management, Forresters Hall, 25–27 Westow Street, London, SE19 3RY, England. *Telephone:* (20) 8771-5271. *Fax:* (20) 8768-6600. *Website:* www.atholestill.com.

MARIN, Ion; Conductor; b. 8 July 1960, Bucharest, Romania. *Education:* Studied at the George Enescu Music School Bucharest, the Mozarteum Salzburg, Accademia Chigiana in Siena and the International Academy, Nice. *Career:* Music Director, Transylvania Philharmonic, 1981, appearing in Romania, East Germany, Czechoslovakia, Greece, Italy and France; Resident Conductor, Vienna Staatsoper, 1987–91, with repertoire from Mozart to Berg; Season 1991–92, in Japan for concerts with Margaret Price and Ruggiero Raimondi, Gala Concert in Prague and Le nozze di Figaro at the Teatro la Fenice, Venice; London debut with the London Symphony Orchestra, 1991, English Chamber Orchestra with Yo-Yo Ma as soloist, 1992; US debut conducting L'Elisir at Dallas 1991, San Francisco, 1992, with Il Barbiere di Siviglia; Led Roman Polanski's production of Les Contes d'Hoffmann at the Opéra Bastille, Paris, 1992; Metropolitan Opera, 1992–93, Semiramide and Ariadne auf Naxos, Magic Flute; Further engagements in L'Italiana in Algeri at Venice, 1992, and with Houston Grand Opera; Concerts with the City of Birmingham Symphony, Philadelphia Orchestra, Santa Cecilia, Rome, BBC Symphony, Rotterdam Philharmonic, Montreal Symphony, 1993; Season 1997 with Scottish Chamber Orchestra, Orchestre National de France and the Yomiuri Nippon Symphony Orchestra, Japan; Tour of Australia with the ABC; Season 1998–99 with Così fan tutte for Nuovo Piccolo, Teatro di Milano, and concerts with the Leipzig, Gewandhaus Orchestra, Dresden Staatskapelle, Swedish Radio Symphony Orchestra; Season 1999–2000 with Orchestre National d'Ile de France, Orchestre Philharmonique de Monte-Carlo and the BBC Scottish Orchestra; Conducted the BBC Scottish Symphony Orchestra at the London Proms, 2002. *Recordings:* Lucia di Lammermoor, with Studer and Domingo, series of Rossini one-acters starting with Il Signor Bruschino; Semiramide, and sacred music for DGG; Various for other major labels including Mozart arias with Barbara Hendricks and the ECO, 1997; Rodrigo and Khachaturian flute concertos with the Philharmonia Orchestra and Patrick Gallois; Opera Arias with the London Symphony Orchestra and Cheryl Studer. *Honours:* Awards Deutsche Schallplatten; Critics Award, 1992, 1994; Nominations for Grammy award. *Current Management:* Askonas Holt Ltd, Lonsdale Chambers, 27 Chancery Lane, London, WC2A 1PF, England. *Telephone:* (20) 7400-1700. *Fax:* (20) 7400-1799. *E-mail:* info@askonasholt.co.uk. *Website:* www.askonasholt.co.uk.

MARINOV, Swetoslav; violinist; b. 21 Sept. 1945, Lom, Bulgaria; m. Elena Maeva 1967; two s. *Education:* Music School of Sofia, Bulgaria, Bulgarian State Conservatoire, Sofia, studied with Vilmoš Tatrai in Budapest, with Mischa Geler in Moscow Conservatoire, with Yfrah Neaman at the Guildhall School of Music and Drama. *Career:* debut as violinist, Orpheus String Quartet, 1969; Performed with the Tilev String Quartet from 1973, and the Bulgarian RT String Quartet, 1975; Leader of Sofia Soloist Chamber Orchestra, 1981 and Leader of Bremerhaven Opera, Germany, 1988; Other concert activity includes violinist and violist of Bulgarian RT String Quartet and Sofia Chamber Orchestra; Concert tours in Europe, Asia, Australia, South America; In duo violin and piano, concerts with Katia Evrova in France, Cycle of Mozart 16 sonatas, 1990, 1991; Cycle of Beethoven 10 sonatas, 1997; In solo viola concert tour with G Tilev, violin, in Sinfonia Concertante by Mozart with Niederheinischen Sinfoniker, Mönchengladbach. *Recordings:* with Radio Sofia, Warsaw, Moscow and Paris. *Honours:* Prizewinner of competition for string quartets in Colmar, 1978 and Evian, France, 1980. *Address:* Rosenweg 5, 27607 Langen, Germany.

MARIOTTI, Alfredo; Singer (Bass-baritone); b. 1936, Udine, Italy. *Career:* Sang in opera throughout Italy, notably at La Scala, Rome, La Fenice, Venice, and Florence; Palermo, 1955, in the premiere of Rota's Il Capello; Treviso, 1984, in Wolf-Ferrari's I Quattro Rusteghi; Las Palmas, 1993, as Donizetti's Dulcamara; Sang the Sacristan in Tosca at Verona, 1998. *Recordings include:* Masetto in Don Giovanni and Don Pasquale; Tosca; Rossini's L'Italiana in Algeri, 1976; La Bohème. *Address:* c/o Arena di Verona, Piazza Bra 28, 37121 Verona, Italy.

MARK, Peter; Director and Conductor; b. 31 Oct. 1940, New York City, USA; m. Thea Musgrave, 2 Oct 1971. *Education:* BA, Musicology, Columbia University, 1961; Juilliard School of Music, with Jean Morel, Joseph Fuchs, Walter Trampler, MS, 1963. *Career:* Boy soprano soloist, Children's Chorus, New York City Opera and Metropolitan Opera, 1953–55; Principal freelance and string quartet violist, Juilliard Orchestra, Princeton Symphony, Trenton Symphony, Tiemann String Quartet, Beaux Arts and Los Angeles String Quartet, Santa Barbara Symphony, Lyric Opera Chicago, 1960–68; Assistant principal violist, Los Angeles Philharmonic Orchestra, 1968–69; Solo Violist, Europe, South America and US tours, 1965–77; General Director, Conductor, Virginia Opera Association, 1975–; Conductor, Chamber Players, Santa Barbara Chamber Orchestra, 1976–77; Guest Conductor, Wolf Trap Orchestra, 1979, New York City Opera 1981, Los Angeles Opera Repertory Theater 1981, Royal Opera House, London, 1982, Hong Kong Philharmonic Orchestra 1984; Jerusalem Symphony Orchestra, 1988; Tulsa Opera, 1988; Opera Nacional de Mexico, 1989; Conductor, local premiere of Porgy and Bess, Buenos Aires and São Paulo, 1992; Guest Conductor, Opera Nacional de Mexico, 1989, 1992; New York Pops, Carnegie Hall, 1991; Orlando Opera Company, 1993; Richmond Symphony, 1993; Conducted La Bohème at the 1996 Torre del Lago Festival; mem, Phi Beta Kappa; Musicians Union, New York, London, Los Angeles, Norfolk, Virginia. *Recordings:* As conductor: Mary, Queen of Scots, 1979; A Christmas Carol, 1980; Handel's Julius Caesar, 1997; Also numerous recordings as violist. *Honours:* Recipient Elias Lifchey Viola Award Juilliard School of Music, 1963; Rosa Ponselle Gold Medal, 1997. *Address:* c/o Virginia Opera, PO Box 2580, Norfolk, VA 23501-2580, USA.

MARKAUSKAS, Arvydas; Singer (Baritone); b. 25 Sept. 1951, Kaunas, Lithuania. *Education:* Studied at the Vilnius Conservatory. *Career:* Sang at the Vilnius Opera from 1979, making his debut as the Count in Lortzing's Der Wildschütz; Guest appearances throughout Russia and eastern Europe and with the Lithuanian Opera in the USA (notably in Chicago); Other roles include Belcore, Posa, Eugene Onegin, Amonasro, Iago, Nabucco and Marcello; Concert repertoire includes Handel's Samson, the War Requiem, Carmina Burana and Kabalevsky's Requiem. *Address:* c/o Lithuania State Opera, Vienuolio 1, 232600 Vilnius, Lithuania.

MARKERT, Annette; Singer (Mezzo-soprano); b. 1957, Kaltensundheim, Germany. *Education:* Studied in Leipzig with Helga Forner and with Hannelore Kuhse and Eleanore Elstermann. *Career:* Debut: British Debut, Dec 1989, in the Alto Rhapsody with the BBC Philharmonic under Kurt Sanderling; Has sung with the Landestheater Halle as Handel's Floridante, Rinaldo and Tamerlano, Gluck's Orpheus and Carmen; Bach oratorios on German radio and oratorio performances and Lieder recitals throughout Germany. *Honours:* Second Prize, Maria Canals Competition, Barcelona, 1985; Handel Prize 1989. *Address:* c/o Landestheater Halle, Universitatsring 24–25, 4020 Halle, Germany.

MARKHAM, Ralph; pianist; b. 1949, Canada. *Education:* Royal Toronto Conservatory of Music, Cleveland Institute of Music with Vronsky and Babin. *Career:* formed Piano Duo partnership with Kenneth Broadway and has given many recitals and concerts in North America and Europe; BBC debut recital 1979 and further broadcasts on CBC television, Radio France Musique, the Bavarian Radio Hilversum in Netherlands; Stravinsky's Three Dances from Petrushka at the Théâtre des Champs Elysées, Paris, 1984; Season 1987–88, included 40 North American recitals; Concert with the Vancouver Symphony and New York debut on WQXR Radio; Season 1988–89 included the concertos for Two Pianos by Mozart and Bruch in Canada and a recital tour of England and

Germany; Recent performances of the Bartók Sonata for two pianos and percussion, with Evelyn Glennie and a 1990–91 tour of North America, Europe and the Far East; Festival appearances include Newport USA 1988. *Recordings:* Duos by Anton Rubinstein; Vaughan Williams Concerto for Two Pianos; Saint-Saëns Carnival of the Animals. *Honours:* Young Artist of the Year, Musical America Magazine, 1980, with Kenneth Broadway. *Current Management:* Robert Gilder & Co., Enterprise House, 59–65 Upper Ground, London, SE1 9PQ, England. *Telephone:* (20) 7928-9008. *Fax:* (20) 7928-9755. *E-mail:* rgilder@robert-gilder.com.

MARKHAM, Richard, ARAM, LRAM, ARCM; pianist; b. 23 June 1952, Grimsby, England. *Education:* private lessons with Shirley Kemp and Max Pirani, RAM; RAM Recital Diploma. *Career:* debut, Queen Elizabeth Hall, 1974; recitals and concerto performances throughout the UK and abroad; several London appearances at Royal Festival Hall, Royal Albert Hall, Queen Elizabeth Hall, Wigmore Hall, Barbican Hall and Purcell Room; The Henry Wood Promenade Concerts; appearances at festivals in Aldeburgh, Bath, Berlin, Cheltenham, Harrogate, City of London, Schleswig-Holstein and York; regular broadcasts of recitals and concerts for BBC and numerous television and radio stations abroad; has performed with the Philharmonia Orchestra, London Symphony Orchestra, RPO, London Philharmonic Orchestra, ECO, SNO, London Mozart Players, Bournemouth Sinfonietta, Hallé, Ulster and BBC Philharmonic and Scottish Symphony Orchestras; frequent appearances and tours with piano duo partner, David Nettle, in Europe, North America, Australia, Japan, Far East and Middle East. *Recordings:* Kabalevsky, Stravinsky and Rachmaninov with Raphael Wallfisch (cello), Bernstein (Arr. Nettle and Markham), Bennett and Grainger (2 pianos); Holst, The Planets (2 pianos) and Stravinsky, Petrushka and Le Sacre du Printemps (piano duet) with David Nettle; Elgar, Holst, Grainger and Rossini with CBSO Chorus; Saint-Saëns Carnival of the Animals with Aquarius; South of the Border, a Latin American Collection with Jill Gomez; Nettle and Markham in England; Nettle and Markham in France; Arnold, Concerto for Two Pianos and Concerto for Piano Duet. *Address:* The Old Power House, Atherton Street, London, SW11 2JE, England. *E-mail:* richardpiano@aol.com. *Website:* www.nettleandmarkham.com.

MÄRKL, Jun; Conductor, Opera Director and Musical Director; b. 1959, Munich, Germany. *Education:* Studied piano, violin and conducting, with degrees in violin and conducting, Music Academy, Hannover, 1978; Further studies with Kees Bakels, Sergiu Celibidache and Gustav Meier, University of Michigan at Ann Arbor, USA. *Career:* Member, Junge Deutsche Philharmonie, 1980–84; Season 1991–94, Principal Conductor and Music Director, Saarland State Theatre; Since 1994 Opera and Music Director, National Theater Mannheim; Conducted performances of Tosca, Marriage of Figaro, and Dvořák's Dmitrij; Conducted premiere of Detlev Glanert's Der Spiegel des grossen Kaisers, 1995; Season 1995–96, London debut at Royal Opera House, Covent Garden, with Götterdämmerung; Season 1996–97, with Bavarian State Opera in Munich, included new production of Smetana's Bartered Bride, Aida, Madama Butterfly, La Traviata, Peter Grimes; With Berlin State Opera, productions of Lohengrin, Salome, The Flying Dutchman, 1996–97; Also engagements in the same season with La Clemenza di Tito in Stuttgart and Falstaff in Bern, Madama Butterfly, Manon, Tales of Hoffmann, Tosca, Turandot and Hindemith's Cardillac; Premiere of Babylon by Detlef Heusinger, Schwetzinger Festspiele, 1997; Tours to Japan and Australia in 1998 and debut at the Metropolitan Opera, New York; Led Berg's Lulu at Mannheim, 1998, also concerts with the Orchestre de Paris and the RSO Copenhagen; Season 1999 debut at the Metropolitan Opera, New York and the Dallas Symphony Orchestra. *Honours:* Conducting Competition winner, German Music Council, 1986; Scholarship for study at Tanglewood with Leonard Bernstein and Seiji Ozawa, with the Boston Symphony Orchestra. *Address:* c/o Nationaltheater Mannheim, Goetheplatz, 68161 Mannheim, Germany.

MARKOV, Albert; Violinist and Composer; b. 8 May 1933, Kharkov, USSR. *Education:* Kharkov Music School; Moscow Gnessin Conservatory; Graduate Master Diploma, 1957; Doctor, 1960. *Career:* Concert Tours in USSR, Eastern and Western Europe, America, Solo with Leningrad Philharmonic, Moscow Philharmonic, major orchestras in Belgium, America, Netherlands, Sweden, England, Denmark, Portugal, Poland, Germany, Yugoslavia and other countries, 1981–; Emigrated to USA 1975, debut with Houston Symphony Orchestra, 1976; Professor, Manhattan School of Music, USA; Artistic Director: Rondo Bennington Music Festival; Founded Albert Markov Music Festival in Nova Scotia, 1995; Art Director, Rondo Bennington Music Festival, Vermont; mem, Rondo Music Society, President; Music Director, Albert Markov Summer Music Festival, Nova Scotia, Canada; NARAS, USA. *Compositions:* Symphony: Kinnor David; Violin Concerto, 1988; Formosa, suite for violin and orchestra; 3 Violin Rhapsodies; 3 Violin Sonatas; Duo-sonata for two violins; Popular Pieces for violin; Paganini Ostinato

(Variations for solo violin); Cadenzas for violin concertos of Mozart, Viotti, Beethoven, Paganini, Brahms; System of violin playing (method); Little Violinist (method); Vocal cycle on A S Pushkin words. *Recordings:* Paganini Concerto No. 2; Other recordings with orchestras and solo compositions by Bach, Veracini, Schubert, Paganini, Prokofiev, Shostakovich. *Publications:* 3 Violin Rhapsodies; Sonata for solo violin; Duosonata for two violins; System of Violin Playing; Violin Technique; Little Violinist (method); Violin Caprices; Cadenzas; Edition of the Tchaikovsky Violin Concerto. *Contributions:* Sovetskaya Musica, USSR; Novoye Russkoe Slovo, Russian Daily, USA. *Honours:* Gold Medal, Violin National Competition, Moscow, 1957; Gold Medal, The Queen Elizabeth Violin Competition, 1959; Ysaye Medal, Belgium. *Address:* 3 Farm Creek Road, Rowayton, CT 06853, USA.

MARKOV, Alexander; Violinist; b. 24 Jan. 1963, Moscow, Russia. *Education:* Central Music School, Moscow; Gnessin Music School; Manhattan School of Music. *Career:* Debut: Carnegie Hall, New York, 1979 (recital debut 1983); Many tours in USA and Europe in virtuoso repertoire, notably concertos and Caprices by Paganini; British debut with BBC Philharmonic, 1993; Wigmore Hall, London, 1997, with Paganini's 24 Caprices. *Recordings include:* Paganini's Concertos Nos 1 and 2, 24 Caprices. *Honours:* Gold Medal Paganini International Competition, 1982. *Address:* c/o Albert Markov, 3 Farm Creek Road, Rowayton, CT 06853, USA.

MARKOVA, Jirina; Singer (Soprano); b. 9 Sept. 1957, Prague, Czechoslovakia. *Education:* Studied at the Prague Conservatory. *Career:* Prague National Theatre from 1979, notably in operas by Mozart, Donizetti, Smetana, Weber and Janáček; Guest appearances in Germany, Austria, New York and Philadelphia; Sang Zerlina in the bicentenary performance of Don Giovanni, Prague, 1987; National Theatre, 1991, as Rusalka in Dvořák's opera, 1991 and in Puccini's Tabarro; Abigail in Nabucco, 2001 (also at Castle Loket festival, 2002–03); Amneris in Aida, at State Opera Prague, 2003; Dir, Childern oper Prag, 1999–. *Recordings include:* Jitka in Smetana's Dalibor, Rusalka, Janáček's Excursions of Mr Brouček. *Address:* National Theatre Prague, PO Box 865, 11230 Prague 1, Czech Republic.

MARKOVA, Juliana; Pianist; b. 8 July 1945, Sofia, Bulgaria; m. Michael Roll, 1 s. *Education:* Sofia Conservatory; Verdi Conservatory Milan with Ilonka Deckers. *Career:* After success in Enescu and Marguérite Long Competitions she performed on both sides of the Atlantic; Berlin Festival, Boston Symphony Orchestra and Andrew Davis and the Los Angeles Philharmonic under Zubin Mehta; Concerto engagements with all major orchestras in the USA and recitals at Lincoln Center NY and in Los Angeles; Recent performances in Atlanta, Cleveland, Chicago, Philadelphia, Detroit, Dallas, Montreal, Toronto and Milwaukee; European tours have included Berlin, Florence and Milan; London concerts with the London Symphony Orchestra, Royal Philharmonic and the Philharmonia, with Claudio Abbado and Simon Rattle; Regional engagements with the City of Birmingham Symphony and Royal Scottish Orchestra; British tour with the Sofia Philharmonic; Season 1991–92 with tour of Japan and debut with the San Francisco Symphony; Repertoire includes concertos by Beethoven, Haydn, Mozart, Prokofiev and Saint-Saëns. *Address:* c/o Lodding, Svensk Konsertdirektia AB, Karfeldsgatan 20, PO Box 5076, S–40222 Göteborg, Sweden.

MARKOVA-MIKHAILENKO, Olga; Singer (Mezzo-Soprano); b. 1950, Russia. *Career:* Many appearances throughout Russia in concert and opera; Kirov Opera, St Petersburg, from 1990 as the Mother Superior in The Fiery Angel, Death in Stravinsky's Nightingale, Valsyevna in the Maid of Pskov by Rimsky-Korsakov and Alkonost in Rimsky's Invisible City of Kitezh; Appearances at San Francisco Opera in Boris Godunov and War and Peace; Sang Khivrya in the British premiere of Prokofiev's Semyon Kotko, with the Kirov at Covent Garden, 2000; Other roles include Fillipyevna in Eugene Onegin, Nezhata in Rimsky's Sadko, Vanya in Ivan Susanin, the Duenna in Prokofiev's Betrothal in a Monastery and Naina in Ruslan and Lyudmila. *Address:* c/o Kirov Opera Mariinsky Theatre, Theatre Square, St Petersburg, Russia.

MARKS, Alan; Concert Pianist; b. 14 May 1949, Chicago, Illinois, USA. *Education:* Studied Piano with Shirley Parnas Adamas, Juilliard School of Music with Irwin Freundlich; BMus, 1971; Studied at Peabody Conservatory Baltimore with Leon Fleischer, 1971–72. *Career:* New York debut in 1971 followed by tour of US schools, prisons and hospitals with violinist Daniel Heifetz; Tours as soloist throughout USA and in Europe and Japan; British debut in 1979; Chamber music performances at the Marlboro and Santa Fe Festivals; Premiered Seven Pieces and Caprichos by Carlos Chavez, 1975, 1976; Teacher at the 92nd Street 'Y' in New York, 1972–80 and Lincoln Center Institute, 1979–81. *Honours:* Winner of Concert Artists Guild Piano Competition, 1970.

MARKSON, Gerhard; German conductor; or *Principal Conductor, Radio Telefís Éireann National Symphony Orchestra*; b. Bensheim an der Bergstrasse. *Education:* Frankfurt Acad. of Music, conducting with Igor Markevitch in Monte Carlo, Franco Ferrara in Rome. *Career:* worked as opera and symphony conductor at opera houses in Augsburg, Oldenburg and Freiburg; Music Dir, Hagen Theatre 1991–98; Principal Conductor, Radio Telefís Éireann (RTE) Nat. Symphony Orchestra 2001–; has conducted world-wide, including Bavarian State Opera (Munich), Hamburg State Opera, Norwegian State Opera (Oslo), St Cecilia Orchestra (Rome), RAI (Turin), Monte Carlo Philharmonic, Bournemouth Symphony Orchestra, Norwegian Radio Symphony Orchestra, Swiss Radio Symphony Orchestra (Basle), Polish Radio Symphony Orchestra (Katowice). *Address:* c/o RTÉ National Symphony Orchestra, Radio Telefís Éireann, Donnybrook, Dublin 4, Ireland. *Website:* www.rte.ie/music/nso/index.html.

MARKUS, Urs; Singer (Baritone); b. 29 Sept. 1941, Villmergen, Aargau, Switzerland. *Education:* Studied in Zürich, Milan and Fribourg. *Career:* Sang as a bass at the Biel-Solothurn Opera, 1979–81, baritone roles at Trier, 1983–86; Engaged at Brunswick 1986–88, Nationaltheater Mannheim from 1988; Guest engagements at Geneva, Nancy and Metz; Roles have included Pizarro and Gluck's Agamemnon, Mozart's Count and Alfonso, Verdi's Amonasro and Iago, Telramund, the Dutchman and Hans Sachs, Escamillo and Gerster's Enoch Arden; Concert appearances throughout Switzerland in Berlin, Venice and Copenhagen.

MARKVART, Jan; Singer (Tenor); b. 30 Aug. 1948, Brno, Czechoslovakia. *Career:* Sang at the Janáček Theatre, Brno, as the Prince in Rusalka, Ismael in Nabucco and Fernando in La Favorita; Turin, 1985, in The Bartered Bride; Buenos Aires, 1986, as Gregor in The Makropulos Case; Prague National Theatre from 1986, notably as Florestan, 1989; Amsterdam, 1988–90, in operas by Janáček; Don José at Bratislava; Theater Luxemburg, 1986–95, as Smetana's Dalibor, Ladislav in The Two Widows and the Prince in Rusalka; Nerone (Nerone, A Boito), State Opera, Prague, 1998; Pinkerton in Madama Butterfly at Tchai-Pei, Taiwan, 1999. *Recordings include:* Stahlav in Smetana's Libuše. *Address:* c/o National Theatre Prague, PO Box 865, 11230 Prague 1, Czech Republic.

MARLEYN, Paul; Concert Cellist; b. 1965, England. *Education:* Studied with David Strange at the Royal Academy of Music, from 1981, with Lawrence Lesser in Boston and Aldo Parisot at Yale University. *Career:* Recital and solo appearances from 1988 throughout Europe, Canada and the USA, Jordan Hall Boston, Merkin Hall NY, Chamber Music East and Cape and Island's Music Festivals; Wigmore Hall, London; Tour of Europe 1985 as solo-cellist with the European Community Youth Orchestra under Claudio Abbado; Radio and television engagements in the United Kingdom, the USA and Switzerland; Tours of Japan, South Korea and Switzerland, 1991. *Honours:* Suggia Scholarship, Dove Prize and Thomas Igloi Trust Prize at the RAM; First Prize, Hudson Valley National String Competition, NY, 1988.

MARLTON, Hilton; singer (tenor); b. 1970, South Africa. *Education:* Guildhall School, London. *Career:* appearances as Mozart's Tamino and Ottavio, the Mad Woman in Curlew River; Bardolph in Falstaff and Triquet in Eugene Onegin; Alfredo at the Covent Garden Festival, the Serenade to Music at the Festival Hall and The Seven Deadly Sins for the BBC; Further roles include Mozart's Basilio; Rossini's Ramiro, Tonio in La Fille du Régiment and parts in Monteverdi's Ulisse; Ferrando and Don Ottavio for the State Theatre, Pretoria; Recitals at St George's, Bristol (songs by Mendelssohn) and elsewhere; Lechmere in Owen Wingrave for Channel 4 TV; Simon the Canaan in Birtwistle's The Last Supper at Glyndebourne, 2001. *Current Management:* Owen White Management, Top Floor, 59 Lansdowne Place, Hove, East Sussex BN3 1FL, England. *Telephone:* (1273) 727127. *Fax:* (1273) 328128. *E-mail:* info@owenwhitemanagement.com.

MAROS, Miklós; composer, teacher and chamber orchestra leader; b. 14 Nov. 1943, Pecs, Hungary; m. Ilona Maros. *Education:* Acad. of Music, Budapest, State Coll. of Music, Stockholm. *Career:* leader, Maros Ensemble; compositions frequently performed in Europe and USA; Composer-in-Residence, West Berlin (DAAD/Berliner Künstler programme); mem. Soc. of Swedish Composers, Int. Soc. for Contemporary Music (Swedish Section), Soc. for Experimental Music and Arts, Royal Swedish Acad. of Music. *Compositions include:* Castratos, opera; Symphonies Nos 1–4; Oolit, chamber orchestra; Divertimento, chamber orchestra; Concerto for Harpsichord and Chamber Orchestra; Concerto for Trombone and Orchestra; Sinfonietta; Concerto for Alto Saxophone and Orchestra; Concerto for Clarinet and Orchestra; Chamber music; Electronic music. *Recordings:* Descort, soprano flute and double bass; Manipulation No. 1, bassoon and live electronics; Divertimento, chamber orchestra; Oolit; Circulation, strings; Dimensions, percussion; Quartet for Saxophones; Symphony No. 1; Stora grusharpan, radio opera; 4 songs from Gitanjali, soprano and chamber ensemble; Concerto for Trombone and Orchestra; Capriccio, guitar; Undulations, alto saxophone and piano; Passacaglia, soprano and organ; Turba, choir; Schattierungen, cello; Praefatio, organ; Concerto for Alto Saxophone and Orchestra; Sinfonia concertante (Symphony No. 3); Trifoglio, harp; Aurora for double wind quintet and windband, 1995; Concerto Grosso for Saxophone Quartet and Orchestra. *Honours:* Lifetime Artists' Award, Swedish Government 1990. *Address:* Krukmakargatan 18, 11851 Stockholm, Sweden.

MARQUEZ, Marta; Singer (mezzo-soprano); b. 1955, San Juan, Puerto Rico. *Education:* Juilliard, New York, and with Tito Gobbi in Florence. *Career:* debut, New York City Opera, as Oscar in Un Ballo in Maschera; sang at Saarbrucken from 1979, notably as Constanze, Frau Fluth, Mimi, Violetta, Susanna and Zdenka in Arabella; Spoleto Festival, 1982, as Sylvie in Gounod's La Colombe; Deutsche Oper am Rhein, Düsseldorf, from 1984, with notable roles including Poppea, Hänsel, Cherubino, Idamantes, Cenerentola and Rosina (Barbiere), and further engagements throughout Germany; Puerto Rico at the Pablo Casals Festival and appearances in Moscow with the Düsseldorf company; other roles include Nedda and Musetta; frequent concert appearances; guest appearances at Royal Opera House, Covent Garden (Zerlina, Musetta), and Bavarian State Opera, Munich (Susanna, Aennchen); sang the title role in the premiere of Klebe's Gervaise Macquart, Düsseldorf, 1996; sang Mascha in Three Sisters by Eötvös at Düsseldorf 1999; Rossini's Isabella 2001. *Address:* Neusserweg 72, 40474 Düsseldorf, Germany.

MARRINER, Andrew Stephen; British clarinettist; b. 25 Feb. 1954, London, England; s. of Sir Neville Marriner and Lady Elizabeth Marriner; m. Elizabeth Ann Sparke 1988; one s. *Education:* King's Coll. Choir School, Cambridge, King's School, Canterbury, Univ. of Oxford, Musichochschule, Hannover, Germany. *Career:* debut, solo chamber and orchestral work 1977–; principal clarinet, London Symphony Orchestra 1986–, Acad. of St Martins 1987–; first performances of pieces written for him by John Tavener 1997, Robin Holloway 1997, Dominic Muldowney 1997; mem. Lords Taverner. *Recordings:* Mozart Quintet and Concerto, London Proms 1997, Weber Concerto, Finzi Concerto, Tavener. *Honours:* Hon. RAM 1995. *Current Management:* Ingpen & Williams Ltd, 7 St George's Court, 131 Putney Bridge Road, London, SW15 2PA, England.

MARRINER, Sir Neville, Kt, CBE, FRCM, FRAM; British music director and conductor; b. 15 April 1924, Lincoln, England; s. of Herbert H. Marriner and Ethel M. Marriner; m. Elizabeth M. Sims 1955; one s. (Andrew Stephen Marriner) one d. *Education:* Lincoln School, Royal Coll. of Music. *Career:* founder and Dir Acad. of St Martin in the Fields 1956–; Musical Dir LA Chamber Orchestra 1969–78; Dir South Bank Festival of Music 1975–78; Dir Meadowbrook Festival, Detroit 1979–84; Music Dir Minn. Orchestra 1979–86, Stuttgart Radio Symphony Orchestra 1984–89, Barbican Summer Festival 1985–87; Fellow, Trinity Coll. of Music, Hong Kong Acad. for Performing Arts. *Recordings include:* Dvořák Serenades, Haydn Violin Concerto in C, Mozart Serenade K361, Il Barbiere di Siviglia, all Schubert's Symphonies, The English Connection (Vaughan Williams' The Lark Ascending, Elgar Serenade and Tippett Corelli Fantasia), Trumpet Concertos (with Hakan Hardenberger), Mendelssohn Piano Works (with Murray Perahia), Mozart Haffner Serenade, Bach Concertos, Suites and Die Kunst der Fuge, Vivaldi's The Four Seasons, Concerti Grossi by Corelli, Geminiani, Torelli, Locatelli and Manfredini, Mozart Symphonies, Concertos, Serenades and Divertimenti, Handel Messiah, Opera overtures and Water and Fireworks music, Die Zauberflöte 1980, Handel Arias (with Kathleen Battle), Il Turco in Italia and Don Giovanni, Verdi's Oberto 1997, Sylvia McNair: Love's Sweet Surrender 1998, Brahms Symphonies 1–4 1998, Schumann Symphonies 1–4 1998, complete Symphonies of Beethoven, Tchaikovsky, Weber, Gounod, Cantatas of Bach (with Fischer-Dieskau, Janet Baker), Haydn Symphonies. *Honours:* Hon. DMus (Hull) 1998, (Royal Scottish Acad.) 1999; Tagore Gold Medal, six Edison Awards (Netherlands), two Mozart Gemeinde Awards (Austria), three Grand Prix du Disque (France), two Grammy Awards (USA), Shakespeare Prize; Kt of the Polar Star 1984, Officier, Ordre des Arts et Lettres 1995. *Address:* c/o Academy of St Martin-in-the-Fields, Raine House, Raine Street, London, E1 9RG, England.

MARSALIS, Wynton; American trumpeter, music administrator and composer; b. 18 Oct. 1961, New Orleans, LA; s. of Ellis Marsalis and Dolores Marsalis; three c. *Education:* Berks. Music Center, Tanglewood, Juilliard School, New York. *Career:* played with New Orleans Philharmonic age 14; joined Art Blakey and the Jazz Messengers 1980; toured with Herbie Hancock 1981; formed own group with brother Branford Marsalis 1982; leader Wynton Marsalis Septet; in addition to regular appearances in many countries with his own jazz quintet, he follows a classical career and has performed with the world's top orchestras; regularly conducts masterclasses in schools and holds private tuition; Artistic Dir Lincoln Center Jazz Dept, New York 1990–. *Compositions:* Soul Gestures in Southern Blues 1988, Blood on the Fields (oratorio) 1994, Jazz/Syncopated Movements 1997. *Recordings include:* All American Hero 1980, Wynton 1980, Wynton Marsalis

1981, Think of One 1983, English Chamber Orchestra 1984, Hot House Flowers 1984, Baroque Music: Wynton Marsalis, Edita Gruberova, Raymond Leppard and the English Chamber 1985, Black Codes (From the Underground) 1985, J Mood 1985, Live at Blues Alley 1986, Tomasi/Jolivet: Trumpet Concertos 1986, Carnaval 1987, Baroque Music for Trumpets 1988, The Majesty of the Blues 1989, Crescent City Christmas Card 1989, Tune in Tomorrow (soundtrack) 1991, Quiet City 1989, 24 1990, Trumpet Concertos 1990, Blue Interlude 1992, Citi Movement 1992, In This House, On This Morning 1992, Hot Licks: Gypsy 1993, On the Twentieth Century 1993, Joe Cool's Blues 1994, Live in Swing Town 1994, In Gabriel's Garden 1996, Jump Start and Jazz 1996, Live at Bubba's 1996, One By One 1998, The Marcial Suite 1998, At the Octoroon Ball: String Quartet No. 1 1999, Big Train 1999, Fiddler's Tale 1999, Reeltime 1999, Sweet Release and Ghost Story 1999, Goin' Down Home 2000, Immortal Concerts: Jody 2000, The London Concert 2000, All Rise 2002, Angel Eyes 2002, The Magic Hour 2004. *Publications:* Sweet Swing Blues on the Road 1994, Marsalis on Music 1995, Requiem 1999. *Honours:* numerous hon. doctorates; Edison Award, Netherlands, Grand Prix du Disque, eight Grammy Awards in both jazz and classical categories, Pulitzer Prize for Music 1997, Algur H. Meadows Award, Southern Methodist Univ. 1997. *Current Management:* Ted Kurland Associates, 173 Brighton Avenue, Boston, MA 02134, USA. *Telephone:* (617) 254-0007. *Fax:* (617) 782-3577. *E-mail:* agents@tedkurland.com.

MARSCHNER, Wolfgang; Violinist; b. 23 May 1926, Dresden, Germany. *Education:* Studied violin, piano, composition and conducting, Conservatory Dresden and Mozarteum Salzburg. *Career:* Debut: At age 9 with Tartini's Devil's Trill sonata; Professor, Folkwang-School, Essexn, 1956; Professor, Music Conservatory, Cologne, 1958; Professor, Music Conservatory, Freiburg, 1963–; Regular Mastercourses in Warsaw and Weimar; Director of Pfluger-Foundation for young violinists, freiburg; International soloist career, concerts in Edinburgh Festival and with Berlin Philharmonic and Royal Philharmonic, London; Premiere, Schoenberg's Violin Concerto in many cities including London, Vienna and Zürich; Founder of: International Ludwig Spohr Violin Competition; Jacobus Stainer Violin Maker's Competition; International Youth Violin Competition; German Spohr Academy; Festival Wolfgang Marschner, Hinterzarten. *Compositions:* Various works for orchestra; 2 concerti for violin and orchestra; Sonata for solo violin; Canto notturno for violin and organ; Rhapsody for viola solo. *Honours:* Kranichsteiner prize for contemporary music, 1954; English record prize for interpretation of Schoenberg's Violin Concerto, Bundesverdienstkreuz, 1986. *Address:* Burgunder Strasse 4, 7800 Freiburg, Germany.

MARSH, David; Singer (bass); b. 29 May 1947, Middlesborough, England. *Education:* Royal Northern College of Music, and with Otakar Kraus. *Career:* English National Opera, Scottish Opera, Gyndebourne Touring Opera, City of Birmingham Touring Opera, English Touring Opera, Opéra de Lyon, Pfalzbau Theatre Ludwigshafen, Singapore Lyric Theatre, Wexford Festival; Roles include Amonasro, Macbeth, Gérard in Andrea Chénier, Don Magnifico, Banquo, Masetto and Commendatore in Don Giovanni, Ramfis, Ferrando in Trovatore, Pantheus in Les Troyens, Dr Grenvil, Pistola in Falstaff, Nourabad in Les Pêcherus de perles, Abimelech in Samson et Delila, Trulove in The Rake's Progress, Quince in A Midsummer Night's Dream, Luther/Crespel in Les Contes d'Hoffmann, Sempronius in Timon of Athens, by Stephen Oliver, The King in Pavel Haas's Sarlatan. *Address:* Music International, 13 Ardilaun Road, London N5 2QR, England.

MARSH, Jane; Singer (Soprano); b. 25 June 1944, San Francisco, USA. *Education:* Studied with Ellen Repp at Oberlin College and with Lili Wexburg and Otto Guth in NY, USA. *Career:* Debut: Spoleto Festival 1965, as Desdemona; Sang in Essen, Hamburg, Moscow, Prague, Naples, Trieste and Johannesburg: Further appearances in Pittsburgh, San Antonio and San Francisco, 1968; Deutsche Oper am Rhein, Düsseldorf, from 1968; Salzburg 1973, in the premiere of Orff's De Temporum fine Comoedia; Often heard as Mozart's Donna Anna, Queen of Night and Constanze. *Recordings:* De Temporum fine Comoedia; The Invisible City of Kitezh; Alfonso und Estrella; Penthesilea by Schoeck; Der Vampyr by Marschner, Voce.

MARSH, Peter (Randall); Violinist, Violist and Conductor; b. 15 June 1931, Glen Ridge, New Jersey, USA; Studied with Hans Letz, Juilliard School, 1946–50, Scott Willits, American Conservatory, 1952, 1966–67, Emanuel Zetlin, University of Washington, 1955–57. *Career:* Teaching experience includes:California Institute of the Arts, 1985–87; Artist-in-Residence, Lecturer, California State University at Fullerton, 1987–90; Professor, Western Washington University, Bellingham, 1990–97; Lecturer, University of Southern California, 1996–; Director of String Chamber Music, University of Southern California Thornton School of Music; Performing career includes: Chamber Music: 1st Violin, Lenox Quartet, 1957–81; 1st Violin, Philadelphia Quartet, 1981–82; 1st Violin, Berkshire Quartet, 1983–85; 1st Violin, Sequoia Quartet, 1985–87; 1st Violin, Southwest Chamber Music Society, 1988–96; Violin/Viola, Picasso Trio, 1992–95; 1st Violin, Pacific Quartet, 1993–96; Orchestra:

1st Violin, Seattle Symphony, 1955–57; Viola/1st Violin, Pittsburgh Symphony, 1957–61; Concertmaster, Seattle Symphony, Seattle Opera, Pacific Northwest Ballet, 1982–83; California Chamber Symphony, Colorado Festival Orchestra, 1987–89; mem, The Bohemians, New York, 1964–. *Recordings include:* As 1st Violinist with Lenox Quartet and Southwest Chamber Music Society: Milton Babbitt, Composition for 4 instruments, 1948; Beethoven, Sextet for string quartet and 2 horns; Beethoven Violin Sonatas 1–10 2001; Beethoven String Quartet Op.18 No.1 and Op.59 No.3; Berger, String Quartet; Haydn, String Quartets op 20, no's 1–6; L Kirchner String Quartet No. 2; Krenek, op 231 for violin and organ, op 237 for string trio; Prokofiev, Quintet op 39 and Overture on Hebrew Themes; Schoenberg, Concerto for string quartet and orchestra, with the London Symphony, and String Trio. *Contributions:* American String Teachers Magazine, whilst Violin Forum Editor, 1988–90. *Address:* 343 Heather Heights Court, Monrovia, CA 91016, USA.

MARSH, Roger; Composer and Lecturer; b. 10 Dec. 1949, Bournemouth, England; m. (1) Christina Rhys, 24 July 1976, 2 s., 2 d., (2) Anna Myatt, 19 Sept 1992, 1 s., 1 d. *Education:* BA, 1971, DPhil, 1975, University of York; Studied with Bernard Rands. *Career:* Harkness Fellow, 1976–78, University of CA, San Diego; Lecturer, Keele University, 1978–88; Lecturer, Senior Lecturer, Professor, University of York; Member of Midland Music Theatre; Director of Black Hair contemporary music ensemble; mem, SPNM Reading Panel, 1991–92; BBC Reading Panel, 1987–. *Compositions:* Not a Soul But Ourselves for 4 Amplified Voices, 1977; The Big Bang, music theatre, 1989; Stepping Out for Piano and Orchestra, 1990; Kagura, 1991; Love on The Rocks, music theatre, 1988; Espace for Orchestra, 1994; Heathcote's Inferno for wind orchestra, 1996; Spin for piano and ensemble, 1997; Canto I for string orchestra, 1999; Chaconne for violin, 1999; Sukeruko for percussion quartet, 2000. *Recordings include:* Not a Soul But Ourselves; Numerous radio broadcasts; CDs: Love on The Rocks and Ferry Music; Heathcote's Inferno, 2001. *Publications:* Various. *Honours:* Arts Council Composition Bursary, 1993. *Current Management:* Novello; Maecenas Music. *Address:* The New Rectory, Everingham, York YO42 4JA, England.

MARSH-EDWARDS, Michael (Richard); Composer and Conductor; b. 7 April 1928, Westgate-on-Sea, Kent, England; m. (1) Stella K Parrott, 9 April 1952, 1 d., (2) Ann Wardleworth, 11 Nov 1971, (3) Srilnuan Suwan, 9 Jan 1981, 1son, 1 d. *Education:* Trinity College, London University, Associate and Licentiate Diplomas, Hon PhD. *Career:* Conductor Luton Bach Orchestra, 1949–63; conductor 1952–63, Vice President, Luton Symphony Orchestra; Director of Music, Luton Industrial Mission and Luton Community Centre, 1957–62; Conductor, Halton Orpheus Choir, 1973–75; Freelance Conductor and lecturer, Consultant, Bangkok Symphony Orchestra; mem, Lfe Member, Former Vice-Chairman, British Music Society and Havergal Brian Society; Composers' Guild of Great Britain; Performing Right Society. *Compositions:* Toccata for Percussion and Orchestra; Variations, 8 percussionists; 3 Studies, 12 percussionists; Dance Overture; Birthday Overture; Revolutionary Overture, 1956; Chester Overture; Celebration Overture; Music 1, 60 strings; Music 2, strings and percussion; Music 3, strings and Brass; Music 4; Oppositions, 2 orchestras; Structures; Fantasy on the Waltz of Diabelli; Thai Dances; Balinese Dances; Petite Suite pour le Tombeau d'Erik Satie; Treurzang; Suite Guernesiase; Concerto for 11 instruments; Horn Concerto; Devouring Time, high voice and piano; Mischevious Ditties, high voice and piano; Elegy on the Name of Havergal Brian, piano or string orchestra; Peter Goldberg Variations, wind quintet; Concertino for harpsichord and string orchestra; Incantations, for flute, oboe, viola and piano; Toccata on One Note, for piano; Numerous other instrumental, vocal and electronic pieces; Music for children. *Publications:* Author of Concert Notes; Author and Presenter of Radio Scripts. *Honours:* Medal, American Biographical Institute, 1986; Alfred Nobel Medal, 1991. *Address:* 5/2440 Muban Prachachuen, Pakred, Nontaburi 11120, Thailand.

MARSHALL, Ingram (Douglas); Composer; b. 10 May 1942, New York, USA. *Education:* BA, Lake Forest College, 1964, Columbia University with Ussachevsky, electronic music, 1964–66, with Morton Subotnick in New York and California, and traditional Indonesian music at the California Institute of the Arts. *Career:* Taught at the California Institute of the Arts until 1974; Performances in Java, Bali and Scandinavia. *Compositions:* Transmogrification for tape, 1966; Three Buchla Studies for synthesizer 1969; Cortez, text-sound piece 1973; Vibrosuperball for 4 amplified percussion 1975; Non Confundar for string sextet, alto flute, clarinet and electronics, 1977; Spiritus for 6 strings, 4 flutes, harpsichord and vibraphone, 1981; Frog Tropes for brass sextet and tape, 1982; Voces resonae for string quartet, 1984. Three Penitential Visions for orchestra, 1987, Raving in the Wind, dance, 1997; Electro-acoustic: Evensongs for string quartet and tape, 1993; Dark Waters, for English horn, tape and electronics, 1995; Sinfonia Kingdom Come for orchestra and tape, 1997; SOE-PA for

guitar with digital delay, 1999. *Address:* ASCAP, ASCAP Building, 1 Lincoln Plaza, NY 10023, USA.

MARSHALL, Margaret Anne, OBE, DRSAMD; British concert and opera singer (soprano); b. 4 Jan. 1949, Stirling, Scotland; m. Graeme Griffiths King Davidson; two d. *Education:* Royal Scottish Academy of Music and Drama. *Career:* debut at Covent Garden, 1980; Vienna Staatsoper 1988, Mozart's Countess; North America Opera debut in Toronto as Vitellia; Performances in Festival Hall, Barbican, Covent Garden; Concerts and Opera in major European events; Has sung Gluck's Euridice and Mozart's Countess at Florence; Sang Contessa in Figaro at La Scala, 1982 and Fiordiligi at Salzburg, 1982–85 and 1990–91; Season 1990–91 with Countess in Hong Kong and Donna Elvira for ENO; Season 1991–92 included Violetta at Frankfurt, Mozart Bicentenary Gala at Covent Garden, followed by Fiordiligi and Vitellia in La Clemenza di Tito at the Salzburg Festival; Sang in Mozart's La Finta Giardiniera at the 1995 Montpellier Festival; Mozart's Countess of Flanders, 1995. *Recordings:* Mozart's C Minor Mass and Haydn's Masses, conducted by Marriner; Vivaldi's Tito Manlio and Canatas, Negri; Handel's Jephtha and Saul; Gluck Orfeo, Muti; Haydn Die Schöpfung and Bach St Matthew Passion, Erato; Pergolesi Stabat Mater, Abbado; Mozart Davidde Penitente and Die Schuldigkeit des Ersten Gebotes; Vaughan Williams Sea Symphony, Virgin Classics; Elgar The Kingdom, Chandos; Hypermestra in Les Danaides by Salieri. *Honours:* 1st prize, Munich International Competition, 1974; James Gulliver Award for Performing Arts in Scotland. *Address:* Woodside Main Street, Gargunnock, Stirling FK8 3BP, Scotland.

MARSHALL, Nicholas; Composer, Musician (piano), Conductor and Teacher; b. 2 June 1942, Plymouth, Devon, England; m. Angela Marshall 1982; one s. one d. *Education:* MA, Univ. of Cambridge, 1964; Royal Coll. of Music, 1964–65. *Career:* Chair. and Artistic Dir, Ashburton Festival 1980–84. *Compositions include:* Section: Partita for Guitar; Three Japanese Fragments for guitar; Seven Folksongs for voice, recorder and piano; Arion and The Dolphins, Junior Operetta; Inscriptions for A Peal of Eight Bells for SATB; Suite for Guitar, Flute, Clarinet, Violin and Cello; Four Haiku for Solo Recorder; Trio for Recorders; Sonatina for Solo Flute; Jump for Flute and Piano; Five West Country Folk Songs for SATB; Two West Country Folk Songs for SATB; A Playford Garland for SATB; The Young King, Children's Opera; Five Country Dances for orchestra, Cool Winds for Cello and Guitar; The Virgin's Song for SATB; Carol for Christmas Eve for SATB. *Recordings:* Cool Winds: original music for cello and guitar; Three Japanese Fragments: Austin Maruri guitar recital; Here we come a-piping, vocal and intrumental music. *Address:* 2 The Mount, Totnes Down Hill, Totnes, Devon TQ9 5ES, England.

MARSHALL, Robert (Lewis); Musicologist; b. 12 Oct. 1939, New York, NY, USA; m. Traute Maass, 9 Sept 1966, 1 s., 1 d. *Education:* AB, Columbia University, 1960; MA, 1962, PhD, 1968, Princeton University; French Horn with Gunther Schuller, High School of Music and Art, New York. *Career:* Faculty Member, 1966–83, Chair, 1972–78, Music, University of Chicago; Visiting professor at Princeton University, 1971–72; Columbia University, 1977; Faculty, 1983–2000, Incumbent Endowed Chair: Louis, Frances and Jeffrey Sachar Professor, Chair, 1985–92, Music, Brandeis University; mem, American Bach Society; Neue Bach-Gesellschaft. *Publications:* The Compositional Process of J. S. Bach, 1972; Studies in Renaissance and Baroque Music in Honour of Arthur Mendel, 1974; Critical Editor, Cantatas for 9th and 10th Sundays after Trinity, 1985; J. S. Bach Cantata Autographs in American Collections, 1985; The Music of J. S. Bach: The Sources, The Style, The Significance, 1989; Mozart Speaks: Views on Music, Musicians and The World, 1991; Eighteenth Century Keyboard Music, 1994, 2nd edn, 2003; Dennis Brain on Record: A Comprehensive Discography, 1996; Bach and Mozart's Artistic Maturity, 1998. *Contributions:* Musical Quarterly; Journal of American Musicological Society. *Honours:* Hon. mem., American Musicological Soc., 2003; Otto Kinkeldey Award, American Musicological Society, 1974; First Incumbent, Harold Spivacke Consultant to Music division, Library of Congress, 1985; ASCAP-Deems Taylor Award, 1990. *Address:* 100 Chestnut Street, West Newton, MA 02465, USA.

MARSHALL, Wayne; Concert Organist, Conductor and Pianist; b. 31 Jan. 1961, Oldham, Lancashire, England. *Education:* ARCM Chetham's School Manchester; FRCO Royal College of Music, 1978–83; Austrian Government Scholarship 1983, to study at the Vienna Hochschule. *Career:* Organ scholar at Manchester Cathedral and St George's Chapel Windsor; Recitals at St Paul's Cathedral, Westminster Abbey, Festival Hall, Leeds and Birmingham Town Halls, and King's College, Cambridge; Tours of the USA and Yugoslavia; Windsor and Hong Kong Festivals; 1986, worked as repetiteur for Glyndebourne production of Porgy and Bess: Appeared as Jasbo Brown the jazz pianist; Assistant Chorus Master at Glyndebourne 1987; 1988–89 Seasons included Promenade Concert debut with the Poulenc Concerto and appearances with the City of Birmingham Symphony under Simon Rattle and the

BBC Symphony under Paul Daniel; Conducted the premiere of Wilfred Joseph's Alice in Wonderland at the Harrogate Festival 1990; Carmen Jones in the West End, London, 1991; Last Night of the 1997 London Proms; Conductor of Porgy and Bess at the Bregenz Festival 1997–98 and at the 1998 London Proms; Duke Ellington Centenary Celebration at the 1999 Proms; Season 2001–02 with Rotterdam Philharmonic Orchestra, Vienna Symphony Orchestra, Bournemouth Symphony Orchestra and BBC Concert Orchestra; Guest conducting in 2002–2003 with Orchestre National de Lyon, BBC Philharmonic, Orquesta Sinfonica de Euskadi and Bochumer Symphoniker; Conducted West Side Story at Bregenz Festival in 2003; Organist in residence at Bridgewater Hall, Manchester; Featured in major celebrity organ recital series worldwide including Suntory Hall, Tokyo, Vienna, Berlin, Paris and New Zealand; As solo pianist appears as recitalist and with orchestras worldwide, and has duo partnership with Kim Criswell and Tasmin Little; Has conducted orchestras including Dallas, Toronto, Winnipeg Symphony Orchestras, City of Birmingham Symphony Orchestra, London Philharmonic, Bournemouth Symphony, Hallé, Munich Radio and Vienna Symphony Orchestras. *Recordings include:* I Got Rhythm; Gershwin Song Book; Rhapsody in Blue; Saint-Saëns Third (Organ) Symphony with Olso Symphony Orchestra and Mariss Jansons. *Current Management:* Askonas Holt Ltd, Lonsdale Chambers, 27 Chancery Lane, London, WC2A 1PF, England. *Telephone:* (20) 7400-1700. *Fax:* (20) 7400-1799. *E-mail:* info@askonasholt.co.uk. *Website:* www.askonasholt.co.uk.

MARSONER, Ingrid; Pianist; b. 1970, Leoben, Austria. *Education:* Hochschule für Musik und Kunst, Graz, 1981; Studied at the Universität für Musik und Darstellende Kunst, Vienna, 1990. *Career:* Teacher at the Universität für Musik, Graz, 1996–; Appearances at the Salzburg Corinthian Summer and Innsbruck Festivals; Peninsula Festival, Los Angeles, Kyoto Chamber Music (Japan) and Mozart Fesivals at Bologna; Repertoire includes J. S. Bach, Partita in C minor; Scarlatti Sonatas; Haydn, Fantasie in C major; Mozart, Fantasie in C minor, Rondo in A minor, Sonatas in A major, C minor and D major; Schubert, Sonatas in A major, A minor, B major, Wandererfantasie in C major, 4 Impromptus; Mendelssohn, Variations sérieuses in D minor op 54; Schumann, Abegg Variations op 1, Papillons, op 2, Kresleriana op 16, Fantasy in C major op 17, Faschingsschwank aus Wien op 32; Pieces by Chopin, Liszt, Berg and Schoenberg; Mendelssohn Double Concerto in G minor; Chamber music includes Beethoven's Archduke Trio; Fauré Piano Quartet in C minor; Schumann, Dichterliebe; César Franck, Sonata in A major; Messiaen, Quartet for the End of Time. *Address:* Kriemhildplatz 7/7, 1150 Vienna, Austria.

MARSTON, Nicholas John, MA, PhD, ARCM, ARCO; Academic and Musicologist; b. 27 Dec. 1958, Penzance, England. *Education:* Humphry Davy Grammar School, Corpus Christi Coll., Univ. of Cambridge. *Career:* Junior Research Fellow, Selwyn Coll., Cambridge 1984–86; British Acad. Post-doctoral Research Fellow, King's College London 1986–89; Lecturer, Exeter Univ. 1989–94; Lecturer, Bristol Univ. 1994–95; Reader, Univ. of Oxford 1995–2001; Reader, Univ. of Cambridge, and Fellow, King's Coll. 2001; mem. Soc. for Music Analysis (vice-pres. and chair., editorial bd), Royal Musical Asscn, American Musicological Soc. *Publications:* Schumann: Fantasie Op. 17, Beethoven's Piano Sonata in E Op. 109, The Beethoven Companion (co-author); contrib. to The Cambridge Companion to Beethoven, 19th Century Music, Music Analysis, Journal of the American Musicological Association. *Address:* King's College, University of Cambridge, Cambridge, CB2 1ST, England (office). *Telephone:* (1223) 331331 (office). *Fax:* (1223) 331115 (office). *E-mail:* njm45@cam.ac.uk (office).

MARTA, Istvan; Composer; b. 14 June 1952, Budapest, Hungary; 2 d. *Education:* Course in Composition in Yugoslavia led by W Lutoslawski, 1979; Diploma in Composition and Teaching from Ferenc Liszt Academy of Music, Budapest, 1981. *Career:* Folk Music Collecting Tour in Moldavia, Romania, 1973; Over 30 pieces of stage and film music composed; Teacher of History of Classical Music and Analysis of 20th Century Music, Jazz Department, Bela Bart ók School of Music, Budapest, 1981–83; Organiser of Planum and Rendezvous, festivals of international contemporary music, 1982 and 1984; Music Director, National Theater, New Theater, Budapest, 1990–95; Director, Art Valley Multicultural Festival, 1995. *Compositions:* Text and Music, stage performance based on Samuel Beckett's radioplay, 1978; King of the Dead, cantata 1979; Christmas Day–24th Lesson, Music for Chamber ensemble, 1980; Our Heats, movements for chamber choir and chamber orchestra, 1983; Visions, ballet performed by the ballet corps of the Hungarian State Opera, 1984; Dolls House Story, composition for percussion instruments, 1985; Workers' Operetta, musical 1985; per quattro tromboni, 1986; Kapolcs Alarm, a videoclip, 1987; Slips and Streams, a ballet for tape, 1989; Doom, A Sigh, string auartet, 1989; The Glassblower's Dream, string quartet, 1990; Anatomy of a Scream, ballet for tape, 1990; Blasting in the Bird Cage for tape, 1990; The Temptation of St Anthony, ballet for tape, 1992; Don't Look

Back, ballet for tape, 1995; Faust, ballet for tape, 1995; Liliomfi, musical play, 1997. *Current Management:* Interkoncert, Budapest. *Address:* Ferenciektere 7–8, 1053 Budapest, Hungary.

MARTIN, Adrian; Singer (tenor); b. 1958, England. *Education:* Studied at the London Opera Centre and the National Opera Studio. *Career:* Debut: With Opera for All as Ramiro and Tonio; Sang small roles at Covent Garden in Parsifal, Salome and Die Zauberflöte, then the Dancing Master in Ariadne and Pong in Turandot; Glyndebourne Festival as Tamino and Idamante; Appearances with English National Opera as Cassio, Alfred, the Steersman, Anatol (War and Peace), Don Ottavio, Vincent (Mireille), Tamino, Ferrando and Rodolfo, Nadir, Jenik in The Makropulos Case and Erik in Fennimore and Gerda; Welsh National Opera as Lensky in Serban's production of Eugene Onegin; Scottish Opera in La Scala di Seta and La Cambiale di Matrimonio by Rossini; Has sung with Opera North as Rodolfo, Alfredo, Camille, Ismaele (Nabucco), Sali in a Village Romeo and Juliet, Tamino, Jacquino, Nadir and Ernesto; Overseas engagements at St Gallen (Hoffmann and Don Ottavio); Hamburg and Zürich (Hoffmann); Paris (Tybalt in Roméo et Juliette at the Opéra) and Queensland (Nadir and Rodolfo at the Lyric Opera); Season 1999–2000 at the Erl Festival, Tyrol, as Alberich in The Ring. *Current Management:* Athole Still International Management, Forresters Hall, 25–27 Westow Street, London, SE19 3RY, England. *Telephone:* (20) 8771-5271. *Fax:* (20) 8768-6600. *Website:* www.atholestill.com.

MARTIN, Andrea; Singer (Baritone); b. 9 March 1949, Klagenfurt, Germany. *Education:* Studied in Vienna and at the Santa Cecilia Academy in Rome; Teachers included Anton Dermota, Hans Hotter, Ettore Campogallian, Mario del Monaco and Giuseppe Taddei; *Career:* Debut: Treviso 1979, as Malatesta in Don Pasquale; Sang with the Wiener Kammeroper and in Klagenfurt, Salzburg, Graz and Munich; Further Italian engagements at Rome, Palermo, Bologna, Venice, Naples and Verona; Ravenna Festival as Michonnet in Adriana Lecouvreur; Has sung in Maria di Rudenz by Donizetti at Venice and Wiesbaden, as Luna in Trovatore at the Dresden Staatsoper; Guest appearances at the Théâtre des Champs-Elysées, Paris, Liège, Barcelona, Lisbon and Vienna; Concert tours of Japan, Korea, the USA and Brazil. *Recordings:* Imelda de Lambertazzi and Alina, Regina di Golconda by Donizetti, Salieri's Axur, and Così fan tutte. *Address:* c/o Teatro La Fenice, Campo S Fantin 2519, 30124 Venice, Italy.

MARTIN, George Whitney, BA, LLB; writer; b. 25 Jan. 1926, New York, USA. *Education:* Harvard Coll., Trinity Coll., Cambridge, Univ. of Virginia Law School. *Career:* practised law 1955–59; writer 1959–. *Publications:* The Damrosch Dynasty, America's First Family of Music 1983, Verdi, His Music, Life and Times (fourth edn) 1992, Aspects of Verdi (second edn) 1993, Verdi at The Golden Gate, Opera and San Francisco in the Gold Rush Years 1993, The Opera Companion (fifth edn) 1997, Twentieth Century Opera, A Guide 1999; contrib. numerous articles on Verdi and his operas in The Opera Quarterly. *Address:* 53 Crosslands Drive, Kennett Square, PA 19348, USA.

MARTIN, Janis; Singer (Soprano); b. 16 Aug. 1939, Sacramento, California, USA; m. Gerhard Hellwig. *Education:* Studied with Julia Monroe in Sacramento and Lili Wexberg and Otto Guth in New York. *Career:* Debut: San Francisco, 1960 as Annina in La Traviata; Returned to San Francisco as Marina, Venus and Meg Page; New York City Opera debut 1962, as Mrs Grose in The Turn of the Screw; New York Metropolitan Opera from 1962–66, at first in mezzo roles then from 1973 as Sieglinde, Marie in Wozzeck and Kundry; Bayreuth Festival 1968–73, as Magdalene, Eva, Sieglinde and Kundry; Chicago 1971, as Tosca; Deutsche Oper Berlin 1971–88; Covent Garden 1973, as Marie; La Scala 1980, as The Woman in Erwartung; La Scala, Marie; Geneva Opera 1985 as Isolde; Other roles include Wagner's Senta, Brünnhilde, Isolde, Venus and Kundry; Tosca; Fidelio, Santuzza and Strauss's Ariadne, Dyer's Wife, Salome, Elektra, and Marschallin; Cologne Opera 1988, as the Dyer's Wife; Turin and Bayreuth, 1989, as Brünnhilde; Sang Beethoven's Leonore at Düsseldorf, 1990; Season 1991–92, as the Götterdämmerung Brünnhilde at Brussels and Senta at Naples; Sang Orpheus at the Accademia di Santa Cecilia, Rome, 1996; Elektra at Catania, 1998; Season 2000 as Strauss's Dyer's Wife at the Munich Staatsoper and as Brünnhilde in Die Walküre for the Vienna Staatsoper. *Recordings:* Adriano in Rienzi; Der fliegende Holländer; Erwartung; Sancta Susanna by Hindemith. *Address:* c/o Deutsche Oper am Rhein, Heinrich-Heine Allee 16, 4000 Düsseldorf, Germany.

MARTIN, Kathleen; Singer (Soprano); b. 28 Feb. 1948, Texas, USA. *Education:* studied at UCLA and at California State University Long Beach. *Career:* Debut: San Francisco Opera as Madama Butterfly; England at the Lubeck Opera, 1974–80, as Fiordiligi, Donna Elvira, Nedda, Mimi, Desdemona, the Trovatore Leonora, Elsa, Tatiana and Katya Kabanova; Sang at the Frankfurt Opera 1980–83, guest engagements at the Theater am Gärtnerplatz, Munich; Sang at Toulouse as Jordane in the 1985 premiere of Landowski's Montségur and appeared at the Paris Opéra, 1987. *Address:* c/o Teatre du Capitole, Place du Capitole, 31000 Toulouse, France.

MARTIN, Marvis; Singer (Soprano); b. 1956, Tallahassee, Florida. *Education:* University of Miami and Manhattan School. *Career:* Sang the Princess in L'Enfant et les Sortilèges, Metropolitan Opera, 1983; Further New York appearances in Boris Godunov, Ariadne auf Naxos, Porgy and Bess, as Clara; Tchaikovsky's Maid of Orleans; Savonlinna Festival, 1992 as Clara and appearances elsewhere as Pamina and Liu in Turandot; Many concert engagements. *Address:* c/o Metropolitan Opera, Lincoln Center, New York NY 19923, USA.

MARTIN, Philip (James); Concert Pianist and Composer; b. 27 Oct. 1947, Dublin, Ireland; m. 22 Aug 1970, 1 s., 1 d. *Education:* St Marys College, Rathmines, Dublin; Patricia Read Pianoforte School, Dublin, Private Studies with Mabel Swainson, Dublin; Royal Academy of Music, London; Private Studies with Louis Kentner, London, and Yvonne Lefèbure, Paris. *Career:* Debut: Wigmore Hall, London, 1970; Regular Performances with major British orchestras; Royal Festival Hall and Royal Albert Hall Debut, 1977; BBC Prom Concerts, 1985, 1987 Recorded live on Omnibus at the Proms, BBC television. *Compositions:* 2 Piano Concertos; Harp Concerto; Beato Angelico, for large orchestra; 3 Piano Trios; Various Chamber Music and over 150 Songs; Symphony, 1999; 2 large choral works. *Address:* Chapel House, Theobalds Green, Calstone Calne, Wiltshire SW11 8QE, England.

MARTINCEK, Dusan; Composer; b. 13 June 1936, Presov, Slovakia; m. Magdalena Kockova, 1961, 1 s. *Education:* Piano and Composition, Bratislava Conservatory, 1951–56; Bratislava Academy of Music and Drama, 1956–61. *Career:* Assistant, Music Theory, 1961–72; Associate Professor, Theory, 1973–86; Freelance Artist, 1987–92; University Professor, Composition, Bratislava Academy of Music and Drama, Bratislava, 1993; mem, Numerous musical institutions. *Compositions include:* Dialogues in the Form of Variations for piano and orchestra, 1961; Simple overture for small orchestra, 1961; 8 piano sonatas, 1967–1981; String Quartet, 1982–84; Animation for 35 solo strings, 1983–86; Continuities for large orchestra, 1987–88; Communications for violin and piano, 1988; Interrupted Silence for large orchestra, 1989–90; Coexistences for String Quintet, 1993; 10 Movements for piano, 1992; New Nocturnes for piano, 1993–94; Dedications for piano, 1997; Verso fine...? for violin solo, 1998; Compositions for flute and piano, for solo guitar, and so on. *Honours:* J L Bella Prize, 1981; Certificate of Merit, 1993; Man of the Year, 1993; Great Minds of the 21st Century, USA, 2002; Cetificate of Award, Switzerland, 2002; Living Legends, Cambridge, 2003; Performances throughout Europe and overseas; Best analyses of his works: Tempo, No. 179 (Boosey and Hawkes); Dusan Martincek: An Introduction to His Music (David Babcock); Zuzana Martina Eova in the Slovak Music, 2002; Complete works kept in the Dr Paul Sacher Foundation in Basel, Switzerland. *Address:* Lipskeho 11, 84101 Bratislava, Slovakia.

MARTINEAU, Malcolm; Pianist; b. 3 Feb. 1960, Edinburgh, Scotland. *Education:* Studied at St Catharine's College, Cambridge, and at the Royal Academy of Music with Kendall Taylor and Geoffrey Parsons; Further study with Joyce Rathbone. *Career:* Has presented own series (complete songs of Debussy and Poulenc), St John's Smith Square; Britten series broadcast Wolf, Wigmore Hall; complete lieder of Hugo Wolf, Edinburgh Festival; has appeared throughout Europe, N America and Australila and at festivals in Aix-en-Provence, Vienna, Edinburgh, Schubertiade, Munich, Salzburg. *Recordings:* Schubert, Schumann and English song recitals with Bryn Terfel; Schubert and Strauss recitals with Simon Keenlyside; recital records with Angela Gheorghiu and Barbara Bonney; Magdalena Kozena; Della Jones; the complete Fauré songs with Sarah Walker and Tom Krause; the complete Britten Folk Songs; the complete Beethoven Folk Songs; accompaniments for Dame Janet Baker, Sarah Walker, Frederica von Stade, Anne Sofie von Otter, Thomas Hampson, Olaf Bär, Karita Mattila, Solveig Kringelborn, Michael Schade, Ian Bostridge, Amanda Roocroft, Joan Rodgers, Sir Thaomas Allen, Ann Murray, Susan Graham, Dame Felicity Lott, Christopher Maltman and Jonathan Lemalu. *Honours:* Walter Gruener International Lieder Competition, 1984. *Current Management:* Askonas Holt Ltd, Lonsdale Chambers, 27 Chancery Lane, London, WC2A 1PF, England. *Telephone:* (20) 7400-1700. *Fax:* (20) 7400-1799. *E-mail:* info@askonasholt.co.uk. *Website:* www.askonasholt.co.uk.

MARTINEZ, Odaline de la; Composer, Conductor and Pianist; b. 31 Oct. 1949, Matanzas, Cuba. *Education:* BFA, Tulane University, 1968–72; Royal Academy of Music, 1972–76; GRSM (Composition and Piano); MMus (Composition), University of Surrey, 1975–77; Postgraduate Research (Computer Music), 1977–80. *Career:* Compositions broadcast by BBC, Radio Istanbul, Radio Cork, Radio Belgrade, KPFA San Francisco; Conductor of Lontano and London Chamber Symphony; Many performances of Contemporary Music; Conducted the premiere of Berthold Goldschmidt's Beatrix Cenci, 1988; Directed series of Latin American concerts on South Bank, 1989; Music Director, Cardiff Festival, 1994, conductor of Dame Ethel Smyth's Opera, The Wreckers, Proms BBC in 1994 (revival after over 50 years); Conducted Lontano at St John's London, 1997; mem, SPNM; Women in Music. *Compositions include:* After Sylvia (Song cycle); Phasing for Chamber Orchestra; A Moment's Madness for Flute and Piano; Sister Aimee, Opera, 1984; Canciones, 1984; 2 American Madrigals for Mixed Chorus; String Quartet, 1985; Cantos de Amor, 1987. *Recordings:* British Women Composers, Vol. I and II, Villa Lobos Chamber and Choral Music, Boulez sans Boulez all on Lorelt label; 2 CDs major revivals of Ethel Smyth: Conifer CD of The Wreckers; Chandos CD of Orchestral Serenade and Double Concertos. *Publications:* Mendelssohn's Sister. *Honours:* First Woman to conduct BBC Prom Concerts at the Royal Albert Hall; Danforth Fellowship; Marshall Scholar; Watson Fellow; National Endowments for the Arts, USA; Joyce Dixie Prize; Villa-Lobos Medal, 1987; Manson Scholarship; Outstanding Alumna Tulane University, FRAM. *Current Management:* Denise Kantor Management. *Address:* c/o Lontano, Toynbee Studios, 28 Commercial Street, London E1 6LS, England.

MARTINEZ, Ruben; Singer (Tenor); b. 1962, Argentina. *Career:* Many opera engagements in South America and Europe, notably in Donizetti's L'Elisir d'amore and Gounod's Roméo et Juliette; also sings chansons by Fauré; Contestant at the 1995 Cardiff Singer of the World Competition; Mozart's Lucio Silla with Opera for Europe in London and elsewhere, 1998. *Address:* Street 27 No. 1221 La Plata (CP 1900), Buenos Aires, Argentina.

MARTINEZ-IZQUIERDO, Ernest; Spanish conductor and composer; b. 11 June 1962, Barcelona. *Education:* diplomas in composition and orchestral conducting. *Career:* debut, Barcelona 1985 with his Ensemble 'Barcelona 216'; Principal Conductor of the Ensemble Barcelona 216; Assistant Conductor of JONDE (Youth Spanish Orchestra), 1985–87; Assistant Conductor of ONE (Spanish National Orchestra), 1988; Assistant Conductor of the Ensemble Intercontemporain, 1988–90; Concerts with foreign orchestras like Philharmonic Orchestra of Minsk, Ensemble Contemporain de Montreal, Orchestra of The Teatro Comunale di Bolonia or Avanti Orchestra of Helsinki; Concerts with the mainly Spanish orchestras as OBC (Symphonic Orchestra of Barcelona), ONE (Spanish National Orchestra), Cadaqués Orchestra, Symphonic Orchestra of Tenerife, Symphonic Orchestra of Granada; As Guest Conductor or with his own Ensemble, he has conducted in the principal European cities as Paris, Prague, Bordeaux, Amsterdam, Palermo, Luxembourg, Madrid, Rome and in some of the most important festivals, Festival Internacional de Alicante, Festival de Torroella de Montgri, Zagreb's Biennal, Festival Castell de Perelada, Festival de Cadaqués, Holland Festival, Helsinki's Biennal, Barcelona's Festival de Musica del Segle XX, Festival Aujourd'hui Musiques of Perpignan; mem, The Associacio Catalena de Compositors. *Compositions:* Música para orquesta de cuerdas, 1986; Música para 10 vcl y orquesta, 1991; Música per a un festival, 1992; Norte-Sur, 1993; Alternanqa, 1995; Fanfare for chamber ensemble, 1995. *Recordings include:* Album de Colien, Spanish and Portuguese Contemporary Piano Music, 1995; Music for the film Metropolis by Martin Matalon, 1995; Composers of Cercle Manuel de Falla, 1995; Xavier Benguerel: 7 Fables de La Fontaine, 1995. *Address:* Muntaner 511 #6, 08022 Barcelona, Spain.

MARTINIS, Carla; Singer (soprano); b. 1921, Danculovice, Yugoslavia. *Education:* Zagreb Conservatory. *Career:* sang first in Zagreb and Prague; New York City Opera, 1950–53, debut as Turandot; Vienna Staatsoper 1951–, debut as Aida, conducted by Karajan; Salzburg Festival, 1951, as Desdemona, conducted by Furtwängler; Paris Opéra, 1951, as Amelia in Un Ballo in Maschera; La Scala Milan, Aix-en-Provence, Naples and Florence, 1952; San Francisco Opera, 1954; sang La Gioconda at Trieste, 1956. *Recordings:* Otello from Salzburg; Donna Anna in Don Giovanni; La Forza del Destino; Tosca.

MARTINO, Donald (James); Composer, Clarinettist, Educator and Publisher; b. 16 May 1931, Plainfield, New Jersey, USA. *Education:* BM, Syracuse University, 1952; MFA, Princeton University, 1954; MA, Harvard University (honorary) 1983; Fulbright Grant for study with Luigi Dallapiciola, Florence, Italy, 1954–55, 1955–56. *Career:* Associate Professor of Music, Yale University, 1958–69; Chairman of Composition, New England Conservatory, 1969–79; Irving Fine Professor, Brandeis University, 1979–82; Walter Bigelow Rosen Professor, Harvard University, 1983–93, Professor Emeritus, 1993–; mem, American Academy of Arts and Letters; American Academy of Arts and Sciences; Founder, American Society of Composers; Broadcast Music Inc. *Compositions include:* Published: Contemplations for orchestra, 1956; Concerto for wind quintet, 1964; Concerto for piano and orchestra, 1965; Notturno, flute, clarinet, violin, violoncello, percussion, piano, 1973; Paradiso Choruses, chorus, soloists, orchestra, tape, 1974; Ritorno for orchestra, 1975; Triple Concerto for clarinet, bass clarinet and contrabass clarinet with chamber ensemble, 1977; Fantasies and Inpromptus, piano solo, 1981; Divertissements for youth orchestra,

1981; String Quartet, 1983; The White Island, chorus, chamber orchestra, 1985; Concerto for alto saxophone and chamber orchestra, 1987; From the Other Side, flute, violoncello, percussion, piano, 1988; Twelve Preludes for piano, 1991; Three Sad Songs, viola and piano, 1993; Concerto for violin and orchestra, 1996; Octet, 1998; Serenata Concertante, 1999. *Recordings include:* Donald Martino: Piano Music; Donald Martino: Chamber Music; Donald Martino: Piano and Chamber Music; Donald Martino: A Jazz Set; Paradiso Choruses; Saxophone Concerto. *Publications:* Editor: 178 Chorale Harmonizations for J. S. Bach: A Comparative Edition for Study, 1984. *Contributions:* The Source Set and its Aggregate Formations, Journal of Music Theory, 1961; Notation in General Articulation in Particular, 1966; An Interview by James Boros, 1991; Perspectives of New Music. *Honours:* Pulitzer Prize, 1974; Kennedy Center-Friedheim Award, 1985; Mark M Horblit Award, Boston Symphony, 1987. *Current Management:* Dantalian Inc, USA. *Address:* 11 Pembroke Street, Newton, MA 02158, USA.

MARTINOTY, Jean-Louis; Stage Director; b. 20 Jan. 1946, Etampes, France. *Career:* Radio producer for ORTF, then critic for L'Humanité; Assistant to Jean-Pierre Ponnelle, notably in works by Mozart and Monteverdi at Zürich; Baroque repertoire includes productions for the Karlsuhe Handel Festival; Production of Ariadne auf Naxos seen at the Paris Opéra 1983, Covent Garden 1985; Produced 3 films about Renaissance and Opera, 1985; General Administrator of the Paris Opéra at the Palais Garnier 1986–89; Productions in season 1994–96 Wagner's Ring at Karlsruhe; Gussmann Opera Seria at Berlin Staatsoper; Cesti's Argia at the Innsbruck Festival. *Honours:* Best Production of the Year, 1980, 1981, 1982, 1983. *Address:* 51310 Joiselle, France.

MARTINOVIC, Boris; singer (bass-baritone); b. 1953, Croatia. *Education:* Juilliard School, New York. *Career:* debut, Avery Fisher Hall New York, in Refice's Cecilia; Charleston 1977, in The Queen of Spades; European appearances at Trieste, Rome and Naples; Teatro Regio Parma in Lucia di Lammermoor, Semiramide, Gerusalemme by Verdi and Roméo et Juliette; Pesaro Festival as Rossini's Mosè, Colline at the Paris Opéra, Vienna and Zürich as Escamillo, at Zürich as Onegin and Pesaro 1991 as Orbazzano in Rossini's Tancredi; Bregenz Festival 1992, Escamillo; Sang in Donizetti's Adelia at Genoa, 1998. *Recordings include:* Prince Igor, Ivan Susanin by Glinka and Boris Godunov, as Rangoni; Crespel in Les Contes d'Hoffmann. *Current Management:* Robert Gilder & Co., Enterprise House, 59–65 Upper Ground, London, SE1 9PQ, England. *Telephone:* (20) 7928-9008. *Fax:* (20) 7928-9755. *E-mail:* rgilder@robert-gilder.com.

MARTINPELTO, Hillevi; Singer (Soprano); b. 9 Jan. 1958, Älvalden, Sweden. *Education:* Studied at the Stockholm Opera School. *Career:* Sang Pamina in Die Zauberflöte with the Folksopera in Stockholm and at the Edinburgh Festival; Norrlands Opera from 1987 in Ivar Hallström's Den Bergtagno, also on Swedish television and at the York Festival; Tatiana in Eugene Onegin and Marguerite; Royal Opera Stockholm debut 1987, as Madama Butterfly; Sang the title roles in Gluck's Iphigénie operas at the Drottningholm Festival, 1989–90; Théâtre de la Monnaie, Brussels, from 1990 as Fiordiligi and the Countess in Le nozze di Figaro; Season 1991–92 with Fiordiligi at the Hamburg Staatsoper, Wagner's Eva at Nice, Donna Anna at Aix-en-Provence; Season 1992–93 included: Don Giovanni, Aix-en-Provence Festival, France; Così fan tutte, Hamburg State Opera, Germany; Das Rheingold, Lyric Opera of Chicago, USA; Le nozze di Figaro, Toulouse Opera, France; Châtelet, Monteverdi and Wagner's Eva in Tokyo with Deutsche Oper Berlin; Further engagements include Verdi's Desdemona in Helsinki; Concert engagements with Dvořák's Requiem, Scottish National Orchestra, 1987; Residentie Orchestra of The Hague in Mozart; Belgian Radio Orchestra; Philharmonia of London in The Creation, conducted by Claus Peter Flor; Sang Donna Anna in Don Giovanni, at Glyndebourne, 1994–; Agathe in Der Freischütz for the Royal Danish Opera at Copenhagen, 1997; Further engagements include: Don Giovanni and Clemenza di Tito (Munich) and Idomeneo (Lausanne); Concert appearances with the National Orchestra of Wales, City of Birmingham Symphony Orchestra, the Gesellschaft der Musikfreunde in Vienna and the Vienna Symphony Orchestra amongst others; Alice Page in Falstaff at the 1998 Proms; London Proms 1999, as The Virgin in The Kingdom by Elgar and Schumann's Scenes from Faust; Elsa in Lohengrin at Gothenburg, 2000; Season 2000–01 as Elsa at Gothenburg, Alice Ford at the Paris Châtelet and Agathe for the Berlin Staatsoper; Recital at the 2001 Edinburgh Festival. *Recordings:* Elettra in Idomeneo, conducted by John Eliot Gardiner; Countess in Figaro with Gardiner; Così fan tutte under Simon Rattle; Alice and Oberon in Falstaff. *Address:* Artists Sekretariat Ulf Tornqvist, Sankt Eriksgatan 100, 2 tr S113 31 Stockholm, Sweden.

MARTINS, Maria de Lourdes; retd academic; b. 26 May 1926, Lisbon, Portugal. *Education:* National Conservatory of Music, Lisbon, Music High School, Munich, Germany, with H. Genzmer, Orff Institute of the Mozarteum, Salzburg. *Career:* piano concerts on nat. and German radio;

television performances in Portugal; debut opera, S Carlos Nat. Theatre, Lisbon 1986; Prof. of Music Education and Composition, Nat. Conservatory in Lisbon 1970–96; founder mem. Portuguese Soc. for Music Education (pres. 1972–77); co-chair. Commission for Music Education; lectures and seminars in Portugal, Argentina, USA, Canada, Japan, Belgium, Germany, Switzerland, Poland and Spain; mem. ISME (mem. of bd), APEM. *Compositions include:* Encoberto de F Pessoa, 1965; O Litoral de A Negreiros, 1971–; Rondó for Wind Orchestra, 1978; Portuguese Christmas Songs for Wind Orchestra, 1978; Portuguese Dances, 1978; Sonatinas 1 and 2 for Piano; Catch, 1981; Ritmite, 1983; Musica de Piano Para Crianças Ed Valentim de Carvalho; Opera: Tres Máscaras, 1983; Simetria for Clarinet Solo, 1984; 4 Poemas de F Pessoa, 1984; Moments of Peace by J Gracen Brown, 1989; II String Quartet, 1989; Concerto de piano, 1990; Divertiment on Mozart Themes, 1991; Kinder Opera 'Donzela Guerreira', 1995; Suite para Quinteto, 1999; Pianoforte and percussion (commissioned by the International Society for Polyaesthetic Education to be played at their symposium in Austria), 1999. *Recordings:* Wind Quartet; 12 Choral Portuguese Songs; Piano Works, pianist Erzsebet Tusa; Historia de Natal. *Publications:* Pizzicato. *Honours:* Composition Prizes: National Prize Carlos Seixas, 1959; JMP, 1960; C Gulbenkian Foundation, 1965, 1971. *Address:* R. Trindade Coelho 108, 2775-293 Parede, Portugal.

MARTINSEN, Tom; Singer (Tenor); b. 1957, Norway. *Education:* Studied in Stockholm with Nicolai Gedda. *Career:* Sang in lyric repertory at Royal Opera, Stockholm, Koblenz Opera, 1985–88; Gelsenkirchen from 1988; Sang Tamino at Dresden, 1992 followed by Hoffmann, 1993; Guest appearances throughout Germany as Mozart's Ferrando; Rossini's Lindoro and Almaviva; Nemorino and Fenton in Falstaff; Modern repertory includes Werle's Drommen om Thérèse; The Two Fiddlers by Maxwell Davies and Norgaard's Siddharta; Sang Hoffmann at Kiel, 1999, Strauss's Narraboth at Dresden, 2001. *Address:* Staatsoper Dresden, Theaterplatz 2, 01067 Dresden, Germany.

MARTINUCCI, Nicola; Singer (tenor); b. 28 March 1941, Tarent, Italy. *Education:* studied with Sara Sforni in Milan. *Career:* debut, Teatro Nuovo Milan 1966, as Manrico; sang at La Scala and at the Teatro La Fenice, Venice; Deutsche Oper am Rhein Düsseldorf from 1973; Florence 1974 as Filippo in a revival of Spontini's Agnese di Hohenstaufen; Verona Arena 1982–86, as Radames, Calaf and Andrea Chénier; Covent Garden debut 1985, as Dick Johnson in La Fanciulla del West; appearances in Dublin, Tehran, Budapest and Salzburg; Rome Opera 1989, as Poliuto; sang Calaf in London 1990; Pollione at Catania, Manrico at Parma; Season 1992 as Enzo in La Gioconda at Rome and Calaf at the Festival of Caracalla; sang Andrea Chénier there 1996; Calaf at Turin 1998; Season 2000–01 as Calaf in Taiwan and Radames at the Macerata Festival. *Recordings:* Turandot, from Verona (video); Donizetti's Poliuto. *Address:* Stafford Law Associates, 6 Barham Close, Weybridge, Surrey KT13 9PR, England.

MARTLAND, Steve; Composer; b. 10 Oct. 1959, Liverpool, England. *Education:* Graduated from Liverpool University, 1981; Royal Conservatory, The Hague, Netherlands, with Louis Andriessen; Tanglewood USA with Gunther Schuller. *Career:* Works with students and musicians outside the classical tradition; Pieces for informal Dutch ensembles, the Jazz Orchestra Loose Tubes and the band Test Department multimedia project for BBC television; Joint premiere of Babi-Yar with the Royal Liverpool Philharmonic and the St Louis Symphony Orchestra; American Invention performed in the USA and Japan; Performances with the Steve Martland Band, including the 1994 South Bank Meltdown Festival (returned 1997). *Compositions:* Remembering Lennon for 7 players, 1981–85; Lotta Continua for orchestra 1981–84; Duo for trumpet and piano 1982; Canto a la Esperanza for soprano, electric guitar and chamber orchestra 1982; Kgakala for piano 1982; Babi Yar for orchestra 1983; Orc for horn and small orchestra 1984; American Invention for 13 players 1985; Shoulder to Shoulder for 13 players 1986; Dividing the Lines for brass, wind band 1986; Remix for jazz ensemble 1986; Big Mac I, II for 4–8 players 1987; Divisions for electronic tape 1986–87; Drill for 2 pianos 1987; Glad Day for voice and ensemble 1988; Albion for tape and film 1987–88; Terra Firma for 5 voices, with amplification and video 1989; Crossing the Border for Strings, 1991; The Perfect Act for ensemble and voice, 1991; Beat the Retreat, for eleven players, 1997; Kick, for eleven players (1995–96); Eternal Delight for eleven players, 1997; Terminal (1998) and Step by Step for 7/8 instruments; Fairest Isle for Counter-tenor and ensemble, 1999. *Honours:* 1981 Mendelssohn Scholarship; 1985 Government Composition Prize, Netherlands. *Address:* Schott and Co Ltd, 48 Great Marlborough Street, London W1V 2BN, England.

MARTON, Eva Heinrich; German opera singer (soprano); b. 18 June 1943, Budapest, Hungary; d. of Bela and Ilona (née Krammer) Heinrich; m. Zoltan Marton 1965; one s. one d. *Education:* Franz Liszt Acad. (Budapest) and with Gerald Mortier and Laszlo Halasz. *Career:* debut, Budapest State Opera, singing there 1968–72; has sung with various opera companies, including Frankfurt Opera 1972–77, Hamburg State

Opera 1977–80, Maggio Musicale Fiorentino (Italy), Vienna State Opera, La Scala (Milan, Italy), Rome Opera (Italy), Metropolitan Opera (New York), Lyric Opera (Chicago), Grand Opera (Houston) and San Francisco Opera (USA), Bayreuth and Salzburg Festivals, Teatro Liceo, Barcelona (Spain), Teatro Colón, Buenos Aires, (Argentina), Royal Opera House Covent Garden, London, (UK), Vienna State Opera, Washington Opera; roles include: Empress in Die Frau ohne Schatten, Salome, all three Brünnhildes in Ring Cycle, Elisabeth and Venus in Tannhäuser, Elsa and Ortrud in Lohengrin, Senta in Der fliegende Holländer, title roles of Turandot, Tosca, Manon Lescaut, Fedora, Gioconda, Aida, Amelia in Ballo in Maschera, Leonora in Il Trovatore, Lady Macbeth in Macbeth, Elisabetta in Don Carlo, Leonore in Fidelio, Maddalena in Andrea Chénier, Leonora in La Forza del Destino; mem. Hungarian Nat. Volleyball team. *Films include:* Turandot, Il Trovatore, Lohengrin, Tannhäuser, Elektra, La Gioconda, Tosca. *Recordings include:* Turandot, Andrea Chenier, Fedora, Bluebeard's Castle, Violanta, Tiefland, Mefistofele, Die Walküre, La Wally. *Honours:* Gold Star, Repub. of Hungary 1989, Bartók Award 1990. *Current Management:* Opéra et Concert, 1 rue Volney, 75002 Paris, France. *Telephone:* 1-42-96-18-18. *Fax:* 1-42-96-18-00. *E-mail:* agence@opera-concert.com. *Website:* www.copera-concert.com; www.evamarton.com.

MARTTINEN, Tauno; Composer; b. 27 Sept. 1912, Helsinki, Finland. *Education:* Studied Music, Viipuri, 1920s; Studied Music, Helsinki, 1930s. *Career:* Director, Hameenlinna Music Institute, 1950–75. *Compositions:* The Cloak, 1962–63; The Engagement, 1964; Burnt Orange, 1968; Maitre Patelin, 1969–72; Shaman's Drum, 1974–76; The Earl's Sister, 1977; The Pharoah's Letter, 1978–80; Song of the Great River, 1982–84; Seven Brothers, 1976–86; Mooses Ooppera, 1990; Ballets: A Portrait of Dorian Gray, 1969; Snow Queen, 1970; The Sun Out of the Moon, 1975–77; The Ugly Duckling, 1976, 1982–83; Orchestra: Symphony No. 1, 1958; Symphony No. 2, 1959; Symphony No. 3, 1960–62; Symphony No. 4, 1964; Symphony No. 7, 1977; Panu, God of Fire, 1966; Symphony No. 8, 1983; Symphony No. 9, 1986; The Maid of Pohjola, 1982; Solo Instrument Concerto for piano and orchestra, 1964; Concerto for flute and orchestra, 1972; Concerto for Clarinet and Orchestra, 1974; Concerto for two pianos and orchestra, 1981; Concerto for piano and orchestra No. 4 Op 241, 1984; Chamber Music: Delta, 1962; Alfa op 16, 1963; Visit to the Giant Sage Vipunen, 1969; String Quartet No. 2, 1971; Divertimento, 1977; Intermezzo, 1977–78; Le Commencement, 1979; Trio, 1982; Solo Instrument: Titisee for piano, 1965; Adagio for organ, 1967; Sonatina for piano; Nore dame, 1970; The Cupola, for organ, 1971; Sonata for piano, 1975; Impression for cello, 1978; Prophet for organ, 1984. *Honours:* Honorary Professor conferred by the State, 1972. *Address:* TEOSTO, Lauttasaarentie 1, 00200 Helsinki 20, Finland.

MARTURET, Eduardo; Conductor and Composer; b. 19 Sept. 1953, Caracas, Venezuela. *Education:* Music Degree, Anglia University; Further studies in Cambridge, Siena and Rome. *Career:* Debut: Caracas in 1978; Artistic Director, Sinfonietta Caracas, 1986; Music Director with Teatro Teresa Carreño, 1984–76, and Orq Sinfonica Venezuela, 1987–95; Has conducted major orchestras in Germany, Netherlands, USA, Scandinavia and Hungary; SPNM, London; American Symphony Orchestra League; Conductors' Guild, USA. *Compositions include:* Canto Llano; Music For Six And Sax; Tres Tiempos; Casa Bonita; Mantra for Orchestra, 1995. *Recordings:* Brahms Complete Symphonies, Overtures and Concertos; With Berliner Symphoniker, Mozart Symphonies and Complete Violin Concertos; Concertgebouw Chamber Orchestra. *Publications:* Casa Bonita: Catalogue of The Exhibition, 1988; Article, Perspectives of Mozart's Symphonic Music, 1991. *Honours:* Orden Diego De Losada, 1992; Best Conductor, 1992; Best Classical Record, 1992; Orden Andres Bello, 1992. *Current Management:* John Gingrich, New York, USA. *Address:* PO Box 2912, Caracas, Venezuela.

MARUZIN, Yuri; Singer (Tenor); b. 8 Dec. 1947, Perm, Russia. *Education:* Studied in Leningrad. *Career:* Debut: Maly Theatre, Leningrad, 1972; Appearances with the Kirov Opera Leningrad, St Petersburg from 1978 notably as Hermann in The Queen of Spades and Dimitri in Boris Godunov and touring to Covent Garden, 1987 as Lensky; Sang the Tsarevich in Rimsky's The Tale of Tsar Saltan at La Scala and Reggio Emilia, 1988; Galitsin in Khovanshchina at the Vienna Staatsoper, 1989; San Francisco Opera as Anatol in War and Peace, Andrei Khovansky in Khovanshchina at Edinburgh, 1991; Bayan in Ruslan and Lyudmila at San Francisco and Palermo, 1995; Other guest engagements at Turin, Nice, Madrid and Toronto; Other roles include Faust, Pinkerton, Rodolfo, Don Carlos, Don Alvaro, Alfredo and the Duke of Mantua; Sang Hermann at Glyndebourne, 1992, 1995; New Israeli Opera, 1997 in Lady Macbeth of the Mtsensk District; Season 2000–01 as Lensky at Miami and Grischa in Rimsky's Invisible City of Kitezh at St Petersburg. *Address:* Kirov Opera and Ballet Theatre, St Petersburg, Russia.

MARVIN, Frederick; Pianist and Musicologist; b. 11 June 1923, California, USA. *Education:* Curtis Institute of Music, Philadelphia; Southern California Conservatory, Los Angeles. *Career:* Debut: Carnegie Hall, 1948; Toured USA, 1949–54; Concerts in every major capital of Europe from 1954, solo recitals, and concert lectures; Masterclasses; Professor of Piano, 1968–, Professor Emeritus and Artist in Residence, 1990, Syracuse University; Season 2000–01: All Soler concert in Greenwich House of Music, New York; Winterthur, Switzerland, Gronau, Germany, Vienna, Austria, Syracuse, New York. *Recordings include:* George Antheil Piano Sonata No. 4; Liszt Album, Sonatas by Moscheles and L Berger; Schubert Album; Three albums of Sonatas by JL Dussek; Sonatas by Soler, 3 albums; 4 Villancicos by A Soler. *Publications:* 63 Sonatas by Soler; Four Villancicos and Salve, Lamentation, Soler; Edited 8 vols Sonatas, and Choral works, Padre Soler; 2 sonatas, J L Dussek; Liederabenende with Martha Mödl, Gebhardt Musikvertrieb, Stuttgart; 13 Sonatas and Fandango, Padre Antonio Soler, 2000. Contributions to music magazines; Article on Padre Antonio Soler, New Grove Dictionary of Music and Musicians, 2000. *Honours:* Carnegie Hall Award, Most Outstanding Debut in New York City, 1948; Schnabel Gold Medal, London, 1955; Orden del Mérito Civil (Commander), Spanish Government, 1969; Croix de Commandeur, Medille de Vermiel, Arts-Sciences, Lettres, France, 1974; Cervantes Medal by the Hispanic Soc. of America, 2000. *Address:* c/o Ernst Schuh, 246 Houston Avenue, Syracuse, NY 13224, USA. *Telephone:* (345)472–6066.

MARVIN, Roberta (Montemorra); Musicologist; b. 29 July 1953, Massachusetts, USA; m. Conrad A Marvin, 30 June 1973. *Education:* BM, Boston Conservatory of Music, 1975; MA, Tufts University, 1986; PhD, Brandeis University, 1992. *Career:* Lecturer, Tufts University, 1991–92; Visiting Assistant Professor, Boston University, 1992–93; Assistant Professor, University of Alabama, 1993–97; Associate Professor, University of Iowa, 1997–; mem, American Musicological Society; Royal Musical Association; Advisory Board, American Institute of Verdi Studies. *Publications:* Artistic Concerns and Practical Considerations in the Composition of I masnadieri, Studi Verdiani 7, 1992; A Verdi Autograph and the Problem of Authenticity, Studi Verdiani 9, 1993; Shakespeare and Primo Ottocento Opera: The Case of Rossini's Otello, The Opera and Shakespeare, 1994; Aspects of Tempo in Verdi's Early and Middle Period Italian Operas, Verdi's Middle Period: Source Studies, Analysis and Performance Practice (1849–59), 1997; Giuseppe Verdi's I Masnadieri, critical edition (editor); The Censorship of Verdi's Operas in Victorian London, Music and Letters, 2001; Verdi's Sinfonia in Re maggiore (Ed). *Contributions:* The New Grove Dictionary of Opera, 1992; and The New Grove Dictionary of Music and Musicians, revised edition; Music Quarterly, 2000. *Honours:* Premio Internazionale 'Giuseppe Verdi', 1991; Fulbright Research Fellowships, 1988, 1993; American Philosophical Society, 1992; NEH Summer Stipend, 1993. *Address:* University of Iowa, School of Music, Voxman Music Building, Iowa City, IA 52242, USA.

MARWOOD, Anthony; British violinist; b. 6 July 1965, London. *Education:* RAM Junior Dept, Guildhall School of Music and Drama. *Career:* Wigmore Hall debut 1987; leader, Raphael Ensemble 1989–98; Prom debut, London 1993; founder mem., Florestan Trio 1995–; première of Sally Beamish's violin concerto 1995, and subsequent premières of works by Judith Weir, Rudi van Dijk, Peteris Vasks and Thomas Adès, including Violin Concerto 2005; Prof. of Violin, Guildhall School of Music and Drama 1999–; appearances at Yellow Barn Festival, Vermont, USA July each year; regular appearances as soloist and dir, Acad. of St Martin in the Fields; collaboration with the South Asian dancer, Mayuri Boonham 1999–. *Recordings:* Schumann Trios (with Florestan Trio, Stanford Concerto), Schumann Sonatas (with Susan Tomes, Coleridge Taylor and Somervell Concertos), Peteris Vasks and Kurt Weill Concertos, Vivaldi's Four Seasons. *Honours:* first prize Shell-LSO competition 1982, Royal Philharmonic Soc. Award (with Florestan Trio). *Current Management:* Owen/White Management, Top Floor, 59 Lansdown Place, Hove, East Sussex BN3 1FL, England. *E-mail:* info@owenwhitemanagement.com (office). *Website:* www.anthonymarwood.com.

MÄRZENDORFER, Ernst; Conductor; b. 26 May 1921, Salzburg, Austria. *Education:* Salzburg Mozarteum with Clemens Krauss. *Career:* conducted opera in Salzburg from 1940; Graz Opera 1945–51; Prof., Salzburg Mozarteum 1951; conductor of the Mozarteum orchestra 1953–58, including tour of the USA 1956; has also conducted at the Teatro Colón, Buenos Aires, the Deutsche Oper, Berlin, the Vienna Staatsoper, Vienna Volksoper, Vienna Redoutensaal, concerts worldwide; recent performances include: Bartók violaconcert and Strauss Symphonia domestica in Nice, Dallpiccola and Cherubini Sinfonia in D at the Todi festival, Rosenkavalier in Vienna, Schweigsame Frau in Dresden, Bruckner's 5th in Nantes-Angers 1998; Johann Strauss Konzert, Schweigsame Frau and Rosenkavalier in Vienna, Schweigsame Frau in Dresden 2000; Ariadne auf Naxos in Vienna, Schumann

Violoncello Konzert and Strauss Sinfonia domestica in Angers-Nantes, and Wagner Siegfried-Idyll and Bruckner's 6th in Klagenfurt 2001; Symphonieorchester des Bayrischen Rundfunks, Strauss Macbeth in München 2002; Beethoven's 9th in Timisoara, Enescu's Oedipe at Bucharest Festival and R. Strauss 2nd Horn Concerto and Sinfonia domestica in Venice 2003. *Recordings:* Haydn Boccherini Violoncello concerts 1965, Haydn, Complete Symphonies 1970–73, Mozart Symphonies 1968–69, Schubert 5 Deutsche Tänze 1968, Mendelssohn Concerto for violin, piano and strings 1968, Rodrigo Concierto Serenada and Boieldieu Concerto 1969, Ginastera Piano Concerto Solo Hilde Somer 1963, J. Strauss Eine Nact in Venedig 1963, Meyerbeer Les Huguenots 1963, Beethoven Egmont Cavalieri Rappresentazione di anima e di corpo 1963, Schreker Der ferne Klang 1963, Pfitzner Das Christelflein 1963, Schmidt Fredigundis 1963, Josef Strauss Waltzes, Polkas, Dances 2000. *Address:* c/o Vienna Volksoper, Währingerstrasse 78, 1090 Vienna, Austria.

MASHAYEKHI, Nader; Composer and Conductor; b. 25 Oct. 1958, Tehran, Iran; m. Gisela Beer, 9 June 1990. *Education:* Studied at Hochschule für Musik, Vienna, Composition, Conducting, Electronic Music. *Career:* Debut: Konzerthaus Festival, Vienna, 1992; Opera performance, Malakut, Vienna Modern, 1997; Pentimento for full orchestra, in Festival Steierische Herbst, 1998; Mise en scène for ensemble in Berlin Philharmonie; mem, Ensemble Wien 2001. *Compositions:* Malakut, opera; Pentimentos, for orchestra; Sonne, for orchestra; Mahler: Das Lied von der Erde, adaptation for ensemble. *Recordings:* Duell for 2 flutes on Tomio and Mari Duo Album; Malakut; Music for flute in the 20th Century; Flute Music, with Gisela Mashayekhi-Beer. *Publications:* Articles in music journals. *Address:* Loudon str 6-8/3, 1140 Vienna, Austria.

MASHEK, Michal; Pianist; b. 17 Sept. 1980, Usti Nad Labem, Czechoslovakia. *Education:* Music Conservatory, Teplice; Music Conservatory in Prague. *Career:* Television documentary, Goldberg Variations; Radio Prague recordings, Goldberg Variations and Beethoven Sonata Op 81a. *Recordings:* Fantaisie and Toccata by B Martinů; Goldberg Variations by J. S. Bach. *Honours:* First Prize, International Piano Competition 'Virtuosi Per Musica di Pianoforte'; First Prize in International Beethoven piano competition. *Address:* Vodarska 128, 40331 Usti nad Labem, Czech Republic.

MASLANKA, David (Henry); Composer; b. 30 Aug. 1943, Maryland, USA. *Education:* Studied at the New England Conservatory 1959–61, Oberlin College, BMus, 1965, and Michigan State University, PhD, 1965–70. *Career:* Teacher, State University of New York at Geneseo, 1970–74; Sarah Lawrence College, 1974–80; Kingsborough College, City University of New York, 1981–90; Freelance Composer, 1990–. *Compositions include:* Orchestra: Symphony No. 1, 1970; Five songs for soprano, baritone and orchestra, 1976; In Lonely Fields, for percussion and orchestra, 1997; Percussion: Crown of Thorns, 1991; Montana Music: Three Dances for Percussion, 1993; Chamber: Duo for flute and piano, 1972; Quintet No. 1 for wind, 1984; Sonata for alto saxophone and piano, 1988; Sonata for horn and piano, 1996; Wind ensemble: Concerto for piano, winds and percussion, 1976; A Child's Garden of Dreams, 1981; Symphony No. 2, 1987; In Memorium, 1989; Symphony No. 3, 1991; Symphony No. 4, 1993; Mass, 1995; Sea Dreams: Concerto for Two Horns and Wind Orchestra, 1997; Vocal: Anne Sexton Songs for soprano and piano, 1975; The Hungry Heart, for chorus, 1996; Black Dog Songs, for tenor and piano, 1996. *Recordings:* David Maslanka Wind Quintets; Wind Music of David Maslanka; Tears; Mass; Percussion Music of David Maslanka; When Angels Speak; Prevailing Winds. *Honours:* MacDowell Colony Fellowships; Grants from National Endowment for the Arts, Martha Baird Rockefeller, ASCAP, National Symphony Orchestra. *Address:* 2625 Strand Avenue, Missoula, Montana 59804, USA.

MASON, Andrew, BMus; British clarinettist; b. 30 Sept. 1977, Kent, England. *Education:* Royal Coll. of Music (Foundation Scholar), 2000; studied with Colin Bradbury, Janet Hilton, Robert Hill, Michael Harris. *Career:* solo performances for Park Lane Group at Purcell Room and Wigmore Hall; solo broadcasts for BBC Radio 3; mem. of Aurora Ensemble, 1997–; performances St David's Hall, Cardiff, Bridgewater Hall, Manchester, Purcell Room (Park Lane Group), St Martin in the Fields, Cheltenham and Chelmsford Festivals; broadcasts and performances for BBC Radio 3; 'Sounds Exciting' education project, 2000–; performs for Live Music Now! with London Clarinet Quartet and the Aurora Ensemble; freelance orchestral musician. *Honours:* Prizewinner with Aurora Ensemble, Music d'Ensemble, Paris Conservatoire, 2001; Thurston Clarinet Prize, Royal Coll. of Music; Roger Fallows Memorial Prize, Royal Coll. of Music. *Address:* 40 Westgate Road, Faversham, Kent ME13 8HF, England. *E-mail:* andrewmason@btinternet.com. *Website:* www.auroraensemble.com.

MASON, Anne; singer (mezzo-soprano); b. 1954, Lincolnshire, England. *Education:* Royal Academy of Music with Marjorie Thomas, National

Opera Studio. *Career:* Welsh National Opera Chorus, 1977–79; Opera North from 1982 as Fenena in Nabucco, and in Madama Butterfly; English National Opera 1983, as a Valkyrie in a new production of Die Walküre; Innsbruch Early Music Festival 1983, in Cesti's Il Tito, conducted by Alan Curtis; Kent Opera and Scottish Opera 1984, in new productions of King Priam by Tippett and Edward Harper's Hedda Gabler; Covent Garden appearances in Carmen, as Mercedes; Otello, Emilia; Das Rheingold, Madama Butterfly, Die Walküre, La Clemenza di Tito, Cenerentola, Rosenkavalier, Traviata and Götterdämmerung; Glyndebourne Tour 1987, as Dorabella in Così fan tutte; Recent engagements as Annius in La Clemenza di Tito at Aix, Casoi fan tutte with Welsh National Opera and as Marcellina in Le nozze di Figaro in Madrid; Season 1992 as Donna Clara in the stage premiere of Gerhard's The Duenna, at Madrid, as Henrietta Maria in I Puritani at Covent Garden and Cornelia in Julius Caesar for Scottish Opera; Second Maid in Elektra at the First Night at the 1993 London Proms; Sang Gertrude in Hansel and Gretel for Scottish Opera, 1996; Minsk Woman in the premiere of Jonathan Dove's Flight, Glyndebourne, 1998; Season 2000–01 as Fricka in Das Rheingold at Edinburgh, Verdi's Fenena for ENO and Mozart's Marcellina for WNO; Concerts in the United Kingdom, Germany, France, Austria and Belgium, notably in The Dream of Gerontius and Verdi's Requiem. *Recordings:* Video of HMS Pinafore; Helen in King Priam; Second Bridesmaid in Le nozze di Figaro, conducted by Solti; Marcellina, Figaro, with Haitink; Emilia di Liverpool, Opera Rara. *Honours:* Gerhardt Lieder Prize, the Recital Diploma and the Countess of Munster Award, at the Royal Academy of Music; Finalist in the 1983 Benson and Hedges Gold Award; ARAM of Royal Academy of Music.

MASON, Barry; British lutenist, classical guitarist and music director; b. 6 Sept. 1947, Cottingham, Yorkshire, England; m. Glenda Simpson 1983. *Education:* Hull College of Technology, Royal Academy of Music with Anthony Rooley and David Munrow, Royal College of Music with Dian Poulton. *Career:* debut, Purcell Room, 1973; Director, Camerata of London, 1974; Director, 1st Early Music Centre Festival, London, 1977; Director, Progress Instruments Tours, Japan, Europe and USA, 1978; The Wicked Lady film, BBC Shakespeare Films: Director, The Guitarist's Companion, 1986; mem, Council Member, Early Music Centre. *Recordings:* Popular Music From The Time of Elizabeth I; The Muses Garden of Delights; Music For Kings and Courtiers'; The Queens Men; Thomas Companion; Elizabethan Ayres and Duets. *Publications:* contrib. to Guitar International; Early Music News; Early Music Magazine; Music in Education. *Honours:* Peter Latham Award for Musicology, Royal Academy of Music, 1971; 1996 Britten Award for Composition. *Current Management:* Francesca McManus, 71 Priory Road, Kew Gardens, Richmond, Surrey TW9 3PH, England.

MASON, Benedict; Composer; b. 21 June 1955, Budleigh, Salterton, England. *Education:* King's College, Cambridge; Study with Peter Maxwell Davies, and with Henri Pousseur in Liège. *Compositions include:* Hinterstoisser Traverse, for 12 players, 1986; Lighthouses of England and Wales, for orchestra, 1987; Oil and Petrol Marks on a Wet Road are Sometimes Held to be Spots where a Rainbow Stood, for 16 voices, 1987; Concerto for the Viola Section, 1990; Self-Referential songs and Realistic Virelais for soprano and 16 players, 1990; Six Rilke songs, 10991; Animals and the origins of Dance, for 21 players, 1992; Music for Concert Halls, Nos 1–10, 1993–97; 2 string quartets, 1987, 1993; Schumann Auftrag: Live Hörspiel ohne Worte, 1994, Opera, Playing Away, 1994; Szene, for female voices, orchestra and sampler, 1998. *Honours:* Winner, Benjamin Britten Composers Competition, 1998; Siemens Stiftungspreis, 1992. Address c/o 7 Gerard Rd, Harrow, Middx, HAI 2 ND, England.

MASON, Marilyn; Organist; b. 29 June 1925, Oklahoma, USA. *Education:* Studied in OK State University, at the University of Michigan, Union Theological Seminary NY, and with Nadia Boulanger, Maurice Duruflé and Arnold Schoenberg. *Career:* Teacher at the University of Michigan, 1947, Chairman of organ department, 1962, Professor 1965; Recital tours of North America, Europe, Australia, Africa and South America; Concerts with the Detroit and Philadelphia Orchestras; 60 Commissions for such composers as Krenek, Cowell, Albright, Ulysses Kay, Sowerby and Ross Lee Finney. *Recordings:* Albums of music by Sessions, Satie, Schoenberg and Virgil Thomson; Recording the music of Pachelbel for the Musical Heritage Society. *Address:* The University of Michigan, School of Music, Ann Arbor, MI 48109, USA.

MASQUELIN, Martine; Singer (Soprano); b. 1957, Paris, France. *Education:* Studied at the Paris Conservatoire. *Career:* Debut: Montpellier, 1982 as Lakmé; Düsseldorf, 1983, as Strauss's Sophie and Rossini's Rosina; Liège, 1988–89 as Julietta and Edvige in Offenbach's Robinson Crusoe; Appearances throughout France as Massenet's Thais and Violetta; Saint Care Festival; Concerts in Paris and elsewhere. *Recordings:* Monteverdi's Poppea; Grétry's Zémire et Azor. *Address:* c/o Opéra Royale de Wallome, 1 Rue des Dominicains, 4000 Liège, Belgium.

MASSARD, Robert; Singer (Baritone); b. 15 Aug. 1925, Pau, France. *Education:* Conservatories of Pau and Bayonne. *Career:* Sang the High Priest in Samson et Dalila at the Paris Opéra, 1952; Thoas in Iphigénie en Tauride at Aix, 1952; Sang Ashton in Lucia di Lammermoor at the Paris Opéra 1957; Glyndebourne 1958, in Alceste; Orestes in Iphigénie en Tauride with the Covent Garden Company at Edinburgh, 1961; Sang Fieramosca in Benvenuto Cellini with the Royal Opera in London; Bolshoi Theatre Moscow 1962, as Rigoletto; La Scala Milan 1967, as Valentin in Faust; Paris 1974, as Sancho Panza in Massenet's Don Quichotte; Other roles include Nero in L'Incoronazione di Poppea, the Count in Capriccio, Milhaud's Orpheus, Escamillo and Ravel's Ramiro. *Recordings:* Iphigénie en Tauride; Mireille; Thais; Rigoletto; Benvenuto Cellini; Raimbaud in Le Comte Ory, Chant du Monde. *Address:* c/o Philips, Polygram Classics, PO Box 1420, 1 Sussex Place, Hammersmith, London W6 9XS, England.

MASSET, Francoise; Singer (Soprano); b. 1970, France. *Education:* Douai Conservatoire; Opera Studio of the Baroque Music Centre, Versailles. *Career:* Appearances throughout France in Chabrier's Une Education manquée, Purcell's Dido and Aeneas and Mozart's Bastien und Bastienne; Chanteuse and Comedienne. *Recordings:* Title role, La Diane de Fontainebleau by Desmarets; Lully's Acis et Galatée; Rameau's Dardanus; Melisse in Gluck's Armide. *Address:* c/o DG Archiv Recordings, 22 St Peter's Square, London W6 9NW, England.

MASSEY, Andrew (John); American (b. British) Conductor; b. 1 May 1946, Nottingham, England; m. Sabra A Todd, 29 May 1982, one s., one d. d. *Education:* BA, Merton College, Oxford University, 1968; MA, Analysis Contemporary Composition techniques, 1969; Dartington Summer School with Hans Keller, Witold Lutoslawski, Luciano Berio. *Career:* Debut: Cleveland, 1978; Assistant conductor, Cleveland Orchestra, USA, 1978–80; Associate Conductor, New Orleans Symphony Orchestra, 1980–86, San Francisco Symphony Orchestra, 1986–; Music director, Rhode Island Philharmonic, 1986–1991; Art adviser, prime guest conductor, Fresno Philharmonic, 1986–; Music Director, 1987–1992; Music Director, Toledo Symphony, Ohio, 1990–2002; Guest appearances with National Symphony, Pittsbsurgh, Vancounver Symphony, Milwaukee Symphony, San Diego Symphony and others; mem. American Federation of Musicians. *Current Management:* John Gingrich Management, PO Box 1515, NYC, NY 10023, USA.

MASSEY, Roy (Cyril); Organist and Choral Conductor; b. 9 May 1934, England; m. Ruth Carol Craddock Grove, 1975. *Education:* BMus, University of Birmingham; Private Study with David Willcocks, FRCO (chm), ADCM, ARCM. *Career:* Organist: St Alban's, Conybere Street, Birmingham, 1953–60; St Augustine's, Edgbaston, 1960–65; Croydon Parish Church, 1965–68; Conductor, Croydon Bach Society, 1966–68; Special Commissioner, Royal School of Church Music, 1964–; Organist to the City of Birmingham Choir, 1954–; Organist, Master of Choristers, Birmingham Cathedral, 1968–74; Director of Music, King Edward's School, Birmingham, 1968–74; Conductor, Hereford Choral Society, 1974–2001; Organist, Master of Choristers, Hereford Cathedral, 1974–2001; Conductor-in-Chief, alternate years Associate Conductor, Three Choirs Festival, 1975–2001; Adviser on Organs to Dioceses of Birmingham and Hereford, 1974–; Led the premieres of Geofrey Burgon's Requiem, Veni Sancte Spiritus by William Mathias, and Te Deum by Paul Patterson; mem, Royal Society of Musicians, 1991. *Honours:* FRSCM 1971, D.Mus (Cantuar) 1991, for distinguished services to Church Music in recognition of work as a Cathedral Organist, as a Conductor of the Three Choirs Festival, and for work and influence in other musical spheres; M.B.E., 1997; Honorary Fellowship of the Guild of Church Musicians, for services to Cathedral Music, 2000. *Address:* 2 King John's Court, Tewkesbury, Gloucestershire, GL20 6EG, England.

MASSIS, Annick; Singer (Soprano); b. 1960, France. *Education:* Studied at the Francis Poulenc Conservatoire, Paris. *Career:* Debut: Toulouse, 1991; Engagements include Ophélie in Hamlet and Philéne in Mignon by Thomas at Compiègne; Rosina, Micaela and Anna in The Merry Wives of Windsor at the Opéra-Comique, Paris; Carolina in Il Matrimonio Segreto at Nantes and Aricie (Hippolyte et Aricie by Rameau) at the Paris Opéra Garnier and the Brooklyn Academy of Music; Lucia di Lammermoor at Rouen and as Countess Adèle in Le Comte Ory at the 1997 Glyndebourne Festival; Season 1997–98 as Gluck's Eurydice and Marie in La Fille du Régiment at Geneva; Bizet's Leila at Toulouse and Countess Adèle at Florence and Montpellier; Season 1998 as Ophelia in Hamlet at Washington and Lucia di Lammermoor at the New York Met; Ophelia's Mad Scene from Hamlet by Thomas at the 1999 London Prom concerts; Season 2000–01 as Lucia di Lammermoor at Barcelona, Amina in Madrid and Philine in Mignon at Toulouse; Title role in first modern performance of Meyerbeer's Margherita d'Anjou (concert), Festival Hall 2002; Lucia di Lammermoor at the Met, 2002; Engaged as the Queen of Shemakha in The Golden Cockerel, San Francisco, 2003;. *Address:* c/o Grand Théâtre de Genève, 11 Boulevard du Théâtre, 1211 Geneva 11, Switzerland.

MASSIS, René; Singer (Baritone); b. 1946, Lyon, France. *Education:* Studied in Lyon and Milan. *Career:* Debut: Marseille 1976, as Silvio in Pagliacci; Sang in L'Heure Espagnole at La Scala (1978) and has appeared throughout France and Italy; Lucca 1985 in Dejanice by Catalani, Paris Opéra 1988, as Valentin in Faust; Paris Opéra-Comique, 1990, in Auber's Manon Lescaut and at Nice Opéra 1990–91, in Wozzeck and as Guglielmo; Other roles include Rossini's Figaro (Glyndebourne Touring Opera, 1989), Mozart's Count, Belcore, Verdi's Ford and Posa, Fieramosca in Benvenuto Cellini, Eugene Onegin and the Marquis in Massenet's Grisélidis; Sang the title role in the premiere of Goya by Prodromidès, Montpellier, 1996; Season 1999–2000 as Tonio in Pagliacci at Nice, Albert in Werther at Lille and Donizetti's Sulpice for Opéra du Rhin, Strasbourg. *Recordings include:* Chausson's Le Roi Arthus (Erato) Iphigénie en Aulide and La Juive (Philips). *Address:* Théâtre de L'Opéra de Nice, 1a 6 Rue St François de Paule, 06300 Nice, France.

MASSON, Askell; Composer and Musician; b. 21 Nov. 1953, Reykjavík, Iceland. *Education:* Reykjavík Children's School of Music, 1961–63; Reykjavík College of Music, 1968–69; Private Studies, London, England, with Patrick Savill, 1975–77; Percussion with James Blades, 1975–76. *Career:* Debut: Icelandic Television playing own music, 1969; Commenced composing 1967; Composer, instrumentalist, National Theatre of Iceland, 1973–75; Producer, Icelandic State Radio, 1978–83; General Secretary, Icelandic League of Composers, 1983–85; Chairman, STEF, Iceland Performing Right Society, 1989–99; Working solely on composition. *Compositions include:* Opera: The Ice Palace, 1995; Sinfonia Trilogia, 1992; Piano Concerto, 1985; Concert Piece for snare drum and orchestra, 1982; Sonata for violin and piano, 1993; Woodwind Quintet, 1991; Trio for piano trio, 1995; Meditation, organ, 1992; Sindur (Sparks), percussion quartet, 1989; Okto November, strings, 1982; Run, orchestra, 1994; chamber Symphony, 1997; Boreas, for tuba, 1999. *Recordings:* Marimba Concerto; Clarinet Concerto; Trio; Sonata; Partita; Hrim; Snow; Helfro and others. *Current Management:* Editions BIM. Switzerland. *Address:* PO Box 821, 121 Reykjavík, Iceland. *E-mail:* askellmasson@hotmail.com. *Website:* www.editions-bim.com.

MASSON, Diego; Conductor; b. 21 June 1935, Tossa, Spain. *Education:* Paris Conservatoire, 1953–59; Study with Leibowitz, Maderna and Boulez. *Career:* Worked as percussionist in Paris with the ensemble Domaine Musicale; Founded Musique Vivante, 1966; Conducted premieres of Stockhausen's Stop and Setz die Segel zur Sonne; Early performances of works by Boulez including Domaines and... explosante fixe... and Berio; Musical Director of Marseilles Opéra and Ballet-Theatre Contemporian, Angers; Guest engagements as orchestral conductor in France, Europe, Australia and New Zealand; Conducted La Bohème for Opera North, 1989, premiere of Caritas by Robert Saxton, 1991; Premiere of Il giudizio Universidale by Claudio Ambrosini at Citti dilastelle, 1996; Conducted Turnage's Greek at the Queen Elizabeth Hall, London, 1998; Premiere of Sally Beamish's Monster, Scottish Opera at Glasgow, 2002. *Recordings:* Boulez, Domaine; Globokar, Fluide and Ausstrahlungen; John Woolrich; Stockhausen Aus den sieben tagen, and Liaison; Keuris Alto saxophone concerto. *Current Management:* Ingpen & Williams Ltd, 7 St George's Court, 131 Putney Bridge Road, London, SW15 2PA, England.

MASTERS, Rachel; Harpist; b. 9 Sept. 1958, Purley, Surrey, England. *Education:* Junior Student, Guildhall School of Music and Drama, 1971–75; National Youth Orchestra, 1972–76; Scholar, Royal College of Music, 1976–80; ARCM, Honours. *Career:* Debut: Wigmore Hall, 22 June 1982; Joint Winner, SE Arts Young Concert Artists Award, 1979; Joint 2nd Prize, Mobil Oil Harp Competition, 1980; Incorporated Society of Musicians Young Concert Artist, 1981; Principal harp in London Philharmonic Orchestra, since 1989; Professor at Royal College of Music. *Recordings:* Mozart Flute and Harp Concerto, with Phillipa Davies, City of London Sinfonia and Richard Hickox; Chandos: Harp pieces by Debussy, Ravel, Glière, Ginastera and Alwyn; Britten: Ceremony of Carols with King's College, Cambridge. *Honours:* Jack Morrison, Elisabeth Coates, Harp Prizes, Royal College of Music. *Address:* 31 Westfield Road, Surbiton, Surrey KT 6 4EL, England.

MASTERS, Robert; Violinist; b. 16 March 1917, Ilford, Essex, England. *Education:* Royal Academy of Music, London. *Career:* Leader, Robert Masters Piano Quartet, 1940–63; Professor of Violin, Royal Academy of Music, London, 1947–64; Leader, Bath Festival Orchestra and Menuhin Festival Orchestra, 1960–75; Leader, London Mozart Players, 1961–78; Director of Music, Yehudi Menuhin School, England, 1968–80; Co-Director, Menuhin Music Academy, Gstaad, Switzerland, 1980–84; Guest Professor, Taiwan Universities, 1980–; Beijing and Shanghai Conservatories of Music, Banff Arts Centre; Artistic Director, Menuhin International Violin Competition, Folkestone, 1983–95; Artistic Director, New Zealand International Violin Competition, 1992; Director of Music, Hattori Foundation for Music and Art, 1992. *Recordings:* Robert Masters Piano Quartet, Fauré Piano Quartets (Argo); Walton Piano

Quartet (Argo); Skalkottas Piano Trio, with Marcel Gazelle and Derek Simpson. *Honours:* FRAM. *Address:* 72d Leopold Road, London SW19 7JQ, England.

MASTERSON, Valerie; Singer (Soprano); b. 3 June 1937, Birkenhead, England; m. Andrew March, 1 s., 1 d. *Education:* Royal College of Music, London; Milan, Won Countess of Munster Scholarship; Gulbenkian Scholarship. *Career:* Performances in Falstaff, Il Turco in Italia and Der Schauspieldirektor, Landestheater, Salzburg; D'Oyly Carte Opera Company including film version of Mikado; Member, English National Opera, 1972–; Roles include, Manon, Traviata, Mimi, Juliet, Louise, Pamina, Gilda, Countess and Susanna in Figaro; Seraglio, Constanza; Cleopatra in Julius Caesar; Mireille; Debut in Covent Garden, 1974, in Das Rheingold; Traviata, Fidelio, We Come To The River by Henze; Semele, Faust (Marguerite), Carmelites, Micaela in Carmen; The King Goes Forth to France (Sallinen); Guest Appearances in Concerts and Opera in many major cities of the world including Paris, Aix, Milan, Munich, New York, Chicago, San Francisco, Barcelona, Geneva, South America; Sang Marguerite in Faust and Mozart's Countess at the London Coliseum, 1990; Fiordiligi for Welsh National Opera and Ilia in Idomeneo for the English Bach Festival at Covent Garden; Season 1992–93 with the Countess at Dublin and the Marschallin at Liège; President of British Youth Opera from 1994; Professor of Singing; Honorary, Academy of Music, London. *Honours:* SWET Award, 1983; C.B.E., 1988; FRCM awarded in 1992; FRCM, 1993; Honorary RAM, 1994. *Address:* c/o English National Opera, St Martin's Lane, London WC2N 4ES, England.

MASTILOVIC, Daniza; Singer (Soprano); b. 7 Nov. 1933, Negotin, Serbia. *Education:* Belgrade Conservatory with Nikola Cvejic. *Career:* Sang operetta in Belgrade, 1955–57; Minor roles at Bayreuth from 1956; Joined Georg Solti at Frankfurt Opera, 1959, debut as Tosca; Guest appearances in Hamburg, Düsseldorf, Zagreb, Vienna and Munich; Teatro Colón Buenos Aires 1972, as Abigaille in Nabucco; Zürich 1973, as Ortrud in Lehengrin; Covent Garden 1973–75, as Elektra; Metropolitan Opera 1975, as Elektra; Commemorated the 50th anniversary of Puccini's death with a performance of Turandot at Torre del Lago, 1974; Landestheater Salzburg 1987, as Clytemnestra in Elektra. *Address:* c/o Landestheater, Schwarstrasse 22, 5020 Salzburg, Austria.

MASTROMEI, Giampietro; Singer (Baritone); b. 1 Nov. 1932, Camoire, Tuscany, Italy. *Education:* Studied in Buenos Aires with Apollo Granforte, Mario Melani and Hilda Spani. *Career:* Sang at the Teatro Colón, Buenos Aires for 13 seasons from 1952; European debut, 1962, appearing in France and Italy, and at the Covent Garden, 1973, as Renato, Un Ballo in Maschera and Amonasro; Verona Arena, 1971–86, as Amonasro and Scarpia; Further appearances at Caracas, Bilbao, Tokyo, Barcelona, Hamburg, Madrid, San Francisco, Dallas and Philadelphia; Also sang Verdi's Iago and Rigoletto and roles in operas by Pergolesi, Scarlatti and Dallapiccola. *Recordings:* Simon Boccanegra; Il Corsaro; Aida.

MASUR, Kurt; German conductor; *Principal Conductor, London Philharmonic Orchestra*; b. 18 July 1927, Brieg, Silesia, Poland. *Education:* Nat. Music School, Breslau, Hochschule für Musik, Leipzig. *Career:* theatre conductor in Erfurt and Leipzig 1948–55, conductor, Dresden Philharmonic 1955–58, Chief Conductor 1967–72; Gen. Musical Dir, Mecklenburg State Theatre 1958–60; Prin. Musical Dir, Komische Oper in East Berlin 1960–64; Musical Dir Dresden Philharmonic 1967–72; Conductor, Leipzig Gewandhaus Orchestra 1970–96, Music Dir 1996–; UK début with New Philharmonia Orchestra 1973; début in USA with Cleveland Orchestra 1974; Music Dir Conductor New York Philharmonic 1991–2002; Prin. Conductor London Philharmonic Orchestra 1991–; Music Dir Orchestre nat. de France 2002–; has toured extensively in Europe and the USA. *Honours:*Freeman of City of Leipzig; Hon. Pres. Kulturstiftung, Leipzig Officier, Légion d'honneur, Bundesverdienstkreuz; Hon. Citizen of Brieg (Poland), Commdr Cross of Merit (Poland) 1999 hon. degrees from seven American univs and Univ. of Leipzig. *Address:* Masur Music International Inc., Ansonia PO Box 231478, New York, NY 10023, USA (office). *Telephone:* (646) 623-5803 (office). *Fax:* (212) 414-8276 (office). *E-mail:* stefana@muasurmusic.com (office). *Website:* www.kurtmasur.com (office).

MASUROK, Yuri; Ukrainian singer (baritone); b. 18 July 1931, Krasnik, Poland. *Education:* Lvov Institute and Moscow Conservatoire. *Career:* Sang at the Bolshoi, Moscow, from 1963, debut as Eugene Oengin; Vienna Staatsoper as Scarpia, Luna and Escamilio; Aix-en-Provence, 1976, as Germont in La Traviata; Covent Garden debut 1975, as Renato in Un Ballo in Maschera; Returned to London as Posa in Don Carlos, Eugene Onegin and Count di Luna; US debut at Metropolitan Opera 1975, with Bolshoi Company; San Francisco, 1977, as Renato; Metropolitan debut as Germont, 1978; Covent Garden 1983 and 1986, as Luna and Germont; Sang at Wiesbaden 1987 as Scarpia, Budapest as Robert in Iolanta, with the company of the Bolshoi Theatre; Gran Teatre del Liceu Barcelona 1989, as Eugene Onegin; Concerts in the United

Kingdom have included Wigmore Hall recitals and Festival Hall concert conducted by Svetlanov; Song repertory includes music by Ravel, Debussy, Schumann and Henze; Other operatic roles include Andrei Bolkonsky in War and Peace, Mazeppa, Rossini's Figaro and Yeletsky in The Queen of Spades; Sang Onegin at Milwaukee, 1992; Scarpia at Metropolitan, New York, 1993 and at Moscow, 1996. *Recordings:* Eugene Onegin, Tosca, The Queen of Spades and Iolanta on Russian labels; Tosca, Il Trovatore and Boris Godunov. *Address:* c/o Bolshoi Theatre, Ochotnyj Rjad 812, 103009 Moscow, Russia.

MATAEVA, Irina; Singer (Soprano); b. 1972, Tumen, Russia. *Education:* St Petersburg Conservatoire, 1995–98. *Career:* Young singers Academy of the Mariinsky Theatre, St Petersburg, from 1998; Roles have included Mozart's Susanna and Barbarina, Tatiana in Eugene Onegin, Natasha in War and Peace, Lisa in la Sonnambula, Zerlina and Sofya in Semyon Kotko by Prokofiev; Appeared with the Kirov Opera in summer season at Covent Garden, 2000; London Proms, 2002. *Honours:* Prizewinner, Gumelev Vocal Competition, 1997. *Address:* c/o Kirov Opera Mariinsky Theatre, Theatre Square, St Petersburg, Russia.

MATEJ, Daniel; Slovak composer; b. 9 March 1963, Bratislava. *Education:* Bratislava Acad. of Music and Drama, Conservatoire National Supérior de Musique, Paris, Koninklijk Conservatorium, The Hague, Dartington Summer Music School, Deutscher Akademischer Austauschdienst residency, Berlin. *Career:* founder contemporary music ensemble, Veni 1987; Lecturer in 20th-Century Music History, Bratislava Coll. of Performing Arts 1996–. *Compositions include:* Lament 1988, Video (Billboards) 1992, Memories of You 1 (14 Variations for J. C.) 1993, Wenn wir in höchsten Nöten sein 2000, Vingt Regards 2000, John King (opera) 2001, Machaut 2001. *Recordings:* Wenn wir in höchsten Nöten sein, (with Opera Aperta Ensemble). *Address:* c/o Music Centre Slovakia, Michalská 10, 815 36 Bratislava 1, Slovakia (office). *Website:* www.hc.sk.

MATHE, Ulrike-Anima; German violinist; b. 5 March 1964, Freiburg. *Education:* studied in Basel, Juilliard School, Konzertexamen Detmold with Tibor Varga, masterclasses. *Career:* debut in New York 1992; extensive chamber music and solo career, Berlin, Cologne, Munich, USA, Australia, Spain, Italy, Switzerland, Prague, Salzburg, Belgium, Netherlands; Repertory: from Vivaldi to Penderecki, with the whole violin concerto repertoire. *Recordings:* Reger Solo sonatas; Korngold violin concerto; Kreisler Pieces. *Publications:* contrib. to coverage of Strad magazine, Fono Forum, NMZ, Stereoplay. *Honours:* First prize, German Music Competition, 1986; First prize, European Youth Competition, 1985; Young Concert Artists Award, 1988; Fifth prize, Queen Elizabeth Competition, 1989. *Current Management:* SKS Russ, Charlottenplatz 17, 70173 Stuttgart, Germany. *E-mail:* ulrike.mathe@debitel.net.

MATHER, Bruce; Composer and Pianist; b. 9 May 1939, Toronto, Canada; m. Pierrette LePage. *Education:* Studied composition at the Royal Conservatory of Music in Toronto, in Paris with Roy Harris, Boulez, Milhaud and Messiaen, Universities of Stanford and Toronto, PhD, 1967. *Career:* Teacher at McGill University Montreal from 1966; Solo piano recitals and piano duet performances with Pierrette LePage. *Compositions:* Five Madrigals for soprano and ensemble, 1967–73; Music for Vancouver, 1969; Musique pour Rouen for string orchestra 1971; Music for Organ, Horn and Gongs, 1973; Eine Kleine Blassermusik, 1975; Au Chateau de Pompariain for Mezzo and Orchestra, 1977; Musique pour Champigny for vocal soloists and ensemble 1976; Ausone for 11 instruments 1979; Musigny for orchestra, 1980; Barbaresco for viola, cello and double bass, 1984; Scherzo for orchestra 1987; Dialogue pour trio basso et orchestre, 1988; Travauz de nuit, for baritone and Chamber orchestra, 1990; Princesse Blanche, opera, 1994; Tallbrem Variations, for 5 percussion and orchestra, 1995. Songs. *Address:* c/o SOCAN, 41 Valleybrook Drive, Don Mills, Ontario M3B 2S6, Canada.

MATHER, Martin; Composer; b. 6 Oct. 1927, Harrow, England (Australian National). *Education:* BA (Hons), University of London, 1948; Royal College of Music, with Herbert Howells and Frank Merrick, 1952–55. *Career:* Resident in Australia from 1956; Public Library of New South Wales, 1958–72; Freelance composer; mem, Fellowship of Australian Composers. *Compositions include:* Last Voyage of Matthew Flanders for soprano, tenor, chorus and orchestra, 1965; ANZAC Requiem for soloists, chorus and orchestra, 1967; Sextet, 1975; Fourteen Lieder for baritone and piano, 1986; Homage to Pushkin for baritone and piano, 1988; Twenty Four Preludes for piano, 1994; Entr'actes for piano solo, 1998. *Recordings include:* ANZAC Requiem, with the Adelaide Symphony Orchestra; Sounds Australian, 1976. *Honours:* Patrons Fund Award, RCM, 1954. *Address:* c/o APRA, 1A Eden Street, Crows Nest, NSW 2065, Australia.

MATHES, Rachel (Clarke); Opera Singer (Soprano) and College Professor; b. 14 March 1941, Atlanta, Georgia, USA. *Education:* BA, Music, Birmingham-Southern College, 1962; MM, Vocal Performance, 1988, DMA, Vocal Performance, 1991, University of South Carolina;

Study at Akademie für Musik und Darstellende Kunst, Vienna, Austria, 1962–63. *Career:* Debut: Aida at Basel, Switzerland, 1965; Deutsche Oper am Rhein, Düsseldorf, Germany, 1965–71; Freelance throughout Europe, 1971–74; Metropolitan Opera, New York, 1974–77, debut as Donna Anna; New York City Opera, 1975, debut as Turandot; Wolf Trap Festival, Verdi's Requiem, 1975; Glasgow Opera, as Donna Anna, 1975. *Recordings:* Highlights from Mozart's Don Giovanni with the Glasgow Opera, 1975. *Address:* c/o Augustana College Music Department, Rock Island, IL 61201, USA.

MATHIESEN, Thomas (James); Musicologist; b. 30 April 1947, Roslyn Heights, New York, USA; m. Penelope Jay Price, 11 Sept 1971. *Education:* BMus, Willamette University, 1968; MMus, 1970, DMA, Honours, 1971, University of Southern California. *Career:* Lecturer in Musicology, University of Southern California, Los Angeles, 1971–72; Professor of Music and Head Musicology Area, 1972–86, Associate Dean, Honours and General Education, 1986–88, Brigham Young University, Provo, Utah; Professor of Music, 1988–96, Distinguished Professor, 1996–, Director of the Center History of Music Theory and Literature, 1998–, David H Jacobs Chair in Music, 1998–, Indiana University; mem., American Acad. of Arts and Sciences, 2001. *Publications:* As Project Director: Thesaurus Musicarum Latinarum, Doctoral Dissertations in Musicology; A Bibliography of Sources for The Study of Ancient Greek Music, 1974; General Editor, Greek and Latin Music Theory, 1982–, 10 vols; Aristides Quintilianus on Music in Three Books: Translation, with Introduction, Commentary and Annotations, 1983; Ancient Greek Music Theory: A Catalogue Raisonné of Manuscripts, 1988 (Duckles Award, 1989); Editor, Festa Musicologica: Essays in Honor of George J Buelow, 1995; Greek Views of Music, 1997; Apollo's Lyre: Greek Music and Music Theory in Antiquity and the Middle Ages, 1999 (Kinkeldey, Berry, and ASCAP-Deems Taylor Awards, 2000); Music in the Mirror: Reflections on the History of Music Theory and Literature for the 21st Century, 2002 (ASCAP-Deems Taylor Award, 2003); Contrib.: New Grove Dictionary of Music and Musicians, 2nd edn, Die Musik in Geschichte und Gegenwart, 2nd edn. *Honours:* Fellowships: NEH 1985–86; Guggenheim, 1990–91. *Address:* 1800 Valley View Drive, Ellettsville, IN 47429-9487, USA.

MATHIS, Edith; Singer (Soprano); b. 11 Feb. 1938, Lucerne, Switzerland; m. Bernhard Klee. *Education:* Studied at the Lucerne Conservatory and in Zürich with Elisabeth Bosshart. *Career:* Debut: Lucerne 1956, in Die Zauberflöte; Sang in Cologne from 1959, Berlin from 1963; Salzburg Debut 1960, in concert; Glyndebourne, 1962–65, as Cherubino and as Sophie in Der Rosenkavalier; Metropolitan Opera debut 1970, as Pamina; Returned to New York as Ännchen in Der Freischütz, Sophie, and Zerlina in Don Giovannia; Covent Garden, 1970–72, as Mozart's Susanna and Despina; Other roles include Ninetta in La Finta Semplice, Salzburg; Beethoven's Marzelline, Debussy's Mélisande, Verdi's Nannetta and Mozart's Aminta; Mozart's Countess; Weber's Agathe, Der Freischütz, Strauss Arabella and the Marschallin in Der Rosenkavalier; Sang in the premieres of Henze's Der junge Lord, Berlin 1965 and Sutermeister's Le Roi Bérenger, Munich 1985; Barcelona 1986, as Agathe; Debut as the Marschallin at the Berne City Opera, 1990; Concert appearances in Baroque music and as Lieder singer; Sang Lieder by Mendelssohn, Brahms and Schubert at the Wigmore Hall, London, 1997. *Recordings:* Le nozze di Figaro; Die Zauberflöte; Fidelio; Die Freunde von Salamanka of Schubert, Die Wildschutz, Lortzing; Frau Fluth, Nicolai's Lustige Weiber von Windsor; Mozart's Ascanio in Alba, Il Re Pastore, Il Sogno di Scipione and Apollo et Hyacinthus; Bach Cantatas; Haydn's Il Mondo della Luna and L'Infedelta Delusa; Handel's Ariodante; Video of Mahler's 4th Symphony, conducted by Bernstein. *Current Management:* Ingpen & Williams Ltd, 7 St George's Court, 131 Putney Bridge Road, London, SW15 2PA, England.

MATORIN, Vladimir; Singer (Bass); b. 1950, Russia. *Education:* Gnessin High School, Moscow, until 1974. *Career:* Sang leading bass roles at the Moscow Music Theatre, 1974–89; Soloist with the Bolshoi Opera from 1991, with Rossini's Basilio, Ivan Susanini, Rene in Iolanthe and Galitsky in Prince Igor; Mussorgsky celebration concerts 1989, Boris Godunov at Geneva and Chicago 1994; Tchaikovsky's Gremin at the Teatro Zarzuela, Madrid; Appearances at the Wexford Festival 1993 and 1995, in Cherivichki by Tchaikovsky and Rimsky-Korsakov's May Night; Songs by Mussorgsky, Rachmaninov and Tchaikovsky at the Deutsche Oper, Berlin, 1995; Season 1998 with Ivan in Glinka's A Life for the Tsar at St Petersburg and Mendoza in Prokofiev's Duenna at Geneva; Sang Boris Godunov with the Bolshoi Opera at the London Coliseum, 1999. *Address:* Allied Artists, 42 Montpelier Square, London SW7 1JZ, England.

MATOUSEK, Bohuslav; violinist; b. 1949, Czechoslovakia. *Education:* Jaroslav Pekelsky Vaclav Snitil; further study with Arthur Grumiaux, Nathan Milstein and Wolfgang Schniderhan. *Career:* soloist with the Tokyo Symphony Orchestra, 1977–78; Co-founder and leader of the Stamic Quartet of Prague 1980; Performances at the Prague Young Artists and the Bratislava Music Festivals; Tours to Spain, Austria,

France, Switzerland, Germany and Eastern Europe; Tour of the USA 1980, debut concerts in the United Kingdom at London and Birmingham, 1983; Further British tours 1985, 1987, 1988, Warwick Arts Festival, and 1989, 20 concerts; Gave the premiere of Helmut Eder's 3rd at the Channel Islands, Festival of Czech Music; Netherlands, Finland, Austria and France; Edinburgh Festival and debut tours of Canada, Japan and Indonesia. *Recordings:* Shostakovich No. 13, Schnittke No. 4, Panton; Dvořák, Martinů and Janáček complete quartets; Haydn Violin Concertos 1–6 Supraphon, Schubet Sonatinas and Grand Duo, Denon; Brahms, Bruch Concertos; Dvořák Concerto; Brahms' Sonatas, Bayuer R E; Dvořák Complete violin and piano; Martinů Duo Concertante; B Martinů Complete violin and piano. *Honours:* with Members of Stamic Quartet: Prizewinner, Winner 1986 ORF, Austrian Radio, International String Quartet Competition followed by live broadcast from the Salzburg Mozarteum; Academie Charles Cros Grand Prix du Disque, 1991, for Dvořák quartets; 1 Prix International Violin Competition Prague, as soloist, 1972. *Current Management:* Robert Gilder & Co., Enterprise House, 59–65 Upper Ground, London, SE1 9PQ, England. *Telephone:* (20) 7928-9008. *Fax:* (20) 7928-9755. *E-mail:* rgilder@robert-gilder.com. *Address:* Dvořákova 311, 25264 Velké Prilepy, Czech Republic.

MATOUSEK, Lukas; Composer, Clarinettist and Performer of Medieval Instruments; b. 29 May 1943, Prague, Czechoslovakia; m. (1) Zuzana Matouskova 1966 (deceased), 2 d, (2) Zdenka Kratka 2002. *Education:* Prague Conservatory of Music; Private Study with Mil Kabelac, Composition; Janáček Academy of Music, Brno. *Career:* Artistic Director, Ars Cameralis Ensemble; Many concerts and recordings for broadcasting and television throughout Europe; Recordings as performer with Ars Cameralis, and of own works; Music Director of CD Label, Studio Matous; Dramaturge of Prague Symphony Orchestra. *Compositions include:* For Orchestra: Radices Temporis; Stories; Concerto for percussion and winds; Metamorphoses of Silence for strings; Fanfare of 17th November for 12 brass; Chamber Music: Sonata for violin and piano; Sonata for double-bass and chamber ensemble; Wind-Quintet; Aztecs for percussion, Intimate Music for viola or cello, Recollection of Mr Sudek for brass-sextet, Sonatina for clarinet and piano; Sonnet Sequence for cello and piano; Shadows and Reflections for chamber ensemble; Min-Kaleidoscope for chamber ensemble; Trio for clarinet, violin and Piano; Vocal: Three Cantatas; Colours and Thoughts; Flower of Paradise; Several Children's Choir Pieces. *Recordings:* CD, Gothic Music in Bohemia; Music of Charles University; Machaut-Chansons; L Matousek: Chamber Music. *Address:* Vápencová 10, 147 00 Prague 4, Czech Republic. *E-mail:* cameralis@volny.cz; cameralis@volny.cz. *Website:* www.musica.cz/matousekl/.

MATSUZAWA, Yuki; Concert Pianist; b. 1960, Tokyo, Japan. *Education:* Studied with: Akiko Iguchi and Hiroshi Tamura at Tokyo University of Fine Arts; Further study with Vladimir Ashkenazy in Europe. *Career:* Concert engagements in Europe, Asia and USA; Radio and television engagements in the United Kingdom, Ireland, Netherlands, Greece, USA, Japan; Irish debut, 1990 with the Berlin Radio Symphony Orchestra; London debut, 1990 at Wigmore Hall; London appearances at: Wigmore Hall, Barbican Hall, St John's Smith Square; Concerto appearances with: Royal Philharmonic Orchestra, BBC Symphony Orchestra, Montreal Symphony Orchestra, Athens Radio Symphony Orchestra, Berlin Radio Symphony Orchestra, NHK Symphony Orchestra, New London Orchestra; Chamber music appearances with Suk Quartet in the United Kingdom and Czechoslovakia and with Martinů Quartet in the United Kingdom; Tours of the United Kingdom and Europe; Concerts with: English Chamber Orchestra, Brno Philharmonic, and Bournemouth Sinfonietta. *Recordings:* Exclusive recording contract with Novalis Records. *Honours:* Prizewinner at such competitions as Queen Elizabeth, Brussels, Maria Canals, Barcelona, and Montreal International, Canada.

MATTEI, Peter; Singer (Baritone); b. 1965, Sweden. *Education:* Studied in Framnas and Stockholm. *Career:* Debut: Drottningholm, 1990 as Nardo in Mozart's Finta Giardiniera's Royal Opera Stockholm, 1991 in the premiere of Backanterna by Daniel Bortz; Drottningholm, 1992–93 in Salieri's Falstaff and Haeffner's Electra; Scottish Opera, 1995 as Don Giovanni; Salzburg Festival, 1996 as Minister in Fidelio; Season 1998 as Mozart's Guglielmo for Scottish Opera and Don Giovanni at Aix; Sang Posa in Don Carlos at Stockholm, 1999; Season 2000–01 as Mozart's Figaro at Glyndebourne, Chorèbe in Les Troyens at the Barbican Hall and as Eugene Onegin in Brussels; Mahler's Symphony of a Thousand at the London Proms, 2002. *Recordings:* Electra; Carmina Burana. *Address:* c/o Scottish Opera, 39 Elmbank Crescent, Glasgow G2 4PT, Scotland.

MATTEUZZI, William; Singer (Tenor); b. 1957, Bologna, Italy. *Education:* Studied with Paride Venturi. *Career:* Debut: Sang Massenet's Des Grieux in Milan; Season 1987 sang Rossini's Ramiro at Bologna, Nemorino at Bergamo and Evander in Alceste at La Scala; Rossini's Comte Ory at Venice, 1988, La Scala, 1991; Pesaro Festival, 1988, in La

Scala di Seta, as Roderigo in Rossini's Otello, 1991; Count Almaviva on Metropolitan Opera debut 1988 and at Barcelona, 1991; Sang Lindoro in L'Italiana in Algeri, at Monte Carlo, 1989; Medoro in Orlando Furioso by Vivaldi at San Francisco; Other roles include Flamand in Capriccio and Ernesto in Don Pasquale. *Recordings:* Francesca da Rimini; Borsa in Rigoletto; Edmondo in Manon Lescaut and in Barbiere di Siviglia; Rossini's Zelmira; Tonio in La Fille du Régiment, Carlo and Goffredo in Rossini's Armida; Sang Lindoro in L'Italiana in Algeri at Parma, 1998. *Honours:* Winner, Caruso International Competition, Milan. *Address:* c/o Teatro alla Scala, Via Filodrammatici 2, 201212 Milan, Italy.

MATTHEW-WALKER, Robert; Musician; b. 23 July 1939, Lewisham, London, England; m. Lynn Sharon Andrews, 27 Dec 1969, 1 s. *Education:* London College of Printing; Goldsmiths' College; London College of Music; Private Composition study with Darius Milhaud, Paris, 1962–63. *Career:* Composer, Record Company Executive, Author, Critic; mem, Performing Right Society; Critics' Circle. *Compositions:* Symphonies 1–6, 1955, 1958, 1959, 1964, 1968 (2); Violin Concerto, 1962; Piano Sonatas 1–4, 1976 (2), 1980, 1982; Piano Trio, 1978; Horn Concerto, 1980; Cello Sonata, 1980; String Quartet, 1980; Sinfonia Solemnis, 1981. *Recordings:* Le Tombeau de Milhaud; Divertimento on a Theme of Mozart. *Publications:* Rachmaninov: His Life and Times, 1980; Madonna–The Biography, 1989; Havergal Brian, 1995; Heartbreak Hotel–The Life and Music of Elvis Presley, 1995; Editor: The Keller Column, 1990; The Symphonies of Robert Simpson, 1991. *Contributions:* Editor, Music and Musicians, 1984–88; National Dictionary of Biography, Musical Times, other publications. *Address:* 1 Exford Road, London SE12 9HD, England.

MATTHEWS, Andrea; Singer (Soprano); b. 6 Nov. 1956, Needham, Massachusetts, USA. *Education:* AB, Princeton University, 1978. *Career:* Debut: Marriage of Figaro as Susanna at Virginia Opera, 1984; Semele in Semele; Gretel in Hansel and Gretel, Virginia Opera; Gilda in Rigoletto, Piedmont Opera; Zerlina in Don Giovanni, Greensboro Opera; Euridice in Orfeo ed Euridice, Violetta in La Traviata, Susanna in Marriage of Figaro, Marie in Bartered Bride and Ilia in Idomeneo at The Stadttheater Aachen, Germany; Other roles: Musetta, Mimi in La Bohème, Pamina in Magic Flute, Lauretta in Gianni Schicchi, Marzelline in Fidelio, Lucy in The Telephone, Marguerite in Faust, Nannetta in Falstaff; Soloist with many orchestras and companies including: St Louis Symphony; Houston Symphony; Baltimore Symphony; Atlanta Symphony; Stuttgart Philharmonic, Prague Autumn Festival, Philadelphia Orchestra, Puerto Rico Symphony, Honolulu Symphony, National Symphony at Wolf Trap, Los Angeles Master Chorale, Dessoff Choirs, Oratorio Society of New York, Mostly Mozart Festival, New Mexico Symphony, Kalamazoo Symphony, Utah Symphony, St Paul Chamber Orchestra, American Ballet Theater, American Symphony, Raleigh Symphony and Cincinnati Symphony; Art-Song recitals in many American States. *Recordings:* Vaughan Williams's Serenade to Music; Handel's Siroe, Muzio, Berenice, Tolomeo; Christmas Album; Victor Herbert's Thine Alone (songs); Ned Rorem's Three Sisters. *Current Management:* Thea Dispeker Artists Representative. *Address:* c/o Thea Dispeker, 59 East 54th Street, New York, NY 10022, USA.

MATTHEWS, Colin; Composer; b. 13 Feb. 1946, London, England. *Education:* Nottingham University; Composition with Arnold Whittall and Nicholas Maw. *Career:* Collaborated with Deryck Cooke on performing version of Mahler's 10th Symphony; Taught at Sussex University, 1972–73, 1976–77; Administrator, Holst Foundation, 1983; Assistant to Britten in last years; Trustee, Britten-Pears Foundation, 1983; Cortège premiered under Bernard Haitink at Covent Garden, 1989, Machines and Dreams by the London Symphony Orchestra, 1991; Founder, NMC Recordings, 1989; Associate Composer, London Symphony Orchestra, 1991–99; Chair, Britten Estate, 2000; Governor, Royal Northern College of Music, 2000; Associate Composer, Hallé Orchestra, 2000, Prince Consort Professor of Compositon, Royal College of Music, 2001. *Compositions:* Ceres for nonet, 1972; Sonata No. 4 for orchestra, 1975; Partita, violin, 1975; Five Sonnets to Orpheus, tenor and harp, 1976; Specula for quartet, 1976; Night Music for small orchestra, 1977; Piano Suite, 1979; Rainbow Studies for quintet, 1978; Shadows in the Water, tenor and piano, 1979; String Quartet No. 1, 1979; Sonata No. 5, Landscape for orchestra, 1977–81; Oboe Quartet, 1981; Secondhand Flames, 5 voices, 1982; Divertimento, double string quartet, string orchestra, 1982; The Great Journey, baritone and ensemble, 1981–86; Toccata Meccanica for orchestra, 1984; Triptych for piano quintet, 1984; Cello Concerto, 1994; Three Enigmas, cello and piano, 1985; String Quartet No. 2, 1985; Suns Dance, 10 players, 1985; Monody for Orchestra, 1987; Two Part Invention for chamber orchestra, 1987–88; Pursuit, 16 players, 1987; Fuga, 8 players, 1988; Cortège for orchestra, 1989; 2nd Oboe Quartet, 1989; Hidden variable, 15 players, 1989; Quatrain, wind, brass and percussion, 1989; Chiaroscuro for orchestra, 1990; Machines and Dreams, full or small orchestra and children, 1990; Broken Symmetry for Orchestra, 1992; Contraflow, 14 players, 1992;

Memorial for Orchestra, 1993; String Quartet No. 3, 1994; Cello Concerto No. 2, 1996; Renewal for chorus and orchestra, 1996; Elegaic Chaconne, for ensemble, 1997; Elegia for 14 players, 1998; Aftertones for chorus and orchestra, 1999; Pluto for orchestra, 1999; Continuum for soprano and ensemble, 2000; Horn Concerto, 2001; Orchestration of seven Debussy Préludes, 2001–03; Estrangements, for chorus, 2002, Vivo for orchestra, 2002. *Recordings:* The Great Journey; Cello Concerto, Landscape; Broken Symmetry, 4th Sonata, Suns Dance. *Honours:* Chamber Music Prize, BBC, 1970; Ian Whyte Award, 1975; Park Lane Group Composer Award, 1983; Royal Philharmonic Society Prize, 1997; Honorary Doctorate, University of Nottingam, 1999. *Address:* c/o Faber Music Ltd, 3 Queen Square, London WC1N 3AU, England.

MATTHEWS, David John, BA; Composer and Writer; b. 9 March 1943, London, England. *Education:* BA Classics, Nottingham University, private study in composition with Anthony Milner. *Career:* Worked with Deryck Cooke on completion of Mahler's 10th Symphony; Assistant to Britten, 1966–70; Artistic Director, Deal Festival, 1989–2003; Artistic Advisor to English Chamber Orchestra; Fifth Symphony premiered at the 1999 London Prom Concerts; mem. British Academy of Composers and Songwriters. *Compositions include:* 5 Symphonies, 1975, 1978, 1983, 1990, 1999; In the Dark Time for orchestra; The Music of Dawn for orchestra; Romanza for cello and small orchestra; Capriccio for two horns and strings; Chaconne for orchestra; From Sea to Sky for small orchestra; Serenade for small orchestra; A Vision and a Journey for orchestra; After Sunrise for orchestra;; Aubade for small orchestra; Oboe Concerto; 2 Violin Concertos; Concerto in Azzurro for cello and orchestra; Variations for strings; Two Pieces for strings; Winter Remembered for viola and strings; Introit for two trumpets and strings; Cantiga for soprano and orchestra; Marina for baritone, basset horn, viola and piano; The Sleeping Lord for soprano, flute, clarinet, harp and string quartet; Winter Passions for baritone, clarinet, string trio and piano; 4 Hymns for chorus; The Company of Lovers for small chorus; The doorway of Dawn for chorus; The Ship of Death for chorus; 10 String Quartets; The Flaying of Marsyas for oboe quintet; Clarinet Quartet; 2 Piano Trios; String Trio; Piano Sonata; Variations for piano; Band of Angels for organ; Three Studies for solo violin; Winter Journey for solo violin; Eight Duos for two violins; 15 Fugues for Violin; Three Roman Miniatures for clarinet; Duet Variations for Flute and Piano; A Little Threnody for cor anglais; The Book of Hours for voice and piano; From Coastal Stations for voice and piano; The Golden Kingdom for voice and piano; Vespers for mezzo soprano and tenor solo, chorus and orchestra; A Congress of Passions for voice, oboe and piano, 1994; Hurrahing in Harvest, for chorus, 1997; Winter Passions for baritone and ensemble, 1999; The Doorway of the Dawn, for chorus, 1999; Aubade for chamber orchestra, 2000; A Congress of Passions for medium voice, oboe and strings, 2000; After Sunrise, for chamber orchestra, 2001; Winter Remembered, for solo viola and strings, 2001; Cello Concerto, Concerto in Azzuro, 2002; Fifteen Fugues for solo violin, 2002. *Recordings:* The Company of Lovers; Romanza; Cantiga; September Music; Introit; The Flaying of Marsyas; A Little Threnody; Winter Journey; Piano Sonata; Symphony No. 4; Piano Trio 1; The Golden Kingdom; In the Dark Time; Chaconne; Three Studies for solo violin; Britten, 2002. *Publications include:* Editor, Mahler, Symphony No 10, 1976; Michael Tippett, 1980; Landscape into Sound, 1992; Editor, Beethoven arr Mahler, String Quartet op 95; Mahler: Rückert Lieder; Britten, 2003. *Contributions:* Tempo, TLS, Musical Times. *Honours:* Hon. DMus 1998. *Address:* c/o Faber Music Ltd, 3 Queen Square, London WC1N 3AU, England.

MATTHEWS, Michael Gough; Pianist and Teacher; b. 12 July 1931, London, England. *Education:* Royal College of Music, open scholarship 1947; ARCM, FRCM 1972; ARCO. *Career:* Debut: Wigmore Hall, 1960; Pianist; Recitals; Broadcasts and concerts in the United Kingdom, Europe and Far East; Adjudicator international competitions; Masterclasses; Lecture Recitals; Piano Teacher; Supervisor; Junior Studies; RSAMD, 1964–71; Royal College of Music; Director, Junior Department and Professor of Piano, 1972–75, Registrar, 1975, Vice-Director, 1978–84, Director, 1985–93, Vice-Pres., 1994; Director Associated Board of the Royal Schools of Music, 1985–93; Director, Royal Music Foundation Inc, USA, from 1985; Consultant to H M the Sultan of Oman, Jaguar Cars Sponsored Concerts; Piano recitals, lectures and masterclasses in the United Kingdom and abroad; mem, Royal Philharmonic Society; Comité d'Honneur Presence de l'Art, Paris; Vice President, RCO; Honorary Vice President, Royal Choral Society; Vice President, Royal College of Music, 1997. *Recordings:* 2 CDs of piano music by Fauré; 8 nocturnes; 9 preludes; 2 barcarolles; Thème et variations; Mazurka; 1 CD of piano music by Brahms: Op 76 and Op 118. *Publications:* Various musical entertainments; Arranger of Educational Music. *Honours:* Gold Medal, RCM, 1953; FRCM, 1972; Prize, Chopin International Piano Competition, 1955; Chopin Fellowship, 1959; FRSAMD, 1986; FRNCM, 1991; Hon GSM, 1987; Hon RAM, 1979. *Address:* Laurel Cottages, South Street, Mayfield, East Sussex TN 20 6 DD, England.

MATTHEWS, Sally; Singer (soprano); b. 1975, England. *Education:* Guildhall School, London; Vilar Young Artist Programme, Covent Garden, 2001. *Career:* debut, Nannetta in Falstaff at Covent Garden, 2000; Season 2000–2001 as Mozart's Fiordiligi for Grange Park Opera and Elisa in Il Re Pastore for the Classical Opera Company; concerts with the Orchestra of St John's, Philharmonia, English Chamber Orchestra and Royal Liverpool Philharmonic Orchestra; First Night of 2001 London Proms in Serenade to Music, by Vaughan Williams; Season 2001–2002 with Debussy's Le Martyre de St Sebastien, with the LSO under Pierre Boulez, and Messiah with the London Philharmonic. *Honours:* Kathleen Ferrier Award, 1999. *Address:* c/o Vilar Young Artists, Royal Opera House, Covent Garden, London, WC2, England. *Telephone:* (20) 7240 1200. *Fax:* (20) 7212 9502.

MATTHUS, Siegfried; Composer; b. 13 April 1934, Mallenuppen, Germany; m. Helga Matthus-Spitzer. *Education:* Deutsche Hochschule für Musik, 1952–58, with Wagner-Régeny; Study with Hanns Eisler at the Germany Academy of Arts. *Career:* Freelance Composer since 1958; Permanent musician for television, radio, film from 1958; Composer-in-Residence at the Komische Oper Berlin from 1964; Works performed in all European Countries, Japan, North and South America, Australia; Since 1991, Artistic Director, Chamber Opera Festival, Rheinsburg; Professor 1985; mem, Academy of Arts, Berlin-West; Bayerischen Akademie der Schönen Künste in Munich. *Compositions:* Operas: Lazarillo vom Tormes, 1964; Der Letzte Schuss, 1967; Noch ein Loffel Gift, Liebling, 1972; Omphale, 1976; Judith, 1982–84; Die Weise von Liebe und Tod des Cornets Christoph Rilke, 1983–84; Graf Mirabeau, 1987–88; Desdemona and her Sisters, 1991–92; Farinelli, 1997; Kronprinz Friedrich, 1998/9; Orchestral: Kleines Orchesterkonzert, 1963; Violin Concerto, 1968; Dresdner Sinfonia, 1969; Piano Concerto, 1970; Serenade, 1974; Cello Concerto, 1975; 2nd Symphony, 1976; Responso, Concerto for Orchestra, 1977; Visions for Strings, 1978; Flute Concerto, 1978; The Wood, Concerto for Kettledrums and Orchestra, 1984; Divertimento for Orchestra, 1985; Oboe Concerto, 1985; The Bride of the Wind, Concerto for Orchestra, 1985; Nächtliche Szene im Park for Orchestra, 1987; Tief ist der Brunnen der Vergangenheit, Four Pieces for Symphonic Orchestra, 1991–92; Sinfonie (Gewandhaussinfonie), 1992–93; Piano Concerto, 1992; Manhattan Concerto, 1993; Concerto for Horn and Orchestra, 1994; Blow out, Concerto for organ and orchestra, 1995; Das Land Phantasien, for orchestra, 1996; Concerto for flute, harp and orchestra, 1998; Ariadne, Dithyrambos for orchestra, 1997; Capriccio for violin and orchestra, 1999; Vocal: Weisen von Liebe, Leben und Tod, (Text R M Rilke), Lieder für Countertenor (Alt) und Orchester, 1993; Vocal: 5 Orchestra Lieder, 1962; Wir Zwei, 1970; 5 Liebeslieder des Catull, 1972; Laudate PACEM, 1974; Vocal: Hyperion-Fragmente, 1978–79; Holofernes-Portrait for Baritone and Orchestra, 1981; Die Liebesqualen des Catull, 1985–86; Nachtlieder für Baritone, String Quartet and Harp, 1987; Wem ich zu gefallen suche-Lieder und Duette für Tenor, Baritone and Klavier, 1987; Chamber: Octet, 1970; String Quartet, 1972; Trio for Flute, Viola and Harp, 1972; Octet, 1989; Windspiele für Violiue, Viola und Violon Cello; Lichte Spiele, 1996; Das Mädchen und der Tod, 1996; Ballet: The Never-ending Story about the Destruction and Deliverance of the Land of Phantasia, 1999. *Honours:* Hanns Eisler Prize, 1969; Arts Prize, DDR, 1970; National Prize, DDR, 1972, 1984. *Address:* Elisabethweg 10, 13187 Berlin, Germany.

MATTILA, Karita; Singer (Soprano); b. 5 Sept. 1960, Somero, Finland. *Education:* Studied in Helsinki with Liisa Linko-Malmio; Pupil of Vera Rozsa from 1984. *Career:* Won 1983 Singer of the World Competion in Cardiff; Concert appearances with Abbado, Albrecht, Colin Davis, Dohnányi, Giulini, Salonen, James levine, George Salti and Sinopoli; Orchestras include: Vienna Philharmonic, Vienna Symphony, Cleveland, London Symphony, Berlin Philharmonic and the Staatskapelle Dresden; Operatic roles include Fiordiligi at the 1985 and 1987 Munich Festivals; Covent Garden debut 1986, as Fiordiligi; Returned for Pamina in Die Zauberflöte; Mozart's Elvira with Washington Opera, US debut; Scottish Opera, Hamburg Opera and Chicago Lyric Opera; Wagner's Eva In Brussels; Sang Emma in Schubert's Fierrabras in Vienna, with Abbado; Other engagements include Elvira and Eva at the Metropolitan Opera, 1990; Sang Ilia in Idomeneo at San Francisco, 1989, Agathe in Der Freishütz at Covent Garden; Sang Donna Elvira at the Vienna Festival, Amelia Grimaldi in Simon Boccanegra at the Geneva Opera, 1991; Sang Sibelius's Hostkvall and Luonnotar at the 1991 Prom Concerts, London; Appeared as Eva in a new production of Die Meistersinger at the Metropolitan, 1993; Sang songs by Grieg at the 1993 Prom Concerts; Appearances at the Salzburg Festival and with the Berlin Philharmonic Orchestra, 1993; Sang Elsa in Lohengrin at San Francisco (1996) and Covent Garden, 1997; Jenůfa at Hamburg and Eva in Die Meistersinger at the Met, 1998; Lohengrin in Paris, 1998; Leonore in Fidelio at Helsinki, 2000; Sang Amelia Grimaldi and Fiordiligi at Salzburg, Leonore at the Met and Tchaikovsky's Lisa and Jenůfa at Covent Garden, 2000–01; Katya Kabanova for San Francisco Opera, 2002. *Recordings:* Portrait Record with Pritchard; Bruckner's Te Deum with Haitink; Così fan tutte and Don Giovanni with Marriner;

Recordings with Abbado and with Gerd Albrecht; Le nozze di Figaro with Mehta and Beethoven's Ninth conducted by Marriner; Five Recital recordings. *Honours:* Lawrence Olivier Nominee for Best Performance, 1997; Evening Standard Award for Best Performance, 1997; Grammy Award for Best Opera Recording, 1998. *Address:* c/o IMG Artists, Lovell House, 616 Chiswick High Road, London W4 5RX, England.

MATTINSON, David; Singer (Bass-baritone); b. 1964, England. *Education:* Choral Scholar, Trinity College, Cambridge; Guildhall School of Music with Thomas Hemsley; Further study with Rudolf Pierney. *Career:* Concert repertoire includes the B minor Mass, Messiah, The Creation, Requiems of Brahms, Verdi and Fauré, The Dream of Gerontius and A Child of Our Time; Appearances with the City of London Sinfonia, the Bournemouth Symphony and the London Philharmonic Orchestras; Further concerts include Elijah at the Albert Hall; Christus in the St Matthew Passion at the Festival Hall; Mozart's Requiem, and Beethoven's Ninth in Koblenz; Song recitals with the accompanist Clare Toomer in Winterreise, Dichterliebe, La Bonne Chanson and the Songs of Travel by Vaughan Williams: Appearances with the New Songmakers and the Mistry String Quartet and at the Buxton, Malvern and Warwick Festivals; Operatic roles include Gualtiero in Musgrave's The Voice of Ariadne, Mozart's Figaro, Germont, and Glover in La Jollie Fille de Perth; Scottish Opera debut 1991, as Zuniga in Carmen; Debut as Mozart's Figaro, Opera North, 1992; Season 1992 as Villotto in Haydn's La Vera Costanza for Garsington Opera and in Billy Budd for Scottish Opera; Sang Mozart's Figaro for Central Festival Opera, 1996. *Recordings:* Bach St John Passion. *Honours:* Gold Medal Rosebowl and the Worshipful Company of Musicians' Silver Medal, GSM; Gold Medal in the 1988 Royal Overseas League Music Competition; Prizewinner, Walter Gruner International Lieder Competition; Elly Ameling International Lied Concours; 1st prize, 1990 BP Peter Pears Award. *Address:* Kaye Artists Management Ltd, Barratt House, 7 Chertsey Road, Woking, Surrey GU21 5 AG, England.

MATTIOTTO, Claudia; Pianist; b. 21 Jan. 1959, Torino, Italy; m. Guido Scano, 1 Aug 1985, 1 s. *Education:* High School for Training of Primary Teachers; Piano Diplomas: Verdi High Conservatory, Torino and Ecole Internationale de Piano, Lausanne, Switzerland; Mozarteum, Salzburg, Austria; Manhattan School of Music, New York, USA; Instituto Liongueres, Barcelona. Spain. *Career:* Debut: Solo, 1981; Piano Duo, 1985; With orchestra, 1988; Concerts in all Italy and in France, Germany, Egypt, India, Slovenia, Romania, Andorra, Greece; Conductor and special teacher in musical courses and seminars; Many European broadcasting appearances; Collaborator in Caleidoscopio Project, 1996–; Concert series A Suon Di Musica, 2000–; President, International Centre for Musical Research. *Recordings:* 4 Steps im 4 Hands, series of 15 weekly programmes, Radiokoper, Monte Carlo, Bucharest, Marseille, Trieste radio and television broadcasts. *Publications:* In Musica, piano teaching methodology text, 1986; Concerto in Famiglia, A Guide for Youngest Muscians, 2003. *Honours:* Dalcroze Teaching Certificate, Manhattan School of Music, 1991; 1st Prize, Genova Competition, 1986. *Address:* Corso Rosselli 105/10A, 10129 Torino, Italy.

MATTON, Roger; Composer; b. 18 May 1929, Granby, Quebec, Canada. *Education:* Studied in Arthur Letondal's class, Conservatoire de musique du Quebec, Montreal; Studied composition under Claude Champagne; Studied under Andree Vaurabourg-Honegger and Nadia Boulanger, Ecole normale superieure de musique; Attended Olivier Messiaen's analysis classes, Conservatoire de Paris; Studied ethnomusicology under Marius Barbeau, National Museum of Canada, Ottawa. *Career:* Joined Archives de folklore, Laval, Quebec; Teacher, History Department, Laval, Quebec City; Ethnological Music, 1963–89; Composer of music having received commissions from Canadian Broadcasting Corporation; l'orchestre symphonique de Quebec, Montreal Symphony Orchestra, Le Grand Theatre de Quebec; mem, Canadian League of Composers. *Compositions:* Orchestral: Danse Bresillienne 1946; Danse Lente 1947; L'Horoscope 1958; Mouvement Symphonique 1, 1960, 11 1962, 111 1974, IV 1978; Pax 1950, Soloists with Orchestra: Concerto pur deux pianos et orchestre, 1964; Concerto pour saxophone et orchestre a cordes 1948; Voices with Orchestra: L'escaouette 1957; Te Deum 1967; Chamber Music: Esquisse pour quatuor a cordes 1949; Etude pour clarinette et piano 1946; Piano: Berceuse 1945; Trois Preludes pour piano 1949; Two Pianos: Concerto pour deux pianos et percussion 1955; Danse bresilienne 1946; Organ: Suite de Paques, 1952; Te es Petrus, 1984. *Recordings:* Berceuse; Concerto pour deux pianos et orchestre; Concerto pour deux pianos et percussion; Danse breilienne; l'horoscope; Movement Symphonique 1, 11; Suite de Paques; Te Deum; Trois Preludes pour piano. *Honours:* Awarded distinction at Seventh Gala du Quebec, Montreal for choral suite l'Escaouette 1965; Received Prix du Disque pour Pierre Mercure for Concerto pour deux pianos et orchestra 1966; Presented with Prix Calixa Lavallee by St Jean Baptiste

Society for contribution to French-Canada 1969. *Address:* c/o SOCAN, 41 Valleybrook Drive, Don Mills, Ontario M3B 2S6, Canada.

MATTSSON, Jack; Composer and Musician; b. 12 Dec. 1954, Aland, Finland. *Education:* Sibelius Academy, 1974–84. *Career:* Debut: Alandskt Requiem for soloists, chorus and orchestra, 1990; Composer, arranger, conductor since 1980; Finnish radio and television, recordings for various record companies, 1986–; Conductor, Swedish Theatre, Helsinki; mem, Clientship in Finnish Teosto. *Compositions:* Alandskt Requiem, 1991; Serenade for basson and strings, 1990; Carating for violin and piano, 1990; Four bagatelles for flute, violin and viola, 1986; Joy and Thoughts for organ, 1992. *Recordings:* Music theatre Katrina for solo voices chorus and orchestra; Finnish Radio Symphony Orchestra, 1998. *Honours:* Alands Culture prize, 1990; Finnish Swedish Culture found, 1987. *Address:* c/o TEOSTO, Lauttasaaventie 1, SF–0020 Helsinki, Finalnd.

MATUSZCZAK, Bernadetta; Composer; b. 10 March 1931, Thorn, Poland. *Education:* Studied with Szeligowski and Sitkowski at the Poznan and Warsaw Conservatoris: Paris with Nadia Boulanger. *Compositions include:* Julia i Romeo, chamber opera, Warsaw 1970; Humanae Voces, radio oratorio, 1972; Mysterium Heloizy, opera, 1973–74; The Diary of a Madman, monodrama after Gogol, Warsaw 1978; Apocalypsis, radio oratorio, 1979; Prometheus, chamber opera after Aeschylus, 1981–83; Quo Vadis, opera after H. Sienkiewicz, 1993–94; Canto funebre, for strings, 1995. *Honours:* Prize-winner at the Young Polish Composers' Competition, 1965; Award winner at the Grzegorz Fitelberg Composers' Competition for Septem Tubae, 1966; Award winner at the competition organized by Jeunesses Musicales for Musica da camera, 1967. *Address:* c/o Society of Authors ZAiKS, 2 Hipoteczna Street, 00 092 Warsaw, Poland. *Telephone:* (4822) 828 17 05. *Fax:* (4822) 828 13 47. *E-mail:* sekretariat@zaiks.org.pl. *Website:* www .zaiks.org.pl.

MATYS, Jiri; Composer; b. 27 Oct. 1927, Bakov, Nachod area, Czechoslovakia. *Education:* Brno Conservatory, studied with Kvapil at the Janáček Acad. of Music, Brno. *Career:* teacher, Janáček Acad. 1953–57; Head of the School of Music, Kralove Pole in Brno 1957–60; Prof. of the Conservatory, Brno; mem. Asscn of Czech Musicians and Scientists (Prague), Moravian Composers Club (Brno). *Compositions:* Viola Sonata 1954, 5 String Quartets 1957–90, Variations on Death for narrator, horn and string quartet of a poem by Milan Kundera 1959, Morning Music 1962, Solo viola sonata 1963, Music for string quartet and orchestra 1971, Suite for viola and bass clarinet 1973, Symphonic Overture 1974, Dialogue for cello and piano 1976, Sonata for Violin Solo No. 1 1977, Divertimento for Four Horns 1981, Suite for flute and guitar 1981, Music for strings 1982, Suite for Wind Quintet 1984, Music for Piano 1985, I Wish You Knew..., mezzo, cello, piano 1985–86, The Urgency of Time, symphonic picture for viola, orchestra and reciter 1986–87, Poetic Movements V, four compositions for four guitars 1988, Tunning 5 compositions for guitar solo 1990, Sonata for Violin Solo No. 2 1991, No. 3 1993, No. 4 1994, No. 5 1995, No. 6 1996, Night Thoughts, a cycle of piano compositions in five parts 1992, Dedicated to a poet, Fantasy for baritone and string quartet 1995, String Trio for violin, viola and violoncello 1996–97, Friendly Sketches for piano 1998, Duo for violin and cello 1999–2000, Music for contrabass solo 2001, Suite for two contrabass 2002, Leaving..., for flute, violin, cello, piano 2002, String Quartet No. 6 2003. *Recordings:* albums: Tunning for Guitar Solo 1990, Music for string quartet and orchestra 1998, String Quartet No. 3 1999, 5 Impromptus for violin and piano 1999, Suite for viola and bassclarinet 2000, Music for Strings 2001, Written by grief into silence..., vocal cycle for mezzo and orchestra 2001. *Honours:* International Award at the Festival of Choral Art, Jihlava 1993, Award, Czech Radio Sacred Music Competition 1994. *Address:* Milénova 2, 638 00 Brno 38, Czech Republic. *Website:* www.musica.cz/comp/matys.htm.

MAUCERI, John F.; Conductor and Music Director; b. 12 Sept. 1945, New York, USA; m. Betty Weiss, 15 June 1968, 1 s. *Education:* MPhil, 1971, BA, 1967, Yale University; Tanglewood, 1972. *Career:* Music Director, Yale Symphony, 1968–74; American Symphony Orchestra, 1984–87; Washington Opera, 1979–82; Kennedy Center, 1973–; Scottish Opera, 1987–93; Consultant, Music Theater, Kennedy Center, 1982–; Co-Producer, On Your Toes, Musical Play, Broadway and London's West End, 1982; Lyric Opera of Chicago debut, La Bohème, 1987; Music Director, WNET Gala of Stars, A Musical Toast, 1987; Conducted, the New York Philharmonic Metropolitan Opera Orchestra and Empire Brass, Carnegie Hall, 1987; British premiere of Weill's Street Scene, 1989; Conducted new production of La Forza del Destino for Scottish Opera, 1990, followed by revivals of Salome and Madama Butterfly; Les Troyens in Glasgow and London; Conducted own edition of Blitzstein's Regina at Glasgow, British Premiere, 1991; Madama Butterfly at Turin, 1996; Turandot at Turin, 1998; Premiere of original version of Weill's Der Weg der Verheissung, Chemnitz, 1999. *Recordings:* Original Cast: Candide, 1973, On Your Toes, 1983; New York City Opera, Candid, 1985; Original Cast, Song and Dance, 1985; My Fair Lady, with Kiri Te

Kanawa and Jerry Hadley. *Contributions:* Opera Magazine, 1985. *Honours:* Antoinette Perry, Outer Critics Circle, Drama Desk Awards, Best Opera Recording, Candide, 1987. *Current Management:* Columbia Artists Management, 165 West 57th Street, NY 10019, USA.

MAULTSBY, Nancy; Singer (Mezzo-Soprano); b. 1970, USA. *Career:* Appearances with Seattle Opera asCharlotte in Werther, Carmen at San Francisco and Erda in Siegfried at Buenos Aires; Further engagements as Carmen for Pittsburgh Opera, Anmeris in Minnesota and Ursula (Béatrice et Benedict) at Santa Fe; Sang The Omniscient Sea-Shell in Die Aegyptische Helena by Strauss for the Royal Opera at the Festival Hall, London, 1998; Concerts include Das Lied von der Erde, the Brahms Alto Rhapsody, Mahler's 2nd symphony (Cleveland Orchestra) and Schoenberg's Gurrelieder, with the Minnesota Orchestra. *Honours:* Marian Anderson and Martin E. Segal Awards, 1993. *Address:* c/o San Francisco Opera, War Memorial House, Van Ness Avenue, San Francisco, CA, USA.

MAUNDER, Charles (Richard Francis); Lecturer, Musicologist and Early Music Practitioner; b. 23 Nov. 1937, Portsmouth, England; m.; three s. *Education:* Jesus College, Cambridge, 1955–61; MA, PhD, Cambridge, 1962. *Career:* Fellow of Christ's College, Cambridge, 1964–; Lecturer at Univesities in Cambridge, London, Reading, Leeds, and in the USA, Philadelphia, Chicago, Northwestern, Northern Illinois, and at musicological conferences, International Mozart Congress, Salzburg, 1991; Performer on the bass viol, Cambridge Consort of Viols, baroque, classical viola, Cambridge Early Music; Violone, concerts in Cambridge and elsewhere include Messiah, St John Passion, Brandenburg Concertos, Bach Christmas Oratorio and Monteverdi Vespers; Has restored early keyboard instruments, including square piano by Johannes Zumpe, London 1766, for Emmanuel College, Cambridge; Instruments built include copies of two-manual harpsichord by Thomas Hitchcock and Mozart's forepiano; Founder of the Cambridge Classical Orchestra, 1990. *Publications:* Mozart's Requiem: On Preparing a New Edition, 1988; Numerous editions of 17th and 189th Century music, including 13 of the 48 vols of J C Bach's Collected Works; Mozart's Requiem K626, C minor Mass K 427 and Vesperae. *Contributions:* Galpin Society Journal, Musical Times, Early Music, Journal of the Royal Musical Association, Music and Letters, Notes, Mozart-Janrbuch. *Address:* 54 High Street, Sawston, Cambridge CB 2 4BG, England.

MAUNDER, Stuart; Stage Director; b. 1957, Australia. *Career:* Productions for Australian Opera include Nabucco, Die Fledermaus, Don Pasquale and Romeo et Juliette; La Traviata, Barber of Seville and Iolanthe for Victorian State Opera; Die Entführung and Don Pasquale for Lyric Opera Queensland; Music theatre pieces by Bernstein, Sondheim and Sullivan throughout Australia; Resident in the United Kingdom from 1990; Staff Director at Covent Garden, reviving La Bohème, L'Elisir d'amore and Guillaume Tell at Lisbon, and featuring in ROH/BBC television Top Score presentations; Pirates of Penzance for D'Oyly Carte Opera; Hoffman, Pasquale, Zauberflöte for Opus Festival, France; Mikado, Fille du Regiment for Opera Pacific, USA; Zauberflöte for British Youth Opera and Figaro for Hong Kong Academy. *Address:* 80 Beckwith Road, London SE24 9LG, England.

MAURER, Elsie; Singer (Mezzo-soprano); b. 1938, Germany. *Career:* Sang at the Aachen Opera from 1963, Pforzheim 1964–67, Frankfurt Opera from 1968; Among her best roles have been Meg Page, Olga in Eugene Onegin and Mary in Fliegender Holländer; Guest appearances at Brunswick, Oldenburg and elsewhere as Ortrud, Amneris, Herodias and Preziosilla; Sang Countess Geschwitz in Lulu for Essen Opera as guest at Barcelona (1969) and Trieste (1971); Also guested at the Vienna State Opera. *Recordings include:* Die Soldaten by Zimmermann (Teldec).

MAURO, Ermanno; Singer (Tenor); b. 20 Jan. 1939, Trieste, Italy. *Education:* Studied at the Toronto Conservatory with Herman Geiger-Torel. *Career:* Debut: Canadian Opera Company 1962, as Tamino in Die Zauberflöte; Sang Manrico in Toronto 1965; Covent Garden from 1967, debut in Manon Lescaut; Guest appearances with Welsh National Opera, Scottish Opera and at Glyndebourne; New York City Opera, 1975 as Calaf in Turandot; BBC television as Paco in La Vida Breve; Metropolitan Opera from 1978, as Canio, Manrico, Ernani, Pinkerton, Paolo in Zandonai's Francesca da Rimini and Des Grieux; La Scala and Rome 1978; San Francisco 1982; Vienna 1983; Brussels 1984, as Manrico; Dallas Opera 1985, as Otello; Other roles include Male Chorus in The Rape of Lucretia; Donizetti's Edgardo, Gounod's Faust, Verdi's Radames, Riccardo, Alfredo and Gabriele Adorno; Don José, Cavaradossi, Dick Johnson and Enzo in La Gioconda; Sang Cavaradossi at the Met 1986, Turiddu 1989; Calaf at the Deutsche Oper Berlin 1987; San Francisco and Barcelona 1989, as Otello and Enzo; Sang Manrico with Zürich Opera 1990, Maurizio in Adriana Lecouvreur at Montreal; Season 1992 at Radames at Dallas, Puccini's Des Grieux at Miami, Calaf at Philadelphia and Turiddu at the Teatro Col ón, Buenos Aires; Sang

Loris in Fedora at Montreal, 1995. *Address:* c/o Metropolitan Opera, Lincoln Center, NY 10023, USA.

MAURUS, Elsa; Singer (Mezzo-Soprano); b. 1968, France. *Education:* Studied with Eugénia Besala-Ludwig, and in Geneva. *Career:* Sang in Le Roi l'a Dit by Delibes at Nantes, then Rossini's Rosina at Rouen, 1994; Opéra d'Aran by Bécaud at the Vienna Konzerthaus, 1994; Concerts include Debussy's Le Martyre, in Rome, Cesar Franck's Les Béatitudes with the Orchesra of Ile de France, Mendelssohn's Erstes Walpurgisnacht at the Théâtre de Champs Elysées and Mozart's Requiem in colmar (1998); Mahler's 2nd and 3rd Symphonies in Japan (1999–2000), the Berlioz Roméo et Juliette in Paris and Poulenc's Carmélites in Italy; Engaged for season 2002 in Ravel's Sheherazade with the Utah symphony, Les Nuites d'été at Lille, as Carmen at Nantes, Nicklausse in Trieste, and Dulcinée in Massenet's Don Quichotte at Marseille. *Address:* c/o Musicaglotz 11, Rue Le Verrier, 75006 Paris, France.

MAUS, Peter; Singer (Tenor); b. 1948, Germany. *Career:* Debut: Bayreuth Youth Festival, 1972, in Wagner's Das Liebesverbot; Sang in the 1981 premiere of Kagel's Aus Deutschland; Bayreuth Festival from 1982, with minor roles in Parsifal and Die Meistersinger; Shepherd in Tristan, 1993; Teacher of Singing at the Hochschule für Kunste in Berlin, from 1987. *Recordings:* Das Liebesverbot; Die Meistersinger; Masses by Schubert, Donizetti Mass and Wolf's Der Corregidor; Esquire in Parsifal, conducted by Barenboim;Deutsche Oper Berlin from 1974, in such character roles as Wenzel in The Bartered Bridge, Sparlich in Lustigen Weiber, Peter Ivanov in Zar und Zimmermann, Pong, the Count in Zimmermann's Die Soldaten, Fatty in Mahagonny and Eljeya in From the House of the Dead; Sang M. Triquet in Eugene Onegin and Mozart's Don Curzio at the Deutsche Oper Berlin 2000. *Address:* c/o Deutsche Oper Berlin, Richard Wagnerstrasse 10, 1000 Berlin 10, Germany.

MAUTI, Nunziata; Singer (Soprano); b. 28 Aug. 1946, Palma Campania, Italy. *Education:* Studied in Naples and with Gina Cigna. *Career:* Debut: Palermo, 1965 aas Liu in Turandot; Appearances throughout Italy including La Scala and the Verona Arena, 1975–85; US debut Dallas, 1973, as Elvira in I Puritana; Chicago, 1978, as Butterfly and Gilda; Metropolitan Opera, 1977–80 in Traviata and Pagliacci; Wiesbaden, 1986, in Zandonai's Giulietta e Romeo, Turin, 1991 as Sulamith in Goldmark's Königin von Sheba; Other roles include Manon and Mozart's Fiordiligi and Donna Elvira; Verdi's Desdemona and Trovatore Leonora. *Address:* Teatro Regio di Torino, Piazza Castello 215, 10124 Turin, Italy.

MAVEL, Regina; Singer (Contralto); b. 1958, Cologne, Germany. *Education:* Cologne Musikhochschule. *Career:* Sang in Die Zauberflöte and Tannhäuser at Dortmund, 1983–84; Essen, 1988 and Munster from 1989 in operas by Bizet, Cornelius and Millöcker; Wiesbaden, 1992–93, in Wagner's Ring; Cologne Opera from 1995; Premiere of Patmos by Schweinitz at Munich, 1990; Other roles include Mary in Der fliegende Holländer and Geneviève in Pelléas et Mélisande; Concerts include Beethoven's Ninth at Bonn, 1994. *Address:* c/o Hessisches Staatstheater, Christian-Zais-Strasse 3–5, Pf. 3247, 6200 Wiesbaden, Germany.

MAW, (John) Nicholas; composer; b. 5 Nov. 1935, Grantham, England; m. Karen Graham 1960; one s. one d. *Education:* Royal Acad. of Music; studies with Nadia Boulanger and Max Deutsch, Paris. *Career:* Fellow Commoner in Creative Arts, Trinity Coll., Cambridge 1966–70. *Compositions include:* operas: One Man Show 1964, The Rising of The Moon 1970, Sophie's Choice 2002; orchestral works: Sinfonia 1966, Sonata for strings and two horns 1967, Serenade for Small Orchestra 1973, 1977, Odyssey 1974–87, Spring Music 1983, The World in the Evening 1988, American Games for Wind Ensemble 1991, Shahnama 1992, Dance Scenes 1995, Voices of Memory, Variations for orchestra 1995; instrumental solos with orchestra: Sonata Notturna for Cello and String Orchestra 1985, Little Concert for oboe, strings and two Horns 1987, Violin Concerto 1993; voice and orchestra: Nocturne 1958, Scenes and Arias 1962, Hymnus, for chorus and orchestra 1995; chamber music: Chamber Music for wind and piano quintet 1962, String Quartet 1965, No. 2 1983, No. 3 1994, Ghost Dances 1988, Piano Trio 1991, Intrada to The Art of Fugue, for string quartet 2002; instrumental music: Sonatina for Flute and Piano 1957, Personae for Piano Nos I–III 1973, Nos IV–VI 1985, Music of Memory for Solo Guitar 1989, Sonata for solo violin 1996, Narration for solo cello 2001; vocal music: 5 Epigrams for Chorus 1960, The Voice of Love for mezzo soprano and piano 1966, Reverdie, 5 songs for male voices 1975, Nonsense Rhymes, songs and rounds for children 1975–76, La Vita Nuova for soprano and chamber ensemble 1979, The Ruin, for double choir and solo horn 1980, Five American Folksongs for high voice and piano 1988, Roman Canticle for medium voice and chamber ensemble 1989, Sweté Jesu 1990, The Head of Orpheus, for soprano and 2 clarinets 1992. *Honours:* Midsummer Prize, Corporation of London 1980, Sudler International Wind Band

Prize 1991, Stoeger Prize for Chamber Music 1993. *Address:* c/o Faber Music Ltd, 3 Queen Square, London, WC1N 3AU, England.

MAX, Robert, GRSM, LRAM, ARAM; British cellist and conductor; b. 7 Feb. 1968, London, England; m. Zoë Solomon 1993; two s. one d. *Education:* Royal Acad. of Music, Royal Northern Coll. of Music, Juilliard School, New York. *Career:* concerts throughout the UK, Europe, North and South America, Russia and the Far East; String Finalist, BBC Young Musician of the Year, 1984; Music Dir for Nonesuch Orchestra, 1993–96, for Zemel Choir, 1994–98, for Pro Corda, 1998–2000; cellist with Barbican Piano Trio. *Recordings include:* Barbican Piano Trio: Mendelssohn D Minor with works by Alan Bush and John Ireland, 1989, Complete Piano Trios of E. Lalo; The Zemel Choir: Liturgical Music of Louis Lewandowski; The English Tradition of Jewish Choral Music Schnittke for ASV; Tchaikovsky and Rachmaninov for Guild. *Address:* 11 Willifield Way, London, NW11 7XU, England.

MAXWELL, Donald; Singer (Baritone); b. 12 Dec. 1948, Perth, Scotland; m. Alison Jayne Norman, 1 d. *Education:* Studied Geography at Edinburgh University. *Career:* Debut: Scottish Opera in Musgrave's Mary Queen of Scots, 1977; Covent Garden debut in Sallinen's The King Goes Forth to France; Performances at La Scala, Paris Opéra, Vienna Staatsoper, Covent Garden, Teatro Col ón, Buenos Aires, Edinburgh Festival, Glydebourne and BBC Proms; Major roles include Falstaff, Iago, Wozzeck, Golaud (all for television); Flying Dutchman, Scarpia, Rigoletto, Gunther, Don Alfonso; World Premieres by Berio, Manoury, Harle, Holt; Season 2000 as Don Alfonso for WNO, Faninal in Der Rosenkavalier at Covent Garden, Rossini's Geronimo for ENO and Britten's Balstrode at La Scala. *Recordings include:* Carmina Burana; Midsummer Night's Dream (Bottom); Lucretia (Tarquinnius); Many appearances and recordings in light music particularly as a Member of Music Box.

MAXWELL DAVIES, Sir Peter, Kt, CBE, MusB, FRCM, FRSAMD, FRNCM; British composer and conductor; *Master of the Queen's Music;* b. 8 Sept. 1934, Manchester, England; s. of Thomas Davies and Hilda (née Howard) Davies. *Education:* Leigh Grammar School, Royal Manchester Coll. of Music, Manchester Univ.; studied with Goffredo Petrassi, Rome 1957 and with Roger Sessions, Milton Babbitt, Earl Kim, Princeton Univ., NJ, USA (Harkness Fellow) 1962–64. *Career:* Dir of Music, Cirencester Grammar School 1959–62; lecture tours in Europe, Australia, USA, Canada, Brazil; Visiting Composer, Univ. of Adelaide 1966; Prof. of Composition, Royal Northern Coll. of Music, Manchester 1965–80 (Fellow 1978); Pres. Schools Music Asscn 1983–, Composers' Guild of GB 1986–, Nat. Fed. of Music Socs 1989–, Cheltenham Arts Festival 1994–96, Soc. for Promotion of New Music 1995–; Visiting Fromm Prof. of Composition, Harvard Univ. 1985; f. and Co-Dir (with Harrison Birtwistle) Pierrot Players 1967–71; f. and Artistic Dir The Fires of London 1971–87; f. and Artistic Dir St Magnus Festival, Orkney Islands 1977–86, Pres. 1986–; Artistic Dir Dartington Summer School of Music 1979–84; Assoc. Conductor and Composer Scottish Chamber Orchestra 1985–94, Composer Laureate 1994–; Conductor and Composer, BBC Philharmonic Orchestra (Manchester) 1992–2001; Assoc. Conductor and Composer Royal Philharmonic Orchestra 1992–2001; apptd Master of the Queen's Music 2004–; mem. Accademia Filarmonica Romana 1979, Royal Swedish Acad. of Music 1993, Bayerische Akad. der Schönen Künste 1998; hon. mem. Royal Acad. of Music 1979, Guildhall School of Music and Drama 1981, Royal Philharmonic Soc. 1987, Royal Scottish Acad. 2001. *Compositions include:* Sonata for trumpet and piano 1955, Alma redemptoris mater for ensemble 1957, St Michael sonata for 17 wind instruments 1957, Prolation for orchestra 1958, Five Klee Pictures for percussion, piano and strings 1959, Five Motets for soli, chorus and ensemble 1959, O Magnum Mysterium for chorus, instruments and organ 1960, Te Lucis ante Terminum 1961, String Quartet 1961, Frammenti di Leopardi for soprano, contralto and chamber ensemble 1962, First Fantasia on John Taverner's In Nomine for orchestra 1962, Veni Sancte Spiritus for soli, chorus and orchestra 1963, Second Fantasia on John Taverner's In Nomine 1964, Ecce Manus Tradentis for mixed chorus and instruments 1964, Shepherd's Calendar for young singers and instrumentalists 1965, Notre Dame des Fleurs 1966, Revelation and Fall for soprano and instrumental ensemble 1966, Antechrist for chamber ensemble 1967, Missa super L'Homme Armé for speaker and ensemble 1968, Stedman Caters for instruments 1968, Nocturnal Dances (ballet) 1969, St Thomas Wake-Foxtrot for orchestra 1969, Worldes Blis 1969, Eram quasi Agnus (instrumental motet) 1969, Eight Songs for a Mad King for male singer and ensemble 1969, Vesalii Icones for dancer and ensemble 1969, Taverner (opera) 1970, From Stone to Thorn for mezzo-soprano and instrumental ensemble 1971, Blind Man's Buff (masque) 1972, Hymn to Saint Magnus for chamber ensemble and mezzo-soprano 1972, Renaissance Scottish Dances 1973, Stone Litany for mezzo-soprano and orchestra 1973, Fiddlers at the Wedding 1974, Miss Donnithorne's Maggot for mezzo-soprano and chamber ensemble 1974, The Kestrel Paced Round the Sun 1975, Ave Maris Stella for chamber ensemble 1975, Three Studies for Percussion

1975, The Blind Fiddler for soprano and chamber ensemble 1975, Stevie's Ferry to Hoy (beginner's piano solo) 1975, Three Organ Voluntaries 1976, Kinloche His Fantassie (with Kinloch) 1976, Anakreontika (Greek songs for mezzo-soprano) 1976, Orchestral Symphony No. 1 1976, The Martyrdom of St Magnus (chamber opera) 1976, Runes from a Holy Island 1977, Westerlings (unaccompanied part songs) 1977, A Mirror of Whitening Light for chamber ensemble 1977, Le Jongleur de Notre Dame (Masque) 1978, The Two Fiddlers 1978, Salome (ballet) 1978, Black Pentecost (for voices and orchestra) 1979, Solstice of Light (for Tenor, Chorus and Organ) 1979, The Lighthouse (chamber opera) 1979, Cinderella (pantomime opera for young performers) 1979, A Welcome to Orkney (chamber ensemble) 1980, Orchestral Symphony No. 2 1980, Little Quartet (string quartet) 1980, The Yellow Cake Revue (for voice and piano) 1980, The Medium 1981, The Bairns of Brugh 1981, Piano Sonata 1981, Little Quartet No. 2 (for string quartet) 1981, Lullabye for Lucy 1981, Brass Quintet 1981, Songs of Hoy (Masque for children's voices and instruments) 1981, The Pole Star 1982, Sea Eagle (for horn solo) 1982, Image, Reflection, Shadow (for chamber ensemble) 1982, Sinfonia Concertante (for chamber orchestra) 1982, Into the Labyrinth (tenor and chamber orchestra) 1983, Sinfonietta Accademica (chamber orchestra) 1983, Unbroken Circle 1984, Guitar Sonata 1984, The No. 11 Bus 1984, One Star, At Last (carol) 1984, Orchestral Symphony No. 3 1984, The Peat Cutters 1985, Violin Concerto 1985, First Ferry to Hoy 1985, An Orkney Wedding, with Sunrise 1985, Sea Runes (vocal sextet) 1986, Jimmack the Postie (overture) 1986, Excuse Me 1986, House of Winter 1986, Trumpet Concerto 1987, Resurrection (opera in one act with prologue) 1987, Oboe Concerto 1988, Cello Concerto 1988, Mishkenot (chamber ensemble) 1988, The Great Bank Robbery 1989, Orchestral Symphony No. 4 1989, Hymn to the Word of God (for tenor and chorus) 1990, Concerto No. 4 for clarinet 1990, Caroline Mathilde (ballet) 1990, Tractus 1990, Dangerous Errand (for tenor soli and chorus) 1990, The Spiders' Revenge 1991, First Grace of Light 1991, Strathclyde Concerto No. 5 for violin and viola, No. 6 for flute 1991, Ojai Festival Overture 1991, A Selkie Tale (music-theatre work for performance by children) 1992, The Turn of the Tide (for orchestra and children's chorus and instrumental groups) 1992, Strathclyde Concerto No. 7 for double bass 1992, Sir Charles his Pavan 1992, Strathclyde Concerto No. 8 for bassoon 1993, A Spell for Green Corn: The MacDonald Dances 1993, Orchestral Symphony No. 5 (Royal Philharmonic Soc. Award for Large-Scale Composition 1995) 1994, Cross Lane Fair (for orchestra) 1994, Strathclyde Concerto No. 9 for six woodwind instruments 1994, The Three Kings (for chorus, orchestra and soloists) 1995, The Beltane Fire (choreographic poem) 1995, The Doctor of Myddfai (opera) 1995, Orchestral Symphony No. 6 1996, Strathclyde Concerto No. 10 for orchestra 1996, Piccolo Concerto 1996, Job (oratorio for chorus, orchestra and soloists) 1997, Mavis in Las Vegas–Theme and Variations 1997, Orkney Saga I: Fifteen keels laid in Norway for Jerusalem-farers 1997, The Jacobite Rising (for chorus, orchestra and soloists) 1997, Piano Concerto 1997, Orkney Saga II: In Kirkwall, the first red Saint Magnus stones 1997, Sails in St Magnus I–III 1998, A Reel of Seven Fishermen 1998, Sea Elegy (for chorus, orchestra and soloists) 1998, Roma Amor Labyrinthus 1998, Reel with Northern Lights 1998, Swinton Jig 1998, Temenos with Mermaids and Angels (for flute and orchestra) 1998, Spinning Jenny 1999, Sails in Orkney Saga III: An Orkney Wintering (for alto saxophone and orchestra) 1999, Trumpet quintet (for string quartet and trumpet) 1999, Mr Emmet Takes a Walk 1999, Horn Concerto 1999, Orkney Saga IV: Westerly Gale in Biscay, Salt in the Bread Broken 2000, Orchestral Symphony No. 7 2000, Orchestral Symphony No. 8 (Antarctic Symphony) 2000, Canticum Canticorum 2001, De Assumtione Beatae Mariae Virginis 2001, Crossing Kings Reach 2001, Mass 2002, Missa Parvula 2002, Naxos Quartet No. 1 2002, Piano Trio 2002, Naxos Quartet No. 2 2003, No. 3 2003, No. 4: Children's Games 2004; has written music for films: The Devils, The Boyfriend and many piano pieces, works for choir, instrumental works and realizations of fifteenth and sixteenth-century composers. *Honours:* several hon. degrees including Hon. DMus (Edin.) 1979, (Manchester) 1981, (Bristol) 1984, (Open Univ.) 1986, (Glasgow) 1993, (Durham) 1994, (Hull) 2001; Hon. DLitt (Warwick) 1986, (Salford) 1999; Hon. DUniv (Heriot-Watt) 2002; Hon. Fellow Royal Incorporation of Architects in Scotland 1994; Olivetti Prize 1959, Koussevitsky Award 1964, Koussevitsky Recording Award 1966, Cobbett Medal for services to chamber music 1989, First Award of Asscn of British Orchestras, for contribs to orchestras and orchestral life in UK 1991, Gulliver Award for Performing Arts in Scotland 1991, Nat. Fed. of Music Socs Charles Groves Award for outstanding contrib. to British Music 1995, Royal Philharmonic Soc. Award for Large-scale Composition (for Symphony No. 5) 1995, Inc. Soc. of Musicians Distinguished Musicians Award 2001; Officier, Ordre des Arts et des Lettres 1988. *Current Management:* Judy Arnold, 50 Hogarth Road, London, SW5 0PU, England. *Telephone:* (20) 7370-2328. *Fax:* (20) 7373-6730. *E-mail:* j.arnold@maxopus.com. *Website:* www.maxopus.com.

MAY, Marius; Cellist; b. 1950, England. *Education:* Studied with Andre Navarra in Paris and with Pierre Fournier in Geneva. *Career:* Debut: Wigmore Hall, 1973, followed by recital and concert appearances throughout the United Kingdom; Festival Hall 1976, with the Schumann Concerto and the Philharmonia Orchestra; Has played in public from age 10, giving a recital at the Royal College of Music, London, and playing the Saint-Saëns A minor Concerto in Edinburgh; Edinburgh and Bath Festivals, 1976; Soloist with leading orchestras in Europe; Several tours of Germany have included Berlin Philharmonic concert 1980; Concerts with Yehudi Menuhin at the Gstaad Festival, Switzerland. Has recently played the Elgar Concerto with the London Philharmonic and the Finzi Concerto at the Three Choirs Festival with the Royal Philharmonic; Has taught at the University of California in Los Angeles; BBC television concerts include the Tchaikovsky Rococo Variations and a Gala from the Edinburgh Festival. *Current Management:* Ingpen & Williams Ltd, 7 St George's Court, 131 Putney Bridge Road, London, SW15 2PA, England.

MAYER, Richard; Composer; b. 9 June 1948, Brno, Czechoslovakia. *Education:* Faculty of Arts, University of Brno; Piano, Composition, Conservatory, Brno; PhD, Musicology, 1975. *Career:* Debut: Brno, 1969, Zlin, 1980; Records of compositions on Czech television and radio; Piano Fantasy, Iceland, the Premiere, USA, 1990; mem, Nordic Society of Prague; Bohemian Music Association; Club of Moravian Composers. *Compositions include:* Sonata for Violin and Piano; Concerto for 2 Pianos and Tromba; Quartet for Clarinet, Violin, Viola and Cello; Variation for Clarinet and Piano; Reykjavík, Sonata for Viola and Cello; Variation for Tromba and Piano; Iceland, Fantasy for Piano Solo; Saga of Northern Night, A Cycle of Compositions for Alto and Bassoon; Drama Musicum Sine Verbis–Chronikon Mundi, 1st Symphony for Chamber Orchestra; Magna Missa Millennia Islandica: Great Magnificent Mass for large orchestra, organ, narrator, solos and choir, dedicated to the forthcoming anniversary of 1000 years of accepting Christianity in Iceland; II Symphony "Icelandic" for Great Orchestra. *Recordings:* Several. *Contributions:* Opus Musicium. *Address:* Cihlarska 14, 602 00 Brno, Czech Republic.

MAYER, William (Robert); Composer; b. 18 Nov. 1925, New York, USA. *Education:* BA, Yale University, 1949; Studied with Roger Sessions at Juilliard, 1949 and at the Mannes College of Music, 1949–52. *Career:* Secretary, National Music Council, 1980. *Compositions:* Stage: The Greatest Sound Around, children's opera, 1954; Hell World children's opera, 1956; One Christmas Long Ago, opera in act, 1964; Brief Candle, micro-opera, 1964; A Death in the Family, opera 1983; The Snow Queen, ballet, 1963; Orchestra: Andante for strings, 1955; Hebraic Portrait, 1957; Overture for an American, 1958; Two Pastels, 1960; Octagon for piano and orchestra, 1971; Inner and Outer Strings for string quartet and string orchestra, 1982; Of Rivers and Trains, 1988; String Quartet and other chamber music; Piano Sonata Choruses and song. *Honours:* Guggenheim Fellowship, 1966; National Institute for Musical Theater Award, 1983. *Address:* ASCAP, ASCAP Building, 1 Lincoln Plaza, NY 10023, USA.

MAYFORTH, Robin; Violinist; b. 1965, USA. *Education:* Studied at the Juilliard School, New York. *Career:* Appearances with I Solisti Veneti, under Claudio Scimone; Co-founded the Lark Quartet, USA; Recent concert tours to Australia, Taiwan, Hong Kong, China, Germany, Netherlands; US appearances at the Lincoln Center, New York, Kennedy Center, Washington DC and in Boston, Los Angeles, Phildelphia, St Louis and San Francisco; Repertoire includes quartets by Haydn, Mozart, Beethoven, Schubert, Dvořák, Brahms, Borodin, Bartók, Debussy and Shostakovich. *Honours:* (With Lark Quartet): Gold Medals at the 1990 Naumberg and 1991 Shostakovich Competitions; Prizewinner, 1991 London International String Quartet, 1991 Melbourne Chamber Music, 1990 Premio Paulio Borciani (Reggio Emilia) and 1990 Karl Klinger (Munich) Competitions. *Current Management:* Sonata, Glasgow Scotland. *Address:* c/o The Lark Quartet, 11 Northpark Street, Glasgow G20 7AA, Scotland.

MAYHEW, Dame Judith, LLM; New Zealand politician and lawyer and academic; b. 18 Oct. 1948, Dunedin; m. 1976 (divorced 1986). *Education:* Otago Girls' High School, Univ. of Otago, NZ. *Career:* barrister and solicitor, NZ 1973, solicitor, England and Wales 1993; lecturer in Law, Univ. of Otago 1970–73; lecturer in Law and Sub Dean, Univ. of Southampton, UK 1973–76, King's Coll. London 1976–89; Dir Anglo-French law degree, Sorbonne, Paris 1976–79; Dir of Training and Employment Law, Titmuss Sainer Dechert 1989–94; Dir of Educ. and Training, Wilde Sapte 1994–99; City and Business Adviser to Mayor of London 2000–; mem. of Court of Common Council Corpn of London 1986–, Chair Policy and Resources Cttee 1997–2002; Special Adviser to Chair. of Clifford Chance 2000–; Dir Gresham Coll. 1990–, London First Centre 1996–, Int. Financial Services London (fmrly British Invisibles) 1996–, London First 1997–, 4Ps 1997–, London Devt Agency 2000, Cross River Partnership; Trustee Natural History Museum 1998–; Gov. Birkbeck Coll. London 1993–; Chair. Royal Opera House, London

2003–. *Honours:* Hon. LLD (Otago) 1998, (City Univ. London) 1999. *Address:* Royal Opera House, Covent Garden, London, WC2E 9DD, England (office). *Telephone:* (20) 7240-1200 (office). *Website:* www .royalopera.org.

MAYNOR, Kevin (Elliott); Singer (Bass); b. 24 July 1954, Mt Vernon, New York, USA. *Education:* Diploma, Manhattan School of Music, 1970–72; BME, Bradley University, 1972–76; MM, Northwestern University, 1976–77; MV, Moscow Conservatory, 1979–80; Indiana University, 1980–83; DM, 1988. *Career:* Debut: Carnegie Hall, 1983 in a concert of Strauss's Die Liebe der Danaë; Avery Fisher Hall as Nocco in Fidelio, 1985; New York City Opera, Akhnaten, 1985; Chicago Lyric Opera; Santa Fe Opera; Virginia Opera; Nashville Opera; Long Beach Opera; Chicago Opera Theater; Mobile Opera Theater; Mobile Opera; Apprenticeship, 1st from the West, Bolshoi Opera, 1979–80; Scottish Opera 1987 and Opera Pacific 1994 as Hunding in Die Walküre. *Current Management:* Herbert Barrett Management. *Address:* 201 Egmont Avenue, Mt Vernon, NY 10552, USA.

MAZURA, Franz; Singer (Bass-Baritone); b. 22 April 1924, Salzburg, Austria. *Education:* Studied with Fred Husler in Detmold. *Career:* Debut: Kassel 1955; Sang at Mainz and Brunswick until 1964; Mannheim 1964–89; Salzburg 1960, in La Finta Semplice; Pizarro in Fidelio, 1970; Member of Deutsche Oper Berlin 1963; Paris Opéra from 1973, as Wagner's Wotan, Alberich and Gurnemanz; Sang Dr Schön in the 1979 premiere of the three-act version of Berg's Lulu; Bayreuth Festival from 1971, as Biterolf, Alberich, Gunther, Gurnemanz, Klingsor and the Wanderer in the 1988 Ring Cycle directed by Harry Kupfer; Hamburg Opera from 1973; Israel Festival, Caeserea, as Moses in Schoenberg's Moses und Aron; Guest appearances in Vienna, Buenos Aires, San Francisco, Nice and Strasbourg; Metropolitan Opera debut 1980, as Dr Schön, returned to New York as Klingsor, Alberich, Gurnemanz, Creon in Oedipus Rex, Pizarro, Doctor in Wozzeck, Frank in Die Fledermaus, Rangoni in Boris Godunov and the Messenger in Die Frau ohne Schatten, 1989; Bayreuth Festival, 1988–89 as Klingsor and the Wanderer; Season 1991–92 as Voland (the Devil), in Höller's Meister und Margarita at Cologne and Klingsor at the Met and the Bayreuth Festival; Narrated Henze's Raft of the Medusa, Festival Hall, London, 1997; Schigolch in Lulu at San Francisco, 1998; Sang Schigolch at Bielefeld and the New York Met, 2001. *Recordings include:* Dr Schön, Jack the Ripper in Lulu (Grammy Award 1980) (Deutsche Grammophon); Gunther in Götterdämmerung (Philips); Schoenberg's Moses (Philips). *Current Management:* Ingpen & Williams Ltd, 7 St George's Court, 131 Putney Bridge Road, London, SW15 2PA, England.

MAZURKEVICH, Yuri (Nicholas); Professor of Violin and Concert Violinist; b. 6 May 1941, Lvov, USSR; m. Dana Mazurkevich, 4 July 1963, 1 d. *Education:* School of Gifted Children, Lvov, 1948–60; Moscow State Conservatoire, with D Oistrakh, 1960–65, Postgraduate course, Artist Diploma; Masters degree in Performance, 1965–67. *Career:* Concert Violinist appeared all over the world; Recorded for Radio Moscow, France, BBC, ABC (Australia), CBC (Canada), Sender Freies (West Berlin), WGBH (Boston) and many others; Assistant Professor, Violin, Kiev State Conservatory, 1967–73; Associate Professor, Violin, University of Western Ontario, 1975–85; Professor of Violin, Chairman of String Department, 1985–; Boston University; Member of Quartet Canada, 1980–; mem, Music Council of Canada. *Recordings:* Works by Beethoven, Paganini, Tartini, Handel, Spohr, Leclair, Prokofiev, Sarasate, Honegger, Telemann and others in Moscow, Toronto and Montreal, Canada. *Honours:* Prize Winner of 3 International Violin Competitions, Helsinki 1962, Munich 1966 and Montreal 1969. *Address:* 56 Mason Terrace, Brookline, MA 02146, USA.

MAZZARIA, Lucia; Singer (Soprano); b. 1964, Gorizia, Poland. *Education:* Studied in Trieste and Rome. *Career:* Debut: Venice 1987, as Mimi; Hamburg Opera 1987, as Mimi, Liu and Micaela; La Scala Milan debut 1988, as Lauretta in Gianni Schicchi, returning as Liu, Euridice and Violetta; Cologne Opera 1991, as Amelia Boccanegra; Further appearances at Monte Carlo, Covent Garden (London), Houston and Vienna; Venice 1990, as Mimi in Leoncavallo's Bohème; Further tours of Russia, Japan and Korea; Sang Desdemona at the 1996 Holland Festival and Micaela in Carmen at Macerata, 1998; Season 2000–01 as Amelia Grimaldi at Macereta, Suor Angelica in Verona and Desdemona in Venice. *Recordings include:* Leoncavallo's Bohème (Nuova Era). *Address:* c/o Opéra et Concert, 1 rue Volney, F–75002 Paris, France.

MAZZOLA, Denia; Singer (Soprano); b. 1956, Bergamo, Italy. *Education:* Studied with Corinna Malatrasi. *Career:* Sang Amina in La Sonnambula at Brescia, then Lucia di Lammermoor, and Adina at Florence and Milan; Landestheatre Salzburg 1984, as Gilda, St Gallen 1985 as Violetta; Sang at the Zürich Opera 1985–87, notably as Elvira in I Puritani; Appearances as Lucia at Naples, 1988–89, New York City Opera; La Scala Milan, 1987, Sole in Fetonte by Jommelli; Further engagements at Houston, Alice Ford, San Francisco, in Maria Stuarda, Bergamo, Amelia in Elisabetta al Castello di Kenilworth by Donizetti,

1989, Reggio Emilia, Violetta, Barcelona, Elvira, 1990 and the 1990 Montpellier Festival, Palmide in a concert performance of Meyerbeer's Il Crociato in Egitto; Sang Mimi at the 1996 Torre del Lago Festival; Season 2000–01 as Manon Lescaut at Catania, Cherubini's Médée for the Macerata Festival and Hélène in Les Vêpres Siciliennes at Schwerin (concert). *Recordings include:* Lucia di Lammermoor, with forces of the San Carlo, Naples (Nuova Era). *Address:* Stafford Law, 6 Barham Close, Weybridge, Surrey KT 13 9 PR.

MAZZOLA, Rudolf; Singer (Bass); b. 1941, Basle, Switzerland. *Education:* Studied in Basle and Zürich. *Career:* Debut: Commendatore in Don Giovanni at St Gallen; Sang at St Gallen until 1971, Basle, 1971–75; Engaged at the Vienna Volksoper from 1975, debut in Wolpert's version of Molière's Le Malade Imaginaire; Sang Osmin in Die Entführung at the Vienna Staatsoper, 1977, returning as Sarastro, Gremin, Pimen, Padre Guardiano and the Grand Inquisitor; Bregenz Festival 1980 and 1984, as Osmin and the Sacristan in Tosca; Salzburg Festival 1981 in the premiere of Cerha's Baal, Paris Opéra 1983, as Truffaldino in Ariadne auf Naxos; Sang the Doctor in Wozzeck at Barcelona 1984, Rossini's Basilio at Liège 1988; Toronto, Don Alfonso in Così fan tutte, 1992; Nice, La Roche, Capriccio, 1993; Created roles in Einem's Tulifant and Krenek's Kehraus um St Stephan, Ronach Theater Vienna, 1990, and sang Mozart's Bartolo at the Theater an der Wien, 1991; Sang the Doctor in Wozzeck at Florence, 1998; Sang Berg's Schigolch and Doctor at the Vienna Staatsoper, 2000. Guest appearances at Frankfurt, Hamburg, Munich, Budapest, Turin and Zürich; Frequent concert and oratorio appearances. *Address:* c/o Staatsoper Opernring 2, 1010 Vienna, Austria.

MAZZUCATO, Daniela; Italian singer (soprano); b. 1 Dec. 1946, Venice. *Education:* Venice Conservatory. *Career:* debut, Teatro Fenice Venice, 1966, as Gilda; Appearances throughout Italy, including 1971 at the Verona Arena, as Oscar; Rome 1990, as Valencienne in The Merry Widow and Mozart's Despina, 1995; Palermo, 1996, as Gluck's Euridice; Guest engagements at La Scala, Oscar, 1977, Düsseldorf, Prague and Berlin; Toulouse 1995, as Musetta in La Bohème; Season 1998 as Despina at Glyndebourne; Casparina in Wolf-Ferrari's Il Campiello at Bologna and Pipsi in Lehar's Eva at Naples. *Recordings:* Vivaldi's Serenata a tre; Medea by Cherubini. *Current Management:* Stage Door, Via Marconi 71, 40122 Bologna, Italy. *Telephone:* (051) 19984750. *Fax:* (051) 19984779. *E-mail:* info@stagedoor.it. *Website:* www.stagedoor.it.

MEAD, Philip (John); Pianist; b. 8 Sept. 1947, Chadwell St Mary, Essex, England; m. Gillian Mead, 2 Aug 1969, 3 d. *Education:* ARCM, Performing 1966, FTCL 1982, LRAM 1968, GRSM 1969, Royal Academy of Music; Honorary degree ARAM, 1993. *Career:* Debut: Purcell Room, 1973; Performances, major festivals, England and overseas; Specialist, 20th century piano music; Commissioned works include works for piano and electronics by Dennis Smalley, Jonathan Harvey, Tim Souster and others; Featured soloist at London South Bank's 1987 Electric Weekend; Soloist, BBC Symphony Orchestra Ives Festival, 1996; Founded the first British Contemporary Piano Competition, Cambridge 1988; Professor, Head of Department of Contemporary Piano, London College of Music and media, 1998–; Repetoire includes Messiaen, Tippett, Stockhausen and George Crumb; Commissioned works for brass and piano, Sackman, Poole, Burrell, Ellerby, Wilkins and Emmerson, 1999–2003; mem, Sonic Arts; Director, Society for the Promotion of New Music; EPTA. *Recordings:* Numerous for BBC and European Stations, including Stephen Montague, Slow Dance on a Burial Ground; Recorded 8 CDs of electronic music;. *Contributions:* Electro Acoustic Music; Classical Piano; Complete piano works of Ives, 2002; Makrokosmos by George Crumb, 2003. *Honours:* 5 prizes, Royal Academy of Music; Research Awards; Prizewinner, Gaudeamus International Competition for Interpreters of Contemporary Music, 1978; ARAM, RAM, 1993; Artistic Director, Contemporary Piano Competition; Fellow of London College of Music and Media, 1998; HonFLCM (Honorary degree London College of Music), 1998. *Address:* 31 Lingholme Close, Cambridge CB 4 3HW, England. *E-mail:* meadpj@hotmail.com.

MEALE, Richard, MBE; composer; b. 24 Aug. 1932, Sydney, Australia. *Education:* New South Wales Conservatorium of Music, University of California at Los Angeles. *Career:* Programme Planning Officer for the Australian Broadcasting Commission, 1962–68; Senior Lecturer in the Department of Music at the University of Adelaide from 1969; Active as Pianist from 1955, notably in the music of Messiaen; mem, Adelaide Festival Centre Trust, 1972; President of the Australian Branch of ISCM, 1977; Chairman of the composition Panel of the Music Board of the Australia Council. *Compositions:* Stage: The Hypnotist Ballet, 1956; Incidental Music to King Lear; Juliet's Memoirs, opera, 1975; Operas Voss, 1986 and Mer de Glace, 1991; Orchestral: Flute Concerto, 1959; Sinfonia for piano and strings, 1959; Homage to Garcia Lorca for double string orchestra, 1964; Images, 1966; Very High Kings, 1968; Clouds Now and Then, 1969; Soon it Will Die, 1969; Evocations, 1973; Viridian, 1979; Symphony, 1994; Instrumental: Divertiemnto for Piano Trio, 1959; Flute Sonata, 1960; Les Alboradas for flute, horn, violin and piano,

1963; Wind Quintet, 1970; Incredible Floridas for flute, clarinet, violin, cello, piano and percussion, 1971; 3 String Quartets, 1974, 1980, 1993; Fanfare for brass ensemble, 1978; Keyboard: Sonatina Patetica, 1957; Orenda, 1959; Coruscations, 1971; Palimpsest, for ensemble, 1998. *Honours:* Composers Fellowship awarded by the South Australian Government 1972–75. *Current Management:* Universal Edition (London) Ltd, 48 Great Marlborough Street, London, W1F 7BB, England. *Telephone:* (20) 7437-6880. *Fax:* (20) 7437-6115.

MECHELEN, Werner van; Singer (Bass-baritone); b. 1961, Turnhout, Belgium. *Education:* Studied under Roland Bufkens, Vocalist's Diploma, Lemmens Institute, Leuven; Masterclasses with Dietrich Fischer-Dieskau, Elisabeth Schwarzkopf, Robert Holl, Mitsuko Shirai, Hartmut Höll, Malcolm King. *Career:* Performances of Passions, Oratorios and orchestral Lieder in Cologne, Geneva, Brussels, Amsterdam, Paris, Barcelona and Tel-Aviv; Has worked with conductors Stefan Soltesz, Sigiswald Kuijken, Ton Koopman, Antonio Pappano, S Varviso, others; Has sung Mozart's Count and Figaro, Guglielmo, Don Giovanni, Leporello, Papageno, also Schaunard in La Bohème, Dandini in La Cenerentola, Belcore in L'Elisir d'amore, Wolfram in Tannhäuser, Animal Trainer and Athlete in Lulu; Guest appearances in Zürich, Liège, Antwerp, Wiesbaden, Braunschweig, Bielefeld, Coburg, Limoges, elsewhere; Sang under direction of Kuijken in Caldara's opera I Disingannati at Innsbruck Baroque Festival, 1993, and with same ensemble performed Don Giovanni, 1995, Pergolesi's Livietta e Tracollo, 1996, Le nozze di Figaro, 1998; Repertoire includes all great lieder-cycles; Often sings to piano accompaniment of Jozef De Beenhouwer, Eric Schneider and others; Conducts Kemp Oratorio Society concerts; Engaged to sing in Wozzeck for La Bastille, Rigoletto for open-air festival in Belgium, Marcello in Liège and Kothner in Meistersinger at Antwerp. *Recordings:* For Belgian and foreign radio and television; Discs with Baroque music; Richard Strauss Lieder. *Address:* Goedeluchtstraat 12, 8420 Wenduine, Belgium. *E-mail:* arioso@skynet.be.

MEDCALF, Stephen; Stage Director; b. 1960, England; m. Susan Gritton, 1 s. *Education:* London Drama Studio. *Career:* Graduated 1983 and became associate director at Glyndebourne 1988, working with Peter Sellars, Peter Hall and Trevor Nunn; Directed in many major international opera houses in France, Portugal, Italy and Australia as well as for Glyndebourne Festival, Opera North, Opera Northern Ireland, The wexford Festival, English Touring Opera, Garsington, Mid Wales Opera (Artistic Adviser) and numerous festivals; Fellow of the Guildhall School of Music and Drama and Resident producer of its opera course; Has directed over 60 opera productions. *Recordings:* Videos: Zauberflöte, Così fan tutte, with John Eliot Gardiner; Le nozze di Figaro, Glyndebourne Festival Opera and Channel 4. *Current Management:* Athole Still International Management, Forresters Hall, 25–27 Westow Street, London, SE19 3RY, England. *Telephone:* (20) 8771-5271. *Fax:* (20) 8768-6600. *Website:* www.atholestill.com.

MEDEK, Ivo; Composer; b. 20 July 1956, Brno, Czechoslovakia; m. Zuzana Medková, 11 Aug 1986, 2 s. *Education:* Computers and Structural Mechanics (Dipl ing), Technical University; Master Composition, 1989, PhD, Composition and Theory, 1997, Janáček Academy of Music and Dramatic Art in Brno. *Career:* About 60 compositions of orchestral, chamber, electro-acoustics music, many recorded on television, broadcasts and festivals in the Czech Republic, Europe and USA, 1990, 1994; Docent of Darmstadt courses, lectures in Brno, Austria, Poland, Netherlands, Portugal; Professor of Janáček Academy of Music in Brno; mem, Camerata Brno 'Q' Society, Czech Music Council. *Compositions:* Adledaivan, 1988; Pangea, 1989; Triads, 1989; Cephedidy, 1991; Flow, 1992; Postludio, 1994; Persofonie, 1995; 11 Gestalten des Mondscheins, 1997; Enlargement, for flute, clarinet, piano, violin and cello, 1999; Crossings, multimedia, 1999; Ancient Stories, 1999; Triax, 2001. *Recordings:* Adai; Adeldaivan; Flow; Cepheidy; Postludio; Fests; Pangea; Wandering in Well-known Landscape; Persofonie. *Publications:* Basic General Composing Principles, 1989; Processuality as a Complex Composing Method, 1996. *Contributions:* About 100 articles, Opus Musicum, Czech Music, The Silence. *Honours:* Czech Music Fund Prize, 1993. *Address:* Sirotkova 67, 61600 Brno, Czech Republic.

MEDEK, Tilo; Composer; b. 22 Jan. 1940, Jena, Thuringia, Germany; s. of the late Willy Müller-Medek and Rosa Gewehr. *Education:* musicology with W. Vetter, E. H. Meyer and G. Knepler, Humboldt Univ., Berlin; composition with R. Wagner-Régeny, German Acad. of Music, East Berlin. *Career:* moved to West Germany, 1977. *Compositions include:* Operas Einzug, 1969; Icke und die Hexe Yu, 1970–71; Appetit auf Frükirschen, 1971; Katharina Blum, 1984–86; Gritzko und der Pan, 1987; Balled David and Goliath, 1972; Orchestral: Triade 1964; Das zögernde Lied, 1970; Flute concerto, 1973; Piccolo Concerto, 1975; König Johann oder Der Ausstieg, for orchestra and organ, 1976; Marimba Concerto, 1977; three Cello Concertos, 1978, 1982, 1984, 1992; Organ Concerto, 1979–80; Violin Concerto, 1980–83; I. Sinfonie (Eisenblatter for organ and orchestra), 1983; II Sinfonie (Rheinische), 1986–88; III.

Sinfonie (Sorbische), 1994–1996 Chamber: Flute Sonata, 1963; five Wind Quintets, 1965–99; String Trio, 1965; Divertissement for wind quintet and harpsichord, 1967; Stadtpfeifes, Schwanengesang for clarinet, trombone, cello and piano, 1973; two Nonett, 1974, 1996; Tagtraum for 7 instruments, 1976; Giebichestein for 8 instruments, 1976; Reliquienschrein for organ and percussion, 1980; Vocal: Altägyptische Liebeslieder for 2 voices and orchestra, 1963; Sintflutbestanden for tenor, horn and piano, 1967; Gethsemane, cantata, 1980; Der Frieden wird immer gefährlicher, for tenor, chorus and orchestra, 1996–98; piano and organ music. *Address:* Rheinhöhe, Westerwaldweg 22, 53424 Remagen-Oberwinter, Germany. *Telephone:* 02228-8175. *Fax:* 02228-8176. *E-mail:* tila@medek.net. *Website:* www.medek.net.

MEDJIMOREC, Heinz; Pianist; b. 1940, Vienna, Austria. *Education:* Studied in Vienna. *Career:* Performances of Haydn and other composers in Vienna and elsewhere from 1968; Co-founder, Hydn Trio of Vienna, 1968 and has performed in Brussels, Munich, Berlin, Zürich, London, Paris and Rome; New York debut in 1979 and has made frequent North American appearances with concerts in 25 states; Debut tour of Japan 1984, with further travels to the Near East, Russia, Africa, Central and South America; Series at the Vienna Konzerthaus Society from 1976, with performances of more than 100 works; Summer Festivals at Vienna, Salzburg, Aix-en-Provence, Flanders and Montreux; Masterclasses at the Royal College and Royal Academy in London, Stockholm, Bloomington, Tokyo and the Salzburg Mozarteum. *Recordings include:* Complete piano trios of Beethoven and Schubert, Mendelssohn D minor, Brahms B major, Tchaikovsky A minor, Schubert Trout Quintet; Albums of works by Haydn, Schumann, Dvořák and Smetana. *Address:* Haydn Trio, Sue Lubbock Concert Management, 25 Courthorpe Road, London NW3 2LE, England.

MEDLAM, Charles; Cellist; b. 10 Sept. 1949, Port of Spain, Trinidad. *Education:* Studied the cello in London, Paris (with Maurice Gendron at the Conservatoire), Vienna and Salzburg (performance practice with Nikolaus Harnoncourt). *Career:* Lectured and played in the resident string quartet at the Chinese University of Hong Kong; Founded London Baroque with Ingrid Seifert 1978; Conducted the first performance of Scarlatti's Une villa di Tuscolo and a revival of Gli Equivoci Sembiante, for the BBC; Season 1990–91 included Dido and Aeneas at the Paris Opéra, Blow and Lully at the Opera-Comique; Aci, Galatea e Polifemo in Spain, Netherlands and England, and cantatas by Handel and Rameau in Austria, Sweden and Germany with Emma Kirkby; Salzburg Festival debut 1991, with music by Mozart; Further festival engagements at Bath, Beaune, Versailles, Ansbach, Innsbruck and Utrecht and 1993 Proms; Founded Romantic Chamber Group of London with Paul Barritt, violin and James Lisney, piano, 1997; Concerts in the United Kingdom, Amsterdam, Barcelona, Evian and the USA. *Recordings:* Marais La Gamme, Theile Matthew Passion, Bach Trio Sonatas, Charpentier Theatre Music, Handel Aci, Galatea e Polifemo, Venus and Adonis, Purcell Chamber Music; Purcell Fantasias, Bach Violin Sonatas, Monteverdi Orfeo, Handel German Arias; A Vauxhall Gardens Entertainment; English Music of the 18th Century; Francois Couperin Chamber Music; The complete trio sonatas of Corelli, Handel, Purcell, Lawes; Gamba sonatas by CPE Bach, harpsichord concertos by JC Bach/WA Mozart; Vivaldi, Trio sonatas Op.1, Christmas Music and Handel Latin Motets with Emma Kirkby, Purcell Fantasias, Couperin's Apotheoses, Rameau Pièces de Clavecin en Concert; Vol. I of the Complete Chamber Music with Piano of Phillip Scharwenka, 1999. *Address:* Brick Kiln Cottage, Hollington, Nr Newbury, Berkshire RG20 9XX, England.

MEDVECZKY, Adam; Conductor; b. 1941, Budapest, Hungary. *Education:* Timpanist Graduate, Bela Bart ók Conservatory; Department of Conducting, Liszt Academy of Music, Budapest, 1968; Masterclass, Maestro Franco Ferrara, Italy. *Career:* Timpanist, Hungarian State Symphony Orchestra for 9 years; Conductor, Budapest State Opera, 1974; Numerous guest appearances in Bulgaria, Germany, Greece, Netherlands, Poland, Italy, Romania, Russia and USA; Professor, Ferenc Liszt Academy, Budapest, 1981–. *Recordings:* Has made numerous recordings. *Honours:* Liszt Prize, 1976; 2nd Prize, Hungarian Television International Concours for Young Conductors, 1974.

MEE, Anthony; Singer (Tenor); b. 9 Sept. 1951, Lancashire, England. *Education:* Studied at the Royal Northern College of Music. *Career:* Debut: Welsh National Opera, 1984 as Ernani; Sang Ernani and Riccardo, 1999–2000 for Welsh National Opera; Gabriele Adorno, Cavaradossi, Nadir and Calaf for English National Opera; Bardolfo in Falstaff at the Berlin Staatsoper; Concerts include Verdi's Giovanna d'Arco, Boito's Mephistopheles and Verdi's Aroldo in London; Season 1999–2000 with Bardolfo at Ferraa Musica, Italy and in Munich. *Recordings:* Weill's Street Scene and Falstaff, conducted by Abbado (DGG). *Address:* c/o Harlequin Agency Ltd, 203 Fidlas Road, Cardiff CF4 5NA, Wales.

MEEK, Clarissa; Singer (Mezzo-soprano); b. 1970, England. *Education:* Guildhall School of Music and Drama. *Career:* Appearances with Scottish Opera in The Merry Widow, Street Scene, Figaro, The Magic Flute, Death in Venice, Jenůfa and Salome; Iolanthe in the opera by Sullivan (also broadcast); Glyndebourne Festival as Madame Larina in Eugene Onegin, Pauline (The Queen of Spades), Glasha (Katya Kabanova) and two roles in the premiere production of Birtwistle's Second Mrs Kong (1994); Season 1996–97 with Haydn's Stabat Mater at Aldeburgh, Thisbe (Cenerentola) in Japan and Maddalena in Rigoletto at Guernsey; Maurya in Hart's Riders to the Sea at Cambridge, 1998; Concerts include Messiah in Hanover and The Dream of Gerontius; Other operas include Les Boréades by Rameau, Tchaikovsky's The Enchantress and Monteverdi's Ulisse (as Penelope). *Honours:* Erich Vietheer Memorial Award at Glyndebourne, 1995. *Address:* c/o C&M Craig Services, 3 Kersley Street, London SW11 4 PR, England.

MEEK, James; Singer (Baritone); b. 29 July 1957, Winchester, England. *Education:* Studied at the Guildhall School of Music. *Career:* Sang for three seasons at the Buxton Festival and appeared as Owen Wingrave at Aldeburgh; Other roles include Escamillo, Rossini's Figaro, Mozart's Count and Guglielmo, Valentin in Faust and the Doctor in Debussy's posthumous Fall of the House of Usher (Queen Elizabeth Hall 1989); Sang in Haydn's La Vera Costanza in Germany; Concert repertoire includes Elijah, the Petite Messe Solennelle, Handel's Judas Maccabaeus (Flanders Festival) Israel in Egypt and Dixit Dominus; Bach's Christmas Oratorio at the Snape Maltings, St John and St Matthew Passions; Britten's War Requiem in Germany and Yugoslavia and the Requiems of Mozart, Fauré and Brahms; Sang Messiah at the National Concert Hall Dublin, Pulcinella at the Barbican and the Missa Solemnis at Guilford Cathedral; Songs by Henri Dutilleux at Aldeburgh and concerts with the Songmakers' Almanac at the Bath, Nottingham, Buxton and Derby Festivals; Recitals on South Bank in the Schoenberg Reluctant Revolutionary Series, 1989 and Schubert directed by Hermann Prey, accompanied by Iain Burnside; Sang Starveling in A Midsummer Night's Dream at Aix-en-Provence, 1992.

MEER, Rud van der; Singer (Baritone); b. 23 June 1936, The Hague, Netherlands. *Education:* Studied oboe and conducting at Royal Conservatory, The Hague; Vocal teachers include Pierre Bernac. *Career:* Debut: As singer, 1967; Played oboe in Hague Philharmonic Orchestra; Teacher at various grammar schools; Conductor of Choir in Netherlands; Recitalist and oratorio soloist in major centres including London, New York, Berlin, Paris, Vienna and Warsaw; Recitals for the BBC and at the Holland, Helsinki and English Bach Festivals; Bregenz Festival and The Belgian Festival of Flanders; Conductors include: Gerd Albrecht, Berio, Michel Corboz, Jean Fournet, Harnoncourt, Leitner, Pritchard and Hans Vonk; Performances with Elly Ameling in New York and London of Wolf's Italienisches Liederbuch and Spanisches Liederbuch; Moscow debut 1988 in the Sviatoslav Richter Festival at the Pushkin Museum; Tour of Russia in May 1989; BBC Recital, 1997; Permanent member of the jury of the International Singing Competiton of Hertogenbosch. *Recordings:* Lieder and Oratorio; 40 Bach Cantatas; Bach's St John Passion. *Honours:* Laureate of International Vocal Competitions of Hertogenbosch, Toulouse and Barcelona; Grand Prix du Disque, 1970 for St John Passion. *Address:* c/o Music International, 13 Ardilaun Road, Highbury, London N5 2QR, England.

MEHNERT, Thomas; Singer (Bass); b. 1966, Chemitz, Germany. *Education:* Studied at the Richard Strauss Conservatory, Munich, from 1991, the Munich Singschule. *Career:* Concert performances at the 1995 Rheingau Music Festival, and the Mozart Festival at Würzburg; Engagements at the Cottbus Opera as Colline, Colas in Mozart's Bastien und Bastienne, the Hermit in Der Freischütz Figaro and Banquo, from 1995; Guest appearances with Netherlands Opera as Pluto in Monteverdi's Orfeo and Fifth Solo Voice in Moses und Aron, under Pierre Boulez (also at the Salzburg Festival); Royal Festival Hall, London, in Moses and Aron with the Philharmonia Orchestra under Christoph von Dohnányi, 1996. *Honours:* Deutsche Buhnvereins Grant, 1993. *Address:* c/o Staatsoper Cottbus, Karl Liebnecht Strasse 136, 7500 Cottbus, Germany.

MEHTA, Zubin; Indian conductor; b. 29 April 1936, Bombay; s. of the late Mehli Mehta and of Tehmina Daruvala Mehta; m. 1st Carmen Lasky 1958 (divorced); one s. one d.; m. 2nd Nancy Diane Kovack 1969. *Education:* Vienna Acad. of Music, studied under Hans Swarowsky. *Career:* first professional conducting in Belgium, Yugoslavia and UK (Liverpool); Music Dir Montreal Symphony 1961–67, Los Angeles Philharmonic Orchestra 1962–78; Music Dir New York Philharmonic Orchestra 1978–91; Music Dir Israel Philharmonic 1969–, appointed Dir for Life 1981; Dir Bavarian State Opera 1998–; conductor at festivals of Holland, Prague, Vienna, Salzburg and Spoleto; debut at La Scala, Milan 1969; conducts regularly with the Vienna and Berlin Orchestras; winner of Liverpool Int. Conductors' Competition 1958; Music Dir Maggio Musicale, Florence 1969, 1986–. *Honours:* Dr hc Tel Aviv Univ., Weizmann Inst. of Science, The Hebrew Univ. of Jerusalem, Jewish Theological Seminary, Westminster Choir Coll., Princeton, Brooklyn Coll., Colgate Univ.; shared Wolf Prize 1996; Commendatore (Italy), Médaille d'Or Vermeil (City of Paris), Commdr des Arts et des Lettres (France), Great Silver Medal of Service (Austria) 1997, Padma Vibhushan (India) 2001. *Address:* Israel Philharmonic Orchestra, 1 Huberman Street, Box 11292, 61112 Tel Aviv, Israel; Orchestra Maggio Musicale, Teatro Communale, Via Solferino 15, 50123 Florence, Italy.

MEI, Eva; Singer (Soprano); b. 3 March 1967, Fabriano, Italy. *Education:* Studied at the Luigi Cherubini Conservatory, Florence. *Career:* Debut: Aspasia in Salieri's Axur, re d'Ormus, Siena, 1989; Sang Mozart's Constanze at the Vienna Staatsoper, 1990; Engaged at Zürich as Donna Anna, Alcina, Mozart's Countess and Luitgarde in Schubert's Des Teufels Lustschloss; Covent Garden debut as the Queen of Night, 1993, Berlin Staatsoper as Violetta; La Scala debut as Amenaide in Tancredi, 1993; Rossini Festival at Pesaro as Fanny in La Cambiale di Matrimonio and Berenice in L'Occasione fa il ladro, 1995–96; Vienna Festival as Genio in Haydn's Orfeo ed Euridice, 1995; Norina in Don Pasquale at Genoa, 1998; Season 2000–01 as Violetta for Zürich Opera, Meyerbeer's Dinorah at Parma, Bellini's Amina at Palermo and Giulietta in Verdi's Un giorno di regno at Bologna; Concert engagements at the Amsterdam Concertgebouw, Queen Elizabeth Hall (London), Academia di Santa Cecilia (Rome) and halls in Buenos Aires, Vienna, St Petersburg and Moscow. *Recordings include:* A Mezzanote, songs by Bellini, Rossini and Donizetti; Rossini's Tancredi and Mozart's Il re Pastore. *Honours:* Caterina Cavalieri Prize at the 1990 Mozart Competition, Vienna. *Address:* c/o Opernhaus Zürich, Falkenstrasse 1, 8008 Zürich, Switzerland.

MEIER, Jaroslav; Composer; b. 7 Dec. 1923, Hronov, Czechoslovakia; m. Marta Kurbelova, 1950, 2 s. *Education:* Organ, Academy of Music, Prague, 1939–44; Organ and Composition, Academy of Music, Bratislava, 1947–49. *Career:* Head of Music Department, Radio Bratislava, 1949–56; Head of Music Department, Czechoslovakia television, Bratislava, 1956–; Music Designer (a lot of television and radio plays and films); mem, Union of Czechoslovak Composers; IMZ. *Compositions:* Opera Erindo (rewriting opera by baroque composer J. S. Kusser); Television opera The Night before Immortality (libretto after A Arbuzov); Opera, The Wooden Shoes (libretto after Guy de Maupassant); Orchestral works, Dances from my Country; Songs from my Country; What a Smell (song cycle based on Stefan Zary's poems); Concerto da Camera for organ and orchestra, 1982. *Recordings:* Chamber Music, Trois Impromptus; Prelude and Double Fugue; Divine Love; The Cycle Nocturnal Songs; Toccata et fuga, Fantasia concertante. *Publications:* Obrazovka pina hudby, (The Screen full of Music), 1970; Johann Sigismund Kusser, 1986. *Contributions:* Slovenska hudba (Slovak Music); Hudebni zivot (Music Life); Czeskoslovenska televize (television weekly paper). *Honours:* Prize of Critics at the International Television Festival The Golden Prague, 1976, for television opera The Night before Immortality. *Address:* Palackého 407, 54931 Hronov, Czech Republic.

MEIER, Johanna; Singer (Soprano); b. 13 Feb. 1938, Chicago, USA; m. Guido Della Vecchia. *Education:* Studied at the University of Miami with Arturo di Filippi and at the Manhattan School with John Brownlee. *Career:* Debut: New York City Opera 1969, as the Countess in Capriccio; Sang with the City Opera as Donna Anna, Senta, Louise and Tosca; Metropolitan Opera from 1976, as Marguerite, Ariadne, the Marschallin, Ellen Orford, Chrysothemis, Elisabeth, Brünnhilde in Die Walküre and Kaiserin; Guest engagements in Seattle, Washington, Philadelphia, San Diego, Ottawa and Chicago; Other roles include Sieglinde, Musetta, Mozart's Countess, Amelia (Un ballo in Maschera), Agathe and Eva; Bayreuth Festival debut 1981, as Isolde; Vienna Staatsoper from 1983, Fidelio and Senta; Tour of Japan 1986, as Isolde and the Marschallin; Barcelona and Buenos Aires 1987, as Elisabeth in Tannhäuser and Chrysothemis; Sang Turandot at Dallas and New Orleans, 1987–88; Ariadne at Trieste, 1988; Pittsburgh Opera, 1989, as Chrysothemis; The Dyer's Wife in Die Frau ohne Schatten at the 1990 Holland Festival; World premiere Les Liaisons Dangereuses at San Francisco Opera, 1994; Retired, 1994; Director, Producer, Black Hills Passion Play. *Address:* c/o Metropolitan Opera, Lincoln Center, NY 10023, USA.

MEIER, Jost; Composer and Conductor; b. 15 March 1939, Solothurn, Switzerland. *Education:* Studied at the Berne Conservatory and with Frank Martin in Netherlands. *Career:* Conducted at the Biel Opera, 1968–79, Basle, 1980–83. *Compositions include:* Sennentuntschi, dramatic legend, Freiburg, 1983; Der Drache, opera in 2 acts, Basle, 1985; Der Zoobar, opera in 4 scenes, Zürich, 1987; Augustin, opera in 4 scenes, Basle, 1988; Dreyfus, opera, Berlin (Deutsche Oper), 1994; Glarus for strings, 1980; Musique for trombone and orchestra, 1986; Musique Concertante, 1989; Esquisses for piano and percussion, 1993; Variations for Viola and Chamber orchestra, 1996; String Quartet, 1988; 2 Clarinet Trios, 1969, 1999; Franz von Assisi for soloists, women's chorus and orchestra, 1996; Galgenlieder for soprano, clarinet, cello and piano,

1996; Music for the Fêtes des Vignerons for soloists, choruses, orchestra and brass bands, 1999. *Address:* c/o Deutsche Oper Berlin, Richard Wagnerstrasse 10, 1000 Berlin, Germany.

MEIER, Waltraud; Singer (Mezzo-soprano); b. 9 Jan. 1956, Würzburg, Germany. *Education:* Studied with Anton Theisen in Würzburg and Dietger Jacob in Cologne. *Career:* Sang in Würzburg from 1976 as Cherubino, Dorabella, Nicklaus in Les Contes d'Hoffmann and Concepcion in L'Heure Espagnole, Mannheim 1978–80, as Carmen, Fricka, Waltraute and Octavian; Dortmund 1980–83, as Kundry in Parsifal, Eboli in Don Carlos and as Santuzza in Cavalleria Rusticana; Guest appearances in Cologne, Hamburg, Buenos Aires, Opera de Paris, Staatsoper Wien, Scala di Milano, San Francisco Opera, Munich, Bayreuth from 1983; Sang Kundry in Götz Friedrich's production of Parsifal, Brangäne in Jean-Pierre Ponelle's Tristan und Isolde, and Waltraute in Harry Kupfer's 1988 production of The Ring; Covent Garden debut 1985, as Eboli, returned to London 1988, as Kundry; Made her Metropolitan Opera debut in 1987 as Fricka in Rheingold and Walküre; Other roles include Azucena (Il Trovatore), Venus (Tannhäuser), the Composer (Ariadne auf Naxos); Sang Venus at Hamburg, 1990; Debut at the Teatro San Carlos, Lisbon, 1990 as Ortrud in Lohengrin; Théâtre du Châtelet, Paris, 1990 as Marguerite in La Damnation de Faust; Sang Waltraute at the Bayreuth Festival, 1988–92, Tchaikovsky's Maid of Orleans at Munich; Season 1992–93 as Kundry at La Scala and the Metropolitan, Berg's Marie at the Théâtre du Châtelet, Paris, and 1993–97 and 1999 as Isolde at Bayreuth; Sang Sieglinde at the Vienna Staatsoper and La Scala, Milan, 1994; Carmen at the Metropolitan, 1997; Isolde at Munich, 1998; Sang Leonore at Munich, and La Scala Milan, 1999; Season 2000–01 as Marie in Wozzeck at La Scala, in Salzburg and Vienna as Isolde, Sieglinde at Bayreuth, Amneris at the Berlin Staatsoper and Les Troyens at Munich, 2001; Wagner's Ortrud at Covent Garden, 2003; Also heard as a concert singer, in Beethoven, Brahms, Mahler and Verdi; New production of Les Contes d'Hoffmann/Giulietta at the Salzburg Festival, 2003; For the season 2003–04 plans to concentrate exclusively on career as lieder and concert singer. *Recordings include:* Opera: Dittersdorf's Doktor und Apotheker; Venus and Kundry; Brahms Alto Rhapsody; Fricka in Bernard Haitink's Die Walküre, Wesendonk and Kindertotenlieder, Missa Solemnis, Mozart Requiem; Wagner recital with the Symphonieorchester des Bayerischen Rundfunks under Lorin Maazel, 1997; Isolde with Barenboim; Leonore with Barenboim; Ortrud with Claudio Abbado; Mahler-Lieder with Maazel, 1998; DVD of Tristan und Isolde, Munich 1998; CD/DVD of Walküre with Zubin Mehta, Munich, 2002. *Honours:* Recipient of several prestigious prizes; Holds titles of Bayerische Kammersängerin at the Bavarian State Opera and Kammersängerin at the Vienna State Opera. *Current Management:* Agentur Dr Hilbert. *Address:* Agentur Dr Germinal Hilbert, Maximilianstr 22, 80539 Munich, Germany. *Website:* www.waltraud-meier.com.

MEIRON, Rhys; Singer (Tenor); b. 1970, Wales. *Education:* Guildhall School, London 1997–99. *Career:* Glyndebourne Festival Chorus from 1998; Sang Edmondo in Manon Lescaut at Glyndebourne, 1999; Concert engagements in London, Guilford, Bournemouth, Toronto and Barbados; English National Opera from 1999, as Major Domo in Der Rosenkavalier, First Armed Man in The Magic Flute and Nadir in The Pearl Fishers. *Honours:* Prizewinner, National Eisteddfod, Wales, 1996–97. *Address:* c/o English National Opera, St Martin's Lane, London, WC2, England.

MEKLER, Mani; Singer (Soprano); b. 1951, Haifa, Israel. *Education:* Studied in Italy. *Career:* Sang Leonora in Il Trovatore at Stockholm and with Welsh National Opera, 1976, 1977; Glyndebourne debut 1978, as First Lady in Die Zauberflöte; Wexford Festival 1979, as Giulia in Spontini's La Vestale; Deutsche Oper am Rhein, Düsseldorf, from 1979 as Janáček's Jenůfa and Mila (Osud) and Chrysothemis; Further appearances at Drottningholm, Zürich and Milan, La Scala (premiere of Testi's Riccardo III, 1987); Other roles include Puccini's Manon Lescaut, Tosca and Butterfly, Strauss's Salome and Ariadne, and Goneril in Reimann's Lear.

MELBY, John B.; Composer; b. 3 Oct. 1941, Wisconsin, USA; m. Jane H. Thompson 1978, 2 s., 1 d. *Education:* Diploma, 1964, BMus, 1966, Curtis Institute of Music; MA, University of Pennsylvania, 1967; MFA, 1971, PhD, 1972, Princeton University. *Career:* Professor of Music, University of Illinois, Urbana. *Compositions include:* ..Of Quiet Desperation for computer-synthesized tape, 1976; Concerto No. 1 for violin and computer-synthesized tape, 1979, No. 2, 1986; Layers for computer-synthesized tape, 1981; Wind, Sand, and Stars for 8 instruments and computer-synthesized tape, 1983; Concerto for violin, English horn and computer-synthesized tape, 1984; Concerto for computer-synthesized tape and orchestra, 1987; Symphony No. 1, 1993; The rest is silence... for organ, 1994; Other concerti, songs and keyboard works. *Recordings include:* 91 Plus 5 for brass quintet and computer-synthesized tape; Forandre: 7 variations for digital computer; Two Stevens Songs for soprano and computer-synthesized tape; Concerto for violin, English

horn and computer-synthesized tape; Concerto No. 1 for violin and computer-synthesized tape; Concerto Nos 1 and 2 for flute and computer-synthesized tape; Chor der Steine; Chor der Waisen. *Publications:* Some recent developments in computer-synthesized music, 1973; Proceedings of the 1975 Music Computation Conference (edited with James Beauchamp), 1976; 'Layers': An approach to composition for computer based upon the concept of structural levels, 1983; 'Computer' Music or Computer 'Music', 1989. *Address:* School of Music, 2136 Music Building, 1114 West Nevada, University of Illinois, Urbana, IL 61801, USA.

MELBYE, Mikael; Singer (Baritone), Stage Director and Designer; b. 15 March 1955, Frederiksberg, Denmark. *Education:* Royal Danish Conservatory, Copenhagen. *Career:* Debut: Guglielmo in Così fan tutte, Royal Danish Opera, 1976; Vast repertoire of mainly lyric baritone roles including Mozart, Rossini, Donizetti, Verdi and Puccini; International debut as Danilo in The Merry Widow at the Spoleto festival, 1981; Has since appeared in opera houses all over the world including La Scala di Milano, The Paris Opéra, Royal Opera House, Covent Garden, Staatsoper, Munich, Hamburgische Staatsoper, Metropolitan Opera; Debut in 1995 as Stage Director and Designer at the Royal Danish Opera in Così fan tutte; Following this was engaged as the Principal Director and Designer for this house; Directed and designed the premiere performance of Turandot at the Royal Danish Opera, 1996; Director, Arabella, in 1997 (Houston, 1998), Magic Flute, 1998 (Boston Lyric, 2000), La Bohème, Royal Danish Opera, 1999, Rigoletto at Santa Fe Opera, 2000; Sets and Costumes for Giselle at the San Francisco Ballet, 1999, La Sylphide for the Royal Swedish Ballet, 1999, and for the National Ballet of China in 1999; Directed Salome for Jutland Opera, 1999, Royal Danish Opera, 2001 and also Capriccio for Royal Danish Opera, 2001; Designed sets and costumes and directed Nutcracker at Tivoli Gardens, 2001; Costumes and sets for Symphony in C (Balanchine) at Royal Danish Ballet, 2000, and Royal Norwegian Ballet, 2001. *Recordings include:* Carmen (Karajan), Die Zauberflöte (Colin Davis). *Honours:* Oberdörfer Preis, Germany; The Golden Pegasus Award, Italy; Gladsaxe Music Award, Denmark; OV Award for best production (Turandot), Denmark; Knighthood from the Danish Queen, 1996. *Address:* c/o Royal Danish Opera, PO Box 2185, DK–1017 Copenhagen, Denmark.

MELCHER, Wilhelm; Violinist; b. 5 April 1940, Hamburg, Germany. *Education:* Studied in Hamburg and Rome. *Career:* Leader of the Hamburg Symphony Orchestra, 1963; Former Member of Karl Munchinger's Stuttgart Chamber Orchestra, Heilbronn; Co-Founder, Melos Quartet of Stuttgart, 1965; Represented West Germany at the Jeunesse Musicales in Paris, 1966; International concert tours from 1967; Bicentenary concerts in the Beethoven Haus at Bonn, 1970; British concerts and festival appearances from 1974; Cycle of Beethoven quartets at Edinburgh Festival, 1987; Wigmore Hall, St John's Smith Square and Bath Festival, 1990; Associations with Rostropovich in the Schubert Quintet and the Cleveland Quartet in works by Spohr and Mendelssohn; Teacher, Stuttgart Musikhochschule. *Recordings include:* Complete quartets of Beethoven, Schubert, Mozart and Brahms; Quintets by Boccherini with Narciso Ypes and by Mozart with Frank Beyer. *Honours:* Grand Prix du Disque and Prix Caecilia, Academie du Disque, Brussels (with Melos Quartet). *Current Management:* Ingpen & Williams Ltd, 7 St George's Court, 131 Putney Bridge Road, London, SW15 2PA, England.

MELIS, György; Singer (Baritone); b. 2 July 1923, Szarvas, Hungary. *Education:* Studied at the Budapest Academy of Music, with Olga Relevhegyi. *Career:* Debut: Budapest Opera 1949, as Morales in Carmen; Many appearances in the major baritone roles of Mozart and Verdi; Sang Don Giovanni at Glyndebourne in 1961, and in Brussels, Berlin and Moscow; Further engagements in Edinburgh, (Bart ók's Bluebeard 1973), Vienna and South America; Sang Don Giovanni at Wiesbaden 1987, as guest with the Hungarian State Opera (Bluebeard at Covent Garden 1989); Also heard in concert and oratorio; Song recitals include music by Bart ók and Kodály. *Recordings:* Kodály's Háry János and Budavari Te Deum; Don Giovanni; Rigoletto; Szokolay's Samson; Title role in Bluebeard's Castle by Bartók, conducted by Fricasy; Scala Milano, Bartók's Bluebeard, 1978. *Honours:* Kossuth Prize 1962. *Address:* Hungarian State Opera, Népöztarsasag utja 22, 1061 Budapest, Hungary.

MELKUS, Eduard; Violinist; b. 1 Sept. 1928, Baden, Austria; m. Marlis Melkus-Selzer, 4 c. *Education:* Studied violin with Ernst Moravec 1942–53, Firmin Touche, Alexander Schaizhet and Peter Rybar; Musicology at Vienna University with Erich Schenk. *Career:* Debut: Vienna 1944; Founded Eduard Melkus Ensemble and Capella Academia, 1965, playing mainly on original instruments of the 18th Century; Professor of Violin and Viola at the Vienna Hochschule für Musik from 1958; Premiered Concerto by Egon Wellesz, 1962; Concerts in all Europe, USA, Australia, Japan, South America; Visiting Professor, University of Georgia, USA, 1973–74, University of Illinois and others;

Lectures and master classes in many Universities all over the world; mem, Ex-President, Austria ESTA. *Recordings:* Concertos by Bach, Tartini, Vivaldi, Haydn; sonatas by Biber, Corelli, Bach, Mozart and Handel; Solo violin music by Bach, Haydn's La Vera Costanza at the Schönbrunn Palace, Vienna, 1984 (television). *Honours:* Kornerpreis 1967; Edison Prize, Prix Academia Charles C Gross; Great Cross of Honour of the Republic of Austria. *Address:* Obere Donaustrasse 57/14, 1020 Vienna 2, Austria.

MELLERS, Wilfrid (Howard); Composer, Author and University Professor (retired); b. 26 April 1914, Leamington, Warwickshire, England; m. (1) Vera Muriel Hobbs, (2) Pauline PeggyLewis, 3 d., (3) Robin Stephanie Hildyard. *Education:* BA (Cantab), 1936; MA (Cantab), 1939; D.Mus, University of Birmingham, 1960; DPhil, City University, 1980; FGSM, 1982; Studied with Egon Wellesz and Edmund Rubbra. *Career:* College Supervisor in English, Lecturer in Music, Downing College, Cambridge, 1945–48; Staff Tutor in Music, Extra-Mural Department, University of Birmingham, 1948–59; Andrew Mellon Professor of Music, University of Pittsburgh, 1960–63; Professor of Music, University of York, England, 1964–81; Visiting Professor, City University, 1984–; Organiser, Attingham Park Summer School of Music, 13 years; Lecturer in Australia, USA, Canada; Work for radio and television; Lecturer at Dartington Summer School, 2001; mem, Sonneck Society. *Compositions:* About 50 including Life Cycle, 3 choirs, 2 orchestras; A May Magnificat; Sun-flower; Rosae Hermeticae; Spells, soprano, chamber ensemble; The Ancient Wound, monodrama; Venery fir Six Plus; Chants and Litanies of Carl Sandberg; Yeibichai, coloratura soprano, scat singer, jazz trio, orchestra, tape (Proms commission). *Recordings include:* Voices and Creatures; The Wellspring of Loves; Rose of May; Life-Cycle; Opus Alchymicum for organ on Modern British Organ Music played by Kevin Bowyer, 1998. *Publications:* 23 books including Studies in Contemporary Music, 1948; Francois Couperin, 1950, revised and expanded edition, 1984; Man and His Music, 2 vols, numerous editions and translations; The Masks of Orpheus, 1987; Vaughan Williams and the Vision of Albion, 1989; Le Jardin Retrouvé: Homage to Federico Mompou, 1990; The Music of Percy Grainger, 1992; Francis Poulenc, 1993; Between Old Worlds and New: Occasional writings on Music, 1998; Singing in the Wilderness, Music and Ecology in the 20th Century, 2002. *Honours:* Honorary DPhil, City University, 1981; Hon FGSM, 1982; O.B.E., 1982; Professor Emeritus, University of York, 1984. *Address:* Oliver Sheldon House, 17 Aldwark, York YO1 7BX, England.

MELLES, Carl; Conductor; b. 15 July 1926, Budapest, Hungary; m. Gertrud Dertnig, 1 s., 1 d. *Education:* Studied in Budapest. *Career:* Conducted more than 100 symphony, radio and opera orchestras including: Hungarian State Orchestra, 1951; Symphony Orchestra of Hungarian Radio and Television; Vienna and Berlin Philharmonic, the New Philharmonic Orchestra, London, the Orchestre National de Paris, the Orchestra of La Scala, Milan; Conducted at many festivals including: Salzburg, Bayreuth, Prague Spring and the Vienna Festwochen; Concert tours of Japan, South Africa, Europe and America; Worked with such distinguished soloists as Annie Fischer, Zino Francescatti, Wilhelm Kempff, Enrico Mainardi and Arthur Rubinstein; Professor, 1976; Honorary Member, Vienna Singakademie, 1978; Regular conductor of the Vienna Symphony Orchestra and on Austrian Radio. *Recordings:* Mozart Piano Concertos K459 and K466 (Ingrid Haebler, Vienna Symphony Orchestra); Il prigioniero by Dallapiccola. *Honours:* Franz Liszt Prize, Budapest, 1956; The Beethoven Medal, 1970; Italian Gramophone Prize, 1974; Honorary Gold Medal, City of Vienna; The Great Silver Badge of Honour, President of Austria. *Address:* Gruenbergstrasse 4, A 1130 Vienna, Austria.

MELLON, Agnès; Singer (Soprano); b. 17 Jan. 1958, Epinay-sur-Seine, France; m. Dominique Visse. *Education:* Studied in Paris and San Francisco. *Career:* Sang with the Paris Opéra and the Opéra-Comique; Later appearances in the Baroque repertoire, notably as Tibrino in Cesti's Orontea at the 1986 Innsbruck Early Music Festival, Eryxene in Hasse's Cleofide, 1987 and Telaire in Rameau's Castor et Pollux at the 1991 Aix-en-Provence Festival; Sang the title role in Rossi's Orfeo at the Queen Elizabeth Hall, London, with Les Arts Florissants, 1990; Sang in Mondonville's Les Fêstes de Paphos at Versailles, 1996. *Recordings include:* Rossi's Orfeo, Cavalli's Xerxes, Lully's Atys, Charpentier's Médée and David et Jonathas, Hasse's Cleofide, Rameau's Anacréon and Zoroastre; Labels include Erato and Harmonia Mundi.

MELLOR, Alwyn; Singer (Soprano); b. 1968, Rawtenstall, Lancashire, England. *Education:* Royal Northern College of Music, with further study in Italy and St Petersburg. *Career:* Roles with Welsh National Opera (from 1992) have included Tatiana, Ginevra in Ariodante, Liu, Fiordiligi, Marguerite; Anne Trulove, and Micaela; Donna Elvira for WNO and Glyndebourne Touring Opera, Fiordiligi at Sante Fe (1997); Concerts include Edinburgh Festival with the Scottish Chamber Orchestra; Die Schöpfung in Amsterdam with the Bach Soloists under

Marc Minkowski, 1993; US debut with the Kansas City Camerata, 1996; Season 1997 with Britten's Spring Symphony (Rotterdam Philharmonic Orchestra under Donald Runnicles); Sang Marenka in new production of The Bartered Bride for Opera North, 1998. *Recordings include:* Elsie in Yeomen of the Guard, with WNO. *Honours:* Awards from the Peter Moores Foundation. *Current Management:* Ingpen & Williams Ltd, 7 St George's Court, 131 Putney Bridge Road, London, SW15 2PA, England.

MELNIKOV, Alexander; Concert Pianist; b. 1973, Russia. *Education:* Moscow Tchaikovsky Conservatory, with Lev Naumov, from 1991. *Career:* Regular guest at international festivals, including the Schleswig-Holstein (Germany), Yehudi Menuhin (Switzerland), Styrian Festival (Austria) and the Bashmet Festival at Bonn; Recitals throughout Europe, America and the Far East, concertos with such conductors as Gergiev, Lazarev and Fedoseyev; Chamber music with Vadim Repin, Boris Pergemenschikov and the Shostakovich Quartet; Performs regularly in Japan in recitals and concertos with the Japan Philharmonic, recitals in Toronto with Vodim Repin (violin); Solo recitals in the USA, Luxembourg, London, Paris and Moscow; Repertoire includes Beethoven, Grieg, Schumann and Schubert. *Honours:* Laureate of the Robert Schumann Competition, Zwickau, 1989; Queen Elisabeth of Belgium Competition, Brussels, 1991. *Address:* c/o IMG Artists, Lovell House, 616 Chiswick High Road, London W4 5RX, England.

MELROSE, Leigh; Singer (Baritone); b. 1972, New York, USA. *Education:* St John's College, Cambridge; Royal Academy of Music. *Career:* Debut: Dancairo in Carmen, for English National Opera; Other roles with ENO Mozart's Count, Papageno, Ned Keene, Junius and Leoncavallo's Rodolfo; roles elsewhere include Rossini's Figaro for New York City Opera; Silvio for Welsh Nat. Opera; Birtwistle's Punch in Porto; Rambo in John Adam's The Death of Klinghoffer (Channel 4 film); Concerts include various BBC Proms; Carmina Burana; Belshazzar's Feast; Friar Lawrence in Berlioz's Romeo et Juliette. *Address:* c/o IMG Artists, Lovell House, 616 Chiswick High Road, London W4 5RX, England.

MENARD, Pierre; Violinist; b. 1945, Quebec, Canada. *Education:* Studied at Quebec Conservatory and at Juilliard with Dorothy DeLay, Ivan Galamian and the Juilliard Quartet. *Career:* Solo appearances in Canada and the USA; Former Concertmaster of the Aspen Festival Orchestra and the Nashville Symphony; Co-Founder and Second Violinist of the Vermeer Quartet from 1970; Performances in most North American centres, Europe, Israel and Australia; Festival engagements at Tanglewood, Aspen, Spoleto, Berlin, Edinburgh, mostly Mozart (New York), Aldeburgh, South Bank, Santa Fe Chamber Music West, and the Casals Festival; Resident Quartet for Chamber Music Chicago; Masterclasses at the Royal Northern College of Music, Manchester; Member of the Resident Artists Faculty of Northern Illinois University. *Recordings:* Quartets by Beethoven, Dvořák, Verdi and Schubert (Teldec); Brahms Clarinet Quintet with Karl Leister (Orfeo). *Honours:* 1st Prize in Chamber Music, Quebec Conservatory; Winner, National Festival of Music Competition; Prix d'Europe from the Quebec Government. *Address:* Allied Artists, 42 Montpelier Square, London SW7 1JZ, England.

MENESES, Antonio; Concert Cellist; b. 23 Aug. 1957, Refice, Brazil. *Education:* Studied with Antonio Janigro in Düsseldorf and Stuttgart. *Career:* Has appeared widely in Europe and America from 1977; Appearances with the Berlin Philharmonic conducted by Karajan, with the London Symphony Orchestra in London and the USA, and with the Israel Philharmonic, Vienna Philharmonic and Concertgebouw Orchestras; Other conductors include Abbado, Previn, Maazel and Muti; Tours of Australia 1984, 1987; Engagements at the Lucerne and the Salzburg Easter Festivals, with the Berlin Philharmonic. *Recordings include:* Brahms Double Concerto, with Anne-Sophie Mutter; Strauss Don Quixote, conducted by Karajan (Deutsche Grammophon). *Honours:* 2nd Prize at International Competitions in Barcelona and Rio de Janeiro; 1st Prize at ARD Competition, Munich, 1977; Gold Medal, Tchaikovsky International Competition, Moscow, 1982.

MENKOVA, Irina; Violinist; b. 1960, Moscow, Russia. *Career:* Co-founder, Glazunov Quartet, 1985; Concerts in the former Soviet Union and recent appearances in Greece, Belgium, Poland, Germany and Italy; Works by Beethoven and Schumann at the Beethoven Haus in Bonn; Further engagements in Canada and Netherlands; Teacher, Moscow State Conservatoire and Resident at the Tchaikovsky Conservatoire; repertoire includes works by Borodin, Shostakovich and Tchaikovsky, in addition to the standard works. *Recordings:* Tchaikovsky on Olympia label. *Honours:* Prizewinner, Borodin Quartet and Shostakovich Chamber Music Competitions, with the Glazunov Quartet. *Current Management:* Sonata, Glasgow, Scotland. *Address:* 11 Northpark Street, Glasgow G20 7AA, Scotland.

MENOTTI, Gian Carlo; Composer and Stage Director; b. 7 July 1911, Cadegliano, Italy; 1 s. (adopted). *Education:* Curtis Institute of Music, Philadelphia, Pennsylvania. *Career:* Went to USA 1928; Member of

Teaching Staff, Curtis Institute of Music, 1941–45; Founder and President, Festival of TwoWorlds, Spoleto, Italy and Charleston, South Carolina. *Compositions include:* Operas: Amelia Goes to the Ball; The Old Maid and the Thief; The Island God; The Telephone; The Medium; The Consul; Amahl and the Night Visitors; The Labyrinth (own libretti); The Saint of Bleecker Street 1954; The Last Savage 1963; Martin's Lie 1964; Help, Help, The Globolinks (Space Opera for Children) 1968; The Most Important Man 1971; Tamu Tamu 1973; Hero 1976; La Loca 1979; Song of Hope (Cantata) 1980; St Teresa 1982; The Boy Who Grew Too Fast 1982; Goya, premiere at Washington Opera 1986; The Wedding, premiere at Seoul, South Korea 1988; The Singing Child, 1993; Ballet: Sebastian; Film: The Medium (Producer); Vanessa (libretto) 1958; The Unicorn, the Gorgon and the Manticore: A Madrigal Fable, Maria Golovin 1959; The Death of the Bishop of Brindisi (Cantata) 1963; Chamber Music Songs: For the Death of Orpheus, for tenor, chorus and orchestra, 1990; Jakob's Prayer, for chorus and orchestra, 1997. *Honours:* Hon BM (Curtis Institute of Music); Guggenheim Award 1946, 1947; Pulitzer Prize 1950, 1955; Kennedy Centre Award 1984; New York City Mayor's Liberty Award, 1986; Hon Association national Institute of Arts and Letters 1953; Richard Tucker Award, 1988. *Address:* ASCAP Building, 1 Lincoln Plaza, NY 10023, USA.

MENTZER, Susanne; Singer (Mezzo-soprano); b. 21 Jan. 1957, Philadelphia, USA. *Education:* Juilliard School, New York and with Norma Newton. *Career:* Debut: Houston Opera 1981, as Albina in La Donna del Lago; Appeared with Dallas Opera 1982, in Gianni Schicchi and Das Rheingold; Washington Opera as Cherubino; Chicago Lyric Opera, Phladelpha Opera and New York City Opera as Rosina in Il Barbiere di Siviglia; Houston Opera as Rossini's Isolier, and at Rossini Festival Pesaro, Italy, the Composer in Ariadne auf Naxos and Giovanna Seymour in Anna Bolena; European debut with Cologne Opera 1983, as Cherubino, later Massenet's Cendrillon; La Scala Milan as Zerlina in Don Giovanni; Vienna Staatsoper as Cherubino; Covent Garden debut 1985, as Rosina, returned as Giovanna Seymour 1988, and Dorabella in Così fan tutte 1989; Metropolitan Opera debut 1989, as Cherubino; Monte Carlo 1988, as Adalgisa in Norma; Sang Octavian at the Théâtre des Champs-Elysées, Paris 1989; Annius in La Clemenza di Tito at La Scala, 1990 and Sesto in the Chicago premiere of Mozart's opera, 1991; Salzburg Festival, Cherubino and Zerlina, Metropolitan Opera, Idamante, 1991; In Les Contes d'Hoffmann as Nicklausse, Octavian in Der Rosenkavalier, Composer in Ariadne auf Naxos, Metropolitan Opera, 1992–93; Geneviève in Pelléas et Mélisande at the Palais Garnier, Paris, 1997; Roméo at the Opéra Bastille; Nicklausse at the Met, 1998; Season 2000–01 as Octavian and Mélisande at the Met, Adalgisa at Covent Garden and Mozart's Idamante at the Dresden Staatsoper. *Recordings include:* Anna Bolena with Sutherland and Bonynge and Bruckner Te Deum on Philips label, Mozart Masses with King's College Choir; Barber of Seville, EMI, (Rosina); Idomeneo, Philips, (Idamante); Don Giovanni, EMI (Zerlina). *Address:* J.M. Poilvé, 16 avenue Franklin D.Roosevelt, F–75008 Paris, France.

MENUHIN, Jeremy; Pianist; b. 2 Nov. 1951, San Francisco, CA, USA. *Education:* Paris with Nadio Boulanger, Israel with Mindru Katz (piano), Vienna with Hans Swarowsky (conducting). *Career:* public performances from 1965; New York recital debut 1984; Berlin Philharmonic 1984; Dame Myra Hess series, Chicago 1985; regular recitals, Kennedy Center (Washington DC), Berlin Philharmonie, Amsterdam Concertgebouw, La Salle Pleyel; US tours with Czech Philharmonic and Prague Chamber Orchestra 1989; guest appearances, San Francisco and Houston Symphonies; European orchestras include BBC, Royal and Amsterdam Philharmonics, Salzburg Mozarteum, Orchestre National de France; 1987–88 season included Windsor Festival concert with English Chamber Orchestra; Beethoven's 1st concerto with Leningrad Philharmonic conducted by Yehudi Menuhin; 1989 European concert tour with Toulouse Chamber Orchestra; chamber music with cellists Colin Carr, Steven Isserlis, Marius May; recitals with sopranos Edith Mahis and Arleen Auger, Aldeburgh 1987; with Hallé Orchestra, Zürich Tonhalle Orchestra, Sinfonia Varsovia 1994; tour of Germany, Czech Republic and Poland with Philharmonia Hungarica (Schumann, Bartók's 3rd Piano Concerto); Bath Festival with English Symphony Orchestra; Beethoven's 5th Piano Concerto with Orchestra of St John's Smith Square; tour of Russia and further concerts throughout Europe 1995; St Nazaire Festival, Wigmore Hall, and other festivals; season 1998–99 toured Germany, Lithuania, Netherlands and France; solo recitals at the Ubeda Festival, Spain and the Ravello Festival in Italy; recent performances include concerts in Brazil and Mexico and recitals in Netherlands, Switzerland and the UK and tours with the Sinfonia Varsovia in Germany. *Recordings include:* works by Schubert, Mozart, Debussy, Beethoven; Bartók's two violin sonatas with father, Yehudi Menuhin; Dvořák Quartets and Quintet with Chilingirian Quartet; Schubert's Late Piano Works 1998. *Honours:* Grand Prix de Disque 1981. *Current Management:* Upbeat Classical Management, PO Box 479, Uxbridge, UB8 2ZH, England.

Telephone: (1895) 259441. *Fax:* (1895) 259341. *E-mail:* info@ upbeatclassical.co.uk. *Website:* www.upbeatclassical.co.uk.

MENZEL, Peter; Singer (Tenor); b. 31 Jan. 1943, Dresden, Germany. *Education:* Studied at the Dresden Muskihochschule. *Career:* Sang with the Dresden Opera from 1968; Berlin Staatsoper from 1977, notably in the 1979 premiere of Leonce und Lena by Dessau; Other roles have included Monostatos, Oronte in Alcina, Jacquino, Mime, Pang in Turandot, the Captain in Wozzeck, and Bardolph; Many concert appearances, notably with the Thomas Choir Leipzig on tour to Switzerland, Italy and Japan. *Address:* c/o Oper Berlin, Unter den Linden 7, 1060 Berlin, Germany.

MERCER, Alexandra; Singer (Mezzo Soprano); b. 12 May 1944, Gravesend, Kent, England; m. Philip Mercer, 2 Oct 1965, twin d. *Education:* Studied with Maestro Antonio and Lina Riccaboni Narducci in Milan, 1963–65, 1967–69; Royal Scottish Academy of Music, 1965–67. *Career:* Debut: Barga Festival, 1970; Has appeared in opera throughout the United Kingdom and Europe, with companies such as English Bach Festival Trust, Kent Opera, Royal Opera House Covent Garden, Opera Rara, and Barber Institute; Roles include Poppea, Despina, Dorabella, Rosina, Hansel, Ascanius, Smeton, Isabella, Mrs Sedley, The Sorceress and Samson; Festival appearances: Barga, 1970, Edinburgh, 1978 and 1979, Bath 1981, Wexford, 1984; Regular appearances in concert, oratorio and recital; BBC Soloist for Radio 3 and 2 with BBC debut in 1984; Artists' Manager. *Recordings:* Opera Rara, 100 Years of Italian Opera 1800–1910. *Honours:* 2 Vaughan Williams Trust Awards, 1972 and 1973. *Address:* 25E Frognal, London NW3 6 AR, England.

MERCER, Gregory; Singer (Tenor); b. 1960, USA. *Career:* Opera appearances at the Metropolitan, New York, Chicago, Sarasota Opera and Dalls; Lawrenceville, NJ, 1988 as Ferrando in Così fan tutte; Monadnock Festival, New York, from 1987; Graz Opera, from 1992, notably as Raffaele in Stiffelio by Verdi, 1994; Concert and broadcast appearances. *Recordings:* Lord Byron by Virgil Thomson. *Address:* Opera Graz, Kaiser Joseph Platz 10, 8010 Graz, Austria.

MERCHANT, Jan; Singer (Mezzo); b. 1960 South Carolina, USA. *Education:* Metropolitan Opera Studio; University of South Carolina. *Career:* Opera engagements in Switzerland, Germany, Netherlands and USA: 1989 with Hannover Opera, Venus in Offenbach's Orpheus in the Underworld; Independent productions: Mephisto in Hervé's Le Petit Faust in Hamburg, Fildama in Cimarosa's Matrimonio Segreto, Countess in Le nozze di Figaro, Maddelena in Rigoletto, Second Dame in Zauberflöte; Concert Soloist with Nord Deutsche Rundfunk in Hamburg, most notably Stabat Mater (Dvořák), Requiem (Mozart); Elijah in Maryland;1995–98, Director of Choral Music, and member of Vocal Staff, Vienna Musical School in addition to guesting. *Address:* c/o Vocal Department, Vienna Musical School, Quellenstr. 102, 1101, Vienna, Austria.

MERIGHI, Giorgio; Singer (Tenor); b. 20 Feb. 1939, Ferrara, Italy. *Education:* Studied at the Rossini Conservatory, Pesaro. *Career:* Debut: Spoleto Festival 1962, as Riccardo in Un Ballo in Maschera; Many appearances on Italian stages, including the Verona Arena and at the Florence Festival (Meyerbeer's Robert le Diable 1968); Covent Garden 1971 and 1974; Metropolitan Opera debut 1978, as Manrico in Il Trovatore; Guest engagements in Berlin, Monte Carlo, Barcelona, Marseilles and Brussels; Geneva 1984, as Pollione in Norma; Wiesbaden Festival 1985, as the Duke of Mantua; Italian television as Pinkerton in Madama Butterfly; Munich and Palermo 1987–88 as Maurizio in Adriana Lecouvreur; Sang Luigi in Il Tabarro at the Met 1989, Maurizio at Bonn; Season 1992 with Don José at Genoa, Andrea Chénier at Turin and concert in memory of Mario del Monaco at the Torre del Lago Festival; Sang Ismaele in Nabucco at Verona, 1996; Gabriele Adorno in Simon Boccanegro at Monte Carlo, 1998; Sang Loris in Fedora at Genoa, 2000. *Address:* c/o L'Opera de Monte Carlo, BP 139, Place du Casino, Monte Carlo, Monaco.

MERILÄINEN, Usko; Composer; b. 27 Jan. 1930, Tampere, Finland. *Education:* Diploma in Composition, Sibelius Academy, 1955. *Career:* Mem, Chairman, Association of Finnish Composers, 1981–92. *Compositions include:* Epyllion for orchestra, 1963; Piano Sonata No. 2, 1966; Papillons for 2 Pianos, 1969; Concerto for Piano and Orchestra No. 2, 1969; Symphony No. 3, 1971; Concerto for 13 Instruments, 1971; Piano Sonata No. 3, 1972; Concerto for Double Bass and Percussion, 1973; Psyche, ballet in 2 acts, (tape), 1973; Piano Sonata No. 4, 1974; Concerto for Cello and Orchestra, 1975; Dialogues for Piano and Orchestra, 1977; Mobile, ein Spiel for Orchestra, 1977; Simultus for 4 Instruments, 1979; (Suvisoitto) Summer Sounds for Flute and Grasshoppers, 1979; Kyma for String Quartet, 1979; Paripeli for Cello and Piano, 1980; Quattro notturni per Arpa, 1984–85;. . . but this is a landscape, Monsieur Dali!, 1986; Exodus for Choir and Orchestra, 1988; Concerto No. 2, Aikaviiva (Timeline) for Orchestra, 1989; Letter to a Cellist for Cello Solo and Ensembles, 1990; Concerto for Guitar and Orchestra, 1991; Piano Sonata No. 5, 1992; String Quartet No. 3, 1992; Geasseija niehku, summer concert for Chamber Orchestra, 1993–94; Fetes d'Henriette for Flute, Cello and Piano, 1995; Kehrä, for orchestra, 1996; Sona, for piano, 1997. *Recordings include:* Visions and Whispers with Mikael Helasvuo on flute; Ku-Gu-Ku, electro-acoustic works; Timeline, Concerto No. 2 under Leif Segerstram; Papillons, Piano Sonatas 2, 4 and 5 with Jaana Kärkkäinen and Ilmo Ranta. *Honours:* Wihuri Foundation International Sibelius Prize, 1965; Prof hc, Doctor hc, Sibelius Academy, 1997. *Address:* Nokiantie 102, 33300 Tampere, Finland.

MERKA, Ivan; Cellist and Musicologist; b. 15 May 1926, Kosice, Czechoslovakia; m., 1 s., 1 d. *Education:* Violoncello, Masaryk Institute of Music and Singing, Ostrava; State Exam for Violoncello teaching, Brno; Musical science and philosophy, Masaryk University, Brno, 1952; Cello, Janáček Academy of Musical Arts, Brno, 1953. *Career:* Deputy Lead Cello, Radio orchestra, Ostrava, 1945–47; Lead violoncello, Opera orchestra of National Moravian-Silesian Theatre, Ostrava, 1953–60; Lead violoncello, Janáček Philharmonic Orchestra, Ostrava, 1960–68; Teacher of violoncello, Janáček Conservatoire, Ostrava, 1953–; Director, Janáček Conservatorie, Ostrava, 1990–92; Lecturer, Janáček Academy of musical arts in Brno, 1970–80; Assistant Professor, Janáček academy of musical Arts, Brno, 1992–; Soloist, concert halls, broadcasting, performed 16 cello concerts; 48 sonatas and suites; 205 other compositions for cello and piano; 884 radio performances; 223 public concerts; Brno quartet, 1948–50; Silesia piano trio, 1946–56; Ostrava string quartet, 1953–88; State ensemble of Janáček Philharmonic Orchestra, 1960–; 509 broadcast transmissions; 2281 public concerts; 200 string quartets; 62 trips abroad; mem, Beethoven Society of the Czech Republic; Board of Directors, Leoš Janáček Foundation. *Publications:* Articles, studies, papers, broadcast transmissions, television scripts with a musical theme, annual reports; Monograph, Violoncello: History, literature, personalities, 1995. *Honours:* Ostrava string quartet Haydn Prize, Budapest, 1959; Zdenka Podhajská Foundation Award, 1997; Senior Prix, 2000; European Gustav Mahler Prize, European Union of the Arts, 2001. *Address:* Mexica 5, 712 00 Ostrava, Czech Republic.

MERRILL, Nathaniel; Stage Director; b. 8 Feb. 1927, Massachusetts, USA. *Education:* Trained with Boris Goldovsky at New England Conservatory of Music and with Gunther Rennert, Herbert Graf and Carl Ebert in Europe. *Career:* Debut: Boston 1952, with the US premiere of Lully's Amadis; Metropolitan Opera New York from 1955, resident stage director from 1960, with productions of Turandot, Meistersinger, Les Troyens, Aida, Rosenkavalier, Adriana Lecouvreur, Luisa Miller, Parsifal, Porgy and Bess, 1985, Il Trovatore, Samson et Dalila and L'Elisir d'amore (collaborations with designer Robert O'Hearn); Other stagings at Strasbourg, Vancouver, Verona, San Francisco, New York City Opera and the Vienna Staatsoper. *Address:* c/o Metropolitan Opera, Lincoln Center, NY 10023, USA.

MERRIMAN, Nan; Singer (Mezzo-soprano); b. 28 April 1920, Pittsburgh, USA; m. Tom Brand. *Education:* Studied with Alexia Bassian in Los Angeles and with Lotte Lehmann. *Career:* Debut in concert, 1940; Opera debut as La Cieca in La Gioconda, Cincinnati, 1942; Sang in Toscanini's NBC broadcasts as Maddalena in Rigoletto, Gluck's Orpheus and Meg Page in Falstaff; Glyndebourne 1953, 1956, as Baba the Turk in The Rake's Progress and Dorabella in Così fan tutte; Sang at Aix-en-Provence as Dorabella, at the Holland Festival and La Scala Milan (1955); Piccola Scala 1958, in the local premiere of Dargomyzhsky's The Stone Guest; Guest engagements in Paris, Geneva, Amsterdam, Chicago and San Francisco. Many appearances in concert. *Recordings include:* Così fan tutte conducted by Karajan (Columbia). *Honours:* 1st Prize, National Federation of Music Clubs, 1943.

MERRITT, Chris; singer (tenor); b. 27 Sept. 1952, Oklahoma City, USA. *Education:* Oklahoma City University, apprentice artist at the Santa Fe Opera. *Career:* Sang in Augsburg as Idomeneo, Rossini's Otello, Rodolfo and Julien in Louise; New York City Opera debut 1981, as Arturo in I Puritani; Appeared in Rossini's Tancredi at Carnegie Hall, Il Viaggio a Reims at the Vienna Staatsoper, Ermione in Naples and Maometto II at San Francisco Opera; Paris Opéra debut 1983, in Rossini's Moise; Sang Uberto in La Donna del Lago at Covent Garden; Season 1985–86 in Il Viaggio a Reims at La Scala, as Rodrigo (La Donna del Lago) in Paris, Idreno in a concert performance of Semiramide at Covent Garden; Leukippos in Daphne at Carnegie Hall; Maggio Musicale Florence 1986, as Benvenuto Cellini; Aeneas in Les Troyens in Amsterdam; Nemorino in L'Elisir d'amore at Orlando, Florida; Opened the 1988–89 season at La Scala in Guillaume Tell by Rossini; Title role in Robert le Diable at Carnegie Hall; Sang in I Puritani at the Rome Opera, 1990; Arnold in a new production of Guillaume Tell at Covent Garden, 1990; Sang Admète in Alceste at the opening of the 1990–91 season at Chicago; Benvenuto Cellini at Geneva, 1992; Season 1992–93 as Leicester in Rossini's Elisabetta at Naples, Arnold at Covent Garden and San Francisco, Rodrigo in La Donna del Lago at La Scala and Conte di Libenskof in Il Viaggio a Reims at Pesaro; Season 1996–97 as Schoenberg's Aron in Amsterdam and Paris and in the premiere of Henze's Venus and Adonis

at Munich; Featured Artists (People No. 183) Opera Magazine Festival issue, 1992; Concert engagements in Verdi's Requiem; Haydn's Creation and the Choral Symphony in Israel; Rossini's Petite Messe Solennelle in Amsterdam; Benvenuto Cellini by Berlioz at the Festival Hall, London under Valery Gergiev, 1999; Sang Lilaque in Henze's Boulevard Solitude at Covent Garden, 2001. *Recordings:* Rossini's Stabat Mater, Ermione and Il Viaggio a Reims; Donizetti's Emilia di Liverpool; I Puritani; Faust, conducted by Michel Plasson. *Current Management:* Askonas Holt Ltd, Lonsdale Chambers, 27 Chancery Lane, London, WC2A 1PF, England. *Telephone:* (20) 7400-1700. *Fax:* (20) 7400-1799. *E-mail:* info@askonasholt.co.uk. *Website:* www.askonasholt.co.uk; www.onatech.com/chris-merritt.

MERTENS, Klaus; Singer (Tenor); b. 25 March 1949, Kleve, Germany; m. Ingrid Mertens, 14 May 1986, 1 s., 3 d. *Education:* Diploma, 1976. *Career:* Numerous radio recordings and television productions; Oratorio Work and Song Recitals, 1976–; mem, Bach-Gesellschaft. *Recordings:* Ranging from Renaissance to 20th Century Composers including Bach complete recordings of all Cantatas, St Matthew Passion, St John Passion and all other major vocal works; Sang the title role in Handel's Riccardo Primo at Magdeburg, 1996. *Address:* Buschhovener Strasse 2, 53347 Alfter, Germany.

MESHIBOVSKY, Alexander; Concert Violinist and Associate Professor; b. 15 April 1949, Kharkov, Russia. *Education:* Special School of Music for Gifted Children, Kharkov, 1955–65; Kharkov Conservatory, 1965–70; Masterclasses with Boris Goldstein, Moscow, 1971–74. *Career:* Concertmaster, Soloist, Moscow Chamber Orchestra, Russian Concert Agency, 1971–72; Soloist, Moscow Concert Agency, 1972–74; Dozent, Innsbruck Conservatory, 1975–76; Concerts in many European Countries, USA; Associate Professor, East Tennessee State University, 1984–; Associate Professor, West Virginia University, 1988. *Compositions:* Paganini Variations; Transcriptions of works by Debussy, Gershwin, Rachmaninov and many others. *Current Management:* Alpha Attractions Inc, New York, USA. *Address:* 82-46 Lefferts Blvd, Apt 2D, Kew Gardens, NY 11415, USA.

MESPLÉ, Mady; Singer (Soprano); b. 7 March 1931, Toulouse, France. *Education:* Studied in Toulouse and with Janine Micheau in Paris. *Career:* Debut: Liège 1953, as Lakmé; Paris Opéra-Comique from 1956, Opéra from 1958, notably as the Queen of Night, Gounod's Juliette, Ophelia in Hamlet, Philine in Mignon, Donizetti's Norina and Lucia and Sophie in Der Rosenkavalier; Aix-en-Provence 1966, as Ariadne; Metropolitan Opera debut 1973, as Gilda; Guest appearances in Buenos Aires, Moscow, Rome and Naples; Concert performances include Schoenberg's Die Jakobsleiter in London, conducted by Boulez. *Recordings:* Lakmé; Socrate by Satie, Barbiere di Siviglia and Guillaume Tell; Operettas by Lecoq, Messager, Planquette, Hahn and Offenbach. *Address:* c/o Conservatoire National de Musique de Lyon, 3 Quai Chauveau, 69009 Lyon, France.

MESSIEREUR, Petr; Violinist; b. 1937, Czechoslovakia. *Education:* Studied at Prague Academy of Art. *Career:* Leader of the Talich String Quartet from 1972; Tours to most European countries, Egypt Iraq, North America, Japan, Indonesia; Chamber Ensemble of the Czech Philharmonnic from 1975; Annual visits to France from 1976; Tours of the United Kingdom 1990–91, with concerts at the Wigmore Hall, appearances at the Bath and Bournemouth Festivals, Queen Elizabeth Hall and on BBC 2's Late Show, with Janáček's 2nd Quartet; Also played Beethoven's Quartet Op 74, the Brahms A minor, Smetana's D minor and works by Mozart in England; Festival appearances in Vienna, Besançon, Dijon, Helsinki, Amsterdam, Prague and Salzburg; Repertoire also includes works by Debussy, Bart ók (complete works recorded by Supraphon), Shostakovich, Ravel and Dvořák. *Recordings include:* For the French companies Sarastro and Calliope, with the complete quartets of Beethoven; Albums for Collins Classics. *Honours:* Grand Prix Charles Cros.

MESSITER, Malcolm; Oboist; b. 1 April 1944, Kingston, Surrey, England; m. Christine Messiter. *Education:* Paris Conservatoire 1967; Royal College of Music, London; ARCM. *Career:* Debut: Purcell Room, London, 1971; Principal Oboe, BBC Concert Orchestra, 1972–77; Solo concert engagements; Many appearances as chamber music player. *Honours:* Royal College of Music Oboe Prize, 1970. *Address:* 67 Crescent Way, Hadley Wood, Herts EN4 0EQ, England.

MESTER, Jorge; Conductor; b. 10 April 1935, Mexico City, Mexico. *Education:* MA, Juilliard School of Music, New York, 1958; Studied with Leonard Bernstein, Berkshire Music Center, Tanglewood, summer 1955; Albert Wolff, the Netherlands. *Career:* Teacher of Conducting, Juilliard School of Music, 1955–67; Music Director, Louisville Orchestra, 1967–79; Music Director, Aspen (Colorado) Music Festival, 1970–; Musical Adviser and Principal Conductor, kansas City (Missouri(Philharmonic Orchestra, 1971–74; Music Director, Casals Festival, Puerto Rico, 1979–; Teacher of Conducting, Conductor of School Ensembles, 1980–; Chairman, Conducting Department 1984–87, Juilliard School; Music Director, Pasadena (California) Symphony Orchestra, 1984–; Guest Conductor in North America and overseas; Chief Conductor of the West Australia Symphony and Principal Guest conductor of the Adelaide Symphony Orchestra; Conducted Der Rosenkavalier at Sydney, 1992. *Recordings:* For Cambridge; Columbia; Composers Recordings Inc; Desto; Louisville; Mercury; Vanguard including Dallapiccola Piccola musica notturna, Hindemith Concert Music for viola and Kammermusik No. 2; Bruch's 2nd Symphony; Penderecki De Natura Sonoris; Shostakovich Hamlet Music; Strauss's Six Songs Op 68; Milhaud Symphony No. 6; Martin Cello Cencerto. *Honours:* Naumburg Award, 1968; Alice M Distwon Award for Conductors, 1985. *Address:* c/o The Juilliard School, Lincoln Center, New York, NY 10023, USA.

MESZOLY, Katalin; Singer (Contralto); b. 1950, Hungary. *Education:* Studied singing under Professor Jenö Sipos, Budapest; Professor Paula Lindberg, Salzburg, Austria. *Career:* Budapest State Opera, 1976–, from debut, leading contralto of Budapest Opera; Performed title role of Carmen 129 times at Budapest and overseas; Azucena, Il Trovatore; Amneris, Aida; Ulrica, Un Ballo in Maschera; Preziosilla, La Forza del Destino, Marfa in Khovanshchina; Judith, Bluebeard's Castle, at La Scala 1981; Sang Britten's Mrs Herring at Budapest, 1988, Herodias in Salome, 1989; Ulrica (Un Ballo in Maschera) for Opéra de Montréal, 1990; Sang in Kodály's Spinning Room at Budapest, 1998; Has appeared in oratorios including Verdi's Requiem, Mozart's Requiem; Gives song recitals; Guest performer in numerous countries and Operas including Milan Scala, Austria, West Germany, Spain, France, Mexico, Egypt and others. *Honours:* Liszt Prize. *Address:* Hungarian State Opera House, Népötarsasag utja 22, 0161 Budapest, Hungary.

METCALF, John Philip, BMus; composer; b. 13 Aug. 1946, Swansea, Wales; m. Gillian Alexander 1972; two s. one d. *Education:* University of Cardiff. *Career:* commissions from Festivals of Cardiff, Swansea and North Wales, Bath and Cheltenham, England and Frankfurt, Germany, also from BBC, Gulbenkian Foundation, London Sinfonietta and Welsh National Opera; Opera, Kafka's Chimp, premiered at Banff, 1996; Artistic Director, Vale of Glamorgan Festival and Artistic Director, Swansea Festival. *Compositions:* Horn Concerto, 1972; PTOC, 1973 Auden Songs, 1973–77; 5 Rags for Charlotte, 1975; Ave Maria, choral, 1977; The Journey, opera, 1981; Music of Changes, orchestra, 1981; Two Carols, 1981; Clarinet Concerto, 1982; The Crossing, music theatre, 1984; The Boundaries of Time, cantata, 1985; Also music for dance, film and television; Piano Trio, 1988; Opera, Tornrak, 1989; Orchestra Variations, 1990; Opera, Kafka's Chimp, 1996; Paradise Haunts, for violin and orchestra, 1995, rev. 1999; Dances from Forgotten Places, for strings, 1999; The Garden of Wales for chorus, 1999; Endless Song, for piano, 1999; 4 other operas. *Honours:* Gulbenkian Dance Fellow, 1973; UK-USA Bicentennial Arts Fellow, 1977–78; University of Wales Creative Arts Fellow, 1984; Hon. Fellow (Univ. of Wales, Lampeter; Royal Welsh College of Music & Drama). *Address:* Ty Yfory, Llanfair Road, Lampeter, Ceredigion SA48 8JZ, Wales. *E-mail:* john@metcalf .demon.co.uk. *Website:* www.johnmetcalf.co.uk.

METCALFE, John; Violist; b. 1964, England. *Education:* Studied at the Royal Northern College of Music with Simon Rowland-Jones, at the Guildhall School of Music, and with Bruno Giuranna at Berlin Hochschule. *Career:* Concerts, Europe, USA, Japan, and on Channel 4 and Canadian television; Principal viola with the Kreisler String Orchestra; Member of Durutti Column, 1984–88; Violist with Duke String Quartet from 1985; Performances in the Wigmore Hall, Purcell Room, Conway Hall and throughout the United Kingdom; With Duke Quartet, tours with Rosas throughout Europe and to Brazil; South Bank series, 1991, with Mozart's early quartets; Soundtrack for Ingmar Bergman documentary The Magic Lantern, Channel 4, 1988; BBC debut feature; Features for French television, 1990–91, playing Mozart, Mendelssohn, Britten and Tippett; Brahms Clarinet Quintet for Dutch Radio with Janet Hilton; Live Music Now series with concerts for disadvantaged people; The Duke Quartet invites... at the Derngate, Northampton, 1991, with Duncan Prescott and Rohan O'Hara; Resident quartet, Rydale Festival, 1991; Residency, Trinity College, Oxford, tours to Scotland and Northern Ireland and concert at the Queen Elizabeth Hall, 1991; Season 1993/94 with Duke Quartet at Casa Manilva Festival, Spain, and tour of the United Kingdom; Founded Factory Classical Label, 1988. *Compositions:* Arranger for Pretenders, Blur, Cranberries, Morrissey, Lloyd Cole; Compositions for television; With Duke Quartet, composing music for Union Dance Co. *Recordings include:* Quartets by Tippett, Shostakovich and Britten (Third); Other albums including music by Dvořák, Barber and Glass; 3 world premieres by Kevin Volans. *Honours:* Martin Musical Trust Award; South East Arts Scholarships. *Address:* 81b Sarsfield Road, London SW12, England.

METTERNICH, Josef; Singer (Baritone); b. 2 June 1915, Hermuhlheim, Nr Cologne, Germany. *Education:* Studied in Berlin and Cologne. *Career:* Sang with the opera chorus at Cologne and Bonn; Solo debut

1945, as Tonio in Pagliacci at the Berlin Stadtische Oper; Covent Garden debut 1951, as the Dutchman; Metropolitan Opera 1953–56, as Carlo (La Forza del Destino), Amfortas, Wolfram, Kurwenal, Tonio, Luna, Renato and Amonasro; Further appearances in Paris, Vienna, Hamburg and Edinburgh; Bayerische Staatsoper Munich from 1954, notably as Johannes Kepler in the premiere of Hindemith's Die Harmonie der Welt (1957) and as Kothner in Die Meistersinger at the reopening of the Nationaltheater, 1963; Professor at the Cologne Musikhochschule from 1965, retired as singer 1971. *Recordings include:* Pagliacci (HMV); Hansel und Gretel (Columbia); Salome (Philips); Lohengrin, Fidelio and Der fliegende Holländer (Deutsche Grammophon).

METTERS, Colin (Raynor); Conductor; b. 22 Jan. 1948, Plymouth, Devon, England; m. Susan Furlong, 28 June 1980, 2 d. *Education:* ARCM, Violin and Conducting, Royal College of Music, 1966–71; Studied Conducting under Vernon Handley and George Hurst, 1966–71; Liverpool Seminar under Charles Groves, 1969; Masterclasses with Nadia Boulanger, 1968. *Career:* Musical Director, Ballet Rambert, 1972–74; Conductor, Sadler's Wells Royal Ballet, 1974–82; Teacher of Conducting, Canford Summer School of Music, 1973–83; Musical Director, East Sussex Youth Orchestra, 1979–; Guest Conductor with London Schools Symphony Orchestra, British Youth Symphony Orchestra, National Centre for Orchestral Studies; Freelance Conductor, 1982–; Director of Conducting, Royal Academy of Music, 1983–; Conducted major British, Provincial and BBC Orchestras; Conducted extensively abroad. *Recordings:* BBC radio and television and various. *Honours:* Honorary RAM conferred at RAM Graduation, 1995. *Current Management:* Helen Sykes Artists Management, 100 Felsham Road, Putney, London SW15 1DQ, England. *Address:* c/o Royal Academy of Music, Marylebone Road, London, NW1 5HT, England.

METTRAUX, Laurent; Composer; b. 27 May 1970, Fribourg, Switzerland. *Education:* Literature Section, St Michael's College; Piano, Violin, Singing, Complete Theoretical Studies with Professor René Oberson, Conservatoire de Fribourg; Composition with Professor Eric Gaudibert, Conducting with Professor S-L Chen, Geneva; Studies in Ancient Music, Musicology, Music History, Organ; Masterclasses. *Career:* Debut: 1st compositions at age 12; Symphonie pour orchestre de chambre first performed by Orchestre de Chambre de Lausanne, conductor Jesus Lopez-Cobos; Directed first performance of his composition Lysistrata; first performance of Concerto for 15 solo strings under Tibor Varga at opening concert, Tibor Varga Festival 1994; Numerous commissions; mem, Swiss Musicians Association, 1995–. *Compositions include:* Concerto for 15 solo strings, 1994; Vers le Soleil Couchant, oratorio, 1995–96; Trio No. 2, for piano, violin and cello, 1995–96; three Concertos for violin, 1996, 1998, 1999; Elògio della Nòtte, after Michelangelo, for bass voice and piano, 1997; Ombre for orchestra, 1995–98; String Trio, 1998; Crucifixion for mixed choir, 1998; Le Cocyte for orchestra, 1999; String Quartet, first performed by Talich Quartet, 1998–99; La plus belle des Lumières, for a cappella mixed choir, 2000; Wind Quintet, 2000; String Quintet, 2001–02; Le Nom Caché, oratorio for the Nat. Swiss Exposition of 2002, 2001–02; Concerto for organ and orchestra, for inauguration of new great organ, Lausanne Cathedral, 2002–03; Complainte, for solo violin, written at request of Shlomo Mintz as set piece for Int. Violin Competition of Sion, 2003; Double-Concerto for violin, pi'pa and orchestra, 2002–04. *Honours:* Symphonie pour orchestre de chambre won 1st Prize and Public Prize, 1st Competition for Young Composers, 1993; Donauschinger Musiktage Prize, 1998. *Address:* Route Principale 160, 1791 Courtaman, Switzerland. *E-mail:* laurent.mettraux@bluewin.ch.

METTRE, Raimundo; Singer (Tenor); b. 1949, Brazil. *Education:* Studied in Berlin and Milan. *Career:* Sang at the Piccola Scala Milan 1982, in Ariodante; Appearances at Zürich as Almaviva and the Duke of Mantua (1985–86), Basle (Rodolfo, 1987), at Rio de Janeiro as Werther and Don José and at Barcelona as Mozart's Ferrando and Don Ottavio; Other roles include Percy in Anna Bolena (at Lisbon), Belmonte (at Tel-Aviv); US debut at Philadelphia, as Ernesto in Don Pasquale; Concert repertoire includes the Verdi Requiem, Puccini's Messa di Gloria, Rossini's Stabat Mater and oratorios by Handel. *Address:* Opernhaus Zürich, Falkenstrasse 1, 8008 Zürich, Switzerland.

METZ, Catherine; Violinist; b. 1965, USA. *Education:* Studied in New York. *Career:* Recitalist, Lincoln Center's Alice Tully Hall, 92nd Street 'Y' and appearances with major orchestras; Chamber Musician at the Santa Fe Festival, Spoleto Festival and Lockenhaus Kammermusikfest and the International Musicians Seminar in Prussia Cove; Co-Founder, Orion Quartet and has given concerts at Washington DC 's Kennedy Center, at Boston Gardner Museum and throughout the USA; Carnegie Hall recital, 1991 and as part of the Centenial Celebration tribute; Concerts as Turku Festival in Finland. *Current Management:* Ingpen & Williams Ltd, 7 St George's Court, 131 Putney Bridge Road, London, SW15 2PA, England.

MEVEN, Peter; Singer (Bass); b. 1 Oct. 1929, Cologne, Germany. *Education:* Studied at the Cologne Musikhochschule with Robert Blasius. *Career:* Debut: Hagen, Westfalen, 1957, as Ferrando in IL Trovatore; Sang in Mainz, Wiesbaden and Oldenburg from 1959; Deutsche Oper Berlin from 1964; Many guest appearances in Germany and engagements in Amsterdam, Basle, Lisbon, Stockholm, Moscow and San Francisco; Covent Garden London, Gurnemanz in Parsifal; Bayreuth 1971, as Fafner; Salzburg 1974, as Sarastro in Die Zauberflöte; Paris Opéra as Daland in Der fliegende Holländer, 1981; Brussels 1983–85, as Kaspar in Der Freischütz and Pogner in Die Meistersinger (also at the Metropolitan 1976–77); Sang Lodovico in Schreker's Die Gezeichneten for Austrian Radio; Sang Hagen and Hunding in the Ring at Geneva, 1988; King Heinrich in Lohengrin at Santiago, 1988; Hagen at the 1989 Holland Festival; Sang Rocco in Fidelio at Düsseldorf, 1990. *Recordings:* Sacred music by Bruckner; Der Freischütz; Mathis der Maler by Hindemith; Fidelio. *Address:* Deutsche Oper am Rhein, Heinrich Heine Allee 16, 4000 Düsseldorf, Germany.

MEWES, Karsten; Singer (Baritone); b. 18 March 1959, Pirna, Saxony, Germany. *Education:* Studied at the Hanns Eisler Musikhochschule Berlin. *Career:* Sang at the Potsdam Opera and the Komische Oper Berlin, 1985–88; Berlin Staatsoper from 1985, notably in the 1989 premiere of Graf Mirabeau by Siegfried Matthus; Season 2000–01 as Iago at Halle and as Schtschelkalov in Boris Godunov at the Komische Oper, Berlin; Guest appearances in Dresden and elsewhere as Mozart's Count, Masetto, Guglielmo and Papageno, Lortzing's Zar, Silvio, Escamillo and Hans Scholl in Udo Zimmermann's Die weisse Rose; Concert repertoire includes works by Bach, Handel, Brahms and Fauré; Lieder recitals in Germany, Finland, Norway, Czechoslovakia, Poland and France. *Honours:* Competition Prize Winner at Zwickau, Verona, Hamburg, Rio de Janeiro, 1985–87.

MEYER, Edgar; Double Bassist and Composer; b. 1968, USA. *Career:* Appearances with concert artists Emanuel Ax (piano) and Yo-Yo Ma (cello), as well as collaborations in cross-over recitals: Neuvo Bluegrass trio with guitarist Russ Barenberg and dobroist Jerry Douglas; Recitals with pianist Amy Dorfman, in classical repertoire and own compositions; Engagements with Bela Flack (Banjo) and Mike Marshall (Mandolin). *Recordings include:* Appalachian Waltz, with Yo-Yo Ma and Mark Connor; Appalachian Journey; Short Trip Home, with Joshua Bell (violin and Mike Marshall), Sony; Transcriptions of the Bach Cello Suites. *Honours:* Grammy Award for Best Crossover Album, 2001. *Address:* c/o IMG Artists, Lovell House, 616 Chiswick High Road, London W4 5RX, England.

MEYER, Felix; Musicologist; b. 24 May 1957, St Gallen, Switzerland; m. Rosmarie Anzenberger, 28 Nov 1986, 1 s., 1 d. *Education:* Musicology, English and German Literature, University of Zürich; PhD, Musicology, 1989; Violin studies in St Gallen; Piano studies with Hans Steinbrecher in St Gallen, Werner Bärtschi in Zürich, Ian Lake in London. *Career:* Secretary, Swiss Youth Music Competition, 1984–85; Curator of Music Manuscripts at Paul Sacher Foundation, Basel, 1986, duties including Director of concert series Klassizistische Moderne, Basel, 1996, and Director of exhibition of music manuscripts at Pierpont Morgan Library, New York City, 1998; Head of the Paul Sacher Foundation, 1999–; mem, Swiss Musicological Society; German Musicological Society; American Musicological Society. *Publications:* A Study of Charles Ives's Concord Sonata, 1991; Editor, contributor, Quellenstudien II: Zwölf Komponisten des 20. Jahrhunderts, 1993; Editor, contributor, Klassizistische Moderne, 1996; Editor, contributor, Settling New Scores, 1998; Editor, facsimile edition of Béla Bartók's Music for Strings, 2000; Co-editor, contributor, 2 facsimile editions of works by Igor Stravinsky. *Contributions:* Music Analysis; Revista de musicología; Neue Zürcher Zeitung; Others. *Address:* Sevogelstrasse 85, 4052 Basel, Switzerland.

MEYER, Henry; Violinist and College Professor; b. 29 June 1923, Dresden, Germany. *Education:* Studied at Prague Music Academy in Paris with George Enescu and at the Juilliard School with Ivan Galamian. *Career:* Co-Founded the Lasalle String Quartet at the Juilliard School, 1949; Many concerts featuring modern composers and the quartets of Beethoven; European debut 1954; Composers who wrote for the ensemble include Hans Erich Apostel, Earle Brown, Henri Pousseur, Mauricio Kagel, György Ligeti, Penderecki and Witold Lutoslawski; Quartet-in-Residence and Professor, Cincinnati College-Conservatory of Music; Quartet disbanded 1988; Has since given masterclasses in the USA, Europe, Israel, Australia and Japan. *Recordings include:* Works by Berg, Schoenberg, Webern and Zemlinsky; Beethoven's Late Quartets; Brahms; Wolf. *Address:* c/o Cincinnati College-Conservatory of Music, Cincinnati, OH 45221, USA.

MEYER, Kerstin, CBE; singer (mezzo-soprano) and rector emerita; b. 3 April 1928, Stockholm, Sweden; m. Björn G. Bexelius 1974 (died 1997). *Education:* Royal Swedish Conservatory, Stockholm, Swedish University College of Opera, Accademia Chigiana, Italy, Mozarteum, Austria. *Career:* debut, Royal Opera, Stockholm, 1952, as Azucena in Il

Trovatore; Orchestra appearances with the Hallé Orchestra; London Philharmonic, Berlin and Vienna Philharmonics, Suisse Romande, Santa Cecilia, Chicago, ABC, BBC, NZBC television; Leading roles in most of the important Houses and Festivals in Europe, North and South America, Far East, such as Royal Opera House Covent Garden, Welsh and Scottish Operas, Glyndebourne and Edinburgh Festivals; La Scala, Milan, La Fenice and Santa Cecilia, Italy, Vienna and Salzburg, Austria; Munich, Berlin, Cologne and Hamburg, Germany; Paris, Marseilles, France, Moscow, Tashkent, Tallinn, Riga, USSR, Metropolitan Opera House, San Francisco, Santa Fe, Tulsa, USA; Teatro Colón, Argentina; Mexico City, Tokyo, Hong Kong; Sang in first British performances of operas by Henze and Einem at Glyndebourne and in the world premieres of operas by Goehr and Searle (Hamburg), Henze's The Bassarids at Salzburg, 1966, and Ligeti's Le Grand Macabre at Stockholm, 1978; President, Swedish University College of Opera, 1984–94; Advisory Director, European Mozart Academy, Kraków and New York, 1994–98; Since retirement teaching vocal interpretation; Giving Masterclasses at the Summer school of Music, Mozarteum, Salzburg; mem, Board Member, STIM; Assessor, HEFCE, London, 1994–95. *Recordings:* Operas, recitals with von Karajan, Barbirolli, Solti, Hans Schmidt-Isserstedt and Sixten Ehrling. *Honours:* Royal Swedish Court Singer, 1963; Swedish Vasa Order; Swedish Litteris et Arbitus; Swedish Illis Quorum, 1994; German Cross of Honour 1st Class; Italian Order of Merit. *Address:* Porsvaegen 48, 16570 Haesselby, Sweden.

MEYER, Krzysztof; Composer, Music Theorist and Pianist; b. 11 Aug. 1943, Kraków, Poland; 1 s., 1 d. *Education:* High School of Music, Kraków; American Conservatory, Fontainebleau. *Career:* Debut: Warsaw in 1965; Professor: High School of Music, Kraków, 1966–87 and High School of Music, Cologne, 1987–; President of Union of Polish Composers, 1985–89. *Compositions include:* Stage Works: Cyberiada, opera, premiere in 1986, The Gamblers, completion of Shostakovich's opera, premiere 1983, The Maple Brothers, children's opera, premiere 1990; Orchestral: 4 Symphonies, Hommage à Johannes Brahms; Musica incrostate; Concertos for: Piano, Violin, Violoncello, 2 for Oboe, Trumpet, Saxophone, 2 for flute, Double concerto for Harp and Cello, Symphony in Mozartean style, Caro Luigi for 4 Cellos and Orchestra; For Choir and Orchestra: Epitaphium Stanislaw Wiechowicz in memoriam, (Symphony No. 2), Symphonie d'Orphée (Symphony No. 3), Farewell Music for Orchestra, 1997; Lyric Triptych for Tenor and Chamber Orchestra, Mass for Choir and Organ; Chamber Works: Clarinet Quintet, Piano Quintet, 10 String Quartets, 1963–94; Piano Trio, String Trio; For Various Ensembles: Concerto Retro; Hommage à Nadia Boulanger, Capriccio, Canzona and Sonata for Cello and Piano; For Piano: 5 Sonatas, 24 Preludes; Solo Sonatas for: Cello, Cembalo, Violin, Flute, Fantasy for Organ. *Recordings include:* String Quartets Nos 1–9; Hommage à Brahms; Symphonies 1–6; Clarinet Quintet; The Gamblers, and others. *Publications:* Dimitri Shostakovich, 1973; Shostakovich, 1995. *Contributions:* Various Journals. *Honours:* Grand Prix, Prince Pierre de Monaco, 1970; Award, Minister of Culture and Art, Poland, 1973, 1976; Medal, Government of Brazil, 1975; Gottfried von Herder Preis, Wien, 1984; Award, Polish Composers Union, 1992; Jurzykowski Foundation, New York, 1993. *Address:* Kurt Schumacher Str 10 W-51, 51427 Bergisch Gladbach, Germany.

MEYER, Paul; Clarinettist and Conductor; b. 5 March 1965, Mulhouse, France. *Education:* Studied at the Paris Conservatoire and the Basle Musikhochschule. *Career:* Debut: Orchestre Symphonique du Rhin, 1978; Concerts in New York, 1984; Formed association with Benny Goodman; Engagements with the Orchestre National de France, BBC Symphony Orchestra, Royal Philharmonic, Tokyo Symphony Orchestra, Salzburg Mozarteum, Suisse Romade, Zürich Tonhalle and ABC Australia; Modern repertory includes works by Boulez (Domains), Gould and Henze; Premiere of Concerto by Gerd Kuhr at the Sinfonia Varsovia, 1994; Premiered Penderecki's arrangement of Viola Concerto, 1996, and the Concerto by Berio, with the Concertgebouw Orchestra, 1997; Tour of the USA with Yo-Yo Ma, Emmanuel Ax and Pamela Frank, playing Brahms and Schoenberg, 1995; Further partnerships with Eric Le Sage, Barbara Hendricks, Gidon Kremer, Maria João Pires, Jean-Pierre Rampal, Rostropovich, Heinrich Schiff and Isaac Stern; Quintet with the Carmina, Cleveland, Emerson and Takacs String Quartets; Concerts as conductor with the Munich CO, English CO and with Carmen in the South of France, 1997. *Recordings include:* Concertos by Mozart, Copland and Busoni, with the English CO; Weber and Fuchs wth the Carmina Quartet; Mendelssohn and Reinecke, with Eric Le Sage. *Honours:* Winner, French Young Artists Competition, 1982; USA Young Artists Competition, 1984. *Address:* Bureau des Concerts Jaques Thelen, Théâtre des Champs Elysées, 15 Avenue Montaigne, 75008 Paris, France.

MEYER, Sabine; Clarinettist; b. 30 March 1959, Crailsheim, Germany. *Education:* Studied with her father, Karl Meyer, with Otto Hermann in Stuttgart and Hans Deinzer in Hanover. *Career:* Joined the Bavarian

Radio Symphony Orchestra from 1983, at first under Herbert von Karajan then Claudio Abbado; Trio partnership with her brother Wolfgang, and Reiner Behle, notably in the Trios with Clarinet by Beethoven and Brahms; Further Collaborations with Pianist Rudolf Buchbinder, Cellist Heinrich Schiff and the Cleveland and Brandis Quartets; Regular concerts in the Divertimenti and Serenades of Mozart with members of the BerlinPhilharmonic; Premieres of Octet for Winds by Edison Denisov, 1991 and the Romance for clarinet and orchestra by Richard Strauss, 1991. *Honours:* Winner, ARD competition at Munich. *Address:* c/o Berlin Philharmonic Orchestra, Philharmonie, Matthäukirchstrasse 1, 1000 Berlin 30, Germany.

MEYER-TOPSOE, Elisabeth; Singer (soprano); b. Copenhagen, Denmark. *Education:* studied in Copenhagen and with Birgit Nilsson in Stockholm. *Career:* debut, Augsburg 1989 as Oxana in Tchaikovsky's Cherevichki; sang the Trovatore Leonora and Arabella at Augsburg; Nuremburg Opera from 1990, as Wagner's Elisabeth and Senta; Weber's Euryanthe, also at Aix en Provence 1993; Copenhagen from 1992 as Ariadne, the Marschallin, Desdemona and Senta; Vienna Staatsoper debut 1995 as Third Norn in Götterdämmerung; US debut 1996 in Strauss's Vier Letzte Lieder at Monterey; sang Ariadne at Maggio Musicale, Firenze, Vienna Staatsoper, Toulouse, Lausanne and Nancy; sang Senta in Vienna Staatsoper, Zürich, Mannheim, Stockholm, Savonlinna, Staatsoper, Berlin, Copenhagen, Verona, Wiesbaden Mai-Festspiele, Santiago de Compostella, Bonn, Malaga; sang Marschallin at the Teatro Colón, Buenos Aires, Trieste, Leipzig, Unter den Linden, Berlin and Sevilla; sang Ingeborg in Heise's Drot og Maske at Arhus 2000; sang Elsa at Torino, Essen; sang Chysothemis at Rome, Verona, Paris in concert; engaged to sing Senta in Rome 2004, Governess in Turn of the Screw in Naples 2005. *Address:* Rosenvangets Sideallé 3, 2100 Copenhagen, Denmark.

MEYER-WOLFF, Frido; Singer (Bass-baritone); b. 22 April 1934, Potsdam, Germany. *Education:* Studied in Berlin, Paris and Hamburg. *Career:* Debut: Stralsund 1955, as Mozart's Figaro; Appearances at Trier, Hamburg, Kassel, Kiel and the Deutsche Oper Berlin; Opéra Comique Paris, 1963, in the premiere of Menotti's The Last Savage; Spoleto Festival, 1964; As Ochs in Der Rosenkavalier; Aix en Provence Festival, 1963, 1964, Marseilles from 1961, Brussels, 1965, Monte Carlo 1967–94, Nice 1962–89, Lausanne 1987; Decorated Chevalier des Arts et Lettres by the French Government, 1985; Direction of open-air theatre Jean Cocteau Cap d'All near Monaco, created and conducted a new chamber orchestra from 1989; Other roles include parts in operas by Verdi, Wagner, Puccini, Strauss, Rossini, Smetana and Moussorgsky; Sang in Wozzeck, Samson et Dalila, and Das Schloss by Reimann, first performance, 1992 at Deutsche Oper Berlin; Frequent concert appearances. *Honours:* Chevalier de l'Ordre des Palmes Academiques, 1997. *Current Management:* Boris Orlob. *Address:* c/o Boris Orlob, Jägerstr. 70, 10117 Berlin, Germany. *Website:* www.meyer -wolff.com.

MEYERS, Anne Akiko; Violinist; b. 1970, San Diego, California, USA. *Education:* Indiana University with Josef Gingold; Colburn School of Performing Arts with Alice and Eleanor Schoenfeld; Dorothy DeLay and Masao Kawasaki at Juilliard School, New York. *Career:* Debut as concerto soloist, age 7; Later appeared with Los Angeles Philharmonic, New York Philharmonic conducted by Mehta and New York String Orchestra at Carnegie Hall; Far East engagements with Japan Philharmonic and NHK Symphony Orchestra; Summer festivals include Aspen, Ravinia, Tanglewood, Hollywood Bowl; Tours: St Louis Symphony with Leonard Slatkin, Australian Chamber Orchestra, Baltimore Symphony with David Zinman, Moscow Philharmonic; Appeared on television with John Williams and Boston Pops; Played with Minnesota Orchestra, Prague Symphony Orchestra, Hallé Orchestra, Orchestre de Paris and Jerusalem Symphony; Appearances in Montreal Symphony, Boston Symphony, St Louis Symphony, Philadelphia Orchestra, Toronto Symphony, Swedish Radio Orchestra, Moscow Philharmonic, Belgian Radio Orchestra; Berlin Radio Symphony. *Recordings include:* Concertos by Barber and Bruch with Royal Philharmonic Orchestra and Christopher Seaman; Lalo Symphonie Espagnole and Bruch Scottish Fantasy with Royal Philharmonic Orchestra, Lopez-Cobos, César Franck and Richard Strauss Sonatas; Mendelssohn with Philharmonia and Andrew Litton; Salût d'Amour for RCA. *Contributions:* Featured, Strad Magazine. *Honours:* Youngest to sign with Young Concert Artists; Sole recipient of Avery Fisher Career Grant, 1993. *Current Management:* ICM Artists, 40 W 57th St, New York, NY 10019; Jasper Parrott, London; Japan Arts, Tokyo. *Address:* Harrison/Parrott Ltd, 12 Penzance Place, London, W11 4PA, England. *Telephone:* (20) 7229 9166. *Fax:* (20) 7221 5042. . *Website:* www .harrisonparrott.com.

MEYERSON, Janice, BA, MM; American singer (mezzo-soprano); b. 12 March 1951, Omaha, NE; m. Raymond Scheindlin 1986. *Education:* Washington Univ., St Louis, Missouri, New England Conservatory. *Career:* Fellowship, Berkshire Music Center (Tanglewood) 1976–77;

Carmen (title role), New York City Opera and Théâtre Royal de la Monnaie, Brussels; Amneris in Aida, Teatro Colón, Buenos Aires and Frankfurt Opera; Santuzza in Cavalleria Rusticana, New York City Opera; Judith in Bluebeard's Castle, New York Philharmonic and Palacio de Bellas Artes, Mexico City; Brangaene in Tristan and Isolde, Leonard Bernstein conducting Philadelphia Orchestra; soloist, Mahler's 3rd Symphony, American Symphony, Carnegie Hall; soloist, Boston Symphony, Milwaukee Symphony, Minnesota Orchestra, New Orleans Symphony, National Symphony, Dallas Symphony, Washington Opera, Houston Grand Opera, Montreal Opera, Opera Co. of Philadelphia, Aspen Festival, Spoleto USA, Marlboro, Tanglewood, Wolf Trap, Schleswig-Holstein Music Festival, Deutsche Oper Berlin, Moscow State Symphony Orchestra; Teatro São Carlo, Lisbon and Vlaamse Opera; Adriano in Rienzi in London 1999; Kabanicha in Katya Kabanova in Dublin 2000; Herodias in Salome, Florida Grand Opera 2003; Barcelona Liceu 2004. *Recordings:* For the Night to Wear (with Boston Musica Viva) 1994. *Address:* 420 Riverside Drive, Apt GC, New York, NY 10025, USA. *E-mail:* Jcmeyerson@aol.com (home). *Website:* www.janicemeyerson.com.

MEYFARTH, Jutta; Singer (Soprano); b. 1933, Germany. *Career:* Sang at Basle in 1955; Aachen Opera 1956–59; Member of Frankfurt Opera from 1959; La Scala Milan debut 1960; Maggio Musicale Florence 1961, as Elsa in Lohengrin; Bayreuth Festival 1962–64, as Freia, Gutrune and Sieglinde; Munich Opera 1965, as Donna Anna; Guest appearances in Buenos Aires, Brussels, Rome, London, Lisbon, Athens, Lyon and Antwerp; Other roles included Wagner's Isolde, The Empress in Die Frau ohne Schatten, Aida, and Martha in Tiefland.

MEYLAN, Raymond; Flautist and Musicologist; b. 22 Sept. 1924, Genava; m. Anne-Marie Bersot, 28 July 1959, 1 d. *Education:* University of Lausanne, 1947; DLitt, University of Zürich, 1967; Studied at Conservatoire of Genava, 1936–1943 and in Paris with Marel Moyse, 1948; Accademia Chigiana, Sienna, with Ruggero Gerlin, 1949–51. *Career:* Debut: 1944; Solo Flute, Orchestra Alessandro Scarlatti, Naples, 1951–54; Pomerriggi Musicali, Milan, 1954–58; Orchestra of Radio Beromünster, Zürich, 1958–70; Basler Orchesten Gesellschaft, Basle, 1971–89; Lecturer in Musicology, University of Zürich, 1969–77; Conductor, Orchestre Académique de Zürich, 1969–77, Orchesterverein Liestal, 1977–91; Studies in archaeology of flutes, 1972–; mem, Swiss Association of Musicians; Swiss Musicological Society; French Society of Musicology. *Compositions:* Le Choix, for voice, choir, flute, vibraphone and marimba, 1979; Notre Dame de Lausanne, for wind, 1986; Bourrasque, for large orchestra in amipheatre, 1987; Cinq Miniatures, for flute and guitar, 1987; Assonances, for scattered orchestra, 1988. *Recordings:* Flute Concertos by Danzi, Widor and Reinecke; Salieri, in Virtuoso Oboe; Bernard Reichel, VDE Gallo; Beethoven, 10 themes and variations, op 107; Telemann, triple concerto, with Zagreber Solisten, A. Janigro, Amadeo and The Bach Guild. *Publications:* The Puzzle of the Music of the Low Dances of the 15th Century, 1969; La Flûte, 1974; Publications on Attaingnant, Mazzocchi, A and D Scarlatti, Sarri, Bach, Nardini, Fischer, Schwindl, Kozeluh, Bellini, Donizetti, other works forthcoming. *Contributions:* Musical and scholarly journals; Musical dictionaries. *Address:* Buchenstr 58, 4142 Münchenstein, Switzerland.

MEZÖ, Laszlo; Cellist; b. 1940, Hungary. *Education:* Franz Liszt Academy, Budapest. *Career:* Cellist of the Bartók Quartet from 1977; Performances in nearly every European country and tours of Australia, Canada, Japan, New Zealand and the USA; Festival appearances at Adelaide, Ascona, Aix, Venice, Dubrovnik, Edinburgh, Helsinki, Lucerne, Menton, Prague, Vienna, Spoleto and Schwetzingen; Tour of the United Kingdom 1986 including concerts at Cheltenham, Dartington, Philharmonic Hall, Liverpool, RNCM, Manchester and the Wigmore Hall; Tours of the United Kingdom 1988 and 1990 featuring visits to the Sheldonian Theatre, Oxford, Wigmore Hall, Harewood House and Birmingham; Repertoire includes standard classics and Hungarian works by Bartók, Durkö, Bozay, Kadosa, Soproni, Farkas, Szabo and Lang. *Recordings include:* Complete quartets of Mozart, Beethoven and Brahms; Major works of Haydn and Schubert (Hungaraton); Complete quartets of Bartók (Erato). *Honours:* With Members of Bart ók Quartet, Kossuth Prize, Outstanding Artists of the Hungarian People's Republic 1981; UNESCO/IMC Prize 1981. *Current Management:* Ingpen & Williams Ltd, 7 St George's Court, 131 Putney Bridge Road, London, SW15 2PA, England.

MICHAEL, Audrey; Singer (Soprano); b. 11 Nov. 1949, Geneva, Switzerland. *Education:* Studied with father, Jean-Marie Auberson, and in Milan and Hamburg. *Career:* Sang with the Hamburg Staatsoper, 1976–81, Deutsche Oper am Rhein Düsseldorf, 1981–86; Guest appearances throughout Europe; Roles have included Gluck's Amor in Orpheus, Ilia (Idomeneo), Mozart's Pamina, Susanna, Countess and Papagena, Elvira (L'Italiana in Algeri), Adina, Lauretta, Zdenka, Mélisande and Elisabeth Zimmer in Elegy for Young Lovers by Henze; Sang at Hamburg in the premieres of Kommen und gehen by Heinz

Holliger, 1978, William Ratcliff by Ostendorf, 1982 and Jakob Lenz by Wolfgang Rihm, 1979; Théâtre Municipal Lausanne, 1991 as Sextus in Gluck's La Clemenza di Tito; Sang Sextus at the Théâtre des Champs Elysées, Paris, 1996; Concert engagements in the Baroque and modern repertory throughout Switzerland and in Berlin, Stuttgart, Paris, Lisbon and Buenos Aires. *Recordings include:* Monteverdi Orfeo, L'Enfant et les Sortilèges, Masses by Schubert and Beethoven; Rigoletto, Luisa Miller and Parsifal; Monteverdi Ballo delle Ingrate and Vespers of 1610. *Address:* c/o Opéra de Lausanne, PO Box 3972, 1002 Lausanne, Switzerland.

MICHAEL, Beth; Singer (Soprano); b. 1962, Gwent, Wales. *Education:* Studied at the Welsh College of Music and Drama and the RAM, London. *Career:* Debut: Pheadra in Cavalli's L'Egisto for Scottish Opera, 1982; Roles with Opera 80/English Touring Opera include Cenerentola, Carmen, Gretel, Frasquita, the Merry Widow and Lucia; Further engagements as Manon Lescaut, Butterfly (Surrey Opera), Tosca (Regency Opera) and at Wexford, Bayreuth and London (English National Opera); Appearances with the Royal Opera, Covent Garden, in Death in Venice, The Cunning Little Vixen, Turandot, Der Rosenkavalier, La Traviata and Die Walküre; Countess Ceprano in Rigoletto, 1997; Many concert appearances, and engagements on radio and television. *Address:* c/o English National Opera (contracts), St Martin's Lane, London WC2N 4ES, England.

MICHAEL, Nadja; Singer (mezzo-soprano); b. 1969, Leipzig, Germany. *Education:* Studied in Stuttgart and in USA with Carlos Montane. *Career:* Debut: Ludiwgsburg Festival 1993, as Third Lady in Die Zauberflöte; Appearances at Wiesbaden as Amastris (Xerxes) and Eustazio (Rinaldo), Dulcinée in Don Quixote at St Gallen and Tchaikovsky's Olga at Glyndebourne; Strauss's Dryad at the Dresden Semper Oper and Handel at the Berlin Staatsoper; Season 1997–98 as Varvara in Katya Kabanova at Covent Garden (debut), Ottavia in Poppea at Munich, Wagner's Venus at Naples and Mahler's Rückert Lieder and Second Symphony; Further concerts include Elijah, Messiah, Berio's Folk Songs and Mahler's Das Lied von der Erde (Swiss television); Appearances in Carmen in Italy and at St Gallen and Tokyo; Sang in Tippett's Midsummer Marriage at Munich, 1998; Sang Hansel in Hansel and Gretel at the Staatsoper in Berlin; Engaged to sing Charlotte in Werther and Carmen at the New National Theatre in Tokyo and at La Monnaie in Brussels; Delilah in Samson and Delilah in Venice; Venus in Tannhäuser in Toulouse and at the Bavarian Staatsoper, Munich, 2000; Season 2000–01 as Carmen in Vienna, Naples and Berlin (Deutsche Oper), Eboli in Don Carlos at Munich and Amneris in Verona. *Current Management:* Askonas Holt Ltd, Lonsdale Chambers, 27 Chancery Lane, London, WC2A 1PF, England. *Telephone:* (20) 7400-1700. *Fax:* (20) 7400-1799. *E-mail:* info@askonasholt.co.uk. *Website:* www.askonasholt.co.uk.

MICHAELS-MOORE, Anthony; Singer (Baritone); b. 8 April 1957, Grays, Essex, England. *Education:* Studied at Newcastle University with Denis Matthews and at Royal Scottish Academy; Further study with Eduardo Asquez and Neilson Taylor. *Career:* Principal Baritone at Covent Garden from 1987 in Jenůfa, Boris Godunov, Turandot, Rigoletto, Pagliacci, Der Freischütz and La Bohème; English National Opera from 1987 as Zurga, Marcello and the Count in new production of Figaro, 1991; Sang Escamillo, Creon in Oedipus Rex and Figaro; US debut with Philadelphia Opera 1989 as Guglielmo, followed by Missa Solemnis in Los Angeles, 1990; Other appearances include: Germont and Posa in new production of Don Carlos in 1993 for Opera North; Concert engagements include Méhul's Uthal conducted by Neeme Järvi; London concert debut in Duruflé Requiem at the Queen Elizabeth Hall; Also sings The Kingdom, Belshazzar's Feast, Carmina Burana, Rossini's Stabat Mater, Elijah and The Creation; Sang Don Fernando in the world premiere production of Gerhard's The Duenna at Madrid, 1992; Season 1992–93 as Marcello and Forester in Vixen at Covent Garden and in a Rossini concert at Turin; Opened 1993–94 season at La Scala as Licinius in La Vestale by Spontini; Lescaut, Belcore and Figaro at Vienna Staatsoper, 1994 and Sharpless and Orestes at Paris Bastille, 1994; Sang Stankar in Stiffelio, and Simon Boccanegra, ROH, 1995; Macbeth in the 1847 version of Verdi's opera at Covent Garden, 1997; St Peter in The Kingdom by Elgar at the 1999 London Proms; for English National Opera: Eugene Onegin 2000; Covent Garden: Ezio in Verdi's Attila, 2000–01 (and at Chicago); at Glyndebourne: Iago, 2001; at Opéra Bastille, Paris: Iago, 2001; Ford; Onegin; Count (Figaro) Montfort; Conte di Luna; at Vienna Staatsoper: Nabucco, Rigoletto, Scarpia, Montforte (Vespin Siciliani); Stankar (Stiffelio); at San Francisco Opera: Onegin, 1996; Posa, 1997; Enrico, 1998; Alfio and Tonio, 2003. *Recordings:* Carmina Burana under Previn with Vienna Philharmonic; La Vestale at La Scala; Die Walpurgisnacht; Szymanowski's Stabat Mater; Puccini Highlights, ROH; Lucia di Lammermoor with Mackerras; Falstaff with Gardiner; La Favorite with Viotti; Aroldo with Luisi; A Masked Ball. *Honours:* Joint Winner of Luciano Pavarotti Opera Company of Philadelphia Competition. *Address:* c/o IMG Artists, Lovell House, 616 Chiswick High Road, London W4 5RX, England.

MICHAILOV, Maxim; Singer (Bass); b. 1961, Moscow, Russia. *Education:* Studied at the Gnessin Conservatory, Moscow. *Career:* Sang with the Bolshoi company, Moscow, from 1987 as Sarastro, Ivan Khovansky in Khovanshchina, Tsar Dodon in The Golden Cockerel and Zaccaria in Nabucco; Edinburgh Festival 1991 on tour with the Bolshoi in Eugene Onegin and Rimsky's Christmas Eve; Guest appearances in opera and concert throughout Russia; Sang Sarastro at Schönbrunn, Vienna, 1996. *Address:* c/o Bolskoi Theatre, 103009 Moscow, C1S, Russia.

MICHALOWSKA, Krystyna; Singer (Mezzo-soprano); b. 13 July 1946, Vilnius, Poland. *Education:* Studied in Gdansk. *Career:* Debut: Bydgoszcz 1970, as Azucena; Engagements in Szczecin, Poznan and Gdansk; Guest appearances in Germany, Bulgaria, Romania, Russia and Czechkoslovakia. Appearances at Bielfeld and elsewhere in Germany from 1980, as Leonora in La Favorita, Carmen, Eboli, Lady Macbeth, Ulrica, Fides, Rosina, Konchakovna, Olga and Larina in Eugene Onegin, Dalila, Laura in La Gioconda, Sara in Roberto Devereux and the Nurse in Die Frau ohne Schatten; Bielefeld 1991, in Yerma by Villa-Lobos, as Ortrud and in the premiere of Katharin Blum by Tilo Medek; Frequent concert appearances. *Address:* c/o Stadtisches Buhnen, Brunnenstrasse 3, 4800 Bielefeld 1, Germany.

MICHELI, Lorenzo; Italian classical guitarist; b. 13 June 1975, Milan; m. Giulia Ichino 2002. *Education:* Accademia Chigiana, Siena, Conservatory of Trieste, Musik-Akademie der Stadt Basel, studied with Paola Coppi in Milan, F. Zigante in Lausanne, with O. Ghiglia. *Career:* debut recital, Milan, 1994; has performed worldwide, as soloist and with orchestra; has given over 250 concerts in Italy, Austria, Spain, Switzerland, the UK, France, Ireland, Croatia, Poland, Germany, Slovenia, Greece, Canada and more than 30 US states, plus Africa and Latin America. *Compositions:* two film and TV soundtracks, including Viaggio Verso Casa (film) 1998. *Recordings:* works by M. Castelnuovo-Tedesco; complete M. Llobet guitar works; Guitar Music by Dionisio Aguado; Three Quartets, op 19 by F. de Rossa; Lorenzo Micheli in Concert at Texas Tech Univ. (video). *Publications:* In Memoriam Michael Tippett, Il Fronimo, 1998; Mauro Giuliani's Guitar Technique and Early Nineteenth-Century Pedagogy (essay, Guitar Forum II), 2004; Miguel Llobet (book), 2004. *Honours:* Guitar competitions worldwide including Alessandria, 1997; Guitar Foundation of America Competition, 1999. *Address:* Via Breguzzo 5, 20148 Milan, Italy. *E-mail:* lorenzo.micheli@libero.it (home). *Website:* www.lorenzomicheli.it (home).

MICHELOW, Sybil; Singer (Contralto) and Voice Coach; b. 12 Aug. 1925, Johannesburg, South Africa; m. Derek Goldfoot, 18 April 1950. *Education:* Music Diploma, Witwatersrand University, South Africa; Private studies with Franz Reizensten (Piano) and Mary Jarred (Singing); LTCL, 1995. *Career:* Debut: London, 1958; Concert performances in the United Kingdom and abroad, especially of Handel's Messiah; Frequent radio and television appearances, notably in Rule Britannia at the Last Night of the Proms; Singing Instructor, Royal Academy of Dramatic Art, 1956–; mem, Royal Society of Musicians of Great Britain, Governor, 1982–85, 1988–93; Incorporated Society of Musicians. *Compositions include:* Incidental music for Royal Academy of Dramatic Art production of Brecht plays Chalk Circle and Mother Courage; Children's stories with music, South African Broadcasting Corporation. *Recordings include:* Music of Court Homes, vol. 4, and Bach Cantatas 78 and 106; Bliss Pastoral; Dallapiccola Sicut Umbra; Dido and Aeneas; Esparanto Songs by Frank Merrick. *Address:* 50 Chatsworth Road, London NW2 4 DD, England. *E-mail:* sybelowgold@amstrad.com.

MICHELS, Maria; Singer (Soprano); b. 1931, Germany. *Career:* Sang at the St ädtische Oper Berlin from 1955 and appeared further in opera at Kiel, Mannheim and Frankfurt; Essen 1963–66, Munich Staatsoper 1966–69, then the Hanover Opera; roles have included Cherubini's Médée, the Queen of Night, Strauss's Sophie and Zerbinetta, Lulu, Lucia di Lammermoor, Musetta and Olympia; Guest appearances at the Vienna and Stuttgart State Operas, Florence and Brussels (in Arabella), Paris Opéra and Barcelona (as Lulu, 1969).

MICHIELS, Jan Prosper; Belgian pianist; b. 10 Oct. 1966, Izegem; m. Inge Spinette 1991. *Education:* Royal Conservatory, Brussels, Hochschule der Künste, Berlin with Hans Leygraf. *Career:* Professor of Piano, Royal Conservatory, Brussels; worked with conductors as Peter Eötvös, Hans Zender, Serge Baudo, Lothar Zagrosek. *Recordings:* Several CDs with works of Brahms, Beethoven, Mendelssohn, Debussy, Ligeti, Huybrechts, Poulenc, Weber, Benjamin, Bartók and Liszt; Ligeti, Etudes I–XIV; Brahms, op 116–119; Debussy, Préludes, Images. *Honours:* Prizewinner, several competitions including Queen Elizabeth Competition, Brussels, 1991. *Address:* Achterstraat 22B, 9310 Meldert (Aalst), Belgium. *E-mail:* janinge@pi.be.

MICHNIEWSKI, Wojciech; Conductor and Composer; b. 4 April 1947, Łódź, Poland. *Education:* Conducting, Theory of Music, Composition, Warsaw Academy of Music, 1966–72; Honours degree with distinction, 1972. *Career:* Assistant Conductor 1973–76, Conductor 1976–79, Warsaw National Philharmonic Orchestra; Artistic Director, The Grand Opera Theatre, Łódź, 1979–81; Musical Director, Modern Stage, Warsaw Chamber Opera, 1979–83; Principal Guest Conductor, Polish Chamber Orchestra and Sinfonia Varsovia, 1984–; Conductor, concerts in most European countries, South America, Asia; Appeared West Berlin Philharmonic Hall, La Scala, Milan, Teatro Colón in Buenos Aires; Participant in numerous international festivals including Steyrischer Herbst, Graz, Austria; International May Festival, Barcelona, Spain; Recontres Musicales, Metz, France; International May Festival, Wiesbaden, Germany; Bemus Festival, Belgrade, Yugoslavia; Dimitria Festival, Thessaloniki, Greece; Warsaw Autumn Festival; Wratisalvia Cantans Music Festival; International Biennale, East Berlin; Polish Chamber Orchestra and Sinfonia Varsovia, 1984–86; General and Artistic Director, The Poznan Philharmonic Orchestra, 1987–; Others. *Recordings:* Gramophone Records; CBS Japan; EMI; Pavane Olympia; Polskie Nagrania Muza; Polton; Tonpress; Radio and television recordings. *Current Management:* Polish Artists Agency PAGART. *Address:* ul Braci Zauskich 3/77, 01 773 Warsaw, Poland.

MICHNO, Alexander; Double Bass Player; b. 29 Nov. 1947, Moscow, Russia; m. Elena Stoliarenko, 18 Oct 1991, 2 d. *Education:* Graduated: Gnesin School of Music, Moscow, 1963; Gnesin College of Music, Moscow, 1966; Gnesin Institute of Music, Moscow, 1971. *Career:* Debut: Moscow, 1969; Teaching at Gnessin College of Music, 1966–, at Gnessin Institute of Music (Academy of Music, 1991–), 1977–; Bassist in Moscow Philharmonic Symphonic Orchestra under K Kondrashin, 1973–80, as Co-Principal Bassist in USSR State Academy Symphony Orchestra under E Svetlanov, 1980–94, as Principal Double Bass in Asturias Symphony Orchestra, Northern Spain, 1994–; Performed as Soloist on Moscow radio and television, giving many recitals and concerts with symphony and chamber orchestras and appearing at International Bass Week in Michaelstein, 1996, 1997, 1998, 1999, Bass Festival 1998 in Reading, England, and Dresden 1999, Germany; Served on Jury for Bass Competitions, USSR, 1980, 1984, Russia, 1988, Kishinev (as Jury Chairman), 1989, Munich, 1991, Kromeriz, 1997; Has given courses in Spain and Germany; mem, British Double Bass Society. *Compositions:* Study for Double Bass, as editor, 1983, 1998. *Recordings include:* Bottesini–Grand Duo, for Violin and Double Bass, 1975; Ivanov–Concerto in the Romantic Style, 1977; Respighi–Concerto a Cinque, 1988; Eccles, Bottesini, Glier and others, with Galina Schastnaja, piano, CD, 1997. *Publications include:* Development of Playing Skills, 1988; History of the Art of Playing the Double Bass, 1988; Musical Heritage of G Bottesini, 1989; Giovanni Bottesini, 1997. *Contributions:* Italian Influences in St Petersburg, in The BIBF Journal, 1999. *Honours:* 1st Prize, International Markneukirchen Double Bass Competition, 1975. *Address:* Ramon y Cajal 2-2-A, 33205 Gijon, Spain.

MIDDENWAY, Ralph, BA; Australian composer, writer and editor; b. 9 Sept. 1932, Sydney, NSW; m., three d. *Education:* Univ. of Sydney, NSW Conservatory. *Career:* music and drama teacher Tudor House School, Moss Vale 1958–64; Theatre Consultant, Sec., Warden Adelaide Univ. Union 1965–77; Theatre Consultant, Gen. Man. The Parks Comomounity Centre 1977–82; mem. Faculty of Music, University of Adelaide 1977–82; music and opera critic 1977–86; freelance writer 1970–; editor 1982–; horticulturist 1989–; Founding Chair. Richard Wagner Soc. of S Australia 1988–2002; Pres. Town and Country Planning Asscn 1973–74; Vice-Pres. S Australian Flowergrowers Asscn 1999–2001; mem. Adelaide Univ. Union, Australian Music Centre, Australasian Performing Right Asscn, Soc. of Editors, Australian Arts Media Alliance, Richard Wagner Soc. of S Australia, S Australian Farmers Fed. *Compositions include:* Missa Omnibus Sanctis, for chorous 1960, Mosaics for 13 brass and two percussion 1970, The Child of Heaven, for chorus, brass sextete and two percussion 1971, Two arias for The Tempest, baritone and orchestra 1980, Stone River, for medium voice and 4 percussion 1984; Stream of Time, for bass clarinet and piano 1984; Sinfonia Concertante for brass quintet and orchestra 1985; Sonata Capricciosa, for piano 1986; Mosaics for orchestra and saxophone ensemble 1986; The Letters of Amalie Dietrich, 1 act opera 1986, Barossa, Singspiel in 2 acts 1988; Stone River, for mezzo-soprano and piano 1989, The Lamentations of Jeremiah, for chorus 1990; The Eye of Heaven, for baritone and string quartet 1991; East River, sonata for piano 1995, The Eye of Heaven, for chorus 2000, Sång Sångars, for 7 solo voices, flute, cello and organ 2002, music for Sure and Certain Hope, epic theatre piece (with playwright Chris Tugwell) 2003; commissions from Univ. of Adelaide Foundation and Adelaide Chamber Orchestra, among others; many recordings. *Publications:* The Enigma of Parsifal, essays (co-ed. and contrib.) 2001, What is Love? (3 one-act plays for young actors) 2004 contrib. to journals, magazines and newspapers in Australia, Canada, UK and USA. *Address:* POB 753, Victor Harbor, S Australia 5211, Australia.

Telephone: (8) 8558-8325. *E-mail:* venteman@comstech.com. *Website:* www.comstech.com/~venteman/.

MIDORI; violinist; b. 25 Oct. 1971, Osaka, Japan; d. of Setsu Goto. *Education:* Juilliard with Dorothy DeLay, Jens Ellerman and Yang-Ho Kim. *Career:* debut, Gala Concert with the New York Philharmonic, 1982; Appearances at the White House, Kennedy Center, Carnegie Hall, the Musikverein, the Philharmonic in Berlin and other major centres; Orchestras include the Berlin Philharmonic, the Boston and Chicago Symphony Orchestras, London Symphony, the Orchestre de Paris, Israel Philharmonic and the Philadelphia Orchestra; Conductors have included Abbado, Ashkenazy, Barenboim, Bernstein (Serenade), Mehta and Rostropovich; Appeared at the Concertgebeow, Amsterdam; Founded the Midori Foundation to promote the learning and education of classical music to children of all ages all over the world; Played the Tchaikovsky Concerto on debut at the London Proms, 1993; Played Barber's Concerto at the 2002 London Proms. *Recordings include:* Dvořák Concerto with the New York Philharmonic; Complete Paganini Caprices; Bartók's Concertos with the Berlin Philharmonic and a live recording of Carnegie Hall Recital Debut (Sony Classical); Encore, released by Sony Classical; Elgar and Franck Violin Sonatas with Robert McDonald; Debossy, Poilenc and Saint-Saëns with Robert McDonald.. *Honours:* Suntory Award, Tokyo, 1994; Avery Fisher Prize, 2001; Musical America Instrumentalist of the year Award, 2002. *Current Management:* ICM Artists, 40 West 57th Street, New York, NY 10019, USA.

MIGENES, Julia; Singer (Soprano); b. 13 March 1945, New York, USA. *Education:* New York High School for Performing Arts and the Juilliard School; Cologne with Gisela Ultman. *Career:* Appeared on Broadway and at the New York City Opera from 1965 (debut in The Saint of Bleecker Street); Vienna Volksoper 1973–78; Roles included Mozart's Despina, Blonchen and Susanna, Schmidt's Esmeralda, Strauss's Sophie and Olympia in Les Contes d'Hoffmann; Metropolitan Opera from 1979, in Mahagonny, Lulu, Pagliacci and La Bohème; Geneva Opera 1983 as Salome; Vienna Staatsoper as Lulu; Television appearances in Germany and on Channel 4, England; Appeared in Francesco Rossi's 1984 film of Carmen; Covent Garden debut 1987, as Manon; Sang Tosca at Earl's Court London, 1991; concert with Domingo at Buenos Aires, 1992; Donizetti's Caterina Cornaro at the Queen Elizabeth Hall, London, 1998; Engaged for premiere of Angels in America by Peter Eötvös, Paris Châtelet, 2004. *Recordings:* Notre Dame; Videos of Carmen and La Voix Humaine. *Honours:* Golden Bambi Awards from German television, 1980, 1981. *Address:* c/o Stafford Law Associates, 6 Barham Close, Weybridge, Surrey KT 13 9 PR, England.

MIHALIČ, Alexander; Slovak composer; b. 7 Aug. 1963, Medzilaborce. *Education:* Košice Conservatory, Bratislava Acad. of Music and Drama, Ecole Normale de Musique, Paris, Conservatoire Nat. de Région, Boulogne, Université de Paris VIII and Ecole de Sciences Sociales, Paris. *Career:* mem. of teaching staff, Institut de Recherche et Coordination Acoustique/Musique, Paris 1992–. *Compositions include:* six prelúdii 1982–83, Forlana 1983, Hudba 1986, Skladba 1987, Music for String Quartet 1988, Kompozicia 1990, Encyclopaedia musicalis (multiple work in progress) 1991–. *Honours:* Prix de Résidence int. electro-acoustic competition, Bourges 1988. *Address:* 8 Résidence les Aigles, 3 rue Adolf Wersand, 93440 Dugny, France. *Telephone:* 1-48-37-79-28. *E-mail:* mihalic@club-internet.fr.

MIHELCIC, Pavel; Composer; b. 8 Nov. 1937, Novo Mesto, Yugoslavia; m. Majda Lovse, 10 April 1965, 2 d. *Education:* Diploma, 1963, Special Class 1967, Academy of Music, Ljubljana. *Career:* Professor, Conservatory of Music, 1982–; Manager, Department of Smyphonic Music, Ljubljana Broadcasting Corporation, 1982–; President, Slovenian Composers Society, 1984–. *Compositions include:* Orchestral works: Bridge for strings; Asphalt ballet; Concerto for horn and orchestra; Sinfonietta; Musique Funèbre for violin and orchestra; Chamber works: Limite; Blow Up; Take-off for piano; Sonatine; Sonata 80; Chorus, 1, 2, 3, 4, 5, 10, 13; Games and Reflections; Double Break; Published by Edition DSS, Ljubljana and Edition Peters, Leipzig; Recorded: Quinta Essentia for brass quintet; Timber-line for chamber orchestra; Exposition and Reflections for 9 horns; Stop-time for horn and chamber orchestra; Team for woodwind quintet; Introduction and Sequences for orchestra; Scenes From Bela Krajina; Fading Pictures; Snow of First Youth for orchestra; Glittering Dusk for Orchestra, 1993; Return to Silence, for Orchestra, 1995; Concerto Grosso, 1997. *Contributions:* Standing Music Critic, Delo, Ljubljana; Zvuk, Sarajevo. *Honours:* Preseren Prize, 1979; Zupancic Prize, 1984. *Address:* Melikova ul 10, 61108 Ljubljana, Slovenia.

MIHEVC, Marko; University Professor; b. 30 April 1957, Ljubljana, Slovenia; m., 1 d. *Education:* Diploma, Academy for Music, University of Ljubljana; Diploma, Hochschule für Musik, Vienna; Master's Degree, Hochschule für Musik, Vienna. *Career:* Debut: Concert for violin and orchestra with Zagreb Philharmonic Orchestra, Ljubljana, 1989;

Symphonic poem Equi, Slovene Philharmonic Orchestra, Ljubljana, 1991; Initiator and Organiser of the Night of Slovene Composers, 1991; Symphonic poem In Signo Tauri, Slovene Philharmonic Orchestra, Ljubljana, 1992; Capricios for Violin and Piano, Vienna, 1993; University career, Professor of Composition and Head of Composition Department, 1994; Symphonic poem Miracula, Slovene Philharmonic Orchestra, Ljubljana, 1994; Cantata Proverbia, Slovene Philharmonic Orchestra, Ljubljana and RTS Choir, 1995; Symphonic poem Alibaba, Slovene Philharmonic Orchestra, Ljubljana, 1995; Cantata Enigmata, Orchestra of Camerata Labacensis and academic choir, 1998; Symphonic poem The Planets, Symphonic Orchestra of RTS, Slovenia, 1998; Concerto for Violin and Orchestra, 1989; Childrens' Opera Aladin and his Wonder Lamp; 5 symphonic poems; 2 cantatas; Symphonic poem Mar Saba, Slovene Philharmonic Orchestra, Ljubljana, 2000. *Address:* Groharjeva 18, 1000 Ljubljana, Slovenia.

MIKHAILOV, Maxim; Singer (Bass-baritone); b. 1956, Moscow. *Education:* Gnessin Institute, Moscow, until 1988. *Career:* Soloist at the Bolshoi Theatre from 1987; Recitalist and guest opera appearances in Italy, Germany, Denmark, Hungary and elsewhere; Season 1993–94 in Rossini's La Scala di Seta and Massenet's Chérubin at the Wiener Kammeroper, in the Mozart Festival at Schönbrunn and in Rachmaninov's Miserly Knight at the Bolshoi; Seaso 1995 with Orlik in Mazeppa at Amsterdam, concert performance of Prokoviev's War and Peace at the Vienna Konzerthaus, and Rimsky's May Night at the Wexford Festival; Season 1996–97 with Prince Khovansky in Khovanshchina at Nantes and Mozart's Masetto at Covent Garden; Sang Giove in Cavalli's Calisto at the Vienna Kammeroper, 1998; Season 2000–01 as Banquo in Oslo and the Mayor in Rimsky's May Night, at Bologna. *Address:* Allied Artists, 42 Montpelier Square, London SW7 1JZ, England.

MIKI, Minoru; Composer; b. 16 March 1930, Tokushima, Shikoku, Japan. *Education:* Studied composition with Ikenouchi and Ifukube at the Toyko National University of Fine Arts and Music, 1951–55. *Career:* Founder and Artistic Director, Ensemble Nipponia, later Pro Musica Nipponia, ensemble of traditional Japanese instruments, 1964; Foreign tours with the Ensemble from 1972; Founded the opera theatre Utaza, 1986; Founded the multi-culture ensemble YUI Ensemble, 1990; Founded the Orchestra Asia, 1993; Founded the Asia Ensemble, 2002; Director, Japan Federation of Composers; Director, Yonden Cultural Foundation. *Compositions include:* Eurasian Triology including Symphony for Two Worlds, 1969–81; Shunkin-Sho, opera in 3 acts, Tokyo, 1975; Ada (An Actor's Revenge), opera in 2 acts, English Music Theatre at the Old Vic, London, 1979; The Monkey Poet, folk opera, 1983; Joruri, opera in 3 acts, St Louis. 1985; Yomigaeru, folk-opera, Tokyo, 1989; Wakahime, opera in 3 acts, Okayama, 1991; Shizuka and Yoshitsune, opera in 3 acts, Kamakura, 1993; The River Sumida/Kusabira, a twin opera, 1995; Pipa Concerto, 1997; The Tale of Geuji, opera in 3 acts, Saint Louis, 2000; Memory of the Eart for Asian soloists and orchestra, 2000. *Recordings:* Works Selections I–VI of Minoru Miki including Eurasian Triology, Camerata Records. *Publications:* The Method of Japanese Instruments, 1995; An Actor's Revenge, 1989. *Honours:* Grand Prize of the National Art Festival, 1970; Giraud Opera Prize for composition of Shunkin-sho, 1976; National Purple Ribbon, 1994; The Order of the Rising Sun, 2000. *Current Management:* Japan Arts Corporation, Tokyo. *Address:* 1-11-6 Higashi Nogawa, Komae-shi, Tokyo 201–002, Japan. *Fax:* 334899341. *E-mail:* m-miki@mtb.biglobe.ne.jp. *Website:* www.m-miki.com. *E-mail:* m-miki@mtb.biglobe.ne.jp. *Website:* www.m-miki.com.

MIKLOSA, Erika; Singer (Soprano); b. 1970, Hungary. *Education:* Studied in Budapest, Philadelphia, USA and Milan, Italy. *Career:* Sang Papagena and Adele in Die Fledermaus and Donizetti's Lucia di Lammermoor at the Opera House, Budapest; Mozart's Queen of Night at Vienna, Berlin, Stuttgart, Cologne, Leipzig and Wiesbaden, 1993–; Other roles include Donizetti's Linda di Chamounix, Stravinsky's Le Rossignol and Oscar in Verdi's Un Ballo in Mascera; Sang the Fiakermilli in Arabella at Zürich, 2000. *Honours:* Winner, International Mozart Competition, Budapest, 1993; European Culture Prize, Zürich, 1995. *Address:* Hungarian National Opera, Andrassy ut 22, 1061 Budapest, Hungary.

MIKULAS, Peter; Singer (Bass); b. 1954, Slovakia. *Education:* Studied at the University of Music and Drama in Bratislava with Viktoria Stracenská. *Career:* Soloist with the Slovak National Theatre in Bratislava, 1978–; Roles have included Kecal, Dulcamara, Gremin, Raimondo, Fiesco, Don Alfonso, Sarastro, Lodovico, Lindorf, Coppelius, Dr Miracle and Dapertutto, Mephisto, Don Pasquale, Banquo, Philip, Don Quichotte, Zaccaria and Golaud; Extensive concert repertoire. Guest appearances in leading European theatres, National Theatre Prague, Berlin Staatsoper, De Nederlandse Opera in Amsterdam; Has sung in Vienna, Salzburg, Paris, London, Liverpool, Birmingham, Madrid, Barcelona, Granada, Rome, Milan, Genoa, Frankfurt, Stuttgart, Hamburg, Copenhagen, Ankara, Budapest, Tokyo, Dallas, Ottowa, Buenos Aires, Rio de Janeiro and at the Prague Spring, Carinthian

Summer and Edinburgh Festivals; Sang Lutobor in Smetana's Libuše at Edinburgh, 1998; Season 2000–01 as Dulcamara at Bratislava and Kolenati in The Makropulos Case at the Met; Collaborated with conductors Ceccato, Bychkov, Pesek, Belohlavek, Solti, Mackerras, Giulini and Altrichter. *Current Management:* Art Agency Ltd, Bratislava; Exclusively in England, Music International, London. *Address:* Art Agency Ltd, Dom novinárov, Zupné ná m 7, 811 03 Bratislava, Slovakia.

MILAN, Susan; Flautist; b. 1947, England; m. 2 s. *Education:* Junior Exhibitioner, Royal College of Music; Studied with John Francis at the Royal College of Music and Geoffrey Gilbert at the Guildhall School of Music; Attended the Marcel Moyse Masterclasses in Switzerland; Graduated from the Royal College of Music with Honours. *Career:* Principal Flute of the Bournemouth Sinfonietta, 1968–1972; Principal Flute and first woman member of the Royal Philharmonic Orchestra, 1974–82; Developed Solo Career; Recording contracts with Hyperion, ASV, Chandos Records, DaCapo, Cala, Omega, Nippon Columbia, Upbeat Records; Many Commissions and first performances from composers including: Nareshe Sohal 1967, Peter Lamb 1970, Robert Saxton 1973, David Morgan 1974, Jindrich Feld 1975, Antal Dorati 1980, Richard Rodney Bennett 1981, 1982, Ole Schmidt 1984, Robert Walker 1987, Carl Davis 1989, Robert Simpson 1991, Roger Steptoe 1995, Edward Cowie 1997, Edwin Roxburgh 2000, Jean Sichler 2001, Cecilia McDowall 2003; Tours world-wide as Soloist and Recitalist; Lady Chairman British Flute Society, 1990–94; Runs two annual masterclass courses; Professor of Flute, Royal College of Music, London; Ensembles: The London Chamber Music Group — Flute, Oboe, Violin, Viola, Cello, Harp, Piano. *Recordings:* Include: Flute Concerto by Ole Schmidt; Saint-Saëns Taratelle; Mozart concertos K313/314 with the English Chamber Orchestra conducted by Raymond Leppard for Chandos; Mozart flute and harp concerto K299, Salieri flute and oboe concerto with the City of London Sinfonia conducted by Richard Hickix for Chandos; La Flute Enchante, French pieces for flute and orchestra, City of London Sinfonia conducted by Richard Hickox; Beethoven Trios with Sergio Azzolini, Ian Brown, Levon Chilingirian and Louise Williams; Saint-Saens Romancevand Prokofiev Sonata in D with Ian Brown. *Publications:* Publishes editions for Educational and Music publishers. *Honours:* Fellowship, Royal College of Music, 1999. *Current Management:* Master Classics Artists Management Ltd, PO305, New Malden, Surrey, KT3 5EX. *Address:* 71 South Lane, New Malden, Surrey, England. *E-mail:* smilan3805@aol.com.

MILANOV, Michail; Singer (Bass); b. 1949, Sofia, Bulgaria. *Education:* Studied in Sofia. *Career:* Sang in Bulgaria from 1974; Throughout Germany from 1977, notably at the Theater am Gärtnerplatz, Munich, from 1988 (Dosifey in Khovanshchina, 1992); Other roles have included Mefistofele, King Philip, Rocco, Hagen, King Mark, and Colline in La Bohème (Verona Arena, 1982); Season 1993 as Sparafucile at Macerata and Dosifey in Munich; Sang the Duc d'Arco in Salvator Rosa for Dorset Opera, 2000; Many concert appearances and lieder recitals. *Address:* c/o Staatstheater am Gärtnerplatz, Gärtnerplatz, W-8000 Munich 5, Germany.

MILANOVA, Stoika; Concert Violinist; b. 5 Aug. 1945, Plovdiv, Bulgaria. *Education:* Studied with father Trendafil Milanova and with David Oistrakh at the Moscow Conservatory. *Career:* Appearances with principal British orchestras from 1970; Engagements in most European countries; Yomiuri Nippon Symphony Orchestra, Japan, 1975; Concerts with the Hallé Orchestra and at the Hong Kong Festival; Tour for Australian Broadcasting Commission, 1976; US and Canadian debuts 1978; Tours of Eastern Europe 1985–86; Duo recitals with Radu Lupu and Malcolm Frager. *Recordings:* Balkanton (Bulgaria), including the complete Brandenburg Concertos with Karl Munchinger and Prokofiev's Violin Concertos; Sonatas with Malcolm Frager. *Honours:* 2nd Prize, Queen Elisabeth Competition, Belgium, 1967; 1st Prize, City of London International Competition (Carl Flesch), 1970; Grand Prix du Disque, 1972. *Current Management:* Terry Harrison Artists Management, The Orchard, Market Street, Charlbury, Oxfordshire OX7 3PJ, England. *Telephone:* (1608) 810330. *Fax:* (1608) 811331. *E-mail:* artists@terryharrison.force9.co.uk.

MILASHKINA, Tamara (Andreyevna); Singer (Soprano); b. 13 Sept. 1934, Astrakhan, USSR. *Education:* Studied with Elena Katul'skaya at the Moscow Conservatory. *Career:* Debut: Bolshoi Theatre 1957, as Titania in Eugene Onegin; Has sung Lisa in The Queen of Spades, Zarina in The Legend of Tsar Saltan, Yaroslavna in Prince Igor and Natasha (War and Peace) with the Bolshoi Company; Guest appearances at La Scala (Lida in La battaglia di Legnano, 1962), Helsinki, Paris, Wuppertal and in North America; Vienna Staatsoper 1971, as Lisa; Deutsche Oper Berlin 1974, as Tosca; Other roles include Fevronia (The Invisible City of Kitezh), Maria (Tchaikovsky's Mazeppa) and Lyuba (Prokofiev's Semyon Kotko) and Verdi's Elisabeth de Valois and Leonora (Il Trovatore). *Recordings include:* Mazeppa, Tosca, The Queen of Spades and The Stone Guest. *Address:* c/o Bolshoi Theatre, Pr Marxa 8/2, 103009 Moscow, Russia.

MILBURN, Ellsworth; Composer; b. 6 Feb. 1938, Greensburg, Pennsylvania, USA. *Education:* Studied with Scot Huston at the University of Cincinnati College-Conservatory of Music, 1956–58, with Roy Travis and Henri Lazarof at the University of California at Los Angeles, 1959–62, and with Milhaud at Mills College in Oakland, 1966–68. *Career:* Teacher, University of Cincinnati College-Conservatory of Music, 1970–75, Rice University, Houston, from 1975. *Contributions:* Opera Gesualdo 1973; 5 Inventions for 2 flutes, 1965; Massacre of the Innocents, chorus, 1965; Concerto, piano and chamber orchestra, 1967; String Trio, 1968; Soli, 5 players on 10 instruments, 1968; String Quintet, 1969; Soli II for 2 players on flutes and double bass, 1970; Voussoirs for orchestra, 1970; Soli III for clarinet, cello and piano, 1971; Soli IV, flute, oboe, double bass and harpsichord, 1972; Violin Sonata, 1972; Lament, harp, 1972; Spiritus mundi for high voice and 5 instruments, 1974. *Address:* Rice University, Shepherd School of Music, PO Box 1892, Houston, TX 77251, USA.

MILCHEVA-NONOVA, Alexandrina; Singer (Mezzo-soprano); b. 27 Nov. 1936, Shoumen, Bulgaria. *Education:* Studied with G Cherkin at the Sofia Conservatory. *Career:* Debut: Warna 1961, as Dorabella in Così fan tutte; Sang at the Bulgarian National Opera in Sofia from 1968; Guest appearances in Vienna, Brussels, Paris, Amsterdam, Berlin (Komische Oper), London and Zürich; Munich 1979 and 1984; Verona Arena 1980 and 1984; Maggio Musicale Florence 1983, in Suor Angelica, Teatro Liceo Barcelona 1983, as Preziosilla in La Forza del Destino; La Scala Milan as Marfa in Khovanshchina, repeated at the Paris Opéra 1984; Geneva 1984, as Adalgisa in Norma; Other roles include Azucena, the Princess in Adriana Lecouvreur, Dalila, Carmen and Cenerentola. *Recordings include:* Carmen, Boris Godunov and Khovanshchina (Balkanton); Aida and songs by Mussorgsky (Harmonia Mundi); Leoncavallo's La Bohème (Orfeo). *Address:* c/o Bulgarian National Opera, Sofia, Bulgaria.

MILES, Alastair; Singer (bass); b. 1961, England. *Education:* flute and voice, Guildhall School and National Opera Studio. *Career:* debut, sang Trulove, in The Rake's Progress, for Opera 80, 1985; appearances from 1986 with Glyndebourne Festival and Touring Opera in Capriccio, Katya Kabanova, The Rake's Progress and Die Zauberflöte; Welsh National Opera as Basilio, Sparafucile, Raimondo and Silva, in Ernani; Royal Opera, Covent Garden in Parsifal, Viaggio a Reims, I Capuleti, Fidelio, Rigoletto, La Cenerentola and La Bohème; other engagements in Vancouver, Amsterdam, San Francisco, Lyon and Deutsche Oper Berlin; concert appearances under Gardiner in Beethoven's Missa Solemnis, Mozart's Requiem, Handel's Saul and Agrippina and Verdi Requiem; under Harnoncourt in Handel's Samson and Bach Cantatas; with Kurt Masur in Elijah and the St Matthew Passion; Berlioz, La Damnation de Faust and Romeo and Juliette under Colin Davis; Bartolo in Figaro under Simon Rattle and the CBSO; Messiah under Helmut Rilling; Damnation of Faust with Myung Whun Chung; Season 1993 in the Choral Symphony under Giulini and title role in Le nozze di Figaro under Harnoncourt for Netherlands Opera; sang Sir George Walton in I Puritani, Met, 1997; sang Philip II in Don Carlos for Opera North 1998; Season 2000 as Gounod's Frère Laurent at Covent Garden, Bellini's Giorgio in Munich, Alvise in La Gioconda for ENO (concert) and in Beethoven's Ninth at the Ravenna Festival; Mendelssohn's Elijah at the London Proms, 2002. *Recordings include:* Lucia di Lammermoor; Saul and Agrippina; Elijah; La Traviata; Rigoletto; Verdi Requiem; Die Zauberflöte; Don Giovanni; Berlioz Roméo et Juliette; Le nozze di Figaro; La Cenerentola. *Current Management:* AOR Management Inc., 6910 Roosevelt Way NE, PMB 221, Seattle, WA 98115, USA.

MILES-JOHNSON, Deborah; Singer (Mezzo-soprano); b. 1965, England. *Career:* Concerts include: Handel's Israel in Egypt on tour to Spain, Elijah in Toronto, St Matthew Passion under Andrew Parrott, Mozart's C Minor Mass at the Barbican and Elgar's Music Makers at Peterborough Cathedral; Opera roles include: Bianca in The Rape of Lucretia, Mrs Peachum in The Beggar's Opera, Madame Popova in Walton's Bear (Thaxted Festival), Orlofsky in Fledermaus (Haddo House) and Mrs Sedley in Peter Grimes; Royal Opera Covent Garden in Birtwistle's Gawain; Dido and Aeneas with the English Bach Festival; Season 1997 with Schubert and Haydn in Switzerland, Handel's Il Parnasso in Festa and Stravinsky's Requiem Canticles with the CBSO under Simon Rattle; Further concerts with Klangforum at the Vienna Konzerthaus (Barraqué's au dela du hasard...) and at the Wigmore Hall with Fretwork: debut there in Upon Silence by George Benjamin. *Recordings include:* Resurrection by Peter Maxwell Davies; Rutti's Magnificat; Pärt's Stabat Mater, with Fretwork, under Parrott. *Address:* 19 Gorham Drive, St Albans AL 1 2HU, England.

MILKINA, Nina; British concert pianist; b. 27 Jan. 1919, Moscow, USSR (now Russian Federation); d. of Jacques and Sophie Milkine; m. Alastair Robert Masson Sedgwick 1943; one s. one d. *Education:* studied under

Leon Conus and Profs Harold Craxton and Tobias Matthay, composition with Glazunov and Sabaniev; Moscow and Paris Conservatoires. *Career:* debut aged 11 with Lamourex Orchestra, Paris; chosen by BBC to broadcast all Mozart's piano sonatas; gave Mozart Bicentennial recital at Edinburgh Int. Festival 1991; int. adjudicator; Hon. Fellow RAM. *Recordings include:* Mozart piano concertos and recitals, Chopin Mazurkas, Scarlatti Sonatas, Mozart and Haydn Sonatas, Brahms piano trios, works by Rachmaninov, Prokofiev, Scriabin, Bach. *Publications:* Works for Piano, Early Compositions. *Address:* 17 Montagu Square, London, W1H 1RD, England. *Telephone:* (20) 7487-4588.

MILLER, Clement A.; Musicologist; b. 29 Jan. 1915, Cleveland, Ohio, USA; m. (1) Jean Miller (deceased), 2 s., 1 d., (2) Nancy Voigt 1983. *Education:* BM, Piano, 1936, MM, Music Theory, 1937, Cleveland Institute of Music; MA, Western Reserve University, 1942; PhD, Musicology, University of Michigan, 1951. *Career:* Instructor, Head of Music Department (History), Dean of Faculty, Acting Director, Cleveland Institute of Music, Ohio, 1937–65; Professor of Music, Fine Arts Department, John Carroll University, 1967–79; mem, American Musicological Society; Renaissance Society of America; Music Library Association; Musica Disciplina. *Publications:* Heinrich Glarean: Dodecachordon, 1965; Franchinus Gaffurius: Musica Practica, 1968; Johannes Cochlaeus: Tetrachordum Musices, 1970; Sebald Heyden: De Arte Canendi, 1972; Hieronymus Cardanus: Writings on Music, 1973; Le Gendre, Maille, Morpain: Collected Chansons, 1981; Nicolaus Burtius: Musices Opusculum, 1983; Co-editor: A Correspondence of Renaissance Musicians, 1990; Commentary and Translation: Musica Practica by Bartolomeo Ramis de Pareia, 1993. *Contributions:* The Musical Quarterly; Journal of the American Musicological Society; Die Musik in Geschichte und Gegenwart; New Grove Dictionary of Music and Musicians. *Honours:* Guggenheim Fellowship, 1974–75; Outstanding Educator of America, 1975. *Address:* 7922 Bremen Avenue, Parma, OH 44129, USA.

MILLER, Sir Jonathan Wolfe, Kt, CBE, MB, BCh; British stage director, film director, physician and writer; b. 21 July 1934, London; s. of the late Emanuel Miller; m. Helen Rachel Collet 1956; two s. one d. *Education:* St Paul's School, St John's Coll., Cambridge and Univ. Coll. Hosp. Medical School, London. *Career:* co-author of and appeared in Beyond the Fringe 1961–64; Dir John Osborne's Under Plain Cover, Royal Court Theatre 1962, Robert Lowell's The Old Glory, New York 1964 and Prometheus Bound, Yale Drama School 1967; Dir at Nottingham Playhouse 1968–69; Dir Oxford and Cambridge Shakespeare Co. production of Twelfth Night on tour in USA 1969; Research Fellow in the History of Medicine, Univ. Coll., London 1970–73; Assoc. Dir Nat. Theatre 1973–75; mem. Arts Council 1975–76; Visiting Prof. in Drama, Westfield Coll., Univ. of London 1977–; Exec. Producer Shakespeare TV series 1979–81; Artistic Dir Old Vic 1988–90; Research Fellow in Neuropsychology, Univ. of Sussex; Fellow, Univ. Coll. London 1981–; mem. RA (fellow), American Acad. of Arts and Sciences. *Productions:* for Nat. Theatre, London: The Merchant of Venice 1970, Danton's Death 1971, The School for Scandal 1972, The Marriage of Figaro 1974, The Wind in the Willows 1990; other productions The Tempest, London 1970, Prometheus Bound, London 1971, The Taming of the Shrew, Chichester 1972, The Seagull, Chichester 1973, The Malcontent, Nottingham 1973, Arden Must Die (opera) 1973, The Family in Love, Greenwich Season 1974, The Importance of Being Earnest 1975, The Cunning Little Vixen (opera) 1975, All's Well That Ends Well, Measure For Measure, Greenwich Season 1975, Three Sisters 1977, The Marriage of Figaro (ENO) 1978, Arabella (opera) 1980, Falstaff (opera) 1980, 1981, Otello (opera) 1982, Rigoletto (opera) 1982, 1984, Fidelio (opera) 1982, 1983, Don Giovanni (opera) 1985, The Mikado (opera) 1986, Tosca (opera) 1986, Long Day's Journey into Night 1986, Taming of the Shrew 1987, The Tempest 1988, Turn of the Screw 1989, King Lear 1989, The Liar 1989, La Fanciulla del West (opera) 1991, Marriage of Figaro (opera), Manon Lescaut (opera), Die Gezeichneten (opera) 1992, Maria Stuarda (opera), Capriccio (opera), Fedora (opera), Bach's St Matthew Passion 1993, Der Rosenkavalier (opera), Anna Bolena (opera), Falstaff (opera), L'Incoronazione di Poppea (opera), La Bohème (opera) 1994, Così fan Tutte (opera) 1995, Carmen (opera) 1995, Pelléas et Mélisande (opera) 1995, She Stoops to Conquer, London 1995, A Midsummer Night's Dream, London 1996, The Rake's Progress, New York 1997, Ariadne auf Naxos, Maggio Musicale, Florence 1997, Falstaff, Berlin State Opera 1998, The Beggar's Opera 1999, Tamerlano, Sadler's Wells, Paris and Halle 2001, Acis and Galatea, Holland Park Opera, London 2003. *Films:* Take a Girl Like You 1969 and several films for television including Whistle and I'll Come to You 1967, Alice in Wonderland 1966, The Body in Question (series) 1978, Henry the Sixth, part one 1983, States of Mind (series) 1983, Subsequent Performances 1986, The Emperor 1987, Jonathan Miller's Opera Works (series) 1997. *Art exhibition:* Mirror Image, National Gallery, London 1998. *Publications:* McLuhan 1971, Freud: The Man, his World, his Influence (ed.) 1972, The Body in Question 1978, Subsequent Performances 1986, The Don Giovanni Book: Myths of Seduction and Betrayal (ed.) 1990, On

Reflection 1998. *Honours:* Hon. Fellow, St John's Coll. Cambridge, Royal Coll. of Physicians 1997, Royal Coll. of Physicians (Edin.) 1998; Dr hc (Open Univ.) 1983, Hon. DLitt (Leicester) 1981, (Kent) 1985, (Leeds) 1996, (Cambridge) 1996; Dir of the Year, Soc. of West End Theatre Awards 1976; Silver Medal (Royal Television Soc.) 1981, Albert Medal (Royal Soc. of Arts) 1992. *Current Management:* IMG Artists, 616 Chiswick High Road, London, W4 5RX, England. *E-mail:* jford@imgworld.com. *Website:* www.imgartists.com.

MILLER, Kevin; Singer (Tenor); b. 1929, Adelaide, Australia. *Education:* Studied at Elder Conservatory, Adelaide. *Career:* Sang with the Australian National Theatre Company, Melbourne in operas by Mozart, Rossini and Vaughan Williams; Studied further in London, and in Rome with Dino Borgiloi and toured with the Australian Opera, 1955; Glyndebourne Festival, 1955–57, as Pedrillo, Monostatos and Scaramuccio in Ariadne auf Naxos; Welsh National Opera from 1958, notably as Rossini's Ramiro, Vanja in Katya Kabanova, Sellem in The Rake's Progress and Offenbach's Orpheus; Toured West Germany and Australia, 1962 with Orpheus in the Underworld and The Rake's Progress. *Recordings:* The Rake's Progress, conducted by the composer.

MILLER, Lajos; Singer (Baritone); b. 23 Jan. 1940, Szombathely; m. Susanna Dobranszky, 31 April 1964, 1 s. *Education:* Diploma, Hungarian State Academy of Music, 1968. *Career:* Debut: Hungarian State Opera House, 1968, in Szokolay's Hamlet; Singer, major companies in Budapest, Vienna, Milan, Rome, Florence, Paris, Toulouse, Aix-en-Provence, Munich, Hamburg, Bonn, West Berlin, Brussels, Liège, Wexford Festival, Glasgow, Liverpool, Houston, Buenos Aires, New York, (Carnegie Hall), Philadelphia, Caracas; Roles include: Verdi Simon Boccanegra, Renato, (Ballo), Luna Il Trovatore, Germont (La Traviata), Rigoletto, Carlo in Ernani, Carlo in Forza, Miller, Giacomo in Giovanna d'Arco; Posa, (Don Carlo); Macbeth, Rolando in Battaglia; Puccini; Scarpia in Tosca, Marcello in Tabarro, Sharpless in Butterfly; Sang Ivo in Berio's La Vera Storia at the Paris Opéra, 1985; Teatro Col ón Buenos Aires 1987, as Grigor, in The Tsar's Bride by Rimsky-Korsakov; Metropolitan 1989–90, as Luna in Il Trovatore; Opéra de Montréal, 1990, as Verdi's Renato; Sang Yeletsky in The Queen of Spades at La Scala Milan, 1990; Kodály's Spinning Room at Budapest, 1998; Season 1999–2000 in the premiere of Szokolay's Savitri and as Germont in La Traviata, at Budapest; Films and television films include: Rigoletto; Pagliacci; Olympiade; Verdi's Ernani; Don Carlos; Simon Boccanegra; Attila; (Ezio); Puccini's Butterfly as Sharpless; Boito, Nerone (Fanuel); Mercadante Il Giuramento, (Manfredo); Verdi baritone arias. *Honours:* Budapest; 3 P. Erkel, 2P. Kodály, 1972; Toulouse, Grand Prize, 4 extra Prizes, Paris, 1974; Budapest, Kossuth Prize, 1980. *Address:* c/o Gergely Arts Ltd, Hollán Ernö ut, 25 1/1, H–1136 Budapest, Hungary.

MILLER, Leta (Ellen); Musicologist, Flautist and Professor; b. 30 Sept. 1947, Burbank, California, USA; m. Alan K. Miller 1969, 1 s, 1 d. *Education:* BA, 1969, PhD, 1978, Stanford University; MM, Hartt College of Music, 1971. *Career:* Professor, University of California, Santa Cruz; Recitalist of baroque and modern flute. *Recordings:* Modern Flute: The Prismatic Flute, by Lou Harrison, David Cope and Gordon Mumma, with Ensemble Nova, 1988; Solstice, Canticle No. 3 Ariadne by Lou Harrison, with A Summerfield Set, 1990; Music of Germaine Tailleferre, 1993; Birthday Celebration by Lou Harrison, 1994; Chansons de Bilitis and other French Chamber Works, by Debussy, 1995; Lou Harrison: Rapunzel and other Works, 1997; La Musique de Germaine Tailleferre, 1999; Baroque Flute: 6 Sonatas for Flute and Continuo and Flute Unaccompanied by CPE Bach, 1988; 6 Sonatas for Flute and Continuo, The Earlier Sonatas, 1990; 4 Sonatas for Flute and Keyboard, 1992; New Music for Early Instruments, 1995; Josef Bodin de Boismortier, Music for 1–4 Flutes, 1996; Antonio Vivaldi: Soprano Cantatas, 1997; Renaissance Flute: Les Plaisirs d'amour–Sixteenth Century Chansons from the French Provinces, 1993; Instant Breath for Solo Flute, Music by Hi Kyung Kim, Centaur Records, 2000; Dancing with Henry: New Discoveries in the Music of Henry Cowell, Mode Records, 2001; Drums Along the Pacific, New Albion Records, 2003; Lou Harrison: works: 1939–2000, Mode Records, 2003. *Publications:* Music in the Paris Academy of Sciences 1666–1793, with A Cohen, 1979; Music in the Royal Society of London 1660–1806, with A Cohen, 1987; Lou Harrison: Composing a World, 1998; Editor: Chansons from The French Provinces 1530–1550, vol. 1, 1980, vol. 2, 1983; Thirty Six Chansons by French Provincial Composers 1529–1550, 1981; Gioseppe Caimo: Madrigali and Canzoni for Four and Five Voices, 1990; Lou Harrison: Selected Keyboard and Chamber Music 1937–1994 (editor), 1998; Lou Harrison in New Grove Dictionary, 2001; Lou Harrison in Musik in Geschichte und Gregenwart, 2002. *Contributions:* Music and Letters, 1985; Journal of The Royal Musical Association, 1990; Studies in the History of Music, 1992; Journal of Musicology, 1993; Early Music, 1995; Current Musicology, 1995; American Music, 1999. *Address:* Music Center, University of California, Santa Cruz, CA 95064, USA.

MILLER, Margaret; Violist; b. 1960, Indiana, USA. *Education:* Studied at Indiana and Wisconsin Universities. *Career:* Principal Violist with the Colorado Springs Orchestra and Co-founded the Da Vinci Quartet, 1980, under the sponsorship of the Fine Arts Quartet; Many concerts in the USA and elsewhere in a repertoire including works by Mozart, Beethoven, Brahms, Dvořák, Shostakovich and Bart ók. *Honours:* (with the Da Vinci Quartet): Awards and grants from the National Endowment for the Arts, The Western States Arts Foundation and the Colorado Council for the Humanities; Artist in Residence, University of Colorado. *Current Management:* Sonata, Glasgow, Scotland. *Address:* 11 Northpark Street, Glasgow G20 7AA, Scotland.

MILLER, Mildred; Opera Singer Recitalist, Impresario and Teacher; b. 16 Dec. 1924, Cleveland, Ohio, USA; m. Wesley W Posvar, 30 April 1950, 1 s., 2 d. *Education:* BMus Cleveland Institute of Music, 1946; Artist's Diploma, New England Conservatory, 1948. *Career:* Debut: Metropolitan Opera, 1951; Metropolitan Opera, 1951–74 as Cherubino, Marriage of Figaro; Octavian, Der Rosenkavalier; Siebel, Faust; Nicklausse, Les Contes d'Hoffman; Suzuki, Butterfly; others: 253 performances in 21 parts; Radio debut, 1952, Telephone Hour; Television debut, 1952, Voice of Firestone; Appearances with all major US opera companies and in Vienna, Berlin, Munich, Stuttgart, Frankfurt, 1959–73; Film, Merry Wives of Windsor; Musical comedy with Pittsburgh Civic Light Opera; Founder Opera Theater of Pittsburgh, 1978; Faculty Carnegie Mellon University, 1990–. *Recordings:* Many recordings with major record labels. *Honours:* 4 Honorary degrees; Distinguished Daughter of Pennsylvania; Grand Prix du Disque; Solo Recital, Nixon White House. *Address:* Opera Theater of Pittsburgh, PO Box 110108, Pittsburgh, PA 15232, USA.

MILLET, Gilles; Violinist; b. 1965, England. *Education:* Studied in London and with Feodor Droujinin, violist of the Beethoven Quartet. *Career:* Many concerts throughout the United Kingdom in works by Shostakovich, Fauré and English composers; Venues include Aldeburgh Festival (Quartet in Residence), Middle Temple (London), Huddersfield and Andover. *Honours:* with members of the Danel Quartet) Prizewinner in competitions at Florence, St Petersburg, Evian and London, 1991–94. *Address:* Manygate Management, 13 Cotswold Mews, 30 Battersea Square, London SW11 3 RA, England.

MILLGRAMM, Wolfgang; Singer (tenor); b. 16 April 1954, Ostseebad Kuhlungsborn, Germany. *Education:* Studied with Gunter Leib in Berlin; Musikhochschule, Berlin. *Career:* Debut: Semperoper in Dresden, 1992 as Graf Elemer in Arabella; Deutsche Staatsoper, Berlin, singing the Steersman in Fliegender Holländer, Walther in Tannhäuser and Alfred in Die Fledermaus; Visited Japan, Hungary and Switzerland with Deutsche Staatsoper; Solo appearances in Yugoslavia, Romania and the former Soviet Union; Chamber Singer in 1988; Sang the Steersman at Bregenz Festival, 1988, 1989, and in concert for Radio France, 1990; Season 1992–93 was engaged at the City of Nuremberg Theatre where he made guest appearance in 1991 as Adolar in Euryanthe; Other roles include: Erik in Holländer, José in Carmen; During that period also sang the Drum Major in Wozzeck and Max in Freischütz; Further appearances: Frankfurt am Main as Alfred in Fledermaus; Parsifal in Nuremberg and Hoffmann at Gärtnerplatz in Munich, 1995; Eleazar in La Juive, Aegisth in Elektra, Florestan in Fidelio at Dortmund in season 1995–96; Season 1998 with Max in Jonny Spielt auf by Krenek at Karlsruhe and Assad in Goldmark's Die Königin von Saba at Dortmund; Season 2000–01 as Manrico at Dortmund, Tristan in Prague and Bacchus at the Theater am Gärtnerplatz, Munich. *Recordings include:* Ariadne auf Naxos and First Prisoner in Fidelio, conducted by Haitink. *Current Management:* Buhnen und Konzertagentur, Sigrid Roslock. *Address:* Eugen-Schonhaar-Strasse 1, 10407 Berlin, Germany.

MILLING, Stephen; Singer (Bass); b. 1965, Denmark. *Career:* Many appearances with the Royal Danish Opera, Copenhagen, and elsewhere in Scandinavia; Repertory includes Die Zauberflöte (Sarastro) and Don Carlos (King Philip); Also sings Lieder by Brahms; Contestant in the 1995 Cardiff Singer of the World Competition; Guest at Covent Garden, London, with the Royal Danish Opera in Prokofiev's Love for Three Oranges; Season 2000–01 as Fasolt and Hunding in The Ring, for Seattle Opera, Landgrave in Tannhäuser at the Deutsche Oper Berlin and as soloist in The Dream of Gerontius with the London SO. *Address:* Sundevedsgade 2, st tv, 1751 Copenhagen V, Denmark.

MILLINGTON, Barry John, BA; Critic and Writer on Music; b. 1 Nov. 1951, Hadleigh, England; m. Deborah Calland 1996. *Education:* Clare Coll., Cambridge. *Career:* editorial staff mem., The New Grove Dictionary of Music and Musicians 1975–76; criticism for Musical Times and newspapers, notably The Times 1977–82, 1988–2001; Reviews Ed. for BBC Music Magazine 1992–2002; Chief Music Critic of Evening Standard 2002–; founder and Artistic Dir of Hampstead and Highgate Festival 1999–2003; dramaturgical advisor on new production of Lohengrin at Bayreuth Festival 1999; mem. Royal Musical Assocn,

Critics Circle. *Publications:* Wagner 1984, Selected Letters of Richard Wagner (ed with Stewart Spencer) 1987, The Wagner Compendium (ed) 1992, Wagner in Performance (ed with Stewart Spencer) 1992, Wagner's Ring of the Nibelung: a Companion (ed with Stewart Spencer) 1993, The New Grove Wagner 2002; contrib. to Oxford Illustrated History of Opera 1994, numerous other publications in newspapers and periodicals. *Address:* 50 Denman Drive South, London, NW11 6 RH, England (home). *E-mail:* bmillin397@aol.com (office).

MILLIOT, Sylvette; Violoncellist and Musicologist; b. 6 June 1927, Paris, France. *Education:* Doctor of Musicology; Studied Violoncello, National Conservatory of Music, Paris. *Career:* Research Assistant, Museum of the National Conservatory of Music, Paris; Soloist, Radio France; Various concert tours; Head of Research, CNRS, French National Centre for Scientific Research in Musicology and Musical Iconography; mem, French Musicology Society; French Society of 18th Century Studies. *Publications:* Documents inédits sur les Luthiers parisiens du XVIIIe siécle, 1970; La Sonate, 1978; Le Violoncelle en France au XVIIIe Siécle, 1981; Le Quatuor, 1986; Marin Marais, 1991; Entretiens Avec André Navarra, 1991; Catalogue descriptif des instruments de Stradivarius et de Guarnerius del Jesù de Charles-Eugène Gand, 1994; History of Parisian Violin Making from the XVIIIth Century to 1960, Vol. I, The Family Chanot-Chardon, 1994, vol. II, The Violin Makers of the XVIIIth Century, 1997. *Contributions:* Revue Française de Musicologie; Recherches sur la Musique française classique; The STRAD; Articles on Lutherie Française, 1992, 1993, 1995, 1998; The Grove Dictionary of Music and Musicians; Die Musik in Geschichte und Gegenwart. *Honours:* 1st Prize for Violoncello, National Conservatory of Music; Héléne Victor Lyon Prize; Solo Artist's Guild Prize. *Address:* 6 Villa de la Reunion, 75016 Paris, France.

MILLO, Aprile; Singer (Soprano); b. 14 April 1958, NY, USA. *Education:* Studied with her parents and with Rita Patané. *Career:* Debut: Salt Lake City 1980, as Aida; Gave concert performances in Los Angeles and made La Scala Milan and Welsh National Opera debuts at Elvira in Ernani; Metropolitan Opera debut 1984, as Amelia Boccanegra; returned to NY as Elvira, Elisabeth de Valois and Aida; Guest appearances in Hamburg and Vienna; Other roles include Leonara in Il Trovatore and La Forza del Destino; Sang Aida and Liu at the Metropolitan 1987, followed by Elvira in Ernani, Elisabeth de Valois and Imogene in Il Pirata; Carnegie Hall 1987, Il Battaglia di Legnano, as Lida, Verona Arena and Caracalla festival 1988–90; Sang Aida at Washington 1990, Luisa Miller at Rome; Season 1991–92, as Marguerite at Chicago, debut, Elisabeth de Valois at the Met and Verona and Aida at the Festival of Caracalla; Sang Maddalena in Andrea Chénier at Rome, 1996; Amelia (Ballo in Maschera) at Palma de Mallorca, 1998 and for Palm Beach Opera, 2001. *Recordings:* Luisa Miller and Don Carlos conducted by James Levine; Met production of Aida on video and DVD; Un Ballo in Maschera. *Address:* c/o S A Gorlinsky Ltd, 33 Dover Street, London W1X 4 NJ, England.

MILLOT, Valerie; Singer (Soprano); b. 1963, France. *Education:* Studied at the Paris Conservatoire. *Career:* Lyon Opéra, 1990–91 in The Three Wishes by Martinů and as Puccini's Musetta; Season 1992 as Gounod's Mireille at Avignon and Sacchini's Antigone at Montpellier; Nancy Opéra 1994, as Elsa in Lohengrin; Montpellier 1993–94, as Offenbach's Giulietta and Brunehild in Reyer's Sigurd; Mme Lidone in Poulenc's Carmélites, Nantes, 1996; Poulenc's La Voix Humaine at Nancy, 1998; Sang Elisabeth de Valois at Dusseldorf, 2000; Frequent concert engagements. *Recordings:* Les Brigands by Offenbach. *Address:* Opéra de Nancy, Rue St Catherine, 54000 Nancy, France.

MILLS, Alan; Composer and Pianist; b. 21 July 1964, Belfast, Northern Ireland. *Education:* Ulster College of Music, 1978–81; Music, Churchill College, Cambridge University, 1983–86; MA (Cantab); Advanced Composition, Guildhall School of Music and Drama, London, 1986–87. *Career:* As Pianist and Accompanist for BBC Radio Ulster, Dutch Television and Radio France, 1987–; Director of Music, Anna Scher Theatre 1989–. *Compositions include:* 25 songs for voice and piano, 1986–; Daybreak over Newgrange for large orchestra and chorus, 1987; Three Irish poems for baritone and small orchestra, 1991; Sonatina for piano, 1993, published 1995; Incantation for trombone and piano, 1993, published 1993; Hymn to the Aten for chamber choir and harp, 1993, published 1994; Capriccio for harpsichord, 1993, published, 1995; Romanza for horn and piano, 1994, published 1995; Epitaph for a cappella double choir, 1995; Psalm 137, for a cappella choir, 1996; Memorial for cello and piano, 1998, published 1999; Three Pieces forpiano solo, 1997–99; Hymn to Inana for a cappella choir, 2000; Three Studies for piano solo, 2001; O Magnum Mysterium for a cappella choir, 2001; In Nomine for String Trio, 2002; Marsyas for solo Flute, 2002. *Recordings:* Hymn to the Aten, by Concert de L'Hostel-Dieu, Lyon. *Address:* 87 Palmerston Road, Wood Green, London N22 4QS, England.

MILLS, Beverly; Singer (Mezzo-soprano); b. 1957, Kent, England. *Education:* Trinity College, and London Opera Studio, with Nancy Evans. *Career:* Debut: Batignano Festival, 1980, as Alessandro in Handel's Tolomeo; Aldeburgh from 1981, as Britten's Nancy and Lucretia; Glyndebourne Touring Opera, 1981, as Cherubino; Sang in Cavalli's L'Egisto for Scottish Opera, 1982, and on tour to Venice and Schwetzingen; Further appearances with Welsh National Opera, and City of Birmingham Touring Opera (Smetana's Two Widows, 1999 and as Debussy's Geneviève, 2000); Other roles include Dorabella, Suzuki in Butterfly, Rosina, Siebel and Cenerentola; Operetta and concert engagements. *Address:* c/o Music International, 13 Ardilaun Rd, London N5 2QR, England.

MILLS, Bronwen; Singer (Soprano); b. 1960, England. *Education:* Studied at London University, The Guildhall School of Music and with Joy Mammon. *Career:* Opera engagements include Dido and Aeneas with Opera Restor'd at the 1986 Edinburgh Festival; Queen Elizabeth Hall 1989 in The Death of Dido by Pepusch and Dibdin's Ephesian Matron; Season 1989–90, with Traviata for New Israeli Opera and Dublin Grand Opera; Elizabeth Zimmer in Henze's Elegy for Young Lovers in London; Norina in Don Pasquale and Madeline in Fall of the House of Usher by Glass in Wales; Donna Anna in Don Giovanni for Opera North, 1992; Man Who Mistook his Wife for a Hat, Michael Nyman, for Music Theatre Wales, 1992–93; Other roles include Mozart's Countess and Fiordiligi, Opera 80, the Governess and Miss Jessel in the Turn of the Screw, and Micaela; Opera North as the Queen of Shemakah in The Golden Cockerel, Strauss's Daphne and Blondchen in Die Entführung; Concert engagements with the Scottish Chamber Orchestra in Handel's Dixit Dominus and Bach's B minor Mass; St Matthew Passion in Stratford and Haydn's Stabat Mater at St John's Smith Square; Mozart's C minor Mass with the Northern Sinfonia, Beethoven's Missa Solemnis at Canterbury Cathedral and the Christmas Oratorio in Belgium; Wexford Festival, 1990, in Handel's L'Allegro, il Penseroso ed il Moderato; Tour of English Cathedrals with London Festival Orchestra in 1991, Messiahs in Germany, Norway in 1992 also Messiahs in Lithuania and Moscow, Kremlin, with Yehudi Menuhin; Further appearances at the Malvern, Music at Oxford, Cambridge and Sully-sur-Loire Festivals. *Recordings:* Solomon by John Blow, Hyperion; Beggar's Opera, Polly Peachum, Hyperion; Dibdin Operas, Hyperion; 100 years of Italian Opera, Opera Rara; Emilia di Liverpool, Opera Rara.

MILLS, Erie; Singer (Soprano); b. 22 June 1953, Granite City, IL, USA. *Education:* National Music Camp, Interlochen, MI; BMus, MA, University of IL; Studied with Karl Trump, Grace Wilson and Elena Nikolai. *Career:* Debut: St Louis 1978, in the US premiere of Martin y Soler's L'Arbore di Diana; Ninette in Love for Three Oranges, Chicago Lyric Opera, 1979; Sang New York City Opera debut as Cunegonde, Candide, 1982; Metropolitan Opera debut, New York as Blondchen, Die Entführung aus dem Serail, 1987; New York recital debut, 1989; Guest appearances with Cincinnati Opera; Cleveland Opera; San Francisco Opera; Minnesota Opera; Opera Society of Washington DC; Santa Fe Opera; Houston Grand Opera; Hamburg State Opera; Teatro alla Scala, Milan; Vienna State Opera; Sang Marie in La Fille du Régiment at New Orleans, 1989, Blondchen in Die Entführung for Opéra de Montréal, 1990; Sang Zerlina at Milwaukee, 1996 and the Queen of Night at New Orleans, 1997; Soloist with many leading orchestras; Numerous recitals; Television appearances; Roles include Rossini's Rosina; Offenbach's Olympia; Donizetti's Lucia; J Strauss's Adele; R Strauss's Zerbinetta. *Recordings:* For New World Records. *Address:* c/o Metropolitan Opera, Lincoln Center, New York, NY 10023, USA.

MILLS, John, ARCM, ARAM, FCLCM; British classical guitarist; b. 13 Sept. 1947, Kingston-upon-Thames, England; m. Jacoba Cornelia; one s. one d. *Education:* Royal Coll. of Music. *Career:* recitalist throughout British Isles 1965–; international debut, Canada 1972; has performed widely overseas, including USA, Australia, New Zealand, Japan, Singapore, Scandinavia, Holland, France, Greece, Italy; work in the chamber music field; specialist teaching areas early guitar (particularly 19th century) and postural difficulties; Prof. at the Royal Acad. of Music and Head of Guitar at the Royal Welsh Coll. of Music and Drama; mem. Musicians' Union, Incorporated Soc. of Musicians, Delius Soc.. *Compositions:* Hommage to Frederick Delius, Suite for Five Guitars, Idyll for Violin and Guitar. *Recordings:* Guitar Music of Five Centuries 1972, Music from the Student Repertoire 1973, 20th Century Guitar Music 1977, John Mills and Raymond Burley 1983, The John Mills Guitar Trio 1981. *Publications:* John Mills Guitar Tutor; contrib. to Classical Guitar Magazine. *Current Management:* Sympathetic Developments, 5 Greenclose Lane, Wimborne, BH21 2AL, England. *Telephone:* (1202) 880331 (office). *Fax:* (1202) 888037 (office). *E-mail:* Graham@symdev.co.uk (office). *Website:* www.pitchperfect.org/johnmills.

MILLS, Richard (John); Composer and Conductor; b. 14 Nov. 1949, Toowoomba, Queensland, Australia. *Education:* University of Queensland; Queensland Conservatorium; Guildhall School of Music, London, England. *Career:* Regular Guest Conductor of all major Australian Orchestras; Artist-in-Residence, Australian Ballet, 1987–88; Artist-in-

Residence, Australian Broadcasting Corporation, 1989–90; Artistic Director, Adelaide Chamber Orchestra, 1991–97; Artistic Adviser, Queensland Symphony Orchestra, 1991–94; Artistic Adviser, Brisbane Biennial International Music Festivals, 1995–97; Artistic Director, West Australian Opera, 1997–. *Compositions:* Principal Works: Music for Strings, Concerti for Trumpet and Percussion; Bamaga Diptych; Fantastic Pantomines; Flute Concerto (written for James Galway); Concerto for Violoncello and Orchestra; Violin Concerto (for Carl Pini, 1992); Summer of the Seventeenth Doll, Opera, 1994; Requiem Diptych for brass quintet, 1997; The Code of Tupsichore, for orchestra, 1997; A Symphony, 1998. *Honours:* National Critics Awards, 1988, 1991; Sir Bernard Heinze Award, 1997. *Current Management:* Arts Management, 180 Goulburn Street, Darlinghurst, New South Wales 2010, Australia. *Address:* 22 Gray Road, Hill End, Queensland 4101, Australia.

MILNE, Hamish; Pianist; b. 27 April 1939, Salisbury, England; m. Margot Gray, 1 s., 2 d. *Education:* Royal Academy of Music, London; Guido Agosti, Rome, Siena. *Career:* Debut: 1963; Concerto, Recital, Chamber Music in the United Kingdom, Europe, USA and USSR; Over 100 BBC Broadcasts; Proms Debut, 1978; Professor, Piano, Royal Academy of Music, London. *Recordings:* Piano works by Chopin, Liszt, Haydn, Medtner, Mozart, Reubke, Schumann, Weber. *Publications:* Bartók, 1981; Heritage of Music, Contributor, 1982. *Contributions:* Medtner-Centenary Appraisal, 1981. *Honours:* Collard Fellowship, 1977; FRAM, 1978. *Address:* 111 Dora Road, London SW19 7JT, England.

MILNE, Lisa; Singer (soprano); b. 1971, Scotland. *Education:* Studied at the Royal Scottish Academy of Music. *Career:* From 1994 appearances throughout Scotland in concert and recital; Member of Scottish Opera from 1994, as Gianetta in L'Elisir d'amore (debut role), Mozart's Susanna, Zerlina and Ilia, the Dew Fairy in Hansel and Gretel and Coryphée in Alceste; Season 1996 in recitals at Covent Garden and Aix en Provence and City of London Festivals; Concerts with the National Youth Orchestra of Scotland, Scottish Chamber, Royal Philharmonic, London Philharmonic and Royal Liverpool Philharmonic Orchestras; Season 1997–98 as Servilia in La Clemenza di Tito for Welsh National Opera, Atalanta in Xerxes at Göttingen and Handel's Rodelinda at Glyndebourne; Nielsen's Springtime on Funen at the 1999 London Proms; With English National Opera as Aennchen in Der Freischütz and Morgana in Alcina, 1999; Season 2000–01 with Marzelline in Fidelio at Glyndebourne and Stravinsky's Anne Trulove for English National Opera; Handel's Samson at the London Proms, 2002; Micaela in Carmen for GTO and Marzelline in Fidelio at Dallas Opera. *Recordings include:* Handel and Vivaldi with the King's Consort; Vaughan Williams Serenade to Music; Land of Hearts Desire; Idomeneo the role of Ilia recorded for EMI; Songs of John Ireland; Songs of Roger Quilter. *Honours:* Maggie Teyte Prize, 1993; John Christie Award, 1996; Royal Philharmonic Society Young Artist Award, 1998. *Current Management:* Askonas Holt Ltd, Lonsdale Chambers, 27 Chancery Lane, London, WC2A 1PF, England. *Telephone:* (20) 7400-1700. *Fax:* (20) 7400-1799. *E-mail:* info@askonasholt.co.uk. *Website:* www .askonasholt.co.uk.

MILNES, Rodney; Music Critic and Magazine Editor; b. 26 July 1936, Stafford, England. *Career:* Music Critic, Queen Magazine, later Harpers and Queen, 1968–87; Opera Critic, The Spectator, 1979–90; Opera Critic, London Evening Standard, 1990–92; Chief Opera Critic, The Times, 1992–2002; Reviews for Opera Magazine from 1971, Associate Editor, 1976; Editor 1986–2000. *Publications:* Numerous opera translations; Under original name, Rodney Blumer, has translated such operas as Osud, Tannhäuser, Rusalka and The Jacobin; Consultant Editor, Viking Opera Guide, 1993. *Address:* 36 Black Lion Lane, London W6 9 BE, England.

MILNES, Sherrill; Opera Singer (Baritone); b. 10 Jan. 1935, Hinsdale, Illinois, USA; m. Nancy Stokes 1969, 1 s., 1 s., 1 d. by first marriage. *Education:* MMus, ED, Drake University, Northwestern University; Studied with Boris Goldovsky, Rosa Ponselle, Andrew White, Hermanes Baer with Goldovsky Opera Company, 1960–65; NY City Opera Company, 1964–67. *Career:* Debut: Metropolitan Opera, NY 1965, as Valentin in Gounod's Faust; Leading Baritone 1965–, as Verdi's Miller, Renato, Amonasro, Don Carlo, Germont, Simon Boccanegra, Iago, Macbeth, Montfort, Paolo, Posa and Rigoletto; Has also appeared in NY as Wagner's Herald, Lohengrin and Donner, Rossini's Figaro, Don Giovanni, Barnaba, Jack Rance, Scarpia, Riccardo in I Puritani and Alphonse in La Favorite; Has performed with all American City Opera Companies and major American Orchestras, 1962–73; Performed in Don Giovanni, Vespri Sicillani and all standard Italian repertory baritone roles; San Francisco Opera; Hamburg Opera; Frankfurt Opera; La Scala, Milan; Covent Garden, London; Teatro Colón; Buenos Aires; Vienna State Opera; Paris Opéra; Chicago Lyric Opera, including Puccini's Scarpia and Verdi's Posa, Boccanegra, Iago and Don Carlo; NYC Opera 1982, as Hamlet in the opera by Thomas, returned 1990; Season 1991–92, with debut as Falstaff, Jack Rance at the Met and

Scarpia at Buenos Aires; Sang Cilea's Michonnet at the Met, 1994; Sang Nemico della patria at the Met Opera Gala, 1996; Season 1998 as Ajax in Antheil's Transatlantic the Minnesota Opera and Scarpia for Palm Beach Opera; Sang Iago in Budapest and Westmoreland in Wolf-Ferrari's Sly at the Teatre Liceo, Barcelona, 2000; mem, Chairman of Board, Affiliate Artists Inc. *Recordings:* 60 Albums, 1967–; Videos of Il Trovatore from the Met; Tosca in the Original Locations. *Honours:* 3 Hon Degrees, Order of Merit, Italy, 1984. *Address:* Metropolitan Opera, Lincoln Center, New York, NY 10023, USA.

MILVEDEN, J. Ingmar G., LPh, PhD; Composer and Assistant Professor; b. 15 Feb. 1920, Gothenburg, Sweden; m. Ulla Milveden; one s. one d. *Education:* musical theory, counterpoint, composition with Dr S. E. Svensson, Uppsala, musicology with Prof. C. A. Moberg; Schola Cantorum Basiliensis, Basel. *Career:* debut, Serenade for Strings, Philharmonic Orchestra of Gothenburg, conductor Issay Dobrowen 1942; Asst Prof. of Musicology, Univ. of Uppsala. *Compositions:* Great Mass for Uppsala Cathedral 1969, Pezzo Concertante for orchestra and soloists 1971, Clarinet Concerto 1972, Now, cantata to Linnean texts for choir and orchestra, Gaudeat Upsalia, cantata for 500th anniversary of University of Uppsala 1977, Musica in honorem Sanctae Eugeniae 1982, Pentatyk for mixed choir 1993, Sonata for violoncello solo 1998, Toccata celebrativa for organ 1999. *Publications:* Zu den liturgischen Hystorie in Schweden. Liturgie und choralgeschichtliche Untersuchungen 1972. *Address:* Torkelsgatan 16B, 753 29 Uppsala, Sweden.

MILYAEVA, Olga; Violist; b. 1967, Moscow, Russia. *Education:* Studied at the Central Music School, Moscow. *Career:* Co-Founder, Quartet Veronique, 1989; Many concerts in the former Soviet Union and Russia, notably in the Russian Chamber Music Series and the 150th Birthday Celebrations for Tchaikovsky, 1990; Masterclasses at the Aldeburgh Festival, 1991; Concert tour of the United Kingdom in season 1992–93; repertoire includes works by Beethoven, Brahms, Tchaikovsky, Bartók, Shostakovich and Schnittke; Resident Quartet, Wilwaukee University, USA. *Honours:* (With Quartet Veronique): Winner, All-Union String Quartet Competition, St Petersburg, 1990–91; Third Place, International Shostakovich Competition, St Petersburg, 1991. *Current Management:* Sonata, Glasgow, Scotland. *Address:* c/o Sonata (Quartet Veronique), 11 Northpark Street, Glasgow G20 7AA, Scotland.

MIMS, Marilyn; Singer (Soprano); b. 1962, USA. *Education:* Studied at Indiana University with Virginia Zeani. *Career:* Sang at Kentucky Opera from 1987 as Lucia and Violetta, New Orleans Opera from 1990 and at the Metropolitan Opera in 1990 as Donna Anna and Fiordiligi; Guest appearances with Hawaii Opera as Constanze in 1988, and Fiordiligi at Santa Fe; Sang at San Francisco Opera, 1990–92 as Donna Anna and Anna Bolena. *Recordings include:* Ortlinde in Die Walküre, conducted by James Levine. *Address:* San Francisco Opera, War Memorial Opera House, San Francisco, CA 94102, USA.

MIN, Lee Huei; Concert Violinist; b. 1982, Singapore. *Education:* University of Michigan, 1991-1995; Yale University School of Music, from 1996, with Erick Friedman. *Career:* Appearances with Washington Symphony and Prague Chamber Orchestras; Inaugurated Singapore Symphony young audience programmes, 2000; Wigmore Hall, London, debut October 2001; Season 2001–2002 with tours of China and elsewhere in Asia; Plays Giuseppe Guarneri Violin, 1704; Resident in London. *Honours:* Winner, Singapore National Music Competition, 1990; Kocian International Violin competition, 1993. *Address:* c/o Wigmore Hall (contracts), Wigmore St, London, W1, England.

MINDE, Stefan P.; Conductor; b. 12 April 1936, Leipzig, Germany; m. Edith Halla, 8 July 1961, 2 s. *Education:* Member of Thomanerchor, Leipzig, 1947–54; MA, Mozarteum, Salzburg, Austria, 1958. *Career:* Debut: State Theatre, Wiesbaden, Germany, Krenek: Life of Orestes; Civic Opera Frankfurt am Main under Sir Georg Solti; Hessisches Staatstheater Wiesbaden under Sawallisch; Principal Conductor at Civic Theatre Trier, Mosel; Berkshire Music Festival at Tanglewood, Massachusetts, USA, with Eric Leinsdorf; Chorusmaster and Conductor, San Francisco Opera; General Director and Conductor at Portland Opera Association, Oregon, 1970–84; Founder, Music Director and Conductor of Sinfonia Concertante, Chamber Orchestra, Portland, Oregon; Guest appearances with New York City Opera, Philadelphia, Pittsburgh, Cincinnati, San Diego, Phoenix, Los Angeles, Seattle, Vancouver, British Columbia, Toronto, Edmonton, Calgary, Lisbon, Portugal, Saarbrucken, Cologne, Nuremberg, Hawaii Opera, Eugene Opera, Utah Opera, Sapporo, Japan and others; Guest Professor at Portland State University, Pacific Lutheran University, Tacoma, Washington and Florida State University; Conducted Wagner's Ring at Flagstaff, Arizona, 1996, engaged to repeat in 1998. *Address:* 1640 SE Holly Street, Portland, OR 97214, USA.

MINDEL, Meir; Composer; b. 25 Dec. 1946, Lvov, Russia; m. Tzippi Bozian 1968; four d. *Education:* harmony, counterpoint, electronic music with Itzhak Saday, 1970–71; Rubin Music Acad., Tel-Aviv, 1971–75; composition with Abel Ehrlich, 1975–77. *Career:* debut, concert in Rubin Acad., Agony for Flute, 1974; radio broadcasts, Israeli Young Composer, The Blue and the White, 1982, Circle, A Maya Prophecy, 1987, Together with... Meir Mindel, An Hour of M. M. Compositions, 1988, Israel Broadcasting Authority; represented Israel at World Festival of Jewish Music, Montréal, Canada, 1983; Genesis with Morli Consort, Israel Defence Forces Army Broadcasting, 1984; attempted to develop a new musical 'language' for recorders; music performed in Israel and abroad; mem., Kibbutz Composers' Organisation (Gen. Dir, Sec.), Israel Composers' League (Sec. of Management and board mem.), Open-Air Museum Project, Kibbutz Negba (founder). *Compositions include:* The Tie, strings, 1980; Grotesque, piano, 1983, recorders, 1985; Genesis, recorders, 1983; A Maya Prophecy, mixed choir a cappella, 1985; Agony, flute, 1986; The Courting Muse, trombone, 1986; Tamar, flute, horn, piano, 1988; Poem, horn, 1988; My City, 2 choirs; The Family Tree, singers ensemble, 1989; Iri, 2 choirs, 1989; Koli, songs, 1989; The Shadow, children's choir, 1989; Murmurs, trumpet, flugelhorn, 1989; Between Rosh Pina and Safed, song; Music for Michal Gretz-Mindel's poem A White Lie, for children's choir, 1994; Symbiosis, for clarinet, bass clarinet and magnetic tape; Circles; The Catch; Where Are You All?; SugiHara, for shakuhachi Japanese bamboo flute, eastern percussion instruments and orchestra, 1995; Sounds of Strings, 18 arrangements for string quartet, 1996. *Recordings:* Negba 40; Bereshit (Genesis), 1987; Song of Songs 85-Duo Beersheba; A Maya Prophecy, Tel-Aviv Philharmonic Choir; Murmurs, A Courting Muse, in Composers in search of their roots; Iri (Acum Prize), 1989; Tamar; Israeli Sounds of Strings, 18 arrangements of folk songs, 1998. *Address:* The Open-Air Museum, Negba, Kibbutz Negba, D.N. Lachish 79408, Israel.

MINEVA, Stefka; Singer, (Mezzo-Soprano); b. 1949, Stara Zagora, Bulgaria. *Education:* Studied in Sofia. *Career:* Debut: Staga Zora 1972, as Berta in Il Barbiere di Siviglia; Sang Suzuki, Olga and Amneris at Stara at Zagora; Sofia Opera from 1977, notably as Marfa in Khovanshchina. Guest appearances throughout Europe; Metropolitan Opera, 1986–88, as Marfa; Sang Konchakovna in Prince Igor at Perugia, 1987, Liubasha in The Tsar's Bridge at Rome and Kabanicha in Katya Kabanova at Florence, 1989; Other roles include Marina in Boris Godunov, Eboli, Adalgisa and Leonora in La Favorita; Sang Fenena in Nabucco at the 1991 Verona Arena. *Recordings:* Rimsky-Korsakov's Vera Sheloga and Prokofiev's War and Peace; Madama Butterfly. *Honours:* Prize Winner, 1976 Sofia and 1977 Osten International Competitions. *Address:* c/o Arena di Verona, Piazza Bra 28, 37121 Verona, Italy.

MINGARDO, Sara; Singer (Contralto); b. 1970, Venice, Italy. *Education:* Academia Chigiana of Siena. *Career:* Many performances at leading Italian opera houses, including Teatro Comunale of Bologna, La Scala Milan, Teatro Comunale Florence, Teatro Regio Turin and Teatro San Carlo, Naples; Further engagements in Puccini's Trittico under Riccardo Chailly, as Emilia in Otello under Claudio Abbado in Berlin and Salzburg (1996); Sang title role in revival of Handel's Riccardo Primo with Les Talens Lyriques under Christophe Rousset at Fontevraud, France, 1995. *Recordings include:* Riccardo Primo (Decca/L'Oiseau Lyre). *Address:* c/o Deutsche Oper Berlin, Bismarckstrasse 35, 1000 Berlin 10, Germany.

MINICH, Peter; Singer, (Tenor); b. 1928, St Polten, Switzerland. *Education:* Studied at the Horak Conservatory, Vienna. *Career:* Debut: St Polten 1951, in Millöcker's Bettelstudent; Engaged at St Gallen 1951–55, Graz, 1955–60; Vienna Volksoper from 1960, notably as Eisenstein in Fledermaus on tour to Japan, 1985; Salzburg Festival 1962–63, in Die Entführung: Other roles have included the Baron in La Vie Parisienne, Paquilo in La Périchole, René in Graf vom Luxembourg by Lehar and Jim Mahoney in Mahagonny; Frequent concert and television appearances. *Address:* c/o Volksoper, Wahringerstrasse 78, 1090 Vienna, Austria.

MINJILKIEV, Bulat; Singer (Bass); b. 1941, Russia. *Education:* Studied in Tashkent and Milan. *Career:* Tashkent Opera in works by local composers, and as Pimen in Boris Godunov, and Gremin; Kirov Opera, St Petersburg from 1987, as Konchak in Prince Igor, Ivan Khovansky in Khovanshchina, and the Inquisitor in The Fiery Angel; Edinburgh Festival, 1991, as Mato in Mussorgsky's Salammbô, Palermo, 1994, as Glinka's Ruslan; Season 1994–95 in Rimsky's Invisible City of Kitezh at the Champs Elysées theatre, Paris, and as Boris in Lady Macbeth by Shostakovich; Sang Kotchubei in Tchaikovsky's Mazeppa at Savonlinna, 1996. *Recordings include:* Khovanshchina, Prince Igor and Sadko. *Address:* Kirov Opera, Mariinsky Theatre, 1 Theatre Square, St Petersburg, Russia.

MINKOFSKI-GARRIGUES, Horst; Concert Pianist, Composer and Professor; b. 23 July 1925, Dresden, Germany; m. Edeltraud Peschke, 1 s., 2 d. *Education:* Music Academy and Conservatory, Dresden; Studies with Professor Herbert Wuesthoff, Romana Lowenstein, Karl Knochenhauer, Hermann Werner Finke, Schneider-Marfels. *Career:*

Debut: State Orchestra, Dresden; Numerous appearances, concerts and radio broadcasts throughout the world. *Compositions:* For Orchestra: Klaviermusik, op 15, Piano Concerto, Variations over a theme by Tchaikovsky, op 8, Expo '67 to 2 pianos and orchestra; For piano solo; Impromptus, Preludes, Sonatinas, Sonata op 23 and Scherzo, op 37; For piano, four hands; Eight Miniatures, op 27, Introduction, Theme and Variations for 2 Pianos and Cello, op 14, Andante for 2 pianos, Expo '67 for 2 Pianos op 28, Pictures of a Child for 2 Pianos op 30; Chamber Music includes: Song Cycle; Love and Deception, op 41, works for flute and piano, organ, op 38. *Recordings:* World Premiere Recording of the Complete works for Piano, four hands by Schubert, 11 albums, in collobration with former student, Lothar Kilian; Also compositions for 4 hands by Beethoven, Brahms, Tchaikovsky, Saint-Saëns, Dvořák and Smetana; With Orchestra: Concerto for 2 pianos by Bach; Concerto in D-Major by Haydn, Klaviermusik, op 15 by Minkofski-Garrigues; Numerous solo and chamber music recordings including Schubert's Sonatas for Violin and Piano with Wolfgang Marschner. *Address:* 205 Edison Ave, St Lambert, Montreal, Quebec J4R 2P6, Canada.

MINKOWSKI, Marc; Conductor; b. 4 Oct. 1962, Paris, France. *Education:* Studied at the Hague Conservatory and at the Pierre Monteux Memorial School, USA. *Career:* Founder of and has performed with, Les Musiciens du Louvre, 1984; Has conducted works by Handel including Riccardo Primo, 1991, for the English Bach Festival and Gluck's Iphigénie en Tauride at Covent Garden; French repertoire includes Charpentier's Malade Imaginaire, Alcyone by Marin Marais, Mouret's Les Amours de Ragonde and Titon et l'Aurore by Mondonville, Rameau's Hippolyte et Aricie, Gluck's Armide; Lully's Phaëton, Opéra de Lyon, 1993; Ariodante by Handel, Welsh National Opera, 1994; Agrippina by Handel, Semper Oper, Dresden, 1994; Dido and Aeneas by Purcell, Houston Grand Opera, 1995; Orchestre de Chambre de Genève, 1995; Amsterdamse Bach Solisten, 1995; Rotterdam Philharmonic, 1995; Idomeneo by Mozart, Opéra de Paris-Bastille, 1996; Orfeo ed Euridice by Gluck, National Opera, Netherlands, 1996; Armide by Gluck, Opéra de Nice, 1996; L'Inganno Felice by Rossini, Poissy, France, 1996; Acis et Galatée, summer tour, 1996; Die Entführung at the 1998 Salzburg Festival; Music Director of the Flanders Opera, from 1997; Le nozze di Figaro at Aix, 2000. *Recordings:* Les Amours de Ragonde by Mouret; Mondonville's Titon et l'Aurore; Stradella's San Giovannia Battista; Grétry's La Caravane du Caire; Alcyone by Marin Marais; Le Malade Imaginaire by Charpentier; Platée by Rameau; Rebel's Les Elemens; Handel's Amadigi; Handel's Teseo; Il Trionfo del Tempo by Handel; Concerti Grossi op 3, by Handel; Rameau's Hippolyte et Aricie, 1994; La Resurrezione by Handel, 1995; Gluck's Armide, 1999. *Honours:* 1st prize, 1st International Concert of Ancient Music, Bruges, 1984. *Address:* c/o VWM, 4 Addison Bridge Place, London, W14 8XP, England.

MINTER, Drew; Singer, (Countertenor); b. 11 Jan. 1955, Washington DC, USA. *Education:* Studied at Indiana University and with Rita Streich, Erik Werba and Marcy Lindheimer. *Career:* Performed in concert with various early music ensembles, including the Waverly Consort of New York; Stage debut as Handel's Orlando at the St Paul's Baroque Festival, 1983; Further appearances in early opera at Boston, Brussels and Los Angeles; Omaha and Milwaukee 1988, as Arsace in Handel's Partenope and Otho in L'Incoronazione di Poppea; Santa Fe 1989, in the US premiere of Judith Weir's A Night at the Chinese Opera and as Endimione in La Calisto by Cavalli; Television appearances include Ptolemeo in Handel's Giulio Cesare, directed by Peter Sellars; Sang the title role in Handel's Ottone, Göttingen, 1992; Endymion in Cavalli's Calisto at Glimmerglass, 1996. *Recordings:* Ottone in Handel's Agrippina and the title role in Floridante, conducted by Nicholas McGegan. *Address:* c/o Glimmerglass Opera, PO Box 191, Copperstown, New York, NY 13326, USA.

MINTON, Yvonne (Fay), CBE; Singer (Mezzo-soprano); b. 4 Dec. 1938, Sydney, Australia; m. William Barclay, 21 Aug 1965, 1 s., 1 d. *Education:* Sydney Conservatorium. *Career:* Soloist with major Australian orchestras; British debut as Rinaldo for Handel Opera Society, London, 1961; In 1964 appeared in premiere of Nicholas Maw's One Man Show; Soloist with Royal Opera, Covent Garden, notably as Mussorgsky's Marina, Mozart's Dorabella, Wagner's Waltraute, Strauss' Octavien and Thea, in premiere of Tippett's Knot Garden, 1970; Has appeared with most major symphony orchestras in the world and at all major opera houses; Sang Octavian at the Metropolitan, (1973); Brangaene at Bayreuth Festival, (1974); Fricka and Waltraute in Centenary Ring, 1976; Octavian at Paris Opéra, 1976; Countess Geschwitz in premiere of the 3 act version of Lulu; Kundry at Covent Garden, in a new production of Parsifal; Waltraute in The Ring, (1988); Sang Fricka in Die Walküre at Lisbon, 1989; Leokadja Begbick in Mahagonny at 1990 Maggio Musicale, Florence; Season 1993–94 as Marguerite in La Damnation de Faust at Wellington and Mme Larina, in Eugene Onegin at Glyndebourne. *Recordings:* Concert recordings with Chicago Symphony Orchestra; BBC Symphony Orchestra and others; Opera recordings include: Rosenkavalier; La Clemenza di Tito;

Wagner's Ring; Tristan and Isolde and others. *Honours:* Honorary RAM, 1977. *Current Management:* Ingpen & Williams Ltd, 7 St George's Court, 131 Putney Bridge Road, London, SW15 2PA, England.

MINTZ, Shlomo; Violinist; b. 30 Oct. 1957, Moscow, USSR; m. Corina Ciacci Mintz, 2 s. *Education:* Diploma, Juilliard School of Music. *Career:* Music Adviser to Israel Chamber Orchestra, 1989–; Conducts and performs with this orchestra in Israel and abroad; Recitals and Chamber Music Concerts throughout the World; Performed with: Israel Philharmonic; Berlin Philharmonic; Vienna Philharmonic; London Symphony; New York Philharmonic; Chicago Symphony; Philadelphia Orchestra; Boston Symphony; Los Angeles Philharmonic; Played the Mendelssohn Concerto with the Royal Philharmonic, London, 1997. *Recordings:* Works by Bach; Bartók; Bruch; Debussy; Dvořák; Franck; Kreisler; Mendelssohn; Mozart; Paganini; Prokofiev; Ravel; Sibelius; Vivaldi; Beethoven; Brahms; Fauré; Lalo; Vieuxtemps. *Honours:* Grand Prix du Disque, 1981, 1984, 1988; Premio Accademia Musicale Chigiana Siena, 1984. *Current Management:* ICM Artists Ltd. *Address:* ICM Artists Ltd, 40 West 57 Street, New York, NY 10019, USA.

MINUTILLO, Hana; Singer (Mezzo-soprano); b. 1963, Jihlava, Czechoslovakia. *Education:* Studied at the Pardubice Conservatory. *Career:* Sang at Liberec in Nabucco, Manon and Rusalka; Opera Studio of the National Theatre Prague from 1989, as Carmen, Rosina and Arsamene in Handel's Serse; Further study in Belgium and with Svatava Subrtova, followed by Mozart's Clemenza di Tito in Darmstadt (1993–94 season) and concert performances of Les Troyens under Michel Plasson in Toulouse and Arhens; Bregenz Festival in Francesca da Rimini and Nabucco; Season 1994–95 as Carmen and The Fox in The Cunning Little Vixen, under Mackerras, at the Théâtre du Châtelet, Paris; Further engagements as the Witch in Rusalka at Essen, The Diary of One who Disappeared, by Janáček, with Peter Schreier in Leipzig, Olga in Eugene Onegin at Amsterdam and Mozart's Annio (Clemenza di Tito) at Wiesbaden; Flowermaiden at Zürich, 1997. *Recordings include:* Rusalka, conducted by Charles Mackerras. *Address:* c/o Opernhaus Zürich, Falkenstrasse 1, 8008 Zürich, Switzerland.

MIREA, Marina; Singer (soprano); b. 1941, Bucharest, Romania; m. *Education:* Bucharest Conservatory. *Career:* sang at the Bucharest National Opera, 1969–, notably as Violetta, Constanze, Pamina, Lucia di Lammermoor, Olympia, Lakmé, Gilda, Norina, Rosina, Rosalinde, Anchen, Caroline, Miss Wordswoord (A. Hering); guest engagements at the Berlin and Budapest State Operas, at Tel-Aviv and in France, Russia, Germany, Greece, Czechoslovakia and Yugoslavia; teacher, Bucharest Music Univ., 1992–, Constanta Ovidius Univ., 1997–. *Address:* Garoafei str., bl. 6, Bucharest, Romania.

MIRFIN, Timothy (Tim); Singer (Bass); b. 1974, England. *Education:* Gonville & Caius College, Cambridge; Royal Academy, and National Opera Studio, London. *Career:* Early roles included Mozart's Figaro (RAM) and Clodomiro in Lotario, for the London Handel Festival; Other roles include Argante in Rinaldo, for Grange Park Opera, Britten's Bottom, and Don Pedro in Beatrice and Benedict; Wigmore Hall debut Nov. 2000, singing Russian songs; Season 2001–2002 with Welsh National Opera, as Publio in La Clemenza di Tito, Fernando in Beethoven's Leonore, and Parson in The Cunning Little Vixen; Also sings Mozart's Masetto and Figaro, Simone in Puccini's Gianni Schicchi; Leporello and Basilio in Barbiere di Siviglia; performances for Edinburgh Int. Festival, 2001, 2002, 2003; Season 2002–03: Engelotti in Tosca and Colline in La Bohème, Welsh Nat. Opera; Sarastro in Magic Flute for Scottish Opera; Collatinus in Rape of Lucretia for Opera East;. *Honours:* Friends of Covent Garden and Countess of Munster Trust Award; Winner , Royal Overseas League Competition, Nat. Mozart Singing Competition. *Current Management:* c/o Askonas Holt, Lonsdale Chambers, 27 Chancery Lane, London WC2A 1PF, England.

MIRICIOIU, Nelly; Singer (Soprano); b. 31 March 1952, Romania. *Education:* Studied in Bucharest and Milan. *Career:* Debut: Sang the Queen of Night in Die Zauberflöte at Iasi, Romania, 1974; Appeared with the Brasov Opera 1975–78; Scottish Opera 1981, as Tosca and Violetta; Covent Garden debut 1982, as Nedda in Pagliacci, returning as Musetta in La Bohème, Marguerite and Antonia in Les Contes d'Hoffmann; Further engagements in Toronto, San Diego, San Francisco, Paris, Rome, Hamburg, Milan La Scala and Verona; Amsterdam 1988 as Rossini's Armida; In 1989 sang Violetta in Monte Carlo and Ravenna and Yaroslavna, Prince Igor, at Munich; Season 1992 as Violetta at Philadelphia; Maria Stuarda, Lucrezia Borgia, Semiramide and Ermione at the Amsterdam Concertgebouw and Amenaide in Tancredi at the Salzburg Festival; Other roles include Puccini's Butterfly, Mimi and Manon Lescaut and Lucia di Lammermoor; Sang Elisabeth in the French verison of Don Carlos, Brussels, 1996; Silvana in Respighi's La Fiamma at Rome, 1998; Season 2000–01 as Isabelle in Meyerbeer's Robert le Diable at the Staatsoper Berlin, Tosca at Covent Garden and Norma in Rome and Florence. *Address:* c/o J. Eddy Artists' Management, Suite 11, The Clivedon, 596 St Kilda Road, Melbourne, Victoria 3004, Australia.

MIROGLIO, Thierry (Jean-Michael); Percussionist; b. 1 Sept. 1963, Paris, France. *Education:* Baccalaureate; Studied Musical Acoustics with Iannis Xenakis, Paris University, Sorbonne; Percussion with J P Drouet and Sylvie Gualda, National Conservatory, Versailles; Harmony and Counterpoint, Chamber Music, National Conservatory of Boulogne, Billancourt. *Career:* Researcher and Soloist with ensembles: Musique Vivante; Atelier Ville d'Avray; Orchestra Opera de Paris; Orchestre Radio France; Musica Insieme, Soloist, concerts in Festivals of Radio France, Angers, Besancon, Orleans, Nice, Salzburg, Athens, Paris, Würzburg, Venice, Bamberg, Rouen, Munich, Trento, Cremona also in South America; Artistic Director, Percussion Season of the French Society of Contemporary Music; Radio broadcasts; Masterclasses, lectures, seminars on the volution of Percussion style from the origin until our time, numerous countries; Masterclasses, South America, 1990; World or Grand Premieres of works of Cage, Ohana, Boucourechiev, Ballif, Pousseur, Denisov, Donatoni, Kelemen, Henze, several dedicated to him; currently Prof. Darius Milhaud Conservatory, Paris; He has recently premiered the latest work of Xenakis for solo percussion and ensemble and the percussion concerti of Marlos Nobre; Recent tours have taken him throughout Europe, Asia, South America ant the USA. *Recordings:* For French, German, Austrian, Italian, Canadian and Greek radio; Has recorded a disc of Saariaho's pieces. *Honours:* 1st prize, Percussion, National Conservatory, Versailles; Prize for Chamber Music, National Conservatory of Boulogne. *Address:* 215 ave Henri Ravera, 92220 Bagneux, France. *Telephone:* 1-46-56-61-00. *Fax:* 1-46-56-61-00. *E-mail:* miroglio@club-internet.fr. *Website:* www .thierrymiroglio-percussion.com.

MIRSHAKAR, Zarrina; composer and teacher; b. 19 March 1947, Dushanbe, Tajikstan. *Education:* Moscow State Conservatory. *Career:* mem. Union of Composers of Tajikstan, 1992; Union of Soviet Composers, 1974–92. *Compositions include:* String Quartet; 24 music pieces for piano; Three Frescos of Pamir for violin and piano, published 1979; Sonata for clarinet solo, published 1982; Sonata for oboe solo; Respiro for violin, chamber orchestra and timpani; Six pieces for piano, published 1987; Music for documentary film, Our Baki; Colours of Sunny Pamir, symphonic poem, published 1989; Sonata for oboe solo; Symphonietta for string orchestra; Symphony for chamber orchestra; Three Inventions for piano quintet. *Recordings include:* 24 music pieces for piano; Sonata for clarinet solo; Sonata for oboe solo; Cycle of songs for children on M. Mirshaker's poems; Six Pieces for flute and clarinet, 1995. *Honours:* Lenin Komsomol Prize Laureate, 1985. *Address:* Pionersky St proezd I 12, 734003 Dushanbe, Tajikstan.

MIRTOVA, Elena; Singer (soprano); b. 1962, South West Siberia, Russia. *Education:* Studied at the Leningrad Conservatory, graduated 1988. *Career:* Debut: Sang at the Musical Academy and Philharmonic Hall in Prague while a student; Sang Maria in Rimsky-Korsakov's The Tsar's Bride in Moscow and Leningrad; Series of concerts in Moscow and Leningrad, 1984; Principal soloist at the Kirov Theatre in Leningrad, St Petersburg, from 1988; Rimsky's Olga and Maria, Tchaikovsky's Tatiana and Iolanta and Violetta; Sang in the 14th Symphony of Shostakovich with the Chamber Orchestra of the Lithuanian Philharmonia at the Berliner Philharmonie, 1989; Sang Iolanta at Frankfurt 1990 and Leonora in Il Trovatore with Omaha Opera 1991. *Honours:* Winner, Glinka Competition, 1984; First prize, Dvořák Voice Competition, Karlovi Vari, 1987; Winner, Fidenza, Parma Verdi Competition, 1990. *Current Management:* Athole Still International Management, Forresters Hall, 25–27 Westow Street, London, SE19 3RY, England. *Telephone:* (20) 8771-5271. *Fax:* (20) 8768-6600. *Website:* www .atholestill.com.

MIRZOYAN, Edward; Composer; b. 12 May 1921, Gori, Georgia, USSR; m. Elena Stepanyan, 1 June 1951, 1 s., 1 d. *Education:* Musical College, Yerevan, 1928–36; Yerevan Conservatoire, 1936–41; Postgraduate, Moscow Concervatoire, 1946–48. *Career:* Debut: Yerevan, 1938; Lecturer, 1949; Professor, 1965–; Head, Chair of Composition, 1972–8, Yerevan Conservatoire; Secretary, 1950–52, Chairman, 1956–; Armenian Composer's Union; Chairman, 1952–56; Armenian Musical Foundation; mem, Armenian and CIS Composers' Societies. *Compositions:* Sako from Lahore, symphonic poem, 1941; Symphonic Dances, suite, 1946; String quartet, 1947; Overture, 1947; Introduction and Perpetuum Mobile; Violin and Orchestra, 1957; Symphony, 1962; Cantatas, 1948, 1949, 1950; Cello Sonata, 1967; Piano pieces, 1983; Epitaph, symphonic poem, 1988; Poem for Cello and Piano, 1995. *Recordings:* Introduction and Perpetuum Mobile; Symphony, Symphonic Dances; String Quartet; Cello Sonata; Romances; Piano Poem. *Current Management:* Armenian Composers' Union. *Address:* c/o Armenian Composers' Union, Demirchyan str, 25, Yerevan 375002, Armenia.

MISHENKINE, Arkadij; Singer (Tenor); b. 1961, Russia. *Education:* Studied in Kazan, at the Moscow Conservatory and the Bolshoi Opera Studio. *Career:* Sang at the Bolshoi Theatre, Moscow, from 1989, Tchaikovsky's Lenski and Jaromir, Rossini's Almaviva, Paolo in Francesca de Rimini by Rachmaninov, Vladimir in Prince Igor, Lykov in The Tsar's Bride by Rimsky, Alfredo, and Antonio in Prokofiev's Betrothal in a Monastery; Guest appearances in France, North America and Japan; Many concert engagements. *Address:* Bolshoi Theatre, 103009 Moscow, Russia.

MISHURA, Irina; Singer (Mezzo-Soprano); b. 1965, Krasnodar, Russia. *Education:* Gnessin Institute, Moscow. *Career:* Appearances with the Moldovan State Opera as Carmen, Amneris, Azucena, Adalgisa in Norma, Ulrica and Princess Eboli (Don Carlos); Mussorgsky's Marina and Marfa, Olga (Eugene Onegin) and Lyubasha in The Tsar's Bride, by Rimsky-Korsakov; European engagements 1998–99, as Carmen and Amneris at the Vienna Staatsoper, and appearances in Munich, Brussels and Tel-Aviv (New Israeli Opera); Rimsky's The Snow Maiden with the Detroit Symphony, Carmen for San Francisco Opera, Dalila at Michigan and Adalgisa for Baltimore Opera; Concerts include Los Angeles Philharmonic under Valery Gergiev and Verdi Gala in Israel; Season 1999–2000 with Carmen in Vienna and Munich, Fricka in Die Walküre for Dallas Opera and Principessa in Adriana Lecouvreur at Trieste; Season 2001–2002 with Carmen, Dalila, Azucena and Amneris at the New York Met, and for Opera Pacific, Washington Opera and Cologne Opera. *Address:* IMG Artists Lovell House, 616 Chiswick High Road, London W4 5RX, England.

MISKELL, Austin; Singer (Tenor) and Professor of Voice; b. 14 Oct. 1925, Shawnee, Oklahoma, USA; m. 2 s. *Education:* Oklahoma City University, 1946–47; Hochschule für Musik, Zürich, 1955–65; Mozarteum of Salzburg, 1955–65; LRAM, Royal Academy of Music, London. *Career:* Featured soloist with Elizabethan Consort of Viols, London, Anglian Chamber Soloists London, Ricecare, Ensemble for Ancient Music, Zürich, Arte Antica Zürich; Musinger Players, New York, 1986–; Sang in 25 countries, 1950–86; Performances with Tonhalle Orchestra, Zürich, Orchestra de la Academia Santa Cecilia Rome, London Symphony Orchestra, Pro Arte, London, Stuttgarter Synfoniker and others; Participant at music festivals including: Sagra Musicale, Perugia, Italy, Settimane Musicali, Ascona, Switzerland, Salzburger Festspiel, Britten, Purcell Festival, Buenos Aires, Mozart Festival, Munich, Bergen Festival, Norway, 1970–80; Assistant Professor of Voice at National University of Columbia, Bogota, 1976–82; Head of Voice at Conservatory of Tolima, Ibague, Columbia, 1978–82; Teacher of Voice, Italian Opera, Teatro Col ón, National Opera Company, Bogota, 1978–82; Lecturer in Voice, University of New Mexico, 1982–84; Professor of Voice, College of Santa Fe, 1982–96. *Address:* c/o College of Santa Fe, Vocal Faculty, Santa Fe, New Mexico, USA.

MISKIMMON, Annilese; stage director; b. 1968, Belfast, N Ireland. *Education:* Christ's College, Cambridge, City University, London. *Career:* Welsh National Opera from 1997, assisting Richard Jones, David Alden and Peter Stein; Assistant to Graham Vick at Glyndebourne, for Manon Lescaut and Così fan tutte, and to Peter Hall for Simon Boccanegra; Production of La Traviata for WNO subject of series with HTV, 2000; further stagings include La Clemenza di Tito for Opera Bordeaux and Figaro at the Peking Conservatory, for WNO; Goehr's Arianna at Cambridge, J.C. Bach's Endimione for Cambridge Classical Opera and Weill operas for the BBC Symphony Orchestra; Season 2000–01 with Hansel and Gretel for San Francisco Opera and Bernstein's On the Town with the BBC Concert Orchestra; Artistic Consultant to Castleward Opera, Ireland. *Honours:* Margot Simon Award, Glyndebourne 2000. *Address:* c/o San Francisco Opera, War Memorial Opera House, 301 Van Ness Avenue, San Francisco, CA 94102, USA.

MISSENHARDT, Gunter; Singer (Bass); b. 29 March 1938, Augsburg, Germany; m. Agnes Baltsa, 1974. *Education:* Studied at the Augsburg Conservatory and with Helge Roswaenge. *Career:* Sang at the Bayerische Staatsoper Munich, 1965–68; Frankfurt, 1968–72; Berne, 1973–78; Appearances from 1978 at Aachen, Bremen and Brussels, 1986; Since 1984, State Opera Vienna (Ochs, Osmin, Varlaam, Colline); 1984, Grand Opéra Paris (Ochs); Covent Garden, London, since 1985, Bartolo, Varlaam, Ochs, Rocco; 1994 Scala di Milano (Osmin); Düsseldorf, 1988; Théâtre des Champs Elysées Paris, 1989, as Ochs in Der Rosenkavalier; Season 1987–88 as the Doctor in Wozzeck at Strasbourg and Schigolch in Lulu at Brussels; Other roles have included Kecal, Osmin, Bett in Zar und Zimmerman, Masetto, Mozart's Figaro and Varlaam in Boris Godunov; Sang Osmin in Die Entführung at Geneva, 1996; Simon in Lortzing's Regina at Karsruhe, 1998; Season 2000 as Osmin at Dresden and Baron Ochs for the Teatre Real, Madrid. *Address:* c/o Deutsche Oper am Rhein, Heinrich Heine Allee 16, 4000 Duseeldorf, Germany.

MITCHELL, Clare; British costume designer and stage designer; b. 1960, England. *Education:* Bristol Old Vic Theatre School. *Career:* Assistant Costume Designer, Royal Shakespeare Company, Stratford; Costumes for premiere of Rebecca by Wilfred Josephs at Leeds, 1983; English National Oper for Madama Butterfly, Scottish Opera Don Giovanni, and Jenůfa in production by Yuri Lyubimov at Zürich and Covent Garden, 1986–93; Costumes and sets for Ulisse by Monteverdi and Handel's Flavio at the Batignano Festival, Rigoletto for Opera 80 and Donizetti's Tudor trilogy for Monte Carlo Opera; Costumes for Traviata at English National Opera, 1996. *Address:* c/o English National Opera, St Martin's Lane, London WC2N 4ES, England.

MITCHELL, Donald (Charles Peter); Writer on Music and Critic; b. 6 Feb. 1925, London, England; m. Kathleen Livingston. *Education:* Durham University, 1949–50, with Arthur Hutchings and A E F Dickinson; PhD, Southampton, 1977. *Career:* Founder, Music Survey, 1947; Co-Editor (with Hans Keller), Music Survey (new series), 1949–52; Music Critic, The Musical Times, 1953–57; Editor of Tempo, 1958–62; Head of Music Department, Faber and Faber, 1958; Managing Director, 1965–76, Vice-Chairman, 1976–77, Chairman, 1977–88, President, 1988–95, Faber Music; Music Staff of Daily Telegraph, 1959–64; Founding Professor of Music, 1971–76, Visiting Professor, 1977–, Sussex University; Chairman Britten Estate Ltd, 1986–2000, Life President 2000–; Trustee, Britten-Pears Foundation, 1986–2000, Trustee Emeritus, 2000–; Governor, Royal Academy of Music, 1988–, Council of Honour, 2000–; Chairman, Performing Right Society, 1989–92; Vice-President, CISAC, 1992–94; Director of study courses at the Britten-Pears School, Snape; Visiting Professor, York University, 1991; Visiting Professor, King's College, London University, 1995–99; Music Adviser for television film: Owen Wingrave, Channel 4, 2001; mem, Honorary Research Fellow, Royal College of Music, 2000. *Publications include:* Benjamin Britten (joint editor with Hans Keller), 1952; The Mozart Companion (joint editor with H. C. Robbins Landon), 1956; Author of 3 vols of a projected 4 on the life and music of Mahler, 1958–85; The Language of Modern Music, 1963; Benjamin Britten, 1913–76: Pictures from a Life (with John Evans), 1978; Britten and Auden in the Thirties, 1981; Benjamin Britten: Death in Venice, 1987; Letters from a Life: Selected Letters and Diaries of Benjamin Britten, vols 1 and 2, 1923–1945 (with Philip Reed), 1991; Cradles of the New: Writings on Music 1951–1991, 1995; The Mahler Companion (with Andrew Nicholson), 1999. *Contributions:* Music Survey, The Chesterian, Tempo, The Times Literary Supplement, Musical Times, Music and Letters, Opera; Articles and broadcasts on Berg, Britten, Hindemith, Mahler, Malcolm Arnold, Mozart, Prokofiev, Reger, Schoenberg, Stravinsky and Weill. *Honours:* Honorary MA (Sussex); Doctor of University of York; Mahler Medal, 1987; Honorary RAM, 1992; C.B.E., 2000. *Address:* 83 Ridgmount Gardens, London WC1E 7AY, England. *E-mail:* mahler@mitchelld.demon.co.uk.

MITCHELL, Geoffrey Roger; British singer (countertenor), conductor and choir manager; b. 6 June 1936, Upminster, Essex, England. *Education:* studied with Alfred Deller and Lucy Manen. *Career:* countertenor, lay clerk, Ely Cathedral, 1957–60; Westminster Cathedral, 1960–61; Vicar-choral, St Paul's Cathedral, 1961–66; Founder and conductor, Surrey University Choir, 1966; Manager, John Alldis Choir, 1966–; Cantores in Ecclesia, 1967–77; Conductor, New London Singers, 1970–86; Professor, Royal Academy of Music, 1974–95; Singing Teacher, King's College, and St John's College, Cambridge, 1975–85; Conductor, Geoffrey Mitchell Choir, 1976–; Conductor, London Festival Singers, 1987–; BBC Choral Manager, 1977–92; Guest Conductor, Camerata Antigua of Curitiba, Brazil. *Recordings:* Various with: John Alldis Choir; Cantores in Ecclesia; Pro Cantione Antigua; 46 recordings with Opera Rara Geoffrey Mitchell Choir; 19 complete operas for Chandos Opera in English Series. *Address:* 49 Chelmsford Road, Woodford, London, E18 2PW, England. *E-mail:* geoffreymitchell@compuserve.com.

MITCHELL, Ian, BMus, GRSM; British clarinettist; b. 14 Feb. 1948, S Yorkshire, England; m. Vanessa Noel-Tod 1970; one s. one d. *Education:* Royal Acad. of Music, London Univ., Goldsmiths' Coll. *Career:* debut in Purcell Room, London 1971; solo appearances throughout the UK, Europe, Middle East, USA, Australia, Democratic People's Republic of Korea and Taiwan; chamber concert performances in Europe; solo broadcasts on BBC and for Swedish, American, Belgian, Austrian and German radio stations; soloist on British television and in films of composers Cornelius Cardew and John Cage; numerous first performances, many works written for him; Dir of Gemini leading chamber ensemble, which is a pioneer in music education; mem., Dreamtiger, Eisler Ensemble of London, Entertainers Clarinet Quartet, AMM, Critical Band Birtwistle; part-time Lecturer in Performance, Exeter Univ., Univ. Dir of Music 1996–; mem. ISM, Clarinet and Saxophone Soc. of Great Britain (chair. 2000–02). *Recordings:* works of Nicola LeFanu (with Gemini), works of Oliver Knussen, Draughtman's Contract, The Masterwork and others (with Michael Nyman Band),

Eisler (with Dagmar Krauze), works by David Lumsdaine, John White, Lindsay Cooper, Philip Grange, Xenakis, Janáček, solo album of music for bass clarinet, music by Geoffrey Poole, numerous chamber ensemble recordings. *Publications:* Structure and Content of Lessons, Preparing for Performance; contrib. to Musical Times, Clarinet and Saxophone, Contact, New Grove Dictionary of Music and Musicians, Music Teacher, Musical Performance. *Honours:* Hon. ARAM 1997. *Address:* 137 Upland Road, East Dulwich, London, SE22 0DF, England. *E-mail:* mitchells@ dulwich1.demon.co.uk. *Website:* www.dulwich1.demon.co.uk/gemini.

MITCHELL, Lee; Composer, Pianist and Educator; b. 27 April 1951, Wilmington, Delaware, USA. *Education:* BMus, Peabody Institute, Johns Hopkins University, 1970; Studies, University of California, Santa Barbara; PhD, University of Berne, Switzerland, 1976. *Career:* Debut: Wilmington, Delaware; Professor, Music Theory and History, Academy of Music, Biel, Switzerland, 1973–76; Professor of Music Theory and History, Peabody Institute, Johns Hopkins University, Baltimore, 1976–86; Chairman, Theory, Hopkins, 1984–86; Adjunct Professor of Music, Goucher College, Towson, Maryland, 1980–83; Lecturer, University of Esztergom, Hungary, 1980, 1981, 1983; Profesor of Music, Johns Hopkins University, School of Continuing Studies, 1986–; Television appearances, Baltimore, 1969; Radio broadcasts, Budapest, 1981, Switzerland, 1993; Piano Concerts, USA, Switzerland, Germany, Netherlands, Greece, Hungary; Compositions performed in the USA, Peru, Europe; mem, Sonneck Society; American Musicological Society. *Compositions include:* Baltimore Reflections for flute and piano, 1989; Variations and Toccata for organ; Fantasy Allegro for flute and organ, 1993; Ballade for violin, viola and piano, 1994; Four Jewish Melodies for clarinet and piano, 1995. *Honours:* Rockefeller Grant in Composition, 1965; Winner, Dame Myra Hess Memorial Concert Series Award, Chicago, 1987; Artist Fellow in Musical Composition, State of Delaware, 1991; Meet the Composer Grants, 1992, 1993, 1994, 1996. *Address:* Comanche Circle/Warwick Park, Millsboro, DE 19966, USA.

MITCHELL, Leona; Singer, (Soprano); b. 13 Oct. 1949, Enid, OK, USA. *Education:* Studied at University of Oklahoma and in Santa Fe and San Francisco; With Ernest St John Metz in Los Angeles. *Career:* Debut: San Francisco, 1972, as Micaela in Carmen; Metropolitan Opera from 1975, as Micaela, Pamina, Puccini's Manon, Liu and Mini, Elvira in Ernani and Leonora in La Forza del Destino; Barcelona 1975, as Mathilde in Guillaume Tell; Guest appearances in Houston, Washington, Stuttgart and Geneva; Covent Garden debut 1980, as Liu in Turandot; Sydney Opera, 1985, as Leonora in Il Trovatore; Nice Opera, 1987 as Salome in Massenet's Hérodiade; Paris Opéra-Comique in Puccini's Trittico, all 3 soprano leads; Verona 1988, Aida; Sang Elvira in Ernani at Parma, 1990, the Trovatore Leonora at the Teatro Col ón Buenos Aires; Season 1992 as Aida for New Israeli Opera; Sang Strauss's Ariadne at the Sydney Opera House, 1997 and Aida at Santiago; Season 1999–2000 as Turandot at Sydney and Elisabeth de Valois in Melbourne. *Recordings:* Gershwin's Bess. *Address:* c/o Teatro Regio, Via Garibaldi 16, 43100 Parma, Italy.

MITCHELL, Madeleine Louise, FRSA, GRSM, ARCM, MMus; British concert violinist; b. 1957, England. *Education:* Royal Coll. of Music, Eastman and Juilliard Schools, New York. *Career:* debut recital, South Bank, London 1984; BBC television Music Time 1979; South Bank recitals include Awards by Park Lane Group, Worshipful Company of Musicians, Kirckman Soc.; numerous solo tours in concertos and recitals in the UK, Germany, Spain, Czechoslovakia, Italy, USA, Canada; world tour, British Council 1989, 1990; Violinist Fires of London 1985–87; numerous int. festival appearances, including ISCM Masters of 20th Century Music, Warsaw, Cardiff, Harrogate, Brighton, Malta, Kiev, Huddersfield, Dartington, Malvern, Aspen, Bath, Belfast, Dvořák CSSR, Schwetzingen, Toronto; soloist on tour with Wurttemberg, Munich Chamber Orchestras, Ulster, Czech Radio Symphony (Plzen), Malaga Symphony of Spain, Acad. of London, London Festival Orchestra, Karlsbad Symphony Orchestra CSSR, Welsh Chamber Orchestra; Wigmore Hall debut recital 1989; solo tour, South America 1991; concertos with City of London Orchestra, QEH, London 1992, Royal Philharmonic Orchestra, London 1993, Polish Radio Symphony 1994, Kiev Radio/Television Orchestra 1994, Ulster Orchestra; tours also include Poland, Ukraine, South Bank recitals 1993, 1994, 1995, 1996, recitals in New York 1994, 1997, Wigmore Hall 1995, 1997, 2001; Prof. of Violin, Royal Coll. of Music, numerous masterclasses worldwide; Artistic Dir, London Chamber Ensemble, BBC Proms 1996, Red Violin Festival, Cardiff 1997, radio and TV broadcasts, Spain 2001; several BBC broadcasts; tour of Australia, Canberra Int. Chamber Music Festival, Artist-in-Residence, and Brazil 1999; apptd Leader, Bridge String Quartet 2001; recital, Lincoln Center, New York, for UK in NY festival 2001; works written for her by Brian Elias, Stuart Jones, Piers Hellawell, Anthony Powers, Vladimir Runshak, James MacMillan, John Woolrich, Michael Nyman, John Hardy, Stephen Montague. *Recordings:* broadcasts in Poland, Ukraine, Hong Kong, Colombia, Australia (ABC and Channel 7 television), Germany, UK (including

BBC radio and television), Singapore, Italy, Canada, Czechoslovakia; Messiaen Quartet for the End of Time (with Joanna MacGregor) 1994; violin sonatas by Goossens, Hurlstone and Turnbull (with Andrew Ball) 2003; Hummel violin sonatas 2003. *Publications:* Tribute to Dorothy DeLay, in The Strad 2002. *Address:* 41 Queen's Gardens, London, W2 3AA, England. *E-mail:* madeleinemitchell@zyworld.com.

MITCHELL, Scott; Pianist; b. 1964, Perth, Scotland. *Education:* Studied at the Royal Academy of Music with Alexander Kelly and John Streets; Further study with members of the Amadeus Quartet. *Career:* Member of the Borante Piano Trio, 1982–; London Performances at the Purcell Room and Wigmore Hall in the trios of Beethoven; Tours to Dublin, Paris and Vienna, Beethoven's Triple Concerto at the 1989 Festival Wiener Klassik; Concerts in Tel-Aviv and Jerusalem with the Israel Piano Trio at the 1988 Dartington Summer School; Season 1990 at the Perth and Bath Festivals, tour of Scandinavia, Russia and the Baltic States; Television appearances on Channel 4 and BSB; Duo partnerships with Laurence Jackson (violin) and Duncan Prescott (clarinet) with concerts at the Wigmore and Purcell Room; Accompanist to Yvonne Howard (mezzo soprano) and Barry Banks (tenor), including tour of France, Spain and Portugal, 1989. *Recordings:* Albums for Chandos with Duncan Prescott and Collins Classics with Jennifer Stinton (flute). *Honours:* Leverhulme Scholarship; English Speaking Union Scholarship; Lisa Fuchsova Prize, Royal Overseas League Competition, 1990. *Current Management:* Scott Mitchell Management. *Address:* The Old Stable, Shudy Camps Park, Shudy Camps, Cambs CB 1 6RD, England.

MITCHINSON, John Leslie, ARMCM, FRMCM; British opera and concert singer (tenor) and administrator; b. 31 March 1932, Blackrod, Lancashire, England; m. Maureen Guy 1958; two s. *Education:* Royal Manchester College of Music, singing with Frederick Cox, Heddle Nash and Boriska Gerab. *Career:* debut in TV series with Eric Robinson, Music for You; Stage debut as Jupiter in Handel's Semele at Sadler's Wells Theatre, 1959; Senior Lecturer, Royal Norther College of Music, 1987–92; Head of Vocal Studies, Welsh College of Music and Drama, 1992–; Many radio, television, concert and opera appearances worldwide, ENO, WNO, Scottish Opera, Basle Opera, Prague Opera; Most of the world's Music Festival; Roles included: Idomeneo, Aegisthus, Luca in From the House of the Dead, Manolios in The Greek Passion; Dalibor, Florestan, Siegmund; Sang Svatopluk Cech in the first British production of Janáček's The Excursions of Mr Brouček, ENO, 1978; Wagner's Tristan and Peter Grimes for Welsh National Opera; Opera North and Buxton Festival, 1983 as Max in Der Freischütz and Gualtiero in Vivaldi's Griselda; Menelaus in Belle Hélène, Scottish Opera, 1995; Banff Arts Centre, Canada, performances of The Raven King (Opera in 2 Parts) by Mervyn Burtch, 1999; Director of Vocal Studies at the Welsh College of Music and Drama, Cardiff. *Recordings:* Mahler 8th Symphony, Bernstein; Mahler 8th Symphony, Wyn Morris; Das Lied von der Erde, Alexander Gibson, Béatrice et Bénédict, Berlioz (Colin Davis); Lelio, Berlioz (Pierre Boulez); Tristan und Isolde, Wagner (Reginald Goodall); Glagolitic Mass, Janáček (Simon Rattle); Glagolitic Mass (Kurt Masur), Gewandhaus Orchestra, 1990; Das Lied von der Erde, Raymond Leppard; Das Lied von der Erde, Horenstein; Dream of Gerontius, Simon Rattle and CBSO. *Honours:* Queen's Prize and Royal Philharmonic Kathleen Ferrier Prize 1956–57; Curtis Gold Medal, RMCM, 1953; Ricordi Opera Prize 1952. *Address:* The Verzons Granary, Munsley, Ledbury, Herefordshire, England.

MITIC, Nikola; Singer, (Bass-Baritone); b. 27 Nov. 1938, Nis, Serbia. *Education:* Studied in Belgrade and with V Badiali in Milan. *Career:* Many appearances at the Belgrade National Opera from 1965; Guest engagements with the company at Copenhagen, 1968, Barcelona, 1972. Further appearances at the Vienna Staatsoper, Philadelphia, 1970; Düsseldorf, Perugia Festival, 1973, Rome 1975 and Dublin; Roles have included Rigoletto, Mozart's Figaro, Eugene Onegin, Mazeppa, Riccardo in I Puritani, Posa in Don Carlos and Enrico in Lucia di Lammermoor. *Address:* c/o Teatro dell'Opera di Roma, Piazza B, Gigli 8, 00184 Rome, Italy.

MITO, Motoko; Violinist; b. 13 June 1957, Kyoto, Japan; m. Yoske Otawa, 17 Mar 1989. *Education:* Toho School of Music, Tokyo; Hochschule Mozarteum, Salzburg, Austria. *Career:* Debut: Salzburg; Concertmaster, International Music Art Society Orchestra, Tokyo, 1980–81; Soloist, International Mozart Week, Salzburg, 1984; Many recitals and appearances with Professor Erika Frieser, Piano, throughout Europe and Japan, 1984–; Member, Salzburger Streichquartett, 1987–. *Recordings:* Preiser Record, 1 Salzburger Streichquartett; Preiser Record, 2 Salzburger Streichquarttet. *Current Management:* Sound Gazely, Tokyo, Japan. *Address:* Kamiyasumatsu 11, Tokorozawa, Japan.

MITTELMANN, Norman; Singer (Opera, Baritone); b. 25 May 1932, Winnipeg, Manitoba, Canada; m. 24 Feb 1979, 2 d. *Education:* Curtis Institute of Music, with Martial Singher, Ernzo Mascherini, diploma,

1959. *Career:* Debut: Toronto Opera Company; Opera houses, Germany; Italy; Austria; Puerto Rico; Canada; USA; Poland; Switzerland; Roles include: Amonasro, (Aida), Zürich, 1967; William Tell, May Festival, Florence, 1969; Rigoletto, Chicago Opera Theatre, 1977; Scarpia, (Tosca), Venice, 1979; John Falstaff, Hamburg and Berlin, 1979; Nelusko, (L'Africaine), San Francisco Opera; Mandryka, (Arabella), La Scala; Sang at Zürich until 1982. *Recordings:* Video of La Gioconda, from San Francisco, 1979. *Honours:* Gellow, Rockefeller Foundation, 1956–59; Award, Fischer Foundation, 1959. *Current Management:* Robert Lombardo Associates, 61 West 62nd Street, Suite F, New York, NY 10023, USA.

MIZELLE, Dary John; Composer; b. 14 June 1940, Stillwater, OK, USA; m. 5 c. *Education:* Studied at the California State University and University of California at Davis, PhD, 1977. *Career:* Professor, University of South Florida, 1973–75, Oberlin College, 1975–79, State University at Purchase, New York, 1990. *Compositions:* Polyphonies, I–III, 1975–78; Polytempus I for trumpet and tape, 1976; Primavera-Heterphony for 24 celli, 1977; Samadhi for quadrophonic tape, 1978; Polytempus II for marimba and tape, 1979; Quanta II and Hymn of the World for 2 choruses and ensemble, 1979; Lake Mountain Thunder for cor anglais and percussion ensemble, 1981; Thunderclap of time, music for a planetarium, 1982; Requiem Mass for chorus, soloists and orchestra, 1982–2002; Sonic Adventures, 1982; Quintet for Woodwinds 1983; Contrabass Quartet, 1983; Indian Summer for string quartet and oboe, 1983; Sounds for orchestra, 1984; Concerto for contrabass and orchestra, 1974–8; Genesis for orchestra, 1985; Blue for orchestra 1986; Percussion Concerto 1987; Parameters for percussion solo and chamber orchestra, 1974–87; Earth Mountain Fire, 1987–; Fossy: A Passion Play, music theatre, 1987; Chance Gives me What I Want, dance, 1988; SPANDA complex of 198 compositions lasting over 13 days, including Transmutations and Metamorphoses, 1989; Silverwind for solo flute, 1990; Polytempus IV Quartet for mallet instruments, 1991; Metacontrasts for clarinet, violin, piano, 1993; Transforms for piano, 1995; Amore for two violins, 1995; Summer Vision a concerto for violin and orchestra, 1996; Endless Melody for orchsestra, 1996; Niagara for large orchestra, 1999; Iguanas for Brass, Percussion and Theatre, 2001; Forbidden Colours for soloistic flute and chamber orchestra, 2000; Illuminations for computer and Chamber Orchestra, 2002; Dream of the Vacationers, chamber opera, 2002. *Address:* ASCAP, ASCAP Building, 1 Lincoln Plaza, NY 10023, USA.

MIZZI, Alfred (Freddie Paul); Musician, Clarinettist; b. 12 Oct. 1934, Valletta, Malta; m. 24 June 1953, 2 d. *Education:* ALCM, 1966. *Career:* Debut: As soloist with the Malta National Orchestra, 1961; Belfast Arts Festival, 1967; Member, World Symphony Orchestra performances in New York, Washington and Florida, 1971; Soloist in concerts in Bucharest, Mannheim, Mozart Castle, Darmstadt, Wigmore Hall and Barbican Centre, London, 1973–83; Concerts in France and Greece as part of the Mediterranean Arts Festival, 1985; Concerts at the Czechoslovakia Arts Festival, 1986; Soloist with: Stamitz Symphony Orchestra, West Germany; Watford Chamber Orchestra, England; Zapadocesky Symphony Orchester, Czechoslovakia and others; Soloist with string quartets: The Brevis String Quartet, Malta; Salzburg String Quartet, Austria; Sinnhoffer String Quartet, West Germany; Quartetto Academica, Romania; The Rasumovsky String Quartet, Great Britain and others; Television appearances and radio broadcasts in Malta, Romania, BBC Germany, USA, France, Greece, Italy; mem, Performing Right Society, London. *Honours:* Phoenicia International Culture Award, 1985; Malta Society of Arts Award, 1986. *Current Management:* Corinthia Group of Companies. *Address:* II Klarinett, Ursuline Sisters Street, G'Mangia, Malta.

MOBBS, Kenneth William; British keyboard player and tutor; b. 4 Aug. 1925, Northamptonshire, England; m. 1st Joyce McNeill 1950; m. 2nd Mary J. Randall 1979; three d. *Education:* Clare College, Cambridge, Royal College of Music, studied with Greville Cooke, M. P. Conway. *Career:* debut organ recital, King's Coll., Cambridge 1949; Lecturer, then Sr Lecturer in Music, Univ. of Bristol 1950–83; freelance keyboard performer, including harpsichord concerto, solo piano, fortepiano recitals and numerous accompaniments on BBC radio; Dir, Mobbs Keyboard Collection. *Compositions include:* Engaged! (comic opera) 1963. *Recordings include:* Mobbs Keyboard Collection Vol. 1, Golden Age of the Clarinet, Twenty Early Keyboard Instruments. *Publications:* contrib. to Encyclopaedia of Keyboard Instruments 1993, Early Music, Galpin Society Journal, English Harpsichord Magazine. *Address:* 16 All Saints Road, Bristol BS8 2JJ, England.

MOE, Bjorn (Kare); Concert Organist; b. 10 Aug. 1946, Hegra, Norway; m. Kristine Kaasa, 21 June 1975. *Education:* Trondheim School of Music, 1963–67; Musik-Akademie der Stadt Basel Abteilung Konservatorium and Schola Cantorum Basiliensis 1968–73, Eduard Muller and Wolfgang Neininger; Paris, Gaston Litaize and Praha, Jiri Reinberger. *Career:* Professor at Trondelag Musik-konservatorium, Trondheim 1973–84; Full-time Concert Organist 1985–; Concerts with the complete works of Olivier Messiaen, the main works of Max Reger and other organ music from all periods though mainly the 20th Century; World premiere of several new works from Switzerland, Iceland and Norway; Co-operates with other arts as theatre, dance and poetry; Organ Expert; Counseller; Arranged Te Deum by Ludvig Nielsen for choir, soloists, strings, brass, percussion and organ, premiere, Ratzenburg, Germany 1971; Transcribed among others Ferruccio Busoni's Fantasia Contrapuntistica for organ, premiere Trondhein, Norway, 1986, and George Gershwin's Rhapsody in Blue for organ, premiere Basle, Switzerland, 1988. *Recordings:* CD with works of Torsten Nilsson, 1999. *Publications:* The Steinmeyer-organ, Trondheim Cathedral, 1996. *Honours:* Numerous scholarships and prizes from many countries; Since 1990 paticipant in the Norwegian government's income guarantee programme for artists. *Address:* Postboks 16, 7221 Melhus, Norway.

MOENNE-LOCCOZ, Philippe; Musician and Composer; b. 21 March 1953, Annecy, France; m. 30 Aug 1986, 3 s. *Education:* Studies in electro-acoustic Composition, 20th century analysis, string bass, contemporary, classical and popular music. *Career:* Debut: At age 10; Teaches aspects of music through animation at special children's centre; Teacher of electro-acoustic Music; Director, Collectif et Compagnie, now known as Musiques Inventives d'Annecy, MIA (studio for research, creative work and music education, renamed), Annecy; Artistic Director, Festival Concert d'Hiver et d'Aujourd'hui, Annecy; International career with Trio Collectif and Solstice ensembles, Canada, Hungary, Netherlands, Switzerland, Spain and the USA; mem, Association for Electro-acoustic Music, Geneva. *Compositions:* Electro-acoustic works: Boucles; Réves opaques; Oscillation; Petit musique du Soir; Mixed works, electro-acoustic and traditional instruments: Le cri des idées sur l'eau; Recontre; Mixage 4; Oscillation No. 1, 2, 6; Inventions, 1991; Chaos for tape only; Aspérites (CDO2), 1992; Fermez la porte, 1992; Limites Extrêmes, 1999; music for theatre: Franz ou les changements profonds, 1997; Les Cris, 2004;. *Recordings:* Réves opaques, cassete C1; Le cri des idées sur l'eau, Radio Suisse Romanda, CDs, Trola, Chutts, 1989; Super Trio with Trio Collectif and Canadian Electronic Ensemble of Toronto, CD; Limites, CD, 2000. *Address:* Le Moulin du Replat, 01130 Le Poizat, France. *E-mail:* philippe.moenne -loccoz@wanadoo.fr. *Website:* pro.wanadoo.fr/philippe.moenne-loccoz/.

MOEVS, Robert (Walter); Composer and Professor; b. 2 Dec. 1920, La Crosse, Wisconsin, USA; m. Maria Teresa Marabini, 1 Oct 1953, 1 s., 1 d. *Education:* BA, Harvard College, 1942; Conservatoire National, Paris, France, 1947–51; MA, Harvard University, 1952. *Career:* Fellow, American Academy in Rome; Professor, Harvard University, USA, 1955–63; Professor, Rutgers, 1964–91; Professor Emeritus, 1991; mem, Founding Member, American Society of University Composers; Executive Committee, International Society for Contemporary Music; National Associate, Sigma Alpha Iota. *Compositions:* Numerous works for solo instruments, chorus, orchestra, chamber music; 6 Symphonic Pieces, 1955–86; 3 String Quartets, 1957, 1989, 1995; Musica da Camera, IV, 1965–97. *Recordings:* Numerous works recorded. *Publications:* Numerous works published in Paris, Italy and USA. *Contributions:* Musical Quarterly; Perspectives of New Music; Journal of Music Theory. *Honours:* Award, National Institute of Arts and Letters, 1956; Recipient, Guggenheim Fellowship, 1963–64; Several ASCAP Awards. *Address:* 1728 Millstone River Road, Hillsborough, NJ 08844, USA.

MOFFAT, Anthony; Violinist; b. 1995, Hexham, Northumberland. *Education:* Royal Academy of Music, with Manoug Parikian. *Career:* Founder member of the Borante Trio, with recitals throughout Europe and Beethoven's Triple Concerto in Vienna; London concerts at the Wigmore Hall and Purcell Room; Solo performances for BBC Radio; Engagements as leader of the BBC Concert Orchestra, Royal Liverpool Philharmonic and National Symphony Orchestra of Ireland; Former Associate Leader of the Hallé Orchestra, Manchester; Leader of the Orchestra of Scottish Opera, from 2000. *Honours:* Marjorie Hayward Prize, RAM. *Address:* c/o Scottish Opera, 39 Elmbank Crescent, Glasgow, G2 4PT, Scotland.

MOFFAT, Julie; Singer (Soprano); b. 1966, Leicester, England. *Education:* Studied at the Royal College of Music, 1984–88, with Marion Studholme; Further study with Pamela Cook and Paul Hamburger. *Career:* Debut: London 1987, in Elliott Carter's A Mirror on Which to Dwell; British premiere of Jonathan Harvey's From Silence, 1989; Appearances with such contemporary music groups as Klangforum Wien, Ensemble Inter Contemporain, Ensemble Moderne of Frankfurt and the BBC Singers; Repertoire has included works by Zender, Barraqué, Webern, Zimmerman, Nono, Beat Furrer and Varèse; Requiem for Reconciliation with Helmuth Rilling at the 1995 Stuttgart Music Festival; Frequent engagements in oratorios by Bach, Beethoven, Haydn, Mozart, Rossini, Mendelssohn and Schubert; Season 1996–97 at the Vienna Konzerthaus, the Bregenz, Salzburg and Schleswig-Holstein Festivals, with the Geneva Chamber Orchestra, at the Berlin Festival and with London Sinfonietta. *Recordings:* Albums with Klangforum Wien, Stuttgarter Bach Akademie and Ensemble Intercontemporain;

Music by Zimmermann and Dallapiccola. *Honours:* Foundation Scholarship to the RCM, 1984. *Address:* Owen/White Management, 39 Hillfield Avenue, London N8 7 DS, England.

MOFFO, Anna; Singer (Soprano); b. 27 June 1932, Wayne, Pennsylvania, USA. *Education:* Studied at the Curtis Institute with E Giannini-Gregory; Rome with Luigi Ricci and Mercedes Llopart. *Career:* Debut: Sang Norina in Don Pasquale at Spoleto in 1955; Madama Butterfly on Italian television, 1956; Sang Mozart's Zerlina at Aix in 1956 and Verdi's Nannetta at Salzburg, 1957; Metropolitan Opera from 1959 as Verdi's Violetta and Gilda, Donizetti's Lucia and Adina, Puccini's Liu, Mozart's Pamina, Massenet's Manon, Gounod's Marguerite and Juliette, the soprano roles in Les Contes d'Hoffmann and Debussy's Mélisande; Covent Garden debut 1964, as Gilda; Guest appearances in Berlin, Vienna and Buenos Aires; Sang Thais at Seattle, 1976 and Adriana Lecouvreur at Parma, 1978. *Recordings:* La Bohème, Le nozze di Figaro, Capriccio, Carmen and Falstaff (Columbia); Lucia di Lammermoor, Hänsel und Gretel, Iphigènie en Aulide; Madama Butterfly, Il Filosofo di Campagna, La Serva Padrona, Luisa Miller (RCA); Film version of La Traviata. *Address:* c/o Metropolitan Opera, Lincoln Center, NY 10023, USA.

MOHLER, Hubert; Singer (Tenor); b. 1922, Augsburg, Germany. *Education:* Studied in Augsburg. *Career:* Sang in the choir of the Augsburg Stadttheater, 1946–52; Appeared in solo roles at Gelsenkirchen, 1952–57; Oberhausen, 1957–61; Augsburg, 1961–64; Many appearances at the Cologne Opera, 1964–89, as Mozart's Pedrillo, Monostatos and Basilio, Mime in the Ring, David in Die Meistersinger, Valzacchi, Rosenkavalier, the Captain in Wozzeck, the character roles in Les Contes d'Hoffmann and Adam in The Devils of Loudun; Many appearances in Germany and abroad as concert singer. *Recordings:* Mozart Masses; Les Brigands by Offenbach. *Address:* c/o Oper der Stadt Köln, Offenbachplatz, 5000 Cologne, Germany.

MOHR, Thomas; Singer (Baritone); b. 17 Oct. 1961, Neumunster, Holstein, Germany. *Education:* Studied in Lubeck, graduating in 1985, and in Hamburg. *Career:* Debut: Lubeck 1984, as Silvio in Pagliacci; Sang at Lubeck and Detmold, 1984–85, Bremen, 1985–87, Nationaltheater, Mannheim, from 1987; Guest appearances at the Schleswig-Holstein Festival, 1987, and at Cologne, Hamburg and Ludwigsburg; Other roles include Mozart's Count and Papageno, Rossini's Figaro, Lortzing'z Zar and Count in Der Wildschütz, Wolfram and Billy Budd; Many concerts and Lieder recitals; Season 2000–01 as Spohr's Faust for Cologne Opera, Moses in the US premiere of Weill's The Eternal Road (Brooklyn Academy, NY) and Mauregato in Schubert's Alfonso and Estrella, at Zürich. *Honours:* Winner, 1984 's-Hertogenbosch Competition; 1985 German Lied Competition, London. *Address:* Nationaltheater, Am Goetheplatz, 6800 Mannheim, Germany.

MOK, Warren; Singer (Tenor); b. 1960, Hawaii. *Education:* University of Hawaii; Manhatten School of Music. *Career:* Appearances at the Deutsche Oper, Berlin, 1988–, as the Duke of Mantua, Alfredo, Rodolfo, Don Carlos, Ferrando, Count Almaviva, Nemorino and Prince Cou-Chong in Das Land des Lächelns; Premieres of Henze's Das verratene Meer and Reimann's Das Scholss; Further engagements at the Vienna and Athens Festivals, Leipzig, Copenhagen and Lisbon Operas; Many companies in the USA; Season 1999–2000 with Calaf in Lithuania, Gabriele Adorno at Martina Franca, Don José in Hong Kong, Alfredo at Shanghai, Verdi's Alvaro at Copenhagen and Manrico for Opéra de Monte Carlo. *Address:* Music International, 13 Ardilaun Road, London N5 2QR, England.

MOLDOVEANU, Eugenia; Singer (Soprano); b. 19 March 1944, Bursteni, Romania. *Education:* Studied at the Ciprian Porumbescu Conservatory and in Bucharest with Arta Florescu. *Career:* Debut: Bucharest 1968 as Donna Anna in Don Giovanni; Guest appearances in Belgrade, Sofia, Athens, Amsterdam, Trieste, Stuttgart, Dresden and Berlin; Repertoire includes roles in operas by Mozart, Verdi and Puccini; Sang Mozart's Countess while on tour to Japan with Vienna Staatsoper, 1986; Season 1987 sang Mozart's Countess at La Scala Milan, Butterfly at Verona and Donna Anna at Turin, Countess, 1989. *Address:* Teatro Regio di Torino, Piazza Castello 215, 10124 Turin, Italy.

MOLDOVEANU, Nicolae; Conductor; b. 20 July 1962. *Education:* Musikhochschule in Zürich, Basel and Bern, Switzerland; Royal Academy of Music, London. *Career:* Violinist, 1982; Repetiteur, conductor, Altmarkt Theatre, former E Germany; worked with orchestras in Switzerland, Germany, UK, South Africa and Romania; Resident Conductor, Bournemouth Orchestra, 1996; Principal Conductor, English Sinfonia, 1998–; Assoc. Guest Conductor, London Mozart Players, 2002–; Associate, Royal Academy of Music, London, 1997. *Honours:* Edwin Samuel Dove Prize and Ricordi Conducting Prize, Royal Academy of Music, London, 1993. *Current Management:* Clarion/Seven Muses, 47 Whitehall Park, London N19 3TW, England.

MOLDOVEANU, Vasile; Singer, (Tenor); b. 6 Oct. 1935, Konstanza, Romania. *Education:* Studied in Bucharest with Constantin Badescu. *Career:* Debut: Bucharest 1966, as Rinuccio in Gianni Schicchi; Stuttgart debut 1972, as Donizetti's Edgardo; Munich Opera from 1976, as Rodolfo and the Duke of Mantua; Deutsche Oper Belin and Chicago Lyric Oper 1977; Hamburg Opera 1978, as Don Carlos; Metropolitan Opera from 1979, as Pinkerton, Turiddu, Gabriele Adorno, Luigi in IL Tabarro and Henri in Les Vêpres Siciliennes; Covent Garden 1979, as Don Carlos; Zürich Opera 1980, in Verdi's Attila; Monte Carlo 1982, in Lucia di Lammermoor; Guest appearances in Helsinki, Brussels, Barcelona, Dresden, Cologne, Frankfurt and Athens; Other roles include Mozart's Don Ottavio, Pedrillo and Tamino; Stuttgart Staatsoper and Nice 1988, as Cavaradossi and as Puccini's Dick Johnson; Sang Pinkerton at Rome, 1990. *Address:* c/o Teatro dell Opera di Roma, Piazza B. Gigli 8, 00184 Rome, Italy.

MOLEDA, Krzysztof; Singer (Tenor); b. 6 April 1955, Poznan, Poland. *Education:* Music High School, Lodz, 1972–75. *Career:* Debut: Sang Wenzel in The Bartered Bride, Lodz, 1975; Sang with Warsaw Chamber Opera, 1978–80, Stettin 1980–82 and Freiberg 1982–83; Dresden Staatsoper from 1983, as Nemorino, the Duke of Mantua, Alfredo, Cassio, Riccardo (Un ballo in Maschera), Fenton, Rodolfo, Pinkerton and Cavaradossi; Guest engagements at Leipzig, Schwerin, Frankfurt an der Oder, Lille and Bratislava; Prague State Opera from 1990; Other roles include Strauss's Elemer (Arabella), Italian Singer (Rosenkavalier) and Narraboth in Salome. *Recordings include:* Rossini's Il Signor Bruschino (Eterna). *Address:* c/o Prague State Opera, Legerova 75, CR-110 00 Praha 1, Czech Republic.

MOLINO, Pippo; Composer; b. 10 June 1947, Milan, Italy; m. Giovanna Stucchi, 22 July 1972, 1 s., 2 d. *Education:* Degree, Composition and Choral Music. *Career:* Debut: Venezia Opera Prima Festival Competition, 1981; mem, SIMC; Societa Italiana Musica Contemporanes. *Compositions:* Replay 1, 11, piano, 1978; Tres, violin and viola, 1978; Litanie, orchestra, 1979; Il Canto Ritrovato, orchestra, 1980; Il Cavalier Selvatico, oratorio, 1981; Cantabile, flute piano, 1983; Jeu, oboe, 1984; Da Lontan, harp, 1985; Per la Festa Della Dedicazione, organ, 1986; Harmonien, wind quintet, 1989; Radici, clarinet, 1991; Ricordando, twelve instruments, 1992; Quintetto, clarinet, string quartet, 1993; Itinerari, string orchestra, 1994; Angelus, soprano, alto and string orchestra, 1997. *Recordings:* Il Pensiero Dominante; Nel Tempo. *Publications:* Articles in La Musica, Musica e Realta, Reggio Emilia, Il Giornale della musica. *Honours:* Rimini Aterforum, 1979; Venezia Opera Prima, 1981; Roodeport International Eisteddfod of South Africa, 1983. *Current Management:* BMG Ariola, Rugginenti. *Address:* Via Pistrucci 23, 20137 Milano, Italy.

MOLL, Kurt; Singer (Bass); b. 11 April 1938, Buir, Germany. *Education:* Studied at Cologne Hochschule and with Emmy Mueller. *Career:* Debut: Lodovico in Otello, Aachen 1961; Sang at Mainz and Wuppertal in 1960s; Bayreuth Festival 1968–, as Fafner, Pogner, Gurnemanz and Marke; Member of the Hamburg Opera from 1970 and took part in the premiere of Bialas's Der gestiefelte Kater at the 1975 Schwetzingen Festival; 1972 Osmin in Die Entführung at La Scala; US debut San Francisco 1974, as Gurnemanz; Covent Garden debut 1977, as Kaspar in a new production of Der Freischütz, Metropolitan Opera debut 1978, as the Landgrave in Tannhäuser; Later sang Beethoven's Rocco, Osmin and Ochs in Der Rosenkavalier; Visited Japan with the Hamburg Opera in 1984; Returned to Covent Garden 1987, as Osmin; San Francisco 1988, Gurnemanz in Parsifal; Metropolitan 1990, as the Commendatore in Don Giovanni, returned 1992, as Gurnemanz; Sang Pogner in Meistersinger at the 1997 Munich Festival; Season 2000 as Wagner's Daland at Covent Garden, the Landgrave and Baron Ochs in Munich and Gurnemanz in Parsifal for San Francisco Opera. *Recordings:* Die Entführung, Der Schauspieldirektor, Parsifal, Der Freischütz, Missa Solemnis, Salome, Tristan und Isolde, Die Lustigen Weiber von Windsor, Der Rosenkavalier (Deutsche Grammophon); St John Passion, Die Zauberflöte, Intermezzo, Abu Hassan, Die Zwillingsbruder, Bastien und Bastienne(Deutsche Grammophon); Don Giovanni, Les Contes d'Hoffmann, Lulu, Le nozze di Figaro, Die Meistersinger, Otello, Der Freishütz, Der fliegende Holländer, Tannhäuser, Winterreise, Video of Die Zauberflöte from the Met. *Address:* c/o Musicaglotz, 11 Rue de Verrier, F–75006 Paris, France.

MOLLER, Niels; Singer (Tenor) and Administrator; b. 4 Sept. 1922, Gorlev, Denmark. *Education:* Studied in Copenhagen, latterly at the Opera School of the Royal Opera. *Career:* Debut: Sang Rossini's Figaro in Copenhagen, 1953; Changed to tenor roles 1959 and sang in Copenhagen until 1975 as Florestan, Tannhäuser, Don José, Aegisthus, Shuisky, the Drum Major in Wozzeck and Zeus in Monteverdi's Ulisse; Bayreuth Festival, 1962–65, as Melot and Erik; Guest appearances at Brussels, Vienna, Oslo, Geneva, Venice, Barcelona, 1968, Lisbon, 1972 and Bordeaux; Baritone roles included Renato in Un Ballo in Maschera, Dandini, and Tarquinius in The Rape of Lucretia; Sang the title role in the premiere of Macbeth by H Koppel and retired as singer, 1975 after appearing as Aegisthus; Director of the Royal Opera Copenhagen 1978–83; Frequent concert engagements. *Recordings:* Schoenberg Gurrelieder; Parsifal, Bayreuth, 1962; Saul and David by Nielsen. *Address:* c/o Det Kongelige Teater, Box 2185, 1017 Copenhagen, Denmark.

MOLLET, Pierre; Singer (Baritone); b. 23 March 1920, Neuchâtel, Switzerland. *Education:* Studied in Neuchâtel, Lausanne and Basle. *Career:* Performed as concert singer in France and Switzerland from 1948; Opéra-Comique, Paris from 1952, notably as Debussy's Pelléas; Aix-en-Provence 1952, in Iphigénie en Tauride by Gluck; Paris Opéra, 1954, in Gounod's Roméo et Juliette; Geneva 1963, in the premiere of Martin's Monsieur de Pourceaugnac, repeated at the Holland Festival; As a concert singer often appeared in the cantatas of Bach and in music by Honegger, which he studied with the composer. *Recordings:* Pelléas et Mélisande, Roméo et Juliette and L'Enfant et les Sortilèges; La Damnation de Faust; Iphigénie en Tauride.

MOLLOVA, Milena; Concert Pianist and Professor of Piano; b. 19 Feb. 1940, Razgrad, Bulgaria; 1 s., 2 d. *Education:* Studied piano with Pavla Jekova; Studied with composer and pianist Dimitar Nenov, 1947; Studied with Professor Panka Pelisheck from 1949; Studied at the Bulgarian Music Academy with Professor Pelischeck from age 14; Studied in the class of Professor Emil Gilels at the Moscow State Conservatory, 1960–61. *Career:* Debut: First piano concert at age 6; Soloist in Sofia State Orchestra with the Beethoven third piano concerto, directed by Professor Sasha Popov; During her education gave numerous concerts in Bulgaria and successful participation in international competitions in Moscow, Paris and Munich; Concert tours in USSR, 1958, 1959, 1960, in Czechoslovakia, Poland, Belgium and Yugoslavia; Appointed Assistant to Professor Pelisheck at the Bulgarian Music Academy, Sofia 1963 and as a concert pianist to the Bulgarian Concert Agency; Conducted own class of young piano students, 1969–; Tour of Japan and Cuba, 1973; Appointed Reader 1976 and Professor 1989 in the Bulgarian Music Academy; To celebrate 40 years on stage, played in Sofia and Varna the whole 32 Beethoven sonatas in 9 concerts; During last few years has conducted Masterclasses in Essen, Germany and Manfredony, Foggia, Italy. *Recordings:* Numerous recordings of piano works from Bach to modern composers.

MOLNAR, András; Singer (Tenor); b. 1948, Hungary. *Education:* Hungarian Radio Children's Choir; Studied singing, 1976. *Career:* Member, Choir of The Hungarian Radio and Television, 1977–78; Soloist at Budapest State Opera, 1979–; Appeared in title roles in Erkel's László Hunyadi, Mozart's Magic Flute, Verdi's Ernani and in La Forza del Destino, Don José in Carmen, 1981–82, Title role in Lohengrin, 1981–82; Invited to sing title role in Theo Adam's new production of Wagner's Lohengrin at Berlin State Opera, 1983; Regular appearances with Budapest State Opera including the premiere of Ecce Homo by Szokolay, 1987; Sang at Teatro Colón Buenos Aires, 1987 as Donello in La Fiamma by Respighi; Budapest 1988–90, in Erkel's Hunyadi László and as Tannhäuser; Frequently participates in oratorio performances; Other performances in: Florestan in Fidelio, Budapest, 1984, Zürich and Graz in 1994; Wagner's Meistersinger at Budapest, 1985, Der fliegende Holländer at Bonn 1986, Zürich, 1987 and Liège in 1995; Tristan at Budapest in 1988, Parsifal in Budapest, 1982 and Antwerp in 1987; Tannhäuser in Rouen, 1992, Limoges in 1994; Radames in Aida, Budapest in 1994; Die Walküre, Budapest with Yuri Simonow, 1995; Sang Siegfried in Götterdämmerung at Budapest, 1998; Lohengrin at Trier, 2001. *Honours:* 1st Prize, Treviso Toti dal Monte International Vocal Competition, 1980; Kossuth Prize–First Hungarian Cultural Prize, 1994. *Address:* c/o Valmalète Concerts, 7 rue Hoche, F–92300 Levallois Perret, France.

MOLNAR, Nicolette; Stage director; b. 1959, London, England. *Education:* Columbia University, New York, USA; Hochschüle für Musik, Hamburg, with Götz Friedrich. *Career:* Staff Director at ENO, 1987–1994; Directed for: Stadttheater Luzern (Elisir d'Amore, 1991); Dublin Grand Opera (Lakmé, 1993); Castleward Opera, Belfast (I Capuleti e I Montecchi, 1995 and Ariadne auf Naxos, 1996); Royal Academy/Royal College of Music, London (Midsummer Night's Dream, 1996); Santa Fe Opera (Così fan tutte, 1997); Orlando Opera (Tosca, 1997, Turandot, 1998 and Fliegende Holländer, 1999); Opera Ontario (Tosca, 1998 and Eugene Onegin, 2001); University of Michigan (Turn of the Screw, 1998 and Cenerentola, 2002); Lyric Opera of Kansas City (Così fan tutte, 1999); Wolf Trap Opera (Don Giovanni, 2000); Atlanta Opera (Così fan tutte, 2000 and Fliegende Hollander, 2002); Co-Opera/Opera Ireland (Madama Butterfly, 2001); Lake George Opera (Entführung aus dem Serail, 2002). *Address:* c/o Pinnacle Arts Management, 889 Ninth Avenue, Suite No. 1, New York, NY 10019, USA.

MOLNAR-TALAJIC, Liljana; Singer (soprano); b. 30 Dec. 1938, Bronsanski, Brod, Yugoslavia. *Education:* Studied in Sarajevo. *Career:* Debut: Sarajevo, 1959, as Mozart's Countess; Sang at Sarajevo and Zagreb, 1959–75; Guest appearances at the Vienna Staatsoper, Florence

and San Francisco, 1969; Philadelphia from 1970, Naples 1971; Verona Arena, 1972–73, as Aida and the Forza Leonora; Sang at Covent Garden, 1975, 1977, Metropolitan Opera, 1976, Aida; Further appearandces at Barcelona, Nice and the Deutsche Oper Berlin, 1977–78, Milan, Rome and Marseilles; Other roles have included the Trovatore Leonora, Amelia in Ballo in Maschera, Desdemona and Norma. *Recordings:* Verdi Requiem. *Address:* c/o Arena di Verona, Piazza Bra 28, 37121 Verona, Italy.

MONELLE, Raymond (John); Critic and University Lecturer; b. 19 Aug. 1937, Bristol, England; m. Hannelore E M Schultz 1964, divorced 1983, 2 d. *Education:* Pembroke College, Oxford; Royal College of Music 1964–66, BMus, London, 1st class honours; PhD, Edinburgh, 1979. *Career:* Senior Lecturer, Bedford College of Physical Education, 1966–69; Lecturer in Music, University of Edinburgh, 1969–; Music Critic, The Scotsman, 1972–88; Music Critic; The Independent, 1986–; Critic, Opera Magazine, 1984–. *Compositions:* Much educational choral music published; Several commissioned works, e.g. Missa Brevis 1979; Cantata, Ballattis of Luve, 1983. *Contributions:* Music Review; Music and Letters; British Journal of Aesthetics; Music Analysis, Comparative Literature, International Review of the Aesthetics and Sociology of Music. *Publications:* Linguistics and Sematics in Music, 1992. *Address:* c/o Opera Magazine, 36 Black Lion Lane, London, W6 9 BE, England.

MONETTI, Mariaclara; Concert Pianist; b. 1965, Italy. *Education:* Studied in Turin, at the Salzburg Mozarteum and at the Conservatories of Venice and Lucerne; Teachers include Geza Anda and Vladimir Ashkenazy. *Career:* Many appearances in 18th Century repertoire throughout Europe; British appearances with the London Symphony at the Barbican and London recitals in the Purcell Room and St John's, Smith Square. *Recordings include:* Mozart concertos K466 and K595, with the Royal Philharmonic; The complete Paisiello Piano Concertos, with the English Chamber Orchestra and a solo CD of the complete piano works of Dallapiccola. *Honours:* Gold Medal, Viotti International Competition. *Address:* Manygate Management, 13 Cotswold Mews, 30 Battersea Square, London SW11 3 RA, England.

MONK, Allan; Singer (Bass-Baritone); b. 19 Aug. 1942, Mission City, British Columbia, Canada. *Education:* Studied in Calgary with Elgar Higgin and in NY with Boris Goldovsky. *Career:* Debut: Western Opera, San Francisco, 1967 in Menotti's The Old Maid and The Thief; Has sung in Portland, St Louis, Chicago, Hawaii and Vancouver; Canadian National Opera, Toronto, 1973 in premiere of Wilson's Abelard and Heloise; Metropolitan Opera from 1976 as Schaunard in La Bohème, The Speaker in Die Zauberflöte, Berg's Wozzeck, Wagner's Wolfram and Verdi's Posa and Ford; Sang Macbeth at Toronto 1986, followed by Carlo in La Forza del Destino; Opéra de Montréal, 1988 as Don Giovanni; Sang Nick Shadow in The Rake's Progress for Vancouver Opera, 1989; Wozzeck and Iago at Toronto in 1990; Sang Simon Boccanegra for Long Beach Opera, 1992. *Recordings include:* Andrea Chénier; La Traviata; Allan Monk with Calgary Philharmonic Orchestra. *Honours:* Artist of the Year, 1983; Officer of The Order of Canada, Canadian Music Council, 1985. *Address:* 97 Woodpark Close SW, Calgary, Alberta, T2W 6H1, Canada.

MONK, Meredith Jane; American composer and director and choreographer; b. 20 Nov. 1942, d. of Theodore G. Monk and Audrey Lois (Zellman). *Education:* Sarah Lawrence Coll. *Career:* Founder and Artistic Dir House Foundation for the Arts 1968–; formed Meredith Monk & Vocal Ensemble 1978–. *Works include:* Break 1964, 16 Millimeter Earrings 1966, Juice: A Theatre Cantata 1969, Key 1971, Vessel: An Opera Epic 1971, Paris 1972, Education of the Girlchild 1973, Quarry 1976, Songs from the Hill 1976, Dolmen Music 1979, Specimen Days: A Civil War Opera 1981, Ellis Island 1981, Turtle Dreams Cabaret 1983, The Games 1983, Acts from Under and Above 1986, Book of Days 1988, Facing North 1990, Three Heavens and Hells 1992, Atlas: An Opera in Three Parts 1991, New York Requiem 1993, Volcano Songs 1994, American Archaeology 1994, The Politics of Quiet 1996, Steppe Music 1997, Magic Frequencies 1998, Micki Suite 2000, Eclipse Variations 2000, Mercy 2001, Possible Sky 2003, Last Song 2003. *Honours:* Dr hc (Bard Coll.) 1988, (Univ. of the Arts) 1989, (Juilliard School of Music) 1998, (San Francisco Art Inst.) 1999, (Boston Conservatory) 2001; Golden Eagle Award 1981, Nat. Music Theatre Award 1986, German Critics' Award for Best Recording of the Year 1981, 1986, MacArthur "Genius" Award 1995, Samuel Scripps Award 1996 and many other awards. *Address:* 228 West Broadway, New York, NY 10013, USA (office).

MONNARD, Jean-François, LLM; artistic director; b. 4 Nov. 1941, Lausanne, Switzerland; m. Lia Rottier. *Education:* Univ. of Lausanne, Music Acad., Lausanne, Folkwang Hochschule, Essen, Germany. *Career:* resident conductor, Kaiserslautern, Graz, Austria, Trier, Aachen and Wuppertal; Music Dir in Osnabruck; Orchestral and opera performances throughout Europe; Artistic Dir, Deutsche Oper Berlin, 1998–; mem., Association Suisse des Musiciens. *Contributions:* articles to professional journals. *Address:* Clavallee 311, 14169 Berlin, Germany.

MONOSOFF, Sonya; Violinist and Professor Emerita; b. 11 June 1927, Ohio, USA; m. Carl Eugene Pancaldo, 8 Dec 1950, 4 d. *Education:* Artists Diploma, Juilliard Graduate School, 1948. *Career:* Debut: New York City, USA; Concerts and Masterclasses: USA, Canada, Europe, Israel, Australia and New Zealand; Professor, Professor Emerita of Music, Cornell University; mem, Early Music America, Steering Committee; American Musical Instrument Society, Editorial Board. *Recordings:* Heinrich Biber, Mystery Sonatas and 1681 Sonatas; JS Bach, Sonatas for Violin and Harpsichord; Mozart, Sonatas. *Contributions:* Notes: Early Music; The New Grove; The Musical Times. *Honours:* Stereo Review, Best Record of the Year (Bach), 1970; Fulbright Lectureship, New Zealand, 1988; Bunting Institute, 1967–68; Smithsonian Institute, 1971. *Address:* 101 Devon Road, Ithaca, New York, NY 14850, USA.

MONOSZON, Boris; Violinist and Conductor; b. 1955, Kiev, Russia. *Education:* Graduate, Moscow Conservatoire, 1979. *Career:* Made several concert tours of European and Latin American countries as concert master, Prague Symphony; Interpreted Concerto for Violin and Orchestra by Sibelius, Royal Festival Hall, London, England. Soloist, Teplice State Philharmonic Orchestra, 1982–. *Honours:* Laureate, Tibor Varga International Competition, Switzerland, 1981.

MONOT, Pierre-Alain; Trumpeter; b. 7 March 1961, Switzerland. *Education:* Diplôme de virtuosité de trompette; Etudes de direction d'orchestre. *Career:* Solo trumpet, Stadtorchester, Winterthur; Chief Conductor, Nouvel Ensemble Contemporain; Guest Conductor, Rousse Philharmonic; Bieler Sinfonieorchester; Orchester des Musikkollegium, Winterthur; mem, Association Suisse des Musiciens. *Compositions:* Stèles for Strings, 1998; Trois Airs de cour for brass quartet and orchestra; Concertino for double bassoon; Concerto for bass trombone. *Recordings:* with the Novus Brass Quartett. *Honours:* First prize, Competition of Union Bank of Switzerland, 1987. *Current Management:* Mrs Esther Herrmann. *Address:* Weinbergstrasse 18, 8001, Zürich.

MONOYIOS, Ann; Singer (Soprano); b. 28 Oct. 1949, Middletown, CT, USA. *Education:* Studied at Princeton University and with Oren Brown. *Career:* Concert performances in Baroque music with the Folger Consort, Washington DC; Stage debut with the Concert Royal of New York, in Rameau's Les Fêtes d'Hébé; European debut at the 1986 Göttingen Festival, in Handel's Terpsichore with the English Baroque Soloists conducted by John Eliot Gardiner; Opéra Comique Paris and Aix-en-Provence Festival, 1987, as Lully's Sangaride (Atys) and Psyché; Sang Elisa in Mozart's Il Re Pastore at the Nakamichi Festival in Los Angeles, 1990; Further engagements at Salzburg, Spoleto and Frankfurt; Season 1999 as Nice in J.C. Bach's Serenata Endimione at Duisburg, and Handel's Theodora at Göttingen. *Recordings:* Iphigénie en Aulide with the Opéra de Lyon; Purcell's Dioclesian and Timon of Athens, 1996.

MONTAGNIER, Jean-Paul C., MA, PhD; French ; b. 28 Sept. 1965, Lyon. *Education:* Univ. of Lyon, Conservatoire National Supérieur de Musique, Paris, Duke Univ., Durham, NC, USA. *Career:* Asst Prof. Music Dept, Nancy 2 Univ. 1992–96, later Prof. of Musicology; Assoc. Prof. Music Dept, Metz Univ. 1996–2000, Dir of Graduate Studies 1996–2000, Chair of Dept 1999–2000; mem. of bd, Société Française de Musicologie 1994–99; sec. to the ed., Revue de Musicologie 1994–; mem. of scientific cttee, CMBV 'Atelier d'étude sur le petit motet'; assoc. mem., CNRS team 'atelier d'étude sur la musique baroque française' 1996; mem. of editorial bd, new critical edition of the works of Jean-Baptiste Lully 1997–; sec., European Science Foundation research programme, 'Musical Life in Europe 1600–1900: Circulation Institutions, Representations' 1998–92; sec., Lully Asscn 1998–; assoc. mem., CNRS team 'Patrimoine musical en France'; mem. of scientific cttee, programme Musica Gallica 2001–; mem. of advisory panel, Eighteenth-Century Music 2002–; Artistic Dir, Ensemble Vocal de la Chartreuse de Bonlieu; mem. Société Française de Musicologie, Int. Musicological Soc., Royal Musical Soc., American Musicological Soc. *Publications:* La Vie l'œuvre de Louis-Claude Daquin 1694–1772, Un Mécène musicien. Philippe d'Orléans Régent 1674–1723, Charles-Hubert Gervais. Un Musicien au service du Régent et de Louis XV; contrib. many articles to journals, conference reviews and programme notes; edns of Marcello's Le Théâtre à la mode, Charpentier's Te Deum, Charpentier's Messe de Minuit, de Mondonville's Jubilate Deo, Gervais' Super flumina Babilonis, Œuvres complètes, Campra's Messe de mort, Du Mont's Magnificat, Madin's Les Messes; contrib. to New Grove Dictionary of Music and Musicians, Die Neue Musik in Geschichte und Gegenwart. *Address:* Université Nancy 2, 23 blvd Albert 1er, 54000 Nancy, France (office). *Telephone:* 3-83-96-71-40 (office). *E-mail:* Jean-Paul.Montagnier@univ-nancy2.fr (office).

MONTAGUE, Diana; Singer, (Mezzo-Soprano); b. 8 April 1953, Winchester, England. *Education:* Studied at the Royal Manchester School of Music with Ronald Stear, Frederic Cox and Rupert Bruce-Lockhard.

Career: Debut: With Glyndebourne Touring Opera 1977, as Zerlina; Member of the Royal Opera Covent Garden, 1978–83, as Laura in Luisa Miller, Kate Pinkerton, Annius in La Clemenza di Tito, Nicklausse, Cherubino and Parseis in Esclarmonde with tour of the Far East; Bayreuth debut 1983, as Wellgunde and Siegrune in Der Ring des Nibelungen, Chicago 1984, in the Missa Solemnis conducted by Solti; Edinburgh Festival 1985, as Mélisande; Salzburg Festival 1986, as Cherubino; Metropolitan Opera debut 1987, Sextus in La Clemenza di Tito; Returned to New York as Dorabella and as Nicklausse in Les Contes d'Hoffman; German operatic debut 1987, Dorabella in a new production of Così fan tutte at the Frankfurt Opera; Appearances with Scottish Opera as Cherubino and Orlofsky and with English National Opera as Cherubino and Prosperina in Monteverdi's Orfeo; Promenade Concerts London 1988, in Pelléas et Mélisande; Glyndebourne Opera 1989, Gluck's Orfeo; Sang The Fox in The Cunning Little Vixen at Covent Garden, 1990; Idamante in Idomeneo at the 1990 Salzburg Festival; Cherubino at the Vienna Staatsoper 1990, Lucio Silla 1991; Glyndebourne 1991 as Sextus in La Clemenza di Tito, also at the Promenade Concerts, London; Season 1992 sang Gluck's Iphigénie en Tauride for Welsh National Opera, and Dorabella for ENO; Sang Isolier in Le Comte Ory at Glyndebourne, 1997; Season 1998 as the Composer in Ariadne auf Naxos for Opera North; Season 2000–01 as Marcellina at Glyndebourne, Octavian in Madrid and Verdi's Meg Page at Covent Garden; Concert engagements in the Mozart Requiem, Bach B Minor Mass, Rossini's Stabat Mater and The Damnation of Faust by Berlioz. *Recordings:* Title role in Iphigénie en Tauride, Mozart's C Minor Mass; Handel arias with Simon Preston and Monteverdi's Orfeo, Deutsche Grammophon; Clothilde in Norma; Cunning Little Vixen; Romeo in I Capuleti e i Montecchi; Armando in Meyerbeer's Il Crociato in Egitto. *Address:* c/o IMG Artists, Lovell House, 616 Chiswick High Road, London W4 5RX, England.

MONTAGUE, Stephen (Rowley); Composer and Pianist; b. 10 March 1943, Syracuse, New York, USA; m. Patricia Mattin, 10 May 1986, 1 s., 1 d. *Education:* AA, St Petersburg Junior College, Florida, 1963; BM, Honours, 1965 MM, Theory, 1967, Florida State University; DMA, Composition, Ohio State University, 1972; Postgraduate work, Conducting, Mozarteum, Salzburg, 1966; Fulbright, Warsaw, Poland, 1972–74; Computer Music, IRCAM, Paris, France, 1982; CCRMA, Stanford University, 1986. *Career:* Debut: Wigmore Hall, London, England. 1975; Warsaw Autumn Festivals, 1974, 1980, 1989, 1991, 1995; Metz Festival, 1976; New Music America, 1987, 1988, 1990; Montague/Mead Piano Plus first tour of the USA, 1986; Frequent European and North American tours to present; Chairman, Sonic Arts Network, United Kingdom, 1987–88; Almeida Festival, London, 1988; Guest Professor, University of Texas at Austin, 1992, 1995, 2000; Featured Composer, Speculum Festival, Norway, 1992; World tours with Maurice Agis' inflatable sculpture, Dreamspace, 1987–2003; Centre Pompidou premiere, 1995; Composer-in-Association with the Orchestra of St John's Smith Square, London, 1995–97; Cheltenham Festival, 1995, 1997, 2001; Ultima 95 Festival, Oslo; Featured Composer at Cambridge Festival, 2000 and at Making New Waves Festival, Budapest, 2001, 2002; Chair, 1993–98, Artistic Director, 1998–99, Society for the Promotion of New Music, 1993–95; British Academy of Composers and Songwriters. *Compositions include:* Eyes of Ambush, 1973; Sound Round, 1973; Paramell Va, 1981; At the White Edge of Phrygia, 1983; String Quartet No. 1, 1989–93; Behold a Pale Horse, 1990; Wild Nights, 1993; Silence: John, Yvar and Tim, 1994; Varshavian Autumn, 1995; Snakebite, 1995; Dark Sun, 1995; Piano Concerto, 1997; Southern Lament, 1997; A Toy Symphony, 1999; Black 'n' Blues, 2000; Bright Interiors III, 2000; When Dreams Collide, 2001; Disparate Dances, 2002. *Recordings include:* CDs: Stephen Montague Orchestra and Chamber Works, 1994; Snakebite, 1997; Silence: John, Yvar and Tim, 1997. *Honours:* Ernst von Dohnányi Award, 1995; 1st Prize, Bourges Electronic Music Competition, 1994; Honorary Fellow Trinity College of Music, London, 2001. *Address:* 2 Ryland Road, London NW5 3EA, England.

MONTAL, Andre; Singer (Tenor); b. 18 Nov. 1940, Baltimore, USA. *Education:* Studied at the Eastman School, The Music Academy of the West at Santa Barbara and the Curtis Institute. *Career:* Debut: American Opera Society New York, 1964, as Tebaldo in I Capuleti e i Montecchi; Has sung at opera houses in Boston, Chicago, Philadelphia, San Francisco and Vancouver; Metropolitan Opera fro m 1974; Further engagements with Australian Opera at Sydney; Other roles have included Donizetti's Ernesto, Nemorino, Tonio and Edgardo, Oronte in Alcina, Gounod's Roméo, Rossini's Almaviva, Lindoro, and Idreno in Semiramide, Mozart's Ferrando, Belmonte and Don Ottavio; Mephistopheles in Prokofiev's Fiery Angel, Verdi's Duke, Pinkerton and the Italian Singer in Rosenkavalier.

MONTALVO, Marisol; American singer (soprano); b. 1970. *Education:* Zürich Opera Studio, Manreo College of Music. *Career:* appearances with Dortmund Opera as Euridice, Flowermaiden in Parsifal and

Sulamith in Goldmark's Königin von Saba; Sang Rossini's Elvira at Chautauqua, Mozart's Barbarina at Sarasto and Musetta in La Bohème for Castel Vocal Arts; Bizet's Frasquita and Nannetta in Falstaff for Regina Opera; Echo in Ariadne auf Naxos and Mozart's Despina in Brooklyn; Susanna for New Rochelle Opera; Season 1999–2000 with Esmeralda in The Bartered Bride at Glyndebourne, Marie in Lortzing's Zar and Zimmermann, Gretel, Micaela in Carmen, and Suzel in Mascagni's L'Amico Fritz. *Address:* c/o Théâtre du Châtelet, 2 rue Edouard Colonne, 75001 Paris, France.

MONTARSOLO, Paolo; singer (bass) and producer; b. 16 March 1925, Portici, Naples, Italy. *Education:* studied with Enrico Conti in Naples and at La Scala Opera School. *Career:* debut, La Scala 1954; Guest appearances in Italy in operas by Rossini, Donizetti, Wolf-Ferrari and Mozart; Bergamo 1955, in a revival of Donizetti's Rita; Verona 1956; Glyndebourne Festival from 1957, as Mustafà in L'Italiana in Algeri, Selim in Il Turco in Italia, and Mozart's Osmin, Leporello and Don Alfonso; Florence, 1966, in Luisa Miller; Deutsche Oper am Rhein, Düsseldorf, 1973; Paris Opéra 1977, as Don Magnifico in La Cenerentola; Geneva Opera 1984, in L'Italiana in Algeri; Engagements in Moscow, Lisbon, New York, Naples and Rio de Janeiro; Sang Don Magnifico at the Berlin Staatsoper, 1987; Mustafà at Covent Garden, debut 1988; Salzburg Festival 1988–89, as Mozart's Bartolo and Don Magnifico; Staged and sang Don Pasquale at the Dallas Opera, 1989, Covent Garden, 1990; Sang Donizetti's Dulcamara at the Royal Opera, 1992; Engaged in Manon Lescaut at the 1997 Glyndebourne Festival. *Recordings:* La Cenerentola; Il Barbiere di Siviglia; Rita and Viva La Mamma; La Serva Padrona; Madama Butterfly.

MONTÉ, Ruth; Concert Harpsichordist, Organist and Pianist; b. 3 Dec. 1958, Galatzi, Romania; m. Noel Monté, 26 Oct 1986. *Education:* Summa cum laude, Academy of Music, Bucharest; Juilliard School of Music, New York; Studies with Rozalyn Tureck, Trevor Pinnock, John Weaver, Peter Husford, Frederick Neemann, Peter Williams, Lukas Foss. *Career:* Debut: Bucharest, Romania, 1973; Bucharest, Romania, 1977, Weimar, Germany, 1978; Television and radio appearances in Romania; Lecturer, Performer, Bach on Harpsichord, Piano, Organ in North America; Lecturer, Performance, 50th Anniversary of the UN, New York Academy of Sciences; mem, Chamber Music America; Early Music and Gramophone. *Recordings:* Integral of Bach's Keyboard Music on Harpsichord, Piano and Organ. *Honours:* Laureate, National Youth Music Festival, Romania, 1973. *Address:* 923 Fifth Avenue #17B, New York, NY 10021, USA.

MONTEBELLO, Benedetto; Conductor; b. 20 May 1964, Rome, Italy; m. Lorena Palumbo, 5 April 1997. *Education:* 1st class degree as Music Historian, La Sapienza University, Rome; Graduated as Guitarist, Bandmaster, Composer and Conductor, 1st class degree, S Cecilia Musical Conservatory, Rome; Specialist courses in Conducting with G Kuhn and D Gatti. *Career:* Debut: Conducted Beethoven's 1st Piano Concerto and 2nd Symphony, Anzio International Festival, 1989; Has conducted major orchestras including Radio Sofia Symphony Orchestra, Burgas National Orchestra, Oradea National Philharmonic Orchestra, Oltenia Philharmonic Orchestra, Craiova, S Cecilia National Academy Symphonic Orchestra, in Italy and abroad; Conducted premiere of G Guaccero's Salmo Metropolitano for large orchestra, based on P P Pasolini's texts, on 20th anniversary of Pasolini's death; Recent performances include Stravinsky's Histoire du Soldât, Ibert's Flute Concerto, Brahms' 1st Symphony, Chopin's 1st and 2nd Piano Concertos, Mussorgsky's Pictures at an Exhibition; Teacher of Conducting, U Giordano Conservatory of Music, Foggia. *Recordings:* Conductor, complete works of G Guaccero; Ennio Morricone's 3rd Concerto for Guitar, Marimba and Orchestra, with S Cecilia National Academy Symphonic Orchestra. *Contributions:* Musical articles in national newspapers; Encyclopaedic items on Treccani. *Honours:* Winner, Rinaldi Prize for Conductors, 1995. *Address:* Via Segesta No. 51, 00179 Rome, Italy.

MONTEFUSCO, Licinio; Singer (baritone); b. 30 Oct. 1936, Milan, Italy. *Education:* studied in Milan. *Career:* debut, Teatro Nuovo, Milan, 1961 as Zurga in Les Pêcheurs de Perles; sang Renato in Un Ballo in Maschera at Florence, 1963, followed by appearances throughout Italy, notably at the Teatro Regio Turin; guest appearances at the Vienna Staatsoper, 1964–, Deutsch Oper Berlin, 1966–; US debut, Philadelphia, 1965; La Scala, Milan, 1970 as Montfort in I Vespri Siciliani; sang at Monte Carlo, 1967–68, Brussels and Strasbourg, 1972–74, Verona, 1972 as Amonasro, Marseilles, 1979; sang Francesco Foscari in I Due Foscari at Turin, 1984 and Posa in Don Carlos, 1985; other roles have included Verdi's Germont, Luna, Rigoletto, Macbeth, Carlos and Ford, Enrico in Lucia di Lammermoor, Alfonso in La Favorita, Marcello, Gérard and Valentin. *Address:* İstanbul Devlet Opera ve Balesi, Atatürk Kültür Merkezi, Taksim, 80124 Istanbul, Turkey.

MONTENEGRO, Roberto; Conductor; b. 18 Sept. 1956, Montevideo, Uruguay. *Education:* Hamburg Musikhochschule; Studied with Guido Santorsola, Gerhard Markson, Aldo Ceccato and Sergiu Celibidache. *Career:* Debut: Santa Barbara Festival Symphony Orchestra, California, 1985; Conducted the world premiere of Francisco Rodrico's Guitar Concerto with the Venezuelan National Orchestra, 1992, and world premiere of Cesar Cano's Piano Concerto with the Spanish National Orchestra, 1993; Teacher of masterclasses in Uruguay and Argentina, Italy (European Community Music High School) and Spain (Santiago de Compostela's International Conducting Masterclasses); Assistant to Aldo Ceccato in Hamburg and Hannover; Jury, Young Concert Artists, New York, USA; Artistic and Musical Director, SODRE, Uruguay, 1991–95; Guest Conductor: Spain, France, Argentina, Venezuela, Czech Republic, USA, Canada, Israel; Shira International Symphony Orchestra in Jerusalem Classical Winter Festival. *Honours:* Man of the Year, American Biographical Institute, 1993; Honorary Member, Young Concert Artists, 1994; Baron, Royal Order of the Bohemian Crown, 1995. *Address:* Avenida del Libertador 1684, Apt 1202, PO Box 1552, Montevideo, Uruguay. *Telephone:* (598–2) 900–5725. *Fax:* (598–2) 900–5725. *E-mail:* montenegrouy@yahoo.com.ar.

MONTGOMERY, Kathryn; Singer, (Soprano); b. 23 Sept. 1952, Canton, Ohio, USA. *Education:* Studied at the University of Bloomington, Indiana. *Career:* Debut: Bloomington 1972, as Elvira in Ernani; Sang at Norfolk from 1978 as Frasquita, and in the premiere of Musgrave's Christmas Carol; European debut at Cologne 1980, as Leonore in Fidelio; Sang at Cologne and Zürich 1980–82, Mannheim 1981–85; Guest engagements at Venice, Edinburgh, Barcelona and Brussels; Metropolitan Opera debut 1985, as Chrysothemis; Pretoria, South Africa, 1984 as Salome; Other roles include Wagner's Elsa, Senta and Sieglinde, Tosca, Donna Anna, Berg's Marie, Donna Elvira and the Empress in Die Frau ohne Schatten; Sang Aksinya in Lady Macbeth of Mtsensk at the Deutsche Oper Berlin, 1988; Frequent concert appearances. *Address:* c/o Deutsche Oper Berlin, Richard Wagnerstrasse 10, 1000 Berlin 1, Germany.

MONTGOMERY, Kenneth; Conductor; b. 28 Oct. 1943, Belfast, Ireland. *Education:* Royal Belfast Academical Institution; Royal College of Music, London. *Career:* Debut: Glyndebourne Festival 1967; Staff Conductor, Sadler's Wells, English National Opera 1967–70; Assistant Conductor, Bournemouth Symphony Orchestra and Sinfonietta from 1970; Conducted Weber's Oberon at Wexford, 1972; Strauss's Ariadne and Capriccio for Netherlands Opera, 1972, 1975; Director, Bournemouth Sinfonietta 1974–76; Covent Garden debut 1975, Le nozze di Figaro; Principal Conductor, Dutch Radio Orchestra from 1976; Musical Director, Glyndebourne Touring Opera 1975–76; Guest appearances with Welsh National Opera, Canadian Opera; Concert performance of Donizetti's Anna Bolena at Amsterdam, 1989; Hansel and Gretel for Netherlands Opera, 1990; Conducted Tosca and The Magic Flute for Opera Northern Ireland at Belfast, 1990; Season 1991 with Alcina for Vancouver Opera, Figaro in Belfast and The Passion of Jonathan Wade for the Monte Carlo Royal Opera (repeated at San Diego, 1996). *Honours:* Silver Medal, Worshipful Company of Musicians, 1963; Tagore Gold Medal, Royal College of Music, 1964. *Address:* c/o Robert Gilders Co, Enterprise House, 59–65 Upper Ground, London SE1 9 PQ, England.

MONTVIDAS, Edgaras; Singer (Tenor); b. 1975, Vilnius, Lithuania. *Education:* Kaunas Music school; Conservatory of Juozas Gruodis and Lithuanian Music Academy; Vilar Young Artists' Programme, Covent Garden, 2001. *Career:* Alfredo, and Donizetti's Arturo for Lithuanian National Opera; Nemorino on tour to Chicago; Concerts include Berlioz Te Deum, Mozart C Minor Mass and Liszt Coronation Mass; Covent Garden debut as Ruiz in Il Trovatore; Sang in Falla's La Vida Breve, London Proms 2002 and as Alfredo at Covent Garden; Engaged as Alfredo for GTO, 2003. *Honours:* Scholarships and Awards in Lithuania and elsewhere. *Address:* c/o Vilar Young Artists, Royal Opera, Covent Garden, London, WC2, England. *Telephone:* (20) 7240 1200. *Fax:* (20) 7212 9502.

MOODY, Howard; Conductor, Pianist and Composer; b. 7 May 1964, Salisbury, Wiltshire, England; m. Emily Blows, 2 d. *Education:* Chorister, Salisbury Cathedral School; Music Scholar, Canford School; Organ Scholar, New College, Oxford; Guildhall School of Music and Drama. *Career:* Artistic Director of the Sarum Chamber Orchestra, 1986–; Worked as conductor with many of the major British orchestras, Netherlands Radio Chorus, Opera Factory, Salisbury Festival Chorus; Keyboard Continuo player for John Eliot Gardiner's Bach 2000 pilgrimage. *Compositions:* Score for Station House Opera, funded by the Arts Council of Great Britain, 1997; Weigh Me The Fire, choral work commissioned by Southern Cathedrals Festival, 1997; Stage works for Bangladesh Festival, 1998 and English National Opera, 2000. *Recordings:* as pianist: Beethoven Cello Sonatas, with David Watkin (cello), recorded on original fortepianos, 1996; Francis Pott Cello Sonata, with David Watkin, 1997; (as conductor) John Surman's Proverbs and songs. *Honours:* FRCO, 1985. *Address:* The Song House, Ashdown Road, Forest Row, East Sussex, RH18 5BW.

MOODY, Ivan (William George); Composer; b. 11 June 1964, London, England; m. Susanna Simoes Diniz, 2 Sept 1989. *Education:* Royal Holloway College, London University; BMus, 1985; Studies with John Tavener, 1984–86. *Career:* Works performed and broadcast in the United Kingdom, Austria, Denmark, Portugal, Italy, Germany, Finland, Estonia, Netherlands, Brazil and USA; Lecturing for music festivals in the United Kingdom, Netherlands and Finland and courses in the United Kingdom and Portugal; Conducting of various choirs in Europe in Orthodox and Renaissance sacred repertoire; Works performed throughout East and West Europe, Brazil and USA. *Compositions include:* Lithuanian Songs, 1986; Cantigas de Amigo; Canticle at The Parting of The Soul; Burial Prayer; Miserere, 1988; Hymn of The Transfiguration; Lament for Christ, 1989; Liturgy of St John Chrysostom, 1991; Cantigas do Mar, 1991; Anamnisis; Hymn of Joseph of Arimathea; Hymn to Christ the Saviour, 1991; Vigil of the Angels, 1991; Passion and Resurrection, 1992; Fables, chamber opera, 1994; Elegia for baritone and ensemble, 1998; Apok-athilosis, Orthodox Vespers of Good Friday, 1999. *Recordings:* As Conductor: Ippolitov–Ivanov, Divine Liturgy, Ikon, Tavener, various works, Ikon. *Publications:* Editions of Renaissance polyphony for Mapa Mundi, 1989, 1991, Chester Music, 1990–, Fundacao Calouste Gulbenkian, 1991. *Address:* c/o Vanderbeek and Imrie Ltd, 15 Marvig, Lochs, Isle of Lewis HS2 9QP, Scotland.

MOOG, Robert Arthur, BS, PhD; American electrical engineer; b. 23 May 1934, Flushing, NY; s. of George Conrad Moog and Shirley Jacobs Moog; m. Ileana Grams; one s. three d.; one step-d. *Education:* Queen's Coll., New York, Columbia Univ., Cornell Univ. *Career:* founder and Pres. R. A. Moog Co. 1954, renamed Moog Music Inc. 1971–77, for the manufacture of electronic musical instruments; Ind. Consultant 1978–84; Vice-Pres. for new product research, Kurzweil Music Systems, Waltham, MA 1985–89; Research Prof. Univ. of NC at Asheville 1989–92; founder and Pres. Big Briar Inc., producing devices for the control of synthesizers 1978–2002; re-purchased rights to Moog Music brand, Chief Tech. Officer Moog Music 2002–; designer of synthisizers, including Moog synthesizer, Minimoog, Polymoog, pedal-operated Taurus system, Memory Moog, Monster Moog; Fellow Audio Engineering Soc.. *Honours:* Dr hc (Lycoming Coll.) 1975, (New York Polytech. Univ.) 1984, (Berkeley Coll. of Music Boston) 2002, (Univ. of the Arts, Philadelphia) 2003; Billboard Magazine Trendsetters Award 1970, NARAS Trustees' Award 1970, Audio Eng Soc. Silver Medal 1980, Seamus Award 1991, Polar Music Prize 2001, NARAS Technical Grammy Award 2002. *Address:* Moog Music, 554-C Riverside Drive, Asheville, NC 28801 (office); 332 Barnard Avenue, Asheville, NC 28804, USA (home). *Telephone:* (828) 251-0090 (office); (828) 254-2750 (home). *Fax:* (828) 254-6233 (office). *E-mail:* bobm@moogmusic.com (office). *Website:* www.moogmusic.com (office).

MOORE, Carman (Leroy); Composer and Conductor; b. 8 Oct. 1936, Lorain, Ohio, USA; Divorced, 2 s. *Education:* BS Music, Ohio State University, 1958; MS Music, Composition, Juilliard School of Music, 1966; Studied composition with Hall Overton, Luciano Berio, Vincent Persichetti. *Career:* Commissioned performances by New York Philharmonic, San Francisco Symphony, Rochester Philharmonic, The Chamber Music Society Of Lincoln Center; Performances by Cleveland Orchestra, Nexus Ensemble, Aeolian Chamber Players; Founder, Composer, Conductor, Skymusic Ensemble, 1978; Taught at Yale School of Music, Queens and Brooklyn Colleges, Manhattanville; Music Critic, Columnist, The Village Voice, 1966–76; Master Composer, Young Choreographers and Composers Project, American Dance Festival, 1986–. *Compositions:* Wildfires and Field Songs; Gospel Fuse; Hit: A Concerto for Percussion and Orchestra; Mass for the 21st Century; Concertos, The Theme is Freedom, for Skymusic Ensemble; Wild Gardens of the Loup Garou, and The Last Chance Planet opera; Paradise Lost, musical; Four Movements for A Five Toed Dragon for Orchestra and Chinese Instruments; Berenice Variations, for clarinet, piano, violin and violoncello; Love Notes to Central Park, mixed media for Skymusic Ensemble, 1996; Journey to Benares, musical, 1999; Gethsemane Park, opera, 1998; Mystery of Tao, chamber music, 2001; God of Peace, music theatre, 2002. *Recordings:* Youth in a Merciful House, Sextet, Folkways; Berenice: Variations on A Theme of G F Handel; Four Movements for A Fashionable 5-Toed Dragon, Hong Kong Trade Development Council; Lyrics to all songs on Felix Cavaliere, Bearsville. *Publications:* Somebody's Angel Child: The Story of Bessie Smith, 1970; Rockit. *Contributions:* Frequently to New York Times, Vogue, others. *Address:* 152 Columbus Avenue, 4R, New York, NY 10023, USA.

MOORE, Diana; Singer (Soprano); b. 1965, England. *Education:* University of Birmingham; Royal Academy of Music. *Career:* Concert appearances in the Saint Matthew Passion and Rossini's Petite Messe at St John's Smith Square; Fauré's La naissance de Venus with The Sixteen, Bach's B minor Mass at the Brighton Festival and La Resurrezione by Handel at Oslo (2001); Psalm 4 by Alexander Goehr

with the New London Chamber Choir and Still Life at the Penguin Café with the Royal Ballet; Janáček's The Diary of One Who Disappeared for English National Opera and in the Netherlands; Season 2001 with Armindo in Handel's Partenope at the Covent Garden Festival (Linbury Theatre) and Purcell's Dido under Trevor Pinnock; Bach's St Matthew Passion at the London Proms, 2002. *Address:* c/o English National Opera, St Martin's Lane, London WC2, England.

MOORE, Dorothy Rudd, BMus; American composer, teacher and singer; b. 4 June 1940, Wilmington, DE. *Education:* Howard High School, Wilmington School of Music, Howard Univ., Washington, DC, American Conservatory, Fontainebleau, France. *Career:* teacher, Harlem School of the Arts, New York 1965–66, New York Univ. 1969, Bronx Community Coll. 1971; private piano, voice, sight singing and ear training instructor, New York 1968–; founding mem., Soc. of Black Composers 1968–75; mem., New York State Council for the Arts 1988–90; Lucy Moten Fellowship 1963; American Music Center grant 1972; New York State Council on the Arts grant 1985; mem. Nat. Endowment for the Arts, Recording and Composers (panel mem. 1986–88), New York Women Composers, New York Singing Teachers' Asscn, American Composers' Alliance, BMI. *Compositions include:* Flight for piano 1956, Symphony No. 1 1962, Songs from the Rubaiyat 1962, Reflections for concert band 1962, Baroque Suite for unaccompanied violoncello 1964, Three Pieces for Violin and piano 1966, Modes for ensemble 1968, Moods for ensemble 1969, Lament for nine instruments 1969, Trio No. 1 1969, From the Dark Tower 1970, Dirge and Deliverance for cello 1970, Weary Blues 1972, Dream and Variations for piano 1974, Sonnets on Love, Rosebuds and Death 1975, In Celebration for chorus 1977, Night Fantasy for clarinet 1978, A Little Whimsy for piano 1978, Frederick Douglass (opera) 1981, Transcension (I Have Been to the Mountaintop) for chamber orchestra 1985, Flowers of Darkness 1988, Voices From The Light for chorus 1997. *Address:* 33 Riverside Drive, 16A, New York, NY 10023, USA.

MOORE, Jonathan; Actor, Writer and Stage Director; b. 1960, England. *Career:* Worked in the Theatre and for Television; Co-librettist and Director of Greek by Mark-Anthony Turnage, premiered at the 1988 Munich Biennale and seen later at the Edinburgh Festival, at the London Coliseum, 1990, directed the version on BBC television; Directed Henze's Elegy for Young Lovers, La Fenice, Venice; Wrote the Libretto for Horse Opera, a television film opera for Channel Four, Music by Stewart Copeland; Staged the premiere of Hans Jürgen von Bose's 63 Dream Palace at Munich, 1990 and the premiere of Michael Berkeley's Baa Baa Black Sheep, Opera North, 1993; British Premiere of Schnitke's Life With an Idiot, ENO London Coliseum, 1995; Further Projects: Libretto and Direction of premiere East and West, by Ian McQueen (Almeida 1995); Libretto and Direction of premiere Mottke the Thief by Bernd Franke, Bonn Opera, 1998; The Nose (Shostakovich), ENO London Coliseum, 1996; Staged the premiere of Macmillan's Inès de Castro, Edinburgh, 1996 and subsequent revivals including a filming by BBS TV and Porto Festival;Directed world premieres of Die Versicherung by Jan Muller-Wieland, Darmstadt, 1999, and Facing Goya by Michael Nyman, Santiago del Compostella and Valencia, 2000; Directed and translated The Magic Flute for Scottish Opera 2002/03 and Three Ways of Dying with Daniel Hope and Uri Caine at the Feldkirch Festival;. *Honours:* Best Libretto Award, Munich, for Greek, 1988; Best Director Award, for 63 Dream Palace, Munich, 1990; Royal Philharmonic Society Award and the Midem Award, Cannes, 1991; Nominated for Olivier Award, for Greek, ENO Coliseum, 1991; BMW Award, for Die Vier Himmelsrichtungen, Munich, 1994. *Current Management:* Ingpen & Williams Ltd, 7 St George's Court, 131 Putney Bridge Road, London, SW15 2PA, England.

MOORE, Kermit; Cellist, Conductor and Composer; b. 11 March 1929, Akron, Ohio, USA; m. Dorothy Rudd, 20 Dec 1964. *Education:* BMus, Cleveland Institute of Music, 1951; MA, New York University, 1952; Paris Conservatory, 1953–56. *Career:* Debut: New York Town Hall, 1949; Cello recitals in Paris, Brussels, Vienna, Cologne, Hamburg, Munich, Geneva, Basel, Amsterdam, Tokyo, Seoul, New York, Boston, Chicago and San Francisco; Guest Conductor of Detroit Symphony, Brooklyn Philharmonic, Symphony of New World; Festival Orchestra at the United Nations; Berkeley (California) Symphony; Dance Theater of Harlem; Opera Ebony. *Compositions:* Music for cello and piano; Music for Viola, percussion and piano; Many Thousand Gone, strings, chorus and percussion; Music for timpani and orchestra; Music for flute and piano; Five Songs for DRM. *Recordings:* Brahms: Sonata in E Minor, Dorothy Rudd Moore; Dirge and Deliverance, Performance Records; Mendelssohn, Sonata in D Major, Kermit Moore: Music for Cello and Piano, Performance Records; Karl Weigl Sonata, Love Song and Wild Dance, Orion records. *Publications:* Chapter in The Music Makers, 1979. *Current Management:* Rud/Mor Corporation. *Address:* 33 Riverside Drive, New York, NY 10023, USA.

MORA, Barry; Singer (Baritone); b. 1944, New Zealand. *Education:* Studied in London with Otakar Kraus and John Matheson. *Career:*

Sang at Gelsenkirchen, 1977–79 as: Verdi's Posa and Luna; Mozart's Speaker and Figaro; Sang at Frankfurt from 1979 as Tamare, in Die Gezeichneten, and Ford, in Falstaff; Festival Hall debut, 1979 as Schumann's Faust; Covent Garden Debut 1980 as Donner, in Das Rheingold; Scottish Opera in 1983 as the Traveller, in Death in Venice; Welsh National Opera from 1986 as Donner, Gunther, The Forester in The Cunning Little Vixen and Frank in Die Fledermaus, 1991; Netherlands Opera, 1991; Engagements at Deutsche Oper Berlin, Zürich Opera, Aachen, Düsseldorf, Barcelona, Wellington and Canterbury, New Zealand; Also sang in 1992: Rosenkavalier, Sydney; La Traviata, Barcelona; Parsifal, Frankfurt; Così fan tutte, Wellington; Un Ballo in Maschera, Brussels; Concert repertoire includes, Puccini's Messa di Gloria, Bach's B minor Mass and St John Passion; Carmina Burana, Stravinsky's Canticum Sacrum, Lieder eines fahrenden Gesellen by Mahler, Lulu at Buenos Aires, Così fan tutte at Barcelona Opera, La Cenerentola, Australian Opera, 1994 and for Opera New Zealand; Current roles with Australian Opera as Dr Schön, in Lulu, Alidoro, in La Cenerentola; Tales of Hoffmann, 1995; Wellington Opera: Ping, in Turandot, 1994; Balstrode, in Peter Grimes, 1995; Father, in Hansel and Gretel, 1995; Season 1999 at Sydney as the Doctor in Wozzeck and in Auckland as Puccini's Sharpless. *Address:* c/o Jennifer Eddy Management, Suite 11, The Clivedon, 596 St Kilda Road, Melbourne, Vicotira 3004, Australia.

MORAN, Robert; Composer; b. 8 Jan. 1937, Denver, Colorado, USA. *Education:* Studied with Hans Erich Apostel and Roman Haubenstock-Ramati in Vienna, Luciano Berio and Darius Milhaud at Mills College. *Career:* Founded and co-directed the New Music Ensemble, San Francisco Conservatory; Performances throughout USA and Europe as Pianist; Lecturer on contemporary music. *Compositions:* Silver and The Circle of Messages, for chamber orchestra, 1970; Emblems of Passage for 2 orchestras, 1974; Angels of Silence for viola and chamber orchestra, 1975; The Last Station of the Albatross, for 1–8 instruments, 1978; Survivor from Darmstadt, 1984; Mixed media works and stage works including Let's Build a Nut House, chamber opera, 1969; Erlösung dem Erlöser, music drama, 1982; LeipzigerKerzenspiel, 1985; The Juniper Tree, 1985; Desert of Roses, 1992; From the Towers of the Moon, 1992; Dracula Diary, 1994; Night Passage, opera, 1995; Remember Him to Me: an Opera, 1996; Entretien Mysterieux, for orchestra, 1996; 4 Partitions for violin and orchestra, 1997; Voce della Fontana, for soprano and ensemble, 1998. *Address:* c/o BMI, 320 West 57th Street, New York, NY 10019, USA.

MORAVEC, Antonin; Violinist and Composer; b. 29 April 1928, Brno, Czech Republic; m. Karla Moravcova, 15 July 1950. *Education:* Conservatory of Brno; Janáček Academy of Musical Art, Brno; Moscow Tchaikovsky Conservatory. *Career:* Prof., Music Academies and Universities: Janáček Academy, Brno, Music Academy Prague, Mastercourses at Kunitachi Music Academy in Tokyo, Tchaikovsky Conservatory in Moscow, Mozarteum in Salzburg, Castle of Pommersfelden in Germany; Member, 35 juries of International Violin Competitions; World-wide soloist of violin concertos. *Compositions:* Snowdrop for Leni Bernstein for violin and piano; Violin Concerto, 2003; Cadenzas for 18 Violin Concertos by Viotti, Haydn, Mozart, Pagannini, Beethoven, Brahms, Slavik and Szymanowski. *Recordings:* Violin Sonatas by Martinů, Shostakowich, Prokofiev; Piano Trio by M Istvan. *Address:* Taussigova 1152, 182 00 Prague 8, Czech Republic.

MORAVEC, Paul; Composer, Professor of Music, Electronic Music Synthesist and Conductor; b. 2 Nov. 1957, Buffalo, NY, USA. *Education:* BA magna cum laude, Music, Harvard University, Cambridge, Massachusetts, 1980; MA Music Composition, 1982, DMA Music Composition, 1987, Columbia University, New York. *Career:* Assistant Professor of Music, Dartmouth College, Hanover, New Hampshire. *Compositions:* Missa Miserere, 1981; Ave Verum Corpus, 1981; Pater Noster, 1981; Sacred Songs, 1982; Three Anthems, 1983; Songs for Violin and Piano, 1983; Music for Chamber Ensemble, 1983; Wings, 1983; Spiritdance, 1984; Innocent Dreamers, 1985; Four Transcendent Love Songs, 1986; Prayers and Praise, 1986; Whispers, 1986; The Kingdom Within, 1987; 3 string quartets, 1986, 1990, 1992; Aubade for strings, 1990; Piano Concerto, 1992; Violin Concerto, 1994; Cello Concerto, 1998; Mood Swings for Piano trio, 1998; Fire/Ice/Air, dramatic cantata, 1998; Tempest Fantasy for solo clarinet and piano trio (Pulitzer Prize) 2004. *Current Management:* JL Music Productions, 250 West 100th Street Suite 104, NY 10025, USA. *Address:* c/o Music Department, Dartmouth College, Hanover, NH 03755, USA.

MORAWETZ, Oskar; Composer and Professor; b. 17 Jan. 1917, Czechoslovakia; m. 1958, 1 s., 1 d. *Career:* Professor of Music, University of Toronto; Orchestral compositions performed frequently by Canadian Orchestras, Canadian Broadcasting Corporation and in USA, Europe and Australia; Among major orchestras abroad, his compositions have been performed by the Philadelphia, Chicago, Detroit, Minneapolis, Indianapolis, Washington and Aspen Festival Orchestras in USA and major orchestras in France, Sweden, Norway, Belgium, Netherlands,

Italy, Czechoslovakia and Greece; Conductors who have programmed his works include, William Steinberg, Zubin Mehta, Karel Ancerl, Kubelik, Walter Susskind, Seiji Ozawa, Adrian Boult, Izler Solomon, Sixten Ehrling and Ernest MacMillan; Artists such as Glenn Gould, Rudolf Firkusny and Anton Kuerti have premiered his piano compositions and Maureen Forrester, Jon Vickers, Louis Marshall, Dorothy Maynor, Louis Quilico and Lillian Sukis have included compositions in programmes in Canada, USA, Europe and Australia. *Compositions:* Memorial to Martin Luther King for cello and orchestra; Sinfonietta For Winds and Percussion, From The Diary of Anne Frank; Fantasy in D; Piano Concerto; Clarinet Concerto, 1989; Tribute to W.A. Mozart, string quartet, 1990; Improvisations of Inventions by J. S. Bach, string quartet, 1992; The Whale's Lament, for piano, 1993. *Recordings:* Many of his compositions have been recorded by various record companies. *Address:* c/o OSA, Cs armady 20, 160-56 Prague 6, Bubenec, Czech Republic.

MORAWSKI, Jerzy; Musicologist; b. 9 Sept. 1932, Warsaw, Poland; m. Katarzyna. *Education:* Theory, 1957, Piano, 1961, Warsaw Conservatory; MA, Institute of Musicology, Warsaw University, 1958; PhD, Institute of Arts, Polish Academy of Sciences, 1970; D habil, Jagiellonian University, Kraków, 1997. *Career:* Assistant, Department of Theory and History of Music, 1956–70, Doctor, Head, History Music Section, 1970–79, Vice-Director, Institute of Arts and Polish Academy of Sciences, 1979–81; Lecturer, Warsaw University, 1968–70; Academy of Catholic Theology, Warsaw, 1970–73; Jagiellonian University, Kraków, 1971–82, 1999–2000; mem, Former Vice-Secretary and President, Polish Composers' Union, Musicological Section. *Publications include:* Research on Liturgical Recitative in Poland, 1973, 1986, 1992, 1995; The Problems of the Tropes Techniques, 1976, 1979; Polish Hymns, 1991; Two Unfamiliar Tonaria from Silesian Antiphonaries dating from the Thirteenth and Fourteenth Centuries, 2002; Editor-in-Chief of serial publications: Monumenta Musicae in Polonia and Musica Medii Aevi; Books: Musical Lyric Poetry in Medieval Poland, 1973; Theory of Music in the Middle Ages, 1979; Liturgical Recitative in Medieval Poland, 1996; Editor, Musica Antiqua Polonica: Anthology, The Middle Ages, 1972; The Rhymed History of St Jadwiga, 1977; The Rhymed History of St Adalbert, 1979; The Polish Cistercian Sequences, 1984; Jan Stefani's Six Partitas for Wind Instruments, 1993; Sursum Corda: Presentation of a Motif, 1999. *Contributions:* Professional publications. *Address:* ul Dluga 24 m 43, 00-238 Warsaw, Poland.

MORDKOVITCH, Lydia; Concert Violinist; b. 1950, Saratov, USSR. *Education:* Studied at the Odessa Conservatory and with David Distrakh in Moscow. *Career:* Emigrated to Israel 1974, later resident in London; British debut 1979, with the Halle Orchestra under Walter Susskind; Appearances with the Philharmonia, London Symphony, London, Royal and Liverpool Philharmonics, Scottish National, City of Birmingham Symphony and all the BBC Symphony Orchestras; US debut with the Chicago Symphony under Solti; Returning to play the Brahms Concerto with the Philadelphia Orchestra under Muti; Promenade Concerts debut 1985, returning 1988 with Szymanowski's 2nd Concerto; Further engagements in Finland, Norway, Italy and the Canary Islands; Conductors include Kurt Sanderling, Stanislav Skrowaczevski, Charles Groves and Marek Janowski. *Recordings:* Shostakovich Concertos with the Scottish National under Neeme Järvi; Complete works for solo violin by Bach; Concertos by Bruch, Prokofiev and Brahms; Moeran Concerto with the Ulster Orchestra under Vernon Handley, Chandos; CD: Solo Sonatas by Ysaÿe. *Honours:* Prize Winner, National Young Musicians Competition, Kiev; Long-Thibaud International Competition, Paris; Gramophone Award for Best Concerto Recording, 1990; Diaspason d'or, France, for Prokofiev Concertos.

MOREHEN, John Manley, JP, MA, PhD, FRCO (Chm), FRCCO, FRSA; British musicologist, organist and conductor; b. 3 Sept. 1941, Gloucester, England; m. Marie Catherine Jacobus 1969; one s. one d. *Education:* Clifton Coll., Bristol, Royal Coll. of Church Music, Croydon, New Coll., Oxford, Coll. of Church Musicians, Washington, DC, USA and King's Coll. Cambridge. *Career:* Asst Dir of Music, St Clement Danes Church, Strand, Hampstead Parish Church, London; keyboard player, Hampstead Choral Soc., Martin Sidwell Choir, London Bach Orchestra 1964–67; Lecturer, Coll. of Church Musicians, Washington Cathedral, American Univ., Washington, DC 1967–68; sub-organist, St George's Chapel, Windsor Castle 1968–72; Lecturer in Music, Univ. of Nottingham 1973–82, Sr Lecturer 1982–89, Prof. of Music 1989–, Head of the School of Humanities 1998–2001; numerous broadcasts as organist, speaker and conductor 1964–; recital tours of Europe and N America; many presentations on computer applications in music at conferences in the UK, USA, Canada, France and the Netherlands; Freeman of the City of London and Liveryman of the Worshipful Company of Musicians 1991; Justice of the Peace, Nottinghamshire 1991; Pres., E Midlands Choirs Charitable Trust 1993–2000; panel mem., Humanitites Research Board 1994–97; HEFCE Subject Assessor, Music 1994–95; Music Adviser to the Commonwealth Scholarship Commission 1996–2000;

Pres., Incorporated Soc. of Musicians 2003–04. *Recordings:* with choirs of New Coll., Oxford and Hampstead Parish Church. *Publications:* numerous critical edns of 16th- and 17th-century English and Italian choral and instrumental music, including vols in the series Early English Church Music, The Byrd Edition, The English Madrigalists, Recent Researches in the Music of the Renaissance; contrib. to most major British and American musical journals and to New Grove Dictionary of Music 1980, 2002, Die Musik in Geschichte und Gegenwart, New Dictionary of Nat. Biography 2004. *Address:* Chestnut Barn, Syerston Hall Park, Newark, Nottinghamshire NG23 5NL, England (home). *Telephone:* (1636) 525068 (office). *E-mail:* John@ Morehen.fsworld.co.uk (home); John.Morehen@Nottingham.ac.uk (office). *Website:* www.nottingham.ac.uk/Music/Morehen.html (office).

MOREL, Francois; Composer; b. 14 March 1926, Montreal, Canada. *Education:* Studied piano with private teacher; Studied composition with Clude Champagne, Conservatoire de Muique, Montreal. *Career:* Working for Radio-Canada writing background music for theatre, radio and television, 1956–81; Professor of composition, orchestration and analysis; l'Ecole de musique, Universite Laval, Quebec City; President of publishing firm, Les Editions Quebec-Musique, Montreal; Received commissions for compositions from Canadian Broadcasting Corporation, First International Festival of Contemporary Music for Wind Symphony Orchestra, Edmonton Symphony Orchestra; McGill Chamber Orchestra, Societe de Musique Contemporaine du Quebec, Guitar Society of Toronto 1976; Olympic Games Committee; Montreal International Competition among others. *Compositions:* Orchestral: Antiphonie 1953; Boreal 1959; Departs 1968–69, Diptyque 1948, revised 1955–56; Esquisse 1947–47; L'Etoile noire 1961–62; Iikkii 1971; Jeux 1976; Litanies 1955–56, revised 1970; Melisma 1980; Le mythe de la roche percee 1960–61; Neumes despace et reliefs 1967; Prismes-anamorphoses 1967; Radiance 1970–72; Requiem for Winds 1962–63; Rituel de l'espace 1958–59; Sinfonia 1963; Spirale 1956; Trajectoire 1967; Instrumental Ensemble: Cassation 1954; Etude en forme de toccate 1965; Quatuor No. 1, 1952, No. 2, 1962–63; Quintette pour cuivres 1962; Rhythmologue 1970; Lumières sculptèes, for wind and 3 percussion, 1992; Les éphemères, for 4 horns and tuba, 1995; Et le crepuscule se trouva libre, for orchestra, 1996; Metamporphoses, for orchestra, 1998; Symphonie pur cuivres 1956. Instrumental Solo and Vocal Solos. *Address:* c/o CAPAC Canada, PRS Ltd, Berners Street, London W1, England.

MORELLI, Adriana; Singer (Soprano); b. 1954, Italy. *Education:* Studied at Regiio Calabria. *Career:* Debut: Spoleto 1978, as Musetta; Sang Sophie in Werther at Bergamo 1979, Lauretta in Gianni Schicchi at Lucca, 1981; Further engagements as Butterfly and Mimi at Spoleto and Lille, Elisabeth de Valois at Dijon, Amsterdam, Amelia, Un Ballo in Maschera, at Trieste; Sang Margherita in Mefistofele and Tosca at Genoa, 1987–88, Giorgetta in Il Tabarro at Florence 1988 and Maria Stuarda at Piacenza, 1990; La Scala debut, 1990, as Nedda in Pagliacci; Sang Silvia in Mascagni's Zanetta at Florence, 1996; Sang Puccini's Giorgetta at Verona, 2000; Stage and concert appearances in South America. *Address:* c/o Teatro alla Scala, Via Filodrammatici 2, Milan, Italy.

MORETTI, Isabelle Cécile Andrée; French harpist; b. 5 May 1964, Lyons. *Education:* studied with Germaine Lorenzini. *Career:* teacher, Conservatoire Nat. Supérieur de Paris 1995–; recital and masterclass tours of USA and Republic of Korea 2004, Estonia and Latvia 2005. *Recordings include:* concertos by Boieldieu, Parish Alvars, Rodrigo, and Ginastera, Debussy: Sonata for flute, viola and harp, Chansons de Bilitis, Prélude à l'après-midi d'un faune. *Honours:* Conservatoire National Supérieur de Paris Premier Prix 1983, first prize in Munich 1983, Bordeaux 1984, Geneva 1986, winner Israel Harp Contest 1988, Nouvelle Académie du Disque Grand Prix 1995, Victoire de la Musique Classique 1996. *Address:* La Hillière, 44470 Thouaré sur Loire, France. *Telephone:* 2-40-77-58-46. *Fax:* 2-40-77-58-46.

MORGAN, Arwel Huw; Singer (Bass); b. 1950, Ystalyfera, Swansea, Wales. *Career:* Joined the chorus of Welsh National Opera in 1978; Solo roles in Wales have included Don Fernando, Fidelio; Ladas in The Greek Passion; Angelotti in Tosca; Hobson, Peter Grimes; The Parson in The Cunning Little Vixen; Created the role of Maskull for New Celtic Opera's Voyage to Arcturus; English National Opera from 1987 in Lady Macbeth of Mtsensk and The Cunning Little Vixen; Toured the United Kingdom 1988, as Osmin in Opera 80s Die Entführung aus dem Serail; Season 1992 as Leporello, and as Carl Olsen, in Weill's Street Scene for ENO; Fabrizio in The Thieving Magpie for Opera North; Sang Leporello in a new production of Don Giovanni for Welsh National Opera, 1996; Zuniga in Carmen at the London Coliseum, 1998; Sang Britten's Snug at the Teatro Nazionale, Rome, 1999. *Recordings:* Polonius in Hamlet by Ambroise Thomas, conducted by Richard Bonynge. *Current Management:* Ingpen & Williams Ltd, 7 St George's Court, 131 Putney Bridge Road, London, SW15 2PA, England.

MORGAN, Beverly; Singer (Soprano); b. 17 March 1952, Hanover, New Hampshire, USA. *Education:* Mt Holyoke College, 1969–71; BMus, Honours, New England Conservatory of Music, 1971–73; MMus, Honours, 1973–75, New York. *Career:* Debut: Recital debut as winner of Concert Artists Guild Award, 1978; Operatic Appearances with Wiener Staatsoper, San Francisco Opera, Netherlands Opera, Opera Company of Boston, Pittsburgh, Omaha and Philadelphia Operas, Kennedy Center in Washington and Scottish National Opera; Sang in the premiere of Glass's Satyagraha at Amsterdam, 1980, and in the US Premiere of Zimmermann's Die Soldaten, Boston, 1982; Other appearances in Bernstein's A Quiet Place at La Scala and in Vienna at Santa Fe in the US Premieres of Henze's English Cat and Penderecki's Die schwarze Maske, 1985, 1988; Scottish Opera as Berg's Lulu, 1987; Other roles include Tatiana and Violetta at Seattle and Fusako in Henze's Das Verratene Meer, Berlin and Milan; Concert appearances with Boston Symphony, San Francisco Symphony, Chamber Society of Lincoln Center, American String Quartet, Marlboro Music Festival, American Composers Orchestra; Performances under Leonard Bernstein, Seiji Ozawa and Herbert Blomstedt. *Recordings:* DGG. *Current Management:* Columbia Artists Management Incorporated, NY, USA. *Address:* c/o Crittenden Division, Columbia Artists Management Incorporated, 165 West 57th Street, NY 10019, USA.

MORGAN, David S.; Composer and Conductor; b. 18 May 1932, Ewell, Surrey, England; m. Crisetta Macleod (divorced), one s. two d.; m. 2nd Una Grimshaw. *Education:* Sydney Grammar School, Sydney Conservatorium, 1946–52; Study in London with Norman Del Mar and Matyas Seiber, 1955–56; BMus, University of Durham, 1970. *Career:* Cor anglais player in the Sydney Symphony Orchestra; Composer and Arranger with the South Australian Department of Education, 1975–93; Commissions from the Adelaide Chamber Orchestra and Musica da Camera, among others. *Compositions include:* 6 Symphonies (1949–99); Mass in B Major, 1948; Horn Concerto, 1957; Violin Concerto, 1957; Concerto for Viola and Strings, 1958; Concerto Grosso No. 2 for string trio and string orchestra, 1978; Sinfonia for 11 string players, 1978; Loss for 4 percussion, 1982; Suite for String Orchestra, Percussion and Piano, 1985; Fun and Games for 4 percussion, 1986; Jubilee Overture, 1986; Harpsichord Sonata, 1992; Concerto for Orchestra No. 1, 1993, No. 2, 1994; Trumpet Concerto, 1995; 2 Harpsichord Concertos. *Address:* 31 Forth Street, Nuriootpa, South Australia, 5355, Australia.

MORGAN, Michael (DeVard); Conductor; b. 17 Sept. 1957, Washington, DC, USA. *Education:* Oberlin College Conservatory of Music; Berkshire Music Centre, Tanglewood, 1977. *Career:* Debut: Operatic, Vienna State Opera, 1982; Apprentice Conductor, Buffalo Philharmonic, 1979–80; Assistant Conductor, St Louis Symphony, 1980–81; Assistant Conductor, Chicago Symphony, 1986–; Guest Conductor: New York and Warsaw Philharmonics, Vienna, Baltimore, Houston, New Orleans Symphony Orchestras; National Symphony, Washington; Deutsche Staatsoper, Berlin; Summer Opera Theater, Washington, DC; Orchestras in Italy, Denmark and Netherlands. *Honours:* 1st prize, Hans Swarowsky International Conductors Competition Vienna, 1980; Prizes in Conducting Competitions at Baltimore, 1974; San Remo, 1975; Copenhagen, 1980. *Current Management:* Sheldon Soffer Management Inc, NY; Alex Saron, Blaricum, Netherlands, Europe. *Address:* 1220 Decatur Street, NW, Washington, DC 20011, USA.

MORGAN, Morris; Singer (Baritone); b. 26 Sept. 1940, Berlin, Germany. *Education:* Studied in Düsseldorf, Cologne and Wiesbaden, 1955–71. *Career:* Sang at Cologne in the 1965 premiere of Die Soldaten by Zimmermann; Kiel Opera 1965–68, notably in the 1965 premiere of Reimann's Traumspiel; Wiesbaden 1968–71, Bern 1971–79, Freiburg 1978–81; Further engagements at Düsseldorf, Mannheim, Stuttgart, Bremen, Saarbrucken, Lubeck and Klagenfurt; Returned to Berne 1985, as Marcello in La Bohème; Concert appearances in baroque music and as Lieder singer. *Recordings include:* Die Soldaten; Zemlinsky's Kleider Machen Leute; Israel in Egypt and Carmina Burana. *Address:* Stadttheater Bern, Nageligasse 1, 3011 Bern, Switzerland.

MORGNY, Bengt-Ola; Singer (Tenor); b. 1959, Sweden. *Education:* Studied in Gothenburg and Berlin. *Career:* Soloist with the Deutsche Oper Berlin from 1986, including premiere of Das Schloss by Reimann, Deutsche Oper Berlin, 1992; Oper de Stadt Köln from 1993 as Mozart's Basilio and Curzio, Jacquino in Fidelio and Wenzel in The Bartered Bride; Royal Opera House, Copenhagen since 1996 as Goro (Butterfly), Pong (Turandot) Brighella (Ariadne), Dr Cajus (Falstaff), Pict von Piels (Le Grand Macabre), Arbace (Idomeneo); Festival at Drottningholm from 1989, as Pedrillo in Die Entführung, Azor in Zémire et Azor by Grétry, and in Soliman II by J M Kraus; Guest appearances at Oslo, Stockholm, Hamburg, Munich, Paris, Monte Carlo and Geneva as Pong (Turandot), Der Bucklige (Frau ohne Schatten), Brussels, Liège, Tel-Aviv and Sarajevo as Harlequin and Soldier (Der Kaiser von Atlantis); Sang Mozart's Pedrillo at Spoleto, 1998; The Scourge of Hyacinth, production of Robert Wilson and Tania Leon, Geneva, Nancy, St Polten (Austria), Teatro Bellas Artes, Mexico City, 2001. *Recordings include:*

Zemlinsky's Der Kreidekreis; Mörder, Hoffnung der Frauen, Hindemith; Das Schloss, Reimann; Video of Die Entführung; Turandot, as Pong, Copenhagen, G Sinopoli; The Handmaid's Tale, P Rouders, The Doctor, CD. *Address:* Det Konglige Teater, Postboks 2185, 1017 Copenhagen, Denmark. *E-mail:* morgny@home.se.

MORINO, Giuseppe; Singer (Tenor); b. 18 Aug. 1950, Assisi, Italy. *Career:* Debut: Spoleto, 1981, as Gounod's Faust; Festival of Martina Franca, 1986, as Idreno in Semiramide; Season 1987 as Admète in Gluck's Alceste at La Scala, Pylades in Rossini's Ermione at Pesaro and the Duke of Mantua at the Vienna Staatsoper; Donizetti's Edgardo at Naples, 1989, Meyerbeer's Raoul at Novara, 1993; Astrologer in Rimsky's Golden Cockerel at Rome, 1995; Other roles include Tebaldo in Bellini's Capuleti, Rossini's Almaviva, Donizetti's Gianni di Parigi and Gounod's Romeo. *Address:* c/o Teatro dell'Opera, Piazza B Gigli 8, 00184 Rome, Italy.

MØRK, Truls; Norwegian cellist; b. 25 April 1961, Bergen; s. of John Mørk and Turid Otterbech; two s. one d. *Education:* studied under his father, with Frans Helmerson at Swedish Radio Music School, in Austria with Heinrich Schiff and in Moscow with Natalia Shakovskaya. *Career:* debut, BBC Promenade Concerts 1989; has since appeared with leading European, American and Australian orchestras, including the Berlin Philharmonic, New York Philharmonic, Philadelphia Symphony, Cincinnati Philharmonic, Rotterdam Philharmonic, London Philharmonic, Pittsburgh Symphony, City of Birmingham Symphony, Orchestre de Paris, NHK Symphony, Royal Concertgebouw and Cleveland, Los Angeles and Gewandhaus Symphony Orchestras; regular appearances at int. chamber music festivals; founder Int. Chamber Music Festival in Stavanger, Artistic Dir–2003. *Recordings include:* Schumann, Elgar and Saint-Saëns concertos, Tchaikovsky Rococo Variations, recitals of cello works by Grieg, Sibelius, Brahms, Rachmaninov and Myaskovksy, Dvořák and Shostakovich cello concertos, Haydn cello concertos with Norwegian Chamber Orchestra, Britten Cello Symphony and Elgar Cello Concerto with Sir Simon Rattle and the City of Birmingham Symphony Orchestra, Britten Cello Suites (Grammy Award 2002). *Honours:* prizewinner Moscow Tchaikovsky Competititon 1982, first prize Cassado Cello Competition, Florence 1983, W Naumburg Competition, New York 1986, UNESCO Prize European Radio-Union Competition, Bratislava 1983. *Current Management:* Harrison/Parrott Ltd, 12 Penzance Place, London, W11 4PA, England. *Telephone:* (20) 7229-9166. *Fax:* (20) 7221-5042. *Website:* www.harrisonparrott.com.

MOROZ, Vladimir; Singer (Baritone); b. 1974, Rechitsa, Ghornel District, Russia. *Education:* Graduated Minsk Academy of Music, 1999. *Career:* Debut: Byelourussian National Opera, 1997, as Eugene Onegin; Young Singers Academy of the Mariinsky Theatre, St Petersburg, from 1999; Repertoire includes Robert in Tchaikovsky's Iolanta, Rossini's Figaro, Enrico (Lucia di Lammermoor), Yeletzky in The Queen of Spades and Andrei Bolkonsky in War and Peace; Sang Andrei, and Mizgir in The Snow Maiden by Rimsky-Korsakov, with the Kirov Opera at Covent Garden, 2000. *Honours:* Prizewinner, International Lysienko Competition, 1997. *Address:* c/o Kirov Opera, Mariinsky Theatre, 1 Theatre Square, St Petersburg, Russia.

MOROZOV, Alexander; Singer (Bass); b. 1950, USSR. *Education:* Studied at the Leningrad Conservatory. *Career:* Joined the Kirov Opera, Leningrad, 1983 and has sung Don Basilio, Mephistopheles, Pimen, Boris Godunov and Surin in The Queen of Spades; Sang at Covent Garden 1987 with the Kirov, as Surin, Pimen and Boris; Tours to Zürich and France; Sang Zemfira's father in a concert performance of Rachmaninov's Aleko at the Santa Cecilia, Rome, 1989; Amsterdam 1989, as Pimen; Dolokhov in War and Peace for Seattle Opera, 1990; Scottish Opera 1990 as Padre Guardiano in La Forza del Destino; Covent Garden company as Basilio, and Fiesco in a new production of Simon Boccanegra conducted by Georg Solti, 1991; Sang in Gala celebrating 125th Anniversary of Feodor Chaliapin's birth in St Petersburg, 1998; Mussorgsky's Boris Godunov at the London Proms, 2002. *Recordings include:* Lord Rochefort in Anna Bolena, 1996. *Honours:* First Prize at competitions in Rio de Janeiro and Moscow, Tchaikovsky International. *Address:* Allied Artists, 42 Montpelier Square, London, SW7 1JZ, England.

MOROZOV, Igor; Singer (Baritone); b. 1948, Moscow, USSR. *Education:* Studied at the Moscow Conservatory. *Career:* First engagement at the Kirov Theatre Leningrad, then sang at the Bolshoi, Moscow, from 1976 as Eugene Onegin, Count Luna, Germont, Yeletzky, The Queen of Spades; Robert in Tchaikovsky's Iolanta; Sang in Shchedrin's Dead Souls at Boston, 1988; Guest engagements in Finland and Hungary as concert and opera atrist; British debut at Covent Garden, 1988; Season 2000–01 at the Deutsche Oper Berlin as Scarpia, Verdi's Miller and Renato, and Rochefort in Anna Bolena; Dubois in Tchaikovsky's Maid of Orleans and Kadoor in Si j'étais Roi at Wexford; Ferdinand in Prokofiev's Duenna at the Bolshoi, Moscow. *Address:* Allied Artists, 42 Montpelier Square, London SW7 1JZ, England.

MOROZOV, Vladimir (Mikhailovich); Opera Singer (Bass); b. 1933, . *Education:* Leningrad Conservatory. *Career:* Soloist with Kirov Opera 1959–, roles include: Varlaam in Boris Godunov; Ivan the Terrible in The Maid of Pskov; Grigory in Quiet Flows the Don; Peter the Great, Peter I; mem, CPSU, 1965–. *Honours:* Glinka Prize, 1974; RSFSR People's Artist, 1976; USSR People's Artist 1981. *Address:* c/o Kirov Opera Company, St Petersburg, Russia.

MORRIS, Colin; Singer (Baritone); b. 17 Nov. 1952, Sheerness, Kent, England. *Education:* BA, 1974, PhD, 1978, Geography, Exeter University; ARCM Performers, 1977; Private Study with Derek Hammond-Stroud. *Career:* Debut: Edinburgh Festival with Kent Opera, 1979; Many concert and recital appearances in the United Kingdom and Netherlands; Lieder repertoire of over 300 songs; Toured the United Kingdom and USA with Pavilion Opera, London Opera Players, Regency Opera, D'Oyly Carte, Crystal Clear Opera; Castleward Opera; Central Festival Opera, Holland Park; Penang Festival; Overseas opera debut, as Bartolo (Rossini), Singapore, 1992; Main roles are Don Alfonso, Leporello, Magnifico, Bartolo, Pasquale, Dulcamara; Falstaff, Rigoletto, Sharpless, Scarpia, Tonio and Alberich; Operetta, especially 'patter' roles in Gilbert and Sullivan. *Recordings:* Several song recitals on BBC, Radio Kent. *Address:* 49 Winstanley Road, Sheerness, Kent ME12 2PW, England. *Telephone:* 1795 664694.

MORRIS, Gareth (Charles Walter); Flautist; b. 13 May 1920, Clevedon, Somerset, England; m. (1) 1954, 1 d.; (2) Patricia Mary Murray, 18 Dec 1975, 1 s., 2 d. *Education:* Bristol Cathedral School and privately; Royal Academy of Music, London. *Career:* Soloist; Professor, Royal Academy of Music, 1945–85; Principal Flautist, Philharmonia Orchestra, London, 1948–72; mem, Royal Society of Arts, Member of Council, Chairman, Music Committee; Royal Society of Musicians, Governor. *Recordings:* Numerous. *Publications:* Flute Technique, 1991; Numerous articles in journals. *Honours:* ARAM, 1945; FRAM, 1949; FRSA, 1967. *Address:* 4 West Mall, Clifton, Bristol BS 8 4BH, England.

MORRIS, James; Singer (bass-baritone); b. 10 Jan. 1947, Baltimore, Maryland, USA; m. Susan Quittmeyer. *Education:* Studied with Rosa Ponselle in Baltimore, with Frank Valentino and Nicola Moscona in New York. *Career:* Debut: Baltimore Civic Opera 1967, as Crespel in Les Contes d'Hoffmann; Metropolitan Opera from 1971, as Mozart's Commendatore and Don Giovanni, 1975; Verdi's Procida, Padre Guardiano, Grand Inquisitor and Philip II, and the villains in Les Contes d'Hoffmann; Glyndebourne debut 1972, as Verdi's Banquo; At the Salzburg Festival he has sung Guglielmo in Così fan tutte and Mozart's Figaro, 1986; Received coaching from Hans Hotter and sang Wagner's Wotan in San Francisco and Vienna 1985; Other roles include Gounod's Mephistopheles, Britten's Claggart and Donizetti's Henry VIII; Sang the Dutchman at the Metropolitan 1989, Mephistopheles and Wotan, also televised, 1990; Sang Mephistopheles at Cincinnati 1990, with his wife as Siebel; Covent Garden 1990, as the Wanderer in a new production of Siegfried; Season 1992, as the Dutchman in New York and at Covent Garden, Claggart in Billy Budd at the Met and Boris Godunov at San Francisco; Sang Iago at the Met, 1995, returned for Mozart's Figaro, 1997; Coppelius in Hoffmann at the Met, 1998; Season 2000–01 as Wotan and the Dutchman at the Met, Don Giovanni in Baltimore and Horace Tabor in Moore's The Ballad of Baby Doe for San Francisco Opera. *Recordings:* Wotan in Ring cycles conducted by James Levine and Bernard Haitink, 1988–90. *Current Management:* Askonas Holt Ltd, Lonsdale Chambers, 27 Chancery Lane, London, WC2A 1PF, England. *Telephone:* (20) 7400-1700. *Fax:* (20) 7400-1799. *E-mail:* info@askonasholt.co.uk. *Website:* www.askonasholt.co.uk.

MORRIS, Joan (Clair); Singer and Teacher; b. 10 Feb. 1943, Portland, Oregon, USA; m. William Bolcom, 28 Nov 1975. *Education:* Gonzaga University, 1963–65; Diploma, American Academy of Dramatic Arts, 1968. *Career:* Debut: Wigmore Hall, 1993; Performed at the Boston Pops, 1976; Polly Peachum in The Beggar's Opera, Guthrie Theatre, Minneapolis, 1979; Soloist, World Premiere of William Bolcom's Songs of Innocence and Experience, Stuttgart Opera, 1984 and at New York Premiere, 1987; Weill Recital Hall, Carnegie Hall, 1987; Soloist, world premiere of William Bolcom's 4th Symphony with the St Louis Symphony 1987; Played the Nurse in world premiere of William Bolcom's Casino Paradise, 1990; Alice Tully Hall, Lincoln Center, 1976, 1977, 1978, 1980, 1983, 1995; Ewart Hall, American University in Cairo, 1988; 20th Anniversary Concert with guest Max Morath at Hunter College, 1993; Church of Santo Spirito, Florence, 1989; Since 1981, Adjunct Associate Professor of Musical Theater at University of Michigan; Azazels, University of Michigan. *Compositions include:* Songs: Carol, 1981; Tears at the Happy Hour, 1983, both with William Bolcom. *Recordings include:* After The Ball: A Treasury of Turn-of-the-Century Popular Songs, 1974; Songs by Ira and George Gershwin, 1978; Blue Skies, 1985; Let's Do It: Bolcom and Morris Live at Aspen, 1989; Orchids in the Moonlight, with tenor Robert White, 1996; 20 albums recorded to date, including Songs of Rodgers and Hart, Jerome Kern and Leiber and Stoller. *Publications:* Contributor to the New Grove

Dictionary of American Music. *Honours:* Grammy Nomination, After the Ball, 1975. *Current Management:* ICM Artists, 40 W 57th Street, New York, NY 10019, USA. *Address:* 3080 Whitmore Lake Road, Ann Arbor, MI 48105, USA.

MORRIS, Robert (Daniel); Composer, Music Theorist and Professor; b. 19 Oct. 1943, Cheltenham, England; m. Ellen Koskoff, 10 June 1979, 1 s., 2 d. *Education:* BM, with distinction, Eastman School of Music; MM 1966; DMA 1969; University of Michigan. *Career:* Instructor, University of Hawaii, 1968–69; Assistant Professor, 1969–75, Director, Yale Electronic Music Studio, 1973–78; Associate Professor, 1975–78; Chairman, Composition Department, 1974–78, Yale University; Associate Professor, 1977–80, Director, Electronic and Computer Music Studio, 1977–80, University of Pittsburgh; Associate Professor, 1980–85; Professor, 1986–, Eastman School of Music. *Compositions:* Continua for Orchestra, 1969; Thunders of Spring Over Distant Mountains, Electronic Music, 1973; In Different Voices for 5 Wind Ensembles, 1975–76; Plexus for Woodwinds, 1977; Passim, 1982; Echanges, piano and computer-generated tape, 1983; Cuts, wind ensemble, 1984; Concerto for piano and strings, 1994. *Recordings:* Phases for two-pianos and electronics; Motet On Doo-dah; Hamiltonian Cycle; Inter Alia; Karuna. *Publications:* Composition with Pitch-Classes: A Theory of Compositional Design, 1986. *Contributions:* Reviews and Articles in Journal of Music Theory, Perspectives of New Music; Musical Quarterly; JAMS; In Theory Only.

MORRIS, Stephen; Violinist; b. 1970, Bridlington, Yorkshire, England. *Education:* Studied with Yfrah Neaman in London and with Manoug Parikian and Maurice Hasson at the Royal Academy of Music. *Career:* Leader of the RAM symphony orchestra 1988; Further study with Howard Davis; Leader of the Pegasus and Thames Chamber Orchestra; As soloist plays Bruch, Bach, Mendelssohn and Lalo; 2nd violin of the Duke String Quartet from 1985; Performances in the Wigmore Hall, Purcel; Room, Conway Hall and throughout the United Kingdom; Tours to Germany, Italy, Austria and the Baltic States; South Bank series 1991, with Mozart's early quartets; Soundtrack from Ingmar Berman documentary and The Magic Lantern, Channel 4 1988; BBC Debut feature; Features for French television 1990–91, playing Mozart, Mendelssohn, Britten and Tippett; Brahms Clarinet Quintet for Dutch Radio with Janet Hilton; Live Music Now series with concerts for disadvantaged people; The Duke Quartet invites… at the Derngate, Northampton, 1991, with Duncan Prescott and Rohan O'Hara; Resident quartet of the Rydale Festival 1991; Residency at Trinity College, Oxford, tours of Scotland and Northern Ireland and concert at the Queen Elizabeth Hall 1991. *Recordings:* Quartets by Tippett, Shostakovich and Britten 3rd for Factory Classics. *Honours:* Awards at the RAM include the John Waterhouse Prize; London Orchestral Society Prize; Poulet Award; Inter-collegiate Quartet Prize. *Address:* c/o Ingrassia, Duke Quartet, Via San Zanobi 7, 1–50018 Scandicci (Fi), Italy.

MORRIS, Wyn; Conductor and Musical Director; b. 14 Feb. 1929, Wales; m. Ruth Marie McDowell 1962; one s. one d. *Education:* Royal Academy of Music; Mozarteum, Salzburg, Austria. *Career:* Apprentice conductor, Yorkshire Symphony Orchestra, 1950–51; Musical Director, 17th Training Regiment, Royal Artillery Band, 1951–53; Founder and conductor, Welsh Symphony Orchestra, 1954–57; Koussevitsky Memorial Prize, Boston Symphony Orchestra, 1957; Observer, on invitation George Szell, Cleveland Symphony Orchestra, 1957–60; Conductor, Ohio Bell Chorus, Cleveland Orpheus Choir, Cleveland Chamber Orchestra, 1958–60; Choir of Royal National Eisteddfod, Wales, 1960–62; London Debut, Royal Festival Hall with Royal Philharmonic Orchestra, 1963; Conductor to Royal Choral Society, 1968–70, Huddersfield Choral Society, 1969–74; Ceremony of Investiture for Prince Charles as Prince of Wales, 1969, Royal Choral Society tour of USA, 1969; Chief Conductor, Musical Director, Symphonica of London, Current: Specialist, conducting works of Mahler. *Recordings:* Des Knaben Wunderhorn, with Janet Baker and Geraint Evans; Das klagende Lied; Symphonies 1, 2, 5, 8; No. 10 in Deryck Cooke's final performing version. *Honours:* August Mann's Prize, 1950; Fellow, Royal Academy of Music, 1964; Mahler Memorial Medal, Bruckner and Mahler Society of America, 1968. *Address:* c/o Manygate Management, 1 Summerhouse Lane, Harmondsworth, Middlesex UB7 0AW, England.

MORRISON, Bryce; Teacher, Pianist, Critic and Lecturer; b. 27 Nov. 1938, Leeds, Yorkshire, England. *Education:* MA (Oxon); MA (Dalhousie); MMus (SMU); Music Scholar, Kings School, Canterbury, 1952; Studied with Ronald Smith, Iso Elinson and Alexander Unisky. *Career:* Has published interviews with most of the world's great pianists including Horowitz, Rubinstein and Clifford Curzon; Jury Member of over 40 international piano competitions; Chairman, First Terence Judd International Award, 1982 and of the Scottish International Piano Competition, 1998; His students have been international prizewinners including first prizes at Santander, Pozzoli and finalist status at Leeds; Has lectured and given Masterclasses world with television appear-

ances in the United Kingdom, USA, Canada and Australia; Extensive broadcasts for BBC, ABC and CBC; also in Poland, USA, and New Zealand; Professor, Royal Academy of Music and visiting Professor at Texas Conservatory for Artists. *Publications:* Published extensively in: The Times; The Times Literary Supplement; Observer; Telegraph; Independent; Gramophone and others; also in America and Australia; Major Contributor to Phaidon Book of The Piano; 2 BBC Talks published by the Oxford University Press; Short biography of Liszt; Written over 300 annotations for Decca, EMI, Sony, DG and others; Personal advisor for testament Records for whom he has weitten perdonal tributes to Schnabel, Edwin Fisher, Solomon, Arrau and others. *Honours:* Held the Corina Frada Pick Chair of Advanced Piano Studies, Ravinia Festival, Chicago, 1988; Honorary ARAM, 1995; Trustee of John Ogdon Foundation, 2002. *Address:* Flat 19, 11 Hinde Street, London W1M 5AQ, England.

MORTIER, Gérard; Belgian music director; *Director-General, Paris Opéra;* b. 25 Nov. 1943, Ghent. *Education:* Univ. of Ghent. *Career:* engaged in journalism and communications 1966–67; Admin. Asst Flanders Festival 1968–72; Artistic Planner, Deutsche Oper am Rhein, Düsseldorf 1972–73; Asst Admin. Frankfurt Opera 1973–77; Dir of Artistic Production, Hamburg Staatsoper 1977–79; Tech. Programme Consultant, Théâtre Nat. de l'Opéra, Paris 1979–81; Dir-Gen. Belgian Nat. Opera, Brussels 1981–91; Dir Salzburg Music Festival 1992–2001; Fellow, Wissenschaftskolleg (Inst. for Advanced Study), Berlin 2001–02; Dir, Kultur Ruhr triennial arts festival 2002; Dir-Gen. Paris Opéra 2004–; mem. Acad. of Arts, Berlin. *Honours:* Dr hc (Univ. of Antwerp), (Univ. of Salzburg); Commdr, Ordre des Arts et des Lettres 2000. *Address:* c/o Opéra National de Paris, 120 rue de Lyon, 75012 Paris, France (office).

MORYL, Richard; Composer and Conductor; b. 23 Feb. 1929, Newark, NJ, USA. *Education:* Studied at Montclair State College, New Jersey and Columbia University, MA 1959; Further study with Boris Blacher and Arthur Berger. *Career:* Teacher, 1960–72; Founder, New England Contemporary Music Ensemble, 1970; Director, Charles Ives Center for American Music, 1979. *Compositions:* Ballons for percussion, orchestra, radios and audience, 1971; Vols for piano, organ and orchestra, 1971; Chroma, 1972; Loops for large orchestra with any instruments, 1974; Strobe for large orchestra with any instruments, 1974; The untuning of the Skies, 1981; The Pond, flute and chamber orchestra, 1984; Instrumental music including Rainbows, I and II, 1982–83 and The Golden Phoenix for string quartet and percussion, 1984; Vocal: Flourescents for 2 choruses, 2 percussion and organ, 1970; Illuminations for soprano, 43 choruses and chamber orchestra, 1970; De morte cantoris for soprano, mezzo and ensemble, 1973; Das Lied for soprano and ensemble, 1975; Stabat Mater, 1982; Come, Sweet Death, chorus and piano, 1983; Mixed media works including Passio avium, 1974; Atlantis, 1976; Visiones mortis, 1977; Music of the Spheres, 1977; An Island on the Moon, 1978; A Sunflower for Maggie, 1979; Music for tape, electronics. *Address:* ASCAP, ASCAP Building, 1 Lincoln Plaza, NY 10023, USA.

MOSCA, Silvia; Singer (Soprano); b. 1958, Italy. *Education:* Studied in Naples. *Career:* Debut: Mantua Teatro Sociale as the Trovatore Leonara; Has sung at opera houses throughout Italy and appeared as Luisa Miller at the Metropolitan 1988; Leonora at Liège and Miami 1988–89; Sang Aida at Buenos Aires and the Savonlinna Festival, 1989; Elvira in Ernani at Rome and Venice, 1989–90. *Address:* c/o Teatro La Fenice, Campo S Fantin 1965, 30124, Venice, Italy.

MOSCATO, Jacques; Conductor and Clarinettist; b. 1945, France. *Career:* Debut: Municipal Orchestra as Clarinettist, 1955; Director, Public concert, Switzerland, 1962; In charge, Music Department, International University, City of Paris from 1968; Director, Charleville Mezières Conservatorium from 1969; Conductor, Concerts in West Germany, Belgium and France, 1971; Guest Conductor, Australian Broadcasting Commission, 1976, 1978; Conductor, Monte Carlo Symphony, the Salle Garnier of Monte Carlo, 1979–94; Guest Conductor, Istanbul Symphonic Orchestra, Symphony Orchestra, Pays Loire, France, 1984, 1989. *Compositions:* Music for film, Symphonic Interdite, 1983; A Music Ballet, Resonances, 1989. *Recordings:* Albums, Symphony No. 2, plus eleven Viennese Dances (Beethoven), 1977, Les Musiciens Monegasquesm, 1981. *Address:* Academie de Musique, Prince Rainier III de Monaco, 1 Boulevard Albert 1er, Monaco.

MOSER, Edda; Singer (Soprano); b. 27 Oct. 1938, Berlin, Germany. *Education:* Studied at the Berlin Conservatory with Hermann Weissenborn and Gerty Konig. *Career:* Debut: Berlin Stadtische Oper 1962, in Madama Butterfly; Sang at Hagen and Bielefeld from 1964; Began musical association with Hans Werner Henze at Brunswick in 1967 and sang in the premiere of Das Floss der Medusa, Vienna 1971; 1968 sang Wellgunde in Das Rheingold at the Salzburg Festival and at the Metropolitan; Later New York appearances as Mozart's Donna Anna, Queen of Night and Constanze, Puccini's Musetta and Liu and Handel's

Armida in Rinaldo, 1984; Guest appearances in Russia, Berlin, Vienna, Salzburg, Aspasia in Mozart's Mitridate at Hamburg (Lucia 1974) and South America; Modern repertory includes music by Nono, Fortner, Zimmermann and Stravinsky, (The Nightingale); Sang Strauss's Ariadne at Rio de Janeiro, 1988; Marie in Wozzeck at the Teatro Valli, Reggio Emilia, 1989. *Recordings:* Der Ring des Nibelungen, Orfeo ed Euridice, Rappresentazione di Anima e di Corpo, Das Floss der Medusa, Deutsche Grammophon; Don Giovanni, also filmed; Idomeneo, Die Zauberflöte, Das Paradies und die Peri, Leonore, Beethoven; Abu Hassan, Der häusliche Krieg by Schubert, Genoveva by Schumann, Die Abreise, (Electrola). *Current Management:* Ingpen & Williams Ltd, 7 St George's Court, 131 Putney Bridge Road, London, SW15 2PA, England.

MOSER, Thomas; Singer (Tenor); b. 27 May 1945, Richmond, Virginia, USA. *Education:* Richmond Professional Institute; Curtis Institute Philadelphia; California with Martial Singher, Gerard Souzay and Lotte Lehmann. *Career:* After success at the 1974 Metropolitan Auditions sang in Graz from 1975; Munich Opera, 1976, as Mozart's Belmonte; Vienna State Opera from 1977, as Mozart's Tamino, Ottavio, Titus and Idomeneo, Strauss's Flamand and Henry; Achilles in Iphigénie en Aulide, conducted by Charles Mackerras; New York City Opera 1979, as Titus; Salzburg Festival 1983, in La Finta Semplice; La Scala Milan, 1985, as Tamino; Rome Opera, 1986, as Achilles; Paris Opéra Comique, 1987 as Mozart's Idomeneo and Tito; Sang the Tenor in the premiere of Berio's Un Re in Ascolto, Salzburg, 1984; Vienna Staatsoper, 1987, as Achilles in Iphigénie en Aulide, Schubert's Fierrabras at the Theater an der Wien, 1988; Sang Florestan in Fidelio at La Scala and Salzburg, 1990; New production of Lucio Silla at Vienna, 1991, the Emperor in Die Frau ohne Schatten at Geneva, 1992; Season 1992–93, with Florestan at Zürich and the Emporor at Salzburg; Sang title role in Pfitzner's Palestrina at Covent Garden, 1997; As concert singer in Beethoven's Choral Symphony and Missa Solemnis, Britten's War Requiem, the Bach Passions, Schmidt's Das Buch mit Sieben Siegeln and Mozart's Requiem; Max in Der Freischütz with the Royal Opera at the Barbican, 1998; Sang Nielsen's David at Ludwigsburg (concert) 1999; Season 2000–01 as Strauss's Emperor at Barcelona and Florestan at the Teatre Real Madrid; Parsifal under Abbado at Edinburgh, 2002; Sang Strauss's Emperor at the Opéra Bastille, 2002. Conductors include Giulini, Colin Davis, Mehta, Leinsdorf, Leopold Hager and Horst Stein. *Recordings:* Roles in Stiffelio, Verdi; Mozart and Salieri, Rimsky-Korsakov; Zaide; La Finta Giardiniera and Don Giovanni, Mozart; Die Freunde von Salamanka, Schubert; Genoveva, Schumann; Oedipus Rex, Stravinsky; Handel's Utrecht Te Deum and Dvořák's Requiem. *Address:* c/o IMG Artists Paris, 54 Avenue Mareau, F–75008 Paris, France.

MOSES, Geoffrey; singer (bass); b. 24 Sept. 1952, Abercynon, Wales. *Education:* Emmanuelle College, Cambridge, Guildhall School of Music and with Otakar Kraus and Peter Harrison. *Career:* debut with Welsh National Opera, 1977, as Basilio in Il Barbiere di Siviglia; Other roles include Seneca, L'Incoronazione di Poppea, Sarastro and Padre Guardiano in La Forza del Destino; Covent Garden debut 1981, in Les Contes d'Hoffmann; Returned in a new production of Otello; Glyndebourne Festival debut 1984; Sang Fiesco in Simon Boccanegra 1986; Brussels Opera in Hoffmann and Boccanegra; Welsh National Opera in Peter Stein's production of Falstaff; Season 1990–91, with WNO in Figaro, Carmen and Falstaff, also on tour to Japan; Sang Professor Millar in the premiere of Friend of the People by David Horne, Glasgow 1999; Created Petrus in The Last Supper, by Birtwistle, Berlin Staatsoper 2000; Concert engagements include: La Damnation de Faust in Frankfurt and the Choral Symphony with the Scottish National Orchestra; Sang in Strauss's Die Liebe der Danaë for BBC Radio 3, conducted by Charles Mackerras. *Recordings:* Rigoletto. *Current Management:* The Old Brushworks, 56 Pickwick Road, Corsham, Wiltshire, England. *Telephone:* (1249) 716716. *Fax:* (1249) 716717. *E-mail:* cphillips@caroline-phillips.co.uk. *Website:* www.caroline -phillips.co.uk.

MOSHINSKY, Elijah; Opera Producer; b. 8 Jan. 1946, Shanghai, China; m. Ruth Dyttman, 1970, 2 s. *Education:* BA, Melbourne University, Australia; St Anthony's College, Oxford University, United Kingdom. *Career:* Original Productions at Covent Garden of: Peter Grimes, 1975; Lohengrin, 1977; The Rake's Progress, 1979; Macbeth, 1981; Samson and Delilah, 1981; Other opera productions include: Wozzeck, 1976; A Midsummer Night's Dream, 1978; Boris Godonuv, 1980; Un Ballo in Maschera, Metropolitan Opera, New York, 1980; Il Trovatore, Australian Opera, 1983; For English National Opera, Le Grand Macabre, 1982; Mastersingers of Nuremberg, 1984; Bartered Bride, 1985; La Bohème, 1988 for Scottish Opera; For Royal Opera: Tannhäuser, 1984; Samson, 1985; Otello, 1986, Die Entführung aus dem Serail, 1987; Productions at National Theatre; Troilus and Cressida, 1976; Productions on the West End; Television film of Michael Tippett's The Midsummer Marriage, 1988; Produced La Forza del Destino for Scottish Opera, 1990; Attila at Covent Garden; Lohengrin revival by Royal Opera 1997 and taken to New York Met, season, 1998; Verdi's Masnadieri for the Royal Opera at

Baden-Baden, Edinburgh and Savonlinna, 1998. *Contributions:* Opera Magazine, 1992, Verdi: A Pox on Post-Modernism. *Address:* 28 Kidbrooke Grove, London SE3 0LG, England.

MOSLEY, George; singer (baritone); b. 1960, England. *Education:* Studied with Laura Sarti at the Guildhall School, at the Academia Chigiana in Siena, the Munich Hochschule für Musik and the National Opera Studio, London. *Career:* Performed in many operas including: Dandini in La Cenerentola, 1987, and Onegin in Tchaikovsky's Eugene Onegin, 1989, both for Opera 80; Orlofsky in Strauss's Die Fledermaus, Scottish Opera, 1990; Marco in Puccini's Gianni Schicchi, 1990, The Sportsman in Delius's Fennimore and Gerda, 1990 and the Duke of Albany in Reimann's Lear, 1991, all for the English National Opera; Patroclus in King Priam, Opera North, 1991; Malatesta in Don Pasquale and Guglielmo in Così fan tutte, 1991 and Dandini in La Cenerentola in 1992, all for Teatro Verdi, Pisa, Italy; Schaunard in La Bohème for Scottish opera, 1993; Ottone in Incoronazione di Poppea and Count in Le nozze di Figaro, both for Teatro Verdi, Pisa, Italy, 1993; Father in Baa Baa Black Sheep for Opera North and BBC television, 1993; Count in Le nozze di Figaro for Concert Hall, Athens, 1993; Papageno in The Magic Flute for Scottish Opera, 1994; Sang Berardo in Riccardo Primo at the 1996 Handel Festival at Göttingen; Schaunard in La Bohème at Hong Kong, 1998; Season 2000–01 with Albert in Werther at Peking, Bellini's Rodolfo in Athens and Thomas' Hamlet at the Teatro Regio, Turin; Josef K in Il Processo for Reggio Emilia and La Piccola Scala, Milan, 2002; Sharpless in Butterfly, Hong Kong, 2002; Don Pedro in Maria Padilla, Buxton Festival, 2003. *Recordings include:* Schumann's Dichterliebe and Liederkreis Op 39; Aeneas in Dido and Aeneas conducted by John Eliot Gardiner; Tavener's Eternity's Sunrise, 2000. *Honours:* First Prize, International Mozart Competition, Salzburg, 1998. *Current Management:* Robert Gilder & Co., Enterprise House, 59–65 Upper Ground, London, SE1 9PQ, England. *Telephone:* (20) 7928-9008. *Fax:* (20) 7928-9755. *E-mail:* rgilder@robert-gilder.com.

MOSUC, Elena; Singer (Soprano); b. 18 Jan. 1964, Iasi, Romania. *Education:* Studied at the George Enescu Conservatory, Bucharest. *Career:* Debut: Tasi Opera 1990, as Mozart's Queen of Night; Further appearances as Lucia di Lammermoor, Gilda and Violetta; Concerts with the Moldau Philharmonic and in Mozart masses at Bucharest; Theater am Gärtnerplatz Munich, Vienna Staatsoper and Deutsche am Rhein 1990, as the Queen of Night; Zürich Opera from 1991, as Lucia and Donna Anna; Season 2000–01 as Luisa Miller and Micaela for Zürich Opera; Offenbach's Olympia in Vienna, Donna Anna for Bonn Opera, Gilda in Warsaw, Violetta for Finnish National Opera and Constanze in Rome. *Address:* Zürich Opera, Falkenstrasse 1, 8008 Zürich, Switzerland.

MOTHERWAY, Fiona; Singer (Soprano); b. 1967, Western Australia. *Education:* Studied in Australia and at the Royal Academy of Music (graduated 1994). *Career:* Performances with British Youth Opera and elsewhere as Fiordiligi; Cambridge Handel Opera Group as Melissa in Amadigi di Gaula; other Handel roles include Semele, Atalanta (Xerxes), Cleopatra and Ginevra (Ariodante); Also sings Mozart's Countess, Susanna and Pamina, Musetta, Gilda and Purcell's Dido; Season 1996–97 with Olympia in Contes d'Hoffman for Stowe Opera and Naiade in Ariadne for Castleward Opera; Concerts include Strauss Four Last Songs, Haydn's Creation and Nelson Mass, Messiah, Bach B minor Mass, Mozart's C minor Mass and Requiem; Mahler's 4th Symphony under Colin Davis; Concert tour of Australia, 1996–97. *Address:* C&M Craig Services Ltd, 3 Kersley Street, London SW11 4 PR, England.

MOTT, Louise; Singer (mezzo-soprano); b. 1971, Barnet, Hertfordshire, England; Graduated 1996, Royal College of Music Opera Department; also studied at Guildhall School of Music and Drama and National Opera Studio, London. *Career:* Opera roles include Bradamante in Alcina, ENO; Annio in La Clemenza di Tito, Welsh Nat. Opera; Edith in Alfred, Agrippina, Ariodante, Sesto in Giulio Cesare, Orlando, Rosmira in Partenope, Serse and Dido in Dido and Aeneas, for The Early Opera Co.; Marlinchen in Roderick Watkins' The Juniper Tree at Munich Bienale; Marguerite in Deirdre Gribbin's Hey Persephone! for Almeida Opera; Emerald in Robin Holloway's Boys and Girls Come Out to Play, and Blind Mary in The Martyrdom of St Magnus, for The Opera Group; Wife/Sphinx/Doreen in Mark Anthony Turnage's Greek, with the London Sinfonietta; Concerts include Mozart's Requiem at the Albert Hall, Messiah at St John's Smith Square, Elgar's Dream of Gerontius and The Music Makers, Dvořák Requiem, Elijah, and the Stabat Maters of Haydn and Rossini; Wigmore Hall debut 1996, with the Young Songmakers' Almanac series; Mozart's Requiem at Bath Abbey, 1997; 2003–04 season: Fidalma in The Secret Marriage and Annina in Der Rosenkavalier for Opera North; Ariodante for English Touring Opera; Madame Larina in Eugene Onegin for Scottish Opera on Tour; Vivaldi Gloria with the Bach Choir, Royal Festival Hall and Royal Albert Hall; Messiah at The Lighthouse, Poole with Bournemouth Symphony Orchestra; UK premiere of Caldara's Amarilli vezzosa with the Orchestra of St John's Smith Square; performances of Mahler

Kindertotenlieder and Mussorgsky Nursery Songs with Hebrides Ensemble. *Honours:* Lies Askonas Singing Prize, Peter Pears Exhibition and Keith Falkner Prize for Bach and Handel, at RCM. *Current Management:* c/o Helen Sykes Artists Management, 100 Felsham Road, Putney, London, SW15 1DQ, England.

MOULDS, Christopher; Conductor and Keyboard Player; b. 1967, Halifax, England. *Education:* Studied at City University, the Guildhall School and Royal College of Music. *Career:* Conducted Figaro and The Rake's Progress at the RCM; Member of Music Staff, English National Opera, 1991–95, working with productions of Billy Rudd, Carmen, Wozzeck, Orfeo, Lohengrin and Street Scene; Harpsichord continuo for ENO's Xerxes and Ariodante; Chorus Master at Glyndebourne Festival from 1995, conducting Figaro 1997; Further engagements with British Youth Opera, Opera Company Tunbridge Wells (Barber and Figaro), European Community Youth Orchestra and London Sinfonietta (as orchestral keyboard player); Conducted The Magic Flute for ENO, 1996, 1997–98. *Address:* Flat 549, Manhattan Buildings, Fairfield Road, London E3 2UL, England.

MOULSON, John; Singer, (Tenor); b. 25 July 1928, Kansas City, Missouri, USA. *Education:* Studied in Atlanta. *Career:* Debut: Berlin Komische Oper 1961 as Cavaradossi; Sang at the Komische Oper until 1982 as Alfredo, Traviata, Hoffmann, the Steersman in Fliegende Holländer, 1969–72, and as Lensky, Gabriele Adorno and Oedipus Rex; Sang at Boston 1988, in the US premiere of Dead Souls by Shchedrin; Further guest engagements in Germany, England, Italy, Poland, Russia and the USA.

MOULT, Daniel Adam Ashbrook, MA, FRCO; Organist; b. 13 Dec. 1973, Manchester, England. *Education:* Manchester Grammar School, St John's Coll., Oxford, Sweelinck Conservatorium, Amsterdam. *Career:* organist and Asst Dir of Music, Coventry Cathedral 1995–2002; visiting organ tutor, Birmingham Conservatoire 2003–; visiting organ tutor, Chetham's, Manchester; organ tutor on Oundle, Salisbury and Amsterdam courses; organ animateur, Bridgewater Hall, Manchester; tutor, Royal Coll. of Music Junior Department, St Giles Int. Organ School, London; concert organist throughout UK and Europe (with repertoire from 14th century to present day); mem. Royal Coll. of Organists, Incorporated Soc. of Musicians, Incorporated Asscn of Organists, British Inst. of Organ Studies. *Recordings:* various recordings for BBC TV and radio 2, 3 and 4, and Dutch radio; organist for four albums from Coventry Cathedral; producer for two albums. *Publications:* contrib. to Choir and Organ, Organists Review, British Institute of Organ Studies Journal. *Honours:* Univ. of Oxford John Betts Organ Scholarship 1994, Durrant, Turpin and Dixon prizes (FRCO) 1993.

MOUND, Vernon; Opera Director; b. 1954, England. *Education:* Studied at London University. *Career:* Has worked with the Royal Opera, the Scottish Ballet, the Swan Theatre, Opera North and the Black Theatre of Prague as Stage Manager; Administrator; Company Manager; Assistant Director; Staff producer at Opera North 1983–88, assisting on new productions and directing revivals; Workshops for children and adults, including community piece Quest of the Hidden Moon; Directed small-scale touring version of Carmen; The Gondoliers for New Sadler's Wells Opera, 1988; Directed the Opera Informal and the Sondheim Workshop at the Royal College of Music, 1989–91; Directed Handel's Ariodante for the Birmingham Conservatoire, 1990, and The Marriage Contract and Le Pauvre Matelot for Morley Opera; Productions of Amahl and the Night Visitors at the Barbican Centre and Alice, the Musical at St Martin-in-the-Fields; La Finta Giardiniera for the Opera Hogskolan in Stockholm, Mar 1991, and Pedrotti's Tutti in Maschera at the Britten Theatre; La Fille du Régiment, 1992; Associate Director Carmen Jones at The Old Vic.

MOUNTAIN, Peter; Violinist; b. 3 Oct. 1923, Shipley, Yorkshire, England; 1 s. 2 d. *Education:* Royal Academy of Music, London. *Career:* Debut: Wigmore Hall, London, 1942; Leader, Soloist, Symphony Orchestra, Tours of Europe and Far East; Member, Boyd Neel Orchestra, Philharmonia Orchestra; Leader, Royal Liverpool Philharmonic Orchestra, 1955–66; Concertmaster, BBC Training Orchestra, 1968–75; Head of Strings, Royal Scottish Academy of Music and Drama, 1975–90; Soloist, Guest Leader, Many British Orchestras; Coach, Youth Orchestras; Adjudicator and Examiner; Committee, Scottish Arts Council; Chairman, Scottish Society of Composers; Incorporated Society of Musicians; Musicians' Union, European String Teachers Association. *Honours:* Fellow, Royal Academy of Music, London, 1963; Fellow, Royal Scottish Academy of Music and Drama, 1988; Honorary LLD, University of Bradford, 1995. *Address:* 93 Park Road, Bingley, West Yorkshire BD 16 4BY, England. *Telephone:* 01274 568762. *Fax:* 01274 220884. *E-mail:* pwmount@blueyonder.co.uk.

MÖWES, Thomas; Singer (Baritone); b. 7 Sept. 1951, Halle, Germany. *Education:* Studied at the Weimar Hochschule. *Career:* Sang as Bass-Baritone at the Magdeburg Opera from 1977, and Baritone roles at Halle from 1988, Leipzig and Dresden from 1990; Roles have included

Busoni's Doktor Faust, Nekrotzar in Le Grand Macabre and Orestes in Elektra; Guest engagements as Basle as Verdi's Posa, and at Frankfurt as Faninal in Der Rosenkavalier; Other roles include Handel's Polyphemus, Don Alfonso, Ottokar in Der Freischütz, Luna, Nabucco, Rigoletto, Wolfram and Escamillo; Season 2000–01 as Kurwenal for Nederlandse Reisopera, Strauss's Faninal at Frankfurt and Reimann's Lear for Essen Opera; Many concert appearances. *Address:* Frankfurt Opera, Frankfurt am Main, Germany.

MOYER, Frederick; Pianist; b. 1957, . *Education:* Curtis Institute of Music; BMus, Indiana University. *Career:* Debut: New York, 1982; Performed in nearly all the states of USA; Frequent tours of Europe, Asia and South America; Solo Appearances with Orchestras include: Philadelphia, Houston, Milwaukee, Boston, Cleveland, Baltimore, Minnesota, St Louis, Dallas, Indianapolis, Pittsburgh, Utrecht, London, Rio di Janeiro, Montevideo, Singapore, Hong Kong, Tokyo and the major orchestras of Australia; Participant of numerous Music Festivals. *Recordings:* 18 commercial recordings for major labels. *Address:* c/o Betsy M Green Associates, Artists Management, 36 Hampshire Road, Wayland, MA 01778, USA.

MOYLAN, William (David); Professor, Composer and Recording Producer; b. 23 April 1956, Virginia, Minnesota, USA; m. Vicki Lee Peterlin, 18 Dec 1976. *Education:* BMus, Composition, Peabody Conservatory, Johns Hopkins University, 1979; MMus, Composition, University of Toronto, Canada, 1980; Doctor of Arts in Theory and Composition, Ball State University, USA, 1983. *Career:* Chairperson, Department of Music, University of Massachusetts, Lowell. *Compositions:* Published works include: On Time–On Age, for soprano, flute, trumpet, piano and four-channel tape, 1978; Concerto for Bass Trombone and Orchestra, 1979; Brass Quintet, for brass quintet and tape, 1979; Two Movements for String Orchestra, 1980; Duo for Flute and Tape, 1980; Seven Soliloquies, for trumpet, 1981; Metamorphic Variations, for clarinet, 1983; The Now, for high voice, horn and piano; Trio for Trombones, for alto, tenor and bass trombones, 1984; Three Interplays for Trumpet Duo, 1984; Wind Quintet No. 2, 1985; Stilled Moments for solo violin, 1988; Evocations for Guitar, 1988; La Liberté, for soprano and piano, 1989; Eroica, a Piano Sonata, 1989; Two Suspended Images, for wind controller, 1990; Ask Your Mama, 1990; The Dream Deferred, for two-channel tape, 1990; Mother Earth and Her Whales, 1993; The Stolen Child, 1995; For a Sleeping Child, 1996. *Publications:* The Art of Recording: The Creative Resources of Music Production and Audio, 1992. *Address:* Department of Music, University of Massachusetts at Lowell, 35 Wilder Street, Suite 3, Lowell, MA 01854, USA.

MOYLE, Richard Michael, MA, PhD; Ethnomusicologist; b. 23 Aug. 1944, Paeroa, New Zealand; m. Linden Averil Evelyn Duncan, 1 s., 2 d. *Education:* Trinity Coll., London, Univ. of Auckland. *Career:* Visiting Lecturer in Anthropology, Indiana University, USA, 1971–72; Assistant Professor in Music, University of Hawaii, 1972–73; Research Fellow, Ethnomusicology, 1974–77, Research Grantee, 1977–82, Australian Institute of Aboriginal Studies; Senior Research Fellow, Faculty of Arts, University of Auckland, New Zealand, 1983–86; Associate Professor of Ethnomusicology and Director of Archive of Maori and Pacific Music, University of Auckland, 1986–. *Recordings:* The Music of Samoa; Traditional Music of Tonga; Compiler, Tonga Today. *Publications:* Fagogo: Fables from Samoa, 1979; Songs of the Pintupi, 1981; Alyawarra Music, 1985; Tongan Music, 1987; Traditional Samoan Music, 1988; Sounds of Oceania, 1989; Polynesian Song and Dance, 1991; Fananga: Fables from Tonga in Tongan and English, Vol. I, 1996, Vol. II, 1998; Balgo: The Musical Life of an Aboriginal Community, 1997. *Contributions:* numerous professional journals. *Address:* Department of Anthropology, University of Auckland, Private Bag 92019, Auckland, New Zealand.

MOYSEOWICZ, Gabriela (Maria); Composer, Pianist and Choir Director; b. 4 May 1944, Lwow, Poland. *Education:* Lyceum of Music, Kraków, Poland, 1962; Academies of Music, Kraków and Katowice, Poland; MA, 1967. *Career:* Debut: Playing own piano concerto, Kraków, 1957; Piano recitals; Public performances of own compositions throughout Poland; Radio appearances, discussions and interviews. *Compositions:* Over 60 works include: Media vita, for 2 violins, cello, soprano and bass recitativ; 9 Moments Musicaux, for piano and strings; Rhapsody No. 1 for piano; Marche Funébre, for cello and piano; Deux Caprices, for violin solo; Ave Maria, for 2 mixed choirs a capella; Sonata No. 1, for cello and piano; Two Canzonas, for viola de gamba solo; Piano Sonata numbers 3 to 8 including the 6th Noumenon and 8th Concatenatio; Sonata Polska, for violin and piano; Alleuja for choir; Credo for 4 voice choir, 1991; Trio for piano, violin and violoncello, 1992, 1993; Discours, ave Mdme H Steingroever, for flute and piano, 1993; Passacaglia for violin, 1994; Shadow symphony for large orchestra; Violin Sonata No. 2; Cello Sonata No. 2; Norwidiana for piano; Churchmusic: Media Vita, Dies irae, Ave Maria, Pater noster, Kyrie, Alleluja, Amen Credo; Memento Mori I and II; Stabat Mater. *Recordings:* Piano recitals and chamber music on German broadcasting. *Address:* Stallupöner Allee 37, 14055 Berlin, Germany.

MOZES, Robert; Violist; b. 1950, Romania. *Education:* Studied at the Cluj Academy of Music and the Tel-Aviv Rubin Music Academy. *Career:* Member of and solo appearances with the Israel Philharmonic; Chamber music concerts in Israel, the USA, Canada and Japan; Co-Founder, Jerusalem String Trio, 1977, performing in Israel and in Europe from 1981; Repertoire includes string trios by Beethoven, Dohnányi, Mozart, Reger, Schubert and Taneyev; Piano Quartets by Beethoven, Brahms, Dvořák, Mozart and Schumann; Concerts with Radu Lupu and Daniel Adni. *Recordings:* Albums for Meridian, Channel Classics Studio, Holland and CDI, Israel. *Address:* c/o Ariën Artists, Jerusalem Trio, de Boeystraat 6, B–2018 Antwerp, Belgium.

MOZHAYEV, Fyodor; Singer (Baritone); b. 1958, Voroshilovgrad, Ukraine. *Education:* Studied at the Kharkov Conservatoire. *Career:* Sang first at the Moldavian State Opera and at the Perm Opera 1982–93; Member of the Bolshoi Opera from 1994, with Mozart's Figaro, 1995; Guest engagements with the Kirov Opera, Kharkov Opera and in Kiev; Has also sung widely in France and in Poland, Budapest and Malta; Other roles include Verdi's Iago, Renato, Luna and Germont, Scarpia, Ruprecht in The Fiery Angel, Lionel in The Maid of Orleans, Escamillo and Rubinstein's Demon; Sang Napoleon in War and Peace at La Scala and Donner in Das Rheingold at St Petersburg, 2000. *Honours:* Prizewinner at 1979 Riga Song Competition. *Address:* Sonata Ltd, 11 North Park Street, Glasgow G20 7AA, Scotland.

MRACEK, Jaroslav (John Stephen), BMus, MA, PhD; academic; *Professor of Music and Musicology Emeritus, San Diego State University*; b. 5 June 1928, Montreal, Canada; m. 1963; two s. *Education:* Royal Conservatory of Music, Toronto, University of Toronto, Indiana University; harpsichord with Willi Apel, John R. White, Paul Nettl, Walter Kaufmann, Bernard Heiden, Marie Zorn; piano with Alberto Guerrero. *Career:* taught instrumental, vocal music English and History at Lisgar Collegiate Institute, Ottawa, Canada, 1953–59; Lecturer: University of Illinois, Urbana 1964–65; Assistant Prof., Associate Prof., Prof., San Diego State University, 1965–91; General Director, the Smetana Centennial, International Conference and Festival of Czechoslovak Music, San Diego State University, 1987; Conducted at Canadian Music Festival, San Diego State University, 1987. *Publications:* Seventeenth-Century Instrumental Dance Music, 1976; 5 articles, New Grove Dictionary of Music and Musicians, 1980; Papers published in proceedings: International Musicological Congress-Bach, Handel, Schütz-Stuttgart, 1985; Musica Antiqua Congress, Bydgoszcz, 1985; Rudolf Firkusny at 75, Musical America, 1987; Smetana Centennial, Musical America, 1985. *Honours:* Rudolf Firkusny Medal 1992. *Address:* 5307 W Falls View Drive, San Diego, CA 92115, USA.

MUCZYNSKI, Robert; Composer and Professor of Music; b. 19 March 1929, Chicago, Illinois, USA. *Education:* BM, 1950, MM, 1952, DePaul University, Chicago; Academy of Music, Nice, France, 1961. *Career:* Visiting Lecturer, DePaul University, Chicago, summers 1954–56; Head of Piano Department, Loras College, Dubuque, Iowa, 1956–58; Visiting Lecturer, Roosevelt University, Chicago, 1964–65; Professor, Head of Composition, University of Arizona, Tucson, 1965–87; Professor Emeritus, 1988–. *Compositions:* Over 40 published works including: Concerto for piano and orchestra; First Symphony; Suite for orchestra; Concerto for alto saxophone and chamber orchestra; 3 Piano Sonatas; 3 piano trios; String trio; Sonatas for cello, for alto saxophone, for flute and piano; Time pieces, for clarinet, piano; Scores for 9 documentary films; Commission: Dream Cycle, for solo piano, 1983; Quintet for winds, 1985; Third Piano Trio, 1986–87; Moments, for flute and piano; Desperate Measures (Paginini Variations for piano). *Recordings:* In release: Compact Disc recordings of Concerto No. 1 for piano and orchestra; A Serenade for Summer; The Three Piano Trios; Trio for violin, viola, cello; Alto Saxophone Concerto; Sonata for flute and piano; Time Pieces for clarinet and piano; Sonata for cello and piano; Symphonic Dialogues for orchestra; Sonata for alto saxophone and piano; Fantasy Trio for clarinet, cello and piano; Complete works for flute. *Honours:* Nominated for Pulizer Prize in Music, 1982. *Address:* 2760 N Wentworth, Tucson, AZ 85749, USA.

MUFF, Alfred; Singer (Bass-Baritone); b. 31 May 1949, Lucerne, Switzerland. *Education:* Studied with Werner Ernst in Lucerne, Elisabeth Grümmer and Irmgard Hartmann-Dressler in Berlin. *Career:* Debut: Don Ferrando in Fidelio, Lucerne, 1974; Member of the opera companies in Lucerne, Linz, Mannheim and since 1986 Zürich; Opera roles include, Philippo II and Grand Inquisitor, Don Carlo; Boris Godunov; Falstaff; Der fliegende Holländer; Barak in Die Frau ohne Schatten; Hans Sachs in Die Meistersinger von Nuernberg; King Marke and Kurwenal in Tristan und Isolde; Appeared as Wotan and Wanderer in Ring des Nibelungen; King Heinrich in Lohengrin; Jochanaan in Salome; Orestes in Elektra; Musiklehrer in Ariadne auf Naxos; Ochs in

Der Rosenkavalier; Morosus in Die scweigsame Frau; Waldner in Arabella; Osmin in Die Entführungl; Albert in Werther; Kezal in Die verkaufte Braut; Dr Schön in Lulu und Dokter in Wozzeck; Pizarro in Fidelio and Scarpia in Tosca at the Opernhaus Zürich, since 1986; Appearances also include: Barak at Milan's La Scala, Munich Festival; Title part of Der fliegende Holländer and Landgraf, Tannhäuser in Barcelona's Teatro del Liceu, Bruckner Festival, Linz, and at the Deutsche Oper Berlin and for a recording; Philip II in the original (French) version of Don Carlo at the Paris Opéra, in the Italian version at the Théâtre de la Monnaie in Brussels and at the Munich State Opera; Stravinsky's Oedipus Rex under Erich Leinsdorf in Geneva; Beethoven's Ninth Symphony at Geneva, Vienna and Basel; Jochanaan, Salome at the Vienna State Opera, at the Semper Oper in Dresden, in Barcelona and at the Festival of Taormina (under Giuseppe Sinopoli); Dvořák's Te Deum, in Vienna and at the Prague Spring Festival; Beethoven's Missa Solemnis on a tour of Switzerland, in Turin, Cologne and Vienna; Mahler's Eighth Symphony in Bonn; Schoenberg's Gurrelieder in Barcelona and Torino; Schnittke's Faust Kantate under Claudio Abbado in Vienna; Haydn's Paukenmesse with the Israel Philharmonic Orchestra under Zubin Mehta; Wotan, Die Walküre at the Munich Opera Festival, at the Vienna State Opera and in a new production at the Cologne Opera; Gurnemanz in Parsifal at the Brucknerfest in Linz; Wanderer in a new production of Siegfried and Wotan in a revival of Rheingold at the Hamburg State Opera; Die Schöpfung under Wolfgang Sawallisch for a television concert and under Nikolaus Harnoncourt for a radio concert; Pizarro, Fidelio under Peter Schneider at the RAI Torino; Barak in a new production of Die Frau ohne Schatten and Morosus in Die schweigsame Frau at the Zürich Opera; Opera roles in the 2003/04 season: Uraufführung L'Upupa by Hans Wwerner Nenze, Salzburger Festspiele; Musiklehrer, Ariadne; Grand Inquisitore; Landgraf; Osmin; Kezal (tschechisch); and Baron Ochs von Lerchenau in Zürich; under Wolfgang Sawallisch; Die Zauberflöte under Armin Jordan; Der fliegende Holländer under Pinchas Steinberg; Die Walküre under Christoph von Dohnanyi, Adorno in Schreker's Die Gezeichneten; Paul Dessau, Hagadah, Lulu Dr Schön for Television under Franz Welser Möst. *Recordings include:* First complete version of Die Frau ohne Schatten under Wolfgang Sawallisch; Die Zauberflöte under Armin Jordan; Der fliegende Holländer unter Pinchas Steinberg; Die Walküre under Christoph von Dohnányi; Adorno in Schreker's Die Gezeichneten; Paul Dessau, Hagadah. *Honours:* Kunstpreis of the City of Lucerne. *Address:* c/o Opernhaus Zürich, Falkenstrasse 1, 8008 Zürich, Switzerland.

MUKERIA, Shalva; Singer (tenor); b. 1965, Georgia, Russia. *Education:* Graduated Odessa Conservatoire, 1991. *Career:* Appearances from 1994 with Odessa Opera as Nemorino, Alfredo, Edgardo, Rodolfo and Werther; From 1996 sang Cassio in Otello as Las Palmas, and Rodolfo for Besançon Opera; Rodolfo and Alfredo on tour in Britain; Sang Bellini's Elvino at Florence, 2000; Season 2000–2001 with Millennium Gala in Dusseldorf, Alfredo for the Royal Opera Copenhagen and the Verdi Requiem in Helsinki; Other concerts include Rossini's Stabat Mater. *Honours:* Winner, Song Competitions at Prague and Tbilisi. *Current Management:* Athole Still International Management, Forresters Hall, 25–27 Westow Street, London, SE19 3RY, England. *Telephone:* (20) 8771-5271. *Fax:* (20) 8768-6600. *Website:* www .atholestill.com.

MULA, Inva; Singer (Soprano); b. 1967, Albania. *Career:* Sang in concert with Placido Domingo at Brussels, Munich and Olso, 1994; Appearances at the Opéra Bastille as Frasquita in Carmen and as Donizetti's Adina and Norina at Los Angeles (1995); Season 1995 as Offenbach's Antonia and Lisette in Puccini's La Rondine at Bonn; Dirce in Cherubini's Médée at Compiègne, 1996; Sang Gilda in Rigoletto at the Verona Arena, 2001. *Honours:* Winner, Georg Enescu Competition, Bucharest, 1991; Grand Prix Madama Butterfly, Barcelona, 1992; Prizewinner, Concours International de Voix d'Opéra Placido Domingo, Paris, 1993. *Address:* c/o Arena di Verona (Festival di Opera), Piazza Bra 28, 37121 Verona, Italy.

MULDOWNEY, Dominic; Composer; b. 19 July 1952, Southampton, England; m. Diane Trevis, 3 Oct 1986, 1 d. *Education:* BA, BPhil, York University. *Career:* Composer in Residence, Southern Arts Association, 1974–76; Composer of Chamber, Choral, Orchestral Works including work for theatre and television; Music Director, National Theatre, 1976–; mem, APC. *Compositions include:* An Heavyweight Dirge, 1971; Driftwood to the Flow for 18 String, 1972; 2 String Quartets, 1973, 1980; Double Helix for 8 players, 1977; 5 Theatre Poems after Brecht: The Beggar's Opera, realization, 1982; Piano Concerto, 1983; The Duration of Exile, 1984; Saxophone Concerto, 1985; Sinfonietta, 1986; Aus Subtilior, 1987; Lonley Hearts, 1988; Violin Concerto, 1989–90; On Suicide, for voice and ensemble, 1989; Un Carnival Cubiste for 10 bass players and metronome, 1989; Percussion Concerto, for Evelyn Glennie, 1991; Oboe Concerto, 1992; Trumpet Concerto, 1993; Concerto for 4 violins and strings, 1994; The Brontes, ballet, 1994; Incidental Music for

Hamlet, 1994; Sonata for 4 violins and strings, 1994; Trombone Concerto, 1995; Dance Suite, for orchestra, 1996; The Volupters Tango, radio opera, 1996; Clarinet Concerto, 1997; The Brontes, suite, 1998; The Fall of Jerusalem, for vocal soloists, choruses and orchestra, 1999; Concerto Grosso, 1997; Music for King Lear, 1997. *Recordings include:* Piano, Saxophone and Oboe Concertos. *Current Management:* Cavlin Music Corp. *Address:* c/o National Theatre, London SE1 1PX, England.

MULLER, Barbel; Singer (mezzo-soprano); b. 1968, Duisburg, Germany. *Education:* Studied at the Frankfurt Musikhochschule and with Laura Sarti and Elsa Cavelti. *Career:* Sang in concert from 1987 and made opera debut at Linz 1991, singing the Composer (Ariadne), Dorabella and Carmen; Further appearances as Sesto (Clemenza di Tito), Orlofsky, Charlotte and Octavian (Strasbourg, 1995); Concert repertoire includes Mozart's Requiem (at Stuttgart), the Christmas Oratorio (Ulm and Amsterdam), St Matthew Passion (Tubingen), Elijah (Zürich) and Bach's B Minor Mass (Frankfurt). *Current Management:* Athole Still International Management, Forresters Hall, 25–27 Westow Street, London, SE19 3RY, England. *Telephone:* (20) 8771-5271. *Fax:* (20) 8768-6600. *Website:* www.atholestill.com.

MULLER, Markus; Singer (Tenor); b. 1958, Saulgau, Germany. *Education:* Studied in Stuttgart with Helmuth Rilling. *Career:* Sang at Dortmund Opera from 1987, Deutsche Oper am Rhein at Düsseldorf from 1991; Roles have included Belmonte and Mozart's Arsace (Idomeneo), Nicolai's Fenton, Tamino, and the Astrologer in Rimsky's Golden Cockerel; Guest appearances at Dresden from 1991, including Belmonte in Die Entführung and Rossini's Almaviva; Premiere of Klebe's Gervaise Macquart at Düsseldorf, 1995; Sang Oronte in Alcina at Dusseldorf, 1999; Many concert appearances. *Address:* Deutsche Oper am Rhein, Heinrich-Heine Alle 16a, 40213 Düsseldorf, Germany.

MÜLLER, Rufus; Singer (Tenor); b. 5 Feb. 1959, Kent, England. *Education:* Choral Scholar, New College, Oxford; Studying with Thomas LoMonaco, New York. *Career:* Worked with many established conductors including: Ivor Bolton, Richard Hickox, Joshua Rifkin, Andrew Parrott and Ivan Fischer; Opera and concert appearances throughout Europe, Japan and the USA; Roles performed include: Bastien in Mozart's Bastien und Bastienne; Aminta in Peri's Euridice; Tersandre in Lully's Roland; Giuliano in Handel's Rodrigo; Lurcanio in Handel's Ariodante; Recitals in Wigmore Hall and Barbican, London, and on radio for BBC, in Munich, Tokyo, Madrid, Utrecht, Salzburg and New York; Recent engagements include Schubert's Die schöne Müllerin, Munich; Jonathan Miller production of St Matthew Passion at Brooklyn Academy of Music; Mendelssohn's St Paul with the Leipzig Gewandhaus Choir; Beethoven's Ninth Symphony and Handel's Messiah with the Swedish Chamber Orchestra; Televised tour of Messiah in Spain with Trevor Pinnock and the English Concert; World première, Rorem's Song Cycle Evidence of Things Not Seen, Carnegie Hall, New York, and Washington DC; St Matthew Passion in Sweden, Germany and Switzerland; Castor in Rameau's Castor et Pollux; Mendelssohn's Elijah in New York; Monteverdi's Il Ritorno d'Ulisse in Athens and Florence; Recital, Musée d'Orsay, Paris; Sang Alessando in Handel's Poro at the 1998 Halle Festival; Further engagements include: Title role in Rameau's Pygmalian, Opera Atelier, Toronto; Evangelist in Bach's St Matthew's passion with the CBSO; Recital, New York Festival of Song, Carnegie Hall. *Recordings include:* Bach's St John Passion; Die Zauberflöte; Beethoven's Choral Fantasia; Dowland's First Book of Airs; Haydn's O Tuneful Voice; 19th Century Songs; The Evangelist in Bach's St Matthew Passion; Telemann's Admiraltätsmusik and Solo Cantatas; Rorem: Evidence of Things Not Seen. *Honours:* GKN English Song Award, 1985; 2nd Prize, Oratorio Society of New York, 1999. *Address:* The Garden Flat, 26 Oliver Grove, London SE25 6EJ, England.

MÜLLER-BRACHMANN, Hanno; German singer (bass-baritone); b. 20 Aug. 1970, Cologne. *Education:* Basle Academy of Music; Staatliche Hochschule für Musik Freiburg; and with Rudolf Piernay, Staatlilche Hochschule für Musik Mannheim. *Career:* Debut: Theater Freiburg, 1992; with Deutsche Staatsoper, Berlin, 1996–, as Donner, Kothner, Biterolf, Mozart's Figaro, Papageno, Leporello, Guglielmo, Orest, Golaud, Tomski, Escamillo; with Bayerische Staatsoper, 1999–, as Fernando, Orest, Guglielmo, Papageno; with Vienna Staatsoper as Guglielmo; with Elliott Carter's opera What Next? under Daniel Barenboim in Berlin, Chicago and New York, 1999–2000; Concert performances under conductors including Kurt Masur, Sir Neville Marriner, Christoph Eschenbach, Sir John Eliott Gardiner, András Schiff; has performed with orchestras including Berlin, London and New York Philharmonics, Concertgebouw Amsterdam, Gewandhaus Leipzig, Acad. of St Martin-in-the-Fields, Chicago Symphony Orchestra and Staatskapelle Berlin; Lieder recitals in Germany, Switzerland, France, Japan and Austria. *Recordings include:* Schubert recital, Bach's Mass in B minor, Mozart's Requiem, Rossini's Petite Messe Solonnelle, Schumann's Der Rose Pilgerfahrt, Telemann's Orpheus, Haydn's Creation, Bach's Christmas Oratorio, Schoenberg's Jakobsleiter (Hänssler), Bach's Cantatas 213 and 214, Wagner's Tannhäuser with

Daniel Barenboim). *Film:* Cosi fan tutte, 2003. *Television:* La Bohème, 2002. *Honours:* 1st Prize, Bundeswettbewerb Gesang, Berlin, 1992, 1994; Meistersingerwettbewerb Nürnberg, 1995; Prix Davidoff, 1995; Brahms Prize, Int. Brahms-Soc. Schleswig-Holstein, 1995. *Current Management:* Askonas Holt Ltd, Lonsdale Chambers, 27 Chancery Lane, London, WC2A 1PF, England. *Telephone:* (20) 7400-1700. *Fax:* (20) 7400-1799. *E-mail:* info@askonasholt.co.uk. *Website:* www .askonasholt.co.uk.

MÜLLER-LORENZ, Wolfgang; Singer (Tenor); b. 24 Nov. 1946, Cologne, Germany. *Education:* Studied in Cologne. *Career:* Sang as Baritone, at the Mannheim Opera, 1972; Engagements at Munich, Nuremburg, Karlsruhe, Frankfurt and Mannheim as Papageno, Rossini's Figaro and Dvořák's Jacobin; Studied further with Hans Hopf and sang at the Graz Opera from 1980 as Lohengrin, Cavardossi, Calaf and Loge; Siegmund and Siegfried in a Ring cycle, 1989; Sang with the Deutsche Oper Berlin on tour to Washington, 1989, and as Bacchus in the original version of Ariadne auf Naxos at the Landestheater, Salzburg, 1991; Other roles have included Otello, Dimitri in Boris Godunov, Parsifal, The Marquis in Lulu, Erik, Herman and Fra Diavolo, Zürich Opera, 1989; Season 2000–01 as Tannhäuser at the Munich Staatsoper and Tristan at Covent Garden; Frequent concert appearances notably in contemporary works. *Address:* c/o Landestheater, Schwarstrasse 22, 5020 Salzburg, Austria.

MULLER-MOLINARI, Helga; Singer (Mezzo-soprano); b. 28 March 1948, Pfaffenhofen, Bavaria, Germany. *Education:* Studied with Felicie Huni-Mihaczek in Munich and with Giulietta Simionato in Rome. *Career:* Sang at Saarbrucken, 1972–73; La Scala Milan, 1975 in L'Enfant et Les Sortilèges, Piccola Scala 1979 in Vivaldi's Tito Manlio; Further appearances at the Salzburg Festival, as Annina, 1983, Barcelona, as Cherubino 1984, Turin as Carmen, 1988 and Monte Carlo, Portrait de Manon by Massenet, 1989; Roles in operas by Rossini, Mozart and other composers at Nancy, Dublin, Pesaro and elsewhere; Trieste 1991 as Werther. *Recordings include:* Der Rosenkavalier, Ariadne auf Naxos, Mozart Requiem, Bruckner Te Deum, Oronte by Cesti, Monteverdi Madrigals; Handel Partenope; L'Arcadia in Brenta by Galuppi, Rossini's Aureliano in Palmira and La Gazza Ladra. *Address:* Teatro Comunale di Trieste, Riva Novembre 1, 34121 Trieste, Italy.

MULLOVA, Viktoria; Violinist; b. 27 Nov. 1959, Moscow, Russia. *Education:* Studied with V. Bronin, Central School of Music, Moscow. *Career:* Appearances with many of the World's most renowned orchestras including: Berlin Philharmonic, London Symphony, Royal Philharmonic, Boston Symphony, Pittsburgh and Toronto Symphonies; Worked with conductors including: Abbado, Boulez, Haitink, Maazel, Marriner, Masur, Ozawa, Previn, Muti; Appeared in many festivals including: Marlboro, Tanglewood, Edinburgh, Lucerne; Appearances with London Symphony Orchestra in Germany, Cleveland Orchestra, Dallas Symphony, Los Angeles Philharmonic, Berlin Philharmonic, Israel Philharmonic; Performances with the Mullova Chamber Ensemble from 1994; Season 1999–2000 concerts with the Israel Philharmonic, Leipzig Gewandhaus, Philadephia, the Philharmonia and the LA Philharmonic; Soloist and Director with the Orchestra of the Age of Enlightenment, Mozart project and solo Bach recitals throughout the United Kingdom, Germany and Italy, 2000; Season 2000–01 tour and recording of Through the Looking Glass, collection of arrangements of the works of Miles Davis, Duke Ellington and the Beatles among others; Mendelssohn's concerto in E minor at the London Proms, 2002. *Recordings include:* Debut release of Tchaikovsky and Sibelius with Ozawa and the Boston Symphony was awarded the Grand Prix du Disque; Vivaldi's Four Seasons with Abbado and the Chamber Orchestra of Europe; Solo works of Bartók, Bach, Paganini; Shostakovich Concerto No. 1 and Prokofiev No. 2 with André Previn and the Royal Philharmonic; Paganini Concerto No. 1 and Vieuxtemps No. 5 with Neville Marriner and the Academy of St Martin in the Fields; Brahms, Violin Concerto, Berlin Philharmonic, Claudio Abbado; Bach Sonatas, Prokofiev Sonata No. 2, Ravel Sonata with Bruno Canino; Brahms Sonatas with Piotr Anderszewski; Bach Violin Concertos with the Mullova Ensemble; Through the Looking Glass with Matthew Barley, Julian Joseph, Paul Clarvis. *Honours:* 1st Prize, Sibelius Competition, Helsinki, 1981; Gold Medal, Tchaikovsky Competition, Moscow, 1982; International Prize of the Accademia Musicale Chigiana in Siena, 1988. *Current Management:* Askonas Holt Ltd, Lonsdale Chambers, 27 Chancery Lane, London, WC2A 1PF, England. *Telephone:* (20) 7400-1700. *Fax:* (20) 7400-1799. *E-mail:* info@askonasholt.co .uk. *Website:* www.askonasholt.co.uk.

MUMELTER, Martin; Violinist; b. 12 May 1948, Innsbruck, Austria; m. Magdalena Pattis, 2 s., 2 d. *Education:* Konservatorium Innsbruck; Philadelphia College of Performing Arts. *Career:* Mainly with 20th Century Music and Wiener Symphoniker, Staatskapelle Berlin, RSO Vienna, Symphony Orchestra des Bayerischen Rundfunks, Bamberger Symphoniker, RTL-Luxemburg, Mozarteum Orchestra Salzburg; Appearances at Musikbiennale Berlin, Bregenzer Festspiele, Sagra musicale Umbra, Edinburgh Fringe Festival, Festwochen der Alten Musik Innsbruck; Recitals: New York at Merkin Hall and Carnegie Recital Hall, 1983 and 1987; Professor of Violin and Director of Orchestra, Konservatorium Innsbruck, 1971–75; Professor of Violin at University Mozarteum, Salzburg, 1986–. *Recordings:* 200 Radio recordings; CDs including complete Ives Sonatas (with Herbert Henck, piano), concerto by Schnittke (Nr 3) Chamber music by Ives, Cage, Bartók. *Publications:* Ums Leben spielen (book), 1994; Several radio plays for Austrian Radio and SRG Zürich. *Honours:* Finalist, Gaudeamus Competition, Rotterdam, 1971; Preis der Kritik Musikbiennale Berlin, 1979; Berlanda Preis des Landes Tirol, 1985. *Current Management:* Hans Adler, Auguste-Viktoria-Straáe 64, 14199, Berlin, Germany. *Address:* Pizachw. 31, 6073 Sistrans, Austria.

MUMFORD, Jeffrey; Composer; b. 22 June 1955, Washington, USA. *Education:* University of California, at Irvine and San Diego; New York, with Elliott Carter. *Career:* Commissions from, Robert Evett Fund of Washington, DC, 1977, Cellist Fred Sherry, 1981, Aspen Wind Quintet, 1983, McKi m Fund, Library of Congress, 1986, New York New Music Ensemble, 1987, Violist Marcus Thompson, 1989, Amphion Foundation for the Da Capo Chamber Players, 1989, Fromm Music Foundation, 1990, Roanoke Symphony Orchestra, 1991; Walter W Naumburg Foundation, 1991, Abel/Steinberg/Winant Trio, 1991, Roanoke Symphony Orchestra, 1992, Cellist Joshua Gordon, 1994, Cincinnati Radio Station WGUC, 1994, National Symphony Orchestra, 1995; Works Extensively Performed in the USA and abroad, including Performances at the Library of Congress, Aspen Music Festival, Bang On A Can Music Festival, Seattle Chamber Music Festival, London's Purcell Room, Helsinki Festival, Musica Nel Nostro Tempo Festival, Milan and by Saint Paul Chamber Orchestra; Meet the Composer/Arts Endowment Commissioning US Program, 1996; Sonia and louis Rothscholl for the Opus 3 Trio, 1998; The Contemporary Music Forum and Philip Berlin, 1999; Artist-in-Residence, Bowling Green State University, 1999–2000; mem, NARAS; Recent commissions include: Radio Station WCLV, Cleveland, 2002, Sharan Leventhal, Violinist, 2001; Rhonda Taylor and David Reminick, saxophonists, 2001; Wendy Richman, violist, 2001; Nncy Ruyle Dodge Charitable Trust, for the Corigliano Quartet, 2000; Cleveland Chamber Symphony, 2000; Phillips Collection (D.C.), Miller Theatre (N.Y.C.), Schubert Club (St. Paul, MN.), for Margaret Kampmeier, 1999. *Compositions include:* Fragments From the Surrounding Evening; A Flower in Folding Shadows, for piano and four hands; Linear Cycles VII, for solo violin; Echoes in a Cloud Box, for violin and cello; Jewels Beyond the Mist; Diamonds Suspended in a Galaxy of Clouds, Soprano Solo; Lullaby, for soprano and piano; In Forests of Evaporating Dawns; A Pond Within the Drifting Dusk; A still radiance within dark air, for piano solo, flute, clarinet, violin, viloncello, 1996; A layer of vivid stillness for cello solo and 12 cellos, 1996; Ringing fields enveloping blue for cello and piano; A window of resonant light, cello piano percussion, 1997; In afternoons of deep and amplified air, string quartet, 1998; Amid the Light of Quickening Memory for orchestra, 2002; The Promise of the Far Hoizon, string quartet, 2002; A Precious Continuity is a day expanding, 2001; Through the Filtering Dawn of Spreading Daybright, 2001; Wending, solo viola, 2001; A Landscape of interior resonances, solo piano, 2001; Revisiting variazioni elegiaci, solo viola, 2001; A Distance of unfolding light, orchestra, 2000; Billowing Pockets brightly layered, cello and chamber orchestra, 2000; As a spray of reflected meadowlight informs the air, alto sax, violin and percussion, 2000; Undiluted days, piano trio, 2000. *Recordings:* A pond within the drifting dusk; The focus of blue light; Fragments from the surrounding evening. *Contributions:* Quadrivium Music Press; Perspectives of New Music. *Honours:* Guggenheim Fellowship; Awards from, Minnesota Composers Forum, American Music Center, Alice M Ditson Fund; Ohio Arts Council Individual Artist Fellowship, 2002; American Academy of Arts and Letters: Academy Award in Music, 2003. *Address:* c/o Theodore Presser Co., 588 North Gulph Road, King of Prussia, PA. 19406, USA.

MUMMA, Gordon; Composer, Performer, Author and Professor of Music; b. 30 March 1935, Framingham, Massachusetts, USA. *Career:* Composer and Performer of electro-acoustic and instrumental music with performances and recordings in North and South America, Europe and Japan; Television and film performances, Germany and USA; Visiting Lecturer, various colleges and universities; Composer and Performing Musician, Sonic Arts Union, New York City, and Merce Cunningham Dance Company, 1966–74; Professor of Music, 1975–95, Professor Emeritus, 1995–, University of California, Santa Cruz; Visiting Professor of Music, University of California, San Diego, 1985–87; mem, Society for Ethnomusicology; Braodcast Music Inc. *Compositions include:* Music from The Venezia Space Theatre; Dresden Interleaf 13 Feb 1945; Mesa; Hornpipe; Schoolwork; Cybersonic Cantilevers; Pontpoint; Than Particle, for percussion and digital computer, 1985; Epifont, for tape, 1985, Begault Meadow Sketches, tape, 1987; Songs Without Words, 1995. *Recordings:* All listed compositions plus performance of music by Robert Ashley, David Behrman, George Cacioppo,

John Cage, Mauricio Kagel and Christian Wolff. *Contributions:* Numerous books and journals including: James Klosty's Merce Cunningham; Appleton and Perera's Development and Practice of Electronic Music; Gilbert Chase's Roger Reynolds: A Portrait; Journal of Audio Engineering Society; Darmstadt Beitrage zur neue Musik; Neuland I; Sound Recording, major article to The New Grove Dictionary of American Music, 1986. *Current Management:* Artservices, 325 Spring Street, New York, NY 10013, USA. *Address:* Porter College, University of California, Santa Cruz, CA 95064, USA.

MUNDT, Richard; Singer (Bass); b. 8 Sept. 1936, Illinois, USA. *Education:* Studied in New York and Vienna. *Career:* Debut: Saarbrucken 1962, as the Commendatore in Don Giovanni; Appearances at Kiel, Dortmond, Darmstadt, Graz, Liège and the Spoleto Festival; American engagements at the New York City Opera, San Francisco, Portland, Chicago and Cincinnati; Other roles have included Mozart's Osmin, Don Giovanni, Figaro and Sarastro, Rocco, Arkel in Pelléas et Mélisande, Ramphis, King Philip, Padre Guardiano and Wagner's Marke, Daland, Fasolt, Pogner, Hunding and Landgrave.

MUNI, Nicholas; Stage Director; b. 1960, USA. *Career:* Artistic Dir, Tusla Opera, 1988–97; has directed over 150 opera productions with leading US companies; Season 1989–90, with Il Trovatore at Seattle, transferring to Houston, Toronto and Vancouver; French version of Verdi's opera at Tulsa, with new production of The Juniper Tree by Philip Glass and Robert Moran; New York City Opera debut with La Traviata, 1991; world premiere of Frankenstein the Modern Prometheus, by Libby Larsen, for Minnesota Opera; US premiere of Rossini's Armida at Tulsa, 1992; complete version of Lulu for Canadian Opera and Ariadne auf Naxos at Opera Theater of St Louis; world premiere of Moran's The Shining Princess at Minnesota, 1993; staging of Norma for Seattle and Houston, Los Angeles, 1996; Artistic Dir, Cincinnati Opera, 1997–, produced Jenůfa there, 1998. *Current Management:* Athole Still International Management, Forresters Hall, 25–27 Westow Street, London, SE19 3RY, England. *Telephone:* (20) 8771-5271. *Fax:* (20) 8768-6600. *Website:* www.atholestill.com.

MUNKITTRICK, Mark; Singer (Bass); b. 1951, Boston, Massachusetts, USA. *Education:* Studied at Fresno State College, California. *Career:* Sang in Carnegie Hall concert performances of Donizetti's Gemma di Vergy and Puccini's Edgar, 1976–77; New York City Opera 1977, as Daland and Pogner; Guest appearances in Washington, Baltimore, Los Angeles and Atlanta, as Leporello, Alfonso, Raimondo and Monteverdi's Seneca; Sang at Karlsruhe, 1978–87, as Mephistopheles, Rocco, Basilio, Kecal, Banquo, King Philip, Ramphis, the Landgrave in Tannhäuser and Fafner; Madrid, 1984, as Handel's Giulio Cesare; Dresden Staatsoper 1989 as Morosus in Die schweigsame Frau; Member of the Stuttgart Staatsoper from 1985; Guest engagements throughout Germany and Europe; Other roles include Arthur in The Lighthouse by Maxwell Davies, Kaspar and Henry VIII in Anna Bolena; Sang Taddeo in L'Italiana in Algeri at Stuttgart, 1996; Sang Angelotti in Tosca at Stuttgart, 1998; Poet in Donizetti's Le Convenienze Teatrali, 2001; Wide concert repertory including bass solo in the Missa Solemnis. *Recordings include:* Gemma di Vergy and Edgar. *Address:* c/o Stuttgart Staatsoper, Oberer Schlossgarten 6, 7000 Stuttgart, Germany.

MUNOZ, Daniel; Singer (Tenor); b. 1951, Buenos Aires, Argentina. *Education:* Studied in Buenos Aires. *Career:* Sang at the Teatro Colón Buenos Aires from 1979, Teatro de la Zarzuela Madrid from 1980; Studied further in Milan and sang from 1982 at opera houses in Spain, Portugal and South America; Nancy Opera 1983, as Cavaradossi, Liège 1986 as Pinkerton and the Berne Stadtheater, 1988; Sang Cornil Schut in Pittore Fiamminghi at Trieste and Calaf at the Szeged Festival, Hungary, 1991; Other roles include Don José, Faust, Werther, Don Carlos and Des Grieux in Manon Lescaut; Sang Andrea Chénier at Buenos Aires, 1996; Canio in Pagliacci at Cape Town, 1998; Sang Verdi's Riccardo at Budapest, 2000; Frequent concert appearances. *Address:* Teatro Comunale, Riva Novembre 1, 34121 Trieste, Italy.

MUNSEL, Patrice; Singer (Soprano); b. 14 May 1925, Spokane, Washington, USA. *Education:* Studied with Charlotte Lange, William Herman and Renato Bellini in New York. *Career:* Debut: Metropolitan Opera 1943, as Philine in Mignon; Sang in New York until 1958, as Adele in Die Fledermaus, Offenbach's Périchole, Lucia di Lammermoor, Rosina, Olympia in Les Contes d'Hoffmann, the Queen of Shemakha, Zerlina, Despina and Gilda; European Tour 1948; Starred in 1953 film Melba; Appeared in musical comedy after leaving the Metropolitan.

MURA, Peter; Conductor; b. 21 June 1924, Budapest, Hungary; m. Rose Tóth, 1 d. *Education:* High School of Music, Budapest. *Career:* Debut: Hungarian State Opera House, 1948; Solo Repetiteur, 1945–, Conductor of the Stagione, 1950–53, Hungarian State Opera House; Director and Chief Conductor, Miskolc National Theatre Opera Company, 1953–57; State Opera Conductor, Warsaw, Poland, 1957–58; Conductor, Silesian Opera, Bytom, Poland, 1958–61; Director and Chief Conductor, Miskolc Symphony Orchestra, Hungary, 1961–84; Conductor, Hungarian State

Opera, 1984–87; Professor, High School of Music, Budapest, 1986–; Conductor, Wiener Kammeroper, 1990–91. *Recordings:* Mozart: Idomeneo Overture and Ballet, Symphony in A, 1974. *Honours:* Ferenc Liszt Prize, 1966; Merited Artist of the Hungarian Republic, 1972. *Address:* Podmaniczky U 63, 1064 Budapest, Hungary. *Telephone:* 1–311–8978. *Fax:* 1–311–8978.

MURGATROYD, Andrew; Singer (Tenor); b. 1955, Halifax, Yorkshire, England. *Education:* Studied singing with Barbara Robotham at Lancaster University and with Rudolf Pierney; Lay-Clerk at Christ Church Cathedral, Oxford. *Career:* Concert engagements include Israel in Egypt for John Eliot Gardiner in Stuttgart, Milan, Paris, Rome, East Berlin and Turin; Handel's Esther for WDR in Cologne and Acis and Galatea for Swiss television; Monteverdi Vespers and Alexander's Feast at Aix-en-Provence; Performances of Bach's St John Passion in London, Cambridge and Spain, and the St Matthew Passion at the Festival Hall, 1990; Debussy's Rodrigue et Chimène in London and Manchester; Beethoven's Ninth with the Hanover Band in London and Germany; Contemporary Music Network Tour with Richard Bernas, 1990; Sang in Haydn's St Nicholas Mass and Stabat Mater at St John's, London, 1997. *Recordings include:* Beethoven's Missa Solemnis and Ninth Symphony (Nimbus); Monteverdi Vespers with The Sixteen (Hyperion); Campra's Tancrède (Erato); Leclair Scylla et Glaucus; John Tavener, We Shall See Him As He Is, (Chandos); Antonio Teixeira, Te Deum (Collins Classics). *Address:* c/o CDI, Lyndhurst, Denton Road, Ben Rhydding, Ilkley, W Yorks, LS29 8QR, England.

MURGU, Corneliu; Singer (Tenor); b. 1948, Timisoara, Romania. *Education:* Studied in Romania, in Florence and with Marcello del Monaco in Treviso. *Career:* Debut: Wiener Staatsoper with Cavalleria Rusticana (Turiddu), 1978; Following appearances until 1982: Deutsche Oper Berlin, Munich, Hamburg, Stuttgart, Düsseldorf, Zürich and Graz; In 1982 made his debut at the Met with Ballo in Maschera (Riccardo); In the same year, appearances in Naples, Rome and Andrea Chénier in Bonn; Norma (Pollione) in Lyon, Carmen and Turandot in Caracalla, Rome, 1983–85; La Scala debut with Aida (Radames), 1986; Andrea Chénier and Samson in Rio de Janeiro and Cavalleria Rusticana in Barcelona, 1987–89; Otello at Opéra Bastille in Paris, 1990; Cavalleria Rusticana/Pagliacci and Carmen in Rotterdam, 1994–95; Debut in Verona with Otello, 1994, and Covent Garden debut with Calaf in Turandot. *Recordings include:* Otello with Renato Bruson, Fanciulla del West with Gwyneth Jones, Cavalleria Rusticana/Pagliacci, Carmen. *Address:* Les Achantes, 6 Avenue des Citronniers, 98000 Monte Carlo.

MURPHY, Aubrey; Violinist; b. 1960, Dublin, Ireland. *Education:* Royal Irish Academy, Yehudi Menuhin School and Indiana University. *Career:* Guest leader from 1992 with Scottish Chamber Orchestra, BBC Ulster Orchestra and Orchestra of the Royal Opera House, Covent Garden (currently a principal); Frequent chamber concerts and member of chamber group playing at country houses and stately homes; Concert Master of the Estonian-Finnish Symphony Orchestra. *Address:* c/o Royal Opera House (orchestra), Covent Garden, London. WC2, England. *Telephone:* (20) 7240 1200. *Fax:* (20) 7212 9502.

MURPHY, Emma, MMus, FTCL; British recorder player and soprano. *Education:* Univ. of Birmingham, Trinity Coll. of Music. *Career:* performances with early music ensembles, including The King's Consort, Ex Cathedra, New London Consort and New Trinity Baroque, and with her own ensemble Da Camera; performances of contemporary music, including Park Lane Group and a duo with marimba; annual recital tours of Japan; Musical Dir, The City Carollers; Countess of Munster Musical Trust Award. *Recordings:* with The King's Consort, Ex Cathedra and Sprezzatura; A Celtic Celebration (with Da Camera). *Publications:* An Introduction to Fontegara and the Art of Divisions. *E-mail:* emma@emmamurphy.co.uk. *Website:* www.emmamurphy.co .uk.

MURPHY, Heidi Grant; Singer (soprano); b. 1962, USA. *Education:* Studied in New York. *Career:* Member of the Met Opera's Young Artist Development Program, from 1988; Met debut in Die Frau ohne Schatten (1989) followed by Xenia (Boris Godunov), Papagena, Oscar, Nannetta, Sophie in Der Rosenkavalier, Soeur Constance (Carmélites), Ilia; Servilia (La Clemenza di Tito), Pamina and Susanna in season 1997–98; Santa Fe debut 1991, as Susanna; European debut at Brussels 1991, in La Favorita, followed by Monteverdi's Drusilla with Netherlands Opera, Mozart's Celia (Lucio Silla) and Ismene (Mitridate) at Salzburg, Servilia at the Paris Opéra and Ilia at Frankfurt; Concerts include Mozart's C Minor Mass (Houston Symphony), Mahler's Eighth Symphony (Atlanta Symphony and Vienna Philharmonic); New York Philharmonic debut 1996, in Honegger's Jeanne d'Arc au Bûcher; Semire in Les Boréades by Rameau at the 1999 London Prom concerts; Sang Strauss's Sophie at the New York Met, 2000; Conductors have included Levine, Ozawa, Robert Shaw, Masur, Michael Tilson Thomas and Charles Dutoit. *Recordings include:* Idomeneo, from the Met (DGG); Haydn's Die Schöpfung (Teldec). *Honours:* Winner, 1988 Metropolitan

National Council Auditions. *Current Management:* Askonas Holt Ltd, Lonsdale Chambers, 27 Chancery Lane, London, WC2A 1PF, England. *Telephone:* (20) 7400-1700. *Fax:* (20) 7400-1799. *E-mail:* info@ askonasholt.co.uk. *Website:* www.askonasholt.co.uk.

MURPHY, Suzanne; Singer (Soprano); b. 15 Oct. 1941, Limerick, Ireland. *Education:* Studied with Veronica Dunne at the College of Music in Dublin, 1973–76. *Career:* Has sung with Welsh National Opera from 1976 as Constanze, Amelia (I Masnadieri and Un Ballo in Maschera), Elisabeth de Valois, Leonora (Il Trovatore), Elvira (Ernani and I Puritani), Violetta, Norma, Lucia di Lammermoor and Musetta; Has sung Constanze and Donna Anna for English National Opera; Donna Anna and the soprano roles in Les Contes d'Hoffmann for Opera North and Constanze for Scottish Opera; German debut 1985, as Norma in a concert performance of Bellini's opera in Munich; Returned 1988 for Amelia (Un Ballo in Maschera); Vienna Staatsoper debut 1987, as Electra in Idomeneo; Invited to return 1988–89 (Armenian Gala Benefit Concert); Has sung Reiza in Oberon at Lyon and Donna Anna at the Aix-en-Provence Festival; North American engagements include Norma at the New York City Opera, Amelia (Ballo), Elvira (Puritani) and Lucia in Vancouver, Fiordiligi, Ophelia (Hamlet) and Violetta in Pittsburgh; Sang Alice Ford in the Peter Stein production of Falstaff for Welsh National Opera (repeated in New York and Milan 1989); Sang Norma for the Dublin Grand Opera Society 1989, Hanna Glawari in The Merry Widow for Scottish Opera; Title role in La Fanciulla del West for Welsh National Opera, 1991; Electra in Idomeneo at the Albert Hall (Proms) and in Wales with WNO, 1991; Season 1992 with Elvira in Ernani and Tosca, in new productions for WNO; Concert appearances in Austria, Sweden, Denmark, Belgium and Portugal; Sang Leonore in Fidelio on South Bank, London, 1989 and at Belfast, 1996; Sang the Kostelnička in Jenůfa at Geneva, 2001. *Current Management:* Ingpen & Williams Ltd, 7 St George's Court, 131 Putney Bridge Road, London, SW15 2PA, England.

MURRAY, Ann; Singer (Mezzo-soprano); b. 27 Aug. 1949, Dublin, Ireland; m. Philip Langridge. *Education:* Studied at the Royal College of Music in Manchester with Frederick Cox and at the London Opera Centre (1972–74). *Career:* Debut: Aldeburgh 1974, with Scottish Opera as Alceste in the opera by Gluck; Wexford Festival 1974–75 as Myrtale in Thaïs by Massenet and Queen Laodicea in Cavalli's Eritrea; English National Opera in Le Comte Ory and as Cenerentola; Covent Garden from 1976, as Cherubino, Siebel (Faust), Ascanio, Tebaldo in I Capuleti e i Montecchi, the Child in L'Enfant et les Sortilèges, Idamante and the Composer in Ariadne auf Naxos; Sang Octavian at Covent Garden 1989 and returned 1991 as Sifare in a new production of Mitridate for the Mozart bicentenary; US debut 1979 with the New York City Opera as Sextus in La Clemenza di Tito, repeating the role at the Metropolitan in 1984; Salzburg Festival 1981, as Nicklausse in Les Contes d'Hoffmann; Glyndebourne Festival 1979, as Minerva in Il Ritorno d'Ulisse, returned to Salzburg 1985 to sing the role in Henze's version of Monteverdi's opera; Milan La Scala 1983 as Dorabella in Così fan tutte, returned 1984 as Cecilio in Mozart's Lucio Silla; In 1989 sang Cenerentola at Salzburg; English National Opera 1990 as Berlioz's Beatrice; Sang Cecilio in a new production of Lucio Silla at the Vienna Staatsoper, 1991; Season 1992–93 appeared as Ruggiero in a new production of Handel's Alcina at Covent Garden, Xerxes for ENO, Cecilio at Salzburg and in The Beggar's Opera at Aldeburgh; Title role in Giulio Cesare at Munich, 1994; Many concert appearances including Stravinsky's Pulcinella at the 1993 London Proms; Season 1996–97 included Brangaene in Munich and Ruggiero at the Vienna Festival; Giulio Cesare for the Royal Opera, 1997; Donizetti's Mary Stuart for ENO, 1998; Season 1999 with music by Lili Boulanger at the London Proms; Sang Gluck's Alceste at Amsterdam, 1999, and Handel's Ariodante in Munich, 2000; London Proms, 2002. *Recordings include:* St Matthew Passion, Handel and Mozart arias, Roméo et Juliette, Mozart's Requiem; Haydn's Stabat Mater; Purcell's Dido and Aeneas; Les Contes d'Hoffmann; Così fan tutte, Videos of Xerxes and Mitridate.

MURRAY, John Horton; Singer (Tenor); b. 1961, Braunschweig, Germany (of American parents); m. Louise Sweet, 3 c. *Education:* Studied at Curtis Institute in Philadelphia and the MET Lindemann Young Artist Devt. *Career:* Debut as David in Meistersinger at Spoleto Festival, 1992; Performances of Stolzing, Don Jose, The Emperor in Frau Ohne Schatten and Aeneas in Les Troyens at the Metropolitan Opera, 1995–; Don Jose, Verona Arena, 1996; Stolzing and Bacchus, Lyric Opera of Chicago, 1998; Menelaus in Strauss's Ägyptische Helena, Royal Opera, Festival Hall, London, 1998; Tichon in Katya Kabanova, 2000; Bacchus in Santa Fe, 1999 and Menelaus, 2001; Apollo and Menelaus at Deutsche Oper Berlin, Parisfal in Edinburgh, Lohengrin at the Liceo, and La Scala debut as Bacchus in 2000; 2001–02 season: as Laca in Jenůfa for Geneva Opera, Paul in Tote Stadt for New York City Opera and Stolzing at Rai Orchestra Sinfonica Naz.; 2002–03 season: Bacchus at Liceo and Rienzi at Antiken Festspiele, Trier; 2003–04 season: Emperor for Metropolitan Opera, Bacchus at Seattle Opera.

Recordings: The Magician in Menotti's Medium; Wagner: Scenes from Lohengrin and Siegfried. *Honours:* National Institute for Music Theater Prizes; George London Award, 1988; Finalist in 1989 Metropolitan National Council Auditions; Musician's Emergency Fund Winner, 1990. *Address:* c/o IMG Artists, Lovell House, 616 Chiswick High Road, London W4 5RX, England. *E-mail:* Johnhortonmurray@aol.com. *Website:* JohnHortonMurray.com.

MURRAY, Niall; Opera Singer (Baritone); b. 22 April 1948, Dublin, Ireland; m. Barbara F M Murray, 1 d. *Education:* Royal Academy of Music, Dublin. *Career:* Debut: Boy Soprano in Pantomime, Dublin; Appearances as Curly in Oklahoma, Dublin, 1970; Opera debut, Bomarzo, Coliseum, London, 1976; Baritone Lead in over 52 musicals including, English National Opera, London; Television and radio appearances, England and Ireland frequently; Also appeared in Cabarets and Musicals, major opera appearances include Papageno, Schaunard, Figaro (Barber of Seville), and Lescaut (Manon); Sang Iago at the Basle City Theatre 1988 (under the name Mario di Mario); Sang Falstaff at Lübeck, 1999. *Recordings:* Niall Murray Sings (Irish Songs); Danilo; The Merry Widow; Robert in La Fille du Régiment. *Address:* c/o English National Opera, London Coliseum, St Martin's Lane, London WC2N 4ES, England.

MURRAY, William; Singer (Baritone); b. 13 March 1935, Schenectady, New York, USA. *Education:* Studied at Adelphi University and in Rome. *Career:* Debut: Spoleto 1957, in Il segreto di Susanna by Wolf-Ferrari; Appearances in Munich, Salzburg, Amsterdam and Frankfurt; Member of the Deutsche Oper Berlin from 1969; Sang Dallapiccola's Ulisse at La Scala in 1970, and took part in the premiere of Nabokov's Love Labour's Lost, Brussels 1973; Other roles include Don Giovanni, Verdi's Macbeth, Luna, Rigoletto and Germont, Puccini's Scarpia and Lescaut, Wagner's Wolfram and parts in We Come to the River by Henze, Orff's Antigonae and Paisiello's Re Theodoro in Venezia. *Honours:* Fulbright Scholarship, 1956; Kammersänger of the Deutsche Oper Berlin. *Address:* c/o Deutsche Oper Berlin, Richard Wagnerstrasse 10, 1000 Berlin, Germany.

MURTO, Matti; Composer, Lecturer and Teacher; b. 12 July 1947, Finland; m., 1 s., 1 d. *Education:* Diploma of Music Theory, Sibelius Academy, 1973; Studied Musicology, University of Helsinki, 1989–91. *Career:* Headmaster of Music Conservatory, Ostro Bothnia, 1980–85; General Manager, Tampere Philharmonic Orchestra, 1985–87; Music Teacher, Hameenlinna Music Schools and Tampere, 1988–90; Headmaster, Savolinna Music School, 1991–; mem, Finnish Composers. *Compositions:* Reel Fantasies for strings, 1980; Aurora Borealis, Prelude for orchestra, 1983; The Fiddlers for Strings, 1988; Concertino for violin and strings, chamber music, solo pieces. *Recordings:* Concertino for violin and strings; Savonlinna Music School SAMCD, 1996; Reel fantasies for strings, Ostro Bothma's Chamber orchestra, 1984; Quartet for flute, clarinet, bassoon, cello and piano, 1997; Many works for accordion. *Publications:* Soivat soinnut, Introduction for harmony, 1994. *Current Management:* Modus Musiikki Ov. *Address:* c/o TEOSTO, Lauttasaarentie 1, SF–00200, Helsinki, Finland.

MUSACCHIO, Martina; Singer (Soprano); b. 11 Feb. 1956, Aosta, Italy. *Education:* Studied in Geneva with Ursula Buckel and in Florence, Munich and Zürich. *Career:* Sang at Zürich Opera 1981–82, Lucerne 1982–85; Guest appearances at Geneva, Düsseldorf, Venice, Mantua, Lausanne and Ravenna; Roles have included Mozart's Susanna, Zerlina, Despina, Pamina and Papagena, Donizetti's Norina and Adina, Martha, Micaela, Euridice, Orff's Die Kluge and Ismene in Honegger's Antigone; Sang Lisetta in La Rondine at Monte Carlo, 1991; Concert appearances throughout Switzerland and in Hamburg, Munich, Stuttgart, Paris, Venice and Madrid, notably in Baroque repertoire. *Address:* c/o Opéra de Monte Carlo, Place du Casino, Monte Carlo.

MUSGRAVE, Thea; Composer; b. 27 May 1928, Edinburgh, Scotland; m. Peter Mark 1971. *Education:* Edinburgh Univ.; Paris Conservatoire under Nadia Boulanger. *Career:* Lecturer, Extra-Mural Department, London Univ., 1958–65; Visiting Prof., Univ. of California, Santa Barbara, USA, 1970; Distinguished Prof., Queen's Coll., CUNY, 1987. *Compositions include:* Chamber Concertos 1, 2 and 3; Concerto for Orchestra, 1967; Clarinet Concerto, 1968; Beauty and the Beast (ballet), 1969; Night Music, 1969; Horn Concerto, 1971; The Voice of Ariadne (chamber opera), 1972–73; Viola Concerto, 1973; Mary Queen of Scots (opera), 1976–77; A Christmas Carol (opera), 1978–79; Harriet, A Woman Called Moses, 1980–84; Peripeteia for orchestra, 1981; An Occurrence At Owl Creek Bridge (radio opera), 1981; Space Play, 1984; The Golden Echo I and II, 1985–86; Rainbow for orchestra, 1990; Wild Winter for ensemble, 1993; Autumn Sonata, concerto for bass-clarinet and orchestra, 1993; Simón Bolívar, opera in 2 acts, 1993; Journey Through a Japanese Landscape, concerto for marimba and wind orchestra, 1993–94; On the Underground Set No. 1–On gratitude, love and madness, SATB, 1994; On the Underground Set No. 2–The strange and the exotic, SATB, 1994; Helios, concerto for oboe and orchestra,

1995; Songs for a Winter's Evening for soprano and orchestra, 1995; On the Underground set No.3 'A Medieval Summer' for chorus, 1995; Phoenix Rising, for orchestra, 1997; Canta, Canta, clarinet and ensemble, 1997; Lamenting with Ariadne, 1999; The Mocking-Bird, for baritone and ensemble. 2000; Pontalba, opera in 2 acts, 2003; Turbulent Landscapes (orchestra), 2004; chamber music; songs; choral music; orchestral music. *Honours:* Koussevitzky Award, 1972; Guggenheim Fellow, 1974–75, 1982–83; Hon. DMus, Council for National Academic Awards, Smith Coll. and Old Dominion Univ.. *Address:* c/o Chester Music/Novello and Co, 8–9 Frith Street, London, W1V 5TZ, England.

MUSOLENO, Rosemary; Singer (Soprano); b. 1965, USA. *Education:* Studied at the Juilliard School, New York, and with Renata Scotto. *Career:* Debut: Opéra de Lyon, as Drusilla in Monteverdi's Poppea; Sang at Lyon as Mozart's Susanna, Cherubino, Servilia and Zerlina; Season 1991 as Poppea at St Etienne and Spoleto, USA; Colorado Opera and Los Angeles, 1994, as Liu in Turandot; Alice Ford in Falstaff for Long Beach Opera; Frequent concert appearances. *Recordings include:* Applausus by Haydn. *Address:* c/o Long Beach Opera, 6372 Pacific Coast Highway, Long Beach, CA 90803, USA.

MUSTONEN, Olli; Concert Pianist and Composer; b. 7 June 1967, Helsinki, Finland. *Education:* Studied piano, harpsichord and composition from age 5; Later studies with Ralf Gothoni, Eero Heinonen (piano) and Einojuhani Rautavaara (composition). *Career:* From 1984, appearances with most major orchestras in Finland and with the Oslo Philharmonic, City of Birmingham Symphony Orchestra and the Royal Philharmonic Orchestra; Festivals include Helsinki, Berlin, Lucerne and Schleswig-Holstein; US debut 1986 at the Newport Festival; Los Angeles Philharmonic at the Hollywood Bowl and New York recital in Young Concert Artists series; London debut April 1987 at the Queen Elizabeth Hall; Concerto performance with the London Philharmonic; Paris debut with the Orchestre de Paris conducted by Kurt Sanderling; 1989 season on Far East tour with the Stockholm Philharmonic and further engagements in the USA; Regular chamber concerts with Heinrich Schiff, Sabine Meyer, Dmitry Sitkovetsky and Steven Isserlis; Soloist in his own two piano concertos; Recital debuts at the Amsterdam Concertgebouw and Chicago's Orchestra Hall, 1990–91; Prom Concerts, London 1991; Nonet for two string quartets and double bass premiered at the Wigmore Hall, 1995; London Proms, 2002. *Recordings include:* Duo recital with Isabelle van Keulen; Shostakovich Preludes and works byAlkan; Prokofiev Concertos; Preludes and Fugues of Bach and Shostakovich; Beethoven Sonatas and Variations. *Honours:* Prizewinner in 1984 Geneva Competition for Young Soloists. *Current Management:* c/o Van Walsum Management, 4 Addison Bridge Place, London, W14 8XP, England.

MUTI, Riccardo; Orchestra Conductor; b. 28 July 1941, Naples, Italy; m., 3 c. *Education:* Milan Conservatory. *Career:* Principal Conductor, Orchestra Maggio Musicale, Florence, Italy, 1969–81 notably in operas by Rossini, Meyebeer, Spontini and Verdi; Principal Conductor, 1973–82, Music Director, 1979–82, Philharmonia Orchestra, London, England; Principal Guest Conductor, 1977–80, Music Director, 1980–92, Philadelphia Orchestra, USA; Music Director, La Scala, Milan, 1986–; Guest Conductor, numerous orchestras, Europe, USA; Conductor of Opera, Florence, Milan, London, Vienna, Munich, Salzburg, Covent Garden debut, Aida, 1977; Conducted I Vespri siciliani at the opening of the season at La Scala, 1989, La Clemenza di Tito and La Traviata 1990; Così fan tutte at the 1990 Salzburg Festival; Season 1992–93 with Parsifal and La Donna del Lago at La Scala, Pagliacci at Philadelphia; Engaged for concert performance of Verdi's Nabucco with the Israel Philharmonic; Season 1996–98 with Gluck's Armide in Milan and Così fan tutte at the Vienna Festival; Fidelio to open the 1999–2000 season at La Scala; Il trovatore, 2001; Engaged for a revival of Salieri's L'Europa riconosciuta, at the reopening of the renovated La Scala theatre, Dec 2004; La Forza del Destino at Covent Garden, 2004. *Recordings:* Symphonic and operatic recordings, EMI, including La Traviata (Scotto) I Puritani (Caballé), Don Pasquale, Attila; Dvořák's Violin Concerto, Scriabin's 1st Symphony; Rigoletto; Guillaume Tell (Studer), Tosca (Vaness). *Honours:* Winner, Guido Cantelli International Contest, 1967. *Current Management:* Columbia Artists Management, New York, USA. *Address:* c/o Columbia Artists Management, 165 West 57th Street, New York, NY 10019, USA.

MUTTER, Anne-Sophie; Concert Violinist; b. 29 June 1963, Rheinfeldin, Germany; m. Dithelf Wunderlich, 1989, (deceased); (2) André Previn, 1 July 2002. *Education:* Studied in Germany and Switzerland with pupils of Carl Flesch. *Career:* Attracted the attention of Karajan at the 1976 Lucerne Festival and appeared at the 1977 Salzburg Festival; British debut 1977, at the Brighton Festival with the English Chamber Orchestra under Daniel Barenboim; US debut with the National Symphony Orchestra of Washington; Moscow debut March 1985; Several return visits to Russia and Eastern Europe; Aldeburgh Festival 1985, playing Beethoven Trios with Rostropovich and Bruno Giurrana;

British concerts with the Philharmonia (Tchaikovsky Concerto) and the Royal Philharmonic under Kurt Masur; Gave the premiere of Luto-slawski's Chaine 2 in 1986; Lullaby for Anne Sophie written for her 1988; Former Chair of Violin at the Royal Academy of Music, London; Played the Brahms Concerto at the London Barbican, 1996; World tour with Beethoven Sonatas, 1998; Premiere of Penderecki's Violin Sonata, Carnegie Hall, 2000. *Recordings include:* Standard repertoire and works by Stravinsky and Lutoslawski (Partita and Chaine); Complete Beethoven Violin Sonatas; Concerto by Berg. *Honours:* Citizen of Honour, Wehr, 1989; Bundesverdienstkreuz First Class, awarded by the Bundespraesident. *Address:* c/o London Symphony Orchestra, Barbican Hall, London, EC1, England.

MYERS, Michael; Singer (Tenor); b. 1955, USA. *Education:* Studied at Curtis Institute, Philadelphia. *Career:* Debut: Central City Opera 1977, in The Bartered Bride; US appearances in Minnesota, Tulsa, Cleveland, San Francisco, Los Angeles and Des Moines; Season 1981–82 as Belmonte in Ottawa, Alfred in Die Fledermaus for Charlotte Opera, Faust for Providence and Virginia Operas and Jenik in Kentucky and Augusta; Highlights of 1982–83 were debuts at the New York City Opera, as Rodolfo, Santa Fe Opera as Quint (Turn of the Screw), Monteverdi's Nerone with Canadian Opera and the Duke of Mantua for Hawaii Opera Theatre; Sang Nick in the premiere of The Postman Always Rings Twice for St Louis Opera (1982) and repeated the role at the 1983 Edinburgh Festival; Scottish Opera debut 1984, as Idomeneo, returning as the Duke in Rigoletto and Cavalli's Orione; Season 1984–85 included Percy to Joan Sutherland's Anna Bolena for Canadian Opera, Flotow's Lionel in Portland and Lord Puff in the US premiere of Henze's The English Cat, at Santa Fe; Season 1985–86 featured debuts with Seattle Opera (Des Grieux in Manon), in Toulouse (Gounod's Roméo), Long Beach Grand Opera (Belmonte), Montpellier (Rimsky's Mozart) and with the Mostly Mozart Festival (Belfiore in La Finta Giardiniera); Active during 1986–87 at Philadelphia (Wagner's Steers-man), Pittsburgh (Edgardo in Lucia di Lammermoor) with the Canadian Opera as Dimitri in Boris Godunov and the Mostly Mozart Festival as Agenore in Il Re Pastore; From 1987 has sung Berg's Painter with the Chicago Opera, the Berlioz Faust with Lyon Opéra, Sergei in Lady Macbeth of Mtsensk with Canadian Opera, Boris in Katya Kabanova at Glyndebourne and Ismael in Nabucco in Philadelphia and New York; Season 1992 as Tom Rakewell at Brussels and Percy in Anna Bolena at Santiago; Tom Rakewell at Madrid, 1996; Donizetti's Edgardo for New Israeli Opera, 1999; Concert engagements include Rossini's Stabat Mater (Cincinnati May Festival) and Huon in Oberon for Radio France. *Honours:* First Prize 1979 Merola Program of the San Francisco Opera. *Address:* c/o Columbia Artists Inc, 165 West 57th Street, New York, NY 10019, USA.

MYERS, Pamela; Singer (Soprano); b. 1952, Baltimore, USA. *Career:* Debut: San Francisco Western Opera, 1977 as Mozart's Countess; Sang the title role in Stephen Oliver's The Duchess of Malfi, Santa Fe 1978; Appearances at New York City Opera from 1979, Scottish Opera 1980–81, as Lucia; Giessen 1981 in the title role of Menotti's La Loca,

Amsterdam 1983 as Mozart's Constanze, Innsbruck Early Music Festival 1984 in Handel's Rodrigo; Sang at Marseille 1988 and 1991 as Desdemona and Ellen Orford; Other roles have included Aennchen in Der Freischütz, Zerlina, Zerbinetta, Micaela, Luisa Miller, Violetta, Liu and Lady Macbeth; Noted concert artist. *Address:* c/o Opera de Marseille, 2 Rue Molière, 1321 Marseille, France.

MYERS, Peter (Joseph); Composer; b. 3 Feb. 1962, Werribee, Victoria, Australia. *Education:* BA (Hons), 1984, MA, 1990, La Trobe University. *Career:* Faculty Member, La Trobe University, 1984–90; Pascoe Vale Girls' Secondary College, 1993–. *Compositions include:* Transforma-tions, for oboe, 1983; Aftermath for concert band Octet for Winds, 1984; Scintilla, for orchestra, 1986; Of Minds and Minds for Ensemble, 1987; Antipathy for mezzo and ensemble, 1988; Towards the Equinox for chamber ensemble, 1986; Vex for violin, 1988; Homage to the Ancient, for trombone, percussion, and piano; Pasar, for piano, 1991; Bilanx for violin, cello, piccolo, clarinet and piano, 1991; Demons Within, for orchestra, 1993; Paroxysms, for string quartet, 1993. *Address:* APRA, 1A Eden Street, Crows Nest, NSW 2065, Australia.

MYERSCOUGH, Clarence, FRAM; violinist; b. 27 Oct. 1930, London, England; m. Marliese Scherer, one s. one d. *Education:* Royal Academy of Music, London, Paris Conservatoire. *Career:* Prof. of Violin, Royal Academy of Music 1964–; soloist, recitalist and chamber music player; appeared in many int. music festivals, including Ascona, Segovia, Madrid, Badajoz and Cardiff; several tours in USA and Far East; broadcasts for BBC, ITV, RTE, HK TV and major European stations; founder mem., Fidelio Quartet; mem. Incorporated Soc. of Musicians, Royal Soc. of Musicians of Great Britain. *Recordings:* String Quartets of Britten, Tippett, Delius, Arriaga; Violin Sonata by Hoddinott with Martin Jones. *Honours:* Winner, All England Violin Competition, National Federation of Music Festivals and Albert Sammons Prize, 1951; 2nd Prize, Carl Flesch International Violin Competition, 1952. *Address:* 17 Salterton Road, London, N7 6BB, England.

MYERSCOUGH, Nadia; Violinist; b. 29 July 1967, London, England. *Education:* Royal Academy of Music, London; Studies with her father, Clarence Myerscough; Indiana University, Bloomington, USA; Studies with Franco Gulli, Rostislav Dubinsky, Luba Edlina, Shigeo Neriki. *Career:* Soloist, Recitalist and Chamber Music Player; Broadcasts on BBC Radio 3, Classic FM and France Music; Appearances at South Bank, Wigmore Hall, City of London Festival, Wexford Festival; Soloist with the Lucerne Festival Strings, London Soloists, Kent Concert Orchestra, Bangkok Philharmonic; mem New Helvetic Society, The Royal Society of Muscians RAM Club. *Recordings:* Dvořák, Suk, Smetana CD; The Festival Strings Lucerne Vivaldi Concerto CD; Chamber Music Works by Alan Rawsthorne. *Honours:* Associate, Royal Academy of Music; B J Dale Prize; Countess of Munster Award; Several scholarships; English Speaking Union Fellowship. *Address:* M&M Management, 17 Salterton Road, London N7 6BB, England. *Telephone:* (20) 7272 2547. *Fax:* (20) 7272 2547.

N

NAAF, Dagmar; German singer (mezzo-soprano); b. 1934, Munich. *Education:* studied in Munich. *Career:* sang in Opera at Freiburg, 1958–63, Munich, 1963–66, Wiesbaden, 1963–66 and Hanover, 1966–70; Engaged at Cologne, 1967–69, Graz, 1970–72, Staatsoper Munich, 1974–76; Guest appearances at Brussels, Berne, Marseilles, Rio de Janeiro, (Amsterdam, Octavian, 1965), Barcelona and Vienna, 1972; Other roles have included Monteverdi's Ottavia, Handel's Cornelia, Gluck's Paride, Dorabella, Brangaene; Strauss's Composer and Clairon; Verdi's Preziosilla, Azucena, Amneris and Eboli; Noted concert artist. *Address:* c/o Bayerische Staatsoper, Postfach 100148, 8000 Munich, Germany.

NADAREISHVILI, Zurab; Composer; b. 4 Jan. 1957, Poti, Georgia; m. Niho Shawdia, 23 November 1985, 1 s., 1 d. *Education:* Theoretical Department, Music School, Poti; Tbilisi State Conservatoire. *Career:* Debut: Tbilisi, 1985; Performed in St Petersburg, 1987, Moscow, 1988, Amsterdam, 1992, USA, 1993; mem, Georgian Composers Union. *Compositions:* 2 String Quartets; Brass Quintet; Orchestral Minatures; Symphonic Poem; Hymns, for chamber orchestra; Variations, for piano; Variations, for piano and orchestra; Instrumental Pieces. *Recordings:* Hymns, for chamber orchestra, 1988. *Publications:* The Way to Music, 1987; Musical Georgia, 1997. *Honours:* Moscow Composers International Competition, 1987; Georgian Composers Union Award, 1992; 3rd Place, Moscow Prokofiev Competition, 1997. *Address:* Street No. 20, fl 41, Tbilisi 380071, Georgia.

NADELMANN, Noëmi; Singer (Soprano); b. 1966, Zürich, Switzerland. *Education:* Studied at Bloomington, Indiana. *Career:* Sang at Lucerne Opera, 1988–89, Zürich and Augsburg (as Norina in Don Pasquale); Theater am Gärtnerplatz, Munich, from 1990, as Zerlina, Blondchen, Aennchen in Der Freischütz, Manon and Zerbinetta; Komische Oper Berlin, 1994–95, as Traviata, Lucia di Lammermoor, Nedda and Musetta; Munich, 1996, as Rosalinde in Die Fledermaus and the title role in Orff's Die Kluge; Further appearances at Venice, Geneva and the Metropolitan, New York debut 2000, as Musetta; Sang Rosalinde for Zürich Opera and Armida in Handel's Rinaldo at the Prinzregententheater, Munich, 2000; Wiener Blut and Die lustige Witwe at Zürich, 2002. *Address:* Theater am Gärtnerplatz 3, 8000 Munich 5, Germany.

NADLER, Sheila; Singer (mezzo-soprano); b. 1945, New York, NY, USA. *Education:* studied at the Manhattan School of Music, at the Opera Studio of the Metropolitan Opera and Juilliard School. *Career:* sang at San Francisco and New York City Opera 1970–72, Baltimore 1972–, notably in 1975 in the premiere of Inez de Castro by Pasatieri, Metropolitan Opera 1976–; sang Anna in Les Troyens at La Scala, 1982, and Clytemnestra in Elektra at Santiago, 1984; further appearances as Fricka and Waltraute in The Ring, at Marseilles, Lyon and Brussels and as Erda, Herodias, Jocasta in Oedipus Rex, Azucena, Ulrica, Mistress Quickly, Cornelia in Giulio Cesare and La Cieca in La Gioconda; sang Clytemnestra in Elektra at Seattle, 1996; as Poulenc's Mme de Croissy, Santa Fe, 1999. *Address:* c/o Baltimore Opera Company, 527 North Charles Street, Baltimore, MD 21201, USA.

NADOR, Magda; Singer (Soprano); b. 16 Dec. 1955, Dorog, Hungary. *Education:* Studied at the Budapest Music Academy. *Career:* Debut: Budapest National Opera, 1979, as Mozart's Constanze; Komische Oper Berlin from 1982, as Mozart's Fiordiligi and Queen of Night, and Gilda in Rigoletto; Guest appearances at Amsterdam (as Adele), Zürich, Düsseldorf and Munich; Vienna Staatsoper, 1986, as Oscar in Un Ballo in Maschera; Queen of Night at Stuttgart and Graz, 1987; Berlin and Wiesbaden, 1991–91, as Isotta in Strauss's Die Schweigsame Frau; Concerts include Salzburg Festival, 1986. *Address:* National Opera House, Nepoztarsarag utja 22, 1061 Budapest, Hungary.

NAEF, Yvonne; Singer (Mezzo-soprano); b. 1965, Switzerland. *Education:* Studied in Zürich, Basle and Mannheim. *Career:* Concert and recital appearances from 1987; Opera debut as Rossini's Cenerentola, followed by an engagement at St Gallen, as Ulrica, Ariodante, Gluck's Orfeo and Sara in Roberto Devereux, from 1992; Wiesbaden from 1993, as Preziosilla, Rosina, Suzuki, Fricka, Brangaene and Adalgisa; Monte Carlo 1994, as Giovanna Seymour in Anna Bolena, and La Scala Milan as Offenbach's Giulietta; Invalid Woman in Schoenberg's Moses and Aron at Amsterdam, Salzburg and the Festival Hall, London (1996); Appearances as Verdi's Amneris at St Gallen, Wiesbaden and the Deutsche Oper Berlin; Concert engagements in Prokofiev's Alexander Nevsky (at Naples), Mahler's Second Symphony (Venice), Bach's B Minor Mass (Lausanne) and Das Lied von der Erde (Toulouse); Bayreuth Festival 1997, as Waltraute and Second Norn, in The Ring; Season 2000–01 as Wagner's Venus at Hamburg, Stravinsky's Jocasta in Brussels, Anna in Les Troyens at Salzburg and Eboli at the Vienna Staatsoper (debut); Azucena at Covent Garden, and returned to

Hamburg for Marina in Boris Godunov. *Honours:* Second Prize, Lieder and Oratorio section, 1987 Maria Callas Competition, at Athens. *Address:* c/o Opernhaus Zürich, Falkenstrasse 1, 8008 Zürich, Switzerland.

NAEGELE, Philipp (Otto); Violinist, Violist and Professor; b. 22 Jan. 1928, Stuttgart, Germany; 1 s. *Education:* BA, Queens College, New York, USA, 1949; MA 1950, PhD 1955, Princeton University, New Jersey. *Career:* Violinist and Violist, Marlboro Music Festival, Marlboro, Vermont, 1950–; Violinist, Cleveland Orchestra, 1956–64; Member, Resident String Quartet, Kent State University, Kent Ohio, 1960–64; Violin Faculty, Cleveland Institute of Music, 1961–64; Assistant Professor, 1964–68, Associate Professor, 1968–72, Professor, 1972–78, William R. Kenan Jr Professor of Music, 1978–2000, Professor Emeritus, 2000–, Smith College, Northampton, Massachusetts; Member, Végh String Quartet, 1977–79; Violist, Cantilena Piano Quartet, concerts USA and abroad, 1980–96; Numerous concerts: Music from Marlboro series, USA, independently, Europe; Residences: National Arts Center, Ottawa; Yehudi Menuhin School, England; Freiburg Hochschule für Musik; Banff Center for the Arts; Rubin Academy, Tel-Aviv University; Teacher, Chamber Music Ensembles, Musicorda Summer School, Mount Holyoke College, 1987–94. *Recordings:* Numerous recordings of violin/viola solos and chamber music, including part of complete recorded edition of chamber works of Max Reger for his centennial, Da Camera, 1973. *Publications:* Gustav Mahler and Johann Sebastian Bach; August Wilhelm Ambros in Grove's Dictionary of Music and Musicians. *Address:* 57 Prospect Street, Northampton, MA 01060, USA.

NAFE, Alicia; Singer (Mezzo-soprano); b. 4 Aug. 1947, Buenos Aires, Argentina. *Education:* Studied in Buenos Aires with Ferruccio Calusio and in Europe with Luigi Ricci and Teresa Berganza. *Career:* Sang in Barcelona after winning competition there, debut in Verdi's Requiem; Sang in Toledo and at the Bayreuth Festival, 1975; Member of the Hamburg Opera, 1977–81; Geneva Opera, 1981, in La Cenerentola; Lyon 1981, in Beatrice et Benedict by Berlioz; Sang Rosina with the Cologne Opera at the 1981 Edinburgh Festival; La Scala 1984, as Idamante in Idomeneo; Covent Garden 1985, as Rosina; Guest engagements in Spain, South America, France, Germany and China; Other roles include Carmen and Dorabella; Sang Adalgisa at Covent Garden, 1987; Metropolitan Opera debut 1988, as Sextus in La Clemenza di Tito and Ramiro in La Finta Giardiniera; Sang Massenet's Charlotte at the Teatro Regio Parma, 1990; Grandmother in La Vida Breve at Madrid, 1998; Also heard in oratorios and as song recitalist. *Recordings:* Mercedes in Carmen and La Vida Breve; Monteverdi Madrigals; Così fan tutte. *Address:* c/o Teatro Regio, Via Garibaldi 16, 43100 Parma, Italy.

NAGANO, Kent (George); Conductor; b. 22 Nov. 1951, Morro Bay, California, USA; m. Mari Kodama, one d. *Education:* BA 1974 and studied with Grosvenor Cooper, University of California, Santa Cruz; MM, San Francisco University, 1976; Studied piano with Goodwin Sammel; Conducting with Laszlo Varga, San Francisco. *Career:* Opera Company of Boston, 1977–79; Music Director, Berkeley (California) Symphony Orchestra, 1978; Assistant to Seiji Ozawa, premiere of Messiaen's St Francois, Paris, 1983; Ojai (California) Music Festival, 1984; Chief Conductor, Opéra de Lyon, 1989–1998; Guest Conductor with many orchestras in the USA and Europe; Conducted Madama Butterfly at Lyon, 1990 followed by Dialogues des Carmélites and a French version of Strauss's Salome; Busoni's Doktor Faust, Vienna Philharmonic, 1990; Associate Principal Guest Conductor of the London Symphony Orchestra, 1990–98; Music Director of the Hallé Orchestra 1991–2000; Season 1992 with Busoni's Turandot at Lyon, Madama Butterfly at Symphony Hall Birmingham (Lyon Company) and The Rake's Progress at Aix-en-Provence; Conducted Carmen at Lyon, 1996; 1997, London Symphony Orchestra, London première of Leonard Bernstein's White House Cantata, the opening of the Barbican's festival Inventing America in 1998 conducting performances of Nixon in China; Concert performances of the four act version of Britten's Billy Budd, Hallé Orchestra, 1998; Salzburg Festival; Messiaen's opera Saint François d'Assise, Deutsches Symphonie- Orchester, Berlin, 1998; Season 1999 with Mahler's Adagio, Berg's Violin Concerto and Beethoven's Seventh at the London Proms; Artistic Director and Chief Conductor, Deutsches Sinfonie Orchester, Berlin, 2000;Deutsches Symphonie-Orchester Berlin, 2000 Residency at the Theatre du Châtelet Paris, World Première of John Adams' El Niño; World première of Kaija Saariaho's opera L'amour de Loin, SWR Baden-Baden Orchestra, 2000; Principal Conductor of Los Angeles Opera, Wagner's Lohengrin, 2001; New production of The Nose, by Shostakovich, for the Berlin Staatsoper, 2002; Zemlinsky's King Kandaules,

Deutsches Symphonie-Orchester, Berlin, 2002; Berkeley Symphony Orchestra, Music Director; Music Director of the Orchestre Symphonique de Montréal, 2006–; Chief Conductor of the Bavarian State Opera, 2006–. *Recordings include:* The Love for Three Oranges, Dialogues des Carmélites, Salome; Chants d'Auvergne; Rodrigue et Chimène; Les Dontes d'Hoffmann; La Bohème; La Damnation de Faust; Billy Budd; Mahler's Symphony Number 3; Turangalila; Trois Soeurs; White House Cantata; El Niño. *Honours:* Co-recipient, Affiliate Artist's Seaver Conducting Award, 1985; Gramophone Magazine Record of the Year Award for The Love of Three Oranges, 1990; Winner, with Opéra de Lyon, the 1995 Grammy Award for Best Opera Recording for Carlisle Floyd's Susannah; Grammy Award for Best Opera Recording for Busoni's Doktor Faust, 2000. *Address:* c/o Deutsches Symphonie Orchester, ROC Gmbh, Hölderlin Strasse 1, 14050 Berlin, Germany.

NÄGELE, Barbara; Recorder Player; b. 16 March 1973, Lustenau, Austria. *Education:* Studied at the Hochschule für Musik und Theater in Zürich, Switzerland, with Kees Boeke and Matthias Weilenmann. *Career:* Member of 'Trio O'Henry' together with Claudia Gerauer and Martina Joos; Appearances (among others) at Bludenzer Tage für Zeitgemässe Musik, Austria, 1997; Festival of Ancient Music, Stary Sacz, Poland, 2000; Festival Musica Nova, Sofia, Bulgaria, 2001; Festival Bohemia-Saxony, Czech Republic, 2001; Cycle of premieres with works of Swiss composers, Zürich, 2000–01; Radio appearances (live recordings): St Peter's Church, Zürich, 1996; Great Hall of the HFMT, Zürich; Radio features: Austrian Radio ORF 1, 1998; Swiss Radio DRS 2, 2000; Bulgarian radio and television, Sofia, 2001; Premieres: Kees Boeke's The Unfolding, 1997; Martin Derungs's A Set of Pieces, 2000; Thomas Müller's Erste Etappe in Richtung farbiger Eindrücke, 2000; Giorgio Tedde's Medio Aevo, 2000; Andreas Nick's Trio pour flûtes à bec, 2000; Annette Schmucki's tatsache. eisschollen. Der unzertrennliche anstoss abweichender labialität, 2001; Gerald Bennett's Textures of Time, 2001. *Honours:* Kiwanis Kammermusik-Wettbewerb, Zürich, 1995; International Recorder Competition, Calw, Germany, 1995; Orpheus Förderpreis, Zürich, 1997; Premio Bonporti, Rovereto, Italy, 1997; Migros Kammermusik-Wettbewerb, Zürich, 1999. *Address:* Neustadt 22, A 6800 Feldkirch, Austria.

NAGELSTAD, Catherine; Singer (Soprano); b. 1967, California. *Education:* San Francisco Conservatory and in Rome. *Career:* As Zdenka in Arabella and Magda in La Rondine, Southern California Festival; European debut as Mozart's Constanze, Hamburg, 1993; Concerts with Placido Domingo in USA and Europe; Staatsoper Stuttgart as Musetta and Mozart's Vitellia; Venus in King Arthur; Tosca and Alcina, 1998–99; Season 1999–2000 with Constanze, Fiordiligi and Poppea, Elisabeth de Valois and Violetta at Stuttgart; Musetta at Covent Garden. *Honours:* Winner, Palm Springs; Pasalena Opera Guild Competitions, 1991–92. *Address:* Music International, 13 Ardilaun Road, London N5 2QR, England.

NAGY, Janos B.; Singer (tenor); b. 1943, Debrecen, Hungary. *Education:* Bartók Conservatory, Budapest. *Career:* Sang with Hungarian Territorial Army choir on tour, 1967–70; Stage debut at Budapest, 1971, as Don José in Carmen; Many performances in operas by Verdi and Puccini; Berlin 1978, in the Verdi Requiem; Warsaw national Opera 1979; Member of Deutsche Oper am Rhein, Düsseldorf from 1981; Other roles include Puccini's Des Grieux, Cavaradossi and Calaf, Verdi's Manrico, Duke of Mantua, and Macduff, Nemorino in L'Elisir d'amore and Pollione in Norma; Guest appearances at opera houses in Germany and Switzerland; Sang Radames with the Deutsche Oper am Rhein, Düsseldorf, 1989. *Recordings:* Boito's Nerone (Hungaroton); Kodály's Te Deum; Psalmus Hungaricus and Missa Brevis; Christus by Liszt; Mosè in Egitto; Szokolay's Blood Wedding; Simon Boccanegra. *Address:* c/o Hungarian State Opera House, Nepöztarsasay utja 22, 1061 Budapest, Hungary.

NAGY, Robert; Singer (Tenor); b. 3 March 1929, Lorain, Ohio, USA. *Education:* Cleveland Institute of Music. *Career:* Metropolitan Opera from 1957, as Canio in Pagliacci, Beethoven's Florestan, Herod in Salome and the Emperor in Die Frau ohne Schatten; With the Met and the New York City Opera (from 1969) has sung in 1000 opera performances; Guest appearances in Chicago, Baltimore, San Diego, Seattle, Montreal and New Orleans; Repertoire includes roles by Wagner, Verdi, Barber, Bizet and Puccini.

NAKAMURA, Tomoko; Singer (Soprano); b. 1961, Japan; m. Uwe Heilmann. *Education:* Studied at Detmold and with Elisabeth Schwarzkopf. *Career:* Debut: Detmold Opera, 1983, as Madama Butterfly; Sang at the Stuttgart Staatsoper from 1986, notably as Mozart's Constanze (also at the Vienna Staatsoper, 1992), Queen of Night and Donna Anna, Olympia in Les contes d'Hoffmann, and Gilda; Numerous concert appearances. *Honours:* Prize Winner, Mozart Competition, Salzburg, 1985. *Address:* Stuttgart Staatsoper, Oberer Schlossgarten 6, 7013 Stuttgart, Germany.

NALL, Cecily; Singer (Soprano); b. 1960, Georgia, USA. *Education:* Studied in USA and Graz, Austria. *Career:* Debut: Spoleto Festival, 1985, as Zerbinetta in Ariadne and Naxos; Season 1986 as Blondchen in Die Entführung at Santiago and Offenbach's Olympia for Miami Opera; Aachen Opera, 1987–91, Darmstadt, 1991–93; Many guest appearances elsewhere in Europe; Cleveland, 1988, as Mozart's Constanze; Cincinnati Opera from 1992, as Olympia, Sophie in Der Rosenkavalier, and Mozart's Susanna (1995). *Address:* Cincinnati Opera Association, Music Hall, 1241 Elm Street, Cincinnati, OH 42510, USA.

NAOURI, Laurent; Singer (Baritone); b. 1964, Paris. *Education:* Studied at Marseille; Guildhall School, London. *Career:* Debut: Guglielmo in Così fan tutte; Lully's Phaeton and Roland at Lyon and Montpellier; Les Contes d'Hoffmann, Metz; Massenet's Des Grieux and Mozart's Figaro, Opéra Bastille, Paris; 1997–98 Season: Jupiter in Orphée aux Enfers, Geneva; Antenor in Rameau's Dardanus; Bottom in A Midsummer Night's Dream, Lyons; Many appearances at Aix-en-Provence Festival; Season 1999–2000 as Melisso in Alcina at the Palais Garnier, Paris, and as Hucscar in Les Indes Galantes by Rameau; the Villains in Les Contes d'Hoffmann at Antwerp. *Recordings:* Hidraot in Gluck's Armide. *Address:* c/o Geneva Opera, Grand Théâtre de Genéve, 11 Boulevard du Théâtre, 1211 Geneva 11, Switzerland.

NASEDKIN, Alexei; Concert Pianist; b. 20 Dec. 1942, Moscow, Russia. *Education:* Studied at Central Music School and the Conservatoire, Moscow. *Career:* Debut: Public concerts from 1951, aged 9; Has toured extensively in Russia and throughout the world, playing works by Haydn, Scarlatti, Mozart, Beethoven, Schubert, Chopin, Prokofiev and Shostakovich; Professor in Piano at Moscow Conservatoire from 1968; Vladimir Ovchinikov has been among his pupils. *Compositions:* Works for piano and orchestra. *Recordings:* Many. *Honours:* Gold Medal at competitions in Vienna and Munich, 1967; Prizewinner at Leeds, 1966, and Moscow, 1962. *Address:* c/o Sonata, 11 Northpark Street, Glasgow G20 7AA, Scotland.

NASH, Graham (Thomas); Conductor; b. 21 June 1952, London, England; Divorced, 1 s. *Education:* LRAM, Royal Academy of Music, 1970–74. *Career:* Debut: Conducting, Royal Albert Hall, 1980, Kraków Radio Symphony Orchestra, Poland, 1988 and London Philharmonic Orchestra, 1985; Conducting, Victor Hochhauser, Opera Gala Nights at Royal Albert Hall, Royal Festival Hall, Barbican, 1980–89; Guest Conductor, London Festival Ballet; Music Director, London City Ballet, 1986–88; Kuopio Orchestra debut in Finland, 1987; mem, Incorporated Society of Musicians. *Compositions:* In Memoriam, Lord Mountbatten for large orchestra, 1979. *Honours:* North London Orchestral Society Prize for Conducting, 1974; Blake Memorial Prize for Flute, Ensemble Prize, 1974. *Address:* 53 Faraday Avenue, Sidcup, Kent DA14 4JB, England.

NASH, Peter Paul; Composer; b. 1950, Leighton Buzzard, Bedfordshire, England. *Education:* Cambridge University, with Robin Holloway. *Career:* Composition Fellow at Leeds University, 1976–78; Composer in Residence at the National Centre for Orchestral Studies, 1983; Producer, BBC Radio 3, 1985–87; Critic and Broadcaster, (presenter of Music Week on Radio 3); Symphony premiered at the 1991 Promenade Concerts, London. *Compositions:* String Trio, 1982; Wind Quintet; Insomnia for chamber ensemble; Etudes for orchestra (On the Beach, Percussion Study, Parting) 1983–84; Figures for harp; Earthquake, scena for narrator and six players, quintet, 1987; Symphony, 1991. *Address:* c/o Faber Music Ltd, 3 Queen Street, London WC1N 3AU, England.

NASH, Rebecca; Singer (soprano); b. 1970, Melbourne, Australia. *Education:* Studied with Dame Joan Hammond in Melbourne; Royal College of Music, London, until 1999. *Career:* Appearances throughout Australia as Pamina, Donna Elvira, Marguerite in Faust, Gilda, Micaela and Nedda (Pagliacci); Mozart's Countess for Opera Australia at Sydney Opera House, 2000; Concerts include Strauss Vier letzte Lieder, under Daniel Harding; Beethoven's Ninth and Egmont under Frans Bruggen with Scottish Chamber Orchestra and The Orchestra of the 19th Century; Mendelssohn's Elijah under Kurt Masur; Verdi Requiem; Ein Deutsches Requiem; Mozart C Minor Mass; Mahler 4; The Creation; Messiah; Handel's Jephtha; Madama Butterfly for Scottish Opera; Barena in Jenufa; Fifth Maid in Elektra; First Maid in Daphne for Royal Opera Covent Garden; Season 2003–04 includes Marschallin in Der Rosenkavalier with ENO; Fifth Maid in Elektra under Donald Runnicles at BBC Proms; concerts with The Orchestra of the 18th Century; Other roles include Desdemona, Arabella, Katya Kabanova and Magda in La Rondine. *Current Management:* Askonas Holt Ltd, Lonsdale Chambers, 27 Chancery Lane, London, WC2A 1PF, England. *Telephone:* (20) 7400-1700. *Fax:* (20) 7400-1799. *E-mail:* info@askonasholt.co.uk. *Website:* www.askonasholt.co.uk.

NASIDZE, Sulkhan; Composer; b. 17 March 1927, Tbilisi, Georgia; m. Lali Surguladze, 20 July 1963, 1 s., 1 d. *Education:* Tbilisi Conservatory. *Career:* Debut: Concerto for Piano and Symphony Orchestra, Tbilisi,

1954; Chamber, Symphony, Chamber-Instrumental, Chamber-Vocal, Choral, Ballet, Film Music Interpreted in Concert Halls and Opera Houses; Television and radio, 1954–97; mem, Union of Composers, Georgia. *Compositions:* Chamber Symphony, 1969; Symphony, Pirosmani, 1977; Symphony, Dalai, 1979; Concerto for violin, cello and chamber orchestra, 1982; Ballet, King Lear, 1988; Concerto for cello and symphony orchestra, 1990; Stringed quartet No. 2, No. 3, Epitaph No. 4, No. 5; Con sordino; Piano concerto No. 3, Autumn Music; Piano Quintet; Piano Quartet, Metamorphosis; Piano Trio, Antiphonia. *Recordings:* Chamber Symphony, Melodia Panton; Symphony, Pirosmani Melodia; Symphony, Passione Melodia; Symphony, Dalai Melodia. *Publications:* Particularities of Gurian Folk Polyphony Songs, 1970; Polyphonic Processes in Z Paliachvifiil Opera, 1971; Some Words About Modern Music, 1974. *Honours:* Shota Rustaveli Prize, Georgia, 1978; State Prize, Russia, 1986. *Address:* Kazbegi Avenue 20, Apt 6, Tbilisi 380077, Georgia.

NASRAWI, Douglas; Singer (Tenor); b. 1960, California, USA. *Career:* Resident in Paris, 1982–; Appearances under conductors William Christie, Kent Nagano, John Eliot Gardiner and Jean-Claude Malgoire; Leading roles in La Clemenza di Tito; Pulcinella by Stravinsky and Lully's Alceste; 1993–94 Season: Ecclitco in Haydn's Il mondo della luna; Premiere Jocaste by Charles Chayne at Rouen; Germanico in Biber's Chi la dura, la vince, Innsbruck and Salzburg; 1998 Season with Hindemith, Toch, Weill, Milhaud bill at Karlsruhe and as Flamingo in Montemezzi's l'Amore dei tre Re at Bregenz. *Recordings:* Osman in Handel's Almira, CPO; Alecton and Apollon in Lully's Alceste; Schütz Symphoniae sacrae; Purcell Songs of Welcome and Farewell. *Address:* c/o Karlsruhe Opera, Baumeisterstrasse 11, 7500 Karlsruhe, Germany.

NASU, Teruhiko, BA, MA, MPhil; University Lecturer; b. 23 Dec. 1960, Tokyo, Japan; m. Machiko; one d. *Education:* Rikkyo Univ., Tokyo, Japan, Univ. of Cambridge. *Career:* part-time lecturer in music, St Gregory's Institute for Religious Music 1991–, Toho Gakuen Junior Coll. 1993–97, Japan Lutheran Theological Coll. 1995–96, Rikkyo Univ. 1996–2000; Lecturer in Music, Senzoku Gakuen Coll. 1996–2000; Assoc. Prof. of Music, Aoyama Gakuin Univ.; mem. Musicological Soc. of Japan, Royal Musical Asscn, Plainsong and Mediaeval Music Soc., Japan Soc. of Liturgical Musicology. *Publications:* The Publication of Byrd's Gradualia Reconsidered, Brio xxxii 1995, On Versus and Versiclus, Grocheio's De Musica: A Japanese Translation 2001. *Honours:* Kan Memorial Scholarship 1984. *Address:* Aoyama Gakuin University 4–4–25 Shibuya, Shibuya-Ku, Tokyo, 150–8366 Japan (office). *Telephone:* (3) 3409-7921 (office). *Fax:* (3) 3409-5414 (office). *E-mail:* tnasu@cl.aoyama.ac.jp (office). *Website:* www.aoyama.ac.jp (office).

NATANEK, Adam (Tadewsa); Conductor; b. 23 July 1933, Kraków, Poland; m. Danuta Daniecka, 27 July 1966. *Education:* Department of Pedagogy, 1957; Department of Composition and Conducting, 1960; Academy of Music, Kraków, 1960. *Career:* Debut: Kraków Philharmonic Orchestra, 1960; Conductor, Lublin Philharmonic Orchestra, 1961–69; Head, Artistic Director, Chief Conductor, 1969–90; First Guest Conductor, Symphonic Orchestra, Valladolid, Spain, 1984–, Artistic Director, Chief Conductor, 1990; Artistic Director Rzeszów Philharmonic and Music Festival in Iancur, Poland; Professor, Marie Curie-Skiodowska University, Lublin, –1992; Member of Jury, numerous music competitions; Appearances throughout Europe, South Korea, Africa, Cuba and Latin America. *Recordings:* Numerous radio and television recordings with orchestras including National Warsaw Philharmonic, Great Symphony Orchestra of Polish Radio and Television, Katowice, Polish Radio and Television Orchestra, Kraków; First world-wide CD recording of Ignacy Feliks Dobrzynski's Piano Concerto with the New Polish Symphony Orchestra. *Contributions:* Promoter and Reviewer, Maria Sklodowska-Curie University, Lublin and Academy of Music, Warsaw and Poznan. *Honours:* Numerous prizes including Commander's Cross of the Order of Polish Revival. *Address:* ul Szczerbowskiego 13/10, 20-012 Lublin, Poland.

NATRA, Sergiu; Composer; b. 12 April 1924, Bucharest, Romania. *Education:* MA, National Music Academy, Bucharest, 1952; Studied Composition with Leo Klepper. *Career:* Commissions of Symphony Works, Chamber Music, Stage and Film Music in Romania; Major commissions in Israel by the Israel Festival, Israel Philharmonic Orchestra, Israel Radio, Israel Composers Fund; Resident in Tel-Aviv from 1961; Professor, Composition; Examiner for higher musical education, Israel Ministry of Education and Culture, 1964–71; Commission for Testimonium, 1968; mem, Honorary Director, World Harp Congress. *Compositions:* 3 Corteges in the Street, 1945; Suite for orchestra, 1948; Sinfonia for strings; Music for violin and harp, Music for harpsichord and 6 instruments, 1964; Music for oboe and strings, 1965; Sonatina for harp, 1965; Song of Deborah, 1967; Variations for piano and orchestra, 1966; Prayer for harp, 1972; Sonatina for trumpet solo, 1973; Sonatina for trombone solo, 1973; Sacred Service, 1976; From the Diary of a Composer, 1978; Variations for harpsichord, 1978; Hours

for mezzo-soprano, violin, clarinet and piano, 1981; Music for harp and three brass instruments, 1982; Divertimento for harp and strings, 1983; Ness Amim, Cantata for solo voices, choir, chamber orchestra with harpsichord, 1984; Music for violin and piano, 1986; Sonatina for piano, 1987; Music for NICANOR for harp solo and chamber ensemble, 1988; Developments for viola solo and chamber orchestra, 1988; Sonata for four harps, 1993; Sonata for harp and string quartet, 1997; Sound Picture, two pianos, 1998. *Recordings:* Suite for orchestra, 1948; Music for harpsichord and 6 instruments; Song of Deborah; Sonatina for harp; Trio for violin, violoncello and piano; Developments, for viola and chamber orchestra. *Address:* 10 Barth St, Tel-Aviv 69104, Israel.

NAUHAUS, Gerd (Ernst Hermann); Musicologist; b. 28 July 1942, Erfurt, Germany; m. Ursula Karsdorf, 15 Aug 1965, 2 s., 1 deceased, 1 d. *Education:* Matriculation, 1961; Diploma, Musical Education, 1965, Diploma, Musicology, 1969, PhD, 1980, Martin Luther University, Halle-Wittenberg. *Career:* Dramaturg at Zwickau Opera House, 1967; Musicologist, 1970–, Vice-Director, 1980–, Robert Schumann House, Zwickau; Director, 1993; mem, Vice-Chairman, Scientific Secretary, Robert Schumann Society, Zwickau; German Musicological Society; Saxon Cultural Council, 1993–2002. *Publications:* Robert Schumann, Diaries and Household Books, complete scholarly edition, vol. III, 1982, vol. II, 1987; Clara Schumann 3 part Songs After Poems by Geibel, 1989; Piano Sonata in G minor, 1991; March in E Flat Major, 1997 (first editions). *Honours:* Schumann Prize, Zwickau Town Council, 1986. *Address:* Robert-Schumann-Haus, Hauptmarkt 5, 08056 Zwickau/Saxony, Germany.

NAYLOR, Peter; Composer; b. 5 Oct. 1933, London, England. *Education:* MA, Cambridge, 1957; BMus, London, 1961; Fellow, Royal College of Organists, London, 1961; Associate, Royal College of Music, London, 1962. *Career:* Lecturer, City Literary Institute, London, 1963–65; Lecturer, Harmony and Counterpoint, History, Royal Scottish Academy of Music and Drama, 1965–71; Organist, Ashwell Festival, Herts, 1964–69; Associate Organist, Glasgow Cathedral, 1972–85; Music Associate, Scottish Opera for Youth, 1975–80; Repetiteur, Shepway Youth Opera, Kent, 1982–85; mem, British Academy of Composers and Songwriters; Scottish Society of Composers. *Compositions:* Symphony in One Movement, Tides and Islands; Beowulf for symphonic wind band; Odysseus Returning, three act opera; Pied Piper, one-act opera; The Mountain People, workshop opera; Earth was Waiting, cantata; Wassail Sing We for SA chorus, piano and percussion; A Hero Dies for 22 voices and clarsach; Movement for organ; Air and Variations for 2 pianos; Clarinet Quintet; Love and Life (5 songs); Carols and Anthems; Daybreak to Starlight, 16 pieces for organ. *Recordings:* Eastern Monarchs, Elizabethan Singers, Louis Halsey and the Choir of St John's College, Cambridge, George Guest; Now the Green Blade Riseth, SATB Choir of Glasgow Cathedral, John R Turner; Clarinet Quintet, Colin Bradbury and the Georgian Quartet. *Honours:* London University Convocation Trust Prize, 1959; Aschenberg Composition Prize, 1959. *Address:* Greenacres, Brady Road, Lyminge, Folkestone, Kent CT 18 8HA, England.

NAYLOR, Steven, BMus, FRAM; Pianist, Accompanist and Vocal Coach; b. 1956, Gwent, Wales. *Education:* University College, Cardiff, at the National Opera Studio and the Royal Academy, LondonFurther piano studies with Geoffrey Parsons. *Career:* Accompanist and opera coach at many venues in the United Kingdom and abroad; Joined Glyndebourne, 1989, Head of Music, 1998–, Dir of Artistic Administration, 1999–; BBC Radio 3 broadcasts; Further engagements at the Wexford and Buxton Festivals, the Munich Festival and the Hans Werner Henze Summer Academy in Germany; Canadian Opera, Singapore Arts Festival, Royal Opera House Covent Garden, English National Opera and Paris (Opéra and Châtelet); Netherlands Opera, Amsterdam. *Honours:* Prizes for piano accompaniment at the RAM, and the Countess of Munster Musical Trust Scholarship; Jani Strasser Award, Glyndebourne, 1993. *Address:* c/o Glyndebourne Festival Opera, Glyndebourne, Lewes, East Sussex BN8 5UU, England. *Telephone:* (1273) 812321 (office). *Fax:* (1273) 815016. *E-mail:* steven.naylor@glyndebourne.com. *Website:* www.glyndebourne.com.

NEARY, Alice; British cellist; b. 15 Dec. 1972, London, England; d. of Martin Gerard James Neary. *Education:* Chetham's School of Music, RNCM with Ralph Kirshbaum, SUNY, Stonybrook with Timothy Eddy. *Career:* debut playing Haydn's C major concerto with the London Symphony Orchestra at the Barbican, 1994; South Bank Show (ITV) appearance in programme on John Tavener, 1995; Wigmore Hall, London, debut, 1999; Recitals for the Park Lane Group Series at the Purcell Room, for BBC Radio 3 and at Bridgewater Hall, Manchester; Concertos with the English CO, in Canada with the Israel Symphony Orchestra (Season 2000), Orchestra of St John's, London, and Royal Liverpool Philharmonic Orchestra; Bach's Solo Suites at St John's 2000; Performances at the International Musicians Seminar, Prussia Cove, with National Tour 2000; Festival engagements at the Manchester International Cello Festival, Santa Fe Chamber Music Festival and

Presteigne Festival (Artist-in-Residence, 1999); Recitals with pianist Gretel Dowdeswell and the Ovid Ensemble, Wigmore Hall recital April 2000. *Recordings include:* Innocence by John Tavener. *Honours:* Pierre Fournier Award, 1988; Silver Medal, 1994 Shell/London Symphony Orchestra Competition; Prize Winner, Adam International Cello Competition, New Zealand, 1997; Countess of Munster Musical Trust. *Address:* 7 Cornwall Avenue, Finchley N3 1LH, England.

NEARY, Martin Gerard James, LVO, MA, FRSCM, FRCO; British organist and conductor; b. 28 March 1940, London; m. Penelope Jane Warren 1967; one s. two d. (including Alice Neary). *Education:* HM Chapels Royal, St James's Palace, City of London School, Gonville and Caius College, Cambridge. *Career:* Assistant Organist 1963–65; Organist and Master of Music 1965–71; St Margaret's Westminster; Professor of Organ, Trinity College, London, 1963–72; Organ Adviser to Diocesan of Winchester, 1972–87; Conductor, Twickenham Musical Society, 1966–72; Founder and Conductor, St Margaret's Westminster Singers, 1967–71; Director of Southern Cathedrals Festival, 1972, 1975, 1978, 1981, 1984, 1987; Organist and Master of Music, Winchester Cathedral, 1972–95, Westminster Abbey, 1988–98; Organ Recitalist and Conductor; Founder and Conductor, Martin Neary Singers, 1972–; Conductor, Wayflete Singers, 1972–; Many organ recitals and broadcasts in England, including Royal Festival Hall and music festivals; has conducted many premieres of music by British composers including John Tavener's Ultimos Ritos, 1979, Jonathan Harvey's Hymn, 1979, and Passion and Resurrection, 1981, with Martin Neary Singers performing Madrigals and Graces at 10 Downing Street, 1970–74; Toured US and Canada, 1963, 1968, 1971, 1973, 1975, 1977, 1979, 1982, 1984; BBC Promenade Concerts, 1979, 1982, 1997; Conductor with ECO, 1978, 1980, 1981; London Symphony Orchestra, 1979, 1980, 1981; Bournemouth Symphony Orchestra and Sinfonietta 1975–; many European tours; Artist-in-Residence, University of California at Davis, 1984; President, Cathedral Organists Association, Royal College of Organists, 1988–90, 1996–98; Consultant, Millennium Youth Choir, 1999–; Conducted The Canterbury Pilgrims by George Dyson at Southwark Cathedral, London, 2000; Founder and Conductor, English Chamber Singers; Director of Music and Senior Organist at First Congregational Church, LA 2001–. *Recordings include:* Lloyd Webber's Requiem. *Honours:* Hon. Citizen of Texas 1971. *Address:* 71 Clancarty Road, Fulham, London SW6 3BB, England.

NEBE, Michael; Cellist and Conductor; b. 28 July 1947, Nordenbeck, Waldeck, Germany. *Education:* Educational Diploma and Teaching Qualifications, Dortmund Conservatorium; MMus, King's College, University of London, England, studied under Thurston Dart, Brian Trowell, Antony Milner, Geoffrey Bush; Licentiate, Royal Academy of Music, studying with Florence Hooton and Colin Hampton; Conducting, private studies in Germany and at Morley College, London under Lawrence Leonard; International Conductors' Seminar, Zlin, Czech Republic, 1991 and 1993 under Kirk Trevor, Jiri Belohlavek and Zdenek Bilek. *Career:* Debut: Wigmore Hall, London, 1977; Member, London Piace Consort, London Piace Duo, both until 1987, Plaegan Piano Quartet; Numerous performances as soloist and chamber music player throughout the United Kingdom; Tours in Germany, Netherlands, USA, Canada, Australia; Conductor and Musical Director of Whitehall Orchestra (The Orchestra of the British Civil Service), 1990–; Associated Conductor, Surrey Sinfonietta until 1994; Founder and Musical Director, Fine Arts Sinfonia of London, 1994–; Appearances as conductor in the United Kingdom, Germany Spain, Turkey; Teacher, conductor, freelance musician, soloist, translator, writer, lecturer and adjudicator; Made numerous live and recorded radio and television appearances, CD recordings; Conducted over 100 British and world Premieres; mem, Dvořák Society; Incorporated Society of Musicians; Musicians' Union. *Publications:* Translation into German, Eta Cohen's Violin Tutor, 1979; Cello Tutor, 1984; Articles for British newspapers and magazines. *Current Management:* Thornton Management. *Address:* c/o Thornton Management, 24 Thornton Avenue, London SW2 4HG, England.

NEBLETT, Carol; Singer (Soprano); b. 1 Feb. 1946, Modesto, California, USA. *Education:* Studied with Lotte Lehmann and Pierre Bernac. *Career:* Sang with Roger Wagner Chorale from 1965; Stage debut as Musetta, New York City Opera 1969; Returned as Marietta in Die Tote Stadt, Poppea, and Margherita and Elena in Boito's Mefistofele; Chicago 1975, as Chrysothemis in Elektra; Veinna Staatsoper debut 1976 as Minnie in La Fanciulla del West, Covent Garden 1977; Metropolitan Opera debut 1979, as Senta in Der fliegende Holländer; Returned as Tosca, Amelia (Un Ballo in Maschera), Manon Lescaut and Alice Ford in Falstaff; Appearances in Dallas, Turin, Leningrad, Pittsburgh, Baltimore and San Francisco; Other roles include Violetta, Minnie in La Fanciulla del West, Mozart's Countess, Charpentier's Louise and Antonia in Les Contes d'Hoffmann; Salzburg Festival as Vitelia in La Clemenza di Tito (has also appeared as Vitelia in Jean-Pierre Ponnelle's film of the opera); Teatro Regio Turin 1987, in Respighi's Semirama;

Sang Mme Lidoine in Les Dialogues des Carmélites at San Diego, 1990; Debut as Norma for Greater Miami Opera 1990; Aida for Cincinnati Opera; Season 1992 as Tosca for Opera Pacific at Costa Mesa, Queen Isabella in Franchetti's Cristoforo Colombo at Miami and as Amelia in Un Ballo in Maschera at Dublin; Sang the title role in Blitzstein's Regina at Costa Mesa, 1990. *Recordings include:* Die Tote Stadt (RCA); La Fanciulla del West (Deutsche Grammophon); La Bohème (HMV). *Address:* c/o Stafford Law Associates, 6 Barham Close, Weybridge, Surrey KT 13 9 PR, England.

NEBOLSIN, Eloar; Pianist; b. 24 Dec. 1974, Tashkent, Uzbekistan. *Education:* Tashkent Uspensky School of Music, 1980–91; Lscuela Superior de Musica, Reina, Sofia, 1991–95. *Career:* Wigmore Hall, London, 1993; New York–92nd Str Y, 1994; Ravina Festival with Riccardo Chailly, Chicago Symphony, 1994; Berlin Philharmonie with V L Ashkenazy, Deutsche Symphony Orchestra, 1995; Avery Fisher Hall with New York Philharmonic and Leonard Slatkin Cleaveland Orchestra, 1996. *Recordings:* Chopin and Liszt Recital; Chopin Piano Concerto No.1, Vladimir Ashkenazy conducting, Deutsche Symphony Orchestra. *Honours:* Concertino Praga Radio Competition; Santander Piano Competition Paloma O'Shea. *Current Management:* Konzertdirection Hans Ulrich Schmid. *Address:* 136-40, 62nd Avn, Flushing, NY 11367, USA.

NEGRIN, Francisco (Miguel); Opera Director; b. 5 June 1963, Mexico City, Mexico. *Education:* Studied cinematography in France notably at Aix-en-Provence. *Career:* Staff Producer at Théâtre Royal de la Monnaie, Brussels; Has assisted directors such as Patrice Chereau, K E Herrmann and Graham Vick; Associations with many opera houses including: Paris Châtelet, Salzburg Landestheater and Seattle Opera; Directed the premiere of his version of Debussy's The Fall of the House of Usher, Christ Church, Spitalfields, 1986, and at London International Opera Festival and Lisbon Opera, 1989; Has produced Werther at Opera de Nice, 1990, Orlando Paladino at Garsington Manor, 1990, La Traviata and the Mozart pasticcio The Jewel Box at Opera North, 1991 being the first outside production to be invited by Glyndebourne to be performed there, 1991, Così fan tutte at Seattle Opera, Don Carlos at Victoria State Opera, Melbourne, L'Heure Espagnole and La Colombe at the Guildhall School of Music, 1993, and Handel's Julius Caesar at Australian Opera in Sydney, 1994 and Melbourne, 1995; World premieres of Tourist Variations and Visitatio Sepulchri by James Macmillan at Glasgow's Tramway and at the Edinburgh Festival, Una Cosa Rara by Martin y Soler at the Drottningholm Festival; Schoeck's Venus at Geneva, 1997; Handel's Partenope for Glimmerglass Opera, New York, 1998. *Recordings:* Julius Caesar on CD and Video. *Current Management:* IMG Artists. *Address:* c/o Diana Mulgan, IMG Artists, Lovell House, 616 Chiswick High Road, London W4 5RX, England.

NÉGYESY, János; Violinist; b. 13 Sept. 1938, Budapest, Hungary. *Education:* Franz Liszt Music Acad., Budapest. *Career:* concert master, Berlin Radio Orchestra, Germany 1970–74; Prof. of Music, Univ. of California San Diego, USA 1979–; soloist in all major European festivals, including Berliner Festwochen, Royan Festival, Donaueschingen, Paris, Witten Chamber Music Festival, Meta Music Festival Berlin, Metz Festival, festivals in New York, San Francisco, Washington, DC, Baltimore, Vancouver, Tokyo, Buenos Aires, Mexico City, Tehran, Helsinki, Stockholm, Zürich, Paris, Torino, Ferrara and Budapest; mem. New York Acad. of Sciences, American Asscn for the Advancement of Science, International Platform Asscn. *Compositions:* latest multimedia works for Electronic Violin System: Digitales 1993, Igitur 1993, en route 1995, Kaleidoscope 3 and 4 (with Adam Findley) 2001, 2003. *Recordings:* All Violin Sonatas by Charles Ives 1975, Dedications to János Négyesy 1978, John Cage: Freeman Etudes I–XVI for solo violin 1984, Personae, Violin Concerto by Roger Reynolds 1992, The Complete Violin Duos by Béla Bartók (with Päivikki Nykter) 1993, The Complete Freeman Etudes for Solo Violin by John Cage 1995, Dedications 2, Solo Violin works written for and dedicated to János Négyesy 1995, Dedications to János Négyesy and Päivikki Nykter, New Works for 2 violins 2000. *Publications:* New Violin Technique 1978. *Address:* University of California San Diego, Department of Music, 9500 Gilman Drive, La Jolla, CA 92093, USA. *E-mail:* jhegyesy@ucsd.edu. *Website:* felix.ucsd.edu/~jnegyesy.

NEIDHART, Elke; Stage Director; b. 1940, Germany. *Education:* Studied at the Stuttgart Drama and Opera School. *Career:* Assistant at the Zürich Stage Opera, 1964; Resident Director of Australian Opera from 1977, staging Fidelio, Cav and Pag, Lohengrin and Salome; Has also staged Fidelio for Lyric Opera of Queensland, Puritani and Flying Dutchman for Victorian State Opera; From 1990, Director of Productions at Cologne Opera, assisting on and restaging The Ring, From the House of the Dead, Don Giovanni, Der Prinz von Homburg and La Finta Semplice; Il Trovatore at Sydney, 1996; Tannhäuser for Opera Australia, 1998. *Current Management:* Athole Still International Management, Forresters Hall, 25–27 Westow Street, London, SE19

3RY, England. *Telephone:* (20) 8771-5271. *Fax:* (20) 8768-6600. *Website:* www.atholestill.com.

NEIGHBOUR, Oliver Wray, BA; fmr Music Librarian; b. 1 April 1923. *Education:* Eastbourne Coll., Birbeck Coll., London. *Career:* Entered Department of Printed Books, BM, 1946; Assistant Keeper in Music Room, 1951; Deputy Keeper, 1976; Music Librarian, Reference Division of The British Library, 1976–85. *Publications:* (with Alan Tyson) English Music Publishers' Plate Numbers, 1965; The Consort and Keyboard Music of William Byrd, 1978; (ed), Music and Bibliography: Essays in Honour of Alec Hyatt King, 1980; Article on Schoenberg in New Grove Dictionary of Music and Musicians, 1980 and 2001; Editor of First Publications of Works by Schumann, Schoenberg and Byrd. *Honours:* Fellow, British Academy. *Address:* 12 Treborough House, 1 Nottingham Place, London W1U 5LA, England.

NEIKRUG, Marc (Edward); Composer and Pianist; b. 24 Sept. 1946, New York City, USA. *Education:* Studied with Giselher Klebe in Detmold 1964–68; Stony Brook State University of New York; MM in Composition 1971. *Career:* Commissions from the Houston Symphony and the St Paul Chamber Orchestra (Consultant on Contemporary Music 1978); Los Alamos premiere at the Deutsche Oper Berlin, 1988; Duo partnership with Pinchas Zukerman; Visited London, 1989; British premiere of Violin Concerto at South Bank and duo recital at the Barbican Hall. *Compositions:* Piano Concerto 1966; Solo Cello sonata 1967; Clarinet Concerto 1967; 2 String Quartets 1969, 1972; Viola Concerto 1974; Suite for cello and piano 1974; Rituals for flute and harp 1976; Concertino for ensemble 1977; Fantasies for violin and piano 1977; Continuum for cello and piano 1978; Cycle for 7 pianos 1978; Kaleidoscope for flute and piano 1979; Eternity's Sunrise for orchestra 1979–80; Through Roses, theatre piece 1979–80; Mobile for orchestra 1981; Violin Concerto 1982; Duo for violin and piano 1983; Los Alamos opera, 1988; Chettro Ketl, for chamber orchestra, 1994; Sonata Concertante for violin and piano, 1994; String Quintet, 1995; Pueblo children's Songs for soprano and piano, 1995; Piano Concerto, 1996. *Honours:* NEA Awards 1972 and 1974; Prizes for Through Roses at the Besancon Film Festival 1981, and the International Film and Television Festival, New York, 1982. *Address:* c/o ASCAP, ASCAP Building, 1 Lincoln Plaza, NY 10023, USA.

NEILL, Stuart; Singer (Tenor); b. 1965, Atlanta, Georgia, USA. *Career:* Sang Rodolfo in La Bohème at San Francisco, 1993 (also at Venice and the Deutsche Oper Berlin); Season 1994–95 as Arturo in I Puritani at Santiago, Geneva, Venice and the Vienna Staatsoper; Dallas Opera, 1996, as Don Ottavio; Other roles include Arnoldo in Guillaume Tell at Amsterdam, 1995, Gualtiero in Bellini's Pirata, Fernando in La Favorita, and Alfredo; Further appearances at the Lyric Opera Chicago, Naples and Nice; Season 1998 as Donizetti's Tonio at Philadelphia and Arnold in Guillaume Tell for Washington Opera; Sang the Italian Tenor in Der Rosenkavalier at the Met, 2000. *Address:* Washington Concert Opera, 1690 36th Street North West, Suite 411, Washington, DC 20007, USA.

NEJCEVA, Liljana; Singer (Mezzo-soprano); b. 1945, Silistra, Bulgaria. *Education:* Studied at the music schools in Ruse and Sofia. *Career:* Sang at the Leipzig Opera 1969, as Amastris in Xerxes, Ulrica, Lady Pamela in Fra Diavolo, Fidalma in Il Matrimonio Segreto and Konchakovna in Prince Igor; Member of Bayerische Staatsoper Munich, 1973–78, as Azucena, Maddalena, Marina in Boris Godunov and Cherubino; Has sung with Nationaltheater Mannheim, 1981–; Guest appearances include Hamburg (as Eboli), Berlin Staatsoper (Dorabella), Vienna Volksoper (Carmen) and Cologne (Suzuki); Also sings Luisa Miller; Travelled to Japan and Cuba; Concert engagements in Munich, Prague, Rome, Frankfurt and Paris. *Address:* Music International, 13 Ardilaun Road, London N5 2QR, England.

NEL, Anton; Pianist and Professor of Piano; b. 29 Dec. 1961, Johannesburg, South Africa. *Education:* BMus, University of the Witwatersand, South Africa, 1983; Performers Diploma, MMus 1984, D.Mus 1986, University of Cincinnati, USA. *Career:* Debut: Carnegie Recital Hall, New York, 1986; Performances with major orchestras including Chicago, Seattle, Cincinnati, Brooklyn; Recitals and chamber music concerts throughout USA, Canada, Europe, Parts of Africa; Recitals in Alice Tully Hall, New York; Barbican Centre and Queen Elizabeth Hall, London; Many appearances at summer festivals including Aspen, Ravinia; Professor of Piano, Eastman School of Music, Rochester, New York; mem, Pi Kappa Lambda. *Recordings:* Saint-Saëns, Carnival of the Animals; Haydn-4 Sonatas. *Honours:* 1st Prize, Walter W Naumburg International Piano Competition; 1st Prize, Joanna Hodges International Piano Competition; Prizes at Leeds and Pretoria International Piano Competition. *Current Management:* Walter W Naumburg Foundation.

NELSON, John; Conductor; b. 6 Dec. 1941, San José, Costa Rica. *Education:* Studies at Juilliard School, New York. *Career:* Conductor, Berlioz's Les Troyens, New York, 1972; Conductor, New York City Opera, 1972–; From 1973 at Metropolitan Opera, conducting Cavalleria Rusticana, Pagliacci, Jenůfa, Il Barbiere di Siviglia, Carmen and L'Incoronazione di Poppea; Conducted US premiere of Britten's Owen Wingrave, Santa Fe Opera; Music Director, Indianapolis Symphony Orchestra, 1977–88; Music Director St Louis Opera, 1981–91, continuing as Principal Guest Conductor; Caramoor Festival, New York; Tour of Europe, 1987; Guest engagements with leading orchestras in North America and Europe; Debut with Lyon Opéra, 1991 conducting Béatrice and Bénédict; Conducted Benvenuto Cellini at Geneva Opera, 1992; Offenbach's The Tales of Hoffmann at the Bastille; Recent productions include Handel's Xerxes, Massenet's Don Quichotte with Chicago Lyric Opera, Béatrice and Bénédict with Welsh National Opera, Faust at Geneva Opera, Benvenuto Cellini with Rome Opera, Don Carlos at Lyon Opéra and A new opera at Lyon Opéra by Marcel Landowski; Verdi's Vespri Siciliani at Rome, 1997 and Handel's Giulio Cesare, 1998. *Recordings:* Béatrice and Bénédict; CD, Bach Arias with Kathleen Battle; Gorecki's Beatus Vir with Czech Philharmonic; Handel's Semele with English Chamber Orchestra and Kathleen Battle, awarded Grammy Award, Best Operatic Recording of 1993; CD of Works of Paul Schönfeld, 1994; Gorecki's Miserere with Chicago Symphony and Chicago Lyric Opera Choruses. *Honours:* Diapason d'Or Award for Erato recording of Béatrice and Bénédict, 1992. *Address:* c/o IMG Artists Europe, Lovell House, 616 Chiswick High Road, London, W4 5RX, England.

NELSON, Judith, BA; singer (soprano); b. 10 Sept. 1939, Chicago, Illinois, USA; m. Alan H. Nelson 1961; one s. one d. *Education:* St Olaf College, Northfield, MN; studied piano 12 years; voice with Thomas Wikman (Chicago), James Cunningham (Berkeley), Martial Singher (Santa Barbara). *Career:* debut, Paris 1973; Radio: BBC, France, Belgium, Netherlands, Germany, Italy, Austria, Scandinavia; Several BBC Promenade Concerts; Television: Series, Music in Time, Open University Handel's Messiah, BBC; ITV; Performances with major symphonies including: San Francisco Symphony; Los Angeles Philharmonic; Baltimore Symphony; Atlanta Symphony; St Louis Symphony. *Recordings:* Various recordings including: Belinda in Dido and Aeneas, Handel's Alceste and La Resurrezione; Haydn: Canzonets and Cantatas, with Koch International. *Honours:* Alfred Hertz Memorial Fellowship, 1972–73; Honorary Doctorate, St Olaf College, 1989. *Current Management:* Tennant Artists, Unit 2, 39 Tadema Road, London, SW10 0PZ, England. *Telephone:* (20) 7376-3758. *Fax:* (20) 7351-0679. *E-mail:* info@tennantartists.demon.co.uk. *Address:* 2600 Buena Vista Way, Berkeley, CA 94708, USA.

NELSON, Richard Lawrence; Surgeon, French Horn Player and Tenor Horn Player; b. 11 Oct. 1946, Evanston, Illinois, USA; m. Susan Jane Berryman, 17 June 1972, 3 s., 2 d. *Education:* BA, Classical Greek, Stanford University, 1968; MD, University of Chicago, 1972; French horn with Paul Navarro, Liss van Pechman, Arnold Jacobs. *Career:* Illinois Brass Band, 1993–2001; mem, North American Brass Band Association; International Horn Society; Historic Brass Society; American College of Surgeons. *Recordings:* Christmas Fantasy; Illinois Brass Band Live; Championship Brass; Shakin' not Stirred. *Publications:* Contributor to, Wind and Song–Arnold Jacobs by Brian Frederickson, 1996. *Honours:* North American Brass Band Champions, 1996, 1997, 1998, 2000, 2001; Order of Brass Band World, 2001. *Address:* 2224 Lincolnwood Drive, Evanston, IL 60201, USA. *E-mail:* e.altohorn@uic.edu.

NELSON, Ron; Composer and Professor of Music; b. 14 Dec. 1929, Joliet, Illinois, USA; m. Helen Mitchell, deceased, 1 s., 1 d. *Education:* BM, 1952, MM, 1953, DMA, 1956, Eastman School of Music, Rochester; Ecole Normale de Musique, Paris, France, 1955–56. *Career:* Professor Emeritus, 1991. *Compositions:* Opera, The Birthday of the Infanta, 1956; The Christmas Story, 1958; Toccata for Orchestra, 1963; What is Man?, 1964; Rocky Point Holiday, 1969; This is the Orchestra, 1969; Prayer for an Emperor of China, 1973; Five Pieces for Orchestra after Paintings of Frank Wyeth, 1975; Four Pieces after the Seasons, 1978; Three Autumnal Sketches, 1979; Mass of LaSalle, 1981; Nocturnal Pieces, 1982; Three Settings of the Moon, 1982; Medieval Suite, 1983; Aspen Jubilee, 1984; Te Deum Laudamus, 1985; Danza Capriccio for saxophone, 1988; Three pieces after Tennyson, 1989; Fanfare for the Hour of Sunlight, 1989; Morning Alleluias, 1989; The Deum Laudamus, 1991; To the Airborne, 1991; Passacaglin (Homage on B-A-C-H), 1992; Lauds (Praise High Day), 1992; Epiphanies, fanfares and chorales, 1994; Chaconne (In memoriam…), 1994. *Address:* Sonoran Highlands, 28412 N 97th Way, Scottsdale, AZ 85262, USA.

NELSSON, Woldemar; Conductor; b. 4 April 1938, Kiev, Ukraine. *Education:* Studied with his father in Kiev, then at the Novosibirsk Conservatory and in Moscow and Leningrad. *Career:* Assistant to Kyrill Kondrashin at the Moscow Philharmonic, 1972; Conducted leading orchestras in the USSR, with such soloists as Rostropovich, David Oistrakh and Gidon Kremer; Emigrated to West Germany 1977 and conducted major orchestras in Hamburg, Munich, Berlin, Frankfurt,

Vienna, London, Geneva, Amsterdam, Tel-Aviv, Jerusalem and Montreal; Directed the premiere of Henze's ballet Orpheus, Stuttgart 1979, and took the production to Washington and the Metropolitan Opera New York; Guest Conductor with Stuttgart Opera from 1980; General Music Director of the State Theatre in Kassel; Has conducted opera productions in Paris, Philadelphia, Japan, Vienna and Barcelona; Bayreuth Festival, 1980–85, Lohengrin and Der fliegende Holländer; Conducted the world premiere of Penderecki's opera Die schwarze Maske, Salzburg 1986; Music Director of the Royal Opera, Copenhagen. *Recordings include:* Lohengrin (CBS); Der fliegende Holländer (Philips). *Honours:* Max Reger Prize. *Address:* c/o Staatstheater Stuttgart, Oberer Schlossgarten 6, 7000 Stuttgart 1, Germany.

NEMETH, Geza; Violist; b. 1930, Hungary. *Education:* Franz Liszt Academy, Budapest. *Career:* Violist of the Bartók Quartet from 1957; Performances in nearly every European country and tours to Australia, Canada, Japan, New Zealand and the USA; Festival appearances at Adelaide, Ascona, Aix, Venice, Dubrovnik, Edinburgh, Helsinki, Lucerne, Menton, Prague, Veinna, Spoleto and Schwetzingen; Tour of the United Kingdom 1986 including concerts at Cheltenham, Dartington, Philharmonic Hall Liverpool, RNCM Manchester and the Wigmore Hall; Tours of the United Kingdom 1988 and 1990, featuring visits to the Sheldonian Theatre Oxford, Wigmore Hall, Harewood House and Birmingham; Repertoire includes standard classics and Hungarian works by Bartók, Durko, Bozay, Kadosa, Soproni, Farkas, Szabo and Lang. *Recordings include:* Complete quartets of Mozart, Beethoven and Brahms; Major works of Haydn and Schubert (Hungaroton); Complete quartets of Bartók (Erato). *Honours:* (with members of Bartók Quartet) Kossuth Prize, Outstanding Artist of the Hungarian People's Republic, 1981; UNESCO/IMC Prize 1981. *Current Management:* Ingpen & Williams Ltd, 7 St George's Court, 131 Putney Bridge Road, London, SW15 2PA, England.

NENDICK, Josephine; Singer (Soprano); b. 1940, Kent, England. *Education:* Studied at the Royal College of Music, the Guildhall School of Music with Audrey Langford. *Career:* Sang first at the Aldeburgh Festival, then premiered works by Boulez and Bo Nilsson at Darmstadt; Has sung with such ensembles as Capricorn, Domaine Musical, Ensemble Musique Nouvelles, Music Group of London, Les Percussions de Strasbourg; Festival engagements at Avignon, Berlin, Cheltenham, London (English Bach), Edinburgh, Prades, Royaun, Warsaw; Conductors include Pierre Boulez, Ernest Bour, Charles Bruck, Colin Davis, Michael Gielen, Norman Del Mar, Bruno Maderna, Manuel Rosenthal; Repertoire includes Berg, Der Wein; Berio Magnificat, Chamber Music, Circles; Four Popular Songs, Sequenza; Boulez Improvisations sur Mallarmé, Le Marteau sans Maitre, Le Soleil des Eaux; Birtwistle Entractes and Sappho Fragments; Bussotti Le Passion selon Sade; Ravel Chansons Medécasses and 3 Poemes de Stephane Mallarmé; Schoenberg Pierrot Lunaire and Das Buch der Hängenden Gärten; Webern Songs Op 8 and Op 13; Bart ók Village Scenes; Works by Barraqué, Smith Brindle, Finnissy, Dillon, Cage, Crumb, Dallapiccola, Stravinsky, Babbitt, Ives and Satie; Sang in Bach's Christmans Oratorio, Berlioz Les Troyens (Ascanius), Delius A Mass of Life; Mahler Das Lied von der Erde, Monteverdi L'Incoronazione di Poppea (Drusilla, at Bremen) and Mozart's Requiem and C minor Mass. *Recordings include:* Boulez Le Soleil des Eaux; Lutyens Quincunx, with the BBC Symphony Orchestra; Barraqué Sequence and Chant après Chant.

NENTWIG, Franz Ferdinand; Singer (Bass-Baritone); b. 23 Aug. 1929, Duisburg, Germany. *Career:* Debut: Bielefeld 1962, as Ottokar in Der Freischütz; Sang in Darmstadt and Hanover and at the Vienna Volksoper, Vience 1983, as Amfortas in Parsifal; Wagner performances in Munich, Berlin and Hamburg; Tour of Japan 1984 with the Hamburg Company; Metropolitan Opera 1984 as Telramund in Lohengrin; Barcelona 1986 also in Lohengrin; Further appearances in Cologne, Frankfurt, Karlsruhe, Stuttgart and Mannheim; Other roles include Pizarro in Fidelio, Escamillo, Strauss's Jochanaan and Mandryka, Mozart's Count and Don Alfonso, Verdi's Rigoletto and Amonasro and Wagner's Dutchman, Wotan and Gunther; Sang Hans Sachs with the Berlin Staatsoper on tour to Japan, 1987; Salzburg Festival and Turin 1987, as Schoenberg's Moses and as Wotan; Sang Dr Schön in Lulu and Dr Vigilius in Schreker's Der ferne Klang, 1988; Wotan in the first Polish production of the Ring, 1989; Brussels 1990, as Shishkov in From the House of the Dead; Sang La Roche in a new production of Capriccio at Covent Garden, 1991; Season 1991–92 as Wotan at Brussels and Beckmesser at Spoleto. *Recordings include:* Schreker's Der Schatzgräber. *Address:* c/o Théâtre Royal de la Monnaie, 4 Leopolstrasse, 1000 Brussels, Belgium.

NERDRUM, Sonja; Opera Singer (Mezzo-soprano); b. 1 Oct. 1953, Bern, Switzerland. *Education:* West London Institute of Higher Education: Singing studies with Eduardo Asquez, Jeffrey Talbot, and subsequently with Françoise Garner. *Career:* Debut: Abbaye de Flaran, Gascogne, as Dorabella in Così fan tutte directed by Jean-Claude Auvray, 1978; Dorabella in Angers, conductor Sylvain Cambreling; Apollo/Mirtillo in

Handel's Il pastor fido at Den Norske Opera, in the Drottningholm production; Giacinta in Mozart's La finta semplice in Batignano, conductor David Parry; Zweite Dame in Die Zauberflöte at Opéra de Montpellier; Dorabella in Oslo Summer Opera, returning as Hermia in A Midsummer Night's Dream; La Baronne in La vie parisienne for English National Opera; Donizetti's Maria Stuarda in Kristiansund; Marcellina in Le nozze di Figaro at Versailles and for Jean-Claude Malgoire at Tourcoing; Puccini's Tosca, touring Middle and Far East; Concert repertoire includes Norwegian, French, Italian, German, English and Russian songs. *Honours:* Honorary RCM, Royal College of Music, 1988. *Address:* c/o K Berg, 39 Avenue Road, London NW8 6 BS, England.

NERSESSIAN, Pavel; Concert Pianist; b. 26 Aug. 1968, Ramenskoye, Moscow, Russia. *Education:* Central Music School, Moscow and Tchaikovsky Conservatory. *Career:* Concert tours of Russia from 1972 and more recent appearances in Spain, Hungary, Italy, France and Ireland; Season 1992–93 in Cannes and Dublin, tour of Japan and appearances in Austria, England, Ireland, Canada, and the USA; Professor of Piano at Moscow Conservatory. *Honours:* 2nd Prize, Beethoven Competition in Vienna, 1985. *Current Management:* Ingpen & Williams Ltd, 7 St George's Court, 131 Putney Bridge Road, London, SW15 2PA, England.

NES, Jard van; Singer (Mezzo-soprano); b. 15 June 1948, Netherlands. *Career:* Debut: Sang in Mahler's 2 Symphony under Bernard Haitink at Concertgebouw, 1983; Appearances in Bach's St Matthew Passion under Nikolaus Harnoncourt and in Mahler's 8th Symphony; Tour of North America with Minnesota Orchestra and Edo de Waart, 1987–88; Further concerts in Paris, London, Oslo, Montreal and Ludwigsburg; Stage debut with Netherlands Opera 1983, as Bertarido in Rodelinda; Double bill of Hindemith's Sancta Susanna and Mörder, Hoffnung der Frauen 1984; Season 1986–87 with parts in Il Ritorno d'Ulisse, Die Meistersinger (Magdalena) and Tristan und Isolde as Brangaene; Sang in Ligeti's Le Grand Macabre at the Paris Châtelet and the Salzburg Festival, 1997; Sang Mrs Sedley in Peter Grimes at Glyndebourne, 2000. *Recordings:* Mozart Requiem, Brahms Alto Rhapsody, Mahler 2nd Symphony and Zemlinsky Lieder; Messiah; Beethoven's Ninth; Handel's Theodora and Das Lied von der Erde. *Address:* c/o Netherlands Opera, Waterlooplein 22, 1011PG, Amsterdam, Netherlands.

NESCHLING, John; Conductor; b. 1945, Rio de Janeiro, Brazil. *Education:* Studied in Vienna with Hans Swarowsky; Further study with Leonard Bernstein in the USA. *Career:* Engagements with the London, Vienna and Berlin Radio Symphony Orchestras, New York and Israel Philharmonic, the Tonhalle, Zürich and the Italian Radio at Naples and Milan; Opera appearances at Berlin (Deutsche Oper and Staatsoper), Stuttgart, Hamburg and Stockholm; Principal Conductor of the San Carlo Lisbon 1981–88; Music Director of the Teatro São Paulo and at St Gallen in Switzerland (Die Zauberflöte 1989); Engaged for Trovatore, Figaro, Pagliacci and Gianni Schicchi at St Gallen; Lucia di Lammermoor, Butterfly, Andrea Chénier and Il Barbiere di Siviglia as guest conductor at the Vienna Staatsoper; Conducted Il Guarany by Gomes at Bonn, 1994 and Der Rosenkavalier at Palermo, 1998. *Recordings include:* Il Guarany, 1996. *Honours:* Winner, International Competition for young conductors in Florence, London Symphony Orchestra International Competition. *Address:* Walter Beloch srl, Artists Management, Via Melzi D'Eril, 26 20154 Milan, Italy.

NESS, Arthur J.; Musicologist; b. 27 Jan. 1936, Chicago, Illinois, USA; m. Charlotte A. Kolczynski 1982. *Education:* BMus, Music Theory, University of Southern California, 1958; AM, Music, Harvard University, 1963; PhD, Musicology, New York University, 1984. *Career:* Assistant Professor, University of Southern California, 1964–76; Associate Professor, Daemen College, 1976–83; Visiting Lecturer, State University of New York, Buffalo, 1983–87; Editor and Music Engraver, 1990–; Former General Editor, Monuments of the Lutenist Art, 1992–94. *Compositions:* Three Poems by Kenneth Patchen, for alto and piano. *Publications:* Lute Works of Francesco Canova da Milano (1497–1543), 1970; The Herwarth Lute Tablatures, 1984; The Königsberg Manuscript (with John M Ward), 1989; The Lute Works of Marco dall'Aguila, 2003. *Contributions:* Major contributor, New Grove Dictionary of Music, 1980, New Harvard Dictionary of Music, 1986; Journal of American Musicological Society; Le Luth et sa Musique II, 1985; Music in Context: Essays for John M Ward, 1985; New Grove Dictionary of American Music, 1986. *Honours:* Fulbright Fellow, University of Munich; Healey Award, 1984. *Address:* 2039 Commonwealth Avenue, Suite 10, Boston, MA 02135, USA.

NESTERENKO, Yevgeniy Yevgeniyevich; Russian singer (bass); b. 8 Jan. 1938, Moscow; s. of Yevgeniy Nikiforovich Nesterenko and Velta Woldearovna Baumann; m. Yekaterina Dmitrievna Alexeyeva 1963; one s. *Education:* Leningrad Eng Inst. and Leningrad Conservatoire (V. Lukanin's class). *Career:* debut as General Ermolov in War and Peace, Maly Theatre, Leningrad 1963; soloist with Leningrad Maly Opera and

Ballet Theatre 1963–67; soloist with Kirov Opera 1967–71; teacher of solo singing at Leningrad Conservatoire 1967–71; soloist with Bolshoi 1971–; mem. CPSU 1974–91; mem. staff, Moscow Musical Pedagogical Inst. 1972–74; Chair. of Singing at Moscow Conservatoire 1975–93, Prof. 1981–93; Prof. Vienna Acad. of Music 1993–; USSR People's Deputy 1989–91. *Roles include:* Boris Godunov, Dosifey (Khovanshchina), Khan Konchak (Prince Igor), Mephistopheles (Faust), Grigori (Quiet Flows the Don), Kutuzov (War and Peace), Filippo II (Don Carlo), Attila, Zaccaria (Nabucco), Don Pasquale, Sarastro (Magic Flute), Bluebeard, Gremin (Eugene Onegin), Ivan Susanin, Old Convict (Lady Macbeth), Don Basilio, Enrico VIII. *Publication:* Thoughts on My Profession 1985. *Honours:* People's Artist of the USSR 1976, Lenin Prize 1982, Melodia Golden Disc 1984, Giovanni Zenatello Prize, Verona 1986, Viotti d'Oro Medal, Vercelli 1981, Chaliapin Prize 1992, Wilhelm Furtwängler Prize, Germany 1992, Austrian Kammersänger 1992, Casta Diva Prize, Russia 2001, Knight of the Opera Prize, Russia 2002. *Address:* Riemergasse 10/14, 1010 Vienna, Austria (home).

NETHSINGHA, Andrew, MA, FRCO, ARCM; Conductor and Organist; b. 16 May 1968, Worcestershire; m. Lucy; one s. one d. *Education:* Royal Coll. of Music, Cambridge Univ. *Career:* asst organist, Wells Cathedral 1990–94; Master of the Choristers and Organist, Truro Cathedral 1994–2002; Musical Dir, Three Spires Singers and Orchestra 1994–2002; Dir of Music, Gloucester Cathedral; Artistic Dir, Three Choirs Festival; Musical Dir Gloucester Choral Soc.; conducted Philharmonia, Royal Philharmonic Orchestra, BBC Concert Orchestra; conducted in China, South Africa, Canada, USA and Europe; organ recitals include at Nôtre-Dame de Paris, Washington National Cathedral; mem. Incorporated Soc. of Musicians, Royal Coll. of Organists. *Recordings:* Magnificat and Nunc Dimittis Vol. 10, Popular Choral Music from Truro, Popular organ music series Vol. 6, The Complete New English Hymnal Vol. 10, Music for a Cathedral's Year. *Address:* 7 Miller's Green, Gloucester, GL1 2BN, England (home). *Telephone:* (1452) 524764 (office). *Fax:* (1452) 300469 (office). *E-mail:* andrew@nethsingha.freeserve.co.uk (office).

NETREBKO, Anna; Russian singer (soprano); b. 1971, Krasnodar. *Education:* Rimsky-Korsakov Conservatory. *Career:* debut, Mariinsky Opera Theatre, St Petersburg 1994, as Susanna; roles include Glinka's Ludmila with Kirov Opera, Gilda in Rigoletto and Kundry in Parsifal at St Petersburg; appearance at Salzburg Festival 1998; tours with Kirov Opera as Pamina and Bizet's Micaela; sang Gilda at Washington 1999, Mimi at San Francisco 1999–2000; concerts with Rotterdam Philharmonic Orchestra include London Proms and Teresa in Benvenuto Cellini, Royal Festival Hall 1999; sang Natasha in War and Peace at St Petersburg and London 2000; other roles include Zerlina and Louisa in Prokovfiev's Betrothal in a Monastery at San Francisco, Rosina, Pamina and Xenia in Boris Godunov, Donna Anna at Salzburg and Mozart's Servilia at Covent Garden 2002. *Recordings:* Glinka's Ruslan and Ludmila. *Honours:* first prize All-Russian Glinka Vocal Competition, Moscow 1993, third prize Rimsky-Korsakov Int. Competition of young opera singers St Petersburg 1996, Costa Diva prize 1998, Golden Sophit prize St Petersburg 1999. *Address:* State Academic Mariinsky Theatre, Teatralnaya pl. 1, St Petersburg, Russia. *Telephone:* 812-114 4004; 812-314 1744.

NETTL, Bruno; Musicologist; b. 14 March 1930, Prague, Czechoslovakia; m. Wanda White, 2 d. *Education:* BA, 1950, MA, 1951, PhD, 1953, Indiana University, Bloomington, USA; MALS, University of Michigan, Ann Arbor, 1960. *Career:* Instructor in Music, 1953–54, Assistant Professor of Music, 1954–56, 1959–64, Wayne State University, Detroit, Michigan; Associate Professor of Music, 1965–67, Professor of Music and Anthropology, 1967–, University of Illinois, Urbana; Visiting Professor of Music, Harvard University, 1990; Distinguished Albert Seay Professor of Music, Colorado College, 1992; Visiting Hill Professor of Music, University of Minnesota, 1995; Benedict Distinguished Visiting Professor of Music, Carleton College, 1996. *Publications include:* Music in Primitive Culture, 1956; An Introduction to Folk Music in the US, 1960; Cheremis Musical Styles, 1961; Theory and Method in Ethnomusicology, 1964; Folk and Traditional Music of the Western Continents, 1965, 2nd edition, 1972; Daramad of Chahargan, A study of the performance practice of Persian music, 1972; Contemporary Music and Music Cultures, with C Hamm and R Byrnside, 1975; Eight Urban Musical Cultures, 1978; The Study of Ethnomusicology, 1983; The Western Impact on World Music, 1965; The Radif of Persian Music, 1987, 1992; Blackfoot Musical Thought: Comparative Perspectives, 1989; Comparative Musicology and Anthropology of Music, 1991; Heartland Excursions: Ethnomusicological Reflections of Schools of Music, 1995; Editor, Ethnomusicology, 1961–65; In the Course of Performance: Studies in the World of Musical Improvisation, 1998. *Address:* 1423 Cambridge Drive, Champaign, IL 61821, USA.

NEUBAUER, Margit; Singer (Mezzo-soprano); b. 1950, Austria. *Education:* Studied in Vienna. *Career:* Sang at Linz Landestheater, 1975–77, notably in 1976 premiere of Der Aufstand by Helmut Eder; Engage-

ments at Frankfurt Opera from 1977, Zürich, 1978–79, Hamburg, 1980–83, Deutsche Oper Berlin, 1982–85; Bayreuth Festival 1981–86, as Sigrune in Die Walküre and a Flowermaiden in Parsifal; US tour with Deutsche Oper, 1985; Roles have included Cherubino, Flosshilde, Brigitte in Korngold's Tote Stadt, Annina, Rosenkavalier and the title role in Miss Jule by Bibalo; Many concert appearances, notably in Baroque music. *Recordings:* Parsifal, Bayreuth, 1985; Bach B minor Mass and Handel Utrecht Te Deum.

NEUENFELS, Hans; Stage Director; b. 1941, Krefeld, Germany. *Career:* Debut: Produced Il Trovatore at Nuremberg, 1974; Frankfurt Opera, 1976–80, with Macbeth, Aida, Die Gezeichneten by Schreker and Busoni's Doktor Faust; Productions at Deutsche Oper Berlin, 1982–86 have included La Forza del Destino, Rigoletto and Zimmermann's Die Soldaten; Paris Opéra 1989 with the premiere of York Höller's Der Meister und Margarita, the last production at the Palais Garnier before the opening of the Opéra Bastille; Il Trovatore at the Deutsche Oper, 1996; Le Prophète by Meyerbeer at the Vienna State Opera, 1998. *Address:* c/o Deutsche Oper Berlin, Bismarckstrasse 35, 1000 Berlin 10, Germany.

NEUGEBAUER, Hans; Singer (Bass) and Stage Director; b. 17 Nov. 1916, Karlsruhe, Germany. *Education:* Studied in Mannheim and Hamburg. *Career:* Debut: Karlsruhe 1946, as Bett in Zar und Zimmermann; Sang Buffo and other roles at Karlsruhe until 1951, Frankfurt Opera, 1951–60, notably as the King in Aida and Mozart's Figaro; Producer of opera from 1955, first at Frankfurt and Heidelberg, then Kassel, 1962–64; Staged premiere of Zimmermann's Die Soldaten at Cologne, Der Rosenkavalier at Glyndebourne, 1965; Guest engagements as Producer at Düsseldorf, Kassel, Mannheim, Basle, Trieste and Chicago. *Address:* c/o Oper der Stadt Koln, Offenbachplatz 5000 Cologne, Germany.

NEUHOLD, Günter; Conductor; b. 2 Nov. 1947, Graz, Austria; m. Emma Schmidt, 1 s. *Education:* Master's degree, 1947; Advanced courses with Franco Ferrara in Rome, Hans Swarowski in Vienna. *Career:* Engaged at various German opera houses, 1972–80, ending as First Kapellmeister in Hannover and Dortmund; Music Director, Teatro Regio di Parma, 1981–86, devoted mainly to Verdi operas and as Chief Conductor, Arturo Toscanini Symphonic Orchestra of Emilia Romagna; Chief Conductor, Musical Director, Flanders Royal Philharmonic Orchestra, Antwerp, 1986–90, with tours, Germany, Italy, the United Kingdom, France; General Music Director, Badisches Staatstheater Karlsruhe, 1989–95, conducting a Richard Strauss cycle and Ring des Nibelungen; General Music Director, Artistic Director, Theater der Freien Hansestadt Bremen and Philharmonische Orchester Bremen, 1995–2002; Concerts with Wiener Philharmoniker, Staatskapelle Dresden, Philharmonic Orchestra Monte Carlo, Tokyo Philharmonic Orchestra, Tokyo Metropolitan Opera, radio orchestras of several German stations, also ORF, RAI, BBC, Radio-Television Moscow, CBC Canada, ABC Australia, National Orchestra of Capitol Toulouse; Operas at Wiener Staatsoper, La Scala, Staatsoper Dresden, Nationaltheater München, Berliner Staatsoper, Deutsche Oper Berlin, Komische Oper Berlin, Oper Leipzig, Staatsoper Hamburg, Grand Théatre Genève, Opéra de Monte Carlo, Capitol Toulouse, Real Madrid, Philadelphia Opera, and tours, USA, Japan, Russia; Appeared Salzburg Festival, 1978, 1980, 1983, 1986, Radio France Festival-Montpellier, Flanders Festival, Musikfestspiele Dresden. *Recordings:* Bach St Matthew Passion; Bartók's Bluebeard's Castle and Concerto for Orchestra; Brahms Symphony No. 1; Berlioz Damnation de Faust; Rolf Liebermann orchestral and vocal works; Mahler Symphonies Nos 1, 2, 3, 5; Puccini Madama Butterfly (vers 1904); Strauss's Dynastie; Wagner: Rheingold, Walküre, Siegfried, Götterdämmerung; Many more. *Honours:* 1st Prize, Contest in Florence, Marinuzzi Contest, San Remo, 1976, Böhm Contest, Salzburg, 1977; 2nd Prize, Swarowski Contest, Vienna, 3rd Prize, Cantelli Contest, Milan, 1977. *Address:* Scheibengasse 14, 1190 Vienna, Austria.

NEUMANN, Gunther; Singer (Tenor); b. 22 Aug. 1938, Stablack, Germany. *Career:* Debut: Potsdam, 1965, as Belmonte; Komische Oper Berlin from 1969, notably as Idomeneo, Lohengrin, Verdi's Riccardo and Alvaro, Pinkerton and Rodolfo; Modern repertory includes Alwa in Lulu, Sergei in Lady Macbeth and Schoenberg's Aron (Cologne, 1995); Guest engagements at the Vienna Staatsoper as Tannhäuser and Volksoper as Vitalino in Handel's Giustino, 1995, Hamburg as Walther von Stolzing, Verona and Tel-Aviv (Handel's Belshazzar, 1995); Other roles include Offenbach's Bluebeard at Covent Garden, 1989, and Grischka in Rimsky's Kitezh at Komische Oper, 1996; Sang Calaf in Berlin, 1998; Season 2000–01 as Herod in Salome at Trier, Shuisky in Boris Godunov at the Komische Oper, Berlin, and Wagner's Loge at Meiningen. *Address:* Komische Oper Berlin, Behrenstrasse 55–57, 10117 Berlin, Germany.

NEUMANN, Veroslav; composer; b. 27 May 1931, Czechoslovakia; m. 1st Jana Hoskova 1958; m. 2nd Hana Kapinusova 1989. *Education:* Acad. of

Musical Arts, Prague. *Career:* Prof., Popular Conservatory, Prague 1969–91; co-owner, Edit Records and Publishing Ltd, Prague 1990–2001; Dir, Prague Conservatoire 1991–. *Compositions:* The Chimney Opera, 1965; Story of the Old Armchair, full-length lyrical comedy opera after Dickens, 1987; Panorama of Prague, 1962; Symphonic Dances for full orchestra, 1984; Little Singers Christmas, 1976; String Quartet, 1969; 5 Dramatic Sequences for cello and piano, 1978; Portraits of a Man, for violin and piano, 1987; The Lament of Ariadne Abandoned, 1970; Atlantis, 1985; Rhymes, 5 Ditties for soprano, flute and piano, 1980; When Birds Fall Silent, 4 Songs for medium-range voice and piano or piano quartet, 1985; Farewell Amadeus!, Sonatina for soprano, flute and piano, 1987. *Honours:* Prize, International Choral Competition, Tours, 1982; Award, Panton Publishing House, Prague, 1987; Czech Composers and Concert Artists Prize, 1987. *Address:* Na Petrinach 1896/31, 162 00 Prague 6, Czech Republic. *E-mail:* velovat@volny.cz.

NEUMANN, Wolfgang; Singer (Tenor); b. 20 June 1945, Waiern, Austria. *Education:* Vocal studies in Essen and Duisburg. *Career:* Debut: Bielefeld 1973, as Max in Der Freischütz; Sang at Augsburg from 1978, Mannheim from 1980; Maggio Musicale Florence 1983, as Tannhäuser; Appearances in Zürich, Bologna, Munich and Hamburg; Other roles include Wagner's Erik, Rienzi, Schoenberg's Aron (at Barcelona), Tristan, Lohengrin and Siegfried, Verdi's Otelo, the Emperor in Die Frau ohne Schatten, Turiddu in Cavalleria Rusticana, Puccini's Calaf and Edgar in Reimann's Lear; Concert repertoire includes Schoenberg's Gurrelieder and Das Lied von der Erde by Mahler; Metropolitan opera debut as Siegfried in the Met's new production of Siegfried by Otto Schenk/James Levine, 1988; Sang the Cardinal in Mathis der Maler at Munich, 1989; Teatro Colón Buenos Aires 1990, as Rienzi in a concert performance of Wagner's opera; Sang Wagner's Erik at the Deutsche Oper Berlin, 2001; Siegfried in Götterdämmerung at Mannheim, 2002. *Current Management:* Ingpen & Williams Ltd, 7 St George's Court, 131 Putney Bridge Road, London, SW15 2PA, England.

NEUWIRTH, Olga, MA; Austrian composer; b. 4 Aug. 1968, Graz. *Education:* Conservatory of Music, San Francisco, USA, Vienna Acad. of Music and Performing Arts, Electroacoustic Inst., studied composition under Erich Urbanner, Elinor Armer, Adriana Hölszky, Tristan Murail and Luigi Nono. *Career:* participant, 'Stage d'Informatique Musicale', IRCAM, Paris; jury mem., Munich Biennale 1994; mem. Composers' Forum, Darmstadt Summer School; composer-in-residence with Koninklijk Philharmonic Orchestra of Flanders, Antwerp, Belgium 2000, Luzerner Festwochen 2002. *Radio music:* Punch & Judy 1994. *Theatre music:* Ein Sportstück 1997, Abenteuer in Sachen Haut 2000, Virus 2000, Ein Sommernachtstraum 2000, Totenauberg 2001, Philoktet 2002, Lost Highway 2003, Der jüngste Tag 2004. *Film score:* The Long Rain 1999. *Compositions include:* Locus... doublure... solos 2001, Ecstaloop 2001, Torsion: transparent variation 2001, Verfremdung/ Entfremdung 2002, Lost Highway 2003. *Recordings include:* Vexierbilder 1993, Loncera Caprifolium 1993, Sans Soleil 1994, Five Daily Miniatures 1994, Spleen 1994, Vampyrotheone 1995, Akroate Hadal 1995, Risonanze! 1996, Pallas/Construction 1996, Hooloomooloo 1996, Bählamms Fest 1997, Photophorus 1997, Todesraten 1997, Nova/ Minraud 1998, Hommage à Klaus Nomi 1998, Ad auras... in memoriam H 1999, Settori 1999, Morphologische Fragmente 1999, Clinamen/ Nodus 1999, The Long Rain 2000, Construction in Space 2000, Inciendo/ fluido 2000, Settori, Quasare/Pulsare. *Honours:* Publicitiy Preis, austro mechana 1994, Ernst von Siemens-Stiftung Förderpreis, Munich, Schleswig-Holstein-Musik-Festival Hindemith-Preis 1999, Ernst Krenek-Preis 1999. *Current Management:* c/o Andrew Rosner, Allied Artists, 42 Montepelier Square, London, SW7 1JZ, England. *Telephone:* (20) 7589-6243 (office). *Fax:* (20) 7581-5269 (office). *Website:* www .olganeuwirth.com.

NEVILLE, Margaret; Singer (Soprano); b. 3 April 1939, Southampton, Hampshire, England. *Education:* Studied with Ruth Packer and Olive Groves in London, Maria Carpi in Geneva. *Career:* Debut: Covent Garden in 1961 in Die Zauberflöte; Appearances at Sadler's Wells, Scottish Opera, Welsh National Opera, Barcelona, Aix, Berlin and Hamburg; Glyndebourne, 1963–64 in Die Zauberflöte and L'Incoronazione di Poppea; Roles included Mozart's Zerlina, Despina and Susanna, Verdi's Gilda, Donizetti's Norina and Humperdinck's Gretel; Sang in the 1967 BBC production of Cavalli's L'Erismena. *Recordings:* Hansel and Gretel. *Honours:* Mozart Memorial Prize, 1962. *Address:* 74 Orchards Way, Highfield, Southampton SO17 1RE, England.

NEVSKAYA, Marina; Organist and Composer; b. 1 Oct. 1965, Moscow, Russia. *Education:* Central Music School, 1984; Moscow Tchaikovsky State Conservatory, 1989; Postgraduate, Moscow Conservatory, 1989–91; Studies, Royal Carillon School, Mechelen, Belgium, 1993–94. *Career:* Debut: Organ Concert, Moscow, 1986; Festival of Young Composers, Moscow, 1985; Recitals, Moscow Conservatory, 1987, 1988, Dnipropetrovsk and Yalta, Ukraine, 1989; Festival of Young

Organists, Polotsk, Byelorussia, 1989; Participation, Organ Forum, Kazan, 1990, International Summer Organ Course, The Organ Art of Flor Peeters, Mechelen, 1990, 1991; International Organ Week, Vlaardingen, Netherlands, 1991, 1993; Recitals, Vlaardingen, 1991, Belaya Tserkov, Ukraine, 1991, 1992, Dnepropetrovsk and Yalta, 1992, Krasnoyarsk, 1993; Concert tours, Belgium and Netherlands, 1993, 1994, Italy, 1993, Siberia, 1994; Recitals, St Petersburg, 1994, Yalta, 1995, 1996, 1999; Organ Soloist Tver Philharmonic, 1992–; Teacher of harmony, polyphony, analysis of musical form and piano, Academy of Fine Arts, Moscow, 1995–; Participation, Yearly Music Festivals, Tver and Moscow; Concert tour in Belgium with choir, 1998; Recitals at the State Big Concert Hall of the Republic of Tatarstan in Kazan, 1998, 1999; Recital at the Organ Festival in Brno, Czech Republic, 1999; Participation in the Days of Russian Culture in Armenia in Yerevan, 1999. *Compositions:* Symphoniette; String Quartet; 2 Piano Sonatas; Sonata for Trumpet and Piano; Sonata for Violin and Organ; Suite for Organ; Poem for Viola and Piano; Vocal and Piano Cycles; Pieces for Wind Instruments; Pieces for Carillon and Other Chamber Works. *Recordings:* Italian, French and German Organ Music of the 17th–18th Centuries; Organ Recital, 5th International Bach Festival, Tver, 1997; Playing in the British Bach Film, 1993. *Address:* Tver Academic Philharmonic, Sovetskaya str 18/43, 170000 Tver, Russia.

NEWAY, Patricia; Singer (Soprano); b. 30 Sept. 1919, Brooklyn, New York, USA; m. Morris Gesell. *Education:* Studied at Mannes College of Music and with Morris Gesell. *Career:* Debut: Chautauqua in 1946 as Fiordiligi in Così fan tutte; New York City Center Opera from 1948 notably as Berg's Marie, in Britten's The Rape of Lucretia and in the 1954 premiere of Copland's The Tender Land; Created roles in Menotti's The Consul in 1950 and Maria Golovin in 1958; Sang at Aix-en-Provence Festival in 1952 in Iphigénie en Tauride, Paris Opéra-Comique, 1952–54 notably as Tosca and Katiusha in Alfano's Risurrezione and with American companies in works by Poulenc, Hoiby and Weisgall; Formed Neway Opera Company in 1960. *Recordings:* The Consul; Cantatas by Buxtehude; Iphigénie en Tauride.

NEWBOULD, Brian (Raby); University Professor; b. 26 Feb. 1936, Kettering, Northamptonshire, England; m. (1) Anne Leicester, 1960, 1 s., 1 d., (2) Ann Airton, 1976, 1 d. *Education:* BA, General Arts, 1957, BMus, 1958, MA, 1961, Bristol. *Career:* Lecturer, Royal Scottish Academy of Music, 1960–65; Lecturer, University of Leeds, 1965–79; Professor of Music, University of Hull, 1979–2001, Prof. Emeritus, 2001–; Numerous talks/interviews on BBC Radio 3, Radio 4, World Service, BBC 2; Also radio stations in USA, Canada, Sweden, Cyprus, Germany, France. *Compositions:* Realisations of Schubert Symphonies No. 7 in E D729, No. 10 in D D936A; Completion of Schubert Symphony No. 8 in B minor D759; Orchestration of Schubert's other symphonic fragments; Completions of Schubert's String Trio, D471, Piano Sonata in C, D840, and other works; Patrick for narrator and small orchestra. *Publications:* Schubert and the Symphony: A New Perspective, 1992; Schubert: The Music and the Man, 1997; Editor, Schubert Studies, 1998, Schubert the Progressive, 2003. *Contributions:* 19th Century Music; Current Musicology; Music Review; Musical Times; Music and Letters; Musiktheorie; Schubert durch die Brille; The Schubertian; Beethoven Newsletter; Notes. *Address:* Department of Music, University of Hull, Hull HU6 7RX, England. *Website:* www.briannewbould.co .uk.

NEWLAND, Larry; Conductor; b. 24 Jan. 1935, Winfield, Kansas, USA; m. Paula Kahn, 18 Feb 1977, 2 d. *Education:* BM, Oberlin Conservatory, 1955; MM, Manhattan School of Music, 1957. *Career:* Violist and keyboard player with New York Philharmonic, 1960–74; Assistant Conductor, New York Philharmonic, 1974–85; Music Director, Harrisburg, Pennsylvania Symphony, 1978–94; Guest Conductor with New York City Ballet and orchestras world-wide, 1974–; Chair, Music Department and Director of Ensembles, Adelphi University, Garden City, New York, 1990–; Faculty, International Opera Workshop, Czech Republic, 1997, Associate Artistic Director, 1998–. *Recordings:* Numerous broadcasts with New York Philharmonic and other orchestras. *Contributions:* Articles in Apprise. *Honours:* Harold Bauer Award, 1957; Koussevitzky Conducting Prize, 1961; Leonard Bernstein Conducting Fellowship, 1962. *Address:* 300 West End Avenue G-B, New York, NY 10023, USA.

NEWLIN, Dika; Musicologist and Composer; b. 22 Nov. 1923, Portland, Oregon, USA. *Education:* BA, Michigan State University, 1939; MA, UCLA, 1941; PhD, Columbia University, 1945; Composition studies with Schoenberg and Sessions. *Career:* Teacher at Western Maryland College, 1945–49; Syracuse University, 1949–51, Drew University, 1952–65, North Texas State University, 1963–75, and Virginia Commonwealth University, 1978–. *Compositions:* Sinfonia for Piano, 1947; Piano Trio, 1948; Chamber Symphony, 1949; Fantasy On A Row for Piano, 1958; Study In Twelve Tones for Viola D'Amore and Piano, 1959; Atone for Chamber Ensemble, 1976; Second-Hand Rows for Voice and Piano, 1978; Three Operas; Piano Concerto; Symphony for Chorus and Orchestra. *Publications:* Bruckner–Mahler–Schoenberg, 1947, 1978; Schoenberg Remembered 1938–76, 1980; Translations of Leibowitz's Schoenberg et s. Ecole, 1949, Schoenberg's Style and Idea, 1951, and Rufer's Das Werk Arnold Schoenberg, 1962. *Address:* Music Dept, Virginia Commonwealth University, 922 Park Avenue, Richmond, VA 23284, USA.

NEWMAN, Anthony; Harpsichordist, Organist, Composer, Fortepianist and Conductor; b. 12 May 1941, Los Angeles, California, USA; m. Mary Jane Flagler, 10 Sept 1968, 3 s. *Education:* BS, Mannes College; MA, Harvard University; DMA, Boston University; Diplome Superieure, Ecole Normale de Musique, Paris. *Career:* Debut: Carnegie Recital Hall; Performing artist in USA and Europe from 1967 with Detroit Symphony, Boston Symphony, Los Angeles Symphony, New York Philharmonic and as conductor with Los Angeles Chamber, Y Chamber, New York, Scottish Chamber, and St Paul Chamber Orchestras; Appearances with Israel Symphony, Calgary Symphony, Colorado Symphony, New Jersey Symphony, Youth Chamber Orchestra and Vienna Boys Choir, and St Stephens Cathedral, Vienna, Kraków Festival, 1991, 1992. *Compositions include:* Concertino for piano and winds; Concerto for viola and strings; Symphony for string orchestra; Grand Hymns Of Awakening for chorus, orchestra and bagpipes; Works for organ solo, piano quintet, quartets for flutes and various smaller works; On Fallen Heroes, sinfonia for orchestra, 1988; Symphony for strings and percussion, 1987; 12 Preludes and Fugues for piano; Symphony No. 1 and 2 for organ solo. *Recordings:* Over 100 including Bach, Baroque and Classical repertoire; On Fallen Heroes, Brandenburg Concerti. *Publications:* Bach and The Baroque, 1985; Symphony No. 1 for Organ and No. 2 for Organ; Three Preludes and Fugues for Organ, 1990; Variations on Bach; 12 Preludes and Fugues for Piano; Sonata for Piano, 1992. *Current Management:* ICM, 40 West 57th Street, New York, NY 10019, USA. *Address:* State University of New York, Purchase, NY 10577, USA.

NEWMAN, Henry; singer (baritone); b. 1950, England. *Career:* roles with Welsh National Opera include Zurga in Les Pêcheurs de Perles, Mozart's Count, Papageno, Don Alfonso and Don Giovanni, Marcello, Germont, Britten's Demetrius, Don Pasquale, Tomsky, Scarpia and Sharpless: Further appearances with English National Opera, Opera North and Scottish Opera. Season 1999–2000 as Foreman of the Mill in Jenůfa at Glyndebourne, Scarpia for Mid Wales Opera, the Forester in The Cunning Little Vixen for City of Birmingham Touring Opera and the Speaker in Die Zauberflöte for London City Opera; radio and television broadcasts.

NEWMAN, Leslie; Flautist; b. 1969, Canada. *Education:* BMus, University of Toronto; MMus, Yale University, with Thomas Nyfenger; Studies with Julius Baker at Juilliard School of Music; Also studied at Mozarteum in Salzburg; Scholarship student with András Adorján, Peter Lukas-Graf and Wolfgang Schulz. *Career:* Debut: Performed Carl Nielsen's Flute Concerto with the Toronto Symphony Orchestra, aged 18; Performances at Lincoln Center's Alice Tully Hall, New York; Salzburg Festival, Wigmore Hall, London; Taiwan's National Concert Hall; Soloist, Toronto Symphony Orchestra Tour to 1988 Winter Olympics Arts Festival at Calgary; Performed major flute concerti with orchestras throughout Canada; Recitalist on BBC Radio 3, England, and CBC Radio in Canada; Duo with pianist John Lenehan, debuted at Wigmore Hall, London, with live BBC broadcast; Appearances at Canadian National Competitive Festival of Music. *Recordings include:* 2 solo CDs; Four concerti with CBC Vancouver Orchestra. *Honours:* Winner, Canadian National Competitive Festival of Music, aged 17; Canada Council Grants; Outstanding Performance Major, Yale University; Top Prizewinner, CBC National Young Performer's Competition; Finalist, New York's Pro Musicis International Competition. *Address:* c/o Latitude 45/Arts Promotion Inc, 109 St Joseph Blvd West, Montreal, Quebec H2T 2P7, Canada.

NEWSTONE, Harry; Conductor; b. 21 June 1921, Winnipeg, Canada; 1 s. *Education:* With Dr Herbert Howells, 1943–45; Guildhall School of Music and Drama, 1945–49; Accademia di Santa Cecilia, Rome, 1954–1956. *Career:* Debut: Chamber Orchestra with Haydn Orchestra at Conway Hall, London, 1949; Full orchestra at Royal Festival Hall Philharmonia Orchestra, 1959; Formed Haydn Orchestra in 1949; BBC broadcasts from 1951 with Haydn Orchestra, London Philharmonic Orchestra, London Symphony Orchestra, Philharmonia, RPO, BBC Symphony and other BBC orchestras; Guest appearances in Berlin, Copenhagen, Hamburg, Budapest, Prague, Jerusalem, Toronto, Vancouver, Victoria BC, Mexico City, Liverpool Philharmonic, London Mozart Players, Jacques Orchestra and Bournemouth Symphony Orchestra; Musical Director of Sacramento Symphony Orchestra, CA, 1965–78; Director of Music, University of Kent, 1979–86; Professor of Conducting at Guildhall School of Music, 1979–87; Visiting Lecturer, University of the Pacific, Stockton, CA, 1988–89. *Recordings:* Bach Brandenburg Concertos; Clavier Concertos with Mindru Katz; Haydn Symphonies, 49, 73, 46, 52; Haydn and Mozart Arias with Jennifer Vyvyan and Peter Wallfisch; Mozart Symphony 41 and Serenata Notturna; Stravinsky Dumbarton Oaks Concerto; Mozart Opera Overtures; Clarinet and Orchestra works by Copland, Arnold, Lutoslawski and Rossini with Gary Gray and Royal Philharmonic Orchestra. *Publications:* Editions of works by Bach, Mozart and Haydn for Eulenburg Edition Miniature Scores, including new edition of Haydn's 12 London Symphonies from 1983–. *Address:* 4 Selborne Road, Ilford, Essex IG1 3AJ, England.

NEWTON, Norma; Singer (Soprano); b. 20 March 1936, Dolgeville, New York, USA. *Education:* Studied in Austin (Texas) and Paris. *Career:* Sang at the Dallas Civic Opera 1962–63, City Opera New York 1964 and 1966 as Donna Elvira and Mozart's Countess; Member of the Kiel Opera, Germany, 1966–72, Graz 1972–73; Sang Butterfly with Welsh National Opera 1973 and appeared widely as guest as Mozart's Pamina, Fiordiligi and Susanna, Eurydice, Katya Kabanova and Berg's Marie; Teacher in Houston from 1980.

NICHITEANU, Liliana; Singer (Mezzo-Soprano); b. 1962, Bucharest, Romania. *Education:* Studied at the Bucharest Academy. *Career:* Numerous engagements including Oslo as Rosina, 1989; Berliner Philharmonie, Fjodor in Boris Godunov, concerts and recordings (CD) with Claudio Abbado, 1993; Vienna, Rossini, Messa di Gloria, 1995; Seasons 1995–97, sang Octavian at Frankfurt; Zerlina at the Mozart Festival, Madrid; Cherubino and Despina with Harnoncourt in Zürich; Sang Te Deum, Bruckner, in Edinburgh Festival concert; Sang at Salzburg Festival with Valery Gergiev; Fatima in Oberon at Zürich, 1998; Der Rosenkavalier as Octavian in Opéra Bastille Paris and in Vienna, 1998, 2000, 2001; Così fan tutte as Dorabella, Munich, 2001 and 2002; Concert repertory: Bach: Magnificat; St John Passion; Brahms Alto Rhapsody; Mahler; Concert appearances world-wide in Bach B minor Mass; Mozart, Requiem and C minor Mass; Mahler, Des Knaben Wunderhorn; Mahler, 8th Symphony; Rossini, Stabat Mater and Messa di Gloria; Hindemith, Die junge Magd, Sieben Lieder for orchestra and alto. *Recordings:* Moussorgsky, Boris Godunov with Claudio Abbado; Mozart's Don Giovanni as Zerlina and in Così fan tutte as Dorabella, both with Alain Lombard. *Honours:* Belvedere Contest, 2 prizes and 6 special prizes, Vienna, 1989; Geneva CIEM contest, 2 prizes and Suisse Prize, 1991. *Current Management:* Rita Schütz, Rütistr 52, 8077 Zürich, Switzerland. *Address:* c/o Zürich Opera, Falkenstrasse 1, 8008 Zürich, Switzerland.

NICHOLAS, James; Cellist; b. 25 Jan. 1957, Valley Stream, New York, USA. *Education:* BM in Cello Performance, 1979, MM, Cello Performance, 1982, Master of Early Music, 1988, D.Mus, 1988, Indiana University. *Career:* Freelance Cellist and Baroque Cellist; Announcer and Producer, Connecticut Public Radio WPKT Meriden, WNPR Norwich and WEDW Stamford and Greenwich. *Compositions:* Concerto for natural horn (Romantic), 1984; Panikhida (Mnemosynon) for Unaccompanied natural horn, 1987; 3 Sonatas for Natural Horn and Piano, 1985, 1993, 1995; Son of Horn Concerto, 1988; Corni Duos, 1991; Grande fantaisie en forme de potpourri, pour cor à pistons en fa et pianoforte (ca 1838), 1991; Psalsima (Chants) for natural horn and small orchestra, 1991; Return of The Shoe Quintet: The Sequel for horn and strings, 1994; Mozart: Horn Concerto in Eb, K370b and 371, a reconstruction, 1994; Mozart: Horn Concerto in E, K494a, a reconstruction, 1995. *Publications:* J. S. Bach–Six Sonatas and Partitas, An Urtext edition for viola, 1986; J. S. Bach–Six suites for Cello, an attempt at an Urtext for viola, 1986; J. S. Bach–Suite No. 6 S1012, a performing version for the 4 stringed cello, 1986; Edition of Horn Concerti from the Lund Manuscript, 1989. *Contributions:* The Horn Call. *Honours:* Performer's Certificate, Indiana University, 1978. *Address:* c/o Birdalone Books, 9245 East Woodview Drive, Bloomington, IN 47401-9101, USA.

NICHOLLS, David (Roy); Musicologist and Composer; b. 19 Nov. 1955, Birmingham, England; m. Tamar Hodes, 28 July 1984, 1 s., 1 d. *Education:* St John's College, Cambridge with Hugh Wood, 1975–78, 1979–84; Degrees: BA, Honours, 1978, MA, 1982, PhD, 1986, all Cantab. *Career:* Keasbey Fellow in American Studies, Selwyn College, Cambridge, 1984–87; Lecturer in Music, 1987–, Senior Lecturer in Music, 1992, Professor of Music, 1995, Keele University; Professor of Music, University of Southampton, 2000. *Compositions include:* Pleiades for 3 groups of instruments, 1979–80; The Giant's Heart for singers and instrumentalists, 1983; 2 Japanese Miniatures for 8 instruments, 1988–89; Winter Landscape with skaters and birdtrap, string quartet, 1989–90; Cantata: Jerusalem, soprano, double choir, double wind band, 1990–91; String Quartet, NMC D006, 1992, Bingham String Quartet. *Publications:* American Experimental Music, 1890–1940, 1990; new edition of Henry Cowell's New Musical Resources, 1995; Contributing Editor, The Whole World of Music: A Henry Cowell Symposium, 1997; Contributing Editor, The Cambridge History of American Music, 1998; Contributing Editor, The Cambridge Companion to John Cage, 2002. *Address:* c/o Department of Music, University of Southampton, Southampton SO17 1BJ, England.

NICHOLLS, Hyacinth; Singer (Mezzo-soprano); b. 10 Sept. 1956, Trinidad. *Education:* Studied at the Guildhall School of Music and the National Opera Studio. *Career:* Sang Cherubino, Octavian, Dorabella, Carmen and Dalilah while a student; Professional debut in 1985 at Wigmore Hall; Sang in the European premiere of Virgil Thomson's Four Saints in Three Acts, Belgium, 1983; Glyndebourne Festival from 1986 in Porgy and Bess, Sang Purcell's Sorceress at Battersea Arts Centre, 1995; L'Enfant et les Sortilèges, Die Entführung, La Traviata, The Electrification of the Soviet Union as Natasha in the premiere, and as Varvara in Katya Kabanova; Tour of Italy in 1989 with Albert Herring; Other roles include Fenina in Nabucco and Humperdinck's Gretel; Sang in the Royal Opera's Garden Venture in 1989; Has performed the role of Carmen for several opera companies including English National Opera's Baylis Programme and the Royal Opera House's Education Programme; Other roles include the title role in Gluck's Orfeo, Dalila, Third Lady (Magic Flute) and Suzuki (Madama Butterfly); Has recently returned from Syria where she sang the role of Dido in a production of Syria's first ever opera; Further roles include Carmen and Serena (Porgy and Bess); Concert repertoire includes Schumann Lieder with recital at St John's with Iain Burnside, Beethoven's Mass in C, the B minor Mass and the St Matthew Passion. *Honours:* Ricordi Opera Prize; Susan Longfield Award; Winner, Maggie Teyte International Competition, 1985. *Current Management:* Helen Sykes Artists Management. *Address:* c/o Helen Sykes Artists Management, 100 Felsham Road, Putney, London SW15 1DQ, England.

NICHOLLS, Rachel; Singer (Soprano); b. 1965, Bedford, England. *Education:* Trinity College of Music; Royal College of Music; London Royal Schools Opera. *Career:* Concerts include Bach's B minor Mass, Mozart's Requiem and Nielsen's 3rd Symphony; Bach's St Matthew Passion and Handel's Apollo e Dafne, with the London Handel Orchestra; Choral Symphony, with the Hanover Band, Dixit Dominus in Birmingham and Messiah at the Albert Hall; Mozart's Mass in C minor (St John Smith's Square); Bach's Magnificat and Saint John Passion, the Brahms and Fauré Requiems, Elgar's Coronation Ode and Poulenc's Gloria; Season 2001 with Handel's L'Allegro for the London Handel Festival, Messiah in Halle, and the Vaughan Williams Sea Symphony at the Brighton Festival; Royal Opera Covent Garden from 2001, as a Flowermaiden in Parsifal and Echo in Ariadne auf Naxos; Other roles include Donna Elvira, Puccini's Lauretta, Maria in Mazeppa, Micaela, Marenka and Mozart's Countess. Recordings include Metella in Handel's Silla (Somm). *Address:* c/o Royal Opera House (contracts) Covent Garden, London, WC2.

NICHOLLS, Simon; Pianist; b. 8 Oct. 1951, London, England; m. Lorraine Wood 1976. *Education:* Junior Exhibitioner, 1963–69, Foundation Scholar, 1969–74, Royal College of Music; Diplomas: GRSM, ARCM and LRAM. *Career:* Performances in London, St John's Smith Square, Wigmore Hall, South Bank, Snape Maltings, Aldeburgh and at music clubs throughout the United Kingdom; Broadcasts on BBC and ITV and Radio; Tours and broadcasts in France, Netherlands, Germany, Ireland, Greece and USA; Piano Teacher at Yehudi Menuhin School, 1976–86 and Professor at Royal College of Music, 1985–Teacher at Birmingham Conservatoire, 2000–; mem, IS M. *Recordings:* Simon Nicholls Plays Scriabin. *Publications:* The Young Cellist's Repertoire, Recital Repertoire for Cellists with Julian Lloyd Webber. *Contributions:* Piano Journal; Music and Musicians; Tempo; Music Teacher, International Piano Quarterly. *Address:* 49 Grove Road, London N12, England.

NICHOLSON, George (Thomas Frederick); Composer, Pianist and Conductor; b. 24 Sept. 1949, Great Lumley, County Durham, England; m. Jane Ginsborg, 14 June 1984, 1 s., 1 d. *Education:* BA, Honours, 1971, DPhil, 1979, University of York. *Career:* Freelance teacher, Guildhall School of Music and Drama, Morley College, London, 1978–88; Recitals with Jane Ginsborg, Soprano and with Philip Edwards, Clarinet, Triple Echo and with John Kenny (trombone); Lecturer, Keele University, 1988–96; Senior Lecturer, Sheffield University, 1996–; mem, British Academy of Composers and Songwriters. *Compositions:* Orchestral Works: 1132; The Convergence of the Twain; Blisworth Tunnel Blues for soprano and orchestra; Chamber Concerto; Cello Concerto; Flute Concerto; Fenestrae; Chamber works include: Winter Music; Ancient Lights; Movements; Stilleven; 3 Nocturnes; Piano Sonata; Brass Quintet; The Arrival of the Poet in the City (melodrama) for actor and 7 musicians; Muybridge Frames for trombone and piano, 1992; Mots Justes for piano solo, 1988–97; Catch; Shailing and Wambling, 2001; Umbra/ Penumbra for trombone and piano; Mister Biberian His Dompe for guitar solo, 2002; Vocal Music includes: Aubade; Vignette; Peripheral Visions; Alla Luna for soprano, clarinet and piano; Letters to the World, 1997–99; Idyll. *Recordings:* String Quartet No. 3; Peripheral Visions; Letters to the World; Spring Songs; Nodus; Mots Justes; Muybridge Frames; Umbra/Penumbra; The arrival of the Poet in the City. *Contributions:* Articles in Composer Magazine. *Honours:* Yorkshire Arts Composers' Award, 1977; Young Composer, Greater London Arts Association, 1979–80; Triple Echo, 4th Prize, Gaudeamus

Competition, Rotterdam, 1982. *Address:* Department of Music, Sheffield University, 38 Taptonville Road, Sheffield S10 2 TN, England. *E-mail:* g-nicholson@shef.ac.uk. *Website:* www.shef.ac.uk/music/staff/gn/gnhomepage.html.

NICHOLSON, Linda; Fortepiano Player; b. 1955, England. *Career:* Member of the London Foretpiano Trio from 1978; Duo with Violinist, Hiro Kurosaki; Solo recitals and concertos, performances of the Viennese classics on original instruments at major festivals and concert series throughout Europe including Italy, Belgium, France, Germany, the United Kingdom and the Netherlands; 12 Concert series of the complete piano trios of Haydn in London 1982, to mark the composer's 250th anniversary; Complete piano trios of Beethoven at the Wigmore Hall in 1987; Season 1991 with Mozart Trios and quartets in London, tour on the early Music Network and lunchtime recitals at the Queen Elizabeth Hall; Played Mozart in Barcelona, Lisbon and Germany; Frequent radio broadcasts. *Recordings:* Complete Trios by Mozart; Trios by Haydn and Beethoven; Mozart Concertos; Complete Violin Sonatas by Mozart, with Hio Kuoselui. *Address:* 21 Clapham Common Northside, London SW4 0RG, England.

NICKLIN, Celia (Mhry); Musician and Oboist; b. 28 Nov. 1941, Malmesbury, Wiltshire, England; m. Howard Gough, 8 Feb 1964, 3 d. *Education:* Royal Academy of Music, London; Hochschule für Musik Detmold, Germany. *Career:* Principal Oboe, City of Birmingham Symphony Orchestra 1962–63, London Mozart Players 1970, Academy of St Martin in the Fields 1970; Professor, Royal Academy of Music, London. *Recordings:* Vaughan Williams, Handel, Vivaldi Oboe Concertos with Academy of St Martin, Mozart with London Mozart Players; Many hundred more. *Honours:* FRAM. *Address:* 19 Park Hill, Carshalton, Surrey SM 5 3 SA, England.

NICOLAI, Claudio; Singer (Baritone); b. 7 March 1929, Kiel, Germany. *Education:* Vocal studies with Clemens Kaiser-Breme in Essen and Serge Radamsky in Vienna. *Career:* Debut: Theater am Gärtnerplatz, Munich, 1954; Early engagements as a tenor then as baritone from 1956; Appearances at Bregenz Festival, Vienna Volksoper and in Stuttgart, Hamburg, Brussels, Munich, Berlin, Paris, London, Stockholm, Oslo, Prague, Bucharest, Budapest, Zürich and Amsterdam; Member of the Cologne Opera from 1964; Sang in the 1965 premiere of Zimmermann's Die Soldaten and visited London in 1969 for the British premiere of Henze's Der Junge Lord; Sang with Oper der Stadt Köln from 1966; Roles include Giovanni, Count, Papageno and Guglielmo; Tel-Aviv in 1984 in Die Zauberflöte, Metropolitan Opera in 1988, sang Don Alfonso at Brussels and Barcelona in 1990 and Don Alfonso under John Eliot Gardiner at Amsterdam in 1992; Professor at the Musikhochschule Cologne; Salzburg Festival, 1976–79; Nozze di Figaro, Giovanni, Vienna Staatsoper; 15 years guest at the Berlin Staatsoper and three times in Japan; Così fan tutte in Paris with J E Gardiner. *Recordings:* Der Freischütz; Die Fledermaus; Die Kluge; Highlights from Die Soldaten. *Address:* c/o Staatliche Hochschule für Musik, Degobertstrasse 38, 5000 Köln 1, Germany.

NICOLESCO, Mariana; Singer (Soprano); b. 28 Nov. 1948, Brasov, Romania. *Education:* Music and Violin in Romania, age 6–18, graduating with Bruch Concerto; Voice with Jolanda Magnoni, Conservatoire Santa Cecilia, Rome; Later with Elisabeth Schwarzkopf and Rodolfo Celletti. *Career:* Debut: Television concert, Voci Rossiniane International Award, Milan, 1972; Sang Violetta in La Traviata, Teatro Comunale, Florence, 1976, Gran Teatro del Liceu, Barcelona, 1976, 1978, 1981, also San Francisco Opera, 1991; Violetta at Metropolitan Opera, 1978, where she also appeared as Gilda in Rigoletto, 1978, and Nedda in Pagliacci, 1979, 1986, Donna Elvira in Don Giovanni, Teatro dell'Opera, Rome, 1984, Munich Staatsoper and Munich Festival, 1986–93, Tokyo, 1988, La Scala, Milan, 1987, 1988, 1993; Also at La Scala, world premiere of Berio's La Vera Storia, 1982, and Un Re in Ascolto, 1986; Dargomishky's Stone Guest, 1983, Mozart's Lucio Silla, 1984, Luigi Rossi's L'Orfeo, 1985, Jommelli's Fetonte, 1988, 3 recitals, 1988–93; Elettra in Idomeneo, Salzburg Festival, 1990, 1991, Japan, 1990, Dresden Semper Oper, 1991; A true dramatic coloratura: Bellini's Beatrice di Tenda, La Fenice, Venice, 1975, Donizetti's Maria di Rohan, Martina Franca Festival, 1988, Elisabeth Queen of England in Roberto Devereux, Monte Carlo, 1992, 1997; Sang at First Christmas Concert in the Vatican, televised world-wide, 1993; Anna Bolena, Munich, 1995; World premiere, Krzysztof Penderecki's Seven Gates of Jerusalem of the Holy City, 1997; Performed at leading opera houses world-wide; Concerts at Royal Festival Hall London, Carnegie Hall New York, Musikverein Vienna, Boston Symphony Hall, Concertgebouw Amsterdam, Teatro Real Madrid, Cleveland Symphony Hall, Teatro alla Scala; Great Conservatory Hall, Moscow. *Recordings:* Bellini: Beatrice di Tenda; Donizetti: Maria di Rohan; Puccini: Simon Boccanegra; Puccini: La Rondine; Mozart: Le nozze di Figaro; World premiere: Meyerbeer cantata Gli Amori di Teolinda, Ravel cantatas Alcyone, Alyssa. *Address:* c/o Wolfgang Stoll, Martius Str 3, 80802 Munich, Germany.

NICOLESCU, Antonius; Singer (Tenor); b. 17 Aug. 1946, Bucharest, Romania. *Career:* Debut: Romanian National Opera, Bucharest, 1971, as Vladimir in Prince Igor; Guest appearances at Athens, Berlin Staatsoper, and Heidelberg; Opéra Bastille, Paris, 1992, as Hoffmann; Berne, 1995, in Zandonai's I Cavalieri di Ekebu, Hamburg, 1996, as Don José; Other roles include Alfredo (Essen, 1994), Pinkerton, Ernesto, Faust, Gerald in Lakmé, Lenky and Don Ottavio. *Address:* c/o Hamburg Staatsoper, Theaterstrasse 34, 20354 Hamburg, Germany.

NICOLET, Aurèle; Flautist and Professor of Music; b. 22 Jan. 1926, Neuchâtel, Switzerland; m. Christiane Gerhard. *Education:* Studied in Zürich with André Jaunet and Willy Burkhard; Paris Conservatoire with Marcel Moyse and Yvonne Drapier. *Career:* First Flute in Winterhur Orchestra, 1948–50; Solo flautist with Berlin Philharmonic, 1950–59; Professor at Berlin Musikhochschule, 1950–65; Later taught in Freiburg and Basle; Concert appearances throughout Europe as soloist with orchestra and with chamber ensembles; Works written for him by composers including Denisov, Takemitsu, Kelterborn and Huber. *Recordings include:* Works by Bach conducted by Karl Richter; Quartets and Concertos by Mozart. *Honours:* First Prize, Paris Conservatoire; First Prize, International Competition at Geneva, 1948; Music Critics' Prize, Berlin, 1963.

NICOLL, Harry; Singer (tenor); b. 1970, Coupar Angus, Perthshire, Scotland. *Education:* Studied at the Royal Scottish Academy of Music and Drama. *Career:* Sang with Scottish Opera Go Round from 1979 as Nemorino, Ferrando, Alfredo and Ramiro; Appearances with Welsh National Opera as Valetto in L'Incoronazione di Poppea, Vasek, the Idiot in Wozzeck and Brighella and the Dancing Master in Ariadne; Sang with English National Opera in Pacific Overtures, Street Scene and The Mikado and with Scottish Opera in their Rossini double bill, as The Lover in the premiere of Judith Weir's The Vanishing Bridegroom in 1990, as Bardolph and as Almaviva; Other engagements with Opera North in Acis and Galatea and L'Heure Espagnole, Park Lane Group in La Finta Semplice, Glyndebourne Touring Opera as Pedrillo in Die Entführung, English Bach Festival in Versailles as Thespis in Rameau's Platée, Kammeroper Berlin in The Lighthouse, Il Re Pastore and Il Matrimonio Segreto; La Fenice Venice in Zaide, Frankfurt and Jerusalem as Roderigo in Otello, Cologne Opera as Vasek, The Bartered Bride, Opera Voor Vlaanderen, Pedrillo in Die Entführung, New Israeli Opera, Tel-Aviv, Idiot in Boris, Vasek in Bartered Bride, and as Almaviva, Barbiere; Théâtre des Champs Elysées as Medor in Roland by Lully; Has sung in several operas at the Batignano Festival; Concert appearances in the United Kingdom and abroad. *Current Management:* Musicmakers International Artists Representation, Tailor House, 63–65 High Street, Whitwell, Hertfordshire SG4 8AH, England. *Telephone:* (1438) 871708. *Fax:* (1438) 871777. *E-mail:* musicmakers@compuserve.com. *Website:* www.operauk.com. *Address:* c/o Ron Gonsalves, 10 Dagnan Road, London SW12 9LQ, England.

NICULESCU, Stefan; Composer, Musicologist and Professor; b. 31 July 1927, Moreni, Romania; m. Colette Demetrescu, 22 June 1952. *Education:* Conservatory of Music, Bucharest; Studio Siemens for Electronic Music, Munich, Germany. *Career:* Debut: Bucharest in 1953; Professor of Compositions and Music Analysis, Bucharest Conservatory of Music; Guest, Deutscher Akademischer Austauschdienst, Berlin, 1971–72. *Compositions:* 3 Symphonies, 1956–84; 3 Cantatas, 1959–64; Unisonos for Orchestra, 1970; The Book With Apolodor, opera for children, 1975; Omaggio a Enescu e Bartók for Orchestra, 1981; Invocatio, for 12 voices, 1989; Axion, for saxophone and women's choir, 1992; Psalmus, for 6 voices, 1993; Deisis, Symphony No. 4, 1995; Litanies, Symphony No. 5, 1997; Umdecimum, for ensemble, 1998. *Recordings:* Formants for Orchestra; Scenes for Orchestra; Symphonies for 15 Soloists; Inventions for Clarinet and Piano; Aphorisms D'Héraclite for Choir; Triplum 2 for Clarinet, Cello and Piano; Ison 1 for 14 Soloists; Ison 2 for Winds and Percussion; Echoes for Violin; Synchronie 1 for 2–12 Instruments; Symphony No. 2; Heteromorphie for Orchestra; Tastenspiel for Piano; Cantos, Symphony No. 3, for saxophone and orchestra, 1990. *Publications:* Co-Author, George Enescu, monography, 1971; Reflections About Music, 1980. *Contributions:* Muzica; Revue Roumaine D'Histoire de L'Art; Arta; Studii de Muzicologie; Muzyka. *Address:* Intrarea Sublocotenent Staniloiu 4, 73228 Bucharest 39, Romania.

NIEHAUS, Manfred; Composer; b. 18 Sept. 1933, Cologne, Germany. *Education:* Studied with Zimmermann at Cologne. *Career:* Dramaturg and Director at Wurttemberg Landesbuhne, Esslingen am Neckar, 1963–65; Editor for Westdeutsche Rundfunk, Cologne from 1967 and freelance composer from 1989; mem, Vice President, DKIV Section, NRW. *Compositions:* Music theatre works Bartleby, Cologne and Berlin, 1967; Die Pataphysiker, Kiel, 1969; Maldoror, Kiel, 1970; Die Badewanne, Bonn, 1973; It Happens, Bonn, 1973; Sylvester, Stuttgart, 1973; Tartarin Von Tarascon, Hamburg, 1977; Die Komponiermaschine, Nuremberg, 1980; Das Verlorene Gewissen, Gelsenkirchen, 1981; Das Christbaumbrettl, Cologne, 1983; Die Geschichte vom riesen und dem Kleinen Mann im Ohr, Emmerich, 1984; Wie es Klingt, Essen, 1993; Narcissus und Echo, 1993; Hermione, 1996; Leda, Cologne 1998; Onkel Peters Gesichten, 1997. *Honours:* Cologne Forderpreis, 1966. *Address:* Simrockstraäe 18, 50823 Köln, Germany.

NIEHOFF, Beatrice; Singer (Soprano); b. 1952, Mannheim, Germany. *Career:* Sang at Karlsruhe and Darmstadt, 1977–82; Later appearances in Hamburg, Zürich, Berlin and Vienna notably as Mozart's Constanze, Countess, Pamina and Fiordiligi, Dvořák's Rusalka, Weber's Agathe and Wagner's Elsa; Modern repertory includes operatic roles in Fortner's Bluthochzeit, Zemlinsky's Der Kreidekreis, Hindemith's Mathis der Maler and Schoeck's Massimilia Doni; In 1988 sang Eva in a new production of Die Meistersinger at Essen and the Protagonist in the German premiere of Berio's Un Re in Ascolto at Düsseldorf; Returned to Düsseldorf in 1989 as Cleopatra in Giulio Cesare by Handel; Sang Strauss's Chrysothemis at Aachen, 1999. *Address:* c/o Deutsche Oper am Rhein, Dusseldorf, Heinrich Heine Allee 16a, D–40213, Dusseldorf, Germany.

NIELSEN, Inga; Danish singer (soprano); b. Holbaek, Seeland; m. Robert Hale. *Education:* Vienna Music Acad. and Musikhochschule Stuttgart. *Career:* performs at Vienna State Opera, La Scala Milan, Covent Garden London, and the opera houses of Munich, Düsseldorf, Hamburg, Stuttgart, Berlin, Paris, Zürich, New York and Buenos Aires; has performed at the festivals of Bayreuth, Munich, Aix-en-Provence, Edinburgh, Holland, Athens, Ludwigsburg, Wexford, Vienna and at the Mostly Mozart Festival in New York; has performed at numerous concerts and recitals and made many TV and radio broadcasts; debut, Gelsenkirchen, Germany 1973; sang in Munster 1974–75, Bern 1975–77; mem., Frankfurt Opera 1978–83, singing Konstanze in Mozart's Die Entführung aus dem Serail, later at the Salzburg Festival and Covent Garden, 1987–89; roles include Schwetzingen in the premiere of Hans Werner Henze's Die Englische Katze, 1983, Donizetti's Lucia in Pittsburgh, Oslo and Hamburg 1984–87, Marguerite in Palermo 1987, Ilia and Fiodiligi in Cologne and Strasbourg 1989, Christine in the Italian premiere of Strauss's Intermezzo in Bologna 1990, Marzelline at Zürich and Gilda at Oslo 1992; Zürich debut as Agathe in Der Freischütz and later as Leonore in Fidelio; sang Salome in Leipzig 1994, Ursula in Hindemith's Mathis der Maler at Covent Garden 1995, Chrysothemis in Elektra in Japan, Feldmarschallin in Der Rosenkavalier at the Royal Opera in Copenhagen 1994, Elsa in Lohengrin and Jenny in Aufstieg und Fall der Stadt Mahagonny at the Hamburg State Opera 1998, Elisabeth in Tannhäuser at the Zürich Opera 1999, the Empress in Die Frau ohne Schatten for the Vienna Staatsoper 2001, Die Frau in Arnold Schönberg's Erwartung at Covent Garden, Senta in Der Fliegende Holländer at the Hamburg State Opera 2003. *Recordings include:* Oberon, Zemlinsky's Geburtstag der Infantin, Schumann's Der Rose Pilgerfahrt, Parsifal, Salome, Don Giovanni, Mozart's Il Re Pastore, Haydn's The Seven Last Words on the Cross; Song of Love (with Robert Hale) 1997, Fidelio 2000, recitals and oratorios. *Honours:* Order of the Dannebrog 1992, Königliche Kammersängerin 1998. *Current Management:* Theateragentur Dr Germinal Hilbert, Maximilianstrasse 22, 80539 Munich, Germany. *Telephone:* (89) 2907470. *Fax:* (89) 29074790. *E-mail:* agentur@hilbert.de. *Website:* www.hilbert.de.

NIELSEN, Svend; Composer; b. 20 April 1937, Copenhagen, Denmark. *Education:* Studied Music, University of Copenhagen; Music Theory, Royal Academy of Music, Copenhagen. *Career:* Debut: Copenhagen, 1962; Teacher, Royal Academy of Music, Århus, 1967–. *Compositions:* Orchestral: Metamorphoses, 1968; Nuages, 1972; Symphony, 1978–79; Nocturne, 1981; Concerto for violin and orchestra, 1985; Nightfall for chamber orchestra, 1989; Symphony No. 2, 1997; Voice and Instruments: Three of Nineteen Poems, 1962; Duets, 1964; Romances, 1970–74; Chamber Cantata, 1975; Sonnets of Time, 1978; Ascent Towards Akseki, 1979; Choral Music: Motets, 1982; Imperia, 1982; Jorden, 1983; Sommerfugledalen for 12 solo singers, 1999; Piano Music: Romantic Piano Pieces, 1974; 5 Inventions, 1983; Chamber: Rondo for flute quintet, 1986; String Quartet, 1987; Black Velvet, Clarinet Quintet, 1988; Variations for double quintet, 1989; Windscapes for brass quintet, 1990; Aria for orchestra, 1991; Aubade for orchestra, 1994; Sinfonia Concertante for cello and chamber orchestra, 1994; Shadowgraphs for 10 instruments, 1995; The Colour Blue, for 3 ensembles, 1998. *Recordings:* Carillons; Sinfonia Concertante; Nightfall. *Honours:* Carl Nielsen Prize, 1981; Lifelong Grant, Danish State, 1982–; Schierbeck Prize, 1995. *Address:* Royal Academy of Music, 8210 Århus V, Denmark.

NIELSEN, Tage; Professor and Composer; b. 16 Jan. 1929, Frederiksberg, Denmark; m. Aase Grue-Sorensen, 14 Oct 1950, 1 s., 2 d. *Education:* Musicology, University of Copenhagen, 1947–55; Additional studies in Israel 1972, Italy 1974, USA 1975. *Career:* Debut: As Composer, 23 October 1949, UNM Festival, Stockholm; Deputy Head of Music Department, Radio Denmark, 1957–63; Director, Professor, Royal Academy of Music, Århus, 1963–83; Chair of Board, Danish State

Art Foundation, 1971–74; Director, Accademia di Danimarca, Rome, 1983–89; Managing Director, The Society for Publication of Danish Music, 1989–93; mem, Danish Composers Society. *Compositions:* Two Nocturnes, piano, 1961; Il gardino magico, orchestra, 1968; Three Character Pieces and an Epilogue, piano, 1972–74; Passacaglia, orchestra, 1981; Laughter in the Dark, opera, 1987–91; Paesaggi, 2 pianos, 1985; Five Opera Fragments, 13 instruments, 1986; The Frosty Silence in the Gardens, guitar, 1990; Lamento and Chorale Fantasy, organ, 1993–95; Laughter in the Dark, opera after V. Nabokov, Arus 1995. *Recordings:* Il giardino magico; Five Opera Fragments. *Publications:* Fra on Langgaard, Alban Berg's Lulu and Lutoslawski and others in Dansk Musiktidsskrift. *Honours:* The Anker Prize, 1975; The Schierbeck Prize, 1992; Wilhelm Hansen Prize, 1998. *Address:* Peter Bangsvej 153, 2000 Frederiksberg, Denmark.

NIEMAN, Alfred (Abbe); Composer and Pianist; b. 25 Jan. 1913, London, England; m. Aileen Steeper, 2 s. *Education:* RAM; RAM; ARAM; FGSM. *Career:* Concert appearances in a two piano team and performances with BBC for 5 years; Professor of Composition and Piano and Lecturer at Guildhall School of Music; mem, CGGB; British Association of Music Therapy; Consultant, National Association for Gifted Children. *Compositions include:* 2nd Piano Sonata; 9 Israeli Folksongs; Paradise Regained for cello, piano and Chinese cymbals; Symphony No. 2; Variations and Finale for piano; Adam, cantata for tenor, 4 trombones, 5 percussion and piano; Various songs; Sonata for guitar, commissioned from Gilbert Biberian through The Arts Council and first performed at Purcell Room in 1986; Soliloquy for solo cello, commissioned by Stefan Popov and first performed at St John's Smith Square in 1986 and a further 6 times in Bulgaria; Suite for piano; Three Expressions for unaccompanied chorus; Chromotempera, concerto for cello and piano. *Recordings:* Canzona for quintet, flute, oboe, clarinet, violin and piano. *Publications:* Schumann; Tension In Music; The Earth It Is Your Shoe for solo guitar. *Contributions:* A Fresh Look at Webern, in The Composer, No. 30. *Honours:* McFarren Gold Medal. *Address:* 21 Well Walk, London, NW3, England.

NIEMELA, Hannu; Singer (Baritone); b. 17 April 1954, Lohtaja, Finland. *Education:* Graduated from Sibelius Academy, Helsinki, 1983; Further study with Kim Borg and Hans Hotter. *Career:* Debut: Zürich Opera in 1985 as Marullo in Rigoletto; Member of Karlsruhe Opera, 1985–89 and Staatstheater Mainz from 1989; Guest engagements at Savonlinna and Schwetzingen Festivals and at Berne, Basle, Mannheim, Dresden, Prague, Leningrad and Strasbourg; Karlsruhe in 1986 in the premiere of Der Meister und Margarita by Rainer Kunad; Other roles have included Mozart's Count, Papageno and Don Giovanni, Gluck's Orestes, Escamillo, Wozzeck and Demetrius in A Midsummer Night's Dream, and Verdi's Macbeth and Falstaff; Sang the title role in the German premiere of Le Roi Arthus by Chausson, Cologne, 1996; Willy Brand in the premiere of Kniefall in Warschau by G Rosenfeld, Dortmund, 1998; Season 2000–01 as Kurwenal and Count Luna at Dortmund and the title role in the premiere of Tüür's Wallenberg; Iago and title role in The Death of Klinghoffer at Helsinki; Noted concert artist. *Address:* c/o Staatstheater, Gutenbergplatz 7, 6500 Mainz, Germany.

NIES, Otfrid; Violinist and Writer on Music; b. 5 May 1937, Giessen, Germany; m. Christel Nies-Fermor, 7 Sept 1961, 2 s., 2 d. *Education:* Violin studies with Max Rostal, 1960–64, and chamber music with Rudolf Kolisch. *Career:* Member of National Theatre Orchestra, Mannheim, 1964–66; Leader, Stadttheaterorchester Hagen, 1966–71 and leader for Staatstheaterorchester Kassel, 1971–; Presentation of music for player piano by Conlon Nancarrow at Documenta 7, Kassel, 1982; Founder of Archiv Charles Koechlin, 1984; mem, Association Charles Koechlin, Paris; Internationale Schoenberg-Gesellschaft, Vienna. *Recordings:* Quintets, Op 80 for piano and strings, Op 156 for flute and harp, by Charles Koechlin; Music for violin and player piano by Conlon Nancarrow. *Publications:* Orchestration of Quartre Interludes, Op 214 for The Ballet Voyages, Op 222, 1947, by Charles Koechlin, 1986. *Contributions:* Many articles on Charles Koechlin in Das Orchester, Neue Zeitschrift fuer Musik, Fonoforum. *Address:* Saengerweg 3, 3500 Kassel, Germany.

NIGG, Serge; Composer; b. 6 June 1924, Paris, France; m. Micheline Nourrit, 1950, 1 d. *Education:* Paris Conservatory with Messiaen, 1941–46; Studied with Leibowitz, 1945–48. *Career:* Freelance Composer; Professor of Orchestration at the Paris Conservatory; President, Societe Nationale de Musique, 1989; Elu membre de l'Academie des Beaux-Arts, 1989; President de l'Academie and President de l'Institut de France, 1995. *Compositions include:* 3 Sonatas for piano; 1 sonata for violin solo; 1 sonata for violin and piano; 4 Mélodies on poems of Paul Eluard; Concerto for viola and orchestra, 1988; 2 Piano Concertos; Concerto for flute and strings; Mirrors for William Blake for orchestra, 1978; Fulgur for orchestra; Million d'Oiseaux d'Or for orchestra; Du Clair au Sombre song-cycle for soprano and orchestra to poems by Paul Eluard; Symphony poems Timour and Pour un poéte captif; 2 Violin concertos, 1957, 1998; Jérome Bosch-Symphony; String quartet, 1982;

Du clair au sombre, for orchestra, 1986; Violin Sonata, 1994; Poéme Pour Orchestre. *Recordings:* 1st Piano Concerto (Orchestre National de France); Violin Concerto (Christian Ferras); Visages d'Axel; Le Chant du Déposédé; Arioso for violin and piano; Poéme for orchestra; Million d'Oiseaux d'Or, Orchestre de Paris; Four Sonatas: No. 1, for piano, No. 2, for piano, No. 3 for solo violin, and No. 4 for violin and piano. *Contributions:* Discours de réception a l'Academie des Beaux Arts, 1990; Revue 'Diapason': Les Quatuors de Bela Bartók, 1991; Communication a l'Academie des Beaux-Arts: Peut-on encore, en 1992, enseigner la composition musicale?; 4 Sonatas. *Publications:* Published discourses from academic seminars and symposia. *Honours:* Officer de l'Ordre du Mérite, Président de l'Académie des Beaux Arts, 1995; Chevalier de la Légion d'honneur; Officier de l'Ordre des Arts et des Lettres; Grand Prix du Disque, 1957, 1967, 1973, 1981 (x2), 1989, 1996; 3 Prix de l'Académie Des Beaux-Arts, 1976, 1983, 1987; Médaille de vermeil de la Ville de Paris. *Address:* 15 bis rue Darcel, 92100 Boulogne sur Seine, France.

NIIMI, Tokuhide; Composer; b. 5 Aug. 1947, Nagoya, Japan. *Education:* Graduated University of Tokyo 1970 and studied at the Tokyo National University of Fine Arts and Music, 1971–78. *Career:* Faculty Member, Toho Gauden School of Music, Tokyo; Board Member, Directors of the Japanese Composers Society; mem, Japanese Federation of Composers. *Compositions include:* Percussion Concerto, 1973; Enlacage I for chorus and orchestra, 1977; Enlacage II for 3 percussionists (1978) and III for 2 marimbas and 2 percussionists (1980); 2 Symphonies, 1981, 1986; Three Valses for piano duet, 1986; 2 Piano Concertos, 1984 and 1993 (Eyes of the Creator); Under Blue Skies, for children's chorus, mixed chorus and orchestra, 1986; Ohju for cello, 1987; Kazane, for clarinet, violin and cello, 1989; Au-Mi for soprano, violin, cello and piano, 1989; Heteorhthmix for orchestra, 1991; Chain of Life for chamber orchestra, 1993; Planets Dance for 6 percussionists, 1993; String Quartet, 1994; Fusui, for small orchestra, 1994; The Cosmic Tree for koto and orchestra, 1996; Soul Bird for flute and piano, 1996; Spiral of the Fire, for orchestra, 1997; Fujin, Raijin, for Japanese big drum, organ and orchestra, 1997; Garden in the Light, for piano quintet, 1997; Towards the Silence, for string orchestra, 1998; Fairy Ring, for clarinet and piano, 1998. *Recordings:* Eye of the Creator; Garden in the Light. *Honours:* Grand Prix of Composition, 8th International Competition of Ballet Music, Suisse Roman, Geneva. *Current Management:* Akira Tanaka, Zen-On Music Co Ltd. *Address:* 1-26-6-303, Chuo, Nakano-ku, Tokyo, Japan.

NIKITIN, Yevgeny; Singer (Bass); b. 1970, Murmansk, Russia. *Education:* St Petersburg Conservatoire. *Career:* Appearances at the Kirov Opera from 1996 (Young Singers' Academy of the Mariinsky Theatre, 1999); Roles have included Mozart's Figaro, Don Giovanni, Rossini's Basilio, Glinka's Ruslan and the Viking Merchant in Sadko by Rimsky-Korsakov; Wagner's Fasolt and Dutchman, Rangoni in Boris Godunov, Rodolfo in La Sonnambula, the Bonze in Madama Butterfly and Ramphis in Aida: Sang Dolokhov in War and Peace and Remeniuk in the British premiere of Prokofiev's Semyon Kotko, with the Kirov Opera at Covent Garden, 2000. *Recordings include:* Boris Godunov. *Honours:* Prizewinner, Pechovsky, Rimsky-Korsakov and Tchaikovsky Competitions, 1996–98. *Address:* c/o Kirov Opera, Mariinsky Theatre, 1 Theatre Square, St Petersburg, Russia.

NIKKANEN, Kurt; Concert Violinist; b. Dec. 1965, Hartford, Connecticut, USA. *Education:* Began violin studies aged 3; Boston University Prep Division with Roman Totenberg; Juilliard School, New York, with Dorothy DeLay, graduated 1986. *Career:* Won first competition, 1976; Carnegie Hall debut, 1978, playing the Saint-Saëns Introduction and Rondo Capriccioso; 1980, played the Paganini 1st Concerto with the New York Philharmonic; Bruch 1st Concerto with the Boston Pops; Appearances with the Hartford Symphony, Colorado Philharmonic, New Jersey Chamber Orchestra and Aspen Chamber Symphony; European debut, 1981, with recital tour of Finland; Cleveland Orchestra debut in the Glazunov Concerto, July 1988; British debut playing the Elgar Concerto with the Royal Liverpool Philharmonic conducted by Libor Pesek, Sept 1988; Toured in Venezuela; Debuted at the Kennedy Center in Washington DC; Further engagements with the Helsinki Philharmonic under James DePreist, and an orchestral/recital tour of Japan; Season 1990–91, made debuts in London, Munich and Barcelona; Season 1991–92, engagements with the San Francisco, New Orleans and Portland Symphonies; Recital debuts in Vancouver, Berlin and Paris; Played the Glazunov Concerto at the 1991 Promenade Concerts, London; 1995, BBC Scottish Symphony, Bergen Philharmonic, Seattle International Festival, Hallé Orchestra, Khumo Festival, Resedentie Orchestra of Holland; Premiered John Adams Concerto in Sweden with the Stockholm Philharmonic, John Adams conducting, January 1995; Season 1996–97 included the Adams Concerto with the Hallé Orchestra, the New Zealand Symphony Orchestra and the Cincinnati Symphony, Dvořák and Brahms on Far East tour; Performed Aaron Jay Kernis' Concerto for violin and guitar at the 1998 Aspen Festival, conducted by Hugh Wolff, and HK Gruber's Violin Concerto,

Nebelsteinmusik performed with the Swedish Chamber Orchestra under the composer's direction in 1999; Gave a recital at Wigmore Hall, London performing Violin Dance, pieces inspired by dance forms; Meditations for flute and strings, 1997; Via Crucis for solo voices, chorus and orchestra, 1997; A Polish Folksong for soprano and orchestra, 1998; Season 2001–02 with New York City Ballet, concerts with Auckland Philharmonic, Eugene Symphony Orchestra and return to Hong Kong Symphony Orchestra. *Recordings include:* Tchaikovsky and Glazunov Concertos. *Current Management:* Harrison/Parrott Ltd, 12 Penzance Place, London, W11 4PA, England. *Telephone:* (20) 7229 9166. *Fax:* (20) 7221 5042. *Website:* www.harrisonparrott.com.

NIKODEMOWICZ, Andrzej; Composer and Pianist; b. 2 Jan. 1925, Lvov, Poland; m. Kazimiera Maria Grabowska 1952, 1 s., 1 d. *Education:* Studied with Adam Soltys, Faculty of Composition, Conservatory of Lvov, 1950; Studied with Tadeusz Majerski, Faculty of Piano, 1954. *Career:* Professor of Composition and Piano, Conservatory of Lvov, 1951–73; Dismissed by reason of religious convictions; 1980–: Professor of Faculty of Music, University of Maria Curie-Sklodowska in Lublin; Professor, Faculty of Church Musicology, Catholic University, Lublin; mem, Polish Composers Society, Society of Authors ZAiKS. *Compositions:* Extensive list of compositions including: Piano works, Ekspresje, 66 miniatures for piano solo, 1959–60; Violin works; Songs for voice and piano; Chamber Concerto, 1968; Composizione sonoristica, for violin, violoncello and piano, 1966–71; Musica concertante per tre for flute, viola and piano, 1966–67; 3 nocturnes for trumpet and piano, 1964; Symphonic music, 1974–75; Concerto for violin and symphony orchestra, 1973; choir music including 500 Polish Christmas carols; Theatre Music, (Pantomime) Glass Mountain, 1969; 35 religious cantatas including: Magnificat for choir of women and orchestra, 1977–78; Evening Offering, 1980; Hear My Cry, O God, 1981; 5 Lullabies for violin and piano, 1991; 4 songs for soprano, trumpet and organ, text: George Herbert, 1992; Variations, Ave maris Stella, for organ, 1993; Concerto for piano and symphony orchestra, 1994; Cantatas: Laudate Dominum, 1985–87, Via Crucis, 1996; Concerto No.2 for piano and symphony orchestra, 2002; Concerto No.3 for piano and symphony orchestra, 2002; Concerto-meditazione for violoncello and symphony orchestra, 2003; Concerto No.4 for piano and symphony orchestra, 2003. *Recordings:* Two cantatas, cycle of songs. *Contributions:* Several reviews in Ruch Muzyczny. *Honours:* Prize of Saint Friar Albert; Mayor of Lublin City Award; The Asscn of Polish Composers Award; Ministry of Culture Award; Artistic Award of the City of Lublin; Diploma and Medal of His Holiness Pope John II Pro Ecclesia et Pontifice. *Address:* ul Paryska 4/37, 20-854 Lublin, Poland.

NIKOLOV, Nikola; Singer (Tenor); b. 1924, Sofia, Bulgaria. *Education:* Studied in Sofia. *Career:* Debut: Varna in 1947 as Pinkerton; Sang at Varna until 1953 then studied further in Moscow and sang at Sofia National Opera from 1955; Appearances in Moscow and Leningrad in the 1950s, La Scala Milan in 1958 as Jenik in The Bartered Bride; Season 1958–60 at Wexford Festival, Vienna Staatsoper and Covent Garden as Radames; New York Metropolitan in 1960 as Don José, State Operas of Berlin and Hamburg and Naples in 1963 as Vasco da Gama in L'Africaine. Sang further in Munich, Barcelona, Geneva, Belgrade, Budapest and Bucharest; Other roles included Manrico, Turiddu, Cavaradossi, Calaf and Don Carlos. *Recordings:* Aida; Carmen; Boris Godunov; L'Africaine. *Address:* c/o Bayerische Staatsoper, Postfach 100148, 8000 Munich 1, Germany.

NIKOLOVA, Zistomira; Singer (mezzo-soprano); b. 10 March 1949, Svilengrad, Bulgaria. *Career:* Sang in opera houses throughout Yugoslavia, as Verdi's Azucena, Eboli and Amneris, Marina in Boris Godunov, Adalgisa in Norma, Carmen, Dalila, Marfa (Khovanshchina) and Clytemnestra; Staatstheater Karlsruhe, 1995–96, notably as Fricka and Waltraute in The Ring; Guest appearances in Moscow, St Petersburg, Mannheim, Leipzig and Marseilles; Numerous concert appearances; Sang Fortunata in Makernas's Satyricon at Zagreb, 1998. *Address:* Karlsruhe Opera, Baumeisterstrasse 11, 7500 Karlsruhe, Germany.

NIKOLSKY, Gleb; Singer (Bass); b. 1959, Moscow, Russia. *Education:* Studied at the Moscow conservatory and at La Scala, Milan. *Career:* Soloist at the Bolshoi Theatre, Moscow, as Verdi's King Philip, Ramphis, Fiesco and Padre Guardiano, Boris, Dosifey, Ivan Susanin and Gounod's Mephistopheles; Guest appearances in Italy, the USA and Zürich (Gremin in Eugene Onegin, 1990); Carnegie Hall 1990, as the Archbishop in Tchaikovsky's The Maid of Orleans; Metropolitan Opera from 1991. *Address:* Bolshoi Theatre, 103009 Moscow, Russia.

NILON, Paul; Singer (Tenor); b. 1961, Keighley, Yorkshire. *Education:* Studied with Frederic Cox at the Royal Northern College of Music. *Career:* Appearances with Opera 80 as Don Ottavio, the Duke of Mantua and Sellem in The Rake's Progress; La Fenice, Venice, as Sellem; Musica nel Chiostro in Batignano, Italy, as Jacquino in Beethoven's Leonora; Has sung Strauss's Scaramuccio and Mozart's Belmonte for

Opera Northern Ireland, 1987–88; Mario and the Magician, Stephen Oliver, world premiere Batignano, 1988; With City of Birmingham Touring Opera has sung Fenton in Falstaff and Mozart's Tamino; Has sung with Opera North from 1988 as Hylas in The Trojans, Kudras (Katya Kabanova), Belfiore (La Finta Giardiniera), Leander in Nielsen's Maskarade (British premiere), Ferrando and Don Ottavio; Engagements with New Israel Opera and English National Opera, 1990–92 as Ferrando, Narraboth (Salome) and Telemachus in The Return of Ulysses; Tamino ENO, 1992–93, Duel of Tancredi and Clorinda; Tamino Scottish Opera, 1992, ENO, 1993; In Ariodante ENO, as Lurcanio, 1993; Many concert appearances; Almaviva, Barbiere, ENO and New Israeli Opera; King Ouf in L'Etoile; Paolino in Secret Marriage; Benedict in Beatrice and Benedict, Welsh National Opera; Pirro in Rossini's Ermione at Glyndebourne 1996; Alfredo for GTO and Grimoaldo in Rodelina (GTO, 1998); Sang Monteverdi's Ulysses at Florence, 1999; Season 2000–01 as Lurcanio in Ariodante at the Munich Staatsoper, with Opera North in Prague as Michel in Martinů's Julietta, Golo in Schumann's Genoveva at Edinburgh and Don Ottavio for ENO. *Recordings include:* L'Assedio di Calais by Donizetti and Vol. II and III in One Hundred Years of Italian Opera (Opera Rara); Medea in Corinta by Mayr; Orazi e Curiazi, Mercadante (Opera Rara). *Current Management:* Ingpen & Williams Ltd, 7 St George's Court, 131 Putney Bridge Road, London, SW15 2PA, England.

NILSON, Göran W.; Conductor and Pianist; b. 5 Jan. 1941, Halmstad, Sweden; m. Catharina Ericson 1965, 1 s., 1 d. *Education:* Royal High School of Music, Stockholm; Further studies in Paris, London and New York. *Career:* Debut: As Pianist at age 15, Stockholm Concert Hall, 1956; As Pianist, tours in Europe and USA; Conductor, Royal Opera, Stockholm, 1963–69; Chief Conductor, Örebro and Gävle, 1974–93; Guest Conductor, Europe, USA, Asia, Mexico and South Africa; mem, Royal Swedish Academy of Music, 1986–. *Recordings:* Many recordings of as Pianist/Conductor, especially Swedish music with several Scandinavian orchestras. *Honours:* Jeton Reward from Royal High School of Music, Stockholm, 1956. *Address:* Tantogatan 47-I, 11842 Stockholm, Sweden.

NILSSON, Anders; Composer; b. 6 July 1954, Stockholm, Sweden; m. Elzbieta Mysliwiec, 11 Feb 1989, 2 d. *Education:* Private musical studies; Music High School, Stockholm, 1971–73; Birkagården Folk High School, Stockholm, 1973–75, 1977–78; Composition, State College of Music, Stockholm, 1979–83. *Career:* Debut: 1st of Trois Pièces pour grand orchestre, with Danish Radio Symphony Orchestra, Copenhagen, 15th Jan 1981; Composer, Conductor, Swedish National Theatre Centre and Stockholm City Theatre, 1975–78; Full-time Composer, 1983–; Represented at International Society for Contemporary Music World Music Days, 1990, 1993, and elsewhere; mem, Swedish Composers' League; International Society for Contemporary Music. *Compositions include:* Trois Pièces pour grand orchestre, 1980–88; Ariel for oboe, tape and string orchestra, 1985; Reflections for soprano and chamber ensemble, 1982; Cadenze for chamber orchestra, 1987; Concerto for organ and orchestra, 1987; Sinfonietta for orchestra, 1992; Divertimento for chamber ensemble, 1991; KRASCH for saxophone quartet and percussion-ensemble, 1993; Concerto Grosso for saxophone quartet and orchestra, 1995; Symphony No. 1, 1996; Mind the Gap, for orchestra, piano concerto, 1997; Concerto for marimba and orchestra, 1998. *Recordings:* Ariel; Cadenze; Concerto for organ and orchestra; Five Orchestral Pieces for piano; Reflections; KRASCH; Divertimento; Aria. *Publications:* Scores: Resonance for piano, 1985; Reflections, 1986; Ariel, 1990; Five Orchestral Pieces for piano, 1993; Mountains for organ, 1994; Divertimento for chamber ensemble, 1995; concerto Grosso for saxophone quartet and orchestra, 1995; Piano Concerto, 1997; Symphony, 1997; Marimba Concerto, 1988. *Contributions:* Numerous articles to Nutida Musik, Swedish magazine for contemporary music. *Honours:* Rosenborg Prize, Gehrmans Music Publishers, 1988; 1st Prize, Grand Prix de Saint-Rèmy-de-Provence, for Mountains, 1992. *Address:* Fyrskeppsvägen 128, 121 54 Johanneshov, Sweden.

NILSSON, Birgit; Soprano; b. 17 May 1918, Karup, Sweden; m. Bertil Nicklasson. *Education:* Stockholm Royal Academy of Music. *Career:* With Stockholm Opera, 1946–58; Sang at Glyndebourne as Mozart's Electra in 1951, Bayreuth, Munich, Hollywood Bowl, Buenos Aires, Florence and Covent Garden London as Brünnhilde, Turandot, Elektra and Isolde, at La Scala Milan, Naples, Vienna, Chicago and San Francisco, Metropolitan Opera, NY, and Moscow; Sang Turandot at Paris in 1968, Tosca at New York in 1968, Elektra at London in 1969 and was particularly well known for her Wagnerian roles as Brünnhilde and Isolde and as Strauss's Elektra, Salome and Dyer's Wife; Appeared at the Met Opera Gala, New York, 1996. Last stage performance in 1982; Gala performances at the Metropolitan in 1983; Gives masterclasses in England and elsewhere; Personal appearance at the Richard Tucker Gala, Covent Garden, 2001. *Recordings include:* Aida; Der Freischütz; Salome; Un Ballo in Maschera; Don Giovanni; Der Ring des Nibelungen; Oberon; Tannhäuser; Tristan; La Fanciulla del West. *Honours:* Medal

Litteris et Artibus, 1960; Medal for Promotion of Art of Music, Royal Academy of Music, Stockholm, 1968; Austrian and Bavarian Kammersängerin; Honorary Member of the Vienna State Opera, 1968; First Commander Order of Vasa, 1974; Honorary Member, Royal Musical Academy, London; Honorary Doctorates; Swedish Gold Medal, CL 18 Illis Quorum. *Address:* c/o Box 527, Stockholm C, Sweden.

NILSSON, Bo; Composer; b. 1 May 1937, Skelleftehamn, Sweden; Divorced, 2 d. *Education:* Piano under Micha Pedersen, 1945–50; Audiology under K G St Clair Renard, 1951–54; Counterpoint and instrumentation under Karl Birger Blomdahl, 1955–57. *Career:* Debut: Composer, Cologne, 1956; Freelance Artist, 1976–; Compositions played world-wide; Author. *Compositions include:* Brief an Gösta Oswald, 1958–59; Drei Szenen, 1960–61; Swedenborg Dreaming for electronic music, 1969; Déjà Vu for woodwind quartet, 1967; Déjà connu, Déjà entendu for wind quintet, 1976; We'll Be Meeting Tomorrow for mixed choir, soprano, celesta and triangles, 1970; Fatumeh for speaker, soloists, mixed choir, electronics and large orchestra, 1973; La Bran for soprano, saxophone, mixed choir, orchestra and electronics, 1975; Fragments for marimba, 5 Thai-gongs, 1975; Floten aus der Einsamkelt for soprano, 9 players, 1976; Bass, bass, tuba solo, 6 Javanian tuned gongs, Chinese gong, 1977; Plexus for brass instruments, piano and percussion, 1979; Wendepunkt-Infrastruktur-Endepunkt, brass quintet, 1981; Autumn Song for baritone and orchestra, 1984; My Summerwind is Yours, for baritone and orchestra, 1984; Brief an Gösta Oswald; Arctic Romance, 1995; A Spirit's Whisper in Swedenborg's Gazebo, 1996; Arctic Air, for orchestra, 2001; Film music; Songs; Jazz. *Recordings:* Introduction and Midsummer Tune; Quantitaten, Raga Rena Rama; Rendez-vous; You; Illness; Walz in Marjoram; Blue-Black Samba; The Last Lass; To Love; Lidingo Airport; Forward Waltz; The Swinging World of Bo Nilsson; The Missile; In The Loneliness of The Night; Ravaillac; A Spirit's Whisper, 1997; Many Others. *Publications:* Spaderboken, 1962; Missilen eller Livet i en mossa, 1994. *Honours:* Christopher Johnson Grand Prize, 1975; Hilding Rosenberg Prize, 1993; Honoré Causa 2000 at the University of Lulea; State Artist's Salary, 1974–. *Address:* Kocksgatan 48, 4 tr, 116 29 Stockholm, Sweden.

NILSSON, Pia-Marie; Singer (Soprano); b. 1961, Sweden. *Education:* Studied at Stockholm College of Music and the State Opera School. *Career:* Debut: Stockholm Folkoperan in 1985 as the Queen of Night; Sang at Royal Opera Stockholm and the Drottningholm Theatre, 1986–88 and Frankfurt Opera from 1989 as Sandrina in La Finta Giardiniera, Servilia in La Clemenza di Tito, Pamina, Oscar in Ballo in Maschera, Gilda and Sophie; French debut in 1991 as Donna Anna at Nancy; Concert engagements in Scandinavia, Italy, Switzerland, Germany and Austria; Engaged as Oscar for the Théâtre de la Monnaie, Brussels, 1995; Season 1994–95, Ring Cycle, Frankfurt; Season 1995–96 as Susanna at Frankfurt; Broadcasting commitments in Scandinavia.

NILSSON, Raymond; Singer (Tenor); b. 26 May 1920, Mosman, Sydney, Australia. *Education:* Studied at the New South Wales Conservatorium and at the Royal College of Music in London. *Career:* After early experience in Australia sang with the Carl Rosa Company, the English Opera Group and Sadler's Wells; Royal Opera House Covent Garden from 1952 as Don José, Alfredo, Germont and Pandarus in Troilus and Cressida; Guest appearances in Wiesbaden and elsewhere in Germany as concert artist, with further tours to USA and Netherlands; Australian tours with the Elizabethan Opera Company in 1958 and Sadler's Wells in 1960; Other roles included Turiddu, Rodolfo, Narraboth in Salome and Luigi in Il Tabarro; BBC performances of Schoenberg's Gurrelieder, Hindemith's Mathis der Maler, Oedipus Rex and Kodály's Psalmus Hungaricus; Sang in Janáček's Glagolitic Mass with ABC, Australia. *Recordings:* Bob Boles in Peter Grimes; Psalmus Hungaricus. *Address:* c/o Australian Opera, PO Box 291, Strawberry Hills, New South Wales 2012, Australia.

NIMSGERN, Siegmund; Singer (Baritone); b. 14 Jan. 1940, St Wendel, Germany. *Education:* Vocal studies with Paul Lohmann and Jakob Staempfli. *Career:* Debut: Lionel in Tchaikovsky's Maid of Orleans, Saarbrucken, 1967; Sang in Saarbrucken until 1971 then Deutsche Oper am Rhein, Düsseldorf, 1971–74; London Promenade Concerts in 1972 as Mephistopheles in La Damnation de Faust; La Scala Milan and Paris Opéra in 1973, Covent Garden in 1973 as Amfortas in Parsifal; Paris, 1977–82 as the Speaker in Die Zauberflöte, Creon in Oedipus Rex, Telramund in Lohengrin and Beethoven's Pizarro; Metropolitan Opera in 1978 as Pizarro and Bayreuth Festival, 1983–85 as Wotan in the Peter Hall production of Der Ring des Nibelungen; Often heard as concert singer; Chicago Lyric Opera in 1988 as Scarpia and sang Wotan in Das Rheingold at Bonn in 1990, Don Pizarro in Fidelio at La Scala and Telramund at Frankfurt in 1991; Sang Creon in Cherubini's Médée at Trier, 1999. *Recordings:* St John Passion by Bach; Masses by Haydn and Hummel; Pergolesi's La Serva Padrona; Cantatas by Bach and Telemann; Bach's Magnificat; St Matthew Passion and Bach B minor Mass; Alberich in Das Rheingold; Mosè in Egitto; Die Schöpfung; Marschner's Der Vampyr. *Current Management:* Ingpen & Williams

Ltd, 7 St George's Court, 131 Putney Bridge Road, London, SW15 2PA, England.

NIRQUET, Jean; Singer (Countertenor), Conductor and Musicologist; b. 15 Aug. 1958, Paris, France. *Education:* Baccalauréat of Sciences; Licence, History, Sorbonne University, Paris; Flute, bassoon, piano and theory studies at Strasbourg Music High School and Conservatory until 1964; Harmony and conducting with Claude-Henry Joubert, singing with Jacqueline Bonnardot at Conservatory of Orléans until 1978; Music analysis with Betsy Jolas, singing with Christiane Eda-Pierre at Conservatory of Paris. *Career:* Engagements at opera houses of Paris, Lyon, Nice, Strasbourg, Karlsruhe and Helsinki; Radio appearances in France, Germany and Netherlands and at numerous festivals; Film for Südwestfunk 2, Pasticcio of Handel-Martinoty, 1985. *Recordings:* Handel's Alessandro; Cavalli's Serse; Charpentier's Vespers of the Annunciation, Te Deum and David et Jonathas; Gilles' Requiem; Prodomidès' H H Ulysse. *Publications:* Rose et Colas de Monsigny, 1982; L'Irato de Méhul, 1984; La Dramaturgie des Opéras de Lully Dans L'Etude des Tempi; Analyse d'Epiphanie d'André Caplet. *Current Management:* Anglo Swiss, London, England; Rainer-Poilvé, Paris, France; Kempf, Munich, Germany. *Address:* c/o Poilvé, 16 avenue Franklin D. Roosevelt, F–7500 Paris, France.

NISHIDA, Hiroko; Singer (Soprano); b. 17 Jan. 1952, Oita, Japan. *Education:* Studied in Tokyo. *Career:* Sang with the Bonn Opera, 1979–81; Appearances at Zürich Opera as Butterfly, Berne, Mimi, St Gallen, Micaela and the Forza Leonora at Berlin, Munich, Cologne, Frankfurt, Düsseldorf, Stuttgart and Mannheim; Sang Butterfly with Opéra de Lyon in 1990; Further guest appearances at San Diego, Enschede and Amsterdam, Vienna Staatsoper; Hamburg; Prague; Sofia; Vancouver; Tokyo; Other roles include Arminda in La Finta Giardiniera, Pamina, Manon Lescaut, Lauretta, Elisabeth de Valois and Kunigunde in Lortzing's Hans Sachs; Concert repertoire includes works by Bach, Handel, Mozart, Schubert, Beethoven, Bruckner and Mahler. *Address:* Magnihalde 11, 9000 St Gallen, Switzerland.

NISHIKAZE, Makiko; Composer and Pianist; b. 22 April 1968, Wakayama, Japan. *Education:* Studied at Aichi University of Fine Arts and Music, 1987–91; Mills College, California, USA, 1991–93; Studies, graduating as MA, Hochschule der Künste, Berlin, Germany, 1994–99. *Career:* Finalist, Forum '93 International Composition Competition, Montreal, 1993; Participant, Darmstadt Summer Course, 1994; Piano solo recitals, Berlin, 1996, 1999; Appeared at Chamber Music Festival in Kanagawa, Japan, 1997; Concerts in New York, Israel, Brazil, and Barcelona, Spain, 1998. *Compositions:* Haiku, for sextet, CD, 1994; Celestial Fruits, for ensemble, 1995; Shades I–V, for piano, 1995–96; Chant I–III, for voice, 1997–98; North Piano I–V, for piano, 1997; Lux, for string quartet 1999; Oratorio for vocal ensemble 2000; Garden, Nocturnal, for ensemble 2001. *Recordings:* Radio recordings, Canada and Germany. *Honours:* Grants from Berlin Senate, 1994; Composition Prize, Stuttgart, 1995; Fellowship, Akademie Schloss Solitude, 1999; State Schleswig-Holstein Prize 2000; State Niedersachsen Prize 2001. *Current Management:* Edition Wandelweiser, Berlin. *Address:* Sophie-Charlotten Strasse 112, 14059 Berlin, Germany.

NISHIYAMA, Ikuko; Pianist; b. 28 Dec. 1976, Tokyo. *Education:* Studies at the Purcell School, London, England, 1982–92; Studies at Hochschule für Musik und Darstellende Kunst in Vienna, Austria, 1993–98. *Career:* Shostakovich Piano Concerto No. 1, with London Gala Orchestra, Royal Festival Hall, London, 1991; Piano recital, Casals Hall, Tokyo, Japan, 1998. *Recordings:* Mozart, Beethoven, Schumann, cd. *Honours:* 3rd Prize, 10th International Beethoven Piano Competition, 1997; 1st Prize, 10th International Chamber Music Competition, Greece, 2000. *Address:* 3–30–18 Ozenji-nishi, Asao-ku, Kawasaki-shi, Kanagawa, 215–0017 Japan.

NISKA, Maralin; Singer (Soprano); b. 16 Nov. 1930, San Pedro, California, USA. *Education:* Studied with Lotte Lehmann. *Career:* Sang widely in California from 1955; Sang at San Diego Opera in 1965 as Mimi in La Bohème, sang Floyd's Susannah with the Met National Company, at New York City Opera in 1967 as Mozart's Countess returning as Turandot, Tosca, Salome and Janáček's Emilia Marty, and at Metropolitan Opera, 1970–77 as Tosca, Musetta and Hélène in Les Vêpres Siciliennes; Italian debut as Marie in Wozzeck at Maggio Musicale Florence, 1978; Other roles have included Violetta, Madama Butterfly, Donna Elvira, Manon Lescaut and Marguerite in Faust.

NISKANEN, Jyrki; Singer (Tenor); b. 12 Feb. 1956, Finland. *Education:* Studied at the Helsinki Sibelius Academy and with Vera Rozsa in London. *Career:* Debut: Tampere, 1986, as Tonio in La Fille du régiment; Sang Alfredo at Helsinki, 1989; Savonlinna Festival, 1992–96, as Florestan and Verdi's Macduff; Théâtre du Châtelet, Paris, 1994, as Siegmund; Florence, 1995, in Zemlinsky's Eine Florentinische Tragödie; Season 1996 as Siegmund at the Vienna Staatsoper, Tristan at Barcelona and Florestan in Rio de Janeiro; Concerts, in Europe and

USA, include Requiems of Mozart and Verdi; Season 1998 as Shostakovich's Sergei at Florence, Alvaro in La Forza del Destino at Savonlinna; Sang Wagner's Lohengrin at Nice, 1998 and Seville, 1999; Tristan in Nice, Washington, Munich and Florence, 2001; Loge and Siegmund at Catania; Beethoven's Ninth at la Scala, 1999, and Gabriele Adorno at Catania. *Address:* c/o Savonlinna Opera Festival, Olavinkatu 35, 57130 Savonlinna, Finland. *E-mail:* sirkka.kuula-niskanen@pp.inet .fi.

NISSEL, Siegmund (Walter); Violinist; b. 3 Jan. 1922, Munich, Germany; m. 5 April 1957, 1 s., 1 d. *Education:* External Matriculation, Honours Degree, London University; Private violin study with Professor Max Weissgarber until 1938, then with Professor Max Rostal in London. *Career:* Debut: With Amadeus Quartet at Wigmore Hall in London, 1948; Founder Member of the Amadeus Quartet; innumerable BBC radio and television and ITV appearances; International concert career; Quartet disbanded in 1987 after the death of the violist Peter Schidlof; mem, ISM; ESTA. *Recordings:* Mozart, Beethoven, Schubert and Brahms Quartets; Benjamin Britten; Brahms Sextets. *Honours:* Honorary DMus, London and York Universities; O.B.E.; Verdienstkreuz für Musik in Germany and Austria; Honorary LRAM. *Address:* 11 Highgrove Point, Mount Vernon, Frognal Rise, London NW3 6PZ, England.

NISSMAN, Barbara; Concert Pianist; b. 31 Dec. 1944, Philadelphia, Pennsylvania, USA. *Education:* BMus, 1966, MMus, 1966, D.Mus Arts, 1969, University of Michigan; Studied with Pianist, György Sandor. *Career:* Debut: American Orchestral Debut with Philadelphia Orchestra, Ormandy, 1971; Appearances with London Philharmonic, Royal Philharmonic, Rotterdam Philharmonic, L'Orchestre de la Suisse Romande, BBC Symphony, Netherlands Chamber, Munich Philharmonic, Bavarian Radio Orchestra; USA; Philadelphia, Pittsburgh, Minnesota, Chicago, Cleveland, St Louis, National, New York Philharmonic Orchestras; With Ormandy, Muti, Mata, Skrowaczewski, Zinman, Slatkin; Concert tours of the Far East, Latin America and Soviet Union; Presented Dutch Premiere of Ginastera Piano Concerto, 1978 in Concertgebouw; Soloist at Gala 60th birthday concert for Ginastera with Suisse Romande, 1976; Third Piano Sonata, 1982, of Ginastera, dedicated to Ms Nissman; Masterclasses given at Moscow, St Petersburg Conservatories, Federal University of Brazil and throughout USA. *Recordings:* Complete Solo and Chamber Music of Alberto Ginastera, 2 vols; Music of Franz Liszt; Complete piano sonatas of Prokofiev, 3 vols; Chopin by Nissman, Beethoven by Nissman, Bartók by Nissman (includes first performance of unpublished 1898 Sonata). *Publications:* Alberto Ginastera – Piano Sonata No. 3, 1982; Bartók and the Piano: A Performer's View (includes CD), 2002. *Address:* Rte 2, Box 260, Lewisburg, WV 24901, USA. *Website:* www.barbaranissman.com.

NITESCU, Adina; Singer (Soprano); b. 1965, Romania. *Education:* Studied at the George Enescu Conservatoire, Bucharest, and in Munich; Stipendium from Georg Solti, 1991–92. *Career:* Roles with the Opera Studio of the Bavarian State Opera included Mozart's Countess and Fiordiligi; Bucharest Opera debut as Mimi in La Bohème, 1993; Further engagements as Donna Anna at Leipzig, Saarbrucken and Essen; Mimi at Cologne and Wiesbaden, Marzelline in Fidelio at the 1996 Bregenz Festival and Gounod's Marguerite at the Deutsche Oper, Berlin, First Lady in Die Zauberflöte, and in Gluck's Armide to open the 1996 season at La Scala, Milan; Glyndebourne Festival 1997, as Manon Lescaut in a new production of Puccini's opera. *Address:* Planie 7, 72764 Reutlingen, Germany.

NITSCHE, Horst; Singer (Tenor); b. 22 March 1939, Vienna, Austria. *Education:* Studied at the Bruckner Conservatory, Linz. *Career:* Sang at the Landestheater Salzburg from 1970, Vienna Staatsoper 1972; Appearances in Vienna (also at Volksoper) as Monostatos, Don Curzio, Jacquino, Zorn in Meistersinger, Flavio in Norma and Missail in Boris Godunov; Sang in the 1976 premiere of Kabale und Liebe by Einem; Salzburg Festival from 1977, in Salome, Don Carlos, Die Zauberflöte and Le nozze di Figaro. *Recordings:* Character roles in Il Trovatore, Der Rosenkavalier, Die Zauberflöte and Don Carlos. *Address:* Vienna Staatsoper, Opernring 2, 1010 Vienna, Austria.

NIXON, Marni; Singer (Soprano) and Teacher; b. 22 Feb. 1930, Altadena, California, USA. *Education:* Studied at the University of Southern California with Carl Ebert, Stanford University with Jan Popper and the Berkshire Music Center with Boris Goldovsky and Sarah Caldwell. *Career:* Has sung in musical comedy, programmes for children's television, concerts, opera and film soundtracks; Provided the singing voices for Deborah Kerr in The King and I, Natalie Wood in West Side Story and Audrey Hepburn in My Fair Lady; Has appeared in Los Angeles, San Francisco, Tanglewood and Seattle as Mozart's Blondchen, Constanze and Susanna, Philine in Thomas' Mignon, and Strauss's Zerbinetta and Violetta; Concert engagements in Cleveland, Toronto, Los Angeles, Israel and London; Modern repertory includes works by Webern, Ives, Hindemith and Stravinsky; Teacher at California

Institute of Arts, 1969–71 and Music Academy of The West, Santa Barbara, from 1980; Appears as Cabaret Artist. *Recordings include:* Webern Complete Works, conducted by Robert Craft. *Address:* c/o Music Academy of The West, 1070 Fairway Road, CA 93109, USA.

NIXON, Roger; Composer; b. 8 Aug. 1921, Tulane, California, USA. *Education:* Studied at University of California, Berkeley, PhD in 1952, notably with Roger Sessions, Arthur Bliss, Bloch and Schoenberg. *Career:* Teacher at Modesto Junior College, 1951–59 and San Francisco State University from 1960. *Compositions:* Opera: The Bride Comes To Yellow Sky, 1968; Orchestral: Air for Strings, 1953, Violin Concerto, 1956, Elegaic Rhapsody for Viola and Orchestra, 1962, Viola Concerto, 1969, San Joaquin Sketches, 1982, California Jubilee, 1982, Golden Jubilee, 1985; Chamber: String Quartet No. 1, 1949, Conversations for Violin and Clarinet, 1981, Music for Clarinet and Piano, 1986; Vocal: Christmas Perspectives for Chorus, 1980, Festival Mass for Chorus, 1980, Chaunticleer for Male Chorus, 1984, The Canterbury Tales for Chorus, 1986, The Daisy for Chorus, 1987; Song Cycles include, A Narative Of Tides for Soprano, Flute and Piano, 1984. *Honours:* Grants and commissions from the San Francisco Festival of The Masses and American Bandmasters Association. *Address:* c/o ASCAP, ASCAP Building, 1 Lincoln Plaza, New York, NY 10023, USA.

NOBLE, Jeremy; Musicologist, Critic and Broadcaster; b. 27 March 1930, London, England. *Education:* Worcester College, Oxford, 1949–53; Private music studies. *Career:* Music Critic for The Times, 1960–63, and The Sunday Telegraph, 1972–76; Research Fellow, Barber Institute Birmingham, 1964–65; Associate Professor at State University of New York, Buffalo, 1966–70 and from 1976; Fellow, Harvard Institute for Renaissance Studies, Florence, 1967–68; Leverhulme Research Fellow, 1975–76; Many broadcasts for BBC Radio 3. *Publications:* Articles on Josquin, Debussy and Stravinsky for the Musical Times; Purcell and The Chapel Royal, in Essays on Music, 1959; Mozart: A Documentary Biography, translation of O Deutsch with E Blom and P Branscombe, 1965; Entries on Josquin and, jointly with EW White, Stravinsky for The New Grove Dictionary of Music and Musicians, 1980. *Address:* Department of Music, State University of New York, Buffalo, NY 14260, USA.

NOBLE, John; Singer (Baritone); b. 2 Jan. 1931, Southampton, England. *Education:* MA (Hons), Cambridge; Privately with Clive Carey and Boriska Gereb. *Career:* Concerts and Oratorio with major orchestras throughout the United Kingdom; Tours in Europe and USA; Guest Artist in opera with Covent Garden and other companies; Many broadcasts for BBC in wide range of music including several first performances; Professor of Singing and Honorary Fellow, Trinity College of Music, London; mem, Past Chairman, Solo Performers, Incorporated Society of Musicians. *Recordings:* Vaughan Williams, The Pilgrim's Progress, title role, conductor Boult; Britten, Albert Herring (Vicar), conductor Britten; Delius, Sea Drift, conductor Groves. *Address:* 185 Syon Lane, Isleworth, Middlesex TW7 5PU, England.

NOBLE, Timothy; Singer (Baritone); b. 22 Feb. 1945, Indianapolis, Indiana, USA. *Career:* Sang supporting roles in Carmen, Turandot and Wozzeck with San Francisco Opera in 1981; Houston Opera from 1982 as Ping, Leporello and Falstaff; Colorado Springs Festival in 1982 as Rigoletto and Fort Worth and Opéra-Comique Paris in 1983 as Sharpless and Germont; Season 1985–86 at Santa Fe in the premiere of John Eaton's The Tempest, as Falstaff in Amsterdam and as Simon Boccanegra at Glyndebourne returning in 1988 as Germont; San Francisco in 1987 as Tomsky in The Queen of Spades, Venice in 1988 in Verdi's Stiffelio; Sang Shaklovity in Khovanshchina at the Metropolitan in 1988 and San Francisco in 1990, returning to New York in 1991 as Leporello; Opera Pacific at Costa Mesa and the Santa Fe Festival in 1991 as Renato and as Jack Rance in La Fanciulla del West; Other roles include William Tell, Amonasro, Macbeth, Iago, Tonio, Alfio, Di Luna and Scarpia; Sang Columbus in the premiere of The Voyage by Philip Glass at New York Metropolitan in 1992; Iago at the 1996 Holland Festival and Rigoletto for Flanders Opera, 1998; Sang Rigoletto, Antwerp and Gent, 1998, and Flying Dutchman at Indianapolis Opera; Iago at Amsterdam, 1999; Sang in Henze's Venus and Adonis at Toronto, 2001; Further engagements in musicals and as concert artist; Professor of Voice, Indiana University, 1999–. *Address:* c/o Caroline Woodfield, ICM, 40W 57th Street, New York, NY 10019, USA.

NOCENTINI, Maria Costanza; Italian singer (soprano); b. 1970. *Education:* Bologna Conservatory. *Career:* appearances as Tebaldo in Don Carlos at Salzburg, Giulia in La Scala di Seta at Reggio Emilia, Berenice in L'Occasione fa il ladro, by Rossini, Donizetti's Adina at Naples, Lisa in La Sonnambula at Rome, Handel's Galatea at Messina, Armida in Rinaldo at Beaume, Clorinda in La Cenerentola at Genoa and Musetta in Munich, Vienna and Santiago; La Scala Milan as Pamina, Nannetta in Falstaff, Bergère in Gluck's Armide, and Mozart's Barbarina; Sophie in Werther at Naples, Modena and Parma; Handel's Semele at Spoleto and Mozart's Countess at Glyndebourne, 2000;

Concerts include Haydn's Die Schöfung, in Santiago. *Honours:* Toti Dal Monte Prize; International Viotti Competition; Miguel Cervantes Prize at Francesco Viñas Competition, Barcelona. *Current Management:* Atelier Musicale Srl, via Caselle 76, 40068 San Lazzaro di Savena, Italy. *Telephone:* (051) 199844 44. *Fax:* (051) 199844 20. *E-mail:* info@ateliermusicale.it. *Website:* www.ateliermusicale.it.

NÖCKER, Hans Gunter; Singer (Bass-Baritone); b. 22 Jan. 1927, Hagen, Germany. *Education:* Studied in Brunswick and with Hans-Hermann Nissen and Willi Domgraf-Fassbaender in Munich. *Career:* Debut: Munster in 1952 as Alfio in Cavalleria Rusticana; Many appearances in Germany particularly at Hamburg, Munich and Stuttgart; Bayreuth Festival, 1958–60, Munich 1963 in the premiere of Egk's Die Verlobung in San Domingo and Schwetzingen 1966 in Gluck's Armide; Sang at Deutsche Oper Berlin in the 1972 premiere of Fortner's Elisabeth Tudor, La Fenice Venice in 1983 as Klingsor in Parsifal, and Berlin in 1984 in the premiere of Reimann's Gespenstersonate; Guest appearances in Florence, Brussels, Palermo, London and Edinburgh; Sang at Munich in the 1986 premiere of D Kirchner's Belshazzar; Sang in Orff's Trionfo di Afrodite at Munich Festival in 1990; Sang in the premiere of Bose's Schlachthof 5, Munich, 1996. *Recordings:* Orff's Trionfo di Afrodite; Oedipus der Tyrann; Götterdämmerung. *Address:* c/o Bayerische Staatsoper, Postfach 745, 8000 Munich 1, Germany.

NODA, Ken; Concert Pianist and Musical Assistant to Artistic Director, Artistic Administration, Metropolitan Opera; b. 5 Oct. 1962, New York, USA. *Education:* Private studies with Daniel Barenboim. *Career:* London debut in 1979 with the English Chamber Orchestra and Daniel Barenboim; Later engagements with the Philharmonia, Berlin Philharmonic, Orchestre de Paris, Rotterdam Philharmonic, New York Philharmonic and Chicago Symphony; Conductors include Abbado, Chailly, Andrew Davis, Kubelik, Leinsdorf, Levine, Mehta, Ozawa and Previn; Recitals in London, Toronto, Chicago, Lincoln Center New York, Hamburg and La Fenice, Venice; Festival appearances at Mostly Mozart, New York, Ravinia and Tanglewood; 1986 debut with the Vienna Philharmonic in Salzburg; Season 1986–87 in concerts with the Berlin Philharmonic, the Hallé and the Philharmonia; 1988 concerts with the Rotterdam Philharmonic playing Mozart under James Conlon, Beethoven's Triple Concerto with Pinchas Zukerman and Lynn Harrell at Ravinia; Toured Japan with Ozawa and the New Japan Philharmonic; Resumed concert career in New York with solo recitals at Metropolitan Museum of Art, 1998, 92nd Street, New York, 1999; Lieder recitals with Jessye Norman in 1998 and Hildegard Behrens, 1999, both at Salzburg Festival. *Address:* c/o Metropolitan Opera, Lincoln Center, New York, NY 10023, USA.

NOEL, Rita; Singer (Mezzo Soprano); b. 21 Nov. 1943, Lancaster, South Carolina, USA. *Education:* Studied at Eastman School, at Queens College, Charlotte, South Carolina and in New York and Vienna. *Career:* Played violin and viola with the Vienna Chamber Orchestra and the Berlin Symphony; Stage debut with the Metropolitan National Opera Company, 1966, as Flora in Traviata; Further appearances at the Theater am Gärtnerplatz Munich, Bielefeld, Amsterdam and Miami; Other roles have included Mozart's Cherubino and Sextus, Cornelia in Giulio Cesare, Carmen, Rosina, Octavian, Nickausse, Azucena and Santuzza; Frequent concert engagements. *Address:* c/o Staatstheater am Gärtnerplatz, Gärtnerplatz 3, 8000 Munich, Germany.

NOLAN, David; Violinist; b. 1949, Liverpool, England. *Education:* Studied with Yossi Zivoni and Alexander Moskowski at the Royal Manchester College of Music; Studied in Russia, 1973–74. *Career:* Debut: Played the Mendelssohn Concerto, 1965; Joined the London Philharmonic Orchestra, 1972, Leader 1976–92; Many appearances with the London Philharmonic Orchestra and other orchestras in concertos by Bach, Beethoven, Brahms, Bruch, Glazunov, Korngold, Mozart, Paganini, Saint-Saëns, Stravinsky, Tchaikovsky and Walton; Leader, Philharmonia Orchestra, 1992–94; Leader, Bournemouth Symphony Orchestra, 1997–2001; Solo Concertmaster, Yomiuri Nippon Symphony Orchestra, Tokyo, 1999–. *Recordings:* The Lark Ascending by Vaughan Williams; The Four Seasons by Vivaldi; Mozart Rondo in C for violin and orchestra with the BBC Philharmonic. *Honours:* RMCM performances, diploma, distinction. *Address:* Flat 1, 34 Craven Street, London WC2N 5NP, England; 5-21-8-2F Nishi-Shinjuku, Shinjuku-ku, Tokyo 160-0023, Japan.

NOLEN, Timothy; Singer (Baritone); b. 9 July 1941, Rotan, Texas, USA. *Education:* Studied at the Manhattan School of Music and with Richard Fredericks and Walter Fredericks. *Career:* Debut: New Jersey Opera Newark as Rossini's Figaro; Sang Marcello in La Bohème with San Francisco Opera in 1968; Appearances in Chicago, Houston, Boston and Minneapolis; European debut at Rouen in 1974 as Pelléas; Sang at Amsterdam in 1974 in the premiere of The Picture of Dorian Gray by Kox, at Cologne, 1974–78 and Paris, Bordeaux, Aix and Nantes as Mozart's Count, Figaro and Guglielmo, Donizetti's Malatesta and Belcore, Monteverdi's Orpheus, and Dandini in La Cenerentola,

Puccini's Gianni Schicchi, the Emperor in The Nightingale by Stravinsky and Ford in Falstaff; Sang in the premieres of Carlisle Floyd's Willie Stark and Bernstein's A Quiet Place, Houston in 1981 and 1983; Further engagements at Florence, Geneva, Miami, New York, City Opera and Philadelphia; Santa Fe Festival in 1992 as Mr Peachum in The Beggar's Opera and Frank in Die Fledermaus; Sang Malatesta at Chicago, 1995; Season 1998 as Somarone in Béatrice and Bénédict at Santa Fe and Don Pasquale at St Louis; Season 2001–02 as Rossini's Don Magnifico at Cincinnati and Trinity Moses in Mahagonny at Genoa.

NONI, Alda; Singer (soprano); b. 30 April 1916, Trieste, Italy. *Education:* Studied in Trieste and Vienna. *Career:* Debut: Ljubljana in 1937 as Rosina in Il Barbiere di Siviglia; Sang first in Yugoslavia then joined the Vienna Staatsoper in 1942; Sang Mozart's Despina and Verdi's Gilda and Oscar; Appeared as Zerbinetta in a 1944 performance of Ariadne auf Naxos to celebrate the 80th birthday of Richard Strauss; Sang in Milan, Rome, Venice and Turin from 1945 and at Cambridge Theatre London in 1946 as Norina in Don Pasquale opposite Marino Stabile; La Scala from 1949 in Cimarosa's Il Matrimonio Segreto and Piccinni's La Buona Figliuola; Sang Zerlina, Nannetta and Papagena with the company of La Scala during its 1950 visit to London; Glyndebourne, 1950–54 as Blondchen, Despina and Clorinda in La Cenerentola; Guest appearances in Berlin, Paris at the Opéra-Comique, Lisbon, Madrid and Rio de Janeiro. *Recordings include:* Ariadne auf Naxos; Don Pasquale; L'Elisir d'amore; Lucia di Lammermoor; Il Matrimonio Segreto; Le nozze di Figaro; La Cenerentola.

NORBERG-SCHULZ, Elisabeth; Singer (Soprano); b. Jan. 1959, Norway. *Education:* Studied at Accademia di Santa Cecilia, Rome, the Pears-Britten School at Snape and with Elisabeth Schwarzkopf in Zürich. *Career:* Gave lieder recitals and sang Britten's Les Illuminations at Snape in 1981; Sang supporting roles in Italy and elsewhere at first, then sang Gilda and Lucia di Lammermoor; Has appeared under such conductors as Georg Solti, Riccardo Muti and Claudio Abbado, notably at La Scala Milan; Sang Musetta in La Bohème with La Scala on a visit to Japan in 1988 and at Rome Opera in 1989 as Barbarina in Le nozze di Figaro; Maggio Musicale Fiorentino in 1989 as Ilia in Idomeneo and sang Pamina in Die Zauberflöte at the Salzburg Landestheater in 1991 as part of the Mozart bicentenary celebrations; Season 1992 as Norina at Naples, Guardian of the Threshold in Die Frau ohne Schatten and Servilia in La Clemenza di Tito at Salzburg; Covent Garden debut 1995, as Liu in Turandot; Sang Cimarosa's Carolina at Rome, 1996; Season 1997–98 as Liu in Turandot and in Rota's Italian Straw Hat at La Scala; Adalgisa in Norma at Rome, 1999; Season 2001 on tour to London and in Europe with Handel's Tamerlano. *Address:* c/o Teatro alla Scala, Via Filodrammatici 2, 20121 Milan, Italy.

NORBY, Erik; Composer; b. 9 Jan. 1936, Copenhagen, Denmark. *Education:* Copenhagen Boys' Choir and Tivoli Band; Copenhagen Conservatory; Diploma in Composition, 1966. *Career:* Teacher, North Jutland Conservatory until 1975 then freelance composer. *Compositions include:* Orchestra: Folk Song Suite, 1962, Music for 6 sextets, 1966, The Rainbow Snake, 1975, Illuminations, Capriccio, 1978, 3 Dances, 1983; Chamber: Illustrations, 1965, Schubert Variations, 1974, Partita, 1981, Tivoli Collage, 1983, Ravel: Le Tombeau De Couperin, 1984; Solo Instrument: 12 Danish Folk Songs for piano, 1961, Chromaticon, partita in 8 movements, 1971, Five Organ Chorales, 1976–78; Choral: March, 1972, Winter Twilight, 1973, Nightingale, 1973, Song Near The Depth Of Spring, 1973, Festival Cantata, on the occasion of the 150th anniversary of Copenhagen Cathedral, 1979, Edvard Munch Triptych, 1978–79; Solo Voice: Two Songs, 1963, Six Shakespeare Sonnets, 1981, 13 Elizabethan Love Songs, The Ballad About My Life, 1984; Music for educational use: Three Suites, 1961, Three Small Suites, 1962, Little Sonatina, Three Humoresques, Evening Song, Suite No. 2, 1963. *Recordings:* Numerous recordings of his work. *Current Management:* Koda, Maltegårdsvej 24, 2820 Gentofte, Denmark. *Address:* Kochsvej 13, 3tv, 1812 Frederiksberg C, Denmark.

NORDAL, Jon; Composer and President, Reykjavík College of Music; b. 1926, Iceland. *Education:* Studied with Arni Kristjansson, Jon Thorarinsson and Dr V Urbancic at Reykjavík College of Music, Iceland; Studies with W Frey and W Burkhard at Zürich, Switzerland, 1949–51 and in Paris and Rome; Darmstadt summer courses, 1956–57. *Career:* President, Reykjavík College of Music. *Compositions:* Orchestral: Concerto Lirico for harp and strings, Concerto for orchestra, 1949, Concerto for piano and orchestra, 1956, Sinfonietta Seriosa, 1956, A Play Of Fragments, 1962, Adagio for flute, harp, piano and strings, 1965, Stiklur, 1970, Canto Elegiaco, 1971, Leidsla, 1973, Epitaphio, 1974, The Winter Night, 1975, Twin Song for violin, viola and orchestra, 1979, Dedication, 1981, Choralis, 1982, Concerto for cello and orchestra, 1983; Chamber: Sonata for violin and piano, Fairy Tale Sisters for violin and piano, Chorale Prelude for organ, 1980, Duo for violin and cello, 1983; Requiem, 1995; From Dream to Dream, string quartet, 1997; Dreaming on a Dormant String, for violin, cello and piano, 1998; My

Faith is but a Flicker, for chorus, 1999; Choir Music: Seven Songs for male chorus, 1955. *Address:* STEF, Laufasveji 40, Reykjavík, Iceland.

NORDEN, Betsy; Singer (Soprano); b. 17 Oct. 1945, Cincinnati, Ohio, USA. *Education:* Studied at Boston University. *Career:* Member of Metropolitan Opera Chorus from 1969; Solo appearances at the Metropolitan from 1972 in Le nozze di Figaro and as Papagena, Elvira in L'Italiana in Algeri, Constance in the Carmélites, Oscar and Despina in Così fan tutte, 1990; Sang in The Cunning Little Vixen at Philadelphia season, 1980–81, Constance at San Francisco in 1983 and Gretel at San Diego, 1985; Many concert appearances. *Address:* c/o Metropolitan Opera, Lincoln Center, New York, NY 10023, USA.

NORDGREN, Pehr (Henrik); Composer; b. 19 Jan. 1944, Saltvik, Finland. *Education:* Studied composition under Professor Joonas Kokkonen, musicology at Helsinki University and composition and traditional Japanese music at Tokyo University of Arts and Music, 1970–73. *Career:* Assistant at Helsinki University. *Compositions include:* Euphonie 1 Op 1, 1967; 7 String Quartets, 1967–92; Ten Ballades To Japanese Ghost Stories By Lafcadio Hearn, 1972–77; As In A Dream, Op 21, 1974; Symphony Op 20, 1974; Autumnal Concerto for traditional japanese instruments and orchestra, 1974; Wind Quintet No. 2, Op 22, 1975; Butterflies, 1977; Summer Music Op 34, 1977; Symphony for strings Op 43, 1978; In Patches, 1978; Piano Quintet Op 44, 1978; In The Palm Of The King's Head for soprano, baritone, chams and orchestra, 1979; Three Cello Concertos, 1980–92; The Lights Of Heaven for soprano, tenor, chorus and ensemble, 1985; Symphony No. 2, 1989; Cronaca for strings, 1991; Concerto for viola, double bass and chamber orchestra, 1994; Violin Concerto, 1994. *Recordings:* Hoichi Earless Op 17; Ballades. *Address:* TEOSTO, Lauttasaarentie 1, 0020 Helsinki 20, Finland.

NORDHEIM, Arne; Composer; b. 20 June 1931, Larvik, Norway. *Education:* Studied with Conrad Baden and Bjarne Brustad at Oslo Conservatory and with Vagn Holmboe in Copenhagen in 1955. *Career:* Critic for Dagbladet of Oslo, 1960–68; Lecturer on and performer of live electronic music; mem, Royal Swedish Academy of Music, 1975; Honorary Member, ISCM, 1996. *Compositions include:* Epigram for string quartet, 1954; String Quartet, 1956; Canzona for orchestra, 1961; Katharsis, ballet on legend of St Anthony for orchestra and tape, 1962; Kimare, ballet, 1963; Epitaffio for orchestra and tape, 1963; Favola, musical play, 1965; Three Responses, 1967; Eco for soprano, chorus and orchestra, 1968; Incidental music for Peer Gynt, 1969; Dinosaurus for accordion and tape, 1971; Doria for tenor and orchestra, 1975; Ballets: Strender, Ariadne And The Tempest, 1974–79; Tempora Noctis for soprano, mezzo, orchestra and tape, 1979; Aurora for soloists, chorus, 2 percussion and tape, 1984; Tenebrae, concerto for cello and orchestra, 1985; Magma for orchestra, 1988; Monolith for orchestra, 1990; Violin Concerto, 1996; Nidaros, oratorium, 1996. *Recordings:* Epitaffio; Doria; Greening; Tempest Suite. *Honours:* Nordic Councils Musical Prize, 1972; Henrik Steffens, 1992; Commander, Royal Order of St Olav, 1997. *Address:* Wergelandsveien 2, 0167 Oslo, Norway.

NORDIN, Birgit; Singer (Soprano); b. 22 Feb. 1934, Sangis, Norrbotten, Sweden. *Education:* Studied at the Stockholm Opera School and with Lina Pagliughi in Italy. *Career:* Debut: Stockholm in 1957 as Oscar in Un Ballo in Maschera; Annual visits to the Drottningholm Opera from 1960 notably in operas by Mozart; Sang at Wexford Festival in 1963 and 1965, and Glyndebourne Festival in 1968 as Blondchen in Die Entführung; Sang Jenny in Weill's Mahagonny at Copenhagen in 1970, Berlin in 1970 as soloist in Bach's St Matthew Passion and Christmas Oratorio; Television appearance as Berg's Lulu and sang the Queen of Night in Bergman's film version of The Magic Flute in 1974; Oratorio engagements in Scandinavia, Germany, England and Austria; Has sung with the Royal Opera Stockholm on tour to Covent Garden in 1990 and the Edinburgh Festival; Other roles include Mozart's Susanna and Pamina, Gilda, Rosina, Sophie in Der Rosenkavalier and Mélisande; Sang Angelica in Handel's Orlando at Stockholm, 2000. *Recordings:* Die Zauberflöte; Madrigals by Monteverdi; Video of Don Giovanni, as Donna Elvira. *Honours:* Swedish Court Singer, 1973. *Address:* c/o Kungliga Teatern, PO Box 16094, 10322 Stockholm, Sweden.

NORDIN, Lena; Singer (Soprano); b. 18 Feb. 1956, Visby, Sweden. *Education:* Studied voice and piano at the College of Music in Malmö and Stockholm, and in Salzburg, Florence and Siena. *Career:* Debut: Verdi's Luisa Miller; Member of soloist ensemble of the Royal Opera in Stockholm, 1987; Has performed numerous roles including: Cleopatra, Donna Anna, Antonia, Lauretta, Marguerite, Constanze, Violetta, Maria Stuarda, Contessa, Nedda, Norma and Sophie; Has also sung at the Drottningholm Court Theatre (Dido, and Regina in Soler's Cosa Rara); Sang Strauss's Daphne in Salzburg and Marguerite at Savonlinna Festival; Has guested Wexford Opera Festival twice, including as Aspasia in Mozart's Mitridate, 1989; Other roles include Adele, Countessa di Folleville in Rossini's Il viaggio a Reims and Donna

Elvira; Has sung as a regular guest in Copenhagen, and also in Dresden, London, Moscow and Seville; Has sung Violetta at the National Opera of Helsinki and Elena in Vespri Siciliani in Darmstadt; Odabella in Verdi's Attila and Die Prinzessin in Schreker's opera Das Spielwerk in Darmstadt, 2003; Concert engagements include performances in USA, France, Germany and in Scandinavia. *Recordings:* Title roles in Berwald's Estrella di Soria, Hallman's Solitär and in Naumann's Gustav Wasa; Carmina Burana; Arias by Mozart, Verdi and Gounod; Mary Stuart, Queen of Scots; CD of Mozart Concert Arias, 1996. *Honours:* Christina Nilsson Prize, 1959; Birgit Nilsson Prize, 1987; Svenska Dagblacket, Prize, 1987; Jussi Björling Prize, 1997; Royal Court Singer, King Carl Gustaf; Litteris et Artibus, King Carl Gustaf, 2003. *Current Management:* Eberhard Gross, Künsteragentur, Germany. *Address:* Östermalmsg 3, 11424 Stockholm, Sweden. *Website:* lenanordinsoprano.homestead.com.

NORDMO-LOVBERG, Aase; Singer (Soprano) and Administrator; b. 10 June 1923, Malselv, Norway. *Education:* Studied with Hjaldis Ingebjart in Oslo. *Career:* Debut: Concert debut in 1948, and operatic debut in 1952 as Imogen in Cymbeline by Arne Eggens; Member of the Royal Opera Stockholm, 1953–69 with debut as Elisabeth in Tannhäuser; Vienna Staatsoper in 1957 as Sieglinde in Die Walküre; Concert appearances in London, Philadelphia and Paris, 1957; Metropolitan Opera, 1959–61 as Elsa in Lohengrin, Eva, Sieglinde and Leonore; Bayreuth Festival, 1960 as Elsa and Sieglinde; Sang at the Stora Theatre Gothenburg in 1963 and 1967 as Elisabeth and Tosca; Engagements at the Drottningholm Court Theatre included Angelica in Handel's Orlando; Professor at the Oslo Music School from 1970 and Director of The Oslo Opera, 1978–81. *Recordings include:* Excerpts from the 1960 Bayreuth Festival. *Honours:* Gold Medal for Singing, Harriet Cohen International Music Award, 1958; Orde Van Oranje-Nassau, 1963; Officer of L'Ordre de Leopold II, 1964; Commander, St Olavs Orden, 1981; Commander, Kungl Nordstjerne Orden, 1986.

NORDSTROM, Hans-Henrik; Composer; b. 26 June 1947, Nakskov, Denmark; m. Anne Kristine Smith, 1 s. *Education:* Royal Danish Academy of Music, Copenhagen, 1965–70. *Career:* Debut: Copenhagen, 1990; mem, Danish Composers Society. *Compositions:* Kybikos (wind band), 1989–90; That Autumn, (orchestra) 1990–91; The Mountains in Monestiés (sinfonietta), 1988; Tripthychos (3 double basses and sinfonietta), 1989–90; Dialogue (tuba and percusion), 1991; Srebrenica (organ), 1993; Tympanon (3 percussion), 1993; Reflections I, (sextet), 1992; Reflections II (violin and harp), 1992; Reflections III (flugelhorn and piano), 1993; Night (choir), 1992; Clockwork and Raindrops (sextet), 1991; Room/Space, String Quartet I, 1991–92, Seven Vignettes from Susaa (sinfonietta), 1994; Andalusian Reflections (piano trio), 1995, Sonata per l'Inverno (piano), 1994–95, String Quartet II (Faroese), 1994; M 31 (clarinet trio), 1995–96; Songlines (sinfonietta), 1995; Carnac (sextet), 1995; Images d'autumne (flute, clarinet, bassoon), 1996; Icelandic Suite (reed quartet), 1996; Fara fram vid (clarinet), 1996; To Winter (saxophone quartet), 1996–97; Sketches from Hirsholmene (sinfonietta), 1997; La Primavera (flute, oboe, bassoon, harpsichord), 1997; La rosa, la noche y el tiempo, 1997; String Quartet III (Norwegian), 1998; Il Quadrato magico (reed quartet), 1998–99; Abstractions (saxophone, percussion), 1998; Entwicklungen (2 accordions), 1998; Flows, 1998 (3 flutes); Fantasy, (bass flute) 1998; Tres Poemas de Federico García Lorca (mezzo, clarinet, cello, harp and percussion), 1998; Birds of Susaa Are Dreaming New Songs (saxophone quartet), 1999; A Dream (flute and harpsichord), 1998–99; Gravures en taille-douce (harpsichord, 1998–99; String Quartet No. 4 (Hebredian), 1999; Asterion (violin), 1999; Mykines (sinfonietta), 2000; Limbo (violin, cello and piano), 2000; Mouvements (piano trio), 2000; Land of Shadows (bass clarinet and percussion), 2000; Light (flute and guitar), 2000; Fluctuations (4 guitars), 2000; Night Glow and Dawn Frosting (soprano and guitar), 2000; Chac (organ), 2001; Lost Traces (saxophone and percussion), 2001; The Twelve Bens (string trio), 2001; In the Woods (violin and sinfonietta), 2001; Nada y todo (recorder quartet), 2001; Imaginations (harpsc.) 2002; "..if a Tone in the Night" (recorder and accordian) 2002; Growth (brass quintet) 2002; Fair Isle (cello, 12 ww and 4 french horns) 2002; Riverrun (Sinfonietta) 2002; Quarks (String Trio) 2002; Tingsomingenting (guitar) 2003; A.L.P. (fl, cl, gt, perc and vl) 2003; Following the Wake (piano trio) 2003; Sketches from Iceland (pno quartet) 2003; Morning Knight (Mezzo, rec., sax and perc) 2003; A.L.P. Too (viola and guitar) 2003; Nuages d'automne (trombone and sinfonietta) 2003–4; Nuvele Italiane (piano) 2004; Nuages Élégique (trombone) 2004. *Recordings:* Many CDs including Hans-Henrik Nordstroem 1 (Portrait CD), 1997; Hans-Henrik Nordstroem 2 (Portrait CD), 1999; Hans Henrik Nordstroem III (Portrait CD), 2001; Hans-Henrik Nordstrøm 4, "In the Woods" (portrait CD) 2003. *Honours:* Grant, Danish Art Foundation, 1990–; Artistic Director, Contemporary Music in Susaa Festivals, held in August every year since 1993–; Danish Composers' Society's Grant 2001; Wilhelm Hansen Foundation's Grant 2003; Composer of the Year 2003 in Bornholm Music Festival; Composer of the Year in Birkeroed, 2004. *Address:* Skovmarksvej 52, Vetterslev, DK–4100 Ringsted, Denmark. *Website:* www.nordstroem.dk.

NOREJKA, Virgilius; Singer (Tenor) and Administrator; b. 22 Sept. 1935, Siaulai, Lithuania. *Education:* Studied in Vilnius. *Career:* Debut: State Opera of Vilnius, 1957 as Lensky in Eugene Onegin; Sang in Lithuania as Alfredo, the Duke in Rigoletto, Werther, Don José, Almaviva and The Prince in The Love For Three Oranges; Guest appearances in Moscow, Leningrad, Kiev and Kharkov; Gave recitals and sang Russian folksongs, in addition to operatic repertoire; Further engagements at the Berlin Staatsoper and in Poland, Bulgaria, Denmark, Finland, Italy, Austria, Hungary, USA and Canada; Sang Radames at Hamburg Staatsoper and also appeared in operas by Lithuanian composers; Director of the Vilnius Opera, 1975–. *Recordings:* Various. *Address:* Av Rómulo Gallegos, Edf Residencias, Santa Rosa, Apt 4-B, Sebucan, Caracas 1071, Venezuela.

NORGÅRD, Per; Composer; b. 13 July 1932, Gentofte, Denmark. *Education:* Degrees in Music History, Music Theory and Composition, Royal Danish Academy of Music, 1952–55; Studied with Nadia Boulanger, Paris, France, 1956–57. *Career:* Teaching positions at Odense Conservatoire, 1958–61, Royal Academy of Music, 1960–65, Royal Academy of Music, Århus, 1965; Terrains Vagues premiered by the BBC Symphony Orchestra, 2001. *Compositions include:* Operas: Gilgamesh, 1971–72, Siddharta, 1974–79, The Divine Circus, 1982; Nuit des Hommes, 1995; Orchestral: Symphony No. 1, 1953–55, Voyage Into The Golden Screen, 1968–69, Twilight, 1976–77, Symphony No. 3 in 2 Movements, 1972–75, No. 4, 1981, No. 5, 1990, Spaces Of Time, 1991; Symphony No. 6, 1999; String and Wind orchestras: Metamorphosis, 1953, Modlys, 1970; Chamber: 8 String Quartets, 1952–97; Fragment V, 1961, Prelude And Ant Fugue (With A Crab Cannon), 1982, Lin for clarinet, cello and piano, 1986; Solo keyboard: Sonata in One Movement, 1953, Canon, 1971; Choral: Evening Land, 1954, Frost Psalm, 1975–76, Interrupted Hymn, Scream, Drinking Song; Piano Concerto, 1995; Terrains Vagues for orchestra, 2001; Solo instruments and orchestra: Between, 3 movements for cello and orchestra, 1985, Helle Nacht, violin concerto, 1987, King, Queen and Ace for harp and 13 instruments, 1989; Percussion: Iching, solo, 1982; 9 Symphonies, 1958–90; Violin Concerto No. 2, 1993; Viola Concerto, 1995; Organ Concerto No. 2, 1996; Elf's Mirror for solo voices, chorus and orchestra, 1996; 9 string quartets, 1955–94. *Recordings:* Much of his work recorded and available on CD. *Honours:* Numerous honours including Nordic Council Prize for Music for opera Gilgamesh, 1974; Sonning Music Prize; Holds several Honorary posts. *Address:* Koda, Maltegårdsvej 24, 2820 Gentofte, Denmark.

NORHOLM, Ib; Composer; b. 24 Jan. 1931, Copenhagen, Denmark. *Education:* The Royal Danish Academy of Music, Copenhagen. *Career:* Music Critic with several major Copenhagen Newspapers; Professor of Composition, The Royal Danish Academy of Music; Organist in Copenhagen. *Compositions include:* Stanzas And Fields; Strofer Og Marker; Trio Op 22; Fluctuations, The Unseen Pan; Exile, Music For A Composition for Large Orchestra; From My Green Herbarium; September-October-November; After Icarus; Tavole Per Orfeo; Invitation To A Beheading, 1965; Isola Bella, 1968–70; Den Unge Park, 1969–70; Day's Nightmare, 1973; Violin Concerto, 1974; Heretic Hymn, 1975; The Garden Wall, 1976; The Funen Cataracts, 1976; Essai Prismatique, 1979; Lys, 1979; Decreation, 1979; The Elements; Moralities–Or There May Be Several Miles To The Nearest Spider; Ecliptic Instincts; Apocalyptic Idylls, 1980; Before Silence, 1980; Haven Med Steir Der Deler Sig, 1982. *Recordings:* Much of his work recroded. *Current Management:* Koda, Maltegårdsvej 24, 2820 Gentofte, Denmark. *Address:* Henningsens Allé 30B, 2900 Hellerup, Denmark.

NORMAN, Daniel; Singer (tenor); b. 1970, England. *Education:* Chorister at Lichfiled Cathedral; Britten-Pears school, with Hugues Cuenod, Anthony Rolfe Johnson and Ernst Haefliger; Royal Academy of Music with Diane Forlano. *Career:* Albert Herring with New Kent Opera; Ariadne auf Naxos with LSO/ Sir Simon Rattle and Paris Opera; Adès's Powder Her Face with Almeida Opera, Aldeburgh Festival, Channel 4, Opera Boston and in Vienna; Monteverdi's Poppea and Ulisse with Bavarian State Opera, Holland; Turn of the Screw with Porto 2000; Acis, Alcina and Arne's Alfred with The Early Opera Company; Concerts and Song recitals in all major venues in Britain. *Recordings:* Billy Budd, LSO/ Hickox; Hyperion Schubert Edition, Graham Johnson; Hugh Wood's Comus, BBCSO/ Davies; Brett Dean's Winter Songs, Berlin Philharmonic Wind Quintet. *Current Management:* Askonas Holt Ltd, Lonsdale Chambers, 27 Chancery Lane, London, WC2A 1PF, England. *Telephone:* (20) 7400-1700. *Fax:* (20) 7400-1799. *E-mail:* info@askonasholt.co.uk. *Website:* www.askonasholt.co.uk.

NORMAN, Jessye, BM, MMus; American concert and opera singer (soprano); b. 15 Sept. 1945, Augusta, GA. *Education:* Howard University, Washington, DC, Peabody Conservatory, University of Michi-

gan. *Career:* operatic debuts with Deutsche Oper, Berlin 1969, La Scala, Milan 1972; title role in Ariadne auf Naxos, 1985; Royal Opera House, Covent Garden, 1972; New York Metropolitan Opera, as Cassandra in Les Troyens, 1983; American debut, Hollywood Bowl, 1972; Lincoln Center, New York City, 1973; First Covent Garden recital, 1980; Debut at Barbican, 1983; Tours include North and South America, Europe, Middle East, Australia and Israel; Many international festivals including Aix-en-Provence, Aldeburgh, Berlin, Edinburgh, Flanders, Helsinki, Lucerne, Salzburg, Tanglewood, Spoleto, Hollywood, Ravinia; Roles include Verdi's Aida, Wagner's Elisabeth and Strauss's Ariadne; Opened the season at Chicago in 1989, as Gluck's Alcestis; Sang Sieglinde in Die Walküre at the Metropolitan, 1990 (also televised); Sang Janáček's Emilia Marty at the Met, 1996; Gave the premiere of Judith Weir's woman. life. song at Carnegie Hall, 2000; La Voix Humaine by Poulenc in Paris, 2002; Concert repertory includes Les Nuits d'été by Berlioz. *Recordings include:* Le nozze di Figaro, La Finta Giardiniera, Fidelio, Carmen, Haydn's La Vera Costanza, Ariadne, Verdi's Un Giorno di Regno and Il Corsaro, Schubert Lieder, Das Lied von der Erde; Alceste, Oedipus Rex, Debussy's La Demoiselle Élue; Mahler's 2nd Symphony; Les Contes d'Hoffmann, Euryanthe; Fauré's Pénélope; Die Walküre; Elektra, conducted by Claudio Abbado. *Address:* c/o Shaw Concerts Incorporated, 1995 Broadway, New York, NY 10023, USA.

NORRINGTON, Sir Roger Arthur Carver, Kt; Musical Director; b. 16 March 1934, Oxford, England; m. (1) Susan Elizabeth McLean, May 1964, divorced 1982, 1 s., 1 d., (2) Karolyn Mary Lawrence, June 1984. *Education:* Westminster; BA, Clare College, Cambridge; Royal College of Music. *Career:* Debut: British, 1962, BBC radio, 1964, Television, 1967, Germany, Austria, Denmark, Finland, 1966, Portugal, 1970, Italy, 1971, France and Belgium, 1972, USA, 1974, Netherlands, 1975, Switzerland, 1976; Freelance Singer, 1962–72; Musical Director for Schütz Choir of London, 1962–, London Baroque Players, 1975–, London Classical Players, 1978–97; Principal Conductor for Kent Opera, 1966–84 and Bournemouth Sinfonietta, 1985–89; Guest Conductor for many British, European and American Orchestras; Many television specials and broadcasts in the United Kingdom and abroad; Conducted the British stage premiere of Rameau's Les Boréades, Royal Academy of Music, 1985, Die Zauberflöte at the 1990 Promenade Concerts and a series of Beethoven Symphonies on BBC television, 1991; Conducted the London Classical Players in Mozart's Prague Symphony and Requiem at Prom Concerts in 1991; Season 1992 with Rossini Bicentenary concert at Fisher Hall, NY; Conducted Beethoven's Missa Solemnis at the Albert Hall, London, December 1995; Mozart's Mitridate at Salzburg (1997) and Haydn songs with the London Philharmonic Orchestra at South Bank; Engaged for Die Zauberflöte at the Vienna State Opera, 2000; Conducted Camerata Salzburg at the London Proms, 2002. *Recordings:* Numerous with London Classical Players including Die Zauberflöte, Beethoven's 2nd and 8th Symphonies, Schütz St Matthew Passion and Resurrection, Bruckner Mass No. 2, and Don Giovanni in 1993. *Contributions:* Occasional articles and reviews in musical journals. *Honours:* Cavaliere, Order al Merito della Repubblica Italiana, 1981; Gramophone Award, 1987; Opus Award, 1987; Ovation Award, 1988.

NORRIS, David Owen, BMus, FRCO, FRAM; British pianist and broadcaster; b. 16 June 1953, Northampton, England; two s. *Education:* Keble College, Oxford, RAM, studied in Paris, France. *Career:* Professor, RAM 1978–; Repetiteur at Covent Garden and Asst MD at RSC–1980; television appearances in Europe and N. America; performances at Wood Promenade Concerts; Chair. of Faculty, Steans Inst. for Singers, Chicago 1992–; Artistic Dir Cardiff Festival 1992–; Gresham Prof. of Music 1993–. *Honours:* first ever Gilmore Artist 1991. *Address:* 60 Old Oak Lane, London, NW10 6UB, England.

NORRIS, Geoffrey; Critic and Musicologist; b. 19 Sept. 1947, London, England. *Education:* ARCM, 1967; BA, University of Durham, 1969; University of Liverpool, 1969–70, 1972–73; Institute of Theatre, Music and Cinematography, Leningrad, 1971. *Career:* Music Critic for The Times, Daily Telegraph; Lecturer in Music History, Royal Northern College of Music, 1975–77; Commissioning Editor, New Oxford Companion to Music, 1977–83; Music Critic, The Daily Telegraph, 1983; Chief Music Critic, 1995–, Daily Telegraph; mem Royal Musical Association; The Critics' Circle. *Publications include:* Encyclopedia of Opera, co-author, 1976; Rachmaninov, 1976, 2nd edition, 1993; Shostakovich: The Man and His Music, co-author, 1982; A Catalogue of the Compositions of S Rachmaninov, co-author, 1982. *Contributions:* New Grove Dictionary of Music and Musicians, 1980, 2001; Musical Times; Music Quarterly; Tempo; Music and Letters; BBC Broadcasts. *Address:* The Daily Telegraph 1 Canada Square, Canary Wharf, London E14 5DT, England.

NORTH, Nigel; British lutenist, classical guitarist and professor of lute; b. 5 June 1954, London, England. *Education:* Guildhall School of Music, Royal College of Music, studied with John Williams, Carlos Bonell,

Francis Baines, Michael Schaffer in Germany. *Career:* performances from 1973 with the Early Music Consort of London, Academy of Ancient Music, Schütz Choir of London and Early Opera Project with Roger Norrington, Kent Opera, English Concert with Pinnock, Taverner Players, London Baroque, Trio Sonnerie, Raglan Baroque Players, and The Sixteen Choir and Orchestra; Professor of Lute at the Guildhall School from 1976; Solo debut at Wigmore Hall in 1977 with Bach recital on lute and played at Bach 300th anniversary concerts in London, 1985 with Maggie Cole; Solo recitals and tours from 1977 world-wide; Accompanist to such singers as Alfred Deller and Emma Kirkby; Summer Academies include The Lute Society of America, 1980–88 and Trio Sonnerie Summer School, 1989; Masterclasses, lectures and workshops in Sardinia, Rome, Venice, Vancouver, New York and San Francisco. *Recordings:* As soloist, music by Robert de Visée, Dowland, Bach and Vivaldi; Albums of Monteverdi, Handel, Purcell, Corelli and Vivaldi with London Baroque, Taverner Players, The English Concert, Academy of Ancient Music, Raglan Baroque Players, Trio Sonnerie and The Sixteen Choir and Orchestra (Monteverdi Vespers, 1988); Music by Bach, 1990s. *Publications:* Lute Music By William Byrd, 1976; Lute Music by Alfonso Ferrabosco, 1979; Continuo Playing on Lute, Archlute and Theorbo, 1987.

NORTH, Roger (Dudley); Composer, Writer and Tutor; b. 1 Aug. 1926, Warblington, Hampshire, England; m. Rosamund Shreeves, 3 April 1965, 2 d. *Education:* Oxford University, 1943–44; Royal Academy of Music, 1947–51; LRAM, 1951. *Career:* Various small choir and orchestra conductorship posts, 1950–56; Evening Institute teaching, 1951–; Morley College, 1963–91; Approximately 100 broadcast talks for BBC, 1960–70; mem, British Academy of Composers and Songwriters. *Compositions:* Sonata for clarinet and piano, published around 1956; Salle d'Attente Suite, 1977; Film Music: Music for Dance and Theatre; 1 Act Opera (performed but not published). *Recordings:* Salle d'Attente, ballet suite, 1977. *Publications:* The Musical Companion, Book I, 1977; ABC of Music (Musical Companion), 1979; Wagner's Most Subtle Art, 1996. *Contributions:* Thematic Unity in Parsifal to Wagner Society Magazine; The Rhinegold–The Music to English National Opera Guide, 1985. *Honours:* William Wallace Exhibition, Royal Academy of Music, 1949; Battison Haynes Prize for Composition, Royal Academy of Music, 1949; Oliviera Prescott Gift for Composition, Royal Academy of Music, 1950. *Address:* 24 Strand on the Green, London W4 3PH, England.

NORTHCOTT, Bayan (Peter); Music Critic and Composer; b. 24 April 1940, Harrow-on-the-Hill, Middlesex, England. *Education:* BA, Dip ED, University College, Oxford; BMus, University of Southampton. *Career:* Music Critic for the New Statesman, 1973–76, Sunday Telegraph, 1976–86 and The Independent, 1986–; mem, Music Section, Critics Circle, 1974–92. *Compositions include:* Hymn to Cybele, 1983; Sextet, 1985; Concerto for horn and ensemble, 1996; Instrumental music and songs. *Contributions:* New Grove Dictionary of Music and Musicians, 1980; Music and Musicians; The Listener; Musical Times; Daily Telegraph; Guardian; Tempo; Dansk Musiktidsskrift; BBC Music Magazine, including articles on Goehr, Tippett, Maw, Davies, Carter, Jonathon Harvey and Poulenc. *Address:* 52 Upper Mall, London, W6, England.

NORUP, Bent; Singer (Baritone); b. 7 Dec. 1936, Hobro, Denmark. *Education:* Studied with Kristian Rils in Copenhagen, with Karl Schmitt-Walter in Munich and with Herta Sperber in New York. *Career:* Debut: Copenhagen in 1970 as Kurwenal in Tristan und Isolde; Sang at The Royal Theatre of Copenhagen, 1970–73, Brunswick, 1973–78, Nuremburg, 1978–, Hannover, 1981–, Bayreuth Festival, 1983, San Antonio Festival, 1985 and guest appearances in leading roles world-wide including Vienna, London, Paris, Hamberg, Berlin, Düsseldorf, Hannover, France, Spain, Netherlands, Poland, Ireland and USA; Roles include Holländer, Telramund, Amfortas, Klingsor, Wotan, Sachs, Pizarro, Jochanaan, Iago, Scarpia, and Borromeo; Sang Telramund in Lohengrin at Venice in 1990, and Klingsor at Århus in 1992; Sang Telramund in Logengrin at Naples, 1995; Ludwigsburg Festival 2000, as Abner in Nielsen's Saul and David (concert); Well known as concert singer. *Recordings include:* Orestes in Elektra. *Address:* Royal Opera, Copenhagen, Denmark.

NOSEDA, Gianandrea; Conductor; b. 1965, Milan, Italy. *Education:* Milan Conservatoire, and with Myung-Wha Chung in Siena. *Career:* Principal Conductor of the Orchestra Sinfonica di Milano, from 1994; Principal Guest Conductor at the Mariinsky Theatre, St Petersburg, 1997; Principal Conductor of the Orquesta de Cadaques and Principal Guest of the Rotterdam Philharmonic, 1999; Repertoire includes La Sonnambula, Der fliegende Holländer, Le nozze di Figaro, Don Carlos and Sleeping Beauty; Conducted the Kirov Ballet at Covent Garden, 2000; Complete Prokofiev Piano Concertos with the Orchestra Sinfonica di Milano; Guest at the Cheltenham Festival, 2000, with the BBC Symphony, at the Teatro Real, Madrid, and the Salle Pleyel, Paris; Principal Conductor, BBC Philharmonic Orchestra, July 2002–; Conducted the BBC Philharmonic at the London Proms, 2002. *Address:* c/o

Kirov Opera, Mariinsky Theatre, 1 Theatre Square, St Petersburg, Russia.

NOSEK, Václav; Conductor; b. 5 April 1921, Stary Plzenec, Czechoslovakia; m. 15 July 1950, 1 d. *Education:* Composition and Conducting, Conservatory; International course with Clemens Krauss, Salzburg. *Career:* debut, Plzeň Theatre; Conductor, Playwright, theatre and opera, Plzeň, Ustí n/L, Brno, Prague National Theatre Ceske Budejovice (South Bohemia); Appeared on radio in operas and concerts, especially 20th music by A. Berg, Schonberg, Prokofiev, Shostakovich, Honegger, Britten, Dessau and other composers; Many premieres of contemporary operas, including Martinů's Les Larmes du Couteau and Les Trois Souhaits, also ballet Le Raid de Veilleux; mem, Societas Janáček. *Recordings:* B. Martinů: Les Trois Souhaits, The Marriage, The Ballets. *Contributions:* Many articles on B. Martinů and L. Janáček to specialist music reviews. *Honours:* Honorary Member, Societas Martinů. *Address:* c/o Prague National Theatre, PO Box 865, 11230 Prague, Czech Republic.

NOSSEK, Carola; Singer (Soprano); b. 10 Feb. 1949, Schwerin, Germany. *Education:* Studied in Dresden and Schwerin. *Career:* Debut: Dresden Staatsoper, 1972, as Nanette in Lortzing's Der Wildschütz; Berlin Staatsoper from 1975, as Marenka in The Bartered Bride, Mozart's Servilia and Despino, Marzelline in Fidelio and Echo in Ariadne; Orff's Die Kluge, 1990, Susanna, 1991, and Nuri in Tiefland, 1995; Guest at Las Palmas Festival and elsewhere; Concert repertory includes songs by Hanns Eisler and Schubert's Lazarus. *Address:* c/o Berlin Staatsoper, Unter den Linden 7, 1060 Berlin, Germany.

NOTARE, Karen; Singer (soprano); b. 1961, USA. *Education:* Manhattan School of Music, New York. *Career:* Debut: Madama Butterfly for New York City Opera, 1987; European debut as Leoncavallo's Zaza, at the 1990 Wexford Festival; Tosca with Greater Miami Opera and the Royal Danish Opera, Mimi at Nice, Desdemona in Hong Kong and Mariella in Mascagni's Piccola Marat at the 1992 Wexford Festival; Bonn Opera from 1994, as Manon Lescaut, Donna Elvira, and Lisa in The Queen of Spades; Concerts with the Pittsburgh and Cincinnati Symphonies, Verdi Requiem with the Eastern Connecticut Symphony Orchestra; Season 1996 with the Trovatore Leonora for Fort Worth Opera, and Tosca with Opera Zuid, Netherlands; Season 1999 as Salome in Dublin and as Santuzza in Auckland. *Current Management:* Athole Still International Management, Forresters Hall, 25–27 Westow Street, London, SE19 3RY, England. *Telephone:* (20) 8771-5271. *Fax:* (20) 8768-6600. *Website:* www.atholestill.com.

NOTT, Jonathan; Conductor; b. 1962, Solihull, England. *Education:* Choral scholar at St John's College, Cambridge, 1981–84; Royal Northern College of Music, 1984–86; National Opera Studio, 1986–87. *Career:* Repetiteur then Conductor at the Frankfurt Opera from 1988; First Kapellmeister of Wiesbaden Opera and Symphony Orchestra 1991–, with repertoire of leading works from composers such as Verdi, Mozart, Puccini, Rossini, Wagner; Conducted premieres of Elektra, Tosca, Aida; Conducted Der Ring des Nibelungen with Siegfried Jerusalem and Janis Martin as part of Centenary Maifestspiele; Music Director, Luzern Opera and Symphony Orchestra, 1997–; Founding Conductor, Dresden Symphoniker, 1998; Guest appearances with major German orchestras, Bergen Philharmonic and London Sinfonietta; Regular concerts with Ensemble Modern and Ensemble Intercontemporain; Russian and French premieres of Henze Requiem; World premieres include Brian Ferneyhough, Wolfgang Rhim and Helmut Lachenmann; Frequent collaborator with Ligeti and a major exponent of his works. *Recordings:* With ASKO Ensemble, Moscow Philharmonic and Luzerner Sinfonieorchester. *Address:* Luzerner Sinfonieorchester, Zentralstrasse 44, 6003 Luzern, Switzerland.

NOVIKOV, Leo; Violinist and Violin Teacher; b. 11 July 1964, Moscow, Russia; m. Tanya Novikov, 1 April 1989, 3 s. *Education:* Moscow State Institute of Music; Music College, Moscow Conservatoire; Special Secondary Music School, Moscow Conservatoire. *Career:* Debut: Solo Recital, Tbilisy Conservatoire, Georgia, with State Chamber Orchestra, 1989; Many solo performances in Moscow, Georgia, Latvia, 1989–92; Solo Performance in television link-up broadcast from Moscow, 1990; Rank and file violinist, Moscow Philharmonic Orchestra, Solo performer with Solo Performers Chamber Orchestra of Moscow Philharmonic, 1990–93; Senior Teacher, Australian Institute of Music, 1993–; Solo performances in Concert Hall of Sydney Opera House, 1996, 1997, and on national television; Conducted first experimental masterclasses on television; mem, Musicians' Union of Australia; Australian String Teachers Association. *Recordings:* First solo CD recording, 1997. *Address:* 915 Anzac Parade, Naroubra, Sydney, NSW 2035, Australia.

NOVOA, Salvador; Singer (Tenor) and Voice Teacher; b. 30 Oct. 1937, Mexico City, Mexico; m. 16 Aug 1968, 3 s., 1 d. *Education:* School of Music, The University of Mexico, 1957–62; Voice with Felipe Aquilera Ruiz, 1957–66; Kurt Baum, 1972–80. *Career:* Debut: As Pinkerton in Madama Butterfly, Mexico Opera Company, 1960; Erik in Der fliegende

Holländer with the Philadelphia Lyric Opera; Several roles in various operas with the New York City Opera including: Don José and Cavaradossi, the title roles in Bomarzo and Don Rodrigo, Faust in Mefistofele and Edgardo in Lucia di Lammermoor; He has appeared with opera companies widely including San Diego Opera, Houston Grand Opera, Boston Opera, Cincinnati Opera, Teatro Col ón, Argentina, Opera Municipal de Marseille, Stuttgart Opera Company, Tehran; His repertoire includes: Radames, Andrea Chénier; Bomarzo (Pier Francesco), Carmen (Don José), Cavalleria Rusticana (Turiddu); Don Rodrigo, Faust, Macbeth, Macduff, Faust in Mefistofele; Pollione in Norma; Samson in Samson and Delilah; Numerous other roles in various operas; Symphonic repertoire includes, Beethoven's Ninth Symphony and Verdi's Messa da requiem. *Recordings:* Bomarzo by Alberto Ginastera, CBS Records. *Honours:* 2nd Prize, Metropolitan Opera Regional Auditions, Mexico City, 1959. *Address:* 4 Cedargate Lane, Westport, CT 06880-3759, USA.

NOVOTNY, Jan; Pianist; b. 15 Dec. 1935, Prague, Czechoslovakia; m. 26 April 1985, 2 d. *Education:* Prague Conservatory, 1950–55; Academy of Music Arts, Prague, 1955–59. *Career:* Debut: Prague, 1954; Concert performances world-wide with frequent appearances at Prague Spring Festival, Festival de Bonaguil, France and on Radio Prague, Bern, Gothenburg, Brussels, Paris and TV Prague; Chairman of the Jury, Smetana Piano Competition, Czech Republic; Head, Piano Classes Department, Prague Conservatory, 1988–95; President, Smetana Society, 1991. *Recordings:* Beethoven's Sonatas Op 10 No3, Op 22, Op 28, Op 31 No. 1; Smetana's Complete Piano Works, 10 records, 7 CDs; Schumann's Phantasie C major Op 17; FX Dussek's Piano Concertos; st Piano Sonatas; Jaroslav Jezek's Complete Piano Works; Ignaz Moscheles' Concerto No. 5 Op 87 in C minor; JL Dussek's Last Piano Sonatas and Piano Concertos with Prague Chamber Philharmonic Orchestra. *Publications:* Smetana: Piano Compositions, in 7 vols, complete edition 1st time in history. *Contributions:* Gramorevue, Prague. *Honours:* State Prize, 1984; Annual Prize of Panton Editor, Prague, 1987. *Address:* 34 Craven Street, Prague 5, 153 00, Czech Republic.

NOWACK, Hans; Singer (Bass); b. 1930, Waldenburg, Germany. *Education:* Completed vocal studies 1956. *Career:* Sang at Heidelberg Opera from 1959, Bielefeld 1961 and Bremen Opera 1963–66; Essen Opera from 1967, with guest engagements at Vienna, Barcelona, Mexico, Venice, Lisbon and New Orleans; Roles have included Osmin, Sarastro, Kaspar in Der Freischütz, Gurnemanz, Hunding, Rocco and Ochs; Further visits to Hamburg, Munich, Berlin and Warsaw, as Jupiter in Rameau's Platée, Marke, the Commendatore, Daland, Boris Godunov and Hindemith's Cardillac. *Address:* Theater Essen, Rolandstrasse 10, W-4300 Essen 1, Germany.

NOWAK, Grzegorz; conductor; b. 1951, Poland. *Education:* Poznan Academy of Music, Eastman School of Music, Rochester, Tanglewood with Bernstein, Ozawa, Leinsdorf and Markevitch. *Career:* Music Director for Slupsk Symphony Orchestra, 1976–80; Won first prize in 1984 at Ansermet Conducting Competition, Geneva; Engagements followed with London Symphony, Montreal Symphony and Orchestre National de France; Has also appeared with orchestras of Rome, Oslo, Stockholm, Copenhagen, Helsinki, Monte Carlo, Jerusalem, Madrid, Lisbon, Baltimore, Cincinnati, San Diego, Vancouver, Ottawa, Tokyo, Hong Kong, Geneva, Zürich, Baden-Baden, Milan, Saarbrücken, Rotterdam, Florence, Göteborg, Malmö, Birmingham, Liverpool, Bournemouth, Manchester, Belfast and Glasgow; Music Director of the Biel Symphony Orchestra, Switzerland; Led the Polish premiere of Simon Boccanegra, Warsaw, 1997. *Recordings:* Ravel's Daphnis et Chloe and Bartók's Dance Suite with the London Symphony Orchestra. *Honours:* American Patronage Prize, 1984; Europaischen Förderpreis für Musik, 1985.

NUCCI, Leo; Singer (Baritone); b. 16 April 1942, Castiglione dei Pepoli, Bologna, Italy; m. Adriana Anelli. *Education:* Studied with Giuseppe Marchesi and Ottaviano Bizzarri. *Career:* Debut: Spoleto in 1967 as Rossini's Figaro; Sang Puccini's Schaunard at Venice in 1975, at La Scala Milan in 1976 as Figaro, at Covent Garden in 1978 as Miller in Luisa Miller and Metropolitan Opera from 1980 as Renato in Un Ballo in Maschera, Eugene Onegin, Germont, Amonasro and Posa in Don Carlos; Sang at Paris Opéra in 1981 as Renato and at Pesaro in 1984 in a revival of Rossini's Il Viaggio a Reims; Wiesbaden in 1985 as Rigoletto, at Salzburg Festival, 1989–90 as Renato, Turin in 1990 as Silvio in Pagliacci and Parma as Di Luna in Il Trovatore; Sang Iago in concert performances of Otello at Chicago and New York in 1991; Season 1992 as Luna at Turin, Tonio at Rome, Iago at Reggio Emilia, the Forza Don Carlo at Florence and Rossini's Figaro at the Festival of Caracalla; Sang Dulcamara at Turin, 1994; Sang Rossini's Figaro at the Verona Arena, 1996; Sang Macbeth at Buenos Aires, 1998; Season 2000–01 as Germont at Verona, Count Luna at La Scala, Verdi's Franesco Foscari for the San Carlo Opera, Naples, and Nabucco at the Vienna Staatsoper. *Recordings:* Donizetti's Maria di Rudenz; Ford in Falstaff; Il Viaggio a Reims;

Aida; Simon Boccanegra; Otello; Rigoletto; Michonnet in Adriana Lecouvreur; Video of Il Barbiere di Siviglia, from the Metropolitan;. *Address:* c/o Allied Artists Agency, 42 Montpelier Square, London SW7 1JZ, England.

NUNEMAKER, Richard E., BS, MM; American clarinettist and saxophonist; b. 30 Nov. 1942, Buffalo, NY; m. Lynda Perkins 1964; one s. one d. *Education:* Performer's Certificate in clarinet, State Univ. of New York Coll. at Fredonia, Univ. of Louisville; studied with Clark Brody, Jerome Stowell, James Livingston, Allen Sigel, William Willett. *Career:* bass clarinet, saxophone, Houston Symphony Orchestra 1967–; clarinet, saxophone, Houston Pops 1970–85; Cambiata Soloists 1970–84; Faculty, clarinet, saxophone, Asst Dir, Wind Ensemble, Univ. of St Thomas, Houston 1970–92; clarinet, saxophone, Music America Chamber Ensemble 1977–92; clarinet, saxophone, Pierrot Plus Ensemble, Rice Univ. 1987–92; clarinet and saxophone concertos with Lawrence Foster, Jorge Mester, Sergiu Comissiona, other conductors; frequent recitalist and soloist with chamber music ensembles on radio and TV, including new music; principal clarinet, Orquesta Filarmonica de la Ciudad de México 1987; Clarinet and Saxophone Opus 90, New Directions in American Chamber Music 1990; Carnegie debut, New and Improvised Music Concert, music of Willian Thomas McKinley 1994; European debut, tour with Camerata Bregenz, conductor Christoph Eberle, Austria 1994; mem. Int. Conference of Symphony and Opera Musicians, American Federation of Musicians, Int. Clarinet Asscn, Houston Composers' Alliance. *Recordings:* From The Great Land, Logo I, America Swings, Stompin' At The Savoy; as exec. producer: Multiplicities, Golden Petals, Magical Place of My Dreams Between Silence and Darkness, The Louisville Project (all contain music for clarinet and saxophone commissioned by Richard Nunemaker). *Publications:* If the Shoe Fits, Scales and Chords (A New Approach for all Instruments). *Honours:* Distinguished Alumni Fellow, Univ. of Louisville 2002. *Current Management:* Lyn-Rich Management, 4114 Leeshire Drive, Houston, TX 77025, USA. *Telephone:* (713) 665-8877. *Fax:* (713) 667-0283. *Address:* 4114 Leeshire Drive, Houston, TX 77025, USA (home). *E-mail:* Rnunemaker@aol.com (home).

NUSSBAUMER, Georg; Composer; b. 24 Aug. 1964, Linz, Austria; m., 1 d. *Education:* Bruckner Conservatory; Sweelinck Conservatory, Amsterdam; Studied recorder with W v Hauwe. *Career:* Work performed at Konzerthaus, Vienna, 1991, 1992, Ciurlionis Museum Kaunas, 1992, Zur Kunst der Klangzucht, Linz, 1993, Unerhörte musik, Berlin, 1996, Ars electronica, Linz, 1996, Atlas mapping, Bregenz, 1997, Melos Ethos Bratislava, 1997, Insel Musik, Berlin, 1997, Schaubühne Berlin, 1999. *Compositions:* Für einen Klavierzyklus, piano, 1994; Organ O Agie, organ, 1991; Introibo ad altare dei, installation, action, ensemble, 1995; AnArmorica, ensemble, 1996; 4 String Quartets, 1997, 1998; Icarusetude/Chopinyonnaise, piano, 1999; Der Hebel des Lichts, installation, 1999. *Recordings:* Lebenssee/3 Männer, with poet Walter Pilar. *Honours:* Prizes and Scholarships from Austrian Government; Casinos Austria Competition, recommendation. *Address:* Ottensheimerstrasse 42, 4111, Walding, Austria.

NYIKOS, Markus Andreas; cellist; b. 9 Dec. 1948, Basel, Switzerland; m. Verena Kamber 1982, one d. *Education:* Musik Akademie, Basel with Paul Szabo; Konservatorium Luzern with Stanislav Apolin; Masterclasses with Zara Nelsova, Pierre Fournier, Sándor Végh and Janáček Quartet. *Career:* cello solo at Festival of Strings Lucerne, 1974–79 and with Philharmonische Virtuosen Berlin, 1983–; Professor, Hochschule der Kunste Berlin, 1979–; Guest Professor at Shanghai Conservatory; Numerous concerts and radio appearances world-wide. *Recordings:* Vivaldi; Cello Concertos with Radio Sinfonie Orchestra Berlin; Brahms Sonatas in E minor and F major, with pianist, Gerard Wyss; Schubert's Arpeggione-Sonata in A minor with Gerard Wyss; With La Groupe Des Six, compositions by Auric, Poulenc, Honegger, and Milhaud, with pianist, Jaroslav Smykal. *Current Management:* Robert Gilder & Co., Enterprise House, 59–65 Upper Ground, London, SE1 9PQ, England. *Telephone:* (20) 7928-9008. *Fax:* (20) 7928-9755. *E-mail:* rgilder@robert-gilder.com.

NYMAN, Michael; British composer; b. 23 March 1944, London, England. *Education:* Royal Acad. of Music, King's Coll. London. *Career:* composer, writer and music critic 1968–78; lecturer 1976–80. *Film and television soundtracks:* Peter Greenaway films: 5 Postcards from Capital Cities 1967, Vertical Features Remake 1976, Goole by Numbers 1976, A Walk Through H: The Reincarnation of an Ornithologist 1978, 1–100 1978, The Falls 1980, Act of God 1980, Terence Conran 1981, The Draughtsman's Contract 1982, The Coastline 1983, Making a Splash 1984, A Zed and Two Noughts 1985, Inside Rooms: 26 Bathrooms, London & Oxfordshire 1985, Drowning by Numbers 1988, Fear of Drowning 1988, Death in the Seine 1988, The Cook, The Thief, His Wife and Her Lover 1989, Hubert Bals Handshake 1989, Prospero's Books 1991; other films: Keep it Downstairs 1976, Tom Phillips 1977, Brimstone and Treacle 1982, Nelly's Version 1983, Frozen Music 1983, The Cold Room 1984, Fairly Secret Army 1984, The Kiss 1985,

L'Ange frénétique 1985, I'll Stake My Cremona to a Jew's Trump 1986, The Disputation 1986, Ballet Méchanique 1986, Le Miraculé 1987, The Man Who Mistook His Wife for a Hat 1987, Monsieur Hire 1989, Out of the Ruins 1989, Le Mari de la coiffeuse 1990, Men of Steel 1990, Les Enfants Volants 1990, Not Mozart: Letters, Riddles and Writs 1991, The Final Score 1992, The Fall of Icarus 1992, The Piano 1993, Ryori no tetsujin 1993, Mesmer 1994, A La Folie (Six Days, Six Nights) 1994, Carrington 1995, Anne no nikki (The Diary of Anne Frank) 1995, Der Unhold (The Ogre) 1996, Enemy Zero 1996, Gattaca 1997, Titch 1998, Ravenous 1999, How to Make Dhyrak: A Dramatic Work for Three Players and Camera, Truncated with Only Two Players 1999, Wonderland 1999, Nabbie no koi (Nabbie's Love) 1999, The End of the Affair 1999, Purely Belter 2000, The Claim 2000, Act Without Words I 2000, That Sinking Feeling 2000, La Stanza del figlio 2001, Haute fidélité 2001, Subtrain 2001, 24 heures de la vie d'une femme 2002, Luminal 2002, The Man with a Movie Camera 2002, On the Trail of John Hunt Morgan 2003, The Actors 2003, Nathalie... 2003, Charged: The Life of Nikola Tesla 2003. *Other compositions:* orchestral: A Handsom, Smooth, Sweet, Smart, Clear Stroke: Or Else Play Not At All 1983, Taking a Line for a Second Walk 1986, L'Orgie Parisienne 1989, Six Celan Songs 1990, Where the Bee Dances 1991, Self Laudatory Hymn of Inanna and Her Omnipotence 1992, The Upside-Down Violin 1992, MGV (Musique à Grande Vitesse) 1993, On the Fiddle 1993, Concerto for Harpsichord and Strings 1995, Concerto for Trombone 1995, Double Concerto 1996, Strong on Oaks, Strong on the Causes of Oaks 1997, Cycle of Disquietude 1998, A Dance he Little Thinks of 2001; chamber music: First Waltz in D, Bell Set No. 1 1974, 1–100 1976, Waltz in F 1976, Think Slow, Act Fast 1981, 2 Violins 1981, Four Saxes (Real Slow Drag) 1982, I'll Stake My Cremona to a Jew's Crump 1983, Time's Up 1983, Child's Play 1985, String Quartet No. 1 1985, Taking a Line for a Second Walk 1986, String Quartet No. 2 1988, String Quartet No. 3 1990, In Re Don Giovanni 1991, Masque Arias 1991, Time Will Pronounce 1992, Songs for Tony 1993, Three Quartets 1994, H.R.T. 1995, String Quartet No. 4 1995; instrumental: Shaping the Curve 1990, Six Celan Songs 1990, Flugelhorn and Piano 1991, For John Cage 1992, The Convertibility of Lute Strings 1992, Here to There 1993, Yamamoto Perpetuo 1993, On the Fiddle 1993, To Morrow 1994, Tango for Tim 1994, Elisabeth Gets her Way 1995, Viola and Piano 1995, Titch 1997; dramatic work: Strange Attractors, The Princess of Milan, A Broken Set of Rules 1984, Basic Black 1984, Portraits in Reflection 1985, And Do They Do 1986, The Man Who Mistook His Wife for a Hat 1986, Miniatures/Configurations 1988, Letters, Riddles and Writs 1991, Noises, Sounds and Sweet Airs 1994, Facing Goya 2000; vocal: A Neat Slice of Time 1980, The Abbess of Andouillets 1984, Out of the Ruins 1989, Polish Love Song 1990, Shaping the Curve 1991, Anne de Lucy Songs 1992, Mozart on Mortality 1992, Grounded 1995, The Waltz Song 1995; Michael Nyman Band: In Re Don Giovanni 1977, The Masterwork/Award-Winning Fishknife 1979, Bird List Song 1979, Five Orchestral Pieces Opus Tree 1981, Bird Anthem 1981, M-Work 1981, Love is Certainly, at Least Alphabetically Speaking 1983, Bird Work 1984, The Fall of Icarus 1989, La Traversée de Paris 1989, The Final Score 1992, AET (After Extra Time) 1996, De Granada a la Luna 1998, Orfeu 1998, The Commissar Vanishes 1999. *Publications:* Libretto for Birtwistle's Dramatic Pastoral, Down by the Greenwood Side 1968–69, Experimental Music: Cage and Beyond 1974; contrib. critical articles to journals, including The Spectator. *Address:* Michael Nyman Ltd, 83

Pulborough Road, London, SW18 5UL, England. *E-mail:* info@michaelnyman.com. *Website:* www.michaelnyman.com.

NYQUIST, Kristian (Benedikt); Harpsichordist and Fortepianist; b. 16 Oct. 1964, Los Angeles, USA; m. Judith Nyquist, 10 Aug 1991, 2 s., 1 d. *Education:* Staatliche Musikhochschule, Karlsruhe, 1983–88; Conservatorie National de Région Rueil-Malmaison, 1988–92. *Career:* Debut: Ernst Toch Saal, Mannheim, Germany, 1986; Concerts as Recitalist, Continuo Player, Duo Partner and Soloist in Germany, France, Belgium, Netherlands, Poland, Czech Republic, Switzerland, Russia, USA, Brazil; mem, Deutscher Tonkunstler-Verband, Stuttgart Section; France Action Musique. *Recordings:* Beethoven Violin Sonatas op. 30, 2001; Hans Werner Henze Complete Works for Harpsichord, 2001, 2004; J.S.Bach Goldberg Variations, 2003; C P E Bach, 5 Sonatas for harpsichord and flute, 1996; J. S. Bach, 5 Flute Sonatas, 1997; D'Anglebert Harpsichord Music, 1998. *Publications:* Realisations of Figured-Bass Parts; Trio-Sonatas by Tartini; Sonata Pastorale by Campioni, Zimmermann, Verlag. *Honours:* 1st Prize, Concours Musical de Region d'Ile de France, 1991; Prague Spring Competition, Honorary Mention, 1994. *Address:* Soonwaldstrasse 27, 55566 Bad Sobernheim, Germany. *Telephone:* +49 6751 6577. *Fax:* +49 6751 6577. *E-mail:* kristian.nyquist@arcor.de.

NYSTEDT, Knut; composer, conductor and organist; b. 3 Sept. 1915, Oslo, Norway; m. Brigit Nystedt 1942; one s. one d. *Education:* Artium, organ with Arild Sandvold, Oslo Conservatory of Music, Ernest White, New York, composition with Bjarne Brustad, Oslo, Aaron Copland, New York. *Career:* debut organist 1938; Guest-Conductor, Oslo Philharmonic, 1945; Organist, Torshov Church, Oslo, 1946–82; Conductor, Norwegian Soloist Choir, 1950–90, performances world-wide; Professor of Choral Conducting, Oslo University, 1964–85. *Compositions:* 5 String Quartets, 1938, 1948, 1955, 1966, 1988; Piano variations, 1948; Symphony for strings, 1950; Lucis Creator Optime, soli, chorus, orchestra, 1968; With Crown and Star, Christmas opera, 1971; Pia memoria, 9 brass instruments, 1971; Music for 6 trombones, 1980; Exsultate, 1980; Mountain Scenes, concert band, 1981; A Hymn of Human Rights, chorus, organ and percussion, 1982; For a Small Planet, chorus, recitation, harp, string quartet, 1982; Sinfonia del Mare, 1983; Ave Maria, chorus, violin solo, 1986; Songs of Soloman, church opera, 1989; Ave Christe, women's chorus, orchestra, 1991; Messa per Percussione, 1991; Concerto Arctandriae, strings, 1991; 4 Grieg Romances, chorus a capella, 1992; The Conch, male quartet with countertenor, 1993; Concerto Sacro, violin, organ, 1993; Miserere, 16-part chorus of mixed voices, 1994; One Mighty Flowering Tree, chorus, brass, 1994; Gebete für Mitgefangene (Bonhoeffer), soprano, organ, 1994; Kristnikvede, 1000th anniversary of Christianity in Norway, chorus, orchestra, 1994; Libertas Vincit, 50th anniversary of liberation from German occupation, recitation, chorus, orchestra, 1994; A Song as in The Night (Esaiah), soprano and baritone solo, chorus and string orchestra, 1996; Magnificat for a New Millennium, chorus, four trombones and percussion, 1997; Apocalysis Joannis, solos, chorus and orchestra, commissioned for Oslo Philharmonic, 1998; Prayers of Kierkegaard, mixed chorus, 1999; The World Became Flesh, chorus, 2000; Reach Out for Peace (Fred Kaan), chorus, 2001; The Shakespeare sonnets, tenor solo, 2002; Psalmus 138, violin solo, chorus and orchestra, 2002; Jesu Sieben Worte, chorus, 2002. *Address:* Vestbrynet 25 B, 1160 Oslo, Norway.

O

OAK, Kilsung; composer; b. 7 May 1942, Tong Yung, Korea; m., 1 s., 2 d. *Education:* MA, Long Island University; DMA, Columbia University. *Career:* The Group for Contemporary Music, 1972; Riverside Dance Festival, 1976; Seoul Symphony orchestra, 1994; mem, ASCAP; The Korean Society of the I-Ching; The Korean Composers Association. *Compositions:* Symphony; Amorphosis; String quartet; Sonata for piano; Duo for violin and piano; Dahn for violin and piano; GHI for violin and piano; The Days of Indong for orchestra. *Recordings:* Amorphosis for soprano and 12 percussionists. *Publications:* Symphony, 1997; Amorphosis, 1997; String quartet, 1995; Sonata for piano, 1998; Duo for violin and piano, 1992; Dahn for violin and piano, 1992; GHI for violin and piano, 1993. *Contributions:* Rappaport Prize, 1971; The Korea Arts and Culture Foundation Award, 1995 and 1998; The Best Film Award by the Korean Film Critics Society, 1996. *Address:* Jong-Gu, Piloon-Dong 32-1, Seoul, Republic of Korea.

OAKLEY-TUCKER, John; Singer (baritone); b. 1959, Canada. *Education:* Guildhall School of Music, Britten-Pears School, Ravel Acad. with Peter Pears, Gerard Souzay, Elisabeth Schwarzkopf and Thomas Hampson; continues to study with David Pollard. *Career:* operatic debut in the title role of Britten's Owen Wingrave, conducted by Steuart Bedford, Aldeburgh, 1984; sang in Glyndebourne Opera Festival Chorus in Jenůfa, Arabella, Le nozze di Figaro and Falstaff, 1988–90; operatic roles include lead role, Tom in Hans Werner Henze's The English Cat, conducted by the composer, Berlin, 1989, Italy, 1990 and Barbican, London, 1991 as part of the Henze BBC Festival; title role in Eugene Onegin, Co-Opera, London, 1993; lead role of Pluto in the world premiere of Hilda Paredes' chamber opera, The Seventh Pip, Mexico City, 1993; Belcore with Island Opera, 1994; English tour with Camberwell Opera as Il Conte, 1994–95, both directed by Mark Tinkler; Pluto in The Seventh Pip, San Diego, 1995; further roles include Don Giovanni, Guglielmo, Papageno, Sid (Albert Herring) and Billy Budd; concert performances include Bach's St John's and St Matthew's Passion, Duruflé's Requiem, Dvořák's Requiem, Elgar's Apostles, Fauré's Requiem, Handel's Messiah, Mozart's Requiem, Orff's Carmina Burana, Rossini's Petite Messe Solennelle and Vaughan Williams Sea Symphony; toured UK, Spain, Portugal, singing Mahler's Kindertotenlieder for the Ballet Rambert, 1988–89; recital debut with Graham Johnson, Schumann's Dichterliebe and English Song, Purcell Room, 1987; performances with the Songmakers' Almanac; Schubert's Winterreise with Nicholas Bosworth, Purcell Room, 1992; recital tour of the Middle East with Iwan Llewelyn-Jones, 1993; Schubert's Die schöne Müllerin with Iwan Llewelyn-Jones, Purcell Room, 1994; other recitals in the UK and abroad; formed duo, Tucker and Rohr, 1996, with pianist Alard von Rohr, performances include Carnegie Hall in New York, 1998 and Konzerthaus, Berlin, 1999. *Recordings:* Tom in Hans Werner Henze's The English Cat (German television), 1991; Pluto in Hilda Paredes' The Seventh Pip (with Arditti String Quartet), 1995; Baritone Solo, Symphony No. 5, Alexander Lokshin conducted by Rudolf Barschai, 1997. *Honours:* AGSM; Countess of Munster Musical Trust Scholarship. *Current Management:* Judith Newton, 75 Aberdare Gardens, London, NW6 3AN, England. *Address:* Sonnenallee 152, 12059 Berlin, Germany.

OBATA, Machiko; Singer (Soprano); b. 23 Feb. 1948, Sapporo, Japan. *Education:* Studied in Tokyo and Cologne. *Career:* Appearances with the Cologne Opera as Mozart's Pamina and Servila, Marzelline in Fidelio, Gretel, Liu and Flora in The Turn of The Screw; Sang the Woodbird in Siegfried in 1991; Guest engagements at Strasbourg, Munich and the Opéra Comique in Paris; Salburg Easter and Summer Festivals in 1991 as Barbarina in Le nozze di Figaro; Sang the Princess in Les Brigands by Offenbach at Colgone, 2001; Frequent concert appearances. *Address:* c/o Oper der Stadt Köln, Offenbachplatz, 5000 Cologne, Germany.

OBERHOLTZER, William; Singer (Baritone); b. 1947, Bloomington, Indiana, USA. *Education:* Studied at Indiana State University. *Career:* Debut: Indiana in 1972 in Herakles by John Eaton; Sang Marcello at St Gallen in 1976 then at Saarbrucken, 1978–81, Gelsenkirchen, 1981–86, and Kassel from 1986, St John in Wolfgang von Schweinitz' Patmos in 1990; Engaged at Munster, 1986–88 and made guest appearances at Düsseldorf as Marcello, Linz, Krefeld and Hannover; Other roles include Mozart's Count and Don Giovanni, Valentin, Renato, Rigoletto, Ford, Paolo, Wagner's Wolfram and Amfortas, Strauss's Jochanaan and Mandryka, and Wozzeck; Season 1998 as Matthes in Weill's Die Burgschaft, at Bielefeld; Sang Dallapiccola's Prigioniero at Bielefeld, 1999; Concert engagements include Bach's St John Passion in Berlin and Carmina Burana. *Address:* c/o Bühnen der Stadt Bielefeld, Brunhenstrasse 3–9, Pf 220, 4800 Bielefeld, Germany.

OBERLIN, Russell; American college lecturer and singer (countertenor); b. 11 Oct. 1928, Akron, OH. *Education:* Juilliard School. *Career:* founding member of New York Pro Musica Antiqua and soloist with many orchestras including New York Philharmonic, Chicago Symphony and Buffalo Philharmonic; Little Orchestra Society, Clarion Concerts, Smithsonian Institute Concert Series, CBS Radio Orchestra; Masterclasses throughout USA; Opera appearances in major roles at Covent Garden in Midsummer Night's Dream, San Francisco Opera, at Edinburgh and Vancouver Festivals and American Opera Society; Solo recitalist throughout USA; Radio and television appearances; Thomas Hunter Professor of Music, Hunter College and The Graduate Center of the City University of New York, 1966–; mem, National Association of Teachers of Singing; Academia Monteverdiana; Founding Board Member, Waverly Consort, Berkshire (Mass) Concert Series, Soho Baroque Opera Company; American Academy of Teachers of Singing. *Recordings include:* A Russell Oberlin Recital; Russell Oberlin, Handel Arias; Russell Oberlin, Baroque Cantatas; Soloist with New York Philharmonic, Handel's Messiah; Bach's Magnificat in D; Soloist with New York Pro Musica, The Play of Daniel; Thomas Tallis's Sacred Music; Josquin des Pres' Missa Pange Lingua; Walton's Façade with Hermione Gingold; Numerous other recordings including recently reissued CDs including: Troubadour and Trouvére Songs. English Polyphony of the 13th and Early 14th Centuries, The French Ars Antiqua and William Byrd Music for Voice and Viols. *Address:* c/o Hunter College, City University of New York, 695 Park Avenue, New York, NY 10021, USA.

OBERMAYR, Christine; Singer (Mezzo-Soprano); b. 30 May 1959, Wiesbaden, Germany. *Education:* Studied in Mainz with Josef Metternich. *Career:* Debut: Theater am Gärtnerplatz Munich in 1983 as Cherubino; Sang a Flowermaiden at Bayreuth Festival in 1984; Roles in Munich have included Hansel, Flotow's Nancy, Nicklausse and Orlofsky; Engagements at Wiesbaden, 1984–89 as Carmen, Emilia, Otello, Olga, Janáček's Fox, the Composer in Ariadne and Ottavio in L'Incoronazione di Poppea; Further appearances at the Theater an der Wien, the Paris Opéra and the Teatro Regio Turin; Sang Lyubasha in Rimsky's Tsar's Bride in 1985 and Mary in Der fliegende Holländer at Naples in 1992; Many concert and lieder performances. *Honours:* Prizewinner in competitions at Vienna, Wiesbaden and Berlin.

OBERSON, René; Composer, Organist and Professor; b. 27 June 1945, La Tour-de-Treme, Fribourg, Switzerland; m. 2 s., 1 d. *Education:* Teachers' Training College, Schools of Music in Fribourg, Berne and Geneva. *Career:* Organist at concerts in Switzerland and abroad notably at Notre-Dame, Paris, France and Symphony Hall, Osaka, Japan; Professor, School of Music, Fribourg. *Compositions include:* L'Exilée (The Exiled Woman), 1983; Concerto for Pan Pipes, 1984; Le Grand Cercle (The Great Circle), 1985; Homo Somniens, 1988; Au Seuil De L'Ere Du Verseau (On The Threshold Of The Era Of Aquarius), 1988; Jumière Divine, Omniprésente, Invulnerable for Organ, 1990; Espoirs for 2 Trumpets, 2 Trombones and Organ, 1990. *Recordings include:* Numerous works have been recorded by the Lausanne Chamber Orchestra, the Berne Symphony Orchestra, Netherlands National of Jeunesses Musicales Orchestra; Also radio recordings. *Contributions:* Has reconstructed the Fourth Concerto for Organ or Harpsichord and String Orchestra by the Swiss composer, Meyer von Schauensee, 1720–1798. *Address:* Pavillon Trobère Miraval, 1756 Lovens, Switzerland.

OBRADOVICH, Aleksandar; Composer and Professor of Composition; b. 22 Aug. 1927, Bled, Yugoslavia; m. Biljana, 2 Aug 1953, 1 s. *Education:* Academy of Music, 1952; Grants to spec. in London and New York. *Career:* Assistant Professor, Associate Professor, Professor, Faculty of Music Art, Belgrade, 1954–91; General Secretary of Union of Composers of Yugoslavia, 1962–66; Rector, University of Arts, Belgrade, 1978–83; President of Senate, 1981–82, President, 1982–83, of Union of Yugoslavian Universities; mem, Society of Serbian Composers. *Compositions:* 8 Symphonies, 5 concertos, 5 cantatas; Wind Of Flame, Green Knight, Stradum, cycles of songs; A Springtime Picnic At Dawn, ballet; Many other symphonic works, 15 vocal, instrumental and chamber works, music for 7 films and for 9 radio dramas; Electronic music and chorale works; Compositions have been performed in 32 different countries. *Recordings:* Radio-Televizja Belgrade. *Publications:* Orchestration I–II, 1978, III in preparation; Electronic Music and Electronic Instruments, 1978. *Contributions:* Over 350 articles and music critiques. *Honours:* 25 Prizes including October Prize of Belgrade in 1959 for Symphonic Epitaph, 4th July Prize in 1972 for IV Symphony and 7th July Prize in 1980 for his whole work. *Address:* Branka Djonovica 8, Belgrade 11 040, Serbia and Montenegro.

OBRAZTSOVA, Elena (Vasilyevna); Singer (Mezzo-soprano); b. 7 July 1939, Leningrad, USSR. *Education:* Leningrad Conservatoire, studied under Professor A Grigorijeva. *Career:* Debut: As Marina in Boris

Godunov, The Moscow Bolshoi Theatre, 1963; Member of the Moscow Bolshoi Theatre, 1964–; Repertoire includes: (Russian) Countess in The Queen of Spades, 1965; Lyubasha in The Tsar's Bride, 1967; Konchakovna in Prince Igor, 1968; Marfa in Khovanshchina, 1968, Lyubava in Sadko, 1979; (Italian and French) Amneris in Aida, 1965; Azucena in Il Trovatore, 1972; Eboli in Don Carlos, 1973, Santuzza in Cavalleria Rusticana, 1977; Ulrica in Un Ballo in Maschera, 1977; Adalgisa in Norma, 1979; Giovanna Seymour in Anna Bolena, 1982; Orfeo in Orfeo and Eurydice, 1984; Neris, Medea, 1989; Leonora in La Favorita, 1992; Aunt Princess in Suor Angelica, 1992, Carmen, 1972, Charlotte in Werther, 1974, Delilah in Samson and Delilah, 1974, Hérodiade, 1990; Opera of the 20th century: Britten's A Midsummer Night's Dream, 1965; Bart ók's Duke Bluebeard's Castle, 1978; Stravinsky's Oedipus Rex, 1980; Respighi, La Fiamma, 1990; Prokofiev's Semyon Kotko, 1970; War and Peace, 1971; The Gambler, 1996; Appearances in most leading Opera Houses of Europe and America; Sang the Princess in Suor Angelica at Venice, 1998; Tours at Venice, throughout Russia and the world; Sang Marina at the London Coliseum with the Bolshoi Opera, 1999; Grandmother in The Gambler at New York Met, 2001; Countess in The Queen of Spades, Washington, 2002;; Prinz Orlofsky in Die Fledermaus, Washington, 2003; Repertoire of recitals includes the music of more than 100 composers of 18th, 19th and 20th centuries; Professor of the Moscow Conservatoire, 1984; Has staged Werther at the Moscow Bolshoi Theatre, 1986; Television appearances inclaude 12 music films; Akhrosimova in War and Peace at Opéra Bastille, 2000; Verdi Requiem, Budapest, 2000. Recordings: Over 50 of operas, oratorios, cantatas, solos of arias and chamber music. Honours: Gold Medals at Competitions, 1962, 1970; Medal of Granados, Spain, 1971; Gold Pen of Critics, Wiesbaden, 1972; State Prize of Russia, 1974; Lenin Prize, 1976; People's Artist of the USSR, 1976; Gold Verdi, Italy, 1978; Memorial Medal of Bart ók, Hungary, 1982; Gold Star, Hero of Labour, 1990; Order For Services to Fatherland, 1999; Minor Planet 4623 Obraztsova, Minor Planet Circular J22503, 1993. Address: c/o Bolshoi Theatre, Moscow, Teatralnaya pl 1, 125009, Russian Federation.

O'BRIEN, Eugene; Composer and Teacher; b. 24 April 1945, Paterson, New Jersey, USA. Education: Studied at University of Nebraska, MM 1969, with Bernd Alois Zimmermann at Cologne, Indiana University with John Eaton and Iannis Xenakis, and Donald Erb at the Cleveland Institute of Music, DMA, 1983. Career: Teacher, 1973–81, Composer-in-Residence, 1981–85, Cleveland Institute; Associate Professor at Catholic University of America in Washington DC, 1985–87, and at Indiana University School of Music, 1987–. Compositions: Orchestral: Symphony, 1969, Cello Concerto, 1972, Dedales for Soprano and Orchestra, 1973, Rites Of Passage, 1978, Dreams And Secrets Of Origin for Soprano and Orchestra, 1983, Alto Saxophone Concerto, 1989; Chamber: Intessitura for Cello and Piano, 1975, Embarking For Cythera for 8 Instruments, 1978, Tristan's Lament for Cello, Allures for Percussion Trio, 1979, Psalms and Nocturnes for Flute, Viola da Gamba and Harpsichord, 1985, Mysteries of the Horizon for 11 Instruments, 1987; Vocal: Requiem Mass for Soprano, Chorus and Wind Ensemble, 1966, Nocturne for Soprano and 10 Instruments, 1968, Elegy for Bernd Alois Zimmermann for Soprano and Ensemble, 1970, Lingual for Soprano, Flute and Cello, 1972; Taking Measures, ballet, 1984. Honours: Guggenheim Fellowship, 1984–85. Address: c/o ASCAP, ASCAP Building, 1 Lincoln Plaza, New York, NY 10023, USA.

OCHMANN, Wieslaw; Singer (Tenor); b. 6 Feb. 1937, Warsaw, Poland. Education: Studied in Warsaw with Gustav Serafin and Sergiusz Nadgryzowski. Career: Debut: Bytom in 1959 as Edgardo in Lucia di Lammermoor; Warsaw Opera from 1964 with roles including Jontek in Halka, Tchaikovsky's Lensky, Cavaradossi, Dmitri in Boris Godunov and Arrigo in Les Vêpres Siciliennes; Guest appearances at the Staatsoper Berlin, Paris Opéra, Covent Garden, Hamburg and Prague; Glyndebourne, 1968–70 as Tamino, Lensky and Don Ottavio; Metropolitan Opera from 1975 as Henri, Dmitri, Lensky and Golitsin in Khovanshchina; Further appearances in Moscow, Chicago, Vienna, San Francisco and Geneva; Sang Grigory in Boris Godunov at the Metropolitan in 1982, Fritz in Schreker's Der Ferne Klang at Brussels in 1988, Hermann in the Queen of Spades and Idomeneo at San Francisco in 1987 and 1989; Sang the Shepherd in Szymanowski's King Roger at Buenos Aires in 1981 and at the Festival Hall London in 1990; Sang Grigory in Boris Godunov at the Berlin Staatsoper, 1996. Recordings: Moniuszko's Halka and Ghost Castle; Penderecki's Requiem and Te Deum; Idomeneo; Mozart's Requiem; Bruckner's D minor Mass; Salome; Jenůfa; Rusalka. Address: c/o San Francisco Opera, War Memorial House, San Francisco, CA 94102, USA.

OCHOTNIKOV, Nikolai; Singer (Bass); b. 1948, Russia. Career: Principal with the Kirov Opera, St Petersburg; Season 1990–91, with Kutuzov in War and Peace for the BBC and in Seattle; Edinburgh Festival, 1991, as Dosifey in Khovanshchina; Sang Boris Godunov at Helsinki and the New York Metropolitan, 1992; Season 1995 as the King in Iolanta at Birmingham and the Prince in Rimsky's Invisible City of

Kitezh with the Kirov at Edinburgh; Other roles include Verdi's King Philip and Glinka's Ivan Susannin. Recordings: Khovanshchina and War and Peace.

O'CONNOR, Gerard; Singer (Bass); b. Co Galway, Ireland. Education: University College, Cork; National Opera Studio, London. Career: Appearances in: Butterfly; Bohème; Figaro; Macbeth for Opera Ireland; Sparafucile in Rigoletto and Cieco in Mascagni's Iris at Holland Park; Il Barbiere di Siliglia by Paisiello, Wexford; Mamirov, Tchaikovsky Enchantress, Brighton; Chelsea Opera in Tannhäuser and Der Freischütz; Britten's Snug at Singapore; Season 1999: with Les Contes d'Hoffmann for Central Festival Opera; Rossini's Basilio for Castleward Opera; Varlaam in Boris Godunov for Opera Ireland; Company House Principal, English National Opera, 2001–; Boris in Lady Macbeth of Mtsensk, ENO and Dublin; Dikoy in Katya Kabanova for Opera Ireland; Croucher in the Silver Tassie, ENO and Dublin. Honours: Guiness Bursary, National Opera Studio, 1994–95. Address: Music International, 13 Ardilaun Road, London N5 2QR, England.

OCTORS, Georges; Conductor; b. 1940, Zaire, Africa. Education: Studied violin at first, then composition with Francis de Bourguignon at the Brussels Conservatory; Conducting studies with André Cluytens. Career: Founded and conducted the Antwerp Bach Society Chamber Orchestra; Assistant to Cluytens at the National Orchestra of Belgium, 1967; Music Director, 1975–83, Resident Conductor, 1983–86, Conductor and Musical Adviser of Gelders Orchestra in Arnhem, 1986–; Musical Director of the Chamber Orchestra of Wallonia, 1990; Guest appearances in Amsterdam, Leningrad, London with London Symphony Orchestra at the Barbican Hall in 1990, and elsewhere; Featured soloists have included Jessye Norman, Yehudi Menuhin, Igor Oistrakh, Uto Ughi, Paul Tortelier, Kyung Wha Chung and Vladimir Ashkenazy. Honours: Winner of various competitions as violinist.

ODINIUS, Lother; Singer (Tenor); b. 1970, Aachen, Germany. Education: Berlin Musikhockschule, 1991–95; Masterclasses with Bernd Weikl and Dietrich Fischer, Dieskau. Career: Debut: Schubertiade at Feldkirch, 1995 in the oratorio Lazarus; Mozart's Pedrillo, Bad Hersfeld Festival, 1995; Brunswick Staatstheater, 1996; Salzburg Festival, 1997; Mozarteum concerts; Further appearances at Stuttgart, Bonn, Vienna Volksoper; Lieder recitals at Paris, Cologne, Hamburg and Frankfurt; Concert tours with Philippe Herreweghe. Recordings: Lucio Vero in Jommelli's Il Vologeso.

ODNOPOSOFF, Ricardo; Violinist and Educator; b. 24 Feb. 1914, Buenos Aires, Argentina; m. (2) Irmtraut Baum, 20 Mar 1965. Education: MMus, High School Music, Berlin, 1932. Career: Violinist, playing in concerts throughout the world, 1932–; Teacher, University of Caracas, Venezuela, 1943–47; Taught summer courses Mozarteum, Salzburg, 1955–60; International Summer Academy, Nice, France, 1959–73; Professor, High School for Music, Vienna, 1956–, Professor Emeritus 1975–; Teacher, High School for Music, Stuttgart, Germany, 1964–94; Music High School, Zürich, 1975–84; mem, Freemason. Honours: Decorated Chevalier des Arts et Lettres, France; Chevalier de l'Ordre Rose Blanche, Finland; Comdr Order of Leopold II, Belgium; Grosses Verdienstkreuz des Verdienstordens, Germany; Mun Hwa Po Chang, South Korea; Medal for Merit, Argentina; Medal of Honor in Silver, City of Vienna, 1979; Ehrenkreuz für Wissenshaft und Kunst i Klasse, Austria; Medal of Merit in Gold, Government Baden-Wurttemberg, West Germany; Gold Ring of Honor by the Wiener Philharmoniker; Honour Member, Academie of Music, Stuttgart. Address: 27 Singerstrasse, 1010 Vienna, Austria.

OEHRING, Helmut; German composer and guitarist; b. 16 July 1961, Berlin. Education: masterclasses at Berlin Akademie der Künste. Compositions include: Coma 1 1991, Documentation 1 (chamber opera) 1993–96, Dokumentaroper (music theatre) 1994–95, Das D'Amato System (dance opera) 1996, Requiem 1998, Silence Moves It 1 and 2, 6ECHS, 7IEBEN and 8CHT, Dramma in Musica: Furcht und Begierde (for deaf soloists, soprano and ensemble) 2002. Recordings include: Dokumentaroper, Requiem. Honours: Deutschlandsender Kultur Hans Eisler prize 1990, WDR Cologne Young Composer's Award 1992, Orpheus Prize, Italy 1994, Hindemith Prize 1997, Schneider-Schott Music Prize 1998. Address: c/o Boosey & Hawkes, Komponisten Abteilung, Lützowufer 26, 10787 Berlin, Germany (office). Website: www.helmutoehring.de.

OELZE, Christiane; Singer (Soprano); b. 9 Oct. 1963, Cologne, Germany. Education: Studied with Klesie-Kelly Moog and Erna Westenberger. Career: Debut: Despina, Ottawa, 1990; Appearances with Neville Marriner, Frans Brüggen, Helmuth Rilling, Roger Norrington, Horst Stein, Nikolaus Harnoncourt, Pierre Boulez, Simon Rattle, Esa-Pekka Salonen, Riccardo Muti, Charles Mackerras, Seiji Ozawa; Roles include: Pamina, in Leipzig, Lyon, Zürich and Hamburg; Konstanze, in Salzburg and Zürich; Anne Trulove at Glyndebourne; Pamina in Zauberflöte and Marzelline in Leonore under John Eliot Gardiner; Regina in Mathis der Maler; Zdenka in Arabella and Zerlina in Don Giovanni at the Royal

Opera House, Covent Garden; Sifare in Mitridate at the Salzburg Festival in 1997; Season 1999 as Debussy's Mélisande at Glyndebourne and the London Proms; Sung with Kurt Masur, Carlo Maria Giulini and Bernard Haitink; as Mozart's Servilia and Pfitzner's Ighino at Covent Garden, Susanna and Olia for Glyndebourne Opera; Sang Strauss's Sophie at Hamburg, 2002. *Recordings:* Goethe-Lieder by Schubert, Wolf; Concert arias and C Minor Mass by Mozart; Webern Songs and Cantatas; Zauberflöte with John Eliot Gardiner; Brahms Requiem with Herreweghe, St Matthew Passion with Ozawa, Carmina Burana with Thielemann; Le nozze de Figaro with Kuijken; Selected Lieder with pianist Rudolf Jansen. *Honours:* Winner, Hugo Wolf Contest 1987. *Address:* c/o Artist Management HRA, Eduart-Schmid-Strasse 30, 81541 Munich, Germany.

OERTEL, Christiane; Singer (Mezzo-Soprano); b. 22 Dec. 1958, Potsdam, Germany. *Education:* Studied at the Leipzig Hochschule, 1975–82. *Career:* Member of the Komische Oper Berlin from 1988 as Cherubino, Olga, Dorabella and Carlotta in Die schweigsame Frau; Debuts at Covent Garden, Hamburg and in 1991 as Cherubino; Hamburg Cherubino; Japan visit with Covent Garden as Cherubino, 1992; Engagement Theater Erfurt, 1982–88; Debut as La Cenerentola, G Rossini, Komische Oper, 1994; Concert with Gewandhaus Leipzig under Kurt Masur; Season 2000–01 at the Komische Oper as Mozart's Annio and Meg Page in Falstaff; Siebel in Faust at the Landestheater, Salzburg; Many concert appearances. *Address:* c/o Komische Oper Berlin, Behrenstrasse 55–57, 10117 Berlin, Germany.

OFENBAUER, Christian, MA; Austrian organist and composer; b. 24 March 1961, Graz. *Education:* Klagenfurt Conservatory, Vienna Musikhochschule. *Career:* organist at Votivkirche, Vienna 1982–87; composer, TheaterAngelusNovus 1982–87; mem. ensemble, Die Reihe 1983–92; freelance ed., Universal Edition 1985–; Visiting Prof. Vienna Musikhochschule 1991–92; Guest Prof. of Composition Univ. Mozarteum Salzburg 1994–97. *Compositions include:* Tod des Hektor 1987, Medea 1990–94, unordentliche inseln/de la motte fouqué-vertonung 1995, Streichquartettsatz 1997, fancies/fancy papers (violin concerto) 1997. *Address:* Burggasse 119/15, 1070 Vienna, Austria.

OGAWA, Noriko; Pianist; b. 28 Jan. 1962, Kawasaki, Japan. *Education:* Tokyo College of Music High School, 1977–80, Juilliard School, New York, 1981–85; Piano studies with Benjamin Kaplan, 1988–. *Career:* Concerto soloist from 1976 playing works by Mendelssohn, Tchaikovsky, Liszt, Schumann and Chopin; New York recital debut in 1982, London Wigmore Hall debut in 1988 playing Schumann's Fantasy and Liszt's Sonata; Recitals throughout England and Ireland, Germany, Spain, France, Scandinavia, USA; Major appearances world-wide include the Harrogate Festival and the Tokyo and Yokohama Festivals; She has recorded several times for the BBC including Tchaikovsky B flat minor and Prokofiev No. 3 Concertos with Rozhdestvensky and the State Symphony Orchestra of the Russian Ministry of Culture; Has appeared outside the United Kingdom with Tokyo Symphony and Philharmonic, the Yomiuri Nippon Symphony Orchestra (with Jan Pascal Tortelier) and the Singapore Symphony; Formed a duo with clarinettist, Michael Collins in 1988, performing at Wigmore Hall and various festivals; 1991 included performances with Philharmonia Orchestra at the Festival Hall, the Ulster Orchestra and Bournemouth Symphony; Gave world premiere of a work by Lyn Davies at Lower Machen Festival and live BBC solo broadcast. *Recordings:* Czerny Etudes; Liszt; Prokofiev; Finzi Bagatelles; Rachmaninov Piano Concertos 2 and 3; Mussorgsky's Pictures at an Exhibition; Takemitsu, Complete solo piano works; Beethoven's Ninth, arranged by Wagner. *Honours:* 2nd Prize, International Music Competition of Japan, 1983; Gina Bachauer Memorial Scholarship, Juilliard, 1984; 3rd Prize, Leeds International Piano Competition, 1987. *Current Management:* Hazard Chase, Norman House, Cambridge Place, Cambridge CB2 1NS, England. *Telephone:* (1223) 312400. *Fax:* (1223) 460827. *Website:* www .hazardchase.co.uk. *Address:* c/o Clarion/Seven Muses, 64 Whitehall Park, London N19 3 TN, England.

OGDON, Wilbur L.; Composer and Professor of Music Theory, Literature and Composition; b. 19 April 1921, USA; m. Beverly Jean Porter 1958, 1 s., 2 d. *Education:* BM, University of Wisconsin, 1942; MA, Hamline University, St Paul, Minnesota, 1947; PhD, Indiana University, 1955; Further study, University of California, Berkeley, 1949–50, Ecole Normale de Musique, 1952–53; Studied composition with Ernst Krenek, Roger Sessions, Rene Leibowitz. *Career:* Professional positions and teaching: University of Texas, 1947–50; College of St Catherine, St Paul, 1956–57; Illinois Wesleyan University, 1957–65; Music Director, Pacifica Foundation, Berkeley, 1962–64; University of Illinois, 1965–66; University of California, San Diego, 1966–; Founding Chair, Music Department, 1966–71; Emeritus, UCSD, 1991–. *Compositions:* 3 Piano Pieces, 1950; Capriccio for Piano, 1952; Seven Piano Pieces, 1987; Voice: 3 Baritone Songs, 1950–56; Two Ketchwa Songs, 1955; Le Tombeau de Jean Cocteau, I, II and III, 1964, 1972, 1976; By the ISAR, 1969; Winter Images, 1981; Summer Images, 1985; The Awakening of

Sappho (chamber opera), 1980; Chorus: Statements; 3 Sea Songs; Instrumental: 7 Pieces and a Capriccio for violin and piano, 1988–89; 6 Small Trios, trumpet, marimba, piano, 1980; 5 Preludes, violin, piano, 1982; 5 Preludes, violin, chamber orchestra, 1985; Capriccio and 5 Comments, symphony orchestra, 1979; Serenade No. 1 for Wind Quintet, 1987; Serenade No. 2 for Wind Quintet, 1990; Palindrome and Variations, string quartet, 1962; 3 Trifles, cello, piano, 1958; Two Sea Chanteys, soprano, baritone and two percussionists, 1988; Four Chamber Songs, soprano with viola, cello, flute, oboe and harp, 1989; Four Tonal Songs, 1988–90; A Modern Fable, 2 soprano, baritone with violin, cello, clarinet, bass clarinet and percussion; 13 Expressions, solo violin and six instruments, 1993; Variation Suite, for violin and viola, 1995–96; Violin Suite, 1998; Three Moon Songs, for baritone and piano, 1998; Five Movements for string quartet, 1999. *Recordings:* The Music of Will Ogdon I, II. *Publications:* Series and Structure, 1955; Horizons Circled (with Ernst Krenek and John Stewart), 1974; How Tonality Functions in Webern's Opus 9, Extempore, 1990; On Webern's Op 27, II, in Journal of Music Theory; An Unpublished Treaties by Rene Leibowitz and How Tonality Functions in Schoenberg's op 11, No. 1, Journal of Schoenberg Institute. *Address:* 482 15th Street, Del Mar, CA 92014, USA.

OGNIVTSEV, Alexander (Pavlovich); Singer (Bass); b. 27 Aug. 1920, Petrovoskoy, Russia. *Education:* Studied at the Kishinev Conservatory. *Career:* Debut: Bolshoi Theatre, Moscow, 1949 as Dosifey in Khovanshchina; Has sung major roles in the Russian bass repertory such as Rimsky Korsakov's Ivan the Terrible and Tchaikovsky's Prince Gremin and Renée in Iolanta; Has also performed Philip II in Don Carlos, Mephistopheles, Don Basilio and the General in Prokofiev's The Gambler (also on the Bolshoi's visit to the Metropolitan in 1975); Sang in the premieres of Shaporin's The Decembrists in 1953 and Kholminov's An Optimistic Tragedy in 1967; Guest appearances in Italy at La Scala, Austria, France, Romania, Canada, Poland, India, Turkey, Hungary and Japan; Appeared in 1953 film version of the life of Shalyapin and sang Aleko in a film of Rachmaninov's opera. *Honours:* People's Artist of Russia, 1965.

OGNOVENKO, Vladimir; Singer (Bass); b. 1957, Russia. *Education:* Studied at the Urals Conservatory. *Career:* Sang at the Sverdlovsk Opera until 1984, then principal at the Kirov Opera, St Petersburg; Season 1991–92 as Bolkonsky in War and Peace at San Francisco, Boris Godunov at Helsinki and Varlaam in Boris Godunov at the New York Metropolitan (as guest with the Kirov); Palermo, 1993, in Rimsky's Sadko, San Francisco, 1995, as Farlaf in Ruslan and Lyudmila; Other roles in Lady Macbeth by Shostakovich, Ivan the Terrible by Rimsky, Prince Igor (as Galitsky) and Il Barbiere di Siviglia; Sang the Grand Inquisitor in Kirov Gala Concert, St Petersburg, 1998; Season 2000–01 in Shostakovich's Lady Macbeth at the Met, as Maljuta in The Tsar's Bride by Rimsky at San Francisco, Chub in Tchaikovsky's Cherevicihi at Cagliari and Galitzky in Price Igor for Houston Opera; Mussorgsky's Boris Godunov at the London Proms, 2002. *Recordings include:* Videos of Prince Igor and Sadko. *Address:* Kirov Opera, Mariinsky Theatre, 1 Theatre Square, St Petersburg, Russia.

OHANESIAN, David; Singer (Baritone); b. 6 Jan. 1927, Bucharest, Romania. *Education:* Studied in Budapest with Aurel Costescu-Duca and in Cluj with Dinu Badescu. *Career:* Debut: Cluj in 1950 in Pagliacci; Sang Tonio at Bucharest in 1952 and remained at the National Opera until 1977 as Verdi's Iago, Rigoletto, Amonasro and Luna, Eugene Onegin, Telramund, Scarpia, Escamillo and Rossini's Figaro, in Meyerbeer's Margherita d'Anjou and Tchaikovsky's Mazeppa; Noted as Enesco's Oedipe, which he sang in Bucharest and as guest abroad; Engagements in Hamburg, Moscow, Prague, Lyon, Paris, Barcelona, Budapest, Leningrad, Warsaw and Tel-Aviv. *Recordings include:* Oedipe and Cavalleria Rusticana. *Publications:* Passion of Music, with I Sava, Bucharest, 1986.

OHANESSIAN, Beatrice, LRAM; Iraqi pianist and composer; b. 1930, Baghdad. *Education:* Inst. of Fine Arts, Baghdad, RAM, London, Juilliard School of Music, NY. *Career:* prin. concert pianist with Iraqi Nat. Symphony Orchestra 1961–95; Head of Piano Dept, Inst. of Fine Arts, Baghdad 1961; teacher, Univ. of Minnesota, Macalester Coll., St Paul 1969–72; taught and performed in Geneva 1972–74; soloist, Minneapolis Symphony Orchestra; resident in USA 1996–. *Compositions:* Fantasy on Iraqi There, Hamurabi Overture, Spring Ballade, Variations on an Armenian Folk Tune, The Door. *Honours:* Frederick Westlake memorial prize, Fulbright scholarship. *Address:* c/o Minnesota Orchestra, Orchestra Hall, 1111 Nicollet Mall, Minneapolis, MN 55403, USA.

OHLSSON, Garrick; American pianist; b. 3 April 1948, White Plains, NY. *Education:* Westchester Conservatory, Juilliard School with Sascha Gorodnitsky, studied with Olga Barabini and Rhosa Lhevinne. *Career:* appears regularly with major orchestras, including New York Philharmonic, Chicago Symphony, Boston Symphony, Philadelphia Orchestra,

Los Angeles Philharmonic and with orchestras in recital series throughout the world. *Recordings include:* Complete Solo Works of Chopin and numerous other recordings. *Honours:* prizewinner at Busoni Piano Competition, Italy 1966, Chopin Int. Piano Competition, Warsaw 1970, Montreal Int. Piano Competition 1970. *Current Management:* ICM Artists Ltd, 8942 Wilshire blvd, Beverly Hills, CA 90211, USA. *Telephone:* (310) 550-4477 (office). *Fax:* (310) 550-4460 (office).

O'HORA, Ronan, GMus; pianist; b. 9 Jan. 1964, Manchester, England; m. Hannah Alice Bell 1991. *Education:* Royal Northern College of Music. *Career:* recitals and concerts in the United Kingdom, USA, Australia, New Zealand, Germany, France, Italy, Austria, Switzerland, Spain, Denmark, Norway, Sweden, Belgium, Netherlands, Portugal, Ireland, Yugoslavia and Czechoslovakia; Concerts with Philharmonia, Royal Philharmonic, BBC Symphony, Hallé, Bournemouth Symphony, Royal Liverpool Philharmonic, BBC Philharmonic, BBC Scottish, Zürich Tonhalle Orchestra, Netherlands Radio Symphony and Chamber Orchestras, Philharmonia Hungaria, Indianapolis Symphony, and Florida Philharmonic. *Recordings:* Concertos by Tchaikovsky, Grieg and Mozart with the Royal Philharmonic Orchestra; Britten complete music for two pianos with Stephen Hough; Numerous radio recordings in the United Kingdom, USA, France, Netherlands, Poland, Czechoslovakia, Portugal and Ireland; Senior tutor at Royal Northern College of Music; Head of Keyboard Studies, Guildhall School of Music and Drama, 1999–. *Recordings:* Over 30 including music of Chopin, Schubert, Brahms and Beethoven. *Honours:* Silver Medal, Worshipful Company of Musicians, 1984; Dayas Gold Medal, 1985; Stefania Niedrasz Prize, 1985; Created Fellow of the RNCM, 1999; Freeman of The City of London, 2000. *Current Management:* Robert Gilder & Co., Enterprise House, 59–65 Upper Ground, London, SE1 9PQ, England. *Telephone:* (20) 7928-9008. *Fax:* (20) 7928-9755. *E-mail:* rgilder@robert-gilder.com. *Address:* 183 Honor Oak Road, Forest Hill, London, SE23 3RP, England.

ÖHRN, Per-Erik, BA; Artistic Director, Opera Singer, Translator and Librettist; b. 18 Oct. 1946, Malmö, Sweden. *Education:* Opera Acad. Göteborg, Univ. of Göteborg. *Career:* opera singer 1972–82; stage dir 1973–; Artistic Dir, NorrlandsOperan, Umeå, Sweden 1988–96, Drottningholms Slottsteater 1996–. *Address:* Drottningholms Slottsteater, Box 15417, Stockholm, S-10765, Sweden (office). *Telephone:* (08) 55693100 (office). *Fax:* (08) 55693101 (office). *E-mail:* dst@dtm.se (office). *Website:* www.dtm.se (office).

OHYAMA, Heiichiro; Violinist, Violist and Conductor; b. 31 July 1947, Kyoto, Japan; m. Gail J Ohyama, 1 s. *Education:* Toho Music High School; Toho College of Music; Guildhall School of Music and Drama; AGSM, Indiana University, USA. *Career:* Debut: New York City, USA; Professor of Music at University of California, Santa Barbara; Assistant Conductor and Principal Violist with Los Angeles Philharmonic; Music Director, Santa Barbara Chamber Orchestra and Crossroads Chamber Ensemble; Music Director and Artistic Director with La Jolla Chamber Music Festival; mem, Musicians Union, England. *Recordings:* Various. *Contributions:* Marlboro Music Festivals; Santa Fe Chamber Music festivals; Round Top Music Festivals. *Honours:* Carl Flesch International Competition, 1968; Indiana University, 1971; Winner, Young Concert Artist, 1975. *Address:* c/o Konsertbolaget AB, Vasagatan 52, 5–11120, Stockholm, Sweden.

OISTRAKH, Igor (Davidovich); Violinist; b. 27 April 1931, Odessa, Russia. *Education:* Music School and State Conservatoire, Moscow; Student at State Conservatoire, 1949–55. *Career:* Many foreign tours, several concerts with father, David Oistrakh, notably in music by Spohr, Leclair and Bach; 60th Birthday Concert at the Barbican Centre, London, 1991 playing concertos by Mozart and Mendelssohn; Played the Shostakovich 1st Concerto at the Festival Hall, 1997. *Honours:* 1st Prize in Violin Competition in Budapest, 1952 and Wieniawski Competition, Poznán; Honoured Artist of RSFSR. *Address:* State Conservatoire, 13 Ulitsa Herzen, Moscow, Russia.

OKADA, Yoshiko; Pianist; b. 5 Oct. 1961, Japan; m. Grzegorz Cimoszko, 1 s. *Education:* Ecole Normale de Musique, Paris, 1976–80; Studied in Paris with Yvonne Loriod, 1980–82, in London with Maria Curcio and in Switzerland with Nikita Magaloff. *Career:* Debut: Carnegie Hall, New York in 1991; Touring in recital and as soloist with orchestras throughout USA, Canada, Poland, Denmark, Belgium, Switzerland and France. *Recordings:* Japan: CDs of Mozart Sonatas and Concertos with Warsaw Chamber Orchestra. *Current Management:* Albert Kay Associates Inc. *Address:* Albert Kay Associates Inc, Concert Artists Management, 58 West 58th Street, New York, NY 10019-2510, USA.

OKE, Alan; Singer (Tenor); b. 1954, London, England. *Education:* Studied at Royal Academy of Music, Glasgow and in Munich with Hans Hotter,. *Career:* Sang first in concert and in oratorios; Stage debut with Scottish Opera; Roles include: Papageno in Die Zauberflöte, Schaunard in La Bohème, and Olivier in Capriccio; Sang in Cavalli's L'Egisto in Frankfurt, Venice and Schwetzingen, 1983; Covent Garden, 1984 in

Taverner by Maxwell Davies; Took part in British premiere of Weill's Street Scene, Glasgow, 1989; Guest appearances with English National Opera and Opera North; Sang Malatesta, in Don Pasquale, Stratford-Upon-Avon, 1990; Sang Macheath in The Threepenny Opera, Leeds, 1990; Season 1992 with Pluto in Orpheus in the Underworld, for Opera North; Tenor roles include Alfredo in La Traviata for Opera North; Gaston in La Traviata for GTO at Glyndebourne, 1996; Season 1998 as Ravel's Gonsalve and Puccini's Rinuccio at Auckland, Shuisky for New Sussex Opera, and in Caterina Cornaro at the Queen Elizabeth Hall, London; Season 2000 as Boris in Katya Kabanova for Opera North and Pinkerton for Castleward Opera. *Recordings include:* Giuseppe in The Gondoliers. *Current Management:* Musichall. *Address:* Vicarage Way, Ringmer, West Sussex BN8 5 LA, England.

OKERLUND, David; Singer (Baritone); b. 1965, Kearney, Nebraska, USA. *Education:* Merola Opera Program, San Francisco. *Career:* Appearances with San Francisco Opera as Don Giovanni, the Herald in Lohengrin, Eugene Onegin and Mozart's Count; Puccini's Sharpless in Tokyo and Guglielmo for Opera Carolina; Season 1998–99 as Stanley in the San Francisco premiere of A Streetcar Named Desire, and Gunther in Götterdämmerung; Germont in La Traviata for Vancouver Opera; Concerts include Carmina Burana, Die Schöpfung by Haydn and the Brahms Requiem. *Honours:* Adler Fellow, 1995. *Address:* Harlequin Agency Ltd, 203 Fidlas Road, Cardiff CF4 5NA, Wales.

OLAFIMIHAN, Tinuke; Singer (Soprano); b. 1961, London, England. *Education:* Studied at the Colchester Institute, at Morley College and the National Opera Studio in London; Further study with Elisabeth Schwarzkopf. *Career:* Debut: Despina at the Queen Elizabeth Hall in 1989 with the National Opera Studio; Has sung Zerlina in Don Giovanni at the Snape Maltings, Messiah with The Sixteen under Harry Christophers and appearances with the Vivaldi Concertante at St John's Smith Square and in the St John Passion at Belfast; Sang Susanna in a production of Figaro by Colin Graham and Barbarina for Opera Northern Ireland and in Aix-en-Provence; Sang Carmina Burana at the Queen Elizabeth Hall in 1990 and Clara in the Covent Garden premiere of Porgy and Bess in 1992. *Honours:* Peter Stuyvesant Foundation Scholarship; Walter Legge/Elisabeth Schwarzkopf Society Award; Finalist, 1988 Richard Tauber Competition.

OLAFSSON, Kjartan; Composer; b. 18 Nov. 1958, Reykjavík, Iceland; 2 d. *Education:* BM, Reykjavic College of Music, 1984; Institute in Sonology, Netherlands, 1984–86; Licentiate of Music, PhD, Sibelius Academy, 1995. *Career:* Debut: Reykjavík, 1985; mem, Society of Composers in Iceland. *Compositions:* Reflex for Orchestra, 1988; Bribraut for Clarinet Trio, 1993; Summary for tape, 1994; Utstrok for Orchestra, 1995. *Recordings:* Reflex for Orchestra; Utstrok for Orchestra; Bribraut for Clarinet Trio; Dimma for Viola and Piano; Summary for Tape; Dark Days for electronics and live performance. *Publications:* Calmus Theory Books, 1, 2, 3, 4. *Contributions:* CALMUS (Calculated Music). *Honours:* Prize, Competition for Young Composers; Grants, Ministries of Iceland and Finland. *Address:* c/o STEF, Laufasvegi 40, 101 Reykjavík, Iceland.

OLAH, Tiberiu; Composer; b. 2 Jan. 1928, Arpasel, Transylvania, Romania; m. Yvonne Olah, 28 Mar 1959. *Education:* Academia de Musica, Cluj, 1946–49; Tchaikovsky Conservatory, Moscow, 1949–54; Composition Diploma, magna cum laude. *Career:* Debut: Trio, Cluj, 1955; Performance of Cantata for Female Choir and Ensemble at Prague in 1963, Warsaw and Budapest in 1966, West Berlin in 1966, West Berlin STB Orchestra in 1967, Darmstadter Ferienkurse in 1968; Performance of Columna by Infinita Orchestra; World's first performance and commissioned works: West Berlin, 1971, Perspectives, Paris, 1971, Ed Salabert's ORTF Orchestra, Translations for 16 Strings, New York Lincoln Center, Washington Kennedy Center, 1974; Time Of Memory to the memory of N and S Koussevitsky, Berlin Festwochen, 1988; Concerto Delle Coppie; Bucharest: The International Week of New Music, 1991; Obelisque For Wolfgang Amadeus for Saxophone and Orchestra, Karlsruhe, Germany, 1992; Concertante commissioned by Land Baden, Wurttemberg. *Recordings:* Numerous. *Publications:* Editor: Muzicale, Bucharest, Salabert, Paris, Schott, Germany, Muzyka, Moscow. *Address:* c/o GEMA, Rosenheimer Str. 11, 81667 Munich, Germany.

OLANO, Miguel; Singer (Tenor); b. 1962, Cenicero, La Rioja, Spain. *Education:* Madrid Conservatory; Florence, with Gino Bechi and at Siena with Carlo Bergonzi. *Career:* Debut: Wels, Austria, 1991, as Rodolfo; Appearances as Puccini's Edgar at Torre del Lago and as Cavaradossi at Vercelli, Bregenz and Salzburg; Season 1995 with Don Carlos at the Paris Châtelet; Further engagements as Puccini's Des Grieux at Livorno and Pisa, Manrico, Pollione (Norma) and Don Carlos at the Amsterdam Concertgebouw; Other roles include Andrea Chénier, Turiddu and Calaf in Turandot; Sang Don Juan in Margarita la Tornera by R. Chapi, opposite Placido Domingo, at Madrid (2000); US debut Washington Opera 2000, as Cavaradossi; Season 2000–01 as Don Carlos and Calaf at Washington; Des Grieux at L'Opéra de Genève. *Address:* c/o Musicaglotz, 11, Rue le Verrier, 75006 Paris, France.

OLCZAK, Krzysztof Robert; Polish composer and accordionist; b. 26 May 1956, Łódź; m. 1980; one s. one d. *Education:* Fr Chopin Academy of Music, Warsaw, Academy of Music, Gdansk. *Career:* solo and chamber concerts in Poland from 1978; Played with National Philharmonic, 1985, 1986 and Bialystok, Gdansk, Koszalin, Łódź, Opole, Poznan, Wroclaw, Austria, Finland, Germany, Italy, Norway, Sweden and Russian Philharmonic Orchestras; Appearances at contemporary music festivals include Styrian Autumn, Austria, Warsaw Autumn, Poznan Spring, Gdansk Encounters of Young Composers; Conservatorium Legnica, 1987, 1991, Musik Biennale, Berlin in 1987, Musica Polonica Nova, Wroclaw in 1988, and Internationale Studienwoche, Bonn in 1991; Tour of Scandinavia with American Waterways Wind Orchestra in 1990; Lecturer at Gdansk Academy of Music. *Compositions include:* Accordion Solos: Manualiter, 1977, Phantasmagorien, 1978, Winter Suite, 1980, Fine Pluie, 1980, Berceuse, 1984, Rondino, 1985, Pozymk for 4 performers, 1982, Sea Spaces for Soprano and Prepared Piano, 1982, Cantata for Soprano, 2 Accordions, 1984, Sinfonietta Concertante for Percussion and Orchestra, 1985–86, Belt The Bellow for Tuba and Accordion, 1986, Trio, Homage to Karol Szymanowski, 1987, Intervals for Organ and 2 Accordions, 1987, Concerto for Accordion and Orchestra, 1989, Concerto Grosso for Wind Orchestra, 1990. *Address:* 11 Listopada 79, 80-180 Gdańsk, Poland.

OLDFIELD, Mark; singer (baritone); b. 1957, Sheffield, England. *Education:* School of Music, Colchester with Rae Woodland, Royal College of Music; further study with Kenneth Woollam. *Career:* operatic work has included Metcalf's Tornrak at Banff Centre in Canada, and Papageno for London Opera Players; London International Opera Festival in 1989 in The Fisherman by Paul Max Edlin; Sang Purcell's Aeneas and Eugene Onegin at the Royal College of Music; Concert repertoire includes the Brahms Requiem, Snape Maltings, Bach's Magnificat, Las Palmas, and Cantata No. 11, Handel's Chandos Anthems with the English Chamber Orchestra under Charles Mackerras, Vaughan Williams's Five Mystical Songs, Carmina Burana, Monteverdi Madrigals and the Brahms Liebeslieder in Northern Italy; Sang Mercurio in Cavalli's La Calisto in Provence; Eiriksdottir's I Have Seen Someone, at the Riverside Studios, London, 1996. *Current Management:* Robert Gilder & Co., Enterprise House, 59–65 Upper Ground, London, SE1 9PQ, England. *Telephone:* (20) 7928-9008. *Fax:* (20) 7928-9755. *E-mail:* rgilder@robert-gilder.com.

O'LEARY, Thomas; Singer (Bass); b. 3 Sept. 1924, Punxsutawney, Pennsylvania, USA. *Education:* Studied with Alexander Kipnis in New York. *Career:* Debut: San Jose in 1947 as Kecal in The Bartered Bride; Sang at Nuremberg, 1960–65, Vienna Volksoper, 1962–75 with further engagements at Munich, Hamburg, Rome, Bologna, Berlin, Barcelona, Zürich, Marseilles and Frankfurt; Appearances at Boston, Baltimore and New Orleans from 1967, Chicago in 1977, and San Francisco, Houston and San Diego; Other roles have included Sarastro, Rocco, King Philip, Zaccaria, Mephistopheles, Arkel, Boris and Pimen in Boris Godunov, Wagner's Mark, Daland, Pogner, Hunding, Hagen and Gurnemanz; Frequent concert performances. *Address:* c/o Volksoper, Wahringerstrasse 78, 1090 Vienna, Austria.

OLEDZKI, Bogdan; Conductor; b. 25 June 1949, Stupsk, Poland; m. Ewa Gtowacka, 12 Aug 1981. *Education:* Warsaw Music Academy, 1974. *Career:* Debut: National Philharmonic Orchestra, Warsaw in 1974; Conductor in Warsaw, Radom and Poznan, 1974–82; Principal Conductor for Rzeszow Philharmonic Orchestra, 1982–84; Conductor for Great Opera, Warsaw, 1984–; Guest Conductor with Philharmonic Orchestra, Poland and Salzburg-Aspecte, Edinburgh and Skopje Festivals. *Current Management:* Polish Artistic Agency (PAGART), Warsaw, Poland. *Address:* Bandrowskiego 8 m 60, 01-496 Warsaw, Poland.

OLEFSKY, Paul; Cellist and Professor; b. 4 Jan. 1926, Chicago, Illinois, USA. *Education:* Studied at Curtis Institute with Gregor Piatigorsky, 1943–47, with Pablo Casals and with Karajan and Monteux (conducting). *Career:* Former First Cellist of Philadelphia Orchestra and Detroit Symphony Orchestra; Concert soloist with leading orchestras in USA and abroad; Recitalist in North America and Europe with solo works by Kodály and Bach and the premieres of works by Milhaud, Tcherepnin, Virgil Thomson and Shapleigh; Professor of Cello and Chamber Music at University of Texas, Austin, 1974–; Concert cellist; Conductor; University Professor; President, Amatius Classics Productions; President, Amatius Classics Foundation; mem, Littlefield Society, University of Texas at Austin. *Recordings:* Complete Beethoven Sonatas; Complete Brahms Trios; Tchaikovsky and Arensky Trios; 4 Vivaldi and Boccherini Concertos with English Chamber Orchestra; Complete Bach Suites and Chaconne; Complete Kodály, Op 4, 7, 8; Shapleigh Sonatas and Quartet; Bartók Concerto; Romanian Dances; Duos; Virgil Thomson Concerto, Ormandy and Philadelphia Orchestras. *Honours:*

Naumberg Award, 1948; Michaels Memorial Award of the Young Concert Artists, 1953. *Current Management:* Amatius Classics Foundation. *Address:* 7603 Yaupon Drive, Austin, TX 78759, USA.

OLEG, Raphaël; Concert Violinist; b. 8 Sept. 1959, Paris, France. *Education:* Paris Conservatoire from 1972 with first prizes for violin and chamber music, 1976. *Career:* International reputation as recitalist and with Europe's major symphony orchestras; Lucerne Festival in 1986 with the Czech Philharmonic and Vaclav Neumann; First Prize in Tchaikovsky International Competition in 1986; British debut in 1987 playing the Brahms Concerto with the London Symphony Orchestra under Jeffrey Tate; 1987 tour of European Festivals with the Orchestre National de France and Lorin Maazel; Engagements with the Concertgebouw under Chailly, Orchestre de Paris under Bychov, the Philadelphia Orchestra under Maazel and the Munich Staatsorchester under Sawallisch; British appearances with the Philharmonia, English Chamber Orchestra, Northern Sinfonia, Scottish Chamber Orchestra and City of London Sinfonia; Japanese debut in 1989 at Suntory Hall; Engagements in 1989–90 season included a tour of Italy with ECO and Tate, and a tour of France and Switzerland with the Academy of St Martin-in-the-Fields and Marriner; Gave recitals at Prague Spring Festival and Paris, concerts with the Orchestre National de France, and Polish Chamber Orchestra; 1990–91 toured Germany with Chamber Orchestra of Europe and Berglund, and Japan with the Nouvel Orchestre Philharmonique. *Address:* Van Walsum Management Ltd, 4 Addison Bridge Place, London W14 8XP, England.

OLEJNICEK, Jiri; Singer (Tenor); b. 11 Feb. 1937, Brno, Czechoslovakia. *Education:* Studied at the Brno Conservatory from 1954. *Career:* Sang at Opava Opera from 1962, and Janáček Opera in Brno from 1964; Roles have included Tamino, Alvaro, Rodolfo, the Prince in Rusalka, Stahlav in Smetana's Libuše and Dmitri in Boris Godunov; Guest appearances in Florence in 1967 and Barcelona as Lensky in 1976; Frequent concert engagements. *Address:* c/o Janáček Opera, Dvořákova 11, 657-70 Brno, Czech Republic.

OLESCH, Peter (Otto); Singer (Bass-Baritone); b. 10 Sept. 1938, Andreashutte, Oberschlesien, Germany. *Education:* Studied in Dresden with Rudolf Bockelmann. *Career:* Debut: Berlin Staatsoper in 1963 as a Flemish Deputy in Don Carlos; Sang at the Berlin Staatsoper until 1982 in such roles as Masetto, Monterone, Bartolo, Pistol, Falstaff, Alberich, Alfio in Cavalleria Rusticana, Vaarlam and Rangier in Penderecki's The Devils of Loudun; Sang at Leipzig Opera in 1989 as Don Pasquale; Many concert performances. *Recordings:* Puntila by Dessau. *Address:* c/o St ädtische Theater, 7010 Leipzig, Germany.

OLIVEIRA, Elmar; Violinist; b. 28 June 1950, Waterbury, Connecticut, USA. *Education:* Hart College of Music, Hartford, CT; Manhattan School of Music. *Career:* Appearances with orchestras including New York Philharmonic, Cleveland, Baltimore, Chicago Symphony, Dallas, Montreal and Moscow Philharmonic. *Recordings include:* Sonata by Husa. *Honours:* First Prize, Naumberg Competition, 1975; Gold Medal, Tchaikovsky International Competition, 1978.

OLIVER, Alexander; Singer (tenor); b. 27 June 1944, Scotland. *Education:* Royal Scottish Acad.; further studies in Vienna and with Rupert Bruce-Lockhart. *Career:* Netherlands Opera from 1971 in The Love For Three Oranges, Intermezzo, Peter Grimes, L'Ormindo and The Turn of the Screw; Scottish Opera in A Midsummer Night's Dream, Wozzeck, The Bartered Bride, Eugene Onegin and Mahagonny; Opera North as Nemorino in L'Elisir d'amore; Glyndebourne Opera in Il Ritorno d'Ulisse, Ariadne auf Naxos and Albert Herring in 1985; Covent Garden in Eugene Onegin, Le nozze di Figaro, Andrea Chénier, Manon and Albert Herring, 1989; Zürich Opera from 1978 in L'Incoronazione di Poppea and Les Contes d'Hoffmann; Brussels Opera in 1982 as Arbace in Idomeneo, returning for the world premiere of Le Passion de Gilles by Boesmans; Antwerp Opera and Canadian Opera debuts in 1983 in Death in Venice and Poppea; La Fenice Venice in Curlew River, La Scala Milan in the premiere of Riccardo III by Flavio Testi and sang Mime in a new production of Siegfried at Covent Garden in 1990; sang Shapkin in From the House of the Dead at Brussels in 1990, and at Salzburg in 1991 in Le nozze di Figaro; sang Schmidt in Werther for Netherlands Opera, 1996; concert engagements with the Concertgebouw Orchestra in the St John and St Matthew Passions of Bach and Stravinsky's Pulcinella; Houston Symphony and Chicago Symphony and frequent appearances with the Songmakers' Almanac. *Recordings include:* Videos of Gilbert and Sullivan's The Sorcerer and Pirates of Penzance.

OLIVER, John (Edward); Composer; b. 21 Sept. 1959, Vancouver, Canada. *Education:* MMus, 1984, D.Mus, 1992, Composition, McGill University, Montreal; BMus Composition, University of British Columbia; Studies: Composition, Guitar, Piano, Voice, San Francisco Conservatory of Music, 1977–79. *Career:* Works performed by: New Music Concerto, Toronto 1982, 87, Vancouver New Music, 1982, 1990, Société de Musique Contemporaine de Quebec, 1989, Canadian Opera Company, 1991; Composer-in-Residence, Banff Centre, Leighton Artist Colony, 1989, 1990 and Music Department, 1990, 1991, Canadian Opera Company, 1989, 1991, Vancouver Opera, 1992–; mem, Society of Composers, Authors and Music Publishers of Canada; American Federation of Musicians; Canadian Electro-acoustic Community. *Compositions:* Gugcamayo's Old Song and Dance, Canadian Opera Company, 1991; El Reposo del Fuego, 1987; Aller Retour, 1988; Marimba Dismembered, 1990; Before the Freeze, 1984. *Recordings:* El Reposo del Fuego; Marimba Dismembered; Before the Freeze. *Publications:* New Music in British Columbia in Soundnotes, Fall, 1992. *Honours:* Canada Council Arts Awards, 1984–87, 1991; 8th CBC National Radio Competition for Young Composers, 1988; Two prizes, 1989 PROCAN Young Composers Competition.

OLIVER, Lisi; Stage Director and Translator; b. 13 Dec. 1951, Frankfurt am Main, Germany. *Education:* BA, Smith College, 1973; ALM Harvard University, 1988; PhD in Linguistics, Harvard University, 1995. *Career:* Stage Manager, Bolshoi Opera US Tour, 1974; Inaugural Gala for President Carter, 1978; Production Stage Manager, Assistant Director, Opera Company of Boston, 1975–78; Assistant Director, Komische Oper Berlin, 1979–80; Director, Opera Company of Boston, Opera New England, Skylight Comic Opera, Des Moines Metro Opera, Atlanta Opera, Baldwin-Wallace Conservatory, Opera Company of the Philippines, Massachusetts Institute of Technology, Wolftrap Farm Park, City of Boston First Night, 1980–90; Director of Opera Studio, New England Conservatory, 1988–90; First projected titles at Bolshoi Opera, 1991; Director, Atlanta Opera Studio, 1989–95; Title Supervisor, Atlanta Opera, Director of Raymond Street Translations, Translation and Titles Rental Company; Professor of Mediaeval Studies and Linguistics, Louisiana State University. *Publications:* Translations of Surtitles used by many American Companies; The Beginnings of English Law, University of Toronto Press, 2002. *Honours:* Yvonne Burger Award, Smith College, 1973; Merit Award, Komische Oper, 1980; National Opera Institute Grant, 1978–80; Whiting Fellowship, Harvard University, 1994–95; Outstanding Graduate Faculty in English, LSU, 1997; Phi Beta Phi Award, LSU, 1998; BP Amoco Award for outstanding undergraduate teaching, 2001. *Address:* 2021 Cedardale Avenue, Baton Rouge, LA 70808, USA. *E-mail:* lolive1@lsu.edu.

OLIVERO, Magda; Singer (Soprano); b. 25 March 1910, Saluzzo, Turin, Italy. *Education:* Studied in Turin with Luigi Gerussi, Luigi Ricci and Ghedini. *Career:* Debut: Turin in 1933 as Lauretta in Gianni Schicchi; La Scala in 1933 in Nabucco; Sang widely in Italy as Adriana Lecouvreur, Puccini's Liu, Suor Angelica and Minnie, Violetta, Zerlina, Poppea and Sophie in Der Rosenkavalier; Retired in 1941 but returned to stage in 1951 to sing Adriana at the composer's request; Sang at Stoll Theatre in London as Mimi in 1952 with further appearances in Edinburgh, Paris, Brussels, Amsterdam and Buenos Aires; Other roles included Fedora, Mascagni's Iris, Zandonai's Francesca, Puccini's Giorgetta and Tosca and parts in operas by Poulenc and Menotti; US debut at Dallas in 1967 as Médée, Metropolitan Opera in 1975 as Tosca. *Recordings:* Turandot; Fedora; Francesca da Rimini; La Fanciulla del West; Il Tabarro; Risurrezione by Alfano; Médée; Madama Butterfly.

OLIVEROS, Pauline; Composer and Performer; b. 30 May 1932, Houston, Texas, USA. *Education:* BA, San Francisco State College, 1957. *Career:* Director, San Francisco Tape Music Center, 1966, Expo '67 Montreal, Canada, 1967, and Expo '70 Osaka, Japan, 1970; Professor of Music, University of California, San Diego, 1970; Summer Olympics, Los Angeles, 1984; Works performed and solo performances world-wide and with numerous orchestras. *Compositions:* Roots For The Moment; Tara's Room; The Well And The Gentle; Tashi Gomang; Rose Moon; Sonic Meditations; Horse Sings From Cloud; Rattlesnake Mountain; Lullaby For Daisy Pauline; Spiral Madala; Bonn Feier; Double Basses At 20 Paces; 3 Songs for Soprano and Piano; To Valerie Solanas and Marilyn Monroe; Jar Piece; Sound Patterns; Njinga the Queen King, music theatre, 1993; From Unknown Silences for ensemble, 1996; Cicada Song, for accordion, 1996; Beyond the Mysterious Silence for low voice and ensemble, 1996. *Recordings:* The Well And The Gentle; The Wanderer; Accordion And Voice; Vor Der Flüt. *Publications:* Software for People, 1984. *Contributions:* Numerous. *Address:* c/o ASCAP, ASCAP Building, 1 Lincoln Plaza, New York, NY 10023, USA.

OLLESON, (Donald) Edward, BA, MA, DPhil; academic and writer on music; *University Lecturer in Music, University of Oxford*; b. 11 April 1937, South Shields, England; m. Eileen Gotto; two s. one d. *Education:* Hertford College, Oxford. *Career:* Assistant Lecturer, Univ. of Hull 1962–63; Research Lecturer, Christ Church, Oxford 1963–66; Faculty Lecturer, Univ. of Oxford 1966–72; Fellow, Merton Coll. 1970–; University Lecturer in Music, 1972–. *Publications:* Editor, Proceedings of The Royal Musical Association, vols 94–100; Essays, with Nigel Fortune and FW Sternfeld, on Opera and English Music in honour of Sir Jack Westrup, 1975; Participation in Everyman Dictionary of Music, 5th edition, 1975; Modern Musical Scholarship, 1978; Co-editor, Music

and Letters, 1976–86. *Address:* Faculty of Music, St Aldate's, Oxford OX1 1DB, England.

OLLI, Kalevi; Singer (Bass-Baritone); b. 1951, Finland. *Education:* Studied at the Sibelius Academy in Helsinki, including Composition with Eino-Johani Rautavaan, 1971–78. *Career:* Sang Silvano in Un Ballo in Maschera at Helsinki in 1977 and sang at the Frankfurt Opera, 1978–84; Appearances at the Savonlinna Festival as the Dutchman and concert engagements, including Lieder recitals, in Germany, Switzerland and elsewhere; mem, Finnish Composers; Finnish Drama Authors. *Recordings:* Complete songs by Rachmaninov; Schumann's Dichterliebe with Toiva Kuula, and Schwanengesang with Ulrich Koneftke. *Honours:* Prizewinner in competitions at Savonlinna, Lappeenranta and Geneva, 1977–81; Sang in Boris Godunov at Royal Opera Stockholm Warlaan, 1997, and at Deutsche Oper Berlin Alberich in Rheingold; Sang whole Ring Cycle in Helsinki, 1996–99; Season 1998 as Alberich in Siegfried at Helsinki; Sang in Sapporo, Japan with Tan Dum and Orchestra Theatre II, 1999. *Address:* c/o Finnish National Opera, PO Box 176, Helsingkatu 58, 00251 Helsinki, Finland.

OLLMANN, Kurt; Singer (Baritone); b. 19 Jan. 1957, Racine, Wisconsin, USA. *Education:* Studied with Gerard Souzay, among others. *Career:* Sang with the Milwaukee Skylight Opera, 1979–82; Engagements in Santa Fe, Washington DC, Milan and Brussels in operas by Debussy and Mozart; Pepsico Summerfare New York in 1987 as Don Giovanni, in the Peter Sellars version of Mozart's opera; Sang under Bernstein in the Viennese premiere of A Quiet Place in 1986 and as Maximilian in a concert performance of Candide at the Barbican in London, 1989; Seattle Opera in 1988 as Mercutio in Gounod's Roméo et Juliette; St Louis Opera, 1989–90, as Purcell's King Arthur and Mozart's Count; Many concert appearances; Season 1992 in On The Town at the Barbican Hall and the title role in the US premiere of Bose's The Sorrows of Young Werther at Santa Fe; Season 1999–2000 for Seattle Opera as the Speaker in Die Zauberflöte and Frédéric in Lakmé. *Recordings:* Count Paris in Roméo et Juliette, conducted by Michel Plasson; Candide and West Side Story conducted by the composer; Mercutio in Roméo et Juliette, under Leonard Slatkin, 1996. *Address:* Opera Theater of St Louis, PO Box 13148, St Louis, MO 63119, USA.

OLMI, Paolo; Conductor; b. 1953, Italy. *Education:* Studied with Massimo Pradella and Franco Ferrara in Rome. *Career:* Frequent appearances with major orchestras in Italy and abroad from 1979; Opera debut at Teatro Communale di Bologna, 1986; Conducted Rossini's Mosè in Egitto at Rome 1988, later at the Bayerische Staatsoper, Munich; Deutsche Oper am Rhein, Düsseldorf, with Traviata, Théâtre des Champs Elysées with Rossini's Guillaume Tell; British debut 1991, with Royal Philharmonic in a concert performance of Nabucco; Bellini's Zaira at Catania, 1990; Concerts at the Schleswig-Holstein Festival, the Philharmonic Berlin, the Frankfurt Alte Oper and the Philharmonie in Munich; English Chamber Orchestra with Rostropovich as soloist; Appointed Principal Conductor of the RAI Rome 1991; Deutsche Oper Berlin 1992 with La Forza del Destino, tour of Italy with the Royal Philharmonic 1993, Verdi Requiem at the Festival Hall 1994; Conducted Mosè at Covent Garden 1994; Madama Butterfly at Copenhagen, 1996; Season 1998 with L'Elisir d'amore at Madrid; Toured Italy with Royal Philharmonic Orchestra, London Philharmonic Orchestra and BBC Symphony Orchestra, 1998–2001; Verdi Requiem with the London Philharmonic Orchestra at the Festival Hall, 2001, Rigoletto in Rotterdam; Ballo in Maschera and Nabucco at Tokyo, 2000–01. *Address:* c/o IMG Artists, Lovell House, 616 Chiswick High Road, London W4 5RX, England.

OLMSTEAD, Andrea Louise, BM, MA; musicologist; b. 5 Sept. 1948, Dayton, Ohio, USA; m. Larry Thomas Bell 1982. *Education:* Hartt Coll. of Music, New York Univ. *Career:* faculty, The Juilliard School 1972–80, Boston Conservatory 1981–; mem. Sonneck Soc.. *Publications:* Roger Sessions and His Music 1985, Conversations with Roger Sessions 1987, The New Grove 20th Century American Masters 1987, The Correspondence of Roger Sessions 1992, Juilliard: A History 1999; contrib. to Journal of the Arnold Schoenberg Institute, American Music, Musical Quarterly, Tempo, Musical America, Perspectives of New Music, Music Library Asscn Notes. *Honours:* Nat. Endowment for the Humanities grants, Outstanding Academic Book, Choice 1986. *Address:* 73 Hemenway Street, Apt 501, Boston, MA 02115, USA. *E-mail:* LBell10276@aol.com. *Website:* www.AndreaOlmstead.com.

OLOF, Theo; Violinist; b. 5 May 1924, Bonn, Germany. *Education:* Studied with Oskar Back in Amsterdam. *Career:* Debut: Amsterdam in 1935; Tours of Europe, the USA and Russia from 1945 as soloist; Leader of the Hague Residentie Orchestra, 1951–71; Duo partnership with Hermann Krebbers included premieres of concertos written for them by Geza Frid, 1952, Henk Badings in 1954 and Hans Kox in 1964; Leader of the Concertgebouw Orchestra, 1974–85; Recitals with pianist, Janine Dacosta, and Gérard van Blerk until 1985 and teacher at the Hague Conservatory; Has given first performances of works by Bruno Maderna and Hans Henkemans. *Address:* de Lairessestraat 12 B, 1071 PA Amsterdam, Netherlands.

OLSEN, Derrick; Singer (Bass-Baritone) and Administrator; b. 30 March 1923, Berne, Switzerland. *Education:* Studied in Berne, Geneva and Lucerne. *Career:* Sang at Grand Théâtre Geneva, 1944–69, Basle, 1950–55, with guest engagements at Holland and Schwetzingen Festivals, Buenos Aires, Milan, Berlin Staatsoper, Zürich, Lucerne and Marseilles; Roles included Mozart's Count, Masetto and Alfonso, Pizarro, Rossini's Basilio and Bartolo, Iago, Germont and Melitone, Wagner's Dutchman, Telramund and Klingsor, Jochanaan, Malatesta and Achilles in Penthesilea by Schoeck; Sang at Basle Opera in 1952 and 1958 in the premieres of Leonore by Liebermann and Titus Feuerfuchs by Sutermeister; Concert premieres of oratorios by Honegger, Cantate de Noel, 1953, Kelterborn and Frank Martin, Mystère de la Nativité, 1958 and Martinů, Gilgamesh, 1958; Sang in the British premiere of Schoenberg's Von Heute auf Morgen, Festival Hall, 1963; Member of the Quatuor Vocale de Genève and Artistic Director of the Radio Orchestra Beromunster at Zürich, 1958–70. *Recordings:* Pelléas et Mélisande; Monteverdi's Combattimento; Sutermeister's Schwarze Spinne; Martin's Le Vin Herbé; Handel's Apollo e Dafne. *Address:* c/o Opernhaus Zürich, Falkenstrasse 1, 8008 Zürich, Switzerland.

OLSEN, Frode; Singer (bass); b. 10 April 1952, Oslo, Norway. *Education:* Studied at Opera State Conservatory in Oslo and Düsseldorf. *Career:* Debut: Düsseldorf, 1982; Sang at Deutsche Oper am Rhein Düsseldorf, 1982–86, notably as Mozart's Masetto and Don Alfonso; Badisches Staatstheater Karlsruhe from 1986, as Sarastro, Pimen, Gremin, Zaccaria, Wagner's Pogner, King Mark and Landgrave, Orestes and Basilio; Guest engagements at: Dresden, Leipzig, Strasbourg, Dortmund, Berne, Vienna, Volksoper, Oslo; Fasolt, in The Ring at Brussels, 1991; Salzburg Festival debut 1992, as a Soldier in Salome; Further appearances as: Sarastro at Brussels, 1992, King Ludwig, in Euryanthe at Music Festival in Aix-en-Provence, 1993, Doctor, in Wozzeck at Frankfurt, Gremin, in Eugene Onegin at the reopened Glyndebourne Opera House, 1994; Other roles include: Raimondo, the Commendatore in Don Giovanni, Colline, Timur, Elmiro in Rossini's Otello; Concert repertoire includes: Verdi's Requiem, Rossini's Petite Messe Solennelle, Stabat Mater, Messiah, Bach's Christmas Oratorio, St Matthew Passion, Elijah, Die Schöpfung; Melchtal in Guillaume Tell in Pesaro-Rossini Festival, 1995; Sang Gurnemanz, in Parsifal for first time, Rouen, France; For 1996 at Glyndebourne, Valens in Handel's Theodora, and Gremin in Onegin; Astradamors in Ligeti's Le grand Macabre with Salonen, and Doktor in Wozzek with Abbado at Salzburger Festspiele, 1997; Season 1998 with Gurnemanz at Brussels, Doktor in Hamburg, 1998; François in first German performance of Messiaen's St François of Assisi, Leipzig; Sang in the premiere of Berio's Cronaco del Luogo 1999; Season 2000–01 as King Mark at Strasbourg, followed by the Dutchman, and Dikoy in Katya Kabanova at Amsterdam. *Recordings:* Astradamors in Le grand Macabre with Salonen; Doktor in Wozzek with Metzmacher. *Current Management:* Athole Still International Management, Forresters Hall, 25–27 Westow Street, London, SE19 3RY, England. *Telephone:* (20) 8771-5271. *Fax:* (20) 8768-6600. *Website:* www.atholestill.com.

OLSEN, Keith, BM, MM; American singer (tenor); b. 1957, Denver, CO. *Education:* San Francisco Conservatory, University of Tennessee, Juilliard School of Music. *Career:* US debut with New York City Opera, 1982, in Die Lustige Witwe; European: Staatstheater Karlsruhe as Rodolfo in 1987; Sang at San Francisco as Capriccio, Helsinki, Los Angeles, Barcelona as Alfredo, Pretoria as Hoffmann and as Rodolfo in Hamburg, London, Arena di Verona, Frankfurt, Düsseldorf, Wiesbaden, Hannover and Toronto, with Manrico in Berlin and Leipzig, Hans in Stuttgart and Macduff in Bologna; Other guest appearances include Radames in Rome and Radio France with Dick Johnson, Turiddu and Hoffmann in Bonn; Film credits include Puccini's Des Grieux, 100th anniversary performance, RAI, Turiddu, South African Broadcasting Corporation and Beethoven's Ninth Symphony with Kurt Masur, Mittel Deutsche Rundfunk; Sang for three years at the Royal Opera House, Covent Garden, with debut as Rodolfo and subsequently as Pinkerton and Boris in Katya Kabanova; (Boris, 1997); Season 1997–98 as Don José at Toulouse and Calaf at Turin. *Recordings:* Giuliano in Handel's Rodrigo; Sang at Palermo Opera as Lensky (1999) and Cavaradossi (2001). *Address:* c/o San Francisco Opera, War Memorial Opera House, San Francisco, CA 94102, USA.

OLSEN, Stanford; Singer (tenor); b. 1959, Salt Lake City, Utah, USA. *Education:* Studied with the Metropolitan Opera Development Program. *Career:* For the Metropolitan Opera in New York has sung Arturo in Puritani, Don Ottavio, Ferrando, Belmonte, Idreno (Semiramide), Count Almaviva, Ernesto and Fenton; European career includes Don Ottavio at the Deutsche Oper Berlin, Rossini's Comte Ory for Netherlands Opera and Belmonte under John Eliot Gardiner; Concert at the Mostly Mozart Festival New York, in Boston and elsewhere for the

Handel and Haydn Society (Messiah and The Creation), for the Berlin Philharmonic (Berlioz Requiem, 1989) and at the Salzburg Festival with the International Bach Academy; New York recital debut at Alice Tully Hall 1990, with Die schöne Müllerin; Season 1993–94 at the Ravinia Festival in Fidelio, with the Houston Symphony in Britten's War Requiem and a tour of Spain with Messiah, conducted by Helmuth Rilling; Sang Iopas in Les Troyens at La Scala, 1996. *Current Management:* Athole Still International Management, Forresters Hall, 25–27 Westow Street, London, SE19 3RY, England. *Telephone:* (20) 8771-5271. *Fax:* (20) 8768-6600. *Website:* www.atholestill.com.

OMACHI, Yoichiro; Conductor; b. 22 Aug. 1931, Tokyo, Japan. *Education:* Studied at Tokyo Academy of Music, 1948–54, with Akeo Watanabe and Kurt Woss; Academy of Music, Vienna with Karl Bohm, Franco Ferrara, and Herbert von Karajan. *Career:* Toured Japan in 1957 with Karajan and the Berlin Philharmonic; Guest conductor with the Berlin Philharmonic, Tonkunstler Orchestra, Vienna, 1959; Chief Conductor, Tokyo Philharmonic Orchestra, 1961; Founded Tokyo Metropolitan Symphony, 1964; Guest conductor with Vienna Symphony Orchestra, 1964–67; Permanent Conductor of the Dortmund Opera, 1968–73; East Asian tour with the Tokyo Philharmonic, 1973; Season 1976–77 conducted Aida at Mannheim, Fidelio in Prague, Madama Butterfly at the Berlin Staatsoper and The Merry Widow in Tokyo; Concerts in Japan, South America, 1978–79; Madama Butterfly at the Vienna Staatsoper in 1980, Permanent Conductor, 1982–84, including Attila on Austrian television and ballet performances; Professor in Opera Faculty at the Tokyo Academy of Music. *Recordings:* Various with the Tokyo Philharmonic.

O'MARA, Stephen; Singer (Tenor); b. 1962, Brooklyn, New York, USA. *Career:* Sang widely in North America, including Turiddu and Radames at the New York City Opera; Vienna Staatsoper from 1991, as Don José and Pinkerton; Deutsche Oper Berlin, 1993, as José; Season 1994–95 as Tom Rakewell at Glyndebourne and Luigi in Il Tabarro at Cologne; Royal Opera, Copenhagen, 1996, as Alvaro in La Forza del Destino; Further appearances at Oslo, and the Bregenz Festival; Season 1998 as Samson at Montpellier and Narr' Havas in the premiere of Fénelon's Salammbô, at the Paris Opéra Bastille; Season 2000–01 as Verdi's Riccardo at Bregenz, Gabriele Adorno at Strasbourg, Radames for Houston Opera and Menelaus in Strauss's Die Aegyptische Helena at Cagliari. *Address:* c/o Opéra de la Bastille, 120 Rue de Lyon, 75012 Paris, France.

OMBUENA, Vicente; Tenor; b. 1949, Valencia, Spain. *Education:* Studied in Valencia. *Career:* Sang at first in concert then with Mainz Opera, 1989–91 as Don José, Erik, Cassio and Lysander in A Midsummer Night's Dream; Sang at Hamburg Staatsoper from 1991 notably as Ernesto in Don Pasquale; Season 2000–01 for New Israeli Opera at Savonlinna as Nemorino and in Tel-Aviv as Macduff; Verdi Requiem in Karlsruhe. *Recordings include:* Franchetti's Cristoforo Colombo. *Address:* Staatsoper Hamburg, Grosse Theaterstrasse 34, Pf 302448, W-2000 Hamburg 36, Germany.

OMILIAN, Jolanta; Singer (Soprano); b. 1956, Warsaw, Poland. *Education:* Studied at the Chopin Academy in Warsaw. *Career:* Debut: Venice in 1979 as Violetta; Sang widely in Germany including Bonn and Dortmund and at the 1985 Macerata Festival as Elisabetta in Roberto Devereux; Sang in Maria Stuarda at Palermo in 1989, Donizetti's Parisina at Basle in 1990 and Norma at Rio de Janeiro; Other roles include Dorabella and Leonora in Trovatore, Amenaide in Tancredi, Fiorilla in Il Turco in Italia, and Anaide in Mosè in Egitto. *Recordings include:* Adriano in Siria by Pergolesi; Il Bravo by Mercadante. *Address:* Montpellier Opéra, 11 Boulevard Victor Hugo, 34000 Montpellier, France.

ONAY, Gülsin; Concert Pianist; b. 1954, Istanbul, Turkey. *Education:* Studied at the Paris Conservatoire with Pierre Sancan and Nadia Boulanger and with Monique Haas and Bernhard Ebert. *Career:* Solo appearances with the Berlin Radio Symphony Orchestra, Austrian, Bavarian and North German Radio orchestras; Copenhagen Symphony, Staatskapelle Dresden, Mozarteum Orchestra Salzburg and the Tokyo Symphony; Repeated tours of west and east Europe, the Far East, in particular Japan; International Festival appearances: Steirischer Herbst, Warsaw autumn, Berliner Festtage, Mozartfest Würzburg, Istanbul Festival, Schleswig-Holstein Festival; Repertoire includes all the concertos of Beethoven, Brahms, Chopin, Liszt, Grieg, Schumann and Rachmaninov and A A Saygun; Mozart K414, K466, K467, K488, K491, K503 and K595 and for 2 pianos and orchestra; Saint-Saëns 2, Tchaikovsky 1, Bartók 2 and 3, Prokofiev 1 and 3, Ravel and Weber F minor; Dvořák piano concerto, de Falla (Nights in Gardens of Spain). *Recordings include:* Solos by Franck, Schubert (Harmonia Mundi); Chopin, Debussy, Ravel (KLAVINS); Bartók. *Address:* Schlossgasse 20, 79112 Freiburg, Germany.

ONCINA, Juan; Singer (Tenor); b. 15 April 1925, Barcelona, Spain. *Education:* Studied in Oran, Barcelona with Mercedes Caspir and in

Milan with Augusta Oltrabella. *Career:* Debut: Barcelona 1946, as Des Grieux in Manon; Sang opposite Tito Gobbi in Il Barbiere di Siviglia at Barcelona; Paris 1949 in Il Matrimonio Segreto; Florence 1949–50, in Cherubini's Osteria Portoghese and Lully's Armide; Glyndebourne 1952–65, as Don Ramiro in Cenerentola, Ferrando, Comte Ory, Scaramuccio in Ariadne auf Naxos, Rossini's Almaviva, Fenton in Falstaff, Don Ottavio, Lindoro in L'Italiana in Algeri and in Anna Bolena; Palermo 1959, in Belini's Beatrice di Tenda; Verdi and Puccini roles from 1963; Guest appearances in Monte Carlo, Venice, Triste and Florence; Vienna Staatsoper 1965; Hamburg 1971–74; Last major role as Cavaradossi, in Vienna, 1976. *Recordings:* Le Comte Ory and La Cenerentola from Glyndebourne; Don Pasquale; L'Arlesiana by Cilea; Un Giorno di Regno by Verdi; Donizetti's Roberto Devereux; Sacchini's Oedipe a Colonne. *Address:* c/o Hamburgische Staatsoper, Gross-Theaterstrasse 34, 2000 Hamburg 36, Germany.

O'NEIL, James; Singer (Tenor); b. 1954, Shawnee, Oklahoma, USA. *Career:* Debut: Santa Fe, 1978, in Salome; Sang at St Gallen and Berne, 1979–82; Bielefeld Opera from 1982, in Fennimore and Gerda by Delius, Schreker's Der singende Teufel and as Eleazar in La Juive; Staatsoper Berlin from 1985, as Arrigo in Les Vêpres Siciliennes, Turiddu and Lohengrin; Rome Opera, 1991, as Leukippos in Daphne by Strauss; Parsifal at Chemnitz, 1992, and Siegfried and Siegmund for Oslo Opera, 1993–96; Los Angeles, 1993, as Strauss's Emperor; Season 1996 as Oedipus Rex, Théâtre du Châtelet, Paris, and the title role in the premiere of Zemlinsky's Der König Kandaules, at Hamburg. *Address:* Hamburg Staatsoper, Grosse Theaterstrasse 34, 20354 Hamburg, Germany.

O'NEILL, Charles; Singer (Tenor); b. 22 Sept. 1930, Ridgefield Park, New Jersey, USA. *Education:* Studied in New York. *Career:* Debut: Fort Worth Opera in 1958 as Radames; Appearances at opera houses in Santa Fe, Cincinnati, Hamburg, Stuttgart, Berlin, Cologne, Frankfurt, Düsseldorf and Zürich; Member of the Theater am Gärtnerplatz Munich, with guest engagements at Toronto, Vancouver, Belgrade and Basle; Other roles have been Florestan, Don José, Don Carlos, Alvaro, Manrico, Otello, Turiddu, Samson, Cavaradossi, Rodolfo, Calaf, Andrea Chénier, Oedipus Rex by Stravinsky, Bacchus and Siegmund.

O'NEILL, Dennis; Singer (Tenor); b. 25 Feb. 1948, Pontarddulais, Wales. *Education:* Studied privately with Frederick Cox, Campogalliani and Ricci. *Career:* State Opera of South Australia, 1975–77, then principal tenor for Scottish Opera; Debuts with Covent Garden in Norma in 1979, Glyndebourne at the Italian Singer in Der Rosenkavalier in 1980, USA at Dallas in Lucia di Lammermoor in 1983, and Vienna Staatsoper as Alfredo in La Traviata in 1983; Has sung internationally including Hamburg, Berlin, Paris, Brussels, Marseilles, Nice, Munich, Cologne, Oslo, Barcelona, Zürich, Chicago, San Francisco, Metropolitan Opera, Vancouver, San Diego and Copenhagen; Long association with the Royal Opera House, Covent Garden in many roles including Rodolfo in La Bohème, the Duke in Rigoletto, Edgardo in Lucia di Lammermoor, Riccardo in Un Ballo in Maschera, and Foresto in Attila; Season 1992 with British Youth Opera Gala at Covent Garden, as Manrico in Munich, Riccardo at the Opéra Bastille and Radames at Tel-Aviv; Covent Garden 1994–95, as Radames in Aida; Season 1998 with Alfredo for the Royal Opera and Macduff at Geneva; Sang Radames at the Met, 1999 and Otello at Hamburg, 2000; Enzo in La Gioconda at ENO (concert) 2000; Season 2000–01 as Calaf at Covent Garden and Manrico for Australian Opera at Sydney. *Recordings include:* Opera Gala Recital, 1991. *Current Management:* Ingpen & Williams Ltd, 7 St George's Court, 131 Putney Bridge Road, London, SW15 2PA, England.

O'NEILL, Fiona; Singer (Soprano); b. 1958, England. *Education:* Studied at the Royal Northern College of Music; Masterclasses at Aldeburgh. *Career:* Solo roles have included Musetta, Norina and Donna Anna for Travelling Opera, Mabel in The Pirates of Penzance for New D'Oyly Carte, Serpetta in La Serva Padrona at the Northcutt Theatre in Exeter, and Salome for the Stockholm Folkopera at the Edinburgh Festival; English National Opera, 1990–91 as Papagena and as Gerda in Fennimore and Gerda; Sang the title role in Lakmé and Louise at the Bloomsbury Theatre and Pedrotti's Tutti in Maschera at the Britten Theatre; Concert engagements include Kurt Weill songs at the Cheltenham and Edinburgh Festivals; Premiere of Goehr's Sing Ariel, at the 1990 Aldeburgh Festival and Handel's Solomon at Birmingham in 1990; Festival Hall debut with the Philharmonia Orchestra in 1990 and debut at the Barbican with the RPO in 1991; Sang Mimi for Castleward Opera, 1996.

ONO, Kazushi; Conductor; b. 1961, Tokyo, Japan. *Education:* National Univ., Tokyo and in Munich with Wolfgang Sawallisch and Giuseppe Patanè. *Career:* Chief Conductor of the Tokyo Philharmonic, 1988, tour of England and Germany, 1994; Chief Conductor of the Zagreb Philharmonic Orchestra, 1988; Music Director, 1990–96; Hamburg Opera debut 1995 with Rigoletto; Music Director of the Karlsruhe Opera from 1996 with Symphonic concerts in charge of the Badisches Staatskapelle; Repertory includes La Traviata, La Bohème; Henze's Junge Lord and The Ring; Norma, Der fliegende Holländer and Schreker's Der Schatzgräber, 2000; Season 1999–2000 with the NDR Symphony in Hamburg and concerts in Frankfurt, Lyon and Bordeaux; British debut with Mahler 8 at Belfast; Further concerts with the BBC and Bournemouth Symphony Orchestra; Boston Symphony Orchestra debut, 1999 with Bartók and Prokofiev; Music Dir of La Monnaie, the Royal Opera House of Belgium, 2002–, producing Elektra by Strauss, I Due Foscari by Verdi, Ballata by Francesconi and Khovanshchina by Mussorgsky; He made his symphonic debut with a performance of Mahler 7. *Address:* c/o IMG Artists, Lovell House, 616 Chiswick High Road, London W4 5RX, England.

OOI, Chean See; Conductor; b. 1965, Malaysia. *Education:* Studied with Volker Wangenheim in Cologne and with W F Hausschild and Dennis Russell Davies. *Career:* Principal Conductor of the Classic Philharmonic Orchestra, Bonn, 1991–94; Guest conductor with German orchestras; Performances of Fidelio and Die Zauberflöte at Bahia, Brazil, 1998, 2000; Resident Conductor of the Malaysian Philharmonic Orchestra, 1997–; Conducting Workshops in Malaysia, Germany and France and with the Jeunesses Musicales World Orchestra; Season 1999–2000 with the Czech Virtuosi and Czech Philharmonic Choir. *Honours:* First Prize, Conductors Competition at Halle, Germany. *Address:* c/o IMG Artists, Lovell House, 616 Chiswick High Road, London W4 5RX, England.

OOSTWOUD, Roelof; Singer (Tenor); b. 16 Jan. 1946, Leeuwarden, Netherlands. *Education:* Studied at University of Toronto and with Louis Quilico. *Career:* Guest appearances in opera throughout North America and in London, Vienna, Paris and Amsterdam; Theater am Gärtnerplatz, Munich, from 1978; North American premiere of Verdi's Stiffelio (title role) with the Opera Company of Boston, 1978; Premiere of Berio's Vera Storia at La Scala, Milan, 1982; Düsseldorf from 1982, notably in Schreker's Die Gezeichneten, Henze's Bassarids (as Dionysus) and as Strauss's Bacchus (1995); Berne, 1992, as Sergei in Lady Macbeth, Coburg, 1996, as Verdi's Otello; Concert and oratorio performances; Sang Oreste in Gluck's Iphigénie en Tauride, Rio de Janeiro, 1997. *Address:* c/o Deutsche Oper am Rhein, Heinrich-Heine Alle 16a, 40213 Düsseldorf, Germany.

OPALACH, Jan; Singer (Bass-Baritone); b. 2 Sept. 1950, Hackensack, New Jersey, USA. *Education:* Studied at Indiana State University. *Career:* Sang at various regional USA operatic centres, New York City Opera from 1980 as Bartolo, Papageno, Schaunard, Kingfisher (Midsummer Marriage) and Leporello; Caramoor Festival, 1980, as Viltotta in the USA premiere of Haydn's La Vera Costanza; St Louis 1986 in USA premiere of Rossini's Il Viaggio a Reims; Sang at Seattle Opera, 1991–92, as the Music Master in Ariadne auf Naxos and Guglielmo in Così fan tutte; New York City Opera, 1991 as the Forester in The Cunning Little Vixen, Mozart's Figaro at Toronto; Sang in Rossini Gala Opera at New York's Fisher Hall, 29 February 1992; New York Premiere, B A Zimmerman's Die Soldaten, Wesener, NYCO, 1992; New York Premiere, Tippett's Midsummer Marriage, King Fisher, 1993; World Premiere, Glass's The Voyage, Metropolitan Opera, 1992; American Premiere, Schnittke's Faust Cantata, American Symphony Orchestra with Botstein; Rossini's Italiana in Algeri, Taddeo, Netherlands Opera; Season 1997–98 in Handel's Serse at the New York City Opera. *Recordings:* Solo Bach Cantatas and Bach Ensemble; 2 world premiere recordings R Beaser's Seven Deadly Sins, D Russell, American Composers' Orchestra (ARGO); Syringa, Elliott Carter; Speculum Musicae (Bridge). *Honours:* NEA Recital Grant, 1986; W M Naumburg Vocalist Award, 1989; Metropolitan Opera Nationals Award; Hertogenbosch Vocalisten Concours, 1981. *Current Management:* Janice Mayer and Associates. *Address:* 201 West 54 Street, Suite 1c, New York, NY 10019, USA.

OPIE, Alan; Singer (Baritone); b. 22 March 1945, Redruth, Cornwall, England. *Education:* Guildhall School of Music, London; London Opera Centre with Vera Rozsa. *Career:* Debut: Sadler's Wells Opera 1969, as Papageno in Die Zauberflöte; Appearances with English National Opera, Welsh National Opera, Aldeburgh Festival and Santa Fe Opera; Other roles include Mozart's Guglielmo, Rossini's Figaro, Verdi's Germont, Britten's Demetrius and Charles Blount (Gloriana) and Massenet's Lescaut; Sang Wagner's Beckmesser with English National Opera 1984 and at Bayreuth, 1987, 1988, Berlin, 1990, Munich, 1994; Sang Germont with ENO, 1990 and the title role in Busoni's Doctor Faust; Glyndebourne Festival 1990, as Sid in Albert Herring; Season 1992 as The Fiddler in Königskinder for ENO, Balstrode in Peter Grimes at Glyndebourne, Melitone in The Force of Destiny and Papageno at the Coliseum; Balstrode at New York Metropolitan, 1994; Panza in Don Quichotte, Paolo in Munich, 1995; Title Role in World premiere of Berio's Outis at Las Scala, Milan in 1996 and again in 1999 and Châtelet, Paris, 1999. Sang Rossini's Taddeo for ENO, 1997; Balstrode in Peter Grimes at the New York Met, 1998; Season 1998 as Don Alfonso at Glyndebourne, Janáček's Gamekeeper at Spoleto and Sharpless in Madama Butterfly at the New York Met; Has sung

Beckmesser in Meistersinger at Munich in 1994, 1996, 1997 and 1998 and Vienna, 1999; Season 2000–01 as Britten's Balstrode at the Vienna Staatsoper, Don Carlo in Ernani for ENO, Don Alfonso at Glyndebourne, Strauss's Faninal at the Met and Germont for the Royal Opera, Covent Garden. *Recordings include:* Maria Stuarda by Donizetti (EMI); The Bear, Rape of Lucretia, Troilus and Cressida, Barber of Seville; Hugh the Drover; Beckmesser in Meistersinger; Balstrode in Peter Grimes; Tonio in Pagliacci; Marcello in La Bohème. *Honours:* Grammies for Balstrode in Peter Grimes, 1996 and Beckmesser in Die Meistersinger, 1997; Nominated for an Olivier Award, Outstanding Achievement in Opera for Falstaff, 1998. *Address:* c/o Allied Artists Agency, 42 Montpelier Square, London SW17 1JZ, England.

OPPENHEIM, David J.; Clarinettist and University Dean (Emeritus); b. 13 April 1922, Detroit, Michigan, USA; m. (1) Judy Holiday, 1948, 1 s., (2) Ellen Adler, 1957, 1 s., 1 d., (3) Patricia Jaffe, 1987. *Education:* Interlochen National Music Camp, Michigan; Juilliard School of Music, New York, 1939–40; University of Rochester Eastman School of Music, 1940–43. *Career:* Director, Masterworks Division, Columbia Records, 1950–59; Producer, Director, Writer, Network News, CBS Television, 1962–68; Executive Producer, Public Broadcasting Laboratory, 1968–69; Co-Producer of Saul Bellow's Last Analysis, Broadway, New York, 1962; Producer of documentary films on Stravinsky and Casals, CBS; Executive Producer, Cultural Programming, Public Broadcasting Laboratory; Clarinet soloist, Prades, France, 1957, San Juan, Puerto Rico, 1959; Performed under Koussevitsky, Toscanini, Leinsdorf, Steinberg, Bernstein, Stokowski, Stravinsky; Performed chamber music with Casals, Serkin and Casadesus; Tony Awards Nominating Committee, 1983–87; Artist-in-Residence, New Mexico, Music Festival; Chamber music performer with Istomin Horzowski. *Recordings:* Brahms Clarinet Quintet with Budapest Quartet; Mozart Clarinet Quintet in A Major with Budapest Quartet; L'histoire du Soldât, Octet, Septet (premiere), conducted by Stravinsky; Bernstein Sonata, clarinet and Leonard Bernstein, piano (dedicated to David Oppenheim); Copland Sextet with Juilliard Quartet; Douglas Moore Quintet with New Music Quartet. *Address:* 1225 Park Avenue 6A, New York, NY 10128, USA.

OPPENS, Ursula; Concert Pianist; b. 2 Feb. 1944, New York City, USA. *Education:* BA, Radcliffe College, 1965; Juilliard School 1966–69, with Rosina Lhevinne, Guido Agosti and Leonard Shure. *Career:* Debut: New York, 1969; Performances with Boston Symphony, New York Philharmonic and other leading American orchestras; Recitals at Tully Hall, Kennedy Center; Appearances at Aspen, Berkshire and Marlboro Festivals; Tours of Europe and US as soloist and as member of Speculum Musicae; Performances of contemporary music; Engagements with the Chamber Music Society of Lincoln Center and the Group for Contemporary Music; Composers who have written for her include Rzeweski, Wolff, Carter and Wuorinen; Teacher at Brooklyn College, City University of New York. *Recordings include:* Busoni, Mozart and Rzewski. *Honours:* Winner, Busoni International Piano Competition, 1969; Avery Fisher Prize, 1976. *Current Management:* Colbert Artists Management, 111 West 57, New York, NY 10019, USA. *Address:* c/o Witmer Management, Leidsegracht 42, NL–1016 CM Amsterdam, Netherlands.

OPRISANU, Carmen; Singer (Mezzo-soprano); b. 1964, Brasov, Romania. *Education:* Studied at the Cluj Music Academy. *Career:* Sang with the Romanian Opera at Cluj, 1986–93, and gave concerts with the Bucharest Radio Symphony Orchestra and the Georges Enescu Philharmonic (tours of Italy and Spain); Bucharest State Opera 1993, as Carmen and Rosina; Lucerne Theatre 1993–96, as Carmen, Suzuki, Isabella in L'Italiana in Algeri, the Composer (Ariadne auf Naxos), Sesto in La Clemenza di Tito and Adalgisa; Season 1995 as Isabella at the Deutsche Oper Berlin and Sigismondo in the German premiere of Rossini's opera, at Wildbad; Charlotte in Werther, Rosina and Maddalena with the Zürich Opera; Season 1997–98, Rosina in Covent Garden and Barcelona, Cenerentola at Hamburg, Pierotto in Linda di Chamonix with La Scala, in Zürich as Fenena in Nabucco and Hänsel; Season 1998–99, Carmen and Charlotte in Amsterdam and Charlotte in Madrid; Season 2000 as Orlofsky for Zürich Opera, Rossini's Isabella for New Israeli Opera and Dulcinée in Don Quichotte at the Opéra Bastille, Paris. *Recordings:* Title role in Sigismondo; Orlofsky in Fledermaus and Elisabetta in Maria Stuerda (Nightingale Classics). *Honours:* Prizewinner at the 1992 Vienna Belvedere Competition and the 1995 Placido Domingo Operalia Competition, in Madrid; Winner, Leonard Bernstein International Oratorio and Song Competition, Jerusalem, 1996. *Address:* c/o Opernhaus Zürich, Falkenstrasse 1, 8008 Zürich, Switzerland.

ORAMO, Sakari; Conductor and Violinist; b. 1966, Helsinki, Finland; m. Anu Komsi. *Education:* Sibelius Acad., Utrecht Conservatoire. *Career:* founder mem. of the Avanti Chamber Orchestra 1982–89; violin leader of the Finnish Radio Symphony Orchestra 1991, co-principal conductor 1994–; further engagements with major Scandinavian orchestras, City of Birmingham Symphony, BBC Symphony and Philharmonic, London

Sinfonietta and Rotterdam Philharmonic; Danish Radio Symphony 1994–, tour of Australia; Principal Conductor, City of Birmingham Symphony 1997, conducting the Sibelius Violin Concerto and Nielsen's Fifth at the London Prom concerts 1999, and conducting at London Proms 2002, 2003. *Current Management:* Harrison/Parrott Ltd, 12 Penzance Place, London, W11 4PA, England. *Telephone:* (20) 7229 9166. *Fax:* (20) 7221 5042. *Website:* www.harrisonparrott.com.

ORBAN, György; Hungarian composer; b. 12 July 1947, Tirgu-Mures, Romania. *Education:* Cluj Conservatory, 1968–73. *Career:* Teacher of Theory, Cluj Conservatory, –1979; moved to Hungary, became Ed., Editio Musica Budapest; Teacher of Composition, Music Acad., Budapest. *Compositions:* orchestra: Five Canons to Poems by Attile Joszef for soprano and chamber ensemble, 1977; Triple Sextet, 1980; 2 Serenades, 1984, 85; 4 Duos with soprano and clarinet, 1979; Soprano and double bass, 1987; Soprano and Violoncello, 1989; Soprano and Violin, 1992; Sonata Concertante for clarinet and piano, 1987; Wind Quintet, 1984; Brass Music for Quintet No. 1, 1987; Sonata for bassoon and piano, 1987; Sonata for violin, 1970; 2 Sonatas for Violin and Piano, 1989, 91; 3 Suites for piano, 1986, 1997, 1998; 4 Piano Sonatas, 1987, 88, 89; chorus and orchestra: Rorarte Coeli, oratorio, 1992; Regina Martyrum, oratorio, 1993; Missa No. 2, 1990, No. 4, 1991, No. 6, 1993; chorus and chamber ensemble: Missa No. 7, 1993; Flower Songs for Female Choir, 1978; Chorus Book in Memory of S A No. 1, 1984; Chorus Book No. 2; Book of Medallions, cycle of 9 choruses, 1987; Stabat Mater, 1987; Passion, oratorio, 1997; Christmas Oratorio, 1998; Sketches from Verona, for orchestra, 1998; 3 string quartets, 1994, 1994, 1998; about 40 Latin motets for mixed and female chorus. *Address:* 1016 Budapest, Mészáros u. 15–17, Hungary.

ORCIANI, Patrizia; Singer (Soprano); b. 1959, Fano, Urbino, Italy. *Education:* Studied at the Bologna Conservatory. *Career:* Debut: Fano in 1983 as Mimi in La Bohème; Has sung widely in Italy notably as Liu at the 1991 Verona Festival and as Handel's Cleopatra at the Valle d'Istria Festival; Sang at the Bonn Opera, 1991–92; Other roles include Donizetti's Adina and Norina, Rossini's Elvira, Micaela and Giulietta in Les Contes d'Hoffmann; Season 1998 as Lucieta in Wolf Ferrari's Il campiello at Bologna and Venus in Tannhäuser at Palermo. *Recordings include:* Cimarosa's L'Italiana in Londra; Nina by Paisiello; Il Signor Bruschino. *Address:* c/o Bonn Opera, Am Boeselagerhof 1, Pf 2440, W-5300 Bonn, Germany.

ORDONEZ, Antonio; Singer (Tenor); b. 27 Oct. 1948, Madrid, Spain. *Education:* Studied in Madrid with Miguel Garcia Barrosa. *Career:* Concert appearances in Spain and USA from 1980; Opera debut at Teatro Zarzuela Madrid 1982, as Pinkerton; Sang Don Carlos at Liège 1986 and at Deutsche Oper Berlin 1988; Teatro Liceo Barcelona 1986, in Pacini's Saffo, with Montserrat Caballé; Further guest appearances as Cavaradossi at Dallas 1987, Calaf at Ravenna Festival 1988 and as Alvaro in La Forza del Destino at Washington 1989; San Francisco Opera 1991 as Foresto in Attila; Other roles include Rodolfo, Deutsche Oper 1989, Alfredo, Riccardo, Gabriele Adorno and Edgardo in Lucia di Lammermoor, Liège 1987; Sang Don José in Carmen at Earl's Court, London 1991. *Address:* c/o San Francisco Opera, War Memorial Opera House, San Francisco, CA 94102, USA.

ORE, Cecilie; Composer; b. 19 July 1954, Oslo, Norway. *Education:* Piano studies at Norwegian State Academy of Music and in Paris; Studied Composition with Ton de Leeuw at Sweelinck Conservatory, Amsterdam, and at Institute of Sonology in Utrecht. *Career:* Frequent performances at Nordic and international festivals; Commissioned by BBC Symphony Orchestra; mem, Society of Norwegian Composers. *Compositions:* Orchestral music: Porphyre, 1986; Nunc et Nunc, 1994; Chamber music: Helices, for wind quintet, 1984; Preasems Subitus, for string quartet, 1989; Erat Erit Est, for ensemble, 1991; Futurum exactum, for string ensemble, 1992; Lex Temporis, for string quartet, 1992; Ictus, for 6 percussionists, 1997; Semper Semper, for saxophone quartet, 1998; Nunquam Non, for ensemble, 1999; Non Nunquam, for string trio, 1999; Cirrus, for string quartet, 2002; Cumulus, for wind trio, 2002; Schwirren for vocal ensemble, 2003; Music for dramatic work: A. – a shadow opera, 2001. *Recordings:* Codex Temporis, 1996; Tempora Mutantur, 2002; A. – a shadow opera, 2003. *Honours:* 1st and 2nd Prize, International Rostrum for Electro-acoustic Music, 1988. *Address:* Ullevålsvn 61 B, 0171 Oslo, Norway.

O'REILLY, Brendan; Violinist; b. 1935, Dublin, Ireland. *Education:* Studied at Belvedere College Dublin, with David Martin at the Royal Academy of Music and with Andre Gertler in Brussels. *Career:* Played with the Radio Eireann String Quartet in Cork, then freelanced with the Royal Philharmonic and the English Chamber Orchestra; Co-founded the Gabrieli Quartet in 1967 touring Europe, North America, the Far East and Australia; Festival engagements in the United Kingdom, including Aldeburgh, City of London and Cheltenham; Concerts every season in London, participation in the Barbican Centre's Mostly Mozart Festival and resident artist at the University of Essex from 1971; Has co-premiered works by William Alwyn, Britten, Alan Bush, Daniel Jones and Gordon Crosse, 3rd Quartet of John McCabe in 1979 and the 2nd Quartets of Nicholas Maw and Panufnik, 1983–80; British premiere of the Piano Quintet by Sibelius in 1990. *Recordings:* 5 CDs including early pieces by Britten, Dohnányi's Piano Quintet with Wolfgang Manz, Walton's Quartets and the Sibelius Quartet and Quintet, with Anthony Goldstone. *Address:* c/o GRMAM, 8 Wren Crescent, Bushey Heath, Herts, WD23 1AN, England.

O'REILLY, Graham (Henry Meredith); Singer, Conductor and Musicologist; b. 4 Sept. 1947, Parkes, New South Wales, Australia; m. (1) Jill Barralet, 2 Sept 1972, divorced, 1 s., 1 d., (2) Brigitte Vinson, 27 Dec 1986, 2 d. *Education:* BA, Honours, University of Sydney, 1968; Associate, Sydney Conservatorium of Music, 1966; Licentiate, Trinity College, London, 1969. *Career:* Debut: Messiah at Sydney Town Hall in 1971; Music Teacher in Sydney, 1970–73; Researcher of late Restoration stage music, 1973–, and pitch in Renaissance vocal music, 1979–; Concert and session singer in London, 1973–82; Director for early music ensembles, 1976–, and for The Restoration Musick, 1980–81, Psallite, 1981–86 and Ensemble européen William Byrd, 1983–; Singing Teacher, 1980–93; Member of Groupe Vocal de France, 1982–86; Solo oratorio and ensemble singer specialising in early music. *Recordings:* With Psallite: Music by Tallis, Byrd and Gibbons and Collected Works of Jon Dixon; With Groupe Vocal de France: Sacred Music of Giacinto Scelsi; With Ensemble William Byrd: English Music of The Seventeenth Century, Vol. 1: Orlando Gibbons, Vol. 2: Welcome Vicegerent, music of Henry Purcell; Palestrina: Canticum Canticorum; Handel: Music for Cannons, Vol. 1; 3 Chandos anthems; Handel: Dixit Dominus, Nisi Dominus; Scarlatti: Musica Sacra; Miserere, (Allegri/Bai, F Scarlatti, Leo); The Last Judgement, Charpentier. *Publications:* Editor, Eccles: Music to Macbeth, Cathedral Music, 1978. *Honours:* Frank Busby Musical Scholarship, Sydney University, 1967. *Address:* 10 rue Massenet, 93600 Aulnay-Sous-Bois, France. *E-mail:* Grabyrdy@aol.com.

ORGONASOVA, Luba; Singer (Soprano); b. 22 Jan. 1961, Bratislava, Czechoslovakia. *Education:* Studied at Bratislava Conservatory. *Career:* Concert and operatic engagements in Czechoslovakia 1979–83; Hagen Opera, West Germany, 1983–88 as Mozart's Ilia and Pamina, Gilda and Violetta, Lauretta and Sophie in Der Rosenkavalier; Guest appearances in Nuremberg, Essen, Hamburg and Zürich; Vienna Volksoper 1988–89; Sang Pamina and Donna Anna at Aix-en-Provence Festival, 1988–89; Opéra de Lyon 1988 as Madame Silberklang in Der Schauspieldirektor; Sang Constanze at Deutsche Oper Berlin and in Lisbon 1991, with concert performances of Die Entführung under John Eliot Gardiner in London and Amsterdam; Other roles include Susanna, Atalanta in Handel's Serse, Marzelline, Cendrillon and Antonia, Les Contes d'Hoffmann; Sang Donna Anna at Chicago, 1995; Season 1999–2000 as Donna Anna at the Opéra Bastille, Gluck's Euridice at Zürich and Elettra in Idomeneo at Salzburg; Concert repertoire includes Janáček's Glagoltic Mass, Bruckner's Te Deum and the Missa Solemnis, all at Zürich, Haydn's Harmonie Mass at Bremen and Oratorios by Bach, Handel and Dvořák. *Recordings:* Die Zauberflöte. *Address:* c/o Chicago Light Opera, 20 North Wacker Drive, Chicago, IL 60604, USA.

ORKIS, Lambert Thomas, BM, MM; American pianist, fortepianist and educator; b. 20 April 1946, Philadelphia, PA; m. Janice Barbara Kretschmann 1972. *Education:* Curtis Institute of Music, Temple Univ. *Career:* world-wide performances; premiered solo works of George Crumb, Richard Wernick, Maurice Wright and James Primosch, including Wernick's Piano Concerto, Washington, DC and Carnegie Hall, New York, with National Symphony Orchestra, conducted by Mstislav Rostropovich 1991; recitals with cellist Mstislav Rostropovich 1981–, with violinist Anne-Sophie Mutter 1988–, with soprano Arleen Augér 1987–90, with soprano Lucy Shelton 1981–, with cellist Han-Na Chang 2001, with violinist Julian Rachlin 2000; founding mem., fortepianist, Castle Trio 1988–; pianist, Smithsonian Chamber Music Soc. 1983–; Honoured Artist, New Aspect International Arts Festival, Taipei, Taiwan 1996; pianist, Library of Congress Summer Chamber Festival 1986–89, American Chamber Players 1986–89, 20th Century Consort 1976–87; soloist with National Symphony Orchestra, Great Performances (PBS) 1983; soloist-in-residence 1983; principal keyboard, National Symphony Orchestra, Washington, DC 1982–; Faculty mem., Temple Univ., Philadelphia; Prof. of Piano, Co-ordinator of Master of Music programme in piano accompanying and Chamber Music 1968–; soloist, National Symphony Orchestra Piano 2000 Festival; trios with Anne-Sophie Mutter and Lynn Harrell 2001–2002; pianist, Bay Chamber Concerts Summer Music Festival 2002–, Kennedy Center Chamber Players 2003–; judge at Carnegie Hall Int. American Music Competition for Pianists 1985, Kennedy Center Friedheim Awards 1991, Trondheim Int. Chamber Music Competition 2003. *Recordings:* solo: Music of Louis Moreau Gottschalk, 1988; Schubert Impromptus, 1990; Schubert Moment Musicaux and 3 Klavierstücke, 1993; George Crumb, A Little Suite for Christmas, Richard Wernick, Sonata for

Piano, 1986; Richard Wernick, Piano Concerto, with Symphony II, composer conducting, 1998; with Anne-Sophie Mutter: Berlin Recital, 1996, Beethoven Cycle of 10 Sonatas for Piano and Violin, 1998; Bartók Sonata No. 2, 1998; with Anner Bylsma: Works by Franchomme and Chopin, 1994, works by Brahms and Schumann, 1995; with Arleen Augér: Schubert Lieder, 1991; with Castle Trio: Beethoven Cycle of Piano Trios, 1989–92; Recital 2000, 2000; A Life With Beethoven (DVD), 2000; The Complete Violin Sonatas (DVD), 2001; Tango, Song and Dance, 2003; Keys to the Future, works of Richard Wernick and James Primosch, 2003. *Publications:* A Journey Back to Beethoven (article) 1998. *Honours:* Grammy Award, Best Chamber Music Performance 1999, Best Classical Album 1999, National Public Radio Critic's Choice Award 1999, Temple University Faculty Award for Creative Achievement 1982. *Address:* PO Box 6023, Arlington, VA 22206-0023, USA. *Telephone:* (703) 998-0791. *Fax:* (703) 998-6531. *E-mail:* orkispiano@lambertorkis.com. *Website:* www.lambertorkis.com.

ORLANDI MALASPINA, Rita; Singer (Soprano); b. 28 Dec. 1937, Bologna, Italy; m. Massimiliano Malaspina. *Education:* Studied with Carmen Melis in Milan. *Career:* Debut: Teatro Nuovo Milan, 1963 as Verdi's Giovanna d'Arco; Sang widely in Italy, and at Covent Garden, London, Munich, Hamburg, Paris, Nice, Barcelona, Vienna and Buenos Aires; Metropolitan Opera debut 1968; Other roles included Puccini's Tosca and Suor Angelica, Wagner's Elsa, Giordano's Maddalena and Verdi's Aida, Odabella, Leonora, Amelia, Abigaille, Desdemona, Luisa Miller, Elisabeth and Lucrezia (I Due Foscari); Also heard in concert. *Address:* c/o Teatro alla Scala, Via Filodrammatici 2, Milan, Italy.

ORLOFF, Claudine; Pianist; b. 6 Jan. 1961, Brussels, Belgium; m. Burkard Spinnier, 1 Oct 1983, 2 s. *Education:* Diplome superieur, Piano, class of J C Vanden Eunden, 1985, Diplome superieur, Chamber Music, class of A Siwy, 1987, Conservatoire Royal de Musique, Brussels; Private studies with B Lemmens, 1985–88. *Career:* Recording for RTB, 1978; Regular appearances as soloist and in chamber music; Often includes contemporary works in recital programmes, including Van Rossum's 12 preludes, 1986; Many concerts on 2 pianos (with Bukard Spinnier), Belgium, France, Germany, including Musique en Sorbonne, Paris, July 1991; Radio engagement, Hommage a Milhaud, live, RTB Brussels, Oct 1992. *Honours:* Ella Olin Prize, Brussels, 1985. *Current Management:* F E de Wasswige Music Management. *Address:* c/o Conservatoire Royale de Musique, 30 Rue de la Régence, B–1000 Brussels, Belgium.

ORMAI, Gabor; Violist; b. 1950, Hungary. *Education:* Studied with Andras Mihaly at the Franz Liszt Academy, Budapest, with members of the Amadeus Quartet and Zoltán Szekely. *Career:* Founder member of the Takacs Quartet, 1975; Many concert appearances in all major centres of Europe and the USA; Tours of Australia, New Zealand, Japan, South America, England, Norway, Sweden, Greece, Belgium and Ireland; Bart ók Cycle for the Bart ók-Solti Festival at South Bank, 1990; Great Performers Series at Lincoln Center and Mostly Mozart Festival at Alice Tully Hall, New York; Visits to Japan 1989 and 1992; Mozart Festivals at South Bank, Wigmore Hall and Barbican Centre, 1991; Bart ók Cycle at the Théâtre des Champs Elysées, 1991; Beethoven Cycles at the Zürich Tonhalle, in Dublin, at the Wigmore Hall and in Paris, 1991–92; Resident at the University of Colorado, Resident at the London Barbican, 1988–91, with masterclasses at the Guildhall School of Music; Plays Amati instrument made for the French Royal Family and loaned by the Corcoran Gallery, Gallery of Art, Washington DC. *Recordings:* Schumann Quartets Op 41, Mozart String Quintets (with Denes Koromzay), Bartók 6 Quartets, Schubert Trout Quintet (with Zoltán Kocsis) Hungaroton; Haydn Op 76, Brahms Op 51, Nos 1 and 2, Chausson Concerto (with Joshua Bell and Jean-Yves Thibaudet); Works by Schubert, Mozart, Dvořák and Bartók. *Honours:* Winner, International Quartet Competition, Evian, 1977; Winner, Portsmouth International Quartet Competition, 1979. *Address:* c/o Phelps, Takaes Quartet, 6 Malvern Road, London, E8 3LT, England.

ORREGO-SALAS, Juan A.; Composer, Professor of Music and Architect; b. 18 Jan. 1919, Santiago, Chile; m. Carmen Benavente 1943, 4 s., 1 d. *Education:* BA 1938, MA 1943, State Uniersity of Chile. *Career:* Conductor, Catholic University Choir, 1938–44; Professor of Musicology, Faculty of Music, State University of Chile, 1942–61; Editor, Revista Musical Chilena, 1949–53; Music Critic, El Mercurio, 1950–61; Director, Instituto de Extension Musical, Chile, 1957–59; Chairman, Music Department, Catholic University, Chile, 1951–61; Professor of Music, Director of Latin American Music Centre, Indiana University, USA, 1961–. *Compositions include:* Orchestral: Variaciones serenas for strings, 1971; Volte for chamber orchestra, 1971; Symphony No. 4, 1966; Violin Concerto, 1983; Second Piano Concerto, 1985; Cello Concerto, 1992; Symphony No. 5, 1995; Sinfonia in One Movement, 1997; Chamber Music: Trio No. 2, 1977; Presencias, 1972; Tangos, 1982; Balada for cello and piano, 1983; Partita, 1988; 2 string quartets, 1957, 1996; Piano Quintetm 1997; Vocal Music: Missa in tempore discordige, 1969; The Days of God, 1974–76; Bolivar for narrator, chorus and orchestra, 1982; The Celestial City, 1992; Stage Music: The Tumbler's Prayer (ballet), 1960; Widows (opera), 1989; Introduction and Allegro Concertante for one piano, four hands and chamber orchestra, 1999. *Publications include:* Latin American Literary Review, 1975; Music of the Americas (co-editor), 1967; Encyclopedia Americana, 1970. *Contributions:* Musical Quarterly; Tempo; Revista Musical. *Address:* 490 S Serena Lane, Bloomington, IN 47401, USA.

ORSANIC, Vlatka; Singer (Soprano); b. 29 Jan. 1958, Zabok, Croatia. *Career:* Sang at Ljubiana Opera from 1979, as Lucia, Gilda, Elvira in I Puritani and Rossini's Rosina; Belgrade, 1981, as Lucia, and guest appearances elsewhere in Yugoslavia; Darmstadt Opera from 1992, as Jenůfa, Rosalinde, Mimi, Mozart's Vitellia and Donna Anna, Tatiana and Traviata; Essen, 1995, as Shostakovich's Lady Macbeth, and Rusalka; Katya Kabanova at Darmstadt, 1996; Vienna Konzerthaus in War and Peace, Janáček's Mr Brouček and Schumann's Genoveva; Komische Oper, Berlin, 1998, as Verdi's Lady Macbeth; As Mozart's Elettra at Salzburg Festspielhaus and as Verdi's Leonora (Trovatore) in Bonn; Sang Shostakovich's Lady Macbeth at Meiningen, 1999 and Verdi's at Leipzig. *Address:* Komische Oper, Behrenstrasse 55–57, 10117 Berlin, Germany.

ORTH, Norbert; Singer (Tenor); b. 1939, Dortmund, Germany. *Education:* Studied in Hamburg and Cologne and at the Dortmund Opera House School. *Career:* Sang in Enschede, Netherlands, then at opera houses in Düsseldorf, Nuremburg, Munich, Paris, Berlin and Stuttgart; Metropolitan Opera 1979, as Pedrillo in Die Entführung; Augsburg 1981, as Max in Der Freischütz; Appearances at the Salzburg and Bayreuth Festivals; Loge in Das Rheingold 1984; Sang Walther in Die Meistersinger at Hanover 1986; Sang Tannhäuser at Kassel 1988, Lohengrin at Hanover and Wiesbaden; Walther in Die Meistersinger at the rebuilt Essen Opera, 1988; Théâtre du Châtelet, Paris 1990, as Walther; Season 1992 as Berg's Alwa at Dresden and Parsifal at Turin; Also heard in the concert hall, as Lieder and oratorio singer. *Recordings:* Die Entführung; Schubert's Die Freunde von Salamanka; Augustin Moser in Die Meistersinger, Bayreuth 1974. *Address:* c/o Niedersächsische Staatstheater, Opernplatz 1, 300 Hannover 1, Germany.

ORTIZ, Cristina; Brazilian concert pianist; b. 17 April 1950, Bahia; d. of Silverio M. Ortiz and Moema F. Ortiz; m. Jasper W. Parrott 1974; two d. *Education:* Conservatório Brasileiro de Música, Rio de Janeiro, Acad. Int. de Piano (with Magda Tagliaferro), Paris and Curtis Inst. of Music, Philadelphia (with Rudolph Serkin). *Career:* New York recital debut 1971; has appeared in concerts with the Vienna Philharmonic, Berlin Philharmonic, the Concertgebouw, Chicago Symphony, New York Philharmonic, Israel Philharmonic, Los Angeles Philharmonic, leading British orchestras and has undertaken many tours of North and South America, the Far East, New Zealand and Japan; appeared with NHK Symphony, the Bergen Philharmonic and Philharmonia under Janowski 1997; has recorded extensively for EMI, Decca, Pantheon, Collins Classics and Pickwick Records; played with conductors including Previn, Mehta, Kondrashin, Ashkenazy, Leinsdorf, Chailly, Masur, Salonen, Colin Davis, Janssons, Fedoseyev, Zinman, Rattle, Järvi and Fürst. *Honours:* First Prize Van Cliburn Int. Competition, Texas 1969. *Current Management:* Harrison-Parrott Ltd, 12 Penzance Road, London, W11 4PA, England. *Telephone:* (20) 7229-9166.

ORTIZ, Francisco; Singer (Tenor); b. 1948, Spain. *Education:* Studied in Barcelona and Madrid. *Career:* Debut: Barcelona 1973, as Foresto in Attila; Further appearances as Foresto in London, Paris, 1974, Madrid and Venice, 1976, Toulouse, 1979; New York City Opera 1973, as Turiddu, Nice 1974, as Radames, Geneva 1975, as Puccini's Des Grieux; Sang Pollione in Norma at Amsterdam, Barcelona and Vienna 1978–80; Théâtre de la Monnaie Brussels 1981, as Cavaradossi, Sydney Opera 1982, as Manrico; Further engagements at Hamburg, Santiago, Ernani 1979, Paris, Rio de Janeiro and the Vienna Staatsoper, Alvaro in La Forza del Destino; Appeared with Canadian Opera Company at Toronto as Pollione 1991; Performances in Zarzuela and as concert artist. *Address:* c/o Canadian Opera Company, 227 Front Street East, Toronto, Ontario MFA 1E8, Canada.

ORTIZ, William; Composer; b. 30 March 1947, Salinas, Puerto Rico; m. Candida Ortiz, 26 Mar 1988, 3 d. *Education:* Puerto Rico Conservatory of Music; MA, PhD, State University of New York, Stony Brook; State University of New York at Buffalo. *Career:* About 100 works for orchestra, chamber ensembles, solo works, songs, opera and electronic music; Composer-in-Residence, Atlantic Center for the Arts; mem, Society of Composers; American Composers Alliance; American Music Center; Composers Forum. *Compositions include:* Tropicalización, 1999; Trio Concertante en 3 Realidades; Unknown Poets from the Full-Time Jungle for soprano and piano, 1992; Loaisai; Nueva York Tropical; Caribe Urbano, for Violin, Viola, Violoncello, 1995; Garabato; A Sensitive Mambo in Transformation; Suspension de Soledad en 3 Tiempos 1990; Rican, street opera, 1991; 2 string quartets 1976, 1987; Graffiti Nuvorican, 1988; Cantilena for guitar, 1996; Montage para

sueño for orchestra, 2001; Fotografia de Héctor, for guitar, 1997; Esta es la tierra de los que aguantan callados y pacientes por un nuevo despertar, Guitar Concierto, 2001; Elogio a la Plena, for Band, 2002. *Recordings:* 1245 E 107th Street; Amor, Cristal y Piedra; William Ortiz Chamber Music; Abrazo; New Music for Four Guitars; Freedom Flight: Guitar Music of Ortiz and Piorkowski. *Publications:* Du-Wop and Dialectics, in Perspectives of New Music, 1988; Musical Snobbism, Latin American Music Conference; Music Critic to San Juan Star. *Honours:* Music Composition Prize, Ateneo Puertorriqueno, 1989; Guest Composer, Latin American Music Festival, Caracas, Venezuela, 1991–92; Premiered Composer, 1995 Casals Festival; Grammy nomination Tropicalización, 2001. *Address:* Plaza de la Fuente, 1275 Calle España, Toa Alta, Puerto Rico 00953. *E-mail:* williamortizupr@yahoo.com. *Website:* www.geocities.com/williamortiz00953.

ORVAL, Francis, DipMus; American horn player and academic; b. 8 Sept. 1944, Liège, Belgium; m. Julie Roy; two s. one d. *Education:* Conservatoire Royal de Musique de Liège, Belgium. *Career:* debut as first solo horn, aged 16, National Orchestra of Belgium, André Clutyens, Conductor; 20 years experience as Principal Horn with major orchestras in Belgium and Luxemburg; Professor, Music Conservatories, Liège and Luxemburg; Co-Director Grétry Music Academy, Liège; Artistic Music Director, Académie Internationale d'Eté de Wallonie; Founder, Organiser, 2 International Horn Competitions, 1977; University Professor, USA, 1983; Has performed as soloist and recitalist around the world; Adjudicator for several competitions; Professor of Horn, Musikhochschule, Trossingen, Germany; mem. International Horn Soc. (fmr officer). *Compositions:* Libre/Free/Frei for horn solo; Champaign for horn and piano; Method for natural horn; Triptych for horn alone; Transcription for horn of Bach's 6 suites for cello. *Recordings include:* Haydn's Concerto for 2 horns; Belgian Contemporary Music; Schumann's Konzertstück; Weber's Concertino; The Berwald and Beethoven Septets with the Uppsala Chamber Soloists; Brahms Horn Trio, with A. Grumiaux and G. Sebok; Bach, 6 Suites for Cello, arrangement for horn; Masterpieces for Horn and Piano with Jean-Claude Vanden Eynden. *Publications:* contrib. articles to Brass Bulletin, Horn Call, Historic Brass Society Journal. *Honours:* First Prize, International music Competition, Louise MacMahon, Lawton, Oklahoma, USA, 1987. *Address:* Boulevard Piercot 14/052, 4000 Liège, Belgium.

OSBORNE, Charles Thomas, FRSL; writer, critic and poet; b. 24 Nov. 1927, Brisbane, Qld, Australia. *Education:* Griffith Univ., studied piano with Archie Day and Irene Fletcher, voice with Vido Luppi and Browning Mummery. *Career:* Asst Ed. London Magazine 1957–66; Asst Literary Dir Arts Council of Great Britain 1966–71, Literary Dir 1971–86; opera critic Jewish Chronicle 1985–; chief theatre critic Daily Telegraph 1986–92; mem. of editorial bd Opera magazine; mem. Critics' Circle, PEN. *Publications* The Gentle Planet 1957, Opera 66 1966, Swansong 1968, The Complete Operas of Verdi 1969, Letters of Giuseppe Verdi (ed.) 1971, The Concert Song Companion 1974, Wagner and his World 1977, The Complete Operas of Mozart 1978, W. H. Auden: The Life of a Poet 1980, The Dictionary of Opera 1983, Letter to W. H. Auden and Other Poems 1984, Giving It Way 1986, The Operas of Richard Strauss 1988, The Complete Operas of Richard Wagner 1990, The Bel Canto Operas of Rossini, Donizetti and Verdi 1994, The Pink Danube 1998; contrib. to anthologies, newspapers and journals, including Opera, London Magazine, Spectator, Times Literary Supplement, Encounter, New Statesman, Observer, Sunday Times. *Honours:* Gold Medal 1993. *Address:* 125 St George's Road, London, SE1 6HY, England.

OSBORNE, Nigel, BA, BMus; British composer; *Reid Professor of Music, University of Edinburgh*; b. 23 June 1948, Manchester, England. *Education:* Univ. of Oxford with Kenneth Leighton and Egon Wellesz, and at Polish Radio Experimental Studio, Warsaw. *Career:* fmr Lecturer Univ. of Nottingham 1978; conducted the premiere of The Sun of Venice, Royal Festival Hall, London 1992; reworking of the Electrification of the Soviet Union on tour with Music Theatre Wales, including Linbury Theatre, Covent Garden, 2002; The Piano Tuner (Linbury Studio, Royal Opera House, London) 2004; currently Reid Prof. of Music, Univ. of Edinburgh; extensive composition for theatre, including Glyndebourne, ENO, Opera Factory, Wuppertal, Hebbel Theatre (Berlin), Shakespeare's Globe (London), the Ulysses Theatre (Istria), BBC Radio 3 and BBC2. *Compositions include:* Seven Last Words cantata (Radio Suisse Romande and Ville de Geneve Opera Prize) 1971, Heaventree for chorus 1973, Remembering Esenin for cello and piano 1974, The Sickle for soprano and orchestra 1975, Chansonier for chorus and ensemble 1975, Prelude and Fugue for ensemble 1975, Passers By for trio and synthesizer 1978, Cello Concerto 1977, I Am Goya for baritone and quartet 1977, Vienna, Zürich, Constance for soprano and quintet 1977, Figure/Ground for piano 1978, Kerenza at the Dawn for oboe and tape 1978, Orlando Furioso for chorus and ensemble 1978, Songs from a Bare Mountain for women's chorus 1979, In Camera for ensemble 1979, Under the Eyes for voice and quartet 1979, Quasi una fantasia for cello

1979, Flute Concerto 1980, Gnostic Passion for chorus 1980, Poem without a Hero for four voices and electronics 1980, Mythologies for sextet 1980, The Cage for tenor and ensemble 1981, Piano Sonata 1981, Choralis I–III for six voices 1981, Sinfonia I 1982, Sinfonia II 1983, Cantata piccola for soprano and string quartet, Fantasia for ensemble 1983, Wildlife for ensemble 1984, Alba for mezzo-soprano, ensemble and tape 1984, Zansa for ensemble 1985, Hell's Angles chamber opera 1985, Pornography for mezzo-soprano and ensemble, The Electrification of the Soviet Union opera after Pasternak 1986, Lumiere for string quartet and four groups of children 1986, The Black Leg Miner for ensemble 1987, Esquisse I and II for strings 1987, Stone Garden for Chamber Orchestra 1988, Zone for oboe, clarinet and string trio 1989, Tracks for two choirs, orchestra and wind band 1990, Eulogy (for Michael Vyner) 1990, Canzona for brass 1990, Violin Concerto 1990, The Sun of Venice (after Turner's visions of Venice) 1991, Terrible Mouth opera 1992, Sarajevo opera 1994, Forest-River-Ocean for carnyx, string quartet and electronics 2002. *Honours:* Netherlands Gaudeamus Prize, Radcliffe Award, Koussevitzky Award of the Library of Congress, Washington. *Address:* c/o Department of Music, Alison House, 12 Nicolson Square, Edinburgh, EH8 9DF, Scotland. *Telephone:* (131) 650-2424. *Fax:* (131) 650-2425. *E-mail:* n.osborne@music.ed.ac.uk.

OSKARSSON, Gudjon; Singer (Bass); b. 1965, Reykjavík, Iceland. *Education:* Studied in Iceland and Italy (Osimo and Milan). *Career:* Member of the Norwegian Opera from 1990, as Colline, Zuniga, Sparafucile and Raimondo (Lucia di Lammermoor); Fafner, Hunding and Hagen in The Ring, 1993–96 (also at Norwich, 1997); Further appearances at Mozart's Commendatore at Glyndebourne and Covent Garden (1996–97), as Raimondo at Munich and Fafner in Das Rheingold at La Scala (1996); Season 1998 with Titurel in Parsifal at Brussels, the Commendatore at Aix and King Mark for Scottish Opera; Concerts include: Tosca and Otello with the Israel Philharmonic Orchestra (1995–97), Act I of Die Walküre with the London Symphony Orchestra, Rocco in Fidelio under Carlo Rizzi and the Berlioz Messe Solennelle with the Gothenburg Symphony Orchestra; Further concerts with the Oslo and Bergen Philharmonics and the Trondheim Symphony Orchestra; Season 2000–01 as Priam in Les Troyens at Salzburg and Fafner in Das Rheingold at Toulouse. *Address:* c/o Norwegian Opera, PO Box 8800, Youngstorget, 0028 Oslo, Norway.

OSKOLKOV, Sergei (Alexandrovich); Composer and Pianist; b. 9 March 1952, Donetsk, Ukraine; m. Natalia Semionovna Oskolkova, 23 April 1986, 2 s. *Education:* Poetry and Painting lessons; Piano class of Galina Sladkovskaya, Donetsk Music College, 1967–71; Piano class of Pavel Serebryakov, 1971–77, Composition class with Vjacheslav Nagovitsin and Yuri Falik, 1976–81, Leningrad Conservatory. *Career:* Debut: As Pianist with Donetsk Philharmonic Orchestra, October 1972; Performance of vocal compositions, Leningrad, 1975; Publishing poetry and selling paintings and graphics, 1972–; Participant as Composer and Pianist at international festivals in Berlin, Kazan, St Petersburg and Kalingrad, 1985; Concert tours, Germany, France, Belgium, Ukraine, Kazakhstan, Latvia; mem, Union of Composers of Russia, 1988. *Compositions:* 2 String Quartets, recorded 1976, 1979; Sinfonietta for string orchestra, recorded 1979; 2 Concertos for piano and orchestra, recorded 1981, 1988; Count Nulin, opera, recorded Leningrad Radio, 1983; Set of Pieces and 2 Sonatas for piano, recorded 1994, published; Music for Russian folk instruments; Music for theatre and film. *Recordings:* Offenbach, Liszt, as pianist with St Petersburg Quartet, CD, 1994; 2nd Piano Sonata and cycle of songs by Oskolkov, 1996; Mussorgsky and Tchaikovsky, as pianist, Radio St Petersburg, 1996. *Address:* St Petersburgsky Prosp 51, ap 5, Petrodvorets, St Petersburg 198903, Russia.

OSOSTOWICZ, Krysia; Violinist; b. 1960, England. *Education:* studied with Yehudi Menuhin and Sándor Végh. *Career:* founder mem. of Chamber Ensemble Domus and leader of the Endymion Ensemble; founder and leader of the Dante String Quartet; many performances as soloist and chamber musician, with repertoire from Baroque to Bartók. *Recordings include:* Les Vendredis, with Dante Quartet. *Current Management:* Connaught Artists Management Ltd, 2 Molasses Row, Plantation Wharf, London, SW11 3UX, England. *Telephone:* (20) 7738 0017. *Fax:* (20) 7738 0909. *E-mail:* classicalmusic@connaughtartists.com. *Website:* www.connaughtartists.com.

OSTEN, Sigune von; Singer (Soprano); b. 8 March 1950, Dresden, Germany. *Education:* Studied in Hamburg and Karlsruhe and with Elisabeth Grümmer and Eugen Rabine. *Career:* Debut: Sang John Cage's Aria at Hanover 1973; Noted interpreter of 20th century repertoire at the Dresden and Salzburg Festivals, the Bonn and Vienna Festivals at Venice, Berlin, Donaueschingen, Madrid, Strasbourg, St Petersburg, Moscow and Tokyo; Concert tours, radio and television recordings of Europe, the USA, Japan and South America and opera engagements at Stuttgart, Wiesbaden, Paris, Venice and Lisbon; Repertoire includes Berg's Marie and Lulu and the Woman in Schoenberg's Erwartung; Shostakovich, Lady Macbeth; Sang Fusako

in Henze's Des verratene Meer at Wiesbaden, 1991 and the Mother in Turnage's Greek, Wuppertal 1992; Worked with composers such as Halffter, Penderecki, Denisov, Messiaen, Cage, Scelsi and Nono; Sang in Orff's De temporum fine comoedia at Munich, 2000. *Recordings:* Penderecki Luke Passion; Messiaen, Harawi; Noche pasiva by Halffter and Dittrich's Engführung; Songs by Ives, Satie, Cage. *Address:* c/o Hessisches Staatstheater, Postfach 3247, 8200 Wiesbaden, Germany.

OSTENDORF, John; Singer (Bass-baritone); b. 1 Nov. 1945, New York, USA. *Education:* Studied at Oberlin College with Margaret Harshaw. *Career:* Debut: Chautauqua Opera 1969, as the Commendatore in Don Giovanni; Appearances at San Francisco, Houston, Baltimore, Toronto and Philadelphia; Amsterdam 1979 in the premiere of Winter Cruise by Henkeman; Repertoire includes Don Alfonso, Basilio, Escamillo, Ramphis in Aida and Handel's Julius Caesar; Many concert performances, notably in the Baroque repertoire. *Recordings:* Bach's St John Passion and Handel's Imeneo, Joshua and Acis and Galatea. *Address:* c/o San Francisco Opera, War Memorial Opera House, San Francisco, CA 84102, USA.

OSTHOFF, Wolfgang; Musicologist; b. 17 March 1927, Halle Saale, Germany; m. Renate Götz, 3 s. *Education:* Frankfurt Conservatory with Kurt Hessenburg and others; Universities of Frankfurt and Heidelberg with H. Osthoff, T. Georgiades and others. *Career:* Assistant Lecturer, Munich University, 1957–68; Professor, 1968–, Emeritus, 1995, Würzburg University; mem, International Musicology Society and others. *Publications:* Das dramatische Spätwerk Claudio Monteverdis, 1960; Beethoven Klavier Konzert c-moll, 1965; Theatergesang und darstellende Musik in der Italienischen Renaissance, 2 vols, 1969; Heinrich Schütz, 1974; Stefan George und 'les deux Musiques', 1989; Briefwechsel Hans Pfitzner-Gerhard Frommel, 1990; Monteverdi's Orfeo, 1995. *Contributions:* musicology journals. *Honours:* Dr hc, University of Rome (La Sapienza) 1999. *Address:* Institut für Musikwissenschaft, University of Würzburg, Residenzplatz 2, 97070 Würzburg, Germany.

ÖSTMAN, Arnold; Conductor and Musical Director; b. 24 Dec. 1939, Malmö, Sweden. *Education:* Studied art history, Lund University; History of music, Paris and Stockholm Universities. *Career:* General Administrator and Artistic Director, Court Theatre, Drottningholm, Sweden, productions there on period instruments include Mozart's Don Giovanni, Così fan tutte, Le nozze di Figaro and Die Zauberflöte; Conducted Mozart's oratorio La Betulia Liberata at La Fenice, Venice, 1982; Series of Purcell's The Fairy Queen throughout Italy; Il Matrimonio Segreto at Cologne Opera, Washington Opera and Sadler's Wells Theatre, London, 1983; Covent Garden Debut, 1984 with Don Giovanni; Il Barbiere di Siviglia, Kent Opera, 1985; Le Siège de Corinthe, Rossini, Paris Opéra, 1985; Conducted Mozart's Lucio Silla, Vienna Staatsoper, 1990; Concerts with Netherlands Radio Chamber Orchestra, Stuttgart Philharmonic, Cologne Orchestra of WDR and Düsseldorf Symphony, 1990–; Season 1992 with Rossini's La Donna del Lago at the Concertgebouw and Orfeo ed Euridice at Drottningholm; Gluck's Alceste at Drottningholm, 1998, returned in 1999 to conduct Mozart's Il re Pastore and in 2000 to conduct a new production of Così fan tutte; Conducted concerts with Minneapolis Symphony Orchestra and Orchestra dell'Arena di Verona; Engaged in 2002 to conduct a new production of Mozart's Die Entführung aus dem Serail at the Flemish Opera in Antwerp and a new production of Die Zauberflöte at Drottningholm. *Recordings include:* Così fan tutte; Le nozze di Figaro; Don Giovanni; Die Zauberflöte; Video recordings of Mozart's operas based on performances at Drottningholm. *Honours:* Edison Prize, Netherlands; Cecilia Prize of Belgian critics; Diapason d'Or; Deutsche Schellplattenpreis. *Current Management:* Haydn Rawstron Ltd, London. *Address:* c/o Haydn Rawstron Ltd, 36 Station Road, London SE20 7BQ, England.

O'SULLIVAN, Cara; Singer (Soprano); b. 1970, Cork, Ireland. *Career:* Engagements with Welsh National Opera as Donna Anna and Violetta; At Garsington for Mozart's Fiordiligi and Constanze; The Queen of Night for Opéra de Nantes, 1999–2000; Helmwige in Die Walküre for the Royal Opera, 1998–99; Concerts include the Verdi Requiem at the Albert Hall; Beethoven's Ninth; Elijah; Messiah in Barcelona with Paul McCreesh; Brahms Requiem; Poulenc's Gloria. *Honours:* Winner, Stanislav Moniuszko Vocal Competition, Warsaw, 1996. *Address:* Harlequin Agency Ltd, 203 Fidlas Road, Cardiff CF4 5NA, Wales.

OTAKA, Tadaaki; Orchestra Conductor; b. 8 Nov. 1947, Kamakura, Japan; m. Yukiko Otaka, 23 Nov 1978. *Education:* Toho-Gakuen School of Music, Japan; Hochschule für Musik, Vienna, Austria. *Career:* Music Faculty, Toho-Gakuen School of Music, 1970–; Prin. Conductor, Tokyo Philharmonic Orchestra, 1981; Prin. Conductor, Sapporo Symphony Orchestra, 1981; Prin. Conductor, BBC National Orchestra of Wales; Promenade Concerts London 1991, with Tchaikovsky's Violin concerto, excerpts from Romeo and Juliet, Tippett's Piano Concerto and Ein Heldenleben; Made his Welsh National Opera debut in 1991 conducting Strauss's Salome; Conducted the BBC in New York and Baltimore at the

United Nations Day concert in 1994; Appointed first Music Adviser and Prin. Conductor, Kioi Sinfonietta, Tokyo; Conducted the Orchestra's debut in 1995; Engaged with Royal Liverpool Philharmonic, Residentie Orchestra, and with concerts with BBC National Orchestra of Wales and BBC Symphony Orchestra; Seasons 1997–98, and 1998–99, included debuts with the London Symphony, Bamberg Symphony and Olso Philharmonic; Director of the Britten-Pears Orchestra, 1998; Conducted the BBC National Orchestra of Wales at the London Proms, 2002; Season 2002–2003 included performances with London Philharmonic Orchestra, City of Birmingham Symphony Orchestra, Bournemouth Symphony Orchestra and Singapore Symphony Orchestra as well as regular commitments with Sapporo Symphony Orchestra and BBC Nat. Orchestra of Wales. *Recordings include:* Rachmaninov Symphonies with BBC National Orchestra of Wales; Further projects with BBC NOW, Yomiuri Nippon Symphony and Kioi Sinfonietta Tokyo. *Honours:* Suntory Music Awd, 1992; Fellowship, Welsh College of Music and Drama, 1993; Honorary Doctorate, Univ. University of Wales. *Address:* c/o BBC National Orchestra of Wales, Broadcasting House, Llandaff, Cardiff CF5 2YQ, Wales.

OTELLI, Claudio; Singer (Bass-baritone); b. 1959, Vienna, Austria. *Education:* Studied at the Vienna Musikhochschule. *Career:* Bregenz Festival, 1986, Vienna Staatsoper, 1989–94; Salzburg Festival, 1986, in Elektra; Rome Opera, 1994, as Alfio and Tonio in Cav and Pag; Season 1996 as Escamillo at Hamburg and Donner in Das Rheingold at La Scala, Milan; Canadian Opera Company, Toronto, 1996, as Orestes in Elektra; Other roles include Wagner's Dutchman and Klingsor, and Carlo in La Forza del Destino; Further appearances at Frankfurt, Berlin, Tokyo and Barcelona; Sang Jochanaan in Salome at Santa Fe, 1998; Season 2000–01 as Ford in Falstaff for the Vienna Staatsoper, Hindemith's Cardillac at Frankfurt, Orestes in Elektra for new Israeli Opera at Savonlinna, Telramund in Essen and Pizarro for Frankfurt Opera (Alfio and Tonio, 2001). *Address:* Santa Fe Opera, PO Box 2408, Santa Fe, NM 87504, USA.

OTEY, Louis; Singer (Baritone); b. 1957, USA. *Career:* Sang in The Rape of Lucretia and La Bohème at Dallas, 1985; Season 1985 with Menotti's The Medium and as Don Giovanni for Victoria State Opera; Sang Sharpless in Butterfly at Chicago and Covent Garden, 1990; Miami Opera from 1992, as Enrico in Lucia di Lammermoor and the Villains in Les contes d'Hoffmann; Season 1994 as Mozart's Count at Costa Mesa and Germont for New York City Opera; Monte Carlo and Cincinnati, 1996, as the Philosopher in Massenet's Chérubin, and Iago in Otello; Sorel in Menotti's The Consul, at the 1998 Spoleto Festival; Season 2000–01 as Francesco in the European premiere of Ginastera's Beatrix Cenci, at Geneva; Pinkerton for Dallas Opera and in the premiere of La Señorita Cristina by Luis de Pablo, at Madrid. *Address:* Cincinnati Opera Association, Music Hall, 1241 Elm Street, Cincinnati, OH 45210, USA.

OTT, Karin; Singer (Soprano); b. 13 Dec. 1945, Wädenswil, Zürich, Switzerland. *Education:* Studied in Zürich and Germany. *Career:* Sang first with the opera house of Biel-Solothurn; Appeared in Mussorgsky's Sorochintsy Fair at Brunswick 1970; Zürich 1970, as Tove in Schoenberg's Gurrelieder; Paris Opéra as the Queen of Night in Die Zauberflöte; Salzburg Festival 1979–81; Venice 1981, in the premiere of Sinopoli's Lou Salomé; Engagements at Stuttgart, Berlin, Zürich, Amsterdam and Vienna; Sang Scoltarella in the premiere of the original version of Henze's König Hirsch, 1985, as Kassel. *Recordings include:* Die Zauberflöte, conducted by Karajan (Deutsche Grammophon). *Address:* c/o Opernhaus Zürich, Falkenstrasse 1, 8008 Zürich, Switzerland.

OTTENTHAL, Gertrud; Singer; b. 1957, Bad Oldesloe, Schleswig-Holstein, Germany. *Education:* Studied in Lubeck. *Career:* Sang at Wiesbaden Opera 1980, Hamburg 1981–82; Engagements at Vienna Volksoper 1982, Salzburg Festival 1984, Vienna Festival 1986–88; Sang Mozart's Countess at Klagenfurt 1984, Komische Oper Berlin 1986, returned to Berlin 1990 as Mimi; Further appearances at Theater am Gärtnerplatz Munich, Barcelona and the Schwetzingen Festival; Other roles include Agathe, Fiordiligi, Sandrina in La Finta Giardiniera, Rosalinde, Antonio and Arianna in Giustino by Handel; Concert repertoire includes works by Bach, Handel, Mozart, Bruckner and Schubert; Sang Elisabeth de Valois at the Komische Oper, Berlin, 1999; Season 2000 as the Queen in Zemlinsky's Der König Kandaules, at the Vienna Volksoper, and Wagner's Gutrune at the Erl Festival, Tyrol. *Recordings:* Werther, Der Rosenkavalier and Der Wildschütz; Mrs Ma in Der Kreidekreis by Zemlinsky; Donna Elvira in Don Giovanni, conducted by Neeme Järvi. *Address:* c/o Komische Oper Berlin, Behrenstrasse 55–57, 1086 Berlin, Germany.

OTTO, Lisa; Singer (Soprano); b. 14 Nov. 1919, Dresden, Germany; m. Albert Blind. *Education:* Dresden Musikhochschukle, with Susane Steinmetz-Pree. *Career:* Debut: Beuthen 1941, as Sophie in Der Rosenkavalier; Sang in Beuthen 1941–44; Nuremburg 1945–46;

Dresden 1946–51; St ädtische (later Deutsche) Oper Berlin from 1951; Took part in the 1965 premiere of Henze's Der junge Lord; Salzburg 1953–57, as Blondchen and Despina; Glyndebourne 1956, as Blondchen in Die Entführung; Guest appearances in Vienna, Milan and Paris; Other roles include Mozart's Papagena and Susanna, Beethoven's Marzelline, and Ighino in Palestrina; Sang at the Deutsche Oper Berlin until 1983; Many engagements as concert singer. *Recordings:* St John Passion by Bach; Der junge Lord; Die Zauberflöte; Così fan tutte.

ÖTVÖS, Csilla; Opera Singer; b. 23 June 1947, Budapest, Hungary; m. Antal Szabados, 23 Aug 1975. *Education:* Liszt Ferenc Academy of Music. *Career:* Debut: Ariadne auf Naxos, Zerbinetta, 1974; More than 48 roles in the Hungarian State Opera include Despina in Mozart's Così fan tutte, Rosina in Rossini's Il Barbiere di Sivigla, Norina in Don Pasquale, Adina in Elisir d'amore; Appearances on Hungarian television, including Lehár's Die Lustige Witwe. *Recordings:* Szép Alom: Hungarian operettas and folk music; Operettcsillogás; International operettas. *Publications:* Contributions to several magazines; Photograph on cover page of Till Géza's Big Book of Operas. *Honours:* Pro Kultúra Hungarica, 1985; Bart ók-Pásztory Prizez, 1992. *Address:* Szt István Krt 13 III, 1955 Budapest, Hungary.

OUE, Eiji; Conductor; b. 1959, Hiroshima, Japan. *Education:* Studied at Toho School of Music and with Bernstein and Ozawa at Tanglewood, from 1978. *Career:* Assistant to Bernstein at concerts in Paris, Vienna and Milan; Music Director of the Erie Philharmonic, Pennysylvania, 1991–95; Associate conductor of the Buffalo Philharmonic Orchestra, 1987–91; Music Director of the Minnesota Orchestra, 1995; Tours through USA and to Europe, 1997–98; Director of the Grand Teton Music Festival in Wyoming, 1997; Further engagements with the New York Philharmonic Orchestra, Philadelphia Orchestra, Oslo Philharmonic Orchestra, Santa Cecilia, Rome, Los Angeles Philharmonic Orchestra; Chief conductor of the NDR SO, Hannover from 1998. *Recordings:* The Rite of Spring and The Firebird by Stravinsky; Strauss Ein Heldenleben and Mussorgsky. *Honours:* Koussevitzky prize, 1980; Hans Haring Gold Medal at the Salzburg Mozarteum, 1981. *Address:* c/o IMG Artists, Lovell House, 616 Chiswick High Road, London W4 5RX, England.

OUNDJIAN, Peter; Violinist; b. 21 Dec. 1955, Toronto, Ontario, Canada. *Education:* Studied at the Juilliard School with Ivan Galamian and Dorothy DeLay. *Career:* Leader of the Tokyo Quartet from 1981; Regular concerts in the USA and abroad; First cycle of the complete quartets of Beethoven at the Yale at Norfolk Chamber Music Festival, 1986; Repeated cycles at the 92nd Street Y (New York), Ravinia and Israel Festivals and Yale and Princeton Universities; Season 1990–91 at Alice Tully Hall and the Metropolitan Museum of Art, New York, Boston, Washington DC, Los Angeles, Cleveland, Detroit, Chicago, Miami, Seattle, San Francisco, Toronto; Tour of South America, two tours of Europe including Paris, Amsterdam, Bonn, Milan, Munich, Dublin, London, Berlin; Quartet-in-Residence at Yale University, University of Cincinnati College-Conservatory of Music. *Recordings:* Schubert's major Quartets; Mozart Flute Quartets with James Galway and Clarinet Quintet with Richard Stolzman; Quartets by Bartók, Brahms, Debussy, Haydn, Mozart and Ravel; Beethoven Middle Period Quartets (RCA). *Honours:* Grand Prix du Disque du Montreux; Best Chamber Music Recording of the Year from Stereo Review and the Gramophone; Four Grammy nominations. *Address:* Intermusica Artists Management, 16 Duncan Terrace, London N1 8BZ, England.

OUSSET, Cécile; Concert Pianist; b. 23 Jan. 1936, Tarbes, France. *Career:* Studied Paris Conservatoire with Marcel Ciampi; Graduated 1950 with First Prize in piano; British debut at Edinburgh Festival 1980; Many appearances with leading orchestras in the United Kingdom and abroad; French debut with the Orchestre de Paris, followed by appearances with all major French orchestras; First recital at the Théâtre des Champs-Elysées in season 1987–88; US debut with the Los Angeles Philharmonic Orchestra, 1984; Later engagements with the Minnesota and Boston Symphony Orchestras; Debut tour of Japan 1984; Repertoire includes Brahms, Beethoven, Rachmaninov and French music; Played Debussy's Preludes on BBC television 1988. *Recordings:* Brahms 2nd Concerto, with the Leipzig Gewandhaus Orchestra; Concertos by Rachmaninov, Liszt, Saint-Saëns, Grieg, Ravel and Mendelssohn; Recitals of Chopin, Liszt and Debussy (EMI). *Honours:* Prizewinner at Van Cliburn, Queen Elisabeth of Belgium, Busoni and Marguerite Long-Jacques Thibaud Competitions; Grand Prix du Disque for Brahms Concerto recording. *Address:* c/o Intermusica Artists' Management, 16 Duncan Terrace, London N1 8BZ, England.

OUZIEL, Dalia; Pianist; b. 28 Sept. 1947, Tel-Aviv, Israel; m. Jerrold Rubenstein, 1 July 1969, 1 s., 1 d. *Education:* Rubin Academy, Tel-Aviv; Royal Conservatories, Mons and Brussels, Belgium. *Career:* Soloist and Chamber Artist; Performs at festivals and is known through her numerous recordings. *Recordings include:* Beethoven Variations, Piano Solo; Mozart Concerti, Double Piano Concerto, Sonatas for Violin and

Piano, complete Piano Duos; Violin-Piano Sonatas of Mozart, Brahms, Fauré, Copland, Ives, Mendelssohn, Ravel, Grieg, Villa-Lobos, others; Piano Trios of Fauré, Schubert, Brahms, Mendelssohn, others; Fauré Piano Quartets; Chausson Concerto; Schubert Trout; Mendelssohn Sextet; Beethoven Lieder. *Address:* Avenue de la Rose des Vents 4, 1410 Waterloo, Belgium.

OVCHINIKOV, Vladimir; Concert Pianist; b. 2 Jan. 1958, Belebey, USSR. *Education:* Studied in Moscow with Anna Artobolevskaya and Alexey Nazedkin. *Career:* International engagements from 1980, including Aldeburgh, Cheltenham, Edinburgh, Lichfield and Schleswig Holstein Festivals; Recitals in London (debut at the Barbican Hall, 1987), Chicago, Toronto, Munich and Rotterdam; Season 1989–, included tour of Japan and London concerto debut with the Philharmonia Orchestra at the Festival Hall; Glyndebourne recital for the Brighton Festival; Western debut in Trio with Alexander Vinnitsky and Alexander Rudin at the Wigmore Hall, May 1989. *Recordings include:* Trios by Rachmaninov and Shostakovich; Tchaikovsky's 1st Piano Concerto, with the London Philharmonic conducted by Yuri Simonov (Collins Classics). *Honours:* Runner up (to Ivo Pogorelich) Montreal Competition 1980; Joint Silver Medal (with Peter Donohoe) Tchaikovsky Competition Moscow 1982; Winner, Leeds International Piano Competition 1987. *Address:* c/o Georgina Ivor Associates, 28 Old Devonshire Road, London, SW12 9RB, England.

OVENS, Raymond; Violinist; b. 14 Oct. 1932, Bristol, England; m. Sheila Margaret Vaughan Williams, 1 s., 1 d. *Education:* Royal Academy of Music; ARAM. *Career:* Debut: Wigmore Hall, London, 1950; Leader, London Symphony Orchestra, 1951; Principal 2nd Violin, Royal Philharmonic Orchestra, 1956; Assistant Leader, 1972; Leader until 1980, BBC Scottish Symphony Orchertra; Leader, Philharmonia Orchestra 1980–85, Orchestra of the English National Opera from 1985; Has played concertos with the BBC Scottish Symphony, the Vancouver Symphony and the Philharmonia Orchestra; Concerts and Recitals for BBC; Leader, Lyra String Quartet; Leader, Ceol Rosh Chamber Group. *Honours:* FRAM.

OVERMAN, Robert; Singer (Baritone); b. 1957, North Carolina, USA. *Career:* Sang at the Landestheater, Salzburg, from 1984; Karlsruhe Opera, 1986–91; Guest appearances at Mannheim, Stuttgart and Zürich; Salzburg Festival, 1987; Leipzig Opera, 1990, as Count Luna; Bonn Opera from 1992, in Le Villi and La Rondine by Puccini, and as Iago; Sang Carlo in La Forza del Destino at Karlsruhe, 1993, and Jack Rance in La Fanciulla del West at Catania, 1995; Other roles include Germont, and Alfio in Cavalleria Rusticana. *Address:* Bonn Opera, Am Boeselagerhof 1, 5311 Bonn, Germany.

OWEN, Barbara, BMus, MMus; American organist and musicologist; b. 25 Jan. 1933, Utica, NY. *Education:* Westminster Choir College, Boston University, North German Organ Academy, Academy of Italian Organ Music. *Career:* Music Director of First Religious Society, Newburyport, 1963–2002; Curator of A.G.O. Organ Library at Boston University, 1985–; Editor of Publications, Westfield Center for Early Keyboard Studies, 2001–Freelance Researcher, Lecturer, Recitalist, Teacher and Organ Consultant; mem, American Guild of Organists; Organ Historical Society, President, 1997–1999; American Musical Instrument Society; British Institute of Organ Studies. *Publications include:* Editions of Music: A Century of American Organ Music, 4 vols, 1975, 1976, 1983, 1991; A Century of English Organ Music, 1979; A Handel Album, 1981; The Candlelight Carol Book, 1981; 4 Centuries of Italian Organ Music, 1994; A Pachelbel Album, 1994; Books written: The Organs and Music of King's Chapel, 1965, 1993; The Organ in New England, 1979; E Power Biggs, Concert Organist, 1987; Co-editor, Charles Brenton Fisk, Organ Builder, 1986; The Registration of Baroque Organ Music, 1997; contrib. to Grove's Dictionary, 6th Edition; Grove's Dictionary of Musical Instruments; New Grove Dictionary of American Music; Harvard Dictionary of Music. *Honours:* A.M.I.S. Curt Sachs Award, 1994. *Address:* 28 Jefferson Street, Newburyport, MA 01950, USA.

OWEN, (Rasmussen) Lynn, BS, MS; American singer (soprano) and voice teacher; b. Kenosha, WI; m. Richard Owen 1960; three s. *Education:* Northwestern University, Juilliard School of Music, Vienna Academy of Music, Austria. *Career:* debut Constanze in Abduction from the Seraglio, New Orleans Opera, USA; La Fanciulla del West (Minnie), Fliegende Holländer (Senta), Metropolitan Opera, New York; Don Carlos (Elisabetta), Forza del Destino (Leonora), Il Trovatore (Leonore), Prince Igor (Jaroslavna), Zürich, Switzerland; Il Trovatore, Turandot, Fidelio (Leonora), Krefeld Opera, Hamburg and Frankfurt, Germany; Fanciulla del West, Central City, Fliegende Holländer, Aspen, USA; Ballo in Maschera, Othello, Calgary, Canada; Il Trovatore, Caracas, Venezuela; Siegfried (Brünnhilde), Art Park, New York; Isolde, Mexico City Opera; Concerts and recitals throughout USA and Europe; US premiere, Strauss, Aegyptische Helene, NY (title role); Frau Ohne Shatten (Dyer's wife; Die Walkuere (Sieglinde) NY; world premieres, US (Owen) Mary Dyer, The Death of the Virgin, Abigail Adams, Rain,(Alice

Tully, New York). *Recordings:* Serenus Records; Vanguard Records; Vienna to Broadway, Aurora, Rain. *Publications:* contrib. to music journals. *Address:* 21 Claremont Avenue, New York, NY 10027, USA.

OWEN, Stephen; Singer (bass-baritone); b. 1961, USA. *Career:* Concert appearances at Carnegie Hall and in Seattle and Honolulu; Dallas, Philadelphia and Cleveland Operas; European debut as Gunther in Götterdämmerung at Salzburg, 1990; Further appearances as Wagner's Dutchman at Kassel, Aachen and Graz; Don Pizarro, Escamillo and Jochanaan; Roles at Aachen Opera have included The Villains in Les Contes d'Hoffmann and Scarpia; Graz Opera as Kurwenal, Amonasro, Orest and Sharpless; Teatro Colón, Buenos Aires, 1993, as the Ring Master in Lulu. *Current Management:* Athole Still International Management, Forresters Hall, 25–27 Westow Street, London, SE19 3RY, England. *Telephone:* (20) 8771-5271. *Fax:* (20) 8768-6600. *Website:* www.atholestill.com.

OWENS, Anne-Marie; Singer (mezzo-soprano); b. 15 Aug. 1955, Jarrow, Tyne and Wear, England. *Education:* Newcastle School of Music, the Guildhall School and the National Opera Studio. *Career:* Sang Gluck's Orpheus, Dido, Dalila and Angelina (La Cenerentola) while student; Professional debut as Mistress Quickly on the Glyndebourne Tour; For English National Opera has sung Charlotte, Rosina, Maddalena, Suzuki (Madama Butterfly), Bianca (The Rape of Lucretia), Solokha in the British premiere of Rimsky-Korsakov's Christmas Eve, 1988, and Magdalene; Covent Garden 1989, as Third Lady in Die Zauberflöte and Rossweise in a new production of Die Walküre; Visit to the Vienna Staatsoper with the company of the Royal Opera, 1992; Sang Jocasta in Oedipus Rex for Opera North, followed by the title role in Ariane and Bluebeard by Dukas, 1990; Season 1992 in Les Contes d'Hoffmann at Covent Garden, as Baba the Turk in The Rake's Progress at Brussels and Preziosilla in The Force of Destiny for ENO; Other roles include Arnalta in Monteverdi's Poppea (Glyndebourne Festival); Clotilde in Norma and the Hostess in Boris Godunov (Royal Opera); Baba the Turk (Brussels); Fidalma in Il Matrimonio Segreto (Lausanne); Sang Venus in a new production of Tannhäuser for Opera North; T Picker's Emmeline at the New York City Opera, 1998; Kundry in Parsifal for Scottish Opera, 2000; Concert appearances with the City of Birmingham Symphony, BBC Symphony, London Mozart Players, Royal Liverpool Philharmonic; Has sung at the London Proms, Aix-en-Provence, San Sebastien, Rouen and Detroit (US debut with Messiah); Season 2000–01 as Kundry for Scottish Opera, Laura in La Gioconda (concert) and Arnalta in Poppea for ENO; Brangaene for Opera North and Azucena in Glasgow. *Current Management:* Hazard Chase, Norman House, Cambridge Place, Cambridge CB2 1NS, England. *Telephone:* (1223) 312400. *Fax:* (1223) 460827. *Website:* www.hazardchase.co.uk.

OWENS, David Bruce; composer; b. 16 Oct. 1950, USA; m. 1974, one s. two d. *Education:* Eastman School, Rochester, NY, Manhattan School, New York. *Career:* mem. ASCAP. *Compositions:* Sonatina for Percussion Solo, 1969; Quartet for Strings, 1969; Encounter for Orchestra, 1970; Gentle Horizon for Chamber Ensemble, 1972; Ricercar for Band, 1978; Concerto for Viola and Orchestra, 1982; The Shores of Peace for Chorus and Chamber Orchestra, 1984; Fantasy on a Celtic Carol for Viola and Piano, 1985; Jonah, opera in 3 acts, 1986–89; One in Heart, processional for Organ or Orchestra or Band, 1988; My Frozen Well for SATB Chorus, 1991; Echoes of Edo for Piano Solo, 1993; Trio for Violin, Horn and Piano, 1995; Double Concerto for euphonium, tuba and orchestra, 1997; Choral, piano, organ pieces and songs. *Contributions:* columns and articles on 20th Century music, also reviews of many books in music; The Christian Science Monitor; Ovation; Musical America. *Honours:* ASCAP/Deems Taylor Award for Distinguished Criticism, for Christian Science Monitor column, Inside 20th Century Music, 1983. *Address:* 75 Travis Road, Holliston, MA 01746, USA.

OXENBOULD, Moffatt; Artistic Director; b. 18 Nov. 1943, Sydney, Australia. *Education:* Studied at the National Institute for Dramatic Art. *Career:* Stage Manager with Elizabethan Trust Opera, 1963–65, Sutherland Williamson Opera, and at Sadler's Wells, London, 1966–67; Planning Co-ordinator with Elizabethan Trust Opera-Australian Opera, 1967–73; Artistic Administrator, Australian Opera, 1974–84; Artistic Director 1984–2000; Productions include: The Rape of Lucretia, 1971, Il Trittico, 1978, La Clemenza di Tito, 1991, Idomeneo, 1994, and Madama Butterfly, 1997; La Bohème, 1999. *Publications:* Joan Sutherland: A Tribute, 1989. *Contributions:* Various Australian publications. *Honours:* Order of Australia, 1985; Dame Joan Hammond Award, 1986. *Address:* c/o Opera Australia, PO Box 291, Strawberry Hills, New South Wales 2012, Australia.

OXLEY, James; Singer (tenor); b. 1964, England. *Education:* Royal College of Music (as Cellist), Oxford University, and with Rudolf Piernay. *Career:* Debut: Royal Albert Hall 1991, under David Willcocks; Concerts include Les Illuminations, and the Brahms Experience on South Bank (1992) and Edinburgh Festival, 1993; Season 1995–96 with Messiah (CBSO and Ulster Orchestras), and Alexander's Feast by

Handel with the Brandenburg Consort; A Child of our Time in Oxford and Sweden, L'Enfance du Christ in Spain, and Britten's War Requiem; Bach's B Minor Mass on tour to France with Le Concert Sprituel; Opera roles include Tamino (at Durham), Ottavio, Rodolfo and Alfredo; Title roles in Britten's Prodigal Son, with Kent Opera; Season 1996–97 with Purcell's King Arthur in France and The Fairy Queen at Schlossbruhl; Werther at Wexford, the Christmas Oratorio under Marc Minkowski, the Missa solemnis at the Festival Hall, London, and Messiah with the CBSO. *Honours:* First Prize at the 1994 International Vocalisten Councours/Hertogenbosch. *Current Management:* Hazard Chase Ltd, Norman House, Cambridge Place, Cambridge, CB2 1NS, England. *Telephone:* (1223) 312400. *Fax:* (1223) 460827. *Website:* www .hazardchase.co.uk.

OZAWA, Seiji; Conductor and Music Director; b. 1 Sept. 1935, Shenyang, China; m. Vera Motoki-llyin, 1 s., 1 d. *Education:* Toho School of Music, Tokyo, Japan, and Tanglewood; studied with Hideo Saito, Eugene Bigot, Herbert von Karajan, Leonard Bernstein. *Career:* One of three assistant conductors, New York Philharmonic, 1961–62 season; Music Director, Ravinia Festival, 1964–68; Music Director, Toronto Symphony Orchestra, 1965–69; Music Director, san Francisco Symphony Orchestra, 1970–76; Artistic Adviser, Tanglewood Festival, 1970–73; Music Director, Boston Symphony Orchestra, 1973–2002; Guest Conductor, major orchestras throughout the world including Philadelphia, Chicago Symphony Orchestras, New York Philharmonic, Berlin Philharmonic, Orchestre de Paris, New Philharmonia, Paris Opéra, Orchestre National de France, La Scala, New Japan Philharmonic, Central Peking Philharmonic, Vienna Philharmonic; Led Boston Symphony Orchestra Cultural Exchange in Peking and Shanghai, China, 1979; Conducted the world premiere of Olivier Messiaen's St Francis of Assisi, Nov 1983, at Paris Opéra, which was subsequently awarded the Grand Prix de la Critique, 1984, in the category of French world premieres; Conducted the Boston Symphony in Beethoven's 8th and the Symphonie Fantastique at the 1991 Promenade Concerts, London; Conducted the Berlin Philharmonic in Russian Nights concert at Moscow, 1995; 50th Anniversary performance of Peter Grimes at Tanglewood, 1996; Leader of the Saito Kinen Festival at Matsumoto, Japan from 1992; Led Krenek's Jonny spielt auf, Vienna 2002. *Recordings:* Philips, Telarc, CBS, Deutsche Grammophon, Angel/EMI, New World, Hyperion, Erato and RCA Records, including the Berg and Stravinsky Violin Concertos (Perlman); Saint Francois d'Assise; Schoenberg's Gurrelieder; Messiaen Turangalila Symphony; Stravinsky Firebird, Rite of Spirng and Petrushka; Ives 4th Symphony; The Queen of Spades (RCA); Mahler Symphony no. 2 with Saito Kinen Orchestra, 2000. *Honours:* Recipient Emmy Award for Outstanding Achievement in Music Direction for Boston Symphony's Evening at Symphony PBS television series; Grand Prix du Disque for recording of Berlioz Roméo et Juliette; 1st Prize, International Competition of Orchestra Conductors, France, 1959, Inouye Sho Award, 1994; Chevalier de la légion d'Honneur, 1997. *Current Management:* Columbia Artists Management LLC, 165 West 57th Street, New York, NY 10019-2276, USA. *Telephone:* (212) 841-9500. *Fax:* (212) 841-9744. *E-mail:* info@cami.com. *Website:* www.cami .com. *Address:* Music Director, Boston Symphony Orchestra, Symphony Hall, 301 Massachusetts Avenue, Boston, MA 02115, USA.

OZIM, Igor; Violinist and Professor of Violin; b. 9 May 1931, Ljubljana, Yugoslavia; m. Breda Volovsel, 1963, 1 s., 1 d. *Education:* State Academy of Music, Ljubljana; Diploma RCM, London; Private study with Max Rostal, London. *Career:* Debut: Ljubljana, 1947; Tours of Europe, USA, South America, Australia, New Zealand and Japan; Broadcasts in all European countries. *Publications:* Editor of numerous contemporary violin works; Editor, Pro Musica Nova, 1974; Editor, Complete Violin Concertos by Mozart, for Neue Mozart Ausgabe, Bärenreiter Edition. *Honours:* Carl Flesch Medal, International Competition, London, 1951; 1st Prize, German Broadcasting Stations International Competition, Munich, 1953. *Current Management:* Konzertdirektion Hörtnagel, Munich, Germany. *Address:* Breibergstrasse 6, 50939 Cologne 41, Germany.

OZOLINS, Arthur Marcelo, BSc; concert pianist; b. 7 Feb. 1946, Lübeck, Germany. *Education:* University of Toronto, Canada, Mannes College of Music, New York, USA; studies with Pablo Casals, Jacques Abram, Nadia Boulanger, Nadia Reisenberg, Vlado Perlemuter. *Career:* debut, Toronto Symphony Orchestra, Toronto, 1961; Soloist with Royal Philharmonic, Hallé Orchestra, Stockholm and Oslo Philharmonic, Leningrad Philharmonic, Montreal Symphony, Toronto Symphony; Recitals, New York, London, Paris, Moscow, Leningrad, Buenos Aires, Sydney, San Paulo; 7 Tours, USSR; Television and radio performances, CBC, BBC, Swedish Radio; Concerto repertoire included works by Bach, Brahms, Beethoven, Mozart (K414, K466 and K503), Rachmaninov, Prokofiev, Tchaikovsky and Tippett (Handel Fantasy); mem, AFM; English Speaking Union. *Recordings:* The Complete Piano Concerti and Paganini Rhapsody of Rachmaninov with Mario Bernardi and the Toronto Symphony plus Dohnányi's Variations on a Nursery Song, Healey Willan's Piano Concerto and Strauss Burleske; Numerous Solo recordings. *Honours:* 1st Prizes, Edmonton Competition, 1968, CBC Talent Festival, 1968; Juno Award, Best Classical Record, 1981; 7 Canada Council Awards. *Current Management:* Robert Gilder & Co., Enterprise House, 59–65 Upper Ground, London, SE1 9PQ, England. *Telephone:* (20) 7928-9008. *Fax:* (20) 7928-9755. *E-mail:* rgilder@robert -gilder.com. *Address:* 159 Colin Avenue, Toronto, ON M5P 2C5, Canada.

OZOLINS, Janis (Alfreds); Violoncellist, Concert Singer and Orchestral Conductor; b. 29 Sept. 1919, Riga, Latvia; m. Adine Uggla, 15 May 1951, 2 s., 1 d. *Education:* Diploma, Solo Violoncello, Conservatory of Latvia, 1944; Studied with Professor E Mainardi, Rome, 1947–48; Studied Composition, Riga, and Royal Academy of Music, Stockholm, Singing Teachers Examination, Stockholm, 1958; Examinations in Musicology, University of Uppsala, 1962. *Career:* Debut: Violoncello, Riga, 1933; Concert radio recitals, solo performances with orchestra, Latvia, Sweden, Denmark, the United Kingdom, Italy, Switzerland; Music Master, 1956–; Conductor, Landskrona Symphony Orchestra, Sweden, 1957; Bass Soloist, Beethoven's 9th Symphony with H Blomstedt, Norrköping, Sweden, 1961; Director, Växjö Municipal School of Music and Municipal Music Dor, Växjö, Sweden, 1964–84; Conductor, operas and ballets, Växjö. *Contributions:* Sohlmans Musiklexicon. *Honours:* National Prize of Latvia, 1944; Culture Prize, Växjö Lions Club, 1976; Royal Gold Medal, Swedish Orchestra National Federation, 1977, 1984. *Address:* Via Sicilia 1, 63039 San Benedetto del Tronto (AP), Italy.

P

PAASIKIVI, Lilli; singer (mezzo-soprano); b. 1970, Finland. *Education:* Royal Academy, Stockholm, and Royal College of Music, London, with Neil Mackie; Further studies with Janet Baker, 1990–94. *Career:* Debut: Noorland Opera 1993, as Ottone in Poppea; Appearances as Savonlinna Festival, for Tampere Opera and Paris Châtelet (Pilgrim in Saariaho's L'amour de loin, 2001); Finnish National Opera from 1998 as Cenerentola, Suzuki, Dorabella, Marguerite (Berlioz Faust) and Rosina; Cordelia in the premiere of Sallinen's King Lear; Season 2002–03 in premiere of Shchedrin's The Enchanted Wanderer, with the New York PO, Alexander Nevsky with the London Philharmonia, Marguerite for Opera North (concert) and Les nuits d'été with the Melbourne SO; Other repertory includes Schoenberg's Gurrelieder (Toronto SO), Mahler's 3rd Symphony, Das klagende Lied and Des Knaben Wunderhorn, the Wesendonck Lieder and Ravel's Shéhérazade. *Recordings:* Kullervo Symphony, The Tempest and The Maiden in the Tower, by Sibelius. *Current Management:* Harrison/Parrott Ltd, 12 Penzance Place, London, W11 4PA, England. *Telephone:* (20) 7229 9166. *Fax:* (20) 7221 5042. *Website:* www.harrisonparrott.com.

PABST, Michael; Singer (tenor); b. 1955, Graz, Austria. *Education:* Studied in Graz and Vienna. *Career:* Principal Tenor at Vienna Volksoper, 1978–84, singing operetta and lyric opera roles; Dramatic repertoire from 1985, including: Max, in Der Freichütz, Munich; Bacchus, at Philadelphia, Stuttgart, Frankfurt and Houston; Lohengrin, at Hamburg and Zürich; Walther, at Cape Town and Trieste; Erik, at La Scala and Buenos Aires; Huon in Oberon, at La Scala; Florestan at the Savonlinna Festival and Siegmund at Liège; Guest appearances at Vienna Staatsoper from 1991, with Florestan, The Drum Major in Wozzeck, Max, Jenik in The Bartered Bride, Erik; Other roles include Hoffmann, Pedro in Tiefland, Luigi in Il Tabarro; Schubert's Fierrabras; Sergei, in Lady Macbeth; Strauss's Matteo, Aegisthus, Burgomaster in Friedenstag and Apollo. *Recordings include:* Heinrich in Schreker's Irrelohe, 1995; Season 1998 in Henze's Venus and Adonis at Genoa and as Bacchus in Ariadne at Toulouse. *Current Management:* Athole Still International Management, Forresters Hall, 25–27 Westow Street, London, SE19 3RY, England. *Telephone:* (20) 8771-5271. *Fax:* (20) 8768-6600. *Website:* www.atholestill.com.

PACE, Patrizia; Singer (Soprano); b. 1963, Turin, Italy. *Education:* Studied at Turin Conservatory. *Career:* Debut: La Scala 1984 as Celia in Mozart's Lucio Silla; Has appeared in Milan as Micaela, Mozart's Despina, Susanna and Zerlina, Oscar, Lisa in La Sonnambula and in premiere Il Principe Felice by Mannino, 1987; Guest appearances at Deutsche Oper Berlin, Spoleto Festival and the Vienna Staatsoper as Oscar and Rossini's Elvira, 1986 and 1988, Gilda, Nannetta in Falstaff and Yniold; Further engagements at Hamburg Staatsoper as Liu, Florence, Genoa, Palermo and Covent Garden 1991 and 1993 as Gilda, and Yniold in Pelléas et Mélisande; Other roles include Rosina, and Sofia in Il Signor Bruschino; Season 1998 at Catania as Gilda and Marzelline; Engaged as Nannetta in Falstaff for the Royal Opera, 1999; Sang Zobeida in Donizetti's Alahor in Granata at Palermo, 1999, Zerlina at La Coruña, 2000. *Recordings:* Barbarina in Le nozze di Figaro and Mozart's Requiem; Mozart's C minor Mass. *Address:* c/o Teatro alla Scala, Via Filodrammatici 2, Milan, Italy.

PACIOREK, Grazyna; Composer; b. 11 Dec. 1967, Zyrardow, Poland. *Education:* Degree in Violin, State School of Music, Warsaw, 1987; Studying Composition under Professor M Borkowski, Academy of Music, Warsaw; International courses for young composers, Polish Section, ISCM, Kazimierz Dolny, Poland, 1989, 1990, 1991; Computer course and workshops, Studio of Electro-acoustic Music, Academy of Music, Kraków, 1991. *Career:* Many performances at the composers concerts in Warsaw (Academy of Music, Royal Castle) and in Kraków, 1987–91; Composed music for film aired on Polish television, 1991; Works presented in radio programme at Gdansk Meeting of Young Composers, Oct 1991 and 5th Laboratory of Contemporary Chamber Music, 1991; mem, Polish Society for Contemporary Music; Polish Composers' Union Youth Circle. *Compositions include:* Monologue for Oboe Solo; Te-qui-la for 6 percussion group; Toccata for violin, cello and piano, string quartet; Muzyka Mapothana for oboe and accordiov; Concert for viola and orchestra; Electronic Music, film music. *Honours:* June 1991, Academy of Music in Warsaw applied to Minister of Culture and Fine Arts for her artistic scholarship in 1991. *Address:* ul Sienkiewicza 28/4, 05-825 Grodzisk Maz, Poland.

PADMORE, Elaine Marguirite, BMus, MA; British opera house director, television producer, broadcaster and singer; *Director of Opera, Royal Opera House;* b. 1945, Haworth, Yorkshire, England. *Education:* Univ. of Birmingham, Guildhall School of Music, studied singing with Helen Isepp. *Career:* Ed. with Oxford University Press; BBC Producer of music programmes and major series for Radio 3; BBC Chief Producer of opera, 1976–82; Artistic Dir, Wexford Festival, 1982–94; radio broadcaster and singer, appearing in concerts and opera; Lecturer in Opera at Royal Acad. of Music, London; Artistic Dir, Dublin Grand Opera, 1989–93; Artistic Dir of Classical Productions, London, 1990–92 with Tosca in 1991 and Carmen in 1992; Artistic Consultant for London International Opera Festival, 1991–92; Dir of Royal Danish Opera, Copenhagen, 1993–2000; Dir of Opera, Royal Opera House, Covent Garden, 2000–; staged Handel's Giulio Cesare for Dublin Grand Opera, 2001. *Publications:* Wagner, in the series The Great Composers, 1970; Chapter on Germany, in Music in The Modern Age, 1973; contrib. to Grove's Dictionary; various British professional journals. *Honours:* Pro Musica Prize, Hungarian Radio, 1975; Prix Musical de Radio Brno, 1976; Hon. Assoc., Royal Acad. of Music, 1981; Sunday Independent Arts Award for Services to Music in Ireland, 1985; Knight of The Royal Danish Dannebrog Order, 1994. *Address:* c/o Royal Opera House, Covent Garden, London, WC2E 9DD, England.

PADMORE, Mark (Joseph); Singer (Tenor); b. 8 March 1961, London, England; m. Josette Simon, 27 Oct 1996. *Education:* Kings College, Cambridge, 1979–82; Studied with Erich Vietheer, Gita Denise, Janice Chapman and Diane Forlano. *Career:* Singer at Major Festivals including Aix-en-Provence, Edinburgh, BBC Proms, Salzburg, Spoleto, Tanglewood, New York; Opera House debuts: Teatro Comunale, Florence, 1992; Opéra Comique, Paris, 1993; Théâtre du Châtelet, 1995; Royal Opera House, Covent Garden, 1995; Scottish Opera, 1996; Opéra de Paris, 1996; Rameau's Zoroatre at the 1998 London Proms; Season 1999–2000 at ENO as Apollo in Monteverdi's Orfeo and the Evangelist in the St John Passion; Jonathan in Saul with the Gabrieli Consort, 2002; London Proms Chamber Music, 2002; Engaged as Handel's Jephtha for WNO, and Iopas in Les Troyens in Paris, under John Eliot Gardiner, 2003. *Recordings:* Chabrier Briseis; Charpentier, Médée; Handel, Messiah; Esther, Samson; Haydn, Masses; Purcell, Fairy Queen and King Arthur; Rameau, Hippolyte et Aricie. *Current Management:* Van Walsum Management. *Address:* 4 Addison Bridge Place, London W14 8XP, England.

PADOUROVA-HAVLAKOVA, Lydie; Singer (Mezzo-Soprano); b. 30 Aug. 1957, Prague, Czechoslovakia; m. Jan Padour, 1 June 1979, 1 s. *Education:* Conservatoire of Prague; University of Music in Prague. *Career:* Debut: National Theatre in Prague, 1986; Prague National Theatre: Janáček's Kata Kabanova (Varvara), Prokofiev's Betrothal in a Monastery (Klara), Tchaikovsky's Queen of Spades (Pavlina and Dafnis), 1987, Mozart's Le nozze di Figaro, as Cherubino, 1988 and Purcell's Dido and Aeneas (Dido). *Recordings:* Arias by Mascagni: Santuzza; Bizet's Carmen; Mozart's Dorabella; Thomas' Mignon; Purcell's Dido; Donizetti's Orsini (Lucrezia Borgia); Complete Opera: Prokofiev's Betrothal in a Monastery. *Current Management:* Na Lysinach 461/30, 14700 Prague, Czech Republic.

PADRÓS, David; Composer and Pianist; b. 22 March 1942, Igualada, Barcelona, Spain. *Education:* Municipal Music School, Barcelona, 1966; Musikhochscule Trossingen, Germany, 1966–69; Konservatorium, Basel, 1969–72; Zürich, Switzerland, 1972–75; Freiburg, Germany, 1976–82. *Career:* Commissions and performances in European Music Festivals; mem, Associacio Catalana de Compositors. *Compositions:* Styx, Chamber Ensemble; Heptagonal, piano; Crna Gora, Chamber Ensemble; Khorva, orchestra; Cal Ligrama (F1 in G, piano); 2 Legendes, organ; Batalla, piano, harpsichord and strings; Musik im Raum, chamber ensemble; Jo-Ha-Kyu, orchestra; Arachne, Chamber ensemble; Maqam, piano; Trajectories, violin; Confluences, brass ensemble, percussion, tape; Chaconne, string quartet, harpsichord; El Sermo de R Muntaner, 4 mixed voices, 4 old wind instruments, organ; Ketjak, pianists quartet; Recordant W A M, clarinet and organ; La Sala de la Suprema Harmonia, chamber ensemble, 1991; Jdeb, recorder quartet, 1992; 6 Differencies, organ, 1992; Ghiza-i-ruh, flute, clartinet, piano, 1993; Nocturne, flute, viola, clarinet, 1992; Gjatams, piano quartet, 1993; Xucla el silenci nocturn, flute, clarinet, violin, cello, 1994; Qawwali, recorder quartet, 1994; Klagelied, piano, 1994; Manas, piano, percussion, wind quintet, 1996; 5 Tankas, mezzo, flute, clarinet, guitar, 1996, Cheops, chamber orchestra, 1997; Sunyata, flute, guitar, 1997;17 Cançons populars catalanes, piano, 1998; Verwandlung, flute quartet, 1999; 3 Poemas sonores, mixed chorus, 1999; El temps segons Rama, orchestra, 1999; Piano Concerto, 2000–01; Acciones y reacciones, flute, piano, 2000; Degung, recorder, vibraphon, 2000; Projeccions, chamber orchestra, 2001. *Recordings:* Musik in Raum, Association of Catalan Composers; Arachne; Confluencies; Chamber Music, 6 works on CD; La Sala de la Suprema Harmonia; Materials; Klagelied; Verwandlung; Complete piano works; 5 Tankas. *Contributions:* Revista Musical Catalana; Revista Quodlibet. *Honours:* Hans-Lenz-Preis, Germany, 1969; Komposition-Preis der Stiftung Landis and Gyr, Switzerland,

1976. *Address:* Rossello 213, 1-1, 08008 Barcelona, Spain. *Telephone:* 93 2170943.

PADROS, Jaime; Composer and Pianist; b. 26 Aug. 1926, Igualada, Spain; m. Eva Marie Wolff, 1962, 1 s., 2 d. *Education:* Baccalaureate, Monastery of Montserrat, Barcelona; Formation, Escolania de Montserrat, 1939–; Piano, organ and musical studies with Dom David Pujol; Piano studies with Frank Marshall and Alicia de Larrocha, Academia Marshall, 1941; Composition with Josep Barbera, Cristobal Taltabull, Barcelona, Darius Milhaud, Paris. *Career:* Debut: As Composer, Ballet Fantasia de circo, 1954; Concerts in all major cities and radio stations in Spain, Paris, Prague and many German cities; First pianist to rediscover several of the works of the 18th Century Spanish Composers Antonio Soler and Narcis Casanoves; First to play complete piano works of Arnold Schoenberg, Alban Berg, Anton Webern and other contemporary composers in Spain; Piano Teacher, Academy of Music, Trossingen, West Germany, 1964–94; Numerous commissioned works, 1954–. *Compositions:* Chamber music for different casts of instruments: Tannkas del somni 1950; Sonata para piano, 1954; Quintet per a quartet d'arc i piano, 1962; Planctus, 1977; Cancionero del lugar, 1978; Policromies, 1980; Several settings of folk songs for choir; Poemas de fragua, 1984; Musica cambiante (piano solo and string orchestra), 1986. *Recordings:* Contrapuntos sobre canciones populares castellanas, 1962; Sternverdunkelung, 1960; Llibre d'alquimies I, 1967; Serenata, 1978; Trama concentrica, 1982; Paseo y contradanza, 1985. *Honours:* Premio Juventudes musicales, 1954; Premi Orfeo catala, 1962. *Address:* Seelengraben 30, 89073 Ulm, Germany.

PAGE, Anne, BMus, DipEd; Organist; b. 2 Dec. 1955, Perth, Australia. *Education:* Univ. of Western Australia, with Maire-Claire Alain at Conservatoire Nationale de Musique, Rueuil-Malmaison, France, with Peter Hurford in Cambridge, and with Jacques van Oortmerssen at the Sweelinck Conservatory, Amsterdam. *Career:* organ recitalist in the UK, Europe, USA and Australia; teacher and course dir; debut Royal Festival Hall, London 1988; directed Cambridge Summer Recitals 1987–94; pioneered revival of serious interest in the harmonium; Prof. of Harmonium at the Royal Coll. of Music, London 2003; mem. Incorporated Soc. of Musicians, British Institute of Organ Studies. *Recordings:* French Music for Harmonium (two vols) 1988, 1990, Sigfrid Karg-Elert: Music for Harmonium 1990, Two Mander Organs 1990, Veni Creator Spiritus: choral and orgam music of Carl Rütti (with Cambridge Voices) 1998, J. S. Bach's Orgelbüchlein 1999, The Willis Organ of Emmanuel United Reform Church 2001, Olivier Messiaen: Livre du Saint Sacrement 2002. *Honours:* Prix d'excellence à l'unanimité, Conservatoire Nationale de Musique 1981. *Address:* 122 Argyle Street, Cambridge, CB1 3LS, England (home). *Telephone:* (1223) 240026 (home). *Fax:* (1223) 573663 (office.) *E-mail:* annepage@waitrose.com (home). *Website:* www.anne-page.co.uk (office).

PAGE, Charlotte; Singer (Soprano); b. 1972, England. *Education:* Royal College of Music, London. *Career:* First niece in Peter Grimes for Covent Garden, Welsh National Opera, 1999; Gretel for Opera Northern Ireland; Frasquita for Central Festival Opera; Zerlina for Pimlico Opera and Offenbach's Hélène, Holland Park; Other roles include Mozart's Despina; Pamina, Second Lady and Cherubino; Clinene in Cavalli's L'Egisto; Mélisande for Atelier Lyrique, Orleans; On tour to France; Further concerts in Tokyo and throughout the United Kingdom. *Address:* Music International, 13 Ardilaun Road, London N5 2QR, England.

PAGE, Christopher (Howard); Medievalist; b. 8 April 1952, London, England; m. Régine Fourcade, 15 Sept 1975. *Education:* BA, English, Oxford University; DPhl, York University. *Career:* University Lecturer in Medieval English, University of Cambridge; Frequent Broadcaster on BBC Radio 3, both as Lecturer and as Director of his Ensemble, Gothic Voices; Presenter of Radio 4 Arts programme, Kaleidoscope. *Recordings:* Directed Gothic Voices in Sequences and Hymns by Abbess Hildegard of Bingen; The Mirror of Narcissus; Songs by Guillaume de Machaut; The Garden of Zephirus; Courtly Songs of the Early 15C; The Castle of Fair Welcome; Courtly Songs of the late 15th Century; The Service of Venus and Mars; A Song for Francesca; Music for the Lionhearted King. *Publications:* (Book) Voices and Instruments of the Middle Ages; Sequences and Hymns by Abbess Hildegard of Bingen; The Owl and the Nightingale: Musical Life and Ideas in France, 1100–1300, 1989; Latin Poetry and Conductors Rhythm in Medieval France, 1997; Music and Instruments of the Middle Ages: Studies in Text and Performance, 1997. *Contributions:* Many academic and scholarly contributions to Early Music; Galpin Society Journal; Proceedings of the Royal Musical Association; New Oxford History of Music; Cambridge Guide to the Arts in Britain; Early Music History; The Historical Harpsichord. *Honours:* British Entrant and Prizewinner, Innsbruck International Radio Prize, 1981; Several Awards for Record of Hildegard; Gramophone Awards for three records; Fellow, Fellowship of Makers and Restorers of Historical Instruments; senior Research Fellow in Music, Sydney Sussex College,

Cambridge. *Address:* Sidney Sussex College, Cambridge University, Cambridge, England.

PAGE, Paula; Singer (Soprano); b. 24 Sept. 1942, Corinth, Mississippi, USA. *Education:* Studied at Indiana University, Bloomington and on a Fulbright Scholarship in Europe. *Career:* Debut: Inez in Il Trovatore, Hamburg, Staatsoper, 1968; Hamburg Staatsoper 1968–72; Appearances at Wuppertal, Aachen, Bremen, Santa Fe, Norfolk, Antwerp, Liège, Bordeaux, Lison, Venice, Düsseldorf; Berlin, Frankfurt am Main Opera from 1983; Repertory includes lyric roles and parts in modern operas, including Staatstheater by Maurizio Kagel; Presently Professor of Voice, Staatliche Hochschule für Musik. *Honours:* Prizewinner, New York Metropolitan Auditions of the Air, 1967; WGN Auditions of the Air, 1967; Geneva International Competition, 1968; s-Hertogenbush Holland, 1968; Martha B Rockefeller Grant, 1977. *Address:* Königsberger Strabe 25, 6239, Germany.

PAGE, Steven; Singer (baritone); b. 1950, England. *Education:* Studied with Margaret Hyde and at the Opera Studio, London. *Career:* Sang Don Alfonso and Nick Shadow with Opera 80, (now English Touring Opera); For English National Opera he has sung the title role in Mozart's Don Giovanni, Tarquinius in The Rape of Lucretia, Albert in Werther, Paolo in Simone Boccanegra, Valentine in Faust and the Count in Marriage of Figaro and most recently the role of Figaro; For Scottish Opera he has appeared as Guglielmo in Così fan tutte, Marcello in La Bohème, Chorèbe in Les Troyens, Ford in Falstaff and the title role of Don Giovanni and the Count in Marriage of Figaro; He has also taken part in four seasons at the Buxton Festival in leading roles and has appeared with Opera Factory as Don Giovanni at the Queen Elizabeth Hall; For Glyndebeourne Touring Opera has sung Nick Shadow in The Rake's Progress, Leporello in Don Giovanni, Anubis in Harrison Birtwistle's The Second Mrs Owen Kong and Coyle in a new production by Robin Philips of Britten's Owen Wingrave; Made his debut Glyndebourne Festival as Nick Shadow in 1994 and returned as Leporello in Don Giovanni and Anubis; Sang Geronio in Rossini's Il Turco in Italia, Garsington, 1996; Season 1999 in Tippett's The Mask of Time at the London Prom concerts. *Address:* c/o Stafford Law Associates, 6 Barham Close, Weybridge, Surrey KT13 9PR, England.

PAGLIARANI, Mario; Swiss composer; b. 27 June 1963, Mendrisio, Ticino canton. *Education:* Conservatorio di Milano, studied with Salvatore Sciarrino. *Compositions include:* Alcuni particolari oscuri 1983, Vie d'uscita 1986, Lucciole o imperi? 1989–90, Paesaggio-Madrigale 1991, Pierrot lunatique 1993, Cappuccetto rosso 1994, Bergweg 1995, Canzone fantasma 1996, Apparizione di Franz Schubert fra le onde 1997, Trio pozzanghera 1998, Rarefatto cantabile 1999. *Recordings:* Alcuni particolari oscuri, Paesaggio-Madrigale, Pierrot lunatique. *Honours:* Musica Ticinensis prize 1987, VI Concurso de obras musicales para Radio prize, Madrid 1995. *Address:* c/o Schweizer Musikedition, Postfach 7851, 6000 Lucerne 7, Switzerland (office). *E-mail:* mail@musicedition.ch (office). *Website:* www.musicedition.ch (office).

PAGLIAZZI, Franco; Singer (baritone, dramatic tenor); b. 8 April 1937, Florence, Italy; m. Denise Serghieva 4 July 1965, 1 s. *Education:* Studied at Centro Lirico del Teatro Comunale, Florence; Studied with Ettore Campogalliani. *Career:* Debut: Cherubini's Elisa, Maggio Musicale Fiorentino, Florence, 1960; As baritone, sang numerous Verdi roles including Rigoletto, Conte di Luna, Amonasro, Iago, Posa, Carlo V; Sang in theatres including Firenze Teatro Comunale, Naples San Carlo, Milan La Scala, Wien Staatsoper, Dublin, Orange Festival, Sofia, Lugano, Brussels, Bielefeld, Amsterdam, Ostrava, Catania, and other venues until 1974; From 1976, singing as dramatic tenor under name Marc Alexander; Sang roles including Enzo, Gabriele, Macduff, Manrico, Don Alvaro, Calaf; Appearances include Barcelona, Teatro del Liceo, Valencia, Rouen, Bordeaux, Braunschweig, Como, Mantova; Recitals in Italy, Switzerland, Japan, until 1998; Sang with conductors such as Muti, Gavazzeni, Bartoletti, G Patanè, Savini, Rivoli, Morelli, Wung Chung. *Recordings:* Conte di Luna in Il Trovatore, 1968; Nello in Donizetti's Pia de Tolomei, 1968; Arias from Il Trovatore, Ernani, Ballo in Maschera, 1963; Un Converso in Cherubini's Elisa, 1960. *Honours:* Competitions, Milan, AS LI CO, 1960; Busseto Voci Verdiane, 1962 Sofia Competition, 1963; First Prize, Vercelli Viotti, 1964. *Address:* Via del Ghirlandaio 24, 50121 Florence, Italy.

PAHUD, Emmanuel; Flautist; b. 1970, France. *Education:* Premier Prix at the Paris Conservatoire, 1990; Further study with Aurèle Nicolet. *Career:* Principal Flute of the Berlin Philharmonic, and many concerts as solo artist appearances at leading international festivals and chamber music societies throughout Europe and Japan; Season 1997–98, Nielsen Concerto with Zürich Tonhalle Orchestra and David Zimman; Recital tour of USA; Mozart Flute and Harp Concerto with Berlin Philharmonic; Tour of Japan including Suntory Hall; Ligeti's Flute and Oboe Concerto with Philharmonia under Heinz Holliger; Season 1998–99, Recital in USA and Japan with Eric le Sage; Mozart

Concerto K313 with Danish National Radio; CPE Bach and Jolivet concertos with the Orchestra d'Auvergne; Wigmore Hall recital with Stephen Kovacevitch; New York Mostly Mozart festival; Salzburg Festival, Mozart Concerto with Berlin Philharmonic and Abbado; Recitalist in International Rising Stars Series in season 1997–98, with concerts at Carnegie Hall and in Europe; Season 1998–99, included concerto appearances with the Vienna Chamber, Zürich Chamber, Budapest Festival, Mostly Mozart Festival, New York and chamber concerts to celebrate the 1999 Poulenc centenary; Season 1999–2000 included concerto performances with the Berlin Philharmonic under Claudio Abbado; The Baltimore Symphony, the London Philharmonic and return recital tours with Eric Le Sage in North America and the Far East. *Recordings include:* Mozart Concertos with the Berlin Philharmonic and Abbado; French repertory with pianist Eric Le Sage. *Honours:* Prize Winner at several international competitions. *Current Management:* Askonas Holt Ltd, Lonsdale Chambers, 27 Chancery Lane, London, WC2A 1PF, England. *Telephone:* (20) 7400-1700. *Fax:* (20) 7400-1799. *E-mail:* info@askonasholt.co.uk. *Website:* www .askonasholt.co.uk.

PAIK, Byung-Dong; Professor; b. 26 Jan. 1936, Seoul, Republic of Korea; m. Wha-ja Woo 1969. *Education:* Shin-Heung High School, Jeon-joo; Coll. of Music, Seoul National Univ.; Stadtliche Hochschule für Musik, Hanover, Germany. *Career:* debut, Annual Korean New Composers Prize with Three Symphonic Chapters 1962; six composition recitals since first recital 1960–; has presented his works several times with National Symphony Orchestra, Seoul Philharmonic Orchestra and other ensembles; Prof., Personnel Management mem., Coll. of Music, Seoul National Univ.; Pres., Perspective Composers Group. *Compositions:* Major works, Symphonic Three Chapters, 1962; Un I, II, III, IV, V, VI for Instrumental Ensemble; Drei Bagetellen für Klavier, 1973; Concerto for Piano and Orchestra, 1974; Veranderte Ehepaar, 1986; In September for Orchestra, 1987; Contra, 1988. *Recordings:* Ein kleine Nachtlied für Violine und Klavier, SEM, Seoul, 1978; Guitariana for two Guitars, SEM, 1984; Byul-Gok 87, Jigu Record Corporation, Seoul, 1987. *Publications:* Musical Theory, 1977; Essays: Seven Fermatas 1979; Essays: Sound or Whispering, 1981; Harmony, 1984; Music for Culture, 1985; College Musical Theory, 1989; The Streams of Modern Music, 1990. *Address:* 214-1 Sangdo 1 dong, Dongjakgu, A-202 Sangdo Villa, Seoul, Republic of Korea.

PAIK, Kun-Woo; pianist; b. 10 May 1946, Seoul, Republic of Korea; m. Son Mi-Ja 1976; one d. *Education:* High School of Performing Arts, New York, Juilliard School of Music, New York, studied with Rosina Lhevine, Ilona Kabos in London, Wihelm Kempff and Guido Agosti in Italy. *Career:* debut as soloist, Grieg Concerto with National Orchestra of Republic of Korea, Seoul, at age of 10; New York Orchestral debut with James Conlon and National Orchestra, Carnegie Hall, 1972; London Debut, 3 recitals, Wigmore Hall, 1974; Recitalist, Alice Tully Hall, New York City, 1971; Recitals, concerts, USA, Europe, South Korea, 1971–; Performed at numerous major festivals, USA and Europe including Berlin, Spoleto, Edinburgh, Paris, Aix-en-Provence; Appearances with major orchestras include London Philharmonic, Paris Orchestre Nationale, Berlin Radio, Suisse Romande, Frankfurt Radio Symphony; US West Coast solo debut with recitals, Los Angeles and San Francisco. *Recordings:* Ravel's complete solo works and 2 concerti, Orfeo and Seon; Moussorgsky's complete piano solo works, RCA; Sonata D960, Schubert, Seon. *Honours:* Special Prize, Dmitri Mitropoulos Competition, 1969; 1st Prize, Walter Naumburg Piano Competition, New York, 1971; Finalist, Leventritt Competition, 1971; Josef Lhevinne Award; Franz Liszt Award. *Address:* 7 rue Villebois-Mareuil, 94300 Vincennes, France.

PAIK, Nam (June); Composer and Performance Artist; b. 20 July 1932, Seoul, South Korea. *Education:* Studied at University of Tokyo; Music theory with Thrasybulos Georgiades in Munich and with Wolfgang Fortner in Munich. *Career:* Worked with Stockhausen at Electronic Music Studio in Cologne, 1958–60; Summer seminars for new music at Darmstadt, 1957–61; Moved to New York 1964, Los Angeles 1970; Performance of music involves total art, including duo recitals with topless cellist Charlotte Moorman in which composer's spine serves as cellist's fingerboard. *Compositions:* Ommaggio a Cage, involving the destruction of piano and raw eggs, and the painting of hands in jet black, 1959; Symphony for 20 Rooms, 1961; Global Groove, high-velocity collage using video tape, 1963; Variations on a Theme of Saint-Saëns for piano and cellist in oil drum; Performable Music, in which performer is required to cut left forearm with a razor, 1967; Opera Sextronique, 1967; Opera Electronique, 1968; Creep into a Whale; Young Penis Symphony, 1970; Earthquake Symphony, with grand finale, 1971; Video Buddha, 1974; The More The Better, 1988; Video Opera, 1993. *Address:* c/o American Music Center, 30 West 26th St, Suite 1001, New York, NY 10010–2011, USA.

PAILLARD, Jean-François; conductor and musicologist; b. 28 April 1928, Vitry-le-Francois, France; m. Anne Marie Beckensteiner; three s.

Education: First Prize in Music History, Paris Conservatoire; Studied conducting with Igor Markevitch, Salzburg; Graduated from the Sorbonne in mathematics. *Career:* Founded the Jean-Marie Leclair Instrumental Ensemble, 1953; Many tours of Europe, USA and the Far East with the Jean-François Paillard Chamber Orchestra, notably in French music of the 17th and 18th centuries; Organiser and Teacher of Conducting Courses, Spring and Summer, France; mem, French Musicological Society; French Society of the 18th Century. *Recordings include:* Bach, Brandenburg Concertos, Suites for Orchestra, Harpsichord Concertos and Musical Offering; Handel Alexander's Feast, Water and Fireworks Music, Dettingen Te Deum, Concertos for oboe, organ and harp; Couperin Les Nations; Delalande Symphonies; Charpentier Te Deum, Magnificat and Messe de Minuit, Baroque trumpet concertos (Maurice André); Rameau Les Indes Galantes; Mozart Divertimenti; Flute and Violin concertos, concerto K 299. *Publications:* La Musique Francaise Classique, 1960, 1973; Archives de la Musique Instrumentale; Archives de la Musique Religieuse. *Honours:* Many Grand Prix du Disque (Academie Charles Cros, Disque Francais Disque Lyrique); Prix Edison, Netherlands; German Record Prize; Gold Record, Japan. *Address:* 23 rue de Marly, 7860 Etang la Ville, France.

PAITA, Carlos; Conductor; b. 10 March 1932, Buenos Aires, Argentina; m. Elisabeth de Quartbarbes, 7 c. *Education:* Studied with Juan Neuchoff and Jacobo Fischer. *Career:* Debut: Teatro Col ón, Buenos Aires; Conducted the National Radio Orchestra in Argentina; Verdi Requiem, 1964, Mahler's 2nd Symphony, 1965; Stuttgart Radio Symphony from 1966; Appearances in London, Paris, Edinburgh and the USA (debut 1979, with the Houston Symphony Orchestra); He has guest conducted orchestras all over the world, including the Washington National Orchestra, the Russian State Orchestra, at the Prague Festival, in Poland, Romania, Bratislava, Slovakia and at the Enesco Festival in Bulgaria and the Flanders Festival in Belgium. *Recordings:* Festival Wagner; Grands Overtures; Verdi Requiem; Beethoven's Eroica Symphony; Rossini Overtures; Mahler's 1st Symphony; Symphonie Fantastique by Berlioz. *Honours:* Grand Prix, Academie Charles Cros, Paris, 1969; Grand Prix de L'Academie Francaise, 1978. *Address:* 15 Chemin du Champ d'Anier, 1209 Geneva, Switzerland.

PAL, Támás; Conductor; b. 16 Sept. 1937, Gyula, Hungary. *Education:* Studied with Janos Viski and Andréas Korody at the Franz Liszt Academy Budapest. *Career:* Conducted the Budapest State Opera 1960–75, notably at the Edinburgh Festival (1973) and the Wiesbaden May Festival (1974); Principal Conductor of the Szeged Symphony Orchestra and Opera, 1975–83; Permanent Conductor of the Budapest Opera, 1983–85; Artistic Director of the open air summer music festival at Budapest, 1987; Has conducted operatic rarities such as Salieri's Falstaff, Liszt's Don Sanche and Il Pittor Parigino by Cimarosa; Directed Aida at Szeged, 1997. *Recordings include:* Liszt Piano Concerto No. 2 with the Hungarian State Orchestra; Brahms Symphony No. 3 and Academic Festival Overture with the Budapest Symphony Orchestra; Il Pittor Parigino (premiere recording). *Address:* c/o Hungarian State Opera House, Nepoztarsasag uta 22, 1061 Budapest, Hungary.

PALACIO, Ernesto; Singer (Tenor); b. 19 Oct. 1946, Lima, Peru. *Education:* Studied in Peru and Milan, Italy. *Career:* Debut: Sang Almaviva in San Remo, Italy, 1972; Sang lyric roles in Milan, Rome, Venice, Trieste, Bologne, Turin, Genoa, Palermo, Naples, Parma, Catania; Guest appearances in London (Covent Garden), New York (Metropolitan and Carnegie Hall), Buenos Aires (Colon), Berlin (Philharmonic), Edinburgh, Marseilles, Bordeaux, Lille, Nancy, Lyon, Strasbourg, Houston, Dallas, Zürich, Düsseldorf, Munich, Caracas, Chile; Other roles include 18 operas of Rossini, Don Giovanni, Così fan tutte, Re Pastore, Die Zauberflöte, Finta giardiniera, Finta Semplice (Mozart); Elisir d'amore, Don Pasquale, La fille du Régiment, Esule di Roma, Torquato Tasso (Donizetti); Sang in a revival of Ciro in Babilonia by Rossini at Savona, 1988; Appeared as Argirio in Tancredi opposite Marilyn Horne at Barcelona, May 1989, Bilbao, Jan 1991; Bonn Opera 1990, as Almaviva. *Recordings:* Mosè in Egitto; Il Turco in Italia; Miserere by Donizetti; Adelaide di Borgogna by Rossini; Vivaldi's Serenata a Tre; Torquato Tasso; Catone in Utica by Vivaldi; Unpublished arias by Rossini, conducted by Carlo Rizzi; Prince Giovanni in Una Cosa Rara.

PALACIO, Pedro (Antonio); Composer; b. 15 April 1961, La Rioja, Argentina; 1 s., 1 d. *Education:* Diplomas: Master of Guitar, 1979, Master of Musical Composition, 1985, Cordoba, Argentina; Master of Composition and Musical Analysis, France, 1987. *Career:* Debut: Variations for Piano performed at National Festival for Contemporary Music, Argentina, 1984; Performance of works: Teatro Colón, Argentina; Festival Antidogma Musica, Italy; Mengano Quartett and WNC Ensemble, Cologne, and Turmheim Ensemble, Germany; Ensemble Stringendo, Ensemble Aleph at Festival of Evreux, BMA Ensemble at Nantes, Wozzeck Trio, ENMD-Montreuil Ensemble, France; World

Music Days Festival, Zürich, Switzerland; Poland Broadcasting Symphony Orchestra; Symphony Orchestra of Cordoba; SACEM, France. *Compositions:* Axis; Triolaid; Quintolaid; Latidos; Yugoslavia Burning; Omphalo; Dämmerung; Laughs of Tokyo; Histoire d'Oiseaux Mathématiques; Quateur à Cordes No. 1, 1998; Cuerdas Vocales, 1998; El tiempo suspendido resonante II, 2000. *Recordings:* Albums: Dämmerung; Laughs of Tokyo; Histoire d'oiseaux mathématiques, Ensemble Aleph; El tiempo suspendido resonante II. *Publications include:* Roman-B for guitar, 1987; Herejía for solo violin, 1998. *Honours:* Essec-Invention, France, 1986; Icons, Italy, 1988; Trinac, Argentina, 1989; André Jolivet, France, 1991; Kazimierz Serocki, Poland, 1996; Alberto Ginastera, Argentina, 1996. *Address:* 56 avenue Jean-Jaurès, 75019 Paris, France.

PALAY, Elliot; Singer (Tenor); b. 18 Dec. 1948, Milwaukee, Wisconsin, USA. *Education:* Studied at Indiana University, Bloomington with Charles Kullmann; Further study with Clemens Kaiser-Breme in Essen. *Career:* Debut: Lubeck 1972, as Matteo in Arabella; Sang in Freiburg, Düsseldorf, Munich and Stuttgart; Komische Oper Berlin 1977, in Aufstieg und Fall der Stadt Mahagonny; Returned to USA and sang at the New York City Opera; Santa Fe and Seattle 1983, as Siegfried in Der Ring des Nibelungen; Antwerp and Ghent 1983, as Siegmund in Die Walküre; Dresden 1984, in Wozzeck; Other roles include Wagner's Tristan and Walther, Verdi's Radames and Ismaele, the Emperor in Die Frau ohne Schatten and Boris in Katya Kabanova; Sang Siegfried with the Jutland Opera at Århus, 1987; Opera roles in Munich from 2000. *Address:* c/o Den Jydske Opera, Musikhuset Arkus, Thomas Jensens Alle, 8000 Århus, Denmark.

PALECZNY, Piotr (Tadeusz); Concert Pianist; b. 10 May 1946, Rybnik, Poland; m. Barbara Kurnik, 31 Mar 1975, 1 s. *Education:* Chopin Music Academy, Warsaw. *Career:* Numerous Concerts with Orchestras including: Chicago Concertgebouw, Zürich Tonhalle, RAI, Gewandhaus, BBC, Santa Cecilia; Recitals on 6 Continents; Masterclasses in Paris, Tokyo, Buenos Aires, Lugano, Warsaw; Jury, International Piano Competitions, Cleveland, London, Warsaw; Professor, Chopin Academy, Warsaw; mem, Chopin Society, Warsaw. *Recordings:* Piano Concertos. *Honours:* Many High Polish State Distinction Prizes of Ministry of Culture, Polish radio and television; Order of Aztec Eagle, Mexico. *Address:* Ligonia 57, 01498 Warsaw, Poland.

PALEY, Alexander; Concert Pianist; b. 9 Jan. 1956, Kishinev, USSR; m. 29 July 1978, 1 d. *Education:* Master's Degree, PhD, Moscow Conservatory. *Career:* Debut: Kishinev, 2 April 1969; Performed with Moscow Virtuosi (V Spivakov), 1985–90; Bolshoi Theatre Orchestra, 1986; With Monte Carlo Philharmonic, 1989; With Colorado Symphony, 1991; Recitals, Châtelet, Paris, 1990, Auditorium de Halles, 1991, Strasbourg, Moscow, Prague, Berlin, Sofia; Appeared with National Symphony Orchestra, Wolf Trap Festival, 1991 and Boston Pops, 1991; Chamber music with Fine Arts Quartet, New York Chamber Soloists also with V Spivakov, Bella Davidovich, Oleg Krysa, D Sitkovetsky and B Pergamentshikov; Musical Director, Cannes-sur-Mer Festival, France. *Recordings:* Talent, Belgium; Liszt, all 4 Mephisto valses, other pieces; National Public Radio, USA; Radio France; Melodia, Moscow, 1990. *Address:* 850 West 176th Street, Apt 4 D, New York, NY 10033, USA.

PALM, Mati-Johannes; Estonian singer (bass); b. 13 Jan. 1942, Tallinn; two c. *Education:* Tallinn Conservatoire, studied in Moscow and at La Scala. *Career:* sang with the Estonian State Opera from 1967, notably as Boris, Basilio, King Philip, Ivan Khovansky, the Dutchman, Silva, Zaccaria, Raimondo, Colline and Gremin; guest appearances from 1980 in Helsinki as Attila, the Savonlinna Festival as the Dutchman, Paris Opéra in 1988 as Pimen, at Karlsruhe in 1992 in Khovanshchina as Dosifei, Buenos Aires from 1991 in Iolanta and Lohengrin; sang King Philip in Don Carlos at Tallinn 1971, 2000; sang Mephistopheles in Boito's Mefistofele and Banquo in Verdi's Macbeth; further appearances in Moscow, St Petersburg, Prague and Berlin; with many concerts, including 55 cantatas and oratorios, including Bach's St John Passion, Handel's Messiah, Mozart's Requiem, Beethoven's Missa Solemnis, Rossini's Stabat Mater, Verdi's Requiem; judge at int. singing competitions; currently soloist, Estonian Nat. Opera and Prof. of Singing, Estonian Acad. of Music. *Recordings:* M. Palm 1972, Aries of Verdi, Romances of A. Kapp and G. Sviridov, Mussorgski's Boris Godunov (Pimen), Two Canatatas of J. S. Bach BWV 78 140, Estonian opera singer Mati Palm, Mati Palm sings Estonian and Italian Songs, A. Kapp's Oratorio Hiob, R. Tobias Oratorio Des Jona Sendung, Verdi's Nabucco (Zaccaria), E. Tubin Barbara von Tiesenhusen (Konguta). *Film recording:* Mati Palm is Singing 1972. *Honours:* gold medal Classical Singing Competition, Sofia, first prize Baltic States Young Singers Competition 1971, G. Ots Prize, silver medal F. Vinase Int. Competition, Barcelona 1972; State Order of White Star, Soviet Union State Prize 1983. *Address:* c/o Estonian National Opera, Estonia Boulevard 4, 10148 Tallinn, Estonia (office). *Telephone:* (372) 683-1230 (office); (372) 51 13

703 (mobile). *Fax:* (372) 631-3080 (office). *E-mail:* mati.palm.001@mail.ee.

PALM, Siegfried; Cellist, Professor of Music and Administrator; b. 25 April 1927, Barmen, Germany; m. Brigitte Heinemann. *Education:* Studied with father and in Enrico Mainardi's masterclasses at Salzburg. *Career:* Principal Cellist, Lubeck City Orchestra, 1945–47, Hamburg Radio Symphony, 1947–62, Cologne Radio Symphony, 1962–67; Played with Hamann Quartet 1950–62; Formed Duo with Aloys Kontarsky 1965; Joined Max Rostal and Heinz Schröter in Piano Trio, 1967; Professor at Cologne Musikhochschule, 1962, Director from 1972; Teacher at Darmstadt from 1962; Has also taught at the Royal Conservatory Stockholm, Dartmouth College USA, Marlboro USA and the Sibelius Academy Helsinki; Intendant of the Deutsche Oper Berlin, 1977–81; Many recitals and appearances with leading orchestras; Engagements at Holland Festival, Warsaw Autumn Festival, Prague Spring Festival and Barcelona Festival; First performances of works by Stockhausen, Zimmermann, Penderecki, Xenakis, Zillig, Blacher, Feldman, Ligeti, Fortner, Yun, Kelemen and Kagel. *Publications:* Pro musica nova: Studien zum Spielen neuer Musik für Cello, 1974. *Honours:* German Record Prize, 1969. *Current Management:* Ingpen & Williams Ltd, 7 St George's Court, 131 Putney Bridge Road, London, SW15 2PA, England.

PALMER, Felicity (Joan); Singer (mezzo-soprano); b. 6 April 1944, Cheltenham, England. *Education:* Guildhall School of Music and Drama; Hochschule Musik, Munich; AGSM, Teacher and Performer; FGSM. *Career:* Debut: Purcell's Dido with Kent Opera, 1971; In USA, Marriage of Figaro, Houston, 1973; At La Scala, Milan in world premiere of Testi's Riccardo III, 1987; Major appearances at concerts in the United Kingdom, America, Belgium, France, Germany, Italy, Russia and Spain; Operatic appearances include: The Magic Flute, 1975, Alcina, Bern, 1977, Idomeneo, Zürich, 1980, Rienzi, ENO, 1983, King Priam, Royal Opera, 1985, Albert Herring, Glyndebourne, 1985; Recitals in Amsterdam, Paris and Vienna, 1976–77; Concert tours to Australasia, Far East and Eastern Europe, 1977–; Sang in Flavio Testi's Riccardo III at Milan, 1987; Has sung Kabanicha at Chicago and Glyndebourne; Sang title role in the stage premiere of Roberto Gerhard's The Duenna, Madrid, 1992; Season 1992 as Klytemnestra for Welsh National Opera and the Countess in The Queen of Spades at Glyndebourne; In 1993 sang Geneviève in Pelléas and Mélisande for Netherlands Opera, and at Orlando and Aix-en-Provence, Fille du Régiment for San Francisco Opera, and Katya Kabonova, Toronto; In 1994 sang in The Rake's Progress, Chicago, Elektra at Dresden and La Scala, Milan; In 1995 sang in Ballo in Maschera at Catania, and in Elektra in Japan with Sinopoli; Klytemnestra in Elektra at Covent Garden, 1997; Season 1999 in Tippett's The Mask of Time at the London Prom concerts; Season 2000 with NY Met debut as Waltraute in Götterdämmerung, Poulenc's Mme de Croissy (also at La Scala) and the Countess in The Queen of Spades at Chicago; London Proms, 2002; Clytemnestra in Elektra, Mrs Lovett in Sweeney Todd, Covent Garden, 2003. *Recordings include:* Messiaen's Poèmes pour Mi, with Pierre Boulez; French songs with John Constable and Simon Rattle with the Nash Ensemble; Andromache in King Priam with David Atherton; Title role in Gluck's Armide. *Honours:* Kathleen Ferrier Memorial Prize, 1970; C.B.E., 1993. *Current Management:* Askonas Holt Ltd, Lonsdale Chambers, 27 Chancery Lane, London, WC2A 1PF, England. *Telephone:* (20) 7400-1700. *Fax:* (20) 7400-1799. *E-mail:* info@askonasholt.co.uk. *Website:* www.askonasholt.co.uk.

PALMER, Larry; Harpsichordist and Organist; b. 13 Nov. 1938, Warren, Ohio, USA. *Education:* Studied at Oberlin College Conservatory and Eastman School at Rochester, DMA 1963; Harpsichord with Isolde Ahlgrimm at Salzburg Mozarteum and with Gustav Leonhardt at Haarlem. *Career:* Recitalist on Harpsichord and Organ throughout the USA and Europe, with premieres of works by such composers as Vincent Persichetti and Ross Lee Finney; Harpsichord Editor of The Diapason from 1969; Professor of Harpsichord and Organ at Southern Methodist University in Dallas, 1970. *Recordings:* Organ works of Distler and harpsichord pieces from the 17th to the 20th centuries. *Publications:* Hugo Distler and his Church Music, 1967; Harpsichord in America: A 20th Century Revival, 1989 (2nd Ed 1992). *Address:* c/o Southern Methodist University, Meadows School of the Arts, Dallas, TX 75275, USA.

PALMER, Peter; Writer on Music and Translator; b. 7 March 1945, West Bridgford, Nottinghamshire, England. *Education:* Exhibitioner in Modern Languages, Gonville and Caius College, Cambridge, 1963–66, MA; Apprentice Stage Director, International Opera Studio, Zürich, 1967–69. *Career:* Founder and Artistic Director, East Midlands Music Theatre; First British stage productions of works by Janáček, Krenek, John Ogdon, Schoeck; Founding Editor, Bruckner Journal, 1997; Visiting Lecturer, Romantic and Modern Swiss Music, Pro Helvetia Foundation, 1998–99; Symposium Speaker, Lucerne Festival, 1999. *Publications:* Translations include: From the Mattress Grave, song cycle by David Blake, 1980; Essays on the Philosophy of Music by Ernst Bloch, 1985; Wagner and Beethoven by Klaus Kropfinger, 1991; Late Idyll: The Second Symphony of Johannes Brahms by Reinhold Brinkmann, 1995; Johann Faustus, libretto by Hanns Eisler in: Hanns Eisler: A Miscellany, 1995. *Contributions:* Die Tat, Zürich; Music and Musicians; Organists' Review; German Life and Letters; Tempo; The Musical Times; New Grove Dictionary of Music and Musicians; Talks for BBC Radio 3. *Address:* 2 Rivergreen Close, Beeston, Nottinghamshire NG9 3ES, England.

PALMER, Rudolph (Alexis); Conductor, Composer and Pianist; b. 5 Aug. 1952, New York City, USA; m. Madeline Rogers, 21 June 1981. *Education:* BA, Russian, French, Bucknell University, 1973; BS, Composition, Mannes College of Music, 1975; MM, Juilliard, Composition, 1977; DMA, Juilliard, Composition, 1982. *Career:* Conducting and Composition Faculty, Mannes College of Music, 1982–; Director, Great Neck Choral Society, 1983–84; Orchestra Director, Horace Mann School, 1988–93; Associate Conductor, Amor Artis Chamber Choir, Fairfield County Chorale; Conductor, North Jersey Music Educators Orchestra, Brewer Chamber Orchestra; Palmer Chamber Orchestra; Palmer Singers; Queen's Chamber Band. *Compositions:* Contrasts for Four Bassoons; O Magnum Mysterium; Commissions: Songs of Reflection; The Vision of Herod; The Immortal Shield; Orchestration of Leonard Bernstein's Touches; Numerous other works for chamber groups, chorus and orchestra, including 2 string quartets, 1 symphony, Dance-Music (a ballet), orchestral overtures and several dramatic cantatas. *Recordings:* Accompanist: Lieder, (by women composers); The Unknown Dvořák; Conductor: Baroque Cantatas of Versailles; The Romantic Handel; Handel's Imeneo; Telemann's Pimpinone; Handel's Berenice; Handel's Siroe; Pergolesi's La Serva Padrona; Handel's Joshua; Handel's Muzio; A Scarlatti's Ishmael; Haydn's La Canterina; Handel Arias, with various artists; Handel's Muzio Scevola; Handel's Alexander Balus; Handel's Deidamia; Handel's Faramondo; Gluck's Il Parnaso Confuso; Chorusmaster, Bach, St John Passion; Handel, Alexander Balus. *Address:* 215 West 88th Street, Apt 7E, New York, NY 10024, USA.

PALOLA, Juhani; Violinist; b. 25 Nov. 1952, Helsinki, Finland; m. Liisa-Maria Lampela, 27 Sept 1977, 2 d. *Education:* Violin Studies, Oulu Music Institute, Sibelius Academy, Privately in Munich with Professor Takaya Urakawa. *Career:* Debut: Soloist, Oulu Symphony Orchestra, 1968; Concerts as Soloist and Chamber Musician, Finland, Sweden, 1968–, Norway, Ukraine, Romania, Albania, Germany, Switzerland, USA, Austria; Professor of Violin, Teachers Training College, Rorschach, Switzerland; First Violin in Arioso Quartet, St Gallen; mem, ESTA. *Recordings:* Several for radio and television; Classic 2000. *Address:* Salen 248, 9035 Grub AR, Switzerland.

PALOMBI, Antonello; Singer (Tenor); b. 1965, Umbria, Italy. *Education:* Studied in Italy. *Career:* Debut: Sang Pinkerton in Germany, 1990; Appearances as Dourmont in La Scala di Seta at Pistoia and as the Duke of Mantua in Austria; Edoardo in La Cambiale di Matrimonio by Rossini at Macerata, Ferrando at Ravenna, Macduff at Livorno and Attalo in Rossini's Ermione in Berlin; Teatro Comunale, Pisa, as Alfredo, Ramiro (La Cenerentola), Don José and Monteverdi's Telemaco (Ritorno d'Ulisse); Nemorino at San Gimmingano, the Duke of Mantua in Tokyo and Sou Chong in Das Land des Lächelns at Florence; Sang Edmondo in a new production of Manon Lescaut at Glyndebourne, 1997; Concerts include Pulcinella, at Pisa and Modena; Fenton in Falstaff at the 1999 London Proms. *Address:* Teatro Comunale G Verdi, Via Palestro 40, 56200 Pisa, Italy.

PAMPUCH, Helmut; Singer (Tenor); b. 1939, Grossmahlendorf, Oberschlesien, Germany. *Education:* Studied at Nuremberg with Willi Domgraf-Fassbaender, 1957–62. *Career:* Sang at Regensburg from 1963; Appearances in Brunswick, Wiesbaden and Saarbrucken; Member of the Deutsche Oper am Rhein, Düsseldorf, 1973–, notably in character and buffo roles; Bayreuth debut 1978, later appeared as Mime in Das Rheingold, 1990; Paris Opéra 1979, in the premiere of the full version of Berg's Lulu, conducted by Pierre Boulez; Has sung Mozart's Monostatos at La Scala 1985, and Mime in Ring cycles at San Francisco 1984–90 and Zürich 1989; Further engagements at the State Operas of Hamburg, Munich and Stuttgart; Deutsche Oper Berlin and the Grand Théâtre Geneva; Sang Mime in Das Rheingold at Bayreuth, 1992 and at Buenos Aires, 1995; Many concert appearances. *Recordings include:* Lulu (Deutsche Grammophon); Das Rheingold (Philips). *Address:* c/o Deutsche Oper am Rhein, Heinrich-Heine Allee 16, 4000 Düsseldorf, Germany.

PAN, Yiming; Pianist and Educator; b. 9 July 1937, Shanghai, China; m. Ying Shi-Zhen 1960, 2 s. *Education:* Piano Department, Central Conservatory of Music, Beijing, 1954–59; Bachelor's degree, 1959; Studied Piano with Li Chang-Sun, C. Stevenska (Poland), D. Klavchenko (USSR), others. *Career:* Teaching Piano, 1959–91, Associate Professor, 1983–90, Deputy Director. Piano Department, 1983–91,

Professor of Piano, 1990–91, Central Conservatory of Music; Came to Singapore, 1991; Piano Professor, LaSalle-SIA, College of Arts; Recitals and concerto concerts, main Chinese cities such as Beijing, Tianjin, Chengdu, Xian; Recital on radio, Central People's Broadcasting, 1984; Joint recitals, Beijing, with Professor Jacob Latiener of Juilliard School of Music and with Professor Razits of Indiana University; Jury Member, National Piano Competitions, China, formerly, and National Music Competitions, Singapore, 1991, 1993, 1995; mem, Resources Panel, National Arts Council of Singapore; Chinese Musicians Association. *Compositions include:* The Youth Piano Concerto, co-composer. *Recordings:* Major works of Beethoven, Chopin, Granados, and many Chinese composers. *Publications:* Author, more than 10 articles about piano performing and teaching; Editor: The Album of 45 Piano Sonatas by Scarlatti, 1st Chinese edition; Foreign Piano Pieces for the Young, vols 1–6. *Honours:* 1st Prize, Piano Competition, Central Conservatory of Music, 1957. *Address:* Blk 38, #14-2406, Upper Boon Keng Road, Singapore 380038, Singapore.

PANAGULIAS, Ann; Singer (Soprano); b. 1963, USA. *Career:* Sang Berg's Lulu at San Francisco, 1989, returned as Natasha in War and Peace; Marzelline in Fidelio and Musetta; Wexford Festival, 1991 as Eleanora in Donizetti's Assedio di Calais; Vancouver, 1992 as Norina, Los Angeles, 1992 as Pamina and Dallas, 1994 as Poppea; Washington Opera, 1995 as Marenka in The Bartered Bride; Guest appearances at Geneva and Bordeaux, as Fiordiligi, and Paris, in Lully's Roland; Santa Fe Opera from 1992, notably in the US premiere of Bose's Werther and the world premiere of D Lang's Modern Painters; Sang Poulenc's Blanche for Portland Opera, 2000. *Address:* c/o Santa Fe Opera, PO Box 2408 Santa Fe, NM 87504, USA.

PANERAI, Rolando; Singer (baritone); b. 17 Oct. 1924, Campi Bisenszio, Florence, Italy. *Education:* studied in Florence with Raoul Frazzi and in Milan with Armani and Giulia Tess. *Career:* debut, Naples in 1947 as Faraone in Rossini's Moses; sang at La Scala from 1951, debut in Samson et Dalila; Venice 1955 in the stage premiere of Prokofiev's The Fiery Angel; Aix in 1955 as Mozart's Figaro; Salzburg from 1957 as Ford in Falstaff, Masetto in Don Giovanni, Guglielmo in Così fan tutte and Paolo in Simon Boccanegra; sang in the Italian premiere of Hindemith's Mathis der Maler, Milan 1957; Covent Garden debut 1960 as Figaro; other roles include Verdi's Luna and Giorgio Germont, Henry Ashton in Lucia di Lammermoor and Marcello in La Bohème; appearances in Verona, Florence, Rome, San Francisco 1958, Moscow, Rio de Janeiro, Athens, Berlin, Munich and Johannesburg; returned to Covent Garden in 1985 as Dulcamara in L'Elisir d'amore; Maggio Musicale Florence 1988 as Puccini's Gianni Schicchi; sang Michonnet in Adriana Lecouvreur at the 1989 Munich Festival; Douglas in Mascagni's Guglielmo Ratcliff at Catania, 1990; returned to Covent Garden 1990, and to Barcelona 1998, as Dulcamara; season 2000–01 with Don Alfonso at the Opéra Bastille and Dulcamara at Frankfurt. *Recordings:* I Puritani; Così fan tutte; Il Trovatore; Falstaff; Il Barbiere di Siviglia; La Bohème; Aida; Verdi's Oberto; Parsifal with Maria Callas.

PANHOFER, Wolfgang; Cellist; b. 6 June 1965, Vienna, Austria. *Education:* Music and Psychology, University; Hochschule Vienna with Benesch and Herzer; Royal Northern College of Music with Ralph Kirschbaum, courses with B Pergamenshikov, W Pleeth, A Schiff, Paul Tortelier. *Career:* Debut: Dvořák Concerto, Grosser Wiener Musik-Vereinssaal; Youngest freelancing member, Vienna Philharmonic; Soloist, most European countries, Japan, USA, Egypt, Korea, Turkey, India, Iran; Concertos with Vienna Symphony Orchestra, Vienna Chamber Orchestra, almost all the Polish orchestras, Bombay Chamber Orchestra, Hamburg Symphony Orchestra, BBC Chamber Ensemble, Cairo Symphony Orchestra; Appearances on BBC television with Paul Tortelier, Polish television with Philharmony Katowice, Austrian television with Franz Welser-Möst; Played with Josef Suk at the 150th Birthday Concert of Dvořák, Wiener Konzerthaus; Schleswig-Holstein Music Festival with Pergamenshikov; Held masterclasses in Europe, USA, Japan, Korea, Egypt, Turkey and Iran; Debut at Carnegie Hall, New York 2000; mem, ESTA; Former President, WUT, Society for Modern Music and Literature. *Recordings:* Contemporary Austrian music, with Vienna J. S. Chamber Orchestra. *Honours:* Sir John Barbirolli Prize, 1984; Anerkennungspreis der Alban Berg Stiftung. *Address:* Gaertnergasse 13, A 2100 Korneuburg, Austria.

PANKRATOV, Vladimir; Singer (bass); b. 1958, St Petersburg, Russia. *Education:* Studied at the St Petersburg Conservatoire. *Career:* Sang with the Kirov Opera in St Petersburg and on tour to Edinburgh, Italy, Sweden, France and Japan in Prince Igor, War and Peace and Khovanshchina; Italian roles include Sparafucile, Philip II, Fiesco, Dulcamara and Basilio; Sarastro, Leporello and Mozart's Commendatore; Guest engagements with Heidelberg Opera until 1995; Debut with Théâtre du Capitole Toulouse, 1996; Concert repertoire includes songs by Borodin, Glinka and Tchaikovsky, and the Requiems of Fauré, Mozart and Verdi; Frequent concerts in Israel, where he also teaches at the Rubin Academy. *Current Management:* Athole Still International

Management, Forresters Hall, 25–27 Westow Street, London, SE19 3RY, England. *Telephone:* (20) 8771-5271. *Fax:* (20) 8768-6600. *Website:* www.atholestill.com.

PANNELL, Raymond; Composer and Pianist; b. 25 Jan. 1935, London, Ontario, Canada. *Education:* Studied piano with Steuermann and composition with Wagenaar and Giannini at Juilliard. *Career:* Taught at Toronto Royal Conservatory from 1959, Directed opera workshops at Stratford Festival, Ontario, 1966; Assistant Director and Resident Conductor at Atlanta Municipal Theater, 1960 and Director of Youth Experimental Opera Workshop, 1969; Co-founder and General Director of Co-Opera Theatre in Toronto, 1975. *Compositions:* Stage works: Aria da Capo, opera in 1 act, Toronto 1963; The Luck of Giner Coffey, opera in 3 acts; Go, children's opera, 1975; Midway 1975; Push, developmental opera in 1 act, Toronto 1976; Circe, masque, Toronto 1977; Aberfan, video opera, CBC 1977; N-E-U-S, radio opera 1977; Souvenirs, opera in 1 act, Toronto 1979; Refugees, vaudeville, Little Rock, Arkansas, 1986 (revised version); The Downsview Anniversary Song-Spectacle Celebration Pageant 1979; Harvest, television opera, CBC 1980; The Forbidden Christmas, musical 1990. *Honours:* Salzburg Television Opera Prize for Aberfan, 1977. *Address:* c/o SOCAN, 41 Valleybrook Drive, Don Mills, Ontario M3B 2S6, Canada.

PANNI, Marcello; Composer and Conductor; b. 24 Jan. 1940, Rome, Italy; m. Jeanne Colombier, 3 Dec 1970, 1 d. *Education:* Roma Liceo Classico; Roma Accademia Santa Cecilia, 1961–65; Paris Conservatoire National Superieur, 1965–68. *Career:* Debut: Venice 1969; Teacher, (Milhaud Chair), Composition and Conducting, Mills College, Oakland, California, USA, 1979–85; Guest Conductor, major stages in Italy; Rome Opera; La Scala, Milan; San Carlo, Naples; La Fenice, Venice; Paris Opéra, 1985; Vienna Staatsoper, 1986; Hamburg Staatsoper, 1977; Zürich, 1986; Berlin Deutsche Oper, 1988; New York Metropolitan Opera House, 1988–1992; London Covent Garden, 1989; Concerts at Roma Accademia Santa Cecilia, 1970–; Radio Symphony Orchestras, Italy; Season 1992 with L'Elisir d'amore at Barcelona and The Fall of the House of Usher by Philip Glass at Florence; Season 1993, Trittico by Puccini; Wildschütz by Lortzing at the opera of Bonn; First Guest Conductor, Bonn Opera, 1993; Musical Director, Bonn Opera, 1994–97, Orchestra i Pomeriggi Musicali, Milan, 1994–97; Nice Opéra, France, 1997–; mem, Accademia Filarmonica Romana. *Compositions:* Klangfarbenspiel, Milan Piccola Scala, 1973; La Partenza dell'Argonauta, Florence, Maggio Musicale, 1976; Opera: Hanjo, Florence, 1994; Il Giudizio di Paride, Bonn, 1996; The Banquet, Bremen, 1998. *Recordings:* Pergolesi Adriano in Siria, Handel Giulio Cesare, Paisiello Nina, Donizetti, La Fille du Régiment, 1997; Rossini, Semiramide, 1999. *Current Management:* Musicagloze 11 rue Le Verrier, 75006 Paris, France.

PANOCHA, Jiri; Violinist; b. 1940, Czechoslovakia. *Education:* Studied at the Prague Academy of Arts. *Career:* Leader of International Student Orchestra in Berlin, under Karajan; Co-founded the Panocha Quartet, 1968; Many concert appearances in Europe, the USA, Canada, Iraq, Mexico, Cuba and other countries; Repertoire includes works by Smetana, Janáček, Dvořák, Martinů, Haydn, Mozart, Beethoven, Schubert, Bartók and Ravel. *Recordings include:* Dvořák late quartets and Terzetto; Haydn Op 33, Nos 1–6, D Major Op 64; Martinů Complete Quartets; Mendelssohn Octet (with Smetana Quartet); Mozart Oboe Quartet, Clarinet Quintet and Horn Quintet; Schubert Quartettsatz D703 (Supraphon). *Honours:* Prizewinner (with members of Panocha Quartet) at Kromeriž, 1971; Weimar 1974; Prague 1975; Bordeaux 1976; Grand Prix du Disque, Paris, 1983 for Martinů recordings. *Address:* Panocha Quartet, Bureau de Concerts J. Mauroy, 19 rue des Primereres, L-2351, Luxembourg.

PANTILLON, Christopher (David); Cellist; b. 26 Jan. 1965, Neuchatel, Switzerland. *Education:* Baccalaureat es Lettres, Humanities, Neuchatel, Switzerland, 1983; Studied with Heinrich Schiff, Conservatory, Basle, 1984–88; Diploma of Cello, 1988; Studied with Valentin Erben, Hochschule für Musik, Vienna. *Career:* Numerous appearances as soloist or chamber player; Member, Trio Pantillon (with 2 brothers); Concerts in Geneva, Zürich, Bern, Vienna, Paris, Rome, England, France, Germany, Netherlands; Appeared on Swiss television and radio; mem, ESTA. *Recordings:* Kabalevsky: Cello-Concerto No. 1 in G Minor. *Honours:* 2nd Prize, Swiss Youth Competition, Lucerne, 1983. *Current Management:* Music Management International. *Address:* La Chanterelle, 2022 Bevaix, Switzerland.

PANUFNIK, Roxanna, FRSA; Composer; b. 1968, London, England. *Education:* Studied at the Royal Academy, with Paul Patterson and Henze. *Career:* BBC Researcher and Presenter; Visiting teacher of composition at various schools in England and Barbados; First ever Composer-in-Residence for the Royal County of Berkshire; Performances of her music at all London's main concert venues and throughout the United Kingdom, Europe, Asia, Antipodes and USA; mem, British Academy of Composers and Songwriters; PRS; MCPS.

Compositions include: Westminster Mass for Westminster Cathedral Choir; Olivia, string quartet; The Music Programme, chamber opera; Leda, ballet; Beastly Tales (words Vikram Seth) for voices and orchestra; Powers & Dominions, harp concertino; Orchestrated Samuel Arnold's opera Inkle and Yarico (1787) for its first modern performance, Barbados, 1997; The Upside Down Sailor, commissioned by Collegiate Wind Ensemble, for narrator and wind nonet, words by Richard Stilgoe. *Recordings:* Angels Sing (all Roxanna Panufnik's religious choral works), The Joyful Company of Singers, Westminster Cathedral Choir; The Upside Down Sailor (for narrator and wind nonet) with Richard Stilgoe & David Campbell's Soundwood Ensemble. *Honours:* ARAM, 1998. *Current Management:* Helen Sykes Artists Management. *Telephone:* (20) 8780-0060. *E-mail:* helen@hsam.unet.com. *Website:* www.roxannapanufnik.com.

PANULA, Jorma; Composer, Conductor and Professor of Conducting; b. 10 Aug. 1930, Kauhajoki, Finland. *Education:* Studied at the Helsinki School of Church Music, at the Sibelius Academy and with Dean Dixon in Lund; Further study with Franco Ferrara at Hilversum, and in Austria and France. *Career:* Conducted at theatres in Lahti and Tampere 1953–58, Helsinki 1958–62; Founded the chamber orchestra of the Sibelius Academy and conducted the Helsinki Philharmonic Orchestra 1965–67 and the Århus City Orchestra in Denmark 1973; Guest appearances in the USSR, USA and Europe; Notable for his interpretations of late Romantic and early 20th Century music; Professor of Conducting at the Sibelius Academy, 1973–; Stockholm Musik Hogskolen, 1981–88; Copenhagen Royal Conservatorium, 1988–91; Professor for many summer courses in conducting including Yale University and Bartók Seminar in Hungary. *Compositions include:* Violin Concerto 1954; Jazz Capriccio for piano and orchestra 1965; Steel Symphony 1969; Choral and vocal works. *Recordings include:* Madetoja's Symphony No. 3 and Opera Pohjalaisia; Englund's Piano Concerto and Palmgren's Piano Concerto No. 2, with the Helsinki Philharmonic (EMI). *Address:* c/o Sibelius Academy, P Rautatiekatu 9, 00100 Helsinki 10, Finland.

PANZARELLA, Anna Maria; Singer (Soprano); b. 1970, France. *Education:* Studied in Grenoble and Geneva, at the Royal College of Music and at the National Opera Studio. *Career:* Debut: Sang Fransquita in Carmen with Geneva Opera; Appeared in La Rondine for Opera North, as Frasquita in Lisbon, and Stephano in Roméo et Juliette at Covent Garden; Season 1995–96 as Puccini's Lauretta in Brussels, First Lady (Die Zauberflöte) at Aix and Amore in the world premiere of Goehr's Arianna at Covent Garden; Season 1996–97 as Donna Elvira for Opera Zürich, Balkis in Haydn's L'Incontro Improvviso at Lausanne and Rameau's Aricie in Paris and New York; Season 1997 as Adèle in Le Comte Ory for GTO and Despina at the Bastille, Paris; Sang Erinice in Rameau's Zoroastre at the Brooklyn Academy of Music and Lyon Opéra, 1998. *Recordings include:* Mozart's Requiem with Les Arts Florissants and William Christie (Erato). *Address:* c/o PG & PM, 7 Whitehorse Close, Royal Mile, Edinburgh, EH8 8BU, Scotland.

PAPAVRAMI, Tedi; Violinist; b. 1965, Tirana Albania. *Education:* Paris Conservatoire, with Pierre Amoyal. *Career:* Many appearances from 1988 in Europe and South Africa; Festival engagements at Montreux, Newport and Schleswig-Holstein; Season 1998–99 in Paris, Monaco, Germany, Italy and Spain; Conductors have included Kurt Sanderling and Zdenek Macal; Season 2000–01 with the Orchestre Philharmonique de Nice, Stuttgart Chamber Orchestra and Istanbul State Symphony; Chamber music partners include Emanuel Pahud (flute), Raphael Oleg (violin) and Gary Hoffman (cello); Debut tour of Japan 2001; with Paganini's 24 Caprices; South American tour with Mozart's Sinfonia Concertante, K364. *Honours:* First Prize, Paris Conservatoire, 1986; Georges Enescu Prize, SACEM, 1992; Winner, Sarasate Competition, Pamplona, 1993. *Address:* c/o Musicaglotz, 11, Rue Le Verrier, 75006, Paris, France.

PAPE, Gerard (Joseph); Composer; b. 22 April 1955, Brooklyn, New York, USA; m. Janet Smarr Pape, 23 Aug 1981, 2 s. *Education:* BA, Columbia, University, 1976; MA, 1978, PhD, 1982, University of Michigan; Studied composition with George Cacioppo and William Albright. *Career:* Director, Composer-in-Residence, Sinewave Studios, 1980–91; Music presented in over 25 Sinewave Studios concerts in Ann Arbor, Michigan; Produced the annual Festival of Contemporary Orchestral, Ensemble and Electronic Music, Ann Arbor, twice, 1986–91; Since 1991, Director, Les Ateliers, UPIC Paris, France (Electronic Music Studio); mem, ASCAP. *Compositions include:* Ivan and Rena for 4 Vocal Soloists and Orchestra, 1984; Cosmos for Large Orchestra, 1985; The Sorrows of The Moon for Baritone and Tape, 1986; Folie à Deux for Violin and Piano, 1986; Exorcism for Baritone and Orchestra, 1986; Catechresis for Soprano and Orchestra, 1987; Cerberus for Organ and Tape, 1987; Vortex (String Quartet No. 2), 1988; Three Faces of Death for Orchestra, 1988; Piano Concerto, 1988; Xstasis for Ensemble and Tape, 1992; 2 Electro-Accoustic Songs for Voice, Flute and Tape, 1993; Le Fleuve du Désir (String Quartet No. 3),

1994; Monologue for bass voice and tape, 1995; Battle for 4 solo voices and tape, 1996; Makbenach for saxophone, ensemble and tape, 1996; Feu Toujours Vivant, for large orchestra and live electronics, 1997; Funeral Sentence, for 2 sopranos and percussion, 1998; Makbenach IV, for trombone and tape, 1998; Fabula for soprano and tape, 1999; Aquarelles for clarinet and tape, 1999; Mon Autre Peau for tape 1999; Les Cenci, opera, 2000–. *Recordings:* Mode 26, 6 pieces of Music by Gerard Pape, 1992; Electro-Acoustic Chamber Works, 1998. *Contributions:* Complexity, Composition, Perception, published in Currents in Musical Thought, 1994; Luigi Nono and his Fellow Travellers in Contemporary Music Review. *Honours:* Various grants to produce the Sinewave series of concerts, Michigan Council for The Arts; Meet The Composer, 1989; 8 ASCAP Standard Awards, 1992–99. *Address:* 62 Rue Michel Ange, 75016 Paris, France.

PAPE, René; Singer (Bass-baritone); b. 4 Sept. 1964, Dresden, Germany. *Education:* Member of Dresden Kreuzchor 1974–81, tours to Japan and Europe; Dresden Musikhochschule from 1981. *Career:* Debut: Berlin Staatsoper 1987, as the Speaker in Die Zauberflöte; Sang in 1989 premiere of Siegfried Matthus's Graf Mirabeau at Berlin Staatsoper and has appeared there and elsewhere in Germany as Mozart's Figaro and Alfonso, Verdi's Banquo, Procida and King in Aida, Gremin in Eugene Onegin and Galitzky in Prince Igor; Guest engagements at Frankfurt and Vienna Staatsoper; Salzburg Festival 1991, as Sarastro in Die Zauberflöte; Many concert appearances, notably in Mozart's Requiem for the bi-centenary performances in 1991; Sang the Speaker in Die Zauberflöte at the Met, 1995; Appeared as King Henry in Lohengrin at Covent Garden, 1997; Season 1998 with Pogner in Die Meistersinger at the Berlin Staatsoper and Verdi's Philip II at Salzburg; Season 2000–01 as King Mark at the Met, Pogner at the Berlin Staatsoper, Leporello for the Salzburg Festival and King Philip in Don Carlos at the Vienna Staatsoper; Season 2002–03 as Massimiliano in I Masnadieri and Heinrich in Lohengrin at Covent Garden. *Address:* c/o Allied Artists Agency, 42 Montpelier Square, London SW7 1JZ, England.

PAPERNO, Dmitry; Concert Pianist and Professor of Piano; b. 18 Feb. 1929, Kiev, USSR; m. Ludmila Gritsay, 21 May 1966, 2 d. *Education:* Honours degree, Moscow Tchaikovsky Conservatory, 1951; Postgraduate, 1955. *Career:* Debut: Recital, Moscow, 1955; Pianist-Soloist, Mosconcert; About 1500 solo recitals and performances in the former Soviet Union, Eastern and Western Europe and Cuba including The USSR State Orchestra, (Moscow, Leningrad and Brussels, Belgium EXPO 1958), Gewandhaus Orchestra, (Leipzig, 1960), Hallé Orchestra, (Manchester, 1967), and many others 1955–76; Numerous concerts in USA, 1977–, also Netherlands, France, Belgium, Majorca and Portugal, 1985–; Sonata recital with Mstislav Rostropovich, Pasadena, California, USA, 1989; Teaching: Moscow State Gnesin Institute, 1967–73; DePaul University, Chicago, USA, 1977–; Full Professor of Piano, 1985; Many masterclasses in the USA and Europe including Tchaikovsky Conservatory, Moscow. *Recordings include:* Melodia, USSR; Works by Chopin, Liszt, Grieg, Schumann, Bach-Busoni, Debussy, Medtner; 2 videotapes for Moscow television: piano recital and Chopin F minor concerto with Moscow Radio and Television Orchestra under Gennady Rozhdestvenski; Selected Works of Scriabin, 1978, and Tchaikovsky's The Seasons, 1982; 5 CDs, USA; Russian Piano Music, 1989; Works of Bach-Busoni, Beethoven, Schubert, Brahms, 1990; Uncommon Encores, 1992; Chopin Live, including the 5th Chopin Competition, Warsaw, 195, 1997; Selected works from the 1960s and 1970s, 1998. *Publications:* 2 books in Russian; Notes of a Moscow Pianist, 1983; Post Scriptum, 1987; Articles and reviews in USSR and USA. *Address:* 2646 North Wayne Unit A, Chicago, IL 60616, USA.

PAPIAN, Vag; Conductor and Pianist; b. 1960, Russia. *Education:* Moscow and St Petersburg Conservatories. *Career:* Performances as piano soloist throughout Russia from 1979; Conducting studies, with Ilia Musin, led to Associate status with the Armenian SO, from 1987 (chief conductor, 1990); Associate Conductor, Been Sheva SO, Israel, from 1990; Music director; Israel Camerata; Soloist and Conductor with the Jerusalem Symphony; Season 2000–2001 with English Chamber orchestra and a tour to Far East; Further conducting engagements with New Japan Philharmonic and Malmö, Trondheim, Lucerne and Valencia Symphonies; Armenian PO, Israel CO, Belgrade SO and Bucharest Virtuosi; Productions of Don Giovanni, Carmen and Nielsen's Saul and David in Israel; Norma for Armenian Opera, 2001; Concerts as pianist in Europe, North and South America and Far East; Accompanist for Maxim Vengerov, violin. *Recordings include:* recitals.

PAPINEAU-COUTURE, Jean; Composer; b. 12 Nov. 1916, Outremont, Québec, Canada; m. Isabelle Baudoin (deceased 1987). *Education:* Conducting with Francis Findley, Composition with Quincy Porter, Piano with Beveridge Webster; BMus, New England Conservatory of Music, Boston, 1941; Composition and Harmony under Nadia Boulanger at Madison, Wisconsin, Lake Arrowhead and Santa Barbara, California. *Career:* Teaching Piano, Jean-de-Brebeuf College, Montreal, 1943–44; Teacher of Music, Conservatoire de Musique et d'Art

Dramatique de la Province de Québec, Montreal, 1946–52; Professor, 1951–, Faculty Secretary, 1952–67, Vice Dean, 1967, Dean, 1968–73, Faculty of Music, University of Montreal; Commissions from Canadian Broadcasting Corporation, Montreal Symphony Orchestra, others. *Compositions include:* Suite Lapitsky, orchestra, 1965; Dialogues, 1967; Sectuor, 1967; Nocturne, 7 instruments, 1969; Oscillations, orchestra, 1969; Chanson de rahit, voice, ensemble, 1972; Obsession, 1973; Trio in 4 movements, 1974; Slano, 1975; Le débat du coeur et du corps de villon, voice, ensemble, 1977; Prouesse, viola, 1986; Nuit Polaire, contralto, 10 instruments, 1986; Vers l'Extinction, organ, 1987; Thrène, violin, piano, 1988; Courbes, organ, 1988; Les arabesques d'Isabelle, flute, cor-d'anglais, clarinet, bassoon, piano, 1989; Celebrations, woodwinds, 5 brass percussions, piano, strings, 1990; Quasipassacaille, C'est bref, organ, 1991; Tournants, organ, 1992; Automne, flute oboe, clarinet, bassoon, horn, string quintet, 1992; Vents capricieux sur le clavier, flute, oboe, clarinet, bassoon, piano, 1993; Chocs sonores, marimba, cymbal and tom; Glanures, soprano, chamber orchestra, 1994; Fantastique, violoncello solo, 1995; Quartet for oboe, violin, cello and piano, 1998. *Recordings:* Many on various labels. *Honours:* Canadian Governor-General's Prize, 1994. *Address:* 4694 Lacombe, Montreal, Quebec H3W 1R3, Canada.

PAPIS, Christian; French singer (tenor); b. 1960, Algrange. *Education:* Paris Conservatoire. *Career:* Glyndebourne Festival Opera from 1992 as Boris in Katya Kababova (1998, also on Tour), Lensky in Eugene Onegin and Gregor in The Makropulos Case (1997); Further engagements as Don Ottavio in Dublin, Massenet's Des Grieux at Lausanne, Tamino throughout France and Berlioz's Bénédict in Toulouse; Werther in France and Netherlands, Alfredo for Opera Zuid, Don José in Bordeaux, Rodolfo in Amsterdam and Vincent in Gounod's Mireille at the Opéra Comique; the Berlioz Faust in Madrid, Matteo in Arabella and Gounod's Roméo at Geneva Opera; Season 1998–99 as Idomeneo in Nantes, Števa in Jenůfa and Berg's Alva in Liège; Wagner's Froh in Geneva and Alim in Massenet's Le Roi de Lahore at St Etienne and Bordeaux.

PAPOULIAS, Althea-Maria; Singer (Soprano); b. 1968, Montreal, Canada. *Education:* Studied at Metill University, Montreal. *Career:* Sang at Cologne Opera from 1993, as Pamina, Gretel and Elvira in L'Italiana in Algeri; Vienna Staatsoper, 1996 as Liu in Turandot; Guest appearances as Agathe in Der Freischütz, Musetta, Puccini's Suor Angelica, Drusilla in Monteverdi's Poppea and Purcell's Dido; Sang Mozart's Fiordiligi for Glyndebourne Touring Opera, 1998; Sang Verdi's Alice Ford at the Vienna Volksoper, 2000; Concerts include songs by Debussy, Ravel and Duparc. *Honours:* Prizewinner, Belvedere Competition, Vienna, 1993. *Address:* c/o Glyndebourne Touring Opera, Glyndebourne, Lewes, East Sussex BN8 5UU, England.

PAPP, Christine; Singer (Mezzo-soprano); b. 1959, Sonneberg, Germany. *Education:* Studied in Weimar, Berlin and Milan. *Career:* Sang at Meiningen Opera, 1983–86; Further appearances at Magdeburg, Potsdam and the Berlin Staatsoper; Frankfurt Opera from 1991 as Verdi's Azucena and Ulrica, Fidalma in Il Matrimonio Segreto, Mozart's Marcellina, Annina in Der Rosenkavalier and Santuzza; Concert repertory includes Beethoven's Ninth; Lieder recital in New York. *Address:* c/o Berlin Staatsoper, Unter den linden 7, 1060 Berlin, Germany.

PAPPANO, Antonio; American conductor and pianist; *Music Director, The Royal Opera, Covent Garden;* b. 30 Dec. 1959, Epping, London; m. Pam Bullock 1995. *Education:* studied in USA with Norma Verrilli, Arnold Franchetti and Gustav Meier. *Career:* Répétiteur and Asst Conductor New York City Opera, Gran Teatro del Liceo, Barcelona, Frankfurt Opera, Lyric Opera of Chicago early to mid-1980s; asst to Daniel Barenboim for Tristan und Isolde, Parsifal and the Ring cycle at Bayreuth Festival 1986; opera conducting debut with Norwegian Opera, Oslo 1987; Music Dir, Norwegian Opera 1990–92; Covent Garden debut conducting La Bohème 1990; Vienna Staatsoper debut conducting new production of Wagner's Siegfried 1993; season 1996 included the original Don Carlos in Brussels and at the Paris Théâtre du Châtelet; season 1997 Salome at Chicago and Eugene Onegin at the Metropolitan; Prin. Guest Conductor Israel Philharmonic Orchestra 1997–2000; seasons 1999–2001 Lohengrin at Bayreuth; has conducted many world-class orchestras, including Berlin Philharmonic Orchestra, Boston Symphony Orchestra, Chicago Symphony Orchestra, Cleveland Orchestra, London Symphony Orchestra, Los Angeles Philharmonic Orchestra, Orchestre de Paris, Oslo Philharmonic Orchestra, Munich Philharmonic Orchestra; Music Dir Théâtre Royal de la Monnaie, Brussels 1992–2002, conducting a wide variety of titles; Music Dir Royal Opera, Covent Garden 2002–; new productions of Ariadne auf Naxos, Wozzeck, Madama Butterfly and Pagliacci, revival of Falstaff 2002–03; Don Giovanni, Aida, Lady Macbeth of Mtsensk, Faust and Peter Grimes in 2003–04; Music Dir Orchestra of the Nat. Acad. of Santa Cecilia, Rome 2005–. *Recordings include:* Puccini's La Rondine (Gramophone Award for Best Opera Recording and Record of the Year 1997), Il Trittico 1999, Britten's The Turn of the Screw (Théâtre Royal de la

Monnaie production) (Choc du Monde de la Musique, Prix de l'Acad. du Disque Lyrique Grand Prix Int., Orphée d'Or) 1999, Werther 1999, Manon Gramophone Award for Best Opera Recording 2001; many recordings as conductor; recordings as pianist with Rockwell Blake, Barbara Bonney and Han-Na Chang. *Current Management:* IMG Artists Paris, 54 avenue Marceau, 75008 Paris, France. *Address:* c/o Royal Opera House, Covent Garden, London, WC2E 9DD, England. *Website:* www.roh.org.uk.

PAQUETTE, Daniel; Professor Emeritus of History of Music; b. 1930, Morteau, Doubs, France; m. Madeleine Mougel 1957, one s. one d. *Education:* National Conservatoire of Dijon, National Conservatoire of Saint Etienne. *Career:* Teacher of Musical Education, Lycées in Angiers, 1952, Dijon, 1953–64; Assistant, Institute of Musicology, University of Strasbourg, 1964–69; Lecturer, University of Dijon, 1970–72; Professor, University of Lyon, 1972–; Head, Musicology Section, Universities of Besançon and Dijon (Audio-visual education), St Etienne; Leader, Philharmonic Choirs of Dijon and Voix Amies Dijon, 1953–64; Leader, University Orchestra, Strasbourg, 1964–69. *Compositions:* Les Dames des Entreportes, symphonic poem; Operetta for children; Les Fantomes du Val au Faon; A cappella choral music based on ancient music of 16th–18th century; Film and chamber music; Films, J J Rousseau et la musique; J Ph Rameau, musicien sensible et savant rigoureux; Oratorio, for 2 choruses, 4 singers, string orchestra, piano, trumpet, based on verses by Lamartine, A Hymn of Peace. *Publications:* L'Instrument de musique dans la Grece Antique, 1984; Jean Phillipe Rameau musicien bourguignon, 1983; Musique baroque, Aspects de la musique en France et à Lyon au XVIII, since 1990; Articles in Dictionaire de la Musique, 1976–86 and Die Musik in Geschichte und Gegenwart, 1999. *Address:* Les Furtins, 71960 Berzé-la-Ville, France.

PARATORE, Anthony; Concert Pianist; b. 17 June 1946, Boston, MA, USA. *Education:* BM, Boston Univ., 1966; BM, MS, Juilliard School, New York, 1970. *Career:* debut, Metropolitan Museum, 1973; guest appearances with New York Philharmonic, Chicago, San Francisco, Detroit, Washington National, Denver, Boston, Indianapolis, Atlanta, San Diego, BBC London, Vienna Philharmonic, Berlin Philharmonic, Vienna Symphony, RAI Orchestra, Nouvel Philharmonique, Warsaw Philharmonic, Amsterdam Philharmonic, Rotterdam Philharmonic, Norwegian Chamber Orchestra, English Chamber Orchestra, Prague Chamber Orchestra, Bavarian Radio Orchestra, London Symphony Orchestra, Munich Chamber Orchestra; festival appearances, mostly Mozart, Salzburg, Berlin, Strauss Tage, Lucerne, Istanbul, Adelaide Festival in Australia, and Spoleto; PBS television special, The Paratores, Two Brothers, Four Hands; NPR radio, All Things Considered and A Note To You; mem., Boston Musicians' Asscn, Dante Alighieri Society. *Compositions:* premieres of new compositions; Wolfgang Rihm, Maskes; Manfred Trojan, Folia; William Bolcom, Sonata for two pianos in one movement. *Recordings:* Pictures at an Exhibition, Mussorgsky; Opera Festival for Four Hands; Mendelssohn Concerti for two pianos and orchestra; Variations for Four Hands; Schoenberg Chamber Symphony op 9; Stravinsky, Sacre du Printemps; Ravel; Bolero, Ma Mère L'Oye, Rapsodie Espagnole; Gershwin; Rhapsody in Blue, Concerto in F; Brahms Liebeslieder Waltzes, opus 52 and 65, Waltzes opus 39; Saint-Saëns, Carnival of the Animals; Variations on a Theme by Haydn Sonata in F minor, opus 34; Points on Jazz, by Dave Brubeck. *Contributions:* Keyboard Classics; Clavier magazine. *Honours:* First Prize, Munich International Music Competition, Duo-Piano Category, 1974; George Washington Honor Medal, 1998. *Current Management:* Konzert-Direktion Hans Adler, Auguste-Viktoria-Strasse 64, 14199 Berlin, Germany. *Telephone:* (30) 825–6333. *Fax:* (30) 826–3520. *Website:* www.musikadler.de.

PARATORE, Joseph D.; Concert Pianist; b. 19 March 1948, Boston, MA, USA. *Education:* BM, Boston Univ., 1970; MS, Juilliard School, 1972. *Career:* debut, Metropolitan Museum of Art, 1973; guest appearances with New York Philharmonic, Chicago Symphony, San Francisco, Detroit, Indianapolis, Atlanta, Washington National, Boston, Denver, San Diego, BBC London, Vienna Philharmonic, Berlin Philharmonic, Vienna Symphony, RAI, Nouvel Philharmonique, Warsaw Philharmonic, Amsterdam Philharmonic, Rotterdam Philharmonic, Norwegian Chamber Orchestra, English Chamber Orchestra, Prague Chamber Orchestra, Bavarian Radio Orchestra, London Symphony, Munich Chamber Orchestra; festival appearances, Lucerne, Istanbul, Adelaide Festival in Australia, Salzburg, Berlin, Strauss Tage, Spoleto, mostly Mozart; television appearances include: WGBH-PBS television special The Paratores, Two Brothers/Four Hands; radio: NPR All Things Considered and A Note to You; mem., Boston Musicians' Asscn, Dante Alighieri Society. *Compositions:* Wolfgang Rihm, Maskes; Manfred Trojan, Folia; William Bolcom, Sonata for two pianos in one movement. *Recordings:* Mussorgsky–Pictures at an Exhibition and Opera Festival for Four Hands; Mendelssohn Concerti for Two Pianos and Orchestra; Variations for Four Hands; Schoenberg, Chamber Symphony op 9; Stravinsky, Sacre du Printemps; Ravel: Bolero, Ma Mère L'Oye,

Rapsodie Espagnole; Gershwin: Rhapsody in Blue, Concerto in F; Brahms: Variations on a Theme by Haydn and Sonata in F minor, Liebeslieder Waltzes Op 52 and 65, Waltzes Op 39; Saint-Saëns, Carnival of the Animals; Points on Jazz, by Dave Brubeck. *Contributions:* Keyboard Classics–The Art of Transcribing Mussorgsky; Clavier magazine–Master Class–Ravel Ma Mère L'Oye. *Honours:* First Prize, Munich International Music Competition, Duo-Piano Category, 1974; George Washington Honor Medal, 1998. *Current Management:* Konzert-Direktion Hans Adler, Auguste-Viktoria-Strasse 64, 14199 Berlin, Germany. *Telephone:* (30) 825–6333. *Fax:* (30) 826–3520. *Website:* www.musikadler.de.

PARDEE, Margaret; American violinist, violist and teacher of violin and viola; b. 10 May 1920, Valdosta, GA; m. Daniel R. Butterly 1944. *Education:* Institute of Musical Art, Juilliard School; studied with Sascha Jacobsen, Albert Spalding, Louis Persinger, Ivan Galamian. *Career:* debut at New York Town Hall, 1952; toured as Soloist and in String Quartet and Duo Recitals as Violinist and Violist, USA; Soloist with Symphony Orchestra; Faculty Member, Juilliard School, 1942–; Concert Master, Great Neck Symphony, New York, 1954–85; Faculty Member and Director, Meadowmount School of Music, 1956–85, 1988–92; Adjunct Professor, Queens College, New York, 1978–, State University of New York, Purchase, 1980–; Jury Member, National and International Competitions; Faculty Member, Estherwood Festival and School, Dobbs Ferry, New York, 1984–85, Estherwood Festival and Summer School, Oneonta State University, 1986; Faculty, Bowdoin Summer Music Festival, Bowdoin College, Brunswick, Maine, 1987; Taught in Conservatory of Music of the Simon Bolivar Orchestra in Caracas, Venezuela, 1988, 1989; Invited to teach in Caracas, Venezuela for Municipal Orchestra and Symphonica, 1991–; On Faculty at Killington Chamber Music Festival, Killington, 1993–. *Address:* c/o Juilliard School, Lincoln Center Plaza, New York, NY 10023, USA.

PARIK, Ivan; Composer; b. 17 Aug. 1936, Bratislava, Czechoslovakia; m. Magdalena Barancoková, 2 Oct 1970, 1 d. *Education:* Completed Composition and Conducting studies, Bratislava Conservatory, 1958; Composition, Academy of Music and Dramatic Arts, Bratislava, 1958–62; Habilitation as Associate Professor of Composition, 1976; Degree of Professor, 1990. *Career:* Debut: Music for 4 strings; Lecturer, 1962–, Pro-Rector, 1990–94, Rector, 1994–97, Academy of Music and Dramatic Arts, Bratislava; Chairman, Music Foundation; Slovak Music Union. *Compositions:* Orchestral including: Music for Ballet, 4 scenes for large orchestra, 1968; Fragments, suite for ballet, 1969; Musica pastoralis for large orchestra, 1984; Music for Flute, Viola and Orchestra, 1987; Two Arias on text fragments of Stabat mater for higher voice and orchestra, 1987; Chamber including: Sonata for flute, 1962; Songs about Falling Leaves for piano, 1962; Time of Departures, diptych for soprano and piano, 1976; Seen Closely Above the Lake for reciter, wind quintet, piano and string quartet, also version for orchestra, 1979; Pastorale for Organ, 1979; Music for Milos Urbásek for string quartet, 1981; Duet for Violas, 1981; How to Drink from a Well, music to poem by Milan Rúfus for reciter and chamber orchestra, 1990; Meditacia, for flute and organ, 1997; Choral including Among the Mountains, ballad for mixed choir, 1973; Electro-acoustic music including: Music to Opening II for flute solo and tape, 1970; In memoriam Ockeghem, 1971; Homage to Hummel, 1980; Scenic and film music including: Fragment, ballet in 1 act on motifs of Kobo Abbe's novel Sand Woman, 1969; King Lear, 1969; Three Sisters, 1981; Medea, 1983; Macbeth, 1992; St Francis of Assisi, 1992. *Publications:* Some Remarks on the Problems of Education in Composition, habilitation thesis, 1974; Co-author, How to Read a Score, 1986; Many articles. *Honours:* Honorary Medal, Slovák Philharmonic Orchestra, 1986; Gold Medal, Academy of Music, Prague, 1997. *Address:* Gajova 17, 81109 Bratislava, Slovakia.

PARIK, Ivan; Conductor; b. 1955, Czechoslovakia. *Education:* Studied with Hans Swarowsky in Vienna and with Arvid Jansons and Kurt Masur in Weimar; Munich Staatsoper with Wolfgang Sawallisch. *Career:* Has appeared with leading orchestras in Czechoslovakia and elsewhere in Eastern Europe; Conductor at Ostrava Opera from 1980, leading works by Mozart, Verdi, Puccini, Weber, Gounod, Wagner, Bizet, Strauss, Shostakovich and Czech composers; Guest Conductor at Vienna Volksoper, notably with The Bartered Bride, Die Entführung, Die Zauberflöte and Dvořák's Jacobin; Guest appearances in Dresden with Rusalka and Lohengrin; Bilbao and Prague with Così fan tutte; Conducted Rigoletto at Gars am Kamp, Austria, 1992; Musical Director of the Klagenfurt Opera from 1992; Concert engagements in works by Mozart, Schubert, Berlioz, Brahms, Dvořák, Janáček, Debussy, Stravinsky and Strauss; mem, Slovak Music Union; ISCM. *Address:* Gajova 17, 81109 Bratislava, Slovakia.

PÂRIS, Alain; Conductor; b. 22 Nov. 1947, Paris, France; m. Marie-Stella Abdul Ahad, 23 June 1973. *Education:* Licence in Law, Paris, 1969; Studied Piano with Bernadette Alexandre-Georges, Ecriture with Georges Dandelot; Conducting with Pierre Dervaux (Licence de concert, Ecole Normale de Musique, 1967), Louis Fourestier, Paul Paray. *Career:*

Debut: 1969; Guest Conductor, with major French orchestras including, Orchestre de Paris, Orchestre National, Orchestre de Lyon, Toulouse, Strasbourg; Performed with various orchestras abroad including, Dresdner Philharmonic, Slovak Philharmonic, Orchestre de la Suisse Romande, Philharmonia Hungarica, Philharmonie George Enesco (Bucharest), Orchestra de la BRT (Brussels), Milan, Saint Petersburg, Germany, Luxembourg, Greece, Iraq, Hong Kong, Granada, Ankara; Assistant Conductor, Orchestre du Capitole de Toulouse, 1976–77; Associate Conductor, 1983–84, Permanent Conductor, 1984–87, Opéra du Rhin, Strasbourg; Producer, Musical Broadcasts for Radio France, 1971–; Professor of Conducting, Strasbourg Conservatory, 1986–89; Regular Conductor, French Season Concerts, Capella Symphony Orchestra and Chorus, St Petersburg, 1996–; mem, Société Française de Musicologie. *Publications:* Dictionnaire des interprètes et de l'interprétation musicale, Paris, Robert Laffont, 1982, 4th edition 1995; Spanish Translation, Turner, Madrid, 1989; German Translation, dtv, Munich, 2nd edition, 1997; Les Livrets d'opéra, Paris, Robert Laffont, 1991; Editor, French Edition of the New Oxford Companion to Music (Dictionnaire encyclopédique de la musique, Robert Laffont 1988) and Baker's Biographical Dictionary of Musicians (Dictionnaire biographique des musiciens, Robert Laffont 1995). *Contributions:* Encyclopaedia Universalis; Retz; Quid; Scherzo; Courrier musical de France; Diapason; La Lettre du Musicien. *Honours:* Licence de concert, Ecole Normale de Musique, Paris, 1967; 1st Prize, concours international de Besançon, 1968. *Address:* 33 Rue de Constantinople, 75008 Paris, France.

PARISOT, Aldo Simoes; Brazilian cellist and teacher; *Samuel Sanford Professor of Music, Yale University;* b. 30 Sept. 1920, Natal; m. Elizabeth Sawyer-Parisot; one s. *Education:* Yale Univ. and private studies with Thomazzo Babini and Ibere Gomes Grosso. *Career:* debut with the Boston Symphony, Berkshire Music Center 1947; principal cellist Pittsburgh Symphony 1949–50; tours of Europe, Asia, Africa, South America and throughout the USA from 1948; plays solo works by Bach and the sonatas of Brahms and Beethoven in recital; joined faculty of Peabody Conservatory 1956–58, Mannes Coll. 1962–66, New England Conservatory 1966–70; Prof. in School of Music, Yale Univ. 1958–, currently Samuel Sanford Prof. of Music; Music Dir Aldo Parisot Int. Cello Course and Competition, Brazil 1977; artist-in-residence, Banff Center for the Arts, Canada 1981–83; has given the premieres of works by Quincy Porter, Villa-Lobos (concerto No. 2 1955), Claudio Santoro (concerto 1963), Leon Kirchner (concerto for violin, cello and orchestra 1960), Alvin Etler (concerto 1971), Yehudi Wyner (De novo 1971) and Donald Martino; formed students at Yale Univ. into the 'Yale Cellos' ensemble. *Address:* The School of Music, Yale University, PO Box 208246, New Haven, CT 06520-8246, USA.

PARKER, Jon Kimura; Concert Pianist; b. 25 Dec. 1959, Vancouver, Canada. *Education:* Masters in Music, 1983 and Doctor of Musical Arts, 1989, Juilliard School; Teachers: Adele Marcus, Lee Kum-Sing, Edward Parker and Marek Jablonski. *Career:* Debut: New York, 1984 and London 1984; Performed with London Symphony, London Philharmonic, Toronto Symphony, Cleveland Orchestra, Minnesota Orchestra, Los Angeles Philharmonic, Philadelphia Orchestra, Scottish National Orchestra, Berlin Radio Symphony, NHK Orchestra, Japan, and all Canadian Orchestras; Recital tours in Europe, Canada, North and South America, Far East and Australia; Command performance for Queen Elizabeth II and Prime Minster of Canada, 1984; Featured on CBC television documentary show The Journal, Local Boy Makes Great in 1985; Benefit performance of Beethoven's Emperor Concerto at Sarajevo, New Year's Eve, 1995; Host of television series, Whole Notes, 1999–. *Recordings:* Tchaikovsky Piano Concerto No. 1; Prokofiev Piano Concerto No. 3 with André Previn and Royal Philharmonic Orchestra, 1986; Solo Piano Music of Chopin, 1987; Two Pianists are Better Than One, with Peter Schickele, 1994; Barber Piano Concerto with Yoel Levi and Atlanta Symphony, 1997. *Honours:* 1st Prize and Princess Mary Gold Medal, Leeds International Piano Competition, 1984; Canadian Governor General's Performing Arts Award, 1996; Officer of the Order of Canada, 1999. Numerous other first prizes in international competitions. *Address:* c/o ICM Artists Ltd, 40 West 57th Street, New York, NY 10019, USA.

PARKER, Moises; Singer (Tenor); b. 1945, Las Villas, Cuba. *Education:* Studied in Munich, at Juilliard School and Verdi Conservatory Milan; Teachers included Tito Gobbi, Richard Holm and Hermann Reutter. *Career:* Debut: New York City Opera 1976 as Don José; Sang at Strasbourg Opera 1978–80 as Tamino, Hoffmann and Ratansen in Roussel's Padmâvatî; Season 1981–82 with Welsh National Opera and Scottish Opera as Rodolfo and Alvaro; Brunswick and Augsburg 1982–83 as Don José and Alvaro; Deutsche Oper Berlin as Pinkerton; Sang Otello at Coburg 1984 and at Stuttgart and Klagenfurt 1989; Theater des Westens Berlin 1988–89, as Gershwin's Porgy, Würzburg 1990 as Bacchus; Member of Kiel Opera from 1988, notably as Turiddu in Cavalleria Rusticana and Win-San-Lui in Leoni's L'Oracolo, 1990;

Sang Tannhäuser at Passau 2000; Concert repertoire includes Messiah, Beethoven's Ninth and the Missa Solemnis, Elijah, Rossini's Stabat Mater and Messe Solennelle, Verdi's Requiem. *Honours:* Prize Winner at 1974 Voci Verdiane Competition at Bussetto, 1975 Francisco Vinas at Barcelona. *Address:* c/o Buhnen des Landeshaupt, Rathausplatz, 2300 Kiel, Germany.

PARKER, Roger; Writer on Music; b. 2 Aug. 1951, London, England. *Education:* Studied at London University with Margaret Bent and Pierluigi Petrobelli. *Career:* Professor at Cornell University, USA, 1982–94; Co-ordinating Editor of Donizetti Critical Edition, 1988; Founding Co-Editor, Cambridge Opera Journal, 1989–98; University Lecturer in Music and Fellow of St Hugh's College, Oxford, 1994–99; Professor of Music and Fellow, St John's College, Cambridge, 1999. *Publications:* Critical Edition of Verdi's Nabucco, 1987; (with A Groos) Giacomo Puccini; La Bohème, 1986, and Reading Opera, 1989; Studies in Early Verdi, 1989; Analyzing Opera: Verdi and Wagner (with C Abbate), 1989; Articles on Verdi and his operas in The New Grove Dictionary of Opera, 4 vols, 1992; Oxford Illustrated History of Opera, editor, 1994; Leonora's Last Act: Essays in Verdian Discourse, 1997. *Honours:* Dent Medal, 1991. *Address:* Faculty of Music, West Road, Cambridge CB 3 9DP, England.

PARKER-SMITH, Jane (Caroline Rebecca); Concert Organist; b. 20 May 1950, Northampton, England; m. John Gadney, 24 October 1996. *Education:* Barton Peveril Grammar School, Eastleigh, Hants, 1959–67; Royal College of Music, 1967–71; Postgraduate Study with Nicolas Kynaston and Jean Langlais, Paris. *Career:* Westminster Cathedral, 1970; Royal Festival Hall, 1975; BBC Promenade Concert, 1972; Solo Recitals, Jyvasklya Festival, Finland, 1977, Stockholm Concert Hall, 1980, Hong Kong Arts Festival, 1988, Roy Thomson Hall, Toronto, 1989, City of London Festival, 1992, Festival Paris Quartier D'Été, 1995, American Guild of Organists Centennial Convention, New York, 1996; Festival Internazionale de musica organistica, Magadino, Switzerland, 1999; Athens Concert Hall, 1999; Cube Concert Hall, Shiroishi, 2000; Lapua Organ Festival, Finland, 2003; American Guild of Organists National COnvention, Philadelphia, 2002, Royal Festival Hall, 2003; Severance Haqll, Cleveland, USA, 2003; mem, Incorporated Society of Musicians; Royal College of Organists; Incorporated Association of Organists. *Recordings:* Widor Symphonies, Music for Trumpet and Organ with Maurice Andre; Liszt Organ Works, Saint-Saëns Organ Symphony No. 3, Janâêek Glagolitic Mass with the City of Birmingham Symphony Orchestra, conductor Simon Rattle; Baroque Organ Concertos with Prague Chamber Orchestra, conductor Steuart Bedford; Popular French Romantics, Armagh Cathedral; Lefébure-Wély Romantische Orgelmusik; Romantic and Virtuoso Organ Works. *Honours:* ARCM, 1966; Winner, National Organ Competition, 1970; LTCL, 1971; Hon FGMS, 1996, Hon FNMSM, 1997. *Current Management:* Karen McFarlane Artists Inc, Cleveland, USA. *Address:* 141 The Quadrangle Tower, Cambridge Square, London W2 2PL, England. *Telephone:* (20) 7262 9259. *Fax:* (20) 7262 9259. *E-mail:* jane@parker-smith.demon.co .uk. *Website:* www. impulse-misic.co.uk/parker-smith.htm.

PARKIN, Simon; Composer, Pianist and Teacher; b. 3 Nov. 1956, Manchester, England. *Education:* Yehudi Menuhin School, 1967–74; BMus, University of Manchester, 1977; Graduate, Royal Northern College of Music, 1978; Associate, Royal College of Music, 1973. *Career:* Performances in St John's, Smith Square, London, Wigmore Hall and Queen Elizabeth Hall, London; Performances as duo-partner in Budapest, Liszt Academy and Berlin (Otto Braun Saal); Resident Pianist at ISM, LDSM and Lenk courses; Compositions performed in London, New York, Frankfurt, Germany; Broadcasts on German radio; Teaching Posts: Royal Northern College of Music; Yehudi Menuhin School. *Compositions:* Ted Spiggot and the Killer Beans (Opera); Le Chant des Oiseaux (choral work); Laughter and Tears (Requiem, choir and orchestra) Piano trio, string quartet, chamber concerto; Composer of several sonatas for solo instruments and piano. *Honours:* Recipient various university and college prizes; Morley College Centenary Concerto Prize for chamber concerto. *Address:* 39 Crompton Road, Burnage, Manchester M19 2QT, England.

PARKINSON, Del R.; Pianist and University Professor; b. 6 Aug. 1948, Blackfoot, Idaho, USA; m. Glenna M Christensen, 6 Aug 1986. *Education:* BM, 1971, MM, 1972, Performers Certificate, 1972, DM, 1975, Indiana University; Postgraduate Diploma, The Juilliard School 1977; Fulbright Hays Grant for graduate study in London, England, 1974–75. *Career:* Debut: Wigmore Hall, London, 1976; Carnegie Recital Hall, New York, 1981; Concerto appearances with Chicago Civic Orchestra, Utah Symphony, Boise Philharmonic and Guadalajara Symphony; Solo recitals in USA, England and Mexico; Chamber Music in USA and aboard Royal Viking Cruise Line; Performer in American Piano Duo, 1984–; Performed with American Piano Quartet throughout USA, Asia and Europe, 1989–95; Teaching Career: Assistant Professor at Furman University, 1975–76, Piano Co-ordinator at Ricks College, 1977–85, Professor at Boise State University, 1985–. *Recordings:*

American Piano Quartet, 1992; American Piano Duo, Celebrating Gershwin, 1998; Mendelssohn Concerto, American Piano Duo, 2004. *Publications:* Selected Works for Piano and Orchestra in One Movement, 1821–53, Indiana University Doctoral Dissertation, 1975. *Contributions:* Record review for Journal of American Liszt Society of Charles Koechlin piano music, 1984. *Honours:* Idaho Governor's Award for Excellence in the Arts, 1988; Idaho Commission on the Arts Career Fellowship, 1997; Boise Mayor's Award for Artistic Excellence, 2001; Boise State Univ. Foundation Scholar Award for Research and Creative Activity, 2003. *Address:* Music Department, Boise State University, Boise, ID 83725, USA.

PARKMAN, Stefan; Choral Conductor and Professor; b. 22 June 1952, Uppsala, Sweden; m. Karin Axelsson; one d. one s. *Education:* Musicology, Uppsala Univ., 1972–74; Royal Coll. of Music, Stockholm, 1978–83; Professorship in Choral Conducting, Uppsala Univ. *Career:* Conductor, Boys' Choir, Uppsala Cathedral 1974–89, Royal Philharmonic Chorus, Stockholm 1985–93, Acad. Chamber Choir of Uppsala 1983–; Chief Conductor, Danish National Radio Choir 1989–2002, Swedish Radio Choir 2002–; freelance appearances with numerous symphony orchestras and ensembles throughout Scandinavia, including the Royal Philharmonic Orchestra and the Royal Opera, Stockholm; regular guest conductor of the BBC Singers (London), Nederlands Kamerkoor (Amsterdam), Rundfunkchor (Berlin); regular teacher of masterclasses and seminars in Sweden and overseas; appearances as a tenor soloist (mainly Evangelist parts) in baroque oratorios and passions. *Recordings:* numerous recordings, particularly for the Chandos label. *Honours:* made Knight of the Dannebrog by Queen Margrethe II, Denmark 1997; Royal Swedish Academy of Music (elected mem.) 1998. *Address:* Uppsala University Choral Centre, PO Box 638, 75126 Uppsala, Sweden. *E-mail:* stefan.parkman@musik.uu.se.

PARMEGIANI, Bernard; Composer; b. 27 Oct. 1927, Paris, France; m., one s. *Career:* Groupe Recherches Musicales from 1959, composer of music for fixed sounds. *Compositions include:* Violostries for violin and tape, 1965; Jazzex, with jazz instrumentalist J.L. Chautemps, 1966; Et Après, with Michel Portal, 1967; electro-acoustic music: 65 works including Capture Ephémère, 1968; L'oeil ecoute, 1970; Pour en finir avec le pouvoir d'Orphée I, 1971–73; Enfer, from Dante, 1972; De natura sonorum, 1974–76; L'écho du miroir, 1980; La création du monde, 1981–1984; Exercisme I, II, III, IV 1985–89; cycle Plain-temps, 1991–93; Sonare, 1996; La Mémoire des Sons, 2000–01; Espèce d'Espace, 2002–03; Numerous scores for film, TV, radio and stage. *Recordings:* La Création du monde; Violostries; La Divine Comédie (Bayle/ Parmegiani); Sonare; Questions de temps; Pop Eclectic, Plate Lunch. *Publications:* L'Envers d'une oeuvre/de natura sonorum, 1982; Portrait Polychrome: Bernard Parmegiani. *Honours:* Grand Prix de l Acad. du Disque, 1979; Prix de la Sacem, 1981; Golden Nica, Ars Electronica of Linz (Austria), 1993. *Address:* c/o GRM/INA, Maison de Radio France, 116 Avenue du Pt Kennedy, 75220 Paris Cédex, France. *E-mail:* parme@ free.fr.

PARMERUD, Ake; Composer; b. 24 July 1953, Lidköping, Sweden. *Education:* Gothenburg Conservatory, from 1978. *Career:* Lecturer in Computer music and composition of Gothenburg, Conservatory, 1987; Lindblad-Studio of University of Gothenburg. *Compositions:* Time's Imaginary Eye, for soprano, tape and slides, 1980; Floden av glas, multimedia, 1978–82; Remaim, orchestra and tape, 1982; Yttringer, soprano and ensemble, 1983; Kren, 1984; Maze, 1985; Yàn, percussion, ensemble and tape, 1985; Isola for chamber orchestra and tape, 1986; Inori, harpsichord and synthesizer, 1987; Les objects obscurs, 1991; Inside Looking Out, computer and ensemble, 1992; Jeux imaginaires, 1993; Stings and Shadows, harp and computer, 1993; Renaissance, 1994; Grains of Voices, 1995; Mirage 1996; Efterbild, computer and orchestra, 1998; The Heart of Silence, multimedia, 1998. *Address:* c/o STIM, Sandhamnsgatan 79, PO Box 27327, S–102 54, Stockholm, Sweden.

PARNAS, Leslie; Concert Cellist and Professor of Music; b. 22 Nov. 1932, St Louis, Missouri, USA; m. Ingeburge Parnas, 2 s. *Education:* Curtis Institute of Music, Philadelphia, with Piatigorsky. *Career:* Debut: New York Town Hall, 1959; Solo Cellist, annual world-wide concert tours with leading orchestras; Director, Kneisal Hall Summer Music School, Blue Hill, Maine; Teacher at the St Louis Conservatory of Music, from 1982; mem, Chamber Music Society of Lincoln Center, New York. *Recordings:* Has recorded for Columbia and Pathé-Marconi Records. *Honours:* Pablo Casals Prize, Paris, 1957; Primavera Trophy, Rome, 1959; Prizewinner, International Tchaikovsky Competition, Moscow, 1962. *Address:* c/o Columbia Artists Management, 165 West 57th Street, New York, NY 10019, USA.

PARR, Patricia (Ann); Pianist and Educator; b. 10 June 1937, Toronto, Canada; two s. *Education:* Curtis Institute of Music, Philadelphia, Pennsylvania, USA; Studied Piano with Isabelle Vengerova; Composition with Gian-Carlo Menotti; Diploma, 1957; Postgraduate studies

with Rudolf Serkin. *Career:* Debut: Toronto Symphony age 9; Soloist with Philadelphia, Cleveland, Pittsburgh, Toronto Orchestras and others; New York Town Hall debut; Soloist and Chamber Musician appeared extensively in Canada and USA; In Trio Concertante toured Australia, 1975 and 1978; Festival appearances include Marlboro, Stratford, Fontana, Marin County, Festival of the Sound; Founding Member, Amici Chamber Ensemble; Faculty, Duquesne University, 1967–74, University of Toronto, 1974–, Royal Conservatory of Music, 1982–90; 16th Season with AMICI, series in Toronto, tours of Mexico, Jamaica, Eastern Europe, Eastern Canada. *Recordings:* Musica Viva Series with Clarinettist Joaquin Valdepenas; With Violinist Lorand Fenyves; With Hornist Eugene Rittich; With Marc Dubois, tenor; 8 CD's as a member of the Amici Chamber Ensemble. *Address:* 1702–71 Charles St E , Toronto, Ontario M4Y 2T3, Canada.

PARRIS, Robert, BS, MS; American composer; b. 21 May 1924, Philadelphia, PA. *Education:* University of Pennsylvania with Peter Mennin and William Bergsma, Juilliard with Ibert and Copland, Berkshire Music Center, Ecole Normale in Paris with Honegger. *Career:* has taught at Washington State College and University of Maryland; George Washington University 1963, Professor, 1976–; commissions from Detroit Symphony Orchestra and the Contemporary Music Forum. *Compositions include:* Orchestra: Symphony, 1952; Piano Concerto, 1953; Concerto for 5 kettledrums and orchestra, 1955; Viola Concerto, 1958; Violin Concerto, 1958; Flute Concerto, 1964; Concerto for trombone and chamber orchestra, 1964; Concerto for percussion, violin, cello and piano, 1967; The Phoenix, 1969; The Messengers, 1974; Rite of Passage, 1978; The Unquiet Heart for violin and orchestra, 1981; Chamber Music for orchestra, 1984; Vocal: Night for baritone string quartet and clarinet, 1951; Alas for the Day, cantata, 1954; Hymn for the Nativity for chorus and brass ensemble, 1962; Dreams for soprano and chamber orchestra; Cynthia's Revell's for baritone and piano, 1979; Chamber: 2 String Trios, 1948, 1951; 2 String Quartets, 1951, 1952; Sonata for solo violin, 1965; The Book of Imaginary Dreams, Parts I and II for ensemble, 1972, 1983; Three Duets for electric guitar and amplified harpsichord, 1984. *Honours:* NEA grants 1974, 1975. *Address:* c/o ASCAP, ASCAP Building, 1 Lincoln Plaza, NY 10023, USA.

PARRISH, Cheryl; Singer (Soprano); b. 6 Nov. 1954, Pasadena, Texas, USA. *Education:* Graduated Baylor University, 1977 and studied at Vienna Musikhochschule, 1978–79. *Career:* Has sung at San Francisco Opera from 1983, as Sophie in Rosenkavalier and Werther and Mozart's Blondchen and Susanna (season 1990–91); Miami Opera, 1987 and 1991, as Ophelia in Hamlet and as Despina; Sang Adele in Die Fledermaus at Toronto, 1987 and San Diego, 1991; Sophie in Der Rosenkavalier at Zürich Opera, 1988 and has guested further at Florence and Santa Fe; Shepherd in Tannhäuser at Austin, Texas, 1996; Frequent concert appearances. *Address:* c/o San Francisco Opera, War Memorial Opera House, San Francisco, CA 94192, USA.

PARROTT, Andrew (Haden); Conductor; b. 10 March 1947, England; m. Emily Van Evera, 1 d. *Education:* Merton College, University of Oxford, 1966–71. *Career:* Guest Conductor around the world; Conductor and Director, Taverner Choir, Consort and Players, 1973–; Assistant to Michael Tippett; Conducted premiere of Judith Weir's A Night at the Chinese Opera; Researcher into performance of pre-classical music; Radio and television broadcasts include the European Broadcasting Union, BBC and US National Public Radio; Recent engagements: conducting Beethoven in Spain, Schubert in Sweden, Bach in Canada; music of the Mannheim School in Mannheim, Zelenka in Prague and Brahms in Bratislava; 2003–04 season: Iphigénie en Tauride with Opera Atelier in Toronto and premiere of Jonathan Dove's children's piece, The Crocodiamond, with Simon Callow and the London Mozart Players; Musical Director, London Mozart Players, 2000–; Music Director, The New York Collegium, 2002–. *Recordings include:* Machaut, Josquin, Tallis, Taverner, Gabrieli, Gesualdo, Monteverdi, Purcell, Vivaldi, Bach, Handel, Mozart; 20th-century music and Christmas music. *Publications:* The New Oxford Book of Carols, co-editor, 1992; The Essential Bach Choir, 2000 (German edn, Bachs Chor: Zum neuen Verständnis, 2003); Various articles on Monteverdi, Purcell and others. *Honours:* Leverhulme Fellowship, 1984–85; Honorary Research Fellow, Royal Holloway, University of London, 1995–; Hon. Senior Research Fellow, Univ. of Birmingham, 2000–. *Address:* c/o Allied Artists, 42 Montpelier Square, London, SW7 1JZ.

PARROTT, Ian; Composer; b. 5 March 1916, London, England; 2 s. *Education:* Royal College of Music, 1932–34. *Career:* Lecturer, Birmingham University, 1946–50; Gregynog Professor of Music, UCW, Aberystwyth, 1950–83; Examiner, Trinity College of Music, London, 1949–; mem, Vice President of Elgar Society, P. Warlock Society; Fellow of the Welsh Music Guild 2003. *Compositions:* 5 symphonies, 1946, 1960, 1966, 1978, 1979; 5 string quartets, 1946, 1956, 1957, 1963, 1994; 4 operas; The Sergeant-Major's Daughter, 1943; The Black Ram, 1953; Once Upon a Time, 1959; The Lady of Flowers, 1981. *Recordings:* String Quartet No. 4 in Contemporary Welsh Chamber Music, Lyrita, 1971;

The Music of Ian Parrott, Tab. 1, 1997; Fanfare Overture, 1998; Prelude and Waltz, 1999. *Publications:* Master Musician Elgar, 1971; Music of Rosemary Brown, 1978; Cyril Scott and His Piano Music, 1992; The Crying Curlew, P Warlock, 1994. *Contributions:* Elgar and P Warlock Society journals and Welsh Music. *Honours:* First prize, Luxor, Royal Philharmonic Society, 1949; Harriet Cohen Award, 1966; J Edwards Award, 1977; J Rooper Prize for String Quartet No. 2, 1983; Glyndwr Award, 1996. *Address:* Henblas Abermad, Aberystwyth, Ceredigion, SY23 4ES, Wales.

PARRY, Susan; Singer (Mezzo-soprano); b. 13 Feb. 1963, Luton, Bedfordshire, England. *Education:* Studied at Birmingham University and the Royal Academy of Music. *Career:* Welsh National Opera from 1987, as the Witch in Hansel and Gretel, and Kate Pinkerton; English National Opera debut 1992, in the premiere of John Buller's The Bacchae; Company Principal with ENO from 1995, as the Kitchen Boy in Rusalka, Brangaene (first major role, 1996), Janáček's Fox, Strauss's Octavian and Composer, and Dorabella, (1997); Concerts include the Brahms Liebeslieder Waltzes under Antal Dorati, Messiah at the Albert Hall and Beethoven's Ninth at the Festival Hall; Season 1996 included concert of Gluck's Iphigénie en Tauride with the Orchestra of the Age of Enlightenment, Covent Garden debut in Alzira, and Tebaldo in Don Carlos at the London Proms; Falla's El Amor Brujo with the BBC Philharmonic Orchestra, Henze's La Cubana with the Ballet Rambert and an orchestration of Alma Mahler Lieder at Maastricht; Imelda in Verdi's Oberto at Covent Garden, 1997, Pierotto in Donizetti's Linda di Chamounix with the OAE and Hansel in concert with the CBSO under Mark Elder; Elizabeth I in new production of Mary Stuart, ENO 1998; Miss Jessel in The Turn of the Screw, Cincinnati (US debut); London Proms, 2002. *Address:* c/o English National Opera, St Martin's Lane, London, WC2, England.

PARSCH, Arnost; Composer; b. 12 Feb. 1936, Bucovice, Moravia, Czechoslovakia. *Education:* Brno Academy, with Miloslav Istvan. *Career:* Founder member of Brno Composers' Group, 1967; Assistant Professor 1971–73, Professor 1990, Janáček Academy of Performing Arts; President of Brno International Music Festival, 1993–. *Compositions:* Sonata, chamber orchestra, 1996; Two symphonies, 1967, 1970; A Sign of Longing, cantata, 1972; Three string quartets, 1969, 1981, 1994; Electric-acoustical; Poetica no. 3, 1967; Transposizioni II, 1969; Polyfonie no. 1, 1979; Metamorphozes of Time, 1989; The King's Ride, cantata, 1984; The Welcoming of Spring, for vocal soloists, chorus and orchestra, 1990; Rapsotietta for 11 strings, 1992; Loneliness for orchestra, 1993; Voice of the River, for nine players, 1994; Hillside for violin and percussion, 1993; Executions and Resurrections, five songs for female voice and piano, 1996; Bridge, orchestra, 1996; Happy Water for cor anglais and cello, 1996. *Address:* c/o OSA, Cs armady 20, 160–56 Praha 6–Buberec, Czech Republic.

PARSONS, Brian Geoffrey, GRSM, ARCM; Singer (tenor); b. 6 Aug. 1952, Luton, England. *Education:* Boston County Music School, Lincolnshire, Royal Coll. of Music, Royal Coll. of Music Opera School. *Career:* Vicar choral, St Paul's Cathedral 1977–79; BBC Singers 1981–83; Groupe Vocal De France 1983–84; Opera 80 (now English Touring Opera) Count Almaviva, Il barbiere di Siviglia 1980; Lindoro, L'italiana in Algeri 1985; Prof. of Singing, Conservatoire National Supérieur de Musique, Lyon 1998–, Guildhall School of Music and Drama 2000–; mem. Incorporated Soc. of Musicians, Asscn of English Singers and Speakers. *Recordings:* Rameau: Castor et Pollux (English Bach Festival, conductor Charles Farncombe) 1983, Rameau: Naïs (English Bach Festival, conductor Nicolas McGegan) 1982. *Honours:* Finalist, National Federation of Music Societies Award 1977, Finalist, Richard Tauber Competition 1982. *Address:* 5 Montrose Avenue, London, NW6 6LE, England (home). *Telephone:* (20) 8969-4880 (home). *E-mail:* bgparsons@aol.com (home).

PÄRT, Arvo; Estonian composer; b. 11 Sept. 1935, Paide. *Education:* Tallinn Conservatory with Heino Eller. *Career:* worked as sound producer for Estonian radio 1957–67; teacher at Tallinn Conservatory 1967–78; emigrated to Berlin 1980; mem. Swedish Royal Music Acad.. *Compositions include:* orchestral music: 3 symphonies 1963, 1966, 1971, Collage über B-A-C-H 1964, Cantus in Memory of Benjamin Britten 1977, Tabula Rasa 1977, Psalom, 1985, 1991, 1995, Festina lente 1988, Trisagion 1992, 1994, Orient and Occident 1999, Lamentate 2002; vocal music: Our Garden 1959 (rev. 2003), Credo 1968, An den Wassern zu Babel sassen wir und weinten… 1976, 1984 and other versions, Summa 1977, several other versions, Missa Syllabica 1977, 1995, 1996, Passio 1982, Te Deum 1984–85, 1992, Stabat Mater 1985, Magnificat 1989, Miserere 1989, Berliner Messe 1990, 1997, Litany 1994, Kanon Pokajanen 1997, Triodion 1998, Como anhela la cierva 1999, Cecilia 2000, Littlemore Tractus 2001, Most Holy Mother of God 2003, In principio 2003; chamber music: Für Alina 1976, Pari intervallo 1976, Fratres 1977 (several other versions), Passacaglia 2003. *Honours:* Hon. DMus (Sydney) 1996; Hon. Dr (Tartu) 1998, (Durham) 2002; Triumph Award (Russia) 1997, Culture Prize 1998, Herder Award (Germany) 2000, Commandeur de l'Ordre des Arts et des Lettres de la République

Française (France) 2001, C. A. Segizzi Composition Trophy (Italy) 2003. *Current Management:* Universal Edition Ltd, 48 Great Marlborough Street, London, W1F 7BB, England. *Telephone:* (20) 7437-6880 (office). *Fax:* (20) 7437-6115 (office). *E-mail:* uelondon@universaledition.com (office). *Website:* www.universaledition.com (office).

PARTRIDGE, Ian H., CBE; Singer (tenor) and Teacher; b. 12 June 1938, London, England; m. Ann Glover 1959, 2 s. *Education:* Clifton College, 1952–56; Royal College of Music, 1956–58; Guildhall School of Music, 1961–63. *Career:* Debut: Bexhill, 1958; Concerts and Recitals World-wide; Covent Garden debut, 1969; Numerous Broadcasts for BBC and World-wide Television; Appearances include, St Nicolas for Thames Television; mem, Garrick Club; Governor, RSM; Director, PAMRA. *Recordings:* Schöne Müllerin, Schubert; Dichterliebe and Liederkreis op 39-Schumann; On Wenlock Edge and Other Songs, V Williams; The Curlew, Peter Warlock; Songs by Fauré, Duparc, Delius, Gurney. *Honours:* Harriet Cohen Award, 1967; Prix Italia, 1977; Hon RAM, 1996. *Address:* 127 Pepys Road, London SW20 8NP, England.

PASATIERI, Thomas; Composer; b. 20 Oct. 1945, New York, USA. *Education:* Studied with Giannini and Persichetti at Juilliard and with Darius Milhaud at the Aspen Music School. *Career:* Freelance Composer, 1965–; Commissions from National Educational Television, Houston Grand Opera, Baltimore Opera, Michigan Opera Theater, University of Arizona, Evelyn Lear and Thomas Stewart. *Compositions:* Operas: The Women, Aspen 1965; La Divine, New York, 1966; Padrevia, New York, 1967; The Trial of Mary Lincoln, NET 1972; Black Widow, Seattle, 1972; The Seagull, Houston, 1974; Signor Deluso, Vienna, 1974; The Penitentes, Aspen, 1974; Inez de Castro, Baltimore, 1976; Washington Square, Detroit, 1976; Three Sisters, 1979; Before Breakfast, New York, 1980; The Goose Girl, Fort Worth, 1981; Maria Elena, Tucson, 1983; Invocations for Orchestra, 1968; Heloise and Abelard for Soprano, Baritone and Piano, 1971; Rites de passage for low voice and Chamber Orchestra, 1974; Three Poems of James Agee, 1974; Far from Love for Soprano, Clarinet and Piano, 1976; Permit Me Voyage, Cantata, 1976; Mass for 4 Solo Voices, Chorus and Orchestra, 1983; The Harvest Frost for chorus and chamber ensemble, 1993; Quintet for flute and strings, 1995; Morning's Innocent, settings of gay and lesbian poets for male voices and ensemble, 1995; Flute sonata, 1997; Piano Music; 400 Songs. *Address:* c/o ASCAP, ASCAP Building, 1 Lincoln Plaza, New York, NY 10023, USA.

PASCAL, Michel; French electro-acoustic composer and academic; b. 12 Oct. 1958, Avignon; m. Maxime Pascal; two d. *Education:* CNSM Paris, CNR Marseille, INA-GRM and IRCAM, Paris with I. Xenakis, H. Dutilleux, W. Lutoslawski and L. Berio. *Career:* debut as asst of Jean Etienne Marie, CIRM, Nice, 1985–87, for studio and Festival of Contemporary Music; Composer in many fields, including acoustic, choir, instrumental, dance music, music for theatre, film, video and television production; as synthesist, performer and creator of the Studio Instrumental, works played on hyperinstruments with live electronics; Prof. of Electro-acoustic Composition, Conservatoire de Nice; mem., SACEM, SACD, Rainbow Across Europe. *Compositions:* Falaises et Emergences, for tape, 1981; Voiles, for choir and synthesizers, 1987; Protos, for symphonic orchestra, 1989; Puissance 3, for string trio, 1997; Puzzle, instrumental acousmatics, 1995–99. *Recordings:* Albums: Contribution to Nausicaa, Centre de la Mer, Boulogne, 1990; Sonic Waters, with Michel Redolfi-Berceuse/Albin Michel, 1990; Repertoires Polychromes, 1999; Puzzle, 1999. Videos: Mille Mêtres sous la Jungle, 1995; Les Grottes ornées de Borneo, 1996. Other: music for Luc Henri Fage's film, French national television. *Publications:* Les Nouveaux Gestes de la Musique 1999. *Address:* Aix en Musique, 3 Place John Rewald, Espace Forbin, 13100 Aix en Provence; rue Sainte Croix, 13480 Cabries, France.

PASCHER, Hartmut; violist; b. 1956, Vienna, Austria. *Education:* Vienna Acad. of Music. *Career:* member of the Franz Schubert Quartet from 1979; Many concert appearances in Europe, the USA and Australia, including the Amsterdam Concertgebouw, the Vienna Musikverein and Konzerthaus, the Salle Gaveau Paris and the Sydney Opera House; Visits to Zürich, Geneva, Basle, Berlin, Hamburg, London, Rome, Rotterdam, Madrid and Copenhagen; Festival engagements include Salzburg, Wiener Festwochen, Prague Spring, Schubertiade at Hohenems, the Schubert Festival at Washington DC and the Belfast and Istanbul Festivals; Tours of Australasia, USA; Frequent concert tours of the United Kingdom: Frequent appearances at the Wigmore Hall and Cheltenham Festival; Teacher of the Graz Musikhochschule; Masterclasses at the Royal Northern College of Music at Lake District Summer Music. *Recordings include:* Schubert's Quartet in G, D877; Complete Quartets of Dittersdorf; Mozart: String Quartet in D, K575, String Quartet in B Flat, K589, Tchaikovsky String Quartets No. 1 and 3 op. 11 D major and op. 30 E flat minor. *Address:* Roatanskygasse 41, 1170 Vienna, Austria.

PASCOE, John; British artistic director; b. 1949, Bath, England. *Career:* debut designed Julius Caesar for English National Opera, also seen in San Francisco, Geneva, the Metropolitan and on television, 1979; Designed Lucrezia Borgia at Covent Garden and Alcina at Sydney, both with Joan Sutherland, Tosca for Welsh National Opera, 1980; Producer and Designer: La Bohème in Belfast, Solomon at the Göttingen Festival, 1984; Producer and Designer: Rameau's Platée in Spoleto Festival, also seen in BAM, New York; Designer: Orlando at San Francisco and Chicago; Così fan tutte in Dallas; Anna Bolena, with Joan Sutherland, in Toronto, Chicago, Detroit, Houston and San Francisco, 1985–86; Designer: Amahl and the Night Visitors; Norma, in Santiago, 1987; Producer and Designer: Anna Bolena at Covent Garden; Norma in Los Angeles and Detroit, both with Joan Sutherland, 1988; Producer and Designer: La Bohème in Bath; Designed: Tosca in Nice; Apollo and Hyacinthus at Cannes Festival, Madrid, Paris, 1991, 1992; Producer and Designer: La Traviata in Bath; Designer: Anna Bolena in Washington, DC, 1993; Founder, Bath and Wessex Opera. *Honours:* Evening Standard Award for Julius Caesar, 1979. *Current Management:* Athole Still International Management, Forresters Hall, 25–27 Westow Street, London, SE19 3RY, England. *Telephone:* (20) 8771-5271. *Fax:* (20) 8768-6600. *Website:* www.atholestill.com.

PASCOE, Keith; Violinist; b. 1959, England. *Career:* Founder Member of the Britten Quartet, debut concert at the Wigmore Hall, 1987; Quartet in Residence at the Dartington Summer School, 1987, with quartets by Schnittke; Season 1988–89 in the Genius of Prokofiev series at Blackheath and BBC Lunchtime Series at St John's Smith Square; South Bank appearances with the Schoenberg/Handel Quartet Concerto conducted by Neville Marriner, concerts with the Hermann Prey Schubertiade and collaborations with the Alban Berg Quartet in the Beethoven Plus series; Tour of South America 1988, followed by Scandinavian debut; Season 1989–90 with debut tours of Netherlands, Germany, Spain, Austria, Finland; Tours from 1990 to the Far East, Malta, Sweden, Norway; Schoenberg/Handel Concerto with the Gothenburg Symphony; Festival appearances at Brighton, the City of London, Greenwich, Canterbury, Harrogate, Chester, Spitalfields and Aldeburg; Collaborations with John Ogdon, Imogen Cooper, Thea King and Lynn Harrell; Formerly resident quartet at Liverpool University; Teaching role at Lake District Summer Music 1989; Universities of Bristol, Hong Kong 1990. *Recordings:* Beethoven Op 130 and Schnittke Quartet No. 3 (Collins Classics); Vaughan Williams On Wenlock Edge and Ravel Quartet (EMI); Britten, Prokofiev, Tippett, Elgar and Walton Quartets (Collins Classics); Exclusive Contract with EMI from 1991. *Current Management:* Ingpen & Williams Ltd, 7 St George's Court, 131 Putney Bridge Road, London, SW15 2PA, England.

PASHLEY, Anne; Singer (Soprano); b. 5 June 1937, Skegness, England; m. Jack Irons, 1 s., 1 d. *Education:* Guildhall School of Music, London. *Career:* Took part as sprinter in 1956 Olympic Games, at Melbourne; Stage debut in Semele, with Handel Opera Society, 1959; Glyndebourne debut 1962, in Die Zauberflöte; Covent Garden debut 1965, as Barbarina in Le nozze di Figaro; Guest appearances with English National Opera, Scottish Opera, Welsh National Opera and at Edinburgh and Aldeburg Festivals; Foreign engagements in France, Germany, Portugal, Spain, Belgium, Italy, Israel; Leading roles in 8 BBC television operas and numerous radio broadcasts; New Opera Company, London, in the British premiere of Hindemith's Cardillac, 1970; mem, Equity. *Recordings include:* La Morte de Cléopâtre, Berlioz; Magnificat, Bach; Albert Herring and Peter Grimes, Britten. *Contributions:* The Listener. *Address:* 289 Goldhawk Road, London W12, England.

PASINO, Gisella; Singer (Mezzo-soprano); b. 1965, Genoa, Italy. *Education:* Studied at Genoa with Maggia Olivero. *Career:* Debut: Padua, 1987 as the Princess in Suor Angelica; Rome, 1987 as Amneris in Aida; Sang Verdi's Preziosilla at Piacenza, 1989; Anacoana in Franchetti's Cristoforo Colombo at Frankfurt, 1991; Season 1995–96 as Carmen at Rotterdam and the Princess in Adriana Lecouvreur at Livorno. *Recordings:* Cristoforo Colombo. *Honours:* Prizewinner, Competitions in Genoa and Milan. *Address:* c/o Netherlands Opera, Waterlooplein 22, 1011 PG Amsterdam, Netherlands.

PASKALIS, Kostas; Singer (Baritone); b. 1 Sept. 1929, Levadia, Boeotia, Greece; m. Marina Krilovici. *Education:* Studied at the National Conservatory Athens. *Career:* Debut: Athens 1954, as Rigoletto; Vienna Staatsoper from 1958, debut as Renato in Un Ballo in Maschera; Tour of North America 1960; Glyndebourne 1964–72, as Macbeth and Don Giovanni; Metropolitan Opera debut 1965, as Don Carlos in La Forza el Destino; Rome Opera 1965–66 as Rigoletto and Posa, in Don Carlos; Salzburg Festival 1966, as Pentheus in the premiere of Henze's The Bassarids; La Scala Milan 1967, as Valentin in Faust; Guest appearances in Leningrad, Kiev, Berlin and Moscow; Sang Nabucco at Brussels 1987; New Jersey Opera 1988, as Don Giovanni; Director of the National Opera of Greece from 1988; Sang Simon Boccanegra for Athens Opera, 1995; Teacher with the European Opera Centre, 1998–.

Recordings: Escamillo in Carmen (HMV); Alfonso in Donizetti's Lucrezia Borgia. *Address:* National Union of Greece, 18-A Harilaou Trikoupi Street, 106 79 Athens, Greece.

PASKUDA, Georg; Singer (Tenor); b. 7 Jan. 1926, Ratibor, Germany. *Career:* Sang small roles in various German theatres from 1951; Bayreuth Festival from 1959, notably as Froh and Mime; Paris Opéra 1960; Bavarian State Opera Munich from 1960, notably in operas by Strauss, Puccini, Lortzing, Wagner, Verdi and Mozart; Munich 1967, as Don Carlos and 1986 in the premiere of V.D Kirchner's Belshazzar; Sang at the Munich Staatsoper until season 1994–95. *Recordings:* Parsifal, Tannhäuser and Arabella; Die Frau ohne Schatten; Das Rheingold and Der fliegende Holländer, from Bayreuth. *Address:* c/o Bayerische Staatsoper, Postfach 745, 8000 Munich 1, Germany.

PASQUETTO, Giancarlo; Italian singer (baritone); b. 1959, Verona. *Career:* sang widely in Italy from 1984 as Alfio in Cavalleria Rusticana, Count Luna, Marcello, Verdi's Miller and Carlo in La Forza del Destino; Metropolitan Opera, New Yok, 1989 as Miller; Season 1993 as Nabucco at Bregenz, Germont at Verona and for New Israeli Opera, 1998; Rigoletto at the Berlin Staatsoper and Tonio in Pagliacci at La Scala, Milan; Further appearances as Guzman in Verdi's Alzira at Parma and at Covent Garden as Rigoletto, 1994; Other roles include Amonasro, Simon Boccanegra, Glyndebourne, 1987; Riccardo in I Puritani; Sang Boccanegra at Munich, 2000. *Recordings include:* Simon Boccanegra, from Glyndebourne 1998. *Current Management:* Il Trittico, Via Rocche 4, 37121 Verona, Italy. *Telephone:* 045 8001500. *Fax:* 045 8046801. *Website:* www.iltrittico.net.

PASQUIER, Bruno; Violist; b. 10 Dec. 1943, Neuilly-sur-Seine, France. *Education:* Studied at the Paris Conservatoire 1957–63 with Etienne Ginot and his father, Pierre Pasquier. *Career:* Mix à Munich, 1965; Queteur à cadas, string quartet, 1972–83; Leader, viola section in the orchestra of the Paris Opéra, 1972; Soloist with the Orchestre National de France, 1984–89; With Regis Pasquier and Roland Pidoux founded the New Pasquier Trio, 1970; Solo performances with leading orchestras in France and abroad; Professor of Viola and of Chamber Music at the Paris Conservatoire, 1983; Plays a Maggilli viola, ca 1620. *Honours:* Chevalier de l'Ordre des Arts et Lettres, 1991. *Address:* c/o Agence Cazeneuve, 5–7 avenue Mac-Mahon, F 75017 Paris, France.

PASQUIER, Regis; Violinist; b. 10 Oct. 1945, Fontainebleau, France. *Education:* Studied at the Paris Conservatoire, gaining first prize in violin and chamber music aged 12; Further study with Isaac Stern. *Career:* Concert tours of Belgium, Netherlands and Luxembourg 1958; New York recital 1960; Many concerts with leading orchestras in Europe and America; Soloist with the Orchestre National de France, 1977–86; With Bruno Pasquier and Roland Pidoux formed the New Pasquier Trio, 1970; Sonata recitals with pianist Jean-Claude Pennetier; Concerto repertoire ranges from standard classics to works by Xenakis and Gilbert Amy (Trajectoires); Plays a Montagnana instrument; Professor of Violin and of Chamber Music at the Paris Conservatoire, 1985. *Address:* Conservatoire National Superieur de Musique, 14 Rue de Madrid, 75008 Paris, France.

PASSOW, Sabine; Singer (Soprano); b. 1960, Essen, Germany. *Education:* Studied in Essen and Hannover. *Career:* Sang in opera at Oldenburg from 1987; Komische Oper Berlin from 1991, as Mozart's Countess, Handel's Cleopatra, Marenka in The Bartered Bride, Micaela and Agathe; Arianna in Handel's Giustino, 1995; Alice Ford in Falstaff, 1996; Guest at the Munich Staatsoper from 1986, notably in Strauss's Daphne and as Ismene in Mozart's Mitridate, 1990; Guest with Komische Oper at Covent Garden, 1989; Tours of Japan, 1991 and 1994; Cleopatra at the Schwetzingen Festival, 1993; Sang Elisabeth in Tannhäuser at Darmstadt, 1994 and at Cottbus in 1999; Sang Anna in Seven Deadly Sins by Brecht/Weill; Concerts of music by Bach; Season 2000–01 as Butterfly at Cottbus, Elisabeth at Saarbrücken, Alice Ford for the Komische Oper and Agathe at the Eutin Festival. *Address:* Komische Oper Berlin, Behrenstrasse 55–57, 10117 Berlin, Germany.

PATAKI, Eva; Pianist; b. 19 Oct. 1941, Budapest, Hungary; m. T Bantay, 27 Aug 1971. *Education:* Diploma, Concert Performance, Pedagogy, Franz Liszt Music Academy, Budapest; Studied with Carlo Zecchi in Salzburg. *Career:* Debut: Recital, Budapest, 1965; Assistant, Mozarteum, Salzburg, 5 years; Coach, Royal Opera, Stockholm, 1967–; Concerts, radio and television, with Helena Doese, Catarina Ligendza, C-H Ahnsjö, Nicolai Gedda, Gösta Winbergh, others, all over Europe and in Moscow, St Petersburg and other venues, 1967–; Teacher of Masterclasses; Producer, concerts at Royal Opera, Stockholm, 1985–. *Recordings:* Several. *Address:* Artistsekretariat Ulf Tornqvist, Sankt Eriksgatan 100 2 tr, 113 31 Stockholm, Sweden.

PATCHELL, Sue; Singer (Soprano); b. 1948, Montana, USA. *Education:* Studied in Montana and at University of California at Los Angeles. *Career:* Engaged at Graz Opera, 1974, Gelsenkirchen, 1979–86; Wiesbaden, 1986–, notably as Elsa in Lohengrin, 1988, and Elisabetta in Don Carlos at Wiesbaden Festival, 1990; Hamburg Staatsoper as Tatiana in Eugene Oengin, Barcelona, 1989 and 1990, as Eva and Chrysothemis, Antwerp Opera as Elisabeth in Tannhäuser and Ariadne; Other roles include Marguerite, Mozart's Countess and Donna Elvira, Frau Fluth and Rosalinde; Sang Isolde at Trieste, 1996; Marietta in Die Tote Stadt at Wiesbaden, 1997; New York Met debut 1999, as Isolde; Sang Leonore at Bonn, 2001, and Isolde at Barcelona, 2002; Concert repertoire includes Das Buch mit Sieben Siegeln by Franz Schmidt. *Recordings:* Das Dunkle Reich by Pfitzner. *Address:* c/o Atholle Still Management, Foresters Hall, 25–27 Westow Street, London, SE19 3RY.

PATON, Iain; Singer (tenor); b. 1960, Scotland. *Education:* Studied at Royal Scottish Academy and with David Keren in London. *Career:* Appearances with Glyndebourne Festival and touring Opera in Capriccio, Death in Venice and Le nozze di Figaro, Don Curzio; Sang in Judith Weir's The Vanishing Bridegroom for Scottish Opera at Glasgow and Covent Garden; Season 1992–93, as Pedrillo in Die Entführung and in The Makropulos Case, season 1993–94, as Vanya in Katya Kabanova, Tamino and the Shepherd in Tristan und Isolde; Sang Leicester in Maria Stuarda for Scottish Opera-Go-Round, 1992; City of Birmingham Touring Opera in Mozart's Zaide; Concert repertoire includes Liszt's Faust Symphony and appearances with Scottish Early Music Consort in Northern Ireland, Germany and Poland; Sang Eurimachos in Dallapiccola's Ulisse for BBC, 1993; Season 1995–96 in Purcell's King Arthur and as Mozart's Pedrillo with Les Arts Florissants and Boris in Katya Kabanova at Dublin; Season 1997 with Ferrando for Flanders Opera and Scottish Opera; Sang Vasek in The Bartered Bride for Opera North, 1998; Sang Don Carlos in Les Indes Galantes by Rameau at the Palais Garnier, Paris, 1999; Season 2000–01 as Grimoaldo in Rodelinda at Göttingen and Lensky for Opera North. *Honours:* Eric Vertier Award, at Glyndebourne. *Current Management:* Askonas Holt Ltd, Lonsdale Chambers, 27 Chancery Lane, London, WC2A 1PF, England. *Telephone:* (20) 7400-1700. *Fax:* (20) 7400-1799. *E-mail:* info@askonasholt.co.uk. *Website:* www.askonasholt.co.uk.

PATRIARCO, Earle; Singer (baritone); b. 1965, USA. *Career:* many concert and recital engagements in Europe and the USA, with songs by Poulenc and Strauss; Opera repertory includes Così fan tutte and The Queen of Spades; Contestant at the 1994 Cardiff Singer of the World Competition. *Current Management:* Askonas Holt Ltd, Lonsdale Chambers, 27 Chancery Lane, London, WC2A 1PF, England. *Telephone:* (20) 7400-1700. *Fax:* (20) 7400-1799. *E-mail:* info@askonasholt.co.uk. *Website:* www.askonasholt.co.uk.

PATTERSON, Paul (Leslie); Composer and Educator; b. 15 June 1947, Chesterfield, England; m. Hazel Wilson, 1981, 1 s., 1 d. *Education:* Royal Academy of Music; FRAM, FRSA, 1980, Hon FLCM, 1997. *Career:* Freelance Composer, 1968–; Art Council Composer-in-Association, English Sinfonia, 1969–70; Director, Contemporary Music, Warwick University, 1974–80; Composer-in-Residence, SE Arts Association, 1980–82, Bedford School, 1984–85; Professor of Composition, 1970–, Head of Composition/20th Century Music, 1985–97, Royal Academy of Music; Artistic Director, Exeter Festival, 1991–97; Composer-in-Residence, 1990–91; Manson Chair of Composition, 1997–; Composer-in-Residence, National Youth Orchestra, 1997–; Visiting Professor of Composition, Christchurch University; mem, RSA. *Compositions:* Te Deum, 1988; Symphony, 1990; The Mighty Voice, 1991; Songs of the West, 1995; Rustic Sketches, 1996; Hell's Angels, 1998; Gloria, 1999; Millennium Mass, 2000; Orchestraland, 2000; Performances world-wide by leading orchestras, soloists, ensembles, also film and television music. *Recordings:* Concerto for Orchestra; Little Red Riding Hood; Mass of Sea; Magnificat, with Bach Choir. *Publications:* Rebecca, 1968; Trumpet Concerto, 1969; Time Piece, 1972; Kyrie, 1972; Requiem, 1973; Comedy for 5 Winds, 1973; Requiem, 1974; Fluorescences, 1974; Clarinet Concerto, 1976; Cracowian Counterpoints, 1977; Voices of Sleep, 1979; Concerto for Orchestra, 1981; Canterbury Psalms, 1981; Sinfonia, 1982; Mass of the Sea, 1983; Deception Pass, 1983; Duologue, 1984; Mean Time, 1984; Europhony, 1985; Missa Brevis, 1985; Stabat Mater, 1986; String Quartet, Harmonica Concerto, Magnificat and Nunc Dimitus, 1986; Te Deum, 1988; Tunnell of Time, 1988; The End, 1989; Violin Concerto, 1992; Little Red Riding Hood, 1993; Magnificat, 1994; Royal Eurostar for the opening Channel Tunnel, 1994; Songs of the West, overture, 1995; Deviations, for String Octet, 2001; City Within, 2000; Cello Concerto, 2002; Jubilee Dances, 2002; Bug for solo harp, 2003; Three Little Pigs, 2004. *Honours:* Medal of Honour, Polish Ministry of Culture, 1986; Leslie Boosey Award, 1996. *Address:* 31 Cromwell Avenue, Highgate, London N6 5HN, England. *E-mail:* musicpp@hotmail.com. *Website:* www.paulpatterson.co.uk.

PATTERSON, Susan; Singer (Soprano); b. 1962, USA. *Career:* Sang widely in USA and made European debut in 1988 with the Welsh National Opera as Violetta; Sang at San Francisco in 1988 and 1991 as Anne Trulove and Constanze; Sang Gilda at Vancouver in 1989 and in Cherubini's Lodoiska at La Scala, 1990–91; Sang at Rome Opera in 1991

as Adèle in Le Comte Ory, Fiordiligi at Cologne and Berenice in Rossini's L'Occasione fa il Ladro at Schwetzingen and Paris; Sang Aspasia in Mozart's Mitridate at Amsterdam in 1992; Magda in La Rondine at St Louis, 1996; Rusalka for ENO, 1998; Frequent concert appearances. *Address:* c/o San Francisco Opera, War Memorial Opera House, San Francisco, CA 94102, USA.

PATTON, Chester; Singer (Bass); b. 1965, Columbia, MS, USA. *Education:* Studied at the San Francisco Conservatory of Music. *Career:* Appearances with San Francisco Opera from 1993, as Don Basilio, the King of Egypt in Aida, First Nazarene in Salome, Colline, Raimondo and Lord Walton in I Puriatni; Bay Area credits include further appearances with West Bay Opera, Opera San José, Pocket Opera and Berkeley Contemporary Opera; Title role in the US premiere of Tippett's King Priam, San Francisco Opera Center; Debut with Opera Pacific as Basilio, Beethoven's Pizarro at Lyon, High Priest in Nabucco at the Opéra Bastille and Timur in Turandot (1997); Hawaii Opera Theater as Ferrando in Trovatore, Sparafucile and Colline. *Recordings include:* Mandarin in San Francisco Opera production of Turandot. *Address:* c/o San Francisco Opera, War Memorial House, Van Ness Avenue, CA 94102, USA.

PAUER, Jiri; Composer and Administrator; b. 22 Feb. 1919, Libusin, Kladno, Czechoslovakia. *Education:* Studied with Alois Haba at Prague Conservatory, 1943–46, and at Academy of Musical Arts. *Career:* Professor of Composition at Prague Academy, 1965–89; Head of Opera at Prague National Theatre, 1951–55, 1965–67, Director 1979–89; Director of Czech Philharmonic, 1958–79. *Compositions include:* Operas: Prattling Slug, for children, 1958; Zuzana Vijirova, 1958; Little Red Riding Hood, Olomouc, 1960; Matrimonial Counterpoints, Ostrava, 1962; The Hypochondriac (after Moliere), Prague, 1970 revised version, Prague, 1988; Swan-Song, monodrama, Prague, 1974; Ballet: Ferdy the Ant, 1975; Orchestral: Comedy Suite, 1949; Bassoon Concerto, 1949; Rhapsody, 1953; Oboe Concerto, 1954; Horn Concerto, 1958; Symphony, 1963; Commemoration, 1969; Trumpet Concerto, 1972; Initials, 1974; Symphony for Strings, 1978; Marimba Concerto, 1984; Suite, 1987; Symphonic Probes, 1990; Chamber: Divertimento for 3 clarinets, 1949; Violin Sonatina, 1953; Cello Sonata, 1954; 4 String Quartets, 1960, 1969, 1970, 1976; Divertimento for Monet, 1961; Wind Quintet, 1961; Piano Trio, 1963; Characters for brass quintet, 1978; Episodes for string quartet, 1980; Trio for 3 horns, 1986; Violin Sonata, 1987; Nonet No. 2, 1989; Green Pieces for trumpet, horn and trombone, 1997; Piano music, cantatas and songs. *Address:* c/o National Theatre, PO Box 865, 11230 Prague 1, Czech Republic.

PAUK, György; Concert Violinist; b. 26 Oct. 1936, Budapest, Hungary; m. 19 July 1959, 1 s., 1 d. *Education:* Franz Liszt Music Academy, Budapest, being youngest pupil of Professors Zathureczki, Weiner and Kodály. *Career:* Many concerts in Hungary and throughout Eastern Europe; Moved to London in 1961 and gave his recital and orchestral debuts there in the same year; Has performed world-wide with all major orchestras of London and on the continent under leading conductors including Pierre Boulez, Antal Dorati, Lorin Maazel, Tennstedt, Georg Solti, Simon Rattle; American debut with Chicago Symphony Orchestra and has played with several US Orchestras; Appearances at such festivals as Aspen, Ravinia, Hollywood Bowl and Saratoga; Formed a trio with Peter Frankl and Ralph Kirshbaum achieving world-wide acclaim; Conductor and soloist with English Chamber Orchestra, Mozart Players and Academy of St Martin-in-the-Fields; Masterclasses; Professor at Royal Academy of Music, London, 1987–; Director, Mozart Bicentenary Festival, 1991; 25th Anniversary concerts with the Pauk-Frankl-Kirschbaum Trio, 1997; Professor, Winterthur-Zürich Konservatorium, 1996–. *Recordings include:* Alban Berg's Chamber Concerto, a Bartók Album and Tippett's Triple Concerto (Record of Year 1983); Complete Sonatas by Handel; Complete Violin Concertos by Mozart; 3 Brahms Sonatas; Mozart Quintets (viola part); All Bartók works for Violin, Piano, Solo Violin and orchestra, (1st Bartók recording nominated for Grammy Award), 1995. *Honours:* Honorary Fellow, Guildhall School of Music; Honorary RAM, 1990; Highest Civilian Award, President of Hungary, 1998. *Current Management:* Vivienne Dimant. *Address:* c/o Tivoli Artists Management, 3 Vesterbrogade, DK–1630 Copenhagen, Denmark.

PAUL, Thomas; Singer (Bass); b. 22 Feb. 1934, Chicago, Illinois, USA. *Education:* Studied at the Juilliard School with Beverly Johnson and Cornelius Reid. *Career:* Debut: New York City Opera 1962, as Sparafucile in Rigoletto; Sang in New York, Pittsburgh, Washington, Vancouver, San Francisco and Montreal as Mozart's Figaro and Sarastro, Pogner in Die Meistersinger, Bart ók's Duke Bluebeard, Padre Guardiano, La Forza del Destino; Ptolemy in Giulio Cesare by Handel; Sang at Central City Colorado in the premiere of Robert Ward's Lady from Colorado, 1964; Many concert performances; Teacher at the Eastman School, Rochester, and the Aspen School, Colorado. *Recordings:* Brander in La Damnation de Faust.

PAULSEN, Melinda; Singer (Mezzo-soprano); b. 1970, USA. *Education:* Swarthmore College; Munich Hochschule; Lieder with Helmut Deutsche. *Career:* Opera Studio of the Bavarian State Theatre, Munich; Appearances at Bregenz Festival, Wratislava Cantans, Poland; Conductors include Helmuth Rilling, Marek Janowski and Roberto Abbado; Ramiro in Mozart's La Finta Giardiniera at Klagenfurt, 1998; Many recital and concert engagements. *Recordings:* Puck in Oberon. *Honours:* Winner, International ARD Competition, Munich, 1992. *Address:* c/o BMG Classic Artists, 69–79 Fulham High Street, London SW6 3JW, England.

PAULUS, Stephen Harrison; Composer; b. 24 Aug. 1949, Summit, New Jersey, USA; m. Patricia Ann Stutzman, 18 July 1975, 1 s. *Education:* Alexander Ramsey High School, 1967; BA, 1971, MA, Music Theory and Composition, 1974; PhD, Music Theory and Composition, 1978, University of Minnesota. *Career:* Co-Founder, Minnesota Composer's Forum, 1973–85; Composer-in-Residence, Minnesota Orchestra, 1983–87; Vice-President, Minnesota Composer's Forum, 1983–; mem, American Society of Composers, Authors and Publishers; Minnesota Composers' Forum. *Compositions:* Operas: The Village Singer; The Postman Always Rings Twice; The Woodlanders, 1984; Harmoonia, opera, 1990; The Woman at Otowi Crossing, 1995; Summer, 1999; Orchestral, Suite from The Postman Always Rings Twice; Symphony in Three Movements; Reflections; Ordway Overture; Concerto for Orchestra; Spectra; Chorus and Orchestra: So Hallow'd Is The Time; Letter For The Times; Canticles, North Shore; Chorus: Too Many Waltzes; Jesn Carols; Echoes Between the Silent Peaks; Chamber Ensembles: Partita for Violin and Piano; Music for Contrasts, String Quartet; Courtship Songs, Flute, Oboe, Cello, Piano; Wind Suite, WW Quartet; Voice, Letters from Colette, Soprano and Chamber Ensemble; All My Pretty Ones, Soprano and Piano; Artsongs, Tenor and Piano; Mad Book; Shadow Book, Tenor and Pianoforte; Three Elizabethan Songs, Soprano and Pianoforte; Visions from Hildegard III for chorus and ensemble, 1996; Toccata for organ, 1996. *Recordings:* So Hallow'd Is The Time, for Chorus, Orchestra and Soloists; Symphony in Three Movements, Neville Marriner/Minnesota Orchestra. *Address:* c/o Opera Theater of St Louis, PO Box 13148, St Louis, MO 63119, USA.

PAUSTIAN, Inger; Singer (Mezzo-Soprano); b. 1937, Denmark. *Education:* Studied in Copenhagen. *Career:* Engaged at Kiel Opera, 1965–67, Hanover, 1967–69, Frankfurt, 1969–78; Guest appearances at Hamburg, 1970, Munich, 1971, and Valencia, 1976, as Ortrud in Lohengrin; Bayreuth Festival, 1968–71, as Siegrune, Wellgunde and a Flowermaiden; Sang at Zürich Opera, 1976–77; Other roles included Monteverdi's Penelope, Mozart's Marcellina, Magdalene, Brangaene, Herodias and the Nurse in Die Frau ohne Schatten; Verdi's Azucena, Amneris and Eboli, Guilietta in Les Contes d'Hoffmann, Larina in Eugene Onegin and Agave (The Bassarids by Henze); Frequent concert performances. *Address:* c/o Opernhaus Zürich, Falkenstrasse 1, 8008 Zürich, Switzerland.

PAUTZA, Sabin; Composer and Conductor; b. 8 Feb. 1943, Calnic, Romania; m. Corina Popa, 2 Oct 1974, 2 d. *Education:* Conducting, Bucharest Academy of Music, 1964; Composition, Accademia Musicale Chigiana, Siena, Italy, 1970. *Career:* Debut: Romanian Athenee, Romania, 1964; Professor of Harmony and Conducting, Iassy Academy of Music, 1965–84; Conductor, Iassy Academy of Music Orchestra, 1969–84; Appearances, Bayreuth Wagner Youth Festival, 1974, 1977, 1978; Carnegie Hall, New York, 1984; Extensively performed as a Conductor in Europe, Australia and North America; Music Director, Conductor, Plainfield Symphony Orchestra, New Jersey, USA, 1987–. *Compositions:* Symphony No. 1, In Memoriam; Symphony No. 2, Sinfonia Sacra; Offering to the Children of the World for double choir; Games I, II, III, IV, V, and VI, for orchestra; 3 String Quartets, 1976, 1977, 1979; Double Concerto for viola, piano and orchestra; Ebony Mass for choir, organ and orchestra; Another Love Story, opera for children; Laudae for chamber orchestra; Five pieces for large orchestra; Nocturnes for soprano and orchestra; Haiku for soprano and chamber orchestra; Simfonietta, 1994; Rita Dove Triptych, 1994; Chimes for percussion instruments, 1995; String Quartet No. 4: Ludus Modalis, 1998; Mood Swings, microcantata for mezzo-soprano and piano on verses by Tristan Tzara; Ode to Hope, cantata for soprano solo, choir and orchestra, dedicated to the New Millennium; Antiphonon Melos–Dramatic oratorio, 1969, revised 1999; Saxophone Concerto 1996, revised 2001; Sonata a Quatro, for strings, 1969 revised 2000. *Recordings:* On Opera Omnia, Vols 1–9, on CD. *Honours:* George Enesco Prize for Composition, Romanian Academy, 1974; Romanian Union of Composers Prize, 1977; Martin Luther King Jr Prize for 'Chimes', 1995; Honorary Doctorate, London Institute for Applied Research. *Address:* 240 Locust Avenue, Locust, NJ 07760, USA.

PAVAROTTI, Luciano, DMus; Italian opera singer (tenor); b. 12 Oct. 1935, Modena; s. of Fernando Pavarotti and Adele (née Venturi) Pavarotti; m. 1st Adua Veroni 1961 (divorced); three d.; m. 2nd Nicoletta Mantovani 2003; one d. *Education:* Istituto Magistrale.

Career: debut as Rodolfo in La Bohème at Reggio nell'Emilia 1961; appearances include Staatsoper Vienna, Royal Opera House, London 1963, La Scala 1965, Edgardo in Lucia di Lammermoor in Miami, USA 1965, Metropolitan Opera House, New York 1968, Paris Opera and Lyric Opera of Chicago 1973, Manrico at the Met 1988, the Duke in Rigoletto 1989, Nemorino in L'Elisir d'amore at Covent Garden 1990, Otello and Nemorino in New York 1991–92, Verdi's Don Carlos at La Scala 1992–93, Cavaradossi at Covent Garden 1992, at the Met 1999, Arvino in I Lombardi at Metropolitan Opera 1994, Gustavus in Ballo in Maschera at Covent Garden 1995, at the Met 1997, Radames at the Met 2001, Tosca at Covent Garden 2002, at the Met 2004; recitals and concerts abroad, including the USA, Europe and fmr USSR, appeared with two other tenors at World Cup Concert, Caracalla, Pavarotti in the Park, London 1991; retd 2004. *Film:* Yes, Giorgio 1981. *Recordings include:* La Bohème, Madama Butterfly, Beatrice di Tenda, Lucia di Lammermoor, La Fille du Régiment, Maria Stuarda, Un Ballo in Maschera, Luisa Miller, Macbeth, Mefistofele, Idomeneo, Aida, Norma, Tosca, Otello, Ti Adoro 2003. *Publications:* Pavarotti: My Own Story (with William Wright), Grandissimo Pavarotti 1986. *Honours:* hon. degree (PA) 1979; Noce d'Oro Nat. Prize, Luigi Illica int. prize, first prize Gold Orfeo (Acad. du Disque Lyrique de France), Grammy Award for best classical vocal soloist 1981, Kennedy Center Honor 2001, and many other prizes; Grand Officer, Italian Repub., Légion d'honneur. *Current Management:* Herbert Breslin, 119 West 57th Street, New York, NY 10019, USA; Via Giardini 941, 41040 Saliceta, Modena, Italy (home).

PAVIOUR, Sir Paul, Kt, MMus; composer and musician (organ); b. 14 April 1931, Birmingham, England. *Education:* studied in London with Herbert Howells, Vaughan Williams and Adrian Boult, University of London. *Career:* Faculty Member, All Saints College, Bathurst, 1969–75; Conductor, Goulburn Consort of Voices, 1975–; commissions from Goulburn Festival of the Arts, Australian Government, and others; Goulburn College of Advanced Education, 1975–84; Organist and Conductor with Argyle Operatic Society, 1977–. *Compositions include:* Horn Concerto, 1970; Missa Australis, 1971; Take Kissing as a Natural Law, for female voices and flute, 1971; Four Carols, 1972; A New Australian Mass, 1973; All Systems Go for chorus and orchestra, 1980; An Urban Symphony (No. 2), 1982; This Endris Nyghte, Christmas Cantata, 1982; Concerto for Oboe, Strings and Percussion, 1983; Symphony No. 5, 1985. *Address:* 4 Beppo Street, Goulburn, NSW 2580, Australia.

PAVLOVSKAYA, Tatiana; Singer (Soprano); b. 1970, Murmansk, Russia. *Education:* Graduated St Petersburg Conservatoire, 1994. *Career:* Engaged with the Kirov Opera, St Petersburg, from 1995; Roles have included Madama Butterfly, Tatiana in Eugene Onegin, Yaroslavna (Prince Igor); Mozart's Countess and Clara in Prokofiev's Betrothal in a Monastery; Further apearances as Paulina in The Gambler by Prokofiev, Natasha in War and Peace, Wagner's Elsa and Maria in Mazeppa; San Francisco Opera debut in Betrothal in a Monastery, under Gergiev; British debut as Maria at Glasgow, with the Kirov, 1999; Sang Sofya in the British premiere of Prokofiev's Semyon Kotko, with the Kirov Opera at Covent Garden, 2000. *Honours:* Winner, International Pechkovsky Vocal Competition; International Competition for Young Singers, Wrocław, Poland. *Address:* c/o Kirov Opera, Mariinsky Theatre, 1 Theatre Square, St Petersburg, Russia.

PAY, Anthony; Clarinettist; b. 21 Feb. 1945, London. *Education:* Studied with John Davies and Wilfred Kealey. *Career:* Debut: Mozart's Concerto with National Youth Orchestra on tour to Europe, 1961; Principal Clarinet of the Royal Philharmonic, 1968–78; London Sinfonietta 1968–83, including the premiere of Henze's The Miracle of the Rose, 1982; Principal with the Academy of St Martin-in-the-Fields (1976–86), Academy of Ancient Music (1983–94) and the Orchestra of the Age of Enlightenment, 1986–; Member of the Nash Ensemble, 1986–93; Teacher at the Guildhall School, London, 1982–90; Frequent concerts as conductor and clarinettist. *Recordings include:* Berio Concertino; Concertos by Weber, Crusell and Mozart; Chamber works by Beethoven (Septet), Schubert (Octet), Mozart and Brahms (Quintets) and others. *Address:* c/o Orchestra of the Age of Enlightenment, 5th Floor, Westcombe House, 56–58 Whitcombe St, London, WC2H 7RW, England.

PAYER-TUCCI, Elisabeth; Singer (Soprano); b. 1944, Germany. *Career:* Sang at the Berne Opera, 1968–70 and at the Cologne Opera until 1976; New York in 1980 as Irene in a concert rendition of Rienzi; Sang the Siegfried Brünnhilde at the Metropolitan, Isolde at Rome and Ariadne at Lisbon; Sang at Verona Festival as Turandot, Brünnhilde at Barcelona and Senta at Rio de Janeiro (1987); Other roles have included Verdi's Amelia in Un Ballo in Maschera, the Forza Leonora, and Santuzza in Cavalleria Rusticana.

PAYNE, Anthony Edward, BA; British composer; b. 2 Aug. 1936, London; s. of the late Edward Alexander Payne and (Muriel) Margaret Payne; m. Jane Manning 1966. *Education:* Dulwich Coll., London and

Durham Univ. *Career:* freelance musical journalist, musicologist, lecturer, etc. with various pubs and BBC Radio, active in promoting "new music", serving on Cttee of Macnaghten Concerts (Chair. 1967) and Soc. for the Promotion of New Music (Chair. 1969–71), composed part-time 1962–73; full-time composer 1973–; tutor in Composition, London Coll. of Music 1983–85, Sydney Conservatorium 1986, Univ. of W Australia 1996; Milhaud Prof., Mills Coll., Oakland, Calif. 1983; Artistic Dir Spitalfields Festival; Composition Tutor Univ. of Western Australia 1996; Contrib. Daily Telegraph 1964–, The Times 1964–, The Independent 1986–, Country Life 1995–; mem. Cttee Asscn Frank Bridge Trust, RVW Trust, MBF Awards and Trusts. *Compositions:* Paraphrases and Cadenzas 1969, Paean for solo piano 1971, Phoenix Mass 1972, The Spirits Harvest for full orchestra 1972, Concerto for Orchestra (Int. Jury Choice for Int. Soc. for Contemporary Music Festival 1976) 1974, The World's Winter for soprano and ensemble 1976, String Quartet 1978, The Stones and Lonely Places Sing (septet) 1979, Song of the Clouds for oboe and orchestra 1980, A Day in the Life of a Mayfly (sextet) 1981, Evening Land for soprano and piano 1981, Spring's Shining Wake for orchestra 1981, Songs and Seascapes for strings 1984, The Song Streams in the Firmament (sextet) 1986, Fanfares and Processional 1986, Half Heard in the Stillness for orchestra 1987, Consort Music for string quintet 1987, Sea Change (septet) 1988, Time's Arrow for orchestra 1990, The Enchantress Plays bassoon and piano 1990, Symphonies of Wind and Rain for chamber ensemble 1991, A Hidden Music 1992, Orchestral Variations: The Seeds Long Hidden 1993, Empty Landscape–Heart's Ease (sextet) 1995, Break, Break, Break for unaccompanied chorus 1996, Elgar's Third Symphony (commissioned by Elgar Trust to complete Elgar's sketches) 1997, Piano Trio 1998, Scenes from The Woodlanders for soprano and ensemble 1999, Of Knots and Skeins for violin and piano 2000, Betwixt Heaven and Charing Cross for unaccompanied chorus 2001, Visions and Journeys for orchestra (British Composers Award 2003) 2001, Poems of Edward Thomas for soprano and piano quartet 2003. *Recordings include:* The Music of Anthony Payne (Gramophone Critics' Choice) 1977. *Publications:* Schoenberg 1968, The Music of Frank Bridge 1984, Elgar's Third Symphony: The Story of the Reconstruction 1998; contrib. to Musical Times, Tempo, Music and Musicians, The Listener, Daily Telegraph, The Times, The Independent, Country Life. *Honours:* Hon. DMus (Birmingham) 2000, (Kingston) 2002; Radcliffe Award 1975, South Bank Show Award 1998, Evening Standard Classical Music Award 1998, New York Critics' Circle Nat. Public Radio Award 1999, Classical CD Award 1999. *Address:* 2 Wilton Square, London, N1 3DL; c/o Boosey & Hawkes, 295 Regent Street, London, W1B 2JH, England. *Telephone:* (20) 7359-1593. *Fax:* (20) 7226-4369. *E-mail:* tony@wiltonsq .demon.co.uk (home).

PAYNE, Nicholas; British opera company director; b. 4 Jan. 1945, Bromley, Kent, England; m. Linda Jane Adamson 1986; two s. *Education:* Eton Coll. and Trinity Coll. Cambridge. *Career:* worked for Paterson Concert Management 1967; Arts Council administration course 1967–68; joined finance dept Royal Opera House, Covent Garden 1968–70; Subsidy Officer, Arts Council 1970–76; Financial Controller, Welsh Nat. Opera 1976–82; Gen. Admin. Opera North 1982–93; Dir of Opera, Royal Opera House 1993–98; Gen. Dir ENO 1998–2002.

PAYNE, Patricia; singer (mezzo-soprano); b. 1942, Dunedin, New Zealand. *Education:* studied in Sydney and London. *Career:* debut at Covent Garden, 1974, as Schwertleite in Die Walküre: returned as Ulrica in Un Ballo in Maschera, Azucena, Erda in Das Rheingold, First Norn in Götterdämmerug and Filippyevna in Eugene Onegin, 1989; Barcelona, 1974–75, as La Cieca in La Gioconda and as Erda; Bayreuth Festival and San Francisco Opera, 1977; La Scala, Milan, 1978 as Ulrica; Verona Festival, 1980; Guest appearances at Frankfurt Opera and the Metropolitan, New York (debut 1980 as Ulrica, sang in La Gioconda, 1983); Has sung Gaea in the British premiere of Strauss's Daphne, Opera North, 1987; Appearances with English National Opera in The Love for Three Oranges, Salome and The Magic Flute; Sang Prokofiev's Princess Clarissa with Opera North at the 1989 Edinburgh Festival; Season 1992 as Herodias in Salome at Wellington; Sang the Witch in Hansel and Gretel and Auntie in Peter Grimes at Wellington, 1996; Concert repertoire includes the Wesendonck Lieder, Bach's St John Passion (in Paris), the Alto Rhapsody and Beethoven's 9th (Spain), Alexander Nevsky and the Mozart Requiem (London, Festival Hall). *Recordings include:* Un Ballo in Maschera and Peter Grimes; Beethoven's Missa Solemnis. *Honours:* Sidney Sun Aria Winner, 1966; Prize Winner, 's-Hertogenbosch Competition, 1972.

PAYNTER, John (Frederick); University Professor; b. 17 July 1931, England; m. 1st Elizabeth Hill, 1956, deceased 1998, 1 d; 2nd Joan Minetta Burrows, 2003. *Education:* GTCL, Trinity College of Music, London, 1952; DPhil, York, 1971. *Career:* Teacher, Primary and Secondary Schools, 1954–62; Lecturer, Music, CF Mott College of Education, Liverpool, 1962–65; Principal Lecturer/Head, Department of Music, Bishop Otter College, Chichester, 1965–69; Lecturer 1969,

Senior Lecturer 1974–82, Professor of Music/Head, Department of Music, University of York, 1982–94; Professor Emeritus, 1994–. *Compositions:* Choral and Instrumental Works including: Landscapes, 1972; The Windhover, 1972; May Magnificat, 1973; God's Grandeur, 1975; Sacraments of Summer, 1975; Galaxies for Orchestra, 1977; The Voyage of St Brendan, 1978; The Visionary Hermit, 1979; The Inviolable Voice, 1980; String Quartet No. 1, 1981; Cantata for the Waking of Lazarus, 1981; The Laughing Stone, 1982; Contrasts for Orchestra, 1982; Variations for Orchestra and Audience, 1983; Conclaves, 1984; Piano Sonata, 1987; Four Sculptures of Austin Wright, for Orchestra, 1991, 1994; String Quartet, No. 2; Time After Time, 1991; Breakthrough, for 2 pianos, 2002; Ouverture d'Urgence, for 2 pianos, 2003. *Publications include:* Sound and Silence, with P Aston, 1970; Hear and Now, 1972; The Dance and The Drum, with E Paynter, 1974; All Kinds of Music, vols 1–3, 1976, vol. 4, 1979; Sound Tracks, 1978; Music in the Secondary School Curriculum, 1982; Sound and Structure, 1992; Editor, Series, Resources of Music; Joint Editor, British Journal of Music Education; Companion to Contemporary Musical Thought; Between Old Words and New: writings on music by W Mellers, 1997. *Honours:* O.B.E., 1985; Honorary GSM, 1986. Leslie Boosey Award, 1998. *Address:* Westfield House, Newton upon Derwent, York YO41 4DA, England.

PAZDERA, Jindrich; Violinist and Conductor; b. 25 July 1954, Zilina, Czechoslovakia; m. 23 Jan 1982, one s. *Education:* Moscow State Conservatory, 1974–79; Violin Class by Leonid Kogan, graduated with honours, 1979. *Career:* Debut: Bratislava, Violin Concerto No. 2, by Karol Szymanowski, with the Slovak Philharmonic Orchestra, 1974; Concerts in 24 countries in Europe, America and Asia, as soloist with orchestras and as a chamber musician (violin and piano, Bohemia Piano Trio); Teacher: Bratislava Secondary Music School, 1983–94; Prague Academy of Arts, 1991–; Reader of Violin, 1995–; Repertoire: 25 violin concertos and many recital programmes; Numerous first performances of contemporary Slovak and Czech works; mem. Slovak Music Association; Czech Association of Music Artists and Scientists; Stamic Quartet (string) 1st Violin 2001–. *Recordings:* CD: As Violinist: Violin Concertos, Vivaldi, 1990; Le Quattro Stagioni, Vivaldi, 1992; Piano Trio works by Beethoven, Dvořák, 1995; Violin works by W A Mozart, 1997; Dvořák, Serenade and Sextet in A major; Schubert complete works for Violin and Piano; As Conductor: Chamber Orchestra works by Suk, Barber, Bruckner and Shostakovich, 1993; live recording violin/piano recital in Kioi Hall Tokyo, Beethoven, Janáček, Martinů, Smetana, 2003; Stamic Quartet, Smetana, Dvořák, Mozart, Schubert, Janáček, 2002–03. *Publications:* A Reconstruction of a W A Mozart's Sinfonia Concertante in A, for Violin, Viola and Cello (K104-320e), A World Premiere, 1991, CD Rec, 1997; Translations of Methodical and Muspsychological Works of Russian Authors (V P Bronin, G Kogan); Selected Chapters from the Method of Violin Playing, 1999. *Honours:* A Frico Kafenda Slovak National Music Award, 1985. *Address:* Luzická 8, 120 00 Prague, Czech Republic. *E-mail:* jindrich@pazdera.biz. *Website:* www.pazdera.biz.

PEACOCK, Lucy; Singer (Soprano); b. 21 June 1947, Jacksonville, Florida, USA. *Education:* North West University, USA, and at the Opera Studio of the Deutsche Oper Berlin. *Career:* Debut: Berlin 1969, as the Milliner in Der Rosenkavalier; Sang in Berlin as Flotow's Martha, Mozart's Pamina, Countess and Servilia, Cavalli's Calisto, Micaela in Carmen and Rosina in Il Barbiere di Siviglia; Guest appearances in Düsseldorf, Vienna, Munich, Hamburg, Turin, Geneva, Paris and London; Bayreuth 1985, as Freia in Das Rheingold and in Die Walküre and Götterdämmerung; Sang Eva in Die Meistersinger at the 1988 Festival; Sang Mathilde in Guillaume Tell at Catania, 1987; Deutsche Oper Berlin as Marenka in The Bartered Bride and as Myrtocle in Die Toten Augen by d'Albert; Created the title role in Desdemona und ihre Schwestern by Siegfried Matthus, Schwetzingen 1992; Princesse de Bouillon in Adriana Lecouvreur at Adelaide, 1994; Gertrud in Hansel and Gretel at the Berlin Deutsche Oper, 1998; Season 2000 at the Deutsche Oper in Die Frau ohne Schatten and Der Rosenkavalier; Television appearances include Martha, in Flotow's opera. *Current Management:* Ingpen & Williams Ltd, 7 St George's Court, 131 Putney Bridge Road, London, SW15 2PA, England.

PEARCE, Alison (Margaret); Singer (soprano); b. 5 Aug. 1953, Bath, England. *Education:* Dartington College of Arts, 1971–72; AGSM, distinction in Performance, Guildhall School of Music and Drama, 1972–77; Certificate of Advanced Musical Studies, 1975–77; With Pierre Bernac, Paris, 1977–78; Gerhard Husch, Munich, 1980–81. *Career:* Debut: Wigmore Hall, London; International soloist, oratorio, concert, opera, recital; Regular performances, all major choirs, orchestras and conductors including Colin Davis, Charles Groves, David Willcocks, James Lockhart, Steuart Bedford, Sylvain Cambreling, Libor Pesek; Major festivals: Three Choirs, Cheltenham, Llandaff, St Davids, Brighton, Flanders, France, Netherlands, Germany, Spain, Norway, Philippines, Poland, Israel; Soloist, world premieres: Sinfonia Fidei (A.

Hoddinott), Six Psalms (D. Muldowney), Music's Empire (J. McCabe); Hell's Angels (P. Patterson), Requiem (J. Bartley); Regular international television and radio appearances include 1995–96 BBC Fairest Isles series, Eugenie (The Rising of the Moon, N. Maw), Diana (The Olympians, A. Bliss), Bronwen, (Bronwen, J. Holbrooke); Television debut, 1982, Hallé Orchestra; British Opera debut, title role in Lucia di Lammermoor, 1982; Other roles include Violetta (La Traviata), Abigaille (Nabucco), Manon (Manon Lescaut), Elisabeth (Tannhäuser), Tosca, Fidelio; Season 2003–04: numerous recitals and opera galas, Mahler 8th, Verdi Requiem, Vaughan-Williams Sea Symphony, Tosca, R. Strauss Four Last Songs, Finzi Dies Natalis, Handel Messiah, Gounod Faust in UK, Italy, Belgium, Netherlands, Germany, Poland, China. *Current Management:* Ariette Drost, Netherlands. *Address:* PO Box 223, Covent Garden, London WC2H 9BY, England. *E-mail:* divapearce@hotmail.com.

PEARCE, Michael; Composer; b. 25 March 1954, Windsor, New South Wales, Australia. *Education:* BA, 1978, BMus (Hons), 1979 (study with Peter Sculthorpe), University of Sydney; Sussex University, with Jonathan Harvey, 1980. *Career:* Faculty Member, New South Wales Conservatory, 1981–; University of Sydney, 1990; Active interest in urban aboriginal music. *Compositions include:* Kynesis, for string quartet, flute, guitar and harpsichord, 1978; Eulogy, for flute, percussion and piano, 1979; Interiors, for violin, cello, flute, carinet and percussion, 1981; Deserts I for 4 percussion, 1982; Deserts II and III for ensembles, 1982–83; Chamber Symphony, 1987; Canciones, for soprano and 7 instruments, 1990; Oh Tierra, Esperame for soprano and piano, 1991; Chamber Symphony No. 2, 1991; Commissions from Synergy and Seymour Group. *Honours:* Sarah Makinson Prize for Composition, 1979. *Address:* c/o APRA, 1a Eden Street, Crows Nest, NSW 2065, Australia.

PEARCE, Michael; Singer (Baritone); b. 1945, Chelmsford, Essex, England. *Education:* Choral Scholar at St John's College, Cambridge; Study with Otakar Kraus and Elizabeth Fleming. *Career:* Concert appearances in China, Canada, Brazil and throughout Europe; Repertory includes Mozart Requiem (at Bruges), Monteverdi Vespers (Maastricht), Bach B Minor Mass (Turin and Edinburgh), Messiah (London and Brighton) and Brahms Requiem (Royal Festival Hall); Haydn's Theresienmesse at Windsor, The Creation at the London Barbican and Schöpfungsmesse at the Queen Elizabeth Hall; Opera roles include Ortel in Meistersinger and 5th Jew in Salome, both at the Royal Opera House, Claudius in Handel's Agrippina with Midsummer Opera, Lysiart in Weber's Euryanthe with New Sussex Opera and Beethoven's Rocco; Season 1996–97 with A Child of our Time by Tippett, the Berlioz Messe Solennelle and Elijah in Norway; Mozart's Requiem and Carmina Burana in Spain; Verdi Requiem at Canterbury Cathedral and Messiah with David Willcocks; Christus in Bach's St John Passion in London, St Matthew Passion at Salisbury and the B Minor Mass at Beverley Minster; Season 1998–99 with Germont for Opera Brava, Mozart's Count for Kentish Opera, Dundas in the premiere of David Horne's Friend of the People; Concerts include Missa Solemnis, B minor Mass, the Dream of Gerontius and A Child of Our Time. *Recordings include:* Handel Coronation Anthems under Simon Preston; Bach B Minor Mass, Edinburgh 1990. *Honours:* Winner, first English Song Award at the Brighton Festival. *Address:* 1 Homelands Copse, Fernhurst, Haslemere, Surrey GU27 3JQ, England.

PEARCE, Richard; Conductor, Organist and Pianist; b. 1965, England. *Education:* Organ Scholar at Trinity College, Cambridge; Guildhall School, London. *Career:* Tours with Trinity College Choir to North America and Far East; Conductor, accompanist and organist throughout Britain, including Purcell Room, Wigmore Hall, and BBC and commercial broadcasts; Accompanist at 1997 Cardiff Singer of the World Competition; Conductor of Whitehall Choir at St John's Smith Square (Handel's Israel in Egypt, 2000), engagements with BBC Singers; Season 1999–2000 with recitals at the Louvre, Paris, and Tokyo; Performances at the London Prom Concerts and in France. *Recordings include:* Stanford, Fauré and Christmas Music, with BBC Singers; Mahler 4th Symphony, with Northern Sinfonia. *Address:* c/o BBC Singers, BBC Broadcasting House, Portland Place, London, W1 1AA, England.

PEARLMAN, Martin; Conductor, Harpsichordist and Composer; b. 21 May 1945, Chicago, USA. *Education:* Studied with Karel Husa at Cornell University (BA 1967) and with Gustav Leonhardt, harpsichord, in the Netherlands, 1967–68; MM in composition with Yehudi Wyner at Yale University (1971) and further harpsichord study with Ralph Kirkpatrick. *Career:* Founder and director of early music group, Banchetto Musicale, 1973 (named Boston Baroque from 1992); Faculty member at University of Massachusetts at Boston, 1976–81; Many tours as harpsichordist in repertory which includes D Scarlatti and Couperin family; US premieres of works by Handel, Rameau and other Baroque composers, as conductor; Handel's Semele at the Kennedy Center, Washington DC, 1995. *Publications include:* Performing editions of Monteverdi's L'Incoronazione di Poppea, Purcell's Comical History of

Don Quixote, and Mozart's fragment, Lo Sposo Deluso; Complete edition of the harpsichord music of Armand-Louis Couperin. *Honours:* Erwin Bodky Award, 1972; Prize-winner at 1974 Bruges Competition. *Address:* c/o Washington Opera (Artists Contracts), John F Kennedy Center for the Arts, Washington DC 20566, USA.

PEARSON, Gail; Singer (Soprano); b. 1970, Neath, Wales. *Education:* Studied at Royal Northern College of Music. *Career:* With Welsh National Opera has sung Gilda, Despina, Oscar (Un Ballo in Maschera), Clorinda (Cenerentola) and Musetta (1999); Jano in Jenůfa at Glyndebourne, Mozart's Barbarina for Scottish Opera and Ninette in La Finta Semplice for the Buxton Festival; Oberto in Handel's Alcina at Zürich and for English National Opera, 1999; Other roles include Mimi, Micaela and Susanna; Concerts at Bournemouth, Aix-en-Provence Festival and Wigmore Hall, London. *Address:* c/o Harlequin Agency Ltd, 203 Fidlas Road, Cardiff CF4 5NA, Wales.

PECCHIOLI, Benedetta; Singer (Mezzo-Soprano); b. 1949, Italy. *Career:* Debut: Piccola Scala, as Clarina in La Cambiale di Matrimonio, 1973; Appearances at Monte Carlo from 1974, Rouen, 1974–75, Maggio Musicale, Florence, 1976–77, in Henze's Il Re Cervo and as Fenena in Nabucco; Spoleto Festival, 1976, as Cenerentola, Geneva, 1980 and 1986, Brussels, 1982 and 1987; Metropolitan Opera debut, 1983, as Rosina; Further engagements at Teatro Regio Turin, Bilbao Festival, Teatro Massimo Palermo and Aix-en-Provence Festival (Meg Page, 1971); Concert appearances in the Ring at Paris, and at Carnegie Hall, New York; La Scala, Milan, 1989, in Rossi's Orfeo; Other roles include Fidalma in Il Matrimonio Segreto, Liseta in Il Mondo della Luna, Erilda in Le Pescatrici by Haydn, Maddalena, Federica in Luisa Miller, Donizetti's Smeton in Anna Bolena and Orsini in Lucrezia Borgia, and Geneviève in Pelléas et Mélisande. *Recordings include:* Il Guiramento by Mercadante; Demetrio e Polibio by Rossini; Donizetti's Pia de Tolomei. *Address:* c/o Teatro alla Scala, Via Filodrammatici 2, Milan, Italy.

PECI, Aleksandër; Composer; b. 24 April 1951, Tirana, Albania. *Education:* Jordan Misja Art Lyceum, Tirana, 1965–69; Tirana Conservatory, 1969–74. *Career:* Musical Director at Përmeti, 1974–77; Composer-in-residence, Tirana Reuve Theatre, 1977–99; Amsterdam International Composers Workshop, 1992. *Compositions:* Sonata, violin and piano, 1972; Suite for flute and strings, 1974; Two cello concertos, 1974, 1982; Variations, horn and orchestra, 1975; The Kids and the Wolf, ballet, 1979; 1st Symphony, vocal soloists and orchestra, 1984; Piano concerto, 1980; Symphony no. 2, 1985–88; Four Rhapsodies for orchestra, 1977–87; Land of the Sun, low voice and orchestra, 1989; Suite for string quartet, 1990; Dialogue Liturgique, 1993; Epic of Gilgamesh for narrator, solo female voices and tape, 1997; Raindrops on Glass, soprano and tape, 1997; Broken Dream, bassoon, 1998; Remodelage piano, 1998; Le paradis des enfants for children's chorus, piano, percussion and ensemble, 1998; Polycentrum for strings, 1999. *Address:* c/o Vereniging Buma, PO Box 725, 1180 AS Amstelveen, Netherlands.

PECKOVA, Dagmar; Singer (Mezzo-Soprano); b. 4 April 1961, Chrudim, Czechoslovakia. *Education:* Studied at Prague Conservatory and in Dresden. *Career:* Sang at Dresden Staatsoper, 1987–, as Cherubino, Rosina and a Dryad in Ariadne auf Naxos; Berlin Staatsoper, 1989–, as Dorabella, Konchakovna in Prince Igor, Hansel, and in Der Kaiser von Atlantis by Ullmann; Guest appearances elsewhere in Germany and in Czechoslovakia; Season 1992 as Jenny in Aufstieg und Fall der Stadt Mahagonny at Stuttgart Staatsoper and Olga in Eugene Onegin at the Théâtre du Châtelet, Paris; Season 1998 as Cherubino for the Royal Opera, London, and Varvara in Katya Kabanova at Salzburg; Season 2000 as Weill's Jenny at Stuttgart, and Pilgrim in the premiere of L'Amour de loin, by Saariaho, at Salzburg; Concert repertoire includes Requiems by Mozart, Dvořák and Verdi, Mahler's 2nd Symphony and Debussy's Le Martyre de St Sebastien. *Address:* c/o Stuttgart Staatsoper, Oberer Schlossgarten 6, 7000 Stuttgart, Germany.

PECORARO, Herwig; Tenor; b. 1959, Bludenz, Switzerland. *Education:* Studied at the Bregenz Conservatory. *Career:* Sang at the Graz Opera, 1985–90 and Bregenz Festival from 1985 as a Priest in Die Zauberflöte and the Steuermann in Fliegende Holländer; Sang at Vienna Staatsoper from 1991 notably as Pedrillo and Steuermann; Other engagements at Nice and the Smetana Theatre in Prague; Appeared at the Vienna Volksoper in 1992 in Dantons Tod; Season 2000–01 as Mozart's Pedrillo at the Vienna Staatsoper and Rosillon in Die Lustige Witwe at Leipzig. *Address:* c/o Vienna Staatsoper, Opernring 2, 1010 Vienna, Austria.

PEDANI, Paolo; Singer (Bass); b. 1930, Italy. *Education:* Studied in Milan. *Career:* Sang in Cherubini's L'Osteria Portoghese and Falla's Vida Breve at La Scala, 1950–51; Appearances at Bologna, Genoa, Trieste and Venice from 1954, Wexford Festival, 1956–59, Spoleto, 1961; Aix-en-Provence Festival from 1959, in Haydn's Mondo della Luna and as Masetto; Venice, 1966, in premiere of La Metamorfosi di Bonaventura by Malipiero; Florence, 1976, in the Italian premiere of Henze's Il Re

Cervo; Guest appearances at Barcelona, Catania, Mexico City and Antwerp; Other roles included Rossini's Alidoro, Don Magnifico, Taddeo and Basilio, Don Pasquale, Don Alfonso, Melitone in La Forza del Destino and Paisiello's Basilio; Character roles from 1970.

PEDERSEN, Laura; Opera singer (Soprano); b. 1969, Sioux City, Iowa, USA. *Career:* Debut: Donna Elvira in Don Giovanni for Tirana Opera, Albania, this production was a cultural gift from the Austrian Government to the Albanian people in 1996; Theatre engagements, Lyric Opera, Cleveland, 1991–94, educational outreach programs, apprenticeships and main stage and leading roles; Cleveland opera, 1990–97, educational outreach programs, mini-residencies, leading roles; Tirana Opera, 1996, mainstage leading role; Tulsa Opera, mainstage role; Bremen Theater, Bremen, Germany, leading roles; Norina, Don Pasquale; Maria, West Side Story; Oscar, The Masked Ball; Amour, Orphée; Susanna, Marriage of Figaro; Adele, Die Fledermaus. *Address:* 347 Morewood PKW, Rocky River, Ohio 44116, USA.

PEDERSON, Monte; Singer (Bass-Baritone); b. 1960, Sunnyside, Washington, USA. *Education:* Studied in USA and with Hans Hotter in Munich. *Career:* Debut: San Francisco Opera, as M Gobineau in Menotti's The Medium, 1986; Engaged at various opera houses in USA and at Bremen, 1987–88, notably as Szymanowski's King Roger; Montpellier and Bregenz, 1988–89, as Wagner's Dutchman; Minister in Fidelio at Orange, Deutsche Oper Berlin and Stuttgart, 1989–90; Sang Pizarro in a new production of Fidelio at Covent Garden, 1990, followed by concert performance at the Festival Hall, conducted by Lorin Maazel; Season 1990–91 as Shishkov in From the House of the Dead at Cologne, Orestes in Elektra at San Francisco and Amfortas at La Scala; Salzburg Festival, 1992, as Shishkov, Houston Opera, 1992, as Amfortas in a production of Parsifal by Robert Wilson; Other roles include Jochanaan in Salome, Basle, 1989, and Angelotti; Sang Nick Shadow at the 1996 Salzburg Festival; Golaud in Pelléas at Brussels, Scarpia at Stuttgart, 1998; Sang Kurwenal at the NY Met, 1999; Season 2000 as Debussy's Golo at Toronto, Orestes in Elektra at the Munich Staatsoper and Britten's Claggart at Cagliari. *Recordings include:* Video of Covent Garden Fidelio. Address Théâtre Royale de la Monnaie, 4 Léopoldstrasse, 1000 Brussels, Belgium.

PEDICONI, Fiorella; Singer (Soprano); b. 1950, Italy. *Education:* Studied at Conservatorio Giuseppe Verdi, Milan. *Career:* Appeared at first in Il Barbiere di Siviglia and I Puritani at opera houses in Italy; Sang Violetta at Glyndebourne, 1988, Gilda at Covent Garden, 1989; Appeared in Bussotti's L'Ispirazione at Turin, 1991, as Sandrina in La Finta Giardiniera at Alessandria; Has also sung in operas by Haydn, Pergolesi, Rossini, Respighi, Cimarosa and Donizetti at such opera centres as La Scala, Milan; San Carlo, Naples; La Fenice, Venice; Teatro dell'Opera, Rome; Grand Théâtre, Geneva; Théâtre des Champs Elysées, Paris, and the Gran Liceo, Barcelona.

PEDUZZI, Richard; stage designer and costume designer; b. 28 Jan. 1943, Argentan, France. *Education:* Academie de Dessin, Paris. *Career:* collaborations with producer Patrice Chéreau have included L'Italiana at Spoleto, 1969, and Les Contes d'Hoffman and Lulu at the Paris Opéra, 1974, 1979; Der Ring des Nibelungen at Bayreuth, 1976; Lucio Silla for La Scala, Théâtre des Amandiers in Nanterre and Théâtre de la Monnaie, Brussels, 1984–85; Co-Artistic Director with Chéreau of Théâtre des Amandiers, 1982–89; Stage designs for Tony Palmer's production of Les Troyens at Zürich, 1990, Don Giovanni at Rome, 1991; Costume designs for War and Peace at San Francisco, 1991, Le nozze di Figaro (designs), Salzburg, 1995. *Address:* c/o Teatro dell'Opera, Piazza B Gigli 8, 00184 Rome, Italy.

PEEBLES, Antony (Gavin Ian); Concert Pianist; b. 26 Feb. 1946, Southborough, England; m. Frances Clark, 1982, divorced 1999, 2 s., 2 d. *Education:* BMus, Trinity College, Cambridge (1968); Piano with Peter Katin. *Career:* Debut: Wigmore Hall, London, 1969; Has given concerts in 125countries; Soloist with London Symphony, Royal Philharmonic, Philharmonia, Hallé, Royal Liverpool Philharmonic, City of Birmingham Symphony, BBC Philharmonic Orchestras and BBC National Orchestra of Wales. *Recordings:* Copland Fantasy; Bartók Studies; Dallapiccola Quaderno Musicale di Anna Libera; Ravel Gaspard de la Nuit, Miroirs, Sonatine, Pavane; Recital of Liszt operatic transcriptions; Schubert Lieder transcribed by Liszt. *Honours:* 1st Prize, BBC Piano Competition, 1971; 1st Prize, Debussy Competition, 1972. *Current Management:* Allegro Artists, Conifers, Roselands Avenue, Mayfield, East Sussex TN 20 6EB, England. *Address:* 130 Roehampton Vale, London SW15 3RX, England.

PEEBLES, Charles (Ross); Conductor; b. 31 Aug. 1959, Hereford, England. *Education:* ARCM, MA (Cantab), Trinity College, Cambridge, 1980; Guildhall School of Music and Drama, 1980–81; Conducting Fellow, Tanglewood, 1982,. *Career:* Orchestras worked with include City of London Sinfonia, City of Birmingham Symphony, Bournemouth Sinfonietta, European Community Chamber Orchestra, London Mozart Players, English Chamber Orchestra, BBC Symphony Orchestra,

Scottish Chamber Orchestra, Nash Ensemble, Composers Ensemble, London Sinfonietta, Vienna Chamber Orchestra; Since 1992 all major orchestras of Spain including Orquesta Nacional de Espana; Opera work includes Opera 80/English Touring Opera, Garsington Opera, Glyndebourne; Broomhill Opera. *Recordings:* Orchestral Works by M Berkeley and Leighton, also Honegger's Amphion; Andrew Toovey, The Juniper Tree, opera. *Honours:* Winner, 1st Prize, 1st Cadaques International Conducting Competition, Spain, 1992. *Current Management:* The Music Partnership Ltd, 41 Aldebert Terrace, London SW8 1BH, England. *Address:* 71 Bartholomew Road, London NW5 2AH, England.

PEEL, Ruth; Singer (Mezzo-soprano); b. 29 March 1966, Rinteln, Germany. *Education:* Royal Northern College of Music. *Career:* Opera roles have included Third Lady in Die Zauberflöte at Geneva and the 1994 Aix Festival, Kate Pinkerton at Antwerp and the Page in Salome at Covent Garden, Kate in Britten's Owen Wingrave for Glyndebourne Touring Opera, the title role in The Rape of Lucretia, under Stuart Bedford, and the Countess of Essex in Gloriana for Opera North; Concerts include recitals in the Covent Garden Festival, Wigmore Hall, Glasgow, Manchester and St John's Smith Square, London (Young Songmakers' Almanac, with Graham Johnson); Concerts include Pergolesi's Stabat Mater at the Barbican Hall, Mahler's 2nd Symphony in Lithuania, Beethoven's 9th in Japan under Ozawa and Holst Songs for the BBC; Beethoven's 9th under Osawa for opening of Winter Olympics, 1998; Mahler 2 in Brisbane, Holst and Brahms recitals for BBC Radio 3. *Recordings:* Brahms recital. *Honours:* Claire Croiza French Song Prize, at the RNCM; Kathleen Ferrier Decca Prize, 1993; Lieder Prize, RNCM. *Address:* Cinema Binatang, 141 King Henry's Road, London NW3 3RD, England.

PEETERS, Harry; Singer (Bass); b. 7 Aug. 1959, Roermond, Netherlands. *Education:* Studied in Maastricht. *Career:* Debut: Vienna Volksoper, 1984 as Rossini's Basilio; Paris Opéra, 1985 in Rossini's Le Siège de Corinthe; Deutsche Oper am Rhein, Düsseldorf, from 1987; Geneva from 1987 as Bluebeard, by Dukas; Seneca in Poppea and the villains in Les Contes d'Hoffmann; San Francisco and Houston, 1992 as Gurnemanz in Parsifal; Season 1994 as Sarastro at Los Angeles and in the premiere of P Schat's Symposium at Amsterdam; Cologne Opera as Escamillo; Orestes in Elektra, 1995; Ariodate in Handel's Xerxes; Other repertory includes Idomeneo, Oedipus Rex, Poliuto by Donizetti and Monteverdi's Orfeo; Season 1998 as Kaspar in Der Freischütz at Cologne; Wagner's Amfortas for Netherlands Opera and Orestes at Catania; Sang Wotan at Münster, 1999; Season 2000–01 at Cologne as Prus in The Makropoulas Case and Alberich in Das Rheingold. *Address:* Cologne Opera, Offenbachplatz, 50505 Cologne, Germany.

PEHRSON, Joseph (Ralph); Composer and Pianist; b. 14 Aug. 1950, Detroit, Michigan, USA; m. Linda Past, 13 July 1985. *Education:* BA 1972, MM 1973, DMA 1981, University of Michigan; Graduate Studies, Eastman School of Music. *Career:* Harmonic Etude for Solo Horn at Merkin Concert Hall, New York, 1988 performed by Francis Orval; Hornucopia by the Francis Orval Horn Ensemble, Budapest, Hungary, 1989; Several works at Greenwich House, New York City, 1992 including Tonreiter, Lewis Carroll Songs, Etheroscape and Windwork; Several works performed by Goliard Concerts at their Warwick Music Festival, New York, 1992 and on tour in USA, 1992–93; Guest composer at University of Akron, 1993; Exhilarations for Clarinet, Cello and Piano was performed by Composers Concordance, 1993; Thanatopsis was performed by Long Island Composers Alliance, 1994; Commission by St Luke's Chamber Ensemble for a piece for trumpet and strings, entitled Trumpet in a New Surrounding, performed 1997 at the Dia Center for the Arts, Manhattan; Commission by the Archaeus Ensemble, Romania, for a new piece for nine players, Wild, Wild, West, performed 1997, Bacau, Romania; Three Piano Pieces by Jeffrey Jacob, in Rees, Germany, 1998; Performance of Lustspiel at University of Colorado, 1998; Performed Exhilarations at University of Chicago, 1998, and Three Arts Club, Chicago, 1998; Tour of Russia, 2001. *Compositions include:* For Orchestra: Chromakkordion, 1995; Chamber Ensemble: Concerto for Horn and 8 Instruments, 1987; Confessions of the Goliards for Tenor Voice, Flute, Violin and Cello, 1992; Hornorarium for Four Horns, 1994; Forest of Winds, for Wind Ensemble, 1994; Trios and duos include: Arecibo for Piano and Percussion, 1976; Exhilarations for Clarinet, Cello and Piano, 1993; Jollity for Violin and Harp, 1994; For Solo Instruments: Three Pianopieces, 1991; Panoply for Solo Flute, 1992; Lake Fantasy for Solo Oboe, 1993; Spectral Harmony, alto sax, horn, 1997; Stringing, violin and piano, 1999; Electronic Pieces, Unheard Verklärte Neunzehn, 2000. *Recordings:* Thanatopsis; Trumpet in a New Surrounding, trumpet and string quartet, 1996; Wild, Wild West, for 7 instruments, 1997; The Nature of the Universe II, for baroque flutes. *Address:* c/o Composers Concordance, PO Box 36–20548 (PABT), New York, NY 10129, USA. *E-mail:* joseph@composersconcordance.org. *Website:* www.composersconcordance.org.

PEINEMANN, Edith; Violinist and Professor; b. 3 March 1939, Mainz, Germany. *Education:* Guildhall School of Music, London; Violin lessons with father, Robert Peinemann, Heinz Stanske, Max Rostal. *Career:* 1st Prize at ARD Competition, Munich; Appearances resulting with Solti, Szell, Steinberg, Karajan, Herbig, Tennstedt, Dohnányi, Boulez, Yan Pascal Tortelier, Kempe, Keilberth, Munch, Barbirolli, Sargent, with leading orchestras world-wide; Carnegie Hall debut with Szell and Cleveland Orchestra, 1965; Festivals including Salzburg, Lucerne, Marlboro Chamber Music; Professor, Academy of Music, Frankfurt, 1976–; Performances of the Beethoven Concerto with the Detroit Symphony, the Mendelssohn in Chicago, and the Pfitzner in Cleveland and with the BBC Philharmonic, 1991. *Recordings:* with DGG. *Honours:* Plaquette Eugene Ysaÿe, Liège. *Address:* c/o Gottschalk Impresario A/S, Tollbugaten 2, N–0152 Oslo, Norway.

PELINKA, Werner; Composer and Pianist; b. 21 Jan. 1952, Vienna, Austria; m. Liliane Flühler, 26 Mar 1976, 2 d. *Education:* Hochschule für Welthandel, Vienna; University of Michigan; Konservatorium der Stadt Wien; MA, Hochschule für Musik und darstellende Kunst, Vienna, 1985; DPhil, University of Vienna, 1985. *Career:* Concerts with horn player Roland Horvath (member of Vienna Philharmonic) as Ensemble Wiener Horn; His own compositions played in Grosser Musikvereinssaal and Grosser Konzerthaussaal in Vienna and on television; Teaching, Konservatorium Wien, Toho-Vienna Music Academy; Since 1992, Manager of Viennese Children's Music Festival, Kinderklang; Formation of a Tomatis Institute in Vienna (training in Paris), 1994–95; Founding mem., Imago. *Compositions:* Op 1–40 e.g. Op 1: Pater Noster; Op 5: Sinfonietta con Corale; Op 9: Trio Reflexionen; Op 14: Passio Silvae; Op 24: Concerto for Jon; Op 28: Die Erbsenprinzessin, Opera after H Chr Andersen (Libretto, Martin Auer), 1995. *Recordings:* Horn und Klavier 4, (with op 2 op 5 and op 8) Werner Pelinka (piano) and Roland Horvath (horn); Österreichische Komponisten der Gegenwart, (with op 12) Brigitte Hübner (contralto), Werner Pelinka (piano); Passio Silvae, (with op 14) with Johannes Jokel (bass voice), Roland Horvath (horn) and Werner Pelinka (piano); Horn und Klavier 5 with op 24; New Music for Orchestra VMM with op 5 (ORF Symphonic Orchestra conducted by Christo Stanischeff, Soloist, Erwin Sükar, Horn); Trio Arabesque op 26 (oboe, bassoon, piano–Tonkünstler Ensemble); Diagonal, concert pieces for strings, op 27, Ruse Philharmonic conducted by Tsanko Delibozov, CD; CD, Musik-Sprache-Dichtung-Musik, with op 9. *Publications:* Die Vertonungen des lateinischen Paternoster der nachklassischen Zeit (Diss 1985, Vienna). *Address:* Gusenleithnergasse 30, 1140 Vienna, Austria.

PELLEGRINI, Maria; Singer (Soprano); b. 15 July 1943, Pescara, Italy. *Education:* Studied at the Opera School of the Royal Conservatory in Toronto. *Career:* Debut: With the Canadian Opera Company as the Priestess in Aida, 1963; Sang Gilda 1965; Appearances in Montreal, Toronto and Vancouver; Sadler's Wells Opera from 1967, Covent Garden from 1968, notably as Violetta, Micaela in Carmen and Madama Butterfly; Guest appearances in Genoa, Bologna, Parma and Trieste and with the Welsh National Opera; US debut Pittsburgh, 1975; Sang Musetta in Ottawa, 1980. *Recordings include:* Carmen.

PELLEGRINO, Ron(ald Anthony); Composer and Performer; b. 11 May 1940, Kenosha, Wisconsin, USA. *Education:* Studied at Lawrence University (BM, 1962) and with Rene Leibowitz and Rudolph Kolisch at University of Wisconsin (PhD, 1968). *Career:* Electronic Music Studio at University of Wisconsin from 1967; Director of the Electronic Music Studios at Ohio State University, 1968–70, and Oberlin Conservatory, 1970–73; Associate Professor at Texas Tech University, Lubbock, 1978–81; Founded electronic music performance ensembles Real Electric Symphony and Sonoma Electro-Acoustic Music Society. *Compositions include:* Electronic and Mixed Media; S&H Explorations, 1972; Metabiosis, 1972; Figured, 1972; Cries, 1973; Kaleidoscope, Electric Rags, 1976; Setting Suns and Spinning Daughters, 1978; Words and Phrases, 1980; Siberian News Release, 1981; Spring Suite, 1982; Laser Seraphim and Cymatic Music, 1982; Tape and Instruments: The End of the Affair, 1967; Dance Drama, 1967; Passage, 1968; Markings, 1969; Leda and the Swan, 1970; Phil's Float, 1974; Wavesong, 1975; Issue of the Silver Hatch, 1979. *Publications include:* An Electronic Music Studios Manual, 1969. *Honours:* National Endowment for the Arts and National Endowment for the Humanities grants for founding the Leading Edge contemporary music series. *Address:* c/o ASCAP, ASCAP Building, 1 Lincoln Plaza, New York, NY 10023, USA.

PELLEKOORNE, Anne; Singer (Contralto); b. 1957, Amsterdam, Netherlands. *Education:* Studied at the Hamburg Musikhochschule. *Career:* Concerts for German television and at Rome under Gerd Albrecht, Hindemith programme; Appearances at Wiesbaden and Zürich in Die Zauberflöte and Die Walküre; Wagner's Ring at Rome; Bavarian State Opera from 1989 in Salome and Der Rosenkavalier and the premiere of Bose's Schlachthof 5, 1996; Concert tour of Brazil, 1996; Sang Angustias in the premiere of Reimann's Bernarda Albas Haus,

Munich 2000. *Address:* Bavarian State Opera, Max-Joseph Platz, 80539 Munich, Germany.

PELLETIER, Louis-Philippe; Pianist and Professor; b. 1945, Montreal, Canada. *Education:* Studies with Lubka Kolessa, Claude Helffer, Harald Boje, Aloys Kontarsky. *Career:* Professor of Piano, Chair, Department of Piano, McGill University. *Recordings:* Piano Works, Bach, Beethoven, Schumann, Brahms, Debussy, Boulez, Messiaen, Stockhausen, Xenakis, Schoenberg, Berg, Webern, Vivier, Papineau-Couture, Garant. *Honours:* 1st Prize, Arnold Schoenberg Piano Competition, Rotterdam, 1979; Artist of the Year, Canadian Music Council, 1980. *Address:* Latitude 45, Arts Promotion Inc, 109 St Joseph Blvd West, Montreal, Quebec H2T 2P7, Canada.

PEČMAN, Rudolf; Czech academic; b. 12 April 1931, Staré Mesto u Frydku (Frydek-Místek). *Education:* Masaryk University, Brno. *Career:* Asst 1955, Docent 1984, Prof. 1990–, Philosophy Faculty, Masaryk Univ.; mem. Czech Music Soc., G-F-Händel-Gesellschaft, Halle (Saale). *Publications:* Josef Myslivecek und sein Opernepilog, Brno, 1970; Beethoven dramatik (Beethoven the Dramatic Composer), Hradec Králové, 1978; Beethovens Opernpläne, Brno, 1981; Josef Myslivecek, Prague, 1981; Georg Friedrich Händel, Prague, 1985; Eseje o Martinů (Essays about Martinů), Brno, 1989; F X Richter und seine 'Harmonischen Belehrungen', Michaelstein/Blankenburg, 1991; Style and Music 1600–1900 (in Czech), Brno 2nd Ed, 1996; The Attack on Antonín Dvořák (in Czech), Brno, 1992; The Stage Works of Ludwig van Beethoven (in Czech), Brno, 1999; Vladimir Helfert (in Czech), Brno, 2003. *Address:* Loosova 12, 638 00 Brno, Czech Republic. *Telephone:* 420 548 520 261.

PEMBERTON JOHNSON, Anne; Singer (Soprano); b. 3 Sept. 1958, New York, NY, USA. *Education:* New England Conservatory and Peabody Institute. *Career:* Sang in Heinz Holliger's Not I at Frankfurt, Paris and Almeida Festival, London; Appearances at Munich in George Crumb's Star Child conducted by Paul Daniel and at Salzburg Festival with the Ensemble Modern under Hans Zender; Premieres of works at Library of Congress and Kennedy Center, Washington DC; Recent engagements of Pli selon Pli by Boulez and Berg's Altenberg Lieder with RAI Milan and BBC Philharmonic Orchestras; Season 1992–93 with Stravinsky's Rossignol in The Hague, conducted by Edward Downes, and opening concert of Luigi Nono Festival of the Venice Biennale, 1993; Other conductors include Matthias Bamert and Peter Eötvös. *Current Management:* Ingpen & Williams Ltd, 7 St George's Court, 131 Putney Bridge Road, London, SW15 2PA, England.

PEÑA, Paco; Flamenco guitarist; b. 1 June 1942, Spain; m. Karin Vaessen 1982; two d. *Education:* Cordoba, Spain. *Career:* flamenco guitarist 1954–; founded Paco Peña Flamenco Co. 1970–, Centro Flamenco Paco Peña, Cordoba 1981–; performed at London Proms 2002. *Honours:* Ramon Montoya Prize 1983. *Address:* 4 Boscastle Road, London, NW5, England.

PENCARREG, Wyn; singer (baritone); b. 1965, Wales. *Education:* Royal Northern College of Music; masterclasses with Geraint Evans, Brigitte Fassbaender and Sherrill Milnes. *Career:* roles at RNCM included Britten's Bottom and John Bunyan in The Pilgrim's Progress, Glyndebourne Chorus from 1993; Sang Masetto with Glyndeburne Tour (1995), Mozart's Don Alfonso with Goldberg Festival Opera, Count for Mid Wales Opera, and Figaro for English Touring Opera; Sang Malcotent in premiere of Jonathan Dove's In Seach of Angels, for Mecklenburg Opera at the Covent Garden Festival, 1996; Season 1998 at the Glyndebourne Festival as Kuligin in Katya Kabanova and Servant in Capriccio. *Honours:* Erich Viether Memorial Award 1995. *Current Management:* Musichall, Vicarage Way, Ringmer, BN8 5LA, England. *Telephone:* (1273) 814240. *Fax:* (1273) 813637. *E-mail:* info@musichall.uk.com. *Website:* www.musichall.uk.com.

PENDACHANSKA, Alexandrina; Singer (Soprano); b. 1970, Bulgaria. *Education:* Studied with her mother, Valeri Popova. *Career:* Debut: Sang in concert at Sofia, 1987, with Violetta's Act 1 aria; Concert tour of West Germany, 1989; Performances of Traviata in Sofia and Bilbao; Performances of Lucia in Cairo and Sofia; Performances of Gilda in a new production of Rigoletto for Welsh National Opera, 1991; Concert engagements with the Sofia Philharmonic and other orchestras in Bulgaria, Moscow and Kiev; Lucia di Lammermoor (title role) in Dublin, Ophelia in Hamlet with Monte Carlo Opera, 1991–92; Sang Marie in La Fille du Régiment at Monte Carlo, 1996; Elisabetta in Donizetti's Roberto Devereux, Naples, 1998; Season 2000 as Donna Anna at Houston, Rossini's Ermione for Santa Fe Opera, Adalgisa in Florence and Lucrezia in Verdi's I Due Foscari at Naples. *Recordings:* Antonida in A Life for the Tsar by Glinka. *Honours:* Second Prize, International Competition, Bilbao, 1988; Winner, 23rd International Dvořák Competition in Prague, 1988; Pretoria Music Competition, 1st Prize, 1990. *Address:* c/o PG & PM, 7 Whitehorse Close, Royal Mile, Edinburgh, EH8 8BU, Scotland.

PENDERECKI, Krzysztof; Composer and Educator; b. 23 Nov. 1933, Debica, Poland; m. Elzbieta Solecka, 1965, 1 s., 1 d. *Education:* State Academy of Music, Kraków, Poland. *Career:* Professor, Kraków Academy of Music, Poland, 1958; Lecturer, Folkwang Academy, Essen, 1966–68; Scholarship to Berlin, Deutscher Akademischer Austausche-dienst, 1968; Principal, Rector, Professor Docent, State Academy of Music, Kraków, 1972–1987; Professor, Yale University, 1973–78; Principal Guest Conductor, NDR-Orchestra, Hamburg, 1988. *Compositions:* Dimensions der Zeit und der Stille, 1960; String Quartet No. 1, 1960; Anaklasis, 1960; Threnos for the Victims of Hiroshima, 1961; Polymorphia, 1961; Canon, 1962; Stabat Mater, 1962; Fluorescences, 1962; Capriccio for Oboe and Strings, 1964; Passio et Mors Domini Nostri Jesu Christi, secundum Lucam, 1966; De natura sonoris I, 1966; Dies Irae, 1967; Capriccio for Violin and Orchestra, 1967; Pittsburgh Overture, 1967; Capriccio per Siegfried Palm, 1968; The Devils of Loudun, Opera, 1969; Quartetto per Archi No. 2, 1968; Kosmogonia, 1970; Prelude, 1971; Utrenja, Grablegung und Auferstehung Christi, for 5 Soloists, 2 Choirs, Orchestra, 1971; De Natura Sonoris No. 2, 1971; Concerto Violoncello and Orchestra, 1966–72; Partita for Harpsichord and Orchestra, 1971; Ecloga VIII, for 6 Singers, 1972; Canticum Canticorum Salominis for 16 Part Chorus and Chamber Orchestra, 1973; Symphonie No. 1, 1973; Magnificat, 1974; Awakening of Jacob, for Orchestra, 1974; Violin Concerto, 1977; Paradise Lost (Rappresenta-zione), 1978; (Christmas) Symphony No. 2, 1980; Te Deum, 1980; Lacrimosa, 1980; Cello Concerto No. 2, 1982; Viola Concerto, 1983; Polish Requiem, 1983–84; The Black Mask, Opera, 1986; Song of Cherubim, 1986; Veni creator, 1987; Symphony No. 4, 1989; String Trio, 1991; Symphony No. 3, 1990–95; Ubu Rex, Opera, 1991; Symphony No. 5, 1992; Sinfonietta per archi, 1992; Flute Concerto, 1992; Clarinet Quintet, 1993; Sinfonietta No. 2 for clarinet and strings, 1994; Violin Concerto No. 2, 1995; The Seven Gates of Jerusalem for soloists, chorus and orchestra, 1997; Credo for soloists, choruses and orchestra, 1998; Sonata for Violin and Piano, 2000; Sextett for clarinet, french horn, string trio and piano, 2000; Concerto grosso for 3 violoncelli and orchestra, 2000–01; Concerto for piano and orchestra, 2001–2002' Largo for violoncello and orchestra, 2003. *Honours:* Many, including: North Rhine-Westphalia Award, 1966; Sibelius Award, 1967; Prix d'Italie, 1967, 1968; 1st Class State Award 1968; Gustav Charpentier Prize, 1971; Gottfried von Herder Prize, 1977; Arthur Honegger Music Award for Magnificat, 1978; Grand Medal of Paris, 1982; Dr L C Mult, Wolf Prize, 1987; Commander's Cross of the Order of Merit of the Federal Republic of Germany, 1990; University of Louisville Grawemeyer Award of Music Composition, 1992; Prize of the International Music Council/ UNESCO for Music, 1993; Crystal Award of Economic Forum, Davos, 1997; Grammy Award for Metamorphosen — Concerto for violin and orchestra no. 2, 1999; Cannes Classical Award as Living composer of the Year, 2000; Prince of Austrias award for the Arts Category, 20001; Staatspreis des Laudes Morelrheim-Westfalen, 2003. *Address:* c/o Schott Musik International, Weihergarten 5, 55116 Mainz, Germany.

PENDLEBURY, Sally; Cellist; b. 1960, England. *Education:* Studied at Chetham's Schhol of Music, in Düsseldorf and at New England Conservatory. *Career:* Led Cello Section of the European Community Youth Orchestra, 1982–85; Member of the Chamber Orchestra of Europe; Recitals with Natalia Gutman and Yuri Bashmet; Co-founded Vellinger String Quartet, 1990; Participated in master classes with Borodin Quartet at Pears-Britten School, 1991; Concerts at Ferrara Musica Festival, Italy and debut on South Bank with London premiere of Robert Simpson's 13th Quartet; BBC Radio 3 Debut, December 1991; Season 1992–93 with concerts in London, Glasgow, Cambridge, at Davos Festival, Switzerland and Crickdale Festival, Wiltshire; Wig-more Hall with Haydn (Op 54, No. 2), Gubaidulina and Beethoven (Op 59, No. 2), Purcell Room with Haydn's Seven Last Words. *Address:* c/o Georgina Ivor Associates (Vellinger Quartet), 66 Alderbrook Road, London SW12 8 AB, England.

PENHERSKI, Zbigniew; Composer; b. 26 Jan. 1935, Warsaw, Poland; m. Malgorzata, 1 s. *Education:* Composers Diploma, Warsaw Conserva-tory of Music, 1959. *Compositions include:* Musica Humana for baritone, choir and symphony orchestra, 1963; Missa Abstracta for tenor, reciting voice, choir and symphony orchestra, 1966; Street Music, chamber ensemble, 1966; Samson Put on Trial, radio opera, 1968; 3 Recitativi for soprano, piano and percussion, 1968; 3M-H1, electronic piece, 1969; Instrumental Quartet, 1970; Incantationi 1 Sextet for Percussion Instruments, 1972; The Twilight of Peryn, opera in 3 parts, 1972; Masurian Chronicles 2, for symphony orchestra and magnetic tape, 1973; Radio Symphony for 2, 1975; Anamnesis for symphony orchestra, 1975; String Play for string orchestra, 1980; Edgar: The Son of Walpor, opera in 3 parts, 1982; Jeux Partis for saxophone and percussion, 1984; 3 impressions for soprano, piano and four percussions, 1985; Scottish Chronicles for symphony orchestra, 1987; The Island of the Roses, chamber opera, 1989; Signals for Symphony orchestra 1992; Cantus for mixed choir, 1992; Signals No.2, 1995; Genesis for bass solo, vocal ensembles, reciting voices, selected instruments and electronic sounds,

1995; Introduction and Toccata for clarinet, trombone, cello and piano, 1998; Little Music for the End of Century for recorder, two percussions, organ and tape, 1999; Cantus II for mixed choir, 2000; Little String Litany for string orchestra, 2002; Lamentations for baritone and string quartet, 2003. *Address:* ul. Krucza 24A, 05–120 Legionowo by Warsaw, Poland. *Telephone:* (22) 7844163. *E-mail:* zpenherski@wp.pl. *Website:* www.zaiks.org.pl.

PENICKA, Miloslav; Australian, (b. Czech) composer; b. 16 April 1935, Ostrava, Czechoslovakia. *Education:* Prague Academy of Music and Arts, 1964, studied with Frantírek Pich and Emil Hlobil. *Career:* Abbotsleigh School, Wahroonga, 1969–75; Percussionist with the Sydney Symphony Orchestra, 1965–69; mem, Full Member, Australian Music Centre; Associate Writer Member, Australian Performing Right Association. *Compositions include:* Symphony, 1964; 4 Overtures, 1972, 1975, 1989, 2003; 2 Orchestral Suites, 1994, 1995; 2 Serenades for small orchestra, 1958, 1961; 2 Piano Concertos, 1963, 1996; Clarinet Concerto, 1977; Divertimento for Violin, Wind, Timpani and Bass, 1963; 3 String Quartets, 1962, 1969, 2002; Clarinet Quintet, 1967; Piano Quartet, 1973; Mosaics for Cor Anglais Quartet, 2003; 2 Piano Sonatas, 1958, 1979; Sonatinas for Violin and Piano, 1978, Cello and Piano, 1991, Piano, 1978; Four Pieces for Flute and Piano, 1977, Oboe and Piano, 1995; Music for String Orchestra: Divertimento, 1972, Sonatina, 1980, Partita, 1987, and Dance Suite, 1991; 3 Piano Cycles, 1990, 1996/2000; Piano pieces, vocal, and theatre music. *Address:* 9 Warraroon Road, Lane Cove 2066, Australia.

PENKOVA, Reni; Singer (Mezzo-soprano); b. 28 Oct. 1935, Tarnovo, Bulgaria. *Education:* Studied with Nadia Aladjem and Elena Doskova-Ricardi in Sofia. *Career:* Debut: Burgas 1960, as Olga in Eugene Onegin; Member of the National Opera Sofia from 1964; Guest appearances in Netherlands and England; Glyndebourne Festival 1971–77 as Olga, Pauline in The Queen of Spades, Dorabella in Così fan tutte and Meg Page in Falstaff; Other roles include Gluck's Orpheus, Cherubino, Octavian in Der Rosenkavalier, Amneris, and Angelina in La Cener-entola; Also heard in concert and oratorio; Member of the Bulgarian National Opera, Sofia, until 1991; Presently, Vocal Professor, State Musical Academie, Sofia; Further roles include Bart ók, (Bluebeard's Castle), Judith, 1975; Britten, (Midsummer Night's Dream), Oberon, 1982; Verdi (Nabucco), Fenena, 1976; Bellini, (Norma), Adalgisa, 1984; Donizetti, (La Favorita), Leonora, 1985; Cilea, (Adriana Lecouvreur), La Princesse de Bouillon, 1987. *Recordings include:* Prince Igor by Borodin (HMV). *Address:* 1202 Bulgaria Blvd, Slivnitza 212-A, Sofia, Bulgaria.

PENN, William (Albert); Composer; b. 11 Jan. 1943, Long Branch, New Jersey, USA. *Education:* Studied with Henri Pousseur and Maurico Kagel at the State University of New York at Buffalo, MA, 1967, and at Michigan State University, PhD, 1971; Further Study at Eastman School with Wayne Barlow. *Career:* Faculty member of Eastman School, 1971–78; Staff Composer at New York Shakespeare Festival, 1974–76; Folger Shakespeare Theatre and Sounds Reasonable Records in Washington from 1975. *Compositions include:* String Quartet, 1968; At Last Olympus, Musical, 1969; Spectrums, Confusions and Sometime for Orchestra, 1969; The Pied Piper of Hamelin, Musical, 1969; Chamber Music No. 1 for Violin and Piano, 1971, for Cello and Piano, 1972; Symphony, 1971; The Boy Who Cried Wolf is Dead, Musical, 1971; Ultra Mensuram 3 Brass Quintets, 1971; The Canticle, Musical, 1972; Inner Loop for Band, 1973; Niagura 1678 for Band, 1973; Night Music for Flute and Chorus, 1973; Miriors sur le Rubaiyat for Piano and Narrator, 1974; Mr.Toad's Wild Adventure for orchestra, 1993; Saxophone Concerto, 1995; The Revelations of St John the Divine, wind ensemble, 1995; Incidental Music and Songs. *Honours:* American Society for Composers, Authors and Publishers Awards and National Endowment for the Arts Fellowship. *Address:* c/o ASCAP, ASCAP Building, 1 Lincoln Plaza, New York, NY 10023, USA.

PENNARIO, Leonard; Concert Pianist; b. 9 July 1924, Buffalo, New York, USA. *Education:* Studied with Guy Maier, Olga Steeb and Ernest Toch. *Career:* Debut: With the Dallas Symphony Orchestra, 1936, playing the Grieg Concerto; Soloist with the Los Angeles Philharmonic, 1939; Played Liszt's E flat Concerto with the New York Philharmonic under Artur Rodzinski, 1943; Tour of Europe, 1952, in the popular Romantic repertory; Chamber Concerts with Jascha Heifetz and Gregor Piatigosky in Los Angeles; Premiered the Concerto by Miklos Rozsa with the LA Philharmonic under Zubin Mehta, 1966.

PENNETIER, Jean-Claude; Pianist and Conductor; b. 16 May 1942, Chatellerault, France. *Education:* Studied at Paris Conservatoire. *Career:* Numerous Solo appearances in Europe and elsewhere, 1968–; Chamber Musician with Regis Pasquier (Violin) and Trio with E Krivine and F Lodeon; Recitals with Piano Four Hands; Duo with Clarinettist Michel Portal 1979–80; Member of such ensembles as Domaine Musical, Musique Vivante, Ars Nova, Itineraire and Musique Plus; Performer of Contemporary Music at the Roayn and La Rochelle Festivals; Has conducted the Ensemble Intercontemporain and the orchestras of

French Radio; Premiered Maurice Ohana's 24 Preludes (1973) and Piano Concerto, 1981; Nikiprovetski's Piano Concerto, 1979; Professor of Chamber Music at the Paris Conservatoire, 1985–. *Honours:* Winner, Prix Gabriel Fauré and International Competition Montreal, 2nd Prize, Long-Triubaud Competition; Winner, Geneva International Competition, 1968. *Address:* Conservatoire National Superieur de Musique, 14 Rue de Madrid, 75008 Paris, France.

PENNISI, Francesco; Composer; b. 11 Feb. 1934, Acireale, Italy. *Education:* University Faculty of Arts, Rome, 1954–55; Further study with Robert W. Mann, 1954–59. *Career:* Co-founder of new music society at Rome, Nuova Consonanza, 1960; Participation in Palermo International New Music Week, 1960–. *Compositions:* A Cantata on Melancholy, 1967; Sylvia Simplex, music theatre, 1972; Fantasia, cello and orchestra, 1997; La vigne di Samaria, chorus and orchestra, 1974; Gläserner Tag, orchestra, 1978; La partenza di Tisies viola and orchestra, 1979; Descrizione dell Isola Ferdinandea, chamber opera, 1983; Per Agamemnone, orchestra, 1983; I mandolini e le chitarre for soprano and ensemble, 1986; Aci il fume, radio opera, 1986; Tre Pezzi, clarinet, viola and piano, 1987–90; Purpureass rosas for two sopranos, baritone and clarinet quartet, 1990; L esequie della luna, music theatre, 1991; Una cartolina da selim (omaggio a Mozart), 1991; The Wild Swans, soprano and ensemble, and Medea dixit, for soprano and ensemble, 1992–93; Tristan, music theatre after Ezra Pound, 1995; Altro efetto di luna, soprano and ensemble, 1996; Scena, flute and orchestra, 1997; Chamber and solo instrumental music. *Address:* c/o SIAE (Sezione Musica), Viale della Letteratum n:30, 00144 Rome, Italy.

PENNY, Andrew (Jonathan); Conductor; b. 4 Dec. 1952, Hull, Yorkshire, England; m. Helga Robinson, 3 Sept 1988, 1 s., 1 d. *Education:* ARNCM, GRNCM, Royal Northern College of Music, Manchester, after Clarinet and Conducting studies; Studied Conducting on Rothschild Scholarship with Charles Groves and Timothy Reynish; Studied with Edward Downes on courses in Netherlands and later at BBC Conductors' Seminar; Clarinet studies with Sydney Fell. *Career:* Conductor of Sheffield Philharmonic Orchestra, 1979–89; Musical Director, Hull Philharmonic Orchestra, 1982–; 2 performances of Mahler 8, 1999 with HPO; Broadcasts with the BBC. *Recordings:* 30 CDs including premiere recordings of Sullivan's ballet and theatre music, symphonies by C Armstrong Gibbs, Edward German and film music by Vaughan Williams and William Walton; Cycle of Malcolm Arnold Symphonies for Naxos with the National Symphony Orchestra, Dublin. *Honours:* Ricordi Prize, Royal Northern College of Music, 1976. *Address:* 14 South Lane, Hessle, East Yorkshire, England.

PENRI-EVANS, David; Composer; b. 18 Jan. 1956, Wrexham, Wales. *Education:* BMus, Centenary Coll. of Louisiana, 1978; PGCE, Univ. of Wales, 1979; MMus, 1983, DMA, 1986, Louisiana State Univ.; FTCL, Trinity Coll., London, 1989; composition with Dinos Constantinides. *Career:* teacher, Victoria Coll., Jersey 1979–81, Portsmouth Grammar School 1987–92; Dir of Music, Elmhurst Ballet School 1992–94, John Lyon School 1995–96, Brooklands Coll., Weybridge 1996–]; Asst Prof. American Univ. in London 1987; Founder Dir, Tempo New Music Festival 1987–94; guest composer, Louisiana Festival of Contemporary Music 1990, 1995, Conservatoire National de Région de Rouen 2000; mem. BMI, Portsmouth District Composers' Alliance (chair.). *Compositions:* many commissions in the UK and USA; Violin Prologue 1982, Brown Studies 1983, Symphony 1983, String Quartet, Dinas Brân 1984, Night Music 1985, Study in Grey, Opera 1985, Death in the Surf 1987, Textures 1990, Sunrise with Sea Monsters 1990, Aurelia 1993, Sift 1994, Five Haiku for Peace 1995, Four Ways of Having Sex in Zero Gravity 2000, Rain Journal 2001. *Honours:* . *Address:* 5 Royston Avenue, Byfleet, Surrey KT14 7PR, England. *E-mail:* dpenrievans@brooklands.ac.uk. *Website:* www.penrievans.free-online.co.uk/DPE_Web_01.

PENROSE, Timothy (Nicholas); Singer; b. 7 April 1949, Farnham, Surrey, England; m. (1) Shirley Margaret Bignell, (2) Carol Heather Oake, 15 Nov 1986. *Education:* Licentiate and Fellow, Trinity College, London. *Career:* Debut: Opera–Holland Festival, 1974; Numerous solo concert appearances throughout the United Kingdom and most European countries; Visits to North and South America; Tours with Pro Cantione Antique of London, Solo Recitals for BBC and European Radio Stations; Concerts with Medieval Ensemble of London and London Music Players; mem, Gentlemen-in-Ordinary, Her Majesty's Chapel Royal, 1972–75; City Glee Club, London. *Recordings:* Handel's Semele; Purcell's The Fairy Queen, with John Eliot Gardiner; Others with Pro Cantione Antiqua, Medieval Ensemble of London, London Music Players and London Early Music Group. *Honours:* Recipient, Greater London Arts Association, Young Musicians Award, 1975. *Address:* c/o Pro Cantione Antiqua, Concert Directory International, Lyndhurst, Denton Road, Ben Rhydding, Ilkley W Yorks, LS29 8QR, England.

PEPER, Uwe; Singer (Tenor); b. 20 May 1939, Hamburg, Germany. *Career:* Debut: Halberstadt, 1966 as Mozart's Pedrillo; Komische Oper Berlin from 1969 as Monostatos and Jacquino in Fidelio, Zürich, Frankfurt and Paris as Jacquino; Pedrillo at the Salzburg Festival, 1990–91; Mime in The Ring at the Salle Pleyel, Paris, 1992; Deutsche Oper Berlin, 1995–96 in Boris Godunov and Andrea Chénier; Sang Guillot in Massenet's Manon, 1998; Sang Jacquino in Fidelio, Strauss's Valzacchi and the Emperor in Turandot at the Deutsche Oper, 1999–2001. *Recordings:* Salome, Die Entführung, Die Zauberflöte. *Address:* Deutsche Oper Berlin, Richard Wagnerstrasse 10, 1058 Berlin, Germany.

PEPI ALÓS, Jorge; Argentine pianist and composer; b. 28 March 1962, Cordoba. *Education:* Acad. Menuhin, Gstaad and studied with Edith Fischer. *Career:* concerto soloist and chamber musician (notably in two-piano duo with Edith Fischer) in Europe, USA and S America; organizer, Festival Int. de Piano de Blonay; teacher, Conservatoire de la Chaux-de-Fonds. *Compositions include:* Septet 1983, Metamorfosis I 1989, La Caccia al tesoro (chamber opera) 1990–92, Extravagario 1993–94, Amalgama 1995, Metamorfosis IV 1995, Amalgama 1995–96, Nachtstücke 1998, Vie Merveilleuse et Burlesque du Café 1999–2000. *Honours:* Orpheus Prize 1987, Association des Musiciens Suisses Prix d'étude 1988, Edition Musicale Suisse composition prize 1991, Soc. Suisse des Auteurs composition prize 1993, first prize Gerona Int. Competition 1995, Grand Prix Gilson 1995. *Address:* 9 rue des Granges, 2300 La Chaux-de-Fonds, Switzerland. *Telephone:* 21 943 31 22. *E-mail:* edith.jorge@tiscalinet.es.

PERAHIA, Murray; American pianist and conductor; b. 19 April 1947, New York, NY; s. of David Perahia and Flora Perahia; m. Naomi (Ninette) Shohet 1980; two s. *Education:* High School of Performing Arts, Mannes Coll. of Music, studied with Jeanette Haien, Arthur Balsam, Mieczyslaw Horszowski. *Career:* debut, Carnegie Hall 1968; won Leeds Int. Piano Competition 1972; has appeared with many of world's leading orchestras and with Amadeus, Budapest, Guarneri and Galimir string quartets; regular recital tours N America, Europe, Japan; Co-Artistic Dir Aldeburgh Festival 1983–89; numerous recordings including complete Mozart Piano Concertos; prin. guest conductor, Acad. of St Martin-in-the-Fields. *Honours:* Dr hc (Univ. of Leeds), Hon. FRCM, FRAM; Kosciusko Chopin Prize 1965, Avery Fisher Award 1975, Gramophone Record Award 1997, Grammy Award 1999; Hon. KBE 2004. *Current Management:* IMG Artists, 22 East 71 Street, New York, NY 10021, USA. *E-mail:* info@imgartists.com. *Website:* www.imgartists.com.

PERDIGAO, Maria Madalena Azeredo; artistic director; b. 28 April 1923, Figueira Da Foz, Portugal; m. Dr José De Azeredo Perdigao; one s. *Education:* Coimbra University, Conservatorio Nacional, Lisbon; studied with Marcel Ciampi, National Conservatory of Paris. *Career:* lectures on musical subjects; Head of Music Department, Calouste Gulbenkian Foundation, 1958–74; created the Gulbenkian Orchestra, 1962, The Gulbenkian Choir, 1964, The Gulbenkian Ballet, 1965 and organized the Gulbenkian Music Festivals, 1958–70; President, International Music Festival of Lisbon, 1983; Piano Recitals and Concert Performances; Assessor to the Ministry of Education for Artistic Education, Lisbon, Portugal, 1978–84; Director of the Department of Artistic Creation and Art Education of The Calouste Gulbenkian Foundation. *Address:* R. Marques de Fronteira, 8, 2ø D, 1000 Lisbon, Portugal.

PEREIRA, Clovis; Composer; b. 14 May 1932, Caruaru, Brazil; m. Rizomar Pereira, 18 Feb 1955, 2 s., 2 d. *Education:* Studies with Guerra Peixe, 1951; School of Arts, Boston University, 1991. *Career:* Debut: Conductor, Lamento e Dansa Brasileira, 1968; Arranger, Radio Jornal do Commercio, 1950; Head, Music Department, Television, 1960; Chairman, Conservatorio Pernambucano de Musica, 1983; Tour of USA as Brazilian Representative and Conductor of University of Paraiba Chorus, 4th International Choir Festival, 1974; Teacher, University da Paraiba, Rio Grande do Norte e Pernambuco, 1994. *Compositions:* Grande Missa Nordestina para Coro, Solistas e Orquestra; 3 Peças Nordestinas; Terno de Pifes; Cantiga; Velame; Cantata de Natal; Poetas Nordestinos, Songs for Voice and Piano; Concertino para Violino e Orquestra de Camara, 1994. *Honours:* 1st Prize, Primeiro Concurso Nacional de e Orq de Camara, 1964; Trofeu Cultural Cidade do Recife, 1997. *Address:* Rua Pe, Bernardino Pessoa, 395 Apt 102, Recife 51020-210, Brazil.

PERENYI, Miklos; Cellist; b. 5 Jan. 1948, Budapest, Hungary. *Education:* Franz Liszt Academy, Budapest, from 1953, with Ede Banda; Accademia di Santa Cecilio, Rome, with Enrico Mainardi; Puerto Rico and Marlboro, with Pablo Casals. *Career:* Professor of Franz List Academy from 1974; Many concerto and recitals appearances in Europe and USA; Concerts with Andras Schiff at the Monlsee International Music Festival; Premiere of Kurtág's Double Concerto, 1990; Plays Gagliano cello of 1730. *Recordings include:* Concertos by Ligeti,

Lutoslawski, Hindemith, Dvořák and Haydn; Sonatas and other chamber music (Hungaraton). *Address:* c/o Franz Liszt Academy, Budapest PO Box 206, Listz Ferenetér 8, H–1391 Budapest VI, Hungary.

PERERA, Ronald (Christopher); Composer; b. 25 Dec. 1941, Boston, Massachusetts, USA. *Education:* Studied with Leon Kirchner at Harvard, MA 1967, and at the electronic studios of Utrecht University. *Career:* Teacher at Syracuse University, 1968–70, Dartmouth College, 1970, Smith College, Northampton, 1971–2002; Elsie Irwin Sweeney Professor of Music Emeritus at Smith College; mem, ASCAP; College Music Society, National Opera Association. *Compositions include:* Instrumental: Piano Suite 1966; Alternate Routes for Electronics, 1971; Fantasy Variations for piano and electronics, 1976; Tolling for 2 pianos and tape, 1979; Choral: Mass, 1967; Three Night Pieces, 1974; Earthsongs, 1983; Songs: Dove sta amore for soprano and tape, 1969; Apollo Circling, 1972; Three Poems of Günther Grass for mezzo, chamber ensemble and tape, 1974; The White Whale for baritone and orchestra, 1981; The Canticle of the Sun for chorus, 1984; The Yellow Wallpaper, chamber opera, 1989; Music for flute and orchestra, 1990; The Saints for orchestra, 1990; The Outermost House, cantata for mixed chorus, narrator, solo soprano and chamber orchestra, 1991; S, opera based on novel by John Updike, 1995. *Recordings include:* Earthsongs; Crossing the Meridian: Chamber Works with Voice; The Outermost House and The Canticle of the Sun; Music for flute and orchestra; Five Summer Songs; The Golden 1 Door. *Publications include:* Co-editor, Development and Practice of Electronic Music, 1975; Sleep Now for High Voice and Piano, 1994 and a further 30 pieces published; The Golden Door, cantata for speaker, mixed chorus and ensemble, 1998; The Araboolies of Liberty Street, opera in one act, 2001. *Honours:* ASCAP Awards for Composition since 1972; Artists Foundation of Massachusetts Fellowship, 1978; Four MacDowell Colony Fellowships, 1974–88; National Endowment for the Arts Grants, 1976, 1988. *Current Management:* Music Associates of America. *Address:* 21 Franklin Street, Northampton, MA 01060, USA. *Website:* www.ronaldperera .com.

PERESS, Maurice; Conductor; b. 18 March 1930, New York, USA; Trumpeter. *Education:* Studied at New York University and Mannes College (conducting with Philip James and Carl Bamberger). *Career:* Played trumpet before appointed by Bernstein as Assistant Conductor of the New York Philharmonic, 1961; Conducted revivals of Candide, Los Angeles, 1966, and West Side Story, New York, 1968; Music Director of the Corpus Christi Symphony Orchestra, 1962–75, the Austin Symphony, 1970–73 and the Kansas City Philharmonic, 1974–80; Guest Conductor in Brussels, Hong Kong, Vienna, Jerusalem and Mexico City; Conducted the premiere of Bernstein's Mass at the opening of the Kennedy Center, Washington DC, 1971, and at the Vienna Staatsoper, 1981; Led the US premiere of Einem's Der Besuch der alten Dame at the San Francisco Opera, 1972; Has orchestrated, edited and conducted jazz music by Duke Ellington, Eubie Blake and Gershwin (60th anniversary concert of the Rhapsody in Blue, New York, 1984); Has taught at New York University, the University of Texas at Austin and Queens College, New York; President, Conductors' Guild of the American Symphony Orchestra League. *Recordings include:* Bernstein's Mass (musical director); Organ Concertos 1 and 2 by Rheinberger, with E Power Biggs and the Columbia Symphony Orchestra. *Address:* Music Faculty, Queen's College, City University of New York, New York, NY, USA.

PEREZ, Jose-Maria; Tenor; b. 1934, Spain. *Education:* Studied in Spain and Switzerland. *Career:* Sang at the Lucerne Opera, 1959–60, then at Innsbruck and Basle; Sang at Graz Opera, 1963–84 in such roles as the Duke of Mantua, Don Carlos, Rodolfo, Calaf, Radames, Cavaradossi, Andrea Chénier, Alfredo and Turiddu; Guest appearances in Switzerland and elsewhere as Vasco da Gamain L'Africaine, by Meyerbeer, Faust, Pelléas, Sergei in Lady Macbeth of Mtensk and Albert Gregor in The Makropulos Case; Also active in operetta at Berlin, Barcelona and Vienna. *Address:* c/o Graz Opera, Vereingte Buhnen, Kaiser Josef Platz 10, 8010 Graz, Austria.

PÉRISSON, Jean-Marie; Conductor; b. 6 Sept. 1924, Arcachon, France. *Education:* Studied with Jean Fournet in Paris and with Igor Markevitch in Salzburg. *Career:* Conducted the orchestra of the Salzburg Mozarteum in Austria and Germany then led the French Radio Orchestra at Strasbourg, 1955–56; Permanent Conductor at the Orchestre Philharmonique of Nice and Musical Director of the Nice Opera; Conducted cycles of The Ring and the French premieres of Katerina Izmailova by Shostakovich in 1964, Elegy for Young Lovers by Henze in 1965 and Prokofiev's The Gambler in 1966; Gave Janáček's Katya Kabanova at the Salle Favart, Paris, and conducted the Monte Carlo Opera, 1969–71; Directed the Presidential Symphony Orchestra, 1972–76, and worked in the French repertory at the San Francisco Opera; Conducted Carmen at Peking in 1982. *Address:* c/o San Francisco Opera, War Memorial Opera House, San Francisco, CA 94102, USA.

PERL, Alfredo; Concert Pianist; b. 1965, Santiago, Chile. *Education:* studied at the Universidad de Chile with Carlos Botto; Cologne Musikhochschule with Günter Ludwig; with Maria Curcio in London. *Career:* concerts throughout South America and Europe, with the Filarmonica de Santiago and the Zagreb Symphony; Liszt Années de Pèlerinage for the BBC 1990; recitals at the Herkulessaal, Munich, May 1991; recital, Queen Elizabeth Hall, London 1992; concerts with the Royal Philharmonic and the Noord-Nederlands Orchestra 1992; Leipzig Gewandhaus recital and in Prague 1993, also US debut with the Florida Philharmonic, a recital at Ravinia; 1993–94 season, recitals in Hamburg, Hannover, Moscow Conservatoire, with the Medici Quartet in London and the Lebanon; 1994–95 season, recitals in Prague, London's Queen Elizabeth and Wigmore Halls, Moscow Conservatoire, Düsseldorf, Bologna; Beethoven sonata series at the Wigmore Hall 1996–97; recital tour of Germany 1997; debut at Royal Albert Hall with BBC Philharmonic Orchestra 1997; Season 1999–2000: recitals at the Wigmore Hall, London, Sudwestrundfunk, Mainz, a Beethoven Sonata cycle in Dortmund, tour of South America with the Deutsche Kammerphilharmonie and Netherlands with the Prokofiev Orchestra; Season 2002–03: debut with Leipzig Gewandhausorchestra at the Barbican, tour of Australia, concerts with the Netherlands Philharmonic Orchestra, Vienna Symphony Orchestra, BBC Welsh, recitals at Sydney Opera House, Wigmore Hall, Teatro Municipal de Santiago de Chile; Season 2003–04: tour of Germany with Orquesta de Málaga, performances at Stuttgart Philharmonic, Munster Symphony; recitals at Wigmore Hall, Bath Festival, Leicester Festival, Rheingau Festival, Schwetzingen Festspiele. *Recordings:* Fantasias by Schumann, Liszt and Busoni; Brahms Sonatas for clarinet and piano, with Ralph Manno; Complete Beethoven sonatas and Diabelli Variations; Grieg Concerto and Szymanowski, Symphonie Concertante; CD, Beethoven Cello Sonatas, with Guido Schieffen; Liszt's 2 piano concertos and Totentanz with BBC Symphony Orchestra under Yakov Kreizberg. *Honours:* Prizewinner at such competitions as Vina del Mar (Tokyo), Ferruccio Busoni at Bolzano and the Beethoven in Vienna; 1st Prize, International Piano Competition in Montevideo. *Current Management:* c/o Harrison Parrott Ltd, 12 Penzance Place, London, W11 4PA, England. *Telephone:* (20) 7229-9166. *Fax:* (20) 7221-5042. *E-mail:* sabine.frank@ harrisonparrott.co.uk. *Website:* www.harrisonparrott.co.uk.

PERLE, George; Composer and Author; b. 6 May 1915, Bayonne, NJ, USA; m. 1st Laura Slobe 1940; m. 2nd Barbara Phillips 1958; two d.; m. 3rd Shirley Gabis Rhoads 1982. *Education:* BMus, DePaul Univ., 1938; MMus, American Conservatory of Music, 1942; PhD, New York Univ., 1956. *Career:* Prof. Emeritus, City Univ. of New York; major compositions performed by Chicago Symphony, Boston Symphony, BBC Symphony, Royal Philharmonic Orchestra, Philadelphia Symphony, San Francisco Symphony, Juilliard Quartet, New York Philharmonic, Bavarian State Radio Orchestra, Da Capo Chamber Players, Cleveland Quartet, Dorian Wind Quintet, Goldman Band; mem. various professional organizations. *Compositions include:* Quintet for strings 1958, Concerto for cello and orchestra 1966, Songs of Praise and Lamentation for soloists, chorus and orchestra 1974, Sonata for cello and piano 1985, Sonata a Cinque 1986, Dance Fantasy for orchestra 1986, Concerto for piano and orchestra 1990, Sinfonietta II 1990, Transcendental Modulations for orchestra 1993, Phantasyplay for piano 1994, Duos for horn and string quartet 1995, Musical Offerings for piano left hand 1998, Nine Bagatelles for piano 1999. *Recordings include:* Concerto No. 2 for piano and orchestra, Two Rilke Songs 1941, Four Wind Quintets 1967–84, Fantasy Variations for piano 1971, Dickinson Songs 1978, Concertino for piano, winds and timpani 1979, Ballade for piano 1980, Six New Etudes for piano 1984, Concerto No. 1 for piano and orchestra 1990, Sinfonietta II 1990. *Publications:* Serial Composition and Atonality 1962, Twelve-Tone Tonality 1977, The Operas of Alban Berg, Vol. I, Wozzeck 1980, Vol. II, Lulu 1985, New Grove Second Viennese School (co-author) 1983, The Listening Composer 1990, The Right Notes 1995, Style and Idea in the Lyric Suite of Alban Berg 1995. *Contributions:* professional journals. *Honours:* Guggenheim Fellowships 1966, 1974, Pulitzer Prize for Wind Quintet IV 1986, MacArthur Fellowship 1986, elected to American Acad. and Inst. of Arts and Letters 1978, American Acad. of Arts and Sciences 1985. *Address:* 138 Ipswich Street, Boston, MA 02215, USA.

PERLMAN, Itzhak; Israeli violinist; b. 31 Aug. 1945, Tel-Aviv; s. of Chaim Perlman and Shoshana Perlman; m. Toby Lynn Friedlander 1967; two s. three d. *Education:* Shulamit High School, Tel-Aviv, Tel-Aviv Acad. of Music and Juilliard School, USA, studied with Ivan Galamian and Dorothy De Lay. *Career:* gave recitals on radio at the age of 10; went to USA 1958; first recital at Carnegie Hall 1963; has played with maj. American orchestras 1964–; has toured Europe regularly and played with maj. European orchestras 1966–; debut in UK with London Symphony Orchestra 1968; toured Poland, Hungary, Far East; played with Israel Philharmonic Orchestra in fmr Soviet Union; appearances at Israel Festival and most European Festivals; Prin. Guest Conductor Detroit Symphony Orchestra 2001–; numerous recordings. *Honours:* Hon. DMus (Univ. of S Carolina) 1982, Dr hc (Yale, Harvard and Yeshivah Univs); several Grammy awards, EMI Artist of the Year 1995, Royal Philharmonic Soc. gold medal 1996; Medal of Liberty 1986, Nat. Medal of Arts 2001. *Current Management:* Askonas Holt Ltd, Lonsdale Chambers, 27 Chancery Lane, London, WC2A 1PF, England; IMG Artists, 22 825 Seventh Avenue, New York, NY 10019, USA.

PERLMAN, Navah; Concert Pianist; b. 1970, USA. *Education:* Studied with Ronit Lowenthal, and with Dorothy DeLay at Juilliard; Graduated Brown University. *Career:* Season 1999–2000 with St Paul Chamber Orchestra, Nashville SO, Philadelphia Orchestra, Pittsburgh SO and Fort Worth Chamber Orchestras; European debut at Ruhr Festival, Bochum, 1999; Further engagements with the Barcelona Symphony, Israel Philharmonic, New Japan PO, and National Orchestra of Mexico; Recital and concerto appearances with Kurt Nikkainen (violin) and Zuill Bailey (cello), including Kennedy Center, Metropolitan Museum, and Ravinia Festival; Beethoven's Triple Concerto throughout USA. *Current Management:* Askonas Holt Ltd, Lonsdale Chambers, 27 Chancery Lane, London, WC2A 1PF, England. *Telephone:* (20) 7400-1700. *Fax:* (20) 7400-1799. *E-mail:* info@askonasholt.co.uk. *Website:* www.askonasholt.co.uk.

PERLONGO, Daniel; Composer; b. 23 Sept. 1942, Gaastra, Michigan, USA. *Education:* Studied with Leslie Bassett and Ross Lee Finney at the University of Michigan (MM 1966) and with Goffredo Petrassi at the Academia di Santa Cecilia, Rome, 1966–68. *Career:* Resident at the American Academy in Rome, 1970–72; Professor of composition and theory at Indiana University of Pennsylvania, 1980–. *Compositions include:* Piano Sonata, 1966; Myriad for orchestra, 1968; Intervals, for string trio, 1968; Missa Brevis, 1968; Movement in Brass, for 12 instruments, 1969; Changes for wind ensemble, 1970; Ephemeron, for orchestra, 1972; Variations for chamber orchestra, 1973; Voyage for chamber orchestra, 1975; 2 String Quartets, 1973, 1983; Ricercar, for oboe, clarinet and bassoon, 1978; A Day at Xochimiloo, for wind quintet and piano, 1987; Lake Breezes, for chamber orchestra, 1990; Piano Concerto, 1992; Arcadian Suite for horn and harp, 1993; Three Songs for chorus, 1994; Shortcut from Bratislava for orchestra, 1994; Two Movements for orchestra, 1995; Sunburst, for clarinet and orchestra, 1995. *Honours:* NEA Fellowships, 1980 and 1995. *Address:* c/o ASCAP, ASCAP Building, 1 Lincoln Plaza, New York, NY 10023, USA.

PERRAGUIN, Hélène; Singer (Mezzo-soprano); b. 7 Sept. 1963, Tours, France. *Career:* Paris Opéra-Comique from 1986 in Die Zauberflöte and Suor Angelica; Season 1988–89 in Massenet's Amadis at St Etienne; Wagner's Ring at the Théâtre du Châtelet, Paris and The Love for Three Oranges at Aix-en-Provence; Opéra Bastille, Paris, 1991 as Pauline in The Queen of Spades; Sang Carmen for Opéra de Lyon, 1996; Leonore in La Favorite at Metz, 1993; Other roles include Mozart's Cherubino and Dorabella; Siebel in Faust and Ursula in Béatrice et Bénédict by Berlioz. *Address:* Opéra de Lyon, 1 Place de la Comédie, 69001 Lyon, France.

PERRETT, Danielle Gillian, MMus, ILTM; Musician and Teacher; b. 2 July 1958, London, England; m. *Education:* RCM Junior Department, Exeter Univ., London Univ. *Career:* musicianship and harp teacher, RCM Junior Department 1980–; debut, Purcell Room 1983; asst examiner, Trinity Coll. London 1988–; harp coach, Kent County Youth Orchestra 1985–; head of harp studies, London Coll. of Music 1996–; Mozart flute and harp concerto with Halstead, Brown, Hanover Band, Wigmore Hall 2001; performances at World Harp Congress, Prague 1999, Geneva 2002; broadcast for BBC World Service 2003; mem. Musicians' Union, Incorporated Soc. of Musicians, FITPRO, United Kingdom Harp Assocn, Clarsach Soc.. *Compositions:* After Debussy, House Music, Lever Harp 2000, A Patchwork Suite, Technical Development for Harpists, Lift off for Harp (with David Gough). *Recordings:* Dussek and the Harp 1993, The Complete Chamber Music and Songs 1996, The Alabaster Box, Elis Pehkonen 2001, Tranquil Haven 2003. *Publications:* harp articles in UK Harp Association Magazine, reviews for BBC Music Magazine, features for World Harp Congress Review, magazines of Victorian Harp Society, South Australian Harp Society, Trinity College, London, Harp Syllabuses; contrib. to Incorporated Society of Musicians Music Journal, Clarsach Society London Branch Publications. *Honours:* Associated Board Sheila Mossman Prize 1974, Clothworkers Company Thomas Aitchison Trust Fund Award 1975, Henry and Lily Davis Trust, Arts Council Award 1982, Royal Overseas Harp Prize 1983, Music for small groups, Arts Council Award 1991, Freedom of Worshipful Company of Musicians 2003. *Current Management:* International Artists' Management, 135 Stevenage Road, Fulham, London, SW6 6PB, England. *Telephone:* (20) 7381-9751 (office). *Fax:* (20) 7381-2406 (office). *Website:* danielleperrett.co.uk (home).

PERRIERS, Danièle; Singer (Soprano); b. 24 June 1945, Beaumont-le-Roger, Eure, France. *Education:* Studied in Paris with Janine Micheau, Roger Bourdin and Fanelu Revoil. *Career:* Debut: Marseille, 1968, as Sophie in Werther; Has appeared in France at the Paris Opéra and the Opéra-Comique, and in Nice, Bordeaux, Lyon, Rouen, Toulouse and Strasbourg; Also engaged at the Grand Théâtre de la Monnaie, Brussels, and in Liège and Monte Carlo; Glyndebourne Festival 1972–73 and 1976, as Despina and Blondchen; Widely known in the Coloratura and light lyrical repertory and in operettas; Sang also in works by Bizet, Boieldieu, Lecocq, Offenbach, Rossini and Richard Strauss. *Recordings:* Les Brigands by Offenbach; Die Entführung, Glyndebourne 1972; L'Amant jaloux by Grétry.

PERRY, Douglas R.; Singer (tenor); b. 19 Jan. 1945, Buffalo, New York, USA. *Career:* Sang at the New York City Opera from 1970 with his debut as Mozart's Basilio, and at Santa Fe Festival from 1971, notably in the US premieres of Reimann's Melusine in 1972 and Weir's A Night at the Chinese Opera in 1989; Sang in the premieres of Glass's Satyagraha at Stuttgart in 1980 and The Voyage at the Metropolitan in 1992; Other modern repertory has included Menotti's Tamu Tamu at Chicago in 1973 and Bernstein's A Quiet Place at Houston in 1983; Has also sung Rameau's Platée, M. Triquet in Eugene Onegin and Scaramuccio in Ariadne auf Naxos; Sang Quint in The Turn of the Screw at Montreal, 1996; Orlofsky in Die Fledermaus at Miami, 1998. *Recordings:* Satyagraha; A Quiet Place. *Address:* c/o Santa Fe Opera, PO Box 2408, Santa Fe, NM 87504, USA.

PERRY, Elisabeth; Concert Violinist; b. 1955, England. *Education:* Graduated, Menuhin School, 1972 and studied further with Dorothy DeLay and Oscar Shumsky at Juilliard. *Career:* Debut: South Bank, London, 1978; Concerts in Cincinnati, Florida, Chicago, Colorado and San Francisco and showings at Carnegie Hall with Alexander Schneider; Bartók's Second Concerto in Chicago; Further engagements in France, Switzerland, Italy and Germany; Leader of Deutsche Kammerakademie, 1982; Concerts in Sviatoslav Richter's Festival of British Music at Moscow and Leningrad, 1987; US premiere of Schnittke's Quasi una Fantasia at Alice Tully Hall and the Berg Chamber Concerto at Queen Elizabeth Hall under Lionel Friend; Recital tour of New Zealand, 1990, and the Berg Violin Concerto in London; Plays a Giovanni Grancini Violin on loan from Yehudi Menuhin. *Recordings include:* Bach's Double Concerto, with Menuhin; Kirschner's Duo for Violin and Piano. *Honours:* Winner, Concert Artists Guild Competition, New York.

PERRY, Eugene; Singer (Baritone); b. 1955, Nashville, Tennessee, USA. *Education:* Studied in New York. *Career:* Debut: Sang St Ignatius in Four Saints in Three Acts by Virgil Thomson, with the Opera Ensemble of New York, 1986; Sang Tarj in premiere of Under the Double Moon, by Anthony Davis, St Louis, 1989; Don Giovanni in the Peter Sellars production of Mozart's opera at Purchase and elsewhere; European debut as Alidoro in La Cenerentola at Nice, 1989; Season 1990–91 at New York City Opera, as Shiskov in US stage premiere of From the House of the Dead and as Stolzius in Die Soldaten by Zimmermann; Appeared as the Devil in Dvořák's Devil and Kate at St Louis, 1990; Théâtre de la Monnaie, Brussels, 1991, as Mamoud in premiere of The Death of Klinghoffer by John Adams (repeated at Brooklyn Academy of Music, New York); Sang Mercutio in Cavalli's Calisto at Glimmerglass Opera, 1996. *Recordings include:* Video of Don Giovanni; The Death of Klinghoffer. *Honours:* George London Award from National Institute of Music Theater, 1986. *Address:* c/o New York City Opera, Lincoln Center, New York, NY 10023, USA.

PERRY, Herbert; Singer (Baritone); b. 1955, Nashville, Tennessee, USA. *Education:* Studied with his twin brother, Eugene, in Texas and Arizona. *Career:* Sang at the Houston and St Louis Operas from 1984; Sang at the Spoleto Festival at Charleston in 1987 as Citheron in Rameau's Platée, at Pepsico Summerfare in 1989 as Leporello in Don Giovanni, at Chicago Opera, Nice and Santa Fe in 1991 in I Puritani, as Mozart's Figaro and as Masetto, and sang Leporello at Toronto in 1992; Sang Mozart's Don Alfonso at Toronto, 1995; Season 1999–2000 in Weill's Die Burgschaft, at Charleston, and the premiere of In the Penal Colony by Philip Glass, for Seattle Opera. *Recordings include:* Video of Don Giovanni, in the production by Peter Sellars. *Address:* Lyric Opera Chicago, 20 North Wacker Drive, Chicago, IL 60606, USA.

PERRY, Janet; singer (soprano); b. 27 Dec. 1947, Minneapolis, Minnesota, USA; m. Alexander Malta. *Education:* Curtis Institute, Philadelphia, with Euphemia Gregory. *Career:* debut Linz 1969, as Zerlina in Don Giovanni; Appearances in Munich and Cologne as Norina (Don Pasquale), Adina (L'Elisir d'amore), Blondchen (Die Entführung), Zerbinetta (Ariadne auf Naxos) and Olympia (Les Contes d'Hoffmann); Guest engagements in Vienna, Frankfurt, Stuttgart and at the Aix-en-Provence Festival; Glyndebourne 1977, as Aminta in Die schweigsame Frau; Numerous opera and operetta films for German television; Salzburg Festival; Sang Zerbinetta in Ariadne auf Naxos, RAI Turin,

1989; Violetta at the 1990 Martina Franca Festival; Season 1992 as Gluck's Eurydice at Bonn and Cleopatra in Giulio Cesare at the Halle Handel Festival. *Recordings:* Papagena in Die Zauberflöte, conducted by Karajan; Falstaff, Der Rosenkavalier, Beethoven's Ninth, Bruckner Te Deum; Nannetta in Falstaff; Egk's Peer Gynt. *E-mail:* janetperry@canada.com. *Website:* www.janetperry.com.

PERRY, Jennifer; Singer (Soprano); b. 1969, Rotterdam, Netherlands. *Education:* Studied at the Royal Academy and the Guildhall School of Music. *Career:* Concerts include Handel's Dixit Dominus on tour with the Tallis Scholars and regular appearances with other leading choral societies; Other repertoire includes Mozart's C minor Mass and songs by Schubert and Duparc; Operatic roles include Despina, Susanna and First Lady. *Address:* c/o Ron Gonsalves Management, 7 Old Town, Clapham, London SW4 0JT, England.

PERRY, Ross; Stage Director and Choreographer; b. 1954, Montreal, Canada. *Education:* Studied in Atlanta and Jacksonville. *Career:* Resident Assistant Director for Houston Grand Opera from 1986, working with such operas as Boris Godunov, Così fan tutte, Turandot, Figaro, Salome and Faust; Assistant at the Los Angeles Music Center with Idomeneo and at Santa Fe and Spoleto; Has worked further as Director and/or Choreographer at Houston, with Hansel and Gretel, The Mikado, Mefistofele and Desert of Roses by Robert Moran; Further engagements with Australian Opera (Così fan tutte, 1992), Victoria State Opera (Carmen) and Washington Opera (Mefistofele, 1995). *Current Management:* Athole Still International Management, Forresters Hall, 25–27 Westow Street, London, SE19 3RY, England. *Telephone:* (20) 8771-5271. *Fax:* (20) 8768-6600. *Website:* www.atholestill.com.

PERTIS, Attila; Pianist; b. 5 March 1966, Budapest, Hungary; m. Monika Egri, 28 June 1991. *Education:* Bartók Conservatory, Budapest; Liszt Music Academy, Budapest; Music Academy, Vienna. *Career:* Performances, Hungarian Days, London, 1989, and Musikverein, Vienna, 1991; Appeared at Budapest Spring Festival and Carinthian Summer Festival, Austria; With Monika Egri founded Egri and Pertis Piano Duo, 1980s; Television and radio recordings, Hungary, Austria, Italy. *Recordings:* For Hungarian radio and television, Austrian radio and television (ORF); CD, Journey Around the World, 1995; Liszt: Opera Fantasies and Transcriptions for two pianos, 1997–98. *Contributions:* Die Presse; Kronen Zeitung; Piano Journal. *Current Management:* Annart Artists Management, Barkács utca 7, 1221 Budapest, Hungary; J A Ellison, International Artists Management, 135 Stevenage Road, Fulham, London SW6 6PB, England; Künstlermanagement Till Dönch, Weimarer Strasse 48, 1180, Vienna. *Address:* Kaltwasserstrasse 1, 3413 Unterkirchbach, Austria.

PERTUSI, Michele; Singer (Bass); b. 1965, Parma, Italy. *Education:* Studied in Parma with Carlo Bergonzi. *Career:* Debut: Modena, as Silva in Ernani, 1984; Appearances at Teatro Donizetti, Bergamo, Ravenna Festival and Teatro Comunale, Bologna; Teatro Regio, Parma, 1987–, notably as Dulcamara, 1992; Season 1992 as Mozart's Count at Orchestra Hall, Chicago, and Figaro at Florence; Sang Talbot in Maria Stuarda at Barcelona, Assur in Semiramide at Pesaro; Other roles include Raimondo in Lucia di Lammermoor, Pagano in I Lombardi, and Rossini's Maometto; Sang Don Giovanni at Lausanne, 1996; Sang in Lucrezia Borgia at La Scala, 1998; Season 2000–01 as Rossini's Selim and Alidoro at Monte Carlo, Mahomet in Le Siège de Corinthe at Pesaro and Don Giovanni at Coruña; the Villiains in Hoffmann, and Alidoro, at Covent Garden, and the Berlioz Mephisto on London's South Bank; Don Alfonso at the Met and Guillaune Tell for the Vienna Staatsoper; London Proms, 2002. *Recordings include:* Mozart's Figaro, Assur, Alidoro, Silva, Lodovico in Otello; La Wally by Catalani. *Address:* c/o Teatro Regio, Via Garibaldi 16, 43100 Parma, Italy.

PERUSKA, Jan; violist; b. 1954, Czechoslovakia. *Education:* studied in Prague with members of the Smetana Quartet. *Career:* co-Founder and Violist of the Stamic Quartet of Prague, 1977; Performances at the Prague Young Artists and the Bratislava Music Festivals; Tours to Spain, Austria, France, Switzerland, Germany and Eastern Europe; Tour of the USA 1980, debut concerts in the United Kingdom at London and Birmingham, 1983; Further British tours, 1985, 1987, 1988 (Warwick Arts Festival) and 1989 (20 concerts); Gave the premiere of Helmut Eder's 3rd Quartet, 1986; Season 1991–92 with visit to the Channel Islands (Festival of Czech Music), Netherlands, Finland, Austria and France, Edinburgh Festival and debut tours of Canada, Japan and Indonesia. *Recordings:* Shostakovich No. 13, Schnittke No. 4; Mozart K589 and K370; Dvořák, Martinů and Janáček complete quartets. *Honours:* (with members of Stamic Quartet): Prize Winner, International Festival of Young Soloists, Bordeaux, 1977; Winner, 1986 ORF (Austrian Radio) International String Quartet Competition (followed by live broadcast from the Salzburg Mozarteum); Academie Charles Cros Grand Prix du Disque, 1991, for Dvořák Quartets. *Current Management:* Robert Gilder & Co., Enterprise House, 59–65 Upper Ground, London, SE1 9PQ, England. *Telephone:* (20) 7928-9008. *Fax:* (20) 7928-9755. *E-mail:* rgilder@robert-gilder.com.

PERUSSO, Mario; Conductor and Composer; b. 16 Sept. 1936, Buenos Aires, Argentina. *Career:* Deputy Conductor at Teatro Colón, Buenos Aires, giving his own opera Escorial in 1989 and Puccini's La Rondine, 1990; Conducted Otello and Turandot at La Plata, season 1990–91. *Compositions include:* Operas: La Voz del Silencio, 1 act, Buenos Aires, 1969; Escorial, 1 act, Buenos Aires, 1989; Sor Juana Ines de la Cruz, 1991–92, premiered, 1993; Guayaquil, lyric drama, 1993; Conducted Tosca at La Plata, 1995. *Recordings include:* La Voz del Silencio. *Address:* c/o Teatro Colón, Buenos Aires, Cerrito 618, 1010 Buenos Aires, Argentina.

PERUZZI, Elio; Clarinettist and Conservatory Teacher; b. 14 Oct. 1927, Malcesine, Verona, Italy. *Education:* Canetti Institute, Vicenza; B Marcello Conservatory, Venice. *Career:* Debut: Olympic Theatre, Vicenza; Soloist with Virtuosi di Roma, Solisti Veneti, Solisti di Milano, 1950–; String Quartets of Milan, Ostrava, Brno, Prague and Zagreb, and with Brno Philharmonic Orchestra, Bozen Orchestra, Padua Chamber Orchestra, Filarmonico di Bologna, 1960–; Founder, Bartók Trio (clarinet, violin, piano), 1958, Piccola Camerata Italian (mediaeval, renaissance and baroque instruments), 1967; Performances, Europe, USA, South America, USSR, Canada, 1960–. *Recordings:* Mozart Clarinet Quintet with Moravian Quartet, 18th and 19th century music with Virtuosi di Roma. *Publications:* Esercizi e Studi Method for Recorder, 1972; Editor, various works including: Sonatas by Robert Valentine for 2 Recorders, 1973; G Rossini Variations for Clarinet and Orchestra, 1978; A Ponchielli's Il Convegno for 2 Clarinets and Piano, 1988. *Honours:* Accademia Tiberina, Rome. *Current Management:* Francesca Diano, Via Vallisnieri 13, 35100 Padova, Italy. *Address:* Via Monte Solarolo 9, 35100 Padova, Italy.

PEŠEK, Libor, KBE; Czech conductor; b. 22 June 1933, Prague. *Education:* Acad. of Musical Arts, Prague, studied with Karel Ancerl, Vaclav Neumann and Vaclav Smetacek. *Career:* founder, Prague Chamber Harmony 1958; Chief Conductor, Slovak Philharmonic Orchestra 1980; Conductor-in-Residence, Czech Philharmonic Orchestra, Prague 1982; Principal Conductor, Artistic Adviser, Royal Liverpool Philharmonic Orchestra, England 1987–; Guest Conductor, Prague Symphony Orchestra; regular guest appearances with Philharmonia Orchestra, London, Oslo Philharmonic, Orchestre de Paris, Chamber Orchestra of Europe, London Symphony Orchestra, BBC Symphony, Dresden Staatskapelle, Netherlands Philharmonic, Los Angeles Philharmonic, San Francisco Symphony, Chicago Symphony; mem. Union of Czech Composers and Performing Artists; Hon. Fellow, Univ. of Central Lancashire 1997. *Recordings include:* Suk's Ripening, Asrael Symphony and Summer's Tale, Wagner's Wesendonck Lieder, Schmidt's 3rd Symphony, Massenet, Werther, complete opera, Bruckner's 7th Symphony, Complete Symphonies of Dvořák, Smetana Ma Vlast, Mahler Symphonies 9 and 10, works by Suk Martinu and Janáček. *Current Management:* IMG Artists Europe, Lovell House, 616 Chiswick High Road, London, W4 5RX, England. *Telephone:* (20) 8233-5800. *Fax:* (20) 8233-5801. *E-mail:* artistseurope@imgworld.com. *Website:* www.imgartists.com.

PESKO, Zoltan; Composer and Conductor; b. 15 Feb. 1937, Budapest, Hungary. *Education:* Diploma, Liszt Ferenc Music Academy, Budapest, 1962; Master Courses in Composing with Goffredo Petrassi, Accademia di S Cecilia, Rome, Italy and in Conducting, Pierre Boulez, Basel, Switzerland and Franco Ferrara, Rome, Italy, 1963–66. *Career:* Debut: As Composer and Conductor, Hungarian television, 1960; Work with Hungarian television, 1960–63; Assistant Conductor to Lorin Maazel, West Berlin Opera and Radio Orchestra, West Berlin, 1969–73; Performances at Teatro alla Scala, 1970; Professor, Hochschule, West Berlin, 1971–74; Chief Conductor, Teatro Communale, Bologna, Italy, 1974–; Conducted Wagner's Ring at Turin, 1988; Concert performance of Mussogsky's Salammbô at the 1989 Holland Festival; Teatro Lirico Milan 1990, premiere of Blimunda by Azio Corghi; Has also led the premieres of Bussotti's Il Catalogo è questo, 1960; Donatoni's Voci, 1974, In Cauda, 1982, Tema 1982, Atem 1985; Jolivet's Bogomile suite 1982; Dies by Wolfgang Rihm, 1985; Fünf Geistliche Lieder von Bach by Dieter Schnebel, 1985; Season 1992 with Der fliegende Holländer at Naples and Le Grand Macabre at Zürich; Conducted Fidelio at Rome, 1996. *Compositions:* Tension, String Quartet, 1967; Trasformazioni, 1968; Bildinis einer Heligen, Soprano and Children's Choir, Chamber Ensemble, 1969; Jelek, 1974. *Recordings:* Various for CBS Italiana. *Contributions:* Melos. *Honours:* Prize for Composition, Academia di S Cecilia, Rome, Italy, 1966; Premio Discografico, for recording debut as Conductor, Italian Critics, 1973. *Current Management:* Musart, 20121 Milan, Via Manzoni 31, Italy. *Address:* 40125 Bologna, Teatro Communale, Largo Respighi, Italy.

PESKOVA, Inna; Violist; b. 1960, Moscow, Russia. *Education:* Studied at Moscow Conservatoire with Alexei Shislov. *Career:* Co-founder, Glazunov Quartet, 1985; Many concerts in Russia and recent appearances in: Greece; Poland; Belgium; Germany; Italy; Works by Beethoven and Schumann at Beethoven Haus in Bonn; Further engagements in Canada and Netherlands; Teacher at Moscow State Conservatoire and Resident at Tchaikovsky Conservatoire; Repertoire includes works by: Borodin; Shostakovich; Tchaikovsky in addition to standard works. *Recordings include:* CDs of the six quartets of Glazunov. *Honours:* With Glazunov Quartet: Prizewinner of Borodin Quartet and Shostakovich Chamber Music Competitions. *Address:* c/o Sonata (Glazunov Quartet), 11 Northpark Street, Glasgow G20 7AA, Scotland.

PETCHERSKY, Alma; Concert Pianist; b. 1950, Argentina. *Education:* Studied with Roberto Caamano in Buenos Aires; Maria Curcio in London and with Magda Tagliaferro and Bruno Seidlhofer of the Vienna Academy. *Career:* Debut: Teatro Col ón Buenos Aires with Bart ók's 3rd Concerto; Concert and broadcasting engagements in Russia, USA, Canada, Spain, Germany, Brazil, Czechoslovakia, Mexico and the Far East; London appearances at the Wigmore Hall. *Recordings:* Works of the German, French and Russian schools, Latin-American and Spanish Romantic Composers; Complete piano music by Ginastera; Recordings for the BBC, London and CBC, Canada. *Current Management:* M Gilbert Management. *Address:* 516 Wadsworth Avenue, Philadelphia, PA 19119, USA.

PETER, Fritz; Singer (Tenor); b. 7 Nov. 1925, Camorino, Switzerland. *Education:* Studied in Winterthur, Zürich and Stuttgart, 1945–55. *Career:* Sang at Ulm Stadttheater, 1955–61, Zürich Opera from 1961, notably in premieres of Martinů's Greek Passion, 1961, Sutermeister's Madame Bovary, 1967, and Kelterborn's Ein Engel kommt nach Babylon, 1977; Guest appearances at Geneva, Lucerne, Munich, Hamburg, Frankfurt, Cologne, Nice, Milan, Helsinki, Vienna and Edinburgh, as Ernesto, Max and Tristan; Many concert performances. *Recordings include:* Monteverdi's Poppea and Ulisse conducted by Nikolaus Harnoncourt. *Address:* Opernhaus Zürich, Falkenstrasse 1, 8008 Zürich, Switzerland.

PETERS, Roberta; Singer (Soprano); b. 4 May 1930, New York City, USA. *Education:* Studied with William Herman in New York. *Career:* Debut: Metropolitan Opera, 1950 as Zerlina in Don Giovanni; With Metropolitan Opera until 1985 as the Queen of Night, Rosina, Mozart's Barbarina, Despina and Susanna, Verdi's Oscar, Nanetta and Gilda, Donizetti's Norina, Lucia and Adina, Strauss's Sophie and Zerbinetta, and Olympia in Les Contes d'Hoffmann; Covent Garden 1951, in The Bohemian Girl, under Beecham; Salzburg Festival 1963–64, as the Queen of the Night; Sang in Leningrad and Moscow, 1972; Other roles included Violetta, Mimi and Massenet's Manon; Sang on Broadway in The King and I, 1973; Appeared with Newark Opera 1989 as Adina in L'Elisir d'amore; Board, National Endowment for the Arts, appointed by George Bush, 1992. *Recordings:* Il Barbiere di Siviglia; Un Ballo in Maschera; Ariadne auf Naxos; Così fan tutte; Die Zauberflöte; Lucia di Lammermoor; Orfeo ed Euridice. *Publications:* Debut at the Met, 1967. *Honours:* National Medal for Arts, presented by President Clinton at the White House, 1998. *Address:* c/o Metropolitan Opera, Lincoln Center, New York, NY 10023, USA.

PETERSEN, Dennis; Singer (Tenor); b. 11 May 1954, Iowa, USA. *Education:* Studied at University of Iowa and with San Francisco Opera's Merola Programme. *Career:* Concert appearances in Mozart's Requiem, Messiah and Bach's Magnificat with St Paul Chamber Orchestra; Haydn's Theresienmesse at Spoleto Festival in Charleston; Sang in Tippett's A Child of Our Time at Carnegie Hall and concerts with New Jersey and Baltimore Symphonies under David Zinman and Calgary Philharmonic under Mario Bernadi; Engagements with San Francisco Opera, 1985–, including: Don Quichotte, Captain in Wozzeck, Mime in Der Ring des Nibelungen, Die Meistersinger, and Tybald in Roméo et Juliette; Lyric Opera of Chicago debut in season 1992–93 as Mime in Das Rheingold under Zubin Mehta; Sang Carlo in Donizetti's Il Duca d'Alba at Spoleto Festival; Season 1994–95 at Chicago Lyric Opera in Boris Godunov, and Mime in Siegfried; Metropolitan Opera in Lady Macbeth of Mtsensk (debut) and as Bob Boles in Peter Grimes; Season 1995–96 at San Francisco Opera in Anna Bolena and Madama Butterfly, Chicago Lyric Opera, Andrea Chénier–The Ring Cycle and Miami Opera in Ariadne auf Naxos; Leo in Antheil's Transatlantic for Minnesota Opera, 1998; Sang Monostatos at the Met, 2000. *Address:* c/o San Francisco Opera, War Memorial House, Van Ness Avenue, San Francisco, CA, USA.

PETERSEN, Marlis; Singer (Soprano); b. 1969, Sindelfingen, nr Stuttgart, Germany. *Education:* Studied with Sylvia Geszty and at the NY City Dance School, Stuttgart. *Career:* Appearances at Nuremberg Opera from 1991, as Aennchen in Der Freischütz, Mozart's Blondchen, Oscar, Adele (Die Fledermaus), Rosina and The Queen of Night; Concert engagements in Porto, Madrid, Milan, Brussels and Amsterdam; Deutsche Oper am Rhein from 1998, as Mozart's Serpetta and Susanna, Marie in La Fille du Régiment and Norina (Don

Pasquale); Season 2000–01 as Lulu at Kassel, Oscar at Bregenz, and Adele at the Opéra Bastille; Covent Garden debut 2002, as Zerbinetta in Ariadne auf Naxos; Sang Lulu at the Vienna Staatsoper, 2002. *Honours:* Prizewinner at Berlin and J. Offenbach Competitions, 1990–91. *Address:* c/o Deutsche Oper am Rhein, Heinrich Heine Allee 16 a, D–40213 Dusseldorf, Germany.

PETERSEN, Nils (Holger); Composer and Minister of the Danish Church; b. 27 April 1946, Copenhagen, Denmark; m. Frances Ellen Hopenwasser, 11 Sept 1971, divorced 1989, 1 s., 1 d. *Education:* Degree in Mathematics, University of Copenhagen, 1969; Postgraduate studies in Mathematics, Universities of Copenhagen and Oslo; Studies in Theology, Copenhagen University; Piano studies with Elisabeth Klein, composition with Ib Norholm; PhD in Theology, University of Copenhagen, 1994. *Career:* Minister of The Danish Church, 1974–; Research Fellow, 1990–, Research Lecturer, 1995, University of Copenhagen; External Professor of Gregorian Studies, University of Trondheim, Norway, 1997–; Freelance Composer with compositions performed on Danish, Swedish, Norwegian and Dutch Radio and on Danish television, at Nordic Music Days and various concerts in many countries; mem, Danish Composers Society; Board of the Nordic Society for Interart Studies. *Compositions:* Piano and Guitar solo works, published and recorded; Fools Play, opera, 1970 first performed in 1985; Vigil for Thomas Beckett, liturgical opera, 1989; Church Cantatas, 1971, 1974 and 1976; Antiphony for Good Friday for 9 Instruments and Voice; 2 Wind Quintets; Solo works for violin, piano and organ; The Lauds of Queen Ingeborg, liturgical opera, 1991; Fragments of a Distant Voice, Electrophonic work for the Danish State Radio, 1992; Concerto for Clarinet in B and Octet, 1994; A Plain Song, piano. *Recordings:* Various instrumental works on major labels. *Publications:* Kristendom i Musikken, 1987; Liturgy and the Arts in the Middle Ages, 1996. *Contributions:* Various articles on Theologico-musical aspects of the western culture in musical and theological papers. *Honours:* Hakon Borresen Memorial Prize, 1993. *Address:* Mimersgade 56, 1 tv, 2200 Copenhagen N, Denmark.

PETERSON, Claudette; Singer (Soprano); b. 15 July 1953, Lakewood, Ohio, USA. *Education:* Studied at San Francisco Conservatory. *Career:* Sang at San Francisco Opera from 1975; Washington Opera, 1979, as Blondchen in Die Entführung, Boston, 1980, as Dunyasha in War and Peace, Chicago, 1982, as Adele in Fledermaus; New York City Opera, 1985–86, as Manon and Lisette in La Rondine; Sang Yum-Yum in The Mikado for Canadian Opera at Toronto, 1986; Other roles have included Lucia (Arizona Opera) and Gilda (Shreveport); Further engagements at Buffalo, Houston, Geneva and Honolulu; Frequent concert appearances. *Recordings include:* Musgrave's A Christmas Carol. *Address:* c/o New York City Opera, Lincoln Center, New York, NY 10023, USA.

PETERSON, John (Murray); Composer; b. 14 Jan. 1957, Wollongong, New South Wales, Australia. *Education:* BMus, honours, 1990, MMus, 1994, Sydney University; PhD, Sydney University. *Career:* Orchestral works performed by Queensland Philharmonic Orchestra, Tasmanian Symphony Orchestra, West Australian Symphony Orchestra, New Zealand Symphony Orchestra and the National Orchestra of Wales; Broadcasts on ABC, Classic FM and BBC Radio 3; Participant, Australian Composers' Orchestral Forum, 1998, 2001; mem, Australian Music Centre; Musicological Society of Australia; Fellowship of Australian Composers. *Compositions:* Ex Tenebris Lux, orchestra, 1989; At The Hawk's Well, music theatre piece, 1990; Walking On Glass, piano solo, 1992; A Voice From The City, voice and small ensemble, 1994; Cyberia, orchestra, 1996; The Still Point, cello and piano, 1997; Diabolic Dance, violin and cello, 1997; Rituals in Transfigured Time, orchestra, 1997; Of Quiet Places, voice and guitar, 1998; Port Kembla, orchestra, 1998; Staring at the Sun, large mixed ensemble, 1998; Drive, alto saxophone and piano, 1998; WiredLife, mandolin duo, 1999; Spike, cello duo, 1999; At the Still Point, viola and piano, 1999; Landmarks, brass quartet, 1999; From Mountains to Sea, mixed sextet, 1999; Moving Fast Through Autumn Light, solo mandolin, 2000; Tallawarra, string quartet, 2000; Encomium, clarinet and cello, 2000; Three Ritual Dances, solo piano, 2000; Illawarra Music, large orchestra, 2000; The Earth That Fire Touches, orchestra, soprano soloist and SATB chorus, 2000; Five Islands, solo piano, 2001; Nocturnalia, orchestra, 2001; New England Dances, Orchestra, 2002; Liquid Steel, String quartet, 2002; Woollungah Dances, three solo clarinets and orchestra, 2002; The velocity of Celebration, mixed ensemble, 2003; Shadows and Light, soprano and tenor solo, SATB chorus, string orchestra and percussion, 2004. *Recordings:* Greenbaum Hindson Peterson, 1995; Drive, 2000; Spike, 2001. *Honours:* Semi-finalist, Masterprize, London, 1997, 2001. *Address:* 67 Kingsclear Road, Alexandria, NSW 2015, Australia.

PETERSONS, Ingus; Latvian singer (tenor); b. 12 Feb. 1959, Gulbene. *Education:* Riga Acad. *Career:* debut in Riga 1985 as Lensky in Eugene Onegin; sang at the Riga Opera as the Duke of Mantua, Alfredo, Don Carlo and Nemorino; sang at Wexford Festival as Arturo in La Straniera by Bellini 1987, Opera North, Leeds as Edgardo in Lucia di Lammermoor 1988; sang Hoffmann at the Folksoperan Stockholm 1991; other roles have included Des Grieux in Massenet's Manon and the Italian Singer in Der Rosenkavalier; sang Rodolfo in La Bohème and Riccardo in Un ballo in maschera at Riga Opera 2004. *Address:* c/o Latvian National Opera, Aspazijas Blvd 3, 1050 Riga, Latvia. *Telephone:* 371 707 3715. *Fax:* 371 722 8930. *E-mail:* info@opera.lv. *Website:* www.opera.lv.

PETIBON, Patricia; Singer (Soprano); b. 1969, France. *Education:* Studied in Paris. *Career:* Appearances with Les Arts Florissants and at the Beaune Festival as Dano in Armida abbandonata by Jommelli and as Argene in L'Olimpiade by Pergolesi; Season 1996-97 as Rameau's Aricie at the Paris Palais Garnier and as Mozart's Blondchen at Strasbourg and Montpellier; Paris Châtelet as Landi's Sant' Alessio; Guest appearances at Aix-en-Provence, La Scala Milan, Buenos Aires and the Wigmore Hall, London; Season 1999 as Zerbinetta at Strasbourg, Lakmé at Toulouse and Gluck's Amor at the Châtelet; Season 2000-01 as Offenbach's Olympia at the Vienna Staatsoper and Zelmira in Haydn's Armida at the Theater an der Wien; Ophélie in Hamlet at Toulouse and Dalinda in Handel's Ariodante in Paris; Frequent concert appearances. *Recordings include:* Stratonice by Méhul, Sant'Alessio by Landi, Die Entführung, Acis and Galatea (Erato); Werther, Haydn's Armida (EMI). *Address:* c/o Opéra et Concert, 1 rue Volney, F-75002 Paris, France.

PETIT, Jean-Louis; Conductor, Harpsichordist and Composer; b. 20 Aug. 1937, Favrolles, France. *Education:* Studied in Paris with Igor Markevitch, Pierre Boulez and Olivier Messiaen. *Career:* Organised and conducted various ensembles in the regions of Champagne, 1958–63 and Picardy, 1964–70; Performances on Radio and Television, tours of Europe and the USA; Co-directed the Paris Summer Festival, 1972–77; Founder member of the contemporary music group Musique Plus; Director of the Association musicale international d'echange (AMIE); Director of the Ecole Nationale de Musique of Ville d'Avray. *Compositions include:* Au-delà du signe for Orchestra; De Quelque Part Effondrée de l'homme for Quartet; Continuelles discontinués for Percussion; (82 Opus) Transcriptions of early music. *Recordings include:* Works by Boismortier, Leclair, Marais, Rameau, Lully, Mouret, Devienne, Campra, Francoeur, Couperin and Mondonville; Roussel's Sinfonietta; Les Troqueurs by d'Auvergne; 2nd Symphonie of Gounod; Chamber Music by Saint-Saëns.

PETKOV, Dimiter; Singer (Bass); b. 5 March 1939, Sofia, Bulgaria; m. Anne-Lise Petkov. *Education:* Sofia Music Academy with Christo Brambarov. *Career:* Debut: Sofia as Ramfis and Zaccaria, 1964; Guest appearances, Glyndebourne Festival, 1968, 1970, as Osmin and Gremin; Rostropovich Festival, Aldeburgh, 1983; Earl's Court, London, 1988; Birmingham Arena, 1991; Daytona Festival with London Symphony Orchestra, 1993; Arena di Verona as Philipp II, 1969, As Zaccaria, 1981, as Ramfis, 1986, 1987; Appearances: Vienna State Opera, 1972–86, 1990, as Philip II, Ramfis, Boris, Khovansky, Mephisto; Madrid, Barcelona, 1978–86, 1990; Chicago, 1980; Bologna, 1980–83, 1988; Catania, Palermo, Lecce, 1981, 1984, 1986; La Scala, Milan, 1981, 1984, 1989; Washington DC, 1982, 1984; Carnegie Hall, New York City, 1982, 1984, 1989; Zürich, Hamburg, Bonn, 1984–85, 1990; Naples, 1984, 1991; Rome, 1987, 1992; Florence, 1986–89, 1991; Monte Carlo, 1986, 1989; Paris, 1986, 1988; Deutsche Oper Berlin, 1988–93; Dallas, 1989, 1993; Opéra Bastille, Paris, 1990–93; Appeared with Berlin Philharmonic, London Symphony Orchestra, National Symphony Washington DC, Boston Symphony Orchestra at Tanglewood, Israel Philharmonic (Zubin Mehta) at Tel-Aviv, Montreal Symphony Orchestra, RAI Orchestras in Milan, Rome, Naples, Orchestre de Paris, Orchestre National de France, Concertgebouw Amsterdam, St Petersburg Philharmonic Jerusalem Symphony, San Francisco Symphony; In demand for all the Verdi bass roles: Philipp, Zaccaria, Fiesco; Bellini, Rossini, Donizetti; Mephisto by Gounod in French repertoire; All main roles in Russian repertoire: Boris Godunov, Ivan Khovansky, Ivan Susanin, others; Sang Shishkov in From the House of the Dead, Opéra du Rhin, 1996; Old Prisoner in Lady Macbeth at Florence, 1998. *Recordings:* EMI, Lady Macbeth of Mtsensk; EMI, Shostakovich 13th Symphony with London Symphony Orchestra; Aleko by Rachmaninov; Khovanshchina by Mussorgsky; Erato, Yolanta by Tchaikovsky, Mussorgsky cycles and Boris arias, 1989; Koch, Shostakovich cycles, 1993; Sony, Boris Godunov, 1992; Verdi Requiem at Eckphrasis Records, New York, 1994; Has sung with such conductors as Abbado, Mehta, Bartoletti, Previn, Molinari-Pradelli, Rostropovich, Ozawa, Rozdestvensky, Prêtre, Bernstein, Pritchard, Maazel and Giulini; Appeared in Werner Herzog's film Fitzcarraldo and sang Ernani at Manaus. *Address:* Rue du Conseil-Général 6, 1205 Geneva, Switzerland.

PETRE, Leonardus (Josephus); Professor of Trumpet; b. 27 Jan. 1943, Saint Triniden, Belgium; m. Maes Arlette, 24 July 1965, 2 s. *Education:* Bachelor of Medicine, University of Leuven, 1962; Music schools of St Trinden en Hasselt, First prizes in Music-Reading and Trumpet; Royal

Music Academy (Conservatoire Royal) Brussels, First Prizes in Music Reading, Transposition, Trumpet and Musical History. *Career:* Teacher of trumpet and several other brass instruments in several music schools; Professor of Trumpet at the Lemmens Institute, Leuven; Many appearances as member of orchestra or soloist on the Belgian and German radio and television; Soloist at many classical concerts in Belgium, France, Netherlands and Germany; Trumpet-Soloist with The New Music Group, and Collegium Instrumentale Brugense; Member of the Xenakis Ensemble, Netherlands; Creator and leader of The Belgian Brass Quintet 2, 1973–79; Conductor of brassband and fanfare; Specialist in playing Bach-trumpet (piccolo) and copies of very old trumpets; mem, International Trumpet Guild. *Recordings:* Several cantatas of J. S. Bach with La Chapelle des Minimes, Brussels. *Contributions:* Several articles concerning the trumpet and brass playing in local music magazines. *Address:* Smoldersstraat 44, 3910 Herk de Stad, Belgium.

PETRENKO, Mikhail; Singer (bass); b. 1976, St Petersburg, Russia. *Education:* St Petersburg Conservatoire. *Career:* Debut: Kirov Opera 1998, as Ivasenko in Prokofiev's Semyon Kotko; Young Singers' Academy of the Mariinsky Theatre, St Petersburg, from 1998; Other roles have included Svetozar in Ruslan and Lyudmila, Mozart's Masetto, Fafner in Das Rheingold and the King of Egypt in Aida; Sang Bermyata in Rimsky-Korsakov's The Snow Maiden, Amsterdam and London (concert performances), 1999–2000; Ivasenko in the British premiere of Semyon Kotko, with the Kirov Opera at Covent Garden, 2000. *Address:* c/o Kirov Opera, Mariinsky Theatre, 1 Theatre Square, St Petersburg, Russia.

PETRI, Michala; Danish musician (recorder player); b. 7 July 1958, Copenhagen; d. of Kanny Sambleben and Hanne Petri; m. Lars Hannibal 1992; two d. *Education:* Staatliche Hochschule für Musik und Theater, Hanover. *Career:* debut aged five, Danish Radio 1964; soloist with Orchestra Tivoli, Copenhagen 1969; over 3,000 concerts in Europe, USA, Japan, Australia and the Far East; numerous appearances at festivals, performances on TV and radio; performs frequently world-wide with lutenist and guitarist, Lars Hannibal; hon. artist, Soro Int. Organ Festival 1992; has inspired and initiated various contemporary compositions by Malcolm Arnold, Vagn Holmboe, Per Norgaard, Thomas Koppel, Daniel Boertz, Gary Kulesha and others; mem. of presidium, UNICEF Denmark; bd mem., Wilhelm Hansen Foundation; Vice-Pres., Cancer Asscn, Denmark. *Recordings:* more than 50 albums, including 12 with the Acad. of St Martin-in-the-Fields, Bach Sonatas and Handel Sonatas with Keith Jarrett, Vivaldi Concertos with Heinz Holliger, Henryk Szeryng, contemporary concerts with English Chamber Orchestra, three albums with Lars Hannibal. *Publications:* ed. of several works for Wilhelm Hansen and Moeck. *Honours:* Jacob Gade Prize 1969, 1975, Critics' Prize of Honour 1976, Nording Radio Prize 1977, Niels Prize 1980, Tagea Brandts Prize 1980, Maarum Prize 1981, Schroder Prize 1982, Deutsche Schallplattenpreis 1997, 2002, Sonning Music Prize 2000, H. C. Lumbye Prize; Knight of Dannebrog 1995. *Address:* Nordskraenten 3, 2980 Kokkedal, Denmark. *Telephone:* 45-86-25-77. *Fax:* 45-86-56-77. *E-mail:* mail@michalapetri.com. *Website:* www.michalapetri.com.

PETRIC, Ivo; Musician, Composer and Conductor; b. 16 June 1931, Ljubljana, Slovenia. *Education:* Music Acad., Ljubljana. *Career:* debut, Piano Trio, 1952; Conductor of Slavko Osterc Ensemble (for contemporary music), 1962–82; Ed.-in-Chief of Composers Editions, 1970–2002; Artistic Dir, Slovenian Philharmonic, 1979–95; mem., Asscn of Slovenian Composers. *Compositions:* orchestral music; concertos for various instruments; chamber music; sonatas for various instruments with piano (three symphonies, 1954, 1957, 1960); Trumpet Concerto, 1986; Dresden Concerto for Strings, 1987; Trois Images, 1973; Dialogues Entre Deux Violons, 1975; Jeux Concertants for Flute and Orchestra, 1978, Toccata Concertante for 4 Percussionists and Orchestra, 1979, Gallus Metamorphoses, 1992; Scottish Impressions, 1994; The Song of Life, 1995; The Four Seasons, 1995; The Autumn Symphony, 1996; Two MacPhadraig's Scottish Diaries for piano, 1996, 2002; Grohar's Impressions II, 1998; Three Places in Scotland, 2002; Autumn Concerto for violin and orchestra, 2003. *Recordings:* 11 CDs of orchestral, chamber and solo music. *Honours:* Slovene State Preseren Foundation Prize, 1971; First Prize, Wieniawski International Composition Competition for Violin, 1975; Ljubljana Prize for Artists, 1977; Oscar Espla International Competition, First Prize, 1984; Kozina Award for six string quartets, 2001. *Address:* Bilecanska 4, 61000 Ljubljana, Slovenia. *E-mail:* ivopetricc@siol.net.

PETRINSKY, Natascha; Singer (mezzo-soprano); b. 1966, Vienna, Austria. *Education:* Studied in Israel. *Career:* Sang Carmen with New Israeli Opera; Appearances from 1995 with Giuseppe Sinopoli (conductor) in the Verdi Requiem, Beethoven's Ninth and Missa Solemnis, in Rome, Mahler's Third (Israel Philharmonic) and Wellgunde in Das Rheingold; Bayreuth Festival 2000, as Kundry in Parsifal; Engagements at Operahaus Halle as Amneris, Azucena and Marie in Wozzeck;

Medea in Cavalli's Giasone at Spoleto USA and Carmen for Finnish Opera; Season 2001–2002 as Britten's Lucretia in Lausanne, Mahler's Second in Singapore, Das Lied von der Erde with the Royal Ballet, Covent Garden, Tchaikovsky's Pauline for Geneva Opera and Janáček's Fox in Paris, Châtelet; Other concerts include Mendelssohn's Elijah, at the Dresden Festival and Mahler's Third in Hong Kong; Further opera roles include Mozart's Donna Elvira and Countess Almaviva. *Current Management:* Athole Still International Management, Forresters Hall, 25–27 Westow Street, London, SE19 3RY, England. *Telephone:* (20) 8771-5271. *Fax:* (20) 8768-6600. *Website:* www.atholestill.com.

PETRO, Janos; Conductor and Chief Music Director; b. 5 March 1937, Repceszemere, Hungary; m. 27 Aug 1959, 1 s., 1 d. *Education:* Conductor and Composer, Academy of Music, Budapest, 1959. *Career:* Debut: As Composer, Vienna, 1959; Opera and Concerts in Budapest, Vienna, Berlin, Dublin, Bratislava, Frankfurt, Hamburg, Graz; Radio Budapest; Vienna Symphonic Record Register; Television Budapest and Vienna; mem, Musicians Alliance, Budapest, President and Member. *Recordings include:* Goldmark: Concerto for Violin and Orchestra; Mendelssohn: Concerto for Violin and Orchestra; Haydn: Scena di Berenice and Concert Arias; P Karolyi; Epilogus; P Karolyi: Consolato; Bizet: Symphony C-major; Bizet: Suite L'Arlesienne; Beethoven: Egmont Overture; Liszt: Les Préludes; Haydn: Symphony No. 104. *Honours:* F Liszt Prize, Conductor, Budapest, 1983; World Young Composer Prize, Vienna, 1959; State Prize, Budapest, 1982. *Current Management:* Interkoncert Budapest, Vorosmarty ter 1, Austrokonzert, Vienna. *Address:* c/o Austroconcert International, Gluckgasse 1, A–1010 Vienna, Austria.

PETROBELLI, Pierluigi, BLitt, MFA; Italian musicologist and writer; *Professor of Music History, University of Rome 'La Sapienza';* b. 18 Oct. 1932, Padua. *Education:* Univ. of Rome, Princeton Univ., Harvard Univ. Summer School, Univ. of California at Berkeley. *Career:* Ed., Rivista Italiana di Musicologia 1968–71, Studi verdiani 1981–; teaching asst 1968–70, Assoc. Prof. of Music History 1970–72, Univ. of Parma; librarian and teacher of music history, Rossini Conservatory, Pesaro 1970–73; Lecturer in Music, King's Coll., London 1973–77; Reader in Musicology, Univ. of London 1978–80; Dir, Istituto di Studi Verdiani, Parma 1980–89, Istituto Nazionale di Studi Verdiani, Parma 1989–; Prof. of Music History, Univ. of Perugia 1981–83, Univ. of Rome 'La Sapienza' 1983–; Chair of Italian Culture, Univ. of California at Berkeley 1988; Lauro de Bosis Lecturer in the History of Italian Civilization, Harvard Univ. 1996; mem. Academia Europaea, American Musicological Soc. (corresponding mem.), Royal Musical Asscn, United Kingdom (foreign hon. mem.), Accademia dei Lincei; mem.: Corresponding member of the American Musicological Society; Hon. mem. of the Royal Musical Association; Zentralinstitut für Mozartforschung, Salzburg; Visitante distinguido, Uiversity of Cordoba, Argentina; Member of the Accademia Nazionale dei Liucei and the Academia Europaea. *Publications:* Thematic Catalog of an 18th-Century Collection of Italian Instrumental Music (held in the Music Library, Univ. of California at Berkeley, with V. Duckles and M. Elmer) 1963, Giuseppe Tartini: le fonti biografiche 1968, Mozart's Il re pastore (critical edn, with Wolfgang Rehm) 1984, Carteggio Verdi-Ricordi 1880–1881 (co-ed.) 1988, Tartini, le sue idee e il suo tempo 1992, Music in the Theater: Essays on Verdi and Other Composers 1994; contrib. to scholarly books and professional journals. *Address:* 34 via di San Anselmo, 00153 Rome, Italy. *E-mail:* petrobel@rmcisadu.let.uniromat.it.

PETROFF-BEVIE, Barbara; singer (soprano) and professor of music; b. 2 June 1934, Hamburg, Germany; m. Joseph Petroff, 17 May 1973, 1 s., 1 d. *Education:* University; Masterclasses, Hochschule für Musik, Hamburg; Opera classes, Bern and Geneva Conservatories; Diploma. *Career:* debut as Constanze in Entführung aus dem Serail, Stadttheater Luneberg 1959, and as Clarice in Haydn's Il mondo della luna, Stadttheater Bern 1960; main appearances include Århus (Denmark), Bern and Geneva (Switzerland), The Hague (Netherlands), Royal Opera Ghent (Belgium), Linz (Austria), Kiel (Germany), Grand Theatre, Geneva; sang as Carolina in Il matrimonio segreto, Gilda in Rigoletto, Blondchen and Constanze in Entführung, Musetta, Sophie in Der Rosenkavalier, Ännchen in Freischütz, Susanna in Figaro, Despina in Così fan tutte, Adele in Die Fledermaus, Rosina in Barbiere di Siviglia and Adina in L'Elisir d'amore; operettas: Maritza in Gräfin Maritza and Evelyne in Graf von Luxemburg. *Address:* 12 rue de Chêne-Bougeries, 1224 Geneva, Switzerland.

PETRONI, Luigi; Singer (Tenor); b. 1970, Italy. *Career:* Debut: Cimarosa's Il Matrimonio segreto, Turin; Appearances in The Civil Wars by Philip Glass; Rossini's Ricciardo e Zoraide and Mavra by Stravinsky; Wexford Festival 1997 as Boemondo in Mercadante's Elena da Fetre; Concerts include Rossini's Stabat Mater with the Oslo Radio Symphony Orchestra, 1997. *Recordings:* Elena da Feltre. *Honours:* Winner, International Enrico Caruso Competition; International Voice Contest, Turin. *Current Management:* Prima International. *Address:* c/o

Prima International, Palazzo Zambeccari, Piazza de Calderini 2/2, 40124 Bologna, Italy.

PETROV, Andrey (Pavlovich); Composer; b. 2 Sept. 1930, Leningrad, Russia. *Education:* Studied at Leningrad Conservatory, 1949–54. *Career:* Editor at Muzgiz Music Publishers, Teacher at Leningrad Conservatory, 1961–63; Chairman of Leningrad/St Petersburg Composers Union from 1964. *Compositions include:* Operas: Peter the First, Leningrad, 1975; Mayokovsky Begins, Leningrad, 1983; Ballets: The Magic Apple Tree, 1953; The Station Master, 1955; The Shore of Hope, 1959; The Creation of the World, 1971; Pushkin: Reflections on the Poet, 1978; The Master and Margarita, ballet, 1987; Orchestral: Pioneer Suite, 1951; Sport Suite, 1953; Radda and Lioko, Symphonic Poem, 1954; Songs of Today, 1965; Poem, in memory of the Siege of Leningrad, 1965; Patriotic vocal music; Film music and popular songs; 2 Symphonies, 1992, 1995; The Time of Christ, Choral Symphony, 1995; String Quartet, 1993. *Honours:* USSR State Prizes. *Address:* c/o MUSICAUTOR, 63 Tzar Assen Str, 1463 Sofia, Bulgaria.

PETROV, Ivan; Singer (Bass); b. 23 Feb. 1920, Irkutsk, USSR. *Education:* Glazunov Music College Moscow, 1938–39, with a Mineyev. *Career:* Sang with Ivan Kozlovsky's opera group from 1939; Concert engagements with the Moscow Philharmonic, 1941; Bolshoi Theatre, Moscow, from 1943; Sang there in the 1953 premiere of Shaporin's The Decembrists; Paris Opéra, 1954, as Boris Godunov; Concert tour of Europe, 1954–55; Other operatic roles include Glinka's Ruslan, Dosifey in Khovanshchina, Mepistopheles in Faust, Verdi's King Philip and Basilio in Il Barbiere di Siviglia. *Recordings:* Eugene Onegin; Rachmaninov's Aleko; Prince Igor; Ruslan and Lyudmila; Boris Godunov; Verdi Requiem; The Tale of Tsar Saltan by Rimsky-Korsakov, Tchaikovsky's Mazeppa and Romeo and Juliette. *Recordings include:* Title role in Prince Igor, conducted by Mark Ermler. *Address:* c/o Bolshoi Theatre, Pr Marxa 8/2, 103009 Moscow, Russia.

PETROV, Marina, MA; Recital Pianist and Piano Lecturer; b. 27 Dec. 1960, Kiev, Russia. *Education:* Central Music School for Gifted Children, Belgrade, Central Music School for Gifted Children, Kiev, College of Music, Belgrade, Moscow Conservatoire, Belgrade Academy of Music. *Career:* debut in Belgrade 1969; recital pianist 1969–; first appearance on television and radio in Belgrade in 1969; subsequently played in Kiev and Moscow; tours in Yugoslavia; has also played in Norway and in the United Kingdom at venues including London, Dartington Hall and Bristol 1990–; lecturer in piano. *Contributions:* The Times. *Address:* 28B Caedmon Road, London N7 6DH, England.

PETROV, Nikolai; Pianist; b. 14 April 1943, Moscow, USSR. *Education:* Graduated Moscow Conservatory, 1967; Postgraduate studies with Yakov Zak. *Career:* Public career from 1962; Many appearances with leading orchestras in Europe, Turkey, Canada, Japan, Mexico, the USA and USSR; Soloist with the Moscow Philharmonic Orchestra from 1968; Often heard in Tchaikovsky and Rachmaninov. *Honours:* Second Prize Van Cliburn International Competition, 1962; Second Prize Queen Elisabeth of the Belgians Competition, 1964. *Address:* c/o Sovinart, Murmansky proezd 18, app. 77, Rus-Moscow, 129075, Russia.

PETROV, Petar Konstantinov; Bulgarian composer and pianist; b. 23 June 1961, Stara Zagora. *Education:* Musical School, St Zagora, State Musical Academy, Sofia. *Career:* debut in New Bulgarian Music, 1984; Manager and Pianist in Chilorch-choire, Sofia, 1988–91; Honorary Professor of Contrapunct in Bulgarian State Academy, 1990–93; Professor of Counterpoint and Composition in Music School, St Zagora; Composition Masterclass of Profesor Anatol Vieru-Rumenia, 1993–95; many appearances as Chamber Pianist with Rosed Idealov–Clarinet, 1990–97. *Compositions:* Sonata, partita for violin solo, 1986; Concerto Piccolo for flute, violin and piano, 1987; The Christian Convert, for organ, 1989; Studies Nos 1–19, for various solo instruments, 1989–99; Ricercare, for three instruments, 1990; Symphony No. 5, alla bulgarese, for electronic instruments, 1998; Dialogues with Mr Galiley, for chamber ensemble, 1997; In Memorium, for piano, 1997; Dewy concerto for clarinet and 3 key instruments, 1997; 6 Mediations for chamber ensemble, 1997; Symphony No. 6 'Because these we are', 1998; Second concerto for Violin (Viola) and Orchestra, 1998; Phantoms in Viennese Forest, six commentaries for piano, 1998; Concerto for Piano and Orchestra, 'In memory of Eric Satie', 1999. *Recordings:* Concerto for Violin and Orchestra No. 1, 1987; Symphony No. 1, Lamento, 1987; Symphony No. 2, Katarsis, 1990; Concerto Piccolo IV, 1994; Dialogues with the Silence, 1994; Estampie, 1994; Symphony No. 3, Momento, 1994; Symphony No. 4, Dona nobis pacem, 1995; Bach Studies for Clarinet, Viola and Piano, 1995; CD, Messages I, 1997; Toccata for Piano, 1997; Messages II, 1999. *Address:* c/o MUSICAUTOR, 63 Tzar Assen Str, 1463 Sofia, Bulgaria.

PETROVA, Elena; Composer; b. 9 Nov. 1929, Modry Kamen, Czechoslovakia; m. Hanus Krupta, deceased, 1 c., deceased. *Education:* Four-term study of Musicology and Aesthetics at the Charles University, Prague; Piano at the High School of Music, Bratislava; Composition, Janáček

Academy of Music, Brno; Studied in USA. *Career:* Debut: Graduation concert (Cantata To Night), Prague, 1970; Works performed at home and abroad (Italy, Germany, Spain, the United Kingdom, Sweden, Russia, USA); Ballet Sunflower staged in Paris and Pilsen; Cooperates with Czech radio and televison and with a Prague art company Lyra Pragensis (organises concerts and poetry readings); Teacher of composition and improvisation at the Ceske Budejovice University and Charles University, Prague. *Compositions include:* 3 Symphonies, 1968, 1972, 1986; Symphonic Interludes, 1983; Si Le Soleil Ne Revenait Pas (full length opera), 1989; Comedy dell'arte for Reciter and Harpsichord (own poems), 1991; 4 String Quartets, 1968, 1972, 1989, 1992; Sun Sonata for soprano and orchestra or piano, 1992; Caprices and Dawning both for female choir a capella, 1993; Etudes for Fourhanded Piano, 1996; 3 Ballets for Orchestra, 1996; Trio for Flute, Clarinet and Piano, 1996; Ballet for Organ and Percussion, 1998; Concerto for Organ and Strings, 1999. *Address:* c/o OSA, CS armady 20, 160–56 Praha 6–Bubenec, Czech Republic.

PETROVA, Petia; Singer (Mezzo-soprano); b. 1970, Sofia, Bulgaria. *Career:* Many appearances in Bulgaria and Germany; In Operas by Rossini, Il Barbiere di Siviglia, La Donna del lago and L'Italiana in Algeri; Engagements with the Hamburg State Opera include Rossini's Rosina, Suzuki in Madama Butterfly and Mercédès in Carmen. *Honours:* Winner of competitions in Sofia and Barcelona; Finalist, Cardiff Singer of the World Competition, 1999. *Address:* c/o Hamburg State Opera, Grosse Theaterstrasse 34, 20354 Hamburg, Germany.

PETROVICS, Emil; Composer and Professor of Composition; b. 9 Feb. 1930, Nagybecskerek, Yugoslavia; 1 d. *Education:* Studied with Ferenc Farkas, Liszt Ferenc Academy of Music, Budapest, Hungary. *Career:* Professor, Academy of Dramatic and Film Arts; Professor of Composition and Head of Composition Faculty, Liszt Academy of Music; Director of Hungarian State Opera, 1986–. *Compositions:* Opera: C'est la Guerre, Lysistrata, Crime and Punishment; Ballet: Salome; Oratorios: The Book of Jonah, 6 cantatas; Cantat No. 7, Pygmalion, 1995; Symphonic Works: Symphony for string orchestra, Concerto for flute and orchestra; Vörösmarty Overture, 1993; Concertio for trumpet and orchestra, 1990; Two Intermezzi for strings, 1997; Chamber Works: String Quartet, Wind Quintet, Cassazione for 5 brass, Passacaglia in Blues for bassoon and piano, Nocturne, Mouvement en Ragtime for 1 and 2 cymbals; String Quartet No. 2, 1991; Three Poems for tenor voice and piano, 1996; All above works recorded; Hungarian Children's Songs for flute and piano, recorded in Canada; Four Self Portraits in Masks for harps; Cantate No. 9, Danube, 1998; Concerto for piano and orchestra, 1999. *Address:* Attila ut 39, Budapest, 1013, Hungary.

PETRUSHANSKY, Boris; Concert Pianist; b. 3 June 1949, Moscow, Russia. *Education:* Studies at Central School of Music and Moscow Conservatoire. *Career:* Many concert tours of Russia and appearances in Italy, Hungary, the United Kingdom, Germany, France, Japan and Australasia; Repertoire includes works by: Beethoven; Brahms; Liszt; Prokoviev; Shostakovich; Schnittke; Gubaidulina; Professor at Academica Pianistica in Italy. *Recordings include:* Works by: Schnikkte; Gubaidulina. *Honours:* Prizewinner in competitions at: Leeds, 1969; Moscow, 1970; Munich, 1971; Casagrande, 1975. *Address:* c/o Sonata, 11 Northpark Street, Glasgow G20 7AA, Scotland.

PETRUTSHENKO, Natalia; Pianist; b. 21 Aug. 1963, Ulan-Ude, Russia. *Education:* Basic Musical Education, Kemerovo; Completed High Music School, Nikolayev, Ukraine, 1983; Diploma with highest honours, graduating from class of Professor Dorenski, 1991, PhD, 1993, Tchaikovsky Moscow Conservatoire. *Career:* Comprehensive repertoire with orchestra and solo; Participant, 1st Rachmaninov International Competition for Pianists, Moscow and International Competition for Young Performers, Japan, 1993; Guest performance tour to Japanese towns; Numerous concerts in major cities in Russia, Ukraine, Belarus, the Baltic States, Bulgaria and Romania; Professor, High Music School, Kurgan, Russia, 1994; Soloist, District Philharmonic Society, Nikolayev, Ukraine, 1995; Living in Varna, Bulgaria, 1996–; European tour in preparation. *Address:* Jen Skobelov str block 19, ap 37, Varna 9000, Bulgaria.

PETUKHOV, Mikhail; Concert Pianist; b. 24 April 1954, Varna, Bulgaria. *Education:* Studied in Kiev and at Moscow Conservatoire with Tatiania Nikolayeva. *Career:* Many concerts in Russia, Italy, Belgium, Netherlands, Czechoslovakia and Germany; Played with Royal Scottish Orchestra, 1992, followed by Tchaikovsky First Concerto with City of Birmingham Symphony under Yuri Simonov; Repertoire has also included works by Purcell, Ravel, Handel, Stravinsky, Mendelssohn, Schumann, Schoenberg and Ives; Professor in Piano at Moscow Conservatoire. *Honours:* 3rd Prize at J. S. Bach Competition, Leipzig, 1972; Queen Elizabeth Competition at Brussels, 1975. *Address:* c/o Sonata, 11 Northpark Street, Glasgow G20 7AA, Scotland.

PEYSER, Joan Gilbert, BA, MA; American musicologist and writer; b. 12 June 1931, New York, NY. *Education:* Barnard Coll., Columbia Univ.

Career: Ed., The Musical Quarterly 1977–84; mem. American Musicological Soc., Music Critics Asscn, PEN. *Publications:* The New Music: The Sense Behind the Sound 1971, revised second edn as Twentieth Century Music: The Sense Behind the Sound 1981, Boulez: Composer, Conductor, Enigma 1976, The Orchestra: Origins and Transformations 1986, Bernstein: A Biography 1987, The Memory of All That: The Life of George Gershwin 1993, To Boulez and Beyond: Music in Europe Since the Rite of Spring 1999; contrib. to periodicals and journals. *Honours:* six ASCAP/Deems Taylor Awards, first prize in the humanities Asscn of American Publishers 1986. *Address:* 19 Charlton Street, New York, NY 10014, USA.

PFAFF, Luca; Conductor; b. 25 Aug. 1948, Olivone, Switzerland; m. Dominique Chanet, 1986, 2 s. *Education:* Basel University; Conservatorio G Verdi, Milan; Musikakademie, Vienna; Accademia Santa Ceàlia, Rome. *Career:* Director, Orchestre Symphonique du Rhin, France; Director, Carme, Milan; Founder, Ensemble Alternance, Paris; Guest Conductor, major orchestras, Europe. *Recordings:* Scelsi; Donatoni; Dusapin, Opera Roméo et Juliette; Mozart, Gran Partita. *Contributions:* Monde de la Musique; Harmonie; Rivista Musicale; Diapason d'Or, 1985; Best CD of 1988; Donatoni, CHOC, Monde de la Musique. *Current Management:* Valmalete, Paris, France. *Address:* c/o Ariën Arts & music, de Boeystraat 6, B–2018 Antwerp, Belgium.

PFISTER, Daniel; Composer; b. 6 Nov. 1952, St Gallen, Switzerland. *Education:* Teachers' Training College, 1970–74; Konservatorium Winterthur (Conservatoire), 1974–78; Teachers' Diploma piano, 1978; Musikhochschule Zürich, music theory with Hans Ulrich Lehmann, 1977–78; Hochschule für Musik und darstellende Kunst in Wien, composition with Prof Alfred Uhl, 1978–84; Diploma composition, 1984; Hochschule für Musik und darstellende Kunst in Wien, conducting with Otmar Suitner, 1984–87. *Career:* Freelance Composer; Private teacher for music theory composition and piano, 1982–; mem, SMPV Schweizerischer Musikpaedagogischer Verband. *Compositions:* Saitenspiel, 1982 for 2 guitars; Concerto for string orchestra, 1982–87; Aeon for soprano and piano, 1983; Aeon for soprano and orchestra, 1983–84; Canto for soprano or flute or saxophone, 1985–88; Canto for soprano (flute), clarinet and vibraphone, 1986; Neun und Zehne auf einen Streich, for guitar, 1988; Touches for flute, oboe, clarinet, bassoon, horn, trumpet, snare drum, gong, xilorimba, vibraphone, guitar, piano, violin, viola, cello, 1988–89; Bruchstuecke aus Touches, 1988, 880 un satiesme, instrument is free, 1988; 12 kleine Odien for flute and guitar, 1987–89; Max and Moritz for reciter and guitar, 1990–91. *Address:* Lehnstrasse 33 9014, St Gallen, Switzerland.

PHARR, Rachel (Elizabeth Caroline); Harpsichordist; b. 15 April 1957, Picayune, Mississippi, USA; m. Bernard Gerard Kolle, 1 Jan 1989. *Education:* BMus Summa Cum Laude, Piano Performance major, 1978, MMus, Piano Performance major, 1980, University of Southwestern Louisiana, Lafayette; Aspen Music School, Aspen Festival, 1980, 1981; MMus, Harpsichord Performace major, Arizona State University, Tempe, 1982; Banff Centre School of Fine Arts, Canada, 1987–89. *Career:* Harpsichordist with Houston Baroque Ensemble, 1983–87, with Texas Chamber Orchestra in Houston, Texas, 1985–87; Numerous concerts, Banff Centre, Banff, Alberta, Canada, 1987–89; Performed at Aspen Music Festival, 1981, Breckenridge Music Institute, 1982, 1983; Featured Soloist in Houston Harpsichord Society's presentation of the entire J. S. Bach Well-Tempered Klavier for Bach Tercentenary, 1985; New Music America concerts, 1986; Tours as Solo Harpsichord, 1986, with Liedermusik Ensemble, 1987; Harpsichord Accompanist, Banff Centre, 1988–89; Radio performances, KLEF, Houston and WWNO, New Orleans; Television performance, NBC-Channel 4, Denver. *Address:* c/o Newton T Pharr, 314 Dodson Street, New Iberia, LA 70560, USA.

PHIBBS, Joseph, MMus, DMA; Composer; b. 1974, London. *Education:* The Purcell School, Harrow, King's Coll., London, Cornell Univ., New York, Britten-Pears Contemporary Music course, Aldeburgh. *Career:* Asst Lecturer in Composition, King's Coll. 1995–96; teaching asst, Cornell Univ.; musical dir and composer for productions at the Wolsey Theatre, Ipswich, of Robinson's Walk 1995, The Devil's Cardinal 1996, Watership Down 1996, Romeo and Juliet 1997, Animal Farm 1997. *Compositions:* orchestral works: Soiree (winner BBC Young Composer's Forum) 1996, Dreams of a Summer Night 2000, In Camera 2001, Lumina (for BBC Last Night of the Proms) 2003; chamber orchestra works: Cayuga (for Faber Millennium Series) 2000; chamber works: Broken Sequence 1996, Char Fragments 1999, Trio Semplice (for Schubert Ensemble Chamber Music 2000 project) 2000, Ritual Songs and Blessings (for London Spitalfields Festival) 2002, La noche arrolladora (for BBC Proms) 2002, Rainland 2004. *Honours:* British Acad. Award, London Univ. 1995; Sage Fellowship 1997, Robbins Composition Prize 1998, Blackmore Prize in Composition 2001, all at Cornell Univ.. *Address:* c/o Faber Music, 3 Queen Square, London, WC1N 3AU, England. *E-mail:* josephphibbs@yahoo.co.uk.

PHILIP, Robert Marshall, MA, PhD, ARCM; music critic; b. 22 July 1945, Witney, Oxfordshire, England; m. Maria Lukianowicz 1976 (divorced 2002); two d. *Education:* Royal College of Music, Peterhouse, Cambridge, University (now Wolfson) College, Cambridge. *Career:* Junior Research Fellow at University Wolfson College, Cambridge, 1972–74; Producer, BBC television, Open University Department, 1976–99; Lecturer in Music, Open University, 2000–; Freelance Music Critic and Broadcast Talks; Early Recordings and Musical Style, 1992; mem, Royal Musical Association. *Contributions:* Records and Recording; BBC Record Review; Broadcast Series includes: The Long Playing Era (Radio 3); The Developing Musician (Radio 3); Composer and Interpreter (BBC World Service); Musical Yearbook (BBC World Service); Vintage Years (Radio 3). *Honours:* Organ Scholarship, Peterhouse, Cambridge, 1964; Visiting Research Fellowship, Open University, 1995–98; ASCAP Deems Taylor Award, 1992. *Address:* The Open University, Walton Hall, Milton Keynes, MK7 6AA, England.

PHILIPPE, Michel; Singer (Bass-baritone); b. 1943, Pau, France. *Education:* Studied at the Paris Conservatoire. *Career:* Sang at the Paris Opéra from 1971; Appearances at the Orange and Aix-en-Provence Festivals, Hamburg Staatsoper, Royal Opera Stockholm, Geneva, Madrid and Rio de Janeiro; Chorèbe and Panthée in Les Troyens at Montreal, 1993; Other roles have included Rossini's Figaro, Marcello, Scarpia, Mozart's Count, Don Giovanni, Valentin in Faust and Iago. *Honours:* Winner, Voix et Musique Concours, Paris, 1971. *Address:* c/o L'Opéra de Montréal, 260 de Maisonneuve Boulevard West, Montreal, Quebec H2X 1Y9, Canada.

PHILIPS, Daniel; Violinist; b. 1960, USA. *Career:* Winner of Young Concert Artists International Auditions and recitalist at Lincoln Center's Alice Tully Hall, 92nd Street 'Y' and appearances with major orchestras; Chamber musician at Santa Fe Festival, Spoleto Festival, Lockenhaus Kammermusikfest and the International Musicians Seminar in Prussia Cove; Co-founded the Orion Quartet and has given concerts at Kennedy Center, Washington DC, at Gardner Museum, Boston and throughout USA; Carnegie Hall recital, 1991 as part of the Centennial Celebration tribute to next 100 years of music making; Concerts at Turku Festival in Finland; Professor of Violin at State University of New York and Faculty member at Aaron Copland School of Music. *Current Management:* Ingpen & Williams Ltd, 7 St George's Court, 131 Putney Bridge Road, London, SW15 2PA, England.

PHILIPS, Leo; Violinist; b. 1960, England. *Education:* Studied at Yehudi Menuhin School and with Sándor Végh, Dorothy DeLay and Shmuel Ashkenasi. *Career:* Concerts as Chamber Musician and Soloist; Former member of the Chamber Orchestra of Europe; Leader and Principal Director of East of England Orchestra; Co-founder Vellinger String Quartet, 1990; Participated in master classes with Borodin Quartet at Pears-Britten School, 1991; Concerts as Ferrara Musica Festival, Italy and debut on South Bank with London premiere of Robert Simpson's 13th Quartet; BBC Radio 3 debut, December 1991; Season 1992–93 with concerts in London, Glasgow, Cambridge, at Davos Festival, Switzerland and Crickdale Festival, Wiltshire; Wigmore Hall with Haydn (Op 54, No. 2), Gubaidulina and Beethoven (Op 59, No. 2), Purcell Room with Haydn's Seven Last Words. *Recordings include:* Elgar's Quartet and Quintet, with Piers Lane. *Address:* c/o Georgina Ivor Associates (Vellinger Quartet), 66 Alderbrook Road, London SW12 8 AB, England.

PHILLIPS, John (Alan); Musicologist; b. 14 April 1960, Adelaide, South Australia, Australia. *Education:* BMus (Hons), 1983, PhD, Musicology, in progress, University of Adelaide; Conducting, Composition, Vienna Konservatorium and Hochschule, 1983–85. *Career:* Active Choral Conductor, Adelaide; Involved on major research project on Bruckner's 9th symphony finale, 1989–, its new performing version completed with Nicola Samale, Rome, May 1991, first performed, Linz, Austria, by Bruckner Orchestra, Dec 1991, first recorded by same orchestra, 1993; Lectures, conference papers, Australia, Europe; Press conferences, Australian, German, Austrian, US newspapers; Interviews, Australian, German, Austrian Radio. *Compositions:* Many unpublished works; Choral arrangements. *Recordings:* Two-piano recording, Bruckner 9th Symphony Finale with Edward Kriek, ABC Radio, Dec 1990. *Publications:* Bruckner's 9th Symphony Revisited. Towards the re-evaluation of a four-movement symphony, dissertation, 1995; Editor: Anton Bruckner: 9th Symphony in D Minor: Finale: Reconstruction of the Autograph Score from the Surviving Manuscripts: Performing Version by Nicola Samale, John A Phillips and Giuseppe Mazzuca, with the assistance of Gunnar Cohrs, 1992; Anton Bruckner Gesamtausgabe: Zu Band IX; Finale: Rekonstruktion der Autograph-Partitur nach den erhaltenen Quellen. a) aller dem Finale der IX Symphonie zugehörigen Manuskripte, 1994. *Address:* 107 Fourth Avenue, Joslin, SA 5070, Australia.

PHILLIPS, Margaret (Corinna); Concert Organist and Harpsichordist; b. 16 Nov. 1950, Exeter, Devon, England. *Education:* Royal College of Music, 1968–72; FRCO; GRSM; ARCM, organ performing with honours; Studied privately with Marie-Claire Alain in Paris, France, 1972–73.

Career: Debut: Royal Festival Hall, 1972; Director of Music, St Lawrence Jewry next Guildhall, London, 1976–85; Professor of Organ and Harpsichord, London College of Music, 1985–91; Tutor in Organ Studies, Royal Northern College of Music, 1993–97, Visiting Tutor, 1997–; Professor in Charge of Organ, Royal College of Music, 1998–; President, Incorporated Association of Organists, 1997–99; Recitals throughout: Europe, USA, Mexico, Australia; Radio broadcasts in: the United Kingdom, Sweden, Denmark, Netherlands, Australia; Performances with: London Choral Society, BBC Singers, The Sixteen and London Mozart Players; Lecturer, English Church and Organ Music; mem, Incorporated Society of Musicians; Royal College of Organists (Council Member). *Recordings:* Festliche Orgelmusik; English Organ Music from Queen Elizabeth I to Queen Elizabeth II; D Buxtehude; Orgelmusik i Karlskoga kyrka; Klosters Orgel; Organ Music of Saint-Saëns; 18th Century English Organ Music; 19th Century English Organ Music; Wesley, Music for Organ; Dances for Organ; Voluntaries and Variations; The Young Bach. *Address:* The Manse, Chapel Lane, Milborne Port, Sherborne DT9 5 DL, England. *E-mail:* phillips.eos@lineone.net.

PHILLIPS, Paul (Schuyler); Conductor; b. 28 April 1956, New Jersey, USA; m. Kathryne Jennings, 23 Nov 1986, 2 d. *Education:* BA, cum Laude, Music, Columbia College, 1978; MA, Composition, Columbia University, 1980; MM, Conducting, College-Conservatory of Music, University of Cincinnati, 1982; Eastman School, 1974–75; Mozarteum, Salzburg, 1977; Aspen, 1979, 1980, 1981; LA Philharmonic Institute, 1982. *Career:* Debut: Conducting Brown Orchestra (with Dave Brubeck Quartet), Carnegie Hall, 1990 (with Itzhak Perlman), Avery Fisher Hall, 1992; Frankfurt Opera, 1982–83; Kapellmeister, Luneberg Stadttheater, 1983–84; Associate Conductor: Greensboro Symphony, 1984–86, Savannah Symphony, 1986–89, Rhode Island Philharmonic, 1989–92; Assistant Conductor, Greensboro Opera, 1984–86; Music Director: Young Artists Opera Theatre, 1984–85, Brown University Orchestra, 1989–, University of Rhode Island Opera Ensemble, 1990–91, Worcester Youth Symphony Orchestra, 1991–97, Holy Cross Chamber Orchestra, 1993–96; Youth Concert Conductor, Maryland Symphony, 1986–99; Director, Savannah Symphony Chorale, 1987–89; Artistic Director, Brown Opera, 1992–; Guest Conductor, Netherlands Radio Chamber Orchestra and Choir, Pro Arte Orchestra of Vienna, US Orchestras; Music Director, Pioneer Valley Symphony, 1994–; Lecturer in Music, Brown University, 1989–. *Address:* Brown University, Box 1924, Providence, RI 02912, USA.

PHILLIPS, Peter; Choral Director; b. 15 Oct. 1953, Southampton, England. *Education:* Studied at Winchester College and an Organ Scholar at St John's College, Oxford. *Career:* Has taught at Oxford University and Trinity College of Music and the Royal College of Music; Founded the Tallis Scholars, 1973 and Gimell Records, 1981; Regular concerts in the United Kingdom and abroad, including USA from 1988 and Australia from 1985; From 1989 the Far East and Promenade Concert debut with Victoria's Requiem; United Kingdom concerts include Bath Festival, 1995; BBC Proms, 1988, 2001, 2003; Three Choirs Festival, 2002; Also conducted BBC Singers, 2003; Collegium Vocale of Ghent, 2003; Documentary features on TV, 1990, 2002; mem, Chelsea Arts Club; MCC. *Recordings include:* Lassus Music for Double Choir; Sarum Chant; John Sheppard Media Vita; Gesualdo Tenebrae Responsories; Cornysh Stabat Mater, Salve Regina and Magnificat; Clemens non Papa Missa Pastores Quidnam vidistis; Victoria Requiem and Tenebrae Responsories; Cardoso Requiem; Josquin Masses; Byrd The Great Service and Three Masses; Medieval Christmas Carols and Motets; Palestrina Masses, 4 CDs; Tallis Complete English Anthems and Spem in Alium; Allegri Miserere and Mundy Vox Patris Caelestis; Taverner Missa Gloria Tibi Trinitas; Russian Orthodox Music; Ikon of Light by John Tavener; CD based on South Bank Show feature; Isaac Missa de Apostolis; Tomkins The Great Service; Tallis Lamentations of Jeremiah; Tallis, Missa Puer Natus; Obrecht, Missa Maria Zart; Live in Rome; Live in Oxford. *Contributions:* The New Republic; Music and Letters; The Listener; The Spectator; The Guardian; Proprietor, The Musical Times, 1995–. *Honours:* (with Tallis Scholars): Record of the Year, Gramophone Magazine, 1987; Gramophone Award for Early Music Record of the Year, 1987, 1991, 1994. *Current Management:* Tallis Scholars, Hazard Chase Ltd, Norman House, Cambridge Place, Cambridge, CB2 1NS, England. *Telephone:* (1223) 312400. *Fax:* (1223) 460827. *Website:* www.hazardchase.co.uk; www.PeterPhillips.info.

PHILLIPS, Richard, BA; Festival Director; b. 15 Sept. 1940, Warwick, England; m. Veronica; two d. *Education:* Oundle School, Univ. of Oxford. *Career:* Sadler's Wells Opera 1966–70; York Arts Asscn 1970–80; Festival Director, Warwick Arts Soc. 1982–, Charlecote Park Festival 1983–98, Norfolk and Norwich Festival 1986–91, Solihull Arts Festival 1990–92, King's Lynn Festival 1997. *Honours:* Hon. Fellow Birmingham Conservatoire 2002. *Address:* Warwick Arts Society, Pageant House, 2 Jury Street, Warwick, CV34 4EW, England (office). *Telephone:* (1926) 497000 (office). *Fax:* (1926) 407606 (office). *E-mail:*

richardp@warwickarts.org.uk (office). *Website:* www.warwickarts.org.uk (office).

PHILLIPS, Todd; Violinist; b. 1968, USA. *Education:* Juilliard School with Sally Thomas and at the Salzburg Mozarteum with Sándor Végh. *Career:* Leader with the Orpheus Chamber Orchestra and solo performances with the Pittsburgh Symphony Orchestra (debut aged 13), the Brandenburg Ensemble, Camerata Academica of Salzburg, and leading American orchestras; Chamber music at the Santa Fe, Marlboro and Mostly Mozart festivals; Joint leader of the Orion String Quartet, with concert tours throughout North America and to London, Vienna and Amsterdam; 'Fourteen Musicians from Marlboro' tours; Season 1996–97 with Chamber Music Society of Lincoln Center, including premiere of George Perle's Quintet for horn and strings; Member of the violin and chamber music faculties at the Mannes School of Music. *Recordings include:* Mozart's Sinfonia Concertante K364, with the Orpheus Chamber Orchestra (DGG). *Current Management:* Ingpen & Williams Ltd, 7 St George's Court, 131 Putney Bridge Road, London, SW15 2PA, England.

PHILOGENE, Ruby Catherine, MBE; British singer (mezzo-soprano); b. 14 July 1965, London, England. *Education:* Curtis Institute, Philadelphia; Guildhall School of Music and Drama. *Career:* Concert engagements with the San Francisco Symphony Orchestra, London Philharmonic and City of London Sinfonia; Season 1994–95 included Mahler 2 with the Liverpool Philharmonic, Messiah under Yehudi Menuhin, Bach B Minor Mass and Schumann's Scenes from Faust with the London Philharmonic Orchestra, Janáček's Glagolitic Mass and Les Nuits d'Eté by Berlioz; Opera appearances as Britten's Hermia (with the London Symphony Orchestra under Colin Davis), in Biber's Arminio at Innsbruck, the Page in Salome (Covent Garden 1997), in Handel's Orlando with the Gabrieli Consort and as Goehr's Arianna; Season 1997–98 as Dorabella in Così fan tutte for Opera North and a new production of Parsifal in Brussels; Other repertory includes the Sorceress in Dido and Aeneas (Staatsoper Berlin) and Smeraldine in The Love for Three Oranges, at Lyon and San Francisco; Carmen for Opera North, 1998; Tokyo debut, with Bach Collegium, 2003; World premiere of Pierre Bartholomé's Oedipe sur la Route, La Monnaie, Paris, 2003; Britten's Midsummer Night's Dream, La Monnaie, 2004; Regular concerts and opera with Rotterdam Philharmonic. *Recordings include:* A Midsummer Night's Dream; Arianna. *Honours:* Winner, Anna Instone Memorial Award, 1990; 1993 Kathleen Ferrier Memorial Prize. *Current Management:* Askonas Holt Ltd, Lonsdale Chambers, 27 Chancery Lane, London, WC2A 1PF, England. *Telephone:* (20) 7400-1700. *Fax:* (20) 7400-1799. *E-mail:* info@askonasholt.co.uk. *Website:* www.askonasholt.co.uk. *Address:* Impulse Art Management, O. Z. Voorburgwal 72–74, 1012 GE, Amsterdam. *Address:* Jacob Marisstraat 97-1, HX1058 Amsterdam, Netherlands; 22 Pine House, Avenue Gardens, Droop Street, London, W10 4EJ, England. *Telephone:* (20) 8400-1721. *Website:* www.philogene.net.

PIA, Claude; Singer (Tenor); b. 1968, Berne, Switzerland. *Education:* Studies with Gina Cigna (Milan), Nicola Gedda (Switzerland) and Edita Gruberova. *Career:* Appearances in Berne, Lucerne and Basle, 1993–96, as Belfiore in Il Viaggio a Reims, the Painter in Lulu, Rossini's Almaviva, Tamino, and Dinna in La Vestale; Season 1996–97 as Ramiro in La Cenerentola at Lille and Mozart's Belmonte at Biel; Season 1997–98 as Rodolfo at Biel, Nikolai's Fenton at Visp, Painter and Negro in Lulu at the Opéra Bastille, Hoffmann at Klagenfurt and Narraboth in Salome at Barcelona; Season 1999–2000 at Lensky in St Etienne, Don Ottavio in Frankfurt, Arbace in Idomeneo at Toulouse and Belmonte for Nice Opéra; Further engagements as Verdi's Fenton in Frankfurt, Belfiore in La Finta giardiniera, and in concerts throughout Europe. *Address:* c/o Theateragentur Dr G. Hilbert, Maximilianstrasse 22, 80539 Munich, Germany.

PIANA, Dominique; harpist, teacher, performer, composer and arranger and writer; b. 5 July 1956, Eupen, Belgium; m. Will Joel Friedman 1985; one s. *Education:* Royal Conservatory of Music, Brussels, Claremont Graduate University, CA. *Career:* Professor of Harp, La Sierra University, Riverside, California, USA, 1982–2001; Professor of Harp, University of Redlands, California, 1985–2001; Holy Names College, Oakland, California, 2001–; As performer: Solo and lecture recitals, Chamber Music, Concerti; California Arts Council Touring Roster, 2000–01; Founder, Pleasanton Chamber Players; mem, American Harp Society, Programme Chairman, 1992 National Conference; American String Teachers Association; World Harp Congress; American Liszt Society; OPERA America. *Compositions:* Mélodies imaginaires, for solo harp, 1995. *Recordings:* Harpiana Productions: Fancy, entertaining music for harp, 1984; Lulling the Soul, Carols of Love and Wonder, 1992; The Harp of King David, Songs of Longing and Hope, 1994; Beyond Dreams, the Spirit of Romanticism, 1996. *Publications:* Contributions to Revue Musicale Belge, Belgium; Lumière, France; Contemplation, The Franz Liszt Anthology for Harp. *Address:* 3078 Camino del Cino,

Pleasanton, CA 94566, USA. *Fax:* (925) 600-1441. *E-mail:* dominiquepiana@comcast.net. *Website:* www.dominiquepiana.com.

PIAU, Sandrine; Singer (Soprano); b. 1969, France. *Education:* Studied with Julius Rudel in Paris and with Rachel Yakar and René Jacobs at Versailles. *Career:* Concert appearances in Bach's Passions and Magnificat under Philippe Herrweghe and Mozart's Exultate Jubilate with Jean-Claude Malgoire; Has also appeared under William Christie in Rossi's Orfeo, Mozart's Davidde Penitente, Campra's Idoménée and Purcell's King Arthur (Covent Garden and Paris, 1995); Has also sung in Purcell's Fairy Queen, Rameau's Les Indes Galantes and Castor et Pollux (at Aix), Handel's Scipione (as Berenice) and Pergolesi's Stabat Mater; Sang Almirena in Handel's Rinaldo under Christophe Rousset, Beaune, 1996; Season 1998 as Antigona in Handel's Admeto on tour to Australia and in Montpellier and Beaune; Season 2000 as Atalanta in Handel's Serse at Dresden, Ismene in Mozart's Mitridate at the Paris Châtelet, and in Handel's Tamerlano at Drottningholm, Stockholm. *Address:* c/o Opéra et Concert, 1 Rue Volney, F–75002 Paris, France.

PICCONI, Maurizio; Singer (Bass-Baritone); b. 1957, Italy. *Education:* Studied at Osimo. *Career:* After winning competitions such as the Concours Bellini in 1983 and the Philadelphia International in 1985, sang widely in Italy; Roles have included Rossini's Taddeo, Gianni Schicchi, Bartolo, Dulcamara, Belcore and Malatesta; Sang at Zürich in 1988 as Sulpice in La Fille du Régiment, at Bonn in 1992 as Leporello and further appearances at Dublin, Bilbao, Amsterdam, Strasbourg and Philadelphia; Sang Rossini's Bartolo at Pavia, 1995; Sang Sulpice in La Fille du régiment at St Gallen, 2000. *Recordings include:* Il Furioso all'Isola di San Domingo by Donizetti. *Address:* c/o Bonn Opera, Am Boeselagerhof 1, Pf 2440 Bonn, Germany.

PICHLER, Guenter; Violinist and Conductor; b. 9 Sept. 1940, Austria. *Education:* Studied in Vienna. *Career:* Leader of the Vienna Symphony Orchestra, 1958; Leader of Vienna Philharmonic, 1961; Professor, University for Music, Vienna, 1963–; Guest Professor, University for Music, Cologne, 1993–; Founder, leader of the Alban Berg Quartet from 1971; Annual concert series at the Vienna Konzerthaus, the QEH London, Théâtre des Champs Elysées, Paris, Opera Zürich, Philharmonie Cologne, Alte Oper Frankfurt and festival and concert engagements world-wide; Associate Artists at the South Bank Centre, London; Conducting engagements include Vienna, Israel, Irish and Norwegian Chamber Orchestras; London Mozart Players, Ensemble Orchestrel de Paris, Orchestre della Toscana, Hallé Orchestra, Deutsche Kammerphilharmonie, Tokyo Osaka and Sendai Philharmonic Orchestras and NHK Orchestra; US appearances: Washington DC, Chicago, Boston, Philadelphia, Los Angeles, San Francisco and New York (Carnegie Hall). *Recordings include:* Complete quartets of Beethoven, Brahms, Berg, Webern and Bartók; Late quartets of Mozart, Schubert, Haydn and Dvořák; Ravel, Debussy and Schumann Quartets; Live recordings from Carnegie Hall (Mozart, Schumann); Konzerthaus in Vienna, Mozart; Complete Beethoven; Brahms, Dvořák, Smetana, Rihm, Schnittke, Berio, Janáček; Opéra-Comique Paris, (Brahms). *Honours:* Grand Prix du Disque; Deutscher Schallplatenpreis; Edison Prize; Japan Grand Prix; Gramophone Magazine Award; International Classical Music Award, 1992; Honorary Member of the Vienna Konzerthaus. *Address:* Intermusica Artists' Management, 16 Duncan Terrace, London N1 8BZ, England.

PICK-HIERONOMI, Monica; Singer (Soprano); b. 1940, Cologne, Germany. *Education:* Studied at Rheinischen Musikschule with Diether Jakob. *Career:* Sang first in Oberhausen, then Gärtnerplatztheater Munich; Sang at Nationaltheater Munich, 1977–88; Has appeared elsewhere in Germany, and in Netherlands, Belgium, Austria and Switzerland; British appearances with Welsh National Opera and Opera North and at Buxton Festival; Roles have included Mozart's Constanze, Donna Anna, Electra, Vitellia and Countess; Verdi's Leonora (Il Trovatore), Luisa Miller, Violetta and Desdemona; Ariadne, the Marschallin, the Empress in Die Frau ohne Schatten and Elektra; Mathilde in Guillaume Tell, Zürich; Prima Donna in Donizetti's Viva la Mamma, Amelia (Ballo in Maschera) and Leonora (Forza del Destino); Concert engagements include Christ at the Mount of Olives by Beethoven, with the Orchestra de Lyon, under Serge Baudo; Season 1988–89 included Donna Anna in Liège and Handel's Belshazzar in Karlsruhe; Puritani at Brescia and Aida at the Verona Arena; Sang with Zürich Opera until 1992. *Address:* Music International, 13 Ardilaun Road, London N5 2QR, England.

PICKENS, Jo Ann; Singer (Soprano); b. 1955, USA. *Education:* Studied in USA and Europe. *Career:* Concert appearances with the Chicago Symphony under Solti, Los Angeles Philharmonic under Kurt Sanderling and Baltimore Symphony; German debut in 1984 appearing later in Porgy and Bess; Toured France in 1987 with the Orchestre Symphonique de Paris, in Verdi's Requiem; British appearances with the Scottish Chamber, Scottish National, Royal Philharmonic, Ulster, Royal Liverpool Philharmonic Orchestras, London Mozart Players, English Chamber and Hallé Orchestras; Conductors include: Antal Dorati, Penderecki, Rattle, Norrington and Libor Pesek; Sang in Liszt's Christus at the Festival Hall, 1990 under Brian Wright, A Child of Our Time under Richard Hickox at the City of London Festival; Concert performance of Nabucco with the Chorus and Orchestra of Welsh National Opera at St David's Hall; Sang in Les Troyens at the Berlioz Festival Lyon with Serge Baudo, Armide at the Buxton Festival and as Purcell's Dido, in France; Other appearances with the Chicago Lyric Opera and in Spain. *Recordings include:* Verdi Quattro Pezzi Sacri with the Chicago Symphony; My Heritage, Negro spirituals and songs by Black American composers with American pianist, Donald Sulzen. *Honours:* Winner of Concours International de Chant, Paris; Benson and Hedges Gold Award for Concert Singers; Metropolitan Regional Auditions, Paris. *Current Management:* Neil Dalrymple, Music International. *Address:* c/o Music International, 13 Ardilaun Road, London, NW3 1RR, England.

PICKER, Martin; Professor and Musicologist; b. 3 April 1929, Chicago, Illinois, USA; m. Ruth Gross, 21 June 1956, 1 s., 2 d. *Education:* PhB, 1947, MA, 1951, University of Chicago; PhD, University of California, Berkeley, 1960. *Career:* Instructor, University of Illinois, 1959–61; Assistant Professor, 1961–65, Associate Professor, 1965–68, Professor, 1968–97, Emeritus Professor, 1997–, Rutgers University; Chairman, Music Department, Rutgers College, 1973–79; mem, American Musicological Society; International Musicological Society. *Publications:* The Chanson Albums of Marguerite of Austria, 1965; Introduction to Music, with Martin Bernstein, 3rd edition, 1966, 4th edition, 1972; Fors Seulement: 30 Compositions, 1981; The Motet Books of Andrea Antico, 1987; Johannes Ockeghem and Jacob Obrecht: A Guide to Research, 1988; Henricus Isaac, A Guide to Research, 1991; New Josquin Edition, vol. 16, 2000; Editor-in-Chief, Journal of the American Musicological Society, 1969–71. *Honours:* I Tatti Fellow, Harvard University, 1966–67; NEH Fellow, 1972–73. *Address:* 3069 Chimney Ridge, Charlottesville, VA 22911, USA.

PICKER, Tobias; Composer; b. 18 July 1954, New York. *Education:* Studied with Charles Wuorinen at the Manhattan School of Music (BM 1976) and with Elliott Carter at Juilliard (MM 1978). *Career:* Composer-in-Residence with the Houston Symphony Orchestra, 1985–87; Commissions from the American Composers Orchestra, San Francisco Symphony Orchestra, St Paul Chamber Orchestra, and Ursula Oppens; Operas, Emmeline, premiered at the Santa Fe Festival, 1996 and Fantastic Mr. Fox, Los Angeles, 1998; Cello Concerto premiered at the London Proms, 2001. *Compositions include:* 4 Sextets for various instruments, 1973, 1973, 1977, 1981; Rhapsody for violin and piano, 1979; 3 Piano Concertos, 1980, 1983, 1986; Violin Concerto, 1981; 3 Symphonies, 1982, 1986, 1989; Serenade for piano and wind quintet, 1983; Piano-o-rama, for 2 pianos, 1984; Encantadas, for narrator and orchestra, 1984; Dedication Anthem for band, 1984; Old and Lost Rivers, for orchestra, 1986; String Quartet, New Memories, 1987; Piano Quintet, 1988; Romances and Interludes, after Schumann, for oboe and orchestra, 1990; Two Fantasies, for orchestra, 1991; Bang, for piano and orchestra, 1992; Violin Sonata, Invisible Lilacs, 1992; And Suddenly it's Evening, for orchestra, 1994; Suite for cello and piano, 1998; Cello Concerto, 2001. *Honours:* Charles Ives Scholarship, 1978; Guggenheim Fellowship, 1981. *Address:* c/o ASCAP, ASCAP Building, 1 Lincoln Plaza, New York, NY 10023, USA.

PICKETT, Philip; Director and Performer of Early Wind Instruments; b. 17 Nov. 1950, London, England. *Education:* Introduced to variety of early wind instruments by Anthony Baines and David Munrow: experienced on recorder, crumhorn, shawm, rackett and others; Professor of Recorder at the Guildhall School of Music, 1972, helping to organise the School's early music department; Fellow of the GSM, 1985; Soloist with leading ensembles, including the Academy of St Martin in the Fields, Polish Chamber Orchestra, London Mozart Players, City of London Sinfonia, London Bach Orchestra and the English Concert; As Director of the New London Consort has appeared at major festivals and concert halls in Finland, France, Germany, Greece, Netherlands, Hong Kong, Israel, Belgium, Spain, Italy, Latin America, Switzerland, USSR and Yugoslavia; British appearances include five Early Music Network tours; Medieval Christmas Extravaganza on the South Bank and concerts for the 21st anniversary of the Queen Elizabeth Hall; Director of the South Bank Summerscope Festival of Medieval and Renaissance Music (Pickett's Pageant), 1988; Regular engagements at the Bath, Edinburgh, King's Lynn, Edinburgh and City of London Festivals; BBC Programmes include music for half the complete Shakespeare play series, BBC 2; Music in Camera showings and regular concerts on Radio 3; Composed music for A Meeting in Vallodolid (Shakespeare and Cervantes) for Radio 3, 1991; Promenade Concerts include Bonfire of the Vanities (Medici Wedding Celebrations of 1539), 1990; Oswald von Wolkenstein concert at the Purcell Room, London, 1997 and Miracles of Mary at the QEH; Engaged to conduct Acis and Galatea for Holland Park Opera, London, 2003. *Recordings include:* Dances from Terpsichore by Michael Praetorius;

Medieval Carmina Burana; The Delights of Posilipo (Neopolitan Dances); Instrumental music by Biber and Schmelzer; Monteverdi Vespers and Orfeo; Cantatas and concertos by Telemann and Vivaldi; Medieval pilgrimage to Santiago; CD of Virtuoso Italian Vocal Music with Catherine Bott: de Rore, Cavalieri, Luzzaschi, G Caccini, Rasi, Gagliano, Marini, Frescobaldi, Monteverdi, F Caccini, Bernardi, Rossi and Carissimi (Il lamento in morte di Maria Stuarda); Biber Requiem. *Address:* c/o Jessica Atkinson, Polygram Classics (Publicity), PO Box 1420, 1 Sussex Place, Hammersmith, London W6 9XS, England.

PIDOUX, Roland; Cellist; b. 29 Oct. 1946, Paris, France. *Education:* Studied at the Paris Conservatoire from 1960, with André Navarra, Jean Hubeau and Joseph Calvet. *Career:* Co-founded the Ensemble Instrumental de France; Played with the orchestra of the Paris Opéra from 1968; Member of the Via Nova Quartet, 1970–78; Joined Regis and Bruno Pasquier, 1972, to form the Pasquier Trio; Directed the record collection Les Musiciens for Harmonia Mundi, 1979; Soloist with the Orchestra National of France, 1979–87; Professor of Cello at the Paris Conservatoire, 1987; Plays a Stradivarius of 1692. *Address:* Conservatoire National Superieur de Musique, 14 Rue de Madrid, 75008 Paris, France.

PIECZONKA, Adrianne, BMus; Canadian singer (soprano); b. 2 March 1963, Poughkeepsie, New York, USA. *Education:* Univ. of Western Ontario; Univ. of Toronto, Opera Division. *Career:* Began European career in 1989 at Vienna Volksoper; mem., Vienna State Opera 1991, sang Countess in Marriage of Figaro; Donna Elvira and Donna Anna in Don Giovanni; Desdemona in Otello; Agathe in Der Freischütz; Eva in Die Meistersinger von Nürnberg; Tatyana in Eugene Onegin; Antonia in Les Contes d'Hoffmann; Die Tochter in Cardillac; Micaela in Carmen; UK operatic debut, Glyndebourne Festival, 1995, Arabella, 1996; Sang Elsa in Lohengrin at Munich State Opera and in Los Angeles and Dresden; Debut at La Scala as Donna Anna, 1999, later as Marschallin in Der Rosenkavalier; Debut Covent Garden as Donna Anna, 2002; Debut at Metropolitan Opera as Lisa in Pique Dame, 2004; Sang Elisabetta in Don Carlo at Salzburg Festival, 2003; Has worked with Riccardo Muti, Claudio Abbado, Sir Colin Davis; Christian Thielemann, Sir Georg Solti; Lorin Maazel, Zubin Mehta; Appears frequently on BBC Radio, CBC and Austrian radio ORF. *Recordings include:* First Lady in Die Zauberflöte conducted by Solti, 1989; Die Fledermaus (Rosalinde), 1997; Complete Richard Strauss Orchestral Songs, 1998; Don Giovanni (Donna Anna), 1999; Millennium Opera Gala, 2000; Aids Gala Berlin, 2003; Don Giovanni (Donna Elvira) for television, video and DVD, 1995. *Honours:* Winner, 's-Hertogenbosch Singing Competition, Netherlands, 1988; Pleine-sur-Mer Singing Competition, France, 1988. *Website:* www.adriannepieczonka.com.

PIERARD, Catherine; Soprano; b. 1960, England. *Career:* Many appearances in the United Kingdom and Europe, with the Jerusalem Symphony Orchestra, City of London Sinfonia, Scottish Chamber Orchestra and Concertgebouw; Opera roles have included Tatiana in Eugene Onegin, Fiordiligi and Donna Elvira with English Touring Opera (1994), Papagena in Die Zauberflöte at the 1990 London Proms, Purcell's Dido (Spitalfields Festival 1993), Gluck's Alceste, Iphigénie and Euridice; Engagements with Roger Norrington in Orfeo at the Bath Festival and Purcell's Fairy Queen in Florence; Drusilla and Fortune in Monteverdi's Poppea under Richard Hickox; Season 1995–96 in Mozart's C Minor Mass, Messiah with the Ulster and London Bach Orchestras and Ravel's Shéhérazade with the Bournemouth Symphony Orchestra; Biber's Arminio at the Salzburg and Innsbruck Festivals, Bach's Magnificat at Ottawa and Handel's Belshazzar with Nicholas Kraemer. *Recordings include:* Monteverdi Arias (Hyperion) Dioclesian and The Fairy Queen (EMI); Britten's Rape of Lucretia (Chandos). *Telephone:* (20) 8995-3226. *Fax:* (20) 8742-7476. *E-mail:* catherinepierard@aol.com.

PIKE, Jeremy; Composer; b. 20 Nov. 1955, London, England; m. Teresa Majcher, 15 Aug 1981, 1 d. *Education:* MA, King's College, Cambridge, 1973–76; Junior Exhibitioner, Royal Academy of Music, 1969–73; Postgraduate Composition and Conducting, Royal Academy of Music, 1976–77; LRAM, Piano, 1979. *Career:* British Council Scholarship to study composition with Henryk Gorecki in Poland, Katowice Academy of Music, 1978–79, and with Tadeusz Baird at the Warsaw Academy, 1979; Director of Contemporary Music, University of Warwick, 1981–; Teaching posts held at, Bedford School, 1981–82 and Stamford School, 1982–. *Compositions include:* Time and Tide, Chorus and Orchestra; 2 Piano Concertos; 2 Chamber Symphonies; Shorter Orchestral Works include, the Voice; Overture; Fugue; 5 String Quartets; Oboe Quartet; Clarinet Quartet; Quintet for 5 Clarinets; Fantasy for Nonet; 6 Piano Sonatas and other Piano works; Guitar Sonata; Vocal works. *Address:* 84 Southern Crescent, Cheadle Hulme, Cheadle, Cheshire, SK8 6HA, England.

PIKE, Julian; Singer (Tenor); b. 1948, England. *Education:* Studied at the Royal College of Music and with Pierre Bernac in France. *Career:*

Sang Don José in Peter Brook's version of Carmen in Paris, Zürich, Stockholm, Copenhagen and New York, 1982–84; Sang Michael in productions of Stockhausen's Donnerstag aus Licht in Netherlands, Germany, Italy and London (Covent Garden, 1985); Tour with the European Community Youth Orchestra under Matthias Bamert, 1985; Wexford Festival, 1985, in Mahagonny; Appearances with Kent Opera in Poppea and Rameau's Pygmalion; Has sung in Henze's English Cat in Frankfurt, at the Edinburgh Festival and for the BBC; Premiere productions of Montag aus Licht in Milan, Amsterdam, Frankfurt and Paris, from 1988; Sang Roderick in The Fall of the House of Usher by Glass with Music Theatre Wales, 1989; Ligeti Festival at the South Bank, 1989; Other roles include the Dancing Master in Ariadne and Piet the Pot in Le Grand Macabre; Season 1992 as Michael in the premiere of Stockhausen's Dienstag aus Licht at Lisbon and later at Amsterdam; Recitals at the Bath, City of London, Camden and Aldeburgh Festivals: repertoire includes, Bach, Monteverdi and contemporary music; Tours of France, Germany, Belgium, Netherlands, Poland, Finland and Austria (Salzburg); Appearances with the Songmakers' Almanac and Fortune's Fire Lute Song Ensemble; Head of Vocal Studies, Birmingham Conservatoire, 1999. *Address:* Birmingham Conservatoire, Paradise Place, Birmingham B3 3HG, England.

PIKE, Lionel John, MA, DPhil, BMus, FRCO, ARCM; Organist and University Lecturer; b. 7 Nov. 1939, Bristol, England; m. Jennifer Parker; two d. *Education:* Bristol Cathedral School, Pembroke Coll., Oxford. *Career:* asst organist, Bristol Cathedral, Royal Holloway Coll., London 1965; Organist and Dir of the Chapel Choir 1969–; Dean of the Faculty of Music, Univ. of London; Senior Lecturer in Music, Royal Holloway Coll.; mem. Purcell Soc. (cttee mem.), Vaughan Williams Soc., Robert Simpson Soc. (fmr chair.), Havergal Brian Soc., Royal Musical Soc., Royal Coll. of Organists. *Compositions:* Monkey Music; The Pilgrim Way; Encircled by Sea; The Lyra Davidica Motets. *Recordings:* with the Chapel Choir of Royal Holloway College 1993–2003. *Publications:* Beethoven, Sibelius and the Profound Logic, Hexachords in late Renaissance Music, Vaughan Williams and the Symphony, Purcell: Symphony Anthems for in The Works of Henry Purcell (ed.); contrib. to Tempo, Music and Letters. *Honours:* Limpus Prize (FRCO). *Address:* Music Department, Royal Holloway (University of London), Egham Hill, Egham, TW20 0EX, England (office). *Telephone:* (1784) 443802 (office). *Fax:* (1784) 439441 (office). *E-mail:* Lionel.Pike@rhol.ac.uk (office). *Website:* www.chapelchoir.co.uk (office).

PILAND, Jeanne; Singer (Mezzo-Soprano); b. 3 Dec. 1945, Raleigh, North Carolina, USA. *Education:* Bachelor's Degree, University of North Carolina; Further studies in New York with Gladys White and Professor Carolyn Grant. *Career:* Debut: New York City Opera, 1972; New York City Opera, 1974–77; Sang at the Deutsche Oper am Rhein from 1977 as Cherubino, Composer, Ariadne, Octavian in Der Rosenkavalier, Silla in Palestrina and the Child in L'Enfant et les Sortilèges; Hamburg from 1981, Munich from 1985; Ludwigsburg Festival 1984, as Dorabella, Vienna Staatsoper, 1984, 1987, 1991 as Composer and Dorabella; Sang the Composer in Paris, Dresden, Hamburg, Vienna, Nice, Monte Carlo, Amsterdam, 1987, Ariadne auf Naxos at Covent Garden and Aix-en-Province, 1985; Returned to Aix 1986 and 1988, as Mozart's Idamante and Sextus, Composer and Octavian; Has appeared as Octavian at Dresden 1986 for 75th Anniversary of World premiere, Cologne, Zürich, Nice 1986, and Monte Carlo 1987, Santa Fe, 1988; Aix-en-Province, Munich, Hamburg 1988, as Idamante and Octavian; Sang Octavia in L'Incoronazione di Poppea Annius, La Clemenza di Tito, at Geneva, 1989; Other roles include Rosina and Cenerentola, Preziosilla, Smeaton (Anna Bolena), Zerlina and Massenet's Charlotte, Rosina, Concepcion, (L'Heure Espagnole), Elena (La Donna del Lago), Marguerite (Damnation de Faust), Clytemnestra, Iphigenia in Aulis, La Scala Milan, Cherubino, 1981; Houston and Los Angeles, Dorabella; Vancouver, Adalgisa, Norma, 1991–Carmen; Sang Charlotte in Werther for Florida Grand Opera, 1996; Olivia in the premiere of Trojahn's Was ihr wollt (Twelfth Night), Munich, 1998; Season 2000 as Neris in Cherubini's Médée at Montpellier (concert) and Eboli in Don Carlos at Dusseldorf; Repertoire includes, Berlioz, Les Nuits d'Eté, Shéhérazade, Mahler's Symphonies and Lied-Cycles. *Address:* c/o Grand Théâtre de Genève, 11 Boulevard de Théâtre, 1211 Geneva 11, Switzerland.

PILARCZYK, Helga; Singer (Soprano); b. 12 March 1925, Schoningen, Brunswick, Germany. *Education:* Studied in Brunswick and Hamburg. *Career:* Brunswick, 1951–54, debut as Irmentraud in Lortzing's Der Waffenschmied; Hamburg Staatsoper, 1954–68, notably as Berg's Marie and Lulu, the Mother in Dallapiccola's Il Prigioniero, Jocasta in Oedipus Rex, Renata in The Fiery Angel; St ädtische Oper Berlin, 1956, in the premiere of Henze's Il Re Cervo; Glyndebourne, 1958, 1960, as the Composer in Ariadne auf Naxos and Columbina in Arlecchino; Covent Garden, 1959, as Salome; US debut Washington, 1960, as the Woman in Erwartung; Metropolitan Opera, 1965, as Marie in Wozzeck. *Recordings:* Erwantung; Pierrot Luniare. *Publications:* Kann Man die

Moderne Opern Singen?, 1964. *Address:* c/o Hamburgische Staatsoper, Grosse-Theaterstrasse 34, 2000 Hamburg 36, Germany.

PILAVACHI, Anthony; Stage Director; b. 1962, Cyprus. *Education:* Guildhall School of Music and Drama, 1984–86. *Career:* Debut: Pergolesi's La Serva Padrona at Monte Carlo, 1983; Director and Assistant at the Bonn Opera, 1987–92, notably with Falstaff (1991); Director and Assistant, Cologne Opera, 1992–95, with Peter Grimes, 1994; Carmen at Bergen (1992); Il Barbiere di Siviglia and Traviata at Bogota (1994); Season 1995 with Un Ballo in Maschera at Freiburg, Carmina Burana at Dresden in the Zwinger Courtyard, Handel's Tolomeo with the Hallé and Lulu at Lubeck, 1996; Season 1997–98 in Freiburg with Orpheus in the Underworld and The Love of Three Oranges, for the reopening of theatre at Freiburg; Tales of Hoffmann at Lubeck; La Traviata at Gothenburg; Madama Butterfly at Lubeck; Engaged for 1998–99 season with Saul at Komische Oper Berlin; Daphne at Deutsche Oper Berlin; Faust at Freiburg; Season 1999–2000, Fliegende Holländer at Frankfurt; Dialogues of Carmelites and The Magic Flute at Freiburg; Seasons 2000–02 directed Cendrillon at Lubeck, Boris Godunov at Hanover, Così fan tutte at Bremen, Onegin at Freiburg, La Bohème at St Gallen, Fanciulla del West at Dessau and Figaro at Oldenburg; Season 2002–03, world premiere of Verdi, Gustavo III at Gothenburg, Sweden, Il Tabarro and Gianni Schicchi at Lübeck, Lohengrin at Bremen, Cavalleria Rusticana and Pagliacci at Dessau; Season 2003–04, Rigoletto at Cottbus, German premiere of Verdi, Gustavo III at Darmstadt, Idomeneo at Oldenburg; Season 2004–05: Entführung aus dem Serail at Oldenburg, Eugene Onegin and Don Giovanni at Cottbus. *Honours:* Princess Grace of Monaco Scholarship, 1983. *Address:* c/o Siemensstrasse 02, 50825 Köln, Germany. *Telephone:* 221 554284. *E-mail:* AnthonyPilavachi@gmx.de.

PILBERY, Joseph; Conductor and Orchestral Administrator; b. 30 March 1931, London, England; m. 1970, 1 s. *Education:* Royal Academy of Music, with Ernest Read; Trinity College of Music, with Trevor Harvey, Peter Gellhorn and Harry Blech. *Career:* Debut: Royal Albert Hall, December 1954; Has given concerts in all major London Concert Halls, notably with the London Mozart Players and the Royal Philharmonic Orchestra; Has conducted all 10 Mahler Symphonies, including the Resurrection Symphony at the Festival Hall; Lectures for the University of Maryland, the Elgar Society and the London Symphony Orchestra Club; Foreign engagements in Zürich, Vienna and the Salzburg Festival, 1982; Repertoire includes Carmina Burana, Sullivan's Golden Legend and Ivanhoe, Aida, La Bohème, Die Meistersinger, The Bartered Bride, Holst's The Perfect Fool, and Tosca; Founded the Vivaldi Concertante, 1983. *Recordings include:* Serious music by Arthur Sullivan, Music Rara, 1975. *Contributions:* Music and Musicians; Classical Music. *Honours:* Diploma, Services to Italian Music, 1989. *Address:* Allegro 35 Laurel Avenue, Potters Bar, Herts EN6 2 AB, England.

PILGRIM, Shirley; Singer (Soprano); b. 1957, London, England. *Education:* Studied at the Royal Academy of Music with Ilse Wolf and Patricia Clark; Further study at the National Opera Studio. *Career:* Sang with the Glyndebourne Festival and Touring Opera choruses; Solo debut as Helena with the Touring Opera, in A Midsummer Night's Dream; Appearances in Hong Kong, and at the Buxton and Wexford Festivals; With Opera East has sung Mimi, and the Female Chorus in The Rape of Lucretia; Scottish Opera as Despina, and cover for various roles; New D'Oyly Carte Opera Carte, Elsie in Yeomen of the Guard and Phyllis in Iolanthe; Oratorio and concert engagements, notably at the Barbican Hall, London, and recitals including lighter American music; Sang in Born Again directed by Peter Hall at the Chichester Festival; Other recent roles include: Countess in The Marriage of Figaro, Fiordiligi in Così fan tutte, Tosca in Tosca, Mimi in La Bohème. *Recordings include:* Solo album: Shirley Pilgrim with Attitude; Duet album–Lloyd Weber. *Honours:* ARCM, 1979; Dip RAM, 1981. *Address:* 85 Chichester Road, Edmonton Green, London N9 9 DH, England.

PILOU, Jeannette; Singer (Soprano); b. July 1931, Alexandria, Egypt. *Education:* Studied with Carla Castellani in Milan. *Career:* Debut: Milan in 1958 as Violetta; Sang widely in Italy as Mélisande, Mimi, Liu, Susanna, Manon, Nedda, Micaela, Marguerite and Nannetta; Appearances in Barcelona, Buenos Aires, Hanover, Hamburg and Wexford; Vienna in 1965 as Mimi; With Metropolitan Opera from 1967–86 with debut as Gounod's Juliette; Covent Garden, 1971 as Madama Butterfly; Sang at Monte Carlo 1973 in the premiere of Rossellini's La Reine Morte; Other roles have included the female leads in Von Einem's Der Prozess, Gluck's Euridice, Marzeline in Fidelio and Magda in La Rondine; US appearances in Houston, Chicago, San Francisco, New Orleans and Philadelphia; Sang Mélisande in Athens, 1998. *Recordings include:* Micaela in Carmen.

PILZ, Gottfried; stage designer and costume designer; b. 1944, Salzburg, Austria; m. Isabel Ines Glathar; one s. *Education:* Academy of Arts, Vienna. *Career:* Assistant at the Vienna State Opera to Wieland

Wagner, Luchino Visconti, Teo Otto, Luciano Damiani, Rudolf Heinrich and others, 1965–69; Assistant to Filippo Sanjust, 1969–72; debut in Reimann's Melusine world premiere at Berlin, Edinburgh and Schwetzingen Festival, staged by Gustav Rudolf Sellner; Operas, Dramatic Theatre and Ballets in Austria, Belgium, the United Kingdom, Netherlands, USA and Switzerland, principal in Germany; Exhibitions in Berlin, Kunsthalle Bielefeld, Düsseldorf, Kunsthalle Kiel and Wuppertal (Reflexe I–III, Aus-Grenzen I–III); debut as a producer with Rameau's Hippolyte et Aricie at Oper Leipzig, 1993; collaborations with John Dew, 1979–92 (Wagner's Ring, Krefeld, 1981–85, The Unknown Repertory at Bielefeld, 1983–91, Les Huguenots Deutsche Oper Berlin, 1987 as well as Royal Opera House, Covent Garden, 1991 and others); With Götz Friedrich (Der Rosenkavalier, Un Ballo in Maschera, Deutsche Oper Berlin, 1993) with Gunther Krämer since 1990 at Kölner Schauspiel, with Nikolaus Lehnhoff at Oper Frankfurt and Leipzig; Munich and Zürich, Henze's new version of Der Prinz von Homburg, 1992 and 1993; With Christine Mielitz, Rienzi at Komische Oper Berlin, 1992, engaged for Henze's The Bassarids at Hamburg State Opera, 1994 and also for 1994 at Oper Leipzig, Moses and Aron staged by George Tabori; Designs for the premiere production of Bose's Schlachthof 5, at the 1996 Munich Festival; Wagner's Ring at Helsinki, 1996–99. *Address:* Leipzig Opera, Augustusplatz 12, 7010 Leipzig, Germany.

PILZ, Janos; Violinist; b. 1960, Hungary. *Education:* Studied at the Franz Liszt Academy of Budapest and with Sándor Devich, György Kurtág and András Mihaly. *Career:* Member of the Keller String Quartet from 1986, debut concert at Budapest, March 1987; Played Beethoven's Grosse Fuge and Schubert's Death and the Maiden Quartet at Interforum 87; Series of concerts in Budapest with Zoltan Kocsis and Deszö Ranki (piano) and Kalman Berkes (clarinet); Further appearances in Nurembourg at the Chamber Music Festival La Baule and tours of Bulgaria, Austria, Switzerland, Italy (Ateforum 88 Ferrara), Belgium and Ireland; Concerts for Hungarian Radio and Television. *Recordings:* Albums for Hungaroton from 1989. *Honours:* 2nd Prize, Evian International String Quartet Competition, May 1988. *Address:* c/o Kunstter-Management T. Dönch, Weimarer Strasse 48, A–1180 Wien, Ausrtia.

PIMLOTT, Steven (Charles); Director of Opera, Theatre, Musicals; b. 18 April 1953, Manchester, England; m. Daniela Bechly, 27 July 1991, 2 s., 1 d. *Education:* MA, English, Cambridge University; Studied Oboe. *Career:* Staff Producer, ENO, 1976; Began long working relationship with opera North, 1978, including productions of Nabucco, The Bartered Bride and Prince Igor; Associate Director, Sheffield Crucible Theatre, 1987–88; Other opera works include: Samson and Delilah, Bregenz, 1988, Carmen, Earls Court, 1989 and La Bohème, 1993; Eugene Onegin for New Israeli Opera; Macbeth, for Hamburg Opera; Coronation of Poppea, 2000; World premiere of Param Vir's Ion, Almeida Opera; Hamlet, 2001; Musicals: Carousel, Royal Exchange Theatre, 1985, Carmen Jones, Sheffield Crucible, 1986, Sunday in the Park with George, National Theatre, 1990; world premiere of Bombay Dreams, London, 2001; Artistic Dir, Chichester Festival Theatre; Savoy Opera. *Honours:* Hon. Assoc. Artist, RSA. *Current Management:* Harriet Cruickshank. *Address:* 97 Old South Lambeth Road, London, SW8 1XU, England.

PINI, Carl; Violinist; b. 2 Jan. 1934, London, England. *Education:* Studied with his father, cellist Anthony Pini (1902–89) and in London. *Career:* Former leader of the Philomusica of London, English Chamber Orchestra and Philharmonia Orchestras (1974–); Leader of the London String Quartet from 1968 and the Melbourne Symphony Orchestra from 1975; Many chamber recitals in English works and the established repertory. *Address:* c/o Melbourne SO, PO Box 9994, Melbourne, VIC 3001, Australia.

PINKHAM, Daniel; Composer; b. 5 June 1923, Lynn, Massachusetts, USA. *Education:* AB, 1943, MA, 1944, Harvard University; Private studies with Nadia Boulanger. *Career:* Faculty Member, New England Conservatory, 1957–; Music Director of King's Chapel, Boston, 1958–2000. *Compositions:* 4 symphonies, 1961, 1962, 1986, 1990; Concertos for trumpet, violin, organ, piano, piccolo; Theatre works and operas; Chamber music; Songs; Electronic music; Television film scores; The Creation of the World, oratorio, 1994; String Trio, 1998. *Recordings:* Christmas Cantata; Signs of the Zodiac; Symphonies 2, 3 and 4; Angels are everywhere; Serenades; Miracles; Epiphanies; Magnificat; Proverbs; Diversions; Concertante for violin and harpsichord soli, strings and celesta; Inter alia; Advent Cantata; Wedding Cantata; String Quartet; Versets; Holland Waltzes. *Address:* 150 Chilton Street, Cambridge, MA 02138-1227, USA.

PINNOCK, Trevor David, CBE, FRCM; Musician, Conductor and Harpsichordist; b. 16 Dec. 1946, Canterbury, Kent, England. *Education:* Canterbury Cathedral Choir School; Simon Langton Grammar School, Canterbury; Foundation Scholarship, Royal College of Music, 1966–68.

Career: Debut: London Solo Debut: Purcell Room, 1968; Galliard Harpsichord Trio (with Stephen Preston, Flute; Anthony Pleeth, Cello), 1966–71; Founder Musical Director, The English Concert, 1972–2003; Recitals throughout Europe, Canada, USA and Japan; Artistic Director and Principal Conductor of the National Arts Centre Orchestra of Canada, 1991–; Conducted Handel's Rodelinda at Karlsruhe, 1998; Season 1999 with Haydn's 49th Symphony and Mozart's Requiem at the London Proms; Monteverdi's Ulisse at Florence, 1999; Conducted St Matthew Passion at the London Proms, 2002. *Recordings:* Over 70 with The English Concert including Bach: Complete Orchestral Works and Harpsichord Concerti; Handel: Messiah; Haydn: Nelson Mass; Haydn: Symphonies; Vivaldi: Concertos; Handel: Acis and Galatea; Purcell: King Arthur; Mozart: Complete Symphonies; Rameau: Complete Keyboard Works; Bach: Partitas, Goldberg Variations; Handel: Harpsichord Suites; Scarlatti: Sonatas. *Honours:* Grand Prix du Musique, Edison Pries, Deutsche Schallplattenpreis, the Gramophone Prize; Officier dans l'Ordre des Arts et des Lettres, 1998; Hon. RAM; Hon. PhD Univ. of Ottawa, 1990; Hon. MusDoc Univ. of Kent. *Current Management:* Askonas Holt Ltd, Lonsdale Chambers, 27 Chancery Lane, London, WC2A 1PF, England. *Telephone:* (20) 7400-1700. *Fax:* (20) 7400-1799. *E-mail:* info@askonasholt.co.uk. *Website:* www.askonasholt.co.uk.

PINSCHOF, Thomas; Flautist; b. 14 Feb. 1948, Vienna, Austria. *Education:* Artist and Teacher Diploma, Conservatorium of Vienna with Camillo Wanausek; Studies with Aurèle Nicolet; Masterclasses with Karl-Heinz Zöller, Jean-Pierre Rampal, Severino Gazzelloni; Postgraduate Studies, Indiana University, USA. *Career:* Debut: Wiener Musikverein, Brahms-Saal, 1965; Member, Vienna Symphony Orchestra, 1971–72; Berkshire Music Festival, Tanglewood, USA (with Scholarship Boston Symphony Orchestra), 1969; Founder, ENSEMBLE I, 1971–; Artist-in-Residence, with ENSEMBLE I, Victorian College of the Arts, Melbourne, Australia, 1976; Acting Head, Woodwind Department, Lecturer in Flute and Chamber Music, Victorian College of Arts, Melbourne, until 1988; Lecturer, Canberra School of Music, Melbourne University. *Recordings:* Deutsche Grammophon, Adel-Cord, Philips. *Publications:* Music editions for various publishers including, own series, Pinschofon, with Zimmermann. *Contributions:* The Flautist; Flutenotes; Musikerzeihung; Österreichishce Musikzeitschrift; Kunst und Freie Berufe. *Honours:* 2nd Prize, International Flute Competition, Severino Gazzelloni, 1975; Alban Berg Foundation Award, 1971; Australia Council Music Board Grantee, 1984–85 for project with Prof Nikolaus Harnoncourt. *Address:* Mozart Circle, Donvale, VIC 3111, Australia.

PINTSCHER, Matthias; Composer; b. 29 Jan. 1971, Marl, Germany. *Education:* Detmold Musikhochschule, Robert Schumann Hochschule, Düsseldorf. *Career:* commissions from Berlin Philharmonic, NDR Symphony Orchestra, Cleveland Orchestra; composer-in-residence to the Nationaltheater, Mannheim 1999–2000; composer-in-residence, Konzerthaus Dortmund 2002–03; première of Thomas Chatterton, opera in two acts, Dresden Oper 1998, L'Espace Dernier, Opéra de Paris 2003. *Compositions:* Choc (Monumento IV) 1996, Fünf Orchesterstücke 1997, a twilight's song 1997, Musik aus Thomas Chatteron 1998, Hérodiade-Fragmente 1999, Sur depart 1999, with lilies white 2000–01, 1 tenebrae 2000–01, en sourdine 2002. *Recordings:* Fünf Orchesterstücke, Musik aus Thomas Chatteron, Choc, Hérodiade-Fragmente, dernier espace avec introspecteur, Départ (Monument III), Figura I und II, Lieder und Schneebilder (Nr 1–4), Janusgesicht, a twilight's song. *Honours:* Foundation Prince Pierre de Monaco 1999, Kompositionspreis der Osterfestspiele Salzburg 2000, Hindemith-Preis from the Schleswig-Holstein Music Festival 2000, Hans Werner Henze Prize (Westfälischer Musikpreis) 2002. *Current Management:* Van Walsum Management, 4 Addison Bridge Place, London, W14 8XP, England. *Telephone:* (20) 7371-4343 (office). *Fax:* (20) 7371-4344 (office). *E-mail:* vwm@vanwalsum.com (office). *Website:* www.vanwalsum.com (office).

PIRES, Filipe; Composer; b. 26 June 1934, Lisbon, Portugal; m. Ligia Falcao, 29 Mar. 1958. *Education:* Piano Superior Course, 1952; Composition Superior Course, 1953, National Conservatory, Lisbon; Piano and Composition, Hannover Music High School, 1957–60. *Career:* Prof. of Composition, Porto National Conservatory, 1960–70; Prof. of Composition, Lisbon National Conservatory, 1972–75; Music Specialist, UNESCO, Paris, 1975–79; Concert tours in Europe (Pianist and Composer); Professor of Composition, Porto High School of Music, 1993–; Artistic Dir Director, National Orchestra, Porto, 1997–99; mem, Vice-President, Portuguese Authors Society. *Compositions:* Figurations I, flute; Sonatine, violin and piano; Piano Trio; Figurations II, piano; Figurations III, 2 pianos; 3 Poems by Fernando Pessoa, high voice and piano; String Quartet; Ostinati, 6 percussionists; Zoocratas, music theatre; Disimulation, for guitar; Brass septet; Epos, orchestra; Ricercare, orchestra; Playing Ludwig, orchestra; Babel, speaker, tenor, baritone, bass, male choir, orchestra; 3 Bagatelles, piano; Partita, piano; Varied song, piano; Stretto, 2 pianos. *Recordings:* Piano Trio; Figurations I; Figurations IV; Ostinati; Figurations III; String Quartet; Canto Ecumenico, tape music; Litania, tape music; Homo Sapiens, tape music; 20 Choral Songs; Portugaliae Genesis, baritone, mixed choir and orchestra; Sintra; Akronos, orchestra; Sonata, piano; Sonorities Studies, piano; Figurations I, flute; Figurations II, piano; Figurations III, 2 pianos; Figurations IV, harp; Sonatine, cello and piano. *Publications:* Theory of Counterpoint and Canon, 1981; Oscar da Silva- Analytical and biographical study; Helena Costa- tradition and renewal. *Honours:* Concours Quatour, Liège 1959; German Industry, Colonia 1959; Alfredo Casella, Naples 1960; Calouste Gulbenkian, Lisbon 1968. *Address:* R Costa Cabral, 2219-4D, 4200 Porto, Portugal.

PIRES, Maria João; Concert Pianist; b. 23 July 1944, Lisbon, Portugal. *Education:* Lisbon Academy of Music with Campos Coelho; Studied composition and theory with Francine Benoit; Further study with Rosl Schmid in Munich and Karl Engel in Hanover. *Career:* First recital aged 4; Concerto debut in Mozart aged 7; Early concert tours of Portugal, Spain and Germany; International career from 1970, with performances in Europe, Africa and Japan; Career interrupted by ill health; British debut, 1986, at the Queen Elizabeth Hall, London; Canadian debut, 1986, with the Montreal Symphony conducted by Charles Dutoit; debut tour of North America, 1988, appearing with the New York Philharmonic, Houston Symphony, Toronto Symphony and the National Arts Centre Orchestra, Ottawa; Season 1988–89 with concerts in Vienna with Claudio Abbado; Munich with Carlo Maria Giulini; Carnegie Hall debut recital; Played Mozart's Concerto K271 at Symphony Hall, Birmingham, 1997; Season 1999 with Beethoven's 4th at the London Prom concerts; Repertoire includes Mozart, Schubert, Schumann, Beethoven and Chopin. *Recordings include:* Complete Mozart Piano Sonatas; Concertos by Mozart. *Honours:* First Prize, Beethoven International Competition, Brussels, 1970; Edison Prize, Prix del l'Academie du Disque Français and Prix de l'Academie Charles Cros for Mozart Sonata Recordings. *Current Management:* Herzberger Artists. *Address:* 't Woud 1, 3862 PM Nijkerk, Netherlands.

PIRONKOFF, Simeon (Angelov); Composer; b. 18 June 1927, Lom, Bulgaria. *Education:* Graduated from State Music Academy at Sofia, 1953. *Career:* Violinist at National Youth Theatre, Sofia, 1947–51, later working as Conductor, Bulgarian Film Studios from 1961, Vice-President of Union of Bulgarian Composers, 1980. *Compositions include:* Opera: Socrates' Real Apology, Monodrama, Sofia, 1967; The Good Person of Szechwan (after Brecht), Stara Zagora, 1972; The Life and Suffering of Sinful Sophronius, Oratorio, Sofia, 1977; The Motley Bird, Ruse, 1980; Oh, My Dream, Ruse, 1987; Orchestral: Symphony for Strings, 1960; Movements for Strings, 1967; Night Music, 1968; Requiem for an Unknown Young Man, 1968; A Big Game for little orchestra, 1970; Ballet Music in Memory of Igor Stravinsky, 1972; Music for Two Pianos and Orchestra, 1973; Concerto Rustico for Cello and Orchestra, 1982; Entrata and Bulgarian Folk Dance, 1983; Lyric Suite for Strings, 1983; In the Eye of the Storm for Tenor and Orchestra, 1986; Symphonic Sketch on a Popular Melody, 1986; Flute Concerto, 1987; Passaglia for Symphonic Orchestra, 1991; Chamber: 3 Trios, 1949, 1950, 1987; 3 String Quartets, 1951, 1966, 1985; Sonata for Solo Violin, 1955; Berceuse for Clarinet and Piano, 1983; Theme and Variations for Violin and Piano, 1985; Symphony for 11 Soloists, 1990; Songs of Life and Death, Poetry of Emily Dickinson for Woman's Voice and Chamber Assembly, 1988; Tree Movements for Harp Solo, 1992; Piano Music, Choruses and Songs; Bosnian Lullaby, 1993; The Green Rain for mixed choir, 1994; Fantanziya for baritone, cello and piano, 1997; Four capriccios by Paganini transcribed for string ensemble; The Memory of a Piano, symphonic music for piano and orchestra; El Tango, variations for symphonic orchestra; Fantasy, on poetry of Heinrich Heine for baritone, piano and cello; The Flight of the Bumblebee, Rimsky-Korsakov, transcription for four saxophones; Film and Theatre Music. *Address:* Vitoscha Blvd 56, 1463 Sofia, Bulgaria.

PISCHNER, Hans; Teacher, Harpsichordist, Musicologist, Intendant and Retired; b. 20 Feb. 1914, Breslau, Germany. *Education:* Musicology studies at University of Breslau; Keyboard studies with Bronislav von Pozniac and Getrud Wertheim; Professor, 1949, PhD, 1961. *Career:* Head of Radio Music Department, 1950–54, Head of Music Department, 1954–56, Ministry of Culture; Representative, Ministry of Culture, 1956–62; Intendant, Deutsche Staatsoper, Berlin, 1963–89; Numerous appearances as soloist and accompanist in Europe, America and Japan, now retired; Chairman, Neue Bach-Gesellschaft, Leipzig. *Recordings:* Numerous works by Bach, both as soloist and continuo player; Bach Sonatas with David Oistrakh; Senior President, International Society for Young Artists, 'Bünneu Reif', 1995–' Bundesverdienstkreuz 1999. *Publications:* Music in China, 1955; Die Harmonielehre Jean-Philippe Rameaus, 1967; Premier en eines Lebens, autobiography, 1986. *Contributions:* Several articles for professional journals. *Honours:* Handel Prize, Halle, 1961; National Prize, 3rd class, 1961; Johannes R Becher, 1962; National Prize, 1st Class; Bundesverdienstkreuz der

Bundesrepublik Deutschland, 1999. *Address:* Friedrichstrasse 105C, 10117 Berlin, Germany.

PITTMAN, Richard (Harding); Conductor; b. 3 June 1935, Baltimore, Maryland, USA; m. 10 Sept 1965, 1 s. *Education:* BMus, Peabody Conservatory, 1957; Private study in conducting with Laszlo Halasz, NY, 1960–63, Accademia Musicale Chigiana, Siena, Italy, 1962, W Brueckner Ruggeberg, Hamburg, 1963–65 and Pierre Boulez, Basel, Switzerland, 1970. *Career:* Instructor, of Conducting and Opera, Eastman School of Music, 1965–68; Teacher of Orchestral Conducting and Orchestra Conductor, New England Conservatory, 1968–85; Guest Conductor of National Symphony, Washington DC, BBC Orchestras, London Sinfonietta, Frankfurt Radio Symphony, Germany, Hamburg Symphony, BBC Concert Orchestra, City of London Symphonia, Ulster Orchestra, Belfast, Nebraska Chamber Orchestra, Lincoln, Dutch Ballet Orchestra, Amsterdam, and Kirov Opera Orchestra, St Petersburg, Russia; Additional Guest Conductor, Banff Arts Festival, Canada; BBC Singers; American Repertory Theatre, Cambridge, Massachusetts; Symphony Orchestra of Ireland, Dublin, 1999; Seattle Symphony, Washington, 2000; Music Director, Boston Musica Viva, 1969–, The Concord Orchestra, 1969–, New England Philharmonic, Boston, 1997–; Guest Conductor, Canadian Opera Co., Toronto, 2000–02. *Recordings:* Music by Ives, Berio, Davidovsky, Harris, Schwantner, Henry Brant, Wilson, Lieberson, Rands, Ellen Taaffe Zwilich, Shifrin, Musgrave, Crawford and Seeger; William Kraft; John Harbison; Ezra Sims. *Honours:* Laurel Leaf Award from American Composers Alliance, New York, 1989; Peabody Conservatory Distinguished Alumni Award, 1996; ASCAP Award for Adventurous Programming (New Zealand Philharmonic), 2003; Chamber Music America/ASCAP Award for Adventurous Programming (Boston Musica Viva), 2004. *Current Management:* Tornay Management, New York. *Address:* 41 Bothfeld Road, Newton Center, MA 02459, USA.

PITTMAN-JENNINGS, David; Baritone; b. 1949, Oklahoma, USA. *Career:* Studied in America, Sang Lensky at Graz Opera in 1977 and was engaged at Bremen, 1981–85; Sang at Paris Opéra, 1982–83, as Don Fernando in Fidelio and Schaunard in La Bohème; Sang Germont at Tel-Aviv in 1988, and Wozzeck at Reggio Emilia in 1989; Member of the Karlsruhe Opera from 1990, singing Amfortas in Parsifal at Strasbourg in 1991; Season 1992 in Dallapiccola's Il Prigioniero, and as Mandryka in Arabella at the Vienna Staatsoper; Other roles have included Guglielmo, the Count in Capriccio, Mozart's Count and Figaro, Lescaut, Chorèbe in Les Troyens, Marcello and Gluck's Orestes; Sang in Schoeck's Venus at Geneva, 1997; Genoa 1998 in Peter Grimes; Season 2000–01 as Wozzeck at Santiago, Scarpia at Buenos Aires and Klingsor for the Edinburgh Festival; Cortez in Die Eroberung von Mexico, by Rihm, at Frankfurt, Orestes at Antwerp and Janáček's Forester in Ghent; Concerts include Beethoven's Ninth, Elijah, Ein Deutsches Requiem and L'Enfance du Christ. *Address:* c/o Staatstheater Karlsruhe, Baumeisterstrasse 11, Pf 1449, W-7500 Karlsruhe, Germany.

PITTSINGER, David; Singer (Bass-Baritone); b. 1962, USA. *Career:* Sang with San Francisco Opera from 1987; Brussels from 1988, as Verdi's Fiesco; Mephistopheles in Faust; Nick Shadow in Stravinsky's Rakes Progress; Shrecker's Der Ferne Klang; Mozart's Figaro and Don Giovanni at Nice, 1991, and Cologne, 1995; Salzburg, 1992, as Orbazzano in Rossini's Tancredi; Vienna Festival as Nick Shadow, 1993, and Lausanne, 1999; Season 1996–97, debuted as Olin Blitch in Carlisle Floyd's Susannah with Vancouver Opera; Performance of Bach's Christmas Oratorio with Amsterdamse Bach Solisten, Netherlands; Season 1997–98, debut at L'Opéra de Montréal, and also Maccerata Festival as Mephistopheles in Gounod's Faust; Boito's Mefistofele for Pittsburgh Opera, 1997, and St Louis, 1998; Season 1998–99, duo-recital with soprano Patricia Schuman including works by Mozart, Verdi, Tchaikovsky, Dvořák, Bowles and Copland; Debut as Four Villains in Offenbach's Les Contes d'Hoffmann for Opera Company of Philadelphia; Sang Publio in La Clemenza di Tito in Paris; Metropolitan Opera in Don Carlo, Rake's Progress, 1998, and as Colline in La Bohème, 1999; Season 2000–01 as Rossini's Alidoro in Brussels, Rossini's Selim in Buenos Aires and Tiresias in Oedipus Rex at Naples. *Recordings:* Simon Boccanegra by Verdi; La Calisto by Cavalli; Susannah by Floyd; Alfonso in Donizetti's Lucrezia Borgia. *Honours:* Grammy Award for Susannah. *Address:* Columbia Artists Management Inc, 165 W 57th St, New York, NY 10019, USA.

PIZARRO, Artur; Concert Pianist; b. 17 Aug. 1968, Lisbon, Portugal. *Education:* Studied with Sequeira Costa in Lisbon and at the University of Kansas; National Conservatory of Music in Lisbon. *Career:* Numerous concert performances in Europe from 1987; London debut 1989, at the Wigmore Hall, followed by concerts with the London Mozart Players at the Queen Elizabeth Hall; Has also played with the RAI-Torino Symphony, the Gulbenkian Orchestra and the Moscow Philharmonic; Rachmaninov's 3rd Concerto with the City of Birmingham Symphony in Leeds and the BBC Symphony under Andrew Davis in London, 1990; Further engagements with the London Symphony (de Burgos), Royal

Liverpool Philharmonic (Pesek), Los Angeles Philharmonic at Hollywood Bowl, English Chamber Orchestra, City of London Sinfonia, Hallé and BBC Symphony (Proms 1991); Recitals in the United Kingdom, Japan, Australia and the USA; Played the Ravel Concerto in G at the 1991 Promenade Concerts, London; Recital in International Piano Series at South Bank, 1997. *Honours:* Winner 1987 International Vianna de Motta Competition, Lisbon; Greater Palm Beach Symphony Invitational Piano Competition, Florida, 1988; First Prize, Harvey Leeds International Pianoforte Competition 1990. *Current Management:* Hazard Chase Ltd, Norman House, Cambridge Place, Cambridge, CB2 1NS, England. *Telephone:* (1223) 312400. *Fax:* (1223) 460827. *Website:* www.hazardchase.co.uk.

PIZER, Elizabeth (Faw Hayden); Composer and Musician; b. 1 Sept. 1954, Watertown, New York, USA; m. Charles Ronald Pizer, 10 July 1974. *Education:* High School Diploma, New York State Regents Diploma, Watertown High School, 1972; Boston Conservatory of Music, Boston, Massachusetts, 1972–75. *Career:* Numerous major concert performances of her compositions internationally including, San Jose State University Symphonic Band, 1979; Members of Honolulu Symphony Orchestra, String Quartet, 1980; Lincoln Center, New York, Charleston, South Carolina; Jacksonville, Florida, Donne in Musica Festival, Rome, 1982; San Francisco Chamber Singers, Nevada City, San Francisco, Berkeley and Ross, California, 1982; Piccolo Spoleto Festival, 1983; University of Michigan, 1983; Mexico City, 1984; Heidelberg, West Germany, 1985; Oakland, California, 1986; Many major broadcasts of compositions, throughout the USA, 1979–86 and a live concert broadcast including pre-recorded material in Australia, 1986. *Compositions:* Expressions Intimes, for Solo Piano, 1975, recorded by pianist Max Lifchitz, 1992; Quilisoly, for Flute and Piano, or Violin and Piano, 1976; Look down, Fair Moon, for Voice and Piano, 1976; Elegy, (formerly known at Interfuguelude) for String Orchestra, or String Quartet or Wind Quartet, 1977; Fanfare Overture, Symphonic Band, 1977–79; Five Haiku, for Soprano and Chamber Ensemble, 1978; Five Haiku II, for Mezzo-Soprano and Piano, 1979; Madrigals Anon, A Capella Choir, 1979; Sunken Flutes, Electronic Tape, 1979; String Quartet, 1981; Lyric Fancies, Solo Piano, 1983; Kyrie Eleison, A Capella Chorus, 1983; Strains and Restraints, solo piano, 1984, recorded by Max Lifchitz, 1992; Nightsongs, voice and piano, 1986; Arlington, electronic tape, 1989; Embryonic Climactus, electronic tape, 1989; Aquasphere, electronic tape, 1990; Elegy in Amber (In Memoriam Leonard Bernstein) string orchestra, 1993, recorded by the Slovak Radio Symphony Orchestra conducted by Robert Stankovsky, 1996. *Address:* 19458 Southshore Road, Point Peninsula, Three Mile Bay, New York, NY 13693, USA.

PIZZARO, Artur; pianist. *Career:* Prof. Guildhall School of Music and Drama, London; has appeared with numerous orchestras, including Philadelphia Orchestra, LA Philharmonic, Baltimore Symphony, NHK Symphony (Tokyo), Montréal Symphony, Toronto Symphony, Hong Kong Philharmonic, Leipzig Chamber Orchestra, Rotterdam Philharmonic, Vienna Symphony, Royal Philharmonic, BBC Symphony Orchestra; has recorded nine solo albums of works by Liszt, Bach-Liszt, Kabalevsky, Rodrigo, Vorisek, Mompou, Shostakovich, Scriabin, Milhaud. *Honours:* winner, Leeds Int. Piano Competition 1990. *Current Management:* Linn Records, Floors Road, Waterfoot, Glasgow G76 0EP, Scotland. *Telephone:* (141) 3035027. *Fax:* (141) 3035007. *E-mail:* info@linnrecords.co.uk. *Website:* www.linnrecords.com.

PIZZI, Pier Luigi; stage director and designer; b. 15 June 1930, Milan, Italy. *Education:* Milan Polytechnic. *Career:* debut designing Don Giovanni at Genoa, 1952; Designs and productions of such Baroque operas as Handel's Ariodante, La Scala, 1982, and Rinaldo (seen at Reggio Emilia, Paris, Madrid and Lisbon); Rameau's Hippolyte et Aricie and Castor et Pollux, Aix-en-Provence, 1983, 1991; Gluck's Alceste for La Scala, 1987; Other work has included Les Troyens, to open the Opéra Bastille at Paris in 1990, followed by Samson et Dalila, 1991; I Capuleti e i Montecchi at Covent Garden, 1984, (revived, 2001); Don Carlos at Vienna, 1989; La Traviata seen at Monte Carlo, Venice and Lausanne; Rossini productions at Pesaro include Otello and Tancredi, 1991; Staged Gluck's Armide at La Scala to open the 1996–97 season; Rossini, Guillaume Tell, Rossini Opera Festival, 1995; Verdi, Macbeth, Arena di Verona, 1997. *Honours:* Légion d'Honneur. *Address:* c/o Opéra de Monte Carlo, MC 98000, Monaco.

PLA GARRIGOS, Adolf; Musician and Pianist; b. 4 Oct. 1960, Sabadell, Spain; m. Roser Farriol. *Education:* Superior Diploma, Public Conservatoire of Barcelona, 1984; Postgraduate, Franz Liszt Academy, Budapest, 1988; Meisterklassen Diploma, Würzburg, Germany, 1992. *Career:* Invited to the International Festivals of Barcelona, Madrid, Havana and St Petersburg, also at Pau Casals Festival in Spain, El Salvador and Prades, France; Appeared in concerts in Italy, Germany and Hungary and on Spanish National Radio, Russian National Radio and Catalan television; mem, Director of Professional Conservatoire of Sabadell, 1989–93, 1996–97; Council Member, Catalan Association of

Performance, 1994–. *Recordings:* CD of music by Schumann, Granados and Ravel as soloist, Ma De Guido, 1995. *Current Management:* Felip Pedrell. *Address:* c/o Felip Pedrell 24, E 08208 Sabadell, Spain.

PLACIDI, Tommaso; Conductor; b. 29 March 1964, Rome, Italy. *Education:* Geneva Conservatory; Vienna Academy of Music; Academia Musicale Chigiana, Siena, Italy. *Career:* Assistant Conductor, London Symphony Orchestra; Guest conductor, in Europe, of the London Symphony Orchestra, Orchestre National du Capitole de Toulouse, Orchestre Philharmonique de Strasbourg, Orchestre Philharmonique des Pays de Loire, Orchestre de la Suisse Romande, Orchestre de Chambre de Lausanne, Wiener Kammerorchester, Orchestra Sinfonica RAI, Turin, Orchestra del Teatro Regio, Turin, Orchestra della Toscana, Florence, Orchestre Sinfonica Haydn Bolzano, Trento, Orchestra of Bratislava Opera House, Philharmonisches Staatorchester Halle, Radio Philharmonie Hannover des NDR, Orchestre Philharmonique de Liège, Orchestre Philharmonique du Luxembourg, Norddeutsche Philharmonie Rostock. *Recordings:* Tchaikovsky's Violin Concerto, Piano Concerto No. 1; Weber's Clarinet Concertos, Münchner Rundfunkorchester, Germany, 1997; Bruch Concerto for Clarinet and Viola, Hannover Radio Philharmonic, 2002. *Honours:* 1st Prize, Besançon Conducting Competition, 1992; 1st Prize, Donatella Flick Conducting Competition, London, 1966. *Current Management:* IMG Artists, London, Konzert-Direktion Hans Adler, Berlin. *Address:* 5 Chemin Taverney, 1218 Geneva, Switzerland.

PLAGGE, Wolfgang (Antoine Marie); Composer and Pianist; b. 23 Aug. 1960, Oslo, Norway; m. Lena Rist-Larsen, 25 June 1993. *Education:* Began Piano, age 5; Piano with Robert Riefling and Jens Harald Bratlie, Norway, Composition with Oistein Sommerfeldt and Johan Kvandal; Piano with Evgenij Koroliev, Composition with Werner Krützfeld, Musikhochschule, Hamburg, graduated 1983. *Career:* Debut: Pianist, Oslo, 1972; 1st published work at age 12; Commissions. *Compositions include:* Music for 2 Pianos, 1982–89; Piano Sonata V, 1985–86, VI, 1988–91; Vesaas-Sange: Baryton og Piano, 1989–90; A Litany for the 21st Century: Sonata for Horn and Piano, 1989; Festival Music, symphonic band, 1989, 1994 Version, symphonic orchestra; Concerto: Horn and Orchestra, 1990; Canzona: Brass Quintet and Pianoforte, 1990; Concerto: Violin and Orchestra, 1991; Concerto: 2 Pianos and Orchestra, 1991; Solarljod: Solsanger fra Norron Middelalder, 1992; Sonata II, Bassoon and Pianoforte, 1993; Hogge i Stein, A Portrait of Trondenes Church and Her People, narrator, choir, 3 soli, orchestra, 1994; Concerto for Trumpet and Orchestra, 1994. *Recordings:* Canzona, Wolfgang Plagge, piano, and Arctic Brass; Bassoon sonata, Robert Ronnes, bassoon, Eva Knardahl, piano; Concerto for Horn and Orchestra, Froydis Reed Wekre, horn, Trondheim Symphony Orchestra, conductor Ole Kristian Ruud; Contemporary Music for Brass: Canzona, Wolfgang Plagge, piano, and Arctic Brass; Eivind Groven; Piano Concerto, Wolfgang Plagge, piano, Trondheim Symphony Orchestra, conductor Ole Kristian Ruud. *Address:* Seljefloyten 39, 1346 Gjettum, Norway.

PLAISTOW, Stephen, ARCM; pianist, critic, broadcaster and radio producer; b. 24 Jan. 1937, Welwyn Garden City, England. *Education:* Clare College, Cambridge. *Career:* freelance journalist 1961–; BBC Music Producer, 1962–74; Chairman British Section of ISCM and Music Section of ICA, 1967–71; Member, Music Panel, Arts Council of Great Britain, 1972–79; Chief Assistant to Controller of Music, BBC, 1974–79; Chairman, British section of ISCM and Arts Council Contemporary Music Network, 1976–79; Editor, Contemporary Music, BBC, 1979–92; Deputy Head of Radio 3 Music Department, BBC, 1989–92; mem. Royal Society of Musicians. *Contributions:* The Gramophone; Guardian; Musical Times; Tempo; Independent; Revista de libros. *Honours:* Lesley Boosey Award, 1994; Hon. RAM. *Address:* 5 Gloucester Court, 33 Gloucester Avenue, London NW1 7TJ, England. *Telephone:* (20) 7485-2693. *Fax:* (20) 7424-0014. *E-mail:* stephen.plaistow@ecosse.net. *Website:* sites.ecosse.net/stephen.plaistow.

PLANCHART, Alejandro (Enrique); Music Historian and Composer; b. 29 July 1935, Caracas, Venezuela; Divorced, 1 d. *Education:* BMus, 1958, MMus, 1960, Yale University School of Music; PhD, Harvard University, 1971. *Career:* Freelance Arranger, Composer, New York and New Haven, 1960–64; Instructor/Assistance Professor, Yale, 1967–75; Associate Professor, University of Victoria, 1975–76; Associate Professor, University of California at Santa Barbara, 1976–; Visiting Professor, Brandeis, 1982–83. *Compositions:* Divertimento for Percussion Trio; Five Poems of James Joyce for Soprano and Piano. *Recordings:* 20 recordings of medieval and renaissance music with the Cappella Cordina, Lyrichord and Musical Heritage Society. *Publications:* The Repertory of Tropes at Winchester, 2 vols, Princeton, 1977; Beneventanum Troporum Corpus, with John Boe co-editor, 10 vols in press. *Contributions:* Guillaume Dufay's Masses: Notes and Revisions, in Musical Quarterly, 1972; Fifteenth Century, Masses: Notes on Chronology and Performance, in Study Musicali 10, 1983; About 50 other titles. *Address:* 1070 Via Regina, Santa Barbara, CA 93111, USA.

PLASSON, Michel; Conductor; b. 2 Oct. 1933, Paris, France. *Education:* Studied at the Paris Conservatoire and in the USA with Leinsdorf, Monteux and Stokowski. *Career:* Musical Director in Metz, 1966–68; Director of the Orchestra and of the Théâtre du Capitole de Toulouse, 1968–83; Operatic performances in Toulouse include Salome, Aida, Die Meistersinger, Faust, Parsifal, Carmen and Montségur by Landowski (world premiere, 1985); Conductor of the Orchestre National du Capitole de Toulouse from 1983; At the Palais Omnisport de Paris-Bercy has conducted Aida, Turandot, the Verdi Requiem and Nabucco, 1984–87; Guest engagements with the Berlin Philharmonic Orchestra, London Philharmonic, Orchestre of the Suisse Romande, and the Gewandhaus Orchestra Leipzig; Paris Opéra, Geneva Opera, State Operas of Vienna, Hamburg and Munich, Zürich Opera, Covent Garden, Metropolitan Opera, Chicago and San Francisco; Principal Guest Conductor of the Zürich Tonhalle Orchestra from 1987; Conducted new production of Guillaume Tell at Covent Garden, 1990; Il Trovatore at the Halle aux Grains, Toulouse, 1990; Faust at the 1990 Orange Festival; Returned to Covent Garden, 1991, Tosca; Season 1991–92 with Lucia di Lammermoor at Munich, Guillaume Tell at Covent Garden, Don Quichotte at Toulouse and Carmen at Orange; Conducted La Forza del Destino at Orange, 1996; Original version of Boris Godunov at Toulouse, 1998; Honorary Conductor for Life of the Orchestre National du Capitole de Toulouse. *Recordings include:* La Vie Parisienne; La Grande Duchesse de Gérolstein; Chausson's Symphony; Saint-Saëns Piano Concertos; Premiere pressings of Roussel's Padmâvati, Magnard's Symphonies and Guercoeur, Symphonic poems by Chausson; Les Pêcheurs de Perles; Faust. *Address:* c/o Orchestre National du Capitole de Toulouse, Halle aux Grains, Place Dupuy, 31000, Toulouse, France.

PLATT, Ian; singer (baritone); b. 1959, Fleetwood, England. *Education:* studied with John Cameron at Royal Northern College of Music. *Career:* sang Rossini's Figaro, Guglielmo, Papageno and Junius in The Rape of Lucretia for Royal Northern College of Music; Professional debut for Kent Opera, in La Traviata and Il Barbiere di Siviglia; Engagements with Opera 80 as Don Magnifico in La Cenerentola and Baron Zeta in The Merry Widow; New Sadler's Wells Opera as Agamemnon in La Belle Hélène; Sang Tom in Henze's The English Cat at Hebbel Theatre, Berlin and toured with Travelling Opera as Schaunard and Mozart's Figaro; Welsh National Opera and Scottish Opera, 1991, in La Traviata; Alcindoro in La Bohème for Glyndebourne Touring Opera, 1991; Pirate King, D'Oyly Carte, 1993; Don Magnifico, Welsh National Opera, 1993–94. *Recordings include:* Il Crociato in Egitto by Meyerbeer, Opera Rara. *Current Management:* Robert Gilder & Co., Enterprise House, 59–65 Upper Ground, London, SE1 9PQ, England. *Telephone:* (20) 7928-9008. *Fax:* (20) 7928-9755. *E-mail:* rgilder@robert-gilder.com.

PLATT, Richard (Swaby); Musicologist; b. 14 May 1928, London, England; m. (1) 2 s., 1 d., (2) Diane Ibbotson, 3 Dec 1977, 1 s., 1 d. *Education:* Associate, Royal College of Art, 1953; Studied privately with Walter Bergmann, 1965–, Hugh Wood, 1966–68. *Career:* Painter, Printmaker, exhibiting at Royal Academy, London Group and others, 1953–61; One man show of works, Leicester Galleries, 1956; Musicologist, specialising in 18th Century English Music, 1969. Editions, William Boyce, 12 Overtures; Thomas Arne, 4 Symphonies; Works by Croft, Roseingrave, Mudge, Fisher; Gli Equivoci, by Stephen Storace; Peleus and Thetis by William Boyce; mem, Royal Musical Association. *Recordings:* Editions of music Boyce (Solomon), Arne and Roseingrave. *Publications:* Contributor of chapters, New Grove, 1980, 2001 and Grove Opera 1992; Theatre Music 1700–1760 in Blackwell's History of Music in Britain vol. 4; The Symphony, 1720–1840, 1983; Semele by John Eccles, Judgement of Paris, 1984, 2000. *Contributions:* BIOS 17, on Gerard Smith Organ Contract; Early Music, Nov. 2000, on Richard Mudge. *Address:* 3 Stratton Place, Falmouth, Cornwall TR11 2ST, England.

PLATT, Theodore; Conductor, Composer, Double Bassist and Harpsichordist; b. 8 Sept. 1937, Moscow, Russia. *Education:* Degree in Double Bass Performance, Composition and Music Education, Ippolitov-Ivanov Conservatory of Music, 1956; Doctorate, Moscow Conservatory of Music, 1962. *Career:* Founder and Director, 4 chamber ensembles including first baroque and classical ensembles in USSR (Moscow), 1968–81, and New York Concertino Ensemble, 1981; Live concerts on major classical music radio stations in US; 8 years as Double Bass Soloist of Moscow Chamber Orchestra under Rudolf Barshay (performance with Gilels, Menuhin, Oistrakh, Rostropoivch, others); Discovered and premiered lost baroque works; Teacher and Coach of String Instruments and Voice; mem, Conductors Guild; College Music Society. *Compositions:* 2 Symphony Concertos; Cycles of Vocal Compositions; 1 Quartet. *Recordings:* Baroque, Romantic and modern works as Double Bass Soloist of Moscow Chamber Orchestra under Rudolf Barshay; Baroque-Early Romantic repertoire (Mozart, Boccherini, Bach, Schubert, others) as Music Director and Soloist with New York Concertino Ensemble. *Address:* c/o ASCAP, ASCAP Building, One Lincoln Plaza, New York, NY 10023, USA.

PLATZ, Robert H. P.; Composer and Conductor; b. 16 Aug. 1951, Baden-Baden, Germany. *Education:* Studies with Wolfgang Fortner, Karlheinz Stockhausen, Francis Travis; IRCAM computer workshop for Composers. *Career:* Founded new music group Ensemble Köln, 1980; Own concert series with Ensemble Köln, 1982; Appeared in new music festivals such as Musik der Zeit WDR and Musica Viva series of Munich, Donaueschingen and La Rochelle; Performed at Salzburg Festival, Metz; All works recorded by Radio Stations in Germany. *Compositions:* Schwelle, Full Orchestra and Tape; Chlebnicov, Ensemble and Tape; Maro and Stille, Soprano, Violin and Piano Solos, plus Ensembles and Choirs; Raumform, Clarinet Solo; Flotenstücke–Seven Pieces for Flute and Ensemble; Requiem for Tape; Pianoforte 2; Closed Loop, Guitar; Verkommenes ufer, opera (texts Heiner Müller); Quartett (Zeitstrahl) for String Quartet, 1986; Dunkles Haus, music theatre, 1991; Grenzgänge Steine, for soprano, 2 pianos and orchestra, 1993; Echo I–V, for ensemble 1994–98. *Publications:* Musikalische Prozesse, 1979; Uber Schwelle, 1980; Uber Schwelle II, 1981; Uber Tasten, 1983; Versuch einer Asthetik des Kleinen, 1984; Blumroder, Nicht Einfach, Aber Neu, 1980; Formpolyphone Musik, 1981; Stegen: Robert HP Platz, 1982; Van den Hoogen: Komplizierte Horbarkeit, 1982; Blumröder: Maro, 1984; Van den Hoogen: Raumform, 1984; Allende-Blin: Uber Chielnicov, 1984; Record Maro, Irvine Arditi, Violin.

PLAVIN, Zecharia; Pianist; b. 7 June 1956, Vilnius (Vilna), Lithuania; m. 12 June 1984, 1 s., 1 d. *Education:* BMus, MMus, Ciurlionis School of Arts, S Rubin Academy of Music, University of Tel-Aviv, Israel. *Career:* Concerts with Israel Philharmonic Orchestra, Jerusalem Symphony Orchestra, Symphonietta of Beer-Sheva, Haifa Symphony Orchestra, others; Recitals on all major stages in Israel; Concerts in Western Europe from 1988; Numerous recordings for Israel Broadcasting Authorities; Work for Israel Concert Bureau Omanuth Laam. *Recordings:* Various. *Publications:* The Metamorphoses by O Partos. *Honours:* 1st Prize, S Rubin Academy of Music Competition, 1978; National François Shapira Prize, 1980; Diploma, Israel Broadcasting Competition, 1985. *Current Management:* International Music Consultants.

PLAZAS, Mary; Singer (Soprano); b. 9 Sept. 1966, Wallingford, England. *Education:* Studied at Royal Northern College of Music with Ava June and at National Opera Studio. *Career:* Solo recitals at Wigmore Hall, Purcell Room, Birmingham Town Hall and Royal Exchange Theatre, Manchester; Concerts at Cheltenham and Aldeburgh Festivals; Opera engagements include Poulenc's La Voix Humaine at Aix-en-Provence, Nannetta at Aldeburgh and Despina for Mid-Wales Opera; English National Opera debut, 1992, as Heavenly Voice in Don Carlos; Opera North, 1992–, as the Gypsy in British premiere of Gerhard's The Duenna, Barbarina and Susanna in Figaro and Tebaldo in Don Carlos; Sang in Opera Factory's Nozze di Figaro for Channel 4 Television and appeared as Echo in Ariadne auf Naxos for Garsington Opera; Joined English National Opera as Company Principal, Aug 1995 and sang Echo in Ariadne auf Naxos, 1997; Tina in premiere of Dove's Flight for GTO at Glyndebourne, 1998; Season 2000–01 as Donna Elvira for GTO and Lauretta in Gianni Schicchi for ENO. *Honours:* Winner, Kathleen Ferrier Memorial Scholarship, 1991. *Address:* c/o Owen-White Management, 14 Nightingale Lane, London N8 7QU, England.

PLECH, Linda; Singer (Soprano); b. 1951, Vienna, Austria. *Education:* Studied in Vienna and at Salzburg Mozarteum. *Career:* Sang as Mezzo at Klagenfurt Opera, 1976–77; Oldenburg, 1980–84; Soprano roles at Kaiserslautern, 1985–86, Hamburg Staatsoper, 1987–88 as Donna Anna and Elisabeth de Valois; Cologne, 1989, as Jenůfa; Bregenz Festival, 1988–89, as Senta in Der fliegende Holländer; Sang the Trovatore Leonora at Deutsche Oper Berlin, 1989, Ariadne auf Naxos at Antwerp; Season 1991–92 as Senta at Geneva, Elisabeth in Tannhäuser at Barcelona; Other roles include Marenka in The Bartered Bride and Giulietta in Les Contes d'Hoffmann. *Address:* c/o Grand Théâtre de Genève, 11 Boulevard du Théâtre, 1211 Geneva, Switzerland.

PLESHAK, Victor (Vasilievich); Composer; b. 13 Nov. 1946, Leningrad, Russia; 2 s. *Education:* Choral College of Chapel; Choir Conductors Department, Composers Department, St Petersburg Conservatoire (with B Tischenko). *Career:* Debut: Many-coloured Balls, song cycle for children, verses by Akimya, Leningrad Radio. *Compositions:* Over 17 musicals and operas including: The Red Imp, musical, 1980; The Knight's Passions, 1981; The Glass Menagerie, opera, 1987; A Tale of a Blot, New Year operetta, 1988; Caution Baba-Yaga, ecological opera; Inspector, an opera after Gogol, 1993; Choral Cycle, About Friendship, Love and Brotherhood, to verses by R Burns, 1983; Over 100 published songs including: V Pleshak, Songs for voice and piano (guitar, accordion), in Soviet Composer, 1988. *Recordings:* The Tale of a Dead Tsarevna and Seven Epic Heroes, opera in 2 acts; The Widow of Valencia, musical after the play by Lope de Vega; Oh These Pretty Sinners, musical farces after Lasage and Rabelais; Puss in Boots, musical after the play by Pierrot; Author of over 150 theatre performances including 30 musicals, and over 400 songs. *Compositions include:* The Turnip, opera after Russian folk tale, 1992; The Canterville

Ghost, musical after story, 1994; Ruslan and Ludmila, after Russian fairy-tale, Pushkin, 1999. *Recordings:* Hymn of St Petersburg Region, 1997; Hymn of St Petersburg University, 1999. *Address:* Gorokhovaya St (formerly Dzerzhinskaya) 53 kv 29, 190031 St Petersburg, Russia.

PLETNEV, Mikhail Vasilievich; Russian pianist, conductor and composer; b. 14 April 1957, Arkhangelsk. *Education:* Moscow State Conservatory with Yakov Flier and Lev Vlasenko (piano), Albert Leman (composition). *Career:* gave recitals and played with orchestras in maj. cities of Russia, Europe, Japan and America; gained reputation as Russian music interpreter; founder and Chief Conductor Russian Nat. Orchestra 1990–99, Hon. Conductor 1999–; tours with orchestra and as piano soloist in various countries; has performed with Haitink, Maazel, Chailly, Tennstedt, Sanderling, Blomstedt, Järvi, Thielemann; also conducted Philharmonia Orchestra, Deutsche Kammerphilharmonie, Norddeutsche Rundfunk Symphony Orchestra, London Symphony OrchestraBerliln Philharmonic, Bayerische Rundfunk Symphony, Orchestre Nat. de France, Israel Philharmonic, San Francisco Symphony and Pittsburgh Symphony; teacher in Moscow Conservatory 1981–1992. *Honours:* First Prize Int. Tchaikovsky competition, Moscow 1978, People's Artist of Russia 1990, State Prize of Russia 1982, 1993. *Current Management:* Columbia Artists Management Ltd, 28 Cheverton Road, London, N19 3AY, England. *Telephone:* (20) 7272-8020. *Fax:* (20) 7272 8991. *E-mail:* info@cami.co.uk. *Address:* Starokonyushenny per. 33, Apt 16, Moscow, Russia. *Telephone:* (095) 241-43-39 (home).

PLISHKA, Paul; Singer (Bass); b. 28 Aug. 1941, Old Forge, Pennsylvania, USA. *Education:* Studied at Montclair State College and with Armen Boyazjian. *Career:* Debut: Paterson Lyric Opera, 1961; Metropolitan Opera from 1967, as King Marke in Tristan, Procida in Les vêpres Siciliennes, Varlaam and Pimen in Boris Godunov, Oroveso in Norman, Leporello and the Commendatore in Don Giovanni, Banquo in the Peter Hall production of Macbeth, and Philip II in Don Carlos; La Scala, 1974, in La Damnation de Faust; San Francisco, 1984, as Silva in Ernani; Teatro Liceo Barcelona, 1985; Orange Festival, 1987, as Phanüel in Massenet's Hérodiade; Sang Daland in Der fliegende Holländer at the Metropolitan, 1989; Procida at Carnegie Hall, 1990; Opera Company of Philadelphia, 1990, as the Mayor in La Gazza Ladra, Fiesco in Simon Boccanegra at the Metropolitan; Grand Park concerts Chicago, in Prince Igor; Season 1991–92 as Giorgio in Puritani at Chicago, the Pope in Benvenuto Cellini at Geneva and Zaccaria at Montreal; Sang Mozart's Bartolo at the Met, 1997; Grand Inquisitor in Don Carlos at Salzburg, 1998; Sang Des Grieux in Manon at the Met, 2001. *Recordings:* Crespel in Les Contes d'Hoffmann and Henry VIII in Anna Bolena; Norma; Le Cid and Donizetti's Gemma di Vergy; Faust; Wurm in Luisa Miller. *Current Management:* Ingpen & Williams Ltd, 7 St George's Court, 131 Putney Bridge Road, London, SW15 2PA, England.

PLOWRIGHT, Jonathan; Concert Pianist; b. 24 Sept. 1959, Doncaster, South Yorkshire, England; m. Diane Shaw, 18 Aug 1990. Education: Birmingham University, 1978–79; Royal Academy of Music, London, 1979–83; Peabody Conservatory, Baltimore, 1983–84. *Career:* Debut: Carnegie Recital Hall, New York, 1984; Purcell Room, South Bank, 1985; World Premiere performance: Constant Lambert Piano Concerto, St Johns Smith Square, 1988; Royal Concert for HRH Princess Alexandra, St James' Palace, 1988; Royal Concert for the Sultan of Oman, 1990; Soloist with all major British orchestras, performed at all major British venues and festivals, and world-wide. *Recordings:* Brahms, solo piano; East European Recital, solo piano; Capital Virtuosi Ensemble; Chopin, solo piano; Paderewski, solo piano; Stojowski, Piano Concertos No. 1 and No. 2. *Honours:* McFarren Gold Medal, Recital Diploma, RAM, 1983; Fulbright Scholarship, 1983; Commonwealth Musician of the Year, 1983; Winner, European Piano Competition, 1989; Associate, Royal Academy of Music, 1990. *Address:* 25 Titian Road, Hove, East Sussex, BN3 5QR, England.

PLOWRIGHT, Rosalind Anne, LRAM; British singer (soprano, mezzo-soprano); b. 21 May 1949, Worksop, England. *Education:* Royal Northern College of Music, Manchester. *Career:* debut as Page in Salome, English National Opera, 1975; Miss Jessell, Turn of the Screw, ENO, 1979; Debut, Covent Garden as Ortlinde, Die Walküre, 1980; With Bern Opera, 1980–81, Frankfurt Opera and Munich Opera, 1981; US debuts, Philadelphia, San Diego, also Paris, Madrid, Hamburg, 1982; La Scala, Milan, Edinburgh Festival, San Francisco, New York, 1983; With Deutsche Oper, Berlin, 1984; Houston, Pittsburgh, Verona, 1985; Teatro Communale, Florence, 1986; Tulsa, Lyon, Buenos Aires, Israel, 1987; Lausanne, Geneva, Bonn, 1988; Copenhagen, Lisbon, 1989; Sang Wagner's Senta at Covent Garden, 1986; Gluck's Alceste at La Scala, Milan, 1987 (followed by Desdemona in London); Season 1988 as Médée in Lausanne, Elisabeth de Valois in Geneva and Norma in Bonn; 1988–89 as Médée and the Trovatore Leonora at Covent Garden; Vienna Staatsoper debut 1990 as Amelia (Un Ballo in Maschera); Season 1990–91 as Lady Macbeth in Frankfurt and Israel, Desdemona in Munich and Tchaikovsky's Tatyana at Pittsburgh; Tosca at Torre del Lago, Italy; Recitals, Concerts, the United Kingdom, Europe, USA; Featured Artist (People No. 180) Opera Magazine, 1992; Season 1992–93, as Elisabeth de Valois at the London Coliseum and Nice, Gioconda for Opera North; Sang Tosca for ENO, 1994; Amneris in Aida for Scottish Opera, 1999; Other Roles: Ariadne; Elizabeth I, Maria Stuarda; Elena, Sicilian Vespers; Manon Lescaut; Aida; Suor Angelica; Giorgetta, Il Tabarro; Violetta, La Traviata; Norma; Madama Butterfly; Maddalena, Andrea Chénier; Leonora, La Forza del Destino; Sang Santuzza at the Berlin Staatsoper, 1996; Engaged as Janáček's Kostelnička, 2003. *Recordings include:* Video of Il Trovatore, Verona 1984. *Honours:* SWET Award, 1979; 1st Prize, 7th International Competition for Opera Singers, Sofia, 1979; Prix, Fondation Fanny Heldy, Academie Nationale du Disque Lyrique, 1985. *Address:* c/o Barratt House, 7 Chertsey Road, Woking, Surrey GU21 5AB, England.

PLOYHAROVA-PREISLEROVA, Vlasta; Singer (soprano); b. 25 Jan. 1928, Zbynice, Klatovy, Czechoslovakia; m. Frantisek Preisler Senior 1972;one s. one d. *Education:* Conservatory of Prague; Corso Academia Musicale Siena, Italy (Gina Cigna), 1960, 1961, 1962, 1963. *Career:* Debut: In Smetana's Bartered Bride at Janáček Theatre, Brno, 1958; Appeared at Theatre Olomouc, 1956–84, Theatre Brno, 1960–64, Theatre Ostrava, 1967–77; Operatic repertoire included: Puccini's Turandot and Madama Butterfly, Strauss's Rosenkavalier (as Sophie), Tchaikovsky's Eugene Onegin, Iolanta, Massenet's Manon, Verdi's Gilda, Bizet's Carmen, Gounod's Marguerite, Gluck's Orfeo and Euridice, Beethoven's Fidelio, Mozart's Don Giovanni, Così fan tutte, Offenbach's Les Contes d'Hoffmann and Janáček's Cunning Little Vixen and From the House of the Dead; also operas by Skroup, Dvořák, Fibich, V. Novak, V. Blodek, B. Martinů, Smetana, Pergolesi, Weber, Rossini, Flotow, J. F. Halévy, Lortzing, Rimsky-Korsakov, Leoncavallo, N. Zajc, A. Honegger; concert repertoire included: Bach's Magnificat, Beethoven's 9th Symphony, Mahler's 4th Symphony. *Honours:* International Competition, Toulouse, France, Silver Medal, 1957. *Address:* Brno, Jánska 16, 60200, Czech Republic.

PÅLSSON, Hans; Pianist and Professor; b. 1 Oct. 1949, Helsingborg, Sweden; m. Eva Pålsson, 14 April 1980. three s., one d. *Education:* Staatliche Hochschule für Musik und Theater, Hanover, Germany, 1968–72; Graduated as Soloist, 1972. *Career:* Debut: Stockholm, Sweden, 1972; Concerts in approximately 20 countries; Performed in 30-part television series Dead Masters, Live Music, 1994–99; Dedicatee of 50 solo pieces and piano concertos; Professor, Lund University, 1987; Juror at international piano competitions, Masterclasses; mem, Royal Swedish Academy of Music. *Recordings:* Approximately 25 CDs. *Honours:* Swedish 1st Prize, Nordic Music Prizes Competition, 1972; Swedish Phonogram Award, 1987. *Current Management:* Svensk Konsertdirektion, Danska Vägen 25B, SE 41274 Gothenburg, Sweden. *Address:* Gotlandsvägen 4, SE 22225 Lund, Sweden.

PLUDERMACHER, Georges; Pianist and Professor of Piano; b. 26 July 1944, Guéret, France. *Education:* Studied with Geneviève Joy and Jacques Fevrier at the Paris Conservatoire; Further study with Geza Anda at Lucerne, 1963–64. *Career:* Many appearances throughout Europe from 1965; Contemporary repertory has included the premieres of Archipel I by Boucourechliev (1967) and Synaphai by Xenakis (1971); Engagements with the Domaine Musical, Musique Vivante and the Orchestra of Paris Opéra; Duos with Yvonne Loriod and chamber music with the Nouveau Trio Pasquier; Professor at the Paris Conservatoire from 1993. *Recordings include:* Complete Sonatas by Mozart; Estampes and Images by Debussy. *Honours:* Second Prize, Leeds International Competition, 1969; First Prize Geza Anda Competition, 1979. *Address:* c/o Dept. Piano, 14 Rue de Madrid, 75008 Paris, France.

PLUISTER, Simon; Dutch composer, conductor and organ and piano teacher; b. 12 Nov. 1913, Obdam; m. Jacoba Maria Leentvaar 1943; one s. one d. *Education:* Amsterdam Conservatory with Hendrik Andriessen and Ernest W. Mulder, studied composition with Daniel Ruyneman, pianoforte with André Jurres. *Career:* debut as composer, Amsterdam, 1936; Composer for Dutch Broadcasting, NCRV, 1950–57; Conductor, The Harold Shamrock Concert Orchestra, Radio Tivoli Orchestra and Vocal Ensemble with instruments, 1955–66; Organ Teacher, Music School, Emmeloord, 1969–79; mem, GENECO (Society of Dutch Composers). *Compositions:* For Orchestra: 15 Psalms and Hymns, 3 Suites, Punch-and-Judy Show, 3 Cascades, Rhapsody in Beer–tonality; For Solo, Choir and Orchestra: Psalm 65, 121, 137, 138, Cantata St Luke 24, Concerto da chiesa The Acts II; 3 Operettas; 2 Works, Voice with Orchestra; 3 Works for String-Orchestra; 75 Works for Small-Orchestra (Short pieces and suites); Concertino for Piano and Orchestra, Ricercare and Ciga for Organ and String-Orchestra; Chamber Music, Donemus, Amsterdam, Netherlands; Music for Pianoforte 2 hds, 4 hds and for 2 Pianofortes; Calvinus Sinfonia for Strings 1987; Commission NCRV; To Silvestre Revueltas, from Mexico, at his death, for Choir (mixed voices) and Orchestra, 1987, (choir singing and speaking); Five Brown Songs, for Soprano, Flute, Alto Saxophone and Pianoforte, 1988; Larghetto for Strings, 1988; The Days after the Crucifixion, Prologue from the Opera,

Bar Abbas, for Soli, Female-Choir and Orchestra, 1986, (also as Cantata); Opera Bar Abbas, for Soli Choir and Orchestra, 1986–88; Concerto da Chiesa for 2 Recorders, V-Cello and Organ, 1990; Ant Brothers (fruit nursery) Musical for Soli Choir and Orchestra, 1990–91; Chronicle of an Eyewitness, Electronic Music for a Broadcast-Play; Super Flumina Babylonis for Soprano-Solo, Male-Choir and Pianoforte, 1992; Ave Verum Corpus and Gloria for Baritone-Solo, Male Choir and Organ, 1992; Duo Facile for Violin, V-Cello; Fantasia for Trio (Violin, Viola and V-Cello), 1993; Requiem for strings, flute, clarinet, sax, trumpet, trombone, organ and choir, 1995. *Address:* Zwartemeerweg 23, 8317 PA Oud-Kraggenburg, Nop, Netherlands.

PLUJNIKOV, Konstantin; Singer (Tenor); b. 1946, Russia. *Education:* St Petersburg Conservatory. *Career:* Sang with the Kirov Opera, St Petersburg from 1971; Roles have included Lensky, Vladimir in Prince Igor, Don Ottavio, the Duke of Mantua, Alfredo, Edgardo, Lucia di Lammermoor, Ernesto, Faust and Lohengrin; Guest appearances with the Kirov Opera at San Francisco, 1993 and La Scala, Milan, as Agrippa in The Fiery Angel by Prokofiev, 1995; Season 1998 as Shuisky in Boris Godunov with the Kirov Opera at Drury Lane, London and the New York Met. *Honours:* Prizewinner at Glinka, Geneva and Bucharest Competitions. *Address:* Kirov Opera, 1 Theatre Square, Mariinsky Theatre, St Petersburg, Russia.

PLUSH, Vincent; Composer; b. 18 April 1950, Adelaide, South Australia. *Education:* BM, University of Adelaide; Studied computer music, University of California, San Diego, USA. *Career:* Staff, Music Department, Australian Broadcasting Commission; Teacher, NSW State Conservatorium of Music, 1973–80; Tutor, Music Department, University of NSW, 1979; Founder, The Seymour Group, University of Sydney, 1976; Consultant for many arts bodies on Federal, State and Municipal levels; Composer-in-Residence, Musica Viva, 1985; Artistic Director, The Braidwood Festival, 1989 and 1991; Composer-in-Residence, ABC Radio, 1987. *Compositions:* Work for Orchestra, Pacifica, 1986, rev 1987; Works for Ensemble: On Shooting Stars-Homage to Victor Jara, 1981; Facing the Danger, 1982; The Wakefield Convocation, 1985; Helices, from The Wakefield Chronicles, 1985; The Love Songs of Herbert Hoover, 1987; Works for Solo Instrument and Ensemble; Aurores, from O Paraguay!, 1979; Bakery Hill Rising, 1980; Gallipoli Sunrise, 1984; FireRaisers, 1984; Works for Brass Band: The Wakefield Chorales, 1985–86; March of the Dalmations, 1987; Works for Narrator and Accompaniment: The Wakefield Chronicles, 1985–86; The Maitland and Morpeth String Quartet, 1979–85; The Muse of Fire, 1986–87; Instrumental Works: Chu no mai, 1974–76; Encompassings, 1975; Chrysalis, 1977–78; Stevie Wonder's Music, 1979; The Wakefield Invocation, 1986; The Wakefield Intrada, 1986; Works for Tape: Vocal Works; Choral Works; Music Theatre Works and Arrangements. *Address:* c/o Australian Music Centre, PO Box 49, Broadway 2007, Australia.

PLUYGERS, Catherine, MMus, ARCM; oboist and artistic director; b. 20 Nov. 1955, Colchester, Essex, England. *Education:* Univ. of London, Royal Coll. of Music, Banff Centre School of Fine Arts, Canada, Goldsmiths Coll. *Career:* freelance orchestral player with BBC, Royal Ballet Orchestra, Ulster Orchestra; Founder Member, Thomas Arne Players, with Purcell Room debut, 1985, Wigmore Hall debut, 1986; Recital tour, oboe and organ music, South Norway, sponsored by Norwegian Arts Council, 1982; Formed New Wind Orchestra (NEWO), 1985 and New Wind Summer School, 1988; Premiered Sonata No. 2, opus 64, oboe and piano, dedicated to self by Dr Ruth Gipps, 1986; BBC World Service broadcast, 1986; NEWO South Bank Premiere, Queen Elizabeth Hall, 1986; 1998 Formed London New Wind Music Festival, and annual festival (Sept. to Nov.) of contemporary wind music. *Compositions:* Gloryland, Mixed Media one woman show on subject of War and The Square, A Mixed Media piece performed in Purcell Room, 1990, by the Group Interartes and Hong Kong City Hall, 1990. *Recordings:* English Music for Oboe and Piano, with accompanist Matthew Stanley, 1984. *Current Management:* New Wind Management Ltd, 119 Woolstone Road, Forest Hill, London, SE23 2TQ, England.

PODLES, Eva; Singer (Mezzo-Soprano); b. 26 April 1952, Warsaw, Poland. *Education:* Studied at the Warsaw Music Academy. *Career:* Debut: Warsaw Chamber Opera in 1975 as Dorabella; After winning prizes at Athens and Geneva in 1977, Moscow in 1978 and Toulouse in 1979, sang widely in Europe as Rosina, Cenerentola and Carmen; Sang at the Metropolitan Opera in 1984 as Handel's Rinaldo, at Trieste and Warsaw as Jaroslavna in Prince Igor, at Covent Garden in 1991 as Edvige in Guillaume Tell, and at the Opéra Bastille, Paris, as Dalila in Samson et Dalila; Other noted roles have been Rossini's Arsace and Isabella, Leonora in La Favorita, Ragonde in Comte Ory and Tancredi (Antwerp, 1991); Sang the Marquis in La Fille du Régiment at La Scala, 1996; Ulrica at Madrid, 1998; Engaged for premiere of Phèdre by Penderecki, New York, 2000; Season 2000–01 as Rossini's Tancredi in Warsaw, Countess Melibea in Il Viaggio a Reims at La Coruña, and Arsace in Semiramide at Liège; Engaged as Eboli at Philadelphia, 2004.

Recordings include: Verdi Requiem; Penderecki's Te Deum. *Address:* c/o Opéra Bastille, 120 Rue de Lyon, 75012 Paris, France.

POGAČNIK, Miha; violinist and music director; b. 31 May 1949, Kranj, Yugoslavia; m. Judith Csik 1974; one s. one d. *Education:* Cologne Conservatory of Music (Musikhochschule), Indiana University School of Music, studied with Veronek, Ozim, Gingold, Rostal, Szeryng. *Career:* over 100 Concerts per season 1977–, in USA, Canada, Mexico, South America, Australia, New Zealand, China, Scandinavia, Western and Eastern Europe; Music Dir Chartres Festival d'Ete 1981–; Pres. and founder, IDRIART International, Geneva (Institute for the Development of Intercultural Relations Through the Arts) now represented in 30 countries 1983–; Music Dir of some 20 IDRIART Festivals on five continents. *Address:* IDRIART, c/o Grad Borl, Ustanova Gandin Fundacija, Dolane 1, 2282 Cirkulane, Slovenia. *E-mail:* miha@mihavision.com. *Website:* www.idriart.org.

POGORELICH, Ivo; Pianist; b. 20 Oct. 1958, Belgrade, Serbia. *Education:* Moscow Conservatory with Aliza Kezeradze. *Career:* international success from 1980, after elimination from the Chopin International Piano Competition; solo recitals and appearances with major orchestras in Europe, USA, Japan, Australasia; plays Chopin, Rachmaninov and other Romantics; records exclusively for Deutsche Grammophon; settled in England 1982; founded Sarajevo Charitable Foundation to raise funds for a new hospital and medical aid for Bosnia 1994. *Recordings include:* Prokofiev's 6th Sonata and Gaspard de la Nuit by Ravel; works by Chopin. *Honours:* first prize, Casagrande Competition at Terni 1978; first prize, Montreal International Competition 1980; created Ambassador of Goodwill at UNESCO in 1987. *Current Management:* Columbia Artists Management Ltd, 28 Cheverton Road, London, N19 3AY, England. *Telephone:* (20) 7272-8020. *Fax:* (20) 7272-8991. *E-mail:* info@cami.co.uk.

POGSON, Geoffrey; Tenor; b. 1966, England. *Education:* Studied at Cambridge and Trinity College of Music. *Career:* Appearances with Glyndebourne Festival in The Queen of Spades in 1995, English National Opera, Scottish Opera and Opera North; Roles include Monostatos, Augustin Moser, Vere in Billy Budd, Quint in The Turn of the Screw and Cornwall in Lear. *Recordings include:* Remendado in Carmen conducted by Abbado.

POHJANNORO, Hannu, MMus; Finnish composer; b. 4 July 1963, Savonlinna. *Education:* Helsinki Conservatory, Sibelius Acad. *Career:* teacher, Sibelius Acad. 1992–93, 1998, Helsinki Conservatory 1992–95, Helsinki Univ. Dept of Musicology 1994–98, Espoo Music Inst. 1996–, Sibelius Acad. electronic music studio 1997–. *Compositions include:* Matkalla 1991, Kuvia, heijastuksia 1992, Eilisen linnut 1994, Saari, rannaton 1994, Korkeina aamujen kaaret 1996, Syksyn huoneet 1997, Kuun kiertoa kohti 1998, Paluu 2000, Ajan reuna 2003, XL 2003–04. *Recordings:* Eilisen linnut, Kuun kiertoa kohti, Ajan reuna. *Address:* c/o Finnish Musici Information Centre, Lauttasaarentie 1, 00200 Helsinki, Finland (office). *E-mail:* hpohjann@siba.fi. *Website:* www.uusinta.com/pohjannoroE.html (office).

POHJOLA, Seppo; Finnish composer; b. 4 May 1965, Espoo. *Education:* Espoo Coll. of Music and Sibelius Acad., Helsinki. *Compositions include:* String Quartet No. 1 1989–91, Pixilated 1992, Daimonion 1994, String Quartet No. 2 1995, Game Over 1996, Vae victis 1997, Taika 1999, Vinha 1999, String Quartet No. 3 2000, Oravan laulu 2000, Tralala 2000, Liebelei 2001, New York New York 2001, Elämän Kevät 2002, Wedding March 2002, Symphony No. 1 2002, Tapiolandia 2003, Ukri 2003. *Honours:* winner Soc. of Finnish Composers New Tone Competition, Kuhmo Chamber Music Festival 2002. *Address:* Esankuja 9, 01400 Vantaa, Finland. *E-mail:* sjpohjola@luukku.com.

POHL, Carla; Singer (Soprano); b. 1942, Johannesburg, South Africa. *Education:* Studied in South Africa and at the Wiesbaden Conservatory. *Career:* Sang at Pforzheim from 1970; Freiburg from 1979, notably as Tosca, Maddalena in Andrea Chénier, Marenka in The Bartered Bride and Stauss's Chrysothemis; Wiesbaden, 1979–81; Deutsche Oper am Rhein, Düsseldorf, from 1981, as Wagner's Elisabeth, Eva and Sieglinde, the Empress in Die Frau ohne Schatten, Strauss's Ariadne and Marschallin, and Leonore in Fidelio; Guest appearances in Mannheim, Berlin, Nancy, Karlsruhe, Stuttgart, Vienna State Opera, Munich State Opera, Milan, Rome and Brunswick; Tour of South Africa, 1985; Deutsche Oper am Rhein 1987, as Rezia in Oberon; Deutsche Oper Berlin and Santiago Chile 1988, as Chrysothemis and Elsa; Sang Wagner's Venus at Cape Town, 2000. *Address:* c/o Deutsche Oper am Rhein, Heinrich-Heine Allee 16, 4000 Düsseldorf, Germany.

POKA, Balazs; Singer (Baritone); b. 1947, Eger, Hungary. *Career:* Soloist with the Hungarian National Opera from 1976 as Rossini's Figaro and Dandini, Valentin, Eugene Onegin, and Carlo in La Forza del Destino; Bregenz Festival 1991 as Escamillo; Season 1993 as Don Giovanni at Madrid and Lisbon, Busoni's Turandot at Opéra de Lyon; Other roles include Germont, Marcello, Renato, Rodrigo and Puccini's Lescaut;

Sang Ping in Turandot; Concert appearances at La Scala, Milan, Palermo, Bergamo, Hamburg, Amsterdam, Antwerp and Rome. *Recordings:* Kodály's Háry János; From Blues to Opera; La Bohème, Puccini; L'Arlesiana, Cilea; Judgement in Jerusalem, Szehely; Petroviks, Crime and Punishment. *Address:* Hungarian National Opera, Audrassy ut 22, 1061 Budapest, Hungary.

POLA, Bruno; Singer (Baritone); b. 1945, Rovereto, Trento, Italy. *Education:* Berlin Conservatory, 1963–68. *Career:* Engaged at Kaiserslautern Opera 1968–71, Kiel 1972–73, Cologne 1974–77, Zürich Opera 1978–81; Recitals and concerts throughout Germany, Netherlands, Switzerland and Austria; From 1982 engagements at such major opera centres as Milan, Rome, Lisbon, Vienna, Munich and Hamburg; Metropolitan Opera from 1988, in Cavalleria Rusticana, Il Barbiere di Siviglia, Gianni Schicci, Rigoletto, Don Giovanni, La Fanciulla del West, Falstaff, Simon Boccanegra, and L'Elisir d'amore; Season 1995–97 in Cavalleria Rusticana and La Forza del Destino at the Met; Aida and Dulcamara at Vienna and Covent Garden; Amonasro in Aida at Santiago, Arena di Verona and Covent Garden; Further opera appearances at Turin, Ascona, Montreal, Pittsburgh, Florence, Geneva and Houston; Melitone in La Forza del Destino at Savonlinna, 1998; Sang Falstaff at the Deutsche Oper, 2000–01. *Address:* Via al Ronco 7, 6933 Muzzano, Switzerland.

POLASKI, Deborah; Singer (Soprano); b. 26 Sept. 1949, Richmond Centre, Wisconsin, USA. *Education:* Conservatory of Music Ohio; American Institute of Music Graz. *Career:* Sang at Gelsenkirchen, Karlsruhe and Ulm from 1976; Further appearances at opera houses in Hanover, Munich, Hamburg and Freiburg; Festival of Waiblingen 1983, in a revival of Croesus by Reinhard Keiser; Oslo 1986, as Elektra; Other roles include Leonore in Fidelio, Wagner's Isolde and Sieglinde and Marie in Wozzeck; Bayreuth Festival, 1988, as Brünnhilde in the Ring cycle directed by Harry Kupfer; Sang Brünnhilde at Rotterdam 1988, Cologne 1990; Stuttgart Staatsoper 1989, as Elektra (also at the Teatro Nuovo Spoleto, 1990); Season 1992 as the Dyer's Wife in Die Frau ohne Schatten at Amsterdam and Brünnhilde at Bayreuth; Sang Brünnhilde in new Ring Cycle at Covent Garden, 1994–95, returned 1997 as Elektra; Sang Isolde under Abbado at Salzburg, 1999; Sang Cassandra and Dido in Les Troyens at Salzburg, 2000; Brünnhilde in Ring Cycles at the Berlin Staatsoper, 2001–02. *Recordings:* Wolf-Ferrari's Sly (RCA); Brünnhilde's Immolation with the Chicago Symphony (Erato). *Address:* Oper der Stadt Köln, Offenbachplatz, 5000 Cologne, Germany.

POLAY, Bruce; Conductor and Composer; b. 22 March 1949, Brooklyn, New York, USA; m. Louise Phillips, 17 Dec 1983, 2 s., 3 d. *Education:* BM, Composition, University of Southern California, 1971; MA, Composition, California State University, 1977; DMA, Instrumental Music, Arizona State University, 1989; Conducting studies with Herbert Blomstedt, Jon Robertson, Murray Sidlin, Alberto Bolet. *Career:* Debut: Conducting: US, Lakewood (California) Chamber Orchestra, 1972; Europe, Filarmonica de Stat Sibiu, Romania, 1993; Music Director, Knox-Galesburg (Illinois) Symphony, 1983–; Professor of Music, Knox College; Recent guest conducting in USA, Romania, Russia, Spain, UK and Ukraine. *Compositions:* Encomium for three-part children's chorus, narrator and orchestra, 1987; Concerto for Tenor Trombone, 1991; Three Word Paintings for a cappella chorus, 1991; Cathedral Images for orchestra, 1993; Concerto-Fantasie for piano and orchestra, 1997; Anniversary Mourning, for a cappella choir, 1996; Sound Images: Pictures for an Exhibition, for solo piano, 1995; Bondi's Journey: An Orchestral Rhapsody after Jewish Themes, 1994; Sinfonia Concertante, 1998; Y'Urning, cycle for soprano, clarinet and piano, 1998. *Recordings:* Cathedral Images, CD, 1996; Y'Urning, 1999; Elegy for solo violin and small orchestra, 2001; Suite of Preludes for Organ, 2002; Illumination for orchestra, 2003. *Honours:* Illinois Orchestra of the Year (Knox-Galesburg Symphony), 1986, 1998; Illinois Conductor of the Year, 1997; Exceptional Achievement Award, Knox College, 1998. *Address:* 1577 N Cherry Street, Galesburg, IL 61401, USA.

POLEGATO, Brett; Singer (Baritone); b. 9 May 1968, Niagara Falls, Ontario, Canada. *Career:* Opera appearances in North America: As Don Pasquale, Papageno, Rossini's Dandini, 1998 and Mozart's Count; European debut at Avignon in title role of Monteverdi's Orfeo; Savonlinna Festival as Silvio in Pagliacci; Engagements with L'Opéra de Montréal, season 1998; Season 2000–01 with Pelléas at Strasbourg and Leipzig, Britten's Ned Keene at La Scala; Concert repertory includes songs by Schubert and Schumann. *Recordings:* Ulbalde in Gluck's Armide; Messiah (Arabesque); Kalman's Die Herzogin von Chicago (Decca); To a Poet, solo recital; Bach Coffee and Peasant Cantates. *Honours:* Finalist, Singer of the World Competition, Cardiff, 1995. *Address:* c/o IMG Artists, Lovell House, 616 Chiswick High Road, London W4 5RX, England.

POLGAR, Laszlo; Singer (Bass); b. 1 Jan. 1947, Somogyszentpal, Hungary. *Education:* Studied at the Franz Liszt Academy of Music, Budapest. *Career:* Sang at the Budapest Opera from 1972, as Rocco,

Osmin, Sarastro and Leporello; Professor of Singing at the Liszt Academy from 1978; Brussels debut 1981, as Colline in La Bohème; Covent Garden debut 1982, as Rodolpho in La Sonnambula; Hamburg Staatsoper as Osmin and Basilio; US debut Philadelphia 1982, as Colline; Has sung Gurnemanz (Parsifal) in Budapest and Berlin; Concert appearances as Bart ók's Bluebeard in Hungary, Ireland, Russia, Italy, France and Canada; Promenade Concerts London 1984, 1987, as Bluebeard and in Pulcinella by Stravinsky; Carnegie Hall New York 1987, in the Choral Symphony; Die Schöpfung and the Dvořák Requiem at La Scala, Milan; Operatic engagements in Paris (Varlaam in Boris Godunov), Vienna, Munich (Leporello, 1984) and Zürich; sang Padre Guardiano in La Forza del Destino at Budapest, 1990; Member of the Zürich Opera from 1991; Season 1992 as Rossini's Basilo at Brussels and Vienna, Bart ók's Bluebeard at the Prom Concerts London; Sang in Schubert's Alfonso und Estrella at the 1997 Vienna Festival; Bart ók's Bluebeard at Aix, 1998; Season 1999–2000 as Wagner in Busoni's Faust at Salzburg, Henry VIII in Anna Bolena for Zürich Opera and Gurnemanz at the Deutsche Oper, Berlin. *Recordings include:* Il Barbiere di Siviglia and works by Haydn and Liszt (Deutsche Grammophon); Alphonse in La favorita by Donizetti. *Honours:* Winner, Dvořák International Singing Competition, 1974; Winner, Hugo Wolf Competition Vienna (1980) and Pavarotti Competition Philadelphia (1981); Liszt Prize, Hungary, 1982. *Address:* c/o Hungarian State Opera House, Népöztársaság utja 22, 1061 Budapest, Hungary.

POLIANICHKO, Alexander; Conductor and Musician (violin); b. 1948, Russia. *Education:* violin studies at the Rostov Conservatory, conducting at the Leningrad Conservatoire, under Ilya Musin. *Career:* violinist with the Leningrad Philharmonic Orchestra, under Evgeny Mravinsky; former Artistic Dir of the St Petersburg Orchestra; Dir of the Opera at the Kirov Theatre; Artistic Dir of the Belorussian CO in Minsk from 1987, and many guest appearances with leading Russian orchestras; conducted the Kirov Company at the 1991 Edinburgh Festival (The Marriage), Los Angeles 1993 (The Nutcracker) and Tel-Aviv 1996 (Khovanshchina); further visits to France, Republic of Korea and Japan; ENO from 1994, with Eugene Onegin and Carmen; Season 1994–95 La Bohème at Oslo, The Fiery Angel in San Francisco and tour of Australia for the ABC; Season 1996 with La Bayadere at the Paris Opéra and in New York, and debut with the Bournemouth Sinfonietta; Principal Conductor, Bournemouth Sinfonietta, 1997–, conducted revival of Eugene Onegin at ENO 1997–98. *Recordings include:* albums for Melodiya. *Current Management:* Ingpen & Williams Ltd, 7 St George's Court, 131 Putney Bridge Road, London, SW15 2PA, England. *Address:* c/o Kanal Griboedora 74–33, 190068 St Petersburg, Russia.

POLIANSKY, Valerig K.; Conductor; b. 19 April 1949, Moscow, USSR; m. Olga P Lapuso, 1 s., 1 d. *Education:* State Conservatoire Tchaikovsky, Moscow, graduated in Choir Conducting, 1971, Orchestra Conducting, 1974. *Career:* Debut: Moscow Operetta; Conducted Shostakovich's Katerina Izmailova at Bolshoi Theatre. *Recordings:* Rachmaninov Vespers, Liturgia of St John Chrysostom, A Schnittke, Choir Concert; A Bruckner, Geistliche motetten, L Cherubini, Requiem in C minor, P Tchaikovsky, Liturgia of St John Chrysostom, Various choruses; Orchestral Serenade. *Contributions:* Soviet Music; Music Life; Music in the USSR. *Honours:* Arezzo Prize for best conductor, 1975; Honoured Artist of the People of Russia until 1996. *Address:* Begovay 4 allegro 3-40, 125040 Moscow, Russia.

POLISI, Joseph W., MA, MMus, DMA; American bassoon player; *President, The Juilliard School;* b. 1947. *Education:* Univ. of Connecticut, Tufts Univ., Yale Univ., Conservatoire Nat. de Paris with Maurice Allard. *Career:* Pres., The Juilliard School, New York; extensive solo and chamber bassoon performances throughout USA; Chair., Seaver Inst., Nat. Endowment for the Arts Conductors' Program; mem. Nat. Cttee on Standards in the Arts; fmr accreditation evaluator for Nat. Asscn of Schools of Music. *Recordings:* A Harvest of 20th Century Bassoon Music 1979. *Honours:* Hon. DMus (Curtis Inst. of Music, Philadelphia) 1990, Dr hc (New England Conservatory) 2001; Hon. mem. Royal Acad. of Music, London, England 1992. *Address:* The Juilliard School, 60 Lincoln Center Plaza, New York, NY 10023, USA.

POLIVNICK, Paul; Conductor; b. 7 July 1947, Atlantic City, New Jersey, USA; m. Marsha Hooks, 20 June 1980. *Education:* BM, Juilliard School of Music, New York, 1969; Aspen Music School, Colorado, summers 1961, 1968, 1970, 1972; Berkshire Music Center, Tanglewood, Massachusetts, summers, 1965, 1966 and 1971; Accademia Musicale Chigiana, Siena, Italy, summer 1969. *Career:* Conductor, Debut Orchestra, Los Angeles, 1969–73; Associate Conductor, Indianapolis Symphony Orchestra, 1977–80; Associate Principal Conductor, Milwaukee Symphony Orchestra, 1981–85; Music Director, Alabama Symphony Orchestra, Birmingham, 1985–; mem, American Symphony Orchestra League. *Recordings:* Several. *Honours:* Honorary Doctorate, Montevallo University, 1986. *Current Management:* Maxim Gershunoff Attractions Inc. *Address:* c/o Alabama Symphony Orchestra, 1814 First Avenue North, Birmingham, AL 35209, USA.

POLLARD, Mark; Composer and Music Director; b. 14 Feb. 1957, Melbourne, Victoria, Australia. *Education:* BA (Hons) 1981, MA 1984, La Trobe University. *Career:* Senior Tutor, La Trobe University, 1983–85; Lecturer, Victoria College of the Arts, 1986–; Music Director of various contemporary ensembles; Commissions from Seymour Group, Australian Chamber Soloists, New Audience, and others. *Compositions include:* Quinque II for tape, 1979; Krebs for piano, 1983; A Sympathetic Resonance for guitar, 1989; Bass Lines for amplified double bass, 1990; Carillon for Sacha for piano, 1991; Two Drummings for Joe, for choir, 1991; The Quick or the Dead, for string quartet, 1992; A View from the Beach, for orchestra, 1994; The Art of Flirting for clarinet, 1994; Inherit the Wind, for English horn, 1994. *Honours:* Spivakovsky Awards, 1993. *Address:* c/o APRA, 1A Eden Street, Crows Nest, NSW 2065, Australia.

POLLASTRI, Paolo; Oboist; b. 12 July 1960, Bologna, Italy; m. Christine Dechaux 1988, 2 d. *Education:* Scientific Diploma, Bologna, 1979; Oboe Diploma, Bologna, 1977; Oboe Diploma 1982, Baroque Oboe Diploma 1982, Brussels; Diploma D'Onore (Accademia Chigiana, Siena), 1977. *Career:* 1st Oboe, Orchestra Giovanile Italiana, 1977; Genova, 1979; Rai Roma, 1981; Orchestra Regionale Toscana-Firenze, 1982–89; Accademia di S Cecilia, Roma, 1989; Solisti Veneti, 1984–89; Television and radio appearances with RAI 1, 2, 3 (Solisti Veneti); Television Australiana (Solisti Veneti); Radio Israeliana (Accademia Bizantina); BBC (Solisti Veneti); Played at Festivals in Montreux, Salzburg, Zagreb and Belgrade, Martigny and Vevey, Toulouse, Paris, Stuttgart, Edinburgh, Sydney, Melbourne and Canberra; Winner of Italian competition to teach in conservatories, 1993; Teacher, Studea di Musica, Fiesole, 1993–. *Recordings:* Numerous recording include: Respighi, Solisti Veneti, Erato; Vivaldi, Oboe concertos, Accademia Bizantina, Frequenz; Malipiero, Respighi, Ghedini, Rota, Woodwind Quintet, Fonè. *Publications:* IDRS, 1998; I Fiati, 1999. *Contributions:* Il Dopo Concerto, 1980–81; The Italian Academy of Woodwinds, 1988–89. *Current Management:* Studio Musica, Viale Caduti in Guerra, 194, 41100 Modena, Italy. *Address:* Via di Mugnana 3, 50027 Strada in Chianti, Florence, Italy.

POLLEI, Paul, BM, MM,' PhD; Pianist and Administrator; b. 9 May 1936, Salt Lake City, UT, USA; m., two c. *Education:* Univ. of Utah, Eastman School of Music, Florida State Univ. *Career:* Prof. of Piano, Brigham Young Univ. 1963–2001; founder of Gina Bachauer International Piano Competition 1976–; creator of American Piano Quartet (2pianos/8hands) 1984–; teacher; soloist; lecturer; speaker; mem. Music Teachers' Nat. Asscn, European Piano Teachers' Asscn, World Federation of Int. Music Competitions. *Recordings:* American Piano Quartet. *Publications:* Essential Technique for the Pianist. *Honours:* The Madeleine Award 2002. *Address:* 138 W Broadway, Salt Lake City, UT, 84101, USA (office). *Telephone:* (801) 2974250 (office). *Fax:* (801) 5219202 (office). *E-mail:* paul@bachauer.com (office). *Website:* www.bachauer.com (office).

POLLET, Françoise; singer (soprano); b. 10 Sept. 1949, Boulogne Billancourt, near Paris, France. *Education:* Versailles Conservatory and in Munich. *Career:* debut, Lubeck, as the Marschallin, 1983; Sang at Lubeck until 1986, as Santuzza, Fiordiligi, Donna Anna, Elisabeth in Tannhäuser, Amelia in Ballo in Maschera, Alice Ford, Giulietta, Ariadne and Arabella: Appearances as Agathe at Marseilles, Vitellia in La Clemenza di Tito at Opéra-Comique, Paris, and Dukas' Ariadne at Théâtre du Châtelet in a production by Ruth Berghaus, 1991; At Montpellier has sung Reizia in Oberon, Meyerbeer's Valentine, Catherine of Aragon in Saint-Saëns's Henry VIII, Elisabeth, and Magnard's Berenice; Hamburg, 1990, in premiere of Liebermann's Freispruch für Medea; Covent Garden, 1991, as Valentine; Sang Ariadne auf Naxos at Toulouse, 1998; Other roles include Cassandra in Les Troyens, at Brussels, and Mozart's Countess; Concert repertoire includes Schumann's Liederkreis and Les Nuits d'Eté by Berlioz; Sang Amelia (Ballo in Maschera) at Venice, 1999, and Geneviève in Chausson's Le Roi Arthus at the 2000 Edinburgh Festival (concert); London Proms, 2002. *Recordings include:* 4th Symphony by Guy Ropartz; La Vièrge in Jeanne d' Arc au Bûcher by Honegger, conducted by Ozawa. *Current Management:* TransArt (UK) Ltd, Cedar House, 10 Rutland Street, Filey, North Yorkshire YO14 9JB, England. *Telephone:* (1723) 515819. *Fax:* (1723) 514678. *E-mail:* transartuk@transartuk.com. *Website:* www.transartuk.com.

POLLETT, Patricia (Engeline Maria); Violist and Associate Professor, University of Queensland; b. 13 Oct. 1958, Utrecht, Netherlands; m. Dr Philip Keith Pollett, 28 Jan 1978, 1 s. *Education:* BMus, Honours, University of Adelaide, 1979; ARCM, Royal College of Music, 1980; Hochschule der Kunst, West Berlin, 1988; Teachers: Beryl Kimber, Peter Schidlof, Margaret Major, Bruno Giuranna. *Career:* Member of I Solisti Veneti, 1983–84; Founder Member of Perihelion, contemporary ensemble; Resident at University of Queensland, 1988–; Concerto Soloist with Gulbenkian Orchestra, Lisbon, 1984, Queensland Philharmonic Orchestra, 1989 and 1995, Queensland Symphony Orchestra, 1990, 1991 and 1994, Sydney Symphony Orchestra, 1991, and Mozart

Symposium at University of Otago, New Zealand, 1991. Commissioned new works for viola by Colin Spiers, Andrew Schultz, Nigel Sabin, Philip Bracanin, Ross Edwards, Colin Brumby (world premiere performances of these works), Robert Davidson, Stephen Cronin, Mary Mageau, Andrew Ford and Elena Kats-Chernin. *Recordings:* Tapestry; Points of Departure; Chamber Music of Andrew Schultz; Anthology of Australian Music; Evocations; Patricia Pollett: Viola Concerti; Solo: Viola Power, Australian works for viola. *Address:* 21 Almay Street, Kenmore, Queensland 4069, Australia.

POLLINI, Maurizio; Pianist and Conductor; b. 5 Jan. 1942, Milan, Italy. *Education:* Studied with Carlo Lonati, and with Carlo Vidusso at the Milan Conservatory. *Career:* Has played with Berlin and Vienna Philharmonic Orchestras, Bayerischer Rundfunk Orchestra, London Symphony Orchestra, Boston, New York, Philadelphia, Los Angeles and San Francisco Orchestras; Has played at Salzburg, Vienna, Berlin, Prague Festivals; Plays Boulez, Nono and Schoenberg, in addition to the standard repertory; Has conducted operas by Rossini at Pesaro from 1981 (La Donna del Lago); World tour with Bach's Well-Tempered Klavier, 1985; Played the 2nd Sonata of Boulez and Beethoven's Diabelli Variations, London 1990; Beethoven Sonata series at the Festival Hall, 1997; Also at La Scala, Carnegie Hall and Vienna; Concert series of his own devising: Salzburg Festival, 1999 and Carnegie Hall, 1999–2001. *Recordings:* For Polydor International, including CDs of Bartók Piano Concertos 1 and 2 (Chicago Symphony/Abbado); Chopin 1st Concerto (Philharmonic/Kletski) and Sonatas Op 35, Op 58; Beethoven Late Sonatas; Brahms Piano Quintet (Quartetto Italiano); Schoenberg piano music; Stravinsky Petrushka Three Movements, Webern Variations, Boulez 2nd Sonata, Prokofiev 7th Sonata. *Honours:* First Prize, International Chopin Competition, Warsaw 1960. *Current Management:* Harrison/Parrott Ltd, 12 Penzance Place, London, W11 4PA, England. *Telephone:* (20) 7229 9166. *Fax:* (20) 7221 5042. *Website:* www.harrisonparrott.com.

POLOLANIK, Zdenek; Composer; b. 25 Oct. 1935, Brno, Czechoslovakia; m. Jarmila Linka, one d., one s. *Education:* Brno Conservatoire; Janáček Academy of Performing Arts, Brno. *Career:* Freelance Composer from 1961–; composed 600 works including concert music and ballet, spiritual music for liturgical purposes and musical scores for film, radio, incidental music, etc; Contributions to journals and books; mem. Prítomnost composers' consortium, Prague. *Compositions include:* Variations for organ and piano, 1956; Sinfonietta, 1958; String Quartet, 1958; Divertimento for 4 horns and strings, 1960; 5 Symphonies, 1961, 1962, 1963, 1969; Concentus resonabilis for 19 soloists and tape, 1963; Musica Spingenta I–III, 1961–63; Mechanism, ballet, 1964; Horn sonata, 1965; Piano Concerto, 1966; Concerto Grosso I and II, 1966, 1988; Missa Brevis, 1969; Song of Songs, oratorio, 1970; Snow Queen, ballet, 1978; Lady Among Shadows, ballet, 1984; Summer Festivities for chorus and 2 pianos, 1985; Christmas Message, 1987; March for wind orchestra, 1990; Easter Way, 14 songs for soprano and ensemble, 1990; Small Mythological Exercises, melodrama, 1991; Ballad for cello and piano, 1992; Christmas Triptych for bugle and 4 trombones, 1993; First One Must Carry the Cross, chamber oratorio for medium voice and synthesizer, 1993; Eulogies, Psalms for chorus, 1993; Psalms for women's chorus, 1993; Cisaŕuv mim (Emperor's Mime), 1993; Chválozpevy, 1994; Spor duše s tělem (Dispute of Soul with Body), 1994; Two Ballads for lower voice, 1995; Prazská legenda (Prague Legend), 1995; Winterballad, 1996; Sexton, 1996; Horka blahoslavenství (Bitter Hallow), 1996; Citadella, 1997; Cycles of Noels for organ, piano, large symphony orchestra, 1997; Dulces cantilenae, 1997; Cantus laetitiae, 1997; Setkání (Ordinario and Proprio), 1997; Musica sacra, 1999; Slavnostní konická mše (Solemn Konical mass), 2000; Baletní epizody (Ballettic episodes), 2001; Interludium, 2001; Missa solemnis, 2001; Capriccio for cello and orchestra, 2002;. *Recordings:* Missa Brevis, CD, 1994; Pastorale for Organ, CD; Liturgical mass, Te Deum, Ave Maria, CD, 1996; Time and Joy of Merrymaking, CD, 1997; Ballad, CD, 1997; What's New, CD, 1997; Snow Queen, CD, 1998; Pierot, CD, 1999; CD Noel's Adventní (Advent), 1999; The Angel's Message to the World; Capriccio for cello and orchestra. *Honours:* Holyš Cyril and Method Decoration; Josef Blaha Prize for Music Composition. *Address:* Osvobození 67, 66481 Ostrovačice, Czech Republic. *Telephone:* (546) 427417. *E-mail:* zdenek.pololanik@tiscali.cz.

POLOZOV, Vyacheslav M.; Singer (tenor); b. 1950, Mariupol, Ukraine, USSR. *Education:* Studied at the Kiev Conservatory. *Career:* Debut: Kiev Opera 1977, as Alfredo in La Traviata; Leading tenor at the Saratov Opera 1978; Leading tenor at Minsk Opera 1980; Bolshoi Opera Moscow, 1982, Alfredo and Turiddu; Sang Pinkerton at La Scala 1986; US debut with Pittsburgh Symphony Orchestra 1986, as Cavaradossi; US stage debut the Chicago Lyric Opera 1986, as Rodolfo in La Bohème; Further appearances at Washington DC (1986, as Lykov, in The Tsar's Bride), New York (Met '1987, as Pinkerton); Palm Springs, as Cavaradossi; San Antonio (as Cavaradossi); Met (as Rodolfo, 1987, summer park concerts); Washington DC, as Dimitri in Boris Godunov;

Season 1987/88 with Calaf in New City Opera, repeated at the Bayerische Staatsoper Munich; Rome Opera as Lykov and the Metropolitan as Verdi's Macduff; Michigan Opera Theatre as Rodolfo in La Bohème, (1988 debut); Further debuts at the San Francisco Opera (1988 as Enzo, in La Gioconda), Carnegie Hall (1988, as Andrea Chénier), Canadian Opera Company (1989 as Cavaradossi), Greater Miami Opera (1989, as Alvaro in La Forza); Sang Pinkerton in San Francisco, 1989, Lyon Opéra (debut 1990), as Pinkerton, repeated in the Greater Miami Opera; appearance, at the 1990 Caracalla Festival, Rome, and Turiddu and Lensky with the Chicago Lyric Opera, 1990; Calaf with the Greater Miami Opera; Cavaradossi in the Houston Grand Opera, 1991; as Lensky in Hamburg; as Don Carlo in Denver at the Opera Colorado. *Recordings include:* Aleko by Rachmaninov (Melodia); Boris Godunov (Erato, under M. Rostropovich), TY broadcast Canadian Opera Company, Tosca. *Honours:* Winner, All-Russia Glinka Competition 1981; Sofia Competition, Bulgaria, 1984 (for the Duke of Mantua); Madama Butterfly Competition, Tokyo, 1987. *Address:* 367 Columbus PKWY, Mineola, NY 11501, USA.

POLSTER, Hermann Christian; Singer; b. 8 April 1937, Leipzig, Germany. *Education:* Univ. of Leipzig. *Career:* Sang with the Dresden Kreuzchor while a boy; Many engagements with the Leipzig Bach Soloists, the chorus of St Thomas's Leipzig and the Leipzig Gewandhaus Orchestra; Guest appearances Berlin; Munich, Frankfurt, Hamburg, Roma, Milano, Torino, Amsterdam (St Matthew Passion); Halle (Shostakovich 14th Symphony); Tokyo, Osaka (Bach: St Matthew and St John Passion, Beethoven's Ninth); Paris (Fidelio), Moscow, Buenos Aires, Rio de Janerio, Aix-en-Provence, Venice, Dubrovnik, Prague (Beethoven's Ninth); Other repertoire includes Monteverdi's Vespers; Buxtehude Cantatas, Telemann Cantatas, Psalms, Serenades; Handel Saul, Acis and Galatea, Samson, Belshazzar, Judas Maccabaeus, Solomon, Jephtha, Hercules and Messiah; Bach Cantatas and Oratorios; Haydn Oratorios; Mozart Masses, Requiem, Solemn Vespers and Die Zauberflöte (Sarastro); Beethoven Missa Solomnis, Mass in C and Christus am Olberg; Mendelssohn Elijah, St Paul, Erste Walpurgisnacht; Schumann Paradies und die Peri; Verdi Requiem; Brahms Ein Deutsches Requiem; Mahler 8th Symphony; Janáček Glagolitic Mass; Stravinsky Oedipus Rex; Wagner Die Meistersinger (Pogner); Tchaikovsky Eugene Onegin (Gremin); Blacher The Grand Inquisitor; Shostakovich 13th Symphony, Songs of Michelangelo; Professur für Gesang Musikhochschule Leipzig, International Masterclasses, Juror in international competitions (Brussels, Moscow, Berlin, Leipzig); mem, Deutscher Musikrat, Bundesverband Deutscher Gesangspädagogen (Vizepräsident); Neue Detusche Bachesellschaft. *Recordings:* St Matthew Passion and Bach Cantatas; Elijah and Orff's Die Kluge; Beethoven: Fidelio (1804 version), Missa solemnis; Shostakovich Michelangelo Songs; Mozart Litaneien; Concert works conducted by Karl Böhm, Karajan, Herbert Kegel, Neville Marriner, Wolfgang Sawallisch and Kurt Masur. *Honours:* Kammersänger, Kunstpreisträger. *Address:* c/o Gewandhausorchester, Augustusplatz 8, 4109 Leipzig, Germany.

POLVERELLI, Laura; Italian singer (mezzo-soprano); b. 1964, Siena. *Education:* Florence and Verona Conservatories. *Career:* appearances at Seattle Opera, Liceu Barcelona, La Scala Milan, Florence, Hamburg, Pesaro and Théâtre des Champs-Elysées, Paris; roles have included Mozart's Sesto, Donna Elvira and Dorabella (Glyndebourne, 2000); Gluck's Orfeo, Verdi's Abigaille and parts in Il Turco in Italia, Le Comte Ory, La Cenerentola, Lucia di Lammermoor, La Traviata and Le nozze di Figaro; Concerts include Rossini and Pergolesi Stabat Mater, Bach's St Matthew Passion and B minor Mass; Season 2000–01 as Dorabella in Così fan tutte, at Glyndebourne, Rossini's Isabella at Venice and Rosina in Paris; La Clemenza di Tito in Munich and Handel's Tamerlano in Florence. *Recordings include:* Le nozze di Figaro and Così fan tutte; Zaida in Il Turco in Italia and Hemon in Traetta's Antigone. *Current Management:* Opéra et Concert, 7 rue de Clichy, 75009 Paris, France. *Website:* www.opera-concert.com.

POMERANTS-MAZURKEVICH, Dana; Concert Violinist and Professor of Violin; b. 11 Oct. 1944, Kaunas, USSR; m. Yuri Mazurekvich, 4 July 1963, 1 d. *Education:* MMus, 1961–65, Artist Diploma 1965–68, Moscow State Conservatory. *Career:* Performed as the Mazurkevich Violin Duo member and also as a soloist in: USSR, Poland, USA, Canada, Australia, England, France, Belgium, East and West Germany, Hong Kong, Taiwan, Switzerland, Italy, Roumania, Mexico and other countries; Recorded for Radio Moscow, France, ABC (Australia), WGGH (Boston); CBC (Canada); BBC (England); Sender Freies (W Berlin), and others. *Recordings:* Works by Telemann, Prokofiev, Honegger, Sarasate, Spohr, Rawsthorne, Wieniawski, Shostakovich, Leclair, Handel and others; Masters of the Bow, Toronto, Canada; SNE, Montreal, Canada. *Current Management:* Robert M Gewald Management. *Address:* School of Music, Boston University, 855 Commonwealth Avenue, Boston, MA 02215, USA.

POMMIER, Jean-Bernard; Concert Pianist and Conductor; b. 17 Aug. 1944, Beziers, France. *Education:* Began piano studies aged 4; later studied with Yves Nat, Eugene Istomin and Eugen Bigot (conducting); 1958–61 Paris Conservatoire. *Career:* Has performed widely from 1962, notably in Europe, the USA, Far East, the USSR, Israel and Scandinavia; Salzburg debut with Karajan 1971; Berlin Philharmonic 1972; US debut in season 1973–74 with the New York Philharmonic and the Chicago Symphony; Engagements with the Concertgebouw under Haitink, the Orchestre de Paris under Barenboim, the St Paul Chamber Orchestra and Zukerman; Festival appearances at Edinburgh, South Bank Music, Ravinia and Mostly Mozart (New York); Director/soloist with English Chamber Orchestra in Salzburg and Vienna and with Scottish Chamber Orchestra in France, Belgium and Netherlands; Season 1987–88 solo appearances with the London Philharmonic, the Hallé and Royal Philharmonic; conducting Bournemouth Symphony and Ulster Orchestras and the Northern Sinfonia on a tour of Spain; Appointed Music Director of the Melbourne Summer Music Festival for 1990; Chamber music with Casals, Schneider, Richter, Oistrakh and Stern and with the Guarneri and Vermeer Quartets; Season 1991–92 appearances with the Northern Sinfonia in North America, Bournemouth Symphony, the Philharmonia and Ulster Orchestra and conducted the Hallé and Royal Liverpool Philharmonic. *Recordings:* Poulenc's Piano Concerto with the City of London Sinfonia and Sonatas by Brahms with Leonard Rose and Jaime Laredo. *Honours:* First Diploma of Honour at the 1962 Tchaikovsky Competition Moscow. *Address:* c/o The Music Partnership Ltd, 41 Aldebert Terrace London, SW1 1BH, England.

POMPILI, Claudio; Composer; b. 12 May 1949, Gorizia, Italy. *Education:* BMus, University of Adelaide, 1983; Study with Richard Meale and Tristram Cary in Australia (1980–82) and with Franco Donatoni and Salvatore Sciarrino in Italy (1984–85); IRCAM studios, Paris, 1984. *Career:* Faculty Member, University of Adelaide, 1983–84, University of New England, 1987–97; Associate Professor and Director, Conservatorium of Music, University of Wollongong, 1998–; Commissions from Duo Contemporain, Perihelion and others. *Compositions include:* Medieval Purity in a Bed of Thorns, for tape, 1981–84; The Star Shoots a Dart, for flute, clarinet, violin and cello, 1985; Polymnia Triptych for soprano and large ensemble, 1986; Songs for Ophelia for soprano, 1989; Scherzo alla Francescana, for double bass, 1990; Trio for violin, guitar and double bass, 1990; Zeitfluss: Teuflicher kontrapunkt, for wind quintet, 1990; Lo spazio stellato si riflette in suoni, for baroque flute, 1990; Ah, amore che se n'ando nell'aria, for clarinet, viola and cello, 1991; String Quartet, 1992; El viento lucha a obscura con tu sueno, 1993; Fra l'urlo e il tacere, for bass clarinet, 1993. *Honours:* Adolf Spivakovsky Scholarship, 1990. *Address:* c/o SIAE (Sezione Musica), Viale della Letteratura n. 30, 00144 Rome, Italy.

PONCE DE LEÓN, Griselda; classical guitarist; b. 1 May 1934, Rosario, Argentina. *Education:* Accademia Musicale Chigiana, Italy, Musica en Compostela, Spain, Fine Arts School, Rosario, studied with Nelly Ezcaray, Maria Luisa Anido, Andres Segovia, Sila Godoy and Narciso Yepes. *Career:* debut in Rosario, 1944; Many concerts for radio and television in Argentina before 1958; First performance of Giuliani's Concerto op 30, with conductor José Rodríguez Fauré, Argentina, 1963; Performances for Radio Televisione Italiana and others, Italy, 1983–93; Concert recording for Cracovia's television, Poland, 1992; Performed in: Teatro Colón, Buenos Aires; El Circolo, Rosario; Municipal, São Paolo, Brazil; Rudaki Opera, Tehran, Iran; Ghione, Rome, Italy; and others; Teacher, Cordoba Conservatory, Argentina; Teacher, Instituto Superior de Musica de la Universidad de Rosario, Argentina; Teacher, Italian Conservatories, Pescara, Potenza and Bologna; Masterclasses and lectures. *Address:* Via le Ballarin 153–int 7, 00142 Rome, Italy. *E-mail:* griselponcedeleon@tiscalinet.it.

POND, Celia (Frances Sophia); Cellist; b. 5 Jan. 1956, London, England; m. Ambrose Miller, 4 April 1981. *Education:* BA 1974–77, MA 1981, Girton College, Cambridge University; LRAM, Royal Academy of Music, London, 1977–78; Staatliche Hochschule für Musik, Rheinland, 1978–81. *Career:* Principal Cello, Artistic Adviser, European Union Chamber Orchestra, 1981–; Many recitals throughout Europe with Trio Gardellino, 1983–86; Cello and Piano Duo, Celia and Mary Pond; Recitals in the United Kingdom and Far East including Hong Kong and Peking; mem, Incorporated Society of Musicians. *Recordings:* Antonio Duni; Cantate da Camera Dedicate Alla Maesta di Giovanni V. *Contributions:* Early Music, 1978; Solo Bass Viol Music in France. *Honours:* Edith Helen Major Prize, Cambridge, 1976; West German Government Scholarship, 1978. *Address:* Hollick, Yarnscombe, N Devon EX31 3LQ, England.

PONDJICLIS, Sophie; Singer (Mezzo-soprano); b. 1968, France. *Career:* Appearances at Florence, the Paris Opéra Bastille, La Scala Milan, Palais Garnier, Hamburg Opera and Marseille; Paris Châtelet in Stravinsky's Les Noces, repeated in Rome; Sang title role in Esther de Carpentras by Milhaud, 1992; Recitals at the Châtelet, Studio Bastille,

Mannheim and Villa Medici in Rome; Further enagements as Carmen, Ruggiero in Alcina and Rossini's Rosina; Season 2000–01 at the Berlin Konzerthaus as Ravel's Enfant, Mozart's Marcellina in Paris, Madrid and Barcelona, Isaura in Rossini's Tancredi at Marseille and Olga in Eugene Onegin at Geneva. *Recordings include:* Stabat Mater by Gouvy. *Honours:* Winner, Toti dal Monte Competition, Treviso. *Address:* c/o Musicaglotz, 11, Rue le Verrier, 75006 Paris, France.

PONIATOWSKA, Irena; Musicologist; b. 5 July 1933, Góra Kalwaria, Poland; m. Andrzej Poniatowski, 14 Nov 1953, deceased 1994, 1 d. *Education:* Diploma, Musicology, Warsaw University, 1962; PhD, 1970; Qualification to Assistant Professor, 1983; Habil; Qualification to Professor, 1994. *Career:* Tutor, 1970, Vice Director, 1974–79; Assistant Professor, 1984, Extraordinary Professor, 1991, Ordinary Professor, 1996, Institute of Musicology, Vice Dean, Faculty of History, 1988–90, 1993–99, Warsaw University; President, Council, 1976–84, Vice President, 1986–91, Chopin Society; President: Congress, Musica Antique Europae Orientalis, Poland, 1988, 1991, 1994, 1997, 2000, 2003; Polish Chopin Academy, 1994; President, Congress Chopin, Warsaw, 1999; President Council Institute of Fryderyk Chopin, 2001–; Editor of many encyclopaedias including: Polish Encyclopaedia of Music, Vols 1–5, 1979–1997. *Publications:* Beethoven Piano Texture, 1972; The Chronicle of the Important Musical Events in Poland 1945–72, 1974; Piano Music and Playing in XIX Century Artistic and Social Aspects, 1991; Dictionary of Music for Schools, 1991, 2nd edition, 1997; History and Interpretation of Music, 1993, 2nd edition, 1995; Editor, Musical Work: Theory History, Interpretation, 1984; Maria Szymanowska 25 Mazurkas, 1993; Editor, Chopin in the Circle of his Friends, vols I–V, 1995–99; Co-editor, J A Hasse und Polen, 1995; Editor 24 Préludes by Fryderyk Chopin, Facsimile edition with commentary, 1999; Henryk Wieniawski Polonaise Brillante pour le violon avec accompagnement de piano op. 4, urtext and critical edition, Poznani 2000; Co-editor Musica antique Europae Orientalis X Acta Musicologica, 1994; Bydqoszoz 1997; Bydqoszoz XI 1999; Bydqoszoz XII, 2003; Editor Chopin and his works in the context of culture vol.1–2 (1065pp.) Krakow 2003; Many articles in collective works. *Contributions:* Muzyka; Ruch Muzyczny; Rocznik Chopinowski; Chopin Studies; Hudobny Život; Quadrivium. *Address:* Filtrowa 63-38, 02-056 Warsaw, Poland.

PONKIN, Vladimir; Conductor; b. 1951, Irkutsk, Siberia, Russia. *Education:* Studied at Gorky Conservatoire and with Rozhdestvensky in Moscow. *Career:* Assistant conductor at Bolshoi Theatre and at Moscow Chamber Theatre; Conductor with Yaroslavl Philharmonic Orchestra, later with Russian State Cinema Orchestra; Guest engagements with St Petersburg Philharmonic and Russian State Academic Symphony Orchestra; Chief Conductor and Music Director of Russian State Maly Symphony from 1991; Music Director of New Moscow State Symphony Orchestra; Has toured to Italy, Hungary, Germany, Austria, Spain and Denmark; Repertoire has included much contemporary music as well as standard works. *Recordings include:* CDs on the Chant du Monde. *Honours:* Winner, 1990 Rupert Foundation Conducting Competition, London. *Address:* c/o Sonata, 11 Northpark Street, Glasgow G20 7AA, Scotland.

PONOMARENKO, Ivan; Baritone; b. 1955, Ukraine, Russia. *Education:* Studied at the Odessa Conservatory and with Irina Arkhipova. *Career:* Sang first with Odessa State Opera Theatre as Escamillo, Don Giovanni, Renato in Un Ballo in Maschera, Germont and Amonasro; Member of the Kiev Opera from 1981 touring with company to Germany, Spain, Netherlands, Hungary, France and Spain; Sang at Strasbourg Festival in 1993 as Nabucco; British debut on tour in 1995; Recitalist with a wide repertoire. *Address:* c/o Sonata Ltd, 11 Northpark Street, Glasgow G20 7AA, Scotland.

PONS, Juan; Singer (Baritone); b. 8 Aug. 1946, Ciutadella, Menorca. *Education:* Studied in Barcelona. *Career:* Sang at the Teatro Liceo Barcelona, at first as a tenor; Covent Garden 1979, as Alfio in Cavalleria Rusticana; Barcelona 1983, Herod in Massenet's Hérodiade; Paris Opéra 1983, as Tonio in Pagliacci; Guest appearances in Munich, Madrid and at the Orange Festival; Verona Arena 1984–85, Amonasro; La Scala Milan 1985, as Rigoletto and as Sharpless in Madama Butterfly; Metropolitan Opera 1986, as Scarpia in Tosca; Well known as Verdi's Falstaff; (Munich Staatsoper 1987), San Francisco and Rome 1989; Also sings Renato in Un Ballo in Maschera and roles in operas by Donizetti; sang Verdi's Germont at Chicago 1988; Sharpless in Madama Butterfly at La Scala, 1990; Barcelona 1989, as Basilio in Respighi's La Fiamma (also at Madrid); Season 1992 as Tonio in Pagliacci at Philadelphia, Scarpia at San Francisco and Luna at Madrid; Sang Amonasro at the Verona Arena, 1994; Tonio at Los Angeles, 1996; Season 1998 as Count of Westmorland in Wolf-Ferrari's Sly at Zürich, and Renato at Milan; Season 2000–01 as Germont in Florence, Amonasro at the Verona Arena, Rigoletto for the Opéra Bastille and Nabucco at the Met. *Recordings:* Aroldo by Verdi; Pagliacci. *Address:* c/o Teatra alla Scala, Via Filodrammatici 2, Milan, Italy.

PONSFORD, David Stewart, MA, PhD, FRCO, ARCM; Organist, Harpsichordist and Musicologist; b. 18 Jan. 1948, Cardiff, Wales. *Education:* Queen's Coll., Taunton, Royal Manchester Coll. of Music, Emmanuel Coll., Cambridge, Cardiff Univ. *Career:* Asst Organist, Wells Cathedral 1971–76; Organist, St Matthew's, Northampton; Conductor, Northampton Bach Choir 1977–79; Cheltenham Bach Choir 1981–88; organ, harpsichord and academic tutor, Birmingham Conservatoire 1982–91; harpsichord and organ tutor, Wells Cathedral School 1986–; Assoc. Lecturer in performance practice, Cardiff Univ. 2000–. *Recordings:* Annus Mirabilis 1684, Harpsichord music by Bach, Handel, Scarlatti and Sandoni 1999, Vive Le Roy, organ music by Bach, Couperin, Gringy from Greyfriars Kirk, Edinburgh 1999, J. S. Bach Clavierübung Part 3 2003. *Publications:* 'The Organ of Gottfried Silbermann' in Choir and Organ 1997, 'Inégalité and Recits: Genre Studies in 17th century French Organ Music' in The Organ Yearbook 1998–99, 'J. S. Bach and the Nature of French Influence' in The Organ Yearbook 2000; contrib. to The Musical Times, Choir and Organ, Organist's Review. *Address:* Ford Cottage, Middle Duntisbourne, Cirencester, Gloucester GL7 7AR, England (home). *Telephone:* (1285) 651995 (home). *Fax:* (1285) 651995 (home). *E-mail:* dsponsford@aol.com (home). *Website:* www .davidponsford.org (office).

PONSONBY, Robert (Noel); Arts Administrator; b. 19 Dec. 1926, Oxford, England; m. Lesley Black, 23 April 1977. *Education:* Trinity College, Oxford, 1948–50; MA Hons (Oxon). *Career:* Staff Member, Glyndebourne Opera, 1951–55; Artistic Director, Edinburgh Festival, 1956–60; General Administrator, Scottish National Orchestra, 1964–72; Controller of Music, BBC, 1972–85; Artistic Director, Canterbury Festival, 1986–88; Administrator, Friends of Musicians Benevolent Fund, 1987–93; Fellow, Royal Society of Arts. *Publications:* Short History of Oxford University Opera Club, 1950. *Contributions:* Numerous magazines and journals. *Honours:* C.B.E., 1985; Honorary RAM, 1975; Janáček Medal, Czech Government, 1980. *Address:* 11 St Cuthbert's Road, London NW2 3QJ, England.

PÖNTINEN, Roland; Swedish pianist and composer; b. 1963, Stockholm; m. Camilla Wiklund, one d. *Education:* Stockholm Royal Music Acad. and with Menahem Pressler, György Sébok and Elisabeth Leonskaya. *Career:* debut, Royal Stockholm Philharmonic Orchestra, playing Franck's Symphonic Variations 1981; many appearances with leading orchestras, including all major Swedish ensembles, Oslo Philharmonic, Los Angeles Philharmonic (Hollywood Bowl), Jerusalem Symphony, BBC Symphony, Tonhalle Orchestra, Zurich, Accademia Santa Cecilia, Rome, Philharmonia Orchestra, Scottish Chamber Orchestra; festival engagements include Bergen, Schleswig-Holstein, Ludwigsburg, Edinburgh, La Roque d'Anthéron Piano Festival, Promenade Concerts, London (playing Grieg Piano Concerto, Ligeti Piano Concerto), Aldeburgh Festival, Berliner Festwochen, Maggio Musicale Fiorentino, Kuhmo Chamber Music Festival; recitals throughout Scandinavia, Western Europe, Japan, Korea, Australia and New Zealand; premiere of composition Blue Water played by Philadelphia Orchestra and Wolfgang Sawallisch, Carnegie Hall 1998; mem. Royal Swedish Acad. of Music. *Compositions:* Blue Winter 1998. *Recordings include:* over 70 albums include as accompanist to singers, playing works by Busoni, Chopin, Janáček, Scriabin Piano Concerto (with Royal Stockholm Philharmonic Orchestra), Rachmaninov's Etudes-Tableaux. *Honours:* Litteris et Artibus medal, for skills in the arts 2001. *Current Management:* Svensk Konsertdirektion, Danska Vägen 25 B, 412 74 Göteborg, Sweden. *Telephone:* (31) 830095. *Website:* www.loddingkonsert.se; www .rolandpontinen.com.

PONTVIK, Peter; Swedish composer, ensemble leader, Musicologist and Music producer; b. 29 April 1963, Copenhagen, Denmark; Grew up in Uruguay; 2 s. *Education:* Composition with Marino Rivero, 1983–86; Musicology, Choir Conducting with Sara Herrera at the National Conservatory, Montevideo, 1984–86; Composition with Sven-David Sandström, Royal Academy of Music, Stockholm, 1989–92, and with Wolfgang Rihm, Academy of Music, Karlsruhe, Germany, as well as early music with Hans-Georg Renner, 1992–94; Ferienkurse für Neue Musik, Darmstadt, 1994. *Career:* Debut: 1st performance of Reencuentro con Misiones for bandoneon at Taller de Música Contemporánea, Montevideo, 1985; Scandinavian UNM Festival: selected works 1990, 1993 and 1994; Founder and Artistic Leader of Ensemble Villancico, Stockholm, 1994–; Radio appearances, several works, Swedish and German Broadcasting, 1994–; mem, FST (Society of Swedish Composers); ISCM; Founder and Artistic Leader of Stockholm Early Music Festival, 2002–. *Compositions:* Amen for mixed choir, 1989; Three Images for Three Recorders, 1990; Candombe for wind orchestra, 1990–91; Yeikó for bandoneon, percussion and dancer, 1992–93; Allelu for mixed choir, 1993; En kort mässa-Missa brevis for choir and brass quintet, 1994; Ur Sagitra, for choir and percussion, 1995–2000; Norr om himlen, song cycle, 2002. *Recordings:* Cancionero de Uppsala 1556 and Music from a Pack of Cards with Ensemble Villancico; ¡A la xácara! — the Jungle Book of the Baroque; Hyhyhyhyhyhyhyhy, the New Jungle

Book of the Baroque (Latin American Baroque Music; Radio and TV productions; Research in early music. *Contributions:* Articles: Codex kellugensis- gåtfult gotländskt musikfynd, 2003. *Honours:* 1st Prize, International Competition for Choir Composition, Tolosa, Spain, 1989; Ivan Lucacic Prize, Varazdin, Croatia with Ensemble Villancico, 2001. *Address:* Tångvägen 9, 1 tr, 126 38 Hägersten Sweden. *Telephone:* +46 8 30 43 29. *E-mail:* peter.pontvik@zeta.telenordia.se..

POOLE, John; Choral Director; b. 1934, Birmingham, England; m. Laura McKirahan, 22 July 1987, 3 s. *Education:* Studied at Oxford University. *Career:* Former Organist of London University Church and Music Director at University College, London; Founded the Bloomsbury Singers and Players; Director of the BBC Singers, 1972–90 and has directed the BBC Symphony Chorus and Singers in many concerts throughout the United Kingdom and abroad; Music Director of the Groupe Vocal de France, 1990–95 and Chief Guest Conductor of the BBC Singers, with frequent performances of modern repertory; Guest Director, world-wide; mem, FRCO. *Recordings:* Giles Swayne, Cry, with BBC Singers; Martin Mass, Britten, A Boy Was Born, BBC Singers, Westminster Cathedral Choristers; Chants d'Eglise with Groupe Vocal de France. *Address:* Le Logis de Thoiré, 79200 La Peyratte, France.

POOT, Sonja; Singer (Soprano); b. 3 Dec. 1936, Gravenzande, Netherlands. *Education:* Studied in Salisbury (Rhodesia), Amsterdam and Vienna. *Career:* Sang at Bonn Opera, 1964–71, notably as Constanze in Entführung, and Donizetti's Lucia and Maria di Rohan; Nuremberg, 1971–73, Stuttgart Staatsoper, 1973–78; Guest engagements at Basle, Amsterdam (Elsa 1978), Vienna Volksoper, Rome, Geneva (Elettra in Idomeneo, 1973), Barcelona and Ottawa; Other roles have included Mozart's Donna Anna, Queen of Night and Pamina, Anna Bolena, Lucrezia Borgia, Violetta, Amelia in Ballo in Maschera and Norina in Don Pasquale; Many concert performances. *Address:* c/o Staatsoper Stuttgart, Oberer Schlossgarten 6, 7000 Stuttgart, Germany.

POPE, Cathryn; Singer (Soprano); b. 1960, England. *Education:* Studied with Ruth Packer at the Royal College of Music; Further study at the National Opera Studio. *Career:* With English National Opera has sung Papagena and Pamina in The Magic Flute, Anna (Moses), Susanna, Zerlina, Sophie (Werther), Leila (The Perl Fishers), Gretel and Werther; Sang Oksana in the first British production of Christmas Eve by Rimsky-Korsakov, 1988; Sang Amor in Orpheus and Euridice for Opera North; Royal Opera Covent Garden as Gianetta (L'Elisir d'Amor), Frasquita (Carmen) and a Naiad (Ariadne auf Naxos). *Recordings include:* Anne Trulove in The Rake's Progress; Barbarina in Le nozze di Figaro; Sang Gretel with Netherlands Opera 1990, Pamina at the London Coliseum; Sang in new productiions of The Marriage of Figaro and Königskinder at the Coliseum, 1991–92; Gilda in a revival of Rigoletto, 1992/93; Featured Artist, Opera Now magazine, Feb 1992. *Recordings include:* Video of Rusalka (as Wood Nymph). *Address:* c/o English National Opera, St Martin's Lane, London WC2, England.

POPE, Michael Douglas, FRSA; Musician, Producer, Choral Conductor and Writer; b. 25 Feb. 1927, London, England; m. 1st Margaret Jean Blakeney 1954, one s.; m. 2nd Gillian Victoria Peck 1967, one s. and one s. *Education:* Guildhall School of Music and Drama. *Career:* served in Army 1945–48; joined BBC 1954, Asst, Music Division 1960, Producer, music programmes and music talks 1966–80; planned and produced many programmes and series with BBC Chorus, subsequently BBC Singers; productions include revivals of works by Elgar, Stanford, Bantock (Omar Khayyám trilogy 1979), Bennett, Rootham, Hurlstone, Boyce (Solomon 1979), Parry (Prometheus Unbound 1980) and other composers; premiere of Everyman, music drama by Kennedy Scott 1977; Missing Music 1972; The Direction of Modern Music 1980; Musical Dir, London Motet and Madrigal Club 1954–93; Guest Conductor, RTE; Hon. Sec., Royal Philharmonic Soc. 1983–85; mem. Royal Musical Asscn. Incorporated Soc. of Musicians, Elgar Soc. (Chair. 1978–88, Vice-Pres. 1988). *Publications include:* King Olaf and the English Choral Tradition in Elgar Studies 1990; contributions to DNB, Royal College of Music Magazine. *Address:* Quarry Farm House, Chicksgrove, Salisbury, Wiltshire SP3 6LY, England.

POPKEN, Ralph; Singer (Counter-tenor); b. 1962, Wilhelmshaven, Germany. *Education:* Studied in Hanover with Emma Kirkby. *Career:* Sang in concerts and oratorios from 1984, in Europe and the USA; Opera debut, Hanover 1989 in Enrico Leone by Steffani; Handel Festival at Göttingen from 1992 in Agrippina, Ottone and Radamisto; Deutsche Staatsoper Berlin, 1992–95 in Graun's Cesare e Cleopatra, Gassmann's L'opera seria; Theater an der Wien, 1998 and 1999–2000; Theater des Westens, Berlin in Chicago (musical); Sang Narciso in Handel's Agrippina at Halle, 1999–2000. *Recordings:* Radamisto, Cesare e Cleopatra; Bach-Cantatas. *Address:* c/o Heide Stock, Ferdinand-Wallbrecht-Str. 13, 30163 Hannover, Germany.

POPLE, Ross; Conductor and Cellist; b. 11 May 1945, Auckland, New Zealand; m. (1) Anne Storrs, 25 June 1965, divorced, 3 s., 1 d., (2) Charlotte Fairbairn, July 1992, 1 s. *Education:* Royal Academy of Music,

London; Recital Medal, Honorary RAM; Paris Conservatoire. *Career:* Debut: London, 1965; Principal Cello, Menuhin Festival Orchestra; BBC Symphony Orchestra, 1976–86; Director of London Festival Orchestra, 1980–; Founder, Cathedral Classics, Festival of Music in Cathedrals, United Kingdom, 1986–; London South Bank series, Birthday Honours, 1988–; Founder and Developer of The Warehouse, Waterloo (home to London Festival Orchestra and recording studio), 1993. *Recordings:* Haydn, Boccherini, Mozart, Mendelssohn, Schoenberg, Vaughan Williams, Holst, Strauss, Arnold, Franck, Bach and others, for various labels. *Address:* Sellet Hall, Stainton, Kendal LA 8 0LE, England.

POPOV, Stefan; Cellist; b. 1940, Bulgaria. *Education:* Studied in Sofia, the Moscow Conservatory with Sviatoslav Knushevitsky and Mstislav Rostropovich, 1961–66. *Career:* Debut: Sofia 1955; Many concert appearances in Europe, North America, Asia notably at London, Moscow, Boston, Florence, Geneva, Dublin, Genoa, Milan, Budapest; Concerto repertoire includes works by Vivaldi, Haydn, Boccherini, Beethoven, Schumann, Dvořák, Brahms, Elgar, Hindemith, Milhaud, Honegger, Kabalevsky and Shostakovich; Don Quixote by Strauss; Respighi Adagio with Variations; Prokofiev Symphonie Concertante; Bloch Schelomo; Sonata collaborations with the pianist Allan Schiller; Has taught at Boston University, the New England Conservatory of Music. *Honours:* Winner of competitions in Moscow 1957, Geneva 1964, Vienna 1967, Florence 1969; 1966 Techaikovsky International Competition, Moscow. *Address:* Sofia-concert, Bulgarian Artistic Agency, 3 Volov Street, Sofia, Bulgaria.

POPOV, Valery; Singer (Tenor); b. 1965, Kharkiv, Ukraine. *Education:* Studied at the Kharkov Institute of Arts. *Career:* Has sung at the Kiev and Kharkov Opera Houses and from 1994 as Principal at the Brno Opera Theatre, Czechoslovakia; Roles have included Cavaradossi, Don Alvaro, Don Ottavio, Don Carlos, Turriddu, Samson and Alfredo; Sang Don José on tour to France in 1992; Further appearances throughout Europe and North America; Jenik in The Bartered Bride at Ostrava, 1998; Sang Meyerbeer's Robert le Diable at Prague, 1999; Robert in Tchaikovsky's Iolanta at Monte Carlo, 2001. *Honours:* Prizewinner, Belvedere International Competition, Vienna. *Address:* c/o Sonata Ltd, 11 North Park Street, Glasgow G20 7AA, Scotland.

POPOV, Vladimir; Singer (Tenor); b. 29 April 1947, Moscow, Russia. *Education:* Studied at Tchaikovsky Conservatory, Moscow. *Career:* Sang at Bolshoi Opera, Moscow, 1977–81; Studied further in Milan and emigrated to USA, 1982, singing Ramirez in La Fanciulla del West at Portland; Metropolitan Opera debut, 1984, as Lensky in Eugene Onegin; Further engagements as Calaf at Houston, 1987, as Cavaradossi at Philadelphia, 1987, as Dimitri in Boris Godunov at Covent Garden, 1988, and Hermann in The Queen of Spades at Washington, 1989; Sang Calaf with Covent Garden Company at Wembley Arena, 1991, Samson at Detroit and Canio in Pagliacci at Buenos Aires, 1992; Other roles include Ernani, Gabriele Adorno, Don José and Radames (San Francisco, 1989).

POPOVA, Valeria; Singer (Soprano); b. 1945, Bulgaria. *Education:* Studied with father Sacha Popov, in Sofia and with Gina Cigna. *Career:* Debut: Sang Lauretta in Gianni Schicchi at National Theatre, Belgrade; Sang at Plovdiv Opera, 1971–76, Sofia from 1976; Guest engagements in former Soviet Union, Germany, Romania and Cuba; Other roles include Violetta, Manon, Mozart's Countess, Jenůfa, Fiordiligi, Marguerite, Donna Anna, Pamina and Leonora in La Forza del Destino; Sang Amelia in Ballo in Maschera at Milwaukee, 1990; Also teacher of singers: d. Alexandrina Pendachanska has been among her pupils. *Recordings include:* Arias by Puccini, Verdi, Massenet and Bellini. *Address:* c/o PG & PM, 7 Whitehorse Close, Royal Mile, Edinburgh, EH8 8BU, Scotland.

POPOVICI, Dorum; Composer; b. 17 Feb. 1932, Resita, Romania. *Education:* Studied in Timosoara, 1944–50, at Bucharest Conservatory, 1950–55, and Darmstadt, 1968. *Career:* Editor of Romanian Radio and Television, 1968. *Compositions:* Operas: Promethu, Bucharest, 1964; Mariana Pineda, lasi, 1969; Interrogation at Daybreak, Galati, 1979; The Longest Night, Bucharest, 1983; Firmness, composed 1989; Orchestral: Triptyque, 1955; 2 Symphonic Sketches, 1955; Concertino for strings, 1956; Concerto for orchestra, 1960; 4 Symphonies, 1962, 1966, 1968, 1973; Poem Bizantin, 1968; Pastorale Suite, 1982; Chamber: Cello sonata, 1952; Violin Sonata, 1953; String Quartet, 1954; Fantasy for String Trio, 1955; Sonata for 2 cellos, 1960; Sonata for 2 violas, 1965; Quintet for piano, violin, viola, cello, clarinet, 1967; Piano Trio, 1970; Madrigal for flute, clarinet, string trio and trombone; Cantatas, piano music, choruses, songs. *Publications include:* Elizabethan Music, 1978: Italian Renaissance Music, 1978. *Address:* Vaselor 3A sect 2, Bucharest, Romania.

PORTELLA, Nelson; Singer (Baritone); b. 1945, Brazil. *Education:* Studied in Rio de Janeiro. *Career:* Sang widely in South America opera houses from 1970, Teatro Liceo Barcelona from 1980, Naples from 1983 and Venice from 1985; Caracalla Festival, 1986, Ravenna, 1988; Roles have included Don Giovanni, Leporello, Masetto, Germont, Iago, Sharpless, the Count in Capriccio and Wozzeck. *Recordings include:* Scarpia, in Tosca (Balkanton); Mascagni's Le Maschere (Cetra).

PORTER, Andrew; Writer on Music; b. 26 Aug. 1928, Cape Town, South Africa. *Education:* MA, Oxford Univ., England. *Career:* wrote for Manchester Guardian 1949, The Times 1951; music critic, Financial Times 1953–74, The New Yorker 1972–92, The Observer 1992–97, Times Literary Supplement 1997–; Ed., The Musical Times 1960–67; Visiting Fellow, All Souls Coll., Oxford 1973–74; Bloch Prof., Univ. of California, Berkeley 1980–81; libretti for The Tempest by John Eaton and The Song of Majnun by Bright Sheng; opera translation performances include Verdi's Don Carlos, Rigoletto, Othello, Falstaff, Macbeth, The Force of Destiny, Nabucco, King for a Day, Wagner's The Ring, Tristan and Isolde, Parsifal, Handel's Ottone, Haydn's Deceit Outwitted and The Unexpected Meeting, Mozart's Mithradates, Lucio Silla, The Abduction from the Seraglio, Idomeneo, The Impresario, The Marriage of Figaro, Così fan tutte, Don Giovanni, The Magic Flute and Titus; Gluck's Orpheus, Richard Strauss's Intermezzo, Rossini's The Turk in Italy and The Voyage to Rheims, Puccini's La Bohème, Schoenberg's Pierrot Lunaire; mem. Royal Musical Asscn (vice-pres.), American Institute of Verdi Studies. *Recordings:* The Song of Majnun, The Ring, Othello, Intermezzo, Pierrot Lunaire (English translation). *Publications:* A Musical Season 1974, Music of Three Seasons 1978, Music of Three More Seasons 1980, Musical Events: A Chronicle 1980–86, two vols 1987, 1991, Verdi's Macbeth: A Sourcebook (ed. with David Rosen) 1984, A Music Critic Remembers 2000. *Contributions to:* Music and Letters, Musical Quarterly, Musical Times, Proceedings of the Royal Musical Association, Atti del Congresso Internazionale di Studi Verdiani. *Honours:* Deems Taylor Award, American Society of Composers, Authors and Publishers 1975, 1978, 1981, National Music Theatre Award 1985, Corresponding Fellow, American Musicological Soc., Words on Music (a Festschrift with contributions from Elliott Carter, Joseph Kerman, Ned Rorem, etc.) 2004. *Address:* 9 Pembroke Walk, London, W8 6PQ, England.

PORTER, David Hugh, BA, PhD; American pianist, harpsichordist and educator; b. 29 Oct. 1935, New York, NY; m. 1st Laudie E. Dimmette 1958 (deceased); three s. one d.; m. 2nd Helen L. Nelson 1987. *Education:* Swarthmore College, Princeton University, Philadelphia Conservatory of Music, studied piano with Edward Steuermann, harpsichord with Gustav Leonhardt. *Career:* debut in Philadelphia, 1955; Piano and Harpsichord Recitals and Lecture-Recitals throughout USA, 1966–; in London and Edinburgh, 1977; Performances on radio and television, 1967–; Professor of Classics and Music, Carleton College, 1962–; President, Carleton College, 1986–87; President, Skidmore College, 1987–98; Visiting Professor of Liberal Arts, Williams College, 1999–; Author: Only Connect: Three Studies in Greek Tragedy, Horace's Poetic Journey, The Not Quite Innocent Bystander: Writings of Eduard Steuermann, Virginia Woolf and Logan Pearsall Smith: an Exquisitely Flattering Duet; Riding a Great Horse: Virginia Woolf and the Hogarth Press. *Publications:* contrib. articles to Music Review and Perspectives of New Music; Numerous articles in classical journals. *Honours:* Steuermann Scholarship, Philadelphia Conservatory of Music, 1955–. *Address:* 5 Birch Run Drive, Saratoga Springs, NY 12866, USA. *E-mail:* ddodger@skidmore.edu.

PORTMAN, Rachel Mary Berkeley; British composer; b. 11 Dec. 1960, Haslemere; m. Uberto Pasolini; three d. *Education:* Worcester Coll., Oxford. *Career:* composer of film and TV scores, for US productions 1992–. *Compositions for film and television:* Experience Preferred... But Not Essential 1982, The Storyteller (TV series) 1986–88, 1990, Life is Sweet 1990, Oranges Are Not the Only Fruit (TV drama) 1990, Antonia and Jane 1991, Where Angels Fear to Tread 1991, Used People 1992, The Joy Luck Club 1993, Benny and Joon 1993, Friends 1993, Sirens 1994, Only You 1994, War of the Buttons 1994, To Wong Foo – Thanks for Everything! 1995, A Pyromaniac's Love Story 1995, Smoke 1995, The Adventures of Pinocchio 1996, Marvin's Room 1996, Emma (Acad. Award 1997) 1996, Addicted to Love 1997, The Cider House Rules 1999, Chocolat 2000, The Emperor's New Clothes 2001, Hart's War 2002, The Truth About Charlie 2002, Nicholas Nickleby 2002, The Human Stain 2003, The Manchurian Candidate 2004, The Little Prince 2004, Because of Winn-Dixie 2005, Flightplan 2005. *Recordings include:* Rachel Portman Soundtracks (compilation album), numerous soundtrack recordings. *Honours:* British Film Inst. Young Composer of the Year Award 1988. *Address:* c/o Bucks Music, Onward House, 11 Uxbridge House, London, W8 7TQ, England (office).

POSCHNER-KLEBEL, Brigitte; Singer (Soprano); b. 1957, Vienna, Austria. *Education:* Studied in Vienna with Gerda Scheyrer and Gottfried Hornik. *Career:* Sang with Vienna Staatsoper, 1982–, Volksoper, 1983–; Guest appearances at Aix-en-Provence Festival, 1988–89, Fiordiligi, La Scala, Milan as Pamina, 1986, Venice, Amsterdam and Tokyo; Sang Susanna in Khovanshchina at Vienna Staatsoper, 1989; Other roles include Hansel, Rosalinde, Esmerelda,

Sophie in Der Rosenkavalier, Xenia in Boris Godunov and Lucy in The Beggar's Opera; Frequent concert appearances. *Recordings:* Khovanshchina; Video of Elektra conducted by Abbado, as a Maidservant. *Address:* c/o Staatsoper, Opernring 2, 1010 Vienna, Austria.

POSPISIL, Juraj; Composer; b. 14 Jan. 1931, Olomouc, Czechoslovakia. *Education:* Studied at the Olomouc School of Music (1949–50), Janáček Academy, Brno (1950–52) and with Cikker at the Bratislava Academy (1952–55). *Career:* Lecturer in theory and composition at the Bratislava Academy of Music and Drama, 1955–91. *Compositions include:* The Mountains and the People, symphonic poem, 1954; Symphonies, 1958, 1963, 1967, 1978, 1986, 1996, 1999; Sonata for strings, 1961; Song About a Man, symphonic variations, 1961; Trombone Concerto, 1962; 4 String Quartets, 1970, 1979, 1985, 1990; Inter Arna, cycle of 3 operas, 1970; Violin Concerto, 1968; Clarinet Concerto, 1972; To Bratislava, for baritone and orchestra, 1973; Symphonic Frescoes I–III, 1972, 1976, 1981; Concerto Eroico, for horn and orchestra, 1973; Chamber Sinfonietta, 1974; November Triptych, for chamber chorus, wind and piano, 1977; 2 Trios for piano, violin and cello, 1977, 1987; Concerto for soprano and orchestra, 1984; Dulcimer Concerto, 1989; Sonata for alto trombone and strings, 1991; Bass Quintet, 1991; The Lord's Prayer of the Hussites, sacred cantata, 1991; Manon Lescaut, scenic drama, 1993; Bass Tuba concerto, 1994; Autumn Bottling, for bass voice and string quartet, 1994. *Address:* c/o SOZA, Rastislavova 3, 821 08 Bratislava, Slovakia.

POSSEMEYER, Berthold; Singer (Baritone); b. 1950, Gladbeck, Westfalen, Germany. *Education:* Studied in Cologne with Josef Metternich. *Career:* Sang at first in concert and gave Lieder recitals, notably at Paris, New York, Jerusalem, Hamburg, Turin and Venice; Stage career from 1978, at first at Oldenburg, then from 1979 at Essen, as Rossini's Figaro, Papageno, Guglielmo, Eugene Onegin and Silvio in Pagliacci; Sang at Gelsenkirchen Opera, 1984–86, then returned to concerts; Repertoire includes works by Bach, Mozart, Mendelssohn and Distler. *Address:* c/o Musiktheater im Rivier, Kennedyplatz, 4650 Gelsenkirchen, Germany.

POSTNIKOVA, Viktoria; Concert Pianist; b. 12 Jan. 1944, Moscow, USSR; m. Gennadi Rozhdestvensky 1969. *Education:* Studied at the Moscow Central School of Music with E B Musaelian, 1950–62; Further study with Yakov Flier at the Moscow Conservatoire. *Career:* Many concert appearances in Europe, Russia and the USA from 1966; Repertoire includes music by Bach, Handel, Scarlatti, Haydn, Mozart, Liszt, Chopin, Mendelssohn, Schumann, Brahms and Rachmaninov; Modern repertoire includes music by Busoni, Ives, Britten and Shostakovich; Played in the British premiere of Schnittke's Concerto for piano duet and orchestra in London 1991. *Recordings:* Tchaikovsky Concertos (Decca); Busoni Concerto and complete piano works by Janáček and Tchaikovsky (Erato); Violin sonatas by Busoni and Strauss (Chandos); Complete piano concertos of Brahms, Chopin and Prokofiev (Melodiya). *Honours:* Prizewinner at competitions in Warsaw (1965), Leeds (1966), Lisbon (1968) and Moscow (1970). *Address:* Allied Artists, 42 Montpelier Square, London SW7 1JZ, England.

POTOCNIK, Tone; Slovenian pianist, organist and ; b. 13 Jan. 1951, Bukovica, Skofja Loka. *Education:* Academy of Music, Ljubljana, Academy of Music, Zagreb, Croatia, Academy of Santa Cecilia, Rome, Conservatoire of Santa Cecilia, Rome, Rome Papal Institute for Church Music, Licenza in Canto Gregoriano, Licenza in Musica Sacra. *Career:* specialised in the piano music of G. Gurdieff and T. de Hartmann, Institute for the Harmonious Development of Man; performances in Italy and the other countries in Europe; Prof. of Gregorian Chant, Piano and Score Play at the Academy of Music in Ljubljana, Slovenia; Founded the 1st School of Gregorian Chant in Slovenia and Shola Cantorum, Cantate Domino; Recording for RTV Slovenia–Cerkveno leto v Gregorijanskem koralu (Church year in Gregorian Chant); Tonus psalmorum; Performs at independent recitals as an organist; Premiere performances of contemporary Slovene composers (L. Lebic, P. Ramovs, L. Vrhunc, M. Gabrijelcic); Soloist and with RTV and Philharmonic orchestra of Ljubljana; Organ and piano accompaniment of instrumental and vocal soloists and chorus. *Recordings:* Eno je dete rojeno, with Komorni zbor Ave (The Child was born, with The Chamber Choir Ave); Ave Maria, with Branko Robinsak–tenor; Music highlights of Baroque, with Norina Radovan, soprano and Tibor Kerekes, trumpet. *Address:* Zabrdo 1, 4229 Sorica, Slovenia.

POTT, Francis (John Dolben); Composer, Pianist and University Lecturer; b. 25 Aug. 1957, Oxfordshire, England; m. Virginia Straker, 19 Sept 1992, 1 s, 1 d. *Education:* Chorister, New College, Oxford; Music Scholar, Winchester College and Magdalene College, Cambridge; Composition with Robin Holloway, Hugh Wood; Piano with Hamish Milne, London; MA, BMus, University of Cambridge. *Career:* Freelance composition/performance; Tutor in Compositional Techniques, Oxford University, 1987–89; Lecturer in Music, St Hugh's College, 1988; Lecturer in Music, Director of Foundation Studies, West London

Institute, 1989–91; John Bennett Lecturer in Music, St Hilda's College, Oxford, 1991–; Visiting Tutor in Composition, Winchester College, 1991–96; Piano recitalist and accompanist; Administrative Head of Music, London College of Music and Media, Thames Valley University, London 2001–2002; Head of Research Development and Composition, London College of Music and Media, 2002–. *Compositions:* Organ: Mosaici di Ravenna, 1981; Empyrean, 1982; Fenix, Music for Lincoln Minster, Organ, Brass, Percussion, Timpani, 1985; Passion Symphony, Christus, 1986–90, premiered Westminster Cathedral, 1991; Toccata for Organ, 1991; choral (church) and other works; Piano Quintet, premiered by The Twentieth Century Consort, Smithsonian Institute, USA, 1993; Solo piano works, Sonata for cello and piano, premiered Wigmore Hall, London, 1996,; A Song on the End of the World, 1999 Elgar Commission, Three Choirs Festival, chorus, orchestra, soloists, organ, texts by Czeslaw Milosz and others, premiere, Worcester Cathedral, 1999; Many television and radio broadcasts; Works performed in 15 countries worldwide; Many sacred choral works and compositions for piano solo. *Recordings:* Christus, organ symphony, 1992; Cello Sonata, David Watkin, 1997. *Publications:* Organ Works, 1989; Christus, organ symphony, 3 vols, 1994–99; Toccata for piano solo, 1999; Cello Sonata, 2000. *Honours:* Gerald Finzi Trust Memorial Award for Composition, 1981; Lloyd's Bank National Composing Competition, 1982; Barclaycard National Composing Competition, 1983; First Prize, 2nd S.S.Prokofiev International Compsing Competition, Moscow, 1997. *Address:* London College of Music and Media, Thames Valley University, St Mary's Road, Ealing, London, W5 5RF; Thurlows, Main Road, Littleton, Winchester, Hampshire SO22 6PS, England. *Telephone:* 020 8231 2569; 01962 885874. *E-mail:* francis.pott@axchange.tvu.ac.uk; fpott@argonet.co.uk. *Website:* www.britishacademy.com/members/pott.htm.

POTURLJAN, Artin (Bedros); Composer; b. 4 May 1943, Kharmanli, Bulgaria; m. Akopjan Anahid Aram, 28 June 1974, 2 s. *Education:* Theoretical Faculty with speciality in Musical Pedagogy, State Academy of Music, Sofia, 1967; Composition at Yerevan State Conservatoire Komitas, 1974. *Career:* First public performance of compositions in Yerevan, Moscow and Tbilisi, 1970–74; Performances of Symphonies Nos 1 and 2 in Sofia, 1976 and 1978; Member of Bulgarian Composers Union, 1978; Regular appearances in New Bulgarian Music Festival, 1980–03; Authorial recital of chamber compositions at Yerevan, Armenia in 1987 and Sofia in 1991, 2003; Performances of Four Spiritual Songs (on themes by Nerses Shnorhali) for organ in Austria at Vienna, Klagenfurt, Anif, 1991, and Friedrichshafen am Bodensee, 1997; Participation in Holland-Bulgarian Music Festival, Sofia, 1992; Teacher of Polyphony and Assoc. Prof. in State Musical Academy, Sofia, 1990–2000; Performances at Salzburg of Arabesques Confessions and Fantasia, Worlds, for two pianos, and participant in symposium West ruft Ost, 1995; Performance of Improvisations for clarinet and piano, Bratislava, Slovakia, 1998; mem, Society for Contemporary Music in Bulgaria, 1992–. *Compositions:* Sonata for violin and piano, 1972; Music for 3 Flutes, 2 Pianos, Tam-Tam and Strings, 1977–78; Klavier Quartet, 2001, Opera, Women's Cry, in one act, 1979; Poem for organ and symphony orchestra, 1980; Chamber Concerto, for piano and strings, 1981; Concerto for violin and symphony orchestra, 1983; Four Spiritual Songs on themes by Nerses Shnorhali, 1988; Klavier Quintet, 1989; Fantasia for piano and symphony orchestra, 1990; Mosaici for symphony orchestra, 1993; Piano Trio, 1995; L'infinito for mezzo soprano solo, baritone solo, chorus and symphony orchestra, poetry by Giacomo Leopardi, 1998; Songs; Concerto for cello and chamber orchestra, 1999; Concerto Grosso '87, 2000; Melomonologue for viola solo, 2003. *Recordings:* Arabesques for piano; The Confession for piano; Kaissa's Temple for piano; Fantasia, Worlds for 2 pianos; Symphony No. 2, documentary; Others on Bulgarian radio; Mosaici, 1994. *Publications:* Geometric Transformations of the Plane and the Space and Invention Polyphony, 1999. *Honours:* 1st Prize in Composition Competition, Pazardjik, 1985; Prizes of Bulgarian Composers Union for Arabesques, 1983 and Violin Concerto, 1989. *Address:* Tsarigradskoshosse Bl 4, Vch B, 1113 Sofia, Bulgaria.

POULENARD, Isabelle; Singer (Soprano); b. 5 July 1961, Paris, France. *Education:* Studied at L'Ecole de l'Opera de Paris. *Career:* Sang at Tourcoing in operas by Mozart, Paisiello, Monteverdi, Scarlatti and Vivaldi, conducted by Jean-Claude Malgoire; Has performed in operas at the festivals of Carpentras and Avignon; Hippolyte et Aricie under William Christie at the Opéra-Comique; Les Dialogues des Carmélites at the Opéra du Rhin; Cesti's Orontea at the Innsbruck Festival, under René Jacobs; Sang Gluck's Iphigénie en Aulide with the City of London Sinfonia at the Spitalfields Festival; Other repertoire includes Paisiello's ll Re Teodoro in Venezia, Handel's Alessandro and Massenet's Grisélidis; Concert appearances throughout France and in Venice, Flanders, Innsbruck and Stuttgart; British engagements at the Barbican, London and for Music at Oxford; Season 1992 as Teutile in the Vivaldi pastiche Montezuma at Monte Carlo and in Conti's Don Chisciotte at the Innsbruck Festival of Early Music; Sang Bita in

Cimarosa's Il Mercato di Malmantile, Opéra du Rhin, 1996. *Recordings:* Music by Cesti, Rameau, Couperin, Schütz, Cavalli, Bach and Vivaldi; Monteverdi's ll Combattimento di Tancredi e Clorinda; Lully's Armide, La Malade imaginaire by Charpentier and Die Zauberflöte (Erato); Handel's Tamerlano (CBS); Le Cinesi by Gluck and Les Indes Galantes by Rameau, (Harmonia Mundi). *Address:* c/o Opéra du Rhin, 19 Place Broglie, 07008 Strasbourg, France.

POULET, Michel; Cellist; b. 1960, France. *Education:* Studied at the Paris Conservatoire with Jean-Claude Pennetier and with members of the Amadeua and Alban Berg Quartets. *Career:* Member of the Ysaÿe String Quartet from 1986; Many concert performances in France, Europe, America and the Far East; Festival engagements at Salzburg, Tivoli (Copenhagen), Bergen, Lockenhaus, Barcelona and Stresa; Many appearances in Italy, notably with the Haydn Quartets of Mozart; Tours of Japan and the USA 1990 and 1992. *Recordings:* Mozart Quartet K421 and Quintet K516 (Harmonia Mundi); Ravel, Debussy and Mendelssohn Quartets (Decca). *Honours:* Grand Prix Evian International String Quartet Competition, May 1988; special prizes for best performances of a Mozart quartet, the Debussy quartet and a contemporary work; 2nd Prize, Portsmouth International String Quartet Competition, 1988. *Address:* c/o Phelps, Ysaÿe Quartet, 6 Malvern Road, London, E8 3LT, England.

POULSON, Lani; Singer (Mezzo Soprano); b. 7 March 1953, Tremonton, Utah, USA. *Career:* Sang as Charlotte, Ramiro, Carmen, Octavian and The Composer, Countess Geschwitz in Lulu; Sung at the Hamburg Staatsoper as Cherubino, Court Theatre at Drottningholm as Sextus in La Clemenza di Tito, Montpellier in 1988 as Dorabella, Stuttgart in 1991 in world premiere, as Andromeda in Perseo ed Andromeda by Sciarrino; Appearances at Essen, Lausanne, Stravanger, Frankfurt, Orleans, Munich, Strasbourg and in Der Rosenkavalier at Mannheim, Tel-Aviv, Budapest and Bonn; Concert repertory includes: The St Matthew Passion, Mozart's Requiem and Beethoven's Mass in C; In season 1993–94 sang performances of Sesto in Dresden, also as part of the Dresden Musikfestspiele; Season 1994–95 included the world premiere of Rihm's Das Schweigen der Sirenen at the Staatstheater in Stuttgart returning to Dresden for futher performances of La Clemenza di Tito; World premiere concert performance of L'Icone Paradoxale by Gerard Grisey, 1996, and also in Strasbourg, Frankfurt and Reggio Emilia; Season 1997–98, Ottavia in L'Incoronazione di Poppea, Utah Opera, and debut as Magdalene in Meistersinger in Lisbon; Season 1998–99, new production of Al gran sole carico d'amore by Luigi Nono at Stuttgart; Mahagonny and Mamma Lucia in Cavalleria Rusticana in Stuttgart, Third Lady in Zauberflöte in Trieste, La Clemenza di Tito and Le Nozze di Figaro in Dresden, debut as Magdalene in Meistersinger in Lisbon, Der Rosenkavalier in Frankfurt and Ottavia L'Incoronazione di Poppea for Utah Opera; Season 1999–2000 included Poppea for Columbus Opera and Al gran sole carico d'amore at Staatstheater in Stuttgart. *Honours:* Prizewinner of the Concours International de Chant de la Ville de Toulouse, 1984; Grand Prizewinner, the first prize Mezzo and winner of the Elly Ameling Prize for Lieder at the 's-Hertogenbosch International Vocal Competition. *Address:* c/o Haydn Rawstron Ltd, 36 Station Road, London SE20 7BQ, England.

POULTON, Robert; Singer (baritone); b. 1960, Brighton, England. *Education:* Studied with Rudolf Piernay, Guildhall School of Music and Drama; Further study, European Opera Centre, Belgium and National Opera Studio, London. *Career:* Sang The Ferryman in Britten's Curlew River for Nexus Opera at the 1986 Bath Festival; Repeated at the Promenade Concerts; With Glyndebourne Touring Opera has appeared in L'Heure Espagnole, L'Enfant et Les Sortilèges, La Traviata, Le nozze di Figaro, Katya Kabanova and Jenůfa, (last two also televised); Oratorio repertoire includes Purcell, Haydn's Creation, Vaughan Williams, Bach's St John Passion, Handel's Messiah, Elgar's The Kingdom and Finzi; Concerts in Singapore, Italy, Belgium and Israel; Created roles of Doctor, Policeman and Stranger in Judith Weir's The Vanishing Bridegroom, Scottish Opera, 1990; Created title role in Gassir the Hero by Theo Loevendie for Netherlands Opera, 1991; ENO Debut, Leander in Love for Three Oranges, 1991; Engaged as Figaro (Mozart) Scottish Opera; Ned Keene, Peter Grimes, Glyndebourne Festival Opera, 1992; Sang Punch in Birtwistle's Punch and Judy for Netherlands Opera, 1993; Count Almaviva in The Marriage of Figaro for ENO, 1994, 1996; Ned Keene, 1992, 1994; (Grimes), ENO, Nantes, Cologne and Copenhagen; Created Mr Dollarama in Birtwistle's The Second Mrs Kong, Glyndebourne Tour 1994 and festival, 1995, and Marcello, 1995; Douphol in Traviata for GTO at Glyndebourne, 1996; Germont Père, 1996, Prus in Makropolus Case, 1997, Glyndebourne Touring Opera; Enrico in Lucia di Lammermoor for Stowe Opera, 1998; Season 1998–99, Father in Hansel and Gretel for Welsh National Opera, also televised for Opera Northern Ireland; Falstaff for Garsington Opera; Season 2000–01 as Eugene Onegin for Grange Park Opera and in the premiere of From Morning to Midnight by David Sawer for ENO. *Recordings:* Baron Zeta in Die Lustige Witwe, 1993; Hugh the Drover;

L'Enfance du Christ. *Honours:* Silver Medal for Singing and Lord Mayor's Prize, Guildhall School of Music. *Current Management:* Musicmakers International Artists Representation, Tailor House, 63–65 High Street, Whitwell, Hertfordshire SG4 8AH, England. *Telephone:* (1438) 871708. *Fax:* (1438) 871777. *E-mail:* musicmakers@compuserve.com. *Website:* www.operauk.com.

POUNTNEY, David; Opera Producer; b. 10 Sept. 1947, Oxford, England. *Education:* Radley College and Cambridge University. *Career:* First opera production Cambridge 1967, Scarlatti's Trionfo dell'Onore; Wexford Festival 1972, Katya Kabanova; Director of Productions for Scottish Opera 1975–80, notably with Die Meistersinger, Eugene Onegin, Jenůfa, The Cunning Little Vixen, Die Entführung and Don Giovanni; Australian debut 1978, Die Meistersinger; Netherlands Opera 1980, world premiere of Philip Glass's Satyagraha; Principal Producer and Director of Productions, English National Opera, 1982–93: work includes The Flying Dutchman, The Queen of Spades, Rusalka, The Valkyrie and Lady Macbeth of Mtsensk; American debut with Houston Opera, Verdi's Macbeth: returned for the world premiere of Bilby's Doll by Carlisle Floyd, Katya Kabanova and Jenůfa; Produced Weill's Street Scene for Scottish Opera, 1989; Other productions include From the House of the Dead in Vancouver, Dr Faust in Berlin and Paris, and The Fiery Angel at the State Opera of South Australia, Adelaide; The Flying Dutchman, Nabucco and Fidelio for the Bregenz Festival, The Excursions of Mr Brouček for the Munich State Opera, the World Premiere of Philip Glass's The Voyage at the Met, and The Fairy Queen for ENO; Completed two libretti, The Doctor of Mydffai and Mr Emmett takes a walk, for Peter Maxwell Davies; Recent engagements include Der Kamkasianische Kreidekreis in Zürich, and A Midsummer Night's Dream in Venice; Season 2002 with Jenůfa for the Vienna Staatsoper and Turandot at Salzburg; Intendant of the Bregenz Festival, 2003; Numerous opera translations from Russian, Czech, German and Italian. *Address:* c/o IMG Artists, Lovell House, 616 Chiswick High Road, London W4 5RX, England.

POUSSEUR, Henri; Composer; b. 23 June 1929, Malmedy, Belgium. *Education:* Studied at the Liège Conservatory, 1947–52; Brussels Conservatory, 1952–53. *Career:* Worked at the Cologne and Milan electronic music studios, notably with Stockhausen and Berio; Taught music in Belgian schools, 1950–59; Founded in 1958 and directed the Studio Musique Electronique APELAC in Brussels; Lecturer in courses of new music, Darmstadt, 1957–67, Cologne, 1962–68, Basle, 1963–64, and the State University of New York at Buffalo, USA, 1966–69; Lecturer at the Liège Conservatory; Professor of Composition, 1971, Director of the Institution, 1975–94; Teacher at Liège University, 1970–94; Directed the organisation of the New Institut de Pedagogie Musicale in Paris; Resident Composer and Lecturer at Leuven Catholic University, 1993–99. *Compositions:* Symphonies, for 15 soloists, 1954; Mobile, for 2 pianos, 1958; Trois visages de Liège, electronic, 1961; Votre Faust, fantasy in the opera genre, with Michel Butor, 1960–68; Petrus Hebraicus, chamber music/theatre, for Schoenberg's centenary, 1973–74; La Rose de Voix, for 4 speakers, 16 solo voices, 4 choirs, 8 instruments, 1982; Traverser la forêt, for speaker, 2 solo voices, chamber choir and 12 instruments, 1987; Dichterliebesreigentraum, for 2 solo voices, 2 solo pianos, choir and orchestra, 1993; Aquarius-Memorial, cycle for solo piano and chamber orchestra, 1994–99; Le village planétaire vu de Nivelles, electro-acoustic programme of 16 hours duration, 2001; Don Juan à Gnide, music theatre, 1996; Suite du Massacre des Innocents, Wind band, 1997;. *Recordings:* CDs: Electronic Works, Traverser la Forêt; Dichterliebesreigentraum; La Guirlande de Pierre; Liège à Paris; Aquarius Memorial; Paraboliques (voltage-controlled electronic music), 1972. *Publications include:* Books: Ecrits d'Alban Berg, selected and translated with commentary, 1956; Fragments théoriques 1 Sur la musique experimentale, 1970; Musique Sémantique Societe, 1972; Die Apotheose Rameaus (Versuch zum Problem der Harmonik), 1987; Schumann le Poète (25 Moments d'une lecture de Dichterliebe), 1993; Musiques Croisées, 1997. *Honours:* Doctor Honoris Causa, Universities of Metz and Lille. *Current Management:* Cebedem, rue d'Arlon 75/77, B01040 Brussels, Belgium; Edizioni Sovini Zerboni, Galleria del Corso 4, I–20722 Milan Italy. *Address:* 38 Avenue Wellington, 1410 Waterloo, Belgium.

POWELL, Christopher (Kit) Bolland; Composer and Lecturer in Music; b. 2 Dec. 1937, Wellington, New Zealand; m. Brigitte Bänninger, 14 Dec 1966, 1 s., 1 d. *Education:* MSc, Diploma of Teaching; BMus. *Career:* Teacher of Mathematics and Music, New Zealand High School, 1962–75; Lecturer, Christchurch Teachers College, 1975–84; Studied in Europe, 1980–81; Has written experimental music for choruses and percussion and 5 song cycle settings of poems by Michael Harlow and 3 major works of experimental music, theatre; Computer Music, Swiss Computer Music Centre, 1985; Atelier UPIC, Paris, 1987; mem, Composers Association of New Zealand; Swiss Tonkünstlerverein. *Compositions:* The Evercircling Light for Choir SATB and Percussion, 1980; Christophorus for Children's Choir and Orchestra, 1981;

Galgenlieder, 1982; Les Episodes for Soprano, Bass Soloists and Orchestra, 1987; Concerto for 2 Violins, String and Percussion, 1989; Hauptsache man geht Zusammen hin, chamber opera, SATB, Speaker and Instrumental Ensemble, 1989–93; Gargantua for Wind Orchestra, 1990. *Recordings:* Devotion to The Small, 1980; The Evercircling Light, 1982; Hubert The Clockmaker, 1982; Whale, 1994; Chinese Songs, 1995. *Publications:* Workbook for University Entrance Prescription, 1973; Musical Design, 1975; Musik mit gefundenen Gegenständen, 1982; Suite for Solo Trombone. *Address:* Nigelstrasse 11, 8193 Eglisau, Switzerland.

POWELL, Claire; Singer (Mezzo-Soprano); b. 1954, Tavistock, Devon, England. *Education:* Royal Academy of Music; London Opera Centre. *Career:* Sang Alceste and Cherubino at Sadler's Wells while with London Opera Centre; London debut recital Wigmore Hall, 1979; Early appearances with Glyndebourne Festival Opera: has sung in Il Ritorno d'Ulisse, Falstaff, La Fedeltà Premiata and A Midsummer Night's Dream; Appearances with Welsh National Opera, Scottish Opera, Opera North and English National Opera, roles include, Berlioz, Didon, Beatrice and Marguerite, Carmen, Verdi's Ulrica and Preziosilla, Mussorgsky's Marina, Mozart's Cherubino and Idamante, Gluck's Alceste and Orfeo, Handel's Cornelia and Cyrus, Ponchielli's Laura, Saint-Saëns's Dalila, Ravel's Concepcion and Tchaikovsky's Pauline; Covent Garden from 1980, Les Contes d'Hoffmann, Midsummer Night's Dream, Otello, Lulu, Rigoletto, Die Zauberflöte, Ariadne auf Naxos, A Florentine Tragedy, Don Carlos (Eboli 1989); Médée (Neris), Rigoletto (Maddalena), Orlofsky, in Die Fledermaus and Samson et Dalila; US debut 1990, as Maddalena at San Francisco; Sang Pauline in The Queen of Spades at Madrid, 1990; Guest appearances in Frankfurt, San Francisco, Barcelona, Madrid, Toronto, Paris, Rome, Brussels, Liège and Lisbon; Sang Eboli in a new production of Don Carlos for Opera North, 1993; April 1995, role of Auntie, Peter Grimes, Royal Opera House; Guest appearances in Munich and Hamburg as Carmen and Eboli, and Lausanne as Mistress Quickly; Title role in Gerhard's The Duenna, Leeds, 1996; Sang Mistress Quickly in new production of Falstaff in Cologne with Conlon and Carsen, 1997; Emilia in new production of Otello in Brussels with Pappano and Decker, 1997; Auntie in Peter Grimes at Tokyo with Otaka, and at Savonlinna with Royal Opera House, new production, San Francisco with Runnicles and Alder, 1998; Mistress Quickly in Hamburg, 1999; Sang Margret in a new production of Wozzeck at Covent Garden, 2002; Concert repertoire includes St Matthew Passion, Verdi Requiem, Das Lied von Erde, La Mort de Cléopâtre, Stabat Mater, Petite Messe Solennelle by Rossini, Messiah and Elijah. *Recordings include:* Title role in The Duenna; Rosenkavalier conducted by Bernard Haitink; Video of Les Contes d'Hoffmann (as Nicklausse) and A Midsummer Night's Dream; El amor Brujo, Der Rosenkavalier, Il Ritorno d'Ulisse in Patria; Video of Otello with Solti, Royal Opera House. *Honours:* Richard Tauber Memorial Prize, 1978; FRAM; ARAM. *Address:* c/o Penelope Marland Artists' Management, 10 Roseneath Road, London SW11 6AH, England.

POWELL, Mel; Composer; b. 12 Feb. 1923, New York, USA; m. Martha Scott, 23 July 1946, 1 s., 2 d. *Education:* BMus, MA, Yale University, 1952; Studied piano with Sara Barg and Nadia Reisenberg; Composition with Paul Hindemith. *Career:* Chairman, Yale University Composition Faculty, 1954–69; Dean, California Institute of The Arts School of Music, 1969–72; Provost (CalArts), 1972–76; Professor and Fellow of The Institute, 1976–; President, American Music Center, 1957–60; Consultant, National Endowment for The Arts, 1970–73; Awarded Honorary Life Membership in Arnold Schoenberg Institute. *Compositions:* Filigree Setting for String Quartet; Haiku Settings for Voice and Piano; String Quartet, 1982; Woodwind Quintet; Modules for Chamber Orchestra; Strand Settings for Mezzo Soprano and Electronics; Duplicates, a concerto for Two Pianos and Orchestra, 1990; Many other orchestral pieces, vocal, chamber music and electronic works including Computer Prelude, 1988; Settings, for chamber orchestra, 1992; Piano Trio, 1994; Sextet, 1996; Six Miniatures for soprano and harp, 1998. *Recordings:* The Music of Arnold Schoenberg and Mel Powell; The Music of Milton Babbitt and Mel Powell; The Chamber Music of Mel Powell; Mel Powell: Six Recent Works. *Publications:* Compositions, essays and articles. *Contributions:* Perspectives of New Music; Journal of Music Theory; American Scholar. *Honours:* Guggenheim Fellowship, 1960; National Institute of Arts and Letters Grant Award, 1964; Works chosen to represent USA in International Society for Contemporary Music Festivals, 1960 and 1984; Pulitzer Prize, 1990. *Address:* c/o California Institute of The Arts, Valencia, CA 91355, USA.

POWER, Patrick; Singer (tenor); b. 6 June 1947, Wellington, New Zealand. *Education:* Studied at Universities of Otago and Auckland, New Zealand; Studied at University of Perugia, Italy. *Career:* Principal lyric tenor with: The Norwegian Opera in Oslo; Gärtnerplatz, Munich and Krefeld; Covent Garden debut, 1983, as the Simpleton in Boris Godunov, followed by Britten's Serenade for the Royal Ballet; Has Sung Alfredo for Kent Opera, Rodolfo and Almaviva for Scottish Opera;

Glyndebourne Festival as Flute and Des Grieux in Manon for Opera North; Wexford Festival in title role of Massenet's Le Jongleur de Notre Dame; Overseas engagements as The Italian Tenor in Rosenkavalier and Fenton for Royal Danish Opera; Don Ottavio, Tamino and Rodolfo in Cologne; Belmonte in New Zealand and at Drottningholm; Le Comte Ory and Huon in Oberon at Lyon and Alceste in Paris; Alfredo, Tamino and Don Ottavio in Canada; Almaviva in San Francisco; Season 1988–89, as Nadir in Les Pêcheurs de Perles in Pisa; Faust with Victorian State Opera; Returned to Australia as Pinkerton, Hoffmann, Rodolfo and the Duke of Mantua; Sang Nadir at Adelaide, 1996; Don José for Welsh National Opera. *Recordings include:* Beethoven's 9th Symphony conducted by Roger Norrington; Balfe's Bohemian Girl conducted by Richard Bonynge; Nadir for Tulsa Opera, 1997; Canio in Pagliacci for Opera Ireland, 1998; Radames in Aida at Nantes, Angers and Rennes, France, Cavalleria rusticana and Pagliacci for Opera New Zealand, Pinkerton in Madama Butterfly for Wellington Opera, 1999. *Current Management:* Athole Still International Management, Forresters Hall, 25–27 Westow Street, London, SE19 3RY, England. *Telephone:* (20) 8771-5271. *Fax:* (20) 8768-6600. *Website:* www .atholestill.com.

POWERS, Anthony; Composer; b. 13 March 1953, London, England. *Education:* Studied with Nadia Boulanger in Paris and with David Blake and Bernard Rands at York. *Career:* Composer-in-Residence, Southern Arts; Composer-in-Residence, University of Wales, Cardiff College. *Compositions include:* Piano Sonata No. 2, 1985–86; Stone, Water, Stars, 1987; Horn Concerto, 1989; Cello Concerto, 1990; String Quartet No. 2, 1991; Terrain for orchestra, 1992; In Sunlight for violin and piano, 1993; Symphony 1994–6; Fast Colours, for ensemble, 1997; Memorials of Sleep, for tenor and chamber orchestra, 1998. *Current Management:* Oxford University Press, London, England. *Address:* Oxford University Press, Music Department, 70 Baker St, London W1M 1DJ, England.

POWTER, Adrian; British singer (baritone); b. 1970, Cambridge, England. *Education:* Royal Northern College of Music with Neil Howlett. *Career:* Britten's Tarquinius and Werther for RNCM; appearances at Glyndebourne as Captain in Manon Lescaut and Philip in Birtwistle's The Last Supper, 2001; Guglielmo and Rossini's Taddeo for the London Opera Players; Figaro in Milhaud's La Mère coupable for Camberwell Pocket Opera, and Dandini in La Cenerentola for Opera Brava; Concerts with the Liverpool Philharmonic and Hallé Orchestra; Messiah at Blackburn and Hereford Cathedrals; Masterclasses with Jonathan Miller on BBC 2, 1998. *Address:* James Black Management, 3/ 26 Denmark Street, London, WC2H 8NN, England. *Telephone:* (20) 7209-0397. *E-mail:* james@jamesblackmanagement.com. *Website:* www .jamesblackmanagement.com.

PRAESENT, Gerhard; Composer and Conductor; b. 21 June 1957, Graz, Austria; m. Sigrid Praesent-Koenig, 2 s. *Education:* Composition and Conducting, University of Music, Graz, 1982 and 1985. *Career:* Debut: Composer, Weiz, 1978; Assistant, 1986–92; Professor, University of Music and Dramatic Arts, Graz, 1992–; over 500 performances of works in 20 countries; Several commissioned compositions for the Vienna Concert Hall, The Austrian Chamber Symphony and the University of Graz among others; Numerous concerts including festivals in Graz, Hong Kong, Vienna; Vice-Pres., Styrian Tone Arts Asscn; mem, ISCM; OEKB; OEGZM. *Compositions:* Oeuvre of over 50 compositions including Symphonic Music: Symphonic Fragment; Hermitage; Configurations; Chaconne; Works for strings: La Tâche, Sonata Regina per SF; Sounds of Wood; Missa for string quartet, A Rayas; Chamber Music: Trio intricato; Sonata del Gesù; Sonata al dente; Marcia funebre, Encore Piece; Vocal music: Song; Fantasy on a Bach-Choral; Missa minima. *Recordings:* 4 dozen radio recordings, Austria; Two CDs, La Tâche, 1997; Sounds of Wood, 1999. *Honours:* Austrian State scholarship; CA Prize; Composition Prize, Berlin; Federal Music Award for Symphonic Fragment, 1992; Reinl prize for La Tâche; Prize of the City of Vienna, 1996; Theodor Koerner prize, 1997. *Address:* Badstr 58, 8063 Eggersdorf, Graz, Austria. *E-mail:* praesent@telering.at.

PRANTL, Pavel, MA; Czech concertmaster and professor of violin; b. 21 April 1945, Susice; m. Martina Maixnerova 1972; two s. *Education:* Conservatory of Music, Kromeriz, Acad. of Musical Arts, Prague, masterclasses with David Oistrakh. *Career:* debut with Czechoslovak Broadcasting Coroporation 1956; mem. first violin group, Czech Philharmonic Orchestra 1967–76, Asst Concertmaster 1976–78; Concertmaster, Artistic Dir, Prague Chamber Orchestra Without a Conductor 1978–80; founder, Artistic Leader, Prague Baroque Ensemble 1973–80; Concertmaster, Singapore Symphony Orchestra 1980–93; guest soloist with Prague Symphony Orchestra 1968, Moravian Philharmonic Orchestra 1975, Radio Plzeň Symphony Orchestra 1977, Singapore Symphony Orchestra 1981–87; numerous tours abroad, including festivals in Salzburg, Montreux, Edinburgh, Würzburg, Japan (Tokyo, Hokkaido), Republic of Korea (Seoul), USA (Cornell Univ., Univ. of California at Los Angeles, San Diego); Head of String

Dept, Hong Kong Acad. for Performing Arts 1993–95; Dir, Singapore Professional String Centre 1995; Concertmaster, Prague Radio Symphony Orchestra 1996, Prague Radio Chamber Orchestra 1996–2000; Artistic Dir and Concertmaster, Czech Philharmonic Chamber Orchestra 1996–. *Recordings:* Ivo Blaha's Violin Concerto 1970, Czech Chamber Music, Czech Classical Violin Concertos 1991. *Honours:* Hon. DFA (London Inst. of Applied Research), Hon. Professorships, Univ. of Bruxelles, Haute Ecole de Recherche, Paris. *Address:* Stanton Management, 45-05 Newtown Road, Astoria, NY 11103, USA. *Telephone:* (718) 956-6092. *Fax:* (718) 956-5385. *E-mail:* TDStanton@ StantonMgt.com.

PRATICO, Bruno; Singer (Bass-Baritone); b. 1962, Aosta, Switzerland. *Education:* Studied at the opera school of La Scala. *Career:* Sang Rossini's Mustafà and Bartolo under Abbado at La Scala; Bologna in 1987 as Belcore, Reggio Emilia in 1988 as Gaudenzio in Il Signor Bruschino; Has sung widely in Italy and guest appearances elsewhere include Opéra de Lyon in 1989, in Salieri's Prima La Musica poi le Parole, and Marseille in 1990 as Leporello; Other repertory includes The Mikado (Macerata Festival), Zurga in Les Pêcheurs de Perles and Geronimo in Cimarosa's Il Matrimonio Segreto; Season 1998 in Don Pasquale at Genoa, La Rocca in Un Giorno di Regno at Parma and Don Magnifico in La Cenerentola at Pesaro. *Recordings include:* Leoncavallo's La Bohème; Lakmé and Paisiello's Don Chisciotte; Cimarosa's I Due Baroni di Rocca Azzurra. *Address:* c/o La Scala Milan, Via Filodrammatici 2, 20121 Milan, Italy.

PRATLEY, Geoffrey (Charles); Accompanist; b. 23 March 1940, Woodford, Essex, England; m. (1) Wendy Eathorne, 27 Mar 1965, 1 d., (2) Vija Rapa, 20 June 1987, 1 d. *Education:* Royal Academy of Music, 1958–63; LRAM, ARCM, 1960; GRSM, 1961; BMus, Dunelm, 1969. *Career:* Numerous Concerts throughout the World with many international artists including Baker, Domingo, Tortelier, Goossens, Brymer, Holmes, Streich and Milanova; Professor, Royal Academy of Music, from 1965–; Professor, Trinity College of Music, 1990–; mem, Incorporated Society of Musicians; Royal Society of Musicians. *Compositions:* Dorothy Parker Poems for female voice and piano, 2000; Six Irish Folk-Songs, for voice and piano; Six English Folk-Songs, for voice and piano. *Recordings:* Ivor Gurney Songs with C Keyte; numerous BBC Recordings for radio and television. *Publications:* Handel Operatic Repertory Bk2: Arias for tenor and piano; Concert Master Series: Book 1–Tchaikovsky Violin Solos with Piano; William Walton's Viola Concerto, new viola/ piano score; Great Orchestral Cello Solos, for cello and piano (2 books); Great Orchestral Violin Solos, for violin and piano; Great Operatic Melodies, arranged for piano duet. *Honours:* ARAM, 1967; FRAM, 1977. *Address:* The Willows, Bambers Green, Bishops Stortford CM 22 6PE, England.

PRATSCHKE, Sinead, MMus; Singer (soprano); b. 1971, Canada. *Education:* Royal Coll. of Music, National Opera Studio. *Career:* operatic roles as Susanna, Poulenc's Thérèse, Handel's Dorinda, Tytania, Euridice, Cunegonde, Valencienne, Barbarina, Despina, Gretel, Musetta; recital appearances at Jubilee Hall, Aldeburgh Festival 1997, Songmakers' Almanac; oratorio performances include Apollo e Daphne, The English Concert at Queen Elizabeth Hall, Mozart's C Minor Mass, Switzerland, Magnificat, National Concert Hall in Dublin, Ireland, St Matthew Passion, National Orchestra of Wales at Brangwyn Hall, Aldeburgh Early Music Festival. *Recordings include:* Handel's Samson and Judas Maccabaeus (Maulbronn Handel Festival, Germany), Rodrigo Centenary Recording, Royal Philharmonic Orchestra, Zélide (Musikfestspiele Sanssouci, Berlin). *Honours:* Canada Council, Countess of Munster, Madeleine Finden, Ian Fleming Trust. *Address:* 70A Stondon Park, Forest Hill, London, SE23 1JZ, England. *Telephone:* (20) 8699-8060. *E-mail:* spratschke@hotmail.com.

PRATT, Stephen (Philip); Composer, Lecturer, Broadcaster and Conductor; b. 15 June 1947, Liverpool, England; m. Monica Mullins, 14 Oct 1972, 1 s., 3 d. *Education:* Certificate of Education, Christ's College, Liverpool, 1965–68; Royal Manchester College of Music, 1968–69; BA, Honours, University of Reading, 1969–71; BMus, University of Liverpool, 1971–72. *Career:* Broadcaster, BBC Radio Merseyside, 1971–; Senior Lecturer in Music, 1972–, Head of Music, 1991–, Liverpool Hope University College; Freelance Conductor, 1975–; Part time Lecturer, Open University, 1976–78; Part time Lecturer, Lancashire Polytechnic, 1983–; Part time Lecturer, Liverpool University, 1984–86; Fellow, University of Liverpool, 1993–; Broadcaster, BBC Radio 3, 1994–; Professor of Music, Gresham College, London, 1997–. *Compositions include:* Star and Dead Leaves; Winter's Fancy, 1978; Some of Their Number for orchestra, 1980; Fruits of The Ground for horn trio, 1982; The Judgement of Paris for orchestra, 1985; Strong Winds, Gentle Airs for concert band, 1987; String Trio, 1988; Uneasy Vespers for mixed choir, soloists and orchestra, 1991; At The Turn of The Year for piano, 1993; About Time for small ensemble with tape, 1995; The Song Within, 1997; Violin Concerto, 1997; Undulations and Other Movements, 1998; Four Studies after John Cage, 1998. *Record-*

ings: Star and Dead Leaves, 1977; 2 of 4 Studies after John Cage, 1998; At the Turn of the Year, 1999; Undulations and Other Movements, 1999. *Contributions:* Arts Alive, 1972–; Reviewer, 1976–78, The Guardian; Classical Music, 1975–78. *Honours:* Chandos Composition Prize, Musica Nova, Glasgow, 1981. *Address:* 9 Wellington Avenue, Liverpool L15 0EH, England.

PRECHT, Ulrika; Singer (Mezzo-soprano); b. 1959, Sweden. *Education:* Studied in Opera Studio 67 and Stockholm State Opera, Stockholm. *Career:* Debut: Royal Opera, Stockholm, as Cherubino, 1990; Sang Dalila with Folkoperan Stockholm, 1991, and Nancy in Martha for Dublin Opera, 1992; Season 1992–93 in Rossini's Il Signor Bruschino at Frankfurt, Eboli in Don Carlos at Stockholm and title role of Carmen at Sodertaleoperan; Concert engagements throughout Scandinavia. *Address:* Nordic Artists Management, Svervagen 76, 11359 Stockholm, Sweden.

PREECE, Margaret; Singer (Soprano); b. 1965, England. *Career:* Appearances with English National Opera as Zerlina, Janáček's Vixen, Ninetta (Love for Three Oranges) and Nymph in Monteverdi's Orfeo; Elisabeth de Valois for Opera-Go-Round, in The Ring Saga for City of Birmingham Touring Opera and Oriana in Handel's Amadigi with Opera Theatre Dublin (also on tour to France); Alice Ford, Fiordiligi and Adina for English Touring Opera; Donizetti's L'Ajo nel Imbarazzo and Provenzale's Lo Schiavo di sua Moglie at Musica nel Chiostro, Batignano; Season 1997 with the Queen of Night for Opera Theatre Dublin and Despina and Papagena for Opera North; British premieres of Kurt Weill's Love Life and Gershwin's Of These I Sing, both recorded for BBC Radio 3; Concerts include Mozart's Davidde Penitente (at Seville), Beethoven's Missa solemnis, Dvořák Requiem and Paul Patterson's Mass of the Sea; Further opera roles include Oscar (Ballo in Maschera), Cordelia in Reimann's Lear, Susanna, Mozart's Countess, Anne Trulove, and Gilda. *Address:* C&M Craig Services Ltd, 3 Kersley Street, London SW11 4 PR, England.

PREGARDIEN, Christoph; Singer (Tenor); b. 18 Jan. 1956, Limburg, Germany. *Education:* Studied at the Frankfurt Hochschule für Musik and in Milan and Stuttgart. *Career:* Sang first with the Limburg Cathedral Choir; Operatic engagements in Frankfurt, Gelsenkirchen, Stuttgart, Ludwigshafen, Hamburg, Antwerp and Karlsruhe; parts include Almaviva, Tamino, Fenton and Don Ottavio; Concert appearances in the festivals of Flanders, Netherlands, Israel, Paris, Aix, Ansbach, Innsbruck and Göttingen; Conductors include Sigiswald Kuijken, Gustav Leonhardt, Ton Koopman, Philippe Herreweghe, Roger Norrington, Ivan Fischer, Hans-Martin Linde, Wolfgang Gönnenwein, Frans Brueggen, Helmuth Rilling, Ferdinand Leitner and Michael Gielen; Sang in production of the St Matthew Passion for Belgian television; Towards Bach and Haydn concert series on London's South Bank, 1989; Sang in L'Infedeltà Delusa by Haydn for Flanders Opera 1990; Debut recital at the Wigmore Hall, London, 1993, returned in Schubert's Winterreise, 1997; Sang in the premiere of Rihm's St Luke Passion, Stuttgart 2000. *Recordings:* Over 100 including St John and St Matthew Passion conducted by Leonhardt; St John Passion, Bach's Magnificant; L'Infedeltà Delusa by Haydn; Mozart Concert Arias conducted by Kuijken; Buxtehude Cantatas and Mozart Requiem under Ton Koopman; Bach Lutheran Masses under Herreweghe; Symphoniae Sacrae by Schütz; Grimoaldo in Rodelinda (Harmonia Mundi); Die schöne Müllerin and Schiller texts by Schubert; Schubert CD: Lieder von Abschied und Reise; Killmayer's Hölderlin cycles; Winterreise, with Andreas Staier; Lieder von Liebe und Tod, with Tilman Hoppstock. *Honours:* Preis der Deutschen Schallplattenkritik; Edison Awards 1995, 1998; Cannes Classical Award, 1995; Diapason d'Or de l'Année, 1996, 1997; Choc de la Musique, 1997; Caecilia-Preis, Belgium, 1998; Orphée d'Or, Academie du Disque Lyrique, Prix Georg Solti, 1998; Preis der Deutschen Schallplettenkritik, Viertekjahresliste, 1999. *Address:* c/o Claudia Nitsche, Gierather Mühlenweg 15, 51469 Bergisch Gladbach, Germany.

PREIN, Johann (Werner); Singer (Bass-baritone); b. 3 Jan. 1954, Trofaiach, Leoben, Austria. *Education:* Studied with Herma Handl-Wiedenhofer in Graz. *Career:* Sang in concerts and recitals from 1979; Stage career from 1984, notably at Graz and Vienna; Bayreuth Festival, 1984–85, as Donner in Das Rheingold; Engaged at Gelsenkirchen from 1986; Guest appearances at the Vienna Staatsoper, Düsseldorf and Barcelona; Wiesbaden 1988, as King Henry in Lohengrin; At Gelsenkirchen in 1989 sang Wagner in the first German production of Busoni's Doktor Faust, in the completion by Antony Beaumont; Other roles include: Mephistopheles (Faust); 4 villains in Les Contes d'Hoffmann; The Speaker in Die Zauberflöte; Biterolf and the Landgrave in Tannhäuser; Wotan in Der Ring des Nibelungen; Achilles in Penthesilea by Schoeck; Season 1998 with the Doctor in Wozzeck at Trieste and Weber's Kuno in Rome; Season 1999 as Strauss's Jochanaan and Faninal at Wiesbaden, followed by Talbot in Maria Stuarda. *Recordings include:* Lieder by Joseph Mathias Hauer (Preiser); Der Konthur in

Schulhoff's Flammen, 1995. *Address:* Musiktheater im Revier, Kennedyplatz, 4650 Gelsenkirchen, Germany.

PREISLER, Frantisek, Sr; Opera Stage Manager and Producer; b. 29 April 1948, Opava, Czechoslovakia; m. Vlastimila Plosharova Preislerova, 8 April 1972, 1 s. *Education:* Janáček Academy, Brno. *Career:* Debut: Smetana's Two Widows at the Theatre Olomouc, 1973; Producer at: Theatre Olomouc, 1973–80; Theatre Maribor, Ljubljana, 1980–83; College Lecturer, Janáček Academy, Brno, 1982–92; Janáček Theatre, Brno, 1983–92; Director, Janáček Opera, Brno, 1985–92; Productions in Czechoslovakia of over 60 operas from the Slav repertoire (Smetana's Bartered Bride, Two Widows and The Secret, Dvořák's Rusalka, Janáček's Jenůfa, Cunning Little Vixen and Kata Kabanova, Mussorgsky's Boris Gudunov and Khovanshchina, Tchaikovsky's Eugene Onegin, Borodin's Prince Igor) and also Bizet's Carmen, Puccini's Madama Butterfly, La Bohème, Gershwin's Porgy and Bess, and Strauss's Rosenkavalier, Mozart's Le nozze di Figaro and Don Giovanni, Gounod's Faust, Rossini's Il Barbiere di Siviglia, Donizetti's L'Elisir d'amore; Verdi's La Traviata; Massenet's Werther, and numerous others; mem, Free Artist. *Honours:* Ljubljana Festival, Porgy and Bess, Estonia, 1982.

PREISLER, Frantisek, Jr; Conductor; b. 23 Oct. 1973, Olomuc, Czechoslovakia. *Education:* Janáček Conservatory, Brno; Janáček Academy, Brno; Vienna, Austria. *Career:* Debut: Janáček's Katya Kabanova, Janáček Theatre Brno, 1993; Chief Conductor of Musical Theatre Karlin, Prague; Conductor in the National Theater, Prague; Chief Conductor of Janáček's Symphony Orchestra, Prague, 1997–; Conducted operas and musicals including Smetana's The Kiss and the Two Widows, Mozart's Così fan tutte, Die Zauberflöte, Don Giovanni, Beethoven's Fidelio, Rossini's Il Barbiere di Seviglia, Verdi's Nabucco, Aida, La Traviata, Rigoletto, Macbeth, Otello and La Forza del Destino, Puccini's Turandot, La Bohème and Tosca, Leoncavallo's Pagliacci, Mascagni's Cavalleria rusticana, Dvořák's Rusalka, Meyerbeer's Les Huguenots, Die Fledermaus. *Recordings include:* B Smetana, Two Widows, radio and television. *Address:* National Theatre of Prague, Ostrovni, Prague 1 11230, Czech Republic.

PREMRU, Raymond (Eugene); Composer and Trombonist; b. 6 June 1934, Elmira, New York, USA; Divorced, 2 d. *Education:* BMus, Composition (Performers), Certificate of Trombone, Eastman School of Music, University of Rochester, New York, 1956. *Career:* Member, Phillip Jones Brass Ensemble, 1960–; Commissions from Cleveland Orchestra (Lorin Maazel), Pittsburgh Symphony (André Previn), Philadelphia Orchestra (Riccardo Muti), Philharmonia Orchestra (Lorin Maazel), London Symphony Orchestra (Previn), Royal Choral Society (Meredith Davies), International Trumpet Guild, York Festival, Cheltenham Festival, Camden Festival, Philip Jones Brass Ensemble; Visiting Professor, Trombone, Guildhall School of Music, Eastman School of Music, Rochester, 1987. *Compositions:* Music from Harter Fell; Quartet for 2 Trumpets, horn and Trombone; Divertimento for Ten Brass; Concertino for Trombone, flute, oboe, clarinet and bassoon; Tissington variations. *Recordings:* Easy Winner, Argo/Decca Records; Modern Brass, Philip Jones Brass Ensemble. *Contributions:* International Trombone Association Journal; Instrumentalist Magazine. *Address:* Eastman School of Music, University of Rochester, 26 Gibbs Street, Rochester, NY 14604, USA.

PRESCOTT, Duncan; Clarinettist; b. 1964, England. *Education:* Studied at the Royal Academy of Music with Anthony Pay, and with Karl Leister. *Career:* Recitals at the Wigmore Hall and on the South Bank; Member of the Nash Ensemble, with whom he has broadcast the Brahms, Reger and Weber Clarinet Quintets; Mozart Clarinet Concerto with the London Sinfonietta and the English String Orchestra; Performances at many jazz venues, including Ronnie Scott's; Member of the Boronte Ensemble and duo partnership with pianist Scott Mitchell; Further engagements in Germany, America, Israel, Russia, Japan, Hong Kong and Italy. *Recordings:* Virtuoso pieces with Scott Mitchell (Chandos). *Honours:* Capitol Radio Music Prize; Lambeth Music Award; Frank Britton Award; Malcolm Sargent Music Award; Scholarships from the Myra Hess Trust, Countess of Munster Trust and the English Speaking Union.

PRESSLER, Menahem; Pianist and Professor of Music; b. 16 Dec. 1923, Magdeburg, Germany; m. Sara Szerzen, 1 s., 1 d. *Education:* Educated in Israel; Studied with Petri and Steuermann. *Career:* Distinguished Professor, Indiana University, USA, 1955–; Soloist under Stokowski, Dorati, Ormandy, Mitropoulos; Co-founder, The Beaux Arts, Trio, 1955, which performs yearly in the Capitals of Europe and Americas; Appearances at Festivals in Edinburgh, Salzburg, Paris; Since 1984 in Residence at the Library of Congress in Washington, DC; Subscription concerts in New York, Metropolitan Museum and at Harvard University. *Recordings:* Most of the Trio Repertoire; More than 50 records for Philips. *Publications:* Several publications. *Honours:* Winner of Debussy Prize in San Francisco; 3 Grand Prix du Disques, Gramophone Record of the Year Award; Prix d'honneur Montreux Prix Mondial Du

Disques. *Current Management:* Columbia Artists Management, New York. *Address:* 1214 Pickwick Place, Bloomington, IN 47401, USA.

PRESTON, Katherine Keenan, BA, MA, PhD; American music historian; *Associate Professor of Music, College of William and Mary;* b. 7 Dec. 1950, Hamilton, OH; m. Daniel F. Preston 1971; one s. *Education:* University of Cincinnati, Evergreen State College, Olympia, WA, University of Maryland, Graduate Center of CUNY. *Career:* taught at University of Maryland, Catholic University, and Smithsonian Institution; Associate Professor, College of William and Mary, Williamsburg, Virginia, 1989–; mem. American Musicological Society; Sonneck Society for American Music. *Publications:* Books: Scott Joplin, Juvenile Biography, 1987; Music for Hire: The Work of Journeymen Musicians in Washington DC 1875–1900, 1992; Opera on the Road: Traveling Opera Troupes in the USA, 1820–1860, 1993; The Music of Toga Plays (Introduction) in Playing Out The Empire: Ben Hur and other Toga Plays and Films, 1883–1908, edited by David Mayer, 1994; Editor of Irish American Theater, Vol. 10 in Series Nineteenth-Century American Musical Theater, 1994. *Contributions:* Various Articles including: The 1838–40 American Concert Tour of Jane Shirreff and John Wilson, British Vocal Stars in Studies in American Music, 1994; Popular Music in the Gilded Age: Musicians' Gigs in Late Nineteenth-Century Washington DC, in Popular Music, 1985; Music and Musicians at the Mountain Resorts of Western Virginia, 1820–1900, in A Celebration of American Music, 1989; Numerous articles in The New Grove Dictionary of American Music, 1986 and The New Grove Dictionary of Opera, 1992. *Address:* 137 Pintail Trace, Williamsburg, VA 23188, USA.

PRESTON, Simon (John); Musician, Organist and Conductor; b. 4 Aug. 1938, Bournemouth, England. *Education:* BA 1961, BMus 1962, MA 1964, King's College, Cambridge University; Fellow, Royal College of Music; Fellow, Royal Academy of Music. *Career:* Sub-Organist, Westminster Abbey, 1962–67; Acting Organist, St Albans Abbey, 1968–69; Organist and Tutor in Music, Christ Church, Oxford, 1970–81; CUF Lecturer in Music, Oxford University, 1972–81; Organist/Master of Choristers, Westminster Abbey, London, 1981–87; Saint-Saëns 3rd Symphony with BBC National Orchestra of Wales at the 1999 London Proms; Member of the Jury for Organ Competitions at: St Albans 1983, Lahti Finland 1985, Bruges Belgium 1986, Dublin Ireland 1990, Calgary Canada 1990; Chairman, Performer of the Year Award (Royal College of Organists), 1988; Patron of the University of Buckingham; Member, Music Panel of the Arts Council, 1968–72; Member, BBC Music Advisory Committee, 1965–67; Royal Society of Musicians; Vice President, Organ Club; Vice President, Organists' Benevolent League; Chairman, Herbert Howells Society; Fellow, Royal Society of Arts. *Recordings:* Organ Music by Handel and Liszt and Masses by Haydn with the Christ Church Choir; Handel: Choral works with Westminster Abbey Choir; Series of Bach's Organ Works; Liszt Fantasia on Ad nos, ad Salutarem Undam, Reubke Sonata on the 94th Psalm; Choral works for Palestrina, Allegri, Anerio, Nanino and Giovannelli. *Honours:* Dr Mann Organ Student, King's College, Cambridge; Honorary Fellow, Royal College of Organists; Edison Award, 1971; Grand Prix du Disque, 1979; International Performer of the Year (New York Chapter of the American Guild of Organists), 1987. *Address:* Little Hardwick, Langton Green, Kent TN 3 0EY, England.

PRESTON, Stephen; Flautist and Choreographer; b. 24 May, 1945, Skipton, Yorkshire, England. *Education:* Studied at the Guildhall School of Music, London (1963–66) with Geoffrey Gilbert; Further study with Wieland Kuijken in Amsterdam. *Career:* Leading flautist with the Academy of Ancient Music, English Baroque Soloists and London Classical Players; Founder members of the English Concert, under Trevor Pinnock; Artistic Director of the MZT Dance Company; Choreographer for many early operas, including works by Gluck and Purcell. *Recordings include:* Concertos by Vivaldi; Trio Sonatas by J. S. Bach. *Address:* c/o MZT, 1 Oast Cottage, Great Maxfield, Three Oaks, Nr. Hastings, East Sussex, TN 35 4NU, England.

PRÊTRE, Georges; French conductor; b. 14 Aug. 1924, Waziers; s. of Emile Prêtre and Jeanne (née Dérin) Prêtre; m. Gina Marny 1950; one s. one d. *Education:* Lycée and Conservatoire de Douai, Conservatoire national supérieur de musique de Paris and Ecole des chefs d'orchestre. *Career:* Dir of Music, Opera Houses of Marseilles, Lille and Toulouse 1946–55; Dir of Music Opéra-comique, Paris 1955–59; Dir of Music, l'Opéra de Paris 1959, Artistic Dir 1966, Dir-Gen. of Music 1970–71; conductor of the symphonic asscns of Paris and of principal festivals throughout the world; also conducted at La Scala, Milan and major American orchestras; Conductor Metropolitan Opera House, New York 1964–65, La Scala, Milan 1965–66, Salzburg 1966; First Visiting Conductor, Vienna Symphony Orchestra 1985–, Opéra Bastille (Turandot) 1997, Opéra-Comique (Pelleas et Melisande) 1998; Turandot at La Scala 2001; concert to celebrate 80th birthday, l'Opéra-Bastille 2004. *Honours:* Officier, Légion d'honneur 1971, Haute Distinction République Italienne 1975, Commdr République Italienne 1980; Europa Prize 1982, Victoire de la musique Award for Best Conductor 1997. *Address:*

c/o Marcel de Valmalete, 7 rue Hoche, 92300 Levallois-Perret (office); Château de Vaudricourt, à Naves, par Castres 81100, France.

PREVIN, André George; American conductor, pianist and composer; b. ((as Andreas Ludwig Priwin)), 6 April 1929, Berlin, Germany; s. of Jack Previn and Charlotte (née Epstein) Previn; m. 1st Betty Bennett (divorced); two d.; m. 2nd Dory Langan 1959 (divorced 1970); m. 3rd Mia Farrow 1970 (divorced 1979); three s. three d.; m. 4th Heather Hales 1982 (divorced); one s.; m. 5th Anne-Sophie Mutter 2003. *Education:* Berlin and Paris Conservatories. *Career:* Music Dir Houston Symphony, US 1967–69; Music Dir and Principal Conductor, London Symphony Orchestra 1968–79, Conductor Emer. 1979–; composed and conducted approx. 50 film scores 1950–65; Guest conductor of most major world orchestras, also Royal Opera House, Covent Garden, Salzburg, Edin., Osaka, Flanders Festivals; Music Dir London South Bank Summer Music Festival 1972–74, Pittsburgh Symphony Orchestra 1976–84, LA Philharmonic Orchestra 1984–89; Music Dir Royal Philharmonic Orchestra 1985–86, Prin. Conductor 1987–92; Conductor Laureate, London Symphony Orchestra 1992–. *Television:* series of television specials for BBC and for American Public Broadcasting Service. *Major works:* Symphony for Strings 1965, Overture to a Comedy 1966, Suite for Piano 1967, Cello Concerto 1968, Four Songs (for soprano and orchestra) 1968, Two Serenades for Violin 1969, Guitar Concerto 1970, Piano Preludes 1972, Good Companions (musical) 1974, Song Cycle on Poems by Philip Larkin 1977, Every Good Boy Deserves Favour (music, drama, text by Tom Stoppard, 1977, Pages from the Calendar (for solo piano) 1977, Peaches (for flute and strings) 1978, Principals 1980, Outings (for brass quintet) 1980, Reflections 1981, Piano Concerto 1984, Triolet for Brass 1987, Variations for Solo Piano 1991, Six Songs for Soprano and Orchestra on texts by Toni Morrison 1991, Sonata for Cello and Piano 1992, The Magic Number (for soprano and orchestra) 1995, Trio for Bassoon, Oboe and Piano 1995, Sonata for Violin 1996, Sonata for Bassoon and Piano 1997, Streetcar Named Desire (opera) 1998, The Giraffes Go to Hamburg (for soprano, alto, flute and piano), Three Dickinson Songs (for soprano and piano), Diversions (for orchestra). *Publications:* Music Face to Face 1971, Orchestra (ed.) 1977, Guide to Music 1983, No Minor Chords: My Days in Hollywood 1992. *Honours:* Hon. KBE 1996; Television Critics' Award 1972; Acad. Award for Best Film Score 1959, 1960, 1964, 1965. *Address:* c/o Columbia Artists, 165 W 57th Street, New York, NY 10019, USA; Barbican Centre, Silk Street, London, EC2Y 8DS, England.

PREVITALI, Fabio; Baritone; b. 1961, Venice, Italy. *Education:* Studied at the Venice Conservatory. *Career:* Debut: Luca in 1987 in Salieri's Falstaff; Sang at Treviso in 1987 as Albert in Werther, Frank in Die Fledermaus and in Linda di Chamounix; Season 1988 at opera houses in Paris, Verona and Reggio Emilia; Other roles in Don Giovanni, Maria Stuarda, La Bohème, Eugene Onegin and Semele. *Recordings include:* Franchetti's Cristoforo Colombo, taped at Frankfurt in 1991. *Address:* Reggio Emilia Opera, Teatro Municipale, Piazzo Martini 7 Luglio, 42100 Reggio Emilia, Italy.

PREVOST, André; Composer; b. 30 July 1934, Hawkesbury, ON, Canada. *Education:* Conservatoire de Musique de Montréal; Studied under Olivier Messiaen at Paris Conservatoire and Henri Dutilleux at Ecole Normale, Paris; Studied electronic music under Michel Philippot, ORTF; Studied under Aaron Copland, Zoltán Kodály, Gunther Schuller and Elliott Carter at Berkshire Music Center, Tanglewood, Massachusetts. *Career:* Professor of composition and analysis, Faculty of Music, University of Montreal; composed music played throughout Canada and also France, USA, England, Yugoslavia, India and New Zealand; commissions have been received from Jeunesse Musicales du Canada, Quintette de Cuivres de Montreal, Charlottetown Festival, Ten Centuries Concerts, Canadian Broadcasting, McGill Chamber Orchestra, l'Orchestre symphonique de Quebec, Communaute Radiophonique des Pays de Langue Francaise, London (Ontario) Symphony Orchestra, Société de Musique Contemporaine du Québec, Canadian Music Centre among others. *Compositions include:* Orchestral: Célébration 1966; Chorégraphie I, 1972, II 1976, III 1976, IV 1978; Cosmophonie 1985; Diallele 1968; Evanescence 1970; Fantasmes 1963; Hommage 1970–71; Ouverture 1975; Scherzo 1960; Soloists with Orchestra: Concerto pour Violoncelle et Orchestre 1976; Le Conte de l'Oiseau 1979; Hiver dans l'Ame 1978; Paraphase 1980; Oboe Concerto, 1993; Chamber Music: Improvisation Pour Violon Seul 1976; Improvisation pour Violoncelle Seul 1976; Improvisation pour Alto Seul 1976; Mobiles 1959–60; Mouvement pour Quintette de Cuivres 1963; Musique pour l'Ode au St Laurent 1965; Mutations 1981; Quatuor 1958, No. 2 1972; Sonate pour Alto et Piano 1978; Sonate No. 1 pour Violoncelle et Piano 1962; No. 2 Pour Violoncelle et Piano 1985; Suite pour Quotuor a Cordes 1968; Triptyque 1962; Trois Pieces Irlandaises 1961; Solo Voice: Geoles 1963; Improvisation pour Voix et Piano 1976; Musique Peintes 1955; Chorus: Ahimsa 1984; Missa de Profundis 1973; Psalm 148 1971; Images d'un Festival for baritone, chorus and orchestra, 1993; Keyboard: Cinq Variations sur un Thème Grégorien 1956; Improvisation pour piano

1976; Variations en passacaille 1984. *Address:* c/o SOCAN, 41 Valleybroo Drive, Don Mills, Ontario M3B 2S6, Canada.

PREY, Florian; Singer (Baritone); b. 1959, Hamburg, Germany. *Education:* Studied with father, Hermann Prey, and at Munich Musikhochschule. *Career:* Gave Lieder recitals and appeared in concert from 1982; Opera debut as the Count in Schreker's Der ferne Klang, Venice, 1984; Sang in a staged version of St Matthew Passion at Teatro La Fenice, 1984; Silvio for Vienna Kammeroper, 1986; Stadttheater Aachen, 1988–, as Harlekin in Ariadne auf Naxos, Falke and Papageno; Writer of stage pieces and film scripts (Montag eine Parodis, 1985). *Address:* c/o Stadttheater, Theaterstrasse 1–3, 5100 Aachen, Germany.

PRIBYL, Luboš; Pianist; b. 29 Oct. 1975, Prague, Czechoslovakia. *Education:* Conservatoire in Prague with Professor Radomír Melmuka, 1990–96; Academy of Music in Prague with Professor Emil Leichner, 1997–. *Career:* Debut: Zlín, performance in the concert of the Zlín Symphony orchestra, 1989–; Recital in the Beethoven festival in Teplice, 1992–; Concerts in Bolzano, Brixen, Italy, 1994; Concert tour in Japan (Tokyo, Sapporo, Obihiro, Asahikava), 1996; Played Tchaikovsky's Concert No. 1, with orchestra of the Prague Conservatoire, 1997; Short portrait on Czech television, 1997. *Recordings:* A few recordings in Czech Radio (Chopin, Tchaikovsky, Rachmaninov, Martinů, Jezek); CD, piano recital (Haydn, Liszt, Semtana, Rachmaninov, Martinů, Jezek). *Honours:* Competition, Virtuosi per musica di pianoforte, Czech Republic, 1st Prize, 1988; Competition 'Citta di Senigallia', Italy, 5th prize, 1991; Beethoven Competition in Hradec nad Moravicí, Czech Republic, 1st Prize, 1992; F P Neglia Competition in Enna, Italy, 2nd Prize, 1993; Dr Václav Holzknecht Competition in Prague, 1st Prize, 1995; Mavi Marcoz Competition in Aosta, Italy, 5th Prize, 1995. *Address:* Smeralova 34, 170 00 Prague 7, Czech Republic.

PRICE, Curtis Alexander, AM, PhD, FRNCM; American musicologist; b. 7 Sept. 1945, Springfield, MO. *Education:* Southern Illinois Univ., Harvard Univ. with John Ward and Nino Pirotta. *Career:* teacher, Washington Univ., St Louis, MO 1974–81; teacher, King's Coll. London 1981, Reader 1985, Prof. 1988; Principal of Royal Acad. of Music, London 1995–; Univ. of London Prof. 2000–; trustee of Musica Britannica and the Handel House Museum; mem. Royal Musical Asscn (Pres. 1999–2002). *Publications include:* The Critical Decade for English Music Drama 1700–1710 1978, Music in the Restoration Theater: with a Catalogue of Instrumental Music in the Plays 1665–1713 1979, Henry Purcell and the London Stage 1984, H. Purcell: Dido and Aeneas (ed.) 1986, Italian Opera and Arson in Late Eighteenth-Century London 1989, The Impresario's Ten Commandments: Continental Recruitment for Italian Opera in London 1763–4 (with J. Milhous and R. D. Hume) 1992, Man and Music: The Early Baroque Era (ed.) 1993, Purcell Studies (ed.) 1995. *Honours:* Hon. RAM, Fellow King's Coll. London. *Address:* Royal Academy of Music, Marylebone Road, London, NW1 5HT, England (office). *Telephone:* (20) 7873-7373. *Fax:* (20) 7873-7374. *E-mail:* go@ram.ac.uk. *Website:* www.ram.ac.uk.

PRICE, Eileen; Singer (Mezzo Soprano); b. Cardigan, Wales; m. Iain McWilliam, 2 s. *Education:* Homerton College, Cambridge; Royal College of Music, London. *Career:* Has performed with all major British orchestras and conductors including Sir Malcolm Sergent, Sir Adrian Bolt, Sworowsky, Bryden Thomson and Sir John Barbirolli; Own radio and television series; Appeared at Citizens Theatre, Glasgow, and Royal Court Theatre, London; Retired Head of Vocal Studies, Welsh College of Music and Drama; Teaches Voice at Junior Guildhall School of Music and Drama, London, and Royal Holloway, University of London; mem, Past Chairman, Association of Teachers of Singing; Association of Teachers of Singing (USA). *Honours:* Jenny Lind Prize, Royal College of Music; Henry Leslie Prize; Clara Butt Prize; Tagore Medal for Most Distinguished Student of the Year. *Address:* 2A Byron Hill Road, Harrow on the Hill, Middlesex HA2 0HY, England.

PRICE, Gwynneth Patricia; Singer (soprano); b. 1945, Bath, England. *Education:* studied in London with E. Herbert-Caesari, and with Parry Jones at Trinity Coll. of Music. *Career:* has sung at opera houses throughout the world, including the Royal Opera House, Covent Garden, as the Priestess in Aida, Fortune Teller in Arabella, Milliner and Duenna in Rosenkavalier, Villager in Jenůfa, 1993; sang title role in Menotti's The Old Maid and The Thief at Norfolk Festival, 1992; Alice in Verdi's Falstaff; concert repertoire includes Verdi's Requiem, conducted by Colin Davis, Tosca, Santuzza in Cavalleria Rusticana; fmr council mem. of the Friends of Covent Garden; founder and Dir, Floriale Singers and Covent Garden Singers; now one of the Britain's leading voice coaches and pronunciation specialists; has made guest appearances on BBC radio. *Honours:* Silver Medallist, 25 Years with Royal Opera. *Address:* 65 Lancaster Grove, Hampstead, London, NW3 4HD, England. *Telephone:* (20) 7794-6455.

PRICE, Henry; Tenor; b. 18 Oct. 1945, Oakland, California, USA. *Career:* Many seasons at the New York City Opera where he sang Telemaco in

Monteverdi's Ulisse, Tamino, Almaviva, Narciso in Il Turco in Italia, Gennaro in Lucrezia Borgia and operetta roles; Other appearances in Philadelphia and Miami, at the US Spoleto Festival and from 1983 in Europe, notably at the Mainz and Linz Operas. *Address:* c/o New York City Opera, Lincoln Center, New York, NY 10023, USA.

PRICE, Janet; Singer (Soprano); b. 1938, Abersychan, Pontypool Gwent, South Wales; m. Adrian Beaumont. *Education:* University of Wales (Cardiff); BMus (1st class honours) and MMus (Wales); LRAM (Singing Performer); ARCM (Piano Performer); LRAM (Piano Accompanist); Special study of French Music with Nadia Boulanger, Paris; Studied Singing with Olive Groves, Isobel Baillie and Hervey Alan. *Career:* Singer in concerts with leading orchestras and conductors throughout the United Kingdom and Western Europe; Numerous premieres, including the Belgian premiere of Tippett's Third Symphony, Festival of Flanders, 1975; Has sung opera with Glyndebourne Festival Opera, Welsh National Opera Company, Kent Opera Company, Opera Rara, Handel Opera Society, Northern Ireland Opera Trust, San Antonio Grand Opera, Texas, BBC television; Has made a speciality of resurrecting neglected heroines of Bel Canto period, being the first person to sing a number of these roles in the modern era; Highlights include: Live commercial recording of Beethoven's 9th Symphony with Haitink and the Concertgebouw Orchestra and Chorus; Tippett's 3rd Symphony with Haitink and the London Philharmonic Orchestra; Stravinsky's Les Noces, with Rozhdestvensky and the BBC Symphony Orchestra and Chorus; Sang role of Hecuba in Kent Opera's production of Tippett's King Priam (video); Professor of Singing, Royal Academy of Music and at Welsh College of Music and Drama, Cardiff. *Recordings:* For several labels. *Contributions:* Haydn's Songs from a Singer's Viewpoint, article to The Haydn Yearbook, 1983. *Honours:* Winner, British Art Council First Young Welsh Singers' Award, 1964; Honorary ARAM, 2000. *Address:* 73 Kings Drive, Bishopston, Bristol BS 7 8JQ, England.

PRICE, Leontyne; Singer (Soprano); b. 10 Feb. 1927, Laurel, Mississippi, USA. *Education:* Central State College, Wilberforce, Ohio and Juilliard School of Music. *Career:* Appeared as Bess (Porgy and Bess), Vienna, Berlin, Paris, London, New York, 1952–54; Recitalist, Soloist, 1954–; Soloist, Hollywood Bowl, 1955–59, 1966; Opera Singer NBC-TV, 1955–58, San Francisco Opera Co, 1957–59, 1960–61, Vienna Staatsoper, 1958, 1959–60, 1961; Recording Artist RCA-Victor, 1958–; Appeared Covent Garden, 1958–59, 1970, Chicago, 1959, 1960, 1965, Milan, 1960–61, 1963, 1967, Metropolitan Opera, New York, 1961–62, 1963–70, 1972, as both Leonoras of Verdi, Madama Butterfly, Fiordiligi, Puccini's Tosca, Minnie, Liu and Manon, Ariadne and Pamina; Paris Opéra as Aida, 1968, Metropolitan Opera as Aida, 1985 (Retired as opera singer but still active in concert). *Recordings:* Numerous recordings, notably The Essential Leontyne Price, 11 CDs, 1996). *Honours:* Fellow, American Academy of Arts and Sciences; Hon D.Mus (Howard University, Central State College, Ohio); Hon DHL (Dartmouth); Hon Dr of Humanities (Rust College, Mississippi); Hon DHum Litt (Fordham); Presidential Medal of Freedom, Order of Merit (Italy), National Medal of Arts, 1985. *Address:* c/o Columbia Artists Management Inc, 165 West 57th Street, New York, NY 10019, USA.

PRICE, Luke; Singer (Tenor); b. 1968, Germany. *Education:* Chorister, Westminster Cathedral; Trinity College, London. *Career:* Appearances at Batignano Festival as Eufemio in Storace's Gli Equivoci; Apprentice in Die Meistersinger for Netherlands Opera and at Covent Garden; Engagements at Opéra de Lyon, Paris Châtelet, Salzburg and Glyndebourne (Festival and Touring); Other roles include Tchaikovsky's Lensky, Arturo in I Puritani and Camille in Die Lustige Witwe; Member of Covent Garden chorus from season 2000–2001; Sang Janissary in revival of Mozart's Die Entführung, 2000. *Address:* c/o Royal Opera House (chorus), Covent Garden, London, WC2, England.

PRICE, Dame Margaret Berenice, DBE; Singer (soprano); b. 13 April 1941, Tredegar, Wales. *Education:* Trinity College of Music, London. *Career:* Debut: Operatic debut with Welsh National Opera in Marriage of Figaro, 1963; Renowned for Mozart Operatic Roles; Has sung in world's leading opera houses and festivals; Many radio broadcasts and television appearances; Major roles include: Countess in Le Nozze di Figaro, Pamina in The Magic Flute, Fiordiligi in Così fan tutte, Donna Anna in Don Giovanni, Constanze in Die Entführung, Amelia in Simon Boccanegra, Agathe in Freischütz, Desdemona in Otello, Elisabetta in Don Carlo, Aida and Norma; Sang: Norma at Covent Garden, 1987, Adriana Lecouvreur at Bonn, 1989, Elisabeth de Valois at the Orange Festival; Sang Amelia Grimaldi in a concert performance of Simon Boccanegra at the Festival Hall, 1990; Season 1993–94 in Ariadne auf Naxos at Opéra de Lyon and Staatsoper Berlin; Retired, 1999; mem, Fellow of The College of Wales, 1991; Fellow of The College of Music and Drama of Wales, 1993. *Recordings:* Many recordings of opera, oratorio, concert works and recitals including, Tristan und Isolde, Le nozze di Figaro, Elgar's The Kingdom, Don Giovanni, Così fan tutte, Judas Maccabaeus, Berg's Altenberglieder, Mozart's Requiem and Die Zauberflöte; Jury Member, Wigmore Hall International Song Competition, 1997. *Address:* Pant Y Wylan, Ceibwr Bay, Moylgrove, Cardigan, SA43 3BU, Wales.

PRICE, Perry; Singer (Tenor); b. 13 Oct. 1942, New York, Pennsylvania, USA; m. Heather Thomson. *Education:* Studied at University of Houston, in London with Otakar Kraus and in New York. *Career:* Debut: San Francisco, as Des Grieux in Manon, 1964; New York (City Opera), Houston, Philadelphia, San Diego and Portland; Sang further at Montreal, Vancouver, Toronto, Lisbon and Stadttheater Augsburg; Other roles have included Mozart's Ferrando, Don Ottavio and Tamino, Rossini's Almaviva and Lindoro, the Duke of Mantua, Edgardo, Nemorino, Faust and Hoffmann; Active in concert and as teacher.

PRICK, Christoph; Conductor; b. 23 Oct. 1946, Hamburg, Germany. *Education:* Studied in Hamburg with Wilhelm Bruckner-Ruggebourg. *Career:* Assistant at the Hamburg Staatsoper; Permanent conductor at Trier Opera, 1970–72, Darmstadt, 1972–74; Musical Director at Saarbrucken, 1974–77, Karlsruhe, 1977–84; Staatskapellmeister at the Deutsche Oper Berlin, 1977–84 (returned to conduct the premiere of Wolfgang Rihm's Oedipus, 1987); Conducted Così fan tutte at Los Angeles 1988 and Arabella at Barcelona, 1989; Music Director, Los Angeles Chamber Orchestra, 1992–95; Conducted Fidelio and Tann-häuser at the Metropolitan, 1992; Music Director City of Hannover, Germany, as of 1993–94 Season; Led Die schweigsame Frau at Dresden, 1998.

PRIDAY, Elisabeth; Singer (Soprano); b. 1955, Buckingham, England. *Education:* Studied at the Royal Academy of Music. *Career:* Joined the Monteverdi Choir 1975: concerts at the Aix Festival, and BBC Promenade; Sang in Handel Opera's Giustino 1983 and Hasse's L'Eroe Cinese at the 1985 Holland Festival; Appearances with Roger Norrington for the Maggio Musicale Florence (Speranza in Orfeo) and Amor in Gluck's Orfeo with the Scottish Chamber Orchestra; Dido and Aeneas with the English Concert in Germany, London and the Brighton Festival Concert performances of Bach's B minor Mass in King's College, Cambridge, Handel's Carmelite Vespers with the European Baroque Orchestra, Alexander's Feast for RAI in Italy and Messiah at the Festival de Beaune in France and also QEH; Monteverdi Vespers in St John's Smith Square, Bristol, St Albans; Concerts in France and England with Chiaroscuro and Climene in Gluck's La Corona at the City of London Festival; Paris 1991 with the Deller Consort. *Recordings:* Bach Motets with the Monteverdi Choir; Purcell's King Arthur, Music for the Chapels Royal and the Fairy Queen; Handel's Israel in Egypt, Semele and Dixit Dominus with the Winchester Cathedral Choir; Motets by Schütz and Monteverdi; Rameau's Les Boréades; Vivaldi Glorias (Nimbus); Dido and Aeneas with Trevor Pinnock and also with John Eliot Gardiner.

PRIESTMAN, Brian; Conductor, Music Director and Professor; b. 10 Feb. 1927, Birmingham, England; m. Ford McClave, 2 Mar 1972, 1 d. *Education:* BMus, 1950, MA, 1952, University of Birmingham; Dipl Sup, Brussels Conservatoire, 1952. *Career:* Has held Musical Director-ships of Royal Shakespeare Theatre and with Symphony Orchestras in Edmonton, Canada, Baltimore, Denver and Miami; Principal Conduc-tor, New Zealand and Malmö Symphony Orchestras; Former, Dean and Professor, University of Cape Town; Artist-in-Residence, University of Kansas, USA; mem, Board Member, Conductors' Guild. *Recordings:* For major recording companies. *Honours:* DHL, University of Colorado, 1972. *Current Management:* Mariedi Anders Artists Management, San Francisco, USA. *Address:* c/o Impresario A/S, Tollbugaten 3, N–0152 Oslo, Norway.

PRIETO, Carlos; Concert Cellist; b. 1 Jan. 1937, Mexico City, Mexico; m. Maria Isabel, 28 Dec 1964, 2 s., 1 d. *Education:* Mexico City Conservatory of Music, under Imre Hartman, 1942–54; Studied with: Pierre Fournier, Geneva, 1978; Leonard Rose, New York, USA, 1981, 1982. *Career:* Member of Trio Mexico, 1978–81; International career as Concert Cellist; Many world tours, USA, Canada, Western and Eastern Europe, USSR, Latin America, China, Japan, India, 1981–; Perfor-mances in Carnegie Hall and Lincoln Center, New York; Kennedy Center, Washington; Salle Pleyel and Salle Gaveau, Paris; Philharmo-nic Hall, Leningrad; Concertgebouw, Amsterdam; Has performed at International Music Festivals; Played at world premieres of many cello concerti including those of Carlos Chavez, Joaquin Rodrigo. *Recordings include:* Complete Bach Suites for Cello Solo, 1985; Works by Paganini, Ponce, Rachmaninov, Fauré, Mendelssohn, Tchaikovsky. *Publications:* Alrededor del Mundo con el Violonchelo (Around the World with the Cello), autobiography, 1987; Russian Letters, 1965. *Current Manage-ment:* Gurtman & Murtha Associates Inc, New York City, USA; Choveaux Management, Mancroft Towers, Oulton Broad, Lowestoft, Suffolk, England. *Address:* c/o Gurtman and Murtha Associates Inc, 450 7th Floor #603, New York, NY 10123-0101, USA.

PRIEW, Uta; Singer (Mezzo-soprano); b. 3 Aug. 1944, Karlovy, Varg, Czechoslovakia. *Education:* Studied at Halle and Leipzig. *Career:* Sang

in opera at Weimar from 1970; Staatsoper Berlin from 1975 as Cenerentola; Selika in L'Africane, 1992; Clytemnestra, 1994; Fricka in Wagner's Ring, 1996; Bayreuth Festival, 1988–96 in The Ring and as Ortrud, Venus and Brangaene; Dresden Staatsoper, 1988 as Kundry; Deutsche Oper Berlin, 1990 as Amneris; Sang Clytemnestra at the Théâtre du Châtelet, Paris, 1996; Brangaene at Monte Carlo, 1998; Berlin Staatsoper 2000–01, as the Kostelnička in Jenůfa, Wagner's Mary and Herodias in Salome. *Recordings:* Video of Götterdämmerung. *Address:* Staatsoper Berlin, Unter den Linden 7, 1060 Berlin, Germany.

PRIMROSE, Claire; Singer (mezzo-soprano); b. 2 Oct. 1957, Melbourne, Victoria, Australia. *Education:* Graduate, Victorian College of Arts; Studied voice with Joan Hammond, Melbourne; Studied interpretation of French Song with Gerard Souzay, Paris. *Career:* Debut: As Mezzo Soprano in Australia; As Soprano from 1990, as the sister in Holloway's Clarissa, English National Opera; Mezzo Soprano: Krista in The Makropolous Case; Meg Page in Falstaff; Mercédès in Carmen; Cornelia, in Giulio Cesare; Title role in Cendrillon at Wexford Festival; Charlotte in Werther at Montpellier; Giulietta in Les Contes d'Hoff-mann at Lille; Salud in La Vida Breve at Liège; Suzuki in Madama Butterfly for Opera North; Orlofsky in Die Fledermaus at the Hong Kong Festival; Dorabella in Così fan tutte; Sesto in La Clemenza di Tito for Opera Forum, Holland; Soprano: Leonore in Fidelio; Medea in Teseo, Athens Festival and Sadler's Wells; Dido in Dido and Aeneas at Bologna; Title role in Alceste, Monte Carlo Festival and Covent Garden; Elettra, in Idomeneo, Valencia Festival, 1991; Chrysothemis, State Opera of South Australia and Festival of Melbourne; Leonore, in Fidelio, Australian Opera, 1992–93; Paris debut as Alceste, at Châtelet; Scandinavian debut as Elettra, in Idomeneo, Helsinki, and with the New Israeli Opera in Tel-Aviv, 1992; Fiordiligi, Lyric Opera of Queensland; Santuzza, Australian Opera, 1994 and 1996; Numerous concert appearances include a Wigmore Hall recital with Roger Vignoles in Berlioz's Roméo et Juliette, Salle Pleyel, Paris, and Leonara, in La Forza del Destino, Scottish Opera.; Sang Verdi's Lady Macbeth at Sydney, 1998; Season 2000–01 as Sieglinde at Brunswick and Senta in Dublin. *Honours:* Winner, Metropolitan Opera Competition; Winner, Pavarotti International Competition, Philadelphia. *Current Manage-ment:* Athole Still International Management, Forresters Hall, 25–27 Westow Street, London, SE19 3RY, England. *Telephone:* (20) 8771-5271. *Fax:* (20) 8768-6600. *Website:* www.atholestill.com.

PRINCE-JOSEPH, Bruce; Conductor, Composer, Organist, Harpsichor-dist and Pianist; b. 30 Aug. 1925, Beaver Falls, Pennsylvania, USA. *Education:* BMusA, Yale University, 1946; MMusA, University of Southern California, 1952; Conservatoire Nationale de Musique, Paris, France, 1953. *Career:* Staff Pianist, Organist, Harpsichordist, New York Philharmonic, 1955–74; Professor, Chairman, Department of Music, Hunter College of the City University of New York, 1955–78. *Recordings:* 6 Sonatas for Violin and Harpsichord, RCA, 1965; Glagolitic Mass, Janáček, 1967, Ode to St Cecilia, Handel, 1958, Columbia Records. *Honours:* Grammy Nomination, 1965, for 6 Sonatas for Violin and Harpsichord; Associate Fellow, Berkeley College, Yale University, 1978–83. *Address:* 6540 Pennsylvania Avenue, Kansas City, MO 64113, USA.

PRING, Katherine; Singer (Mezzo-Soprano); b. 4 June 1940, Brighton, England. *Education:* Studied at the Royal College of Music with Ruth Packer; Further study with Maria Carpi in Geneva and Luigi Ricci in Rome. *Career:* Debut: Geneva 1966, as Flora in La Traviata; Sang at Sadler's Wells from 1968, notably as Carmen, Dorabella, Poppea, Eboli, Azucena and Waltraute; Sang in the 1974 British stage premiere of Henze's The Bassarids; Covent Garden debut 1972, as Thea in The Knot Garden; Bayreuth 1972–73, as Schwertleite in Die Walküre; Glynde-bourne 1978, as Baba the Turk in The Rake's Progress; Other modern roles included Kate in Owen Wingrave and Jocasta in Oedipus Rex; Retired 1982. *Recordings:* Fricka and Waltraute in The Ring conducted by Reginald Goodall; The Magic Fountain by Delius. *Address:* c/o Trafalgar Perry Ltd, 4 Goodwin's Court, St Martin's Lane, London WC2N 4LL, England.

PRING, Sarah; Singer (soprano); b. 1962, England. *Education:* Studied at Guildhall School, in Florence with Suzanne Danco, and with Johanna Peters. *Career:* Sang Norina, Susanna, Concepcion and Martinů's Julietta while a student in London, the Trovatore Leonora in Belgium; Professional debut at Glyndebourne, 1988, as Alice in Falstaff, returning as Barena in Jenůfa; Glyndebourne Touring Opera as Glasha in Katya Kabanova, First Lady in Die Zauberflöte and Dorabella; Opera North debut, 1989, as Concepcion, Scottish Opera, 1991, as Mimi; Concert appearances at Festival Hall (Jenůfa), Greenwich Festival (Judas Maccabaeus), Belfast (Beethoven's Ninth) and Purcell Room; Sang Gluck's Euridice for Opera West, 1991; English National Opera debut, 1993, Princess Ida, Don Pasquale; ENO, 1993, Norina, Don Pasquale; ENO, 1994, Nannetta, Falstaff, also Glyndebourne Touring Opera, Second Niece, Peter Grimes. 1995, Second Niece, Paris Châtelet; Covent Garden debut 1996 as a Rhinemaiden in Götterdämmerung;

Berta in Il Barbiere di Siviglia, 1997–98. *Honours:* Joint winner, 1990 John Christie Award. *Current Management:* Musicmakers International Artists Representation, Tailor House, 63–65 High Street, Whitwell, Hertfordshire SG4 8AH, England. *Telephone:* (1438) 871708. *Fax:* (1438) 871777. *E-mail:* musicmakers@compuserve.com. *Website:* www.operauk.com.

PRINGLE, John; Singer (Baritone); b. 17 Oct. 1938, Melbourne, Victoria, Australia. *Education:* Studied Singing in Melbourne and with Luigi Ricci in Rome. *Career:* Debut: Australian Opera, as Frank in Die Fledermaus, 1967; Many appearances with Australian Opera as Mozart's Don Giovanni and Leporello, Count and Papageno, Verdi's Posa, Ford, the Lescauts of Puccini and Massenet, Rossini's Barber, Britten's Death in Venice, Mozart's Figaro, Don Alfonso, Debussy's Golaud; Nick Shadow in The Rake's Progress, Andrei in War and Peace, Janáček's Forester and Robert Storch in Intermezzo (Glyndebourne, 1983); Also sings Olivier in Capriccio and appeared at Paris, Brussels and Cologne, 1980–85; Sang Beckmesser in Meistersinger for Australian Opera, 1988–89, Comte de Nevers in Les Huguenots, 1990; Appeared in Los Angeles and San Diego, 1992; Gianni Schicchi at Sydney, 1995 and sang Prus in The Makropulos Case at Sydney, 1996; Don Alfonso at Sydney, 1997–98; Teatro Regio, Turin, as Musiklehrer, 1998; Conjoint Professor of Vocal Studies, Newcastle University Conservatorium, 1998–; Sang Don Alfonso at Sydney, 2001. *Recordings include:* Video of Les Huguenots; Videos of Intermezzo and Love for Three Oranges (both Glyndebourne); Die Meistersinger (Australian Opera). *Honours:* Member, Order of Australia, 1988. *Address:* c/o Australian Opera, PO Box 291, Strawberry Hills, New South Wales 2012, Australia.

PRIOR, Benjamin; Singer (Tenor); b. 1943, Venice, Italy. *Career:* Sang widely in Italy from 1967, with Edgardo at La Fenice Venice in 1969; Wexford Festival, 1971, in La Rondine and Vienna Staatsoper, 1972, as Verdi's Riccardo; Barcelona 1971, as Percy in Anna Bolena, San Francisco 1980 (Alfredo), Buenos Aires 1981 (Pinkerton) and New Orleans Opera 1981–88; Sang Pinkerton at Verona (1983) and has also sung Verdi's Rodolfo (Luisa Miller) and Foresto, Nemorino, Faust, Macduff, the Duke of Mantua and Des Grieux. *Address:* Opera di Verona, Piazza Bra 28, 37121 Verona, Italy.

PRITCHARD, Edith; Singer (Soprano); b. 1962, Edmonton, Canada. *Education:* Studied at University of Toronto and Royal Northern College of Music. *Career:* Represented Canada at the 1991 Cardiff Singer of the World Competition; Sang Fiordiligi at the 1991 Glyndebourne Festival and the Countess in Cornet Rilke by Siegfried Matthus with the 1993 Glyndebourne Tour; Other roles include First Lady in Die Zauberflöte at Covent Garden, 1992–93, Licenza in Mozart's Sogno di Scipione at Buxton Festival and the Heavenly Voice in Don Carlos for Opera North. *Honours:* Brigitte Fassbaender Prize for Lieder, Royal Northern College of Music, and 1992 John Christie Award, Glyndebourne. *Address:* c/o 'Glen Craig', Llangollen Road, Trevor, Llangollen LL20 7 TN, Wales.

PRITCHARD, Gwyn (Charles); Composer, Conductor and Cellist; b. 29 Jan. 1948, Richmond, Yorkshire, England; m. Claudia Klasicka, 23 June 1967, 2 d. *Education:* Royal Scottish Academy of Music and Drama, 1966–69; Studied cello with Joan Dickson, Composition with Dr Frank Spedding; DRSAM. *Career:* Director of Music, Salisbury Cathedral School, 1969–70; BBC contract for documentary Young Composer, 1972–73; Freelance cellist and member of various chamber ensembles 1973–78; Artistic Director and Conductor, Uroboros Ensemble, 1981–; Founded Reggello International Festival of Music, Italy, 2003; Compositions performed world-wide including Warsaw Autumn Festival, Mexico Festival, Huddersfield Contemporary Music Festival, International Composers Forum, USA, Eastern and Western Europe, and Australia; Featured Composer at Southampton International New Music Week, 1989; mem, Society for the Promotion of New Music. *Compositions:* Concerto for Viola and Orchestra, 1967, revised 1984; Tangents, 1970; Spring Music for Chamber Orchestra, 1972; Enitharmon, 1973; Becoming, 1974; Five pieces for Piano, 1975; Ensemble Music for Six, 1976; Nephalauxis, 1977; Strata, 1977; Jardenna, 1978; Objects in Space, 1978; Mercurius, 1979; Duo, 1980; Earthcrust, 1980; Visions of Zosimos, 1981; Sonata for Guitar, 1982; Moondance, 1982; Lollay, 1983; Dramalogue, 1984; Chamber Concerto, 1985; Madrigal, 1987; La Settima Bolgia, 1989; Eidos, 1990; Janus, 1991; Wayang, 1993; Demise, 1994; Break Apart, 1995; Raum Greift Aus, 1996; Forse Mi Stai Chiamando, 1997; From Time to Time, 2000; Features and Formations, 2003. *Current Management:* Camerata Artists. *Address:* 40 Woolstone Road, London SE23 2SG, England.

PROBST, Dominique (Henri); Percussionist, Composer and Conductor; b. 19 Feb. 1954, Paris, France. *Education:* Baccalaureate, Philosophy Studies, La Sorbone, Paris, 1971; Paris Conservatoire National Superieur de Musique, 1st Prize Percussion, 198; Prize, Composition, Lili and Naida Boulanger Foundation, 1979. *Career:* As Musician at La Comédie

Francaise, and many other great Parisian theatres, 1974–; Titulary Member, Concert Colonne and Ensemble Percussion 4; Assistant, CNSM, Paris, 1978–; Professor, Levallois Conservatory of Music, 1984–. *Compositions:* Numerous pieces for Theatre: King Lear, 1978; Dom Juan, Berenice, 1979; Macbeth; Les Caprices de Marianne, Les Plaisirs de L'Ile Enchantée, 1980; Les Cenci, 1981; Marie Tudor, 1982; L'Esprit des Bois; Dialogues des Carmélites, 1984; La Mouette, L'Arbre des Tropiques, Le Cid, 1985; L'Hote et le Renegat; Thomas More' Richard de Gloucester' Bacchus, 1987; Ascese-A-Seize, 6 percussion players; Les Plaisirs de l'Ile Enchantee, for recorder, violin, guitar and percussion; Coda and Variation IV, guitar. *Contributions:* Professional journals including La Revue Musicale. *Honours:* Prize Marcel Samuel Rousseau, Académie des Beaux-Arts of Paris, 1986, for Opera, Maximilien Kolbe. *Address:* 39 Rue Durantin, 75018 Paris, France.

PROBST, Wolfgang; Singer (Bass-baritone); b. 16 Nov. 1945, Neuhausen, Germany. *Education:* Studied in Munich with Marianne Scheck. *Career:* Staatsoper Stuttgart from 1971 as King Philip in Don Carlos, Wotan in The Ring, in the premiere of Glass's Akhnaten (1984), and as Bartók's Bluebeard (1996); Guest at Munich as Wotan, Jochanaan and Wagner's Dutchman; Orange Festival, 1979, as Klingsor, Dallas, 1980, as Wotan (US debut); Sang Orestes in Elektra at Buenos Aires, 1987, and Boris Godunov at Basle, 1990; Trieste, 1992–94, as Hans Sachs and Kaspar in Der Freischütz; Sang Pizarro in Fidelio at Stuttgart, 1998; Season 2000–01 at Stuttgart in the premiere of Adriana Hölszky's Giuseppe e Sylvia, and in Donizetti's La Convenienze Teatrali and I Pazzi per progetto. *Recordings include:* Video of Der Freischütz, from Stuttgart. *Address:* Staatsoper Stuttgart, Oberer Schlossgarten 6, 70173 Stuttgart, Germany.

PROCHAZKOVA, Jarmila; Musicologist; b. 27 Feb. 1961, Trebic, Czechoslovakia. *Education:* Piano, Conservatoire in Brno; Mašaryk University in Brno; Faculty of Musicology. *Career:* Scholarship-holder of the Leoš Janáček Fund, practice at Janáček Archives; Custodian, Janáček Archive of the Music History Department of Moravian Museum in Brno; mem, Commission to edit Janáček's Musical Works. *Publications:* Leoš Janáček, Album for Kamila Stösslova, in Czech and German, 1994, in English, 1996; Jarmil Prochazkova, Bohumir Volny, Leoš Janáček, born in Hukvaldy, Czech and English versions, 1995. *Contributions:* About 20 on Janáček's composition method, folk inspirations, sociological aspects; On The Genesis of Janáček Symphony Dunaj, 1993; Leoš Janáček and the Czech National Band, 1995. *Address:* Foltynova 6, 635 00, Brno, Czech Republic.

PROCTER, Norma; fmr singer (contralto); b. 15 Feb. 1928, Cleethorpes, Lincolnshire, England. *Education:* vocal studies with Roy Henderson, musicianship with Alec Redshaw, Lieder with Hans Oppenheim and Paul Hamburger. *Career:* London debut at Southwark Cathedral, 1948; Specialist in concert works, oratorio and recitals; Appeared with all major festivals in the United Kingdom and Europe; Operatic debut as Lucretia in Britten's Rape of Lucretia, Aldeburgh Festival, 1959, 1960; Covent Garden debut in Gluck's Orpheus, 1961; Performed in Germany, France, Spain, Portugal, Norway, Sweden, Denmark, Finland, Netherlands, Belgium, Austria, Israel, Luxembourg, South America; Conductors include: Bruno Walter, Bernstein, Rafael Kubelik, Karl Richter, Pablo Casals, Malcolm Sargent; Charles Groves, David Willcocks, Alexander Gibson, Charles Mackerras, Norman del Mar and Bernard Haitink; President, Grimsby Phil Society. *Recordings include:* Messiah; Elijah; Samson; Mahler's 2nd, 3rd and 8th Symphonies, Das klagende Lied; Hartmann 1st Symphony; Julius Caesar Jones-Williamson; Nicholas Maw's Scenes and Arias; BBC, Last Night of the Proms; Premiere recording Brahms, Mahler, Ballads; Songs of England with Jennifer Vyvyan, 1999; Premiere release of 1957 recording of Britten's Canticle II Abraham and Isaac, with Peter Pears and Benjamin Britten (in Benjamin Britten: The Rarities), 2001. *Honours:* Honorary RAM, 1974. *Address:* 194 Clee Road, Grimsby, Lincolnshire DN32 8NG, England.

PROKINA, Elena; Soprano; b. 16 Jan. 1964, Odessa, Russia. *Education:* Studied in Odessa and at the Leningrad Theatre Institute and Leningrad Conservatory. *Career:* Kirov Theatre Leningrad from 1988 as Emma in Khovanshchina, Violetta, Marguerite, Natasha in War and Peace (seen on BBC television), Tatyana, Desdemona, Pauline in The Gambler, Jaroslavna in Prince Igor, Iolanta and Maria in Mazeppa; Tours with the Kirov Company in Europe and Kirov Gala at Covent Garden, 1992–; Appearances in Los Angeles as Donna Anna, and Lina in Stiffelio; Lisbon and Sydney as Tatiana; Shostakovich No. 14 with the London Symphony Orchestra under Rostropovich, 1993; Covent Garden debut in 1994 as Katya Kabanova in a production by Trevor Nunn, returning 1995 as Desdemona; Katya at Covent Garden in 1997; Verdi's Amelia Grimaldi at Glyndebourne, 1998; Sang in Rachmaninov's Aleko at the 1999 London Prom concerts; Season 1999–2000 for Zürich Opera as Tatiana in Eugene Onegin, Giselda in I Lombardi, Lucrezia (I Due Foscari) and Tosca; Elisabeth de Valois, 2001; Amelia Grimaldi at Sydney and Marie in Wozzeck for Dallas Opera, 2000. *Current*

Management: Askonas Holt Ltd, Lonsdale Chambers, 27 Chancery Lane, London, WC2A 1PF, England. *Telephone:* (20) 7400-1700. *Fax:* (20) 7400-1799. *E-mail:* info@askonasholt.co.uk. *Website:* www .askonasholt.co.uk.

PROMONTI, Elisabeth; Opera Singer (soprano); b. 9 July 1942, Budapest, Hungary; one s. *Education:* diploma, Choir Conducting Faculty, Franz Liszt Music Acad., Budapest; diploma, Opera, Lied, Oratorio, Akad. Mozarteum, Salzburg; studied with Zoltan Zavodsky, Viorica Ursuleac, Friederike Baumgartner, Elisabeth Grümmer International Opera Studio, Opera Zürich, 1970–71. *Career:* debut, as Aida, Bielefeld Municipal Theatre, 1967; sang such roles as Aida, Amelia, Desdemona, Elisabeth, Donna Anna, Pamina, Countess, Elsa and Marie at opera houses of Bielefeld, Oberhausen, Kiel, Bremen, Heidelberg, Bordeaux, Vienna, Zürich, 1967–75; Concert Singer, 1975–; appearances on radio and television; tours in Europe, USA and Canada; Dir, Swiss Kodály Institute, 1983–95; Pres., Swiss Kodály Society, 1991–96; Dir, Concorde Opera Management Ltd, Vienna, 1998–. *Recordings:* Zoltán Kodály, Epigrammes, 1991; Folk Songs Arranged by Great Composers, 1993. *Address:* Hagenberggasse 25/4, 1130 Vienna, Austria.

PROSTITOV, Oleg; Composer; b. 7 Sept. 1955, Stavropol, Russia; m. Grishina Lyudmila, 22 May 1976, 1 s., 1 d. *Education:* Rimsky-Korsakov State Conservatoire, Leningrad (Petersburg), 1979; Postgraduate courses with Professor Mnatsakanyan, pupil of Shostakovich, Leningrad (St Petersburg) Conservatoire, 1983. *Career:* Debut: Stavropol, 1972; Participant of 3 international music festivals, Baku, 1987; Sofia, 1990; St Petersburg, 1991; Sonata-fantasy, Amadeus; mem, Union of the Composers of Russia, since 1979. *Compositions:* 5 symphonies, 2 piano concertos, a violin concerto, 5 children's musicals, a great number of chamber and vocal instrumental works (sonatas, suites, string quartets, cantatas, romances), about 100 songs. *Recordings:* Sonata-fantasy, Amadeus; Sonata for trombone, violin and piano performed in Moscow, St Petersburg, Florida, Stuttgart, Paris, A Black Man, monopera for baritone, mixed choir, large symphony orchestra based on the poem by S Esenin. *Honours:* 1st Prize for vocal cycle on the poems by S Esenin for baritone and piano, Young Musicians' Competition, Leningrad (St Petersburg), 1978. *Current Management:* Chairman, Krasnoyarsk Department, Union of the Composers of Russia. *Address:* Krasnoyarsky Rabochy, 124-A Apt 25, 660095 Krasnoyarsk, Russia.

PROTSCHKA, Josef; German singer (tenor); b. 5 Feb. 1946, Prague, Czechoslovakia. *Education:* Philology and Philosophy at Universities of Tubingen and Bonn; Cologne Musikhochschule with Erika Köth and Peter Witsch. *Career:* Giessen, 1977–78, Saarbrücken, 1978–80, leading tenor at Cologne Opera from 1980, singing all main tenor parts in Ponnelle's Mozart cycle, Lionel (Martha), Tom Rakewell, Faust, Max, Lensky, Jenik in The Bartered Bride, José, Hermann (Queen of Spades), Loge, Erik, Eisenstein; Freelance from 1987; Important debuts: Salzburg Festival and Vienna State Opera (Hans), 1985; La Scala and Semperopera Dresden (José), 1986; Bregenz Festival (Hoffmann), Maggio Musicale, Florence (Flamand) and Zürich Opera, 1987; Wiener Festwochen (Fierrabras-Schubert), 1988; Hamburg State Opera as Florestan and Elis in Schreker's Schatzgräber, 1989, Idomeneo, 1990; Royal Opera, Brussels, 1989, as Florestan and Lohengrin, 1990; Florestan at Covent Garden and Tokyo NHK, 1990; US debut, Houston (Song of the Earth), 1991; Now appears regularly on stage at festivals and opera houses with leading conductors and producers; Also lieder recitals, concerts, radio and television productions; Professor, Hochschule für Musik Köln, Aachen Division, and Det Kongelige Danske Musikkonservatoriet, Copenhagen, 1993–. *Recordings include:* Haydn Die Schöpfung; Schubert Fierrabras; Schubert Schöne Müllerin; Mendelssohn Lieder, complete; Fidelio (Florestan) and Flying Dutchman (Erik) with Vienna Philharmonic and Dohnányi; Mozart Lieder, complete; Videos: Fidelio, Covent Garden; Tales of Hoffmann, Bregenz Festival; Fierrabras, Theater an der Wien; Schatzgräber, Hamburg Opera; Missa solemnis, Uracher Musiktage; Lieder recital, Urach. *Address:* Ringstrasse 17B, 50765 Köln, Germany.

PROUVOST, Gaetane; Violinist; b. 21 July 1954, Lille, France; m. Charles de Couessin, 6 July 1985, 2 s. *Education:* Baccalaureate; 1st Prize, Violin and Chamber Music, Cycle de Perfectionnement, Conservatoire National Superieur; Studied: With Ivan Galamian, Juilliard School of Music, New York; Chigiana, Siena, Italy; With D Markevitch, Institut des hautes etudes musicales, Montreux; Pupil of Zino Francescatti. *Career:* Debut: Carnegie Hall, 1974; Soloist with Radio-France Orchestra, Orchestre Lamoureux, Bucharest Philharmonic; Gdansk Philharmonic, Ensemble Intercontemporain, Ensemble Forum; Performed under conductors J Conlon, K Nagano, G Bertini, P Boulez, A Tamayo, S Baudo, R Kempe; Recitals with M Dalberto, N Lee, P Barbizet, B Rigutto, A Queffelec; Premiered: Olivier Greif's Sonate; M Rateau's Offrande lyrique, Paris, 1984; Participated in Etienne Perrier's film Rouge Venitien; Professor, Conservatoire National Superieur de Musique, Paris; mem, Alumni Association of Conservatoire National Superieur de Musique, Paris. *Recordings:* Prokofiev, Sonatas op 80 and

94 for violin and piano (with A R el Bacha); Szymanowski, Complete works for violin and piano; Zino Francescatti's Works. *Publications:* Biography of Zino Francescati. *Honours:* Prizewinner, Carl Flesch International Competition, London; Award for Best Record, France, 1987. *Current Management:* Ch de Covessin, France. *Address:* 7 rue des Volontaires, 75015 Paris, France.

PROUZA, Zdenek; Cellist; b. 3 Aug. 1955, Prague, Czechoslovakia; m. Katherine H Allen, 25 April 1987. *Education:* Conservatory of Music, Prague; Academy of Performing Arts, Prague; Hochschule für Musik, Wien; Mozarteum, Salzburg; Accademia Musicale Chigiana, Siena. *Career:* Debut: Recital debut in Prague, 1973; Principal Cellist with Czech Chamber Orchestra and Nurnberg Symphony Orchestra; Co-Principal with Vienna Chamber Orchestra and Munich Chamber Orchestra; Solo appearances in Czechoslovakia, West Germany, Belgium, France, Italy, Austria, USA and Canada; mem, American Cello Society. *Recordings:* Pauer, Radio Prague; Suk, Czech television; Suk, ORTF; Vivaldi, RAI; Saint-Saëns, Colosseum; Musical Heritage Society. *Honours:* Concertino Praga, 1970; Beethoven Cello Competition, 1972; Czech Cello Competition, 1976; Contemporary Performance Award, Czech Music Foundation, 1977, 1978. *Current Management:* The Added Staff. *Address:* 820 West End Avenue, Suite 3C, New York, NY 10025, USA.

PROVOST, Serge; Composer, Performer and Professor; b. 1952, Saint-Timothée de Beauharnois, Quebec, Canada. *Education:* Studied composition and analysis under Gilles Tremblay, organ with Bernard Lagacé; Studied writing, electracoustics, orchestration, piano and harpsichord, Conservatoire de Musique, Montréal 1970–79; Studied composition and analysis under Claude Ballif, Paris 1979–81. *Career:* Professor of analysis, Trois-Rivières and Hull Conservatories; Took part in Banff Centre's Composers Workshop 1979 and Rencontres Internationales de la Jeunesse at Bayreuth Festival; given organ recitals in France, Germany and Canada. *Compositions include:* Les Isles du Songe, for choir, orchestra and percussion; Cretes, a piece for 2 harpsichords which Swiss duo Esterman-Gallet commissioned and played in 1980; Tetrarys, 1988, saxophone, harp, flute, piano; Les Jardins Suspendus, 1989, 4 ondes martenots, piano. *Honours:* Won 1st Prize in composition for choir, orchestra and percussion with Les Isles du Songe, 1979; Won First Prize in analysis at Conservatoire de Paris 1981. *Address:* c/o SOCAN, 41 Valleybrook Drive, Don Mills, Ontario M3B 2S6, Canada.

PROWSE, Philip; British stage director and stage designer; b. 29 Dec. 1937, Worcestershire, England. *Education:* Slade School of Fine Art, London. *Career:* teacher at Birmingham College of Art and Slade School of Fine art; Designed ballets for Covent Garden, followed by Orfeo ed Euridice, 1969, and Ariadne auf Naxos, 1976; Director of Citizens Theatre, Glasgow, 1970–; Produced and Designed Handel's Tamerlano for Welsh National Opera, 1982, and Les Pêcheurs de Perles for English National Opera, 1987; Designs for Jonathan Miller's production of Don Giovanni at English National Opera, 1985 and The Magic Flute for Scottish Opera; Work as Producer and Designer for Opera North includes Orfeo ed Euridice, Die Dreigroschenoper and Aida, 1986, British premiere of Strauss's Daphne, 1987, and La Gioconda, 1993; Staged the house premiere of Verdi's Giovanna d'Arco, Covent Garden, 1996 (also at Opera North, 1998); Professor, Slade School, University College London, 1999–. *Address:* c/o The Citizen's Theatre, Gorbals Street, Glasgow, G5 9DS, Scotland.

PRUETT, Jerome; singer (tenor); b. 22 Nov. 1941, Poplar Bluff, Missouri, USA. *Education:* Studied with Thorwald Olsen in St Louis and with Boris Goldovsky in West Virginia. *Career:* Debut: Carnegie Hall New York 1974, in a concert performance of Donizetti's Parisina d'Este; Sang with New York City Opera then followed a career in Europe: Vienna Volksoper, 1975, in the premiere of Wolpert's Le Malade Imaginaire; Théâtre de la Monnaie Brussels, 1983, as Julien in Louise and as Boris in Katya Kabanova; Geneva Opera, 1984, as Debussy's Pelléas; Sang at Nancy, 1984, in Henze's Boulevard Solitude; Other roles include Mozart's Belmonte and Tamino, Nicolai's Fenton, Tonio in La Fille du Régiment and Ernesto in Don Pasquale; Amsterdam and Paris, 1988, as Boris in Katya Kabanova and Faust; Sang Ferrando in Così fan tutte at the Gran Teatre del Liceu Barcelona 1990; Sang Alfredo and Gounod's Faust for Opera North, 1996. *Recordings:* Louise (Erato).

PRUNELL-FRIEND, Agustin; Singer (Tenor); b. 1969, Tenerife, Canary Islands. *Education:* Guildhall School, London. *Career:* Debut: As Ramiro in Cenerentola at Madrid, 1996; Appearances as Fenton in Falstaff at Ischia and in Lully's Bourgeois Gentilhomme for English Bach Festival at Covent Garden; Nettuno and Sterope in Cavalli's Orione at Venice and Maderna's Venetian Journal, 1998; Berio's Coro at Geneva and Ramiro in Cenerentola for Opera New Zealand, 1998; Season 1999–2000 with Don Ramiro at Savona, Almaviva for Grange Park Opera, Narciso in Il Turco in Italia throughout Italy, Thomson's Four Saints for La Fenice and Hidalgo's Celos aún del aire matan at

Madrid; Concerts including Haydn's Creation in Mexico, 1997, Carmina Burana on tour in Germany, 1998, Bach's Passions, Messiah, Mozart's Requiem and C minor Mass. *Address:* 79 Sterling Gardens, London SE14 6DU England. *Telephone:* 07736 046767. *E-mail:* aprunellfr@aol .com. *Website:* www.prunell-friend.com.

PRUSLIN, Stephen Lawrence, BA, MFA; pianist and writer on music; b. 16 April 1940, Brooklyn, NY, USA. *Education:* Brandeis Univ., Princeton Univ., studied piano with Eduard Steuermann. *Career:* Taught at Princeton until 1964, then moved to London; Recital debut as pianist at Purcell Room, South Bank, 1970; Concert appearances with BBC Symphony and Royal Philharmonic; Recital accompanist to Bethany Beardslee, Elisabeth Söderström and Jan DeGaetani; Appearances with London Sinfonietta and the Fires of London (Co-founder), 1970–87; Repertoire has included works by Elliott Carter, Maxwell Davies (premiere of Piano Sonata), late Beethoven, Bach and John Bull; Collaborated with Davies on music for Ken Russell's film The Devils and has written other film and theatre music, including Derek Jarman's The Tempest; Articles on contemporary music, translation of Schoenberg's Pierrot Lunaire and librettos for Birtwistle's Monodrama, 1967, and Punch and Judy, 1968; Libretto for Craig's Progress by Martin Butler. *Recordings include:* albums as solo and ensemble pianist. *Publications include:* Peter Maxwell Davies: Studies from Two Decades (editor), London, 1979. *Current Management:* Universal Edition (London) Ltd, 48 Great Marlborough Street, London, W1F 7BB, England. *Telephone:* (20) 7437-6880. *Fax:* (20) 7437-6115.

PRYCE-JONES, John; Conductor; b. 1946, Wales. *Education:* Studied in Penarth and Worcester and at Corpus Christi College, Cambridge (Organ Scholar). *Career:* Assistant Chorus Master and Conductor at Welsh National Opera, 1970–; Freelance conductor in the United Kingdom and abroad until 1978; Chorus Master and Conductor with Opera North, 1978–; Head of Music, Scottish Opera, 1987; Debut with English National Opera in The Mikado; Music Director of The New D'Oyly Carte Opera, 1990–92; First US visit of the Company with The Mikado and The Pirates of Penzance; Artistic Director of the Halifax Choral Society; Has conducted the Oslo Philharmonic, the Bergen Symphony and the Norwegian Broadcasting Orchestra; Debut with Icelandic Opera, 1991, with Rigoletto; Principal Conductor and Musical Director, with Northern Ballet Theatre, 1992; Rigoletto, with Opera North, 1992; La Bohème with Welsh National Opera, 1993; Conducted CBSO, BBC National Orchestra of Wales. *Recordings:* Pirates of Penzance; Mikado; Iolanthe; Gondoliers. *Honours:* ARCO; MA. *Address:* 4 Croft Way, Menston, West Yorkshire CS29 6LT, England.

PRYOR, Gwenneth; Concert Pianist; b. 7 April 1941, Sydney, New South Wales, Australia; m. Roger Stone, 10 Dec 1972, 1 s., 1 d. *Education:* Diploma, New South Wales Conservatorium of Music; ARCM, Royal College of Music. *Career:* Debut: Wigmore Hall, London; recitals and concerts in major cities in United Kingdom, Europe, North and South America and Australia; Many records and radio broadcasts, both solo and chamber music; Teaching, Morley College; mem, Incorporated Society of Musicians; Royal Society of Musicians. *Recordings:* Moussorgsky's Pictures at an Exhibition; Schumann's Carnaval and Papillons; Gershwin's Rhapsody in Blue and Concerto; With clarinettist Gervase de Peyer; Malcolm Williamson Concertos. *Honours:* Prize for Most Outstanding Student, New South Wales Conservatorium, 1960; 1st Prize, Australia House, 1963; Gold Medal, Royal College of Music, 1963. *Current Management:* Michael Harrold Artist Management. *Address:* c/o 13 Clinton Road, Leatherhead, Surrey, KT 22 8NU, England.

PRZYBYLSKI, Bronislaw Kazimierz; Composer; b. 11 Dec. 1941, Łódź, Poland. *Education:* Studied at the Łódź Stage College of Music, 1964–69, with Boleslaw Szabelski in Katowice, and with Roman Haubenstock-Ramati at the Vienna Hochschule für Musik, 1975–76. *Career:* Faculty Member, Łódź State College of Music, from 1964. *Compositions include:* Wind Quintet, 1967; String Quartet, 1969; Quattro Studi for orchestra, 1970; Suite of Polish Dances, 1971; Scherzi musicali for strings, 1973; Midnight, monodrama for actor and chamber ensemble, 1973; Concerto Polacco for accordion and orchestra, 1973; Voices for 3 actors and chamber ensemble, 1974; Requiem for soprano, 2 reciters, boys' chorus and orchestra, 1976; Sinfonia da Requiem, 1976; Arnold Schoenberg In Memoriam for string quartet, 1977; Sinfonia Polacca, 1974–78; The City of Hope, for bass, chorus and 2 orchestras, 1979; Sinfonia-Affresco, 1982; Concerto for harpsichord and strings, 1983; Return, quasi symphonic poem, 1984; Miriam, ballet, 1985; Concerto Classico for accordion and orchestra, 1986; The Dragon of Wawel, ballet, 1987; Lacrimosa 2000 for strings, 1991; Autumn Multiplay for 6 instruments, 1994; Sinfonia-Anniversario, 1995; Missa Papae Joannis Pauli Secundi, 1998; Solo songs; Choruses. *Address:* c/o Society of Authors ZAiKS, 2 Hipoteczna Street, 00 092 Warsaw, Poland. *Telephone:* (4822) 828 17 05. *Fax:* (4822) 828 13 47. *E-mail:* sekretariat@ zaiks.org.pl. *Website:* www.zaiks.org.pl.

PTASZYNSKA, Marta; Composer and Percussionist; b. 29 July 1943, Warsaw, Poland; m. Andrew Rafalski, 9 Nov 1974, 1 d. *Education:* Acad. of Music, Warsaw; Acad. of Music, Poznań; Studied composition with Nadia Boulanger and Olivier Bourdan in Paris and electronic music at Centre Bourdan, ORTF; Cleveland Institute of Music. *Career:* Performances at international festivals including ISCM World Music Days, and international conventions; Radio and television appearances in Poland and USA; Teacher of Composition and Percussion at Warsaw Higher School of Music and Prof. of Composition in USA, including Indiana University in Bloomington, Northwestern Univ., Cincinnati College Conservatory, Univ. of California in Berkeley and Santa Barbara; Prof. of Composition, Univ. of Chicago, 1998–; Commissions from American and European orchestras, chamber groups and major institutions including Chicago Symphony Orchestra, Cincinnati Symphony Orchestra, Polish Chamber Orchestra, Sinfonia Varsovia, Polish TV, BBC, Nat. Opera in Warsaw; and for musicians including Yehudi Menuhin, Ewa Podles, Keiko Abe, Evelyn Glennie. *Compositions:* Spectri Sonori for Orchestra, 1973; Siderals for 10 Percussionists, 1974; Un Grand Sommeil Noir, 1977; Dream Lands, Magic Spaces, 1978; Die Sonette an Orpheus, 1981; Winter's Tale, 1984 (Int. Rostrum of Composers at UNESCO Award, 1985); Marimba Concerto, 1985; Moon Flowers, 1986; Oscar of Alva, opera on G.G.Byron's poem, 1972 (revised 1986; Polish Radio and TV Award); Songs of Despair and Loneliness, 1988–89; Saxophone Concerto, 1988; Poetic Impressions, 1991; Holocaust Memorial Cantata, 1992; Spider Walk, 1993; Mister Marimba, opera for children, 1993–96; Liquid Light for mezzosoprano, piano and percussion, 1995; Concerto Grosso, 1996; Letter to the Sun, 1998; Inverted Mountain for orchestra, 2001; Mosaics for string quartet, 2002; The Drum of Orfeo for percussion and orchestra, 2003. *Recordings:* Polskie Nagraina; Un Grand Sommeil Noir, 1979; La Novella D'Inverno, 1985; Moon Flowers, 1986; Space Model; Epigrams; Many archive recordings at Polish Radio and also Moon Flowers at BBC in 1986. *Publications:* Many works published. *Contributions:* Cum Notis Variorum. *Honours:* Officer Cross of Repub. of Poland, 1995; Alfred Jurzykowski Ward, New York, 1997; Polish Government Award, 2000. *Address:* c/o ASCAP, ASCAP Building, On Lincoln Plaza, New York, NY 10023, USA.

PUDDY, Keith; Music Professor, Clarinettist and Researcher; b. 27 Feb. 1935, Wedmore, England; m. Marilyn Johnston, 14 Feb 1970, 1 s. *Education:* Studied at Royal Academy of Music, London. *Career:* Principal Clarinet for Hallé Orchestra under Barbirolli, at age 23; Returned to London for solo and chamber music; Former member of The Gabrieli Ensemble, The Music Group of London, The New London Wind Ensemble; Now plays with The London Wind Trio and London Music Phoenix; Awarded Leverhulme Trust Fellowships in 1983 and 1988 to study and research clarinets; Principal Clarinet and Wind Adviser on period instruments to the New Queen's Hall Orchestra, London; Performs and records on both modern and period instruments; Professor at the Royal Academy of Music and Trinity College of Music, London; Member of the London Wind Trio and NSW Queen's Hall Orchestra; Freelance Clarinettist, playing solo and chamber and also performing on early period instruments. *Recordings:* Major chamber repertoire on various labels; Brahms Sonatas; Brahms Quintet; Mozart Concerto; Mozart Quintet; Beethoven Septet; Numerous solo period recordings. *Honours:* Honorary FTCL, 1970; FRAM, 1995. *Address:* 20 Courtnell Street, London W2 5BX, England.

PUERTO, David Del; Composer; b. 30 April 1964, Madrid, Spain; m. Karin Anita Burk, 24 June 1991; one s. *Education:* Private studies in Madrid with: Alberto Potin (guitar); Jesus Maria Corral (harmony); Francisco Guerrero (composition); Luis de Pablo (composition). *Career:* Major works in: Almeida Festival, London, 1985; Ensemble Intercontemporain Season, Paris, 1989; Geneva Summer Festival, 1989; Alicante Festival, 1991, 1996; Ars Musica Festival, Brussels, 1992, 1993, 1996; Gaudeamus Week, Amsterdam, 1993, 1996; Takefu Festival, Japan, 1993; Premiere of Concerto for Violin and Orchestra in Madison, Wisconsin, 1998; Composer-in-Residence, Young Spanish National Orchestra, 1999; Works performed at Strasbourg Festival, 1999; premiere of chamber opera Sol de Invierno, Teatro San Joao, Portugal 2002; premiere of String Quartet, Liceo de Cámara de Madrid 2002; premiere of Symphony No. 1 Boreas, Festival de Canarias 2005. *Compositions:* Corriente Cautiva for Orchestra, 1991; Concerto for Oboe and Chamber Ensemble, 1992; Etude, for wind quintet, 1993; Vision Del Errante, for 12 mixed voices, 1994; Concerto for Marimba and 15 Instruments, 1996; Concerto For Violin and Orchestra, 1997; Intermezzo for String Orchestra, 1998; Fantasía Primera for Orchestra, 1998; Mito, for 13 instruments, 1999; Fantasía Segunda for orchestra, 1999; Sol de Invierno, scene for mezzo, baritone and six percussionists, after Ibsen; String Quartet 2002, Alio Modo (for piano) 2002, Advenit 2003, Sobre la Noche (for soprano and accordion) 2003; Symphony No. 1, Boreas 2004, Symphony No. 2 (for piano and orchestra) 2005. *Recordings:* Concerto for Oboe, by Ernest Rombout, Xenakis Ensemble and Diego Masson (conductor); Invernal and En La Luz, by Orquestra

Del Teatre Lliure, Conductor, J Pons; Consort, by Quartet de Bec Frullato; Verso III, by José Vicente (percussion); Verso I, Isabelle Duval (flute); Chamber Music, featuring M. Bernat (marimba), E. Rombout (oboe), A. Sukarlan (piano), F. Panisello (conductor); Complete Piano Music/Accordion Duos/Una Suite para Leo, feturing A. Sukarlan (piano), M. Bernat (percussion), C. Gurriarán (soprano), A. L. Castaño (accordion), J. Libardo (saxophone). *Address:* Azurita, 9 El Giujo, 28260 Galapagar, Madrid, Spain. *E-mail:* davidelpuerto_mp@yahoo.es.

PUGH, William; Singer (Tenor); b. 1 July 1949, Scotland. *Education:* Studied at Oxford and St Andrew's Universities and the London Opera Centre; A pupil of the Spanish tenor, Eduardo Asquez. *Career:* Appearances in opera throughout Germany from 1981: Hildesheim, 1981–84; Oberhausen, 1984–86, Oldenburg, 1986–91, Saarbrücken, 1991–94 (as Werther, Mozart's Titus, Eisenstein, Danilo and Libenskof in the German premiere of Il Viaggio a Reims by Rossini); Subsequently as guest artist in Mannheim: 1994, Schaum der Tage (Denisov); 1995, Il Viaggio a Reims; 1998–2000, the Painter in Lulu (Berg); Essen: 2000, Faust (Gounod); Bielefeld, 1993–94: Faust (Spohr) (recording) and the German premiere of The Duenna by Gerhard; Other roles have included Belmonte, Ferrando, Don Ottavio, Almaviva, Hoffmann, Don José, Alfredo, the Duke of Mantua, Edgardo and Rodolfo. *Address:* Lupinenstrasse 3a, 26125 Oldenburg, Germany.

PULESTON, Faith; Singer (Mezzo-soprano); b. 1942, England. *Education:* Studied with Eva Turner at the Royal Academy of Music and in Germany. *Career:* Sang at the Saarbrucken Opera from 1966, Deutsche Oper am Rhein at Düsseldorf from 1968; Roles have included Carmen, Eboli, Fricka and Mozart's Sextus; Bayreuth Festival, 1970–71, as Grimgerde, and Verdi's Amneris at Covent Garden; Sang Brangaene at the Stadttheater Hagen, 1991. *Address:* Stadttheater Hagen, Elberfelderstrasse 65, W-5800 Hagen, Germany.

PULIEV, Michael; Singer (Bass-baritone); b. 27 March 1958, Sofia, Bulgaria. *Education:* Studied in Sofia with Boris Christoff. *Career:* Sang at the National Opera, Sofia, 1984–86, then gave concerts in Bulgaria, China, Korea, Germany and Switzerland; Sang at Stadttheater Bern, 1986–87 and at Liège-, as Mars in Orphée aux Enfers, Frère Laurent in Roméo et Juliette and roles in Mascagni's Nerone, Die Zauberflöte, Le nozze di Figaro, La Traviata and Andrea Chénier. *Honours:* Winner, Bulgarian young singers competitions; Prizewinner, Maria Callas Competition at Athens, 1984, Geneva International, 1987.

PURCELL, Kevin (John); Composer, Author and Conductor; b. 9 Sept. 1959, Melbourne, Victoria, Australia. *Education:* BA (Music), La Trobe University, 1980; MMus, University of Melbourne, 1991; GradDipMus, New South Wales Conservatory, 1993; Janáček Academy, Brno, 1994; Composition with Brenton Broadstock, 1989–91; Conducting with Myer Fredman, 1993. *Career:* Conductor in Australia and England; Faculty Member, University of Melbourne, 1990–92; Resident in London. *Compositions include:* Symphony No.1 The Monk of St Evroul, 1990; Three Brass Monkeys, for trumpet, horn and bass trombone, 1990; An Umbrella for Inclement Weather, for flute, oboe and clarinet, 1991; Kite Songs for a Crescent Moon, for mezzo and large ensemble, 1992; Symphony No. 2 The Enchanter of Caer-Myrddin, 1992; The Thirty-Nine Steps, one-act chamber opera, 1993–95. *Honours:* Charles Mackerras Conducting Award, 1995. *Address:* c/o APRA, 1A Eden Street, Crows Nest, NSW 2065, Australia.

PURVES, Christopher; Singer (bass-baritone); b. 1960, England. *Education:* Choral scholar at King's College, Cambridge. *Career:* Appearances with English and Welsh National Operas and Opera Northern Ireland as Mozart's Figaro, Leporello, Masetto, the Speaker and Papageno; Other roles include Don Pasquale, the Sacristan in Tosca, Dandini in La Cenerentola, Janáček's Forester and Melibeo in La Fedeltà Premiata (Garsington, 1995); Melot in Tristan and Isolde for Scottish Opera, 1998; Concerts with such conductors as Colin Davis, Pesek, Rattle, Hickox, Christophers and Herreweghe. *Recordings include:* Israel in Egypt, with Gardiner; Purcell and Charpentier albums. *Current Management:* Hazard Chase, Norman House, Cambridge Place, Cambridge CB2 1NS, England. *Telephone:* (1223) 312400. *Fax:* (1223) 460827. *Website:* www.hazardchase.co.uk.

PURVS, Arvids; Conductor, Composer and Music Critic; b. 22 March 1926, Mengele, Latvia; m Marija Falkenburgs 1952; one d. *Education:* violin, conducting and composition at private lessons; attended music seminars at Univs of Waterloo and Halifax, Canada. *Career:* Music Dir, St Andrew's Latvian Lutheran Church Choir, Toronto, Canada, 1958–; Conductor, Women's Choir, Zile, Toronto, 1974–; conductor at over 40 Latvian Song Festivals in the USA, Canada, Australia and Europe, leading orchestras and massed choirs of up to 4,000 voices, as in the Festival at the Royal Albert Hall, London, 1977 and in the XXth National Song Festival, Riga, Latvia, 1990; mem., Toronto Latvian Concert Asscn (pres. 1967–), Latvian Song Festival Asscn in Canada. *Compositions include:* Cantata of Psalms for soloists, chorus, orchestra and organ, 1956; Calling of the Bells for chorus and orchestra 1972,

Toward the Light for chorus, speaker, orchestra and organ, 1975; Time, cantata for chorus, string orchestra, timpani and organ, 1980. *Publications:* Pa skanosu vasaru (My Musical Summers), 2000. *Honours:* Music Award, The Arts Foundation of the Asscn of Latvians in the Free World, 1977, 2001; Order of Three Stars, Latvian Republic, 1997. *Address:* 65 Rivercove Drive, Etobicoke, ON M9B 4Y8, Canada.

PUSAR, Ana; Singer (soprano); b. 1954, Celje, Yugoslavia. *Education:* Studied in Celje and at School of Music, Ljubljana. *Career:* Sang in Ljubljana from 1975 as Rosina, Manon, Tatiana, Dido, Nedda, Micaela, Desdemona and Poppea; Berlin Komische Oper, 1979–85; Appearances at the State Operas of Berlin and Dresden; Guest appearances in Japan, Prague, Moscow, Leningrad, Edinburgh, Venice and Madrid; Roles have included: Mozart's Fiordiligi and Countess, Agathe, Ariadne, Elsa, Madama Butterfly and Ellen Orford; Sang the Marschallin at reopening of Dresden Semper Oper, 1985, Vienna Staatsoper from 1986 as Donna Anna, Arabella, Agathe and the Marschallin, Munich Staatsoper in Daphne, as the Countess in Figaro and Capriccio and Donna Anna; Has also sung in Barcelona, Venice, Hamburg, Montreal, Geneva, Stuttgart, Lisbon, Toulouse, Graz and Cologne; Season 1992 with Sieglinde in Die Walküre at Bonn; Concert appearances in most major European centres; Has worked with such conductors as Peter Schneider, Gerd Albrecht, John Pritchard, Nikolaus Harnoncourt and Lorin Maazel; From 1992 sang: Tatiana at Venice, 1993, Katya Kabanova at Zürich, 1994 and Graz, 1994 in Stiffelio, as Lina; Gertrud at Palermo, 1995; Sang Mozart's Countess at Ljubljana, 2000. *Recordings include:* Der Rosenkavalier, Semper Opera; Bontempi Requiem; Dvořák Stabat Mater; Così fan tutte; Hugo Wolf, Lieder, 1990; Rachmaninov Lieder and Romances; Orfeo, 1994. *Honours:* Winner, Toti dal Monte Competition and Mario del Monaco Competition, 1978; National Award of Slovenia, 1979. *Current Management:* Music International. *Address:* c/o Music International, 13 Ardilaun Road, London N5 2QR, England.

PUSHEE, Graham; Singer (Counter-tenor); b. 1954, Sydney, Australia. *Education:* Studied in London with Paul Esswood and Schola Cantorum Basiliensis, Basel, Switzerland. *Career:* Debut: Sydney, 1973, as Oberon in A Midsummer Night's Dream; Concerts in Australia, 1973–77; Handel Festivals at Karlsruhe in Orlando, Poro, Scipione, Belshazzar and Admeto; Paris Opéra, 1987, as Giulio Cesare; Australian Opera at Sydney as Ruggiero in Alcina, 1990, Opera North, 1993, as Andronico in Handel's Tamerlano; Turin, 1995, as Oberon and Staatsoper Berlin, 1996, as Endimione in Cavalli's La Calisto; Further appearances in operas by Gluck (as Orpheus), Cesti (Orindo in L'Orontea at Basle, 1990), Monteverdi and Stradella; Handel's Giulio Cesare for Opera Australia, 1997, and for Houston Grand Opera and at Karlsruhe; Rinaldo for Opera Australia; Semele for Berlin Staatsoper and Innsbruck Festival; In La Calisto at the Salzburg Festival, Barcelona, Brussels (La Monnaie) and Lyon; Season 2000–01 as Giulio Cesare at Sydney, in the premiere of Tatiana by Azio Corghi for La Scala Milan, and in Handel's Tamerlano at Halle. *Recordings include:* La Calisto; Handel Arias; Vivaldi, Solo Sacred Works. *Address:* c/o Australian Opera, PO Box 291, Strawberry Hills, NSW 2012, Australia.

PUSZ, Ryszard; Percussionist and Teacher; b. 5 Feb. 1948, Frille, Germany; m., 1 s., 3 d. *Education:* Studied with Richard Smith, Elder Conservatorium, and with George Gaber, Indiana University. *Career:* Music teacher 1970–73; Worked in Education Department of South Australia Music Branch 1974–86; Head of Percussion, School of Music, ACTAFE 1986–; Commissioned and premiered over 50 works for Percussion, and performed Australian premieres of numerous works of prominent overseas composers; Arranged many pieces for Percussion Solo and Ensemble; Orchestral Percussionist with Australian Youth Orchestra, 1964–70, Adelaide Symphony Orchestra, Adelaide Chamber Orchestra, 1964–90; Performed as Soloist with many orchestras and ensembles including Hungarian Youth Orchestra, Adelaide Symphony Orchestra, Prague Conservatory Percussion Ensemble, Stuttgart Musikhochschule Percussion Ensemble, Corpus Christi Percussion Ensemble (USA) at numerous festivals including International Percussion Festival, Bydgoszcz (Poland), Adelaide Festival of Arts, Banff Festival (Canada), International Barossa Music Festival, Perkusja 2001, Warsaw (Poland), as well as at major music academies and concert halls throughout Europe, USA, the Far East, and Australia; Has conducted various percussion ensembles and other performing groups; Discovered and developed a new, one-handed tremolo technique, applied in existing and new commissioned pieces; Has worked with filmmakers, theatre directors, and visual artists to produce performance projects for educational puproses and other productions; Music Director COME OUT '93 Festival; Pioneered the teaching of instrumental music by Distance Mode in Australia; Founded The Percussion Society of Australia, Adelaide Percussions, Sonitus, Drumworks and Percusson (a double father-son percussion quartet). *Compositions include:* Baltika (Steelband); Drumworks Quintet for 75 Players; Keep on Drummin!; Three Camps Thrice; ForE (multiple perscussion solo); Tsunami (Taiko ensemble). *Publications:* Percussion: A Comprehensive Approach; Time and Again: Essentials of Percussion Practice. *Honours:* Sounds Australian Awards for Most Significant Contribution by a South Australian to the Presentation of Australian Music, and Australia Council Fellowship to present Australian compositions overseas. *Address:* School of Music, Adelaide Institute of TAFE, 279 Flinders Street, Adelaide, SA 5000, Australia. *E-mail:* rpusz@camtech.net.au.

PUTILIN, Nikolai; Singer (baritone); b. 1953, Russia. *Career:* Principal with the Kirov Opera at the Mariinsky Theatre, St Petersburg; Roles have included Verdi's Iago, Posa, Rigoletto, Amonasro, Germont and Don Carlo (Forza); Scarpia, Escamillo, Eugene Onegin, Figaro, Tomsky (The Queen of Spades), Rubinstein's Demon, Prince Igor, Ruprecht (The Fiery Angel), Rangoni (Boris Godunov) and Mizgir in The Snow Maiden; Guest with the Kirov at the Metropolitan New York, Milan, Hamburg and Japan; Edinburgh Festival, 1995, in Rimsky's Sadko and Invisible City of Kitezh; Boris Godunov at the 1995 Birmingham Festival, and the posthumous premiere of Karetnikov's Apostle Paul's Mystery; Scarpia at the 1995 Savonlinna Festival; Drury Lane, London, 1997, with the Kirov Company, as Boris; Don Carlo in La Forza del Destino at St Petersburg, 1998; Season 2000–01 as Barnaba in La Gioconda at the Deutsche Oper Berlin, Mussorgsky's Shakloviti on tour with the Kirov Opera at Covent Garden (also as Tchaikovsky's Mazeppa); Tomsky in The Queen of Spades in Chicago and London, with futher appearances at Monte Carlo and San Franscisco in Iolanta and Simon Boccanegra. *Current Management:* Askonas Holt Ltd, Lonsdale Chambers, 27 Chancery Lane, London, WC2A 1PF, England. *Telephone:* (20) 7400-1700. *Fax:* (20) 7400-1799. *E-mail:* info@askonasholt.co.uk. *Website:* www.askonasholt.co.uk.

PUTKONEN, Marko; Singer (Bass); b. 1947, Finland. *Education:* Studied at the Sibelius Academy, Helsinki. *Career:* At the Finnish National Opera has sung Mozart's Bartolo, Nicolai's Falstaff, in Katerina Izmailova, Sallinen's Red Line and the 1990 premiere of Rautavaara's Vincent (as Gauguin); Guested at Los Angeles, 1992, in the premiere of Kullervo by Sallinen; Further guest appearances at the Savonlinna Festival (Rocco, 1992), Zürich and Geneva. *Address:* Finnish National Opera, 23–27 Bulevardi, 00180 Helsinki, Finland.

PUTNAM, Ashley; Singer (Soprano); b. 10 Aug. 1952, New York, USA. *Education:* University of Michigan, with Elizabeth Mosher and Willis Patterson. *Career:* Norfolk Opera, Virginia, from 1976 as Donizetti's Lucia and the title role in the US premiere of Musgrave's Mary Queen of Scots; NYC Opera debut, 1978, as Violetta; Later sang Bellini's Elvira, Verdi's Giselda, Thomas' Ophelia and Donizetti's Maria Stuarda; European debut 1978 as Musetta at Glyndebourne; Returned for Arabella 1984; Lucia with Scottish Opera; Mozart's Fiordiligi at Venice and for BBC television, Sifare in Mitridate at Aix, Donna Anna in Brussels and Countess Almaviva in Cologne; Covent Garden debut 1986, as Janáček's Jenůfa; Appearances at Santa Fe in Thomson's The Mother of us All and in the title role of Die Liebe der Danaë, 1985; Metropolitan Opera debut 1990, as Donna Elvira; Florence 1990, as Katya Kabanova; Sang Ellen Orford in Peter Grimes at the Geneva Opera and Vitellia in La Clemenza di Tito at the 1991 Glyndebourne Festival; Season 1991–92 as Fusako in the US premiere of Henze's Das Verratere Meer, at San Francisco, and the Marshallin at Santa Fe; Eva in Die Meistersinger at Cleveland, 1995; Sang St Teresa I in Thomson's Four Saints in Three Acts, Houston and Edinburgh, 1996; Concert engagements with the Los Angeles Philharmonic, New York Philharmonic and Concertgebouw Orchestras; Regular concerts at Carnegie Hall. *Recordings:* The Mother of us All; Mary Queen of Scots; Musetta in La Bohème. *Address:* c/o Los Angeles Opera, 135 N. Grand Ave, Los Angeles, CA 90012, USA.

PUTTEN, Thea van der; Singer (Soprano); b. 1950, Eindhoven, Netherlands. *Education:* Studied at the Hague Conservatory. *Career:* Sang in the 1980 Holland Festival and with Netherlands Opera in La Cenerentola, Hansel and Gretel, Die Zauberflöte and La Vie Parisienne; Nedda in Pagliacci, 1985; Komische Oper Berlin, 1988, as Donna Elvira, and in the 1986 premiere of Ketting's Ithaka, at the opening of the Amsterdam Muziektheater; Many concert engagements; Teaches singing at the Royal Conservatory, The Hague. *Recordings include:* Die Zauberflöte. *Address:* Netherlands Opera, Waterlooplein 22, 1001 PS Amsterdam, Netherlands.

PÜTZ, Ruth-Margret; Singer (Soprano); b. 26 Feb. 1931, Krefeld, Germany. *Education:* Studied with Bertold Putz in Krefeld. *Career:* Debut: Cologne 1950, as Nuri in Tiefland by d'Albert; Sang at Hanover 1951–57; Stuttgart from 1957, notably as Gilda and Zerbinetta; Bayreuth Festival 1960, as Waldvogel; Salzburg Festival 1961, as Constanze in Die Entfuhrung; Russian Tour with the Capella Coloniensis 1961; Hamburg Staatsoper 1963–68; Guest appearances in Buenos Aires, Helsinki, Frankfurt, Munich, Nice, Rome, Venice, Naples and Barcelona; Other roles included Cimarosa's Carolina, Mozart's Susanna, Pamina and Despina, Lucia di Lammermoor, Rosina, Adina, Norina in Don Pasquale, Violetta, Musetta, Liu in Turandot and Sophie in Der Rosenkavalier. *Recordings:* Bach's Magnificat; Die Lustigen Weiber von Windsor; Lortzing's Undine; Il Barbiere di Siviglia; Queen of Night in Die Zauberflöte; Trionfo by Orff. *Address:* c/o Bayerische Staatsoper, Postfach 745, 8000 Munich 1, Germany.

PUUMALA, Veli-Matti; Finnish composer; b. 18 July 1965, Kaustinen. *Education:* Sibelius Acad., Helsinki, Accademia Musicale Chigiana summer course with Franco Donatoni, Siena. *Compositions include:* Scroscio 1989, Verso 1991, Ghirlande 1992, Line to Clash 1993, Tutta via 1993, String Quartet 1994, Chant Chains 1995, Chains of Camenae 1996, Soira 1996, Chainsprings 1997, Umstrichen vom Schreienden 1997–98, Taon concerto for double bass 1998–2000, Hommages Fugitives 2000–01, Seeds of Time piano concerto 2004, Credenza 2005. *Current Management:* c/o Fennica Gehrman, PO Box 158, 00121 Helsinki, Finland. *E-mail:* info@fennicagehrman.fi (office). *Website:* www.fennicagehrman.fi (office).

PUYANA, Rafael; Harpsichordist; b. 4 Oct. 1931, Bogotá, Colombia. *Education:* Studied under Wanda Landowska. *Career:* Now lives in France but gives performances throughout the world; Festival appearances at: Berlin; Ansbach; Netherlands; Aldeburgh; Harrogate; Besançon; Aix-en-Provence; BBC television, 1985, with Sonatas by Scarlatti. *Recordings:* Records for major recording companies. *Address:* c/o Miss M Garnham, 8 St George's Terrace, London, NW1 8XJ, England.

PY, Gilbert; Singer (Tenor); b. 9 Dec. 1933, Sete, France. *Career:* Debut: Verviers, Belgium, 1964 as Pinkerton in Madama Butterfly; Paris Opéra from 1969, notably as Manrico, Don José, Samson, Florestan, Tannhäuser, Lohengrin and in La Damnation de Faust; Paris Opéra-Comique 1969, in the title role of Les Contes d'Hoffmann; Nice Opéra in the local premiere of Sutermeister's Raskolnikov; Toulouse 1970, in Gounod's La Reine de Saba; Guest appearances in Vienna, Munich, Verona, Florence, Barcelona, New Orleans and Budapest; Turin 1973, as Lohengrin; Sang at the 1987 Orange Festival as Jean in Massenet's Hérodiade; Aeneas in Les Troyens at Marseilles 1989. *Recordings include:* Carmen (RCA); La Vestale by Spontini. *Address:* c/o Opéra de Marseille, 2 rue Moliére, 1323 Marseille Cédex 01, France.

PYATT, David; Horn player; b. 1973, England. *Career:* former Principal Horn, National Youth Orchestra and National Youth Chamber Orchestra of Great Britain; from 1988 has performed with the London Symphony and Halle Orchestras, English Chamber Orchestra and London Mozart Players; tours of Germany and Japan with the BBC National Orchestra of Wales; played the Second Concerto by Strauss at the 1993 London Proms; repertoire ranges from Telemann, Haydn and Mozart to contemporary composers; broadcast on BBC and independent television and radio; Season 1998–99 included debut at Salzburg Festival, concert with Deutsche Symphonie Orchestre, Berlin, and Promenade Concerts with BBC Symphony Orchestra; Season 2001–02 with concerts in London and Europe, as soloist in Britten's Serenade; Principal Horn, London Symphony Orchestra. *Recordings include:* Strauss Concerti; Britten Serenade; Mozart Concerti. *Honours:* Gramophone Magazine's Young Artist of the Year, 1996. *Current Management:* Askonas Holt Ltd, Lonsdale Chambers, 27 Chancery Lane, London, WC2A 1PF, England. *Telephone:* (20) 7400-1700. *Fax:* (20) 7400-1799. *E-mail:* info@askonasholt.co.uk. *Website:* www.askonasholt .co.uk.

Q

QUARTARARO, Florence; American singer (soprano); b. 31 May 1922, San Francisco. *Education:* studied with Elizabeth Wells in San Francisco, Pietro Cimini in Los Angeles. *Career:* debut at Hollywood Bowl 1945, as Leonora in Il Trovatore; Metropolitan Opera from 1946 as Micaela (Carmen), Pamina, Verdi's Violetta and Desdemona and Nedda (Pagliacci); San Francisco 1947, as Donna Elvira in Don Giovanni; guest appearances at Philadelphia and elsewhere in the USA; Arena Flagrea, Naples 1953 as Margherita in Mefistofele; many concert appearances.

QUASTHOFF, Thomas; Singer (Baritone); b. Nov. 1959, Hildesheim, Germany. *Education:* Studied with Charlotte Lehmann in Hanover and with Carol Richardson; Law degree at the University of Hanover. *Career:* Many appearances at the world's leading concert halls in Oratorio and Lieder; Season 1995 with US debut at the Oregon-Bach Festival and Japan debut with the Internationale Bachakademie under Helmuth Rilling; Season 1995–96 at the Schleswig-Holstein Festival, the Herkulessaal in Munich and in Paris and Madrid; Britten's War Requiem at the Edinburgh Festival under Donald Runnicles; Season 1996–97 with the English Chamber Orchestra, Berlin Philharmonic under Rattle and the Chamber Orchestra of Europe under Abbado; Schubert Bicentenary concerts 1997, including Wigmore Hall recital and Winterreise for television; Sang in Mahler's Des Knaben Wunderhorn at the Edinburgh Festival, 2002; Engaged as Don Fernando in Fidelio, Salzburg 2003. *Recordings include:* Bach Cantatas (Bayer); St John Passion and Schumann Lieder (BMG); Schubert Goethe-Lieder, Fidelio under Colin Davis and Mozart Arias (BMG); Des Knaben Wunderhorn, by Mahler, with Anne Sofie von Otter, 2001. *Honours:* Grand Prix Gabriel Fauré, Paris, for Schumann Lieder. *Current Management:* Ingpen & Williams Ltd, 7 St George's Court, 131 Putney Bridge Road, London, SW15 2PA, England.

QUEFFÉLEC, Anne; Concert Pianist; b. 17 Jan. 1948, Paris, France; m. 2 c. *Education:* Studied at the Paris Conservatoire and in Vienna with Paul Badura-Skoda, Jörg Demus and Alfred Brendel. *Career:* Solo recitals and orchestral concerts from 1969 in Europe, Japan, USA, Israel and Canada; Conductors include James Conlon, Rudolf Barshai, Colin Davis, Pierre Boulez, Theodor Guschlbauer, Charles Groves, Heinz Holliger, Armin Jordan, Raymond Leppard, David Zinman, Neville Marriner, Jerzy Semkov, Neeme Järvi, J E Gardiner and Stanislav Skrowaczewski; British appearances with all the BBC Symphony Orchestras, the Royal Liverpool Philharmonic, Bournemouth Symphony, Hallé, Scottish Chamber, Northern Sinfonia, Royal Philharmonic, City of Birmingham Symphony, Paris National Orchestra, Lille, Philharmonique de Strasbourg, Tokyo NHK Orchestra, Hong Kong Philharmonic, Gothenburg Symphony and the London Symphony; Concerts at the Proms in London, Cheltenham, Bath, King's Lynn Festivals; Chamber music recitals with Pierre Amoyal, Augustin Dumay, Régis Pasquier, Frederic Lodéon, the Chilingirian Quartet, Endellion Quartet and Imogen Cooper (piano duo). *Recordings:* Works by Scarlatti, Chopin, Schubert, Liszt, Ravel, Mendelssohn, Fauré, Hummel and Debussy; Complete solo works of Satie and Ravel, Dutilleux, Poulenc's Concerto for Two Pianos. *Honours:* 1st Prizes for piano and for chamber music at the Paris Conservatoire, 1965, 1966; Winner, Munich International, 1968; 5th Prize, Leeds International, 1969; Victoire de la Musique Awards, Best French Classical Artist of the Year, 1990; Chevalier de la Légion d'Honneur, France, 1997; Officier de l'ordre du Mérite, 2002. *Address:* 15 Avenue Corneille, 78600 Maisons Lafitte, France.

QUELER, Eve; Conductor and Director of Opera; b. 1 Jan. 1936, New York, USA; m. Stanley N Queler, 1 s., 1 d. *Education:* High School of Music and Art, NY; City University of New York; Mannes College of Music, New York; Graduate Conducting studies with Joseph Rosenstock, at American Institute of Conducting under auspices of St Louis Symphony, with Walter Susskind and Leonard Slatkin and at Concours de Monte Carlo with Igor Markevitch and Herbert Blomstedt. *Career:* Founder, Director and Conductor of Opera Orchestra of New York, 1968–; National Opera Orchestra workshop created for her by University of Maryland, 1978; Guest Conductor for Cleveland and Philadelphia Orchestras, symphonies of Edmonton, Toledo Jacksonville, Kansas City, New Jersey, Hartford, Chautauqua, Montreal, Puerto Rico and Colorado Springs, Michigan Chamber Orchestra and Fort Wayne Philharmonic; Opera Companies include Gran Teatro Liceo, Barcelona, St Louis, Chattanooga, Providence, Shreveport, San Diego, Sydney Australia, Opera South, Opéra de Nice, Oberlin Opera Festival in Lyon, Opera Metropolitan in Caracas, National Theatre of Czechoslovakia, Orchestra Lyrique on Radio France and New York City Opera; conducted Rossini's Armida at Carnegie Hall, 1996. *Recordings include:* Puccini's Edgar; Donizetti's Gemma di Vergy; Verdi's Aroldo; Boito's Nerone. *Contributions:* An American Conductor in Prague.

Honours: Martha Baird Rockefeller Fund for Music Study Grant, 1970; Honorary Doctorates from Russell Sage College, 1978 and Colby College, 1983. *Current Management:* Herbert Barrett Management, 1776 Broadway, Ste 504, New York, NY 10019, USA. *Address:* Vincent and Robbins Associates, 124 East 40th Street, Ste 304, New York, NY 10016, USA.

QUILICO, Gino; Singer (Baritone); b. 29 April 1955, New York, USA. *Education:* Graduated University of Toronto 1978; Vocal studies with Lina Pizzolongo and his father. *Career:* Canadian debut 1978, in a television performance of The Medium; Member of the Paris Opéra from 1980, in operas by Rossini, Britten, Poulenc, Puccini, Gounod, Massenet, and Gluck; British debut with Scottish Opera at the 1982 Edinburgh Festival, as Puccini's Lescaut; Covent Garden debut 1983, as Valentin in Faust; later London appearances as Puccini's Marcello, Donizetti's Belcore, Rossini's Figaro, Escamillo and Posa in Don Carlos (1989); Aix-en-Provence Festival 1985 and 1986, as Monteverdi's Orfeo and Mozart's Don Giovanni; Metropolitan Opera debut 1987, as Massenet's Lescaut; Malatesta in Don Pasquale at Lyon; Sang Dandini in La Cenerentola at the 1988 and 1989 Salzburg Festivals; Rome Opera 1990, as Riccardo in I Puritani; Sang Gluck's Oreste at the 1994 Vienna Festival; Sang Iago at Cologne, 1996; Sang Escamillo at Metropolitan Opera and Munich Festival, 1997; Zurga in Les Pêcheurs de Perles at Chicago and Barber of Seville in Seville, 1998; Season 1999–2000 as Donizetti's Enrico at Los Angeles, Massenet's Lescaut for La Scala, Iago in Montreal and Escamillo at the Munich Staatsoper. *Recordings include:* Lescaut in Manon (EMI); Dancairo in Carmen (Deutsche Grammophon); Mercutio in Roméo et Juliette (EMI); Marcello in La Bohème and Malatesta in Don Pasquale (Erato); Video of 1988 Salzburg Cenerentola. *Address:* c/o IMG Artists, Lovell House, 616 Chiswick High Road, London W4 5RX, England.

QUILLA CROFT, Howard; Singer (Baritone); b. 1966, Huddersfield, England. *Education:* Royal College of Music, London; National Opera Studio. *Career:* Debut: Mozart's Count, for the Opera Company, 1993; Appearances with Glyndebourne Touring Opera 1993–4, as Don Giovanni, A Captain in Eugene Onegin and Fiorello in Il Barbiere di Siviglia; Glyndebourne Festival 1994, in Eugene Onegin; Further engagements as Escamillo in Carmen for British Youth Opera, and Fiorello for Opera Northern Ireland. *Honours:* Cuthbert Smith and Agnes Nicholls Trophy; Kirkless Young Musician of the Year. *Address:* c/o Glyndebourne Touring Opera, Glyndebourne, Lewes, Sussex BN8 5UU, England.

QUING, Miao; Singer (mezzo-soprano); b. 1955, China. *Education:* Peking Conservatory. *Career:* Sang Carmen under the direction of Jacqueline Brumaire at Peking, 1982; Studied further at the Nancy Conservatoire and sang Butterfly from 1986 at Basle, Berlin, Lausanne, Toulon and Covent Garden; Guested with the Peking Opera at Savonlinna as Carmen, sang Donna Elvira at Brunswick (1991) and in Ariadne and Zauberflöte at the Bonn Opera; Many concert engagements. *Address:* Oper der Stadt Bonn, Am Boeselagerhof 1, Pf 2440, 5300 Bonn, Germany.

QUINN, Andrea, BA; British conductor and music director; b. 22 Dec. 1964; m. Roderick Champ 1991; one s. two d. *Education:* Royal Acad. of Music, London, Nottingham Univ.; Bartók Int. Seminar, Hungary. *Career:* Music Dir London Philharmonic Youth Orchestra 1994–97, Royal Ballet 1998–2001; Music Dir New York City Ballet 2001–; has conducted London Symphony Orchestra, London Philharmonic, Philharmonia, Royal Philharmonic, Hallé, Scottish Chamber, Northern Sinfonia, London Mozart Players and other leading orchestras in UK, Australia, Hong Kong, Sweden, Norway, Italy, Singapore; operas and music theatre pieces conducted include Misper (Glyndebourne), Four Saints in Three Acts (ENO), Harrison Birtwistle's Pulse Shadows (UK tour), Royal Opera House debut conducting Royal Ballet's Anastasia and on tour Cinderella in Turin and Frankfurt and Swan Lake in Japan, China and N America; Fellow Trinity Coll. of Music 2000, Assoc. Royal Acad. of Music 2001. *Dance:* conducted world premiere of Saint-Saens's Carnival of the Animals (choreography Christopher Wheeldon) 2003, Double Feature (Susan Stroman) 2004. *Current Management:* Nicholas Curry, Clarion/Seven Muses, 47 Whitehall Park, London, N19 3TW, England. *Address:* New York City Ballet, New York State Theater, New York City, NY (office); 325 North Broadway, Nyack, NY 10960, USA (home). *Telephone:* (212) 870-5570 (office); (20) 7272-4413. *E-mail:* nick@c7m.co.uk (office). *Website:* www.nycballet.com (office).

QUINN, Gerard; Singer (Baritone); b. 1962, Irvine, Scotland; m. Heather Lorimer, 1 d. *Education:* Studied flute at Napier College, Edinburgh; Singing at The Royal Northern College of Music, Manchester with Patrick McGuigan; The National Opera Studio, London; In Vienna with

Otto Edelmann and presently with Iris Dell'Acqua. *Career:* Early appearances as Golaud in Pelléas et Mélisande, Escamillo, Mozart's Count and Junius in The Rape of Lucretia; Buxton Festival Opera 1985; Glyndebourne Festival debut 1987, in Capriccio; Glyndebourne Tour, 1988, in La Traviata; Scottish Opera debut 1989, Donner, (Das Rheingold); English National Opera debut 1990, as Pantaloon, (The Love for Three Oranges), also for New Israeli Opera; Royal Opera, Covent Garden debut Flemish Deputy, (Don Carlo), 1989; Meru, (Les Huguenots), 1991 and in 1994 Le Comte in the British premiere of Massenet's Chérubin; Welsh National Opera debut, 1993, Enrico, (Lucia di Lammermoor), 1995, Father, Hansel and Gretel, Germont, (La Traviata); Bath and Wessex Opera, title role Rigoletto, 1994; English Touring Opera, 1994, Marcello, La Bohème; European Chamber Opera 1993, Count di Luna, Il Trovatore (also recorded), 1994 Count Alamaviva, Le nozze di Figaro and Rigoletto; Crystal Clear Opera, Sharpless, Madama Butterfly, 1995; Other roles performed include Nabucco, Germont, Ford, Michele in Il Tabarro, Tonio, Pagliacci, Zurga in The Pearl Fishers, Malatesta, Don Pasquale, Danilo in The Merry Widow, Don Giovanni and Eugene Onegin; Sang Rolla in I Masnadieri for the Royal Opera in Savonlinna, 1997; Concert repertoire includes Elijah, Carmina Burana, Sea Symphony, Dream of Gerontius, Brahms Requiem and Britten's War Requiem. *Address:* c/o International Opera and Concert Artists, 75 Aberdare Gardens, London NW6 3AN, England.

QUITTMEYER, Susan; Singer (Mezzo-soprano); b. 1955, USA; m. James Morris. *Education:* Studied at Wesleyan University, Illinois, and at the Manhattan School of Music. *Career:* Sang with the America Opera Project, notably in the premiere of John Harbison's A Winter's Tale, at San Francisco, 1979; Guested at St Louis (debut in a revival of Martin y Soler's L'Arbore di Diana, 1978), and sang further at San Francisco from 1981; Sang in Montreal from 1983, Los Angeles 1984; Santa Fe 1984–88, notably in the US premiere of Henze's We Come to the River; Further US appearances in Philadelphia, Cincinnati and San Diego; Sang the Messenger in Monteverdi's Orfeo at Geneva (1986) and Sesto in Giulio Cesare at the Paris Opéra, 1987; Further European engagements as Octavian for Netherlands Opera, Cherubino and Annius at Munich and Zerlina at the Vienna Staatsoper; Salzburg Festival debut 1991, as Idamantes in Idomeneo; Concerts with the Los Angeles Philharmonic and the Symphony Orchestras of Oakland, Sacramento and San Francisco; Metropolitan Opera from 1987 as Nicklausse in Les Contes d'Hoffmann and Dorabella; Sang Varvara in Katya Kabanova and Siebel with James Morris, 1991; Other roles include Meg Page, Cherubino, the Composer in Ariadne, Carmen, Pauline (The Queen of Spades) and Zerlina (Miami 1988); Engaged as Siebel at San Francisco, 1995; Many concert appearances. *Address:* c/o Metropolitan Opera, Lincoln Center, New York, NY 10023, USA.

QUIVAR, Florence; Singer (Mezzo-Soprano); b. 3 March 1944, Philadelphia, USA. *Education:* Philadelphia Academy of Music; Juilliard School New York. *Career:* Concert appearances with the New York, Los Angeles and Israel Philharmonics, the Cleveland, Philadelphia and Mostly Mozart Festival Orchestras and the Boston Symphony; Conductors include Mehta, Bernstein, Leinsdorf, Boulez, Muti and Colin Davis; Metropolitan Opera debut 1977, as Marina in Boris Godunov: returned to New York for Jocasta (Oedipus Rex); Isabella (L'Italiana in Algeri), Fides (Le Prophète) and Serena in Porgy and Bess; Guest appearances in Berlin, Florence, Geneva, Montreal and San Francisco; Recent engagements include La Damnation de Faust in Geneva, the Wesendonk Lieder in Madrid and London, the Verdi Requiem with the Philharmonia Orchestra, Mahler's 3rd Symphony with the New York Philharmonic and performances with the Berlin Philharmonic under Giulini; Festival appearances with the Israel Philharmonic in Salzburg, London, Lucerne, Florence and Edinburgh; Sang Ulrica in Un ballo in maschera at the 1990 Salzburg Festival (also televised); Season 1990/91 with Mahler's 2nd and 3rd symphonies (La Scala and New York, and in Japan); Met Opera as Federica in Luisa Miller; Gurrelieder under Zubin Mehta; London Proms 1991, in The Dream of Gerontius; Sang in the Met Opera Gala concert, 1996; Goddess in the premiere of La Amistad by A Davis, Chicago, 1998; Sang Brangaene at Houston, 2000. *Recordings:* Rossini's Stabat Mater (Vox); Mahler's 8th Symphony under Seiji Ozawa (Philips); Mendelssohn's Midsummer Night's Dream (Deutsche Grammophon); Berlioz's Romeo and Juliet (Erato); Virgil Thomson's Four Saints in Three Acts (Nonesuch); Verdi Requiem; Un ballo in maschera conducted by Karajan (Deutsche Grammophon); Luisa Miller (Sony); Schoenberg's Gurrelieder. *Address:* Kaye Artists Management, Barratt House, 7 Chertsey Road, Woking, Surrey GU21 3 AB, England.

R

RABES, C.-A. Lennart; Pianist, Harpsichordist, Organist and Conductor, Lecturer, Editor and Examiner; b. 1938, Eskilstuna, Sweden. *Education:* Music Academy, Zürich; Accademia Chigiana, Siena; ARCM, London; Studied Piano with Professor S Sundell, Stockholm, E Cavallo, Milan, B Siki, Zürich, M Tagliaferro, Paris; J von Karolyi, Munich; Studied Conducting with Paul von Kempen, Siena, Adrian Boult, London; BA, Music, Pacific Western University, Los Angeles, California, 1992. *Career:* Debut: As Pianist and Conductor, Stockholm, 1951; Performances in major cities of Europe, Canada and USA; Many recordings for Swedish, Austrian, French, Swiss and German broadcasting companies; Director, International Liszt Centre, Stockholm; Organist, various churches, Munich, 1960–66, Swiss Church, London, 1966–78; Founder, Musical Director, Deal Summer Music Festival, Deal, Kent, England, 1981–83, Sabylund Festival, Sweden, 1985–; Repetiteur at Norrlandsopera, Umea, 1985–88; Has given concerts at historical places including on Wagner's Erard at the Wagner Museum, Tribschen, Lucerne, Switzerland, 1985; Lecturer for research associations, universities radio and conservatories; Examiner, Associated Board, Royal Schools of Music, London; Working at Operastudio 67, Stockholm. *Recordings:* Piano works by Liszt. *Publications:* Liszt's Scandinavian Reputation, in Liszt and His World, 1998. *Address:* Synalsvagen 5, 16149 Bromma, Stockholm, Sweden.

RABIN, Shira; Violinist; b. 1 April 1970, Tel-Aviv, Israel. *Education:* Studied at the Juilliard School with Dorothy DeLay. *Career:* Debut: Played with the Israel Philharmonic 1979; Appeared in the International Huberman Week with Isaac Stern and the Israel Philharmonic 1983; Toured Europe 1983, Canada coast-to-coast tour 1985; Played with Henryk Szeryng during Israel Philharmonic Jubilee Season 1987; Soloist in the Stradivarius Year in Cremona; Israel representative in Italian Nights of Music with Zubin Mehta; Gala concert at Carnegie Hall with Isaac Stern; Musical Discovery of 1989 in Italy, after recital debut in Milan; German debut Feb 1991, with the Bavarian Radio Symphony Orchestra; US debut 1992 with the Philadelphia Orchestra under Riccardo Muti; Further concerts with the Pittsburgh Orchestra under Lorin Maazel. *Address:* c/o Israel Philharmonic Orchestra, PO Box 11292, 1 Huberman St, 61112 Tel-Aviv, Israel.

RABSILBER, Michael; Singer (Tenor); b. 8 Sept. 1953, Stassfurt, Magdeburg, Germany. *Education:* Studied at Leipzig Musikhochschule. *Career:* Debut: Stadttheater Halle 1980 in Wagner-Régeny's Die Burger von Calais; Sang at Halle until 1984 then joined the Komische Oper Berlin, with guest appearances in Leipzig and Dresden; Roles have included Mozart's Belmonte and Don Ottavio, Lensky, Ferrando Tamino, Max in Der Freischütz, Nicolai's Fenton and Pinkerton; Sang Zhivny in a production by Joachim Herz of Janáček's Osud, Dresden 1991; Florestan in Fidelio at the Komische Oper, 1997; Season 2000 as Fenton in Berlin and Tamino at the Loreley Festival; Frequent concert engagements. *Address:* c/o Komische Oper Berlin, Behrenstrasse 55–57, 1086 Berlin, Germany.

RACETTE, Patricia; Singer (Soprano); b. 1967, San Francisco, USA. *Education:* Studied with the Merola Opera Program, San Francisco. *Career:* Has sung with the San Francisco Opera from 1990, as Alice Ford, Rosalinde, Freia, Micaela, Mimi, Antonia and Mathilde in Guillaume Tell, 1997; Other roles include Musetta for Netherlands Opera and at the Metropolitan (1994), Ellen Orford for Vancouver Opera and Gluck's Iphigénie en Tauride at Saint Louis; Further appearances with the New York City and Vienna State Operas; Concerts include the Messa per Rossini and Stephen Albert's Flower in the Mountain, at San Francisco; Sang Emmeline Mostover in the premiere of Tobias Picker's Emmeline, Santa Fe, 1996, Mathilde at Washington, 1998; Sang Violetta and Offenbach's Antonia at the Met, 1999; Season 2000–01 as Ellen Orford at La Scala, Luisa Miller for San Francisco Opera and Jenůfa in Washington; Poulenc's Blanche at the Met, 2003. *Address:* c/o IMG Artists, Lovell House, 616 Chiswick High Road, London W4 5RX, England.

RADETA, Zdenko; Composer and Conductor; b. 16 Sept. 1955, Kragujevac, Yugoslavia; m. Miroslava Jankovic, 28 Sept. 1980, 2 s., 1 d. *Education:* Department of Composition and Orchestration and Department of Conducting, Faculty of Music, Belgrade; Advanced studies at Tchaikovsky Conservatoire, Moscow, 1991–92. *Career:* Debut: Four Sketches for chamber ensemble, 1974; Singer in Choir, Radio Television Belgrade; Producer, Radio Belgrade; Professor of Harmony and Counterpoint, Mokranjac Intermediate School, Belgrade; mem, Association of Composers of Serbia; SOKOJ. *Compositions:* 9 Piano pieces, 1972–90; Solo songs, 1974–84; 12 works for choirs, 1974–87; 1st String Quartet, 1980; Caleidoscope for 15 strings, 1985; Caleidoscope 2 for symphony orchestra, 1988; Gloomy Songs, Cyclus songs for voice, cor anglais and piano, 1998. *Recordings:* Permanent recordings for Radio Television Belgrade including Caleidoscope 2, 1st String Quartet, Remembrance for flute and piano, Wedding for mixed choir, and ballet Verities; Gloomy Songs, 1999. *Honours:* October Prize, City of Belgrade, 1974; SOKOJ Awards, 1983, 1984; 6 Awards from Association of Composers of Serbia. *Address:* Jurija Gagarina 186/4, 11070 Belgrade, Serbia and Montenegro.

RADIGUE, Eliane; Composer; b. 24 Jan. 1932, Paris, France; m. Arman, 17 Feb 1953, divorced 1971, 1 s., 2 d. *Education:* Studied with Pierre Schaeffer, Pierre Henry; School of the Arts, New York University, University of Iowa, California Institute of the Arts, USA. *Career:* Work with electronic sounds on tape; Recent performances: Salon des Artistes Decorateurs, Paris; Foundation Maeght, St Paul de Vence; Albany Museum of the Arts, New York; Gallery Rive Droite, Paris; Gallery Sonnabend, New York; Gallery Yvon Lambert, Paris; etc; Festivals including: Como, Italy; Paris Autumn; Festival Estival, Paris; International Festival of Music, Bourges, France; New York Cultural Center; Experimental Intermedia Foundation, New York; Vanguard Theater, Los Angeles; Mills College, Oakland, California; University of Iowa; Wesleyan University; San Francisco Art Institute. *Compositions include:* Environmental Music, 1969; OHMNT-Record Object, 1971; Labyrinthe Sonore, tape music, 1971; Chry-ptus, 1971; Geelriandre, 1972; Biogenesis, 1974; Adnos, 1975; Adnos II, 1980; Adnos III, 1982; Prelude a Milarepa, 1982; 5 songs of Milarepa, 1984; Jetsun Mila, 1986. *Recordings:* Songs of Milarepa, New York; Mila's Journey Inspired by a Dream; Jetsun Mila, New York. *Contributions:* Musique en Jeu, 1973; Art Press, 1974; Guide Musical, 1975. *Address:* 22 rue Liancourt, 75014 Paris, France.

RADNOFSKY, Kenneth (Alan); Saxophonist; b. 31 July 1953, Bryn Mawr, Pennsylvania, USA; m. Nancy Abramchuk, 1 May 1977, 2 d. *Education:* BM cum laude, University of Houston, Texas; MM, with honours, New England Conservatory of Music, Boston. *Career:* Carnegie Hall debut, 1985 Performance of Gunther Schuller Saxophone Concerto written for Radnofsky; European debut, 1987 with Leipzig Gewandhaus Orchestra as first ever Saxophone Soloist under direction of Kurt Masur; First ever saxophone soloist with Dresden Staatskapelle Orchestra and Pittsburgh Symphony Orchestra; Solo works premiered or dedicated to Radnofsky by Milton Babbitt, Donald Martino, Gunther Schuller, Morton Subotnick, Lee Hoiby, David Amram, Alan Hovhaness and John Harbison; Saxophonist with Boston Symphony, 1977–; Soloist with BBC, Boston Pops and numerous USA orchestras. *Recordings:* Soloist with New York Philharmonic in Debussy Rhapsody with Masur on Teldec, 1996; Bass clarinet in Schoenberg Kammersymphonie with Felix Galimir. *Contributions:* Numerous articles in Saxophone Journal. *Honours:* Appointed youngest member of Faculty, New England Conservatory, 1976. *Address:* PO Box 1016, E Arlington, MA 02174, USA.

RADOVAN, Ferdinand; Singer (baritone); b. 26 Jan. 1938, Rijeka, Yugoslavia. *Education:* Studied in Belgrade. *Career:* Debut: Belgrade National Opera 1964 as Germont; Sang at Ljubljana 1965–67, Graz 1967–74, Dortmund 1974–77; Guest appearances at Vienna Volksoper, Düsseldorf, Essen, Bordeaux and Prague and the State Operas of Hamburg and Munich; Returned to Yugoslavia 1977; Other roles have included Escamillo, Mozart's Count and Don Giovanni, Verdi's Rigoletto, Nabucco, Amonasro, Renato, Luna and Iago; Prince Igor, Scarpia, Barnaba in La Gioconda, Nélusko in L'Africaine, Jochanaan, Enrico, Gérard and Milhaud's Christophe Colombe; Concert and oratorio engagements. *Address:* Slovensko Narodno Gledalisce, Zupancicava 1, 61000 Ljubljana, Slovenia.

RAE, Caroline (Anne); Pianist and Musicologist; b. 7 Jan. 1961, Leeds, England; m. Peter Whittaker, 20 Aug 1993, two s. *Education:* BA, 1982, MA, 1986, DPhil, 1990, Somerville College, Oxford; Hochschule für Musik und Theater, Hannover, Germany, 1985–88, DiplMus (Distinction), 1988; Piano studies with Fanny Waterman, David Wilde, Yvonne Loriod-Messiaen, masterclasses with Karl-Heinz Kämmerling; French Government Scholarship, 1982–83; ARCM, 1984. *Career:* Debut: 1982; As pianist: Recitals, lecture-recitals, chamber music, masterclasses in the United Kingdom, Germany and France; Two-piano duo with Robert Sherlaw Johnson; Appearances for BBC television and Channel 4; As musicologist: College Tutor, Oxford University, 1984–88; Lecturer in Piano, Oxford Polytechnic, 1984, 1988; Lecturer, Department of Music, University of Wales, Cardiff, 1989–; Radio France Broadcast, 1992; Visiting Lecturer, University of Rouen, France, 1993; University of Köln, 2000; mem, Royal Musical Association. *Publications:* The Music of Maurice Ohana, Aldershot, 2000; Articles on 20th Century French music published in English, French and German. *Contributions:* New Grove Dictionaries; Musical Times; Cahiers Debussy; Les Cahiers du CIREM; NZM; Revista Musica; Contemporary Composers. *Address:*

School of Music, Corbett Road, Cardiff University, CF10 3EB, Wales. *Telephone:* (29) 2087 4391. *Fax:* (29) 2087 4379. *E-mail:* rae@cardiff.ac .uk.

RAE, (John) Charles Bodman, MA, PhD, DMus, ARCM, FCLCM, FRSA; composer; b. 10 Aug. 1955, Catterick, England; m. Dorota Kwiatkowska 1984. *Education:* Cambridge University, Chopin Academy of Music, Warsaw; piano with Fanny Waterman; composition with Edward Cowie, Robert Sherlaw Johnson and Robin Holloway. *Career:* Broadcaster: Contributions as Writer, Presenter for BBC Radio 3 including Glocken, Cloches, Kolokola (six-hour series on European Bells); An Affair with Romanticism, features on Penderecki and Lutoslawski; Lecturer, Composition and Analysis, 1979–81, 1983–92, Head of School of Creative Studies, 1992–97, City of Leeds College of Music; Visiting Composer, University of Cincinnati College-Conservatory of Music, Ohio, USA, 1993; Director of Studies, Royal Northern College of Music, Manchester, 1997–2001; Elder Professor of Music, and Director/Dean of the Elder Conservatorium of Music, University of Adelaide, 2001–; mem, Royal Musical Association; Fellow, Royal Society of Arts; British Academy of Composers and Songwriters. *Compositions:* Six Verses of Vision, 1976; String Quartet, 1981; Jede Irdische Venus, 1982; Fulgura Frango, 1986; Donaxis Quartet, 1987. *Publications:* The Music of Lutoslawski, 1994, rev. 1999; Muzyka Lutoslawskiego, 1996; Bells in European Music. *Honours:* Fellowship, Leeds College of Music, 1999. *Address:* c/o Elder Conservatorium of Music, Elder Hall, University of Adelaide, SA 5005, Australia.

RAEKALLIO, Matti Juhani, DMus; pianist and professor; b. 14 Oct. 1954, Helsinki, Finland; m. 1st Sinikka Alstela 1977 (divorced 1996); m. 2nd Lara Lev 1998; one s. one d. *Education:* Turku Inst. of Music, private lessons with Maria Diamond Curcio, London, and with Dieter Weber, Vienna Music Acad., Austria, Leningrad Conservatory, Sibelius Acad., Finland. *Career:* debut as orchestra soloist, Turku 1971; solo, Helsinki 1975; extensive tours with all professional Finnish symphony orchestras, 1971–; recitals in Nordic countries 1971–, in Finland 1975–, in Central Europe 1979–; Recitals in USA, 1981–, in Japan, 1990–; First American tour as orchestra soloist with Helsinki Philharmonic Orchestra, 1983; Visiting Professor, Western MI University, 1984–85; Recitals in Helsinki Festival, 1981–97, Savonlinna Opera Festival, 1988–2000; Various Other Finnish and central European Festivals; Beethoven Complete Sonatas in 8 Finnish cities, 1989–91; Concerto repertoire includes over 60 works for Piano and Orchestra; Professor, Royal Swedish College of Music, Stockholm, 1994–1995; Associate Professor, Sibelius Academy, Helsinki, 1994–2001, full Professor, 2001; Member, commission for research of culture and society (Academy of Finland), 1998–2000; Board of Directors, Society for Finnish Concert Soloists.. *Recordings include:* Complete Prokofiev Sonatas; about 20 albums; numerous for the archives of the Finnish Broadcasting Company. *Contributions:* several Finnish journals of music. *Address:* c/o Sibelius Academy, Pl 86, 00251, Helsinki, Finland.

RAFFAELLI, Piero; Italian violinist and violin teacher; b. 8 April 1949, Cesena; m. Santarelli Mariangela 1975; two d. *Education:* G. B. Martini Conservatory of Music, Bologna, masterclasses with various teachers. *Career:* debut 1968, Italy; radio appearances in Italy and Norway; Italian and European Concerts with Ensemble l Cameristi di Venezia; Solo Concerts with Capella Academica of Vienna, Italy; Chamber Music Group Layer and Soloist, Italy; Europe, North America with Italian Ensembles, 1971–73; Leader, Guitar Trio Paganini (also a viola player); Duo Recitals, Barcelona, Vienna, Berlin, Olso, Trondheim, Greece, Italy; Violin Teacher, Conservatory of Music, Bologna, 1978–. *Recordings:* With Ensemble E Melkus; Wien; Solo Violin Works by M Kich (Yugoton) dedicated to him, 1981; Contemporary Violin Chamber Music Recording, 1982. *Publications:* Revisions of Violin Works in First Printing for Zanibon and Violoncelo, 1979; A Vivaldi Concerto F 1 n 237 in D for violin, strings, cembalo, 1980; N Paganini 3 Duetti Concertani for Violin and Violoncello, 1982. *Address:* Via Filli Latini 112, 47020, S. Giorgio di Cesena, Italy.

RAFFALLI, Tibère; Singer (Tenor); b. 1954, Corsica. *Career:* Sang Gabriele Adorno in Simon Boccanegra at Glyndebourne, 1986 (Gonzalve in L'Heure Espagnole, 1987); Bologna, 1987, as the Berlioz Faust, Montpellier, 1989, as Floresky in Cherubini's Lodoiska; Season 1990–91 as La ërte in Hamlet by A Thomas at Turin, Julien in Louise at Liège and Berlioz's Bénédict for Opéra de Lyon; Strasbourg, 1991, as Manalois in Martinů's Greek Passion; Other roles include Edgardo in Lucia di Lammermoor and Massenet's Werther. *Recordings include:* L'Heure Espagnole. *Address:* Opéra de Lyon, 1 Place de la Comédie, 69001 Lyon, France.

RAFFANTI, Dano; singer (tenor); b. 5 April 1948, Lucca, Italy. *Education:* La Scala School. *Career:* debut at La Scala School 1976, in Bussotti's Nottetempo; Verona 1978, in Orlando Furioso: Dallas 1980, in the US premiere of Vivaldi's opera; San Francisco 1980, as Almaviva in Il Barbiere di Siviglia; Houston 1981–82, as Giacomo in La Donna del

Lago by Rossini; Metropolitan Opera from 1981, as Alfredo, Rodolfo, the Duke of Mantua, Edgardo, Goffredo in Handel's Rinaldo and the Italian Singer in Der Rosenkavalier; Teatro San Carlos Naples and Covent Garden, 1983 and 1984, as Tebaldo in I Capuleti e i Montecchi by Bellini; Guest appearances in Hamburg, Berlin, Santiago, Bilbao and at the Landestheater Salzburg; Maggio Musicale Florence 1989, as Idomeneo; Sang the Duke of Mantua at Turin, Dec 1989; Florence 1990, as Ugo in Donizetti's Parisina; Season 1992 as Cléomène in Le Siège de Corinthe by Rossini at Genoa. *Recordings include:* Fra Diavolo (Cetra); I Capuleti e i Montecchi; La Donna del Lago.

RAFFEINER, Walter; Singer (Tenor); b. 8 April 1947, Wolfsberg, Germany. *Education:* Studied in Vienna and Cologne. *Career:* Debut: Sang at Hagen in Germany as a Baritone; Sang at Darmstadt as a Tenor, 1979 and appeared at Frankfurt from 1980 as Max, Parsifal, Florestan, Stolzius in Die Soldaten and the Painter and Negro in Lulu; Sang at Rouen and the Paris Opéra 1982, as Siegmund and Lohengrin; Guest appearances in Hamburg, Freiburg, Vienna, Düsseldorf and Munich; Salzburg Festival 1986, as Silvanus Schuller in the premiere of Penderecki's Schwarze Maske; Appeared as Siegmund with the Kassel Opera at the restored Amsterdam Opera House; Other roles have included Tristan, Pedro in Tiefland, Ivanovich in The Gambler, Sergei in Katerina Izmailova, Shuisky, Herod, Yannakos in Martinů's Greek Passion and Tichon in Katya Kabanova; Sang in the premiere of Lampersberg's Einöde der Welt, Bonn, 1995; Sang in the premiere of Gute Meine böses spiel by Karl-Wieland Kurz, Schwetzingen 2000. *Recordings:* Drum Major in Wozzeck.

RAFFELL, Anthony; Singer (Baritone); b. 1940, London, England. *Career:* Sang first with a touring company with the works of Gilbert and Sullivan; Opera debut at Glyndebourne 1966, in Werther by Massenet; Sang at Gelsenkirchen, Karlsruhe and Bremen; Debut, Covent Garden as Pantheus in The Trojans, 1969; Member of the Stuttgart Opera from 1985; Metropolitan Opera debut 1983, as Kurwenal, in Tristan und Isolde, returning as Hans Sachs, 1985; Appearances in Ring Cycles with the English National Opera and in Seattle; Further appearances as Klingsor in Turin, Wotan in Genoa, Jochanaan in Rio de Janeiro, Falstaff in Lisbon and at Parma, Trieste and Nancy; Metropolitan Opera 1989, as Gunther, in Götterdämmerung; Sang Telramund at Buenos Aires, 1991; Regularly at Vienna State Opera, Hamburg, Berlin and Stuttgart; More recently in Buenos Aires in Tales of Hoffmann, as a guest, 1993; Sang Wotan/Wanderer at Wiesbaden, 1994, Jochanaan in Switzerland, 1996 and Telramund and Wotan in Prague, 1997. *Recordings:* Video of Der Ring des Nibelungen, conducted by James Levine. *Current Management:* SK Management, 5 Meadscroft, 15 St John's Road, Eastbourne, BN20 7NQ, England.

RAFTERY, J. Patrick; Singer (baritone); b. 4 April 1951, Washington DC, USA. *Education:* Studied with Armen Boyajian. *Career:* Debut: Chicago Lyric Opera 1980, as Shchelkalov in Boris Godunov; European debut 1982, at the Théâtre du Châtelet, Paris, as Zurga in Les Pêcheurs de Perles; Glyndebourne 1984, as Guglielmo; Santa Fe, New Mexico, 1984 in Verdi's Il Corsaro and Gwendoline by Chabrier; Covent Garden debut 1985, as Mozart's Count; Further appearances with the New York City Opera and in Hamburg, Brussels, and Cologne; Santiago 1988, as Luna in Il Trovatore; Rome Opera 1988, as Puccini's Lescaut; Sang Belcore in L'Elisir d'amore at Genoa in 1989; Other roles include Escamillo, Mercutio (Roméo et Juliette), Eugene Onegin, Valentin (Faust), Yeletsky in The Queen of Spades and Rossini's Figaro; Sang Rossini's Figaro at Vancouver, 1991; Matho in the premiere of Fénelon's Salammbô, Paris Opéra Bastille, 1998; Sang Mozart's Lucio Silla at Lausanne, 2001.

RAGACCI, Susanna; Singer (Soprano); b. 1959, Stockholm, Sweden. *Education:* Studied in Florence. *Career:* Sang first at Rome as Rossini's Rosina, then appeared at Florence, Venice, Palermo, Turin and La Scala Milan; Sang Gilda in Dublin and at the Wexford Festival in Cimarosa's Astuzie Femminili; Opera de Wallonie at Liège 1987–88 as Rosina and as Egloge in Mascagni's Nerone; Sang at Bologna in the 1987 Italian premiere of Henze's English Cat and at Florence as the Italian Singer in Capriccio; Théâtre du Châtelet, Paris, 1992 as Sofia in Il Signor Bruschino. *Recordings:* Vivaldi's Catone in Utica and La Caduta di Adamo by Galuppi; I Pazzi per Progresso by Donizetti; L'Elisir d'amore.

RAGATZU, Rosella; Singer (Soprano); b. 1964, Cagliari, Sardinia. *Education:* Studied at the Cagliari Conservatory and with Magda Olivero and Claudio Desderi. *Career:* Sang Fiordiligi at Spoleto (1987) and Donna Anna at Treviso, 1989; Toured Italy, 1990, as Mozart's Countess and sang this role with Donna Anna at the 1991 Macerata Festival; Further guest appearances at the Leipzig Opera, Teatro Regio Turin (in Don Carlos) and at Frankfurt in a concert of Franchetti's Cristoforo Colombo (1991), as Queen Isabella; Mozart's Countess at Turin, 1998; Season 2000 as Mme Cortese in Il Viaggio a Reims at Liège and Rossini's Mathilde at the Vienna Staatsoper. *Honours:* Winner,

1987 Concorso Sperimento di Spoleto and 1989 Concorso Toti dal Monte, Treviso.

RAGIN, Derek Lee; Singer (Counter-tenor); b. 17 June 1958, West Point, New York, USA. *Education:* Arts High School, Newark, New Jersey; Newark Boys Chorus School, 1969–72; Piano Scholarship, Newark Community Center of Arts, 1970–75; Piano, BM, MMT, Oberlin Conservatory of Music, 1980. *Career:* Debut: Opera–Festwoche der Alten Musik, Innsbruck, Austria, 1983; Recital debut, Wigmore Hall, London, 1984; Debut recital, Aldeburgh Festival, 1984; Sang title role in Handel's Tamerlano, at Lyon Opéra, France, and at Göttingen Handel Festival; BBC debut recital, 1984; Debut at the Metropolitan Opera in Handel's Giulio Cesare, September 1988; Recitals and Oratorio continued in Frankfurt, Munich, Stuttgart, Cologne, Venice, Milan, Bologna, New York, Amsterdam, Maryland Handel Festival, London, Washington DC, Atlanta, Boston, San Francisco; Made Salzburg debut in Gluck's Orfeo, 1990; Gluck's Orfeo in Budapest, 1991; Season 1992 in Conti's Don Chisciotte at Innsbruck and as Britten's Oberon at Saint Louis; Sang in Ligeti's Le Grand Macabre at the Paris Châtelet and the Salzburg Festival, 1997; Hasse's Attilio regolo at Dresden, 1997; Sang in Legrenzi's La divisione del mondo at Innsbruck, 2000. *Recordings:* Role of Spirit in Purcell's Dido and Aeneas 1985; Title role in Handel's Tamerlano, 1985; Handel's Flavio and Tolomeo in Giulio Cesare; Handel's Saul; Vivaldi Cantatas. *Current Management:* Colbert Artists Management, New York, USA. *Address:* 106 1/2 9th Avenue, Newark, NJ 07107, USA.

RAGNARSSON, Hjalmar (Helgi); Composer; b. 23 Sept. 1952, Isafjordur, Iceland; m. Sigridur Asa Richardsdottir, 2 s., 1 d. *Education:* Isafjordur School of Music, 1959–69; Reykjavík College of Music, 1969–72; BA, Brandeis University, USA, 1974; Rijksuniversiteit Utrecht-Instituut voor Sonologie, Netherlands, 1976–77; MFA, Cornell University, USA, 1980. *Career:* Rector, Iceland Academy of the Arts, 1999–; mem, Composers Society of Iceland, President 1988–92; President, Federation of Icelandic Artists, 1991–98. *Compositions include:* Six songs to Icelandic Poems for voice and chamber ensemble, 1978–79; Romanza for flute, clarinet and piano, 1981; Canto for mixed choirs and synthesizer, 1982; Mass for mixed choir, 1982–89; Trio for clarinet, cello and piano, 1983–84; Five Preludes for piano, 1983–85; Tengsl for voice and string quartet, 1988; Spjotalög for orchestra, 1989; Raudur Thradur, ballet music for orchestra, 1989; Rhodymenia Palmata, chamber opera, 1992; Concerto for organ and orchestra, 1997; Music for theatre including Icelandic National Theatre and Reykjavík Municipal Theatre; Music for films: Tears of Stone, 1995; No Trace, 1998; Music for television films, Iceland State Television Service and Swedish State Television. *Recordings:* Conductor, Icelandic Choral works with the University Choir of Iceland; Own choral works for Hljomeyki Chamber Choir. *Publications:* Jon Leifs, Icelandic Composer: Historical Background, Biography, Analysis of Selected Works, MFA thesis, 1980; A Short History of Icelandic Music to the Beginning of the Twentieth Century, 1985; Film script: Tears of Stone, co-author, 1995. *Address:* Laekjarhjalli 22, 200 Kopavogur, Iceland.

RAICHEV, Rouslan; Conductor; b. 2 May 1924, Milan, Italy. *Education:* Studied the piano in Milan, then with Leopold Reichwein, Emil Sauer and Karl Böhm in Vienna (until 1944). *Career:* Assistant at the Vienna Staatsoper 1942–43; Chief Conductor at the Königsberg Opera 1943–44; Conductor of the Varna Opera, Bulgaria, 1946–48; Conductor of the Sofia Opera 1948–89 (Musical Director 1981–89); Conducted the State Orchestra of Plovdiv 1968 and directed stage works at the Schleswig-Holstein Festival 1974–78; Guest conductor at the Vienna Staatsoper, La Scala Milan and the Paris Opéra. *Recordings include:* Rachmaninov Aleko.

RAIMONDI, Gianni; Singer (Tenor); b. 13 April 1923, Bologna, Italy. *Education:* Studied with Gennaro Barra-Caracciolo and with Ettore Campogalliani in Milan. *Career:* Debut: Bologna 1947, as the Duke of Mantua; Sang Pinkerton at Budrio, 1947; Bologna 1948, as Ernesto in Don Pasquale; Florence 1952, in Rossini's Armida, with Callas; London, Stoll Theatre, 1953; Naples 1955, in the premiere of Madame Bovary by Pannain; La Scala Milan from 1956, notably as Alfredo and as Lord Percy in Anna Bolena, opposite Callas, and in Mosè and Semiramide (1958, 1962); US debut San Francisco 1957; Verona Arena from 1957; Guest appearances in Vienna from 1959, Munich from 1960; Metropolitan Opera from 1965, as Rodolfo, Cavaradossi and Faust; Hamburg Staatsoper 1969–77; Other appearances in Paris 1953, Chicago, Dallas, Lisbon, Edinburgh, Geneva, Zürich and Helsinki; Other roles included Gabriele Adorno, Ismaele (Nabucco), Arrigo in Les Vêpres Siciliennes, Pollione, and Edgardo. *Recordings:* La Favorita (Cetra); La Traviata (Deutsche Grammophon); Linda di Chamounix; Maria Stuarda, with Callas; I Puritani; Armida. *Address:* c/o Teatro alla Scala, Via Filodrammtatici 2, Milan, Italy.

RAIMONDI, Ruggero; Singer (bass); b. 3 Oct. 1941, Bologna, Italy; m. Isabel Maier. *Education:* Student, Theresa Pediconi, Rome, 1961–62;

Armando Piervenanzi, 1963–65. *Career:* Debut: Spoleto, 1964; Appeared Rome Opera; Principal opera houses in Italy; Metropolitan Opera, 1970; Munich; La Scala; Lyric Opera Chicago; Paris Opéra; Sang Don Giovanni at Glyndebourne, 1969, and throughout the world; Covent Garden, 1972, as Fiesco in Simon Boccanegra; Vienna Staatsoper, 1982, as Don Quichotte; Hamburg, 1985, as Gounod's Mephisto in Faust; Sang Selim in Il Turco in Italia; Chicago, 1987, as Mozart's Count; Pesaro, 1985 and Vienna as Don Profondo in Il Viaggio a Reims; Sang in the opening concert at the Bastille Opéra, 1989; 25th Anniversary Celebration live at the Barbican Hall, 1990; Scarpia in a live televised Tosca from Rome, 1992; Rossini's Mosè at Covent Garden, 1994; Donizetti's Don Pasquale; Iago in Otello, Salzburg, 1996; 4 Devils in Les Contes d'Hoffmanni; Verdi's Falstaff at the Berlin Staatsoper, 1998, and at Salzburg, 2000; Season 2000–01 as Pizzetti's Thomas Becket at Turin, Don Quichotte for Washington Opera and Don Pasquale for Zürich Opera. *Recordings:* 2 Verdi Requiems; Complete operas Attila, I Vespri Siciliani, La Bohème, Aida, Don Carlos, Forza de Destino, Il Pirata, Norma, Don Giovanni, Carmen, Nozze di Figaro, Mosè, Italiana in Algeri, Boris Godunov, Pelléas et Mélisande, Turandot, Barbiere di Siviglia, Cenerentola, Simon Boccanegra, Macbeth, Nabucco, I Lombardi, Tosca; Don Giovanni in Joseph Losey's film of Mozart's opera; Escamillo in Francesco Rosi's Carmen; Maurice Béjart's 6 Characters in Search of a Singer; Boris in Zulawsky's film Boris Godunov; Played in Alain Resnais' Life is a Bed of Roses; Opera production since 1986. *Honours:* Recipient, Competition Award, Spoleto, 1964; Commdr des Arts et des Lettres, Officier de la Légion d'honneur, France; Grand Ufficiale Della Repubblica, Italy; Chevalier de l'Ordre de Malte; Commandeur du Mérite Culturel, Monaco; Citizen of Honour, City of Athens, Greece. *Address:* 140 bis rue Lecourbe, 75015 Paris, France.

RAIMONDO, Ildiko; Singer (Soprano); b. 11 Nov. 1962, Arad, Romania. *Education:* Studied at the Arad Conservatory. *Career:* Sang at Chemnitz from 1983 and from 1988 at the Vienna Kammeroper, in Dresden and at the Landestheater Linz; Bregenz Festival 1991 (as Micaela) and further appearances at the Vienna Volksoper and Staatsoper; Other roles have included Mozart's Zerlina, Susanna, Despina and Pamina, Sophie in Der Rosenkavalier and Walter in La Wally; Concerts include Masses by Mozart and Rossini, Die Schöpfung, the Verdi Requiem and Ein Deutsches Requiem; Marzelline in Fidelio at the 1996 Edinburgh Festival; Eurydice in Leopold I's Il figliol prodigo, Vienna, 1997. *Address:* c/o Staatsoper Vienna, Opernring 2, 1010 Vienna, Austria.

RAITIO, Pentti; Composer and Music Educator; b. 4 June 1930, Pieksamaki, Finland. *Education:* Studied composition with Joonas Kokkonen, 1961–63; Erik Bergman, 1963–66; Diploma, Sibelius Academy, Helsinki, 1966. *Career:* Director, Hyvinkaa School of Music, 1967–; Chairman, Lahti Organ Festival, 1981–85; Association of Finnish Music Schools, 1986–. *Compositions:* Orchestral: 13, 1964; Audiendum, 1967; 5 Pieces for String Orchestra, 1975; Petandrie, 1977; Noharmus, 1978; Noharmus II, 1980; Canzone d'autunno, 1982; Flute Concerto, 1983; Due figure, 1985; Yoldia arctica, 1987; Chamber: Small Pieces for brass instruments, 1984; Wind Quintet, 1975; Nocturne for violin and piano, 1977; Vocal: 3 Songs for soprano, 1962; The River, 7 Songs for soprano and 7 instruments, 1965; Along the Moonlit Path, 3 songs for soprano and 4 instruments, 1965; Orphean Chorus, 3 songs for baritone and men's chorus, 1966; 3 Songs for baritone and string quartet, 1970; One Summer Evening for men's chorus, 1971; Song for men's chorus, 1972; Song for a Rain Bird for baritone and piano, 1974; I'm Looking at the River, 6 songs for women's or youth chorus, 1986. *Address:* c/o Hyvinkaa School of Music, 05800 Hyvinkaa, Finland.

RAJNA, Thomas; Pianist, Composer and Lecturer; b. 21 Dec. 1921, Budapest, Hungary. *Education:* 1944–47 Liszt Academy of Music with Kodály, Sándor Veress and Leo Weiner; Royal College of Music with Herbert Howells and Angus Morrison. *Career:* Professor of Piano and Composition, Guidhall School of Music, 1963; Lecturer, Keyboard History and Studies, University of Surrey, 1967; Senior Lecturer at Cape Town University from 1970; Appointed Associate Professor, 1989; Numerous performances as pianist in Europe and South Africa of music by Stravinsky, Messiaen, Scriabin, Liszt, Granados and Rajna; Launched New Rajna CD label Amarantha Records, 2001. *Compositions include:* Dialogues for clarinet and piano, 1947; Preludes for piano, 1944–49; Music for cello and piano 1957; Capriccio for keyboard 1960; Piano Concerto No. 1 1962; Movements for strings 1962; Cantilenas and Interludes for orchestra 1968; Three Hebrew Choruses, 1972; Four African Lyrics for high voice and piano 1976; Piano Concerto No. 2, 1984; Concerto for harp and orchestra, 1990; Amarantha (opera) 1991–95; Video Games, 1994; Rhapsody for clarinet and orchestra, 1995; Fantasy for violin and orchestra, 1996; Suite for violin and harp, 1997; Stop all the Clocks, Four Songs on Poems by W H Auden, 1998; The Creation – A Negro Sermon for choir, 2000; Tarantulla for violin and piano, 2001; Valley Song, opera, 2004. *Recordings:* Complete piano works of Stravinsky and Granados; works by Messiaen, Bartók,

Scriabin, Liszt and Schumann; Rajna: Piano Concerto No. 1; Music for violin and piano; Preludes for piano; Serenade for 10 wind instruments, piano and percussion; Divertimento Piccolo for orchestra; Piano Concerto No. 2; Concerto for harp and orchestra; The Hungarian Connection, music by Dohnányi and Rajna, 1997; Rajna: Amarantha; Stop All the Clocks; Video Games. *Publications:* Suite for violin and harp, 1998, (premiered at the 7th World Harp Congress, Prague, 1999); Harp Concerto/Tarantulla for violin and piano. *Address:* 10 Wyndover Road, Claremont, Cape 7708, South Africa.

RAKOWSKI, Andrzej; Musicologist and Acoustician; b. 16 June 1931, Warsaw, Poland; m. Magdalena Jakobczyk, 30 Dec 1972, 1 s., 2 d. *Education:* MSc, 1957, DSc, 1963, Warsaw Univ. of Technology; PhD, Warsaw Univ., 1977; MA, State College of Music in Warsaw, 1958. *Career:* Professor of Musical Acoustics, 1963–2001, Prof. Emeritus, 2001–; President, 1981–87, Chopin Academy of Music, Warsaw; Part-time Professor, Institute of Musicology, Warsaw University, 1987–2003; Chair. of Musicology, A. Mickiewicz Univ., 1997–; mem, Polish Music Council, Vice President, 1984–89; Union of Polish Composers; Polish Academy of Sciences, President of Acoustical Committee, 1996–; European Society for Cognitive Sciences of Music, President, 2000–03. *Publications:* Categorical Perception of Pitch in Music, 1978; The Access of Children and Youth to Musical Culture, 1984; Over 100 articles on music perception and music acoustics to international, American and Polish journals. *Honours:* Polish State Award, Golden Cross of Merit, 1973; Order of the Revival of Poland, Bachelor's Cross, 1983, Officer's Cross, 2002. *Address:* Fryderyk Chopin Academy of Music, Okolnik 2, 00-368 Warsaw, Poland. *E-mail:* rakowski@chopin.edu.pl.

RAMEY, Phillip; Composer; b. 12 Sept. 1939, Elmhurst, Illinois, USA. *Education:* Studied composition with A. Tcherepnin at the International Academy of Music in Nice (1959) and at De Paul University, Chicago (BA 1962); Further study with Jack Beeson at Columbia University, New York (MA 1965). *Career:* Program Editor for the New York Philharmonic, 1977–93; Freelance composer, with premieres at New York, Boston, Sacramento, Chicago, London, Aldeburgh Festival, Tangier, Vilnius, Montreux; Vice Pres. USA, The Tcherepnin Soc., 2002–. *Compositions include:* 5 Piano Sonatas, 1961, 1966, 1968, 1988, 1989 (for left hand); Concert Suite for piano and small orchestra, 1962 (revised, reorchestrated and expanded 1984 as Concert Suite for piano and orchestra); Music, for brass and percussion, 1964; Orchestral Discourse, 1967; Night Music, for percussion, 1967; Suite for violin and piano, 1971; 3 Piano Concertos, 1971, 1976, 1994; A William Blake Trilogy for soprano and piano, 1980; Moroccan Songs to Words of Paul Bowles, for high voice and piano, 1982–86; Concerto for horn and strings, 1987; Rhapsody for cello, 1992; Trio Concertant for violin, horn and piano, 1993; Tangier Portraits, for piano, 1991–99; La Citadelle for horn and piano, 1994; Praeludium for 5 horns, 1994; Color Etudes for piano, 1994; Gargoyles for horn, 1995; Elegy for horn and piano, 1995; Nightfall, Aria for flute and piano, 1996; Concertino for 4 horns, timpani and percussion, 1996; Sonata-Ballade for 2 horns and piano, 1997; Dialogue for 2 horns, 1997; Phantoms (Ostinato Etude) for piano, 1997; Sonata for harpsichord, 1998; Effigies for viola and piano, 1998; Lyric Fragment for flute and harpsichord (or piano), 1998; Tangier Portraits for piano, 1991–99; Lament for Richard III for piano, 2001; Color Etudes for piano and orchestra (arranged from Color Etudes for piano), 2002; Orchestral Epigrams, 2002; Winter Nocturne for piano, 2003; Orchestration of Aaron Copland's Proclamation for piano as Proclamation for orchestra, 1985. *Publications:* Irving Fine: His Life in Music, 2001. *Address:* 825 West End Avenue, Penthouse F, New York, NY 10025, USA.

RAMEY, Samuel; Singer (bass-baritone); b. 28 March 1942, Kolby, Kansas, USA. *Education:* Wichita State University, with Arthur Newman; New York with Armen Boyajian. *Career:* Debut: New York City Opera 1973, as Zuniga in Carmen: returned as Mephistopheles (Gounod and Boito), Attila, Don Giovanni, Henry VIII (Anna Bolena) and Massenet's Don Quichotte; Glyndebourne debut 1976, as Mozart's Figaro; Nick Shadow in The Rake's Progress 1977; Guest appearances in Hamburg, San Francisco, Chicago and Vienna, as Colline in La Bohème, Figaro, and Arkel, in Pelléas et Mélisande; Covent Garden debut 1982: returned to London for a concert performance of Semiramide, 1986 and as Philip II in Don Carlos, 1989; Metropolitan Opera debut 1984, as Argante in Rinaldo, 1986–87 as Walton in I Puritani and Escamillo; Pesaro 1984, in a revival of Rossini's Il Viaggio a Reims; Bartók's Bluebeard 1989, at the Met; Pesaro Festival 1986 (Maometto II) and 1989 (La Gazza Ladra); Munich 1988, as Mephistopheles; Don Giovanni at Salzburg from 1987, Metropolitan and Maggio Musicale, Florence 1990; Season 1992/93 as Attila at San Francisco and Geneva, Rossini's Basilio at the Met, Philip II in Venice and New York, the Hoffman Villains and Berlioz Mephistopheles at Covent Garden, and Nick Shadow at Aix-en-Provence; Sang Mephistopheles in a new production of Faust at the Vienna Staatsoper, 1997; Other roles include the villains in Les Contes d'Hoffmann, Verdi's Renato and Banquo, and

Mozart's Leporello; Covent Garden, 1997, as Verdi's Fiesco and Oberto; Philippe in Don Carlo at the Paris Opéra Bastille, 1998; Season 2000–01 as Verdi's Zaccaria at Houston; Attila for the Chicago Lyric Opera and Rossini's Mustafà at the Met; Engaged for Don Quichotte, 2001. *Recordings:* Bach B Minor Mass, I Due Foscari, Un Ballo in Maschera, Ariodante, Lucia di Lammermoor, Maometto II, Petite Messe solenelle, Haydn's Armida (Philips); Le nozze di Figaro, The Rake's Progress (Decca); Il Turco in Italia, La Donna del Lago (CBS); Il Viaggio a Reims, Don Giovanni (Deutsche Grammophon). *Current Management:* IMG Artists, Lovell House, 616 Chiswick High Road, London, W4 5RX, England. *Telephone:* (20) 8233-5800. *Fax:* (20) 8233-5801. *E-mail:* artistseurope@imgworld.com. *Website:* www.imgartists.com.

RAMICOVA, Dunya; Costume Designer; b. 1950, Czechoslovakia. *Education:* Studied at Yale School of Drama. *Career:* Has collaborated with Director Stephen Wadsworth on Jenůfa and Fliegende Holländer for Seattle Opera, Fidelio for Scottish Opera and La Clemenza di Tito for Houston Grand Opera; Costume designs for Peter Sellars production of Die Zauberflöte and The Electrification of the Soviet Union at Glyndebourne, Tannhäuser at Chicago, Nixon in China for Houston and St François d'Assise at Salzburg, 1992; Premiere of The Voyage by Philip Glass at the Metropolitan, 1992, production by David Pountney; Covent Garden, 1992, costumes for Alcina; Costumes for the house premiere of Mathis der Maler, Covent Garden, 1995, Tan Dun/Peter Sellars Peony Pavilion, Vienna, 1998. *Address:* c/o Metropolitan Opera, Lincoln Center, New York, NY 10023, USA.

RAMIREZ, Alejandro; Singer (Tenor); b. 2 Sept. 1946, Bogota, Columbia. *Education:* Qualified as Doctor of Medicine, then studied singing at Conservatory of Bogota; Further study at the Musikhochschule Freiburg, 1973–75; Completed studies with Annelies Kupper in Munich and Gunther Reich in Stuttgart. *Career:* Sang in Pforzheim, 1975–77, Kaiserslautern, 1977–80; Member of Mannheim Opera, 1980–82, Frankfurt from 1982; Covent Garden, London, 1984 as Nemorino in L'Elisir d'amore; Vienna Staatsoper, 1985 as Alfredo; Salzburg Festival in 1985 in the Henze/Monteverdi Il Ritorno d'Ulisse; Other roles include Belmonte, Don Ottavio, Tamino, Ferrando, Jacquino in Berlin 1984, Elvino in La Sonnambula, Rossini's Almaviva and Lindoro, Strauss's Narraboth and Flamand, Rodolfo and Edgardo; Concert repertoire includes the Evangelist in the Bach Passions, and works by Handel, Bruckner, Schumann, Dvořák, Beethoven and Verdi; Bavarian State Opera as Don Ottavio, Frankfurt, 1980–85; La Scala Milan in 1988 as Henry Morosus in R Strauss's Schweigsame Frau, 1990; Season 1992 as Rodolfo at Bonn and Tamino at Düsseldorf; Professor of Singing at the Musikhochschule of Mannheim, Germany; Sang Pollione in Norma at Karlsrune, 2000. *Recordings include:* Schumann's Manfred; St John Passion and Christmas Oratorio by Bach; Sacred Music by Schubert, Mendelssohn and Charpentier; The Seven Last Words by Schütz; Mozart's Nozze di Figaro under Riccardo Muti. *Address:* Andersenstrasse 55, 68259 Mannheim, Germany.

RAMIRO, Yordi; Singer (Tenor); b. 1948, Acapulco, Mexico. *Career:* Debut: Mexico City, 1977, as Pinkerton; Sang at the Vienna Staatsoper from 1978 and guested at the San Francisco Opera, 1979, as Rinuccio in Gianni Schicchi; Further appearances at Seattle as Alfredo, Barcelona as Rodolfo (1980) and Mexico City as Edgardo; Strasbourg, 1983, as Gounod's Roméo; Covent Garden, 1984, in Der Rosenkavalier and Arturo in I Puritani at the 1985 Bregenz Festival; Metropolitan Opera debut, 1985, as Paco in La Vida Breve; Other roles include Ernesto in Don Pasquale, Nemorino, the Duke of Mantua and Tebaldo in I Capuleti by Bellini. *Recordings include:* Rigoletto and La Traviata (Naxos). *Address:* c/o Staatsoper Vienna, Opernring 2, 1010 Vienna, Austria.

RAMSAY, Dervla; Northern Irish singer (mezzo-soprano); b. 25 Aug. 1970, Derry, N Ireland. *Education:* Guildhall School of Music and Drama, London; Studies with Renata Scotto and Margarita Rinaldi. *Career:* debut, sang Volpino in Haydn's Lo Speziale, Bagno di Lucca, 1994; Janissary in Mozart's Die Entführung at Covent Garden, 2000; Countess Ceprano in Rigoletto; Page in Wagner's Lohengrin; Train bearer in Strauss's Elektra, Royal Opera House, Covent Garden; mem. Royal Opera Chorus, 1999–. *Honours:* Winner, Ulster Bank's Music Foundation Award for Young Musicians, 1993; Concorso Internazionale di Bagna di Lucca, 1994. *Address:* c/o Royal Opera House (chorus), Covent Garden, London, WC2, England.

RAN, Shulamit; Composer; b. 21 Oct. 1949, Tel-Aviv, Israel. *Education:* Studied in Tel-Aviv, and with Norman Dello Joio (composition) at the Mannes College of Music, New York (graduated 1967); Further study with Dorothy Taubman and Ralph Shapey. *Career:* Prof. of Composition, University of Chicago; Composer-in-Residence, Chicago Symphony 1991–97, Lyric Opera of Chicago, 1994–97; Visiting Professor at Princeton University, 1987; Works performed by orchestras include Chicago Symphony, Cleveland Orchestra, Philadelphia Orchestra, Israel Philharmonic, American Composers Orchestra; Baltimore Symphony, Orchestre de la Suisse Romande, Jerusalem Symphony,

New York Philharmonic and many others. *Compositions include:* O the Chimneys for mezzo-soprano and tape, 1969; Concert Piece for piano and orchestra, 1971; Ensembles for Seventeen, for soprano and 16 instruments, 1975; Double Vision for woodwind quintet, brass quintet and piano, 1976; Apprehensions for voice, clarinet and piano, 1979; Excursions for piano trio, 1981; Verticals for piano, 1982; 2 String Quartets, 1984, 1989; Concerto da Camera I for woodwind quintet, 1985; Concerto for orchestra, 1986; Concerto da Camera II for clarinet, string quartet and piano, 1987; Symphony, 1990; Mirage for 5 players, 1990; Chicago Skyline for brass and percussion, 1991; Inscriptions for violin, 1991; Legends for orchestra, 1993; Three Fantasy Movements for cello and orchestra, 1993; Invocation, for horn, timpani, and chimes, 1994; Between Two Worlds: The Dybbuk, opera, 1994–95, (premiered at Chicago, 1997); Soliloquy for piano trio, 1997; Vessels of Courage and Hope for orchestra, 1998; Voices for flautist with orchestra, 2000; Supplications for chorus and orchestra, 2002; Violin Concerto, 2003. *Honours:* Fellowships the Guggenheim Foundation, 1977, 1991; Koussevitzky Foundation; Nat. Endowment for the Arts; American Acad. of Arts and Letters; Pulitzer Prize (for Symphony No. 1, 1991); First Prize, Kennedy Center Friedheim Awards, 1992. *Address:* University of Chicago Dept of Music, 1010 East 59th Street, Chicago IL 60637, USA.

RANACHER, Christa; Singer (Soprano); b. 12 Dec. 1953, Dollach in Kärnten, Austria. *Education:* Studied in Vienna and attended master classes by Mario del Monaco and Elisabeth Schwarzkopf. *Career:* Sang at Regensburg, 1984–85, Monchengladbach from 1985, Leonore in Fidelio, 1989; Further appearances at Gelsenkirchen, Mannheim, Munster, Hannover, the Deutsche Oper Berlin, Staatsoper Munich and Zürich; Season, 1992, as Salome at Dusseldorf and Shostakovich's Katerina Izmailova at Berne; Other roles include Mozart's Countess and Donna Anna, Agathe, Marenka in The Bartered Bride, Senta, and Ada in Wagner's Die Feen, Tosca, Santuzza, Zdenka, Arabella, Judith in the opera by Siegfried Matthus, Sophie in Cerha's Baal and Andromache in Troades by Reimann; Sang Stella in Goldschmidt's Der Gewaltige Hahnrei, Bonn, 1995; Noted concert performer; Season 2000 as Andromache in Troades, at Berlin, and Amélia in Clara by Hans Gefors, for Berne Opera. *Address:* c/o Stadttheater Bern, Nägeligasse 1, CH–3011 Berne, Switzerland.

RANCATORE, Desirée; Singer (Soprano); b. 1972, Sicily. *Education:* Studied with Margaret Baker-Genovesi. *Career:* Debut: Mozart's Barbarina at the 1996 Salzburg Festival; Appearances at Bologna in Figaro, at Parma in L'Arlesiana and as Frasquita in Carmen at Genoa; Flowermaiden in Parsifal at Florence and the Opéra Bastille, Paris; Sophie in Der Rosenkavalier at Palermo and Gilda at the San Francisco Opera, 2000–01; Covent Garden debut as Nannetta in Falstaff, repeated at the Vienna Staatsoper; Further engagements in Don Carlos at Salzburg and Die Zauberflöte at the Bastille; Blonde in Die Entführung at Salzburg and in film conducted by Charles Mackerras. *Recordings:* DVD of Nannetta in Falstaff, Covent Garden. *Honours:* Winner, 1996 Maria Caniglia Competition. *Address:* c/o Opéra Bastille, 120 Rue de Lyon, 75012 Paris, France.

RANDLE, Thomas; Singer (Tenor); b. 21 Dec. 1958, Hollywood, California, USA. *Education:* Studied at the University of Southern California. *Career:* Concert appearances in the USA and Europe with the London Philharmonic Orchestra, Boston Symphony Orchestra and the Leipzig Radio Symphony Orchestra; Conductors include Helmuth Rilling, Gennadi Rozhdestvensky, Michael Tilson Thomas and André Previn; Has sung Berg and Stravinsky, and the US and world premieres of works by Tippett, Heinz Holliger and William Kraft, with the Los Angeles Philharmonic; Often heard in Bach, Handel and Mozart; Bach's Christmas Oratorio in Leipzig; Operatic repertoire includes all the major tenor roles of Mozart, Rossini and Donizetti, and French roles of Massenet and Thomas; British debut as Tamino in Nicholas Hytner's production of The Magic Flute (English National Opera, 1988, returned, 1989); European opera debut at the Aix-en-Provence Festival, France, in Purcell's The Fairy Queen; Sang Monteverdi's Orfeo at Valencia, 1989; Ferrando in Brussels and with Scottish Opera; Sang Tamino at Glyndebourne, 1991; Sang Dionysius in the premiere of John Buller's The Bacchae and as Pelléas, English National Opera, 1992; Sang title role in reduced version of Pelléas et Mélisande with Peter Brook in Paris and European tour, Netherlands Opera in world premiere of Peter Schaat's opera Symposion, based on Life of Tchaikovsky, in 1994; Season 1994 returned to English National Opera to sing Tippett's King Priam and appeared in Britten's Gloriana at Covent Garden; Fairy Queen at ENO, 1995; Sang Idomeneo for Scottish Opera, 1996 and Mozart's Lucio Silla at Garsington, 1998; Recent engagements include: Tom Rakewell in The Rake's Progress with Netherlands Opera; Title role in Hasse's Solimano at the Staatsoper, Berlin, and Alfredo in La Traviata for Opera North; Sang in the premiere of The Last Supper by Birtwistle, Berlin Staatsoper, 2000; Season 2000–01 as Schubert's Fierrabras at Buxton, Loge in The Rheingold for ENO, Berlioz's

Bénédict for WNO and in Handel's Tamerlano at Halle; Handel's Samson at the London Proms, 2002. *Recordings:* Purcell's Fairy Queen with Les Arts Florissants; Tippett's The Ice Break with London Sinfonietta; Britten's War Requiem with BBC Scottish Symphony Orchestra; Luigi Nono, Canti di Vita e d'Amore with Bamberg Symphony Orchestra; Mozart's Requiem with German National Youth Orchestra; Handel's Esther with Harry Christophers and The Sixteen; Requiem of Reconciliation with Helmuth Rilling and the Israel Philharmonic Orchestra; Handel's Messiah with the Royal Philharmonic Orchestra; Handel's Samson with Harry Christophers and the Symphony of Harmony and Invention. *Address:* c/o IMG Artists Europe, Lovell House, 616 Chiswick High Road, London W4 5RX, England.

RANDOLPH, David; Conductor, Author, Lecturer and Broadcaster; b. 21 Dec. 1914, New York, NY, USA; m. Mildred Greenberg, 18 July 1948. *Education:* BS, City College of New York; MA, Teachers College, Columbia University. *Career:* Conductor, The Masterwork Chorus and Orchestra, The St Cecilia Chorus and Orchestra, at Carnegie Hall, Avery Fisher Hall, Kennedy Center, Washington DC; Numerous choral works including: Bach's B Minor Mass, St Matthew Passion St John Passion, Magnificat, Christmas Oratorio, Brahms' Requiem, Schicksalied, Mozart's Requiem, Vaughan Williams's Sea Symphony and Hodie, Dona Nobis Pacem, and Mass in G Minor, Haydn's Mass in Time Of War, Orff's Carmina Burana, Beethoven's Mass in C and Missa Solemnis, Mozart's Mass in C Minor, Mendelssohn's Symphony No. 2, Elijah and Die erste Walpurgisnacht, Poulenc's Gloria, Kodály's Te Deum, 171 Complete performances of Handel's Messiah; Haydn, St Cecilia Mass; Dvořák, Requiem; Guest Conductor: The Philharmonia Orchestra, Barbican Centre, London, Brahms' Requiem, 1988; Pre-concert Lecturer: New York Philharmonic, Cleveland Orchestra, Vienna Symphony Orchestra; Conductor, David Randolph Singers; Season 2000–01 with Beethoven's Ninth and The Music Makers by Elgar; Season 2001–02, Rachmaninoff's The Bells. *Compositions:* A Song for Humanity, Edward, 1936; Andante for Strings, 1937. *Recordings:* Works by: Monteverdi, Schütz, Handel's Messiah; Writer, Narrator, The Instruments of the Orchestra, CD, 1995; Madrigals of Weelkes, Bateson, Wilbye, Gesualdo, 13 Modern American Madrigals. *Publications:* This Is Music: A Guide to The Pleasures of Listening, 1964, new edition, 1997. *Address:* 420 East 86th Street, Apt 4C, New York, NY 10028-6456, USA.

RANDOVÁ, Eva; Singer (mezzo-soprano); b. 31 Dec. 1936, Kolin, Czechoslovakia. *Education:* Studied with J. Svanova at Usti nad Labem, and at the Prague Conservatory. *Career:* Sang first at Ostrava, as Eboli, Carmen, Amneris, the Princess in Rusalka, and Ortrud; Prague National Opera from 1969; Nuremberg and Stuttgart from 1971; Bayreuth Festival from 1973, as Gutrune, Fricka and Kundry; Salzburg Festival, 1975, Eboli in Don Carlos, conducted by Karajan; Covent Garden debut, 1977, as Ortrud; Returned to London as Marina, Venus, the Kostelnicka in Jenůfa, 1986, and Azucena in a new production of Il Trovatore, 1989; Metropolitan Opera, 1981, 1987, as Fricka and Venus; Orange Festival, 1985, as Marina in Boris Godunov; Vienna, 1987, in Rusalka; Sang Ortrud at San Francisco, 1989, Stuttgart, 1990; Sang Marina in Boris Godunov at Barcelona, 1990; Season 1992 as Clytemnestra at Athens; Covent Garden, 1994, as Kabanicha in Katya Kabanova (returned 1997); Sang Erda in Siegfried at Stuttgart, 1999; Grandmother in Jenůfa at Covent Garden, 2001; Frequent concert engagements; Jury Member, 1999 Cardiff Singer of the World Competition. *Recordings:* Bach cantatas; Santuzza in Cavalleria Rusticana; Mahler's Resurrection Symphony; Glagolitic Mass by Janáček; Šarka by Fibich; The Cunning Little Vixen and Jenůfa, conducted by Charles Mackerras. *Current Management:* Askonas Holt Ltd, Lonsdale Chambers, 27 Chancery Lane, London, WC2A 1PF, England. *Telephone:* (20) 7400-1700. *Fax:* (20) 7400-1799. *E-mail:* info@askonasholt.co.uk. *Website:* www.askonasholt.co.uk.

RANDS, Bernard, MMus; British composer and conductor; b. 2 March 1935, Sheffield, Yorkshire, England. *Education:* Univ. of Wales, Bangor; studied in Italy with Dallapiccola, Boulez, Maderna and Berio. *Career:* instructor in the music dept, York Univ. 1968–74; Fellowship in Creative Arts, Brasenose Coll., Oxford 1972–73; Prof. of Music, Univ. of California, San Diego 1976; Visiting Prof., California Inst. of the Arts, Valencia 1984–85; worked at electronic music studios in Milan, Berlin, Albany (New York), Urbana; appearances as conductor of new music, notably with the London Sonor ensemble; founder mem., music theatre ensemble CLAP. *Compositions:* Serena, music theatre, 1972–78; Orchestral: Per Esempio, 1968; Wildtrack I–III, 1969–75; Agenda, 1970; Mesalliance, 1972; Ology for jazz group, 1973; Aum, 1974; Serenata 75b, flute, chamber orchestra, 1976; Hirath, cello, orchestra, 1987;... Body and Shadow..., 1988; Instrumental: Espressioni, series of piano pieces, 1960–70; Actions for Six, 1962; Formants I, II, 1965–70; Tableau, 1970; Memo 1–5, solo pieces, 1971–75; Deja I, 1972; As all get out, 1972; Etendre, 1972; Response, double bass, tape, 1973; Scherzi, 1974; Cuaderna for string quartet, 1975; Madrigali, 1977; Obbligato, string quartet, trombone, 1980;... In the Receding Mist..., flute, harp, string trio, 1988; 2 String Quartets, 1974, 1994; Vocal: Ballad 103, 1970–73; Metalepsis 2 for mezzo, 1971; Lunatici, soprano, ensemble, 1980; Dejà 2, soprano, ensemble, 1980; Sound Patterns, various combinations with voices; Canti del Sole, tenor, orchestra, 1983; London Serenade, 1984; Le Tambourin, suite 1, 2, 1984; Ceremonial, 1, 2, 1985–86; Serenata 85, 1985; Requiescat, soprano, chorus, ensemble, 1985–86;... Among the Voices..., chorus, harp, 1988; Canzoni per Orchestra, 1995; Symphony, 1995; Cello Concerto, 1996; Triple Concerto, 1997; Requiescant for soprano, chorus and orchestra, 1997; Opera commission for the Aspen Festival, 1999. Honours:Hon. Fellow, Univ. of Wales, Bangor 2003; Pulitzer Prize for Canti del Sole 1984. Current Management: Universal Edition (London) Ltd, 48 Great Marlborough Street, London, W1F 7BB, England. Telephone: (20) 7437-6880. Fax: (20) 7437-6115. Website: www.bernardrands.com.

RANGEL(-LATOUCHE), César; Concert Pianist and Pedagogue; b. 3 April 1950, Caracas, Venezuela; m. María Cristina Graterol, 1 April 1995, 1 s. Education: Bachelor of Music, Juilliard School of Music, New York; Master of Music, Doctor of Music, Piano Performance, Indiana University; Diploma in Performance, Conservatory Juan Manuel Olivares. Career: Debut: Carnegie Recital Hall, New York; Extensive performances throughout USA; Invited by President of Venezuela to recital tour throughout the country; Repertoire includes: Bach's Goldberg Variations; Complete cycle, Beethoven Sonatas; Chopin, 24 Preludes and Etudes; Ravel's Gaspard de la Nuit; Stravinsky's Petrouchka; Performed Bartók's Second Piano Concerto, International Festival, Caracas; Television and radio appearances include Spain Radio and Television TVE, BBC; Performed Beethoven's Fifth Concerto with the Venezuelan Symphony Orchestra under Irwin Hoffmann; Recent engagements include concert at Konzerthaus in Berlin with Beethoven's Fifth Piano Concerto, with Berliner Symphoniker under Eduardo Marturet; Teacher, Piano Performance, Master's Programme, Simón Bolívar University, Caracas. Recordings: Chopin Etudes op 10, 25; Schubert Sonatas in G major and B Flat major; Beethoven Sonatas op 109, 110, 111; Beethoven's Emperor Concerto. Address: Calle Loma Larga 30, Los Guayalitos, Baruta, Caracas 1081, Venezuela.

RANGELOV, Svetozar; Singer (Bass); b. 1967, Bulgaria. Education: Graduated, State Musical Academy, Sofia, 1994. Career: Many concert and opera engagements in Bularia and elsewhere in Europe; Opera debut as Ferrando in Il Trovatore with the Bulgarian National Opera, 1995; Repertory also includes Le nozze di Figaro, Verdi's Vespri Siciliani and songs by Glière, Cui and Borodin; Contestant at the 1995 Cardiff Singer of the World Competition. Address: j.k. Druzba, bl.43, entr 7, ap 114, Sofia 1592, Bulgaria.

RANKI, Dezsö; Pianist; b. 8 Sept. 1951, Budapest, Hungary. Education: Béla Bart ók Conservatory; Ferenc Liszt Academy of Music; Graduated with distinction, 1973. Career: Has given numerous guest performances including: Kremlin Conservatory, Moscow, USSR; Royal Festival Hall, London, England; Deputised for Rubinstein in Milan and for Benedetti-Michelangeli at Menton; Appearances at International Festivals of Antibes, Helsinki, Lucerne, Menton, St Moritz, Paris and Prague; Carinthian Summer Festival, Ossiach, Villach; Solo part, Bernstein's The Age of Anxiety, Carinthian Festival, 1975; Regular appearances world-wide. Honours: Kossuth Prize; Liszt Prize; 1st Prize, Robert Schumann International Piano Competition, Zwickau, 1969; Recipient, 1st Prizes, National Piano Competitions, 1965, 1967, 1969.

RANKINE, Peter (John); Composer and Conductor; b. 11 March 1960, Queensland, Australia. Education: BMus, Queensland Conservatory, 1984; GradDipMus, 1985; MMus, University of Queensland, 1996. Career: Faculty Member, University of Queensland, 1987; Queenland University of Technology, 1988–94; Commissions from Queensland Wind Soloists, Australian Broadcasting Commission, Dance North, Opera Queensland, Canticum and others. Compositions include: Bunyip!, chamber opera, 1985; Three Movements for Orchestra, 1986; Eulogy for wind quintet, 1987; Symphonia Dialectica, 1988; From Fire by Fire for Wind octet, 1989; Celtic Cross for violin and chamber orchestra, 1990; Time and the Bell: Clarinet Concerto, 1990; John Brown, Rose, and the Midnight Cat, for ensemble, 1992; Surya Namaskar, Chaand Namaskar, for horn and percussion, 1993; Please No More Psalms, ballet score, for oboe, clarinet, percussion, violin and cello, 1994; Media Vita, for choir, clarinet, trombone and percussion, 1997. Honours: Sounds Australian Awards, 1990–91. Address: 3/15 Bellewe Terrace, St Lucia, Qld 4067, Australia.

RAPER, Marion (Eileen); Pianist and Accompanist; b. 18 Feb. 1938, Birmingham, England; m. 28 July 1962, divorced 1979. Education: Licentiate, Royal Academy of Music, 1957–59; University of London Teaching Certificate, Goldsmiths' College, University of London, 1959–61; BA, Honours, Open University; M.A. Manchester University. Career: Recitals throughout England with singers and instrumentalists; Broadcasts for BBC and Capital Radio; Teaching, Leeds College of

Music; Masterclasses; Tour of Canada with Jennifer Hillman, piano duo, 1987; Appearances on television (ITV and Channel 4); Second tour of Canada with Jennifer Hillman, 1989; mem, Incorporated Society of Musicians; Royal Soc. of Musicians. Address: 3 Cavendish Drive, Guiseley, Leeds LS20 8DR, England. Telephone: 01943 873060. E-mail: Marion.Raper@btinternet.co.uk.

RAPF, Kurt; Conductor, Musician and Composer; b. 15 Feb. 1922, Vienna, Austria; m. Ellen Rapf, 2 Dec 1961, one d. Education: Graduate in Piano, Organ and Conducting, Music Academy, Vienna. Career: Founder and Conductor, Collegium Musicum Wien (Vienna String Symphony), 1945–56; Assistant Conductor to Hans Knappertsbusch, Opera House Zürich, Switzerland; Accompanist for famous singers and instrumentalists; Director of Music, Innsbruck, 1953–60; Broadcast and television activities; Numerous tours in Europe, USA, Canada, Middle and Far East; Many appearances at festivals in Europe, Asia and America; Professor, Chief of Music Department, City of Vienna, 1970–87; Head of Austrian Composers' Guild, 1970–83; Founder and Music Director of Vienna Sinfonietta, 1986; Lecturer and jury participations. Compositions: Over 190 works for orchestra, choir, chamber orchestra, organ and piano solo, chamber music and vocal works include: 6 symphonies, 1976–2001; 2 operas; Passio Aeterna, 1979; Poem Symphonic, 1981; Reqium, 2000. Recordings: Over 70 records as conductor, harpsichordist, organist, pianist, and composer. Honours: Various. Address: Bossigasse 35, 1130 Vienna, Austria.

RAPHANEL, Ghilaine; Singer (Soprano); b. 19 April 1952, Rouen, France. Education: Studied at the Rouen Conservatory and at the Paris Conservatoire with Janine Micheau. Career: Sang Rosina in Il Barbiere di Siviglia at the Opera Studio of the Paris Opéra; Stadttheater Basle from 1980 as Gilda, Constanze, Juliette, Manon, and Titania in A Midsummer Night's Dream; Guest appearances in Lyon and Nantes; Hamburg Staatsoper, 1985, as the Queen of Night and Zerbinetta; Aix-en-Provence Festival, 1985, Zerbinetta; Sang at Mézières, 1988, as Amor in Orfeo ed Euridice; At Nancy, 1989, as Susanna. Recordings include: Pousette in Manon, L'Etoile by Chabrier; Fiorella in Les Brigands by Offenbach; Marguérite de Valois in Les Huguenots; Sang Nicolai's Frau Fluth at the Paris Opéra-Comique, 1995–96. Address: c/o Opéra de Nancy et de Lorraine, Rue Ste Catherine, 54000 Nancy, France.

RAPPE, Jadwiga; Singer (Contralto); b. 1957, Poland. Education: Studied in Warsaw and Breslau. Career: Sang at first in concert and made stage debut at Warsaw in 1983; Has sung throughout Europe in concert, notably with masses by Mozart, Bach and Beethoven and Szymanowski's Stabat Mater; Performances of Erda in Wagner's Ring at the Deutsche Oper Berlin, Warsaw and Covent Garden from 1988; Concerts of La Gioconda in Amsterdam and Strauss's Daphne (as Gaea) in Geneva, 1990–91; Other roles include Ulrica, Orpheus and Juno in Semele; Countess in The Queen of Spades for Scottish Opera, 1998; Season 2000–01 as Gaea in Daphne for the Deutsche Oper Berlin and Erda in Siegfried for Geneva Opera. Address: Warsaw National Opera, Grand Theatre, Place Teatrainy 1, 00-950 Warsaw, Poland.

RASILAINEN, Jukka; Singer (Bass-baritone); b. 1959, Helsinki, Finland. Education: Studied in Rome and Helsinki. Career: Debut: Savonlinna Festival, 1983, as Leporello; Lahti, 1984, as Rossini's Basilio; Dortmund Opera from 1986, as Verdi's Zaccaria and Ferrando, Galitzky in Prince Igor and Wozzeck; Karlsruhe, 1990, as Masetto and the Commendatore, in Don Giovanni; Vienna Staatsoper, 1991, as Wagner's Dutchman, Dresden, 1992–95, as Kaspar in Der Freischütz, Pizarro and Kurwenal; Finnish National Opera, 1996, as Wotan in Das Rheingold; Other roles include the Villains in Les contes d'Hoffmann, Scarpia, Amonasro and Jochanaan; Sang Strauss's Mandryka and Orestes at the Dresden Staatsoper, 1999; Season 2000–01 as Wagner's Wanderer at Mannheim, Wotan for the Zürich Opera and Jochanaan in Salome at Dresden. Address: c/o Finnish National Opera, PO Box 176, Helsingkatu 58, 00251 Helsinki, Finland.

RASMUSSEN, Karl Aage; Composer, Conductor and Professor of Music; b. 14 Dec. 1947, Kolding, Denmark; m. Charlotte Schiotz. 7 May 1975. Education: Composition with Per Norgaard, degrees in Music History, Theory and Composition, Academy of Music, Arhus. Career: Teacher: Academy of Music, Århus, 1970–, Royal Academy, Copenhagen, 1980–; Director, Conductor, Chamber Ensemble, The Elsinore Players, 1975–; Numerous duties at the New Music Department, Danish Radio, co-editing The Danish Music Magazine; Lectures, many European countries, USA; Artistic Director, NUMUS Festival, Århus, also Esbjerg Ensemble (1991–); mem, Danish Music Council; Danish Arts Foundation. Compositions include: Stage: Jephta, two-act opera, 1976–77; Majakovskij, two-act scenic concert piece, 1977–78; Jonas, musical play for radio, 1978–80; 'Our Hoffmann', opera, 1986; The Sinking of the Titanic, opera, 1994; Orchestral: Symphony Anfang und Ende, 1973; Contrafactum, concerto for cello and orchestra, 1980; A Symphony in Time, 1982; Movements on a Moving Line, 1985; Phantom Movements,

1989; Litania, 1994; Cosmology According to Chagall, piano and chamber orchestra, 1996; Blissful Music for violin and orchestra, 1997; Chamber: Protocol and Myth, 1971; Genklang, 1972; A Ballad of Game and Dream, 1974; Lullaby, 1976; Berio Mask, 1977; Le Tombeau de Père Igor, 1977; Parts Apart, 1978; Capricci e Dance, 1979; Italiensk Koncert, 1981; Ballo in Maschera, 1981; Pianissimo Furioso, 1982; A Quartet of Five, 1982; Solos and Shadows, 1983; Fugue/Fuga (Encore VIII), 1984; Surrounded by Sales, 1985; Still, string quartet, 1988; Solo instrument: Invention, 1972; Antifoni, 1973; Paganini Variations, 1976; Fugue/Fuga, 1984; Triple Tango, 1984; Etudes and Postludes, piano, 1990; I Will See a Rose at the end of the Path, string quartet, 1994; Vocal: Love Is In The World, 1974–75; One And All, 1976; Encore Series I–XI, 1977–85; Gebet for soprano and string quartet, 1996; Resurrexi...... for soprano, mezzo and chamber orchestra, 1997; Praise, for 4 voices, 1998. *Recordings:* String Quartets, Arditti String Quartet; A Symphony in Time, Danish Radio Symphony Orchestra; Movements on a Moving Line, Speculum Musicae. *Honours:* Carl Nielsen Prize, 1991. *Address:* Brokbjerggaard, 8752 Oestbirk, Denmark.

RASMUSSEN, Paula; Singer (Mezzo-soprano); b. 1965, California, USA. *Career:* Concert appearances with San Francisco Symphony under Nicholas McGegan in Bach Cantatas, the Los Angeles Master Chorale in Messiah, Bruckner's Te Deum and Pergolesi's Magnifict and with José Carreras in Dublin, 1992; Opera engagements as Nancy T'ang in the Peter Sellars production of Nixon in China at Los Angeles, Paris and Frankfurt; Lola in Cavalleria Rusticana with Long Beach Opera; Nancy in Albert Herring, Hansel, Anna in Les Troyens, Hippolyta in Midsummer Night's Dream and the Composer in Ariadne auf Naxos with the Los Angeles Music Center Opera; Sang Handel's Serse at Cologne, 1996 and Geneva, 1998; Season 2000 as Carmen at Cologne, Handel's Serse in Dresden and Cherubino for the New York City Opera. *Honours:* Regional Winner, 1992 Metropolitan Opera Competition. *Address:* c/o IMG Artists, Lovell House, 616 Chiswick High Road, London W4 5RX, England.

RATH, John Frédéric, BA; British opera and concert singer (bass); b. 10 June 1946, Manchester, England. *Education:* Manchester University, RNCM, Opera School at Basle; studied with Elsa Cavelti, Max Lorenz and Otakar Kraus. *Career:* debut as Ramphis in Aida, RNCM; Appearances with: English Music Theatre Company, Glyndebourne Festival, Touring Company Royal Opera House, Covent Garden, La Fenice, Venice, Maggio Musicale in Florence; Roles include: Masetto in Don Giovanni, Argante in Handel's Rinaldo, Sparafucile in Rigoletto, Escamillo and Zuniga in Carmen; Recently in Peter Brook's La Tragèdie de Carmen in Paris, its European tour and New York as Escamillo; Kent Opera: Rocco in Fidelio; Nexus Opera: The Traveller in Britten's Curlew River at Wells Cathedral and filmed by BBC 2; Edinburgh Festival: Jochanaan in Salome; English Bach Festival: Charon in Handel's Alceste; Appearances at various festivals; Principal Bass with D'Oyly Carte Opera; Concert and oratorio work throughout Europe including notable performances of Handel's Theodora in London, Spain and Italy, Bach Cantatas in NY and concert performances including Wotan in Das Rheingold and Die Walküre; Opera North: The Doctor in Berg's Wozzeck, 1993; Sarastro in Mozart's The Magic Flute, 1994; Nourabad in Bizet's Les Pêcheurs de Perles, 1995; Created a new English version of Schubert's Winter Journey with the poet Miriam Scott and performed it; Sang Herod in Stradella's San Giovanni Batista, Batignano, 1996; Satyr and Cythéron in Rameau's Platée in Berkeley, California, and Ferrando in Il Trovatore for Opera South in Cork, Ireland, 1998; Sang 2nd Soldier in Salome and the Poet in Salieri's Prima la musica poi le parole for Oper Frankfurt, 1999; Ashby in La Fanciulla de l'West for Opera Zuid, Maastricht; King Philip, Don Carlos; Pizarro, Fidelio; Golaud, Pelléas et Mélisande for Stadtsoper Bremerhaven, 2002–03; Sebastiano d'Alberts Tiefland; Wicks Booth, Sondheim Assassins; Iago, Otello and bass-baritone roles in Contes de Hoffman, also for Bremerhaven, 2003–04. *Recordings:* The Gondoliers and Iolanthe with the D'Oyly Carte. *Address:* Cwmilechwedd Fawr, Llanbister, Powys LD1 6UH, Wales.

RATJU, Adrian; Composer and Musicologist; b. 28 July 1928, Bucharest, Romania. *Education:* Studied harmony, counterpoint and compositions at the Bucharest Conservatory, 1950–56; Summer course at Darmstadt, Germany, 1969. *Career:* Professor at the Bucharest Conservatory from 1962; Executive Committee of the Union of Composers and Musicologists, Bucharest, from 1968. *Compositions include:* 2 String Quartets, 1956, 1988; 2 Symphonies, 1961, 1977; Concerto for oboe, bassoon and orchestra, 1963; Three Madrigals for chorus, after Shakespeare, 1964; Diptych for orchestra, 1965; Partita for wind quartet, 1966; Impressions for ensemble, 1969; Fragment of a Triumphal Arch for Beethoven for soprano, clarinet and piano, 1970; Six Images for orchestra, 1971; Transfigurations, for piano, clarinet and spring trio, 1975; Trio for flute and oboe and clarinet, 1980; Sonata a Cinque, for brass quintet, 1984; Sonata for solo violin, 1985; Trio for piano, clarinet and guitar, 1987; Piano Concerto, 1988; Echoes, for vibraphone and marimba, 1989;

Violin Sonata, 1991; Convergences, for piano, clarinet and percussion, 1994; Hommage a Erik Satie, for voice and piano, 1994. *Honours:* Six composition prizes from the Union of Composers and Musicologists, 1967–93. *Address:* c/o UCMR , Calea Victoriei 141, Sector 1, Bucharest, Romania. *Telephone:* 0040212127966. *Fax:* 0040212107211. *E-mail:* ucmr@itcnet.ro.

RATTAY, Evzen; Cellist; b. 1945, Czechoslovakia. *Education:* Studied at the Prague Academy of Arts. *Career:* Cellist of the Talich String Quartet from 1962; Tours to most European countries, Egypt, Iraq, North America, Japan, Indonesia; Chamber Ensemble of the Czech Philarmonic from 1975; Annual visits to France from 1976; Tours of the United Kingdom, 1990–91, with concerts at the Wigmore Hall, appearances at the Bath and Bournemouth Festivals, Queen Elizabeth Hall and on BBC 2's Late Show, with Janácek's 2nd quartet; Also played Beethoven's Quartet Opus 74, the Brahms A minor, Smetana D minor and works by Mozart in England; Festival appearances in Vienna, Besançon, Lucerne, Helsinki, Amsterdam, Prague and Salzburg; Repertoire also includes works by Debussy, Bartók (complete quartets recorded), Shostakovich, Ravel and Dvořák. *Recordings include:* Complete quartets of Beethoven; Albums. *Honours:* Grand Prix Charles Cros. *Address:* c/o Clarion/Seven Muses, 64 Whitehall Park, London N19 3 TN, England.

RATTI, Eugenia; Singer (Soprano); b. 5 April 1933, Genoa, Italy. *Education:* Studied with her mother. *Career:* Concert tour with Tito Schipa, 1952; Stage debut, 1954, in Sestri Levante; La Scala Milan from 1955, as Lisa in La Sonnambula, and in the premiere of Milhaud's David, 1955, and Dialogues des Carmélites, 1957; Holland Festival, 1955, 1961, as Nannetta and Adina; Edinburgh Festival, 1957, Il Matrimonio Segreto; Holland Festival, 1970, in Haydn's La Fedelta Premiata; Returned to Glyndebourne, 1973 and 1976, as the Italian Singer in Capriccio; Other roles include Zerlina in Don Giovanni, Susanna, Rosina, Musetta and Oscar. *Recordings:* Un Ballo in Maschera; Il Matrimonio Segreto; Aida; La Sonnambula; Don Giovanni, conducted by Leinsdorf. *Address:* c/o La Scala Opera, Via Drammatici 2, 20121 Milan, Italy.

RATTLE, Sir Simon, Kt, CBE; British conductor; *Chief Conductor and Artistic Director, Berlin Philharmonic Orchestra;* b. 19 Jan. 1955, Liverpool; m. 1st Elise Ross 1980 (divorced 1995); two s.; m. 2nd Candace Allen 1996. *Education:* Royal Acad. of Music. *Career:* won John Player Int. Conducting Competition 1973; has conducted Bournemouth Symphony, Northern Sinfonia, London Philharmonic, London Sinfonietta, Berlin Philharmonic, LA Philharmonic, Stockholm Philharmonic, Vienna Philharmonic, Philadelphia Orchestra, Boston Symphony orchestras, etc.; debut at Queen Elizabeth Hall, London 1974, Royal Festival Hall, London 1976, Royal Albert Hall, London 1976; Asst Conductor, BBC Symphony Orchestra 1977–80; Assoc. Conductor, Royal Liverpool Philharmonic Soc. 1977–80; Glyndebourne debut 1977, Royal Opera, Covent Garden debut 1990; Artistic Dir, London Choral Soc. 1979–84; Prin. Conductor and Artistic Adviser, City of Birmingham Symphony Orchestra (CBSO) 1980–90, Music Dir 1990–98; Artistic Dir South Bank Summer Music 1981–83; Jt Artistic Dir Aldeburgh Festival 1982–93; Prin. Guest Conductor, LA Philarmonic 1981–94, Rotterdam Philharmonic 1981–84; Prin. Guest Conductor Orchestra of the Age of Enlightenment 1992–; Chief Conductor and Artistic Dir Berlin Philharmonic Orchestra 2002–; Hon. Fellow St Anne's Coll. Oxford 1991. *Honours:* Hon. DMus (Liverpool) 1991, (Leeds) 1993; Edison Award (for recording of Shostakovich's Symphony No. 10) 1987, Grand Prix du Disque (Turangalîla Symphony) 1988, Grand Prix Caecilia (Turangalîla Symphony, Jazz Album) 1988, Gramophone Record of the Year Award (Mahler's Symphony No. 2) 1988, Gramophone Opera Award (Porgy and Bess) 1989, Int. Record Critics' Award (Porgy and Bess) 1990, Grand Prix de l' Acad. Charles Cros 1990, Gramophone Artist of the Year 1993, Montblanc de la Culture Award 1993, Toepfer Foundation Shakespeare Prize (Hamburg) 1996, Gramophone Award for Best Concerto recording (Szymanowski Violin Concertos Nos 1 and 2), Albert Medal (RSA) 1997, Choc de l'Année Award (for recording of Brahms Piano Concerto Op. 15) 1998, Outstanding Achievement Award, South Bank Show 1999, Diapason Recording of the Year Award (complete Beethoven Piano Concertos) 1999, Gramophone Award for Best Opera Recording (Szymanowski's King Roger) 2000, Gramophone Awards for Best Orchestral Recording and Record of the Year (Mahler's Symphony No. 10) 2000, Comenius Prize (Germany) 2004; Officier, Ordre des Arts et des Lettres 1995. *Current Management:* Askonas Holt Ltd, Lonsdale Chambers, 27 Chancery Lane, London, WC2A 1PF, England. *Telephone:* (20) 7400-1700. *Fax:* (20) 7400-1799. *E-mail:* info@askonasholt.co.uk. *Website:* www.askonasholt.co.uk. *Address:* Berlin Philharmonie Orchestra, Philharmonie, Matthäckirchstrasse 1, 14057 Berlin, Germany (office).

RAUCH, Wolfgang; singer (baritone); b. 27 Jan. 1957, Cologne, Germany. *Education:* Studied in Cologne with Josef Metternich and in Italy with Mario del Monaco. *Career:* Sang with the Deutsche Oper am Rhein Düsseldorf from 1984, member of the Bayerische Staatsoper Munich from 1987; Guest appearances at La Scala Milan, the State Operas of Vienna and Hamburg and the Deutsche Oper Berlin; Sang Papageno in Mozart bicentenary performances of Die Zauberflöte at Barcelona and Bonn, 1991; Other roles include Lortzing's Tsar, Marcello, Mozart's Guglielmo and Figaro, Count Perruchetto in Haydn's La Fedeltà Premiata, Silvio, Lionel in Tchaikovsky's The Maid of Orleans, Strauss's Count in Capriccio and Harlekin and the Herald in Lohengrin (Hamburg, 1998); Season 2000–01 as Puccini's Marcello at Hamburg, Strauss's Spirit Messenger at Barcelona and Lescaut in Henze's Boulevard Solitude for Covent Garden; Frequent concert and broadcasting engagements. *Address:* c/o Hamburgische Staatsoper, Grosse Theaterstrasse 34, 20354 Hamburg, Germany.

RAUNIG, Arnold; Singer (Counter-tenor); b. 1956, Klagenfurt, Germany. *Education:* Member of the Vienna Boys' Choir, 1966–72, studied at the Linz Conservatoire and with Kurt Equiluz in Vienna. *Career:* Many appearances in Baroque music throughout Europe, notably in works by Bach, Handel and Mozart in Vienna, Berlin and Hamburg; Repertoire includes Mozart's Ascanio in Alba and Idomeneo, Handel's Radamisto and Xerxes, Cesti's Pomo d'Oro and The Fairy Queen; Wiesbaden Festival, 1992, in the premiere of Der Park by Hans Gefors; Sang Creon in the premiere of Medea by Osca Strasnoy, Spoleto 2000. *Address:* c/o Wiesbaden Opera, Hessisches Staatstheater, Christian-Zais-Strasse 3-5, Pf 3247, W-6200 Wiesbaden, Germany.

RAUTAVAARA, Einojuhani; Composer; b. 9 Oct. 1928, Helsinki, Finland; m. Sini Koivisto, 18 Aug 1984. *Education:* MA, University of Helsinki; Sibelius Academy, 1950–57; Juilliard School of Music with Vincent Persichetti, New York, USA, 1955–56; Tanglewood Music Center with Aaron Copland and Roger Sessions, 1955–56; Ascona, Switzerland with Vladimir Vogel, 1957; Kölner Musikhochschule with Rudolf Petzold, Germany, 1958. *Career:* Lecturer, Music Theory, Sibelius Academy, 1966–76; Art Professor, Finland, 1971–76; Professor of Composition, Sibelius Academy, 1976–90. *Compositions:* 8 Operas including Thomas (1985), Vincent, 1990 and Rasputin, 2002; 2 Choir-Operas; 8 Symphonies; Concerti for cello, piano, flute, violin, organ, double bass, clarinet and harp; Cantus Arcticus concerto for birds and orchestra; Cantatas; Chamber Music; String Quintet 1997; 4 String Quartets; Piano Music, Songs and other works. *Recordings include:* Thomas, opera; Vincent, opera; Aleksis Kivi, opera; The House of the Sun, Opera; 8 Symphonies, Ondine Company; Angel of Dusk, concerto for Double Bass and Orchestra; Vigilia, orthodox Mass; Cantus Arcticus; Piano Concertos 1, 2 and 3; Naxos; Symphony 6; Symphony 7; Organ Concerto; Flute Concerto. *Publications:* Libretti for operas: Kaivos, 1957; Thomas, 1986; Vincent, 1986; House of the Sun, 1990; Gift of the Magi, 1993; Alexis Kivi, 1995; Omakuva, memoirs, 1989; Rasputin, 2001. *Current Management:* Boosey & Hawkes, London. *Address:* Puolipäivankatu 4A9, Helsinki 16, Finland. *E-mail:* erautava@sivoa.fi.

RAUTIO, Nina; Singer (soprano); b. 21 Sept. 1957, Bryansk, Russia. *Education:* Studied at Leningrad Conservatoire. *Career:* Sang first at the Leningrad State Theatre, 1981–87; Bolshoi Opera from 1987; Western debut with Bolshoi Company at Metropolitan and the Edinburgh Festival 1991, as Tatiana and as Oksana in Rimsky's Christmas Eve; Season 1992, as Manon Lescaut at La Scala, conducted by Lorin Maazel, Verdi Requiem at Rome, Aida at the Savonlinna Festival and in concert performances conducted by Zubin Mehta; Sang with the Pittsburgh Symphony on tour to Seville Expo 92 and as Elisabetta in Don Carlo to open the season at La Scala; Season 1993–94, as Lisa in The Queen of Spades at the Opéra Bastille Paris, Ballo in Maschera and Aida at Covent Garden, Verdi Requiem at Florence and the Festival Hall, Beethoven and Mahler in Pittsburgh, Desdemona at the Orange Festival, the Glagolitic Mass at La Scala and Amelia Boccanegra at Florence; Season 1994–95, as Aida at the Staatsoper Berlin and Amelia Boccanegra at Florence and Turin; Season 1995–96 Metropolitan Opera debut as Aida; Sang Aida at the Verona Arena, 1996, and the Trovatore Leonora at Geneva, 1998; Sang Tosca at Glasgow, 2000. *Recordings:* Manon Lescaut; Verdi Requiem; Guillaume Tell; Norma. *Current Management:* Athole Still International Management, Forresters Hall, 25–27 Westow Street, London, SE19 3RY, England. *Telephone:* (20) 8771-5271. *Fax:* (20) 8768-6600. *Website:* www.atholestill.com.

RAWLINS, Emily, BMus; opera and concert singer; b. 25 Sept. 1950, Lancaster, OH, USA; m. 1982. *Education:* Indiana University, Curtis Institute of Music, Hochschule für Musik, Vienna. *Career:* debut in Basel, Switzerland; Basel Stadttheater, 1973–77; Deutsche Oper am Rhein, 1977–82; Debuts, Theater der Stadt Bonn, 1975, National Theater, Mannheim, 1976, Theater der Stadt Köln, 1977, Städtische Bühnen, Dortmund, 1979, Städtische Bühnen, Augsburg; San Francisco Opera, 1980; American premiere, Lear, Salzburg Festival, world premiere of Baal, 1981; Vienna Staatsoper, 1981; Teatro Nacional de São Carlos, Lisbon, 1982; Grand Théâtre de Genève, 1982; Houston Grand Opera, 1983; American premiere of Anna Karenina, Los Angeles

Opera Theater, 1983; Appeared on television, ZDF Germany, 1981, 1982, ORF, Austria, 1981; Film appearances in Bartered Bride and Fra Diavolo, 1983, and Baal, 1984; Vienna State Opera, 1985; ORF with Wiener Symphoniker; Concert Opera Association, 1986; World premiere of Das Schloss, Opera National, Brussels, 1986; Sang Third Norn in Götterdämmerung at Cologne, 2000. *Recordings:* Baal (singing part of Sophie) 1985. *Address:* c/o Alferink, Appololaan 181, 1077 AT Amsterdam, Netherlands.

RAWNSLEY, John; Singer (Baritone); b. 14 Dec. 1949, England. *Education:* Royal Northern College of Music. *Career:* Debut: Glyndebourne Touring Opera, 1975; Later sang Verdi's Ford and Stravinsky's Nick Shadow on tour, Mozart's Masetto, Rossini's Figaro and Puccini's Marcello at Glyndebourne; Covent Garden debut, 1979, as Schaunard in La Bohème; French debut at Nancy in 1980, as Tonio in Pagliacci; English National Opera from 1982, as Amonasro and as Rigoletto in Jonathan Miller's production of Verdi's opera; Tour to the USA, 1984; Italian debut, 1985, as Verdi's Renato in Trieste; La Scala Milan, 1987, as Tonio; Guest engagements at the Vienna Staatsoper, San Diego, Barcelona, Bilbao, Brussels and Geneva: Roles include Paolo Albiani (Simon Boccanegra), Macbeth, Papageno, Don Alfonso and Taddeo in L'Italiana in Algeri; Sang Rigoletto at Turin, 1989; Simon Boccanegra in a concert performance at the Festival Hall, 1990; Season 1992 as Rigoletto at Oslo and the Coliseum, and in The Beggar's Opera at the Aldeburgh Festival; Sang Falstaff for Opera Zuid, Netherlands, 1994. *Recordings:* Rigoletto; Masetto in Don Giovanni; Videos of Così fan tutte, Il Barbiere di Siviglia, La Bohème and Rigoletto. *Address:* c/o Kaye Artists Management, Barratt House, 7 Chertsey Road, Woking, Surrey GU21 5 AB, England.

RAXACH, Enrique; Dutch composer; b. 15 Jan. 1932, Barcelona, Spain. *Education:* studied in Darmstadt with Messiaen, Boulez, Stockhausen and Maderna, 1959–66. *Compositions include:* Estudis for strings, 1952; Six Movements for orchestra, 1955; Polifonias, for strings, 1956; Metamorphose I–II for orchestra, 1956–58; Metamorphose III for 15 solo instruments, 1959; Columna de fuego for orchestra 1958; Fluxion, for 17 players, 1963; Syntagma, for orchestra, 1965; Fragmento II for soprano, flute and 2 percussionists, 1966; Textures for orchestra, 1966; Inside Outside for orchestra and tape, 1969; Paraphrase for mezzo-soprano and 11 players, 1969; 2 String Quartets, 1961, 1971; Rite of Perception, electronic tape music, 1971; Interface for chorus and orchestra, 1972; Scattertime for 6 players, 1972; Sine Nomine for soprano and orchestra, 1973; Figuren in einer Landschaft for orchestra, 1974; Chimaera for bass clarinet and tape, 1974; Erdenlicht for orchestra, 1975; Aubade for percussion quartet, 1979; The Hunting in Winter for horn and piano, 1979; Am Ende des Regenbogens, for orchestra, 1980; Careful with that… for clarinet and percussionist, 1982; Chalumeau for clarinet quartet, 1982; Ode for flute and string trio, 1982; Vortice for 9 clarinets, 1983; …hub of ambiguity, for soprano and 8 players, 1984; Opus Incertum for chamber orchestra, 1985; Calles y sueños, for chamber orchestra, 1986; Obsessum for bassoon and 9 accordions, 1988; Nocturno del hueco for chorus, large ensemble and tape, 1990; Danses Pythiques for harp, 1992; Decade for bass clarinet and accordion, 1992; 12 Preludes for piano, 1993; Reflections inside, electronic tape music, 1994; Piano Concertino, 1995; Neumes for percussion sextet, 1996; Nocturnal Stroll for flute orchestra, 1996; Chapter Three for orchestra, 1997. *Address:* c/o Vereniging BUMA, PO Box 725, 1180 AS Amstelveen, Netherlands.

RAYAM, Curtis; Singer (Tenor); b. 4 Feb. 1951, Belleville, Florida, USA. *Education:* Studied at the University of Miami with Mary Henderson Buckley. *Career:* Debut: Miami, 1971, in Manon Lescaut; Appearances in Dallas, Houston and Jackson Opera South; European debut at the Wexford Festival, 1976, in Giovanni d'Arco by Verdi, returning as the Sultan in Mozart's Zaide and as Wilhelm Meister in Thomas' Mignon; Boston, 1979, as Olympion in the US premiere of Tippett's The Ice Break, conducted by Sarah Caldwell; Amsterdam, 1981, as Massenet's Werther; Further engagements at Salzburg, Paris, Frankfurt and Venice; La Scala, 1985, in Handel's Alcina, returning 1988 as Orcane in Fetonte by Jommelli; Spoleto, 1988, as Creon in Traetta's Antigone; Other roles include Rossini's Otello and Cleomene (L'Assedio di Corinto), Mozart's Idomeneo, Belmonte and Mitridate, Irus in Il Ritorno d'Ulisse, Nemorino and Puccini's Pinkerton and Rodolfo; Sang Titus April in the premiere of Buchuland by Roelof Temmingh, Pretoria, 1998. *Recordings include:* Treemonisha by Scott Joplin; Da-ud in Die Aegyptische Helena by Strauss. *Honours:* Finalist, Metropolitan Auditions, 1972; Winner, Dallas Competition, 1974.

RAYMOND, Deborah; Soprano; b. 26 Nov. 1951, Chicago, Illinois, USA; m. Nando Schellen, 19 June 1991. *Education:* BMus, School of Music, University of Iowa; Private studies with Jean Kraft, Bill and Dixie Neill, Pauline Tinsley, Virginia Zeani. *Career:* Debut: Netherlands Opera, Amsterdam, 1983; Leading roles: Salome at Staatsoper Dresden, 1988, at Aachen, 1989, at Salt Lake City, Utah, 1993, at Charlotte, North Carolina, 1994, with Arizona Opera at Tucson and Phoenix, 1995; Marie in Wozzeck, at Coburg, 1989, at Spoleto Festival, USA, 1997; Woman in Erwartung, with Netherlands Radio Symphony Orchestra, 1988, in Indianapolis, 1994; Zoë in Stephen Climax (Hans Zender), La Monnaie Opera, Brussels, 1990; Eine Diene in Reigen (Ph Boesmans/Luc Bondy), La Monnaie, Brussels, 1991–93 (Strasbourg and Paris); Tatiana in Eugene Onegin, with the Bolshoi Opera of Belorus at Minsk, 1993; Mimi in La Bohéme, USA, 1994, 1996, 1997; Title role in Tosca, USA, 1996, 1998, 2000; Nedda in Pagliacci, USA, 1997–98; Cio-Cio San in Madama Butterfly, USA, 1997–99; Appears often in concerts and recitals, in USA 1996, 1997, 1999, 2000, 2001; Voice teacher at Northern Arizona University, Flagstaff AZ as of 2001. *Recordings include:* Reigen (Philippe Boesmans-Bondy). *Current Management:* Sara Tornay and Blythe de Blasis. *Address:* c/o Sara Tornay, 155 W 72nd Street, New York, NY 10023, USA.

REA, John; Composer; b. 14 Jan. 1944, Toronto, Ontario, Canada. *Education:* Studied with John Weinzweg at University of Toronto and Milton Babbitt at Princeton. *Career:* Teacher at McGill University, 1973, Dean of the Faculty of Music, 1986–91; Composer-in-Residence at Mannheim, 1984; Founder Member of the Montreal music society Les Evénements du Neuf. *Compositions:* Music theatre pieces: Les Jours, ballet, 1969; The Prisoner's Play, opera, 1973; Hommage à Richard Wagner, 1988; Com-possession, 1980; Le Petit Livre des Ravalet, opera, 1983; Offenes Lied, operatic scenes, 1986; Operatic scenes based on Dante's Inferno and Poe's Morella, 1990–93; Orchestral: Hommage à Vasarely, 1977; Vanishing Points, 1983; Over Time, 1987; Time and Again, 1987; Chamber: Clarinet Sonatina, 1965; Sestina, 1968; Prologue, Scene and Movement for soprano, viola and 2 pianos, 1968; Tempest, 1969; What You Will for piano, 1969; La Dernière Sirène for ondes martenot, piano and percussion, 1981; Les Raison des Forces Mouvantes for flute and string quartet, 1984; Some Time Later for amplified string quartet, 1986; Vocal: Litaneia for chorus and orchestra, 1984. *Address:* c/o McGill University, Faculty of Music, Strathcona Music Building, 555 Sherbrooke Street West, Montreal, Quebec H3A 1E3, Canada.

READ, Gardner; Composer and University Professor; b. 2 Jan. 1913, Evanston, Illinois, USA. *Education:* BMus, 1936, MMus, 1937, Eastman School of Music; Composition with Jan Sibelius, Finland, 1939, Aaron Copland, Tanglewood, 1941, others; Piano, Organ, Conducting, Theory, various masters. *Career:* Teacher, Composition, Theory, 1940–; Professor, Composition, Music Theory, Composer in Residence, 1948–, Emeritus, 1978–, School of Fine and Applied Arts, Boston University; Guest Conductor, major orchestras including Boston Symphony, 1943, 1954, Philadelphia Orchestra, 1964; Originator, Host, weekly educational radio series Our American Music, 1953–60; Orchestral works performed by major orchestras, USA and abroad. *Compositions:* Numerous, orchestral, chamber, solo, organ, piano, choral, vocal, including Villon, opera, 1967; Many commissions such as: Passacaglia and Fugue, 1938; A Bell Overture, 1946. *Recordings:* Night Flight, 1942; Toccata Giocosa, 1953; Los Dioses Aztecas, 1982; De Profundis, 1985, 1991; Preludes on Old Southern Hymns, 1985, 1990; Symphony No. 4, 1986; Sonata Brevis, 1986; Works for Organ, 1989; Invocation, 1991; Sonata da Chiesa, String Quartet No. 1, Sononic Fantasia No. 1, Fantasy-Toccata, Five Aphorisms, all 1995; Phantasmagoria, 1996; Epistle to the Corinthians; The Hidden Lute; By-Low; My Babe; Concerto for piano and orchestra, 1997; Gardner Read: The Art of Song, 1999. *Publications include:* Thesaurus of Orchestral Devices, 1969; Music Notation, 2nd edition, 1969; Contemporary Instrumental Techniques, 1976; Modern Rhythmic Notation, 1978; Style and Orchestration, 1979; Source Book of Proposed Music Notation Reforms, 1987; 20th-Century Microtonal Notation, 1990; Compendium of Modern Instrumental Techniques, 1993; Gardner Read: A Bio-Bibliography by Mary Ann Dodd and Jayson Engquist, 1995; Pictographic Score Notation, 1998; Orchestral Combinations: The Science and Art of Instrumental Tone-Color, 2002. *Address:* 47 Forster Road, Manchester, MA 01944, USA.

REANEY, Gilbert; Professor; b. 11 Jan. 1924, Sheffield, England. *Education:* Licentiate, Royal Academy of Music, 1946; BA 1948, BMus 1950, MA 1951, Sheffield University; Sorbonne University, Paris, France, 1950–53. *Career:* Performer, BBC and tours of the United Kingdom and the continent, 1952–88; Research Fellow, Reading University, 1953–56, Birmingham, 1956–59; Director of London Medieval Group, 1958–; Visiting Professor, Hamburg University, Germany, 1960; Associate Professor, University of California, Los Angeles, 1960–62, Full Professor, 1963–97; mem, Royal Musical Association; American Musicological Society; Plainsong and Medieval Music Society. *Publications:* Early 15th Century Music, 7 vols, (10 vols for Corpus Scriptorum de Musica), 1955–83; Catalogue, Medieval Polyphonic Manuscripts to 1400, 2 vols, 1966, 1969; The Music Theory of John Hothby, 1989. *Contributions:* Assistant and Co-editor of numerous articles in Musica Disciplina, 1956–97; General Editor of

Corpus Scriptorum de Musica. *Address:* 1001 Third Street, Santa Monica, CA 90403, USA.

REARICK, Barbara; Singer (Mezzo-soprano); b. 1960, USA. *Education:* Studied at Manhattan School of Music and at Britten-Pears School with Nancy Evans and Anthony Rolfe Johnson. *Career:* Concert and opera performances in the United Kingdom and USA; British debut, 1987, at Aldeburgh Festival as Britten's Lucretia; Sang Copland's Old American Songs with Lukas Foss, piano, at the Snape Concert Hall; Other repertoire includes Messiah, Lieder eines fahrenden Gesellen, L'Enfance du Christ and Britten's Charm of Lullabies orchestrated by Colin Matthews, all at Snape; Ravel's Chansons Madécasses, Haydn Masses with the Orchestra of St John's Smith Square and Handel's Dixit Dominus at the Norfolk and Norwich Festival, American popular songs there, 1992, with Richard Rodney Bennett; Operatic repertoire includes Meg Page, Chautauqua Opera, Suzuki in Opera Delaware and Annina in Rosenkavalier in New York City Opera; Member of the Britten-Pears Ensemble, with performances throughout the United Kingdom and USA. *Address:* c/o Owen-White Management, 14 Nightingale Road, London N8 7QU, England.

REAUX, Angelina; Singer (Soprano); b. 1959, Houston, Texas, USA. *Career:* Sang in various New York night clubs and was discovered by Leonard Bernstein; Sang Mimi in La Bohème at Rome, 1987, and recorded the role with Bernstein; New York Academy of Music, 1989, as Dido by Purcell, Musetta at Boston and Despina at the Kentucky Opera, 1993; Other roles include Pamina, Nedda and the Woman in La Voix Humaine; Sang The Queen of Sparta in La Belle Hélène for L'Opéra Français de New York, 1996. *Recordings include:* La Bohème; Street Scene by Weill and Blitzstein's Regina. *Address:* c/o Kentucky Opera, 631 South Fifth Street, Louisville, KY 40202, USA.

REAVILLE, Richard; Singer (Tenor); b. 1954, England. *Career:* Appearances with English National Opera, Welsh National Opera, Scottish Opera and Mid Wales Opera; Glyndebourne Festival and Tour, London Opera Players and festivals in the United Kingdom, France and Germany; Roles have included Jacquino in Fidelio, Mozart's Monostatos and Arbace, Britten's Peter Grimes and Albert Herring and Herod in Salome; Wagner's Loge, Froh and David, and Don José on tour to the Far East (1996); Concerts throughout Europe, including engagements with the BBC Philharmonic Orchestra, Danish Radio Symphony Orchestra, Belgian State Orchestra, Odense Philharmonic, Weimar Staatskapelle and various chamber ensembles; Mahler's Das Lied von der Erde with the Rander Orchestra (Denmark), Puccini's Messa di Gloria with the Ostrava Philharmonic Orchestra and Ligeti's Le Grand Macabre with the Odense Symphony Orchestra (1996–97); Sang Second Judge in Param Vir's Broken Strings, Glasgow, 1998. *Address:* c/o Tivoli Artists, 3 Vesterbrogade, DK–1630 Copenhagen, Denmark.

RECHBERGER, Herman; Finnish composer and performer; b. 14 Feb. 1947, Linz, Austria; m. (1) Ilse Maier, 1966, 1 s., 1 d., (2) Soile Jaatinen, 1972, 1 s., 2 d. *Education:* Graphic Arts, Linz, 1967; Teaching degree, Classical Guitar, Recorder, 1973, Diploma, Composition, 1976, Sibelius Academy, Helsinki. *Career:* Music Teacher, Choir Conductor, 1975–79; Producer of Contemporary Music, Artistic Director of Experimental Studio, Finnish Broadcasting, 1979–84; State Grant, 1985–; Recitals of new recorder music, most European countries, Russia, Cuba, USA; Performed own works, ISCM Music Days, Helsinki and Stockholm, 1978, Athens, 1979, Warsaw, 1992, and Helsinki Biennale, 1981, 1983; Frequent performances and tours with ensembles Poor Knights; Guest Composer for Hungarofilm at Hungarian Broadcasting Company's Electronic Music Studio, 1985, and Slovak Radio (Rustle of Spring), 1986; Composer-in-Residence. *Compositions include:* Orchestral: Consort Music 1, 2, 4, 5; The Garden of Delights; Venezia; 3 guitar concertos; Goya; Cello Concerto, 1999; Operas: The Nuns; Laurentius nunc and semper, 1998; The Night of Wishes, 2000; Ballet, The Changeling Princess, 1997; Radiophonic works: The Rise of Mr Jonathan Smith; Magnus Cordius, entries in a diary; Vocal music: Vanha Linna; Hades; Dunk; Notturno inamorata; Seis Canciones de anochecer; Musica Picta for small children; Tape music: Cordamix; Narod; KV-622bis; Moldavia; Rustle of Spring; Multimedia: Zin Kibaru; Firenze 1582; Survol; La Folia; Chamber music: Consort Music 3 for brass nonet; El Palacio del Sonido for 3 guitars; Consort Music 6 for 12 recorders; Musical graphics and pictographic scores for educational purposes; Many arrangements and reconstructions of early music and Ancient Greek music, e.g. the world's first opera, Jacopo Peri's Euridice. *Recordings include:* The King's Hunt, Esa-Pekka Salonen, French horn; Cordamix; Rasenie järi, Rustle of Spring; The Garden of Delights, Austrian RSO, conductor Leif Segerstam; Consort Music I, Clas Pehrson, recorders, Swedish RSO, conductor Leif Segerstam. *Address:* Laajavuorenkuja 5 B 11, 01620 Vantaa, Finland.

RECHNAGEL, Axel; Organist and Cantor; b. 27 March 1936, Århus; m. 2 d. *Education:* Århus Cathedral School, 1954; University of Århus, 1955–59; State Academy of Music, Århus, 1960; Vienna, Austria, 1959;

USA, 1969. *Career:* Organist, Ringkobing, 1961; Organist and Kantor, Nyborg, Denmark, 1965; Retired 1999; mem, Dansk Organist og Kantor Samfund; Det danske Orgelselskab. *Compositions:* Koncert for Orgel, 1968. *Recordings:* Concerto for Organ, 1993. *Publications:* Concerto For Organ, The Society for the Publication of Danish Music, 1998; Co-author, Nyborg Vor Frue Kirke 1388–1988. *Honours:* Toccata for Organ, Odense, Denmark, 1996. *Address:* Grejsdalen 5, 5800, Nyborg, Denmark.

RECTANUS, L. Hans; Professor of Music; b. 18 Feb. 1935, Worms, Germany; m. Elisabeth Zilbauer, 1 s., 1 d. *Education:* Civic Music Academy and University, Frankfurt/Main; Academy of Music and Interpretive Art, University of Vienna; School for Protestant Church Music, Schlüchtern/Hesse; PhD, University of Frankfurt, 1966. *Career:* Teacher (Music, German Literature) for Gymnasium, 1960–63; Lecturer and Assistant, University of Frankfurt/Main, 1963–66; Lecturer, 1966–71, Professor, 1971–, Teachers' College, Heidelberg; mem, Präsidium, Hans Pfitzner Society, Munich; Society for Music Research, Cassel; Society of Professional Choirmasters. *Compositions:* Edited: Hans Pfitzner String Quartet in D minor; Trio for violin, violoncello and piano. *Publications:* Leitmotiv und Form in den Musikdramatischen Werken Hans Pfitzners, 1967; Neue Ansätze im Musikunterricht, 1972; Hans Pfitzner, Sämtliche Lieder mit Klavierbegleitung, vol. I, 1980, vol. II, 1983. *Contributions:* Die Musikforschung; Riemannmusiklexikon; Studien zur Musikgeschichte des 19 Jahrhundert; Mitteilungen der Hans Pfitzner-Gesellschaft; Festchrift H. Osthoff; Renaissance-Studien; Zeitschrift für Musik-Pädagogik; Lexikon der Musikpädagogik; Pfitzner-Studien. *Honours:* Kritiker-Preis, 1956; Recipient, Music Director, Organist Prizes. *Address:* Schlittweg 31, 6905 Schriesheim/Bergstr, Germany.

REDEL, Kurt; Conductor and Flautist; b. 8 Oct. 1918, Breslau, Germany. *Education:* Studied flute, conducting and composition at the Breslau Hochschule für Musik. *Career:* Conductor and flute soloist from 1938; Professor at Salzburg Mozarteum, 1938; Professor at the Music Academy Detmold, 1943; Debut as flautist outside Germany at Menton, 1950; Founded the Munich Pro Arte Orchestra, 1952; Conducted at Festival de Royaumont and the Semaines Musicales in Paris, 1953; Founder and Artistic Director of the Easter Festival at Lourdes; Conductor of the Mozart Chamber Orchestra of Salzburg. *Recordings include:* Bach's Brandenburg Concertos, Orchestral Suites, Die Kunst der Fuge, Musikalisches Opfer, Harpsichord and Violin Concertos, Magnificat, Masses and Cantatas; Telemann Concertos for flute, oboe, trumpet, viola and violin, St Mark Passion and St Matthew Passion; Vivaldi Four Seasons and other concertos; Concerti Grossi by Handel, Torelli, Corelli, Scarlatti, Stölzel; Music by Marais, Couperin, Caldara, Carissimi and Marcello; Mozart Symphonies, Divertimenti, and Concertante K364; Solo flautist in Mozart Sonatas, Quartets and Concertos; Schubert 4th Symphony with the Czech Philharmonic.

REDEL, Martin (Christoph); Composer; b. 30 Jan. 1947, Detmold, Germany. *Education:* Studied with Kelterborn and Gishele Klebe at Detmold, 1964–69, and with Isang Yun in Hanover. *Career:* Faculty, Detmold Hochschule, from 1971; Professor of Composition, 1979; Rector 1993; President of Jeunesses Musicales, 1992. *Compositions include:* String Quartet, 1967; Strophen, for orchestra, 1970; Epilog for baritone, flute and guitar, 1971; Dispersion, for ensemble, 1972; Kammersinfonie II, 1972; Konfrontationen, for orchestra, 1974; Correspondences, for 2 percussion, 1975; Interplay for ensemble, 1975; Mobile, for oboe, clarinet and bassoon, 1976; Concerto for Orchestra, 1978; Espressioni, for woodwind quintet, 1980; Traumtanz for percussion and strings, 1981; Bruckner Essay for orchestra, 1982; Clarinet Quintet, 1988; Visions Fugitives for accordion and percussion, 1993; Teamwork, for 17 instruments, 1997; Vivo, for 4 percussion, 1997. *Publications:* Grundlagen des Kadenzspiels im Tonsatzunterricht (Berlin, 1975). *Honours:* Arthur Honegger Prize. *Address:* c/o German Music Information Centre, Weberstrasse 59, 53113 Bonn, Germany.

REDGATE, Christopher (Frederick); Oboist and Lecturer; b. 17 Sept. 1956, Bolton, Lancashire, England; m. Celia Jane Pilstow, 3 Oct 1981, 2 s. *Education:* Chetham's School of Music, Manchester; Royal Academy of Music, London. *Career:* Solo and chamber performances, England, Europe, USA; Many performer-in-residence courses for composersl; Artist-in-Residence, Victorian College of the Arts, Melbourne, Australia, including recitals, lectures, recordings, 1983; Toured Canada, 1985; American debut, Pittsburgh International Festival of New Music, 1986–92; Professor of Oboe, Darmstadt International School for Contemporary Music, 1978–2003; Performed regularly with the Phoenix Wind Quintet, Krosta Trio, Exposé, Lontano; Broadcasts, radio in the United Kingdom and Netherlands; Television; Many works written or commissioned for him by Michael Finnissy, James Clarke, Roger Redgate and others. *Recordings:* Pascilli for oboe; Platinium Fiction by Luca Francescin; Lost Lard, oboe music of Michael Finnissy; Quintets by Redgate, Fox and Clarke; Ferneyhough's Allegebrah and

Coloratura. *Address:* 1 Batten Place, Sandford-on-Thames, Oxfordshire OX4 4SZ, England.

REDGATE, Roger; Composer; b. 3 June 1958, Bolton, England. *Education:* Chetham's School of Music, Manchester; RCM, London, with Edwin Roxburgh; Freiburg Hochschule, with Brian Ferneyhough. *Career:* Co-founder, with Richard Barrett, Ensemble Exposé, 1984; Northern Arts Fellow in Composition; Universities of Durham and Newcastle, 1989–92; Lecturer in Composition Goldsmiths' College, London, 1997–. *Compositions include:* 2 String Quartets, 1983, 1985; Eidos for piano, 1985; Eperons for oboe and percussion, 1988; Vers-Glas for 14 amplified voices, 1990; Inventio, for ensemble, 1990; Celan Songs, for soprano and ensemble, 1991–4; Beuys for piano, 1992; Feu la Cendre, for cello, 1992; Scribble for ensemble, 1992; Eurydice, multimedia, 1993; Iro/ku, for prepared piano, 1994,... still... for bass flute, violin, viola and cello, 1995. *Honours:* Darmstadt Kranich-Steiner Prize for composition, 1988. *Address:* c/o Music Department, Goldsmiths' College, University of London, New Cross, London SE14 6NW, England.

REDOLFI, Michel; Composer; b. 8 Dec. 1951, Marseilles, France. *Education:* Studied I Marseilles and at the University of San Diego, 1973–84. *Career:* Co-founder, Groupe de Musique Electroacoustique, Marseilles, 1969; Director, Centre International de Recherche Musical, Nice, 1986–; Development of concept of sub-aquatic concerts, in California and France; Also sound installations for public buildings in Austria, Germany, Netherlands and France. *Compositions include:* Pacific Tubular Waves (1978), Immersion (1979), Too Much Sky (1986), Volare (1987) and Desert Tracks (1988), all for tape; Sub-aquatic works: Sonic Waters (1981–91), Crysallis (1992) and Virtual Lagoon (1997); Multi-media: L'ecume de la nuit (1984), La Galaxie du Caiman (1990) and Matu Pan (1993); Sound Installations Les murs ont la parole (Paris, 1984), Phoenix, Jardin de s. (Nice, 1990), Hurricane (Paris, Disneyland, 1991), Pavillon de Monaco (Seville, 1992) and Atlanticum (Bremerhaven, 1996); Electronic, with tape; Nausicaa (1991), Jungle (1991), Portrait (1993), Songes drolatiques (1994), and Millennium (1995). *Honours:* Prix Luigi Russolo, 1978; Prix Ars Electronica, 1994, 1996. *Address:* Centre de la Musique Contemporain, 16 Place de la Fontaine auz Lions, 75019, Paris, France.

REE, Jean van; Singer (Tenor); b. 7 March 1943, Kerkrade, Netherlands. *Education:* Studied with Else Bischof-Bornes in Aachen and Franziska Martienssen-Lohmann in Düsseldorf. *Career:* Debut: Mainz, 1963, in Zar und Zimmermann; Sang in Basle, Augsburg and Cologne; Guest appearances in Amsterdam, Hamburg, Hanover, Salzburg and Frankfurt; Augsburg, 1971, in the premiere of Rafael Kubelik's opera on the life of Titian, Cornelia Faroli; Teatro Regio Turin, 1983, in Lulu; Antwerp and Ghent, 1984, as Matteo in Arabella; Other roles include Don Ottavio, Hoffmann, Count Almaviva, Alfredo, and Mephistopheles in Doktor Faust by Busoni; Metropolitan Opera, 1978, as Bicias in Massenet's Thaïs; Sang Berg's Alwa at Barcelona and Vienna, 1987; Sang the Captain in Wozzeck at Enschede, Netherlands, 1993. *Recordings include:* Les Brigandes, by Offenbach. *Address:* c/o Staatsoper, Opernring 2, 1010 Vienna, Austria.

REECE, Arley; Singer (Tenor); b. 27 Aug. 1945, Yoakum, Texas, USA. *Education:* Studied at North Texas State University with Eugene Conley and at Manhattan School of Music. *Career:* Debut: Sang Assad in Die Königin von Saba by Goldmark with the American Opera Society at Carnegie Hall, 1970; Sang with Dallas Civic Opera, Shreveport Symphony, Philadelphia Lyric Opera, Kentucky and Connecticut Opera Associations, Opera Society of Washington and at Lake George Festival; European debut in Prokofiev's The Gambler at Wexford Festival, Ireland, 1973; New York City debut, 1974, as Bacchus; European engagements in Netherlands, Belgium, France including Berlioz Festival, Germany including East and West Berlin, Spain, Italy, Austria, Poland and Switzerland; Appearances in Canada and Iran; British appearances with the Northern Ireland Trust, Scottish Opera, Welsh National Opera and at Edinburgh and Wexford Festivals; Broadcasts: Cardillac (RAI Italy), The Gambler (BBC), Oberon, Ariadne auf Naxos and Wozzeck (Radio France), Tristan und Isolde, Macbeth (Netherlands Radio), Schmidt's Das Buch mit Sieben Siegeln and Dallapiccola's Job (WDR), From the House of the Dead (CBC Canada), Turandot (Radio Warsaw), Tannhäuser (Spanish Radio, Barcelona), Wozzeck (BBC Scotland), Lohengrin (Radio Espana); Television appearances: Lohengrin (Spanish television), Concert celebrating the 100th Anniversary of Richard Wagner (Polish television), Das Kleine Mahagonny and Il Ritorno d'Ulisse in Patria (TV Schweiz); Season 1989–90 sang Siegmund and Siegfried in Ring cycles for Warsaw Opera, St François d'Assise for Polish radio and television; Lohengrin, Calaf and Samson at Wiesbaden. Other roles include Otello, Canio and Manrico; Sang Don José in Carmen for the first time at the National Theatre in Weimar in 1993; In 1995 sang Parsifal and Tenor Soloist in the Mahler 8th Symphony for the first time at the Brisbane Biennial Festival in Australia. *Recordings include:* Il Ritorno d'Ulisse. *Address:* Martin Luther 63, 46284 Dorsten, Germany.

REEDER, Haydn (Brett); Composer, Pianist and Conductor; b. 27 Feb. 1944, Melbourne, Victoria, Australia. *Education:* BMus, University of Melbourne, 1965; MA, La Trobe University, 1991. *Career:* Editor for Universal Edition, Schott and Chester, music publishers, 1970–82; Lecturer, La Trobe University, 1984–88; Commissions from Elision and Melbourne Windpower, 1987–88. *Compositions include:* Mandala Rite for clarinet and guitar, 1982; Strad Evarie, for cello and piano, 1984; Temi Distratti for trombone, cello and percussion, 1985; Sirens' Hotel, chamber opera, 1986; Masks for piano, 1986; Clashing Auras for wind octet, 1989; Dance in a Mirror of Time, for 7 instruments, 1989; Chants at Play with Solid Background, 1990; Glances Repose, for violin, 1990; Draw neat to the Bell for guitar, 1990; Piano Pieces 1–3. *Honours:* Primo, Citta di Trieste Orchestral Competition. *Address:* c/o APRA, 1A Eden Street, Crows Nest, NSW 2065, Australia.

REEKIE, Jonathan; Music Administrator; m., two c. *Career:* company co-ordinator, Glyndebourne Opera 1988–91; Musica nel Chiostra, Batignano; founded Almeida Opera 1992; Chief Exec., Aldeburgh Productions 1997–; Trustee of Arts Foundation. *Address:* Aldeburgh Productions, Snape Maltings Concert Hall, Snape, Suffolk IP17 1SP, England (office). *Telephone:* (1728) 687100 (office). *Fax:* (1728) 687120 (office). *E-mail:* enquiries@aldeburgh.co.uk (office). *Website:* www .aldeburgh.co.uk (office).

REES, Jonathan; Violinist and Director; b. 1963, England. *Education:* Studied at the Yehudi Menuhin School and with Dorothy DeLay at Juilliard. *Career:* Student engagements at the Windsor, Gstaad and Llandaff Festivals and three tours of the Netherlands; Later recitals at the Bath, City of London, Brighton, Henley and Salisbury Festivals; Concerto soloist with the Bournemouth Sinfonietta, Philharmonia, London Soloists Chamber Orchestra and the Royal Philharmonic; Concerts with the Academy of St Martin in the Fields at Carnegie Hall, the Festival Hall and at St Martin's Church; Beethoven's Concerto with the Bournemouth Sinfonietta, 1990; Director of the Scottish Ensemble: concerts in Edinburgh, elsewhere in Scotland and in Austria, Belgium, France, Germany, the Netherlands, Norway and North and Central America; Festivals include Berlin, Guelph, Prague, Sofia, Cheltenham and Edinburgh; Royal Command Performances at the Palace of Holyrood House and at Balmoral. *Honours:* Prizewinner, 1978, BBC Young Musician of the Year Competition; 1st Prize, Royal Overseas League Competition, 1979.

REEVE, Stephen; Composer; b. 15 March 1948, London, England. *Education:* Composition class of Henri Pousseur, Liège Conservatoire, 1971–72. *Career:* Major commissions, BBC South, 1975, Institute for Research and Co-ordination in Acoustics and Music, 1980, Institute of Contemporary Arts, Londn, 1985; mem, Performing Right Society. *Compositions:* The Kite's Feathers, 1969–70; Japanese Haikai for mezzo and ensemble; Colour Music for woodwind quartet, 1970; Poème: Couleurs du Spectre for orchestra with optional light projection, 1972–73; Summer Morning by a lake full of colors, an expansion of Schoenberg's Farben, for large orchestra, 1974; Aux régions éthérées for 3 chamber groups, 1975–76; Grande thèse de la petite-fille de Téthys, an ethnic encyclopaedia for solo cello, 1980–87; L'Oracle de Delphes, music-theatre for brass quintet, 1985; Strophe for solo rock and 4 classical guitars, 1985–86; Les fées dansent selon la mode double, scene for 3–5 dancer-percussionists and 6–10 or more actor extras, 1988–89; O que Zeus apparaisse à l'horizon for gamelan ensemble and tape, 1989–90; Volontaires d'Icare for harpsichord trio, 1995. *Address:* 73 Knightsfield, Welwyn Garden City, Herts AL 8 7JE, England.

REEVES, Paul; Singer (Bass); b. 1970, England. *Education:* Guildhall School, London, with Rudolf Piernay; National Opera Studio. *Career:* Roles at GSMD included Budd in Albert Herring, Pasquale in The Aspern Papers by Argento and Rossini's Basilio; Appearances at Mozart's Publio for the Glyndebourne Tour, Colline in La Bohème and Speaker in The Magic Flute for British Youth Opera; Ramphis in Aida for Ashleyan Opera, Mozart's Bartolo for Opera Box and Sarastro in Die Zauberflöte for Kentish Opera; Season 2001 with the King in Raymond Gubay's Aida at the Albert Hall, and Matthew in Birtwistle's The Last Supper at Glyndebourne; Recitals at the Wigmore, Fairfield and Blackheath Halls. *Honours:* Richard Lewis-Jean Shanks Award; Tillett Trust Award. *Address:* c/o Glyndebourne Festival Opera, Lewes, Sussex BN8 5UU, England. *Telephone:* 01273 812321. *Fax:* 01273 812783.

REGAZZO, Lorenzo; Singer (Bass); b. 1968, Venice, Italy. *Education:* Studied with Regina Resnik and Sesto Bruscantini. *Career:* Many appearances at the Rossini Festival, Pesaro, in La Scala di Seta, La Cenerentola and L'Ingano felice; Salzburg Festival as Publio in La Clemenza di Tito and in Les Boréades by Rameau, conducted by Simon Rattle; Further engagements in L'Italiana in Algeri at Munich and Venice, La Gazza Ladra, Rossini's Zelmira (Lyon) and Il Viaggio a Reims (Bologna); Royal Opera House 2000–01, as Publio, Alidoro in La Cenerentola and Lorenzo in I Capuleti e i Montecchi; Performances in Don Giovanni at Vienna, Milan and Brussels, Handel's Agrippina in Paris and as Mozart's Figaro at the 2001 Salzburg Festival; Concerts with the Berlin Philharmonic, under Claudio Abbado. *Address:* c/o Opéra Bastille, 120 Rue de Lyon, 75012 Paris, France.

ŘEHÁNEK, František; Philologist, Musicologist and Teacher; b. 13 Sept. 1921, Mistek, Czechoslovakia; m. Marie Řehánková-Motáčková, 17 April 1954, 1 s. *Education:* Philosophical Faculty of Charles University in Prague, Czech and English Languages; Music School at Mistek, Philosophical Faculty of University in Brno, Musicology and Music Education, PhD, Brno, 1967; Music Education: Gabriel Stefánek and Josef Muzika, violin. *Publications include:* Janáček's Teaching of Harmony, dissertation, 1965; Harmonic Thinking of Leoš Janáček, 1993; The Diatonic Modes with Leoš Janáček, 1994, published in Hudebni Věda (Musicology), 2003; Leoš Janáček and the Whole-Tone System, 1998; Fourth Chords of Leoš Janáček, 1999. *Contributions:* Modality in Janáček's Music Theory, in Colloquium Probleme der Modalität, Leoš Janáček heute und morgen, Brno 1988, 1994; Leoš Janáček's Sonata for Violin and Piano, 1988; Modality in the Works of Vitezslav Novák, in Zprávy Spolecnosti Vitezslava Nováka 17, Brno 1990; To the Problem of Modality with Bohuslav Martinů, in Colloquim Bohuslav Martinů, His Pupils, Friends and Contemporaries, 1990, 1993; Alois Hába's Wallachian Suite in Zpávy Spolecnosti Vitězslava Nováka 25, 26, 1995; On Harmonic Thinking of Leoš Janáček, 2001, in Hudebni Věda (Musicology), 2002; Association of Musical Artists and Scientists, Prague; Czech Society of Musicology. *Address:* František Řehánek, Vlnařská 692, 460 01 Liberec VI, Czech Republic.

REHNQVIST, Karin; Composer; b. 21 Aug. 1957, Stockholm, Sweden; m. Hans Persson 1982, one d., two s. *Education:* Swedish Royal Academy of Music, Stockholm, with Gunnar Bucht, Pär Lindgren and Brian Ferneyhough. *Career:* Conductor, Stans Kör choir, 1976–; mem., Society of Swedish Composers, 1985–; Royal Acad. of Music, Sweden. *Compositions include:* Stråk for strings, 1982; Dance for piano, 1984; Davids nimm, 3 female voices, 1984; Kast, for strings, 1986; Songs from the Saga of Fatumeh, for male chours, 1988; Here I am, Where are you? for girls' voices, 1989; Violin Concerto, Skrin, 1990; The Triumph of Being for girls' voices, 1990; Lamento for orchestra, 1993; Sun Song, for female voice, speakers and chamber orchestra, 1994; Visletens lov for mixed chorus, 1996; Arktis Arktis! for orchestra, 2000–01; On the Far Side, concerto for clarinet and orchestra, 2002; Teile dich Nacht for mixed choir and solo female voice, 2002; Ljus av ljus (Lumière source de lumière) for children's choir and symphony orchestra, 2003. *Publications:* Young People – New Music, an introduction to composition. *Honours:* Läkerol Arts Award, 1996; Expressen's Spelmannen Prize, 1996; Christ Johnsson Prize, 1997; City of Stockholm Honour Prize, 1999; Kurt Atterberg Prize, 2001; Litteris et Artibus, 2002. *Address:* Swedish Music Information Centre, 79 Sandhamnsgatan, 10254 Stockholm, Sweden. *Website:* www.editionreimers.se/tt/kr; www.mic.stim.se.

REIBEL, Guy; Composer; b. 19 July 1936, Strasbourg, France. *Education:* Studied with Messiaen and Serge Wigg. *Career:* Groupe de recherches musicales, 1963–; Lecturer in electro-acoustic music at the Paris Conservatoire; Founded Atelier des Choeurs, Radio France, 1976; Director, Groupe Vocal de France, 1986–90, with many premieres; Adviser to Cité De la Musique, La Villette, 1983–89; Professor of Composition, Paris Conservatoire, 1976; Collaborations with Pierre Schaeffer. *Compositions include:* Musaiques for 2 voices, percussion and orchestra, 1987; Fugitivement à la surface de l'eau, for ensemble, 1989; Variations cinétiques, ensemble, 1989; Etudes de flux, for orchestra, 1990; Métaphores, for soprano and two guitars, 1991; Le coq et le renard, for flute and chorus, 1991; La Marseillaise des Mille, for 500 voices and orchestra, 1992; Calliphores, for 12 voices, 1995; Musique en Liesse, for 12 brass and 2 percussion, 1995; Trois Epigrammes de Clément Marot, chorus, 1996; Surface Légèrement spérique, for tape, 1996; Mamemimomusiques, for orchestra, 1997. *Publications include:* Essais sur l'idée musicale, 1997. *Address:* Centre de Musique Contemporain, 16 Place de la Fontaine, 75019 Paris, France.

REICH, Steve; Composer; b. 3 Oct. 1936, New York, USA; m. Beryl Korot, 30 May 1976, 1 s. *Education:* BA, Honours, Philosophy, Cornell University, 1957; Studied composition with Hall Overton, 1957–58 and at Juilliard School of Music with William Bergsma, Vincent Persichetti, 1958–61; MA in Music, Mills College, CA, with Darius Milhaud, Luciano Berio, 1963; Studied African drumming, 1970, Balinese Gamelan Semar Pegulingan, 1974 and Hebrew Cantillation, 1976. *Career:* Formed own ensemble with 3 others, 1966 now with 18 or more members performing world-wide; More than 300 concerts 1971–87; Composer of music, played by major orchestras in USA and Europe also choeographed by leading dance companies; BBC Prom Concert featuring his music, 1995; mem, American Academy of Arts and Letters, 1994; Bavarian Academy of Fine Arts, 1995. *Compositions include:* (recorded) Come Out, 1966; Drumming, 1971; Music for 18 musicians, 1976; Telhillim, 1981, 1982, 1994; The Desert Music, 1984; New York Counterpoint, 1985; Sextet, 1985; Three Movements, 1986; The Four Sections, 1987; Different Trains for string quartet and tape,

1988; Co-Commission in 1993 by Vienna Festival, Holland Festival, Hebbel Theater, Berlin, Serious Speakout and The South Bank Centre, London, Festival d'Automne, Paris, Theatre de la Monnaie, Brussels and Brooklyn Academy of Music, Next Wave Festival for The Cave, a new form of opera with video; A collaboration with video artist Beryl Korot; Nagoya Marimbas, 1994; City Life, 1995; Proverb, for 3 sopranos, 2 tenors, 2 vibraphones and 2 electronic keyboards, 1995; Three Tales, for 2 sopranos, 3 tenors and ensemble, 1998; Triple Quartet, for string quartet and tape, 1999; Know what is above you, for 4 female voices and percussion, 2000. *Publications include:* Writing About Music, 1974, French edition 1981, Italian edition, 1994; Writings on Music 1965–2000, 2001. *Contributions:* Various journals. *Honours:* Guggenheim Fellow, 1978; Commandeur, Ordre des Arts et des Lettres, 2000; Composer of the Year, Musical America Magazine, 2000; Montgomery Fellowship, Dartmouth College, 2000; Shuman Prize, Columbia University, 2000; Many awards and grants. *Current Management:* Allied Artists Management, London and Elizabeth Sobol, IMG Artists, 22 East 71st Street, NY 10021, USA. *Address:* 258 Broadway, Apt 7E, New York, NY 10007, USA.

REICHERT, Manfred; Conductor; b. 5 May 1942, Karlsruhe, Germany. *Education:* Studied at the Karlsruhe Hochschule, 1961–65; Musicology at the University of Fribourg/Breisgau, 1966–67. *Career:* Producer at South West German Radio, Baden-Baden, 1967–83; Founded the chamber group Ensemble 13, 1973; Directed the festivals Wintermusik and Musik auf den 49ten at Karlsruhe, 1980 and 1983; Artistic Director of the Festival of European Culture at Karlsruhe, 1983–87; Teacher at the Hochschule für Musik at Karlsruhe from 1984; Conducted the premieres of Hans-Jürgen von Bose's Variations for Strings, 1981, Wolfgang Rihm's Chiffre-Zyklus, 1988, and Gejagte Form, 1989.

REID-SMITH, Randall; Singer (Tenor); b. 1959, Barboursville, West Virginia, USA. *Education:* Studied in Cincinnati and New York. *Career:* Sang in concert and opera at Santa Fe, Dayton and Michigan; Roles have included Don José, Rodolfo and Pinkerton; Brunswick Opera from 1990, as Don Ottavio, Rossini's Almaviva, Fenton in Falstaff and Nemorino; Dortmund Opera from 1993, as Tamino, Ferrando and the Duke of Mantua; Sang Don Ottavio at Aachen, 1995; Guest appearances at Leipzig, Madrid, Vienna and Bregenz. *Address:* c/o Dortmund Opera, Kuhstrasse 12, 4600 Dortmund, Germany.

REIMANN, Aribert; Composer and Pianist; b. 4 March 1936, Berlin, Germany. *Education:* Berlin Hochschule für Musik with Boris Blacher (composition), Ernst Pepping (counterpoint) and Rausch (piano), 1955–59; Studied musicology at the University of Vienna, 1958. *Career:* Professor of the Contemporary Lied at the Hamburg Musikhochschule, 1974–83, Berlin Hochschule der Künste, 1983; Freelance composer, notably of operas; Accompanist to Dietrich Fischer-Dieskau in Lieder recitals; London premieres, Lear and The Ghost Sonata, 1989; Opera Das Schloß premiered at the Deutsche Oper Berlin, 1992, Bernarda Albas Haus premiered at the Bavarian State Opera, Munich, 2000; mem, Berlin Akademie der Künste, 1971; Bayerische Akademie der Schönen Künste, 1976; Freie Akademie der Künste, Hamburg, 1985; Order 'Pour le Mérite' for Science and Art, 1993; Grand Cross with Star for Distinguished Service of the Order of Merit, 1995; Commander of the Ordre du Mérite Culturel, Monaco, 1999; 'Goldene Nadel' of the German Association of Playwrights, 1999. *Compositions:* Operas: Ein Traumspiel (Strindberg), 1964; Melusine, 1970; Lear (Shakespeare), 1978; Die Gespenstersonate (Strindberg), 1983; Troades (Euripides), 1985; Das Schloß (Kafka), 1992; Bernarda Albas Haus, 2000; Ballet: Stoffreste, 1958, revised as Die Vogelscheuchen, 1970; Orchestral: Elegie for orchestra, 1957; Cello Concerto, 1959; Monumenta, for wind and percussion, 1960; Piano Concerto No. 1, 1961, No. 2, 1972; Sinfonie (from the opera Ein Traumspiel), 1964; Rondes for string orchestra, 1967; Loqui, for orchestra, 1969; Music from the ballet Die Vogelscheuchen, 1970; Variations for orchestra, 1975; Sieben Fragmente, 1988; Neun Stücke, 1993; Concerto for violin, cello and orchestra, 1988–89; Violin Concerto, 1995–96; 9 Stücke, 1993; Violin Concerto, 1997; Vocal: Ein Totentanz, baritone, chamber orchestra, 1960; Hölderlin-Fragments, soprano, orchestra, 1963; 3 Shakespeare Sonnets, baritone, piano, 1964; Epitaph, tenor, 7 instruments, 1965; Verra la Morte, cantata, 1966; Inane, soprano, orchestra, 1968; Zyklus, baritone, orchestra, 1971; Lines, soprano, strings, 1973; Wolkenloses Christmas, Requiem for baritone, cello, orchestra, 1974; Lear, symphony for baritone, orchestra, 1980; Unrevealed, baritone, string quartet; Tre Poemi di Michelangelo, 1985; Neun Sonette der Louize Labé; Chacun sa Chimère, for tenor and orchestra, 1981; Three Songs (poems by Edgar Allan Poe), 1982; Requiem, soprano, mezzo, baritone, orchestra, 1982; Ein apokalyptisches Fragment, for mezzo, piano and orchestra, 1987; Orchestration of Schumann's Gedichte der Maria Stuart, 1988; Lady Lazarus, for soprano solo, 1992; Eingedunkelt, for alto solo, 1992; Nightpiece (James Joyce) for soprano and piano, 1992; Schubert's Mignon Lieder, for soprano and string quartet, 1995; Kumi Ori, for baritone and orchestra, 1999; Drei Gedichte der Sappho, for soprano

and 9 instruments, 2000; Chamber: Piano Sonata, 1958; Canzoni e Ricercare for flute, viola and cello, 1961; Cello Sonata, 1963; Nocturnos, for cello and harp, 1965; Reflexionen, for 7 instruments, 1966; Spektren, for piano, 1967; Variationen, for piano, 1979; Invenzioni, for 12 players, 1979; Solo for cello, 1981; String Trio, 1987; Auf dem Weg, for piano, 1989–93; Solo for viola, 1996; Metamorphosen, for 10 instruments, 1997; Solo for clarinet, 2000. *Honours:* Berlins Arts Award for Music (Young Generation), 1962; Rome Prize, 1963; Schumann Prize, Düsseldorf, 1964; Stuttgart Award for Young Composers, 1966; Critics Award for Music, Berlin, 1970; Grand Cross for Distinguished Service of the Order of Merit, 1985; Ludwig Spohr Prize of Braunschweig, 1985; Prix de composition musicale, Fondation Prince Pierre de Monaco, 1986; Bach Prize of the Free Hanseatic City of Hamburg, 1987; Order of Merit of the state of Berlin, 1988; Frankfurt Music Award, 1991. *Current Management:* Schott Musik International GmbH & Co KG. *Address:* c/o Yvonne Stern, Schott Musik International GmbH & Co KG, Weihergarten 5, 55116 Mainz, Germany.

REINEMANN, Udo; Singer (Baritone); b. 6 Aug. 1942, Lubeck, Germany. *Education:* Studied at Krefeld, the Vienna Academy of Music and with Erik Werba and W Steinbruck at the Salzburg Mozarteum, 1962–67. *Career:* Debut: Song recital at Bordeaux, 1967; Gave more recitals, then studied further with Germaine Lubin in Paris and with Otakar Kraus in London; Many performances in Lieder, opera and oratorio; Founded a vocal quartet, 1975, with Ana-Maria Miranda, Clara Wirtz and Jean-Claude Orliac (Lieder Quartet); Sang in the premiere of Adrienne Clostre's opera Nietzsche, 1978; My Chau Trong Thuy by Dao, 1979. *Recordings include:* Vocal quartets by Haydn; Lieder by Clara Schumann and Richard Strauss; Posthumous Lieder by Hugo Wolf. *Honours:* 1st Prize for concert singing, Vienna Academy of Music, 1967.

REINER, Thomas; Composer; b. 12 Aug. 1959, Bad Homburg, Germany (Australian resident from 1979). *Education:* BA, La Trobe University, 1983; Study with Hans Werner Henze, 1984–86, Barry Conyngham and Peter Tahourdin, 1987–89; MMus, University of Melbourne, 1990; PhD, University of Melbourne, 1996; Electronic and computer music studies, 1997–. *Career:* Staff Member, University of Melbourne, 1990–91, and Monash University, 1993–98. *Compositions include:* Journey and Contemplation for guitar and ensemble, 1987; Moth and Spider for alto saxophone and percussion, 1988; Paraphrase, Surge and Response, for orchestra, 1988; Bali Suite, for ensemble, 1989; Fantasy and Fugue for trombone, 1989; Kalorama Prelude for piano, 1989; Schumannianna: An Orchestration of Robert Schumann's Mondnacht, 1991; Baby Orang Utan for piano, 1991; Words for 6 solo voices, 1992; Three Sketches for cello, 1993; Construction in Time for guitar and piano, 1993; Oblique for flute, 1994; Flexious for flute and guitar, 1995–96; Septet for chamber ensemble, 1996; Grace Notes for B flat clarinet, 1997. *Publications:* Author of articles on musical time and electronic dance music. *Honours:* Prizes in the International Witold Lutoslawski Composers Competition, 1992; Dorian Le Gallienne Composition Award, 1994; Albert H Maggs Composition Award, 1995; International Borwil Composer's Competition, 1997. *Address:* c/o APRA, 1A Eden Street, Crows Nest, NSW 2065, Australia.

REINHARDT, Rolf; Conductor; b. 3 Feb. 1927, Heidelberg, Germany. *Education:* Studied piano with Frieda Kwast-Hodapp and composition with Wolfgang Fortner. *Career:* Conducted Opera in the Heidelborg, Stuttgart, Darmstadt 1948–1957; GMD Oper und Konzerte in Trier (1959–1968) Assistant Bayreuth 1954–57; 1968–1992 Leiter der Opernabteilung Hochschule für Musik und Darstellende Kunst Frankfurt/M; 1973–1983 Leiter das Hachchores Köln; Zahlreiche Schallplatten und Kundfunkautnahmen. *Recordings:* Bach's Magnificant, Cantatas and Concertos for harpsichord and violin; Haydn Sinfonia Concertante and Concertos for trumpet, Horn and oboe; Mozart Violin Concertos, Concertante K297b, Thamos King of Egypt and Litaniae Lauretanae; Handel Organ Concertos and Silete Venti; Stamitz Viola Concerto, Sinfonia Concertante; Bartók 1 and Brahms 2 Piano Concertos, with György Sandor; Mozart Bastien and Bastienne, La Finta Giardiniera; Bartók Music for Strings, Percussion and Celesta, Wooden Prince and Miraculous Mandarin; Beethoven Egmont; Schumann Cello Concerto, Violin Fantasia, Konzertstück for four horns and D minor Introduction and Allegro; Dvořák and Goldmark Violin Concertos, with Bronislav Gimpel; Lieder accompanist for Fritz Wunderlich. *Honours:* Two Grand Prix du disque by Durante (6 Concerto grossi) and Bartok (Wooden Prince/ Miraculous Mandarin); Lieder accompnist u.a. for Fritz Wunderlich. *Address:* Staatliche Hochschule für Musik, Escherheimer Landstrasse 33, Postfach 2326 Frankfurt, Germany.

REINHARDT-KISS, Ursula; Singer (Soprano); b. 3 Nov. 1938, Letmathe, Sauerland, Germany. *Education:* Studied with Ellen Bosenius in Cologne and Irma Beilke in Berlin. *Career:* Debut: Saarbrücken, 1967 as Marie in Der Waffenschmied; Sang in Saarbrücken until 1969 then Aachen, 1969–71; Guest appearances in Lubeck, Cologne, Zürich, Antwerp, Milan, Copenhagen and Rome; Drottningholm in 1983 in Il

Fanatico Burlato by Cimarosa; Komische Oper Berlin as Susanna and Lulu, and Dresden Staatsoper as Aminta in Die schweigsame Frau; Sang at Graz in 1985, in Angelica Vincitrice di Alcina by Fux, returning in 1987 in the premiere of Der Rattenfänger by Cerha; Also sings Salomé in Hérodiade by Massenet. *Recordings:* Sacred Music by Mozart; Lazarus by Schubert; Epitaph for Garcia Lorca, by Nono. *Address:* c/o Vereinigte Bühnen, Kaiser Josef Platz 10, 8010 Graz, Austria.

REINHART, Gregory; Singer (Bass); b. 1955, USA. *Career:* Sang at Tourcoing, 1981, in Paisiello's Il Re Teodoro, Innsbruck, 1982 and 1987, in Cesti's Oronte and Semiramide; King of Scotland in Ariodante at Nancy (1983) and in Henze's English Cat at the Paris Opéra-Comique, 1984; Nice, 1986, as Henry VIII in Anna Bolena and at Aix-en-Provence as Ismenor in Campra's Tancrède; London concert performances of Poppea and Moses und Aron, 1988; Opéra-Bastille Paris, 1990, as Panthé in Les Troyens and Santa Fe, 1992, as Mozart's Commendatore; Sang Basil Hallward in the premiere of Lowell Liebermann's The Picture of Dorian Gray, Monte Carlo, 1996; Other roles include Lord Robinson in Il Matrimonio Segreto, Monteverdi's Seneca, Huascar in Les Indes Galantes and Douglas in Rossini's Donna del Lago; Sang Claudio in Handel's Agrippina at Halle, 1999; Premiere of K.... by Philippe Manouri at the Opéra Bastille, Paris, 2001. *Recordings:* Handel's Tamerlano; Tancrède by Campra; Rameau's Zoroastre; Messiah. *Address:* c/o Cédelle, 78 Boulevard Malesherbes, F–75008 Paris, France.

REITER, Alfred; Singer (Bass); b. Dec. 1965, Augsburg, Germany. *Education:* Studied at Munich Music Academy and with Astrid Varnay and Hans Hotter. *Career:* Debut: Wiesbaden State Theatre, 1995 as Lefort in Lortzing's Zar und Zimmermann; Performances of Mozart's Sarastro at the Deutsche Oper Berlin, Ludwigsburg Festival, Vienna and Lisbon; Monteverdi's Seneca at Nuremberg and Stuttgart; Hans Schwarz and Titurel in Parsifal at the Bayreuth Festival, Pogner in Meistersinger at Nuremberg, Fafner in Siegfried at Geneva and in Das Rheingold at the Vienna Staatsoper; Royal Opera Covent Garden 2001–02 as Titurel and as Peneios in Strauss's Daphne (concert); Season 2002–03 as Sarastro in Salzburg, Paris and London, Timur in Turandot at San Francisco and Gurnemanz in Cardiff, Geneva and Bologna; Concerts include Haydn's Die Schöpfung (Ludwigsburg 2000) and Beethoven's Missa Solemnis (Philadelphia, 2001). *Current Management:* Balmer & Dixon Management AG, Kreuzstrasse 82, 8032 Zürich, Switzerland. *Telephone:* (43) 244-8644. *Fax:* (43) 244-8649. *Website:* www.badix.ch.

RELYEA, John; Singer (baritone); b. 1970, Canada. *Education:* Studies with Jerome Hines. *Career:* Appearances from 1995 with San Francisco Opera as Colline, and Mozart's Figaro; Metropolitan Opera as Alidoro in La Cenerentola and in Die Meistersinger and Lucia di Lammermoor; Escamillo at the Paris, Hamburg and Munich Operas; Concerts include Elijah in San Francisco, Bach's B minor Mass with the Cleveland Orchestra and Magnificat in Philadelphia; Beethoven's 9th and Messiah with the Pittsburgh SO; Verdi Requiem under Antonio Pappano in Brussels and Frankfurt; Mozart's C minor Mass with the Boston SO, and Requiem in Pittsburgh (season 2001–02); Further engagements at Covent Garden in La Bohème, Semele and Lucia di Lammermoor. *Honours:* Winner 1995 Merola Grand Finals, San Francisco. *Current Management:* Askonas Holt Ltd, Lonsdale Chambers, 27 Chancery Lane, London, WC2A 1PF, England. *Telephone:* (20) 7400-1700. *Fax:* (20) 7400-1799. *E-mail:* info@askonasholt.co.uk. *Website:* www .askonasholt.co.uk.

REMEDIOS, Alberto; Singer (Tenor); b. 27 Feb. 1935, Liverpool, England. *Education:* Studied in Liverpool with Edwin Francis and at The Royal College of Music. *Career:* Debut: Sadler's Wells Opera, 1957 as Tinca in Il Tabarro; Has sung at Sadler's Wells, English National Opera in many roles; Toured Australia with Joan Sutherland, 1965; At Covent Garden from 1965, as Dimitri in Boris Godunov, Erik, Florestan, Mark in The Midsummer Marriage, Siegfried, Bacchus and Max; Camden Theatre, 1968 in Adriana Lecouvreur by Cilea; BBC radio, 1970, as Huon in Oberon; Sang Mozart's Don Ottavio in South Africa, 1972; US debut as Dimitri and Don Carlos, at San Francisco; Metropolitan Opera debut in 1976 as Bacchus; Scottish Opera in 1983 as Walther in Die Meistersinger; Performances of Otello, Siegmund, Florestan and Radames for Australian Opera; Sang in Schoenberg's Gurrelieder at Melbourne, 1988; Concert repertoire also includes Mahler's 8th Symphony at Promenade Concerts in London; Returned to Scotland in 1989 as Stravinsky's Oedipus; Sang in Reginald Goodall's Memorial Concert, London, 1991; Appeared in Janáček's The Excursions of Mr Brouček at London Coliseum, 1992 and sang Tristan in concert performances of Wagner's Opera at Nashville, Tennessee, 1993; Siegmund in Die Walküre, 1999. *Recordings include:* The Ring of the Nibelung, conducted by Reginald Goodall (reissued by Chandos, 2001). *Honours:* Prizewinner, Sofia International Competition, 1963; C.B.E., 1981. *Address:* The Master-singers, 15 David Avenue, Wickford, Essex SS11 7BG, England.

REMEDIOS, Ramon; Singer (Tenor); b. 9 May 1940, Liverpool, England. *Education:* Studied at the Guildhall School of Music, the National School of Opera and the London Opera Centre. *Career:* Has sung with Opera For All, Scottish Opera, Welsh National Opera and European companies; Notably as Alfredo, Macduff, Ismaele in Nabucco, Grigory/Dimitri, Don Ottavio, the Duke of Mantua, the Painter in Lulu, Skuratov (From the House of the Dead), Tamino and Almaviva; English National Opera: Alfredo, Rodolfo, Don José, Pinkerton, Paris in La Belle Hélène, Smith in the British premiere production of Christmas Eve (1988) and Lensky in Eugene Onegin; Covent Garden, 1990, as Uldino in a new production of Attila; Television appearances in Top C's and Tiaras, and The Word by Rick Wakeman; Season 1992 as Sir Bruno Robertson in I Puritani at Covent Garden; Concert engagements include operatic arias in Glasgow, a Viennese Evening at the Festival Hall and Verdi's Requiem (Royal Festival Hall, Mar 1991). *Recordings include:* The Word, with the Eton College Choir; Kalman's Countess Maritza with New Sadler's Wells Opera; A Suite of Gods, songs by Rick Wakeman. *Honours:* School Tenor Prize, Ricordi Prize and Countess of Munster Trust, Guildhall School of Music; Finalist, Kathleen Ferrier Competition. *Address:* c/o The Master-singers, 15 David Avenue, Wickford, Essex SS11 7BG.

REMENIKOVA, Tanya; cellist and cello teacher; b. 31 Jan. 1946, Moscow, USSR; m. Alexander Braginsky. *Education:* Moscow Conservatoire, studied with Prof. Rostropovich. *Career:* regular appearances in recitals and with various orchestras, including Israel Philharmonic, Orchestra National de Belgique; Foreign tours: Europe, Taiwan, People's Republic of China; New York debut, 1979; Radio: BBC, RTB (Belgium), WFMT (Chicago), WQXR (New York); North American tours: Chicago, New York, Washington, DC, Minneapolis, Los Angeles, elsewhere; Professor of Cello, School of Music, University of Minnesota; Artist-in-Residence, Churchill College, Cambridge, 1981, 1986; Premieres of Stephen Paulus, American Vignettes, 1988; mem, College Music Society; American String Teachers' Association. *Recordings:* Stravinsky, Suite Italienne; Shostakovich, Sonata op 40; Britten, Sonata in C; Rachmaninov, Sonata Op 19; Grieg, Sonata Op 36. *Honours:* Gold Medal, Gaspar Cassado Cello Competition, 1969; Eugene Ysaye Award for Musical Contribution, Brussels, 1979. *Address:* 4141 Dupont Avenue South, Minneapolis, MN 55409, USA.

REMEŠ, Vaclav; violinist; b. 1950, Czechoslovakia. *Education:* Prague Conservatory. *Career:* founder mem., Prazak String Quartet 1972; tour of Finland 1973, followed by appearances at competitions in Prague and Evian; concerts in Salzburg, Munich, Paris, Rome, Berlin, Cologne and Amsterdam; tour of the UK 1985, including Wigmore Hall debut; tours of Japan, the USA, Australia and New Zealand; tour of the UK 1988, and concert at the Huddersfield Contemporary Music Festival 1989; recitals for the BBC, Radio France, Dutch Radio, the WDR in Cologne and Radio Prague; appearances with the Smetana and LaSalle Quartets in Mendelssohn's Octet. *Honours:* 1st Prize, Chamber Music Competition of the Prague Conservatory, 1974; Grand Prix, International String Quartet Competition, Evian Music Festival, 1978; 1st Prize, National Competition of String Quartets in Czechoslovakia, 1978; Winner, String Quartet of the Prague Spring Festival, 1978.

REMMERT, Birgit; Singer (Alto); b. 1966, Germany. *Education:* Studied at the Detmold Musikhochschule with Helmut Kretschmar. *Career:* Sang in Beethoven's Ninth under Nikolaus Harnoncourt in London, 1991, and again under Giulini in Stockholm, 1994; Further concerts include Mendelssohn's Walpurgisnacht in Graz, Biber's Requiem and Vespers under Harnoncourt in Vienna, the song cycle Sunless by Mussorgsky, in Amsterdam, and Das Lied von der Erde under Philippe Herreweghe at the Théâtre des Champs-Elysées, Paris; Holland Festival 1992, as Martha in Tchaikovsky's Iolantha, Hamburg, 1993 as Erda in the Ring and Ulrica at Dresden; Zürich Opera, 1994, as Dalila, Suzuki and Third Lady in Die Zauberflöte; Other repertory includes Mahler's Eighth and Das klagende Lied (with Chailly at the Concertgebouw), Mahler 3rd Symphony with Simon Rattle in Birmingham and the Nurse in Monteverdi's Poppea at Salzburg Festival; Mahler's Second with the CBSO under Rattle at the 1999 London Proms; Sang Fricka in Das Rheingold and Die Walküre at the Bayreuth Festival, 2000; Mahler's Symphony of a Thousand at the London Proms, 2002. *Recordings include:* Beethoven's Ninth; Lieder by Brahms, Clara Schumann and Tchaikovsky; Bach Cantatas with Peter Schreier; Bruckner, Te Deum and F Minor Mass with Welser-Möst. *Honours:* Lieder Prize at the Palma d'oro Competition, Ligure.

RENDALL, David; Singer (Tenor); b. 11 Oct. 1948, London, England. *Education:* Studied at the Royal Academy of Music and at the Salzburg Mozarteum. *Career:* Debut: Glyndebourne Touring Company, 1975, as Ferrando in Così fan tutte; Covent Garden from 1975, as the Italian Tenor in Der Rosenkavalier, Almaviva, Matteo, Rodolfo, Des Grieux in Manon and Rodrigo in a new production of La Donna del Lago by Rossini (1985); Glyndebourne Festival, 1976, Ferrando, returned as Belmonte and Tom Rakewell (1989); English National Opera from 1976, as

Leicester in Mary Stuart, Rodolfo, Alfredo, Tamino and Pinkerton; European debut at Angers, 1975, as the High Priest in Idomeneo; North American debut, Ottawa, 1977, as Tamino; New York City Opera, 1978, Rodolfo and Alfredo; San Francisco debut, 1978, Don Ottavio; Metropolitan Opera from 1980, as Ottavio, Ernesto, Belmonte, Idomeneo, Lenski, Ferrando, Alfred in Die Fledermaus and Mozart's Titus; Lyon Opéra, 1983, in the title role of La Damnation de Faust by Berlioz; Further engagements in Amsterdam, Berlin, Paris, Milan, Hamburg, Tel-Aviv, Turin, Washington, Vienna, Dresden, Chicago, Santa Fe and Munich; Other operatic roles include Gounod's Faust (Palermo) and the Duke of Mantua; Many concert appearances in Europe and the USA; Sang the Duke of Mantua and Matteo at Covent Garden, 1989/90; Cavaradossi with English National Opera, 1990; Season 1992 as Don Antonio in the stage premiere of Gerhard's The Duenna (Madrid), Pinkerton at the Coliseum and for Welsh National Opera; Genoa 1996–97, as Hoffmann and Don José; Otello for ENO, 1998; Sang Wagner's Erik at Toronto and Cavaradossi for Covent Garden, 2000. Recordings: Maria Stuarda; Così fan tutte; Ariodante; Mozart's Requiem; Beethoven's Missa solemnis; Madama Butterfly; Bruckner's Te Deum. Honours: Young Musician of the Year Award, 1973; Gulbenkian Fellowship, 1975. Address: c/o IMG Artists, Lovell House, 616 Chiswick High Road, London W4 5RX, England.

RENICK, Therese; Singer (Mezzo-soprano); b. 1963, St Louis, Missouri, USA. Education: Studied in Vienna with Hilde Zadek. Career: Debut: Würzburg, 1985, in Der Barbier von Bagdad by Cornelius; Krefeld Opera, 1985–88, as Carmen and Azucena; Essen from 1989, as Verdi's Eboli, and Amneris, and Mozart's Dorabella; Salzburg, 1987–88, in Schoenberg's Moses und Aron; Season 1995–96 as Ortrud in Lohengrin at Dessau and in the premiere of Bose's Schlachthof 5 at Munich; Other roles include Santuzza, Venus in Tannhäuser and Fenena in Nabucco (Munich, 1996); Concerts include the Requiems of Mozart and Verdi, and Beethoven's Ninth. Address: Bayerische Staatsoper, Max-Joseph Platz, 80539 Munich, Germany.

RENICKE, Volker; Conductor and Professor; b. 3 July 1929, Bremen, Germany; m. Rey Nishiuchi, 5 April 1975. Education: Nordwest-deutsche Musikakademie, Detmold, 1950–54; Accademia Chigiana, Siena, with Paul van Kempen. Career: In Korea, 1991, with Korean Symphony Orchestra in the Korean Orchestral Festival; Tokyo Mozart 200 Anniversary of Death, Idomeneo, 1991; In Seoul Opera Favorita and Fidelio at National Theatre, 1992; International Festival in Tsuyama, Japan, Mozart Tito, 1993; Salzburg Mozart Requiem, 1993; Guest conducting and concerts in England, France, Germany, Netherlands, Luxembourg, Switzerland, Italy, Yugoslavia and Korea; Concerts with all major Japanese orchestras; In Korea with Seoul Philharmonic Orchestra and Korean Symphony Orchestra; Zauberflöte and Traviata in Opernhaus Köln, 1995; mem, Kojimachi Rotary Club, Tokyo. Recordings: With Jörg Demus and NHK Orchestra members; Piano concertos of Bach, Haydn, Mozart, Debussy, Franck, Fauré; With Karl Suske, violin, and NHK Orchestra members; Recordings of Vivaldi and Bach; Humperdinck's Hansel and Gretel, in Japanese, with Yomiuri Orchestra. Current Management: Christoph Schellbach, Representation of Classical Musicians in Europa, Lutherstrasse 7, D 34117 Kassel, Germany. Address: 5-26-15 Okuzawa, Setagaya-ku, 158 Tokyo, Japan.

RENNERT, Jonathan; Organist, Conductor and Writer; b. 17 March 1952, London, England; m. Sheralyn Ivil 1992. Education: St. Paul's School, London; Foundation Scholar, Royal Coll. of Music; Organ Scholar, St John's Coll., Cambridge; Stewart of Rannoch Scholar in Sacred Music, Univ. of Cambridge; MA (Cantab); FRCO; ARCM; LRAM. Career: numerous organ recitals, radio and television appearances world-wide; Dir of Music, Holy Trinity Church, Barnes, London, 1969–71; Musical Dir, Cambridge Opera, 1972–74; Dir of Music, St Jude's, Courtfield Gardens, London; Conductor, American Community Choirs in London, 1975–76; Acting Dir of Music, St Matthew's, Ottawa, Canada, 1976–78; Dir of Music, St Michael's, Cornhill, City of London, Musical Dir, St Michael's Singers, 1979–; Musician-in-Residence, Grace Cathedral, San Francisco, 1982; Conductor, Elizabethan Singers, 1983–88; Festival Dir, Cornhill Festival of British Music, 1982–88; Admin., International Congress of Organists, Cambridge, 1987; Course Dir and Chair., Central London District Cttee, Royal School of Church Music, 1995–; Musical Dir, London Motet and Madrigal Club, 1995–; Dir of Music, St Mary-at-Hill, City of London, and Dir, St Mary-at-Hill Baroque Chamber Orchestra and Bach Cantata Series, 1996–; Master of the Reigate Choristers (from St Mary's Choir School), 1997–2000; Moderating and Training Examiner, Associated Board of the Royal Schools of Music; mem., Incorporated Society of Musicians (Warden, Performers' and Composers' section, 2002–03), Worshipful Company of Musicians (Master, 2003–04). Recordings: various as solo organist, conductor, organ accompanist and harpsichord continuo player. Publications: William Crotch (1775–1847): composer, teacher, artist, 1975; George Thalben-Ball: a biography, 1979. Honours: FRCCO (hc).

Address: 46 Doods Road, Reigate, Surrey RH2 0NL, England. Telephone: (1737) 244604. E-mail: jonathanrennert@hotmail.com.

RENNERT, Wolfgang; Conductor; b. 1 April 1922, Cologne, Germany; m. (1) Anny Schlemm, 1958, (2) Ulla Berkewicz, 1971, divorced 1975, 1 s. Education: Mozarteum, Salzburg, 1940–43, 1945–47. Career: Debut: Düsseldorf Opera, 1948, Un Ballo in Maschera; Conducted Düsseldorf Opera, 1947–50, Kiel, 1950–53; Assistant Conductor, Frankfurt Opera, 1953–67; Music Director, Staatstheater am Gärtnerplatz, Munich, 1967–72; Permanent Guest Conductor, Staatsoper, Berlin, 1972–; General Music Director and Opera Director, National Theatre, Mannheim, 1980–85; Conducted Arabella at Covent Garden, London; Mozart's Il Rè Pastore and Wagner's Parsifal at Rome, 1988, Die Zauberflöte and Walküre at Dallas; Arabella, Wozzeck and Nozze di Figaro at San Francisco; Teatro São Carlos, Lisbon, 1989, Die Walküre; Staatsoper, Berlin, 1990; Komische Oper Berlin, Silent Woman (Strauss), 1990; Permanent Guest Conductor, Staatsoper, Dresden, 1990–; Season 1992 with Arabella at Dresden; Cunning Little Vixen, 1994; Jenůfa, 1996; Principal Guest Conductor, Portuguese Symphony Orchestra, Lisbon, 1999–; Engaged to conduct Tannhäuser at the Deutsche Oper Berlin, 2003. Recordings: Several labels. Current Management: Allied Artists Agency, 42 Montpelier Square, London SW7 1JZ, England.

RENTOWSKI, Wieslaw (Stanislaw Vivian); Composer and Organist; b. 23 Nov. 1953, Bydgoszcz, Poland; m. Magdalena Kubiak, 5 Sept 1985, 1 s. Education: MA, Psychology, University of Łódź, 1978; MA, Organ, Academy of Music, Łódź, 1985; MA, Composition, Fr Chopin Academy of Music, Warsaw, 1987; MMus, Composition, Louisiana State University School of Music, 1991. Career: Debut: Carnegie Hall, Lagniappe for 8 instruments, 1991; Compositions performed at: International Festival of Contemporary Music, Warsaw Autumn, 1984, 1986, 1987, 1989; Internationale Sinziger Orgelwoche, Bonn, 1989, 1990; Festival International de Lanaudière, Canada, 1989; International Festival of Contemporary Music, Baton Rouge, USA, 1990, 1991; Organist, many performances and recordings including solo recitals and chamber concerts in Warsaw, Banff, Toronto, Bayreuth, Baton Rouge and New Orleans. Compositions: Por dia de anos, published in 1987 and 1989; Chorea minor, published 1989. Recordings: Anagram, 1986; Wayang, 1989; Por dia de anos, 1990; Anagram, 1986; Wayang, 1989. Contributions: Intellectual music harmony, article to Ruch Muzyczny national musical magazine, Poland, 1989. Address: Louisiana State University School of Music, Baton Rouge, LA 70803, USA.

RENZETTI, Donato; Conductor; b. 30 Jan. 1950, Milan, Italy. Education: Studied at the Conservatorio Giuseppe Verdi, Milan. Career: Assisted Claudio Abbado in Milan, then conducted the Verdi Requiem in Salzburg; Gave Rigoletto at Verona in 1981 and has since worked at most Italian opera houses; Conducted the premiere of Corghi's Gargantua at Turin, 1984; Paris Théâtre Musical, Macbeth; Conducted La Sonnambula at the Chicago Lyric Opera, 1988, and Le nozze di Figaro at Rome, 1989; Bonn Opera and Teatro Fenice, Venice, 1990, with Il Barbiere di Siviglia and Ernani; Has given orchestral concerts in Italy and elsewhere; Conducted Turandot at the 1996 Macerata Festival and at Dallas, 1998. Honours: Prizewinner at the Gino Marinuzzi International Competition, 1976; Bronze Medal, Ernest Ansermet Competition at Geneva, 1978; Guido Cantelli Prize at Milan, 1980. Address: c/o Teatro dell'Opera, Piazza Beniamino Gigli 8, 00184 Rome, Italy.

RENZI, Emma; Singer (Soprano); b. 8 April 1926, Heidelberg, Transvaal, South Africa. Education: Studied at the College of Music in Kapstad, at the London Opera Centre, with Santo Santonocito in Catania and with Virginia Borroni in Milan. Career: Debut: Karlsruhe, 1961, as Sieglinde; Has sung in major cities world-wide including La Scala, Milan, Genoa, Lisbon, Buenos Aires, Barcelona, Edinburgh, Mexico City, Johannesburg, Naples, Rome and Munich; Italian Radio, 1977, in Parisina by Mascagni; Verona Arena, 1989; Other roles include Norma, Aida, Amelia (Un Ballo in Maschera), Tosca, Leonora (Il Trovatore), Turandot, the Duchess of Parma in Doktor Faust, Abigail, Lady Macbeth, Elisabeth, and Countess Almaviva; Head Pretoria Technikon Opera School, 1981–91; Senior Lecturer in Singing, Witwatersrand University, 1992–2003. Recordings: Emma Renzi: A Tribute. Honours: Vita Award, 1986; OMSS, 1987; Nederburg Special Award, 1993; ATKV Award, 1995. Address: 39 Auckland Avenue, Auckland Park, Johannesburg 2092, Gauteng, South Africa.

REPIN, Vadim Valentinovich; Russian violinist; b. 31 Aug. 1971, Novosibirsk, Siberia; s. of Viktor Antonovich Repin and Galina Georgievna Repina; m. Nato Gabunia (divorced). Education: Novosibirsk Music School with Zakhar Bron. Career: toured Europe since 1985; debut in London (Barbican) 1988, in USA 1990; performances with the Royal Concertgebouw, Suddeutscher Rundfunk, Royal, Israel and St Petersburg Philharmonic Orchestras, NHK, Tokyo Metropolitan, Hallé, and Kirov Orchestras, Berlin and Sydney Symphony Orchestras; USA appearances with the Cleveland, Chicago, Minnesota Symphonies and Los Angeles Philharmonic; season 1996–97 with New York Philharmonic; worked with conductors including Menuhin, Bychkov, Gergiev, Prêtre, Rozhdestvensky, Jansons and Boulez; chamber music partners include Boris Berezovsky, Bella Davidovich and Alexander Melnikov; lives in Germany. *Recordings include:* Shostakovich No. 1 and Prokofiev No. 2 with the Hallé Orchestra under Nagano, Tchaikovsky and Sibelius Concertos with the London Symphony under Krivine, Prokofiev Violin Sonatas and Five Melodies with Berezovsky. *Honours:* Veniawsky competition winner, Poznan 1982, Tibor Varga competition winner, Mion 1985, Queen Elizabeth competition winner, Brussels 1990. *Current Management:* Interclassica Music Management, Schönburgstrasse 4 Vienna, A 1040, Austria. *Telephone:* (20) 8233-5800 (office). *Fax:* (20) 8233-5801 (office).

REPPA, David; Set Designer; b. 2 Nov. 1926, Hammond, Indiana, USA. *Education:* Professional training at the Metropolitan Opera, 1957–58. *Career:* Debut: Designed Le nozze di Figaro for North Shore Opera, New York, 1960; Has worked with Sarah Caldwell's Opera Company of Boston and in Miami and San Francisco; Debut with the Metropolitan Opera, 1974, Duke Bluebeard's Castle and Gianni Schicchi; Other designs include Aida, 1976, Dialogues des Carmélites, 1977, and Don Carlos, 1979; As staff scenic designer has worked with most Metropolitan Opera scenic designers, supervising painting and construction of sets and adapting productions for the company's former spring tours. *Address:* c/o Metropolitan Opera, Lincoln Center, New York, NY 10023, USA.

REPPEL, Carmen; Singer (Soprano); b. 27 April 1941, Gummersbach, Germany. *Education:* Studied at the Hamburg Musikhochschule with Erna Berger. *Career:* Debut: Flensburg, 1968, as Elisabeth de Valois; Has sung in Hanover, Hamburg, Frankfurt, Cologne, Mannheim, Wiesbaden and Kassel; Bayreuth Festival, 1977–80, as Freia and Gutrune, and in Die Walküre and Parsifal; Wuppertal, 1983, in a concert performance of Schwarzschwanenreich by Siegfried Wagner; San Francisco, 1983, as Ariadne auf Naxos; Sang Mozart's Electra at Stuttgart, 1985; Hamburg and Vienna, 1985, as Leonore and Chrysothemis; Munich Opera, 1986, as Andromache in the premiere of Troades by Reimann; Zürich Opera, 1986, Salome; Further appearances in Berlin, Zürich, Barcelona, Milan and Tokyo; Other roles include Fiordiligi, Donna Anna, Mélisande, Mimi, Liu, Marenka in The Bartered Bride, Violetta, Desdemona, Leonora in Il Trovatore, Ariadne, Salome, Elsa and Sieglinde; Sang in Flavio Testi's Ricardo III at La Scala, 1987; Sieglinde in Die Walküre at Bologna, 1988; Strauss's Ariadne and Salome, Turin, 1989; Salome at the Torre del Lago festival, 1989. *Recordings include:* Freia and Gerhilde in Der Ring des Nibelungen, from Bayreuth; Les Troyens by Berlioz; Chrysothemis in Götz Friedrich's film version of Elektra.

RESA, Neithard; Violist; b. 1950, Berlin, Germany. *Education:* Studied in Berlin with Michel Schwalbe, Cologne with Max Rostal, USA with Michael Tree. *Career:* Prizewinner of German Music Foundation, 1978; Principal Viola of Berlin Philharmonic, 1978; Co-founded the Philharmonia Quartet, Berlin, giving concerts throughout Europe, USA and Japan; British debut, 1987, playing Haydn, Szymanowski and Beethoven at Wigmore Hall; Bath Festival, 1987, playing Mozart, Schumann and Beethoven; Other repertoire includes quartets by Bartók, Mendelssohn, Nicolai, Ravel and Schubert; Quintets by Brahms, Weber, Reger and Schumann. *Address:* Cimbernstr 34A, 14129 Berlin, Germany.

RESCIGNO, Nicola; Opera Conductor and Artistic Director; b. 28 May 1916, New York City, USA. *Education:* Italian Jurisprudence Degree, Rome. *Career:* Debut: Brooklyn New York Academy of Music, 1943; Co-Founder, Artistic Director, Chicago Lyric Opera, 1954–56; Presented American Debut of Maria Callas; Co-Founder/Artistic Director, Dallas Civic Opera (The Dallas Opera), 1957–; Regularly presents American debuts; past debuts include Sutherland, Vickers, Berganza, Montarsolo, Caballé, Knie, Domingo, Olivero, Dimitrova, W Meier; Instrumental in presenting baroque opera including American professional stage premieres of Handel's Alcina, Monteverdi's L'Incoronazione di Poppea, Samson, Giulio Cesare, and Vivaldi's Orlando Furioso; Guest Conductor: San Francisco, Metropolitan (debut 1978, Don Pasquale)-Chicago Lyric, Cincinnati, Philadelphia, Washington, Tulsa, Houston, at the Metropolitan Opera has conducted Donizetti's Don Pasquale and L'Elisir d'amore, Rossini's Italiana in Algeri and Verdi's La Traviata; Guest Conductor in Canada, South America, Italy, Portugal, the United Kingdom, Switzerland, Austria and France; Conducted the premiere of Argento's The Aspern Papers, Dallas, 1988; Werther at Rome, 1990; Aida at the 1990 Caracalla Festival, Rome; Season 1991 with Il Barbiere di Siviglia at Philadelphia. *Current Management:* CAMI Conductors Division.

RESICK, Georgine; Singer (Soprano); b. 1953, USA. *Education:* Studied with George London. *Career:* Sang Sophie in Werther at Washington;

Cologne Opera from 1981 as Marzelline in Fidelio, Oscar, Adina (L'Elisir d'amore) and Anne Trulove; Chicago Opera, 1984, as Blondchen in Die Entführung; Drottningholm Festival, 1985, as Mozart's Susanna and Constanze; Carolina in Il Matrimonio Segreto at Paris and Edinburgh; US appearances from 1986, including Hilde Mack in Henze's Elegy for Young Lovers at Long Beach Opera, 1996. *Recordings include:* Così fan tutte; Video of Le nozze di Figaro. *Address:* Long Beach Opera, 6372 Pacific Coast Highway, Long Beach, CA 90803, USA.

RESNIK, Regina; Singer (Mezzo-soprano); b. 30 Aug. 1924, New York, NY, USA; m. (1) Harry W Davies, 1947, 1 s., (2) Arbit Blatas, 1975. *Education:* Hunter College, New York. *Career:* Debut: Concert, Brooklyn Academy of Music, 1942; Appeared as Leonore in Fidelio, Mexico City, 1943; With New York City Opera, 1944–45; Debut as Leonora in Il Trovatore, 1944, with company, 1946–, Metropolitan Opera, New York; Conducted seminars on opera, New School for Social Research; Subsequently sang at venues including Chicago Opera Theater and San Francisco Opera; Bayreuth debut, as Sieglinde, 1953; London debut, 1957; Has sung at Vienna, Berlin, Stuttgart, Buenos Aires, Paris, Marseilles and Salzburg; Directed Carmen, Hamburg State Opera, 1971; San Francisco, 1972, as Claire in the US premiere of Der Besuch der alten Dame by Einem; Returned, 1982, as the Countess in The Queen of Spades; Produced and acted in Falstaff, Teatr Wielki, Warsaw, Poland, 1975. *Recordings include:* Carmen; Clytemnestra in Elektra, Mistress Quickly (Falstaff) and Sieglinde in Die Walkure (Bayreuth, 1953). *Honours:* President's Medal, Commandeur, Arts et Lettres, France. *Address:* 50 West 56th Street, New York, NY 10019, USA.

RESS, Ulrich; Singer (Tenor); b. 29 Oct. 1958, Augsburg, Germany. *Education:* Studied at Augsburg Conservatory, 1975–78, with Leonore Kirchstein from 1979. *Career:* Sang at Stadttheater Augsburg, 1979–84, notably as Idamante and Rossini's Almaviva; Engaged at Bayerische Staatsoper from 1984, as Mozart's Pedrillo and Monostatos, Verdi's Bardolph and Macduff, Beppe in Pagliacci and Pong in Turandot; Sang the Steersman and Strauss's Truffaldino at Munich, 1991; Guest appearances at Bayreuth and Barcelona, 1988–89, as David in Meistersinger, Strasbourg and Nice, Jacquino, 1989; Munich Staatsoper 2000–01 in Carmen, Tannhäuser, Katya Kabanova, Falstaff and Arabella. *Recordings:* Young Servant in video of Elektra conducted by Abbado; Bardolph in Falstaff conducted by Colin Davis; Massimilia Doni by Schoeck. *Address:* c/o Bayerische Staatsoper, Postfach 100184, 8000 Munich 1, Germany.

REUTER, Rolf; Conductor; b. 7 Oct. 1926, Leipzig, Germany. *Education:* Studied at the Dresden Hochschule für Musik, 1958–61. *Career:* Repetiteur and conductor at Eisenach, 1951–55; Musical Director at Meinigen, 1955–61; Leipzig Opera, 1961–73 (Generalmusikdirektor from 1963); Music Director at Weimar, 1979–80, Komische Oper Berlin, 1981–94; Professor of Music and Conductor of the orchestra at the Hanns Eisler Hochschule, Berlin; Guest conductor in Cuba, France, Germany, Yugoslavia, Czechoslovakia, Tokyo, Houston, Rome, Buenos Aires, Copenhagen, Moscow and Prague; Gave Der Ring des Nibelungen at the Paris Opéra, 1978, and Tristan und Isolde at the Berlin Staatsoper; Gave the premieres of Guayana Johnny by Alan Bush (1966) and Judith by Siegfried Matthus (1975); Visited Covent Garden and Wiesbaden, 1989, with the company of the Komische Oper, conducting The Bartered Bride and Judith; Conducted a new production of Der Freischütz at the Komische Oper, 1989; Le nozze di Figaro for New Israeli Opera, 1992. *Recordings include:* Beethoven's incidental music for Egmont; Handel: Oratorio L'Allegro, il Moderato ed il Penseroso; Hans Pfitzner: Das Herz and Das Dunkle Reich; Siegfried Matthus: Judith and Hyperion Fragmente; Berlioz: Lélio and Symphonie Fantastique; Mozart: Divertimenti and Oboe Concerto; Festliche Weihnachtskonzerte (Corelli, Telemann, Tartini, Locatelli). *Honours:* Honorary Member, Oper Leipzig; Honorary Member, Komische Oper Berlin. *Current Management:* Berliner Konzertagentur. *Address:* c/o Berliner Konzertagentur, Dramburgerstrasse 46, 12683 Berlin, Germany.

REVERDY, Michèle; Composer; b. 12 Dec. 1943, Alexandria, Egypt; 1 d. *Education:* Literature, Sorbonne, Paris; Counterpoint with Alain Weber, Analysis with Claude Ballif, Composition with Olivier Messiaen, Paris Conservatory; Casa de Velazquez, Madrid. *Career:* Teaching, lycées, 1965–74; Professor of Analysis, regional and municipal conservatories, 1974–83; Producer, Radio-France, 1978–80; Professor, Class of Analysis, Paris Conservatory, 1983–. *Compositions include:* Kaleidoscope for harpsichord and flute, 1975; Number One for guitar, 1977; Météores for 17 instruments, 1978; L'Ile aux Lumières for solo violin and string orchestra, 1983; Scenic Railway for 16 instruments, 1983; La Nuit Qui Suivit Notre Dernier Dîner, chamber opera, 1984; Triade for guitar, 1986; Trois Fantaisies de Gaspard de la Nuit for choir or 12-voice ensemble, 1987; Sept Enluminures for soprano, clarinet, piano and percussion, 1987; Propos Félins for string orchestra and children's choir, 1988; Le Cercle du Vent for orchestra, 1988; Vincent, opera based on the life of Vincent Van Gogh, 1984–89; Le Précepteur, opera (Jakob Lenz) for coloratura soprano, soprano, mezzo-soprano, contralto, 3 tenors, 2 baritones, 3 basses and 20 instruments. *Recordings:* CD, Michèle Reverdy (Scenic Railway, Sept Enluminures, Météores, Fugure, Kaleidoscope); Triade, CD Rafael Andia, guitar; Le Château, 1980–86, Opera for 9 soloists, 2 choirs (men and children), orchestra, text from Franz Kafka. *Publications:* L'oeuvre pour piano d'Olivier Messiaen, 1978; Histoire de la Musique Occidentale, 1985; L'oeuvre pour orchestra d'Olivier Messiaen, 1988. *Address:* 75 rue des Gravilliers, 75003 Paris, France.

REX, Christopher; Cellist; b. 2 Jan. 1951, Orlando, Florida, USA; m. Martha Anne Wilkins, 30 Nov 1985, 1 s., 1 d. *Education:* Bachelor of Music, Curtis Institute of Music, Philadelphia, Pennsylvania, 1972; Graduate studies with Leonard Rose, Juilliard School, New York. *Career:* Debut: Premiered Stephen Paul's Double Concerto with brother Charles, Lincoln Center, New York; 7 years with Philadelphia Orchestra, 1972–79; Principal Cello, Atlanta Symphony, 1979–; Principal Cello, New York Philharmonic, 1988 European tour; Founding Member, Georgian Chamber Players; mem, NARAS; AFM. *Recordings:* Saint-Saëns, Muse and Poet with Martium Philharmonic. *Publications:* Editor, Mussorgsky's Pictures at an Exhibition; Art work for Choral Journal. *Honours:* First cellist to win Young Artist Competition, American Federation of Music Clubs, 1979. *Address:* 1237 Woods Circle NE, Atlanta, GA 30324, USA.

REY, Isabel; Singer (Soprano); b. 1966, Valencia, Spain. *Education:* Studied at the Valencia Conservatory with Ana Luisa Chova and in Barcelona with Juan Oncina and Tatiana Menotti. *Career:* Debut: Bilbao, 1987, as Amina in La Sonnambula; Madrid as Ilia in Idomeneo and Vienna in concerts of Mozart's Exultate Jubilate; Ascanio in Alba (Fauno); Handel's Saul and Beethoven's Ninth; Zürich Opera, 1991–, as Susanna in Le nozze di Figaro, Gilda in Rigoletto, Adina in L'Elisir d'amore; Juliette in Roméo et Juliette, Marie in La Fille du Régiment; Susanna with Harnoncourt, Nederlandse Opera, 1993, 1994; Concerts with José Carreras world-wide, 1993–; Sang Susanna in a new production of Figaro at Zürich, 1996 and at Madrid, 1998; Sang Gilda and Lucia di Lammermoor at Zürich, Susanna at La Coruña, 2000. *Recordings:* Nozze di Figaro (Erato); With José Carreras, Zarzuela Arias and duets. *Address:* Opernhaus Zürich, Falkenstrasse 1, 8008 Zürich, Switzerland.

REYMOND, Valentin; Conductor; b. 1954, Neuchâtel, Switzerland. *Education:* Studied at Conservatories of Bienne and Zürich. *Career:* Assistant at the Grand Théâtre Geneva; Has assisted such conductors as Jean-Marie Auberson, Horst Stein, Armin Jordan and Roderick Brydon; Music Director of Opéra Décentralisé; Concert and broadcast appearances with Orchestre de la Suisse Romande and Orchestre de la Radio Suisse Italienne, Orchestre de Chambre de Toulouse, Krasnoyarsk Symphony Orchestra (Siberia), Russian State Symphony Orchestra; Operatic appearances: Traviata (Opéra de Lucerne); Rape of Lucretia (Opéra Décentralisé and Opéra de Lausanne); Albert Herring (Bern Opera, Opéra de Lausanne and Opéra de Nantes); Les Pêcheurs de Perles (Dublin Opera); Les Mamelles de Tirésias, Das Rheingold, Die Walküre, Le Roi Malgré Lui (Opéra de Nantes); L'Etoile (Opera North); Iphigénie en Aulide for Opera North, 1996. *Address:* Music International, 13 Ardilaun Road, London N5 2QR, England.

REYNOLDS, Anna, FRAM; British opera and concert singer (mezzo-soprano); b. 5 June 1931, Canterbury, England. *Education:* Royal Academy of Music, studied with Prof. Debora Fambri. *Career:* Italy from 1958 in operas by Rossini, Donizetti and Massenet; Appearances at many international festivals including Spoleto, Edinburgh, Aix-en-Provence, Salzburg Easter Festival, Vienna, Tanglewood; Bayreuth Festival, 1970–75, as Fricka, Waltraute and Magdalena; Has sung with leading orchestras all over the world including Chicago Symphony, New York Philharmonic, Berlin Philharmonic and London Symphony; Appearances in opera performances at New York Metropolitan, La Scala Milan, Covent Garden, Bayreuth, Rome, Chicago Lyric Opera, Teatro Colón, Buenos Aires, Teatro Fenice, Venice and many others; Teacher of singing. *Recordings:* notably cantatas by Bach. *Address:* 37 Chelwood Gardens, Richmond, Surrey TW9 4JG, England.

REYNOLDS, Julian; Conductor and Pianist; b. 1962, London, England. *Education:* Vienna Hochschule für Musik and with Albert Ferber. *Career:* Debut: Wigmore Hall recital, 1981; Pianist with European Community Youth Orchestra, 1980–85; Assistant musical director at Netherlands Opera, 1986–94, conducting Bluebeard's Castle by Bart ók, Luisa Miller and Mozart's Mitridate; A Midsummer Night's Dream, 1993; Kirov Opera, St Petersburg, with La Traviata and Le nozze di Figaro; Otello at Stuttgart and The Cunning Little Vixen at Maastricht; Concerts throughout the United Kingdom and the Netherlands; Season 1998–99 with Haydn's Seasons at Melbourne and Luisa Miller at Mainz; Associate Conductor of Netherlands Opera from 1999, with L'italiana in

Algeri, Figaro and L'Elisir d'amore; Recital appearances with Barbara Bonney and Kiri Te Kanawa; Ravel's Ma Mère l'Oye, and own orchestrations of Alma Mahler Songs. *Address:* c/o IMG Artists, Lovell House, 616 Chiswick High Road, London W4 5RX, England.

REYNOLDS, Roger (Lee); Composer; b. 18 July 1934, Detroit, Michigan, USA; m. Karen Jeanne Hill, 11 April 1964, two d. *Education:* BSE, Physics, University of Michigan; BM, Music Literature, MM, Composition, University of Michigan. *Career:* Faculty member, University of California at San Diego, 1969–; George Miller Visiting Professor, University of Illinois, 1971; Founding Director, Center for Music Experiment, University of California at San Diego, 1972–77; Visiting Professor, Yale University, 1981; Senior Research Fellow, ISAM, Brooklyn College, 1985; Valentine Professor of Music, Amherst College, 1988; Rothschild Composer-in-Residence, Peabody Conservatory of Music, Baltimore, 1992–93. *Compositions:* Some 100 compositions including: Dreaming, 1992; Symphony (The Stages of Life), 1991–92; The Emperor of Ice Cream, 1961–62; Visions, 1991; Transfigured Wind, I–IV, 1984–85; Voicespace I–V, 1975–86; Odyssey, 1989–93; last things I think, to think about, 1994; Watershed I, III, IV, 1995; The Red Act Arias, 1997; Justice, 1999–2001. *Recordings:* About 60 on CD or DVD including: Whispers Out of Time; Transfigured Wind IV; Coconino... a shattered landscape; The Ivanov Suite; Versions/Stages I–V; Voicespace I, III, IV, V; Variation; Archipelago, Personae; Odyssey; First Custom Designed Classical DVD, Watershed, 1998. *Publications:* 4 books: Mind Models: New Forms of Musical Experience, 1975; A Searcher's Path: A Composer's Ways, 1987; A Jostled Silence: Contemporary Japanese Musical Thought, 1992–93; Form and Method: Composing Music,2002. *Honours:* Pulitzer Prize in Music, 1989, National Institute of Arts and Letters Award, 1971. *Current Management:* Graham Hayter, Contemporary Music Promotions. *Address:* 624 Serpentine Drive, Del Mar, CA 92014, USA. *Website:* www.rogerreynolds.com.

REYNOLDS, Verne Becker; Composer and Horn Player; b. 18 July 1926, Lyons, Kansas, USA. *Education:* BM, 1950, Cincinnati Conservatory of Music; MM 1951, University of Wisconsin; Further study with Herbert Howells at the Royal College of Music, London. *Career:* Horn player with the Cincinnati Symphony Orchestra, 1947–50, and first horn of the Rochester Philharmonic, 1959–68; Faculty Member, University of Wisconsin, 1950–53, Indiana University School of Music at Bloomington, 1954–59, and Eastman School of Music at Rochester, 1959–95. *Compositions include:* Violin Concerto, 1951; Saturday with Venus, overture, 1953; Serenade for 13 wind instruments, 1958; Flute sonata, 1962; String Quartet, 1967; Concertare I–V, for various instrumental combinations, 1968–76; Horn sonata, 1970; Violin Sonata, 1970; Ventures for orchestra, 1975; Events for trombone choir, 1977; Scenes Revisited for wind ensemble, 1977; Festival and Memorial Music, for orchestra, 1977; Trio for horn, trombone and tuba, 1978; Fantasy-Etudes I–V for various wind instruments, 1979–92; Concerto for band, 1980; Cello Sonata, 1983; Quintet for piano and winds, 1986; Brass Quintet, 1987; Songs of the Season for soprano, horn and piano, 1988; Trio for oboe, horn and piano, 1990; Clarinet sonata, 1994; Letter to the World for soprano and percussion, 1994; Concerto for piano and wind ensemble, 1996; Concerto for orchestra, 1997; String Quartet, 1998; Sonata for viola and piano, 1998. *Publications:* Horn handbook, 1997. *Address:* 102 Southern Parkway, Rochester, NY 14618, USA.

RHODES, Cherry; Educator, Concert Organist and Adjunct Professor; b. 28 June 1943, Brooklyn, New York, USA; m. Ladd Thomas. *Education:* BMus, Curtis Institute of Music, Philadelphia, Pennsylvania, 1964; HS Music, Munich, studied with Karl Richter, 1964–67; Private Study with Marie-Claire Alain and Jean Guillou, Paris, 1967–69; Summer schools, Harvard and University of Pennsylvania, 1961, 1962, 1963. *Career:* Soloist, Philadelphia Orchestra, South German Radio Orchestra, Chamber Orchestra of French National Radio, Pasadena Chamber Orchestra, Phoenix Symphony Orchestra; Los Angeles Philharmonic; First American to win an international organ competition, Munich; Recitals, Lincoln Center, New York City, Notre Dame, Paris, Royal Festival Hall, London, Los Angeles Music Center, Milwaukee Performing Arts Center, Orchestra Hall, Chicago, Meyerson Symphony Center, Dallas; Numerous appearances at national and regional conventions of AGO; Performances, several Bach festivals; International festivals Bratislava, Nuremberg, Paris, St Albans, Luxembourg, Vienna and throughout Poland; Gave opening recital on new organ at John F Kennedy Center in Washington DC; Broadcast performances in USA, Canada and Europe; Adjudicator for national and international organ-playing competitions. *Publications:* Editor, Ascent for Organ by Joan Tower; Co-editor, Prelude and Variations on Old Hundredth by Calvin Hampton. *Address:* Thornton School of Music, University of Southern California, Los Angeles, CA 90089-0851, USA.

RHODES, Jane; Singer (Soprano); b. 13 March 1929, Paris, France; m. Roberto Benzi, 1966. *Career:* Debut: Marguerite in La Damnation de Faust, Nancy, 1953; Sang Renata in the first (concert) performance of The Fiery Angel by Prokofiev; Sang in the 1956 premiere of Le Fou by

Landowski; Paris Opéra from 1958, as Marguerite, Carmen, Salome, and Kundry, 1974; Metropolitan Opera, 1960, Carmen; Aix-en-Provence, 1961, in L'Incoronazione di Poppea; Paris Opéra-Comique, 1968, in L'Heure Espagnole and La Voix Humaine; Also sang in Duke Bluebeard's Castle by Bart ók. *Recordings:* Carmen; La Juive by Halévy; Mireille by Gounod; Margared in Le Roi d'Ys by Lalo; The Fiery Angel; Public Opinion in Orphée aux Enfers.

RHODES, Michael; Singer (baritone), Actor and Teacher; b. 13 Aug. 1923, Brooklyn, New York, USA; m Anne Foegen. *Education:* BA, Dartmouth College; Juilliard School of Music; Mannes School; New York College of Music; Actors Studio; Private Study, Voice with Robert Weede, Guiseppe De Luca, Apollo Granforte. *Career:* Debut: New York City Opera, Jochanaan, Salome, 1947; Concert Debut: Carnegie Hall, New York Philharmonic, Stokowski, Boris and Elektra with Mitropoulis; New York City Opera; Berlin Staatsoper; Deutsche Oper, Berlin; Opera National, Paris; La Scala, Milan; Royal Opera Amsterdam; Royal Opera, Copenhagen; Théâtre de la Monnaie, Brussels; Monte Carlo Opera; Rome Opera; Australian Opera, Sydney; Theatre Liceu, Barcelona; Bolshoi, Moscow; Broadway: Carousel, Oklahoma, Most Happy Fella; Radio: NBC Concerts with Toscanini; RAI Wozzeck with Karajan; Masterclasses: Milan, Paris, Barcelona; mem, American Guild of Musical Artists; Deutsche Bühnen Genossenschaft. *Honours:* Commander Italian Republic, 1955, Commander Legion of Honor, 1958; Bellas Artes, Spain, 1960. *Address:* Januarius-Zickstr 1, 54296 Trier, Germany.

RHODES, Phillip (Carl); Composer; b. 6 June 1940, Forest City, North Carolina, USA. *Education:* Studied with Iain Hamilton at Duke University (BA 1962); Composition with Donald Martino and Mel Powell, theory with Gunther Schuller and George Perle at Yale University (MM 1963). *Career:* Composer-in-Residence and faculty member at Louisville, 1969–72; Composer-in-Residence and Andrew W Mellon Professor of the Humanities at Carleton College, Northfield, Minnesota, from 1974; President of Carleton College Music Society, 1985–87. *Compositions include:* Four Movements for chamber orchestra, 1962; Remembrance for symphonic wind ensemble, 1967; About Faces, ballet, 1970; Divertimento for small orchestra, 1971; String Trio, 1973; Museum Pieces, for clarinet and string quartet, 1973; Quartet, for flute harp, violin and cello, 1975; On the Morning of Christ's Nativity, cantata, 1976; Ceremonial Fanfare and Chorale, for 2 brass choirs, 1977; Wind Songs for children's chorus and Orff instruments, 1979; In Praise of Wisdom, for chorus and brass choir, 1982; Nets to Catch the Wind, for chorus and percussion, 1986; The Gentle Boy, opera, premiered 1987; The Magic Pipe, opera, 1989; Wedding Song, for soprano, violin and organ, 1990; Reels and Reveries, variations for orchestra, 1991; Mary's Lullaby, for soprano, violin and organ, 1993; Chorale and Mediatationa (O Sacred Head Now Wounded) for women's voices and organ, 1995; Fiddle Tunes, for violin and synthesized strings, 1995; Solo instrumental pieces. *Address:* c/o ASCAP, ASCAP Building, 1 Lincoln Plaza, New York, NY 10023, USA.

RHODES, Samuel; Violist; b. 13 Feb. 1941, Long Beach, New York, USA; m. 30 Dec 1968, 2 d. *Education:* BA, Queens College, New York City; MFA, Princeton University. *Career:* Debut: Carnegie Recital Hall, 1966; Faculty of Tanglewood and participant of Marlboro Festival, 1960–; Member of Juilliard String Quartet, 1969–; Faculty Juilliard School, 1969 Appeared: Great Performances, PBS television, 1977; Hindemith: The Viola Legacy 3 Concert Series, Carnegie Recital Hall, 1985; CBS Sunday Morning, 1986; Rcitals: Library of Congress, Washington DC, Juilliard School, Participant in International Hinemith Viola Feativial, New York Chapter, 1996–. *Compositions:* Quintet for string quartet and viola. *Recordings:* Schoenberg Quartets; Complete Beethoven Quartets; Mozart-Haydn Quartets; Complete Bartók Quartets; Schubert and Dvořák Quartets; Guest Artist with Beaux Arts Trio; 4 Carter Quartets; Berg Lyric Suite; Complete Hindemith Quartets; Mendelssohn Op 12, Op 13; Hindemith Four Viola Solo Sonatas. *Honours:* 3 Grammy Awards, 1971, 1976, 1985. *Address:* c/o The Juilliard School, Lincoln Center, 144 West 66th St, New York, NY 10023, USA.

RHODES, Teddy Tahu; Singer (baritone); b. 1965, New Zealand. *Education:* Studied with Maud Adams Taylor; Guildhall School, London, with Ruldoph Piernay and David Harper. *Career:* Debut: Dandini in La Cenerentola with Opera Australia, 1998; Season 1999 with Sharples for Canterbury Opera, Marcello and Silvio (Pagliacci) for Opera New Zealand; Season 2000–2001 as Mozart's Count and Britten's Demetrius for Opera Australia; US debut as Joe in the premiere of Jake Heggie's Dead Man Walking, San Francisco; Season 2001–2002 as Guglielmo, Belcore and the Herald in Lohengrin for Opera Australia, Escamillo and Marcello for Dallas Opera; Stanley in Previn's A Streetcar Named Desire for Austin Opera. *Honours:* Represented New Zealand at 1999 Cardiff Singer of the World Competition. *Current Management:* Askonas Holt Ltd, Lonsdale Chambers, 27 Chancery Lane, London, WC2A 1PF, England. *Telephone:* (20) 7400-1700. *Fax:*

(20) 7400-1799. *E-mail:* info@askonasholt.co.uk. *Website:* www .askonasholt.co.uk.

RHYS-DAVIES, Jennifer; Singer (Soprano); b. 8 May 1953, Panteg, Gwent, Wales. *Education:* Studied at Trinity College of Music, London. *Career:* Appearances with Welsh National Opera as the Forester's Wife in The Cunning Little Vixen, Fortune in Poppea, Miss Jessel in Turn of The Screw, also in Dresden and Leipzig, First Lady in Die Zauberflöte and Donna Elvira; Further appearances as Constanze for Opera 80 and Donna Anna for Kent Opera on tour to Valencia; Opera North as Sandrina in La Finta Giardiniera, Aloysia in the Mozart-Griffiths pastiche; Sang Semiramide and Sieglinde at Nuremberg, Queen of Night for Dublin Grand Opera and Scottish Opera, 1993; Covent Garden and English Nationa Opera debut in 1993 as Berta in Barbiere di Siviglia and Mrs Fiorentino in Street Scene; Concert engagements in Beethoven's Mount of Olives and Haydn's Seasons at Dublin, Handel's Dixit Dominus and Poulenc's Gloria for Stuttgart Radio, Haydn's Orlando Paladino at Garsington; Sang Clorinda in Cenerentola at Royal Opera House, The Duenna in Der Rosenkavalier, Amaltea in Moses, Queen of Night in Stuttgart, Lady Macbeth for WNO and Nuremberg; Italian Singer in Capriccio at Glyndebourne, 1998; Season 2000–01 as Mozart's Marcellina at Garsington and Elettra at Basle. *Recordings:* As Berta in Barber of Seville; Various recordings for Opera Rara. *Honours:* Kennedy Scott Prize and Rowland Jones Memorial Award, Trinity College. *Address:* c/o Glyndebourne Festival Opera, Glyndebourne, Lewes, Sussex BN8 5UU, England.

RHYS-EVANS, Huw; Singer (Tenor); b. 1959, Tregaron, Ceredigion, Wales. *Education:* Studied, Royal Academy of Music; Studied, National Opera Centre. *Career:* Wide range of operatic engagements; Sang Ferrando in Così fan tutte, America, France, the Netherlands and Majorca; Pedrillo in Die Entfuhrung aus dem Serail, France; Tamino, Die Zauberflote, North Netherlands Philharmonic Orchestra; Ernesto, Don Pasquale; Ismaele Nabucco, Welsh National Opera; Vivaldo Mendelssohn's Die Hochzeit des Camacho, Flanders Festival; First Jew, Salome, Bastille Opéra; Celebrated singer of oratorio; Evangelist in Bach's passions, Netherlands, Leith Hill Music Festival; B Minor Mass, Besançon; Messiah, St Martin-in-the-Fields; The Royal Albert Hall; Singapore Symphony Orchestra; Nelson Mass, Teatro La Fenice, Venice; Elijah, Singapore; Amsterdam Baroque Orchestra; Les Musiciens du Louvre; Evangelist in Bach's St John Passion, Leith Musical Festival, Southwark Cathedral; Evangelist in Bach's St Matthew Passion; Arias, St Matthew Passion, Zupthen, Netherlands; The Seasons, Rochester Cathedral; Elijah, St Paul's Festival Choir; Messiah, Harrogate; Jonathan Saul, Darmstadt, Germany; Pang, Turandot, Mid-Wales Opera; Count Almaviva, The Barber of Seville, Opera North; Idreno in Semiramide, Chelsea Opera Group; Monteverdi Vespers, Mozart Requiem; Belfiore Il viaggio a Reims, Amiens and Versailles; Ottavio in Don Giovanni, 1999 Perth Festival of the Arts; Belmonte in Seraglio, The Opera Project. *Recordings:* Stabat Mater; Ferrando; Pedrillo; Orff. *Address:* 609A Kenton Lane, Harrow Weald, Middlesex HA3 7HJ, England.

RIBARY, Antal; Composer; b. 8 Jan. 1924, Budapest, Hungary. *Education:* Diploma in Art History, Pazmany Peter University of Budapest; Diploma in Composition, Academy of Music, Budapest. *Career:* Debut: 2 Michelangelo songs, 1947; The Divorce of King Louis (one-act opera) performed at the Hungarian State Opera House, 1959. *Compositions include:* Pantomime Suite; Hellas Cantata; Requiem for the Lover; Six Lines from the Satyricon; Concerto Grosso; Five Quartets; Four Violin and Piano Sonatas; King Louis Divorces, opera; Two Michelangelo Songs; Five Shakespeare Sonnets; Five Villon Songs; Symphonies I–VII, 1960–84; De Profundis/Motetta; Two Poems for choirs; Rest C G Rossetti; Chant pour 8 Ligne/Baudelaire; Two Piano Concertos, 1979–80; In manuscript: Symphonies V–XII; In Memoriam Charles Beaudelaire; Six portraits imaginaires de Charles Moreas; Four Piano Concertos; Masks and Churches in Spain, suite for orchestra; Two Spanish Songs for voice and piano. *Recordings:* The Music of Antal Ribary, vols 1, 2 and 3; Sonata for Alto and Piano; Six Staves from Satyricon, 1980. *Publications:* Music Criticism 1960–70. *Address:* Felka 3, 1136 Budapest, Hungary.

RIBNIKOV, Alexei (L'vovich); Composer; b. 17 July 1946, Moscow, Russia. *Education:* Moscow Conservatory, 1969–75; Director, Russian State Symphony, 1986–87; Founded Ribnikov Theatre Studio, Moscow, 1990. *Compositions include:* Theatre Pieces: The Star and Death of Joachino Murieti, 1976; Tuno and Avos, 1980; Liturgy for the Catechumens, 1991; A Night Song, ballet, 1997; 2 piano sonatas, 1962, 1966; 2 symphonies, 1969, 1974; Russian overture, 1967; The Jester, Capriccio for orchestra, 1968; Concerto for string quartet and orchestra, 1971; Piano Concerto, 1971; Bayan Concerto, 1972; Performance of works throughout Russia and in USA, France, the United Kingdom and Germany. *Address:* c/o Centre for Russian Music, Music Dept., Goldsmiths' College, New Cross, London SE14 6NW, England.

RICCARDI, Franco; Singer (Tenor); b. 1921, Italy. *Career:* Debut: Naples, 1947, as Pinkerton; Has sung widely in Italy, and notably at La Scala Milan from 1954, as Monostatos, Missail, Goro, Pang, and Bardolph; Rome Opera, 1963, as David in Die Meistersinger; Caracalla Festival and Verona Arena, 1968–69; Sang at Dallas Opera, 1970, Martina Franca Festival, 1982; Other roles have included Borsa in Rigoletto, Arturo in Lucia di Lammermoor, Cassio and Shuisky. *Address:* c/o Teatro alla Scala, Via Filodrammatici 2, 20121 Milan, Italy.

RICCI, Ruggiero; American violinist; b. 24 July 1918, San Francisco; s. of Pietro Ricci and Emma Bacigalupi; m. 1st Ruth Rink 1942; m. 2nd Valma Rodriguez 1957; m. 3rd Julia Whitehurst Clemenceau 1978; two s. three d. *Education:* under Louis Persinger, Mischel Piastro, Paul Stassévitch and Georg Kulenkampff. *Career:* début with Manhattan Symphony Orchestra, New York 1929; first tour of Europe 1932; served USAF 1942–45; Prof. of Violin, Univ. of Mich. 1982–87, Hochschule für Musik, Mozarteum, Salzburg, Austria 1989–2002; played first performances of the violin concertos of Ginastera, Von Einem and Veerhoff; specializes in violin solo literature. *Recordings:* over 500 recordings, including the first complete recording of Paganini Caprices. *Publications:* Left Hand Violin Technique 1987. *Honours:* Cavaliere Order of Merit (Italy). *Current Management:* Intermusica, 16 Duncan Terrace, London, N1 8BZ, England. *Address:* 1143 May Drive, Palm Springs, CA 92262, USA. *Telephone:* (760) 320–9785 (home).

RICCIARELLI, Katia; Singer (Soprano); b. 16 Jan. 1946, Rovigo, Italy; m. Pippo Baudo, 1986. *Education:* Studied at the Benedetto Marcello Conservatory, Venice. *Career:* Debut: Mantua, 1969, as Mimi in La Bohème; Sang Leonora in Il Trovatore at Parma in 1970; After winning the 1971 New Voices Competition on television appeared throughout Italy; US debut at the Chicago Lyric Opera, 1972, as Lucrezia in I Due Foscari; Covent Garden, 1974, La Bohème and as Amelia in Un Ballo in Maschera, 1975; Metropolitan Opera from 1975, as Mimi, Micaela in Carmen, Desdemona, Luisa Miller and Amelia; Guest appearances in Moscow, Barcelona, Berlin, New Orleans and Verona; At Pesaro has sung in revivals of Rossini's Il Viaggio a Reims and Bianca e Falliero (1985–86); Other roles include Donizetti's Caterina Cornaro, Maria di Rohan, Lucrezia Borgia, Bellini's Imogene (Il Pirata) and Giulietta (I Capuleti e i Montecchi); Returned to Covent Garden, 1989, as Elisabeth de Valois in Don Carlos; Théâtre du Châtelet, Paris, 1988, as Gluck's Iphigénie en Tauride; Pesaro Festival, 1988, as Ninetta in La gazza ladra; Sang Desdemona at the Met and Covent Garden, 1990, Maria Stuarda at Reggio Emilia; Geneva, 1990, as Amenaide in Rossini's Tancredi; Season 1992/93 as Wolf-Ferrari's Susanna at Monte Carlo and Rosalinde in Fledermaus at Catania; Gave opera recital at Ljubljana, 1994; Sang Handel's Agrippina at Palermo, 1997; Giordano's Fedora at Lecce, 1998. *Recordings:* Roles in Suor Angelica and Simon Boccanegra; I Due Foscari (2); Tosca; Il Battaglia di Legnano; Il Trovatore; La Bohème; Luisa Miller; Falstaff; Un Ballo in Maschera; Don Carlos; Aida; Turandot; Carmen; Il Viaggio a Reims; La Donna del Lago; I Capuleti e i Montecchi; Anacréon; Tancredi; I Lombardi; Appears as Desdemona in the film of Otello directed by Franco Zeffirelli. *Address:* c/o Teatro Massimo, Palermo, Via R. Wagner 2, 90139 Palermo, Italy.

RICH, Alan; Music Critic, Editor and Author; b. 17 June 1924, Boston, Massachusetts, USA. *Education:* AB, Harvard University, 1945; MA, University of California, Berkeley, 1952; Studied in Vienna, Austria, 1952–53. *Career:* Assistant Music Critic, Boston Herald, 1944–45; New York Sun, 1947–48; Contributor, American Record Guide, 1947–61; Saturday Review, 1952–53; Musical America, 1955–61; Teacher of Music, University of California, Berkeley, 1950–58; Programme and Music Director, Pacifica Foundation FM Radio, 1953–61; Assistant Music Critic, New York Times, 1961–63; Chief Music Critic and Editor, New York-Herald Tribune, 1963–66; Music Critic and Editor, New York World-Journal-Tribune, 1966–67; Contributing Editor, Time magazine, 1967–68; Music and Drama Critic and Arts Editor, 1979–83, Contributing Editor, 1983–85; California magazine; General Editor, Newsweek magazine, 1983–87; Music Critic, Los Angeles Herald-Examiner, 1987–; Teacher, New School for Social Research, 1972–75, 1977–79; University of Southern California School of Journalism, 1980–82; California Institute of the Arts, 1982–; Artist-in-Residence, Davis Center for the Performing Arts, City University of New York, 1975–76. *Publications:* Careers and Opportunities in Music, 1964; Music: Mirror of the Arts, 1969; Simon and Schuster Listener's Guide to Music, 3 vols, 1980; The Lincoln Center Story, 1984. *Contributions:* Numerous articles and reviews to various journals. *Address:* c/o Los Angeles Herald-Examiner, 1111 S Broadway, Los Angeles, CA 90015, USA.

RICH, Elizabeth; Concert Pianist; b. 8 Feb. 1931, New York City, USA; m. Joel Markowitz, 30 June 1952, 2 s., 1 d. *Education:* Juilliard School of Music; Scholarships at ages 7–18. *Career:* Debut: New York Philharmonic Auditions, Young People's Concert, Carnegie Hall, 1949; English premiere of Clara Schumann Piano Concerto, Beethoven Choral Fantasy, Queen Elizabeth Hall, London, 1985; Complete Cycle, Mozart Piano Sonatas, NY, 1984–85; Guest artist at Mt Desert Festival of

Chamber Music, 1987–91, 1993, 1994 and 1995; 4th Recital, Alice Tully Hall, Lincoln Center, 1993; Mozart Concerto and Bach Concerto, St Martin's in the Field, London Chamber Soloists Orchestra, 1993; Opened Mozart Days at the Prague Festival in the Dvořák Hall, Prague, 1997; Schumann Concerto, Bridgeport Symphony, January 25th, 1997; Mozart recital at Weill Hall, Carnegie Hall, 2000; Weill Hall Recital, April 15th , 2004; 'In Their Own Words', Bach, Schumann, Weber, Beethoven; Mozart Piano Concerto, K271, Purcell Room, London Chamber Soloists Orchestra, October 12th, 2001; Schumann Concerto, Kalamazoo Symphony, February 18th, 2001. *Contributions:* Article in Piano Today, Winter 2001, Playing Late Mozart. *Recordings:* For Dutch radio; Schumann CD for Connoisseur Society, 6 Noveletten and Carnaval, 1992; 2 Piano Concerti of Carl Maria von Weber, Clara Schumann Concerto, Janáček Philharmonic Orchestra, 1995; Haydn and CPE Bach, 1998; Complete Mozart Sonatas, vols I–III, 2000–01, vol IV, 2004;. *Current Management:* Liegner Management. *Address:* c/o Liegner Management, PO Box 884, New York, NY 10023, USA.

RICHARD, André; Composer and Conductor; b. 18 April 1944, Berne, Switzerland. *Education:* Studied in Geneva, and in Freiburg with Klaus Huber and Brian Ferneyhough, 1975–78. *Career:* Director, Freiburg Institute for New Music, 1980–; Horizonte Concert Series, Freiburg, until 1989; co-founder, Freiburger Solistenchor, 1983, with concerts of works by Luigi Nono, and others; Director of experimental studio at Heinrich Strobel Foundation, from 1989. *Compositions include:* Ritornelle, for 3 precussion instruments, 1976; Cinque, for piano, 1979; Trilogie, for flute, oboe and harpsichord, 1981; String Quartet, 1982; Etude sur la carré rouge, for chamber ensemble, 1984–6; Echanges, for orchestra and live electronics, 1986; Musique de rue (Street Music) for 6 instruments and tape, 1987; Glidif for bassoon, clarinet, 2 doublebasses and live electronics, 1990. *Publications include:* Articles on the music of Luigi Nono, 1991, 1993. *Address:* c/o SUISA, Rue de l'Hopitâl 22, Case Postele 409, 2001 Neuchâtel, Switzerland.

RICHARDS, Denby; Music Critic, Author and Lecturer; b. 7 Nov. 1924, London, England; m. Rhondda Gillespie, 29 May 1973. *Education:* Regent Street Polytechnic, London. Self-taught Piano and 50 years attending concerts and studying scores. *Career:* Early writing on Kensington News, then Music Critic to Hampstead and Highgate Express for 30 years; Contributor to Music and Musicians from first issue, 1952; Editor, 1981–84; Opera Editor, 1984–; Editor, Musical Opinion, 1987–; Many radio and television appearances in the United Kingdom, USA, Scandinavia, Australia; Lecturer including Seminar Course on History and Function of Western Musical Criticism at Yale University, USA; Programme Notes and Record Sleeves; mem, The Critics' Circle; Royal Overseas League; Zoological Society of London. *Publications:* The Music of Finland, 1966. *Contributions:* Music and Musicians; Records and Recording; Musical Opinion; New Film Review; Parade; Other journals in the United Kingdom and internationally. *Address:* 2 Princes Road, St Leonards-on-Sea, East Sussex TN 37 6EL, England.

RICHARDS, Timothy; Singer (Tenor); b. 1970, Wales. *Education:* Royal Northern College of Music and with Dennis O'Neill. *Career:* Concerts throughout the United Kingdom and Europe including Messiah, the Mozart and Verdi Requiems, The Creation and Rossini's Stabat Mater; Opera roles include Alfredo for Welsh National Opera, The Duke of Mantua at Innsbruck and Cassio in Otello at Basle; Season 1999–2000 with Macduff in Leipzig and Rodolfo, Nemorino and Fenton for Dresden Opera; Other roles include Tamino, British Youth Opera, Belmonte and Verdi's Ismaele. *Address:* Harlequin Agency Ltd, 203 Fidlas Road, Cardiff CF4 5NA, Wales.

RICHARDSON, Carol; Singer (Mezzo-soprano); b. 1948, California, USA. *Education:* Studied at Occidental College, Los Angeles, with Martial Singher in Philadelphia and in New York. *Career:* Debut: Klagenfurt, 1973, as Nicklausse in Hoffmann; Sang at Kiel from 1975, Bayreuth Festival, 1976–81, in Parsifal; Engagements at Bern Stadttheater until 1984, Cenerentola at Bielefeld, 1988; Other roles have included Dorabella and Cherubino, Rosina, Orlofsky, Nancy in Martha, Lola and Zerlina; Further guest appearances at Hamburg, Gelsenkirchen, Karlsruhe and Hanover; Noted concert performer; Season 1998 at ENO in Purcell's Fairy Queen and the premiere of Dr Ox's Experiment by Gavin Bryars. *Address:* c/o English National Opera, St Martin's Lane, London WC2N 4ES, England.

RICHARDSON, Marilyn; Singer (Soprano) and Stage Director; b. 1936, Sydney, New South Wales, Australia; m. (1) Peter Richardson, 1954, 3 c., (2) James Christiansen, 1974, 3 step-c. *Education:* Diploma, New South Wales Conservatorium of Music. *Career:* Australian premiere of Schoenberg's Pierrot Lunaire, ISCM concert, Sydney, 1958; Debut with Basler Theater, Switzerland, 1972, Lulu; Salome, debut with The Australian Opera, 1975, Aida; Roles and operas include Four Sopranos in Tales of Hoffmann, Marschallin, Countess, Donna Anna, Katya Kabanova, Queen of Spades, Otello, Eva, Sieglinde, Elsa, Mimi,

Rosalinda, Merry Widow, Laura in Voss, Leonore (Fidelio), Isolde, 1990, and Tosca, 1992; Emilia Marty in The Makropulos Case, 1996; Has appeared with all State Companies; The Excursions of Mr Brouček, Fiordiligi, La Traviata, Madama Butterfly, Midsummer Marriage; Desdemona, Marguerite, Mistress Ford, Senta, Alcina, Cleopatra; Soloist in a huge range of concert music, including Australian premieres of about 400 songs and vocal works; Directed Les Pêcheurs de Perles at Adelaide, 1996. *Honours:* Churchill Fellowship, 1969; Australian Council Creative Fellowship, 1991; Joan Hammond Award, 1993; Honorary D.Mus, University of Queensland, 1993. *Address:* Australian Opera, PO Box 291, Strawberry Hills, NSW 2012, Australia.

RICHARDSON, Mark; singer (bass-baritone); b. 1966, England. *Education:* Royal Manchester College of Music. *Career:* English National Opera Company Principal as Lamoral in Arabella, Masetto, Colline in La Bohème and France in Reimann's Lear, Varlaam in Boris Godunov, Leporello; Other roles in War and Peace, Der Rosenkavalier, Rimsky's Christmas Eve and The Pearl Fishers, Ariodate in Xerxes, Donald in Billy Budd, Hobson in Peter Grimes, Parson in The Cunning Little Vixen; Niklausse in Dr Ox's Experiment; Season 1995–96 as Bizet's Zuniga and Nourabad; Guest appearances at Buxton, as Mustafà in L'Italiana in Algeri, Welsh National Opera (Angelotti and Rossini's Basilio) and the Bergen Festival (Sparafucile in Rigoletto); Sang Frank Maurrant in the Italian premiere of Street Scene, in Turin. *Current Management:* Robert Gilder & Co., Enterprise House, 59–65 Upper Ground, London, SE1 9PQ, England. *Telephone:* (20) 7928-9008. *Fax:* (20) 7928-9755. *E-mail:* rgilder@robert-gilder.com.

RICHARDSON, Meryl; Singer (soprano); b. 1965, England. *Education:* Royal Northern College of Music, with Neil Howlett; Further study with Philip Thomas and Jeffrey Talbot. *Career:* Appearances with English National Opera as Musetta, and as Helmwige in Die Walküre, 2001–2002; Title role in British premiere of Barber's Vanessa and Brünnhilde in Die Walküre (chamber version) for the Covent Garden Festival; Other roles include Lady Macbeth (Buxton Festival), Leonora in La Forza del Destino, Anna Bolena and Elvira in Ernani; Concerts include Vier letzte Lieder, Mozart's C minor Mass, Tippett's A Child of our Time and the Verdi Requiem; Aksinya in Lady Macbeth of Mtsensk for ENO, 2002. *Current Management:* Athole Still International Management, Forresters Hall, 25–27 Westow Street, London, SE19 3RY, England. *Telephone:* (20) 8771-5271. *Fax:* (20) 8768-6600. *Website:* www.atholestill.com.

RICHARDSON, Stephen; Singer (bass); b. 1965, Liverpool, England. *Education:* Studied at the Royal Northern College of Music. *Career:* Has sung at Glyndebourne and with GTO, English and Welsh National Opera, Scottish Opera and Kent Opera; Roles have included Mozart's Osmin, Sarastro and Commendatore, Colline, Sparafucile, Silva in Ernani and Rossini's Basilio; US debut with Messiah at Carnegie Hall and other concerts with leading British orchestras Montreal Philharmonic Orchestra and Prague Symphony Orchestra; Premieres of Tavener's Eis Thanaton, Resurrection and Apocalypse, with other works by Gerald Barry, Birtwistle (Punch and Judy), Knussen, Mason and Casken; Festival appearances at Aldeburgh, BBC Proms, Vienna, Hong Kong, Boston and Brussels; Season 1996–97 with Colline and Sparafucile for Welsh National Opera, Daland with Chelsea Opera Group and Tiresias in Oedipus Rex for the BBC; Baron Ochs for ENO, 1999; Season 2000–01 as Casken's The Golem at the Aspen Festival, Mr. Flint in Billy Budd at Covent Garden and Fafner in The Rhinegold for ENO; Oliver Knussen's Where the Wild Things Are and Higglety, Pigglety, Pop! at the London Proms, 2002. *Current Management:* Harrison/Parrott Ltd, 12 Penzance Place, London, W11 4PA, England. *Telephone:* (20) 7229 9166. *Fax:* (20) 7221 5042. *Website:* www .harrisonparrott.com.

RICHTER, Marga; Composer; b. 21 Oct. 1926, Reedsburg, Wisconsin, USA. *Education:* Juilliard School, New York, from 1945, with Rosalyn Tureck, William Bergsma and Vincent Persichetti (MS 1951). *Career:* Freelance Composer, with premieres of her music at Salzburg, Chicago, Cannes, Cologne, Tucson, Atlanta, Brookville and New York. *Compositions include:* Clarinet sonata, 1948; Piano Sonata, 1954; 2 Piano Concertos, 1955, 1974; Aria and Toccata for viola and strings, 1957; String Quartet, 1958; Abyss, ballet, 1964; Bird of Yearning, ballet, 1967; Requiem for piano, 1978; Blackberry Vines and Winter Fruit for orchestra, 1976; Spectral Chimes/Enshrouded Hills for three orchestral quintets and orchestra, 1980; Düsseldorf Concerto for flute, viola, harp, percussion and strings, 1982; Seacliff Variations for piano, violin, viola, cello, 1984; Lament for Art O'Leary for soprano voice, 1984; Out of Shadows and Solitude for orchestra, 1985; Qhanri-Tibetan Variations for cello and piano, 1988; Quantum Quirks of a Quick Quaint Quark, I–III for orchestra, organ and piano, 1992–93; Variations and Interludes on Themes from Monteverdi and Bach, concerto for piano, violin, cello and orchestra, 1993; Riders to the Sea, opera in one act, 1996; Choruses and songs. *Recordings include:* Qhanri; Lament for Strings; Sonata for Piano; Seacliff Variations; Out of Shadows and Solitude; Spectral

Chimes/Enshrouded Hills; Landscapes of the Mind II; Sonora for 2 clarinets and piano; Variations and Interludes on Themes from Monteverdi and Bach. *Honours:* Annual ASCAP Awards, 1966–2002; NEA Fellowships, 1978, 1980. *Address:* 3 Bayview Lane, Huntington, NY 11743, USA.

RICHTER de VROE, Nicolaus; Composer and Violinist; b. 1 Feb. 1955, Halle, Germany. *Education:* Violin studies at the Moscow Conservatory, 1973–78; Composition with Goldmann at the Berlin Akademie der Künste, 1980–83. *Career:* violinist with the Bavarian Radio Symphony, 1988–; co-founder of XSEMBLE, Munich, 1990. *Compositions include:* Tetra, series I–III, for differentiated quartets, 1984–91; Durchlässige Zonen I, for 13 instruments, 1985; String Quartet, 1986. Zu Fuss nach Island, graphic music, 1986; Isole de Rumore, for orchestra, 1988; Frag In Memorian Luigi Nono, for ensemble, 1990; Decemberhelft, for alto flute, guitar, cello and percussion, 1990; Naiss' orchestr' ance, 1992; Engfernt: Tänze, for ensemble, 1993; Shibuya movements for orchestra, 1993; Air't'rance, for ensemble, 1997; Éraflures, violin concerto, 1997. *Address:* c/o German Music Information Centre, Weberstr. 59, 53113 Bonn, Germany.

RICKARDS, Steven, BMusEd, MM, DM; American singer (countertenor), composer and music educator; b. 1955. *Education:* Florida State University, Tallahassee, Indiana University, Bloomington, Oberlin College Baroque Performance Institute, Indiana University, Bloomington, Guildhall School of Music and Drama, London. *Career:* concert engagements with the Waverly Consort (New York), Chicago's Music of the Baroque, Concert Royal, New York, Arts Musica and Chanticleer; British appearances with the Ipswich Bach Choir and at the East Cornwall Bach Festival; Tour of Ireland with the Gabrieli Consort and world-wide recitals with lutenist Dorothy Linell; Has toured France and Michigan with Messiah 1981–82; Carnegie Hall debut 1987, with the Oratorio Society of New York; Boston Early Music Festival in Handel's Teseo and Santa Fe Opera as Ariel in the premiere of John Eaton's The Tempest (1985); Sang with the Opera Company of Philadelphia as Apollo in Death in Venice; Recent revivals of Handel's Siroe in New York, Locke's Psyche in London, Hasse's L'Olimpiade in Dresden and Mondonville's De Profundis at Harvard; Sang in John Adams' El Niño at the Châtelet Theatre in Paris, 2000; Teaches singing at University of Indianapolis and Butler University, USA. *Compositions:* A Christmas Vision; All Good Gifts; Calm on the List'ning Ear of Night; Come Let Us Sing To The Lord; Come Thou Long Expected Jesus; Little Lamb; As the Lyre to the Singer; Behold the Tabernacle of God; Breathe on Me, Breath of God; Angels Did Sing. *Recordings include:* Bach cantatas 106 and 131 with Joshua Rifkin; St John Passion by Bach; Gradualia by Byrd with Chanticleer; Medarse in Siroe by Handel; Mass in B Minor by Bach; Buxtehude Project Vol. I Sacred Cantatas; T Campion Songs; J Dowland Songs. *Current Management:* John Gingrich Management, PO Box 1515, New York, NY 10023, USA.

RICKENBACHER, Karl Anton; Conductor; b. 20 May 1940, Basle, Switzerland; m. Gaye Fulton, 21 July 1973. *Education:* Opera and Concert Conducting Degree, Konservatorium Berlin; Studies with von Karajan and Pierre Boulez. *Career:* Debut: RIAS Berlin; Assistant Conductor, Zürich Opera, 1966–69; 1st Kapellmeister St ädt Bühnen Freiburg, 1969–75; Music Director of Westphalian Symphony, 1976–85; Principal Conductor of BBC Scottish Symphony, 1978–80; Featured in, Karl Anton Rickenbacher Conducts, BBC Scotland and appeared in Olivier Messiaen–Chronochromie, on Bavarian television; Concerts for ZDF Germany and Swiss, Belgian and French television; Since 1985, Freelance Guest Conductor in Europe, North America, Japan, Australia and Israel in opera and concert repertoire. *Recordings:* Over 50 titles with London Philharmonic, Bavarian Radio Symphony, Bamberg Symphony, Berlin Radio Symphony RSB, Budapest Radio Symphony. *Honours:* Grand Prix du Disque, for Milhaud CD, 1993; Diapason d'Or, for Messiaen CD, 1994; Cannes Classical Award, for Hartmann CD, 1994; Echo Award for R. Strauss CD, 1999; Echo Award for O. Messiaen CD, 2000. *Current Management:* TransArt (UK) Ltd, Cedar House, 10 Rutland Street, Filey, YO14 9JB, North Yorkshire, England. *Telephone:* (1723) 515819. *Fax:* (1723) 514678. *E-mail:* transartuk@transartuk .com. *Website:* www.transartuk.com. *Address:* Oriole, 1822 Chernex-Montreux, Switzerland.

RIDDELL, Alistair (Matthew); Composer and Computer Technologist; b. 22 June 1955, Melbourne, Victoria, Australia. *Education:* BA (Hons), 1981, MA, 1989, La Trobe University (PhD 1993); Graduate Studies, Princeton University, 1989–93. *Career:* Fellowships at Princeton and La Trobe Universities, 1989–95. *Compositions include:* (Most with Computer-Processed Sound) Ligeti-Continuum, 1982; Studies in Perception, Context and Paradox: Three-Existential Constellations: Canon in 6 Voices, 1982; Bach-Inventio No. 4, 1982; Atlantic Fears, 1983; Core Image (four 4), 1983; Atmisfearia, 1989; Entering 2–12, 1990; Third Hand, 1991; Idyll Moment, 1991; Heavy Mouse, 1992; Z Says, 1993; Triptychos, 1995. *Recordings:* CD, 42, 1997. *Honours:* AC Artists and

New Technology Program Grant, 1987. *Address:* 12 Napier Street, Fitzroy, Victoria 3065, Australia.

RIDDELL, David; Conductor; b. 1960, Elgin, Scotland. *Education:* St Andrew's University; Guildhall School, London. *Career:* Engagements for Den Jyske Opera, Denmark, in La Périchole, Butterfly, Cenerentola, The Pirates of Penzance, Paganini and Reesen's Farinelli (1992); Don Giovanni for Århus Summer Opera, 1989–90, followed by Il Barbiere di Siviglia, 1991; Die Fledermaus for Odense Symphony Orchestra, 1992; British appearances with La Forza del Destino for Scottish Opera, Eugene Onegin for Opera 80 and Rimsky's Mozart and Salieri at the Royal Scottish Academy of Music; Regular concerts at the Guildhall School; Season 1996 with Bach's Christmas Oratorio for the Randers Chamber Orchestra, and Burns International Festival Concert with the Northern Sinfonia in Scotland.

RIDDER, Anton de; Singer (Tenor); b. 13 Feb. 1929, Amsterdam, Netherlands. *Education:* Studied at the Amsterdam Conservatory with H Mulder and J Keyzer. *Career:* After Dutch stage debut in 1952 sang in Karlsruhe from 1956, Munich Theater am Gärtnerplatz, 1962–66, with Cologne Opera in the premiere of Zimmermann's Die Soldaten in 1965 and at the Edinburgh Festival in 1972; Guest appearances in London, Germany and Amsterdam; Bregenz Festival in 1974 as Don José, Glyndebourne Festival in 1979 as Florestan in the Peter Hall production of Fidelio under Haitink, and Salzburg Festival in 1985 in Capriccio. *Recordings:* Busoni's Doktor Faust; Capriccio; La Traviata; Lucia di Lammermoor.

RIEBL, Thomas; Violist; b. 1956, Vienna, Austria. *Education:* Studied at the Vienna Academy of Music and with Peter Schidlof and Sándor Végh. *Career:* Led the violas of the World Youth Orchestra, 1972; Solo debut at the Vienna Konzerthaus in 1972 and has since appeared with leading orchestras in Europe and North America including the Chicago Symphony, Helsinki Radio, Bournemouth Symphony, Los Angeles and Vienna Chamber Orchestras; Conductors include Abbado, Walter Weller, Andrew Davis, Horst Stein, Erich Bergel and Edo de Waart; Festival appearances at Salzburg, Vienna, Aspen, Ravinia, New York, Munich, Lockenhaus and Carinthian Summer Festival; Concerts with the Juilliard Quartet, Gidon Kremer and Jessye Norman (Brahms Lieder Op 91); Founder Member of the Vienna Sextet; Professor of Viola at the Musikhochschule, Mozarteum, at Salzburg from 1983. *Recordings include:* Brahms Lieder Op 91 with Brigitte Fassbaender and Irwin Gage. *Honours:* Prizewinner at international competitions at Budapest in 1975 and Munich in 1976; Ernst Wallfisch Memorial Award at the International Naumberg Viola Competition in New York, 1982.

RIEDEL, Deborah; Singer (Soprano); b. 31 July 1958, Sydney, New South Wales, Australia. *Education:* Studied at the Sydney Conservatorium and in London. *Career:* Sang Hansel with Western Australian Opera, 1986, followed by Meg Page and Thomas' Mignon, Mimi and Countess Maritza; The Australian Opera from 1988, as Zerlina, Micaela, Juliette, Susanna, Elvira and Violetta; Appearances with the Victorian State Opera as the Drummer in Ullmann's Emperor of Atlantis, Nayad in Ariadne auf Naxos, Leila (Les Pêcheurs de Perles), Marguerite in Faust; London engagements as Freia in Das Rheingold, Mimi and Elvira at Covent Garden; Teresa in Benvenuto Cellini at Geneva Opera, Bastille (Paris), and Rome; Sang Elvira at Bordeaux, Violetta in the Netherlands, Amina in La Sonnambula at San Diego, California 1994, the Countess at Montpellier, Adina in L'Elisir d'amoreGounod's Marguerite in Faust at Geneva; Donna Anna in Munich and Vienna; Concert engagements as Mariana in Il Signor Bruschino at the Festival of Flanders; Mozart Coronation Mass, Bordeaux, Child of Our Time with London Symphony Orchestra NY Philharmonic; War Requiem (Britten) in London and Prague; Miss Solemnis, Beethoven in Prague, Beethoven in Tenerife, Royal Albert Hall, London; Rossini's Petite Messe Solennelle; Scarlatti's St Cecilia Mass and frequent appearances with the Australian Pops Orchestra; Mozart's Vespers for the Rantos Collegium and Messiah for the ABC in Melbourne and Sydney; Mendelssohn's Midsummer Night's Dream and Mozart Exultate Jubilate with the Sydney Symphony Orchestra and Strauss's Four Last Songs for the Australian Ballet and ABC Perth and Adelaide; Season 1997 with Maria Stuarda in Sydney and Donna Anna at the Met; Alice Ford in Falstaff at San Diego, 1998; at Sydney as the Trovatore Leonora, Donna Anna and Elettra in Idomeneo for Welsh Nat. Opera and Opera Australia; the Marschallin for WNO and Tosca in Adelaide; Fidelio in Tours and Reims; Margerite in Faust for Opera Australia; In concert in Barcelona and Bergen (Messiaen's Poème pour Mi) and Sydney; in recital with Richard Bonynge. *Recordings include:* Paganini and Giuditta, Die Herzogm von Chicago, Requiem Embriaco, Power of Love, Gypsy Princess (video). *Honours:* Winner, Australian regional final of the Metropolitan Opera Auditions; Dame Sister Mary Leo Scholarship; Dame Mabel Brookes Fellowship; Aria Award, Sydney Sun, 1986. *Address:* c/o Harlequin Agency Ltd, 203 Fidlas Road, Cardiff, CF14 5NA, England.

RIEDELBAUCH, Vaclav; Composer; b. 1 April 1947, Dysina, near Plžn, Czechoslovakia. *Education:* Prague Conservatory, 1962–73; Further study with Franco Donatoni in Siena and Lutoslawski in Poland. *Career:* Lecturer, later Docent, Prague Academy; Artistic Director, Prague National Theatre 1987–89; Director of Panton, music publishing, 1993–96. *Compositions include:* Symphony, 1972; Cathedrals, for organ, 1972; Symphony with Refrain, 1973; Concerto, Battle for Organ and orchestra, 1973; Wedding Songs for female voices and mixed chorus, 1978; Pastorali e Trenodie, wind octet, 1978; Songs and Games from Shakespeare, for 6 voices, 2 violins, oboe and cello, 1979; Macbeth, ballet, 1979–82; Vision, Fantasy for orchestra, 1984; Episode, for wind band, 1987; String Quartet no. 1, 1987; Temptation and Deed, for orchestra, 1988; 2 Piano Trios, 1991, 1995; Private Flights, 2nd Wind Quintet, 1995–99. *Address:* c/o Music Information Centre, Besednc 3, 11800 Prague, Czech Republic.

RIEGEL, Kenneth; Singer (Tenor); b. 19 April 1938, Womelsdorf, Pennsylvania, USA. *Education:* Manhattan School of Music; Berkshire Music Center; Metropolitan Opera Studio. *Career:* Debut: Santa Fe Festival in 1965 as the Alchemist in the US premiee of Henze's König Hirsch; San Francisco Opera, 1971, Metropolitan Opera, NY, 1973, Vienna State Opera, 1977, Paris Opéra, 1979 as the Painter in the premiere of the three-act version of Lulu, La Scala, 1979, Hamburg State Opera, 1981, Geneva Opera, 1981, Deutsche Oper, West Berlin, 1983, and Bonn Opera, 1983; Sang the Leper in the premiere of Messiaen's St François d'Assise, Paris, 1983, at Brussels Opera, 1984, and at Royal Opera Covent Garden, 1985 in Der Zwerg by Zemlinsky; Appeared in film, Don Giovanni, directed by Joseph Losey, 1988, and at Stuttgart in 1989 as Dionysos in The Bassarids by Henze; Season 1992 as Herod in Salome at Covent Garden and Salzburg; Season 1996 with Aegisthus at Salzburg and the Inquisitor in Dallapiccola's Prigioniero at Florence; Herod in Salome at Santa Fe, 1998; Title role in the premiere of K…. by Philippe Manouri at the Opéra Bastille, Paris, 2001. *Recordings:* Der Zwerg; Damnation of Faust; Florentinische Tragoedie; Don Giovanni; Lulu; Mahler Symphony No. 8; Berlioz's Requiem. *Honours:* Nominated for Olivier Award for Best Individual Performance in an Opera, 1985. *Current Management:* SAFIMM Corporation. *Address:* c/o SAFIMM Corporation, 250 West 57th Street, Suite 1018, New York, NY 10107, USA.

RIFKIN, Joshua, BS, MFA; American conductor, musicologist and composer; b. 22 April 1944, New York; s. of Harry H. Rifkin and Dorothy Helsh; m. Helen Palmer 1995; one d. *Education:* Juilliard School and New York, Göttingen and Princeton Univs. *Career:* Musical Adviser, Assoc. Dir Nonesuch Records 1963–75; Asst, Assoc. Prof. of Music, Brandeis Univ. 1970–82; Dir The Bach Ensemble 1978–; Visiting Prof. New York Univ. 1978, 1983, 2000, Yale Univ. 1982–83, Princeton Univ. 1988, Stanford Univ. 1989, King's Coll. London 1991, Univ. of Basel 1993, 1997, Ohio State Univ. 1994, Univ. of Dortmund 1996, Schola Cantorum Basiliensis 1997, 2001, Univ. of Munich 2000; Fellow, Inst. for Advanced Study, Berlin 1984–86; guest conductor English Chamber Orchestra, Los Angeles Chamber Orchestra, St Louis Symphony Orchestra, St Paul Chamber Orchestra, Scottish Chamber Orchestra, BBC Symphony Orchestra, Bayerische Staatsoper, San Francisco Symphony Orchestra, City of Glasgow Symphony Orchestra, Jerusalem Symphony Orchestra, Prague Chamber Orchestra); contributed to the revival of interest in the ragtime music of Scott Joplin; as a musicologist has researched Renaissance and Baroque music. *Recordings:* Bach Mass in B minor 1982, Bach Magnificat 1983, numerous Bach cantatas 1986–2001, Rags and Tangos 1990, Haydn Symphonies 1994, Silvestre Revueltas 1999, rags by Scott Joplin, Mozart Posthorn Serenade, fanfares and sonatas by Pezel and Hammerschmidt, sonatas by Biber, vocal music by Busnois, Josquin. *Publications:* articles on Haydn, Schütz, Bach and Josquin in The Musical Times, Musical Quarterly and other journals, and in the New Grove Dictionary of Music and Musicians. *Honours:* Dr hc (Univ. of Dortmund) 1999; Gramophone Award 1983. *Address:* 61 Dana Street, Cambridge, MA 02138, USA. *Telephone:* (617) 876-4017 (office). *Fax:* (617) 441-5572 (office). *E-mail:* jrifkin@compuserve.com.

RIGACCI, Susanna; Singer (Soprano); b. 1959, Stockholm, Sweden. *Education:* Studied in Florence. *Career:* Debut: Rome Opera, as Rossini's Rosina; Appearances in opera throughout Italy, and guest at Dublin as Gilda in Rigoletto; Wexford Festival in Cimarosa's Astuzie Femminili; Season 1987 in the Italian premiere of Henze's English Cat, at Bologna, and in Capriccio at Florence; Season 1991–92 as Weber's Aennchen at Liège and Sofia in Rossini's Il Signo Bruschino at the Paris Théâtre du Châtelet. *Recordings include:* Vivaldi's Catone in Utica; L'Elisir d'amore. *Address:* c/o Via Giambologna 3a, 50132 Florence, Italy.

RIGAL, Joel; French pianist and fortepianist; b. 17 Aug. 1950, Castres. *Education:* Master Degree, Musicology, University of Paris-Sorbonne; Graduate, Aix en Provence and Marseilles Conservatories; Piano and Fortepiano Studies with Pierre Barbizet and Paul Badura-Skoda,

Vienna. *Career:* Debut: Vienna Theatre, 1979; Performances in Paris: Châtelet, 1983, Gaveau, 1987, Musée de la Villette, 1997–; Purcell Room, London, 1981–; Opera, Cairo, 1989–; Bibliotek Theatre, Rotterdam, 1991–; Budapest Strings Orchestra, Budapest, 1995; several television and radio appearances. *Recordings:* with Nadine Palmier: Mozart, Complete Works for Piano Duet and 2 Keyboards; French Music, The Golden Age; Schubert, The Final Masterpieces. *Publications:* Le clavier bien partagé (teaching manual), 1993; contrib. to Marsyas. *Current Management:* c/o Bureau de Concerts Maurice Werner, 17 rue du Quatre Septembre, 75002, Paris, France.

RIGBY, Jean; Singer (Mezzo-Soprano); b. 22 Dec. 1954, Fleetwood, Lancashire, England; m. J Hayes, 1987, 3 s. *Education:* Birmingham School of Music with Janet Edmunds; Royal Academy of Music with Patricia Clark; National Opera Studio, London. *Career:* Member of English National Opera from 1982; Roles include Mercédès in Carmen, Maddalena, Marina in Boris Godunov, Blanche in The Gambler, Britten's Lucretia and Magdalena in The Mastersingers; Octavian, Rosenkavalier; Helen, King Priam; Concert performance of Lady Essex in Gloriana with Chelsea Opera Group; Festival Hall debut in the Verdi Requiem and Covent Garden debut as Thibault in Don Carlos in 1983; Glyndebourne Festival in 1985 as Mercédès, and Zürich in 1986 as Cornelia in Handel's Giulio Cesare; Sang Penelope in The Return of Ulysses with ENO in 1989 and 1992, Ursula in Beatrice and Benedict, 1990, and at Glyndebourne in 1990 as Nancy in Albert Herring; Season 1992–93 as Amastris in Xerxes, Rossini's Isabella at Buxton and Nicklausse in Les Contes d'Hoffmann at Covent Garden and San Diego; Cenerentola, Garsington Opera; Rosina, Barber; Mahler's 2nd Symphony at the Festival Hall, 1997; Season 1999 as Geneviève in Pelléas et Mélisande at Glyndebourne and the London Proms; Edvige in Rodelinda at Glyndebourne and Helena in King Priam for ENO; London Proms, 2002. *Recordings include:* Video of English National Opera's Rigoletto; Glyndebourne, Albert Herring/Carmen; Lucretia, Xerxes. *Honours:* Friends of Covent Garden Bursary; Countess of Munster Scholarship; Worshipful Company of Musicians' Medal; Royal Overseas League Competition, 1981; Young Artists Competition, ENO, 1981; ARAM, 1984; FRAM, 1989. *Address:* Park House, 33 Brackley Road, Towcester, Northants, NN12 6 DH.

RIHM, Wolfgang; composer; b. 13 March 1952, Karlsruhe, Germany. *Education:* Hochschule für Musik Karlsruhe, with Eugen W Velte, studied with Stockhausen in Cologne and Klaus Huber in Freiburg. *Career:* Teacher at the Karlsruhe Hochschule für Musik, 1973–78; Freelance Composer; From 1985 Professor of Composition at Musikhochschule Karlsruhe, British premiere of Jakob Lenz in London in 1987, Die Eroberung von Mexiko premiered at the Hamburg Staatsoper, 1992. *Compositions include:* Operas: Deploration, 1974, Jakob Lenz, 1978, Oedipus, 1987; Die Eroberung von Mexico, 1992; Orchestral: Three Symphonies, 1969–76, Sub-Kontar, 1975–76, La Musique Creuse Le Ciel for 2 pianos and orchestra, 1979, Monodram for cello and orchestra, 1983, Medea-Spiel, 1988, Passion, 1989, Schwebende Begegnung, 1989, Dunkles Spiel, 1990; La lugubre gondola for orchestra, 1992; Vers une symphonie fleuve, I–IV, 1994–8; Musik für oboe und orchester, 1994; Styx und Lethe for cello and orchestra, 1998; Marsyas, for trumpet and orchestra, 1998; Musick für Klarinette und orchester, 1999; Vocal: Hervorgedunkelt for mezzo and ensemble, 1974, Umhergetrieben Aufgewirbelt, Nietzsche Fragments for baritone and mezzo, chorus and flute, 1981, Lowry-Lieder (Wondratschek), 1987, Song Cycles for soprano and orchestra, Frau, Stimme for soprano and orchestra, 1989, Mein Tod, Requiem In Memoriam Jane S, 1990; Abschiedsstücke for female voice and 15 instruments, 1993; Raumauge for chorus and 5 percussion, 1994; Deutsches Stück mit Hamlet, for mezzo, baritone and orchestra, 1997; In doppelter Tiefe for mezzo, alto and orchestra, 1999; Chamber: Paraphrase for cello, percussion and piano, 1972, Ländler for 13 strings, 1979, 10 string quartets, 1970–97, Gebild for trumpet, strings and percussion, 1983, Duomonolog for violin and cello, 1989; Music for voice and piano, organ and piano. *Current Management:* Universal Edition (London) Ltd, 48 Great Marlborough Street, London, W1F 7BB, England. *Telephone:* (20) 7437-6880. *Fax:* (20) 7437-6115.

RILEY, Dennis; Composer; b. 28 May 1943, Los Angeles, USA. *Education:* Universities of Colorado, Illinois and Iowa (Phd, 1973), notably with George Crumb and Ben Johnston. *Career:* Lecturer at California State University at Fresno, 1971–74, and Columbia, New York, 1974–78. *Compositions include:* Concertante music 1–4, for ensembles, 1970, 1972, 1974, 1978; 4 Choral Cantatas, 1966–80; Wedding Canticle for baritone and viola, 1968; Elegy: in Memoriam David Bates for cello and strings, 1975; Seven Songs on Poems of Emily Dickinson for soprano and orchestra, 1982; Noon Dances for chamber orchestra, 1983; Symphony, 1984: Operas Rappaccini's Daughter, and Cats' Concert, 1984; Five Poems of Marilyn Hacker for soprano and ensemble, 1986. *Honours:* Guggenheim Fellowship; NEA Grants;

Forum Foundation Commission. *Address:* c/o ASCAP, ASCAP Building, 1 Lincoln Plaza, New York, NY 10023, USA.

RILEY, Howard, BA, MA, MMus, MPh; British musician (piano) and composer; b. 16 Feb. 1943, Huddersfield, Yorkshire, England. *Education:* Univ. of Wales, Indiana Univ., USA, York Univ. *Career:* festival, club, TV and radio appearances as solo and group pianist, throughout Europe and N America 1967–; Creative Assoc., Centre of the Creative and Performing Arts, Buffalo, NY, USA 1976–77; Bicentennial Arts Fellowship 1976. *Recordings include:* Facets 1983, For Four On Two Two 1984, In Focus 1985, Live At The Royal Festival Hall 1985, Feathers 1988, Procession 1990, The Heat Of Moments 1991, Beyond Category 1993, The Bern Concert 1993, Inner Mirror 1996, Making Moves 1997, Short Stories 1998, One to One 1999, Synopsis 2000, Overground 2001, Airplay 2001. *Publications:* The Contemporary Piano Folio 1982. *Address:* Flat 2, 53 Tweedy Road, Bromley, Kent BR1 3NH, England. *Telephone:* (20) 8290-5917.

RILEY, Terry Mitchell, MA; American composer and pianist and raga singer; b. 24 June 1935, Colfax, CA; s. of Wilma Ridlofi and Charles Riley; m. Ann Yvonne Smith 1958; three c. *Education:* San Francisco State Univ., Univ. of California, studied with Duane Hampton, Adolf Baller and Pandit Pran Nath. *Career:* Creative Assoc., Center for Creative and Performing Arts, Buffalo 1967; taught music composition and N Indian raga at Mills Coll. 1971–83; freelance composer and performer 1961–; launched Minimal Music Movt with composition and first performance of In C 1964; Guggenheim Fellowship 1980. *Compositions include:* The Harp of New Albion for solo piano in just intonation, Sunrise of the Planetary Dream Collector, Sri Camel, The Ten Voices of the Two Prophets, Chorale of the Blessed Day, Eastern Man, Embroidery, Song from the Old Country, G-Song, Remember This Oh Mind, The Ethereal Time Shadow, Offering to Chief Crazy Horse, Rites of the Imitators, The Medicine Wheel, Song of the Emerald Runner, Cycle of five string quartets, Trio for violin, clarinet and cello 1957, Concert for two pianos and tape 1960, String Trio 1961, Keyboard Studies 1963, Dorian Reeds for ensemble 1964, In C 1964, A Rainbow in the Curved Air 1968, Persian Surgery Dervishes for electronic keyboard 1971, Descending Moonshine Dervishes 1975, Do You Know How it Sounds? for low voice, piano and tabla 1983, Cadenza on the Night Plain for string quartet 1984, Salome Dances for Peace string quartet 1988, Jade Palace for orchestra and synthesiser 1989, Cactus Rosary for synthesiser and ensemble 1990, June Buddhas for chorus and orchestra 1991, The Sands for string quartet and orchestra 1991, Four Woelfi Portraits for ensemble 1992, The Saint Adolf Ring chamber opera 1993, Ritmos and Melos 1993, El Hombre string quartet 1993, Ascension for solo guitar 1993, The Heaven Ladder for piano four hands 1996, Three Requiem Quartets 1997, Autodreamographical Tales for narrator and instruments 1997. *Address:* 13699 Moonshine Road, Camptonville, CA 95922, USA. *Telephone:* (916) 288-3522. *Fax:* (916) 288-3468.

RILLING, Helmuth; Conductor, Chorus Master, Organist and Professor of Music; b. 29 May 1933, Stuttgart, Germany; m. Martina Greiner 1967; two d. *Education:* studied Staatliche Hochschule für Musik, Stuttgart, 1952–55, composition with Johann Nepomuk David; studied organ with Fernando Germani, Conservatorio di Santa Cecilia, Rome; studied conducting with Leonard Bernstein, New York. *Career:* Founder and Dir, Gächinger Kantorei, Stuttgart, 1954–; Organist and Choirmaster, Gedächtniskirche, Stuttgart, 1957–98; London debut as organist in 1963, as conductor 1972; taught organ and conducting, Berliner Kirchenmusikschule, Berlin-Spandau and Dir, Spandauer Kantorei, 1963–66; Founder, Bach-Collegium Stuttgart 1965–; Prof. of Conducting, Staatliche Hochschule für Musik, Frankfurt, 1966–85; Dir, Frankfurter Kantorei, 1969–81; Co-founder and Artistic Dir, Summer Festival (now Oregon Bach Festival), Eugene, USA, 1970–; taught at Indiana Univ., Bloomington, USA, 1976–77; Founder and Dir, Sommer Acad. Johann Sebastian Bach Stuttgart, 1979–99, Internationale Bachakademie Stuttgart, 1981–, Bach Acads, Tokyo, Buenos Aires, 1983, Santiago de Compostela, Spain, Prague, Kraków, Moscow, Budapest, Caracas; Chief Conductor, Real Filarmonía de Galicia, Santiago de Compostela, Spain, 1996–2000; Founder, Stuttgart Festival Choir and Orchestra , 2001–; world wide international appearances with own ensembles and as guest conductor and guest prof.; regular co-operation with Israel Philharmonic Orchestra, Cleveland Orchestra, Boston Symphony Orchestra, Minnesota Orchestra, LA Philharmonic, Toronto Symphony Orchestra, New York Philharmonic, Vienna Philharmonic Orchestra, Münchner Philharmoniker, Radio-Sinfonieorchester Munich; mem, Kungl. Musikaliska Akad., Stockholm, 1993. *Recordings:* Cycle of Bach Cantatas with the Frankfurter Kantorei, the Gächinger Kantorei and the Figuralchor of Stuttgart, 1970–84; Motets, Lutheran Masses, Choral Preludes and Orgelbüchlein by Bach; Magnificats by Schütz, Bach, Monteverdi and Buxtehude; Carissimi's Jephte and Judicum Salomonis; Handel's Belshazzar; Telemann's Ino and Pimpinone; Mozart's Concertos K364 and K190, Mass K317 and Vesperae Solennes de Confessore; Geistliche Chormusik, St Matthew

Passion, Symphoniae Sacrae and Cantiones Sacrae by Schütz; Messiaen's Cinq Rechants; Edition Bachakademie, The Complete Works of Bach (172 CDs), 1998–2000, Credo, by Penderecki and Wolfgang Rihm's Deus Passus, 2001–02. *Publications:* Johann Sebastian Bach, Matthäus-Passion, Einführung und Studienanleitung, 1975; Johann Sebastian Bachs h-moll-Messe, 1975. *Honours:* Grand Prix du Disque, 1985; Hon. DFA, Concordia Coll., USA, 1990; UNESCO/IMC Music Prize, 1994; Theodor Heuss Prize, 1995; International Prize Compostela, 1999; Dr hc, Univ. of Oregon, 1999; Cannes Classic Award, 1999; Grammy Award for Best Choral Performance, 2000; Hanns Martin Schleyer Prize, 2001. *Address:* c/o Internationale Bachakademie Stuttgart, Presse- und Öffentlichkeitsarbeit, Johann-Sebastian-Bach-Platz (Hasenbergsteige 3), 70178 Stuttgart, Germany (office). *Telephone:* (711) 619210 (office). *Fax:* (711) 6192123 (office). *E-mail:* pr@bachakademie.de (office). *Website:* www.bachakademie.de (office).

RIMMER, John (Francis); Composer; b. 5 Feb. 1939, Auckland, New Zealand. *Education:* University of Auckland; Further study with John Weinzweig in Toronto. *Career:* Lecturer at University of Auckland, 1974–; Founder of electro-acoustic music studio; Chair in Music, 1995. *Compositions include:* Symphony, 1968; Electro-acoustic: Composition nos 1–10, 1968–77; Seaswell, 1978; Projections at Dawn, 1985; Fleeting images, 1985; Beyond the Saying, 1990; A Vocalise for Einstein, 1991; La Voci di Galileo, 1995; Pacific Soundscapes with Dancing, 1995; Viola Concerto, 1980; Meeting Place for orchestra, 1984; Gossamer for 12 strings, 1984; with the Current, for ensemble, 1986; Symphony, the Feeling of Sound, 1989; Cloud Fanfares for orchestra, 1990; Millennia for brass ensemble, 1991; Bowed Insights, string quartet, 1993; The Ripple Effect, for ensemble, 1995; Flashes of Iridescence for piano, 1995; A Dialogue of Opposites, for cello, 1997; Memories, for youth orchestra, 198; Galileo, chamber opera, 1999. *Address:* Music Department, University of Auckland, Private Bag, Auckland, New Zealand.

RINALDI, Alberto; Singer (Baritone); b. 6 June 1939, Rome, Italy. *Education:* Studied at the Accademia di Santa Cecilia, Rome. *Career:* Debut: Spoleto in 1963 as Simon Boccanegra; Teatro Fenice Venice in 1970 as Rossini's Figaro; Appearances in Milan, Rome, Naples, Paris, Rio de Janeiro, Ghent, Florence and Aix-en-Provence; Edinburgh Festival in 1973; Glyndebourne Festival in 1980 as Ford in Falstaff; Sang Mozart's Count on tour to Japan with the company of the Vienna Staatsoper, 1986; Sang at the Berlin Staastoper in 1987 as Dandini in La Cenerentola; Pesaro and Cologne, 1988–89 in Il Signor Bruschino and Il Cambiale di Matrimonio; Bonn Opera in 1990 as Rossini's Figaro; Sang Blansac in La Scala di Seta at the 1990 Schwetzingen Festival; Season 1992 as Blansac at Cologne and Paris; Sang Geronio in Rossini's Il Turco in Italia, Brussels, 1996; Don Pasquale at Brussels, 1998; Season 2000–01 as Belcore at the Vienna Staatsoper and Rambaldo in Puccini's La Rondine at Rome. *Recordings:* Masetto in Don Giovanni; Il Matrimonio Segreto; Il Campanello; Pagliacci; Video of La Scala di Seta. *Address:* c/o Oper der Stadt Köln, Offenbachplatz, 5000 Cologne, Germany.

RINALDI, Margarita; Singer (Soprano); b. 12 Jan. 1933, Turin, Italy. *Education:* Studied in Rovigo. *Career:* Debut: Spoleto in 1958 as Lucia di Lammermoor; La Scala Milan in 1959 as Sinaide in Mosè by Rossini; Dublin in 1961 as Carolina in Il Matrimonio Segreto and Gilda; Verona Arena in 1962 and 1969; US debut at Dallas in 1966 as Gilda; Glyndebourne Festival in 1966 as Carolina; Bregenz Festival in 1974 and 1980 in Un Girono di Regno and as Alice Ford; Further appearances in Barcelona, Chicago, San Francisco, Wexford, Rome, Naples and Turin; Other roles include Amina, Norina, Linda di Chamounix, Marie in La Fille du Régiment, Bertha in La Prophète, Sophie, Ilia, Fiordiligi, Violetta, Oscar and the Marschallin; Maggio Musicale Florence, 1977–78 as Amenaide in Tancredi and Helena in A Midsummer Night's Dream; Retired from stage in 1981; Many concert engagements. *Recordings:* Lucia di Lammermoor; Rigoletto; Le Prophète; La Scala di Seta; L'Africaine; Ilia in Idomeneo.

RINGART, Anna; Singer (Mezzo-Soprano); b. 15 Jan. 1937, Paris, France. *Education:* Studied with Irene Joachim and Marguerite Liszt in Paris; Hamburg Musikhochschule with Frau Anders-Mysz-Gmeiner. *Career:* Sang at such German opera centres as Lubeck, Koblenz, Düsseldorf and Hamburg; Sang at the Paris Opéra from 1973 under Karl Böhm, Pierre Boulez, Seiji Ozawa and Georg Solti, in a repertoire extending from Mozart to Schoenberg's Moses und Aron; Appeared in the 1985 premiere of Docteur Faustus by Konrad Boehmer; Opéra-Comique in 1988 as the Nurse in Boris Godunov; Has sung at many festivals of contemporary music notably with the group Contrasts. *Address:* c/o Théâtre National de Paris, 8 Rue Scribe, 75009 Paris, France.

RINGBORG, (Hans) Patrik Erland; conductor; b. 1 Nov. 1965, Stockholm, Sweden. *Education:* Stockholm Institute of Music, Royal College of Music, Stockholm, further studies in Vienna and London. *Career:* debut Ystad Summer Opera, Akhnaten by Glass, 1989; Städtische

Bühnen, Freiburg, Bizet's Carmen, 1992; Royal Opera, Stockholm, triple bill with Scheherazade, 1993; Conductor and Coach since 1987, Swedish Radio Choir, 1988, Sächsische Staatsoper, Dresden, 1988, Royal Opera, Stockholm, 1989–93 (including television), Canadian Opera Company, 1992, 2nd Kapellmeister and Studienleiter, Städtische Bühnen Freiburg, 1993–95; Co 1st Kapellmeister, Städtische Bühnen Freiburg, 1995–. *Honours:* British Council Fellow, 1987; Major Scholarship, Royal Academy of Music, Stockholm, 1987; Music Fellowship, Swedish-American Foundation, 1990; 1st R-U, First Competition for Opera Conductors, Royal Opera, Stockholm, 1997. *Current Management:* Nordic Artist, Stockholm, Sweden, Künstleragentur Markow, München, Germany. *Address:* Hindenburgstrasse 28, 79102 Freiburg in Breisgau, Germany.

RINGBORG, Tobias; violinist and conductor; b. 2 Nov. 1973, Stockholm, Sweden. *Education:* Royal Univ. Coll. of Music, Stockholm with Harald Thedéen, Juilliard School, New York. *Career:* debut, Tchaikovsky Concerto, with Royal Stockholm Philharmonic Orchestra, 1994; Appearances with every Swedish Symphony and Chamber Orchestra; Recitals throughout Europe and USA, including Concertgebouw, Amsterdam; National Gallery of Art, Washington DC; Several appearances and concerts for Swedish Television and Radio; Solo performances in Germany, Hungary and the USA; Brahms Concerto with Orchestre Nationale de Belgique, Brussels, 1995; Tour with Polish Radio Chamber Orchestra, Beethoven Concerto; Plays 18th Century Gagliano violin on loan from Swedish Academy of Music; engagements as conductor in Sweden 1999–. *Recordings:* Joseph Marx: Sonata in A major; Romantic Swedish Violin Concertos; Strindberg and Music; Numerous recordings for Swedish Broadcasting Corporation. *Honours:* Soloist Prize, Royal Swedish Academy of Music, 1994; First Prize, Concourt International de Musique de Chimay, Belgium, 1995. *Address:* c/o Svenska Konsertbyrån AB, Jungfrugatan 45, 11444 Stockholm, Sweden.

RINGHOLZ, Teresa; Singer (Soprano); b. 30 Dec. 1958, Rochester, New York, USA. *Education:* Studied at the Eastman School, Rochester and in San Francisco. *Career:* Debut: Western Opera Theatre, San Francisco in 1982 as Gilda; Toured in the USA then sang in Europe from 1985 with debut at Strasbourg as Zerbinetta; Cologne Opera from 1985 as Liu, Sophie, Susanna, Despina, Pamina and Sandrina in La Finta Giardiniera; Sang at the Salzburg Festival, 1987–88 and at Tel-Aviv with the Cologne Opera Company; Further appearances in opera and concert throughout Germany, France and Switzerland; Other roles include Gretel, Oscar, Lauretta, Micaela, Marzelline and Adele in Die Fledermaus; Season 1992 as the Wife in the premiere of Schnittke's Life With an Idiot, Amsterdam, and as Fanny in Rossini's La Cambiale di Matrimonio, Paris; Most recently sang at the Kennedy Center with the Washington Opera in 1994 as Susanna in Le nozze di Figaro; Violetta in Bogota and Fiordiligi in Barcelona, Seville and the Hamburg Staatsoper; Sang Gluck's Alceste at Drottningholm, 1998; Tatiana in Eugene Onegin at Osnabrück, 2000. *Address:* St Apernstrasse 20, 50667 Cologne, Germany.

RINGO, Jennifer; Singer (Soprano); b. 1965, USA. *Education:* University of Iowa; Juilliard School, New York; Merola Opera Program; Houston Grand Opera Studio. *Career:* Appearances with San Francisco Opera, Houston Opera, Maggio Musicale (Florence) Grand Théâtre de Genève and Canadian Opera Company; Poulenc's La Voix Humaine in New York and Cologne; Other repertory includes Der Zwerg by Zemlinsky, Wozzeck and Enescu's Oedipe; Concerts in Vienna, Berlin, Nice, Barcelona and Rotterdam; Festival engagements at Aspen, Caramoor, Ravina, Tanglewood and Hollyowood Bowl; Season 2000–01 with Britten's Ellen Orford at Tours, Berg's Lulu Symphonie at Aspen, Donna Elvira and Mozart's Countess at Lisbon and Ullmann's Kaiser von Atlantis at Cincinnati. *Address:* c/o Musicaglotz, 11 rue Le Verrier, 75006 Paris, France.

RINKEVICIUS, Gintaras; Conductor; b. 20 Jan. 1960, Vilnius, Lithuania. *Education:* Studies at St Petersburg and Moscow Conservatoires. *Career:* Assistant conductor of Lithuanian Philharmonic Orchestra, 1979; Music Director of Lithuanian State Symphony Orchestra from 1988; Tours with Moscow Radio Orchestra to: Italy; Spain; Austria; Finland; Yugoslavia; Worked with such soloists as Natalia Gutman, Peter Donohoe, Oleg Kagan and Vladimir Ovchinikov; Repertoire includes music by: Dvořák, Mahler, Poulenc, Orff, Honegger, Prokoviev, Elgar and John Adams, in addition to standard works; Appearances with Lithuanian State Opera, notably conducting Nabucco in Paris, 1992; Guest engagements with Russian State Symphony, Moscow Philharmonic and St Petersburg Philharmonic Orchestras; Performed Wagner's Flying Dutchman, in Vilnius, 1995; Turandot with the Latvian National Opera at the Albert Hall, London, 1998. *Honours:* Winner, All-Union Conducting Competition at St Petersburg Conservatoire; Third Prize, Herbert von Karajan Conducting Competition, 1985; Second Prize, in Janos Ferencsik Competition, Budapest, 1986. *Address:* c/o Sonata, 11 Northpark Street, Glasgow G20 7AA, Scotland.

RINTZLER, Marius; Singer (Bass); b. 14 March 1932, Bucharest, Romania. *Education:* Studied at the Bucharest Conservatory with A Alexandrescu. *Career:* Debut: Bucharest in 1964 as Basilio in Il Barbiere di Siviglia; Member of the Deutsche Oper am Rhein, Düsseldorf; Has also sung at Covent Garden, Drottningholm, Edinburgh in Die Soldaten in 1972, and Cologne; Glyndebourne Festival, 1967–79 as the Commendatore, Enrico in Anna Bolena, Osmin, Bartolo, La Roche in Capriccio and Morosus in Die schweigsame Frau; Metropolitan Opera, 1973–74 as Alberich; Geneva in 1974 as Osmin; Further appearances in Rio de Janeiro, San Francisco, Stockholm and Oslo; Sang in the US premiere of Penderecki's Die schwarze Maske, Santa Fe, 1988; Concert engagements in sacred music by Bach. *Recordings:* Bruckner F minor Mass; Beethoven Mass in C; Bach Cantatas; Madama Butterfly; Shostakovich's 13th Symphony; Orlando by Handel; Tamerlano by Handel; Video of Il Barbiere di Siviglia.

RIPPON, Michael (George); Singer (Bass-Baritone); b. 10 Dec. 1938, Coventry, Warwickshire, England. *Education:* MA, St John's College, Cambridge, 1957–60; Royal Academy of Music, 1960–63; ARAM. *Career:* Debut: Handel Opera Society in 1963 as Nireno in Giulio Cesare; Sang in the 1967 London premiere of Puccini's Edgar; Covent Garden Opera in 1969; Sang Leporello with Welsh National Opera in 1969; Glyndebourne Festival, 1970–73 in Die Zauberflöte, Le nozze di Figaro, The Queen of Spades and The Visit of The Old Lady; Has also sung with English National Opera, Scottish Opera, Handel Opera, Boston Opera, New York City Opera and PACT, Johannesburg, and at most leading music festivals and societies in the United Kingdom and abroad; Sang in the premieres of Maxwell Davies's The Martyrdom of St Magnus in 1977, Le Jongleur de Notre Dame in 1978, The Lighthouse in 1980 and Black Pentecost in 1982, and as Merlin in Hamilton's Lancelot in 1985; Benoit in La Bohème at Hong Kong, 1998. *Recordings:* Belshazzar's Feast; Bach Cantatas and B minor Mass; Mozart's Requiem; Purcell's Ode to St Cecilia; Handel's Israel in Egypt; Schoenberg's Moses und Aron; Vaughan Williams's Hugh The Drover; Holst's The Wandering Scholar; Mathias' This Worlds Joie; Salome.

RISHTON, Timothy (John); Organist and Musicologist; b. 14 Aug. 1960, Lancashire, England; m. Tracy Jane Hogg, 11 July 1987, 2 s., 1 d. *Education:* BA Music, University of Reading; Certificate in Welsh; MMus, University of Manchester, England; PhD University of Wales; Associate, Royal College of Organists. *Career:* Numerous recitals worldwide including complete Stanley series, London, 1981 and complete Bach Trio Sonatas, London and Salford, 1983; Complete Bach organ works, Norway, 1988–89; Concert tours in Central Europe, the Arctic, Scandinavia, the Far East and USA; 1st performance of Smethergell Harpsichord Concerto, Tadley, 1983; Dedicatee of new compositions by Henning Somevvo and Hans-Olav Lien; Lectures, Boxhill Summer School annually 1985–90, University of Oxford 1986 and 1987; University of Reading, 1988; Norwegian Music Conservatoire, Trondheim, 1993–; Many public lectures in English, Welsh and Norwegian (some broadcast); Many radio and television broadcasts for HTV, S4C, NRK (Norway) and BBC, 1984–; University of Wales, Bangor, Wales, 1984–87, 1989–91; Organist and Master of Choristers, Collegiate Church of St Cybi, Holyhead and Parish Churches of Holy Island, Anglesey, 1984–87; University of Tromso, 1998–; Reader in Performance Practice at Tromso, 2001. *Compositions:* Organ Works. *Recordings:* with Aled Jones, 1985; Organ Works of the Eighteenth-Century, 1986; From Many Lands, 1991; Walther and Bach arrangements of Albinoni and Vivaldi, 2001; Contemporary Norwegian Organ Music, 2001. *Compositions:* Organ works published in Norway, Sweden and Germany. *Publications:* Aspects of Keyboard Music; Essays in Honour of Susi Jeans, 1986; Organist in Norway, 1989; Liturgisk orgelspill, (various editions) 1995; Voll Kyryje, 1996. *Address:* 6315 Innfjorden, Norway.

RISLEY, Patricia; Singer (Mezzo-soprano); b. 12 Jan. 1968, South Carolina, USA. *Education:* Indiana University and Chicago Lyric Opera Center for American Artists. *Career:* Chicago Lyric Opera from 1995, as Siebel in Faust and in Berio's Un re in ascolto, Die Walküre, Die Zauberflöte and Norma; Metropolitan Opera from 1998 as Tebaldo in Don Carlo, Thisbe in Cenerentola and Mercédès in Carmen; European debut 1997 in Die Sieben Todsünden by Weill at Florence; Further roles include Mozart's Dorabella at St Louis, Farnace in Mitridate for Wolf Trap Opera and Cherubino at the Deutsche Oper, Berlin; Diana in La Calisto and Cesti's Orontea for Music of the Baroque, Gounod's Stephano and Meg Page in Falstaff at Chicago and Munich. *Current Management:* Balmer & Dixon Management AG, Kreuzstrasse 82, 8032 Zürich, Switzerland. *Telephone:* (43) 244-8644. *Fax:* (43) 244-8649. *Website:* www.badix.ch.

RISSET, Jean-Claude; Composer and Researcher; b. 13 March 1938, Le Puy, France; m. Rozenn Cornic, 2 children. *Education:* Ecole Normale Supérieure; studied composition with André Jolivet. *Career:* Bell Laboratories, USA, 1964–69; Centre National de la Recherche Scientifique, 1979–72 (Dir of Research, 1985–); head of computer dept at

IRCAM, Paris, 1975–79, with Pierre Boulez; fmr Composer-in-Residence, MIT and Stanford, USA. *Compositions include:* Little Boy, tape, 1968; Mutations I, tape, 1969; Dialogues, for 4 instruments and tape, 1975; Inharmonique, soprano and tape, 1977; Moments Newtoniens, for 7 instruments and tape, 1977; Mirages, 16 instruments and tape, 1978; Filtres, for 2 pianos, 1984; Sud, 1985; Dérives, for chorus and tape, 1985–87; Phases, for orchestra, 1988; Electron Positron, 1989; Duet for One Pianist, 1989; Lurai, for celtic harp and computer, 1991; Triptyque for clarinet and orchestra, 1991; Une aube sans soleil, soprano and percussion, 1991; Invisibles/Invisible soprano and computer, 1994; Mokee, for bass, piano and tape, 1996; Contre Nature, percussion and tape, 1996; Elementa, for tape, 1998; Escalas, for orchestra, 2001; Resonant Sound Spaces, 2002. *Recordings:* Works appear on 24 Cds. *Publications:* in Science, Musique en jeu, Esprit, Critique, Contemporary Music Review, Perspectives of New Music, Pour la Science, etc. *Honours:* Grand Prix National de la Musique, France, 1991; Médaille d'Or du CNRS, 1999; Hon. DMus Univ. of Edinburgh 1994, Univ. of Cordoba, Argentina 2000. *Address:* Laboratoire de Mécanique et d'Acoustique, CNRS, 31 chemin Joseph Aiguier, 13402 Marseille Cédex 20, France. *E-mail:* jcrisset@lma.cnrs-mrs.fr.

RITCHIE, Anthony (Damian); Composer; b. 18 Sept. 1960, Christchurch, New Zealand. *Education:* Ph.D on Bartók, Canterbury University; Liszt Academy, Budapest, composition with Attila Bozay. *Career:* Lecturer, Canterbury University, 1985–87; Composer-in-Schools, Christchurch, 1987; Mozart Fellowship at Otago University, 1988–89; Composer-in-Residence, Southern Sinfonia, 1993–94; Lecturer, Otago University, 2001. *Compositions include:* Concertino for piano and strings, 1981; Piano Concerto, Autumn, 1985; Shintaro San, brass band, 1986; Beginnings, for orchestra, 1987; Music for Tristan for piano, 1988; The Hanging Bulb, for orchestra, 1989; To Face the Night Alone for baritone, chorus and orchestra, 1990; As Long as Time, for unaccompanied Choir, 1991; Berlin Fragments for soprano and piano, 1992; Flute Concerto, 1993; Symphony No.1 'Boum' 1993; Viola Concerto, 1994; Star Fire, opera, 1995; A Bugle will Do, for orchestra, 1995; Then I Understood, for choir and orchestra, 1996; Guitar Concerto, 1996; The Eagle has Landed, one-act opera, 1997; From the Southern Marches, for choir and orchestra, 1997; Revelations, for orchestra, 1998; Symphony No. 2 'The Widening Gyre', 1999; Ahua for Choir and Orchestra, 2000; 24 Preludes for Piano, 2002; String Quartet No.2, 2002; 'Qaartet', a chamber opera, 2003; Timeless Land, for orchestra and film, 2003. *Recordings:* Music for Tristan, SOUNZ finemusic CDseries; The Hanging Bulb, for orchestra, Continum Records; Flute Concerto, Koch; Viola Concerto, Atoll Records; As Long as Time, Viva Voce Cd 'Snapshots'; 24 Preludes for Piano, Bellbird Music. *Address:* Music Department, University of Otago, Box 56, Dunedin New Zealand. *E-mail:* anthony.ritchie@xtra.co.nz. *Website:* www.anthonyritchie.co.nz.

RITTERMAN, Dame Janet Elizabeth, DSCM, BMus, MMus, FTCL, PhD; academic; *Director, Royal College of Music;* b. 1 Dec. 1941, Sydney, Australia; m. Gerrard Peter Ritterman. *Education:* NSW State Conservatorium, Sydney, Australia, King's Coll. London. *Career:* Sr Lecturer in Music, Middlesex Polytechnic 1975–79, Goldsmith's Coll., London 1980–87; Head of Music, Dartington Coll. of Arts 1987–90; Dean (Academic Affairs), Dartington Coll. 1988–90; Visiting Prof. in Music Education, Univ. of Plymouth 1993–; Dir, Royal Coll. of Music 1993–; mem. Incorporated Soc. of Musicians, Royal Musical Asscn, Royal Soc. of Musicians, Soc. for Education, Music and Psychology Research, Worshipful Company of Musicians. *Publications:* articles in music journals; contrib. to books on performance and pedagogy. *Address:* Royal College of Music, Prince Consort Road, London, SW7 2BS, England (office). *Telephone:* (20) 7591-4363 (office). *Fax:* (20) 7591-4356 (office). *E-mail:* jritterman@rcm.ac.uk (office). *Website:* www.rcm.ac.uk (office).

RIVA, Ambroglio; Singer (Bass); b. 1951, Ignazio, Milan, Italy. *Career:* Debut: Teatro Nuovo Milan, 1975, in Lucia di Lammermoor; Has appeared widely in Italy, notably in La Bohème at Verona (1980) and at the Verona Arena in Aida and Carmen; Sang in Donizetti's Martyrs at Bergamo, in Anna Bolena at Brescia and Sparafucile in Rigoletto at Ferrara; Valle d'Istria Festival, 1985, as Polyphemus in Acis and Galatea; Maggio Musicale Florence, 1990, as Angelotti in Tosca; Further appearances at Salzburg, Würzburg and Berlin. *Address:* c/o Teatro Comunale, Via Solferino 15, 50123 Florence, Italy.

RIVENQ, Nicolas; Singer (Baritone); b. 1958, London, England. *Education:* Studied with Madame Bonnardo in Paris, at the Orléans Conservatory and with Michel Sénéchal at the School of The Paris Opéra; Further study with Nicola Rossi-Lemeni at Indiana University. *Career:* Sang major roles in such operas as Boris Godunov, La Traviata and Don Giovanni at Indiana; 1984–85 season as Sulpice in La Fille du Régiment, Guglielmo, Marcello and Jupiter in Orphée aux Enfers, and Christus in Bach's St Matthew Passion; Recitals in Moscow and Leningrad in 1984 and sang Bach Cantatas with English Chamber

Orchestra in London and Edinburgh; Sang in Lully's Atys under William Christie at the Paris Opéra in 1986 and on tour to Tourcoing, Versailles and New York, 1988; Schwetzingen and Karlsruhe Festivals in 1988 with Tarare by Salieri under Jean-Claude Malgoire, Paris Opéra, 1989; Season 1989 with Rameau's Platée at Montpellier and Don Giovanni for Opera Northern Ireland; 1990–91 included Osman and Adario in Les Indes Galantes at Aix, Mozart's Count in Toulouse and performances of La Clemenza di Tito by Gluck at Tourcoing; Cherubini's Anacréon with The Orchestra of The Age of Enlightenment, 1992; Sang Sallustia in Pacini's L'Ultimo giorno di Pompei, Martina Franca, 1996; Turin 1998 in Bernstein's Candide; Sang Ambassadeur in Madame de, by Damase, at Geneva, 2001. *Address:* c/o Opéra et Concert, 1 rue Volney, F–75002 Paris, France.

RIVERS, Malcolm; Singer (baritone); b. 1940, England. *Education:* Royal College of Music. *Career:* Appearances with English National Opera in various roles including Alberich in The Ring, Escamillo in Carmen, and Marullo in Rigoletto; Sang in Troilus and Cressida and La Fanciulla del West at Covent Garden, Germont in La Traviata and Alberich in Seattle, numerous other appearances; Sang Sullivan's Pirate King and Pooh-Bah with the D'Oyly Carte Company, 1989; Alberich in The Ring at Falstaff, Arizona, 1996; mem., RSC. *Current Management:* Athole Still International Management, Forresters Hall, 25–27 Westow Street, London, SE19 3RY, England. *Telephone:* (20) 8771-5271. *Fax:* (20) 8768-6600. *Website:* www.atholestill.com.

RIZZI, Carlo; Italian conductor; *Music Director, Welsh National Opera*; b. 19 July 1960, Milan. *Education:* Milan Conservatoire, studied with Vladimir Delman in Bologna, Accademia Chigiana with Franco Ferrara. *Career:* debut, Milan Angelicum in Donizetti's L'Aio nell'Imbarrazzo 1982; conducted Falstaff, Parma 1985 and widely in Italy with Rigoletto, La Traviata, Tancredi, Donizetti's Torquato Tasso, Beatrice di Tenda, La Voix Humaine, Don Giovanni, L'Italiana in Algeri and Salieri's Falstaff; British debut at Buxton Festival with Torquato Tasso 1988; Netherlands Opera debut with Don Pasquale and productions of Fra Diavolo and Norma at Palermo 1989; Royal Philharmonic debut 1989, London Philharmonic debut 1990, Philharmonia debut 1991; Australian Opera with Il Barbiere di Siviglia and Lucrezia Borgia 1989–90; Tosca for Opera North and La Cenerentola at Covent Garden 1990; concert repertoire includes symphonies by Tchaikovsky and works by Haydn, Mozart, Beethoven and French composers; regular guest in Italy and Netherlands; US opera debut with Il Barbiere di Siviglia 1994; Don Giovanni and La Bohème for WNO 1996; Tristan and Isolde at Oxford and Bristol 1999; conducted Semiramide in Pesaro 2003; conducted Nabucco at the Met, I vespri siciliani in Zurich, Un ballo in maschera in Turin, Ariadne auf Naxos for WNO, Mefistofele in Amersterdam, Falstaff in Strasburg and Madama Butterfuly in Seville 2004; Music Dir, WNO 1992–2001, 2004–. *Recordings:* L'Italiana in Algeri, Donizetti's Il Furioso sull'Isola di San Domingo, Rossini's Ciro in Babilonia, Paisiello's La Scuffiara, Piccinni's La Pescatrice, Arias for tenor and orchestra by Rossini (with Ernesto Palacio), Schubert, Liszt and Debussy with the London Philharmonic and Philharmonia. *Current Management:* Allied Artists, 42 Montpelier Square, London, SW7 1JZ, England; Prima International Artists Management, Piazza de' Calderini 2/2, 40124 Bologna, Italy. *Address:* c/o Welsh National Opera, Wales Millennium Centre, Bay Chambers, West Bute Street, Cardiff, CF10 5GG, Wales. *Website:* www.wno.org.uk.

RIZZI, Lucia; Singer (Mezzo-soprano); b. 1965, Turin, Italy. *Education:* Studied architecture and music in Turin. *Career:* Appearances throughout Italy, in Tokyo and at the Aldeburgh Festival, under such conductors as Myung Wha Chung, Gianandrea Gavazzeni and Semyon Bychkov; Operas include Monteverdi's Poppea, Pergolesi's Frate 'nnamorato and Vivaldi's Farnace; Roles include Mozart's Fiordiligi, Dorabella and Sesto, Clarice in La Pietra del Paragone and Rossini's Roggiero (Tancredi) and Cenerentola (both at Zürich, 1996–97); Further engagements in Luisa Miller, Falstaff, Boris Godunov, Lady Macbeth of the Mtsensk District (in Florence), Stravinsky's Rossignol and Les Noces (Monte Carlo) and the Italian premiere of Tchaikovsky's Cantata Moscow, at Genoa; Other concerts in music by Vivaldi, Mahler and Schoenberg, at most Italian music centres; Sang Rosmene in a revival of Pergolesi's Il prigionero superbo, Jesi, 1998. *Recordings include:* Rossini Rarities. *Address:* c/o Opernhaus Zürich, Falkenstrasse 1, 8008 Zürich, Switzerland.

RIZZO, Francis; Stage Director and Administrator; b. 8 Nov. 1936, New York, NY, USA. *Education:* BA, Hamilton College, 1958; Yale University School of Drama, 1958–60. *Career:* American Director, Spoleto Festival of Two Worlds, 1968–71; Artistic Administrator, Wolf Trap Farm Park for The Performing Arts, 1972–78; Artistic Director, the Washington Opera, 1977–87; As director staged productions for New York City Opera, Houston Grand Opera, Washington Opera, Wolf Trap, Opera Theater of St Louis, Santa Fe Opera, Baltimore Opera, Teatro Verdi, Trieste, Michigan Opera Theater, Théâtre Municipal, Marseilles;

mem, American Guild of Musical Artists. *Contributions:* Opera News. *Address:* 590 West End Avenue, New York, NY 10024, USA.

ROARK-STRUMMER, Linda; Singer (Soprano); b. 1952, Tulsa, Oklahoma, USA. *Education:* Studied at Tulsa University. *Career:* Sang Dorabella at St Louis in 1977; Engaged at Hannover, 1979–80, Linz, 1980–86 as Regina in the 1983 Austrian premiere of Lortzing's opera and in the premiere of In Seinem Garten Liebt Don Perlimpin Belinda by B Sulzer; New York City Opera in 1985 as Giselda in I Lombardi; Over 150 performances of Verdi's Abigaille, notably at the Deutsche Oper Berlin in 1987, Ravenna in 1988 and Montreal and Verona in 1992; La Scala Milan in 1988 as Lucrezia in I Due Foscari; Sang Krasava in a concert performance of Smetana's Libuce in New York; Other roles include Lina in Stiffelio, the Forza and Trovatore Leonoras, Arabella, Jenůfa and Antonia; Guest engagements at Hamburg, Krefeld, Milwaukee and Venice; Sang Norma for Opera Hamilton at Toronto in 1991; Turandot at Portland, 1996; Poulenc's Mère Marie at Portland, 2001. *Address:* Opera Hamilton, 2 King Street West, Hamilton, Ontario L6P 1A1, Canada.

ROBBIN, Catherine; Singer (mezzo-soprano); b. 28 Sept. 1950, Toronto, Canada. *Career:* many appearances in Baroque music; sang in Messiah with English Baroque Soloists under Gardiner, Bach's B minor Mass with Monteverdi Choir and Handel's Orlando at the 1989 Promenade Concerts; opera performances include Olga in Eugene Onegin at Opéra de Lyon, Purcell's Dido and Handel's Orlando, (role of Medoro) with Acad. of Ancient Music and Handel's Xerxes at Carmel Bach Festival; collaborations with Trevor Pinnock, Hogwood, Andrew Davis, John Nelson, Jukka-Peka Saraste and Charles Dutoit; repertoire includes Les Nuits d'Été by Berlioz, Mahler's Lieder eines Fahrenden Gesellen and Rückert Lieder, Elgar's Sea Pictures and the Brahms Alto Rhapsody; many recitals in Canada and the USA and appearances at Aldeburgh Festival and with the Songmakers' Almanac; sang the title role in the North American premiere of Handel's Floridante in Toronto, 1990; Annius in La Clemenza di Tito at the Queen Elizabeth Hall, London, 1990; sang in Handel's Rinaldo at Blackheath and Bromsgrove, 1996. *Recordings include:* Beethoven's Mass in C and Missa Solemnis; Messiah under Gardiner; Berlioz Songs, also Gardiner; Haydn's Stabat Mater with Trevor Pinnock and the English Concert; Orlando under Hogwood; Mahler Song Cycles. *Honours:* Gold Award at the International Benson and Hedges Competition, Aldeburgh, England. *Current Management:* Caroline Phillips Management, The Old Brushworks, Pickwick Road, Corsham, Wiltshire, SN13 9BX, England. *Telephone:* (1249) 716716. *Fax:* (1249) 716717. *E-mail:* cphillips@caroline-phillips .co.uk. *Website:* www.caroline-phillips.co.uk/robbin.

ROBBINS, Julien; Singer (Bass); b. 14 Nov. 1950, Harrisburg, Pennsylvania, USA. *Education:* Studied, Philadelphia Academy of Vocal Arts, and with Nicola Moscona in New York. *Career:* Debut: Philadelphia 1976, in Un Ballo in Maschera; Engagements at Santa Fe, Miami, Washington and Chicago; Metropolitan Opera from 1979, as Ramphis, Colline, Gremin and Don Fernando in Fidelio; Deutsche Oper Berlin 1990, as Abimelech in Samson et Dalila; Sang Masetto at the Metropolitan, 1990; World premiere, The Voyage, by Philip Glass, Metropolitan Opera (Second Mate and Space Twin), Nightwatchman in Meistersinger, 1993; Deutsche Oper, Berlin, Don Giovanni, 1992, 1993, Escamillo, 1993, Turandot, (Timur) 1992; Staatsoper Berlin, Barber of Seville, Basilio, 1992; 1993 Deutsche Oper, Berlin, Figaro in The Marriage of Figaro; Season 1994 at San Diego as Count Rodolfo in La Sonnambala at Lisbon as Escamillo in Carmen and the Dresdner Festival, Messiah; Le Comte Ory, Le Gouverneur, Glyndebourne, 1997–98; Alidoro in La Cenerentola, Achilles in Giulio Cesare for Metropolitan, 2000; Don Alfonso in Così fan tutte for Metropolitan Opera, 2001. *Recordings:* Salome, First Soldier, Berlin Philharmonic, 1991; Doctor, La Traviata, Metropolitan Opera, 1992. *Current Management:* c/o Martha Munro, Munro Artist Management, 786 Dartmouth Street, South Dartmouth, MA 02748, USA. *Address:* 2805 Windy Hill Road, Allentown, PA 18103-4663, USA.

ROBERTI, Margherita; Singer (Soprano); b. 1930, Davenport, Iowa, USA. *Education:* Studied at Hunter College and the Mannes School of Music, New York; Further study in Italy, 1956. *Career:* Debut: Teatro Alfieri Turin, 1957, as Leonore in Il Trovatore; Appeared at Covent Garden in 1959 as Tosca; La Scala debut in 1959 as Abigaille in Nabucco; Engagements at the Verona Arena from 1959; Metropolitan Opera debut in 1962 as Tosca; Edinburgh Festival in 1963 as Luisa Miller and Glyndebourne Festival in 1964 as Lady Macbeth; Other roles include Elisabeth de Valois, Amelia in Un Ballo in Maschera, Hélène in Les Vêpres Siciliennes and Odabella in Atilla; Guest appearances as concert artist in England and North America. *Recordings include:* Elena in Donizetti's Marino Faliero.

ROBERTS, Brenda; Singer (Soprano); b. 16 March 1945, Lowell, Indiana, USA. *Education:* Studied at Northwestern University, Evanstown with Hermann Baer; Further study with Lotte Lehmann, Gerald

Moore and Josef Metternich in Germany. *Career:* Debut: Staatstheater Saarbrucken, 1968 as Sieglinde in Die Walküre; German appearances at Düsseldorf, Essen, Frankfurt, Nuremberg, Wiesbaden and Wuppertal; Member of the Hamburg Staatsoper; Bayreuth Festival in 1974 as Brünnhilde in Siegfried; Sang Isolde at Kassel in 1983; American engagements in Baltimore, Chicago, Baltimore and San Francisco; Metropolitan Opera debut in 1982 as the Dyer's Wife in Die Frau ohne Schatten; Other roles include Salome at Vienna in 1984 and Salome at Bremen in 1986, Wagner's Senta and Elsa, Verdi's Elisabeth de Valois, Aida, Lady Macbeth, Leonora and Violetta, Mozart's Donna Elvira and Countess, Puccini's Tosca, Giorgetta and Turandot, Santuzza and Lulu; Sang in a concert performance of Die Bakchantinnen by Egon Wellesz at Vienna in 1985; Kiel Opera in 1990 as Elektra and the title role in the premiere of Medea by Friedhelm Dohl; Sang Schoenberg's Erwartung at Palermo, 2000. *Address:* Buhnen Landeshaupstadt, Rathausplatz, 2300 Kiel, Germany.

ROBERTS, Deborah; Singer (Soprano); b. 1952, England. *Education:* Studied at Nottingham University, editing and interpreting Renaissance Baroque music; Further study with Andrea von Ramm in Basle. *Career:* Has sung with the Tallis Scholars on tours to Europe, Australia and the USA, appearing at most major festivals; Guest concerts with the Deller Consort and the Consort of Musicke; Frequent engagements with Musica Secreta notably in the Early Music Centre Festival, the Lufthansa Festival of Baroque Music and at the National Gallery; Early Music Network tour of Britain with programme Filiae Jerusalem, sacred music for women's voices by Monteverdi, Carissimi, Cavalli, Viadana, Grandi and Marco da Gagliano; Other repertoire includes works by Marenzio, Wert, Luzzaschi, Luigi Rossi and the women composers Francesca Cacini and Barbara Strozzi; Participation in lecture-recitals and workshops on performance practice and ornamentation. *Recordings:* With Musica Secreta, as musical director, Luzzaschi Madrigals for 1–3 Sopranos; Ensemble Music of Barbara Strozzi, 1994; Over 30 recordings with Tallis Scholars. *Honours:* Prizewinner, Bruges Early Music Competition, 1981. *Address:* 84 Devonshire Road, London SE23 3SX, England.

ROBERTS, Dorothy (Elizabeth); Concert Pianist; b. 1930, Brisbane, Queensland, Australia; Divorced, 1 s. *Education:* Studies at Sydney Conservatorium of Music, including Piano, Harmony, History of Music, Form of Music, Chamber Music; Clara Schumann technique with Adelina de Lara, London. *Career:* Music concerts at Balliol College, Oxford, Purcell Room, South Bank, London; Performed Liszt's Piano Concerto in E Flat with London Symphony Orchestra at Royal Albert Hall, London; Other concerto performances with the Hallé Orchestra, Northern Sinfonia Orchestra and London Bach Players; Recitals in London, the United Kingdom provinces, Glasgow, Germany, Australia, France, Netherlands, Canada; Television appearance with the Hallé Orchestra; Other television appearances with Richard Bonynge, 2 pianos, including playing with the BBC Orchestra. *Honours:* AMusA; LMus; Honorary DLit, Bradford University, 1995; Recently confirmed as the only Grand Pupil of the Clara Schumann piano-playing tradition. *Current Management:* Lee Reid Concerts. *Address:* Alveley House, 17 Lindum Road, Lincoln LN2 1NS, England.

ROBERTS, Eric; Singer (baritone); b. 16 Oct. 1944, Conway, North Wales. *Career:* Debut: Opera debut as Papageno with Welsh National Opera; Has sung with various British companies as: Guglielmo; Falke; Mozart's Figaro, Count and Trinity Moses, in Mahagonny, Scottish Opera; English National Opera in Pacific Overtures and the British premiere of Rimsky's Christmas Eve, 1988; D'Oyly Carte Opera Company, 1988–90; Further appearances as: Don Alfonso for Opera North; Bartolo and Britten's Redburn for Scottish Opera; Don Isaac in the British premiere of Gerhard's The Duenna; Haly, in L'Italiana in Algeri at Dublin; Eugene Onegin, for Opera Omaha, Nebraska, 1993; Australian debut as Bartolo, Lyric Opera of Queensland, 1992; Sang Don Isaac in Gerhard's The Duenna, Leeds, 1996; Concert engagements in Britten's War Requiem at Belgrade and L'Enfant et les Sortilèges at Rotterdam. *Current Management:* Athole Still International Management, Forresters Hall, 25–27 Westow Street, London, SE19 3RY, England. *Telephone:* (20) 8771-5271. *Fax:* (20) 8768-6600. *Website:* www.atholestill.com.

ROBERTS, Kathleen; Singer (Soprano); b. 9 Oct. 1941, Hattiesburg, Mississippi, USA. *Education:* Studied at Mississippi College, at Texas Christian University and in Zürich and Darmstadt. *Career:* Debut: St Gallen in 1967 as Violetta; Appearances at opera houses in Zürich, Geneva, Cologne and Frankfurt; Member of the Darmstadt Opera as Marzelline in Fidelio, Micaela, Aennchen in Der Freischütz, Mozart's Pamina, Susanna and Constanze, Gretel, Martha and Mimi; Modern repertoire has included Luise in Henze's Der Junge Lord and Laetitia in The Old Maid and The Thief by Menotti; Many concert appearances; Teacher of Singing in Darmstadt and elsewhere.

ROBERTS, Paul (Anthony); Concert Pianist; b. 2 June 1949, Beaconsfield, England; 2 s. *Education:* BA, Honours, University of York, 1970; Royal Academy of Music, London. *Career:* Juror, International Debussy Piano Competition, France, 1982, 1984; Cycle of Complete Debussy Piano Music at Purcell Room, London in 1984; World premiere of Maurice Ohana's piano etudes in a live broadcast for Radio France, 1986; Premieres of Ohana work for BBC in 1984, 1986 and 1988; World premiere of original piano score of an unpublished opera by Debussy, Rodrigue et Chimène, BBC Radio 3 in 1988; Lecturer, Professor of Piano at Guildhall School of Music, 1985–; Director, International Piano Summer School, SW France; Music at Ladevie. *Publications:* Book reviews for Times Educational Supplement, Composer, and Revue Musicale, Paris. *Current Management:* Management USA, Pat Zagelow, 3420 NE 21st Avenue, OR 97212, USA. *Address:* 10 Montague Road, London E8 2HW, England.

ROBERTS, Stephen (Pritchard); Singer (Baritone); b. 8 Feb. 1949. *Education:* Scholar, Associate, 1969, Royal College of Music; Graduate, Royal Schools of Music, 1971. *Career:* Professional Lay-Cleric, Westminster Cathedral Choir, 1972–76; Sings regularly in London, the United Kingdom and Europe, with all major orchestras and choral societies; Has sung in USA, Canada, Israel, Italy, Hong Kong, Paris, Poland, Spain, Singapore and South America; Opera roles include: Count in Marriage of Figaro, Falke in Die Fledermaus, Ubalde in Armide, Ramiro in Ravel's L'Heure Espagnole, Aeneas in Dido and Aeneas, Don Quixote in Master Peter's Puppet Show, Mittenhofer in Elegy for Young Lovers by Henze; Television appearances include Britten's War Requiem, Weill's Seven Deadly Sins, Delius's Sea Drift, Handel's Jephtha and Judas Maccabaeus, Penderecki's St Luke Passion at 1983 Proms, Walton's Belshazzar's Feast at 1984 Proms; Has worked with many orchestras specializing in authentic Baroque; Concert and oratorio performer singing all major baritone roles by JS Bach, Mozart, Handel, Elgar and Britten, also the choral symphonies by Mahler and Beethoven; Sang in Bach's St Matthew Passion at the Festival Hall, 1997; Professor at Royal Schools of Music, Vocal Faculty, 1993–. *Recordings include:* Numerous, many with King's College and St John's College, Cambridge, and Bach Choir of London including: St Matthew Passion, Punch and Judy with London Sinfonietta, The Apostles with London Symphony Orchestra, Caractacus with London Symphony Orchestra, Requiem with RPO, Messiah, Alexander's Feast, Carmina Burana with Berlin RSO, St Luke Passion, King Priam with London Sinfonietta, and A Sea Symphony; Dyson Canterbury Pilgrims; 2 CDs of English Songs. *Address:* 144 Gleneagle Road, London SW16 6 BA, England. *E-mail:* SRobertsBaritone@aol.com. *Website:* www .StephenRoberts.uk.com.

ROBERTS, Susan; Singer (Lyric-Coloratura Soprano); b. 1960, USA; m. Dimitry Sitkovetsky (qv), 26 July 1983. *Career:* Sang at first at the Bielefeld Opera then in Wiesbaden and Frankfurt; Has sung Blonchen in productions of Die Entführung by Ruth Berghaus in Frankfurt, Giorgio Strehler in Bologna, Jean-Pierre Ponnelle in Cologne and Giancarlo del Monaco in Bonn; Sang Minette in the premiere of Henze's English Cat at Frankfurt and again in Edinburgh and for the BBC; Further appearances at the Bayreuth and Orange Festivals and other German theatres; Paris Opéra in 1988 in the premiere of La Celestina by Maurice Ohana; Season 1990–91 as Blondchen for Netherlands Opera and Zan in Blitzstein's Regina for Scottish Opera; Concert engagements with radio orchestras in Vienna, Turin and Berlin, the National Orchestra of Spain, Orchestre Philharmonique Paris, Orchestre de Lyon and the Düsseldorf Symphonic; Recitals at the Vassa, Lockenhaus and Schleswig-Holstein Festivals; Season 1992 as Handel's Agrippina at the Buxton Festival; Sang in Param Vir's Snatched by the Gods at the Almeida Theatre, 1996; Sang Poulenc's Thérèse for Grange Park Opera, 1999. *Honours:* Martha Baird Rockefeller Foundation Grant; Laureate Winner, Concours International Musicale, Geneva. *Address:* Music International, 13 Ardilaun Road, London N5 2QR, England.

ROBERTS, Winifred; Violinist; b. 1930, Lismore, New South Wales, Australia; m. Geraint Jones. *Education:* Royal College of Music; Studied with Antonio Brosa and Albert Sammons. *Career:* National Gallery Concerts, England; Promenade Concerts; 3 Choirs Festival; Lake District Festival; Salisbury Festival; Manchester Festival; Soloist, Festival Hall and Queen Elizabeth Hall; Tours of Italy, Spain, USA; BBC Radio and Television appearances; Professor of Violin, Royal Academy of Music, now retired; Advanced Performers Class, Morley College, London, now retired; Private Teaching; Adjudicating and acting as Outside Examiner at Music Colleges and Schools. *Recordings:* History of Music; Biber Sonata; Vivaldi Double Concerto; Harpsichord and Violin Sonatas with husband. *Honours:* Tagore Gold Medal, 1st Prize, Violin Playing, Royal College of Music; Honorary RAM, 1983. *Address:* Flat 25, Circus Lodge, Circus Road, London NW8 9JL, England. *Telephone:* (20) 7289-5391.

ROBERTSON, Christopher; Singer (Baritone); b. 1964, USA. *Education:* Studied in San Francisco (member of the 1987 Merola Opera Program). *Career:* Many appearances at Leading Opera Houses in North America and Europe; Metropolitan Opera, season 1992–93, as Marcello and Sharpless in Butterfly; Don Giovanni, 1995–96; European debut as Guglielmo at Frankfurt Opera, followed by Mozart's Count at Munich, Egberto in Verdi's Aroldo at Covent Garden, and Oreste in Gluck's Iphigénie en Tauride at the Berlin Staatsoper; Prus in The Makropulos Case at Vancouver, Germont for English National Opera (1996) and Amonasro for San Francisco Opera (1997); Further engagements as Donner in Das Rheingold at Valencia, Count Luna with Florida Grand Opera, 1997 and Rigoletto with San Francisco Opera, also in 1997, Renato in Un Ballo in Maschera at Seattle and for Flanders Opera, and in Belgium, New Orleans, Montreal, Rio de Janeiro, Madrid and Santiago. *Honours:* Robert Jackson Memorial Grant, Richard Tucker Music Foundation. *Address:* c/o Metropolitan Opera, Lincoln Center, NY 10023, USA.

ROBERTSON, Duncan; Singer (Tenor); b. 1 Dec. 1924, Hamilton, Scotland; m. Mary Dawson, 24 June 1950, 1 s., 1 d. *Education:* Diploma SNAM, Gold Medal, 1945; LRAM, 1946 Royal College of Music, London; FGSM, 1975; Fellow Emeritus GSM, 1979. *Career:* Varied career in Oratorio including appearances in most European countries; Opera mostly at Glyndebourne and Scottish Opera, also Covent Garden, Sadler's Wells, English Opera Group, Welsh Opera, Handel Opera; Many broadcasts ranging from light music to Radio 3; Some television, recordings and recital work; Sang in Canticum Sacrum by Stravinsky, 1st performance in the United Kingdom conducted by Robert Craft, 1956; Appeared in Oedipus Rex by Stravinsky, with Jean Cocteau as narrator and conducted by Stravinsky, 1959; Sang in Benjamin Britten's 50th Birthday Concert, 1963; Sang with Giulini conducting, performance of Schubert's Mass in E Flat, televised from the Edinburgh Festival, 1968; Professor of Singing, Guildhall School of Music and Drama, London, 1966–77; Lecturer in Singing, Royal Scottish Academy of Music and Drama, Glasgow, 1977–88. *Address:* Heathers, 5 The Driftway, Upper Beeding, West Sussex BN44 3JX, England.

ROBERTSON, John; singer (tenor); b. 20 Sept. 1938, Galashiels, Scotland. *Education:* Sedburgh and Edinburgh Universities. *Career:* regular appearances with Scottish Opera; 850 performances in 50 roles including Ferrando, Tamino, Ottavio, Albert Herring and Almaviva; Has toured with the company to Austria, Germany, Switzerland, Yugoslavia, Poland, Portugal and Iceland in The Turn of the Screw, The Rape of Lucretia and A Midsummer Night's Dream; Appearances at Edinburgh as Tannhäuser and in Le nozze di Figaro; Has directed the Edinburgh Opera in La Traviata, L'Elisir d'amore and La Sonnambula; Oratorio and concert work throughout Scotland and on BBC and Scottish television; Teaches voice in Glasgow and Edinburgh and at the School of Vocal Studies at the Royal Northern College of Music, Manchester. *Recordings include:* Le nozze di Figaro. *Current Management:* Tennant Artists, Unit 2, 39 Tadema Road, London, SW10 0PZ, England. *Telephone:* (20) 7376-3758. *Fax:* (20) 7351-0679. *E-mail:* info@tennantartists.demon.co.uk.

ROBERTSON, Stewart (John); Conductor, Pianist and Music Director; b. 22 May 1948, Glasgow, Scotland. *Education:* Royal Scottish Academy of Music, 1965–69; Bristol University, 1969–70; Vienna Academy, 1975; Salzburg Mozarteum, 1977; Teachers: Otmar Suitner and Hans Swarowsky for conducting, and Denis Matthews for piano. *Career:* Assistant Chorus Master, Scottish Opera, Edinburgh Festival Chorus, 1968–69; Chorus Master, London City Singers, 1970–72; Conductor for Cologne Opera, 1972–75; Music Director, Tanz Forum, Zürich Opera, 1975–76; Scottish Opera Touring Company, 1976–79; Assistant Conductor, Oakland Symphony Orchestra, 1985–86; Music Director and Principal Conductor, Glimmerglass Opera, NY, 1987–; Guest Conductor for SNO, and BBC Scottish Symphony Orchestra, CBSO Swiss-Italian Radio Symphony Orchestra, San Jose Symphony Orchestra, Utah Symphony Orchestra, Britt Festival, Long Beach, Portland, Sacramento, Kentucky Opera, Arkansas Opera and Montreal Opera; Season 1998 with L'Elisir d'amore for Florida Grand Opera and Thomson's The Mother of us All for Glimmerglass Opera; Artistic Dir, Opera Omaha 2005–. *Current Management:* John Miller, Robert Lombardo Associates, NY, USA. *Address:* 81 Poppy Road, Carmel Valley, CA 93924, USA.

ROBINS, Brian Martin; Writer and Lecturer; b. 2 Jan. 1940, Cheltenham, England; pnr Anne Young, one d. *Education:* Univ. of London. *Career:* classical record retailer 1957–90; Adult Education lecturer 1984–87; freelance writer and lecturer 2001–; mem. Royal Musical Asscn, Soc. for Eighteenth-Century Music. *Publications:* The John Marsh Journals, Catch and Glee Culture in Eighteenth Century England, 'The Catch and Glee in 18th century provincial England', in Concert Life in Eighteenth-Century Britain; contrib. to New Grove Dictionary of Music and Musicians 2000, New Dictionary of National Biography 2004, Early Music, The Journal of the Royal Musical Association, Fanfare (USA), Goldberg Early Music Magazine (Spain).

Honours: Andrew W. Mellon Fellowship 1994, British Acad. Exchange Fellowship to Huntington Library, San Marino, CA 2000. *Address:* Bière, 71190 Broye, France (home). *Telephone:* (385) 543163 (home). *E-mail:* BrianRob13@wanadoo.fr (home).

ROBINSON, Dean; Singer (Bass); b. 20 Aug. 1968, Bathurst, Australia. *Education:* Studied in Australia and Royal Northern College of Music. *Career:* Opera engagements at Covent Garden in Don Carlos, Die Meistersinger, Lohengrin, Palestrina (also at Metropolitan Opera) and Ariadne auf Naxos; for English National Opera Colline in La Bohème, 2nd Soldier in Salome, Pluto in Orfeo and created role of Passauf in Gavin Bryers' Dr Ox's Experiment; Colline, Mr Ratcliffe in Billy Budd and Angelotti for Welsh Nat. Opera; Sparafucile and Sarastro for Scottish Opera; Colline, Sparafucile and Don Giovanni with Mid Wales Opera; Claudio in Agrippina, Polyphemus in Acis and Galataea, and King of Scotland in Ariodante, for The Early Opera Company; Death in The Emperor of Atlantis for Mecklenburgh Opera; with English Touring Opera Sarastro, and Comte de Grieux in Manon; Concerts include St John Passion at Westminster Abbey, Mozart Requiem with Eric Ericsson, Messiah with Sir John Eliot Gardiner and the English Baroque Soloists, L'enfance du Christ with Kent Nagano, Verdi's Requiem with Sir David Willcocks. *Recordings:* Don Pedro in Beatrice et Benedict with Sir Colin Davis and the London Symphony Orchestra; Masetto in Don Giovanni; Duca d'Argile in La Prigione di Edimburgo for Opera Rara and appearances on several Opera Rara recital discs. *Film:* First Officer in The Death of Klinghoffer for Channel 4 TV. *Address:* c/o Harlequin Agency Limited, 203 Fidlas Road, Cardiff, CF14 5NA, Wales. *E-mail:* deanrobinson@orange.net.

ROBINSON, Ethna; Singer (mezzo-soprano); b. 20 June 1956, Dublin, Ireland. *Education:* Studied in Birmingham and at the Guildhall School, London. *Career:* English National Opera from 1984, as Rosette in Manon and in the British premiere of Akhnaten by Glass; Premieres of Birtwistle's The Mask of Orpheus, 1986, and Harvey's Inquest of Love, 1993; Other roles have included Mozart's Dorabella and Cherubino, Hansel, Olga in Eugene Onegin, Berlioz's Béatrice, Margret in Wozzeck, and Pauline in The Queen of Spades; Tour of Russia with ENO, 1990; Season 1998 as The Prioress in Suor Angelica for ENO, and Third Lady in The Magic Flute; Season 2000–01 as St Theresa III in Thomson's Four Saints in Three Acts, for ENO, and Larina in Eugene Onegin for Opera North. *Recordings include:* Video of ENO Mikado. *Current Management:* Owen/White Management, Top Floor, 59 Lansdowne Place, Hove, East Sussex, BN3 1FL, England.

ROBINSON, Faye; Singer (Soprano); b. 2 Nov. 1943, Houston, Texas, USA. *Education:* Studied with Ruth Stewart at Texas Southern University and with Ellen Faull in New York. *Career:* Debut: New York City Opera, 1972, as Micaela; Has sung Violetta, the Queen of Shemakha and Liu in New York; Washington Civic Opera in 1973 as Violetta and Juliette; Jackson, FL, 1974–75 as Desdemona and Adina; Aix-en-Provence in 1975 in Der Schauspieldirektor and La Serva Padrona; Engagements in Houston, Barcelona and Frankfurt; Buenos Aires in 1980 in Les Contes d'Hoffmann; Schwetzingen Festival in 1981 as Elektra in Idomeneo; Paris Opéra and Bordeaux in 1982 as Juliette and Luisa Miller; Other roles include Constanze, Norina and Oscar; Sang in the premiere of The Mask of Time in Boston, 1984 and in the first British performance of Tippett's oratorio; Cologne in 1988 as Constanze. *Recordings:* Mahler's 8th Symphony; The Mask of Time. *Address:* c/o Houston Grand Opera, 510 Preston Avenue, Houston, TX 77002, USA.

ROBINSON, Gail; Singer (Soprano); b. 7 Aug. 1946, Meridian, Mississippi, USA. *Education:* Studied at Memphis State University and with Robley Lawson. *Career:* Debut: Memphis, 1967 as Lucia in Lammermoor; Appearances in Berlin, Munich and Hamburg; Sang with Metropolitan Opera from 1970, in Die Zauberflöte and as Gilda, Adina, Oscar, Marie in La Fille du Régiment, Rosina and Gretel; Director, Metropolitan National Council Auditions and now Director, Metropolitan Young Artist Development Program. *Honours:* Winner of Metropolitan's National Council Auditions, 1966. *Address:* c/o Metropolitan Opera, Lincoln Center, New York, NY 10023, USA.

ROBINSON, Michael (Finlay); Professor of Music (retd); b. 3 March 1933, Gloucester, England; m. Ann James, 28 Dec 1961, two s. *Education:* BA, 1956, BMus, 1957, MA, 1960, DPhil, 1963, Oxford University. *Career:* Teacher, Royal Scottish Academy of Music, 1960–61; Music Lecturer, Durham University, 1961–65; Assistant Professor, 1965–67, Associate Professor, 1967–70, McGill University, Montreal, Canada; Music Lecturer, 1970–75, Senior Lecturer in Music, 1975–91, Head of Music Department, 1987–94, Professor of Music, 1991–94, Emeritus Professor of Music, 1995–, University of Wales College of Cardiff, Wales. *Compositions:* 2 String Quartets, 1972, 1974; A Pretty How Town, baritone and eight instrumentalists, 1983; Fantasy for unaccompanied cello, 1997; Other chamber music and songs. *Publications:* Opera Before Mozart, 1966, 2 later editions; Naples and

Neapolitan Opera, 1972, American reprint, 1984, Italian edition, 1985; Giovanni Paisiello, a thematic catalogue of his works, vol. 1, 1991, Vol. 2, 1993. *Contributions:* Proceedings of the Royal Musical Association; New Grove; Chigiana; Studi Musicali; Soundings; Music and Letters; The Alternative Endings of Mozart's Don Giovanni, in 'Opera Buffa in Mozart's Vienna', 1997. *Address:* Northridge House, Usk Road, Shirenewton, Monmouthshire NP16 6RZ, Wales. *E-mail:* 101770 .1352@compuserve.com.

ROBINSON, Paul; Singer (Baritone); b. 1970, England. *Education:* Chorister and Choral Scholar, Kings College, Cambridge; Royal College of Music. *Career:* Concerts include St John Passion at the London Bach Festival, Bach's Magnificat at Bristol Cathedral, Monteverdi Vespers in Vancouver, St Matthew Passion for Italian Radio and Schubertiade Recital at the Wigmore Hall; Mozart's Coronation Mass with the Royal Flanders Philharmonic Orchestra, Purcell's Indian Queen with the Academy of Ancient Music, Messiah with the CBSO and Haydn's Mariazeller Mass at Canterbury Cathedral; Opera Roles include The Speaker in The Magic Flute for Opera West, Mangus in Tippett's Knot Garden and Janáček's Poacher and Britten's Demetrius for the RAM; Season 1997–98 with the Brahms Requiem in London, Bach's Christmas Oratorio in Oxford, St John Passion with the Royal Liverpool Philharmonic Orchestra, Carmina Burana at Bristol and Handel's Joshua with the Academy of Ancient Music. *Recordings:* Many Albums with King's College Choir; Robert in Hugh the Drover by Vaughan Williams.

ROBINSON, Peter; Conductor; b. 1949, England. *Education:* Studied music at Oxford. *Career:* Assistant Organist, Durham Cathedral; Associated with the Glyndebourne Festival Opera, 1971–73; Head of Music Staff and Resident Conductor, Australian Opera, 1973–80; Assistant Music Director, English National Opera, 1981–89, conducting Le nozze di Figaro, Don Giovanni, Die Zauberflöte, Così fan tutte, Otello, Rigoletto, The Mastersingers, Madama Butterfly, Orfeo, Maria Stuarda, The Mikado, Carmen, Werther, Hansel and Gretel, Simon Boccanegra and The Turn of the Screw; Appearances for Kent Opera with The Beggar's Opera and Don Giovanni, and the Scottish Opera with The Pearl Fishers; Conducted Così fan tutte in a production for BBC television; Has conducted in Australia; Le nozze di Figaro, Victoria State Opera, 1987; Die Entführung VSO, 1989; Così fan tutte, The Australian Opera, 1990; Don Giovanni, State Opera of South Australia, 1991; Engagements with Opera Factory (Marriage of Figaro also for television), 1991; Figaro at Adelaide, 1997; Symphony concerts with the London Symphony, London Mozart Players and London Sinfonietta; Concerts with the Melbourne and Sydney Symphony Orchestras, 1988–90; Sound and Video recordings with Lesley Garrett for Silva Screen Records and BBC television; Conducted The Magic Flute for British Youth Opera, 1996. *Current Management:* Marks Management Ltd. *Address:* c/o 14 New Burlington Street, London W1X 1FF, England.

ROBINSON, Sharon; Concert Cellist; b. 2 Dec. 1949, Houston, Texas, USA; m. Jaime Laredo 1976. *Education:* North Carolina School of the Arts, 1968; University of Southern California, 1968–70; BM, Peabody Conservatory of Music, 1972. *Career:* Debut: New York in 1974; Member of Kalichstein-Laredo-Robinson Trio from 1976; Soloist at Marlboro Music Festival, Mostly Mozart Festival and South Bank Festival in London, Edinburgh Festival, Madeira Bach Festival, Helsinki Festival and Tivoli Gardens; Commissioned and premiered Ned Rorem's After Reading Shakespeare, for solo cello and premiered Alan Shulman's Kol Nidrei for cello and piano, William Bland's Rhapsody for cello and piano, and Robert Blake's Cello Sonata; mem, Violoncello Society of America. *Recordings:* Vivaldi Sonatas; Fauré's Elegy; Debussy Sonata; Rorem's After Reading Shakespeare; Beethoven's Triple Concerto; With Kalichstein-Laredo-Robinson Trio, Mendelssohn and Brahms Trios; Duos for Violin and Cello with Jaime Laredo. *Honours:* Avery Fisher Award, 1979; Levintritt Award, 1975; Pro Musicis Foundation Award, 1974. *Current Management:* Askonas Holt Ltd, Lonsdale Chambers, 27 Chancery Lane, London, WC2A 1PF, England. *Telephone:* (20) 7400-1700. *Fax:* (20) 7400-1799. *E-mail:* info@askonasholt.co.uk. *Website:* www.askonasholt.co.uk.

ROBINSON, Timothy; Singer (Tenor); b. 1968, England. *Education:* Studied at New College Oxford (Choral Scholar) and with William McAlpine at the Guildhall School. *Career:* 1996 concerts include Mozart's Davidde Penitente at Seville, Messiah in Singapore, Weber's Euryanthe at the Queen Elizabeth Hall, South Bank, and Proms debut as Jupiter in Semele, under William Christie; Opera roles include Kudrjash in Katya Kabanova for Glyndebourne Touring Opera, Fenton and Scaramuccio (Ariadne auf Naxos) for English National Opera and Jupiter at the Aix-en-Provence Festival (French premiere, 1996); Member of the Royal Opera, in such operas as Nabucco, Traviata and Fedora; Sang in the British premiere of Pfitzner's Palestrina, 1997; Season 1997–98 in Katya Kabanova at Glyndebourne and in Turandot at the Paris Opéra; Other roles include Don Ottavio, Tamino and Alfredo, with Travelling Opera; Arminio in Verdi's Masnadieri for the

Royal Opera, 1998; Sang St John in The Kingdom by Elgar at the 1999 London Prom concerts; London Proms, 2002. *Recordings include:* Bach's Magnificat; Vaughan Williams Serenade to Music; Beethoven Cantatas. *Address:* 11 Gilmore Road, Lewisham, SE13 5AD.

ROBISON, Paula; Flautist; b. 8 June 1941, Nashville, Tennessee, USA; m. Scott Nickrenz, 1 d. *Career:* Founding Artist Member, Chamber Music Society of Lincoln Center; Joint Recitalist with pianist Ruth Laredo and Guitarist Eliot Fisk; Soloist, New York Philharmonic, Atlanta, American and San Francisco Symphony Orchestra; Recitalist at numerous venues including Carnegie Hall and Kennedy Center and Wigmore Hall in January 1990; Commissioned and premiered Kirchner's Music for Flute and Orchestra with the Indianapolis Symphony, Toru Takemitsu's I Hear the Water Dreaming, Robert Beaser's Song of the Bells; Numerous television appearances including Live from Lincoln Center, 1984–85; Christmas at the Kennedy Center; Sunday Morning, CBS Television; For 10 years (1978–1988) Co-Director of Chamber Music, Spoleto Festival at Charleston, South Carolina, and Spoleto, Italy; Blue Ridge Airs II, flute and orchestra, Kenneth Frazelle, 1991; Soloist, London Symphony Orchestra, Michael Tilson Thomas, 1995; I Solisti Veneti, Claudio Scimone, 1995. *Recordings:* Has made many recordings including, Flute Music of the Romantic Era; The Sonatas for Flute and Harpsichord by J. S. Bach (complete) and G F Handel (complete) with Kenneth Cooper; Release for Music Masters: American Masterworks for flute and piano. *Current Management:* Shaw Concerts. *Address:* c/o London Symphony Orchestra, Barbican Centre, Silk Street, London, EC 2, England.

ROBLES, Marisa; Concert Harpist; b. 4 May 1937, Madrid, Spain; m. David Bean, 29 Oct 1985, 2 s., 1 d. *Education:* Real Conservatorio de Musica, Madrid, gaining Honours, 1953. *Career:* Debut: Spain, 1954; Settled in the United Kingdom and appeared on many television programmes; London concert debut, 1963; Solo recitals and major orchestral appearances in the United Kingdom, Europe, Japan, Australia, Canada, USA, South America, with most London orchestras, New York Philharmonic; Professor, Real Conservatorio de Musica, Madrid, 1958–63; has worked with Zubin Mehta, Kurt Masur, Rafael Frühbeck de Burgos, Mstislav Rostropovich, Yehudi Menuhin, James Galway and Isaac Stern; Professor, Royal College of Music, London, 1973–; Artistic Director: World Harp Festival, Cardiff, Wales, 1991, World Harp Festival II, 1994; took part in TV series CONCERTO! with James Galway and Dudley Moore, 1994; mem, International Harp Association; Royal Overseas League; United Kingdom Harp Association; Vice-President, Spanish Association of Harpists. *Compositions:* Narnia Suite; Music for Narnia Chronicles; Irish Suite; Basque Suite for flute and harp. *Recordings:* with James Galway, Mozart Concerto for Flute and Harp and Clair de Lune, Music of Debussy; Harp Concertos with The Acad. of St Martin in the Fields and Iona Brown; Rodgrigo Concerto de Aranjuez; solo: The World of the Harp; The Chronicles of Narnia narrated by Michael Hordern, music composed and performed by Marisa Robles. *Honours:* Fellow, Royal College of Music, 1983. *Current Management:* Clarion/Seven Muses, 47 Whitehall Park, London N19 3TW, England. *Address:* 38 Luttrell Avenue, London SW15 6PE, England.

ROBLOU, David, ARAM, Dip RAM, LRAM, ARCM, ARCO; Conductor, Harpsichordist, Organist, Pianist and Vocal Coach; b. 23 Dec. 1949, London, England. *Education:* Royal Acad. of Music, masterclasses with Nadia Boulanger (London) and Kenneth Gilbert (Antwerp). *Career:* Artistic and Musical Dir, Midsummer Opera; Prof., Guildhall School of Music and Drama 1974; mem. Musicians' Union, Incorporated Soc. of Musicians. *Recordings:* numerous chamber music recordings with New London Consort, including harpsichord solo, J. S. Bach: Brandenburg Concerto No. 5. *Current Management:* Sounds Lyrical Artists Management, 109 Algernon Road, London, SE13 7AP, England. *Telephone:* (20) 8244-5789 (office). *Fax:* (20) 7652-0070 (office). *E-mail:* sounds.lyrical@ntlworld.com (office).

ROBOTHAM, Barbara; Musician and Singer; b. 15 Jan. 1936, Blackpool, England; m. Eric Waite, 30 Aug 1958, 1 s. *Education:* ARMCM Teachers Diploma with distinction, 1957, Performers Diploma with distinction, 1959, Royal Manchester College of Music. *Career:* Appearances with all major British Orchestras; Festival appearances include Three Choirs Festival, Cheltenham, Haydn-Mozart Festival, Gulbenkian Lisbon, and Bordeaux France; Concerts include Paris, Madrid, Barcelona, Prague, and Frankfurt; Principal Lecturer at Royal Northern College of Music and Professor of Voice at Lancaster University; mem, Incorporated Society of Musicians. *Recordings:* Stravinsky's Cantata on Old English Texts; Walton's Gloria. *Honours:* Imperial League of Opera Prize and Curtis Gold Medal, 1958; 1st Prize, Liverpool Philharmonic International Singers Competition, 1960; 2nd Prize, Concours International de Geneva, 1961; Honorary Fellowship, Royal Manchester College of Music, 1967; Honorary Fellowship, Royal Northern College of Music, 1992; Honorary Fellowship, University of Central Lancashire, 1998.

Address: 49 Blackpool Road North, St Annes on Sea, Lancashire, England.

ROBSON, Christopher; British opera and concert singer (counter-tenor); b. 9 Dec. 1953, Falkirk, Scotland; m. Laura Carin Snelling 1974 (divorced 1984); one s. (with Samantha Lambourne). *Education:* Cambridge College of Arts and Technology, Trinity College of Music, London with James Gaddarn, studied with Paul Esswood and Helga Mott. *Career:* debut in Handel's Samson, Queen Elizabeth Hall, London, 1976; Opera debut, Handel's Sosarme, Barber Institute, Birmingham, 1979; Principal roles, Kent Opera, Phoenix Opera, Handel Opera Society, Royal Opera Covent Garden (Semele), 1988–; English National Opera (Orfeo, Xerxes, title role in Julius Caesar and Akhnaten, Lear), Frankfurt State Opera, Berliner Kammeroper (Orlando title role), Houston Grand Opera, New York City Opera, Opera Factory Zürich, Opera Factory-London Sinfonietta, Nancy Opera, Innsbruck Tiro-lertheater; Sang at major festivals, the United Kingdom, France, Spain, Austria, Netherlands, USA, Switzerland, Germany, Poland, and BBC Proms; Concerts throughout the United Kingdom and Europe; Broad-casts, BBC, SFB, WDR, ORF, DRS, Radio France Musique; Monteverdi Choir, 1974–84; London Oratory Choir, 1974–80; The Spieglers, 1976–82; St George's Theatre Company, 1976; Westminster Cathedral Choir, 1980–85; Kings Consort, 1981–86; New London Consort, 1986–; Sang in Xerxes on ENO Russian tour, 1990; Season 1992–93, Ptolemy (Julius Caesar) for Scottish Opera, Polinesso (Ariodante) for ENO, Andronicus (Tamerlano) for Karlsruhe, Ezio title role, Berliner Kammeroper; Season 1993–94, Tamerlano title role, Opera North, Arsamenes (Xerxes), ENO, Apollo (Death in Venice), Liège, Oberon (Midsummer Night's Dream), Covent Garden Festival, Tolomeo (Giulio Cesare); Season 1994–95, Oberon, ENO; Season 1995–96, Arsamenes, Chicago Lyric Opera, Vlaamse Oper Antwerp, Bayerische Staatsoper Munich, Oberon, Ravenna Festival; Season 1966–97, Didimus (Theo-dora), Glyndebourne Touring Opera; Season 1997–98, Orlofsky (Fle-dermaus), Munich; Season 1998–99 World premieres at Lunn's The Maids, Lyric Theatre, London and Dove's Flight at Glyndebourne Opera; Season 1999–2000, Polinesso (Ariodante), Munich; Engaged for season 2001–2002 as Baba the Turk in The Rake's Progress, Munich; film Hell for Leather directed by Dominik Scherrer; World premier of Hans Jurgen von Bose K-Projekt 12/14, a one-man opera commissioned by the Bavarian State Opera to open the 2003 Opernfestspiel. *Television appearances include:* A Night with Handel (Channel 4/NVC/Warner Music), Xerxes (ThamesTV/Channel 4/RM Arts/Arthaus), Hail Bright Cecilia (Channel 4/EMI), The Rake's Progress and Rodelinda (both Bayerische Rundfunk), Flight (Channel 4). *Recordings include:* Resur-rection, Maxwell Davies; Psyche, Locke; Ezio, Handel; Artaxerxes, Arne; Magnificat, Bach; Xerxes, Handel; Vivaldi Gloria, Decca; Jonathan Dove, Flight, Chandos. *Honours:* Opernfestspiel Preis, Munich, 1997; Bayerische Kammersaenger, 2003. *Address:* c/o Music International, 13 Ardilaun Road, London N5 2QR, England. *E-mail:* chrisopera@lineone.net.

ROBSON, Elizabeth; Singer (Soprano); b. 1938, Dundee, Scotland; m. Neil Howlett. *Education:* Studied at Royal Scottish Academy of Music and in Florence. *Career:* Debut: Sadler's Wells in 1961 as Micaela; Appearances at Covent Garden throughout the 1960s as Musetta, Zdenka, Sophie, Susanna, Pamina, Marzelline and Nannetta in Falstaff; Guest appearances with Scottish Opera as Zerlina and at the 1967 Edinburgh Festival as Anne Trulove in The Rake's Progress; Sang also at Aix-en-Provence and La Scala Milan; Noted concert artist. *Recordings:* Marzelline in Fidelio.

ROBSON, Nigel; Singer (Tenor); b. 1955, Argyllshire, Scotland. *Educa-tion:* Royal Northern College of Music with Alexander Young. *Career:* Sang with the Glyndebourne Festival Chorus and English National Opera from 1981 as Monteverdi's Orfeo and in the premiere of Birtwistle's The Mask of Orpheus, 1986; British stage premiere of Weill's Der Protagonist; Sang Ferrando in Così fan tutte and in David Freeman's production of Falstaff, in the premiere of Michael Finnissy's The Undivine Comedy and in Tippett's Songs for Dov conducted by Tippett, La Finta Giardiniera for Opera North and Don Ottavio in Don Giovanni for Opera Factory; Idomeneo at Munich (1996) and sang in new production of Monteverdi's Ulysses for Opera North, 1997 Appearances with the Monteverdi Choir and Orchestra including tours of Italy, Germany and France; Performances of Monteverdi's Vespers in Venice and Orfeo in Spain as well as Idomeneo in Lisbon, Paris, Amsterdam and London; Sang Handel's Jephtha at the Handel Festival in Göttingen and the Holland Festival; Sang the Anonymous Voice in the British premiere of Tippett's New Year at Glyndebourne in 1990; Concerts at the Festival Hall with Janáček's Glagolitic Mass, with the Ensemble Intercontemporain in Paris and with the London Sinfonietta in Henze's Voices in 1991; Season 1992 as Claggart in Billy Budd for Scottish Opera and Nero in The Coronation of Poppea for Opera Factory; Other recent roles have included the title role in Idomeneo at the Bayerische Staatsoper; Ulisse in Il Ritorno d'Ulisse in Patria and

Pandarus in Walton's Troilus and Cressida for Opera North; Laca in Jenůfa for WNO, 1998; Season 2000–01 as Peter Grimes at Maastricht, Golo in Schumann's Genoveva at Garsington and Britten's Captian Vere for Canadian Opera at Toronto. *Recordings include:* Handel's Tamer-lano; Alexander's Feast and Jephtha; Tippett's Songs for Dov; Stravinsky's Renard; Arbace in Idomeneo; Britten's The Rape of Lucretia; Walton's Troilus and Cressida. *Current Management:* Ingpen & Williams Ltd, 7 St George's Court, 131 Putney Bridge Road, London, SW15 2PA, England.

ROBSON, Richard; Singer (Bass); b. 1964, County Durham, England. *Education:* Guildhall School with Otakar Kraus; Further Study with Arlene Randazzo. *Career:* Debut: Badger in The Cunning Little Vixen and Antonio in Figaro, at Glyndebourne; Speaker in The Magic Flute and Gremin in Eugene Onegin, for Kent Opera; Debut with Wiener Kammeroper as Rossini's Basilio, 1990; Festival Engagements at Vienna Schonbrunn, Barcelona, Brighton, Hong Kong and Edinburgh; Colline and Sparafucile in Rigoletto for Bath and Essex Opera; Wexford Festival, 1994–95, in Rubinstein's The Demon and as Il Cieco in Mascagni's Iris; Further Appearances in Iris at Rome and Munich and with the Chelsea Opera Group; Season 1996–97 with Ramfis in Aida for Norwegian Opera and return to Wexford; Concerts include Elgar's Apostles at Canterbury Cathedral, Rossini's Petite Messe in Strasbourg, Verdi Requiem in Croydon and Mozart's Requiem on Tour to Germany; Creon in Cherubini's Médée and Frederico in Verdi's Battaglia di Legnano (St John's Smith Square and Chelsea Opera Group).

ROCHAIX, François; stage director; b. 2 Aug. 1942, Geneva, Switzer-land. *Education:* University of Geneva, Berliner Ensemble, East Berlin. *Career:* founded the Atelier de Genève, 1963, actor and director; Director of the Théâtre de Carouge, 1975–81; Produced The Turn of The Screw and Death in Venice at Geneva in 1981 and 1983, La Traviata for Opera North in 1985, Cardillac and Parsifal at Berne, 1988–89, Der Ring des Nibelungen, 1985–87, and Die Meistersinger in 1989 at Seattle; Production of Tristan und Isolde for Opéra Lyon in 1990; Dialogues des Carmélites at Geneva, 1993. *Address:* 7 Vy aux Vergnes, 1295 Mies, Switzerland.

ROCHAT, Michel; Conductor; b. 29 Jan. 1931, Switzerland; m. Josette-Marie Rochat, 4 April 1959, 2 d. *Education:* Master's degree, Clarinet, Conservatoires of Lausanne, Geneva, and Paris in class of Maestro Cahuzac; Master's degree, Conducting, Basel Musikakademie. *Career:* Taught Clarinet, Switzerland, 1952; Conducting, Switzerland, 1960; Played Clarinet, Basel Contemporary Music Group, 1968–72; Professor, Director, Conservatoire Supérieur, Lausanne, 1963–83; Guest Con-ductor, Belgium, Bulgaria, Italy, Greece, Romania, Russia, Switzerland, Venezuela, 1976–85; General Music Director, Conductor, Izmir National Symphony Orchestra, Guest Conductor, National Symphony Orchestra, Istanbul, 1982–85; Professor, National Institute of Arts and National Academy of Arts, Taiwan, 1985–; Conductor: Taiwan, Taipei City and Kaohsiung Symphony Orchestras, Taipei Bach Orchestra, Artist's Ensemble, 1985–, Hwa Shing Children's Chorus, 1989–90, Rong Shing Chorus, 1993–96, Asia International Festival for Contemporary Music, 1994, Dan Tie Orchestra, 1995–, Music Camp for Chinese Music, Ilan, 1996, Lan Yang Chinese Ensemble, performing at International Children's Festival and Taipei Chinese Music Festival, 1996, Lan Yan Chinese Ensemble, Taiwanese Opera Ilan, 1996–; Guest Conductor, Taipei Municipal Chinese Orchestra, 1993–, Experimental Chinese Orchestra, Taipei, Taichung and Kaohsiung tours, 1997; mem, Swiss Musicians Association. *Compositions:* Taiwanese operas: 7 words, Kavalan Story, Kavalan Princess, Ataya Song, 1996, 1997, 1998, 1999; Arranged Taiwanese songs; The Mouse Bride Children, Taiwanese Opera, 2000; Hymns for Taoist Association, 2000; Music, Dance and Theater, Opera Ballet, 2001; Improvisation and Dance, flute and piano; Alleluia, choir and brass; Amen for choir, brass and organ; Christmas Songs, choir, brass and organ, 2002. *Recordings:* Masterpieces of Chinese Music, 1995; Chinese Contemporary Music, 1995; Chinese Music for the Young, 1996. *Publications:* To Know Tonality, 1995; Clarinet for Beginners, 1996; Introduction to Conducting, 1996; Rudiments of Intervals and Notation, 1996. *Address:* Route de la Vuy 8, 1305 Penthalaz, Switzerland. *E-mail:* rochat31@freesurf.ch. *Website:* home.kimo.com.tw/mrochat31/index.htm.

ROCHBERG, George; Composer; b. 5 July 1918, Paterson, New Jersey, USA; m. Gene Rosenfeld, 18 Aug 1941, 1 s., 1 d. *Education:* BA, Montclair Teachers College, 1939; Mannes School of Music, 1939–42; BM, Curtis Institute of Music, 1948–54; MA, University of PA, 1949. *Career:* US Army, World War II, Purple Heart; Faculty, Curtis Institute; Director of Publications, Theodore Presser Company, 1951–60; Chair, Music Department, 1960–68, Professor of Composition, 1960–79, Annenberg Professor of Humanities, 1979–, University of Pennsylvania; Work in progress: Chromaticism: Symmetry in Atonal and Tonal Music. *Compositions include:* 6 Symphonies; 5th Symphony commissioned for and premiered by Georg Solti and Chicago Symphony; 6th Symphony commissioned for and premiered by Lorin Maazel and Pittsburgh

Symphony, also in Leningrad, Moscow and Warsaw, 1989; 7 String Quartets, 1952–79; Violin, Oboe and Clarinet Concertos; Piano solos, trios, quartet and quintet; Various chamber works; The Confidence Man, opera, libretto by Gene Rochberg; Clarinet Concerto commissioned by the Philadelphia Orchestra, 1994–95; Circles of Fire, for 2 pianos, 1996–97; Eden : Out of Time and out of Space, chamber concerto for guitar and six players, 1997; Sonata Seria for piano solo, 1998; Three Elegiac Pieces for piano solo, 1998. *Recordings:* Violin Concerto; Oboe Concerto; Black Sounds; Blake Songs; Caprice Variations; Chamber Symphony; La Bocca della Verita; Serenate d'Estate; Tableaux; 12 Bagatelles; Three Piano Trios; String Quartets Nos 3, 4, 5 and 6; Symphony No. 2; Symphony No.5; Restored Version of Violin Concerto; Phaedra. *Publications:* Aesthetics of Survival, 1984, 2004. *Contributions:* Critical Enquiry; New Literary History; Polarity in Music, in Proceedings of the American Philosophical Society, Philadelphia, 1997. *Address:* Dunwoody Village, 3500 West Chester Pike, Newtown Square, PA 19073-4168, USA.

ROCHE, Elizabeth Barbara Winifred, BA; Musicologist and Music Critic; b. 12 March 1948, Southport, England; m. Jerome Roche (deceased), one d. *Education:* Univ. of Durham. *Career:* research on 18th-century German Catholic Church Music with Denis Arnold; research on rise of interest in early music in Britain from 1870 onwards; assisted Jerome Roche's work on 17th-century north Italian church music; mem. Royal Musical Asscn. *Publications:* A Dictionary of Early Music (with Jerome Roche); contrib. to New Grove Dictionary of Music and Musicians, New Oxford Companion to Music, The Musical Times, Early Music. *Address:* 31 Sideling Fields, Tiverton, EX16 4AG, England (home). *Telephone:* (1884) 254051 (home).

ROCHESTER, Marc; Music Journalist, Organist, Conductor and Adjudicator; b. 28 April 1954, London, England; m Magdelene Teresa de Rozario, 1998. *Education:* BMus, MA, PhD, University of Wales, 1972–77; FTCL; ARCM; LRAM. *Career:* Music Critic, Western Mail, 1975–80; Correspondent, Organists review, Musical Times, 1980–89, Independent, 1987–, Gramophone, 1989; Sub-organist, Bangor Cathedral, 1978–80; Organist and Master of Choristers, Londonderry Cathedral, 1980–82; Music Tutor, New University of Ulster, Northern Ireland, 1980–84; Solo Recitalist; Choral Conductor; Examiner, Associated Board, Royal Schools of Music, Trinity College London, Northern Ireland Schools Examinations Council; University of London; Lecturer, Putra University, Malaysia, 1997–99; Programme Co-ordinator and Organist, Dewan Filharmonik Petronas, Kuala Lumpur. *Compositions:* Hymn tunes; Various church music. *Recordings:* Soloist, 20th Century British Organ Music, 1983; Conductor, Hymns of C F Alexander, Derry Cathedral Choir, 1981; Accompanist, Beaufort Male Voice Choir, 1977, 1978, Leila Carewe (soprano), 1980; A European Organ Tour. *Publications:* Frank Martin at Golgotha, 1977; Editor, catalogue, Traditional Welsh Musical Instruments. *Contributions:* Articles on 20th century music. *Address:* 48 Jalan Bayan 4, 47100 Puchong Jaya, Malaysia.

ROCKWELL, John Sargent; Music Critic; b. 16 Sept. 1940, Washington DC, USA. *Education:* BA, Harvard College, 1962; MA, 1964, PhD, 1972, University of California, Berkeley. *Career:* Music and Dance Critic for Oakland Tribune, CA, 1969, and Los Angeles Times, 1970–72; Music Critic for New York Times, 1972–; mem, Past Treasurer, US Music Critics' Association. *Publications:* All American Music: Composition in Late 20th Century, 1983; Sinatra: An American Classic, 1984. *Contributions:* Numerous books and magazines. *Address:* c/o Music Department, New York Times, 229 West 43rd Street, New York, NY 10036, USA.

RODAN, Mendi; Conductor and Professor; b. 17 April 1929, Jassy, Romania; m. Judith Calmanovici, 2 c. *Education:* BMus, MA, Academy of Music, Arts Institute. *Career:* Permanent Conductor for Radio and Television Orchestra, Bucharest, 1953–58; Founder and Permanent Conductor of Jerusalem Chamber Orchestra; Chief Conductor, Music Director, Jerusalem Symphony, 1963–72; Music Director for Israel Sinfonietta, 1977–91; Music Director and Permanent Conductor of Orchestre National Belge, 1983–89; Music Director, IDF Educational Corp Chamber Orchestra, 1990–92; Laureate Conductor of Israel Sinfonietta, 1991–; Associate Conductor, Israel Philharmonic Orchestra, 1993–97; Guest Conductor for Israel Chamber Ensemble, Jerusalem Symphony, Israeli New Opera, Haifa Symphony; Concert tours world-wide with orchestras including Oslo Philharmonic, Vienna Symphony, Berlin Radio Symphony, London Symphony, London Philharmonia, Frankfurt Radio, Stockholm Philharmonic and Berlin Radio Symphony; Adviser at Jerusalem International Music Centre and Head of Jerusalem Academy of Music and Dance, 1985–94; Music Director and Chief Conductor, Israel Symphony Orchestra, 1997–; Member of the International Jury for Composition and Conducting, Poland, Israel, Italy; Professor for Orchestra Conducting and Ensembles at Rochester University, Eastman School of Music Guest appearance in Europe, USA and South America; With the China National Symphony Orchestra and with orchestras in the USA (Toledo,

Passadena, Oklahoma, Bloomington and Rochester) and in Mexico, Venezuela, the Far East and Australia. *Honours:* Order of Distinction, The Republic of Italy; Fr Peleg Prize 1997 Musician of the Year, Israel; Honorary Citizenship of Tuscon Arizona, USA. *Address:* Israel Symphony Orchestra, 16 Jabotinsky, Jerusalem 75229, Israel.

RODDE, Anne-Marie; Singer (Soprano); b. 21 Nov. 1946, Clermont-Ferrand, France. *Education:* Studied at the Conservatory of Clermont-Ferrand and at the Paris Conservatoire with Irene Joachim and Louis Nougera. *Career:* Sang at Aix-en-Provence in 1971 as Amor in Orfeo ed Euridice, Yniold in Pelléas et Mélisande at Paris in 1972, in Cantate Nuptial by Milhaud and The Nightingale by Stravinsky; Sang in Hyppolite et Aricie at Covent Garden, Falstaff, Cherubini's Médée, and Rosenkavalier at Paris Opéra House, Pelléas et Mélisande at Rome Opera House, Pearl Fishers at Stockholm Opera, Magic Flute debut in 1991 at La Bastille Opéra, Magic Flute at Montreal and Bonn Opera; Appearances in Amsterdam in Le nozze di Figaro and at Zürich and Barcelona; Many appearances in the Baroque repertory including London Bach Festival in Les Boréades by Rameau; Other roles include Zerbinetta, Oscar, Nannetta, Ravel's Child and Dirce in Médée, Paris Opéra in 1986; Sang Frasquita in Carmen at Florence, 1993. *Recordings:* Les Indes Galantes by Rameau; Handel's Xerxes; Lully's Le Triomphe d'Alcide; Les Boréades; Honegger's Jeanne d'Arc au Bûcher; Messiah; Songs by Debussy; Avietta di Camera by Rossini; Songs by Widor; Works by Bellini, Donizetti and Gluck.

RODEN, Anthony; Singer (Tenor); b. 19 March 1937, Adelaide, Australia; m. Doreen Roden. *Education:* Associated Australian Insurance Institute; Licenciate, Adelaide Conservatory. *Career:* Debut: Glyndebourne, England; Appearances at Glyndebourne and Netherlands Festivals, English, Welsh and Scottish National Operas, Opera North, Prague National Opera, Krefeld Opera, Victorian State Opera, Covent Garden in Peter Grimes, Freiburg Opera, Hamburg, Madrid and Barcelona; Numerous concerts for BBC, British, Italian and Dutch Orchestras; Sang Samson and Tannhäuser in Melbourne in 1992, Mahler's 8th Symphony, Royal Liverpool Philharmonic Orchestra, and Florestan for Glyndebourne; Mahler, Das Lied von der Erde, Taiwan; Vitek in The Makropulos Case at Glyndebourne, 1995; Sang Vitek at Hamburg, 2000; Principal Tutor, Royal Northern College of Music. *Recordings include:* Britten War Requiem, Dresden Philharmonic Orchestra under Herbert Kegel. *Honours:* John Christie Award, 1971; Opera Prize, Adelaide Conservatory. *Current Management:* Patricia Greenan. *Address:* 33 Castlebar Road, Ealing, London W5 2DJ, England.

RODERICK JONES, Richard (Trevor); Composer, Conductor, Pianist and Musicologist; b. 14 Nov. 1947, Newport, Gwent, Wales; m. Susan Ann Thomason, 1992. *Education:* Associate, Royal College of Music, 1967; Graduate, Royal Schools of Music, 1969; MMus, University of Bristol, 1989. *Career:* Head of Music, South Warwickshire College, Stratford-upon-Avon, 1970–79; Extramural Tutor, University of Birmingham, 1971–79; Musical Director, National Youth Theatre of Wales, 1978–87; Tutor, Welsh College of Music and Drama, 1979–93; Extramural Tutor, University College, Cardiff, 1980–93, 1997–; External Tutor, University of Oxford, 1993–95; Visiting Lecturer, Birmingham Conservatoire, 2001–02; Composer in Residence, Alcester Grammar School, 2002–; Fellow, Royal Society of Arts. *Compositions:* Piano concerto; 3 symphonies; 3 chamber concertos; 3 sinfoniettas; Numerous choral works including oratorio Altus Prosator, Missa Sarum; Numerous chamber works including 2 piano trios, a piano quartet; Stage works including: Me and My Bike, opera (BBC commission); Chanticleer, church opera; Altar Fire, scenic celebration; Game Circle, scenic cantata; Over 30 scores for television and stage. *Honours:* Cobbett Prize, Royal College of Music, 1970. *Address:* 2 Primrose Court, Moreton-in-Marsh, Gloucestershire GL56 0JG, England.

RODESCU, Julian; Singer (Bass); b. 1 May 1953, Bucharest, Romania; m. Barbara Govatos, 4 June 1983. *Education:* BMus, MMus, Juilliard School; Teachers: Giorgio Tozzi, William Glazier, Jerome Hines, Hans Hotter and Daniel Ferro. *Career:* Debut: Plutone in Monteverdi's Il Ballo delle Ingrate with Brooklyn Opera, 1980; Carnegie Hall debut in 1989 with Rostropovich in world premiere of Shostakovich's Rayok; Teatro alla Scala with Riccardo Muti in 1991, Boston Symphony with Seiji Ozawa in Boston Symphony Hall, Carnegie Hall and Tanglewood; Appearances with Miami Opera, New York City Opera, Knoxville Opera, Aachen Stadttheater, Kennedy Center in Washington DC, Alice Tully Hall, WHYY-TV Philadelphia, WQXR, WNCN New York, Central City Opera and Opera Delaware. *Recordings:* Shostakovich's Rayok; Tchaikovsky's Queen of Spades; Bortniansky's Complete Vocal Concerti. *Honours:* Winner of Luciano Pavarotti Competition, 1988. *Current Management:* Ann Summers International. *Address:* 1420 Locust Street, Philadelphia, PA 19102, USA.

RODGERS, Joan, CBE; Singer (Soprano); b. 4 Nov. 1956, Whitehaven, Cumbria, England; m. Paul Daniel, 1988. *Education:* Studied at the

Royal Northern College of Music with Josef Ward and with Audrey Longford. *Career:* Opera debut as Pamina at the 1982 Aix-en-Provence Festival; Engagements at the Ponnelle-Barenboim Mostly Mozart Festival in Paris as Zerlina, and with the English National Opera as Nannetta in Falstaff; Israel Mozart Festival as Susanna and Despina, Turin Opera as Ilia in Idomeneo, Covent Garden debut in 1983 as the Princess in L'Enfant et les Sortilèges and has returned as Xenia in Boris Godunov, Echo in Ariadne auf Naxos, Zerlina in 1988 and Servilia in La Clemenza di Tito in 1989; Glyndebourne debut in 1989 as Susanna in an authentic version of Le nozze di Figaro under Simon Rattle; Promenade Concerts in 1989 as soloist in Mahler's 4th Symphony, featured on BBC television's Omnibus programme; Sang at Munich Opera and Covent Garden, 1990–91 as Pamina, Mélisande in a concert performance at Madrid, Susanna and Despina at the Maggio Musicale and with the Chicago Symphony Orchestra, Mozart's Countess for English National Opera and Handel's Cleopatra for Scottish Opera in 1992; Season 1992 as Yolanta in Tchaikovsky's opera for Opera North at the Edinburgh Festival and as Susanna at Florence; Sang Mélisande for Opera North, 1995; Many recitals and concert appearances in the United Kingdom, including Anne Trulove in The Rake's Progress at the Festival Hall, 1997; Governess in Britten's Turn of the Screw for the Royal Opera, 1997, 2001; Sang Handel's Theodora at the 1997 Glyndebourne Festival and in Mozart's Grabmusik at the Britten Theatre, London, 1998; Sang Blanche in Dialogues des Carmélites for Netherlands Opera; Countess in Figaro, La Monnaie, Brussels, 2001; Ginevra in Ariodante, ENO and Munich, 2000–01. *Recordings:* 3 Da Ponte operas with Barenboim and Berlin Philharmonic; Tchaikovsky, Rachmaninov and Mozart. *Contributions:* People, No. 216, Joan Rodgers: Opera Magazine, Dec 1995. *Honours:* Kathleen Ferrier Memorial Scholarship, 1981; Peter Moores Foundation Scholarship; Royal Philharmonic Society's Award Singer of 1997; Evening Standard Opera Award, 1997. *Current Management:* Ingpen & Williams Ltd, 7 St George's Court, 131 Putney Bridge Road, London, SW15 2PA, England.

RODGERS, Sarah Louise, BA, FRSA; Composer; b. 15 April 1953, Aylesbury, England. *Education:* Walthamstow Hall, Sevenoaks, Nottingham Univ. *Career:* composer 1982–; Chair., Composers' Guild of Great Britain 1992–95; Dir, MCPS 1996–; founding Dir, British Acad. of Composers and Songwriters 1999–; concert chair., British Asscn of Composers and Songwriters 1999–; trustee, British Music Information Centre 1997–. *Compositions:* Spanish Sonata 1990, The Roaring Whirl 1992, Saigyo 1995, The King of the Golden River 2000, The Fire will Blaze Again 2003. *Recordings:* The Roaring Whirl 1995, The King of the Golden River 2000. *Publications:* contrib. to Music Journal (Incorporated Society of Musicians), The Works (British Association of Composers and Songwriters). *Current Management:* Impulse Music Consultants, 18 Hillfield Park, London, N10 3QS, England. *Telephone:* (20) 8444-8587 (office). *Fax:* (20) 8245-0358 (office). *E-mail:* impulse@impulse-music.co.uk (office). *Website:* www.impulse-music.co.uk (office).

RODRIGUEZ, Robert Xavier; Composer; b. 28 June 1946, San Antonio, TX, USA. *Education:* MM, Univ. of Texas, Austin, 1969; DMA, Univ. of California, Los Angeles, 1975; further study with Jakob Druckman at Tanglewood and Nadia Boulanger in Fontainebleau/Paris; master-classes with Elliott Carter and Bruno Maderna at Tanglewood. *Career:* faculty mem., Univ. of Southern California, 1973–75, Univ. of Texas, Dallas, 1975–; Composer-in-Residence, Dallas Symphony Orchestra, 1982–85, San Antonio Symphony Orchestra, 1996–98. *Compositions include:* 2 Piano Trios, 1970, 1971; Canto for soprano, tenor and chamber orchestra, 1973; Favola Concertante for violin, cello and strings, 1975 (revised 1977); Variations for violin and piano, 1975; Transfigurationis Mysteria for soloists, narrator, chorus and orchestra, 1978; Favola Boccaccesca, 1979; Estampie, ballet for orchestra, 1981; Semi-Suite for violin and orchestra, 1981; Suor Isabella, Opera, 1982; Trunks for narrator and orchestra, 1983; Oktoechoes for orchestra, 1983; Seven Deadly Sins for wind ensemble, 1984; Tango, chamber opera, 1985; Varmi'ts! for narrator, chorus and orchestra, 1985; Monkey See, Monkey Do, children's opera, 1986; The Ransoms of Red Chief, children's opera, 1986; A Colorful Symphony for narrator and orchestra, 1987 We the People for narrator, chorus and orchestra, 1987; The old Majestic, opera, 1988; Invocations of Orpheus, trumpet concerto, 1989; A Gathering of Angels for orchestra, 1989; Les Niais Amoureux for chamber ensemble, 1989; Fantasia Lussuriosa for piano, 1989; Ursa: Four Seasons for double bass and orchestra, 1990; Frida, opera, 1991; Pinata for orchestra, 1991; Tango di Tango for orchestra, 1992; The Song of Songs for actor, soprano and chamber ensemble, 1992; Meta 4 for string quartet, 1994; Hot Buttered Rumba for orchestra, 1993; Mascaras for cello and orchestra, 1994; Adoracion Ambulante (Con Flor y Canto), folk celebration for soloists, mariachis, percussion ensemble, chorus and orchestra, 1994; Scrooge for bass-baritone, chorus and orchestra, 1994; Concerto Grosso, 1997; Forbidden Fire for bass-baritone, chorus and orchestra, 1998; Sinfonia à la Mariachi for double orchestra, 1998; Bachanale for orchestra, 1999; The Last Night of Don Juan for actors, singers, dancers, puppets and orchestra, 2000; The

Tempest for actors and orchestra, 2001; Incidental Music for A Midsummer Night's Dream, 2001; Decem Perfectum for wind ensemble, 2002; Flight for narrator and orchestra, 2003. *Honours:* Guggenheim Fellowship, 1976; Prix de Composition Prince Pierre de Monaco, 1971; Prix Lili Boulanger, 1973; Goddard Lieberson Award, American Acad. and Inst. of Arts and Letters, 1980. *Address:* c/o ASCAP, ASCAP Building, 1 Lincoln Plaza, New York, NY 10023; c/o G. Schirmer, 257 Park Avenue South, New York, NY 10010, USA.

ROE, Betty, LRAM, ARCM, ARAM, LTCL, FTCL; Composer and Singer (soprano); b. 30 July 1930, London, England; m. John Bishop (deceased), one s. two d. *Education:* Royal Acad. of Music. *Career:* organist and choirmaster, including Kensington 1958–68, 1978–88; Music Dir, London Acad. of Music and Dramatic Art 1968–78; professional soprano 1962–; John Aldiss Singers, St Clement Dane Chorale; founded NorthKen Chorale; Musical Dir of NorthKen Concerts 1980–; founded Thames Publishing, specializing in English vocal music and books about British composers; festival adjudicator 1960–; Associated Board examiner; mem. Equity, Incorporated Soc. of Musicians, Assoc of Teachers of Singing, Performing Artists' Media Rights Assoc, Assoc of English Singers and Speakers. *Compositions:* four chamber operas, musicals, cantatas, organ music, music theatre entertainments, choral music, piano, flute and other instrumental music, much of it for schools and young people. *Recordings:* Music's Empire, The Music Tree, The Family Tree. *Publications include:* Songs from the Betty Roe Shows (four vols), Pubs are People Places, Serious: Noble Numbers, Music's Empire, Conversation Piece for Horn and Piano. *Address:* 14 Barlby Road, Kensington, London, W10 6AR, England (home). *Telephone:* (20) 8896930 (office). *Fax:* (20) 8896930 (office). *E-mail:* br@robish.fsnet.co .uk (office). *Website:* bettyroe.com (office).

ROEBUCK, Janine; Singer (Mezzo-soprano); b. 1954, England. *Education:* Royal Northern College of Music; Paris Conservatoire with Regine Crespin; National Opera School, London; Studying with Gita Denise. *Career:* Appearances in La Buona Figliola, Buxton; As Rossini's Isabella for Opera 80; Lucille in The Silken Ladder for Scottish Opera; Mozart's Dorabella and Maddalena in Rigoletto for Pavilion Opera; Eduige in Handel's Rodelinda at Batignano; English Bach Festival in Dido and Aeneas and Gluck's Alceste, Monte Carlo and Covent Garden; Operetta with D'Oyly Carte, until 1982, New Sadler's Wells Opera; Shows with Richard Baker and Marilyn Hill Smith and BBC broadcasts; Mahler's Rückertlieder with Scottish Ballet; Concerts in Coventry and Peterborough Cathedrals. *Recordings:* Rodgers and Hammerstein, Love Songs; Kiss Me Kate; The King and I. *Address:* 55A Thorparch Road, London SW8 4SX, England.

ROESEL, Peter; Pianist; b. 2 Feb. 1945, Dresden, Germany; m. Heidrun Bergmann, 1 s., 1 d. *Education:* Completed study with Bazkirov and Oborin, Moscow Conservatory, 1964–69. *Career:* Debut: With Berlin Symphony, 1964; Regular appearances with leading European and American orchestras, 1966–; Performances at major festivals including Salzburg, Berlin, Edinburgh, Prague, London Proms, Hollywood Bowl. *Recordings:* Over 50 including complete concerti by Weber, Beethoven, Schumann and Rachmaninov, complete piano works by Brahms, major piano sonatas by Mozart, Beethoven, Schubert and Schumann, various chamber music works. *Current Management:* Berliner Konzertagentur Monika Ott, Dramburger Str. 46, 12683 Berlin, Germany. *Address:* Malerstr. 25, 01326 Dresden, Germany.

ROGÉ, Pascal; French pianist; b. 6 April 1951, Paris; two s. *Education:* Paris Conservatoire, private studies with Lucette Descaves, Pierre Pasquier and Julius Katchen. *Career:* début Paris 1969, London 1969; specialist in Ravel, Poulenc, Debussy, Satie; soloist with leading orchestras; exclusive recording contract with Decca, London. *Honours:* Premiers Prix for Piano and Chamber Music at the Paris Conservatoire 1966, First Prize Marguerite Long-Jacques Thibaud Int. Competition 1971, Grand Prix du Disque and Edison Award 1984, Gramophone Award for Best Instrumental Recording 1988, Best Chamber Music Recording 1997. *Current Management:* Clarion/Seven Muses, 47 Whitehall Park, London, N19 3TW, England. *Website:* www.c7m.co.uk. *Address:* Lorentz Concerts, 3 rue de la Boétie, 75008 Paris, France; 17 avenue des Cavaliers, 1224 Geneva, Switzerland.

ROGER, David; Stage Designer; b. 1950, England. *Career:* For Opera Factory in London designed La Calisto, The Knot Garden, Osborne premiere of Hell's Angels, Birtwistle premiere of Yan Tan Tethera in 1986, a conflation of Gluck's Iphigenia operas, Ligeti's Adventures and Nouvelles Adventures, Mahagonny Songspiel, Così fan tutte, Don Giovanni, Reimann's The Ghost Sonata and The Marriage of Figaro in 1991; Other work has included Le Grand Macabre by Ligeti at Freiburg, Akhnaten by Philip Glass and The Return of Ulysses at English National Opera, La Bohème for Opera North and Manon Lescaut for Opéra-Comique in Paris; Madama Butterfly at the Albert Hall, 1998. *Address:* c/o English National Opera, St Martin's Lane, London WC2, England.

ROGERS, Lesley-Jane, ARAM; Singer (soprano); b. 25 April 1962, Bristol, England; m. Robin Daniel 1988, 1 step-s., 1 step-d. *Education:* Royal Academy of Music, 1981–85; Harry Farjeon Prize, Harmony, 1982; LRAM (Pianoforte Teachers), 1983; Ella Mary Jacob Prize, Singing, 1983; GRSM Honours, 1984; Greta G M Parkinson Prize, Piano, 1984; LRAM (Singing Teachers), 1985. *Career:* Performed extensively in the fields of oratorio and solo cantatas and is also a contemporary music specialist; Particularly wide oratorio repertoire incorporating standard and unusual works; Hundreds of solo cantatas, especially Bach and Telemann; Performances of contemporary music such as Ligeti's Aventures and Nouvelles Aventures; Several world premieres, including Fédélé's La chute de la maison Usher with Ensemble Intercontemporain; mem, Life Member, National Early Music Association; British Actors' Equity Association. *Recordings:* Handel Tamerlano (highlights), role of Asteria, European Community Baroque Orchestra, director Roy Goodman, TéléDiffusion de France, live recording, 1990; Caldara Madrigals and Cantatas, Wren Baroque Soloists, 1992; Caldara Motets, Wren Baroque Soloists, 1994; Peter Maxwell Davies Resurrection, role of electronic soprano, BBC Philharmonic Orchestra, conductor Davies, 1994; Peerson Private Musicke, Wren Baroque Soloists, 1994; Carl Rütti Choral Music, conductor Stephen Jackson, BBC Symphony Chorus, 1995; Percy Grainger, Jungle Book, The Love Song of Har Dyal, Choir and Orchestra of Polyphony, Hyperion, 1996; Sadie Harrison, Taking Flight, 2000; The Soprano Sings Schubert Lieder, piano Christopher Ross, 2002; Julia Usher Sacred Physic, 2002; Celtic Magic, recorders John Turner, piano Keith Swallow, 2003. *Address:* The Old Rectory Coach House, High Street, Bourton-on-the-Water, Gloucestershire GL54 2AP, England. *Telephone:* (1451) 821481. *E-mail:* info@lesleyjanerogers.demon.co.uk. *Website:* www.lesleyjanerogers.demon.co.uk.

ROGERS, Nigel David, BA, MA; British singer (tenor), conductor and teacher; b. 21 March 1935, Wellington, Shropshire, England. *Education:* King's Coll., Cambridge, private musical tuition in Rome and Milan, Hochschule für Musik, Munich. *Career:* began professional career with quartet, Studio der Frühen Musik, 1961; operatic debut at Amsterdam in 1969; sang in Monteverdi's Ulisse and Orfeo under Harnoncourt at Vienna and Amsterdam, 1971, 1976, Poppea at Amsterdam under Leonhardt in 1972 and Il Combattimento at Milan under Berio in 1973; sang in British premiere of Arden Must Die by Goehr at Sadler's Wells in 1974 and the title role in Handel's Teseo at Warsaw in 1977; conducting from 1985; directed and sang in the serenata La Gloria di Primavera by Alessandro Scarlatti, 1996. *Recordings:* some 70 recordings, including Monteverdi's 1610 Vespers and Orfeo, John Dowland Lute Songs, 1988, Sigismondo d'India, 1991, Florentine Intermedi of 1589, Dido and Aeneas, Songs of Henry Lawes, 1994; Symphonie Sacrae of Schütz, 1995; Monteverdi, Vespers of 1610, 1996. *Contributions:* various magazines and academic publications; Chapter on Voice, in Companion to Baroque Music, 1991. *Honours:* Hon. RCM 1980. *Address:* 13 Victoria Road, Deal, Kent CT14 7AS, England (home).

ROGG, Lionel; Organist and Composer; b. 21 April 1936, Geneva, Switzerland; m. Claudine Effront, 1957, 3 s. *Education:* Geneva Conservatory; Piano with Nikita Magaloff; Organ with Pierre Segond. *Career:* Complete Bach organ works in 10 recitals, Victoria Hall, Geneva, 1961; Concerts (organ, harpsichord) world-wide; Interpretative courses, USA, the United Kingdom, Switzerland, Austria, Japan, Italy. *Compositions include:* Organ: 12 chorales; Variations, Psalm 91, 1983; Introduction, ricercare, toccata; Cantata, Geburt der Venus; Also: Face à face, 2 pianos; Missa Brevis, chorus and orchestra; Concerto for organ and orchestra, 1992. *Recordings:* Complete Bach organ works; Art of Fugue; Complete Buxtehude organ works; Rogg Plays Reger; Rogg Plays Rogg (organ compositions); Du Mage, Clérambault. *Publications:* Improvisation Course for Organists. *Honours:* Grand Prix du Disque, 1970; Deutscher Schallplatten Preis, 1980; Doctor honoris causa, University of Geneva. *Address:* 38A route de Troinex, 1234 Vessy, Geneva, Switzerland.

ROGLIANO, Marco; Violinist; b. 26 Nov. 1967, Rome, Italy; m. Ciccozzi Antonella, 1 s. *Education:* Conservatory Santa Cecilia, Rome; Mozarteum of Salzburg; Academy W Stauffer. *Career:* Debut: Helsingborg Concert Hall Playing Sibelius Violin Concerto fo 47 with the Helsingborg Symphony Orchestra, 1989; Casals Hall, Tokyo, 1991, Paris, 1993, Moscow, 1993; With the Radio Symphonic Orchestra of Moscow, 1994; Milan, 1995; Rome, 1996; Munich, 1997; Numerous Radio and Television Appearances in France, Bulgaria, Sweden. *Recordings:* Salvatore Sciarrino, 1947; 6 Caprieei for Solo Violin, 1976; Angelo Ragazzi; 3 Violin Concertos; Franz Adolf Berwald; The Violin Concerto. *Contributions:* Musical Journals and Magazines. *Address:* Lorenzo il Mgnifico 15, 06162 Rome, Italy.

ROGNER, Heinz; Conductor; b. 1929, Leipzig, Germany. *Education:* Studied composition and piano with Egon Boelsche and Hugo Steuer in Leipzig. *Career:* Repetiteur and Conductor at the German National Theatre in Weimar; Teacher, Leipzig Musikhochschule, 1954–58; Principal Conductor for Great Leipzig Radio Orchestra, 1959–63; General Musical Director, Deutsche Staatsoper Berlin, 1962–73; Chief Conductor of the Berlin Radio Symphony Orchestra, 1973 with tours to Eastern Europe, Austria, Sweden, France, Belgium, Switzerland, Germany and Japan; Regular Guest Conductor for Yomiuri Nippon Symphony Orchestra from 1978, Principal Conductor, 1984. *Recordings:* Strauss Horn Concertos; Weber's Abu Hassan and Eine Nacht in Venedig, with the Dresden Staatskapelle; Trumpet Concertos by Torelli, Grossi, Fasch and Albinoni; Schubert's 7th Symphony, arranged by Weingartner, and 9th Symphony; Reger's Romantic Suite and Symphonic Prologue; Beethoven's Cantata on the Accession of Leopold II, Die Glorreiche Augenblick and Vestas Feuer; Strauss's Duet Concertino and Preludes to Palestrina by Pfitzner. *Honours:* National Prize, 1975; Gerhardt Eusler Gold Plakette, 1979; Professor, 1981.

ROGOFF, Ilan; Israeli concert pianist and conductor; b. 26 July 1943, s. of Boris Rogoff and Sofija Rogoff; m. Vesna Zorka Mimiça 1985; two d. *Education:* Israel Acad. of Music, Royal Conservatoire, Brussels, Mannes Coll., Juilliard School, New York. *Career:* has played all over Israel, Europe, N. America, Latin America, S. Africa, Japan and Far East with Israel Philharmonic Orchestra and many other orchestras; plays mostly works by Romantic composers including Beethoven, Schumann, Brahms, Chopin, Liszt, César Franck, Rachmaninov, Tchaikovsky, Piazzolla; has performed twentieth-century and contemporary works including world premiere of concerti by John McCabe and by Ivan Erod; has performed with various chamber music groups including Enesco Quartet, Orpheus Quartet, Amati Trio, Festival Ensemble, Matrix Quartet, soloists of Vienna Chamber Orchestra and Vienna Philharmonic Orchestra; conducting début 1985, with Israel Philharmonic 1988; radio performances and TV appearances in UK, Spain, Austria, Germany, Israel, Canada, USA, SA, Colombia, Ecuador, Venezuela and Argentina; lectures and recital/lectures, masterclasses; Trustee Tel-Aviv Museum; f. Ilan Rogoff Foundation, Colombia to provide medical care to children of poor families. *Recordings include:* Chopin in Mallorca, Chopin Concerti (version for piano and string quintet), Portraits by Schumann, numerous works by Bach–Busoni, César Franck, Schumann, Schubert, Chopin, Beethoven and Liszt, transcriptions for piano solo of works by Astor Piazzolla. *Publications:* Transcriptions for Piano Solo of Works by Astor Piazzolla, Ed Two Chopin Concerti for Piano and String Quartet; articles on music published in Scherzo magazine (Madrid). *Honours:* various int. awards. *Address:* Estudio/Taller, Calle Bartomeu Fons 13, 07015 Palma de Mallorca, Spain. *Telephone:* (71) 707016. *Fax:* (71) 707703. *E-mail:* ilanrogoff@telefonica.net. *Website:* www.infonegocio.com/ilanrogoff.

ROGOSIC, Marko; Composer and University Professor of Music; b. 6 April 1941, Podgorica, Yugoslavia. *Education:* History of Arts and Philosophy; BA, MA in Music, Musical Academy in Belgrade; Specialisations and study tours throughout Europe including London, Paris and Moscow. *Career:* Professor of Music; Chief Editor, first Montenegrin Musical Herald; President, Association of Composers of Montenegro; mem, League of Composers' Association of Yugoslavia; President, Montenegrin Association of Composers. *Compositions:* Seashore Water-Colour for clarinet and piano; Sonata in C-minor for piano; Sonata Fantasy for violin and piano; Concerto for contrabass and orchestra; Shepperds' Game for oboe or violin and piano; Suite for flute and fiddlers; Music for ballet Vladimir and Kosara. *Recordings:* Sonata for Piano; Concerto for Contrabass and Orchestra; Seashore Water-Colour. *Publications:* Methodics of Music Education, reader for students, 1981; Monograph of Association of Composers, 1996; Anthology of Soloist and Chamber Music of Montenegrin Composers, 1998. *Contributions:* Numerous in professional journals. *Address:* Dahna 15, 81000 Podgorica, Serbia and Montenegro.

ROHAN, Jiri; Double Bass Player; b. 11 Jan. 1965, Prague, Czechoslovakia; m. Dana Skrovankova, 13 June 1992, 1 d. *Education:* Conservatory, Prague; Academy of Music, Prague; 10 years Piano Studies, Art Academy, Prague; 6 years Double Bass Study, Prague Conservatory; 4 years Double Bass Studies, Academy of Music, Prague. *Career:* Debut: Solo Concert with Symphony Orchestra, Prague, 1985; Czech Philharmonic Orchestra, 1983–85; Suk Chamber Orchestra, 1988–91; Munich Philharmonic Orchestra, 1990; Czech String Ensemble, 1992; Prague String Quintet, 1993–97; Osaka Symphonic, 1994. *Recordings:* Over 40 CDs with Several Symphonic Orchestras; Over 10 CDs with Suk Chamber Orchestra; 2 CDs with Czech String Ensemble; 3 CDs with Prague String Quintet; CD with Czech Chamber Orchestra. *Publications:* Psychological Aspects of Music Listening, 1993. *Address:* Mahenova 168/7, 150 00 Prague 5, Czech Republic.

ROHNER, Ruth; Singer (Soprano); b. 18 Sept. 1935, Zürich, Switzerland. *Education:* Studied in Winterhur and Amsterdam. *Career:* Sang at the Opera of Biel-Solothurn, 1960–61, Vienna Kammeroper, 1960–62 and engaged at Zürich opera from 1962 notably in the premieres of Sutermeister's Madame Bovary in 1967 and Kelterborn's Ein Engel Kommt Nach Babylon in 1977; Many performances in the lyric and coloratura repertory and in the first local performances of Burkhard's Ein Stern Geht auf Jakob and Krenek's Karl V; Guest engagements at Berne, Basle, the State Operas of Hamburg and Munich, Düsseldorf, Strasbourg, Helsinki and Châtelet Paris; Festival appearances at Lausanne, Wiesbaden and Athens; Noted concert artist in oratorio and lieder. *Address:* c/o Zürich Opera, 8008 Zürich, Switzerland.

ROHRL, Manfred; Singer (Bass); b. 12 Sept. 1935, Augsburg, Germany. *Education:* Studied at the Augsburg Conservatory and with Franz Kelch and Margarethe von Winterfeld. *Career:* Debut: Augsburg in 1958 as Masetto; Member of the Deutsche Oper Berlin notably in the 1965 premiere of Der Junge Lord by Henze; Guest appearances in Brussels, Nancy, Düsseldorf, Geneva, Zürich, Zagreb and Edinburgh; Netherlands Opera in 1984 as Leporello; Sang Waldner in Arabella at the Deutsche Oper Berlin in 1988, and Dr Kolenaty in The Makropulos Case in 1989; Many performances in the buffo repertory; Sang Taddeo in L'Italiana in Algeri with the Deutsche Oper in 1992; Mozart's Bartolo at Glyndebourne, 1994; Sang Bartolo at the Deutsche Oper, 2000. *Recordings:* Various. *Address:* c/o Deutsche Oper Berlin, Richard Wagnerstrasse 10, 1000 Berlin 1, Germany.

ROJAS, Rafael; Singer (Tenor); b. 15 Sept. 1962, Guadalaja, Mexico. *Education:* University of Guadalajara, Royal Scottish Academy and Northern College of Music. *Career:* Student roles included the Duke of Mantua, Manrico, Tamino, Rodolfo, Roberto Devereux and Ernani; Engagements in Guadalajara City and Mexico City; US Debut as Alfredo in Traviata, Seattle, followed by Rafael Ruiz in El Gato Montes for Washington Opera; Concerts include the Verdi Requiem with the Jerusalem Symphony Orchestra and the Hallé Orchestra; Lambeth Palace, London, Monmouth Cathedral, and the Glasgow Mayfest; Season 1997–98 as La Vida Breve at Nice, Pinkerton for Glimmerglass Opera, USA, Werther at Boston, Rodolfo and Nemorino at Seattle and Verdi's Macduff for Houston Opera; Season 2002–02 as Alfredo at Boston, Riccardo at Bregenz, Dick Johnson for Opera Zuid and Rodolfo at Melbourne; Don Carlos in Leipzig and Cavaradossi for Opera North. *Honours:* Domingo Prize at 1995 Placido Domingo Competition. *Address:* c/o IMG Artists, Lovell House, 616 Chiswick High Road, London W4 5RX, England.

ROLAND, Claude-Robert; Conductor, Organist and Composer; b. 19 Dec. 1935, Pont-de-Loup, Belgium; m. Anne-Marie Girardot, 6 Sept 1963, 1 s. *Education:* Athénée Royal; Academy of Music, Châtelet; Conservatories in Liège, Paris, Brussels, with Messiaen and Defossez. *Career:* Organist, Notre Dame Church, Wasmes, 1955–63, and Basilica Charleroi, 1963–67; Professor, Brussels Conservatory, 1972–; Organist: Works of Hoyoul, Lohet, Dumont, Buston, Schlick, Froidebise, Guillaume, Quatrefages; Conductor: Satie, Prokofiev, Guillaume, RTBF. *Compositions:* Over 100 works including Demain seulement, on poems by Alain Grandbois; Preludes, piano, 1962; Rossignolet du bois, orchestra, 1971; Rondeau, organ, 1979; Thriller, trumpet and piano, 1984; Datura 281, piano, 1987; Ricordanza, bass-clarinet and piano, 1989; Music for Molière, Labiche, Turgenev and Ghelderode. *Recordings:* Compositeurs Liegeois, organ; Alpha; Musique Au Chateau, organ and brass; Musica Magna. *Publications:* Orgues en Hainaut, 1966. *Contributions:* Musique Vivante; Feuillets du Spantole; Hainaut-Tourisme, UWO. *Address:* 59 Rue Lebeau, 1000 Brussels, Belgium.

ROLANDI, Gianna; Singer (Soprano); b. 16 Aug. 1952, New York, USA; m. Andrew Davis. *Education:* Studied with her mother and with Ellen Faull and Max Rudolf. *Career:* Debut: Sang Offenbach's Olympia in Les Contes d'Hoffmann at the New York City Opera in 1975; Metropolitan Opera in 1979 as Sophie, later singing Olympia, Stravinsky's Nightingale and Zerbinetta; Glyndebourne debut in 1981 as Zerbinetta returning in 1984 as Zdenka in Arabella and Susanna; English National Opera in 1983 as Cleopatra in Giulio Cesare; San Diego in 1984 as Ophelia in Hamlet by Thomas; Sang Lucia di Lammermoor at San Francisco in 1986, and Curiazio in a performance of Cimarosa's Gli Orazi e i Curizai, to mark the 200th anniversary of the French Revolution, at Rome Opera in 1989; Other roles include Gilda, the Queen of Night and parts in operas by Donizetti at the New York City Opera; Sang Despina at Chicago, 1993; Concert tour of the USA with the BBC Symphony Orchestra, 1996. *Address:* c/o Teatro dell'Opera, Piazzo Beniamino Gigli 8, 00184 Rome, Italy.

ROLFE JOHNSON, Anthony; Singer (tenor); b. 5 Nov. 1940, Tackley, Oxfordshire, England. *Education:* Guildhall School of Music, London. *Career:* Debut: With the English Opera Group in 1973 in Tchaikovsky's Iolanta; European career from 1977 as Lensky and Mozart's Titus with Netherlands Opera, Hamburg State Opera, La Scala as Mozart's Lucio Silla and in Geneva and at the Edinburgh Festival as Aschenbach in Death in Venice; With English National Opera roles have included Tamino, Ferrando, Monteverdi's Ulysses, Britten's Male Chorus and Essex; Sang Jupiter in Semele at Covent Garden; US concerts with Chicago Symphony under Solti, Boston Symphony Orchestra under Ozawa, New York Philharmonic under Rostropovich and the Cleveland

Orchestra under Rattle; Other conductors include Marriner, Norrington, Boulez, Haitink, and Abbado; Salzburg debut in 1987 in Schmidt's Das Buch mit Sieben Siegeln, returning in 1991 in title role in Idomeneo; Season 1992–93 as Monteverdi's Ulisse and Orfeo for ENO, Lucio Silla at Salzburg, Oronte in a new production of Handel's Alcina at Covent Garden, Peter Grimes in the first season of the reopened Glyndebourne Opera and Aschenbach at the Metropolitan, 1994; Male Chorus in The Rape of Lucretia, Glyndebourne, 1996; Grimes with the Royal Opera at Savonlinna, 1998; Sang Polixenes in the premiere of Wintermärchen by Boesmans, Brussels 1999; Oedipus Rex at Antwerp, and in Handel's Tamerlano at Drottningholm, 2000. *Recordings:* Handel's Acis and Galatea; Saul, Hercules, Jephtha, Alexander's Feast, Esther, Solomon, Semele and Messiah; Mozart's Lo Sposo Deluso; Haydn's Il Mondo della Luna and Stabat Mater; Mozart's Apollo et Hyacinthus and La Finta Semplice, from the Salzburg Mozartwoche; Bach's St John and St Matthew Passion; Mozart's Zauberflöte, La Clemenza di Tito, Idomeneo; Haydn's Creation, Seasons, Peter Grimes, Samson, Oedipus Rex, Orfeo, War Requiem. *Current Management:* Askonas Holt Ltd, Lonsdale Chambers, 27 Chancery Lane, London, WC2A 1PF, England. *Telephone:* (20) 7400-1700. *Fax:* (20) 7400-1799. *E-mail:* info@askonasholt.co.uk. *Website:* www.askonasholt.co.uk.

ROLL, Michael; Pianist; b. 17 July 1946, Leeds, England; m. Juliana Markova, 1 s. *Education:* Piano studies with Fanny Waterman. *Career:* Debut: Royal Festival Hall in 1958 playing Schumann Concerto with Malcolm Sargent; Regular appearances with major British orchestras; Played at Hong Kong Festival with London Philharmonic and toured Japan with the BBC Symphony; Also toured Netherlands, Germany, Switzerland, Spain and Eastern Europe; Tours of Russia and Scandinavia in recital and with orchestra; Conductors include Boulez, Giulini, Leinsdorf, and Previn; Visits to Aldeburgh, Bath, Edinburgh, Granada and Vienna Festivals; US debut in 1974 with Boston Symphony Orchestra conducted by Colin Davis; 1987–88 season with recitals in Milan, East Berlin, Dresden, Leipzig and London; Prof. Folkwang Hochschule, Essen, Germany 1987; 1988–89 season with London Symphony, Scottish National, Hallé, Bournemouth Symphony, Helsinki Philharmonic and Hong Kong Philharmonic Orchestras; Recitals in London, Milan, Leipzig, Berlin and Dresden; Played concertos in the 1990 Promenade Concerts, with Kurt Masur in Leipzig and London and Valery Gergiev in Leningrad and the United Kingdom; 1991–92 season played concertos with Skrowaczewski and the Hallé, BBC Philharmonic, BBC Scottish Orchestras and Leipzig Gewandhaus, recitals in the International Piano Series at the Queen Elizabeth Hall and at the Klavierfestival Ruhr in Germany with Helsinki Philharmonic under Comissiona, for the English Chamber Orchestra at the Barbican and his New York debut recital in 1992; performed complete cycle of Beethoven piano concertos with London Mozart Players, Barbican 1995; Cologne Philharmonic Orchestra (debut) 2002; Major Australian tour 2002. *Recordings include:* Beethoven Piano Concertos (complete cycle). *Current Management:* Terry Harrison Artists Management, The Orchard, Market Street, Charlbury, Oxfordshire OX7 3PJ, England. *Telephone:* (1608) 810330. *Fax:* (1608) 811331. *E-mail:* artists@terryharrison.force9.co.uk.

ROLLAND, Sophie; cellist; b. 18 July 1963, Montreal, Canada. *Education:* Conservatoire de Musique du Quebéc, Montreal with Walter Joachim, studied with Nathaniel Rosen in New York, Pierre Fournier in Geneva and William Pleeth in London. *Career:* debut with Montreal Symphony Orchestra under Charles Dutoit, 1982; regular appearances throughout Canada with all major orchestras including the Montreal, Toronto and Vancouver Symphony Orchestras; Toured in USA, France, Spain, England, Wales, Germany, Switzerland, Bulgaria, Hungary, Yugoslavia, Finland and China; Frequent guest at international chamber music festivals including Kuhmo, Dubrovnik and Parry Sound; Duo partnership with pianist, Marc-André Hamelin since 1988; 1990–91 season includes Beethoven cycle in New York at Carnegie Hall in 1991, Washington DC, Montreal with broadcast for CBC, and in London at Wigmore Hall in 1991 and broadcast for BBC; Plays a 1674 cello by Petrus Ranta of Brescia. *Honours:* Premier Prix à l'Unamanité Montreal; Study awards from the Canadian and Quebec Governments; Prix d'Europe, Canada; 1st Prize, Du Maurier Competition; Virginia P Moore Prize, Canada Arts Council, 1985. *Address:* 27 Cleveland Avenue, London W4 1SN, England.

ROLOFF, Elisabeth, BA, MA; concert organist; b. 18 Feb. 1937, Bielefeld, Germany. *Education:* Berlin High School of Music, Bremen Conservatory of Music, Cologne High School of Music, Royal College of Music, London. *Career:* Organist and Choirmaster, Christ Church, Hannover, Germany, 1968–74; Titular Organist, German Church, Paris, France, 1974–82; Concerts throughout Europe, Israel and USA; Faculty, Rubin Academy of Music, Jerusalem, Israel, 1983–; Titular Organist, Redeemer Church, Jerusalem, 1983–; Main Appearances: Europe: Alte Oper, Frankfurt; Royal Festival Hall, London; King's College Chapel, Cambridge, England; St Ouen, Rouen; Notre Dame, La Madeleine, Chartres

Cathedral, France; Switzerland, Italy, Hungary, Romania; USA; Boston, Salt Lake City, Philadelphia; Russia: St Petersburg; Volgograd; International Organ Festivals: Bach Organ Festival, Jerusalem; Sorø, Denmark; Orléans, France; Tallinn, Estonia; Riga, Latvia; Prague, Kiev, São Paulo, Montevideo, Buenos Aires; Mexico; Radio appearances: Germany, Israel, Norway; mem, Association Jehan Alain; Internationale Mendelssohn-Stiftung, eV. *Recordings:* Organ works by Pachelbel, Buxtehude, J. S. Bach and Mozart; Organ Landscape Jerusalem. *Honours:* Decree of International Letters for Cultural Achievement, 1996. *Current Management:* International Music Consultants, PO Box 45401, Tel-Aviv 61453, Israel. *Address:* 28, Ha-Palmah Street, Jerusalem 92542, Israel.

ROLOFF, Roger (Raymond); Singer (Baritone); b. 22 Feb. 1947, Peoria, Illinois, USA; m. Barbara A Petersen, 19 Mar 1982. *Education:* BA, magna cum laude, English, IL Wesleyan University, 1969; MA, Illinois State University, 1972; Graduate study in English, SUNY, Stony Brook; Private voice study with Sam Sakarian, New York City, 1975–; Vocal and Dramatic coaching with teachers including Hans Hotter. *Career:* Debut: Deertrees Opera Theatre, Maine, 1975; Operatic roles include Wotan and Wanderer in The Ring, Jochanaan in Salome, and Ruprecht in Prokofiev's Fiery Angel; Appearances with English National Opera, Deutsche Oper Berlin, Seattle, Kentucky, Dallas, San Diego and New York City Operas, Niederschsische Staatsoper Hannover, Hawaii Opera Theater, Houston Grand Opera and major orchestras in USA and Canada; Concert appearances in Milwaukee, Boston, Los Angeles, Germany and Switzerland; Sang the Dutchman in a concert performance of Der fliegende Holländer at Boston in 1990, and Telramund in Lohengrin at Nice in 1990. *Address:* International Music Consultants, PO Box 45401, Tel-Aviv 61453, Israel.

ROLTON, Julian; Pianist; b. 1965, England. *Career:* Co-founded the Chagall Piano Trio at the Banff Centre for The Arts in Canada, resident artist; Debut concert at the Blackheath Concert Halls in London, 1991; Further appearances at Barbican's Prokofiev Centenary Festival, Warwick Festival and the South Place Sunday Concerts at Conway Hall in London; Purcell Room recitals in 1993 with the London premiere of Piano Trios by Tristan Keuris, Nicholas Maw and Dame Ethel Smyth, composed 1880; Premiere of Piano Trio No. 2 by David Matthews at Norfolk and Norwich Festival in 1993; Engaged for Malvern Festival in 1994. *Address:* South Bank Centre, c/o Press Office (Pamela Chowhan Management), London SE1, England.

ROMANENKO), Yelena; Singer (Mezzo-Soprano); b. 1951, Kharkov, Russia. *Education:* Studied at the Institute of Arts at Kharkov. *Career:* Participated in the foundation of an opera programme with the State Opera Company of Kharkov; Many performances in Russia and on tour in Europe and America, as Santuzza, Azucena, Eboli, Carmen, Dalila and Marfa in Khovanshchina; British debut on tour with the National Opera of the Ukraine in 1995, as Marina in Boris Godunov and Fenena in Nabucco; Concert recitalist in German, Czech and Russian works. *Address:* c/o Sonata Ltd, 11 North Park Street, Glasgow G20 7AA, Scotland.

ROMANOVA, Nina; Mezzo-Soprano; b. 1946, Leningrad, Russia. *Education:* Studied with Vera Sopina at Leningrad Academy of Music. *Career:* Performed at Pushkin Theatre in Kishinov then from 1976 member of the Maly Theatre Leningrad, now St Petersburg; Roles have included Rosina in Barber of Seville, Azucena in Il Trovatore, Eboli in Don Carlo, Lady Macbeth, Carmen, Olga in Eugene Onegin, The Countess and Polina in The Queen of Spades, Marina in Boris Godunov and Marfa in Mussorgsky's Khovanshchina; Concerts include Alexander Nevsky by Prokofiev in Verona, St Matthew Passion, St John Passion, Mass in B minor by Bach, Mozart's Requiem, Verdi's Requiem, and Mahler's 2nd and 8th Symphonies; Guest performances with St Petersburg Mussorgsky State Academic Opera and Ballet Theatre, formerly Leningrad Maly Theatre, as member of the Opera Company; Sang in Italy at Palermo, Modena, Reggio Emilia, Parma, Ferrara, Ravenna and Catania, in France at Paris, Cannes and Nantes, New York and in Japan at Tokyo, Osaka, Hiroshima and Iokogama, Greece, Portugal and Netherlands; Sang in Rimsky's Invisible City of Kitezh at Bregenz, 1995. *Address:* Maly Opera and Ballet Theatre, St Petersburg, Russia.

ROMBOUT, Ernest; Dutch oboist; *Professor of Oboe, Conservatory of Music, Utrecht;* b. 30 Aug. 1959; m. Anne-Lou Langendyk 1995; one s. one d. *Education:* Staatliche Hochschule für Musik, Freiburg, Germany and studied with Heinz Holliger. *Career:* debut at Concertgebouw, Amsterdam 1983; soloist in major halls in Amsterdam, Berlin, Moscow, Munich, Lisbon, Paris, Zürich; festivals include Biennale of Venice, Donaueschinger Musiktage, Ludwigsburger Festspiele, Festival of New Music Middelburg, Takefu Festival, Japan, Summer Festival, Avignon, Summer Festival, Los Angeles; Prof. of Oboe, Conservatory of Music, Utrecht 1985–; masterclasses and workshops in Netherlands, Russia, Austria and Liechtenstein 1993–; mem. of jury, Int. Oboe Competition (CIEM), Geneva 1998. *Recordings:* solo: Oboe Concertos, Haydn,

Mozart, Theme and Variations by J N Hummel with the Concertgebouw Chamber Orchestra; Oboe Concertos by L Francesconi, D del Puerto; Omaggio all'Opera Lirica, arrangements of works by Rossini, Bellini, Donizetti, Verdi and others for oboe and harp with harpist Erika Waardenburg. *Honours:* Prize Winner Ancona Competition of Winds, Italy 1979. *Address:* Oude Eemnesserstraat 34, 1221 HL Hilversum, Netherlands. *E-mail:* erombout@tiscali.nl.

ROMERO, Angel; classical guitarist and conductor; b. 17 Aug. 1946, Malaga, Spain; one s. two d. *Education:* studied guitar with Celedonio Romero, conducting with Soltan Rushnia, Eugene Ormandy, Morton Gould, Ather Fiedler. *Career:* debut, Lobero Theatre, Santa Barbara, California, 1958; First classical guitarist to perform at the Hollywood Bowl at West Coast premiere of Joaquin Rodrigo's Concerto de Aranjuez with the Los Angeles Philharmonic; Performances with the Boston Symphony, Chicago Symphony, Philadelphia Orchestra, New York Philharmonic, Cleveland Orchestra, Orquesta National de Espana, Berlin Philharmonic, Concertgebouw-Amsterdam; Halls include Carnegie Hall, Musikverein-Vienna, Orchestra Hall, Chicago; Performed for both Presidents Jimmy Carter and Richard Nixon, also the Pope at the Vatican; Television appearances include the celebration of the 500th anniversary of Columbus' discovery at the United Nations with the Orquesta National de Espana, 1992; Also with Arther Fiedler and the Boston Pops; Performed with conductors including Eugene Ormandy, Raymond Leppard, Neville Mariner, Jesús López Cobos, Rafael Frühbeck de Burgos, Eduardo Mata, Giuseppe Patanè, Morton Gould, André Previn; Conducted the Academy of St Martin-in-the-Fields, Pittsburgh Symphony Orchestra, San Diego Symphony Orchestra. *Compositions:* movie score for Bienvenido-Welcome. *Recordings:* Guitar Concertos; Concerto de Aranjuez; Giuliani Guitar Concertos; Vivaldi Concertos; Villa Lobos and Schifrin Guitar Concertos; Touch of Class; Angel Romero plays Bach; Granados 12 Spanish Dances. *Honours:* Mexican Academy Award (Ariel) for best original score. *Address:* c/o Konzertveranstaltungen Andreas Schlessl, Postfach 810952, 81909, Munich, Germany.

ROMERO, Angelo; Singer (Bass-baritone); b. 30 May 1940, Cagliari, Sardinia. *Education:* Studied in Rome. *Career:* Debut: Opera di Camera, Rome, as Monteverdi's Orfeo, 1966; Appearances throughout Italy, including Rome, Milan and Verona Arena (1982); Raimbaud in Le Comte Ory at Venice, 1988, Dandini in Cenerentola at Parma, 1990, and Geronimo in Il Matrimonio Segreto at Lausanne, 1993; Further guest appearances at Buenos Aires, Cincinnati, Geneva and Aix-en-Provence; Sang Cimarosa's Maestro di Capella for Rome Opera, 2001. *Recordings include:* Le Maschere by Mascagni; Donizetti's Gianni di Parigi. *Address:* c/o Opera de Lausanne, PO Box 3972, 1002 Lausanne, Switzerland.

ROMERO, Patricia; Pianist; b. 20 Sept. 1953, Mexico City, Mexico; m. David Hanesworth; one s. *Education:* Conservatorio Nacional de Música, Mexico City, 1965–72; Trinity Coll., London, 1972–76; studies with Louis Kentner, 1976–85. *Career:* debut, Wigmore Hall, London, June 1976; performed widely in the UK, Spain, Switzerland, Italy, France, Greece and the Middle East; London appearances: Purcell Room, Wigmore Hall, Fairfield Halls, St John's Smith Square, Leighton House; performances with Orquesta Sinfonia del Bajio, Orquesta de la Universidad de Guadalajara, Orquesta Sinfonia de Coyoacan; radio broadcasts in Mexico City, Guadalajara and for the BBC; performed complete piano works of Maurice Ravel at the Purcell Room, London, July 1994; tours of Australia, New Zealand, Scandinavia and Russia, 1998; tours of Argentina and Brazil, 1999; concert with the Philharmonic of the University of Hertfordshire, 1999; tour of Turkey, Greece, Italy, France and Spain, 2000, Spain and the Canary Islands, 2001; concerts in the Arcadia and Oriana, 2002; mem., European Piano Teachers Asscn (UK), Incorporated Society of Musicians (Performers Section); ILAMS. *Honours:* First Prize Yamaha, 1971; Maud Seton Pianist Prize, London, 1975. *Current Management:* Maureen Lunn Management, Top Farm, Parish Lane, Hedgesley, Buckinghamshire, SL2 3JH, England. *Address:* 114 Woodcote Grove Road, Coulsdon, Surrey CR5 2AF, England.

ROMERO, Pepe; classical guitarist; b. 8 March 1944, Malaga, Spain. *Education:* studied classical and flamenco styles with his father. *Career:* moved to USA 1958 and joined family guitar quartet, giving some 3,000 concerts in America, Australia, South America and Europe from 1970; Solo European tour in 1982 followed by performances in Rome, Madrid, Budapest, Stockholm, Amsterdam, Paris, Vienna, Berlin, London and Copenhagen; Festival appearances at Osaka, Bergen, Istanbul, Rome and Luxembourg; Has premiered the Concerto Andalou and the Concierto Para una Festa by Rodrigo, 1967, 1973, and the Concerto Iberico by Torroba; Professor of the Guitar Department, University of Southern California, Los Angeles, San Diego from 1982. *Recordings:* Five Rodrigo Concertos with the Boccherini Guitar Quintets and the Giuliani Concerti Op 65 and Op 70; Spanish Songs with Jessye Norman. *Address:* c/o Schlote GmbH, Danreitergasse 4, 5020 Salzburg, Austria.

ROMIG, James, MA, PhD; Composer; b. 5 Aug. 1971, Long Beach, CA, USA. *Education:* University of Iowa; Rutgers University. *Career:* Teacher, University of Iowa; Teacher, Rutgers University; Conductor and Music Director, Society of Chromatic Art; Conductor of new-music ensembles, Luna Nova and Frankenstein's Monster; Assistant Music Director and Conductor of Helix, Rutgers University new-music ensemble; Played percussion with the Joffrey Ballet, the Handel and Haydn Society of Boston and the Symphony Orchestra, Percussion Ensemble and Center for New Music at the University of Iowa; commissions/works performed by many US ensembles and orchestras; Prof., Bucknell Univ., 2001–02; Western Illinios Univ., 2002–; lectures at several US univs; mem, ASCAP; American Music Center; Society for Music Theory; Pi Kappa Lambda National Music Honor Society. *Compositions:* Trio for orchestra, 1998; Spin, for flute, violin, violoncello, percussion, 1999; Variations for string quartet, 1999; Piano trio for violin, violoncello, piano, 1997; Six Pieces, for string orchestra, 1996. *Publications:* How to Listen to a New Pice of Music, A Conversation with Milton Babbitt, Parametric Counterpoint: Babbittonian Ideals in Composition and Performance. *Honours:* Finalist, Civic Orchestra of Chicago, First Hearing, 1998; ASCAP Standard Award, 1998–2003; Finalist, Rudolph Nissim Award, ASCAP Foundation, 2002; Meet the Composer grant, 2003. *Address:* Western Illinois University, Dept of Music, Macomb IL 61455, USA. *Telephone:* (309) 298-1338 (office). *E-mail:* jromig@jamesromig.com (home). *Website:* www.jamesromig.com (office).

RONCO, Claudio; Cellist and Composer; b. 16 Sept. 1955, Torino, Italy; m. Lone K Loëll, 17 Sept 1983, 2 s. *Education:* MA in Music, Student of Anner Bylsma and Christophe Coin, Conservatorio Music, Torino. *Career:* Debut: Como with the Clemencic Consort of Vienna, 1982; Soloist with the Clemencic Consort, Vienna, 1982–; Hesperion XX, Ensemble 14, for ZDF, 1991; Television programme on Jewish music and Solo recital for Radio Canada, Montreal. *Compositions:* Tombeau de Mr Farinelli for violin, violoncello and harpsichord, 1994; Serenata Pastorale for 3 voices, violin, violoncello, harpsichord. *Recordings:* Several recordings with Hesperion XX, Clemencic Consort; First recording of Veracini, Bonporti, Lanzetti; Paganini; Gade, Heise trios. *Address:* Cannaregio 3023, Venice 30121, Italy.

RONCONI, Luca; Stage Director; b. 8 March 1933, Susah, Tunisia. *Education:* Graduated, Accademia d'Arte Drammatica, Rome, 1953. *Career:* Began as an actor then directed plays; Opera debut in 1967 with Jeanne d'Arc au Bûcher by Honegger and Busoni's Arlecchino at Turin; Later work has included revivals of neglected operas by Purcell, Jommelli, Cimarosa and Rimsky-Korsakov, The Tsar's Bride; Founding Director of theatre laboratory at the Teatro Metastasio, Prato, 1977; Produced Così fan tutte at Teatro La Fenice, 1983, Piccinni's Iphigénie en Tauride at Bari, 1985, seen also in Paris and Rome; Teatro alla Scala with Rossi's Orfeo in 1985 and Cherubini's Lodoiska in 1990; Productions of Don Giovanni in 1990 and I Vespri Siciliani at Bologna, Rossini's Ricciardo e Zoraide at the 1990 Pesaro Festival; Staged Rossini's Otello at Brussels, 1994 and Cenerentola at Pesaro, 1998; Modern repertory includes stagings of works by Stockhausen, Berio and Globokar; Director of the Teatro Stabile at Turin from 1989. *Address:* c/o Teatro alla Scala, Via Filodrammatici 2, Milan, Italy.

RONGE, Gabriela Marie; singer (soprano); b. 3 July 1957, Hanover, Germany. *Career:* Sang in opera at Heidelberg from 1982, and Osnabruck from 1983 notably as Fiordiligi and Hanna Glawari; Further engagements at Hanover, 1985–87, Cologne, 1989, Frankfurt, Bonn, the Deutsche Oper Berlin and Brunswick; Bayerische Staatsoper Munich from 1987 as the Marschallin, Elsa, Eva and Agathe; Frankfurt in 1987 as Gluck's Iphigénie en Tauride, Paris Opéra in 1989 as Eva, and Isabella in Wagner's Das Liebesverbot at Palermo in 1991; Sang Aida at Schwerin, 1999; Brünnhilde in the Ring at Graz and Senta at the Deutsche Oper Berlin; Noted interpreter of Lieder. *Address:* c/o Teatro Massimo Bellini, via Perrotta 12, 95131 Catania, Italy.

RONI, Luigi; Singer (Bass); b. 22 Feb. 1942, Vergemoli, Lucca, Italy. *Education:* Studied with Sara Sforni Corti in Milan. *Career:* Debut: Spoleto in 1965 as Mephistopheles in Faust; Sang in Milan, Rome, Turin, Venice, Palermo, Florence and Naples; Moscow in 1973 with La Scala Company; Guest appearances in Vienna, Munich, Berlin, London, Paris, New York, Chicago, Dallas and Houston; Orange Festival in 1984 as the Grand Inquisitor in Don Carlos; Other roles include Mozart's Commendatore and Mussorgsky's Dosifey; La Scala in 1987 as Lodovico in Otello; Sang MacGregor in Mascagni's Guglielmo Ratcliff at Catania, 1990, Rossini's Basilio at Bonn, and Festival d'Orange in 1990 as the Grand Inquisitor in Don Carlos. *Recordings include:* Aida; Don Giovanni; Fernand Cortez by Spontini; Zaira by Bellini; Otello. *Address:* c/o Teatro Massimo Bellini, 95100 Catania, Italy.

ROOCROFT, Amanda; Singer (Soprano); b. 9 Feb. 1966, Coppull, Lancashire, England. *Education:* Studied at the Royal Northern College of Music with Barbara Robotham. *Career:* Operatic debut as Sophie in Der Rosenkavalier with Welsh National Opera, 1990; Has developed close associations with Covent Garden, the Bayerische Staatsoper, Munich and the Glyndebourne Festival; Roles include: Fiordiligi, The Countess, Amelia in Simon Boccanegra, Desdemona, Mimi, Handel's Cleopatra and Janáček's Katya; Met debut in New York as Donna Elvira in 1997 and returned to sing the Countess in 1999; Sang Chausson's Poème de l'Amour et de la Mer at the 1999 London Prom concerts and Desdemona at Munich, 1999; Sang Katya Kabanova at Covent Garden, 2001; Desdemona at Covent Garden, 2001; role debut as Wagner's Eva, 2002; Sings in recitals and concerts throughout Europe and the USA with many leading conductors. *Recordings include:* Debut album, Amanda Roocroft; Mozart and his Contemporaries; Mahler Symphony No. 4 with Simon Rattle; Così fan tutte with John Eliot Gardiner; Vaughan Williams' Sea Symphony with Andrew Davis. *Honours:* Decca-Kathleen Ferrier Prize, 1988; Charles Heidsieck Award, Royal Philharmonic Society, 1991. Honorary Fellowship RNCM, 1998. *Current Management:* Ingpen & Williams Ltd, 7 St George's Court, 131 Putney Bridge Road, London, SW15 2PA, England.

ROOLEY, Anthony; Lutenist, Director and Lecturer; b. 10 June 1944, Leeds, Yorkshire, England. *Education:* Guitar, Royal Academy of Music, 1965–68. *Career:* Teacher, guitar, lute, Royal Academy of Music, 1968–71; With James Tyler founded Consort of Musicke, 1969; As director and lutenist, many early music concerts, Europe, Middle East, USA; Sole director, 1971–, often giving concerts of Renaissance theme; Appearances, BBC, French and German television and radio; International festivals, Europe, Scandinavia, USA; Concerts with sopranos Emma Kirby, Evelyn Tubb, alto Mary Nichols, tenor Andrew King, Simon Grant, Joseph Cornwell (Consort of Musicke members), bass David Thomas, tenor Paul Agnew, other early music specialists; Music-theatre includes staging of Le Veglie di Siena (music by Orazio Vecchi), Copenhagen, London, 1988; Collaboration with Italian commedia dell'arte actors La Famiglia Carrara in Marriage of Pantelone; Promenade Concert, 1988, based on settings of poet Torquato Tasso; Concerts, Tel-Aviv, New York, 1988; Co-director with Arjen Terpstra, new record label Musica Oscura; Teacher, Japan, Padova, Basle, Dartington, promoting Renaissance Attitudes to Performance; Co-director with Don Taylor, video Banquet of the Senses: Monteverdi's Madrigali Erotici; mem, Viola da Gamba Society; Galpin Society; Wine Society; Royal Society of Arts. *Recordings include:* Madrigals by Monteverdi, de Rore, Marini, Porter, Pallavicino, Marenzio, d'India; L'anime del Purgatorio (Stradella); Madrigals and Fantasias, Psalms and Anthems (John Ward); Arie Antiche, The Mad Lover (The Orpheus Circle); The Dark is my Delight (Women in Song); Maurice Greene: Songs and Keyboard works (The Handel Circle); The Mistress, The Mantle, Orpheus, Sound the Trumpets from Shore to Shore (Purcell). *Publications include:* A New Varietie of Lute Lessons, record, book, 1975; The Penguin Book of Early Music, record, book, 1979; Performance: Revealing the Orpeus Within, 1990;. *Contributions:* Lute Society Journal; Early Music; Guitar. *Address:* 13 Pages Lane, London, N10 1PU, England.

ROOSENSCHOON, Hans; South African composer; b. 17 Dec. 1952, The Hague, Netherlands. *Education:* Pretoria Conservatory, 1969–71, 1974–75; Royal Academy of Music, London, with Paul Patterson, 1977–78; D.Mus, University of Cape Town, 2001. *Career:* Production Manager, South African Broadcasting Corporation, Johannesburg, 1980–95. *Compositions:* Suite for oboe and piano, 1973; Ekstase for chorus and orchestra, 1975; Cantata on Psalm 8, 1976; Tablo for orchestra, 1976; Sinfonietta, 1976; Katutura for orchestra, 1977; Palette for strings, 1977; Mosaiek for orchestra, 1978; Ars Poetica for baritone, chorus and orchestra, 1979; Psalm 23 for choirs, 1979; Firebowl for chorus, 1980; Ikonografie, Anagram and Architectura, all for orchestra, 1983–86; Horizon, Night-Sky and Landscape for strings, 1987; Chronicles for orchestra, 1987; Clouds Clearing for strings, 1987; Mantis, Ballet Suite, 1988; Circle of Light for orchestra, 1989; Die Sonnevanger, for orchestra, 1990; The Magic Marimba, 1991; Mbira for chorus, 1994; Trombone Concerto, 1995; String Quartet, 1995; Keyboard, Organ and Electronic Music. *Address:* c/o SAMRO, PO Box 31609, Braamfontein 2017, Johannesburg, South Africa.

ROOT, Deane (Leslie); Musicologist, Museum Curator, Teacher, Librarian and Editor and Author; b. 9 Aug. 1947, Wausau, Wisconsin, USA; m. Doris J Dyen, 27 Aug 1972, 2 d. *Education:* New College, Sarasota, Florida; University of Illinois. *Career:* Faculty, University of Wisconsin, 1973; Editorial Staff, New Grove Dictionary of Music and Musicians, 1974–76; Research Associate, University of Illinois, 1976–80; Visiting Research Associate, Florida State University, 1981–82; Curator, Stephen Foster Memorial and Adjunct Assistant Professor in Music, University of Pittsburgh, 1982–96, Chair of Music Dept, 2002–(05); Heinz Chapel Administrator 1983–95; Director of Cultural Resources 1990–94, Adjunct Associate Professor 1992–96, Professor of Music, Director of Center for American Music, 1998–, University of Pittsburgh; President, Sonneck Society for American

Music, 1989–93; Delegate American Council of Learned Societies, 1996–99. *Recordings:* Proud Traditions; Musical Tribute to Pitt. *Publications:* American Popular Stage Music 1860–1880; Music of Florida Historic Sites; Co-Author, Resources of American Music History; Co-Editor, Music of Stephen C Foster; Series Editor, Nineteenth Century American Musical Theater, 16 vols, 1994; Voices Across Time: American History through Song, 2004. *Contributions:* New Grove Dictionary of Music and New Grove Dictionary of American Music; American National Biography; Various journals, yearbooks, conference proceedings. *Telephone:* (412) 624-4126. *Fax:* (412) 624-4186. *E-mail:* dlr@pitt.edu*Address:* Dept of Music, University of Pittsburgh, Pittsburgh, PA 15260, USA.

ROOTERING, Jan-Hendrik; Singer (Bass); b. 18 March 1950, Wedingfeld, Nr Flensburg, Germany. *Education:* Studies with his father, Hendrikus Rootering, a voice teacher; Further education at Musikhochschule Hamburg. *Career:* Debut: Colline in La Bohème, 1980; Engagements include Concerts, Opera Performances and Lieder Recitals as well as numerous recordings with such conductors as Sawallisch, Muti, Levine, Abbado, Marriner, Davis and others; Appearances at Munich State Opera, Vienna State Opera, Berlin Deutsche Oper, Amsterdam, Geneva, Hamburg State Opera, London's Covent Garden, New York's Metropolitan Opera, Chicago's Lyric Opera, San Francisco Opera and Milan's La Scala. *Recordings:* Beethoven Ninth Symphony conducted by Bernstein, 1989; Fasolt in Das Rheingold; Sang Gurnemanz in Parsifal at the Opéra Bastille, Paris, 1997; La Roche in Capriccio at the Metropolitan, 1998New York Met 2000, as Sarastro and Daland; Hans Sachs at Covent Garden, 2002. *Honours:* Honorary Title of Bavarian Kammersänger, 1989; Honorary Title of Professor with the Hochschule für Musik in Munich, 1994. *Address:* 45 West 67th Street, Apt 26C, New York, NY 10023, USA.

ROREM, Ned; Composer; b. 23 Oct. 1923, Richmond, Indiana, USA. *Education:* American Conservatory, Chicago with Leo Sowerby; Northwestern University, 1940–42; Curtis Institute Philadelphia, 1943; Juilliard School New York, 1946; Masters Degree, Juilliard, 1948; Private studies with Thomson and Copland. *Career:* Lived in Morocco 1949–51, and in France, 1951–57; Composer-in-Residence University of Buffalo 1959–61, University of Utah 1966–67; Curtis Institute 1980–; Manhattan School of Music, 1985–; Yale, 1998–; President of the American Academy of Arts and Letters, 2000–03. *Compositions:* 3 Symphonies, 1951, 1956, 1959; 4 String Quartets, 1948, 1950, 1990, 1994; Design for orchestra, 1953; A Childhood Miracle, opera, 1955; The Poets' Requiem, 1955; The Robbers, opera, 1958; Eleven Studies for Eleven Players, 1960; Ideas for orchestra, 1961; Lift up your Heads, for chorus and wind, 1963; Lions (A Dream) for orchestra, 1963; Miss Julie, opera, 1965; Letters from Paris for chorus and orchestra, 1966; Sun, 8 poems for high voice and orchestra; Water Music for clarinet, violin and orchestra, 1966; Bertha, one-act opera, 1968; War Scenes for voice and piano, 1969; 3 Piano Concertos, 1950, 1951, 1969; Little Prayers for soprano, baritone and orchestra, 1973; Air Music, variations for orchestra, 1974; Serenade on Five English Poems, 1975; Hearing, 5 scenes for singers and 7 instruments, 1976; Sunday Morning for orchestra, 1977; The Nantucket Songs, 1979; Remembering Tommy, concerto for piano, cello and orchestra, 1979; After Reading Shakespeare for solo cello, 1980; The Santa Fe Songs, voice and piano quartet, 1980; After Long Silence for soprano, oboe and strings, 1982; An American Oratorio, 1983; Winter Pages, for 5 instruments, 1982; Whitman Cantata, 1983; Violin Concerto, 1984; Septet, Scenes from Childhood, 1985; Organ Concerto, 1985; End of Summer, for violin, clarinet and piano, 1985; String Symphony, 1985; Homer (Three Scenes from the Iliad) for chorus and 8 instruments, 1986; Goodbye My Fancy chorus, soloists, orchestra, 1988–89; The Auden Poems, Tenor and Piano Trio, 1989; Swords and Plowshares, 4 vocal soloists and orchestra, 1991; Piano Concerto for left-hand and orchestra, 1992; Hundreds of songs and 12 song cycles; Cor anglais concerto, 1995; String Quartet No. 4, 1995; Evidence of Things not Seen, 365 songs to texts by 24 authors, 1997; Double Concerto, for violin, cello and orchestra, 1998; Evidence of Things Not Seen, 36 songs for four voices and piano, 1999; Aftermain for voice and trio, 2002; Cello Concerto, 2002; Flute Concerto, 2002, Mallet Concerto, 2003. *Publications:* Prose: Paris Diary, 1966; Music From Inside Out, 1966; New York Diary 1967; Music and People, 1968; Critical Affairs, 1970; The Later Diaries, 1974; Pure Contraption, 1974; Setting the Tone, 1980; The Nantucket Diary, 1985; Settling the Score, 1988; Knowing When to Stop, 1994; Other Entertainment, essays, 1995; Dear Paul, Dear Ned; Lies, A Diary (1986–99), 2001; A Ned Rorem Reader, 2002. *Honours:* Pulitzer Prize for Air Music, variations for orchestra, 1976; American Society of Composers, Authors and Publishers Foundation Lifetime Achievement Award. *Address:* c/o ASCAP, ASCAP Building, 1 Lincoln Plaza, New York, NY 10023, USA.

RORHOLM, Marianne; Singer (Mezzo-Soprano); b. 1960, Denmark. *Education:* Opera Academy at Copenhagen. *Career:* Debut: Royal Opera, Copenhagen as Cherubino; Season 1984–85 sang Olga, Lola

and Rosina at Copenhagen and as the Sorceress in Dido and Aeneas at Paris Opéra; Frankfurt Opera, 1985–88 as Rosina, Dorabella, Sextus in La Clemenza di Tito, Nicklausse and Octavian; Sang Cherubino with the Israel Philharmonic under Daniel Barenboim and at the 1987 Ludwigsburg Festival; Bayreuth Festival in 1988 as a Flowermaiden in Parsifal; Season 1988–89 included US debut with the Indianapolis Symphony under Raymond Leppard, a concert at Carnegie Hall, Cherubino at Glyndebourne and Isolier in Le Comte Ory for Netherlands Opera; Regular appearances with the Deutsche Oper am Rhein, Düsseldorf, and Basle Operas; Season 1992 as Annius in La Clemenza di Tito at Toulouse, Varvara in Katya Kabanova at Bonn, Purcell's Dido at Brussels and the Berlioz Marguerite at Amsterdam; Season 2000 as Offred in the premiere of The Handmaid's Tale by Paul Ruders, at Copenhagen, and Carlotta in Die schweigsame Frau, at Århus; Concert repertory includes Mahler's Das Lied von der Erde. *Recordings include:* Kate Pinkerton in Madama Butterfly; Salome under Giuseppe Sinopoli; Dryad in Ariadne auf Naxos; Sang Verdi's Preziosilla at Copenhagen, 1996 and Nicklausse in Les Contes d'Hoffmann at Dublin, 1998. *Honours:* Carl Nielsen Scholarship, 1984; Elisabeth Dons Memorial Prize, 1985. *Current Management:* Ingpen & Williams Ltd, 7 St George's Court, 131 Putney Bridge Road, London, SW15 2PA, England.

ROS MARBA, Antoni; Conductor; b. 2 April 1937, Barcelona, Spain. *Education:* Barcelona Conservatory; Studied orchestral conducting with Eduard Toldra, Celibidache at Accademia Chigiana, and Jean Martinon at Düsseldorf. *Career:* Debut: Barcelona in 1962; Principal Conductor, 1965–68, and later as Principal Guest Conductor and Artistic Consultant for Spanish Radio and Television Orchestras, for City of Barcelona Orchestra, 1967–77, Spanish National Orchestra, 1978–81, and Netherlands Chamber Orchestra, 1979–86; Principal Guest Conductor for Netherlands Chamber Orchestra since it joined with Netherlands Philharmonic Orchestra, 1986–; Further appearances and tours world-wide including Europe, North and South America, Japan, and China and with orchestras such as Berlin Philharmonic Orchestra; Recently developed international career as an opera conductor with special success at Teatro de la Zarzuela, Madrid, and Gran Teatro del Liceu, Barcelona; Appointed Musical Director at National Opera Theatre Real, Madrid, 1989; Season 1992 with the stage premiere of Gerhard's The Duenna at Madrid, repeated for Opera North; Idomeneo for Scottish Opera, 1996. *Recordings include:* Haydn's Seven Last Words on the Cross; Others with Victoria de Los Angeles, Teresa Berganza, English Chamber Orchestra and Netherlands Chamber Orchestra. *Honours:* National Music Prize of Spain, Ministry of Culture, 1989; Arthur Honegger International Recording Prize for Seven Last Words on the Cross; Cross of St Jordi Generalitat de Cataluna. *Address:* c/o Teatro Real, Plaza de Isabel II s/n, 28013 Madrid, Spain.

ROSAND, Aaron; Violinist and Teacher; b. 15 March 1927, Hammond, Indiana, USA. *Education:* Studied with Marinus Paulsen, 1935–39, Leon Samenti, 1940–44, and Efrem Zimbalist, 1944–48. *Career:* Debut: With the Chicago Symphony under Frederick Stock playing the Mendelssohn Concerto, 1937; Played at New York Town Hall in 1948; European debut at Copenhagen in 1955; Tours of Europe, the Far East and Russia; Appearances with leading orchestras in the USA; Repertoire includes concertos by Lalo, Ries, Vieuxtemps, Joachim, Hubay and Wieniawski; Taught at the Academie Internationale d'Eté in Nice from 1971, Peabody Conservatory, Baltimore and Mannes College, NY, and Curtis Institute, Philadelphia, 1981–; Plays a Guarneri del Gesu of 1741. *Recordings:* 15 CD recordings. *Honours:* Chevalier Pour Mérite Cultural et Artistique, 1965; Gold Medal of the Foundation Ysaÿe, Belgium, 1967. *Current Management:* Jacques Leiser Artist Management. *Address:* c/o Jacques Leiser Artist Management, The Del Prado, 666 L/Pas Street, Suite 602, San Diego, CA 92103, USA.

ROSCA, Andreaiana; Pianist and Professor; b. 19 Nov. 1961, Bucharest, Romania; m. Alexandru-Ioan Geamana, 14 July 1984. *Education:* Music High School Dinu Lipatti, 1968–80; Bucharest University of Music, 1982–86; Masterclasses with Bernard Ringeissen and Roger Vignoles. *Career:* Debut: At age 16 with Philharmonic Orchestra Ploiesti, Romania, playing Mozart's C minor concerto; Concerts in Romania with major orchestras including The Radio and Television Orchestra; Numerous recordings for radio and television; Recitals in Romania, Belgium; Played at Verbier Festival, and in Poland and Japan; Repertoire includes Beethoven Piano Concertos; Liszt; Mozart; Schumann; Brahms; Cycles of lieder and Romanian music such as Enesun; Accompanist for International Singing Competition for Radio Cologne, Germany; EPTA, Romania; Dinu Lipatti Foundation. *Recordings:* For Radio Cologne, Lieder and Romanian piano repertoire. *Honours:* National Prizes, 1979, 1980, 1982, 1986; Accompaniment Prize, Bianca, 1993. *Address:* 23 Principatele Unite, Sector 4, 7051 Bucharest, Romania.

ROSCA, Marcel; Singer (Bass); b. 1948, Bucharest, Romania. *Career:* Sang at the National Opera, Bucharest, from 1970; Guest appearances at the Bolshoi Theatre, Moscow, and in Poland, China and Korea; Gelsenkirchen Opera from 1980, Essen, 1987; Roles have included King Philip in Don Carlos, Boris Godunov, Gremin, Wagner's Hunding and Fafner, Osmin and Mozart's Commendatore (1995); Berlin Staatsoper, 1991, as Arkel in Pelléas and Sparafucile in Rigoletto; Vienna Staatsoper as Sarastro; Other roles include Mephistophele (in Paris), Rocco, and Pagno in I Lombardi (Zürich); Sang Rocco in the 1806 version of Fidelio, Amsterdam, 1997; Sang at Essen 1998–2000 as Peneios in Daphne, Waldner in Arabella, Rocco, King Heinrich in Lohengrin, Don Pasquale and Gounod's Mephisto; Walter in Luisa Miller, 2001; Concerts throughout Europe and South America in the Verdi Requiem and Beethoven's Ninth. *Address:* Essen Opera, Rolandstrasse 10, 4300 Essen 1, Germany.

RÖSCHMANN, Dorothea; Singer (soprano); b. 1969, Flensburg, Germany. *Education:* Studied in Germany and with Vera Rozsa in London. *Career:* Member of the Deutsche Staatsoper Berlin, appearing as Papagena, Iris (Semele) and Sophie in Der Rosenkavalier (1997); Salzburg Festival from 1995, as Susanna and in concert; Further engagements as Zerlina at Tel-Aviv, Handel's Dorinda (Orlando) at Halle, Monteverdi's Drusilla (at Munich) and Dorina in Caldara's I Disingannati at the Early Music Festival Innsbruck; Other roles include Weber's Ännchen (at Berlin and Munich), Handel's Arianna (Giustino) at Göttingen and Servilia in La Clemenza di Tito, at the 1997 Salzburg Festival; Season 1998 with Susanna at Salzburg and Donizetti's Norina at Brussels; Sang Nannetta in Falstaff at Salzburg, 2001; Season 2001–02 as Anne Trulove at the Munich Festival, Elmire in Keiser's Croesus, Staatsoper Berlin, Griselda (Scarlatti), Nannetta, Pamina, Zerlina and Fiordiligi; Covent Garden debut as Pamina, 2003; Concerts at Carnegie Hall, the Vienna Musikverein, Leipzig Gewandhaus, Hamburg Musikhalle and Semperoper, Dresden. *Recordings include:* Pergolesi's Stabat Mater and Keiser's Masaniello Furioso; Messiah with Paul McCreesh and Bach's Secular Cantatas with Reinhard Goebbel (DGG); Bach's Weihnachtsoratorium and Telemann's Orpheus with René Jacobs (Harmonia Mundi). *Current Management:* Askonas Holt Ltd, Lonsdale Chambers, 27 Chancery Lane, London, WC2A 1PF, England. *Telephone:* (20) 7400-1700. *Fax:* (20) 7400-1799. *E-mail:* info@askonasholt.co.uk. *Website:* www.askonasholt.co.uk.

ROSCOE, Martin; Pianist; b. 3 Aug. 1952, Halton, Cheshire, England. *Education:* Royal Manchester College of Music with Marjorie Clementi and Gordon Green. *Career:* Appearances at Cheltenham, Bath, Leeds, and South Bank Music Festivals; Performances at Royal Festival Hall, Queen Elizabeth Hall, Royal Albert Hall, and Wigmore Hall in London with Hallé, City of Birmingham, Royal Philharmonic, Royal Liverpool Philharmonic, Northern Sinfonia, London Mozart Players, and BBC Philharmonic Orchestras; Tours of Australia, Middle East and South America; Further appearances at Harrogate Festival with Scottish National Orchestra, BBC, and Welsh Symphony Orchestras; Played at the Promenade Concerts with BBC Symphony Orchestra in 1987, and with French Philharmonic Orchestra in 1989; Recitals with violinist Tasmin Little, notably in the Kreutzer Sonata; mem, Incorporated Society of Musicians; Musicians Union. *Recordings:* Many for BBC Radio 3 including Piano Concertos of Berwald, Liszt, Beethoven, Stravinsky, Fauré, Vaughan Williams, and Shostakovich; Solo works by Beethoven; Complete Sonatas of Schubert, Debussy, Liszt and Bartók; Concertos by Strauss and Szymanowski; Solo commercial recordings with music by Liszt. *Honours:* Davas Gold Medal, 1973; Silver Medal, Worshipful Company of Musicians, 1974; British Liszt Piano Competition, 1976; Sydney International Piano Competition, 1981. *Current Management:* Hazard Chase, Norman House, Cambridge Place, Cambridge CB2 1NS, England. *Telephone:* (1223) 312400. *Fax:* (1223) 460827. *Website:* www.hazardchase.co.uk.

ROSE, Gregory; Conductor; b. 18 April 1948, Beaconsfield, England. *Education:* BA, Magdalen College, Oxford University, 1967–70; Trained Violinist, Pianist and Singer. *Career:* Conductor, Founder of Singcircle, Circle, 1977–; Music Director, London Jupiter Orchestra, 1986–; Conductor, Reading Festival Chorus, 1984–88; Conductor, London Concert Choir, 1988–96; Conductor, Reading Symphony Orchestra, 1986–91; Conductor, National Youth Choir of Wales, 1986–89; Conducted BBC Concert Orchestra, Ulster Orchestra, Estonian National Symphony Orchestra, Netherlands Radio Chamber Orchestra, BBC Singers, Nederlands Kamerkoor, Groupe Vocal de France, WDR Choir, Steve Reich and Musicians, London Philharmonic, Odense Symfonieorkester and Latvian Filharmonia; Series Director, Cage at 70, Almeida Festival, 1982 and Reich at 50, Almeida Festival, 1986; Conducted Thomson's Four Saints in Three Acts, Spitalfields, 1996 and the British stage premiere of Goldschmidt's Beatrice Cenci, 1998. *Recordings:* Hyperion, Mouth Music, Stockhausen's Stimmung, Wergo, Son Entero by Alejandro Viñao; Continuum, music by Simon Emmerson; October Music, music by Trevor Wishart; Chandos, music by Janáček; Numerous recordings for BBC radio and television, Channel 4, ITV and European radio stations. *Publications:* Various compositions.

Current Management: Connaught Artists Management Ltd, 2 Molasses Row, Plantation Wharf, London, SW11 3UX, England. *Telephone:* (20) 7738 0017. *Fax:* (20) 7738 0909. *E-mail:* classicalmusic@connaughtartists.com. *Website:* www.connaughtartists.com. *Address:* 57 White Horse Road, London E1 0ND, England.

ROSE, John (Luke); Composer, Pianist, Lecturer, Teacher and Writer and Conductor; b. 19 July 1933, Northwood Hills, Middlesex, England. *Education:* University of London, Trinity College of Music, 1954–58; BMus, London, 1957; LMusTCL, 1957; PhD, Wagner's Musical Language, London, 1963. *Career:* Debut: Oxford University, 1958; Extension Lecturer in Music, University of Oxford, 1958–66; Lecturer, Teacher and Examiner (United Kingdom, USA, Newfoundland, Canada, Fiji, New Zealand, Australia, India), Trinity College of Music, 1960–; Part-time Teacher, St Marylebone Grammar School, 1963–66; Staff Tutor, Department of Extra-Mural Studies, University of London, 1966–84. *Compositions:* Symphony No. 1, The Mystic, BBC Philharmonic, 1982; Piano Concerto, BBC Northern and Scottish Orchestras, 1977; Overture Macbeth, BBC Scottish Symphony Orchestra, 1977; Symphony No. 2, 1985; Symphonic Dances, Hallé Orchestra; String Quartet; Part-songs; 2 Piano Sonatas; Various piano works; Blake's Songs of Innocence; The Pleasures of Youth, cantata; Hymns and Anthems; Apocalyptic Visions for piano; St Francis, musical play, 1985; Violin Concerto, BBC Philharmonic, 1987; Odysseus, opera, 1987. *Publications:* Wagner's Tristan and Isolde: A Landmark in Musical History, introductory essay to libretto book, English National Opera Guide No. 6, 1981; Ludwig, Wagner and the Romantic View, essay and lecture, Victoria and Albert Museum Exhibition. *Honours:* Hon. Fellow Trinity Coll., 1961; Royal Philharmonic Soc. Prizewinner twice for 1st and 2nd symphonies; mem. Association of Univ. Teachers and The British Acad. of Composers. *Address:* Kalon, 113 Farnham Road, Guildford, Surrey GU2 7PF, England.

ROSE, Jürgen; Stage Designer; b. 25 Aug. 1937, Bernburg, Germany. *Education:* Studied acting and painting in Berlin. *Career:* Ballet designs for the Stuttgart Ballet, 1962–73; Collaborations with director, Otto Schenk for Don Carlos and Die Meistersinger in Vienna, Simon Boccanegra and Der Rosenkavalier at Munich and Così fan tutte in Berlin; Bayreuth Festival in 1972 and 1990 with Tannhäuser and Der fliegende Holländer, in productions by Götz Friedrich and Dieter Dorn; Salome and Die Entführung in Vienna, Lucia di Lammermoor and Lohengrin in Hamburg; Premiere of Isang Yun's Sim Tjong at Munich in 1972; Designed Die Zauberflöte for the Munich Opera and the 1981 Ludwigsburg Festival; Le nozze di Figaro for the 1997 Munich Festival; Bayreuth Festival, Tristan and Isolde (1999), Met New York, Premiere of H.W. Henze's L'Upupa, Salzburg Festival, 2003; Own direction in own stage-and costume designs: La Traviata (1994), Die Zauberflöte (1996), Bonn Opera/Don Carlo (2000) and The Cunning Little Vixen (2002) Munich Opera. *Recordings include:* Video of Munich production of Die Zauberflöte. *Address:* c/o Bayerische Staatsoper, Postfach 100148, 8000 Munich 1, Germany.

ROSE, Peter; Singer (bass); b. 1961, Canterbury, Kent, England. *Education:* University of East Anglia; Guildhall School of Music with Ellis Keeler; National Opera Studio. *Career:* Debut: As Commendatore in Don Giovanni with Glyndebourne Opera in Hong Kong, 1986 and on tour; Welsh National Opera, 1986–89 as Bartolo, Basilio, Prince Gremin in Eugene Onegin, Angelotti in Tosca, Osmin, Tutor in Count Ory and Marke in Tristan; Glyndebourne Touring Opera as Don Inigo in L'Heure Espagnole, Osmin and Basilio; Maggio Musicale Florence as Commendatore; Scottish Opera as Narbal in Les Troyens; Sang in La Damnation de Faust in Chicago, BBC Proms and Salzburg Festival with Chicago Symphony under Solti; English National Opera as Angelotti and Bottom; Covent Garden debut 1988 as Lord Rochefort in Anna Bolena then Cadmus in Semele, Bonze in Madama Butterfly, Lodovico in Otello, Nightwatchman in Meistersinger; Kecal in The Bartered Bride, Chicago Lyric Opera, Commendatore, Gessler in Guillaume Tell and Basilio at San Francisco, 1991–92; Also sang Walther in Luisa Miller, Amsterdam, 1st Nazarene in Salome, Salzburg, Bottom at Aix-en-Provence, Commendatore at Covent Garden in 1993, Mustafà (Italiana), Amsterdam, Pimen in Boris Godunov at New Israeli Opera, Ramfis in Aida, Hunding in Walküre, Berlin Staatsoper, in 1994 and Dosifei in Khovanshchina, Hamburg; Other roles include Fasolt in Rheingold; Bottom at the Met; Sang in Pfitzner's Palestrina at Covent Garden, 1997; Engaged for Rachmaninov's Aleko at the 1999 London Prom concerts; Season 2000 as Silva in Ernani for ENO and King Mark in Tristan at Covent Garden; Britten's Claggart at Cologne, 2001; Ravel's Le Heure espagnole at the London Proms, 2002. *Recordings include:* Nozze di Figaro with Barenboim and the Berlin Philharmonic; Video of Clemenza di Tito for Glyndebourne; Salome with Dohnányi; Seven Deadly Sins (also on video); Barber of Seville (with Peter Moores); Beatrice Cenci, Goldschmidt; Ballo in Maschera, Teldec. *Current Management:* Askonas Holt Ltd, Lonsdale Chambers, 27 Chancery Lane, London, WC2A 1PF, England. *Telephone:* (20) 7400-1700. *Fax:*

(20) 7400-1799. *E-mail:* info@askonasholt.co.uk. *Website:* www .askonasholt.co.uk.

ROSEBERRY, Eric Norman; Musician and Writer; b. 18 July 1930, Sunderland, England; m. 1st Elspeth Mary Campbell 1952, four d.; m. 2nd Frances Jill Sharp 1969. *Education:* BA, BMus, University of Durham; PhD, University of Bristol, 1982. *Career:* Director of Music, Stand Grammar School for Boys, Manchester, 1953–58; County Music Organiser, Huntingdonshire, 1958–64; Music Assistant, BBC London, 1964–69; Radcliffe Lecturer in Music, University of Sussex, 1969–72; Lecturer for University of Bristol Extra-Mural Department, 1972–; Senior Lecturer in Music, Bath College of Higher Education, 1972–85; Director of Music, Bath Symphony Orchestra, 1977–89; Founder Director of Apollo Ensemble of Bath, 1989; ARCO, 1999; mem, Royal College of Organists. *Publications:* Faber Book of Christmas Carols and Songs, 1969; Dmitri Shostakovich: His Life and Times, 1982; Essays appearing in, Of German Music, 1976, The Britten Companion, 1984, Benjamin Britten Death in Venice, Cambridge Opera Handbooks, 1987; Shostakovich's Musical Style, USA, 1990; Shostakovich and Britten in Shostakovich Studies, 1995; On Mahler and Britten, 1995; Essays in The Cambridge Companion to Britten, 1999. *Contributions:* Articles and reviews in Tempo, The Listener, Music and Musicians, Music and Letters, Musical Times, CD Review; Programme Notes for BBC Symphony Concerts, Aldeburgh Festival and the Proms; Sleeve notes for Chandos Records; Broadcast talks on BBC Radio 3. *Honours:* Class FM Red Award for outstanding contribution to classical music, 2002. *Address:* The Toll House, Marshfield, Chippenham, Wiltshire SN14 8JN, England.

ROSELL, Lars-Erik; Composer and Organist; b. 9 Aug. 1944, Nybro, Sweden. *Education:* Organ Student, 1963–69; Composition with Ingvar Lidholm, Stockholm Royal College of Music, 1968–71. *Career:* Teacher, Counterpoint, Composition, Stockholm Royal College of Music, 1972–, Professor from 2001; Freelance Organist, Performances of Contemporary Music. *Compositions include:* Terry Riley for 3 Pianos, 1970; Poem in the Dark for mezzo and ensemble, 1972; After the Fall, Dramatic Scene Based on Arthur Miller, for vocal soloists and ensemble, 1973; Visiones Prophetae, Biblical Scene, 1974; Musik for cello and string orchestra, 1975; Ordens källa, Scenic Cantata, 1980; Tillfälligt avbrott, chamber opera, 1981; Organ Concerto, 1982; Amédée, chamber opera, 1987; Five Aphorisms, cello solo, 1990; Fantasia Concertante for cello and orchestra, 1992; The Illusionist, chamber opera, 1996; Three Orchestral Songs for soprano and baritone, 1999; Out of the Shadows, chamber opera, 2001; Choir music, chamber music and other stage music. *Recordings:* Lars-Erik Rosell, In Between. *Address:* Gnejsstigen 2, 19633 Kungsängen, Sweden. *E-mail:* lars-erik.rosell@kmh.se.

ROSEN, Charles, PhD; American pianist and writer; b. 5 May 1927, New York, NY; s. of Irwin Rosen and Anita Gerber. *Education:* Juilliard School of Music, Princeton Univ., Univ. of S. California. *Career:* studied piano with Moriz Rosenthal and Hedwig Kanner-Rosenthal 1938–45; recital début, New York 1951; first complete recording of Debussy Etudes 1951; première of Double Concerto by Elliott Carter, New York 1961; has played recitals and as soloist with orchestras throughout America and Europe; has made over 35 recordings including Stravinsky: Movements with composer conducting 1962, Bach: Art of Fugue, Two Ricercares, Goldberg Variations 1971, Beethoven: Last Six Sonatas 1972, Boulez: Piano Music, Vol. I, Diabelli Variations, Beethoven Concerto No. 4, 1979, Schumann: The Revolutionary Masterpieces, Chopin: 24 Mazurkas 1991; Prof. of Music, State Univ. of NY 1972–90; Guggenheim Fellowship 1974; Messenger Lectures, Cornell Univ. 1975, Bloch Lectures, Univ. of Calif., Berkeley 1977, Gauss Seminars, Princeton Univ. 1978; Norton Prof. of Poetry, Harvard Univ. 1980–81; George Eastman Prof., Balliol Coll., Oxford 1987–88, Prof. of Music and Social Thought, Univ. of Chicago 1988–96. *Publications:* The Classical Style: Haydn, Mozart, Beethoven 1971, Beethoven's Last Six Sonatas 1972, Schoenberg 1975, Sonata Forms 1980, Romanticism and Realism: The Mythology of Nineteenth-Century Art (with Henri Zerner) 1984, The Musical Language of Elliott Carter 1984, Paisir de jouer, plaiser de penser 1993, The Frontiers of Meaning: Three Informal Lectures on Music 1994, The Romantic Generation 1995, Romantic Poets, Critics and Other Madmen 1998, Critical Entertainment: Music Old and New 2000, Beethoven's Piano Sonatas: A Short Companion 2001, Piano Notes 2003; contrib. to books, newspapers and journals. *Honours:* Hon. DMus (Trinity Coll., Dublin 1976, Leeds Univ. 1976, Durham Univ.); Dr hc (Cambridge) 1992; Nat. Book Award 1972, Edison Prize, Netherlands 1974. *Current Management:* John Gingrich Management Inc, PO Box 1515, New York, NY 10023, USA.

ROSEN, Jerome (William); Composer, Clarinettist and Professor of Music; b. 23 July 1921, Boston, Massachusetts, USA; m. Sylvia T Rosen, 1 s., 3 d. *Education:* MA, University of California, Berkeley, 1948; Special student at National Conservatory of Paris; Studied with Darius Milhaud, 1949–50. *Career:* Professor of Music and Director of Electronic Studio at University of California, Davis, 1963–; mem, American Composers' Alliance; Musicological Society. *Compositions include:* Sonata for Clarinet and Cello, 1954; 2 String Quartets, 1953 and 1965; Suite for 4 Clarinets, 1962; Three Songs for Chorus and Piano, 1968; Clarinet Concerto, 1973; Serenade for Clarinet and Violin, 1977; Calisto And Melibea, chamber opera, 1978; Campus Doorways for Chorus and Orchestra, 1978; Music for 2 Clarinets, 1980; Fantasy for Violin, 1983; Concertpiece for Clarinet and Piano, 1984; Sextet Sine Nomine, 1996; Emperor Norton of the USA, 1997;. *Contributions:* Various musical journals and articles in Grove's Dictionary of Music and Musicians. *Honours:* George Ladd Prix de Paris, 1949–51; Fromm Foundation, 1952; Guggenheim Fellowship, 1958. *Address:* Department of Music, University of California, Davis, CA 95616, USA.

ROSEN, Nathaniel (Kent); Cellist; b. 9 June 1948, Altadena, California, USA; m. Margo Shohl. *Education:* Studied with Eleonore Schoenfeld in Pasadena and with Piatigorsky at the University of Southern California, Los Angeles. *Career:* Assistant to Piatigorsky, 1966–76; Solo debut with the Los Angeles Philharmonic, 1969; New York debut, 1970, Carnegie Hall; Principal Cellist, Los Angeles Chamber Orchestra, 1972–76; Pittsburgh Symphony Orchestra, 1977–79; Professor, University of Illinois at Champaign-Urbana, 1988–94; Professor, Manhattan School of Music, 1981–88, 1994–; Appearances with leading American and European Orchestras and as Recitalist and in Chamber Music. *Recordings:* Complete music for Cello and Piano by Chopin; Shostakovich Cello Concerto No. 1; Brahms Sonatas; Bach Suites. *Address:* c/o Manhattan School of Music, Cello Faculty, 120 Claremont Ave, New York, NY 10027, USA.

ROSEN, Robert (Joseph); Composer and Performer; b. 20 May 1956, Melfort, Saskatchewan, Canada; m. Deborah Alpaugh, 18 Aug 1979, 2 s., 1 d. *Education:* BMus, Distinction, University of Alberta, 1977; Advanced Music Studies Programme of Banff Centre, 1979–81; Darmstadt Summer Course, 1982; Studied composition with Violet Archer and Bruce Mather; Worked for short periods with John Cage, R Murray Schafer, Witold Lutoslawski, Iannis Xenakis and Morton Feldman; National Choreographic Workshop, Vancouver, 1985. *Career:* Broadcasts as performer on CBC National Radio; Compositions performed in Canada, Sweden, Germany, Netherlands, France, Spain, USA, Italy and Australia by such notable performers as Robert Aitken, Jean-Pierre Drouet and Alan Hacker; Founding Member of performing ensemble, Fusion 5; Created film scores for documentaries produced by Helios Pictures for the National Film Board of Canada; Assistant Director of Music Programs at the Banff centre for The Arts from 1991; Musical Director of Kokoro Dance. *Compositions:* From Silence for Piano and Orchestra; String Quartet, 1979; Krikos, l, 1980, ll, 1982; Enigmas From The Muse; Meditation No. 1 for Flute, Violin and Cello, No. 2 for Small Orchestra, No. 4 for 2 Pianos, No. 5, Mosaic for Flute and Piano, No. 6 for Piano, No. 7, Coro for 24 Voices; In Anticipation Of Beautiful Shadows for 7 Cellos; Mi Istakistsi for Flute, Percussion and String Quartet; Zero To The Power for Violin, Cello, Taiko Percussion and Electronics; Stones for 2 Sopranos, Tuba and Percussion; Canyon Shadows: Stones; Animals for 2 Sopranos, Alpenhorn and Tuba, 1993. *Publications:* Canadian Composers at Banff, Celebration, Canadian Music Centre. *Address:* c/o SOCAN, 41 Valleybrook Drive, Don Mills, Ontario M3B 2S6, Canada.

ROSEN, Rudolf; Singer (Baritone); b. 1960, Switzerland. *Education:* Berne Academy of Music, with Jakob St ämpfli. *Career:* Many concert engagements in Oslo, Stuttgart, Leipzig, Munich, Zürich and Geneva; conductors have included Neeme Järvi, John Nelson, Helmuth Rilling and Michel Corboz; Further engagements at Tel-Aviv and Mexico City; Heilbronn and Salzburg Festivals, 1996–97; concert repertoire from Lieder to Oratorios; Stuttgart State Opera from 2001, including engagement as Don Giovanni, 2002. *Honours:* Prizewinner, Internaional Music Competition, Geneva (1997), ARD Music Competition Munich (1998) and Belvedere Song Competition, Vienna. *Address:* c/o Theateragentur Dr G. Hilbert, Maximilianstrasse 22, Munich, Germany.

ROSENBAUM, Victor; Pianist, Conductor and Administrator; b. 19 Dec. 1941, Philadelphia, Pennsylvania, USA; 2 d. *Education:* BA (Hons), Brandeis University, 1964; MFA, Princeton University, 1967; Aspen Music School, 1957–60; Piano with Leonard Shure and Rosina Lhevinne; Composition with Roger Sessions, Earl Kim and Edward T Cone. *Career:* Solo performances in USA, Japan, Brazil, Israel and Russia; Chamber performances with artists Leonard Rose, Roman Totenberg, Arnold Steinhardt; Cleveland, Vermeer, New World Quartets; Tully Hall; Town Hall, New York; Jordan Hall, Boston; Conductor, Concerto Company chamber orchestra; Former faculty member of Eastman School of Music, Brandeis University; Faculty Member, New England Conservatory; Director, Longy School of Music, Cambridge, Massachusetts. *Compositions:* For voice, piano, chorus, chamber ensemble and theatre pieces. *Recordings:* John Harbison Trio. *Address:* c/o Longy School of Music, 1 Follen Street, Cambridge, MA 02138, USA.

ROSENBOOM, David; Composer and Electronic Instrument Technician; b. 9 Sept. 1947, Fairfield, Iowa, USA. *Education:* Studied with Gordon Binkerd, Salvatore Martirano and Kenneth Gaburro, University of Illinois, Urbana. *Career:* Co-Founder, President, Neurona Co, New York, 1969–71; Teacher, York University, Toronto, 1972–79, Mills College, Oakland, 1979–; Head, Music Department, 1984, Darius Milhaud Chair in Music, 1988, Dean of Music, California Institute of the Arts, 1990. *Compositions include:* The Brandy of the Damned, music theatre, 1967; How Much Better if Plymouth Rock Had Landed on the Pilgrims, 1972; On Being Invisible, 1976; In the Beginning I–IV, for Various Instrumental Combinations, 1978–80; Future Travel for Piano, Violin and Computer Music System, 1982; Champ Vital, 1987; systems of Judgement, Tape Collage, 1987; Predictions, Confirmations and Disconfirmations, 1991; Extended Trio, 1992; It Is About To... Sound, Interactive Computer Music Installation, 1993; On Being Invisible II: Hypatia Speaks to Jefferson in a Dream, Multimedia Piece, 1995; Brave New World: Music for the Play, 1995. *Publications include:* Biofeedback and the Arts: Results of Early Experiments, 1975; Extended Musical Interface with the Human Nervous System: Assessment and Prospectus (study of Leonardo), 1990. *Address:* c/o ASCAP, ASCAP Building, 1 Lincoln Plaza, NY 10023, USA.

ROSENKRANZ, Helge; violinist; b. 1962, Austria. *Career:* member of Franz Schubert Quartet, Vienna, 1989–; many concert engagements in Europe, USA, and Australia including Amsterdam Concertgebouw, Vienna Musikverein and Kozerthaus, Salle Gaveau, Paris and Sydney Opera House; Visits to Zürich, Geneva, Basle, Hamburg, Rome, Rotterdam, Madrid and Copenhagen; Festival engagements include Salzburg, Wiener Festwochen, Prague Spring, Schubertiade at Hohenems, Schubert Festival in Washington DC, Belfast and Istanbul; tours of Australasia, Russia and USA; Frequent concert tours to the United Kingdom; Featured in Concerto by Spohr with Royal Liverpool Philharmonic, Liverpool and Festival Hall, London; many appearances at Wigmore Hall and at Cheltenham Festival; Masterclasses at Royal Northern College of Music and Lake District Summer Music. *Recordings include:* Schubert's Quartet in G, D877; Complete Quartets by Dittersdorf. *Address:* Steingasse 27, 5020 Salzburg, Austria.

ROSENSHEIN, Neil; Singer (Tenor); b. 27 Nov. 1947, New York, USA. *Education:* Studied in New York. *Career:* Debut: Florida Opera in 1972 as Almaviva in Il Barbiere di Siviglia; Sang in Washington, Dallas, Boston and Santa Fe; European debut at Vaison-la-Romaine in 1980 as Almaviva; Further appearances in Geneva, Zürich and Paris; Covent Garden debut in 1986 as Lensky in Eugene Onegin; Chicago Lyric Opera in 1988 as Alfredo in La Traviata; Sang in the premiere of The Aspern Papers by Dominick Argento, Dallas, 1988; Berlioz Festival at Lyon in 1989 as Benvenuto Cellini; Other roles include Mozart's Tamino and Belmonte, Verdi's Fenton and Don Carlos, Massenet's Des Grieux and Werther at Turin, Sydney and Metropolitan in 1989, and Števa in Jenůfa; Season 1992–93 at the Metropolitan as Faust, Werther, Alfredo in Traviata and Léon in the premiere of Corigliano's The Ghosts of Versailles; Sang the Berlioz Faust at Turin in 1992 and Peter Grimes at Sydney; Sang Cavaradossi at Santa Fe, 1994. *Recordings:* Eugene Onegin. *Address:* c/o Metropolitan Opera, Lincoln Center, New York, NY 10023, USA.

ROSKELL, Penelope; Pianist; b. 1960, Oxford, England; m. Richard Griffiths, 26 Oct 1985. *Education:* GMus (RNCM) Honours, PPRNCM, Royal Northern College of Music; Private study with Guido Agosti in Rome. *Career:* Solo pianist with tours world-wide at invitation of the British Council; Concerts regularly in Europe, Scandinavia, USA, Africa, Asia, Middle and Far East; Broadcasts on BBC Radio 3, WFMT Radio Chicago and British and Polish television; Professor of Piano at London College of Music; Recitals at Wigmore Hall and Purcell Room; Concerto engagements include recording with Oxford Pro Musica; Tours with Manchester Camerata and the Bournemouth Sinfonietta under Simon Rattle. *Honours:* Winner of British Contemporary Piano Competition. *Current Management:* Helen Sykes Artists Management. *Address:* c/o Helen Sykes Artists Management, 100 Felsham Road, Putney, London SW15 1DQ, England.

ROSS, Christopher; Pianist (accompanist and chamber musician) and Conductor; b. 1961, England. *Career:* Has worked with such musicians as soprano Jennifer Smith, cellist Raphael Wallfisch, violinist Dona Lee Croft (tour of the USA) and José Carreras (2 albums); Many performances in France, Germany, Switzerland, Portugal, Namibia, Japan, Korea, India, Malaysia and all London's concert halls; Conducted Le Nozze di Figaro in Switzerland and Mozart's Requiem Mass in London, 2003. *Honours:* Accompanist's Prize, Richard Tauber Competition; Accompanist's Prize, NFMS competition (twice). *E-mail:* chris_ross@ntlworld.com.

ROSS, Elinor; Singer (Soprano); b. 1 Aug. 1932, Tampa, Florida, USA. *Education:* Studied with Zinka Milanov in New York. *Career:* Debut: Cincinnati Opera in 1958 as Leonora in Il Trovatore; Guest appearances in Boston, Chicago, Baltimore and Philadelphia; Sang at Carnegie Hall in the 1968 US premiere of Verdi's Alzira; Metropolitan Opera from 1970 with debut as Turandot; European engagements at La Scala, Bologna, Palermo, Vienna, Budapest, Zagreb, Verona and Florence; Other roles include Bellini's Norma, Verdi's Aida, Elisabetta, Amelia, Lady Macbeth and Abigaille, Mozart's Donna Anna, Puccini's Tosca and Giordano's Maddalena; Sang Tosca at the Metropolitan in 1973, and the Trovatore, Leonora at Buenos Aires in 1974; Frequent concert appearances. *Address:* c/o Metropolitan Opera, Lincoln Center, New York, NY 10023, USA.

ROSS, Elise; Singer (soprano); b. 28 April 1947, New York, USA; m. Simon Rattle (divorced). *Career:* Sang with the Juilliard Ensemble, New York and the Los Angeles Philharmonic Orchestra from 1970; Performances of music by Berio in USA and Europe (Passagio in Rome); Tour of Europe with the London Sinfonietta and appearances at Royan and Bath Festivals and in Venice and Warsaw; Sang in Bussotti's Passion Selon Sade and Le Racine at La Scala in 1991; Concerts with the Ensemble Intercontemporain, Paris from 1976; Repertoire includes Berlin Cabaret songs, lieder by composers of the Second Viennese School, Chansons by Ravel and Debussy and lieder by Mozart, Schumann and Strauss; Shostakovich Symphony 14 with the Los Angeles Philharmonic and Ensemble Intercontemporain; Has sung Cherubino for Opera North and for Long Beach Opera; Sang Marie in Wozzeck at Los Angeles in 1989, Mélisande with Netherlands Opera and Berlioz's Romeo and Juliette, Rotterdam, 1993.

ROSS, Walter; Composer; b. 3 Oct. 1936, Lincoln, Nebraska, USA. *Education:* MMus, University of Nebraska, 1962; DMA, Cornell University, 1966, with Robert Palmer. *Career:* Music Faculty, University of Virginia, 1967–. *Compositions:* Concerto for brass quintet and orchestra, 1966; Five Dream Sequences for percussion quartet and piano, 1968; 2 Trombone Concertos, 1970, 1982; Canzona I and II for brass instruments, 1969, 1979; In the Penal Colony, Opera, 1972; 3 Wind Quintets, 1974, 1985, 1989; A Jefferson Symphony, for tenor, chorus and orchestra, 1976; Concerto for wind quintet and strings, 1977; String Trio, 1978; Nocturne for strings, 1980; Violin Sonata, 1981; Concerto for bassoon and strings, 1983; Suite No. 1 for chamber ensemble, 1983; Concerto for oboe, harp and strings, 1984; 3 Brass Trios, 1985, 1986, 1986; Concerto for flute, guitar and orchestra, 1987; Sinfonia Concertante for strings, 1987; Oil of Dog, for brass quintet and actor, 1988; Concerto for euphonium, brass and timpani, 1988; Scherzo Festivo, for orchestra, 1992; Summer Dances for oboe and marimba, 1992; Clarinet Concerto, 1994; Harlequinade for 5 wind instruments and piano, 1994; Vocal Music, including Songs and Choruses. *Address:* c/o ASCAP, ASCAP Building, 1 Lincoln Plaza, New York, NY 10023, USA.

ROSSBERG, Dieter; Conductor; b. 1952, Hamburg, Germany. *Education:* Studied at the Hamburg Academy, with Horst Stein, György Ligeti, Götz Friedrich and August Everding. *Career:* Principal Conductor/Kapellmeister and Deputy General Music Director in various opera houses in Germany and Austria, 1975–92; Since 1973 has appeared as a guest conductor for opera concert and radio productions (NHK-Tokyo, Bayerische Rundfunk-München, Radio Hilversum, NDR, Danish and Norwegian Broadcasting Corporation) and festivals in Germany: Berlin, Bonn, Cologne, Essen, Hamburg, Hannover, Frankfurt and Munich and abroad: Austria, Canada, Denmark, Estonia, France, Finland, Hungary, Italy, Japan, Tokyo, Monaco, Netherlands, Norway, Slovenia, Sweden, Switzerland, Turkey; Has worked with many noted instrumentalists and singers including René Kollo, Gegam Grigorian, Ingvar Wixell, Peter Mattei and stage directors and choreographers such as John Neumier; Performed as a freelance conductor, 1992–; More than 90 different operas in 1000 performances with a wide concert repertoire; Has conducted many world premieres. *Address:* Lottbeker Platz 4, 22359 Hamburg, Germany.

RÖSSEL-MAJDAN, Hildegard; Singer (Contralto); b. 30 Jan. 1921, Moosbierbaum, Austria; m. Karl Rossel-Majdan, 1 d. *Education:* HS for Music and Dramatic Art, Vienna. *Career:* Concert and oratorio singer under leading Austrian and foreign conductors, 1948–; Member of Vienna State Opera, 1951–71; Professor, University for Music and Dramatic Art, Vienna, 1971–91; Concerts, opera and oratorio in Europe, USA and Japan; Lecturer in Austrian seminaries and in Japan; President of Goetheanistic Konservatory and Waldorfpedagogical Akademy. *Recordings:* Various. *Address:* Agnesgasse 13, Vienna, Austria.

RÖSSLER, Almut; Organist and Choral Director; b. 12 June 1932, Beveringen, Germany. *Education:* Studied organ with Michael Schneider at Detmold and Gaston Litaize in Paris; Piano with Hans Richter-Haaser and choral direction with Kurt Thomas. *Career:* Performances of music by such contemporary composers as André Jolivet, Giselher Klebe (Organ Concerto, 1980) and Olivier Messiaen; Premieres of Le Mystère de la Sainte Trinité in 1972 and Le Livre du Saint Scarement in 1986;

Kantor at the Johanneskirche Düsseldorf and Professor of Organ at the Robert Schumann Conservatory; Founder and Director of the Johannes-Kantorei, giving a capella work and performing in oratorios; Director of Messiaen Festivals at Düsseldorf, 1968, 1972, 1979 and 1986; Masterclasses in Japan and at Yale University. *Honours:* Organist of The Year, Yale University, 1986. *Address:* Staatliche Hochschule für Musik Rheinland, Robert Schumann Institut, Fischerstrasse 110, 4000 Düsseldorf, Germany.

ROST, Andrea; Singer (Soprano); b. 1965, Hungary. *Education:* Studied in Budapest until 1989. *Career:* Debut: Budapest National Opera, 1989, as Gounod's Juliette; Made further appearances in Hungary and sang Verdi's Nannetta at Enschede (1991), Susanna at St Gallen and Zerlina at Cologne; Vienna Staatsoper from 1991, notably as Rosina; Sang the Voice of the Falcon in Die Frau ohne Schatten at the 1992 Salzburg Festival; Covent Garden debut, 1995, in Le nozze di Figaro; Sang Mozart's Pamina at La Scala, 1996; Sang Donizetti's Linda di Chamounix at the Festival Hall, 1997; Pamina at La Scala and Budapest, 1998; Sang Lucia di Lammermoor at the Met, 1999; Giulietta in Hoffmann at the Palais Garnier, 2000; Adina, Gilda and Violetta at La Scala, 2001. *Address:* c/o Staatsoper Vienna, Opernring 2, 1010 Vienna, Austria.

ROSTROPOVICH, Mstislav; Cellist, Pianist and Conductor; b. 27 March 1927, Baku, Russia; m. Galina Vishnevskaya, 15 May 1955, 2 d. *Education:* Moscow Conservatory. *Career:* Debut: Russia in 1941, international in 1948; Conducting debut in 1961; Professor at Moscow and Leningrad Conservatories; Music Director for National Symphony Orchestra, Washington DC, 1977; Opera engagements include The Queen of Spades at San Francisco in 1975 and Eugene Onegin at Aldeburgh in 1979, Rimsky's Tsar's Bride at Washington DC in 1986 and Prokofiev's The Duenna at the Royal Academy of Music in London, 1991; Lolita, Royal Opera, Sweden, 1994; Prokofiev and Shostakovich wrote concertos for him and Britten the 3 Cello Suites and Cello Symphony; Premiered the Shostakovich Cello Sonata, concertos by Bliss, Lutoslawski, Christobal Halffter in 1986 and Panufnik in 1992; As Conductor has premiered works by Bernstein, Landowski, Mennin's 9th Symphony, Walton's Prologue and Fantasia and Penderecki's Polish Requiem; Season 1992 with the premieres of Gubaidulina's opera-oratorio-ballet, Orazione per l'era di Acquario at Genoa and Schnittke's Life With an Idiot at Amsterdam; Conducted The Golden Cockerel at the Barbican Hall in London, 1992 and the premiere of Schnittke's Gesualdo at the Vienna Staatsoper, 1995; 70th Birthday Concerts at the Barbican, and elsewhere, 1997; Conducted new production of Mazeppa at La Scala, 1999; mem, Academy of St Cecilia, Rome; Royal Academy of Music, England. *Recordings include:* CDs of Beethovens Triple Concerto and Dvořák's Cello Concerto; Britten's Cello Symphony; Mozart Flute Quartets; Boris Godunov. *Honours:* Over 30 honorary degrees; Stalin Prize; Lenin Prize; People's Artist; Commander Legion of Honour, France; Medal of Freedom from 10 countries; Fellow, Royal College of Music; K.B.E., 1987. *Current Management:* Ronald A Wilford, Columbia Artists Management Inc. *Address:* 165 West 57 Street, New York, NY 10019, USA.

ROTH, Daniel; Organist and Composer; b. 31 Oct. 1942, Mulhouse, France. *Education:* Studied at the Paris Conservatoire, 1960–70 with Maurice Duruflé, Rolande Falcinelli, Henriette Puig-Roget and Marcel Bitsch; Further study with Marie Claire Alain. *Career:* Organist at Sacre-Coeur, Paris, 1963–85; Organist at Saint-Sulpice, 1985–; Professor of Organ at Marseille Conservatoire, 1973–79, later at Strasbourg Conservatoire; Visiting Professor at the Summer Academy at Haarlem, Holland; Professor at Catholic University and Resident Artist at the National Shrine, Washington DC, 1974–76; Professor at the Saar-brücken Musikhochschule, 1988; Professor of Organ, Musikhochschule, Frankfurt am Main, 1995–. *Compositions include:* Several works for organ published by Leduc, Bärenreiter, Schott (Mainz), Novello, and for flute and organ, choir and organ (Missa Brevis) published by Schott. *Recordings include:* Works by Bach, Liszt, Franck, Guilmant, Boëly, Saint-Saëns, Widor, Vierne, Dupré, and Jolivet with Erato, Philips, Arion, Pathé-Marconi EMI, Motette, Wergo (Schott) and Priory. *Honours:* Florent Schmitt prize awarded for his compositions by the Academy des Beaux Arts (Institut de France). *Address:* Église Saint Sulpice, 75006 Paris, France. *Website:* www.danielrothsaintsulpice.org.

ROTH, David (Robert); Violinist; b. 9 March 1936, Stockton-on-Tees, County Durham, England; m. Ruth Elaine West, 22 July 1963, 2 s. *Education:* University of Edinburgh, 1953–54; Royal Academy of Music, 1954–59; LRAM. *Career:* Debut: West Linton, Peebles, Scotland, 1954; With Netherlands Chamber Orchestra, Amsterdam, 1960–64; Played Bloch Sonata No. 1, Kol Israel Radio, Tel-Aviv, 1962; Deputy Leader, Northern Sinfonia Orchestra, Newcastle upon Tyne, 1966–68; 2nd Violin, Allegri String Quartet, 1969–99; Teaching at University of Southampton; mem, Incorporated Society of Musicians; Musicians Union. *Recordings:* With Allegri String Quartet for Open University; Many recordings for various labels. *Honours:* MMus, Hull, 1975; ARAM;

D.Mus, Nottingham, 1994; D.Mus, Southampton. *Address:* 16 Oman Avenue, London NW2 6BG, England.

ROTHENBERGER, Anneliese; Singer (Soprano); b. 19 June 1924, Mannheim, Germany; m. Gerd Dieberich, 1954. *Education:* Mannheim Musikhochschule with Erika Muller. *Career:* Debut: Koblenz in 1943; Hamburg Staatsoper, 1946–73 notably as Blonde in Die Entführung, Verdi's Oscar and Lulu; Visited Edinburgh with the company in 1952 for the British premiere of Hindemith's Mathis der Maler; Vienna Staatsoper from 1953, Salzburg from 1954 in the premiere of Liebermann's Penelope and Die Schule der Frauen; Also sang Papagena in Die Zauberflöte, Zdenka in Arabella, Sophie in Der Rosenkavalier and Flaminia in Haydn's Il Mondo della Luna; Glyndebourne, 1959–60 as Sophie; Metropolitan Opera debut in 1960 returning as Susanna, Oscar and Sophie; Zürich in 1967 in the premiere of Sutermeister's Madame Bovary; Tour of Russia in 1970. *Recordings:* Le nozze di Figaro; Die Fledermaus; Martha; Der Wildschütz; Die Entführung; Arabella; Gluck's Le Cadi Dupé; Sophie in 1960 film version of Der Rosenkavalier; Lulu (title role) conducted by Leopold Ludwig. *Publications:* Melodie Meines Lebens, autobiography, 1972. *Address:* c/o Hamburgische Staatsoper, Grosse-Theaterstrasse 34, 2000 Hamburg 36, Germany.

ROTZSCH, Hans-Joachim; Singer (Tenor); b. 25 April 1929, Leipzig, Germany; Educator. *Education:* Institute for Church Music at the Musikhochschule Leipzig, 1949–53; Organ study with Gunter Ramin; Vocal studies with P Losse and P Polster in Leipzig. *Career:* Many concerts and recordings of sacred music in Germany, Switzerland, Austria, Poland, Russia and Czechoslovakia; Appearances at the Leipzig Opera from 1961 and Kantor at St Thomas's School, Leipzig, from 1972; President of the Bach Committee, East Germany, 1983. *Recordings:* Bach Cantatas; St Luke Passion by Schütz; Dessau's Das Verhör des Lukullus; Mendelssohn's Elijah.

ROUILLON, Philippe; Singer (Baritone); b. 1955, Paris, France. *Education:* Studied at the Conservatoire National Supérieur de Paris; Ecole d'Art Lyrique de l'Opéra de Paris. *Career:* Performed Golaud in Pelléas et Mélisande and High Priest of Dagon in Samson et Dalila, Vienna; Chorèbe in Les Troyens, Ruprecht in The Fiery Angel, Orest in Elektra, Renato in Un Ballo in Maschera, the High Priest of Dagon, The High Priest in Alceste and Thoas in Iphigénie en Tauride in Paris; Ruprecht, High Priest of Dagon, Gellner in La Wally and Escamillo in Carmen at Amsterdam; Jochanaan in Salome, Lisbon and Strasbourg; Guillaume Tell in Liège; Samson et Dalila and Les Contes d'Hoffmann in Zürich; Frequent appearances in Germany in a variety of leading baritone roles; Close collaborations with Festival of Bregenz, Austria; Further engagements include: Rigoletto in Leipzig, Tel-Aviv and Hamburg, Pagliacci in Hamburg, Macbeth and Guillaume Tell in Liège, Tosca in Amsterdam and Ballo in Maschera in Bregenz; Season 2000–01 as Macbeth at the Munich Staatsoper, Thaos in Iphigénie en Tauride at Salzburg and Scarpia for Bonn Opera. *Recordings include:* Thaïs by Massenet; Saint François d'Assise by Messiaen with Kent Nagano; Chant de Paix by Landowski; Henry VIII by Saint-Saëns; Le Déluge by Saint-Saëns; Lélio and La Damnation de Faust by Berlioz. *Honours:* First Place, Prix Opéra and Prix de Public, international competition in Verviers, 1979; First Prize, Rio de Janeiro Competition, 1983.

ROULEAU, Joseph-Alfred, OC; Canadian singer (bass); b. 28 Feb. 1929, Matane, Québec, Canada. *Education:* studied singing with Edouard Wooley and Albert Cornellier, with Martial Singher at Conservatoire de Musique du Québec, in Milan with Mario Basiola and Antonio Narducci and further studies in Montréal with Ruzena Herlinger and Rachaele Mori. *Career:* debut, Montréal Opera Guild in 1951 in Un Ballo in Maschera; as Colline in La Bohème in Montreal in 1955; as King Philip in Don Carlos, New Orleans 1955–56; sang at Royal Opera House Covent Garden 1956–92, in 850 performances of over 45 operas; sang in the 1957 production of Les Troyens and in Turandot, Aida, Rigoletto, Simon Boccanegra, Don Giovanni and Billy Budd; Paris Opéra in 1960 as Raimondo in Lucia di Lammermoor, returning from 1974–79 as Tituriel in Parsifal, Don Quichotte, Abimelech in Samson et Dalila, Crespel, Contes d'Hoffman; from 1966–71 three tours of USSR, singing in 12 cities, including Moscow and Leningrad; guest appearances in USA, UK, Germany, Netherlands, Italy, Romania, Hungary, France, Belgium, Ireland, Switzerland, Israel, Argentina, Chile, Brazil, South Africa and Australia; in Toronto in 1967 premiere of Harry Summer's Louis Riel; festival appearances at Edinburgh, Aldeburgh, Glynde-bourne, Bath, Leeds, London, Wexford, Paris and New York, Empire State Festival; other roles include Arkel in Pelléas et Mélisande, Sarastro, Boris Godunov, Osmin in Die Entführung, Daland in Der fliegende Holländer and Oroveso in Norma, Philippe II in Don Carlo, Dosifei in Khovanshchina, Mephisto, Basilio in Barber of Seville, Mephistopheles in Faust; sang Don Marco in Menotti's The Saint of Bleecker Street at Philadelphia in 1989, Trulove in The Rake's Progress for Vancouver Opera 1989, The Prince in Adriana Lecouvreur for L'Opéra de Montréal in 1990 and Mozart's Bartolo with Vancouver Opera 1992; worked with Pavarotti, Domingo, Te Kanawa, Baker,

Gobbi, Christoff, Vickers, Sutherland, Callas, De Los Angeles, Jones, Taddei, Schwarzkopf and others; sang under Solti, Maazel, Levine, Dutoit, Davies, Stravinsky, Boulez, Ozawa, Plasson, Bernardi et Decker and others; concerts and recitals with int. orchestras; Prof., Univ. of Québec 1980–98; Pres., Jeunesses Musicales du Canada 1989–, Prix Joseph Rouleau for Vocal Art named for him 1995; founder and mem. of bd, Concours Musical Int. de Montréal 2002–; mem., numerous competition judging panels 1973–. *Films:* Au Pays de Monsieur Zom (title role); worked with Zeffirelli, Visconti, Gielgud, Ronconi and Chéreau. *Recordings include:* Sémiramide; Roméo et Juliette, Gounod; L'Enfance du Christ; Lucia di Lammermoor; Renard, Stravinski; Don Carlos; Aïda; Il Trovatore; French Operatic arias; Metropolitan Opera, New York, 1984–88; San Francisco Opera, 1984–89; Boris Godunov, title role (Prix Félix, 2000). *Honours:* Hon. Pres., 65th Concours OSM 2004; Officier de l'Ordre du Canada 1977; Officier de l'Ordre nat. du Québec 1999; Dr hc (Québec à Rimouski); Prix Archambault 1967; Silver Medal, Royal Opera House Covent Garden 1977; Prix du Quebec 1990; Panthéon de l'art lyrique du Canada 1992; Médaille du mérite exceptionnel des Jeunesses Musicales du Canada 1995; Prix Opus Hommage, Conseil québecois de la musique 2003. *Address:* 7 Roosevelt, Suite 20, Ville Mont-Royal, Québec, QC H3R 1Z3, Canada.

ROUSE, Christopher (Chapman); Composer; b. 15 Feb. 1949, Baltimore, Maryland, USA; m. Ann Jensen, 28 Aug 1983, 1 s., 2 d. *Education:* BMus, Oberlin Conservatory, 1971; Private study with George Crumb, 1971–73; MFA, DMA, Cornell University, 1977. *Career:* Assistant Professor, University of Michigan, 1978–81; Assistant Professor, 1981–85, Associate Professor, 1985–91, Professor, 1991–, Eastman School of Music; Composer-in-Residence, Indianapolis Symphony Orchestra, 1985–86; Composer-in-Residence, Baltimore Symphony Orchestra, 1986–88. *Compositions:* Ogoun Badagris, 1976; Ku-Ka-Ilimoku, 1978; Mitternachtslieder, 1979; Liber Daemonum, 1980; The Infernal Machine, 1981; String Quartet, 1982; Rotae Passionis, 1982; Lares Hercii, 1983; The Surma Ritornelli, 1983; Gorgon, 1984; Contrabass Concerto, 1985; Phantasmata, 1985; Phaethon, 1986; Symphony No. 1, 1986; Jagannath, 1987; String Quartet No. 2, 1988; Bonham, 1988; Iscariot, 1989; Concerto per corde, 1990; Karolju, 1990; Violin Concerto, 1991; Trombone Concerto, 1991; Violoncello Concerto, 1992; Flute Concerto, 1993; Symphony No. 2, 1994; Envoi, 1995; Compline, 1996; Guitar Concerto, 1999. *Honours:* Friedheim Award, Kennedy Center, 1988; Guggenheim Fellowship, 1990; Academy of of Arts and Letters Award, 1993; Pulitzer Prize, 1993.

ROUSSET, Christophe; French harpsichordist and conductor; b. 12 April 1961, Avignon. *Education:* studied with Huguette Dreyfus, Kenneth Gilbert, Bob van Asperen and Gustav Leonhardt, chamber music with the brothers Kuijken and Lucy van Dael. *Career:* frequent solo appearances in France and throughout Europe concertos with La Petite Bande, Musica Antiqua Köln, Acad. of Ancient Music; Asst for Les Arts Florissants; collaborations with artists, including William Christie, Agnès Mellon, Wieland Kuijken and Christopher Hogwood; conducts Les Arts Florissants, Il Seminario Musicale and other ensembles; founded Les Talens Lyriques (title from Rameau's Les Fêtes d'Hébé) 1991–, giving many performances of Baroque Opera; revival of Handel's Riccardo Primo at Fontevraud, France 1995; Handel's Admeto at Beaune and Montpellier and in Australia 1998; Wigmore Hall concerts 1999. *Recordings include:* Harpsichord Music by Bach, Rameau and Gaspard le Roux; Handel's Scipione and Riccardo Primo, Jommelli's Armida Abbandonata; Les Fêtes de Paphos by Mondonville; Mozart's Mitridate; Antigona by Traetta; The complete keyboard works of Couperin; Rameau, Overtures. *Honours:* First Prize Bruges Competition 1983, Gramophone Award 1998. *Address:* c/o Les Arts Florissants, 2 rue Saint Pétersbourg, 75008 Paris, France.

ROUTH, Francis (John); Composer, Pianist and Writer; b. 15 Jan. 1927, Kidderminster, England; m. (1) Virginia Anne Raphael, 1 September 1956, (2) Diana Florence Elizabeth Cardell Oliver, 1 Nov 1991, 2 s., 2 d. *Education:* BA 1951, MA 1954, King's College, Cambridge; FRCO, LRAM, Royal Academy of Music; Private Study with Matyas Seiber. *Career:* Appeared as Pianist, occasionally Conducted in London and elsewhere, South Bank, Radio Broadcasts; Founder, Director, Redcliffe Concerts, 1963–64. *Compositions:* A Sacred Tetralogy, 1959–74; Dialogue for violin and orchestra, 1968; Double Concerto, 1970; Sonata for solo cello, 1971; Spring Night, 1971; Symphony, 1972; Cello Concerto, 1973; Mosaics, 1976; Oboe Quartet, 1977; Fantasy for violin and pianoforte, 1978; Scenes for orchestra, 1978; Vocalise, 1979; Concerto for ensemble I, 1982, II 1983; Tragic Interludes for oboe, 1984; Celebration for piano, 1984; Elegy for piano, 1986; Oboe Concerto, 1986; Poeme Fantastique for piano and orchestra, 1986–88; Four Marian Antiphons for organ, 1988; Romance, 1989; Woefully Arranyed, for soloists, choir and orchestra, 1990; Fantasy Duo for violin and piano, 1990; Romanian Dance, 1990; Concerto for ensemble III, 1991; Suite for string orchestra, 1992; Clarinet Quintet, 1994; Capriccio, 1995; Scenes for orchestra II, 1997; Triumphal March, 1997; Suite for Tbilisi,

Concerto for ensemble IV, 1997; Divertimento for string quartet, 1998; Angels of Albion Scenes, for Piano III, 1998; Bretagne, Scenes for piano IV, 1998; Sonata Festiva, Scenes for Piano V, 1999. *Recordings:* A Sacred Tetralogy, Organ, Christopher Bowers-Broadbent, 1984; Celebration, Elegy, Piano, Jeffrey Jacob, 1986; Oboe Quartet, Tragic Interlude, Oboe Robin Canter with Redcliffe Ensemble, 1992; A Woman Young and Old, soprano Margaret Field, 1995; Clarinet Quintet, clarinet Nicholas Cox with Redcliffe Ensemble, 1995; On a Deserted Shore, 1996; Four Marian Antiphons, Exultet Coelum Laudibus, 1998; Divertimento for string quartet, Bochmann Quartet, 1998; Scenes for piano III and IV, 1999; Symphonic Variations, 2003. *Publications:* The Organ, 1958; Contemporary Music, 1968; The Patronage and Presentation of Contemporary Music, 1970; Contemporary British Music, 1972; Early English Organ Music, 1973; Stravinsky, 1974. *Contributions:* Various journals and The Annual Register, 1980–; Editor, Composer, 1980–88;. *Address:* 68 Barrowgate Road, Chiswick, London W4 4QU, England.

ROUTLEY, Nicholas; Conductor, Composer and University Lecturer; b. 26 June 1947, England; m. Margo Adelson, m. 26 May 1982, 1 s., 2 d. *Education:* George Heriot's, Edinburgh; St John's College, Cambridge; Piano studies with Peter Feuchtwanger; Conducting with Hans Heimler, Franco Ferrara. *Career:* Debut: Pianist, Wigmore Hall, 1979; Conductor, Taiwan Symphony Orchestra, 1984; University of Cambridge, 1973–75; University of Sydney, 1975–; University of Hong Kong, 1982–85, 1990–93; mem, Musicological Society of Australia. *Compositions:* Sicut Lilium, for choir and vibraphone, 1996; Sanctus, for choir and percussion, 1996; Like Snow, 5 songs for voice and piano, 1997; Icarus For Orchestra, 1997; Mycenae Lookout for baritone solo, choir, 2 pianos and percussion, 1998. *Recordings:* The Hermit of Green Light (Australian vocal music), 1983; Monteverdi Vespers of 1610, 1989; Josquin, 1994; Clare MacLean, The Complete Choral Music, 1995; Josquin, Secular Music, 1996. *Publications:* A Practical Guide to Musica Ficta, 1985; Arianna Thrice Betrayed (Gordon Athol Anderson Memorial Lecture), 1998; Symphony, 2000. *Contributions:* 2 articles on Debussy's Preludes in Musicology Australia, 1992, 1993. *Address:* Department of Music, University of Sydney, NSW 2006, Australia.

ROWLAND, Christopher (Selwyn); Violinist, Teacher and Quartet Leader; b. 21 Dec. 1946, Barnet, Hertfordshire, England; m. Elizabeth Attwood, 18 Dec 1982, 1 s. *Education:* BA, MA, Trinity College, Cambridge, 1965–68; Associate, Royal Academy of Music, 1980; D.Mus, Bucknell University, PA, 1981. *Career:* Performed live on radio throughout the United Kingdom and Europe and regularly in North America; Supervisor of Chamber Music, Tutor in Violin, Royal Northern College of Music, Manchester; Violinist for contemporary music group, Lumina; Leader of Sartori Quartet, 1970–74 and Fitzwilliam Quartet, 1974–84, with tours to Russia in 1976 and 1978. *Recordings:* Many. *Publications:* Shostakovich–Man and Music, 1982. *Contributions:* Music Times; Soviet Music; Berlioz Bulletin. *Honours:* Numerous prizes at Royal Acadey of Music and Cambridge University; Grammy Awards and Grand Prix du Disque. *Address:* Fountain House, Low Street, Burton-in-Lonsdale, Via Carnforth, Lancashire, England.

ROWLAND, Gilbert; Harpsichordist and Organist; b. 8 Oct. 1946, Glasgow. *Education:* Harpsichord and Organ, Royal College of Music, 1965–69; Masterclasses, Dartington. *Career:* Debut: Wigmore Hall, 1973; Harpsichordist, Wigmore Hall, 1973, 1975; Harpsichordist, Purcell Room, 1979, 1982, 1983, 1985; Harpsichordist, Greenwich Festival, 1975–84; Berlin, 1985; Many recitals in North England; Radio performances at BBC Concert Halls, 1977–78; Broadcasts, French harpsichord Music, 1984; Scarlatti Sonatas, 1986; Soler Sonatas, 1983; mem, ARCO; ARCM. *Recordings:* Scarlatti Sonatas; Rameau keyboard works; Soler Sonatas; Complete Handel Suites, forthcoming. *Contributions:* Article on Scarlatti for NEMA, 1985. *Address:* 418 Brockley Road, Brockley, London SE4 2 DH, England.

ROWLAND, Joan (Charlotte); Pianist and Teacher; b. 7 May 1930, Toronto, Canada; m. John Michael Thornton, 5 May 1956, 3 s., 1 d. *Education:* BA, English, Columbia University, NY, 1970; Piano study with Mona Bates in Toronto, 1938–48, theoretical studies at Royal Conservatory of Music, 1940–46 and piano study with Eduard Steuermann at Juilliard School, NY, 1952–56. *Career:* Debut: With the Toronto Symphony under Ernest MacMillan in 1942; Recital debut in New York in 1948; Solo recitals in Canada, USA and Europe and for Canadian Broadcasting Corporation since 1942; 2 Tours of USA and London with Columbia Canadian Trio and toured with Reginald Kell Players; Soloist for various orchestras including Toronto Symphony, Wiesbaden Orchestra, Mozarteum Orchestra, Mozart Festival Orchestra, and San Francisco and Buffalo Symphonies; Toured with Piano Duo Schnabel in USA and Europe, 1981–95. *Recordings:* Schubert Grand Duo and B flat Variations, Mozart Sonata in F major, Schubert E minor Sonata, Schubert Fantasy in F minor and Variations in A flat, all with Piano Duo Schnabel; Solo recording of Schumann Fantasy and Carnaval. *Publications:* Playing Four-Hands: A Pilgrim's Progress,

The Piano Quarterly, 1986–87. *Honours:* 1st Prize, Kranichsteiner Modern Music Competition, Darmstadt, Germany, 1954; 1st Prize, Mozarteum Piano Competition, Salzburg, 1955. *Address:* 285 Riverside Drive No. 4A, New York, NY 10025, USA.

ROWLAND-JONES, (Simon) Christopher; violist and composer; b. 8 Sept. 1950, Colchester, England. *Education:* Royal College of Music. *Career:* debut Carnegie Hall, 1979; Chilingirian String Quartet, 1971–78, 1992–; Nash Ensemble, Villiers Piano Quartet; Chameleon; Arenski Ensemble; Professor and Chamber Music Co-ordinator, Royal College of Music; mem, Musicians Union; Performing Right Society. *Compositions:* 2 String Quartets; Piano Quartet; String Trio; Rivers Gods; Seven pieces for Solo Viola; String Quintet (Painting by Numbers), 1998. *Recordings include:* Dale, Phantasy and Suite; Bloch, Suites; Schubert, Schumann and Beethoven; Bach Solo Cello Suites, vol. 1, suites 1–3, after own edition/transcription. *Publications:* Transcription of Bach Cello Suites, 1998. *Address:* 77 The Vineyard, Richmond, Surrey TW10 6AS, England.

ROWLANDS, Carol; Singer (Mezzo-Soprano); b. 1960, Newcastle upon Tyne, England. *Education:* Hull University; Studied at the Royal Northern College of Music with Andrew Field and Peter Alexander Wilson. *Career:* Appeared with Scottish Opera, 1982–90 in L'Egisto, The Magic Flute, Le nozze di Figaro, Rigoletto, Il Trovatore, Lulu, Madama Butterfly and Salome; Has also understudied Mozart's Cherubino, Puck in Oberon, Wellgunde in Das Rheingold, Clairon in Capriccio, Judith in Bluebeard's Castle in 1990 and Didon in Berlioz's The Trojans for Scottish Opera; Performed Santuzza in Scottish Opera Go Round's autumn tour of Pagliacci and Cavalleria Rusticana in 1989; For University College sang Tigrana in Edgar by Puccini, also performed the title role of Regina by Blitzstein for Scottish Opera, Santuzza in Cavalleria Rusticana for Opera South, the Mother in Amahl and the Night Visitors for Opera West, Suzuki in Madama Butterfly at Isle of Man, and concert performances in the title role of Orfeo with John Currie Singers; Season 1992–93 as Cherubino in Marriage of Figaro in Malta, Waltraute in Die Walküre for Scottish Opera, Marcellina in Marriage of Figaro for Scottish Opera, Second Lady in The Magic Flute for Scottish Opera, Marcellina for Opera Factory and the title role in Carmen for Regency Opera; Sang Mrs Grose in The Turn of the Screw for Broomhill Opera, 1996; Birtwistle's Judy for Theatre Wales at the Queen Elizabeth Hall, London, 1998; Judy in Punch and Judy for Music Theatre Wales, 1998; Mother Jeanne in Les Dialogues des Carmelites for Welsh National Opera, 1999; Baba the Turk in The Rake's Progress for English Touring Opera 2000; Throttlethumper in The Wondrous Tale of Fanferlizzy Sunnyfeet by Schwertsik for Broomhill Opera 2001; Berta in The Barber of Seville, Holland Park, 2001; Tisbe in La Cenerentola for Opera Northern Ireland; Mrs. Grose in The Turn of The Screw for Broomhill Opera, 2001 and Nationale Reisopera, Netherlands, 2002; Suzuki in Madama Butterfly for London City Opera USA Tour, 2003; Despina in Così fan tutte for Longborough Opera, 2003. *Honours:* John Scott Award for contribution to Scottish Opera 1989. *Address:* Flat A, 3 The Boundary, Seaford, East Sussex BN25 1DG England. *Telephone:* 01323 491082. *E-mail:* carol.rowlands@tiscali.co .uk.

ROXBURGH, Edwin; Conductor, Composer and Oboist; b. 6 Oct. 1937, Liverpool, England. *Education:* RCM 1957–60, with Herbert Howells and Terence McDonagh; Further study with Nadia Boulanger and Luigi Dallapiccola and at St John's College, Cambridge. *Career:* Principal oboe of Sadler's Wells Opera, 1964–67, and soloist in contemporary music (Berio's Sequenza VII); Teacher of composition at RCM, 1968–; Founded 20th Century Ensemble of London, 1969. *Compositions include:* Night Music for soprano and orchestra, 1969; How Pleasant to Know Mr. Lear, for narrator and chamber orchestra, 1971; A Mosaic for Cummings, for 2 narrators and orchestra; Montage for orchestra, 1977; At the Still Point of the Turning World for amplified oboe and electronics, 1978; Voyager, for wind instruments, 1989. *Honours:* Cobbett Medal, 1970. *Address:* British Music Information Centre, 11 Stratford Place, London W1, England.

ROZARIO, Patricia; Singer (Soprano); b. 1960, Bombay, India; m. Mark Troop, 1 d. *Education:* Guildhall School of Music with Walter Gruner; Pierre Bernac, St Jean de Luz; National Opera Studio; Study with Vera Rozsa from 1980. *Career:* Concerts with Songmakers' Almanac, including tour to USA; Solo recitals, South Bank London, elsewhere; Frequent performances of Bach, Handel, Mozart; Vaughan Williams Serenade to Music, 1988 Proms; Schumann's Paradies und der Peri at Madrid, with Gerd Albrecht; Appeared at Bath and Edinburgh Festivals; Operatic roles include Giulietta (Jommelli's La Schiava Liberata), Netherlands Opera, Gluck's Euridice for Opera North, Mozart's Bastienne and Pamina for Kent Opera, Ilia on Glyndebourne tour, Ismene in Lyon production of Mitridate and Zerlina at Aix; Statue in Rameau's Pygmalion and Purcell's Belinda for Kent Opera; Florinda in Handel's Rodrigo at Innsbruck; Nero in L'Incoronazione di Poppea and Massenet's Sophie; Concert performance, Il Re Pastore, Queen

Elizabeth Hall; World premiere of John Casken's Golem, as Miriam, Almeida Festival, London; Wexford Festival, 1989, Ismene; Created title role in premiere of Tavener's Mary of Egypt, Aldeburgh, 1992; Season 1992–93, in Monteverdi's Il Combattimento, English National Opera and Haydn's L'infedeltà delusa, Garsington Opera; 1993–94, Wexford Festival, tour of Germany with BBC National Orchestra of Wales/Otaka, Hong Kong Philharmonic; World premiere of Tavener's Apocalypse, BBC Proms, 1994–95, recital in Lebanon, Purcell Room with Nash Ensemble; Romilda in Serse at Brussels, 1996; Sang Les Illuminations at St John's, London, 1997; Handel's Triumph of Time and Truth at the 1999 London Prom concerts. *Recordings:* Mahler Symphony No. 4, London Symphony; Songs of the Auvergne, conductor John Pritchard; Haydn Stabat Mater, conductor Trevor Pinnock; Golem; Tavener: We shall see him as he is, Mary of Egypt, To a child dancing in the wind; Spanish Songs; Britten Rape of Lucretia. *Honours:* British Song Prize, Barcelona; Maggie Teyte Prize; Sängerforderungspreis, Salzburg Mozarteum; Gold Medal, Guildhall School of Music; Gramophone Award, Golem, 1991. *Address:* c/o Stafford Law, 6 Barham Close, Weybridge, Surrey, KT 13 9 PR, England.

ROZE, Jeanine Michèle; French music promoter; b. 19 Aug. 1943, Aurillac (Cantal); d. of Henri Roze and Chana Roze (née Bernholc). *Education:* Lycée Lamartine, Paris, Univ. of Paris-IV Sorbonne. *Career:* Publicity Ed. Maillard agency 1962–63, Artistic Sec. 1964–75; artistic agent 1975–88; promoter of concerts etc. 1998–; creator and organizer Sunday morning concerts at Théâtre de Châtelet 1975, of Alban Berg quartet 1988–, of piano on the Champs-Elysées 1991–, at Théâtre de Champs-Elysées, in La Comédie des Champs-Elysées, of recitals by Jessye Norman at Pleyel 1990, 1991. *Publications include:* Schubert, album de famille (co-ed.) 1992, Musique en têtes (series of 16 musical post cards, ed.) 1992. *Honours:* Chevalier, Ordre des Arts et des Lettres. *Address:* 17 rue du Colisée, 75008 Paris, France. *Website:* www.jeanine -roze-production.com.

ROZHDESTVENSKY, Gennady (Nikolayevich); Conductor; b. 4 May 1931, Moscow, Russia; m. Viktoria Postnikova, 1969. *Education:* Moscow Conservatory, with Nikolay Rozhdstvensky and Lev Oborin. *Career:* Debut: Bolshoi Theatre, 1951 with The Nutcracker; Conducted at the Bolshoi, 1951–70 and as Principal Conductor from 1964–70, with productions including Spartacus, Prokofiev's War and Peace and A Midsummer Night's Dream; London debut in 1956; Principal Conductor of the Symphony Orchestra of All-Union Radio and Television, 1961–; Gave works by Prokofiev, Hindemith, Berg, Martinů and Sergei Slonimsky; Conducted Boris Godunov at Covent Garden, 1970; Artistic Director of Stockholm Philharmonic Orchestra, 1974; Chief Conductor of BBC Symphony Orchestra, 1978–81, Vienna Symphony Orchestra, 1981–; Conducted the premiere of Smirnov's Jacob's Ladder at the Queen Elizabeth Hall, 1991 with London Sinfonietta; Returned to Covent Garden in 1991 with Boris Godunov; Idomeneo at Finlandia Hall, Helsinki, 1991; Eugene Onegin for European Union Opera, 1998. *Honours:* People's Artist of the RSFSR, 1966; Lenin Prize, 1970. *Address:* Allied Artists Agency, 42 Montpelier Square, London SW7 1JZ, England.

ROZSA, Pál; Composer; b. 14 March 1946, Szombathely, Hungary; m. Éva Molnár, 28 Jan 1977, 2 d. *Education:* Chemical Engineering, Moscow State University; Private tuition, Composition, Sándor Szokolay and Zsolt Durkó. *Career:* Works performed in France, Italy, Germany, Sweden, Denmark, Poland, Austria, the United Kingdom, Canada, USA, South Africa, Hong Kong; Many works commissioned by renowned musicians; mem, Hungarian Composers Union, 1984–; Hungarian Music Society, 1990–. *Compositions:* Around 400 works including symphonic works, concertos, 5 operas, 7 string quartets, wind quintets, brass music, songs, oratorios and cantatas, church music, wind band, transcriptions of classical works. *Recordings:* 4 records; Many recordings for Hungarian Radio; 1 opera recorded by Hungarian Television. *Honours:* 15 works awarded 1st, 2nd or 3rd prizes at international or national composers competitions. *Address:* Zsókavár u.2 XI/50, Budapest XV, 1157, Hungary. *Telephone:* (36) 1418-4547. *E-mail:* erozsa@office.mta.hu.

RUBENACKER, Jutta; German violinist; *Professor of Violin, Hochschule für Musik und Theater, Hannover;* b. 25 May 1955, Karlsruhe, Germany; one s. *Education:* violin lessons and masterclasses. *Career:* mem., Bartholdy Quartet, Ensemble Neublang, Art Ensemble, Das Neue Ensemble, Rubernadzer Quartet, Duo Parlando; solo violist of the Sudwestdeubahe Kammer Orchester, Chamber Orchestra of Southwest Germany; concerts as soloist and chamber music, played mainly in Europe; masterclasses in Norway; many performances with Tatjana Prelevic, Xaver Thoma, David Wilde, Johannes Schollhorn, Stefan Schleiermacher, Tatjana Kumarova, Yougi Pagh-Pan, Sofia Gubaiduluia, Wolfgang Rihm; Prof. of Violin, Hochschule für Musik und Theater, Hannover 1993–. *Honours:* Hessischer Rundjunk-Preis 1974, Art and Promotion for music, Nieder Sadisen 1998. *Address:* Helmstedter Str 1, 30519 Hannover, Germany.

RUBENS, Sibylla; Singer (Soprano); b. 1970, Germany. *Education:* Studied at Trossingen and Frankfurt Musikhochschule; Further study with Elise Cavelti in Basle. *Career:* Frequent Concerts with Helmuth Rilling and Bachakademie Stuttgart, including Tour of Japan, 1995 with Mozart's C Minor Mass; Bach's St John Passion under Rilling and Philippe Herreweghe, 1996; Deutsche Symphony Orchestra Berlin under Ashkenazy and Janowski, in Mendelssohn's Lobesgesang and Schumann's Scenes from Faust; Season 1997–98 with the Fauré Requiem and Poulenc's Stabat Mater at the Concertgebouw, Amsterdam, Ein Deutsches Requiem in Stuttgart and a tour of Messiah with the Windsbache Knabenchor; St John Passion under Ton Koopman, The Creation with Michael Schonwandt and tour with the group Tafelmusik; Other engagements in Italy, France, Czech Republic, Poland and Norway; Opera includes Mozart's Pamina and Beethoven's Marzelline. *Recordings include:* Schubert's Lazarus, arranged by Denisov (Hänssler); Mozart's Requiem (Harmonia Mundi). *Address:* Kunstler Sekretariat am Gasteig, Rosenheimerstrasse 52, 81699 Munich, Germany.

RUBIN, Cristina; Singer (Soprano); b. 1958, Milan, Italy. *Education:* Studied at the Milan Conservatoire and the opera school of La Scala. *Career:* Debut: Bergamo in 1985 as Mimi; Sang Anna in Puccini's Le Villi at Torre del Lago and Trieste; Sang at Teatro Goldoni in Venice as Agata in Il Flamino by Pergolesi, Trieste in 1987 as Suzel in L'Amico Fritz, as Mimi at Zürich in 1986 and Mozart's Countess at Piacenza; Concerts with Beethoven's Missa Solemnis, Schumann's Manfred and Mendelssohn's Lobesgesang Symphony. *Address:* c/o Teatro alla Scala, Via Filodrammatici 2, 20121 Milan, Italy.

RUCKER, Mark; Singer (Baritone); b. 1957, Chicago, USA. *Career:* Debut: Cincinnati, 1985, as Amonasro, in Aida; Philadelphia, 1986, as Verdi's Renato, New York City Opera, 1988, as Rigoletto; European debut at Nice, 1989, as Tonio in Pagliacci; Vienna Staatsoper, 1993, as Alfio in Cavalleria Rusticana; Verdi's Macbeth at New Orleans and Enrico in Lucia di Lammermoor for Portland Opera, 1994; Rigoletto for Milwaukee Opera, 1996; Season 2000 as Rigoletto at Miami and Amonasro in Amsterdam; Concerts include Messiah, Elijah and Donna nobis pacem by Vaughan Williams. *Recordings include:* Amonasro in Aida. *Honours:* Winner, Pavarotti Competition at Philadelphia, 1985. *Address:* Milwaukee Opera Company, 820 East Knapp St, Milwaukee, WI 53302, USA.

RUDAKOVA, Larisa; Singer (soprano); b. 1964, Russia. *Career:* Many performances in Russia and Eastern Europe in operas by Rossini (Il Barbiere di Siviglia), Donizetti (Lucia di Lammermoor), Charpentier (Louise) and Glinka (Ruslan and Lyudmila); Also sings Rossini's Bel raggio lusinghier (Semiramide); Contestant at the 1995 Cardiff Singer of the World Competition; Sang Antonina in Glinka's A Life for the Tsar, St Petersburg, 1998. *Current Management:* Askonas Holt Ltd, Lonsdale Chambers, 27 Chancery Lane, London, WC2A 1PF, England. *Telephone:* (20) 7400-1700. *Fax:* (20) 7400-1799. *E-mail:* info@askonasholt.co.uk. *Website:* www.askonasholt.co.uk.

RUDEL, Julius; Conductor; b. 6 March 1921, Vienna, Austria. *Education:* Vienna and Mannes School of Music in USA. *Career:* Rehearsal Pianist for New York City Opera; Conductor for Johann Strauss's The Gypsy Baron, NY, 1944, with overall command, 1957, and was responsible for many premieres of works by American and foreign composers, and for revivals of many neglected operas; Guest Conductor for La Scala Milan, Covent Garden, Teatro Col ón in Buenos Aires, Vienna State Opera and the opera houses of Berlin, Munich, Paris and Hamburg; Conducted Rigoletto at the Metropolitan in 1989, Hamlet by Thomas at Chicago in 1990, and Der Rosenkavalier at Toronto in 1990; Season 1992 conducted La Bohème at Bonn, Don Carlo at Nice and Tosca at Buenos Aires; Conducted Faust at the Met, 1996; Die Zauberflöte for Los Angeles Opera, 1998. *Recordings include:* Julius Caesar by Handel; The Merry Widow by Lehar; Silverlake by Kurt Weill; Ginastera's Bomarzo; Works by Massenet, Donizetti, Offenbach, Verdi, Bellini, Boito and Charpentier; Many television recordings. *Honours:* Julius Rudel Award established in his honour for young conductors, 1969.

RUDENKO, Bela Andreyevna; Singer (soprano); b. 18 Aug. 1933, Bokovo-Antratsit, Ukraine, Russia. *Education:* Studied at the Odessa Conservatory with Olga Blagovidova. *Career:* Debut: Odessa in 1955 as Gilda in Rigoletto; Sang at Kiev from 1965 notably as Glinka's Ludmila, Rosina in Il Barbiere di Siviglia, Lakmé and Natasha in War and Peace; Bolshoi Theatre Moscow from 1972; Also successful in operas by Ukranian composers. *Recordings include:* Ruslan and Ludmila and A Life for The Tsar, by Glinka. *Honours:* State Prize of USSR. *Address:* c/o TG Shevchenko Theatre, Ul Vladimirskaya 50, Kiev, Ukraine.

RUDERS, Poul; Danish composer; b. 27 March 1949, Ringsted, Denmark; m. Annette Gerlach. *Education:* Royal Danish Music Acad. *Career:* performances with all major Danish symphony orchestras; performances by London Sinfonietta, Ensemble Intercontemporain, Speculum Musicae, New York Philharmonic, Philharmonia, Capricorn, Lontano;

Psalmodies for Guitar and Ensemble, 1990, and frequent performances of works at several international festivals; mem. Danish Composers' Guild, SPNM, England. *Compositions:* Major orchestral pieces: Capriccio Pian E Forte, 1978, Manhattan Abstraction, 1982, Thus Saw St John, 1984, The Drama Trilogy: Dramaphonia, Monodrama, Polydrama, 1987–88, Himmelhoch-Jauchzend zum Tode betrübt, symphony, 1989, Violin Concerto No. 2, 1991, Gong for Orchestra, 1992; Symphony No. 2, 1997; Chamber works: String Quartet No. 1, 1971, No. 2, 1979, Four Compositions, 1980, Greeting Concertino, 1982, 4 Dances in one movement, 1983, Vox In Rama, 1983; Concerto in Pieces (commissioned by BBC Symphony Orchestra), 1995; The Handmaid's Tale (opera commissioned by the Royal Theatre Copenhagen), 2000; Kafkas's Trial (opera with libretto by Paul Bentley, commissioned by The Royal Opera Co., Copenhagen), 2001–03; Listening Earth (commissioned by Berlin Philharmonic), 2002; Final Nightshade (commissioned by New York Philharmonic), 2003; Numerous solo pieces for various instruments. *Recordings include:* Four Dances, with London Sinfonietta conducted by Oliver Knussen, 1983–89; Corpus Cum Figuris, commissioned by Ensemble Intercontemporain, 1984–90; Corpus Cum Figuris: Point PCD 5084, Violin Concerto No. 1 Unicorn-Kanchana, 9114, Psalmodies: Bridge 9037, Symphony: Chan 9179. *Honours:* Royal Philharmonic, London, Charles Heidsieck Prize, 1991. *Current Management:* c/o Chester Music, 8–9 Frith Street, London, W1 5TZ, England. *E-mail:* poulmus.ruders@mail.tele.dk. *Website:* www.poulruders.net.

RUDY, Mikhail; Concert Pianist; b. 3 April 1953, Tashkent, USSR. *Education:* Moscow Conservatory with Jakov Flier. *Career:* After winning prizes at competitions in Leipzig and Paris he made his western debut in 1977, playing Beethoven's Triple Concerto in Paris with Rostropovich and Stern; Guest appearances with the Berlin Philharmonic, Orchestre de Paris, Concertgebouw, Boston Symphony, Montreal Symphony Orchestra, London Philharmonic and Toronto Symphony; US debut 1981 with the Cleveland Orchestra conducted by Lorin Maazel; Festivals include Schleswig-Holstein, Berlin, Tanglewood, Lockenhaus and Vienna; Salzburg Easter Festival, 1987 with Karajan; Chamber music concerts with the Amadeus Quartet until 1987, Guarneri Quartet and Vienna Philharmonic Wind Ensemble; London debut with the London Symphony Orchestra under Michael Tilson Thomas, 1988; Promenade Concerts 1989, Prokofiev's 2nd Concerto; Subject of French television Documentary Le grand Echiquier, 1989; Debut with Dresden Staatskapelle, 1991; Season 1991–92 with concerts in Cleveland and Munich; Returned to Russia, 1990, concerts with the St Petersburg Philharmonic; Music Director, St Riquier Festival; Waldbühne Concert with Berlin Philharmonic and Mariss Jansons, 1994; Janáček, Stravinsky and Schubert concert at the Wigmore Hall, London, 1997. *Recordings include:* Brahms and Ravel recital (EMI); Concertos by Rachmaninov and Tchaikovsky with St Petersburg Philharmonic and Mariss Jansons; Shostakovich Piano Concerto No. 1 with Berlin Philharmonic; Stravinsky: integral of Petroushka ballet (Transcriptions: Stravinsky/Rudy); Wagner: Siegfried Idyll; 2 piano improvisations with jazz pianist Micha Alperin. *Honours:* Chevalier des Arts et des Lettres, Prizewinner, 1971 Bach Competition, Leipzig; First Prize, Marguérite Long Competition, Paris, 1975; Grand Prix du disque Liszt, Budapest; Grand Prix du Disque Acad. Charles Cros (Scribiane); Grand Prix, Acad. Française (Rachmaninov concerti with Mariss Jansons; Symanovski recital); Deutsche Schalplatte Kritik Preis (Shostokovich). *Current Management:* Harrison/Parrott Ltd, 12 Penzance Place, London, W11 4PA, England. *Telephone:* (20) 7229 9166. *Fax:* (20) 7221 5042. *Website:* www.harrisonparrott.com.

RUDZINSKI, Witold; Composer, Musicologist and Pedagogue; b. 14 March 1913, Siebiez, Russia; m. Nina Rewienska, 26 Dec 1958, 1 s., 2 d. *Education:* Phil Mag, University of Wilno, 1936; Conservatory M Karlowicz Wilno, 1937; Studies with Nadia Boulanger and Charles Koechlin, Institut Gregorien, Paris, France, 1938–39. *Career:* Debut: 1936; Head, Music School Swieciany, Poland, 1937–38; Conservatory Wilno, 1939–42; Professor, Cons Lódz, 1945–47; Director of Music Department, Ministry of Culture, Warsaw, 1947–48; Academy of Music, Warsaw, 1957–; Dr hon causa, Chopin's Academy of Music Warsaw. *Compositions:* Operas: Janko Muzykant (Janko The Fiddler), 1951; Commander of Paris, 1957; The Dismissal of Grecian Envoys, 1962; Sulamith, 1964; The Peasants, 1972; The Ring and The Rose, 1982; The Yellow Nightcap, 1969; Oratorios: The Roof of the World, 1960; Gaude Mater Polonia, 1966, The Circle of Psalms 1987, Madonna 1991; Litany to the Holy Virgin of Ostra Brama, 1994; Symphonic Music: Musique Concertante for piano and orchestra, 1958; Pictures from Holy Cross Mountains, 1965; Concerto Grosso for percussion with string orchestra, 1970; Chamber Music: Sonata for viola and pianoforte, 1946; Flute Quintet, 1954; Deux Portraits des Femmes for voice and string quartet, 1960; To Citizen John Brown, voice and chamber ensemble, 1972; Duo Concertante for percussion, 1976; Sonata Pastorale for violin and pianoforte, 1976; Instrumental: Variations and Fugue for percussion, 1966; Quasi una sonata for pianoforte, 1975; Sonata per clavicembalo,

1978; Dialogue for saxophone and piano; Pleiades, sonata for clarinet and piano, 1987; Songs: Incidental music. *Recordings:* Sonata for viola and pianoforte; Janko Muzykant Muza; Musique Concertante for pianoforte and orchestra; The Roof of the World and Pictures from Holy Cross Mountains; Odprawa posłów greckich; Gaude Mater Polonia; Children Songs. *Publications:* Music for Everybody, 1948, 1966; Stanislaw Moniuszko, Principal Biography in 2 vols, 1954–61; Moniuszko's Correspondence, 1969; Moniuszko, Popular Mongr, 1978; What Is Opera? 1960; Béla Bartók Musical Technique, 1965; How to Listen to Music, 1975; Treatise on Musical Rhythm, 2 vols, 1987. *Address:* Narbutta 50 m 6, 02541 Warsaw, Poland.

RUDZINSKI, Zbigniew; Composer; b. 23 Oct. 1935, Czechowice, Poland; m. Ewa Debska, 13 July 1965, 1 d. *Education:* Warsaw University, 1956; MA, Composition Diploma with distinction, State High School for Music, Warsaw, 1956–60. *Career:* Professor of Composition, 1973–, Head of Composition Department, 1980–81, Rector (director), 1981–84, Academy of Music, F Chopin, Warsaw; President, Warsaw District, Polish Composers' Union, 1983–85, Secretary General, 1985–. *Compositions include:* Orchestral: Sonata for 2 String Quartets, Piano and Kettle Drums, 1960, Contra Fidem, 1964, Moments Musicaux l, 11, 111, 1965–68, Music By Night, 1970; Vocal/instrumental works: Four Folk Songs for soprano and piano, 1955; Sonata for clarinet and piano, 1958; Trio for 2 clarinets and bassoon, 1958; Epigrames for flute, choir and percussion, 1962; String Trio, 1964; Study for C for ensemble ad libitum, 1964; Impromptu for 2 pianos, 1968; Symphony for men's choir and orchestra, 1969; Requiem for the Victims of Wars for choir and orchestra, 1971; Tutti E Solo for soprano, flute, french horn and piano, 1973; Strings in the Earth for soprano and string orchestra, 1983; Three Romantic Portraits for 12 saxophones; Chamber: Quartet for 2 Pianos and Percussion, 1969, Sonata for Piano, 1975, Campanella for Percussion Ensemble, 1977, Tritones for Percussion Ensemble, 1979; Opera: The Mannequins, 1981, The Book Of Hours, songs for mezzo-soprano and piano trio, 1983, Das Sind Keine Träume, songs for mezzo-soprano and piano, 1986; Three Pictures at an Exhibition for flute, piano and vibraphone, 1996. *Address:* ul Poznanska 23 m 26, 00-685 Warsaw, Poland.

RUFFINI, Alessandra; Singer (Soprano); b. 1961, Italy. *Education:* Studied at the Milan Conservatory. *Career:* Sang Arianna in Vivaldi's Giustino in 1985 and appeared as Gilda at Treviso and Rovigo in 1987; Sang at Vicenza in 1988 as Elena in Gluck's Paride e Helena, Palermo in 1991 as Mariana in Wagner's Das Liebesverbot, and at Rome Opera in 1992 as Rossini's Adina and Leila in Les Pêcheurs de Perles; Other roles include Amina in La Sonnambula (Cremona, 1988) and Adina in L'Elisir d'amore (Piacenza 1992); Sang Pauline in Donizetti's Les Martyrs, Nancy, 1996. *Recordings include:* Rosina in Morlacchi's Il Barbiere di Siviglia; La Locandiera by Salieri; La Cecchina by Piccinni. *Address:* Rome Opera, Teatro dell'Opera, Piazza B Gigli 8, 00184 Rome, Italy.

RUFO, Bruno; Singer (Tenor); b. 1941, Italy. *Career:* Debut: Spoleto in 1965 as Pinkerton; Many appearances at La Scala Milan, Rome, Naples and as Radames in 1981 at Verona Arena; Further engagements at Bologna, Parma, Hamburg, Munich, Vienna, the Deutsche Oper Berlin and Düsseldorf; Sang Manrico at Liège, and Samson in season 1986–87; Television appearances have included Verdi's Ernani. *Address:* c/o Opéra Royal de Wallonie, 1 Rue des Dominicains, 4000 Liège, Belgium.

RUGGEBERG, Claudia; Singer (Contralto); b. 1955, Hamburg, Germany. *Education:* Studied in Hamburg with Judith Beckmann. *Career:* Many appearances throughout Germany in concerts and recitals; Guest engagements at the Hamburg and Oldenburg Operas, Bregenz Festival, 1985–86 in Die Zauberflöte and Gelsenkirchen and Stuttgart in 1987 in La Gioconda and Die Soldaten; Sang in Eugene Onegin at Zürich in 1991 and has appeared elsewhere including Barcelona, Bologna, Cologne and Krefeld; Has sung mainly in opera houses of Hamburg, Bonn, Cologne, Stuttgart, Aalto-Theater Essen; Ring Production (Erda), Dessau, Die Verurteilung des Lukullus, Handel, Giulio Cesare, 1992–97; Teatro Liceo Barcelona: Schoenberg Moses und Aron, Götterdämmerung, Walküre, Eugene Onegin; Teatro Communale Bologna: Walküre (Riccardo Chailly); Teatro alla Scala Milano, Elektra (Giuseppe Sinopoli), 1994; Asia-Concert tour with the Staatskapelle Dresden, Giuseppe Sinopoli: Elektra in Japan and Taiwan, 1995; Sang at Marseille, 1997 and Toulouse, 1999; Professor at the Essen Musikhochschule, 1990–. *Recordings:* CDs: Braunfels: Die Verkündigung, 1994; Schoeck, Rohm, Shostakovich Lieder, 1997. *Address:* Wesselswerth 50, 45239 Essen, Germany.

RUITUNEN, Esa; Singer (Baritone); b. 1949, Finland. *Education:* Studied at the Sibelius Academy, Helsinki, 1974–80. *Career:* Vicar at the Temppelaukio Church at Helsinki, 1975–84; Appearances in Lieder recitals and concerts of sacred music throughout Scandinavia and Northern Europe and in the USA; Opera engagements at Helsinki and Savonlinna as Monterone, Escamillo, Pizarro, Enrico in Lucia di Lammermoor, Klingsor and Valentin; Appeared as guest at Essen in

Merikanto's Juha and at Los Angeles in 1992 in the premiere of Sallinen's Kullervo; Sang Alberich in Das Rheingold at Helsinki, 1996; King Fisher in The Midsummer Marriage at Munich, 1998; Season 1999–2000 as Grigoris in The Greek Passion by Martinů, at Bregenz and Covent Garden; Enescu's Oedipe at the Deutsche Oper Berlin and the General in the premiere of Maria's Love by Kortekangas, at Savonlinna. *Address:* Finnish National Opera, Blvd 23–27, 00180 Helsinki, Finland.

RUK-FOCIC, Bozena; Singer (soprano); b. 31 Oct. 1937, Zagreb, Yugoslavia. *Education:* Studied with Zlatko Sir in Zagreb. *Career:* Debut: Basle in 1960 as Micaela in Carmen; Member of Croatian National Opera, Zagreb; Guest appearances in Bucharest, Athens, Roma, Palermo, Naples, Trieste, Genoa, Luxembourg, Netherlands, Graz, Bern, Belgrade, Vienna, Berlin, Stuttgart, Hamburg and at Covent Garden (as Eva in Die Meistersinger); La Scala as Sieglinde in Walküre in 1970 and in the Italian premiere of Dallapiccola's Ulisse; Further engagements in Kiev, Budapest, Houston, Pittsburgh, Seattle, Washington, Zürich, Geneva, Barcelona and Salzburg; Other roles include Jaroslavna in Prince Igor, Alceste, Madama Butterfly, Mozart's Countess, Verdi's Leonora and Aida, Wagner's Elsa, Elisabeth and Sieglinde, Strauss's Ariadne and Weber's Agathe, Desdemona in Otello, Tosca, Elisabetta in Don Carlos, Manon, Arabella, Marguerite in Faust, and Amelia in Simon Boccanegra; Many appearances as concert singer.

RUMBOLD, Ian Francis, BMus; Editor; b. 29 March , Grantham, England; m. Valerie Proctor. *Education:* King's School, Grantham, Lincolnshire, Univ. of Birmingham, Jesus Coll., Cambridge. *Career:* Research Fellow, Clare Hall, Cambridge 1981–83; Sir James Knott Research Fellow, Newcastle upon Tyne 1983–85; freelance editing and teaching 1985–86; Lecturer in Music, Univ. of Exeter 1986–87; Research Assoc. (New Berlioz Edition) Univ. of Manchester 1987–99, Royal Coll. of Music 1999–2003; mem. Royal Musical Asscn. *Publications:* Editions for New Berlioz Edition Vols 14, 15, and 22b; contrib. to The New Grove Dictionary of Music and Musicians, The New Oxford Companion to Music and many journals. *Address:* 33 Selly Wick Drive, Selly Park, Birmingham, B29 7JQ, England (home). *Telephone:* (121) 472-4994 (home). *Fax:* (121) 472-4994 (home). *E-mail:* ianrumbold@aol .com (home).

RUNDGREN, Bengt; Singer (Bass-Baritone); b. 21 April 1931, Karlskrona, Sweden. *Education:* Studied with Arne Sunnegaard and Ragnar Hulten in Stockholm. *Career:* Sang in operetta then made opera debut as the Commendatore, Stockholm in 1962; Member of the Royal Opera, Stockholm until 1969; Sang Osmin in Die Entführung at Drottningholm, 1965–67; Member of Deutsche Oper Berlin from 1969, often being heard as Leporello in Don Giovanni; Metropolitan Opera in 1974 as Hagen, repeating the role at Bayreuth in the 1976 centenary production of The Ring; Sang the Commendatore in Don Giovanni at Stockholm in 1988; Fafner in Siegfried at Helsinki, 1998; Also heard as concert singer. *Honours:* Swedish Court Singer, 1975. *Address:* c/o Finnish National Opera, PO Box 176, Helsingkatu 58, 00251 Helsinki, Finland.

RUNGE, Peter-Christoph; Singer (baritone); b. 12 April 1933, Lubeck, Germany. *Education:* Studied with Lilly Schmidtt de Giorgi in Hamburg. *Career:* Debut: Flensburg in 1958 as Guglielmo in Così fan tutte; Sang in Wuppertal, 1959–64, Deutsche Oper am Rhein, Düsseldorf, 1964–; Roles include Monteverdi: Orfeo; Mozart: Count, Figaro, Guglielmo, Papageno, Alfonso, Speaker, Rossini's Cenerentola, Dandini, Barber, Raimbaud, Le Comte Ory; Donizetti: Belcore, Malatesta; Strauss repertoire, Harlekin, Musiklehrer and Olivier, Barbier; Puccini: Turandot, Marcello and Scaunard in La Bohème; Wagner: Beckmesser and Wolfram; Berg: Wozzeck; Glyndebourne Opera, 1966–73, 1982, 1983 as Papageno, Pelléas and Amida in the Leppard/Cavalli L'Ormindo, 1967–68; Edinburgh Festival in 1972 in the British premiere of Zimmermann's Die Soldaten as Stolzius, and Corpo in Cavallieri's Rappresentione; Guest appearances in Vienna Staatsoper, Brussels, Stockholm, Amsterdam, Warsaw, Bolshoi, Berlin, Hamburg and Zürich, Bogota, Verona, Paris, Nice, Buenos Aires, Berlin, Salzburg; Scottish Opera, 1970–74; World Premiere of Goehr's Behold the Sun, Düsseldorf in 1985 and BBC production; Udo Zimmermann's Schüsterfrau, Düsseldorf 1987; Wexford Festival in 1990 as Major Max von Zastrow in The Rising of The Moon by Maw; Dresden Festival, 1997–98 as Parmenione in Rossini's L'Occasione; Concert artist often heard in classical and contemporary repertoire; Oratorios and Missae include Bach, Handel, Mozart, Schubert, Bruckner, Brahms, Mendelssohn, War Requiem by Britten, Lucas Passion by Penderecki; Radio concerts and recordings with BBC London, Edinburgh, Paris, Berlin, Hamburg, Munich, Cologne, Milan, Rome, Madrid, Stockholm, Brussels and Netherlands; Teacher, Music High Schools in Düsseldorf and Aachen, also gives Masterclasses. *Recordings include:* Cavalli's L'Ormindo; Music by Monteverdi, Schütz and Bach; Handel's Apollo and Dafne; Auber's Manon Lescaut. *Honours:* Kammersänger, 1990; Honorary Professorship, 1996. *Current Management:* Athole Still

International Management, Forresters Hall, 25–27 Westow Street, London, SE19 3RY, England. *Telephone:* (20) 8771-5271. *Fax:* (20) 8768-6600. *Website:* www.atholestill.com.

RUNKEL, Reinhild; Singer (Mezzo-Soprano); b. 25 Dec. 1943, Volkach am Main, Germany. *Education:* Studied in Wuppertal. *Career:* Sang at the Nuremberg Opera, 1975–82; Guest engagements at Lisbon, Reggio Emilia, Paris and San Francisco, 1985, and Florence as Magdalene in Meistersinger in 1986; Salzburg Festival in 1987 in Moses and Aron by Schoenberg; Sang Fricka in Ring performances at Bologna, Stuttgart and Cologne, 1987–88; Appearances at the Zürich Opera from 1985 as Herodias, Fricka and Clytemnestra in a Ruth Berghaus production of Elektra in 1991; Stuttgart Staatsoper in 1992 as Begbick in Aufstieg und Fall der Stadt Mahagonny; Other roles include Erda, Waltraute, Brangaene, Lyon 1990, Jocasta in Oedipus Rex and the Nurse in Die Frau ohne Schatten; Fricka in Die Walküre for Netherlands Opera, 1998; Sang the Nurse in Die Frau ohne Schatten at La Scala and Munich, 1999; Clytemnestra in Elektra in Sydney and at the Savonlinna Festival, 2000; Frequent concert appearances. *Recordings include:* Fortune Teller in Arabella and Nurse in Die Frau ohne Schatten conducted by Solti; Beethoven's 9th. *Address:* c/o Zürich Opera, Falkenstrasse 1, 8008 Zürich, Switzerland.

RUNNICLES, Donald; Conductor; b. 16 Nov. 1954, Edinburgh, Scotland. *Education:* Studied at Edinburgh and Cambridge Universities and at the London Opera Centre. *Career:* Repetiteur at the Mannheim National Theatre from 1980, debut with Les Contes d'Hoffmann; Kapellmeister from 1984, conducting Fidelio, Le nozze di Figaro, Un Ballo in Maschera, Die Walküre and Parsifal; Principal conductor at Hanover from 1987, leading Salome, Jenůfa, Tosca, Don Giovanni, Werther; Regular engagements with the Hamburg Staatsoper: Turandot, The Bartered Bride, Die Zauberflöte, Manon Lescaut, Carmen, Don Carlos, Zar und Zimmermann, Il Trovatore, Il Barbiere di Siviglia, L'Elisir d'amore, Lady Macbeth of Mtsensk; General Music Director at Freiburg from 1989: Lady Macbeth, Billy Budd, Peter Grimes; Assisted James Levine at Bayreuth, then conducted Lulu at the Metropolitan, 1988, followed by Die fliegende Holländer, 1990, and Die Zauberflöte; Conducted The Ring at San Francisco, Summer, 1990; Vienna Staatsoper from season, 1990–91, with Il Barbiere di Siviglia, Don Giovanni, Madama Butterfly, La Traviata and Prince Igor; Glyndebourne debut 1991, with Don Giovanni; Musical Director of San Francisco Opera from 1992; Season 1992–93 with Lady Macbeth of the Mtsensk District at Vienna Volksoper; The Fiery Angel, Guillaume Tell, Boris Godunov at San Francisco; Don Giovanni at Munich; Tannhäuser at Bayreuth; Der Ring des Nibelungen at Bayreuth; Other repertoire includes Idomeneo at Hanover; Der Freischütz; Symphonic engagements in Darmstadt, Odensee, St Gallen, Copenhagen and with NDR Orchestra, Hamburg; Season 1997–98 at San Francisco with Death in Venice, Le nozze di Figaro, and Pelléas et Mélisande; Engaged for Billy Budd and the Ring at the Vienna State Opera, 2001; Led new prodction of Katya Kabanova at San Francisco, 2002; Conducted Schoenberg's Gurrelieder at the London Proms, 2002; Tristan und Isolde (over 3 concerts) for the BBC SO, 2002–03. *Current Management:* Athole Still International Management, Forresters Hall, 25–27 Westow Street, London, SE19 3RY, England. *Telephone:* (20) 8771-5271. *Fax:* (20) 8768-6600. *Website:* www.atholestill.com.

RUNSWICK, Daryl; Composer, Musician and Singer; b. 12 Oct. 1946, Leicester, England. *Education:* MA, hons, Music, Corpus Christi College, Cambridge, 1964–67. *Career:* Musical Director, Footlights Club, 1966–67; Jazz Bass Player, especially with C Laine and J Dankworth, 1968–82; Concert Bass Player, especially with London Sinfonietta, 1970–82; Session Player, bass, bass guitar, keyboards, 1970–81; Arranger, Record Producer, especially King's Singers, 1971–; Composer of film and television music, 1976–; Tenor Singer in Electric Phoenix, 1983–; Musical Director, Green Light Music Theatre Company, 1990–; Professor of Composition and Media Studies, Trinity College of Music, London. *Compositions:* Scafra Preludes; 6 Episodes forming a Threnody; Moto interrotto/Ripresso; Mouth Symphony; Four by Five; I Am A Donut; Four Nocturnes; Main-Lineing; From Two Worlds; Cool>Warm>Hot. *Recordings:* With Electric Pheonix including: Berio, Cage, Nordheim, Wishart; With London Sinfonietta including: Songs for Dov, Agon, King Priam; With Nash Ensemble including: The Soldier's Tale. *Current Management:* Faber Music Ltd. *Address:* 34A Garthorne Road, London SE23 1EW, England.

RUOFF, Axel D.; Composer; b. 24 March 1957, Stuttgart, Germany. *Education:* State University for Music, Stuttgart and Academy for Music, Kassel, 1975–84; Diplomas in Piano and Music Theory, cum laude, 1979 and Diploma for Composers, 1984; National University for Fine Arts and Music, Tokyo, Japan, 1985–87. *Career:* Head of Department, Stuttgart Music School, 1981–88; Lecturer, State University for Music, Trossingen, 1985–87; Concurrently Guest Professor in Composition at Morioka College in 1988, selected for the Forum for Young Composers, Berlin; Fellowship from the Art Foundation of

Baden, Württemberg; Fellowship from the Japanese Ministry of Culture for study at the National University for Fine Arts and Music in Tokyo; Professor at State University for Music, Stuttgart, 1992. *Compositions:* Prozession for Orchestra, 1983; Concerto for flute and orchestra, 1984; Correlations, cello solo, 1983; Jemand In Vorbeigehen for voice and piano, 1984; Via Dolorosa for organ, 1985; Fassaden for violin solo, 1985; String Quartet, 1986; Salomo-Variations for choir, 1986; Nacht Und Träume for orchestra, 1987–88; String Quartet No. 2, 1988; Piano Concerto, 1989. *Recordings:* Various records; Broadcasts for German, other European and Japanese stations. *Publications:* Publishing contracts with Edition Moeck, Con Brio in Berlin and Celle and Mieroprint in Münster. *Honours:* Valentino Bucchi, Rome, 1985, 1987; 1st Prize, ICONS, Torino, 1988; 2nd Prize, Ensemblia, Mönchengladbach, 1986; 1st Prize, Corciano, Perugia, 1991. *Address:* Möhringer Land Str 53, 7000 Stuttgart 80, Germany.

RUOHONEN, Seppo; Singer (Tenor); b. 25 April 1946, Turku, Finland. *Education:* Studied in Helsinki, with Luigi Ricci in Rome and with Anton Dermota in Vienna. *Career:* Debut: Helsinki in 1973 as Alvaro in La Forza del Destino; Appearances with Finnish National Opera as Verdi's Duke and Manrico, Tchaikovsky's Lensky and Hermann, and Don Ottavio; Savonlinna in 1977 in The Last Temptations by Kokonen, with Sallinen's The Red Line, repeated at the Metropolitan, NY in 1983; San Diego Opera as Riccardo in Un Ballo in Maschera; Returned to Savonlinna in 1983 as Don Carlos and as Erik in Der fliegende Holländer; Has sung at Frankfurt from 1978 and made guest appearances in Berlin, Dresden, Leeds, Glasgow, Stuttgart and Wiesbaden as the Duke of Parma in Doktor Faust, Puccini's Cavaradossi, Luigi and Pinkerton, and Jenik in The Bartered Bride; Sang Florestan at the 1992 Savonlinna Festival; Inquisitor in Dallapiccola's Il Prigioniero for Tampere Opera, 1996. *Recordings include:* The Last Temptations.

RUPP, Andrew; Singer (baritone); b. 1970, England. *Education:* St John's College, Cambridge and with Linda Esther Gray. *Career:* Concerts with The Sixteen, The Cardinall's Musick and the Tallis Scholars; Repertoire includes Mozart and Fauré Requiems, Messiah, Bach's Christmas Oratorio, St Matthew Passion and B minor Mass; British premiere of Prokofiev's Eugene Onegin on South Bank; Glyndebourne Festival in Le Comte Ory, Dove's Flight, and as John in Birtwistle's The Last Supper; Somnus and Apollo in Semele by Eccles, Junius in The Rape of Lucretia for Opera de Caen and Purcell's Aeneas at Aix; European tour as the Ferryman in Britten's Curlew River; Mozart's Count for Kentish Opera and tour with the Gabrieli Consort 2001. *Current Management:* Athole Still International Management, Forresters Hall, 25–27 Westow Street, London, SE19 3RY, England. *Telephone:* (20) 8771-5271. *Fax:* (20) 8768-6600. *Website:* www .atholestill.com.

RUSHTON, Julian (Gordon); University Professor; b. 22 May 1941, Cambridge, England; m. 1968, 2 s. *Education:* Studied at Trinity College, Cambridge and Magdalen College, Oxford. *Career:* University Lecturer, University of East Anglia, 1968–74; University of Cambridge, 1974–81; West Riding Professor, University of Leeds, 1982–2002; Emeritus Professor, 2002–; mem, Chairman Musica Britannica; President, Royal Musical Association, 1994–99; American Musicological Society (Corresponding Member), 2000; Elgar Society; Schubert Institute, UK. *Publications:* Berlioz: Huit Scènes de Faust, La Damnation de Faust, editions; The Musical Language of Berlioz; Classical Music: A Concise History; WA Mozart: Don Giovanni; WA Mozart: Idomeneo; Berlioz: Roméo et Juliette; Elgar: Enigma Variations, 1999; The Music of Berlioz, 2001. *Contributions:* New Grove Dictionary of Music and Musicians; Various books and professional journals; New Grove Dictionary of Opera. *Address:* School of Music, University of Leeds, Leeds LS2 9JT, England.

RUSSELL, Ken; Stage Producer; b. 3 July 1927, Southampton, England. *Education:* Nautical College, Pangbourne; Choreography with Nicolai Sergueff of the Marinsky Ballet, St Petersburg. *Career:* Films for BBC and ITV, 1959–70 including studies of Elgar, Debussy, Prokofiev, Delius, Vaughan Williams, Martinů and Richard Strauss; Feature films include The Music Lovers (Tchaikovsky), Mahler, and The Devils with music by Peter Maxwell Davies; First opera production was The Rake's Progress at the 1982 Maggio Musicale in Florence; Other productions include Zimmermann's Die Soldaten for Opéra de Lyon in 1983, Madama Butterfly at Spoleto in 1983, L'Italiana in Algeri at Geneva in 1984, La Bohème at Macerata Festival in 1984, Faust at Vienna in 1985 and Mefistofele at Genoa in 1987; He has directed his production of Butterfly in Houston and Melbourne, and Gilbert and Sullivan's Princess Ida at the London Coliseum in 1992. *Honours:* Prix Italia for his symbolic portrait of Vaughan Williams, 1985.

RUSSELL, Lynda; Singer (Soprano); b. 1963, Birmingham, England. *Education:* Studied in London with Meriel St Clair and in Vienna with Eugene Ludwig. *Career:* Has sung with Glyndebourne Opera as the

Queen of Night, Fortuna in Monteverdi's Ulisse and Marzelline in Fidelio; Opera engagements at Barcelona, Madrid, Nice, Venice, Vicenza, Rome, Bologna and Strasbourg; British appearances as Handel's Partenope and with Opera North and English National Opera; Trieste in 1990 as Donna Elvira; Concert showings at the festivals of Athens, Barcelona, Granada, San Sebastian, Cuence, Venice, Berne, Munich and Siena; Brahms Requiem under Jesus Lopez-Cobos and Beethoven's 9th with Walter Weller; Has sung Mozart's oratorios Davidde Penitente and Betulia Liberata in Italy; Further repertoire includes Wolf's Italienisches Liederbuch, Beethoven's Missa Solemnis under Weller, and Ah, Perfido, Mozart's Exultate and Coronation Mass; Mozart bicentenary concerts in London, Birmingham, Winchester and Lahti in Finland in 1991; Season 1996–97 with Bach's Jauchzet Gott in Vienna, Britten's Illuminations in Scotland, Mozart's Requiem with the Ulster Orchestra, and Dalila in Handel's Samson with The Sixteen; Sang Xanthe in Die Liebe der Danaë by Strauss at Garsington, 1999. *Recordings:* Handel Dixit Dominus with The Sixteen.

RUSSELL, Malcolm Howard Alexander, FRCO, GRSM, ARAM, LRAM; Musician; b. 17 Oct. 1945, Long Eaton, England; m. Judith Russell; three d. *Education:* Royal Acad. of Music; postgraduate study with Peter Hurford, Harald Vogel, Piet Kee and Ewald Kooiman. *Career:* educational work 1969–94; founded several choirs; conductor, Phoenix Singers 1976–96; 'The Bach Experience' Complete Organ Works of J. S. Bach 1991–94; founder and Artistic Dir, East Anglian Acad. of Organ and Early Keyboard 1997; complete performances of Bach Clavieruburg III in England and Netherlands 1999–2000; recent cycles of Handel Concertos and Mendelssohn Sonatas; organ, harpsichord, clavichord recitals in UK, Italy and the Netherlands; mem. British Inst. of Organ Studies, Incorporated Soc. of Musicians, British Clavichord Soc.. *Recordings:* Bach from Framlingham 1997. *Publications:* contrib. to Organists' Review, Choir and Organ. *Address:* 14 Norfolk Crescent, Framlingham, Woodbridge, Suffolk, IP13 9EW, England (home). *Telephone:* (1728) 724456 (office). *E-mail:* russell.org.acad@ macunlimited. net (office).

RUSSO, William; Composer; b. 25 June 1928, Chicago, Illinois, USA. *Education:* Studied with Lenni Tristano, 1943–46, John Becker, 1953–55 and Karel Jirak, 1955–57. *Career:* Trombonist and Chief Composer, Arranger with the Stan Kenton Orchestra, 1950–54; Taught at the Manhattan School of Music, 1958–61 and formed and conducted the Russo Orchestra, Columbia College Chicago, 1965–67 and Antioch College, 1971–72; Founded and directed the Center for New Music and Free Theatre at Columbia College, 1965–75; Returned to teaching at Columbia in 1979. *Compositions include:* Operas: John Hooten, BBC, 1963, The Island, BBC, 1963, Land of Milk and Honey, Chicago, 1967, Antigone, Chicago, 1967, A Cabaret Opera, New York, 1970, Aesop's Fables, Chicago, 1971, The Shepherds' Christmas, Chicago, 1979, Isabella's Fortune, New York, 1974, Pedrolino's Revenge, Chicago, 1974, A General Opera, Chicago, 1976, The Pay Off, Chicago, 1984, Talking To The Sun, Chicago, 1989; Ballets: The World Of Alcina, 1954, Les Deux Errants, Monte Carlo, 1956, The Golden Bird, Chicago, 1984; 2 Symphonies, 1957 and 1958; Music for Blues and Jazz Bands, Rock Cantatas and Sonata for Violin and Piano, 1986. *Publications include:* Composing Music: A New Approach, 1988. *Address:* c/o ASCAP, ASCAP Building, 1 Lincoln Plaza, New York, NY 10023, USA.

RUT, Josef; Violinist and Composer; b. 21 Nov. 1926, Kutná Hora, Czechoslovakia; m. Dr Milada Rutová, 14 Feb 1953 (died 2001), 1 s. *Education:* Studied with Professor Bedřich Voldan; State Conservatory of Music, Prague. *Career:* Debut: Prague in 1951; Violinist for Radio Prague Symphony Orchestra, 1953–83; Composer from 1983; mem, Society of Czech Composers. *Compositions:* 49 compositions based on own 12 note tonal theory. *Recordings:* Sonata for double bass and strings; String Quartets No. 1 and 2; Symphonies No. 2 and 3; Sonata for winds No. 1; Wind Quintet; Concerto for violin and orchestra; Duo for violin and violoncello; Concerto for horn and strings; Variations for orchestra; Sonate for piano; Concerto for trumpet and strings; Sonate for violin and piano; String Quartet No. 3 with tenor solo on the words of St Paul; Sonata for viola and piano; Duo for violins; Variations for violoncello and piano; Meditation over Kyrie eleison for violin, viola and violoncello. *Publications:* Studies for two violins; Small Dialogues for trumpet and trombone; Five Little Pieces for flute and piano; 12 Note Tonal Theory, 1969; Die Musik und ihre Perspektive vom Gesichtspunkt der Relativitätstheorie (International Review of the Aesthetics and Sociology of Music), 1980; Manual of Rhythm, with Jan Dostal, 1979 and 1984; Beitrag zur übersichtlicheren Notierung des Rhythmus, 1982; The Relativistic Theory of Musical Motion, 1990; Search for Order as the Inspiration for Music Creation – Philosophy of Music, 2000. *Address:* Zborovská 40, 15000 Prague 5, Czech Republic.

RUTHERFORD, James; Singer (Bass); b. 1970, England. *Education:* Durham University; Royal College of Music, with Margaret Kingsley; National Opera Studio, London, 1998–99. *Career:* Appearances as Falstaff for British Youth Music Opera, Nick Shadow, Caronte in Orfeo

for Kent Opera, and Rossini's Don Magnifico for Clonter Opera; Marziano in Alessandro Severo and Tullio in Arminio for the London Handel Society; Christus in St Matthew Passion and Handel's L'Allegro ed il Moderato, 2001; Concerts include Telemann's Don Quichotte with the Orchestra of the Age of Enlightenment, Verdi and Brahms Requiems, Haydn's Creation with the Britten Sinfonia and St Matthew Passion at St George's Church, Hannover Square; Messiah at Salisbury Cathedral, the Missa Solemnis at Exeter Cathedral and the B minor Mass at St John's Smith Square; Season 2000–01 with Mozart's Figaro for Opera North and Welsh National opera, The Dream of Gerontius with the Hallé Orchestra and L'Allegro ed il Moderato for the London Handel Festival; Season 2001–2002 as First Shepherd in Daphne and Kothner in Die Meistersinger, at Covent Garden. *Address:* c/o Royal Opera House (Contracts), Covent Garden, London, WC2.

RUTMAN, Neil; Pianist; b. 12 July 1953, California, USA. *Education:* BMus, San Jose State University, 1976 with Aiko Onishi; MMus, Piano Performance, Eastman School of Music, University of Rochester, 1977; Student of Cecile Genhart; DMA, Piano Performance, Peabody Institute of The Johns Hopkins University, 1983, under Ellen Mack; Private piano studies with Leon Fleisher, Frank Mannheimmer and Gaby Casadesus. *Career:* Debut: US debut at Carnegie Hall in 1985; London debut at Wigmore Hall in 1985; Washington DC debut at Phillips Gallery in 1985; Associate Professor of Piano at Goucher College, Baltimore, 1983–; Masterclasses on interpretation of French piano music of Fauré, Debussy, and Ravel, at Chateau de la Gesse, Toulouse, France, University of Colorado, Denver, 1986, and Wright State University, Dayton, OH, 1986; Recitalist at Chateau de la Gesse in 1985, at Cheltenham International Festival of Music in 1986 and soloist for Denver Symphony in 1986; US State Department recital tour of Yugoslavia and soloist for Metropolitan Orchestra at Carnegie Hall in 1986; Recitalist at Merkin Hall, NYC with 3 recitals of the music of Ravel, Debussy, Fauré and Poulence with American premiere each evening, 1987. *Recordings:* 3 Movements of Petrouchka by Stravinsky; 2 Mozart Piano Concerti, K482 and K414; Préludes Book 1 and 2 by Debussy. *Current Management:* Thea Dispeker, NYC, USA. *Address:* 20990 Valley Green Dr, Apt 700, Cupertino, CA 95014-1846, USA.

RUTTER, Claire; Singer (Soprano); b. 1972, South Shields, County Durham, England. *Education:* Studied at the Guildhall School of Music and the National Opera Studio. *Career:* Sang in Birtwistle's Yan Tan Tethera for Opera Factory (1986) and Donna Anna for British Youth Opera; Violetta for Welsh National Opera (1994) and Scottish Opera from 1995, as Mozart's Countess, Terinka in The Jacobin, and Violetta; Other roles include Tatiana, Mimi and Alice Ford; Further appearances at the Buxton and Chester Festivals, at the Wigmore Hall and in South America and South Africa; Sang Mozart's Elettra for Scottish Opera, 1996 and Violetta, 1998; Sang Mimi at Hong Kong, 1998; Sang Gilda for ENO and WNO, 1999; La Gioconda for Opera North and Donna Anna in London, 2000–01. *Address:* c/o Scottish Opera, 39 Elmbank Crescent, Glasgow, G2 4PT, Scotland.

RUTTER, John; Composer and Conductor; b. 24 Sept. 1945, London, England; m. Joanne Redden, 1980, 2 s., 1 d. *Education:* MA, BMus, Clare College, Cambridge. *Career:* Director of Music, Clare College, Cambridge, 1975–79; Lecturer, Open University, 1975–88; Honorary Fellow, Westminster Choir College, Princeton, 1980; Founder, Director, Cambridge Singers. *Compositions include:* The Falcon, 1969; Gloria, 1974; The Piper of Hamelin, 1980; Requiem, 1985; Magnificat, 1990; Unaccompanied choral work, I my best beloved's am, for the BBC's Sounding the Millennium series, premièred at Canterbury Cathedral 1999 by the BBC Singers under Stephen Layton; Many carols, anthems and songs; Edited and recorded original version of Fauré's Requiem, 1984. *Recordings include:* Many including his own Requiem with Cambridge Singers and City of London Sinfonia. *Publications:* Edited the first three volumes in the Oxford Choral Classics series, Opera Choruses (1995) and European Sacred Music (1996), and Christmas Motets (1999). *Honours:* D Mus Lambeth, 1996. *Address:* c/o Oxford University Press, Great Clarendon Street, Oxford OX2 6DP, England.

RUUD, Ole Kristian; Conductor; b. 2 Oct. 1958, Oslo, Norway; m. Karen Johnstad Ruud, 26 Mar 1988, 2 s. *Education:* Norwegian Academy of Music, 1979–83; Sibelius Academy, 1984–85. *Career:* Debut: Radio Concert, Oslo Philharmonic Orchestra, 1985; Chief Conductor, North Norwegian Chamber Orchestra, 1986–89; Chief Conductor, Trondheim Symphony Orchestra, 1987–95, Norrkoping Symphony Orchestra, 1996–99; Touring Concerts with Trondheim Symphony Orchestra, Germany, 1988, 1995, Bergen Philharmonic, Germany, 1991, Jeunesse Musicale Orchestra, Europe, 1993, Berlin, 1996, Stockholm Chamber Orchestra, Japan, 1995, 1999; Professor of Conducting at Oslo Academy, 1999–. *Recordings:* Norwegian Composers: Oslo Philharmonic, Trondheim Symphony, Stavanger Symphony Orchestra; International Composers: Swedish Radio Symphony Orchestra, Norrkoping Symphony Orchestra, Bergen Philharmonic, Trondheim Symphony. *Honours:* E

Grieg Prize, 1992; Norwegian Newspaper Best Review Prize, 1993; Lindeman Prize, 1994; Johan Halvorsen Prize, 1996.

RUZICKA, Peter; Composer and Intendant; b. 3 July 1948, Düsseldorf, Germany. *Education:* Piano, Oboe and Composition, Hamburg Conservatory, 1963–68; PhD, 1977, Munich and Berlin. *Career:* Intendant, Berlin Radio Symphony Orchestra, 1979–87; Fellow, Bavarian Academy of Fine Arts, Munich, 1985; Free Academy of Arts, Hamburg, 1987. *Compositions:* Esta Noche, for the victims of the Viet Nam War, 1967; Antifone-Strofe for 25 strings and percussion, 1970; Elis, for mezzo, oboe and orchestra, 1970; Sonata for solo cello, 1970; 3 string quartets, 1970, 1970, 1992; Metastrophe for 87 instrumentalists, 1971; Sinfonia for 25 strings, 16 vocalists and percussions, 1971; Outside-Inside, Music Theatre, 1972; In Processo di Tempo for 26 instrumentalists and cello, 1972; Versuch, 7 Pieces for strings, 1974; Stress for 8 percussion groups, 1972; Einblendungen for orchestra, 1973–77; Feed Back for 4 orchestral groups, 1974; Torso for orchestra, 1974; Emanazione Variations for flute and 4 orchestral groups, 1975; Zeit for organ, 1975; Stille for cello, 1976; Abbruche for orchestra, 1977; Gestalt and Abbruch for voices, 1979; Impuls zum Weitersprechen for viola and orchestra, 1981; Satyagraha for orchestra, 1985;… der die Gesange zerschlug for baritone and ensemble, 1985; Metamorphosen uber ein Klangfeld von Joseph Haydn, for orchestra, 1990; Vier Gesänge nach Fragmenten von Nietzsche, for mezzo and piano, 1992; Klangschatten for string quartet, 1992; Tallis, for orchestra, 1993;… Inseln, randlos, for violin, chamber orchestra and chorus, 1994; Music Premiered at Gottingen, Stuttgart, Berlin, Hilversum, Hamburg, Munich, Vienna and Savonlinna. *Address:* Alphonsstrasse 17, 22043 Hamburg, Germany.

RUŽICKÁ, Rudolf; Composer and Teacher; b. 25 April 1941, Brno, Czechoslovakia; m. Bozena Ruzickova, 7 July 1967, 2 s. *Education:* Composition studies, Brno Conservatory and Janáček Academy of Performing Arts. *Career:* Composer; Professor of Composition and Music Theory, Brno and Kromeriz Conservatories, Brno State University, Janáček Academy; President, Society for Electro-acoustic Music in the Czech Republic; Chairman of the Jury of Musica Nova Competition. *Compositions:* Over 100 instrumental, chamber, vocal, electro-acoustic and computer compositions, including 3 cantatas, 5 symphonies, 6 concertos, 10 suites. *Recordings:* Approximately 60 compositions recorded for CD, gramophone, radio, television. *Publications:* Use of Computers in Creating Works of Art. *Contributions:* Numerous articles on music theory of computer composition and automatic notation, to various publications. *Honours:* Numerous honours, prizes and awards for electro-acoustic and computer music. *Address:* Serikova 32, 637 00 Brno, Czech Republic. *E-mail:* ruzicka@fi.muni.cz.

RUŽICKOVÁ, Zuzana; Harpsichordist; b. 14 Jan. 1928, Plzeň, Czechoslovakia; m. Viktor Kalabis. *Education:* Prague Academy of Music. *Career:* Has appeared widely in Europe from 1956; Co-founder with Vaclav Neumann of the Prague Chamber Soloists: performances 1962–67; Formed duo with violinist Josef Suk, 1963; Teacher at Prague Academy from 1962; Chairman International Competitions, Prague Spring Festival; mem, Member Directories, Neue Bachgesellshaft Leipzig; Honorary Member for Life, British National Early Music Association. *Recordings:* Complete keyboard works of J. S. Bach; Concertos by Benda; Sonatas D. Scarlatti, B. Martinů; Concert pour Clavecin, Bach and his Predecessors; J. S. Bach: Concerti. *Honours:* Winner, Munich International Competition, 1956; Grand Prix du Disque, 1961; Supraphon Grand Prix, 1968, 1972; Artist of Merit, 1968; State Prize Czechoslovak Republic, 1970; National Artist, 1989.

RYABCHIKOV, Victor; Pianist; b. 13 Feb. 1954, Tashkent, Uzbekistan; m. Golovina Irina, 31 Oct 1987, 1 d. *Education:* State Music Conservatory, Tashkent, 1972–79; Moscow Conservatory, 1977–79. *Career:* Concert as soloist and with orchestra in various cities across Russia from 1979 and in France, Switzerland, the United Kingdom, Sweden, Netherlands, Italy, South Africa and Germany from 1993; Numerous appearances on television and radio in Russia, Sweden and Switzerland; Founding Vice-President of Glinka Society, Moscow, 1997; Artistic Director, Glinka Festival, Moscow, 1997; Wigmore Hall debut, 2000. *Recordings:* CD, Russian Piano Music of XIX Century; Mikhail Glinka–Complete Piano Music in 3 Vols; Complete Piano Music by Borodin and Kalinnikov; Piano Music by Anton and Nikolai Rubinstein; Live recording, Chopin in Stockholm, 1999; Tchaikovsky – The Seasons and other piano pieces; Moments musicaux by Schubert and Rachmaninov. *Radio:* Writer/presenter, series of 14 broadcasts on Russian 19th century composers, Radio Orphei, 2002–03. *Honours:* Winner, 5th Republic Competition of Piano and Special Prize, Union of Composers, Russia, 1976; Pianist of the Year, APN, Moscow, 1992. *Current Management:* Tyndale-Biscoe Promotions, Stockholm. *Address:* Barvikha 21-7, Odinzovski R-N, Moscow 143083, Russia.

RYABETS, Oleg; Singer (Male Soprano); b. 28 June 1967, Kiev, Ukraine. *Education:* Kiev State Conservatory and Moscow State Academy of Music, 1988–94, with Professors K Radchenko and Z Dolukhanova. *Career:* Debut: Soprano part in Schnittke's Symphony No. 2 with Great Symphony Orchestra conducted by G Rozhdestvensky, Bolshoi Moscow State Conservatory Hall, 1990; Professional stage performer, 1977–; Soloist, State Boys Choir and State Chapel Choir of Kiev, performing in European countries, 1977–90; Sang with Vivaldi State Chamber Orchestra in 17–19th century music programme in Russian and Italian tours, 1990–93; Soprano role in Pergolesi's Stabat Mater, Moscow and Prague, 1992–93; Amour in Gluck's Orpheus, Hermitage Theatre, St Petersburg, 1993; Concerts and recitals in Moscow and St Petersburg, including special recital dedicated to 1st and only official visit to Russia by Queen Elizabeth II, Tchaikovsky Great Concert Hall, Moscow, 17 Oct 1994; Performed in Petersburg's Seasons Music Festival and Ludwigsburg Festival conducted by W Gönnenwein, sang in recital at French Embassy, Vienna, and appeared as Count Myshkin in world premiere of V Kobekin's NFB at Sacro Art Festival, Bochum and Ludwigsburg, Germany, 1995; Lenin in world premiere of The Naked Revolution by D Soldier, New York, 1997; Aminta in Galuppi's Il Re Pastore, Italy, 1998. *Recordings:* Solo Soprano, Stabat Mater by G Pergolesi, 1993; Italian music of 17–18th centuries, Mr Soprano sings Bel Canto, 1996; King Solomon's Song, cantata composed for O Ryabets by V Kobekin. *Honours:* Audio tape with his voice preserved next to only recorded castrato singer Sgnr A Mareschi in British National Sound Archives, London, 1996–.

RYAN, Barry; Singer (Tenor); b. 1956, Australia. *Education:* Graduated with Honours, the NSW Conservatorium Opera School 1981. *Career:* Principal tenor with Cologne Opera 1988–92; Australian Opera debut 1993, as David in Die Meistersinger (returned 1998 as Laca in Jenůfa, under Charles Mackerras); Season 1996–97 with Royal Opera debut, in Peter Grimes, as Armand in Henze's Boulevard Solitude at Basle and Froh in Das Rheingold at La Scala; Erik in Der fliegende Holländer for Australian Opera and as return to Covent Garden, in Elektra and Katya Kabanova; Concerts included 1988 Australian Bicentennial at Drury Lane, London, the Mozart Requiem in Bergen, Beethoven's Ninth in Tokyo and Hindemith's Cardillac at the Amsterdam Concertgebouw (1997); Further appearances at the Opéra-Comique and the Komische Oper, Berlin; Sang Alfred in Die Fledermaus at Sydney, 2000. *Honours:* Awards at the Shell Aria, Metropolitan Opera Auditions and Marten Bequest for Singing. *Address:* c/o Australian Opera, PO Box 291, Strawberry Hills, NSW 2012, Australia.

RYAN, Kwamé; conductor; b. 1976, Canada. *Education:* Oakham School, England, Gonville and Caius Coll., Cambridge; further studies with Peter Eötvös. *Career:* concert tours of Austria, France and Hungary with Peter Eötvös; Asst to Lothar Zagrosek at Stuttgart Opera 1998–99; Music Dir, Freiburg Opera 1999–2003, leading Tosca, Katya Kabanova, Der fliegende Holländer, Eugene Onegin, Fidelio and Nixon in China, Goebbels' Surrogate Cities, Fidelio and Maderna's Hyperion; season 2001–02 with Three Sisters by Eötvös at Opéra de Lyon, Nono's Prometeo in Lisbon and Brussels and Surrogate Cities by Heiner Goebbels at Freiburg; season 2002–03 with premiere of Percussion Concerto by Tüür, Grisey's Les Espaces Acoustiques at Lyon; season 2003–04 with Hartmann's Simplicius Simplissimus at Stuttgart State Opera; debut with Paris Nat. Opera with premiere of L'espace derniere by Matthias Pintscher 2004, UK debut at the Edinburgh Festival 2004; guest appearances at many festivals, including Salzburg, Strasbourg Musica, Berlin Biennale, Budapest Spring Festival, Metapher in Stuttgart, Donaueschingen Musiktage, Wien Modern, Wittener Tage für Neue Musik, Rhine Music Festival in Cologne and the Festival d'Automne in Paris; he has worked with many orchestras and ensembles, including the Bavarian, Baden-Baden, Freiburg, Stuttgart and Saarland Radio Symphonies, the Hungarian State Orchestra, the Netherlands Radio Chamber Orchestra, the Luxembourg Philharmonic Orchestra and the Sudfunkchor Stuttgart. *Current Management:* Harrison/Parrott Ltd, 12 Penzance Place, London, W11 4PA, England. *Telephone:* (20) 7229-9166. *Fax:* (20) 7221-5042. *Website:* www.harrisonparrott.com.

RYBARSKA, Lydia; Singer (Soprano); b. 1958, Czechoslovakia. *Career:* Sang Rusalka at the National Theatre, Prague; Season 1988–89 as Luisa Miller at Philadelphia and Amelia in Un Ballo in Maschera at Zürich; Guest with the Slovak National Opera at Edinburgh, 1990, in Prince Igor (as Jaroslavna) and Suchon's The Whirlpool; Bregenz Festival, 1993, as Abigaille in Nabucco; Bratislava, 1996, as Margherita in Mefistofele; Further appearances at the Paris Opéra Bastille (as Amelia) and Stuttgart; Concerts include Beethoven's Ninth in London and the Missa Solemnis in Vienna. *Address:* Slovak National Opera, Gorkeho 4, 81506 Bratislava, Slovakia.

RYDL, Kurt; Singer (Bass); b. 8 Oct. 1947, Vienna, Austria. *Education:* Studied in Vienna and Moscow. *Career:* Debut: Stuttgart in 1973 as Daland in Der fliegende Holländer; Guest appearances in Venice, Barcelona and Lisbon; Sang at Bayreuth Festival in 1975; Vienna Staatsoper from 1976 as Rocco in Fidelio, Zaccaria in Nabucco, Procida in Vêpres Siciliennes, Mephistopheles in Faust, King Philip in Don Carlos, Kecal in The Bartered Bride, the Landgrave in Tannhäuser and Marke in Tristan und Isolde; Salzburg Festival in 1985 in Il Ritorno d'Ulisse by Henze/Monteverdi; Tour of Japan with Vienna Staatsoper in 1986; Sang Baron Ochs in Turin and at Monte Carlo and Florence in 1987 and 1989; Salzburg Festival, 1987–89 as Mozart's Osmin, and La Scala Milan in 1990 as Rocco; Sang Pimen at Barcelona and Rocco at the 1990 Salzburg Festival; Season 1991–92 as Titurel at La Scala, Verdi's Zaccaria at the Vienna Volksoper, Ramfis in Aida at Tel-Aviv, Padre Guardiano at Florence and the Grand Inquisitor at the Verona Arena; Sang Hagen in Götterdämmerung at Covent Garden, 1995; returned 1997, in Pfitzner's Palestrina; Grand Inquisitor at Edinburgh, 1998; Season 2000–01 as Baron Ochs at the Deutsche Oper Berlin, Mozart's Osmin in Geneva, Dodon in The Golden Cockerel at Bregenz and Wagner's Pogner at Covent Garden; Morosus in Die schweigsame Frau at the Vienna Staatsoper and Wagner's Hagen (concert) in Sydney. *Recordings include:* Salome; Opera scenes by Schubert; Alceste; Manon Lescaut. *Address:* c/o Staatsoper, Opernring 2, 1010 Vienna, Austria.

RYHANEN, Jaako; Singer (Bass); b. 2 Dec. 1946, Tampere, Finland. *Education:* Studied in Helsinki. *Career:* Member of the Finnish National Opera at Helsinki from 1974; Appearances at the Savonlinna Festival and in Moscow and New York with the Helsinki Company; Further engagements in Madrid, Hamburg, Berlin, Munich, Zürich and Stuttgart; Paris Opéra in 1987, as Daland, and at Monte Carlo in 1988; Season 1991 as Daland at Munich, Titurel in Parsifal at Tampere and Mozart's Bartolo at Helsinki; Sang Daland at Santiago in 1992, and Sarastro at the Savonlinna Festival; Sang Fiesco in the original version of Simon Boccanegra at Covent Garden, 1997; Wagner's Daland at Lille, 1998; Season 2000–01 as Verdi's Banquo for Cologne Opera, Fiesco and Boris Godunov in Helsinki and Sarastro at Savonlinna; Boris for the Deutsche Oper am Rhein; Concerts with the Israel Philharmonic and throughout Scandinavia. *Address:* Finnish National Opera, Bulevardi 23–27, 00180 Helsinki 18, Finland.

RYSANEK, Lotte; Singer (Soprano); b. 18 March 1928, Vienna, Austria. *Education:* Vienna Conservatory with Richard Grossman. *Career:* Debut: Klagenfurt in 1950 as Massenet's Manon; Member of the Vienna Staatsoper as Marzelline in Fidelio, Marguerite in Faust, Pamina, Fiordiligi, Marenka in The Bartered Bride and Donna Elvira, and parts in operas by Wagner and Verdi; Guest appearances at the Vienna Volksoper in Graz, Berlin, Düsseldorf and Hamburg; Sang at Bayreuth in 1958; Well known in operetta and as a concert singer. *Recordings include:* Roles in operetta. *Address:* c/o Staatsoper, Opernring 2, 1010 Vienna, Austria.

RYSSOV, Michail; Singer (bass); b. 25 Aug. 1955, Crimea, Russia. *Career:* Principal Bass at the Opera in Minsk, 1983–87, in Don Giovanni, Don Carlos, Aida, La Forza del Destino, Macbeth, Nabucco, I Vespri Siciliani, Faust, Eugene Onegin, Boris Godunov, Mefistofele; Treviso, 1989, as the Commendatore in Don Giovanni; Has recently sung Ramfis at the Deutsche Oper Berlin and at the Verona Arena; Philip II at Deutsche Oper am Rhein, Düsseldorf; Prince Gremin and The Inquisitor in Don Carlos, at La Fenice, Venice; Sang Ramfis in Aida at the 1996 Verona Arena. *Honours:* Winner, Glinka Competition, 1984; International Verviers Competition, Belgium, 1987; International Ettore Bastianini Competition, Siena, 1988; International New Voice Competition in Pavia and the Toti dal Monte Competition in Treviso, 1989; Season 2000 as Verdi's Padre Guardiano at Verona and Procida at St Gallen; Kutzman in the premiere of Tatiana by Azio Corghi, at La Scala. *Current Management:* Athole Still International Management, Forresters Hall, 25–27 Westow Street, London, SE19 3RY, England. *Telephone:* (20) 8771-5271. *Fax:* (20) 8768-6600. *Website:* www .atholestill.com.

RZEWSKI, Frederic (Anthony); Composer and Pianist; b. 13 April 1938, Westfield, Massachusetts, USA; m. Nicole Abbeloss, 3 c. *Education:* BA, Harvard University, 1958, study with Thompson and Piston; MFA, Princeton University, 1960, study with Sessions and Babbitt; Italy, 1960–61 with Dallapiccola. *Career:* Pianist and teacher in Europe from 1962; Played in the premieres of Stockhausen's Klavierstuck X and Plus Minus; Co-founded electronic ensemble, Musica Electronica Viva, Rome, 1966; Returned to New York in 1971; Professor of Composition at the Royal Conservatory, Liège from 1977; Visiting Professor of Composition at Yale University in 1984. *Compositions:* For Violin, 1962; Composition for 2, 1964; Nature Morte for instruments and percussion, 1965; Zoologischer Garten, 1965; Spacecraft, 1967; Impersonation, audiodrama, 1967; Requiem, 1968; Symphony, 1968; Last Judgement for trombone, 1969; Falling Music for piano and tape, 1971; Coming Together for speaker and instruments, 1972; Piano Variations On The Song No Place To Go But Around, 1974; The People United Will Never Be Defeated, 36 variations for piano, 1975; 4 Piano Pieces, 1977; Satyrica for jazz band, 1983; Una Breve Storia D'Estate for 3 flutes and small orchestra; A Machine for 2 pianos, 1984; The Invincible Persian Army for low voice and prepared piano, 1984; The Persians for 4 voices, actors and ensemble, 1985; The Triumph of Death, oratorio, 1988; Roses, for 8 instruments, 1989; Piano Sonata, 1991; The Road, for piano, 1995–98; Scratch Symphony, 1997; Spiritus, for recorder and percussion, 1997. *Recordings:* As pianist, numerous items of contemporary music. *Address:* c/o ASCAP, ASCAP Building, 1 Lincoln Plaza, New York, NY 10023, USA.

S

SAARI, Jouko Erik Sakari; Conductor and Musical Director; b. 23 Nov. 1944, Stockholm, Sweden; m. Raija Syvänen, 1 s., 1 d. *Education:* Sibelius Academy, 1962–68; Music Science, Helsinki University, 1965–67; Organist degree, 1966; Music Education degree, 1966; Conservatory degree in Trumpet, 1966; Conducting, Indiana University, USA, 1969–70; Music Director degree, 1966; Church Music Division degree, 1968; Conducting Diploma, 1968. *Career:* Musical Director, Helsinki Opera Society, 1971; Conductor, Tampere City Orchestra, 1973–74; Chorus Master, 1974–75, Conductor and Coach, 1976–78, National Opera Finland; Musical Director, Lahti Symphony Orchestra, 1978–84; Conductor, Gothenburg Opera House, Stora Teatern, 1984–85, Guest Conductor, 1985–88; Broadcast recordings with Finnish Radio Symphony Orchestra, 1971, 1973–75 and with Swedish Radio Symphony Orchestra, 1974, 1976–77; Concerts in USA, Canada, Germany, Hungary, Denmark, Sweden and Finland; Guest Conductor, Hämeenlinna Symphony Orchestra, 1989–93; Appearances on Swedish Radio and on Finnish Radio and Television; Freelance Conductor and Organist. *Compositions:* For Brass Band recorded with Töölö Brass Band; For voice, choir, organ and trumpets published by Sulasol, Finland. *Address:* Laaksokatu 5B23, 15140 Lahti, Finland.

SAARIAHO, Kaija; Composer; b. 14 Oct. 1952, Helsinki, Finland; m. Jean-Baptiste Barriere 1984; one s. one d. *Education:* Sibelius Acad., Helsinki; studied with Brian Ferneyhough and Klaus Huber at the Freiburg Hochschule für Musik. *Career:* freelance composer of orchestral and instrumental music with live electronics and computers; music performed in most major festivals, including Salzburg Festival 1996; Graalthéatre for violin and orchestra, performed at the 1995 London Proms; mem. Finnish Composers' Soc.. *Compositions:* Verbledungen 1984, Lichtbogen 1986, Du Cristal...à la fumée 1988–90, Graalthéatre 1994, Château de l'âme 1995, Oltra mar 1998, Miranda's Lament, for soprano and ensemble 1998, Neiges, for 8 cellos 1998, L'amour de loin, opera 2000, British premiere of L'amour de loin at the Barbican Hall, London 2002, Nymphea Reflection, for orchestra 2001, Orion, for orchestra 2002, Aile du Songe, for flute and ensemble 2001, Cinq Reflects, for soprano, baritone and orchestra 2001, Terrestre, for flute and ensemble 2002. *Honours:* Prix Italia 1989, Prix Art Electronica 1989, Suomi Prize 1995, Chevalier de l'ordre des Arts et des Lettres 1997, hon. mem., Swedish Music Acad. 1999; Winner, Grawemeyer Award for Music 2003 for Opera L'Amour de Loin. *Address:* c/o Chester Music, 8–9 Frith Street, London, W1V 5TZ, England.

SAARINEN, Eeva-Liisa; Singer (Mezzo-Soprano); b. 1951, Finland. *Education:* Studied at the Sibelius Academy, Helsinki, from 1972. *Career:* Sang throughout Northern Europe from 1981 in concerts and recitals; Stage debut at Helsinki in 1983 as Cherubino; Further roles with the Finnish National Opera have been Rosina, Cenerentola, the Composer in Ariadne auf Naxos, Marja in Merikanto's Juha, and Hansel; Has sung in the premieres of Sallinen's The King Goes Forth to France at Savonlinna in 1984 and Kullervo at Los Angeles in 1992; Fricka in Das Rheingold at Helsinki, 1996; Sang in the premiere of Luther by Kari Tikka, Helsinki 2000. *Recordings include:* Kullervo Symphony by Sibelius. *Address:* c/o Finnish National Opera, Blvd 23–27, 00180 Helsinki, Finland.

SAARMAN, Risto; Singer (tenor); b. 25 Jan. 1956, Jyvaskyla, Finland. *Education:* Sibelius Academy in Helsinki, 1983. *Career:* Finnish National Opera from 1984, at first as M Triquet in Eugene Onegin; Beppe; Borsa in Rigoletto; Don Curzio; Later sang: Tamino, Don Ottavio, Ferrando, Belmonte, Almaviva, Lensky and Albert Herring; Savonlinna Festival and Opéra de Lyon, 1987, as Tamino and Belmonte; Aix-en-Provence, 1990, as Belmonte and Almaviva; Sang Jacquino at the 1992 Savonlinna Festival; Concert engagements in the St John and St Matthew Passions; Masses by Haydn, Handel, Mozart and Beethoven; L'Enfance du Christ by Berlioz and Mendelssohn's Second Symphony; Lieder repertoire includes: Dichterliebe; Die schöne Müllerin; Songs by Strauss. *Current Management:* Athole Still International Management, Forresters Hall, 25–27 Westow Street, London, SE19 3RY, England. *Telephone:* (20) 8771-5271. *Fax:* (20) 8768-6600. *Website:* www.atholestill.com.

SABBATINI, Giuseppe; Singer (Tenor); b. 11 May 1957, Rome, Italy. *Education:* Studied Double Bass at the Santa Cecilia Conservatory, Rome; Private study in Singing. *Career:* Debut: As Opera Singer, Edgardo in Lucia di Lammermoor at Spoleto, 1987; Played double bass in various Italian orchestras; Following opera debut, has sung in Faust, La Bohème, Werther, Massenet's Manon, Linda di Chamounix, La Traviata, Rigoletto, I Puritani, L'Elisir d'amore, Les Pêcheurs de Perles, Eugene Onegin, Idomeneo, Maria Stuarda, Les Contes d'Hoffmann, La Favorita, Falstaff; Guillaume Tell; Dom Sébastien, by Donizetti; Roméo et Juliette; Performances at main

theatres such as Teatro alla Scala, Milan, Vienna Staatsoper, Opéra-Bastille, Paris, Covent Garden, London, Chicago Lyric Opera, Suntory Hall, Tokyo, Carnegie Hall, New York City, Hamburg Staatsoper, San Francisco Opera; Gran Teatre del Liceu, Barcelona; Japan Opera Foundation Tokyo; Sang in Massenet's Thais at Nice, 1997; Engaged as Arnold in Guillaume Tell at the Vienna Staatsoper, 1998; Season 1998 as Gounod's Roméo at Turin and Donizetti's Roberto Devereux at Naples; Concert repertoire includes: Rossini's Stabat Mater, Rome, 1991, Bologna, 1992; La Damnation de Faust, Florence, 1995; La Damnation de Faust in London and New York both in 1996; Stabat Mater in Amsterdam, 1997; Sang Massenet's Werther at Parma and Des Grieux at La Scala, 1999; Season 2000–01 as Mozart's Mitridate at the Paris Châtelet, Lensky at the Vienna Staatsoper and Alfredo at Covent Garden; Beethoven's Ninth at the Ravenna Festival, Nemorinio for La Scala and Des Grieux at the New York Met (debut). *Recordings include:* La maga Circe; Gala Opera Concert–l'arte del belcanto; Le Maschere, by Mascagni; Canzone Sacre; Mozart Gala–Suntory Hall, Tokyo; Simon Boccanegra; La Bohème; Don Giovanni; Messe Solennelle; Recital; Mitridate, re di Ponto. *Address:* c/o Prima International Artists Management, Palazzo Zambeccari, Piazza de'Calderini 2/2, 40124 Bologna, Italy.

SABIN, Nigel; Composer and Clarinettist; b. 25 Nov. 1959, England (Resident in Australia from 1974). *Education:* BMus hons, University of Adelaide; Manhattan School of Music, 1992, with David Del Tredici; Study with Richard Meale in Australia. *Career:* Musician-in-Residence, University of Queensland, 1988–95. *Compositions:* Job's Lament for clarinet, 1984; Inner-City Counter-Points, for clarinet, viola, cello and piano, 1989; Four Studies for flute, clarinet, violin and guitar, 1990; Points of Departure for violin, viola, piano and clarinet, 1991; Time and Motion Studies: Postcards From France for clarinet and viola, 1991; Voyages to Arcadia for small orchestra, 1992; Terra Australia for soprano and ensemble, 1992; Another Look At Autumn, for piano, 1993; Faint Qualm for piano, 1993; Love Songs for orchestra, 1993; Angel's Flight for small orchestra, 1994. *Honours:* ASME Young Composers Award, 1981, 1984. *Address:* c/o APRA, 1A Eden Street, Corws Nest, NSW 2065, Australia.

SACCÀ, Roberto; Singer (tenor); b. 12 Sept. 1961, Sendehorst, Westfalen, Germany. *Education:* Musikhochschule of Stuttgart and Karlsruhe. *Career:* sang in Germany from 1985 and in Israel, Switzerland, France and England; concert tour of Brazil, 1987 with appearances at Teatro Municipal Rio de Janeiro; Stadttheater Würzburg, 1987–88, Wiesbaden from 1988; sang at the Fermo Festival as Leandro in a 1990 revival of Paisiello's Le Due Contese; debut at La Scala, Milan with Henze's Das Verratene Meer, 1990; Brussels and Salzburg Festival in Ulisse by Dallapiccola, 1993, and Vienna, Musikvereinsaal, 1993; mem. of Zürich Opera, 1994–97; in 1994 sang Le Pêcheur in Le Rossignol at Salzburg Festival, and in Mozart's Der Schauspieldirektor under Harnoncourt; Season 1994–95 as Rinuccio in Puccini's Gianni Schicchi Bruxelles under Pappano, Vienna, title role of Orfeo, Alessandro in Mozart's Il Re Pastore under Harnoncourt, Don Ramiro in a new production of La Cenerentola, Don Ottavio in Don Giovanni and Almaviva in Il Barbiere di Siviglia; Fidelio under Solti in the Salzburg Festival; Sang in Handel's Alcina at the 1997 Vienna Festival; Season 1998 as Mozart's Ferrando at Glyndebourne and Lindoro in Paisiello's Nina at Zürich, with Cecilia Bartoli; Season 1999 in Zürich as Oberon under Gardiner, Don Ottavio and Ramiro in Cenerentola; Berlin with Leukippos in Daphne under Thielemann and Don Ottavio in Baltimore; sang Alfredo in Traviata in Cologne and Munich and Tamino in The Magic Flute under Runniclers at San Francisco, 2000, and Nemorino in L'Elisir d'amore there in 2001; sang Haydn's Orfeo at Covent Garden, 2001; Traviata and Magic Flute in Vienna; Berbiere in Paris; Sang Tamino in Seville, 2002, 2003; Rinuccio, Opéra Bastille, and Tokyo under Ozawa, Entfuhrung Munich, 2004; Inauguration concert of Le Fenice, Venice under Muti, 2004; Tokyo Bohéme under Ozawa; Entfuhrung Berlin; Traviata under Mehta in Munich; Rigoletto in Chile; Inauguration Performance La Fenice with La Traviata under Maazel in Venice. *Recordings:* Handel's Messiah; Capriccio with Vienna Philharmonic; Meistersinger von Nürnberg; Il Re Pastore; Don Giovanni and Cosí fan tutte under Harnoncourt and several solo CDs. *Contributions:* Openwelt, Orpheus; Opernglas, Merker. *Honours:* winner, Opera Prize in Geneva, Switzerland, 1989. *Current Management:* Mag Kurt-Walther Schober, Opernring 8-13, 1010 Vienna, Austria. *Website:* www.roberto-sacca.com.

SACCO, P. Peter; Composer and Singer (tenor); b. 25 Oct. 1928, Albion, New York, USA. *Education:* Pupil of Vivian Major and William Willett at Fredonia State University; Eastman School of Music, 1953–58 with Barlow, Rogers and Hanson; MM, 1954, DMus, 1958. *Career:* Studied composition with Wolfgang Niederste-Schee in Frankfurt, 1950–52; Clarinettist with 4th Division Infantry Band; Music Faculty of San Francisco State University, 1959–80; Visiting Professor at University of Hawaii, 1970–71; Concert Tenor. *Compositions:* Dramatic: Jesu, oratorio, 1956, Midsummer Night's Dream Night, oratorio, 1961, Mr Vinegar, chamber opera, 1967, Solomon, oratorio, 1976; Orchestral: Symphony No. 1, 1955, No. 2, The Symphony Of Thanksgiving, 1965–76, No. 3, The Convocation Symphony, 1968, Piano Concerto, 1964, Four Sketches on Emerson Essays, 1963, 2 Piano Sonatas, 1951, 1965, Violin Concerto, 1969–74, Moab Illuminations, for solo piano, 1972, 5 Songs for mezzo-soprano and strings; Chamber: Clarinet Quintet, 1956, String Quartet, 1966, Variations On Schubert's An Die Musik for piano four hands, 1981; 60 Solo songs, 25 choruses, four cantatas and 11 anthems.

SACCOMANI, Lorenzo; Singer (Baritone); b. 9 June 1938, Milan, Italy. *Education:* Studied in Milan with Vladimiro Badiali and Alfonso Siliotti. *Career:* Debut: Avignon in 1964 as Silvio in Pagliacci; Sang the Herald in Lohengrin at Venice then appeared in many Italian houses, notably La Scala, Milan, in operas by Puccini, Gounod, Massenet and Verdi; London in 1972 in a concert performance of Caterina Cornaro by Donizetti; US debut at Dallas in 1972 as Henry Ashton in Lucia di Lammermoor; Sang at Verona Arena in 1983, and Geneva in 1985 as Guy de Montfort in Les Vêpres Siciliennes; Further appearances in Frankfurt, New York, Chicago and Buenos Aires; Other roles include Escamillo, Zurga in Les Pêcheurs de Perles and Verdi's Nabucco, Germont, Ezio in Attila, Amonasro, Rigoletto, Luna and Francesco in I Masnadieri; Season 1998 as Gérard in Andrea Chénier at Monte Carlo. *Recordings include:* Caterina Cornaro; Pagliacci.

SACHS, (Stewart) Harvey; Canadian writer; b. 8 June 1946, Cleveland, OH, USA; m. 1st Barbara Gogolick 1967 (divorced); one s.; m. 2nd Maria Cristina Reinhart 2001; one d. *Education:* Cleveland Institute of Music, Oberlin College Conservatory, OH, Mannes College of Music, NY, Conductors' Workshop, University of Toronto. *Career:* Conducting, Peterborough Symphony Orchestra, Canada, 1972–75; Guest Conductor, Pomeriggi Musicali, Milan, Italy, 1977; Angelicum, Milan, 1977; Canadian Opera Touring Company, 1979; CBC Vancouver Chamber Orchestra, 1982, 1984; Orchestre Symphonique de Québec, 1984; Toronto Chamber Players, 1984, 1985; Full-time Writer, 1985–; numerous documentaries for radio. *Television:* Toscanini – The Maestro (documentary), for Bravo, PBS and other networks worldwide. *Publications:* Toscanini, biography, 1978; Virtuoso, 1982; Co-author Plácido Domingo's My First 40 Years, 1983; Music in Fascist Italy, 1987; Arturo Toscanini from 1915 to 1946: Art in the Shadow of Politics, exhibition catalogue, 1987; Reflections on Toscanini, 1991; Rubinstein: A Life, biography, 1995; Co-author Sir Georg Solti's Solti on Solti (Memoirs), 1997; Ed. and translator, The Letters of Arturo Toscanini, 2002; contrib. to The New Yorker, TLS, New York Times. *Honours:* Fellow, John Simon Guggenheim Foundation, 1981, Cullman Center for Scholars and Writers, The New York Public Library, 1999–2000. *Current Management:* Denise Shannon Agency, Suite 1603, 20 West 22nd Street, New York, NY 10012, USA. *Telephone:* (212) 414-2911. *Fax:* (212) 414-2930. *E-mail:* dshannon@deniseshannonagency.com.

SACKMAN, Nicholas; Composer; b. 12 April 1950, London, England. *Education:* Dulwich College, Nottingham University and Leeds University with Alexander Goehr. *Career:* Ensembles and Cadenzas performed in 1973 at the International Gaudaemus Week and the BBC Young Composers' Forum; A Pair of Wings for 3 Sopranos and Ensemble premiered at the 1974 ISCM Festival and Ellipsis for Piano and Ensemble premiered at Leeds Festival in 1976; Doubles for 2 Instrumental Groups and Flute Concerto commissioned by the BBC and String Quartet by the Barber Institute of Fine Arts, Birmingham; Alap for Orchestra premiered by the BBC Philharmonic Orchestra in 1983 and Hawthorn for Orchestra premiered at the 1993 London Proms; Taught in London and is now Senior Lecturer at the Music Department of Nottingham University. *Compositions include:* Simplicia, musical for schools, 1980; The World A Wonder Waking for mezzo-soprano and ensemble, 1981; The Empress of Shoreditch, musical for schools, 1981; Holism for viola and cello, 1982; Time-Piece for brass quintet, 1982–83; Piano sonata, 1983–84; Corronach for ensemble, 1985; Sonata for trombone and piano, 1986; Paraphrase for wind, 1987; Flute concerto, 1988–89; String Quartet No. 2, 1990–91; Hawthorn for orchestra, 1993, revised 1994; Scorpio for multi-percussion and piano, 1995; Caccia for piano and orchestra, 1998; Koi for four flutes, 1999; Meld for piano, brass and percussion, 1999; Sextet for wind, 2000; Way Back When, for orchestra, 2000; Ballo, for ensemble, 2002; Mosaic, for orchestra, 2002; Fling, for flute, cello and piano, 2002; Cross hands, for piano, 2002; Puppets, for four percussionists, 2003; Vivace, for small orchestra, 2004. *E-mail:* nicholas@sackman.co.uk. *Website:* www.sackman.co.uk.

SADÉ, Gabriel; Singer (Tenor); b. 1959, Romania. *Education:* Studied in Israel and at the Guildhall School, London. *Career:* New Israeli Opera at Tel-Aviv from 1986, as Nemorino, Alfredo, Rodolfo, Faust and Pedrillo;

Seattle Opera, 1991, as Don Ottavio; Stuttgart Staatsoper from 1992, as Jim Mahonney, Rodolfo and the Duke of Mantua; Tel-Aviv, 1994–95, as Dmitri in Boris Godunov and in the premiere of Tal's Josef; Cologne Opera, 1995–96, as Lensky and Pinkerton; Other roles include Cavaradossi at Dresden, 1994, and Stuttgart, 1998, and Don José at Bologna and Modena; Season 2000–01 as Radames at Cincinnati and Alpha in the premiere of Alpha and Omega by Gil Shohat, in Tel-Aviv. *Recordings include:* Verdi's Requiem.

SADIE, Julie Anne, BA, BMus, MA, PhD; cellist, viola da gamba player, lecturer and writer on baroque music; b. 26 Jan. 1948, Eugene, OR, USA; m. Stanley Sadie 1978; one s. one d. *Education:* University of Oregon, Cornell University, City University. *Career:* taught at the Eastman School of Music, Rochester, New York, 1974–76; Freelance Musician, Lecturer and Writer on Baroque Music; Lecturer in Baroque Music, King's College, University of London, 1982; Lecturer in Early Music, Royal College of Music, London, 1986–88; Editor, The Consort: European Journal of Early Music, 1993–; Administrator of The Handel House Trust Ltd, 1994–98; mem, Royal Musical Association; American Musicological Society; Viola da Gamba Society of Great Britain; American Viola da Gamba Society; Museums Association; Musical Collections Forum; Ford Foundation Fellowship, 1970–74. *Recordings:* as member of orchestra, with the Academy of Ancient Music in Mozart's Paris Symphony and with the English Bach Festival in Rameau's Castor et Pollux. *Publications:* The Bass Viol in French Baroque Chamber Music, 1980; Companion to Baroque Music (editor), 1991; The New Grove Dictionary of Women Composers (edited with Rhian Samuel), 1994; with Stanley Sadie, Calling on the Composer: a Guide to European Composer Museums and Memorials, 2003; contrib. to Gramophone; The Musical Times; Early Music; Chelys; Proceedings of the Royal Musical Association. *Address:* The Manor, Cossington, Somerset, TA7 8JR, England.

SADIE, Stanley; Writer on Music; b. 30 Oct. 1930, Wembley, Middlesex, England; m. (1) Adèle Bloom, 10 Dec 1953, deceased 1978, 2 s., 1 d., (2) Julie Anne McCornack, 18 July 1978, 1 s., 1 d. *Education:* Gonville and Caius College, Cambridge, 1950–56; BA 1953, MusB 1953, MA 1957 and PhD 1958; BMus, Oxford. *Career:* Professor, Trinity College of Music, 1957–65; Writer and Broadcaster, 1957–; Music Critic for The Times, 1964–81; Editor, Musical Times, 1967–87; Musical Adviser, Granada television series Man and Music, 1984–90; President, Royal Musical Association, 1989–94; Critics Circle; International Musicological Society, President, 1992–97. *Publications:* Handel, 1962; Mozart, 1965; Pan Book of Opera, with A Jacobs, 1964, 1985; Beethoven, 1967, and Handel, 1968, in The Great Composers; Handel Concertos, 1972; Editor, The New Grove Dictionary of Music and Musicians, 20 vols, 1980; Mozart, 1982; Editor, The New Grove Dictionary of Musical Instruments, 3 vols, 1984; Stanley Sadie's Music Guide/ The Cambridge Music Guide, with A Latham, 1985; Co-editor, The New Grove Dictionary of American Music, 4 vols, 1986; Mozart Symphonies, 1986; Stanley Sadie's Brief Music Guide, 1987; Editor, The Grove Concise Dictionary of Music, 1988; History of Opera (New Grove Handbook) 1989, Man and Music, 8 vol. social history, 1989–93; Co-editor, Performance Practice (New Grove Handbook), 2 vols, 1990; Co-editor, Music Printing and Publishing (New Grove Handbook), 1990; Editor, New Grove Dictionary of Opera, 4 vols, 1992; Editor, New Grove Book of Operas, 1996; Editor, New Grove Dictionary of Music, 2nd edition, 29 vols, 2001; with Julie Anne Sadie, Calling on the Composer: a Guide to European Composers and Musicians Museums and Memorials, 2004. Many reviews and articles in Musical Times, Opera, Gramophone. *Honours:* Honorary RAM, 1982; Honorary LittD, 1982; C.B.E., 1982; FRCM, 1994; Corresponding Member, American Musicological Society, 1996. *Address:* The Manor , Cossington, Somerset, TA 7 8JR, England.

SAÉDEN, Erik; Singer (Baritone); b. 3 Sept. 1924, Vanersborg, Sweden; m. Elisabeth Murgard. *Education:* Studied at the Royal College of Music, Stockholm and at the Royal Opera School; Private studies with Arne Sunnegardh, Martin Ohman and W Freund. *Career:* Royal Opera Stockholm from 1952 as Mozart's Figaro and Count, Wagner's Sachs, Beckmesser, Pogner, Dutchman and Wolfram, Verdi's Iago, Renato, Macbeth, Germont, Ford and Nabucco; Berg's Wozzeck, Stravinsky's Nick Shadow, Tchaikovsky's Eugene Onegin, Busoni's Faust and the title role in Dallapiccola's Il Prigionierlo; created leading roles in Blomdahl's Aniara, Werle's Drommen om Thérèse, Berwald's Drottningen av Golconda, Dallapiccola's Ulisse (1968), Rosenberg's Hus med Dubbel Ingang and Ligeti's Le Grand Macabre, (1978); Guest Appearances at Bayreuth, Edinburgh, Covent Garden, Montreal; Also Savonlinna as Father Henrik in Singoalla; recorded the role in complete recording of Singoalla; mem, Stockholm Academy of Music. *Recordings include:* The Speaker in Bergman film version of Die Zauberflöte; Swedish Romances, Schubert's Winterreise. *Honours:* Swedish Court Singer; Order Litteris et Artibus. *Address:* Höglidsv 17 A, 182 46 Enebyberg, Sweden.

SAFFER, Lisa; Singer (Soprano); b. 1964, USA. *Career:* Philadelphia Opera, 1987–88, as Flora in The Turn of the Screw, Susanna, and Poppea in Handel's Agrippina; Los Angeles Opera, 1990, as Mozart's Re Pastore; Handel Festival at Göttingen, 1992–93, as Poppea, in Ottone as Teofana, and Polinessa in Radamisto; English National Opera, 1996, and Opéra Bastille, Paris, 1994, as Marie in Zimmermann's Die Soldaten; Season 1996 as Cavalli's Calisto for Glimmerglass Opera, USA, and Despina in Così fan tutte at Philadelphia; Season 1998 as Handel's Partenope for Glimmerglass Opera; Sang Xanthe in Die Liebe der Danaë by Strauss at Avery Fisher Hall, NY, 2000; Almirena in Handel's Rinaldo for New York City Opera; Lulu in a new production of Berg's opera for ENO, 2002. *Recordings include:* Handel's Agrippina, Judas Maccabaeus and Radamisto. *Address:* c/o Glimmerglass Opera, PO Box 191, Cooperstown, NY 13326, USA.

SAHL, Michael; Composer; b. 2 Sept. 1934, Boston, Massachusetts, USA. *Education:* Studied with Israel Citkowitz, 1947–57; BA, Amherst College, 1955; MFA, Princeton University with Sessions, 1957; Berkshire Music Center and Florence in 1957 on a Fulbright Fellowship. *Career:* Buffalo/Lukas Foss Ensemble, 1965–66; Lincoln Center Repertory Company, 1966; Organist, Spencer Memorial Church; Pianist/arranger for Judy Collins, 1968–69; String Quartet, 1969; Music Director, WBAI-FM, 1972–73; Music theatre works, 1975; Tango Project with William Schimmel, 1981; Film work, 1963–. *Compositions include:* String Quartet, 1969; Doina, violin and jazz trio, 1979; Boxes, opera, 1980; Symphony 1983, big band with electric violin, 1983; Tango from Exiles Cafe, for piano solo, 1984; Dream Beach, opera, 1987; Jungles, for electric violin, electric guitar, piano, bass and drums, 1992; John Grace Ranter, opera, 1996; Trio, violin, cello and piano, 1997. *Recordings:* Tropes on the Salve Regina; A Mitzvah for the Dead; Symphony 1983; Doina; Prothalamium; Exiles Cafe Tango; New album, White Rabbit, 1997. *Publications:* Making Changes: A Practical Guide to Vernacular Harmony, 1977. *Honours:* Prix Italia, 1980 for Civilizations And Its Discontents; Nominated for Academy Award, 1990; Seagrams Award in Opera for Boxes; Nominated for Grammy, 1982. *Address:* c/o ASCAP, ASCAP Building, 1 Lincoln Plaza, New York, NY 10023, USA.

SAINSBURY, Lionel; Composer; b. 2 June 1958, Wiltshire, England. *Career:* Adjudicator, European Piano Teachers' Assen Composers Competition, 2001; mem., British Acad. of Composers and Songwriters, Performing Right Soc., Mechanical Copyright Protection Soc.. *Compositions:* Twelve Preludes for piano premiered by Jack Gibbons, St John's Smith Square, 1987, featured in composer's own performance on Classic FM, 1993; Cuban Dance No. 2 for violin and piano premiered by Tasmin Little and Piers Lane, Wigmore Hall, 1993; Two Nocturnes for strings premiered by William Boughton and the English String Orchestra, Malvern, 1994; Fiesta for two pianos performed by Jeremy Filsell and Francis Pott, Grocer's Hall, London, 1995; Violin Concerto first broadcast by Lorraine McAslan with the BBC Concert Orchestra conducted by Barry Wordsworth, BBC Radio 3, 1995; South American Suite for piano premiered by Jack Gibbons, Holywell Music Room, Oxford, 1996; Two Cuban Dances (arranged for piano four hands) premiered by Black/Katayama duo, Nuits Musicales de Beynac-en-Périgord, 1998; Soliloquy for solo violin premiered by Oliver Lewis, Dartington International Summer School, 1998; Incantation for piano premiered by the composer, St John's Coll., Oxford, 2000; Cuban Fantasy for piano broadcast in composer's own performance on BBC Radio 3, 2002; public premiere of Violin Concerto given by Lorraine McAslan with the Bournemouth Symphony Orchestra conducted by Adrian Lucas, Worcester Three Choirs Festival, 2002. *Recordings:* Cuban Dance No. 2 on 'Tchaikovskiana', Tasmin Little/John Lenehan, 2003; Two Nocturnes for strings on British String Miniatures Vol. 5, Royal Ballet Sinfonia/Gavin Sutherland, 2004. *Honours:* Mendelssohn Scholarship, 1980. *Address:* Boot Cottage, Brook End, Chadlington, Chipping Norton, Oxfordshire OX7 3NF, England. *Website:* www.lionelsainsbury.com. .

SAINT-CLAIR, Carol; Singer (Soprano); b. 1951, Texas, USA. *Education:* Studied at Texas State University. *Career:* Sang at the Gelsenkirchen Opera, 1977–82, Klagenfurt, 1982–87 and Osnabruck Opera from 1987; Guest appearances throughout Germany and South America in such roles as Mimi, Marzelline in Fidelio, Euridice, Blanche in The Carmelites, Donna Anna and Tatiana in Eugene Onegin; Frequent concert appearances. *Address:* c/o Osnabruck Opera, St ädtische Buhnen, Osnabruck GmBH, Domhof 10–11, 4500 Osnabruck, Germany.

ST HILL, Krister; Singer (baritone); b. 1957, Sweden. *Career:* debut, sang Escamillo in 1982; Roles in Sweden have included Sancho Panza in Massenet's Don Quichotte, Belcore and Nick Shadow in The Rake's Progress at Malmö City Theatre, Lord Sidney in Rossini's Il Viaggio a Reims, Bohème, Ned Keene, Peter Grimes, Valentin, Faust and Wolfram in Tannhäuser; Sang at Garsington Opera, Oxford, as Ernesto in Haydn's Il Mondo della Luna, at Houston as Donny in the premiere of New Year by Tippett in 1989, Glyndebourne Opera in 1990 in the British premiere of New Year and lieder recitals in Scandinavia and abroad which included Wigmore Hall recitals with Elisabeth Söder-

ström. *Recordings include:* three solo albums; Title role in Jonny Spielt Auf by Krenek; Hindemith's Requiem. *Current Management:* Nordic Artists Management, Sveavagen 76, 11359 Stockholm, Sweden.

SAKAMOTO, Ryûichi, MA; Japanese composer, musician and actor; b. 17 Jan. 1952, Tokyo; m. Akiko Yano 1979. *Education:* Shinjuku High School, Composition Dept, Tokyo Fine Arts Univ. *Career:* began composing at age of ten; mem. group Yellow Magic Orchestra 1978–83; worked with David Sylvian 1982–83; solo recording artist, composer 1982–; conductor, arranger, music for Olympic Games opening ceremony, Barcelona, Spain 1992. *Film appearances:* Merry Christmas Mr Lawrence 1982, The Last Emperor 1987, New Rose Hotel 1998. *Film soundtracks:* Daijôbu, mai furendo 1983, Merry Christmas Mr Lawrence 1982, Koneko monogatari 1986, The Last Emperor (with David Byrne and Cong Su, Acad. Award) 1987, Ôritsu uchûgun Oneamisu no tsubasa 1987, The Laser Man (title song) 1988, The Handmaid's Tale 1990, The Sheltering Sky 1990, Tacones lejanos 1991, Topâzu 1992, Wuthering Heights 1992, Wild Palms (TV series) 1993, Little Buddha 1993, Rabbit Ears: Peachboy 1993, Wild Side 1995, Snake Eyes 1998, Love is the Devil 1998, Gohatto 1999, Poppoya (theme) 1999, Alexei to izumi 2002, Derrida 2002, Femme Fatale 2002, Los Rubios 2003. *Recordings include:* albums: Thousand Knives 1978, B-2 Unit 1980, Hidariudeno (A Dream Of The Left Arm) 1981, Coda 1983, Ongaku Zukan (A Picture Book Of Music) 1984, Illustrated Musical Encyclopedia 1984, Esperanto 1985, Miraiha Yarô (A Futurist Chap) 1986, Media Bahn Live 1986, Oneamisno Tsubasa (The Wings Of Oneamis) 1986, Neo Geo 1987, Playing The Orchestra 1988, Tokyo Joe 1988, Sakamoto Plays Sakamoto 1989, Grupo Musicale 1989, Beauty 1989, Heartbeat 1991, Neo Geo (with Iggy Pop) 1992, Sweet Revenge 1994, Soundbites 1994, Hard To Get 1995, 1996 1996, Music For Yohji Yamamoto 1997, Smoochy 1997, Discord 1998, Love Is The Devil 1998, Raw Life 1999, Intimate 1999, Space 1999, BTTB 1999, Gohatto 1999, Complete Index of Gut 1999, Cinemage 2000, Casa 2002; singles: Bamboo Houses (with David Sylvian) 1982, Forbidden Colours (with David Sylvian) 1983, Field Work (with Thomas Dolby) 1986, Risky 1988, We Love You 1991, Moving On 1994, Prayer/Salvation 1998, Anger 1998. *Current Management:* David Rubinson Management, PO Box 411197, San Francisco, CA 94141, USA.

SAKS, Gidon; Singer (Bass baritone); b. 5 Jan. 1960, Rechovot, Israel. *Education:* Studied at Univ. of Capetown, Royal Northern College of Music with John Cameron, Univ. of Toronto with Patricia Kern; Int. Opera Studio, Zürich. *Career:* Debut: Stratford Festival Canada as The Mikado; Sang with Canadian Opera Company in Magic Flute, Belle Helene, Fanciulla del West, Poppea, Barbiere di Siviglia, Carmen, Merry Widow, Tales of Hoffmann, La Bohème, Anna Bolena, Fliegende Hollander, Luisa Miller, Beatrice et Benedict and Boris Godunov; Gelsenkirchen Opera in Hero und Leander, Punch and Judy, Der Freischütz, Poppea, Gianni Schicchi, Die Zauberflöte, Im Weissen Rossl, Die Blinden (world premiere), L'Italiana in Algeri, Barbiere di Siviglia, Der Rosenkavalier; Bielefeld Opera in Der Zauberflöte, Das Wunder der Heliane, Der Singende Teufel, La Juive, Verlorene Ehe von Katharina Blum (world premiere), Die Bakchantinnen, Street Scene, Ariadne auf Naxos; New Israeli Opera in La Bohème and Bartered Bride; Ariadne auf Naxos in Madrid; L'Incoronazione di Poppea in Brussels; Billby Budd, Don Giovannik Giulio Cesare and Magic Flute for Scottish Opera; Billy Budd and Don Carlo in Geneva; Billy Budd, Fanciulla del West, Rigoletto, Semele with Vlaamse Opera; Boris Godunov in Dublin and Das Liebesverbot in Wexford; Fidelio and Freischutz at Berlin Staatsoper; Fidelio and Nozze di Figaro with Welsh Nat. Opera; Borish Godunov, Freischutz, Rake's Progress and Twilight of the Gods with English Nat. Opera; Harvey Milk in Houston, New York and San Francisco; Luisa Miller USA; Fidelio in Florence and Helsinki; Don Carlo in Palermo; Billy Budd, Salammbo and L'Espace Dernier at Bastille Paris; Nozze di Figaro in Cincinnati; Concerts include Berliner Festwochen with Fischer Dieskau and Ashkenazy in Franck's Beatitudes, Shostakovitch 13th Symphony in Liverpool, Execution of Styenka Razin in Florence with Bychkov and Verdi Requiem in Toronto; As Dir and Designer: Puny Little Life Show in Cape Town; Wozzeck, Cavalleria Rusticana, Happy End and Don Giovanni in Manchester; Paisiello Barbiere in Gattierres, Grande Macabre in Vienna; Cosí fan Tutte, Eugene Onegin, Don Giovanni and Carmen for Aberdeen Int. Youth Festival; teaches singing privately and in masterclasses. *Recordings:* Hercules; Billy Budd; Pilgrim's Progress; Silbersee; Ferne Klang; Der Kreidekries; Opera Gala; Harvey Milk. *Address:* c/o Harlequin Agency Ltd, 203 Fidlas Road, Llanishen, Cardiff CF14 5NA, Wales.

SALA, Ofelia; Singer (Soprano); b. 1970, Valencia, Spain. *Education:* Valencia Conservatoire; Courses with Victoria de los Angeles, Elly Ameling and Renata Scotto. *Career:* Appearances in opera and concert at Leipzig, Lyon, Munich (Prinzregententheater), Vienna, Barcelona and Prague; Repertoire includes Sophie in Der Rosenkavalier, Pamina, Gretel, Oscar, and Henze's Elizabeth Zimmer; Angel in Messiaen's St

François d'Assise, at Leipzig 1998, in Outis by Berio at La Scala, Gilda (Bonn Opera) and Mozart's Servilia (Netherlands Opera, 2000); Engaged with the Deutsche Oper Berlin, from 2001; Concerts include the Requiems of Brahms and Mozart, Haydn's Creation, Vivaldi's Gloria and Mozart's C minor Mass. *Honours:* Prize Winner, Montserrat Caballé, Francisco Viñas and Vervier Competitions. *Address:* c/o Theateragentur Dr G. Hilbert, Maximilianstrasse 22, 80539 Munich, Germany.

SALAFF, Peter; Violinist; b. 1942, USA. *Career:* Member of the Cleveland Quartet, 1968–92, with regular tours of the USA, Canada, Europe, Japan, Russia, South America, Australia, New Zealand and the Middle East; Faculty, Eastman School Rochester and in residence at the Aspen Music Festival, co-founding the Center for Advanced Quartet Studies; Tour of Russia and 5 European countries in 1988; Season 1988–89 with appearances at the Metropolitan Museum and Alice Tully, New York; Concerts in Paris, London, Bonn, Prague, Lisbon and Brussels; Appearances at Salzburg, Edinburgh and Lucerne Festivals; Many complete Beethoven Cycles and annual appearances at Lincoln Center's Mostly Mozart Festival; In addition to standard works his repertory has included performances of works by Ives, John Harbison, Sergei Slonimsky, Samuel Adler, George Perle, Christopher Rouse and Toru Takemitsu. *Recordings:* Repertoire from Mozart to Ravel and collaborations with Alfred Brendel in Schubert's Trout Quintet, Pinchas Zukerman and Bernard Greenhouse with Brahms' Sextets, Emmanuel Ax, Yo-Yo Ma and Richard Stoltzman. *Address:* Eastman School of Music, 26 Gibbs Street, Rochester, NY 14604, USA.

SALERNO-SONNENBERG, Nadja; Violinist; b. 10 Jan. 1961, Rome, Italy. *Education:* Curtis Institute of Music (came to USA 1969); The Juilliard School. *Career:* Television, CBS 60 minutes; 60 minutes II; Sunday Morning; NBC 's National News; The Tonight Show; A and E's Artist of the Week; PBS' Live from Lincoln Center; Backstage/Lincoln Center; The Charlie Rose Show; City Arts; PBS/BBC Series the Mind; PBS Sesame Street; Subject of documentary: Speaking in Strings, 1999. *Recordings include:* Speaking in Strings; Humoresque; Night and Day; Bella Italia; It Aint Necessarily So; Vivaldi The Four Seasons; Nadja Salerno-Sonnenberg, Sergio and Odair Assad.. *Honours:* Violin Competition, Walter W Naumburg International, 1981; Avery Fisher Career Grant, 1983; Ovation Award for Mendelssohn/Massenet/Saint Saëns, 1988; Avery Fisher Prize, 1999. *Current Management:* ICM Artists Ltd. *Address:* c/o M L Falcone, Public Relations, 155 West 68th Street, Suite 1114, New York, NY 10023, USA. *Telephone:* 212 580 4302.

SALKELD, Robert, ARCM; teacher, examiner and editor; b. 16 April 1920, Newcastle upon Tyne, England; two s. one d. *Education:* Royal Grammar School, Newcastle upon Tyne, Newcastle Conservatoire of Music, Royal Coll. of Music. *Career:* Head of Music Dept, Collingwood School, Peckham 1957–60; tutor, Morley Coll. 1950–69; Prof., London Coll. of Music 1961–69, examiner 1961–82; extensive work at festivals, summer schools and courses 1949–72; mem. Royal Musical Asscn. *Publications:* Play the Recorder Series, Concert Pieces; contrib. to Music in Education 1954–76. *Honours:* Hon. FLCM 1977. *Address:* c/o HSBC, 58 High Street, Winchester, SO23 9BZ, England (office).

SALLINEN, Aulis; Composer; b. 9 April 1935, Salmi, Finland. *Education:* Studied with Aarre Merikanto and Joonas Kokkonen, Sibelius Academy, Helsinki. *Career:* Teaching post, Sibelius Academy; Administrator, Finnish Radio Symphony Orchestra, 1960–70; Board Member, Finnish National Opera; Chairman, Teosto Professor of Arts (life appointment by Finnish Government); mem, Finnish Composers' Association, Secretary, Chairman. *Compositions include:* Mauermusik, 1962; Elegy for Sebastian Knight, 1964; Cadenze, 1965; Quattro per Quattro, 1965; Notturno, 1966; Violin Concerto, 1968; String Quartet No. 3, 1969; Chaconne, 1970; String Quartet No. 4, 1971; Sonata for solo cello, 1971; Symphony No. 1, 1971; Suite Grammaticale, 1971; Four Dream Songs, 1972; Symphony No. 2, 1972; The Horseman, opera, 1973; Songs for the Sea, 1974; Symphony No. 3, 1975; Chamber Music I, 1975; Chamber Music II, 1976; Cello Concerto, 1976; The Red Line, opera, 1978; Dies Irae, 1978; Symphony No. 4, 1979; Song Around a Song, 1980; The Iron Age; Shadows; The King goes forth to France, 1984; Symphony No. 5, 1985; Kullervo, opera, 1988; Symphony No. 6, 1989; The Palace, opera, 1993; King Lear, opera, 1999; Symphony no. 7, 2000; The Hobbitt, ballet, 2000; Symphony no 8 (Autumnal Fragments), 2001; Concerto for horn and orchestra, 2002. *Recordings:* Major works on Swedish and/or Finnish label. *Honours:* Wihuri International Sibelius Prize, 1983; Admitted to Membership, Royal Swedish Music Academy, 1983. *Address:* TEOSTO, Lauttasaarentie 1, 00200 Helsinki 20, Finland.

SALMENHAARA, Erkki; Composer and Musicologist; b. 12 March 1941, Helsinki, Finland. *Education:* Studies, Sibelius Academy, Helsinki with Joonas Kokkonen and Vienna with Ligeti, 1963; PhD, University of Helsinki, 1970. *Career:* Faculty Member, University of Helsinki, 1963–; Chairman, Society of Finnish Composers, 1974–76. *Compositions:* 4 Symphonies, 1962, 1963, 1963, 1972; 2 Cello Sonatas, 1960–69, 1982;

Elegy for 2 string quartets, 1963; Wind Quintet, 1964; Requiem Profanum, 1969; Quartet for flute, violin, viola and cello, 1971; Nel Mezzo Del Cammin Di Nostra Vita, for orchestra, 1972; The Woman of Portugal, Opera, 1972 (premiered Helsinki 1976); Suomi-Finland, Unsymphonic Poem, 1967; Canzonetta per Archi, 1972; Illuminations for orchestra, 1972; Horn Concerto, 1973; Sonatine for 2 violins, 1973; Canzona per piccola, orchestra, 1974; Poema for violin or viola and strings, 1976; Introduction and Chorale for organ and orchestra, 1978; String Quartet, 1978; Lamento per orchestra d'archi, 1979; Concerto for 2 violins and orchestra, 1980; Sonatine for flute and guitar, 1981; Violin Sonata, 1982; Sonatella for piano four hands, 1983; Adagietto for orchestra, 1982; Sinfonietta per archi, 1985; Introduction and Allegro for clarinet, cello and piano, 1985; Cello Concerto, 1987; Isle of Bliss for baritone, soprano and orchestra, 1990; *Publications include;* The History of Finnish Music, 1995. *Address:* c/o TEOSTO, Lauttasaarentie 1, 00200 Helsinki, Finland.

SALMINEN, Matti; Singer (Bass); b. 7 July 1945, Turku, Finland. *Education:* Sibelius Academy in Helsinki, and in Rome. *Career:* Debut: Helsinki Opera in 1969 as King Philip in Don Carlos; Sang in Cologne, Zürich and Berlin, 1972–76 in the principal bass parts; La Scala Milan in 1973 as Fafner and at Savonlinna Festival in 1975 as the Horseman, Sarastro, Philip, Don Carlos, Daland and Ramphis; Sang at Bayreuth from 1978 as Daland, the Landgrave, Titurel, King Mark and in The Ring operas; Metropolitan Opera from 1981 as King Mark, Rocco, Osmin, Fasolt, Fafner, Hunding and Hagen; Sang in Berlin in 1985 and Munich in 1987 as Fasolt, Hunding and Hagen; Prince Khovansky in 1984 at San Francisco and 1988 in Barcelona, and Boris Godunov in 1984 at Zürich and 1985 in Barcelona; Sang in Zürich in the Ponnelle productions of L'Incoronazione di Poppea, Die Zauberflöte and Die Entführung and several principal bass parts in Vienna, Hamburg, Paris, Chicago and Tokyo; Sang Hunding in Die Walküre at the Metropolitan in 1990, also televised, Rocco in Fidelio at the Los Angeles Music Center, Daland at the 1990 Savonlinna Festival; Season 1992–93 as Daland at the Metropolitan, Rocco at Zürich and Savonlinna, King Philip at the Deutsche Oper Berlin and Sarastro at the Savonlinna Festival; Sang the Landgrave in Tannhäuser at Savonlinna, 1996; Sang Padre Guardiano in La Forza del Destino at Savonlinna, 1998; Season 2000–01 as Wagner's Hagen at the Deutsche Oper Berlin, Daland at Liège, King Mark for the Salzburg Festival, Gurnemanz for Washington Opera and Hunding in Zürich; Title role in the premiere of Sallinen's Lear, at Helsinki; Engaged for the premiere of Rautavaara's Rasputin (title role) at Helsinki, 2003. *Recordings:* St Matthew Passion; The Landgrave in Tannhäuser; The Ring; Sallinen's The Horseman; Daland; Mozart's Requiem; Osmin; Sarastro. *Current Management:* Ingpen & Williams Ltd, 7 St George's Court, 131 Putney Bridge Road, London, SW15 2PA, England.

SALMON, Philip; singer (tenor); b. 1960, England. *Education:* Royal College of Music. *Career:* debut recital at the City of London Festival followed by the St Matthew Passion with the Rotterdam Philharmonic, Beethoven's 9th with the Ulster Orchestra and Netherlands Philharmonic, and Mozart's Requiem with the Florida Philharmonic; Sang in Massenet's La Vièrge at St Etienne in 1991; Operatic repertoire includes Mozart's Tamino and Belmonte for Pavilion Opera and Debussy's Pelléas at Marseille and Strasbourg, 1990–91; Sang Belmonte in Die Entführung at the Buxton Festival in 1991 and Albert Herring at St Albans; Sang Tamino at the Gaiety Theatre, Dublin, 1996. *Honours:* Young Musicians Recordings Prize. *Current Management:* Robert Gilder & Co., Enterprise House, 59–65 Upper Ground, London, SE1 9PQ, England. *Telephone:* (20) 7928-9008. *Fax:* (20) 7928-9755. *E-mail:* rgilder@robert-gilder.com.

SALOMAA, Petteri; Singer (Baritone); b. 1961, Helsinki, Finland. *Education:* Studied at the Sibelius Academy and with Hans Hotter and Kim Borg. *Career:* Debut: Finnish National Opera, Helsinki 1983, as Mozart's Figaro; Appeared at the Ludwigsburg and Schwetzingen Festivals, 1984; Wexford Festival 1985, as the King in Ariodante; Drottningholm from 1986, as Leporello and Nardo in La Finta Giardiniera; Geneva Opera 1987, as Papageno and Amsterdam 1988, as Masetto, conducted by Nikolaus Harnoncourt; North American debut 1988, with Messiah in San Francisco, followed by Figaro with Michigan Opera; Season 1989–90 at Freiburg Opera as Faninal, Ned Keene, the Father in Hansel and Gretel and in Purcell's King Arthur; 1989–91 at Freiburg Opera as Billy Budd, Posa, Ned Keene and Belcore, 1991 at Frankfurt Opera as Papageno and Guglielmo, 1993 as Conte Robinson in Il matrimonio Segreto; Sang in Purcell's King Arthur at the Châtelet and Covent Garden, 1995; Other roles include Oreste in Iphigénie en Tauride, Posa, Billy Budd and Albert in Werther; Sang Silvio in Pagliacci with Tampere Opera, 1996; Sang in premiere of Bergman's The Singing Tree, Helsinki, 1995; Season 2000–01 in Legrenzi's La Divisione del Mondo, Swetzingen and Innsbruck Festivals; Captain in Death of Klinghoffer, by John Adams, Helsinki, 2001. *Recordings include:* Beethoven's Ninth Symphony; La Finta Giardiniera; The Fiery

Angel by Prokofiev, and Peer Gynt with the Berlin Philharmonic; Le nozze di Figaro; Mendelssohn Elijah. *Honours:* 1st Prize, National Singing Competition at Lappeenranta, 1981. *Address:* Festium Agency, Partiotic 34, 00370 Helsinki, Finland.

SALOMAN, Ora (Frishberg); Musicologist and Professor of Music; b. 14 Nov. 1938, Brooklyn, New York, USA; m. Edward Barry Saloman, 1 July 1968. *Education:* PhD in Musicology, MA in Musicology, AB in Music, Columbia University, New York; Studied violin with Vladimir Graffman and Ivan Galamian, chamber music with Raphael Hillyer, Claus Adam and William Kroll. *Career:* Chairman, Department of Music, 1978–84, Professor of Music, Baruch College and The Graduate Center, City University of New York; Visiting Scholar in Residence, Queen's University, Ontario, Canada, 1999; mem. Editorial Advisory Board, American Music, 1995–97. *Publications:* Beethoven's Symphonies and J. S. Dwight: The Birth of American Music Criticism, 1995; Essay in Music and Civilisation: Essays in Honor of Paul Henry Lang, 1984; Essay in Music and the French Revolution, 1992; Essay in Mainzer Studien zur Musikwissenschaft: Festschrift Walter Wiora, 1997. *Contributions:* Acta Musicologica; Musical Quarterly, 1974, 1992, 1996; Music and Man; American Music, 1988, 1990; International Review of the Aesthetics and Sociology of Music, 1989; The Journal of Musicology, 1992; The New Grove Dictionary of Opera, 1992; St James International Dictionary of Opera, 1993; Journal of the Royal Musical Association, 1994; American National Biography; Reader's Guide to Music, 1999; Encyclopaedia of New England Culture, 2001; Revised New Grove Dictionary of Music and Musicians, 2001; Dictionary of Literary Biography; Die Musik in Geschichte und Gegenwart, 2001; The Opera Quaterly, 2003. *Honours:* National Endowment for the Humanities Fellowship, 1989. *Address:* 14 Summit Street, Englewood, NJ 07631, USA. *E-mail:* ora_saloman@baruch.cuny.edu.

SALONEN, Esa-Pekka; Conductor; b. 30 June 1958, Helsinki, Finland. *Education:* Qualified French Horn player by age 19. *Career:* Composer, 1970–; Conducting Composer, 1980; Conducted performances of Mahler's 3rd Symphony with Philharmonia Orchestra, London, 1983; Music Director, Los Angeles Philharmonic Orchestra, 1992–; Chief Conductor of Swedish Radio Symphony Orchestra, 1985; Principal Guest Conductor, Philharmonia Orchestra, London, and Oslo Philharmonic Orchestra; Led first performance of Robert Saxton's The Circles of Light, 1986; Conducted Messiaen's St François d'Assise at the Salzburg Festival, 1992; Hindemith's Mathis der Maler at Covent Garden, 1995; Ligeti concerts at South Bank, London, 1997; Conducted the Los Angeles Philharmonic at the London Proms, 2002. *Compositions:* Horn Music l, 1976; Cello Sonata; Nachtlieder, 1978; Goodbye, 1980; Concerto for Saxophone and Orchestra; Auf der ersten Blick und ohne zu wissen; Giro; Baalal; Yta l and ll; Meeting; Wind Quintet; Floof; Mimo ll; Mania, for cello and orchestra, 2000; Foreign Bodies for orchestra, 2001; Insomnia, for orchestra, 2002. *Recordings include:* Lutoslawski's Third Symphony; Numerous works by Stravinsky; Sibelius' Symphony No. 5; Messiaen's Turangalîla Symphonie; Mahler's 4th Symphony; Recordings with various orchestras including the London Sinfonietta (Le Grand Macabre, 1999) the Philharmonia Orchestra and the Los Angeles Philharmonic Orchestra. *Current Management:* Van Walsum Management. *Address:* c/o Van Walsum Management, 4 Addison Bridge Place, London W14 8XP, England.

SALTA, Anita; Singer (Soprano); b. 1 Sept. 1937, New York, USA. *Education:* Studied in New York. *Career:* Debut: Jacksonville 1959, as Aida; Appearances at such German Opera House Centres as Stuttgart, Wuppertal, Nuremberg, Dortmund, Kassel, Essen and Hanover; Other roles have included Gluck's Alceste, Mozart's Countess, Donna Elvira and Fiordiligi, Marguerite, the Trovatore and Forza Leonoras, Traviata, Desdemona, Hélène and Elisabeth de Valois; Tatiana, Antonida in A Life for the Tsar, Marenka, Mimi, Butterfly, Santuzza, Elsa, Eva, Chrysothemis, the Marschallin and Katerina Izmailova; Many concert appearances. *Address:* c/o Theatre, Rolandstrasse 10, 4300 Essen, Germany.

SALTER, Richard; Singer (Baritone); b. 12 Nov. 1943, Hindhead, Surrey, England. *Education:* Studied at Royal College of Music, London, then at the Vienna Academy of Music with Christain Moeller, Ilse Rapf and Anton Dermota. *Career:* Sang with King's Singers and gave concert performances; Opera debut Darmstadt 1973; Sang further in Frankfurt and at Glyndebourne; Kiel Opera 1979, as Don Giovanni; Guest appearances in Berlin and Hanover; Hamburg Staatsoper 1979, as Lenz in the premiere of Wolfgang Rihm's Jakob Lenz; Sang Beckmesser at the Paris Opéra, 1988; Hamlet in Rihm's Die Hamletmaschine at Hamburg; Season 1992–93 as the Master in Höller's Meister und Margarita at Cologne and Cortez in the premiere of Rihm's Die Eroberung von Mexico at Hamburg; Sang Coupeau in the premiere of Klebe's Gervaise Macquart, Düsseldorf, 1996; Berg's Wozzeck at Montpellier, 1998; Season 2000–01 as Beckmesser at Nuremberg; Dr Schön in Lulu at Dusseldorf and Bielefeld. *Recordings:* Jakob Lenz, on

Harmonia Mundi. *Address:* c/o Hamburgische Staatsoper, Grosse Theaterstraase 34, 2000 Hamburg 36, Germany.

SALTER, Robert; Violinist; b. 1960, England. *Education:* Wells Cathedral School and Guildhall School, London, with David Takeno. *Career:* Founder member of the Guildhall String Ensemble, with concerts in Europe, the Far East and North America; Solo engagements at the Barbican and Wigmore Halls, London and elsewhere in England and Europe; Leader of Glyndebourne Touring Opera, 1992–; Guest Leader with the English Chamber Orchestra, London Pro Arte and orchestra of the Royal Opera (debut with Giulio Cesare at the Barbican, 1997). *Recordings:* many albums with the Guildhall String Ensemble. *Honours:* Prizes for solo and chamber music performance, GSMO.

SALTER, Timothy, MA, LRAM, ARCO; Composer, Conductor and Pianist; b. 15 Dec. 1942, Mexborough, Yorkshire, England. *Education:* St John's Coll., MTC, London Univ. *Career:* Musical Dir of The Ionian Singers; pianist (chamber music) on tours in the UK and internationally; conductor and pianist on recordings and broadcasts; Prof., Royal Coll. of Music; founded Usk Recordings to promulgate new and neglected works 1995. *Compositions:* instrumental works, chamber music, songs, choral works and orchestral works. *Recordings include:* many choral and piano works, two string quartets and other chamber music, including Fantasy on a Theme by J. S. Bach for Piano, String Quartets Nos 1 and 2, Abstractions for oboe trio, Variations 1986; English folk song arrangements; Katharsios for chorus, piano and percussion; Perspectives, set two, for piano. *Address:* 26 Caterham Road, London, SE13 5AR, England. *Website:* www.timothysalter.com.

SALVADORI, Antonio; Singer (Baritone); b. 1950, Venice, Italy. *Education:* Studied at the Conservatorio Benedetto Marcello, Venice. *Career:* Sang first in Il Barbiere di Siviglia and Pagliacci; La Scala 1977, in Luisa Miller, with Caballé and Pavarotti; Verona Arena fro m 1978, notably as Amonasro (1988); Marcello and Belcore at La Scala 1987–88, tour with the company to Japan 1988; Has sung Rossini's William Tell in Milan, Linz, Nice, Zürich and New York (concert performance at Carnegie Hall); Vienna Staatsoper 1988, as Ezio in Attila; Sang Simon Boccanegra at Cremona, 1990; Other appearances at Chicago, Venice (Gerard in Andrea Chénier), Turin and Hamburg (Don Carlo in Ernani); Sang Iago at Palermo, 1999. *Address:* c/o Opernhaus Zürich, Falkenstrasse 1, 8008 Zürich, Switzerland.

SALVATORI, Roberto; Singer (Baritone); b. 1970, Trinidad. *Education:* Studied, Guildhall School, London, England and the Britten/Pears School at Aldeburgh; Masterclasses with Sena Jurinac and Sherrill Milnes. *Career:* Roles with Pavilion Opera have included Mozart's Don Giovanni, Count and Guglielmo, Rossini's Figaro, Donizetti's Enrico in Lucia di Lammermoor, Dr Malatesta and Belcore; Germont and Scarpia with European Chamber Opera, Sid in Albert Herring at Aldeburgh and Berkely in Marschner's Vampyr for BBC television; Principal with English National Opera from 1995, with Ping, Escamillo and Marcello (La Bohème) in first season; Stolzius in the British company premiere of Zimmerman's Soldaten, 1996; Season 1998–99 as Marcello and Escamillo for ENO and in Massenet's Esclarmonde for Chelsea Opera Group; Sang Iago in Verdi's Otello at ENO and Jochanaan in Salome at the Spier Festival in South Africa. *Honours:* Scholarship from the Countess of Munster Trust. *Current Management:* Penelope Marland Artists' Management. *Address:* c/o ENO Press Office, English National Opera, St Martin's Lane, London WC2N 4ES, England.

SALWAROWSKI, Jerzy (Hubert); Conductor and Musical Director; b. 7 Sept. 1946, Kraków, Poland; m. Ewa Czarniecka, 19 Sept 1976, two s. *Education:* Kraków Music High School, Conducting and Composition, Graduated 1970; Warsaw Chopin Music Academy, docent symphony and opera conducting, 1997. *Career:* Assistant Conductor, Kraków Philharmonic Choir, 1970–71; Second Conductor, Opole Philharmonic Orchestra, 1972–78; Second Conductor, Katowice-Silesian Philharmonic, 1978–81; Substitute Art Director, Silesian Philharmonic, 1982–84; Substitute Art Director, Polish Radio National Symphony Orchestra, 1985–; Guest Conductor, Łódź Great Opera House, tours in Europe; Artistic Director, Pomeranian Philharmonic Orchestra, 1988–90; Artistic Director, Lublin State Philharmonic Orchestra, 1991–93; Artistic Director, Szczein Symphony Orchestra and Torunn Chamber Orchestra; Principal Guest Conductor, Szczecin Philharmonic Orchestra, Torun Chamber Orchestra; Artistic Dir, of festival, Torun: Music and Architecture; Tours in Europe (France, Portugal, Spain, Germany) with symphony and opera music; Prof., Paderewski Music Acad. Poznan, 1999–; Dir, Orchestra and Opera Conductorship Inst.. *Compositions:* Transcriptions and theatre music. *Recordings:* All Gershwin's Pieces for piano and orchestra, with A Ratusinski; All Symphonic Poems by M Karlowicz; J Sibelius: En Saga and Violin Concerto, with V Brodski, for Musical Heritage Society, first digital in Poland; H Wieniawski, Violin Concerto, with V Brodski; Mozart CD, All Church Sonatas with Pomeranian Philharmonic Orchestra and Karol Golebiewski, 1988; Lessel, Grand Rondeau and Piano Concerto, with

Silesian Philharmonic and Jerzy Sterczynski, 1992; Mendelssohn, Hebrides Overture, Violin Concerto and 4th Symphony (Italian) with Krzysztof Jakowicz, 1997; Permanent recording for Polish radio and television over 250 each year; Television concerts, television cycles, Musical Drawing Room. *Publications:* New Elaborations of Karlowicz Scores in PWM Edition. *Contributions:* Permanent Reviews. *Honours:* Gold Plate Award, for Gershwin Album, 1993. *Address:* ul. Wietnamska 63B, 40-765 Katowice, Poland.

SALZMAN, Eric; Composer and Writer on Music; b. 8 Sept. 1933, New York, USA. *Education:* BA, Columbia College, Columbia University, 1954; MFA, Princeton University, 1956; Teachers include Otto Luening, Ussachevsky, Jack Beeson, Roger Sessions and Milton Babbitt; Continued studies in Europe with Petrassi in Rome and Darmstadt. *Career:* Music critic for the New York Times, 1958–62, New York Herald Tribune, 1963–66; Teacher at Queen's College, NY, 1966–68; Director, New Images of Sounds, series of concerts at Hunter College; In 1970 founded Quog Music Theater, to explore new ideas in the performing arts; Co-founder and Artistic Director of American Music Theater Festival with Marjorie Samoff, Philadelphia, 1983–. *Compositions include:* String Quartet, 1955; Flute Sonata, 1956; Inventions for orchestra, 1959; Verses and Cantos for 4 voices, instruments and electronics, 1967; Larynx Music, dance piece with tape, 1968; The Conjurer, multimedia spectacle, 1975; Civilization and its Discontents, opera buffa for radio, 1977; Noah, spectacle, 1978; The Passion of Simple Simon, for performance at the Electric Circus in Greenwich Village; Variations on a Sacred Harp Tune for harpsichord, 1982; Boxes, radio opera with Michael Sahl, 1983; Big Jim and the Small-Time Investors, music theatre, 1985; The Last Words of Dutch Schulz, music theatre, 1996; Body Language, mixed media, 1996; Adaptation of Gershwin's Strike up The Band, 1984. *Publications include:* 20th Century Music: An Introduction, 1967, new edition, 1987; Civilization and Its Discontents and Making Changes, a handbook of vernacular harmony, both with Michael Sahl; The New Music Theater, 1998. *Address:* American Music Theater Festival, 1 Franklin Plaza, Philadelphia, PA 19103, USA.

SAMARITANI, Pier Luigi; stage designer, costume designer and opera director; b. 29 Sept. 1942, Novare, Italy. *Education:* Accademia de Brera, Milan, Centre d'Art Dramatique, Paris. *Career:* debut as Director, Werther, Florence, 1978; Assisted Stage Designer, Lila de Nobili, Paris; Set Designer, Théâtre du Gymnase, Paris 1962, Teatro dell'Opera, Rome 1964; Dance Design for American Ballet Theatre, 1980; Stage Designer for many companies in USA and Europe; Exhibited Stage Designs Spoleto Festival, 1972; Ernani at the Met and Eugene Onegin for the Lyric Opera of Chicago/Werther in Vienna, Paris and Florence, Butterfly in Berlin (1987); Season 1992 with Andrea Chénier at Florence and Turin and Die Meistersinger at Spoleto. *Current Management:* Herbert H. Breslin Inc., 119 W 57th Street, New York, NY 10019, USA.

SAMPSON, Carolyn; Singer (soprano); b. 1974, England; m. *Education:* Univ. of Birmingham, 1995. *Career:* opera includes Amor in The Coronation of Poppea (ENO), Tanterabogus in The Fairy Queen (ENO in London and on tour to Barcelona), La Musica and Euridice in Orfeo (Barbican, London), Antonia in The Tales of Hoffmann at the St Endellion Festival, First Niece in Peter Grimes for Opéra National de Paris; concert engagements with City of London Sinfonia, Manchester Camarata, Le Chapelle Royale, ChorwerkRuhr, Il Giardino Armonico, Music of the Baroque Chicago, RIAS Kammerchor, Holland Sinfonia, Sonnerie, The King's Consort (including US tour, 2001), The Sixteen, Ex Cathedra, Halle Orchestra, Scottish Chamber Orchestra, Collegium Vocale, Gent, Washington Bach Consort, The Royal Concertgebouw Orchestra, Freiburg Baroque Orchestra, The English Concert, Orchestra of the Age of Enlightenment, Le Concert d'Astrée, The Gabrieli Consort, Orchestre des Champs Elysées; festival appearances include BBC Proms, Mostly Mozart (New York), Beaune, Leipzig, Saintes, Halle, Salzburg, Istanbul; recitals in the Proms Chamber Music series, The Wigmore Hall, BBC Wales, BBC Scotland, and the Hampstead and Highgate Festival, London. *Recordings include:* Kuhnau, Knüpfer, Vivaldi, Monteverdi, Zelenka, Lalande, Rameau, Bach, Orfeo, Buxtehude, Carmina Burana. *Current Management:* Caroline Phillips Management, The Old Brushworks, 56 Pickwick Road, Corsham, Wiltshire, SN13 9BX, England. *Telephone:* (1249) 716716. *Fax:* (1249) 716717. *E-mail:* cphillips@caroline-phillips.co.uk. *Website:* www.caroline-phillips.co.uk/sampson.

SAMSING, Boris (Leon); Violinist; b. 31 Dec. 1943, Copenhagen, Denmark; m., 1 s., 1 d. *Education:* Funen Academy of Music; Bern and Prague. *Career:* Debut: Funen Academy, 1963; Member, Sonderjylland Symphony Orchestra, 1964–69; Principal, Sjaelland Symphony Orchestra, 1969–75; Member, Kontra Quartet, 1973–; principal, Danish Radio Symphony Orchestra, 1975–; Representative ensemble af the Danish State, 1989–92; Teacher, Royal Danish Academy of music; Toured all over the world with Kontra Quartet; Workshops as a violinist

with Kontra Quartet. *Recordings:* Carl Nielsen; Per Norgaard; Rued Langgaard; Vagn Holmboe; Niels W Gade; Poul Ruders; Hans Abrahamsen; Mozart; Schubert; Tchaikovsky; 33 recordings with the Kontra Quartet. *Honours:* Peder Moller Award; Nominations of the Nordic Council; The Gramophone Recording of the Year; Danish Musicians Union Award. *Address:* Vejlemosevej 10, 2840 Holte, Denmark.

SAMSON, (Thomas) James, BMus, MMus, PhD, LRAM; university teacher; b. 6 July 1946, Northern Ireland. *Education:* Queen's University, Belfast, University College, Cardiff. *Career:* Research Fellow in Humanities, University of Leicester, England, 1972–73; Lecturer in Music, 1973–86, Reader in Musicology, 1986–91, Professor of Musicology, 1991–94, University of Exeter; Badock Professor of Musicology, University of Bristol, 1994–2002; Professor of Music, Royal Holloway, University of London, 2002–; mem, Council Member, Royal Musical Association. *Publications:* Music in Transition, 1977; The Music of Szymanowski, 1980; The Music of Chopin, 1985; Chopin Studies, 1988; Man and Music, vol. 7, The Late Romantic Era, 1991; The Cambridge Companion to Chopin, 1992; Chopin: The Four Ballades, 1992; Chopin Studies 2 (with John Rink), 1994; Chopin, Master Musicians series, 1996; The Cambridge History of Music, 2002. *Contributions:* Rocznik Chopinowski, Journal of the American Musicological Society, Nineteenth-Century Music, Tempo, Journal of Musicology, Music Analysis, Music and Letters, Musical Times. *Honours:* Szymanowski Centennial Medal, 1982; Order of Merit, Polish Ministry of Culture, 1990; Fellow of the British Academy, 2000. *Address:* Music Department, University of Bristol, Royal Fort House, Tyndall Avenue, Bristol BS8 1VJ, England.

SAMUEL, Gerhard; Conductor, Composer and Professor of Music; b. 20 April 1924, Germany. *Education:* BM, Eastman School of Music; MM, Yale University. *Career:* Conductor, Ballet Ballads on Broadway, 1947–48; Attached to Cultural Attache, American Embassy, Paris, 1948–49; Associate Conductor and Violinist, Minneapolis Symphony, 1949–59; Director and Conductor, Collegium Musicum, Minneapolis Civic Opera, 1949–59; Director and Conductor, San Francisco Composers Forum, 1959–71; Music Director Oakland Symphony Orchestra, 1959–71; Music Director/Conductor, San Francisco Ballet, 1960–70; Guest Conductor, San Francisco Opera; Conductor, Ojai Festival, 1971; Associate Conductor, Los Angeles Philharmonic Orchestra, 1970–73; Director and Conductor, Ojai Festival, 1971; Conductor of Orchestra and Opera and Director of Conducting Program, California Institute of the Arts, 1972–76; Director of Orchestral Activities, College-Conservatory of Music, University of Cincinnati, 1976–97; Conductor, Music Director, Cincinnati Chamber Orchestra, 1983–91; Guest Conductor, USA, South America, Mexico, Canada, the Philippines, England, Belgium, France, Germany, Norway, Sweden, Russia, China, Poland and Switzerland; Chief Guest Conductor, Oakland Ballet Company, 1983–86; Conducted the premiere of Harold Blumenfeld's Seasons in Hell, Cincinnati, 1996; Music Director, Cosmopolitan Orchestra, New York City, 1997–. *Compositions:* Over 70 including: Requiem for Survivors, orchestral, 1973; Looking at Orpheus Looking, orchestral, 1971; Out of Time, A Short Symphony, 1978; Chamber Concerto for flute in the Shape of a Summer, orchestral, 1981; Emperor and the Nightingale, small ensemble, 1980; Fanfare for a Pleasant Occasion, small ensemble, 1981; Thoughts For Sandy on His Birthday, small ensemble, 1983; Harlequin's Caprice, solo harpsichord, 1980; On the Beach at Night Alone, orchestral, 1980; The Naumburg Cadenza, solo violin, 1985; Nocturne on an Impossible Dream, small ensemble, 1986; Nicholas and Concepcion, orchestral, 1987; As Imperceptibly as Grief, orchestral, 1988; Christ! What are Patterns For?, small ensemble, 1988; Henry's Cadenza, solo violin, 1989; Apollo and Hyacinth, small ensemble, 1989; After a Dirge, small ensemble, 1993; His Cincinnati Philharmonia Orchestra participated in the 1989 Mahler Cyle, Châtelet Theatre, Paris, and Festival 98 in Lisbon; In Search of Words, orchestral, 1995. *Current Management:* Corbett Arts Management, San Francisco, California, USA. *Address:* c/o ASCAP, ASCAP Building, One Lincoln Plaza, New York, NY 10027, USA.

SAMUELSON, Mikael; Singer (Baritone); b. 9 March 1951, Stockholm, Sweden. *Education:* Studied with Birgit Stenberg and Erik Werba. *Career:* Has sung in Sweden from 1968 in opera, oratorio, music theatre and films; Royal Opera Stockholm as Rossini's Figaro; Drottningholm Theatre 1987 and 1989, as Mozart's Figaro and Papageno; Sang in Die Schöpfung 1988; Appearances with the Stockholm Music Drama Ensemble in Pagliacci, Mahagonny and Death in Venice; Television engagements in Drömmen om Thérèse by Werle and Kronbruden by Rangströ m; Has appeared as cabaret artist in Sweden and Finland. *Address:* c/o Drottningholms Slottsteater, PO Box 27050, 102 51 Stockholm, Sweden.

SANCHEZ, Ana Maria; Singer (Soprano); b. 1966, Elda, Alicante, Spain. *Education:* Studied at the Alicante Conservatory and in Madrid with Isabel Penagos and Miguel Zanetwi. *Career:* Sang in concerts and recitals in Spain, France and Germany; Stage debut as Abigaille in

Nabucco at Palma (1994) followed by Donna Anna at Valencia and elsewhere; Mathilde in Guillaume Tell at Lisbon, Leonora in La Forza de destino at Barcelona and Chrysothemis in Elektra at Valencia; Sang the Trovatore Leonora at Zürich, season 1996–97, and has appeared further in Roberto Devereux and Tannhäuser in Bibao, Salud in La Vida Breve at Malaga and in Don Giovanni at Hamburg; Engaged to return to Valencia 1998, as Gutrune in Götterdämmerung; Concerts include the Verdi Requiem and song recitals. *Honours:* Prizewinner in competitions at Bilbao and Enna (Italy), 1992–93. *Address:* c/o Opernhaus Zürich, Falkenstrasse 1, 8008 Zürich, Switzerland.

SAND, Annemarie; Singer (Mezzo-Soprano); b. 26 Nov. 1958, Copenhagen, Denmark. *Education:* Studied at the Royal Academy of Music and the National Opera Studio. *Career:* Appeared with English National Opera from 1987 as the Page in Salome, Linetta in The Love of Three Oranges, and Dryad in Ariadne auf Naxos; Welsh National Opera, 1989 as the Composer in Ariadne, conducted by Charles Mackerras; Other roles include Mother Goose in The Rake's Progress, Nancy in Albert Herring, Charlotte, Octavian, Hansel and the Mother in Amahl and the Night Visitors; Many concert appearances including Mozart's Requiem at the Teatro San Carlo, Naples, and 12 concerts in Denmark, 1989; Season 1992 as Kate Pinkerton for ENO and in Oliver's Mario and the Magician at the Almeida Theatre; Season 1993 included BBC Proms debut in The Wreckers, Ethyl Smyth. *Honours:* Elena Gerhardt Lieder Prize; Minnie Hauk Prize; Clifton Prize for Best Recital. *Address:* c/o English National Opera, St Martin's Lane, London, WC2, England.

SAND, Malmfrid; singer (soprano); b. 1955, Oslo, Norway. *Education:* studied in Oslo and London. *Career:* debut, sang Pamina in Die Zauberflöte at Oslo; Appearances as Fiordiligi in Brussels, London and at the Bath Festival; Irene in Tamerlano for Orpheus Opera and Isaura in Jérusalem by Verdi for BBC Radio 1983; Wexford Festival 1983, as the Queen in Marschner's Hans Heiling, returning as Donna Anna in Gazzaniga's Don Giovanni and in Busoni's Turandot; Recent engagements as Electra in Idomeneo for the English Bach Festival and Manon for Dorset Opera, 1991; Concert Repertoire includes Vivaldi Gloria, Messiah, Dvořák's Requiem; Concerts and Recitals in Scandinavia, the USA and Europe, notably with the Stavanger Symphony, the Oslo NRK Symphony and the Harmonien Symphony Orchestra of Bergen; Sang Mrs Maurrant in Weill's Street Scene, Turin, 1995. *Current Management:* Robert Gilder & Co., Enterprise House, 59–65 Upper Ground, London, SE1 9PQ, England. *Telephone:* (20) 7928-9008. *Fax:* (20) 7928-9755. *E-mail:* rgilder@robert-gilder.com.

SANDEL, Marina; Singer (Mezzo-soprano); b. 1959, Stuttgart, Germany. *Education:* Studied in Frankfurt and Stuttgart, and with Brigitte Fassbaender. *Career:* Concert appearances in Europe and Israel from 1984; Essen Opera from 1989, with guest engagements in opera at Karlsruhe, Mannheim and Ludwigsburg; Roles have included Dorabella, Hansel, Laura in La Gioconda (Bremen, 1996) and Octavian in Der Rosenkavalier; Essen, 1996, in the premiere of Bibalo's Miss Julie and as Nicklausse in Les contes d'Hoffmann. *Address:* c/o Essen Opera, Rolandstrasse 10, 4300 Essen 1, Germany.

SANDERLING, Kurt; Conductor; b. 19 Sept. 1912, Arys, Germany. *Education:* Studied privately while working as répétiteur with the Berlin St ädtische Oper, 1931. *Career:* Left Germany, 1936, and was Conductor of the Moscow Radio Symphony Orchestra, 1936–41; Leningrad Philharmonic Orchestra, 1941–60; Chief Professor of conducting and orchestral classes at the Leningrad Conservatory; Berlin Symphony Orchestra, 1960–77; Dresden State Orchestra, 1964–67; Guest appearances at the Prague, Warsaw, Salzburg and Vienna Festivals; British debut, 1970, with the Leipzig Gewandhaus Orchestra; New Philharmonia Orchestra, 1972–; Recent visits to Japan, USA, Canada, Australia and New Zealand; Conducted the Los Angeles Philharmonic at Symphony Hall, Birmingham, 1991; Haydn's 39th Symphony and Shostakovich No. 8; Retired, 2002. *Recordings:* All Beethoven's Symphonies with the Philharmonia Orchestra, 1981; Beethoven's Piano Concertos (Gilels); Complete Symphonies of Brahms and Sibelius; Prokofiev Sinfonia Concertante (Rostropovich); Mozart Divertimento K334, Concertos K216 (Kogan) and K466 (Richter); Haydn Symphonies 88, 45, 104, 1982–87; Bruckner's 3rd Symphony and Shostakovich Nos 8, 10 and 15. *Honours:* Soviet Award of Honoured Artist; National Prize of the German Democratic Republic, 1962, 1974. *Address:* The Music Partnership Ltd, 41 Adlebert Terrace, London, SW8 1BH.

SANDERLING, Michael; Concert Cellist; b. 1967, Berlin, Germany. *Education:* Studied at the Berlin Musikhochschule. *Career:* Principal of the Leipzig Gewandhaus Orchestra, 1987–92; Solo career from 1992, notably with the Boston Symphony Orchestra, Los Angeles Philharmonic Orchestra, Berlin and Bamberg Symphonies, Philharmonia, Royal Philharmonic Orchestra and Tonhalle Zürich; Chamber concerts with the Trio Ex Aequo at the Schleswig-Holstein, Lucerne and Salzburg Festivals. *Honours:* Prizewinner at the Maria-Canals Competition

Barcelona, JS Bach Competition Leipzig and ARD Competition, Munich. *Address:* c/o World-wide Artists, 6 Petersfield Crescent, Coulsdon, Surrey CR5 2JQ, England.

SANDERLING, Thomas; Conductor; b. 2 Nov. 1942, Nowosibirsk, USSR. *Education:* School of the Leningrad Conservatory; German High School of Music, East Berlin. *Career:* Debut: Conducted Berlin Symphony Orchestra, 1962; Chief Conductor, Reichenbach, 1964; Music Director, Opera and Concerts, Halle, Democratic Republic of Germany, 1966; Permanent Guest Conductor, German State Opera, Berlin, 1978–; Moved to West Germany in 1983; Has conducted at most major centres in Germany and throughout Europe including Stockholm, Oslo, Helsinki, Milan, Rome, London, Salzburg and Amsterdam; Gave the German premiere of Shostakovich's Symphonies 13 and 14 with Berlin Radio Symphony Orchestra, 1969, and A Petterson's 8th Symphony in 1979; Outstanding success with productions of Magic Flute and Marriage of Figaro at Vienna State Opera, 1979; Has worked with Rotterdam Philharmonic, Bournemouth Symphony Orchestra, Philharmonia (London), Vienna Symphony Orchestra and in Nice, Vancouver, Rochester, New Zealand, Japan, Israel and Australia, with recent productions of Figaro (Nice) and Don Giovanni (Austria and Helsinki). *Recordings:* Shostakovich: Michelangelo cycle (recording premiere) and Symphonies 2 and 4; Handel: Alexander's Feast and Italian Cantatas; Wolfgang Strauss: Symphony No. 1; Udo Zimmermann: Ein Zeuge der liebe. *Honours:* Berlin Critics' Award, 1970. *Address:* The Music Partnership Ltd, 41 Adlebert Terrace, London, SW8 1BH.

SANDERS, Ernest H.; Musicologist; b. 4 Dec. 1918, Hamburg, Germany; m. Marion Hollander 1954, 1 s., 1 d. *Education:* MA, Music Historical Musicology, 1952, PhD, in the same, Columbia University, 1963. *Career:* Department of Music, Columbia University, Lecturer, 1954–58, Instructor, 1958–61 and 1962–63, Assistant Professor, 1963–65 and 1966–67, Associate Professor, 1967–72, Professor, 1972–86, Chairman, Department of Music, 1978–85. *Publications:* English Polyphony of the Thirteenth and Early 14th Centuries (Polyphonic Music of the Fourteenth Century Vol. XIV, 1979); Vols XVI and XVII, co-editor. *Contributions:* Numerous articles dealing with aspects of mediaeval polyphony in Journal of the American Musicological Society; The Musical Quarterly; Acta Musicologica; Archiv für Musikwissenschaft; Music and Letters; Musica Disciplina; The New Grove Dictionary; Various Festschriften; Most of these collected in French and English Polyphony of the 13th and 14th Centuries–The Notation of Notre-Dame Organa Tripla and Quadrupla, forthcoming; 3 articles on Beethoven's Opp 125 and 123. *Honours:* Fulbright Research Scholarship, 1965–66 (England); Guggenheim Fellowship (supplementary), 1965–66; ACLS Fellowship, 1969–70; Senior Research Fellowship, National Endowment for the Humanities, 1973–74. *Address:* 885 West End Avenue 8B, New York, NY 10025-3524, USA.

SANDERS, Graham; Singer (tenor); b. 1963, Chichester, England. *Education:* London College of Music, and in USA with James King and William Johns. *Career:* Appearances at Bonn Opera as Roderigo in Otello (debut role), Laca in Jenůfa and Florestan in Fidelio; Bremen Opera 1994-2000, as Wagner's Erik and Walther, Bacchus in Ariadne auf Naxos and Canio in Pagliacci; Further engagements as Siegmund in Die Walküre at Graz, Kiel and Darmstadt, Laca at Dresden and Polixenes in Ein Wintermärchen by Boesmans at Braunschweig; Season 2001–2002 as Otello at Budapest and Siegfried for Scottish Opera; Engaged for Götterdämmerung at Edinburgh, 2003. *Current Management:* Athole Still International Management, Forresters Hall, 25–27 Westow Street, London, SE19 3RY, England. *Telephone:* (20) 8771-5271. *Fax:* (20) 8768-6600. *Website:* www.atholestill.com.

SANDISON, Gordon; Singer (Baritone); b. 1949, Aberdeen, Scotland. *Education:* Studied at the Royal Scottish Academy. *Career:* Has sung with Scottish Opera from 1973 as Papageno, the Figaros of Rossini and Mozart, Malatesta, Don Giovanni, Belcore, Don Alfonso, Falstaff, Marcello; Covent Garden debut, 1984, as Fléville in Andrea Chénier, followed by Mandarin, Morales, Starveling, Montano, Masetto and the Doctor and Shepherd in Pélleas et Mélisande; Further appearances with English National Opera, Théâtre du Châtelet Paris, Opera Northern Ireland and the Glyndebourne, Wexford and Edinburgh Festivals; Sang in Carmen at Earls Court, London and on Tour to Japan; Rossini's Bartolo for ENO, 1995; Sang Frank in Die Fledermaus for Opera Holland Park, 1998; Season 2000–01 as the Mayor in Jenůfa at Glyndebourne and Rossini's Bartolo for ENO. *Address:* c/o Phoenix Artists Management, 6 Windmill Street, London, W10 1HF, England.

SANDON, Nicholas (John); Musicologist; b. 16 Feb. 1948, Faversham, Kent, England; m. Edith Virginia Edwards, 1 July 1975, 1 step-s., 2 step-d. *Education:* Studied, 1967–71, BMus, 1970, University of Birmingham; PhD, University of Exeter, 1983. *Career:* Lecturer in Music, 1971–86, Head, Music Department, 1983–86, Professor of Music, 1993–, University of Exeter; Professor of Music, Head, Music Department, University College, Cork, Ireland, 1986–93; mem, Royal Musical

Associatiion; Plainsong and Medieval Society, Council Member; Henry Bradshaw Society. *Publications:* John Sheppard's Masses, 1976; Oxford Anthology of Medieval Music, 1977; The Use of Salisbury, 1986–99; Many other editions of English church music; General Editor of Antico Edition. *Contributions:* Early Music; Music and Letters; Musica Disciplina; Proceedings of the Royal Musical Association; Royal Musical Association Research Chronicle; Musical Times; Music Review; The Consort; BBC Radio 3; Journal of Theological Studies. *Honours:* University Scholar at Birmingham, 1967–70. *Address:* Department of Music, University of Exeter, Exeter EX4 4PD, England.

SANDOR, György; Pianist and Conductor; b. 21 Sept. 1912, Budapest, Hungary. *Education:* Piano Student, Liszt Academy, Budapest, Hungary; Piano Student of Bart ók; Composition Student of Kodály. *Career:* Appearances with the orchestras of Vienna, Baden-Baden, New York Philharmonic Orchestra and the Philadelphia Orchestra; Has performed at numerous music festivals world-wide; Concert tours, Mozarteum, Salzburg and the Assisi Festival; Gave the first performance of Bart ók's 3rd Piano Concerto, Philadelphia, 1946; Judges International Piano Competitions; Holds Masterclasses. *Recordings:* Has made numerous recordings including Bartók and the Baroque. *Publications:* On Piano Playing, 1981. *Honours:* Grand Prix du Disque.

SANDSTRÖM, Sven-David; Composer; b. 30 Oct. 1942, Motala, Sweden; m. Gudrun Sandströ m. *Education:* Stockholm University, 1963–67; State College of Music, 1968–72 with Lidholm; Further study with Ligeti and Norgard. *Career:* Joined Faculty of State College of Music Stockholm, 1980. *Compositions:* Stage: Strong Like Death, Church opera, 1978; Hasta O Beloved Bride, chamber opera, 1978; Emperor Jones, music drama, 1980; Incidental Music for Strindberg's Dream Play, 1980; Ballet Den elfte gryningen, 1988; Music, ballet, 1995; The City, opera, 1998; Vocal: Pictures, 1969; Intrada, 1969; In the Meantime, 1970; Around a Line, 1971; Through and Through, 1972; Con tutta Forza, 1976; Clumination, 1977; Agitato, 1978; The Rest is Dross, 1980; Guitar Concerto, 1983; Invignings fanfar, 1988; Cello Concerto, 1989; Piano Concerto, 1990; Percussion Concerto, 1994; Concerto for recorder, harpsichord and strings, 1996; Soft Music for clarinet strings and percussion, 1996. Chamber: String Quartet, 1969; Mosaic for string trio, 1970; 6 Character Pieces, 1973; Metal, Metal for 4 percussionists, 1974; Utmost, premiered by Pierre Boulez, London 1975; Within for 8 trombones and percussion, 1979; Drums for timpani and 4 percussionists, 1980; Spring Music for percussion, 1997; Vocal: Inventions for 16 voices, 1969; Lamento, 1971; Birgitta-Music I, 1973; Expression, 1976; A Cradle Song/The Tiger, after Blake, 1978; Requiem, for the child victims of war and racism, 1979; Agnus Dei, 1980; Piano and organ music; Moses, Oratorio, 1997.

SANDVE, Kjell Magnus; Singer (Tenor); b. 1957, Karmoy, Norway. *Education:* Studied at the Oslo State Opera School, 1979–82. *Career:* Sang at the Nationaltheater Weimar, 1982–84 and Norwegian National Opera at Oslo from 1983, with guest appearances at Copenhagen, Opéra Bastille as Hylas in Les Troyens, the Staatsoper Berlin as Belmonte in 1989, and at Munich as Sifare in Mitridate in 1990; Other roles include Don Ottavio, Ferrando, Nemorino, Alfredo, Lensky and Nielsen's David; Sang Verdi's Macduff at Oslo, 2000. *Recordings include:* Songs by Grieg. *Address:* Norwegian National Opera, PO Box 8800 Youngstorget, 0028 Oslo, Norway.

SANGER, David John, FRCO, ARCM, FRAM; Organ Recitalist; b. 17 April 1947, London, England. *Education:* Eltham Coll., Royal Acad. of Music. *Career:* international tours as organ recitalist, notably in Scandinavia; performances at Proms and Royal Festival Hall; jury mem. of many international competitions; consultant for new organs and restorations (notably Exeter Coll., Oxford and Usher Hall, Edinburgh). *Compositions include:* liturgical music, carols, organ music. *Recordings include:* complete organ symphonies of Louis Vierne, complete organ works of César Franck, complete organ works of J. S. Bach (in progress). *Publications:* Organ Tutor 'Play the Organ' Vols 1 and 2, editions of Willan: Introduction, Passacaglia and Fugue, Pepusch: Voluntary in C, Lefébure-Wély: Favourite Organ Music (two vols); contrib. to Organists' Review, The Organ. *Honours:* first prize, St Albans International Organ Festival 1969, first prize, International Organ Competition, Kiel, Germany 1972. *Address:* Old Wesleyan Chapel, Embleton, CA13 9YA, England (home). *Telephone:* (17687) 76628 (home). *Fax:* (17687) 76628 (home). *E-mail:* david.sanger@virgin.net (office). *Website:* www .davidsanger.co.uk (office).

SANT, Cecile van de; Singer (mezzo-soprano); b. 1970, Netherlands. *Education:* Sweelinck Conservatory, and in New York; Studies with Regine Crespin, Charlotte Margiono and Robert Holl. *Career:* Appearances at the Göttingen Festival in cantatas by Handel and Vivaldi, and as Tauride in Handel's Arianna in Creta; Sang Gualtiero in Bononcini's Griselda at Utrecht and Handel's Tamerlano in Amsterdam; Other roles include Amastre in Xerxes, Monteverdi's Nerone, Jezibaba in Rusalka, Gluck's Orfeo, and Cherubino; Concerts include Mahler's Lieder eines

fahrenden Gesellen and Knaben Wunderhorn, Elijah, Les Nuits d'été, the Alto Rhapsody and sacred music by Bach; Haydn's Seven Last Words at the Concertgebouw. Amsterdam; Season 2000–2001 with Cenerentola at Kaiserslautern, Unulfo in Rodelinda at Göttingen and Messenger in Monteverdi's Orfeo at Munich; Olga in Eugene Onegin for Opera North, and Rosina for Opera Holland Park, London. *Current Management:* Athole Still International Management, Forresters Hall, 25–27 Westow Street, London, SE19 3RY, England. *Telephone:* (20) 8771-5271. *Fax:* (20) 8768-6600. *Website:* www.atholestill.com.

SANTE, Sophia (Maris Christina) van; Singer (Mezzo-soprano); b. 11 Aug. 1925, Zaandam, Netherlands. *Education:* Studied at the Amsterdam Muziekclyceum with van der Sluys and Ruth Horna; Further studies with Marietta Amstad in Italy. *Career:* Many appearances from 1960 with the Amsterdam Opera as the Woman in Schoenberg's Erwartung, Marie in Wozzeck and Judith in Duke Bluebeard's Castle; Also sang in the Dutch premieres of Henze's Der Junge Lord and Dallapiccola's Il Prigioniero. *Recordings include:* Der Rosenkavalier.

SANTI, Nello; Conductor; b. 22 Sept. 1931, Adria, Rovigo, Italy. *Education:* Studied at the Liceo Musicale in Padua and with Coltro and Pedrollo. *Career:* Debut: Teatro Verdi, Padua, 1951, Rigoletto; Conductor of the Zürich Opera from 1958; Covent Garden debut, 1960, with La Traviata; Vienna Staatsoper and Salzburg Festival debuts, 1960; Metropolitan Opera, 1962, Un Ballo in Maschera; Regular appearances from 1976; La Scala, Milan, 1971; Paris Opéra, 1974; Guest engagements in Berlin, Munich, Florence, Geneva, Lisbon and Madrid, in the operas of Rossini, Bellini, Donizetti, Verdi, Puccini and Mascagni; Orchestral concerts with L'Orchestre National, Paris; RIAS, West Berlin, and the Munich Philharmonic; New Philharmonia Orchestra and the London Symphony; Returned to Covent Garden, 1982, La Fanciulla del West; Conducted Aida in a new production by Vittorio Rossi; Conducts regularly at the Metropolitan Opera House, New York, Arena di Verona and throughout Italy and Germany; Rigoletto at Verona, 1997 and Nabucco at Zürich, 1998; Season 2003/04 includes: Barbiere di Siviglio, Nabucco, Tosca and Rigoletto with the Opera House of Zurich, Donizetti's Don Pasquale in Montecarlo, new productions of Bellini's I Capuleti e Montecci at the Opera of Rome and Verdi's Nabucco at the Summer Festival of Caracalla in Rome and a new production of Puccini's La Bohème at the Teatro San Carlo di Napoli. Concert Engagements include a summer concert with the Philharmonic Orchestra of Montecarlo , symphonic concerts with the Oslo Philharmonic Orchestra and further concerts with the NHK Symphony Orchestra in Tokyo. *Recordings:* Pagliacci; L'Amore dei Tre Re; Complete Verdi tenor arias, with Carlo Bergonzi; Aria recitals with Placido Domingo; Videos of Otello, La Bohème, Nabucco, Rigoletto, Andrea Chénier, Falstaff and the Verdi Requiem. *Honours:* Medallion de la Cité de Zürich; Commendatore of the Republic of Italy. *Address:* Wildbachstrasse 77. CH-8008 Zürich Switzerland.

SANTUNIONE, Orianna; Singer (Soprano); b. 1 Sept. 1934, Sassolo, Modena, Italy. *Education:* Studied in Milan with Carmen Melis and Renato Pastorino. *Career:* After debut as Giordano's Fedora sang in Rome, Genoa, Bologna, Trieste, Naples, Parma and Palermo; Covent Garden, London 1965, as Amelia in Un Ballo in Maschera and Elisabeth de Valois; Further appearances in Nice, Rouen, Turin, Venice, Munich, Hamburg, Amsterdam, Dallas, Philadelphia and Cincinnati; Verona Arena, 1967–77; Other roles include Desdemona, Elsa, Medea, Santuzza, Nedda, both Leonoras of Verdi, Mathilde in Guillaume Tell, Francesca da Rimini, Tosca, Madama Butterfly and Aida. *Recordings include:* Madame Sans-Gêne by Giordano; Pimmalione by Donizetti; Otello and Lohengrin for Italian television. *Address:* c/o Arena di Verona, Piazza Bra 28, 37121 Verona, Italy.

SAPAROVA-FISCHEROVA, Jitka; Opera Singer (Soprano); b. 7 April 1964, Brno, Czechoslovakia; m. Miroslav Fischer, 19 Oct 1991, 1 d. *Education:* High School of Musical Art. *Career:* Debut: Mozart's Zauberflöte; Soloist of Chamber Orchestre, Baroque and Renaissance Music, Musica Aeterna, 1985–86; Soloist of Slovak National Theatres Opera from 1986; Operas include: Faust; Le nozze di Figaro; Rigoletto; Suor Angelica; Carmen; mem, Association of Slovak Theatres. *Recordings:* Rigoletto; La Sonnambula. *Honours:* 1st Prize, 1985 Competition of M Schneider Trnausee; Laureate of Singing Competition of Antonín Dvořák. *Address:* Dankovskeho 14, 811 03 Bratislava, Slovakia.

SARADJIAN, Vagram; Cellist; b. 15 July 1948, Yerevan, Armenia. *Career:* Debut: Yerevan, Armenia, 1956; US debut, Carnegie Hall, 1994; Winner of Russian National Competition aged 18; Won several major contests including Tchaikovsky International Competition, 1970; Geneva International Cello Competition, 1975; Recitals performed around the world in halls including: Gaveau in Paris; La Scala in Milan, Victoria Hall in Geneva, Musikverein in Vienna, Teatro Col ón in Buenos Aires, Carnegie Hall in New York, Great Hall of the Moscow Conservatory, Leningrad Philharmonic Hall; International tours playing with conductors including Gergiev, Khachaturian, Kondrashin,

Svetlanov, Rostropovich, Shostakovich, Temirkanov; Premiered works by composers including Alexander Tchaikovsky, Gia Kancheli, Karen Khachaturian; Appearances include: Valery Gergiev's Stars of the White Nights Festival in St Petersburg; Extensive tour of Argentina and Uruguay; Extensive European tour with Maxim Vengerov and Vag Papian; Engaged for performances in Chicago, Los Angeles, Philadelphia, tours in Russia, Switzerland, Poland and Germany; Taught at Connecticut College, New London, Connecticut and Oberlin Conservatory, Oberlin, Ohio; Faculty, Aaron Copland School of Music, Queens College, City University of New York and Pierchase Conservatory (SUNY); Professor of Violoncello, University of Houston, Texas. *Recordings:* Karen Khachaturian Cello Concerto (USSR Symphony Orchestra); Saint-Saëns, Concerto No. 1; Tchaikovsky Rococo Variations; Dvořák's Concerto in B Minor, op 104 (Moscow Philharmonic); Karen Khachaturian, Sonata for Cello and Piano; Eduard Mirzoian–Sonata for Cello and Piano. *Honours:* Fourth Prize, Tchaikovsky International Competition, Moscow, 1970; Gold Medals, Geneva Prize Winner, Switzerland, 1975; International Music Festivals in Sofia, 1976, Prague, 1980; First Prize, Aram Khachaturian International Music Awards, New York, 1990.

SARASTE, Jukka-Pekka; Conductor; b. 22 April 1956, Heinola, Finland. *Education:* Studied Violin and Conducting at the Sibelius Academy, Helsinki. *Career:* Debut: 1980 with the Helsinki Philharmonic; Conductor, jointly with Okku Kamu, Helsinki Philharmonic, on 1983 tour of USA; Appointed Principal Guest Conductor of the Finnish Radio Symphony Orchestra, 1985; Principal Conductor and Music Director from 1987; Principal Conductor, Scottish Chamber Orchestra, 1987–91; Music Director of the Toronto Symphony from 1994; Tours to France, Finland and the Far East; Guest Conductor with orchestras in Minnesota, Vienna, Rotterdam, Munich and Toronto; Conducted the Finnish Radio Symphony Orchestra at the 1991 and the Scottish Chamber Orchestra at the 1992 Promenade Concerts, London. Season 1999–2000 Orchestra Philharmonique de Radio France, Orchestre de Paris and the Pittsburgh Symphony; Conducted the BBC Symphony Orchestra at the 1999 Proms in Schumann's Piano Concerto and Nielsen's 3rd Symphony; Conducted Merikanto's Juha at Savonlinna, 2002. *Recordings:* Mozart Symphonies Nos 32, 35, 36 with the Scottish Chamber Orchestra; Sibelius Symphonies; Debussy La Mer and Images with the Rotterdam Philharmonic, Mahler 5th Symphony and Nielsen's Symphonies Nos 4 and 5 with the Finnish Radio Symphony Orchestra. *Address:* c/o CAMI Berlin, Albrechtstrasse 18, 10117 Berlin, German.

SARBU, Eugene; Violinist; b. 6 Sept. 1950, Pietrari, nr. Rimnicu Vilcea, Romania. *Education:* Following studies in Bucharest and Paris joined Curtis Institute, Philadelphia, for further study with Ivan Galamian; Later at Juilliard, New York, and with Nathan Milstein in Zürich. *Career:* Made first solo appearance aged 6; Won National Festival of Music Award in Bucharest, 1958; Regular solo recitals and concerts in England; Promenade Concert debut, 1982; Performances in USA, Europe, Australia and South America; Far East tour 1987–88, with the New Japan Philharmonic in Tokyo; Plays a Cremonese Violin by Tomasso Balestieri made in 1756. *Recordings:* Sibelius Concerto for EMI with the Hallé Orchestra, 1980; Vivaldi's Four Seasons and Mozart Concertos with European Master Orchestra, 1988. *Honours:* Winner, Paganini and Carl Flesch Competitions, 1978; George Enescu Medal, 1995. *Address:* c/o Hispania Clásica S.L., Los Madrazo 16 bajo, 28014 Madrid, Spain.

SARDI, Ivan; Singer (Bass); b. 7 July 1930, Budapest, Hungary. *Education:* Studied with Antonio Mekandri at the Martini Conservatory Bologna. *Career:* Debut: Brescia 1951, as Padre Guardiano in La Forza del Destino; Sang in Naples, Bologna, Genoa, Trieste and Catania, as Mozart's Masetto and Bartolo and in Operas by Verdi; Glyndebourne 1956, as Don Alfonso; Further appearances in Florence, Milan and Lisbon; Staatsoper Munich, 1956–61; Member of the Deutsche Oper Berlin from 1961; Concerts in Munich, Hamburg, Vienna and elsewhere in Europe; Sang Schigolch in Lulu at Dresden, 1992. *Recordings:* Don Giovanni, Le nozze di Figaro, Verdi Requiem, Der junge Lord by Henze; Sparafucile in Rigoletto; Guillaume Tell. *Address:* c/o Deutsche Oper Berlin, Richard Wagnerstrasse 10, 100 Berlin 1, Germany.

SARDINERO, Vincenzo; Singer (Baritone); b. 12 Jan. 1937, Barcelona, Spain. *Education:* Studied at the Liceo Conservatory in Barcelona. *Career:* Sang first in operettas and Spanish zarzuelas; Opera debut Barcelona 1964, as Escamillo; In 1967 sang Germont in La Traviata at Barcelona and in Lucia di Lammermoor at La Scala, Milan; New York City Opera 1970, as Tonio in Pagliacci; Covent Garden debut 1976, as Marcello in La Bohème; Further appearances Lisbon, Rome, Vienna, Madrid, Lyon, Paris, Munich, Hamburg, Basle, Budapest and the Aix-en-Provence Festival; Season 1991–92 as Marcello at Barcelona and Rigoletto at Palma; Other roles include Nottingham in Roberto Devereux, Valentin (Faust), Alphonse XI (La Favorite) and Verdi's Renato, Posa and Luna. *Recordings include:* L'Amico Fritz; L'Atlantida;

Turandot; Manon Lescaut; Lucia di Lammermoor; Un Giorno di Regno; La Navarraise by Massenet; Edgar by Puccini; La Straniera by Bellini.

SARFATY, Regina; Singer (Mezzo-soprano); b. 1932, Rochester, New York, USA. *Education:* Studied at the Juilliard School, New York. *Career:* Sang with New Mexico Opera from 1948; Santa Fe Opera from 1957, notably in the 1968 US premiere of The Bassarids by Henze; New York City Opera from 1958, as Cenerentola, Maria Golovin in the opera by Menotti, Jocasta (Oedipus Rex) and Dorabella; Frankfurt Opera from 1963, as Carmen and Octavian; Sang Octavian at Glyndebourne, 1960, and returned in 1984, as Adelaide in Arabella; Sang Mme de Croissy in Dialogues des Carmélites at Baltimore, 1984; Member of the Zürich Opera, notably as the Countess Geschwitz in Lulu and in the premiere of Die Erretung Thebens by Kelterborn, 1963. *Recordings:* Excerpts from Die Walküre, conducted by Stokowski; The Rake's Progress, conducted by Stravinsky, and the Choral Symphony, conducted by Bernstein.

SARGON, Simon A.; Composer, Pianist and Music Director; b. 6 April 1938, Bombay, India; m. Bonnie Glasgow 1961, 1 d. *Education:* BA, Brandeis University, 1959; MS, Juilliard School, 1962. *Career:* Debut: Carnegie Hall, with Jennie Tourel, 1963; Musical Staff, New York City Opera, 1960; Associate Conductor, Concert Opera, 1962–68; Pianist for concerts of Jennie Tourel, 1963–71; Faculty Member, Juilliard School, 1967–69; Chairman, Voice, Rubin Academy, Jerusalem, 1971–74; Faculty, Hebrew University, Jerusalem, 1973–74; Director of Music, Temple Emanu-El, 1974–; Faculty, SMU, 1983–. *Compositions:* Patterns in Blue, 1976; Elul: Midnight, 1980; Praise Ye the Lord, 1980; Sing His Praise, 1981; The Queen's Consort, 1982; Lord Make Me to Know My End, 1985; Voices of Change, commission, 1988; Symphony No. 1, Holocaust, premiered by Dallas Symphony, 1991; Jump Back; Before the Ark. *Recordings:* Music for French Horn and Piano; Huntsman, What Quarry; Deep Ellum Nights. *Publications:* Shemà; At Grandmother's Knee, 1995; Waves of the Sea, 1995. *Address:* 3308 Dartmouth Avenue, Dallas, TX 75205, USA.

SÁRI, József; Composer; b. 23 June 1935, Lenti, Hungary; m. 2 d. *Education:* Ferenc Liszt Academy of Music, Budapest; Composition; Choral conducting. *Career:* Tutor, Music School, Budapest, 1962–71; Freelance Composer, Germany, 1971–84; Teacher of Music Theory, F Liszt Academy, 1984; Director of department, 1992; Adviser at Hungarian Radio, 1997; Composer's Portrait, broadcast by three major radio stations, Germany, 1992. *Compositions:* Fossils, 1974; String Quartet, 1975; Alienated Quotations for 2 pianos, 1982; Symbols, 1978; Attributes, 1990; Questions for Hillel, 1996; Concertino, 1992–95; Zenith, 1995; Parallel Lines which Cross before the Infinite, for flute and strings, 1997; Con Spirito for orchestra, 1998; Sonnenfinsternis, opera, 2000. *Recordings:* Time Mill; Farewell to Glenn Gould; Four Inventions; Fossils; Legend; His complete works for flute; works for dulcimer and brass instruments. *Honours:* Erkel Prize, 1991; Bartók Pásztory Prize, 1995; Artist of Merit, 1998. *Address:* 2011, Budakalasz, Szent Laszlo 41, Hungary. *Website:* www.bmc.hu/sari.

SARICH, Paul; Composer and Percussionist; b. 18 Sept. 1951, Wellington, New Zealand. *Education:* BSc, Victoria University of Wellington, 1971; Study with Leonard Salzedo and James Blades, 1981. *Career:* Percussionist, Various Australian Bands and Orchestras, 1973–93; Lecturer, Victoria College of the Arts, 1991–; New Notations, London, 1994–95. *Compositions:* Fantasia in G Minor for violin, 1981; Sonata for side drum and 3 percussion, 1981; Fantasia on a fragment of Martinů, for orchestra, 1982; Chaconne in B Flat for tuba, 1986; Concerto for bass trombone and orchestra, 1986; Antiphons for 2 percussions, 1986; Divertimento for viola, cello, double bass and percussion, 1986; Five in the Afternoon, trumpet, keyboards and percussion, 1986; Dance Suite for 3 tubas, 1987; Concerto da Camera, for percussion and strings, 1988; Music for tubes and sticks, 1988; Songs of Light and Shade for soprano and ensemble, 1989; Concerto Pieces for timpani and piano, 1990; Percussion Mass, 1991; The Illusionist for bass and piano, 1992; Fiesta, for soprano, timpani, 4 percussion and flamenco dancers, 1993; Essay for brass quintet and 8 tubas, 1993; Austranimalia for chorus, bass, percussion and piano, 1994; Invocation and dance for saxophone and clarinet trio, 1994; Three Neruda Love Songs for soprano and ensemble, 1994. *Address:* c/o APRA, 1A Eden Street, Crows Nest, NSW 2065, Australia.

SARROCA, Suzanne; Singer (Soprano); b. 21 April 1927, Carcassonne, France. *Education:* Studied at the Toulouse Conservatoire, 1946–48. *Career:* Debut: Carcassonne 1949, as Massenet's Charlotte; Sang Carmen in Brussels, 1951; Paris Opéra and Opéra-Comique from 1952, as Tosca, Rezia, Marina (Boris Godunov), Aida, Marguerite in La Damnation de Faust, Leonore and Octavian 1957, 1966; Also sang in Les Indes Galantes by Rameau; Guest appearances in Marseille, 1961 (Donna Anna), Rome 1965 (Elisabeth de Valois) and in Buenos Aires, Geneva, New York, London, Lisbon, Strasbourg and Toulouse; Salzburg Festival 1968, in Cavalieri's La Rappresentazione di Anima e di Corpo;

Further engagements in Rio de Janeiro, Hamburg and Vienna; Modern repertoire included La Voix Humaine by Poulenc and Schoenberg's Erwartung; Director of the Centre d'art Lyrique at Strasbourg, 1983–85.

SASAKI, Ken; Concert Pianist; b. 14 Sept. 1943, Sendai, Miyagi, Japan. *Education:* Studied at University of Arts, Tokyo and at Warsaw Conservatoire; Attended Masterclasses of Vlado Perlemuter in Paris and Danuta Lewandowska in Warsaw. *Career:* Given many concerts in France, Poland, Netherlands, Switzerland, Austria, Germany, Japan; British debut 1972, at the Wigmore Hall; Coast to coast tour of the USA, 1979; Queen Elizabeth Hall, London, 1986 playing Bach's 1st Partita, Gaspard de la Nuit and Chopin's 2nd Sonata; Further appearances with the Warsaw Chamber Orchestra and the Berlin Octet; Other repertory includes Concertos by Bach (D minor) and Beethoven (C minor and G major); Mozart K449 and K466; Chopin No. 1 and Schumann; Ravel in G; Rachmaninov Nos 1 and 3; Mozart Sonatas K310, K311; Chopin Sonatas, Etudes Ballades, Nocturnes, Preludes and Polonaise; Schumann Fantasie Op 17, Fantasiestücke, Etudes Symphoniques and Kreisleriana; Ravel Miroirs and Le Tombeau de Couperin; Debussy Images and Suite Bergamasque; Prokofiev 3rd and 7th Sonatas and Scriabin Etudes; Scarlatti Sonatas. *Recordings include:* Chopin Etudes. *Honours:* Stefanie Niekrasz Prize, 1984.

SASS, Sylvia; Singer (Soprano); b. 21 July 1951, Budapest, Hungary. *Education:* Studied at the Liszt Academy Budapest with Ferenc Revhegyi. *Career:* Debut: Budapest State Opera 1971, as Frasquita in Carmen; First major role as Gutrune, 1972; Sang Giselda in I Lombardi, 1973 and repeated the role at Covent Garden, 1976; Sofia 1972, Violetta (also at Aix-en-Provence 1976); Scottish Opera debut 1975, Desdemona; At the Budapest Opera 1977, sang in the premiere of Mózes by Zsolt Durkó; Metropolitan Opera 1977, Tosca; Guest engagements at the State Operas of Hamburg and Munich and at the Paris Opéra and La Scala Milan; Other roles include Norma, Penelope (Il Ritorno d'Ulisse), Tatiana, Elvira (Ernani), Alceste, Odabella (Attila), Medea, Santuzza, Elisabeth de Valois, Lady Macbeth, Donna Elvira and Donna Anna, Countess Almaviva, Mimi, Manon Lescaut, Turandot, Adriana Lecouvreur, Nedda (Pagliacci), Juliette and Marguerite by Gounod, and Salome (Budapest 1989); Has sung Bartók's Judith on BBC television and in Montpellier and Metz, 1989; Many concert performances in music by Strauss and Wagner; Modern repertoire includes Sogno di un Tramonto d'Autunno by Malipiero; Wigmore Hall debut 1979, in songs by Strauss and Liszt; Invited to return for András Schiff's Beethoven-Bartók series, Sept 1990; Season 1993, as Adriana Lecouvreur at Budapest. *Recordings include:* Don Giovanni, Arias by Puccini and Verdi, Liszt and Bartók songs (Decca); Verdi Stiffelio, Il Trittico, Duke Bluebeard's Castle by Bartók (Philips); Wagner Wesendonck Lieder, Vier Letzte Lieder by Strauss, Medea, Ernani, I Lombardi, Macbeth, Attila, Faust, Mózes by Durkó, Erkel's Hunyadi László (Hungaroton).

SASSON, Deborah; Singer (Soprano); b. 1955, Boston, Massachusetts, USA; m. Peter Hofmann, 1983, divorced 1990. *Education:* Studied at Oberlin College with Ellen Repp and Helen Hodam; New England Conservatory, Boston with Gladys Miller. *Career:* Debut: Hamburg Staatsoper 1979, as Maria in West Side Story; Sang at the Stadttheater Aachen, 1979–81; Guest appearances in Hamburg, Berlin, Venice and San Francisco; Has sung at the Bayreuth Festival from 1982; Other roles include Norina, Adina, Gilda, Rosina, Despina and Zerlina. *Recordings include:* Arias and Duets with Peter Hofmann; Mahler's 8th Symphony, from Tanglewood. *Address:* c/o PO Box Bayreuther Festspiele, 8580 Bayreuth 1, Germany.

SATANOWSKI, Robert Zdzislaw; Conductor and Music Director; b. 20 June 1918, Łódź, Poland; m.; two s. *Education:* Technical Univ., Warsaw 1935–39, Theory of Music and Conducting, Acad. of Music, Łódź, Poland 1951. *Career:* debut, Łódź State Philharmonic 1951; Conductor, Lubin State Philharmonic 1951–54; Artistic Dir, Principal Conductor, Bydgoszcz State Philharmonic 1954–58; Gen. Music Dir, Staedtische Oper Karl Marx Stadt/former and later Chemitz 1960–62; Gen. and Artistic Dir, State Opera Poznan 1962–69; founder and Artistic Dir, Poznan Chamber Orchestra 1963–69; Gen. Music Dir, Staedtishe Buehnen Krefeld-Moenchengladbach 1969–76, State Opera House, Kraków 1975–77, State Opera House, Wroclaw 1977–82, Grand Theatre Warsaw/National Opera 1981–91; Conductor, Aachen Opera 1991–92; Guest Conductor, operatic works, Staatsoper Vienna, Dresden, Berlin, Bolshoi Moscow State Opera Bucharest, Operhaus Dresden, Oslo Opera House, Opera House Seattle, USA, National Opera House Genoa, Royal Opera Liège, Zagreb Opera House, Istanbul Festival; symphony concerts in Paris, London, Moscow, Berlin, Dresden, Leipzig, Bucharest, Genoa, Stockholm, Gothenburg, Leningrad, Tehran, Ankara, Madrid, Vienna, Düsseldorf and Warsaw. *Compositions:* symphony, chamber and vocal works composed –1958. *Recordings:* with National Philharmonic, Warsaw, Warsaw Grand Theatre Orchestra, State Symphony Orchestra, Poznan, Poznan Chamber Orchestra, mainly Polish, classi-

cal and contemporary, symphony and operatic works; Halka, 1998. *Address:* Teatr Wielki, ul Moliera 3/5, 00-950 Warsaw, Poland.

SATO, Shunske; Violinist; b. 1984, Tokyo, Japan. *Education:* Juilliard School, New York, with Dorothy DeLay, from 1995. *Career:* Debut: Philadelphia Orchestra, 1994; Appearances with the St Petersburg Philharmonic under Yuri Temirkanov, National Symphony Orchestra, with Christopher Hogwood, Baltimore and Minnesota Orchestras, and elsewhere in USA; Season 2000–01 with the Mariinsky Orchestra under Gergiev, the Beethoven Concerto at the Bonn Festival, European tour with the St Petersburg Symphony Orchestra, Munich Radio Orchestra under Zdenek Macal, Swiss debut recital in Basle, and Italian concert with Riccardo Muti. *Address:* c/o Musicaglotz, 11, Rue Le Verrier, 75006 Paris, France.

SATOH, Somei; Composer; b. 19 Jan. 1949, Sendai, Japan. *Education:* Studied in Japan. *Career:* Freelance Composer in Advanced Idioms, including Non-Western Techniques and Instruments; Resident in New York, 1983–84. *Compositions include:* Hymn for the Sun for 2 pianos and tape delay, 1975; Cosmic Womb, 1975; Incarnation I and II, 1977–78; The Heavenly Spheres Are Illuminated by Light, for soprano, piano and percussion, 1979; Birds in Warped Time I and II, 1980; Lyra for 2 harps, percussion and strings, 1980; Sumeru I and II, 1982, 1985; A Journey Through Sacred Time, 1983; Naohi for piano, 1983; Hikari for trumpet and piano, 1986; Shirasagi for string quartet, 1987; Stabat Mater for soprano and chorus, 1987; A Gate into Infinity for violin, piano and percussion, 1988; Homa for soprano and string quartet, 1988; Towards the Night for strings, 1991; Kami No Miuri for mezzo and 7 instruments, 1991; Burning Meditation, for baritone, harp, tubar bells and string quartet, 1993 (revised version, New York, 1995); Lanzarote for soprano saxophone and piano, 1993. *Address:* c/o JASRAC, 3-6-12 Uehara, Shibuya-ku, Tokyo 151, Japan.

SAULESCO, Mircea (Petre); Violinist; b. 14 Sept. 1926, Bucharest, Romania; m. (1) 3 c., (2) Gunilla Sandberg-Saulesco, 1 c. *Education:* Bucharest Conservatory; Diploma, Bucharest Musical Academy, 1944; Studied with various masters including Iosif Dailis, Garbis Avachian, Georges Enesco and Jacques Thibaud; Studied Piano and Composition with various masters. *Career:* Debut: Bucharest, 1941; Member, Bucharest Radio Symphony Orchestra, 1938–50; Founder, Saulesco String Quartet, 1945; Member 1950–58, Leader 1957–58, Bucharest State Philharmonic Orchestra Georges Enesco; Numerous chamber music and solo concerts in Eastern Europe until 1958; Member and one of the Leaders, Symphony Orchestra, Swedish Broadcasting Corporation, 1958–89; Founder, Swedish Saulesco Quartet, 1962; Co-Founder, Leygraf (piano) Quartet, 1965; Numerous television and radio appearances; Various foreign concert tours; mem, Mazer Society for Chamber Music. *Recordings include:* Alfven Violin Sonata; Mozart Piano Quartets No. 1 G minor and No. 2 E flat major; Atterberg String Quartet op 11; Verdi, String Quartet E minor. *Honours:* Swedish Record Prize, Grammis, 1970, 1972; Austrian Mozart Prize, 1974. *Address:* Pepparkaksgrand 26, 128 66 Sköndal, Sweden.

SAUNDERS, Arlene; Singer (Soprano) and Teacher; b. 5 Oct. 1935, Cleveland, Ohio, USA. *Education:* Baldwin-Wallace College and New York. *Career:* Debut: Operatic, as Rosalinde with National Opera Company, 1958; New York City Opera debut as Giorgetta in Il Tabarro, 1961; European debut as Mimi, Teatro Nuovo, Milan, 1961; Joined Hamburg State Opera, 1964; Also sang Pamina, Glyndebourne Festival, England, 1966 and Louise, San Francisco Opera 1967, Beatrix Cenci (world premiere) with the Washington DC Opera Society 1971, Eva, Metropolitan Opera 1976, Minnie, Royal Opera Covent Garden, London 1980; Farewell operatic appearances as the Marschallin, Teatro Colón, Buenos Aires, 1985; Other roles were Natasha (War and Peace), Nadia in The Ice Break (US premiere Boston, 1979), Mozart Donna Elvira and Fiordiligi, Wagner's Sieglinde, Elsa, Senta and Elisabeth, Tosca, Manon, Arabella and the Countess in Capriccio; Teacher, Rutgers University, New Jersey and Abraham Goodman School, New York, 1987–. *Honours:* Gold Medal, Vercelli Vocal Competition; Kammersängerin, Hamburg State Opera, 1967.

SAUNDERS, Christopher; Singer (Tenor); b. 1971, Queensland, Australia. *Education:* University of Queensland and the Guildhall School, London. *Career:* Appearances with Opera Queensland from 1993, including Ernesto in Don Pasquale and Aufidio in the local premiere of Mozart's Lucio Silla; Other roles include Jacquino for English Touring Opera, Tobias in Sweeney Todd for Opera North, Ferrando in Così fan tutte, and Jupiter in Handel's Semele; Concerts include Britten's Serenade at the Barbican Hall and Britten's St Nicolas. *Honours:* The Hammond Prize, Queensland. *Address:* Harlequin Agency Ltd, 203 Fidlas Road, Cardiff CF4 5NA, Wales.

SAUNDERS, Jenny; Singer (soprano); b. 1970, England. *Education:* Studied with Marjorie Thomas at the Royal Academy of Music and with Mary Thomas. *Career:* Concerts include Mozart's C Minor Mass in Canterbury Cathedral, Mendelssohn's Elijah in Scotland, the Christmas Oratorio in Oslo and the Brahms Requiem at the St Endellion Easter Festival; Further engagements with Messiah and Carmina Burana at the Albert Hall, Gounod's St Cecilia Mass and the Fauré Requiem at the Festival Hall and Mendelssohn's Midsummer Night's Dream with the Academy of St Martin in the Fields; Appearances with the Opera Company as Helen in Mefistofele and Mozart's Barabarina and Susanna; Season 1996–97 as Zerlina for Opera East, in Dido and Aeneas at Covent Garden and The Fairy Queen on tour to Spain and Greece; Despina for Country Opera and Nannetta for Palace Opera; 1997 concerts at St John's Smith Square (Exsultate Jubilate and St Matthew Passion) St Paul's Cathedral (Vivaldi's Gloria) and Wells Cathedral (Haydn's Creation); Papagena with Opera Factory; Season 1998 with the Sandman and Dew Fairy in Hansel and Gretel for Palace Opera. *Honours:* Winner, Soprano Section, 1992 Great Grimsby International Singers Competition. *Current Management:* Hazard Chase Ltd, Norman House, Cambridge Place, Cambridge, CB2 1NS, England. *Telephone:* (1223) 312400. *Fax:* (1223) 460827. *Website:* www .hazardchase.co.uk.

SAUNDERS, Rebecca; Composer; b. 19 Dec. 1967, London. *Education:* Studied with Wolfgang Rihm in Karlsruhe, 1991–94, and with Nigel Osborne in England, 1994–97. *Career:* Freelance composer in New York, Brussels, Berlin and elsewhere. *Compositions include:* Behind the Velvet Curtain for trumpet, piano, harp and cello, 1992; Into the Blue for clarinet, bassoon, percussion; piano, cello and double bass, 1996; Two pieces based on Molly Bloom's Monologue, from Ulysses, 1996; String Quartet, and double bass, 1998; Cinnabar, for ensemble, 1999; Duo for viola and percussion, 1999. *Honours:* Prize Winner, Berlin Academy at Art (1995) and Siemens Foundation (1996). *Address:* c/o Edition Peters, 10–12 Backes St, London N1 6DN, England.

SAUTER, Lily; Singer; b. 16 Nov. 1934, Zürich, Switzerland. *Education:* Studied in Milan and Zürich. *Career:* Sang at the Deutsche Oper am Rhein Düsseldorf, 1961–64; Zürich Opera, 1965–66; Stuttgart Staatsoper, 1964–83; Guest appearances at the State Operas of Hamburg and Munich, Berlin, Frankfurt, Barcelona, Venice, Milan, Genoa and Edinburgh; Roles have included Mozart's Susanna, Blondchen and Despina, Rosina, Martha, Norina, Adina, Marzelline, Lortzing's Gretchen and Marie, Musetta, Nannetta, Sophie in Der Rosenkavalier, Aennchen, and Regina in Mathis der Maler; Television appearances in Germany and Switzerland. *Address:* c/o Staatsoper Stuttgart, Oberer Schlossgarten 6, 7000 Stuttgart, Germany.

SAVAGE, Stephen (Leon); Concert Pianist, Conductor and Teacher; b. 26 April 1942, Hertford, England; 2 s. *Education:* Vienna Akademie with Bruno Seidlhofer; Royal College of Music with Cyril Smith. *Career:* Debut: Wigmore Hall, London, 1966; Concerts, Radio, Television, Recordings in England, Canada, Australia, Japan; Concertos with Boult, A Davis, Zollman and others including 1st Australasian performance, Lutoslawski Concerto 1989; Director, Brisbane Tippett Festival 1990; Dedicatee of major works by Justin Connolly and Roger Smalley; Professor of Piano and Co-Director, 20th Century Ensemble, Royal College of Music, 1967–81, Artistic Director, Conductor, Griffith University Ensemble, Brisbane, Australia; Master Teacher to Australian National Academy of Music, Melbourne; Frequent Residencies include, Universities of Adelaide, Toronto, Hong Kong, Guildhall School of Music, Royal Academy of Music, Royal College of Music (Honorary Associate Professor); Noted for performances of classical repertoire and 20th Century Music including important first performances. *Recordings:* Roger Smalley, Accord for 2 Pianos with the Composer; Tippett, sonatas 1 and 3; Beethoven Sonatas Op 109, 110, 111. *Honours:* Dannreuther Prize, 1964; Hopkinson Medal, Worshipful Company of Musicians, Medal, 1965; Recommendation of Tippett Sonatas 1 and 3 by Gramophone, 1986. *Address:* c/o Queensland Conservatorium of Music, Griffith University, PO Box 28, Brisbane, Albert Street, 4002 Brisbane, Australia.

SAVARY, Jerome; Stage Director; b. 27 June 1942, Buenos Aires, Argentina. *Education:* Studied in Paris. *Career:* Stagings of Operettas by Offenbach and Johann Strauss at the Geneva Opera, 1982–91; La Scala Milan, 1983–92, with a revival of Cherubini's Anacréon, the Premiere of Corghi's Blimunda, and Attila; Don Giovanni at Rome, 1984; Die Zauberflöte at Bregenz, 1985, followed by Les Contes d'Hoffmann and Carmen; Directed Le Comte Ory for the Opéra de Lyon, 1988, and War and Peace for San Francisco Opera, 1991; La Cenerentola for Geneva and the Palais Garnier, Paris, 1996; Le Comte Ory for Glyndebourne, 1997; Macbeth at Buenos Aires, 1998. *Address:* c/o Teatro Alla Scala, Via Filodrammatici 2, Milan, Italy.

SAVASKAN, Sinan (Carter); Composer and Conductor; b. 11 Aug. 1954, England; m. Sarah Carter, 2 s., 2 d. *Education:* PhD, University of York; MMus, University of Surrey; BA Hons, University of London, Middlesex; Diploma Studies , Chiswick Music Centre. *Career:* Composer of orchestral, chamber and performing arts related music; Conductor and member of London based ensembles; Contemporary Arts Ensemble;

Battersea Orchestra; Deputy Director of Music, Westminster School, London; Works featured at the 2002 International Rostrum of Composers, Paris; mem, British Academy of Composers and Songwriters; Association of Professional Composers; Executive Committee Member of British Academy of Composers and Songwriters PRS; MCPS. *Compositions:* String Quartet No. 3, Panic in Needle Park, commissioned and premiered by Balanescu String Quartet, 1990; Anthems for the Sun No. 2 for organ, played by Martin Ball, Westminster Abbey, 1994; Three Dances for chamber orchestra, BBC Philharmonic Forum Award Winner, 1997; Symphony No. 2, commissioned and premiered by BBC Symphony Orchestra, 1997; Symphony No. 3, commissioned and premiered by SEM Orchestra, New York, 1998. *Recordings:* Intercontinental Communication Disaster 1877; String Study No. 3. *Contributions:* Regular contributor to The Times Supplements. *Honours:* Dio Award (ACGB), 1985; BBC Symphony Orchestra Commission, 1997; Winner, Foundation for Contemporary Performance Arts, USA, 1998. *Current Management:* Sarah Moyse Artist Management. *Address:* 27 Dorchester Court, London SE24 9QX, England.

SAVCHENKO, Arkadiy Markovich; Belarusian opera singer (baritone); b. 6 April 1936, Vitebsk, Byelorussia; s. of Mark Iosifovich Savchenko and Marfa Stratonovna Savchenko; m. Glasova Serafima Semienovna 1977; two s. *Education:* Moscow Conservatoire. *Career:* soloist with Byelorussian (now Belarus) Bolshoi Theatre 1960–; Faculty mem., Prof., Vocal Dept, Belarus Acad. of Music 1987–. *Roles include:* Yevgeny in Tchaikovsky's Yevgeny Onegin, Kizgaylo in Smolsky's Ancient Legend, Telramund in Wagner's Lohengrin, Malatesta in Donizetti's Don Pasquale, Jermon in Verdi's Traviata, Valentin in Gounod's Faust, Rigoletto in Verdi's Rigoletto, Renato in Verdi's A Masked Ball, Zurga in Bizet's Pearl Fishers, Almaviva in Mozart's The Marriage of Figaro, Tomsky, Eletsky in Tchaikovsky's Queen of Spades, Gryaznoy in Rimsky-Korsakov's The Tsar's Bride, Don Giovanni in Mozart's Don Giovanni, Amonasro in Verdi's Aida, Di Luna in Verdi's Trovatore, Rodrigo in Verdi's Don Carlos, Sharpless in Puccini's Madame Butterfly, Escamillo in Bizet's Carmen, Figaro in Rossini's The Barber of Seville, Prince Igor in Borodin's Prince Igor, Bolkonsky in Prokofiev's War and Peace, Alfio in Mascagni's Cavalleria Rusticana etc., Iago in Verdi's Otello, Robert in Tchaikovsky's Iolanta, Mizgir in Rimsky-Korsakov's Snowmaiden, Tonyo in Leoncavallo's Pagliacci. *Honours:* People's Artist of USSR 1985. *Address:* Bolshoi Teatr, 1 Parizhskaya Kommuna Square, 220029 Minsk (Theatre); 8–358 Storozhovskaya Str., 220002 Minsk, Belarus (home). *Telephone:* (17) 219-22-01 (Theatre); (17) 239-15-51 (home). *Fax:* (17) 34-05-84.

SAVIDGE, Peter; Singer (baritone); b. 1952, Essex, England. *Education:* Cambrdge University. *Career:* Debut: English Music Theatre, 1976, as Papageno; Appearances with Opera North as Mozart's Count, Storch in Intermezzo, Don Giovanni, Valentin, Nardo in La finta giardiniera, Sharpless (Butterfly), Eugene Onegin; Welsh National Opera as Papageno, Marcello, Danilo, and Rossini's Figaro; Lescaut in Massenet's Manon, Ned Keene in Peter Grimes and the Baron in Massenet's Chérubin at Covent Garden, 1994; Seven baritone roles in Death in Venice at Nancy and Liège; Belcore (L'Elisir d'amore) at Opéra Comique, Paris; Ned Keene at Genoa, Strasbourg and Cologne; Season 1999–2000 world premiere of A Friend of the People by Horne at Scottish Opera; Count at Garsington; L'Anima del Filosofo by Haydn at Lausanne; Season 2000–01, title role in world premiere of Abélard et Heloïse for Strasbourg and Paris; 2003: Chnegos in Punch and Judy; Birtwistle in Porto; Gunther in Götterdämmerung for Scottish Opera and at Edinburgh Festival; Sang Szymanowski's Stabat Mater with Rotterdam Philharmonic, under Valerie Gergier, 2003. *Recordings include:* Britten's Albert Herring and Handel's Hercules; Mr Coyle in Channel 4's television film of Britten's Owen Wingrave, 2001; Bantock songs with David Owen Norris. *Current Management:* Musicmakers International Artists Representation, Tailor House, 63–65 High Street, Whitwell, Hertfordshire SG4 8AH, England. *Telephone:* (1438) 871708. *Fax:* (1438) 871777. *E-mail:* musicmakers@compuserve.com. *Website:* www.operauk.com. *Address:* 1, The Bank, Little Compton, Moreton-in-Marsh, Gloucestershire GL56 0RX, England.

SAVOIE, Robert; Singer (Baritone); b. 21 April 1927, Montreal, Canada. *Education:* Studied with Pauline Donalda in Montreal and with Antonio Narducci in Milan. *Career:* Debut: Teatro Nuovo Milan 1953, as Scarpia; Sang with many seasons for L'Opéra de Montréal and made guest appearances with the Paris Opéra and the Opéra du Rhin Strasbourg; Opera houses in Nice, Toulouse, Lyon, Marseille, Dallas, Washington, Pittsburgh and London; Other roles have been Mozart's Leporello, Don Giovanni, Count Figaro and Guglielmo; Escamillo; Verdi's Iago, Amonasro and Ford in Falstaff; Puccini's Gianni Schicchi and Sharpless; Golaud in Pelléas et Mélisande, Albert in Werther and Ramiro in L'Heure Espagnole; Artistic Director, City of Lachine, Quebec, Canada, now retired; The Lachine Music Festival; Vocal teacher at the Music Faculty, McGill University of Montreal; President, Founder, L'Orchestra Metropolitan of Montreal. *Recordings include:* Posa in the French version of Don Carlos. *Publications:* Memoires: Figaro-ci Figaro-la, 1998. *Honours:* Officer of the Order of Canada; Dr hc in Music, University of Moncton, Canada; Dr hc in Laws, Concordia Univ., Canada. *Address:* 2100 Du Calvados, St Bruno, Quebec J3V 3K2, Canada.

SAVOVA, Galina; Singer (Soprano); b. 1945, Sofia, Bulgaria. *Career:* Sang first at the Sofia Opera before an international career at the opera houses of Rome, Naples, Karlsruhe and Bologna; Metropolitan Opera debut 1982, as Amelia in Un Ballo in Maschera; Other roles include Chrysothemis (Elektra), Puccini's Minnie, Turandot and Tosca, Amelia (Simon Boccanegra), Yaroslavna in Prince Igor and Leonore; In 1989 sang Aida at the Teatro São Carlos, Lisbon; Chicago Lyric Opera, 1992 as Turandot; Season 2000–01 as Frosja in Semyon Kotko by Prokofiev, with Kirov Opera at Covent Garden, and Mme Blanche in Prokofiev's The Gambler at the New York Met. *Address:* c/o Stafford Law, 6 Barkham Close, Weybridge, Surrey KT 13 9 PR.

SAVOVA, Olga B.; Russian actress and singer (mezzo-soprano); b. 14 Nov. 1964, Leningrad; m. Yefimov Dmitri; two s. *Education:* Leningrad State Inst. of Music Theatre and Cinematography, Leningrad State Conservatory. *Career:* actress at Leningrad Tovstonogov Drama Theatre –1995; singer at Mariinsky Opera Theatre (Kirov Opera) 1995–; repertoire includes Verdi's Requiem, Emilia in Othello, Eboli in Don Carlos, Flora in La Traviata, Carmen, Amneris and Preziosilla, Olga in Eugene Onegin, Prokofiev's Semyon Kotko, Azucena in Il Trovatore, Marfa in Tsar's Bride, Bobilikha in Rimsky-Korsakov's The Snow Maiden, Blanche in The Gambler by Prokofiev, Lyubov in Mazeppa, Marina Mnishek in Boris Godunov, Hélène in War and Peace, Paulina in The Queen of Spades and Teresa in La Sonnambula; performances in France, Belgium, Holland, Italy, Japan, China and Israel. *Honours:* Voci Verdiani International Competition prizewinner, Italy 1992. *Address:* St Petersburg State Academic Mariinsky Opera Theatre, Teatralnaya pl.1, St Petersburg 130000, Russia (office).

SAWALLISCH, Wolfgang; Conductor and Pianist; b. 26 Aug. 1923, Munich, Germany. *Education:* Studied at the Munich Academy. *Career:* Repetiteur at Augsburg; Conducted Hansel and Gretel on 1947 debut; Joint winner of prize for duos at 1949 Geneva International Competition; General Music Director at Aachen, 1953–58; Wiesbaden, 1958–60; Cologne, 1960–63; Bayreuth debut 1957, Tristan und Isolde; Later conducted Tannhäuser and Der fliegende Holländer there; London 1957, with Schwarzkopf in a Lieder programme and conducting the Philharmonia Orchestra; 1961, Principal Conductor, Vienna Symphony Orchestra and Hamburg Philharmonic Orchestra; US debut 1964; General Music Director, Bavarian State Opera Munich, 1971–92, Philadelphia Orchestra, 1993; Covent Garden debut with the Munich company 1972, conducting operas by Strauss; Lieder programmes with Dietrich Fischer-Dieskau and Hermann Prey; Solo performances as pianist in works by Mozart and Beethoven; Conducted a new production of Strauss's Friedenstag at the Munich Festival, 1988; Mathis der Maler and Dantons Tod, 1990; Arabella at La Scala, 1992; Last new production as Chief Conductor of the Bavarian State Opera, Henze's Der Prinz von Homburg, 1992. *Recordings:* Operas by Strauss, Mozart and Wagner (Die Meistersinger, 1994); Orchestral music by Schubert, Mendelssohn and Beethoven; Video of The Ring, from Munich, 1989. *Address:* c/o Bayerische Staatsoper, Postfach 745, 8000 Munich 1, Germany.

SAWER, David; Composer; b. 14 Sept. 1961, Stockport, England. *Education:* Univ. of York; DPhil studies with Richard Orton; further studies with Mauricio Kagel in Cologne. *Career:* music performed by the London Sinfonietta and Music Projects, London; commissions from MusICA 1986, the Kirklees Metropolitan Council, the 1988 Almeida Festival, King's Lynn Festival, BBC Singers, and BBC Symphony Orchestra; directed premiere productions of Kagel's Pas de Cinq and Kantrimiusik (Huddersfield Festival 1983, 1984) and as soloist in Kagel's Phonophonie at the 1987 Summerscope season on the South Bank; music for radio and theatre productions; Composer in association with the Bournemouth Orchestras, 1995–96; opera, From Morning to Midnight, premiered by ENO, 2001. *Compositions:* Music theatre: Etudes for 2–6 actors/musicians, 2 trumpets, percussion, 1984; Food of Love for actress and piano, 1988; The Panic, chamber opera, for 4 voices and 6 instruments, 1990–91; From Morning to Midnight, opera, 7 scenes, Sawer, from G. Kaiser: Von morgens bis mitternachts, 1998–2001; Orchestral: Byrnan Wood for large orchestra, 1992; The Memory of Water for 2 violins and strings, 1993; Trumpet Concerto, 1994; Tiroirs for chamber orchestra, 1996; The greatest happiness principle, 1997; Musica Ficta for chamber orchestra, 1998; Piano Concerto, 2002; Vocal: Rhetoric for soprano, viola, cello and double bass, 1989; Songs of Love and War for 24 voices, 2 harps and 2 percussion, 1990; Sounds: Three Kandinsky poems for chorus, 1996, 1999; Stramm Gedichte for chorus, 2001; Chamber: Solo Piano for piano, 1983; Cat's-Eye for chamber ensemble, 1986; Take Off for instrumental ensemble, 1987; Good Night for flute and piccolo, harp, violin, viola and cello, 1989; The Melancholy of Departure for piano, 1990; Hollywood

Extra for chamber ensemble, 1996; Between for harp, 1998. *Recordings include:* Byrnan Wood; The Melancholy of Departure; Songs of Love and War. *Contributions:* New Grove Dictionary of Opera, entry on Kagel. *Honours:* DAAD Scholarship, 1984–85; Sony Radio Award, for Swansong, 1990; Fulbright-Chester-Schirmer Fellowship in Composition, 1992–93; Paul Hamlyn Foundation Award, 1993; Arts Foundations's Composer Fellowship, 1995; British Acad. of Composers and Songwriters Award, 2003. *Current Management:* Allied Artist Agency, 42 Montpelier Square, London, SW7 1JZ, England. *E-mail:* info@alliedartists.co.uk.

SAWYER, Philip (John); Lecturer, Organist and Continuo Player; b. 3 Feb. 1948, Birmingham, England; m. (1) Judith Susan Timbury, 9 Jan 1981, (2) Patricia Anne McAlister, 3 Feb 1996. *Education:* Royal College of Music, 1966–68; ARCM, 1966; ARCO, 1967; Peterhouse, Cambridge, 1968–71; BA, Honours, 1971; MA, 1975; Organ study in Amsterdam with Piet Kee, 1970; Study at the Nice Conservatoire with René Saorin, 1973–74; MMus, 1986. *Career:* Assistant Director of Music, Trent College, 1971–73; Lecturer, 1975–, Head of the School of Music, 1987–99, Napier University (formerly Napier College/Polytechnic); Organist, Choirmaster: St Cuthbert's Parish Church, Edinburgh, 1975–78, Nicolson Square Methodist Church, Edinburgh, 1978–83, Director of Music, St Andrew's and St George's Church, Edinburgh, 1983–86; Director of Music, St Mary's Collegiate Church, Haddington, 1999–; Organ recitals: Westminster Abbey, Notre Dame, Paris, Nice Cathedral, Monaco Cathedral, St Laurens, Alkmaar, St Bavo's RC Cathedral, Haarlem, Hillsborough Parish Church, N Ireland; Universities of: St Andrews, Edinburgh, Glasgow, Aberdeen; Cathedrals: Edinburgh, Glasgow, Dundee; Founder and Director, Edinburgh Organ Week; First performances of newly-commissioned organ works by Alan Ridout and others; 1st Performance of The Seven Sacraments of Poussin by John Mcleod in Edinburgh, Glasgow and London, 1992; Appearances as Continuo Player with: Scottish Chamber Orchestra, Scottish Baroque Ensemble; Conductor, Scottish Chamber Choir, 1994–97. *Recordings:* Solo Organ recitals for BBC Radio 3 and Radio Scotland; Harpsichord Continuo with Scottish Chamber Orchestra, conductor, Gibson, with music by Handel; BBC Radio Scotland recording of 1st performance of The Seven Sacraments of Poussin, Edinburgh, 1992. *Contributions:* Various to journals of British Institute of Organ Studies. *Address:* The Ian Tomlin School of Music, Napier University, Craighouse Road, Edinburgh EH10 5 LG, Scotland.

SAXTON, Robert, BMus, DMus; British composer; b. 8 Oct. 1953, London, England. *Education:* St Catharine's Coll., Cambridge, Worcester Coll., Oxford, studied privately with Elisabeth Lutyens and Luciano Berio, Univ. of Oxford. *Career:* Lecturer, Bristol Univ. 1984–85; Fulbright Arts Award, Visiting Fellow Princeton Univ., USA 1985–86; Head of Composition, Guildhall School of Music and Drama 1990–98; Head of Composition, RAM, London 1998–99; Univ. Lecturer and Tutorial Fellow, Worcester Coll., Oxford; mem. Royal Soc. of Musicians. *Compositions include:* orchestral: Ring of Eternity 1982, Concerto for Orchestra 1984, Viola Concerto 1986, In The Beginning 1987, Elijah's Violin 1988, Music to Celebrate the Resurrection of Christ 1988, Violin Concerto 1989, Cello Concerto 1992, Ring, Time for wind orchestra 1994; ensemble: Piccola Musica per Luigi Dallapiccola 1981, Processions and Dances 1981; vocal: Cantata No. 3 1981, Éloge for soprano and ensemble 1981, Chaconne for double chorus 1981, Caritas (opera) 1991, Paraphrase on Mozart's Idomeneo 1991; chamber: Chiaroscuro for percussion 1981, Piano Sonata 1981, Fantasiestuck for accordion 1982, The Sentinel of the Rainbow for sextet 1984, A Yardstick to the Stars 1994; choral: I Will Awake the Dawn 1987, At the Round Earth's Imagined Corners 1992, Psalm, a song of ascents 1992, O Sing unto the Lord a New Song 1993, Canticum Luminis for choir and orchestra 1994, Fanfare for the Golden Wedding Anniversary of Queen Elizabeth II, Songs, Dances and Ellipses 1997, Prayer Before Sleep 1997, Music for St Catharine 1998, Sonata on a Theme of William Walton for cello 1999, A Yardstick to the Stars 2000, The Dialogue of God and Zion for chorus and double bass 2000, Invocation, Dance and Meditation 2001, The Child of Light (carol), …From a Distant Shore…2001, Alternative Canticles 2002, Five Motets for nine voices 2003. *Publications:* The Process of Composition from Detection to Confection 1998; contrib. Where Do I Begin? (article in Musical Times) 1994, reviews in TLS. *Address:* Worcester College, Oxford, OX1 2HB, England.

SAYER, Roger (Martin); Organist; b. 1 May 1961, Portsmouth, England; m. Nancy Sayer, 4 October 1986, one s., one d. *Education:* Royal College of Music, 1979–84; Organ Scholar, St Paul's Cathedral, London, 1980–84. *Career:* Organist and Dir of Music, Rochester Cathedral; Prof. of Organ, Trinity College of Music; Dir of Music, Rochester Choral Soc.; Organ concerts in many parts of the world; Examiner, Associated Board of the Royal Schools of Music; Adjudicator, National Federation of Music and Drama; mem, Honorary FNMSM; ARCM; FTCL; LRAM. *Recordings:* Great European Organs; Hallgrimskirja, Iceland; Rochester Cathedra, A Classic Selection, Magnificat and Nunc Dimitus; A

Choral Portrait, Vaughan Williams. *Honours:* Winner, International Organ Competition, St Albans, 1989; Winner, Organ Prizes, Royal College of Music, 1989. *Address:* 7 Minor Canon Row, Rochester, Kent ME1 1ST, England. *E-mail:* rms2001@bigfoot.com.

SAYERS, Gavin; singer (tenor); b. 7 Jan. 1962, England. *Education:* Guildhall School of Music with Johanna Peters and Maureen Morelle. *Career:* sang Arturo in a concert performance of Lucia di Lammermoor, British premiere of Nino Rota's La Notte di un nevrastenico at Morley College, 1990; Concert repertoire includes Puccini's Messa di Gloria; Hiawatha's Wedding Feast by Coleridge-Taylor; Haydn's Nelson Mass and Maria Theresa Mass; Messiah and Mozart Mass in C; Hymn of Praise by Mendelssohn (2nd Symphony); Elijah (Harrow Choral 1990); Britten's Serenade (East Surrey Orchestra 1991) performed in a variety of amateur operatic performances.

SAYLOR, Bruce; Composer; b. 24 April 1946, Philadelphia, USA. *Education:* Studied at the Juilliard School of Music with Hugo Weisgall and Roger Sessions; Accademia di Santa Cecilia in Rome with Petrassi and Evangelisti, CUNY Graduate School with Weisgall and George Perle. *Career:* Instructor, Queens College, 1970–76, NY University, 1976–79; Professor, Queens College, 1979–, Composer-in-Residence, Chicago Lyric Opera, 1992–94. *Compositions include:* Ballets Cycle; Inner World Out; Wildfire; Notturno for piano and orchestra; Woodwind Quartet; Symphony in Two Parts, Turns and Mordents for flute and orchestra; Duo for violin and viola; St Elmos Fire for flute and harp; Lyrics for soprano and violin; Love Play for mezzo and ensemble; Song from Water Street for mezzo; See You in the Morning, mezzo and ensemble; Orpheus Descending, opera in two acts; My Kinsman, Major Molineux, opera in one act; Songs from Water Street; See You in the Morning; Jessye Norman at Notre-Dame; A Scattering of Salts, concerto for piano and chorus, 1997; Dreams for 2 choruses and orchestra, 1998; Visions of Dante for piano, 1999; The Scrimshaw Violin, opera in one act, 2000; The Book in Your Hearts, for mezzo, baritone, chorus, orchestra, 2000; Cantos from The Inferno, for clarinet and piano, 2000; Prod Music of the Storm, for children's chorus and orchestra, 2002; Dante's Violin, 2001; Good News! for soprano, chorus and orchestra, 2003; Swimming with Yevgeny, for mezzo and ensemble, 2003; It had Wings, for mezzo and orchestra, 1989; With Anthems Sweet for chorus and orchestra; Archangel, for orchestra. *Recordings:* Jessye Norman; In the Spirit, 1997. *Publications include:* The Writings of Henry Cowell. *Address:* 318 W 85 Street, New York, NY 10024, USA.

SCALCHI, Gloria; Singer (mezzo-soprano); b. 23 July 1956, Trieste, Italy. *Education:* Studied with Iris Adami Corradetti and with Joseph Metternich in Munich; Seminars at the Rossini Academy in Pesaro. *Career:* Sang Angelina in La Cenerentola at Catania, 1988; Further appearances at the Rome Opera as Emma in Rossini's Zelmira, conducted by Philip Gossett, and as Andromaca in Rossini's Ermione; Concertgebouw Amsterdam as Maffio Orsini, in Lucrezia Borgia; Verona as Rosina and Angelina; Bologna as Sinaide in Mosè; Carnegie Hall, Ermione; San Francisco, Zelmira; Monte Carlo, Roberto Devereux; Paris, Rossini's Petite Messe Solennelle and Vivaldi's Juditha Triumphans; Musikverein Vienna, Cherubini's D Minor Requiem; Rossini Festival Pesaro, 1990, as Somira in Ricciardo e Zoraide; Season 1996 as Verdi's Preziosilla at the Met and Pippo in La Gazza Ladra at Palermo; Season 1998 as Donizetti's Léonor at Rome and Rosina at Genoa; Season 1999–2000 as Hassem in Donizetti's Alahor in Granata, at Palermo, Rossini's Isabella at the Deutsche Oper Berlin and Fenena in Nabucco at the Verona Arena. *Recordings include:* Juditha Triumphans. *Current Management:* Athole Still International Management, Forresters Hall, 25–27 Westow Street, London, SE19 3RY, England. *Telephone:* (20) 8771-5271. *Fax:* (20) 8768-6600. *Website:* www.atholestill.com.

SCALTRITI, Roberto; Singer (Baritone); b. 1969, Modena, Italy. *Education:* Graduate, The G B Martini Conservatory in Bologna; The School of Music of Fiesole; Studying with Ryland Davies;. *Career:* Debut: Philadelphia 1986, as Alcindoro in La Bohème; Appearances as Schaunard in Hamburg, as Masetto at Glyndebourne and the Festival Hall (1996, under Solti), Mozart's Count in Amsterdam and at the Opéra of Nice; Figaro with the Welsh National Opera, Publio in La Clemenza di Tito at the Théâtre des Champs-Elysées; Further roles in La Gazza Ladra (Nantes), Cimarosa's Maestro di Cappella (Florence) and Handel's Rinaldo (Beaune Festival); Season 1996–97 with Belcore at Lyon Opéra, Guglielmo and Don Giovanni in Amsterdam, Alidoro in La Cenerentola at Genoa; Don Giovanni produced by Peter Brook and conducted by Claudio Abbado in Aix en Provence; Monteverdi's Orfeo in Florence for the season 1998–99. *Recordings include:* Rigoletto with Riccardo Chailly; La Traviata with Zubin Mehta; Handel's Riccardo I with Christophe Rousset; Masetto in Don Giovanni, under Solti; Belcore in L'Elisir d'amore; Amadeus and Vienna–Arias with Christophe Rousset. *Honours:* Winner, 1985 Opera Company of Philadelphia Luciano Pavarotti International Voice Competition. *Address:* c/o IMG Artists, 54 Avenue Marceau, 75008 Paris, France.

SCANDIUZZI, Roberto; Singer (Bass); b. 14 July 1958, Treviso, Italy. *Career:* Debut: Sang Bartolo in Mozart's Figaro under Riccardo Muti at La Scala, 1982; Appearances in Opera at Paris, Munich, Hamburg, Amsterdam, Venice, Rome, US Debut in Verdi's Requiem, 1991; Sang Fiesco in a new production of Simon Boccanegra at Covent Garden, 1991; Other conductors have included Patanè, Giulini, Colin Davis; Festival engagements 1992 at Florence as Padre Guardiano in La Forza del Destino, Ramfis at Caracalla and Philip II and Zaccaria at Verona; Sang Zaccaria at Zürich, 1998; Season 2000–01 at the Munich Staatsoper as Verdi's Banquo, King Philip and Fiesco, Boito's Mefistofele in Vienna, Cherubini's Creon at Montpellier (concert) and Verdi's Attila at Frankfurt (concert); Verdi Requiem in Verona, Dresden and Florence; Other roles include Silva, Attila, Mefistofele and Don Giovanni. *Recordings include:* Aida conducted by Mehta, I Puritani, Turandot and Simon Boccanegra. *Address:* c/o Theateragentur Dr G. Hilbert, Maximilianstrasse 22, D–80539 München, Germany.

SCARABELLI, Adelina; Singer (Soprano); b. 1950, Milan, Italy. *Education:* Studied in Brescia. *Career:* Sang at the Piccola Scala, Milan from 1977; La Scala Milan from 1981, debut as Barbarina in Le nozze di Figaro; Salzburg Festival, 1984–85, as Despina and the Italian Singer in Capriccio; Florence 1988, as Lauretta in Gianni Schicchi; Rome Opera 1989, as Aminta in Mozart's Il re Pastore and as Susanna; She sang Zerlina in Don Giovanni at Parma in 1989; Other roles include Mozart's Servilia (La clemenza di Tito) and Ismene (Mitridate), Verdi's Oscar and Nannetta, Puccini's Musetta and Liu, and Micaela in Carmen; Season 1996 as Rachelina in Paisiello's La Molinara at Bologna, and Olga in Fedora at La Scala; Anaide in Rota's Italian Straw Hat at Milan. *Address:* c/o Teatro Dell'Opera, Piazza Beniamino Gigli 8, 00184 Rome, Italy.

SCAUNAS MARKOS, Simona; Pianist; b. 12 Nov. 1965, Rimnicu Vilcea, Romania. *Education:* Baccalaureate Diploma, High School of Art, George Enescu, Bucharest, 1984; Conservator of Arts and Music, George Enescu, Iasi. *Career:* Recitals at Romanian Athene, Bucharest, 1989 and in other cities of Romania; Participant in Young Talents Piatra-Neamt; Museum of Republic, 1987–88; Concerts with: Bacau Symphony Orchestra, 1987 and Craiova Oltenia Philharmonic Orchestra, 1988; Radio appearances in musical programmes and with recitals, 1987 and 1988; Television, 1987; Participant in Young Talents Festival, 1984, 1986, 1987, 1988; Piano recitals and Chamber Music collaboration in German cities of Darmstadt, Erfurt, Freiburg, Gotha, Heiligenstadt, Nordhausen, Osnabrück, Sonderhausen, also in Poland and Italy; International Masterclasses for Pianists. *Recordings:* Radio appearances, 1989 and 1990. *Address:* Morgenröte Str 7, 99734 Nordhausen, Germany.

SCEBBA, Miguel (Angel); Pianist, Composer and Professor of Music; b. 6 Nov. 1948, San Martin, Buenos Aires, Argentina. *Education:* National Conservatory of Music, Buenos Aires, 1972; Postgraduate work at Tchaikovsky Conservatory, Kiev, 1974–76, Moscow, 1977–78. *Career:* Debut: Piano soloist with Orchestra of San Martin, Buenos Aires, Beethoven Concerto No. 3, 1966; Concerts in more than 15 countries in the world, among them: Two major tours in USSR, 1981, 1985; International festival, Settembre Musicale Triestino, 1983; Numerous appearances in Germany, 1986–90, on Radio RIAS-Berlin, Tübingen, Konstanz; Theater Colon, Buenos Aires, 1992; Artist-in-Residence, Miami University, Ohio, USA, 1994–97; Full Professor, National University of San Juan, Argentina; 2 tours in Europe, 2000. *Compositions:* Four symphonies, 1987, 1996, 1998, 1999, recorded by National University of San Juan; Organ Book, 1975; 10 string quartets; 5th Symphony, 2001. *Recordings:* Piano solo, Schumann, sonata op 22, Debussy, l'Isle Joyeuse, Ginastera sonata No. 1, Con Anima, São Paulo, Brazil, 1989; Argentina Musical, 1997; Liszt B minor sonata. *Address:* Dominguito 1572, 5400 San Juan, Argentina. *E-mail:* miguel.scebba@interredes.com.ar.

SCHAAF, Jerrold Van Der; Singer (Tenor); b. 1952, Battle Creek, Michigan, USA. *Education:* Studied at the University of Michigan. *Career:* Sang at the Aachen Opera, 1977–80, at Essen, 1980–83, and at Stuttgart Staatsoper, 1987–93 notably as Checchi in Henze's König Hirsch, Janáček's Steva, Tamino, Wagner's Steuermann and Don Ottavio; Guest at Frankfurt in 1983 as Hylas in Les Troyens and elsewhere in Germany in Jommelli's Fetonte; Sang at Vienna Staatsoper from 1989 notably as Tamino. *Recordings include:* Die Entführung; Die Soldaten. *Address:* c/o Staatsoper Wien, Opernring 2, 1010 Vienna, Austria.

SCHAAF, Johannes; stage director; b. 7 April 1933, Bad Cannstatt, Germany; m. Stella Kleindienst. *Education:* studied medicine. *Career:* Worked at the Stuttgart Schauspielhaus, then directed plays in Ulm and Bremen; Further theatre work at Munich (Twelfth Night), Vienna and Salzburg (Beaumarchais, Buchner and Lessing); Director of award winning films from 1967 (with some acting) and television programmes featuring Sviatoslav Richter, Edith Mathis, Peter Schreier and Dietrich

Fischer-Dieskau; Opera productions have included Les Contes d'Hoffmann (Vienna Volksoper), Idomeneo (Vienna Staatsoper), Eugene Onegin (Geneva and Bremen) and Capriccio and Die Entführung (Salzburg); Produced Le nozze di Figaro at Covent Garden 1987 and was invited to return for Così fan tutte and Idomeneo (1989), Don Giovanni 1992; Also engaged for Fidelio (1989) and Die Frau ohne Schatten (1992) at Geneva Opera, The Nose by Shostakovich at Frankfurt (1990) and Schreker's Der Ferne Klang at Brussels; Engaged to produce Boris Godunov to open the New Israel Opera House, 1994; Season 1995–96 with Simon Boccanegra at Stuttgart; Le nozze di Figaro at Confidencen, Stockholm, 1998; Directed Katya Kabanova for San Francisco Opera, 2002. *Publications:* contrib. to Geo, on subjects including Chinese Opera.

SCHACHTSCHNEIDER, Herbert; Singer (Tenor); b. 5 Feb. 1919, Allenstein, Germany. *Education:* Studied at the Musikhochschule Berlin. *Career:* Sang at the Stadttheater Flensburg from 1953; Further engagements at Mainz and Essen; Holland Festival 1958; Cologne Opera 1959–72; Sang at the Festival Hall, London 1963, in the British premiere (concert) of Schoenberg's Von Heute auf Morgen; Roles included Florestan, Walther, Tannhäuser, Lohengrin, Parsifal, Radames, Don Carlos, Cavaradossi and Don José; Guest appearances in Germany and elsewhere in Europe; Professor at the Musikhochschule Saarbrücken from 1975. *Address:* Musikhochschule des Saarlandes, Bismarckstrasse 1, Saarbrücken, Germany.

SCHADE, Michael; Singer (Tenor); b. 23 Jan. 1965, Geneva, Switzerland. *Education:* Curtis Institute. *Career:* Early experience as Ernesto in Belgium and Rameau's Pygmalion with Opera Atelier in Toronto; Professional debut in 1990 as Jacquino with the Pacific Opera of British Columbia; Sang Tamino at Bologna, 1991; Appeared as Iago in Rossini's Otello at Pesaro; Vienna Staatsoper debut in 1991 as Almaviva; Season 1991–92 as Alfred in Fledermaus at Geneva, Almaviva with Edmonton and Canadian Operas, Ernesto with Vancouver Opera and Elvino in La Sonnambula at Macerata; Season 1992–93 as Jacquino in San Francisco and the Chevalier in Dialogues des Carmélites at Geneva; Sang Roderigo in Otello, 1993; Engaged by Vienna Staatsoper as Ferrando, Almaviva, Nemorino, Tamino and Nicolai's Fenton; Salzburg Festival in 1994 in a staged version of Mozart Arias; Cologne Opera as Telemaco in Monteverdi's Ulisse and Elvino at Trieste; Sang Tamino, 1995, Haydn's Creation, 1995 and Fidelio, 1995; Oedipus Rex at Toronto, 1997; Sang Tamino at Salzburg, 1997, and La Scala, 1998; Appeared in Merry Widow at Paris Opéra in 1998 and as Alfred in Fledermaus at the Metropolitan Opera in 1998–99; Concert repertoire includes Beethoven's Missa Solemnis, The Creation, The Seasons and Bach's St Matthew Passion, Mozart's Requiem, Carmina Burana, Schumann's Paradies und die Peri under John Eliot Gardiner and Elijah with the Cleveland Orchestra; Wagner's David at Chicago, 1999, Ottavio at Los Angeles, Vienna and Ravenna, 1999; Season 2000–01 at the Met as Rossini's Almaviva and Tamino, Henry in Die schweigsame Frau at the Vienna Staatsoper, Cherubini's Jason at Salzburg (concert) and Idomeneo at Dresden. *Recordings include:* Haydn's Maria Theresa Mass under Trevor Pinnock; The Creation and The Seasons; St Matthew Passion, Elijah, St Paul under Rilling; Die Zauberflöte under Gardiner; Mozart Requiem under Abbado. *Current Management:* IMG Artists. *Address:* c/o IMG Artists, Lovell House, 616 Chiswick High Road, London W4 5RX, England.

SCHADLER, Elisabeth; Pianist; b. 10 Nov. 1963, Feldbach, Styria, Austria. *Education:* Private lessons, at 15 years, Hochschule für Musik, Graz; Masterclasses. *Career:* Concerts and recitals at Vienna Konzerthaus and Musikverein; Many European countries with Vienna Chamber Orchestra, Graz Symphony Orchestra; Notable partners; Festivals; Teacher, Kunstuniversität, Graz, 1987–; Member, EPTA, Austria; Professorship at the Conservatory Klagenfurt, 1999–. *Recordings:* Double concertos for violin, piano and orchestra, 1996. *Honours:* Second prize, International Competition Vercelli, 1985; Second prize, International Schubert Competition, Dortmund, 1987; Winner, International competition, Schubert and Music of the 20th Century, Graz, 1989; Third prize, Lied. *Address:* Friedrichgasse 29, 8010 Graz, Austria.

SCHAEFER, Peter; Composer and Musician (Sitar); b. 14 Sept. 1956, Sydney, New South Wales, Australia. *Education:* BA, 1977, BMus, hons 1984, University of Sydney; DCA, University of Wollongong, 1998; Study with Peter Sculthorpe, Barry Conyngham Ustad Ali Akbar Khan, Ashok Roy. *Career:* Faculty Member, New South Wales Conservatory, 1984–90; University of Wollongong, 1990–92; Founding Member of Peter Schaefer Ensemble; Performer of Indian and electro-acoustic music. *Compositions:* Toward, for string quartet, 1980; See, for synthesizer and/or computer and digital delay, 1983; Petal... Silence, For 2 pianos and tape, 1983; Chien... Still, for orchestra, 1984; Spans, for ensemble and tape, 1989; Time Breathing, Dance Theatre, for ensemble and ape, 1990; Quartet Vibra, for string quartet and tape, 1991; Open/Secret, Music Theatre, for children, 1994; Expans Series (I–VII), for ensemble and tape, 1990–; Tao Streams, orchestra project,

1995–. *Honours:* 2 MBS-FM Radiophonic Tape Composition Prize, 1985. *Address:* c/o APRA, 1A Eden Street, NSW 2065, Australia.

SCHAEFFER, Boguslaw (Julien); Composer; b. 6 June 1929, Lwow, Poland. *Education:* Studied Composition with Arthur Malawski in Kraków and Musicology with Jachimecki at the Jagiello University in Kraków, 1940–53; Studied further with Luigi Nono, 1959. *Career:* Director of the record library of Polish Radio in Kraków, 1952; Music Critic, 1953–59; Professor of Composition, Academy of Music, Kraków, from 1963; At the Hochschule für Musik und darstellende Kunst Mozarteum, from 1985 (1989 OH Prof); Experimental studio of Polish Radio in Warsaw, 1965–68; Director and Professor at the Internationale Akademie für Neue Komposition in Schwaz, 1993. *Compositions include:* Concerto for 2 Pianos, 1951; Music for string quartet, 1954; Sonata for solo violin, 1955; Permutations for 10 instruments, 1956; 20 Models for piano, 1954–2000; Extremes for 10 instruments, 1957; 10 String Quartets, 1957, 1964, 1971, 1973, 1986, 1993, 1997, 1998, 1999, 2000; Movimenti for piano and orchestra, 1957; 8 Pieces for piano, 1954–58; Monosonata for 6 string quartets (ISCM, Vienna), 1959; Equivalenze sonore for percussion and chamber orchestra, 1959; Concerto Breve for cello and orchestra, 1959; Concerto for string quartet, 1959; Topofonica for 40 instruments, 1960; Non-Stop for piano (8 hours playing time at premiere 1964); Musica for harpsichord and orchestra, 1961; 4 Pieces for string trio (ISCM, Copenhagen), 1962; Musical Ipsa, 1962; Expressive Aspects for soprano and flute, 1963; Collage and Form for 8 jazz musicians and orchestra, 1963; Audiences I–V for various performers, 1964; Collage for chamber orchestra, 1964; Howl, monodrama after poem by Allen Ginsburg, 1966; Decet for harp and 9 instruments, 1966; Piano Concerto, 1967; Media for voices and instruments, 1967; Jazz Concerto (SIMC, Boston), 1969; Synectics for 3 performers, 1970; Algorithms for 7 performers, 1970; Thema for tape, 1970; Texts for orchestra, 1971; 15 Elements for 2 pianos, 1971; Variants for wind quintet, 1971; Confrontations, 1972; Conceptual Music, 1972; Concerto for 3 pianos, 1972; Bergsoniana for soprano and ensemble, 1972; Neues for 3 violins, 1972; Symphony in 9 movements, 1973; Tentative Music for 159 instruments, 1973; Synhistory for tape, 1973; Antiphona for tape, 1975; Missa elettronica, 1975; Iranian Set, 1976; Spinoziana, action music, 1977; Gravesono for wind instruments and percussion, 1977; Self-Expression for cello, 1977; Matan for 3 percussionists, 1978; Kesukaan for 13 strings, 1978; Miserere for soprano, choir, orchestra, organ and tape, 1978; Jangwa for double bass and orchestra, 1979; Te Deum for voices and orchestra, 1979; Maah for orchestra and tape, 1979; Berlin '80' for piano and tape, 1980; Cantata, 1980; Autogenic Composition, 1980; Introductions and an Epilogue for small orchestra, 1981; Duodrama for alto saxophone and percussion, 1981; Euphony for double bass, 1981; Stabat mater for soprano, alto, descant choir, strings and organ, 1983; Organ Concerto, 1984; 4 Sonatas for organ solo (Vier Jahreszeiten) (ISCM, Manchester), 1985–86; Lieder for voice and orchestra, 1986; Saxophone Concerto 1986; Kwaiwa for violin and computer, 1986; Missa Sinfonica, 1986; Miniopera, 1988; Missa Brevis for choir, 1988; Doppelkonzert for 2 violins and orchestra, 1988; Concerto for percussion, piano and orchestra, 1988; Kammersymphonie, 1988; Concerto for soprano and orchestra, 1988; Sinfonia, 1988; Liebesblicke, opera, 1989; Piano Concerto No. 3, 1990; Violin Concerto, 1988; Oboe Concerto, 1992; Symphony No. 4, 1993; Leopolis for violin and orchestra, 1994; Love Song for string orchestra, 1994; Orchestral and Electronic Changes for amplified solo instruments and orchestra, 1994; Concerto for saxophone quartet and orchestra, 1995; Clarinet Concerto, 1995; Concerto for soprano, saxophone and string orchestra, 1995; Sinfonietta for 16 instruments, 1996; Flute Concerto, 1996; Dialogues for two pianos, 1996; Sinfonia/Concerto for 15 solo instruments and orchestra, 1996; Salve Regina for soprano, organ and orchestra, 1996; Concerto for violin, piano and orchestra, 1997; Viola Concerto, 1997; Symphony in One Movement, 1997; Monophonie I for 16 flutes, 1997; Enigma for orchestra, 1997; Musica dell'Avvenire for percussion orchestra, 1997; Movimento Sinfónico for 88 instruments, 1997; Adagio for orchestra, 1998; Bassoon Concerto, 1998; Transparencies for orchestra, 1998; Piano Quintet, 1998; Max Ernst Variations for saxophone, accordion, piano and computer, 1998; Piano Concerto, 1999; Missa in honorem Beatae Virginis Mariae for voices and orchestra, 1999; Monophonie VI for 17 saxophonists, 1999; Four Psalms for choir, soprano saxophone and orchestra, 1999; Ephuys Josbe for piano, percussion and computer, 2000; De profundis for soprano and chamber orchestra, 2000; Nine Studies on themes of Max Ernst, 2000; SeaHarb for saxophone and oboe (ISCM, Yokohama), 2000; Harp Concerto, 2001; Vibraphone Concerto, 2001. *Publications include:* Classics of Dodecaphonic Music, 1961, 1964; Lexicon of 20th Century Composers, 1963, 1965; Music of the 20th Century, 1975; History of Music, Styles and Authors, 1979; Introduction to Composition (In English), 1975; History of Music, 1987; 20th Century Composers, 1990. *Address:* Bsiedle Kolorowe 4, 31938 Kraków, Poland.

SCHÄFER, Christine; Singer (Soprano); b. 3 March 1965, Frankfurt, Germany. *Education:* Studied at the Berlin Musikhochschule and with

Arleen Auger and Aribert Reimann. *Career:* Has sung widely in concert from 1988, notably with such ensembles as the Windsbacher Knaben Chor and the Berlin Philharmonic Choir; Sang Zerbinetta in Ariadne auf Naxos in Munich; Opera engagements at Brussels from 1991 as Papagena, Zerlina and Gilda; San Francisco debut as Sophie in 1993 and returned in 1994 as Zdenka; Pamina and Elisa in Il Re Pastore at Netherlands Opera; Pierrot Lunaire at the Châtelet and Berlin Staatsoper; Sang title role in Berg's Lulu at Salzburg (1995, 1999) and Glyndebourne (1996); Sang Constanze at the 1998 Salzburg Festival; Sang Gilda in Rigoletto at Covent Garden, 2001 (also televised); New York Met debut as Lulu, 2001. *Honours:* Prizewinner at the Mozart Competitions in Vienna and Rome in 1991. *Address:* c/o IMG Artists, Lovell House, 616 Chiswick High Road, London W4 5RX, England.

SCHÄFER, Markus; Singer (Tenor); b. 13 June 1961, Andernach am Rhein, Germany. *Education:* Studied in Koblenz, Karlsruhe. *Career:* Sang at the Zürich Opera from 1985; Hamburg, 1986; Deutsche Oper am Rhein, Düsseldorf, from 1987; Sang Fenton in Die Lustige Weiber von Windsor at Duisburg, 1991; Damon in Acis and Galatea at the Queen Elizabeth Hall; Other concerts include the Evangelist in Bach's Passions; Messiah, Elijah, St Paul, Die Schöpfung and Rossini's Stabat Mater; Opera roles include Paisiello's Almaviva, Pedrillo, Ramiro and Caramelo in Eine Nacht in Venedig; Mozart's Ferrando at the Berlin Staatsoper, 1997; Tamino at the Berlin Komische Oper, 1999. *Recordings include:* St Paul, Mendelssohn's Christus, Beethoven's Mass in C, Haydn's L'Infedeltà Delusa; Mozart's Mass K139. *Address:* c/o Deutsche Oper am Rhein, Heinrich Heine Allee 16, 4000 Düsseldorf, Germany.

SCHAFER, Raymond (Murray); Composer, Writer on Music and Educationist; b. 18 July 1933, Sarnia, Ontario, Canada. *Education:* Studied at the Toronto Conservatory with Guerrero (piano) and Weinzweg (composition). *Career:* Worked freelance for the BBC in Europe, 1956–61; Founded Ten Centuries Concerts 1961, Toronto; Artist-in-Residence, Memorial University, Newfoundland, 1963–65; Simon Fraser University British Columbia, 1965; Research into acoustic ecology from 1971. *Compositions:* Concerto for harpsichord and 8 instruments, 1954; Minnelieder for mezzo and wind quintet, 1956; Sonatina for flute and keyboard, 1958; In Memoriam: Iberto Guerrero for strings, 1959; Protest and Incarceration for mezzo and orchestra, 1960; Brebeuf for baritone and orchestra, 1961; Canzoni for Prisoners, orchestra, 1962; Untitled Composition for orchestra, 1963; Loving/Toi, music theatre, 1963–66; Requiems for the Party Girl, 1966; Threnody, 1966; Kaleidoscope for multi-track tape, 1967; Son of Heldenleben for orchestra and tape, 1968; From the Tibetan Book of the Dead for soprano, chorus and ensemble, 1968; Yeow and Pax for chorus, organ and tape, 1969; No Longer than Ten Minutes for orchestra, 1970; Sappho for mezzo and ensemble, 1970; String Quartet, 1970; Okeanos for 4-track tape, 1971; In Search of Zoroaster for male voice, chorus, percussion and organ, 1971; Music for the Morning for the World, 1970; Beyond the Great Gate of Light, 1972; Arcana for low voice and ensemble, 1972; East for chamber orchestra, 1972; Paria I–X music theatre, 1969–97; North White for orchestra, 1972; String Quartet No. 2, Waves, 1976; Adieu Robert Schumann for alto and orchestra, 1976; Hymn to the Night for soprano and orchestra, 1976; Cortège for orchestra, 1977; Apocolypsis, music theatre, 1980; RA, multimedia piece based on the Egyptian God, 1983; Flute Concerto, 1985; String Quartet No. 4, 1989; Tristan and Iseult, for vocal soloists, 1992; Accordion Concerto, 1993; String quartets Nos 5 and 6, 1989, 1993; The Falcon's Trumpet, 1995; Musique pour la parque Fontaine, for 4 bands, 1995; Viola Concerto, 1997; Seventeen Haiku, for chorus, 1997. *Publications include:* Edition of Ezra Pound's Opera Le testament de Francois Villon, 1960; British Composers in Interview, 1963; Ezra Pound and Music, 1977; The Thinking Ear, 1986. *Honours:* Canada Council Grants, 1961, 1963; Ford Foundation Award, 1968; Canadian Music Council Medal, 1972; Donner Foundation Grant, 1972; Guggenheim Fellowship, 1974.

SCHAFF, Gabriel (Jacob Gideon Polin); Violinist; b. 9 Nov. 1959, Philadelphia, Pennsylvania, USA; m. Nancy McDill, 18 Dec 1988, 1 d. *Education:* BMus, 1981, Assistant teaching for Erick Friedman, 1979–81, Manhattan School of Music, New York City, 1981; Additional Studies, New School of Music and Temple University, Philadelphia; Studies with Norman Carol, Philadelphia Orchestra. *Career:* Extensive symphonic, opera, ballet and chamber music performances at Lincoln Center, Carnegie Hall and throughout Metropolitan New York City; Violin Soloist in Soviet-American Exchange Concerts organised by Claire Polin with performances in Philadelphia, New York, Moscow, Leningrad and Helsinki, 1979–88; Several commissions and premieres of works by US and Russian composers. *Recordings:* Recording on numerous labels; North/South Consonance. *Address:* c/o Manhattan School of Music, Violin Faculty, 120 Claremont Avenue, New York, NY 10027, USA.

SCHAGIDULLIN, Albert; Opera Singer (bass); b. 1 May 1966, Baschkizia; m., 1 s. *Education:* Moscow Conservatory, 1988–92. *Career:* Debut: Dublin, Enrico Grand Opera, 1991; Hamburg State Opera, 1993–97; Easter and Summer Festival, Salzburg, 1993, 1994; Visited Tokyo with Vienna State Opera, 1994; Salzburg, 1998; Opera di Roma, 1994; Bregenz Summer Festival, 1995–96; Messa di Gloria, Vienna Symphony, 1996; Oslo Philharmonic, 1996; Munich Staatsoper, 1997; Lyon Opéra, 1998. *Recordings:* Boris Godunov; Three Sisters by Peter Eötvös. *Publications:* F Times, 1991; Hamburger Abendblatt, 1992; Corriere della Sera, 1994; Salzburger Nachrichten, 1995. *Contributions:* Opera International, 1998; Opern Glas, 1998. *Honours:* Special prize for best young singer, Francisco Viñas Competition, Barcelona, 1990; 3rd prize, Maria Callas Competition, Athens, 1991; 2nd prize, Belvedere Competition, Vienna, 1991; 2nd prize, CIEM Competition, Geneva, 1991; 1st prize, Vervier Competition, 1991; Winner, Pavarotti Competition, Philadelphia. *Current Management:* Askonas Holt Ltd, Lonsdale Chambers, 27 Chancery Lane, London, WC2A 1PF, England. *Telephone:* (20) 7400-1700. *Fax:* (20) 7400-1799. *E-mail:* info@askonasholt.co .uk. *Website:* www.askonasholt.co.uk.

SCHARFENBERGER, Tobias; Singer (Baritone); b. 1 Sept. 1964, Grafelfing, Munich, Germany. *Education:* Studied in Hannover and Karlsruhe. *Career:* Sang at Stuttgart, 1991 in the premiere of Perseo e Andromeda by Sciarrone; Deutsche Oper am Rhein at Düsseldorf as Ottakar in Der Freischütz and in Krenek's Orpheus; German premiere of Schnittke's Life with an Idiot, Gelsenkirchen, 1991; Bielefeld Opera from 1995 as Papageno, Siegfried in Schumann's Genoveva and in the local premiere of Weir's Blond Eckbert, 1996; Season 1999–2000 as Nicomedes in Zemlinsky's König Kandaules at Cologne and as Kilian in Der Freischütz at the Komische Oper Berlin; Concert and oratorio appearances. *Address:* Bielefeld Opera, Bruhnenstrasse 3–5, 4800 Bielefeld, Germany.

SCHARINGER, Anton; Singer (Baritone); b. 5 March 1959, Austria. *Education:* Studied at Vienna Conservatory. *Career:* Sang with the Salzburg Landestheater, 1981–83, Vienna Volksoper from 1987; Sang Dr Falke in Fledermaus at Amsterdam, 1987; Mozart's Figaro at Ludwigsburg, 1989; Salzburg Festival, 1991; Guest appearances at Cologne, Zürich; Other roles include, Masetto and Guglielmo; Sang the Captain in Gurlitt's Wozzeck at Florence, 1998; Many concert engagements, notably in sacred works by Bach; Television appearances include Bass Solos in the St Matthew Passion, with the Neubeuern Choral Society and the Munich Bach Collegium. *Recordings include:* Die Zauberflöte with Les Arts Florissants, 1996; Masetto in Don Giovanni; Mozart's L'Oca del Cairo. *Address:* c/o Zürich Opera, Falkenstrasse 1, 8008 Zürich, Switzerland.

SCHARLEY, Denise; Singer (Mezzo-soprano); b. 1923, France. *Education:* Studied at the Paris Conservatoire. *Career:* Debut: Paris Opéra Comique 1942, as Geneviève in Pelléas et Mélisande; Appeared at the Opéra Comique until 1947, as Carmen, Dulcinée, Charlotte and Mignon; Sang at the Théâtre de la Monnaie, Brussels, 1947–48; Sang in Rome as Carmen; Paris Opéra from 1951, as Maddalena in Rigoletto, Dalila, Amneris, Wagner's Erda, Fricka and Mary; Puck in Oberon, Bellone in Les Indes Galantes and Madame de Croissy in the local premiere of Les Dialogues des Carmélites; Guest appearances in Geneva, Lyon and Barcelona; Marseilles 1961, as the Countess in The Queen of Spades. *Recordings include:* Werther and Carmen; Carmélites; L'Enfant et les Sortilèges. *Address:* c/o Théâtre National, 8 Rue Scribe, 75009 Paris, France.

SCHÄRTEL, Elisabeth; Singer (Contralto); b. 6 Oct. 1919, Weiden, Oberpfalz, Germany. *Education:* Studied with Helma Rodgier and Wilma Kaiser and with Anna Bahr-Mildenburg in Munich; Further study with Henny Wolff in Hamburg. *Career:* Sang first at Regensburg, then at Freiburg; Brunswick, 1951–57; Bayreuth Festival from 1954, as Mary in Der fliegende Holländer, Erda, Magdalene and Waltraute; Cologne Opera from 1960 (sang in the premiere of Zimmermann's Die Soldaten, 1965); Appearances in Florence, Lisbon and Vienna as Adelaide in Araballa, Magdalene and Brangaene; Deutsche Oper Berlin as Kundry, Brangaene and the Kostelnicka in Jenůfa; Concert Recitals, 1973. *Recordings:* Der fliegende Holländer; Der Zigeunerbaron.

SCHASCHING, Rudolf; Singer (Tenor); b. 12 April 1957, Engelhartszell, Austria. *Education:* Studied at the Vienna Musikhochschule, 1978–83. *Career:* Sang at the Saarbrucken Opera from 1983 as Tamino, Don Ottavio, Pinkerton, Cassio, Max, Oedipus Rex and Idomeneo; Sang Loge, Siegmund and Siegfried, 1987–90; Guest appearances at the Vienna Staatsoper as Aegisthus in 1992, Zürich and elsewhere; Concerts include Beethoven's Ninth, Bruckner's Te Deum and Haydn's Seasons. *Address:* c/o Staatsoper Wien, Opernring 2, 1010 Vienna, Austria.

SCHAUERTE-MAUBOUET, Helga (Elisabeth); Organist; b. 8 March 1957, Lennestadt, Germany; m. Philippe Maubouet, 22 July 1988, 1 d. *Education:* BA, (Abitur), St Franziskusschule, Olpe, 1976; State Examinations, Philosophy and Pedagogy, University of Cologne, 1982; Music and Artistic Maturity, 1982, Organ Playing, 1985, Musikhochschule, Cologne; Conservatory of Rueil-Malmaison, France,

1983. *Career:* Debut: Public appearance as organist, aged 10; Chief Organist at local parish church, aged 13; Organist, German Church, Paris, 1982–; Organ Teacher, Conservatory Paris, 9th arrondisseiment and in Andresy; Recitals, lectures, master classes, Europe and USA, including Royal Academy of Music, London, University of Michigan, USA; Radio performances, Germany, France, and Denmark; Concerts include: Performance, integral of Jehan Alain's and Buxtehude's organ works, Paris, 1986; 1st Performance, Jean Langlais' organ works, Bach and Miniature II and Mort et Resurrection. *Recordings:* Integral of Jehan Alain's Organ Works; Poulenc Organ Concerto; Works of Langlais, Vierne, Dupré, Boëllmann, Dubois, J. S. Bach, Homilius, Walther, Kittel, Kellner, Buttstett, Armsdorff, Muthel and Max Reger; Complete Organ Works of Buxtehude. *Publications:* Jehan Alain: Das Orgelwerk, Eine monographische Studie, 1983; Jehan Alain: L'Homme et l'Oeuvre, 1985; Deutsche und französische Weihnachtslieder, 1997; Noël dans la tradition, Traditionelle Weihnacht, 1997; Boëllmann: Complete Organ Works, Vols I & II, 2002, 2003; Vol. III, 2004; Handbuch Orgelmusik, 2002. *Address:* 25 rue Blanche, 75009 Paris, France. *Website:* www.orguefrance.org/schauerte.htm.

SCHAVERNOCH, Hans; Stage Designer; b. 1955, Australia. *Education:* Studied at the Vienna Akademie. *Career:* Has designed productions of Erwartung, Iphigénie en Aulide, Elektra and La Clemenza di Tito in Vienna; Tannhäuser and Werther at Hamburg, Orfeo and Die Zauberflöte at the Komische Oper Berlin; Collaborations with Producer Harry Kupfer in Berlin, at Salzburg for the premiere of Penderecki's Die schwarze Maske and the 1988 Ring des Nibelungen at Bayreuth; Metropolitan Opera with Der fliegende Holländer, Erwartung and Bluebeard's Castle; Paris Opéra with Der Rosenkavalier, Il Trittico, and Katya Kabanova; Royal Opera Covent Garden designs include Ariadne auf Naxos; Followed by Così fan tutte, Idomeneo, Elektra and La Damnation de Faust; Other designs include Alceste at Versailles, Pelléas et Mélisande at Cologne, Liszt St Elisabeth in Vienna, Parsifal and the Ring at the Berlin Staatsoper and Khovanshchina in Hamburg; Rimsky's Legend of the Invisible City of Kitezh at the Bregenz Festival and Komische Oper, Berlin, 1995–96; Boris Godunov at the Vienna Volksoper. *Address:* c/o Deutsche Staatsoper, Unter der Linden, Berlin, Germany.

SCHEIBNER, Andreas; Singer (Baritone); b. 18 Jan. 1951, Dresden, Germany. *Education:* Studied in Dresden with Gunther Leib. *Career:* Debut: Gorlitz 1972, as Dr Caius in Die Lustige Weiber Von Windsor; Sang at Butzen, 1974, Stralsund 1976–79, Postdam 1979–83; Engaged at the Dresden Staatsoper from 1983; Roles have included Mozart's Don Giovanni, Guglielmo, Papageno, Belcore, Eugene Onegin, Count Luna, Silvio, Marcello, Lortzing's Zar and Kilian in Der Freischütz; Concert appearances in Austria, Netherlands, Poland and throughout Germany; Season 1999–2000 as the Count in Capriccio at Dresden, Barbier in Die schweigsame Frau for the Vienna Staatsoper, and Jochanaan in Salome at Zagreb; Hans Sachs in Madrid, 2001. *Recordings include:* Der Freischütz, conducted by C Davis; Bach Cantatas. *Address:* c/o Semper-Oper, 8012 Dresden, Germany.

SCHEIDEGGER, Hans Peter; Singer (Bass); b. 23 Feb. 1953, La Bottiere, Jura, Switzerland. *Education:* Studied at Berne University and in Essen with Jakob St ämpfli and Paul Lohmann. *Career:* Debut: Geneva Opera 1983, as Curio in Giulio Cesare, conducted by Charles Mackerras; Has appeared at Lucerne and elsewhere in Switzerland as Fiesco (Simon Boccanegra), Britten's Theseus and Collatinus, Bart ók's Duke Bluebeard, Zuniga, Leporello, Walter (Luisa Miller), Trulove (The Rake's Progress) and Rocco; Has sung at Karlsruhe from 1986, as King Henry (Lohengrin), Gremin, the Commendatore, Sarastro, Pogner and the Doctor in Wozzeck; Other roles include Zoroastro in Handel's Orlando, Publio in La Clemenza di Tito, and Ferrando in Il Trovatore; Sang Rocco and King Marke at Basle, 1990; Concert repertoire includes Bach Cantatas, B minor Mass, St John Passion and Christmas Oratorio; Beethoven Missa Solemnis; Dvořák Requiem, Te Deum and Mass in D; Haydn Schöpfung, Jahreszeiten, Harmonie and Nicholas Masses; Salve Regina; Handel Messiah, Saul and Hercules; Mozart Requiem and other Masses; Schubert Mass in A flat and G; Graun Der Tod Jesu; Keiser Markus Passion; Telemann Matthew and Luke Passions; Conductors have included Armin Jordan, Horst Stein, Jeffrey Tate, Roderick Brydon, Kurt Sanderling, Charles Farncombe, Wolfgang Gönnenwein and David Lloyd-Jones; Sang Wotan and the Wanderer at Hannover, 1999; Season 2000–01 as Enkidu in the premiere of Gilgamesh by V.D Kirchner, Monteverdi's Seneca, Rangoni in Boris Godunov and Strauss's Orestes. [Change address to]: Staatstheater Hannover, Opernhaus, Opernplatz 1, 30159 Hannover, Germany. *Address:* Badisches Staatstheater, Baumeisterstrasse 11, 7500 Karlsruhe, Germany.

SCHEJA, Steffan; Concert Pianist; b. 1950, Sweden. *Education:* Studied at the Stockholm College of Music, Juilliard School, New York. *Career:* Debut: Concert with Swedish Radio Symphony Orchestra, 1962; New York debut 1972, followed by concerts with the French Radio Symphony Orchestra, Philharmonia Hungarica, Munich Philharmonic, English Chamber Orchestra, NHK Symphony Tokyo and the major Scandinavian Orchestras; Solo Recitals and Lieder Accompanist to Håkan Hagegard, Barbara Bonney and Barbara Hendricks; Director of Chamber Music Festival at Gotland, from 1986; Broadcasting engagements, tours of Europe, the USA and Asia; Recital programmes with Violinist Young Uck Kim. *Recordings include:* Albums as Concert Soloist and as Recitalist. *Address:* c/o Gottschalk Impresario A/S, Tollbugaten 3, N–0152 Oslo, Norway.

SCHELLE, Michael; Composer and Music Educator; b. 22 Jan. 1950, Philadelphia, Pennsylvania, USA; m. Joyce Tucciarone, 15 Jan 1972, 1 s., 1 d. *Education:* BA, Villanova University, 1972; BM, Butler University, 1974; MM, Hartt School of Music, University of Hartford, 1976; PhD, University of Minnesota, 1980; Private study with Aaron Copland, 1976–77. *Career:* Teaching Assistant, Hartt School of Music, University of Hartford, 1974–77; Instructor, Teaching Associate, University of Minnesota School of Music, 1977–79; Instructor, Carleton College, 19679; Instructor of Music 1979–81, Assistant Professor 1981–87, Associate Professor 1987–, Composer-in-Residence 1981–, Director, New Music Ensemble 1981–, Jordan College of Fine Arts, Butler University; Guest Composer, Lecturer, various universities and colleges, with orchestras and at festivals. *Compositions:* Stage: The Great Soap Opera, chamber opera, 1988; Orchestral: Lancaster Variations, 1976; Masque–A Story of Puppets, Poets, Kings and Clowns, 1977; El Medico, 1977; Pygmies for youth orchestra and tape, 1982; Pygmies II for youth orchestra and speaker, 1983; Golden Bells for orchestra and chorus, 1983; Completion of an unfinished score by N Dinerstein; Oboe Concerto, 1983; Swashbuckler!, 1984; Concerto for 2 pianos and orchestra, 1986; Kidspeace for orchestra and voices, 1987; (restless dreams before) The Big Night, 1989; Symphonic Band: King Ubu, 1980; Cliff Hanger March, 1984; Seven Steps from Hell, 1985; Chamber Music; Piano Pieces; Vocal Music includes: Swanwhite–Letters to Strindberg from Harriet Bosse, cycle for soprano and piano, 1980. *Honours:* Many composition awards and prizes, various commissions including Indianapolis Symphony Orchestra, Buffalo Philharmonic Orchestra, Kansas City Symphony. *Address:* 5939 N Rosslyn Ave, Indianapolis, IN 46220, USA.

SCHELLEN, Nando; Artistic Director, Stage Director; b. 11 Oct. 1934, The Hague, Netherlands; m. Deborah Raymond, 19 June 1991. *Career:* Director Nederlandse Operastichting, Amsterdam, 1969–87; Stage Director from 1982, with debut at Holland Festival with The Magic Flute, 1982, American continent debut, 1983 with Lohengrin at Toronto and Edmonton for the centennial of Richard Wagner's death; directed productions of Eugene Onegin in 1986, and The Merry Wives of Windsor 1987 in Germany, and Salto Mortale, 1989, and Our Town, 1990 in Netherlands; Nabucco 1999 Bulgaria/Netherlands; Background managerial, musical and theatrical; Produced 14 World premieres during his engagement at Netherlands Operastichting, also initiated major policy changes there including expansion of season from initially 90 to 165 performances; General Artistic Director of Sweelinck Conservatory of Music, Amsterdam, 1991–93; General Artistic Director of Indianapolis Opera, USA, 1993–96; Director of Opera Workshop at Oberlin Summer School at Casaimaggiore, 1998–; Director of Opera Theater at Northern Arizona University, Flagstaff, Arizona, USA, 2000–; Directed in USA: The Telephone, 1993, 2001; Rigoletto, 1994; Erwartung, 1994; Salomé, 1995; Ariadne auf Naxos, 1996; Così fan tutte, 1997, 1998, 2001; Samson et Dalila, 1998; Don Giovanni, 2000; Into the Woods, 2000; La Voix Humaine 2001; The Magic Flute, 2001; Little Night Music, 2002; Director of Opera Workshop at Oberlin Summer School at Casalmaggiore, 1998–. *Address:* 3841 Woodridge Way, Flagstaff, AZ 86004, USA.

SCHELLENBERGER, Dagmar; Singer (soprano); b. 8 June 1958, Oschatz, Germany. *Education:* Studied with Professor Ilse Hahn at Musikhochschule, Dresden. *Career:* From 1984 with Komische Oper, Berlin, singing: Donna Anna, in Dargomyzhsky's The Stone Guest; Eurydice, in Orfeo ed Eurydice; Rosalind (1995); Guest artist in many German theatres including Dresden, as Aennchen in Freichütz and Laura in Weber's Die drei Pintos; In Leipzig as Hanna in The Merry Widow; Berlin Staatsoper as Agathe in Der Freischütz; Susanna in Le nozze di Figaro, at Hamburgische Staatsoper; US debut as Eurydice with Komische Oper Berlin and as Elena, in Donna del Lago, 1992; Opera of Bordeaux debut as Woglinde, in Das Rheingold; Italian debut with RAI Roma; In France: Beethoven 9th, Bordeaux, 1992; Title role in L'incoronazione di Poppea, Opéra de Marseille, 1993; Other engagements include: Countess in Le nozze di Figaro for Opera Northern Ireland; Anne in Marschner's Hans Heiling, Netherlands Opera; All four sopranos, Contes d'Hoffmann, Komische Oper Berlin; Donna Anna, in Don Giovanni, 1993; Adina, in L'Elisir d'amore; Norina in Don Pasquale; Webern Cantatas with Beethoven Academy, Antwerp and Brussels; Brahms, Ein Deutsches Requiem with Berlin Philharmonic; Messiah with Cleveland Orchestra; Donna Anna at Strasbourg Festival; Sang Anna Maria Strada in the premiere of Farinelli by Matthus,

Karlsruhe, 1998; Season 2000–01 as Volkhova in Rimsky's Sadko at Venice and as Lehar's Hanna Glawari at the Leipzig Gewandhaus. *Recordings include:* Mozart's Bastien und Bastienne; Hasse's Mass with Capriccio; Handel's L'Allegro, il penseroso ed il moderato; Mozart's Kleinere Kirchenwerke; Solo Recital of Mozart Arias; Marenka in The Bartered Bride. *Honours:* Winner, Dvořák International Voice Competition, 1982; Kammersängerin, German Government, 1988. *Current Management:* Athole Still International Management, Forresters Hall, 25–27 Westow Street, London, SE19 3RY, England. *Telephone:* (20) 8771-5271. *Fax:* (20) 8768-6600. *Website:* www.atholestill.com.

SCHEMTSCHUK, Ludmilla; Singer (Mezzo-soprano); b. 14 Sept. 1946, Donetsk, Ukraine. *Education:* Studied at the Odessa Conservatory. *Career:* Sang at the Minsk Opera from 1970; Bolshoi Theatre Moscow from 1978, as Pauline (The Queen of Spades), Azucena, Amneris, Eboli, Dorabella, Ortrud, Fricka, Carmen and Charlotte (Werther); Has sung at the Vienna Staatsoper from 1985 as Laura in La Gioconda, Marina (Boris Godunov), Ulrica and Marfa in Khovanshchina; Guest appearances at the Verona Arena (Azucena 1985), Munich, Hamburg, Caracalla Festival, Rome and Stuttgart (Santuzza 1987); Countess in The Queen of Spades at Buenos Aires, 1995; Sang with Kirov Opera in Tchaikovsy's Mazeppa, as Lyubov, 1998; Season 2000 as Solokha in Tchaikovsky's Cherevichki, at Cagliari, and Ulrica at Barcelona; Concert tours of Finland, Bulgaria and Hungary. *Recordings include:* Video of La Gioconda with Domingo. *Address:* c/o Staatsoper, Opernring 2, 1010 Vienna, Austria.

SCHENK, Otto; Opera Producer; b. 12 June 1930, Vienna, Austria. *Education:* Studied acting with Max Reinhardt and production at the Unversity of Vienna. *Career:* Debut: First opera production Die Zauberflöte, Salzburg Landestheater, 1957; Don Pasquale at the Vienna Volksoper, 1961; Vienna Festival 1963, Dantons Tod and Lulu; Salzburg Festival 1963, Die Zauberflöte and Der Rosenkavalier; Jenůfa at the Vienna Staatsoper 1964; Chief Stage Director from 1965; Further productions include Macbeth and Der Freischütz; Opera productions in Frankfurt, Berlin, Munich (Der Rosenkavalier 1975) and Stuttgart; Metropolitan Opera from 1970; Tosca, Fidelio, Tannhäuser, Les Contes d'Hoffmann, Arabella and Der Ring des Nibelungen (1986–88); La Scala Milan 1974, Le nozze di Figaro; Covent Garden 1975, Un Ballo in Maschera; Savonlinna Festival 1991, The Bartered Bride; Elektra and Die Meistersinger at the Metropolitan, 1992–93. *Recordings include:* Video of Der Ring des Nibelungen, from the Metropolitan. *Address:* c/o Bayerische Staatsoper, Postfach 745, 8000 Munich 1, Germany.

SCHERLER, Barbara; Singer (Contralto); b. 10 Jan. 1938, Leipzig, Germany. *Education:* Studied at the Berlin Musikhochschule and with Margarete Barwinkel. *Career:* Sang at Frankfurt 1959–64; Cologne Opera 1964–68; Deutsche Oper Berlin from 1968, notably in the 1984 premiere of Gespenstersonate by Reimann; Guest appearances in London, Brussels, Lisbon, Mexico City, Zürich and Venice; Noted concert artist, particularly in works by Bach. *Recordings:* Bach Cantatas; Masses by Mozart; Penthesilea by Schoeck.

SCHERMERHORN, Kenneth (DeWitt); Conductor and Composer; b. 20 Nov. 1929, New York, USA; m. (1) Lupe Servano, 1957, 2 d., (2) Carol Neblett, 1975, 1 s. *Education:* Artists Diploma; Highest Honours, New England Conservatory of Music. *Career:* Assistant Conductor, New York Philharmonic, 1959; Music Director, American Ballet Theatre, 1957–70; Music Director, New Jersey Symphony, 1963–68; Music Director, Milwaukee Symphony, 1968–80; Music Director, Nashville Symphony, 1984–; Music Director, Hong Kong Philharmonic, 1985–; Guest, San Francisco Opera; Boston, Cleveland, San Francisco, Philadelphia, New York Symphonies, et al. *Honours:* S Koussevitzky Memorial Award; Honorary Doctorate, Ripon College. *Address:* c/o Nashville Symphony, 200 10th Avenue S, Suite 448, Nashville, TN 37203, USA.

SCHEUERELL, Douglas Andrew; Musician and Teacher; b. 31 May 1948, Madison, Wisconsin, USA; m. Victoria Ann Scheuerell, 4 Aug 1992, 1 s. *Education:* Bachelor of Music with distinction, University of Wisconsin, Madison, 1971; Teaching certificate K-12, Wisconsin, California and Oregon; Ali Akbar College of Music, San Rafael, California; Ali Akbar Khan, Swapan Chaudhuri, 1981–98; Jnan Prakash Ghosh, 1985–86; Workshops with Samir Chatterjee. *Career:* Musician, Madison, 1966–74; Intern Choral Director, Sun Prairie High School, Wisconsin, 1970; Recording Artist, Stas WHA and WHA-TV, Madison, 1973–74; Musician, Composer, Missing Link Theatre Company, Berkeley, California, 1977–78; Faculty Member, East Bay Centre for the Performing Arts, Berkeley, 1977–78; Family Light Music School, Sausalito, California, 1978; Elizabeth Waters Dance Ensemble, Albuquerque, New Mexico, 1979–80; Accompanist, University of New Mexico School of Dance, Albuquerque, 1979–80; Tabla soloist and accompanist, North Indian classical music, 1988–; Tabla tutor, Eugene, Oregon, 1988–93; Faculty Member, University of Oregon School of Music, Eugene, 1993–; Residencies in California schools National Endowment for the Arts, 1977–78; Performance grantee, Lane Regional Arts

Council, Eugene, 1989; Faculty Development grantee, University of Oregon, Eugene, 1996; Performances for Percussive Arts Society; Asia Society. *Recordings:* Badger A Go-Go; Vanish Into Blue. *Address:* 65 N Lawrence Street, Eugene, OR 97401, USA.

SCHEVCHENKO, Larissa; Singer (Soprano); b. 1952, Kiev, Russia. *Education:* Graduated St Petersburg Conservatoire, 1976. *Career:* Appearances with the Kirov Opera, St Petersburg, from 1976 as Aida, Olga in The Maid of Pskov by Rimsky-Korsakov, Lisa in The Queen of Spades and Maria in War and Peace; Other roles include Tatiana, Leonora (Il Trovatore), Mimi and Maria in Tchaikovsky's Mazeppa; Sang with the Kirov Opera in London, 1999–2000, as Katerina in Lady Macbeth of Mtsensk (Barbican Hall) and Maria in War and Peace (Covent Garden). *Honours:* Grand Prix in Holland, 1978 and Gold Medal in Belgium, 1979; Glinka All-Union Competition; Honoured Artist of the Republic and People's Artist of Russia. *Address:* c/o Mariinksy Theatre, 1 Theatre Square, St Petersburg, Russia.

SCHEXNAYDER, Brian; Singer (Baritone); b. 18 Sept. 1953, Port Arthur, Texas, USA. *Education:* Studied at the Juilliard School New York. *Career:* Sang in Operas by Verdi and Puccini while at Juilliard; Metropolitan Opera from 1980 as Ashton (Lucia di Lammermoor), Marcello (La Bohème), Guglielmo and Lescaut in Manon Lescaut; Paris Opéra 1982–83, as Marcello; Sang Marcello at the Metropolitan 1989, Valentin in Faust, 1990. *Address:* c/o Metropolitan Opera, Lincoln Center, New York, NY 10023, USA.

SCHIAVI, Felice; Singer (Baritone); b. 4 July 1931, Vimercate, Italy. *Education:* Studied with Riccardo Malipiero in Monza and with Carlo Tagliabue, Carlo Alfieri and Enrico Pessina in Milan. *Career:* Has sung widely in Italy from 1955, notably at Rome, Parma, Bologna, Trieste, Naples, Milan and Venice; Verona Arena, 1977; Vienna Staatsoper 1984, as Paolo in Simon Boccanegra; Further appearances in Nice, Marseille, Edinburgh, Prague, Barcelona, Moscow, Munich, Glasgow, Cardiff and Warsaw; Other roles include Amonasro, Renato, Luna, Iago, Posa, Don Carlos (La Forza del Destino), Simon Boccanegra, Scarpia, Gerard, Barnaba and Escamillo. *Address:* c/o Vienna Staatsoper, Opernring 2, 1010 Vienna, Austria.

SCHIDLOWSKY, Leon; Composer; b. 21 July 1931, Santiago, Chile. *Education:* Studies, National Conservatory, Santiago, 1940–47 and Germany, 1952–55. *Career:* Founded Performance Group, Agrupacion Tonus, for the Promotion of New Music; Teacher, Santaigo Music Institute, 1955–63; Professor, Composition, University of Chile, 1962–68; Emigrated to Israel, 1969; Faculty Member, Rubin Academy, Tel-Aviv. *Compositions:* Jeremias for 8 mixed voices and strings, 1966; String Quartet, 1967; Wind Quintet, 1968; Sextet, 1970; Bai Yar for strings, piano and percussion, 1970; Rabbi Akiba, Scenic Fantasy, 1972; Images for strings, 1976; Lux in Tenebris for orchestra, 1977; Adieu for mezzo and chamber orchestra, 1982; Missa in Nomine Bach for chorus and 8 instruments, 1984; Trilogy for orchestra, 1986; Ballade for violin and orchestra, 1986; Piano Quartet, 1988; String Quartet No. 2, 1988; Laudatio for orchestra, 1988; Kaleidoscope for orchestra, 1989; Trio In Memoriam Vruno Maderna, 1990; Sealed Room for 12 instruments, 1991; Silvestre Revueltas, Oratorio, 1994; Am Grab Kafkas for woman singer playing crotales, 1994; I Will Lay My Hand Upon My Mouth, for orchestra, 1994; Dybbuk, opera, 1994; Laudate, for chorus, 1995; Absalom, for orchestra, 1996; Before Breakfast, monodrama, 1997; Lamento for soprano, string quartet and percussion, 1998. *Address:* c/o Ministry of Education and Culture, Music Department, Hashalum Street 23, PO Box 131, Even Yehuda 40500, Israel.

SCHIEFERSTEIN, Eva; Pianist and Harpsichordist; b. 17 March 1955, Büdesheim, Germany. *Education:* Sociology, Political Science, Ludwig Maximilians University, Munich; Studied at Richard Strauss Konservatorium, Munich, and Salzburg Mozarteum; Masterclasses with Elisabeth Leonskaja, Peter Feuchtwanger and others. *Career:* Debut: Municipal Hall, Friedberg, Germany, 1983; Specialised in contemporary music, lied accompaniment and chamber music; Chamber concerts, Meran, 1984, Berlin, 1986, Bayreuth, 1989, Reims, 1991, Dresden, 1992, Wartburgkonzerte, 1997, Salzburg, 2002, elsewhere; Concertised at Festivals for Contemporary Music, Bacau, Romania, 1994, Bucharest, Romania, 1995, Belgrade, Yugoslavia, 1998; Recorded for Bavarian Broadcasting Station, Deutschland Radio, SWF Radio; mem, European Piano Teachers Association; GEDOK; Committee Member, Münchner Tonkünstlerverband. *Recordings:* as pianist/harpsichordist of Munich Flute Trio: Musik in Sanssouci; Oper im Salon; Meisterwerke barocker Kammermusik; Noble Tafelmusik; as soloist: Klaviernacht; Carl Maria von Weber: Tänzerische Klaviermusik; Musik am Hofe August des Starken (Music at the court of August the Strong); Friedrich der Grosse (Flute Music from Sanssouci). *Honours:* Special Prize as Lied Accompanist, Brahms Competition, Hamburg, 1985. *Address:* Baldurstr 31, 80637 Munich, Germany. *Telephone:* 089 1576614. *Fax:* 089 1576614.

SCHIEMER, Gregory, BMus, PhD; Composer, Electronic instrument designer and Academic; b. 16 Jan. 1949, Dunedoo, New South Wales,

Australia. *Education:* University of Sydney; Control Data Institute; Macquarie Univ. *Career:* Computer Technician, Digital Equipment Australia, 1976–81; Lecturer in Composition, New South Wales Conservatorium, 1986–2002; Senior Lecturer in Music Technology, Faculty of Creative Arts, Univ. of Wollongong; mem., Int. Computer Music Asscn. *Compositions include:* (most with purpose-built electronics) Laotian Wood for piccolo, flute, alto flute, soprano saxophone, tenor saxophone and harp, 1970–72; Brolga for computer generated tape, 1973; Iconophony for piano, 1973; Body Sonata for theremin controlled analogue electronics, 1974; A Rain Poem for theremin controlled digital synthesiser, 1975; Ground-Harp for theremin controlled analogue electronics, 1977; Karamojan Wood for 2 marimbas, 1978; Mandala I and II for Tupperware Gamelan, 1981–82; Porcelain Dialogue for Tupperware Gamelan, 1982–83; Monophonic Variations for percussion and interactive MIDI system, 1986; Music for Shreelata for percussion, Tupperware Gamelan and computer generated tape, 1986; Polyphonic Variations for percussion and interactive MIDI system, 1988; Spectral Dance for MIDI Tool Box and Tupperware Gamelan, 1991; Talk-Back Piano for MIDI Tool Box and Disklavier, 1991; Voltage-Control Piano Studies for MIDI Tool Box and Disklavier, 1991; Token Objects for MIDI Tool Box and Tupperware Gamelan, 1993; Machine Dance for MIDI Tool Box and clarinet, 1994; Shantivanam for carnatic violin and MIDI Tool Box, 1995; Shantivanam II for veena and A4 MIDI Tool Box, 1996; Vedic Mass for 2 sopranos and 2 mezzo-sopranos, 19998; Transposed Hexanies for computer generated tape, 2000–01; Tempered Dekanies for computer generated tape, 2002; Tampatablatarangalila for tabla and MIDI Tool Box, 2002; A Dekany In Memorian for computer generated tape, 2003. *Honours:* Various Grants, University of Sydney, 1990–95; Australia Council Composer's Fellowship for musical instrument design at CSIRO Division of Radiophysics, 1994; Australian Research Council Collaborative Project for musical applications of 3D audio with Lake Technology, 1997; Australian Research Council Discovery Project for mobile J2ME musical instrument development, 2003–05; Research Infrastructure Grant for 3D audio, Univ. of Wollongong, 2003. *Address:* Faculty of Creative Arts, Building 25, University of Wollongong, 2522, Australia. *Telephone:* (2) 4221-3584. *Fax:* (2) 4221-3301. *E-mail:* schiemer@uow.edu.au.

SCHIFF, András; Hungarian pianist; b. 21 Dec. 1953, Budapest; s. of Odon Schiff and Klara Schiff (Csengeri); m. Yuuko Shiokawa 1987. *Education:* Franz Liszt Acad. of Music, Budapest with Pal Kadosa, Gyorgy Kurtag and Ferenc Rados, private lessons with George Malcolm, England. *Career:* recitals in London, New York, Paris, Vienna, Munich, Florence; concerts with New York Philharmonic, Chicago Symphony, Vienna Philharmonic, Concertgebouw, Orchestre de Paris, London Philharmonic, London Symphony, Philharmonia, Royal Philharmonic, Israel Philharmonic, Berlin Philharmonic, Cleveland, Philadelphia, Washington Nat. Symphony; played at Salzburg, Edinburgh, Aldeburgh, Feldkirch Schubertiade, Lucerne and Tanglewood Festivals; f. Musiktage Mondsee Festival 1989 (Artistic Dir 1989–98); f. own orchestra Cappella Andrea Barca 1999. *Recordings include:* Bach Goldberg Variations, Bach Partitas, Bach Piano Concertos, Mendelssohn Concertos 1 and 2, all the Schubert Sonatas, Schubert Trout Quintet, Schumann and Chopin 2, all the Mozart Concertos, Bach Two-and Three-part Inventions, Bach Well-Tempered Klavier, Beethoven Violin and Piano Sonatas with Sandor Vegh, Beethoven Piano Concertos, Bartok Piano Concertos, Tchaikovsky Piano Concerto, Bach English Suites (Grammy Award 1990), Bach French Suites, Lieder with Peter Schreier, Robert Holl and Cecilia Bartoli, etc.. *Television:* The Wanderer – A Film About Schubert with Andras Schiff (BBC Omnibus, narrator), Chopin with Andras Schiff (BBC Omnibus, narrator). *Honours:* Prizewinner at 1974 Tchaikovsky Competition in Moscow and Leeds Piano Competition 1975, Liszt Prize 1977, Premio della Accad. Chigiana, Siena 1987, RPS/Charles Heidsieck Award for best concert series of 1988–89, Wiener Flotenuhr 1989, Bartok Prize 1991, Royal Philharmonic Soc.'s Instrumentalist of the Year 1994, Claudio Arrau Memorial Medal 1994, Kossuth Prize 1996, Sonning Prize, Copenhagen 1997), Penna d'Oro della Città di Vicenza 2003. *Current Management:* Terry Harrison Artists Management, The Orchard, Market Street, Charlbury, Oxfordshire OX7 3PJ, England. *Telephone:* (1608) 810330. *Fax:* (1608) 811331. *E-mail:* artists@terryharrison.force9.co.uk (office). *Website:* www.terryharrison.force9.co.uk (office).

SCHIFF, Heinrich; Concert Cellist and Conductor; b. 18 Nov. 1951, Gmunden, Austria. *Education:* First studied piano then cello with Tobias Kuhne in Vienna and André Navarra in Detmold. *Career:* Prizewinner at competitions in Vienna, Geneva and Warsaw; Soloist with Vienna Philharmonic, Concertgebouw, Stockholm Philharmonic, BBC Symphony and Royal Philharmonic Orchestra; Season 1988–89 with Berlin, Israel and Los Angeles Philharmonics; Conductors include Haitink, Chailly, Masur and Previn; Recent British engagements with the London Philharmonic and Academy of St Martin in the Fields at the Festival Hall; Tokyo Metropolitan Orchestra in Manchester and London

playing the Elgar Concerto; Schumann Concerto with the Philharmonia Orchestra and Sinopoli; Northern Sinfonia and City of London Sinfonia as soloist and conductor; Lutoslawski Concerto with the composer conducting the Philharmonia; Artistic Director of the Northern Sinfonia, 1990–96; Has also conducted (from 1984) the Vienna Symphony Orchestra and the Stockholm and Scottish Chamber Orchestras; Played the Schubert String Quintet with the Alban Berg Quartet, London, 1997; British premiere of Friedrich Cerha's Concerto, London Proms, 1999. *Recordings:* Deutsche Schallplatenpreis 1978, as Artist of the Year; Bach's Solo Suites; Philips contract from 1986; Schumann's Concerto with the Berlin Philharmonic and Haitink; Prokofiev's Sinfonia Concertante with the Los Angeles Philharmonic and Previn; Concertos by Vivaldi, Haydn, Dvořák and Lutoslawski. *Address:* c/o Van Walsum Management Ltd, 4 Addison Bridge Place, London W14 8XP, England.

SCHILDKNECHT, Gregor; Singer (Baritone); b. 18 Oct. 1936, Biel, Switzerland. *Education:* Studied in Vienna at the Academy of Music with Adolf Vogel, with Domgraf Fassbänder in Nuremberg and Carino in Düsseldorf. *Career:* Sang at the Oldenburg Opera, 1965–67, Coburg, 1968–73, Detmold, 1973–74, Krefeld, 1974–77, and Bielefeld, 1977–80; Guest engagements from 1980 at the Berlin Staatsoper, Hamburg, Düsseldorf, Karlsruhe, Geneva, Amsterdam, Brussels and Prague; Roles have included parts in operas by Mozart, Donizetti, Rossini; Verdi's Luna, Rigoletto, Germont, Macbeth, Posa, Amonasro and Carlo in La Forza del Destino; Wolfram, Scarpia, the villains in Hoffmann and Mandryka in Arabella; Concert engagement in Germany, Netherlands and Switzerland. *Address:* Gregor Schildknecht, 2555 Brügg bei Biel, Switzerland.

SCHILLER, Allan; Concert Pianist; b. 18 March 1943, Leeds, Yorkshire, England. *Education:* Associate, Royal College of Music, Performance and Diploma, 1959; Moscow Conservatoire. *Career:* Debut: Hallé Orchestra with John Barbiroli, Leeds Town Hall, 1954; Edinburgh Festival, Scotland, 1954; Promenade Concert, London, 1957; Subject of Philpott File, television documentary; Toured in Canada, Europe, Russia; Professor, Guildhall School of Music; mem, Incorporated Society of Musicians; Bristol Savages. *Recordings:* Recital, 1958; Chopin and Mozart; Bridge and Elgar Quintets with Coull Quartet; Complete Chopin Waltzes. *Honours:* Harriet Cohen Medal, 1966. *Address:* 14 Lilymead Avenue, Knowle, Bristol 4, Avon, England.

SCHILLER, Christoph; Concert Violist; b. 17 May 1951, Zürich, Switzerland; m. Louise Pelerin 1981, 1 s. *Education:* Realgymnasium Zürichberg; Matura, 1970; University of Zürich; North Carolina School of Arts, 1972–73; Accademia Chigiana, Siena, Italy; Nordwestdeutsche Musikakademie, Detmold, Germany. *Career:* Violist of New Zürich String Quartet, 1973–88 with tours in Europe, Israel, Scandinavia and North and South America; Viola soloist with orchestras throughout Europe; Professor at the Zürich and Basle Conservatories; Founder and Artistic Director of Ensemble Mobile, 1989–. *Recordings:* Charles Koechlin, Viola Sonata; Willy Burkhard, works for viola; Giacinto Scelsi, Solo and Chamber Music; String Quartets by Brahms, Mendelssohn, Debussy, Ravel, Dvořák, Grieg and Haydn; Chamber works by various Swiss composers. *Honours:* Soloist's Prize of Swiss Musicians Association, 1976. *Current Management:* Pro Musicis, Silvia Ackermann, Rütistrasse 38, 8032, Zürich, Switzerland. *Address:* Bombachstr 21, 8049 Zürich, Switzerland.

SCHIML, Marga; Singer (Mezzo-soprano); b. 29 Nov. 1945, Weiden, Germany; m. Horst Laubenthal. *Education:* Studied with Hanno Blaschke in Munich and with Hartmann-Dressler in Berlin. *Career:* Debut: Basle Opera 1967, in Tigrane by Hasse; Has sung in Vienna, Munich, Graz, Basle and Zürich; Appearances at the Orange and Salzburg Festivals; Bayreuth Festival 1981, 1986, as Magdalene in Die Meistersinger and in Parsifal and Der Ring des Nibelungen; Sang at Turin 1986, as Fricka in Das Rheingold; Maggio Musicale Florence 1989, Annina in Der Rosenkavalier. *Recordings:* Puck in Oberon, La Clemenza di Tito; Mozart Masses, Der Ring des Nibelungen; Choral Symphony; Masses by Weber. *Address:* c/o Festspielhaus, 8580 Bayreuth, Germany.

SCHIPIZKY, Frederick (Alexander); Composer, Conductor, Bassist and Teacher; b. 20 Dec. 1952, Calgary, Alberta, Canada; m. Ruth Fagerburg (violinist), 4 Aug 1984. *Education:* BMus, Composition, University of British Columbia, 1974, study with Elliot Weisgarber and Jean Coulthard; Private study with Harry Freedman and Sophie Eckhardt-Gramatte Courtenay, 1974 and with Murray Adaskin at Victoria Conservatory, 1975–76; MMus in Composition and Double Bass at Juilliard School, NY, 1976–78, with Roger Sessions, David Diamond and David Walter; D.Mus in Music Composition, University of Toronto, 1994, with John Beckwith and John Hawkins. *Career:* Appearances on CBC radio and television with Vancouver Symphony Orchestra, and as Composer, Conductor and Bassist; Bassist for Vancouver Symphony Orchestra; Teacher of Theory and Composition at Vancouver Academy of Music; Faculty, Courtenay Youth Music Centre, 1986; Performed with Montreal Symphony Orchestra; Faculty, Douglas College since 1989; Performed with Esprit Orchestra and Arraymusic; mem, Associate Composer, Canadian Music Centre; Canadian League of Composers. *Compositions:* Symphonic Sketches, 1977; Fanfare for The Royal Visit, 1983; Divertimento for string orchestra, 1983; Symphony No. 1, 1985, commissioned by Vancouver Symphony Orchestra for Japan tour 1985; Symphony No. 2, 1988; From Under The Overture, 1990; Aurora Borealis, 1992; Concerto for contrabass and orchestra, 1994. *Address:* 5390 Larch Street, Vancouver, British Columbia, V6M 4C8, Canada.

SCHIRMER, Astrid; Singer (Soprano); b. 8 Nov. 1942, Berlin, Germany. *Education:* Studied at the Berlin Musikhochschule with Johanna Rakow and Elisabeth Grümmer. *Career:* Debut: Coburg, 1967, as Senta in Der fliegende Holländer; Has sung at the Hanover Opera and widely in Germany, notably in Cologne, Mannheim, Berlin, Stuttgart and Nuremberg; Guest appearances in Barcelona and Zürich; Other roles include Santuzza, Leonore, Brünnhilde, Aida, Amelia (Un Ballo in Maschera), Sieglinde, Ariadne, Arabella, Tosca, Turandot and Lady Billows in Albert Herring; Many concert appearances.

SCHIRMER, Ulf; Conductor; b. 1959, Germany. *Education:* Studied in Bremen and in Hamburg with Horst Stein and Christoph von Dohnányi. *Career:* Assistant to Lorin Maazel at the Vienna Staatsoper and from 1984 conducted Berio's Un Re in Ascolto, Erwartung, Lulu and Henze's Orpheus there; Music Consultant from 1993–95, leading Ariadne, Tannhäuser, Rosenkavalier, Fidelio, Katya Kabanova, Figaro, Parsifal and Cardillac, also Raymonda (with Rudolf Nureyev); Antigone (Orff) at Salzburg Festival, 1989; Bregenz Festival from 1994, with Der fliegende Holländer, Nabucco, Fidelio and Martinů's Greek Passion; Music Director at Wiesbaden, 1988–91; Concerts with the Vienna Philharmonic from 1992; Engagements with the Berlin Philharmonic from 1993; Principal Conductor, Danish National Radio Symphony Orchestra, 1995–; From 1995/6 season, engagements with London, Israel and Rotterdam Philharmonics and Pittsburgh, St Louis and Gothenburg Symphony Orchestras; Nielsen's Maskarade and Berg's Lulu with the Danish Radio Symphony Orchestra; Schubert Bicentenary concert in Copenhagen, 1997; Tristan, 1997 and Ring, 2001, in Graz; Rosenkavalier and Lulu at the Bastille in Paris; Professor of Music Analysis, Academy of Music, Hamburg. *Recordings include:* Capriccio, with Te Kanawa (Decca), Lulu (Chandos); Maskarade (2 Grammy nominations). *Address:* c/o Artists Management Zürich, Rütisstrasse 52, 8044 Zürich-Gockhausen, Switzerland.

SCHIRRER, René; Singer (Bass-baritone); b. 1957, France. *Education:* Studied in Strasbourg, Basle and Salzburg. *Career:* Sang with the Groupe Vocal de France and with Lyon Opéra from 1983; Edinburgh Festival, 1985; in Pelléas et Mélisande and Chabrier's Etoile; Aix-en-Provence, 1987 in Lully's Psyché, Karlsruhe, 1990, as Rangoni in Boris Godunov and Montreal, 1993 in Les Troyens; Herald in Lohengrin at Lyons, 1995; Appearances with Opéra du Rhin, Strasbourg, including title role in Honegger's Les Aventures du Roi Pausole, 1998; Other roles include Peter Quince, Zaccaria in Nabucco and Rossini's Basilio; Sang Gounod's Frère Laurent at Strasbourg and Indra in Le Roi de Lahore by Massenet at St Etienne, 1999–2000. *Recordings:* Le Roi Arthus by Chausson, Iphigénie in Aulide, Handel's Tamerlano and Leclair's Scylla et Glaucus. *Address:* Opéra du Rhin, 19 Place Broglie, 67008 Strasbourg Cédex, France.

SCHLAEPFER, Jean-Claude; Composer and Teacher; b. 11 Jan. 1961, Geneva, Switzerland. *Education:* Conservatoire supérieur du Musique, Geneva; Academy of Music, Paris with Betsy Jolas, Diplomas in Musical Education and Musical Culture. *Career:* Composer; Professor, Department of Harmony and Analysis at the Conservatoire supérieur de Musique; Professor, Department of Musical Languages, University of Geneva. *Compositions include:* 3 Caprices, for violin in memory of N Paganini, 1988; 5 Pieces for orchestra, in homage of Anton Webern, 1988; Impressions, 1988, debut by L'Ensemble Orchestral de Geneve, under the direction of Laurent Gay, Jan 1989; Dialogues, for violoncello, debut by Christian Secrétan, Istanbul, March 1989; Stabat Mater for soprano, choir and orchestra 1990, performed by L'Orchestre de la Suisse Romande and Le Choeur de La Psalette de Genève; Soloist, Naoko Okada, in Geneva, 1991; 7 Preludes for two pianos, debut at Lausanne in May 1991 by Denise Duport and Gui-Michel Caillat; Motets for soprano, harp and violin, de gambe, 1992; Three Dreams on poems by Georg Trakl for narrator, soprano, alto, wind quintet, string quartet, piano, 1992; Instanes II for solo horn for the International Competition of Music in Geneva, 1993; Visibili et Invisibili, 1994; La Rose de Jérico, 1995; L'Impossible Absence, 1995. *Recordings:* Impressions; Stabat Mater and 7 Preludes for two pianos, Radio Suisse Romande. *Address:* c/o SUISA, Bellabastrasse 82, CH–8038, Zürich, Switzerland.

SCHLEE, Thomas (Daniel); Composer, Organist and Festival Director; b. 26 Oct. 1957, Vienna, Austria; m. Claire Aniotz, 24 May 1986, 1 s., 1 d. *Education:* Theresianische Akademie Wien, Hochschule für Musik, Vienna; Composition and Organ, Conservatoire National Supérieur de Musique, Paris, France; University of Vienna: Dr phil, Musicology, History of Arts, Theresianische Akademie Wien, University of Vienna. *Career:* Many organ concerts, Europe, USA and former USSR; Participant, various international festivals; Music Dramaturg, Salzburger Landestheater, 1986–89; Teacher, Wiener Musikhochschule and University Salzburg, 1988–90; Artistic Director of the Bruckner Lall Linz and International Bruckner Festival, 1990–98; Project director of La Cite Céleste by the Guardini Foundation, Berlin; President of the Foundation from 1998–2001; Nominated Music Director of the Brucknerhaus Linz, Upper Austria, 1990; Vice-Director, International Beethoven Festival, Bonn, 1999; Nominated Director of Carinthian Summer Festival, Austria, 2004; mem. governing body of the Guardini Foundation. *Compositions:* Organ, vocal, instrumental and orchestral music; Edited Bärenreiter, Leduc, Lemoine, Choudens, Combre, Schola Cantorum Doblinger, Universal Edition, Billaudot, Butz, Schola Cantorum;. *Recordings:* Radio and television recordings, various European countries including: Messiaen at La Trinité; E Reuchsel. *Publications:* La Cité céleste–Olivier Messiaen, 1998. *Contributions:* Books: Ecrivains Français et l'Opéra (Legende de Tristan, Tournemire), 1986; Studien zur Wertungsforschung 20 ('Cinq Rechants' by Messiaen), 1988; Meilensteine der Musik, 1991; Numerous music journals; Editor, Universal Organ series; Almanach zum Internationalen Beethovenfest Bonn 1999, 2000; Les Solitudes de Jean Françaix, 2001. *Honours:* Chevalier des Arts et des Lettres, 1991; Joaquin Rodrigo Medal, 1997; Landeskulturpreis für Musik Oberösterreich, 1998; Kirchenmusikpreis der Staat Neuss, 2002; Förderungspreis des Österr. Bundeskanzleramtes, 2003. *Address:* Hofmühlgasse 7a/7, 1060 Vienna, Austria.

SCHLEMM, Anny; Singer (Mezzo-soprano); b. 22 Feb. 1929, Neu-Isenburg, Frankfurt, Germany. *Education:* Studied with Erna Westenberger in Berlin. *Career:* Sang at the Berlin Staatsoper and the Berlin Komische Oper from 1949; Cologne Opera 1950–51; Has sung at Frankfurt Opera from 1951; Guest appearances in Hamburg, Munich and Berlin; Glyndebourne 1954, as Zerlina; Bayreuth Festival 1978–86, as Mary in Der fliegende Holländer; Netherlands Opera Amsterdam 1978, Herodias and Clytemnestra; Cologne 1981, as the Kostelnicka in Jenůfa; Covent Garden debut 1984, Madelon in a new production of Andrea Chénier; Other roles include Susanna, Desdemona, the Marschallin, Octavian and Marenka in The Bartered Bride; Sang Clytemnestra in Elektra at Stuttgart, 1989; Modern repertoire has included Miranda in Martin's The Tempest, Europera I and II by Cage (premiere at Frankfurt 1987), Mumie in Reimann's Gespenstersonate and Mother in Cerha's Baal (Vienna 1992); Sang the Countess in The Queen of Spades for Opera Flanders (1999) and Mamma Lucia in Cavalleria Rusticana at Frankfurt, 2001. *Recordings:* Madama Butterfly, Pagliacci; Hansel und Gretel; Der fliegende Holländer from Bayreuth; Video of Andrea Chénier. *Address:* 6078 Neeu-Isenburg, Graf-Folke-Bernasotte, Str 12, Germany.

SCHLESINGER, John; Stage Director; b. 16 Feb. 1926, London, England. *Education:* Studied at Oxford. *Career:* Film Actor then Director; Associate Director of the National Theatre London; Debut as Opera Producer, Les Contes d'Hoffmann at Covent Garden, 1980; Staged Der Rosenkavalier at Covent Garden, 1984; Un Ballo in Maschera at the 1989 Salzburg Festival.

SCHLICK, Barbara; Singer (Soprano); b. 21 July 1943, Würzburg, Germany. *Education:* Musikhochschule Würzburg; Paul Lohmann in Wiesbaden; Further study in Essen. *Career:* Engaged by Adolf Scherbaum for his Baroque Ensemble in 1966; Concert engagements in Munich, Hamburg, Rome, Geneva, Paris, Prague, Leningrad and New York; Russian tour 1971 and tour of the USA and Canada with the Chamber Orchestra of Paul Kuentz in 1972; Tour of Israel and USA 1975–76 with the Monteverdi Choir under Jürgen Jürgens; Festival appearances in Aix, Paris, Berlin, Kassel and Herrenhausen; Sang at the Göttingen Handel Festival 1980, York Early Music Festival 1988, CPE Bach's Die Letzten Leiden; Further appearances at the Haydn series on South Bank with the Orchestra of the Age of Enlightenment and in Mozart's Requiem with the Amsterdam Baroque Orchestra; Repertoire includes Carissimi's Jephte; Vivaldi's Gloria; Passions and Cantatas by Bach; Handel's Messiah, Acis and Galatea and Caecilia Ode; Haydn's Creation and Seven Last Words, Mozart's Requiem and Stravinsky's Cantata; Songs by Dowland, Purcell, Handel, Scarlatti and Haydn. *Recordings include:* Gagliano's La Dafne; Bach's St Matthew Passion; Jephtha by Reinthaler; Hasse's Piramo e Tisbe; Handel's Giulio Cesare and Rosalinda. *Address:* Greingstrasse 9, 8700 Würzburg, Germany.

SCHMALFUSS, Peter; Pianist and Professor of Piano; b. 13 Jan. 1937, Berlin, Germany; m. Sylvia Heckendorn, 7 Mar 1966. *Education:* Staatliche Hochschule für Musik, Saarbrücken with Walter Gieseking,

Alexander Sellier, Adrian Aeschbacher; Studied with Wilhelm Kempff, Beethoven Seminary, Positano, Italy. *Career:* Appearances as soloist and with orchestras in over 40 countries since 1960; Premieres of contemporary works; Many concert tours to Asia and North Africa; Concerts and participation on many Music Festivals in 4 continents, China, 1989, South America, 1990, Canada and USA, 1992, Japan, 1993. *Recordings:* Works of R Schumann, Grieg, Chopin, Smetana, Szymanowski, Mozart, Beethoven, Debussy. *Publications:* Editor of educational literature for piano. *Honours:* Title, Honorary Professor of the State Institute of Education, Moscow, 1993.

SCHMECKENBECHER, Jochen; Singer (Baritone); b. 1967, Heidelberg, Germany. *Education:* Studied at Cologne with Kurt Moll. *Career:* Sang at Hagen Opera, 1990–93, as Mozart's Count and Dandini in Cenerentola; The Count in Lortzing's Wildschültz; Komische Oper Berlin from 1993 as Papegano, Silvio and Schaunard, and in Rimsky's The Tale of Tsar Saltan; Further engagements at Hamburg, Bonn, the Châtelet, Paris and Geneva Opera; Season 1997–98 with Papageno at Dallas Opera; Frequent concert appearances. *Address:* Komische Oper Berlin, Behrenstrasse 55–57, 10117 Berlin, Germany.

SCHMID, Benjamin; Violinist; b. 13 Sept. 1968, Vienna, Austria. *Education:* Music Universities, Salzburg, Vienna, Philadelphia; Diploma, Curtis Institute, Magister Artium, Salzburg. *Career:* Debut: Salzburg Festival, 1986; Over 500 concertos and recitals, St Petersburg Orchestra, Paris, London, Berlin, Vienna, in Europe, USA, Canada and Japan; Chamber music and violin solo recitals, radio and television appearances in Europe, USA and Canada; Professional Jazz Player; Repertory includes more than 50 concertos from Baroque to Contemporary music; The Three Great Cycles for violino-solo; Most of the important duo sonatas from 18th and Contemporary Music. *Recordings:* Concertos: All of Bach; 3 Mozart; Haydn C Major; Brahms D major; Violin concerto; Violin solo, Bach, 6 sonatas and partitas; Paganini; Ysaÿe, 6 sonatas, recitals; Brahms, Ravel, Kreisler solo recital. *Honours:* First prizes, Concours-Menuhin, Paris, 1985; Leopold Mozart, Augsburg, 1991; Carl-Flesch-International, 1992; Guest Professor, Hochschule Mozarteum, Salzburg, 1996–98. *Address:* Ziegelstadelstrasse 19A, 5026 Salzburg, Austria.

SCHMID, Patric (James); Artistic Director; b. 12 April 1944, Eagle Pass, Texas, USA. *Education:* San Francisco State College. *Career:* Founded Opera Rara 1970 and has given British Premieres in Stage and Concert Performances, including Donizetti's Maria di Rudenz, Maria Padilla, Rosmonda D'Inghilterra, Le Convenienze Teatrali, Francesca di Foix and La Romanziera; Mercadante's Orazi e Curiazi and Virginia, Offenbach's Robinson Crusoe, Pacini's Maria Tudor; World Premiere of Donizetti's Gabriella di Vergy, Belfast 1978, and Offenbach pasticcio Christopher Columbus, Belfast 1976. *Recordings:* Donizetti Ugo, Conte di Parigi, Maria Padilla, Emilia di Liverpool, L'Assedio di Calais; Robinson Crusoe and Christopher Columbus; 100 Years of Italian Opera, Anthology. *Contributions:* Opera Magazine. *Honours:* MRA Award; Best Opera Recording; Best Recording of the Year. *Address:* 25 Compton Terrace, London N1 2 UN, England.

SCHMID-LIENBACHER, Edith; Singer (Soprano); b. 1959, St Andra, Kartnen, Germany. *Education:* Studied at Klagenfurt and Vienna. *Career:* Vienna Volksoper from 1985, as Janáček's Vixen, Leila in Les Pêcheurs de perles and Lauretta in Gianni Schicchi; Bregenz, Aix and Salzburg Festivals, 1985, 1989, 1993; as Papagena in Die Zauberflöte; Sang Mozart's Susanna at Cologne, 1996; Other roles include Fortuna in Handel's Giustino, Despina, Adele in Die Fledermaus and Christel in Der Vogelhändler; Sang Mozart's Constanze at the Vienna Volksoper, 2001. *Recordings:* Die Zauberflöte. *Address:* c/o Wiener Volksoper, Wahringerstrasse 78, A–1090 Vienna, Austria.

SCHMIDT, Andreas; Singer (Baritone); b. 30 July 1960, Düsseldorf, Germany. *Education:* Studied in Düsseldorf with Ingeborg Reichelt and in Berlin with Dietrich Fischer-Dieskau. *Career:* Debut: Deutsche Oper Berlin 1984, as Malatesta in Don Pasquale; Has sung in Berlin as Guglielmo, Lortzing's Zar, Wolfram in Tannhäuser and the title role in the premiere of Oedipus by Wolfgang Rihm, 1987; Sang in the premiere of Henze's Das verratene Meer, May 1990; Covent Garden London from 1986, as Valentin and Guglielmo; Further appearances in Munich, Vienna, Paris, New York and Hamburg; Concert appearances in Israel, Europe and North and South America under Colin Davis, Carlo Maria Giulini, Abbado, Gardiner, Barenboim, Harnoncourt, Ozawa, Mazur, Wolfgang Sawallisch, Leonard Bernstein and Giuseppe Sinopoli; Season 1989–90 sang Mephistopheles in La Damnation de Faust at the Barbican Hall; Wolfram in Hamburg and the Herald in Lohengrin at Berlin; Papageno in concert with the London Classical Players at the Proms; Oliver in Capriccio at the Salzburg Festival; Other roles include Posa, Marcello, Mozart's Count, Hindemith's Mathis, Amfortas and Don Giovanni; Brahms Centenary concert at the Wigmore Hall, London, 1997; Beckmesser at the Berlin Staatsoper, 1998; Season 2000–01 as Wolfram at Hamburg, Kurwenal for the Berlin Staatsoper and

Beckmesser and Amfortas at Bayreuth; Premier of St Luke Passion by Rihm at Stuttgart, Amonasro in Berlin and the title role in the premiere of Celan by Peter Ruzicka, at the Dresden Semperoper. *Recordings include:* Brahms and Fauré Requiems; Des Knaben Wunderhorn by Mahler; St Matthew Passion; Tannhäuser; Faust; Die Frau ohne Schatten; Das Rheingold; Così fan tutte; Bach B minor Mass; St Matthew Passion by CPE Bach; Hansel and Gretel; Die Zauberflöte; Schubert Lieder. *Address:* c/o R & B Agentur, Plankengasse 7, A–1010 Vienna, Austria.

SCHMIDT, Anne-Sophie; Singer (Soprano); b. 1968, France. *Education:* Strasbourg Conservatoire. *Career:* Debut: Aminta in Mozart's Il Re Pastore and Fiordiligi at Marseille, 1990; Appearances in Figaro and Boris Godunov at the Opéra Bastille, and as Italian Singer in Capriccio at the Salzburg Festival; Berlin Staatsoper in Honegger's Jeann d'Arc au Bûcher, in Haydn's I Pescatrici at Toulouse, as Donna Elvira at Nancy and Poulenc's Blanche de la Force at Toronto: also seen at Savonlinna and the London Proms; Season 1995 as Mélisande at Marseilles, followed by performances at the Paris Châtelet, Turin, Bucharest and Bologna; Further engagements in Werther, opposite Alfredo Kraus, at Seville, and concerts with leading European orchestras; Sang Susanna at Compiègne (1997) and Poulenc's La Voix Humaine, 2000. *Recordings include:* Arias from operas by Gounod and Massenet and Mélodies by Satie (Harmonia Mundi). *Address:* c/o Musicglotz, 11, rue le Verrier, 75006 Paris, France.

SCHMIDT, Annerose; Pianist and Professor; b. 5 Oct. 1936, Wittenberg, Germany. *Education:* Studied with Hugo Steurer, Hochschule für Musik, Leipzig, 1953–58. *Career:* Debut: Wittenberg, 1945; Numerous engagements as Soloist with major orchestras including: Gewandhaus Orchestra, Leipzig; Dresden State Orchestra; Royal Philharmonic Orchestra, London; New Philharmonic Orchestra, London; Cleveland Orchestra; Chicago Symphony Orchestra; Tonhalle Orchestra, Zürich; Danish Radio Symphony Orchestra, Copenhagen; Concertgebouw Orchestra, Amsterdam; Residentie Orchestra, The Hague; NHK (Japan Broadcasting Orchestra) Symphony Orchestra, Tokyo; Many festival appearances including Salzburg, Holland, Prague Spring, Berlin, Dresden, Warsaw Autumn; Professor, Hochschule für Musik Berlin, 1986–; Television appearances include Beethoven's 5th Piano Concerto; Rector, Hanns Eisler Hochschule für Musik, Berlin, 1990–. *Recordings:* Many as soloist with orchestra and as recitalist. *Honours:* Diploma, International Chopin Competition, Warsaw, 1954; 1st Prize, International Robert Schumann Competition, Zwickau, 1956; Artist's Prize, 1961; National Prize, 1965; Gold Bart ók Medal, 1974. *Address:* Friedrich-Engels-Damm 131, Bad Saarow 75521, Germany.

SCHMIDT, Carl (Brandon); Professor of Music and Director of Graduate Studies; b. 20 Oct. 1941, Nashville, Tennessee, USA; m. Elizabeth Jane Kady, 25 June 1967, 2 s., 1 d. *Education:* AB, Stanford University, 1963; AM 1967, PhD 1973, Harvard University; Diploma, Fontainebleau School of Music, 1961; Conducting with Boulanger, Solfège-Dieudonné. *Career:* Debut: Conducting, Stanford, California 1963, London, 1971; Assistant Professor, Wabash College, 1970–73, Bryn Mawr College 1973–79; Professor, The University of the Arts, 1978–. *Publications:* Antonio Cesti: Il Pomo d'oro (Music for Acts III and V from Modena, Biblioteca Estense, Ms Mus E 120), Recent Researches in the Music of The Baroque Era, Vol. 42, 1982; A Catalogue raisonné of the Literary Sources for the Tragédies Lyriques of Jean-Baptiste Lully; General Editor, Jean-Baptiste Lully: The Collected Works; The Music of Francis Poulenc (1899–1963): A Catalogue; Jean-Baptiste Lully: Actes du colloque/Kongressbericht; The New Grove Dictionary of Opera, 1992; Journal of Musicology. *Address:* 250 South Broad Street, Philadelphia, PA 19120, USA.

SCHMIDT, Emma; Pianist; b. 8 Feb. 1944, Vienna, Austria; m., 1 s. *Education:* Master degree, Hochschule für Musik, Graz, Austria; Masterclasses, Salzburg and Siena. *Career:* Teacher; College of Music, Graz and Hannover; Soloist in Austria, Portugal, South America, Germany and Italy; Recitals and chamber music in Vienna, Salzburg, London, Berlin, Hamburg, Düsseldorf, Hannover, Brussels, Warsaw, Belgrade, Segovia, Zagreb, Moscow, Rome, Milan, Turin and Florence; Several tours in Hong Kong and Korea; Radio productions across the world; Television concerts. *Recordings include:* La Ricordanza by Carl Czerny; George Gershwin's Rhapsody in Blue and 3 Preludes; Leoš Janáček, Piano Sonata and On the Overgrown Path I; Scott Joplin, Ragtimes; Alfred Schnittke, Concerto for Piano; Erwin Schulhoff's Concerto for piano; Franz Schubert, Winterreise; Smetana, Bohemian Dances; Alexandre Tansman, Sonatine Transatlantique; P I Tchaikovsky, Piano Trio. *Honours:* Bösendorfer Prize, Vienna, 1969; First prize, Vittorio Gui Chamber Music Competition, Florence, 1979. *Address:* Scheibengasse 14, 1190 Vienna, Austria.

SCHMIDT, Erika; Singer (Soprano); b. 12 Jan. 1913, Quirnheim, Germany. *Education:* Studied in Frankfurt. *Career:* Sang at Frankfurt 1935–67 in operas by Mozart, Weber, Verdi, Strauss and Wagner; Guest appearances throughout Germany; Paris Opéra 1941; Holland Festival 1958, Von Heute auf Morgen by Schoenberg, conducted by Hans Rosbaud; Glyndebourne Festival 1965, as the Marschallin; Lieder recitals; Oratorio performances. *Address:* Staatliche Hochschule für Musik, Escherheimer Landstrasse 33, Postfach 2326, Frankfurt, Germany.

SCHMIDT, Hansjürgen; Composer; b. 26 Aug. 1935, Jena-Burgau, Germany; m. Annemarie Illig, 11 July 1959, 2 s. *Education:* Studied Philosophy at Friedrich-Schiller University, Jena; Musical Theory, Franz Liszt Hochschule Weimar, 1968; Diploma as Composer; MMus, Akademie der Künste Berlin, 1979. *Career:* Freelance composer in Jena from 1970; Lectureship in Theory of Music in Weimar, 1986–87; Lectureship at Volkshochschule in Erlangen since 1990; mem, Union of Composers, Thüringen. *Compositions:* Winterpastorale, 1976; Streichquartett II, 1979; Schwanengesang, 1983; Nachtstück and Toccata, 1987; Sinfonie III, 1989. *Recordings:* Nachtstück and Toccata, 1995; Chthulu Suite; Schütz-Fantasie, electronic music. *Honours:* Kunstpreis of the District of Gera, 1980. *Address:* Siedlung Sonnenblick 1, 07749 Jena, Germany.

SCHMIDT, Manfred; Singer (Tenor); b. 27 June 1928, Berlin, Germany. *Education:* Studied with Jean Nadolovitch and with Herbert Brauer in Berlin. *Career:* Concert Singer from 1956; Many Radio Concerts; From the Bielefeld Opera moved to Cologne 1965, singing Ernesto, Ottavio, Tamino, Almaviva and other lyric roles; Sang at the Festivals of Salzburg, Holland, Perugia, Flanders and Prague; Guest appearances in London, Paris and Milan. *Recordings include:* Opera excerpts. *Address:* c/o Musikhochschule Berlin, Ernst-Feuter-Platz 10, D–10587 Berlin, Germany.

SCHMIDT, Ole; Conductor and Composer; b. 14 July 1928, Copenhagen, Denmark. *Education:* Royal Academy of Music, Copenhagen; Conducting studies abroad with Albert Wolff, Sergiu Celibidache, Rafael Kubelik. *Career:* First compositions played while at university, notably ballet Behind the Curtain, Royal Theatre Copenhagen; Conductor, Royal Danish Opera and Ballet, 1959–65; Principal Conductor, Danish Radio Orchestra, 1971; Artistic Director, Principal Conductor, Århus Symphony Orchestra, 1979–85; Guest, major European orchestras; Often with London Symphony, notably Brian's Gothic Symphony, 1980; Prom with Philharmonia; BBC Symphony debut, 1977, since conducting all BBC regional orchestras; Royal Liverpool Philharmonic and Hallé debuts, 1978; US debut, 1980, Oakland Symphony; Many modern Danish music performances in Europe; Chief Guest Conductor, Royal Northern College of Music, 1986–89; Interim Chief Conductor, Musical Adviser, Toledo Symphony, Ohio, 1989–; 1st production in Czech in England of Janáček's From the House of the Dead, Royal Northern College of Music, 1989. *Compositions:* Ballets: Fever, Behind the Curtain, Ballet in D; Opera Exhibition; 2 Symphonies, 1955, 1958; Concertos, Horn, Trumpet, Trombone, Flute, Piano, Accordion, Violin, Tuba, Guitar; 6 String Quartets, 1966–97; Music for the silent film by Carl Dreyer, The Passion of Joan of Arc, 1983; Millennium Fanfare 2000 for military band, 1999. *Recordings:* Complete symphonies of Nielsen with London Symphony Orchestra; Bentzon Symphonies 3–7, Piano Concerto No. 4, Flute Concerto No. 2, 5 Mobiles for orchestra; Sibelius Finlandia, Karelia Suite and Violin Concerto with the Hallé; Langgard Symphony No. 6, 10 and Antichrist. *Address:* Mariot, Gazax et Bacarrisse, 32230 Marciac, France.

SCHMIDT, Peter-Jurgen; Singer (Tenor); b. 25 Jan. 1941, Meiningen, Germany. *Education:* Studied in Weimar. *Career:* Debut: Weimar 1968, as Oberto in Alcina; Sang at Weimar until 1980, Staatsoper Berlin from 1981, notably in 1989 premiere of Graf Mirabeau by Siegfried Matthus; Guest appearances in concert and opera at London, Oslo, Linz, Salzburg, Graz and Germany, Japan and Korea; Schwetzinger Festival 1989, as Bacchus in Ariadne auf Naxos; Other roles include Don José, Hoffmann, Radames, Walther Von Stolzing, Lohengrin and Laca in Jenůfa; Season 1999–2000 at Chemnitz and the Brooklyn Academy of Music in the premiere production of Weill's The Eternal Road. *Recordings include:* Levins Muhle by Udo Zimmermann and Graf Mirabeau. *Address:* c/o Staatsoper Berlin, Unter Den Linden 7, 1086 Berlin, Germany.

SCHMIDT, Werner Albert; Composer and Educator; b. 29 July 1925, Bad Kissingen, Germany. *Education:* Studied Philosophy with Ernesto Grassi; Musicology and old German Language and Literature, University of Munich, graduated 1969; Conducting and Composition under Hans Rosbaud, Joseph Haas and Karl Höller, Academy of Music, Munich, 1946–50; Masterclass Diploma in Composition, 1950; Pedagogic State Examination, State Academy of Music, Munich, 1972; Further studies with Carl Orff, Karl A Hartmann (composition) and Kurt Eichhorn (conducting); PhD. *Career:* Freelance Composer in Munich (Musica Viva, Munich, 1954); Worked as Pianist with symphony and jazz orchestras; Music Teacher, Grammar School and Junior Music School in Wangen/Allgau; Head of City Orchestra; Teacher of Music

Theory, 1975–91, Professor, 1980–92, State Academy of Music, Mannheim; mem, Several professional organizations; Deutsche Johan-Strauá Gesellschaft. *Compositions include:* Kassation, for strings, 1947; Partita, for piano, 1948; Sonata per il pianoforte, 1949; Sonate, Das Ballett, for violin and piano, 1950; Tollhausballade, for speaker and chamber orchestra, 1952, new edition without speaker, 1956; Tre Pezzi drammatici per archi, 1953–54; Symphony 'Aufstand der Massen' (Praeludium und Toccata) for large orchestra, 1953–55; Concerto grosso, for jazz combo and wind ensemble, 1955–56; Hieroglyphik, for large orchestra, 1956–57; Faszination, music for a filmic ballet, for 2 percussionists, 1957; Positiv-Negativ-Synthesis, for 4 instrumental respect vocal groups, 1958; Apokalypsis, for large orchestra, speaker and 6 vocalists, 1982–86. *Publications:* Theorie der Induktion, 1974. *Honours:* Achievement Awards, Bavarian Academy of Fine Arts, Munich; Composition Prize, Competition of German Composers' Association. *Address:* Herzogstr 20, 68723 Schwetzingen, Germany.

SCHMIDT, Wolfgang; Singer (Tenor); b. 1955, Kassel, Germany. *Education:* Studied at the Frankfurt Musikochschule. *Career:* Sang first with the Pocket Oper Nuremburg, then at the Court Theatre Bayreuth, 1982–84; Kiel 1984–86; Dortmund from 1986, notably as Otello and as Siegfried in Wagner's Opera; Appearances at the Eutin Festival 1983–87, as Tamino, Max and Huon in Oberon; Bregenz Festival 1989, as Erik in Fliegende Holländer; Bayreuth 1992, as Tannhäuser; Further engagements at Essen, Karlsruhe, Hanover, Stuttgart; Sang First Armed Man in Die Zauberflöte at the 1991 Salzburg Festival; Tristan at the Opéra Bastille, Paris, 1998; Season 1999 as Siegfried at San Francisco, Loge, Siegmund and Siegfried in Hannover; Walther and Florestan for the Deutsche Oper am Rhein; Siegfried and Siegmund at the Berlin Staatsoper and Cologne, 2000; Sang Siegfried at the 2002 Bayreuth Festival; Concert Repertoire includes the Missa Solemnis with appearances in Mexico City, Parma, Prague. *Recordings include:* Die Zauberflöte; Weill's Lindberghflug. *Address:* c/o Opernhaus Kuhstrasse 12, 4600 Dortmund, Germany.

SCHMIEGE, Marilyn; Singer (Mezzo-soprano); b. 1955, Milwaukee, Wisconsin, USA. *Education:* Studied at Valparaiso University, BMus; MMus at Boston University; Further study at the Zürich Opera Studio. *Career:* Debut: Wuppertal as Dorabella, 1978; Theater am Gärtnerplatz, Munich as Cherubino, Rosina, Hänsel, Orlovsky, 1978–82; Teatro La Fenice, Venice, 1981; Aix-en Provence as Zaide in Il Turco in Italia, 1982; Munich Radio 1982 as Dido by Jan Novák conducted by Kubelik, 1982; Düsseldorf as Cherubino, 1983; La Scala title role in Orfeo by Rossi, 1983; Vienna Staatsoper debut as Rosina, later as Octavian, the Composer, 1985; Stuttgart as Charlotte in Werther, later as Lady Macbeth of Mtensk, Marguerite in Berlioz's Damnation de Faust, 1985; Aldeburgh Festival in Das Lied von der Erde, 1985; Hamburg Staatsoper as the Composer and Rosina, 1985, later as Venus in Tannhäuser; Dresden Staatsoper as the Composer, Octavian, 1986, later as Kundry; New York Philharmonic with Novák's Dido, 1986; Cologne as Lady Macbeth, 1988; Munich Staatsoper Octavian, 1988 later as Cherubino, Jeanne d'Arc, Silla in Palestrina, Dorabella, Venus, 1991; Carmen at Berlin Komische Opera, 1991; Judith in Berlin Schauspielhaus, 1993; Amsterdam as Marie in Wozzeck and at the Paris Châtelet as Waltraute in Götterdämmerung, 1994; Sang Marie in Wozzeck at Catania, 1996; Kundry in Parsifal for Nationale Reisopera, Netherlands, 1998; Season 1999–2000 as Countess Geschwitz in Lulu at Liège and Sieglinde for the Vienna Staatsoper. *Recordings include:* Vivaldi's Catone in Utica, Galuppi's La Caduta d'Adamo; Haydn Cantatas and Orfeo ed Euridice; Cherubino in Mozart's Figaro, directed by Colin Davis; Dido by Novák, directed by Kubelik; Schreker Die Gezeichneten; Mélodies of Gabriel Fauré, 1994.

SCHNAPKA, Georg; Singer (Bass); b. 27 May 1932, Schlesisch Ostrau, Czechoslovakia; m. Elisabeth Schwarzenberg. *Education:* Studied at the Bruckner Conservatory Linz with Andreas Sotzkov. *Career:* Debut: Heidelberg 1954, as Repela in Wolf's Der Corregidor; Sang 1964–85 at the Vienna Volksoper in the buffo repertory, also appeared with the Vienna Staatsoper; Guest appearances in Hamburg, Munich, Stuttgart, Saarbrucken, Düsseldorf, Wuppertal, Cologne and Frankfurt; Further engagements in Florence (Maggio Musicale), Venice, Amsterdam, Strasbourg, Lisbon, Bucharest and Zürich; American centres include New York City Opera, Baltimore and Washington DC; Main roles have included Philip II in Don Carlos, Daland, Fafner, Hunding, Sarastro, Pimen, Osmin, Leporello, Nicolai's Falstaff, Baron Ochs and Rossini's Bartolo; Many concert engagements. *Address:* Opernhaus, Kuhstrasse 12, 4600 Dortmund, Germany.

SCHNAUT, Gabriele; Singer (Mezzo-soprano, Soprano); b. 24 Feb. 1951, Mannheim, Germany. *Education:* Studied in Frankfurt with Elsa Cavelti, in Darmstadt with Aga Zah-Landzettel and in Berlin with Hannelore Kuhse. *Career:* Sang in Stuttgart from 1976; Darmstadt, 1978–80; Member of the Mannheim Opera from 1980; Bayreuth Festival from 1977, as Waltraute, Venus and Sieglinde, Chicago 1983, as Fricka in a concert performance of Die Walküre; Dortmund 1985, as Isolde; Has sung at Stuttgart, Frankfurt, Hamburg, Barcelona, Rome and Warsaw; Covent Garden debut 1989, as Sieglinde in a new production of Die Walküre conducted by Bernard Haitink; Sang in Düsseldorf and Hamburg 1989, as Lady Macbeth and Els in Schreker's Der Schatzgräber; Brünnhilde in Die Walküre at Cologne, 1990; Bayreuth 1987–89, as Ortrud in Lohengrin; Sang Isolde at San Francisco, 1991, Elektra at the Opéra Bastille, Paris, 1992; Sang the Walküre Brünnhilde at the 1997 Munich Festival, Isolde at Catania, 1996; Other roles include Octavian, Sextus (La Clemenza di Tito), Dorabella, Carmen, Brangaene, Kundry and Marie in Wozzeck; Season 1998 as Isolde at Cologne and 1999 as Elsa at Bayreuth; Sang Isolde at Covent Garden, 2000; Season 2001–02 as Isolde at Amsterdam, Turandot at the Vienna Staatsoper and Brünnhilde in new productions of Die Walküre and Siegfried at the Munich Staatsoper. *Recordings include:* St Matthew Passion by Bach; Sancta Susanna and Lieder by Hindemith. *Address:* c/o Theateragentur Dr G. Hilbert, Maximillian-Strasse 22, D–80539 München, Germany.

SCHNEBEL, Dieter; Composer; b. 14 March 1930, Lahr, Germany. *Education:* Studied at the Freiburg Hochschule für Musik, at Darmstadt and the University of Thubingen, 1952–56. *Career:* Active in the Lutheran Church, from 1976; Professor of Experimental Music and Musicology at the Berlin Hochschule für Musik; Work with the experimental theatre group Die Maulwerker, from 1978; Collaborations with Director Achim Freyer on Maulwerke and Cage-up. *Compositions include:* Music Theatre Maulwerke, 1968–74, Laut-Gesten-Laute, Zeichen-Sprache and St Jago (Music and pictures on Kleist 1989–91); Orchestral, Compositio 1956, revised 1964; Webern Variations 1972; Canones, 1975; In motu proprio, 1975; Diapason, 1977; Orchestra, 1977; Schubert-Phantasie, 1978; Wagner-Idyll, 1980; Thanatos-Eros, 1982; Sinfonie-Stucke, 1985; Beethoven-Sinfonie, 1985; Mahler Moment for strings, 1985; Raumklang X, 1988; Chamber, Reactions, 1961; Visable Music I, 1961; Nostalgie for Conductor, 1962; Espressivo, music drama for pianist, 1963; Concert sans orchestre for piano and audience, 1964; Ansclage-auschlage, 1966; Quintet, 1977; Pan for flute, 1978; Monotonien for piano and electronics, 1989; Vocal, Fur Stimmen (... missa est) for chorus, 1961; Glossolalie 61, 1961; Bach-Contrapuncti for chorus, 1976; Jowaegerli for 2 speakers, voices and chamber ensemble, 1983; Lieder ohne Worte, 1980–86; Missa Dahlemer Messe, 1984–87; Sinfonie X for orchestra, 1992; Majakowskis Tod, chamber opera, 1987; Totentantz, ballet-oratorio, 1989–94; Motetus II for two choruses, 1997; Ekstasis for soprano, chorus and orchestra, 1997; Museumstücke I/II for mobile voices and instruments; Produktionprozesse series, 1968–75; Graphic works including mo-no: Musik Zum Lesen, 1969. *Publications include:* Study of Stockhausen's early works: Mauricio Kagel, Cologne, 1970; Denkbare Musik: Schriften 1952–72, Cologne, 1972; Anschläge-Ausschläge, Essays, 1993. *Address:* Hektorstr. 15, 10711 Berlin, Germany.

SCHNEEBERGER, Hansheins; Violinist; b. 16 Oct. 1926, Berne, Switzerland. *Education:* Studied at the Berne Conservatory, with Carl Flesch in Lucerne and with Boris Kamensky. *Career:* Debut: 1946, in the Swiss premiere of Bart ók's Second Violin Concerto; Teacher at the Biel Conservatory, 1948–58; Basle Musikakademie, 1961–91; Leader of String Quartet, 1952–59, and the North German Symphony Orchestra, Hamburg; Premieres of Martin's Violin Concerto and Bart ók's First concerto (1952, 1958, with Paul Sacher); Further performances of music by Klaus Huber, Heinz Holliger and Elliott Carter. *Recordings include:* Schumann Sonatas and concerto; Bach Sonatas and Partitas for solo violin, Bartók Sonata for solo violin. *Address:* c/o Basle Musikakademie, Leonhardsstrasse 6, 4501 Basle, Switzerland.

SCHNEIDER, David E.; Musicologist and Clarinettist; b. 14 June 1963, Berkeley, California, USA; m. Klára Móricz 1994. *Education:* AB cum laude, Harvard University, 1985; MA, 1990, PhD, 1997, University of California at Berkeley; Private Clarinet studies with Donald Carrol, Leon Russianoff, Pasquale Cardillo, Greg Smith and Robert Marcellus; Chamber Music study with Nancy Garniez, Leon Kirchner and György Kurtag. *Career:* Member, Alaria Chamber Ensemble, New York City, 1986–88; Valentine Professor of Music, Amherst College, Amherst, Massachusetts, 1997–; mem, American Musicological Society. *Recordings:* Copland Clarinet Concerto, 1988. *Publications:* Bartók and Stravinsky, 1995; The Culmination Point as a Fulcrum Between Analysis and Interpretation, 1996; Expression in the Time of Objectivity: Nationality and Modernity in Five Concertos by Béla Bartók, PhD dissertation; A Context for Béla Bartók on the Eve of World War II, 1997. *Honours:* American Musicological Society 50 Fellowship, 1996. *Address:* Amherst College, Box 2258 Music, Amherst, MA 01002-5000, USA. *E-mail:* deschneider@amherst.edu.

SCHNEIDER, Gary M.; Conductor and Composer; b. 1950, USA. *Career:* Founder, Music Director and Principal Conductor of the Hoboken Chamber Orchestra; Debut in Europe at the International Zelt Musik Festival in Freiburg; New York debut with the American Composers Orchestra performing his Concerto for Jazz Clarinet and Orchestra; Has

also conducted the Chamber Symphony of Princeton, and the New York Festival Orchestra; Artist-in-Residence at Denison University, Ohio and Composer-in-Residence at the Rockport (Massachusetts) Chamber Music Festival. *Compositions include:* Sonata for solo cello, 1976; String Quartet, 1977; Study for a Ballet, for piano, 1981; Piano Sonata, 1989; Nocturne for bassoon and strings, 1988; The Bremen Town Musicians, 1989; The Tell-Tale Heart and The Voice of Eternity for soloists and ensemble. *Publications:* compositions have been published by leading publishers. *Address:* c/o ASCAP, ASCAP Building, 1 Lincoln Plaza, New York, NY 10023, USA.

SCHNEIDER, Gundula; Singer (mezzo-soprano); b. 1965, Dresden, Germany. *Education:* Studied in Karlsrule and at Dresden Music Academy; Masterclasses with Brigitte Fassbaender and Sena Jurinac. *Career:* Appearances from 1997 with Dortmund Opera as Carmen, the Composer in Ariadne auf Naxos, Hansel, and Orlovsky in Die Fledermaus; Guest engagements in Dresden, Strasbourg and the Komische Oper Berlin as Annio in La Clemenza di Tito; Cherubino at Dusseldorf and Bellini's Adalgisa at Kassel; Festival engagements at the Dresdner Musikfestspiele and Rossini Festspiele Bad Wildbad; Recitals at the Paris Opéra-Comique, Liederhalle Stuttgart and Carnegie Hall, New York. *Current Management:* Athole Still International Management, Forresters Hall, 25–27 Westow Street, London, SE19 3RY, England. *Telephone:* (20) 8771-5271. *Fax:* (20) 8768-6600. *Website:* www.atholestill.com.

SCHNEIDER, Peter; Conductor; b. 26 March 1939, Vienna, Austria. *Education:* Academy for Music and Dramatic Art, Vienna; conducting with Hans Swarowsky. *Career:* Sang with the Wiener Sängerknaben as a boy; Head of Studies at the Landestheater Salzburg from 1959 (conducting debut with Handel's Giulio Cesare); Principal Conductor in Heidleberg, 1961, Deutsche Oper am Rhein, Düsseldorf, from 1968; Performances of operas by Janáček, Berg, Wagner, Mozart, Verdi and Dallapiccola; Guest Conductor in Warsaw, Florence and Edinburgh; Music Director in Bremen 1978–85, Mannheim 1985–87; Bayreuth Festival from 1981; Der fliegende Holländer, Der Ring des Nibelungen and Lohengrin; Conducted the Vienna Opera in Der Rosenkavalier on its 1986 tour of Japan, and the Vienna Philharmonic at the Salzburg Festival; Further appearances as a Conductor of opera in Vienna, Berlin, London, Bologna, Barcelona and Madrid; Concerts in San Francisco; Die Soldaten by Zimmermann at the Vienna Staatsoper, 1990; Conducted Tristan und Isolde in Japan 1990 and San Francisco, 1991; Music Director of the Bavarian State Opera, Munich, 1993; Led Walküre and Meistersinger at the 1997 Munich Festival; Lohengrin at Barcelona, 2000. *Current Management:* Ingpen & Williams Ltd, 7 St George's Court, 131 Putney Bridge Road, London, SW15 2PA, England.

SCHNEIDER, Urs; Conductor and Music Director; b. 16 May 1939, St Gallen, Switzerland. *Education:* Violin Diploma, Zürich Conservatory; Conducting with Rafael Kubelik, Igor Markevitch, Otto Klemperer. *Career:* Debut: With own orchestras at age 15; Founder, Conductor, Artistic Director, Ostschweizer Kammerorchester, Camerata Helvetica; Guest Conductor, USA; Music Director, Camerata Stuttgart; Music Director, Camerata Academica Salzburg; Chief Conductor, Music Director, Haifa Symphony Orchestra; Concerts, operas, radio and television; Guest Conductor, numerous major orchestras and Opera Houses all over the 5 continents; Over 3500 performances in 70 countries; Member, Jury of the Concours des Jeunes Chefs d'Orchestre, Festival International de Besançon; Jury of Conductors' Competition, Silvestri, Bucharest; Principal Conductor, Artistic Director, National Taiwan Philharmonic Orchestra; First Guest Conductor of Prague Chamber Soloists; mem, Swiss Musicians Association; Schweiz Berufsdirigenten Verband. *Recordings:* 50 records. *Honours:* Cultural Prize, City of St Gallen. *Address:* Gattestrasse 1B, 9010 St Gallen, Switzerland. *Telephone:* 4171 2223980. *Fax:* 4171 2223889. *E-mail:* urs .schneider.conductor@freesurf.ch.

SCHNEIDER, Victoria, BM, MM; opera and concert singer (soprano); b. 28 Oct. 1952, Reading, PA, USA; m. Riccardo Malipiero 1988 (deceased). *Education:* Eastman School of Music, Rochester, NY. *Career:* debut Staatsoper Stuttgart, Germany 1981; regular collaboration with Staatsoper Stuttgart and many concert appearances throughout Germany 1981–85, increased activity, Italy 1984–; appearances at Teatro alla Scala, Milan, Teatro Comunale di Bologna, Teatro dell'Opera di Roma, Teatro dell'Opera di Genova; many concerts with major Italian orchestras, Santa Cecilia, Rome, with Radio Orchestras (RAI) of Milan, Turin, Naples; Festival Wien Modern 1992; Paris debut at Théâtre du Châtelet 1993; Berg's Altenberg-Lieder and Der Wein with Staatsorchester Saarbrücken 1995; engagement with Frankfurt Opera 2000; concert repertoire ranges from baroque to contemporary, including Handel's Messiah, Beethoven's Mass in C Major and Missa Solemnis, Mozart's Mass in C Minor, Mahler's Kindertotenlieder, many Strauss Orchesterlieder, Wagner's Wesendoncklieder, Berg's Sieben Frühe Lieder, Shostakovich's Seven Lyrics of Alexander Blok, Dallapiccola's An Mathilde and Commiato; many world premieres with works by R. Malipiero, S. Sciarrino, Donatoni, Gentilucci, Guarnieri and others; numerous concerts, including Schoenberg's op 10 with Arditti String Quartet 1989, Elliott Carter with the Ensemble Contrechamps and the Nieuw Ensemble 1998, 1999, Shostakovich and Beethoven with the Ensemble Recherche 1999–2000, Bach with the Orchestra Sinfonica Abruzzese 2000, Verdi and Schoenberg with the Quartetto di Fiesole 2001. *Radio recordings include:* Vara Radio (Netherlands), Sud-deutscher Rundfunk (Stuttgart), Bayerischer Rundfunk (Munich), Radio Bremen, RSI (Lugano), Italian National Radio RAI. *Address:* Via Stradella 1, 20129 Milan, Italy.

SCHNEIDER-SIEMSSEN, Gunther; stage designer and set designer; b. 7 June 1926, Augsburg, Germany; m. Eva Mazar 1969; four c. *Education:* Akademie für Kunst, Munich. *Career:* film designer, 1946–51; Head Designer, Landestheater, Salzburg, 1951–54; Head Designer, Marionetten Theater, Salzburg, 1951–; State Theater, Bremen, 1954–; Designed Der Ring des Nibelungen at Covent Garden, 1962–64; Guest Designer numerous opera houses; Professor, Stage Design, International Summer Academy Fine Arts, Salzburg, 1968–87; Designer, Salzburg Festival, 1965–89; Designer, Easter Festival, 1967–89; Notable productions include Boris Godunov, Tristan und Isolde, Die Frau ohne Schatten and Berio's Un Re in Ascolto; Designer Met Opera New York and cities in USA, including the Ring in New York (also televised and recorded 1990); Stage Director in South Africa, USA, Germany, Austria and Slovenia, 1982–; President, Society of the Stage of the Future; Rotary. *Publications:* contrib. to professional journals. *Honours:* Fellow, MIT, USA, 1980–85. *Address:* 4 Schlickgasse, Vienna, Austria.

SCHNEIDERMAN, Helene; singer (mezzo-soprano); b. 1955, Fleming-ton, NJ, USA. *Education:* Westminster Choir Coll., Princeton, Univ. of Cincinnati Coll. *Career:* sang at Heidelberg Opera 1982–, Stuttgart 1984–, with guest appearances at Düsseldorf, Munich, Orlando and New York City Opera; season 1990 with the Rossini Festival at Pesaro and Smeaton in Anna Bolena at the Concertgebouw; other roles have included Monteverdi's Penelope Isabella, Carmen and Rosina at Stuttgart; Covent Garden season 1995–96, as Cherubino and Dorabella; appearances with conductors, including Bernard Haitink, Salzburg 1993, Bernstein, Arias and Barcarolles, Bonn, Solti, and Alberto Zedda, Pesaro; season 1998 with Cenerentola for New Israeli Opera. *Recordings include:* Copland's Eight Poems of Emily Dickinson. *Current Management:* Robert Gilder & Co., Enterprise House, 59–65 Upper Ground, London, SE1 9PQ, England. *Telephone:* (20) 7928-9008. *Fax:* (20) 7928-9755. *E-mail:* rgilder@robert-gilder.com.

SCHNITZLER, Michael; Violinist; b. 1940, California. *Education:* Studied in Vienna Music Academy. *Career:* Member and soloist in the chamber orchestra Wiener Solisten, 1963–67; First concertmaster of Vienna Symphony, over 1000 concerts, touring USA, Japan and Europe; Appearances as soloist under Giulini, Abbado, Sawallisch and Jochum; Performances of Haydn and other composers in Vienna and elsewhere from 1968; Co-Founder, The Haydn Trio of Vienna 1968 and has performed in Brussels, Munich, Berlin, Zürich, London, Rome, Paris; New York debut 1979 and has made frequent North American appearances with concerts in 25 States; Professor of Violin at Vienna Music University, 1983–; Debut tour of Japan, 1984 with further travels to the Near East, Russia, Africa, Central and South America; Series at the Vienna Konzerthaus Society from 1976, with performances of more than 100 works; Summer Festivals at Vienna, Salzburg, Axi-en-Provence, Flanders and Montreux; Masterclasses at the Royal College and Royal Academy of London, Stockholm, Bloomington, Tokyo and the Salzburg Mozarteum; Leader of Vienna Johann Strauss Orchestra, 2000–; Master classes at the University of Indiana, Bloomington, Eastman School, Rochester, Mozarteum, Salzburg, RAM, RCM, London, Sweden, Holland and Japan; Juror at international competitions in Vienna, Salzburg and Osaka. *Recordings:* Complete Piano Trios of Beethoven and Schubert, Mendelssohn D Minor, Brahms B Major, Tchaikovsky A Minor, Schubert Trout Quintet; Albums of Works by Haydn, Schumann, Dvořák and Smetana. *Address:* Sternwartestrasse 58, A-1180 Wien Austria.

SCHOLL, Andreas; Singer (countertenor); b. 10 Nov. 1967, Eltville Germany. *Education:* Kiedriche Chorbuben, as Choir Member; Schola Cantorum Basiliensis, with René Jacobs, 1987–93. *Career:* Debut: Paris recital, 1993; Concerts include Vivaldi's Stabat Mater with Ensemble 415 of Switzerland, Messiah with Les Arts Florissants at Aix, Bach's Christmas Oratorio and Masses, with Philippe Herreweghe, St John Passion in Berlin and B Minor Mass with the Stuttgart Kammerchor; London Prom Concerts, 1996, with Bach Magnificat and excerpts from Handel's Julius Caesar (Collegium Vocale); Other Festival Engagements at Versailles, Saintes, Santiago, Aix and Lucerne; Season 1997–98 with recitals at the Wigmore Hall, Cologne Philharmonie, Concertgebouw Amsterdam and the Sydney Festival; Tours with La Petite Bande (Bach Cantatas) the Gabrieli Consort (Handel's Solomon) and with Collegium Vocale to Europe and Japan; Sang Bertarido in

Handel's Rodelinda for the 1998 Glyndebourne Festival; Pergolesi's Stabat Mater at the 1999 London Proms; Handel's Saul on tour with the Gabrieli Ensemble, 2002. *Recordings:* Messiah with William Christie, Deutsches Barocklieder, Vivaldi Stabat Mater, English Lute and Folksongs, Caldara Maddalena ai peide di Cristo, Bach Christmas Oratorio and Cantatas; Handel's Solomon. *Honours:* Conseil de l'Europe and Foundation Claude Nicolas Ledoux, 1992. *Current Management:* Harrison/Parrott Ltd, 12 Penzance Place, London, W11 4PA, England. *Telephone:* (20) 7229 9166. *Fax:* (20) 7221 5042. *Website:* www.harrisonparrott.com.

SCHOLLUM, Benno; Singer (Baritone); b. 1953, Klagenfurt, Austria. *Education:* Studied at the Vienna Musikhochschule with Josef Greindl and with his father, Robert Schollum; Masterclasses in New York and Vienna with Sena Jurinac and others. *Career:* Has performed in Austria and elsewhere in operettas by Lehar, Johann Strauss, Milloecker and Offenbach; Operas by Mozart, Britten, Lortzing, Mascagni; Lieder by Loewe, Schubert, Wolf, Strauss, Grieg, Brahms and others; Oratorios include Schmidt's Das Buch mit Sieben Siegeln, the Brahms Requiem and Cantatas and Masses by Bach and Mozart; Festival appearances at Vienna, Antibes, Carinthian Summer and Gstaad; Guest Engagements in France, Yugoslavia, Italy, USA, South America, South Africa, Germany, Netherlands and Luxembourg; Berlin Philharmonic debut in Herbst by Antal Dorati; British debut, 1991 with the English Symphony Orchestra in Arias by Mozart; Stage roles include Papageno; Teacher at the Vienna Musikhochschule from 1983. *Recordings:* Schubert's Winterreise with Graham Johnson; Beethoven's Symphony No. 9 with Yehudi Menuhin. *Publications:* Sprecherziehung in der Praxis der Gesangsausbildung, 1993. *Honours:* MA, 1993. *Current Management:* Eleanor Hope, London. *Address:* 9 Southwood Hall, Wood Lane, London N6 5UF, England.

SCHOLZ, Andreas; Singer (Baritone); b. 14 Dec. 1964, Leipzig. *Education:* Felix Mendelssohn Musikhochschule, Leipzig, 1985–91. *Career:* Sang at Leipzig Opera from 1991, as Zuniga in Carmen, Schaunard, Guglielmo, Lortzing's Tsar Peter, Rossini's Figaro and Sander in Grétry's Zémire et Azore; Further appearances in Schoen-berg's Moses and Aron and Hiller's Der Jagd; Dresden Opera as the Constable in Strauss's Friedenstag; Soloist with the Leipzig Gewand-haus Orchestra; Further concerts in Munich and Berlin. *Honours:* Prizewinner at Competitions in Karlovy Vary and Berlin, 1990. *Address:* Oper Leipzig, Opernhaus Augustusplatz 12, 7010 Leipzig, Germany.

SCHOLZE, Rainer; Singer (Bass); b. 13 May 1940, Sudetenland Germany. *Education:* Studied at the Cologne Musikhochschule. *Career:* Sang in the Chorus of the Lübeck Stadt Theatre, 1962–66; Discovered by Gerd Albrecht and sang small roles; Studied further and sang solo at Lübeck from 1966–70; Engaged at Brunswick, 1970–71; Kassel, 1971–81; Appeared at Kiel 1981–83 and made guest outings to Munich, Dresden, Hamburg; Has often appeared in operas by Mozart, Rossini, Lortzing and notably as Baron Ochs. *Recordings include:* Masetto in Don Giovanni; Reinmar in Tannhäuser; Larkens in Fanciulla del West.

SCHOMBERG, Martin; Singer (Tenor); b. 7 Nov. 1944, Hoxter, Westfalen, Germany. *Education:* Studied at the Hamburg Musi-khochschule with Jakob St ämpfli. *Career:* Debut: Mainz 1972, as Lenski in Eugene Onegin; Many appearances at the Opera houses of Cologne, Hamburg, Düsseldorf; Zürich Opera in lyric roles and in the 1974 premiere of Ein Wahrer Held by Klebe; Concert engagements at the Salzburg Festival and elsewhere; Roles have included Mozart's Belmonte, Ottavio and Tamino, Nencio in Haydn's L'Infedeltà Delusa, Florindo in Le Donne Curiose by Wolf-Ferrari, the Italian Tenor in Rosenkavalier and Alfred in Fledermaus. *Address:* Opernhaus Zürich, Falkenstrasse 1, 8008 Zürich, Switzerland.

SCHONBACH, Dieter; Composer; b. 18 Feb. 1931, Stolp, Pomerania, Germany. *Education:* Studied in Detmold and Freiburg with Gunter Bialas and Wolfgang Fortner. *Career:* Music Director of the Bochum Schauspielhaus, 1959–73; Has also worked at theatres in Munster and Basle. *Compositions include:* Die Geschichte von einem Feuer, mixed-media show with puppet, 1970; Bedrohung und Uberleben, multimedia opera, Cologne, 1971; Hysteria-Paradies Schwarz, mixed-media show after The Tempest, Wiesbaden, 1971; Hymnus II-Morgen nach dem Feuer, mixed-media show, Munich, 1972; Come S Francesco, Munster, 1979; Divina Comedia (Dante), multimedia show, Düsseldorf, 1985; Barocke Prunkoper, Come Signori... nach Lully, 1985–87, Versailles; Reineke Fuchs, musiktheater nach Goethe, Baden-Baden, 1988; Barocke Prunkoper, Il Pomo D'oro, nach Cesti, Vienna, 1989; Fläche und Raum zur Musik, after Wassily Kandinsky, 1996; Farben und Klange, in memory of Kandinsky for orchestra, 1958; Piano Concerto, 1958; Canticum Psalmi Resurrectionis, 1959; Kammermusik for 14 instruments, 1964; Hoquetus for 8 wind instruments, 1964; Revised form of Così fan tutte by Mozart for 6 instruments, 1992; Cover over piano concerto by Mozart (K491) for great orchestra, 1999. *Honours:*

Joint Winner, Stamitz Prize of Stuttgart, 1972. *Address:* GEMA, Postfach 80 07 67, 81607 Munich, Germany.

SCHONBECK, Uwe; Singer (Tenor); b. 1961, Essen, Germany. *Education:* Studied at the Essen Musikhochschule. *Career:* Appearances at Krefeld Opera from 1985; Frankfurt 1990 and at the Deutsche Oper am Rhein at Düsseldorf; Geneva 1991 as Mime in The Ring, also at Frankfurt, 1995; Vienna Staatsoper, 1993 as Herod in Salome; Salzburg, 1994 as Sellem in The Rake's Progress; Munich 1996 as Billy II in the premiere of Bose's Slaughterhouse Five; Other roles include Arnalta in Monteverdi's Poppea; Rameau's Platée and Nemorino; Modern repertory includes Troades by Reimann; Judith by Matthus; Macbeth by Bibalo. *Recordings:* Stephen Climax by Hans Zender. *Address:* c/o Bavarian State Opera, Max-Joseph-Platz, 80530 Munich, Germany.

SCHONBERG, Stig Gustav; Composer and Organist; b. 13 May 1933, Vastra Husby, Sweden. *Education:* Studies, Stockholm Musikhogskolan, 1953–60 (composition studies with Lars-Eric Larsson, Karl-Birger Blomdahl); Organ studies with Flor Peeters, Belgium. *Career:* Freelance Composer with performances throughout Sweden; Many Concert Tours and Church Performances throughout Scandinavia, Europe, USA and Japan as Organist. *Compositions include:* Introduction and Allegro for strings, 1959; Concerto for organ and strings, 1962; Sinfonia Aperta, 1965; 3 Concertino for strings, 1966; Madeleine and Conrad, ballet, 1967; Fantasia for strings, 1967; String Quartets, 1961–84; Impromptu Visionario for orchestra, 1972; Flute Sonata, 1974; Concerto for 2 flutes and strings, 1976; Symphony No. 2, 1977; Pastoral for horn and organ, 1979; Concerto for organ and orchestra, 1982; Missa Coralis, 1983; Missa da Pacem, 1985; Concerto for organ and brass orchestra, 1987; Sonata alla ricercata for organ and violin, 1989; Bassoon Concerto, 1992; Te Deum for choir and strings, 1993; Gloria, 1994; Sinfonie III, 1996; Variations on a Swedish folktune for string orchestra, 1999; Prince Hat under the Earth, children's opera, 1999; Choruses; Songs. *Address:* c/o STIM, Sandhamnsgatan 79, PO Box 27327, 102 54 Stockholm, Sweden.

SCHÖNE, Wolfgang; Singer (Bass Baritone); b. 9 Feb. 1941, Bad Gandersheim, Germany. *Education:* Studied with Naan Pold in Hanover and Hamburg, Diploma in 1969. *Career:* Winner of awards from 1966 at Bordeaux, Berlin, Stuttgart and 's-Hertogenbosch; Concert tours and lieder recitals in Belgium, Netherlands, France, Denmark, USA, Mexico, Argentina and England; Appeared in film, The Chronicle of Anna Magdalena Bach; Opera career from 1970 at the State Operas of Stuttgart, Vienna and Hamburg, notably as Guglielmo, Wolfram and Count Eberbach in Der Wildschütz by Lortzing; Schwetzingen Festival 1983 as Tom, in the premiere of The English Cat by Henze; Komische Oper Berlin in 1984 as Golaud in Pelléas et Mélisande; Sang in the 1984 reopening of the Stuttgart Opera, as Don Giovanni; Season 1988–89 sang Gunther at Turin, Alidoro in Cenerentola at Salzburg and Barak at Cologne; Hamburg in 1990 as Wolfram; Sang Orestes and Pentheus in The Bassarids at Stuttgart in 1989; Sang Wolfram in Hamburg in 1990, the Count in Capriccio at 1990 Salzburg Festival, Dr Schön in Lulu at the Paris Châtelet, 1992; Amfortas in Parsifal at the Opéra Bastille, Paris, 1997; Gunther in Götterdämmerung for Netherlands Opera, 1998; Season 2000–01 as the Wanderer in Siegfried at Stuttgart, Prus in The Makropulos Case at Hamburg, Amfortas in the Albert Hall, London, Strauss's Barak in Barcelona and Marschner's Hans Heiling for the Deutsche Oper, Berlin; Hans Sachs at Hamburg, 2002. *Recordings:* Bach Cantatas; St Matthew Passion by Schütz; Theresienmesse by Haydn; Bach B minor Mass; Doktor und Apotheker by Dittersdorf; Giulio Cesare by Handel; Lulu; Video of Der Freischütz.

SCHØNWANDT, Michael; Conductor; b. 10 Sept. 1953, Copenhagen, Denmark; m. Amalie Malling, 23 Mar 1991. *Education:* BMus, Musicology, Copenhagen University, 1975; Conducting and Composition, Royal Academy of Music, London, England, 1975–77. *Career:* Debut: Copenhagen, 1977; Concerts throughout Europe, Debut Royal Danish Opera, 1979; Guest Conductor: Covent Garden, London, Paris Opéra, Wiener Staatsoper, Bayreuth Festival; Principal Guest Conductor, Théâtre Royal de la Monnaie, Brussels, 1984–87; Principal Conductor, Collegium Musicum, Copenhagen, 1981–; Principal Guest Conductor, Nice Opera, 1987–91; Danish Radio Symphony Orchestra, 1989–2000; Principal Conductor, Berliner Sinfonie Orchestra, 1992–98; Permanent Conductor, Vienna State Opera, 1990; Conducts regularly in London (Philharmonia, BBC), Paris, (Orchestre Philharmonique), Vienna, Berlin; Music Director Royal Danish Opera and Orchestra, 2000–. *Recordings:* More than 50 CDs include: Mozart Piano Concertos and Violin Concertos; Beethoven Piano Concertos; Niels W Gade Complete Symphonies; Kuhlau's Lulu, Complete Opera; Schoenberg and Sibelius Pelléas and Mélisande, Berlioz Requiem; Richard Strauss: Salome, complete opera; Weyse: Complete Symphonies; Nielsen: Complete Symphonies. *Honours:* Numerous Musical Prizes, Denmark; Knighthood from HM Queen of Denmark, 1997; Carl Nielsen Prize, 1997. *Current Management:* Ingpen & Williams Ltd, 7 St George's

Court, 131 Putney Bridge Road, London, SW15 2PA, England. *Address:* Svalevej 24, 2900, Hellerup, Denmark.

SCHOPPER, Michael; Singer (Bass-baritone); b. 1942, Passau, Germany. *Education:* Munich Musikhockschule. *Career:* Debut: Bach's Christmas Oratorio under Karl Richter, 1968; Many appearances in concerts and opera in the Baroque and classical repertory; In Europe and North and South America; Founded ensemble Musica Poetica, for performance of Renaissance and Baroque music, 1974; Sang Monteverdi's Seneca at Montpellier, 1989; and in Cavalli's Giasone at the Châtelet, Paris; Innsbruck Festival 1990–93 in Cesti's L'Orontea, as Sancho Panza in Conti's Don Chisciotte and Monteverdi's Seneca and Nettuno; Frankfurt, 1994 as Pfalzgrafen in Holzbauer's Gunther von Schwarzburg and Polyphemus in Handel's Acis and Galatea at Göttingen; Magdeburg, 1996 in the title role of Telemann's Der neumodische Liebhaber Damon. *Recordings:* Giulio Cesare and Bach cantatas; Bach Matthew Passion; Telemann's Pimpinone; Winterreise; Poppea and Stradella's San Giovanni Batista; Keiser's Masaniello Furioso; Gunther von Schwarzburg. *Address:* c/o Konzertbüro Andreas Braun, Sülzgürtl 86, D–50937 Köln, Germany.

SCHOTT, Howard (Mansfield); Musicologist and Harpsichordist; b. 17 June 1923, New York, NY, USA. *Education:* BA, 1943, JD, 1948, Yale University; DPhil (Oxon), 1978; Studied Applied Music at Mannes College, NY; Musicology with Barry Brook, Emanuel Winternitz, HC Robbins Landon, City University of New York, Leo Schrade, Yale, Joseph Kerman and John Caldwell at Oxford; Keyboard with Ralph Kirkpatrick at Yale and Hans Neumann at Mannes College; Composition with Richard Donovan and Luther Noss at Yale. *Career:* Lecturer at New England Conservatory, Boston, MA, 1988–; Lectures at Oxford, King's College London, Harvard, Yale (Sanford Fellowship), 1979), Cornell, Paris, and City University of New York; Consultant to Boston Early Music Festival, East Nakamichi Festival, also Victoria and Albert Museum and Metropolitan Museum of Art. *Publications:* Playing The Harpsichord, 1971, 3rd edition, 1979, Italian edition, 1982, German edition, 1983; Oeuvres Complètes De J J Froberger, 1980–; Editor, The Historical Harpsichord Series, 1984–; Catalogue of The Musical Instruments in The Victoria and Albert Museum, I: Keyboard Instruments, 1985. *Contributions:* Many articles in The New Grove Dictionary and New Harvard Dictionary of Music; Regularly to The Musical Times and to Early Music, including The Harpsichord Revival, and From Harpsichord to Pianoforte. *Address:* Brook House, Suite 402, 44 Washington Street, Brookline, MA 02146, USA.

SCHRANZ, Karoly; Violinist; b. 1950, Hungary. *Education:* Studied with András Mihaly at the Franz Liszt Academy in Budapest, with members of the Amadeus Quartet and Zoltán Szekely. *Career:* Founder Member of the Takacs Quartet, 1975; Many concert appearances in all major centres of Europe and USA; Tours of Australia, New Zealand, Japan, South America, England, Norway, Sweden, Greece, Belgium and Ireland; Resident at the London Barbican, 1988–91, with masterclasses at the Guildhall School of Music; Visits to Japan in 1989 and 1992; Bartók Cycle for the Bartók-Solti Festival at South Bank in 1990; Great Performers Series at Lincoln Center and Mostly Mozart Festival at Alice Tully Hall, NY; Appeared at Mozart Festivals at South Bank, Wigmore Hall and Barbican Centre in 1991; Bartók Cycle at the Théâtre des Champs Elysées in 1991, and Beethoven Cycles at the Zürich Tonhalle, in Dublin, at the Wigmore Hall and in Paris, 1991–92; Plays Amati instrument made for the French Royal Family and loaned by the Corcoran Gallery, Gallery of Art, Washington DC. *Recordings:* Schumann Quartets, Op 41; Mozart String Quintets, with Denes Koromzay; Bartók 6 Quartets; Schubert Trout Quintet, with Zoltán Kocsis; Haydn Op 76; Brahms Op 51, Nos 1 and 2; Chausson Concerto, with Joshua Bell and Jean-Yves Thibaudet; Works by Schubert, Mozart, Dvořák and Bartók. *Honours:* Winner, International Quartet Competition, Evian, 1977; Winner, Portsmouth International Quartet Competition, 1979. *Address:* c/o Phelps, Takacs Quartet, 6 Malvern Road, London, E8 3LT, England.

SCHREIBMAYER, Kurt; Singer (Tenor); b. 1953, Klagenfurt, Germany. *Education:* Studied at the Graz Musikhochschule. *Career:* Sang at Graz, 1976–78, then at the Vienna Volksoper; Further appearances at the Theater am Gartnerplatz Munich, 1987–88, Deutsche Oper am Rhein Düsseldorf from 1987, Hamburg Staatsoper and the Zürich Opera; Théâtre Royal de la Monnaie, Brussels from 1987 as Steva in Jenůfa and Luka in From The House of the Dead in 1990; Bayreuth Festival engagements, 1986–90, as Froh, Walter von der Vogelweide and Parsifal; Returned to Vienna Volksoper in 1988 as Max in Der Freischütz; Has sung at Liège as Lohengrin, 1988–89; Other roles include Fra Diavalo, Babinsky in Shvanda the Bagpiper, Pedro in Tiefland, Gomez in Die drei Pintos, Wenzel in Zemlinsky's Kleider Machen Leute, and parts in operettas; Sang in Mona Lisa by Max von Schillings at the Vienna Volksoper, 1996 and Dimitri in Boris Godunov, 1998; Season 2000 as Shuisky in Boris Godunov and Zemlinsky's König

Kandaules at the Vienna Volksoper, Siegmund in Graz. *Address:* c/o Théâtre Royal de la Monnaie, 4 Leopoldstrasse, 1000 Brussels, Belgium.

SCHREIER, Peter; Singer (tenor) and Conductor; b. 29 July 1935, Gauernitz, Near Meissen, Germany. *Education:* Sang in Dresden Kreuzchor as a child then studied with Polster in Leipzig and with Winkler at the Dresden Musikhochschule, 1956–59. *Career:* Debut: Dresden Staatsoper in 1961 as First Prisoner in Fidelio; Lyric tenor at the Staatsoper Berlin and in Hamburg, Vienna, London and Munich in operas by Mozart, Rossini, Weber, Wagner and Lortzing; Sang Mozart's Ferrando at Sadler's Wells Theatre, London in 1966 and Tamino at the New York Metropolitan in 1968; Also celebrated as Mozart's Belmonte and Ottavio, Tchaikovsky's Lensky, Verdi's Fenton, Wagner's David and Loge and Strauss's Leukippos; Sang at Salzburg Festival from 1967; Sang in the premiere of Orff's De Temporum Fine Comoedia in 1973 and Dessau's Einstein in 1974; Well known as the Evangelist in Bach's Passion and in concert works by Handel, Haydn, Beethoven, Berlioz and Mendelssohn; Many lieder recitals notably in song cycles by Schubert and Schumann; Debut as conductor with the Berlin Staatskapelle in 1970; First song recital at Wigmore Hall in 1989; Conducted Mozart's Mitridate at the Cuvilliés Theater in Munich, 1990; Lieder recitals for the Schubert Bicentenary, 1997; Retired as opera singer, 2000, with Tamino at the Berlin Staatsoper, but continued as concert singer, and conductor. *Recordings include:* St Matthew Passion; Haydn's Die Jahreszeiten; CPE Bach Mark Passion; Das Buch mit Sieben Siegeln; Das Lied von der Erde; Die Zauberflöte; Così fan tutte; Der Freischütz; Lortzing's Der Wildschütz; Berlioz Requiem; Mendelssohn's Elijah; Mozart's Requiem, as conductor; many Lieder recordings. *Current Management:* Askonas Holt Ltd, Lonsdale Chambers, 27 Chancery Lane, London, WC2A 1PF, England. *Telephone:* (20) 7400-1700. *Fax:* (20) 7400-1799. *E-mail:* info@askonasholt.co.uk. *Website:* www.askonasholt.co.uk.

SCHRÖDER, Jaap; Violinist; b. 31 Dec. 1925, Amsterdam, Netherlands; m. Agnès Jeanne Françoise Lefèvre, 3 d. *Education:* Diploma, Amsterdam Conservatory; 1st Prize, Ecole Jacques Thibaud, Paris, 1948. *Career:* Debut: Holland 1949; Leader, Radio Chamber Orchestra, 1950–63; Founder, Chamber Music ensembles Quadro Amsterdam, and Concerto Amsterdam, 1962, Quartetto Esterhazy 1973–81; Smithson String Quartet, 1983; Professor of violin, Amsterdam Conservatory, Yale School of Music, Basel Schola cantozum; mem, Netherlands String Quartet, 1952–69. *Recordings:* Numerous recordings on major record labels. *Address:* Gerard Brandtstraat 18, Amsterdam, Netherlands.

SCHRÖDER-FEINEN, Ursula; Singer (Soprano); b. 21 July 1935, Gelsenkirchen, Germany. *Education:* Studied with Maria Helm in Gelsenkirchen, then at the Folkwang School, Essen. *Career:* Gelsenkirchen 1961–68, debut as Aida and sang Gershwin's Bess, Handel's Cleopatra, Beethoven's Leonore and Verdi's Oscar; Deutsche Oper am Rhein, Düsseldorf, 1968–72; New York Metropolitan debut 1970, as Chrysothemis and Elektra; Bayreuth 1971, as Senta, Ortrud, Kundry and Brünnhilde; Wagner's Ortrud and Strauss's Dyer's Wife at Salzburg; British debut at the 1975 Edinburgh Festival, as Salome; Other roles include Puccini's Tosca and Turandot, Wagner's Isolde, Janáček's Jenůfa, Gluck's Alceste and Strauss's Elektra. *Recordings:* Roles in Korngold's Violanta and Marschner's Hans Heiling.

SCHRÖTER, Gisela; Singer (Mezzo-soprano); b. 19 Aug. 1933, Sardenhnen, East Prussia, Germany. *Education:* Studied at the Berlin State Conservatory and with Rudolf Dittrich at the Studio of the Dresden Staatsoper. *Career:* Debut: Dresden 1957, as a page in Lohengrin; Sang at the Dresden Staatsoper until 1964 in the mezzo and dramatic soprano repertory, notably as the Dyer's Wife in Die Frau ohne Schatten; Bayreuth Festival 1959, as a Flowermaiden in Parsifal; Berlin Staatsoper from 1964, as Carmen, Octavian and the Composer in Ariadne; Guest appearances in Barcelona, Lausanne, Bratislava, Vienna, Hamburg, Prague, Budapest, USA and Soviet Union; Guested with the Staatsoper in North America as Sieglinde, Kundry, the Composer and Marie in Wozzeck; Sang Herodias, Salome, in Berlin 1987; Many Concert appearances. *Recordings:* Hansel and Gretel, Der Wildschütz; Wozzeck; Schumann's Genoveva. *Address:* c/o Deutsche Staatsoper, Unter den Linden 7, 1086 Berlin, Germany.

SCHROTT, Thomas; Violinist; b. 24 Nov. 1966, Milan, Italy. *Education:* Milan Conservatory; Parma Conservatory A. Boito; Mannes College of Music, New York; Masterclasses, Mozarteum, Salzburg; Centre International de Formation Musicale, Nice; Accademia Musicale Chigiana, Siena; Scuola di Musica di Fiesole. *Career:* Played extensively in Italy; Associazione Amici del Teatro all Scala; Pomeriggi Musicali di Milano; Ravello Festival; Sagra Musicale Umbra; Bologna Teatro Comunale; Piccolo Teatro Studio, Milano; Accademia Musicale Pescarese; Many concerts in USA, Japan, Switzerland, Germany, Austria, France, Finland, Romania, South Africa, India, Bahrain, Mauritius, Turkey; Soloist, various orchestras; mem., Festival Strings Lucerne, 1995–; Performs regularly at major European festivals; Principal violin,

Sentieri Selvaggi, Milan; Performer (with Daniel Bosshard), complete cycle of J. S. Bach's sonatas for violin and harpsichord. *Recordings:* Chamber music by Chopin. *Address:* via Treviglio 17, 20128 Milano, Italy. *E-mail:* thschrott@libero.it.

SCHUBACK, Thomas; Conductor and Pianist; b. 1943, Sweden. *Education:* Studied at the Stockholm College of Music. *Career:* Conductor, Royal Opera Stockholm from 1971; productions at the Drottningholm Theatre include L'Incoronazione di Poppea, L'Arbore di Diana by Martin y Soler, Mozart's Così fan tutte and Gluck's Paride ed Elena; Musical Director of Lyric Opera of Queensland from 1982; Guest Appearances with San Diego Opera and at Sydney and Copenhagen; Season 1992–93 included performances with the Drottningholm Theatre at the Barbican Centre, London; Concerts with major Swedish Orchestras and elsewhere in Scandinavia, USA and Australia; Lieder Accompanist to Gösta Winbergh, Barbara Bonney and others; Professor of Vocal Coaching, State Oper School, Stockholm. *Recordings include:* Electra by Haeffner. *Current Management:* Ulf Tornqvist Artists Management. *Address:* St Eriksgatan 100, 113 31 Stockholm, Sweden.

SCHUBEL, Max; Composer; b. 11 April 1932, New York, USA. *Education:* Graduated, New York University, 1953; Further Composition Study with Frank Martin. *Career:* Freelance Composer, Many Performances Throughout North America; Founded OPUS ONE, 1966, for the Recording of New and Unfamiliar Concert and Electronic Music. *Compositions:* Insected Surfaces, Concerto for clarinet and 4 instruments, 1965; Exotica, for cello and harpsichord, 1967; 3 String Quartets, 1968, 1980, 1981; Everybody's Favourite Rag, for piano, 1979; Divertimento for piano, trumpet and chamber orchestra, 1980; B Natural, for prepared piano, 1980; Guale for orchestra, 1984; Punch and Judie, for chamber orchestra, 1985; The Spoors of Time for viola and piano, 1986; Scherzo for orchestra, 1987; Septet, 1988; Super Scherzo, for chamber orchestra, 1989; String Quintet, 1989; Sygnet for orchestra, 1995; Cyrèniäde for voice and orchestra, 1997; Elation, for cello, voice and orchestra, 2000; April's Ascension into Blue Destiny, 2003; Aurora Angelica for orchestra, 2003; Rhapsody for English Horn, cello and orchestra, 2003; Toccatina for piano, 2003; Trio for violin, cello and piano, 2000. *Honours:* Residencies at the MacDowell Colony, Ossabaw Island and Wolf Trap; Grants from Nat. Endowment for the Arts, Ford Foundation, Martha Baird Rockefeller Foundation. *Address:* Box 604, Greenville, ME 04441, USA.

SCHUDEL, Regina; Singer (Soprano); b. 1964, Zürich, Switzerland. *Education:* Berlin Hochschule and Opera Studio of the Vienna Staatsoper. *Career:* Debut: Vienna, 1988 as Quiteria in Die Hochzeit des Camacho by Mendelssohn; Berlin Kammeroper from 1988, as Leda in Europa und der Stier by Helge Jorus and in Henze's Elegy for Young Lovers; Sang Rosina in Paisiello's Il Barbiere di Siviglia; Guest appearances at Krefeld, the Bregenz Festival and throughout Germany and Switzerland; Many concert and recital engagements; Leipzig Opera from 1991. *Recordings:* Die Hochzeit des Comacho; Das Wunder der Heliane by Korngold; Wozzeck by Manfred Gurlitt. *Address:* c/o Leipzig Opera, Augustusplatz 12, 7010 Leipzig, Germany.

SCHUDEL, Thomas; Canadian composer; b. 8 Sept. 1937, Defiance, Ohio, USA. *Education:* BSc, 1959, MA, 1961, Ohio University; Composition Studies with Leslie Bassett and Ross Lee Finney, University of Michigan, DMA 1971. *Career:* Faculty Member, University of Regina, Canada, 1964–; Bassoonist, Regina Symphony Orchestra, 1964–70. *Compositions:* Set No. 2, for brass and wind quintets, 1963; Violin Sonata, 1966; String Quartet, 1967; 2 Symphonies, 1971, 1983; Variations, for orchestra, 1977; Winterpiece, for chamber orchestra and dancers, 1979; Triptych, for wind ensemble, 1979; A Dream Within a Dream, for chorus, 1985; A.C.T.S, for narrator and ensemble, 1986; Dialogues, for trombone and percussion, 1987; Concerto, for piccolo, strings and percussion, 1988; Concerto, for alto trombone and chamber orchestra, 1990; An Emily Dickinson Folio, for soprano and ensemble, 1991; Trigon, for 2 saxophones and percussion, 1992; A Tangled Web, for chamber orchestra, 1993; The Enchanted Cat, children's operetta, 1993; Pick Up The Earth, Gold and Rose, and Another Love Poem, all for chorus, 1994; Sinfonia Concertante, for saxophone quartet and band, 1994. *Honours:* 1st Prize, 1972 City of Trieste International Competition. *Address:* 149 Shannon Road, Regina, SK S4S 5H6, Canada.

SCHULLER, Gunther Alexander; American composer, conductor, music educator and record producer; b. 22 Nov. 1925, New York, NY; s. of Arthur E. Schuller and Elsie (Bernartz) Schuller; m. Marjorie Black 1948 (died 1992); two s. *Education:* St Thomas Choir School, New York, Manhattan School of Music. *Career:* Principal French horn, Cincinnati Symphony Orchestra 1943–45, Metropolitan Opera Orchestra 1945–59; teacher, Manhattan School of Music 1950–63, Yale Univ. 1964–67; Head Composition Dept, Tanglewood 1963–84; Music Dir First Int. Jazz Festival, Washington 1962; active as conductor since mid-1960s with maj. orchestras in Europe and USA; reconstructed and orchestrated Der

Gelbe Klang by De Hartmann/Kandinsky; Pres. New England Conservatory of Music 1967–77; Pres. Nat. Music Council 1979–81; Artistic Co-Dir, then Artistic Dir Summer Activities, Boston Symphony Orchestra, Berkshire Music Center, Tanglewood 1969–84, Festival at Sandpoint 1985–98; founder and Pres. Margun Music Inc. 1975–2000, GM Records 1980; mem. American Acad. of Arts and Sciences, American Acad. of Arts and Letters. *Compositions include:* Horn Concerto No. 1 1945, Vertige d'Eros 1946, Concerto for cello and orchestra 1946, Jumpin' in the Future 1946, Quartet for Four Brasses 1947, Oboe Sonata 1947, Duo Concertante for cello and piano 1947, Symphonic Study (Meditation) 1948, Trio for Oboe, Horn, Viola 1948, Symphony for brass and percussion 1950, Fantasy for Unaccompanied Cello 1951, Recitative and Rondo for violin and piano 1953, Dramatic Overture 1951, Five Pieces for Five Horns 1952, Adagio for flute, string trio 1952, Music for Violin, Piano and Percussion 1957, Symbiosis for violin, piano, percussion 1957, String Quartet No. 1 1957, Contours 1958, Woodwind Quintet 1958, Spectra 1958, Concertino for jazz quartet and orchestra 1959, Seven Studies on Themes of Paul Klee 1959, Conversations 1960, Lines and Contrasts for 16 horns 1960, Abstraction for jazz ensemble 1960, Variants on a Theme of Thelonious Monk 1960, Music for Brass Quintet 1960, Contrasts for woodwind quintet and orchestra 1961, Variants (ballet with choreography by Balanchine) 1961, Double Quintet for woodwind and brass quintets 1961, Meditation for concert band 1961, Concerto for piano and orchestra 1962, Journey into Jazz 1962, Fantasy Quartet for four cellos 1963, Threnos for oboe and orchestra 1963, Composition in Three Parts 1963, Five Bagatelles for Orchestra 1964, Five Etudes for orchestra 1964, The Power Within Us 1964, Five Shakespearean Songs for baritone and orchestra 1964, String Quartet No. 2 1965, Symphony 1965, American Triptych (on paintings of Pollock, Davis and Calder) 1965, Sacred Cantata 1966, Gala Music concerto for orchestra 1966, The Visitation (opera) 1966, Movements for flute and strings, Six Renaissance Lyrics, Triplum I 1967, Study in Textures for concert band 1967, Diptych for brass quintet and orchestra 1967, Shapes and Designs 1968, Concerto for double bass and orchestra 1968, Consequents for orchestra 1969, Fisherman and his Wife (opera) 1970, Concerto da Camera No. 1 1971, Capriccio Stravagante 1972, Tre Invenzioni 1972, Three Nocturnes 1973, Five Moods for tuba quartet 1973, Four Soundscapes 1974, Triplum II 1975, Violin Concerto 1976, Concerto No. 2 for horn and orchestra 1976, Diptych for organ 1976, Concerto No. 2 for orchestra 1977, Concerto for contrabassoon and orchestra 1978, Deaï for three orchestras 1978, Sonata Serenata 1978, Octet 1979, Concerto for trumpet and orchestra 1979, Eine Kleine Posaunenmusik 1980, In Praise of Winds symphony for large wind orchestra 1981, Concerto No. 2 for piano and orchestra 1981, Symphony for organ 1981, Concerto Quaternio 1984, Concerto for alto saxophone 1983, Duologue for violin and piano 1983, On Light Wings piano quartet 1984, Piano Trio 1984, Concerto for viola and orchestra 1985, Concerto for bassoon and orchestra 1985, Farbenspiel Concerto No. 3 for orchestra 1985, String Quartet No. 3 1986, Chimeric Images 1988, Concerto for string quartet and orchestra 1988, Concerto for flute and orchestra 1988, Horn Sonata 1988, On Winged Flight: A Divertimento for Band 1989, Chamber Symphony 1989, Five Impromptus for English horn and string quartet 1989, Impromptus and Cadenzas for chamber sextet 1990, Song and Dance for violin and concert band 1990, Concerto for piano three hands 1990, Violin Concerto No. 2 1991, Brass Quintet No. 2 1993, Reminiscences and Reflections 1993, The Past is the Present for orchestra 1994, Sextet for left-hand piano and woodwind quintet 1994, Concerto for organ and orchestra 1994, Mondrian's Vision 1994, Lament for M 1994, Blue Dawn into White Heat concert band 1995, An Arc Ascending 1996, Ohio River Reflections 1998, A Bouquet for Collage 1988, Fantasia Impromptu for flute and harpsichord 2000, Quod Libet for violin, cello, oboe, horn and harp 2001, String Quartet No. 4 2002, Concerto da Camera No. 2 2002, String Trio 2003, Encounters for jazz orchestra and symphony orchestra 2003. *Publications:* Horn Technique 1962, Early Jazz: Its Roots and Musical Development, Vol. I 1968, Musings: The Musical Worlds of Gunther Schuller 1985, The Swing Era: The Development of Jazz 1930–45 1989, The Compleat Conductor 1997. *Honours:* Hon. DMus (Northeastern Univ.) 1967, (Colby Coll.) 1969, (Ill. Univ.) 1970, (Williams Coll.) 1975, (Rutgers Univ.) 1980, (Oberlin Coll.) 1989, (Fla State Univ.) 1991; Creative Arts Award, Brandeis Univ. 1960, Nat. Inst. Arts and Letters Award 1960, Guggenheim Grant 1962, 1963, ASCAP Deems Taylor Award 1970, Rogers and Hammerstein Award 1971, William Schuman Award, Columbia Univ. 1989, McArthur Foundation Fellowship 1991, McArthur'Genius' Award 1994; Gold Medal American Acad. of Arts and Letters 1996, Order of Merit, Germany 1997, Max Rudolf Award 1998, Pulitzer Prize in Music 1999. *Address:* 167 Dudley Road, Newton Center, MA 02459, USA. *Telephone:* (617) 332-6398. *Fax:* (617) 969-1079.

SCHULTE, Eike (Wilm); Singer (Baritone); b. 13 Oct. 1939, Plettenberg, Germany. *Education:* Studied at Cologne Musikhochschule with Joseph Metternich and at the Salzburg Mozarteum. *Career:* Member of the

Deutsche Oper am Rhein Düsseldorf, 1956–69, Bielefeld Opera, 1969–73 and Hessisches Staatstheater Wiesbaden, 1973–88; Sang the Herald in Lohengrin at Bayreuth, 1988 and toured Japan with the Bayreuth Festival Company, 1989; Munich Staatsoper from 1989 as Faraone in Mosè by Rossini, the Father in Hansel and Gretel and Schtschelkalov in Boris Godunov; Baritone role in staged performances of Carmina Burana, 1990; Sang Beckmesser in Die Meistersinger at the Paris Opéra and in Munich; Guest engagements in Vienna, Hamburg, Cologne, Bonn, Trieste, Rome and Brussels, notably as Figaro and Rigoletto; Sang Kurwenal in Japan in 1990 conducted by Peter Schneider, Mahler's 8th Symphony with the London Philharmonic under Klaus Tennstedt in 1991; Season 1991–92 included: Lohengrin at Vienna State Opera, Zemlinsky, VARA Holland and Brahms Requiem with Hamburg Philharmonic; Season 1993–94 included: Hansel and Gretel, Rosenkavalier and Meistersinger in Munich, Ariadne auf Naxos in Cologne and Rigoletto in Tel-Aviv; Season 1994–95 included: Gunther in a new Ring production at Paris, Tannhäuser at Bayreuth Festival and debut with the Philadelphia Orchestra in Ariadne auf Naxos in Philadelphia and Carnegie Hall, New York; Sang the Herald in Lohengrin at the Accademia di Santa Cecilia, Rome, 1996 and at New York Met, 1998; Also in 1998–1999 sang Meistersinger at the Deutsche Oper Berlin; Alidoro in Cenerentola in Dresden, Rosenkavalier at the Munich Opera Festival and Parsifal in Chile; Season 1999–2000 debuts with Gunther at La Scala, Herald in Lohengrin at Florence Opera and Beckmesser at the Lyric Opera, Chicago; Season 2002–03 with Meistersinger at the Royal Opera House in London and the Vienna State Opera, Die Zauberflöte and Der Rosenkavalier in Munich, Götterdämmerung at the Tenerife Festival, Fidelio in Milan and Monte Carlo, Lohengrin in Berlin and La Cenerentola in San Fransisco. *Recordings include:* Die Meistersinger conducted by Sawallisch; Video of Mahler's 8th Symphony; CDs: Berlioz's L'enfance du Christ, Wagner's Lohengrin, Beethoven's 9th, Haydn's Creation and Wagner's Das Rheingold. *Address:* c/o Haydn Rawstron Ltd, 36 Station Road, London SE20 7BQ, England.

SCHULTZ, Andrew; Composer and University Professor; b. 18 Aug. 1960, Adelaide, South Australia. *Education:* Composition studies with Colin Brumby; BMus, Queensland University, 1982; Composition Studies with George Crumb, Conducting with Richard Wernick, University of Pennsylvania, USA, 1983; Composition with David Lumsdaine, MMus, Kings College, London, England, 1986; PhD, Queensland University, 1987. *Career:* Head of Composition and Music Studies, Guildhall School of Music and Drama and Visiting Professor, Faculty of Creative Arts, University of Wollongong, New South Wales; Compositions performed and broadcast widely, Australia, USA, Europe; Commissions, University of Melbourne, Perihelion, Seymour Group, Elision, Flederman, Queensland Philharmonic Orchestra, Hunter Orchestra, Sydney Symphony Orchestra, 4 MBS-FM, Duo Contemporain, Musica Nova; Discography includes: Garotte, 1981, on Tropic of Capricorn, Qld Symphony Orchestra, CD; Barren Grounds on Tapestry, CD; Ekstasis on Australian Vocal Music, 1992, CD; Chamber Music of Andrew Schultz, CD. *Compositions:* Spherics, flute, trombone, 1 percussion, piano, synthesizer, cello, 1985; Stick Dance, clarinet, marimba, piano, 1987; Sea-Change piano, 1987; Black River, opera, 1988; Barren Grounds, clarinet, viola, cello, piano, 1990; Ekstasis, 1990, 6 solo voices; Calling Music, 1991, chamber orchestra; The Devil's Music, 1992, large orchestra; Diver's Lament, large orchestra, 1995; Violin Concerto, 1996; In Tempore Stellae, Symphony No. 1, choir and orchestra, 1998; Going Into Shadows, 3-act opera, 2000. *Honours:* Composer Fellowship, Australia Council Music Board, 1982; Queensland University Medal, 1982; Fulbright Award, 1983; Commonwealth Postgraduate Research Award, 1983; Commonwealth Scholarship and Fellowship Plan Award, 1985; Albert H Maggs Composition Award, 1985; Hilda Margaret Watts Prize, Kings College London, 1986; Australian National Composers Opera Award, 1988; Composer Fellowship, Australia Council, 1990; APRA Classical Composition of the Year, 1994. *Address:* Professor of Composition, University of Wollongong, NSW 2522, Australia. *E-mail:* info@andrewschultz.net. *Website:* www.andrewschultz.net.

SCHULZ, Gerhard; Violinist; b. 23 Sept. 1951, Austria. *Education:* Studied in Vienna, Düsseldorf and USA. *Career:* 2nd violin of the Alban Berg Quartet from 1978; Many concert engagements, including complete cycles of the Beethoven Quartets in 15 European cities 1987–88, 1988–89 seasons; Bart ók-Mozart cycle in London, Vienna, Paris, Frankfurt, Munich, Geneva and Turin, 1990–91; Annual concert series at the Vienna Konzerthaus and festival engagements world-wide; Associate Artist at the South Bank Centre, London; US appearances in Washington DC, San Francisco, NY, Carnegie Hall. *Recordings:* Complete quartets of Beethoven, Brahms, Berg, Webern and Bartók; Late quartets of Mozart, Schubert, Haydn and Dvořák; Ravel and Debussy quartets; Live recordings from Carnegie Hall, Mozart, Schumann; Konzerthaus in Vienna, Brahms; Opéra-Comique Paris, Brahms. *Honours:* Grand Prix du Disque; Deutsche Schallplatenpreis;

Edison Prize; Japan Grand Prix; Gramophone Magazine Award. *Address:* Intermusica Artists' Management, 16 Duncan Terrace, London N1 8BZ, England.

SCHULZ, Walther; Cellist; b. 1940, Vienna, Austria. *Education:* Studied in Vienna. *Career:* Debut: New York 1979; Debut Tour of Japan 1984; Performances of Haydn and other composers in Vienna and elsewhere from 1968; Co-Founder of the Haydn Trio of Vienna, 1968 and has performed in Brussels, Munich, Berlin, Zürich, London, Paris and Rome; Frequent North American appearances with Concerts in 25 States; Further travels to the Near East, Russia, Africa, Central and South America; Series at the Vienna Konzerthaus Society from 1976 with Performances of more than 100 works; Summer Festivals at Vienna, Salzburg, Aix en Provence, Flanders and Montreux; Masterclasses at the Royal College and Royal Academy in London, Stockholm, Bloomington, Tokyo and the Salzburg Mozarteum. *Recordings:* Complete Piano Trios of Beethoven and Schubert, Mendelssohn D Minor, Brahms B major, Tchaikovsky A Minor, Schubert Trout Quintet; Albums of Works by Haydn, Schumann, Dvořák, Smetana. *Address:* c/o Gerhild Baron Artists, Dornbacher Strasse 4/111/2, A–1170 Wien, Austria.

SCHUMAN, Patricia; singer (soprano); b. 4 Feb. 1954, Los Angeles, USA. *Education:* Santa Cruz University, CA. *Career:* Sang minor roles with San Francisco Opera then appeared with the Houston Opera and in a touring company; Engagements at the NYC Opera, the Paris Opéra, Teatro La Fenice Venice and in Washington DC; Sang on tour with Peter Brook's version of Carmen; Théâtre de la Monnaie Brussels from 1983 as Dorabella, Zerlina, and as Angelina in La Cenerentola; St Louis 1986 and in US premiere of Il Viaggio a Reims by Rossini; Théâtre du Châtelet, Paris 1989, in the title role of L'Incoronazione di Poppea; Miami Opera and Long Beach Opera 1989, as Antonia in Les Contes d'Hoffmann and as Mozart's Countess; Seattle Opera 1990, as Blanche in Les Dialogues des Carmélites; Has also sung at the Vienna Staatsoper and in the concert hall; Metropolitan Opera debut, Donna Elvira, 1990; The Voyage, by Glass, 1996; Covent Garden debut 1992, as Donna Elvira; Salzburg Festival 1997, in La Clemenza di Tito, also at Covent Garden, 2000; Sang Schumann's Genoveva in Leeds and London, 2000; Alice Ford in Falstaff at Cologne and Covent Garden, 2001. *Recordings:* Roggiero in Rossini's Tancredi; Messiah, Handel; Video of Monteverdi's Poppea, Schwetzingen 1993, title role. *Address:* c/o PG & PM, 7 Whitehorse Close, Royal Mile, Edinburgh, EH8 8BU, Scotland.

SCHUNK, Robert; Singer (Tenor); b. 5 Jan. 1948, Neu-Isenburg, Frankfurt, Germany. *Education:* Studied with Martin Grundler at the Frankfurt Musikhochschule. *Career:* Sang at Karlsruhe 1973–75; Bonn Opera 1975–77; Dortmund 1977–79; Bayreuth Festival from 1977, as Siegmund, Erik and Melot; Hamburg Staatsoper 1981, as the Emperor in Die Frau ohne Schatten; Bregenz Festival 1983, Max in Der Freischutz; Engagements in Munich, Vienna, Frankfurt, London, Cologne and Berlin; Tour of Japan with the Hamburg Staatsoper 1984; Sang Florestan at the Met and Naples, 1986–87; Siegmund in New York and Munich, 1987, 1989; Emperor in Die Frau ohne Schatten and Vladimir in Prince Igor at Munich, 1989; Sang Wagner's Erik at Naples, 1992; Florestan in Fidelio at Catania, 1998. *Recordings:* Erik in Der fliegende Holländer, from Bayreuth.

SCHURMANN, Gerard; Composer and Conductor; b. 19 Jan. 1924, Kertosono, Java; m. Carolyn Nott, 26 May 1973, 1 d. *Education:* Composition with Alan Rawsthrone; Piano with Kathleen Long; Conducting with Franco Ferrara. *Career:* Aircrew, 320 Squadron, RAF, 1941–45; Acting Netherlands Cultural Attaché, London, 1945–48; Resident Orchestral Conductor, Radio Hilversum, 1948–51; Freelance Composer/Conductor, 1950–; Guest Conductor, France, Italy, Spain, Switzerland, Czechoslovakia, Germany, Netherlands, Scandinavia, Ireland, USA; mem, Performing Right Society; American Society of Composers, Authors and Publishers; MCPS; APC; AMPAS; BAFTA; Composers' Guild of Great Britain; Phyllis Court Club. *Compositions include:* Orchestral: 6 Studies of Francis Bacon, 1969; Variants, 1970; Attack and Celebration, 1971; Piano Concerto, 1972–73; Violin Concerto, 1975–78; The Gardens of Exile, concerto, cello, orchestra, 1989–90; Man in the Sky, 1994; Concerto for orchestra, 1994–95; Man in the Sky, 1996; Chamber, instrumental: Serenade, 1971; Contrasts, 1973; Leotaurus, 1975; Wind Quintet, flute, oboe, clarinet, horn, bassoon, 1976; 2 Ballades for piano, 1, Hukvaldy, 2, Brno, 1981; Duo, violin, piano, 1984; Quartet for piano and strings (violin, viola, cello, piano), 1986; Ariel, oboe, 1987; Quartet No. 2 for piano and strings, 1997; String Quartet, 2003; Vocal, choral: Song cycle, Chuenchi, 1966; Summer is Coming, madrigal, SATB, unaccompanied, 1970; The Double Heart, cantata, SATB, unaccompanied, 1976; Piers Plowman, opera cantata, 2 acts, 1979–80; Nine Slovak folk songs, high voice, piano or orchestra, 1988; Six Songs of William Blake, 1997; Gaudiana, Symphonic Studies for orchestra, 1999–2002; Trio for clarinet, cello and piano, 2001. *Recordings:* 6 Studies of Francis Bacon; Variants;

Chuench'i; The Double Heart; Claretta; Piers Plowman; The Gardens of Exile; Piano Concerto; Violin Concerto; Concerto for Orchestra; Duo for violin and piano; Attack and Celebration; The Film Music of Gerard Schurmann; The Gambler; Man in the Sky. *Contributions:* Introductory essay to 3 vols on Alan Rawsthorne, 1984; Essay about working on the music for the film Lawrence of Arabia, 1990. *Honours:* Numerous. *Current Management:* The Marion Rosenberg Office. *Address:* 3700 Multiview Drive, Hollywood Hills, Los Angeles, CA 90068, USA.

SCHÜTZ, Siiri; Pianist; b. 26 July 1974, Berlin, Germany. *Education:* Carl Phil E. Bach Gymnasium, Berlin, 1985–91; studied with Annerose Schmidt at the Hochschule für Musik, Berlin, 1991–96; Diploma at the Hochschule für Musik, Hanns Eisler, Berlin, 1996; studied with Leon Fleisher at the Peabody Conservatory, Baltimore, 1996–98; Musikhochschule, Cologne. *Career:* performed in place of Claudio Arrau in the Cologne Philharmonic and Murray Perahia in Düsseldorf, debut with the Berlin Philharmonic Orchestra, conducted by Claudio Abbado (this concert was recorded and used in the film, The First Year), 1991; further concerts include the Schleswig Holtstein Festival, the Schwetzinger Mozart Festival and the Ruhrfestspiele, with the Tonhalle Orchestra Zürich, the Bern Symphony Orchestra, and the Berlin Rundfunk Symphony Orchestra; played chamber music during the Berliner Festwochen, 1993, and in the Faust cycle of the Philharmonic Orchestra in Berlin, 1997. *Honours:* First Prize in the International Piano Competition, Aussig, 1989; Jütting Award, Stendhal, Germany, 1996; Jürgen Ponto Stiftung fellowship; Studienstiftung des Deutschen Volkes fellowship. *Current Management:* Konzert-Direktion Hans Adler, Auguste-Viktoria-Str. 64, 14199 Berlin. *Telephone:* (30) 825–6333. *Fax:* (30) 826–3520. *Website:* www.musikadler.de. *Address:* Üderseestr. 17, 10318 Berlin, Germany. *Telephone:* (30) 5038–1718. *E-mail:* atischuetz@aol.com. *Website:* www.siiri-schuetz.de.

SCHWAGER, Myron August; Professor of Music; b. 16 March 1937, Pittsfield, Massachusetts, USA; m. (1) Katharine Lake, Sept 1961, 1 s., 1 d., (2) Laurie Beth Lewis, June 1982. *Education:* Massachussetts Institute of Technology, 1955–56; BMus, Boston University, 1958; MMus, New England Conservatory of Music, 1961; MA, PhD, Harvard University, 1970. *Career:* Worcester Community School of the Performing Arts; Jesuit Artists Institute, Italy; Chair, Department of Music, Hartt School of Music, University of Hartford, Connecticut, 1974–; Former Principal Cellist, Springfield Symphony Orchestra; Appearances with Cambridge Society for Early Music, Boston Chamber Players, Consortium Musicale, Hawthorne Trio, Hartford Chamber Orchestra, and Karas String Quartet; Revived and reconstructed Francesco Cavalli's La Virtu de'strali d'Amore, Venice, 1642 at Wadsworth Atheneum, Hartford, 31 July–1 Aug. 1987. *Contributions:* The Creative World of Beethoven, 1971; Current Musicology; Music and Letters; Early Music; Musical Quarterly. *Address:* 30 Hoskins Road, Bloomfield, CT 06002, USA.

SCHWANBECK, Bodo; Singer (Bass-Baritone); b. 20 July 1935, Scherwin, Germany. *Education:* Studied with Franz-Theo Reuter in Munich and with KH Jarius in Stuttgart. *Career:* Debut: Detmold 1959, as Varlaam in Boris Godunov; Has sung in Frankfurt, Hamburg, Munich, Manheim, Düsseldorf, and Lisbon and at the NYC Opera, Zürich Opera 1967, in the premiere of Madame Bovary by Sutermeister; French television as Mustafà in L'Italiana in Algeri; Théâtre de la Monnaie, Brussels, 1986; Sang at Madrid 1988, in Lulu; Brussels 1990, in From the House of the Dead; Covent Garden 1990, as Waldner in Arabella; Sang Antonio in Figaro with the Royal Opera on tour to Japan, 1992; Other roles include Baron Ochs, Osmin, Alfonso, Pizarro, Leporello, Mephistopheles, Nicolai's Falstaff, Don Pasquale, Dulcamara, Golaud, Don Magnifico and Wozzeck; Sang in Lulu at Palermo, 2001; Frequent concert appearances. *Address:* c/o Theatre Royal de le Monnaie, 4 Leopoldstrasse, 1000 Brussels, Belgium.

SCHWANEWILMS, Anne; Singer (mezzo-soprano); b. 1965, Gelsenkirchen, Germany. *Education:* Cologne Musikhochschule, with Hans Sotin. *Career:* member, Cologne Opera Studio 1990–92, Cologne Opera 1993–95; freelance engagements 1995–; recent engagements haver included Die Walküre in Essen and Klagenfurt, Sieglinde/Walküre in Freiburg, Die Zauberflöte in Trieste (with Arnold Östman) and Salome with the Cologne Radio Symphony Orchestra; debut at the Bayreuth Festival in 1996 in roles of Gerhilde (Die Walküre) and Gutrune (Götterdämmerung) whilst covering the role of Kundry and has been reinvited to Bayreuth each year since; returned to Turin in 1998 to perform Gutrune and 3rd Norn in concert performances of Götterdämmerung; season 1999–2000 with Sieglinde at Bonn and Berlin, Senta at Lübeck, Adriano and Gutrune at Berlin; a new production of Götterdämmerung at Stuttgart and her first performance of Senta at the Hamburg State Opera 2000; recent concerts have included Zemlinsky's Der Zwerg with the Gürzenich Orchestra in Cologne, Mahler's Symphony No. 8 in Udine and a concert at the Kongresshalle in Lübeck (Weber/Schubert/Rubinstein) with Erich Wächter; further engagements with return visits to Bayreuth and concerts in Japan, Die

Walküre (Gerhilde) in Hamburg, Hänsel und Gretel (Hexe) in Stuttgart, Wagner's Rienzi (Adriano) at the Komische Oper in Berlin, Die Walküure (Sieglinde) in Bonn, role of Judith in Barbe Bleue at the Brussels Opera and at the Schouwbund in Rotterdam, Beethoven's Symphony No. 9 in Leipzig for MDR and Wesendoncklieder (in the Mottl edition) in Freiburg; sang Beethoven's Leonore at the Châtelet 2002; Weber's Euryanthe at the London Proms 2002; engaged at Glyndebourne 2002–03, as Weber's Euryanthe and Mozart's Electra; Covent Garden debut as Chrysothemis in Elektra 2003; Ariadne in Ariadne auf Naxos, Covent Garden 2004. *Recordings:* Elektra. *Current Management:* Haydn Rawstron Ltd, 36 Station Road, London, SE20 7BQ, England.

SCHWANTER, Joseph, BM, MM, DM; composer; b. 22 March 1943, Chicago, USA. *Education:* American Conservatory of Music, Chicago, Northwestern University. *Career:* Faculty mem., Eastman School of Music, Rochester 1970–, (Prof. of Composition 1980); composer-in-residence, St Louis Symphony 1982–85, Cabrillo Music Festival 1992. *Compositions:* Chronicon, for bassoon and piano, 1968; Consortium I and II, for flute and ensemble, 1970–71; Modus Caeliestis, for orchestra, 1973; Elixir, for flute and 5 players, 1975; And the Mountains Rising Nowhere, for orchestra, 1977; Canticle of the Evening Bells, for flute and 12 players, 1977; Wild Angels of the Open Hills, Song Cycle, for soprano and ensemble, 1977; Aftertones of Infinity, for orchestra, 1978; Sparrows, for soprano and chamber ensemble, 1979; Wind Willow, Whisper, for chamber ensemble, 1980; Dark Millennium, for orchestra, 1981; Through Interior Worlds, for ensemble, 1981; Distant Runes and Incantations, for piano and orchestra, 1984; Someday Memories, for orchestra, 1984; Witchnomad, Song Cycle, for soprano and orchestra, 1984; Dreamcaller, Song Cycle, for soprano, violin and chamber orchestra, 1984; A Sudden Rainbow, for orchestra, 1984; Toward Light, for orchestra, 1986; Piano Concerto, 1988; Freeflight, for orchestra, 1989; A Play of Shadows, Fantasy, for flute and orchestra, 1990; Velocities, for marimba, 1990; Percussion Concerto, 1991 (premiered 1995); Through Interior Worlds, Ballet, 1992 (concert version 1994); Symphony 'Evening Land' for soprano and orchestra, 1995; In Memories Embrace... for strings, 1996. *Honours:* Pulitzer Prize 1979.

SCHWARTNER, Dieter; Singer (Tenor); b. 6 Feb. 1938, Plauen, Germany. *Education:* Studied in Dresden. *Career:* Debut: Plauen in 1969 as the Baron in Der Wildschütz; Sang at Plauen until 1972, then at Dresden, 1972–78, and Dessau, 1978–79; Member of the Leipzig Opera from 1979 singing Ligeti's Le Grand Macabre and the Duke of Parma in Busoni's Doktor Faust in 1991; Guest appearances in Dresden and at the Berlin Staatsoper; Other roles have included Tamino, Faust, Max, Lionel in Martha, Florestan, Don José, Alvaro in La Forza del Destino and Walther von Stolzing; Many concert engagements. *Address:* c/o Stadtische Theatre, 7010 Leipzig, Germany.

SCHWARTZ, Elliott; Composer, Author and Professor; b. 19 Jan. 1936, Brooklyn, New York, USA; m. Dorothy Feldman, 26 June 1960, 1 s., 1 d. *Education:* Studied, Columbia University, New York; Bennington Composers' Conference. *Career:* Professor of Music and Department Chair, Bowdoin College, Brunswick, Maine, USA, 1964–; Professor of Composition, Ohio State University, 1985–86, 1988–91; Visiting Appointment, Trinity College of Music, London, 1967–; University of California, San Diego, 1978–79; Robinson College, Cambridge, England, 1993–94, 1999. *Compositions:* Timepiece 1794 for chamber orchestra, 1994; Rainbow for orchestra, 1996; Alto Prisms for 8 violas, 1997; Mehitadel's Serenade for saxophone and orchestra, 2001; Voyager for orchestra, 2002. *Recordings:* Grand Concerto; Extended Piano; Mirrors; Texture for Chamber Orchestras; Concert Piece for Ten Players; Chamber Concerto; Cycles and Gongs; Extended Clarinet; Dream Music with Variations; Celebrations/Reflections for Orchestra; Memorial in Two Parts; Chiaroscuro; Elan; Aerie for 6 flutes; Equinox for orchestra. *Publications:* The Symphonies of Ralph Vaughan Williams; Contemporary Composers in Contemporary Music; Electronic Music; A Listeners Guide; Music Ways of Listening, Music since 1945. *Address:* PO Box 451, South Freeport, ME 04078, USA. *E-mail:* eschwart@bowdoin.edu. *Website:* www.schwartzmusic.com.

SCHWARTZ, Sergiu; Israeli/American concert violinist and conductor and pedagogue; b. 1957, Romania. *Education:* studied with Dorothy DeLay, Juilliard School, New York, Yfrah Neaman, Guildhall School, London, Rami Shevelov, Rubin Academy, Tel-Aviv, Stefan Gheorghiu, Romania; additional studies with Sándor Végh, Felix Galimir, Leon Fleisher, Isaac Stern and Sergiu Celibidache. *Career:* New York debut at Carnegie Recital Hall; London debut at Wigmore Hall in the Outstanding Israeli Artists series; North American debut at the Museum of Fine Arts, Montreal; soloist with over 200 leading orchestras in Europe, Israel and throughout the USA, including Dresden Staatskapelle, Jerusalem Symphony, London Symphony, Sarajevo, Dresden and Slovak Philharmonics, European Community Chamber Orchestra, National Orchestra of Mexico, Florida Philharmonic and Chicago's Grant Park Festival Orchestra and with numerous distin-

guished ensembles in the USA and world-wide; collaborations in performances with conductors, including Segiu Commissiona, James Judd, Peter Maag, Giuseppe Sinopoli and Bruno Weil; performances in major concert halls including Lincoln Center, Carnegie Recital Hall and 92nd Street Y (New York), Kennedy Center (Washington, DC), and Barbican Hall, Queen Elizabeth Hall and Wigmore Hall (London); frequent guest at int. music festivals, including Aspen, Newport, Bowdoin, Interlochen (USA), Israel, Switzerland, Finland, England, France, Romania and Bulgaria; conductor with European Community Chamber Orchestra, Concentus Hungaricus, Sarajevo Philharmonic, Israel Camerata Orchestra, Lynn Univ. Philharmonia and String Orchestra; broadcasts for major radio and TV stations, including the BBC, NPR and CNN; master classes conducted at music schools, colls and univs throughout the USA, including Interlochen Arts Acad., UCLA, Oberlin Conservatory, Eastman School, San Francisco Conservatory, Idyllwild Arts Acad., New York's La Guardia School for the Performing Arts, RAM (London), Reina Sofia Acad. of Music (Madrid) and Rubin Acad. of Music (Jerusalem); master courses in Romania, Bulgaria, Switzerland, Netherlands, Germany, Israel; judge in international violin competitions, including Tchaikovsky (Moscow), Pablo Sarasate (Spain), Henryk Szeryng (Mexico), Wieniawski (Poland), Novosibirsk (Russia), Int. Texaco-Sphinx (USA) and other competitions in France, Italy, Canada and the USA; teaching position, artist faculty, Conservatory of Music, Lynn Univ., Boca Raton, FL. *Recordings:* Works by Sibelius, Svendsen, Grieg, Spohr, Debussy, Schumann, R. Strauss, Bloch, Enescu, Smetana, Khachaturian, Millhaud, for Vox, Gega, Naxos, Arcobaleno, Romeo Records, Nonesuch, CBS and Discover/Koch International. *Honours:* America-Israel Cultural Foundation Award, Nat. Endowment for the Arts Solo Recitalist Fellowship, Nat. Foundation for the Advancement of the Arts; prizewinner, int. violin competitions in the USA, England, Switzerland and Chile. *Address:* C/o Joanne Rile Artists Management, 801 Old York Road, Noble Plaza, Suite 212, Jenkintown PA 19046 USA. *E-mail:* sergiuschwartz@aol .com. *Website:* members.aol.com/sergiuschwartz.

SCHWARZ, Gerard; American conductor; b. 19 Aug. 1947, Weehawken, NJ; m. Jody Greitzer 1984; two s. two d. *Education:* Professional Children's School, Juilliard School. *Career:* joined American Brass Quintet 1965; Music Dir Erick Hawkins Dance Co. 1966, Eliot Feld Dance Co. 1972; Co-Prin. Trumpet, New York Philharmonic 1973–74; Founding Music Dir Waterloo Festival 1975; Music Dir New York Chamber Symphony 1977–, LA Chamber Orchestra 1978–86; est. Music Today series, Merkin Concert Hall, New York 1981 (Music Dir 1988–89); Music Adviser Mostly Mozart Festival, Lincoln Center, New York 1982–84, Music Dir 1984–; Music Adviser Seattle Symphony 1983–84, Prin. Conductor 1984–85, Music Dir 1985–2001; Artistic Adviser Tokyu Bunkamura's Orchard Hall, Japan 1994–; Music Dir Royal Liverpool Philharmonic Orchestra Sept. 2001–; Guest Conductor, Cosmopolitan Symphony, Aspen Festival Chamber, Tokyo Philharmonic, Residentie, The Hague, St Louis Symphony, Kirov, St Petersburg, Royal Liverpool Philharmonic and Vancouver Symphony Orchestras, City of London Symphonia and London Mozart Players; has conducted many US orchestras and the Hong Kong Philharmonic, Jerusalem Symphony, Israeli Chamber and English Chamber Orchestras, London Symphony, Helsinki Philharmonic and Monte Carlo Philharmonic Orchestras, Ensemble Contemporain, Paris and Nat. Orchestra of Spain; operatic conducting début, Washington Opera 1982; has also conducted Seattle Opera 1986, San Francisco Opera 1991 and New Japan Philharmonic 1998; numerous recordings for Delos, Nonesuch, Angel and RCA labels; numerous TV appearances. *Honours:* Hon. DFA (Fairleigh Dickinson Univ., Seattle Univ.); Hon. DMus (Univ. of Puget Sound); named Conductor of the Year 1994 by Musical America Int. Directory of the Performing Arts; Ditson Conductor's Award, Columbia Univ. 1989; has received two Record of the Year Awards, one Mumms Ovation Award. *Address:* Royal Liverpool Philharmonic Orchestra, Philharmonic Hall, Hope Street, Liverpool, L1 9BP, England.

SCHWARZ, Hanna; Singer (Mezzo-soprano); b. 15 Aug. 1943, Hamburg, Germany. *Education:* Studied in Hamburg, Hanover and Essen. *Career:* Debut: Hanover 1970, as Maddalena in Rigoletto; Eutin 1972, as Carmen; Member of the Hamburg Staatsoper from 1973; Guest appearances in Zürich (1975–), San Francisco (1977–), Vienna, Paris (Preziosilla 1977), Deutsche Oper Berlin (Cherubino 1978); Munich Staatsoper 1974, 1980, 1984; Bayreuth Festival 1976–85, as Fricka and Erda; sang in the first complete performance of Berg's Lulu, Paris Opéra 1979; Holland Festival 1985, as Brangaene in Tristan und Isolde; Paris 1987, as Cornelia in Giulio Cesare; Sang Fricka in Das Rheingold at Bonn and Cologne, 1990; Season 1992 as Orpheus and Fricka at Bonn; Sang Fricka at the New York Met, 1996–97; Mephistophila and Helen in the premiere of Schnittke's Historia von D Johann Fausten, Hamburg, 1995; Sang Brangaene at Cologne, 1998; Season 2000–01 as Fricka in the Ring and Berg's Countess Geschwitz at the Met; Waltraute at Cologne, the Nurse in Die Frau ohne Schatten at Dresden and Herodias for the Hamburg Staatsoper. *Recordings include:* Die Zauberflöte, The

Queen of Spades, Lulu, Mahler's Rückert Lieder, Apollo et Hyacinthus by Mozart, Die Lustige Witwe; Les Contes d'Hoffmann, Humperdinck's Königskinder, Die Heimkehr aus der Fremde by Mendelssohn; Rhinedaughter in The Ring; Fricka in the Bayreuth Ring; Martha in Schubert's oratorio Lazarus; Mother in Hänsel und Gretel. *Address:* c/o Theateragentur Dr G. Hilbert, Maximillianstrasse 22, D–80539 München, Germany.

SCHWARZENBERG, Elisabeth; Singer (Soprano); b. 23 Sept. 1933, Vienna, Austria; m. Georg Schnapka. *Education:* Studied in Vienna. *Career:* Debut: Deutsche Oper am Rhein, Düsseldorf, 1956, as Eva in Die Meistersinger; Sang in Munich, Paris, Brussels, Nice, Turin, Dublin, Geneva and Zürich; Many appearances at the Vienna Volksoper; Düsseldorf 1957, in the premiere of Die Räuber by Klebe; Salzburg Festival 1961, in the premiere of Das Bergwerk zu Falun by Wagner-Régeny; Bayreuth 1962–72; Teatro San Carlo Lisbon 1967; Other roles included the Marschallin and Donna Elvira. *Address:* c/o Volksoper, Währingerstrasse 78, 1090 Vienna, Austria.

SCHWARZKOPF, Dame Elisabeth, MusD; Singer (soprano); b. 9 Dec. 1915, Jarotschin, Poland; m. Walter Legge 1953 (died 1979). *Education:* Berlin Hochschule für Musik, later with Maria Ivogün. *Career:* debut, Berlin Städtsiche Oper 1938 as a Flowermaiden in Parsifal; recital debut Berlin 1942; joined the Vienna Staatsoper 1944 and visited Covent Garden 1947; until 1959 sang Mozart's Pamina and Susanna, Wagner's Eva, Puccini's Mimi and Butterfly, Strauss's Sophie and Marschallin and Massenet's Manon in London; Salzburg Festival 1947–64, debut as Mozart's Susanna; created Anne Trulove in The Rake's Progress at Venice in 1951 and sang in the premiere of Orff's Trionfi at La Scala Milan 1953; US debut San Francisco 1955, as Marenka in The Bartered Bride; appeared in operas by Mozart at the Chicago Lyric Opera in 1959; Metropolitan Opera debut 1964, as the Marschallin; other opera roles included Debussy's Mélisande, Mozart's Donna Elvira and Fiordiligi, Wagner's Elisabeth and Elsa, Gounod's Marguerite and Verdi's Gilda; concert repertoire included Bach's Passions, oratorios by Handel and Haydn, the Requiems of Verdi and Brahms, Tippett's A Child of Our Time and the Four Last Songs of Strauss; particularly noted as a singer of Lieder; retired from opera 1972 and from concerts in 1975; gave master classes in Europe and America. *Recordings:* many operatic roles on Columbia; also recorded for Telefunken, Electrola, Olympic, Urania and Cetra including Don Giovanni; Figaro, Così fan tutte, Rosenkavalier, Capriccio, Falstaff, Turandot (as Liu), Die Meistersinger (Bayreuth 1951), St Matthew Passion (Klemperer); Les Contes d'Hoffmann (as Giulietta); Die Zauberflöte (First Lady); Die Fledermaus; Lieder recitals under the direction of Walter Legge. *Honours:* Grosses Verdienst-Kreuz der Bundesrepublik Deutschland. *Address:* Kammersängerin, Rebhusstrasse 29, 8126 Zumikon, Switzerland.

SCHWEEN, Astrid; Cellist; b. 1960, New York, USA. *Education:* Studied at the Juilliard School. *Career:* Soloist with The New York Philharmonic; Co-founder of the Lark String Quartet; Recent concert tours to: Australia; Taiwan; Hong Kong; China; Germany; Netherlands; US appearances at: The Lincoln Center, New York; Kennedy Center, Washington; Boston; Los Angeles; Philadelphia; St Louis; San Francisco; Repertoire includes: Quartets by Haydn, Mozart, Beethoven, Schubert, Dvořák, Brahms, Borodin, Bartók, Debussy and Shostakovich. *Honours:* Gold Medals at the 1990 Naumberg, 1991 Shostakovich Competitions; Prizewinner at the: 1990, Premio Paulio Borciani; 1990, Karl Klinger; 1991 London International String Quartet; 1991, Melbourne Chamber Music Competitions. *Address:* c/o Sonata (Lark Quartet), 11 Northpark Street, Glasgow G20 7AA, Scotland.

SCHWEIGER, Stephanie (Kreszenz Berta); Composer; b. 19 Dec. 1964, Regensburg, Germany. *Education:* Piano lessons and choir-singing from 1970; Studied Philosophy and Musicology in Regensburg, Munich and Berlin, 1986–91; Studied Composition at the Hochschule der Künste Berlin, with Gösta Neuwirth, Walter Zimmermann and Dieter Schnebel. *Career:* First compositions, 1980; Composer and Pianist in experimental ensemble, 1983–88; Appeared on radio at Westdeutscher Rundfunk, Sender Freies Berlin and other stations; Her works performed regularly, 1992–; Recent performances, 1998–, include at Darmstadt summer courses and at festivals in Rome, Paris, Berlin, Leipzig and elsewhere; Cooperated with Anna Clementi, Barre Bouman, ConGioco Ensemble, Accroche Note, Barbara Thun, Ariane Jessulat and others; mem, Freunde Guter Musik, Berlin, 1998. *Compositions:* 1au9tu9mn3 for 4 instruments and dancer, 1993; ekloge for mezzo-soprano, viola, guitar and percussion, 1996–97; frango phragmón for accordion, 1996–97; Skira for flute, violoncello, accordion, 1997; exilata for soprano and clarinet or bassoon, 1998; Film music: Nine pieces of music (One more time before I die), 1990; Die Vergessenen, 1997. *Recordings:* Sp19ri9ng one, 1991; Solo für Ebba, 1995. *Honours:* Commission from Berlin Senate, 1993; Commissions from G-Lock, Passau, 1994–98. *Address:* Barbarossastrasse 5, 10781 Berlin, Germany.

SCHWEIKART, Dieter; Singer (Bass); b. 9 Jan. 1942, Iserlohn, Germany. *Education:* Studied in Wuppertal with Becker-Brill and with Thomas Lo Monaco in Rome. *Career:* Sang in Saarbrucken from 1964; Appearances at Düsseldorf, Krefeld and Bonn; Hanover from 1976; Has sung in Dortmund, Hamburg, Frankfurt, Helsinki, Florence, Copenhagen and Cologne; Bayreuth Festival 1983–86, as Hans Foltz in Die Meistersinger and as Fafner in Der Ring des Nibelungen; Sang Daland in Der fliegende Holländer at Naples, 1992; Crespel in Les Contes d'Hoffmann at Cologne, 1998; Season 2000–01 at Cologne as Fafner and Sarastro. *Address:* c/o PO Box 100262, Bayreuther Festspiele, 8580 Bayreuth, Germany.

SCHWEINITZ, Wolfgang von; Composer; b. 7 Feb. 1953, Hamburg, Germany. *Education:* American University in Washington, DC, 1968–69; Hamburg Hochschule für Musik, 1971–75, with György Ligeti. *Career:* Center for Computer Research in Music and Acoustics, Stanford University, California, 1975–76; Resident Composer, German Academy, Rome, 1978–79; Opera 'azione musicale' Patmos Premiered at Munich, 1990; Guest Professor in composition, Weimar, 1994–96. *Compositions:* 2 Symphonies, 1973, 1974; Mozart Variations, for orchestra, 1976; String Quartet, 1977; Die Brücke, for tenor, baritone and chamber orchestra, 1978; Piano Concerto, 1979; Papiersterne Song Cycle, for mezzo and piano, 1981; Englische Serenade, for 6 wind instruments, 1984; Mass, for soloists, chorus and orchestra, 1984; Music for 4 saxophones, 1984; Patmos, azione musicale, 1990; Morgenlied, for flute, 1990;... wir aber singen, Symphonic Cycle in 3 Parts, for cello and orchestra, 1992, 1995, 1996; Franz and Morton for piano trio, 1993–94; O-Ton Automne, Linguistikherbst, song on a poem by Oskar Pastior for soprano and piano, 1996; Helmholtz-Funk for 8 computer-controlled sine generators and 2 ringmodulated pianos with natural tuning, 1997; Klang auf Schön Berg La Monte Young for string trio and live-electronic ring modulation, 1999; JUZ (eil Jodelschrei) for amplified tenor trombone and CD or hard disk recorder, 1999. *Honours:* Schneider-Schott Prize for Young Composers, 1986; Plöner-Hindemith Preis, 1988. *Address:* Eisenbahnstrasse 12, 10997 Berlin, Germany.

SCHWEIZER, Alfred; Composer; b. 4 Nov. 1941, Sevelen, Switzerland. *Education:* University of Berne; Berne Conservatory; Music Academy of Basle; Swiss Centre for Computer Music. *Career:* Professor, Winterthur Conservatory, 1970–71; Professor, 1971–2003, Acting Director, 1979–80, Biel Conservtory; Manager, Classic 2000, 1982–; mem, Schweizerischer Tonkünstlerverein; Schweizerischer Musikpädagogischer Verband. *Compositions:* 4 pieces for orchestra; 2 Concertinos for Violin and Strings; Metamusic for Percussion and Strings; Concerto for Piano and Orchestra; Concerto for Swiss folk instruments and small Orchestra; Canon for open Orchestra; The Year in Naïve Music; Christmas Music; Woodwind Quintet; Music for Piano Nos 1–7; Music for Guitars Nos 1–6; Music for Viola; Dorian Song for male voice, cello, piano; Phrygian Song for female voice, cello, piano; Lydian Song for female voice, violin, piano; Septet for flute, clarinet, piano, violin, viola, voice; Music for Brass Nos 1 and 2; Hip Hop for Wind Ensemble; Music for Christian, brass and two keyboards. *Recordings:* Orchestral Pieces Nos 1, 2, 3; Piano Concerto; Concertinos for Violin and Strings; Quartet ATON, open music; Alpine Sounds for four horns; Music for Piano Nos 1, 2, 3,4,5,6,7,8; Metamusic; Music for Guitars Nos 1, 2, 3, 4,5,6. *Honours:* Second Prize, International Composers Competition, Sanremo; Recognition Prize, Pro Arte Foundation, Berne; Recognition Prize, Canton Berne; Culture-Prize, City of Biel, 2001. *Address:* PO Box 17, CH-2513 Twann, Switzerland. *E-mail:* classic2000@bluewin.ch.

SCHWEIZER, Daniel; Conductor; b. 6 Nov. 1953, Herisau, Switzerland; m. Michiko Tsuda, 4 Oct 1980, 2 s. *Education:* Zürich Konservatorium 1972–76; Cello, Musikhochschule Essen, 1976–77; Conducting, Musikhochschule Freiburg, 1979–81. *Career:* Debut: With Zürich Symphony Orchestra, 23 Nov 1981; Concerts Founder, Zürich Symphony Orchestra, 1981; Concerts at festivals in Spain and Estoril, Portugal; Guest conductor, Germany, Czechoslovakia, Italy, France, Austria, Singapore, Korea, USA, Mexico, Estonia; mem, Schweizerischer Tonkünstlerverein. *Recordings:* Jecklin: Paul Muller, orchestral works; Motette: Marcel Dupré, Symphony G minor op 25, Dupré Concerto op 31 Demessieux op 9, Jongen Symphonie Concertante op 81, Classic 2000; Alfred Schweizer, orchestral works. *Contributions:* Neue Zürcher Zeitung. *Address:* Buecheneggstrasse 31, 8906, Bonstetten, Switzerland.

SCHWEIZER, Verena; Singer (Soprano); b. 9 May 1944, Solothurn, Switzerland. *Education:* Studied at the Zürich Conservatory, in Frankfurt, Basle with Elsa Cavelti, in Aachen and Freiburg and in Mannheim with Anna Reynolds. *Career:* Sang at Aargau 1971–72, Mainz 1973–75, Dortmund 1975–83; Sang at Freiburg from 1985 and guested at Stuttgart (1986 as Jenůfa, 1990 as Marenka in The Bartered Bride); Ludwigsburg 1984–89, as Fiodriligi and Mozart's Countess; Further appearances in Leeds (with the Dortmund Opera), Geneva, Cologne, Düsseldorf and Wiesbaden; Other roles include Susanna, Zerlina, Marcellina, Adina, Gilda, Micaela, Nannetta, Mimi, Sophie in Der Rosenkavalier, Anne Trulove and Desdemona; Concert engagements in Paris, Rome, Buenos Aires and Copenhagen; St Gallen 1983, in the premiere of P Huber's Te Deum. *Recordings include:* Christmas Oratorio by Saint-Saëns; Magnificat and other sacred music by Vivaldi (Erato); Cosi fan tutte (Harmonia Mundi); Hindemith's Cardillac (Wergo). *Address:* c/o Staatstheater Stuttgart, Oberer Schlossgarten 6, 7000 Stuttgart, Germany.

SCHWENNIGER, Aurelia; Singer (Mezzo-Soprano); b. 1938, Austria. *Career:* Sang at the Landestheater Linz, 1962–64, Augsburg, 1964–66, and at the Nationaltheater Mannheim, 1968–78; Roles have included Zenobia in Handel's Radamisto, Rosina, Fenena in Nabucco, Eboli, Amneris, Magdalene, the Composer in Ariadne auf Naxos, Silla in Palestrina, Janáček's Fox and Tchaikovsky's Maid of Orleans; Guest appearances at the Vienna Staatsoper, Rome and Cologne Operas and the Teatro San Carlos at Lisbon. *Address:* Mannheim National Theater, Nationaltheater Am Goetheplatz, 6800 Mannheim, Germany.

SCHWETS, Stanislav; Opera Singer (bass); b. 28 Jan. 1974, Ekaterinburg, Russia. *Education:* Studied under Professors P. Gluboky and V. Chachava, Moscow State Conservatory, 1992–97. *Career:* Debut: Banquo in Verdi's Macbeth, Dublin Opera, 1996; Filmed in Masterclass by Galina Vishnevskaya, Moscow, 1993; Frequent broadcasts on Russian television; Sang Rogozhin and David in world premieres of N. F. B. and Young David by V. Kobekin, at Sacro Art Festival, Germany, 1995, 1997; Sang in Te Deum by Handel and in Mass in B flat by Mozart, conducted by W Gönnenwein at Lüdwigsburger Festival, 1996; Sang Daland in Der fliegende Holländer for Metz Opera, France, 1997, and with Maryinsky company, conducted by Valery Gergiev in Toulouse and Madrid, Nov 1997; 1998 engagements with Basilio in Rossini's Il Barbiere di Siviglia and Leporello in Don Giovanni at Frankfurt Opera, Daland with Maryinsky Theatre conducted by Gergiev in Lisbon, and Pimen in Boris Godunov at Dublin. Has sung in concerts with V Chachava in Moscow, St Petersburg and other Russian cities; Performed in Ekaterinburg in recital with Elena Obraztsova and Vazha Chachava. *Honours:* Grand Prix and Special Prize, Belvedere International Singers Competition, Vienna, 1994; Prizewinner, Rimsky-Korsakov International Singers Competition, St Petersburg, 1996. *Current Management:* Askonas Holt Ltd, Lonsdale Chambers, 27 Chancery Lane, London, WC2A 1PF, England. *Telephone:* (20) 7400-1700. *Fax:* (20) 7400-1799. *E-mail:* info@askonasholt.co.uk. *Website:* www.askonasholt.co.uk.

SCIAMA, Pierre; Singer (Countertenor); b. 1960, England. *Education:* Studied, Guildhall School with David Pollard and David Roblou, and at the GSM Early Music Course. *Career:* Sang Reason in Cavalieri's La Rappresentazione di Anima e di Corpo, Morley College, 1987; Purcell's Fairy Queen at the GSM conducted by William Christie; Sang in Rameau's Pygmalion at the Queen Elizabeth Hall and in Gluck's Alceste at Covent Garden and in Monte Carlo; Acis and Galatea with Midsummer Opera in Tours and at St John's Smith Square, London, 1989; Appeared in Dido and Aeneas with the Early English Opera Society and as Apollo in Grabu's Albion and Albanus; Armindo in Handel's Partenope with Midsummer Opera.

SCIARRINO, Salvatore; Composer; b. 4 April 1947, Palermo, Italy. *Education:* Studied with Tulio Belfiore, 1964, and attended electronic music sessions at the Accademia di Santa Cecilia in Rome, 1969. *Career:* Artistic Director of Teatro Comunale in Bologna; Teacher in Milan, Florence and Citta del Castello; Milan Conservatory from 1974. *Compositions:* Instrumental pieces; Berceuse for orchestra 1967; Quartetto 1967; Da un divertimento 1970; Sonata du camera 1971; Arabesque for 2 organs 1971; Rondo for flute and orchestra 1972; Romanza for viola d'amore and orchestra 1973; Variazioni for cello and orchestra 1974; 2 Piano Trios, 1974, 1986; 2 Quintetes, 1976, 1977; Clair de Lune for piano and orchestra 1976; Kindertotenlied for soprano, tenor and chamber orchestra 1978; Flos Forum for chorus and orchestra 1981; Nox apud Orpheum for 2 organs and instruments 1982; String Trio 1983; 3 Piano Sonatas 1976, 1983, 1986; Violin Conceto, Allegoria nella notte 1985; Morte di Borromini for narrator and orchestra 1989; Florence, 1978; Lohengrin, 'azione invisible', Milan 1983; Perseo e Andromeda, Stuttgart 1991; Opera Luci Miei Traditrici, Schwetzingen, 1998; Infinito nero, theatre, 1998; Notturni for piano, 1999; Cantare con silenzio, for chorus, flute and percussion, 1999; Settimo quartetto, for string quartet, 1999. *Address:* c/o Staatstheater Stuttgart, Oberer Schlossgarten 6, 7000 Stuttgart, Germany.

SCIBELLI, Carlo; Singer (Tenor); b. 1970, New York. *Career:* Appearances throughout USA and Europe as Pinkerton, the Duke of Mantua, Faust, Rodolfo, Count Almaviva and Nemorino; Telemaco in Monteverdi's Ulisse; Lurciano in Ariodante; Fracasso in Mozart's Finta Semplice and Vladimir in Prince Igor; Season 1998–99, with Don Ottavio at Turin; Macduff at Cagliari and Alfredo at Covent Garden; Season 1999–2000, with Eduardo in Un giorno di regno for the Royal Opera, in Rosenkavalier at San Francisco and I Lombardi at Santiago.

Address: c/o San Francisco Opera, Van Ness Avenue, War Memorial House, San Francisco CA 94102, USA.

SCIMONE, Claudio; Conductor and Musicologist; b. 23 Dec. 1934, Padua, Italy. *Career:* Studied with Franco Ferrara, Dmitri Mitropoulos and Carlo Zecchi., Founded the chamber ensemble I Solisti Veneti 1959; performances of 18th and 19th century Italian music, Mozart, Schoenberg and modern works (Donatoni, Bussotti, Malipiero and others); Tours of USA, Europe and Japan; wrote for La gazzetta del Veneto, 1952–57; Taught at Venice Conservatory, 1961–67; Chamber Music at Verona Conservatory, 1967–74; since then Director of Padua State Conservatory of Music; Permanent Conductor and Artistic Director of the chamber orchestra, Conducted Il Barbiere di Siviglia at Caracalla, 1992 and at the Verona Arena, 1996. *Recordings:* More than 200 recordings with I Solisti Veneti and other orchestras (London Philarmonia, Royal Philharmonic, English Chamber Orchestra, Bamberger Symphoniker, others), including L'Elisir d'amore (Ricciarelli, Carreras); Vivaldi flute concertos and Orlando Furioso; Concerti Grossi by Albinoni, Corelli and Geminiani; Marcello La Cetra; Italian flute and oboe concertos; Rossini string sonatas and Mozart's Salzburg Divertimenti; Operas by Rossini, including Zelmira, 1990. *Publications:* Editions of concertos by Tartini; Complete edition of Rossini; Segno, Significato, Interpretazione 1974; Numerous articles in music journals. *Honours:* Elizabeth Sprague Coolidge Memorial Medal 1969; Grammy record award (Los Angeles); several Grand Prix du Disque de l'Academie Charles Cros, Academie du Disque Lyrique and others. *Address:* Piazzale Pontecorvo 6, 35100 Padova, Italy.

SCOGNA, Flavio (Emilio); Composer and Conductor; b. 16 Aug. 1956, Savona, Italy; m. Fiorenza Iademarco, 1993, 2 s. *Education:* N Paganini Conservatory, Genoa; Graduated in Music, University of Bologna, 1980; Conducting with Franco Ferrara, Rome. *Career:* His works performed in major international venues including Italian Radio (Rome, Naples), Centre Pompidou (Paris), Vienna Konzerthaus, and broadcast, RAI, BBC, Radio France, ORF, BRT; Many commissions, Italian Radio, Vienna Konzerthaus, Pomeriggi Musicali of Milan; Conductor, musical groups, national and international orchestras such as RAI, Accademia Nazionale di St Cecilia, Israel Symphony Orchestra, Radio Broadcasting of Spain, Hungarian State Symphony Orchestra; Appearances on Italian Radio, Teatro Massimo, Palermo, Teatro Opera Roma, Teatro Comunale, Firenze; Teaching, several Italian conservatories such as S Pietro a Maiella, Naples, and G Rossini, Pesaro. *Compositions include:* Arioso per Guillermo, 1984; Serenata, ensemble, 1984, new version, 1988; Anton, one-act opera, 1984, new version, 1988; Incanto, string trio, 1985; Come un'onda di luce, oboe, clarinet, violin, viola, cello, 1985; Canto del mare, flute, violin, cello, 1985; Cadenza seconda, piano, 1986; Sinfonia concertante, orchestra, 1986–87; Frammento, after Mario Luz's poem, soprano, piano, 1987; La mar, marimba, 1987; Concertino, 10 instruments, 1987; Tre invenzioni, piano, 1988; Risonanze, string quartet, 1988; Fluxus, orchestra, 1988; Verso, 3 winds, 3 strings, 1988; Rifrazioni, soprano, orchestra, 1989; Alternanze, piano, strings, 1989; Musica reservata, strings, orchestra, 1990; Salmo XII, mezzo-soprano, baritone, orchestra, 1990; Relazioni, ensemble, 1991; La memoria perduta, two-act opera, 1991–93; Diaphonia, viola, orchestra, 1992; Trame, trumpet, 1993; Aulos, oboe, 1993; Concentus, for orchestra, 1994–95; Amadeus Mio Caro, for chamber orchestra, 1998. *Recordings:* As Conductor: Planc, chamber ensemble; Serenata; Incanto; Anton; Alternanze and many others for leading recording companies. *Address:* Via Gradoli 56, 00189 Rome, Italy.

SCORSIN, Giuseppe; Singer (Bass); b. 6 July 1961, Treviso, Italy. *Education:* Studied at Cremona University and the Verdi Conservatory, Milan. *Career:* Debut: Treviso 1990, as Bartolo in Le nozze di Figaro; Appearances at Monte Carlo in Gianni Schicchi, at Rovigo in La Bohème and La Scala in Franchetti's Cristoforo Colombo; Zürich Opera from 1992, in Semiramide, Butterfly, Lohengrin, The Rape of Lucretia, Macbeth, Salome, Otello, Roméo et Juliette and Die Zauberflöte; Lucerne Opera as Philip II in Don Carlo and at Lugano in Mendelssohn's Die Erste Walpurgisnacht; Further roles include Bellini's Oroveso, Rossini's Don Basilio and Ferrando in Il Trovatore, Pistola in Falstaff; Season 1996 in The Gambler at La Scala, as Orbazzano in Tancredi at Winterthur, and Don Basilio throughout Italy; Zürich Opera 1997–98: Sparafucile in Rigoletto; Il Prefetto in Linda di Chamounix (also at Bologna), Raimondo in Lucia di Lammermoor; Ashby in La fanciulla del West; Fabrizio in Wolf-Ferrari's Il Campiello at Bologna, 1998. *Honours:* Winner, 1990 Toti dal Monte Competition, Treviso. *Address:* Via Castellana 1/E, 31100 Treviso, Italy.

SCOTTO, Renata; Singer (Soprano); b. 24 Feb. 1933, Savona, Italy; m. Lorenzo Anselmi. *Education:* Studied at the Giuseppe Verdi Conservatory, Milan, with Emilio Ghiriardini. *Career:* Debut: Teatro Nuovo Milan 1953, as Violetta; Sang at La Scala from 1954 as Donizetti's Amina, Lucia and Adina and as Helena in I Vespri Siciliani; London debut Stoll Theatre 1957, as Adina, Mimi, Violetta and Donna Elvira; Edinburgh Festival 1957, as Amina in La Sonnambula; US debut

Chicago 1960, Miami; Covent Garden debut 1962, as Butterfly; Metropolitan Opera from 1965, as Lucia, Verdi's Gilda, Helena, Luisa Miller, Desdemona, Elisabeth de Valois and Lady Macbeth, Norma and Adriana Lecouvreur and in Puccini's Trittico; Directed Butterfly at the Metropolitan 1986 and sang there for the last time in 1987; Returned to Edinburgh 1972, with the Palermo company in Bellini's La Straniera; Guest appearances as Anna Bolena in Dallas and in Verdi's Requiem at the Verona arena; Sang in The Medium by Menotti and Poulenc's La Voix Humaine at Turin, 1999. *Recordings:* Roles in: Pagliacci, Cavalleria Rusticana, Lucia di Lammermoor, La Traviata, La Bohème, Edgar, Adriana Lecouvreur, Andrea Chénier, Robert le Diable, La Straniera, I Lombardi, I Capuleti e i Montecchi, La Sonnambula. *Publications:* More than a Diva, autobiography, 1984. *Address:* c/o Opéa et Concert, 1 Rue Volney, F–75002 Paris, France.

SCOVOTTI, Jeannette; Singer (Soprano); b. 5 Dec. 1933, New York City, USA. *Education:* Studied at the Juilliard School, New York. *Career:* Debut: Metropolitan Opera 1962, as Adele in Die Fledermaus; Teatro Col ón Buenos Aires 1963–65; Munich Staatsoper 1965; Sang at the Hamburg Staatsoper 1966–77, as Mozart's Zerlina and Despina, Aminta in Die schweigsame Frau, Donizetti's Lucia and Norina, and in the premiere of Krenek's Sardakai; Many engagements at opera houses elsewhere in Europe; Other roles include Olympia, Gilda, The Queen of Night, Zerlina, Aminta in Die schweigsame Frau, Zerbinetta, Constanze and Carolina in Il Matrimonio Segreto; Boston Opera 1977, in the US premiere of Ruslan and Ludmila by Glinka; Sang Costanza in a concert performance of Vivaldi's Griselda, London, 1978. *Recordings:* Les Contes d'Hoffmann; Castor et Pollux by Rameau; Eine Nacht in Venedig; Les Huguenots; Rinaldo by Handel; Die drei Pintos by Weber/Mahler; Die schweigsame Frau. *Address:* c/o Hamburgische Staatsoper, Grosse Theaterstrasse 34, 2000 Hamburg 36, Germany.

SCUDERI, Vincenzo; Singer (Tenor); b. 1961, New York, USA. *Education:* Studied in New York and with Franco Corelli. *Career:* Long Island Opera, Pinkerton, Turiddu, Rodolfo; Appearances at Plovdiv and Zürich as Ishmaele in Nabucco and as Radames, 1987–89; Sang the Duke of Mantua on tour throughout France, 1989; Sang arias from Chénier and Fanciulla del West in Tribute Concert to Franco Corelli, Purchase, New York, 1991; Radames at the Baths of Caracalla, 1991. *Address:* Opera de Marseille, 2 Rue Moliére, 1321 Marseille Cédex 01, France.

SCULTHORPE, Peter (Joshua); Composer; b. 29 April 1929, Launceston, Tasmania. *Education:* Melbourne University Conservatory of Music; Wadham College Oxford with Egon Wellesz and Edmund Rubbra. *Career:* Teacher at Syndey University from 1963; Composer in Residence Yale University, 1966; Visiting Professor, Sussex University, 1972–73. *Compositions:* Stage: Sun Music, ballet 1968; Rites of Passage, opera 1973; Quiros, television opera, 1982; Tatea, music theatre piece 1988; Orchestral: Irkanda IV for violin and strings, 1961; Small Town 1963–76; Sun Music I–IV 1965–67; Music for Japan, 1970; Rain 1970; Lament for strings 1976; Port Essington for string trio and strings 1977; Mangrove 1979; Guitar Concerto 1980; Piano Concerto, 1983; Little Suite for Strings, 1983; Sonata for Strings, 1983; Earth Cry, 1986; Second Sonata for Strings, 1988; At the Grave of Isaac Nathan, 1988; Darwin Marching, 1995; Great Sandy Island, 1998; Rockpool Dreaming for soprano saxophone and strings, 1998; Cello Dreaming for cello, strings and percussion, 1998; Gondwana Land for strings, 1999; My Country Childhood, for strings, 1999; Quamby, for chamber orchestra, 2000; Instrumental: The Loneliness of Bunjil for string trio 1954; 15 String Quartets 1947–99; Sonata for viola and percussion, 1960; Tabuh Tabuhan for wind quintet and percussion 1968; How the Stars were Made for percussion ensemble, 1971; Landscape for piano quartet 1980; Songs of Sea and Sky for clarinet and piano, 1987; Vocal: Sun Music for Voices and Percussion, 1966; Love 200 for rock band 1970; Ketjak for six male voices with tape echo, 1972; The Songs of Tailitnama for high voice, 6 cellos and percussion, 1974; Child of Australia for chorus, soprano, narrator and orchestra, 1987; Maranoa Lullaby, for mezzo and string quartet, 1996; Love Thoughts, for two speakers, soprano and five instruments, 1998. Piano Music; Music for the film Burke and Wills, 1985; Postcard from Nourlangie to Clapham Common, 1993; From Saibai, 1993; Memento Mori for orchestra, 1993; From Ubirr, for string quartet and didjeridoo, 1994. *Honours:* Order of the British Empire, 1977; Doctor of Letters, University of Tasmania, 1980, 1985 APRA Award for his Piano Concerto. *Address:* c/o Faber Music Ltd, 3 Queen Square, London WC1N 3AU, England.

SEAMAN, Christopher; Conductor; b. 7 March 1942, Faversham, Kent, England. *Education:* Canterbury Cathedral Choir School, 1950–55; The King's School Canterbury, 1955–60; ARCO, ARCM, King's College, Cambridge, 1960; MA 1963. *Career:* Principal Timpanist, London Philharmonic Orchestra, 1964–68; Assistant Conductor, BBC Scottish Symphony Orchestra, 1968–70; Principal Conductor, BBC Scottish Symphony Orchestra, 1971–77; Principal Conductor, Northern Sinfonia, 1973–79; Chief Guest Conductor, Utrecht Symphony Orchestra,

1979–83; Conductor-in-Residence, Baltimore Symphony Orchestra 1987–98; Opened the 1995 Bergen Festival with Elgar's King of Olaf; Further concerts with the Rotterdam Philharmonics, Detroit and Houston Symphony Orchestras and the Prague Symphony Orchestra; Music Director, Naples (Florida) Philharmonic Orchestra, 1993–; Music Director Elect of Rochester Philharmonic Orchestra, 1998–. *Honours:* FGSM 1972. *Current Management:* Harrison/Parrott Ltd, 12 Penzance Place, London, W11 4PA, England. *Telephone:* (20) 7229 9166. *Fax:* (20) 7221 5042. *Website:* www.harrisonparrott.com.

SEARS, Nicholas; Singer (Tenor); b. 1965, Australia. *Education:* Trinity College, Cambridge; Guildhall School of Music, London. *Career:* Performed as a baritone singing major roles with the Welsh National Opera, Opera North, English National Opera, Scottish Opera and La Monnaie, Brussels; Concert appearances with the Songmakers' Almanac, the London Philharmonic Orchestra, the London Symphony Orchestra and the BBC Symphony and Philharmonic Orchestras; Having changed to tenor, made debut as the Chevalier in Poulenc's Dialogues des Carmélites at Aldeburgh and has since sung Achilles (King Priam) in Antwerp, Lysander (Midsummer Night's Dream), Essex and Spirit of the Mask (Gloriana), Telemachus (Ulisse) and Agenore (Re Pastore) for Opera North, Chevalier (Carmélites) Lucano (Poppea) for Welsh National Opera, Damon (Acis and Galatea) in Frankfurt, Grimoaldo (Rodelinda) for OTC in Ireland, High Priest (Idomeneo), Aufidio (Lucio Silla) and Da-ud (Die Aegyptische Helena) for Garsington, Sailor (Dido and Aeneas) at Covent Garden, and Shepherd (Orfeo) in Lugano; Further engagements for Opera North, Pluto (Orfeus in the Underworld), Grimaldo (Rodelinda) in New York, Gloriana in Barcelona, and Handel's Il Trionfo di Tempo e del Disinganno in Italy, Spain, Mexico, France and Belgium; Sang in Rodelinda at the 2000 Buxton Festival. *Recordings:* On this Bleak Hut by Philip Grange with the Gemini Ensemble; Lysander (Dream); Spirit of the Mask in Gloriana for the BBC. *Address:* 84 Algernon Road, Ladywell, London SE13 7AW, England.

SEBASTIAN, Bruno; Singer (Tenor); b. 1947, Udine, Italy. *Education:* Studied with Mario del Monaco. *Career:* Debut: Venice in 1969 in Donizetti's Belisario; Sang widely in Italy from 1970 notably as Arnold in Guillaume Tell at Florence, Wagner in Boito's Mefistofele at Caracalla and Radames at Verona; Sang Cavaradossi at Brussels in 1976, Otello at Basle, Manrico at Boston and the Metropolitan Opera, and Edgardo at Barcelona in 1987; Other roles include the Duke of Mantua, Macduff and Calaf (Helsinki, 1991); Sang Cavaradossi at the Prague State Opera, 2000. *Address:* Deutsche Oper Berlin, Bismarckstrasse 35, 1 Berlin 10, Germany.

SEBESTA, Ronald; Clarinettist; b. 22 July 1967, Senica, Czechoslovakia. *Education:* Diploma, Bratislava Conservatory, 1987; Studies, 1988–93, Diploma, 1993, Postgraduate study, Clarinet in the 20th century–virtuality and reality, 1995–, Academy of Music, Bratislava; 8 months study, Boulogne Conservatory, France, 1991–92. *Career:* Co-founder, VENI ensemble for contemporary music, with concerts in Bratislava (Evenings of New Music Festival), Prague, Berlin, Vienna, Perugia, Bucharest; Projects (workshops and concerts) with Younghi Pagh Paan, Siegfried Palm, Hans Deinzer, Louis Andriessen, James Tenney, Hugh Davies; Solo performance of Giacinto Scelsi's Kya, 1990; VENI ensemble recording for Die Hessische Rundfunk in Frankfurt, 1993; 1st Clarinettist, Slovak Radio Symphony Orchestra, Bratislava; Solo performance at Wien Modern Festival, 1994; Co-founder of Vapori del Cuore, improvising group, 1994; Solo performance of Mozart and Brahms Clarinet Quintets, 1995; 1st Clarinet, Cappela Istropolitana, chamber orchestra, Bratislava, 1995–; Co-founder, Opera Aperta ensemble, for classical and contemporary chamber music, 1997–; Solo performances of Mozart Clarinet Concerto, 1997–; mem, International Society for Contemporary Music, Slovak Section. *Recordings:* 2 CDs of VENI ensemble, 1990, 1992; Third CD, VENI ensemble, with music by Daniel Matej, 1995; CD of Opera Aperta ensemble, Postminimal set 2002; CD of Vapori del Cuore, Alpine Songs 2003. *Publications:* Clarinet quintet as a formation of chamber music and its place in the chamber music of classical-romantic tradition, diploma thesis, 1993. *Address:* Fandlyho 1, 81103 Bratislava, Slovakia. *E-mail:* info@operaaperta.com. *Website:* www.operaaperta.com.

SEBESTYEN, Janos; Organist and Harpsichordist; b. 2 March 1931, Budapest, Hungary. *Education:* Diploma, Ferenc Liszt Academy, Budapest. *Career:* Recitals, radio and television in Hungary; Tours with organ and harpsichord recitals throughout Europe, USA, Japan and Philippines; Radio recordings; Organ Four Hand Duo with István Lantos; Founder and Leading Professor of Harpsichord Faculty, Academy of Music, Budapest, 1970–; Musical feature programme series, Radio Budapest; President of Jury, International Liszt Organ Competition, Budapest, 1983, 1988 and 1993; Member of the Jury Organ Competition S Elpidio, Italy, 1998; Member of the Jury International Harpsichord Competition, Paris, 1976, Prague, 1999; President of the Jury First International Harpsichord Competition, Budapest, 2000.

Recordings: Over 85 records, including Complete Organ Works of Liszt. *Publications:* Musical Conversations with Miklós Rózsa, 1979;... those Radio years 1925–1995, 1995. *Honours:* Erkel Prize, 1967; Liszt Prize, 1974; Merited Artist, 1982; Cavaliere of the Italian Republic, 1984; Commander of the Order Infante Dom Henrique, Portugal, 1996; Officer of the Order, Isabelle la Católica, Spain, 1999; Cavalier of the Order of the Southern Cross, Brazil, 2000; Royal Order of the Nordic Star, Sweden, 2000; Hungarian Order Officers Cross, 2000; Ufficiale of the Italian Repub., 2003. *Address:* Fillér-u. 48, 1022 Budapest, Hungary. *Website:* jsebestyen.org.

SECUNDE, Nadine; Singer (soprano); b. 21 Dec. 1953, Independence, Ohio, USA. *Education:* Oberlin Conservatory and Indiana University School of Music with Margaret Harshaw; further study in Germany on a Fulbright Scholarship. *Career:* Engaged first at the Hessisches Staatstheater Wiesbaden; Member of the Cologne Opera, where her roles have been Katya Kabanova, Elsa, Agathe, Elisabeth, Chrysothemis and Ariadne; Vienna Staatsoper debut as Sieglinde, Hamburg Staatsoper as Katya; Bayreuth Festival debut 1987, as Elsa in a Werner Herzog production of Lohengrin; returned 1988, as Sieglinde in the Harry Kupfer production of Der Ring des Nibelungen; Covent Garden and Chicago 1988, as Elsa and Elisabeth; returned to London 1990, as Chrysothemis; Sang Elisabeth at Munich, 1994, (also televised); Concert engagements include the Choral Symphony with the Los Angeles Philharmonic, conducted by Previn, and with the Orchestre de Paris under Barenboim; Penderecki's Dies Irae with the Warsaw Philharmonic; Sang Chrysothemis at Covent Garden (1997), and in the 1997 Munich premiere of Henze's Venus and Adonis; Netherlands Opera 1998 as Brünnhilde in Götterdämmerung; Sang Chrysothemis at Munich (2000) and Isolde at the Teatro Colón, Buenos Aires; Brünnhilde at Bilbao, 2002. *Current Management:* Ingpen & Williams Ltd, 7 St George's Court, 131 Putney Bridge Road, London, SW15 2PA, England.

SEERS, Mary; Singer (Soprano); b. 1958, England. *Education:* Studied at Girton College, Cambridge (choral exhibitioner) and in Rome and London. *Career:* Appearances with the Landini Consort, the Consort of Musique, The Scholars and the Hilliard Ensemble; Festival engagements at Aix-en-Provence, Schleswig-Holstein and Greenwich; Tour of the United Kingdom and Italy 1988 with Pärt's St John Passion; Concerts in Sydney and Tokyo 1989 with John Eliot Gardiner and the Monteverdi Choir; Concerts include Bach B minor Mass, Wrocław (Poland) with City of London Sinfonia; Other repertoire includes Mozart's C minor Mass, the Monteverdi Vespers (Bruges Festival), Messiah (St Martin in the Fields) and music by Finzi and Purcell; Further engagements at the Almeida, Cheltenham and Orkney Festivals and concerts with the Scottish Chamber Orchestra and the East of England Orchestra; US concerts in Chicago and New York, Pärt's St John Passion; Opera: with Music Theatre Wales, role of Madeleine in Philip Glass, The Fall of The House of Usher; Festivals: Warsaw Contemporary Music Festival (Pärt Passio), 1992; Television: Took part in BBC 2 documentary with English Chamber Orchestra and Corydon Singers; Monteverdi Vespers with The Sixteen. *Address:* c/o Music Theatre Wales, 5 Llandaff Road, Cardiff, CF11 9NF, Wales.

SEGAL, Uriel; Conductor; b. 7 March 1944, Jerusalem, Israel; m. Illana Finkelstein, 1 s., 3 d. *Education:* Studied violin from age 7; Rubin Academy of Music, Israel; Conducting with Mendi Rodan at the Guildhall School of Music, London. *Career:* Debut: With Seajillands Symphony Orchestra, Copenhagen, 1969; Assistant Conductor, working with George Szell and Leonard Bernstein, New York, Philharmonic Orchestra, 1969–70; Chief Conductor, Philharmonica Hungarica, 1981–85; Principal Conductor, Bournemouth Symphony, 1980–83; Guest appearances with the Hamburg and Israel Philharmonics, Chicago Symphony, Spanish National Orchestra, London Symphony and Philharmonic, Philharmonia, French Radio Philharmonic, Montreal and New Zealand Symphony. Stuttgart Radio Symphony, RAI Rome, Hallé Orchestra, Scottish National; Chief Conductor of the Israel Chamber Orchestra from 1982; Music Director of the Chautauqua Festival (New York State) and Chief Conductor of the Osaka Century Orchestra, Japan; Opera experience includes Der fliegende Holländer at Santa Fe, 1973, and Il re Pastore, Opéra de Nice; Madama Butterfly at Tel-Aviv, season, 1995–96. *Recordings include:* Stravinsky's Firebird Suite and Symphony in C, with the Suisse Romande Orchestra; Mozart Piano Concertos with Radu Lupu and the English Chamber Orchestra; Schumann's Piano Concerto with Ashkenazy and the London Symphony; Beethoven Piano Concertos with Rudolf Firkusny and the Philharmonia. *Honours:* 1st Prize, Mitropoulos Conducting Competition, New York, 1969. *Current Management:* Terry Harrison Artists Management, The Orchard, Market Street, Charlbury, Oxfordshire OX7 3PJ, England. *Telephone:* (1608) 810330. *Fax:* (1608) 811331. *E-mail:* artists@terryharrison.force9.co.uk.

SEGERSTAM, Leif; Conductor and Composer; b. 2 March 1944, Vasa, Finland. *Education:* Violin, Piano, Conducting, Composition, Sibelius Academy, Helsinki until 1963; Conducting diploma, Juilliard School of Music, New York, USA, 1964; Postgraduate Diploma, 1965. *Career:* Debut: Violin soloist Helsinki, 1963; Conductor, Royal Opera Stockholm, 1968–72 and Musical Director, 1971–72; 1st Conductor, Deutsche Oper Berlin, 1972–73; General Manager Finnish National Opera, 1973–74; Chief Conductor ORF (Austrian Radio) Vienna 1975–82; Musical Director, Finnish Radio Symphony Orchestra, Helsinki, 1977–87: Principal Guest Conductor from 1987; General Music Director, Staatsphilharmonie Rhenland-Pfalz 1983–89; Honorary Conductor, 1989; Conductor of the Danish Radio Symphony Orchestra from 1988; Chief Conductor of the Helsinki Philharmonic Orchestra, 1995–; Led Tannhäuser at the 1997 Savonlinna Festival and began a new Ring cycle at Stockholm with Das Rheingold; Conducted Die Walküre and Siegfried at Helsinki, 1998; mem, Royal Academy of Music, Sweden. *Compositions include:* Divertimento for strings 1963; 6 Cello Concertos; 3 Piano Concertos; 57 Symphonies 1977–98 (nos. 20–25 to be given without conductor); 8 Violin Concertos; 6 Double Concertos; Many works for orchestra under title Composed orchestral works called Thought, the most famous being, Monumental Thoughts, Martti Tavela in memorium; Orchestral Diary Sheets, 5 Songs of Experience after Blake and Auden for soprano and orchestra 1971; 28 String Quartets; 3 Piano Trios; 4 String Trios; Episodes for various instrumental combinations. *Recordings:* Works by Mahler, Sibelius, Brahms, Scriabin, Petterson, Schnittke, Rott, Ruders, Koechlin, Schmitt, Roussel, Caplet, Roger-Ducasse and own compositions. *Honours:* Second Prize with Symphony IV, Sibelius, 1991; Record of the Year, Sibelius III symphony (Chandos), 1992. *Address:* c/o Jankko, Tölögatan 7 A5, 00100 Helsinki, Finland.

SEIFERT, Gerd-Heinrich; Horn player; b. 17 Oct. 1931, Hamburg, Germany; m. 29 June 1957, 3 s., 1 d. *Education:* Music High School, Hamburg, 1944–49; Studied horn with Albert Doscher. *Career:* Debut: Soloist, Horn Concerto (Strauss), 1948; Substitute, Hamburg Philharmonic Orchestra, 1947–49; Solo Horn, Düsseldorfer Symphoniker, 1949–64; Solo Horn, Bayreuth Festival, 1961; Solo Horn, Berlin Philharmonic Orchestra, 1964–; Performed with Düsseldorfer Waldhorn Quartett, also 13 Bläser Philharmonic Orchestra and Philharmonic Octet, Berlin; Teacher of Horn, Music High School, Berlin, 1970–. *Recordings:* With Berlin Philharmonic Orchestra/Octet (Hindemith); Octet, Nonet (Spohr); Serenade for 13 Wind instruments by Mozart, and other Chamber music; Concert Piece for 4 horns (Schumann). *Contributions:* Brass Bulletin. *Honours:* 1st Prize, ARD Competition, Munich, 1956; 125 Siegfried Calls at Bayreuth Festival since 1961; Grand Prix du Disque. *Address:* Xantenerstrasse 1, 1000 Berlin 15, Germany.

SEIFERT, Ingrid; Violinist; b. 1952, Austria. *Education:* Studied violin in Salzburg and Vienna. *Career:* Played with the Concentus Musicus, Vienna and studied further in Netherlands; With Charles Medlam co-founded London Baroque, 1978; With London Baroque led the first performance of Scarlatti's Una Villa di Tuscolo and a revival of Gli Equivoci Sembiante, for the BBC; Season 1990–91 included: Dido and Aeneas at Paris Opéra; Music by Blow and Lully, Opéra Comique; Aci, Galatea e Polifemo in Spain, Netherlands and England; Cantatas by Handel and Rameau in Austria, Sweden and Germany, with Emma Kirkby; Other recent repertoire includes: Charpentier Messe de Minuit; 4 Violin music by Telemann, Vivaldi and Wassenaar; Bach Brandenburg Concertos; Monteverdi Tancredi and Clorinda; Salzburg Festival debut, 1991, with music by Mozart; Further festival engagements at Bath, Beaune, Versailles, Ansbach, Innsbruck and Utrecht. *Recordings:* Marais La Gamme; Theile Matthew Passion; Bach Trio Sonatas; Charpentier Theatre Music; Handel Aci, Galatea e Polifemo; Blow Venus and Adonis; Purcell Chamber Music, (Harmonia Mundi); Purcell Fantasias; Bach Violin Sonatas; Monteverdi Orfeo; Handel German Arias; A Vauxhall Gardens Entertainment; English Music of the 18th Century; François Couperin Apotheose de Lulli, Corelli Chamber Music; Complete Trios of Handel, Purcell; Chamber Music by Lawes; Pachelbel, Complete Chamber Music; Vivaldi Sonatas op. 1; Handel Latin Motets, with Emma Kirkby; Bach Trio sonatas; Couperin Apotheose de Lulli, Corelli etc; Rameau Pièces de Clavecin en concert. *Address:* Brick Kiln Cottage, Hollington, Near Newbury, Berkshire RG20 9XX, England.

SEIFFERT, Peter; Singer (Tenor); b. 4 Jan. 1954, Düsseldorf, Germany; m. Lucia Popp, 1986, deceased 1993. *Education:* Studied at the Robert Schumann Musikhochschule Düsseldorf. *Career:* Sang first with the Deutsche Oper am Rhein Düsseldorf in Der Wildschütz and Fra Diavalo; Member of the Deutsche Oper Berlin from 1982, notably as Lensky, Jenik in The Bartered Bride, Huon (Oberon) and Faust; Bayerische Staatsoper Munich 1983, as Fenton in Die Lustigen Weiber von Windsor: has returned in Der Barber von Bagdad by Cornelius and as Narraboth and Lohengrin; Vienna Staatsoper and La Scala Milan debuts 1984; Covent Garden debut 1988, as Parsifal in a new production of Wagner's opera conducted by Bernard Haitink; Season 1988/89 sang Faust at the Deutsche Oper Berlin and Lohengrin in Munich (repeated 1990); Sang at Salzburg 1992, as Narraboth; Concert engagements include Mozart's Requiem with Giulini in London, and the Choral Symphony with Muti in Philadelphia; Sang Walther von Stolzing in Die Meistersinger at the 1996 Bayreuth Festival; Season 1998 with Max in Der Freischütz at Rome; Season 2000–01 as Lohengrin at the Deutsche Oper Berlin, Walther in Munich in, Rienzi in Dresden and Erik for Zürich Opera; Parsifal at Bayreuth, 2002. *Recordings:* Elijah; Zar und Zimmerman; Matteo in Arabella, conducted by Jeffrey Tate; Die Fledermaus, conducted by Domingo; Gianni Schicchi (Patanè); Erik in Der fliegende Holländer, conducted by Pinchas Steinberg; The Choral Symphony (Muti) and Mozart's Mass in C Minor with Levine; Mendelssohn's Lobgesang and Beethoven's Symphony No. 9 with Sawallisch; Solo Records of Operetta; Solo Record of Opera; Freischitz; Fidelio; Liszt, Faust Symphony, conducted by Simon Rattle. *Honours:* Kammersänger of the Bavarian State Opera. *Address:* Bavarian Staatsoper, Maximilianstrasse, Munich, Germany.

SEIFRIED, Reinhard; Conductor; b. 25 July 1945, Freising, Germany; m. Fenna Kügel, 31 Oct 1991, 2 d. *Education:* Hochschule für Musik in Munich, trade examination and master class for conducting; Assistant Conductor with Rudolf Kempe, Rafael Kubelik, Karl Richter, Leonard Bernstein. *Career:* Debut: Conductor in Staatstheater am Gärtnerplatz, Munich, 1976; Conductor, Nürnberg, 1986; Chief Conductor, Remscheider Symphoniker, 1991; Music Director, and Chief Conductor of Oldenburgisches Staatsorchester, 1993–; Guest Conductor, Europe, Japan and USA. *Recordings:* Mendelssohn-Bartholdy, all symphonies with Irish National Symphony Orchestra, Dublin; Smetana, Ma Vlast, with Slovak State Philharmonic Košice. *Current Management:* FAME Management, Claudius Hirt, Lucerne. *Address:* Oldenburgisches Staatstheater, Theaterwall 18, 26122 Oldenburg, Germany.

SEILER, Mayumi; Violinist; b. 1963, Japan (German/Japanese parentage). *Education:* Studied in Japan and at the Salzburg Mozarteum, with Sándor Végh. *Career:* Concerts with the Australian Chamber Orchestra, Hong Kong Philharmonic, Royal Philharmonic, and the Academy of St Martin in the Fields at the 1994 London Proms. *Recordings include:* Concertos as director/soloist with the City of London Sinfonia (Virgin Classics). *Honours:* Christina Rechter Steiner Prize, Salzburg Mozarteum. *Address:* City of London Sinfonia, 11 Drum Street, London E1 12H, England.

SEILTGEN, Annette; Singer (Mezzo-Soprano); b. 26 June 1964, Wuppertal, Germany. *Education:* Leopold Mozart Conservatory in Augsburg and the Studio of the Bavarian State Opera. *Career:* Kassel Opera, 1990–92, as Rosina, Wellgunde in The Ring and Strauss's Composer; Theater am Gärtnerplatz, Munich, 1992–96; as Hansel, Cherubino, Rosina and Cornet in Matthus's Die Weise von Liebe und Tod; Guest appearances from 1989 at Mannheim, Heidelberg, Bielefeld, and Hannover notably as Octavian in Der Rosenkavalier; Deutsche Oper am Rhein at Düsseldorf from 1996, with Andronico in Handel's Tamerlano, 1998; Guest appearance in Madrid at the Theatro Real as Sextus in Mozart's La Clemenza di Tito, 1999; Season 1999–2000 as Dusseldorf as Olga in Three Sisters by Peter Eötvös, Ruggiero in Alcina and three roles in Lulu; Guest appearances in Nice and Santiago de Chile; Other roles include Don Ramiro in La finta giardineira by Mozart. *Address:* c/o Deutsche Oper am Rhein, Operhaus Düsseldorf, Heinrich-Heine-Alle 16a, 40213 Düsseldorf, Germany.

SEIPP, Joachim; Singer (BassBaritone); b. 1956, Pohlheim, Germany. *Education:* Frankfurt Musikhochschule, Milan and Vienna with Milkana Nikolova. *Career:* Sang at Kiel Opera, 1982–86; Karlsruhe 1985–86; Hanover 1986–91; Landestheater Innsbruck from 1991; Repertoire; Marquese di Posa, Rigoletto, Iago, Scarpia, Wotan in Rheingold, Four Villains in Les Contes d'Hoffmann, Carmina Burana by Carl Orff, Germont, Ford in Falstaff and Mozart's Count; Title role in Dallapiccola's Il Prigioniero; Guest appearances at the Ludwigsburg Festival as the Count, 1987 and 1989; Sang at Wiesbaden in Henze's Das verratene Meer, 1990; Der Kaiser von Atlantis by Victor Ullmann, La Monnaie, Brussels; Sang at Innsbruck as Iago (1999) and Albert in Werther, 2001; Der Fliegende Holländer in Domstufen Festival in Erfurt under the direction of Werner Herzog; Further roles include Kurwenal in Tristan und Isolde and Pizarro in Fidelio under Brigitte Fassbaender and Conte Luna in Il Trovatore and Amonasro in Aida; Concert repertory includes Schubert's Schwanengesang, Wolf's Italian Song Book and all great oratorios and major concert pieces. *Address:* c/o Landestheater Innsbruck, Rennweg 2, 6020 Innsbruck, Austria.

SEIVEWRIGHT, (Robert) Peter, BA, MA; concert pianist and lecturer; b. 11 July 1954, Skipton, England. *Education:* Worcester College, Oxford; FRCO Diploma, Royal Northern College of Music with Ryszard Bakst. *Career:* Tutor, University of Keele, 1979–83; Instructor in Music, University of Leicester, 1980–84; Lecturer in Music, Royal Scottish Academy of Music and Drama, 1984–; University Pianist, University of Strathclyde, 1990–93; Concerts throughout the United Kingdom, Ireland, Norway, Germany, Belgium, Denmark (eight recital tours), Latvia, Estonia, Viet Nam, Australia (five concert tours) and China,

including Huddersfield Contemporary Music Festival 1983, 1984, Tivoli Concert Hall and Århus Festival, Denmark, 1986, Munch-Museum, Oslo, 1986; Heilbronn International Piano Forum 1993, Germany International Masters of the Keyboard series, Bruges, Belgium, 1994, International All-Stars Piano Festival, Liepaja, Latvia, 1997, Concerto appearances with leading orchestras including Hallé Orchestra, Bradford Chamber Orchestra, Scottish Sinfonietta, Strathclyde Sinfonia, Paragon Ensemble, Liepaja Symphony Orchestra, recordings BBC Scotland, BBC Radio 3, Radio Denmark, 3MBs and ABC (Australia). *Recordings include:* Contemporary Scottish Piano Music; Complete Piano Music of Carl Nielsen, 2CDs, 1995; Piano Music by Victor Bendix, 1998; Complete Piano Sonatas of Baldassare Galuppi 1706–1785, 10 CDs; Variations and Fugue on a theme of Telemann and Variations and Fugue on a theme of Bach by Max Reger, 1999. *Current Management:* Tivoli Festival Agency, 20 H. C. Andersens Boulevard, Copenhagen V, Denmark. *Address:* The Old Joinery, Lintfieldbank, Coalburn, Lanarkshire ML11 0NJ, Scotland.

SELBIG, Ute; Singer (Soprano); b. 18 Aug. 1960, Dresden, Germany. *Education:* Dresden Musikhochschule until 1985. *Career:* Sang with Dresden Kreuzchor; Tours of Japan, 1988 and Canada, 1991; Member of Dresden Opera from 1985, as Zerlina, Nannetta, Aennchen in Der Freischütz, Musetta, Susanna, Sophie in Der Rosenkavalier, Pamina and Fiordiligi; Guest appearances throughout Europe and at Los Angeles and St Louis; Zdenka in Arabella at Geneva, 1994; Guardian of the Threshold in Die Frau ohne Schatten at Dresden, 1997; Season 2000–01 at Dresden as Donna Elvira, Pamina, Marzelline in Fidelio and Ilia in Idomeneo (concert). *Recordings:* Mozart Arias; Sacred Music by Mozart; Das Lied von der Glocke by Bruch. *Honours:* Prizewinner in competitions at Prague and Leipzig. *Address:* c/o Semper Oper Dresden, Theaterplatz 2, 01067 Dresden, Germany.

SELBY, Kathryn Shauna, BA, MM; concert pianist; b. 20 Sept. 1962, Sydney, Australia. *Education:* Sydney Conservatorium of Music, Bryn Mawr College, PA, Curtis Institute of Music, Juilliard School of Music. *Career:* debut, YMCA, 92nd Street, NY, 1981; Wigmore Hall in London in 1987; Appearances with Sydney Symphony Orchestra, Philadelphia Orchestra, Pittsburgh, St Louis and Cincinnati Symphony Orchestras, Calgary and Erie Philharmonic, Indianapolis Symphony Orchestra, Shreveport Symphony Orchestra, among others; As Chamber Musician at Spoleto Festival, Australia in 1986, Marlboro Music Festival, Caramoor Festival, Concerto Soloists of Philadelphia, Hartford Chamber Orchestra, Kennedy Center Washington; Founding Member of Selby, Pini, Pereira Trio, Australia with appearances and tours, Musica Viva in Australia, 1985, 1987; ABC Film, Mozart in Delphi with Australian Chamber Orchestra for ABC Australia; Recitals in New York, Washington DC, Seattle, Portland, Pittsburgh, Philadelphia, Sydney, London and Munich.

SELBY, Philip; Composer; b. 6 Feb. 1948, United Kingdom; m.; one s. *Education:* composition studies with G. Petrassi, C. Camilleri and K. Stockhausen; Royal Manchester Coll. of Music. *Career:* debut, composer, first performance of From the Fountain of Youth, for guitar and chamber orchestra, Royal Spa Centre, Leamington 1975; guitarist soloist, Birmingham Town Hall 1966; Royal Albert Hall, London 1970; All India Radio and television, Pakistani television, Youth Palace, Tehran, Istanbul Univ.; musical works performed internationally; mem. British Acad. of Composers and Songwriters; Inc. Soc. of Musicians; Performing Rights Soc.. *Compositions:* Suite for guitar, 1965–67; Music for Golden Leaves, 1971–72; Portrait of Django for guitar, 1972; Two Meditations for piano, 1972–74; Symphonic Dance for orchestra, 1973; Ten Little Studies for guitar, 1973–76; Fantasia for guitar, 1974; Rhapsody for piano and orchestra, 1975; A Nature Meditation for violin and small orchestra, 1976; Guitar concerto, 1976–77; Sonatina for piano, 1978; Spirit of the Earth for flute, 1978; Branch Touches Branch for small orchestra, 1979; Isa Upanishad for double chorus and orchestra, 1979–87; Fountain of Youth ballet, 1981–82; Greek Suite for oboe, 1981; Siddhartha, 1981–84; Logos for trumpet, 1982; Symphony of Sacred Images for soprano and bass soloist, double chorus and orchestra, 1986–92; Ring out ye bells, 1988; Anthem for Gibraltar, unison voices and organ, 1994; Beatus Vir, Motet, 1995; String quartet no.1, 1996–97; Autoritratto Vittorio Alfieri for soprano, violin and guitar, 1998; Piano Sonata, 1998–99; Agape for solo violin, 2001–02; Agape II for solo viola, 2002. *Honours:* Chevalier Ordre Souverain et Militaire de la Milice du Saint Sépulcre, 1988. *Address:* Hill Cottage, via Maggio 93, 00068 Rignano Flaminio, Rome, Italy. *Telephone:* (761) 507945.

SELEZNEV, Georgi; Singer (bass); b. 21 Oct. 1938, Tbilisi, Georgia. *Education:* Studied at Toilisi and the Leningrad Conservatory. *Career:* Bass Soloist at the Maly Opera Leningrad, 1972–78; Appearances with the Bolshoi Opera Russia, 1978–, on tour to Western Europe and USA; Solo debut in the West as Konchak and Galitzky in Prince Igor at Trieste, 1985; Returned as Dosifei, in Khovanshchina; Title role in Salammbô by Mussorgsky for RAI in Rome; Appeared in all international tours of Bolshoi Company in recent years; Engagements such as: Verdi Requiem under Chailly, with Royal Concertgebouw Orchestra in Amsterdam; Oroveso, with Joan Sutherland as Norma, at Opera Pacific and with Michigan Opera; Boris at Wiesbaden Festival; Pimen at Opéra du Rhin, Strasbourg, repeated at Bordeaux, 1993; Returned to Bordeaux as Timur, in production of Turandot, director Alain Lombard, 1994; Boris Godunov at St Petersburg, 1997. *Recordings include:* Salammbô; Oroveso in Norma. *Honours:* Lenin Prize. *Current Management:* Athole Still International Management, Forresters Hall, 25–27 Westow Street, London, SE19 3RY, England. *Telephone:* (20) 8771-5271. *Fax:* (20) 8768-6600. *Website:* www.atholestill.com.

SELIG, Franz-Josef; Singer (Bass); b. 11 July 1962, Germany. *Education:* Studied at the Cologne Musikhochschule with Claudio Nicolai. *Career:* Concert Tours of Italy, Germany, France, Switzerland, Netherlands and Turkey; Engaged at the Essen Opera from 1989, as the King in Aida, Herr Reich in Die Lustige Weiber von Windsor and Sarastro in Die Zauberflöte; Sang Mozart's Speaker at Frankfurt, 1991, and Fafner in Das Rheingold at Covent Garden; USA debut in Fidelio at San Francisco, 1995; St John Passion with Solti, 1997–98; Season 1998 with Mozart's Sarastro, and Samiel and Hermit in Der Freischütz at La Scala; Season 1999–2000 as Mozart's Commendatore at La Scala and the Vienna Staatsoper, Camillo in the premiere of Wintermärchen by Boesmans, at Brussels, and King Marke for the Deutsche Oper Berlin. *Recordings include:* Die Zauberflöte; Sacred Music by Mozart.

SELLARS, Peter, BA; American theatre and opera director; b. 27 Sept. 1957, Pittsburgh, PA. *Education:* Harvard Univ. *Career:* Dir Boston Shakespeare Co. 1983–84; Dir and Man. American Nat. Theater at J. F. Kennedy Center, Washington, DC 1984–; Artistic Adviser, Boston Opera Theatre 1990; Fellow MacArthur Foundation, Chicago 1983. *Productions include:* Ajax, Armida, Così fan tutte, The Death of Klinghoffer, Die Zauberflöte, Don Giovanni, The Electrification of the Soviet Union, Le Grand Macabre, Idomeneo, The Lighthouse, The Marriage of Figaro, Mathis der Maler, Merchant of Venice, The Mikado, El Niño, Nixon in China, Orlando, The Rake's Progress, Saul and Orlando, St Francois d'Assise, Tannhäuser, Theodora, Zangezi. *Address:* American National Theater, Kennedy Center, Washington, DC 20566, USA.

SELLHEIM, Eckart; Pianist, Fortepianist and Accompanist; b. 29 Oct. 1939, Danzig. *Education:* Hamburg Conservatory; Piano, Accompanying, Musikhochschule, Cologne; Concert Diploma, 1963; Musicology, Music History, History of Art, Theatre, Cologne University. *Career:* Lecturer, Rheinische Musikschule, Cologne, 1963–69; Professor, Piano, Musikhochschule, Cologne, 1969–83; Piano, Piano Chamber Music, University of Michigan, Ann Arbor, USA, 1983–89; Piano Accompanying, Director of Accompanying, Arizona State University, Tempe, 1989–; Concert tours: Germany, Austria, England, France, Spain, Italy, Poland, Netherlands, USA, Latin America, Middle East; Duo with Friedrich-Jürgen Sellheim, Cello, 1965–; Several 100 Radio recordings, Germany, Europe, USA. *Recordings include:* With Fr J Sellheim, Cello: Mendelssohn, 2 Cello Sonatas; 2 Variations Concertantes; Lied Ohne Worte, 1976; Brahms, 2 Cello Sonatas, 1977; Schumann, Fantasiestücke, Adagio und Allegro, Stücke im Volkston, 1978; Schubert, Arpeggione-Sonata, Chopin, Cello Sonata, Polonaise Brillante, Grand Duo Concertant, 1980; Ravel, Violin Sonata, 1985; Transcriptions of Chopin, Bach, Weber, Gluck, Schumann, Schubert, Rakoczi March, also Brahms Transcriptions by Max Reger and Theodor Kirchner, 1990. *Publications:* Editor, Spielbuch für Klavier. *Contributions:* Friedrich Gruetzmacher, 1966; Oskar von Pander, 1968; Instrumentale Ausbildung-Klavier, 1980; Die Klavierwerke W Fr Bachs, Concerto, 1984. *Address:* 2416 West Nopal Avenue, Mesa, AZ 85202, USA.

SELLICK, Phyllis Doreen, OBE, FRAM, FRCM, LRAM; piano teacher; b. 1911, Essex, England; m. Cyril Smith (deceased); one d. *Education:* Glenarm Coll., Ilford, Royal Acad. of Music. *Career:* debut at Wigmore Hall in 1930s; solo performances throughout British Isles and in Paris and Brussels; duo performances with (late) husband Cyril Smith in British Isles, Europe, Middle and Far East, and New Zealand; following Cyril Smith's stoke during a British Council tour in 1956, which paralysed his left arm, Phyllis and Cyril performed duos for three hands; compositions dedicated to Phyllis Sellick include ones by Arthur Bliss, Gordon Jacob, Michael Tippett and Ralph Vaughan Williams; mem. Incorporated Soc. of Musicians. *Recordings:* several with Cyril Smith. *Telephone:* (20) 8876-5143 (office).

SELTZER, Dov; Composer, Conductor, Orchestrator and Musician; b. 26 Jan. 1932, Iasi, Romania; m. Grazielle Fontana, 15 May 1968, 1 step-s. *Education:* Piano, Theory, privately, 1944–47; Piano, General Music, Haifa and Tel-Aviv Conservatory, 1949–50; Composition with Mordecai Setter, 1950–53, with Herbert Bruen, 1952–54; Diploma, Composition, Mannes College of Music, 1958; BS, Music, State University of New York, 1960. *Career:* Music Director, Composer, Israel Army Nachal Theatrical Group, 1950–53; Music Teacher, Afek School, Haifa;

Arranger, Music Director, Oranim Zabar Folk Singers and Theodore Bikel for Elektra, Columbia Co, USA, 1956–58; Music Teacher, Mannes College of Music, New York, 1958–60; Freelance Composer, Conductor for theatre, musicals, films, records, Israel, USA, France, Italy, England, Germany, elsewhere; Conducted Israel Philharmonic and Jerusalem Symphony Orchestra, concert of his music, 1987; Music Director, Conductor, Three Penny Opera film version, 1988;. *Compositions include:* 15 musicals including: The Megillah, 1966; Kazablan, 1967; I Like Mike, 1968; To Live Another Summer, 1971; Comme la neige en été, 1974; Stempeniu, symphonic poem, 1985; This Scroll, cantata for Ben Gurion centenary, 1986; Music for Thieves In The Night, German television series, 1988; The Assisi Underground; Hassidic Rhapsody, violin solo, symphonic orchestra, 1989–90; The Gold of the Ashes, rhapsodic poem, 1991–92; Notre Dame de Paris, opera after novel by Victor Hugo, 1993–94; Lament to Yitzhak (requiem in memory of Yitzhak Rabin) world premiere, 1998, Mann Auditorium Tel-Aviv, Zubin Mehta conducting the Israel Philharmonic Orchestra. *Address:* 19 Netiv Hamazalot, Jaffa, Israel.

SELWAY, Emma; Singer (Mezzo-soprano); b. 1970, England. *Education:* Royal Academy, London; National Opera Studio. *Career:* Debut: Kate Pinkerton in Madama Butterfly for English National Opera, 1995; Sang Cefisa in Rossini's Ermione at Glyndebourne, 1995 (Musician in Manon Lescaut, 1999); Glyndebourne Tour 1996 and 1999, as Mozart's Dorabella and Sesto; Further engagements as Dorabella for Opera North, Idamante for Opera Northern Ireland and Cenerentola for Welsh National Opera; Sang Charlotte in Die Soldaten by Zimmermann, and Strauss's Octavian for English National Opera; Concerts include Debussy's Le Martyre de St Sebastian (Hallé Orchestra) and Mahler's 2nd symphony, with the Jersey Symphonic Orchestra; Anna in Weill's Seven Deadly Sins at Batignano. *Address:* c/o English National Opera, St Martin's Lane, London, WC2, England.

SEMENCHUK, Ekaterina; Singer (Mezzo-soprano); b. 1976, Minsk, Russia. *Education:* Minsk Music School; Byelorussian Music Academy; St Petersburg Conservatoire. *Career:* Young Singers' Academy of the Mariinsky Theatre, St Petersburg, from 1999; Roles have included the Nurse and Olga in Eugene Onegin, Marta in Iolanta, Puccini's Suzuki, Lyubasha in The Tsar's Bride by Rimsky-Korsakov and Pauline in The Queen of Spades; Sang Lehl in Rimsky's The Snow Maiden and Sonya in War and Peace with the Kirov Opera at Covent Garden, 2000. *Honours:* Diplomas for opera and recital singing, International Dvórak Competition, Prague, 1997; Winner, International Obraztsova competition, 1999. *Address:* c/o Kirov Opera, Mariinsky Theatre, 1 Theatre Square, St Petersburg, Russia.

SEMKOW, Jerzy (Georges); Conductor; b. 12 Oct. 1928, Radomsko, Poland. *Education:* 1948–51 State High School Kraków with Arthur Malawski; 1951–53 Leningrad Conservatory with Boris Khaikin; Further studies with Bruno Walter, Tullio Serafin. *Career:* Assistant to Mravinsky at the Leningrad Philharmonic 1954–56; Bolshoi Theatre 1956–58; 1959–62 Artistic Director and Principal Conductor of the Warsaw National Opera; 1966–76 Principal Conductor of the Danish Royal Opera, Copenhagen; US debut 1968, with the Boston Symphony Orchestra; Guest appearances with the Chicago Symphony, New York Philharmonic, Cleveland Orchestra; National Orchestra, Washington, Pittsburgh Symphony and others; British debut 1968, with the London Philharmonic; Covent Garden 1970, Don Giovanni; Music Director St Louis Symphony 1976–79; Artistic Director RAI Rome 1979–. *Recordings:* Late Romantic music and contemporary Danish works; Nielsen's Helios overture and Violin Concerto; Chopin 1st Piano Concerto; Boris Godunov and Prince Igor; Schumann Symphonies and Manfred overture; Scriabin 2nd Symphony (London Philharmonic), Mozart's Symphonies Nos 33 and 36. *Address:* c/o ICM Artists, 40 West 57 Street, New York, NY 10019, USA.

SEMMINGSEN, Tuva; Singer (mezzo-soprano); b. 1970, Denmark. *Education:* Royal Danish Opera, with Ingrid Bjoner and Anthony Rolfe Johnson. *Career:* Appearances as Cherubino in Figaro at Copenhagen and Venice, 2001; British debut in La Gazzetta by Rossini at Garsington; Delia in Il Viaggio a Reims and Sesto in Handel's Giulio Cesare for the Royal Danish Opera; Other roles include Britten's Hermia, Dorabella, Meg Page in Falstaff and Rossini's Isabella; Concert repertory includes Mozart's Requiem, Vivaldi's Juditha Triumphans (King's Consort, 2002), the Magnificats of Bach and Buxtehude, Pergolesi's Stabat Mater, St John and Matthew Passions; Season 2002–03 as Rosina in Il Barbiere di Siviglia for Royal Danish Opera. *Recordings include:* Vivaldi Sum in Medio Tempastatum and Jubilate (Hyperion). *Current Management:* Harrison/Parrott Ltd, 12 Penzance Place, London, W11 4PA, England. *Telephone:* (20) 7229 9166. *Fax:* (20) 7221 5042. *Website:* www.harrisonparrott.com.

SEMPERE, José; Singer (Tenor); b. 9 Jan. 1955, Catalonia, Spain. *Education:* Barcelona Conservatory; La Scala Opera School, Milan. *Career:* Debut: Ford in Salieri's Falstaff, Parma, 1987; Appearances at

Modena, Ferrara, Rome and Reggio Emilia; Season 1991–92 as the Duke of Mantua at Covent Garden, London, in Auber's Masaniello at Ravenna and Ernesto in Don Pasquale at Naples; Guest appearances at Oslo, 1989 as Rodolfo and at Bergamo, Donizetti's Poliuto, 1993; Madrid as Edgardo in Lucia di Lammermoor; Sang at St Etienne, 1993 and as Duke of Mantua at Verona, 1994; Arturo in I Puritani, Vienna Staatsoper and Lisbon, 1995–96; Sang Don Pedro in Persiani's Ines de Castro at Jesi, 1999. *Recordings:* Poliuto. *Address:* c/o Teatro San Carlos, Rua Serpa Pinto 9, 1200 Lisbon, Spain.

SENATOR, Ronald, BMus, PhD, FTCL; British composer; b. 17 April 1926, London, England; m. Miriam Brickman 1986. *Education:* Univ. of Oxford with Egon Wellesz, London Univ. with Arnold Cooke, Trinity Coll. of Music. *Career:* Ed. of review, Counterpoint 1947–50; Prof. of Composition, Guildhall School of Music 1981; fmr Sr Lecturer in Music, Univ. of London; Visiting Prof., Univs of Queensland and Melbourne, Australia, CUNY and MIT, USA, Toronto and McGill Univs, Canada, and Tel-Aviv Univ., Israel; founding mem. Montserrat Composers' Asscn for Sacred Music; founding dir Nat. Asscn of Music Theatre; mem. PRS, ASCAP, BAC&S, BMI. *Compositions:* Insect Play, Echoes, Pageant of London, Trotsky, Kaddish for Terezin, Basket of Eggs, Streets of London, Francis and the Wolf, Mobiles, Spring Changes, My Animals, Sun's in the East, Poet to his Beloved, Holocaust Requiem 1990; incidental music for film and theatre, including Lightning (film), Siberia (play). *Publications:* General Grammar of Music 1975, Musicolor 1975, The Gaia of Music, Requiem Letters (autobiog.). *Address:* 81 Hillcrest Avenue, Yonkers, NY 10705, USA. *E-mail:* contact@ronaldsenator.com. *Website:* www.ronaldsenator.com.

SENDEROVAS, Anatolijus; Composer; b. 21 Aug. 1945, Uljanovsk, Russia; 1 d. *Education:* Graduated from the Lithuanian Academy of Music (Vilnius), 1967; Postgraduate studies at the Rubin Israel Academy of Music (Tel-Aviv University), 1990; St Petersburg N. Rimski-Korsakoff Conservatory, 1967. *Career:* International Arts Manager, 2002; Berliner Morgeupost, 2002. *Compositions:* A Maiden and Death (ballet), staged at the Lithuanian Opera and Ballet Theatre, Vilnius, 1982; Symphony No. 2 (Music, St Petersburg), 1984; Mary Stewart (ballet), staged at the Vanemuine Theatre, Tartu, Estonia, 1988; Two Songs of Shulamith, for voice and piano, 1992; Der Tiefe Brunnen for voice and 5 instruments, 1993; Simeni Kahoteam al Libeha; Paratum cor Meum, Concerto for Cello, Mixed Choir, Piano (Clavinova) and Symphony Orchestra, 1995; Simeni Kahotam al Libeha (Set Me As A Seal on Your Heart) for soprano, bass, percussion solo and symphony orchestra, 1995; Shma Israel (Hear O Israel) for cantor, male choir and symphony orchestra , 1997; Cantus I, Cantus II for cello solo, 1997; Concerto in Do for Cello and Symphony Orchestra, 2002, Premiered Young Euro Classic, Berlin, 2002 by D. Geringas and the Lithuanian Symphony Orchestra, conducted by Robertas Servenikas. *Recordings:* Simeni Kahotam al libeha (Set me as a seal on your heart); Shma Israel; Concerto in Do. *Publications:* Berliner Zeitung, 1977; Ruch Muzyczny, 1978; Frankfurter Allegmeine Zeitung, 1982; Festival Zeitung, 1992; The Independent, 2003; International Arts Manager, 2002; Die Welt, 2002; Der Tagesspiegel, 2002. *Honours:* Laureate of the Lithuanian National Award, Europeian Composers Prize, 2002; Lithuanian Grand Duke Gediminas Order Bearer; 2nd Prize Winner at the International Composers Competition in Prague, 1993; Sertificate holder at the International W.Lutoslawski Contest, Kil, Sweden, 1994; Lithuanian National Award, 1997; European Composers Prize, Berlin, 2002 for Concerto in Do for Cello and Symphony Orchestra. *Address:* Lakstingalu 5, 15173 Nemencine, Vilnius reg, Lithuania. *Telephone:* +370 6 9999 576. *Fax:* +370 5 2370 995. *E-mail:* asenderovas@yahoo.com. *Website:* www.mie.lt/c_senderovas.htm..

SÉNÉCHAL, Michel; Singer (Tenor); b. 11 Feb. 1927, Tavery, France. *Education:* Studies, Paris Conservatoire. *Career:* Debut: Théâtre de la Monnaie, Brussels, 1950; Many Appearances at the Paris Opéra and Opéra Comique and elsewhere in France; Roles have included Ferrando, Don Ottavio, Tamino, Hylas in Les Troyens, Rossini's Almaviva and Comte Ory; Successful in Such Character Roles as Rameau's Platée (Aix 1956, Brussels Opéra Comique 1977), Erice in Cavalli's L'Ormindo (Glyndebourne), M. Triquet in Eugene Onegin, Valzacchi and Scaramuccio in Ariadne auf Naxos; Glyndebourne Debut, 1966, as Gonzalve in L'Heure Espagnole; Salzburg Festival 1972–88, notably as Mozart's Basilio; Metropolitan Opera debut 1982, as the Villains in Les Contes d'Hoffmann, returned 1997 and 2002, as Basilio; Season 1985 with the premieres of Landowski's Montségur at Toulouse and Boehmer's Docteur Faustus at the Paris Opéra; Director, Opera School at the Opéra, 1980–. *Honours:* Officier de l'Ordre National de la Légion d'Honneur; Officier de l'Ordre des Arts et des Lettres; Commandeur de l'Ordre du Mérite National. *Address:* c/o Metropolitan Opera, Lincoln Center, New York, NY 10023, USA.

SENIA, Paul (Anthony); Composer and Conductor; b. 26 Aug. 1925, Brooklyn, New York, USA; Divorced, 1 s., 3 d. *Education:* MM and MA, Composition, Theory, Juilliard School of Music, 1948; DMA, Composi-

tion, Los Angeles Conservatory, 1961; PhD, Music History, Toronto, 1971. *Career:* Debut: Saint-Saëns Piano Concerto, Carnegie Hall, 1939; Conductor, Los Angeles Conservatory Orchestra, 1960–62; Founder, Conductor, Simi Valley Symphony, 1964–67; Musical Director, Conductor: Los Angeles Civic Arts Symphony, 1964–; Los Angeles Pops Symphony, 1969–; American Theatre of the Opera, 1974–; New American Chamber Strings, 1980; British debut, Gershwin Concerto in F with Leeds Symphony; West Coast premieres, Eugene Zador's operas Christopher Columbus, 1976, Inspector General, 1978, Jehu, 1980; Guest Conductor, US Symphony orchestra: American Korean, Philadelphia, Rochester, Utah, Detroit and Miami Philharmonic, Bank of America Radio Orchestra and Boston Pops, European Symphony, Leeds, Chesterfield, Harrogate Chamber Orchestra (England), Brussels Symphony. *Compositions:* Work for piano, strings and vibraphone; Art Songs, 1945; 42 string quartets, 1948–60; Fisherman and the Mermaid, ballet, 1952, opera, 1954; Variety Suite for orchestra, 1953; Piano Suite (Belle South), 1953; 3 Piano Sonatinas, 1954; Brass Processional, 1956; Choral works, 1956–70; Divertimento, strings, 1961; Symphony No. 1, based on Psalm 23, with soloists and choruses, 1966; 3 Woodwind Quintets, 1968, 1991; 2 Cello Sonatas, 1973; 3 Violin Sonatas, 1969–1972; Crystals, ballet, 1993; Triple Concerto, violin, viola, cello, 1995. *Address:* c/o Sienna Enterprises, 5337 Northridge Drive, Palmdale, CA 93551, USA.

SENN, Marta; Singer (mezzo-soprano); b. 1958, Switzerland. *Education:* Legal Training in Columbia; Musical study in USA. *Career:* Rosina and in title role of Rossi's Orfeo, at several American Opera Houses and La Scala, 1984; Charlotte in Stuttgart, Paris, Hamburg and Nantes; Giulietta in Les Contes d'Hoffmann in Madrid; Isabella in Rome; Massenet's Dulcinée at the Liceo, Barcelona; US tour with Placido Domingo; Annius in La Clemenza di Tito and Rossini's Angelina at the Salzburg Festival, 1988; Season 1988–89, as Sara in Roberto Devereux at Naples and Meg in new production of Falstaff at Bologna; Fenena in Nabucco and Verdi's Preziosilla at Verona Arena; Carmen at Munich State Theatre; Carmen at Stuttgart State Theatre; Liceo, Barcelona, Olympics Arts Festival; Charlotte in Werther; Concerts and recording role of Salud, in La Vida Breve, Venezuela and Minnesota Orchestra, 1993; Debut role of Carmen, Paris Opéra, 1994; Charlotte, in Lisbon and Rome; Dorabella in Toulon and Fidalma in Il Matrimonio Segreto at Bologna; Season 1996 as Charlotte at Naples. *Recordings include:* Maddalena in Rigoletto, from La Scala, conducted by Riccardo Muti; Musetta, in La Bohème, at Venice; Lola in Cavalleria Rusticana; Salud in La Vida Breve, Mata conducting, 1993; El Amor Brujo, original version. *Honours:* Winner, Concours International de Paris, 1982; 1st Prize, Baltimore Opera National Auditions, 1982. *Current Management:* Athole Still International Management, Forresters Hall, 25–27 Westow Street, London, SE19 3RY, England. *Telephone:* (20) 8771-5271. *Fax:* (20) 8768-6600. *Website:* www.atholestill.com. *Address:* Fedeli Opera International, via Montegrappa 3, 40121 Bologna, Italy; Musicagliotz, SARL, 11 Rue La Verrier, 75006 Paris, France; Robert Lombardo Associates, 61 West 62nd Street, Suite 6F, New York, NY 10023, USA.

SEOW, Yitkin; Pianist; b. 28 March 1955, Singapore. *Education:* Yehudi Mehuhin School, 1967–72; LRSM, 1967; Royal College of Music, 1972–75. *Career:* Debut: Wigmore Hall, 1968; Televised Prom, 1975; Royal Festival Hall, Philharmonia, 1975; Berlin Radio Symphony Orchestra, Hong Kong Arts Festival, 1977; Royal Philharmonic Orchestra, London Promenade Concert, 1982; Television, BBC Scottish Orchestra, 1985; Russia Tour, BBC National Orchestra of Wales, 1988; St Petersburg Philharmonic, 1998mem, ISM. *Recordings:* Satie Piano Works: Janáček Piano Works; Debussy; Rachmaninov Cello Sonata; Yellow River Concerto (Gold Disc); Bartók Quartet as Violist, 1972 (with Nigel Kennedy). *Honours:* Winner, BBC Piano Competition, 1974; Rubinstein Prize, Tel-Aviv, 1977. *Address:* 8 North Terrace, London SW3 2 BA, England.

SEQUI, Sandro; Stage Director; b. 10 Nov. 1933, Rome, Italy. *Education:* Studied Literature and Philosophy at Rome University. *Career:* Directed La Sonnambula at the Teatro La Fenice Venice, 1961; Staging of I Puritani seen at Florence, 1971, Metropolitan 1976, Rome 1990; Guillaume Tell at Florence 1972, Les Contes d'Hoffmann at Dallas 1975; Staged the premiere production of Mannino's Il Principe Felice at La Scala, 1987; Rigoletto at the Chicago Lyric Opera, 1991; Fille du Régiment, Metropolitan, 1995–. *Address:* Lungotevere Sanzio 1, 00153 Rome, Italy.

SERBAN, Andrei; Opera Producer; b. 21 June 1943, Bucharest, Romania. *Education:* Theatre Institute, Bucharest. *Career:* Worked on theatre productions with Peter Brook in New York and Paris; Opera debut with Welsh National Opera, Eugene Onegin; returned for I Puritani, Rodelinda, and Norma; Produced Die Zauberflöte in Nancy, 1979; Alcina at the New York City Opera; Staging of Turandot for the Royal Opera was seen in Los Angeles and London in 1984; Premiere of The Juniper-Tree by Philip Glass for Baltimore Opera, 1985; Fidelio at Covent Garden and Prokofiev's Fiery Angel for Geneva and Los Angeles;

Don Carlos in Geneva and Bologna; Permanent post with the Boston Repertory Theatre; Produced Prince Igor at Covent Garden 1990; The Fiery Angel seen at the Holland Festival 1990; I Puritani in London, 1992; Tales of Hoffmann, Vienna Opera, 1993; Adriana Lecouvreur, Zürich Opera, 1994; Lucia di Lammermoor, Paris, Bastille Opéra, 1995; Love of Three Oranges, Paris, Paris Conservatory, 1995; Staged Massenet's Thais at Nice, 1997; L'Italiana in Algeri at the Palais Garnier, Paris, 1998; Les Indes Galantes, 1999–2000. *Current Management:* Diana Mulgan, IMG Artists. *Address:* c/o Théâtre National de L'Opéra de Paris, 8 rue Scribe, F–75009 Paris, France.

SERBO, Rico; Singer (Tenor); b. 9 May 1940, Stockton, California, USA. *Education:* Studied in San Francisco. *Career:* Debut: San Francisco 1965 as Ramiro in Cenerentola; Sang in Opera at Seattle, Santa Fe and San Francisco, Europe from 1970, notably with Netherlands Opera and at Koblenz, Essen and the Theater am Gärtnerplatz Munich; Further engagements at San Diego, New York City Opera, Houston, Toronto and Vancouver; Sang at New Orleans, as Arvino in the US premiere of I Lombardi; Deutsche Oper and Theater des Westens Berlin, and at Belfast; Other roles have included Mozart's Ferrando and Tamino, Almaviva, Ernesto, Fenton, Alfredo, Tom Rakewell, Rodolfo, Boito's Faust, Lord Barrat in Der Junge Lord and Tony in Elegy for Young Lovers. *Recordings include:* Donizetti's L'Assedio di Calais.

SERDIUK, Nadezhda; Singer (Mezzo-Soprano); b. 1975, Moscow, Russia. *Education:* Tchaikovsky Conservatoire, Moscow. *Career:* Young Singers' Academy at the Mariinsky Theatre, St Petersburg, from 1999; Masterclasses with Christa Ludwig, Marilyn Horne and Renata Scotto at the Metropolitan Opera Young Singers' Programme; Roles with Kirov Opera have included Gluck's Orfeo, Olga in Eugene Onegin, Nadezhda in Vera Sheloga by Rimsky-Korsakov and Lyubava in Sadko; Sang Beautiful Spring in Rimsky's Snow Maiden with the Kirov at Amsterdam and London (Covent Garden), 1999–2000; Other roles include Lyubasha in Rimsky's The Tsar's Bride. *Honours:* Prizewinner, International Glinka and Rimsky-Korsakov Vocal Competitions, 1998; Participant in the 1999 Cardiff Singer of the World Competition. *Address:* c/o Kirov Opera, Mariinsky Theatre, 1 Theatre Square, St Petersburg, Russia.

SEREBRIER, José, MA; American conductor and composer; b. 3 Dec. 1938, Montevideo, Uruguay; s. of David Serebrier and Frida Serebrier (née Wasser); m. Carole Farley 1969; one d. *Education:* Univ. of Minn., Curtis Inst. of Music, Phila. *Career:* started conducting at age of 12; went to USA 1956; studied composition with Aaron Copland and Vittorio Giannini, Curtis Inst., Phila 1956–58 and conducting with Antal Dorati and Pierre Monteux; guest conductor in USA, S America, Australia and Europe; Assoc. Conductor American Symphony Orchestra, with Leopold Stokowski 1962–68; conducted alongside Leopold Stokowski world première of Charles Ives' Fourth Symphony, Carnegie Hall, New York 1964; conducted first performance in Poland of Charles Ives' Fourth Symphony 1971 and premieres of over 100 works; Composer-in-Residence with Cleveland Orchestra 1968–70; Music Dir Cleveland Philharmonic Orchestra 1968–71; Artistic Dir Int. Festival of Americas, Miami 1984–, Miami Festival 1985– (also Founder). *Compositions:* Solo Violin Sonata 1954, Quartet for Saxophones 1955, Pequeña música (wind quintet) 1955, Symphony No. 1 1956, Momento psicológico (string orchestra) 1957, Solo Piano Sonata 1957, Suite canina (wind trio) 1957, Symphony for Percussion 1960, The Star Wagon (chamber orchestra) 1967, Nueve (double bass and orchestra) 1970, Colores mágicos (variations for harp and chamber orchestra) 1971, At Dusk, in Shadows (solo flute), Andante Cantabile (strings), Night Cry (brass), Dorothy and Carmine (flute and strings), George and Muriel (contrabass), Winter (violin concerto) 1995, Winterreise (for orchestra) 1999; composed music for several films; all compositions published and recorded; over 175 recordings to date. *Television includes:* int. TV broadcast of Grammys Ceremony, LA 2002, conducting suite from Bernstein's West Side Story. *Publications:* orchestration of 14 songs by Edvard Grieg 2000, orchestration of Gershwin's works 2002. *Honours:* Nat. Endownment for Arts Comm. Award 1969, Ditson Award for Promotion of New Music, Columbia Univ. 1980, Deutsche Schallplatten Critics' Award 1991, UK Music Retailers' Asscn Award for Best Symphony Recording (Mendelssohn symphonies) 1991, Diapason d'Or Recording Award, France, Best Audiophile Recording (Scheherazade), Soundstage 2000, BMI Award, Koussevitzky Foundation Award. *Address:* 20 Queensgate Gardens, London, SW7 5LZ, England. *Fax:* (212) 662-8073 (office). *E-mail:* caspil23@aol.com (office). *Website:* www.naxos.com (office).

SEREMBE, Gilberto; Conductor and Professor of Orchestral Conducting; b. 17 Dec. 1955, Milan, Italy; m. Elisabetta Brusa, 3 May 1997. *Career:* Professor of Composition, Brescia Conservatorio, 1979–81; Assistant, Teatro alla Scala, Milan, 1980; Professor of Orchestral Rehearsing: Mantova Conservatorio, 1982–83, Conservatorio G Verdi, Milan, 1984–86, Brescia Conservatorio, 1986–88, Genoa Conservatorio, 1989–97; Professor of Orchestral Conducting, International Superior

courses, Accademia Musicale Pescarese, 1988–; Professor/Conductor, Orchestra of the Conservatorio di Brescia, 1997–; Guest Conductor: Pomeriggi Musicali Orchestra, Milan, 1976–77, 1980–83, 1987, 1990, 1992, 1994, AIDEM Orchestra, Firenze, 1979, Angelicum Chamber Orchestra, Milan, 1980–83, San Remo Symphony Orchestra, 1980–87, Teatro Massimo Symphony Orchestra, Palermo, 1986–88, Orchestra Regionale della Toscana, Florence, 1986–88, 1995, Stradivari Orchestra, Milan, 1991–92, and Hungarian tour, 1991, Teatro Regio Symphony Orchestra, Turin, 1991, Toscanini Symphony Orchestra, Parma, 1993, Brescia Symphony Orchestra, 1996, 1998, 1999, Orchestra Sinfonica Triveneta, 1997–98, Filarmonia Veneta of Teatro Comunale, Treviso, 1997; Orchestra Stabile di Bergamo, 1998; Orchestra Sinfonia di Pescana, 1999, 2001, 2003; Abroad: Gothenburg Symphonic Orchestra, Sweden, 1989, BRT Radio Television Symphony Orchestra, Brussels, 1991, Turku Philharmonic, Finland, 1991, Tirana Radio and Television Symphony Orchestra, Albania, 1994–95, Summer Stage in Conducting, Valencia, Spain, 1999. *Current Management:* Via Zanella 43/1, 20133 Milan, Italy.

SERENI, Mario; Singer (Baritone); b. 25 March 1928, Perugia, Italy. *Education:* Studied at the Accademia di Santa Cecilia in Rome and at the Accademia Chigiana, Siena. *Career:* Debut: Florence 1953, in Lualdi's Il Diavolo nel Campanile; Sang in The Stone Guest by Dargomyzhsky, Florence, 1954; Palermo 1955, as Wolfram in Tannhäuser; Metropolitan Opera from 1957: almost 400 performances in 26 roles, including Gerard, Sharpless, Germont, Amonasro, Belcore and Marcello; Vienna 1965, Verona Arena 1965–74; Further engagements in London, Chicago, Dallas, Houston, London, Milan and Buenos Aires. *Recordings:* Madama Butterfly; Andrea Chénier; La Bohème; Cavalleria Rusticana; Elisir d'amore; Aida; La Traviata; Ernani; Turandot; Lucia di Lammermoor. *Address:* c/o Arena di Verona, Piazza Bra 28, 37121 Verona, Italy.

SERKIN, Peter; Pianist; b. 24 July 1947, New York, USA. *Education:* Lessons in music and piano with Blanche Moyse and Luis Battle; Curtis Institute for six years studying with Lee Luvisi, Mieczyslaw Horszowski and his father, Rudolf Serkin; Further lessons and studies with Ernst Oster, Marcel Moyse and Karl Ulrich Schnabel. *Career:* Public concerts from the age of twelve; Mozart Concertos at the Marlboro Festival and concerts with Alexander Schneider; Premiered Peter Lieberson's Piano Concerto No. 1 (Piano Quintet, 1997), commissioned by the Boston Symphony under Seiji Ozawa, 1985; Also premiered works by Hans Werner Henze, Oliver Knussen, Toru Takemitsu, Alexander Goehr, Luciano Berio and others; Plays music by Bach, Mozart, Beethoven, Brahms, Schoenberg and Stravinsky; Premiered Peter Lieberson's 2nd Piano Concerto 1998; Teaches at the Tanglewood Music Center annually; mem, Faculty Member of the Juilliard School of Music and the Curtis Institute of Music. *Recordings include:* Music by Webern, Messiaen, Berio, Goehr, Henze and Takemitsu. *Honours:* Prize for Outstanding artistic achievement from the Premier Internazionale Accademia Musicale Chigiana. *Address:* Kirshbaum Demler & Associates, 711 West End Avenue, Suite 5KN, New York, NY 10025, USA.

SERMILÄ, Jarmo Kalevi, MA; Finnish composer and musician (trumpet, flugelhorn); b. 16 Aug. 1939, Hämeenlinna; m. Ritva Vuorinen 1962. *Education:* Helsinki Univ., Sibelius Acad. *Career:* worked for Finnish broadcasting co. (YLE), Artistic Dir YLE Experimental Studio 1973–79; Pres. Finnish Section, Int. Soc. for Contemporary Music 1975–79; composer-in-residence, Hämeenlinna 1977–82; freelance composer 1982–; Artistic Dir, Time of Music Contemporary Music Festival, Viitasaari 1987–99; state grant for composition 1990; mem. Soc. of Finnish Composers (vice-pres. 1981–). *Compositions include:* A Circle of the Moon, Allegria, At Bizarre Exits, La Place Revisitée, Labor, Manifesto, Merlin's Mascarade (ballet), Mimesis 2, Movimenti, On the Road, Pentagram, Quattro Rilievi, Random Infinities, Technogourmet, Train of Thoughts, Wolf Bride (ballet). *Honours:* Janacek Medal 1978, Hämeenlinna City Music Prize 1981, Smetana Medal 1984, Häme Provincial Art Cttee Award 1988. *Address:* Niittykatu 7 A 7, 13100 Hämeenlinna, Finland. *Website:* www.sermila.net.

SEROV, Edward; Symphony Orchestra Conductor; b. 9 Sept. 1937, Moscow, Russia; Guenrietta Serova, 29 June 1961, 2 s. *Education:* Gnessin Institute, Moscow, 1954–59; Tchaikovsky Conservatoire, Kiev, 1958–61; Rimsky-Korsakov Conservatoire, Leningrad, 1961–64. *Career:* Debut: Kiev Opera, 1960; Conductor, Leningrad Philharmonic Orchestra, 1961–68, 1985–90; Founder, Chief Conductor, Uljanovsk Philharmonic, 1968–77; Chief Conductor, Leningrad Chamber Orchestra, 1974–85; Founder, Chief Conductor, Volgograd Philharmonic Orchestra, 1987–; Professor, Leningrad (now St Petersburg) Conservatoire, 1987–; Chief Conductor, Odense Symphony Orchestra, Denmark, 1991–96; Chief Conductor Saratov Philharmonic Orchestra, 1995–; Foreign Tours: Japan, USA, France, Germany, Austria, Spain, Sweden, Norway, Finland, Denmark, Czechoslovakia, Hungary, Yugoslavia, others. *Recordings include:* works of Webern, Tishchenko, Arensky, Mozart, Rubenstein, Tchaikovsky, Prokofiev, Sviridov, Purcell, Tartini,

Bartók, Slonimski, Hindemith, Mendelssohn, Bach, Nielsen, Rossini, Ginastera, Shostakovich, Rodrigo, Elgar, Suk, Schumann, Spohr and Schubert. *Contributions:* The Exploit of Service to Music; The Soviet Music Magazine, 1980; About Conductor's Art, The Soviet Music, 1980; The original Symphonic Narration, The Music Life magazine, 1984; Meditation about G Sviridov to book on Sviridov; Others. *Honours:* People's Artist of Russia Honorary Title, President of Russia, 1990; Order of Honour, President of Russia, 1998. *Address:* Warschawskaja str 124 kw 95, St Petersburg 196 240, Russia.

SERRA, Enric; Singer (Baritone); b. 24 July 1940, Barcelona, Spain. *Education:* Studied in Barcelona. *Career:* Debut: Teatro del Liceo Barcelona, 1966, as Morales in Carmen; Has sung in Spain (Madrid, Valencia, Bilbao and Barcelona) from 1969, notably as Falstaff, Scarpia, Escamillo, Enrico, Belcore and Alcandro in Pacini's Saffo, 1987; Guest engagements in Zürich, Cologne, Nice, Tours, Naples, Venice, Bogota and Caracas, as Don Pasquale, Rossini's Figaro, Alfonso (La Favorita) and Don Carlos in La Forza del Destino; At Schwetzingen as Italiana in Algeri and Lescaut in Manon Lescaut and at Barcelona, 1990;; Don Magnifico in La Cenerentola at Hamburg, 1998; Sang Belfiore in Haydn's Il mondo della luna at Maastricht, 1999; Other roles include Mozart's Leporello and Alfonso, Escamillo, Valentin in Faust, Scarpia, and Verdi's Count Luna; Concert repertoire includes Falla's L'Atlantida (Madrid 1977); Rossini's Barbiere at München's Bayerische Staatsoper, 1989, and also at the New York Metropolitan Opera, 1997–98; Further roles include: Massenet's Mandy, Marcello, Albert, Michonet and Grand Prêtre from Saint-Saëns' Samson et Dalila; Concerts in Madrid's Teatro Real, Barcelona's Palau Musica, Paris' Salle Pleyel and ORTF, London's Royal Festival Hall, Rome's RAI, Tokyo's Suntory Hall and Granada's Music Festival. *Recordings include:* Madama Butterfly, with Caballé; Tosca with Aragall; Italiana in Algeri. *Address:* Gran Teatro del Liceo, Sant Pau I bis, 08001 Barcelona, Spain.

SERRA, Luciana; Singer (soprano); b. 4 Nov. 1946, Genoa, Italy. *Education:* Genoa Conservatoire and with Michele Casato. *Career:* debut, Budapest Opera 1966, in Cimarosa's Il Convito; mem. of Tehran Opera 1969–76; sang Gilda in Rigoletto at Genoa 1974; Bologna 1979, in La Sonnambula; Covent Garden 1980, as Olympia in Les Contes d' Hoffmann; Rossini's Aureliano in Palmira at Genoa 1980; Hamburg 1982 and La Scala Milan 1983, as Lucia; US debut at Charleston as Violetta; Chicago Lyric Opera 1983 as Lakmé; Parma 1986 as Lucia; Rossini Opera Festival Pesaro 1987 in L'Occasione fa il Iadro (Rossini); Vienna 1988 as the Queen of Night; Maggio Musicale Florence 1989, as Elvira in I Puritani; sang Gilda at Turin 1989, Hanna Glawari at Trieste 1990; Santiago 1990, as Donizetti's Marie; Schwetzingen Festival 1990, in Fra Diavolo at La Scala and Pamira in Le Siège de Corinthe at Genoa; sang Olympia at Genoa 1996; other roles include Rosina, Fiorilla; Ophelia, Philine; Bellini's Giulietta; Norina; Adina; Linda di Chamounix and Marie in La Fille du Régiment; Season 1998 with Gounod's Juliette at Palermo and Puccini's Lauretta at Torre del Lago; Rossini's Rosina at Santiago, 2000; concert appearances in pre-classical works and music by Vivaldi, Mozart, Rossini and Rimsky-Korsakov. *Recordings:* Zerline in Fra Diavolo (Cetra); Torquato Tasso by Donizetti; Die Zauberflöte; Les Contes d'Hoffmann; Don Pasquale, Barbiere di Siviglia, Gianni di Parigi; Fille du Régiment; La Scala di Seta and L'Occasione fa il Ladro. *Current Management:* Allied Artists Agency, 42 Montpelier Square, London, SW7 1JZ, England.

SERRAIOCCO, Danielo; Singer (Bass); b. 1960, San Giovanni Teatino, Italy. *Education:* Accademia di Santa Cecilia, Rome. *Career:* Debut: Spoleto, 1987 as Raimondo in Lucia di Lammermoor; Sang at Spoleto in Così fan tutte, Don Carlos, Mahagonny and L'Italiana in Algeri; Savonna, 1988 in a revival of Rossini's Ciro in Babilonia; Season 1990 as Wurm in Luisa Miller at Rome, in La rosa bianca e la rose rossa by Simone Mayr and in Britten's The Rape of Lucretia at Naples; Santa Domingo, 1992, as Columbus in the premiere of 1492 by A Braga; Concerts include Bach and Mozart at Florence; Puccini's Messa di Gloria and Mozart's Requiem in London; Schubert's Mass in G, Rome. *Recordings:* Angelotti in Tosca; La Fanciulla del West. *Address:* Teatro San Carlo, Via S Carlo, 80132 Naples, Italy.

SERVADEI, Annette Elizabeth, BMus; pianist; b. 16 Oct. 1945, Durban, Natal; m. 1972 (divorced 1981); one s. one d. *Education:* studied with pianist mother, further studies in Milan, Detmold, Salzburg, London with Ilonka Deckers, Schilde, Hilda Dederich, Ilona Kabos, Carlo Zecchi, Klaus Schilde, Wilhelm Kempff. *Career:* first radio broadcast aged 10; concert debut with Durban Symphony Orchestra aged 12; debut, Wigmore Hall, London 1972; recitals and concertos in UK, Western Europe, USA, Africa; frequent radio and television broadcasts; Sr Piano Tutor, UOFS Bloemfontein 1974, Wits Univ., Johannesburg 1977–81; festival adjudicator, lecture recitals, masterclasses; played world premiere, Tavener's Palintropos, London 1980; resumed career after heart surgery 1988; championed music of Sibelius and Dohnanyi; career further interrupted by stroke 1997–2003, resumed public performances, specialising in Mozart 2003–; mem., Inc. Soc. of

Musicians. *Recordings:* Britten and Khachaturian Piano Concertos with London Philharmonic Orchestra, 1987; Mendelssohn, Schumann and Brahms piano pieces; Sibelius complete piano music (five CDs), 1994–96; Dohnányi Piano, Vols 1 and 2. *Honours:* UK Sibelius Soc. Artist of the Year 1993. *Address:* 3 Bournemouth Drive, Herne Bay, Kent CT6 8HH, England. *E-mail:* annetteservadei@tiscali.co.uk.

SERVILE, Roberto; Singer (Baritone); b. 1959, Genoa, Italy. *Education:* Studied with Paride Venturi. *Career:* Sang Don Carlos in Ernani at Modena and Marcello with Bohème at Treviso, 1984; Marcello with Pavarotti at Philadelphia, 1986; Rome Opera, 1989 in a revival of Rossini's Zelmira and 1994 as Enrico in Lucia di Lammermoor; Genoa, 1990 as Luna in Il Trovatore, Macerata, 1992 as Germont; Further appearances at Naples, from 1993, Santiago, 1994 and Hamburg, 1995; Season 1996 as Osaka in Mascagni's Iris at Rome and Azo in Donizetti's Parisina at Wexford; Season 1997–98 as Enrico at La Scala; High Priest in Samson and Delilah, Eugene Onegin at Turin and Nottingham in Roberto Devereux at Naples; Other roles include Verdi's Posa, Macbeth and Ford, Oreste in Iphigénie en Tauride, Escamillo, Belcore and Zurga in Les Pêcheurs de Perles; Season 2000–01 as Count Luna at Parma, Puccini's Lescaut at Catania and Belfiore in Verdi's Un giorno di regno at Bologna. *Recordings:* Il Trovatore; Il Barbiere di Siviglia. *Address:* c/o Turin Opera, Piazza Castello 215, 10124 Turin, Italy.

SESTAK, Zdenek; Composer; b. 10 Dec. 1925, Citoliby, Czechoslovakia; m. Marie Zatecka, 2 Sept 1950, 1 s., 1 d. *Education:* Gymnasium, Louny, 1936–44; Conservatorium de la Musique, Prague, 1945–50; PhD, Charles University, Faculty of Philosophy, 1945–50. *Career:* Professor of Music, 1952–57; Freelance Composer, 1957–; Dramaturge, Centre for Symphonic Music, Radio Czechoslovakia, Prague, 1968–70; mem, Association of Music Artists Tchèques. *Compositions include:* Symphonie II, 1970, III, 1971, IV, 1979, V Chronos, 1978 and VI L'Inquietude Eternelle du Coeur, 1979; Cycle des Cantates Spirituels sur les Textes de psaume, 1972–92; Concert for string orchestra, 1974; String Quintet, Concentus musicus, 1975; Sonata Symphonica, 1976; Sonata da Camera, 1978; Concerto for violin: Sursum corda, 1981; Concerto for viola: Meditations de Socrates, 1982; Memoria, La Fresque Symphonique de Variation, 1983; Fatum, Vocale-Symphonique Fragment d'Apriès Sophocles, 1983; Concerto for violin: Jean le Violiniste, 1985; Queen Dagmar, oratorium, 1989; Les Cycles des Chants sur Vers de Villon, Michelangelo Buonarotti, Hora, Macha, Jelen, Sefl, King Salamon, Le Testament Ancien (Book of Ecclesiasticas); Evocations Paschales for trumpet and organ, 1992; Sonata for trumpet and organ, Dies Laetitiae, 1993; String Quartet VI, Variations de Mácha, 1993; String Quartet VII, Soliloquia, 1994; Herakleitos (Movimenti musicali per novem stromenti a fiato), 1998; String Quartet IX, Sisyfos, 1999; String Quintet No. 2, Conscientia temporis, 2000; String Sextet, Laus Vitae, 2001. *Publications:* La Musique de Maîtres de Citoliby de 18 Siècle, 1968, 1985. *Address:* Pracska 2594-87, 106 00 Prague 10, Czech Republic.

SEXTON, Timothy A. P., BMus, DipEd; Australian composer, conductor and singer (bass-baritone); b. 10 Aug. 1960, McLaren Vale, SA; m. Suzanne Walker 1984; one s. one d. *Education:* Elder Conservatorium of Music, Univ. of Adelaide, studied composition with Richard Meale and Bozidar Kos, conducting with Shalom Ronly-Riklis, Gianluigi Gelmetti and David Porcelijn. *Career:* debut, conducted Tasmanian Symphony Orchestra, 1994; debut as bass soloist, world premiere of Propriocepts Symphony, 1997; Australian premiere of Flamma Flamma, 1998; debut as conductor, Don Pasquale, Riders to the Sea, Mavra, SOSA, 1998; The Mikado, SOSA, Mahogonny Songspiel, Treemonisha, 1999; The Turn of the Screw, SOSA, 2001; Akhnaten, Sweeney Todd, SOSA, 2002; mem., Music Arrangers' Guild of Australia. *Compositions:* Newcastle Coal Cantata; Escape of the Chrysalids (opera); Whispering Winds (choral song cycle); The Hole in the Sky (cantata). *Recordings:* Australia, Be Proud; Fanfare; A Universal Christmas. *Publications:* contrib. to Sounds Australian; Sing Out; many opera programmes throughout Australia. *Honours:* Henry Krips Memorial Conducting Scholarships, 1994, 1997. *Address:* PO Box 332, Birdwood, SA 5234, Australia.

SFIRIS, Konstantin; Singer (Bass); b. 1958, Waltessinikon, Arcadia, Greece. *Education:* Athens National Conservatory; Cologne Musikhochschule. *Career:* Sang at the Vienna Staatsoper 1981–87; Graz Opera from 1986, notably in the premieres of Der Rattenfänger by Cerha and Rashomon by Makayo Kuba; Guest appearances in opera and concert at Bregenz, Barcelona, San Francisco and Geneva; Sang Sparafucile in Rigoletto at Liège, 1989; Other roles include Philip II and the Grand Inquisitor in Don Carlos, Zaccaria in Nabucco, Procida (I Vespri Siciliani), Hunding in Die Walküre and Pimen in Boris Godunov; Wide concert repertory. *Honours:* Winner, Treviso International Competition, 1981. *Address:* c/o Vereinigte Buhnen, Kaiser Josef Platz 10, A-8010 Graz, Austria.

SGOURDA, Antigone; Singer (Soprano); b. 6 June 1938, Saloniki, Greece. *Education:* Athens Conservatory; Vienna Music Academy.

Career: Sang at Bonn Opera 1960–62, Essen 1962–66; Glyndebourne Festival 1962–63, as Fiordiligi, and First Lady in Die Zauberflöte; Festival appearances at Schwetzingen, Holland and Athens (1971–73); Zürich Opera 1968–82, notably in operas by Mozart, including Lucio Silla; Frankfurt Opera 1968–82; Guest engagements at Dusseldorf, Vienna, Stuttgart and Munich (Israel tour, 1974); Sang Donna Anna in Don Giovanni at Edinburgh 1973 and Philadelphia 1977; Other roles have included Tatiana, Verdi's Amelia (Ballo in Maschera), Alice Ford, Violetta, and Aida; Katya Kabanova, Elizabeth I in Donizetti's Roberto Devereux, Arabella and Ariadne. *Recordings include:* Don Giovanni (HMV); Beatrice di Tenda by Bellini (Fonit). *Address:* c/o Opernhaus Zürich, Falkenstrasse 1, CH-8008 Zürich, Switzerland.

SHABALTINA, Svitlana; Pianist and Harpsichordist; b. 3 Feb. 1948, Kiev, Ukraine. *Education:* Kiev Music School; Gnessin Academy of Music, Moscow; Postgraduate course at Gnessin Academy of Music. *Career:* Debut: Kiev International Festival of the Contemporary Music, 1982; Early Music Festival, Kraków, 1990; Kiev International Festival, Ukraine and the World of Baroque; Bach's Concertos for 2 harpsichords with Elizabieta Stefanska and the Kiev Chamber Orchestra, Kiev Organ Hall, 1994; Recital of Slav Composers music, Germany, 1994; Played music of Russian and Ukraine composers for piano and flute, Tolouse, France, 1996; Baroque music for harpsichord and flute, Teatro Regio di Torino, Italy, 1998; Recital harpsichord music, Kiev Philharmonic Hall, 1998; Professor of piano and harpsichord, Ukraine. *Recordings:* Ukraine early and contemporary music for Kiev radio and television, 1972–98; Music for harpsichord on CD, 1997; Beethoven sonata op 111, Schumann Kreisleriana op.16, Luboš Fiser Sonata 4 for piano on CD, 1998. *Honours:* Special diplomas as a best accompanist, Ukraine Cello competition, Kcharkow, 1984; International Cello competition, Kyshynev, 1985. *Address:* St Prytysko-Mykilska 2 Apt 26, Kiev 254070, Ukraine.

SHADE, Ellen; Singer (Soprano); b. 17 Feb. 1948, New York, USA. *Education:* Studied at the Juilliard Opera Center and with Cornelius Reid; Further study at the Sanata Fe Opera, 1969. *Career:* Debut: Frankfurt 1972, as Liu in Turandot; Sang Micaela at Pittsburgh 1972 (US debut); Further engagements in Cincinnati, Milwaukee, Dallas and New Orleans; Chicago 1976, as Emma in Khovanshchina, returning as Eve in the premiere of Penderecki's Paradise Lost, 1978; Metropolitan Opera debut, as Eva in Die Meistersinger; New York City Opera, 1981, Donna Elvira; Sang in Paradise Lost at La Scala in 1979 and has made further European appearances at Hamburg, Brussels, Vienna (Florinda in Schubert's Fierrabras, conducted by Abbado), and Geneva (Katya Kabanova, 1988); Returned to the Metropolitan as Sieglinde in Die Walküre, conducted by James Levine; Season 1992 as the Empress in Die Frau ohne Schatten, at Amsterdam and Salzburg; Other roles include Verdi's Alice Ford, Wagner's Elsa and Freia, Climene in Cavalli's Egisto and Agathe in Der Freischütz; As a concert singer has appeared with the New York Philharmonic, the Chicago Symphony and the Orchestras of Boston, Cleveland, Los Angeles, Minnesota, St Louis, Pittsburgh and the National Symphony and in Europe with the Radio Orchestras of Frankfurt, Berlin, Stuttgart, Baden-Baden, Rome and Turin; Invited to teach French Art Song with the Ravinia Festival in Chicago; Revival of Die Frau ohne Schatten in Amsterdam; Aida with the Metropolitan Opera; Sang Arabella at Covent Garden, 1996. *Recordings include:* Hans Pfitzner Cantata Von Deutscher Seele with the Frankfurt Radio Orchestra conducted by Horst Stein; Television recordings include Strauss's Empress and Saffi in Der Zigeunerbaron. *Address:* c/o IMG Artists, Lovell House, 616 Chiswick High Road, London W4 5RX, England.

SHADE, Nancy Elizabeth; American opera and concert singer (soprano); b. 31 May 1949, Rockford, IL. *Education:* De Pauw University, Indiana University; studied voice with Vera Scammon. *Career:* debut at Kentucky Opera Theatre, 1968, as Leonora in Il Trovatore; Lulu, Frankfurt Opera; Countess in Figaro, Hamburg State Opera; Manon Lescaut, Munich State Opera; Marguerite in Faust, San Francisco Opera; Madama Butterfly, New York City Opera; Marie in Die Soldaten, Lyons; Santa Fe 1984, in the US premiere of Henze's We Come to the River; Stuttgart 1988, as Marie in Die Soldaten (repeated Vienna 1990); Sang Schoenberg's Erwartung at the Prague State Opera, 2000. *Honours:* First prize, National Metropolitan Auditions, 1968. *Current Management:* Thea Dispeker, 59 E 54th Street, New York, NY 10022, USA.

SHAGUCH, Marina; Singer (Soprano); b. 1964, Krasnodar, Russia. *Education:* Studied at the Arts School in Maikop and at St Petersburg State Conservatoire. *Career:* Sang at the Kirov Opera Theatre in season 1991–92, notably in Mussorgsky's Sorochinsky Fair and Il Trovatore; Concert debuts at Grand Hall of the Moscow Conservatoire; Glinka Capella in St Petersburg; Further appearances throughout Russia, USA, Germany, Wales; Concert repertoire has included works by Handel, Mozart, Rimsky, Schumann, Schubert, Wolf, Dvořák and Brahms; Performed in The Legend of the Invisible City of Kitezh with

Kirov Opera at the Barbican, 1995. *Honours:* Winner, Mussorgsky All Russia and Glinka National Singing Competitions; Second Prize, Tchaikovsky International Competition. *Address:* c/o Sonata, 11 Northpark Street, Glasgow G20 7AA, Scotland.

SHAHAM, Gil; Concert Violinist; b. 19 Feb. 1971, Champaign-Urbana, Illinois, USA. *Education:* Studied at the Rubin Academy in Jerusalem, in Aspen and at Juilliard with Dorothy DeLay. *Career:* Debut: Concert with the Jerusalem Symphony Conducted by Alexander Schneider; Appeared with the Israel Philharmonic under Zubin Mehta, 1982; Engagements with the New York Philharmonic; Season, 1987–88 with the London Symphony Orchestra at the Barbican, Bavarian Radio Orchestra in Munich, the RAI Turin and Recitals at La Scala and in Munich; Debut with the Philadelphia Orchestra and Tour of South America, 1988; Season, 1988–89 with the Berlin Philharmonic, Orchestre de Paris, Frankfurt Symphony and the Philharmonia under Sinopoli; Bruch and Sibelius Concertos with the London Symphony Orchestra, 1989; Recital Debut at the Wigmore Hall, London, 1990; Season 1995–96 with the Israel Philharmonic, the London Symphony Orchestra, CBSO, Vienna Symphony Orchestra and the Philharmonia Orchestra; Recitals throughout Europe and the Far East. *Recordings include:* Bartók Concerto No. 2 (Boulez/Chicago Symphony Orchestra); Messiaen's Quartet for the End of Time. *Honours:* First Prize, 1982 Claremont Competition, Israel. *Current Management:* Harrison/Parrott Ltd, 12 Penzance Place, London, W11 4PA, England. *Telephone:* (20) 7229 9166. *Fax:* (20) 7221 5042. *Website:* www.harrisonparrott.com.

SHAMEYEVA, Natalia; Harpist; b. 30 Dec. 1939, Moscow; m., 1 s. *Education:* Moscow Middle Special Music School; Musical Pedagogical Institute; Postgraduate courses, Moscow Conservatory. *Career:* Soloist, Moscow Concert Organisation, 1962–70; Solo Harpist, 1970–85; Principal Harpist, 1985–2003, Bolshoi Theatre Orchestra; Teacher, Moscow Conservatory, 1967–70; Teacher, Musical Pedogical Institute, 1977–79; Teacher, Russian Academy of Music, 1985; Assistant Professor, 1996. Performances on radio stations; Masterclasses, USA, Holland, Switzerlandthe United Kingdom, Japan and Italy; Performances on major stages in Moscow; World premieres of Schnittke's Concerto for oboe, harp and orchestra; Baltin's Bylina for harp and orchestra; Ulyanich's Dreamings for harp, flute, saxophone and viola; First performances in Russia of Quintets by Villa-Lobos, V.d'Indy; A. Roussel, A. Caplet, Quartet by Haydn; mem, Association of Russian Harpists; World Harp Congress. *Recordings include:* solo and chamber compositions for harp. *Publications:* The History of Development of Harp Music in Russia, Moscow, 1994; The Development of Harp Music in Russia, Bloomington, 1997; V Dulova, Creative portrait, Moscow, 1975; In Dulova's book, The Art of Harp Playing. *Honours:* Master of Art Criticism, 1992; Honoured Artist of Russia, 1993; 2nd prize, Laureat of the all Union Competition, 1963; 3rd prize, International Harp Contest, Israel, 1965; 1st prize, USA, 1969; International Woman of the Year, for Services to Music, IBC, Cambridge. *Address:* Harpa 242, Liapidevskogo 14-68, Moscow 125581, Russia. *Telephone:* (95) 456-9196. *Fax:* (95) 504-4500.

SHAMIR, Michal; Singer (Soprano); b. 1960, Tel-Aviv, Israel. *Education:* Studied at the Rubin Academy of Music, Tel-Aviv, and in London. *Career:* Operatic debut at Gluck's Euridice; Followed by Cherubino and Elvira in L'Italiana in Algeri; European debut at Hamburg as Susanna, followed by Pamina, Gretel and Frasquita; Geneva Opera 1987, as Larissa in the premiere of La Forêt by Liebermann; Appearances with Frankfurt Oper as Susanna, Despina, Gilda, Marzellina and Jenny in Mahagonny; Has returned to Tel-Aviv for Violetta, Nedda and Marguerite; Basle Opera in Zemlinsky's Der Zwerg; Member of the Deutsche Oper Berlin; Concert repertoire includes Lutoslawski's Chantefleurs et Chantefables, performed with the composer in San Francisco and Helsinki; British debut as Violetta in La Traviata with Opera North, 1994; First Tatiana in Eugene Onegin at Lausanne, Switzerland, 1994; Violetta in Tel-Aviv, 1998; Sang Jenůfa at Essen and Omega in the premiere of Alpha and Omega, by Gil Shohat for New Israeli Opera, 2001. *Address:* c/o Valmalète, Bureau de Concerts, 7 rue Hoche, F–92300 Levallois Perret, France.

SHANAHAN, Ian (Leslie); Composer; b. 13 June 1962, Sydney, New South Wales, Australia. *Education:* BMus, University of Sydney, 1986; Study with Eric Gross and Peter Sculthorpe. *Career:* Faculty Member, Department of Music, University of Sydney, 1994–; New South Wales Conservatory, 1989–94; Commissions from Roger Woodward, 1993 and others. *Compositions:* Echoes/Fantasies for bass clarinet and percussion, 1984; Arcturus Timespace for amplified mandolin and percussion, 1987; Solar Dust for mandolin, 1988; Cycles of Vega for clarinet and 2 percussions, 1988–90; Lines of Light for amplified recorders and percussion, 1991–93; Ritual Canons for 4 tubas, 1982–93; Dimensions Paradisim for alto flute, 1993; Arc of Light, for piano, 1993; Gate of Remembrance, for amplified piano, 1993. *Honours:* Adolf Spivakovsky Prize, 1991. *Address:* c/o APRA, 1A Eden Street, Crows Nest, NSW 2065, Australia.

SHANE, Rita (Frances); Opera, Concert Singer (Soprano); b. 1940, New York City, USA; m. Daniel F Tritter, 1 s. *Education:* BA, Barnard College; Private Study, Beverly Peck Johnson, Bliss Hebert, Elisabeth Schwarzkopf; Santa Fe Opera Apprentice Program; Hunter College Opera Workshop. *Career:* Appearances with, Metropolitan Opera, Chicago Lyric, San Francisco, New York City Opera, most American companies; La Scala, Vienna Staatsoper, Bavarian State Opera, Turin, Strasbourg, Scottish, other opera houses in Europe, South America; Orchestras of Philadelphia, Cleveland, Cincinnati, in USA, Santa Cecilia, Vienna, in Europe, Israel Philharmonic; Festivals, Salzburg, Vienna, Munich, Glyndebourne, Perugia, Aspen; Mostly Mozart, Canada; Roles at Met Opera New York include the Queen of Night, Lucia, Berthe in Le Prophète, Pamira in The Siege of Corinth, Verdi's Gilda, Oscar and Violetta; Recitals; Television, CBC Canada, Bayerische Rundfunk, Germany; Sang title role in the premiere of Argento's Miss Havisham's Fire, New York City Opera, 1979; American premieres of Henze's Elegy for Young Lovers (Hilda Mack), New York, Schat's Houdini (Cecelia) at Aspen and Reimann's Lear (Regan), San Francisco; Professor of Voice, Eastman School of Music, Rochester, New York; Aspen School of Music and Festival, Colorado; Hamamatsu, Japan; Juilliard School, New York. *Recordings:* Highlights from Handel's Athalia; Highlights from Handel's Rinaldo; Complete works of Schoenberg, vol. 2; R Strauss, Brentano Songs, Op 68 with orchestra (Louisville Premiere); Various private recordings including, Les Huguenots, Die Zauberflöte; Professor of Voice, Eastman School of Music, Rochester, New York. *Address:* c/o Daniel F Tritter, 330 West 42nd Street, New York, NY 10036 USA.

SHANKAR, Anoushka; Indian sitar player and conductor; b. 9 June 1981, London; d. of Sukanya and Ravi Shankar. *Education:* San Dieguito Acad., San Diego, Calif., USA. *Career:* professional debut in New Delhi 1995 at age of 13; signed to Angel/EMI Classics 1997; performances since then at major concert halls in India, Europe, USA and Asia, including tours with Ravi Shankar ensemble; first solo tour in 2000; fundraising concerts for the Tibet Foundation Peace Garden 2000, Ramakrishna Centre, Kolkata 2000, Siri Fort Auditorium, New Delhi (conducting debut) 2001, World Economic Forum, New York 2002, Rainforest Foundation Benefit Concert, Carnegie Hall 2002. *Recordings include:* Anoushka 1998, Anourag 2000, Live at Carnegie Hall 2002; contributions to albums by Ravi Shankar. *Film:* Dance Like a Man 2003. *Publication:* Bapi, The Love of My Life (pictorial biog. of Ravi Shankar) 2002. *Honours:* House of Commons Shield 1998, Nat. Council on Youth Leadership Award 1998, San Dieguito Acad. Award Winner 1999. *Current Management:* Sulivan Sweetland, 28 Albion Street, London, W2 2AX, England. *Telephone:* (20) 7262-0333. *Fax:* (20) 7402-5851. *E-mail:* info@sulivansweetland.co.uk. *Website:* www.sulivansweetland.co.uk; www.anoushkashankar.com.

SHANKAR, Ravi; Indian sitar player and composer; b. 7 April 1920, Varansi; m. Sukanya Rajan 1989; two d. (Anoushka Shankar and Norah Jones) one s. (deceased). *Education:* studied under Ustad Allauddin Khan of Maihar. *Career:* fmr Dir of Music All-India Radio and founder of the Nat. Orchestra; founder and Dir, Kinnara Schools of Music, Mumbai 1962, Los Angeles 1967; Visiting Lecturer Univ. of Calif. 1965; concert tours in Europe, USA and the East, major festivals include Edinburgh, Woodstock, Monterey; appeared in film, Raga 1974; elected to Rajya Sabha (Upper House) 1986; Fellow Sangeet Natak Akademi 1977. *Compositions include:* Concerto No. 1 for Sitar and Orchestra 1971, No. 2 1981, Ghanashyam (opera-ballet, premiered by City of Birmingham Touring Opera) 1989, Kalyan 2001, Mood Circle 2002. *Soundtracks:* for film: Pather Panchali, The Flute and the Arrow, Nava Rasa Ranga, Charly, Gandhi, Chappaqua; for television: Alice In Wonderland. *Recordings include:* Concertos 1 and 2 for Sitar and Orchestra, Raga Jageshwari 1981, Homage To Mahatma Ghandhi 1981, West Meets East (with Yehudi Menuhin and others), In London (live) 1999, In New York 2000, Full Circle: Carnegie Hall 2000, In San Francisco 2001, Collected 2001. *Publications:* My Music, My Life (auto biog.) 1968, Rag Anurag (Bengali), Ravi: The Autobiography of Ravi Shankar (with others) 1995, From India 1997, Mantram: Chant of India 1997, Raga Jogeshwari 1998. *Honours:* numerous hon. degrees; Silver Bear of Berlin 1966; Award of Indian Nat. Acad. for Music, Dance and Drama 1962; Award of Padma Bhushan 1967, Padma Vibhushan 1981, Deshikottam 1981, Int. Music Council UNESCO Award 1975, Ramon Magsaysay Award 1992, Praemium Imperiale 1997, Polar Music Prize 1998, Bharat Ratna (Jewel of India) Award 1999; Grammy Award 2000; Hon. KBE 2001; ISPA Distinguished Artists Award 2003. *Current Management:* Sulivan Sweetland, 28 Albion Street, London, W2 2AX, England. *Telephone:* (20) 7262-0333. *Fax:* (20) 7402-5851. *E-mail:* info@sulivansweetland.co.uk. *Website:* www.sulivansweetland.co.uk.

SHANKS, Donald; Singer (Bass-Baritone); b. 5 July 1940, Brisbane, Australia. *Career:* Sang first in operettas by Gilbert and Sullivan, then toured Australia with the Williamson-Sutherland Opera Company; From 1964 has sung with the Australian Opera, Sydney in over 70 roles including Boris in Boris Godunov, Don Pasquale, Phillip in Don Carlos, Baron Ochs in Rosenkavalier, Osmin, Zaccaria, Nabucco, Raimondo in Lucia di Lammermoor, Prince Gremin in Eugene Onegin, Gurnemanz, Parsifal; Sang at Covent Garden in 1974 and Paris Opéra in 1976; Various roles with Queensland Lyric Opera and Victoria State Opera; Season 1996 as Rocco in Fidelio, Zaccaria in Nabucco, Daland in Der fliegende Holländer, Sarastro in The Magic Flute in Sydney for the Australian Opera; Parson/Badger in The Cunning Little Vixen, 1997. *Honours:* O.B.E., 1976; AO, 1987. *Address:* c/o The Australian Opera, PO Box 291, Strawberry Hills, Sydney 2012, Australia.

SHAO, En; Conductor; b. 1954, Tianjin, China. *Education:* Piano studies from age 4, violin from 5; Peking Centre Music Conservatory and Royal Northern College of Music. *Career:* Deputy Principal Conductor of the Chinese Broadcasting Symphony Orchestra and Principal Guest Conductor of the Central Philharmonic Orchestra of Ogina and the National Youth Orchestra; Engagements in Europe from 1988; Associate Conductor of the BBC Philharmonic Orchestra, 1990; Principal Conductor and Artistic Adviser of the Ulster Orchestra, 1993; Guest Appearances with the Bournemouth Symphony, Northern Sinfonia, Royal Liverpool Philharmonic and other BBC orchestras; London debut 1992 with the London Symphony Orchestra; European engagements with the Oslo Philharmonic, the Berlin Symphony and the Czech Philharmonic; Prague Autumn Festival, 1993; Concerts with the ABC Orchestras in Australia and the Hong Kong Philharmonic; North American showings with the Toronto Symphony and the Colorado and Vancouver Symphonies; Royal Philharmonic Orchestra debut, 1994; Helsinki Philharmonic. *Honours:* Lord Rhodes Scholarship; First Edward Van Beinum Scholarship; Winner, Sixth Hungarian Television Conductors Competition. *Current Management:* IMG Artists, Lovell House, 616 Chiswick High Road, London W4 5RX, England.

SHAPERO, Harold (Samuel); Pianist, Teacher and Composer; b. 29 April 1920, Lynn, Massachusetts, USA. *Education:* Studied piano with Eleanor Kerr; Composition with Nicolas Slonimsky, Malkin Conservatory, Boston 1936–37; with Ernst Krenek, 1937, with Walter Piston, Harvard University, 1938–41; With Paul Hindemith, Berkshire Music Center, Tanglewood, summers 1940, 1941; Nadia Boulanger, Longy School of Music, 1942–43. *Career:* Pianist; Teacher 1952–, Founder-director, electronic music studio, Brandeis University. *Compositions:* Orchestral: 9-minuted Overture, 1940; Serenade, 1945; Symphony for classical orchestra, 1947; Sinfonia: The Travelers Overture, 1948; Concerto, 1950; Credo, 1955; Lyric Dances, 1955; On Green Mountain for jazz ensemble, 1957; for orchestra, 1981; Partita for piano and small orchestra, 1960; Trumpet Concerto, 1995; Chamber: String Trio, 1938; 3 Pieces for flute, clarinet and bassoon, 1939; Trumpet Sonata, 1940, String Quartet, 1941; Violin Sonata, 1942; 3 Improvisations for piano and synthesizer, 1968; 3 Studies for piano and synthesizer, 1969; 4 Pieces for piano and synthesizer, 1969; 4 Pieces for piano and synthesizer, 1970; Six for Five, woodwind quintet, 1994; Piano: Sonata for 4-hands, 1941; 3 sonatas, all 1944; Variations, 1947; Sonata, 1948; American Variations, 1950; Vocal: 4 Baritone Songs, 1942; 2 Psalms for chorus, 1952; Hebrew Cantata for soprano, alto, tenor, baritone, chorus and 5 instruments, 1954; 2 Hebrew Songs for tenor and piano, 1970, also for tenor, piano and string orchestra, 1980. *Recordings:* Several compositions recorded. *Honours:* American Prix de Rome, 1941; Naumburg Fellowship, 1942; Guggenheim Fellowships, 1947, 1948; Fulbright Fellowship, 1948. *Address:* c/o Music Department, Brandeis University, MA 02254, USA.

SHAPIRO, Joel; Concert Pianist and Teacher; b. 28 Nov. 1934, Cleveland, Ohio, USA. *Education:* AB, Columbia College, New York City; Private study with Beryl Rubinstein and Frank Sheridan; Brussels Royal Conservatory with Stefan Askenase; Premier Prix avec Distinction, 1959. *Career:* debut, New York City, 1963; As a Soloist with Royal Philharmonic Orchestra, 1968; Extensive annual concert tours including piano recitals, concertos and chamber music in the world's leading music centres; Numerous radio and television broadcasts; Professor of Piano, University of Illinois, 1970–93; Professor of Piano and Prorektor, Staatliche Hochschule für Musik, Leipzig, 1994–; Artistic Director International Summer Music Academy, Leipzig, 1999–. *Honours:* Winner, Young Concert Artists International Auditions, New York City, 1961; 1st Prize, Darche Competition, Brussels, 1962; Harriet Cohen International Bach Award, London, 1963; Awards from The International Institute, 1964 and Rockefeller Foundation, 1965. *Address:* Hochschule für Musik, Grassistrasse 8, 04107 Leipzig, Germany.

SHAPIRRA, Elyakum; Conductor; b. 1926, Tel-Aviv, Israel. *Education:* Studied with Bernstein and Koussevitzky at Tanglewood and the Juilliard School. *Career:* Assistant with the San Francisco Symphony Orchestra; Conducted the New York Philharmonic on tours to Canada and Japan, 1960–61; Associate Conductor of the Boston Symphony Orchestra 1962–67; Guest conductor with leading orchestras in England (1968) and the USA; Chief Conductor of the Malmö Symphony

Orchestra, Sweden, 1969–74; Chief Conductor of the South Australian Symphony Orchestra at Adelaide, 1975; Has conducted opera in Scandinavia. *Recordings include:* Bruckner's F minor Symphony and G minor Overture with the London Symphony Orchestra.

SHARAF, Hisham; Iraqi musician (clarinet); *Artistic Director, Baghdad Symphony Orchestra. Education:* Baghdad School of Folk Music and Ballet;*Address:* Iraqi National Symphony Orchestra, Baghdad Convention Center, Green Zone, Baghdad, Iraq.

SHARNINA, Ljubov; Singer (Soprano); b. 1962, Moscow, Russia. *Education:* Studied at the Gnessin Institute, Moscow. *Career:* Sang at the Nemirovitsch-Danschenko Theatre Moscow from 1986, notably as Tatiana, Lisa, Iolanta, Nedda, Lisa in La Battaglia di Legnano, Zemfira in Rachmaninov's Aleko and Imogene in Bellini's Pirata; Guest engagements as Aida at Birmingham and Manchester, Desdemona at Aachen in 1990, the Trovatore Leonora at Leipzig in 1991, and Maria in Tchaikovsky's Mazeppa at Amsterdam in 1991; Many concert appearances in Cologne, Vienna, St Petersburg and North America. *Address:* Bolshoi Theatre, 103009 Moscow, Russia.

SHARP, Norma; Opera Singer (Soprano); b. 1945, Shawnee, Oklahoma, USA; m. Jens Niggemeyer, 1 s. *Education:* Kansas University, USA; Hochschule für Musik, Hamburg, Cologne. *Career:* 1970–77 Permanent Member of the opera houses of Regensburg, Augsburg, Karlsruhe as Lyric Soprano; Since 1978 freelance Opera Singer, regular guest at Berlin, Hamburg, Munich, Frankfurt, Cologne, Düsseldorf, Vienna; Further Guest Appearances at Dresden, Hannover, Stuttgart, Amsterdam, Antwerp, Ghent, Zürich, Basel, Bern, Geneva, Milan, Rome, Naples, Madrid, London, Glasgow, Prague, Budapest; Festivals: Bayreuth 1977–81, Glyndebourne, Vienna; Concerts throughout Europe with conductors including Pierre Boulez, Carlo Maria Giulini, Marek Janowski, Neville Marriner, Wolfgang Sawallisch, Giuseppe Sinopoli, Horst Stein; Professor of Voice, Hochschule für Musik, Hanns Eisler, Berlin, 1992–. *Recordings:* Tales of Hoffmann; Peer Gynt; Ring of the Nibelung; Tannhäuser. *Current Management:* Marguerite Kollo, Berlin. *Address:* Seestr 119, 13353 Berlin, Germany.

SHAULIS, Jane; Singer (Mezzo-Soprano); b. 1950, New Jersey, USA. *Education:* Studies, Philadelphia Academy and Curtis Institute. *Career:* Appearances with New York City Opera, 1977–90; Metropolitan Opera, 1990–, Notably in the premieres of The Ghosts of Versailles by Corigliano and The Voyage by Glass; Further New York appearances in Idomeneo, Elektra, Die Zauberflöte, The Ring, I Lombardi, Arabella and Peter Grimes; Season 1996–97 as Mozart's Marcellina, Mdme. Larina in Eugene Onegin and Marthe in Faust; Glyndebourne, 1990–, as Nan in New Year by Tippett and Ragonde in Le Comte Ory, 1997; Other Roles include Amneris at Buffalo, Azucena and Herodias for Kentucky Opera and the Countess in Andrea Chénier at Chicago; Fricka, Erda and Waltraute in The Ring at Artpark. *Address:* c/o New York Metropolitan Opera, Lincoln Center, New York, NY 10023, USA.

SHAVE, Jacqueline; Violinist; b. 1960, England. *Career:* Co-Founded the Brindisi String Quartet at Aldeburgh, 1984; Wigmore Hall Debut 1984, with Peter Pears; Concerts in a wide repertory throughout the United Kingdom and in France, Germany, Spain, Italy and Switzerland; Festival Engagements at Aldeburgh, Arundel, Bath, Brighton, Huddersfield, Norwich and Warwick; First London Performance of Colin Matthews 2nd Quartet, 1990; Quartet by Mark Anthony Turnage, 1992; Many BBC Recitals and Resident Artist with the University of Ulster. *Recordings include:* Quartets by Britten, Bridge and Imogen Holst; Works by Pierné and Lekeu. *Honours:* Prize Winner at the Third Banff International String Quartet Competition. *Address:* c/o Owen/White Management, 14 Nightingale Lane, London N8 7QU, England.

SHAVERZASHVILI, George; composer and pianist; b. 4 Aug. 1950, Tbilisi, Georgia; m.; one d. *Education:* State Conservatory, Tbilisi. *Career:* debut, piano 1970, composer 1980, Tbilisi; Concerts at Tbilisi, Moscow, St Petersburg, Tallinn, Budapest, Bratislava; Professor, State Conservatory, Tbilisi; mem, Georgian Composers Union, 1986. *Compositions:* Quintet for piano and string quartet; 3 Sonatas for piano; 2 Concerts for piano and orchestra, 1984, 1991; 2 Concertos for violin, 1990, 1995; Sonata for violin; Trio for piano, flute and clarinet, 1997; Alegg for string orchestra, 1998; 2 piano fantasies, 1998, 1999; Mass for chorus and orchestra, 1999; Maestoso for piano, 2000; Clouds for symphony orchestra, 2003. *Address:* Mosashvili Street 8, Ap 6, 380062 Tbilisi, Georgia.

SHAW, Kenneth; Singer (Bass-baritone); b. 1955, Georgia, USA. *Career:* Debut: New Orleans, 1980, as Morales in Carmen; Appearances at New Orleans and Kentucky Operas as Mozart's Count, Germont and Escamillo, 1989; Scarpia and Nilakantha in Lakmé; season 1986–87 as Sharpless in Butterfly at New York City Opera; Mefistofele at Three Cities Opera; Concert of Jenůfa at Carnegie Hall, 1988; Saratoga Festival, New York as Marcello; Other roles include Jochanaan in Salome; Sarastro, Kentucky Opera, 1998. *Recordings:* Jenůfa. *Address:* c/o Kentucky Opera, 101 South 8th Street, Louisville KY 40202, USA.

SHAW, Teresa; Singer (Mezzo-soprano); b. 1965, England. *Education:* Studied at the Royal Academy of Music. *Career:* Concert appearances in Debussy's Le Martyre de Saint Sebastien with the London Philharmonic under Kurt Masur; Vivaldi's Gloria with Richard Hickox; Handel's Dixit Dominus and Haydn's Nelson Mass conducted by David Willcocks; The Dream of Gerontius at the York and Ripon Festival, 1991; The Apostles and the Glagolitic Mass at Canterbury; Operatic roles include Octavian, Third Lady in Die Zauberflöte, Dorabella (Opera Factory) and Female Chorus in Goehr's Triptych; Season 1991 included Purcell Room, Conway Hall and Wigmore Hall recitals; Premiere production of The Death of Klinghoffer by John Adams in Lyon and Vienna; Season 1992 in title role of Oliver's Beauty and the Beast, at Portsmouth; Season 1996 as the Composer in Ariadne auf Naxos for Castleward Opera. *Recordings include:* Sorceress in Dido and Aeneas and Brahms Liebesliederwalzer, conducted by John Eliot Gardiner. *Honours:* Winner, Great Grimsby International Singing Competition, 1989.

SHCHEDRIN, Rodion Konstantinovich; Russian composer; b. 16 Dec. 1932, Moscow; s. of Konstantin Mikhailovich Shchedrin and Konkordia Ivanovna Shchedrin; m. Maya Plisetskaya 1958. *Education:* Moscow Conservatoire. *Career:* Chair. RSFSR (now Russian) Union of Composers 1973–90; USSR People's Deputy 1989–91; mem. Acad. of Fine Arts, Berlin, Bavarian Acad. of Fine Arts. *Compositions include:* operas: Not Only Love 1961, Dead Souls (operatic scenes in three acts) 1976, Lolita (after V. Nabokov) 1994; ballets: Humpbacked Horse 1960, Carmen Suite 1967, Anna Karenina 1972, The Seagull 1980, Lady with a Lapdog 1985; for orchestra: three symphonies 1958, 1965, 2000, 5 concertos for orchestra 1963, 1968, 1988, 1989, 1998; Self-Portrait 1984, Stykhira 1988, Old Russian Circus Music 1989; 6 concertos for piano and orchestra 1954, 1966, 1973, 1992, 1999, 2003, Concerto for cello and orchestra 1994, Concerto for trumpet and orchestra 1995, Two Tangos by Albéniz for orchestra 1996, Concerto dolce for viola and string orchestra 1997; other: Poetoria 1974, Musical Offering for organ and nine soloists 1983, The Sealed Angel (Russian Liturgy) 1988, Nina and the Twelve Months (musical) 1988, Piano Terzetto 1996, Concerto Cantabile (for violin and strings) 1997, Preludium for 9th Symphony by Beethoven 1999, Lolita-serenade 2001, Parabola concertante (for cello and strings) 2001, Dialogue with Shostakovich 2001, The Enchanted Wanderer (concert opera) 2002, Tanja-Katya 2002, My Age, My Wild Beast 2003; works for chamber orchestra, piano, violin, organ and cello and song cycles, music for theatre and cinema. *Honours:* Hon. mem. American Liszt Soc., Int. Music Council, Hon. Prof., Moscow Conservatoire; Lenin Prize, USSR and Russian State Prizes, Russian Union of Composers Prize, Shostakovich Prize, Beethoven Soc. Prize. *Address:* Theresienstrasse 23, 80333 Munich, Germany (home); 25/9, Tverskaya St, apt. 31, 103050 Moscow, Russia (home). *Telephone:* (89) 285834 (Munich); (095) 299-72-39 (Moscow). *Fax:* (89) 282057 (Munich).

SHEBANOVA, Tatiana; Pianist; b. 12 Jan. 1953, Moscow, USSR; m. 18 Sept 1986, 1 s. *Education:* Undergraduate and Postgraduate Studies, Main Music School, Moscow Conservatory. *Career:* Represented Moscow Conservatory, various International competitions and meetings; Live concert performances include appearances in Czechoslovakia, Belgium, France, Germany, Switzerland, Italy, Netherlands, Greece, Portugal, Austria and many tours: Japan, Philippines, Yugoslavia, Poland, Spain; Repertoire includes about 30 recitals, about 30 piano concertos; 1st interpretation of Bach's 12 choral preludes in Feinberg's transcription, Moscow Conservatory; Teaching, Warsaw and Bygdoszoz Academies of Music, Poland. *Recordings:* Works by Tchaikovsky, Chopin (many), Szymanowski, Rachmaninov, Bach, Debussy, Brahms.

SHEERIN, Mairead; Singer (Soprano); b. 1972, England. *Education:* Birmingham Conservatoire; Royal College of Music, with Margaret Kingsley. *Career:* Concert engagements in Haydn's Paukenmesse and Harmoniemesse, Elijah, Mozart's Requiem and Coronation Mass, Messiah, the Fauré Requiem and Monteverdi's Vespers; European tour with the St Matthew Passion, as soloist with the English Concert under Trevor Pinnock, 2001; London Handel Festival, 2001, as Clelia in Muzio Scevola; Other roles include Serpetto in La Finta Giardiniera, Ravel's Enfant, Purcell's Sorceress and Yum-Yum in The Mikado. *Honours:* D'Oyly Carte Scholar, at the London Royal Schools Opera. *Address:* c/o Royal College of Music (vocal faculty) Prince Consort Road, London SW7, England.

SHEFFIELD, Philip; Singer (tenor); b. 1960, Kenya. *Education:* Studied at Cambridge University, Guildhall School and Royal College of Music; Further Study with Philip Langridge and Malcolm King. *Career:* Season 1989–90 in L'Incoronazione di Popea at Brussels, Hans Jürgen von Bose's 63: Dream Palace at Munich and Capriccio at Glyndebourne; Cavalli's Egisto for the Berlin Kammeroper, Scaramuccio at Antwerp and the Count in Die Tote Stadt in Netherlands; Other Repertoire Encludes Mozart's Ferrando and Tamino, and Agenore in Il Re Pastore;

Lensky, Tamino, and Belmonte for Lucerne Opera; Recent Concert performances include Britten's Nocturne with the Berlin Symphony Orchestra in the Philharmonie, and again in Montepulciano, Haydn's L'isola disabitata in the Vienna Konzerthaus with Heinz Holliger, Alexander Goehr's Eve Dreams in Paradise with the BBC Philharmonic, Henze's Kammermusik 1958 in Amsterdam, Schreker's Der Schatzgraeber for the Dutch Radio Philharmonic Orchestra in the Amsterdam Concertgebouw, Stravinsky's Renard with the Ensemble Modern in Frankfurt, Berlin and Vienna, Bach's St John Passion (Evangelist) with the North Netherlands Orchestra, Berio's Sinfonia in Leningrad and Messiah in Antwerp with the Royal Flanders Philharmonic; Also many appearances throughout the United Kingdom including Monteverdi's Orfeo at the Proms, Poppea in the QEH and Bach's B Minor Mass in Canterbury, all with Roger Norrington; Recent operatic performances include Ferrando in Così fan tutte; Shere Khan and Harry in Baa Baa Black Sheep; Chevalier in Der Ferne Klang; Belmonte in Die Entführung; Tamino in Die Zauberflöte; Lensky in Eugene Onegin; Sang Theseus in Goehr's Arianna at Cambridge, 1996; Janáček's Schoolmaster (Vixen) at Birmingham, 1998. *Recordings include:* Berio's Sinfonia with Pierre Boulez; Baa Baa Black Sheep for BBC and Radio with CD to follow; Tippett's Midsummer Marriage for Thames television and 63 Dream Palace for Bayerischer Rundfunk. *Current Management:* Musicmakers International Artists Representation, Tailor House, 63–65 High Street, Whitwell, Hertfordshire SG4 8AH, England. *Telephone:* (1438) 871708. *Fax:* (1438) 871777. *E-mail:* musicmakers@ compuserve.com. *Website:* www.operauk.com.

SHELLEY, Howard; Concert Pianist and Conductor; b. 9 March 1950, London, England; m. Hilary Macnamara, 1975, one s., one step-s. *Education:* Highgate School Music Scholar; Royal College of Music Foundation Scholar with Harold Craxton, Kendall Taylor, Lamar Crowson and Ilona Kabos; ARCM, Honours, 1966, ARCO, 1967. *Career:* First television appearance at age 10 playing Bach and Chopin; Adult debut, Wigmore Hall, London, 1971; Televised Henry Wood Prom debut 1972; 2 Piano partnership with Hilary Macnamara, 1976–; International solo pianist; Conducting debut, 1985 with London Symphony Orchestra, Barbican Hall, London; Performed world's first cycle of complete solo piano works of Rachmaninov, Wigmore Hall, 1983; Edward Cowie, Brian Chapple and Peter Dickinson have written concertos for him; Principal Guest Conductor of the London Mozart Players, 1992–98; Music Director and Principal Conductor, Uppsala Chamber Orchestra, 2000–. *Recordings include:* the complete solo piano music of Rachmaninov (9 vols) and complete Rachmaninov song-cycle (3 vols); Chopin Preludes/Sonatas/Scherzi/Impromptus; Schumann Carnaval/Kinderszenen; Hummel solo piano works; Complete piano concertos of Rachmaninov; Piano concertos of British composers, Alwyn, Dickinson, Ferguson, Rubbra, Tippett and Vaughan Williams; Piano concertos and rhapsodies for piano and orchestra of Gershwin; Piano concertos of Balakirev, Lyapounov, Korngold (Left Hand); Dohnányi Nursery Variations; Hindemith's Four Temperaments; Szymanowski's Symphony No. 4; Messiaen's Turangalîla; Conducting from the keyboard the Mendelssohn piano concertos, Hummel piano concertos (3 vols) and Mozart piano concertos Nos 9, 12, 13, 14, 17, 19, 20–24, 27; Moscheles Piano Concertos (2 vols); Cramer Piano Concertos; Conducting the Royal Philharmonic Orchestra, Mozart symphonies 35 and 38 and Schubert symphonies 3 and 5. *Honours:* Chappell Gold Medal and Peter Morrison Prize, 1968; Dannreuther Concerto Prize, 1971; Silver Medal, Worshipful Company of Musicians, 1971; Honorary FRCM, 1993. *Current Management:* Caroline Baird Artists. *Address:* c/o Caroline Baird Artists, Pinkhill House, Oxford Rd, Eynsham, Oxon, OX29 4DA England.

SHELTON, Lucy; Singer (Soprano); b. 22 Feb. 1954, Pomona, California, USA. *Education:* Pomona College and New England Conservatory. *Career:* Has performed as recitalist, soloist with orchestra and performer in opera from 1980; Sang Jenifer in Thames television's production of Tippett's Midsummer Marriage, Jan 1989; Other operatic roles have been Euridice in Gluck's Orfeo, Salud in La Vida Breve and appearances in Dallapiccola's Il Prigioniero, Mozart's Zaide, Milhaud's Médée and John Corigliano's The Ghost of Versailles; Concert appearances throughout the US and Europe; Repertoire includes music of all periods, from Monteverdi and Bach to Boulez, and Schoenberg (Erwartung) and many first performances of works written specially for her by such composers as Carter, Goehr, Knussen, Maw and Schwantner; Has taught at the Eastman School of Music and the Cleveland Institute of Music. *Honours:* Walter W Naumburg Competition (as member of the Jubal Trio) and in 1980 as winner of the International Solo Vocal Competition; National Endowment for the Arts Award. *Current Management:* Ingpen & Williams Ltd, 7 St George's Court, 131 Putney Bridge Road, London, SW15 2PA, England.

SHENG, Bright; composer; b. 6 Dec. 1955, Shanghai, China. *Education:* Shanghai Conservatory, 1976–; Queens College, City University of New York and Columbia University, 1982–, with Chou-Wen Chung, Mario

Davidovsky, George Perle and Hugo Weisgall. *Career:* freelance composer with many performances throughout the USA; Commissions from Peter Serkin and Gerard Schwarz; Opera, The Song of Majnun, with libretto by Andrew Porter, written for the Chicago Lyric Opera, 1992 (former Composer-in-Residence); Resident, Seattle Symphony Orchestra, 1992–94. *Compositions:* Three Pieces, for orchestra, 1982; Trio, for flute, harp and cello, 1982; Five Pieces, for oboe and cello, 1983; 2 String Quartets, 1984; Suite for piano, 1984; Four Poems From the Tang Dynasty, for mezzo and piano, 1984; Adagio, for chamber orchestra, 1987; Three Poems From the Sung Dynasty, for soprano and chamber orchestra, 1987; H'un (Lacerations): In Memoriam, 1966–76, for orchestra, 1987; Three Pieces for viola and piano, 1987; My Song, for piano, 1988; Three Chinese Love Songs, for soprano, viola and piano, 1988; Three Chinhai Folk Songs, for chorus, 1989; Four Movements, for piano trio, 1990; The Song of Majnun, Opera, 1992; Prelude, for orchestra, 1994; The Silver River (musical, libretto by David Henry Hwang) 1997, Madame Mao (opera) 2003.

SHEPPARD, Craig; Concert Pianist; b. 26 Nov. 1947, Philadelphia, USA. *Education:* Studied at the Curtis Institute of Music and the Juilliard School of Music. *Career:* Senior Artist-in-Residence, University of Washington, Seattle; Teacher, Yehudi Menuhin School, Surrey, 1978–88; Teacher, University of Lancaster, 1979–81; Teacher, Guildhall School of Music and Drama, 1981–86; Concert Experience as Soloist in most American and all the major British, German and Italian Orchestras; Conductors have included Georg Solti, James Levine, Leonard Slatkin, Michael Tilson Thomas, Pritchard, Neeme Järvi and Charles Mackerras; Television appearances on PBS America and BBC England. *Recordings:* Liszt; Rachmaninov; Rossini; Jolivet. *Honours:* Arthur Rubinstein Prize; Silver Medal, Leeds International Pianoforte Competition; Dealey Award; Young Musicians Foundation of Los Angeles 1st Prize. *Address:* c/o School of Music, University of Washington, Seattle, WA 98195-3450, USA.

SHEPPARD, Honor; Singer (soprano); b. 1931, Leeds, Yorkshire, England; m. Robert Elliott, 1 s., 1 d. *Education:* Royal Manchester College of Music; FRMCM. *Career:* Recitalist and Oratorio singer; Appearances at major British and European Festivals; First Soprano with the Deller Consort, specialising in 17th and 18th Century Music; Extensive tours of North and South America, Canada and Europe from 1961; Many broadcasts; Tutor in vocal Studies at the Royal Manchester College of Music, since 1987. *Recordings include:* Belinda in Dido and Aeneas, conducted by Alfred Deller; The Fairy Queen, The Indian Queen and King Arthur; Handel's Acis and Galatea. *Honours:* Curtis Gold Medal, Royal Manchester College of Music. *Address:* The Firs, 27 The Firs, Bowdon, Cheshire WA14 2TF, England.

SHEPPARD, Kerrie; Singer (Soprano); b. 1970, Mansfield, England. *Education:* Studied at the Guildhall School and the National Opera Studio. *Career:* Appearances as Mimi in La Bohème at the Mananan Festival; Premiere production of Birtwistle's The Second Mrs Kong at Glyndebourne; Other roles include Micaela, Donna Elvira, Fiordiligi in Così fan tutte; Concerts include engagements with the Bangkok Symphony, Exultate Jubilate by Mozart at Chichester, Beethoven's Mass in C at the Fishguard Festival, Carmina Burana; Concerts with the Liverpool Philharmonic and Bournemouth Symphony Orchestras. *Honours:* Decca prize, 1995 Kathleen Ferrier Competition. *Address:* Harlequin Agency Ltd, 203 Fidlas Road, Cardiff CF4 5NA, Wales.

SHEPPARD, Peter; Violinist; b. 1965, England. *Education:* Studied at the Royal Academy with Sidney Griller and Erich Gruenberg, and in Boston with Louis Krasner. *Career:* Played Henze's 2nd Concerto at London's Barbican in 1991 and has performed works by Judith Weir, Dmitri Smirnov and David Matthews; Further concerts at the Wigmore Hall, Tokyo's Suntory Hall, in Istanbul and throughout Spain; Duo partnership with pianist Aaron Shorr in works by Satie, Ustvolskaya, Berg and Bartók; Principal Lecturer at the Royal Academy of Music from 1993 and leader of the Kreutzer Quartet. *Address:* c/o Royal Academy of Music Strings Faculty, Marylebone Road, London, NW1 5HT, England.

SHERE, Charles; Composer and Writer on Music; b. 20 Aug. 1935, Berkeley, California, USA; m. Lindsay Remolif Shere. *Education:* Graduated, University of California at Berkeley, 1960 and studied music at the San Francisco Conservatory. *Career:* Music Director at California radio stations, 1964–73; Instructor at Mills College, Oakland, 1973–84 and Critic for the Oakland Tribune, 1972–88. *Compositions include:* Fratture for 7 instruments, 1962; Small Concerto for piano and orchestra, 1964; Ces desirs du vent des Greogoriens for tape, 1967; Nightmusic for diminished orchestra, 1967; Handler of Gravity for organ and optional chimes, 1971; Music for Orchestra (Symphony), 1976; Tongues for poet, chamber orchestra and tape, 1978; String QuartetNo. 1, 1980; The Bride Stripped Bare by Her Bachelors, Even, opera, 1981 and 1984; Certain Phenomena of Sound for soprano and violin, 1983; Concerto for Violin with Harp, Percussion and Small

Orchestra, 1985; Requiem with oboe, 1985; Ladies Voice, chamber opera, 1987; Symphony in 3 Movements, 1988; I Like it to be a Play for tenor baritone, bass and string quartet, 1989; Sonata: Bachelor Machine for piano, 1989; What Happened, chamber opera after Gertrude Stein (trilogy with Ladies Voices and I Like it to be a Play); Three more Stein songs for soprano, violin, piano and bass clarinet, 1997; Trio for violin, piano and percussion, 1997;. *Contributions:* EAR (monthly new-music magazinee), which he co-founded and published. *Address:* c/o ASCAP, ASCAP Building, 1 Lincoln Plaza, New York, NY 10023, USA.

SHERLOCK, Elizabeth; British double bassist and viola da gamba player; b. 27 April 1946, Hillingdon, Middlesex. *Education:* Royal Coll. of Music. *Career:* debut, Purcell Room with the Helicon Ensemble, viola da gamba 1972; Oviedo, playing Dittersdorf Sinfonia Concertante, double bass 1994; mem. of Collegium Sagittarii and Helicon Ensemble 1967–72; principal cellist of St Cecilia Orchestra, Norwich, Celtic Sinfonia, South Wales, Ryedale Festival Orchestra; changed to bass in 1989; mem. of Asturias Symphony Orchestra, Spain 1991–; founder mem. of ensemble, La Ghironda, specialising in early music. *Publications:* contrib. to British and int. Bass Forum magazine. *Honours:* Lesley Alexander Prize for Violoncello 1965–66. *Address:* Calle Jorge Tuya 4-1c, La Corredoria, Oviedo 33011, Asturias, Spain.

SHERMAN, Alexandra; Singer (mezzo-soprano); b. 1970, St Petersburg, Russia. *Education:* Studied in Jerusalem and at Victorian College of the Arts, Melbourne; Royal College of Music, with Margaret Kingsley. *Career:* Concert engagements include Bach's Passions, Elijah, Messiah, Mozart's Requiem and Vivaldi's Gloria; Lieder eines fahrenden Gesellen in Melbourne and Sydney, Les Nuits d'été and Elgar's Sea Pictures; Season 1999 included Prokofiev's Alexander Nevsky with the Queensland Symphony Orchestra, Pergolesi's Stabat Mater, and Russian Songs at St John's Smith Square; Season 2000–01, with Messiah in Manchester, B minor Mass in York, Schubert's A flat Mass with the London Mozart Players and Mahler's 2nd Symphony in Melbourne; London Handel Festival 2001, as Guido in Flavio and Irene in Muzio Scevola; European tour with the Academy of Ancient Music in Bach's Magnificat, 2001. *Honours:* Queen's Trust for Young Australians Award; Joan Sutherland Award. *Current Management:* Musicmakers International Artists Representation, Tailor House, 63–65 High Street, Whitwell, Hertfordshire SG4 8AH, England. *Telephone:* (1438) 871708. *Fax:* (1438) 871777. *E-mail:* musicmakers@compuserve.com. *Website:* www.operauk.com. *Address:* c/o Royal College of Music (Vocal Faculty), Prince Consort Road, London SW7, England.

SHERRATT, Brindley; Singer (bass); b. 1965, England; m. 2 children. *Education:* Royal Academy of Music. *Career:* Debut: Welsh National Opera, as Leporello; Appearances as Wurm in Luisa Miller at Lausanne, Commendatore in Don Giovanni and Basilio in Barbiere for Garsington Opera and the King in Ariodante for Reisopera, Netherlands; Concerts include St Matthew Passion (London Proms, 2002), Les Noces by Stravinsky under Boulez in Paris, The Creation with Trevor Pinnock at the Lucerne Festival and Messiah with Robert King in the USA; Bach Cantatas and Haydn Masses with John Eliot Gardiner; Season 2001–02 with Plutone in Haydn's Orfeo and Publio in La Clemenza di Tito at Covent Garden; Season 2002–03 as Melisso in Alcina at the New York Met, Verdi's Ferrando and Gremin in Eugene Onegin for Welsh National Opera and Britten's Theseus at La Monnaie, Brussels; Concerts with Gardiner and Christophe Rousset; Sarasto for ENO, Commendatore and Claudio in Agrippina for Santa Fe Opera; Hobson in Peter Grimes in Saltzburg with the Berlin Philharmonic and Sir Simon Rattle. *Current Management:* Musicmakers International Artists Representation, Tailor House, 63–65 High Street, Whitwell, Hertfordshire SG4 8AH, England. *Telephone:* (1438) 871708. *Fax:* (1438) 871777. *E-mail:* musicmakers@compuserve.com. *Website:* www.operauk.com.

SHICOFF, Neil; singer (tenor); b. 2 June 1949, New York, USA; m. Judith Haddon. *Education:* Juilliard School with Jennie Tourel. *Career:* debut, Kennedy Center Washington as Narraboth in Salome 1975; Metropolitan Opera 1976–, as Rinuccio in Gianni Schicchi, Verdi's Duke of Mantua, Tchaikovsky's Lensky, Massenet's Werther, Offenbach's Hoffmann and Massenet's Des Grieux; European career from 1976; Don Carlos in Amsterdam, Alfredo and Cilea's Maurizio at the Munich Opera; Macduff in a BBC version of Macbeth and the Duke of Mantua at Covent Garden 1988; At La Scala he has sung Lensky and at the Paris Opéra Don Carlos; Gounod's Roméo for French television; Chicago Lyric Opera debut 1979; San Francisco 1981; Sang Cavaradossi at Stuttgart, 1990; Debut at Barcelona as Hoffmann, 1990; Returned to Covent Garden, 1993, as Pinkerton; Don José at the Opéra Bastille, Paris, 1997; Eléazar in La Juive at the Vienna Staatsoper, 1999; Season 2000–01 at the Met as Hoffmann and Manrico, Don José at the Deutsche Oper Berlin, Donizeti's Edgardo for Zürich Opera and Britten's Captain Vere at the Vienna Staatsoper; Engaged as Eléazar at the Met, 2002–03. *Recordings:* Macduff and the Duke of Mantua for Philips; Foresto in Attila, conducted by Muti. *Current Management:* Theateragentur Dr Germinal Hilbert, Maximilianstrasse 22, 80539 Munich, Germany.

Telephone: (89) 290 7470. *Fax:* (89) 290 74790. *E-mail:* agentur@hilbert .de. *Website:* www.hilbert.de; www.shicoff.com.

SHIFRIN, Kenneth (Ken) Allen, BA, PhD; lecturer, tenor trombonist, alto trombonist, tenor tubist and bass trumpeter and music publisher; b. 25 Aug. 1952, Washington, DC, USA. *Education:* Duke University, Durham, NC, Univ. of Oxford. *Career:* Debuts: US/British premiere of Leopold Mozart Konzert für Posaune, 1974, 1996; World premiere of D to A for Ken Shifrin and Digital Analogue by David Maves; Associate Principal Trombone, Israel Philharmonic, 1976–77; Co-Solo Trombone, Radio Sinfonie Stuttgart, 1977–78; Principal Trombone, Israel Radio Symphony, 1978–92; Principal Trombone, City of Birmingham Symphony Orchestra, 1982–94; Posaune Voce Trio, 1994–; Publisher, Director, Virgo Music, 1987–; Leopold Mozart, Concerto for Alto Trombone, British Premiere, 1996, Czech Premiere, 1997; Leopold Mozart, Agnus Dei, British Premiere, 1996; Wolfgang Amadeus Mozart, Jener Donnerworte Kraft, 1996; Elizabeth Raum, Three Jazz Moods, British and USA Premieres, 1997; Word, St Thomas Sonata, Premier, 1999; Guest artist, Dvořák International Music Festival; Malta International Arts Festival; Masterclasses presented including Prague, Vienna, Manchester, University of Illinois, Duke University and Washington, DC; British Academy Research Board Fellowship, 1998–2001; Academy of Sciences of the Czech Republic Scholar Exchange Fellowship, 1998–2001. *Honours:* James Ingham Halstead Scholar, Oxford University; Oxford University Press Music and Letters Award. *Address:* 47 Colebank Road, Hall Green, Birmingham B28 8EZ, England.

SHIH, Patricia; Concert Violinist; b. 1971, Canada. *Education:* Studied in Vancouver and with Josef Gingold at Indiana University. *Career:* Season 1987 with recitals in Warsaw and at the Carnegie Hall, New York; Many appearances with leading orchestras in the USA and Europe; Prokofiev's 2nd Concerto with the Toronto Symphony Orchestra, 1994. *Honours:* Prize Winner at Seattle Young Artists Festival, 1985 and Wieniawski Competition, Warsaw, 1986. *Address:* c/o Worldwide Artists, 6 Petersfield Crescent, Coulsdon, Surrey CR5 2JQ, England.

SHILAKADZE, Shavleg; Composer and Conductor; b. 21 Feb. 1940, Tbilisi, Georgia; m. Liana Shilakadze, 25 Jan 1964, 2 s., 1 d. *Education:* Z Paliashvili Special Music School; Viola and Composition at V Saradjishvili Conservatoire, Tbilisi; Conducting at Rimsky-Korsakov State Conservatoire, Leningrad. *Career:* Debut: Composition, Tbilisi, 1959; Conducting, Tbilisi, 1967; Founder, Ensemble Camerata Tbilisi; Concerts at Tbilisi, Moscow, Leningrad, Kiev, Minsk, Tallinn, Vilnius and elsewhere, 1978–85; Founder, Art Director, chamber orchestra Concertino Tbilisi, 1988–; Concerts at Tbilisi, Germany, 1990, 1991, 1993, 1995, 1996, 1997 Spain, Mar, Oct–Nov, 1993, Switzerland, 1996; 1997; London, Edinburgh, 1998; Professor, Tbilisi Conservatoire; mem, Union of Georgian Composers. *Compositions include:* Sonata for viola and piano; Epitaph, chamber symphony; From Ancient Georgian Poetry, cantata; Concerto for oboe and chamber orchestra; 2 symphonies; Pages of Love, cantata; Concerto for bassoon and chamber orchestra; Concerto giocoso for 3 trumpets and percussion. *Recordings:* R Gabitchvadze's Chamber Symphony No. 4, 1980; G Djaparidze's Chamber Symphony, 1983; Sh Shilakadze's Epitaph, 1983; Camerata Tbilisi, conductor Sh Shilakadze. *Publications:* Articles: About Tbilisi's musical life, 1982; The unity of creative forces, 1984. *Address:* 20 T Tabidze st, 380079 Tbilisi, Georgia.

SHILLING, Eric; Singer; b. 12 Oct. 1920, London, England; m. Erica Johns, 2 c. *Education:* Guildhall School of Music; Royal College of Music; Further study with Walter Hyde and Frank Titterton in London. *Career:* Debut: Sadler's Wells, 1945 as Marullo in Rigoletto; In Operas by Smetana, Wagner, Mozart, Donizetti, Rossini and Janáček; Television apearances in Die Fledermaus, Orpheus in the Underworld, The Visitation, Trial by Jury and A Tale of Two Cities; Sang in the British Stage premiere of Prokofiev's War and Peace, London Coliseum, 1972; Further appearances in operas by Wagner, Mozart, Donizetti, Rossini, Puccini, Strauss, Prokofiev, Penderecki and Reimann; Premieres, Story of Vasco by Crosse and Clarissa by Holloway; Somarone in a new production of Beatrice and Benedict; mem, ISM; Council Equity. *Recordings:* Has recorded for major record labels. *Honours:* Opera Prize, Royal College of Music; ARCM, 1946; Worshipful Company of Musicians, Sir Charles Santley Memorial Prize, 1991. *Address:* 49 Belgrave Road, Wanstead, London E11 3QP, England.

SHILLITO, Helen Claire, BMus; British horn player; b. 18 Oct. 1975, Newcastle-upon-Tyne, England. *Education:* Royal College of Music, London, with Julian Baker, Tim Brown and Susan Dent; Franz Liszt Acad., Budapest, with Adam Friedrich; CESMD, Saintes, France, with Claude Maury and Martin Murner (natural horn). *Career:* Co-founder of Aurora Ensemble (wind quintet), 1995, giving wind quintet performances at ORF studios, Vienna, Purcell Room (London), English Music and Cheltenham International Festivals, South Bank Rimsky-Korsakov Festival and International Akademie Prag-Wien-Budapest; Co-founded

Ensemble Piros (wind and strings), 2002, Alla Caccia (horn, violin and piano trio), 2003; Joined Broadwood Ensemble (wind and piano), 2002; Launched outreach education scheme Sounds Exciting, 2000; Has played with The Acad. of St Martin-in-the-Fields, BBC Symphony Orchestra, Northern Sinfonia, City of London Sinfonia, Scottish Symphony Orchestra, Scottish Ballet, Welsh Nat. Opera and (on the natural horn) with Europa Galante and Orchestre Champs-Elysées; mem. (with Aurora Ensemble) Live Music Now!. *Television:* The Aurora Ensemble, Channel 4 Wales, 2002. *Radio:* with Aurora Ensemble: BBC Radio 3 Young Artists' Forum Broadcasts, 1999. *Honours:* Prague-Vienna-Budapest Internationale Sommerakademie scholarship winner (with Aurora Ensemble), 1997 and 1997; Winner, Outstanding Musicians Series (with Aurora Ensemble) at St Martin-in-the-Fields, 1998 and 1999; Prizewinner, European Music d'Ensemble Competition, Paris, 2001; Winners, Manchester Mid-day Concert Series, 2003; Winners, Park Lane Group Series, 2004. *Address:* 40 Westgate Road, Faversham, Kent ME13 8HF, England (office); 47 Salisbury Gardens, Jesmond, Newcastle-upon-Tyne NE2 1HP, England. *Telephone:* (7885) 540950 (office); (1795) 532432 (home). *E-mail:* auroraensemble@hotmail .com (office); helenshillito@ukonline.co.uk (home). *Website:* www .auroraensemble.com (office).

SHIMELL, William; Singer (Baritone); b. 23 Sept. 1952, Ilford, Essex, England. *Education:* Guildhall School of Music with Ellis Keeler; National Opera Studio until 1979;. *Career:* Debut: English National Opera 1980, as Masetto: later sang Schaunard in La Bohème, Mercutio in Romeo and Juliet, Papageno and Don Giovanni; Opera North in Le nozze di Figaro, The Cunning Little Vixen and The Rake's Progress; Scottish Opera in Cavalli's L'Egisto; Kent Opera as Guglielmo in Così fan tutte; Glyndebourne from 1983, in Cenerentola and Figaro; Welsh National Opera debut 1984, as Don Giovanni; Geneva, Vienna Staatsoper and La Scala Milan as Figaro; Paris Opéra in La Gazza Ladra; San Francisco Opera as Nick Shadow; Covent Garden debut as Guglielmo, 1988; Concert appearances on South Bank and elsewhere in the United Kingdom; London Promenade Concerts 1989, as Figaro; Sang Malatesta in Don Pasquale at Amsterdam and Covent Garden, 1990; Capriccio San Francisco, 1990; Capriccio, Covent Garden, 1991; Lodoiska, La Scala, 1991; Ravenna Festival, Lodoiska, La Muette di Portici (Auber), 1991; Così, Covent Garden and on tour to Japan, 1992; Raimbaud in Le Comte Ory for Netherlands Opera, Marcello in London; Television engagements in L'Enfance du Christ and Mozart series with Jane Glover; Title role, Don Giovanni, Zürich Opera, 1992 and 1993; Sang in The Rake's Progress at the Festival Hall, 1997, and Mozart's Count at Tel-Aviv; Sang the Count at the Deutsche Oper Berlin and La Coruña Festival, 2000. *Recordings include:* Cherubini's Lodoiska, conducted by Muti; Title role: Don Giovanni, Riccardo Muti, Vienna Philharmonic, Bach B minor Mass, Solti, Chicago Symphony. *Current Management:* IMG Artists, Europe. *Address:* c/o IMG Artists, Europe, Lovell House, 616 Chiswick High Road, London W4 5RX, England.

SHIMIZU, Takashi; Violinist; b. 13 Jan. 1953, Yokosuka, Japan; m. Harue Shimizu, 18 Aug 1973, 1 s. *Education:* Yokosuka High School; University of Southern California, USA; Guildhall School of Music, London, England. *Career:* Debut: Tokyo; Performed with the Royal Philharmonic Orchestra, BBC Philharmonic Orchestra, London Mozart Players, City of Birmingham Symphony Orchestra, The Hague Philharmonic; Many television appearances in France, Belgium, Spain, USSR and Japan. *Recordings:* For international record labels. *Honours:* Bronze Medal, Queen Elizabeth Competition; 2nd Prize and Beethoven Sonata Prize, Carl Flesch Competition; 1st Prize, Granada International Competition. *Current Management:* John Wright. *Address:* 18 Alyth Garden, London NW11, England.

SHIN, Youngok; Singer (soprano); b. 1961, Republic of Korea. *Education:* Juilliard School, New York. *Career:* Debut: Spoleto Festival, USA, 1989 as Mozart's Susanna; Metropolitan Opera, New York, from 1990 as Gilda in Rigoletto and roles in Rossini's Semiramide and Bellini's Bianca e Fernando at Catania, 1991; Oscar in Ballo in Maschera at Paris Opéra Bastille, 1991; Gilda at Covent Garden, 1994; Season 1995–96, as Lucia di Lammermoor at Toronto and Elvira in I Puritani at Turin; Other roles include Leila in Les Pêcheurs de Perles. *Recordings:* Bianca e Fernando; Semiramide; Ave Maria. *Address:* c/o Metropolitan Opera, Lincoln Center, New York NY 10023, USA.

SHINALL, Vern; Singer (baritone); b. 22 June 1936, St Louis, USA. *Education:* Indiana University, Bloomington, with Charles Kullman. *Career:* Debut: Kansas City Opera, as Scarpia in Tosca, 1964; Appearances at opera houses in Philadelphia, Boston, Houston, New Orleans and St Paul; Main career at New York City Opera; Roles have included Escamillo, Pizarro in Fidelio, Rigoletto, Amonasro, Count Luna, Mephistopheles in Faust and Barnaba in La Gioconda; Wagner's Dutchman, Telramund and Wotan, Don Giovanni and the baritone roles in Les Contes d'Hoffmann; Modern repertoire includes John Proctor in The Crucible by Robert Ward and Olin Blitch in Susannah by Carlisle

Floyd; Many concert engagements. *Address:* c/o New York City Opera, NY Theater, Lincoln Center, New York, NY 10023, USA.

SHINOZAKI, Yasuo; Conductor; b. 19 Feb. 1968, Kyoto, Japan; m. 12 April 1998. *Education:* Toho-Gakuen Music University, 1986–90; Toho-Gakuen Music Graduate School, 1990–92; Toho-Gakuen Conducting Course, 1992–94; Vienna National Music University, Austria, 1995–98. *Career:* Debut: With Bolzano and Trento Orchestra, in Trento, Italy, 1993; Opera debut, Tokyo, 1993; Conducted Bolzano and Trento Orchestra, 1993, Szeged Symphony Orchestra, 1996, Tokyo City Philharmonic Orchestra, 1998, Shinsei (Japan) Symphony Orchestra, 1999. *Honours:* Winner, 2nd Prize, 3rd Antonio Pedrotti International Conducting Competition (1st Prize not awarded), 1993. *Address:* c/o Shinsei Symphony Orchestra, Maruishi Building, 3–16–4 Nishi Ikebukuro, Toshima-Ku, Tokyo 171, Japan.

SHIRAI, Mitsuko; Singer (Contralto); b. 1952, Japan. *Education:* Studied in Stuttgart. *Career:* Appearances in Europe, Israel, Japan and USA; Recitals with piano accompanist Hartmut Holl and concerts with the Berlin Philharmonic, New Japan Philharmonic, Atlanta Symphony, Nouvel Orchestre Philharmonique de Paris and the Vienna Symphony; Conductors include Chailly, Inbal, Ahronovitch, Ferencic and Sawallisch; Repertoire includes Mahler Symphony No. 8, Berlioz Les Nuits d'Été, Berg 7 Early Songs, Hindemith Das Marienleben, Complete vocal works of Webern, Schubert Winterreise and Lieder by Brahms, Wolf and Schumann; Concert performances of Mozart's Lucio Silla, Wagner's Das Liebesverbot and Ariane et Barbe-Bleue; Opened Suntory Hall Tokyo with Alexander Nevsky by Prokofiev; Stage debut Frankfurt 1987, as Despina in Così fan tutte; Masterclasses with Hartmut Holl at the Savonlinna Festival, Schleswig-Holstein Festival, Aldeburgh Festival, in Switzerland and USA and at Isaac Stern's Music Centre in Jerusalem. *Recordings:* Mozart, Schumann and Brahms Lieder (Capriccio); Bach, Mozart and Spohr Lieder; Sacred music by Mozart (Philips); Frauenliebe und-leben by Schumann; Lieder by Mendelssohn and Schumann. *Honours:* Winner of Competitions in Vienna, 's-Hertogenbosch, Athens and Munich; Winner, Robert Schumann Prize, Zwickau, 1982.

SHIRASAKA-TERATINI, Chieko; Singer (Mezzo-soprano); b. 1956, Tokyo, Japan. *Education:* Studied in Tokyo, and Hamburg Musikhochschule, 1977-80. *Career:* Many opera appearances from 1981, notably at Bremerhaven and Bonn; Guest engagements at Hamburg, Innsbruck, Bremen and Montpellier; Roles have included Octavian, Hansel, Siebel in Faust, Mozart's Annio, Suzuki in Madama Butterfly, Verdi's Eboli, Preziosilla and Fenena (Nabucco); Ottavia in L'Incoronazione di Poppea, and Rossini's Rosina and Isabella; Many concert and rectial appearances, notably in USA, Japan, Poland and Netherlands. *Honours:* Prizewinner, 1980 's-Hertogenbosch Competition. *Address:* c/o Bonn Opera, Am Boeselagerhof 1, Pf 2440, D-53111 Bonn, Germany.

SHIRLEY, George (Irving); Singer (Tenor); b. 18 April 1934, Indianapolis, Indiana, USA; m. Gladys Ishop, 24 June 1956, 1 s., 1 d. *Education:* BS, Education, Wayne State University, Detroit, Michigan, 1955. *Career:* Debut: Turnau Opera Players, Woodstock, New York, 1955 (Eisenstein in Die Fledermaus); Appearances: Teatro Nuovo, Milan, Italy; Teatro Della Pergola, Florence, Italy, 1960; New York City Opera, Metropolitan Opera, Santa Fe Opera, 1961; Opera Society of Washington, 1962; Teatro Col ón, Buenos Aires, 1964; La Scala, Milan, 1965; Glyndebourne Festival, 1966; Scottish Opera, Royal Opera, Covent Garden, 1967; Netherlands Opera, 1975; L'Opéra de Monte Carlo, 1976; San Francisco Opera, Chicago Lyric Opera, 1977; Deutsche Oper, Germany, 1983; Roles have included Puccini's Rodolfo, Mozart's Ferrando, Tamino, Don Ottavio and Idomeneo, Debussy's Pelléas, Wagner's Loge and David and Donizetti's Lord Percy; Additional Festivals: Guelph, Ottawa (Canada), Berkshire, Ravinia, Saratoga, Spoleto (USA and Italy), Edinburgh; Orchestras include: New York Philharmonic, Chicago, Detroit and Los Angeles Symphonies; Philadelphia Orchestra and several others; Sang Herod in Salome at Detroit, 1996; Professor of Music (Voice) at the University of Michigan School of Music, Ann Arbor, 1992–; Director, Vocal Arts Division, 1999–; Appeared as Eumeto in Monteverdi's Ulisse at Glimmerglass, 1999. *Recordings:* Many recordings of Stravinsky, Mozart, Haydn; Così fan tutte; Pelléas et Mélisande, Oedipus Rex and Renard; Orlando Paladino and Idomeneo. *Contributions:* Opera News. *Address:* c/o University of Michigan School of Music, Vocal Division, Ann Arbor MI 48109, USA.

SHIRLEY-QUIRK, John, CBE, BSc, DipEd; concert and opera singer (baritone); b. 28 Aug. 1931, Liverpool, England; m. 1st Patricia May Hastie 1955 (died 1981); one s. one d.; m. 2nd Sara Van Horn Watkins 1981 (died 1997); one s. two d. (one deceased). *Education:* Liverpool University; studied singing with Austen Carnegie and Roy Henderson. *Career:* Created roles in all Britten operas since Curlew River, notably Mr Coyle, Owen Wingrave and Traveller, Death in Venice (Covent Garden, Metropolitan Opera, New York, USA); Performances with

Scottish Opera and all major orchestras throughout Europe and America; Created role of Lev in The Ice Break by Tippett; Sang Folk songs by Britten at the 1991 Aldeburgh Festival; Narrator in Hans Krása's Verlobung im Traum at Washington, 1996; Sang in Vaughan Williams Five Tudor Portraits, with the London Symphony Orchestra at the Barbican, 1997; Visiting Artist, Carnegie Mellon University, Pittsburgh, Pennsylvania, USA, 1994–98; Teacher of Voice at Peabody Conservatory, Baltimore, Maryland, USA, 1991–; mem. ISM. *Recordings:* Numerous recordings of English songs, Lieder and especially of Britten's works for Decca; Messiah, A Child of Our Time, Die Jahreszeiten, Bach B minor Mass, Dido and Aeneas; A Village Romeo and Juliet, The Kingdom, The Pilgrim's Progress, Beethoven's Ninth. *Honours:* Hon RAM, 1973; Mus Doc (HC), Liverpool, 1976; D. Univ. Brunel, 1981. *Current Management:* Herbert Barrett, 1776 Broadway, Suite 1610, New York, NY 10019, USA. *Address:* 6062 Red Clover Lane, Clarksville, MD 21029-1272, USA.

SHKOLNIKOVA, Nelli; Violinist; b. 8 July 1928, Zolotonosha, Ukraine; m. (1) Boris Sokolov, deceased, (2) Alexander Gul, 14 Dec 1989. *Education:* Music studies, BMus, MMus, Moscow Conservatory, 1949–57; Honours degree in Violin. *Career:* Concert tours in USSR, Austria, Australia, Bulgaria, Czechoslovakia, France, Finland, Hungary, East Germany, Canada, USA, Norway, New Zealand, Japan, 1953–; Appeared with conductors such as Kondrashin, Rozhdestvensky, Munch, Cluytens, Sanderling, Masur, Ormandy; Professor of Violin at Indiana University School of Music, USA; mem, American String Teachers' Association. *Recordings:* Tchaikovsky–Concerto in D op 35; Mozart–Concerto No. 4 in D K218; Mendelssohn–Concerto in E Minor; Beethoven–Sonata No. 2 in A major op 12 No. 2, Sonata No. 8 in G major op 30 No. 3; Copland–Sonata in G major; Handel–Sonata No. 1 in A major, Sonata No. 3; Pieces by Paganini, Prokofiev and others. *Contributions:* Reviews in Le Figaro, New York Post, Berliner Morgenpost, Arbeiderbladet, Pravda, others. *Honours:* Grand Prix at Marguerite Long-Jacques Thibaud Competition, Paris, France, 1953; Honoured Artist of Russian Republic, 1978. *Address:* 2814 St Remy Circle, Bloomington, IN 47401, USA.

SHKOSA, Enkelejda; Singer (Mezzo-soprano); b. 29 Sept. 1969, Tirana, Albania. *Education:* Studied at the State Conservatory, the Academy of Fine Arts, Tirana; Giuseppe Verdi Conservatory, Milan. *Career:* Many appearances at La Scala, Milan, Naples, Turin, Barbican Centre London (under Colin Davis), Strasbourg Cathedral (Pergolesi Stabat Mater) and the Rossini Festival, Pesaro; Season 1997–98 with Maddalena at the Opéra Bastille, Paris, Stockholm, Amsterdam, Bologna, Monte Carlo and Brussels. *Honours:* Winner, Leyla Gencer Competition, Istanbul, 1995. *Address:* c/o Pentagramma, Via Bicetti De' Buttinoni 1, 20156 Milan, Italy.

SHMITOV, Alexei; Concert Organist and Pianist; b. 1957, Moscow, Russia. *Education:* Studied at the Moscow Conservatoire, with Roisman and Nikolayeva. *Career:* Many concerts in Russia as organist and pianist; Piano concertos by Bach in Vilnius, Lithuania, and the Sonatas for violin and harpsichord and violin with Viktor Pikaisen; Organ recitals in: Lithuania; Estonia; Latvia; Bach Festival in West Berlin; Recitals with the tenor Alexei Martynov in music by Bach, Handel, Scheidt, Schütz, Mendelssohn, Schumann and Verdi; Recitals at the Prokofiev Centenary Festival in Scotland, 1991; Organ Repertoire includes works by Bach, Widor, Taneyev, Liszt and Shostakovich. *Honours:* 2nd Prize, Organ Competition in Dom Zu Speyer, Germany. *Address:* c/o Sonata, 11 Northpark Street, Glasgow G20 7AA, Scotland.

SHOKOV, Vladimir; Cellist; b. 1950, Crimea, Russia. *Career:* Co-founder, Rachmaninov Quartet, 1974, under auspices of the Sochi State Philharmonic Society, Crimea; Many concerts in Russia, and from season, 1975–76, tours to: Switzerland; Austria; Bulgaria; Norway; Germany; Participation in the 1976 Shostakovich Chamber Music Festival at Vilnius, and in festivals in Moscow and St Petersburg; Repertoire has included works by: Haydn, Mozart, Beethoven, Bartók, Brahms, Schnittke, Shostakovich, Tchaikovsky and Meyerovich. *Honours:* Prizewinner at the first All Union Borodin String Quartet Competition. *Address:* c/o Sonata, 11 Northpark Street, Glasgow G20 7AA, Scotland.

SHORE, Andrew, BA; British concert and opera singer (baritone); b. 30 Sept. 1952, Oldham, England; m. Fiona Macdonald 1976; three d. *Education:* University of Bristol, Royal Northern College of Music, London Opera Centre. *Career:* as stage manager and singer, Opera For All, 1977–79; debut as Antonio in Marriage of Figaro, Kent Opera, 1981; English National Opera debut, 1988, as Don Alfonso in Così fan tutte; Covent Garden debut, 1992, as Trombonok in Rossini's Il viaggio a Reims; Paris Opéra debut, 1995, as Sacristan in Tosca; US debut, 1996, as Dulcamara in L'Elisir d'amore, at San Diego; Principal roles with all British opera companies and in Paris, Lyon, Hamburg, Barcelona, Amsterdam, Copenhagen, Brussels, Vancouver, Ottawa, Tel-Aviv; Particularly known for Falstaff, Don Pasquale, Dulcamara, Don

Alfonso, Papageno, Bartolo, Gianni Schicchi, and in the serious repertoire for Wozzeck, King Priam and Šiškov in Janáček's House of the Dead; Gianni Schicchi for ENO, 1998; Season 2000–01 as Janáček's Kolenaty at Hamburg, Mozart's Bartolo at Glyndebourne and Tippett's King Priam for ENO; Engaged as Hans Sachs for Opéra de Nantes, 2003. *Recordings:* Bartolo in Barber of Seville; Sacristan in Tosca; Benoit and Alcindoro in La Bohème; Dulcamara in L'Elisir d'amore; Title role in Don Pasquale; Video recording of Kolenaty in Janáček's Makropulos Case. *Current Management:* Ingpen & Williams Ltd, 7 St George's Court, 131 Putney Bridge Road, London, SW15 2PA, England.

SHORE, Clare; Composer; b. 18 Dec. 1954, Winston-Salem, North Carolina, USA. *Education:* BA cum laude with honours, Music, Wake Forest University, 1976; MMus, University of Colorado, 1977; DMA, Juilliard School of Music, 1984; Studied with Annette LeSiege, Wake Forest University, Charles Eakin and Cecil Effinger, University of Colorado, David Diamond, Vincent Persichetti and Roger Sessions, Juilliard School. *Career:* Teaching: Fordham University, Manhattan School of Music, University of Virginia, and George Mason University, 1981–; Numerous commissions; Works performed in Carnegie Recital Hall, Alice Tully Hall, Lincoln Center, Merkin Concert Hall, Spoleto Festival, Charleston, The Barns of Wolf Trap, National Gallery of Art, throughout USA and abroad. *Compositions:* All works published by leading music publishers. *Recordings include:* July Remembrances, CD; Nightwatch; Oatlands Sketches. *Honours:* Contemporary Records Society Grant, 1988. *Current Management:* E C Schirmer Music Company Inc. *Address:* 12329 Cliveden Street, Herndon, VA 22070, USA.

SHOSTAKOVICH, Maxim; Conductor; b. 10 May 1938, Leningrad, USSR. *Education:* Leningrad Conservatory, 1961–62; Moscow Conservatory. *Career:* Debut: London Philharmonic Orchestra, 1968; Assistant Conductor, Moscow Symphony Orchestra, 1964; Moscow State Symphony Orchestra, 1966; Principal Conductor, Moscow Radio Symphony Orchestra; Toured Canada with USSR State Symphony Orchestra, 1969; Guest Conductor, Europe, North America, Japan and Australia; Pianist, including Piano Concerto No. 2 by Shostakovich; Conducted New Orleans Symphony until 1991; Led Lady Macbeth of Mtsensk at Hamburg, 1990; Dmitri Shostakovich concert with the Philharmonia at the Festival Hall, London, 1997. *Recordings:* Ballet compositions, including Bolt, The Age of Gold, suites, music for films Zoya, Pirogov with Bolshoi Theatre Orchestra; Shostakovich's Violin Concerto No. 1, Shostakovich's Symphony No. 5, Suites on Verses of Michelangelo, 1971; Shostakovich's Cello Concerti, 1984.

SHRAPNEL, Hugh (Michael); Composer; b. 18 Feb. 1947, Birmingham, England. *Education:* Eltham College, 1960–65; Royal Academy of Music, 1966–69; Goldsmiths' College, London, 1984–88; BMus. *Career:* Scratch Orchestra, 1969–72; Promenade Theatre Orchestra, 1970–72; People's Liberation Music, 1975–79; Co-Founder of Redlands Consort, 1992 specialising in new music; Compositions widely performed in London, provinces and abroad including: Wigmore Hall, 1968; Purcell Room, 1970; San Diego, 1974; Conway Hall, 1986 and 1993; University of Redlands, Texas, 1986 and 1989; Leighton House, 1989, 1990, 1991; Slaughterhouse Gallery, 1991; Appointed Composer-in-Residence at Music Works, London; mem, British Academy of Composers and Songwriters; Performing Right Society. *Compositions:* Oakley St, 1971; Variations for viola, 1984; Unity, 1991; Cat Preludes, 1994; South of the River, 1993–95; West Pier, 1997; Many works for piano and educational music. *Honours:* Lady Holland prize for composition, 1969. *Current Management:* STR Music Marketing & Management. *Address:* 27A Shooters Hill Road, Blackheath, London SE3 7AS, England.

SHTODA, Daniil; Singer (Tenor); b. 1977, St Petersburg, Russia. *Education:* Glinka Capella; St Petersburg Conservatoire. *Career:* Debut: Sang Fyodor in Boris Godunov at the Marrinksy Theatre while a child; Young Artists' Academy of the Mariinksy Theatre, from 1998; Repertoire has included Lensky in Eugene Onegin, Elvino (La Sonnambula), The Indian Guest in Sadko by Rimsky-Korsakov and Tsar Berendai in The Snow Maiden (concert) with the Kirov Opera at Covent Garden, 2000; Wigmore Hall recital, March 2002; London Proms, 2002. *Honours:* Winner, Mario Lanza Vocal Competition; 3rd Rimsky-Korsakov and 11th Tchaikovsky Competitions. *Address:* c/o Mariinsky Theatre, 1 Theatre Square, St Petersburg, Russia.

SHTOKOLOV, Boris; Singer (Bass); b. 19 March 1930, Kuznetsk, Russia. *Education:* Studied at the Sverdlovsk Conservatory. *Career:* Joined Sverdlovsky Opera, 1951, remaining until 1959; Appearances with the Kirov Opera from 1959, as the Miller in Dargomyzhsky's Russalka, Glinka's Ruslan, Dosifei in Khovanshchina, Gremin, Rossini's Basilio and Boris Godunov; Sang Andrei Sokolov in the Premiere of Dzerzhinsky's Destiny of a Man, Moscow, 1961; Mephisto in Gounod's Faust, Galitsky in Borodin's Prince Igor, Ivan Susanin in Glinka's Life for the Tsar. *Recordings include:* Boris Godunov and Ruslan and Lyudmila, from the Kirov; Highlights from Destiny of a Man; Burn My

Star, Russian Songs and Romances (1984). *Honours:* People's Artist of the USSR; Glinka Prize; State Prize of the USSR. *Address:* c/o Kirov Oper and Ballet Theatre, St Petersburg, Russia.

SHULMAN, Andrew; Cellist and Conductor; b. 1960, London, England. *Education:* Studies at the RAM and the RCM (Joan Dickson and William Pleeth). *Career:* Principal cellist of the Philharmonia (5 years) followed by solo and conducting career; repertoire includes concertos by Dvořák, Elgar, Beethoven (Triple), Vivaldi and Haydn; Strauss's Don Quixote and Bloch's Schelomo; Founder member of the Britten Quartet, debut concert at the Wigmore Hall, 1987; Quartet in Residence at the Dartington Summer School, 1987, with quartets by Schnittke; Season 1988–89 in the Genius of Prokofiev series at Blackheath and BBC Lunchtime Series at St John's Smith Square; South Bank appearances with the Schoenberg/Handel Quartet Concerto conducted by Neville Marriner, concerts with the Hermann Prey Schubertiade and collaborations with the Alban Berg Quartet in the Beethoven Plus series; Tour of South America 1988, followed by Scandinavian debut; Season 1989–90 with debut tours of Netherlands, Germany, Spain, Austria, Finland; Tours from 1990 to the Far East, Malta, Sweden, Norway; Schoenberg/Handel Concerto with the Gothenburg Symphony; Festival appearances at Brighton, the City of London, Greenwich, Canterbury, Harrogate, Chester, Spitalfields and Aldeburgh; Collaborations with John Ogdon, Imogen Cooper, Thea King and Lynn Harrell; Formerly resident quartet at Liverpool University; Teaching role at Lake District Summer Music 1989; Universities of Bristol, Hong Kong 1990; Conductor of various orchestras including RCM String Ensemble, Proteus Orchestra, Norfolk Youth Orchestra, Leicester Symphony Orchestra, Britten-Pears Orchestra, Ambache Chamber Orchestra, Salomon Orchestra. *Recordings:* Beethoven Op 130 and Schnittke Quartet No. 3; Vaughan Williams On Wenlock Edge and Ravel Quartet; Britten, Prokofiev, Tippett, Elgar and Walton Quartets; Vivaldi Concertos; Solo Disc, Delius and Dyson. *Honours:* Piatigorsky Artist Award in Boston, USA, 1989–90. *Address:* c/o The Ambache, 9 Beversbrook Rd, London, N19 4QG, England.

SHUTOVA, Marina; Singer (mezzo-soprano); b. 1961, Moscow, Russia. *Education:* Studied at the Tchaikovsky Conservatory, Moscow, and with Judith Beckmann in Hamburg. *Career:* Has sung with the Bolshoi Opera at Moscow from 1981; La Scala Milan debut 1989, as Clara in Prokofiev's Duenna (repeated at Edinburgh and Glasgow with the Bolshoi in 1990); Metropolitan Opera debut 1991, as Olga in Eugene Onegin; season 1992/93 as Amneris at Düsseldorf, Azucena at Liège and concerts in Hamburg; Season 1995/6 as Sonia in War and Peace in Vienna, Dalila at Toulon and Maddalena in Rigoletto at Orange; Other roles include Solocha in Rimsky's Christmas Eve (Edinburgh 1992). *Current Management:* Athole Still International Management, Forresters Hall, 25–27 Westow Street, London, SE19 3RY, England. *Telephone:* (20) 8771-5271. *Fax:* (20) 8768-6600. *Website:* www.atholestill.com.

SHUTTLEWORTH, Anna Lee, ARCM, BA; Cellist; b. 2 May 1927, Bournemouth, England; m. David Sellen. *Education:* St Christopher's School, Hampstead, Talbot Heath School, Bournemouth, Royal Coll. of Music, Boise scholarship to study with Pablo Casals and Enrico Mainardi. *Career:* cellist in Vivien Hind Quartet 1947; played with Philomusica, Jacques, Boyd Neel and BBC Concert Orchestras; broadcasts as soloist; recitals in London with Bernard Roberts in Purcell Room; Prof., Royal Coll. of Music 1967–96; examiner, Associated Board of the Royal Schools of Music 1969–96; cellist in Georgian Quartet and Leonardo Piano Trio with David Roth, Maureen Smith and Ian Brown; cello and piano recitals with John Thwaites 2003; mem. European String Teachers Assocn, Incorporated Soc. of Musicians, Musicians' Union. *Recordings:* cello continuo on recordings by Alfred Deller. *Publications:* Playing the Cello 1971; contrib. to ESTA and NEEMF Magazines 2001–03. *Honours:* Leslie Alexander Prize (RCM). *Address:* 1 Buckingham Road, Leeds, LS6 1BP, England (home). *Telephone:* (113) 2758509 (home).

SICHKIN, Emilian (Boris); Composer; b. 14 Aug. 1954, Kiev, Ukraine. *Education:* Moscow Conservatory of Music; Gorky Conservatory of Music; Gnesins College of Music; Private lessons with Professor Berlin; Audio Institute of America; School for the Media Arts; Diplomas in Recording Engineering, Synthesizers and Computers. *Career:* Debut: Carnegie Hall, 1991; Performances include Winds of Freedom at Carnegie Hall, 1991; Concerto for Astronauts, 1988, 1989; Piano Recital, Carnegie Hall, 1988; Television appearance, All My Children, ABC television; Broadcast appearances on WQXR, Voice of America, WNBC, WBAI, Heart of Space; mem, ASCAP; American Composers Forum. *Compositions:* Concerto for Astronauts; Winds of Freedom, symphonic suite; Ballet, The Demon; Romeo and Juliet, symphonic tragedy; Little Mermaid, symphonic overture. *Recordings:* Concerto for Astronauts; Romeo and Juliet. *Address:* 35-20 21 St, Suite 6C, L.I.C., NY 11106, USA.

ŠICHO, Robert; singer (tenor); b. 1967, Prague, Czechoslovakia. *Education:* State Conservatory, Prague, Music Acad., Prague, studied with Jana Jonasová. *Career:* soloist of the State Opera, Prague; appearances in many major theatres in the Czech Republic; frequent guest, Austria, Belgium, Norway, Netherlands, Germany, Greece, Switzerland, Japan; operatic roles include Ferrando in Così fan tutte, Tamino in Die Zauberflöte, Almaviva in Il Barbiere di Siviglia, Alfredo in La Traviata, Lensky in Eugene Onegin, Leandro in Busoni's Arlecchino, Prince in Rusalka, Hoffmann in Les contes d'Hoffmann, Turiddu in Cavalleria rusticana and Don José in Carmen; operetta roles include Rosillon in Die Lustige Witwe, title role in Paganini and Octavio in Giuditta (Lehar), Caramello in Eine Nacht in Venedig, Bárinkay in Der Zigeunerbaron (J. Strauss) and Paris in Offenbach's La Belle Hélène; extensive concert repertoire includes Mozart's Requiem, Verdi's Requiem, Orff's Carmina Burana, Beethoven's Ninth, Rossini's Messe Solennelle and Stabat Mater and Telemann's Die Tageszeiten. *Recordings include:* Caramello in Strauss's Ein Nacht in Venedig 1990, Telemann's Die Tageszeiten, for Czech radio and television 1995, Carmina Burana for radio and television 1998, Charpentier's Te Deum, for radio and television 1999. *Address:* Otavska 1677, PSD-25101 Ricany, Czech Republic.

SICILIANI, Alessandro; Conductor and Composer; b. 5 June 1952, Florence, Italy. *Education:* Studied piano, conducting and composition at the Milan Conservatoire and the Accademia Chigiana in Siena (conducting with Franco Ferrara). *Career:* Many appearances at leading opera centres in Italy, notably Rome, Naples, Palermo and Florence; Further engagements in Marseilles, Barcelona, Nice, Liège, New Orleans and Philadelphia; Metropolitan Opera debut 1988, with Pagliacci and Cavalleria Rusticana; Symphonic engagements throughout the USA, Far East and Europe; From 1988 principal guest conductor of the Teatro Col ón, Buenos Aires, and of the Teatro Municipal, São Paulo; From 1992 Music Director of the Columbus, Ohio, Symphony Orchestra. *Compositions include:* Cantata; L'Amour peintre (ballet); Giona, oratorio. *Address:* Columbus Symphony Orchestra, 55 East State Street, Columbus, OH 45210, USA.

SIDLIN, Murray; Conductor; b. 6 May 1940, Baltimore, Maryland, USA. *Education:* BA 1962, MM 1968, Peabody Conservatory, Maryland; Further study with Sergiu Celibidache at the Accademia Chigiana, Siena, 1961–62 and with Donald Grout and Karel Husa at Cornell University, 1963–65. *Career:* Assistant conductor at the Aspen Music Festival, 1970–71; Assistant at the Baltimore Symphony, 1971–73; Resident Conductor with the National Symphony Orchestra in Washington DC, 1973–77; Music Director of the New Haven (Connecticut) Symphony Orchestra, 1977–88; Music Director of the Tulsa Philharmonic, 1978–80 and directed the conducting fellowship programme at the Aspen Festival, 1978–93; Music Director, Long Beach, California, Symphony Orhchestra, 1980–88; Conductor of the American Music Concerts for the Chevron Corporation, 1987–92; Resident Conductor with the Oregon Symphony Orchestra, Portland, 1994–. *Address:* c/o Kaylor Management Inc, 130 West 57th Street, Suite 8G, New York, NY 10019, USA.

SIDOROVA, Svetlana; Singer (Mezzo-Soprano); b. 1970, St Petersburg, Russia. *Education:* St Petersburg Conservatoire and in Italy with Alberto Zedda and Carlo Bergonzi; Further study with Christa Ludwig. *Career:* Appearances from 1992 in Vienna, Paris, Berlin and Bologna (Janacek's Makropulos Case, 1994); Italiana in Algeri at the Pesaro Festival and Jocasta in Oedipus Rex at St Petersburg; Verdi's Amneris at Cologne, Kundry in Parsifal for the Kirov Opera and Eboli in Don Carlos at Essen; Sang in Pacini's L'Ultimo giorni di Pompeii at the Martina Franca Festival and Falla's Atlantida at Granada; Concerts include the Brahms Alto Rhapsody, Bach's Magnificat, Rossini's Stabat Mater (at Pesaro), Beethoven's Ninth and Alexander Nevsky by Prokofiev (Bologna); Other opera roles include Carmen, Ulrica, Maddalena and Olga in Eugene Onegin (Deutsche Oper, Berlin). *Honours:* Prizewinner at Competitions in Athens, Sienna, Brussels, Tokyo and Barcelona. *Address:* c/o Theateragentur Dr G. Hilbert, Maximilianstrasse 22, 80539 Munich, Germany.

SIEBER, Gudrun; Singer (Soprano); b. 1953, Germany. *Education:* Studied at the Düsseldorf Opera Studio. *Career:* Member of the Deutsche Oper am Rhein Düsseldorf 1974–83; Deutsche Oper Berlin from 1977, notably in the 1984 premiere of Reimann's Gespenstersonate; Sang at the Bayerische Staatsoper Munich, 1978–84, in operas by Gluck, Mozart and Lortzing; Schwetzingen Festival 1980 and 1982, Salzburg Festival, 1981, 1984 and 1986 as Papagena in Die Zauberflöte; Also sang Papagena at the Théâtre des Champs-Elysées, Paris, 1987; Sang in a double bill of Il Maestro di Capella (Cimarosa) and La Serva Padrona at the Deutsche Oper foyer, 1990; Other roles include Marie in Zar und Zimmermann; Amour in Hippolyte et Aricie and Kristen in Miss Julie by Bibalo; Sang Papagena and Marie in Lortzing's Zar und Zimmermann at the Deutsche Oper Berlin, 1999; Shepherd in Tannhäuser 2001; Many concert appearances. *Recordings include:*

Schumann's Manfred (Schwann). *Address:* c/o Deutsche Oper Berlin, Richard Wagnerstrasse 10, 1000 Berlin, Germany.

SIEBERT, Isolde; German singer (soprano); b. 1960, Hunfield, Hesse. *Education:* studied in Fribourg. *Career:* mem. of the Basle Opera 1982–85; sang at Darmstadt 1985–87, debut as Zerbinetta; Hanover Opera from 1987, as Blondchen, Susanna, Gretel, Tytania in A Midsummer Night's Dream, and Papagena; Bregenz Festival and Liège 1986, 1988, as the Queen of Night in Die Zauberflöte; sang in the 300th anniversary performance of Steffani's Enrico Leone, Hanover 1989; many concerts and recital appearances; sang La Reine de la nuit in Die Zauberflote, Beaune 2004, Europa in Europa riconosciuta, La Scala, Milan 2004. *Recordings include:* Dvořák's Biblical Songs Op99 2002, Von Winter's Clarinet Concerto and Aria 2004. *Address:* c/o Orfeo, Chandos House, Commerce Way, Colchester, Essex CO2 8HQ, England.

SIEDEN, Cyndia; Singer (Soprano); b. 10 Sept. 1954, Glendale, California, USA. *Education:* Studied at Olympia, Washington, and with Elisabeth Schwarzkopf. *Career:* Sang Cunegonde in Candide for New York City Opera, 1989; Sang Sifare in Mozart's Mitridate at the 1989 Wexford Festival, the Queen of Night in Toulon, Adele in Fledermaus for Scottish Opera and Offenbach's Olympia at Seattle; Salzburg Festival debut as Amor in Orfeo ed Euridice, conducted by John Eliot Gardiner; Appearances with the Bayerische Staatsoper Munich as Rosina, Helena in the premiere of Reimann's Troades, 1986, Zerbinetta and Fiakermilli in Arabella; Further engagements at Nice as Blondchen and Aminta in Die schweigsame Frau at Palermo; Sang Xenia in a concert performance of Boris Godunov conducted by Abbado, 1984, Verdi's Oscar for Washington Opera, Donizetti's Marie with Florida Opera West, Nannetta at Omaha and Fido in the US Professional premiere of Britten's Paul Bunyan, at St Louis; Season 1990/91 as Blondchen at the Théâtre du Châtelet, Paris, and on tour to Amsterdam, London, Lisbon and Stuttgart; Recent appearances as the Queen of Night at the Opéra Bastille, Paris, and Lucia di Lammermoor at Seattle; Zerbinetta for English National Opera and at the Vienna Staatsoper, season 1992/93 with Sophie in Der Rosenkavalier at the Châtelet; Sang in Mozart's Mitridate at Salzburg, 1997; Handel's Rodelinda at Halle, 1996; Sang Gilda in Rigoletto for Flanders Opera, 1999; Season 2000–01 as the Queen of Night for ENO and Gilda for Vlaamse Opera, Antwerp; Sang Morgana in Alcina at Göttingen, 2002; Concert repertoire includes Mozart's C minor Mass (Cleveland Orchestra), Carmina Burana, Bach's St John Passion at the Concertgebouw under Frans Brüggen, and Candide at the Barbican Centre, London. *Recordings include:* Guardian of the Threshold in Die Frau ohne Schatten, conducted by Sawallisch (EMI); Orfeo ed Euridice (Philips); Die Entführung aus dem Serail. *Address:* c/o Opera voor Vlaanderen, Schouwburgstrasse 3, B–900 Ghent, Belgium.

SIEGEL, Jeffrey; Concert Pianist; b. 18 Nov. 1942, Chicago, Illinois, USA; m. Laura Mizel, 20 May 1973, 1 s., 1 d. *Education:* DMA, Juilliard School of Music, 1971; Studies with Rudolph Ganz, Rosina Lhevinne, Franz Reizenstein, Ilona Kabos. *Career:* Debut: Soloist, Chicago Symphony, 1958; Soloist with Orchestras of New York, Philadelphia, Boston, Cleveland, Los Angeles, London Symphony, London Philharmonic, Royal Philharmonic, Philharmonia, BBC Orchestras; NHK Orchestra of Japan; Nacionale Orchestra of Buenos Aires, Teatro Colón; Berlin Philharmonic; Recitals in Carnegie Hall, Festival Hall, Concertgebouw, Brussels, Berlin, Munich, Zürich, Tokyo, Tel-Aviv, Oslo, Stockholm; Television appearances; Frequent radio appearances. *Compositions:* Cadenza for Mozart C Minor Concerto. *Recordings:* Dutilleux Sonata and Hindemith Third Sonata; Gershwin Complete Works for Piano and Orchestra with St Louis Symphony, 1974; Solo works of Rachmaninov. *Honours:* Silver Medal, Queen Elizabeth Competition, Brussles, 1968; Honorary Doctorate, National College of Education, Evanston, Illinois, 1976. *Current Management:* ICM Artists Management. *Address:* c/o Kansai Opera Group, 3–3–9 Bingo-Cho, Chyno-Ku, Osaka, Japan.

SIEGEL, Laurence (Gordon); Conductor; b. 23 July 1931, New York, NY, USA; m. 15 Oct 1959, 1 d. *Education:* BA, City College of New York, 1953; MM, New England Conservatory, Boston, 1955; Studied under Boris Goldovsky and Leonard Bernstein, Berkshire Music Center, Tanglewood, 1953, 1955. *Career:* Conductor, NBC Symphony, Carnegie Hall concerts including tribute to Fritz Kreisler; Appeared with Honolulu Orchestra, Shreveport Festival Orchestra, Alexandria Symphony, Jacksonville Symphony and Opera Company, Connecticut Grand Opera Company; Director, Miami International Music Competition, Theater of Performing Arts, Miami Beach, 7 seasons; World-wide conducting includes Orquesta Sinfonica del Salvador, Orquesta Sinfonica de Las Palmas, Spain, Manila Metro Philharmonic Orchestra and Opera Association, Teatro Sperimentale di Spoleto Orchestra, Belgrade Symphony, Filharmonica de Stat Oradea-Romania; Regularly conducts RAI Milan Orchestra; Music Director, Conductor, Puccini Festival Orchestra, Italy, 1984, Pan American Sinfonica, 1991–, also Festival of the Continents, Key West, Florida; Music Director, North Miami Beach

Orchestra; Guest Conductor, Kensington Symphony (California), São Paulo Symphony, Brazil, Orquesta Sinfonica Ciudad Asuncion, Paraguay (1994); Chief Conductor, Sakai City, Osaka Opera, Japan; Numerous operas include Così fan tutte, Faust, Butterfly, Tosca, La Bohème, La Traviata, Otello, Rigoletto, Die Fledermaus, Ernani, Il Trovatore, Suor Angelica, Hansel and Gretel, Samson and Delilah, La Périchole, Elisir d'amore, Carmen (1991, 1992), Merry Widow (1992–). *Recordings:* Tchaikovsky Album with New Philharmonia Orchestra, London; Others with London Symphony, London Philharmonic and Royal Philharmonic Orchestras and London Festival Orchestra. *Honours:* Numerous citations and medals of honour; D.Mus, 1993. *Current Management:* Pan American Sociedad de Artisias. *Address:* 5225 La Gorce Drive, Miami Beach, FL 33140, USA.

SIEGEL, Wayne; Composer; b. 14 Feb. 1953, Los Angeles, USA; m. 22 Mar 1980, 1 s., 1 d. *Education:* BA, Music Composition, University of California, Santa Barbara, 1975; Diplomeksamen, Composition, Royal Danish Academy of Music, Århus. *Career:* Active as Composer and Performer, Europe and USA, including many radio and television broadcasts and numerous commissions; Major performances include: Danish Radio Festival, Copenhagen, 1980; Nordic Music Days, Helsinki, 1980; German Radio, 1981; New Music America, Chicago, 1982; Warsaw Autumn, 1984; Nordic Music Days, 1984; Rostrum, Stockholm, 1988; Wigmore Recital Hall, 1997; Sydney Opera House, 1998, 1999; Cunningham Dance Studio, New York, 1999; mem, Administrative Director, West Jutland Symphony and Chamber Ensemble, 1984–86; Director, Danish Institute of Electro-acoustic Music, 1986–. *Compositions:* String Quartet, 1975–79; East LA for 4 Marimbas or 2 guitars, 1975; Narcissus ad fontem, 1976; Mosaic, 1978; Autumn Resonance, 1979; Domino Figures, 1979; Music for 21 Clarinets, 1980; Watercolor, Acrylic, Watercolor, 1981; Polyphonic Music, 1983; 42nd Street Rondo, 1984; Devil's Golf Course, 1985; Last Request, 1986; Cobra, 1988; Tracking, 1991; Livstegn (opera) 1994; Jackdaw, 1995; Movement Study, 1996; Savannah, 1997. *Recordings:* String Quartet and Watercolor, Acrylic, Watercolor; Autumn Resonance and Domino Figures; East LA Phase; 42nd Street Rondo. *Contributions:* Danish Music Periodical, Nutida Musik, Contemporary Music Review. *Honours:* Danish Art Council 3-Year Grant for Composition, 1978–81. *Address:* DIEM, The Concert Hall Århus, DK 8000 Århus, Denmark.

SIEGELE, Ulrich; Musicologist; b. 1 Nov. 1930, Stuttgart, Germany. *Education:* DPhil, Tuebingen University, 1957. *Career:* Lecturer in Musicology, 1965–71, Professor of Musicology, 1971–95, Tuebingen University. *Publications:* Die Musiksammlung der Stadt Heilbronn, 1967; Kompositionsweise und Bearbeitungstechnik in der Instrumentalmusik Johann Sebastian Bachs, 1975; Bachs theologischer Formbegriff und das Duett F-Dur, 1978; Zwei Kommentare zum Marteau sans maître von Pierre Boulez, 1979; Beethoven/Formale Strategien der späten Quartette, 1990; Die Orgeln des Musikwissenschaftlichen Instituts im Pfleghof zu Tuebingen, 1992. *Contributions:* Articles in periodicals, collections by several authors, and musical encyclopaedias including Bach, Das Wohltemperierte Klavier I; Ulrich Siegele zum 70 Geburtstag (biog.), 2002. *Address:* Am Hasenborn 2A, 61389 Schmitten, Germany.

SIEPI, Cesare; Singer (Bass-Baritone); b. 10 June 1923, Milan, Italy. *Education:* Studied privately and at the Milan Conservatory. *Career:* Debut: 1941, as Sparafucile in Rigoleto at Schio; La Fenice Venice 1946 as Silva in Ernani; La Scala Milan 1946–58, notably as Donizetti's Raimondo, Verdi's Grand Inquisitor, Wagner's Pogner and as Mefistofele and Simon Mago in the 1948 Boito celebrations conducted by Toscanini; New York Metropolitan, 1950–74, principally as Mozart's Don Giovanni and Figaro; Also sang Philip II in Don Carlos, Gounod's Mephistopheles, Verdi's Padre Guardiano, Ramfis, Silva, Zaccaria and Fiesco; First Wagner role in German was Gurnemanz, 1970; Sang Don Giovanni at Salzburg in the 1950s (also filmed) and on his Covent Garden debut, 1962; Appeared as Roger in Verdi's Jérusalem at Parma in 1985. *Recordings:* Don Giovanni, Mefistofele and L'Amore dei tre Re (RCA); Le nozze di Figaro, Don Giovanni, La Gioconda, Rigoletto, La Forza del Destino, La Bohème, Il Barbiere di Siviglia, Lucia di Lammermoor; Faust; Boris Godunov, La Juive, Don Carlos (New York Met, 1950, Myto), La Favorita, Ernani and Norma on various other labels; Five complete recordings of Don Giovanni, including Salzburg film, released 2002. *Address:* c/o Metropolitan Opera, Lincoln Center, NY 10023, New York.

SIERRA, Roberto; Composer and Music Educator; b. 9 Oct. 1953, Vega Baja, Puerto Rico. *Education:* Puerto Rico Conservatory of Music; Graduated, University of Puerto Rico, 1976; Royal College of Music, London; University of London, 1976–78; Institute of Sonology, Utrecht, 1978; Studied with Gyorgy Ligeti, Hamburg Hochschule für Musik, 1979–82. *Career:* Assistant Director, 1983–85, Director, 1985–86, Cultural Activities Department, University of Puerto Rico; Dean of Studies, 1986–87, Chancellor, 1987–, Puerto Rico Conservatory of Music. *Compositions:* Salsa on the C String for cello and piano, 1983;

Salsa for wind quintet, 1983; Cantos Populares for chorus, 1983; Cinco bocetos for clarinet, 1984; El Mensajero de Plata, chamber opera, 1984; Concerto Nocturnal for harpsichord, flute, clarinet, oboe, violin and cello, 1985; Jubilo for orchestra, 1985; Memorias Tropicales for string quartet, 1985; Dona Rosita for mezzo-soprano and wind quintet, 1985; El sueno de Antonia for clarinet and percussion, 1985; Invocaciones for voice and percussion, 1986; Cuatro ensayos orquestales for orchestra, 1986; Glosa a la sombra.for mezzo-soprano, viola, clarinet and piano, 1987; Essays for wind quintet, 1987; Mano a mano for 2 percussionists, 1987; El Contemplado, ballet, 1987; Glosas for piano and orchestra, 1987; Introduccion y Descarga for piano, brass quintet and percussion, 1988; Dascarga for chamber ensemble or orchestra, 1988; Entre terceras for 2 synthesizers and computer, 1988; Tributo for harp, flute, clarinet and string quartet, 1988; Bayoán, oratorio, 1991–3; Trio Tropical, for violin, cello and piano, 1991; Evocaciones, for violin and orchestra, 1994; Lux Aeterna, for chorus, 1996; Alegriá for orchestra, 1996; Cuentos, for chamber orchestra, 1997; Concerto for percussion and orchestra, 1998; Piano Pieces; Harpsichord pieces. *Recordings:* Number of works recorded. *Honours:* Several commissions; Many works performed in USA and Europe. *Address:* c/o Conservatorio de Musica de Puerto Rico, Apartado 41227, Minillas Station, Santurce, Puerto Rico 00940, USA.

SIFFERT (TRAVASSOS), Henrik; Dramatic Tenor, Opera Singer and Singing Teacher; b. 20 Sept. 1959, Porto Alegre, Brazil. *Education:* Psychology and Sociology, University Gama Filho, Rio de Janeiro; Conservatory H. Villa-Lobos, Rio de Janeiro; Musikhochschule, Cologne, Germany; Musikhochschule, Karlsruhe, Germany; Studied with Dieter Jacob in Cologne, Aldo Baldin in Karlsruhe, Floriana Cavalli in Milan, James King in Munich and Rina del Monaco in Pesaro. *Career:* Debut: As Baritone: Teatro Municipal Rio de Janeiro, 1978; As Dramatic Tenor: Youth Festival Bayreuth, as Max in Der Freischütz by Weber; Baritone, German television; Tonio in Pagliacci, ZDF, 1984; Schicchi in Gianni Schicchi, Puccini, Sudwestfunk television; International Festival, Wiesbaden, Gonzales in Guarany, Carlos Gomes, Teatro Municipal do Rio de Janeiro, and others; Recorded leider, operas, Zarzuelas and oratorios for German radio; Dramatic tenor, 1988; Lord Cecil, Bonynge, del Monaco, Liceo de Barcelona, 1990; Otello, Parsifal, Ismaele, and others; Recitals with orchestra and piano; Teacher, Department of Voice, Conservatory of Colmar, France; Creator, Artistic Director, European Academy of Singing, Guebwiller, Alsace, France. *Current Management:* Walter Beloch, Milan, Italy. *Address:* 1 rue des Tourneurs, 68000 Colmar, France.

SIGHELE, Mietta; Singer (Soprano); b. 1944, Rovereto, Italy; m. Veriano Luchetti. *Education:* Studied in Milan and Rome. *Career:* Debut: Sang Butterfly at Spoleto; Appearances at opera houses throughout Italy and in Vienna, Barcelona, Buenos Aires, Montreal, Chicago, Dallas and New Orleans; Verona Arena from 1979, as Micaela in Carmen; Ravenna Festival, 1986 and Torre del Lago, 1989 as Butterfly; Metropolitan Opera, 1989 as Micaela; Season 1991 as Liu in Turandot, at Verona and Prioress in The Carmelites at Rome; Engagements in operas by Mozart, Janáček, Wagner and Tchaikovsky. *Recordings:* Priestess in Aida; Meyerbeer's L'Africaine, Florence, 1971.

SIGMUNDSSON, Kristinn; Singer (Bass-Baritone); b. 1 May 1951, Reykjavík, Iceland. *Education:* Studied at Academy of Music in Vienna and in Washington DC. *Career:* Member of Wiesbaden Opera from 1989 as Don Giovanni, the Speaker in Die Zauberflöte and Eugene Onegin; Royal Court Theatre Drottningholm, 1989–90 as Agamemnon and Thoas in Gluck's Iphigénie operas; Season 1990–91 includes: Geisterbote in Die Frau ohne Schatten at the Concertgebouw, Beethoven's 9th with the Essen Philharmonie and St John Passion in the Hague; Recital at the Stratford-upon-Avon Scandinavian Festival; Malcolm in La Donna del Lago for Vara Radio, Netherlands, 1992; Concert appearances with the Dutch Radio Orchestra, the Rotterdam Philharmonic and the NDR Symphony Orchestra, Hamburg; Season 1991–92 included: Don Giovanni at Stuttgart Opera, Mozart's Requiem at Drottningholm and Barber of Seville at Geneva; Season 1993–94 included: Alidoro and Speaker in Geneva, Mathis der Maler in Barcelona and Lady Macbeth of Mtsensk at the Maggio Musicale in Florence; Sang in a new production of The Bartered Bride at the Grand Théâtre in Geneva, 1994; Sang Mephistofeles in La Damnation de Faust at the Opéra National in Paris; Colline in 1996; Sang Klingsor in Parsifal at the Opéra Bastille, Paris, 1997; Season 1997–98 as Rossini's Mustafà at Dresden, the Hermit in Der Freischütz for the Royal Opera at the Barbican and Grand Inquisitor in Don Carlos at the Opéra Bastille, Paris; Season 2000 as Banquo at Cologne, Cherubini's Creon at Salzburg (concert) and Rossini's Mustafà for the Vienna Staatsoper; Season 2001–02 engagements included Barbiere at the Paris Bastille, Don Giovanni in Munich and Berlin, Lucia di Lammermoor in Munich, Die Walküre and Parsifal in Cologne and Eugene Ongin in Hamburg, Nabucco at the Arena di Nimes; Season 2002–03 with Der Rosenkavalier and a revival of Walküre in Cologne, Meistersinger at Covent Garden, Gounod's Faust, Parisfal, Der fliegende Holländer, Meister-

singer and La Juive at the Opéra National de Paris, La Damnation de Faust in San Francisco, Don Giovanni in Munich, Don Carlos in Dallas, Der Rosenkavalier in Dresden and Die Walküre in Naples. *Recordings include:* Commendatore in Don Giovanni, conducted by Arnold Östman. *Honours:* Prizewinner, Belvedere Singing Competition in Vienna, 1983; Winner, Philadelphia Opera Competition, 1983. *Address:* c/o Haydn Rawstron Ltd, 36 Station Road, London SE20 7BQ, England.

SIGURBJORNSSON, Thorkell; Composer; b. 16 July 1938, Reykjavík, Iceland. *Education:* Reykjavík College of Music; Continuing Studies in USA. *Career:* Creative Associate, State University of New York, USA, 1973; Research Musician, Centre for Music Experiment, University of California, San Diego, 1975; Head of Theory and Composition, Reykjavík College of Music, Iceland, 1968–74; Bukolla, 1974; Wiblo, 1976; Cadensa and Dance; Seascape; Albumblatt, 1975; The Bull Man, ballet music; Caprice, 1986; Chamber Music: Differing Opinions; Intrada, 1971; For Renee, 1973; A Short Passion Story; Hasselby Icelandic Folk Songs, 1976; Ballade, 1960; Happy Music, 1971; Kissum, 1970; Copenhagen Quartet; For Better or Worse, 1975; Solstice, 1976; Auf Meinen Lieben Gott, 1981; Three Faces of Pantomine, 1982; Choir Music: Ode, 1975; Five Laudi, 1973; Beginning, 1978; Hosanna Son of David; Palm Sunday, 1978; The Artificial Flower; Seven Christmas Songs; David 121, 1984; Evening Prayers, 1983; Children's Music: Seven Songs from Apaspil; Apaspil, opera, 1966; Velferd; Four Icelandic Folk Songs; Three Songs; Gigjuleikur; The Ugly Duckling, 1981; The Last Flower, 1983; Electronic Music: La Jolla Good Friday I, 1975; La Jolla Good Friday II, 1975; fipur, 1971; Race Track, 1975; Trifonia for orchestra, 1990; Missa Brevis, 1993; Visit, string quartet, 1993; Life, Dreams and Reality, for orchestra, 1993; Runes, for horn and orchestra, 1994; The Girl in the Lighthouse, children's opera, 1997; Symphony, 1998; Wheel of Fortune, chamber opera, 1998; President, Icelandic League of Composers. *Address:* c/o STEF, Laufasvegi 40, 101 Reykjavík, Iceland.

SIKI, Bela; Pianist; b. 21 Feb. 1923, Budapest, Hungary; m. Yolande Oltramare, 18 Sept 1952, 1 s., 1 d. *Education:* University of Budapest; Academy Franz Liszt, Budapest; Conservatoire de Genève, Switzerland. *Career:* Numerous concert tours world-wide; Appearances with major orchestras around the world; Extensive concert tours and master classes in Japan, Australia, USA and Canada, 1988. *Recordings:* Has made numerous recordings including music by Bach, Ravel, Liszt (B minor sonata), Beethoven (late sonatas) and Bartók. *Publications:* Piano Literature, 1981. *Honours:* Liszt Competition, Budapest, 1942, 1943; Concours International d'Executions Musicales, Geneva, 1948. *Address:* School of Music, University of Washington, Seattle, WA 98195, USA.

SIKORA, Elizabeth; Singer (Soprano); b. 1950, Edinburgh, Scotland. *Education:* Studied at the Royal Scottish Academy and at Elsa Mayer Lismanns Opera Workshop. *Career:* Appearances with the Royal Opera Covent Garden in London and on Tour to Los Angeles, La Scala Milan, Japan, Korea and Greece; Solo Roles in Die Meistersinger, Butterfly, Die Frau ohne Schatten, Manon Lescaut, Parsifal, Rigoletto and Simon Boccanegra; Sang in the British premieres of Henze's Pollicino and Menotti's The Boy Who Grew Too Fast; Appearances as Carmen in Oundle and Germany with Royal Opera Education; Annina in La Traviata at the Albert Hall. *Address:* c/o Scottish Opera, 39 Elmbank Crescent, Glasgow, G2 4PT, Scotland.

SILJA, Anja; Singer (Soprano) and Director; b. 17 April 1940, Berlin, Germany. *Education:* Studied with Egon van Rijn. *Career:* Concert at the Berlin Titania Palace aged 10; Stage debut Brunswick 1956, as Rosina; Stuttgart from 1958, Frankfurt from 1959; Sang the Queen of Night at Aix, 1959; Bayreuth Festival, 1960–67, as Senta, Elsa, Eva, Elisabeth, and Venus; London debut at Sadler's Wells Theatre, 1963, as Leonore; Member of the Stuttgart Staatsoper from 1965; Covent Garden debut 1969, as Leonore: returned as Cassandre in Les Troyens, Senta, and Marie in Wozzeck; Metropolitan Opera debut 1972: returned as Salome, Marie and Kostelnicka (Jenůfa); Vienna Staatsoper 1959–(roles included: Queen of Night, Salome, Elektra, Lulu) Paris Opéra 1964–, as Salome; Glyndebourne Opera debut 1989, as the Kostelnicka; Sang the Nurse in Die Frau ohne Schatten at San Francisco, 1989; 1990 debut as opera producer at Brussels; Covent Garden, 1993, in Jenůfa; Sang Janáček's Emilia Marty at Glyndebourne, 1995; Season 1997 in The Makropulos Case at Glyndebourne and as Herodias at Covent Garden; Sang the Kostelnicka at Zürich, 1998 and at Covent Garden, 2001; Sang Geschwitz in Lulu at Düsseldorf, 2000; Season 2000–01 in Reimann's Lear at Turin, Clytemnestra at Madrid, in Lulu and Salome (Herodias) at Amsterdam, Erwartung at Aix and The Bassarids in Amsterdam; Engaged in Pierrot Lunaire by Schoenberg at Aix, 2003. *Recordings:* Der fliegende Holländer, Tannhäuser, Lohengrin and Parsifal from Bayreuth; Lulu and Wozzeck. *Address:* c/o Artists Management Zürich, Rütistr 52, 8044 Zürich, Switzerland.

SILLA, Frederick; Singer (Tenor) and Composer; b. 1948, Vienna, Australia. *Education:* Studied at the Vienna Musikhochschule with

Friedrich Cerha and Anton Dermota. *Career:* Sang first at the Stadttheater Krefeld, then appeared at Opera Houses in Ulm, Kiel, Munster and Gelsenkirchen; Opera, Jagdszenen aus Niederbayern, premiered at Karlsruhe 1979; Member of the Staatstheater am Gärtnerplatz Munich from 1985; Roles have included Mozart's Ottavio, Tamino, Ferrando and Belmonte, Nemorino and Hoffmann; Modern Repertoire includes parts in The Lighthouse by Maxwell Davies, Jakob Lenz by Wolfgang Rihm and Die Veruteilung des Lukullus by Dessau; Guest Engagements in Pisa, Venice and Madrid, Concert appearances in Germany and elsewhere. *Address:* c/o Staatstheater am Gärtnerplatz, Gärtnerplatz 3, 8000 Munich, Germany.

SILLS, Beverly; Singer (Soprano) and Opera Director; b. 25 May 1929, Brooklyn, New York, USA. *Education:* Studied with Estelle Liebing from age 7. *Career:* Often sang on radio commercials as a child, with name Bubbles; Opera debut as Frasquita in Carmen, Philadelphia Civic Opera 1946; San Francisco Opera 1953, as Elena in Mefistofele; New York City Opera 1955–79 as Charpentier's Louise, Mozart's Donna Anna, Gounod's Marguerite, the heroines in Les Contes d'Hoffmann, Massenet's Manon, Donizetti's Tudor Queens and Bellini's Elvira; Success as Cleopatra in a version of Handel's Giulio Cesare led to engagements in Vienna (Mozart's Queen of Night 1967), La Scala (Pamira in Rossini's L'Assedio di Corinto 1969), and Covent Garden (Donizetti's Lucia 1970); Opera Company of Boston 1971–; Metropolitan Opera debut 1975, as Pamira; also sang Massenet's Thais, Donizetti's Norina and Violetta at the Met; Retired from opera 1979, in Menotti's La Loca; Director, New York City Opera, 1979–89; Chair of the Lincoln Center for Performing Arts, 1994. *Recordings:* Giulio Cesare; Lucia di Lammermoor; La Traviata; Les Contes d'Hoffmann; Manon; Thais; Maria Stuarda; Don Pasquale; Roberto Devereux; L'Assedio di Corinto; Rigoletto; I Capuleti e i Montecchi; Norma. *Publications:* Beverly: an Autobiography, (New York, 1988). *Address:* c/o Lincoln Center for the Performing Arts, 70 Lincoln Center Plaza, New York, NY 10023, USA.

SILVA, Stella; Singer (Mezzo-soprano); b. 6 Jan. 1948, Buenos Aires, Argentina. *Education:* Studied in Buenos Aires and at Vercelli, Italy. *Career:* Debut: Bordeaux 1969, as Preziosilla in La Forza del Destino; Many appearances in Opera Houses at Parma, Lyon, Nice, Strasbourg, Hamburg, Vienna, Berlin, Barcelona and Buenos Aires; Verona Arena, 1973–74, as Amneris; Other roles have included Carmen, Ulrica, Eboli, Azucena, Adalgisa, Charlotte, Dalila and Ortrud; Laura in La Gioconda, Leonora, Gluck's Orpheus and Holofernes in Vivaldi's Juditha Triumphans; Frequent Concert Appearances.

SILVA-MARIN, Guillermo (Osvaldo); Singer (Tenor) and Artistic Director; b. 11 April 1944, Ponce, Puerto Rico. *Education:* BA, University of Puerto Rico; Diploma, Opera, University of Toronto. *Career:* Artistic Director, Metropolitan Music Theatre, Scarborough, 1976–79; Founder and Artistic Director, Toronto Operetta Theatre, 1985; Founder, Summer Opera Lyric Theatre, 1986; General Manager, Opera in Concert, 1994; Staged over 21 operas and operettas including Donizetti's Elixir of Love, Rossini's Barber of Seville, Lehar's Land of Smiles, Offenbach's La Vie Parisienne and Strauss's Gypsy Baron with the Toronto Operetta Theatre, Summer Opera Lyric Theatre, Opera de San Juan and Sault Ste Marie Opera; 16 performances as tenor with the Canadian Opera Company, including Richard Strauss's Ariadne auf Naxos and Leoncavallo's Pagliacci; Appearances with Opera Lyra, Cincinnati Opera Association, New York City Opera, Metropolitan Opera, Mexico State Symphony, Toronto Symphony, Edmonton Symphony, Puerto Rico Symphony, Carnegie Hall, Canadian Broadcasting Corporation, CFMX-FM include Stravinsky's Oedipus Rex, Strauss's Die Fledermaus, Zeller's The Bird Seller and Puccini's La Bohème. *Current Management:* VKD International Artists, 9 Vernham Avenue, Willowdale, Ontario M2L 2B1, Canada.

SILVASTI, Jorma; Singer (Tenor); b. 9 March 1959, Leppavirta, Finland. *Education:* Studied at Savonlinna from 1975, Sibelius Academy Helsinki, 1978–81, Frankfurt, 1981–83. *Career:* Appearances with the Finnish National Opera at Helsinki from 1980; Frankfurt 1981–82, Krefeld, 1982–85; Karlsruhe, 1985–88; Savonlinna Festival from 1983 as Jenik (Bartered Bride), the Steersman in Fliegende Holländer and Tamino; Premiere of Veitsi by Paavo Heikinen, 1989; Sang Ottavio at the Vienna Volksoper, 1988, Henry Morosus in Schweigsame Frau at Dresden, 1989; Further engagements at Essen, Karlsruhe and Bremen; Created Kimmo in Sallinen's Kullervo with the Company of Finnish National Opera at the Dorothy Chandler Pavilion, Los Angeles, 1992; Other roles include Ferrando, Fenton, Gluck's Pylades, Almaviva, Steva in Jenůfa, Lensky, Belmonte (Vienna State Opera, 1993) Nemorino, Alfredo; Noted Concert and Oratorio Performer; Gregor in premiere of Sansibar by E Meyer at Schwetzingen with Bavarian State Opera Munich, 1994; Faust at the Dorothy Chandler Pavilion, Los Angeles; Further engagements: Stuttgart, Düsseldorf, Frankfurt, Hannover, Hamburg, Munich, Vienna State Opera; Sang Petruccio in The Palace, by Sallinen, at the 1996 Savonlinna Festival; Sang Parsifal at Brussels, 1998; Season 2000–01 as Berg's Alwa at the Vienna Staatsoper,

Manolios in Martinů's The Greek Passion at Covent Garden and Edmund in the premiere of Sallinen's Lear, for Finnish National Opera; Laca in Jenůfa at Covent Garden, 2001; Dvořák's Stabat mater at the London Proms, 2002. *Address:* Finnish National Opera, Bulevardi 23–27, 00180 Helsinki, Finland.

SILVER, Sheila; Composer; b. 3 Oct. 1946, Seattle, Washington, USA. *Education:* Studied at the University of Washington, Seattle (1964–65) and in Paris at the Institute for European Studies, 1966–67; BA 1968 University of California at Berkeley; Stuttgart Hochschule für Musik, with Ligeti and PhD 1976 at Brandeis University (study with Alfred Berger, Lalo Schifrin and Harold Shapero); Tanglewood 1972, with Further study at Paris and London. *Career:* Freelance composer, with performances throughout the United states; Has worked with film including scores Alligator Eyes and Dead Funny; Teacher of composition then Professor of Music at SUNY, Stony Brook, from 1979. *Compositions include:* String quartet, 1977; Galixidi, for orchestra, 1977; Dynamis for horn, 1979; Canto for baritone and chamber ensemble, 1979; Chariessa for soprano and orchestra, after Sappho, 1980; Two Elizabethan Songs for chorus, 1982; Ek Ong Kar for chorus, 1983; Dance Converging, for viola, horn, piano and percussion, 1987; The Thief of Love, opera, 1987; Window Waltz for bass clarinet, horn, strings, harpsichord, piano and percussion, 1988; Song of Sarah for string orchestra, 1988; Cello Sonata, 1988; Oh, Thou Beautiful One, for piano, 1989; Dance of wild Angels, for chamber orchestra, 1990; Six Préludes pour piano, 1991; Three Preludes for orchestra, 1992; To the Spirit Unconquered trio for violin, cello and piano, 1992; Transcending three songs for Michael Dash, in memoriam, 1995; From Darkness Emerging, harp and string quartet, 1995; Piano Concerto, 1996 Four Etudes and a Fantasy, string quartet No. 2, 1997; Winter Tapestry, for chamber ensemble, 1998. *Recordings include:* To the Spirit Unconquered; Fantasy Quasi Theme and Variation. *Address:* PO Box 292, Spencertown, NY 12165, USA.

SILVERMAN, Faye-Ellen, BA, MA, DMA; composer, pianist, writer and educator; b. 2 Oct. 1947, New York, NY, USA. *Education:* Mannes College of Music, Barnard College, Harvard University, Columbia University. *Career:* Teaching Assistant, Columbia University, 1972–74; Adjunct Assistant Professor, City University of New York, 1972–77; Assistant Professor, Goucher College, 1977–81; Graduate Facility, Department of Music History and Literature, Peabody Institute, Johns Hopkins University, 1977–85; Faculty, Center for Compositional Studies, Aspen Music Festival, 1986; College and Extension Faculty at Mannes College of Music since 1991, the Eugene Lang Faculty since Autumn 2000; Works performed live and/or on radio and television in many countries. *Compositions include:* Kalends for brass quintet, 1981; Trysts for 2 trumpets, 1982; Volcanic Songs for harp, 1983; Restless Winds for woodwind quintet, 1986; Adhesions for orchestra, 1987; A Free Pen, a cantata for narrator, soloists, chorus and chamber ensemble, 1990; Journey Towards Oblivion for soprano, tenor and chamber ensemble, 1991; Azure Skies for violin, cello and harp, 1993; Connections for clarinet, cello and marimba, 1994; Just For Fun for chamber orchestra, 1994; Mariana for mezzo-soprano, clarinet and piano, 1995; At The Colour Cafe, for brass choir, 1997; Dialogue Continued horn, trombone, tuba, 2000; Reconstructed Music, Piano Trio, 2002; Over 65 published compositions with Seesaw Music Corporation. *Recordings:* Oboe-sthenics by James Astryniec; Zigzags by Velvet Brown; Passing Fancies, Restless Winds and Speaking Alone by Aspen Music Festival Contemporary Ensemble under Stephen Mosko. *Publications:* 20th Century Section of the Schirmer History of Music. *Address:* 330 West 28th Street 7G, New York, NY 10001, USA. *E-mail:* FayeNote@post.harvard.edu. *Website:* www.cmc.net/member/faye_silverman.

SILVERMAN, Stanley (Joel); Composer; b. 5 July 1938, New York, USA. *Education:* Studied at Mills College; Columbia University, 1958–59 and Berkshire Music Centre, 1961. *Career:* Writer of Incidental Music for Plays, Composer of Operas. *Compositions include:* Operas and Musical Plays, Elephant Steps, Tanglewood, 1968; Dr Selavy's Magic Theatre, Stockbridge, 1972; Hotel for Criminals, Stockbridge, 1974; Madame Adare, New York Opera, 1980; The Columbine String Quartet Tonight, Stockbridge, 1981; Up from Paradise, New York, 1983; The Golem, 1984; Africanaus Instructus, New York, 1986; A Good Life, Washington, 1986; Black Sea Follies, Stockbridge, 1986; Love and Science, 1990. *Address:* c/o ASCAP, ASCAP Building, 1 Lincoln Plaza, New York, NY 10023, USA.

SILVERSTEIN, Joseph; Violinist and Conductor; b. 21 March 1932, Detroit, Michigan, USA. *Education:* Studied with Reynolds and Zimbalist, Curtis Institute of Music, Philadelphia, 1945–50; with Gingold and Mischakoff. *Career:* Houston Symphony Orchestra; Denver Symphony Orchestra; Philadelphia Orchestra; Member, 1955–62, Concertmaster, 1962–83, Assistant Conductor, 1971–83, Boston Symphony Orchestra; Faculty Member, Berkshire Music Center, Tanglewood; Boston University; Interim Music Director, Toledo (Ohio)

Symphony Orchestra, 1979–80; Principal Guest Conductor, Baltimore Symphony Orchestra, 1981–83; Music Director, Utah Symphony Orchestra, Salt Lake City, 1983–; Chautauqua (NY) Symphony Orchestra, 1987–; Guest conductor with various orchestras. *Recordings:* As violinist and conductor. *Honours:* Winner, Queen Elisabeth of Belgium competition, 1959; Naumburg Foundation Award, 1960. *Address:* c/o Utah Symphony Orchestra, 123 West South Temple, Salt Lake City, UT 84101, USA.

SILVESTRELLI, Andrea; Singer (bass); b. 1966, Ancona, Italy. *Education:* Rossini Conservatory, Pesaro. *Career:* Debut: Rodolfo in La Sonnambula at Spoleto, 1989; Sang Fiesco in Simon Boccanegra (1989), Banquo in Macbeth at Jesi and the Commendatore at Bologna and Rome; Season 1992-93 as Colline at Naples, the Monk in Don Carlos at La Scala and Baldassare in La Favorita at Philadelphia; Macerata Festival as Monterone in Rigoletto, Sarastro in Die Zauberflöte; Commendatore in Don Giovanni for the Holland and Ludwigsburg Festivals, Scottish Opera and in Toulouse (1995-96); Florence 1996 in Il Prigioniero by Dallapiccola and Capello in Bellini's I Capuleti at the Opéra Bastille; Season 1999-200 as Verdi's Lodovico at Munich, Oroveso in Norma at Geneva and Sparafucile (Rigoletto) at the Chicago Lyric Opera; Concerts in Italy and elsewhere. *Recordings include:* Don Giovanni; Don Carlos; Mahler's 8th Symphony. *Address:* c/o Teatro Comunale di Firenze, Via Solferino H. 15, 50123 Florence, Italy.

SILVESTRINI, Roberta; Conservatory Professor and Composer; b. 3 Jan. 1964, Milan, Italy; m. Lorenzo Brunelli, 21 July 1996. *Education:* G Rossini Conservatory, Pesaro; G B Martini Conservatory, Bologna; Composition with Franco Donatoni at Chigiana and S Cecilia Academies; Film Music with Ennio Morricone, 1991. *Career:* Debut: Institut Français, Naples, 9 Oct 1987; Collaborated with international solists, theatrical companies, national and foreign ensembles; Works performed at major venues and festivals including La Fenice Venice, Carnegie Hall New York, Harvard University, Gaudeamus Amsterdam, Academies S Cecilia and Chigiana; Broadcasts, RAI radio and television, Bayerische Rundfunk, others; Director, San Giovanni Choir; Professor, Fermo State Conservatory of Music; mem, Artistic Director, Association for Ancient and Contemporary Music. *Compositions include:* La toile d'araignée for flute quartet, 1989; Charmant for double bass, 1990; Agité, double bass, 1991; Crescendo intenso, violin, viola, cello, vibraphone, marimba, 1992; Energique, piano, 1993; Nuances éclatantes for saxophone quartet, 1993; Animé, viola, 1993; Pour Toi, guitar, 1994; Epaisseurs No. 2, 4 flutes, 2 pianos, 1995; Sursauts, 2 percussionists, 1995; L'Acquata, narrator, piano, 1998; Spruzzi d'onde for string quartet, 1998; Monsiue Oz Nerol le Fou, bass clarinet, 1999. *Recordings:* Animé; Effet unique; Spruzzi d'onde; La toile d'araignée; Toccata, antique organ; L'Acrobata, harp, ad lib narrator. Publications; Various. *Honours:* Finalist, Premio 900 Musicale Europeo, 1987; SIAE Scholarship, 1991. *Address:* Via della Marina 16, 60010 Montignano di Senigallia (AN), Italy.

SILVESTROV, Valentin Vasilyevich; Ukrainian composer; b. 30 Sept. 1937, Kiev. *Education:* Kiev State Conservatory (pupil of B. Lyatoshinsky). *Career:* author of compositions performed in USSR and many countries of Europe and in USA. *Compositions include:* 5 symphonies for large symphony orchestra 1963–82, Symphony for baritone with orchestra Echo Momentum on verses of A. Pushkin 1987, string quartets 1978, 1988, Dedication – symphony for violin and orchestra 1991, Mertamusica for piano and orchestra 1992, numerous chamber ensembles, piano pieces, vocal cycles, choruses. *Honours:* S. Koussevitsky Prize (USA) 1967, Prize of Gaudeamus Soc. (Netherlands) 1970. *Address:* Entuziastov str. 35/1, Apt. 49, 252147 Kiev, Ukraine (home). *Telephone:* (44) 517-04-47 (home).

SIMA, Gabriele; Singer (Mezzo-soprano); b. 1955, Salzburg, Austria. *Education:* Studied at the Salzburg Mozarteum and the Vienna Musikhochschule. *Career:* Sang in the Baroque repertoire with the Viennese ensemble Spectaculum and studied with Nikolaus Harnoncourt from 1979; Opera Studio of the Vienna Opera, 1979–82; Has sung at the Vienna Staatsoper from 1982, Tebaldo in Don Carlos, 1989; Salzburg Festival from 1980, notably as Johanna in the premiere of Cerha's Baal, 1981 and in the 1984 premiere of Berio's Un Re in Ascolto; Guest appearances at the Hamburg Staatsoper and at Zürich, Berlin from 1988; Opera and Concert tour of Japan, 1989; Other roles include Rosina, Cherubino, Octavian, Siebel, Annio (Titus), Idamante in Idomeneo, Feodor (Boris), Dorabella (Così), Zerlina; Season 2000–01 as Giunone in Legrenzi's La divisone del mondo, at Innsbruck and Schwetzingen; Handel's Agrippina at Graz and Carlotta in Die schweigsame Frau for the Opéra Bastille. *Recordings:* Handel's Jephtha (Telefunken); Tannhäuser, as Shepherd (Schwann); Barbiere di Siviglia, as Berta (Abbado). *Address:* Staatsoper, Opernring 2, 1010 Vienna, Austria.

SIMCOCK, Iain Hamilton, FRCO; British organist; b. 13 March 1965, Hemel Hempstead, England. *Education:* Solihull School, Christ Church Coll., Oxford, St Georges Chapel, Windsor Castle. *Career:* recitals for major venues all over the United Kingdom and Europe; Sub-organist of Westminster Abbey and Assistant Master of Music, Westminster Cathedral; Frequent broadcaster for BBC Radio 3; Recitals at Nôtre Dame de Paris, Strasbourg Cathedral, Proms Royal Albert Hall; Frequent tours of Scandinavia, Germany and France; mem, Royal College of Organists. *Recordings:* Christus; Vièrne Symphonies. *Publications:* contrib. articles on Music of Louis Vièrne for the Musical Times. *Honours:* Second Grand Prix, Chartes International Organ Competition. *Address:* 12 Vincent Square Mansions, Walcott Street, London SW1P 2NT, England.

SIMIC, Goran; Singer (bass); b. 14 Oct. 1953, Belgrade, Yugoslavia. *Education:* Studied at the Music High School of Belgrade and Sarajevo. *Career:* Sang in opera at Sarajevo 1978–84; Member of the Vienna Staatsoper from 1984, notably as Wurm (Luisa Miller), Timur, Sparafucile, the Commendatore, Colline, Pimen, Titurel and Rossini's Basilio; Guest appearances in Russia, Japan, Yugoslavia and the USA; Salzburg Festival from 1986, notably as Horn in Un Ballo in Maschera, conducted by Karajan and by Solti (1990); Other roles include Padre Guardiano, Ramphis; The Grand Inquisitor, Ferrando, Kecal in The Bartered Bride, Raimondo (Lucia di Lammermoor) and Konchak in Prince Igor; Season 2000–01 in Vienna as Mozart's Bartolo, Gremin in Eugene Onegin and Timur in Turandot. *Recordings include:* Un Ballo in Maschera (Deutsche Grammophon); Khovanshchina conducted by Abbado; Anselmus in Schreker's Irrelohe, 1995. *Honours:* Prizewinner in competitions at Busseto 1981, Moscow 1982 and Philadelphia 1985. *Address:* Staatsoper, Opernring 2, 1010 Vienna, Austria.

SIMIONATO, Giulietta; Singer (Mezzo-soprano); b. 12 May 1912, Forli, Italy. *Education:* Rovigo with Ettore Locatello and Padua with Guido Palumbo. *Career:* Debut: As Lola in Cavalleria Rusticana, Montagana, 1928; Sang in premiere of Pizzetti's Orsèolo, 1933; La Scala Milan 1936–66, notably as Thomas' Mignon, Massenet's Charlotte, Rossini's Isabella, Rosina and Cenerentola, Donizetti's Giovanna Seymour and as Valentine in Meyerbeer's Les Huguenots; Sang in premiere of Falla's L'Atlantida 1962; British debut 1947, as Mozart's Cherubino at Edinburgh; Royal Opera House Covent Garden 1953 as Bellini's Adalgisa and Verdi's Amneris and Azucena, opposite Callas; US debut San Francisco 1953; Chicago 1954–61; Metropolitan Opera debut 1959, as Azucena; Last appearance as Servilia in La Clemenza di Tito, Piccola Scala 1966. *Recordings:* Il Matrimonio Segreto; Cavalleria Rusticana; La Cenerentola; Il Barbiere di Siviglia; L'Italiana in Algeri; Il Trovatore; La Favorita; Rigoletto; La Gioconda; Falstaff; Aida; Un Ballo in Maschera; Carmen; Gluck's Orpheus; Meyerbeer's Valentine and in partnership with Maria Callas. *Address:* 29/C Via di Villa Grazioli, Rome, Italy.

SIMON, Abbey; Concert Pianist; b. 8 Jan. 1922, New York, NY, USA; m. Dina Levinson Simon, 28 July 1942, 1 s. *Education:* Graduate, Curtis Institute of Music, Philadelphia, Pennsylvania. *Career:* Debut: Town Hall, New York, as winner of Walter W Naumberg Award, 1940; Concert tours in recital and with orchestra on six continents, 1940–; Professor of Piano, Juilliard School of Music, New York City; Cullen Chair for Distinguished Professor, University of Houston, Texas. *Recordings:* Complete Chopin repertoire for solo piano and orchestra; Complete Ravel repertoire for solo piano and orchestra; All Rachmaninov's works for piano and orchestra plus transcriptions; Beethoven and Mozart Woodwind quintets Mendelssohn Variations and Songs Without Words; Many other recordings include the Piano Virtuoso and works by Schumann, Brahms and Liszt. *Honours:* First Prize, Walter W Naumburg Piano Competition; Best Recital of the Year, Federation of Music Clubs, New York; National Orchestral Award; Elizabeth Sprague Coolidge Medal, London; Harriet Cohen Foundation, London. *Current Management:* Gurtman & Murtha Associates Inc, New York City. *Address:* 45 Chemin Moise Deboule, 1209 Geneva, Switzerland.

SIMON, Geoffrey; Conductor; b. 3 July 1946, Adelaide, South Australia, Australia. *Education:* Studied at Melbourne University, the Juilliard School and Indiana University. *Career:* Guest appearances with leading orchestras, 1974–; Music Director, Australian Sinfonia, London; Music Director, Albany Symphony Orchestra, New York, 1987–89; Music Director, Cala Records, London, 1991–; Artistic Adviser, 1993–94, Music Director, 1994–, Sacramento Symphony, California; Regular concerts with The London Philharmonic, London Symphony and English Chamber Orchestras; Other engagements with the Munich, Israel and New Japan Philharmonic Orchestras, the American, City of Birmingham, Sapporo and Tokyo Metropolitan Symphonies, the Orchestras of the Australian Broadcasting Corporation and the Australian Opera; Conducted the Royal Philharmonic Orchestra in the premiere of Paul Patterson's 1st Symphony at the Cheltenham Festival; mem, Vice-President, Stokowski Society, 1993–. *Recordings:* Music by French composers of the 1920s and rare music by Respighi and Tchaikovsky; Patterson's Mass of the Sea; The Warriors and other works by Percy Grainger; Music by Debussy, Ravel, Respighi, Brahms,

Borodin, Mussorgsky, Saint-Saëns and Barry Conyngham; The London Cello Sound–the 40 cellos of the London Philharmonic, Royal Philharmonic Orchestra, BBC Symphony Orchestra and the Philharmonia Orchestra, similarly, the London Violin Sound, the London Viola Sound and the London Trombone Sound. *Honours:* Prize Winner, John Player International Conductor's Award, 1974; Prix de la Ville de Paris, Académie du Disque Français, 1985; Gramophone Award for Respighi recordings. *Address:* c/o Cala Records Ltd, 17 Shakespeare Gardens, London N2 9LJ, England.

SIMON, Laszlo; Pianist and Professor; b. 16 July 1948, Miskolc, Hungary; m. Sabine Simon, 1978, 2 d. *Education:* Musica; education in Stockholm, Hannover, New York. Teachers: Hans Leygraf, Ilona Kabos, Claudio Arrau. *Career:* Debut: 1966; Appearances in Hamburg, Rome, Stockholm, Helsinki, Oslo, Berlin, Tokyo, Seoul, London, Porto, Professor, Karlsruhe State Academy, 1977–; Professor, Hochschule der Kunste, Berlin, 1981–; Stockholm 1988–; Masterclasses at Murashino Academy in Tokyo, 1988–. *Recordings:* Liszt; Clementi; Kodály; Schubert; de Frumerie; Velte. *Honours:* III Prize Busoni Competition, I Prize Casagrande Competition. *Current Management:* Konsertbolaget, Stockholm. *Address:* Hochschule der Kunste Berlin, Fasanenstr 1, 1000 Berlin, Germany.

SIMONEAU, Léopold; Singer (Tenor); b. 3 May 1928, Quebec, Canada; m. Pierette Alarie, 1946. *Education:* Studied in Montreal with Salvator Issaurel and with Paul Althouse in New York. *Career:* Debut: Montreal, Varietées Lyriques, in 1941 as Hadji in Lakmé; Sang in Montreal as Wilhelm Meister, Tamino and Ferrando, and Central City Colorado, Philadelphia and New Orleans; Sang in Paris at Opéra-Comique in 1949 in Mireille by Gounod, Aix-en-Provence in 1950 in Iphigénie en Tauride; Glyndebourne Festival, 1951–54 as Don Ottavio and Idamante; Paris in 1953 as Tom Rakewell in the French premiere of The Rake's Progress; La Scala debut in 1953, and Vienna Staatsoper in 1954; Visited London's Festival Hall with the Vienna Company in 1954; Salzburg Festival, 1956–59 as Don Ottavio and Tamino; Chicago Lyric Opera in 1959 as Alfredo; Taught in Montreal after retirement from stage; Director of the Opéra de Quebec from 1971. *Recordings:* Die Zauberflöte; Die Entführung; Così fan tutte; Don Giovanni; Orphée et Eurydice; Idomeneo; Iphigénie en Tauride; Berlioz's Requiem. *Publications:* L'art du Bel Canto, 1995. *Address:* c/o San Francisco Conservatory of Music, 1201 Ortega Street, CA 94122, USA.

SIMONELLA, Liborio; Singer (Tenor); b. 10 Jan. 1933, Cordoba, Argentina. *Education:* Studied in Buenos Aires with Mario Melani and Angel Celega. *Career:* Debut: Teatro Col ón, Buenos Aires, as Roberto in Le Villi by Puccini, 1967; Sang Jason in the premiere of Medea by Guidi-Drei, 1973; Teatro Col ón, Rio de Janeiro and Santiago as Verdi's Alfredo and Duke of Mantua, Don José, Andrea Chenier, Hoffmann, Rodolfo and Cavaradossi; Season 1984 as Saint-Saëns's Samson at Santiago and Pierre in War and Peace at the Teatro Col ón; Other roles have included Canio in Pagliacci and Aegisthus in Elektra; Many concert engagements. *Address:* Teatro Col ón, Cerrito 618, 1010 Buenos Aires, Argentina.

SIMONETTI, Riccardo; Singer (Baritone); b. 10 Jan. 1970, Leigh, Lancashire, England. *Education:* Royal Northern College of Music, with Robert Alderson. *Career:* Sang Rodimarte in Scarlatti's Il Trionfo d'Onore at Liège, Trento, Caen and Brussels; English National Opera from 1996, notably as Bill in Mahagonny (debut role) and Papageno; Ping in Turandot at Nice, Albert in Werther for English Touring Opera, Britten's Demetrius for the Broomhill Trust and Belcore for Clonter Farm Opera; Season 1997 with Mozart's Count for English Touring Opera and a principal contract with ENO; Season 1998 with ENO in The Tales of Hoffmann and the premiere of Dr Ox's Experiment by Gavin Bryars; Concerts include the St Matthew Passion with the Liverpool Philharmonic Orchestra, Messiah under David Willcocks and concerts with the Liverpool Philharmonic Choir. *Honours:* Winner, Anne Ziegler/ Esso Award, 1993. *Address:* c/o IMG Artists, Lovell House, 616 Chiswick High Road, London W4 5RX, England.

SIMONOV, Yuri (Ivanovich); Conductor; b. 4 March 1941, Saratov, USSR. *Education:* Studied at the Leningrad Conservatory with Kramarov (viola) and Rabinovich (conducting). *Career:* Debut 1953, conducting school orchestra; Led several opera productions while a student; Principal Conductor of the Kislovodsk Philharmonic 1968–69; Assistant Conductor of the Leningrad Philharmonic 1968–69; Principal Conductor of the Bolshoi Theatre, Moscow, from 1970: Toured with Prince Igor to the Metropolitan Opera 1975; Premieres include Shchedrin's ballet Anna Karenina, 1972; Teacher at the Moscow Conservatory from 1975; Frequent Guest Conductor with British orchestras; Performances include: Das Rheingold, at Bolshoi Theatre, 1979; Eugen Onegin by Tchaikovsky, 1982 and La Traviata, 1986, Covent Garden; Mahler Festival in Paris with London Philharmonic Orchestra, 1989; The Queen of Spades, Bastille Opéra, Paris, 1993; Concert tours of Japan with NHK Orchestra, 1993–95; Der Ring des

Nibelungen, Budapest Opera House, 1995–98; Shostakovich Symphony No. 4, with BNO, 1996. *Recordings include:* Glinka, Ruslan and Lyudmila, opera with the Bolshoi; Anna Karenina, ballet with the Bolshoi; Wagner, excerpts and overtures; Mahler, Symphony No. 1, with RPO; Tchaikovsky, Romeo and Juliet and 1812 Overture; Prokofiev, Romeo and Juliet and Lieutenent Kijé. *Honours:* Winner, Accademia di Santa Cecilia Competition, Rome, 1968; Artist of Merit of the USSR 1983. *Address:* Allied Artists Agency, 42 Montpelier Square, London SW7 1JZ, England.

SIMPSON, Dudley (George); Composer, Conductor and Pianist; b. 4 Oct. 1922, Melbourne, Victoria, Australia; m. Jill Yvonne Bathurst, 8 Oct 1960, 1 s., 2 d. *Education:* Studied piano with Vera Porter, Victor Stephenson, Melbourne University; Orchestration with Elford Mack, Melbourne, Dr Gordon Jacob, England; Composition with John Ingram, Australia. *Career:* Debut: 1st and 2nd M D Borovansky Ballet, Royal Ballet, Covent Garden; Guest Conductor, Royal Ballet, Covent Garden, 1960–62; Principal Conductor at British and European major festivals including: Monte Carlo, Nice, Athens and Middle East, 1961–63; 2 World tours with Dame Margot Fonteyn and Rudolph Nureyev, 1962–64; Conducted Tokyo Philharmonic Orchestra, Ballet Festival, 1985; Conducted premiere of own work Class, Ballet at Covent Garden, 1986. *Compositions:* The Winter Play, ballet, Sadler's Wells Royal Ballet; Here We Come, ballet, transcription for Orchestra, Canadian National Ballet; Ballet, Class, Royal Ballet School; Marguerite and Armand for Fonteyn and Nureyev, transcription for Orchestra; The Pastoral Symphony; Numerous television themes and incidental music including Shakespeare Canon for BBC; A Trilogy of Psalms for Choir. *Honours:* Diploma of Music (Hons). *Address:* 6 Tristania Grove, Menai, New South Wales, 2234, Australia.

SIMPSON, Marietta; Singer (Mezzo-soprano); b. 1954, Philadelphia, USA. *Education:* Temple University and in New York State. *Career:* Sang in concert with the Atlanta Symphony Orchestra and in Dallas, Los Angeles, Cincinnati and Detroit; Virginia Opera, 1985 as Pat in the premiere of Harriet, a Woman Called Moses by Thea Musgrave; Glyndebourne Festival, 1986–87; As Maria in Porgy and Bess, also at Covent Garden in 1992; Sang Alto Rhapsody by Brahms at Carnegie Hall, 1988; Virgil Thomson's Four Saints in Three Acts at Houston, Edinburgh and San Diego, 1996. *Recordings:* Porgy and Bess; Mendelssohn's Elijah. *Address:* c/o Houston Opera, 510 Preston Avenue, Houston TX 77002, USA.

SIMS, Ezra; Composer; b. 16 Jan. 1928, Birmingham, Alabama, USA. *Education:* BA, Birmingham Southern College, 1947; BMus, Yale University School of Music, 1952; US Army Language School, 1953; MA, Mills College, 1956. *Career:* Music Director, New England Dinosaur Dance Theatre, 1968–74; Member, Theory Faculty, New England Conservatory, 1976–78; President, Dinosaur Annex Music Ensemble, 1977–81; Composer; Lecturer at Mozarteum, 1992–93. *Compositions include:* Twenty Years After, 1978; All Done From Memory, 1980; Ruminations, 1980; Phenomena, 1981; Sextet, 1981; Solo After Sextet, 1981; Quartet, 1982; Pictures for an Institution, 1983; String Quartet No. 4, 1984; Night Unto Night, 1984; The Conversions, 1985; Solo in Four Movements, 1987; Quintet, 1987; Flight, 1989; Night Piece, 1989; Concert Piece, 1990; Duo, 1992; Invocation, 1992; Stanzas, 1995; Duo, 1996; Kumo Sudare, 1999; String Quartet No. 5, 2001; If I told Him, 1996; Musing and Reminiscence, 2003. *Recordings include:* Sextet; String Quartet No. 2, 1962; Elegie–nach Rilke; Third Quartet; Quintet; Night Piece; Flight; Solo in Four Movements; Concert Piece; Come Away. *Publications:* Selected works, Frogpeak Music 1998; as I was saying..., Corpus Microtonole, 1987. *Contributions include:* Apologia pro Musica Sua, Jaarboch, 1992; Stichting Huyghens-Fokker; Reflections on This and That, in Perspectives of New Music, vol. 29 No. 1; Yet Another 72-Noter, in Computer Music Journal, vol. 12 No. 4. *Address:* Rosalie Calabrese Management. *E-mail:* rcmgt@yahoo.com. *Address:* 229 Hurley Street #2, Cambridge, MA 02141, USA. *E-mail:* ezrsims@aol.com.

SIMSON, Julie, BMusEd, MMus; American singer (mezzo-soprano) and academic; b. 13 Feb. 1956, Milwaukee, WI. *Education:* Western Michigan University, University of Illinois. *Career:* New York recital debut, Weill Recital Hall, Carnegie Hall 1989; radio appearance, The Listening Room, New York Times Radio 1989; Lyric Opera Cleveland debut as Minerva in The Return of Ulysses 1991; Opera Colorado debut as Emilia in Otello 1991; other opera appearances with Santa Fe Opera, Dallas Civic Opera, Opera Colorado, Houston Opera Association; appeared as soloist with Milwaukee, Des Moines, Missoula, Denver, Cheyenne symphonies; George Crumb Festival featuring Ancient Voices of Children, Prague, Czech Republic; solo recital at Prague Spring Festival 1994; sang Suzuki in Madama Butterfly at Colorado Opera Festival 1999; La Dama in Macbeth for Opera Colorado 1999; soloist in Mahler's 2nd Symphony with the Omaha Symphony Orchestra 1999; Assoc. Prof. of Voice, University of Colorado. *Recordings:* Horatio Parker's Hora Norissima; Mahler's 8th Symphony.

Honours: Mozart Prize, International Belvedere Competition, Vienna, 1985; Winner, East and West Artists International Competition for Carnegie Hall Debut; National 2nd Place Winner, NATS Artist Award. *Address:* University of Colorado-Boulder, College of Music, Campus Box 301, Boulder, CO 80309-0301, USA.

SINGER, Malcolm (John); Composer and Conductor; b. 13 July 1953, London, England; m. Sara Catherine Nathan, 15 July 1984. *Education:* Magdalene College, Cambridge; Studied with Nadia Boulanger, Paris and Gyorgy Ligeti, Hamburg. *Career:* Teacher, Yehudi Menuhin School; Department of PCS, Guildhall School of Music and Drama; Teacher of Composition, Guildhall School of Music and Drama and The Yehudi Menuhin School; Director of music, The Yehudi Menuhin School of Music, 1998–; mem, APC; British Academy of Composers and Songwriters. *Compositions:* Time Must Have a Stop for orchestra and piano solo, 1976; The Icarus Toccata for piano duet, 1979; A Singer's Complaint, 1979; Making Music for narrator and orchestra, 1983; Nonet for strings, 1984; Sonata for piano, 1986; Yetziah, Music for Dance, 1987; Piano Quartet, 1989; York, a cantata, 1990; Kaddish for a cappella choir, 1991; Honk, for Ugly Culture, 1992; A Hopeful Place, for Yehudi Menuhin's 80th Birthday, 1996; Dragons, 1998. *Publications:* Articles of self by R Rollin in Musical Quarterly and K Potter in Musical Times. *Contributions:* Composer. *Address:* 29 Goldsmith Avenue, London W3 6HR, England.

SINIMBERGHI, Gino; Singer (Tenor); b. 26 Aug. 1913, Rome, Italy. *Education:* Studied at the Academia di Sant Cecilia, Rome. *Career:* Sang at the Berlin Staatsoper, 1937–44; Italy, 1944–68, notably as Ismaele in Nabucco; Sang in the Italian premiere of Hindemith's Long Christmas Dinner and appeared in Milan, Venice and at the Caracalla Festival; Frankfurt 1960 in Monteverdi's Orfeo, RAI Italian Radio 1970, in Rossini's La Donna del Lago. *Recordings include:* Massenet's Thérèse; La Donna Del Lago, Donizetti Requiem; Nabucco.

SINYAVSKAYA, Tamara; Singer (Mezzo-soprano); b. 6 July 1943, Moscow, Russia. *Education:* Moscow Conservatory; Opera Studio of La Scala, 1973-4. *Career:* Debut: Bolshoi, Moscow, as Ratmir in Glinka's Ruslan and Lyudmila, 1965; Sang Ratmir at La Scala 1973 and made festival appearances at Wiesbaden and elsewhere on tour with the Bolshoi, 1987; Verona Arena 1987, as Konchakovna in Prince Igor; Seattle Opera 1990-91 as Erda in The Ring; Other roles have included Carmen, Princess in Dargomizsky's Rusalka, Ljubschi in The Tsar's Bride and Liubava in Sadko, both by Rimsky-Korsakov; Blanche in The Gambler and Prosia in Semyon Kotko, both by Prokofiev; Many concert engagements. *Recordings include:* Operas by Glinka, Tchaikovsky and Mussorgsky; Songs by Glazunov and Tchaikovsky. *Honours:* Winner, Competition at Sofia, 1968. *Address:* c/o Bolshoi Theatre, 103009 Moscow, Russia.

SIPPOLA, Una; Singer (Mezzo-soprano); b. 1959, Janakkala, Finland. *Education:* Sibelius Academy, Helsinki. *Career:* Debut: Helsinki, 1985 as Amneris in Aida; Savonlinna Festival from 1986; Freiburg Opera from 1989, notably as Jane Seymour in Anna Bolena, 1991–92; Season 1992 at Hagen as Lizzie Borden in Jack Beeson's opera; Deutsche Oper am Rhein from 1993, as Eboli in Don Carlos, Venus in Tannhäuser; Laura in La Gioconda and Brangaene and Kundry; Bayreuth Festival, 1995 as Venus; Dresden Staatsoper, 1996 and 1998 as Brangaene and Amneris; Deutsche Oper Berlin from 2000, as Ortrud and other dramatic repertory; Many concert appearances. *Recordings:* Rossini's Petite Messe. *Address:* Dresden State Opera, Theaterplatz 2, 01067 Dresden, Germany.

SIRKIA, Raimo; Singer (Tenor); b. 7 Feb. 1951, Helsinki, Finland. *Education:* Studied at the Sibelius Academy in Helsinki, 1977–80 and in Rome and London. *Career:* Has sung at the Savonlinna Festival from 1982, and Kiel Opera from 1983 as Tamino, Lionel in Martha, Pollione and Cavaradossi; Sang dramatic roles at Dortmund Opera from 1985 as Riccardo, Manrico, Otello, Alvaro, Walther, Parsifal, Don José, Bacchus, Huon in Oberon, Narraboth and Vladimir in Prince Igor; Guest appearances at the Deutsche Oper am Rhein and member since 1991, Dresden, Stuttgart, Braunschweig, Karlsruhe, Basle, Stockholm, Copenhagen, Bordeaux and the Deutsche Oper Berlin (as Manrico in 1989); Hanover, Essen, Hamburg (Calaf in 1992); Member of the Finnish National Opera at Helsinki from 1989 singing Edgardo and Alfredo there and at Tallinn in 1990; Sang at Savonlinna in 1990 as Radames and as Erik in Der fliegende Holländer; Sang Idomeneo at the Finlandia Hall, Helsinki in 1991; Has appeared as a guest soloist at many important opera houses throughout Europe; Role of Canio at the Royal Opera House in Stockholm followed by new production of Pagliacci in Tampere, Finland, 1996; Debut as Tannhäuser in the Savonlinna Opera Festival's new production in 1996 and as Siegmund in the same year; Siegfried in new production of Wagner's Ring at the Finnish National Opera in 1997; Sang Siegmund at Helsinki, 1998; Season 2000–01 as Macduff at the Deutsche Oper Berlin, Tristan at Darmstadt, Manrico and Otello for Finnish National Opera; Frequent

concert appearances. *Recordings:* Jää mun lähellein, 1984; Opera Arias, 1992; Amado mio, 1994; Juha, 1995; Symphony No. 8 Mahler, 1994; Der fliegender Holländer, video, 1989. *Address:* PO Box 176, SF 00251 Helsinki, Finland.

SISA, Hans; Singer (Bass); b. 1947, Linz, Austria; m. Sophia Larson. *Education:* Salzburg Mozarteum. *Career:* Appearances at the Theater am Gärtnerplatz, Munich, Bregenz Festival, Essen, Kiel and Lucca; Roles have included Verdi's Padre Guardiano, Fiesco, Ferrando and Sparafucile; Rossini's Basilio, Donizetti's Raimondo, Mozart's Count and King Henry in Lohengrin; Sang Nicolai's Falstaff at Basle, 1989, and Sarastro at Graz, 1995; Season 1999–2000 included Salome at Graz, Beethoven's 9th Symphony at Aachen, Freischütz at Savonlinna and the Landgraf in Tannhäuser at Baltimore, USA; Further engagements in Rheingold and Götterdämmerung at Graz, 2001; Other roles include Bellini's Oroveso, Berkley in Der Vampyr by Marschner and the Hermit in Der Freischütz; Many concert appearances, including Mahler's Das Klagende Lied, for Italian Radio. *Address:* c/o Graz Opera Vereinigte Buhnen, Kaiser Josef Platz 10, 8010 Graz, Austria.

SISMAN, Elaine (Rochelle); Musicologist; b. 20 Jan. 1952, New York City, USA; m. Martin Fridson, 14 June 1981, 1 s., 1 d. *Education:* AB, Cornell University, 1972; MFA, 1974, PhD, 1978, Princeton University. *Career:* Instructor, 1976–79, Assistant Professor, 1979–81, University of Michigan; National Endowment for The Humanities Fellowship, 1981–82; Assistant Professor, 1982–90, Associate Professor, 1990–94; Professor, Columbia University, New York, 1995–. *Publications:* Haydn and The Classical Variation, 1993; Mozart's Jupiter Symphony, 1993; Haydn and His World, 1997. *Contributions:* Haydn Studies, 1981; Small and Expanded Forms: Koch's Model and Haydn's Music, in Musical Quarterly, 1982; Haydn Kongress, Vienna, 1982, 1986; The Orchestra: Origins and Transformations, 1986; The New Harvard Dictionary of Music, 1986; Haydn's Theater Symphonies, Journal of the American Musicological Society, 1990; Brahms and the Variation Canon, 19th Century Music, 1990; Pathos and the Pathétique, Beethoven Forum, 1994; Genre, Gesture and Meaning in Mozart's Prague Symphony, 1997; After the Heroic Style, Beethoven Forum, 1997. *Address:* Columbia University, Department of Music, 611 Dodge Hall, New York, NY 10027, USA.

SITKOVETSKY, Dmitry; Violinist; b. 27 Sept. 1954, Baku, Ukraine; m. Susan Roberts 1983. *Education:* Moscow Central Music School, 1961–72; Moscow Conservatory, 1972–77; Artistic Diploma, Juilliard School, USA, 1977–79. *Career:* Debut: Berlin Philharmonic, 1980, Chicago Symphony, 1983, London Proms, 1986, New York Philharmonic, 1988; Music Director, Korsholm Music Festival, Vaasa, Finland, 1984; Guest Soloist at Salzburg, Edinburgh, Berlin, Vienna, Ansbach, Helsinki, Istanbul, Newport, Spoleto and Mostly Mozart Festivals, with Berlin, Munich, Royal London, and Rotterdam Philharmonics, Chicago, Cincinnati, Detroit, Toronto, Montreal, London, Vienna, Munich Radio, BBC, NHK and Tokyo Symphonies and Cleveland Orchestra, Orchestre de Paris and Orchestre de la Suisse Romande; Promenade Concerts London in 1989 with concertos by Beethoven and Tchaikovsky; Played the Elgar Concerto at the 1990 Proms, and Brahms in 1991; ASCAP, 1986–. *Compositions:* Transcription of Bach, Goldberg Variations for String Trio, 1984 and for String Orchestra, 1994. *Recordings include:* Grieg's Complete Sonatas for Violin and Piano with Bella Davidovich; Bach Sonatas and Partitas for Solo Violin, 1985; Mozart Violin Concerti with English Chamber Orchestra, 1986; Schubert Complete Piano Trios with G Oppitz and D Geringas, 1986; Brahms Complete Sonatas for Violin and Piano, 1987; Prokofiev Violin Concertos Nos 1 and 2 with London Symphony Orchestra under Colin Davis, 1988. *Honours:* 1st prize, Concertino Praha, 1966; 1st prize, International Fritz Kreisler Competition, Vienna, 1979; Avery Fisher Career Grant, NYC, 1983.

SITSKY, Larry; Composer, Pianist, Musicologist, Teacher and Broadcaster; b. 10 Sept. 1934, Tientsin, China; m. 8 Feb 1961, one s., one d. *Education:* Graduated, 1956, Postgraduate Studies, 1956–58, New South Wales State Conservatorium, Sydney, Australia; Studied with Egon Petri, San Francisco Conservatory of Music, USA, 1959–61; Higher Doctorate in Fine Arts, Australian National University, 1997. *Career:* First recital aged 11; Lived Australia, 1951–; Many recitals including contemporary Australian music, USA, 1959–61; Numerous commissions; Piano Teacher, Queensland State Conservatorium of Music, Guest Lecturer, Queensland University, 1961–65; Head, Keyboard Studies, 1966–78, Department Head, Composition, Electronic Music, 1978–81, Department Head, Composition, Musicology, 1981–, Canberra School of Music, ACT; External Examiner, Composition, Piano Performance, Australian Universities and Colleges of Advanced Education; Artistic Director, Bi-Centennial Recording Project; Director, Australian Contemporary Music Ensemble; Composer-in-Residence, University of Cincinnati, USA, 1989–90; Director, Conference Music and Musicians in Australian Culture 1930–1960, Sept 1993; Promotion to Reader, 1993; Granted Personal Chair, Australian National University, 1994. *Compositions:* Numerous including: The Jade Flute; The

Secret Doctrine: 7 Epigrams for percussion duo, 1995; Opera, The Golem, 1994; Signor Locatelli Visits Russia, for violin ensemble, 1995; Beowulf Sonata for double bass and piano, 1997; Sonatinetto for oboe and piano, 1997; Bone of My Bones, 5 love lyrics for voice and piano; Enochian, Trio No. 7 for 2 cellos and piano, 1999; Five Violin Concertos (1971–98); Symphony in Four Movements, 2000; Operas, Lenz, De Profundis, Fiery Tales; De Profundis (1982) and Three Scenes from Aboriginal Life (1988); Concertos for various instruments; Keyboard music. *Recordings:* Numerous for major record labels; The Golem, 3 CD set; Piano concerto; Chamber instrumental music. *Publications include:* Music of the 20th Century Avante Garde; Australian Piano Music of the 20th Century; The repressed Russian Avant-Garde 1900–1929, book; Busoni and the Piano, book; Editor, Complete piano music of Roy Agnew; Anton Rubinstein, book, 1998. *Address:* 29 Threlfall Street, Chifley, ACT 2606, Australia.

SITU, Gang; Composer; b. 6 Dec. 1954, Shanghai, China. *Education:* Shanghai Teachers' University, 1978; Master of music in Composition, 1988; Music and Arts Institute of San Francisco. *Career:* Instructor in Music Theory, Music Department, Shanghai Teachers' University, 1979–85; Music Director, Chinese Cultural Productions, 1990–; Composer-in-Residence, Alexander String Quartet, 1998–2000; BMI, American Composers Forum; National Association of Composers; The Society of Composers Inc. *Compositions:* Symphonic Suite, 1988; Circle Series for Dance, 1992–94; Double Concerto for Violin and Erhu, 1994; Common Ground, 1994; Songs From the Land, San Francisco Suite, 1997; String Quartet No. 1, 1998; Rondo–String Quartet No. 2, 2000; Strings Calligraphy, 2000; String Symphony, 2000. *Recordings:* Sunlight, 1994; Dynaities, 1996; Concerto for Violin, Erhu and Strings, 1998; Songs from the Land, 1998. *Honours:* Commissioning awards, Ross McKee Foundation, 1994; SF California Art Commission, 1996; Composers Fellowship, Californian Arts Council, 1995; Compoer-in-Residence, Meet the Composer, 1998. *Address:* 1286 Pacific Avenue, San Francisco, CA 94109, USA.

SIUKOLA, Heikki; Singer (Tenor); b. 20 March 1943, Finland. *Education:* Studied at the Sibelius Academy, Helsinki. *Career:* Sang in Opera at Tempere and Helsinki; Engaged at Wuppertal 1972–79; Krefeld 1980–83; Season 1989 as Erik at Oslo, Siegmund in Naples and Tristan at Basle and Nancy; Sang Tristan at Lyon 1990; Tannhäuser at Montpellier 1991; Other roles include, Andrea Chénier, Alfredo, Cavaradossi, Don Carlos, Pinkerton, Dick Johnson, and Hoffmann; Florestan in Fidelio, Lohengrin, Parsifal and Bacchus; Sang Samson for Palm Beach Opera, 1998; Sang Tristan at Strasbourg and Buenos Aires, 2000; Siegmund at the Vienna Staatsoper. *Address:* c/o Opéra et Concert, 1 rue Volney, F–75002 Paris, France.

SIXTA, Jozef; Composer; b. 12 May 1940, Jicin, Czechoslovakia. *Education:* Bratislava Conservatory, 1955–60, High School of Music, Bratislava, 1960–64; Postgraduate studies in Paris, 1971. *Career:* Lecturer at University of Music and Drama, Bratislava; mem, Slovak Music Union. *Compositions:* Symphony No. 1, 1964; String Quartet No. 1, 1965; Asynchronie, 1968; Noneto, 1970; Flutes Quartet 1972; Solo for piano, 1973; Recitativo for violin solo, 1974; Octeto, 1977; Piano Sonata, 1985. *Recordings:* Variations for 13 instruments, 1967; Asynchronie, 1968; Noneto, 1970; Punctum Contra Punctum, 1971; Flutes Quartet, 1972; Solo for piano, 1973; Octeto, 1977; Piano Sonata, 1985; String Quartet No.2, 1985; Music for four Players, 1988; Symphony No.2, 1991; Trio for 3 clarinets, 1992; Musica, for ensemble, 1994. *Honours:* Prague Spring Festival Composition Competition, 1966; Radio Tribune UNESCO, Paris, 1970; Haydn Festival Competition, Austria, 1987; Jan Leveslav Bella Prize, 1987 and 1990. *Address:* Riazanska 68, 83102 Bratislava, Slovakia.

SJÖBERG, Gitta-Maria; Singer (Soprano); b. 1957, Sweden. *Education:* Århus Conservatory and Opera Studio. *Career:* Debut: Sang Mimi in La Bohème at Århus, 1987; Appearances with Jutland Opera, Århus and Royal Opera Stockholm as Desdemona, Madama Butterfly and Donna Elvira; Season 1989-90 as Micaela in Carmen at Stockholm and Amelia in Simon Boccanegra at Malmö; Guest appearances at Umea as Amelia in Un Ballo in Maschera; Royal Opera Stockholm 1996, as Butterfly; Season 1999-2000 as Mimi and Butterfly at Bonn Opera, Emilia Marty in The Makropulos Case at Dusseldorf. *Address:* c/o Svenska Konsertbyram AB, Jungfrugatan 45, S–11444, Stockholm, Sweden.

SJÖBERG, Johan-Magnus (Göran); Organist, Cantor and Composer; b. 7 June 1953, Östra Grevie, Sweden; m. Cajsa Finnström, 4 June 1983, 1 s., 1 d. *Education:* Organist-Cantor, 1972; Music Pedagogue, 1975; Choir Pedagogue, College of Music, Malmö, 1981. *Career:* Music Director, Sankt Hans Church, Lund, 1974–; Performed at Poznán Spring Festival, 1989, Warsaw Autumn Festival, 1992, Festival for Contemporary Church Music, Sweden, 1993; mem, Swedish Composers' Society. *Compositions:* Face It for wind quintet and tape; Via Dolorosa for flute and tape; Windows for chamber orchestra and tape; String Quartet 1 (Reverse); Around for flute and choir; Choral works.

Recordings: Composer of: Windows, Basic Music; Ave Maria Stella and Ave Maria; Five; Reverse, 1995. *Honours:* Culture Award, Lund, 1988. *Address:* Flygelvägen 307, 224 72 Lund, Sweden.

SJÖHOLM, Monica; Singer (Soprano); b. 1945, Sweden. *Education:* Studied at the Stockholm Music High School. *Career:* Sang at Vastenda and with the Ensemble Sangens Makt, from 1972; Norrlandsoperan, Umea, from its foundation 1974, notably in L'Italiana in Algeri, as Donna Elvira, Rosina and Amelia (Un Ballo in Maschera); Other roles have included Alice Ford, Begbick in Weill's Mahagonny, Ragnhild in Den bergtagna by Ivan Hallströ m, Flora in The Medium, and in Fortunato by Ian MacQueen, 1993; Frequent concert appearances throughout Scandinavia. *Address:* c/o Norrlandsoperan, PO Box 260, S-901 08 Umea, Sweden.

SJÖSTEDT, Sten; Singer (Tenor); b. 1945, Malmö, Sweden. *Education:* Studied in Malmö, and at the Salzburg Mozarteum, 1966-69. *Career:* Debut: Trier Opera 1969, as Rodolfo in La Bohème; Malmö Opera 1969-74, notably in a revival of Dal Male il bene, by Abbatini; Stora Theatre, Gothenburg, from 1974; Guest appearances at San Diego (Ferrando, 1971), Oslo (as Massenet's des Grieux) and Århus (as Hoffmann); Other roles have included Tamino, Manrico, Riccardo (Un Ballo in Maschera), Lensky and Faust; Modern repertory has included the title role in The Voyage of Edgar Allan Poe, by Dominick Argento. *Recordings include:* Tintomara, by Werle (Philips). *Address:* c/o (Stora Theatre), Göteborgs Opera, Christina Nilssons Gatan, S-A11 04 Göteborg, Sweden.

SKALICKI, Wolfram; Stage Designer; b. 1938, Vienna, Austria; m. Amrei Skalicki. *Education:* Studied in Austria. *Career:* Stage designs for San Francisco Opera from 1962, The Rake's Progress, The Ring (1967–72), Aida, Lady Macbeth of Mtsensk, L'Africaine, Andrea Chénier and Salome; Collaborations with costume designer Amrei Skalicki at the Vienna Burgtheater, Volksoper and Staatsoper; Productions in Lyon, Munich, Toronto, Buenos Aires, Hamburg, Miami, Athens and Geneva; Operas have included Lulu, Boris Godunov, Tristan und Isolde, Death in Venice, Hérodiade and Giovanna d'Arco; Andrea Chénier at the Metropolitan, Boris at Pittsburgh, Falstaff for Canadian Opera, Ariadne at Los Angeles; The Queen of Spades in Santiago and Elektra for Seattle Opera; Exhibitions at Bayreuth, Vienna, Zürich, New York and San Francisco; Professor at the University for Music and the Performing Arts, Graz. *Address:* c/o San Francisco Opera, War Memorial House, Van Ness Avenue, San Francisco, CA 94102, USA.

SKARECKY, Jana (Milena); Composer and Teacher; b. 11 Nov. 1957, Prague, Czechoslovakia; 2 d. *Education:* BMus, Honours Composition, Wilfrid Laurier University, Ontario, Canada, 1980; ARCT, Piano Performance, Royal Conservatory of Music, Toronto, 1984; MMus, Composition, University of Sydney, Australia, 1987. *Career:* Composer; Teacher, piano and theory, Canada, USA, Australia, 1977–; Faculty, Piano Theory, Royal Conservatory of Music, Toronto, Canada; Faculty, Halton Waldorf School, Canada; Compositions performed in North America, Europe, Australia and Japan; mem, Canadian League of Composers; Association of Canadian Women Composers; Canadian Music Centre. *Compositions include:* Sea Window, brass quintet, 1983; 3 Movements on Bach Themes, trumpet and strings/trumpet and organ, 1984; Oresteia, solo double bass, 1986; Rose of Sharon, solo harp, 1985; Night Songs, 4 percussionists, 1986; The Sign of the Four, solo tenor recorder, 1986; Aquamarine, orchestra, 1986; Dayspring, mezzo-soprano, piano, 1987; Lullabies, voice, 1988; Flame of Roses, flute, cello, piano, 1989; The Living Wind, mezzo, flute, cello, harp, 1990; Consort Royal recorder quartet, 1990; Sonata for viola and piano, 1992; La Corona, 3 motets, 1993; Sinfonia Lauretta, string orchestra, 1994; Into the Centre of Our Heart, chamber ensemble, 1994; The Eye of the Phoenix for cello, 1995; Water, Fire, Air and Earth for piano, 1996; Streams for large orchestra, 1997; The Foundation Stone for piano, 1999; Green and Gold for soprano and piano, 2001; Song of Life, SATB choir, 2001; Planet Earth for soprano and piano, 2002; Numerous choral works. *Recordings:* Flame of Roses, on Spinners of Starlight CD produced by the Ardeleana Trio. *Publications include:* On Her Wings, 1993, solo organ; Love Is Come Again, SATB choir, 1995. *Address:* 2318 Bonner Road, Mississauga, Ontario L5J 2C6, Canada.

SKARENG, Per; Swedish classical guitarist; b. 28 June 1959, Gavle; m.; two d. *Career:* debut playing Concierto de Aranjuez, 1985; Swedish Radio Symphony; Stockholm Royal Philharmonic Orchestra, 1991; Norrkoping Symphony Orchestra, 1992; Estonia Symphony Orchestra, 1993; Gavleborgs Symphony Orchestra, 1993; Concierto para una Fiesta, 1984; Wigmore Hall, London, 1993; Toured Argentina, Cuba, Estonia and Switzerland; Concerts in Tallinn, Finland, with Pietersaari Symphony Orchestra; Macedonian Philharmonic Orchestra, Skopje; 8 recital programmes; Teacher, Music College, Vaasa, Finland; Senior Master, Royal College of Music, Stockholm; Guest lecturer, Music College in Stockholm, Oslo and Copenhagen; Artistic Director, International Guitar Festival, Galve. *Recordings:* El Colibri; Dag Wiren Little Serenade; CD with flautist Tobias Carron, 1995; CD with Tobias

Carron with South American and Spanish music, 1998. *Address:* c/o Svenska Konterybyran AB, Kerstin Hammarstrom, Executive Director, Jungfrugatan 45, 114 44 Stockholm, Sweden.

SKELTON, Stuart; Singer (Tenor); b. 1968, Australia; Studied in Australia, Cincinnati and San Francisco. *Career:* Debut: Alfredo for Rockdale Opera Company, Australia; Appearances with San Francisco Opera from 1996–, in Hamlet, Lohengrin, Carmen, Hoffman, Salome and Aida; Australian Opera debut 1993, in Die Meistersinger; Basilio and Don Curzio in Figaro for Western Opera Theater tour, 1995; Title role in Argento's The Aspern Papers for San Francisco Opera Center '96 Showcase production; Concerts include opera highlights with Louisville Symphony Orchestra and the Verdi Requiem with the Lubbock, Texas, Symphony Orchestra. *Honours:* Winner, Marianne Mathy Award and McDonald Aria Award, Australia. *Address:* c/o San Francisco Opera, War Memorial House, Van Ness Avenue, San Francisco, CA 94102, USA.

SKEMPTON, Howard; Composer, Accordionist and Music Publisher; b. 31 Oct. 1947, Chester, England. *Education:* Studied with Cornelius Cardew, 1960s. *Career:* Freelance Composer; Visiting Lecturer in Composition at the University of Adelaide, South Australia, 1991; Concerto for oboe and accordion premiered and toured by Camerata Roman of Sweden, 1997; Visiting Professor in Music at De Montfort University, 2000; mem, British Academy of Composers and Songwriters. *Compositions include:* Lento for orchestra, 1990; Concerto for hurdy gurdy and percussion, 1994; Gemini Dances for flute, clarinet, violin, cello, percussion and piano, 1994; Shiftwork for percussion quartet, 1994; Chamber Concerto, 1995; We Who With Songs, for chorus and organ, 1995; Winter Sunrise, string trio, 1996; Delicate, Ballet, 1996; The Flight of Song for chorus, 1996; Two Poems of Edward Thomas, for choir, 1996; Into My Heart an Air that Kills, for soprano, piano, 2 violins, viola and cello, 1996; Concerto for oboe and accordion, 1997; Clarinet Quintet, 1997; Hot Noon in Malabar, for soprano and piano trio, 1997; Ballade for saxophone quartet and strings, 1997; Concertante for violin and strings, 1998; Prelude for orchestra, 1999; The Voice of the Spirits, for choir, 1999; He Wishes for the Cloths of Heaven, for choir, 1999; Murallennium for choir and wind band, 2000; The Bridge of Fire, for choir, 2001; Sarabande for string orchestra, 2002; Rise up, my love, for choir, 2002; Emerson Songs for soprano and baritone, 2003; That Music Always Round Me for choir and orchestra, 2003; Magnificat and Nunc Dimittis (The Edinburgh Service) for treble voices and organ, 2003; Eternity's Sunrise for flute, clarinet, harp and string quartet, 2003; Numerous piano pieces, including Images (1989);. *Address:* c/o Repertoire Promotion Department, Oxford University Press, 70 Baker Street, London W1U 7DN, England. *E-mail:* repertoire.promotion.uk@oup.com.

SKETRIS, Paul; singer (bass); b. 2 June 1960, Sarnia, Canada. *Education:* Univ. of Toronto, and Freiburg. *Career:* sang at Frankfurt Opera, 1991–93, Magdeburg, 1993–2004, as Sarastro, Gremin, King Phillip, Hunding, Rocco, Daland, Mephisto, Mozart's Bartolo and Alfonso, Fafner and Henry, in Lohengrin; Premiere of Goldschmidt's Beatrice Cenci, 1994; Guest at Toronto, Vancouver, Hamilton and Japan (tour, Aida, 2003) opera houses and Aldeburgh Festival; Concerts include Beethoven's Ninth, Shostakovich's 14th Symphony, Bach's B minor Mass and Christmas Oratorio, Messiah, Mozart Requiem and Verdi Requiem; Canadian music features in his recital programmes. *Recordings:* Winterreise, 2000; Christmas music (Stille Nacht), 2003. *Address:* c/o Magdeburg Theatre, Universitätsplatz 13, Pf 1240, 39104 Magdeburg, Germany. *Website:* www.paulsketris.de.

SKINNER, John York, BMus, LRAM; Singer (counter-tenor); b. 5 March 1949, York, England; m. 1st Juanesse Adele Reeve 1970 (divorced); m. 2nd Janet Lesley Budden 1976; two d. *Education:* York Minster Song School, Colchester Institute, RAM, London. *Career:* debut, Kassel Opera, West Germany; broadcasts on BBC, WDR, NDR, ORTF and Italian radio; opera appearances at Royal Opera House Covent Garden, La Scala Milan, Scottish Opera, Festival Ottawa and English Music Theatre. *Recordings:* works of John Dowland with Consort of Musicke; Handel's Partenope; other Mediaeval, Renaissance and Baroque music. *Honours:* Hon. mem., Royal College of Music 1982; ARAM, 1984. *Address:* Principal, Bermuda School of Music, PO Box HM 3149, Hamilton HMNX, Bermuda.

SKOGLUND, Annika; Singer (Mezzo-Soprano); b. 5 Nov. 1960, Vanersborg, Alvsborg, Sweden. *Education:* Studied at Royal Academy of Music, Gothenburg and London. *Career:* Sang Cherubino at Drottningholm 1988, followed by Suzuki at the Royal Opera in Stockholm; Returned to Drottningholm as Ramiro in La Finta Giardiniera and made Italian debut at Venice as Isolier in Le Comte Ory; Further engagements as Cherubino at Oslo, Suzuki in Stockholm and the Countess in Maw's The Rising of the Moon at the 1990 Wexford Festival; Concert repertoire includes the Lieder eines Fahrenden Gesellen with Oregon Symphony; Songs of the Auvergne and Kindertotenlieder and Das Lied von der Erde.

Recordings include: Video of La Finta Giardiniera. *Current Management:* Nordic Artist AB. *Address:* Sveavagen 76, 113 59 Stockholm, Sweden.

SKOLOVSKY, Zadel; Concert Pianist; b. 17 July 1926, Vancouver, Canada; m. Alice Glass, 29 July 1947, divorced 1953. *Education:* Piano, Conducting, Violin, various teachers including last (and youngest) student, Leopold Godowsky; Graduate Diploma, Curtis Institute of Music, Philadelphia, USA. *Career:* Debut: Solo Recital as Winner, Naumburg Award, New York Town Hall; Orchestral with New York Philharmonic, Carnegie Hall; Solo appearances, most great orchestras world-wide including New York Philharmonic, Philadelphia, Chicago, San Francisco, Toronto, London Philharmonic, Royal Philharmonic, BBC Symphony, French National Orchestra, Lamoureux, Israel Philharmonic, under conductors including Monteux, Munch, Bernstein, Maazel, Leinsdorf, Kubelik, Kletzki; Appearances, Mexico, South America, many world capitals; Allied Arts Piano Series, Chicago; Aaron Richmond Celebrity Series, Boston; Eaton Series, Toronto; Stage and television; Teaching, Professor of Music, 1975–87, Professor Emeritus, 1987–, Indiana University. *Recordings:* Various performances on major record labels. *Current Management:* Self. *Address:* 240 East 79th Street, Apt 10-A, New York, NY 10021, USA.

SKOVHUS, Bo; Singer (baritone); b. 22 May 1962, Ikast, Denmark. *Education:* Århus Music Coll., Copenhagen Royal Acad., and in New York. *Career:* debut, Vienna Volksoper 1988, as Don Giovanni; many Lieder recitals in such centres as Edinburgh, Tanglewood, the Vienna Konzerthaus, Paris, Osaka, London and Amsterdam; appearances as Don Giovanni at the Vienna Staatsoper and Schonbrünn, Deutsche Oper Berlin, 1995, Edinburgh Festival and the Hamburg Opera; Wagner's Wolfram and Olivier in Capriccio at Vienna, Mozart's Count in Munich and at San Francisco, 1997, Opéra de Paris, Lustige Witwe, Danilo, 1997, and Don Giovanni, Guglielmo at the Ravenna Festival, Wozzeck at Hamburg, 1997–98, and concert of Mahler Lieder with the Israel Philharmonic, 1999; Covent Garden, 1997, as Guglielmo; concerts include Mahler's Lieder eines fahrenden Gesellen and Des Knaben Wunderhorn, Edinburgh 1995; sang at the Metropolitan in Fledermaus, Eisenstein, 1998, and Mozart's Count in 1999, Hindemith's Requiem with the Berlin Philharmonic, Mendelssohn's Walpurgisnacht at Salzburg, 1992, and Elijah in Munich; with Lieder recitals in Japan, Washington DC, New York, Milan, Vienna and Amsterdam, 1997–98; with the Vienna Staatsoper, 1997–2001, for Barbier in Schweigsame Frau by Strauss, Wolfram, Mozart's Count and Don Giovanni, Danilo in Die lustige Witwe (also in Paris, Palais Garnier, 1997) and Billy Budd; debut in Chicago with The Queen of Spades, 2000, and in Barcelona with Billy Budd, 2001; Billy Budd in original version of Britten's opera, Vienna, 2001; title role in Krenek's Jonny spielt auf, Vienna Staaatsoper, 2002; Kurwenal in Tristan at Glyndebourne, 2003. *Recordings include:* Fidelio under Harnoncourt; Carmina Burana under Mehta; Britten's War Requiem; Le Nozze di Figaro; Don Giovanni conducted by Mackerras; Don Giovanni conducted by Michael Halasz; Schoeck's Venus; Schwanengesang by Schubert; Schumann's Die Dichterliebe Liederkreis Op 24; Oberon; Zemlinsky's Lyrische Sinfonie, conducted by Claus Peter Flor; Zemlinsky's Lyrische Sinfonie, conducted by James Conlon; Wolf Eichendorff Lieder; Schubert, Die Schöne Müllerin; Berg's Wozzeck; Blackford's Mirror of Perfection; Lehar's Die lustige Witwe; Leoncavallo's I Pagliacci; Lortzing's Der Waffenschmied; Mahler's Das Lied von der Erde; Nielsen's Maskarade; Spohr's Faust; Strauss' Die Orchesterlieder; Arienalbum. *Honours:* Kammersänger, Austria, 1997. *Current Management:* Balmer & Dixon Management AG, Kreuzstrasse 82, 8032 Zürich, Switzerland. *Telephone:* (43) 244-8644. *Fax:* (43) 244-8649. *Website:* www.badix.ch.

SKRAM, Knut; Singer (Baritone); b. 18 Dec. 1937, Saebo, Norway. *Education:* Montana University and voice with George Buckbee; European studies with Paul Lohmann in Wiesbaden, Luigi Ricci in Rome and Kristian Riis in Copenhagen. *Career:* Oslo Opera from 1964 with debut as Amonasro in Aida; In 1967 won first prize in Munich Radio International Competition; Sang at Glyndebourne Festival, 1969–76, as Mozart's Guglielmo, Papageno and Figaro; Così fan tutte for French television in 1977; Sang at Aix-en-Provence, 1977–, in operas by Mozart and at Spoleto Festival in Italy from 1978; Concert appearances in Europe and America with regular broadcasts on television and radio in Scandinavia; Sang at Lyon in 1984 as Tchaikovsky's Eugene Onegin; Sang Jochanaan in Salome with the Berlin Staatsoper on tour to Japan in 1987, Amfortas, Amonasro and Kurwenal in Berlin, 1988–89 and appeared as Pizarro in Tel-Aviv and Buenos Aires in 1988; Bolshoi Opera debut in 1988 as Scarpia; Season 1989–90 sang in The Makropulos Case at the Deutsche Oper Berlin, Amfortas at the Spoleto Festival, Charleston, and Don Giovanni at Trieste; Sang Hans Sachs at Nice in 1992; Sang the Wanderer in Mike Ashman's production of Siegfried, Oslo, 1996; Season 1999–2000 as Scarpia at the Opéra-Comique, Paris, Creon in Oedipus Rex at Brussels.

Recordings include: Video from Glyndebourne Festival of Le nozze di Figaro in 1973; Many recitals of Norwegian Songs.

SKRIPKA, Sergei (Ivanovich); Conductor; b. 5 Oct. 1949, Kharkiv, Ukraine; m. Skripka Evgenija, 11 Oct 1975, 2 d. *Education:* Graduated as Chorusmaster, Kharkov Institute of Arts, 1972; Graduated in Conducting Opera and Symphony Orchestras from Moscow State Conservatoire (studied under Professor Leo Ginzburg), 1977; Master's Degree, 1979. *Career:* Debut: Zhukovsky Symphony Orchestra, 1975; First performance in the USSR of R Keiser's St Markus Passion with the Moscow Chamber Orchestra, 1982; Tour with the Zhukowsky Symphony Orchestra, 1991; Britten's War Requiem in Berlin, 1991; Mozart's Requiem and Beethoven's 9th Symphony, with the Russian State Symphony Orchestra of Cinematography, Frankfurt am Main, 1992; mem, Professional Society of Cinematography, 1988. *Recordings:* Cello Concertos by Glièr and Mosolov with S Sudzilovsky (cello), 1996; Russian Overture and Symphonies Nos 2 and 4 by Shebalin. *Honours:* Honourable Person in Russian Arts, 1993; Artistic Leader and Main Conductor of the Russian State Symphony Orchestra of Cinematography; Professor of the Russian Academy of Music (Gnessin's Institute), 1997; People's Artist of the Russian Federation, 1998. *Address:* ul Isakovskogo 12-1-208, 123181 Moscow, Russia.

SKRIVAN, Zvonimir; Conductor; b. 12 Aug. 1938, Prague, Czechoslovakia; m. 1964, 1 d. *Education:* Academy of Music Arts in Prague. *Career:* Debut: Il Barbiere di Siviglia, Olomouc, 1967; Albert Herring; Jakobin; Dalibor, Devil and Kate; Bartered Bride, Jenůfa; Aida; Rigoletto; La Traviata; Un Ballo in Maschera; Lucia di Lammermoor; Faust; La Gioconda; Idomeneo; Così fan tutte; Le nozze di Figaro; Fidelio; Other operas and ballets in the Moravian Theatre in Olomouc, 1967–97; also National Theatre, Prague; Collaboration with Moravian Philharmonia Orchestra, Olomouc, Simon Boccanegra, Suor Angelica, Gianni Schicchi and Orfeo ed Euridice; mem, Association of Music Artists; Society of Music Theatre. *Recordings:* The Bell by Donizetti, Czech television, and operas, arias and duets for Czech radio. *Honours:* The Prize of Oldrich Stibor, 1976, 1983; Prize of Prague Opera Festival for Lucia di Lammermoor, 1995, Idomeneo, 1997. *Address:* Dobnerova Str N 20, 77900 Olomouc, Czech Republic.

SKROWACZEWSKI, Stanislaw; Conductor and Composer; b. 3 Oct. 1923, Lwow, Poland (USA 1960–); m. Krystyna Jarosz, 6 Sept 1956, 2 s., 1 d. *Education:* Diploma, Philosophy, University of Lwow, 1945; Diplomas, Composition, Conducting, Lwow Academy of Music, 1945, Kraków Academy 1946; LHD, Hamline University 1963, Macalester College 1972, Univ. of Minnesota, 1979, USA. *Career:* Pianist 1928–, Composer 1931–, Violinist 1934–, Conductor 1939–, Guest Conductor, Europe, USA, Canada, South America, Japan, Australia, 1947–; Permanent Conductor, Music Director: Wroclaw Philharmonic 1946–47, Katowice National Philharmonic 1949–54, Kraków Philharmonic 1955–56, Warsaw National Philharmonic 1957–59; Minnesota Orchestra 1960–79; Principal Conductor, Musical Adviser, Hallé Orchestra, Manchester, United Kingdom, 1984–92; Musical Adviser, St Paul Chamber Orchestra, 1986–87; mem, Polish and American professional associations. *Compositions include:* 1st symphony and overture written and played (Lwow Philharmonic), aged 8; 4 symphonies, prelude and fugue for orchestra, 1948; Overture, 1947; Cantiques des Cantiques, 1951; String Quartet, 1953; Suite Symphonique, 1954; Music at Night, 1954; Ricercari Notturni, 1978; Concerti for clarinet and orchestra, 1980; Violin Concerto, 1985; Concerto for orchestra, 1985; Fanfare for orchestra, 1987; Chamber Concerto, 1992; Passacaglia Immaginaria, 1995; Musica à Quattro, 1998; Also music for films, theatre, songs. *Recordings:* Numerous including Schubert 5, 8 and 9 symphonies; Chopin music for piano and orchestra (Weissenberg); Lalo and Schumann cello concertos (Starker); Beethoven 5th and Brahms 2nd piano concertos (Bachauer); Ravel orchestral works (Minnesota Orchestra); Brahms, 4 Symphonies; Bruckner, all 11 Symphonies (Cannes Award, 2001); Shostakovich, No. 1, 5, 6 and 10 Symphonies; Stravinsky and Prokofiev, all ballets; Mahler, No. 4 Symphony; Berlioz, Fantastique; Beethoven overtures and incidental music. *Honours:* National prize, artistic achievement, Poland, 1953; 1st prize, St Cecilia International Concours for Conductors, Rome, 1956; Numerous awards, compositions, Poland, Belgium, USSR, USA; Honorary LHD, University of Minnesota; Order of Polnia Restituta, Commander and White Star, Poland, 1999. *Address:* PO Box 700, Wayzata, MN 55391, USA.

SKRZYPCZAK, Bettina, DMus; Polish composer, musicologist and music journalist; b. 25 Jan. 1962. *Education:* Poznań Acad. of Music, Basle Musikakademie Studio for Electronic Music. *Career:* Lecturer in Music History, Theory and Aesthetics of Music, Univ. of Lucerne, Switzerland 1995–, Prof. 2002–; Lecturer, Internationale Ferienkurse für Neue Musik, Darmstadt, Germany 2004. *Compositions include:* Sonata for two pianos 1985, What is Black, What is White 1987, Lob der Erde 1991, String Quartet 1993, 'SN 1993 J' 1995, Oboe Concerto 1996, Piano Concerto 1998, Mouvement 1999, Miroirs 2000, Vier Figuren 2001, String Quartet No. 4 2003, Lettres 2004. *Recordings include:* Portrait Bettina Skrzypczak with String Quartet No. 3 (DVD), Portrait Bettina Skrzypczak (including Scène, Miroirs, Toccata sospesa, 'SN 1993 J', Fantasie, Piano Concerto). *Honours:* awards at Zagreb Music Biennale competition for young composers 1988, Tadeusz Baird competition, Warsaw 1990, Mannheim Int. Competition for Women Composers 1994, Basle Förderpreis 1996, Riehen Kulturpreis 2004. *E-mail:* info@bettina-skrzypczak.com. *Website:* www.bettina-skrzypczak.com.

SKWORTSOW, Alexander; Violinist; b. 24 May 1944, Novosibirsk, Russia; m. 2 s., 1 d. *Education:* School for Musically Gifted Children, Novosibirsk; Masterclass, Leningrad Conservatory. *Career:* Debut: Novosibirsk Symphony Orchestra; Concertmaster: Leningrad Concert Orchestra; Primarius String Quartet, St Petersburg; First Concertmaster: Lubecker Symphony; Vancouver Symphony; Various orchestras throughout Western Europe; Soloist in Canada, USA, Germany and Western Europe. *Compositions:* Various cadenzas for violin concertos. *Recordings:* Yuri Boutsko trio, Holocaust commemorative CD, award winning; Musica with works by Liszt, Enescu and Paganini. *Contributions:* Das Orchester; Lubecker Nachrichten. *Honours:* Twice obtained first prize in National Music competition for USSR. *Current Management:* Starling Artist Management. *Address:* Augustinushof 130, 1216 LH Hilversum, Netherlands.

SLABBERT, Wicus; Singer (Baritone); b. 1941, Kroonstad, South Africa. *Education:* Studied at the University of Pretoria, BA, Fine Arts; With Josef Metternich in Germany. *Career:* Sang in German repertory at Düsseldorf from 1968 and Italian from 1973; Appearances at Essen, 1974–79 as Germont, Don Carlo, Rigoletto, Don Giovanni, Count Almaviva in Figaro, Scarpia, Jochanaan, Mandryka and Beckmesser; Staatsoper Kassel from 1979 notably as Macbeth, Iago, the Villains in Hoffmann and Dr Schön; Guest engagements at the Bregenz Festival from 1988 in Les Contes d'Hoffmann and Der fliegende Holländer, at Düsseldorf, Stuttgart, Theater am Gärtnerplatz Munich and Pretoria; Member of the Vienna Staatsoper since 1991 with performances as Boris in Lady Macbeth of Mtsensk and as Nabucco in 1992; Festival engagements at Edinburgh, Florence, Stockholm and Warsaw; Sang at Teatro Colón Buenos Aires in 1992 as Wagner's Dutchman, Alberich in the Ring and Tosca; Vienna Volksoper 1996, in Mona Lisa by Max von Schillings; Shostakovich's Boris in Bonn, 1998; Season 2000 as Falstaff, Nick Shadow and Gyges in Zemlinsky's Der König Kandaules, at the Veinna Volskoper; Dutchman at Dusseldorf. *Recordings include:* Bohni in Zemlinsky's Kleider Machen Leute. *Address:* c/o Staatsoper, 1010 Vienna, Austria.

SLADE, Julian (Penkivil); Author and Composer; b. 28 May 1930, London. *Education:* BA, Trinity College, Cambridge; Bristol Old Vic Theatre School, 1951. *Career:* Joined Bristol Old Vic Company as Musical Director, 1952; Wrote and composed, Christmas in King Street (with Dorothy Reynolds, James Cairncross), Bristol, 1952; Composed music for, Sheridan's The Duenna, Bristol, 1953; Transferred to Westminster Theatre, London, 1954; Wrote and composed, The Merry Gentleman (with Dorothy Reynolds), Bristol, 1953; Composed incidental music for, The Merchant of Venice, 1953; Wrote musical version, The Comedy of Errors for television, 1954 and for Arts Theatre, London, 1956; Wrote, Salad Days (with Dorothy Reynolds), Bristol, and Vaudeville, London, 1954, Duke of York's, 1976; Free As Air, Savoy, London, 1957; Hooray for Daisy!, Bristol, 1959; Lyric, Hammersmith, 1960; Follow That Girl, Vaudeville, London, 1960; Wildest Dreams, 1960; Vanity Fair (with Alan Pryce-Jones, Robin Miller), Queens Theatre, London, 1962; Nutmeg and Ginger, Cheltenham, 1963; Sixty Thousand Nights (with George Rowell), Bristol, 1966; The Pursuit of Love, Bristol, 1967; Composed music for songs in: As You Like It, Bristol, 1970; A Midsummer Night's Dream and Much Ado About Nothing, Regents Park, 1970; Adapted AA Milne's Winnie the Pooh, Phoenix Theatre, 1970, 1975; music and lyrics, Trelawny, Bristol, then London West End, 1972; Out of Bounds, 1973; Wrote, Now We are Sixty (with Gyles Brandreth), Arts Theatre, Cambridge, 1986–; Revival, Nutmeg and Ginger, New Orange Tree Theatre, Richmond, 1991; Revival, The Comedy of Errors, Grays Inn Hall, 1994; Revival, Salad Days, Vaudeville, London, 1996; revival of Follow that Girl, Theatre Museum, Covent Garden, 70th birthday concert, Theatre Museum, 2000; revival of Vanity Fair, Theatre Museum, 2001. *Honours:* Gold Badge of Merit, BASCA, 1987. *Address:* 86 Beaufort Street, London SW3 6BU, England.

SLAMA, František; Czech cellist and viola da gamba player; b. 19 Nov. 1923, Herálec; three s. two d. *Education:* Conservatory of Prague, Chamber of Instrumental Music with Václav Talich, Academy of Music and Dramatic Arts of Prague. *Career:* debut playing Schumann's Concerto A Minor (with Czech Philharmonic Orchestra), Rudolfinum Hall, Prague, 1952; Cellist in Talich's Czech Chamber Orchestra, 1946–48; Member, Czech Philharmonic Orchestra, 1951–; Soloist and Continuo Player of two of the first European ensembles of Ancient music, Pro Arte Antiqua and Ars Rediviva, 1951–; Ars Rediviva had 45 years' subscription concerts cycle of Baroque music at Rudolfinum Hall,

Prague (6 concerts annually; Repertoire of over 300 compositions of Czech and European Masters), festivals in Czechoslovakia, Germany, Spain, Italy, Austria, Sweden; Radio and television broadcasts and recordings with J. P. Rampal, M. André, O. Peter, A. Adorján. *Recordings:* Purcell's Phantasy Upon One Note, 1959; Musical Offering, 1969, radio, 1985; Brandenburg Concertos, 1965; J D Zelenka, Lamentationes, 1970; J. S. Bach's Concerto G Minor for Viola da gamba, 1981; C. P. E. Bach's Sonatas, 1994; Series on viola da gamba and Jordi Savall, for Czech Radio Prague, 1995. *Address:* Na Sumave 1, 150 00 Prague 5, Czech Republic.

SLATFORD, Rodney (Gerald Yorke); Musician (Double Bass) and Publisher; b. 18 July 1944, Cuffley, Hertfordshire, England. *Education:* Royal College of Music with Adrian Beers. *Career:* Principal Bass with Midland Sinfonia, the Academy of St Martin-in-the-Fields and English Chamber Orchestra until 1981; Edited and published 100 works for his own Yorke Edition, devoted to double bass literature; Founder member of Nash Ensemble and guest appearances with leading string quartets; Tours to Australia, New Zealand and The Far East; 1st Double Bass recital at Sydney Opera House; Lectures in USA; Professor in Residence at Kusatsu International Summer Academy in Japan, 1984; Teaching at the Toho Academy in Tokyo and at the Conservatoire in Peking; Professor at Royal College of Music, 1974–84; From 1984, Head of School of Strings at Royal Northern College of Music, Manchester; Fellow RNCM, 1987; Established teaching method for double bass, 1978; Founder of the Yorke Trust to promote the training of young bassists; Director and Founder, RNCM Junior Strings project, 1991; Chairman, European String Teachers Association, 1992; Regular Presenter of Radio 3, 1993. *Recordings include:* Rossini's Duetto in solo record with Academy of St Martin-in-the-Fields. *Publications:* The Bottom Line, 1985. *Contributions:* Woman's Hour; A Word in Edgeways; One Pair of Ears; Mainly for Pleasure, Radio 3; The Strad Magazine; New Grove Dictionary of Music and Musicians, 1980. *Address:* 31 Thornhill Square, London N1 1BQ, England.

SLATINARU, Maria; Singer (Soprano); b. 25 May 1938, Jassy, Romania. *Education:* Studied at the Bucharest Conservatory with Arta Florescu and Aurel Alexandrescu. *Career:* Debut: Bucharest in 1969 as Elisabeth de Valois; Appearances as guest at Mannheim, Stuttgart, Zürich, Wiesbaden and Düsseldorf; Sang at Basle and Florence in 1983 as Giorgetta in Il Tabarro, Strasbourg in 1984 as Elisabeth in Tannhäuser and has sung Tosca in San Francisco, Dallas in 1988 and elsewhere; Other roles include Verdi's Abigaille and Amelia in Simon Boccanegra, Leonore in Fidelio, Wagner's Sieglinde, Senta and Elsa, Santuzza and Puccini's Turandot, Minnie and Manon Lescaut.

SLATKIN, Leonard Edward; American conductor and pianist; b. 1 Sept. 1944, Los Angeles, CA; s. of Felix Slatkin and Eleanor Aller; m. Linda Hohenfeld 1986; one s. *Education:* Indiana Univ., Los Angeles City Coll., Juilliard School; studied violin, piano, viola, composition, conducting. *Career:* debut Carnegie Hall 1966; Founder, Music Dir and Conductor St Louis Symphony Youth Orchestra 1979–80, 1980–81; Asst Conductor Youth Symphony of New York, Carnegie Hall 1966, Juilliard Opera, Theater and Dance Dept 1967, St Louis Symphony Orchestra 1968–71, Assoc. Conductor 1971–74, Music Dir and Conductor 1979–96; Prin. Guest Conductor Minn. Orchestra 1974–, Summer Artistic Dir 1979–80; Music Dir New Orleans Philharmonic Symphony Orchestra 1977–78; Music Dir Nat. Symphony Orchestra, Washington DC 1996–2001; Prin. Conductor BBC Symphony Orchestra 2000–04; guest conductor with orchestras world-wide, including most major US orchestras, Montreal, Toronto, Vienna, Vienna State Opera, London Symphony, London Philharmonia, English Chamber, Concertgebouw, Royal Danish, Stockholm, Scottish Nat., NHK Tokyo, Israel, Berlin, Stuttgart Opera; festivals include Tanglewood, Blossom, Mann Music Center, Mostly Mozart and Saratoga. *Honours:* five hon. degrees; two Grammy Awards. *Address:* c/o BBC Symphony Orchestra, Maida Vale Studios, Delaware Road, London, W9 2LG, England (office). *Telephone:* (20) 7765-5751 (office).

SLÄTTEGAARD, Tordi; Singer (Tenor); b. 3 Aug. 1933, Liungbyholm, Småland, Sweden. *Education:* Royal Music Academy, Stockholm. *Career:* Debut: Royal Opera, Stockholm, 1963, as Alfredo in La Traviata; Drottningholm Festival, Sweden, from 1964, as Mozart's Ferrando, Belmonte and Tamino, and Silvio in Handel's Il Pastor Fido; Rossini's Almaviva at Oslo, 1996; Appearances at the Stockholm Royal Opera and as guest at Copenhagen, Edinburgh and elsewhere; Other roles have included Orontes in Handel's Alcina, Don Ottavio, Ernesto in Don Pasquale, the Duke of Mantua, Giasone in Cherubini's Médée, and Hoffmann; Stockholm 1976, as Boris in the Swedish premiere of Katya Kabanova by Janáček; Frequent concert appearances in Scandinavia. *Address:* c/o Royal Opera, PO Box 16094, s-10333 Stockholm, Sweden.

SLAVICKY, Milan; Czech composer, producer, writer on music and lecturer; b. 7 May 1947, Prague; m. Eva Hachova 1972; two s. *Education:* Charles Univ., Prague, Janáček Acad. of Music Arts, Brno.

Career: Sr Music Producer of Classics, Supraphon 1973–81; Producer of Electro-acoustic Music, Radio Prague 1981–82; freelance composer and producer 1982–90; Asst Prof., Film Faculty 1990–94, Composition 1994–97, Assoc. Prof. 1997–2001, Prof. 2002–, Academy of Music Arts, Prague; Asst Prof. 1990–97, Assoc. Prof. 1997–2001, Prof. 2002–, Musicology, Charles Univ.; lectures given throughout Europe and many papers presented at congresses; compositions performed widely at leading festivals and broadcast world-wide. *Compositions:* orchestral: Hommage à Saint-Exupéry, Terre des hommes, Porta coeli, Two chapters from the Revelation, Ich dien, Synergy' Concerto: Way of the Heart for violin, wind and percussion, Requiem; chamber: Musica lirica, Musica notturna, Brightening I–IV, Dialogues with the Silence string quartet; organ music and compositions for solo instruments; vocal: Stay with Us, Sweet Loving for soprano and ensemble, Media Vita for soprano and viola, Veni Sancte Spiritus for soprano and ensemble, Electro-acoustic: In Praise of Harpsichord, Variations on a Laser Ray, Brightening V or Prague Autumn, Adventus. *Recordings:* over 550 albums as producer for many labels. *Publications:* Interviews from the House of the Artists, Gideon Klein: A Fragment of Life and Work. *Honours:* Carl-Maria-von Weber Prize, Dresden 1976, 1979, Second Prize Competition from Czech Ministry of Culture 1980, Prize of Brasilia 1985, Czech Music Critics' Award 1992. *Address:* Lukesova 39, 142 00 Prague 4, Czech Republic. *E-mail:* milan.slavicky@iol.cz.

SLAVKOVA, Maria; Singer (Soprano); b. 1958, Tarnova, Bulgaria. *Career:* Sang at the National Opera, Sofia, from 1987; Mainz Opera from 1984 and Mannheim from 1990, as La Gioconda, Tosca, Senta, Leonore in Fidelio, Aida, Butterfly, Odabella in Attila and Margherita in Mefistofele; Guest appearances at Munich as Smetana's Marenka and Tokyo (Santuzza); Gelsenkirchen, 1995, as Leonore (also at Leipzig, 1996), Brunswick, 1994, as Elisabeth in Tannhäuser; Wagner's Sieglinde at Hamburg and Abigaille in Nabucco at Vienna; Venus and Elisabeth in Tannhäuser at Limoges and Toulon. *Address:* c/o Mannheim Opera, Mozartstr 9, 68161 Mannheim, Germany.

SLAWSON, A. Wayne; Composer and Professor of Music; b. 29 Dec. 1932, Detroit, Michigan, USA. *Education:* BA in Mathematics, 1955, MA in Music Composition, 1959, University of Michigan; PhD in Psychology, Harvard University, 1965. *Career:* Assistant Professor of Theory of Music, Yale School of Music, Connecticut, 1967–72; Associate Professor, 1972–84, Chair, Department of Music, 1972–78, Professor of Music, 1984–86, University of Pittsburgh, Pennsylvania; Professor of Music, 1986–, Chair Department of Music, 1996–, University of California, Davis. *Compositions:* Electronic music works: Wishful Thinking About Winter, 1966, Variations for 2 violins, 1977, Colors, 1981, Greetings, 1985, Quatrains Miniature, 1986, If These Two Tolled, computer music, 1990, Interpolations of Dance for string quartet, 1992, Grave Trunks for computer music and video tape, with Harvey Himelfarb, 1992, Warm Shades, an octet for singers and woodwinds, 1993, Match for orchestra, 1994; Dual II for computer synthesised, speech derived sound and sound poet, 1997; Autumn rounds for computer synthesised, speech derived sound, 1999. *Publications:* Sound Color, 1985; Rap soft for computer-synthesized speech-derived sound, 2000. *Contributions:* Book Reviewer for Journal of Music Theory, 1986. *Honours:* Fellow, American Council of Learned Societies, 1978–79; Outstanding Publication Award, Society for Music Theory. *Address:* c/o Music Department, University of California, Davis, CA 95616, USA.

SLEPKOVSKA, Denisa; Singer (Mezzo-soprano); b. 1965, Košice, Czechoslovakia. *Education:* Košice Conservatory. *Career:* Appearances with Slovak National Opera at Bratislava, with guest appearances in Greece, Austria, Germany, Edinburgh, Spain and Jerusalem; Concerts at Munich, Passau and Baden-Baden, 1992–95; Repertory includes Puccini's Suzuki, Mozart's Apollo and Cherubino, Verdi's Maddalena and Fenena; Nicklausse in Les Contes d'Hoffmann, Rossini's Rosina and Vlasta in Sárka by Fibich, Recordings include: Respighi's Bella dormente and Lucrezia. *Address:* Music International, 13 Ardilaun Street, London N5 2QR, England.

SLIMACEK, Jan; Composer; b. 31 July 1939, Kelc, Czechoslovakia; m. Marie Chvatikova 1964, two d. *Education:* Prague Conservatory. *Career:* debut, Symfonietta for Strings, Tape Recording Czech Radio; Music Director, Radio Plzeň, 1967–; Sonatina for strings, Northern Music Festival, Ontario, 1988, Vassa, 1992; Divertimento for flute and piano, Inter Music Festival, Brno, 1983, Graz Wien, 1993; Quattro Intermezzi per Orchestra Gera, 1983, Musical Festival Rostow Don, 1988; Concertino for accordion, electravox and orchestra gera, 1976, Nuremberg 1982, Bern, 1983; Dramatic Picture Szczecin, Weimar, 1979; Piano Quartet, Warsaw, 1977; Three Etudes for piano, Bristol, 1981; Professor of Music, Gymnasium Plzeň, 1993–; mem, Association of Musicians and Musicologists. *Compositions include:* Piano Quartet; Sonatina for strings; Three Etudes for piano; Dramatic Picture; Songs for children's choir and piano; Variations for strings and harpsichord. *Recordings include:* Quattro Intermezzi per orchestra; The Victory Overture for orchestra; Musica per orchestra; Three Miniatures for chamber orchestra; Music per ottoni. *Address:* Mohylová 109, Plzeň 312 06, Czech Republic.

SLONIMSKY, Sergey; Composer and Teacher; b. 12 Aug. 1932, Leningrad, Russia; m. 1958, 1 s. *Education:* Graduated, Composition with Professor Evlakhov, 1955, Piano with Professor Nilsen, 1956, Postgraduate, 1957–58, Leningrad (now St Petersburg) Conservatoire. *Career:* Teaching Faculty, music theory and composition, 1958–, Professor, 1976–, St Petersburg Conservatoire; Board, CIS Composers' Union; Board, St Petersburg Branch, CIS Composers' Union. *Compositions:* Wide variety of musical forms and genres including 10 symphonies, 1958–95; orchestral and vocal; Chamber works; Opera, ballet; Songs and choral pieces; Titles include: Carnival Overture, 1957; Concerto Buffa, chamber orchestra, 1966; Antiphones, string quartet, 1969; Virinea, opera, 1969; Icarus, ballet in 3 acts, 1973; Master and Margarita, chamber opera in 3 acts, 1970–85; Merry Songs, piccolo, flute and tuba, 1971; Sonata for Violoncello and Piano, 1986; Works performed widely; Opera Mary Stuart performed at 1986 Edinburgh Festival, USSR and abroad; Hamlet, opera, 1990–94; Cerch: dell'Inferno, secondo Dante, 1992; 24 Preludes and Fugues for Piano, 1994; Opera, Ivan the Terrible, 1994 (premiered at Samara, 1998); 24 Preludes and Fugues for piano, 1995; King Lear, opera after Shakespeare, 2001. *Recordings:* Numerous. *Publications:* Thesis, book, Symphonies of S Prokofiev; Many works published in Russia and abroad. *Honours:* Winner, M I Glinka State Prize, 1983; People's Artist of Russia, 1987. *Address:* St Petersburg Conservatoire of Music, Teatrainaya Ploshchad, St Petersburg, Russia.

SLORACH, Marie; Singer (Soprano); b. 8 May 1951, Glasgow, Scotland. *Education:* Royal Scottish Academy of Music and Drama. *Career:* Member of the Scottish Opera, 1974–81 with roles including Marzelline in Fidelio, Marenka in The Bartered Bride, Zerlina in Don Giovanni, Eva in Die Meistersinger, Tatiana in Eugene Onegin, Fiordiligi in Così fan tutte and Jenifer in The Midsummer Marriage; Sang at Wexford Festival in Wolf-Ferrari's I Gioelli della Madonna and Smetana's The Kiss; Sang with English National Opera as Lisa in The Queen of Spades and Donna Elvira in Don Giovanni, Glyndebourne Touring Opera as Mozart's Donna Anna and Electra and Amelia in Simon Boccanegra; Opera North in Carmen, Die Meistersinger, Katya Kabanova and Così fan tutte, Dorset Opera as Gabriella di Vergy and Giovanna d'Arco and Australian Opera in Sydney as Amelia; Sang Ellen Orford in a new production of Peter Grimes for Opera North in 1989; Concert engagements with the Hallé, Liverpool Philharmonic and Scottish National Orchestras, London Mozart Players and London Sinfonietta. *Address:* c/o Music International, 13 Ardilaun Road, Highbury, London, N5 2QR, England.

SLOVAK, Ladislav; Conductor; b. 10 Sept. 1919, Bratislava, Czecholsovakia. *Education:* Studied at the Bratislava Conservatory, then the Academy of Music with Vaclav Talich, 1949–53, and Leningrad with Yevgeni Mravinsky, 1954–55. *Career:* Music Producer of the Czech Broadcasting Company at Bratislava, 1946–61; Conducted the Symphony Orchestra of Radio Bratislava, 1955–61 and Slovak Philharmonic Orchestra, 1961–81; Tours of Germany, the United Kingdom and France; Tours with the Czech Philharmonic Orchestra to China, India, Japan, New Zealand and Russia in 1959 and the USA in 1967; Chief Conductor of the Prague Symphony Orchestra, 1972–75 and of the South Australia Symphony Orchestra at Adelaide in 1966 and 1972–73; Conducted the premieres of works by Alexander Moyzes, Eugen Suchon, Dezider Kardos and other Slovak composers; Conductor and Professor at the Academy of Music Bratislava. *Recordings include:* Tchaikovsky Symphonies with the Czech and Slovak Philharmonics; Shostakovich Symphonies Nos 2 and 9; Bartók Music for Strings, Percussion and Celesta; Prokofiev 5th Symphony; Music by Kubik, Ryba, Suchon, Cikker and Kardos; Shostakovich Complete Symphonies with the Symphony Orchestra of Radio Bratislava. *Address:* Banicka 3, 81104 Bratislava, Slovakia.

SLUYS, Jozef; organist; b. 22 Oct. 1936, Gaasbeek, Belgium; two s. one d. *Education:* Lemmens Inst., Malines, Royal Conservatoire of Music, Brussels. *Career:* Prof. of Organ, Lemmens Inst., Louvain –1987; Dir, Acad. of Music, Schaerbeek, Brussels 1968–95; organist, Cathedral of SS Michael and Gudule, Brussels; Artistic Dir, Cathedral Concert series and Brussels Int. Organ Week; founder, Dir, Historical Concerts, Church of Our Blessed Lady, Lombeek; recitalist; performed on radio and television, Belgium and abroad; appearances in many European countries; toured former Soviet Union 1987, USA, Zaire, New Zealand, South Africa; represented Belgium at first World Organ Festival, Cambridge, England. *Recordings:* On the Walcker organ in Riga, works of F. Mendelssohn 1987; Organ works of Belgian composers A. De Boeck, E. Tinel, J. N. Lemmens, J. Jongen, Flor Peeters; Chamber music of Marcel Dupré; J. S. Bach works on organs of Gottfried Silbermann; Romantic Music of Belgian Composers, works for organ (Van Bever, Brussels) viola, violin, piano and cello 1999. *Address:* Domstraat 8, 1602 Vlezenbeek, Belgium.

SMALLEY, Denis (Arthur); Composer; b. 16 May 1946, Nelson, New Zealand. *Education:* BMus, Dip Mus, University of Canterbury, 1967; BMus Honours, Victoria University of Wellington, 1969; Diplôme de Musique Electro-Acoustique et de Recherche Musicale, Paris Conservatoire, 1972; DPhil, University of York, England. *Career:* Head of Music, Wellington College, 1969–71; Northern Music Critic, The Guardian, 1972–75; Composition Fellow, 1975–76, Senior Lecturer, Music, 1976–94, University of East Anglia, Norwich, England; Professor of Music and Head of Department, City University, London, 1994. *Compositions:* Gradual, 1974; Pentes, 1974; Ouroboros, 1975; Pneuma, 1976; Darkness After Time's Colours, 1976; Chanson de Geste, 1978; The Pulses of Time, 1979; Word Within, 1981; Vortex, 1982; Tides, 1984; Clarinet Threads, 1985; O Vos Omnes, 1986; Wind Chimes, 1987; Piano Nets, 1990; Valley Flow, 1992; Névé, 1994; Empty Vessels, 1997; Base Metals, 2000; Ringing Down the Sun, 2002. *Recordings:* Gradual; Pentes; Chanson de Geste; The Pulses of Time; Pneuma; Vortex Tides; Clarinet Threads; Wind Chimes; Piano Nets; Valley Flow; Névé; Base Metals; Empty Vessels; Tides; Pentes. *Publications:* Spectro-Morphology and Structuring Processes, The Language of Electro-Acoustic Music, 1986; The Listening Imagination: Listening in the Electro-acoustic Era, 1992, 1996. *Contributions:* Does Acousmatic Music Exist?, in Musiques et Recherches, 1991; Spatial Experience in Electro-acoustic Music, in Musiques et Recherches, 1991; Defining Transformations, in Interface, 1993; Defining Timbre, Refining Timbre, in Contemporary Music Review, 1994; Spectromorphology: Explaining sound shapes, in Organised Sound, 1997; Établissement de cadres relationels pour l'analyse de la musique postschaefférienne in Ouïr, Écouter, Comprendre Apriles Schaeffer, 1999. *Honours:* Fylkingen Prize, 1975; 1st Prize, Bourges Electro-acoustic Awards, 1983; Special Prize, International Confederation of Electro-acoustic Music, 1983; Prix Ars Electronica, 1988. *Address:* Music Department, City University, Northampton Square, London EC 1V 0HB, England.

SMALLEY, Roger; Composer and Pianist; b. 26 July 1943, Swinton, Manchester, England. *Education:* Studied at the Royal College of Music with Fricker and White; Later study with Walter Goehr at Morley College and with Stockhausen in Cologne. *Career:* Composer-in-Residence at King's College Cambridge, 1967; Co-founded and directed a four-man group, Intermodulation, 1970, disbanded in 1976; Has specialised as pianist in the music of Stockhausen; Appointed to University of Western Australia in 1976 as teacher, composer and performer. *Compositions include:* Piano Pieces I–V, 1962–65; Septet for tenor, soprano and ensemble, 1963; Variations for strings, 1964; Gloria Tibi Trinitas l for orchestras, 1965; Missa Brevis, 1967; Missa Paraodia l for piano, 1967; The Song Of The Highest Tower for solo voices, chorus and orchestra, 1968; Transformation l for piano and ring modulator, 1969; Pulses for 5 x 4 players, 1969; Melody Study ll for 4–12 players, 1970; Beat Music for 4 electronic instruments and orchestra; Zeitenbenen for ensemble and four-track tape, 1973; Accord for 2 pianos, 1974–75; 6 Modular Pieces for 4 flutes, 1977; William Derrincourt, entertainment for baritone, male chorus and ensemble, 1977; String Quartet, 1979; Konzertstuck for violin and orchestra, 1980; Symphony, 1980–81; Movement for flute and piano, 1980; The Narrow Road to the Deep North, music theatre, 1983; Piano Concerto, 1985; Strung Out for 13 solo strings, 1988; Ceremony l for percussion quartet, 1987; Piano Trio, 1991; Poles Apart, for ensemble, 1992; The Southland for double chorus and Antipodean ensemble 1986; rev. 1993; Chimera for orchestra, 1994; Figures in a Landscape, for ensemble, 1994; Music for an Imaginary Ballet, for percussion, 1994; Close to the Edge, for orchestra, 1995. *Publications include:* Essays on Stockhausen, Debussy, Messiaen and Peter Maxwell Davies for Musical Times and Tempo. *Address:* c/o Music Department, University of Western Australia, Perth, Western Australia, Australia.

SMALLWOOD, Robert; Composer; b. 22 July 1958, Melbourne, Australia. *Education:* BMus, University of Melbourne, 1980; Accademia Chigiana, Siena, 1985; Study with Barry Conyngham and Nigel Butterley. *Career:* Freelance Composer; Musician-in-Residence, Orange City, 1987–90. *Compositions include:* Trio Sonatina for 2 clarinets and piano, 1976; Discovery for orchestra, 1979; Sunshine Disaster for choir and band, 1981; Reminiscences for clarinet and percussion 1982; Kyrie, 1984; Elements for speaker, children's chorus and band, 1985; Wake up my Soul for children's and adult choirs, and orchestra, 1987; Living Land, for chorus, children's choir and ensemble, 1988; Three Little Poems for speaker, for flute, clarinet and cello, 1980; Psalm 150 for soprano, chorus, strings, piano and organ, 1991; Three Greek Dances, for flute/piccolo, clarinet and string quartet, 1993. *Honours:* Twin Cities Church Musicians Competition, 1992. *Address:* c/o APRA, 1A Eden Street, Crows Nest, NSW 2065, Australia.

SMEDING, Marten; Singer (Tenor); b. 1960, Netherlands. *Career:* Appearances at Théâtre de la Monnaie, Brussels, in Salome, Khovanshchina, Parsifal and Otello, season 1999–2000; Holland Festival, 1996, in Enescu's Oedipe; Netherlands Opera from 1992, in Samson et Dalila,

Parsifal and The Carmelites; Strauss's Bacchus at Frankfurt and Gounod's Faust in Romania; Concerts include Evangelist in the Bach Passions, Lieder by Schubert and Schumann, and Janáček's Diary of One who Disappeared; Pompeo in Benvenuto Cellini with the Rotterdam Philharmonic Orchestra at the Festival Hall, London, 1999. *Honours:* Semi-finalist at 's-Hertogenbosch Singers' Competition, Netherlands.

SMEETS, Roger; Singer (Baritone); b. 1959, Maastricht, Netherlands. *Education:* Studied at the Maastricht Conservatory. *Career:* Has sung with Netherlands Opera from 1984, including the 1985 premiere of Wintercruise by Henkemans; Komische Oper Berlin as Don Giovanni, Eugene Onegin and Wagner's Dutchman; Opera Zuid in Kerkrade, Netherlands, from 1990, notably as Mozart's Figaro; Major roles in recent years with Netherlands Opera; Steuermann in Tristan at Amsterdam, 2001. *Address:* Netherlands Opera, Waterloodein 22, 1011 PG Amsterdam, Netherlands.

SMETANIN, Michael; Composer; b. 1 Oct. 1958, Sydney, Australia. *Education:* BM, Composition, New South Wales State Conservatorium of Music, 1981; Australian Broadcasting Corporation's orchestral summer schools, 1981 and 1982; Composition study with Louis Andriessen at Royal Conservatorium, The Hague. *Career:* Composer in Residence, Musica Viva, 1988. *Compositions:* Ensemble: Per Canonem, 1982, revised 1984, Lichtpunt, 1983, The Speed Of Sound, 1983, Ladder Of Escape, 1984, Track, 1985, Vault, 1986, Bellvue ll, 1987, Fylgir, 1989, Spray, 1990, Strange Attractions, 1991; Orchestral: After The First Circle, 1982, Black Snow, 1987, Zyerkala, Blitz, 1989; Women and Birds in Front of the Moon, 1991; Vocal: 3 Songs, 1981, The Skinless Kiss Of Angels, for mezzo, baritone and ensemble, 1992; Tubemakers, 1995; Adjacent Rooms, 1992; Children's music: Music for Children and Dancers, 1988; Instrumental and keyboard: Afstand, 1983, Sting, 1987, Stroke, 1988. *Recordings:* Works on CD; Ladder Of Escape; Spray; Sting. *Address:* c/o Australian Music Centre, PO Box N690, Grosvenor Street, Sydney 2000, Australia.

SMIETANA, Krzysztof, FGSM; Musician and Violinist; b. 11 Oct. 1956, Kraków, Poland. *Education:* Secondary High School of Music; Kraków Acad. of Music; ASS postgraduate course, Guildhall School of Music and Drama, London. *Career:* debut, 1974; appearances with major orchestras such as London Symphony Orchestra, Philharmonia, BBC Symphony Orchestra; performed at 1997 Proms Festival; numerous broadcasts for BBC Radio 3 and Polish National Radio; very active in chamber music; leader with orchestras such as Chamber Orchestra of Europe, London Symphonietta and London Symphony Orchestra; violinist in London Mozart Trio; Prof. of Violin at Guildhall School of Music and Drama. *Recordings:* Brahms – Sonatas for Violin and Piano, with Caroline Palmer; Panufnik – Violin Concerto, with London Musici; Fauré Violin Sonatas, with John Blakely, piano; Stravinsky – Violin Concerto, with Philharmonia, conducted by Robert Craft. *Honours:* Prizes at competitions: Thibaud, Paris; Kreisler, Vienna; Flesch, London; Brahms, Hamburg; Lipizer, Gorizia.

SMIRNOV, Dmitri Nikolayevich; Composer; b. 2 Nov. 1948, Minsk, USSR; m. Elena Firsova 1972; two c. *Education:* studied with Nikolai Sidelnikov, Edison Denisov, Yuri Kholopov at Moscow Conservatoire, 1967–72; studied with Philip Herschkowitz (privately). *Career:* Ed., Sovetsky Kompositor publishing house, 1973–80; freelance composer, 1980–; operas Tiriel and The Lamentations of Thel (after William Blake)(chamber) performed in Freiburg and Almeida Theatre, London; Symphony No. 1 The Seasons in Tanglewood, 1989; oratorio A Song of Liberty premiered in Leeds, 1993; Prof., Composer-in-Residence, Keele Univ., 1993–98; Oratorio Song of Songs premiered in Geneva, 1998; Visiting Fellow at Goldsmiths College of Music, London, 2002–. *Compositions include:* Five piano sonatas, 1967, 1980, 1992, 2000, 2001; three violin sonatas, 1969, 1979, 1997; two piano concerti, 1971, 1978; six string quartets, 1973, 1985, 1993 (two), 1994, 1998; two piano trio, 1977, 1992; three symphonies, 1980, 1982, 1995; three violin concerti, 1990, 1995, 1996; two cello concerti, 1992, 2001; Songs of Destiny, voice, organ, 1980; Six Poems by William Blake, voice, Organ; Dirge Canons, ensemble; Serenade, ensemble, 1981; Farewell Song, viola, harp; Fantasia, saxophone quartet; The Night Rhymes, voice, orchestra, 1982; Two Ricercares for strings, 1993; Tiriel, 1985; Partita, solo violin, 1985; Thel, 1986; Mozart Variations, orchestra; The Visions of Coleridge, voice, ensemble, 1987; The Songs of Love and Madness, voice, ensemble, 1988–92; Angels of William Blake, piano, 1988; Blake's Pictures, visionary ballet, ensemble, 1988–92; From Evening to Morning, mixed chorus, 1990; Trinity Music, clarinet, violin, piano, 1990; A Song of Liberty, 1991; Three Blake's Songs, voice, ensemble, 1991; Job's Studies, solo clarinet, 1991; Wonderful Stories, voice, ensemble, 1991; The Angels of Albion, piano, 1991; Diptich, organ, 1992; Orcades, solo flute, 1992; Piano Quintet, 1992; Ariel's Songs, voice, ensemble; Magic Lamb, voice, ensemble; The Bride in Her Grave, an opera, 1995; Between Scylla and Charybdis, for strings; Song of Songs for soprano, tenor, chorus and orchestra, 1997; MMass; Opus 111 for

clarinet, cello and piano; Twilight for voice and ensemble, 1998; Three Quarks for Muster Msrk, percussion; Portrait for wind ensemble; Shadows in Light for viola and harp, 1999; Well Tempered Piano, 2000 (completed); Saga fopr solo cello; Innocence of Experience for tape, 2001; Metaplasms I and II for Piano; The Stony Path for voice, cello and piano, 2002; Triple Concerto No.2 fopr violin, harp and double-bass with orchestra; Dream Journey for voice, flute and piano, 2003. *Articles:* On Webern, Boulez, Ligeti, Ferneyhow, Birtwhistle, Shostakovich, Denisov, Schnittke, Gubaidulina etc.. *Publications:* The Book on Philip Herschkowitz: A Geometer of Sound Crystals (in English), Verlag Ernst Kuhn, Berlin, 2003. *Honours:* First Prize for Solo for Harp, Maastricht, 1976. *Current Management:* Boosey & Hawkes PLC, 295 Regent Street, London, W1B 2JH, England. *Telephone:* (20) 7299-1919. *Fax:* (20) 7299-1991. *E-mail:* dmitrismirnov@ntlworld.com (home).

SMIRNOV, Oleg; Cellist; b. 1950, Moscow, Russia. *Education:* Studied at the Moscow Conservatoire with Professor Kosolapova. *Career:* Co-founder, Amisted Quartet, 1973 (now Tchaikovsky Quartet); Many concerts in Russia with a repertoire including works by: Haydn, Mozart, Beethoven, Schubert, Brahms, Tchaikovsky, Borodin, Prokofiev, Shostakovich, Bart ók, Barber, Bucchi, Golovin, Tikhomirov; Recent concert tours to: Mexico, Italy and Germany. *Recordings include:* Recitals for the US Russian Company Arts and Electronics. *Honours:* Prizewinner at the Béla Bart ók Festival and the Bucchi Competition. *Address:* c/o Sonata (Tchaikovsky Quartet), 11 Northpark Street, Glasgow G20 7AA, Scotland.

SMIT, Henk; Singer (Bass-baritone); b. 1937, Netherlands. *Education:* Toronto and Amsterdam Conservatories. *Career:* Sang at Netherlands Opera from 1963 as Puccini's Lescaut, Pistol in Falstaff, Rossini's Bartolo and Don Magnifico, Verdi's Ramphis, Zaccaria and Simon Boccanegra; Pizarro, the Dutchman, Speaker in Die Zauberflöte and the Man in Schoenberg's Die glückliche Hand; Premiere of Otto Ketting's Ithaka, 1986; Tel-Aviv, 1984, as Tiresias in Oedipus Rex, Paris Opéra, 1985, as Varlaam in Boris Godunov, Amsterdam, 1986, in Zemlinsky's Der Kreidekreis; Sang Falstaff at Enschede, 1990, and Wagner's Klingsor at Montpellier, 1995; Concerts throughout Europe and the USA; Season 1998 as Dikoy in Katya Kabanova at Salzburg and Alberich in Siegfried and Götterdämmerung at Amsterdam. *Address:* c/o Netherlands Opera, Waterlooplein 22, 1011 Amsterdam, Netherlands.

SMITH, Carol; Singer (Soprano); b. 1960, Huddersfield, England. *Education:* Guildhall School and National Opera Studio. *Career:* Appearances at Glyndebourne in Albert Herring and L'Enfant et les Sortilèges; Melissa in Handel's Amadigi for Dublin Opera Theatre at Prague, Paris and Warsaw; Handel's Solomon at the Prague Spring Festival and Tamerlano at Melbourne and Lisbon; Recitals include Carnegie Hall and the Aldeburgh Festival; Concerts with the Philharmonia, London Mozart Players, Hallé Orchestra and Berlin Symphony Orchestra; Mozart's C minor Mass at Tenerife and Henze's Der Prinz von Homburg (as Natalie) for the BBC; Season 1999 with Haydn's Seasons for City of London Sinfonia and Beethoven's 9th for Northern Sinfonia. *Recordings include:* Rossini's Ricciardo e Zoraide. *Honours:* Concert Artists Guild Award, New York.

SMITH, Catriona; Singer (Soprano); b. 1963, Scotland. *Education:* Studied at the Royal Scottish Academy and the University of Toronto, Opera Division. *Career:* Sang Britten's Lucretia and Miss Wordsworth at the Banff Summer Arts Festival in 1988, Cathleen in Riders to the Sea by Vaughan Williams at Toronto and Pamina for British Youth Opera; Wigmore Hall recital debut in 1988; Sang at Kent Opera as Juno in The Return of Ulysses; Festival engagements include Aldeburgh in Goehr's Triptych and English Bach Festival in Idomeneo; Sang Clorinda in La Cenerentola at Covent Garden in 1991 and engaged at the Stuttgart Staatsoper, 1991–95; Other roles include Mozart's Countess, Rossini's Berta, Dido, Frasquita, Susanna and Barbarina in Le nozze di Figaro; Roles in Stuttgart include Pamina, Gilda, Nayad, Sophie in Der Rosenkavalier, Erénoira (world premiere) and Zerlina; Madeline in Debussy's Fall of the House of Usher, 1996; Morgana in Alcina at Stuttgart, 1998; Season 2000–01 as Offenbach's Olympia, at Stuttgart, and Norina in Donizett's I Pazzi per progetto. *Honours:* Winner, Maggie Teyte Competition, 1987. *Address:* c/o Stuttgart Staatsoper, Oberer Schlossgarten 6, 7000 Stuttgart, Germany.

SMITH, Craig; Singer (Baritone); b. 1960, England. *Education:* Studied at the Royal Northern College of Music, with Nicholas Powell. *Career:* Roles at the RNCM included Sharpless, Pandolfe in Cendrillon, Zurga in Les Pêcheurs de Perles and Lionel in The Maid of Orleans by Tchaikovsky; Cecil in Jonathan Miller's production of Maria Stuarda at Buxton and Smirnov in Walton's The Bear, at Los Angeles; Zürich Opera from 1995, as Morales in Carmen, Paris in Roméo et Juliette and the Wig Maker in Ariadne auf Naxos; Other roles include Nabucco (Bad Hersfeld, 1996) and Sharpless, with the Royal Liverpool Philharmonic; Concert repertory includes CPE Bach's Magnificat, Rossini's Petite

Messe Solennelle at Winchester Cathedral, L'Enfance du Christ at the Queen Elizabeth Hall, London, Carmina Burana at the Royal Concert Hall, Glasgow, and in Terra Pax by Frank Martin, at Schaffhausen and Ravensburg. *Honours:* Peter Moores Foundation and Robert Stanley Ford Scholarships. *Address:* Portland Wallis Artists' Management, 50 Great Portland Street, London W1N 5AH, England.

SMITH, Daniel W., BM, MA; bassoon player; b. 11 Sept. 1939, New York, NY, USA; m. Judith Smith 1961; one s. one d. *Education:* Manhattan School of Music, Columbia University, Mannes College of Music. *Career:* debut at Carnegie Recital Hall, New York; European debut, Wigmore Hall, London; Soloist on recordings and in concert with English Chamber Orchestra, I Solisti di Zagreb, Royal Philharmonic Orchestra, Orchestra da Camera di Santa Cecilia, New York Virtuosi Chamber Symphony, Santa Cruz Symphony, Rome Festival Orchestra, Florida Chamber Symphony, New York String Ensemble, AIH Roma Orchestra; Recitals: BBC Concert Hall, London; Carnegie Recital Hall, New York; Wigmore Hall, London; Merkin Concert Hall, New York; Bruno Walter Auditorium, New York; Diligentia Hall, The Hague; Atalier, Belgium; Distinguished Artists Series, Long Island, New York; B'nai Brith Festival, Purcell Room, London; Premiered Contrabassoon Concerto of Gunther Schuller with Santa Cruz Symphony. *Recordings:* Vols 1–6 (37 concerti), Antonio Vivaldi with English Chamber Orchestra and I Solisti di Zagreb; 3 Bassoon Concertos with English Chamber Orchestra; Bassoon Bon-Bons with Royal Philharmonic Orchestra; English Music for Bassoon and Piano with pianist Roger Vignoles; Vols 1 and 2, 18th Century Bassoon concerti with Ravina Chamber Ensemble; Vivaldi Concerti with Ravina Chamber Ensemble; Music for Bassoon and String Quartet with Coull String Quartet; 5 Bassoon Concertos with English Chamber Orchestra.

SMITH, Jennifer; singer (soprano) and academic; *Professor of French Mélodie and German Lied, Royal College of Music;* b. 13 July 1945, Lisbon, Portugal; 1 s., 1 d. *Education:* Lisbon Conservatory and French Lycé, Lisbon; Privately with Winifred Radford, London; Pierre Bernac, London and Paris; Hans Keller, London. *Career:* Debut: Sang Jephtha, Carissimi, Lisbon, 1966; Sang in Europe before moving to England, 1971; Operatic roles have included Countess Almaviva for Welsh National, Scottish and Kent Operas; Gluck's Orfeo at the Wexford Festival; Rameau's Les Boréades and Hippolyte et Aricie at Aix-en-Provence; L'Incoronazione di Poppea conducted by Leonhardt; Aminta in Il Re Pastore, Lisbon; Cybelle in Lully's Atys at the Opéra-Comique Paris and in New York; Electra in Mozart's Idomeneo, Lisbon, 1995; Praskovia Ossipovna in Shostakovich The Nose, Lausanne; Foresta's Wife and Screech Owl in Janáček The Cunning Little Vixan, ROH, debut 2002; Concert repertoire includes works by Bach, Handel, Poulenc, Purcell, Britten and Berlioz (Les Nuits d'Eté); Appearances with the English Chamber Orchestra, London Bach Orchestra, the English Concert, Steinitz Bach Players and the Orchestra of the Age of Enlightenment; Conductors include Rattle, Willcocks, Leppard, Pinnock, Gardiner, Boulez, Mackerras and Kempe; Tour of Europe with the B Minor Mass, conducted by Frans Brueggen; Song recitals in Portugal, France, Germany, Switzerland, Belgium and England; Television appearances include Scarlatti's Salve Regina with George Malcolm, Handel's Judas Maccabaeus conducted by Norrington and Purcell's Come, Ye Sons of Art Away and Tony Palmer's film of Purcell; Sang the Queen of Night (Mozart Experience, London) conducted by Norrington, QEH 1989; Rameau at Versailles (Flore and Nais) with the English Bach Festival, 1989; Season 1992 as Music in Monteverdi's Orfeo at ENO, Iphigénie en Tauride with the English Bach Festival at Covent Garden and in Conti's Don Chisciotte at Innsbruck; Sang the Queen of Night with Hamilton Opera, 1996; Title Role in the first performance since 1744 of Artaserse by Terradellas, Barcelona, 1998; mem, Royal Society of Musicians. *Recordings:* Bach Mass in B Minor, Magnificat/Corboz, Cantata 208; Carissimi Jephté; Falla Retablo de Maese Pedro and Psyche/Rattle; Gabrieli Sacrae Symphoniae; Handel Hercules and L'Allegro/Gardiner, Il Trionfo del Tempo, Silete Venti/Pinnock, Messiah, Amadigi; Haydn Mariazeller Mass and Little Organ Mass/Guest; Lully Dies Irae, Miserere and Te Deum/Paillard; Rameau's Nais/McGegan, Castor et Pollux/Farncombe and Les Boréades/Gardiner; Purcell King Arthur, Indian Queen and Fairy Queen/Gardiner, Come Ye Sons of Art/Pinnock; Vivaldi Gloria and Kyrie/Corboz, Beatus Vir and Dixit Dominus/Cleobury; Schubert Lieder; Platée (Rameau), Titon et l'Aurore (Mondonville) Alycone (Marais) Il Trionfo del Tempo (Handel), La Resurrezione (Handel), all with Marc Minkowski; Xerxes (Handel) with McGegan; Orphée aux enfers (Offenbach), with Minkowski; French Cantatas; Saudade, amor e morte, with Manuel Morais; Ottone (Handel) with Robert King; King Alfred (Arne); Chants de L'âme (Greif) with the composer at the piano. *Current Management:* Helen Sykes Artists Management, 100 Felsham Road, Putney, London SW15 1DQ, England. *Address:* 3 Gumleigh Road, London W5 4UX, England.

SMITH, Lawrence (Leighton); Conductor and Pianist; b. 8 April 1936, Portland, Oregon, USA; m. (1) 2 s., (2) Kathleen Dale, 4 June 1976, 1 d.,

1 step-s., 1 step-d. *Education:* BM, Music, Mannes College of Music, New York, 1959; Studied piano with Ariel Rubstein, Portland and Leonard Shure, New York. *Career:* Teacher at Mannes College of Music, 1959–62, University of Texas, 1962–63, Boston University, 1963–64, Curtis Institute of Music, 1968–69 and California Institute of The Arts, 1970–72; Professional debut as pianist in 1962; Assistant to Erich Leinsdorf, Berkshire Music Center, Tanglewood, Massachusetts, 1962–64; Assistant Conductor with Metropolitan Opera, New York, 1964–67; Music Director with Westchester Symphony Orchestra, New York, 1967–69; Principal Guest Conductor with Phoenix Symphony Orchestra, Arizona, 1971–73; Music Director with Austin Symphony Orchestra, Texas, 1972–73 and Oregon Symphony Orchestra, Portland, 1973–80; Artistic Adviser, Principal Guest Conductor, North Carolina Symphony Orchestra, Raleigh, 1980–81; Music Director, San Antonio Symphony Orchestra, 1980–85 and Louisville Orchestra, 1983–, and at Music Academy of the West, Santa Barbara, California, 1985–; Guest Conductor with various orchestras in the USA and abroad; mem, American Federation of Musicians. *Recordings:* Various. *Honours:* 1st Prize, Dimitri Mitropoulos International Conducting Competition, New York, 1964. *Address:* c/o Louisville Orchestra, 609 West Main Street, Louisville, KY 40202, USA.

SMITH, Malcolm; Singer (Bass); b. 22 June 1933, Rockville Center, New York; M. Margaret Younger. *Education:* Oberlin Conservatory and Indiana University, Bloomington. *Career:* Debut: Inquisitor in Prokofiev's The Fiery Angel, New York City Opera, 1965; Sang at the City Opera until 1970, New York Metropolitan from 1975; Guest appearances at Chicago, Seattle, Houston, Miami and San Francisco; Deutsche Oper am Rhein, Dusseldorf, from 1972, with further engagements in Milan, Vienna and throughout Germany; Season 1985-86 as Ramphis in Aida at Cincinnati and Fafner in Das Rheingold at Turin; Paris Théâtre du Châtelet, as Mephisto in Schumann's Faust and Salzburg Festival 1986 in the premiere of Die schwarze Maske by Penderecki; Dusseldorf 1991, as Drago in Schumann's Genoveva; Season 2000-2001 as Debussy's Arkel at Cincinnati, the Grand Inquisitor (Don Carlos) and Mussorgsky's Pimen at Dusseldorf; Further roles in operas by Beethoven, Rossini, Mussorgsky and Wagner (King Marke at Trieste, 1969). *Recordings include:* Tristan und Isolde, Das Rheingold, War and Peace, Oedipus Rex, Mahler's 8th Symphony. *Address:* c/o Deutsche Oper am Rhein, Heinrich Heine Allee 16a, D-40213 Dusseldorf, Germany.

SMITH, Maureen (Felicity); Violinist; b. Leeds, England; m. Geoffrey Rivlin, 27 Aug 1974, 2 d. *Education:* Royal Manchester College of Music; Indiana University, USA. *Career:* Debut: Royal Festival Hall in 1961; Soloist with most leading British orchestras; Debut at London Promenade Concerts in 1965; Regular broadcasts for BBC Radio 3 and numerous television appearances; Appearances at major festivals including Aldeburgh and Leeds, Brighton, Cheltenham, English Bach and Three Choirs; Professor of Violin, Royal College of Music, 1997, appointed Deputy Head of Strings, 2002; mem, European String Teachers Association; Hon. ARAM, 1996. *Recordings:* Mendelssohn Violin Concerto; Milhaud Duos; Brahms and Mahler Piano Quartets; Mozart and Haydn violin and viola duos. *Honours:* BBC Violin Competition, 1965; Gulbenkian Foundation Fellowship, 1966; Leverhulme Fellowship, 1966. *Address:* 8 Heath Close, London, NW11 7DX, England. *E-mail:* riv@dircon.co.uk.

SMITH, Richard Langham; Reader in Music; b. 10 Sept. 1947, London, England. *Education:* BA, Hons, Music, University of York; Further study with Edward Lockspeiser and at Amsterdam Conservatory. *Career:* Harpsichordist; Musicologist, specialising in French Music; Lecturer, University of Lancaster until 1979, City University in London, until 1995; University of Exeter, 1995–; Visiting Professor of Music, Gresham College, 2003–04. *Compositions:* Reconstruction of Debussy's unpublished opera, Rodrigue et Chimène premiered at Opéra de Lyon in 1993. *Publications:* Translator and Editor, Debussy on Music, 1977; With R Nichols: Debussy, Pelléas et Mélisande, Cambridge Opera Handbook, 1989; Debussy Studies, 1997; Editor Debussy: Rodrigue et Chimène, Durand, 2003. *Contributions:* Numerous articles and reviews on Debussy in journals including Music and Letters, Times Literary Supplement, 19th Century Music, Cahiers Debussy, Musical Times, The Listener, Early Music, The Strad, Frequent Broadcaster, BBC Radio 2, 3 and 4, and France Musique. *Honours:* Chevalier de L'ordre des arts et des lettres. *Address:* Higher Summerlands, 4 Longlands, Dawlish, Devon EX7 9NE, England.

SMITH, Robert Dean; Singer (Tenor); b. 1965, Kansas, USA. *Education:* Pittsburgh State University and Juilliard, New York. *Career:* Lyric-baritone roles in German opera houses early in career; Tenor repertoire has included Wagner's Walther, Parsifal and Lohengrin, Verdi's Don Carlo and Manrico, Enzo in La Gioconda and Beethoven's Florestan; Don José, Pinkerton, Cavaradossi, Des Grieux in Manon Lescaut, Offenbach's Hoffmann and Kardinal Albrecht in Mathis der Maler by Hindemith; Bayreuth Festival 1997–2002, as Walther von Stolzing and

Siegmund in Die Walküre; Further engagements in Vienna, Paris, Barcelona, Tokyo and Berlin; Season 2000–01 with Die Meistersinger at the Royal Opera, Beethoven's Missa Solemnis at Carnegie Hall and Walther at San Francisco; Engaged as Siegmund in Tokyo and as Bacchus in Ariadne auf Naxos, 2002; Other concerts include the Verdi Requiem, The Dream of Gerontius and Rossini's Petite Messe. *Address:* c/o Theateragentur Dr G. Hilbert, Maximilianstrasse 22, 80539 Munich, Germany.

SMITH, Roger; Cellist; b. 1945, England. *Career:* Principal Cello with the Academy of St Martin in the Fields and member of the Academy of St Martin's Octet; Teacher at the Menuhin School; Co-Founder and Cellist of the re-constituted London String Quartet giving performances throughout the United Kingdom of English works and the recognised repertory. *Address:* c/o Academy of St Martin in the Fields Chamber Ensemble, Station House, Staverton, Totnes, Devon, TQ9 6 AG.

SMITH, Trefor (Leslie); Pianist; b. 4 July 1948, Aberdeen, Scotland. *Education:* MA Honours, Music, Aberdeen University, 1970; BMus, Liverpool University, 1971; Associate (Performance), Royal Manchester College of Music, 1973; Concert Examination, State College of Music, Hamburg; Further studies with Wilhelm Kempff, Vlado Perlemuter, Paul Badura-Skoda and Hans Leygraf. *Career:* Numerous appearances in Germany, the United Kingdom, France, Italy, Spain, Norway, Ireland, Austria, USA, India, Turkey, Poland and Russia; Various radio recordings; Staff and Professor of Piano, Musikhochschule, Hamburg. *Recordings:* 2 records of Piano Music by Theodore Kirchner (1823–1903); 2 CDs of Brahms Piano Sonatas and Beethoven Piano Sonatas; Radio recordings for North German Radio, RTE Dublin and NRK Oslo. *Address:* c/o Barbara Dennerlein, Newtone Management & BEBAB Records, Andreas-Wagner-Str. 39 A, 85640 Putzbrunn (Solalinden), Germany.

SMITH, Wilma; Violinist; b. 1960, New Zealand. *Education:* Studied at the New England Conservatory. *Career:* Leader of the Boston based Lydia Quartet; Co-founded the New Zealand String Quartet under the auspices of the Music Federation of New Zealand; Debut concert in Wellington in 1988; Concerts at the Tanglewood School in the USA, The Banff International Competition in Canada and performances with the Lindsay Quartet at the 1990 International Festival of The Arts; Soloist with the New Zealand Symphony Orchestra and Artist-in-Residence at Victoria University; Tour to Australia in 1990 for Music Viva Australia; Tours of New Zealand in 1992 and concerts in New York in 1993. *Recordings include:* Various.

SMITH-LOMBARDINI, Maryelizabeth Anne; Opera Singer and Artistic Director; b. 1 Sept. 1957, Norfolk, Virginia, USA; m. Danilo Lombardini, 30 Oct 1987. *Education:* BMus, 1979, MMus, 1980, University of Michigan, Ann Arbor; G Verdi Conservatory, Milan, Italy, 1980–83; La Scala Opera Studio, 1982–84, Diploma; Apprentice, Vienna State Opera, Austria, 1984–86. *Career:* Debut: Azio Corghi's Gargantua, Teatro Regio, Turin, 1984; Specialist in 20th century music; Vienna State Opera and Genoa Opera debuts, 1985; La Scala, 1991, in leading role in Henze's Das Verratene Meer, returning 1992 as Andromeda in Sciarrino's Perseo e Andromeda, 1993 for Donatoni's Il Velo Dissolto, 1996 for Berio's Outis; Catania and Venice debuts, 1997; Concert activity includes regular appearances at La Fenice, Venice; Artistic Director, Laboratorio Lirico, Sicilian Chamber Music Society, 1994–96; Professor, A Scontrino State Music Conservatory, Trapani, 1995–96; Artistic Director, Operalaboratorio, City of Palermo Foundation Teatro Massimo-Ars Nova, 1997–; Directo, Palermo-Detroit Cultural Exchange for Opera (Young Artists), 1998–. *Recordings:* La Griselda, Vivaldi; Stabat Mater, Boccherini. *Current Management:* Agentia Lirica Internazionale, Milan. *Address:* Via del Celso 95, 90134 Palermo, Italy.

SMITH-MAXER, Carolyn; Singer (Soprano); b. 1945, Oklahoma City, USA. *Education:* Studied in Chicago. *Career:* Debut: Basle Opera 1967, as Gilda in Rigoletto; Sang as Komische Oper Berlin from 1969, notably as Gershwin's Bess; Staatsoper Berlin 1974, in the premiere of Kunad's Sabellicus; Dresden Staatsoper 1976, as Mozart's Constanze; Appeared at the Frankfurt Opera until 1984 and sang at Bremen 1989-90; Frequent opera and concert engagements in Chicago; Repertory has included soubrette and coloratura roles, in addition to Negro spirituals. *Address:* c/o Bremen Theater, pf. 101046, D-2800 Bremen, Germany.

SMITHERS, Don (Le Roy); Music Historian; b. 17 Feb. 1933, New York, USA; m. (2) 1 Sept 1967, 1 d.; 1 s. and 1 d. from previous marriage. *Education:* BS, Music, Physics and Philosophy, Hofstra University, 1957; Seminars in Musicology, New York University, 1957–58; Studied Renaissance and Reformation History, Columbia University, New York, 1958; PhD, History of Music, University of Oxford, England. *Career:* Associate Professor, Department of Fine Arts and School of Music, Syracuse University, 1966–75; Lectures and papers on Baroque ornament, Festival Books, the history of music and musical instruments and the history of musical performance for various groups, colleges and universities; Solo concert performances on Baroque trumpet, cornetto,

and various Renaissance wind instruments; Co-founder, First Musical Director and sometime conductor of Oxford Pro Musica, Oxford, 1965–. *Recordings:* About 50 solo and ensemble recordings with various European and American groups including New York Pro Musica, The Leonhardt Consort, Concentus Musicus Wien and Early Music Consort of London. *Publications include:* The Music and History of the Baroque Trumpet Before 1721, 1973; A Catalogue of Telemann's Music with Brass, 1995. *Contributions:* Many articles to professional journals and book chapters. *Honours:* Research Fellow and study with Professor Arthur Mendel, Princeton University, 1978; The Japan Foundation Grantee; ASECS/Folger Institute Fellowship, 1984. *Address:* 55 Van Houten Fields, West Nyack, NY 10994, USA.

SMITKOVA, Jana; Singer (Soprano); b. 26 Dec. 1942, Prague, Czechoslovakia. *Education:* Studied at the Prague Conservatory and Music Academy. *Career:* Debut: Liberec, 1967, as Nancy in Martha by Flotow; Sang with the Brno Opera, 1968–70, Ceske Budejovice, 1970–73; Member of the Komische Oper Berlin from 1973, debut as Katya Kabanova; Frequent guest appearances in Dresden, notably as Agathe in Der Freischütz at the 1985 reopening of the Semper Opera House; Has also sung at the National Theatre, Prague, and in other East European centres; Sang Ludmila in Harry Kupfer's production of The Bartered Bride at Covent Garden, 1989, on visit with the company of the Komische Opera; Other roles include Pamina, Puccini's Butterfly and the leading role in Die Kluge by Orff. *Recordings include:* Opera sets for two recording companies; Der Freischütz and Beethoven's Ninth. *Honours:* Prize of the Prague Spring Festival, 1963. *Address:* Leipzigerstr 41 06/08, 10117 Berlin, Germany.

SMITS, Stefanie; Opera Singer (Soprano); b. 13 Sept. 1966, Speyer, Rhein. *Education:* German Abitur in French and German, 1986; Studied at Hochschule für Musik, Karlsruhe, with Diploma in Music Pedagogy; Diplomas for opera and for lied and oratorio, Hochschule für Darstellende Kunst und Musik, Frankfurt/Main. *Career:* Debut: Telemann Festival, Magdeburg, as Nigella in Der neumodische Liebhaber Damon, 1996; Donna Anna in Don Giovanni in Berlin, 1997; Debut with Norske Opera Oslo as Tosca in Kristiansand, 1998; Dame in George Taboris's production of Magic Flute in Berlin, 1998; Guest performance as Suor Angelica at Frankfurt, 1999; Engaged with Landestheater Coburg to sing Mimi in La Bohème, Arabella, Rosalinde in Fledermaus and Manon by Massenet. *Recordings:* Der neumodische Liebhaber Damon with La Stagione Frankfurt with DLF Köln. *Honours:* Scholarship, Stiftung Frederique Brion, Basel, 1991; Silver Medal, Maria Callas Competition, Athens, 1997. *Current Management:* Karin Müller Kunstconsulting PR, Kulturmanagement GmmbH, 10117 Berlin, Germany.

SMOLKA, Jaroslav; Musicologist and Composer; b. 8 April 1933, Prague, Czechoslovakia; m. Jara Popelová, 8 Sept 1956, 1 s., 1 d. *Education:* Musicology, Charles University, Prague, 1951–56; Composition, Academy of Performing Arts, Prague. *Career:* Recordings Director of LP Supraphon, 1956–62, and then Panton, 1969–72; Assistant, 1962, Docent (Assistant Professor), 1968, Professor of History and Theory of Music, 1991; Leader of Development for Theory and History of Music Academy of Performing Arts, Prague; mem, Atelier 9O, The Society of Czech Composers and Musicologists. *Compositions:* The Play About Teeth, chamber comic opera, 1977–78; The Cock is Sitting Over the Cloud, cycle of female choruses, 1964; Choral Overture, for orchestra, 1982; The Dialog of Forms, symphony for large orchestra, 1989; String Quartet No. 2, 1963–65; Sonata for Pianoforte No. 2 Kontrasty, 1978–79; The Mist of Depression, for viola solo, 1982; Just Don't Be Afraid, concerto for cello and large orchestra. *Publications:* Ladislav Vycpálek: His Evolution as a Composer, 1960; Ceská hudba našeho stoleti, 1961; Ceská kantáta a oratorium, 1970; The Fugue in the Czech Music, 1987; Smetanova vokálni tvorba (The Vocal Music of Bedrich Smetana), 1980; Smetanova symfonická tvorba (The Symphonic Music of Bedrich Smetana), 1984; Dejiny hudby (History of Music, Leader of Authors team), 2001. *Address:* Nad Bertramkou 4, 15000 Prague 5, Czech Republic.

SMOLYANINOVA, Soya; Singer (soprano); b. 1960, Russia. *Education:* Studied at the Gnessin Institute, Moscow. *Career:* Appearances at the Bolshoi Opera from 1986, as Tatiana, Lisa in The Queen of Spades, Emma (Khovanshchina), Yaroslavna (Prince Igor), the Trovatore Leonora, Tosca and Desdemona; Guest appearances at Leipzig, Dresden and the Deutsche Oper Berlin, as Amelia, Tosca and Tatiana; Soloist with the Gewandhaus Orchestra, Leipzig, and other leading orchestras; Semper Oper Dresden from 1995, as Abigaille in Nabucco, Madama Butterfly and the Forza Leonora; Season 1996 as Leonora and Tosca at Antwerp; Engaged as Turandot, 1998. *Current Management:* Athole Still International Management, Forresters Hall, 25–27 Westow Street, London, SE19 3RY, England. *Telephone:* (20) 8771-5271. *Fax:* (20) 8768-6600. *Website:* www.atholestill.com.

SMYTHE, Russell; Singer (baritone); b. 19 Dec. 1949, Dublin, Ireland. *Education:* Studied at Guildhall School of Music and London Opera Centre. *Career:* English Music Theatre Company from 1976 as: Tom Jones, Dandini and Ballad Singer in Stephen Oliver's Tom Jones, Rossini's Cenerentola and Britten's Paul Bunyan; Welsh National Opera from 1977 as Billy Budd, Onegin, Papageno, Count Almaviva and Rossini's Figaro; Covent Garden from 1983 as Malatesta in Don Pasquale, Falke in Der Fledermaus and Guglielmo; has sung with English National Opera: Pelléas, Papageno, Figaro, Tarquin in The Rape of Lucretia, Prince Andrei in War and Peace; Hamburg Staastoper from 1980 as Guglielmo, Figaro, Papageno and in Ariadne and Pelléas; Vienna from 1982 as The Count in Der Wildschütz, Harlequin and Falke; Paris Opéra from 1985 as Harlequin and Apollon in Alceste by Gluck; Brother in Dr Faust; North American debut 1986 as Papageno at Vancouver; Sang in Oberon at Lyon and in La Finta Giardiniera, Amsterdam, Berlin and Brussels; Buxton Festival 1988 as Donizetti's Torquato Tasso; Sang Rossini's Figaro for Opera North, 1989; Don Giovanni, Dublin, 1990; Frankfurt: Finta, 1990; Basel Opera as Orestes in Iphigénie en Tauride, Germont in Traviata and Belcore in L'Elisir d'amore, 1991; Catania: Papageno; Madrid: Ned Keene, in Peter Grimes; ENO: Albert, in Werther; Season 1992 included Ping in Turandot, Antwerp, Eugene Onegin, Tel-Aviv; Season 1993–94 Onegin, Scottish Opera; Orfeo, Monteverdi, Nancy; Season 1994–95 included Henri de Valois in Le Roi Malgré Lui for Opera North; Balstrode in Peter Grimes, Scottish Opera, The Forester, Cunning Little Vixen, Opera Zuid: (Maastricht) Sharpless in Madama Butterfly for Welsh National Opera; Season 1995–96 included Peter, Hansel and Gretel for Scottish Opera; Shishkov in House of the Dead for Opéra du Rhin, Strasbourg; Season 1996–97 as Apollo in Orfeo for Netherlands Opera and Ned Keen in Peter Grimes at La Monnaie; Season 1998–99 at De Vlaamse Opera as Ping in Turandot, Aeneas in Dido and Aeneas, and Arbace in Idomeneo. Concert engagements include Berlioz's L'Enfance du Christ with the Hallé Orchestra and Messiah at Valencia; Recently sang in Orfeo for English Bach Festival and Shishkov in From the House of the Dead, BBC Symphony Orchestra. *Recordings:* Nardo, Brussels Opera; Thésée in Hippolyte et Aricie, Rameau, Archiv; Extensive recording for Radio 3; Video Disc of Menotti's The Telephone. *Current Management:* Athole Still International Management, Forresters Hall, 25–27 Westow Street, London, SE19 3RY, England. *Telephone:* (20) 8771-5271. *Fax:* (20) 8768-6600. *Website:* www.atholestill.com.

SNIPP, Peter; singer (baritone); b. 1964, London, England. *Education:* Guildhall School. *Career:* appearances as Masetto with Opera North and in the title role of the premiere of Judith Weir's The Vanishing Bridegroom for Scottish Opera; Eugene Onegin for Kentish Opera and in Zaide and Les Boréades for City of Birmingham Touring Opera; Principal with English National Opera from 1994, singing Malatesta, Harlequin (Ariadne), Guglielmo and Patroclus in King Priam; Concerts include the War Requiem in Finland, Carmina Burana under Jane Glover and the Steersman in Tristan with the London Philharmonic Orchestra; Sang in Henze's Prince of Homburg for ENO, 1996, as Papageno, 1998 and as Figaro in Le Nozze in 1999. *Recordings include:* Il Barbiere di Siviglia, with ENO. *Current Management:* Robert Gilder & Co., Enterprise House, 59–65 Upper Ground, London, SE1 9PQ, England. *Telephone:* (20) 7928-9008. *Fax:* (20) 7928-9755. *E-mail:* rgilder@robert-gilder.com.

SNOWMAN, Nicholas; Music Administrator; b. 18 March 1944, London, England; m. Margo Michelle Rouard, 1983, 1 s. *Education:* Magdalene College, Cambridge. *Career:* Founder and Administrator of Cambridge University Opera Society, 1965–67; Assistant to Head of Music Staff, Glyndebourne Festival Opera, 1967–69; Co-founder and General Manager of London Sinfonietta, 1967–72; Director, Department Artistique, Institut de Recherche et de Co-ordination Acoustique-Musique (IRCAM), Paris, France, 1972–86; Co-founder and Conseiller Artistique Ensemble Intercontemporain, Paris, 1976–92; Member of Music Committee, Venice Biennale, 1979–86; Artistic Director, Projects, 1980, 1981, and 1983, Festival d'Automne de Paris; Initiator and Member of Steering Committee, National Studio for Electronic Music at South Bank, 1986–92; General Director, Arts, South Bank Centre, London until 1998; Responsible for the 1988–89 series, The Reluctant Revolutionary: Arnold Schoenberg His Work and His World; Director of the Glyndebourne Festival, 1998–2000. *Publications:* Co-editor, The Best of Granta, 1967; The Contemporary Composers, 1982–; Introductions and articles in Orchestre de Paris, Centre Pompidou, Festival d'Automne Programme Books. *Honours:* Chevalier, L'Ordre des Arts et des Lettres, 1985; Chevalier dans l'ordre National du Mérite, France, 1995.

SNYDER, Barry; Concert Pianist and Teacher; b. 6 March 1944, Allentown, Pennsylvania, USA. *Education:* BM, Master's Degree, Performance and Literature, Artist Diploma in Piano, Eastman School of Music, University of Rochester. *Career:* Debut: Soloist with Allentown Symphony Orchestra; Has performed throughout the USA, Canada, Europe, Poland, South America and Asia; Appearances with orchestras of Montreal, Atlanta, Houston, Baltimore, National, Detroit and Kraków in Poland, with such conductors as Sixten Ehrling, David Zinman, Charles Dutoit, Robert Shaw, Leopold Stokowski; Chamber music with Jan DeGaetani, Dong-Suk Kang, Zvi Zeitlin, Ani Kavafian, Bonita Boyd, Cleveland Quartet, Composers' Quartet, Eastman Brass Quintet, New York Brass Quintet; Founding Member of Eastman Trio with tours to Europe and South America; Professor of Piano, Eastman School of Music, 1970–; Has given masterclasses with solo recitals. *Recordings:* 38 CDs including Dohnányi, solo recording; Dohnányi chamber works with Cleveland Quartet; Complete cello music of Fauré with Steven Doone, cellist; Stephen Jaffe's Two Piano Sonata with Anton Nel. *Address:* 166 Orchard Drive, Rochester, New York, NY 14618-2344, USA.

SOBEHARTOVA, Jitka; Singer (Soprano); b. 1950, Czechoslovakia. *Education:* Studied in Prague. *Career:* Sang in operetta at the Karlin Music Theatre, Prague; Opera roles at Usti nad Labern 1977-84, including Marenka in The Bartered Bride, Susanna, and Marguerite in Faust; National Theatre, Prague, from 1984, notably as Zerlina in Don Giovanni, Musetta (La Bohème), Aennchen (Der Freischütz) and roles in operas by Dvořák and Smetana; Many concert appearances in Eastern Europe. *Recordings include:* The Cunning Peasant by Dvořák (Supraphon). *Address:* National Theatre, PO Box 865, 112 30 Prague 1, Czech Republic.

SOBOLEVA, Galina; Cellist; b. 1960, Moscow, Russia. *Education:* Studied at Moscow Conservatoire with Valentin Berlinsky. *Career:* Member of the Prokofiev Quartet (founded at Moscow Festival of World Youth and the International Quartet Competition, Budapest); Many concerts in former Soviet Union and on tour to Czechoslovakia, Germany, Austria, USA, Canada, Spain, Japan and Italy; Repertoire includes works by Haydn, Mozart, Beethoven, Schubert, Debussy, Ravel, Tchaikovsky, Bart ók and Shostakovich. *Address:* c/o Sonata (Prokofiev Quartet), 11 Northgate Street, Glasgow G20 7AA, Scotland.

SOCCI, Gianni; Singer (Bass); b. 19 March 1939, Rome, Italy. *Education:* Studied at the Accademia di Santa Cecilia in Rome and with Franco Cavara. *Career:* Debut: Piccolo Teatro Comico Rome in 1965 as Achmed in Paisiello's Il Re Teodoro in Venezia; Sang in the buffo repertory at opera houses in Milan, Rome, Naples, Florence, Turin, Venice, Genoa and Trieste; Guest appearances in Brussels, Copenhagen, Toulouse, Strasbourg, Paris, Cologne, Frankfurt, Philadelphia, Montreal, Quebec, Monte Carlo and Barcelona; Many performances in operas by Mozart, Cimarosa, Rossini and Donizetti; Sang at Teatro Lirico Milan in 1975 in the premiere of Al Gran Sole Carico d'Amore by Luigi Nono; Concert engagements in Italy and elsewhere.

SÖDERSTRÖM, Elisabeth (Anna); Singer (Soprano) and Administrator; b. 7 May 1927, Sweden; m. Sverker Olow, 1950, 3 s. *Education:* Singing Studies, Andrejewa de Skilonz and Stockholm Opera School. *Career:* Royal Opera, Stockholm, 1950–; Appearances: Salzburg, 1955, Glyndebourne, 6 times between 1957–79 as the Composer in Ariadne, Octavian and Leonore, in Fidelio; Metropolitan Opera, New York, 8 times between 1959–87; Frequent concert and television appearances in Europe and USA; Tour, Russia, 1966; Roles included: Fiordiligi, in Così fan tutte, Countess and Susanna, in Figaro, Countess, in Capriccio, Christine, in Intermezzo; 3 Leading roles: Der Rosenkavalier, 1959, Janáček's Emilia Marty and Jenůfa, Mélisande; Sang at Dallas, 1988, in premiere of The Aspern Papers by Argento; Artistic Director, Drottningholm Court Theatre, 1993–97; Sang the Countess in The Queen of Spades at the Met, 1999; Member, Judging Panel, Cardiff Singer of The World, 1991; Presented, Drottningholm Theatre Saga at Barbican Hall, London, 1992; Professor, 1996–. *Publications:* I Min Tonart, 1978; Sjung ut Elisabeth, 1986. *Honours:* Honorary Academician, Royal Academy of Music; Court Singer, Sweden, 1959; Order of Vasa; Stelle della Solidarieta, Italy; Prize, Best Acting, Royal Swedish Academy, 1965; Literis et Artibus Award, 1969; Commander, Order of Vasa, 1973; Commandeur des Arts et des Lettres, 1986; C.B.E.; Named Professor by the Swedish Government. *Address:* Drottningholms Slottsteater, Box 27050, 10251 Stockholm, Sweden.

SÖDERSTRÖM, Gunilla; Singer (Mezzo-soprano); b. 1943, Stockholm, Sweden. *Education:* Royal Music Academy, Stockholm, with Kerstin Thorborg and Käthe Sundströ m. *Career:* Debut: Drottningholm Festival, 1969, as Lisetta in Haydn's Il mondo della luna; Sang at Valstena 1969-72, notably in a revival of Da male il bene by Abbatini; Appearances at Malmö 1971-73 and Royal Opera Stockholm from 1973, including the premiere of Tintomara by Werle; Rotaunda Theatre Stockholm, 1994 in the premiere of Peter Bengtson's Jungfrurna; Other roles have included Carmen, Eboli in Don Carlos, Gluck's Orpheus, Bianca in The Rape of Lucretia, Olga in Eugene Onegin, and Rossini's Cenerentola. *Address:* c/o Royal Opera, PO Box 16094, S-10322 Stockholm, Sweden.

SOFFEL, Doris; Singer (Mezzo-Soprano); b. 12 May 1948, Hechingen, Germany. *Education:* Early studies as violinist, then voice with Marianne Schech in Munich, 1968–73. *Career:* Bayreuth Youth Festival in 1972, in Das Liebesverbot; Stuttgart State Opera, 1973–76; Sang Waltraute at Bayreuth and began career as a concert artist; Noted in Bach and other Baroque music; Sang at Bregenz Festival in 1977 as Puck in Oberon; Sang Monteverdi's Poppea in Toronto in 1983 and took part in the Hamburg premiere of JC Bach's Amadis de Gaule; Sang at Covent Garden in 1983 as Sextus in La Clemenza di Tito and Orlovsky in Die Fledermaus; Fricka (Solti/Hall), Bayreuth Festival, 1983; Mahler 3rd (Tennstedt), New York Carnegie Hall, 1983; Sang in the world premiere of Reimann's Troades in Munich, 1986; Sang Octavian in a production of Der Rosenkavalier at the renovated Brussels Opera House, and Angelina in La Cenerentola at the Berlin Staatsoper in 1987; L'Italiana in Algeri/Isabella, Schwetzingen, Zürich, Cologne, 1987; Television appearances include Das Lied von der Erde in 1988; Sang in the premiere of Penderecki's Ubu Rex at Munich in 1991; Season 1992 as Cassandra in Reimann's Troades at Frankfurt and Elizabeth in Donizetti's Maria Stuarda at Amsterdam; Verdi's Preziosilla at Munich in 1994; Bartók's Bluebeard's Castle (Judith), Deutsche Oper Berlin (Kout/Friedrich), 1994; Werther (Charlotte) at Parma with Alfredo Kraus and Damnation of Faust at Munich, 1995; Returned to London 1997 for Mahler/Brahms recital at St John's Smith Square; Season 2000–01 as Kundry at the Deutsche Oper Berlin; Frick and Waltraute for Cologne Opera, Countess Geschwitz in Palermo and Schoeck's Penthesilea for the Maggio Musicale, Florence; Ortrud in Lohengrin at Bologna, 2002. *Recordings include:* Bach Cantatas and Magnificat; Flotow's Martha; Lortzing's Der Wildschütz; Haydn's St Cecilia Mass; Das Liebesverbot; Schumann's Requiem; Zemlinsky's Eine Florentinische Tragödie; Troades; Parsifal; Mahler No. 2; Beethoven's Missa Solemnis; Wolf's Der Corregidor; Mahler 3; Mahler 8; Kindertotenlieder; Lieder eines fahrenden Gesellen; Mahler's Rückertlieder; Virtuoso Arias, Anna Bolena. *Current Management:* Ingpen & Williams Ltd, 7 St George's Court, 131 Putney Bridge Road, London, SW15 2PA, England.

SOGNY, Michel; Artistic Director, Manager, Composer and Author; b. 21 Nov. 1947, Pau, France. *Education:* Doctor of Philosophy, Paris; Masters Degree in Psychology and Literature; Ecole Normale de Musique de Paris. *Career:* Debut: Piano recital of own compositions, Paris, 1990; Book on Liszt, 1975; New Piano method, 1978; Producer, International recitals of gifted pupils; Founder, Paris Piano School, 1974; Numerous radio and television programmes; Television film on Liszt, 1982; Educational methods adopted by ILO, Geneva, 1985; Creation of Michel Sogny Foundation for young and talented underprivileged children, 2000; mem, Treasurer of French Association Franz Liszt, Paris, 1972. *Compositions:* Numerous concert pieces for piano; Numerous didactic compositions for piano. *Recordings:* Michel Sogny Live at Espace Cardin, 1990; Prolegomenes to a Musical Eidetic; Michel Sogny Live at Villa Schindler. *Publications:* Admiration Créatrice Chez Liszt, 1975; La Methode eu Questions, 1984; Le Methode eu Action, 1987. *Contributions:* Tribune de Genève, 1993; Record critique in classical review Harmony, Paris, 1980. *Honours:* Peace Medal of UN, New York, 1986; Honorary diploma from UNESCO for his work, 1995. *Address:* Villa Schindler, Obermarkstr 45, 6410 Teifs, Austria.

SOHAL, Naresh; Composer; b. 18 Sept. 1939, Harsipind, Punjab, India. *Education:* University of Punjab; London College of Music; Leeds University. *Career:* Asht Prahar performed by London Philharmonic Orchestra under Norman del Mar at the Royal Festival Hall in 1970; BBC have commissioned four major works including The Wanderer, first performed during the 1982 Promenade Concerts, under Andrew Davis; From Gitanjali commissioned by Philharmonic Society of New York, first performed by New York Philharmonic Orchestra under Zubin Mehta in 1985; Represented the West in 2 East-West encounters in the Netherlands and Bombay in 1983; Television credits include music score for Sir William in Search of Xanadu for Scottish television and three episodes of Granada television's series, End of Empire, 1985; Member of BBC 's Central Music Advisory Committee and the equivalent committee in Scotland; mem, Society for the Promotion of New Music. *Compositions include:* Orchestral: Indra-Dhanush, 1973, Dhyan l, 1974, Tandava Nritya, 1984; Chamber and instrumental: Shades I, 1974, Shades II, 1975, Shades III, 1978, Chakra, 1979, Shades IV, 1983, Brass Quintet No. 2, 1983; Vocal and choral: Inscape, 1979, The Wanderer, 1981, From Gitanjali, 1985; Maya, music theatre, 1997; Satyagraha for orchestra, 1997. *Contributions:* Tempo Magazine. *Address:* c/o British Music Information Centre, 11 Stratford Place, London, W1, England.

SOHN, Sung-Rai; Violinist and Conductor; b. 23 Sept. 1950, Seoul, Republic of Korea; m. Patricia Esposito Gilleran 1980, 1 s., 3 step-d. *Education:* BM, Peabody Conservatory of Music (full scholarship student of Berl Senofsky), Baltimore, Maryland, USA; MFA, Sarah Lawrence College (scholarship student of Dorothy DeLay); Quartet

Seminar, Juilliard School of Music. *Career:* Debut: As a winner of Artists International Competition and Jack Kahn Music Award, Carnegie Recital Hall, New York City, 1980; Founder, Music Director/Conductor, Philharmonic Lawrencia Chamber Orchestra; Founder, 1st Violinist, Laurentian String Quartet; Appeared: Korean National television (KBS Radio); WNYC, New York, in Rising Star, Live, and the Bosendorfer Concert Series; The Listening Room, WQXR, New York; NPR, USA; MaineTelevision Network; Kansas Television Network; Sendai Television Network, Japan; Toured Canada, USA, Europe, Africa, Asia. *Recordings:* Barber String Quartet Op 11; Rochberg String Quartet No. 3; C P E Bach Concerto in A major; Ginastera Piano Quintet. *Publications:* Careers in Music, 1980. *Address:* 69 Mile Road, Suffern, NY 10901, USA.

SOJAT, Tiziana; Singer (Soprano); b. 28 April 1955, Rome, Italy. *Education:* Studied with her mother, Alda Noni, and Elisabeth Schwarzkopf. *Career:* Debut: Dublin in 1984 as Elsa in Lohengrin; Sang Mimi at Ljubljana in 1984; Concert performances of Dido and Aeneas and Gianni Schicchi at Lausanne in 1985; Sang with the company of San Carlo, Naples, in Pergolesi's Stabat Mater at New York; Croatian National Opera at Zagreb in 1988 as Sieglinde in Die Walküre; Marseilles in 1989 as Elena in Mefistofele; Engaged at Karlsruhe Opera from 1989, notably as Butterfly and Arabella; Concert performances at Turin, Dubrovnik, Rome and Milan; Freelance career, giving several concertts and Liederabende in Tokyo, one of which for the Richard Strauss Society of Japan, 1995–. *Recordings include:* Lieder by Wolf, Schumann, Liszt and Mahler; CD War Songs by Franz Lehar and Kurt Weill, 1996. *Address:* Badisches Staatstheater, Baumeisterstrasse 11, 7500 Karlsruhe, Germany.

SOJER, Hans; Singer (Tenor); b. 20 March 1943, Innsbruck, Austria. *Education:* Studied with Franziska Lohmann. *Career:* Debut: Innsbruck in 1967 as David in Meistersinger; Sang at Innsbruck until 1971, Bonn, 1971–73, Wiesbaden, 1973–81, and Hanover, 1981–; Roles in operas by Rossini, Donizetti, Mozart, Wagner and Strauss, at Graz, Cologne, Mannheim, Düsseldorf, Frankfurt, Berlin, Lisbon and Karlsruhe; Sang at Bregenz and Schwetzingen Festivals; Sang the Steersman and Narraboth at Barcelona in 1988, Ernesto at Kiel and Count Riccardo in Wolf-Ferrari's Quattro Rusteghi at Hanover in 1991; Concert repertoire includes Beethoven's 9th and cantatas and Passions by Bach. *Recordings include:* Brighella in Ariadne auf Naxos. *Address:* c/o Niedersachsische Staatstheater, Opernplatz 1, 3000 Hanover, Germany.

SOKOL, Ivan; Organist; b. 15 June 1937, Bratislava, Slovakia; m. Gertrud Bethke, 14 Sept 1990. *Education:* Hochschule für Musik, Prag. Studium; Laureat Prague Spring; Leipzig Bachwettbewerb Preisträger. *Career:* Debut: Prague; Concerts in Europe, Asia, USA and Mexico; Television and radio appearances; Director for International Orgelfestival Kosice, Slovakia; mem, Director of the Josef-Gresak Organ Festival, Bardejov; Ehrenbürger von Kosice, Slovakia. *Recordings include:* Complete organ works of Bach, Handel, Mendelssohn, Mozart, Brixi, Brahms, Reger, Hindemith 1, 2, 3, Sonata, Slovak Music, Poulenc-Concerto for Organ and Orchestra, Saint-Saëns, 3 Symphony, Janáček, Glagolitic Mass; Czech Music; French Organ Music, Franck, Mulet, Messiaen and Dupré; Romantic Organ Works: Mendelssohn-Bartholdy, Liszt and Reger; Orgel Musik zur Weihnacht; Mozart, Church Sonatas and Works for Organ. *Honours:* 2 Prizes, Stadt Košice; National Prize, Verdienter Künstler. *Address:* Trencianska 5, 82109 Bratislava, Slovakia. *Telephone:* (2) 55576068.

SOKOLOV, Grigory; Pianist; b. 18 April 1950, Leningrad, Russia. *Education:* Special Music School; Entered St Petersburg Conservatory, 1968. *Career:* First recital at age 12; Regular performances throughout Europe, North America and the Far East; Worked with Philharmonia London and Ulster Orchestra under Yan-Pascal Tortelier; Appeared with Orchestra of the Bolshoi under Alexander Lazarev at Edinburgh Festival; Has played with many foreign orchestras including Leipzig Gewandhaus, Dresden Philharmonic, Munich Philharmonic, Bamberg Symphony, Warsaw Philharmonic, Zürich Tonhalle, Vienna Symphony, Helsinki Radio Symphony, Amsterdam Concertgebouw and Philharmonic Orchestra of La Scala Milan, with such conductors as Inbal, Flor, Järvi, Stein, Saraste, Groves, Rozhdestvensky, Pinnock, Rowicki, Kondrashin, Svetlanov, Lombard, Barshai, Weller, Blomstedt and Chailly; Recitals in Paris, Vienna Musikverein, Munich, Berlin, Frankfurt, Salzburg, Helsinki, Copenhagen, Milan, Rome, New York Carnegie Hall and Tokyo; Recital at the Edinburgh Festival, 1999; Repertoire ranges from Byrd, with some pieces also from Leonine and Palestrina to Schoenberg including Rameau, Bach, Beethoven, Mozart, Chopin, Schubert, Ravel, Rachmaninov, Scriabin; Prokofiev. *Recordings include:* Beethoven Sonatas Op 90 and Op 110 and the Diabelli Variations; Chopin Preludes; Bach's The Art of Fugue and Sonatas by Prokofiev, Rachmaninov and Scriabin. *Honours:* First Prize, 3rd International Tchaikovsky Piano Competition, at age 16, 1966. *Address:* c/o Artists Management Company, Via Valverde 32, 37122 Verona, Italy.

SOKOLOV, Ivan Glebovitch; Russian composer, pianist and educator; b. 29 Aug. 1960. *Education:* Gnesin Musical College, composition with Nik Sidelnikov, piano with Lev Maumov. *Career:* Assistant Probationer under Nik Sidelnikov, 1984–86, Moscow Conservatoire; Concerts, as soloist and with others in Moscow, Leningrad, Sverdlovsk, Kharkov, Briansk, Tashkent, Alma-Ata, Lvov and Tallinn among others, 1985–; Repertoire includes Stockhausen, Cage, Crumb, Scriabin, Shostakovich, Prokofiev, Debussy and Brahms; Festival appearances include Moscow Autumn, 1987–90, Alternative, 1988–90, Festival of Music in Russia and Germany, 1990, and Schleswig-Holstein Music Festival, Hamburg, 1991; Solo concert, playing Chopin in 1991; Teacher of Composition at Musical College, 1986–; Leader of classes in Instrumentation and Musical Score Reading at Moscow Conservatoire, 1988–. *Compositions include:* 10 Pieces for flute and piano, 1983; The Night, cantata, 1983; Rus Pevutchaya, cantata, 1985; Blazhenstvo I Beznadezhnos, vocal cycle, 1986; Volokos for piano, 1988; Sonata for flute and piano, 1988; 13 Pieces for piano, 1988; Eshtche, 7 pieces for piano, 1989; Knigy Na Stole for piano, 1989; Zvezda for soprano and piano, 1990; O, flute solo, 1990; Korably V More for 2 pianos, 1990; Igra Bez Natchala I Konza for percussion, 1991; Mysli O Rachmaninove for piano, 1991; Summer for narrator, actress and strings, 1994; Opera-Cryptophonics, 1995; KA-24 Non-Preludes, for piano and percussion ensemble, 1995; Secret Letters for violin, viola, piano and synthesizer, 1995; I. Sokolov, for fortepiano, 1997. *Address:* uliza Staryi Gaiy, dom 1, korpus 1, Kvartira 116, 111539 Moscow, Russia.

SOKOLOV, Vladimir; Clarinettist; b. 21 Feb. 1936, Uckshor, Republic of Komi, Russia; m. Irina Sokolova. *Education:* City of Siktivkar Music School, Republic of Komi, 1950–54; Orchestra Faculty, Moscow Conservatory, 1954–59;. *Career:* Debut: With Moscow Conservatory Symphony Orchestra at the Grand Hall, Moscow Conservatory, 1955; Clarinettist, Radio and Television Symphony Orchestra, 1960–63; Clarinettist, USSR State Symphony Orchestra, 1963–92; Clarinettist, Russian National Symphony Orchestra, 1992–94; Teacher, 1973–, Professor, 1992–, Moscow Conservatory; Teacher, Central Music School, 1977–; Professor, Korean National Institute of Arts, Seoul, 1994–. *Recordings:* Concertos by Mozart, Krommer and Weber; Sonatas by Brahms, Glinka, Grechaninov, Artemov, Saint-Saëns, Poulenc; Works by French composers; Duets, Trios, Quartets, Quintets by Mozart, Beethoven, Brahms, Glinka, Khachaturian, Power. *Address:* Presnensky Val h 40, Apt 41, 123557 Moscow, Russia.

SOLARE, Juan Maria; Composer and Pianist; b. 11 Aug. 1966, Buenos Aires, Argentina. *Education:* Conservatorio Nacional, Buenos Aires; Postgraduate studies, Musikhochschulen, Cologne and Stuttgart. *Career:* Professor, Conservatorio, Tandil, 1986–93; Compositions performed at Ferienkurse, Darmstadt, 1992, 1994 and 1998. *Compositions:* Chamber opera Veinticinco de Agosto, 1983; Neverness, string quartet; Passacaglia uber Heidelberg, trio; Pope for voice; An Angel of Ice and Fire, orchestra. *Publications:* Musica y Ajedrez, Planteo de un metodo, 1998; El encuentro de Mahler y Freud, 1996. *Contributions:* Columnist of Clasica, 1990–; Doce Notas, 1996–; Interviews with diverse musicians. *Address:* Adam-Stegerwald Str 15, 51063, Cologne, Germany.

SOLBIATI, Alessandro; Composer; b. 5 Sept. 1956, Busto Arsizio, Italy; m. Emuanuela Piemonti, 2 Feb 1985, 1 s., 1 d. *Education:* 2 Years, Faculty of Classics, University of Milan; Diploma in Piano and in Composition, Conservatory G. Verdi, Milan. *Career:* Debut: Biennale, Venice, 1981; Numerous commissions from Teatro alla Scala, RAI, French Ministry of Culture, Radio France, Mozarteum, South Bank of London, Gulbenkian Foundation, Lisbon, University of Paris; Performances at numerous festivals including Lille, Avignon, Strasbourg, Radio France Presences, 1992, 1994, 1997, Huddersfield, England, Wien Modern, Holland Festival, Zagreb, Musicale of Florence, Sydney, Maastricht, Moscow. *Compositions:* Trio d'archi, 1981; Sonata, 1986; Nel deserts, 1986; Canto per Anita, for cello and instruments, 1992; Quartetto con lied, for string quartet and child's voice, 1992; Inno, radiophonic production, 1997; Sinfonia, for orchestra, 1998; Sonata, for piano, 1998. *Recordings:* Solbiata: Chamber Recordings, 1999; Nel Deserto, oratorio and ensemble; Quartetto con Lied, Quartetto Borciani; Trio, Trio Matisse; Tre pezzi, for guitar, Filomena Moretti; Tre pezzi, for guitar, Halasa; Inno. *Publications:* Progettualita Pormale nell'Ultimo Moderna, in Studies in Bruno Maderna, 1989. *Contributions:* Journals and periodicals. *Honours:* First Prize, International Composition Award, Turin, 1980; First Prize, International Composition Award, RAI-Paganini, Rome, 1983; Targa d'Argento, Prize Saint Vincent, 1983. *Address:* Viale Argonne 39, 20133 Milano, Italy.

SOLDH, Anita; Singer (Soprano); b. 26 Sept. 1949, Stockholm, Sweden. *Education:* Studied at Stockholm University and with Erik Saéden from 1969; Further study at the Stockholm and Vienna Music Academies, 1971–75, and with Luigi Ricci in Rome. *Career:* Sang with Norrlands Opera, 1975–77, notably as Britten's Lucretia and Mozart's Countess, Royal Opera Stockholm from 1977 with debut as Eva in Die Meister-

singer, returning as Senta, Elizabeth, Arabella, Octavian, Chrysothemis, Mozart's Countess, Elvira, Vitelia and Pamina, Tchaikovsky's Tatiana and Maid of Orleans; Concert tours of the USA, Brussels and Europe in 1984, as Cherubino; Bayreuth Festival, 1983–84 as Freia in Das Rheingold; Sang Elsa in Lohengrin at Stockholm in 1989 and First Lady in Die Zauberflöte at the Drottningholm Court Theatre, and the Queen in Vogler's Gustaf Adolf och Ebba Brahe in 1990; Season 1991–92 as Agave in the premiere of Backanterna by Daniel Börtz, production by Ingmar Bergman, and at Drottningholm in Haeffner's Electra and as Gluck's Eurydice; Concert repertoire includes Schoenberg's Erwartung, Berg's Frühe Lieder and Haydn's Schöpfung. *Recordings:* Video of Idomeneo from Drottningholm, as Elettra. *Address:* c/o Kungliga Teatern, PO Box 16094, 10322 Stockholm, Sweden.

SOLÉN, Christer; singer (tenor); b. 1939, Gustavs, Finland. *Education:* Royal Music Academy, Stockholm, and with Luigi Ricci in Rome. *Career:* Sang at Herrenhausen 1969-70, as Sextus in Handel's Giulio Cesare; Norrlandsoperan at Umea from 1974, as Rossini's Lindoro, Don Ottavio, Male Chorus in The Rape of Lucretia; Folksoperan Stockholm from 1981, as Pinkerton, Radames and Tamino; Stora Theatre Gothenburg in The Lighthouse by Peter Maxwell Davies (1984) and title role in The Voyage of Edgar Allan Poe, by Argento; Other roles have included Hoffmann, Fatty in Weill's Mahagonny, Oedipus Rex, and Eufemio in Gli Equivoci, by Storace; Many concert appearances throughout Europe.

SOLLBERGER, Harvey; Composer, Conductor and Flautist; b. 11 May 1938, Cedar Rapids, Iowa, USA. *Education:* BA 1960, University of Iowa; Composition with Jack Beeson and Otto Luening at Columbia University, New York (MA 1964). *Career:* Co-founded the Group for Contemporary Music, New York 1962; Regular tours as flautist and conductor; Faculty Member, Columbia University 1966–82; Manhattan School of Music, 1972–83; Indiana University School of Music 1983–92; Professor of Music at the University of California, San Diego, from 1992; Music Director, La Jolla Symphony Orchestra, 1998–. *Compositions include:* Chamber Variations for 12 players, 1964; Music for Sophocles's Antigone, electronic, 1966; Musica Transalpina, 2 motets for soprano, baritone and 9 players, 1970; Folio, 11 pieces for bassoon, 1976; Sunflowers, for flute and vibraphone, 1976; Music for Prepared Dancers, 1978; Interrupted Night for 5 instruments, 1983; Double Triptych for flute and percussion, 1984; Persian Golf, for strings, 1987; Aurelian Echoes for flute and alto flute, 1989; Passages, for soloists, chorus and orchestra, 1990; The Advancing Moment for flute, clarinet, violin, cello, piano and percussion, 1993; CIAO, Arcosanti for 8 instruments, 1994; In Terra Aliena for 5 soloists and orchestra, 1995; Grandis Templum Machinae for soprano, mezzo, baritone, chorus and 21 Instruments, 1996; To the Spirit Unappeased and Peregrine, for flute and clarinet, 1998; New Millennium Memo for solo flute, 2000. *Honours:* Guggenheim Fellowships, 1969, 1973. *Address:* Department of Music 0326, University of California, San Diego, La Jolla, CA 92093, USA. *E-mail:* hsollberger@ucsd.edu.

SOLODCHIN, Galina; Violinist; b. 29 April 1944, Tientsin, China. *Education:* Studied at the New South Wales Conservatorium. *Career:* Freelance musican, including member of Delmé Quartet from 1967; Many performances in the United Kingdom and Europe in the classical and modern repertory; Concerts at the Salzburg Festival and the Brahms Saal of the Musikverein Vienna; Season 1990 included Haydn's Seven Last Words in Italy and elsewhere, three Brahms programmes at St John's Smith Square with Iain Burnside on piano; Concerts at St David's Hall in Cardiff with Quartets by Tchaikovsky and Robert Simpson including premiere of his 13th Quartet; Appearances in Bremen, Hamburg and Trieste followed by festival engagements in 1991; Other repertory includes works by Paul Patterson, Daniel Jones, Wilfred Josephs, Iain Hamilton and Bernard Stevens. *Recordings include:* Haydn's Seven Last Words; Vaughan Williams's On Wenlock Edge; Gurney's Ludlow and Tame; Simpson Quartets 1–9 and String Trio; Daniel Jones 3 Quartets and Bridge No. 2; Bliss's No. 1 and 2; Josef Holbrooke Piano Quartet and Clarinet Quintet; Brahms Clarinet Quintet; Dvořák F major Quartet; Verdi Quartet; Strauss A major Op 2; Hummel No. 1, 2 and 3; Bernard Stevens Theme and Variations and Quartet No. 2 and Lyric Suite for String Trio; Beethoven Op 74 and Op 95; Favourite Encores. *Address:* c/o 33 Whittingstall Road, Fulham, London SW6, England.

SOLOMON, Maynard Elliott, BA; American music historian and writer; b. 5 Jan. 1930, New York, NY; m. Eva Georgiana Tevan 1951; two s. one d. *Education:* Brooklyn Coll., CUNY, Columbia Univ. *Career:* co-founder, co-owner, Vanguard Recording Soc. Inc 1950–86; teacher, CUNY 1979–81; Visiting Prof., SUNY at Stony Brook 1988–89, Columbia Univ. 1989–90, Harvard Univ. 1991–92, Yale Univ. 1994–95; Scholarly Adviser, Beethoven Archive, Bonn 1995–; Graduate Faculty, Juilliard School 1998–; Associate Editor, American Imago 1976; mem. PEN. *Contributions:* articles in Beethoven Jahrbuch: Music and Letters, Musical Quarterly: 19th Century Music, Journal of the American Musicological Society. *Publications:* Marxism and Art 1973,

Beethoven 1977, 1998, Myth, Creativity and Psychoanalysis 1978, Beethoven Essays 1988, Mozart: A Life 1995, Some Romantic Images in Beethoven 1998, Late Beethoven: Music, Thought, Imagination 2003. *Honours:* ASCAP–Deems Taylor Awards 1978, 1989, 1995, Kinkeldey Award American Musicological Soc. 1989, hon. mem. 1999, 2000. *Address:* 1 W 72nd Street, Apartment 56, New York, NY 10023, USA.

SOLOMON, Yonty; Pianist; b. 6 May 1938, Cape Town, South Africa. *Education:* BMus, Cape Town University, 1958; Studied with Myra Hess in London and with Charles Rosen in USA. *Career:* Debut: London in 1963; Concert appearances with leading orchestras in Europe, USA, Canada, South Africa, Israel and Romania; First performances of works by Bennett, Joseph, Merilaainen and Sorabji; Repertoire also includes works by Bach (Goldberg variations), Schoenberg, Albeniz, Janáček, Ives, Granados, Debussy and Shostakovich; Duos with violinist, Sylvia Rosenberg and cellist, Radu Aldulescu; Appearance on ITV programme in honour of Sorabji; Professor at the Royal College of Music; Masterclasses at Prussia Cove, Cornwall and at Nottingham University. *Recordings include:* Music by Sorabji; 14 Studies by Wilfred Josephs; Sonatas for Cello and Piano by Prokofiev and Fauré with Timothy Hugh for the BBC, 1991. *Honours:* Beethoven International Award, 1963. *Address:* c/o Basil Douglas Artists Management, 8 St George's Terrace, London NW1 8XJ, England.

SOLTESZ, Stefan; Conductor; b. 6 Jan. 1949, Nyiregyhaza, Hungary. *Education:* Studied at the Vienna Hochschule für Musik with Dieter Weber, Hans Swarowsky, Reinhold Schmidt and Friedrich Cerha. *Career:* Conductor at the Theater an der Wien, Vienna, 1971–73; Coach and Conductor at Vienna Staatsoper, 1973–83; Salzburg Festivals, 1978, 1979, 1983 being assistant to Karl Böhm, Christoph von Dohnányi and Karajan; Guest Conductor of the Graz Opera, 1979–81; Permanent Conductor of the Hamburg Staatsoper, 1983–85 and Deutsche Oper Berlin 1985–97; General Music Director of the State Theatre at Brunswick, 1988–93; Music Director of the Flanders Opera, Antwerp/ Ghent, 1992–97 Guest Conductor with the Opéra Royale de Wallonie at Liège, Bavarian State Opera in Munich, Bonn Opera, Leipzig Opera, Vlaamse Opera Antwerp, Stuttgart State Theater, Nederlandse Oper at Amsterdam, Festival de Radio France et Montpelleier, Aix-en-Provence, Paris Opéra, Vienna State Opera, Frankfurt Opera, Semper Opera, Dresden, Teatro Bellini, Catania, Hamburg Opera, Teatro Colón, Buenos Aires, Washington Opera, Kennedy Center and ROH, London; Toured Japan with the German State Opera Unter den Linden, 1990; Concerts in Bologna, Hamburg, Mexico City, Naples, Paris, Salzburg, Turin, Vienna, Munich, Essen, Berlin, Karlsruhe, Hannover, Basel and Zagreb among others; Since 1997 Artistic Director of the Aalto Musiktheater in Essen and Music Director of the City of Essen, Germany. *Recordings include:* Swan Lake Excerpts with Vienna Symphony; La Bohème with Lucia Popp and Francisco Araiza; Opera Arias with Lucia Popp; Opera Arias with Grace Bumbry; Don Giovanni, by Giuseppe Gazzaniga, with Munich Radio Orchestra; The Chalk Circle by Alexander Zemlinsky; Orchestral Songs by Hugo Wolf with Dietrich Fischer-Dieskau. *Address:* Aalto Musiktheater Essen, Opernplatz 10, 45128 Essen, Germany.

SOLUM, John (Henry); Concert Flautist, Writer and Educator; b. 11 May 1935, New Richmond, Wisconsin, USA; m. Millicent Hunt, 30 July 1960, two s. *Education:* BA, Princeton University, 1957; Private Studies in flute with William Kincaid, Philadelphia, 1953–58; Flute, Harmony, Counterpoint, Composition, Musicology, various teachers. *Career:* Debut: Solo, 1953; Soloist, Philadelphia Orchestra, 1957; New York debut recital, 1959; Soloist, Chamber Music Player, 37 countries on 5 continents, including Asia, 1968, 1969, 1976, Latin America, 1978, 1979, 1980; USSR, 1983 and 14 New York recitals; Guest appearances with orchestras in over 50 cities; Many Radio Broadcasts; Festivals, Europe, North America; Teacher: Vassar College, 1969–71, 1977–; Indiana University, 1973; Oberlin Conservatory, 1976; Co-Director: Bath Summer School of Baroque Music, England, 1979–89; Connecticut Early Music Festival, 1982–99. *Compositions:* Cadenzas, Mozart's Flute Concertos. *Recordings:* Ibert, Jolivet, Honegger Flute Concertos, 1975; 2 Malcolm Arnold Flute Concertos, 1977; Romantic Music for Flute and Orchestra, 1978; Mozart Flute Concertos, 1980; Telemann Duets, 1981; Bach Flute Sonatas, 1988; Vivaldi Bullfinch Concerto, 1992; Bach, Handel, Telemann Trio Sonatas, 1992; Sonatas by Telemann, Handel, Vinci, Scarlatti, J C Bach, C P E Bach, Mozart, 1994; Works by Kupferman, Laderman, Beeson, Luening, Kraft and Nowak, 1994; Handel Trio Sonata in C Minor, 1995; Hummel's chamber arrangements of Mozart symphonies 35 and 36, 1997; Shadow by David MacBride, 1995; Works by J.S.Bach, C.P.E.Bach, W.F.Bach and J.C.Bach, 2001; Trio Sonatas by de la Barre, Hotteterre, Couperin, Leclair, 2003; Music composed for Lord Abingdon by Haydn, Abel, Gretry, J.C. Bach, 2003. *Publications:* The Early Flute, 1992. *Address:* 10 Bobwhite Drive, Westport, CT 06880, USA. *E-mail:* jhsolum@optonline.net.

SOLYOM-NAGY, Sandor; Singer (Baritone); b. 21 Dec. 1941, Siklos, Hungary. *Education:* Ferenc Liszt Academy of Music, Budapest, 1960.

Career: Budapest State Opera, 1964–; Numerous guest performances in Berlin, Brussels, Bratislava, Prague, Cologne, Barcelona, Moscow, Leningrad, Genoa, Rome, The Hague, Rotterdam, Paris, Rio de Janeiro, São Paulo, Sofia, Varna and Vienna; Frequent guest appearances with Bavarian State Opera at Munich in Germany and Vienna State Opera in Austria and Japan; Regular guest artist at Bayreuth Festival from 1981 including Grail Knight in Parsifal in 1992; Sang Palatine Gara in Erkel's Hunyadi László at Budapest in 1989; Sang Amonasro at Budapest, 2000. *Recordings:* Numerous records including Liszt's Christus Oratorio, The Legend of Elisabeth, Via Crucis, Goldmark's The Queen of Sheba, Agamemnon in Gluck's Iphigénie en Aulide, the title role in Kodály's Háry János and in Strauss's Guntram and Respighi's La Fiamma. *Honours:* Liszt Prize, 1972; Merited Artist of Hungary, 1977; Hector Berlioz Prize, French Record Academy; Grand Prix, French Record Academy; Charles Cros Prize; Golden Orpheus Prize, French Record Academy; Excellent Artist of Hungary, 1987; Kossuth Prize, 1998. *Address:* c/o Budapest State Opera, Budapest, Hungary.

SOMACH, Beverly; Violinist; b. 17 Jan. 1935, New York, NY, USA; m. S George Silverstein, 20 August 1959, 2 s., 2 d. *Education:* BS, Columbia University, 1956; Certificate of Completion of Studies with Jascha Heifetz, University of California, Los Angeles, 1959. *Career:* Recitals, Town Hall, Carnegie Hall, Lincoln Center, Alice Tully Hall, New York City; Recitals in London (Wigmore Hall, Purcell Room), Edinburgh, Glasgow, Stockholm, Copenhagen, Zürich, Paris, Tokyo, Hong Kong, Montreal; Soloist with Orchestra: New York Philharmonic, Chicago Symphony, Los Angeles Symphony, American Symphony, Orchestra Luxembourg. *Recordings:* For Newport Classic, Heritage Society, Radio Free Europe, Voice of America. *Contributions:* New York Times; Musical America. *Current Management:* Seymour F. Malkin Management.

SOMARY, Johannes (Felix); Musician; b. 7 April 1935, Zürich, Switzerland; m. Anne Van Zandt, 20 July 1963, 2 s., 1 d. *Education:* BA, Yale University, 1957; MMus, Yale School of Music, 1959. *Career:* Debut: As Conductor with Washington Square Music Festival, New York, 1960; Founder, Music Director and Conductor of Amor Artis, New York City, 1962–; Chairman, Arts and Music Department, Horace Mann School, New York City, 1971–2002; Conductor for Fairfield County Chorale, 1975–, Great Neck Choral Society, 1982–94, Taghkanic Chorale, 1992–99; Artist-in-Residence at St Jean Baptiste Church, 1985–; Music Dir, St Patrick's Cathedral, 2001–03; Appeared as Guest Conductor at Madeira Bach Festival, 1985, Dubrovnik Music Festival, 1986, Sion Music Festival, Switzerland, 1990, with Polish radio and television Orchestra, 1990, and with Royal Philharmonic, London, New Orleans Philharmonic, others; Composition commissions include This Is Life, oratorio for Jefferson Music Festival, 1994, The Ultimate Quest, for Great Neck Choral Society, Liturgy in E-flat, for Blessed Sacrament Fathers' Centennial Celebration, and Te Deum, for Benedictinus, premiered in Rome, 2000; Violin Concerto, premiered in St Petersburg, Russia, 2004; mem, American Choral Directors' Association; Chorus America; American Symphony Orchestra League. *Recordings include:* Handel's Messiah, Theodora, Jephtha, Semele, Bach's Mass in B Minor, and St Matthew Passion as Conductor with the English Chamber Orchestra; Additional recordings of works by Haydn, Tchaikovsky, Schütz, Mozart, Prokofiev, Kurt Weill; Mozart's Requiem (Amor Artis Chorus and Orchestra), 1996; Haydn's Creation, 1998; Vivaldi's Four Seasons; Handel's Acis and Galatea; Saint-Saëns's Requiem. *Current Management:* MPL, c/o Michael Leavitt, 170 West 74th Street, New York, NY 10023, USA. *Address:* 620 West 254th Street, Bronx, New York, NY 10471, USA.

SOMFAI, László; Musicologist; b. 15 Aug. 1934, Jászladány, Hungary; m. Dorrit Révész-Somfai, 1 s., 1 d. *Education:* Diploma in Musicology, Ferenc Liszt Academy of Music, Budapest, 1958; Doctor of Musicology, Hungarian Academy of Sciences, Budapest, 1982. *Career:* Music Librarian at National Széchényi Library, Budapest until 1962; Head of Budapest Bartók Archives, Institute for Musicology, Hungarian Academy of Sciences, 1972–; Professor of Musicology, Ferenc Liszt Academy of Music, 1980–; mem, Zentralinstitut der Mozartforschung, Salzburg; Joseph Haydn Institut, Cologne; Corresponding Member, Hungarian Academy of Sciences; Corresponding Member, American Musicological Society and British Academy; Last President, International Musicological Society. *Publications:* Co-author, Haydn als Opernkapellmeister, 1960; Joseph Haydn: Sein Leben in Zeitgenössischen Bildern, 1966, English edition, 1969; Anton Webern, 1968; The Keyboard Sonatas of Joseph Haydn, Hungarian edition, 1979, English edition, 1995; 18 Bartók Studies, 1981; Béla Bartók: Composition, Concepts and Autograph Sources, 1996; Studies on Haydn, Liszt, Stravinsky, Webern and Bartók; Critical editions in Mozart Neue Ausgabe, Gluck Neue Ausgabe, Musica Rinata; Editor, Documenta Bartókiana. *Address:* Falk Miksa u 12, V4, 1055 Budapest, Hungary.

SON, Dang Thai; Pianist; b. 1950, Hanoi, Viet Nam. *Education:* Diploma, 1976; Moscow Tchaikovsky Conservatory, 1983. *Career:* Appearances at

Several Major Festivals, including, Berlin, Geneva, Ravinia, Miami, Paris, Brescia, Bergamo, Cannes, Prague Spring, Dubrovnik, Bratislava, Russian Winter, December Nights, Chopin Festival of Nohant, Ruhr Piano Festival; Tour of North America, 1989; Played with World-Famous Orchestras including, Leningrad Philharmonic, Montreal Symphony, BBC Philharmonic, Dresden Philharmonic, Staatskapelle Berlin, Oslo Philharmonic, Warsaw National Philharmonic, Prague Symphony, NHK Symphony, Helsinki Philharmonic, Sydney Symphony, Hungarian Symphony, Moscow Philharmonic; Appearances with the Virtuosi of Moscow, the Polish, Moscow and Zürich Chamber Orchestras and with Sinfonia Varsovia; Honorary Professor, Kunitachi Music College, Tokyo. *Honours:* Gold Medal, 10th International Chopin Piano Competition, Warsaw, 1980. *Address:* c/o Latitude 45, Arts Promotion Inc, 109 St Joseph Blvd West, Montreal, QC H2T 2P7, Canada.

SONDEREGGER, Peter; Swiss composer and musician; b. 2 Oct. 1960, St Gallen. *Education:* Konservatorium Basel with Jacques Wildberger, Musikhochschule Karlsruhe, Germany with Wolfgang Rihm. *Career:* performer of 16th- and 17th-century music. *Compositions:* Delirien I–III, chamber ensembles and live electronics, 1981–83; Piano Concerto No. 1, 1985; Tombeau per tre Clarinetti, 1985; Eclairs Errants, piano and orchestra, 1986–87; Webern-Variations to Symphony Op 21, for orchestra, 1987; Zeit, Verjüngendes Licht, clarinet, viola and guitar, 1987–88; 73 Pezzi Degli Scrovegni, piano, 1989–90; Missa Incontri, piano trio, 1990–91; Auslöschung, for panflute and double-string quartet, 1991; Conductus II, violin and organ, 1993–94; Various other compositions for chamber ensembles, piano solo, guitar Solo; Quaenam sit divina caligo, for female voices and violins, 1994; La Mallorquina, for violin and piano, 1995; Conductus IV for 2 saxophones. *Recordings:* Tombeau per tre Clarinetti; Zeit, Verjüngendes Licht. *Honours:* scholarships to Heinrich Strobel-Stiftung des Südwestfunks 1986, Schweizerischer Tonkünstlerverein 1987. *Address:* Unterdorf 10, 4203 Grellingen, Switzerland.

SONDHEIM, Stephen Joshua, BA; American composer and lyricist; b. 22 March 1930, New York, NY; s. of Herbert Sondheim and Janet Fox. *Education:* George School, Newtown, PA, Williams Coll., Williamstown, MA, private instruction. *Career:* Pres. Dramatists' Guild 1973–81, Council mem. 1981–; Visiting Prof. of Drama and Musical Theatre, Univ. of Oxford Jan.–June 1990; mem. American Acad. and Inst. of Arts and Letters 1983–. *Compositions:* television: Topper (co-author) 1953, Evening Primrose (music and lyrics) 1967; lyrics: West Side Story 1957, Gypsy 1959, Do I Hear a Waltz? 1965, Candide 1973; music and lyrics: A Funny Thing Happened on the Way to the Forum 1962, Anyone Can Whistle 1964, Evening Primrose 1966, Company 1970, Follies 1971, A Little Night Music 1973, The Frogs 1974, Pacific Overtures 1976, Sweeney Todd 1978, Merrily We Roll Along 1981, Sunday in the Park with George 1984, Into the Woods (Drama Critics' Circle Award 1988) 1986, Follies 1987, Assassins 1991, Passion 1994, Wise Guys 2001; anthologies: Side by Side by Sondheim 1976, Marry Me a Little 1980, You're Gonna Love Tomorrow 1983, Putting It Together 1993; screenplays: (with Anthony Perkins) The Last of Sheila 1973, Birdcage 1996, Getting Away Murder 1996; film scores: Stavisky 1974, Reds 1981, Dick Tracy 1989; incidental music: The Girls of Summer 1956, Invitation to a March 1961, Twigs 1971. *Honours:* Antoinette Perry Awards for Company 1971, Follies 1972, A Little Night Music 1973, Sweeney Todd 1979; Drama Critics' Awards 1971, 1972, 1973, 1976, 1979; Evening Standard Drama Award 1996; Grammy Awards 1984, 1986; Nat. Medal of Arts 1997, Praemium Imperial 2000. *Current Management:* c/o John Breglio, 1285 Avenue of the Americas, New York, NY 10019, USA.

SONEK, Frantisek; Pianist and Conductor; b. 12 April 1933, Opava, Czechoslovakia; m. Lubomíra Záskodná, 1 Aug 1959, 2 d. *Education:* Piano and conducting at Conservatory in Ostrava; Conducting at Janáček Academy of Music Arts in Brno (JAMU). *Career:* Debut: Ballet, Fairy-tale about John by Oskar Nedbal in Theatre Ostrava (as conductor), Czech Republic; Teacher at Conservatories of Ostrava and Brno, 1965–69; Then Janáček Academy of Music Arts (JAMU) in Brno mainly as Pianist-Choral Répétiteur, 1969–; Also Pianist-Choral Répétiteur in Opera House of Opava, 1960–64: Conductor-Assistant, Janáček Opera in Brno (music of Smetana, Dvořák, Janáček, Bizet, Moniuszko, Rimsky-Korsakov, Tchaikovsky); mem, Chief and Conductor of Amateur Symphony Orchestra of Railwaymen in Brno, 1978–. *Recordings:* Janáček's operas Jenůfa and Excursions of Mr Brouček. *Contributions:* JAMU: About Janáček's Glagolitic Mass and its Problems, 1972. *Address:* Milénova 12, Brno 38, Czech Republic 63800.

SONNTAG, Ulrike; Singer (Soprano); b. 1959, Esslingen, Germany. *Education:* Studied with Eva Sava and Dietrich Fischer-Dieskau; Hartmann-Dressler. *Career:* Debut: Sang Oriane in Amadis de Gaul by J C Bach as guest with the Hamburg Staatsoper, 1983; Sang at the Stadttheater Heidelberg, 1984–86; Nationaltheater Mannheim, 1986–88; Has appeared in concerts all over Europe, festivals of

Salzburg, Vienna, Berlin, Frankfurt, Schwetzingen and in the USA (Los Angeles), China, Brazil, Japan; Member of the Stuttgart Opera from 1988, as Euridice, Susanna, Donna Elvira, Marcellina, Pamina, Marie, Ännchen, Micaela, Nedda, Frau Fluth, Gretel, Sophie in Der Rosenkavalier and Helena (A Midsummer Night's Dream); Sang Aennchen in Der Freischütz at the 1989 Ludwigsburg Festival; Member of Vienna State Opera for 1991–94, repertoire including Susanna, Pamina, Micaela, Zdenka, Musetta; Pamina, 1992; Freischütz production, Trieste, 1994; Wildschütz production, Cologne, 1994; Lieder tour, Moscow and St Petersburg, 1994; Guest appearances: Deutsche Oper, Berlin; Frankfurt, Belinda, Marcellina, Musetta; Monte Carlo, Ännchen, 1990; Cairo, Rosina in Haydn's La Vera Costanza, 1990; Trieste, Ännchen, 1994, Euridice, 1995; Tel-Aviv Opera with Der Freischütz, 1996; Appeared in Don Giovanni at Berlin in 1997; Season 1998 in Cagliari with Wagner's Die Feen and with Carmen at St Margarethen in Austria. *Recordings include:* Bach Cantatas; Bach: B minor Mass with Rilling; Mignon lieder, Schubert, Schumann, Wolf; Milhaud, songs and chamber music; Hindemith: Das Unaufhörliche; Bach; Video of Der Freischütz. *Address:* Steigstrasse 21, 71394 Kernen, Germany.

SOOTER, Edward; Singer (Tenor); b. 8 Dec. 1934, Salina, Kansas, USA. *Education:* Studied at the Friends University in Wichita with Elsa Haury, Kansas University with Joseph Wilkins and the Hamburg Musikhochschule with Helmut Melchert. *Career:* Debut: Bremerhaven, 1966, as Florestan; Sang in Kiel, Karlsruhe, Wiesbaden, Munich, Frankfurt and Cologne; Metropolitan Opera from 1979, as Florestan, Tannhäuser, Otello, Aeneas in Les Troyens, Walther, Tristan and Lohengrin; Sang Siegmund in Ring cycles at Seattle; New Orleans Opera, 1992, as Florestan; Other roles include Parsifal, Don José, Canio, Aegisthus, Manrico, Ernani, Samson, and Babinsky in Schvanda the Bagpiper; Sang Siegmund at Flagstaff, 1996. *Address:* c/o Thea Dispeker Artists' Management, 59 E 54th, New York, NY 10021, USA.

SOPRONI, Jozsef; Composer; b. 4 Oct. 1930, Sopron, Hungary. *Education:* Studied at the Budapest Academy of Music, 1949–56. *Career:* Faculty Member at Bela Bartók School, Budapest, from 1957; Professor, Budapest Academy of Music, from 1977 (on faculty from 1962); Rector at Budapest Academy 1988–94. *Compositions include:* Concerto for Strings 1953; 10 String quartets, 1958–94; Carmina polinaesiana cantata for women's chorus and ensemble, 1963; Ovidi metamorphoses, for soprano, chorus and orchestra, 1965; 2 Cello concertos, 1967, 1984; 6 Symphonies, No. 1 1975, No. 2 The Seasons 1977, No. 3 Sinfonia da Requiem, for soloists, chorus and orchestra, 1980, No. 4 1994, No. 5 1995, No. 6, 1995; Horn sonata, 1976; Six Bagatelles for wind quintet, 1977; Late Summer Caprices for string trio and piano, 1978; 2 violin sonatas, 1979, 1980; Violin Concerto, 1983; Comments on a Theme by Handel, for orchestra, 1985; Antigone, opera, 1987; Three Pieces for orchestra, 1988; Magnificat for soloists, chorus and orchestra, 1989; Missa Scarbantiensis, 1991; Missa Choralis, 1992; Missa super B-A-C-H, 1992; Litaniae Omnium Sanctorum, 1993; Pslam XXIX for chorus, organ, trumpet and trombone, 1993; Missa Gurcensis for chorus and ensemble, 1994; Te Deum, for soloists, chorus and orchestra; Livre d'orgue, 9 pieces, 1994; 12 Piano sonatas, 1996–98; Piano concerto, 1997; Chamber Concerto No. 2, for 12 instruments, 1998; Das Marienleben, for soprano and piano, 1998. Piano Music, songs and choruses. *Address:* II Pajzs-u 22/b, 1025, Budapest, Hungary.

SORDELLO, Enzo; Singer (Baritone); b. 20 April 1927, Pievebovigliano, Macerata, Italy. *Education:* Studied at the Torino Conservatory and Scuola di Perfezio namento per Giovani Artisti del Teatro Alla Scala of Milan. *Career:* Debut: Teatro Toselli in Cueno as Enrico in Lucia di Lammermoor, 1952; La Scala, 1954–75, as Cinna in La Vestale opposite Callas; Later appeared in Milan as Belcore, Albert in Werther, Gerard in Andrea Chénier in 1955 and as Tonio; Sang at Metropolitan Opera in 1956 as Marcello, Malatesta, Enrico and Ashtou, Vienna Staatsoper in 1959, Stoll Theatre in London in 1960 and Glyndebourne Festival, 1961–62, as Belcore; Frequent broadcasts on RAI. *Recordings include:* La Fanciulla del West; La Vestale, Pagliacci; Madama Butterfly; Lucia di Lammermoor. *Publications:* Enzo Sordello, Autobiografia-Verità di vu Baritono (Il "Fattaççio" Çallas-Sordello-Metropolitan of New York). *Address:* Villa America, 12018 Roccavione, Cueno, Italy.

SORENSON VON GERTTEN, Iwa (Cecilia); Singer (Soprano); b. 5 Sept. 1946, Gothenburg, Sweden; m. Gustf von Gertten, 5 July 1980, 2 s. *Education:* Music Conservatory, Gothenburg, 1966–74; Staatliche Hochschule für Musik, Cologne, 1970–71; Trained as Singer, Singing Teacher and Organist, School of Theatre and Opera, Gothenburg, 1974–75, 1976–77. *Career:* Debut: Malmö, Sweden, as Norina in Donizetti's Don Pasquale, 1978; Opera soloist at Malmö Stadsteater, 1978–79 and Royal Opera of Stockholm, 1979–; Major roles include Rosina in The Barber of Seville, Musetta in La Bohème, Sophie in Der Rosenkavalier, Zdenka in Arabella, Fiordiligi in Così fan tutte, Susanna in The Marriage of Figaro, Blonde in The Abduction from the Seraglio, Aminta in Il Re Pastore, Violetta in La Traviata, Marguerite in Faust, and Olympia in Tales of Hoffmann; Roles in operettas include Adele in Die Fledermaus, Laura in Der Bettelstudent by Millöcker, Josephine in HMS Pinafore, and Fiametta in Boccaccio by Von Suppé; Concert repertoire includes Handel's Messiah and Judas Maccabaeus, Haydn's Creation, Mendelssohn's Elijah, and Mozart's Requiem and Mass in C minor; Recitals with piano of German Lieder, French Art Songs, Swedish repertoire and contemporary music. *Recordings:* Mostly 19th and 20th Century Swedish Music. *Honours:* 3 Gramophone Prizes, 1983, 1984, 1985. *Address:* Hogbergsgatan 26B, 11620 Stockholm, Sweden.

SOROKINA, Elena; Pianist and Music Historian; b. 6 April 1940, Moscow, USSR; m. Alexander Bakhchiev, 28 Nov 1962, 1 d. *Education:* Graduated, Central School of Music, 1958; MA, Performance, MA, History of Music, 1963, PhD, 1965, Moscow State Conservatory. *Career:* Debut: Duet concert (with husband), Mozart, Schubert, Central Arts House, Moscow; Professor, 1965–, Chief, Chair of Russian Music History, 1992–, Moscow State Conservatory; Regular duet performances, Beethoven, Mozart, Weber, Schumann, Schubert, Brahms, Glinka, Borodin, Rachmaninov, other Russian composers, music genres, history of Moscow Conservatory, 1969–; Series of television programmes, chamber music concerts, 1970s; Tours lecturing on Russian music, France, Austria, Latin America; International/national festivals of music, Moscow, Leningrad (with husband); Mozart International Festival, Tokyo (1991); English tour (Cambridge, London), Soviet and British modern piano duets; Concerts with husband, Israel, Italy, Germany, USA, 1992–93; 8 programmes, all Schubert piano duets, with husband; Piano duo festivals, Novosibirsk and Ekaterinburg, 1993–95; Works dedicated to her and husband by Boyarsky, Lubovksy, Fried, Manukyan and Moore. *Recordings include:* Piano duets with husband: Rachmaninov; Russian Salon Piano Music; Mozart; Schubert; Music of France; Weber, Schumann, Mendelssohn; V Persichetti; Bartók, Lutoslawski; Enescu; Albums: Music of Old Vienna; J. S. Bach, his family and pupils; Music for 6 and 8 hands (with G Rozhdestvensky, V Postnikova). *Publications:* Piano Duet (history of genre), 1988. *Address:* 4-32 Koshkin Str, Moscow 115409, Russia.

SOTIN, Hans; Singer (Bass); b. 10 Sept. 1939, Dortmund, Germany. *Education:* Studied privately with FW Hetzel; Dortmund Musikhochschule with Dieter Jacob. *Career:* Debut: Essen in 1962 in Der Rosenkavalier; Hamburg Staatsoper, 1964–, in the standard bass repertory and in the premieres of operas by Penderecki, Klebe, Blacher, Von Einem and Kelemen; Visits with Hamburg Company to New York, Montreal, Rome, Stockholm and Edinburgh; In 1970 sang in Beethoven's Choral Symphony at the United Nations; Glyndebourne debut in 1970 as Sarastro in Die Zauberflöte; Sang at Bayreuth Festival from 1972 as the Landgrave, Pogner, Titurel and Gurnemanz, New York Metropolitan from 1972 as Sarastro and as Hunding and Wotan in Die Walküre, Covent Garden debut in 1974 as Hunding and La Scala Milan in 1976 as Baron Ochs in Der Rosenkavalier; Sang Ochs at Covent Garden in 1986, Lodovico in Otello at the Metropolitan Opera in 1988, and Landgrave in Tannhäuser at Hamburg in 1990; Sang at Bayreuth, 1989–92, as Gurnemanz and Daland; Season 1992 as the Landgrave at Berlin and Barcelona; Sang Rocco in Fidelio at Catania, 1998; Sang Wotan at the Vienna Staatsoper and La Roche in Capriccio at Amsterdam, 2000; Often heard as concert singer, notably in music by Bach. *Recordings include:* Tannhäuser; Aida; Fidelio; Salome; Così fan tutte; Die Walküre; St Matthew Passion; Beethoven's Christ at the Mount of Olives; The Devils of Loudun; Mahler's 8th Symphony; Parsifal; Paukenmesse, Haydn. *Honours:* Forderpreis des Landes NRW; Friedrich Oberdörfer Preis, Hamburg; Kammersänger, Hamburg. *Address:* c/o Opéra et Concert, 1 Rue Volney, F–75002 Paris, France.

SOUDANT, Hubert; Conductor; b. 16 March 1946, Maastricht, Netherlands. *Education:* Studied at the Maastricht Conservatory, with Franco Ferrara in Italy and at Netherlands Radio Course in Hilversum. *Career:* Assistant Conductor with the Hilversum Radio Orchestra, 1967–70; Has conducted the Orchestra of Radio France and the Nouvel Orchestre Philharmonique, with which he gave the French premiere of Mahler's 10th Symphony at Strasbourg in 1979; In 1980 conducted the premieres of Rene Koering's opera Elseneur and the Nana Symphonie by Marius Constant; Conductor of the Symphony Orchestra of Utrecht, 1982; Musical Director with Orchestra Sinfonica dell'Emilia Romagna Arturo Toscanini, Parma, 1988; Guest conductor in England, Germany, Belgium, Italy, Scandinavia, South Africa and Japan; Conducted Ernani at Parma in 1990 and Berlioz's Faust at Turin in 1992. *Recordings:* Tchaikovsky 4th and 6th Symphonies and Romeo and Juliet with the London Philharmonic; Liszt Piano Concertos with the London Philharmonic Orchestra. *Honours:* Winner, International Competition for Young Conductors at Besançon, 1971; 2nd Prize, Herbert von Karajan International Conducting Competition, 1973; First Prize, Guido Cantelli International Conducting Competition, Milan, 1975. *Address:* c/o Baron Artists, Dornbacher Strasse 41/11/2, A–1170 Vienna, Austria.

SOUKUPOVA, Vera; Singer (Contralto); b. 12 April 1932, Prague, Czechoslovakia. *Education:* Studied in Prague with L Kaderabek and A Mustanova-Linkova. *Career:* Has sung in concert from 1955; Stage debut in 1957 at Pilsen; Member of the Prague National Opera from 1960; Tour of Russia in 1961 and sang Dalila in Bordeaux; Guest appearances in Vienna, France and Switzerland; Sang at State Operas of Hamburg and Berlin, 1969–71; Prague National Opera in 1983 as Radmila in Smetana's Libuše. *Recordings:* Erda in The Ring; Dvořák's Stabat Mater; Lieder by Mahler; Choral Symphony; Libuše; The Brandenburgers in Bohemia; The Bride of Messina by Fibich; Oedipus Rex; Janáček's Glagolitic Mass. *Address:* c/o National Theatre, PO Box 865, 112 30 Prague 1, Czech Republic.

SOUNOVA, Daniela; Singer (Soprano); b. 17 May 1943, Prague, Czech Republic. *Education:* Studied in Prague. *Career:* Debut: Sang at the National Theatre Prague, from 1973, notably in the 1974 premiere of Coriolanus by Jan Cikker and lyric roles in operas by Mozart, Smetana, Bizet, Puccini and Prokofiev; Guest appearances at Bologna and the Edinburgh Festival; Sang Donna Elvira in the bi-centenary performances of Don Giovanni, in Prague, 1987; Savonlinna Festival 1991, in Dvořák's Rusalka; Many concert and recital engagements. *Recordings include:* Rusalka, The Jacobin by Dvořák, The Bride of Messina by Fibich, and Don Giovanni (Supraphon); Mahler's 8th Symphony (Ariola–Eurodisc). *Address:* c/o National Theatre, PO Box 865, 11230 Prague 1, Czech Republic.

SOUSA DIAS, Antonio de; Composer; b. 13 Nov. 1959, Lisbon, Portugal. *Education:* Superior Course in Composition at Lisbon Conservatory, with Constança Capdeville; University of Paris VIII with Horacio Vaggione; Further studies in electronics and musicology. *Career:* Partner in performance groups, ColecViva, directed by Constança Capdeville, as direction assistant, sound synthesis and percussion since 1985; and Opus Sic; Since 1992, collaboration with Grupo Música Nova, directed by Cândido Lima; Professor in composition and electro-acoustics at the Escola Superior de Música, Lisbon; Deputy director of Escola Superior de Música de Lisboa, 1995–2001. *Compositions:* Estudos para Decoração de Interiores for synthesizers controlled by computer, 1987; Para dois pianos, nos 1 & 2, 1986, 1992; Estilhaços, incidental music, 1989; Mise en page, tape, 1990; O Jardim das Chuvas de Todo o Sempre for flute, clarinet, guitar, harp, percussion, piano, 2 violins, viola and cello, 1991; Rumbinação, Definitivamente! for 2 flutes, oboe, 2 clarinets, soprano, viola, cello and piano, 1994; 5 Circunstancias for clarinet and piano, 1995; Komm, tanz mit mir ! for five instruments, 1997; Gamanço tape, 1997; Natureza Morta com Ruídos de Sala, Efeitos Especiais e Claquete, for tape, 1997; há dois ou, music theatre, 1998; ...há dois ou..., musical theatre, 1998; Le blanc souci de notre toile for oboe and cello, 1998; uma sombra também, for clarinet and electronics, 1999; Uma Nuvem Também for clarinet and Max/Roland S-760, 1999; Estranho movimento, tape, 2000; Dói-me o luar for flute, clarinet, harp, vibraphone, piano, 2 violins, viola, cello, 2001; Têtrês for tape, 2001; Quand trois poules vont au champ for tape, 2002; Trois Chansons Inachevées for Soprano, Tenor sax and tape, 2003; Ressonâncias-Memórias for flute, clarinet, vibraphone, piano, violin, viola, cello and tape, 2003; Music for film: Santo António do Todo o Mundo, 1996; Chá Forte com Limão, 1993; O Altar dos Holocaustos, 1992; A Maldição de Marialva, 1989; Transparências em Prata, 1988; Fernando Lanhas, Os Sete Rostos, 1988; Os Emissáros de Khálom, 1987; Os Abismos da Meia-Noite, 1984; Short Movies: Nature Morte/ Stilleben, 2004; Processo Crime 141/53, 2000; Detectim, 1991; Theatre: Rumor, 1996; Estilhaços, 1989. *Publications:* Translatins MusicV files to Csound format with the help of OpenMusic (www.ircam.fr/equipes/repmus/OMBook); Transcription de fichiers MusicV vers Csound au travers de OpenMusic in Actes des 10es Journées d'Informatique Musicale, Montbéliard; Autómatos da Areia, 1978–1984. *Address:* Al. Linhas de Torres, 155 — 4Dto 1750–142 Lisboa Portugal.

SOUSTROT, Marc; Conductor; b. 15 April 1949, Lyon, France. *Education:* Studied trombone at the Lyon Conservatoire, 1962–69, and conducting with Manuel Rosenthal at the Paris Conservatoire, 1969–76. *Career:* Assistant to André Previn with the London Symphony Orchestra, 1974–76; Deputy Conductor, 1976, then Musical Director of the Orchestre Philharmonique of the Loire; Artistic Director of the Nantes Opera, 1986–90; Conducted the premieres of Claude Baliff's Fantasio Grandioso in 1977, 1st Piano Concerto by Maurice Ohana in 1981, and Concerto for Orchestra by Alain Louvier, 1987; Conducted Tristan and Isolde at Nantes, 1989, Manon Lescaut, 1990, Les Contes d'Hoffmann at Geneva in 1990, and Carmen at the Bregenz Festival, Austria; Conducted Rheingold at Bonn, 1997. *Recordings:* Trumpet Concertos with Maurice André; Music by Franceschini, Scarlatti, Vivaldi, Tartini and Telemann with the Monte Carlo National Opera Orchestra. *Honours:* Winner, Rupert Foundation Competition for Young Conductors, London, 1974; International Competition at Besançon, 1975. *Address:* Orchestra of Bonn, Germany.

SOUTHAM, Ann; Composer; b. 4 Feb. 1937, Winnipeg, Manitoba, Canada. *Education:* Composition at the Royal Conservatory of Music, Toronto; electronic music at the University of Toronto. *Career:* Associated with the Toronto Dance Theatre and other modern dance companies, and Arraymusic and other concert music ensembles and soloists. *Compositions:* Throughways: Improvising Music, for ensemble, 1988; In a Measure of Time for two pianos, 1988; Song of the Varied Thrush, for string quartet, 1991; The Music so Far for clarinet and piano, 1992; Webster's Spin, for strings, 1993; Remembering Schubert, for piano, 19993; Full circles, for trumpet, violin, vibraphone and piano, 1996; Electro Acoustic: Emerging Ground, 1983; Tuning, and Re-Tuning, for Viola and tape 1982, 1985; Music for Slow Dancing, 1985; Fluke Sound, 1989; Figures for solo piano and string orchestra, 2002. *Address:* c/o SOCAN, 41 Valleybrook Drive, Don Mills, Ontario, M3B 2S6, Canada.

SOUTHGATE, Sir William David, Kt; Conductor and Composer; b. 4 Aug. 1941, Waipukarau, New Zealand. *Education:* Otago University and the Guildhall School of Music. *Career:* Freelance Composer in London and guest musical director of the Royal Shakespeare Company; Conductor and Arranger for the Phoenix Opera Company; Musical Director of the Wellington Youth Orchestra from 1977; Musical Director of the Christchurch Symphony Orchestra from 1984; Has conducted operas by Rossini, Verdi and Johann Strauss for the Wellington and Canterbury Opera Companies; Prsenter of music programmes on New Zealand radio and television; Toured Finland as Conductor, 1986, Sweden and Finland, 1989; Debut with Honolulu Symphony, 1989; Tour of New Zealand with the Royal New Zealand Ballet Company, 1989; Premieres of children's opera Faery Tale and Cello Concerto in New Zealand, 1990; Also engaged for the Dunedin Sinfonia, New Zealand, 1991; St Matthews Chamber Orchestra, New Zealand, 1991; SWF Sinfonia Orchestra, Spohr Competition, Baden-Baden, 1991; Christchurch Symphony Orchestra, New Zealand, 1991; New Zealand Symphony Orchestra, 1992. *Recordings include:* Second Symphony. *Honours:* Guildhall School conducting prize; 2nd prize, Besançon Conducting Competition.

SOUZA, Ralph de; Violinist; b. 1959, England. *Career:* Founder Member and Second Violinist of the Endellion String Quartet, 1979; Many concerts in Paris, Amsterdam, Frankfurt, Munich, Salzburg and Rome; Appeared at the South Bank Haydn Festival in 1990, the Wigmore Hall Beethoven Series in 1991 and the Quartet Plus Series on South Bank in 1994; Quartet-in-Residence at Cambridge University from 1992 and Residency at MIT, USA, 1995. *Recordings include:* Works by Haydn, Bartók, Dvořák, Walton and Smetana. *Current Management:* Hazard Chase Ltd, Norman House, Cambridge Place, Cambridge, CB2 1NS, England. *Telephone:* (1223) 312400. *Fax:* (1223) 460827. *Website:* www .hazardchase.co.uk.

SOUZA, Rodolfo Coelho de; Composer; b. 8 Aug. 1952, São Paulo, Brazil. *Education:* degree, University of São Paulo, 1968–79; Masters degree, 1994; Electronic music at the University of Texas, Austin, 1996–98. *Career:* Co-director, Santos and São Paulo New Music Festival, 1984–93; Director of Symposium at Winter Festival of Campos do Jordão, 1998–93; Chiarosuro premiered by the American Composers Orchestra, 1996. *Compositions:* Phantasiestück for string quartet, 1982; Carnavalia, for orchestra, 1983; Rébus, for piano, 1985; Galáxias for piano and orchestra, 1998; Diálogos for marimba and vibraphone, 1998; Oblique Rain, for ensemble, 1992; Luminosidades, for orchestra, 1993; Fractal Landscapes, for ensemble, 1993; Chiaroscuro, for piano, tape and two percussionists, 1995; Invariants, for wind quintet and piano, 1995; What Happens Beneath the City While Janis Sleeps, electro-acoustic, 1997. *Address:* c/o SBAT, Rua da Quintanda 194-1o, Caixa Postal no. 1503, Rio de Janeiro (GB), Brazil.

SOVERAL, Isabel; Composer; b. 25 Dec. 1961, Oporto, Portugal. *Education:* Lisbon Conservatory, 1984-88, with Joly Braga Santos; NY State University at Stony Brook, from 1988. *Career:* Lecturer at the University of Aveiro. *Compositions:* Contornos, I, for two clarinets (1987), II, for oboe and bassoon (1987), III, for four clarinets (1990); Pensando, enredano sombras, for low voice and orchestra, 1991; Quadramorphosis (1993); Anamorphoses I, for clarinet and tape (1993), II, marimba, vibraphone and tape (1994), III, violin and tape (1995), IV, cello and tape (1997), V, for string quartet (1997); Le Navigateur du soleil incandescent, for baritone, chorus, orchestra and tape, 1998; Un Soir, for baritone and ensemble, 1998. *Address:* c/o SPA, Av. Duque de Loulé 31, 1098 Lisbon Codez, Portugal.

SOVIERO, Diana; Singer (Soprano); b. 1952, USA. *Career:* Sang first at St Paul in 1974 appearing as Lauretta in Gianni Schicchi and as Massenet's Manon; Joined the New York City Opera in 1976 and sang further at Miami, San Francisco and Chicago; Metropolitan Opera debut in 1986 as Juliet in Roméo et Juliette; European engagements at Paris, Rome, Florence, Milan, Vienna and Hamburg; Geneva in 1988 as Gretchen in Doktor Faust by Busoni, Philadelphia and San Diego in 1988 as Margherita in Mefistofele and Marguerite in Faust; Sang Juliet and Manon at Montreal in 1989; Covent Garden debut in 1989 as Nedda; Season 1992 as Tosca with Opera Pacific at Costa Mesa, Puccini's Trittico heroines at Dallas, Manon Lescaut at Miami and Adriana Lecouvreur at Sydney; Other roles include Puccini's Butterfly and Mimi, Leila in Les Pêcheurs de Perles and Norina in Don Pasquale; Sang Maddalena in Andrea Chénier at Seattle, 1996 and Monte Carlo 1998; Tosca for Palm Beach Opera, 1998. *Address:* c/o Seattle Opera Association, PO Box 9248, Seattle, WA 98109, USA.

SOYER, David; Cellist; b. 24 Feb. 1924, Philadelphia, Pennsylvania, USA. *Education:* Studied with Emanuel Feuermann and Pablo Casals. *Career:* Played with Bach Aria Group, Guilet Quartet, New Music Quartet and Marlboro Trio; Performed in chamber music with Rudolf Serkin at Marlboro Festival and prompted by Alexander Schneider to co-found the Guarneri String Quartet in 1964; Many tours of American and Europe notably with appearances at the Spoleto Festival in 1965, to Paris with Arthur Rubinstein and London in 1970 in the complete quartets of Beethoven; Noted for performances of the Viennese Classics and works by Walton, Bartók and Stravinsky; Season 1987–88 included tour of Japan, concerts at St John's Smith Square, and Queen Elizabeth Hall in London; Faculty at Curtis Institute, Philadelphia and the University of Maryland. *Recordings include:* Mozart's Quartets dedicated to Haydn; Complete Quartets of Beethoven; With Arthur Rubinstein, Piano Quintets of Schumann, Dvořák and Brahms; Piano Quartets by Fauré and Brahms. *Honours:* Edison Award for Beethoven Recordings, 1971; Honorary Doctorates at University of South Florida and State University of New York; Many Grammy Awards for recordings. *Address:* 6 W 77th Street, New York, NY 10024, USA.

SOYER, Roger; Singer (Bass); b. 1 Sept. 1939, Thiais, France. *Education:* Studied at the Paris Conservatoire with Georges Daum and Georges Jouatte. *Career:* Sang at the Paris Opéra from 1963; Sang at La Scala Milan in 1963 as Tirésias in Les Mamelles de Tirésias by Poulenc, Aix-en-Provence Festival from 1965 as Pluto in Monteverdi's Orfeo, Don Giovanni, Don Basilio and Arkel, Paris in 1965 in Rameau's Hippolyte et Aricie, Wexford Festival in 1968 in La Jolie Fille de Perth by Bizet and US debut at Miami in 1973 as Frère Laurent in Roméo et Juliette by Gounod; Sang at Paris Opéra from 1972 in the premiere of Sud by Stanton Coe, and as Don Giovanni, Procida in Les Vêpres Siciliennes, Ferrando in Il Trovatore, Colline and Mephistopheles, Metropolitan Opera in 1972 and Edinburgh Festival in 1973 as Don Giovanni in a new production of Mozart's opera under Daniel Barenboim; Guest appearances in Cologne, Brussels, Geneva, Chicago, Lisbon, Prague, San Antonio and Salzburg; Sang Rodolfo in La Sonnambula at Geneva in 1982, Sulpice in La Fille du Régiment at Dallas in 1983 and sang in L'Heure Espagnole at Turin in 1992. *Recordings:* Les Troyens and Benvenuto Cellini conducted by Colin Davis; Les Pêcheurs de Perles; L'Enfance du Christ; Mozart's Requiem; Lakmé; Werther; Maria Stuarda by Donizetti; Pelléas et Mélisande; Dardanus by Rameau; David et Jonathas by Charpentier. *Address:* c/o Grand Théâtre de Genève, 11 Boulevard du Théâtre, 1211 Geneva 11, Switzerland.

SPACAGNA, Maria; Singer (Soprano); b. 1951, Rhode Island, USA. *Education:* Studied at the New England Conservatory. *Career:* Sang with Dallas Opera from 1977, New York City Opera, 1978, St Louis Opera, 1982, and Detroit, 1986; Sang Puccini's Liu at Toronto in 1983 and appeared at Santa Fe, New Orleans and Trieste in 1987; Debut at La Scala Milan in 1988 as Butterfly; Sang at Spoleto Festival in 1988 as Ismene in Traetta's Antigone, sang Mimi for New Orleans Opera in 1989, Liu and Butterfly at Costa Mesa California and Greater Miami Opera in 1990; Appearances at Memphis, the Cologne Opera and elsewhere as Violetta, Susanna, Zerlina, Norina, Gilda, Marguerite, Rusalka, Micaela, Lauretta and Mascagni's Lodoletta; Sang Madama Butterfly at Santa Fe, 1996 and at Montreal 1997; Active concert career. *Address:* c/o Greater Miami Opera Association, 1200 Coral Way, Miami, FL 33145, USA.

SPAGNOLI, Pietro; Singer (Bass-baritone); b. 1958, Rome, Italy. *Career:* Member of Sistine Chapel Choir, and sang in concert; Stage debut Martina Franca, 1987, as Gaffredo in Bellini's Il Pirata, and returned as Achillas in Giulio Cesare and Mangetto in La buona figliuola by Piccinni; La Scala from 1991; Season 1991–92 as Leporello at Prague and Publio in La Clemenza di Tito at the Salzburg Festival; Rome Opera, 1995, as Don Alfonso and Paris Palais Garnier, 1996, as Alidoro in La Cenerentola; Other roles include Rossini's Bartolo and Dandini, Belcore in L'Elisir d'amore and Talbot in Giovanna d'Arco; Sang Mozart's Figaro at Turin, 1998; Sang Rossini's Dandini at Monte Carlo, Taddeo for New Israeli Opera, and Don Alfonso at Aix, 2000. *Recordings include:* L'Elisir d'amore; Rossini's Tancredi. *Address:* c/o Turin Opera, Piazza Castello 215, 10124 Turin, Italy.

SPAHLINGER, Mathias; Composer; b. 15 Oct. 1944, Frankfurt, Germany. *Education:* Studied composition and music education with Erhard Karkoschka and Konrad Lechner. *Career:* Lecturer at the

Hochschule der Kunst, Berlin, 1978-81; Professor of Karlsruhe Hochschule für Musik, 1983-90; Professor of Composition at Freiberg, 1990-. *Compositions:* Morendi, for orchestra, 1974; éphémène, for percussion and piano, 1977; Extension, for violin and piano; String Quartet, 1982; Inter-mezzo, for piano and orchestra, 1986; Passage/ Paysage, for orchestra, 1990; Und als wir, for 54 strings, 1993; Gegen unendlich, for ensemble, 1995; Akt, eine Treppe Herabsteigend, for trombone, bass, clarinet and orchestra, 1998. *Honours:* Boswil Foundation Prizes. *Address:* c/o GEMA, Rosenheimer Str. 11, 81677 Munic, Germany.

SPANO, Robert; Conductor and Pianist; b. 1970, Conneaut, OH, USA. *Education:* Oberlin Conservatory; Curtis Institute with Max Rudolf. *Career:* Music Director of the Atlanta SO and Brooklyn PO; Director of Festival of Contemporary Music at Tanglewood, 2003–04; Appearances with Symphonies of Boston, Houston, San Francisco and Chicago; Opera engagements at Santa Fe (US premiere of Saariaho's L'amour de loin, 2002), New York (Saariaho's Château de l'âme) and Houston (Eugene Onegin); Season 2002–03 with the Cleveland and St Louis Symphonies, L'Amour de loin with the BBC SO and the City of Birmingham SO; Further modern repertory includes El Niño, by Adams, Del Tredici's Child Alice and Billy Budd (Seattle Opera); Chamber musician (piano) with members of American orchestras. *Recordings include:* Rimsky-Korsakov Scheherazade and Vaughan Williams A Sea Symphony, with the Atlanta SO(Telarc). *Address:* c/o Harrision Parrott Ltd, 12 Penzance Road, London, W11 4 PA, England. *Telephone:* (20) 7229 9166. *Fax:* (20) 7221 5042.

SPARNAAY, Harry (Willem); Bass Clarinettist; b. 14 April 1944, Amsterdam, Netherlands; m. Roswitha Sparnaay-Mol. *Education:* Amsterdam Conservatory. *Career:* Debut: Amsterdam in 1969; Performances with many leading orchestras including the BBC Symphony, Rotterdam Philharmonic, ORTF, Concertgebouw and Radio Chamber Orchestra Hilversum; Soloist at festivals of Warsaw, Zagreb, Graz, Madrid, Poitiers, Witten, Como, Paris, Naples and the ISCM World Music Days at Boston, Athens and Bonn; Concerts in Europe and America; Professor of Bass Clarinet and Contemporary Music at Sweelinck Conservatory, Amsterdam-Rotterdam Conservatory and Royal Conservatory, The Hague; Composers who have written for him include Donatoni, Ferneyhough, Bussotti, Isang Yun and Barry Anderson (premiere of ARC), 1987; Appeared at Hudderfield Festival in 1987 with Time And Motion Studies by Ferneyhough; Tour of the United Kingdom in 1989 on the Contemporary Music Network, playing Echange by Xenakis. *Recordings:* Bass Clarinet Identity; Harry Sparnaay/Lucien Goethals; Composers' Voice; Music by Thon Tbuynel; Music by Earle Brown; Bass Clarinet Idenitity 2; The Garden of Delight. *Honours:* First Prize, Bass Clarinet Soloist, International Gaudeamus Competition, 1972. *Address:* Z Buiten Sparne 120, 2012 AD Haarlem, Netherlands.

SPASOV, Bozhidar; Composer and Musicologist; b. 13 Aug. 1949, Sofia, Bulgaria. *Education:* Moscow Conservatory, 1970-76, with Edison Denisov. *Career:* Lecturer at Sofia Academy of Music, from 1976; Folkwang Hochschule, Essen, 1990 -; Music performed at Festivals in Dresden, Essen, Darmstadt and Rome. *Compositions:* The Bewitched, chamber opera, 1975; Sinfonie, 1978; Konzertmusik for wind, percussion and two pianos, 1982; Dialog I for two ensembles, 1983; Glagolitic Concerto, for mezzo, harpsichord and 13 strings, 1984; The Beginning, for mezzo and ensemble, 1987; De Profundis, for ensemble, 1988; Violin Concerto, 1988; Prabel 12 for chamber ensemble 1992; Oboe Concerto, 1995; Sandglass for trombone, keyboard and electonics, 1996; The Flight of the Butterfly, for mezzo, flute and harpsichord, 1997. *Address:* c/o MUSICATOR, 63 Tsar Assen Str, 1463 Sofia, Bulgaria.

SPEECH, Bernadette; Composer; b. 1 Jan. 1948, Syracuse, USA. *Education:* Columbia University, NY, and in Siena with Franco Donatoni, 1976; State University of NY, Buffalo, with Morton Feldman. *Career:* Administrator of the Composers Forum, 1988-94 and The Kitchen, 1995-. *Compositions:* Shattered Glass, for percussion, 1986; Telepathy Suite, for speaker and ensemble, 1998; Inside Out, for piano, 1987; Les ordes pour quatre, string quartet, 1988; Resoundings, piano four hands, 1990; It Came to me in a Dream, for baritone and ensemble, 1990; Trio des trois, I–III, 1991–92; Angels in the Snow, for piano, 1993; Woman without Adornment, for speaker and ensemble, 1995; Parallel Windows–Unframed, for piano and orchestra, 1995. *Address:* c/o ASCAP, ASCAP Building, One Lincoln Plaza, New York, NY, 10023, USA.

SPEISER, Elisabeth; Singer (Soprano); b. 15 Oct. 1940, Zürich, Switzerland; m. Hans Jecklin, 2 c. *Education:* Academy of Music, Winterhur. *Career:* Debut: Zürich; Concerts in all European countries, North and South America; Guest at many festivals; Many concerts with Karl Richter; Opera debut as Pamina in Die Zauberflöte, Ludwigsburger Schloss Festspiele, 1972–73; Glyndebourne Festival, 1973; Mélisande, St Gallen, 1974; Euridice, Ludwigsburger Schloss Festspiele,

1975; Many Lieder recitals with Irwin Gage; Television and radio appearances in Germany, Italy, Switzerland; Glyndebourne Festival as Euridice, 1982; mem, Swiss Tonkunstlerverband. *Recordings include:* Secular Cantatas and Geistliche Lieder by JS Bach; Caecilien Mass by Haydn; Carissimi Cantatas; Berg/Schoenberg Lieder; Gluck's Orfeo ed Euridice; Schubert, Lieder, 1984 and 1989; Brahms, Lieder, 1985; Haydn's Arianna a Naxos and English songs, CD, 1987. *Address:* Au Village, CH 1742 Autigny, Switzerland.

SPELINA, Karel; Violist; b. 2 Nov. 1936, Czechoslovakia; m. Marie Husickova, 7 June 1958, 2 d. *Education:* Graduated, Technical College, 1955; Graduated, Conservatory of Music, Plzeň, 1967. *Career:* Debut: With Plzeň Radio Quartet, 1963; Principal Viola, Plzeň Radio Orchestra, 1962–70; Principal Viola, Czech Philharmonic Orchestra, 1970–; Member, Ars Rediviva Ensemble, 1970–; Member, Martinů Piano Quartet, 1979–; Professor, Prague Conservatory, 1994–; Has played concertos and orchestral works by Berlioz, J. Reicha, A. Vranitzky, J. V. Stamitz, J. K. Vanhal, J. S. Bach, Martinů, other composers; Sonatas and chamber music by Bach and sons, Telemann, Handel, Mendelssohn, Hindemith, Brahms, Shostakovich, Martinů, Honegger, Milhaud, and others; AHUV, Prague; Teacher, Sándor Végh International Chamber Music Academy. *Recordings:* Sonatas of C. P. E. Bach and W. F. Bach; Sonatas of A. Honegger and D. Milhaud; Sonatas of Hindemith; Concertos of Josef Reicha; Complete Sonatas of J. K. Vanhal, first World Recording, 1997. *Honours:* City of Plzeň Prize, 1968. *Address:* Sturova 32/1153, 14200 Prague 4, Czech Republic.

SPEMANN, Alexander; Singer (Tenor) and Composer; b. 1 June 1967, Wiesbaden, Germany. *Education:* Studied with Gertie Charlent at the Peter Cornelius Conservatory, Mainz and with Martin Grundler at the Frankfurt Musikhochschule. *Career:* Debut: Tenor solo in Beethoven's Ninth, Milan, 1989; Stage debut as First Armed Man in Die Zauberflöte at Wiesbaden; Many concert and opera appearances at Essen, Vienna, Stuttgart, Cologne, Frankfurt, Munich and Hamburg; Engaged with Bonn Opera from 1993–97, singing Kronthal in Lortzing's Wildschütz, and making debut in a Wagner role as Erik in Der fliegende Holländer; Freelance Film and Theatre music composer, including music for the Hessiche Staatstheater, Wiesbaden; Engaged with Darmstadt since 1997 as young heroic tenor, singing Son-Chong in Land des Lächelns, Don José in Carmen and many other roles; Sang Berg's Alwa at Mainz, 1999; Season 2000–01 as Florestan in the 1805 version of Fidelio, Don José and Herod in Salome. *Recordings include:* Count Rudolf in Weber's Silvana (Marco Polo); Jenik in The Bartered Bride, with the orchestra of North German Radio. *Honours:* Winner, Robert Stolz Competition, Hamburg 1996. *Address:* c/o NWB Apollon & Hermes, PR-Arts-Media Services Production, Im Floegerhof 12, 53819 Neunkirchen/Cologne, Germany.

SPENCE, Patricia; Singer (Mezzo-soprano); b. 12 Jan. 1961, Salem, Oregon, USA. *Education:* Studied in San Francisco. *Career:* Debut: San Francisco Opera as Anna in L'Africaine; Has performed the Princess in Suor Angelica, Mother Goose in The Rake's Progress and Meg Page in Falstaff at San Francisco; New York City debut, 1988, as Rosina; Opera Colorado, 1989 as Mistress Quickly; European debut as Edwige in Guillaume Tell at Verona followed by Mozart's Requiem at St Petersburg, Malcolm in La Donna del Lago at La Scala, 1992, and Cenerentola with Phoenix Opera, Arizona; Further engagements as Farnace in Mitridate at St Louis, Tsaura in Tancredi at La Scala, Lola at the Arena di Verona, Cenerentola at Covent Garden, (United Kingdom debut, 1993), and Ramiro in La Finta Giardinera for Welsh National Opera; recitals at Göttingen and Hesse Handel Festivals, further Handel performances with Nicholas McGegan and appearances with San Francisco, Detroit, St Louis and Sacramento Symphonies, and Fresno and Mexico City Philharmonics; Sang Handel's Poro at the Halle Festival, 1998. *Recordings include:* Flora in La Traviata; Handel's La Resurrezione, Messiah and Ottone, conducted by McGegan. *Honours:* Il Cenacolo Award in the 1987 Merola Opera Programme, San Francisco Opera Centre. *Current Management:* Neil Funkhauser. *Address:* c/o San Francisco Opera, War Memorial Opera House, San Francisco, CA 94102, USA.

SPENCE, Toby; Singer (Tenor); b. 1968, England. *Education:* Choral scholar at New College, Oxford; Opera School of the Guildhall School. *Career:* Debut: Barbican Hall with the Gothenburg Symphony Orchestra in The Tempest by Sibelius; Concerts with RIAS Berlin in Handel's Theodora, at the Wigmore Hall in Schubertiade series and at the Brighton Festival in the Missa Solemnis; Further concerts include the St Matthew Passion, with Frans Brueggen, Die Schöpfung by Haydn and On Wenlock Edge, by Vaughan Williams (Cheltenham Festival); Other orchestras include the Bournemouth Symphony Orchestra, Royal Philharmonic and Cleveland Orchestra; Season 1995–96 included Welsh National Opera debut, as Idamante in Idomeneo, Pane in La Calisto under René Jacobs at Brussels, and in Verdi's Alzira at Covent Garden; Season 1996–97 at the Salzburg Festival in Mitridate, as Tamino at Brussels and with the Israel Philharmonic and San Francisco

Symphony Orchestras; Sang in Roméo et Juliette by Berlioz at the London Festival Hall, 1999; Jacquino in Fidelio at the Paris Châtelet, 2002. *Recordings include:* Albums with DGG, Decca, BMG and EMI; St Matthew Passion (Philips Classics). *Address:* 408 The Royle Building, 23–41 Wenlock Road, London, N1 7SH.

SPERSKI, Krzysztof; Violoncellist and Teacher; b. 11 June 1942, Kraków, Poland; m. Janina Duda, 24 June 1967, divorced 1986, 1 s. *Education:* MA (cello class of Professor R Suchecki), Academy of Music, Gdansk, 1969; Doctorate (Adjunct qualification), Academy of Music, Poznan, 1978; Habilitation (Docent qualification), Academy of Music, Łódź, 1985. *Career:* Debut: Debut recital by Association of Polish Artist Musicians, Gdansk, 1964; Soloist of symphony concerts, recitals, chamber concerts in Poland and foreign concert tours, Finland, the United Kingdom, Sweden, Germany, Romania, Bulgaria, Iceland, Czechoslovakia, Austria, Greece, Italy, Denmark, Lithuania, Peru, Switzerland, Netherlands, Belgium, Russia, Chile; Professor of Cello, Academy of Music, Gdansk; Guest Professor, Music Masterclasses, Mynä m äki, Finland, 1976, International Music Seminar, Kozani, Greece, 1990–99, Masterclasses Santiago, Chile, 1998–2000, Lima, Peru, 2000; mem, Association of Polish Artist Musicians. *Recordings:* Radio and television recordings; CD, Slavic Music, 1994; Music Treasures of Gdansk, 1997. *Publications:* About faults of position, left and right hand of young cellists, 1979; Characteristics of Musical Utterance, 1981; Remarks of Performing Violoncello Baroque Music in the Light of Traditions and Contemporary Requirements, 1988; Polish Violoncello Pedagogic Literature, 1988. *Honours:* Award for Polish Culture, 1979; Distinction of Merit, Town of Gdansk, 1981; Gold Cross of Merit, 1985. *Address:* ul Goralska 55/A/9, 80-292 Gdańsk, Poland.

SPICKA, Daniel (Hilarius); Music Festival Art Director, Early Music Instrument Maker and Collector; b. 5 Feb. 1939, Prague, Czechoslovakia; m. The Hon Victoria W Reilly, 13 Jan 1973, 2 d. *Education:* Architecture, Czech Technical University, Prague, 1956–62; Evening course in Conducting, Prague Conservatoire, 1960–63; Private studies of Piano, Viol, Classical Guitar. *Career:* Debut: With Vejvanovsky Consort, Prague, 1959; With Camerata RSX, 1977; Valtice Baroque Festival, 1989; Founder, Camerata RSX, 1st authentic Renaissance Consort in Bohemia; Co-Founder of Valtice Baroque Opera Festival, South Moravia, Czech Republic; Performances on Czech and Austrian television, BBC and Czech Radio; Dramaturg of Valtice Baroque Opera Festival, 1989–; Noted for introducing authentic Early Music performances to Czech music scene, by bringing books, magazines, recordings and plans of instruments from the West to former Czechoslovakia; mem, Czech Music Society, Early Music Branch. *Recordings:* Gagliano–La Dafne, 1992; Monteverdi–Balli, 1994. *Contributions:* Various Czech music magazines, 1982–; Articles on Valtice Festival in The Independent, 1990, Die Presse, 1990, 1992, The Times, 1992. *Current Management:* Avant Promotion. *Address:* U Mrázovky 7, 15000 Prague 5, Czech Republic.

SPIERS, Colin James, BA; Australian composer and pianist; b. 24 July 1957, Brisbane, Qld. *Education:* Queensland Conservatorium. *Career:* Faculty mem., Univ. of Queensland 1980–90, Newcastle Conservatorium 1990–; founding mem., Perihelion Ensemble; solo pianist, recital accompanist and composition teacher. *Compositions include:* Fantasy on Theme of Keith Jarrett for piano 1987, Divertimento for strings 1987, Tales from Nowhere for piano 1988, Sonata for solo viola 1988, Day of Death and Dreams for tenor and piano 1989, UWJ for viola and piano 1991, Flecks for piano 1991, Cadenzas and Interludes for string orchestra 1991, Deranged Confessions, Desperate Acts, Divine Symmetry, Delicate Games piano sonatas 1990–98, ZYJ for trumpet and piano 1993, Music, Like the Dark Husk of Earth, Abiding for string orchestra 1994, NSJ for clarinet, bassett-horn and piano 1995, Mutations for piano 1996, five Bagatelles for piano 1996–97, Sonata for cello and piano 1999, The Last Thoughts of Prokofiev for piano 2003, Blue into Blue for orchestra 2004, Collide for orchestra 2004. *Honours:* Queensland Conservatorium Medal of Excellence 1979, Jean Bogan Composition Prize 1995. *Address:* 16 Kimian Avenue, Waratah West, NSW 2298, Australia (home). *Telephone:* (02) 49218925 (office). *E-mail:* Colin.Spiers@newcastle.edu.au (office).

SPIESS, Ludovico; Singer (Tenor); b. 13 May 1938, Cluj, Romania. *Education:* Studied at the Budapest Music Academy and in Milan with Antonio Narducci. *Career:* Debut: Galati in 1962 as the Duke of Mantua; Sang operetta at the Bucharest Operetta Theatre, 1962–64; Bucharest Opera from 1964 with debut as Cavaradossi; Sang at Salzburg Festival in 1967 as Dmitri in Boris Godunov conducted by Karajan, Vienna Staatsoper from 1968 with debut as Smetana's Dalibor, Verona Arena in 1969 as Calaf in Turandot, Covent Garden debut in 1973 as Radames, and Bregenz Festival in 1974 as Don José; Appearances at Metropolitan Opera and in Hamburg, Houston, Buenos Aires, San Francisco, Naples and Berlin; Other roles include Florestan, Rodolfo, Lohengrin and Otello. *Recordings:* Boris Godunov; Iphigénie en Aulide; Khovanshchina. *Address:* c/o Staatsoper, Opernring 2, 1010 Vienna, Austria.

SPIEWAK, Tomasz, BEd; Australian (b. Polish) pianist and composer; b. 12 Sept. 1936, Kraków; s. of Antoni Spiewak and Janina Mermon; one s. one d. *Education:* State Primary and Secondary Music School, Kraków, Jagiellonian Univ., Kraków and Univ. of Melbourne, Australia. *Career:* full-time teacher, Box Hill Coll. of Music, Melbourne, Australia 1982–2001; two years in Polish army ensemble, Desant as pianist, composer and arranger; five years in Polish comedy theatre, Wagabunda as musical dir, pianist, composer, arranger and bandleader; two years in Polish radio and TV orchestra as pianist, composer and arranger; pianist, organist and arranger in a quartet, toured through Scandinavia 1971–74; currently part-time teacher of aural training, Defence Force School of Music, Melbourne. *Compositions include:* Quartet for Saxophones in four movements 1988, 11 studies for marimba 1988–94, three marimba duets 1988–94, six preludes for vibraphone 1988–95, Sonatina for B flat saxophone and piano 1990, Duo Sonata for tenor and baritone saxophones 1990, Trio for alto and baritone saxophones and piano 1991, Sonata for trombone and piano 1992, Roller Coaster for violoncello 1996, pieces for bassoon and piano 1996, Floral Suite for alto saxophone and piano 2000, Scherzetto for baritone saxophone and piano 2000, Walking Dance for baritone saxophone and piano 2000, Second Quartet for saxophones, featuring baritone saxophone 2000, Kaleidoscope for alto saxophone and piano 2002, Blue Ride for alto saxophone and piano 2002, Palindrome for saxophone quartet 2003, Quartet for Saxophones No. 3 (from Rag to Funk) 2003, six pieces for saxophone solo 2004, six pieces for clarinet solo 2004. *Publications:* Aural Training for Musicians and Music Students Vols I–IV 1991–96, The Performing Ear (with Jenni Hillman) 2001, Vocalises for Modern Singers Vols I–III 2002. *E-mail:* tspiewak@bigpond.net.au.

SPIEWOK, Stephen; Singer (Tenor); b. 1 Dec. 1947, Berlin, Germany. *Education:* Musikhochschule, Weimar, and with Johannes Kemter in Dresden. *Career:* Debut: Weimar 1971, as Nicolai's Fenton; Dresden Staatsoper 1971-80, notably in the 1979 premiere of Vincent, by Kunad; Leipzig Opera and Berlin Staatsoper 1980-90, including the 1984 premiere if Kunad's Amphitryon; Ludwigsburg Festival 1989, as Ephrain in the premiere of Judith, by S. Matthus; Sang Arbace in Idomeneo at the Komische Oper, Berlin, and Morosus at Wiesbaden (Die schweigsame Frau, by Strauss); Guest appearances throughout Europe and in Japan as Tamino, the Duke of Mantua, Števa in Jenůfa, and Andres in Wozzeck; Many concert engagements. *Address:* c/o Komische Oper, Behrenstrasse 55-S7, D-10117 Berlin, Germany.

SPILLER, Andres; Oboist and Conductor; b. 24 Dec. 1946, Buenos Aires, Argentina; m. Marcela Magin, 2 s., 1 d. *Education:* Conservatorio Nacional; Private studies, Hochschule für Musik, Cologne, Germany; Summer courses with Heinz Holliger, Bruno Maderna, Franco Ferrara, Michael Gielen, Volker Wangenheim. *Career:* Assistant Conductor, National Symphony Orchestra and Oboe Soloist; Oboe Soloist, Camerata Bariloche and Soloist of Bach Academy, Buenos Aires; Conductor, La Plata Chamber Orchestra; Performed with Koeckert Quartet in Munich; Other European appearances include Madrid, Rome and Radio Zürich; Toured America and Europe with Camerata Bariloche; Professor of Oboe and Chamber Music. *Recordings:* Death of an Angel; Tango. *Honours:* DAAD Fellowship for study in Germany; Sociedad Hebraica Prize; 2nd Prize, Promaciones Musicales; Premio Konex, 1989, 1999. *Address:* Medrano 47, 5øA, 1178 Buenos Aires, Argentina.

SPINK, Ian; Emeritus Professor; b. 29 March 1932, London, England; m. 7 c. *Education:* BMus, London, 1952; MA, Birmingham, 1958. *Career:* Lecturer, Senior Lecturer, University of Sydney, New South Wales, 1962–68; Senior Lecturer, Reader, Professor, London University (RHUL), 1969–97; Emeritus Professor, 1997–, Dean of Faculty of Arts, 1973–75 and 1983–85; Dean of Faculty of Music, University of London, 1974–78; Member of Senate, 1975–81. *Publications include:* The English Lute-Songs, Vol. 17, 1961, 2nd edition, 1974, Vol. 18, 1963, Vol. 19, 1966; An Historical Approach to Musical Form, 1967; Editor, English Songs 1625–1660, Musica Britannica, Vol. 33, 1971; English Song, Dowland to Purcell, 1974, revised edition, 1986; Editor, Arne, The Judgement of Paris, Musica Britannica, Vol. 42, 1979; Purcell, A Song for the Duke of Gloucester's Birthday, 1695, Purcell Society Edition, Vol. 4, 1990; The Seventeenth Century, Blackwell History of Music in Britain, Vol. 3, 1992; Purcell, Timon of Athens, Vol. 2, 1994; Restoration Cathedral Music, 1660–1714, 1995; Purcell, Dramatic Music Part II vol. 20, 1998; Henry Lawes, Cavalier Songwriter, 2000; Purcell, Catches, Vol. 22a, 2000; Purcell, Duets, Dialgoues and Trios, Vol. 22B, 2001. *Address:* Royal Holloway, University of London, Egham, Surrey TW20 0EX, England.

SPINNLER, Burkard; Pianist; b. 17 July 1954, Goldbach, Germany; m. Claudine Orloff, 1 Oct 1983, 2 s., 1 d. *Education:* Staatsexamen, Musikhochschule Würzburg, with J von Karolyi, 1978; Diplome Superieur, Brussels Royal Conservatory, with J Cl Vanden Eynden, 1982; Ecole de Maitrise Pianistique, 1981–84; Private studies with Eduardo del Pueyo in Brussels. *Career:* Debut: With University Orchestra at

Würzburg in 1978; Recording for Bavarian Radio in 1979, for Belgian Radio RTB, 1984; Appearances as soloist and in chamber music in Germany, Belgium and France; Special L Godowsky commemorative programme, 1989; Regular concerts on 2 pianos with Claudine Orloff, including Musique en Sorbonne, Paris, 1991; Live radio engagement, Hommage à Milhaud, RTB Brussels in 1992 and 1999; Private research of Liszt unpublished works and 136 unedited letters of Francis Poulenc; Teaches at Brussels Conservatory, 1985–; Further live recordings for Belgian and French radio in 1995 and 1998. *Publications:* Zur Angemessenheit Traditionelles Formbegriffe in der Analyse Mahlerscher Symphonik, in Form und Idée in G Mahlers Instrumentalmusik, 1980. *Current Management:* F E de Wasseige Music Management. *Address:* 109 Avenue E Van Becelaere, 1170 Brussels, Belgium.

ŠPITKOVA, Jela; violinist; b. 1947, Czechoslovakia. *Education:* Bratislava Conservatory and in Vienna with Riccardo Odnoposoff, Prague Coll. of Music, Tchaikovsky Conservatory Moscow with David and Igor Oistrakh. *Career:* has performed with leading Czech Orchestras and in 40 other countries, including South and North America and Africa; recitals in Paris, Rome, Moscow, Berlin, Prague, Amsterdam and Vienna; television and radio recordings in Spain, Norway, Denmark, Austria, France, Finland and Russia; Leader of the Mozarteum Orchestra 1980; teacher at the Music Acad. in Vienna; soloist with the Slovak Philharmonic in Bratislava; repertoire includes concertos by Tchaikovsky, Brahms, Beethoven, Sibelius, Mendelssohn, Mozart, Bach and Haydn, Lalo Symphonie Espagnole, Sonatas by Brahms, Beethoven, Franck, Schumann, Prokofiev, Mozart, Handel, Debussy and Dvořák; Concertmaster, Mozarteum Orchestra in Salzburg 1980–94; teacher of violin, Music Acad., Vienna 1985–. *Recordings:* Mendelssohn Violin Concerto in E Minor; Bruch Violin Concerto; Chausson, Poème; Tchaikovsky Serenade Melancholique; Brahms Sonata No. 3; Ravel's Tzigane; Sibelius Violin Concerto; Suchon Sonatine op 11; Haydn Violin Concerto in C Major; Dittersdorf Violin Concerto in G Minor. *Honours:* 3rd Prize, National Youth Festival, Sofia, 1968; 3 Prizes in international violin competition, Tibor Varga, Switzerland, 1969; 3rd Prize, international competition, Emily Anderson, Royal Philharmonic Society, London, 1969. *Address:* Belopotockeho 2, 81105 Bratislava, Slovakia.

SPIVAKOV, Vladimir Teodorovich; Russian violinist and conductor; b. 12 Sept. 1944, Ufa, Bashkiria; m. Satinik Saakyants; three d. *Education:* Moscow State Conservatory, postgraduate with Yury Yankelevich. *Career:* studied violin since age of six with B. Kroger in Leningrad; prize winner in several int. competitions including Tchaikovsky, Moscow; Founder and Conductor Chamber Orchestra Virtuosi of Moscow 1979–; Founder and Artistic Dir Music Festival in Colmar, France 1989–; Artistic Dir and Chief Conductor Russian Nat. Symphony Orchestra 1999–2003; founder, Artistic Dir and Chief Conductor Nat. Philharmonic Orchestra of Russia 2003–; Guest Conductor of several orchestras including Chicago Symphony Orchestra, LA Philharmonic, London Symphony Orchestra, English and Scottish Chamber Orchestras; f. Int. Charity Foundation 1994. *Recordings:* more than 20 CDs on Capriccio, RCA Victor Red Seal and BMG Classics including works by Brahms, Berg, Chausson, Franck, Prokoviev, Ravel, Tchaikovsky, Richard Strauss, Schubert, Sibelius, Shostakovich. *Honours:* Les Insignes de Chevalier de la Légion d'Honneur 1994 USSR State Prize 1989, USSR People's Artist 1990, Triumph Prize, Nat. Cultural Heritage Award, Russia's Artist of the Year 2002, First Prize Montreal Competition, Marguerite Long St Jacques Thibaud Competition, Paris, Nicolo Paganini Int. Violin Competition, Genoa, Int. Tchaikovsky Competition, Moscow. *Address:* c/o Columbia Artists Management, 165 West 57th Street, New York, NY 10019, USA (office); Vspolny per. 17, Apt 14, Moscow, Russia. *Telephone:* (095) 290-23-24 (Moscow); 1-45-25-50-85 (Paris). *Fax:* 1-45-25-04-60 (Paris).

SPOORENBERG, Erna; Singer (Soprano); b. 11 April 1926, Yogyakarta, Java. *Education:* Studied in the Netherlands with Julius Rontgen and Aaltje Noordewier-Reddingius. *Career:* Debut: Hilversum concert in 1947 with Mozart's Motet Exsultate Jubilate; Opera debut at the Vienna Staatsoper in 1949; Sang in Vienna, Hamburg in 1962, Düsseldorf and Amsterdam in operas by Mozart and as Debussy's Mélisande, and at Bordeaux in 1964 in La Dame Blanche by Boildieu; Concert tours of Germany, South Africa, Russia, Austria and Scandinavia; US debut at Lincoln Center in New York in 1967; Recital partnership with the pianist, Geza Frid. *Recordings:* Pelléas et Mélisande conducted by Ansermet; Die Schöpfung; Mahler's 8th Symphony; Bach Cantatas; Masses by Haydn.

SPOTORNO, Marianangela; Singer (Soprano); b. 1970, Rome. *Education:* First studied cello, then singing with Magda Laszlo and Elio Battaglia. *Career:* Debut: Elisabetta in Cimarosa's Il Matrimonio Segreto, for the Walton Trust at Ischia and in Scotland, 1992; Sang in Offenbach's Barbe-bleue at Bologna and Messina, Mozart's Fiordiligi and Susanna at Cagliari; Sang the title role in Manon Lescaut at the Glyndebourne Festival, 1997, and engaged 1997–98 as Antonia in L'Elisir d'amore; Concerts include: Beethoven's Christus am Olberge, at

Treviso, and opera concert with Domingo in Finland; Sang the voice of the soprano Guiditta Pasta for Italian television film of the life of Giulio Ricordi. *Address:* c/o Teatro Massimo Bellini, Via Perrotta 12, 95131 Catania, Italy.

SPRATLAN, Lewis; Composer; b. 5 Sept. 1940, Miami, Florida, USA. *Education:* Composition studies with Yehudi Wyner, Gunther Schuller and Mel Powell at Yale University (BA, 1962, MM, 1965); George Rochberg and Roger Sessions at Tanglewood, 1966. Career Faculty Member, Pennsylvania State University, 1967–70; Amherst College from 1970 (Chairman of Music Department, 1977–94, Professor from 1980). *Compositions include:* Missa Brevis, 1965; Cantate Domine for men's chorus, winds and tape, 1968; Serenade for 6 instruments, 1970; Moonsong for chorus and ensemble, 1970; Two Pieces for orchestra, 1971; Woodwind quintet, 1971; Fantasy for piano and chamber ensemble, 1973; Ben Jonson for soprano, violin and cello, 1974; Life is a Dream, opera, 1977; Coils for ensemble, 1980; String Quartet, 1982; When Crows Gather for 3 clarinets, violin, cello, and piano, 1986; Hung Monophonies for oboe and 11 instruments, 1990; Night Music for violin, clarinet and percussion, 1991; In Memorian for soloists, chorus and orchestra, 1993; A Barred Owl baritone and 5 instruments, 1994; Concertino for violin, cello and double baritone and 5 instruments, 1994; Concertino for violin, cello and double bass, 1995; Psalm 42, for soprano, baritone and ensemble, 1996. *Address:* c/o ASCAP, ASCAP Building, 1 Lincoln Plaza, New York, NY 10023, USA.

SPRATT, Geoffrey (Kenneth); Musician; b. 16 Sept. 1950, London, England; m. 1st Frances Vivien Spratt, two s. 2nd Elizabeth Searls. *Education:* BA, Honours with Distinction in Practical Work, 1973; PhD, University of Bristol, 1980. *Career:* Professional freelance flute and viola player with Cyprus Broadcasting Company Orchestras, 1969–70, and various British Orchestras, 1970–76; Part-time Tutor, Open University, 1973–76 and University of Bristol, 1974–76; Lecturer in Music, University College, Cork, Ireland, 1976–92; Founder-Conductor, UCC Choir and Orchestra, 1976–92; Conductor, UCC Choral Society, 1978–86, Madrigal '75 Chamber Choir; Director, Cork School of Music, 1992–; Founder-Conductor, Irish Youth Choir and the Fleischmann Choir of the Cork School of Music; Conductor, Canticum Novum Chamber Choir; Guest Conductor: National Symphony Orchestra of Ireland, RTE Concert Orchestra, RTE Chorus, RTE Chamber Choir, Irish Chamber Orchestra and Galway Baroque Singers; Chairman, Association of Irish Choirs and Cork Orchestral Society; Council, Music Teachers' Association of Ireland, 1977–. *Recordings:* Choral music of Séamas de Barra sung by the Irish Youth Choir and Madrigal '75; Sacred Choral Music of Angel Climent sung by the Irish Youth Choir. *Publications:* Catalogue des oeuvres de Arthur Honegger, Geneva and Paris, 1986; Co-author with M Delannoy, Honegger, Geneva and Paris, 1986; The Music of Arthur Honegger, Cork, 1987. *Honours:* Napier Miles Prize, Bristol University, 1972. *Address:* Director, Cork School of Music, Union Quay, Cork, Ireland. *E-mail:* gspratt@cit.ie.

SQUIRES, Shelagh; Singer (Mezzo-soprano); b. 17 Aug. 1936, England. *Education:* Guildhall School, London. *Career:* Debut: Glyndebourne 1968, in Die Zauberflöte; Sang Cherubino for Phoenix Opera, 1969; Sadler's Wells/English National Opera from 1972, as Mozart's Marcellina, Tisbe in Cenerentola, Filippevna in Eugene Onegin, Emilia in Othello, and Mamma Lucia in Cavalleria Rusticana; Appearances in the first local stage performances of War and Peace; Penderecki's The Devils of Loudun, Janáček's Osud (1984), Christmas Eve by Rimsky-Korsakov, and the premiere of Robin Holloway's Clarissa (1990); Other roles in The Ring of the Nibelung, as Rosette in Manon, Jezibaba in Rusalka and Mrs Sedley in Peter Grimes. *Recordings include:* Othello, The Ring (EMI); Video of Gloriana. *Address:* c/o English National Opera, St Martin's Lane, London, WC2, England.

SRABRAWA, Daniel; Violinist; b. 1948, Kraków, Poland. *Education:* Studied with Z Slezer in Kraków. *Career:* Leader of Kraków Radio Symphony Orchestra, 1979; Joined Berlin Philharmonic Orchestra in 1983 and became leader in 1983; Co-founder of the Philharmonic Quartet Berlin giving concerts throughout Europe, USA and Japan; British debut in 1987 playing Haydn, Szymanowski and Beethoven at Wigmore Hall; Played at Bath Festival in 1987 with Mozart, Schumann and Beethoven Op 127; Other repertoire includes quartets by Bart ók, Mendelssohn, Nicolai, Ravel and Schubert, and quintets by Brahms, Weber, Reger and Schumann. *Address:* c/o Vogtr Artists, Philharmonia Quartet, 1714 Stockton St, Suite 300, San Francisco, CA 94133–2930, USA.

SRAMEK, Alfred; Singer (Bass); b. 5 April 1951, Nichtelbach, Vienna, Austria. *Education:* Studied with Ludwig Weber and Hilde Zadek. *Career:* Has sung with the Vienna Staatsoper from 1975 in Palestrina and as Don Pasquale, Dulcamara, Beckmesser, Masetto, Leporello and Figaro; Sang at Salzburg Festival from 1976, and Bregenz Festival in 1982; Season 2000–01 at the Vienna State Opera in Lulu, Figaro (as Bartolo), Wozzeck and Billy Budd; Dulcamara in L'elisir d'amore; Many concert appearances. *Recordings:* Lohengrin; Wozzeck; Don Giovanni; Ariadne auf Naxos; Die Lustigen Weiber von Windsor; Karl V by Krenek; Video of Wozzeck, as First Workman, conducted by Abbado. *Address:* c/o Staatsoper, Opernring 2, 1010 Vienna, Austria.

STAAHLEN, Torhild; Norwegian Singer (mezzo-soprano); b. 25 Sept. 1947, Skien; m. Neil Dodd 1975. *Education:* Music Conservatory, Oslo; National Opera School. *Career:* debut, Oslo, as Suzuki in Madama Butterfly, 1971; has sung 65 roles from the mezzo-alto repertoire, including the title role in Carmen, Octavian in Der Rosenkavalier, Azucena in Il Trovatore, Ulrica in Un Ballo in Maschera, Amneris in Aida, Erda in Das Rheingold, Waltraute in Götterdämmerung, La Principezza in Suor Angelica, Olga in Eugene Onegin, Prince Orlovsky in Die Fledermaus, and Valencienne in The Merry Widow; character roles include Heriodas in Salome, Marcellina in The Marriage of Figaro, La Vecchia Madelon in Andrea Chenier, and The Secretary in Jeppe by Geir Tveitt; frequent radio and television broadcasts; sings many oratorios including the Bach Passions and Handel's Messiah; concert repertoire includes Brahms' Alto Rhapsody, Wagner's Wesendonck Lieder, Beethoven's Ninth Symphony, Mahler's Second and Fourth Symphonies, Elgar's Sea Pictures, Heise's Bergljot, Handel's Samson, and Pergolesi's Stabat Mater; guested in Sweden, Denmark, Finland, Germany, England, Scotland and the USA; has sung under conductors including Heinrich Hollreiser, Paavo Berglund, Maurice Handford, Heinz Fricke, Antonio Pappano, Michael Schönwandt, Silvio Varviso, Erich Wächter, and Berislav Klobuchar; mem., Norsk Musikerforbund, Norsk Operasangerforbund. *Recordings:* Expression, 1991. *Honours:* State Artist's Stipendium, Fund for Performing Artists; Prize of Honour, Friends of Music in Telemark, 1981; City of Oslo Cultural Stipendium; Vel Medal, Norway. *Address:* Breidablikkveien 24, 1167 Oslo, Norway.

STAAR, René; Composer and Violinist; b. 30 May 1951, Graz, Austria. *Education:* Sibelius Academy, Helsinki, 1968-69; Vienna Hochschule für Msuik, 1963-79, with Hans Swarowsky and Roman Haubenstock – Ramati, Violin with Nathan Milstein in Zürich. *Career:* Co-founder, Ensemble Wiener College 1986; Member of Vienna PO, from 1988; Director of Graz-Petersburg Ensemble, 1993; Founder, Ensemble Wien-Paris, 1996. *Compositions:* Structures I-VI, for various ensembles, 1981-82; Just an Accident, Requiem, 1985; Das wachsende Schloss, for violin and orchestra, 1986; Bagatellen auf den Namen György Ligeti, for piano, 1989-96, Metamorphosen eines labyrinths for violin and strings, 1991; Versunkene Träume, for string quartet, 1993; Metropolitan Midnight Music, 1993; Heine Fragments, for soprano, baritone and ensemble, 1997; Monumentum pro Thomas Alva Edison, for violin, guitar and double bass, 1998. *Address:* c/o AKM, Baumanstrasse 10, 1031 Wien, Postfach 259, Austria.

STABELL, Carsten; Singer (Bass); b. 5 Sept. 1960, Trondheim, Norway. *Education:* Studied at the Norwegian Opera School, Oslo. *Career:* Debut: Oslo in 1984 as the King in Aida; Sang at Stuttgart Opera from 1986 as Osmin, Sarastro, the Commendatore, Pietro in Simon Boccanegra and the Hermit in Der Freischütz; Sang Rustomji in Philip Glass's Satyagraha in 1990; Concert repertoire includes Bach's Magnificat and St John Passion, Messiah, Judas Maccabaeus, Acis and Galatea, Die Schöpfung, the Requiems of Mozart and Verdi and Liszt's Christus; Engaged as the Commendatore at Opera Geneva and Sarastro at the Opéra de Paris Bastille in 1991, and in Perseo e Andromeda by Sciarrino at La Scala Milan in 1992; Season 1998 with Oroveso in Norma at Philadelphia and Fafner in Siegfried for Netherlands Opera; Sang Fasolt at Edinburgh, Daland in Ghent, King Marke for Houston Opera and Banquo at the Vienna Staatsoper, 2000–01. *Address:* c/o Staatstheater Stuttgart, Oberer Schlossgarten 6, 7000 Stuttgart 1, Germany.

STABLER, Gerhard; Composer; b. 20 July 1949, Wilhelmsdorf, Germany. *Education:* Studied at Detmold Music Academy, 1968–70 and with Nicolaus Huber (composition) and Gerd Zacher (organ) at the Essen Hochschule, 1970–76; Further courses with Stockhausen, Kagel and Ligeti, at Cologne and Darmstadt. *Career:* Stanford University computer music centre, 1983, 1986; Faculty Member, Essen Hochschule 1989–94; Concert, lecture tours and guest professorships in Europe, Asia and North and South America from 1985. *Compositions include:* Drüber, for 8 screamers, cello and tape, 1972; Das Sichere ist nicht sicher, spiral rondo for 8 instruments and tape, 1982; Schatten Wilder Schmerzen, for orchestra, 1985; Warnung mit Liebeslied for harp, accordion and percussion, 1986;... strike the ear... for string quartet, 1988; October for flute, violin and double bass, 1988; Den Müllfahren von San Francisco, for 17 instruments, 1990; Ungaretti Lieder for mezzo or baritone and percussion, 1990; Sünde, Fall, Beil, opera after Catherine Howard by Dumas, 1992; Traum 1/9/92, for soprano saxophone, cello, piano and ensemble, 1992; CassandraComplex, music theatre, 1994; (Apparat), for chorus, clarinet, accordion, double bass and percussion, 1994; Karas.Krähen, for tape, 1994; Winter, Blumen, for countertenor, or solo string instruments, 1995; Internet, various works for solo instruments or chamber music ensembles, 1995–98; Spuren, for

saxophone quartet, 1995; Dali, for piano solo, 1996; Poetic Arcs, for ensemble, 1996; Cassandra, music for dance, 1996; Burning Minds, for 12 voices, 1997; Bridges, for mezzo and accordion, 1997; Ausnahme.Zustand for orchestra, 1998; Time for Tomorrow, theatre music, for voice percussion and tape, 1998; Metal Seasons for violin solo, brass ensemble, percussion and airplanes, 1999. *Honours:* Cornelius Cardew Memorial Prize, London, 1982; Fellowship in composition, Heinrich-Strobel-Stiftung, 1985–86; Niederdachsen Scholarship, 1987–88; Japan Foundation Scholarship, 1994. GEMA, Rosenheimer Str 11, 81667 Munich, Germany.

STACY, Thomas; Oboist and English Horn Player; b. 15 Aug. 1938, Little Rock, AR, USA. *Education:* Studied in New York. *Career:* Solo English Horn with the New York PO, from 1972; Guest engagements with leading orchestras throughout America; Commisioned and premiered works by Stanislav Skrowaczewski, Gunther Schuller, Ned Rorem (1994) and Vincent Persichetti; Lecturer at the Juilliard School, NY, masterclasses at the Royal Academy, London and throughout Asia, Director of Stacy English Horn Seminar. *Recordings include:* Concertos by Rorem and Persichetti. *Address:* c/o New York Philharmonic Orchestra, 10 Lincoln Center Plaza, Broadway at 65th Street, New York, NY 10023, USA.

STADELMANN, Christian; Violinist; b. 1958, Berlin, Germany. *Education:* Studied with Charlotte Hampe and Thomas Brandis in Berlin. *Career:* Former Member of the Junge Deutsche Philharmonie and Co-founder of its Chamber Orchestra; Member of the Berlin Philharmonic 1985, leader of the 2nd violins, 1987; Second Violinist of the Philharmonia Quartet, Berlin, 1986; Many concerts with the Quartet in all European major cities and regular tours to the USA, Japan and South America. *Recordings include:* Quartets by Reger, Beethoven, Shostakovich, Szymanowski, Janáček for leading recording companies. *Address:* c/o Berlin Philharmonisches Orchester, Herbert von Karajan Strasse 1, 10785 Berlin, Germany.

STADLER, Irmgard; Singer (Soprano); b. 28 March 1937, Michaelbeuern, Salzburg, Austria. *Education:* Studied at Salzburg Mozarteum and Vienna Academy of Music. *Career:* Debut: Stuttgart 1962, as Micaela; Salzburg Festival 1961–62, in Idomeneo, Mozart's Requiem 1962–63; Glyndebourne Festival 1967–72 as Sicle in L'Ormindo, Donna Elvira, Juno in La Calisto and the Composer (Ariadne auf Naxos); Member of Stuttgart Opera since 1963; Guest appearances in Vienna, Munich, Berlin, Lisbon, Venice and Rome; Most important roles: Elvira, Cherubino, Fiordiligi, Elektra (Idomeneo), Octavian and Marschallin, Eva, Gutrune, Alice, Agathe, Marenka (Bartered Bride), Rusalka, Jenůfa, Katya Kabanova, Lisa (Queen of Spades), Tatiana, Marina and Marie in Wozzeck; Concert appearances in sacred music by Bach, Mozart, Bruckner and Lieder Recitals; Sang Theresa in the premiere of Giuseppe & Sylvia by Adriana Hölszky, Stuttgart, 2000. *Address:* c/o Staatstheater Stuttgart, Oberer Schlossgarten 6, D-70173 Stuttgart, Germany.

STADLMAIR, Hans; Conductor; b. 3 May 1929, Neuhofen, Austria. *Education:* Studied at the Vienna Academy of Music, 1946–52 with Clemens Krauss and Alfred Uhl and in Stuttgart, 1952–56 with Johann Nepomuk David. *Career:* Conducted the Stuttgart Chorus and became conductor of Munich Chamber Orchestra, 1956; Tours of Europe, North and South America, Asia, Africa, Canada and India; Has conducted own realisation of the Adagio from Mahler's 10th Symphony. *Compositions:* Concerto Profano for Violin, Cello and Orchestra; Concerto Capriccioso for two Flutes and Orchestra (composed for A Nicolet and J Pierre Rampal); Adagietto for Strings, Ecce Homo, 5 Novelletten for Strings; Sinfonia: 'Da Pacem Domine' für Alphorn, Röhrenglocken and Strings, 1988; Lacrimae Metamorphosen for Strings; Essay for clarinet and strings. *Recordings:* W A Mozart, Piano Concertos Nr 8 KV246, Lützow and Nr 9 KV271, Jeunehomme; F Danzi: Phantasie on La ci darem la mano from Don Giovanni, K Stamitz; Concerto for Clarinet Nr 3 B flat (E Brunner–Clarinet); Haydn's Seven Last Words; Scarlatti Il Giardino di Amore; Mozart Bassoon Concerto, Clarinet Concerto and Violin Concerto K219; Vivaldi Four Seasons; Koch-Schwann: Hans Stadlmair. *Contributions:* Riemann Musiklexikon. *Honours:* Medaille: München Leuchtet, 1989; Bundesverdienstkreuz am Bande, 1989; Musikpreis der Stadt München, 1994. *Address:* Dachauerstr 175, 80636 München, Germany.

STADLMAIR, Vincent; Cellist; b. 1959, Vienna, Austria. *Education:* Vienna Acad. of Music. *Career:* mem. of the Franz Schubert Quartet, Vienna from 1983; many concert engagements in Europe, USA, and Australia including appearances at the Amsterdam Concertgebouw, the Vienna Musikverein and Konzerthaus, the Salle Gaveau Paris and the Sydney Opera House; visits to Zürich, Geneva, Basle, Berlin, Hamburg, Rome, Rotterdam, Madrid and Copenhagen; festival engagements include Salzburg, Wiener Festwochen, Prague, Spring Schubertiade at Hohenems, the Schubert Festival at Washington DC and the Belfast and Istanbul Festivals; tours of Australasia, Russia and USA; frequent concert tours of the UK; featured in the Quartet Concerto by Spohr with the Liverpool Philharmonic in Liverpool at the Festival Hall; many appearances at the Wigmore Hall and Cheltenham Festival; teacher at the Vienna Conservatory and Graz Musikhochschule; masterclasses at the Royal Northern Coll. of Music, Lake District Summer Music. *Recordings include:* Schubert's Quartet in G, D887; Complete Quartets of Dittersdorf; Mozart's String Quartet in D, K575, and String Quartet in B flat, K589.

STAEHELIN, Martin; Musicologist; b. 25 Sept. 1937, Basel, Switzerland; m. Elisabeth Schenker. *Education:* Diploma, Teacher Querflöte, 1962, School Music Diploma, 1963, Music Academy, Basel; PhD, University of Basel, 1967. *Career:* Teacher of Latin, Greek and Music, Basel, 1963; Musicology Teacher, University of Zürich, 1971–76; Head of Beethoven Archives, Bonn, Germany, 1976–84; Teacher, 1976–77, Professor, 1977–83, University of Bonn; Professor, University of Göttingen, 1983–; Honorary Director of J. S. Bach Institut, Göttingen, 1992; mem. Akad. der Wissenschaften, Göttingen, 1987, Academia Europaea, London, 1995; Emeritus Univ., Göttingen, 2002. *Publications:* Editor, H Isaac, Messen, 1970, 1973; Der Grüne Codex der Viadrina, 1971; Die Messen Heinrich Isaacs, 3 vols, 1977. *Contributions:* Archiv für Musikwissenschaft; Die Musikforschung; Fontes Artis Musicae; Schweizer Beiträge zur Musikwissenschaft; Tijdschrift van de Vereniging voor Nederlandse Muziekgeschiedenis; Schweizerisches Archiv für Volkskunde. *Address:* Musicology Seminar of Georg August University, Kurze Geismarstrasse 1, 37073 Göttingen, Germany.

STAFFORD, Ashley (George); Counter-Tenor; b. 3 March 1954, Holland, near Oxted, Surrey, England; m. Shauni Lee McGregor, 4 June 1977, 2 s. *Education:* Westminster Abbey Choir School, 1963–68; Trinity School Croydon, 1968–72; Christchurch, Oxford, Choral Award, Academical Clerkship, 1972–75; BA, Honours, 1975, MA, 1978; Certificate of Education, London, 1976; Studied with Douglas Guest, at Oxford under Simon Preston, and vocal training with Hervey Alan, 1968–72, Paul Esswood, 1972–76, Helga Mott, 1976–80, and Jessica Cash, 1980–93. *Career:* Debut: Purcell Room, 1975; Sang in opera at Aix-en-Provence, Lyon, Oxford and London and in concert at major festivals throughout Europe, in Sydney and Melbourne, 1989, Japan, 1987 and 1989, Taiwan in 1989, USA and Canada including Bath, Edinburgh, Three Choirs, Berlin, Rome, Venice, Madrid, Barcelona, Lisbon, New York, Boston and Ottawa, 1980–86; Sang in Judith Weir's A Night at the Chinese Opera for Kent Opera; Many appearances on radio and on television including Messiah in France; Visiting Professor of Voice at Royal College of Music, London in 1989; mem. Incorporated Society of Musicians; Equity; Committee, Royal Society of Musicians. *Recordings include:* Purcell's Ode to St Cecilia, King Arthur, From the Nativity of Time (Songs sacred and secular); Handel's Israel in Egypt, Dettingen Te Deum; Valls's Mass Scala Aretina; Motets by Bach, Power, Dunstable and Josquin; Haydn's Nelson Mass; Scarlatti's Stabat Mater; Schütz's Muzikalisches Exequien; Handel's Alexander's Feast. *Honours:* Young Musician, Greater London Arts Association. *Address:* Fenton House, Banbury Road, Chipping Norton, Oxon OX7 5AW, England.

STAHL, David, BA, MA, MM; American symphony and opera conductor; b. 4 Nov. 1949, New York, NY; m. Karen Doss Stahl 1989; one s. two d. *Education:* Queens College, CUNY. *Career:* debut at Carnegie Hall, New York, 8 Dec 1973; Assistant Conductor, New York Philharmonic, 1976, and Cincinnati Symphony Orchestra, 1976–79; Music Director, St Louis Philharmonic, 1976–81; Broadway and international tour of West Side Story, 1980–82; Charleston (South Carolina) Symphony Orchestra, 1996–; Guest Conductor, Pittsburgh, Atlanta, Dallas, Indianapolis, St Louis, Buffalo, Baltimore, Long Beach, Edmonton, New World, San Jose, Winnipeg, and Louisville Symphonies; New York City Opera, Spoleto Festival, Lake George Opera, Dayton, Detroit, Hawaii and Tulsa opera companies; Overseas: RAI orchestra, Rome, Teatro Massimo, Palermo, Teatro Comunale, Genoa, Festival of two worlds, Spoleto, Orchestre Colonne, Paris, Orchestra del Sodre, Montevideo and Seoul (South Korea) Philharmonic, Toronto Symphony Orchestra, Montreal Opera, Washington Opera; Stadtheater National Mannheim, Darmstadt, Bernstein Festival in the Concertgebouw, Amsterdam; Principal Guest Conductor, Bavarian Staatstheater am Gaertnerplatz; Guest Conductor: NDR Symphony, Hamburg; Bamberg Symphony; Staatskappelle Dresden; L'Orchestre National de Lyon; Helsinki Philharmonic; Düsseldorf Symphony; Berlin Symphony Orchestra; Munich Philharmonic, Radio Symphony Orchestra of Stuttgart, Radio Philharmonie, Hannover; Chief Conductor Bavarian Staatstheater am Gaertnerplatz, 1999–. *Recordings:* Proto concertos for double bass; Portraits in Blue and Grey with Charleston Symphony; Poulenc Double Piano Concerto. *Honours:* ASCAP Award for Adventuresome Programming; Order of the Palmetto (highest award in South Carolina). *Current Management:* Colbert Artists Management Inc., 111 W 57th Street, New York, NY 10019, USA. *Address:* 14 George Street, Charleston, SC 29401, USA.

STAHLAMMER, Semmy; Musician and Violinist; b. 5 March 1954, Eskilstuna, Sweden. *Education:* Soloist Diploma, Royal Music College, Stockholm, 1972; Juilliard School of Music, USA, 1972–74; BMus, Curtis Institute of Music, 1975–79; Studied with Jaime Laredo, Ivan Galamian, Felx Galimir, Isidore Cohen, Szymon Goldberg, Paul Makanowitsky, Josef Silverstein, Josef Gingold, Nathan Milstein, Isaac Stern and Henryk Szeryng. *Career:* Debut: With Stockholm Philharmonic Orchestra, 1964; First Concertmaster of Stockholm Royal Opera, 1979–83; Artistic Director, Chamber Music in The Mirror Hall, 1982–; Artistic Director, Chamber Music in The Parks, 1986–; Teacher at Stockholm Royal Music College, 1987–. *Recordings:* Collections of Swedish 20th century music; Alfred Schnittke's Labyrinths; JS Bach's Sonatas and Partitas for Solo Violin. *Honours:* Winner of JS Bach International Violin Competition, Washington DC, 1985. *Address:* Norr Málarstrand 24, 112 20 Stockholm, Sweden.

STAHMER, Klaus Hinrich; Composer; b. 25 June 1941, Stettin, Poland. *Education:* Hamburg Musikhochschule, 1960-69. *Career:* Lecturer of Würzburg Hochschule für Musik 1969, Professor from 1979; Director of Würzburg New Music Studio, from 1989. *Compositions:* Quasi un requiem, for speaker and string quartet, 1974; Espace de la solitude (ballet), 1977; Multiples, concertino for three percussion and orchestra, 1977; Four Transformations, electronic, 1983; Soundscape, sound sculptures, 1985; Momentaufnahmen, for speaker and ensemble, 1986-89; Kristall-gitter, electronic, 1992; Weg nach Innen, for organ and percussion, 1992; Wie ein Still-stand der Zeit, for harp and strings, 1995; Noa, Noa for ensemble, 1996; Sacred Site, for piano, 1996; Herr der Winde, sound sculpture 1996. *Honours:* Würzburg Arts Prize, 1995. *Address:* c/o GEMA, Rozenheimerstr, 11, 8166 Munich, Germany.

STAICU, Paul; Conductor, Professor and Horn Player; b. 7 June 1937, Bucharest, Romania; m. Irina Botez, 6 July 1963, 1 s. *Education:* Graduate Diploma in Horn, Prague Academy of Music, 1961; Graduate Diploma at Vienna Academy of Music, with conductor Hans Swarowsky. *Career:* Debut: As Horn Soloist, 1954 and as Conductor, 1963, Bucharest Radio and Philharmonic Orchestra; Horn Soloist, 1954–79; Solo Horn with Bucharest Philharmonic, 1961–69; Chief Conductor of Chamber Orchestra, 1966; Professor of Chamber Music, 1966–; Camerata, 1978; H von Karajan Foundation, Medal with Camerata, orchestra, 1974; Professor of Horn, 1969–89, Chief Conductor of Symphony Orchestra, Bucharest Music Academy, 1975–78; Chief Conductor, Symphony and Chamber Orchestra, Constanta Romania, 1978–79; Professor, Conservatoire of Music, Montbeliard, France, 1990; Director, School of Music, Exincourt, France, 1990; Chief Conductor, Ensemble Orchestral Montbeliard, France, 1992; Television and radio performances in Romania and abroad; Summer classes at Bayreuth, Gourdon, Europe, USA and Canada tours; Membership, Munich and Prague International Music Competitions. *Recordings:* No. 3, Beethoven Horn Sonata; Mozart and Beethoven Quintets; Mozart's Horn Concertos as Soloist and Conductor; Haydn Concertos as Conductor; Haydn Symphonies 100–103 as Conductor; Radio: Beethoven Symphony No. 4, Schoenberg Verklärte Nacht and Shostakovich's Symphony No. 14. *Publications:* Studiu introductiv si exercitii zilnice pentru corn (Introductory studies and daily exercises for horn).

STAIER, Andreas; Harpsichordist and Pianist; b. 13 Sept. 1955, Göttingen, Germany. *Education:* Baccalaureate in Göttingen; Studies in Piano, Harpsichord, Chamber Music in Hanover and Amsterdam. *Career:* Harpsichordist in Musica Antiqua, Köln, 1983–86; Professor, Schola Cantorum, Basle, Switzerland, 1987–96; Concerts in USA, Europe and Australia. *Recordings:* Haydn Piano Sonatas; J. S. Bach Harpsichord Works; CPE Bach Harpsichord Works; Chamber Music; Lieder; D Scarlatti; L Dussek; Schubert and Schumann, Piano solo works, concertos and lieder; Mozart Piano Sonatas. *Current Management:* Claudia Nitsche, Jean Michel Forest,. *Address:* Franzstr 19, 50931 Cologne, Germany.

STALDER, Hans Rudolf; Clarinettist and Musician; b. 9 July 1930, Zürich, Switzerland; m. Ursula Burkhard, 11 April 1957. *Education:* Konservatorium, Zürich; Bayerische Staatskonservatorium, Würzburg, Germany; Private studies with Louis Cahuzac, Paris. *Career:* International Soloist on clarinet, Bassethorn and Chalumeau, also with Chamber Music groups including: Stalder Quintet, Zürich Chamber Ensemble, Zürich Clarinet Trio; Teacher at Musik Akademie, Basle and Schola Cantorum Basiliensis; mem, Schweizerischer Tonkunstlerverein. *Recordings include:* First recording of Mozart Clarinet Concerto in original version with Bassetclarinet, 1968; Bassethorn Concerto from A Rolla; Das Chalumeau ein Portrait. *Address:* Wengi 2, 8126 Zumikon, Switzerland.

STALLMAN, Robert; Flautist; b. 12 June 1946, Boston, Massachusetts, USA; m. Hannah Woods, 26 Sept 1981. *Education:* BMus, 1968, MMus, 1971, New England Conservatory of Music; Paris Conservatoire, France, 1968–69. *Career:* Major solo appearances include Library of Congress (Washington), Carnegie Hall, Weill Hall, Alice Tully Hall,

Avery Fisher Hall (New York), Symphony Hall (Boston), Salle Pleyel (Paris), Suntory Hall (Tokyo), Wigmore Hall (London); Radio and television appearances, nationwide USA, Canada, France and Spain; Guest Artist appearances include American Symphony, Mostly Mozart Festival, Netherlands and Suk Chamber Orchestras, Lincoln Center Chamber Music Society, Chamber Orchestra of Philadelphia, Speculum Musicae, Muir, Mendelssohn, Martinů and Orion String Quartets; Festivals, Brazil, Canada, Czech Republic; Finland, France, Netherlands, Japan, USA; Founder, Artistic Director, Cambridge Chamber Players and Marblehead Music Festival, 1976–96; Composers for whom he has premiered works include Elliott Carter, Richard Danielpour, Stephen Dodgson, Robert Helps, John Harbison, Karel Husa, William McKinley, Alexander St. Lawrence; Teaching: Aaron Copland School of Music, Queen's College, New York, 1980–; Académie Internationale d'Eté, Nice, France, 1985; Boston Conservatory, 1986–90; New England Conservatory, 1978–82; Masterclasses, USA, Canada, Mexico, England, France, Germany; Japan; Editor of flute repertoire, International Music Co, New York, 1984–; also, G Schirmer, New York, 1996–. *Recordings:* Blavet Sonatas; Incantations (20th century solo flute works); Gypsy Flute; Handel Sonatas; Leclair Sonatas; Bach Sonatas; The American Flute; Schubert Sonatas; The Nightingale in Love (French Baroque music); Telemann Concerti; Vivaldi Concerti; Dodgson Concerto with the Northern Sinfonia; McKinley Concerto with the Prism Orchestra. *Publications:* 40 include Flute Workout, 1995; The Flutist's Détaché Book, 1997. *Address:* 1530 Locust Street, #11A, Philadelphia, PA 19102, USA. *Website:* flute@robertstallman.com.

STAMENOVA, Galina; Violinist; b. 5 Oct. 1958, Sofia, Bulgaria. *Education:* Musical studies from age 5 with her mother; Studies with Dorothy DeLay, Juilliard School of Music, New York. *Career:* Debut: With André Previn and London Symphony Orchestra at Royal Festival Hall; American debut with Dallas Symphony in 1984; Performances with most leading British orchestras, Antwerp Philharmonic and orchestras in Bulgaria; Radio and television appearances in Bulgaria, Netherlands, the United Kingdom and Belgium; Accomplished recitalist having appeared at Harrogate and Aspen Music Festivals, live on BBC and Radio VARA in Netherlands and several other European countries. *Recordings:* Saint-Saëns No. 3, Chausson-Poème, Sofia Radio Orchestra with Vassil Stefanov conducting. *Honours:* Several first prizes for young violinists. *Address:* 33 Greinstraat, 2060 Antwerp, Belgium.

STAMM, Harald; Singer (Bass); b. 29 April 1938, Frankfurt am Main, Germany. *Education:* Studied with Franz Fehringer. *Career:* Debut: Gelsenkirchen, 1968; Sang at Cologne and Frankfurt, Hamburg Staatsoper, 1975, in the premiere of Der Gestiefelte Kater by Bialas; Many appearances in German opera houses and in Budapest Venice, Rome and Nice; Metropolitan Opera from 1979; Salzburg Festival 1985, in the Henze version of Monteverdi's Ulisse; Bregenz Festival 1986, as Sarastro in Die Zauberflöte; Other roles include: Mozart's Commendatore, Beethoven's Rocco, Verdi's Grand Inquisitor and Zaccaria, Wagner's Daland, Marke, Fasolt and Hunding and Massenet's Don Quixote; Covent Garden debut in 1987 as Raimondo in Lucia di Lammermoor; Sang the King in Schreker's Der Schatzgräber at Hamburg, 1989, King Henry in Lohengrin at Brussels and Lisbon, 1990; Season 1992 as Gurnemanz at Eseen; King Henry in Lohengrin at Hamburg, 1998; Hamburg State Opera 1999–2000, as Arkel in Pelléas and Wagner's Landgrave. Also heard in recital and concert. *Recordings:* Lieder by Liszt and Franz; Vier Ernste Gesänge by Brahms; Dittersdorf's Doktor und Apotheker; Schumann's Manfred; Massimila Doni by Schoeck. *Honours:* Nominated Kammersänger by Hamburg Opera, 1989; Professor at Hochschule der Künste Berlin, 1993. *Address:* c/o R & B GmbH, Plankengasse 7, A–1010 Vienna, Austria.

STÄMPFLI, Jakob; Singer (Bass); b. 26 Oct. 1934, Berne, Switzerland. *Education:* Studied at the Berne Conservatory and in Frankfurt with Paul Lohmann. *Career:* Gave concerts in Germany while still a student; Sang with the Chorus of St Thomas's Leipzig, conducted by Gunter Ramin; Many performances of sacred music by Bach in Europe, USA and Japan; Sang also with the Schola Cantorum Basiliensis; Lieder recitals with music by Brahms, Schubert and Schumann; Professor at the Saabrücken Musikhochschule from 1960 then at the Hamburg Musikhochschule. *Recordings:* Cantatas by Buxtehude; Bach Cantatas; Monteverdi's Orfeo; Christmas Oratorio; St Matthew Passion and Magnificat by Bach; Plutone in L'Orfeo conducted by Michel Corboz. *Address:* c/o Hochschule für Musik, Harvestehuderweg 12, 2000 Hamburg 13, Germany.

STANDAGE, Simon; Violinist; b. 8 Nov. 1941, High Wycombe, Buckinghamshire, England; m. Jennifer Ward, 15 Aug 1964, 3 s. *Education:* Studied at Cambridge; Violin studies with Ivan Galamian in New York, 1967–69. *Career:* Associate member of the London Symphony Orchestra and deputy leader of the English Chamber Orchestra; Appointed Leader of the English Concert in 1973; Leader of the Richard Hickox Orchestra and the City of London Sinfonia; Founded the Salomon Quartet in 1981 giving performances of 18th century

repertoire on original instruments; Teacher of Baroque violin at the Royal Academy of Music from 1983; Founded Collegium Musicum 90 in 1990; Associate Director of Academy of Ancient Music, 1991–95; Professor of Baroque Violin, Dresdner Akademie für Alte Musik, 1993–. *Recordings:* Vivaldi op 8 (including Four Seasons), op 3 (L'Estro Armonico), op 4 (La Stravaganza), op 9 (La Cetra), J. S. Bach Violin Concertos, Leclair complete concertos, Mozart and Haydn complete violin concertos, Mozart mature string quartets and quintets, Haydn quartets opp 17, 20, 33, 42, 50, 54/55, 64, 71/74, 77 and 103. *Address:* 106 Hervey Road, London SE3 8BX, England.

STANDFORD, Patric; Composer; b. 5 Feb. 1939, Barnsley, Yorkshire, England; m. Sarah Blyth Hilton. 2 s., 1 d. *Education:* GGSM, London, 1963; FGSM, London, 1973; MMus, London, 1979; Studied with Rubbra, Mendelssohn Scholarship, extended studies, Malipiero in Italy; Lutoslawski in Poland; Stanley Glasser at London University. *Career:* Professor of Composition, Guildhall School of Music, London, 1969–80; Head of Music Leeds University at Bretton Hall, 1980–93. *Compositions include:* 6 symphonies, 1971–95; Taikyoku for 2 pianos and percussion, 1976; A Christmas Carol Symphony, 1978; Variations for orchestra, 1979; Cello Concerto; Violin Concerto; Christus Requiem, oratorio; 2 string quartets; Choral and instrumental works; Villon, opera; Ballet scores: Celestial Fire and Reflexions; Film and video music; Clarinet Quintet; The Prayer of St Francis for chorus and orchestra, 1996; Concertino for harpsichord and orchestra, 1998; The Emperor's Orchestra, for narrator and orchestra, 2001. *Recordings:* The Prayer of St Francis (Hungariton); A Christmas Carol Symphony (Naxos); Ballet Suite Celestial Fire (ASV). *Contributions:* (Features, concert and CD reviews) Yorkshire Post; Choir and Organ; Yorkshire Artscene; Classic CD; BBC Music Magazine; Music and Vision. *Honours:* City of Geneve Ernst Ansermet Aware, 1987; Budapest International Composers' Award, 1997; Belgian International ClarinetFest Prize, 1999. *Address:* c/o 17 Bradford Road, Wakefield, West Yorkshire WF1 2RF, England. *E-mail:* standford@rtsmusic.demon.co.uk.

STANHOPE, David; Composer, Conductor and Horn Player; b. 19 Dec. 1952, Sutton Coldfield, England (Resident in Australia from 1958). *Education:* Studied in Melbourne. *Career:* 2nd Horn, Australian Symphony Orchestra, 1970; Conductor with Australian Opera from 1986 (gave Berg's Lulu in season 1994). *Compositions include:* Quintet No. 3 for brass quintet, 1983; The Australian Fanfare for 9 trumpets in 3 choirs, 1983; Four Concert Studies for 4 trombones, 1985; Felix Randall, for high voice and piano, 1986; Concerto for Band, 1988; Droylsden Wakes for wind or brass band, 1990; Folksongs for Band, 1990–91; Endpiece for orchestra, 1991; Three Poems for soprano and string orchestra; String Songs; Three Folksongs for brass quintet. *Honours:* Prize Winner, International Horn Society Composition Contest, 1979. *Address:* c/o APRA, 1A Eden Street, Crows Nest, NSW 2065, Australia.

STANHOPE, Paul Thomas; Composer; b. 25 Nov. 1969, Wollongong, NSW, Australia. *Education:* BA (Hons), University of Sydney, 1992; MA (Hons), University of Wollongong, 1994; Study with Peter Sculthorpe, 1995–96. *Career:* Faculty Member, University of Wollongong, 1994–95; University of Sydney, 1995–. *Compositions include:* Liquid Marimba for tape, 1991; Morning Star for string quartet, 1992; Missa Brevis for chorus, 1992; The Taste of Midnight for flute, piano and clarinet, 1993; Morning Star II and III for ensemble, 1993; Kandeyala for orchestra, 1994; Satz for mandolin quartet, 1994; Rin, for tape, 1994; Snap, for clarinet, 1994; Geography Songs for chorus, 1994–95; No More than Movement. . . or Stillness, for tape, 1995; Kraftwerk Overture, for string orchestra, 1995; Rain Dance for violin, 2 violas and cello, 1995; Stars Sounding for orchestra, 1996. *Honours:* Australian Voices Festival Young Composers Award, 1995. *Address:* c/o APRA, 1A Eden Street, Crows Nest, NSW 2065, Australia.

STANKOV, Angel (Mirchov); Concert Violinist, Conductor and Violin Duo Chamber Player (with Josif Radionov); b. 28 April 1948, Sofia, Bulgaria; m. Meglena Stankova, 1 d. *Education:* State High School; Bulgarian State Music Academy, Sofia; Specialised in London with Professor Parikian of the Royal Academy of Music. *Career:* Debut: Pleven Philharmonic Orchestra, Beethoven Concerto, 1970; Regular appearances with Sofia Phiharmonic Orchestra and foreign orchestras; Appearances on Bulgarian radio and television; Concert Master, Sofia Philharmonic, 1981–2000; Live recital, Hague Radio, 1991; North France and Soviet television appearances, 1991; Foreign tours to almost all European countries and Cuba; International Music Festivals, Llandaff, the United Kingdom, 1975, Brno, Czechoslovakia, 1989, Warsaw, Bydgoscz and Crete, Greece, 1983; Professor of Violin and Chamber Music, Sofia State Music Academy; Performer as soloist and as member of violin duo with Josif Radionov; First Violin of the Sofia Quartet, 2002; Teaching one term at the North Carolina School of the Arts, 2003; Recitals in the USA, 2003. *Recordings:* Bulgarian radio and television; BBC London; BBC Oxford; Hague Radio; Prague Radio; Some concertos specially dedicated to the Violin Duo by outstanding Bulgarian and foreign composers, also individual pieces; Conducted all

Beethoven Symphonies Cycle, 1999–2000. *Honours:* First Prize and Gold Medal, First International Chamber Music Festival, Osaka, 1993; Nominated Artist of the Year, Bulgaria, 1997. *Address:* 58 William Gladstone Street, 1000 Sofia, Bulgaria.

STANKOVYCH, Yevhen Fedorovych; Composer; b. 19 Sept. 1942, Svaliava, Ukraine. *Education:* Kiev Conservatory, 1963-70. *Career:* Works performed throughout Russia and in USA and Asia; Composer-in-residence at Berne, 1996. *Compositions:* Prometheus, ballet, 1985; Five Symphonies, 1973, 1975, 1976, 1977, 1980; String Quartet, 1973; Dictum, for ensemble, 1987; Black Elegy, for chorus and orchestra, 1991; Kaddish-Requiem, for tenor, bass, chorus and orchestra, 1991; Music for Heavenly Musicians, woodwind quintet, 1993; Requiem for Those Who Died of Famine, 1993; Sonata, for clarinet, 1996; Elegy, string quartet, 19997; Ave Maria, for orchestra, 1997; May Night, and The Night before Christmas, ballets after Gogol. *Address:* c/o RAO, 6a B. Bronnaya, Moscow 103670, Russia.

STANTCHEV, Ognian Nikolov; Violist and Professor; b. 1937, Sofia, Bulgaria. *Education:* Graduated, State Academy of Music, Sofia, 1960; Specialization, Chamber Music with Joseph Calvet, Paris Conservatory, 1967; Specialization, Tchaikovsky Conservatory, Moscow, Russia, 1976. *Career:* Lecturer, 1962–81, Assistant Professor, 1981–88, Professor, 1988–, State Academy of Music, Sofia; First Viola, Sofia Philharmonic Orchestra, 1962–66; Violist, Orpheus Quartet, 1966–72; Violist, Tilev Quartet, Bulgarian National Radio, 1972–78; First Viola, Sofia Philharmonic Orchestra, 1979–88; Violist, Sofia Quartet, Bulgarian National Radio, 1988–93; Numerous concerts and many broadcasts of chamber music, especially string quartets; Numerous concert tours in Czech Republic, Hungary, Germany, Austria, Poland, France, Italy, England, USA and Greece; Holds Masterclasses, Summer Academy Prague-Vienna-Budapest, 1997–; Jury Member, viola competition in Vienna, 1998; mem, Union of Musicians, Bulgaria. *Recordings:* Shostakovich Sonata for viola and piano; Debussy string quartet op 10; Prokofiev string quartet op 50; Four quartets for flute and strings, Mozart; Mozart quartet K 458; Haydn op 76 No. 2; Borodin string quartet No. 1; Sofia String quartet; For Bulgarian Radio: Britten, Lachrimae op 48; Hindemith, Meditation. Prizewinner, international competitions in Helsinki for stringed instruments, 1962; Second Prize, Stringed Quartet Competition, Kolmar, France, 1978. *Address:* Drujba 2, bl 206, en 3, ap 57, Sofia 1582, Bulgaria.

STANZELEIT, Susanne; Violinist; b. 1968, Germany. *Education:* Studies with Leonid Kogan and at Folkwang Hochschule in Essen (diploma 1989) and with Yfrah Neaman at the Guildhall School of Music; Masterclasses with Nathan Milstein, Sándor Végh and György Kurtag at Prussia Cove. *Career:* Recitals throughout Germany, Italy, Hungary, Netherlands, Canada, USA and England; Concerto appearances with leading orchestras, leader of Werethina Quartet (Haydn, Mendelssohn and Bart ók at Purcell Room, 1993) and Prometheus and Ondine Ensembles; Purcell Room Recital, 1993 with Julian Jacobson, playing Strauss, Schubert's C Major Fantasy and Beethoven, Op 96; Broadcasts with BBC Radio 3, teaching and performing with the Paxos Festival in Greece, Dartington Summer School (1993) and International Bart ók Festival in Hungary. *Recordings:* Bartók's music for violin and piano, Delius sonatas for violin and piano, Stanford, Bantock, Dunhill. *Address:* c/o Encord Concerts, Caversham Grange, The Warren, Mapledurham, Berks RG4 7TQ, England.

STAPP, Olivia; Singer (Mezzo-Soprano); b. 30 May 1940, New York, USA. *Education:* Studied with Oren Brown in New York and Ettore Campogalliani and Rodolfo Ricci in Italy. *Career:* Debut: Spoleto Festival in 1960 in L'Amico Fritz; Sang in Vienna, Berlin, Wuppertal, Turin and Basle; Sang at Indiana University at Bloomington in the 1971 premiere of Eaton's Heracles; Sang at New York City Opera from 1972 notably as Carmen and Norma, Metropolitan Opera from 1982 as Lady Macbeth and Tosca, Paris Opéra in 1982, La Scala Milan, 1983–84 as Turandot and Electra in Idomeneo, and Geneva in 1985 as Elena in Les Vêpres Siciliennes; Other roles include Verdi's Ulrica and Mistress Quickly, Santuzza, Dorabella, Isabella, Rosina, Idalma in Il Matrimonio Segreto and Jocasta in Oedipus Rex; Sang Lady Macbeth at Geneva and Venice in 1986, Elektra and Abigaille at Frankfurt and Zürich, 1988–89, at Paris in 1989 in La Noche Triste by Prodomidès, and sang Shostakovich's Katherina at Hamburg in 1990. *Recordings include:* Cyrano de Bergerac by Alfano.

STAREK, Jiri; Conductor; b. 25 March 1928, Mocovice, Czechoslovakia; m. Eva Itis, 18 Feb 1964, 1 s. *Education:* Studies at State Conservatory of Music, 1939–40; Private music studies, 1940–45; Graduate, Academy of Music Arts, Prague, 1950. *Career:* Conductor and Chief Conductor, Czech Radio, Prague, 1953–68; Chief Conductor and Music Director of Chamber Orchestra Collegium Musicum Pragense, 1963–68; Guest Conductor for many international symphony orchestras; Artistic Leader, Sinfonietta RIAS, Berlin, 1976–80 and Chief Conductor for Trondheim Symphony Orchestra, Norway, 1981–84; Professor and

Head of Conductor's Class, Music Academy, Frankfurt am Main, 1975–97; Dean, Artistic Department, 1980–90; Principal Guest Conductor, ABC West Australia Symphony Orchestra, 1988–90; General Music Director of the Pfalztheater Kaiserslautern, Germany, 1989–92; After 22 years in exile returned to Prague, conducting Czech Philharmonic Orchestra, State Philharmonic Orchestra, Brno, Janáček Philharmonic Orchestra, Ostrava, Prague Symphony Orchestra, Radio Symphony Orchestra Prague, 1990–; Chief Conductor, State Opera Prague, 1996–; Appearances at many leading international music festivals including Salzburg, Prague, Berlin, Schleswig-Holstein; mem, Czech Society of Arts and Sciences; Dvořák Society, London; Schubert Society, Prague. *Recordings:* Radio and CD recordings with Prague Symphony Orchestra FOK, Radio Symphony Orchestra Prague, Sinfonietta-RIAS, Berlin, Radio Symphony Orchestra Stuttgart, Frankfurt, Munich. *Honours:* OIRT Award, Z Sestak: Vocal Symphony, 1964; Czech Radio Awards for operas: W Egk: Columbus, Shostakovich: The Nose, Dallapiccola: The Prisoner, 1966–67; Czech Music Council Award, 1997. *Address:* Brunnenweg 18, 61352 Bad Homburg vdh, Germany.

STARKER, Janos; American cellist and academic; *Distinguished Professor of Cello, School of Music, Indiana University;* b. 5 July 1924, Budapest, Hungary; s. of Margit Starker and Sandor Starker; m. 1st Eva Uranyi 1944 (divorced); one d.; m. 2nd Rae Busch 1960; three d. *Education:* Franz Liszt Acad. of Music, Budapest. *Career:* Solo Cellist, Budapest Opera House and Philharmonic Orchestra 1945–46; Solo Cellist, Dallas Symphony Orchestra 1948–49, Metropolitan Opera Orchestra 1949–53, Chicago Symphony Orchestra 1953–58; Resident Cellist, Indiana Univ. 1958–, Prof. of Music 1961, now Distinguished Prof. of Cello; inventor of Starker bridge for orchestral string instruments; worldwide concert tours. *Publications:* Method 1964, Bach Suites 1971, Concerto Cadenzas, Schubert-Starker Sonatina, Bottermund-Starker Variations, Beethoven Sonatas, Beethoven Variations, Dvořák Concerto; numerous magazine articles, essays and record cover notes. *Honours:* Hon. mem. American Fed. of Musicians, Royal Acad. of London 1981, Indiana Acad. of Arts and Sciences, American Acad. of Arts and Sciences; Chevalier Ordre des Arts et Lettres 1997; Hon. DMus (Chicago Conservatory) 1961, (Cornell Coll.) 1978, (East West Univ.) 1982, (Williams Coll.) 1983, (Lawrence Univ.) 1990; Grand Prix du Disque 1948, George Washington Award 1972, Sanford Fellowship Award, Yale 1974, Herzl Award 1978, Ed Press Award 1983, Kodály Commemorative Medallion, New York 1983, Arturo Toscanini Award 1986, Indiana Univ. Tracy Sonneborn Award 1986, Indiana Gov.'s Award 1995, Medal of Paris 1995, Grammy Award 1998, Indiana Univ. Pres.'s Medal for Excellence 1999, Pres. of Hungary's Gold Medal 1999. *Current Management:* Colbert Artists, 111 West 57th Street, New York, NY 10019, USA. *Address:* c/o Department of Music, Office MA155, Indiana University, Bloomington, IN 47405-2200, USA. *E-mail:* starker@indiana.edu. *Website:* www.music.indiana.edu.

STAROBIN, David Nathan, BM; American classical guitarist; b. 27 Sept. 1951, New York, NY; m. Rebecca Patience Askew 1975; one s. one d. *Education:* Peabody Conservatory, studied with Manuel Gayol, Abert Valdes Blain and Aaren Shearer. *Career:* debut at Carnegie Recital Hall, New York, 1978; European at Wigmore Hall, London, 1979; Played the premiere performances of over 200 new compositions written for him including solo works, concerti and chamber music; Composers who have written for him include Elliott Carter, Charles Wuorinen, Barbara Kolb, David Del Tredici, Tod Machover, Milton Babbitt, Roger Reynolds, Robert Saxton, Mel Powell, Elisabeth Lutyens, Lukas Foss, Poul Ruders, George Crumb and Mario Davidovsky; Member of Speculum Misicae. *Recordings:* New Music with Guitar, vols 1, 2, 3 and 4; A Song From The East, music from Russia and Hungary; Twentieth Century Music for Voice and Guitar; Newdance. *Publications:* Editor: Looking for Claudio, 1978, Three Lullabies, 1980, Changes, 1984, Acrostic Song, 1983. *Honours:* AFIM Award Best Solo Classical Album, Newdance, 1999. *Current Management:* Bridge Records Inc, GPO Box 1864, New York, NY 10116, USA.

STARYK, Steven S.; violinist, concertmaster and professor; b. 28 April 1932, Toronto, Canada; m. 1963; one d. *Education:* Royal Conservatory of Music, Toronto; private studies in New York. *Career:* debut in Toronto; Concert Master, Royal Philharmonic, London, Concertgebouw Amsterdam, Chicago Symphony and Toronto Symphony; Professor of Violin, Amsterdam Conservatory, Oberlin Conservatory, Northwestern University, University of Victoria and Academy of Music, Vancouver; Visiting Professor at University of Ottawa and University of Western Ontario; Professor, Royal Conservatory of Music, Toronto; Faculty of Music, University of Toronto; Professor and Head String Division, University of Washington, Seattle, USA, 1987–98; Organiser of Quartet Canada; Extensive concert tours, radio and television appearances in North America, Europe and the Far East. *Recordings:* 190 compositions on 45 albums. *Publications:* Fiddling with Life (biog., co-author) 2000. *Honours:* Canada Council Arts Awards, 1967, 1975; Shevchenko Medal, 1974; Queen Elizabeth Centennial Award, 1978; Honorary DLitt, York

University, Toronto, 1980; Distinguished Teaching Award, University of Washington, Seattle, 1995; Professor Emeritus, 1997. *Address:* 12068 E Bella Vista Cr, Scottsdale, AZ 85259, USA.

STAUFFER, George Boyer; Musicologist and Organist; b. 18 Feb. 1947, Hershey, Pennsylvania, USA; m. Marie Caruso, 26 May 1985, one s. *Education:* BA, Dartmouth College, 1969; PhD, Columbia University, 1978; Organ study with John Weaver and Vernon de Tar. *Career:* Director of Chapel Music and Organist, Columbia University, 1977–99; Adjunct Assistant Professor of Music, Yeshiva University, 1978–79; Assistant, Associate and Professor of Music, Hunter College and Graduate Center, City University of New York, 1979–2000; President, American Bach Society, 1996–2000; Dean, Mason Gross School of the Arts, Rutgers University, 2000–. *Publications:* Author, Organ Preludes of J. S. Bach, 1980 and J. S. Bach: Mass in B minor, 1997; Co-editor, J. S. Bach as Organist, 1986; Editor, The Forkel–Hoffmeister and Kuhnel Correspondence, 1990, and Bach Perspectives 2, 1996; Co-author, Organ Technique: Modern and Early, 2002; General Editor, Yale Music Masterworks series. *Contributions:* Early Music; Musical Quarterly; Bach-Jahrbuch. *Address:* 30 Euclid Avenue, Hastings-on-Hudson, NY 10706, USA.

STEANE, John Barry; British music journalist and writer; b. 12 April 1928, Coventry, England. *Education:* Univ. of Cambridge. *Career:* teacher of English, Merchant Taylors' School, Northwood 1952–88; reviewer, Gramophone 1973–, Musical Times 1988–, Opera Now 1989–. *Publications:* Marlowe: A Critical Study 1964, Dekker: The Shoemaker's Holiday (ed.) 1965, Tennyson 1966, Jonson: The Alchemist (ed.) 1967, Marlowe: The Complete Plays 1969, Nashe: The Unfortunate Traveller and Other Works 1972, The Grand Tradition: Seventy Years of Singing on Record 1973, Opera on Record (co-author, three vols) 1979–85, Song on Record (co-author, two vols) 1986–88, Choral Music on Record 1991, Voices: Singers and Critics 1992, Elisabeth Schwarzkopf: A Career on Record (with Alan Sanders) 1995, Singers of the Century (three vols) 1996, 1998, 2000, The Gramophone and the Voice 1999; contrib. to The New Grove Dictionary of Music and Musicians 1980, 2001, The New Grove Dictionary of Opera 1992. *Address:* 32 Woodland Avenue, Coventry, CV5 6DB, England.

STEBLIANKO, Alexei; Tenor; b. 1950, Russia. *Education:* Studied at the Leningrad Conservatory. *Career:* Has sung at the Kirov Theatre Leningrad as Lensky (debut), Radames, Manrico, Don José, Des Grieux, Andrei in Mazeppa, Herman in The Queen of Spades, Andrei Khovansky, Dmitri in Boris Godunov, Cavaradossi, Lohengrin, Canio and Pierre Bezukhov in War and Peace; Tours of Europe with the Kirov Company, including Covent Garden debut as Hermann in 1987; Sang at La Scala in 1982 as Aeneas in Les Troyens, and Covent Garden, 1989–90 as Jason in Médée, Vladimir in Prince Igor, both being new productions, and Manrico; Season 1992 as Otello at Reggio Emilia; Television appearances include Prince Igor, also on video; Sang Herman in The Queen of Spades at Bonn, 1996; Season 2000 as Pierre in War and Peace, as guest with the Mariinsky Company at Covent Garden; Mussorgsky's Boris Godunov at the London Proms, 2002. *Address:* Allied Artists, 42 Montpelier Square, London, SW7 1JZ, England.

STEDRON, Milos; Composer; b. 9 Feb. 1942, Brno, Czechoslovakia. *Education:* Musicology and music theory at Brno Academy, 1965–70. *Career:* Researched Janáček's music and worked in administration at the Moravian Museum in Brno, 1963–72; Teacher of theory at University of Brno from 1972. *Compositions include:* Operas: The Apparatus, after Kafka, 1967, Culinary Cares, Brno, 1979, The Chameleon, Or Josef Fouche, Brno, 1984; Ballets: Justina, 1969, Ballet Macabre, 1986; Annals of the Predecessors of the Avant-garde, chamber orchestra, 1997; Orchestra: Concerto for Double Bass and Strings, 1971, Diagram for Piano and Jazz Orchestra, 1971, Music for Ballet, 1972, Wheel, symphony, 1972, Cello Concerto, 1975, Sette Villanelle for Cello and Strings, 1981, Musica Concertante for Bassoon and Strings, 1986, Lammento for Viola and Orchestra, 1987; Chamber: Musica Ficta for Wind Quintet, 1968, String Quartet, 1970, Trium Vocum for Flute, Cello and Drums, 1984, Danze, Canti and Lamenti for String Quartet, 1986;Qudra, for ensemble, 1992; Trio for violin, cello and piano, 1993; String Quartet, 1994; Dances of King Lear, for cello, early music instruments and percussion, 1996; Vocal: Mourning Ceremony, cantata, 1969, Vocal symphony for Soprano, Baritone and Orchestra, 1969, Attendite, Populi, cantata for Chorus and Drums, 1982, Dolorosa Gioia Ommaggio á Gesualdo, Madrigal Cantata, 1978, Death Of Dobrovsky, cantata-oratorio, 1988; Missa Sine ritu, for mezzo and cello, 1996; Solo instrumental music and piano pieces. *Address:* c/o OSA, Cs armady 20, 160-56 Prague 6, Bubenec, Czech Republic.

STEELE-PERKINS, Crispian; Trumpeter; b. 18 Dec. 1944, Exeter, England; m. Jane Elisabeth Mary, 6 April 1995. *Education:* Guildhall School of Music. *Career:* Many appearances in the Baroque repertoire at the Barbican and Royal Festival Halls with the City of London Sinfonia and the English Chamber Orchestra; Sadler's Wells Opera, 1966–73;

Royal Philharmonic, 1976–80; Played Haydn's Trumpet Concerto at the 1982 Edinburgh Festival; Performances on the Natural Trumpet with The King's Consort, The English Baroque Soloists, The Taverner Players and The Parley of Instruments; Professor of Trumpet at Guildhall School of Music, 1980; Workshops and masterclasses as preludes to concert presentations; Season 1989–90 in Boston, Tokyo, Lisbon, Stuttgart and Gstaad; British festival engagements at Edinburgh, the Proms, City of London, Cambridge, Chester, Dartington, Leeds and Glasgow; US tour in 1988 and tour of Japan in 1990; King's Consort, 1985–; Full-time Trumpet Soloist, 1990–; Bach's Magnificat with The Sixteen at QEH, London, 2000; mem, Royal Society of Musicians. *Recordings:* Participation in over 700 recordings including 13 solo albums; Mr Purcell's Trumpeter with the City of London Sinfonia under Richard Hickox; Messiah featuring English trumpet of Handel's time; Shore's Trumpet, EMI; Let the Trumpet Sound, Carlton Classics; 6 Trumpet Concertos, Carlton Classics; 80 Film tracks. *Contributions:* Articles in Historic Brass Journal.

STEFANESCU, Ana Camelia; Singer (Soprano); b. 8 June 1974, Bucharest, Romania. *Education:* Dinu Lipatti High School of Music, Bucharest; University of Music, Bucharest studying with Professor Andreiana Rosca. *Career:* Romanian National Opera, as Lucia di Lammermoor, Rosina, the Queen of Night in Die Zauberflöte, Zerbinetta, and Zerlina; Season 1997–98 as the Queen of Night at the Teatro Comunale, Florence, and at the Vienna State Opera; Deutsche Staatsoper, Berlin; Concerts and recitals in Romania, Poland, France, Netherlands, Luxembourg, the United Kingdom, Belgium and Switzerland; Season 1998–99 new productions in Berlin Deutsche Staatsoper with René Jacobs including Narsea in Solimano by Adolf Hasse; Concerts with José van Dam, José Carreras, performances at Teatro Real in Madrid and with the National Orchestra of Spain, several International Festivals; Roles include: Adina from L'elisir d'amore, Adele from Strauss' Die Fledermaus, the Fire, the Princess and the Lark from Ravel's l'Enfant et sortileges, Sophie from Massenet's Werther and Gilda from Verdi's Rigoletto. *Recordings:* Many recordings for Romanian radio and television, and WDR in Cologne. *Honours:* Prize Winner, Verviers International Competition and the Queen Elisabeth International Music Competition, Belgium; The Romanian Critics Award, 1997; Finalist of the Placido Domingo Competition, 1998. *Address:* c/o IMG Artists, Lovell House, 616 Chiswick High Road, London W4 5RX, England.

STEFANESCU-BARNEA, Georgeta; Romanian pianist and academic; *Professor, Ciprian Porumbescu Conservatory;* b. 25 April 1934, Satu-Mare; m. Jean Barnea 1958; two s. *Education:* Lyceum, Cluj, G. H. Dima Academy of Music, Cluj, Ciprian Porumbescu Conservatory, Bucharest, additional studies in Weimar, Germany, Switzerland, France. *Career:* piano teacher, Music Lyceum 1957–60; Univ. Lecturer, Ciprian Porumbescu Conservatory, Bucharest 1960–91, Univ. Reader 1991–, Prof. 1995–; numerous concerts and piano recitals in Romania, Germany, Switzerland, Czechoslovakia, England; appearances on Romanian radio and television, Radio Weimar, Suisse Romande Radio, Geneva. *Publications include:* Mihai Burada–Homage Album (three vols) 1993, Martian Negrea–Piano Pieces 1994, Romanian Sonatines for Piano (ed., two vols) 1994, many other pedagogical albums by H. Herz, Schubert, Grieg, Chopin, Haydn, Mozart and Beethoven, Romanian Pieces for Piano of the XIXth Century (ed., two vols) 1975, Romanian Sonatines for Piano (ed.) 1985, Lieds of Romanian Contemporary Creation (ed., two vols) 1987, Little Pieces for Piano Four Hands (ed., three vols) 1989, Album of Little Romanican Pieces for Piano 1997. *Address:* Str Compozitorilor Nr 32, Bl F8, Apt 24 Sect Vl, 77353 Bucharest 66, Romania; c/o Conservatorul Ciprian Porumbescu, Strada Stribei Vodá 33, 70732 Bucharest, Romania (office).

STEFANOVIC, Ivana; Composer; b. 14 Sept. 1948, Belgrade, Yugoslavia. *Education:* Belgrade Academy of Music, and with Gilbert Amy in Paris. *Career:* Radio Belgrade from 1976, founder of Sound Workshop (1985) and head of Music Production, 1990. *Compositions:* Hommage à François Villon, for voices and early instruments, 1978; Fragment of a Possible Order, for two pianos and ensemble, 1979; Interpretation of a Dream for flute, two speakers and tape, 1984; Lingua/Phonia/Patria, 1989; Psalm, for mezzo and choir, 1990; Isadora, ballet, 1992; Tree of life, for strings, 1997. *Address:* c/o SOKOJ, PO Box 213, Mišarska 12–14, 1100 Belgrade, Serbia and Montenegro.

STEFANOWICZ, Artur; Singer (Counter-Tenor); b. 1968, Szczecin, Poland. *Education:* Graduated from the Chopin Academy of Music, where he studied singing under Jerzy Artysz in 1991 and then continued his studies with Paul Esswood and Jadwiga Rappe. *Career:* Appearances from 1990 with the Warsaw Chamber Opera in Mozart's Ascanio in Alba, Apollo et Hyacinthus and Mitridate; Since 1991, appearances with orchestras and ensembles such as Orchestra Teatro La Fenice, Sinfonia Varsovia, Warsaw National Philharmonic, DSO Berlin, Capella Savaria, Musica Aeterna, Comnattimento Consort Amsterdam, Il Fondamento, Collegium Instrumentale Brugense, Les

Arts Florissants, Netherlands Wind Ensemble, Orchestra of the Age of Enlightenment, Akademie für Alte Musik; Engagements include Warsaw and Budapest Chamber Opera, Opéra Comique Paris, Opéra Marseille, Théâtre des Champs Elysées, Théâtre du Châtelet, Opéra du Rhin, Florida Grand Opera, Miami, New York City Opera, Concertgebouw and De Nederlandse Opers Amsterdam, De Doelen Rotterdam, De Vlaamse Opera, Deutsche Staatsoper Berlin etc.; Festival engagements at Halla, Warsaw and Bratislava and concerts with the Vienna Philharmonic, Clemencic Consort and Ensemble Mosaique; Sang Ottone in Monteverdi's Poppea for Netherlands Opera in 1995; Various Mozart roles, including Farnace in Mitridate Re di Ponto, 1995; Recital at the Lincoln Center, New York with the Polish Chamber Orchestra, 1996 and the roles of Ottone at the Massachusetts Music Festival and Orlofsky in Austria, also in 1996; Repertoire includes Mozart's Ascanio, Farnace, Apollo, Handel's Arsamenes from Xerxes, Tolomeo from Julio Cesare, Polinesso from Ariodante, Unulfo from Rodelinda, Tamerlano, Didymus from Theodore, Orlando, Orfeo and Monteverdi's Ottone from L'Incoronazione di Poppea. *Recordings include:* Mozart operatic arias for the Polskie Nagrania company, with the Warsaw Symphony Orchestra and Karol Teutsch; Stabat Mater by Pergolesi, and by Vivaldi; Recital for Polish Radio with the Hedos Ensemble, 1994; Orlofsky in Die Fledermaus for BMG/Arte Nova Classics; Vespro della Beata Vergine by Monteverdi for Erato; Christmas Cantatas by Bach and Stölzel for Forlane; The Roes' Room by Josef Skrzek and Lech Majewski for Polygram, Cantatas by Handel and Vivaldi for Koch. *Honours:* Venanzio Rauzzini Prize for the best counter-tenor at the Mozart Singing Competition in Vienna. *Address:* Helen Sykes Artists Management, 100 Felsham Road, Putney, London SW15 1DQ, England.

STEFANSSON, Finnur (Torfi), MA; Composer; b. 20 March 1947, Iceland; m. 1st, two s., one d., 2nd, two d., 3rd Steinunn Johannesdottir, 18 Aug. 2002. *Education:* University of Iceland, 1972; University of Manchester, 1974; Reykjavík College of Music, 1985; University of California, 1989. *Career:* Government and Law, Iceland; Member of Parliament, 1978; Ombudsman, Ministry of Justice, 1980; Lecturer, Reykjavík College of Music, 1991–94; Music Critic, 1991–94; Composer, 1994–; mem. Icelandic Society of Composers. *Compositions:* Works for Full Orchestra: Piece I, 1986; Piece II, 1988; Piece III, 1992; Piece IV, 1995; Piece V, 1997; Piece VI, 2001; Piece VII, 2003; Opera: The Shinbone and the Shell, 1992; Oratoria: The Seventh Word of Christ, 2003; Concertos: Concerto for violin and orchestra, 1996; for clarinet, bassoon and orchestra, 1991; Concerto Grosso, 1992; Chamber Music: String quartets, 1989, 1994, 1998; Wind quintets, 1993, 1996; Violin and piano, 1985, 1998; Flute and piano, 2001; Clarinet and piano, 1993; Piano Solo, 1987, 1995, 1997; Choral: My mother said, 1999; Cradle song, 1996; Christmas night, 2001; Solo songs to Icelandic and English texts. *Recordings:* Waves in the field, 2000. *Current Management:* Iceland Music Information Center. *Address:* Vesturfold 44, 112 Reykjavik, Iceland. *E-mail:* fts@li.is.

STEFFEK, Hanny; Singer (Soprano); b. 12 Dec. 1927, Biala, Poland. *Education:* Studied at the Vienna Music Academy and the Salzburg Mozarteum. *Career:* Sang in concert from 1949 with opera debut in 1951; Sang at the Graz Opera from 1953 then the Frankfurt Opera, and at the Munich Staatsoper, 1957–72; Salzburg Festival, 1950–55 as Papagena, Ilia and Blondchen, Covent Garden in 1959 as Sophie in Der Rosenkavalier, Aix-en-Provence in 1960 and Teatro Fenice Venice in 1962; Sang at the Vienna Staatsoper, 1964–73; Sang Christine in the British premiere of Intermezzo by Strauss at Edinburgh in 1965. *Recordings include:* Despina in Così fan tutte; Das Buch mit Sieben Siegeln by Franz Schmidt. *Address:* c/o Bayerische Staatsoper, Postfach 745, 8000 Munich 1, Germany.

STEFFENS, Walter; Professor and Composer; b. 31 Oct. 1934, Aachen, Germany. *Education:* Basic music education with Toni and Max Spindler; Conducting with Rolf Agap; Music theory and composition with Klussmann, Maler and Philipp Jarnach at Musikhochschule Hamburg; Musicology, phonetics, theology, arts and general history at University of Hamburg. *Career:* Dozent (lecturer) in Composition and Music Theory at Hamburg Conservatorium, 1962–69; Professor of Composition and Music Theory, masterclasses, Hochschule für Musik, Detmold, 1969–. *Compositions:* Operas: Eli, librettos by composer, after Mystery of The Sorrow of Israel by Nelly Sachs, Dortmund, 1967; Under Milk Wood, English and German versions, librettos by composer, after Dylan Thomas, Hamburg State Opera, 1973, 1977 Staastheater Kassel opening; Grabbes Leben, librettos by Peter Schütze, Landestheater Detmold, 1986, Hamburg State Opera; Der Philosoph, libretto by Schütze, Landestheater Detmold, 1990; Die Judenbuche, libretto by Schütze, after Annette von Droste-Hülshoff, Dortmund, 1993, Gelsenkirchen during the New Music Theatre Days; Bildvertonugen, over 50 individual musical settings after paintings by Bosch, Marc Chagall, Klee, Picasso, Soto and others, Kassel, 1977 and 1992; Chamber music, Lieder, Concertos, Symphonies, ballet music and oratorio. *Address:* Rosenstr 15, 32756 Detmold, Germany.

STEFIUK, Maria; Singer (Soprano); b. 1967, Kiev, Ukraine. *Education:* Studied at the Kiev State Conservatoire. *Career:* Debut: Kiev Opera in 1982 as Violetta; Many appearances in Kiev, Moscow and St Petersburg as Lucia, Zerlina, Marguerite de Valois, Mimi, Leila in Les Pêcheurs de Perles and Marfa in The Tsar's Bride; Guest engagements in Dresden, Madrid, Wiesbaden, London, Paris, Washington, Tokyo and Sydney, including many concert appearances; Sang at La Scala Milan in Sorochintsy Fair by Mussorgsky. *Address:* c/o Sonata Ltd, 11 North Park Street, Glasgow G20 7AA, Scotland.

STEGER, Ingrid; Singer (Soprano and Mezzo-Soprano); b. 27 Feb. 1927, Roding, Germany. *Education:* Studied in Munich at the Musikhochschule. *Career:* Debut: As Azucena in Passau, 1951; Sang in opera at Augsburg, 1952–54, Kassel, 1954–59, Trier, 1958–60 and Oberhausen from 1960; Further engagements at Berlin Staatsoper, 1965–68, Parma and Venice, 1965 and 1968, Salzburg Easter Festival, 1967, Graz, 1974–75 and Karlsruhe, 1975–77; Sang Elektra at San Francisco in 1973 and appeared further at the state operas of Vienna, Hamburg and Stuttgart; Sang until 1986 in such roles as Rodelinda, Leonore, Senta, Elsa, Ortrud, Elisabeth, Isolde, Kundry, the Composer in Ariadne, Lady Macbeth, Amneris, Amelia in Un Ballo in Maschera, Santuzza, Turandot, Judith in Bluebeard's Castle and Schoeck's Penthesilea. *Recordings include:* Die Walküre conducted by Karajan. *Address:* c/o Stuttgart Staatsoper, Oberer Schlossgarten 6, 7000 Stuttgart, Germany.

STEIGER, Anna; Singer (Soprano); b. 13 Feb. 1960, Los Angeles, California, USA. *Education:* Guildhall School of Music, London; Further study with Vera Rozsa and Irmgard Seefried. *Career:* Associated with Glyndebourne Opera from 1983 singing Micaela on tour in 1985, Poppea at the 1986 Festival and in the 1987 premiere production of Osborne's The Electrification of the Soviet Union; Sang at Lausanne Opera in 1985 in La Cenerentola, Opera North in 1986 as Musetta, Covent Garden Opera from 1987 in Parsifal and Jenůfa, English National Opera in The Makropulos Case, and Geneva Opera as Concepcion in L'Heure Espagnole; Sang Despina in Così fan tutte for Netherlands Opera in 1990, and Eurydice in Milhaud's Les Malheurs d'Orphée at the Queen Elizabeth Hall in 1990; Season 1991–92 as Despina at Stuttgart, a Hooded Figure in the premiere of Osborne's Terrible Mouth at the Almeida Theatre, and Zerlina for Netherlands Opera; Sang in Verdi's Un Giorno di Regno for Dorset Opera, 1994; Sang the Marquise in La Fille du régiment at St Gallen, 2000; Concert engagements include BBC recitals, Clarissa's Mad Scene by Holloway with the London Symphony, Les Illuminations with Bournemouth Sinfonietta and Fauré's Requiem with Scottish National Orchestra. *Recordings:* Poème de L'Amour et de La Mer by Chausson, with the BBC Scottish Symphony Orchestra. *Honours:* Peter Pears Award, 1982; Richard Tauber Award, 1984; John Christie Award, 1985. *Address:* c/o Stadtheater St Gallen, Museumstrasse 24, CH–9000 St Gallen, Switzerland.

STEIGER, Rand; Composer and Conductor; b. 18 June 1957, New York, USA. *Education:* New York High School of Music and Art, 1972–75; Percussion and Composition at the Manhattan School of Music (BMus 1980); California Institute of the Arts, with Brown, Subotnick and Powell (MFA 1982); Yale University with Elliott Carter, Betsy Jolas and Jakob Druckman; Further study at IRCAM, electronic music studios, Paris. *Career:* Faculty, University of Costa Rica, 1984–85, California Institute of the Arts, 1982–87 and University of California at San Diego, from 1987; Conductor and Director of contemporary music performances with SONOR at San Diego and with the Los Angeles Philharmonic New Music Group; From 1981 member new-music ensemble E.A.R., based at California Institute of the Arts. *Compositions include:* Brave New World for voices and electronics, 1980; Dialogues II for marimba and orchestra, 1980; Quintessence for 6 instruments, 1981; Currents Caprice, electronic, 1982; Kennedy Sketches for marimba and vibraphone, 1982; In Nested Symmetry for 15 instruments and electronics, 1982; Tributaries for chamber orchestra, 1986; Tributaries for Nancarrow, for six computer-controlled pianos, 1987; ZLoops for clarinet, piano and percussion, 1989; Mozart Tributary for clarinet quintet, 1991; The Burgess Shale for orchestra, 1994; Resonant Vertices, for ensemble, 1996; Frames, for ensemble, 1998; Diaspora for cello and percussion, 1999; Lemma I and II, for percussion and electronics 1997, 1999. *Honours:* First Composer Fellow of the Los Angeles Philharmonic, 1987–88. *Address:* c/o ASCAP, ASCAP Building, 1 Lincoln Plaza, New York, NY 10023, USA.

STEIN, Caroline; Singer (Soprano); b. 1963, Germany. *Education:* Musikhochschule, Cologne. *Career:* Debut: Würzburg Municipal Theatre; Sang with Wiesbaden State Opera from 1989, as Adele, Zerlina and The Queen of Night, Hannover Opera 1991-99, as Adina, Norina, Olympia, Sophie in Der Rosenkavalier, Zerbinetta, Susanna, and Venus in Ligeti's Le Grand Macabre; Further engagements at the Komische and Deutsche Operas, Berlin, and at Leipzig, Lisbon, Dresden and Munich; Blonde in Die Entführung at Quebec and Covent Garden (2000); Flower Maiden in Parsifal at Bayreuth, and roles in Henze's

König Hirsch at Hannover and Rihm's Die Eroberung von Mexico at Frankfurt; London Proms Concerts, 2000-2001. *Address:* Semper Oper, Dresden, Theaterplatz 2, D-01067 Dresden, Germany.

STEIN, Horst; Conductor; b. 2 May 1928, Elberfeld, Germany. *Education:* Studied at the Cologne Musikhochschule. *Career:* Conducted first at Wuppertal, then at the Hamburg Staatsoper, 1951–, and Berlin Staatsoper, 1955–61; Opera Director in Mannheim, 1963–70; Conducted the South American premiere of Schoenberg's Gurrelieder at Buenos Aires in 1964; Bayreuth Festival from 1969 with Parsifal and Der Ring des Nibelungen; Principal Conductor at the Vienna Staatsoper, 1970–72; Music Director at the Hamburg Staatsoper, 1972–79; Director of the Hamburg Philharmonic, 1973–76; Has conducted Tristan und Isolde in Buenos Aires, Der fliegende Holländer in Sofia and Parsifal at the Paris Opéra; Conductor of the Orchestre de la Suisse Romande, 1980–85; Director of the Bamberg Symphony from 1985, Basle Symphony from 1987; Conducted Fidelio at the 1990 Salzburg Festival; Parsifal at the Opéra Bastille, Paris, 1997; Often heard in the symphonies of Bruckner. *Address:* c/o Bamberger Symphoniker, Altes Rathaus, Postfach 110 146, 8600 Bamberg, Germany.

STEIN, Peter; Stage Director; b. 1 Oct. 1937, Berlin, Germany. *Career:* Worked with Munich Kammerspiele from 1964 directing Saved by Edward Bond in 1967; Directed plays by Brecht in Munich, Goethe and Schiller in Bremen; Co-founded the Berlin Schaubuhne Company in 1970 and was Artistic Director until 1985; Debut as opera director with Das Rheingold in Paris, 1976; For Welsh National Opera has directed Otello in 1986, Falstaff in 1988, Pelléas et Mélisande in 1992 and Peter Grimes in 1999; Director of Drama at Salzburg Festival, 1992–97; Staged Schoenberg's Moses and Aron at Salzburg, 1996; Engaged for Simon Boccanegra, 2000. *Recordings include:* Videos of Welsh National Opera productions, as director for television.

STEINAUER, Mathias; Composer; b. 20 April 1959, Basel, Switzerland; m. Elena Gianini, 3 June 1991. *Education:* Teaching Diploma, Piano, with P Efler, Teaching Diploma, Composition Theory, with R Moser, R Stuter, J Wildberger, Musik-Akademie, Basel, 1978–86; Private Study with G Kurtág, Budapest. *Career:* Various concerts of own music, radio productions, film music, 1982–; Founder, Komponisten Forum, 1982; Teacher of Music theory, and composition at the Hochschule für Musik and Theater Winterthur, Zürich, 1986. *Compositions include:* Music for xylophone, marimba and 2 musical boxes, 1984; Musik in fünf Teilen for 3 cellists and 2 percussionists, 1985; Andante for percussion trio, 1985; Vier Klangbilder for baritone, large orchestra, female choir, 18 recorders, words by H Erni, 1986; Visions for 12 wind instruments, 2 percussionists, piano, 1987; Drei Skizzen for string quartet, 1987; Duat, 14 signs for chamber orchestra. 1988;... wir Risse im Schatten..., concerto for flute and orchestra, 1988–89; Blutenlese for 2 choirs, soprano, children's voice, ensemble, words by 12 authors, 1990–91; Undici Duettini for violin and viola, 1991; Speculum Sibyllinum, 1992; Omaggio ad Italo Calvino for clarinet, horn, violin and piano, 1993; Il rallentamento della sarabanda for piano, percussion and orchestra, 1993–95; Die gehaubte Braut, a little wedding music for mezzo-soprano and organ, 1994; Jahreszeiten for percussion trio, 1994; Alta fedeltà for 2 violins and tape, 1996; Rumori cardiacl for flute, clarinet, violin, cello and piano, 1996; Nacht, pipe dreams for chamber orchestra; Koren Fantasie, 1997. *Recordings:* For various radio stations in Switzerland. *Address:* c/o Konservatorium Winterhur, Tossertobelstrasse 1, CH 8400 Winterhur, Switzerland.

STEINBACH, Heribert; Singer (Tenor); b. 17 May 1937, Duisberg, Germany. *Education:* Studied in Düsseldorf, and in Cologne with Clemens Glettenberg. *Career:* Sang at the Cologne Opera, 1964–66, and Staatstheater Karlsruhe, 1966–68; Member of the Deutsche Oper am Rhein Düsseldorf, 1968–76, and Munich Staatsoper, 1977–80; Sang at Bayreuth Festival, 1971–76 as Froh and Melot; Guest engagements at the Paris Opéra in 1976 and 1978, and Lisbon and Barcelona in 1978; Sang Loge in Das Rheingold at the 1979 Maggio Musicale Florence and again at the Teatro Col ón Buenos Aires in 1982; Sang Tristan at Lausanne in 1983, Walther von Stolzing at the Metropolitan in 1985 followed by Siegfried at Kassel; Sang at Teatro Regio Turin, 1987–88 as Siegmund in Die Walküre; At the first season of the new Musiektheater Rotterdam in 1988 sang Siegfried in Der Ring des Nibelungen; Sang Herod in Salome in 1989 at Lyric Opera of Queensland. *Recordings:* Pfitzner's Palestrina; Tristan und Isolde conducted by Bernstein; Die Soldaten by Zimmermann. *Address:* c/o Hochschule für Musik Rheinland, Vocal Faculty, Robert-Schumann-Institut, Fischerstrasse 110, D–40416 Dusseldorf, Germany.

STEINBERG, Pinchas; Conductor; b. 12 Feb. 1945, New York, USA. *Education:* Studied in New York and at Tanglewood; Composition studies with Boris Blacher in Berlin. *Career:* Took part in the 1964 Tanglewood Festival and became Professor and Assistant at the University of Indiana; Associate Conductor at the Lyric Opera Chicago from 1967, making his debut with Don Giovanni; Conducted leading

orchestras in Europe from 1972; Conducted at the Frankfurt Opera from 1979 and has led performances in Stuttgart, Hamburg and Berlin and at Covent Garden, Paris Opéra and the San Francisco Opera; Musical Director at Bremen, 1985–89, Chief Conductor at the Verona Arena in 1989 and Conductor of the Austrian Radio Symphony Orchestra notably in Janáček's Everlasting Gospel and Dvořák's Te Deum in 1990; Appeared at Bregenz Festival in 1990 with Catalani's La Wally and conducted Rossini's Tancredi at the 1992 Salzburg Festival; L'amore dei tre re at the 1994 Montpellier Festival; Further opera includes Rienzi for Radio France, Rigoletto at Orange, Nabucco at the Opéra Bastille, Tosca at Houston and Trovatore in Geneva; Un Ballo in Maschera at Monte Carlo, 1998; Die Walküre at Toulouse, 1999. *Honours:* Winner, Florence International Conductors' Competition, 1972. *Address:* c/o Poilvé, 16 avenue Franklin D. Roosevelt, F–75008 Paris, France.

STEINBERGER, Birgit; Singer (soprano); b. 1967, Berghausen, Salzach, Austria. *Education:* Studied with Wilma Lipp in Salzburg, Charlotte Lehmann in Hannover and with Kurt Widmer. *Career:* Debut: Heidelberg 1991, as Serpetta in La Serva padrona by Pergolesi; Sang at Basle Oper 1992-1994, then at Vienna Volks and State Operas, as Susanna, Marzelline in Fidelio, Papagena, Marie in Lortzing's Zar and Zimmermann, Nicolai's Anne, and Musetta in La Bohème; Operetta roles include Franziska in Wiener Blut, Rosalinde in Die Fledermaus and Lehar's Valencienne. *Honours:* Prizewinner. Hugo Wolf Competition, Stuttgart, 1990. *Address:* c/o Volksoper, Währingerstrasse 78, A-1090 Vienna, Austria.

STEINECKER, Anton; Composer; b. 9 Dec. 1971, Bratislava, Slovakia (then Czechoslovakia). *Education:* Studied Viola and Double Bass at the Bratislava Conservatory, 1986–91; Studied Double Bass at the Kromeríž Conservatory, Czech Republic; Private studies in composition with Tadeáš Salva, 1993–95; Academy of Music and Drama, Bratislava with Jozef Sixta and Dušan Martincek, 1993–98; Acadmey of Music and Drama, Prague with Svatopluk Havelka and Juraj Filas; Jerusalem Rubin Academy of Music and Dance with Mark Kopytman, 1998–2000; Doctorate course at Academy of Music and Drama, Bratislava with Dušan Martincek and Vladimír Bokes, 1999–. *Career:* Debut: Ground for Oboe and Viola, Mirfach Concert Hall, Bratislava, 1993; works performed at festivals in Slovakia, Czech Repub., Germany, Russia, Israel, France, Austria and Poland; Lecturer, Acad. of Arts, Banská Bystrica, Slovakia, 2001–02; mem, Slovakian Composers League. *Compositions:* Piano Trio, 1994; Jaj, Bože môj!f for a capella SATB Choir, 1994; Invention, in memoriam Tadeáš Salva for Violin, Viola and Cello, 1994–95; Impressions I–VIII for Piano, 1995–96; Moments musicaux for String Trio, 1996; Notturno to Ján Steinecker for Horn, 1996; String Quartet No. 1, 1996–98; Variants for Clarinet, 1998; String Trio, 1998–99; Memories for Percussion, 1999; Wind Quintet, 2000; String Quartet No. 2 Choral Variations, 2000; Es umfingen mich die Wogen des Todes Cantata for Baritone, SATB Choir and Chamber Orchestra, 2000; Chamber Opera in Four Scenes (libretto by Daniila Charms), 2001; String Quartet No. 2 Preludium – Fragmente, 2001–02; Preludium for violoncello, 2001–02; Notturni for cimbalom, 2001–03; Preludium e Quasi una passacaglia for string orchestra, 2002; Impressions for clarinet, 2002; Quasi una sonata for cimbalom, 2003–04; Quintet for cimbalom and string quartet, 2003. *Recordings:* Ground for Oboe and Viola, Slovak Radio, 1994; String Trio, Slovak Radio, 2001. *Contributions:* Slovak Music, 1998. *Honours:* Third Prize at the Year of Slovak Music Composition Competition (for Jaj, Bože m ôj!). *Address:* Tolsteho 2, 81106 Bratislava, Slovakia.

STEINER, Elisabeth; Singer (Mezzo-Soprano); b. 17 March 1935, Berlin, Germany. *Education:* Studied in Berlin with Frida Leider. *Career:* Sang at the St ädtischen Oper Berlin from 1961 with debut in Blacher's Rosamunde Floris; Sang at Salzburg Festival in 1962 as Artemis in Gluck's Iphigenia in Aulis; Discovered by Rolf Liebermann and engaged for the Staatsoper Hamburg; Sang in many premieres there including Von Einem's Der Zerrissene in 1964, Penderecki's The Devils of Loudun in 1969, Kelemen's Der Belagerungszustand in 1970 and Stefen's Under Milk Wood in 1973; Appeared often at Bayreuth and in guest engagements at the Maggio Musicale Florence, Metropolitan Opera, New York and La Scala Milan; Sang at Vienna Staatsoper in 1980 in the premiere of Jesu Hochzeit by Gottfried von Einem; Sang the Countess in Lortzing's Wildschütz, Hamburg, 1994. *Recordings:* Roles in Tiefland, Die Fledermaus, The Devils of Loudun, Rienzi and Eine Nacht in Venedig. *Address:* c/o Staatsoper, Opernring 2, 1010 Vienna, Austria.

STEINER, Frederick, BM, PhD; Composer, Conductor and Musicologist; b. 24 Feb. 1923, New York, NY, USA; m. Shirley Laura Steiner; two d. *Education:* Institute of Musical Art, New York, Oberlin Conservatory of Music, Ohio, Univ. of Southern California. *Career:* composer, conductor, radio in New York; Music Director, radio programmes This Is Your FBI, To Los Angeles 1947, many other radio programmes; worked for Columbia Broadcasting System 1950; Lecturer, History and Art of Film Music, University of Southern California, 1984–89, College of Santa Fe,

1990–93; mem Acad. of Motion Picture Arts and Sciences, American Musicological Soc., AFofM, ASCAP, Soc. of Composers and Lyricists, Film Music Society (bd of advisers). *Television music compositions include:* Andy Griffith, Danny Thomas, Gunsmoke, Have Gun Will Travel, Hogan's Heroes, Rocky and Bullwinkle Show, Movie of the Week, Fractured Fairy Tales, Rawhide, Star Trek, Twilight Zone, Hawaii Five-O, Dynasty, Amazing Stories, Tinytoons, Perry Mason theme, Dudley Doright theme. *Film music compositions include:* Della, First To Fight, Hercules, The Man From Del Rio, Run For The Sun, St Valentine's Day Massacre, Time Limit, Shipwreck, The Color Purple. *Other compositions:* Navy Log March, Five Pieces for String Trio, Tower Music for brass and percussion, Pezzo Italiano for cello and piano, Act Without Words for percussion ensemble, Indian music for viola and piano; transcriptions. *Recordings:* King Kong (conductor, motion picture score by Max Steiner), Great American Film Scores, Music from the Television Series Star Trek. *Publications:* foreword, in Music on Demand (R. R. Faulkner) 1983, Music for Star Trek, in Wonderful Inventions (Iris Newsom) 1985, Fred Steiner on Film Music, in Film Score (Tony Thomas) 1991, Interlude, in Hollywood Holyland (Ken Darby) 1992, Arthur Honegger's Les Ombres: Fragment of a Lost Score, in The Rosaleen Moldenhauer Memorial: Music History from Primary Sources (eds Jon Newsom and Alfred Mann) 2000; contributions to: Journal of the Arnold Schoenberg Institute, Film Music Notebook, Quarterly Journal of the Library of Congress, New Grove Dictionary of American Music, Dictionary of American Biography, New Grove Dictionary of Music and Musicians, album sleeve notes. *Honours:* City of Los Angeles Special Recognition Certificate, Award of Merit, Film Music Soc.. *Address:* 1086 Mansion Ridge Road, Santa Fe, NM 87501, USA.

STEINER, Paul; Singer; b. 19 Aug. 1948, Horgen, nr. Zürich, Switzerland. *Education:* studied with Elsa Cavelti in Basle, and Adalbert Kraus in Stuttgart. *Career:* many appearances in opera houses in Switzerland, notably at Paolino in Il Matrimonio Segreto, Milford in Rossini's Cambiale di matrimonio, Marquis in Zar und Zimmermann by Lortzing; concert engagements throughout Germany and Switzerland in repertory from Baroque to contemporary music; many premiere performances, including Une songe d'une nuit d'été, by R. Gerber, Biel 1984. *Recordings include:* Cantatas by Mozart and Schubert; Markus Passion, attributed to Bach (Collegium Musicum); Lieder by Othmar Schoeck. *Address:* c/o Stadttheater Biel, Burggasse 19, 2502 Biel, Switzerland.

STEINHARDT, Arnold; Violinist; b. 1 April 1937, Los Angeles, California, USA. *Education:* Studied at the Curtis Institute, Philadelphia, with Ivan Galamian. *Career:* Debut: With Los Angeles Philharmonic, 1951; Assistant Concertmaster, Cleveland Orchestra under George Szell; Performed in chamber music with Rudolf Serkin at the Marlboro Festival and prompted by Alexander Schneider to co-found the Guarneri String Quartet, 1964; Many tours of America and Europe, notably in appearances at the Spoleto Festival in 1965, to Paris with Arthur Rubinstein and London in 1970, in the complete quartets of Beethoven; Noted for performances of Viennese classics, works by Walton, Bartók and Stravinsky; Season 1987–88 included opening concert in New Concert Hall at Shufmotomo Festival, Japan and British appearances at St John's Smith Square and Queen Elizabeth Hall; Faculty Member of Curtis Institute at University of Maryland. *Recordings include:* Mozart's Quartets dedicated to Haydn; Complete Quartets of Beethoven; With Arthur Rubinstein, Piano Quintets of Schumann, Dvořák and Brahms; Piano Quartets by Fauré and Brahms. *Honours:* Edison Award for Beethoven recordings, 1971.

STEINSKY, Ulrike; Singer (Soprano); b. 21 Sept. 1960, Vienna, Austria. *Education:* Studied with Margaret Zimmermann, Hilde Zadek and Waldemar Kmentt in Vienna. *Career:* Many performances as Constanze in Die Entführung while a student; Debut at the Vienna Staatsoper in 1983 as the Queen of Night; Has also sung in Die Zauberflöte with Cologne Opera in Tel-Aviv, Covent Garden in Los Angeles in 1984 and at the 1985 Bregenz Festival; Appeared with the Bayerische Staatsoper Munich, 1984–90 and at Zürich from 1985 as Zerline in Fra Diavolo in season 1989–90; Further guest engagements at Cologne, Dortmund, Barcelona as Fiakermilli in Arabella in 1989 and at Hamburg in 1990; Season 1992 as Fiakermilli at La Scala; Other roles include Adele in Die Fledermaus, Musetta, Zerlina, Pamina, Despina, Aennchen and Papagena; Has also sung in operettas by Oscar Straus, Lehar and Millöcker; Concert performances of Così fan tutte, Don Giovanni and Mozart's La Finta Giardiniera; Sang Pamina at the Loreley Fstival, 2000. *Recordings:* Die Fledermaus. *Address:* c/o Wiener Staatsoper, 1010 Vienna, Austria.

STEJSKAL, Margot; Singer (Soprano); b. 9 Feb. 1947, Engelsdorf, Leipzig, Germany. *Education:* Studied in Weimar and at Leipzig Musikhochschule with Hannelore Kuhse. *Career:* Debut: Cottbus as Musetta in 1975; Sang in opera at Cottbus until 1977, Staatsoper Dresden, 1977–80, and Chemnitz, 1980–84; Sang Sophie in Der Rosenkavalier at the opening of Semper Oper Dresden, 1985; Guest

appearances at Berlin Staatsoper and elsewhere in Germany; Other roles have included Blondchen, Susanna, Nannetta and Adele in Die Fledermaus; Many concert appearances. *Recordings include:* Der Rosenkavalier. *Address:* c/o Semper Oper Dresden, 8012 Dresden, Germany.

STELLA, Antonietta; Singer (Soprano); b. 15 March 1929, Perugia, Italy. *Education:* Studied at the Accademia di Santa Cecilia, Rome. *Career:* Debut: Leonora in Il Trovatore, Spoleto, 1950; Rome debut, 1951, as Leonora in La Forza del Destino; Germany from 1951, in Stuttgart, Wiesbaden and Munich; Sang as guest all over Italy; Verona Arena and La Scala debuts, 1953; At the New York Metropolitan (debut 1956) she sang Aida, Butterfly, Tosca, Elisabeth de Valois (Don Carlos), Violetta and Amelia (Un Ballo in Maschera); At Naples in 1974 sang in the premiere of Maria Stuarda by de Bellis. *Recordings:* Roles in Verdi's Simon Boccanegra, Un Ballo in Maschera, Don Carlos, Il Trovatore, Aida and Il Battaglia di Legnano; Donizetti's Linda di Chamounix; Puccini's La Bohème and Tosca; Giordano's Andrea Chénier.

STEMME, Nina; Singer (Soprano); b. 1966, Stockholm, Sweden. *Education:* Studied in Stockholm and sang Rosalind, Euridice and Mimi there. *Career:* Stockholm Royal Opera, 1994, as Cherubino, Stora Theatre Gothenburg as Donna Elvira and Butterfly; Bayreuth Festival 1994–95, as Freia in Das Rheingold; Cologne Opera from 1995, as Pamina, Butterfly, Mozart's Countess, and Mimi (1998); Sang Katerina in Martinů's Greek Passion at Bregenz, 1999; Elsa at Basle and Tosca for Cologne Opera; Season 2000–01 as Senta at Antwerp, Marguerite for the Savonlinna Festival, Manon Lescaut for ENO and Tatiana in Brussels, Senta at the New York Met; Engaged as Elisabeth in Tannhäuser at the Deutsche Oper, Berlin, 2003; Many concert appearances. *Honours:* Winner, 1993 Placido Domingo Competition; Finalist, 1993 Cardiff Singer of the World Competition. *Address:* c/o English National Opera, St Martin's Lane, London, WC2.

STENE, Randi; Singer (mezzo-soprano); b. 1967, Norway. *Education:* Studied at the Norwegian State Academy of Music, Oslo, and the Opera Academy, Copenhagen. *Career:* Salzburg Festival from 1992, in Salome and Dallapiccola's Ulisse; Premiere of Reigen by Boesmans at Brussels, 1993; Season 1993–94 as Octavian at the Théâtre du Châtelet, Paris, and Dorabella at the Royal Opera, Copenhagen; Season 1995–96 with Cherubino at Covent Garden, Olga in Eugene Onegin at the Opèra Bastille, Paris, and Carmen in Brussels; Returned to London 1997, as Silla in a new production of Palestrina by Pfitzner; Hansel at the Théâtre du Châtelet, Paris, 1997; Concert repertory includes Szymanowski's Stabat Mater (London Proms, 1996), Dvořák's Requiem (Edinburgh Festival, 1996), Missa Brevis by Bach (Salzburg), the Christmas Oratorio, Zemlinsky's Maeterlinck Lieder and Falla's Three Cornered Hat (with the Berlin Symphony Orchestra); Schubert's A-flat Mass with the Oslo Philharmonic Orchestra and Sibelius's Kullervo Symphony with the Stockholm Philharmonic Orchestra. *Recordings include:* Vivaldi Cantatas; Opera Arias with Kathleen Battle; Salome, under Christoph von Dohnányi; Kullervo Symphony. *Honours:* Finalist, 1991 Cardiff Singer of the World Competition. *Current Management:* Askonas Holt Ltd, Lonsdale Chambers, 27 Chancery Lane, London, WC2A 1PF, England. *Telephone:* (20) 7400-1700. *Fax:* (20) 7400-1799. *E-mail:* info@askonasholt.co.uk. *Website:* www.askonasholt.co.uk.

STENZ, Markus; Conductor; b. 28 Feb. 1965, Bad Neuenahr, Germany. *Education:* Studied at the Cologne Musikhochschule in Salzburg, with Gary Bertini and Noam Sheriff. *Career:* With Ozawa and Bernstein at Tanglewood, 1988; Association with Hans Werner Henze includes Elegy for Young Lovers at Venice, 1988, and The English Cat in Berlin, 1989; Premieres of Das Verratene Meer (Berlin, 1990) and Venus und Adonis (Munich, 1997); Musical Director of the Montepulciano Festival, 1989–92; Conducted Figaro at Los Angeles 1994 and Hamburg, 1996; English National Opera debut 1995, Don Giovanni; Principal Conductor of the London Sinfonietta from 1994, leading it at the 1994 Proms in Music by Kurtag, Ives and Xenakis; Season 1993–94 with the Berlin Symphony Orchestra, Scottish Chamber Orchestra and BBC Symphony Orchestra; Season 1994–95 included debuts with the Hallé Orchestra, Royal Stockholm Philharmonic, and Philharmonic of Rotterdam, Helsinki and Hamburg; Debut appearances with the Sydney and Melbourne Symphony Orchestras in season 1995–96 and Prom concert with Weill's Der Silbersee; Other operas include Henze's Bassarids in Hamburg (1994), Hans Zender's Stephen Climax in Brussels and Weill's Mahagonny in Stuttgart; Season 1997–98 included debuts with the Minnesota Orchestra and the Chicago Symphony Orchestra; Chief Conductor and Artistic Director, Melbourne Symphony Orchestra, 1998–. *Current Management:* Ingpen & Williams Ltd, 7 St George's Court, 131 Putney Bridge Road, London, SW15 2PA, England.

STEPANOV, Oleg; Pianist; b. 2 May 1956, Riga, Latvia; m. Natasha Vlassenko 1981, 1 d. *Education:* Undergraduate, Postgraduate, Moscow Tchaikovsky Conservatory. *Career:* Appeared as duo with Cellist Daniel Shafran; Appeared solo and as Chamber Music Player in Germany,

Italy, Hungary, Sweden, Poland, Cuba, Bulgaria, Russia, Hong Kong and Australia; Lecturer in Piano, Queensland Conservatorium, Griffith University, Brisbane, Australia; Founder, Artistic Director, The Lev Vlasenko Piano Competition, Brisbane. *Honours:* First Prize, Grand Prize, Vittorio Gui Chamber Music Competition, Citta di Firenze, Italy, 1988. *Address:* 26 Ninth Ave, St Lucia, Brisbane, Qld 4067, Australia.

STEPHAN, Erwin; Singer (Tenor); b. 23 June 1949, Worms, Germany. *Education:* Studied in Frankfurt, Osnabruck and Karlsruhe; Further study with James King. *Career:* Debut: Flensburg, 1978; Sang in opera at Luneburg, Coburg and Giessen; Saarbrucken, 1984–86 in debut as Florestan and sang Tannhäuser from 1985, notably at Dortmund, Bremen, Geneva and the 1986 Orange Festival; Freiburg in 1987 as Otello, Huon in Oberon at Catania and Max in Der Freischütz at Cologne; US debut in 1989 as Walther von Stolzing at Seattle; Other roles have included Don José and Ismaele in Nabucco; Opera performances at Semper Oper Dresden and concert showings in France, Austria, Switzerland, Japan and South America. *Address:* c/o Semper Oper Dresden, 8012 Dresden, Germany.

STEPHEN, Pamela (Helen); Singer (Mezzo-soprano); b. 1965, England; m. Richard Hickox. *Career:* Debut: Cathleen in The Rising of the Moon, Wexford, 1990; Appearances with Opera North as the Composer in the Mozart/Griffiths Jewel Box, Cherubino, Donna Clara in Gerhard's Duenna and Cynthia in Benedict Mason's Playing Away (Munich and London); Prince in Massenet's Cenrillon for WNO, Dafne in Peri's Euridice at Batignano and Juno in Semele for the City of London Festival; Season 1999–2000 with Sonya in War and Peace at Spoleto, Verdi's Maddalena for Los Angeles Opera, and Nero in Agrippina by Handel; Concerts including Haydn's Nelson Mass at the London Proms, Britten's Phaedra with the Los Angeles CO and Dream of Gerontius for the Scottish National Orchestra; Elgar's Sea Pictures at Lisbon.

STEPHENSON, Donald (James); Singer (Tenor); b. 15 Feb. 1947, Leeds, England; Divorced. 1 s., 1 d. *Education:* Royal Manchester College of Music, 1969–71; Diploma, ARCM, with Honours, Singing and Teaching, 1972; National Opera Studio, 1982–83; Diploma, ITEC, 1992. *Career:* English National Opera, 1972–75; English Opera Group, 1975; English Music Theatre, 1976–78; Freelance Opera Singer, 1978–; Festival appearances in the United Kingdom and Europe; Film, Death in Venice, Benjamin Britten, English Music Theatre; Regular television and radio appearances; Principal Tenor, Welsh National Opera; Roles include: Radames, in Aida, Don José, in Carmen, title role in Parsifal, Siegmund in Die Walküre, Max in Der Freischütz; Glyndebourne and Aldeburgh Festivals; Numerous British premieres; World premieres include: No. 11 Bus, Peter Maxwell Davies, London, Rome and New York, 1985; Other appearances include Freiburg Opera in roles including Alwa in Lulu, 1986, Erik in Fliegende Holländer, 1988; Scottish Opera: Florestan in Fidelio, 1984, Red Whiskers in Billy Budd, 1987; Opera North: Mark, Midsummer Marriage, Tippett, 1985, Wiesbaden, 1986; Florestan, Fidelio at Regensburg and Kaiserslautern Operas, 1987–88; Hoffmann, in Tales of Hoffmann, Stockholm, 1990, First Jew, in Salome, ENO, 1991, Bob Boles in Peter Grimes, 1992; Missa Solemnis, RAH, 1992; Sang Filaura in Cesti's Il Pomo d'Oro at Batignano, 1998; mem, Equity; International Therapy Education Council. *Honours:* Arts Council Scholarship to study with Otakar Kraus, 1974. *Address:* 55 Milner Street, York, YO24 4 NJ, England.

STEPHENSON, Michael; Saxophonist; b. 16 Nov. 1963, Charlotte, North Carolina, USA; m. Cheryl Ann Swanson, 6 August 1988. *Education:* BMus, North Carolina School of Arts; MMus, Ithaca College. *Career:* Debut: New Century Saxophone Quartet, Carnegie Hall, New York City, 1993; White House; Ambassador Auditorium; Boston Symphony Hall; Concertgebouw, Amsterdam; Kennedy Centre. *Recordings:* With New Century Saxophone Quartet: Drastic Measures; Main Street, USA; Home Grown; New Century Christmas; Standard Repertoire. *Current Management:* Robert Besen, Besen Artists. *Address:* 102 Prince Road, Greenville, NC 27858, USA.

STEPHINGER, Christoph; Singer (Bass); b. 4 June 1954, Herrshing, Germany. *Education:* Studied at Munich Hochschule and the Opera Studio of Bayerische Staatsoper; Further study with Kurt Moll. *Career:* Sang at Bielefeld Staadttheater, 1982–86, Staatstheater Hannover from 1986; Guest appearances at Düsseldorf, Dortmund, Karlsruhe, Hamburg, Berlin, Nice and Spleto; Roles have included Wagner's Guernemanz, King Henry, Pogner and Daland, Mozart's Commendatore, Osmin, Sarastro and Alfonso, Kecal in The Bartered Bride and Jim in Maschinist Hopkins by Max Brand (at Bielefeld); Concert repertoire includes Herod in L'Enfance du Christ by Berlioz, with the Gächinger Kantorei under Helmuth Rilling in 1989; Sang Fasolt and Hunding in new productions of Das Rheingold and Die Walküre at Hannover in 1992; Season 1999–2000 as Leporello at the Theater am Gärtnerplatz, Munich, and Lothario in Mignon. *Address:* c/o Niedersachsische Staatstheater, Opernplatz 1, 30159 Hannover, Germany.

STEPTOE, Roger Guy, BA, ARAM; British composer, pianist and teacher; *Professor of Harmony, Analysis, Ecole Nationale de Musique, de Danse et l'Art Dramatique;* b. 25 Jan. 1953, Winchester, Hampshire, England. *Education:* Univ. of Reading, Royal Acad. of Music. *Career:* debut as composer at Purcell Room 1977, as pianist at Wigmore Hall 1982; first Vaughan Williams Composer-in-Residence, Charterhouse 1976–79; Prof. of Composition, Royal Acad. of Music 1980–91; US debut as composer and pianist at Federal Hall, NY 1991; Administrator of Contemporary Music Projects, Royal Acad. of Music 1989–91, for Int. Composer Festivals 1991–93; Prof. of Harmony, Analysis, Ecole Nationale de Musique, de Danse et l'Art Dramatica, Brive-la-Gaillarde, France 2001–; French debut as pianist and composer, Salle Cortot, Paris 2003; mem. Incorporated Soc. of Musicians. *Compositions include:* opera: King of Macedon (libretto by Ursula Vaughan Williams) 1979; orchestral: Dance Music for Symphonic Brass 1976, Two Miniatures for strings 1977, Oboe Concerto 1982, Tuba Concerto 1983, Clarinet Concerto 1989, Cello Concerto 1991, Cheers 1993, Impressions Correziennes 1999, This Side of Winter 2002; choral: Two Madrigals 1976, In Winter's Cold Embraces Dye (cantata for soprano, tenor, chorus and chamber orchestra) 1985, Life's Unquiet Dream (cantata for baritone, chorus and chamber orchestra) 1992; chamber: String Quartet No. 1 1976, No. 2 1985, No. 3 2002, No. 4 2003, Clarinet Quintet 1981, Four Sonnets for brass quintet 1984, Oboe Quartet 1989, Piano Quartet 2001; vocal: Aspects for high voice and piano 1978, Chinese Lyrics for soprano and piano 1982, Chinese Lyrics for mezzo or counter-tenor and piano 1983, The Bond of the Sea for bass-baritone and piano 1983, Five Rondos for soprano, baritone and piano 1989, Sonnets to Delia for baritone and piano 1993; instrumental: Three Preludes for piano 1976, Piano Sonata No. 1 1980, No. 2 1988, No. 3 2003, Prelude for guitar 1981, Equinox for piano 1981, Violin Sonata No. 1 1981, No. 2 1986, In the White and the Walk of the Morning (five poems for two guitars) 1989, Prelude La Dame de Labenche 2001, Prelude for viola and piano 2002, Clarinet Sonata 2003. *Address:* c/o Stainer & Bell Ltd, Victoria House, 23 Gruneison Road, London, N3 1DZ, England (office); 7 rue Jean Gentet, 19140 Uzerche, France (home). *E-mail:* post@stainer.co.uk (office); roger.steptoe@nordnet.fr (home).

STERN, David; Conductor; b. 1965, USA. *Career:* Music Director of the Philharmonisches Orchester, Westphalen, 1995: Principal Guest Conductor, 1998–; Music Director of the European Academy of Music, Aix-en-Provence, 1997–2000; Led the Philharmonia Orchestra, London, at the Albert Hall in a Yehudi Menuhin Memorial Concert; collaborations with the Peking Festival and several orchestras in China; Principal Guest Conductor of Opéra de Rouen, 2001–; Season 2000–01 with the Gurzenich Orchestra and the Royal Flanders Orchestra; Regular appearances with period instrument orchestra Concerto Köln, including tours of Europe and USA, 2002–2003. *Address:* c/o IMG Artists, Lovell House, 616 Chiswick High Road, London, W4 5RX.

STERNBERG, Jonathan; Conductor; b. 27 July 1919, New York, USA; m. Ursula Hertz, 15 Oct 1957, 1 s., 1 d. *Education:* AB, Washington Square College, NY Univ. (NYU); 1939; NYU Graduate School, 1940; Harvard Summer School, 1940; Juilliard School of Music; Manhattan School of Music; Private conducting study with Leon Barzin, 1946 and Pierre Monteux 1946–47. *Career:* Initial engagements, Nat. Youth Administration Symphony Orchestra, 11940–42; Shanghai Municipal Symphony, 1945–46; Professional debut: Vienna Symphony Orchestra, 1949; Guest Conductor, major orchestras and opera cos worldwide, 1950–; Conductor, Halifax Symphony Orchestra, Nova Scotia, 1957–58; Musical Dir, Royal Flemish Opera, 1962–66, Harkness Ballet, 1966–68, Atlanta Opera and Ballet, 1968–69; Visiting Professor of Conducting, Eastman School of Music (Univ. of Rochester), 1969–71; Professor, Temple Univ. College of Music, 1971–89, Professor Emeritus; Lecturer, Chestnut Hill College (Philadelphia), 1989–92; Faculty, International Conductors Workshop and masterclasses, Zlin, Marienbad, Karlsbad (Czech Republic), Kharkov (Ukraine), Philadelphia, New York, 1992–2003; Conducted premiere performances in Europe, S Africa, China and USA of music by Bloch, Ives, Rorem, Blackwood, Persichetti, Prokofiev, Messiaen, Lajtha, von Einem, Diamond, Skrowaczewski, Hindemith; Musical/Artistic Dir, Philadelphia Bach Festival, 2003; mem., Int. Arts Medicine Asscn, Vice Pres., 1981–85; Bartok Soc. of America, Vice Pres., 1972–78; Conductors Guild, Vice Pres., 1991–96. *Recordings:* 50 recordings including: several symphonies, Nelson Mass, Mozart Posthorn Serenade, several cantatas, Rossini Stabat Mater, Prokoviev Piano Concerto No. 5 (Brendel), Mozart Piano Concerti (Badura-Skoda), Schubert Symphonies Nos 2, 4, 5; Bassett Variations for Orchestra, Ives Set of Pieces, Telemann Pimpinone. *Publications:* Scores and parts, Journal of the Conductors Guild, 1983–2000. *Honours:* Citation Award for Outstanding Service to American Music, 1972; Faculty Research Award, Temple Univ., 1983; Distinguished Alumnus Award Third Street Music School Settlement, 1988; Conducting Teacher of the Year, Maestro Soc., 2001; Hon. Life Mem., Conductors Guild, 2003. *Address:* 5 West Chestnut Hill Avenue, Philadelphia, PA 19118, USA.

STERNKLAR, Avraham; Pianist, Composer and Educator; b. 21 Oct. 1930, Trieste, Italy; m. Evelyn Katz, 10 July 1953, one s. *Education:* Piano with L Kestenberg and composition with P Ben Haim, Israel; Juilliard School of Music, New York, USA, 1949–54; Piano with J Friskin and E Steuermann; Composition with V Giannini; Graduate work, chamber music. *Career:* Debut: Tel-Aviv, Israel; Recitals, broadcasts and performances with Israel Philharmonic, Jerusalem Symphony; Music Correspondent, Israel Broadcasting Service, 1949–52; Film; Siena Pianoforte, numerous concerts throughout USA, Canada and Europe as soloist, chamber music and as soloist with orchestras; Guest performer at Festivals; Lecturer at seminars and workshops; Specialist in Contemporary Music; Premiered many works several of which are now recorded; Faculty Member, Chamber Music Workshop, sponsored by Training Orchestra, Long Island and New York University; Appeared in concerts with Mischa Elman, Ruggiero Ricci, Oscar Shumsky, Zvi Zeitlin, Tossy Spivakovsky, Jascha Horenstein, the Hofstra String Quartet and the Bayview Chamber Players; Associate Professor of Piano Performance at Aaron Copland School of Music, Queens College, 1992. *Compositions:* For Piano: Sonatinas, Sonata, Trapezium, Etudes, A Promise Fulfilled,a set of 10 piano pieces based on the paintings of Tea Sternklar, The General Schwarzkopf March, works for one piano four hands and for two pianos; Violin and Piano sonata, Cello and Piano sonata, Clarinet and Piano sonata; Introduction and Dance for Flute and Piano, songs, chamber music, choral works, recorder works, 12 duets for 2 violins, educational music; Etudes for Piano; Sonatina for Flute, Oboe and Bassoon, Silhouttes for solo Harp. *Honours:* Recipient of 17 Meet the Composer Awards; 3 Best of the Year Awards from the Piano Quarterly Magazine. *Current Management:* E Florence. *Address:* 14 Jerold Street, Plainview, NY 11803, USA. *E-mail:* composers@sprynet.com. *Website:* www.clearstarinternational.com/asbio.html.

STEUERMAN, Jean Louis; Concert Pianist; b. 16 March 1949, Rio de Janeiro, Brazil; m. Monica Laport, 14 Aug 1981, 2 s. *Career:* Debut: Rio de Janeiro, 1963; Appearances world-wide with major orchestras with British debut in 1976; Recent engagements with Royal Philharmonic under Menuhin, Britten's Concerto at Athens Festival, with London Symphony Orchestra under Abbado and Liverpool Philharmonic and Gewandhaus Orchestra under Masur; Played Bach's D minor Concerto at the 1985 Promenade Concerts in London; Tour of Japan in 1989 with Stuttgart Chamber Orchestra, Schumann's Concerto with the Hallé Orchestra; Season 1989–90 season included recital at Salle Gaveau in Paris, Mendelssohn's G minor Concerto with Florida Philharmonic Orchestra and Tippett's Concerto with Helsinki Philharmonic; Further tours of Switzerland, with EC Youth Orchestra under James Judd, Italy and Japan, with the Gustav Mahler Youth Orchestra of Vienna, Czechoslovakia and Ireland; Recitals in San Francisco and Scotland; Chamber music concerts with leading instrumentalists notably at the Menuhin Festival in Gstaad and Kuhmo Chamber Music Festival. *Recordings include:* Bach Partitas; Italian Concerto; French Overtures; Chromatic Fantasia and Fugue; Capriccio; Preludes and Fugues; Concerti; Scriabin Sonatas 3, 4 and 5. *Honours:* 2nd Prize, Leipzig Bach Competition, 1972. *Address:* c/o London Artists, 10 Guild Street, Stratford-upon-Avon, Warwickshire, CV 37 6RE, England.

STEVENS, Risë; Singer (Mezzo-Soprano); b. 1 June 1913, New York, USA. *Education:* Juilliard School with Anna Schoen-Rene; Study in Europe with Marie Gutheil-Schoder and Herbert Graf. *Career:* Sang at Prague Opera in 1936 as Mignon in Thomas's opera, as Strauss's Octavian in 1938 at the Vienna Staatsoper and at the Teatro Col ón, Buenos Aires, at Glyndebourne Festival in 1939 as Dorabella and Cherubino, and at Metropolitan Opera, 1938–61 as Mignon, Carmen, Dalila, Orfeo, Ponchielli's Laura and Mussorgsky's Marina, 337 performances in New York and on tour; Sang in Chicago and San Francisco in 1940, Paris Opéra in 1949 as Octavian, and Glyndebourne in 1955 as Cherubino; Retired from stage in 1965 and became Director of the Metropolitan National Company until 1967, and President of the Mannes College of Music, 1975–78; Adviser to the Metropolitan's Young Artists Development Programme. *Recordings:* Carmen; Le nozze di Figaro; Orpheus and Euridice; Die Fledermaus. *Address:* c/o Metropolitan Opera, Lincoln Center, New York, NY 10023, USA.

STEVENSON, Robert (Murrell); Professor of Music; b. 3 July 1916, Melrose, New Mexico, USA. *Education:* AB, University of Texas, 1936; Piano at Juilliard School of Music, New York; Composition and musicology at Yale University; Private lessons in composition with Stravinsky, 1939, piano with Artur Schnabel, 1940; PhD, Eastman School of Music, Rochester, NY, 1942; Theology degrees, Harvard and Princeton; BLitt, Musicology, Oxford University, United Kingdom, 1954. *Career:* Instructor at University of Texas, 1941–43, 1946; US Army Chaplain, 1942–46; Recitals as concert pianist in USA and the United Kingdom, 1942–47; Lecturer of Church Music at Westminster Choir College, NJ, 1946–49; Music Faculty, 1949–, Professor of Music, 1961–, Faculty Research Lecturer, 1981–, University of California, Los Angeles; Visiting Professor to various universities. *Compositions include:* Orchestral, works performed by Philadelphia Orchestra, conducted by Leopold Stokowski; Pieces for piano, clarinet and piano, organ, mixed chorus. *Publications:* Prolific writings especially on Latin American, Spanish and Portuguese music, Italian Renaissance, and Baroque including Music In Mexico, Historical Survey, 1952, Patterns of Protestant Church Music, 1953, Cathedral Music in Colonial Peru, 1959, Spanish Cathedral Music in The Golden Age, 1961, Renaissance and Baroque Musical Sources in the Americas, 1970, Guide to Caribbean Music History, 1975, Antologia da Música Portuguesa 1490–1680, 1984; Francisco Barbieri, 1986. *Contributions:* Over 400 articles in New Grove Dictionary, 1980; Numerous contributions to prestigious journals and books. *Honours:* Research and teaching awards and fellowships; Honorary Degrees. *Address:* Department of Music, University of California, 405 Hilgard Avenue, Los Angeles, CA 90024, USA.

STEVENSON, Ronald; Composer, Pianist and Writer on Music; b. 6 March 1928, Blackburn, Lancashire, England; m. Marjorie Spedding, 18 Aug 1952, 1 s., 2 d. *Education:* Royal Manchester College of Music, 1945–48; Accademia di Santa Cecilia, Rome, 1955. *Career:* Debut: Albert Hall Proms in 1972 with own 2nd Piano Concerto; Senior Lecturer in Composition at University of Cape Town, 1963–65; 12 Busoni programmes on Radio 3, 1973; Busoni documentary on BBC television, 1974; mem, Royal Society of Musicians, United Kingdom; Composers' Guild; Savile Club; Scottish Arts Club. *Compositions include:* Prelude, Fugue and Fantasy on Busoni's Faust for Piano, 1949–59; Harpsichord Sonata, 1968; Peter Grimes Fantasy for Piano, 1970; 9 Haiku for Soprano, Tenor and Piano, 1971; Violin Concerto, The Gypsy, 1979 commissioned by Menuhin; St Mary's May Songs, song cycle, poems by Chaucer, Tennyson, Rossetti, Joyce for Soprano and String Orchestra premiered in Edinburgh, 1988; Cello Concerto, commissioned by RSNO, 1995; A Carlyle Suite, for piano, 1995; Many settings for voice and piano and for chorus of Scottish folk songs; Transcriptions of works by Purcell, Bach, Chopin, Berlioz, Delius, Britten, Berg and Grainger. *Recordings:* Stevenson plays Stevenson piano works; Passacaglia on DSCH; Grainger's Salute to Scotland; Cathedrals in Sound; Taken into the Mountains; Piano Concertos 1 and 2; Piano Music from Scotland; The Essence of Busoni; Twentieth Century Operatic Fantasias; Busoni for Two Pianos; In memoriam John Ogdon; Essentially Scottish; In memoriam Benjamin Britten; Eurocantica; Twentieth Century Scottish Choral Music. *Publications:* Numerous publications for piano; Western Music: A Brief Introduction, 1971; Editor, Bernhard Ziehn: Canonical Studies, 1976; Editor, Time Remembered, a symposium for the 80th birthday of Alan Bush, 1981; The Paderewski Paradox, 1992; Biography: Ronald Stevenson, a musical biography, by Malcolm MacDonald, 1989. *Contributions:* Various publications and many learned journals. *Honours:* Harriet Cohen International Music Award for 1966 Busoni Centenary radio broadcasts; Fellow, RNCM. 1966; Honorary Fellow, RIAS, 1992; DUniv, Stirling, 1996; HonD.Mus, Aberdeen, 1998; LLD, Dundee, 1998. *Address:* Townfoot House, Main Street, West Linton, Peeblesshire EH46 7EE, Scotland.

STEWART, Donald George, MusB; American musician (clarinet), composer and music industry executive; b. 8 Jan. 1935, Sterling, IL; m. Susan Ann Trainer 1963 (divorced 1979); one d. *Education:* Indiana Univ., Manhattan School of Music, School of Jazz, studied with Ray Harris, Bernhard Heiden, Gunther Schuller, clarinet with Russianoff, Cioffi and Moyse. *Career:* second clarinet, Birmingham Symphony Orchestra, Alabama 1954–56, Florida Symphony, Orlando 1963; played with numerous jazz ensembles, including Ornette Coleman, David Baker, Sammy Davis 1957–65; freelance copyist 1958–88; woodwind in various orchestras, New York 1967–72; founder, Boehm Quintette, New York 1968–88, debut at Carnegie Recital Hall 1972; over 1,000 chamber music concerts, festival appearances, with Boehm Quintette and other groups; music asst, New York State Council on Arts 1970–74; panellist, Vermont Council on the Arts 1976–78; founder 1978, bd mem., treasurer 1982, Chamber Music America; founder, pres., Trillenium Music Co 1986–; pres. 1987–89, bd mem. 1985–95, Opera North, Norwich, VT; bd mem., Vermont Symphony Orchestra 1989–93; mem. ASCAP, American Federation of Musicians, American Soc. of Music Copyists (bd of dirs 1970–87, treasurer 1984–87), American Music Centre, Music Publishers' Asscn, Retail Print Music Dealers' Asscn. *Compositions:* Seven Little Etudes for orchestral woodwind section, A Book of Sliding Things for eight trombones, tuba and bass, Gesualdo Stanzas for large ensemble, 200-bar Passacaglia, two string quartets, Sonata No. 1 for horn and piano, No. 2 for wind quintet, String Quartet Nos 1 and 2, Saxophone Quartet, Brass Quintet, Duet for Flute and Bass Clarinet, Violin Sonata, Never Leave Me Blue for SSAATTBB, piano and string bass, Piccolo Concerto 1973, August Lions, for youth orchestra 1978, Song of Arion 1985, First Blue Symphony, for large orchestra 1988, Book of Sliding Things 1989, Green Mountain Christmas Card, opera 1993, Never Seek To Tell Thy Love, for voice and ensemble 1998, Duo for violin and cello 1999, Sinfonia for Strings and Percussion 2000, A

Quartet of Flutes 2003; transcriber, composer, arranger. *Recordings include:* three records with Boehm Quintette; Marlboro Recordings; Music of Arthur Berger. *Current Management:* 192 Belknap Brook Road, PO Box 88, Tunbridge, VT 05077, USA. *Website:* www.trillmusic .com.

STEWART, Jeffrey; singer (tenor); b. 1970, England. *Education:* Guildhall School and National Opera Studio. *Career:* appearances with Opera North in The Thieving Magpie and The Magic Flute (Tamino); Nadir in The Pearl Fishers for ETO and Narraboth in Salome for ENO; Edgardo for European Chamber Opera and Ernesto at Düsseldorf; Other roles include Don José at Dartington, Števa in Jenůfa, Maurizio in Adriana Lecouvreur, 1999, the duke of Mantua and Mozart's Ferrando; Season 1999–2000 as Count Ivrea in Un giorno di regno, and Italian Singer in Der Rosenkavalier, for the Royal Opera; Concerts include Bach's B minor Mass, The Dream of Gerontius and Mozart's Requiem. *Current Management:* Robert Gilder & Co., Enterprise House, 59–65 Upper Ground, London, SE1 9PQ, England. *Telephone:* (20) 7928-9008. *Fax:* (20) 7928-9755. *E-mail:* rgilder@robert -gilder.com.

STEWART, Murray; Conductor; b. 1954, London, England. *Education:* Studied at Trinity Hall, Cambridge (as organ scholar) and with Daniel Roth in Paris; Conducting studies with Meredith Davies and Charles Mackerras. *Career:* As organist recorded the complete works of Franck and and works by Vierne; Artistic Director and Principal Conductor of the London Pro Arte Orchestra and London Pro Arte Baroque Orchestra, conducted premieres by Ropartz, Langlais, Sallinen, Kokkonen, Szymanowski, Howells, Patterson, Chapple, Hellawell, Burgon, Blake, Hakim, Walker and Leighton; Guest conducting engagements with the Philharmonia Orchestra, Bournemouth Symphony Orchestra, Bournemouth Sinfonietta, Ulster Orchestra, City of London Sinfonia, East of England Orchestra, and with the Prague Radio Symphony Orchestra and the Musici de Praga; Studio recordings for the BBC with the BBC Concert Orchestra; Conductor of the East London Chorus; Formerly conductor of the Collegium Musicum of London, Bristol Choral Society and Finchley Children's Music Group. *Recordings include:* Works by Jean Langlais, and Mozart's Requiem; Complete orchestral works of Maurice Duruflé with the BBC Concert Orchestra. *Address:* 17b St Augustine's Avenue, South Croydon, Surrey CR2 6JN, England. *Fax:* (20) 8688-2901. *E-mail:* m.stewart@londonproarte.co.uk. *Website:* www.londonproarte.co.uk.

STEWART, Thomas; Singer (Baritone); b. 29 Aug. 1926, San Saba, Texas, USA; m. Evelyn Lear, 1955. *Education:* Juilliard School of Music, New York, with Mack Harrell. *Career:* Debut: In 1954 as La Roche in the first US performance of Strauss's Capriccio, at Juilliard; Sang at New York City Opera in 1954 as the Commendatore in Don Giovanni; European career from 1956 at Berlin Städtische Opera, 1957–66; Sang at Bayreuth, 1960–72 as Amfortas, Donner, Gunther, the Dutchman and Wotan in The Ring, Covent Garden, 1960–78 as Escamillo in Carmen, Gunther, Don Giovanni and the Flying Dutchman, Metropolitan Opera, 1966–, as Ford in Falstaff, Wagner's Wotan, Kurwenal and Sachs, Debussy's Golaud, Verdi's Iago, Britten's Balstrode, Almaviva and the villains in Les Contes d'Hoffmann; Sang at Santa Fe Opera as Cardillac in the first US performance of Hindemith's opera, at Washington in 1972 in A Village Romeo and Juliet, and at New York City Center in Donizetti's Maria Stuarda; Many appearances with his wife, notably at San Francisco in Eugene Onegin 1971 and Reimann's Lear in 1981; Sang at Maggio Musicale Florence in 1988 as Balstrode in Peter Grimes, Falstaff at Louisville, KY in 1988, San Francisco in 1989, and Boston Opera in 1990 as the Speaker in Die Zauberflöte. *Recordings:* Die Walküre; Lohengrin; Der fliegende Holländer; Götterdämmerung; Parsifal; Die Kluge; Iphigénie en Aulide; Jonny Spielt Auf; Das Rheingold. *Current Management:* Ingpen & Williams Ltd, 7 St George's Court, 131 Putney Bridge Road, London, SW15 2PA, England.

STICH-RANDALL, Teresa; Soprano; b. 24 Dec. 1927, West Hartford, Connecticut, USA. *Education:* Hartford School of Music; Columbia University, New York. *Career:* While at college in New York created Gertrude Stein in Thomson's The Mother Of Us All in 1947 and the title role in Luening's Evangeline in 1948; Season 1949–50 sang Priestess in Aida and Nannetta in Falstaff conducted by Toscanini; European debut at Florence in 1951 as the Mermaid in Oberon; Sang at Salzburg Festival in 1952 in concert with arias by Mozart, at Vienna Staatsoper, 1952–, Aix-en-Provence Festival, 1953–71 as Mozart's Pamina, Constanze, Countess, Donna Anna and Fiordiligi; Chicago Lyric Opera debut in 1955 as Gilda; Sang at Metropolitan Opera, 1961–65 as Fiordiligi and Donna Anna; Concert performances of works by Bach and Handel, retired in 1971. *Recordings:* Così fan tutte; A Life for The Tsar; Falstaff; Aida; Hercules; Orpheus and Euridice; Rodelinda; Le nozze di Figaro; Don Giovanni; Beethoven's 9th Symphony; Brahms Requiem; Mozart's Coronation Mass. *Honours:* Austrian Kammersängerin, first American to be so honoured, 1962.

STILES, Frank, BSc, BMus, LGSM, AGSM; British composer, conductor and violist; b. 2 April 1924, Chiswick, London, England; m. 1st Estelle Lewis 1969; m. 2nd Elizabeth Horwood 1988. *Education:* Imperial Coll., Durham Univ., Paris Conservatoire. *Career:* Principal Conductor, Priory Concertante of London; composer-in-residence, Protoangel Visions, Normanby by Spital, Lincolnshire 2003–; mem. Composers' Guild of Great Britain, Incorporated Soc. of Musicians, Royal Soc. of Musicians, Asscn for British Music (chair.), British Acad. of Composers and Songwriters. *Compositions:* Dramatic Cantata, Masada, Song Cycle Mans' Four Seasons, Triple Concerto, Mirage for solo piano, Concoid organ work, In Memoriam choral work, five symphonies, seven concertos, other orchestral works, works for string orchestra, five string quartets, trios, duos and solo works, various other chamber, choral and vocal works, Four Miniatures for solo clarinet, Fantasia for 12 violas, The Great Lakes symphonic suite, Sonata No. 3 for viola and piano 2005. *Recordings:* Guitar Sonata, String Quartet No. 3, Keyboard Sonata, Concerto For Five, First Piano Concerto, Equinox for Solo Piano, Sonata for Solo Violin No. 2 2000, Sonata for Violin and Piano No. 2 2000, String Quartet No. 6 2001. *Publications:* contrib. to Composer, Musician. *Honours:* City of London Prize for Composition 1955. *Address:* 43 Beech Road, Branston, Lincoln LN4 1PP, England.

STILLER, Andrew (Philip); Composer; b. 6 Dec. 1946, Washington, District of Columbia, USA; Ernestine Steiner, 25 May 1975. *Education:* BA, Zoology, University of Wisconsin, 1968; MA, 1972, PhD, 1976, Composition, State University of New York. *Career:* Center of Creative and Performing Arts, 1971–73; Decapod Wind Quintet, 1975; Age of Reason Ensemble, 1981; Buffalo New Music Ensemble, 1984–85; Network for New Music, 1986–89; Solo shows, Buffalo, 1979, 1972, 1973, 1976; Works also heard at 2nd and 3rd North American New Music Festivals, 1984, 1985; Consultant, New Grove Dictionary of Opera, 1990; Founder and Director, Kallisti Music Press, 1991–; mem, American Society of Composers, Authors and Publishers. *Compositions:* Orchestral: Periodic Table of Elements; Foster Song; Magnification: Procrustean Concerto, 1994; Chamber music: Numerous works including Sonata, Chamber Symphony; Also various pieces, keyboard and vocal. *Recordings:* A Descent into the Maelstrom; The Mouse Singer; A Periodic Table of the Elements; The Water is Wide, Daisy Bell; Sonata a3 pulsatoribus. *Publications:* Handbook of Instrumentation, 1985; Buffalo Philharmonic Orchestra, 1985. *Contributions:* Opus; Philadelphia Inquirer; Buffalo News; Revised New Grove Dictionary of Music and Musicians; New Grove Dictionary of Opera; Musical Quarterly; Musical America. *Address:* 810 South Saint Bernard Street, Philadelphia, PA 19143, USA.

STILWELL, Richard (Dale); Singer (Baritone); b. 6 May 1942, St Louis, Missouri, USA; m. (1) Elizabeth Louise Jencks, 21 Mar 1967, (2) Kerry M McCarthy, 22 Oct 1983. *Education:* Anderson College, Indiana; BA, Indiana University School of Music, Bloomington, 1966; Studied voice with F St Leger, P Mathen and D Ferro. *Career:* Debut: St Louis Grand Opera in 1962 as Silvio in Pagliacci; First appearance as Pelléas at New York City Opera in 1970; British debut as Ulysees in Il Ritorno d'Ulisse in Patria, Glyndebourne Festival, 1973; Metropolitan Opera debut in 1975 as Guglielmo; Guest artist at Houston Grand Opera, Paris Opéra, Netherlands Opera, Chicago Lyric Opera, Washington Opera Society and Berlin Deutsche Oper; Appearances as soloist with leading US orchestras; Operatic repertory includes Don Giovanni, Don Pasquale and Eugene Onegin; Created roles in Pasatieri's The Seagull and Ines de Castro and Argento's The Aspern Papers; Sang Malatesta at Dallas in 1989, Sharpless in Madama Butterfly at Lyon in 1990 and at Chicago in 1992; Season 1992 as Mozart's Count at Dallas, Don Alfonso at Seattle and Sharpless with Opéra de Lyon at Symphony Hall, Birmingham; Sang the Doctor in Barber's Vanessa, Dallas, 1994; Washington Opera 1997, in The Ballad of Baby Doe; Sang the Poet in the US premiere of Lindholm's A Dream Play, Santa Fe 1998; Season 2000–01 as Mr. Redburn in Billy Budd and Balstrode in Peter Grimes, at Los Angeles and Seattle; mem, American Guild of Musical Artists. *Recordings:* Various. *Honours:* National Society of Arts and Letters Award, 1963; Young Artists Award, St Louis, 1963; Fisher Foundation Award, Metropolitan Opera Auditions, 1965; Honorary D.Mus, Knox College, 1980. *Current Management:* Columbia Artists Management Inc, 165 West 57th Street, New York, NY 10019, USA.

STOCKER, Markus; Violoncellist; b. 2 April 1945, Basel, Switzerland; m. Mei-Lee Ong, 21 Mar 1975, 2 d. *Education:* University of Basel; Teachers and soloist diplomas under August Wenzinger, Academy of Music, Basel. *Career:* Debut: At London, Paris, Vienna, Berlin, New York, Tokyo, Beijing; Concerts throughout Europe, USA, Far East, Israel and Russia; Performed at Lucerne, Salzburg and Menuhin Festivals, Marlboro and Lockenhaus; Appearances with Rudolf Serkin, Martha Argerich, Sándor Végh, Gidon Kremer; Professor at Winterhur and Zürich Conservatories; Piano Trio with violinist Wanda Wilkomirska and pianist Werner Genuit, 1985; European premiere, Cello Concerto by Oscar Morawetz, Memorial of Martin Luther King, Zürich,

1995; Professor of Cello, Queensland Conservatorium, Brisbane, 1995–; mem, Association of Swiss Musicians; Indooroopilly LC. *Recordings:* Live recording of Bach Suites; Mendelssohn, Complete Works for Cello and Piano; Swiss composers: Martin and Honegger; Rachmaninov and Shostakovich with Victor Yampolsky, 1994. *Honours:* 1st Prize, Bloomington, IN, USA, 1972; Grand Prix, Maurice Marechal International Cello Competition, Paris, 1972; Soloists Prize, Association of Swiss Musicians, 1973. *Address:* 11 Tarcoola Street, St Lucia, Brisbane, Qld 4067, Australia.

STOCKHAUSEN, Karlheinz; German composer; b. 22 Aug. 1928, Mödrath bei Cologne; s. of Simon Stockhausen and Gertrud Stupp; m. 1st Doris Andreae 1951; one s. three d.; m. 2nd Mary Bauermeister 1967; one s. one d. *Education:* Cologne Nat. Music Conservatory, Univs. of Cologne and Bonn. *Career:* worked with Olivier Messiaen and with the "Musique Concrète" Group in Paris 1952–53; with Westdeutscher Rundfunk Electronic Music Studio, Cologne 1953–, Artistic Dir 1963–77; first composition of purely electronic music (Studie 1 for sinewaves) 1953; Co-ed. Die Reihe (Universal Edn) 1954–59; lecturer at the Int. Summer School for New Music, Darmstadt 1955–74; concert tours throughout the world since 1958; Founder and Artistic Dir Cologne Courses for New Music 1963–68; f. ensemble for live electronic music 1964–; Int. World Fair Expo 70, Osaka; Prof. of Composition Staatliche Hochschule für Musik, Cologne 1971–77; Stockhausen annual courses for composers and interpreters of music, Kürten 1998–; mem. Royal Swedish Acad., Akad. der Künste, Berlin, American Acad. and Inst. of Arts and Letters and others; Assoc. mem. Acad. royale des sciences, des lettres et des beaux arts (Belgium) 2004. *Compositions:* 296 works including Chöre für Doris 1950, Drei Lieder (alto voice and chamber orchestra) 1950, Choral (chorus) 1950, Sonatine (violin and piano) 1951, Kreuzspiel (oboe, clarinet, piano, 3 percussion) 1951, Formel (orchestra) 1951, Etude (musique concrète) 1952, Schlagtrio 1952, Spiel (orchestra) 1952, Punkte (orchestra) 1952 (new version 1962), Klavierstücke I–IV 1952–53, Kontra-Punkte (ten instruments) 1952–53, Elektronische Studien 1953–54, Klavierstücke V–X 1954–61, Zeitmasze (five woodwind) 1955–56, Gruppen (three orchestras) 1955–57, Klavierstück XI 1956, Gesang der Jünglinge (electronic) 1955–56, Zyklus (percussionist) 1959, Refrain (three players) 1959, Carré (four orchestras and four choruses) 1959–60, Kontakte (piano, percussion and/or electronic sounds) 1959–60, Originale (musical theatre) 1961, Momente (soprano, four choral groups and 13 instrumentalists) 1962–64, Plus Minus 1963, Mikrophonie 1 (tam-tam, two microphones, two filters and potentiometers) 1964, Mixtur (orchestra, four sine-generators and ring-modulators) 1964, Mikrophonie II (choir, Hammond organ and four ring-modulators) 1965, Stop (orchestra) 1965, Telemusik (electronic music) 1966, Solo (melodic instrument and feedback) 1966, Adieu (wind quintet) 1966, Hymnen (electronic and concrete music with or without soloists) 1966–67, Prozession (tam-tam, viola, electronium, piano, filters and potentiometers) 1967, Ensemble (process planning) 1967, Kurzwellen (six players) 1968, Stimmung (six vocalists) 1968, Aus den sieben Tagen (fifteen compositions of intuitive music) 1968, Musik für ein Haus (process planning) 1968, Spiral (soloist with short-wave receiver) 1968, Dr. K-Sextett 1969, Fresco (four orchestral groups) 1969, Hymnen Dritte Region (electronic music with orchestra) 1969, Stop (ensemble) 1969–73, Pole (two players/singers) 1970, Expo (three players/singers) 1970, Mantra (two pianists) 1970, Sternklang (park music for 5 groups instrumentalists/singers), Trans (orchestra) 1971, Für kommende Zeiten (17 texts of intuitive music) 1968–70, Alphabet for Liège (13 musical pictures for soloists and duos) 1972, 'Am Himmel wandre ich' (12 American Indian songs) 1972, Ylem (19 or more players) 1972, 'Atmen gibt das Leben' (choir with orchestra or tape) 1974, Inori (Adorations for soloists and orchestra) 1973–74, Herbstmusik (4 players) 1974, Musik im Bauch (six percussionists and music boxes) 1975, Tierkreis (12 melodies of the star-signs) 1975, Harlekin (clarinet) 1975, The Little Harlequin (clarinet) 1975, Sirius (electronic music and trumpet, bass-clarinet, soprano and bass) 1975–77, Amour (5 pieces for clarinet or flute) 1976, Jubiläum (for orchestra) 1977, In Freundschaft 1977, Licht, die sieben Tage der Woche (for solo voices/ instruments, dancers, choir, orchestra, ballet, electronic and concrete music) 1977–2000, an operatic cycle that includes Donnerstag aus Licht 1981, Samstag aus Licht 1984, Montag aus Licht 1988, Dienstag aus Licht 1991, Freitag aus Licht 1996, Mittwoch aus Licht 1998 and other scenes for a combination of forces, Sonntag aus Licht Lichter – Wasser (for soprano, tenor and orchestra with synthesizer) 1999, Litanei 97 (for chorus) 1997, Engel-Prozessionen for choir a capella 2002, Düfte-Zeiten for 7 vocalists, boy's voice and synthesizer 2003, Hoch-Zeiten for choir and orchestra 2003; over 130 records; from 1991 a complete CD edn of all his works was being released. *Publications:* Texte zur Musik (10 vols) 1952–62, 1963–70, 1970–77, 1977–84, 1984–91, Stockhausen on Music – Lectures and Interviews 1989, Towards a Cosmic Music 1990, Stockhausen beiden international Ferienkurse in Darmstadt 1951–96. *Honours:* Hon. PhD (Freie Univ. Berlin) 1966; Hon. DPhil (Queen's Univ., Belfast) 2004; Hon. mem. Royal Acad. of Music, London; Hon.

Patron Sonic Arts Network, UK; many prizes including Preis der deutschen Schallplattenkritik 1964, Grand Prix du Disque 1968, Diapason d'Or 1983, UNESCO Picasso Medal 1992, Polar Music Prize 2001, German Music Publrs Society Award for score Michaelion 2002, for score Stop and Start 2004; Bundesverdienstkreuz (1st Class), Commdr, Ordre des Arts et des Lettres (France) 1985. *Address:* Kettenberg 15, 51515 Kürten (office); Stockhausen-Verlag, 51515 Kürten, Germany. *Telephone:* (2268) 1813 (office). *Fax:* (2268) 1813 (office). *E-mail:* stockhausen-verlag@stockhausen.org (office). *Website:* www.stockhausen.org (office).

STOCKHAUSEN, Markus; Trumpeter and Composer; b. 2 May 1957, Cologne, Germany. *Education:* Cologne Hochschule für Musik. *Career:* Debut: K-H Stockhausen's Sirius, Washington DC, 1976; Participation in the premieres of Aries (1977) and the Licht cycle of operas; Donnerstag (Michaels Reise um die Erde, 1981), Samstag (oberlippentanz, 1984) and Dienstag (Invasion und Pietà, 1991); Jazz collaborations including the group Possible Worlds, 1995–; Duo partners include the pianist Majella Stockhausen (b Cologne, 1961); Film and theatre music composition with brother, Simon Stockhausen (b Bensberg, 1967); Lecturer at Cologne Hochschule für musik, from 1996. *Recordings include:* Michaels Reise um die Erde (DGG); New Colours of Piccolo Trumpet (1993); Clow and Jubilee (1996). *Address:* Hochschule für musik, Dagobertstrasse 38, 50668 Cologne, Germany.

STOCKIGT, Janice Beverley, BMus, MMus, PhD; musicologist; b. 14 July 1938, Melbourne, Vic., Australia. *Education:* University of Melbourne. *Career:* mem. American Musicological Society; Australian Musicological Society; International Musicological Society. *Publications:* Die 'Annuae Literae' der Leipziger Jesuiten 1719–1740: Ein Bach-Dokument, 1992; Zpráve o návsteve císare Karla VI. s choti v Klementinu v roce 1723, 1992; Einflüsse auf Zelenkas Kompositionsstil am Beispiel seiner Vesperpsalm-Vertönungen von etwa 1725 bis 1730, 1993; Jan Dismas Zelenka's Setting of Psalm 150: Chvalte Boha Silného, 1995; The Life and Afterlife of Jan Dismas Zelenka, 1996; Indications of the Original Performances of Zelenka's Vespers Psalms, published as Hinweise auf die Originalaufführungen von Zelenkas Vesperpsalmen, 1997; The Transmission of Prague Vespers Sources to Dresden by Zelenka: An Example of a Group of Anonymous Settings, published as Die Übertragung Prager Vesperquellen nach Dresden durch Zelenka: Ein Beispiel anhand einer Gruppe anonymer Vertonungen, 1997; Music as a Proselytizing Force of the Jesuits in Saxony, 1998; The Prague Sources of Zelenka's Vespers Psalm Collection, 1998; Szenen in Zelenka's Vespers Psalm Settings, 1998; Jan Dismas Zelenka (1679–1745): A Bohemian Musician at the Court of Dresden, 2000. *Contributions:* The Oxford Companion to Australia; The New Grove Dictionary of Music and Musicians. *Honours:* Chancellor's Prize, University of Melbourne, 1994; Harbison-Higinbotham Research Scholarship for 1994; Woodward Medal, University of Melbourne 2001; Derek Allen Prize, British Academy, 2001. *Address:* c/o Faculty of Music, University of Melbourne, Parkville, Vic. 3052, Australia.

STØDLE, Tori; Pianist; b. 1 July 1942, Oslo, Norway; m. Hakon Stodle 1975; one s. one d. *Education:* studied with Robert Riefling in Oslo, Jurgen Uhde in Stuttgart, and Adele Marcus in New York. *Career:* debut, Oslo in 1970 and New York in 1990; recitals in Norway, UK, Germany, Russia, Italy, Netherlands, Denmark and USA; several television and radio programmes for Norwegian broadcasting; guest artist at major music festivals, including Chamber Music Festival at Tromso, Bergen Festival and North Norwegian Festival; piano soloist for world premieres of Ketil Vea's Piano Concertos Nos 1 and 3; Music from the Top of the World, recital of music by 19th- and 20th-century Norwegian composers, sponsored by various Norwegian organizations, Weill Recital Hall, Carnegie Hall, New York 1990; The Dream of a Sound, television portrait 1991; promotes new music; works dedicated to her by several Norwegian composers; Assoc. Prof. of Piano, North Norwegian Music Conservatory, Tromso; mem. of two Norwegian music asscns, European Piano Teachers' Asscn. *Recordings:* Music From The North, Music From The Top Of The World, Berg, Bibalo and Brahms 1996, Landscapes in Music (works by Norwegian composer David Monrad Johansen) 2000. *Honours:* Northern Lights Prize 1991. *Address:* Fogd Dreyersgt 21, 9008 Tromso, Norway. .

STOIANOV, Konstantin; Violinist; b. 1950, Russia. *Education:* Studied at the Antwerp Conservatory from age 9 and in Berlin and Würzburg. *Career:* Numerous solo appearances with leading orchestras; Radio broadcasts in Belgium, France and Italy; Leader of the Royal Philharmonic Orchestra of Flanders: Co-Leader of the London Philharmonic, 1990; Professor at the International Menuhin Academy at Gstaad.

STOICA, Adrian-Oliviu; Pianist; b. 27 Oct. 1955, Cluj-Napoca, Romania; m. Marcela-Iustina Stoica, 1 Sept 1979. *Education:* Musical studies, Piano with Georg Sava and Harald Enghiurliu, Chamber Music with Ferdinand Weiss, 1974–78, graduated, 1978, George Dima Academy of

Music, Cluj; Masterclasses, 1 year; MA degree equivalent; Masterclasses, Weimar, Germany, 1975, 1977, with Rudolf Kehrer. *Career:* Debut: Played Mozart's Concerto in C major, K 415, with Oradea Symphony Orchestra, 1972; Permanent Piano Soloist, Sibiu State Philharmonic Orchestra, 1989–91; Recitals; Guest Soloist, concerts with all philharmonic orchestras in Romania; Tours abroad: Washington DC, Midland-Odessa (Texas), New York, 1979, Boston, Massachusetts, 1993, 1994, New Jersey, 1994, Galesburg and Monmouth, Illinois, 1996, USA; Thuringia, 1979, Hannover-Langenhagen, 1994, 1996, Germany; Czech Republic, 1984; Poland, 1985; Russia and Baltic Republics, 1986, 1989; Valencia, Spain, 1992, 1994; Lecturer, University of Music, Bucharest. *Recordings:* Paul Richter: Op 58, Concerto in C minor for piano and orchestra, and op 121, Variations for piano and orchestra. *Honours:* Full Scholarship to George Dima Academy of Music; Fellowship, Romanian Ministry of Culture. *Address:* Bd Magheru No. 9, ap 133, 70161 Bucharest, Romania.

STOJADINOVIC-MILIC, Milana; Composer; b. 13 July 1962, Belgrade, Yugoslavia; m.; two s. *Education:* Composition, Belgrade Faculty of Music, 1987; postgraduate studies, 1994. *Career:* debut, String Quartet Melodia, Radio Belgrade Programme for Classical Music, 1985; Prof. of Harmony and Analysis, High School for Music, Belgrade; Asst, Dept of Music Theory, Faculty of Music, Belgrade; live performances at festivals in Yugoslavia, Slovenia, Croatia, Germany, Italy, Bulgaria, Greece, UK; mem., Assn of Composers of Serbia. *Compositions:* Melody for string quartet, 1985; Dream, for flute and piano, 1986; Mimicry for symphony orchestra, 1987; Aurora Borealis for symphony orchestra, 1989; Duo Symbolico for piano and symphony orchestra, 1994; Kaleidoscope for wind quintet, 2001; Tango Sentimental for violin, double bass, accordion and piano (in memory of Astor Piazzola), 2002; Haven't You Forgotten Something? for flute and bassoon, 2002; Tears, a cycle of songs for unusual trio: voice (soprano), alt-flute and piano, first live performance, Belgrade, 2003. *Recordings:* Albums: Aurora Borealis, 1989; Duo Simbolico, 1995; Contemporary Music from the Balkans, 1999; Kaleidoscope, on The International Review of Composers, 2002; Tango Sentimental, on New Tango After Piazzola, 2002. *Honours:* three annual Assn of Composers of Serbia awards, 1985, 1986, 1988; two International Festival of Composers awards, 1992, 1994; Belgrade October Prize, 1987; Vasilije Mokraniac Prize, 1989; Josip Slavenski Prize, 1987. *Address:* Palmoticeva 5/15, 11000 Belgrade, Serbia and Montenegro. *Telephone:* (11) 3232765.

STOJANOVIC, Milka; Singer (soprano); b. 13 Jan. 1937, Belgrade, Yugoslavia. *Education:* Studied at La Scala Opera School and with Zinka Milanov. *Career:* Sang with Belgrade National Opera from 1960, notably at Edinburgh Festival in 1962 and at Oslo and Lausanne in 1968 and 1971; Further appearances at Graz, 1962, Metropolitan Opera, 1967–68, Vienna, Bari, Munich, Cologne and Barcelona, 1970–71; Opera and concert engagements in Denmark, England, Hungary, Hamburg, Frankfurt, Dresden, Berlin, Zürich, Oslo, Copenhagen, Helsinki, Rome, Venice, Bologna, Palermo, Syracuse, Valencia, Athens, Ankara, Cairo, Caracas, Russia, Sofia, Budapest, Bucharest, and Czechoslovakia; Also festival appearances at Prague Spring and Salzburg; Roles have included Verdi's Aida, Desdemona and Amelia in Un Ballo in Maschera, Leonore, Mimi, Liu, Mozart's Countess, La Gioconda, Marenka, Santuzza and Tatiana; Roles in Verdi's Simon Boccanegra, Traviata and Vespri Siciliani, Madama Butterfly, Fidelio, Lohengrin, Tchaikovsky's Queen of Spades, Borodin's Prince Igor. *Address:* c/o Narodno Pozoriste, Francuska 3, 11000 Belgrade, Serbia and Montenegro.

STOJANOVIC-KUTLACA, Svetlana; Harpsichordist; b. 2 May 1957, Skopje, Macedonia; m. Djuro Kutlaca, 23 Feb 1980, 1 d. *Education:* Completed Secondary Music School, 1975; BA, Piano, 1981, BA, Harpsichord, 1991, MA, Harpsichord, 1993, Faculty of Music Art, Belgrade; Masterclasses with Huguette Dreyfus, France, 1989, 1990, Colin Tilney, England, 1996; Curso de perfeccionamiento with Genoveva Galvez, Madrid, 1989–90; Specialisation with Paul Simmonds, Brighton, England, 1996, 1997. *Career:* Debut: Harpsichord recital, Real Conservatorio Superior da Musica, Madrid, April 1990; Performed J. S. Bach's D minor Concerto, 5th Brandenburg Concerto, and Rameau's Pièces de clavecin en concerts, Belgrade, 1991; Cycle of 4 concerts and lectures on Improvisation, Folklore, Description, Polyphony, Belgrade, 1992; Over 50 harpsichord recitals, Yugoslavia, 1992–97; Harpsichord recitals, Aranjuez and Alcala de Henares, Spain, 1993, Brighton and Lewes, England, 1996; Repertoire includes works by Frescobaldi, Couperin, Rameau, Scarlatti, Soler, J. S. Bach, Balbastre; Teaches harpsichord, Josip Slavenski High School, Belgrade. *Recordings:* Vivaldi's Four Seasons, CD, 1993; Balbastre's Premier Livre de Clavecin, tape, 1994; For Radio Belgrade: Cycle of 4 concerts and lectures, Improvisation, Folklore, Description, Polyphony, 1992, Bach Goldberg Variations, 1995, Frescobaldi, Picchi, Froberger, F Couperin, D Scarlatti, M Kuzmanovic, 1997. *Publications:* The elements of Spanish folklore music in Domenico Scarlatti's harpsichord sonatas,

MA thesis. *Address:* Branicevska 11, 11000 Belgrade, Serbia and Montenegro.

STOKER, Richard, FRAM, ARAM, ARCM; British composer and conductor and writer and poet and painter; b. 8 Nov. 1938, Castleford, Yorkshire, England; s. of the late Capt. Bower Morrell Stoker and of Winifred Harling; m. 1st Jacqueline Margaret Trelfer (divorced 1985); m. 2nd Dr Gillian Patricia Watson 1986. *Education:* Breadalbane House School, Castleford, Huddersfield Coll. of Music with Harold Truscott, Coll. of Art, Royal Acad. of Music, composition, conducting with Maurice Miles and Sir Lennox Berkeley, private study with Nadia Boulanger, Paris. *Career:* performance debut with BBC Home Service 1953, Nat. and Int. Eisteddfods, Wales 1955–58; conducting debut 1956; asst librarian, London Symphony Orchestra 1962–63; Prof. of Composition RAM 1963–87 (tutor 1970–80); composition teacher St Paul's School 1972–74, Magdalene Coll., Cambridge 1974–76; Ed. The Composer magazine 1969–80; apptd Magistrate, Inner London Commission 1995–2003, Crown Court 1998–2003; Adjudicator, Royal Philharmonic Soc. Composer's Award, Cyprus Orchestral Composer's Award for the Ministry of Culture 2001–; mem. Composers' Guild 1962– (mem. exec. cttee 1969–80); founder mem. RAM Guild Cttee 1994– (hon. treas. 1995–); founder mem. European-Atlantic Group 1993–; mem. Byron Soc. 1993–, Magistrates' Asscn 1995–2003, English and Int. PEN 1996–; mem. and treas. Steering Cttee Lewisham Arts Festival 1990, 1992; founder-mem. Atlantic Council 1993, RSL, Creative Rights Alliance 2001–. *Art:* two exhbns. *Compositions include:* four symphonies 1961, 1976, 1981, 1991; 12 nocturnes; two jazz preludes; overtures: Antic Hay, Feast of Fools, Heroic Overture; three string quartets, three violin sonatas, Partita for Violin and Harp, Sonatina for Guitar, two piano sonatas, three piano trios, A York Suite for piano, Piano Variations, Piano Concerto, Partita for Clarinet and Piano, Wind Quintet; organ works: Partita, Little Organ Book, Three Improvisations, Symphony; Monologue, Passacagalia, Serenade, Petite Suite, Nocturnal, Festival Suite; choral works and song cycles: Benedictus, Ecce Homo, Proverb, Psalms, Make Me a Willow Cabin, Canticle of the Rose, O Be Joyful, A Landscape of Truth; piano works: Zodiac Variations, Regency Suite, A Poet's Notebook; vocal works: Music That Brings Sweet Sleep, Aspects of Flight, Four Yeats Songs, Four Shakespeare Songs, Johnson Preserv'd (three-act opera), Thérèse Raquin, Chinese Canticle, Birthday of the Infanta; music for film and stage includes Troilus and Cressida, Portrait of a Town, Garden Party, My Friend – My Enemy. *Publications:* Portrait of a Town 1970, Words Without Music 1974, Strolling Players 1978, Open Window – Open Door (autobiog.) 1985, Tanglewood (novel) 1990, Between the Lines 1991, Diva (novel) 1992, Collected Short Stories 1993, Sir Thomas Armstrong – A Celebration 1998, Turn Back the Clock 1998, A Passage of Time 1999; contrib. to anthologies, including Triumph, Forward, Outposts, Spotlight, Strolling Players, American Poetry Soc. publications, reviews and articles for periodicals, including Records and Recording, Books and Bookmen, Guardian, Performance, The Magistrate, poems in numerous anthologies and internet publications; contrib. to Oxford Dictionary of Nat. Biography 2004 (adviser 2003–). *Honours:* BBC Music Award 1952, Eric Coates Award 1962, Dove Prize 1962, Nat. Library of Poetry (USA) Editors' Choice Award 1995, 1996, 1997. *Address:* Ricordi & Co. (London) Ltd, 210 New King's Road, London, SW6 4NZ, England (office). *Telephone:* (20) 7371-7501. *Fax:* (20) 7371-7270.

STOKES, Harvey, BM, MM, PhD; composer and professor of music; b. 14 Sept. 1957, Norfolk, Virginia, USA; m.; one s. two d. *Education:* East Carolina University, University of Georgia, Michigan State University. *Compositions:* 4 string quartets; Dominion Fragments; Ethnic Impressions; Concerto No. 2 for oboe and strings; 2 piano sonatas; Values and Proposals no.6; Music for 12 Trumpets; In Memoriam SCA; Sonata for Violin and Piano; Sonata for Cello and Piano; 4 symphonies; Quintet No. 3 for Winds; Three Psalm Fragments; The Triumphant Men for wind ensemble, New York, 2003; Sonata for Viola and Piano, 4 Movements, New York, 2001. *Recordings:* Harvey J. Stokes: String Quartet no.1; String Quartet No. 2; String Quartet No. 3; The Oxford String Quartet. *Publications:* A Selected Annotated Bibliography on Italian Serial Composers 1989, Compositional Language in the Oratorio the Second Act 1992. *Honours:* New England Conservatory New Works Competition, 1st Prize, 1983; Lancaster Summer Arts Festival/1983 Orchestral Composition Contest, 1st Prize. *Address:* 1412 Hastings Drive, Hampton, VA, USA 23663. *Telephone:* (757) 727 5410 (office); (757) 850 6456 (home). *E-mail:* harvey.stokes@hamptonu.edu (office); hstok1412@aol.com (home).

STOLL, David Michael, MA (Oxon), ARAM, FRSA; British composer; b. 29 Dec. 1948, London, England. *Education:* Worcester Coll., Oxford, Royal Acad. of Music, London. *Career:* Music Dir, Greenwich Young People's Theatre 1971–75; subsequently freelance; Dir, British Acad. of Composers & Songwriters (fmr chair.), British Music Rights; education work includes: leading the Dept for Education and Skills-commissioned project, 'Building Music'; commissioned by UK Govt to write a book on the teaching of music composition in primary schools; consultant on music and creativity in schools; mem., Incorporated Soc. of Musicians. *Compositions:* concert music: Piano Quartet 1987, Sonata for 2 Pianos 1990, Piano Sonata 1991, String Trio 1992, Fanfares and Reflections (sextet) 1992, String Quartet No. 1 1994, Monument 1995, The Bowl of Nous (cantata) 1996, False Relations (opera) 1997, Motet in Memoriam 1998, Midwinter Spring (symphonic poem) 1998, String Quartet No. 2 1999, Cello Concerto 2000, Octave Variations (tuba quartet) 2001, The Path to the River (octet) 2001, Cello Sonata 2001, Fools by Heavenly Compulsion (String Quartet No. 3) 2002, Sonnet (for string orchestra) 2002, Pot-Pourri (for orchestra) 2002, Theatre Dreams (for brass quintet) 2003, A Colchester Suite (for pipes) 2003; media music: commissions include several signature tunes and much media and library (production) music; for theatre: several scores, including Teller of Tales (musical, co-composer), As You Like It (RSC production) 2003. *Recordings:* Chamber Music 1993, The Shakespeare Suite 2000, String Quartets 2001, The Fair Singer 2002, Fools by Heavenly Compulsion 2004. *Publications:* contrib. several articles on music, philosophy and related subjects. *Honours:* Hadow Open Scholarship in Composition to Worcester Coll., Oxford 1967. *E-mail:* info@davidstoll.co.uk. *Website:* www.impulse-music.co.uk/stoll.htm; www.creative-confidence.com.

STOLL, Klaus; Double Bass Player; b. 24 May 1943, Rheydt, Germany. *Education:* Cologne Musikhochschule. *Career:* Member of Niederrheinische Sinfoniker, 1959-65; Berlin Philharmonic from 1965, Principal Bass 1992-; Professor at Salzburg Mozarteum, 1990-; Premieres include Skalkottas Concerto and concertos for cello and double bass by Harald Genzmer and Helmut Eder; Many duo recitals with cellist Jörg Baumann, as Philharmonisches Duo Berlin, 1981-94; Further engagements with András Schiff, Heinz Holliger, Ruggiero Ricci and Viktoria Mullova; Plays Maggini Bass of 1610. *Publications include:* Repertoire Philharmonisches Duo Berlin (ed). *Address:* c/o Berlin Philharmonic Orchestra, Herbert Von Karajan Str, D-10785 Berlin, Germany.

STOLLERY, Pete, BMus, MA, PhD, PGCE, FRSA; Composer and University Lecturer; b. 24 July 1960, Halifax, England; m. Catherine Sutcliffe, 22 Oct 1988, two s., one d. *Education:* University of Birmingham. *Career:* Frequent radio broadcasts around the world; mem, Chair of Sonic Arts Network, 1996–2000. *Compositions:* Shortstuff, 1993; Shioum, 1994; Altered Images, 1995; Onset/Offset, 1996; Peel, 1997; ABZ/A, 1998; Thickness, 2000; Vox Magna, 2003. *Recordings:* All the above. *Contributions:* Editor of Journal of Electro-acoustic Music. *Honours:* Musica Nova, 1994; CIMESP, 1997; Pierre Schaeffer Award, 1998; Musica Nova 2003. *Address:* University of Aberdeen, Hilton Campus, Hilton Place Aberdeen AB24 4FA (office). *Telephone:* (1224) 274601 (office). *E-mail:* p.stollery@abdn.ac.uk (office). *Address:* 3 Whitehills Cottages, Monymusk, Inverurie, Aberdeenshire AB 51 7SS, Scotland (home). *Telephone:* (1467) 651425 (home). *Website:* www.petestollery .com (home).

STOLTZMAN, Richard (Leslie); Clarinettist; b. 12 July 1942, Omaha, Nebraska, USA; m. Lucy Chapman. *Education:* BA, Ohio State University, 1964; MM, Yale University, 1967; Teachers included Donald McGinnis, Kalmen Opperman and Keith Wilson. *Career:* Debut: Metropolitan Museum, New York; Taught at the California Institute of the Arts, Valencia, 1970–75; Program Director, 1971–74, and Board Member of Western Region of Young Audiences; Co-founder with Peter Serkin, Ida Kavafian and Fred Sherry of chamber group, Tashi, 1973; Mozart concert debut at Carnegie Hall, 1976; Performed with Amadeus Quartet at the Aldeburgh Festival, 1978, and New York Philharmonic with James Levine, 1979; Performances with the Cleveland, Emerson, Guarneri, Tokyo and Vermeer Quartets; Concert programmes with transcriptions and commissioned pieces; Debut at the Promenade Concerts in London with Mozart's Concerto, 1989; Premiere of Rautavaara Concerto with BBC and Leonard Slatkin, 2003. *Compositions:* Edition of Schubert's Arpeggione Sonata, Sonatinas in A minor, D385 and D384; Saint-Saëns's Romanza for Clarinet and Harp. *Recordings include:* World premiere Toru Takemitsu's Fantasma/ Cantos with BBC Wales; Brahms and Weber Quintets with Tokyo Quartet; Mozart, Beethoven and Brahms Trios with Yo-Yo Ma and Emmanuel Ax; Schubert and Schumann with Richard Goode; Laser Disc, Vienna Konzerthaus, 1791, 1891, 1991–Mozart, Brahms, Takemitsu, with Rafael Frubeck de Burgos; Finzi Concerto and Bagatelles with Guildhall Concerti for Richard Stoltzman by Einar Englund, Lukas Foss, William T McKinley with Berlin Radio Orchestra under Lukas Foss; Steve Reich, New York Counterpoint. *Honours:* Avery Fisher Prize, 1977 and 1986; Yale University Order of Merit; Grammy Award, 1983, 1996; Emmy Award for Copland Concerto Video. *Address:* c/o Frank Salomon Associates, 201 West 54th Street 4C, New York, USA.

STONE, Carl (Joseph); Composer and Radio Producer; b. 10 Feb. 1953, Los Angeles, CA. *Education:* California Institute of the Arts, with Morton Subotnick. *Career:* Independent Composers Association, from 1974; Director of KPFA Radio; Performances and lectures throughout

Japan, 1989. *Compositions:* (Electro-Acoustic) Thoughts in Stone, 1980; Ho ban, with piano, 1984; Wave Heat, 1984; Samanluang, 1986; Shing Kee, 1986; Jang toh, 1988; Chao nue, 1990; Noor mahal, 1991; Kamiya bar, 1992; Acid Karaoke, 1994; Electric Flowers, with pipa, 1994; Mae ploy, with string quartet, 1994; The Wagon Wheel, with pipa, 1995; Sampling Neurosis 1996; Wei fun, 1996. *Honours:* Asian cultural Council Grant, 1989. *Address:* c/o ASCAP, ASCAP Building, One Lincoln Plaza, New York, NY 10023, USA.

STONE, Elisabeth; Cellist; b. 1975, England. *Education:* Royal College of Music, with Simon Rowland-Jones and Chillingirian Quartet. *Career:* Co-founded Tavec String Quartet at RCM, 1999; Frequent performances at music society venues throughout Britain; London engagements at Queen Elizabeth Hall, St Martin in the Fields and Serpentine Gallery (BBC Proms); National Gallery, 2001, performing Schubert's Octet as member of Piros Ensemble (founded 2000); Workshops and other educational projects, notably in the North East of Britain. *Honours:* Prizewinner Music d'ensemble competition, Paris, 2001; Rio Tinto Ensemble Prize; Helen Just String Quartet Prize. *Address:* c/o Royal College of Music, Prince Consort Road, London, SW7 2 BS, England.

STONE, William; Singer (Baritone); b. 1944, Goldsboro, North Carolina, USA. *Education:* Studied at Duke University and University of Illinois. *Career:* Sang at first in concert and oratorios; Opera debut as Germont in La Traviata in 1975 at Youngstown, Ohio; European debut in 1977 at Spoleto Festival in Napoli Milionaria by Nino Rota, and New York City Opera debut in 1981; Sang at Lyric Opera Chicago in 1978 as Adam in the premiere of Penderecki's Paradise Lost and again at La Scala in 1979; Maggio Musicale Florence in 1979 as Wozzeck, as Orestes in 1981, at Opéra Comique in Paris in 1984 as Purcell's Aeneas, Aix-en-Provence in 1987 as Ford in Falstaff; Further guest engagements at Trieste, Rome, Naples and Brussels as Germont, Paolo and Simone in Simon Boccanegra; Many appearances at the New York City Opera including Mozart's Count in 1990 and sang at Santa Fe in 1980 in the US premiere of Schoenberg's Von Heute auf Morgen; Sang at Wexford Festival in 1989 as the Templar in Marschner's Der Templer und die Jüdin; Other roles include Rossini's Figaro, Enrico, Malatesta, Verdi's Ezio and Posa, Zurga, Albert in Werther, Golaud, Alfio and Eugene Onegin; Sang the title role in the US stage premiere of Busoni's Doktor Faust, New York City Opera, 1992; Sang Wozzeck at the 1994 Spoleto Festival; Sharpless in Butterfly at Chicago, 1998; Concert repertoire includes the St Matthew Passion, Messiah, Missa Solemnis, Beethoven's 9th and Ein Deutsches Requiem. *Recordings:* Mussorgsky's Salammbô; Hindemith's Requiem; Walton's Belshazzar's Feast; Robert Ward's Arias and Songs; Bach B minor Mass; Mahler's Symphony No. 8; Schubert's Mass in G; Bach's Magnificat; Mozart's C minor Mass; Video of Messiah with Robert Shaw. *Address:* c/o Columbia Artists Management Inc, Arbib-Treuhaft Dn, 165 West 57th Street, New York, NY 10019, USA.

STOROJEV, Nikita; Singer (bass); b. 9 Nov. 1950, Harbin, China. *Education:* Studied at Tchaikovsky Conservatoire, Moscow. *Career:* Bolshoi Theatre, Moscow, from 1978, as Pimen, Prince Igor, Gremin, Basilio and fafner; Appearances from 1983 at Vienna, Paris, Rome, Florence, Berlin, London, New York, San Francisco and Toronto; Repertoire has included Verdi's Zaccaria, Ramphis and Grand Inquisitor, Sarastro, Mephistopheles, Boris Godunov and Ivan Khovansky; Sang in Prokofiev's War and Peace at San Francisco, Rimsky's Mozart and Salieri at the Komische Oper in Berlin and Montreal, 1992; Rimsky's Ivan the Terrible at the Rome Opera, 1993, followed by Verdi Requiem at the Festival Deauville and Tchaikovsky's Iolanta at Dresden Festival; Song Recitals with David Ashkenazy and concert features with the Songs and Dances of Death at Festival Hall, 1991, and Gorecki's Beatus Vir at New York. *Recordings include:* Shostakovich 13th and 14th Symphonies; War and Peace; Gorecki's Beatus Vir and Songs of the Forest by Shostakovich; Mozart and Salieri. *Honours:* Diaposon d'Or and Choc de la Musique. *Current Management:* Athole Still International Management, Forresters Hall, 25–27 Westow Street, London, SE19 3RY, England. *Telephone:* (20) 8771-5271. *Fax:* (20) 8768-6600. *Website:* www.atholestill.com.

STOTT, Kathryn Linda, ARCM; British pianist; b. 10 Dec. 1958, Nelson, Lancs.; d. of Desmond Stott and Elsie Cheetham; m. 1st Michael Ardron 1979 (divorced 1983); m. 2nd John Elliot 1983 (divorced 1997); one d. *Education:* Yehudi Menuhin School (under Marcel Ciampi, Vlado Perlemuter, Louis Kentner) and Royal Coll. of Music, London (under Kendall Taylor). *Career:* fifth prizewinner, Leeds Int. Piano Competition 1978; debut Purcell Room, London 1978; has since performed extensively in recitals and concertos both in UK and in Europe, Far East, Australia, Canada and USA; ten appearances at Henry Wood Promenade concerts; Dir Fauré and the French Connection Festival, Manchester 1995, Piano 2000, Manchester 2000, Piano 2003, Manchester 2003. *Recordings:* 20 recordings, including premieres of concertos by George Lloyd and Michael Nyman. *Honours:* Martin Scholarship 1976, Churchill Scholarship 1979, Croydon Symphony Award, Chappell

Medal, Royal Amateur Orchestral Soc. Silver Medal 1979; Chevalier, Ordre des Arts et Lettres 1996. *Current Management:* Hazard Chase, Norman House, Cambridge Place, Cambridge CB2 1NS, England. *Telephone:* (1223) 312400. *Fax:* (1223) 460827. *Website:* www .hazardchase.co.uk. *Address:* c/o Jane Ward, 38 Townfield, Rickmansworth, Hertfordshire WD3 7DD, England (office). *Telephone:* (1923) 493903. *Fax:* (1923) 493903. *E-mail:* ward.music@ntlworld.com (office). *Website:* www.kathrynstott.com (office).

STOUT, Alan Burrage, MA; Composer; b. 26 Nov. 1932, Baltimore, MD, USA. *Education:* John Hopkins Univ., Peabody Conservatory, Univs of Copenhagen and Washington, Seattle, with Vagn Holmboe, Wallingford Riegger and Henry Cowell. *Career:* Music Department at Northwestern University, 1962–; George Lieder, Second Symphony, Fourth Symphony and Passion premiered by the Chicago SO. *Compositions:* 10 String Quartets, 1953–62; 4 Symphonies, 1959–1970; George Lieder for baritone and orchestra, 1962; Cello Sonata 1965; Solo for soprano and orchestra, 1968; Nocturnes for mezzo, speaker and ensemble, 1970; Pulsar for brass and timpani, 1972; Passion, for orchestra, 1975; Five Visages de Laforgue for soprano and orchestra, 1997; Pilva for orchestra and organ, 1983; Tryptich for female voices, chorus and orchestra, 1983; Waves of Light and sound, for chamber orchestra, 1993; Brass Quintet, 1997; Stele, for organ, 1997. *Address:* c/o ASCAP, ASCAP Building, One Lincoln Plaza, New York, NY 10023, USA.

STOYANOV, Boyko (Stoykov); Composer, Conductor, Pianist and Music Teacher; b. 4 May 1953, Sliven, Bulgaria; m. Rikako Akatsu, deceased, 2 d. *Education:* Bulgarian State Academy of Music, Sofia, 1974–75; Frederick Chopin Academy of Music, Warsaw, Poland, 1975–82; Toho Gakuen School of Music, Tokyo, Japan, 1981–82. *Career:* Conductor, Varna Philharmonic Orchestra, 1983–; Iwaki Symphony Orchestra, Japan, 1984–; Private music school, Iwaki Musica, 1984; Tokyo debut with Tokyo Symphony Orchestra, 1986; Conducted with Tenerife Symphony Orchestra, 1991–; Kaguyahime, opera for children, premiered in Vienna, 1993; Broadcasts on Bulgaria Radio Varna, Japan Fukushima Central Television, TV V and NHK, Radio RFC, Poland Radio, Austria Television; mem, Piano Teachers National Association, Japan; Japan Computer Music Association. *Honours:* 1st Prize, Folk Song Section, Bulgarian National Folk Music Competition, 1959; Varna Prize for Popular Song, 1965; 2nd Prize for Conducting and Arrangement, Bulgarian National Folk Music Competition, 1972; Distinction, Wroclaw Arrangement Competition, 1979; International Composers Competition, 1985; International Electro-acoustic Music Competition, 1990. *Address:* 35 Baba, Nishiki-machi, Iwaki City, Fukushima 974-8232, Japan.

STOYANOVA, Krassimira; Singer (Soprano); b. 1969, Bulgaria. *Education:* University of Plovdiv, Bulgaria. *Career:* Debut: Violetta in La Traviata at Opava, 1994; Appearances at the National Theatre, Sofia, from 1995 as Gilda, Susanna, Cecilia in Il Guarany and Delia in Fosca, both by Gomes, Rachel in La Juive; Mozart's Vitellia and Ilia (Idomoneo); Vienna Staatsoper from 1998 as Micaela, and in other roles; Further engagements as Mozart's Countess at Helsinki, Rachel in Tel-Aviv and Nedda in Pagliacci in Buenos Aires; Season 2001–2002 as Donna Anna at Covent Garden, Carmen (Micaela) with the Bavarian Staatsoper and Valentine in Les Huguenots at Carnegie Hall, New York; Concerts include Beethoven's Ninth Symphony, conducted by Philippe Herreweghe in Europe and Japan, and under Riccardo Muti at the Ravenna Festival. *Address:* c/o Theateragentur Dr G. Hilbert, Maximilianstrasse 22, 80539 Munich, Germany.

STRAESSER, Joep; Composer; b. 11 March 1934, Amsterdam, Netherlands. *Education:* Studied musicology at Amsterdam University, 1952–55, and with Ton de Leeuw at Amsterdam Conservatory. *Career:* Lecturer at Utrecht Conservatory, 1962–89. *Compositions include:* Opera, Uber Erich, performed in concert at the Royal Conservatory in The Hague, 1987; 22 Pages after John Cage for ensemble and voices, 1965; Summer Concerto for oboe and chamber orchestra, 1967; Musique pour l'homme for 4 voices and orchestra, 1968; Ramasiri for soprano and instruments, 1968 Missa for chorus and wind Instruments, 1969; Spring Quartet for string quartet, 1971; Intersections V-2 for bass clarinet and piano, 1975; Splendid Isolation for organ, 1977; Longing for the Emperor for soprano and instruments, 1981; Signals and Echoes for bass clarinet and orchestra, 1982; All perishes for flute and soprano, 1985; Motetus for chorus, 1987; Symphony for strings, 2nd symphony, 1989; Chamber Concerto l, 1991; Symphony No. 3 for orchestra, 1992; Gedanken Der Nacht (RM Rilke) for mezzo soprano, 1992; To The Point for 2 marimbas, 1993; Chamber Concerto No. 3, 1993; Madrigals 1-2-3 for 4–6 part chamber choir, 1993; Duo Piccolo for flute and harp, 1995; Briefings, 12 preludes for piano, 1996; Fische 4+1 songs for mezzo-soprano flute and piano, 1996; Romance for violin and piano, 1997; Sinfonia per organo, 1998; Liederfür Dich, 1999; Sonata Grande for cello and piano, 1999; Sans Détours for flute and piano, 2000; Quattro Canzoni for mixed choir, flute, harp and trombone, 2001. *Recordings:* Just for One; Ramasasiri, Spring Quartet, Intersections V-2, Signals

and echoes, A Solo for Alkaios, Gedanken der NachtSymphonie Nr 3; Sonata a Tre; Madrigals 1-2-3, Motetus, Herfst der Musiek, Madrigals IV, Cinq étu des légièrees, Splendid Isolation, Faites vos jeux. *Publications:* Number of essays on musical subjects among which his analyses of works of Anton Webern are prominent; Article on composer Jacques Bank, 1988–89. *Honours:* Matthjs Vermeulen Prize for Uber Erich M, 1988. *Address:* Donemus, Paulus Potterstraat 16, 1071 C2 Amsterdam, Netherlands.

STRAHAN, Derek; Composer, Actor and Writer; b. 28 May 1935, Penang, Malaysia. *Education:* BA, Cambridge University, 1956. *Career:* Commissions from Band Assocation of New South Wales, Sydney Ensemble, Sydney Youth Orchestra, Sydney Conservatorium of Music, Canberra School of Music, and others; Writer, Director and Actor for films and television. *Compositions include:* String Quartet: The Key, 1980; Clarinet Quintet: The Princess, 1980; The Quay for orchestra, 1986; Piano Trio in F minor, 1987; Rose of the Bay, song cycle for mezzo-soprano, clarinet and piano; Sydney 200 for orchestra, 1988; China Spring for cello and piano, 1989; Two Suites for cello, 1991; Atlantis for flute and piano, 1992; Atlantis Variations for piano, 1993; Eden in Atlantis for soprano, flute and piano, 1994; Voodoo Fire for clarinet, percussion and keyboards, 1995; Clarinet Concerto, 2001; Opera libretto, Eden in Atlantis, 2002; Calypso In Exile, for soprano and wind quintet, 2003. *Recordings:* 20 albums of concert works and film music. *Address:* PO Box 1003, Marrickville, NSW 2204, Australia. *E-mail:* dstrahan@revolve.com.au. *Website:* www.revolve.com.au.

STRAKA, Peter; Tenor; b. 22 Feb. 1950, Zlin, Czechoslovakia. *Education:* Düsseldorf Conservatory; Cologne Music High School; Artistic development, International Opera Studio, Zürich. *Career:* Member, Zürich Opera; Guest at many opera houses and in concert; Appearances include New York Metropolitan debut as Boris and Kudryasch in Katya Kabanova under Charles Mackerras, 1991, returning as Boris, 1999; Season 1991–92 as Alwa in Lulu at the Châtelet, Paris, Titus in La Clemenza di Tito in Nice; Florestan at Zürich Opera, 1992, also Berlin State Opera, Covent Garden, Nice, Paris; Returned to the Châtelet as Lenski in Eugene Onegin; Lurcano in Monteverdi's Poppea, Salzburg Festival, 1993; Opened Season 1993 as Erik in Der fliegende Holländer at Bastille Opéra, Paris, then Loge in Rheingold at the Châtelet, Boris at Zürich; Mazal and Petrik in Janáček's Excursions of Mr Brouček and Narraboth in Salome under Mackerras at Bavarian State Opera, Munich, 1995; Erik at Munich State Opera and Zürich, Boris at the Bastille, Alwa in Copenhagen programme, Oedipus in Oedipus Rex at Zürich, 1996; Prince in Rusalka at Zürich Opera, Laca in Jenůfa at Amsterdam Opera for Holland Festival's 50th Anniversary, Mahoney in Mahagonny at the Bastille, 1997; Laca in Zürich, Siegmund in Walküre at Caracas Opera, 1998; Season 2000–01 at Zürich Opera as Elemer in Arabella, Narraboth, and Berg's Alwa; Boris in Katya Kabanova at the Munich Staatsoper; Concerts with London Philharmonia, Munich Philharmonic under Celibidache, Bavarian Radio Orchestra under Colin Davis, Concentus Musicus Wien under Harnoncourt, other leading orchestras and conductors; Concert repertoire includes Mahler's 8th Symphony, Janáček's Glagolitic Mass and Our Father, Beethoven Ninth, Zivny in Janáček's Osud, Bruckner's Te Deum, Puccini's Messa di Gloria, Stravinsky's Oedipus, Bach B minor Mass, Richard Strauss Lieder. *Recordings:* Several operatic and concert performances. *Address:* Ränkestrasse 34, 8700 Küsnacht, Switzerland.

STRANGE, (John) Allen, MA; composer; b. 26 June 1943, Calexico, CA, USA. *Education:* California State University, Fullerton, University of California at San Diego with Harry Partch, Pauline Oliveros and Kenneth Gaburro. *Career:* co-founder, electronic music performances groups Biome (1967–72) and Electronic Weasel Ensemble, 1974; President of International Computer Music Association, 1993–98. *Compositions:* Soundbeams, for ensemble and electronics, 1977; Second Book of Angels, for string quartet and tape, 1979; Santa Fe, string quartet, 1980; Velocity Studies, for violin and tape, 1983; Sleeping Beauty, 1989; Ursa Major, tape, 1989; Antigone, theatre music, 1989; Cygnus, kinetic sculpture, 1992; Phoenix and the Harlequin, tape, 1995; Physical States, theatre, 1996; Chimera, for orchestra and tape, 1997; The Phoenix Set, tape, 1999; Goddess, for violin and electronics, 1999. *Address* c/o ASCAP, ASCAP Building, One Lincoln Plaza, New York, NY 10023, USA.

STRANZ, Ulrich; Composer; b. 10 May 1946, Neumarkt St Veit, Bavaria, Germany. *Education:* Munich Musikhochschule, with Günter Bialas, 1968–72. *Career:* Performances of music throughout German-speaking Europe. *Compositions:* Déjà vu, for oboe d'amore and chamber orchestra, 1973; Tachys, for solo strings and orchestra, 1974; Klangbild, for orchestra, 1976; Musik für Klavier und Orchester no. 1, 1978–82, no, 2 1992; Four String quartets, 1976, 1981, 1993, 1999; Auguri, for viola and small orchestra, 1981; Janus, for violin, piano and 13 wind instruments, 1986; Piano Trio, 1986; Symphony no. 1 1990; Aus dem Zusammenhang. for eesemble, 1997; Der Sinn des Lebens for soprano, flute, violin and viola, 1998; Music for Two Violoncelli and Orchestra,

1999. *Address:* c/o GEMA, Rozenheimer Str. 11, 81667 Munich, Germany.

STRASHKO, Yevgeny; Singer (Tenor); b. 1967, Crimea, Russia. *Education:* Graduated St Petersburg Conservatoire, 1998; Musikhochschule Graz and Salzburg. *Career:* Appearances with the Kirov Opera, St Petersburg, from 1995 as Tamino, Alfredo, Steersman in Der fliegende Holländer and Young Gypsy in Rachmaninov's Aleko; Further roles include Tchaikovsky's Lensky and Herman, Dimitri in Boris Godunov, Kuragin in War and Peace and Prokofiev's Semyon Kotko; Sang in Rimsky-Korsakov's Snow Maiden (Concert) with the Kirov Opera at Covent Garden, 2000; Also appears as Genarro in Prokofiev's Maddalena and gives recitals of Russian German and Italian songs. *Honours:* Prizewinner at competitions in Russia, Germany and Sweden. *Address:* c/o Kirov Opera, Mariinsky Theatre, 1 Theatre Square, St Petersburg, Russia.

STRATAS, Teresa Anastasia Strataki, OC; Canadian opera singer; b. 26 May 1938, Toronto, Ont.; d. of Emmanuel Stratas and Argero Stratakis; m. Tony Harrison. *Education:* Univ. of Toronto. *Career:* began singing career in nightclubs in Toronto; début at Toronto Opera Festival 1958; won audition to Metropolitan Opera, New York 1959; performances there include Berg's Lulu, Jenny in Brecht and Weill's Mahagonny, Suor Angelica, Lauretta and Giorgetta in Il Trittico; major roles in opera houses worldwide include Paris (Lulu 1979), Brussels (Lulu 1988), Boston (Mimi 1989), Chicago (Mélisande 1992); appeared as Violetta in Zeffirelli's film of La Traviata 1983; appeared in Broadway musical Rags 1986; cr. role of Marie Antoinette in Ghosts of Versailles, premièred Metropolitan Opera, NY 1992; Il Tabarro and Pagliacci at the Met 1994. *Honours:* LLD hc (McMaster Univ.) 1986, (Toronto) 1994, (Rochester) 1998, (Juilliard School of Music), (Royal Conservatory of Music); Canadian Music Council Performer of the Year 1979, Drama Desk Award for Leading Actress in a Musical on Broadway 1986–87, Gemini Award for Best Supporting Actress (for Under the Piano) 1997, 3 Grammy Awards. *Current Management:* Vincent & Farrell Associates, 157 W 57th Street, Suite 502, New York, NY 10019, USA. *Address:* The Ansonia, 2109 Broadway, New York, NY 10023, USA (office).

STRATE, Petra-Ines; Singer (Soprano); b. 7 Sept. 1945, Jessen an der Alster, Germany. *Education:* Magdeburg Musikhochschule, and with Gunther Leib, Dresden. *Career:* Debut: Magdeburg 1971, as Pamina in Die Zauberflöte; Sang at Magdeburg until 1973; Halle Opera from 1973, Leipzig Opera from 1984; Guest appearances throughout Germany as Mozart's Countess, Donna Anna and Fiordiligi, Agathe in Der Freischütz, and Liù in Turandot; Many appearances in operas by Handel at the Halle Festival; Often heard in oratorios by Bach, Haydn and Handel. *Address:* c/o Oper Leipzig, Augustusplatz 12, D-7010 Leipzig, Germany.

STRAUCH, Jacek; Singer (Baritone); b. 1953, London, England. *Education:* Studied at the Royal College of Music and National Opera Studio in London. *Career:* Debut: Kent Opera in 1978 as Rigoletto; Sang in opera at Würzburg, 1980–82, and Saarbrucken, 1982–85; Guest appearances in Modena and Pretoria, South Africa in 1985; Berne Opera in 1987 as Wozzeck, English National Opera in 1988 as Alfio and as Jaroslav Prus in The Makropulos Case; Season 1988–90 as Amfortas, Iago and the Hoffmann Villains at Brunswick, Kurwenal at Saarbrücken and Gunther in Götterdämmerung; Other roles include Mozart's Count; Broadcast engagements in Germany, England and Norway; Sang Pacheco in the premiere of Macmillan's Ines de Castro, Edinburgh, 1996; Season 2000–01 as Wotan in The Ring at Graz, followed by Nicolai's Falstaff, Verdi's Renato at Barcelona and Tomsky in The Queen of Spades for the Munich Staatsoper. *Honours:* Winner, Kathleen Ferrier Competition, 1978; Prizewinner, Belvedere International at Vienna, 1984. *Address:* c/o Grant Rogers Management, 8 Wren Crescent, Hertfordshire WD23 1AN, England.

STRAUSSOVA, Eva; Singer (Soprano); b. 7 June 1934, Cheb, Czechoslovakia. *Education:* Studied with Elisa Stunzner and with Rudolf Dittrich at the Dresden Opera Studio, 1956–59. *Career:* Debut: Landestheater Dessau in 1959 as Helmwige in Die Walküre; Sang at Dessau until 1963, notably as Eva in Die Meistersinger, then joined the Staatsoper Berlin in major roles including Wagner's Elisabeth and Gutrune, Amelia in Un Ballo in Maschera, Donna Anna, Turandot, Elektra, Fiordiligi, Leonore and Katerina Izmailova; Guest engagements in Zürich, Berne, West Germany, Russia and Austria; Sang Isolde at Aachen Opera. *Recordings:* Various albums.

STREATFIELD, Simon; Violist and Conductor; b. 3 May 1929, Windsor, Berkshire, England; m. Elizabeth Winship, 2 d. *Education:* Eton College; Royal College of Music, London. *Career:* Principal Viola, Sadler's Wells Opera, 1953–55, London Symphony Orchestra, 1956–65 and Vancouver Symphony Orchestra, Canada, 1965; Assistant Conductor, 1967, Associate Conductor, 1972–77, Music Director and Conductor of the Vancouver Bach Choir, 1969–81; Season 1970–71 included concerts with the City of Birmingham Symphony, the Royal

Choral Society, the BBC and with the Vancouver Bach Choir in Netherlands; Visiting Professor at Faculty of Music, University of West Ontario, 1977–81; Conductor, Regina Symphony Orchestra, Canada, 1981–84; Conductor, Manitoba Chamber Orchestra, 1982–; Conductor, Quebec Symphony Orchestra, 1984–; Has also conducted the National Arts Centre Orchestra in Ottawa, the Danish Radio Symphony, the Oslo Philharmonic and the Belgian Radio Symphony. *Recordings include:* Telemann Viola Concerto; Berlioz Harold en Italie.

STREET, Tison; Composer and Violinist; b. 20 May 1943, Boston, MA, USA. *Education:* Harvard University, with David Del Tredici and Leon Kirchner (MA 1971). *Career:* Lecturer at Berkeley, 1971–72, Harvard University, 1979-83, and Boston University, 1995-; Co-leader of the Boston Ballet Orchestra, 1992-97. *Compositions:* String Quartet, 1972; String Quintet, 1974; Adagio for oboe and strings 1977; Montsalvat for orchestra, 1980; Divertimento for piano, 1983; Six Fantasies on a Hymm Tune for string quartet, 1984; Violin Concerto 1986; Fantasia, for six cellos, 1988; Bright Sambas, for orchestra, 1993; Symphony no. 2, 1993; Ave maris stella, for chorus, 1994; The Jewel Tree, ballet, 1998. *Honours:* Prix de Rome, 1973; Guggenheim Fellowship 1981; Commissions from the New York PO and Boston Ballet. *Address:* c/o ASCAP, ASCAP Building, One Lincoln Plaza, New York, NY 10023, USA.

STREHLE, Wilfried; Violist; b. 1947, Stuttgart, Germany. *Education:* Studied at Stuttgart and Detmold Hochschulen. *Career:* Violist with Sudfunk-Sinfonie-Orchester at Stuttgart; Soloist with Chamber Orchestra Tibor Varga until 1971 then Principal Violist with Berlin Philharmonic Orchestra; Co-Founded Brandis String Quartet in 1976 with chamber concerts in Paris, Munich, Hamburg, Milan, Tokyo and London, and appearances with Wiener Singverein and Berlin Philharmonic; Festival engagements at Edinburgh, Tours, Bergen, Salzburg, Lucerne, Florence and Vienna; Co-premiered the 3rd Quartets of Gottfried von Einem and Giselher Klebe in 1981 and 1983, and the Clarinet Quintet of Helmut Eder in 1984. *Recordings include:* Albums in the standard repertory from 1978; Recent releases of Quartets by Beethoven, Schulhoff, Weill and Hindemith, and the Schubert String Quintet. *Honours:* European Chamber Music Award, 1997. *Address:* c/o Berlin Philharmonie, Herbert-von-Karajan-Straase 1, 10785 Berlin, Germany.

STREIT, Kurt; Singer (Tenor); b. 14 Oct. 1959, Itazuke, Japan. *Education:* Studied at the University of New Mexico with Marilyn Tyler. *Career:* Member of apprentice programmes at San Francisco and Santa Fe, also at the Texas Opera Theater; Appearances with the Milwaukee Skylight Comic Opera and in Dallas; European career with the Hamburg Staatsoper singing in operas by Mozart, Donizetti and Rossini; Guest appearances at Schwetzingen in 1987, Aix-en-Provence in 1989, Salzburg in 1989 and at Glyndebourne as Tamino in the 1990 production of Die Zauberflöte by Peter Sellars; Has also sung at opera houses in Vienna, Munich, Brussels, Leipzig, Düsseldorf and San Francisco (1990); Covent Garden debut in 1992 as Ferrando; Concert engagements with the London Symphony, Orchestre National de France, St Petersburg Philharmonic, Hamburg Staatsorchester and the English Chamber Orchestra; Promenade Concerts in London in a 1990 concert performance of Die Zauberflöte; Sang Orfeo in Haydn's Orfeo ed Euridice at South Bank, London, 1997; Belmonte at Covent Garden, 1996; Grimoaldo in Rodelinda at Glyndebourne, 1998; Season 2000–01 as Mozart's Tito for the New York City Opera, Almaviva in Seattle, Rossini's Ramiro in Los Angeles and Cassio in Otello at Covent Garden. *Recordings include:* Gluck's Echo et Narcisse; Ferrando in Così fan tutte (also at Glyndebourne in 1990), with Daniel Barenboim and the Berlin Philharmonic; Die Entführung aus dem Serail. *Address:* c/o IMG Artists, Lovell House, 616 Chiswick High Road, London W4 5RX, England.

STRINDBERG, Henrik; Composer; b. 28 March 1954, Kalmar, Sweden. *Education:* Stockholm Royal College of Music, with Gunnar Bucht, Brian Ferneyhough and Sven-David Sandströ m. *Career:* Assistant to Sandströ m, 1985–87; Computer music programs at IRCAM, Paris, 1987–89. *Compositions:* In Yellow and Red, suite for orchestra, 1979; String Quartet, 1982; Hustle and Bustle, for ensemble, 1984; Scenario, for wind band, 1984; Petite chronique berlinoise, two pianos, 1984; Bambu, electro-acoustic, 1984; Midsommar, for soprano and ensemble, 1986; The First Lay about Gudrun, for mezzo and guitar, 1987; Within Trees, for orchestra, 1988; Etymology, for piano, string quartet, soprano, saxophone and double bass, 1990; Two Pianos, 1992; Nattlig Madonna, for chamber orchestra, 1994; Clarinet Concerto, 1998. *Address:* c/o STIM. Sandhamnsgatan 79, PO Box 29327, S–102 54 Stockholm, Sweden. *Telephone:* 0046 8783 8800. *Fax:* 0046 8662 6275.

STROE, Aurel; Composer; b. 5 May 1932, Bucharest, Romania. *Education:* Bucharest Conservatory, 1951–56; Darmstadt summer courses, 1966–69, with Ligeti, Stockhausen and Maurico Kagel. *Career:* Reader in Composition at Bucharest Conservatory, 1962–; Professor at Mannheim Hochschule für musik, 1986–93; Commissions from Royan

Festival, French Ministry of Culture and Kassel Opera. *Compositions:* Le Paix, opera after Aristophanes 1973; String quartet, 1973; Clarinet Concerto, 1976; Le Jardin des Structures for trombone and tape, 1976; Les Choephores music theatre, 1977; Missa Puerorum, 1983; Piano sonata no. 2, 1983, no. 3 1993; Agememnon, music theatre, 1983; Eumenides, opera after Sophocles, 1985; Accords et continues, for orchestra, 1988; Capricci e Ragas for violin and chamber orchestra, 1990; L'Enfant et le Diable, opera, 1990; Mozart Sound Introspection, string trio, 1994; Préludes lyriques, for orchestra, 1999. *Address:* c/o UCMR, Calea Victoriei 141, Sector 1 Bucharest, Romania. *Telephone:* 40212127966. *Fax:* 40212107211. *E-mail:* umcr@itcnet.ro.

STROHM, Reinhard; Musicologist; b. 4 Aug, 1942, Munich, Germany. *Education:* Studied in Munich, and in Berlin with Carl Dahlhaus, 1961–71. *Career:* Co-editor of Wagner Collected Edition, 1970–82; Lecturer at King's College, London, 1975–83; Professor at Yale University 1983–90; King's College 1991–96; Heather Professor of Music at Oxford University from 1996. *Publications include:* Zu Vivaldis Opern schaffen, 1975; Hasse, Scarlatti, Rolli, 1975; Die italienische Oper in 18 Jahrhundert, 1979, rev. 1991; Essays on Handel and Italian Opera (contrib. 1985); Music in Late Medieval Bruges, 1985, rev. 1900; The Rise of European Music (1380–1500), 1993; Drama per musica; Italian Opera Seria of the Eighteenth Century, 1997; Song Composition in the 14th and 15th Centuries: Old and New Questions, 1997; Editions of Wagner's Rienzi and Tannhäuser, Giustino by Vivaldi. Honours include: Dent Medal of the Royal Musical Association, 1997. *Address:* Heather Professor of Music, Faculty of Music, St Aldate's, Oxford, OX1 1 DB, England.

STROPPA, Marco; Composer; b. 8 Dec. 1959, Verona, Italy. *Education:* Verona, Milan and Venice Conservatories; Michigan Institute of Technology 1984–86, computer music. *Career:* Composer and researcher at IRCAM, electronic music studios, Paris, from 1982; Professor of Composition, Stuttgart Musikhochschule, from 1997. *Compositions:* Traiettoria, with piano, 1984; Etude pour Pulsazioni, for 18 instruments, 1985–89; Spirali, with string quartet, 1988; Träumen vom Fliegen, ballet, 1990; Leggere il decamerone, 1990; Miniature estrose, piano, 1991–95; Danza per miniature estrose, ballet, 1995; Auras, 1996; Upon a Blade of Grass, for piano and orchestra, 1996. *Honours:* Kompositionpreis, Salzburg Easter Festival, 1996. *Address:* c/o SIAE (Sezione Musica), Viala della Letteratura 30, 00144 Rome (EUR), Italy.

STROW-PICCOLO, Lynn; Singer (Soprano); b. 17 June 1947, Waterburg, Connecticut, USA. *Education:* Studied at Hartford University and with Carlo Alfieri in Parma. *Career:* Debut: Siena Opera, 1975; Season 1976-77 as Leoncavallo's Zaza for RAI, and guest appearances in San Diego, and Turin; Further engagments at New Orleans, Santiago, Miami, Oslo and Marseille; Norma in Bellini's opera at Covent Garden, 1987; La Scala, Vienna Staatsoper and elsewhere in Europe as Maria Stuarda, both Leonoras of Verdi, Elisabeth in Don Carlos, Desdemona, Odabella and Amelia (Un Ballo in Maschera); Manon Lesaut, Mascagni's Isabeau, and Sieglinde in Die Walküre. *Honours:* Winner Giuseppe Verdi Competition at Bussetto, 1974. *Address:* c/o Teatro alla Scala, Via Filodrammatici 2, 20121 Milan, Italy.

STRUCKMANN, Falk; Singer (Baritone); b. 23 Jan. 1958, Heilbronn, Germany. *Education:* Studied at the Stuttgart Musikhochschule. *Career:* Debut: Kiel, 1985; Kiel Opera, 1985–89, Basle Opera, 1991; Vienna State Opera, 1990, as Scarpia and Escamillo; Berlin State Opera from 1992, as Amfortas, the Wanderer in Siegfried, the Dutchman, Pizarro and Jochanaan in Salome; Bayreuth Festival from 1993 as Kurwenal, Donner, Gunther and Amfortas; Kurwenal and Wotan at the Vienna State, Oslo and Marseille; US debut Chicago, 1995, as Orestes in Elektra (concert); New York Metropolitan debut, 1997, as Wozzeck; La Scala, 1997, as the Wanderer; Berlin Staatsoper, 1996 and 1998, as Telramund and Hans Sachs; Other roles include Barak in Busoni's Turandot, Rangoni in Boris Godunov and Bart ók's Bluebeard; Sang Kurnwenal at Florence, Wozzeck at the Berlin Staatsoper and Strauss's Barak in Vienna, 1999; Season 2000–01 as Gunther for Cologne Opera, Pizarro at the Met, Hans Sachs in Madrid, Wagner's Dutchman and Wotan in Berlin. *Recordings include:* Tristan und Isolde, and Lohengrin conducted by Barenboim; Video of Parsifal, Berlin 1992; Bluebeard's Castle, under Eliahu Inbal. *Address:* c/o Music International, 13 Ardilaun Road, London N5 2QR, England.

STRUMMER, Peter; Canadian/American (b. Austrian) singer (bass-baritone); b. 8 Sept. 1948, Vienna, Austria; m. Linda Roark. *Education:* Cleveland Inst. of Music. *Career:* debut as Antonio in Le Nozze di Figaro with the Atlanta Symphony Orchestra 1972; Metropolitan Opera debut as Beckmesser 1985; debut with New York City Opera as the Sacristan in Tosca 1998–99; season 1999–2000 engagements included San Francisco Opera as Benoit/Alcindoro in La Bohème and as Borov in Giordani's Fedora for the Domingo Gala, New York City Opera as Don Prudenzio in Il Viaggio a Reims and as the Sacristan in Tosca, De Brétigny in Manon with Milwaukee's Florentine Opera Company, the

Sacristan in Tosca with Manitoba Opera, Geronte in Manon Lescaut with Opera Pacific, and a concert performance as Alberich in Das Rheingold with L'Opéra de Montréal; season 2001–02 included appearances at San Francisco Opera as the Sacristan in Tosca and as Bogdanovic in The Merry Widow, New York City Opera as the Sacristan in Tosca and as Colonel Vandeveer in John Philip Sousa's The Glass Blowers, Opera Colorado as the Sacristan in Tosca, and Florentine Opera as Faninal in Der Rosenkavalier; season 2002–03 engagements included New York City Opera as Talpa in Il Tabarro and as Simone in Gianni Schicchi, Dr Bartolo in Il Barbiere di Siviglia with New York City Opera, Mustafa in L'italiana in Algeri with L'opéra de Montréal, Sulpice in La Fille du Régiment with Opera Ontario, and Benoit/ Alcindoro in La Bohème with Utah Opera; season 2003–04 engagements include San Francisco Opera as Benoit/Alcindoro in La Bohème and as the Badger in The Cunning Little Vixen, New York City Opera in the title role of Don Pasquale and as Candy in Of Mice And Men, Florentine Opera and Opera Lyra Ottawa in the title role of Don Pasquale, and New Orleans Opera as Alberich in Das Rheingold; other roles include Baron Zeta in The Merry Widow, Beckmesser in Die Meistersinger von Nürnberg, Bottom in A Midsummer Night's Dream, Dansker in Billy Budd, Dikoj in Katya Kabanova, Don Alfonso in Così fan Tutte, Don Magnifico in La Cenerentola, Dr Bartolo in Le Nozze di Figaro, Dulcamara in L'Elisir d'Amore, Fabrizio in La Gazza Ladra, Frank in Die Fledermaus, Kecal in The Bartered Bride, Leporello in Don Giovanni, Mamma Agatha and the Impresario in Viva la Mamma, Melitone in La Forza del Destino, Raimbaud and the Gouverneur in Le Comte Ory, Shishkov in From the House of the Dead, the Mayor in Jenůfa, the Music Master in Ariadne auf Naxos, the Parson in The Cunning Little Vixen, Varlaam in Boris Godunov; numerous radio and television broadcasts, including Melitone in La Forza del Destino and the Sacristan in Tosca (CBC) and the Music Master in Ariadne auf Naxos (PBS). *Recordings:* Devilshoof in The Bohemian Girl, with Central City Opera. *Current Management:* Pinnacle Arts Management/ Uzan Division, 889 Ninth Avenue, Suite 1, New York, NY 10019, USA. *Telephone:* (212) 397-7926. *Fax:* (212) 397-7920. *E-mail:* Vuzan@ pinnaclearts.com. *Website:* www.peterstrummer.com.

STRYCZEK, Karl-Heinz; Singer (Baritone); b. 5 May 1937, Nichelsdorf, Germany. *Education:* Leipzig Musikhochschule. *Career:* Debut: Dresden-Radebeul, 1964, as Germont; Dresden Staatsoper from 1966, Berlin Staatsoper, 1970; Premiere of Levins Muhle by U Zimmermann at Dresden, 1973; Guest appearances at Paris Opéra, Helsinki, Wiesbaden and Barcelona (Telramund in Lohengrin, 1992); Dresden, 1992 and 1994, in Hoffmann and as Oger in Reimann's Melusine; Other roles include Pizarro, Wozzeck, Scarpia, Mozart's Count, Amonasro, Iago and Carlos in La Forza del Destino; Dresden Staatsoper 2000–01 as the Speaker in Die Zauberflöte, and in the premiere of Celan, by Peter Ruzicka; Many concert and oratorio engagements. *Recordings include:* Donner in Das Rheingold; Die Kluge and Carmina Burana. *Address:* Dresden Semper Oper, Theaterplatz 2, 01067 Dresden, Germany.

STUART, Debra; Singer (Mezzo-Soprano); b. 1969, Scotland. *Education:* Studied at the Royal Scottish Academy and the Guildhall School of Music. *Career:* Opera appearances at Covent Garden, English National Opera and with the English Touring Opera; Roles include Mozart's Annius and Dorabella, Rosina, Meg Page and Britten's Hermia; Concerts with Frans Brüggen and the Songmakers' Almanac; Sang in A Midsummer Night's Dream at Aldeburgh in 1995 and festival engagements at Aix-en-Provence and Bordeaux; Further repertoire includes Les Nuits d'Été (BBC); Sang Luca in the premiere of Woolrich's In the House of Crossed Desires, Cheltenham, 1996.

STUBBS, Stephen; chitarrone player, archlute player and ensemble director; b. 1951, Seattle, WA, USA. *Career:* Director of Tragicomedia, ensemble performing in the Renaissance and Baroque repertory; Concerts, the United Kingdom and leading European early music festivals; Gave Stefano Landi's La Morte d'Orfeo at the 1987 Flanders Festival; Francesca Caccini's La Liberazione di Ruggiero dall'Isola d'Alcina at the 1989 Swedish Baroque Festival, Malmö; Conducted Monteverdi's L'Incoronazione di Poppea for Norrlands Opera in Umeå, Sweden, 1993; Conducted Monetverdi's L'Orfeo at Netherlands Opera, Amsterdam, 1995. *Compositions:* Pegasus and the Griffin, one-hour chamber opera for three singers and chamber ensemble, libretto by Peter Bockström, performed Malmö, 1994. *Recordings:* Solo lute recordings, David Kellner's XVI. Auserlesene Lauten-Stücke; J. S. Bach and S L Weiss Lute Suites; With Tragicomedia, Proensa (Troubadour songs); My Mind to Me a Kingdom (Elizabethan ballads); A Musicall Dreame (duets from Robert Jones 1609 collection); Orpheus I Am (masque and theatre music by Robert Johnson and William Lawes); Sprezzatura (Italian instrumental music); Il Ballo dell'Ingrate (and other theatrical music by Monteverdi); The Notebook of Anna Magdalena Bach; Le Canterine Romane (music for 3 sopranos by Luigi Rossi); Concert programmes including all recorded repertoire and other 17th and 18th century music including Orpheus Britannicus (best of

Purcell's secular music for up to 5 singers, violins and oboes); Purcell, Songs of Welcome and Farewell, Tragicomedia, 1995. *Publications:* contrib. L'Armnonia Sonora: continuo orchestration in Monteverdi's L'Orfeo, to Early Music, 1994. *Current Management:* Robert White Artist Management, 182 Moselle Avenue, London, N22 6EX, England.

STUCKY, Steven; Composer and Conductor; b. 7 Nov. 1947, Hutchinson, Kansas, USA. *Education:* BM, 1971, Baylor University; MFA, 1973, DMA, 1978, Cornell University (with Karel Husa); Conducting with Daniel Sternberg. *Career:* Faculty of Cornell University from 1980; Chairman of the music department at Cornell, 1992–97; Composer-in-Residence with the Los Angeles Philharmonic, 1988–. *Compositions include:* Two Holy Sonnets of Donne for mezzo, oboe and piano, 1982; Sappho Fragments for mezzo and ensemble, 1982; Voyages, for voice and wind orchestra, 1984; Double Concerto, for violin, oboe and chamber orchestra, 1985; Concerto for Orchestra, 1987; Threnos for wind ensemble, 1988; Son et Lumière for orchestra, 1988; Angelus for orchestra, 1989; Serenade for wind quintet, 1989; Impromptus for orchestra, 1991; Four Poems of A. R. Ammons for baritone and ensemble, 1992; Funeral Music for Queen Mary, arrangement of Purcell, 1992; Ancora, for orchestra, 1994; Fanfares and Arias for wind ensemble, 1994; Concerto for 2 flutes and orchestra, 1994; Pinturas de Tamayo, for orchestra, 1995; Cradle songs, 1997; Concerto Mediterraneo, 1998; Ad Parnassum, 1998; American Muse, 1999; Nell'ombra, nella luce, 2000; Partita-Pastorale, 2000; Etudes, concerto for recorder and chamber orchestra, 2000; Skylarks, 2001; Noctuelles, orchestration of Ravel, 2001; Concerto for percussion and wind orchestra, 2001; Whispers, 2002; Colburn Variations, 2002; Spirit Voices for percussion and orchestra, 2002–03; Second Concerto for Orchestra, 2003; Jeu de timbres, 2003; Sonate en forme de préludes, 2003–04. *Publications include:* Lutoslawski and his Music, 1981. *Honours:* Fellowships including Guggenheim Foundation, 1986; Goddard Lieberson Fellowship, American Acad. of Arts and Letters, 2002. *Current Management:* Theodore Presser Co, 588 North Gulph Road, King of Prussia, PA 19406, USA.

STUDEBAKER, Thomas; Singer (Tenor); b. 1970, Illinois, USA. *Career:* Debut: St Louis Opera, 1995; Appearances throughout USA, including engagements with the Metropolitan (Ruiz in Il Trovatore); Sang Narraboth in Salome at Santa Fe, 1998; Season 1999–2000 with appearances at Montreal and Seattle. *Honours:* Finalist in 1999 Singer of the World Competition, Cardiff. *Address:* c/o Metropolitan Opera, Lincoln Center, New York, NY 10023, USA.

STUDER, Cheryl; Singer (Soprano); b. 24 Oct. 1955, Midland, Michigan, USA. *Education:* Studied in USA and with Hans Hotter in Vienna. *Career:* Concert engagements in USA then sang with the Munich Staatsoper from 1980, notably as Marenka in The Bartered Bride; Darmstadt, 1983–85 in Mozart roles and as Bizet's Micaela, Strauss's Chrysothemis and Wagner's Irene and Eva; Berlin Deutsche Opernhaus from 1985; Bayreuth debut in 1985 as Elisabeth in Tannhäuser, returning in 1988 as Else in Lohengrin; Paris Opéra in 1986 as Pamina in Die Zauberflöte; Covent Garden, 1987–88 as Elisabeth and Elsa; Sang Sieglinde and the Empress in Die Frau ohne Schatten at La Scala in 1987; Metropolitan debut in 1988 as Micaela; Season 1989 sang Chrysothemis at Salzburg and Vienna, Lucia at Philadelphia; Opening night of season at La Scala, 1989 as Hélène in I Vespri Siciliani; Sang Elsa at Vienna in 1990 opposite Domingo; Deutsche Oper Berlin in 1990 as Salome; Sang Mozart's Elettra at the 1990 Salzburg Festival, Donna Anna at Vienna; Season 1992–93 as Lehar's Giuditta at Vienna Volksoper, the Empress in Die Frau ohne Schatten and Madame Cortesa in Il Viaggio a Reims at Salzburg; Covent Garden in 1994 as Aida; Sang Beethoven's Leonore at the at the 1996 Salzburg Festival; Sang Senta and Sieglinde at Bayreuth, 1999–2000; Season 2000–01 as Arabella at Zürich, the Marschallin at the Met and Strauss's Empress for the Dresden Staatsoper. *Recordings:* Zemlinsky's Der Zwerg; Sieglinde in Haitink recording of Die Walküre; Aida and Tannhäuser; Salome; Guillaume Tell; I Vespri Siciliani; Attila; La Traviata; Die Zauberflöte; Lohengrin; Lucia di Lammermoor. *Address:* c/o Deutsche Oper Berlin, Richard Wagnerstrasse 10, 1000 Berlin, Germany.

STUDER, Ulrich; Singer (Baritone); b. 27 Aug. 1945, Bern, Switzerland. *Education:* Studied at Bern Conservatory and Musikhochschule Munich. *Career:* Many appearances at Opera Houses in Italy, Netherlands (The Hague), Austria (Innsbruck), Australia and Czechoslavakia; Concert and Broadcast engagements in Switzerland, Germany and France, notably in Bach's Sacred Music and contemporary works by Burkhard, Milhaud and Huber; Recitals featuring German Lieder and French Chansons; Opera performances at Bern, 1979–83, and at Basle, Lausanne and Munich; Roles have included Morales in Carmen, Belcore, Malatesta, Valentin, Creonte in Haydn's Orfeo, Masetto, Suppé's Boccaccio and Monteverdi's Orfeo; Season 2000–01 at Halle as Don Alfosno, Escamillo, and Elmiro in Rossini's Otello (concert). *Recordings include:* Cantatas by Bach and Charpentier; Messe des Morts by Gilles; Cantatas by Vivaldi; Elviro in Handel's Serse; Lully's

Armide; Erode in Stradella's San Giovanni Battista. *Address:* c/o Opern- and Konzertsänger, Mittelstrasse 14–15, 06108 Halle/Saale, Germany.

STUDNICKA, Vladimir; Composer and Music Director; b. 24 Aug. 1935, Czechoslovakia; 2 d. *Education:* Completed Composition studies, 1957, and Classical Guitar Performance, 1966, Conservatory of Music. *Career:* Debut: Suite for Orchestra performed by Janáček Philharmonic Orchestra in 1957; Teacher at Music School, 1961–75; Music Director, Radio Ostrava, 1975–; Works as a Conductor; Established and conducted the Beskydska Muzika Harmonic Folk Orchestra. *Compositions:* All kinds especially concert pieces for orchestra, adaptations of folk songs of the Janáček region, and chamber and symphony works including: Suite for Orchestra, 1957; The May Dance, recorded, Prague Radio, 1973; The Beskydy Nocturno, Radio Ostrava, 1984; The Ondra's Dance, Radio Ostrava, 1985; Salut JV Stich-Punto for 12 Horns, Radio Ostrava, 1986. *Recordings include:* Radio recordings of many smaller pieces. *Publications:* The Round, 1985; The Song Of The Rising Sun by Wilhelm Halter, 1990; Slazsky Dance Musikvarlag Rundal, 1993. *Address:* ul Prof Jana Soupala 1607, 70800 Ostrava-Poruba, Czech Republic.

STUMPF, Peter (Daniel); Cellist; b. 16 Jan. 1963, Syracuse, New York, USA. *Education:* BM, Curtis Institute of Music, 1985; Artist Diploma, New England Conservatory, 1990; Teachers: David Wells, Orlando Cole, Lawrence Lesser. *Career:* Debut: Boston Symphony Orchestra, Symphony Hall, Boston, 1979; Participant at Marlboro Music Festival, 1985–; Tours with Music From Marlboro; Member, Philadelphia Chamber Music Society Players, 1994–; Piano Trio with Mitsuko Uchida and Mark Steinberg, 1995–; Solo recitals at the Jordan Hall, Boston, 1989–90, Phillips Collection, Washington DC, 1991, 1994, 1996, Corcoran Gallery, Washington DC, 1997; Solo appearances at: Aspen Festival, Colorado, 1984; Boston Philharmonic, 1989; Virginia Symphony, 1992; National Repertory Orchestra, 1992; Philadelphia Orchestra Chamber Music Series, 1990–; Chamber Music with Wolfgang Sawallisch in Carnegie Hall and Concertgebouw; Teaching Chamber Music at the Curtis Institute of Music, 1994–. *Honours:* Second Prize, Evian International String Quartet Competition, 1983; First Prize, Aspen Concerto Competition for Cello, 1984; First Prize, Washington International Competition, 1991; Serving on Board of Trustees for Yellow Barn Festival, Putney, Vermont, USA, 1995–. *Address:* 400 South Sydenham Street, Philadelphia, PA 19146, USA.

STUMPHIUS, Annegeer; Singer (Soprano); b. 1963, Netherlands. *Career:* Glyndebourne Touring Opera, 1987, as Fiordiligi; Munich Festival, 1988, as Europa in Strauss's Die Liebe der Danaë; Sang Britten's Helena at Glyndebourne, 1989; First Lady in Die Zauberflöte, 1991; Season 1991 as Vitellia in La Clemenza di Tito at Enschede and Zürich, Ilia in Idomeneo at Amsterdam; Season 1993–94 as Ellen Orford at Munich and Vitellia at Dresden; Munich, 1996, as Echo in Ariadne and Naxos; Jenůfa at Hildesheim, 2001; Further engagements as Donna Anna at Dresden, Jenůfa at Hildesheim, Mozart's Countess at Salzburg and Donna Elvira at Munich; Wellgunde and Helmwige in Munich Ring, under Zubin Mehta. *Recordings include:* Bach B minor Mass; Haydn's Seasons, under Helmuth Rilling; Mendelssohn Lobgesang; Bach St John Passion; Gluck Pilgrims to Mecca. *Current Management:* Agentur Haase, Munich. *Address:* c/o Bavarian State Opera, Max-Joseph-Platz, 80539 Munich, Germany.

STUPPNER, Hubert; Composer; b. 18 Jan. 1944, Trodena, nr. Bolzano, Italy. *Education:* Bolzano Conservatory and University of Padua (Doctorate, 1965); Darmstadt 1970–74, with Ligeti, Xenakis and Stockhausen. *Career:* Founded International Festival of Contemporary Music at Bolzano, 1975; Director of Bolzano Conservatory, from 1981. *Compositions:* Historia Naturalis, for soprano, mezzo, six voices, two flutes and two percussion, 1976; Totentanz, chamber opera, 1978; Die Stimme der Sylphiden for orchestra, 1979; Quasi una Sinfonia, 1981; Chamber concerto, 1981–84; String quartet no. 1, 1984, no. 2 1987, no. 3 1990; Symphony no.1, 1985; Piano Concerto, 1984; Chamber Symphony, 1986; Symphony no. 2 1986; Café Eros, theatre, 1986; Salomes Tanz for soprano and orchestra, 1988; Bergkristall, for violin and piano, 1989; Hiob, oratorio, 1991; Folk Songs for soprano and ensemble, 1994; Corrida, for orchestra, 1996. *Address:* c/o SIAE (Sezione Musica), Viale della Letteratura n.30, 00144 Rome, Italy.

STUR, Svetozar; Conductor and Composer; b. 21 Feb. 1951, Bratislava, Czechoslovakia; m. Nadezda Sturova, 12 November 1977. *Education:* Graduate, conservatoire in Bratislava, 1972; Graduate, Academy of Music and Performing Arts, Bratislava, 1977. *Career:* Debut: Taras Bulba by Janáček with the Slovak Philharmonic Orchestra, Bratislava, 1977; Artistic Head of Orchestra, Slovak Folklorist Ensemble, Lucnica, 1972–77; Assistant Conductor, Slovak Philharmonic Orchestra, Bratislava, 1977–79; First Conductor, Cairo Conservatoire Orchestra, 1979–80; Conductor, Symphony Orchestra of Czech Radio, Bratislava, 1980–81; Recording Own Compositions for Films and Television with Fisyo Orchestra, Prague, 1980–; Assistant Conductor, Slovak National

Theatre, Bratislava, 1980–87; Conductor, Slovak State Folk Ensemble, Bratislava, 1988–90; Freelance Composer, for films, television and theatre, 1991–. *Address:* Grosslingova 28, 811 09 Bratislava, Slovakia.

STURROCK, Kathron; Pianist; b. 17 July 1948, Bournemouth, England. *Education:* Studied at the Royal College of Music and with Alfred Brendel in Vienna; Further study with Mstislav Rostropovich in Moscow. *Career:* Concert and television appearances throughout Europe and in North America, India and Australia; Regular performances for the BBC and concerts in the major London halls; Director, the chamber music ensemble, The Fibonacci Sequence; Has taught at Morley College, the Royal College of Music, Royal Academy of Music and the Birmingham School of Music; Artist in Residence at the Brisbane Conservatoire, 1987; British Council tour of Oman in 1989; BBC recitals include Schubert's Wanderer Fantasy, Beethoven Op 109, and Rawsthorne Ballade; Prom debut in 1994 in Rawsthorne 2 Piano Concerto with Piers Lane. *Recordings include:* Bliss Viola Sonata with Emanuel Vardi; Beethoven Spring Sonata; Brahms Violin and Viola Sonatas; Cello Sonatas by Beethoven, Schnittke, Shostakovich and Kabalevsky; Songs by Rebecca Clarke with Patricia Wright; Chamber Works of Alan Rawsthorne; Songs by Sir Arthur Bliss. *Honours:* Sofia International Opera Competition, as accompanist; Martin Musical Scholarship Fund and The Countess of Munster Award, RCM. *Address:* 81 Lacy Road, London SW15 1NR, England.

STUTZMANN, Natalie; Singer (Contralto); b. 6 May 1965, Suresnes, France. *Education:* Nancy Conservatory; Studied singing with her mother, Christiane Stutzmann, with Hans Hotter and at the Paris Opéra School. *Career:* Sang in recitals and concerts at London Wigmore Hall, Paris Théâtre Champs-Elysées, New York Carnegie Hall; La Scala, Milan; Amsterdam Concertgebouw; Berlin Philharmonie, Vienna Musikverein, Tokyo Suntory Hall; Sang Mozart's Ombra Felice at the Salzburg Festival, 1994; Gluck's Orpheus at Lyon, 1998; Giulio Cesare by Handel at Bordeaux, 1999. *Recordings include:* Schumann complete lieder, Fauré, Debussy, Ravel, Chausson, mélodies, Handel and Mozart Arias, Bach Cantatas and Passions, and Brahms Alto Rhapsody; Handel Amadigi. *Address:* c/o Opéra et Concert, 1 Rue Volney, F–75002 Paris, France.

SUART, Richard (Martin); Singer (Baritone); b. 5 Sept. 1951, Blackpool, England; m. Susan Cook, 1981, 2 s., 1 d. *Education:* Sang in choir of St John's College; Studied at Royal Academy of Music. *Career:* Roles in contemporary opera include: The Black Minister in Le Grand Macabre, Der Gatte in Reigen at Amsterdam, Dad/Café Manager in Greek for English National Opera; Old Musician in Broken Strings (Param Vir) for Netherlands Opera; Chaplinoperas (Mason) throughout Europe with Ensemble Modern; Eight Songs for a Mad King in London, Paris, Helsinki, Milan and Strasbourg; Stan Stock in Playing Away (Mason) also French Ambassador in Of Thee I Sing (Gershwin) for Opera North; Other roles include: Frank in Die Fledermaus, Benoit and Alcindoro in La Bohème for English National Opera; and Don Inigo Gomez in L'Heure Espagnole for Grange Park Opera; Savoy Opera performances include the patter roles in Gilbert and Sullivan, particularly Ko-Ko (The Mikado), in London, Venice, New York; Presents one-man show, As A Matter of Patter. *Recordings include:* Most of the Savoy Operas, Candide, A Midsummer Night's Dream, The Geisha, The Rose of Persia, The Fairy Queen and Ligeti's Le Grand Macabre. *Honours:* ARAM, 1991. *Current Management:* Musichall, Vicarage Way, Ringmer, BN8 5 LA, England. *Address:* Yardley Bank, 29 Yardley Park Road, Tonbridge, Kent TN 9 1 NB, England.

SUBEN, Joel Eric, BMus, MFA, PhD; American conductor, composer and academic; b. 16 May 1946, New York, NY; m. 1st Judith Ann Gundersheimer 1979 (divorced 1985); m. 2nd Linda Rodgers 1993. *Education:* Eastman School of Music, Brandeis University, Hochschule Mozarteum, Salzburg, studied conducting with Jacques-Louis Monod. *Career:* Music Director and Permanent Conductor of Peninsula Symphony of VA, 1982–87; Guest Conductor includes: Silesian Philharmonic Orchestra, Poland, 1986 and 1994, New Jersey Composers Orchestra, 1987–, Polish Radio National Symphony Orchestra, 1993, Janáček Philharmonic Orchestra, 1994 and 1996, Slovak Radio Symphony Orchestra, Bratislava, 1995 and North Bohemian Philharmonic Orchestra, Czech Republic, 1996; Director of Orchestras, College of William and Mary, VA, 1983–92; Artistic Director, Brooklyn Heights Music Festival, 1986; Guest Lecturer, NY Philharmonic Pre-Concert Lecture Series, 1989–; Music Director, Composers Chorus, 1992–; Music Adviser, Wellesley Philharmonic, MA, 1993–. *Compositions include:* Gesualdo Triptych, for String Orchestra, 1984; Symphony in Old Style for Orchestra, 1987; Concerto Classico for Flute and Small Orchestra, 1991; Breve Sogno for Large Orchestra, 1993. *Publications:* Debussy and Octatonic Pitch Structure, University Microfilms, 1980. *Current Management:* Linda Rodgers Associates, 628 Bloomfield Street, Hoboken, NJ 07030, USA.

SUBLETT, Virginia; Singer (Soprano); b. 29 July 1952, Kansas City, Kansas, USA. *Education:* BMus, Louisiana State University, Baton Rouge, 1974; Master of Arts in Music, University of California at San Diego, 1994; Doctorate of Musical Arts, UCSD, 1997; Private vocal study with Carol Webber, Isabel Penagos, and Michael Jackson Parker. *Career:* Sang the Queen of Night in The Magic Flute (Mozart), New York City Opera and San Diego Opera; La Princess and La Rossignol in L'Enfant et les Sortilèges (Ravel), New York City Opera; Nannetta in Falstaff (Verdi), Tytania in A Midsummer Night's Dream (Britten), and Oberto in Alcina (Handel), Los Angeles Opera; Ismene in Mitridate (Mozart) and Servilia in La Clemenza di Tito (Mozart), L'Opéra de Nice; Numerous appearances as soprano soloist with Los Angeles Philharmonic Orchestra, San Diego Symphony Orchestra, Illinois Symphony Orchestra, New Jersey Symphony Orchestra, and Los Angeles Baroque Orchestra; Founder and Co-conductor of Cappella Gloriana vocal ensemble, 1996; Member of Adjunct Faculties at University of California at San Diego and University of San Diego, 1992; Director of Choral Scholars and University-Community Choir at UCSD, 1997–99; mem, American Guild of Musical Artists, National Association of Teachers of Singing; American Choral Directors' Association. *Current Management:* Classical Performing Artists Management. *Address:* c/o CPAM, 3760 29th Street, San Diego, CA 92104, USA.

SUBOTNICK, Morton; Composer, Clarinettist, Conductor and Teacher; b. 14 April 1933, Los Angeles, California, USA; m. Joan La Barbara, 18 Dec 1979, 1 s. *Education:* BA, Composition, University of Denver, 1958; MA, Mills College, 1960. *Career:* Various appearances as Clarinettist and Conductor; Teacher at Mills College, 1959–66 and New York University, 1966–69; Co-founder and Director of San Francisco Tape Music Center, 1961–65; Music Director for Ann Halprin Dance Company, 1961–67 and Lincoln Center Repertory Theater, 1967–68; Co-Director of Composition Program and the Center for Experiments in Art, Information and Technology at California Institute of Arts, Valencia, 1969–; Composer-in-Residence at Deutscher Akademischer Austauschdienst, West Berlin, 1979–80; Various visiting professorships. *Compositions include:* Orchestral: Lamination for Orchestra and Tape, 1968, Before The Butterfly, 1975, Place, 1978, Liquid Strata for Piano, Orchestra and Electronics, 1982, In Two Worlds, concerto for Saxophone, Electronic Wind Controller and Orchestra, 1987–88, All My Hummingbirds Have Alibis for Flute, Cello, Midi Piano, Midi Mallets and Computer, CD-ROM, 1991, first piece of music composed specifically for CD-ROM; Jacob's Room, chamber opera premiered at the American Music Theater Festival, Philadelphia in 1993; Various mixed-media scores; Tape Pieces; Chamber music; Vocal scores; Instrumental works with electronics; Incidental music; Making Music, computer, 1996; Intimate Immensity for 2 voices, instruments and electronics, 1997; Echoes from the Silent Call of Girona, for string quartet and computer, 1998. *Recordings:* Several. *Honours:* Fellow, Institute for Advanced Musical Studies, Princeton University, 1959, 1960; National Endowment for the Arts Grant, 1975; American Academy and Institute of Arts and Letters Award, 1979; Brandeis University Creative Arts Award, 1983; Many commissions. *Address:* 121 Coronado Lane, Santa Fe, NM 87501, USA.

SUBRTOVA, Milada; Opera Singer (Dramatic Soprano); b. 24 May 1924, Lhota, Kralovice, Czechoslovakia; m. Jan Hus Tichy. *Education:* Business School, Prague; Private studies with tenor Zdenek Knittl, Prague. *Career:* Debut: As Giulietta in Offenbach's Les Contes d'Hoffmann, Theatre 5 May, Prague; Opera and concerts, Czechoslovakia including National Theatre Prague and Czech Philharmonic, Prague, Italy, Poland, Romania, Bulgaria, England, Yugoslavia, Switzerland, Spain, Iceland, Germany, Netherlands, Austria; Recitals, songs and opera arias of romantic composers, Radio Prague; Roles included: 3 female roles (Hoffmann); Norma, Dona Anna (Don Giovanni), Constanze (Entführung), Fiordiligi (Così fan tutte), Pamina (Die Zauberflöte), Gilda (Rigoletto), Violetta (La Traviata), Elisabeth (Don Carlo), Abigaille (Nabucco), Mimi (La Bohème), Butterfly, Tosca, Turandot, Santuzza (Cavalleria), Charpentier's Louise, Marguerite (Faust), Micaela (Carmen), Woman (Poulenc's La Voix Humaine), Ännchen and Agathe (Der Freischütz), Elsa (Lohengrin), Sieglinde (Die Walküre), Tatyana (Eugene Onegin), Marenka (Bartered Bride), title roles in Libuše, Rusalka, Jenůfa, many others; Concerts include Beethoven's 9th; Bach, B minor mass; Martinů, Gilgamesh; Honneger, Jeanne d'Arc; Janáček, Glagolitic Mass; Schoenberg, Gurreleider; Mahler's 4th; Dvořák, Stabat Mater; Berlioz, Damnation of Faust. *Recordings:* Portrait recital; Complete operas: At Well, Blodek, conductor Frantisek Skvor, 1959; Rusalka, conductor Zdenek Chalabala, 1960; The Devil's Wall, conductor Zdenek Chalabala, 1961; Libuše, conductor Jaroslav Krombholc. *Honours:* 1st Prize, International Vocal Competition, Prague Spring Festival, 1954. *Address:* Belohorska 70, 16900 Prague 6, Czech Republic.

SUHONEN, Antti; Singer (Bass-Baritone); b. 5 Nov. 1956, Nurmes, Finland. *Education:* Studied at Sibelius Academy and at the National

Opera Studio, Helsinki and at the International Opera Studio, Zürich; Masterclasses with Charles Farncombe, Herbert Brauer and Victoria de los Angeles. *Career:* Made debut at Zürich, 1986, engaged at Karlsruhe, 1987–91, and at Helsinki from 1991–; Made guest appearances at Dresden, Wiesbaden, Hanover and Mannheim and also at Munich State Opera, Berlin State Oera, Essen and Royal Opera in Copenhagen; Karlsruhe, 1989, in shared premiere of Graf Mirabeau by Siegfried Matthus; Appearances at Helsinki and elsewhere as Mozart's Leporello, Masetto, Figaro and Alfonso, Sparafucile, Dulcamara, Basilio, Varlaam and Rangoni in Boris Godunov, Melitone in La Forza del Destino, Méphistopélès in Gounod's Faust; Sang Klaus in premiere of Linkola's Elina, Helsinki, 1992 and Fruitseller in Bergman's The Singing Tree in Helsinki, 1995; With Berlin State Opera, Wagner's Ring, Kupfer and Barenboim, 1996; Savonlinna Festival, 1992, as Don Fernando in Fidelio; Bluebeard in Bart ók's Bluebeard's Castle, 1994; Season 1999 with the Israel Philharmonic Orchestra under Zubin Mehta in Ariadne auf Naxos, Chicago Symphony orchestra under Pierre Boulez in Schoenberg's Moses und Aron and the Finnish National Opera in Wagner's Ring; Season 1999–2000 as Wagner's Gunther in Helsinki and the Forester in The Cunning Little Vixen, for the Deutsche Oper Berlin; Guest appearances at Deutsche Oper, Berlin, 2000–; Alongside his opera career he frequently appears as soloist in numerous concerts. *Recordings:* Rautavaara: Thomas, 1986, Sampo, 1995; Mozart: Die Zauberflöte, 1988; Pacius: Kung Karls Jagd, 1991; Sang Ossip in The Palace, by Sallinen, at the 1996 Savonlinna Festival. *Address:* c/o Finnish National Opera, Helsinginkatu 58, SF 00260 Helsinki 18, Finland.

SUITNER, Otmar; Conductor and Musical Director; b. 16 May 1922, Innsbruck, Austria; m. Marita Wilckens. *Education:* Innsbruck Conservatory; Salzburg Mozarteum, 1940–42, under Ledwinka; Studied Conducting with Clemens Krauss. *Career:* Debut: Landestheater, Innsbruck, 1942; Musical Director, Remscheid, Germany, 1952–57; Musical Director of the Pfalz Orchestra, Ludwigshafen, 1957; Guest appearances in Vienna, Munich, Hamburg and Berlin; Chief Conductor of the Dresden Staatsoper and Staatskapelle, 1960; Musical Director of the Staatsoper, East Berlin, 1964–71; Conducted the premieres of Dessau's Puntilla (1966), Einstein (1974) and Leonce und Lena (1979); Tours with the Berlin company to Paris, Warsaw, Cairo and Lausanne; Bayreuth Festival, 1964–69, Der fliegende Holländer, Tannhäuser and Der Ring des Nibelungen; Engagements at the San Francisco Opera from 1969; Honorary Conductor of the Tokyo NHK Symphony Orchestra, 1973; Professor, Hochschule für Musik, Vienna, 1977–. *Recordings include:* Figaro, Così fan tutte, Salome, Die Entführung, Il Barbiere di Siviglia; Palestrina with Peter Schreier, 1989; Lortzing's Die Opernprobe and Gluck's Der betrogene Cadi (CPO 1998). *Honours:* Commendatore, Gregorius Order, 1973; Austrian Ehrenkreuz für Wissenschaft und Kunst, 1982. *Address:* c/o Widerhofer Platz 4/48, 1090 Vienna, Austria.

SUK, Josef; Violinist; b. 8 Aug. 1929, Prague, Czechoslovakia; m. Marie Polakova. *Education:* Conservatory of Music in Prague; Prague Academy, 1951–53. *Career:* Debut: 1940; Western European engagements from 1948 in Paris and Brussels; Leader of Prague Quartet, 1951–52; Joined Suk Trio, 1952; Leader of orchestra at Prague National Theatre, 1953–55; Soloist with Czech Philharmonic Orchestra, US debut 23 Jan 1964 with the Cleveland Orchestra; British debut, 1964 at the Promenade Concerts playing Mozart and Dvořák; Formed duo with Zuzana Ružicková in 1963 and a trio with Janos Starker and Julius Katchen, 1967–69; Duos with Jan Panenka, piano; Founded Suk Chamber Orchestra, 1974; Teacher at the Vienna Hochschule für Musik, 1980–; Played at the Bath Festival, 1991; mem, Antonin Dvořák Foundation; Prague Spring Foundation; President, Castle Sirin Foundation. *Recordings:* Numerous on major record labels. *Honours:* Grand Prix du Disque Paris, 1960, 1966, 1968, 1974; State Prize, 1964; Artist of Merit, 1970; Edison Prize, 1972; Wiener Flotenuhr, 1974; National Prize, 1977; President, Antonin Dvořák Foundation; President, Prague Spring Foundation; Golden Disco Supraphon, 1986. *Address:* Karlovo Namesti 5, 120 00 Prague 2, Czech Republic.

SUKIS, Lilian; Singer (Soprano); b. 29 June 1939, Kaunas, Lithuania. *Education:* Toronto University. *Career:* Debut: Toronto 1964, as Lady Billows in Britten's Albert Herring; Metropolitan Opera from 1965, notably as Pamina in Die Zauberflöte; Bayerishe Staatsoper, Munich, and elsewhere in Germany from 1969, as Violetta, Mozart's Countess and Fiordiligi, Micaela in Carmen, Liu in Turandot, and Verdi's Luisa Miller; Sang Strauss's Daphne at Munich, and in the 1972 premiere of Sim Tjong by Isang Yun. *Recordings include:* Ascanio in Alba, by Mozart (Philips); Die Lustige Weiber von Windsor (Decca); Mozart's La finta giardiniera (DGG). *Address:* c/o Bayerische Staatsoper, Max-Josephs-Platz, D-8-539 Munich, Germany.

SULEIMANOV, Stanislav; Russian singer (bass); b. 1945, Baku. *Education:* Baku Conservatory. *Career:* sang at the Bolshoi Theatre Moscow from 1977; since 1989 also the creator of the first Contract

Musical Theatre 'Forum'; repertoire includes: Boris and Varlaam in Boris Godunov, Rimsky's Salieri, Scarpia in Tosca, Malatesta in Rachmaninov's Francesca da Rimini, Boris in Lady Macbeth, Pontius Pilate in Master and Margarita by S. Slonimsky; guest appearances throughout Russia, USA, Japan, Netherlands, Belgium, Luxembourg, Italy, Spain, Greece and Germany; concerts and Lieder recitals. *Address:* Halturinskaja str 4-1-58, 107392 Moscow, Russia.

SULLIVAN, Ghillian; Singer (Soprano); b. 1954, Adelaide, South Australia. *Education:* Studied with Audrey Langford, in London. *Career:* Debut: Opera 80 in 1980, as Mozart's Countess; Season 1981–82 as Britten's Tytania for GTO and Donizetti's Adina for Opera North; Fiordiligi at Sydney, 1983; Leeds, 1983–84, in the premiere of Rebecca by W Josephs, and the English premiere of Krenek's Jonny spielt auf; Wiesbaden and Aachen, 1985–86, as Constanze; Cologne, 1987 as Musetta; Victoria State Opera debut, 1986, as Donna Elvira; English National Opera from 1989, including tour of Russia; Principal Guest Artist at Opera Australia from 1985 to the present day; Many major roles including Traviata, Lucia, Gilda, Donna Anna and Rosalinde; Guest appearances at all State companies and with Sydney Symphony Orchestra; Sang Bizet's Leila and Rosalinde in Die Fledermaus at Sydney, 2000; Concert and oratorio engagements. *Recordings:* First solo CD, Vocal Gems. *Address:* c/o Jenifer Eddy Artists Management, Suite 11, The Clivedon, 596 St Kilda Road, VIC 3004, Australia.

SULZEN, Donald; Pianist and Accompanist; b. 17 Feb. 1955, Kansas City, Kansas, USA. *Education:* Honour Graduate, Ecole Normale de Musique de Paris, 1976; MMus, University North Texas, 1980. *Career:* Performed at major festivals throughout the world; Regular appearances with well-known singers such as Julie Kaufmann, Michiè Nakamaru, Anna Caterina Antonacci, Daphne Evangelatos, Doris Soffel, Marilyn Schmiege, Ofelia Sala, James Taylor, Laura Aikin and Thomas Cooley; Pianist of Munich Piano Trio, 2001–; Television and radio performances for Bayerischer Rundfunk Munich, WDR Cologne, Radio France Paris, RAI 1 Rome, Nippon TV Tokyo, RAI 3 Naples; Teaching at Richard Strauss Conservatory and Hochschule für Musik, Munich. *Recordings:* Gabriel Fauré Melodies with Marilyn Schmiege; Johannes Brahms Lieder und Duette with Julie Kaufmann and Marilyn Schmiege; George Enescu Cello Sonatas with Gerhard Zank; Franz Liszt Songs–Schmiege; Hans Pfitzner Lieder with Julie Kaufmann; Songs of John Duke with James Taylor and works of Alberto Ginastera including solo piano pieces, 2 CDs (Orfeo). *Honours:* Prix du Choc, from Le Monde de la Musique, for the Fauré recording with Marilyn Schmiege, 1994. *Address:* Baaderstr. 19, 80469 Munich, Germany.

SUMEGI, Daniel; Singer (bass); b. 1965, Australia. *Education:* studied in Australia, Venice, San Francisco, Vienna, New York. *Career:* appearances with San Francisco Opera from 1991 in La Traviata, Andrea Chénier, A Midsummer Night's Dream, Der Rosenkavalier, Capriccio, Il Trovatore, Fiery Angel, Die Meistersinger, Pique Dame, Tannhäuser, King Priam, Salome and Aida; La Bohème at the Golden Gate Theatre 1996; world premiere in Asdrubila, Barcelona Olympic Games, 1992; Season 1994–95 with Hermit in Freischutz at Trieste, Sarastro at Victoria State Opera; Season 1995–96 with Ramfis and Rossini's Basilio for Australia Opera, Gounod's Mefisto and Verdi's Banquo for Holland's Reiseopera, Britten's Theseus at Turin, Gremin for Victorian State Opera; Seneca in Monteverdi's Poppea for Glimmerglass Opera at Brooklyn Acad., Ratcliffe in Billy Budd at the Opéra Bastille and Alonso in Il Guarany for Washington Opera; Season 1996–97 Ramphis and the Commendatore for Victoria State Opera, Basilio for Opera Australia, Commendatore in Oviedo, and Sarastro in Die Zauberflöte for Bonn Opera; Season 1997–98 Colline and Saint Saens Old Hebrew for Opera Australia, Banquo at Houston, Peter Grimes and Boris Godunov at Metropolitan Opera, Sant Saens High Priest at Palm Beach, Billy Budd at Opera Bastille, Lady Macbeth of Mtsensk at Opera Nantes; Season 1998–99 with Faust at Opera Australia, Wagner's Hagen at State Opera of South Australia, The Crucible and Boris for Washington, Pizzaro at Utah, Mefisto in Minneapolis and Fafner in Sydney; Season 1999–2000 with I Lombardi in Santiago de Chile, Ramphis and the Commendatore in Houston, I Puritani's Georgio, Tosca's Scarpia and Otello's Lodovico in Washington and Baron Ochs for WNO; Season 2000–01 as Fiesco for Opera Australia and Mahler's 8th for Olympic Games, Scarpa in Adelaide, Mozart's Speaker in San Diego, Verdi's Grand Inquisitor in DC and Richard Tucker Gala at Covent Garden; Season 2001–02 as Wagner's Klingsor in Adelaide, Hoffmann Villains and Kurwenal for Opera Australia, Opera de Montreal Gala Concert, Don Carlo at the Met, Wagner's Pogner in Antwerp and Daland in San Diego; Washington Opera Japan Tour of Tosca, Otello and Sly; Season 2002–03 as Scarpia at WNP, Medea's Creonte in Montpellier, Puccini's Timur in Dallas, Daland in Minneapolis, Escamillo for Opera Australia, Elijah for Sydney Phiharmonia and Stiffelio's Jorg for Minneapolis, Daland at Austin Lyric and Escamillo at WNO; Season 2003–04: Messiah in Minnesota, Dutchman in Sydney and Austin. *Honours:*

Winner: 1987 Melbourne Sun Aria, 1987; Sydney McDonald's Aria, 1994; Met Opera National Council Auditions, 1994; Sullivan Foundation Grant, 1994; Finalist of 1992 Pavarotti and 1995 Placido Domingo Operalia Competition. *Current Management:* Vincent & Farrell Associates, 165 East 83 No. 5E, New York, NY 10028, USA; Ingpen & Williams Ltd, 7 St George's Court, 131 Putney Bridge Road, London, SW15 2PA, England.

SUMMERLY, Jeremy, BA, MMus; Conductor and Musicologist; b. 28 Feb. 1961, Stoke-on-Trent, England. *Education:* Lichfield Cathedral School, Winchester Coll., Univ. of Oxford, London Univ. *Career:* Studio Man., BBC Radio 1982–89; Lecturer in Academic Studies, Royal Acad. of Music 1989–95; Head of Academic Studies, Royal Acad. of Music 1996–; Conductor, Oxford Camerata 1983; Conductor, Schola Cantorum of Oxford 1990–96; freelance writer and presenter for BBC Radio, including Record Review and CD Review (BBC Radio 3) 1990–, The English Cadence (BBC Radio 3) 1995, Choir Works (BBC Radio 3) 1996–98, Front Row (BBC Radio 4) 2002–; organist, Christ Church, Chelsea 1999–2002; debut as conductor at BBC Promenade Concerts, July 1999; mem. Royal Musical Asscn, American Musicological Soc.. *Recordings:* Schütz: Christmas Story 1995, J. S. Bach: Magnificat 1995, Fauré Requiem 1994, Handel: Coronation Anthems 2002. *Publications:* Gaudete: Medieval Songs and Carols 1999, Passetime with Good Company: Medieval Songs 2002, Fair Oriana: Elizabethan Madrigals 2002; contrib. to Early Music, The Musical Times, Choir and Organ, Leading Notes, Classic CD. *Honours:* European Cultural Prize (Basel) 1995, Hon. ARAM 1997, Hon. FASC 2002. *Current Management:* Sigma Management, Suite 729, 78 Marylebone High Street, London, W1V 5AP, England. *Telephone:* (20) 7381-4692 (office). *Fax:* (20) 7460-0742 (office). *E-mail:* sigma@camerata.demon.co.uk (office). *Website:* www.camerata.demon.co.uk (office).

SUMMERS, Hilary; Contralto; b. 1965, Newport, Gwent, Wales. *Education:* Reading University, Royal Academy of Music and the National Opera Studio. *Career:* Concert appearances at Festival Hall, Barbican Centre, Purcell Room and St John's Smith Square; Sang in The Dream of Gerontius with Liverpool Philharmonic and Henze's Novae de Infinito Laudes with London Sinfonietta; Other modern repertory includes Schoenberg's Pierrot Lunaire and works by Berio, Stravinsky, Webern, Berg, Rihm and Jonathan Harvey; Opera debut as a Valkyrie in Die Walküre for Scottish Opera in 1992; Has also sung in Die Königskinder for English National Opera and appeared as Britten's Lucretia, Ursule in Béatrice et Bénédict, Cornelia in Giulo Cesare, Mercédès in Carmen, Gaea in Daphne, Martha in Mefistofele and Anna in Les Troyens; Sang Medoro in Handel's Orlando at the Brooklyn Academy of Music, 1996; Season 1998 as Trasimede in Handel's Admeto at Beaune and Montpellier and in Australia; Sang Stellea in the premiere of Carter's What Next?, Berlin Staatsoper 1999; Schwetzingen and Innsbruck 2000, in Legrenzi's La divisione del mondo; Created the role of Irma in Peter Eotvos' opera Le Balcon at the Aix Festival, 2002. *Recordings include:* Messiah with the King's College Choir. *Honours:* The Worshipful Company of Musicians Silver Medal; Shinn Fellowship, Royal Academy of Music; Recital Diploma, Royal Academy of Music. *Current Management:* Ingpen & Williams Ltd, 7 St George's Court, 131 Putney Bridge Road, London, SW15 2PA, England.

SUMMERS, Jonathan; Singer (Baritone); b. 2 Oct. 1946, Melbourne, Australia. *Education:* Studied with Bettine McCaughan in Melbourne and with Otakar Kraus in London. *Career:* Debut: Kent Opera in 1975 as Rigoletto; Royal Opera House Covent Garden company member, 1976–86; roles include: High Priest in Samson et Dalila, Figaro, Papageno, Balstrode, Marcello, Demetrius, Silvio, Sharpless, Paolo, Ford, Nabucco and Iago; Other British appearances include: English National Opera as Rodrigo, Renato, Macbeth, Boccanegra, Onegin, Kurwenal; Scottish Opera as Count Almaviva and Don Giovanni; Opera North as the High Priest, Onegin and Amonasro in Aida; Glyndebourne as Ford in Falstaff. Welsh National Opera, Germont Pére and Kurwenal; European engagements at Hamburg, Munich, Florence, Las Scala, Avignon, Paris Opéra and Geneva; American and Australian engagements include: Metropolitan Opera in 1988, debut Australian Opera in 1981, Sydney Opera in Le nozze di Figaro; Season 1994 at Australian Opera, Sydney as Germont and appearances in Chicago, London, Toulouse and Lausanne; Season 1995 included Michele, Il Tabarro in Trittico with the Australian Oper, Sydney, Don Carlo and Kurwenal for ENO and Nabucco with WNO; Season 1996 included Nabucco in Melbourne, Germont, La Traviata, for Scottish Opera and Figaro in The Marriage of Figaro with ENO; Season 1997 as Amonasro with Opera North; Iago with Royal Opera House and Scarpia in Tosca at Spear Festival, South Africa; Season 1998 included Traviata with the New Israeli Opera and WNO, Balstrode in Peter Grimes with the Royal Opera at Savonlinna and Amfortas in Parsifal with ENO; Season 1999 included Kurwenal in Tristan and Isolde with WNO, the title role in Wozzeck with Opera Australia and Balstrode in Peter Grimes with ENO; Season 2000–01 with Opera North, as Barnaba in La Gioconda,

and Simon Boccanegra; Season 2001 included Amfortas in Parsifal with State Opera of South Australia; Pere Germont in La Traviata with Israeli Opera; Season 2002 included Prus in Vec Makropulos with Houston Grand Opera, Scarpia in Tosca with Buhnen der Stadt, Cologne, Alfio and Tonio in Cavalleria Rusticana and Pagliacci with Opera Australia, Scarpia in Tosca with Opera Australia. *Recordings include:* Peter Grimes; Samson et Dalila; The Bohemian Girl; Sea Symphony; Carmina Burana; Videos of Samson et Dalila, Il Trovatore and Nabucco. *Address:* c/o Patricia Greenan, 19b Belsize Park, London NW3 4DU, England. *E-mail:* patricia@greenanartists.fsnet.co.uk.

SUMMERS, Patrick; Conductor; b. 1960, San Francisco, USA. *Education:* Indiana University School of Music. *Career:* Conducted Season Preview Concerts with the San Francisco Opera, from 1989; Opera Center Showcase productions include Handel's Ariodante, Reimann's Ghost Sonata and Shield's Rosina; Projects for the Merola Opera Program include Bohème, Butterfly, Pasquale and Falstaff; Lucia di Lammermoor for the Western Opera Theater; As Music Director of the San Francisco Opera Center has led Carmen and Bohème on tour to Japan (1991, 1993) and La Fille du Régiment for the Opera Guild (1994); Performances with the San Francisco Opera include Tosca, the US premiere of Rossini's Ermione and the local premiere of his Otello; La Traviata and Così fan tutte; Associated with the Shanghai Conservatory of Music in productions of Rigoletto and Don Pasquale; Asian premiere of Tosca at the Shanghai Opera House; Italian debut in season 1993–94, with Manon Lescaut for Rome Opera, and Canadian debut with Lucia di Lammermoor at Calgary; Australian debut with Cenerentola at Sydney and Melbourne, 1994; L'Incoronazione di Poppea for Dallas Opera (1995) and Tosca at Lisbon. *Honours:* Named Outstanding San Franciscan by the San Francisco Chamber of Commerce, 1991. *Current Management:* Askonas Holt Ltd, Lonsdale Chambers, 27 Chancery Lane, London, WC2A 1PF, England. *Telephone:* (20) 7400-1700. *Fax:* (20) 7400-1799. *E-mail:* info@askonasholt.co.uk. *Website:* www.askonasholt.co.uk.

SUNDIN, Nils-Göran; Music Director, Composer and Author; b. 18 May 1951, Växjö, Sweden. *Education:* Diploma, Choirmaster and Organist, Lund, 1968; Master's Degree, Musical Theory, Pedagogy of Musical Theory, Stockholm State School of Music; PhilCand, Musicology, History of Literature and Fine Arts, Stockholm University; PhD, Philosophy of Music, USA, 1988; MedCand, Lund University. *Career:* Lecturer in Music Theory and Interpretation at Stockholm State College of Music and Edsberg College of Music, Sollentuna, 1975–85; Lecturer in Music History at Stockholm University, 1976; Music Critic, Svenska Dagbladet, 1977–81; Executive Music Chief, Kronoberg Music Foundation, Växjö, 1987–; mem, STIM; Sveriges Författaförbund; New York Academy of Sciences; International Musicological Society. *Compositions:* Numerous for piano, chamber music, voice, choir and orchestra including: Symphony For Peace for Orchestra and Choir with poems by Dag Hammarskjöld, commissioned for The Great Peace Journey, Invitazione, Emmanuel Swedenborg In Memoriam, 1988, Concerto St George for Piano and Orchestra, 1990; Violin Concerto, 1994. *Publications:* Books include: Musical Interpretation in Performance, 1983, Bilder Ur Musikens Historia, 1984, Musical Interpretation Research, 1984, MIR vols I–II, 1984, Aesthetic Criteria of Musical Interpretation in Contemporary Performance, 1994. *Contributions:* About 300 articles and reviews in numerous publications including Nutida Musik, Bonniers Musiklexikon, Sohlmans Musiklexikon. *Address:* c/o STIM, Sandhamnsgatan 79, PO Box 27327, S–10254 Stockholm, Sweden.

SUNDINE, Stephanie; Singer (Soprano); b. 1954, Illinois, USA. *Education:* Studied in Illinois and New York. *Career:* Sang with the New York City Opera, 1981–84 as Ariadne, Santuzza and Margherita in Boito's Mefistofele; Sang the title roles in the US premieres of Prokofiev's Maddalena at St Louis in 1982 and Judith by Siegfried Matthus at Santa Fe in 1990; Best known as Strauss's Salome at Covent Garden (debut) in 1988, Metropolitan Opera (debut) in 1990 and Welsh National Opera in 1991; Sang Isolde at Nantes in 1989 and Fusako in the premiere production of Henze's Das Verratene Meer at the Deutsche Oper Berlin in 1990; Other roles include Janáček's Emilia Marty, Tosca, La Gioconda and Elsa; Sang the Foreign Princess in Rusalka at San Francisco, 1995. *Address:* c/o San Francisco Opera, War Memorial House, Van Ness Avenue, San Francisco, CA, USA.

SUNDMAN, Ulf (Johan); Organist and Musical Director; b. 27 Feb. 1929, Stockholm, Sweden; m. Anna-Greta Persson, 10 July 1954, 1 d. *Education:* Hogre Organistexamen, 1949; Hogre Kantorsexamen, Musiklararexamen, 1951; Diplom Organ Playing, 1974; Royal Academy of Music, Stockholm; International Academy for Organ, Haarlem, Netherlands, 1967. *Career:* Organist, Skelleftea St Olovs Church, 1954–81; Organist, Gavle Heliga Trefaldighets Church, 1981–94; Organ concerts in Sweden, Finland, Norway, Germany, Austria, Netherlands, Switzerland, France, Italy, Spain, Czechoslovakia, Poland, USSR, 1974, 1976, 1979, Denmark and Belgium; Organ Music Festivals, Gottingen,

West Germany, 1972, 1987, Vilnius, USSR, 1974, Madrid, 1982, Naples, Toulon, 1983, Ratzeburg, 1985, Verona and Asola, 1986, Buren 1987, Gottingen 1987, Zug 1988, Biella 1988; Concerts on Radio Sweden and Radio Netherlands. *Recordings:* Soviet (Melodia) Sweden (Proprius), (Opus 3). *Honours:* PA Berg Medal, Royal Academy of Music, Stockholm; Culture Prize of the Town of Skelleftea 1972, Province of Vasterbotten 1973, Gavle 1994. *Address:* N Köpmangatan 22A, 803 21 Gavle, Sweden.

SUNNEGARDH, Thomas; Singer (Tenor); b. 11 July 1949, Stockholm, Sweden. *Education:* Studied at The Royal School of Music in Stockholm. *Career:* Sang at Vadstena Academy, 1978–79; Appeared in Die Fledermaus and Der Vogelhändler with National Touring Company; Royal Opera Stockholm from 1982 as Albert Herring, Walther von der Vogelweide, Taverner, Ferrando, Fra Diavolo, Tamino and Steuermann in Der fliegende Holländer; Has sung Lohengrin in Stockholm, Moscow with Bolshoi, Wiesbaden and Stuttgart conducted by Silvio Varviso, 1990; Macduff at the Bergen Festival, 1988; Other roles include Florestan, Erik and Parsifal in Denmark and Antwerp, and parts in Iphigénie en Aulide and Genoveva at Deutsche Oper am Rhein, and Die Meistersinger at Nice, 1992; Season 1991–92 sang Lohengrin at Barcelona, Parsifal at Århus, Die Meistersinger at Nice Opera, Der fliegende Holländer at Royal Opera Covent Garden, Das Lied von der Erde with London Philharmonic Orchestra; Season 1992–93 with Meistersinger at Brussels, Deutsche Oper Berlin, Munich, Tokyo, Stuttgart, Dutchman/Erik in Munich, Parsifal in Essen and Deutsche Oper Düsseldorf, Lohengrin in Frankfurt, Berlin, Tokyo and Toulouse; Season 1993–94 in Lohengrin in Frankfurt, Der fliegende Holländer in Munich, and Walter in Stuttgart; Season 1994–95 with Walter von Stolzing in Stuttgart, Fidelio and Lohengrin in Düsseldorf and Toulouse; Sang Paul in Korngold's Die tote Stadt at Stockholm, 1996; Engaged for Lohengrin in Seville and concert performances of Wozzeck with the Swedish Radio Symphony Orchestra and Rheingold at the Canary Islands Festival; Season 2001–02 with Capriccio in Stockholm, Tannhäuser in Gothenburg; Berg's Alwa and Rhiengold/Loge in San Francisco, a Wagner Gala Concert in San Diego, concert performances of Fidelio in Lübeck, performances of Beethoven IX at the Gewandhaus in Leipzig, concerts for RAI Torino (Bach's Magnificat and Chapentier's Te deum) and a new production of Gefors' Clara at the Royal Opera Stockholm; Season 2002–03 with The Bells by Rachmaninov at Malmö and Tristan in Gothenburg, and further performances of Tannhäuser at the Royal Opera Stockholm. *Recordings:* Role of Froh with Cleveland Orchestra under Christoph von Dohnányi, 1993. *Address:* Artistsekretariat ulf Törnquist, Sankt Eriksgatan 100, 2 tr., S-113 31 Stockholm Sweden.

SUNSHINE, Adrian; Conductor and Teacher; b. 1940 New York City, USA; m. Sheila Genden, 1 s., 1 d. *Education:* San Francisco State University; University of California, Berkeley; Private instrumental studies with Gabriel Sunshine (father), Janet Hale, Georg Gruenberg, Herman Reinberg; Conducting teachers: Pierre Monteux, Leonard Bernstein, Paul Klecki. *Career:* Performances: Philharmonia (London); BBC Orchestras; BBC Opera; São Carlos Opera (Lisbon); Bournemouth, Berlin, Leningrad, Cleveland, Geneva, Paris, Vienna, Philharmonia Hungarica, Athens, Budapest, Bucharest, Cluj, Lausanne, Lugano, Amsterdam, Denmark, Sweden, Poland, Miami, San Francisco, Buenos Aires, Rio de Janeiro, São Paulo, Caracas, Mexico City, Israel, Ankara, Madrid, Barcelona, Bilbao, Luxembourg, Bangkok, Kuala Lumpur, Tai Pei; Festivals include: Blossom, Athens, São Paulo, Montreux-Vevey, Ascona, London, Cheltenham, Gulbenkian, Reims, Lille, Seville, Romania, Chamonix, San Sebastian, Sion, Cadiz; Previously Founder-Conductor, San Francisco Chamber Orchestra; music director, Gulbenkian Orchestra, Lisbon; Principal Guest Conductor, Romania; Director Crete International Festival; Music director, London Chamber Players; Co-conductor, Camerata Budapest; Permanent Guest conductor, Bucharest Philharmonic Orchestra; Previously Visiting Professor, Bowling Green State University, Ohio; Guest Lecturer, University of London Institute of Education; Director, Orchestra-in-Residence Music Programme, Middlesex University, London; Visiting Lecturer, Smith College, Massachusetts; Visiting Professor, Romanian Academy of Music; mem, Conductors' Guild. *Recordings:* Works by Schoenberg, Shostakovich, Perera, Wheelock and Ives. *Publications:* Various articles on music. *Current Management:* Armonia, Santander, Spain; Bureau de Concerts Camile Kiesgen, 252 Faubourg St Honore, 75008 Paris, France. *Address:* PO Box 84, London NW11 8 AL, England.

SURJAN, Giorgio; Singer (bass); b. 21 Oct. 1954, Rijeca, Yugoslavia. *Education:* Studied in Ljubljana and at the Opera School of La Scala. *Career:* Sang in Yugoslavia from 1977; La Scala, 1980, in a concert version of Mussorgsky's Salammbô; Pesaro Festival, 1984 and 1987, in Il Viaggio a Reims and Ermione; Aix Festival, 1988, as Publio in La Clemenza di Tito and Astarotte in Rossini's Armida; Season 1991–92 as Rossini's Alidoro at Covent Garden, Gluck's Thoas at La Scala and Frère Laurent in Gounod's Roméo et Juliette at Martina Franca; Season

1995–96 as Polidoro in Rossini's Zelmira at Pesaro, Fiesco in Simon Boccanegra at Turin, and the Villains in Hoffmann at Genoa; Season 1998 as Balthasar in La Favorita at Rome, Governor in Le Comte Ory at Florence, Banquo at Genoa and Escamillo at Macerata; Season 2000–01 as Monteverdi's Seneca in Florence, Rossini's Mosè in Verona, Rodolfo in La Sonnambula at Palermo, Alfonso (Luzrezia Borgia) in Bologna and Walter in Luisa Miller for Opéra Lausanne. *Recordings include:* La Forza del Destino; Anna Bolena; Salammbô. *Address:* c/o Teatro Comunale di Firenze, Via Solferino 15, 50123 Florence, Italy.

SUSA, Conrad; Composer; b. 26 April 1935, Springfield, Pennsylvania, USA. *Education:* BFA, Carnegie Institute of Technology at Pittsburgh, 1957; Juilliard School, New York, with William Bergsma and Vincent Persichetti. *Career:* Composer in Residence at the Old Globe Theatre, San Diego, 1959–60; Music Director of APA-Phoenix Repertory Company in New York, 1961–68, and the American Shakespeare Festival in Stratford, CT, 1969–71; Dramaturg of the Eugene O'Neill Center in Connecticut, 1986–. *Compositions include:* Operas: Transformations, Minneapolis, 1973, Black River: A Wisconsin Idyll, St Paul, 1975, The Love Of Don Perlimplin, Purchase, NY, 1984; The Dangerous Liaisons, 1994, rev. 1997; The Wise Women, church opera, 1994; A Sonnet Voyage, symphony, 1963; Choral: Dawn Greeting, 1976, The Chanticleer's Carol, 1982, Earth Song, 1988; A Midnight Clear, 1992; Piano pieces. *Address:* c/o ASCAP, ASCAP Building, One Lincoln Center, New York, NY 10023, USA.

SUSHANSKAYA, Rimma; Concert Violinist; b. 1950, Leningrad, Russia. *Education:* Studied at Leningrad and Moscow Conservatoires with David Oistrakh; PhD. *Career:* Emigrated to America in 1977 and has given many concerts there, in South America, throughout Russia and in Europe; Orchestras include Czech, Moscow, and St Petersburg Philharmonic Orchestras and Prague Radio Symphony Orchestra; Orchestral and recital tours of Russia, Finland and Czechoslovakia; London recital debut in 1987 at the Wigmore Hall, followed by Tchaikovsky's Concerto with the Royal Liverpool Philharmonic Orchestra and the City of Birmingham Symphony Orchestra; Based in the United Kingdom, residing in London, Stratford and New York. *Honours:* First Prize, Prague International Competition; Ysaye Medal. *Address:* Manhattan, 5 Lock Close, Kingfisher Court, Stratford-upon-Avon, Warwickshire, CV 37 6TY, England.

SUSS, Reiner; Singer (Bass); b. 2 Feb. 1930, Chemnitz, Germany. *Education:* Member of the Thomas Choir, Leipzig, 1939–48; Hochschule für Musik Leipzig, 1948–53. *Career:* Sang with Radio Leipzig, 1953–56 and the opera company at Bernburgan Der Saale, 1956–57 with debut in Tiefland by d'Albert; Sang at Theater der Stadt Halle, 1957–59 notably as Ochs in Der Rosenkavalier and member of the Staatsoper Berlin from 1959 as Leporello, Beckmesser, Nicolai's Falstaff, Kecal in The Bartered Bride, Varlaam and Baculus in Der Wildschütz; Dr Bartolo in Barbiere, Kovalyov in The Nose by Shostakovich, Don Pasquale, and Osmin in Entführung; Guest engagements at the Vienna Staatsoper and in Budapest, Helsinki, Lyon, Lausanne, Florence, Moscow, Prague, Warsaw and Tokyo. *Recordings include:* Tannhäuser conducted by Franz Konwitschny; Tosca; Der Wildschütz; La Serva Padrona; Mozart's Zaide; Die Kluge and Der Mond by Orff; Don Pasquale. *Address:* c/o Deutsche Staatsoper, Unter den Linden 7, 1086 Berlin, Germany.

SUSTIKOVA, Vera; Musicologist; b. 9 Jan. 1956, Uh Hradiste, Czechoslovakia; m. Sustik Jaroslav, 15 July 1982, 1 d. *Education:* Philosophical Faculty, Charles University in Prague, PhD, 1982; Conservatory in Brno (Guitar); Guitar-Masterclasses with Professor Cotsiolis (Greece); Musicology at the PF of Charles University in Prague. *Career:* Debut: Muzeum of Czech Music in Prague; 100 let spolecen pusobeni smetanova dila, Prague, 1984; Bedrich Smetana, 1824–1884, Prague, 1994; Opera and song without Singing Musical Melodram, Stanford, California, 1996; Fibich-Melodrama-Art nouveau, Prague 2000; Author of major exhibitions: History of Czech Musical Culture, 1986; Smetana-Dvořák, Litomyšl, 1988; B Smetana's Memorial in Benatky n j, 1991; Bedrich Smetana, Legend of My Country, Montreal, Ottawa, Toronto, 1994; Zdeněk Fibich 1850–1900, Prague 2000/2001; Dramaturgist and director of Concert tour with melodramas of Zdeněk Fibich, Los Angeles, San Francisco, Stanford, Portland, Vancouver, Montreal, Toronto, New York, 1996; Founder and dramaturgist of International Workshops of Melodrama, from 1997; International Festival of Cncert Melodrama, Prague from 1998; International Zdeněk Fibich Competition in the interpretation of melodrama, in Prague, from 1999. *Publications include:* Bedrich Smetana–Legend of My Country, 1994; Zdenek Fibich–Master of Scenic Melodrama, 1996; Zdeněk Fibich 1850–1900, 2000; Zdeněk Fibich Concert Melodramas Christmas Eve and Water Sprite (Noten Edition), 2003. *Address:* Pstrossova 35, Prague 1, 11008, Czech Republic.

SUTER, Jeremy Langton, MA, FRCO, ARCM; Organist; b. 3 March 1951, London, England; m. Susan; two d. *Education:* Royal Coll. of Music, Magdalen Coll., Oxford. *Career:* Organist and Choirmaster, All Saints,

Northampton 1975–81; Asst Organist, Chichester Cathedral 1981–91; Master of Music, Carlisle Cathedral 1991–; mem. Royal Coll. of Organists, Incorporated Soc. of Musicians. *Address:* 6 The Abbey, Carlisle, CA3 8TZ, England (home). *Telephone:* (1228) 526646 (home). *Fax:* (1228) 547049 (office). *E-mail:* jeremy.suter@virgin.net (home).

SUTER, Louis-Marc, PhD; Musicologist and Emeritus Professor; b. 2 Feb. 1928, Fribourg, Switzerland; m. Monique Suter 1955; four s. *Education:* chemistry and pedagogic studies, Univ. of Fribourg; musical and musicological studies, Conservatory of Geneva and Berne Univ. *Career:* debut, 1955; International Academic Orchestra, Salzburg; Lausanne Chamber Orchestra; Suisse Romande Orchestra; Prof. of Musicology, Univ. of Berne; mem. International Society for Musicology, Société Suisse de Musicologie, Association Suisse des Musiciens. *Publications:* Four concert works of Serbian composers 1989, Norbert Moret, compositeur 1993, Le langage musical de l'Europe occidentale 1998. *Contributions:* Claude Debussy: 'Pour les accords', Etude No. 12 pour piano, in Revue Musicale de Suisse Romande, 1983; Ronsard: 'Les Amours' de 1552 mises en musique, in Actes du Colloque de Neuchâtel, 1985, Droz 1987; Pelléas et Mélisande in Performance, in Debussy in Performance, 1999; Les graduels en la, 1999. *Address:* Route du Pré-de-L'Ile 1, 1752 Villars-sur-Glâne, Switzerland.

SUTHERLAND, Dame Joan, DBE; Singer (soprano); b. 7 Nov. 1926, Sydney, New South Wales, Australia; m. Richard Bonynge, 1954. *Career:* Came to London, 1951, to study at the Royal College of Music; Richard Bonynge became her accompanist and musical adviser; Engaged as Member of Covent Garden Opera Company, with first role as First Lady in The Magic Flute, 1952; In early years sang Amelia in A Masked Ball, Aida, Eva in The Mastersingers, Gilda in Rigoletto, Desdemona in Othello, Agathe in Der Freischütz, Olympia, Giulietta, Antonia, and Stella in Tales of Hoffmann; Sang Jenifer in the premiere of Tippett's The Midsummer Marriage, 1955; Became an international star with Covent Garden performance of Lucia di Lammermoor, 1959; Sang at Covent Garden in operas including I Puritani, Dialogues of the Carmelites, Lucia di Lammermoor, Norma; Sang in world's major opera houses including Paris, Vienna, La Scala, Hamburg, Buenos Aires, Metropolitan New York, Chicago Lyric, San Francisco, Australian Opera in Sydney, Glyndebourne, and in Edinburgh, Leeds and Florence Festivals; Specialised in bel canto operas, particularly of Rossini, Donizetti and Bellini, and operas of Handel, as well as in 19th century French repertoire; Sang Haydn's Euridice at the 1967 Edinburgh Festival; With husband was responsible for bringing back into standard repertoire previously more obscure works such as Esclarmonde, Le roi de Lahore, Semiramide, Les Huguenots, of French and Italian composers; Retired, 1990; Last operatic role Marguerite de Valois in Les Huguenots for Australian Opera, 1990; Sang as guest in Die Fledermaus at Covent Garden. *Recordings:* Lucia di Lammermoor, Alcina, La Sonnambula, Faust, Semiramide, I Puritani, Les Huguenots, Turandot, La Traviata, Les Contes d'Hoffmann, Don Giovanni, Don Pasquale, Adriana Lecouvreur, Le Roi de Lahore, Rodelinda, Athalia, Norma, Anna Bolena, La Fille du Régiment; The Midsummer Marriage, 1955; Haydn's Orfeo, 1967. *Publications include:* Autobiography, 1997. *Honours:* Commander, Order of Australia, 1975; Commander, Ordre National du Mérit, France; recipient of Kennedy Center Honors 2004, depicted on two Australian postage stamps 2004. *Current Management:* Ingpen & Williams Ltd, 7 St George's Court, 131 Putney Bridge Road, London, SW15 2PA, England.

SUTHERLAND, Rosalind; Singer (Soprano); b. 8 May 1963, Lennox-town, Glasgow, Scotland. *Education:* Qualified as a nurse; Studied at London College of Music and with Joseph Ward at Royal Northern College of Music. *Career:* Appearances with Royal Northern College of Music in Suor Angelica, L'Elisir d'amore and Madama Butterfly; Sang Pamina with Liverpool Mozart Orchestra, Bournemouth Sinfonietta and Scottish National Orchestra; Recent engagements with Welsh National Opera as Madama Butterfly, Tatyana and Liu, and Mimi for New Israeli Opera; English National Opera debut season, 1993–94 as Mimi (repeated with Welsh National Opera, 1996); Sang Butterfly at Golden Gate Theatre, San Francisco, 1997; Season 1998–99 sang title role in new production of Jenůfa, Mimi in La Bohème and Nedda in Pagliacci for Welsh National Opera; Governess in The Turn of the Screw at Minnesota Opera; Engaged to sing in La Bohème at San Francisco Season 1999–2000 as Carmen at WNO and Madama Butterfly for Opera North. *Honours:* Peter Moores Scholarship and winner of the Anne Ziegler Prize for a Singer Showing Outstanding Promise. *Address:* c/o IMG Artists, Lovell House, 616 Chiswick High Road, London W4 5RX, England.

SUTTER, Ursula; Singer (Mezzo-Soprano); b. 26 March 1938, Berne, Switzerland. *Education:* Studied in Berne and Stuttgart. *Career:* Sang at Biel-Solothurn, 1961–63, Trier, 1963–64, Essen, 1964–66 and engaged at Stuttgart Staatsoper, 1966–85, notably in the premiere of Orff's Prometheus in 1968; Guest appearances at State Operas of Vienna, Munich and Hamburg, Cologne, Nuremberg and Düsseldorf;

Further engagements at Bucharest, Lisbon, Monte Carlo, Essen and Schwetzingen Festival (premiere of Henze's The English Cat in 1983); Roles have included Dorabella, Cherubino, Rosina, Isabella, Maddalena, Preziosilla, Magdalene in Meistersinger, the Composer in Ariadne and Britten's Lucretia. *Address:* c/o Stuttgart Staatsoper, Oberer Schlossgarten 6, 7000 Stuttgart, Germany.

SUWANAI, Akiko; Concert Violinist; b. 1959, Tokyo, Japan. *Education:* Studied at the Toho Gakuen School of Music College, with Dorothy DeLay at Juilliard and Cho-Liang and Cho-Liang at Columbia University, New York. *Career:* Many concert engagements since becoming the youngest ever winner of the Tchaikovsky Competition, Moscow; Conductor have included Bychkov, Rostropovich, Rozhdestvensky, Ozawa, Marriner, Conlon, Previn, Svetlanaov and Temirkanov; Boston Symphony debut 1996, and performances with the Orchestre de Paris, Cincinnati, Pittsburgh and Seattle Symphonies and Academy of St Martin in the Fields; Ravinia and Evian Festivals, recital at the Amsterdam Concertgebouw and concert with the Toho Gakuen Orchestra at Carnegie Hall; Further engagements with the State Symphony of Russia, Russian National Orchestra and Budapest Symphony; Tours of Japan and South America. *Recordings include:* Concertos No. 1 by Bruch and Scottish Fantasia, with Neville Marriner (Phillips Classics, 1997); The Winners Gala at the Tchaikovsky Competition at Moscow; Prizewinner at the 35th International Paganini Violin Competition, the fourth International Japan Competition and the Queen Elizabeth International Competition, Belgium. *Current Management:* Ingpen & Williams Ltd, 7 St George's Court, 131 Putney Bridge Road, London, SW15 2PA, England.

SUZUKI, Hidetaro; Violinist and Conductor; b. 1 June 1937, Tokyo, Japan; m. Zeyda Ruga, 16 May 1962, 2 s., 1 d. *Education:* Toho School of Music, Tokyo, 1953–56; Curtis Institute of Music, Philadelphia, Pennsylvania, USA, 1956–63; Studied with Efrem Zimbalist. *Career:* Debut: Tokyo, 1951; Concertmaster, Quebec Symphony, Canada, 1963–78; Professor, Conservatory of Province of Quebec, 1963–79; Professor, Laval University, 1970–79; Concertmaster, Indianapolis Symphony, Indiana, USA, 1978–; Concert appearances as soloist, recitalist, conductor, the United Kingdom, Western Europe, Soviet Union, Central America, USA, Canada, Japan, South East Asia; Director of Chamber Music Series Suzuki and Friends, 1980. *Recordings:* Beethoven Sonatas; Hidetaro Suzuki Encore Album; Franck, Ravel Sonatas; Beethoven Piano Trios, Marlboro Festival; 3 CDs of violin/piano repertoires with pianist Zeyda Ruga Suzuki. *Honours:* Laureat, Tchaikovsky International Competition, 1962; Laureat, Queen Elizabeth International Competition, 1963, 1967; Laureat, Montreal International Competition, 1966; Served as Jury Member, Montreal International Competition, 1979; International Violin Competition, 1982, 1986, 1990, 1994. *Address:* 430 West 93rd Street, Indianapolis, IN 46260, USA.

SVANIDZE, Natela; Composer; b. 4 Sept. 1926, Akhaltsikhe, Georgia; m. Peter Tomadze, 15 June 1952, 1 d. *Education:* Studies at Tbilisi State University, French Literature; Graduated from the Tbilisi State Conservatoire, 1951. *Career:* Debut: Symphonic poem, Samgori, conducted by Odyssey Dymitriady, Tbilisi, 1951; Performances: Improvisation, violin, piano, 1956; Fairytale, piano, Tbilisi, 1960; Kvarkvare, symphonic poem, conducted by Lile Kilaze, Radio Tbilisi, 1963; Burlesque, symphonic poem, conducted by Lile Kiladze, Tbilisi, 1966; Symphony No. 1, conducted G Rozdestvensky, Radio Moscow, Paris, Belgrade, 1969; Pirosmani, oratorio, conducted by Lile Kiladze, Tbilisi, 1972, by Kataeff, Moscow, 1974 and by Provatoroff, Samara, 1976; Professor of the Georgian State Institute of Theatre and Cinema, Tbilisi; mem. Board member, The Georgian Composers' Union. *Compositions:* Symphony No. 1, for strings, piano and percussion instruments, 1967; Lamentatia Georgica, oratorio for speaker, female sextet, two choruses, instruments and tape, 1974; Symphony No. 2, for big orchestra, 1983; Gaul-Gavkhe, cantata, mixed choruses, big orchestra, 1995; Monodrama for voice, piano, cassa a pedal, piatto and tape, 1999. *Honours:* Honoured Art Worker of the Georgian SSR, 1981; Professor, 1991. *Current Management:* Professor of the Institute of Theatre and Cinema, Tbilisi. *Address:* Griboedoff Str 4, Apt 7, 380 008, Tbilisi, Georgia.

SVARC-GRENDA, Ivana; Pianist; b. 17 Feb. 1970, Yugoslavia. *Education:* Music Academy in Zagreb; Peabody Conservatory of Music, Baltimore; Hochschule der Kunste, Berlin; Mozarteum, Salzburg. *Career:* Winner of the Kosciuszko Chopin Competition, New York; Winner Croatian National Artists Competition; Solo appearances at Carnegie Recital Hall; Lincoln Center Library, New York; Kennedy Center, Washington DC; Philharmonie Berlin; Alte Oper Frankfurt; Chamber Music appearances, Salle Cortot, Paris; Philharmonie Berlin; Schauspielhaus Berlin; Glinka Hall, St Petersburg; Orchestra appearances with Zagreb Philharmonic, Solisti di Zagreb and Croatian Chamber Orchestra; Berlin Symphony Orchestra; Gives master courses at International Summer school, Hvar, Croatia. *Recordings:* Cello-piano duo with Monika Leskovar. *Honours:* Milka Trnina prize for the best

Croatian Musician, 1996; Porin award for the best Croatian recording, 1996. *Address:* Kastlenstr 26A, 81827 Munchen, Germany.

SVECENY, Jaroslav; Concert Violinist; b. 8 Dec. 1960, Hradec Kralove, Czechoslovakia; m. Monika Svecena. *Education:* Studied at the Prague Conservatoire and the Prague Academy of Arts with Vaclav Snitil; Masterclasses with Nathan Milstein at Zürich and Gidon Kremer at Kuhmo. *Career:* Concert appearances in Germany, Spain, France, Italy, the United Kingdom, Finland, Denmark, USA, Russia, Poland, Hungary and Romania; Participated in several festivals in Berlin, Constance, Helsinki, Bilbao, Madrid, Granada, Havana, Prague, Leipzig and Palermo; Repertoire includes Concertos by Dvořák, Beethoven, Brahms, Mozart, Bach, Vivaldi, Haydn, Reicha and Martinů, Reicha Complete Works for Violin and Piano, Benda 24 Capriccios (only artist with this repertoire), and sonatas by Brahms, Beethoven, Dvořák, Benda, Handel and Ysaÿe. *Recordings include:* Reicha 4 Sonatas, Grand Duo Concertante and Rondo; Sonatas by Benda, Stamitz, Corelli, Handel and Tartini; Vivaldi Four Seasons. *Honours:* Winner, Pablo de Sarasate International Violin Competition. *Address:* c/o Czech Arts & Concert Agency, Korunni 60, CZ–12000 Praha-Vinohrady, Czech Republic.

SVEINSSON, Atli Heimir; Composer, Conductor and Administrator; b. 21 Sept. 1938, Reykjavík, Iceland. *Education:* Studied at the Reykjavic College of Music and with Petzold and BA Zommermann at the Cologne Hochschule für Musik; Composition studies with Pousseur and Stockhausen at Darmstadt and Cologne. *Career:* Freelance composer and conductor throughout Iceland and Scandinavia; Chairman, Society of Icelandic Composers, 1972–83. *Compositions include:* Tautophony, for orchestra, 1967; Flower Shower, for orchestra, 1973; Flute Concerto, 1975; Septet, 1976; Twenty-One Sounding Minutes for flute, 1980; Bassoon Concerto, Trobar Clus, 1980; The Silken Drum, opera, 1982; Trombone Concerto, Jubilus, 1984; Recitation, for piano and orchestra, 1984; Bicentennial, for string quartet, 1984; Trio, for violin, cello and piano, 1985; The Night on our Shoulders, for soprano, alto, women's chorus and orchestra, 1986; Dreamboat, concerto for violin, harpsichord and orchestra, 1987; Vikivaki, television opera, 1990; Opplaring, for soprano and wind instruments, 1991; Dernier Amour, chamber opera, 1992; Rockerauschen, Bruit des Robes for chamber orchestra, 1993; Poem to the Virgin Mary, for chorus, 1995; The Isle of Moonlight, 1995, performed Peking, 1997; Signs of Fire, for piano and wind, 1995; Discords, for cello, strings and piano, 1997; Independent People, incidental music, 1999; The Conversion of Iceland, opera, 2000. *Honours:* Nordic Council Prize, 1976. *Address:* c/o STEF, Laufasvegi 40, 101 Reykjavík, Iceland.

SVENDEN, Birgitta; Singer (Mezzo-Soprano); b. 20 March 1952, Porjus, Sweden. *Education:* Studied at the Stockholm Opera School. *Career:* Has sung at the Royal Opera in Stockholm as Cherubino, Olga and Erda; Sang a Rhinemaiden in The Ring under Solti at Bayreuth in 1983, at Nice Opéra from 1985 in Carmen and as Meg Page and Anna in Les Troyens; Created Queen Christina in Hans Gefors' opera in 1988; Sang at Metropolitan Opera from 1988 as Erda in Das Rheingold and Siegfried and Maddalena in Rigoletto, Seattle Opera in 1989 as Magdalena in Die Meistersinger, Ravinia Festival Chicago in Mahler's 3rd Symphony under James levine, and at La Scala, Munich and San Francisco in 1990 as Magdalena, Erda and First Norn; Covent Garden debut in 1990 in a new production of Siegfried under Bernard Haitink; Sang at Théâtre du Châtelet, Paris, as Margret in a production of Wozzeck by Patrice Chéreau under Daniel Barenboim; Engaged for BBC Philharmonic in Verdi's Requiem in 1991, Gürzenich Orchestra in Mahler's 3rd in 1992, and Los Angeles Philharmonic in Mahler's 3rd; Sang in Eugene Onegin and Die Meistersinger at Metropolitan Opera in 1993; Season 1993 with Mahler's 3rd at Boston and Carnegie Hall under Ozawa, Mahler's 3rd and 8th at Rome and Rotterdam under Conlon, Missa Solemnis at Paris under Solti, and Octavian in Der Rosenkavalier at Paris Châtelet; Season 1994 with new Ring productions at Bayreuth, Covent Garden and Cologne; Season 1996–97 as Wagner's Magdalena at Bayreuth, Erda at the Met; Season 2000–01 as Erda in Das Rheingold at the Met and Brigitta in Die tote Stadt at Strasbourg; mem. Royal Swedish Academy of Music. *Recordings:* Das Rheingold; Mahler; Elgar; Siegfried; Zemlinsky. *Honours:* Royal Court Singer (Hovsångerska) 1995 by King of Sweden. *Address:* Artistsekretariat Ulf Törnqvist, Sankt Eriksgatan 100, 2tr, 113 31, Stockholm, Sweden.

SVENSSON, Peter; Singer (Tenor); b. 1963, Vienna, Austria. *Career:* Sang in the 1988 Vienna Festival under Claudio Abbado; Season 1991–92 at the Prague State Opera, as Wagner's Rienzi and Zemlensky's Der Zwerg and Eine Florentinische Tragödie; Lucerne, 1993, as Strauss's Bacchus (also at Cologne); Sang Tannhäuser at Prague, 1994, and Claudio in Das Liebesverbot by Wagner at Wexford; Season 1995–96 as Hermann in The Queen of Spades at Mainz, Tannhäuser at Meinigen and in the premiere of The Marx Sisters at Bielefeld; Guest appearances as Siegmund at the Châtelet, Paris, and as Max in Der Freischütz, Florestan and Strauss's Herod; Sang Oedipus Rex at

Naples, 2001. *Address:* c/o Buhnen der Stadt Bielefeld, Bruhnenstrasse 3–9, Pf 220, 4800 Bielefeld, Germany.

SVETE, Tomaz; Composer and Conductor; b. 29 Jan. 1956, Ljubljana, Slovenia. *Education:* Graduated in Composition, 1980 and Conducting, 1981, Academy of Music, Ljubljana; Studied with Professor F Cerha, Hochschule für Musik und Darstellende Kunst, Vienna, Diploma with Distinction, 1986; Studies in conducting with Otmar Suitner, Diploma 1988 and electro-acoustic music with Dieter Kaufmann, Vienna; Magister Artis of the Hochschule für Musik und Darstellende Kunst, Vienna, 1989. *Career:* Debut: 1st composition performance, Ljubljana, 1978; Works performed in: Ljubljana, Skopje, Opatija, Zagreb-Music Biennial, Vienna, Salzburg, Prague, Brno-Moravian Autumn, Amsterdam, Rotterdam, Middleburgh, Torino, Trieste, Klagenfurt, Spittal-Drau, Tirana, Leipzig, Melk, St Pölten- Niederösterreich International; Conductor of Slovene Philharmonic and Pro Arte Orchestras, of Singkreis Währing, Vienna and Brno Radio Symphony Orchestra; Professor of Composition, Karl Prayner Conservatory, Vienna; Concert of own works in Brahmssaal, Musikverein, Vienna; Freelance Composer in Vienna; Docent for composition at Pedagogical Faculty, Maribor, Slovenia; Guest Professor for Composition, University of Hartford, Connecticut, 1999–2000. *Compositions include:* Requiem, 1991; The Rape from Laudach Sea, opera, 1993; Isomerisms for Chamber Ensemble; Rappresentazione Sacra for Double Bass Solo and Flute Quartet, Ljubljana, 1994; Sonata Solaris for Violoncello and Piano, Salzburg, 1994; Sacrum Delirium, cantata for Soloists, Chorus, Ensembles and Orchestra (Italian Prize), 1994; Hommage à Slavko Osterc for Piano, Ljubljana, 1995; Evocazione, soprano and chamber ensemble, 1995; Poet and Rebellion, opera, 1996; Concert de la Nuit, double bass, violin, harp and orchestra, 1997; Kriton, opera after Plato, 2000. *Recordings:* Jugoton, 1986 and Kriton. *Address:* Prusnikova 2, SL-2000 Maribor, Slovenia.

SVETLEV, Michail; Singer (Tenor); b. 6 March 1943, Sofia, Bulgaria. *Education:* Studied at the Sofia Conservatoire. *Career:* Debut: Passau in 1971 as Manrico; Appearances in Munich, Hamburg, Berlin and Vienna, and La Scala Milan in 1979; US debut as Riccardo in Un Ballo in Maschera at Washington DC in 1980; Further US appearances at Houston in 1980, San Francisco in 1980 and 1983, and Philadelphia in 1982; Sang Dmitri in Boris Godunov at Covent Garden in 1983 and has appeared elsewhere as Verdi's Radames and Gabriele Adorno, Andrea Chénier and Cavaradossi; Season 1985–86 as Hermann in The Queen of Spades at Marseilles and Lykov in Rimsky's The Tsar's Bride at Monte Carlo; Other roles include the Duke of Mantua, Don Carlos, Bacchus, Lensky, Edgardo and the Prince in Rusalka. *Address:* c/o Opéra de Monte Carlo, Place du Casino, Monte Carlo.

SVOBODA, Tomas; Composer, Pianist, Conductor and Professor of Music; b. 6 Dec. 1939, Paris, France; m. Jana Demartini, 9 Oct 1965, 1 s., 1 d. *Education:* Degree in Percussion, 1956, Composition, 1958, Conducting, 1962, Conservatory of Music, Prague, Czechoslovakia; Degree in Composition, University of Southern California, USA, 1969. *Career:* Debut: FOK Prague Symphony Orchestra, Symphony No. 1, Op 20, 1957. *Compositions:* Symphonies 1–6; Overture of the Season, Op 89; Festive Overture, Op 103; Nocturne for orchestra, Op 100; Serenade for orchestra, Op 115; Sinfonietta (à la Renaissance), Op 60; Reflections for orchestra, Op 53; Concerto for piano and orchestra, Op 71; Concerto for violin and orchestra, Op 77; Ex Libris, Op 113; Child's Dream for children's choir and orchestra, Op 66; Concerto for chamber orchestra, Op 125; Journey, cantata for mezzo-soprano, baritone, choir and orchestra, Op 127; Dance Suite for orchestra, Op 128; Concerto No. 2 for piano and orchestra, Op 134; Concerto for marimba and orchestra, Op 148; Meditation for oboe and strings, Op 143, 1993; Rememberance, Chorale for trumpet and orchestra, Op 152a, 1997; 121 chamber pieces include Children's Treasure Box for piano, 1977–78; Woodwind Quintet Op 111, 1983–97; Duo Concerto for trumpet and organ; 53 keyboard compositions. *Recordings:* Symphony No. 4 (Apocalyptic), Op 69; Ex Libris, Op 113, for orchestra; CD recording (Mirecourt Trio), Passacaglia and Fugue for piano trio, Op 87; Concerto for chamber orchestra, Op 125; Trio for flute, oboe and bassoon Op 97; Concerto for Marimba and Orchestra, Op.148; Concerto No.1&2 for Piano and Orchestra; Overture of the Season for ORchestra; Symphony No.1 (Of Nature) for Orchestra; Autumn for Piano. *Publications:* Chaconne for Strings, Op.166a; Oriental Echoes, for String Orchestra, Op.140; Prelude and Fugue for String Orchestra, Op.172; Swing Dance, for Orchestra, Op.135a; Aria for Soprano and four instruments, Op.153; Autumn, for Koto, Op.110; Brass Quintet, Op.112; Celebration of Life, Cantata on Aztec Poetry, op.80; Chorales from 15th Century for English Horn and Strings, Op.52f; Chorale in E flat for Piano Quintet (homage to Aaron Copland) Op.118; Concealed Shapes for two Pianos, Xylophone and Marimba, Op.163; Concertino for Oboe, Brass Choir and Timpani, Op.46; Czernogorsk Fugue for Choir, Op.14; Duo for Xylophone and Marimba, Op.141; Farewell Matinee for Brass Quintet, Op.160; Five Studies for Two Timpanists, Op.160; Forest Rhythms for Flute, Viola and Xylophone, Op.150; Intrata for Brass Quintet, Op.127a; March of the Puppets for Guitar, Xylophone and four Temple Blocks, Op.95; Morning Prayer, for four Percussion, Op.101; Nocturne for Organ four hands, Op.155; Nocturne for Piano, Op.84; Offertories for Organ Vol. I, Op.52a; Partita in D for Viola da Gamba and Harpsichord, Op.161; Quartet, for four French Horns, Op.145; Sonata for Guitar, Op.99; Sonata for Violin and Piano, Op.73; Storm Session, for Electric Guitar and Bass Guitar, Op.126; String Quartet No.2, Op.102; Suite for Piano and 5 Percussionists, Op. 83; Veritas Veritatum, for Men's Choir, Op.129a; Wedding March, for Organ, Op.94. *Honours:* ASCAP Foundation/ Meet the Composer Award, 1985; Oregon Governor's Arts Award, 1992; American Record Guide, 2001 Critics Choice Award for Piano Trios CD. *Current Management:* Thomas C Stangland, Portland, USA. *Address:* c/o Thomas Stangland Co, PO Box 19263, Portland, OR 97201, USA. *E-mail:* info@TomasSvoboda.com. *Website:* www.TomasSvoboda .com.

SVORC, Antonin; Singer (Bass-Baritone); b. 12 Feb. 1934, Jaromer, Czechoslovakia. *Education:* Studied with Jan Berlik in Prague. *Career:* Debut: State Theatre of Liberec as Pizarro in Fidelio, 1955; Member of the National Theatre, Prague, from 1958; Visited Edinburgh with the company in 1964 in the British premiere of From the House of the Dead by Janáček; Guest appearances at the Berlin Staatsoper and in Vienna, Paris, Dresden, Cologne, Düsseldorf, Kassel, Zürich, Trieste, Venice and Barcelona; Sang in Prague in 1974 in the premiere of Cikker's Coriolanus and as Chrudos in Libuše at the 1983 reopening of the National Opera; Sang as guest at the Paris Opéra in 1988 in From the House of the Dead. *Recordings:* Operas by Smetana including Dalibor and Libuše. *Honours:* National Artists of Czechoslovakia, 1985. *Address:* c/o National Theatre, PO Box 865, 112 30 Prague 1, Czech Republic.

SWAFFORD, Jan (Johnson); Composer; b. 10 Sept. 1946, Chattanooga, Tennessee, USA. *Education:* Harvard College; Yale School of Music; Tanglewood. *Career:* Teacher at: Boston University, Goddard College, Hampshire College, Amherst College, Tufts University. *Compositions:* Passage, 1975; Peal, 1976; Landscape With Traveller, 1981; Shore Lines, 1982; Labyrinths, 1983; Music Like Steel Like Fire, 1983; In Time Of Fear, 1984; Midsummer Variations, 1985; Chamber Sinfonietta, 1988; They Who Hunger, 1989; Requiem in Winter, 1991; Iphigenia Choruses, 1993. *Recordings:* Midsummer Variations; They Who Hunger, 1993. *Publications:* The Vintage Guide to Classical Music, 1992; A Life of Charles Ives, in progress; A Life of Brahms, in progress. *Contributions:* Articles and reviews to Symphony; New England Monthly; Musical America; Yankee. *Address:* 37 Magnolia Avenue 1, Cambridge, MA, USA.

SWANSTON, Roderick Brian; Professor of Music Theory; b. 28 Aug. 1948, Gosport, England. *Education:* Music Scholar, Stowe School, 1961–66; Royal College of Music, 1966–69; Organ Scholar at Pembroke College, Cambridge, 1969–71; MA; BMus; Graduate, Royal Schools of Music; Fellow, Royal College of Organists; Licentiate of Royal Academy; Associate of Royal College of Music. *Career:* Organist at Christ Church, Lancaster Gate, 1972–77, and St James, Sussex Gardens, 1977–80; Conductor of Christ Church Choral Society, 1973–80; Part-Time Tutor at University of London, Department of Extra Mural Studies, 1972–; Academic Adviser in Music to Birkbeck College, University of London, Centre for Extra Mural Studies, 1987–; Visiting Lecturer for many organizations including English National Opera, Royal Opera House, Covent Garden, BBC, Oxford University and Goldsmiths' College. *Compositions:* A Time There Was for Tenor, Choir and Strings; Let Us Gather Hand In Hand for Choir and Brass à 5, recorded by BBC. *Recordings:* Organ recital from Framlingham Parish Church. *Publications:* Concise History of Music. *Address:* Royal College of Music, Prince Consort Road, London SW7, England.

SWAYNE, Giles; Composer; b. 30 June 1946, Hitchin, Hertfordshire, England. *Education:* Ampleforth, Trinity Coll. Cambridge; RAM, London; studies with Nicholas Maw, Harrison Birtwistle, Oliver Messiaen; conducting course at Siena 1968. *Career:* early work performed by SPNM and at Aldeburgh and Bromsgrove Festivals; Orlando's Music and Pentecost Music performed by several major orchestras; opera repetiteur at Wexford Festival 1972–73 and Glyndebourne 1973–74; teaching staff at Bryanston School 1974–76; first major int. success with composition Cry for 28 voices for BBC premiered London 1980, later 1988, Proms 1983, 1994, also Amsterdam Concertgebouw 1982, Vienna Modern Festival and Stuttgart 1997; companion piece Havoc premiered Proms 1999; visited West Africa in 1980 to study the music of the Jola people of Senegal and The Gambia; lived in Ghana 1990–96; teaches composition Cambridge Univ.; mem. PRS, APC, MCPS. *Compositions include:* Six Songs of Love & Lust, La Rivière 1966, The Kiss 1967, Sonata for String Quartet 1968, Three Shakespeare Songs (SATB choir) 1969, Chamber Music for Strings, Four Lyrical Pieces for Cello and Piano 1970, The Good Morrow (mezzo and piano), Paraphrase (organ), String Quartet No. 1 1971, Trio (flute,

oboe and piano), Canto for Guitar 1972, Canto for Piano, Canto for Violin 1973, Orlando's Music for Orchestra, Synthesis (2 pianos) 1974, Scrapbook (piano), Canto for clarinet, Duo (violin and piano), Charades (school orchestra) 1975, Suite for guitar, Pentecost-Music for Orchestra, Alleluia! (SA choir, harp, percussion) 1976, String Quartet no. 2 1977, A World Within, ballet with tape 1978, Phoenix Variations (piano), Cry for 28 amplified voices 1979, The Three Rs (primary school orchestra), Freewheeling (violin, viola, bass) 1980, Count-Down (SATB choir), Canto for Cello 1981, Rhythm Studies 1 & 2 (school percussion), Magnificat (SATB choir) 1982, Riff-Raff (organ), A Song for Haddi (ensemble) 1983, Le Nozze di Cherubino (opera), Symphony for Small Orchestra, Naaotwa Lalà (for orchestra) 1984, Missa Tiburtina for SATB choir 1985, Into the Light (ensemble), Solo for Guitar 1986, godsong (mezzo & ensemble), Nunc Dimittis (SATB choir and organ), O Magnum Mysterium (treble voices and organ) 1986, Tonos for ensemble 1987, Veni Creator I & 2 (SATB choir and organ), Songlines for Flute and Guitar, The Coming of Saskia Hawkins (organ) 1987, Harmonies of Hell (large ensemble), The Song of Leviathan (large orchestra) 1988, No Quiet Place (SA choir and ensemble), No Man's Land for solo bass voice, SATB choir, ensemble 1990, Circle of Silence for 6 male voices 1991, Zebra Music (piano), The Song of the Tortoise (narrator, SATB, small orchestra) 1992, The Owl & the Pussycat I (narrator, ensemble), String Quartet no. 3 1993, Fiddlesticks (violin & bass), Goodnight, Sweet Ladies (soprano & piano), Squeezy (accordion) 1994, All about Henry (string orchestra), The Tiger (SATB choir), Communion Service in D (congregation and organ), A Convocation of Worms (countertenor & organ) 1995, Two romantic songs (SATB choir), Ophelia drowning (flute & SATB choir), The Silent Land (cello & 40-part choir) 1996, Tombeau (piano), Beatus vir (SATB choir & organ), Mr Leary's Mechanical Maggot (string orchestra), Chinese Whispers (organ & orchestra), Miss Brevissima (SATB choir), Petite Messe Solitaire (SATB choir & unison voices), Echo (violin & piano) 1997, Winter Solstice Carol (flute & SATB choir), Groundwork (theorbo) Merlis Lied (voice & piano) 1998, The Flight of the Swan (flute & SATB choir), Havoc (24 voices, countertenor, ensemble & small orchestra) 1999, Perturbèd Spirit (countertenor & organ), Canto for flute, The Akond of Swat (2 narrators & ensemble) 2000, Mancanza (solo guitar & orchestra), The Murder of Gonzago (wind quintet) 2001, Epitaph and Refrain (ensemble) 2002, The Owl & the Pussycat II (treble voices & piano), Midwinter (SATB choir), Sangre viva (trumpet & piano) 2003, Stabat mater (SATB choir and soloists), Stations of the Cross Book I (organ), Mr Bach's Bottle-Bank (organ) 2004. *Address:* Gonzaga Music, 43 Victor Road, London, NW10 5XB, England. *E-mail:* giles@havocry.ndo.co.uk.

SWEENEY, William; Composer; b. 5 Jan. 1950, Glasgow, Scotland. *Education:* Royal Scottish Academy 1967–70; Royal Academy of Music, London, 1970–73, with Harrison Birtwistle and Alan Hacker. *Career:* Lecturer on Composition at the University of Glasgow. *Compositions:* Three Poems from Sangschaw for soprano, three clarinets and piano, 1977; Maqam for orchestra, 1984; Sunset Song, for orchestra, 1986; The Heights of Macchu Picchu, for soprano, harp and percussion, 1988; The New Road, for tenor saxophone and orchestra, 1989; El Pueblo, for baritone and ensemble, 1989; Concerto Grosso, for nine clarinets, strings and timpani, 1990; St, Blane's Hill, for orchestra 1991; A Set for the Kingdom, for strings, 1991; Two Lyrics, for two sopranos and chorus, 1992; A Drunk Man Looks at the Thistle, for speaker baritone and ensemble, 1992; The Woods of Rassay for soprano, baritone and orchestra, 1993; Seeking Wise Salmon, for soprano, clarinet, trombone and two synthesizers, 1994; October Landscapes, for orchestra, 1994; The Lost Mountain, for wind band, 1996; All that Came in the Coracle, for mezzo and ensemble, 1999. *Address:* c/o PRS Ltd, 29–33 Berners St, London, W1T 3 AB, England. *Telephone:* (20) 7580 5544. *Fax:* (20) 7306 4455.

SWEET, Sharon; Singer (Soprano); b. 16 Aug. 1951, New York, USA. *Education:* Studied with Margaret Harshaw at the Curtis Institute, Philadelphia and with Marinka Gurewich in New York. *Career:* Sang in private recitals at Philadelphia then appeared in the title role in concert performance of Aida at Munich, 1985; Dortmund Opera, 1986–88, debut as Elisabeth in Tannhäuser; Deutsche Oper Berlin from 1987, notably as guest in Zürich and Japan as Elisabeth and in the Ring; Paris Opera and Hamburg, 1987 as Elisabeth de Valois; Season 1987–88 as Desdemona in Brunswick, Dvořák's Stabat Mater at the Salzburg Festival, Gurrelider in Munich under Zubin Mehta and Wagner's Elisabeth at the Vienna Staatsoper; Norma in a concert performance of Bellini's opera at Brussels, 1988; US debut as Aida at San Francisco in 1989; Season 1992 as Aida in Dallas and the Trovatore Leonora at Orange; Sang in the house premiere of Verdi's Stiffelio at the Metropolitan Season, 1993–94 returned 1997, as Aida; Aida at Covent Garden, 1995, returned as Turandot, 1997; Norma at Rome, 1999; Sang Turandot at the Dresden Staatsoper, 2001. *Recordings include:* Verdi's Requiem. *Address:* c/o IMG Paris, 54 Ave Marceau, F–75008 Paris, France.

SWENSEN, Joseph; Conductor; b. 4 Aug. 1960, New York, USA. *Education:* Studied violin at the Juilliard School with Dorothy DeLay; Conducting studies with Paavo Berglund, Jorge Mester, Otto-Werner Mueller and Lawrence Foster; Studied piano with Christian Sager and Thomas Schumacker. *Career:* Guest Conductor with the City of Birmingham Symphony, Hallé Orchestra, BBC Symphony, St Louis Symphony, Indianapolis Symphony, New World Symphony, Dallas Symphony and Royal Stockholm Philharmonic; Principal Guest Conductor, Stockholm Chamber Orchestra, 1994–; Lahti Symphony Orchestra, 1995–; Appointed Principal Guest Conductor BBC National Orchestra of Wales, 2000–; Principal Conductor of the Scottish Chamber Orchestra, 1996–2005; Premiere of Rautavaara's Autumn Gardens and the Eroica Symphony with the Scottish Chamber Orchestra at the 1999 London Proms; Conducted a new production of The Marriage of Figaro at the Royal Danish Opera, 1999; Conducted the BBC National Orchestra of Wales at the London Proms, 2002. *Recordings include:* Shostakovich 14 with Tapiola Sinfonietta; Bach and Mendelssohn Violin Concertos with Robert McDuffie and Scottish Chamber Orchestra. *Address:* c/o Victoria Rowsell, Van Walsum Management Ltd, 4 Addison Bridge Place, London W14 8XP, England.

SWENSEN, Robert; Singer (Tenor); b. 1961, USA. *Career:* Sang at the New Jersey Festival, 1987 and 1988, as Rossini's Count and Britten's Lysander; Season 1990 with Tybalt in I Capuleti e i Montecchi at Geneva and Nadir in Les Pêcheurs des Perles at the Paris Opéra-Comique; Carnegie Hall, New York, 1992, as George Brown in La Dame Blanche by Boieldieu: Matsumato Festival, 1993, as Oedipus Rex and Amenofi in Nabucco at Venice; Season 1995–96 in Mozart's Mitridate at Turin and Gianetto in La Gazza Ladra at Palermo; Concerts include Mozart's Requiem at Cologne. *Recordings include:* Bach's St John Passion; Haydn's Orfeo ed Euridice; Bach's Christmas Oratorio; Oedipus Rex, also on video. *Address:* c/o Teatro Regio de Torino, Piazza Castello 215, 10124 Turin, Italy.

SWENSON, Ruth-Ann; Singer (soprano); b. 25 Aug. 1959, New York, USA. *Career:* Debut: San Francisco 1983, as Despina; Sang soubrette roles with the San Francisco Opera, 1983–93; Donizetti's Adina at Seattle (1984) and Despina at Geneva; Nannetta at Amsterdam (1987), Mozart's Ilia at Toronto and Inez in L'Africaine at San Francisco; Metropolitan Opera debut, 1991, as Zerlina, followed by Gilda; Washington Opera 1989–90, as Lucia and Rosina, Dallas 1989–92, as Norina and Susanna; Detroit 1990, as Gounod's Juliette, Cologne and Schwetzingen 1991, as Mozart's Constanze; Covent Garden debut 1996, as Handel's Semele; Sang Bellini's Elvira at the Met, 1997; Season 1999–2000 at the Met as Lucia di Lammermoor and all four soprano roles in Les Contes d'Hoffmann; Pamyra in Le Siège de Corinthe at the Pesaro Festival, 2000, Baby Doe at San Francisco and Massenet's Manon for the Met, 2001; Rosina in 2001; Engaged as Semele at Covent Garden, 2003; Modern repertory includes Argento's The Voyage of Edgar Allan Poe (Chicago, 1990) and Moore's The Ballad of Baby Doe (Long Beach Opera, 1987). *Recordings include:* Video of L'Africaine. *Current Management:* Askonas Holt Ltd, Lonsdale Chambers, 27 Chancery Lane, London, WC2A 1PF, England. *Telephone:* (20) 7400-1700. *Fax:* (20) 7400-1799. *E-mail:* info@askonasholt.co.uk. *Website:* www.askonasholt.co.uk.

SWERTS, Piet; Composer; b. 14 Nov, 1960, Tongeren, Belgium. *Education:* Lemmens Institute, Leuven; Masterclasses with Witold Lutoslawski. *Compositions:* Four String Quartets, 1982, 1985, 1991, 1993; Paysages Métaphysiques, for orchestra, 1982; Three Piano Concertos, 1984, 1986, 1991; Yoshiwara for soprano and 14 instruments, 1986; Marcuspasie (St Mark Passion), 1988; Rotations for piano and orchestra, 1988; Magma, concerto for violin, cello and strings, 1989; Two Symphonies, 1990, 1997; Rapsodia, for bassoon and string quartet, 1991; Zodiac, for violin and orchestra, 1993; Cello Concerto, 1996; Les Liaisons Dangereuses, theatre music, 1996; Songs and keyboard music. *Honours:* Lemmens Tinel Prize, for piano and composition; Flor Baron Peeters and Camille Huysmans prizes. *Address:* c/o SABAM, Rue d'Arlon 75–77, B–1040 Brussels, Belgium. *Telephone:* 0055 21286 4017. *Fax:* 0022 21286 5068.

SWIERCZEWSKI, Michel; Conductor; b. 1960, France. *Education:* Studied with Jean-Claude Hartemann in Paris and Charles Mackerras at the Vienna Hochschule. *Career:* Made debut in 1976 and was then assistant conductor to Pierre Boulez and Peter Eötvös at the Ensemble Intercontemporain, 1983–85 and for Claudio Abbado at La Scala, including the premiere of Nono's Prometeo, 1985–86; Paris Opéra in 1986 with Georges Prêtre; Has conducted such contemporary music ensembles as Itineraire, Musique Oblique, Antidogma and New Music Ensemble, giving many premieres; Guest engagements in France, Germany, Italy, Spain, Portugal and Australia; Conducted Die Fledermaus at Lyon, 1996. *Recordings:* La Conférence des Oiseaux by Michael Levinas; Works by Roussel with the Gulbenkian Foundation Orchestra; Complete Symphonies of Méhul. *Honours:* Finalist, 1984 Tanglewood International Conducting Competition; Prize, Villa Medicis

Hors Les Murs. *Current Management:* Agence Thelen, 15 avenue Montaigne, 75008 Paris, France.

SWINGLE, Ward (Lamar); Choral Conductor, Composer, Arranger and Clinician; b. 21 Sept. 1927, Mobile, Alabama, USA; m. Françoise Demorest, 23 Sept 1952, 3 d. *Education:* BM, MM, Piano Major, Cincinnati Conservatory of Music, 1947–51; Masterclasses with Walter Gieseking at Saarbrücken, Germany, 1951–53. *Career:* Solo piano recitals and accompanist, 1953–55; Conductor of Ballets de Paris, France, 1955–59; Founded Swingle Singers, a world-wide touring concert group, 1963; Numerous radio and television appearances with Swingle Singers in most major capitals and about 2000 concerts around the world, 1963–91. *Compositions:* Over 100 arrangements and compositions for the Swingle Singers. *Recordings:* About 30 with the Swingle Singers including Bach's Greatest Hits, Going Baroque, and Luciano Berio's Sinfonia. *Honours:* 5 Grammy Awards, 1964, 1965, 1966, 1970; Grand Prix du Disque, 1964; Edison Award, 1970. *Current Management:* Piers Schmidt, 45a Chalcot Road, London, NW1 8LS, England. *Address:* c/o ASCAP, ASCAP Building, One Lincoln Plaza, NY 10023, USA.

SWINNEN, Peter; Belgian composer; b. 31 Jan. 1965, Lier. *Education:* Royal Conservatory, Brussels, Muziekkapel Konigin Elisabeth, Waterloo, masterclasses with Michael Finnissy and Brian Ferneyhough. *Career:* taught cello at music schools 1990–97; teacher of analysis, Royal Conservatory, Brussels 1992–, of music technology 2002–, of composition 2004–; software development for aural training at Leuven Univ. 1997–2004; for musical analysis at Brussels Univ. 2004–; freelance work for BRTN-television; frequent performances of live electronics with various ensembles. *Compositions include:* Diorama 1989, FugaEneas 1990, Escurial 1991, The Petrifying Blue (chamber opera) 1992, Hombre alado 1995, The Black Lark's Ballad (symphonic poem, tribute to Frank Zappa) 1995, Een pimpelpaarse wiebelfiets 1996, La Vieille dame et la fille nomade 1998, Toaminá'k 1998, Sinfonia I 1998, Ciaccona 2000, Annotazione 2000, Pas-de-deux 2001, Maitre Tsa (mini opera for children) 2003. *Compositions for films:* Andres 1992, Het Verhoor 1998, The Voice of the Violin 1998. *Recordings include:* Ciaccona, The Black Lark's Ballad, Quar'l. *Honours:* Prijs CERA – Jeugd en Muziek Vlaanderen 1991, Prov. of Antwerp Prijs voor Muziekcompositie 1992, Prix de Musique Contemporaine, Québec 1997, winner Queen Elisabeth Int. Music Competition Nat. Composition Contest, Belgium 1997, 2001. *Address:* Frans Gasthuislaan 33/4, 1081 Brussels, Belgium. *Telephone:* (2) 425-24-18. *E-mail:* info@peterswinnen.be. *Website:* www.peterswinnen.be.

SYDEMAN, William; Composer; b. 8 May 1928, New York, USA. *Education:* Mannes College, with Roy Travis, and Hartt College (1948–58); Further studies with Goffredo Petrassi and Roger Sessions. *Career:* Lecturer at Mannes College, 1959–70; Rudolf Steiner College, CA, from 1980; Commissions from Boston SO and Chamber Music Society of Lincoln Center. *Compositions:* Three Concertos da Camera, for violin and orchestra, 1959, 1960, 1965; Piano Sonata, 1961; Homage to L'Histoire du Soldât, 1962; Three Studies for Orchestra, 1959, 1963, 1965; Music for Viola, Winds and Percussion, 1996; Concerto for piano four hands and orchestra, 1967; Full Circle, for three solo voices and ensemble, 1971; 18 Duos for two violins, 1976; Duo, for violin and cello, 1979; A Winter's Tale, incidental music, 1982; Sonata for violin and piano, 1987; Duo for cello and double bass, 1992; Duo for oboe and piano, 1996; Jonathan's Trombone, 1996. *Address:* c/o ASCAP, ASCAP Building, One Lincoln Plaza, New York, NY 10023, USA.

SYLVAN, Sanford; Singer (Baritone); b. 1952, USA. *Career:* Debut: Concert with New York Philharmonic Orchestra, under Pierre Boulez, 1977; Sang at the Marlboro Festival from 1982 and collaborated with Peter Sellars as Handel's Orlando, as Mozart's Don Alfonso, 1986, and Mozart's Figaro, 1987; Premieres of Nixon in China by John Adams at Houston, 1987, and The Death of Klinghoffer at Brussels, 1991; Albert Hall, London, 1990, as Xun in Tippett's The Ice Break; Glyndebourne, 1994, as Leporello; Houston, New York and Edinburgh, 1996, as St Agnatius in Virgil Thomson's Three Saints in Four Acts; Klinghoffer at Barbican Hall, London, 2002; London Proms, 2002. *Recordings include:* Nixon in China and The Death of Klinghoffer. *Address:* c/o Houston Opera Association, 510 Preston Avenue, Houston, TX 77002, USA.

SYLVESTER, Michael; Singer (Tenor); b. 21 Aug. 1951, Noblesville, Indiana, USA. *Education:* Studied with Margaret Harshaw at Bloomington. *Career:* Sang Radames and Pinkerton at Stuttgart, 1987, at Cincinnati Opera from 1987 as Pinkerton and Sam in Floyd's Susannah, New York City Opera debut in 1987 as Rodolfo in La Bohème and further engagements at La Scala and Santiago as Pinkerton in 1990, Paris Opéra as Pollione in Norma, Hamburg Staatsoper as Rodolfo and Don José, and Vienna Staatsoper as Cavaradossi; Covent Garden debut in 1990 as Samson, followed by Gabriel Adorno in a new production of Simon Boccanegra in 1991; Sang at Bregenz Festival in 1990 as Hagenbach in La Wally, and at Metropolitan Opera in debut, 1991, as

Rodolfo in Luisa Miller followed by Don Carlos in 1992; Appearances as Radames at Deutsche Oper Berlin, Chicago, Orange Festival and Seattle in 1992; Further engagements at Bonn as Bacchus in 1990, San Francisco as Calaf, Venice as Don Carlos and Geneva as Foresto in Attila; Sang Radames at the Met, 1996–97; Season 2000–01 as Eleazar in La Juive for New Israeli Opera, Giasone in Cherubini's Médée at Montpellier, Calaf at the Met, Gabriele Adorno for Australian Opera and Puccini's Dick Johnson in Toronto. *Recordings include:* Title role in Oberon; Don Carlos conducted by James Levine; Video of Simon Boccanegra from Covent Garden with Solti conducting. *Address:* c/o Metropolitan Opera, Lincoln Center, New York, NY 10023, USA.

SYNKOVA, Milada; Pianist, Harpsichordist, Opera Repetiteur at the Opera of the Slovak National Theatre and Tutor at the Academy of Music Arts; b. 16 May 1933, Bratislava, Czechoslovakia. *Education:* Conservatoire of Music, Brno; University of Bratislava, 1951–63. *Career:* Debut: Slovak National Theatre, Bratislava, 1963; Concerts World-wide; Harpsichordist, Pianist and Assistant to Professor Viktor Málek, Conductor of the Chamber Orchestra Camerata Slovaca, 1969–; Singer, Pianist and Assistant to Professor Ladislav Holásek, Conductor of the Bratislava City Choir, 1973–; Performed in chamber orchestras in Edinburgh, Jerusalem, Budapest and Seoul; Co-operates regularly (with Professor Milau Sládek) with The Mime Theatre ARENA in Bratislava; Taught professional training courses in piano, singing and Czech music at Sungshin Women's University, Seoul, Korea, 2000. *Recordings:* For Czechoslovak Radio, Television, Live Cycle for Slovak television, CD. *Address:* Salviova 52, 82101 Bratislava 2, Slovakia.

SYRUS, David; Conductor; b. 1945, England. *Education:* Oxford University and the London Opera Centre. *Career:* Repetiteur at the Royal Opera, Covent Garden, from 1971; Head of Music Staff from 1981, Head of Music and Assistant Conductor from 1993; Operas have included Ariadne auf Naxos, Die Zauberflöte, and Le nozze di Figaro; Assistant Conductor at the Bayreuth Festival for seven reasons, at Salzburg from 1991; Guest Conductor with Israeli Ballet, Garden Venture, at St John's Smith Square and the Ludlow Festival; Continuo player and an accompanist in Lieder recitals; Conducted Jenůfa at Covent Garden, 2001. *Recordings:* EMI, BMG and Phonogram. *Current Management:* Athole Still International Management, Forresters Hall, 25–27 Westow Street, London, SE19 3RY, England. *Telephone:* (20) 8771-5271. *Fax:* (20) 8768-6600. *Website:* www.atholestill.com.

SZABADI, Vilmos; Violinist; b. 10 March 1959, Budapest. *Education:* Liszt Academy of Music. *Career:* Debut: 2nd violin concerto, Bart ók Festival, Royal Festival Hall, London, 1988; Regular performer, Finland; Masterclasses in Finland, Greece and Hungary; Royal Philharmonic Orchestra; BBC Philharmonic; RTE Concert Orchestra, Ireland; Played at Wigmore and Barbican Halls, RFH, London; St David's, Cardiff; Ulster, Belfast; National Concert Hall, Dublin; Concertbegouw, Amsterdam; RAI Auditorium, Torino; Auditorio Nacional, Madrid; Châtelet, Conservatoire, Paris; Konzerthaus, Vienna; Liederhalle, Stuttgart; Helsinki, Finlandia, New York, Washington, Toronto, Montreal, Israel, Turkey, South Korea, Taiwan; Performed at celebration in honour of Georg Solti's 80th birthday, Buckingham Palace, 1992; Stradivarius serie, Spanish Royalty, Madrid, 1995; Artistic Director, Castle Chamber Music Festival, Hungary. *Recordings:* Dohnányi violin concertos, CD; Royal Festival Hall, London; Recorded for many radio and television stations; 21 CDs. *Honours:* Winner, 33rd Midem Festival's World Best Performance Prize, Cannes, 1999; Hungaroton Prize; First Prize, Hungarian Radio Competition; Jenö Hubay; 3rd Prize, Jean Sibelius, 1985; Franz Liszt Prize, 1993. *Website:* www.szabadi.com.

SZABO, Peter; Concert Cellist; b. 1965, Romania. *Education:* Studied at the Kolozsvar Academy, Budapest. *Career:* Played the Dvořák Concerto at Weimar 1981, with the Jena Philharmonic and is soloist with the Concentus Hungaricus and Budapest Festival Orchestra; Soloist and Chamber Musician in USA, Mexico, South Korea and throughout Europe; Recitals and recordings with pianist Denes Varjon. *Recordings:* Albums for Electrecord, Naxos and Hungaroton. *Address:* World-wide Artists, 6 Petersfield Crescent, Coulsdon, Surrey CR5 2JQ, England.

SZALONEK, Witold (Jozef); Composer; b. 2 March 1927, Czechowice, Poland; m. Beata Zygmunt, 23 April 1963, 2 s. *Education:* Diploma of Music, Lyceum Katowice, 1949; Diploma with Distinction, MA, Composition, High School of Music, Katowice, 1956; Studied with Nadia Boulanger in Paris, 1962–63. *Career:* Debut: Katowice in 1954; Assistant at High School of Music, Katowice, Poland, 1956–61; Adjunct Professor, 1961–67, Profesor of Composition, 1967–75, Rector, 1972–73; Professor of Composition and Theory, High School of Arts, Berlin West, 1973–; Lecturer at universities and high schools of music in Munster, Osnabruck, Heidelberg, Mannheim, Arhus, Helsinki, Graz, Kraków, Warsaw, Jyväskylä and Turku; Lecturer, Viitasaari. *Compositions include:* Pastorale for oboe and orchestra; Symphonic Satire; Les Sons for orchestra; Musica Concertante for double bass and orchestra;

Confessions for speaker, choir and orchestra; Sonata for cello and piano; Proporzioni l for flute, viola and harp; ++++ for 1–4 Instruments ad Arco; Connections for chamber ensemble; DP's Five Ghoulish Dreams for saxophone; Alice's Unknown Adventures In The Fairy Land Of Percussion; Nocturne for baritone, harp and string orchestra; Elegy for clarinet and piano; Litany for choir, 1996; Three preludes for piano, 1996; Chaconne-Fantasie for violin, 1997; Pegasus and Medusa for flute and french horn, 1997; Miserere for 12 voice choir, 1997; Three Obereks for guitar, 1998; Bagattellae di Dahlem for flute and piano, 1998 Berceuse for Celesta for piano, 1998; Hautbois mon amour for oboe and orchestra, 1999. *Recordings:* Mutanza for Piano; Improvisations Sonoristiques for Clarinet, Trombone, Cello and Piano; Piernikiana for Tuba Solo; Concertino for Flute; Les Sons; Mutazioni for Orchestra; Musica Concertante for Double Bass and Orchestra; Little B-A-C-H Symphony for Orchestra; Connections; O Pleasant Earth, cantata for Voice and Orchestra. *Honours:* Doctor honoris causa Wilhelmsuniversität, Münster, Germany, 1990; Award of the Composers Society for the Year, 1994. *Address:* Hittorfstr 12, 14195 Berlin, Germany.

SZE, Jean Yi-Ching; Composer and Zheng Performer; b. 14 May 1956, Shanghai, People's Republic of China. *Education:* graduate, Shanghai Conservatory of Music 1984; BA, College of St Elizabeth, USA, 1988; MA, Virginia Tech, USA, 1992. *Career:* also organic chemist; mem. American Music Center, American Society of Composers, Authors and Publishers, American Chemical Society. *Compositions:* Shi, string quartet; Mountain, electric violin, zheng, bamboo flute; Autumn, string orchestra, with bamboo flute; Flute Solo; Eastern View and Tradition Suite, violin and zheng; A Spring Morning at Miao Mountain, bamboo flute and zheng; Three Poems of Tang Dynasty, soprano, bamboo flute, yang qing, zheng, ban hu and pipa; The Sword and the Silk, 2000; The Pearl and the Thread, 2001; Nature for violin and piano, 2003. *Honours:* Second Prize, Shanghai National Music Competition 1983. *Address:* 13 Joann Court, Monmouth Junction, NJ 08852, USA.

SZEGEDI, Aniko; Pianist; b. 22 March 1938, Budapest, Hungary; m. J Szavai, 20 Dec 1966, 1 d. *Education:* F Liszt Academy of Music, Budapest. *Career:* Debut: Piano Concerto, Chopin, Budapest Academy of Music, 1961; Concerts include: Budapest, 1966, Vienna Brahms Saal, 1969; Leningrad, Kiev, 1974, Dresden, London, 1974, Berlin, 1983. *Recordings:* Beethoven, Eroica Variations; Haydn, Sonatas, Beethoven, Piano Concerto, Triple Concerto (with D Koracs and M Pereuy). *Honours:* 3rd Prize, International Schumann Piano Concerts, Zwickau, 1963; F Liszt Prize, Budapest, 1973. *Address:* Szt Istvan krt 16, 1137 Budapest, Hungary.

SZEGHY, Iris; Composer; b. 5 March 1956, Presov, Czechoslovakia; m. Pedro Zimmermann. *Education:* Composition and piano, Conservatory, Kosice, 1971–76; Composition, 1976–81, ArtD, Music, 1986–89, Acad., Bratislava. *Career:* Resident Composer, Akad. Schloss Solitude, Stuttgart, 1992–93; Visiting Composer, Univ. of California, San Diego, 1994; Composer-in-Residence, Hamburg State Opera, 1995, Kunstlerhauser Worpswede, 1999; several portrait concerts, Hamburg, San Diego, Stuttgart, Bremen; participation in many festivals of music; Composer-in-Residence, Künstlerhaus Boswil, Switzerland, 2001, Künstler Wohnung Stein am Rhun, Switzerland, 2002. *Compositions:* Concerto for violoncello and orchestra, 1989; Homewards for symphony orchestra, 1997; De Profundis for voice and 2 melodic instruments, 1990; Midsummer Night's Mystery for 2 percussionists, 1992; Musica folklorica for clarinet, percussion and piano, 1996; Tableaux d'un parc for chamber ensemble, 2000; Pro Helvetia Zürich, 2001; for Künstlerhaus Boswil, 2003; Vielleicht, dass uns etwas aufginge, for soprano and string orchestra, 2003. *Recordings:* broadcasts on Slovak radio stations in Bratislava, Kosice, and Radio Bremen, SWR Stuttgart, MDR Leipzig; albums: Music Fund; Opus; Portrait, 2001. *Honours:* several composition scholarships. *Address:* Nürenbergstrasse 17, 8037 Zürich, Switzerland.

SZEMZO, Tibor; Composer and Performer; b. 7 Feb. 1955, Budapest, Hungary. *Education:* Budapest Academy. *Career:* Composes diverse groups; Performs with quartet, Group 180; Solo performances; Ensemble, The Gordian Knot, 1998; Written 12 records; Written works for films; Performed: Contemporary Music Week, Budapest, 1981–; Autumn Festival, Paris, 1982; Steyerischer Herbst, Austria; New Music America, Houston, 1986; Donaufest, St Polten, 1988; Dokumenta, Kassel; Wiener Festwochen, 1988; Ars Electronica, Linz, 1988 and 1989; Urban Aboriginal Festival, Berlin, 1992; NIPAF, Nagano, 1993; Music Now from Hungaary, Yoahama, 1994; Warsaw Autumn Festival, Poland, 1995; Unsung Music, 1996; Izumiwaka '96, Tokyo; Zona Europa de Est, 1996; Romania Literatur Im Marz, Vienna and other countries. *Recordings:* Water Wonder, 1983; Snapshot From the Island, 1987; Private Exits, 1989; Meteo/The Dreams of Eckermann, 1990; Sub-Carpathia, 1981; Ain't Nothing But a Little Bit of Music for Moving Pictures, 1992;; The Conscience/Narrative Chamber Pieces, 1993; Duo, 1984; The Last Hungarian PVC, 1994; The Sex Appeal of Death/Airy

Wedding, 1994; Tractatus, 1995; Symultan, 1997; Relative Things, 1998. *Address:* 2093 Budajeny, Kossuth Str 43, Hungary.

SZETO, Caroline; Composer; b. 15 Sept. 1956, Australia. *Education:* BMus (Hons) 1988, MMus (Hons) 1994, University of Sydney; Study with Peter Sculthorpe, from 1985. *Career:* University of Sydney, 1990–91; Commissions from ABC, 1991, Sydney Metropolitan Opera, 1993, Song Company 1994, 1997; Sydney Mandolins, 1995, 1997; Commissions from Bernadette Balkus and Michael Kieran Harvey, 1999. *Compositions include:* Three Pieces for Guitar, 1984; Catalogue for string quartet, 1985; C.C. 33 for concert band, 1985; Sheng for orchestra, 1986; Images of Li Po for ensemble, 1987; Missa Brevis, 1987; Energy for orchestra, 1990; Study No. 1 and 2 for tuba, 1990; Moon on Night's Water for piano, 1990; Lament of the Boobook for computer-based instruments, 1991; Yunny's Treat, for piano, 1991; ABC Fanfare for orchestra, 1992; In A Garden for computer-based instruments, 1992; A Game For Violin, 1992; The Third Station of the Cross for clarinet, double bass and percussion, 1993; The Sweet Apple, for 6 vocal soloists, 1994; Energy II for orchestra, 1994; Mandolin Dance, 1995; Prelude for mandolin ensemble, 1997; Monkeys Cry for 6 vocal soloists and 2 percussionists, 1997; Cycles for guitar, 1997; Mandolin Concerto, 1998–99; Buffo for bassoon and piano, 1998; Toccata for two pianos, 1999; Cello Dance for cello and piano, 1999; Impulse, for oboe, clarinet, French horn and bassoon, 2000. *Recordings:* Yunny's Treat, 1993; Mandolin Dance, 1996; Energy for Orchestra, 1997; ABC Fanfare for Orchestra, 1997; Moon on Night's water, 1998; Prelude, 1999. *Honours:* Ignaz Friedman Memorial Prize, 1985; Donald Peart Memorial Prize, 1986; 2 First Prizes, City of Sydney Eisteddfod, 1991; Composer Fellowship, Australia Council for the Arts, 1994. *Address:* PO Box 163, Mosman, NSW 2088, Australia.

SZEVERENYI, Ilona; Music Professor and Dulcimer Player; b. 12 Aug. 1946, Gyula, Hungary; m. Ferenc Gerencser, 25 Mar 1967. *Education:* Studied with Ferenc Gerencser, Liszt Ferenc Academy of Music, Budapest, graduating 1968. *Career:* Regular concerts as Soloist and with her chamber orchestras, Hungary and throughout Europe, 1968–; Founder, dulcimer duo, 1972; Numerous recitals, France, Germany, Italy; Premieres of more than 70 works including 3 concertos by contemporary composers; With her students founded Pantaleon, ensemble for 4 dulcimers, 1996; Teaching, Béla Bart ók Music Secondary School, 1986–, Liszt Ferenc Academy of Music, 1989–; Developed curriculum for low, medium and advanced levels of dulcimer instruction. *Compositions:* Several published compositions for dulcimer. *Recordings include:* Pieces for 2 dulcimers, 1980; Contemporary works for dulcimer solo, 1986; CD with selection from J. S. Bach's pieces arranged for dulcimer solo, 1995; Lachrymae, a CD featuring the music of J. Dowland, S.L. Weiss and J.S.Bach's solo works, Hungarton, 2003; Participant in records of 10 composers. *Publications:* Co-author, Cimbalon Tutor, 1982; Publications in field of music education. *Contributions:* Parlando music journal. *Address:* Krecsanyi utca 12, 1025 Budapest, Hungary.

SZIGETI, István; Composer; b. 16 Oct. 1952, Budapest, Hungary; Orsolya Srauleno, 2 d. *Education:* Béla Bart ók Conservatory, Budapest, study with Miklós Kocsár and Sándor Szokolay; Electro-acoustic music with Zoltán Pongrácz at Ferenc Liszt Academy of Music. *Career:* Worked for Hungarian Radio, 1975–; Musical Editor, 1982–; Artistic Director, Electro-acoustic Music Studio, Hungarian Radio HEAR Studio, 1994; Head of Young Composers Group, Budapest, 1986–89; Presidium, Hungarian Composer's Union. *Compositions include:* Souvenir de K, 1981; Elka. *Honours:* Special Prize, International Composers Competition, GMEB Electro-acoustic Music Centre, Bourges; Kodály Scholarship, 1984; Lajtha Prize, 1999. *Address:* Hungarian Radio, 1800 Budapest, Hungary.

SZILAGYI, Karoly; Singer (Baritone); b. 1949, Oradea Mare, Romania. *Education:* Studied at the Cluj Conservatory. *Career:* Sang Morales and Rigoletto at the Cluj Opera, then engaged at the Gelsenkirchen Opera 1980–85, Essen 1985–89; Guest appearances at the Vienna Staatsoper, Zürich Opera and St Gallen and throughout Germany, Hungary and Austria; Liège 1990, as Rigoletto; Also sings in operas by Donizetti and Puccini; Sang Coppelius in Les Contes d'Hoffmann at Essen, 1996; Sang Verdi's Miller at Essen, 2001. *Address:* c/o Essen Opera, Theater Essen, Rolandstrasse 10, W-4300 Essen 1, Germany.

SZIRMAY, Marta; Singer (Mezzo-Soprano); b. 1939, Kaposvar, Hungary. *Education:* Studied at the Budapest Conservatory. *Career:* Member of the Hungarian State Opera from 1964 singing the mezzo repertory in operas by Wagner and Verdi, and Cologne Opera from 1976; Covent Garden debut in 1977 as Clytemnestra in Elektra with later London appearances as Erda in Das Rheingold and Mistress Quickly in Falstaff; Further appearances in Hamburg, Berlin, Vienna, Barcelona, Venice and Naples; Sang at Salzburg Festival in 1985 as Ericles in Il Ritorno d'Ulisse by Monteverdi, arranged by Henze; Other roles include Gaea in Daphne, Gluck's Orpheus and Brangaene in Tristan and Isolde; Season

1992 in Corghi's Blimunda at Turin. *Address:* c/o Teatro Region di Turino, Piazza Castello 215, 10124 Turin, Italy.

SZMYTKA, Elzbieta; Singer (Soprano); b. 1956, Prochowice, Poland. *Education:* Studied in Kraków, 1975–82 with Helena Lazarska. *Career:* Sang at the Kraków Opera from 1978 then at Bytom and Wroclaw; Toured to West Germany and Luxembourg as Blondchen in Die Entführung; Sang widely in Western Europe from 1983 notably at Ghent, Antwerp and Brussels as Despina, Blondchen and Serpina, and as Nannetta, 1987–88; Sang at Aix-en-Provence Festival, 1987–88 as Nannetta and as Servilia in La Clemenza di Tito, Holland Festival in 1987 as Serpina in La Finta Giardiniera, at the Vienna Staatsoper in 1988 as Papagena, and in Amsterdam and Antwerp in 1989 as Gilda and Zerbinetta; Sang at Glyndebourne Festival in 1991 as Ilia in Idomeneo and Servilia in La Clemenza di Tito, Salzburg Summer Festival in 1992 as Alyeya in From the House of the Dead and Mozartwoche in 1993 as Cinna in Lucio Silla; Sang Vitellia in Gluck's La Clemenza di Tito at the Théâtre des Champs-Elysées, Paris, 1996; Other roles include Susanna, Norina and Aennchen in Der Freischütz; Engaged for Mozart's Lucio Silla and Entführung at the 1997 Salzburg Festival; Season 1999–2000 as Mozart's Elettra at Lyon, Mélisande in Toronto and Donna Anna for the Berlin Staatsoper. *Recordings include:* La Finta Giardiniera; Despina in Così fan tutte; Mozart Arias; Die Entführung; Il Matrimonio Segreto; Music by Szymanowski conducted by Simon Rattle.. *Address:* c/o PG & PM, 7 Whitehorse Close, Royal Mile, Edinburgh, EH8 8BU, England.

SZOKOLAY, Sándor; Composer; b. 30 March 1931, Kunágota, Hungary; m. (1) Sari Szesztay, 1952, (2) Maja Weltler, 1970, 4 s., 1 d. *Education:* Studied with Szabo and Farkas at the Budapest Music Academy, 1950–57; Composition department graduate in 1957. *Career:* Music teacher, Budapest Conservatory, 1952–55; Musical Adviser and Editor at Hungarian Radio, 1955–59; Composition Teacher at Budapest Music Academy, 1959–66; Musical Adviser for Hungarian television, 1966–; mem, Chairman of Hungarian Kodály Society. *Compositions:* Dramatic: The Ballad of Horror, ballet, 1961, Blood Wedding, opera, 1964, Hamlet, opera, 1968, Sacrifice, ballet, 1973, Ecce Homo, passion-opera, 1987; Margaret, Victim Sacrificed for the Country, opera, 1996; Savitri, opera, 1999; Orchestral: Concert Rondo for Piano and Strings, 1955, Violin Concerto, 1956, Piano Concerto, 1958, Trumpet Concerto, 1969, Oratorios, The Fire of March, 1958 and Isthar's Descent Into Hell, 1960, Negro Cantata, 1962, Deploration, Requiem in Memory of Poulenc, 1964, The Power of Music, choral fantasy with orchestra; Chamber: Sonata for Solo Violin, 1956, String Quartet, 1973. *Honours:* Erkel Prize, 1960, 1965; Kossuth Prize, 1966; Paris International Dance Festival Golden Star Prize for Best Composition, 1967; Merited Artist, 1976; Honoured Artist, 1986; Bart ók-Pasztory Prize, 1987. *Current Management:* Martin Perdoux, 5014 Chaparral Way, San Diego, CA 92115, USA.

SZÖLLÖSY, Andras; Composer and Music Historian; b. 27 Feb. 1921, Szaszvaros, Transylvania; m. Eva Kemenyfy. *Education:* Academy of Music, Budapest with Kodály, 1939–44; Accademia di Santa Cecilia, Rome, with Petrassi, 1947–48; PhD, University of Budapest. *Career:* Academy of Music Budapest from 1950. *Compositions:* Ballets: Improvisations on the Fear 1963, Pantomime 1965; Sons of Fire 1977; Orchestral: Concerto for piano, brass, percussion and strings, 1957; Concerto for Strings, 1968; Trasfigurazioni, 1972; Musica concertante, 1973; Musica per orchestra, 1973; Sonorita, 1974; Concerto for harpsichord and strings, 1978; Tristia (Maros Sirato) for Strings, 1983; Concerto No. V (Lehellet), 1975; Chamber Music: Pro Somno Igoris Stravinsky Quieto for small ensemble, 1978; Fragments for Mezzo-soprano, flute and viola; Suoni di tromba for trumpet and piano, 1983; Musiche per ottoni for brass instruments, 1983; Quartetto di tromboni, 1986; Quartetto per archi, 1988; Elegy (dixtuor), 1992; Passacaglia, Achatio Mathe in Memoriam for string quartet and cello solo, 1997; Addio for Violin solo and Strings, 2003; Choral Works: Fabula Phaedri, 1982; In Phariaeos, 1981; Plactus Mariae, 1982; Miserere, 1984. *Publications:* Arthur Honegger 1960, 1980; Editor of various writings by Bartók and Kodály; Critical edition of Bartók's writings, 1967. *Honours:* First Prize, UNESCO International Rostrum of Composers, Paris, 1970; Kossuth Prize, 1985; Bart ók-Pasztory Prix, 1986, 1998; Commendeur de L'Ordre des Arts et Lettres, 1987. *Address:* Somloi ut 12, 1118 Budapest, Hungary.

SZONYI, Erzsebet; Composer and Music Educator; b. 25 April 1924, Budapest, Hungary. *Education:* Budapest Music Academy, 1942–47; Paris Conservatoire, 1948 with Aubin, Messiaen and Nadia Boulanger. *Career:* Teacher of Music Education at Budapest Music Academy, 1948–81, prompted the Kodály Method in Hungary and elsewhere. *Compositions include:* Operas: Dalma, 1953, The Florentine Tragedy, Meiningen, 1960, Le Malade Imaginaire, Budapest, 1961, Joyful Lament, Budapest, 1980, Break In Transmission, Szeged, 1982, Elfrida, 1985; Other: 2 Piano Sonatinas, 1944 and 1946; 2 Divertimentos, 1948 and 1951; Piano Sonata, 1953; Organ Concerto, 1958; Trio for Oboe,

Clarinet and Bassoon, 1958; Musica Festiva for Orchestra, 1964; 3 Ideas In 4 Movements for Piano and Orchestra, 1980; Sonata for Double Bass and Piano, 1982; Evocatio for Piano and Organ, 1985; Choral works. *Publications include:* Methods of Musical Reading and Writing, 4 vols, Budapest, 1953–65, English translation, 1972; Study of Kodály's Teaching Methods, Budapest, 1973. *Honours:* Erkel Prize, 1959; Award of the Hungarian Republic, 1993; Apáuzai Csere János Prize, 1994; Bartók-Pásztory Prize, 1995; Order of Excellent Artist, 2000; Pro Renovanda Culturae Hungariae, Kodály Prize, 2001. *Address:* c/o Artisjus, Mészárosu 15-17, 1539 Budapest 114, PO Box 593, Hungary.

SZÖRENYI, Suzana; Pianist and Lecturer; b. 23 Oct. 1929, Bucharest, Romania; m. Corneliu Radulescu, 26 Sept 1968 (divorced). *Education:* Diploma, C Porumbescu Bucharest National University of Music1954; Piano Studies with Dusi Mura and Music Forms with Tudor Ciortea. *Career:* Debut: Recital, Romanian Atheneum, Bucharest, 1946; Professor by the Music Academy, Bucharest; Soloist, Symphony Concertos, Piano Solo Recitals, Piano Duets, Lieder, Chamber Music, Tours abroad; Recordings for Romanian Broadcasting, from Romanian and Universal repertoire; Premieres of recorded and stage performances of Romanian music by George Enescu, Constantin Silvestri, Hilda Jerea, Dan Constantinescu, and others; Premieres of works by Beethoven, Brahms, Schumann and Mendelssohn in Romania; Television films with famous pages of the pianistic literature; Participation in George Enescu International Festival, Bucharest–11th Edition, September 1988; Tour abroad: Germany and Switzerland, with Cornelia Binonzetti (violin), 1991; Also to Austria, 1996; Participation in the Gala, first EPTA Congress in Romania, Constanto, 1992; Interpretation of Nietzsche's works; Lieder, violin, piano and four hands works; Participation as accompanist at several international contests with singers and instrumentalists in France, Switzerland, Poland, Hungaria, Russia, Czech Republic and Romania; Participation as soloist with the G. Enescue Philharmonie Orchestra in the opening concert of the International Piano Competition and Festival, Dinu Lipattis, in Bucharest, 1995. *Recordings:* Lieder by Brahms with Marta Kessler; Romanian Lieder with Emilia Petrecu; Romanian Dances for two Pianos by Dinu Lipatti with Hilda Jerea; Beethoven's complete works for piano–four hands; Symphony Concertante for Two Pianos and String Orchestra by Dinu Lipatti, and George Enescu's works for piano–four hands with Corneliu Radulescu; Original four-hands works by Brahms, Schumann, Mendelssohn-Bartholdy and Max Reger (with Corneliu Radulescu). *Contributions:* Musica Revue; Elore, Newspapers. *Honours:* A life dedicate to music award from the M.Jora society of Music Critics, 2000. *Current Management:* Academia de Muzica Bucuresti, Str Stirbei Voda 33, Romania. *Address:* Colentina 37-VI/26, 72.245 Bucharest 10, Romania.

SZOSTTEK-RADKOVA, Krystina; Singer (Mezzo-Soprano); b. 14 March 1933, Katowice, Poland. *Education:* Studied at the Katowice Conservatory with Faryaszevska and Lenczevska. *Career:* Debut: Katowice in 1960 as Azucena in Il Trovatore; National Opera Warsaw from 1962 as Eboli, Amneris, Ortrud, Kundry and other roles in the dramatic mezzo repertory; Guest engagements in Vienna, Hamburg, Berlin, Prague, Sofia, Belgrade, Moscow and Leningrad; Sang at Paris Opéra in 1981 as Ulrica in Un Ballo in Maschera, Grand Théâtre, Geneva, in 1983 as Herodias in Salome and appeared at the Théâtre de la Monnaie, Brussels, and the Opéra de Lyon in operas by Verdi and Wagner; Sang Fricka in The Ring at Warsaw in 1988; Concert tours of France and South America. *Recordings:* Many opera albums and works by Penderecki and Tadeusz Baird. *Address:* Teatr Wiekli, Plac Teatrainy, 00-076 Warsaw, Poland.

SZUCS, Marta; Singer (Soprano); b. 1964, Hungary. *Education:* Studied violin at first, then singing in Budapest. *Career:* Sang in concert in Hungary and abroad, 1976–78; Guest appearances at Hamburg Staatsoper and Frankfurt from 1979; Member of the Hungarian National Opera from 1981 with debut as Gilda; Further engagements at Vienna Staatsoper, La Traviata's Violetta, 1985–87, Scottish Opera as Gilda in 1984 and Anna in Anna Bolena in 1989, Liège, 1986–87 as Lucia di Lammermoor, and Monte Carlo in 1988 in Cimarosa's Il Pittore Parigino; Sang Anaide in Moïse et Pharaon by Rossini at Budapest in 1992. *Address:* c/o Hungarian State Opera House, Nepoztarsasag utja 22, 1061 Budapest, Hungary.

SZYMAŃSKI, Paweł; Composer; b. 28 March 1954, Warsaw, Poland. *Education:* Warsaw Acad. of Music with Tadeusz Baird; Vienna with Roman Haubenstock-Ramati. *Compositions:* String quartet 1975, Partitas I–IV for orchestra 1977–86, Gloria, for female chorus and orchestra 1979, 10 Pieces, for sting trio 1979, La folia, tape 1979, Appendix, for ensemble 1983, Lux Aeterna, for chorus and ensemble 1984, Trope, for piano 1986, Through the Looking Glass I and II for chamber orchestra 1987, 1994, III for harpsichord and string quartet 1995, A Study of Shade, for chamber orchestra 1989, Quasi una Sinfonietta 1990, Miserere, for male voices and ensemble 1993, Piano Concerto 1994, Sonata for piano 1995, Recalling a Serenade, for clarinet and string quartet 1996, Muzyska filmowa 1996. *Address:* c/o ZAiKS, 2 Hipoteczna Street, 00 092 Warsaw, Poland. *Telephone:* (4822) 828 17 05. *Fax:* (4822) 828 13 47. *E-mail:* sekretariat@zaiks.org.pl. *Website:* www .zaiks.org.pl.

TABACHNIK, Michel; Conductor and Composer; b. 10 Nov. 1942, Geneva, Switzerland; m. Sabine Tabachnik, 24 June 1981, 2 s., 1 d. *Education:* Piano, Conducting, Writing, Composition; Assistant of Markevitch and Boulez. *Career:* Debut: BBC, London; National Orchestra, Paris; Berlin Philharmonic; Conducting all major orchestras including: NHK Tokyo; Orchestre de Paris; Israel Philharmonic; Berlin Philharmonic; Philharmonic, London; St Cecilia, Rome; Suisse Romande, Geneva; Concertgebouw, Amsterdam. *Compositions:* Cosmogonie for orchestra; Haisha for choir and orchestra; Le Pacte des Onze for choir and orchestra; L'Arch for soprano and orchestra; Concerto for Piano; Quatuor; Les Perseides for orchestra. *Recordings:* Schumann, Grieg, Lalo, Saint-Saëns; Xenakis. *Address:* 1985 Villaz-La Sage, Switzerland.

TABAKOV, Emil; Conductor and Composer; b. 1947, Bulgaria. *Education:* Bulgarian State Conservatory, degree in conducting, composition and double bass. *Career:* Founded and conducted the Bulgarian State Conservatoire Chamber Orchestra of Sofia, 1977; Director of the Sofia Soloists Chamber Orchestra, 1979–, touring Bulgaria, Europe, Asia, Latin America, Australia and the USA; Principal Conductor of the Sofia Philharmonic Orchestra, 1985 with tours of the USA, Japan, Hong Kong, South America and the United Kingdom; Guest Conductor in Denmark, Sweden, Germany, Poland, Brazil, Romania, Greece and France; Conducted The Queen of Spades at Turin, 1998. *Compositions:* Concerto for Double Bass and Orchestra; Turnovgrad Velki; 1393 Cantata; Concerto for Percussion; Three Symphonies. *Recordings:* Mozart, The Complete Church Sonatas; Works by JS Bach, Handel, Haydn, Mendelssohn, Shostakovich, Britten and Schoenberg (with the Sofia Soloists); Complete Symphonies of Mahler, Rachmaninov and Bruckner (with the Sofia Philharmonic Orchestra). *Honours:* Prizewinner, Nikolai Malko International Competition for Young Conductors, Copenhagen, 1977. *Address:* c/o Teatro Regio di Torino, Piazzo Castello 215, 10134 Turin, Italy.

TACHEZI, Herbert; Organist, Harpsichordist and Composer; b. 12 Feb. 1930, Wiener Neustadt, Austria. *Education:* Vienna Music Academy. *Career:* Teacher at Vienna Secondary Schools, 1952–67; Vienna Academy 1958, Professor from 1972; Performances with the Vienna Soloists and Solisti di Zagreb, from 1960; Keyboard soloist with the Concentus Musicus, 1964–; Organist of the Vienna Hofmusikkapelle, 1974; Concert tours throughout Europe and in the USA. *Compositions:* Sacred vocal music, keyboard works, chamber and orchestral music. *Recordings include:* Handel Organ Concertos; Organ works by J. S. and C. P. E Bach. *Honours:* Theodor Körner Prize, Vienna, 1965. *Address:* c/o AKM, Baumannstrasse 10, 1031 Wien, Postfach 259, Austria. *Telephone:* 00431 717 140. *Fax:* 00431 717 14107.

TACUCHIAN, Ricardo; Composer and Conductor; b. 18 Nov. 1939, Rio de Janeiro, Brazil; m. Maria de Fátima G. Tacuchian, 2 s. *Education:* Bachelor in Piano, Universidade do Brasil, 1961; Bachelor in Composition and Conducting, Universidade Federal do Rio de Janeiro, 1965; Postgraduate studies in Conducting, 1965, Postgraduate studies in Composition, 1966, Universidade Federal do Rio de Janeiro; Doctor of Musical Arts in Composition, University of Southern California, USA, 1990. *Career:* Composer and Conductor; Titular Professor UFRJ, Retired in 1995; Titular Professor, UNIRIO, 1995–; Visiting Professor, State University of New York at Albany, 1998, Universidade Nova de Lisboa, 2002–3; Pro-Reitor of UNIRIO, 1999–2000, Titular Conductor, UNIRIO Chamber Orchestra, 2002–04; Life mem., Brazilian Music Acad., 1981. *Compositions:* More than 150 works among symphonic pieces, cantatas, chamber music, instrumental soli and tape music. *Publications:* O Requiem Mozartiano de José Maurício, Revista Brasileira de Música 19, 1991; Estrutura e Estilo na Obra de Béla Bartók. Revista Brasileira de Música, v. 21 (1994–95), 1–17; Música pós-moderna no final do século; Pesquisa e Música, No. 2 (1995), 25–40; Fundamentos Teóricos do Sistema-T; Debates: Cadernos do Programa de Pós-graduação em Música, 1, 1997, 45–68. *Contributions:* More than 60 papers published in Brazilian music journals. *Address:* Rua Carlos Góis 327, ap. 702, 22440-040 Rio de Janeiro, RJ, Brazil. *E-mail:* rtacuchi@cybernet.com.br.

TADDEI, Giuseppe; Singer (Baritone); b. 26 June 1916, Genoa, Italy. *Education:* Studied in Rome. *Career:* Debut: Rome in 1936 as The Herald in Lohengrin; Sang in Rome until 1942 as Alberich and Germont and in Dallapiccola's Volo di Notte; Sang at Vienna Staatsoper, 1946–48 as Amonasro, Rigoletto and the Figaros of Mozart and Rossini, Cambridge Theatre in London, 1947, as Scarpia and Rigoletto, Salzburg Festival in 1948 as Mozart's Figaro, and La Scala, 1948–61 as Malatesta, the villains in Les Contes d'Hoffmann and Pizarro; Sang Wagner's Dutchman, Gunther and Wolfram elsewhere in Italy, and Mozart's Papageno and Leporello; US debut at San Francisco in 1957 as Macbeth; Sang at Chicago in 1959 as Barnaba, Teatro Masimo Palermo in 1959 in Beatrice di Tenda by Bellini and Covent Garden, 1960–67, as Macbeth, Rigoletto, Iago and Scarpia; Sang at Bregenz Festival, 1968–71, as Falstaff, Dulcamara and Suplice in La Fille du Régiment, Vienna Staatsoper in 1980 in Il Tabarro, Metropolitan Opera debut in 1985 as Falstaff, Vienna Staatsoper in 1986 as Scarpia, to celebrate 70th birthday, and sang Gianni Schicchi at Torre del Lago in 1987; Appeared at Stuttgart Staatsoper in 1990 as Falstaff. *Recordings:* La Bohème; Ernani; Un Ballo in Maschera; Guillaume Tell; Rigoletto; Falstaff; Don Giovanni; Il Maestro di Capella; Andrea Chénier; Le nozze di Figaro; Così fan tutte; L'Elisir d'amore; Mosè in Egitto; Linda di Chamounix; Falstaff; Tosca; Macbeth. *Address:* c/o Staatstheater Stuttgart, Oberer Schlossgarten 6, 7000 Stuttgart 1, Germany.

TADDEI, Ottavio; Singer (tenor); b. 15 July 1926, Tuscany, Italy. *Education:* Studied in Siena. *Career:* Debut: Sienna, as Rodolfo in La Bohème, 1953; Sang the Duke of Mantua and Edgardo at Rome, 1954; Appearances at Milan, Florence, Modena and San Jose in Costa Rica; Teatro San Carlo, Naples, 1959, as Mateo in Conchita by Zandonai; Sang at Teatro Comunale in Florence from 1960, and made tours of the Netherlands, Turkey and England; Many broadcasts for Italian radio, RAI including The Queen of Spades in 1963; Sang in Hamburg, Nuremberg and Frankfurt from 1966 notably as Pinkerton; Sang in Monteverdi's Poppea at Rome, 1966. *Address:* Teatro Comunale di Firenze, Via Solferino 15, 50123 Florence, Italy.

TADEO, Giorgio; Singer (Bass); b. 2 Oct. 1929, Verona, Italy. *Education:* Studied in Parma with Ettore Campogalliani and at the Opera School of La Scala, Milan. *Career:* Debut: Palermo in 1953 as Mephistopheles in Faust; Sang at Turin, Rome, Florence and Trieste as well as La Scala; Sang at Verona Arena in 1955 and 1973–74; Covent Garden debut in 1974 as Don Pasquale; Further engagements at Buenos Aires, Mexico City, Dallas, Chicago, Paris and Salzburg. *Recordings include:* Tosca; Andrea Chénier conducted by Chailly; Leonore by Paer; Antonio in Le nozze di Figaro; Manon Lescaut.

TAGLIASACCI, Monica; Singer (Mezzo-soprano); b. 1959, Turin, Italy. *Education:* Studied in Venice. *Career:* Sang in Rossini's Tancredi at Turin and at La Scala in Rossini's Il Viaggio a Reims, I Lombardi and Die Frau ohne Schatten; Suzuki in Butterfly at Ravenna, Verona and Zürich; Guest appearances at the Vienna Staatsoper in L'Italiana in Algeri, at Philadelphia as Dorabella and at Florence as Pantalis in Boito's Mefistofele; Bayerische Staatsoper at Munich, 1991–91; Sang Teresa in La Sonnambula at Rome, 1996. *Address:* c/o Bavarian State Opera, Max Joseph Platz, Pf 100148, 8000 Munich 1, Germany.

TAGLIAVINI, Franco; Singer (Tenor); b. 29 Oct. 1934, Novellara, Reggio Emilia, Italy. *Education:* Studied at Liceo Musicale Vercelli and with Zita Fumagalli-Riva. *Career:* Debut: Teatro Nuovo Milan in 1961 as Canio in Pagliacci; Bologna in 1962 as Pinkerton; Sang Edgardo in Lucia di Lammermoor at Tunisia, and at Rome Opera as Dmitri in Boris Godunov, Cavaradossi and Lensky; US debut in 1964 as Ismaele in Nabucco and Calaf in Turandot at San Francisco; Sang Alfredo for Dallas Opera in 1965; La Scala debut in 1965 in Mosè by Rossini; Sang at Royal Opera House, Covent Garden, 1967–76 as Pollione, Cavaradossi, the Duke of Mantua and Macduff, and Chicago Lyric Opera, 1969–73 as Turiddu, Calaf, Pinkerton, Alfredo and Riccardo in Un Ballo in Maschera, I Due Foscari and Maria Stuarda; Appearances at the Metropolitan Opera, NY in Norma, Un Ballo in Maschera, Tosca, Vespri Siciliani and Macbeth; Guest appearances in Munich, Paris, Berlin, Vienna, Parma, Geneva, Zürich, Verona and Brussels; Other roles include Enzo in La Gioconda, Don Carlos, Don José, Des Grieux in Manon Lescaut, Paolo in Francesca da Rimini and Maurizio in Adriana Lecouvreur; Sang Rodolfo in Luisa Miller at Brussels in 1982; Retired in 1989. *Recordings include:* Te Deum by Berlioz; Madame Sans-Gêne by Giordano; Olympie by Spontini; Adriana Lecouvreur and Francesca da Rimini for Italian television.

TAGLIAVINI, Luigi (Ferdinando); Organist, Harpsichordist and Musicologist; b. 7 Oct. 1929, Bologna, Italy. *Education:* Studied at the Conservatoires of Bologna and Paris with Marcel Dupré (organ) and Riccardo Nielsen (composition); PhD, University of Padua, 1951. *Career:* Teacher of Organ, 1952–54, Librarian, 1953–60, at Martini Conservatory, Bologna; Organ Professor at the Monteverdi Conservatory, Bolzano, 1954–64; Founder and Co-editor from 1960 of L'Organo; Many concert appearances in Europe and North America playing the harpsichord and organ; Visiting Professor at Cornell University, 1963 and SUNY, Buffalo, 1969; Director of the Institute of Musicology at Fribourg University, 1965, Professor from 1971; Editor of Monumenti di Musica Italiana. *Recordings include:* Two-Organ Works with Marie-Claire Alain. *Contributions:* Neue Mozart-Ausgabe, 3 vols: Ascanio in

Alba, Betulia Liberata, Mitridate Re di Ponto; Articles in L'Organo, Musik in Gesicht und Gegenwart, Ricordi, La Musica, Larousse de la Musique.

TAHOURDIN, Peter, LTCL, MMus; Composer; b. 1928, England. *Education:* Studied composition with Richard Arnell, Trinity College of Music, London, graduated in 1952; Postgraduate studies at Toronto University, Canada, 1966–67. *Career:* Visiting Composer at University of Adelaide, 1965; Staff, Faculty of Music, University of Melbourne, 1973–88; Chairman, Composers Guild of Australia, 1978–79; mem, Australian Performing Right Association; Fellowship of Australian Composers. *Compositions:* Orchestral: Sinfonietta No. 1, 1952, No. 2, 1959, Diversions for orchestra, 1958–59, Symphony No. 1, 1960, No. 2, 1968–69, No. 3, 1979, No. 4, 1987, Fanfares And Variations, A Festival Overture, 1983; Symphony No. 5, 1994; Cello and orchestra: Sinfonia Concertante, 1966; Ensemble: Three Pieces for wind quintet, 1959, Quartet for oboe and strings, 1963, Celebration, 1979, Quartet for strings, 1982, Raga Music 3–Elision, 1988, Trio for clarinet, piano and cello, 2003; Instrumental: Sonata for clarinet and piano, 1962, Dialogue No. 1, 1971, No. 2, 1976, No. 3, 1978, No. 4, 1984, Raga Music 4 for Two, 1990, Music for solo viola, 2001, Music for solo bassoon, 2002; Piano: Capriccio, 1963; Exposé, 1995; Vocal: Raga Music 1, The Starlight Night, 1985; Choral: Seven Gnomic Verses, 1968, King Oswald's Victory, 1970; Music Theatre: Ern Malley–A Dramatic Testament, 1975–76; Stage: Inside Information, 1 act opera, 1955, Illyria, 1 act ballet, 1965; Heloise and Abelard, chamber opera in two acts, 1991; The Tempest, opera in three acts after Shakespeare, 2000; Works for tape and education works. *Recordings:* CD, Exposé: The Chamber Music of Peter Tahourdin, 1998. *Address:* c/o Australian Music Centre, PO Box N690, Grosvenor Place, New South Wales 1220, Australia.

TAÏRA, Yoshihisa; Composer; b. 3 March 1937, Tokyo, Japan. *Education:* studied in Tokyo and with Messiaen at the Paris Conservatoire. *Career:* Lecturer at Ecole Normale de Musique, Paris; music performed by the Ensemble Intercontemporain, in Tokyo and Tanglewood and throughout Europe. *Compositions:* Hierophonie II for 15 instruments, 1970, III for four flutes 1971; Stratus, for flute and harpsichord and 22 strings, 1971; Trans-Appearance for 29 instruments, 1977; Delta for chamber orchestra, 1981; Pénombres I-IV, for various instruments, 1981–91; Tourbillon for six percussions, 1984; Polydère, for orchestra, 1987; Monodrame I for percussion (1984), II for bassoon (1986), III for guitar (1988); Hexaphonie, for string sextet, 1992; Pentamorphe, wind quintet, 1993; Filigrane for flute and piano, 1994; Réminiscence flute concerto, 1998. *Honours:* Lily Boulanger Prize, 1971; Prix Florent Schmitt, 1985; Officier, Ordre des Arts et des Lettres.

TAKACS, Klara; Singer (Mezzo-Soprano); b. 24 April 1945, Hungary. *Education:* Studied at the Ferenc Liszt Academy Budapest. *Career:* Has sung at the Hungarian State Opera from 1973 notably as Orpheus, Adalgisa, Goldmark's Königin von Saba, Cenerentola and Cherubino; Guest appearances at Europe's leading opera houses and concert halls; Sang with the Vienna Staatsoper on a tour to Japan in 1986, Teatro Colón Buenos Aires in 1987 as Charlotte and as Eudossia in La Fiamma by Respighi and sang Mozart's Marcellina at the 1992 Salzburg Festival. *Recordings:* Médée by Cherubini with Sylvia Sass; Die Königin von Saba; Boito's Nerone; Hunyádi Lászlo by Erkel; Haydn's Apothecary; Mozart's Requiem; Liszt's Legend of Saint Elizabeth; Missa Solemnis by Beethoven; Mahler Lieder eines Fahrenden Gesellen; Kodály's Háry János; Sacred Music by Haydn. *Honours:* Prizewinner, Erkel International Singing Competition, Budapest, 1975; Liszt Prize Laureate; Grand Prix de L'Academie du Disque, Paris, 3 times. *Address:* c/o Hungarian State Opera, Nepoztarsasag utja 22, 1061 Budapest, Hungary.

TAKACS, Tamara; Singer (Mezzo-Soprano); b. 1950, Hungary. *Education:* Studied with Joszef Reti at the Ferenc Liszt Academy in Budapest until 1978. *Career:* Has sung at Hungarian State Opera House from 1978 as Vivaldi's Griselda, Orpheus, Mozart's 2nd Lady and Dorabella, Verdi's Azucena, Maddalena, Ulrica, Emilia, Mrs Quickly and Eboli, Wagner's Waltraute and Magdalena, Charlotte and Carmen; Sang Orzse in Kodály's Háry János in 1988; Appeared as Judit in Duke Bluebeard's Castle at Covent Garden in 1989 on a visit with the Hungarian State Opera; Season 1992 as Public Opinion in Orphée aux Enfers, at Budapest; Concert repertoire includes Purcell's Ode for St Cecilia's Day, Vivaldi's Stabat Mater, Gloria, Juditha Triumphans and Nisi Dominus, Donizetti and Verdi Requiems, Messiah and Rossini's Stabat Mater. *Recordings:* Numerous albums. *Address:* Hungarian State Opera, Nepoztarsasag utja 22, 1061 Budapest, Hungary.

TAKÁCS-NAGY, Gabor; Violinist; b. 17 April 1956, Budapest, Hungary. *Education:* Studied with András Mihaly at the Franz Liszt Academy, Budapest, with members of the Amadeus Quartet and Zoltán Szekely. *Career:* Founder member of the Takács Quartet in 1975; Many concert appearances in all major centres of Europe and USA; Tours of Australia, New Zealand, Japan, South America, England, Norway, Sweden,

Greece, Belgium and Ireland; Bartók Cycle for the Bartók-Solti Festival at South Bank, 1990; Great Performers Series at Lincoln Center and Mostly Mozart Festival at Alice Tully Hall, New York; Visits to Japan in 1989 and 1992; Mozart Festivals at South Bank, Wigmore Hall and Barbican Centre in 1991; Bartók Cycle at the Théâtre des Champs Elysées in 1991; Beethoven Cycles at the Zürich Tonhalle, in Dublin, at the Wigmore Hall and in Paris, 1991–92; Resident at the University of Colorado, and at the London Barbican, 1988–91, with masterclasses at the Guildhall School of Music; Plays Amati instrument made for the French Royal Family and loaned by the Corcoran Gallery, Gallery of Art, Washington DC. *Recordings:* Schumann Quartets Op 41; Mozart String Quintets with Denes Koromzáy; Bartók 6 Quartets; Schubert Trout Quintet with Zoltán Kocsis; Haydn Op 76; Brahms Op 51, Nos 1 and 2; Chausson Concerto with Joshua Bell and Jean-Yves Thibaudet; Works by Schubert, Mozart, Dvořák and Bartók. *Honours:* Winner, International Quartet Competition, Evian, 1977; Winner, Portsmouth International Quartet Competition, 1979. *Address:* 22 Tower Street, London WC2H 9 NS, England.

TAKEZAWA, Kyoko; Concert Violinist; b. 1977, Japan. *Education:* studied with Dorothy DeLay, Juilliard School. *Career:* concerts with Philadelphia Orchestra and Charles Dutoit, New York Philharmonic, BBC Symphony Orchestra under Andrew Davis, Leipzig Gewandhaus orchestra; and London Symphony Orchestra with Tilson Thomas. Many appearances with leading orchestras in Europe, North America and Japan; Mainly Mozart Festival, New York, 1999; Co-director of Suntory Festival Soloists of Suntory Hall, Tokyo, including collaborations with Isaac Stern (violin), Yo-Yo Ma (cello), Wolfgang Sawallisch (piano) and Josef Suk (violin); Royal Concertgebouw Orchestra, Amsterdam, with the Elgar Violin Concerto, conducted by Leonard Slatkin, 2001; Szymanowski's Violin concerto No.1 at the London Proms, 2002; Chamber music performances in Europe and North America; Juror Indianapolis Violin Compeition 2002. *Recordings include:* Elgar Concerto, with Bavaria Radio Symphony Orchestra under Colin Davis; Bartok's Second Violin Concerto with London Symphony Orchestra under Michael Tilson Thomas; both Mendelssohn Concertos, with Bamberg Symphony Orchestra under Klaus Peter Flor (RCA Victor Red Seal); Barber's Violin Concerto with the Saint Louis Symphony Orchestra under Leonard Slatkin. *Honours:* Gold Medal Second Quadrennial Int. Violin Competition 1986, Winner Indianapolis Violin Competition, Idemitsu Award for Outstanding Musicianship. *Address:* c/o IMG Artists, Lovell House, 616 Chiswick High Rd, London W4 5RX, England.

TAKOVA, Davina; Singer (soprano); b. 1968, Sofia, Bulgaria. *Career:* appearances with Sofia Opera from 1992, with guest appearances at La Scala, as the Queen of Night and Lucrezia Borgia, and the Royal Opera as Rimsky's Queen of Shemakha and Violetta 2001; Gilda at Geneva, Rome, Frankfurt and Detroit; Lucia di Lammermoor at Bergamo, Florence, Amsterdam Concertgebouw and Tel-Aviv; Teatro Real, Madrid, in revival of 1660 opera by Juan Hidalgo, Celos aun del aire matan; Violetta in Berlin, Munich, Hamburg and Verona (Arena); season 2001–02 as Pamyre in Rossini's Le Siège de Corinthe at Lyon, Bellini's Elvira at Trieste and Violetta at Geneva. *Honours:* Winner, Francisco Vinas Computation 1993, Toti del Monte Competition 1994.

TAL, Josef; Israeli composer; b. 18 Sept. 1910, Pinne, now Poland; m. 1940, one s. *Education:* Hochschule für Musik, Berlin. *Career:* Dir, Jerusalem Acad. of Music, Israel 1948–52, Centre for Electronic Music 1961; Head of Musicology Dept, Incumbent Arthur Rubinstein Cathedra, Hebrew Univ., Jerusalem 1965; mem. Berlin Acad. of Arts, 1975; hon. mem. American Acad. and Inst. of Arts and Letters. *Compositions include:* Eight Operas: Saul At Ein Dor, 1957, Ammon And Tamar, 1961, Ashmedai, 1971, Massada 967, 1973, Die Versuchung, 1976, Der Turm, 1987, Der Garten, 1988, Josef, 1993; 6 Symphonies, 6 Piano Concertos and 5 Concertos for different instruments; Requiem: The Death Of Moses; Chamber Music Works, Vocal Music, Cantatas; Psychodrama Die Hand. *Recordings:* Else, hommage; three Essays for Piano. *Publications:* Autobiography, 1984; Ars Nova in the third Millennium, 2000. *Honours:* three Engel Prizes, Tel-Aviv Municipality; Unesco Fellowship, 1957; Israel State Prize, 1971; Art Prize of the City of Berlin, 1975; Wolf Prize, 1982; Verdienstkreuz 1 Klasse, BDR, 1984; Commandeur de l'Ordre des Artes et des Lettres, France, 1985. *Address:* 3 Guatemala Street, Jerusalem 96704, Israel.

TALARICO, Rita; Singer (Soprano); b. 30 May 1941, Rome, Italy. *Education:* Studied in Rome with Gabriella Besanzoni and at the Accademia di Santa Cecilia with Maria Teresa Pediconi. *Career:* Debut: As Eleonora in Il Furioso all'Isola di San Domingo by Donizetti, at the 1967 Spoleto Festival; Has sung at leading Italian opera houses and in Lyon, Rouen, Montreal, New York and Philadelphia; Other roles include Elvira in I Puritani, Amina in La Sonnambula, Leila in Les Pêcheurs de Perles, Mimi, Violetta, Medora in Il Corsaro, Elsa, Agathe, Donna Anna, Susanna, Countess Almaviva, Marguerite, Carolina in Il Matrimonio Segreto and Margherita in Mefistofele; Sang at La Scala in 1985 in

Orfeo by Luigi Rossi. *Recordings include:* Il Furioso all'Isolo di San Domingo.

TALBOT, Michael Owen, BA, BMus, PhD, ARCM, FBA; writer; *Emeritus Professor of Music, University of Liverpool;* b. 4 Jan. 1943, Luton, Bedfordshire, England; m. Shirley Mashiane 26 Sept. 1970; one s. one d. *Education:* Royal Coll. of Music, London, Clare Coll., Cambridge. *Career:* Lecturer 1968–79, Sr Lecturer 1979–83, Reader 1983–86, James and Constance Alsop Prof. of Music 1986–2003, Emeritus Prof. of Music 2003–, Univ. of Liverpool; mem. Royal Musical Asscn, Società Italiana di Musicologia; corresponding Fellow, Ateneo Veneto. *Publications:* Vivaldi 1978, Albinoni: Leben und Werk 1980, Antonio Vivaldi: A Guide to Research 1988, Tomaso Albinoni: The Venetian Composer and his World 1990, Benedetto Vinaccesi: A Musician in Brescia and Venice in the Age of Corelli 1994, The Sacred Vocal Music of Antonio Vivaldi 1995, Venetian Music in the Age of Vivaldi 1999, The Musical Work: Reality or Invention (ed.) 2000, The Finale in Western Instrumental Music 2001, The Business of Music (ed.) 2002; contrib. to professional journals, including Early Music, Music and Letters, Music Review, Musical Times, Journal of the Royal Musical Association, Soundings, The Consort, Note d'Archivio, Händel Jahrbuch, Informazioni e Studi Vivaldiani, Studi Vivaldiani, Journal of Eighteenth Century Music. *Honours:* Cavaliere del Ordine al Merito, Italy 1980, Oldman Prize 1990, Serena Medal 1999. *Address:* c/o School of Music, The University of Liverpool, Liverpool, L69 7WW, England. *Fax:* (151) 794 3141 (office). *E-mail:* mtalbot@liv.ac.uk (office).

TALICH, Jan; Violist; b. 30 Oct. 1945, Pilzen, Czechoslovakia. *Education:* Studied at the Prague Conservatory. *Career:* Co-founded the Talich Quartet in 1961; After success in competitions at Komeriz and Belgrade gained title of Laureate by the Association of International Music Festivals in Bayreuth; Moved from leader of Talich Quartet to Violist in 1972; Appearances in Europe and North America, Egypt, Iraq, Indonesia and Japan; Annual visits to France from 1976 including the complete Beethoven quartets; Engagements with festivals and music clubs in the United Kingdom; Played at Wigmore Hall in London in 1991 with the quartets of Smetana, Beethoven's Op 74, Brahms A minor and Mozart D minor, and at Bath and Bournemouth Festivals in 1991; Played at Queen Elizabeth Hall in 1991, and Janáček's 2nd Quartet for BBC 2's The Late Show. *Recordings:* Various albums. *Address:* c/o Clarion–Seven Muses, 64 Whitehall Park, London N19 3 TN, England.

TALLEY-SCHMIDT, Eugene; Singer (Tenor) and Professor of Voice and Chairman of Voice Department, Houston Baptist University; b. 10 Feb. 1932, Rome, Georgia, USA; m. Jeanette Lombard Pecorello, 22 Nov 1960, 2 s. *Education:* San Diego State College; Indiana University; Opera Arts, Atlanta, GA; Teatro dell'Opera, Rome, Italy; Diploma, Teatro Lirico, Spoleto, Italy; Voice study with Ethel Wilkerson, Rome, GA, John Walsh and Raoul Couyas, San Diego, CA. *Career:* Debut: USA debut as Jenik in The Bartered Bride at San Diego, CA; European debut as Fritz in L'Amico Fritz at Spoleto, Italy; Leading Tenor with Deutsche Oper am Rhein, Düsseldorf, Staatsoper Hamburg, Wuppertal and Munster Operas; Sang over 50 leading tenor roles at opera houses in USA and Europe; Television and radio performances in Europe and America; Performed at international festivals and appeared with Atlanta, Birmingham, Mobile, Miami, Palm Beach, Indianapolis, Rome, and San Diego Symphony Orchestras. *Recordings:* Robert Schumann, Complete Duets for tenor and soprano. *Address:* 3506 Oyster Cove Drive, Missouri City, TX 77459, USA.

TALMI, Yoav; Conductor and Composer; b. 28 April 1943, Kibbutz Merhavia, Israel; m. Er'ella Talmi, 2 Sept 1964, 1 s., 1 d. *Education:* Diploma, Rubin Academy of Music, Tel-Aviv, 1961–65; Postgraduate Diploma, Juilliard School of Music, New York, 1965–68; Summer study courses with Walter Suskind, Aspen, 1966; Bruno Maderna, Salzburg, 1967; Jean Fournet, Hilversum, 1968; Eric Leinsdorf, Tanglewood, 1969. *Career:* Co-Conductor, Israel Chamber Orchestra, Tel-Aviv, 1970–72; Artistic Director and Conductor, Gelders Symphony Orchestra, Arnhem, 1974–80; Principal Guest Conductor, Munich Philharmonic Orchestra, 1979–80; Music Director and Principal Conductor, Israel Chamber Orchestra, 1984–88; Music Director, New Israeli Opera, 1985–89; Music Director, San Diego Symphony, USA, 1989–96; Guest Conducting with the Berlin and Munich Philharmonics, London Symphony and Philharmonia, London and Royal Philharmonics, Amsterdam's Concertgebouw, Israel and New Japan Philharmonics, Vienna Symphony, St Petersburg and Oslo Philharmonics, Tonhalle Orchestra, Zürich, Detroit, Pittsburgh, Houston, Dallas and St Louis Symphonies; Los Angeles and New York Chamber Symphonies. *Compositions:* Elegy for strings, timpani and accordion; Dreams for choir a capella; Music for flute and strings; Overture on Mexican Themes, (recorded by Louisville Orchestra); 3 monologues for flute solo, (published); Inauguration Fanfare for brass ensemble. *Recordings:* Bruckner: Symphony No. 9, Oslo Philharmonic; Tchaikovsky Symphony No.1, Quebec Symphony Orchestra; Glière Symphony No.3, San Diego; Rachmaninov's Isle of the Dead; Brahms; Sextet-4 Serious Songs, San

Diego Symphony; Tchaikovsky and Schoenberg with the Israel Chamber Orchestra; Bloch, Barber, Puccini and Grieg with the Israel Chamber Orchestra; Berlioz: Overtures; Symphonie Fantastique, Romeo and Juliet, San Diego Symphony; Harold in Italy with San Diego Symphony; Works for Flute and Piano with Erella Talmi. *Honours:* Koussevitzky Memorial Conducting Prize, Tanglewood, USA, 1969; Rupert Foundation Conductors' Competition, London, 1973; Boskovitch Prize for Composition, Israel, 1965; Ahad Ha'am Award LA Centre for Jewish Culture and the American-Israel Cultural Foundation, 1997. *Current Management:* ICM Artists Ltd, 40 W 57 Street, New York, NY 10019, USA. *Address:* PO Box 1384, Kfar Saba 44113, Israel. *E-mail:* talmi@netvision.net.il.

TALVI, Ilkka Ilari; violinist and concertmaster; b. 22 Oct. 1948, Kuusankoski, Finland; m. Marjorie Kransberg 1984; three d. *Education:* Sibelius Academy, Helsinki with Arno Granroth, Univ. of Southern California, USA with Jascha Heifetz, Curtis Institute of Music with Ivan Galamian, with Riccardo Odnoposoff in Vienna and Gabriel Bouillon in Paris. *Career:* debut with orchestra aged 10; recital debut aged 15, Helsinki; Performances as soloist and recitalist in Europe and USA; Lecturer at Sibelius Academy, Finland, 1969–75 and at Pori School of Music, 1970–76; Concertmaster with Malmö Symphony, Sweden, 1976–77; Working in motion picture business at Los Angeles, USA, 1977–85; Principal with Los Angeles Chamber Orchestra, 1979–85; Guest Concertmaster, 1983–85, Concertmaster, 1985–, Seattle Opera; Concertmaster, Waterloo Festival, New Jersey, 1988–. *Recordings include:* Klami Violin Concerto, Albert Im Concordiam. *Honours:* numerous honours and prizes in Finland. *Address:* 3456 10th Avenue W, Seattle, WA 98119, USA.

TAMAR, Iano; Singer (Soprano); b. 15 Oct. 1963, Kashbergi, Georgia. *Education:* Studied at the Tbilisi Conservatory. *Career:* Sang at the Tbilisi Opera from 1989; Best known in the title role of Rossini's Semiramide, which she has sung at the Pesaro Festival, under Alberto Zedda and at the Zürich Opera (1992); Has also sung the Rossini Stabat Mater at Dresden, Natasha in War and Peace, Mozart's Countess and Amelia (Ballo in Maschera); Sang Ottavia in Pacini's L'Ultimo giorno di Pompei, Martina Franca Festival, 1996; Lady Macbeth at Naples, 1998 and Fiordiligi at Miami; Sang Fausta in Massenet's Roma at Martina Franca, 1999; Season 2000–01 as Amelia (Ballo in Maschera) at Bregenz, Lady Macbeth for the Deutsche Oper Berlin, Donna Anna at La Coruña and Elvira in Ernani at the Vienna Staatsoper. *Address:* c/o Zürich Opernhaus, Falkenstrasse 1, 8008 Zürich, Switzerland.

TAMASSY, Eva; Singer (Contralto); b. 19 March 1937, Budapest, Hungary. *Education:* Studied with Geza Laszlo in Budapest and with Gerda Heuer and Kurt Schneider in Germany. *Career:* Debut: Hungarian State Opera in 1951 as Maddalena in Rigoletto; Sang at the Cologne Opera, Deutsche Oper am Rhein and the State Operas of Hamburg, Vienna, Munich and Stuttgart; Further engagements in Hanover, Nuremberg, Paris, Nancy, Nice, Lisbon, Bucharest, Prague, Rome, Venice, Naples and Berne; Other roles have been Carmen, Dalila, Verdi's Azucena, Amneris, Ulrica and Eboli, Wagner's Erda, Fricka, Waltraute and Brangaene, Konchakovna in Prince Igor and Marina in Boris Godunov, Mary Louise in Háry János, the Queen in Szokolay's Hamlet, and Clytemnestra in Elektra; Many concert appearances. *Address:* Caesart Str 70/A, 50968 Cologne, Germany.

TAMAYO, Arturo; Conductor; b. 3 Aug. 1946, Madrid, Spain. *Education:* Studied at the Royal Conservatoire Madrid, harmony with A Barrera, and composition with Francisco Cales and Gerardo Gombau. *Career:* Gave concerts in Spain from 1967; Studied further with Pierre Boulez at Basle and at the Musikhochschule Fribourg-in-Brisgau; Studied conducting with Franc Travis, 1971–76, and composition with Wolfgang Fortner and Klaus Huber; Assisted Huber at Fribourg from 1974 and directed concerts of contemporary music; Frequent appearances at the Deutsche Oper Berlin from 1982 notably with the 1983 premiere of Wolfgang Rihm's ballet, Tutuguri; Conducted the premiere of Kelterborn's Ophelia at the 1984 Schwetzingen Festival, and Maurice Ohana's La Celestine at the Paris Opéra in 1988; Théâtre des Champs Elysées in Paris, 1990 with the local premiere of La Noche Triste by Jean Prodomidès; Graz 1996, Busoni's Doktor Faust. *Address:* c/o Théâtre des Champs Elysées, 15 Avenue Montaigne, 75012 Paris, France.

TAMBERG, Eino; Composer; b. 27 May 1930, Tallinn, Estonia. *Education:* Studied with Eugen Kapp at Tallinn Conservatory, graduated 1953. *Career:* Music Supervisor for Estonian Radio then Teacher at Estonian Conservatory, 1967–; Professor, 1983. *Compositions include:* Operas: The Iron House, 1965, Cyrano de Bergerac, 1976 Soaring, 1983 and The Beings, 1992; all premiered in Tallinn; Ballets: Ballet Symphony, Schwerin, 1960, The Boy and The Butterfly, Tallinn, 1963 and Joanna Tentata, Tallinn, 1971; Orchestral: Concerto Grosso, 1956, Symphonic Dances, 1957, Toccata, 1967, Trumpet Concerto, 1972, 4 Symphonies, 1978, 1986, 1989, and 1998; Concerto for Mezzo Soprano and Orchestra, 1986, Alto Saxophone Concerto, 1987; Clarinet Concerto, 1996; 2nd Trumpet Concerto, 1997; Chamber: String Quartet, 1958, 2 Wind Quintets, 1975, 1984; Vocal: Moonlight Oratorio, 1962, Fanfares of Victory, cantata, 1975, Amores, oratorio, 1981; Songs and piano pieces. *Honours:* People's Artist of the Estonian SSR, 1975. *Address:* EE 0001 Tallinn, Lauteri 7-23, Estonia.

TAMBOSI, Olivier; Opera Director; b. 7 July 1963, Paris, France. *Education:* Vienna Music Academy. *Career:* Formed Neue Oper Wien, 1988 and was Artistic Director until 1993; Productions included Medea, Die Zauberflöte, Macbeth, Pimpinone by Telemann, Don Pasquale and Lulu; Artistic Director at Klagenfurt Opera, 1993–96 with Manon Lescaut, Death in Venice, Così fan tutte, Cav and Pag, Les Contes d'Hoffmann and Rigoletto; Productions from 1996 include Der Rosen-kavalier and Lulu at Mannheim; Macbeth at Strasbourg and Bohème and Jenůfa at Hamburg; Season 1999–2000 with Pelléas et Mélisande at Linz, Falstaff for the Lyric Opera of Chicago; Tristan at Berne; Katya Kabanova in Hamburg; Mozart's Die Entführung in Klagenfurt; Season 2000–01 with Jenůfa at Covent Garden and Saariaho's L'Amour de Loin at Berne; Engaged for Lulu at Klagenfurt (2002), Un Ballo in Maschera at Chicago (2003), Jenůfa, Met Opera, New York, (2003); Luisa Miller at Covent Garden (2003) and Falstaff at Salzburg (2004). *Address:* c/o IMG Artists, Lovell House, 616 Chiswick High Road, London W4 5RX, England.

TAMULENAS, Eva; Singer (Mezzo-soprano); b. 1943, Narva, Estonia. *Education:* Studied in Milwaukee and Vienna. *Career:* Sang at first with the Royal Opera Copenhagen and from 1977 at Gelsenkirchen; Roles have included Hansel, Rosina, Orlofsky, Olga, Maddalena and the title role in Miss Julie by Antonio Bibalo; Einem's Der Besuch der alten Dame (1991); Sang Third Lady in Die Zauberflöte at Gelsenkirchen, 2000; Many concert engagements. *Address:* Gelsenkirchen Opera, Musiktheater im Revier, Kennedyplatz, Pf 101857, W-4650 Gelsen-kirchen, Germany.

TAMULIONIS, Jonas; Composer; b. 10 Jan. 1949, Alytus, Lithuania; Divorced, 2 s. *Education:* Graduated from the Faculty of Music of the Vilnius Pedagogical Institute, 1970; Composition with Professor Eduardos Balsys at the Lithuanian State Conservatoire, 1976. *Compo-sitions include:* For string quartet: Two Quartets, 1973, 1982; Diary, 1978; For string orchestras: Concertino, 1974; Toccata Diavolesca, 1988; Pastoral Suite, 1990; Three symphonies, 1976, 1978, 1986; For wind orchestra: Festive Overture, 1987; Spanish Rhapsody, 1981; Sonatas: for two guitars, 1978, two pianos, 1979, two birbynes (Lithuanian folk wind instrument), 1988; For chamber orchestra: Epitaph, 1981; Cantatas: I Sing of Lithuania, 1981; Children's Earth (verse by J Marcinkevicius), 1988; To My Motherland (verse by J Mikstas), 1989; Sinfonia Rustica, 1989; Oratorio: Six Dedications To The Town (text by various Lithunanian poets, 1985; Reminiscence for two violins and two accordions, 1989; Recollection for glass instruments, 1992; Trio for flute, viola, guitar and piano, 1993; Vocal music includes: Seven Love Elegies for soprano and chamber ensemble, 1982; Summer Psalms for soprano and piano (verse by J Marcinkevicius), 1985; Three Prayers for baritone and piano, (verse by B Brazdzionis), 1989; For Choir: Single Words, 1980; The Tears of Ablinga, 1984; Tres retratos con sombra (verse by F García Lorca), 1992; Los juegos, 1997; For accordion: Sonatina, 1978; Metamorphoses, 1984; Polyphonic Pieces, 1990; Ten Etudes, 1995; For guitar: Eleven preludes, 1982; Suite of Intervals, 1987. *Recordings:* CD: On The Coast, 1990; Numerations, Patterers, 1992; Ex Anima, 1994; Home Psalames, 1995; The Sea, 1996. *Honours:* 2nd Prize, Symphony No. 1, Moscow, Russia, 1967; 1st prize, Canciones de la Tierra, Spain, 1995; 1st Prize, Oda al Atlántico, Spain, 1997; 1st Prize, Los juegos, Spain, 1997. *Address:* Tauro 8-11, 2001 Vilnius, Lithuania.

TAN, Dun, MA; Chinese composer; b. 18 Aug. 1957, Si Mao, Hunan Province; s. of Tan Xiang Qiu and Fang Qun Ying; m. Jane Huang 1994; one s. *Education:* Cen. Conservatory of Music, Beijing and Columbia Univ., USA. *Career:* violist, Beijing Opera Orchestra 1976–77; Vice-Pres. Cen. Conservatory of Music 1978–; works performed by major orchestras in China and at festivals world-wide; four recordings of his major orchestral works, oriental instrumental music, chamber music and electronic music issued by China Nat. Recording Co.; works also include 14 film scores for US and Chinese films, six modern ballet scores, music for several stage plays; orchestral piece commissioned by Inst. for Devt of Intercultural Relations Through the Arts, USA for Beijing Int. Music Festival 1988; Artistic Dir Fire Crossing Water Festival Barbican Centre, London 2000. *Film scores:* Aktion K 1994, Nanjing 1937 1995, Fallen 1997, In the Name of the Emperor 1998, Wo hu cang long (Crouching Tiger Hidden Dragon) (Grammy Award 2001, Acad. Award 2001, British Acad. Film Award 2001, Classical BRIT Contemporary Music Award 2001) 2000, Ying xiong (Hero) 2002. *Compositions:* orchestral works: Li Sao (symphony) 1979, Five Pieces in Human Accent for piano 1980, Feng Ya Song for string quartet 1982, Fu for two sopranos, bass and ensemble 1982, Piano Concerto 1983, Symphony in two movements 1985, On Taoism for orchestra 1985, Traces for piano 1989, Eight Colours for string quartet 1989, Silk Road for soprano and

percussion 1989, Orchestral Theatre I: Xun 1990, Soundshape 1990, Silent Earth 1991, Jo-Ha-Kyu 1992, Death and Fire: Dialogue with Paul Klee 1992, Orchestral Theatre II: Re 1992, CAGE for piano 1993, Circle for four trios, conductor and audience 1993, The Pink 1993, Autumn Winds for instruments and conductor ad lib 1993, Memorial Nineteen for voice, piano and double paper 1993, Orchestral Theatre III: Red 1993, Yi concerto for cello 1994, Heaven, Earth, Mankind symphony for the 'Bian Zhong' bronze bells (composed in celebration of the Hong Kong handover) 1997, 2000 Today: A World Symphony for the Millennium: A Musical Odyssey for the Ages 1999, Water Passion after St Matthew 2000, The Map concerto for cello, video and orchestra 2003; opera: Out of Beijing 1987, Nine Songs 1989, Marco Polo 1994, Peony Pavilion 1998, Tea 2002. *Honours:* second place Weber Int. Chamber Music Composi-tion Competition, Dresden 1983, Suntory Prize 1992, Grawemeyer Award 1998, Musical America Composer of the Year 2003. *Address:* 367 W 19th Street, Suite A, New York, NY 10011, USA (office). *Telephone:* (212) 627-0410 (office). *Fax:* (917) 606-0247 (office). *E-mail:* tan_dun@ hotmail.com (office). *Website:* www.tandun.com (office).

TAN, Lihua; Conductor; b. 22 Oct. 1955, Jiangsu, China; m. Lumin Qiao, October 1980, 1 d. *Education:* Graduated, Shanghai Conservatory of Music. *Career:* debut, conducting Bruch's Violin Concerto and Dvořák Symphony No. 9, Wuhan Orchestra, Wuhan, China; Conductor, Chinese Ballet, 1990–96; Conductor, China Central Philharmonic Symphony Orchestra, 1993–; Music Director, Principal Conductor, Beijing Symph-ony Orchestra; Chinese premieres include: Pines of Rome, Dvořák Symphony No. 7, Prokofiev Symphony No. 5; Guest conducting appearances include: New York Youth Symphony, Seattle Federal Way Symphony, Russian National Symphony; Venues include New York City's Avery Fisher Hall, Lincoln Center; Moscow's Tchaikovsky Conservatory of Music. *Recordings:* Beethoven Symphony No. 5; Brahms Symphony No. 4, with Beijing Symphony Orchestra; Dvořák Symphony Nos 8 and 9; Haydn Symphony No. 94; Mendelssohn, Saint-Saëns and Tchaikovsky Violin Concertos, China Central Philharmonic Symphony Orchestra. *Publications:* Article, Conducting Technique and Instrumental Performance, 1988. *Current Management:* Bary Plews, Australia. *Address:* Beijing Symphony Orchestra, No. A-1 Eight Poplar, Shuang Jing, Chao-Yang District, Beijing 100022, People's Republic of China.

TAN, Melvyn; Musician (Harpsichord, Fortepiano); b. 13 Oct. 1956, Singapore. *Education:* Studied at the Yehudi Menuhin School, Surrey from 1968; Teachers include Vlado Perlemuter and Nadia Boulanger; Royal College of Music from 1978, where he made a special study of performing practice. *Career:* International appearances in the keyboard works of Baroque, Classical and early Romantic composers; Played piano until 1980 then turned to harpsichord and fortepiano; Engage-ments with the Academy of Ancient Music, the English Chamber Orchestra, Royal Philharmonic and London Classical Players; Tour of USA in 1985; Series of Beethoven concerts 1987 with Roger Norrington and the London Classical Players; Flanders Festival, 1988 followed by South Bank Beethoven Plus series; Appearances during 1989 at the Bath Festival, Holland Festival, Midsummer Mozart Festival, San Francisco and the Beethoven Experience with the London Classical Players in Purchase, New York; In season 1990 visited France, Germany, Japan, Australia, San Francisco, Vancouver and New York, Carnegie Hall; Played the Schumann Concerto at the Queen Elizabeth Hall, London, 1990; Debut at the Paris Opéra, 1991; Debut concerts as director of The New Mozart Ensemble in Britain, France, Netherlands and Hong Kong; Repertoire includes: Weber, Mendelssohn, Chopin and earlier music. *Recordings:* Beethoven's Waldstein and Appassionata Sonatas; Schubert's Impromptus; Beethoven's Concertos and Choral Fantasia conducted by Roger Norrington. *Address:* c/o Valerie Barber Management Ltd, Fifth Floor, 24 Chancery Lane, London WC2A 1LS, England.

TANAKA, Karen, BA; Japanese composer; b. 7 April 1961, Tokyo. *Education:* Tōhō Gakuen School of Music, Tokyo, studied with Berio in Florence, IRCAM composition technology course. *Career:* Visiting Assoc. Prof., Univ. of California at Santa Barbara. *Compositions include:* Anamorphose (piano concerto) 1986, Crystalline I, II and III 1988, 1995–96, 2000, Hommage en cristal 1991, Initium 1993, Metallic Crystal 1994–95, Echo Canyon 1995, Metal Strings 1996, The Song of Songs 1997, Frozen Horizon 1998, Guardian Angel 2000. *Honours:* Gaudeamus Prize 1987. *Current Management:* G. Schirmer Promotion Department, 257 Park Avenue S, 20th Floor, New York, NY 10010, USA. *Website:* www.schirmer.com (office).

TANG, Muhai; Conductor; b. 10 July 1949, Shanghai, China. *Education:* Music Conservatory at Shanghai; Music Hochschule, Munich, Ger-many; Masterclass Diploma. *Career:* Conducted the Berlin Philharmo-nic, London Philharmonic, Orchestre de Paris, San Francisco Symphony, Montreal Symphony, Santa Cecilia Orchestra, Rome, Tonhalle Orchestra Zürich, Helsinki Philharmonic, Hallé Orchestra, Scottish National Symphony Orchestra, National Symphony Orchestra of Spain, Mozarteum Orchestra Salzburg, Polish Chamber Orchestra, Oper Orchestra Hamburg, Frankfurt, Munich, Bonn, Monte Carlo, Radio Symphony Orchestra Munich, Berlin, Hamburg, and Cologne; Chief Conductor of Peking Central Philharmonic and Gulbenkian Orchestra of Lisbon; Classic Aid Television Gala Concert, UN Geneva, 1986. *Current Management:* Askonas Holt Ltd, Lonsdale Chambers, 27 Chancery Lane, London, WC2A 1PF, England. *Telephone:* (20) 7400-1700. *Fax:* (20) 7400-1799. *E-mail:* info@askonasholt.co.uk. *Website:* www.askonasholt.co.uk. *Address:* c/o Keils, Treibjagdweg 31, 1 Berlin 37, Germany.

TANGGAARD, Svend Erik; Composer and Writer; b. 25 Jan. 1942, Copenhagen, Denmark; m. Margit Bendtsen, 29 Feb 1980, 2 d. *Education:* Piano and Composition studies with Helge Bonnen, Copenhagen, 1962–67; Studies in Munich, 1968–70. *Career:* Debut: Royal Academy of Fine Arts, 1962; Performances of own works by Danish Radio Symphony Orchestra, Aalborg Symphony Orchestra, Southern Jutland Symphony Orchestra, Odense Symphony Orchestra and Moritz Fromberg Quartet; Several transmissions on Danish Radio, NDR and Swedish Radio; Performances at the Art Association, Gronningen and other art galleries. *Compositions:* 5 Symphonies; Concerto for orchestra; 12 String Quartets; 3 Fuga String Quartets op 150; Piano, Violin (2), Viola, Cello, Oboe, Flute, Trumpet and Clarinet Concertos; Overtures Nos 1 and 2, for chamber orchestra; Concertos Nos 1, 2 and 3, for 14 wind instruments, 2 double basses and percussion, and Concerto, for violin, viola and orchestra; Vox Humana, for orchestra, soprano, bass and tape recorder; The Bells, for orchestra and reader; Songs, 3 Wind Quintets; 3 Solo Cello Suites; 2 Solo Violin Sonatas, Piano Sonata, Day and Night; 3 Italian Prayers, for mezzo-soprano and viola; 3 Cantatas, for tenor and wind quintet; 25 Selected Songs From Omar Khayyam's Rubaiyat, for basso and 3 instruments; Songs for small ensembles; Memoria Futuris, Nos II and III, for string orchestra, 1997, Nos IV and V, for wind quintet, 1998; Opus 200, String Quartet No. 16, 1999. *Address:* Nikolaj Plads 7, 4, 1067 Copenhagen K, Denmark.

TANGUY, Eric; French composer; b. 27 Jan. 1968, Caen. *Education:* Caen Conservatoire, Darmstadt Ferienkurse, Conservatoire Nat. Supérieur de Musique, Paris. *Career:* composer-in-residence, Champagne-Ardenne 1995, Lille 1996, Orchestre de Bretagne 2001–03. *Compositions include:* Avènement de la ligne 1988, Alloys 1988, Océan N.Y. Fantaisie 1989, Azur B 1990, Azur C 1990, Towards 1991, Wadi 1992, Solo 1993, Concerto pour violon 1990, Towards 1991, Concerto pour flûte et 16 instruments 1992, Célébration de Marie-Madeleine 1995, Le Jardin des délices 1996, Éclipse 1999, Concerto for cello and orchestra No. 2 2000, Chronos (opera) 2002, Ouverture 2002. *Honours:* Darmstadt Stipendienpreis 1988, Villa Medici extra-mural prize 1989, Paris Conservatoire first prize for composition 1991, Darmstadt Kranichstein Musikpreis 1992, Institut de France André Caplet Prize 1995, SACEM Hervé Dugardin Prize 1997. *Address:* c/o Patricia Alia, Editions Salabert, 5 rue du Helder, 75002 Paris, France (office).

TANGUY, Jean-Michel; Flautist; b. 15 Nov. 1944, France. *Education:* French Baccalaureate, Lycee Français, Berlin; Jean-Pierre Rampal, Nice, Paris; Aurèle Nicolet, Berlin; Freiburg, Breisgau Staatliche Hochschule für Musik. *Career:* Debut: Orchestra der Beethovenhalle, Bonn, Germany; Performances with Bonn Orchestra, Rotterdam Philharmonic, Orchestre National de Belgique, Brussels; Chargé de Cours Conservatoire Royal de Bruxelles; Professor of Flute, Hochschule für Musik, Heidelberg-Mannheim, 1992–; mem, Jury Member, International Flute Competition, Jean-Pierre Rampal, 1994, 1998; Guest Member, National Flute Convention, Chicago, 1986, Atlanta, 1999. *Recordings:* Telemann Flute Concertos; Heidelberger Chamber Orchestra, JS Bach Trios, CPE Bach–Sonatas; JS Bach–Flute Sonatas; Sommermusik with Belgian Windquintett. *Honours:* Prize, International Music Competition, Geneva, 1973; Scholarship, DAAD; Masterclasses: Belgium, France, Italy, Germany, Austria, Korea. *Address:* 17 rue Guimard, 1040 Brussels, Belgium.

TANYEL, Seta; Concert Pianist; b. 1950, Istanbul. *Education:* Studied at Vienna Hochschule for Musik with Dieter Weber and with Louis Kentner in London. *Career:* Orchestral and recital debuts in New York, Philadelphia, Detroit and London in 1978; Extensive touring in Europe, the Middle East, Russia and the USA performing with such orchestras as the Vienna Symphony, Israel Philharmonic, Stuttgart Philharmonic, the Philharmonia and London Symphony Orchestra; Taught at Yehudi Menuhin School in London from 1986–1989; A pianist with an international reputation in both standard and lesser-known Romantic piano repertoire, recent performing projects include the long overdue revival in the piano music of Xaver Scharwenka. *Recordings include:* Shostakovich, Khachaturian, Poulenc and Bax 2-piano works (Chandos); Brahms and Beethoven solo recital; Grieg and Schumann Piano Concertos with London Symphony Orchestra/Fruhbeck de Burgos; Brahms Piano Concerto No. 1 with the Philharmonia/Vaclav Neumann; Scharwenka Piano Concerto No. 1 and Chopin Piano Concerto No. 1 with the Philharmonia/Rizzi; Chopin, Sharwenka and Moszkowski solo

recitals; Scharwenka chamber works with piano (Complete) (Collins Classics). *Honours:* Prizewinner at International Beethoven Competition in Vienna in 1973, at first Arthur Rubinstein Piano Master Competition in Israel in 1974 and at Queen Elisabeth of Belgium Competition in 1975. *Address:* c/o Philharmonia Orchestra (Artist Contracts), 1st Floor, 125 High Holborn, London, WC1V 6QA, England.

TAPPY, Eric; Singer (Tenor); b. 19 May 1931, Lausanne, Switzerland. *Education:* Studied with Fernando Carpi in Geneva, Ernst Reichert in Salzburg and Eva Liebenberg in Hilversum. *Career:* Debut: Strasbourg in 1959 as the Evangelist in Bach's St Matthew Passion; Concert performances of Milhaud's Les Malheurs d'Orphée and Martin's Le Mystère de la Nativité and Monsieur de Pourceaugnac; Sang in the premiere of Klaus Huber's Soliloquia in 1962; Stage debut at Opéra-Comique Paris in 1964 as Rameau's Zoroastre; Sang at Herrenhausen in 1966 as Monteverdi's Orfeo, Geneva Opera in 1966 in the premiere of Milhaud's La Mère Coupable, and Hanover in 1967 in L'Incoronazione di Poppea; Covent Garden debut in 1974 in the title role of La Clemenza di Tito; US debut in 1974 as Don Ottavio at San Francisco returning in Poppea and as Idomeneo, 1977–78; Sang at Rome Opera in 1980 as Titus; Appearances in Chicago, Drottningholm, Aix-en-Provence, Salzburg as Tamino, Amsterdam, Lyon, Brussels and Lisbon; Other roles include Schoenberg's Aron, Pelléas, Lysander in A Midsummer Night's Dream, Don Ramiro, Lensky and Stravinsky's Oedipus; Concert repertoire includes music by Handel, Haydn, Campra, Carissimi, Vivaldi, Bach, Berlioz and Schütz; Retired in 1982. *Recordings include:* Monteverdi's Orfeo and Poppea; Zoroastre; Pelléas et Mélisande; Die Jahreszeiten by Haydn; Die Zauberflöte; La Clemenza di Tito.

TARASCHENKO, Vitalij; Singer (Tenor); b. 1953, Kyrgyzstan, USSR. *Career:* Sang in opera at Moscow and Warsaw; Florence, 1990, as Prince Vsevolod in Rimsky's Kitezh; Dimitri in Boris Godunov at Bologna; Bregenz Festival, 1993, as Andrei in Mazeppa and Ismaele in Nabucco; Season 1993–94 as Calaf at Hamburg and Amsterdam, Turiddu at the Vienna Staatsoper and Hermann in The Queen of Spades at the Paris Opéra Bastille; Venice and Zürich, 1995, as Andrei and Lensky in Eugene Onegin; Member of the Bolshoi Opera, Moscow, from 1992; Other roles include Vladimir in Prince Igor, Gabriele Adorno in Simon Boccanegra, and Cavoradossi; Season 1997–98 as Prince Guidon in Rimsky's Tsar Saltan, at Florence, and Paolo in Rachmaninov's Francesca da Rimini, at St Petersburg; Sang Dimitri in Boris Godunov with the Bolshoi Company in London, 1999; Season 1999–2000 as Ugo in Mascagni's Parisina, at Montpellier, and Tchaikovsky's Herman for WNO. *Address:* c/o Bolshoi Opera, Bolshoi Theatre, 103009 Moscow, Russia.

TARASSOVA, Marianna; Singer (Mezzo-Soprano); b. 1962, St Petersburg, Russia. *Education:* St Petersburg Conservatoire; Masterclasses at Aldeburgh, 1992. *Career:* Appearances with the Kirov Opera from 1993, as Carmen, Amneris, Cherubino, Olga in Eugene Onegin, Purcell's Dido, Konchakovna in Prince Igor and Blanche in The Gambler by Prokofiev; Other roles include Lyubava in Sadko and Young Boy in The Invisible City of Kitezh, both by Rimsky-Korsakov, Polina in The Queen of Spades, Marfa (Khovanshchina) and Clara in Prokofiev's Betrothal in a Monastery; Concert repertory includes Mahler Symphony no. 3, the Verdi Requiem and songs by Shostakovich for mezzo and orchestra; Recitals and concerts in the USA, and world-wide tours with the Kirov Opera, including summer season at the Royal Opera, Covent Garden, 2000. *Address:* c/o Kirov Opera, Mariinsky Theatre, 1 Theatre Square, St Petersburg, Russia.

TARBUK, Mladen; Composer, Conductor and Producer; b. 19 July 1962, Sarajevo; m. Jasna Cizmek, 29 Jan 1994, 2 s. *Education:* Diploma, Conducting, Music Academy, Zagreb, 1987; Diploma, Conducting, Hochschule für Musik und darstellende Kunst, Graz, 1988; Postgraduate Study, Conducting, Hochschule für Musik und darstellende Kunst, Vienna, 1991–92; Diploma, Composition, Music Academy, Zagreb, 1994. *Career:* Das Rheingold, Elektra and many other operas and ballets, Croatian National Opera, Zagreb, 1990–91; Premiere, Udo Zimmermann's White Rose, Slovenian National Theatre, Maribor, 1991; World Premiere, Schwertsik's Café Museum, Deutschlandsberg, 1993; Concert of composers from Alpe-Adria region, Moscow Autumn festival, 1996; Concert of Croatian music composers, Symphonic Orchestra of Croatian Radio and Television, broadcast by European Broadcasting Union, 1998; World Premiere, Villardi's Judas, Brussels, 1999; World Premiere, Medida del tiempo, conducted by Friedrich Cerha, 1991; Performance of Zildjian Concerto, World Music Days, Manchester, 1998; Chief Conductor, Symphonic Wind Orchestra, Croatian Military Forces, 1992–99; Principal Conductor, Symphonic Orchestra of Croatian Radio and Television, 1999; Lecturer, 1989, Senior Lecturer, 1997, Assistant Professor of Music Theory, 1997, Zagreb Music Academy. *Compositions include:* A tre for string trio, 1990; Discusiones amorosas, for choir, 1993; Zildjian Concerto, for percussion and orchestra, 1995. *Recordings:* Zildjian Concerto, Sticks&Strings&Winds, recorded by Honey & Rock; Croatian Masses. *Address:* Katicev Prilaz 7, 10010 Zagreb, Croatia.

TARLING, Judith; Violinist and Violist; b. 1947, England. *Career:* Leader of the Parley of Instruments; Frequent tours of the United Kingdom and abroad including the British Early Music Network; Performances in Spain, France, Germany, Sweden, Netherlands, Poland, Czechoslovakia, USA and Colombia; US debut at New York in 1988; Many concerts with first modern performances of early music in new editions by Peter Holman; Numerous broadcasts on BBC Radio 3 and elsewhere; English Eighteenth Century Music such as Dr Arne at Vauxhall Gardens, William Boyce's Solomon, and John Stanley 6 Concertos in seven parts, Op 2, these works performed with Crispian Steele-Perkins on trumpet and Emma Kirkby as soprano, among others; Principal Viola of Brandenburg Consort, Director, Roy Goodman with recordings including Bach Brandenburg Concertos and Suites; Handel arias, flute concertos by Quantz and C. P. E. Bach; Principal Viola of the Hanover Band, 1981–2002, with numerous recordings including complete symphonies of Beethoven, Schubert and Haydn. *Recordings:* Repertoire includes Renaissance Violin Consort Music such as Music by Michael Praetorius, Peter Philips, music for Charles I by Orlando Gibbons and Thomas Lupo, Baroque Consort Music by Monteverdi and Matthew Locke anthems, motets and ceremonial music, Purcell Ayres for Theatre, Georg Muffat's Armonico Tributo sonatas of 1682, Heinrich Biber's Sonate tam Aris, Quam Aulis Servientes of 1676, Vivaldi sonatas and concertos for lute and mandolin, concertos for recorders, and JS Bach's Hunt Cantata, No. 208; Italian and German sacred music with Robin Blaze. *Publications:* Baroque String Playing for ingenious learners, 2000. *Address:* 3 North Street, Punnetts Town, Heathfield, East Sussex, England. *E-mail:* judytarling@btinternet.com.

TARR, Edward (Hankins); Trumpeter and Musicologist; b. 15 June 1936, Norwich, Connecticut, USA. *Education:* Studied trumpet with Roger Voisin in Boston, 1953 and with Adolph Herseth in Chicago, 1958–59; Musicology with Leo Schrade in Basle, 1959–64. DPhil, University of Hamburg, 1986. *Career:* Founded the Edward Tarr Brass Ensemble, 1969, giving many performances of Renaissance, Baroque and contemporary music in Europe and the USA; Early repertoire includes the trumpet works of Torelli; Modern repertoire includes works by Kagel, Stockhausen and Krol; Has collaborated on the reconstruction of early instruments with the German firm Meinl and Lauber and the Swiss firm Adolf Egger and Son; Teacher of Trumpet at Rheinische Musikschule Cologne, 1968–70; Teacher of Cornett and Natural Trumpet at the Schola Cantorum Basiliensis, 1972–2001; Teacher of Trumpet at the Basle Conservatory, 1974–2001; Teacher of Baroque Trumpet at Musikhochschule Karlsruhe, 2001– (Prof., 2003), Musikhochschule Lucerne, 2002–; Teacher of Brass Ensemble, Musikhochschule Frankfurt am Main, 2003–; Director of the Trumpet Museum in Bad Säckingen, Germany, 1985–2003. *Publications include:* Die Trompete, 1977; Over 70 articles in The New Grove (1980 and 2000 editions); Performing editions of Baroque, Classical and Romantic Music. *Honours:* DrMus hc (Oberlin College), 2003. *Address:* c/o Trumpet Museum, PO Box 1143, 79702 Bad Säckingen, Germany.

TARRÉS, Enriqueta; Singer (Soprano); b. 18 March 1934, Barcelona, Spain. *Education:* Studied at the Barcelona Conservatory with Concepcion Callao de Sanchez Parra. *Career:* Debut: Valencia in 1956 as the Trovatore Leonora; Sang in Spain notably at the Teatro Liceo, Barcelona, Basle and Wuppertal Opera, 1960–64, Glyndebourne in 1962 and 1964 as Ariadne and Elettra in Idomeneo, and Hamburg Staatsoper from 1964, visiting Sadler's Wells in 1966 as the Empress in the first British performance of Die Frau ohne Schatten by Strauss; Engaged with Düsseldorf, Cologne and Stuttgart Operas; Sang at Metropolitan Opera in 1973 as Mimi, Lausanne in 1983 as the Marschallin, Verona in 1984 as Carmen, and sang the Mother in Luis de Pablo's El Viajero Indiscreto at the Teatro de la Zarzuela at Madrid in 1990; Frequent concert appearances. *Recordings:* Falla's Atlantida; Orff's Trionfi; Les Huguenots; Idomeneo. *Address:* c/o Arena di Verona, Piazza Brà 28, 37121 Verona, Italy.

TARUSKIN, Richard (Filler); Musicologist and Critic; b. 2 April 1945, New York City, USA. *Education:* PhD, Columbia University, 1975. *Career:* Teacher at Columbia University, 1973–87; Professor at University of California, Berkeley, 1987; Music Critic for Opus and The New York Times. *Publications include:* Opera and Drama in Russia, Ann Arbor, 1981; Study of Stravinsky and articles on the 15th Century Chanson, the Early Music Movement and on Russian Music. *Contributions:* Articles on Russian Composers and Operas, in new Grove Dictionary of Opera, 4 vols, 1992; Text and Act: Essays on Music and Performance, 1995; Stravinsky and the Russian Traditions: a Biography of the Works through Mavra, 1996. *Address:* University of California, Music Department, Morrison Hall, Berkeley, CA 94720, USA.

TARVER, Kenneth; Singer (Tenor); b. 1965, Detroit, USA. *Education:* Oberlin College Conservatory and Yale University School of Music. *Career:* Stuttgart Staatsoper 1994–97, as Tamino, Ferrando, Almaviva and Lindoro; Tamino in Don Giovanni at Aix-en-Provence, Milan,

Stockholm and Tokyo, 1998; Season 2000–01 at Covent Garden, London, as Fenton in Falstaff and Roderigo in Otello by Rossini; Further appearances at the Deutsche Oper and State Opera, Berlin, and the New York City Opera; Concerts include Bach's St Matthew Passion, conducted by Chailly and Berlioz series in London, conducted by Colin Davis, 2000; Roméo et Juliette, Béatrice et Bénédict and Les Troyens; London Proms, 2002. *Recordings:* DVD of Falstaff, Covent Garden, 2000. *Honours:* Winner, Metropolitan Opera National Competition. *Address:* c/o Deutsche Oper Berlin, 10 Richard Wagnerstrasse, 100 Berlin, Germany.

TASKOVA, Slavka; Singer (Soprano); b. 16 Nov. 1940, Sofia, Bulgaria. *Education:* Studied at the Accademia di Santa Cecilia with Gina Cigne and in Milan with Lina Pagliughi. *Career:* Debut: Milan in 1966 as Rosina in Il Barbiere di Siviglia; Has sung in Venice, Bologna, Berlin, Munich, Paris, Vienna, Sofia, Warsaw and Zagreb; Sang at Schwetzingen Festival in 1971 in the premiere of Reimann's Melusine, Teatro Lirico Milan in 1975 in the premiere of Nono's Al Gran Sole Carico d'Amore, and Genoa in 1983 as Violetta. *Recordings include:* Anacréon by Cherubini. *Address:* c/o Teatro Carlo Felice, 16100 Genoa, Italy.

TASSEL, Charles Van; Singer (Baritone); b. 28 Aug. 1937, New York, USA. *Education:* Studied in New York and with Luigi Ricci, Rome. *Career:* Debut: Contemporary Chamber Players, Chicago, in Weisgall's Purgatory, 1967; Sang at Bremerhaven Opera 1968–71, Kassel 1971–75, Wiesbaden and Hamburg Staatsoper; Appearances with Netherlands Opera from 1975, notably as Guglielmo, Enrico in Lucia di Lammermoor, Verdi's Ford, and Nabucco, and Yeletsky in The Queen of Spades; Holland Festival 1983, as the man in Mörder, Hoffnung der Frauen, by Hindemith; Further engagments as Escamillo, Mozart's Count, Marcello, Verdi's Posa, Jochanaan in Salome, and Demetrius in A Midsummer Night's Dream; Sang Mussorgsky in the premiere of Symposion by Peter Schat, Amsterdam, 1994; Teacher at the Sweelinck Conservatory; Frequent concert appearances. *Recordings include:* Die Zauberflöte (Erato); Schreker's Die Gezeichneten (Marco Polo); Messiaen's St François d'Assise (KRO). *Address:* c/o Netherlands Opera, Waterlooplein 22, 1011 PG Amsterdam, Netherlands.

TATE, Jeffrey; Conductor; b. 28 April 1943, Salisbury, Wiltshire, England. *Education:* Christ's College Cambridge; St Thomas' Hospital London; MA, MB, BChir, Cantab; London Opera Centre. *Career:* Assistant to Boulez at Bayreuth and Paris, 1976–80; Opera debut at Gothenburg in 1978 with Carmen; Metropolitan debut in 1980 with Lulu, returning for Der Rosenkavalier, Wozzeck and Lohengrin; Covent Garden debut in 1982 in La Clemenza di Tito, becoming Principal Conductor, 1986–; Principal Guest Conductor for Geneva Opera, 1984–, Orchestre National de France, 1989–, and Royal Opera House, 1991–; Principal Conductor with English Chamber Orchestra, 1985; Conducted new production of Henze's realization of Monteverdi's Il Ritorno d'Ulisse at Salzburg Festival in 1985 and the premiere of Liebermann's La Fôret at Geneva in 1987; Works regularly with many leading orchestras including the London Symphony, Boston Symphony, and Orchestre de la Suisse Romande; Music Director for Rotterdam Philharmonic 1991–; Principal Guest Conductor of Orchestra Nazionale RAI, 1998–2001 (Oedipus Rex and Die Meistersinger); Season 1991–92 included Mozart's Zaide in Amsterdam and at the Barbican Hall, Le nozze di Figaro and Fidelio at Covent Garden and Weill's Mahagonny at Geneva; Led new production of Parsifal for Bonn Opera, 1997; Led The Ring at Adelaide, 1999; Engaged for Der Rosenkavalier in Milan, 2003. *Recordings:* Various with such orchestras as English Chamber, Dresden Staatskapelle and Royal Opera House. *Honours:* SWET Opera Award, 1984; Honorary Fellowship, Christ's College Cambridge, 1988; C.B.E., 1990; Chevalier des Arts et des Lettres, 1990. *Current Management:* Columbia Artists Management Inc, 165 West 57th Street, New York, NY 10019, USA; Artists Management Zürich, 8044 Zürich Rutistrasse 52, Switzerland. *Address:* c/o Betty Scholar, Secretary, Royal Opera House, Covent Garden, London WC2, England.

TATTERMUSCHOVA, Helena; Singer (Soprano); b. 28 Jan. 1933, Prague, Czechoslovakia. *Education:* Studied at the Prague Conservatory with Vlasta Linhartova. *Career:* Debut: Ostrava in 1955 as Musetta; National Theatre Prague from 1959; Visited Edinburgh with the company in 1964 and 1970 in the British premieres of Janáček's From The House Of The Dead and The Excursions of Mr Brouček; Guest appearances at opera houses in Barcelona, Brussels, Amsterdam, Warsaw, Naples, Venice and Sofia; Repertoire included works by Janáček, Smetana, Mozart, Puccini and Strauss; Also sang in concert. *Recordings:* Orfeo ed Euridice; Trionfi by Orff; The Makropulos Case; From the House of the Dead; Glagolitic Mass; The Cunning Little Vixen. *Address:* Detska 13, 100 00 Prague 10, Czech Republic.

TATUM, Nancy; Singer (Soprano); b. 25 Aug. 1934, Memphis, Tennessee, USA; m. Wiley Tatum. *Education:* Studied with Zelma Lee Thomas in Memphis and with Samuel Margolis and Wiley Tatum in New York. *Career:* Debut: Saarbrucken in 1962 as Santuzza; Has sung in Paris,

Geneva, Lyon, Minneapolis, Vancouver and Sofia; Member of the Deutsche Oper am Rhein, Düsseldorf, from 1964, and Metropolitan Opera from 1973; Further appearances in Budapest, Bucharest, Zagreb, Brussels and Amsterdam; Repertoire includes major roles in operas by Wagner and Verdi.

TAUB, Robert David; Concert Pianist; b. 25 Dec. 1955, New York, NY, USA; m. Tracy Elizabeth Milner 1983. *Education:* AB, Princeton Univ., 1977; MMus, 1978, DMA, 1981, Juilliard School. *Career:* concert pianist performing throughout the USA, Europe, Asia and Latin America with orchestras including the MET Opera Orchestra, Boston Symphony Orchestra, LA Philharmonic, BBC Philharmonic, Philadelphia Orchestra; Concerto and solo repertoire covering the Baroque to contemporary music; numerous works composed for him by Milton Babbitt, Mel Powell, Jonathan Dawe, David Bessell, Ludger Brummer and others; performances broadcast live on nat. radio including BBC, RTE, NPR. *Recordings:* Beethoven, Complete Piano Sonatas; Scriabin, Complete Piano Sonatas; Milton Babbitt, Piano Works, Three Compositions; Schumann, Davidsbündlertänze and two Liszt transcriptions; Mel Powell, Duplicates: Concerto for 2 Pianos, 1990; Persichetti, Piano Concerto; Sessions, Piano Concerto; Bartók, Sonata; Shifrin, Responses; Kirchner, Sonata. *Television:* featured in US nat. TV special The Big Idea. *Publications:* Playing the Beethoven Piano Sonatas (book); contributions to many music journals. *Current Management:* California Artists Management, 41 Sutter Street, Suite 420, San Francisco, CA 94104-4903, USA. *Telephone:* (415) 362-2787. *E-mail:* don@calartists .com. *Website:* www.calartists.com.

TAUTU, Cornelia; Composer; b. 10 March 1938, Odorhei, Romania; m. Valentin Curocichin, 6 Aug 1976, 1 d. *Education:* Ciprian Porumbescu Conservatory, Bucharest; Postgraduate studies at Long Island University, NY, USA, 1971–72. *Compositions:* Film Music: Tragic Holiday, Stage Music for: Prometheus (Aeschylus), La Locandiera (Goldoni), Medees (Seneca), Cherry Orchard (Chekhov); Symphonic: Counterpoint for String Orchestra, Segments for String Orchestra, Inventions for Piano and Orchestra, Dice, symphonic sketch, Palingenesia–Poem For 1907 for Orchestra; Engravings for Orchestra, Sinfonietta, Symphony No. 1, 1907, 1987, Concerto for Piano and Orchestra, 1989; Chamber: Concerto for 12 Instruments, Inventions for Piano, Collage for String Quartet, Carol Echoes, quintet for Flute, Oboe, Clarinet, Bassoon and Horn, Homage For Peace for String Quintet, Sonata, Trio for Flute, Piano and Harp, 8 progressive pieces for piano, 1988, Three Lieder, rhymes, by M Eminescu; Choral: Triptych 1991; Dixatuor, for ensemble and percussion, 1993; Inventions No.2 for piano and orchestra, 1996; Palingenesia, septet, 1996. *Address:* c/o UCMR-ADA, Cala Victoriei 141, 71102 Bucharest, Romania.

TAVENER, Alan; Conductor, Organist and Manager; b. 22 April 1957, Weston-Super-Mare, Avon, England; m. Rebecca Jane Gibson, 30 Aug 1980. *Education:* Organ Scholar, Brasenose College, Oxford, 1976–79; ARCO/ARCM 1978, graduated with BA Honours, Music, 1979; Subsequently gained MA degree. *Career:* Director of Music, University of Strathclyde, 1980–; Founder Director, Cappella Nova, 1982–; Conducted several world premieres of new choral works, including John Tavener's Resurrection, Glasgow, 1990; and James MacMillan's Seven Last Words, Glasgow, 1994. *Recordings:* Robert Carver, the Complete Sacred Choral Music, 3 CDs, 1990; Scottish Medieval Plainchant, Columba, most Holy of Saints, 1992; Twentieth Century Scottish Choral Music, 1992; Sacred Music for Mary Queen of Scots, 1993; Sacred Music of Robert Johnson, 1996; Scottish Medieval Plainchant, The Ceremonies of St Kentigern, 1997; Now Let Us Sing: A Scottish Christmas, 1998. *Address:* Director of Music, University of Strathclyde, Livingstone Tower, Richmond Street, Glasgow G1 1XH, Scotland.

TAVENER, Sir John, Kt; Composer and Professor of Music; b. 28 Jan. 1944; m. (1), divorced 1980, (2) Maryanna Schaefer, 1991, 2 d. *Education:* Royal Academy of Music, LRAM. *Career:* Professor of Music, Trinity College of Music, 1969–; mem, Russian Orthodox Church. *Compositions:* Piano Concerto; Three Holy Sonnets (Donne); Cain and Able (first prize Monaco); The Cappemakers; Three Songs of T. S. Eliot; Grandma's Footsteps; In Memoriam Igor Stravinsky; Responsorium in memory of Annon Lee Silver; The Whale; Introit for March 27th; Three Surrealist Songs; In Alium; Akhmatova Requiem; Ultimos Ritos, 1972; Thérèse (opera), 1972; A Gentle Spirit (opera), 1977; Kyklike Kinesis; Palin; Palintropos; Canticle of the Mother of God; Divine Liturgy of St John Chrysostum; The Immurement of Antigone; Lamentation, Last Prayer and Exaltation; Six Abbasid Songs; Greek Interlude; Sappho; Lyrical Fragments; Prayer for The World; The Great Canon of St Andrew of Crete; Trisagion; Risen!; Mandelion; The Lamb, carol; Funeral Ikos; Doxa; Lord's Prayer; Mandoodles; Towards the Son; 16 Haiku of Seferis; Ikon of Light; Orthodox Vigil Service; Two Hymns to the Mother of God; Eis Thanaton; Nativity; Angels; Love Bade Me Welcome; Panikhida, (orthodox funeral service); Ikon of St Cuthbert; Magnificat and Nunc Dimittis (Collegium Regale); Akathis of Thanksgiving; Meditation on the Light; Wedding Prayer; Many Years;

Acclamation; The Protecting Veil, for cello and orchestra; Ikon of St Seraphim; God is With Us; Hymn to the Holy Spirit; The Tyger; Apolytikion for St Nicholas; The Call; Let Not the Prince be Silent; Resurrection, 1989; The Hidden Treasure for String Quartet, 1989; The Repentant Thief for clarinet and strings, 1990; Mary of Egypt, chamber opera, 1991, premiere at Aldeburgh Festival in 1992; We Shall See Him as He Is, 1992; Annunciation, 1992; Theophany, 1993; The Apocalypse, 1993; Song for Athene, 1993; The World is Burning, 1993; The Myrrh-Bearer, 1993; Akhmatova Songs, 1993; Innocence, 1994; Agraphon, for soprano Patricia Rozario and string orchestra, 1995; Feast of Feasts, 1995; Prayer to the Holy Trinity, 1995; Let's Begin Again, 1995; Syvati, 1995; Vlepondas, 1996; The Hidden Face, 1996; Diodia, for string quartet, 1997; Fear and Rejoice, O People, 1997; My Gaze is Ever upon You, for violin and tape, 1998; Eternity's Sunrise for soprano and ensemble, 1998; Music for Millennium celebrations at Millennium Dome, London, 2000; In One Single Moment, 2000; The Gentle Light, 2000; Ekstasis, 2001; Epistle of Love, 2001; Glory for God for his Transient Life, 2001; Mahatmatar, 2001; Song of the Cosmos, 2001; Lamentation and Praises, 2002; The Second coming, 2002; In Memory, 2002, Ikon of Eros, 2002; Lament for Jerusalem, 2002; Mother and Child, 2002; Butterfly Dream, 2002; Maya and Atma, 2002; Elizabeth Full of Grace, 2002; Exhortion and Kohima, 2003; Supernatural Songs, 2003. *Honours:* Honorary Doctorate for Sacred Music, New Delhi, 1990; Honorary Member, Anglo-Hellenic Society; Honorary Vice President, Composers Guild; Honorary Member, Friends of Mount Athos; The Gramophone Award for Best Contemporary Recording, 1992; The Apollo Award for Contribution to Greek Culture, 1993; Honorary FRAM; Honorary FTCL; Patron of Cricklade Festival; Biography, John Tavener–Glimpses of Paradise by Geoffrey Haydon, 1995. *Address:* c/o Chester Music Ltd, 8–9 Frith Street, London W1V 5TZ, England.

TAYLOR, Ann; Singer (Mezzo-soprano); b. 1966 Wrexham, North Wales. *Education:* Royal Northern College of Music, Guildhall School and the National Opera Studio. *Career:* Appearances with Opera North as Ramiro in La Finta Giardiniera, Feodor in Boris Godunov (also at the London Proms), Cherubino, and Donna Clara in the British premiere of Gerhard's The Duenna; Dorabella, Ramiro, Phoebe in Yeomen of the Guard and Handel's Ariodante for Welsh National Opera; Kristina in The Makropulos Case and Oreste in La Belle Hélène for Scottish Opera, Rosina and Mozart's Annius for Glyndebourne Touring Opera; Premiere of Berkeley's Baa Baa Black Sheep at the 1993 Cheltenham Festival; Schumann's Manfred at Monnaie, Brussels, and Cherubino for the Bavarian State Opera; Concerts include Chabrier's La Sulamite at the Queen Elizabeth Hall, Schumann's Scenes from Faust at the 1994 Edinburgh Festival, Les Nuits d'Eté, and Nancy in Albert Herring under Steuart Bedford; Season 1997 with Hänsel for Opera Zuid, and Glyndebourne Festival debut, as Kate in Owen Wingrave; Sang the Stewardess in the premiere of Jonathan Dove's Flight for GTO at Glyndebourne, and also GFO (television) 1998 and Rosina in the Barber of Seville for Opera North; Pippo in The Thieving Magpie and Varvara in Katya Kabanova with Opera North, 1999, and Sarah in Tobias and the Angel for Almeida Opera; Concert, Les Noces, Stravinsky Ensemble Modern, Barbican. *Recordings include:* The Duenna; Baa Baa Black Sheep; Albert Herring; Flight by Jonathan Dove; Messiah, with Hallé Orchestra. *Current Management:* Ingpen & Williams Ltd, 7 St George's Court, 131 Putney Bridge Road, London, SW15 2PA, England.

TAYLOR, Daniel; Singer (Counter-Tenor); b. 1969, Canada. *Education:* Studied at McGill University and at the University of Montreal. *Career:* Concerts with Tafelmusik, Netherlands Radio Chamber Orchestra, Dallas Symphony Orchestra, Portland Baroque, Winnipeg and Quebec Symphonies, Kammerchor Stuttgart and American Bach Soloists; Repertoire includes Messiah (at Göttingen), St Matthew Passion (Berkeley), King Arthur (with Les Violons du Roi), and Rodelinda; Sang Bertarido in Rodelinda at Broomhill and Halle, 1996; Tolomeo in Giulio Cesare at Rome, 1998; Handel's Israel in Egypt at the London Proms, 2002. *Recordings include:* Jommelli, La Didone Abandonata, and Zelenka Missa Omnium Sanctorum.

TAYLOR, Hilary; Singer (Soprano); b. 1970, Melbourne, Australia. *Education:* Melbourne Conservatorium and Victorian College of Arts; National Opera Studio, London. *Career:* Appearances with Victorian State Opera, Australian Opera, Glyndebourne and Salzburg Festivals, and Raymond Gubbay productions; Concerts with Tasmanian and Melbourne Symphonies and BBI Classic Café recitals from the Floral Hall, Covent Garden; Royal Opera engagements in Der Rosenkavalier, The Greek Passion by Martinů, Turandot and Die Entführung. *Honours:* Opera foundation Australia Shell Covent Garden Scholarship, 1996. *Address:* Royal Opera House (chorus), Covent Garden, London, WC2, England.

TAYLOR, James; singer (tenor); b. 1966, Dallas, TX, USA. *Education:* Texas Christian University, Munich Hochschule with Adalbert Kraus. *Career:* debut as Tony in West Side Story, with the Fort Worth Symphony Orchestra 1990; opera appearances in Stuttgart (Monteverdi's Ulisse and Fliegende Holländer) and the Grand Priest in Idomeneo at Brussels; Concerts include: Bach's St Matthew Passion in Munich, and the St John Passion with the Vienna Philharmonic; Beethoven's Missa Solemnis, Mendelssohn's Elijah and Bach Cantatas, conducted by Philippe Herreweghe; season 1997 with Mozart's Requiem at Zürich and Bach's B Minor Mass with the Cleveland Orchestra under Christoph von Dohnányi. *Recordings include:* Orff's Catulli Carmina, Bach's Magnificat and Mass in A (with Helmuth Rilling), Missa solemnis and Mendelssohn's St Paul (Herreweghe). *Address:* Kunstler Sekretariat, Rosenheimerstrasse 52, 81669 Munich, Germany.

TAYLOR, Paul Wegman; Conductor; b. 30 Sept. 1954, Cleveland, Ohio, USA. *Education:* Private violin lessons aged 6–16 years old, with grandfather Willem Wegman; School orchestras; Youth orchestras; Family recitals; Studied horn from 15 years old; Studied at Juilliard with John Chambers and John Cerminaro; New York Freelance including solo horn, Greenwich Symphony Orchestra, extra New York Philharmonic, Metropolitan Opera and numerous other engagements including chamber music, 1975–83; Conducting studies, David Gilbert, Maurice Peress, Walter Hugler, 1986–, San Francisco State University; Juilliard School; Queens College, City University of New York. *Career:* Kammerphilharmonie Budweis CR Wiener Oper Theater, 1992–94; Conductor of Choirs and Amateur Orchestras in Zürich, 1993–2000; Guest Conductor, Tonhalle Orchestra, 1994; Founder, Conductor, Mauritius Ensemble, Switzerland, 1995–; Thuner Stadtsorchester, Switzerland, 1998; Artistic Director, Jakobstads Orchestra, Finland, 2000; Teacher of Horn, Uster, Switzerland; mem, Conductors Guild; International Horn Society. *Recordings:* Hornist with the New York Philharmonic: Ein Heldenleber, Strauss; Ring Excerpts, Wagner. *Honours:* Winner, Conducting Competition, Biel, Bienne Summer Academy, 1994; Guest engagement: Kammerphilharmonie, Budweis, CR, 1995. *Current Management:* Sirkka Varonen Artists. *Address:* Vasterbyvagen 222, 68560 Eegmo, Finland.

TAZZINI, Rinaldo; Producer, Director and Artistic Director; b. 15 Feb. 1942, New York City, USA; m. Helen Neswald, 15 Sept 1965, 1 s., 2 d. *Education:* High School of Music and Art, New York City; BA, Music, Hunter College; Mannes School of Music with Paul Berl and Carl Bamberger; Conservatorio di Cherubini with Cecilia Castelana-Zotti, Florence, Italy; Accademia di Chigiana with Gino Bechi; Accademia di Santa Cecilia with Tito Gobbi. *Career:* Sang at New York City Opera, 1971–72, Teatro dell'Opera, Rome, Italy, 1972–74, Teatro Massimo Bellini at Catania in 1974, and Teatro Lonigo in 1974; Artistic Director and Director of Productions at Brooklyn Opera Society, USA, 1977–; Madama Butterfly at Japanese Garden in New York City, being the first opera for television shot on location in USA, 1980; Producer, Director of the George Gershwin Festival Tour in 1982; Creator, Director, Hot Rags Musical at Lincoln Center in 1983. *Address:* c/o Bernard Lewis, Director of Communications, The Brooklyn Opera Society, Borough Hall, Brooklyn, NY 11201, USA.

TCHISTJAKOVA, Trina; Singer (mezzo-soprano); b. 1965, Moscow, Russia. *Education:* Graduated from the Gnesin Russian Academy of Music, Moscow, 1989. *Career:* Soloist with the Theatre Studio of the Gnesin Academy, from 1988; Principal with the Moscow Municipal Theatre, from 1990 (tour of Italy 1991, as Ratmir in Glinka's Ruslan and Lyudmila); Season 1994–95 Marina in Boris Godunov at Liège, the Verdi Requiem at Lincoln Center, New York, and Ruslan and Lyudmila at Carnegie Hall; Marfa in Khovanshchina at the Bolshoi, 1995; Season 1996–97 as Marina at Turin and Salzburg; Eugene Onegin and The Queen of Spades at Trieste; Kirov Opera St Petersburg as Cherubino, Marguerite in La Damnation de Faust, Amneris and Eboli; Concert repertory includes Skriabin's 1st Symphony (in Sweden and Germany), Beethoven's Ninth and Prokofiev's Alexander Nevsky (with the Philharmonia Orchestra). *Recordings include:* Verdi Arias; Azucena in Il Trovatore. *Honours:* Winner, Viñas Singing Competition, Barcelona, 1993. *Current Management:* Askonas Holt Ltd, Lonsdale Chambers, 27 Chancery Lane, London, WC2A 1PF, England. *Telephone:* (20) 7400-1700. *Fax:* (20) 7400-1799. *E-mail:* info@askonasholt.co.uk. *Website:* www.askonasholt.co.uk.

TEAR, Robert; Singer (tenor) and Conductor; b. 8 March 1939, Barry, South Wales; m. 2 d. *Education:* King's College, Cambridge. *Career:* Debut: With English Opera Group, 1963; Sang as Lensky in Eugene Onegin, Covent Garden; From 1970 as Dov in The Knot Garden (premiere), Lensky, Paris (King Priam), Wagner's Froh and Loge, Tom Rakewell, Admetus in Alceste, Rimbaud in Tavener's Thérèse (premiere 1979), David, Jupiter in Semele; The Director in British premiere of Berio's Un re in Ascolto, 1979, Shuisky (Boris Godunov), 1991, and the Schoolmaster (Cunning Little Vixen), 1990; Sang in world premiere of Tippett's Mask of Time with Boston Symphony Orchestra; Salzburg Festival, 1985, as Eumetus in the Henze/Monteverdi Ulisse; Season 1990–91 with the War Requiem in Detroit and The Mask of Time in London; The Turn of the Screw at Montpellier and Peter Grimes with Geneva Opera; Beethoven and Tippett in Florida and Los Angeles; Title

role in premiere of Ubu Rex by Penderecki at Munich; Mephisto in the Covent Garden premiere of Prokofiev's Fiery Angel, 1992; Season 1994/ 95 as Janáček's Mr Brouček at Munich, Captain Vere in Billy Budd in Geneva, Figaro and The Rake's Progress at Glyndebourne, Loge (Das Rheingold) at the Royal Opera House, Covent Garden, and Herod (Salome) at Hamburg Opera; Sang in Pfitzner's Palestrina at Covent Garden, 1997; Large repertoire in opera and lieder; Created roles in Britten's Burning Fiery Furnace and Prodigal Son; Well known Mime in Das Rheingold in London and Bayreuth; Other roles include Peter Grimes, Matteo (Arabella); Appeared in Europe at Paris Opéra including premiere of three-act version of Berg's Lulu, La Scala Milan, and Salzburg; Regular guest of great US orchestras such as Boston, Chicago, Los Angeles and New York Philharmonic; Tippett's The Mask of Time at 1999 London Prom concerts (also televised); Conducting debut in Minneapolis, 1985, subsequently conducting many orchestras including London Mozart Players, Northern Sinfonia, English Chamber Orchestra, Philharmonia, BBC National Orchestra of Wales, Royal Liverpool Philharmonic and Royal Scottish National Orchestra; Artistic Director, Vocal faculty of London Royal Schools of Music, 1992–94; Holds the Chair of International Singing at the Royal Academy of Music; Sang Arthur in Birtwistle's Gawain at Covent Garden and Captain Vere in Los Angeles, 2000; Mozart's Basilio for WNO, 2001. *Recordings include:* Mahler (orch Schoenberg) Das Lied von der Erde, with Premiere Ensemble and Mark Wigglesworth. *Honours:* Honorary Fellow, King's College, Cambridge; C.B.E., 1984. *Current Management:* Askonas Holt Ltd, Lonsdale Chambers, 27 Chancery Lane, London, WC2A 1PF, England. *Telephone:* (20) 7400-1700. *Fax:* (20) 7400-1799. *E-mail:* info@askonasholt.co.uk. *Website:* www.askonasholt.co.uk.

TEARE, Christine; Singer (Soprano); b. 1959, Isle of Man. *Education:* Royal Academy of Music, with Marjorie Thomas; Further study with Rudolf Piernay. *Career:* Debut: Welsh National Opera, Cardiff, as Donna Anna, 1983; Covent Garden, 1983, as Helmwige, Ortlinde and Third Norn in The Ring; Season 1985–6 as a Flower Maiden in Parsifal for English National Opera, and Donna Anna for Opera North; Welsh National Opera 1985–89 as Mozart's Countess, Amelia (Ballo in Maschera), Third Norn in Götterdämmerung, Berta (Barbiere di Siviglia) and the Empress in Die Frau ohne Schatten; Broadcasts with the BBC. *Recordings include:* Osud by Janáček, and Parsifal (ENO and WNO; EMI). *Address:* c/o Stafford Law, 6 Barham Close, Weybridge, Surrey, KT 13 9 PR, England.

TEDE, Margery; Singer (Mezzo-Soprano); b. 1940, USA. *Education:* Studied at San Francisco State College, Madrid Conservatory and the Hochschule für Musik in Berlin. *Career:* Sang with the San Francisco Opera as Fricka, Amneris, Azucena, Judith in Bluebeard's Castle, Jocasta and Herodias in Salome; Sang Countess Carolina in the local premiere of Henze's Elegy for Young Lovers, conducted by Christopher Keene; Lake Tahoe Summer Music Festival as Susan B Anthony in Virgil Thomson's The Mother of Us All; Concert appearances with the San Francisco Symphony under Seiji Ozawa and in Mozart's Coronation Mass in New York; Sang in opera, concerts and recitals in Europe, Central America, Alaska and the South Pacific; Sang the world premiere of Roger Nixon's Three Transcendental Songs in New York and songs by Charles Ives in Hamburg; Now retired as singer and active as teacher. *Honours:* International Scholarship from the Federation of Music Clubs. *Address:* Steorra Enterprises, 243 West End Avenue, Suite 907, New York, NY 10023, USA.

TEITELBAUM, Richard (Lowe); Composer, Performer and Teacher; b. 19 May 1939, New York City, USA. *Education:* BA, Haverford College, 1960; MMus, Yale University School of Music, 1964; Mannes School, 1960–61; Accademia di Santa Cecilia, Rome, 1964–65; Composition with Luigi Nono in Venice, 1965–66; Wesleyan University World Music Program, 1970–71. *Career:* Founding Member, Musica Electronica Viva, Rome, 1966; Instructor at California Institute of the Arts, 1971–72; Founder and Director, Electronic Music Studio, Art Institute of Chicago, 1972–73; Co-Director and Visiting Professor, York University, Toronto, 1973–76; Soloist at Berlin Philharmonic Hall, Concertgebouw, Centre Pompidou, and WDR Cologne among others, 1984–86; Visiting Professor, Vassar College, Full Professor, Bard College, 1988–89; mem, American Music Center; Composers Forum; College Music Society; International Computer Music Society. *Compositions include:* Intersections for Piano, 1964; In Tune for Live Electronics, 1966; Digital Piano Music, 1983; Concerto Grosso for Robotic Pianos, Winds, Trombone and Synthesizers; Iro Wa Nioedo for 20 Buddhist Monks; Golem, interactive opera, 1989–94; Dal Niente, for midi piano, sampler and computer, 1997. *Recordings include:* Hi Uchi Ishi, 1977; Time Zones, 1977; Concerto Grosso, 1987; Golem, Cyberband, Live at Merkin Hall. *Honours:* Fulbright Scholarships, Italy, 1964–66, Japan, 1976–77; Meet the Composer/NEA Grant, Mary Flager Cary Trust, 1976, 1979, 1988. *Address:* 250 Cold Brook Road, Bearsville, NY 12409, USA.

TELLEFSEN, Arve; Violinist; b. 13 Dec. 1936, Trondheim, Norway. *Education:* Studied with Arne Stoltenberg, Henry Holst and Ivan

Galamian, New York, 1960. *Career:* Numerous recitals and concerts in Europe; Professor of The Academy of Music in Oslo from 1973; Tour of Norway in 1985 with the RPO under Ashkenazy; Oslo Philharmonai concerts in 1987 with Mariss Jansons, Neeme Järvi and Esa-Pekka Salonen; British engagements with David Zinman, Jerzy Maksymiuk, Marek Janowski, Okko Kamu, Vernon Handley and Kurt Sanderling; Festival concerts at Schleswig-Holstein, Lockenhaus and Montreux; Founded Oslo Chamber Music Festival in 1989; Season 1997 premiered the Concerto by Nordheim, with the Oslo Philharmonic Orchestra. *Recordings include:* concertos by Nielsen, Shostakovich, Berwald, Aulin, Valen, Sinding, Svendsen and Sibelius; Beethoven and Grieg Sonatas; Bruch and Beethoven concertos with the London Philharmonic Orchestra; Shostakovich 1 and Sibelius with the Royal Philharmonic. *Honours:* First Prize, Princess Astrid's Competition for Young Norwegian Artists, 1956; Harriet Cohen International Award, 1962; Awarded the prize of Bergen Festival, 1964; Grieg Prize, 1973.

TEMESI, Maria, (Maria Toth); Singer (soprano); b. 1957, Szeged, Hungary. *Education:* Studied at Franz Liszt Academy; At Szeged, Piano; Singing Teacher, Opera Singer diplomas, Budapest; Masterclasses at Weimar Music Academy and Mozarteum, Salzburg. *Career:* Debut: Budapest State Opera as Elsa, in Wagner's Lohengrin, under G Patanè, 1982; Appearances: Staatsoper Hamburg, Oper der Stadt Köln, Semperoper Dresden, Staatsoper Berlin, Komische Oper Berlin, Opernhaus Zürich, Teatro Farnese Parma, Teatro de la Zarzuela Madrid, Opéra de Nice, Théâtre du Capitole Toulouse, Opera Company of Philadelphia, Smetana Theatre Prague, Herodes Atticus Ampthitheatre Athens, Opernhaus Graz, Montevideo Teatro Solis, Uruguay; Main Roles: Vitellia in La Clemenza di Tito, Adriana Lecouvrer, Tatiana, Lisa in The Queen of Spades, Amelia in Ballo in Maschera, Leonora in Trovatore, Elisabeth de Valois, Elena in Vespri Siciliani, Desdemona, Alice in Falstaff, Elsa in Lohengrin, Eva in Meistersinger, Elisabeth in Tannhäuser, Estrella in Schubert's Alfonso und Estrella, Sieglinde in Die Walküre, Mimi in La Bohème and Manon in Manon Lescaut; Brünnhilde in Götterdämmerung at Budapest, 1998; Concert performance of Guntram by Strauss, Manhattan Cable television, NY; Götterdämmerung (Gutrune); Mahler's 2nd Symphony under Dorati; Handel's Messiah under Gönnenwein; La Clemenza di Tito conducted by John Pritchard, Cologne; Liederabenden, Budapest Music Academy; Lisbon Fundacao Calouste Gulbenkian; Cairo Academy of Arts; Beethoven: Missa Solemnis (Milano, RAI); Verdi: Requiem; Dvořák, Requiem; Britten: War Requiem (Zagreb); Rossini: Stabat Mater; Pergolesi: Stabat Mater. *Recordings:* Liszt, Missa Choralis; Mahler, 8th Symphony. *Honours:* Prizewinner in competitions in Athens, 1979, Toulouse, 1980; 1st Prize, Rio de Janeiro, 1981; Winner, Pavarotti Competition, Philadelphia, 1985; Szekely Mihaly Plaquette, Budapest, 1995. *Address:* Templom u 22, 1028 Budapest, Hungary.

TEMIRKANOV, Yuri; Conductor; b. 10 Dec. 1938, Nalchik, Caucasus, Russia. *Education:* Leningrad Conservatory for Talented Children, 1953–56; Leningrad Conservatory of Music, graduated as violinist in 1962 and conductor in 1965. *Career:* Conductor of Leningrad Opera and all major Soviet orchestras, 1968–; Director, Leningrad Symphony Orchestra, 1969 touring extensively; Artistic Director of Kirov Opera in 1977; Has conducted Berlin Philharmonic, Vienna Philharmonic, Dresden State Orchestras, and Orchestre de Paris; Following London debut with The Royal Philharmonic Orchestra in 1977 worked with Philharmonia, City of Birmingham, and Royal Liverpool Philharmonic Orchestras; Principal Guest Conductor with RPO, 1979; Conducted the BBC Symphony Orchestra in Italy and Russia in 1987, and the Philadelphia, Boston and New York Orchestras in USA; Artistic Director of the Leningrad (now St Petersburg) Philharmonic, 1988; Conducted The Queen of Spades for RAI, Turin, in 1990; Principal Conductor of the Royal Philharmonic Orchestra from 1992; Recent seasons have included Tchaikovsky Cycle with St Petersburg Philharmonic in Japan and Europe and tours of USA and Germany with the Royal Philharmonic; Conducted and produced Eugene Onegin at San Francisco, 1997; Tchaikovsky's 1st Symphony at 2001 London Prom concerts; Music Director, Baltimore Symphony Orchestra, 2000–. *Honours:* 1st Prize, National Conducting Competition, Russia, 1968. *Current Management:* IMG Artists (Europe). *Address:* c/o IMG Artists (Europe), Lovell House, 616 Chiswick High Road, London W4 5RX, England.

TEMPERLEY, Nicholas; American musicologist; b. 7 Aug. 1932, Beaconsfield, England; m. Mary Dorothea Sleator, 17 Sept 1960, 1 s., 2 d. *Education:* ARCM, Royal College of Music, 1952; BA, BMus, MA, PhD, King's College, Cambridge University, 1952–59. *Career:* Assistant Lecturer, Music, Cambridge University and Fellow, Clare College, Cambridge, 1961–66; Assistant Professor, Musicology, Yale University, USA, 1966–67; Associate Professor 1967–72, Professor 1972–96, Professor Emeritus, 1996–, Chairman Musicology Division 1972–75, 1992–96, University of Illinois. *Publications include:* Books: Raymond and Agnes, Edward J Loder, performed Cambridge, 1966; Symphonie

Fantastique, Berlioz, New Berlioz Edition, 1972; English Songs 1800–60, Musica Britannica Vol. 43, 1979; London Pianoforte School 1766–1860, 20 vols, Garland, 1984–87; Haydn's Creation, with authentic English text, 1987; Music of English Parish Church, 2 vols, 1979; Athlone History of Music in Britain, vol. 5, Romantic Age, 1981; Haydn: The Creation, 1991; Co-Editor, The Hymn Tune Index, 4 vols, 1998; Bound for America: Three British Composers, 2003. *Contributions:* numerous musical journals; New Grove Dictionary. *Address:* 805 West Indiana Street, Urbana, IL 61801, USA.

TENENBOM, Steven; Violist; b. 1965, USA. *Education:* Curtis Institute of Music with Michael Tree and Karen Tuttle. *Career:* soloist with the Brandenburg Ensemble and Rochester Philharmonic Orchestra, guest artist with the Guarneri Quartet, Beaux Arts Trio and Chamber Music Society of Lincoln Center; festival engagements at Chamber Music Northwest, Aspen, music from Angel Fire and Bravo Colorado; violist with the Orion String Quartet, including concerts throughout North America and in Europe; Brahms and Schubert evening in season 1996–97 at Lincoln Center, and opening night Gala in honour of Marilyn Horne; faculty mem. at Mannes Coll. of Music and Hartt School of Music, New York. *Current Management:* Ingpen & Williams Ltd, 7 St George's Court, 131 Putney Bridge Road, London, SW15 2PA, England.

TENNFJORD, Oddbjorn; Singer (bass); b. 1941, Oslo, Norway. *Education:* Studied at the Bergen and Oslo Conservatories, in Essen with Clemens Kaiser-Breme, in Rome with Luigi Ricci and in London with Roy Henderson. *Career:* Has sung with the Norske Opera Oslo from 1971 as Osmin, Don Pasquale, Basilio, Falstaff, Pogner, Boris Godunov, Sarastro, Wotan, King Marke, Gremin and Fiesco; Concert and opera engagements for Norwegian radio and television, in Germany, Italy, Poland, Sweden, Denmark, Israel, Yugoslavia, France and USA; Appearances with Scottish Opera as The Commendatore, Daland, Sarastro and Fafner; Bologna in 1988 and Ravenna Festival in 1989 as the Grand Inquisitor in Don Carlos; Sang with Scottish Opera as Fafner in Das Rheingold and the Commendatore and as Daland at Oslo in 1989; Numerous guest appearances world-wide include: Baron Ochs and Daland in Montpellier, Daland in Cologne, Tokyo, Barcelona and Las Palmas, Baron Ochs in Osaka, The Grand Inquisitor in Bologna and Ravenna, Sarastro, Fafner, The Commendatore and Frank (Die Fledermaus) with the Scottish Opera; Since 1994 freelance: Gurrelieder with Mariss Jansons and the Oslo Philharmonic Orchestra, King Marke in Brussels with Antonio Pappano, Duke Bluebeard with Neeme Järvi and Gothenburg Symphony Orchestra, Vespri Siciliani, Rheingold and Die Walküre at Den Norske Opera; Season 1996–97 included Baron Ochs at Deutsche Oper, Berlin, Boris Godunov at Kungliga Operan, Stockholm, Marke and Commendatore in Brussels and Der Friedenstag and Don Giovanni at Sächsische Staatsoper, Dresden; Season 1998–99, Sang Wagner's Klingsor at Brussels, Baron Ochs at Royal Opera, Stockholm, Daland at Hamburg Staatsoper and The National Opera, Oslo. *Address:* Olaf Bulls Vei 32, 0765 Oslo, Norway.

TENSTAM, Ulrica; Singer (Mezzo-soprano); b. 1963, Sweden. *Education:* Gothenburg 1983–87, Opera Studio Stockholm, 1987–89. *Career:* Debut: Oslo 1987, as Ramiro in Mozart's La finta giardiniera; Drottningholm Festival from 1989, as Klytemnestra in Gluck's Iphigenie en Aulide, and other roles; Stockholm Folkoperan as Rossini's Rosina; Royal Opera Stockholm from 1992, as Rosina, Nicklausse in Les Contes d'Hoffmann and Dalila; Ystad Opera 1993, as the Mother in Szokolay's Blood Wedding; Hermia in A Midsummer Night's Dream; Other roles include Gluck's Orpheus (Stockholm, 1991); Frequent concerts throughout Scandinavia. *Address:* Kungliga Teater, PO Box 16094, S–103 22 Stockholm, Sweden.

TENZI, Fausto; Singer (Tenor); b. 1 April 1939, Lugano, Switzerland. *Education:* Studied in Milan. *Career:* Sang at La Scala Milan, Théâtre des Champs Elysées, Paris, Teatro Comunale, Bologna and in Florence, Lucerne, Aachen and Perugia; Engaged at Buxton Festival, England and made concert appearances in Rome, Paris, Berlin, Moscow, Leningrad and North America; Other roles include Don José, Edgardo, Manrico, Don Carlos, Pinkerton, Rodolfo, Turiddu and Ivan Khovansky in Khovanshchina. *Recordings include:* The Queen of Spades; Scriabin's 1st Symphony.

TERAMOTO, Mariko; Japanese musicologist; b. 6 June 1948, Tokyo. *Education:* BA, Musashino Coll. of Music, Tokyo, 1971; MA, National Univ. of Fine Arts and Music, Tokyo, 1973; PhD, Univ. of Frankfurt am Main, 1978. *Career:* Lecturer, National Univ. of Fine Arts and Music 1985–89, 1996–97; Asst Prof. 1984–87, Prof. 1988–97, Meisei Univ.; Lecturer 1984–97, Asst Prof. 2001–, Prof. 2002–, Musashino Coll. of Music; mem. International, American and Japanese Musicological Soc., Gesellschaft für Musikforschung, Internationale CMv Weber-Gesellschaft, Internationale Heinrich Schütz Gesellschaft. *Publications:* Die Psalmmotettendrucke des Johannes Petrejus in Nürnberg 1983, Katalog der Musikdrucke des Johannes Petrejus in Nürnberg 1993. *Contributions:* Journal of the Japanese Musicological Soc., musicological reference books. *Address:* 2-10-16 Shimo-ochiai, Shinjuku-ku, Tokyo 161-0033, Japan. .

TERENTIEVA, Nina; Singer (Mezzo-soprano); b. 1950, Russia. *Education:* Leningrad State Conservatory. *Career:* Sang with the Kirov Opera as Olga in Eugene Onegin, Marina (Boris Godunov) and Gounod's Siebel; Bolshoi Opera as Amneris, Marfa in Khovanshchina and Carmen; Vienna Staatsoper from 1987, as Azucena and Eboli, Azucena and Marina at La Scala, Ulrica at Munich, Berlin and Buenos Aires; Eboli in Don Carlos at Los Angeles (1990) and San Francisco (1992); Amneris in Aida at Berlin, Hamburg, Munich, and the Royal Opera Covent Garden (1996); Further appearances at the Metropolitan Opera, Washington Opera, and with the Canadian Opera Company; Season 1997 with Amneris for San Francisco Opera; Frequent concert appearances and recitals in Russia. *Address:* c/o Vienna State Opera, Opernring 2, 1010 Vienna, Austria.

TEREY-SMITH, Mary; Musicologist, Opera Conductor and Vocal Coach; b. 1933, Budapest, Hungary; m. C A C Smith, deceased. *Education:* BMus, Conducting and Composition, Liszt Academy of Music; MA, Music Literature, University of Vermont, USA; PhD, Musicology, Eastman School of Music, University of Rochester. *Career:* Debut: Conductor, Tatabanya Symphony Orchestra, Budapest, 1951; Vocal coach, then assistant conductor, Hungarian State Opera, 1950–56; Resident conductor, Tatabanya Symphony Orchestra, 1951–56; Vocal Coach, Toronto Royal Conservatory Opera School, Canada, 1957–58; Assistant Professor, 1967–72, Associate Professor, 1972–85, Professor of Music History and Literature, 1985–2001, Western Washington University; Director, Opera Workshop, 1967–75, Director of the Collegium Musicum Ensemble, 1969–2001, Western Washington University; Five biannual European summer tours with the Collegium Musicum, 1990–2000, performing in Hungary, Italy, Austria, Switzerland, Liechtenstein, Slovakia and Romania; Musical advisor and conductor of Capella Savaria, with tours in Baroque music; Research Project: the church music of Gregor J. Werner. *Recordings:* Conductor of 2 CDs: Four Orchestral Suites from Operas by J P Rameau with the Capella Savaria Baroque Orchestra, 1996; Director of Syrens, Enchanters and Fairies- 18th Century Overtures from the London Stage with the Capella Savaria Baroque Orchestra; Thomas Arne- The Complete Solo Cantatas; G.J.Werner:Masses and Offertories composed for the Esterházy Family. *Publications:* Selection of published articles and studies: Editor, French Baroque Orchestral Dances, by Jean-Philippe Rameau, Canada 1986; Orchestral Practice in the Paris Opéra, 1690–1764, and the Spread of the French Influence in Europe, in Studia Musicologica xxxi, 1989; International Dictionary of Opera: Rameau: Les Boréades, essay, 1993; D Dragonetti in England by F Palmer, review for Notes; Passio Jesu Christi by F F Fasch in The Fasch Yearbook, 1997; Alfred Planyavsky's The Baroque Bass Violon; One Hundred years of Violoncello by Valerie Walden and the Cambridge Companion to the Cello, editor, R Stowell; Reviews for Music and Letters. *Honours:* Prof. Emer. from Wester Washington University, 2001. *Address:* Department of Music, Western Washington University, 516 High Street, Bellingham, WA 98225–9107 USA.

TERFEL JONES, Bryn, CBE; British singer (bass baritone); b. 9 Nov. 1965, Pantglas, Snowdonia, Wales; s. of Hefin Jones and Nesta Jones; m. Lesley Halliday 1987; three s. *Education:* Ysgol Dyffryn Nantlle, Penygroes, Gwynedd and Guildhall School of Music and Drama. *Career:* debut, WNO as Guglielmo 1990; sang Mozart's Figaro at Santa Fe Opera and ENO 1991; Royal Nat. Opera, Covent Garden debut as Masetto in Don Giovanni 1992, repeated on tour to Japan; sang at Salzburg Festival as the Spirit Messenger in Die Frau ohne Schatten, and as Jochanaan in Salome 1992, returning as Leporello in Patrice Chéreau's production of Don Giovanni 1994; further appearances at Vienna Staatsoper as Mozart's Figaro 1993, at Chicago as Donner in Das Rheingold, debuts at New York Metropolitan Opera 1994, Sydney Opera House 1999, and frequent guest soloist with Berlin Philharmonic Orchestra; sang in the Brahms Requiem under Colin Davis and at Salzburg Easter Festival under Abbado (Herbert von Karajan In Memoriam) 1993; sang Nick Shadow in The Rake's Progress for WNO 1996, Figaro at La Scala 1997, Scarpia for Netherlands Opera 1998, Falstaff at the reopening of the Royal Opera House, Covent Garden 1999; 4 male roles in Les Contes d'Hoffmann, and Don Giovanni, both at Metropolitan Opera, New York, and Nick Shadow in The Rake's Progress for San Francisco Opera 1999–2000; London Proms 2002; baritone roles in Les Contes d'Hoffmann at the Opéra Bastille, Sweeney Todd in Chicago, and Falstaff and Don Giovanni at Covent Garden 2002–03; Mephistopheles in Faust, Wotan in Das Rheingold and Die Walküre at Covent Garden 2004; many concert appearances in Europe, USA, Canada, Japan and Australia; Pres. Nat. Youth Choir of Wales, Festival of Wales; Vice-Pres. Llangollen Int. Eisteddfod; Founder, Faenol Festival 2000. *Recordings include:* Salome, Le nozze di Figaro, An Die Musik, Wagner Arias, Britten's Gloriana, Beethoven's Ninth Symphony, Brahms' Requiem, Schwanengesang, Cecilia and Bryn, If

Ever I Would Leave You, Handel Arias, Vagabond (Caecillia Prize 1995, Gramophone People's Award 1996) 1995, Opera Arias (Grammy Award for best classical vocal performance) 1996, Something Wonderful (Britannia Record Club Members' Award) 1997, Don Giovanni 1997, Bryn (Classical BRIT award for best album 2004) 2003. *Honours:* Hon. Fellow, Univ. of Wales, Aberystwyth, Welsh Coll. of Music and Drama, Univ. of Wales, Bangor; Hon. DMus (Glamorgan) 1997; White Robe, Gorsedd; recipient, Kathleen Ferrier Scholarship 1988; Gold Medal Award 1989; Lieder Prize, Cardiff Singer of the World Competition 1989; Young Singer of the Year, Gramophone magazine 1992; British Critics' Circle Award 1992; Newcomer of Year, Int. Classic Music Awards 1993, Classical BRIT award for best male artist 2004. *Current Management:* Harlequin Agency, 203 Fidlas Road, Cardiff, CF14 5NA, Wales. *Telephone:* (29) 2075-0821. *Fax:* (29) 2075-5971.

TERRACINI, Lyndon; Singer (Baritone); b. 1950, Australia. *Education:* Studied in Australia. *Career:* Debut: With Australian Opera at Sydney Opera House as Sid in Albert Herring, 1976; Sang in London in 1983 as Ivan in Brian Howard's Inner Voices; Sang Daniello in the local premiere of Krenek's Jonny Spielt Auf in 1984; US debut in 1984 at the Cabrillo Music festival in Australian Folksongs; German debut in the title role in Hans Zender's Stephen Climax at Frankfurt; Italian debut as Sancio Panza in the world premiere of Henze-Paisiello Don Quischotte at the Montepulciano Festival; Has sung with Opera Factory Zürich as Agamemnon and Orestes in the Iphigenias by Gluck; Sang Der Alte in Reimann's Ghost Sonata and Landsknecht in Hartmann's Simplicius Simplicissimus; Appearances in Ullmann's posthumous The Emperor of Atlantis and as Marcello in La Bohème and Byron in the premiere of Richard Meale's La Mer de Glace at Sydney, 1991; Sang Don Giovanni in Adelaide in 1991 and appearances with Opera Factory London as Figaro on stage and on film for Channel 4 television; Sang the title role in the premiere of Casanova Confined, by Andrew Ford, Barossa Festival, Australia, 1996. Concert repertoire includes Syringa by Elliott Carter, with Collegium Musicum, Zürich, and El Cimarrón by Hans Werner Henze. *Address:* Performing Arts, 6 Windmill Street, London W1 1HF, England.

TERRANOVA, Vittorio; Singer (Tenor); b. 18 June 1945, Licata, Sicily. *Education:* Studied in Milan. *Career:* Debut: Mantua 1970, as Arturo in I Puritani; Many appearances at opera houses throughout Italy, and at the Spoleto and Florence (Maggio Musical) festivals; Rosini's Almaviva at Amsterdam, 1971; Guest engagements at the Vienna Staatsoper, Bregenz festival, Teatro Col ón Buenos Aires, New York City Opera and Chicago Lyric Opera; Other roles have included Verdi's Fenton, Alfredo and the Duke of Mantua, Nadir in Les Pêcheurs de Perles, Don Ottavio, Ferrando, Faust, and Lyonel in Martha; Further roles in operas by Donizetti (Alamiro in Belisario, Buenos Aires), Cimarosa and Paisiello; Many concert engagements. *Address:* c/o New York City Opera, Lincoln Center, New York, NY 10023, USA.

TERVO, Markku; Singer (Bass); b. 1955, Helsinki, Finland. *Education:* Sibelius Academy, Helsinki; Further study with Hendrik Rootering. *Career:* Sang with Finnish National Opera, 1977–79, Karlsruhe Opera 1981–86, Krefeld 1986–89 and Freiburg, 1989–94; Returned to Karlsruhe, 1994; Roles have included Mozart's Osmin and Sarastro, Rossini's Basilio, Verdi's Ferrando, Sparafucile and King Philip (Don Carlos); Wagner's Daland and Hagen, and Claggart in Billy Budd; Guest engagements throughout Germany, and in Luxembourg; Concerts throughout Europe, notably Bach's Christmas Oratorio, St John Passion and Magnificat, L'Enfance du Christ by Berlioz, the Verdi Requiem and Shostakovich 13th Symphony (Babi-yar). *Recordings include:* Götterdämmerung (Bella Musica). *Address:* c/o Staatstheater Karlsrhe, Baumesterstrasse 11Pf 1449, D–7550 Karlsruhe, Germany.

TERZAKIS, Dimitri, DipMus; Greek composer; b. 12 March 1938, Athens. *Education:* Hellenic Conservatory, Athens, Cologne Musikhochschule with Zimmermann. *Career:* co-founder, Greek Soc. for Contemporary Music 1966; Lecturer, Robert Schumann Inst., Düsseldorf 1974; teacher of composition, Düsseldorf Hochschule 1987–93, Berne Hochschule 1990–94, Felix Mendelssohn Musikhochschule, Leipzig 1994–. *Compositions include:* Ikona for strings 1963, Oboe Concerto 1968, Okeaniden for chorus and orchestra 1968, Ichochronos (electronic) 1968, Torquemada (opera) 1976, Circus Universal (chamber opera) 1976, four string quartets 1969, 1976, 1982, 1990, Tropi for orchestra 1976, Passionen (oratorio) 1979, Erotikon for soprano and three instruments 1979, Lachesis for orchestra 1984, Hermes (opera) 1984, Brass Quintet 1984, Six Monologues for soprano and orchestra 1985, Violin Concerto 1986, Das sechste Siegel for chorus and ensemble 1987, Per aspera ad Astra for orchestra 1990, Ikaros-Daidolos for soprano quartet and brass orchestra 1990, Der Holle Nachklang II for soprano and organ 1993, Daphnis und Chloe for soprano and viola 1994, Lieder ohne Worte for soprano 1994, Alto saxophone concerto 1995. *Address:* c/o AEPI, Fragoklissias and Samou Street 51, 151 25 Amaroussio, Athens, Greece.

TERZAKIS, Zachos; Singer (Tenor); b. 1945, Athens, Greece. *Education:* Degree in Geology, University of Athens; Studied voice at Apollonion Odeon, Athens, 1969. *Career:* Engaged at National Lyric Theatre of Athens, roles included Alfredo in La Traviata, Pinkerton in Madama Butterfly and Elvino in Sonnambula; Sang in Athens Festival; Greek radio and television appearances; German debut as Turiddu in Cavalleria rusticana, Kiel, 1978; Engaged in Bielefeld, roles included Cassio in Otello, Singer in Rosenkavalier and Tamino in Magic Flute, 1979–82; Member, Nuremberg-Opera, roles included Rodolfo in Bohème, Almaviva in Barbiere di Siviglia and Adorno in Simon Boccanegra, 1982–87; Since 1987, freelance opera singer, appearances in many European venues including Opernhaus Zürich, Staatsoper Berlin, Volksoper Wien and National Opera Athens; sang Hoffman at Bregenz Festival, 1987; Other festival appearances include Luzerner Festwochen and Casals Festival in Puerto Rico; Debut as Titus in Staatsoper Vienna, and Jason in Medea by Mikis Theodorakis in Bilbao, 1991; Teatro dell Opera, Rome, as Rudolf von Habsburg in Mayerling, 1993; Numerous concert recitals including Tivoli Copenhagen, Concert House Stockholm and Palais des Beaux Arts, Brussels; Staging Director, Medea, at Meiningen, 1995, and German translator; Numerous radio broadcasts. *Recordings:* Greek opera, Mother's Ring by Kalomiris, tenor solo, 1985; Penderecki's Polish Requiem, 1992; Missa Solemnis; Lehar's Operetta Highlights; Die lustige Witwe; Markopoulos's Orpheus Liturgy. *Honours:* Gold Medal of Excellence, Apollonion Odeon, Athens, 1976; First Prize, Maria Callas Scholarship Competition, 1976; Grammy Award nomination, 1992. *Address:* Bergstrasse 15, 91086 Falkendorf, Germany.

TERZIAN, Alicia; Composer, Conductor, Lecturer and Musicologist; b. 1 July 1934, Cordoba, Argentina; Divorced, 1 d. *Education:* Philosophical Studies, National University of Argentina; Research in Musicology, Latin American music; Private study in Conducting with Mariano Drago. *Career:* Debut: Premiere of String Quartet, Wagneriana Association, Buenos Aires, 1955; Organizer, Argentine Music Council of UNESCO, and also Jeunesses Musicales; Over 2000 lectures on 20th Century music history world-wide; Organizer, Foundation Encuentros Internacionales de Musica Contemporanea, 1968; Founder, Grupo Encuentros, to promote Latin American music; Performances for television and radio and over 400 concerts world-wide; As composer, works performed world-wide by leading soloists, orchestras and chamber ensembles. *Compositions include:* Stage: Hacia la luz, ballet, 1965; Bestiela, theatre music, 1981; El enano, theatre music, 1964; Orchestral works: Three Pieces for strings, orchestra of guitar quartet, 1954; Concertio para violin, 1955; Atmosferas, symphonic band, 1969; Carmen Criaturalis, solo horn, string orchestra and percussion, 1971; Off the Edge, baritone, string orchestra and percussion, 1992; Chamber Music: Y cuya luy es como la profunda oscuridad, group and tape, 1982; Les yeux fertiles, mezzo and group with percussion, 1997; Au dela des rêves, for piano, clarinet and violin, 2001; Instrumental: Libro de canciones de Federico Garcia Lorca for voice and piano, 1954; Atmosferas, duo piano, 1969; Yagua ya yuca, solo percussion, 1992; Canto a Vahan for piano and tape, 1996; Offer to Bach, for organ, 2000; Le viol des anges for 4 to 6 percussionists, 2000/01; Multimedia: Sinfonia Visual en dos movimientos, tape and slides, 1972; Canto a mí misma, string orchestra, tamtam and electronic sound transformation and loudspeakers in concert hall, 1986; Buenos Aires me vas a matar, 1990; Frémissement, organ and tape, 2000. *Recordings:* Violin Concerto, Voces and Canto a mi misma, 1997; Toccata for Piano; Juegos para Diana. *Honours:* Hon. mem., Int. Music Council, 2003; First Prize of Municipality of Buenos Aires, 1964; Francisco Solano Award, 1968; Outstanding Young Musicians Prize, Argentina, 1970; Nat. Fund for the Arts Prize, 1970; First Nat. Prize for Music, 1982; Gomidas Int. Prize, 1983; Médaille des Palmes Académiques, France, 1992; St Sahuk and St Mesrop Medals, Pope Vasken I of Armenian Church, 1992; Alberto de Castilla Medal of Columbia, 1994; Mozart Medal, Int. Music Council, 1995. *Address:* Santa Fe 3269-4B, Buenos Aires 1425, Argentina. *E-mail:* aterzian@aliciaterzian.com.ar. *Website:* www.aliciaterzian.com .ar.

TERZIAN, Anita; Singer (Mezzo-Soprano); b. 12 Oct. 1947, Strasbourg, France. *Education:* Studied at the Juilliard School, New York with Jennie Tourel. *Career:* Debut: Brussels in 1973 as Rosina; Has appeared at many operatic centres in Europe and the USA: Opéra du Rhin, Strasbourg, Brussels, Liège and San Francisco Opera; Best known in such coloratura mezzo repertoire as Rossini's Isabella and Sinaide in Mosè, Elisetta in Il Matrimonio Segreto and Sesto in La Clemenza di Tito; Other roles include Carmen, Charlotte, Olga, Orlofsky and Konchakovna in Prince Igor; Many concert appearances. *Recordings include:* Title role in Handel's Serse. *Address:* c/o Opéra du Rhin, 19 Place Broglie, 67008 Strasbourg Cédex, France.

TETZLAFF, Christian; Violinist; b. 29 April 1966, Hamburg, Germany. *Education:* Studied at the Lubeck Conservatory with Uwe-Martin Haiberg and in Cincinnati with Walter Levine. *Career:* Debut at the Berlin Festival and with the Cleveland Orchestra followed by regular appearances with the Berlin and Vienna Philharmonic, London Symphony Orchestra, City of Birmingham Symphony Orchestra, Orchestra Philharmonie de Paris, Gewandhausorchestra Leipzig, Munich Philharmonic, NHK Orchestra Tokyo, the New York Philharmonic, Boston and Chicago Symphonies and Academy of St Martin in the Fields; Season 1996–97 with the Houston Symphony Orchestra under Eschenbach and the Boston Symphony Orchestra under Franz Welser-Möst; Brahms Double Concerto and Shostakovich No. 1 with the Bavarian Radio Symphony Orchestra; Bach Sonatas and Partitas in Brussels and Paris 1997; Vienna Philharmonic concert at the 1997 Salzburg Festival; Chamber music series at the Vienna Konzerthaus: has collaborated with Leif Ove Andses, Yo-Yo Ma, Sabine Meyer and Heinrich Schiff; Beethoven's Concerto at the 1999 London Prom concerts; Berg's concerto at the London Proms, 2002; Has worked with many distinguished conductors including Boulez, Dohnanyi, Eschenbach, Gatti, Harding, Herreweghe, Paavo Jarvi, Levine, Nagano, Salonen, Saraste, Slatkin, Tilson Thomas and Vanska. *Recordings include:* Bach Sonatas and Partitas; Mozart Violin Concertos, with the Deutsche Kammerphilharmonie; Complete works for Violin and Orchestra by Sibelius. *Honours:* Recordings of the Bach Sonatas and Partitas and Sibelius's complete works for violin and orchestra were both awarded the Diapason d'Or. *Current Management:* Harrison/Parrott Ltd, 12 Penzance Place, London, W11 4PA, England. *Telephone:* (0)20 7313 3511. *E-mail:* matt.fretton@harrisonparrott.co.uk. *Website:* www.harrisonparrott.com.

TEZIER, Ludovic; Singer (Baritone); b. 1968, Marseilles, France. *Education:* Studied in Paris and Switzerland. *Career:* Engagements with Lyon, Marseilles, Tours and Bordeaux Opéras; Opéra-Comique, Paris, as Don Giovanni, Marcello, Escamillo, Harlequin (Ariadne auf Naxos), Sharpless, and Britten's Demetrius; Season 1996–97 in Handel's Radamisto and as Frédéric in Lakmé at Marseilles, Guglielmo at Bordeaux; Mozart Count, Marcello and Belcore at Lyon; Season 1997–98 as Malatesta, and Mercutio in Roméo et Juliette, at Bordeaux, with Escamillo, Don Giovanni and Talbot in Donizetti's Maria Stuarda at the Opéra-Comique; Glyndebourne 1997–98, as Comte Ory in a new production of Rossini's opera. *Address:* c/o Opera de Bordeaux, Grand Théâtre Municipal, Place de la Comédie, 33074 Bordeaux, France.

THALLAUG, Edith; Singer (Mezzo-Soprano); b. 16 June 1929, Oslo, Norway. *Education:* Studied with Giurgia Leppee and Joel Berglund in Stockholm. *Career:* Debut: Stage debut as actress in 1952; Song recital in Oslo in 1959; Stage debut as Dorabella at Gothenburg in 1960; Sang at Royal Opera Stockholm from 1964 notably as Carmen, Cherubino, Rosina, Bradamante in Alcina, Maddalena in Rigoletto, Eboli, Azucena, Amneris, Venus, Fricka, Waltraute, Octavian and The Composer in Ariadne, Judith in Bluebeard and Miss Julie; Frequent appearances at the Drottningholm Court Theatre from 1964; Sang at Glyndebourne Festival in 1971 as Dorabella, Basle in 1976 in Schoenberg's Gurrelieder and on Swedish television as Carmen; Guest engagements in Oslo, Copenhagen, Moscow, USA, Japan, Korea, Germany, La Scala Milan, Italy, Paris, Prague and Vienna. *Recordings include:* CD: Songs by De Falla, Montsalvatge, Ravel and many other recordings of Scandinavian Songs; Opera Arias, Songs by Grieg, and duets with Gösta Winbergh. *Honours:* Critic Prizes for La Cenerentola, Oslo, 1972; Court Singer, 1976; Grieg Prize, 1978; Drottingholm Court Theater, Gold Medal, 1979; Litteris et Artibus, 1982. *Address:* c/o Kongliga Teatern, PO Box 16094, 10322 Stockholm, Sweden.

THANE, Amanda; Singer (Soprano); b. 1960, Australia. *Education:* New South Wales Conservatorium of Music, Sydney. *Career:* Roles with the Australian opera since 1983 include Fiordiligi, Violetta, Marzelline, Constanze, Mimi, Norina, Pamina, Mozart's Countess, Micaela, Lauretta, Antonia, Leila, Nedda, Liu, Valentine (in Joan Sutherland's farewell performance of Les Huguenots), Governess, Maria Stuarda, Eva, Euridice and Gilda; Additional roles sung with other Australian companies include: Madama Butterfly, Rosalinde, Alice Ford, Marenka and Suor Angelica; Royal Opera House Covent Garden debut season 1991–92 as Valentine in new production of Les Huguenots and Antonia in Les Contes d'Hoffmann; Other roles at Royal Opera include Mimi, Lina in Verdi's Stiffelio and Amelia (Boccanegra); European debut 1993, as Lina in Stiffelio with Opera Forum, the Netherlands; Donna Elvira in Don Giovanni for Grand-Théâtre de Bordeaux; Many concert appearances throughout Australia, United Kingdom, Europe, USA, Japan and Korea; Teacher of Voice in London. *Honours:* Prizewinner, Metropolitan Opera Auditions, New York; Winner, ABC Instrumental and Vocal Competition; Queen Elizabeth II Silver Jubilee Award for Young Australians; Australian Music Foundation Award, London, Churchill Fellowship, 1990 (Australia). *Address:* c/o 70 Chandos Avenue, London W5 4ER, England.

THAW, David; Singer (Tenor); b. 19 June 1928, New York, USA; m. Claire Watson, deceased 1986. *Education:* Studied at Columbia University, with Giovanni Martinelli in New York and Giuseppe Pais in Milan.

Career: Debut: Vichy in 1950 as Vincent in Mireille; Sang at the Theater am Gärtnerplatz Munich from 1955, with debut as the Duke of Mantua, Frankfurt am Main Opera from 1958 with debut as Lenski in Eugene Onegin and a visit to London with the company in 1963 in Fidelio, Salome and Die Entführung, Bayreuth Festival in 1961 as Froh in Das Rheingold and member of the Bayerische Staatsoper Munich from 1963; Guest appearances in Berlin at Deutsche Oper and Staatsoper, Hanover and elsewhere; Sang at Salzburg Festival, 1964–68, and Munich in 1986 in the premiere of Belshazzar by VD Kirchner; Many appearances in musicals notably as Professor Higgins in My Fair Lady. *Address:* c/o Bayerische Staatsoper, Postfach 745, 8000 Munich 1, Germany.

THEBOM, Blanche; Singer (Mezzo-Soprano); b. 19 Sept. 1918, Monessen, Pennsylvania, USA. *Education:* Studied with Margharete Matzenauer and Edyth Walker in New York. *Career:* Debut: Sang in concert from 1941; Stage debut in 1944 at Philadelphia with the Metropolitan Opera as Brangaene; Sang in New York until 1966 as Marina, Eboli, Baba the Turk, Herodias, Orlofsky and in Wagner roles as Venus and Fricka; Sang at Chicago in 1946 as Brangaene, San Francisco Opera, 1947–59 with debut as Amneris, Glyndebourne in 1950 as Dorabella, Covent Garden in 1957 as Dido in the first British professional performance of Les Troyens and a tour of Russia in 1958; Directed the Atlanta Opera Company, 1967–68; Professor at the University of Arkansas. *Recordings:* Tristan und Isolde, conducted by Furtwängler; The Rake's Progress.

THEISEN, Kristin; Singer (Soprano); b. 13 Jan. 1955, Oslo, Norway. *Education:* Studied German, Oslo University, 1 year; Vocal Pedagogic studies, Music Conservatorium, Oslo for 4 years; Norwegian State Opera School, 3 years; Studied in Vienna, Salzburg and Bayreuth; Teachers: Erna Skaug, Ingrid Bjoner, Kim Borg, Anna Reynolds and Jean Cox. *Career:* Debut: Recital, Oslo, 1979; As opera singer, Leoncavallo's Nedda, Gelsenkirchen, 1982; Has appeared in Hamburg, Frankfurt, Nuremberg, Catania, Strasbourg, Eutin, Basel and Lubeck; Television, radio and film in Norway, Austria and Poland; Important opera roles: Agathe in Freischütz, Rezia in Oberon, Susanna in Figaro, Giulietta in Hoffmann, Ellen Orford in Peter Grimes, Euridice in Orpheus and Euridice, Sieglinde in Walküre, Senta in Holländer; mem, Leader of The Norwegian Opera Singer Society. *Recordings:* Zigeunerlieder with Audin Kayser, piano; Irmgard in Franz Schreker's opera Flammen, conducted by Frank Strobl. *Current Management:* Kollo, Berlin and Heissler-Remy, Düsseldorf. *Address:* Sarbuvollveien 8A, 1322 Hovik, Norway.

THEODOLOZ, Annelise; Singer (Soprano); b. 1954, Switzerland. *Education:* Violin pupil of Carl Flesch and Tibor Varga at early age; Award-winning graduate, Lausanne Conservatory and Guildhall School of Music and Drama, London. *Career:* Debut: As Dorabella in Così fan tutte and Dalila in Samson et Dalila, National Hungarian Opera under conductor János Kovács; Has performed as Soloist in major concert halls and on radio, with Orchestre de la Suisse Romande, Israel Chamber Orchestra, Bach Solisten Amsterdam, Orchestre National de Lyon and many others all over Europe, in Middle East, Japan and Canada; Works with conductors such as Michel Corboz, Jesus Lopez-Cobos, Zoltán Nágy, Helmut Rilling; French debut as Bradamante in Handel's Alcina. 1998; Further roles include Berlioz's Béatrice et Bénédict in Nancy and Tours under M Ossonce; Debut as soprano lirico spinto with Leonora's aria from Verdi's La Forza del Destino at Geneva, 2000. *Current Management:* Catherine Schoendorff Félix. *Address:* c/o Catherine Schoendorff Félix, Avenue du Tribunal-Fédéral 25, 1005 Lausanne, Switzerland.

THEURING, Günther; Conductor and University Professor; b. 28 Nov. 1930, Paris, France. *Education:* choirboy, Vienna; univ. studies in law and musicology; studied orchestral conducting with Hans Swarowsky and choir conducting with Ferdinand Grossmann, at Univ. of Music. *Career:* Regens Chori at St Rochus Church, Vienna, 1950; Conductor, Vienna Acad. Chorus, 1954; founder, Conductor, Vienna Jeunesse-Chorus, 1959; Conductor, Contraste Ensemble for Contemporary Music, 1971; concerts with Munich, Leipzig and Berlin Radio Choirs, Rias Chamber Choir, Berlin, Danish Radio Choir, Copenhagen, ORF Choir, Vienna, others; Conductor, orchestras including Vienna Symphony Orchestra, ORF Symphony Orchestra, Tonkünstler Orchester Wien, Mozarteum Orchestra, Salzburg, Orchestra Scala, Milan, Jerusalem Symphony Orchestra; Gewandhausorchester, Leipzig, Danish Radio Orchestra, Copenhagen, Leipzig Radio Orchestra, Prague Symphony, Slovakian Philharmonic, Bratislava, and Vienna Chamber Orchestra; Artistic Dir, Vienna master courses, 1971–; Prof. Ordinarius, Univ. of Music, Vienna, 1973–; Music Dir, Alpbach European Forum, –1982; Artistic Dir, First World Symposium for Choral Music, held in Vienna 1987. *Recordings include:* concert extracts. *Honours:* First prize, Choir Competition, Arezzo, 1956; Gold Badge of Service, Republic of Austria, 1970; Cross of Honour for Science and Arts, Republic of Austria, 1984; Ferdinand Grossmann Prize, 1999. *Address:* Landstrasser Hauptstrasse 67, Vienna 1030, Austria. *E-mail:* guenther.theuring@aon.at.

T'HEZAN, Helia; Singer (Soprano); b. 23 Aug. 1934, Rieumes, France. *Education:* Studied at the Toulouse Conservatoire and the Musikhochschule, Berlin. *Career:* Debut: Bordeaux in 1958 in Armide by Lully; Sang at the Paris Opéra and the Opéra-Comique from 1959, Covent Garden in 1965 in the title role of Gluck's Iphigénie en Tauride, Glyndebourne in 1966 as Charlotte in Werther, and Monte Carlo in 1973 in the premiere of La Reine Morte by Rossellini; Has sung at Lyon, Marseille, Geneva, Rome, Trieste, Turin, Lisbon and Philadelphia; Sang at the Paris Opéra in 1988 as Juno in Orphée aux Enfers. *Recordings include:* Manon by Massenet. *Address:* Théâtre National, 8 Rue Scribe, 75009 Paris, France.

THIBAUD, Pierre; Trumpeter; b. 22 June 1929, Proissans, France. *Education:* Studied violin and trumpet at the Bordeaux Conservatoire; Premier Prix for cornet playing at the Paris Conservatoire. *Career:* Principal Trumpet with the Orchestre de Paris Opéra, Ensemble Ars Nova, Domaine Musicale, Musique Vivante, Musique Plus and the Chamber Orchestra Fernand Oubradous; Further experience with the Concerts Lamoureux, Concerts Colonne and Musique de la Garde Republicaine; Founded the Brass Quintet Ars Nova and collaborations with the Société des Concerts du Conservatoire and IRCAM (electronic music studios), Paris; Concert appearances with leading European orchestras in the standard classics; Also plays music by Marius Constant, Xenakis, Messiaen, Varèse, Berio and Enesco; Professor of Trumpet at the Paris Conservatoire, 1975. *Recordings:* Brandenburg Concerto No. 2; Concertos by Haydn, Hummel and Telemann. *Address:* Conservatoire National Superieur de Musique de Paris, 209 Avenue Jean-Jaures, 75019, Paris, France.

THIBAUDET, Jean-Yves; Concert Pianist; b. 7 Sept. 1961, Lyon, France. *Education:* Lycée Musical, Lyon; Lycée St Exupéry, Lyon; Conservatory of Music, Lyon; National Conservatory of Music, Paris. *Career:* Debuts and appearances throughout the world; Recitals, New York, Chicago, Washington DC, Los Angeles, San Francisco, London, Paris, Milan, Amsterdam; Played with Montreal, St-Louis National, Indianapolis, New World and Boston Symphonies, Cleveland Orchestra, Chicago Symphony, Philadelphia Orchestra, New York Philharmonic, Toronto Symphony, Los Angeles Philharmonic, Concertgebouw Orchestra, Orchestre de Paris, Ensemble Orchestral de Paris, Rotterdam Philharmonic, Stuttgart Radio Orchestra; Participated in Spoleto Festivals, USA, Italy, Australia; Regular guest, Chamber Music Society, Lincoln Center; Debut appearances at Casals and Schleswig-Holstein Festivals; Hollywood Bowl, 1989; played Debussy and Chopin at the Wigmore Hall, London, 1997; Mendelsohn's G Minor Concerto at the 1999 London Prom concerts; London Proms, 2002. *Recordings:* Numerous including music by Ravel, Liszt, Chopin; Violin sonatas by Debussy, Franck, Fauré, with Joshua Bell; Chausson concerto for piano, violin and string quartet (Takacs); Ravel Trio (Bell, Isserlis); Liszt works for piano and orchestra (Montreal Symphony); Ravel: Complete solo piano works; Messiaen: Turangalila Symphony (Concertgebouw Orchestra). *Current Management:* Mastroinni Associates, 161 West 61st Street, Ste 17E, New York, NY 10023, USA. *Address:* c/o M L Falcone, Public Relations, 55 West 68th St, Ste 1114, New York, NY 10023, USA.

THIEDE, Helga; Singer (Soprano); b. 6 Feb. 1940, Berlin, Germany. *Education:* Berlin Musikhochschule. *Career:* Debut: Schwerin 1967, as Marina in Wolf-Ferrari's Quattro Rusteghi; Sang at Schwerin until 1971, Dessau 1972–84 and Dresden Staatsoper from 1984; Roles have included Leonore in Fidelio (1989), Chrysothemis in Elektra (also at Berlin Staatsoper and Kiel), Ariadne, the Marschallin, Wagner's Eva and Elisabeth, Eglantine in Euryanthe, the Mother in Dallapiccola's Il Prigioniero, and the Kostelnička in Jenůfa (1996); Many concert engagements throughout Germany. *Address:* c/o Semper Opera, Theaterplatz 2, D–01607 Dresden, Germany.

THIELEMANN, Christian; German conductor; b. 1 April 1959, Berlin. *Education:* Berlin Hochschule für Musik, Karajan Foundation Orchestra Acad., Berlin. *Career:* musical coach in Berlin, with Karajan from 1979, at Berlin, Salzburg and Munich; asst to Daniel Barenboim at Paris, Berlin and Bayreuth; Principal Conductor, Deutsche Oper am Rhein Düsseldorf 1985; Music Dir, Nuremberg Opera 1988–92; American debut season 1991–92, with Elektra at the San Francisco Opera; Der Rosenkavalier at the New York Met 1993, Arabella 1994; regular concerts with the New York Philharmonic Orchestra and Philadelphia and Minnesota Orchestras; British debut with Jenůfa at Covent Garden 1988, returning for Elektra 1994 and the British premiere of Pfitzner's Palestrina 1997; further opera includes Capriccio in Florence, The Makropulos Case in Bologna, Don Giovanni in Berlin and Lohengrin on tour to Japan with the Deutsche Oper Berlin; season 1996 with Otello in Bologna (Principal Guest Conductor), Tristan and Meistersinger with the Deutsche Opera; further concerts with the Chicago Symphony Orchestra, Philharmonia Orchestra and the Munich Philharmonic Orchestra; Strauss's Aegyptische Helena for the Royal Opera at the Festival Hall 1998; returned to Covent Garden with Palestrina 2001; Gen. Music Dir, Deutsche Oper Berlin 1997–2004,

Guest Dir 2004–. *Recordings include:* Wagner and Strauss, with René Kollo; Beethoven Cantatas, orchestral music by Wagner, Strauss and Pfitzner, Schumann 2nd Symphony and Beethoven Nos 5 and 7; Video of Arabella, from the Met, with Kiri Te Kanawa. *Current Management:* Columbia Artists (Conductors Division), 165 West 57th Street, New York, NY 10019, USA.

THIEME, Helga; Singer (Soprano); b. 27 Feb. 1937, Oberlengsfeld, Germany. *Education:* Studied in Frankfurt. *Career:* Sang in opera at Basle, 1962–65, Bielefeld, 1965–67, Wiesbaden, 1967–68, Hamburg, 1968–83, notably in the premieres of The Devils of Loudun by Penderecki in 1969 and Josef Tal's Ashmedai in 1971, Bremen, 1974–76, St Gallen from 1980 and Zürich, 1984–85; Guest engagements at Berne, Deutsche Oper Berlin, state operas of Munich and Stuttgart, Düsseldorf, Vienna Volksoper, Barcelona and Cologne; Roles have included Susanna, Zerlina, Despina and the Queen of Night, Norina and Adina, Lortzing's Gretchen and Marie, Gilda, Aennchen, Marenka, Sophie in Der Rosenkavalier, Isotta in Die schweigsame Frau and Ida in Henze's Junge Lord. *Recordings include:* The Devils of Loudun. *Address:* c/o Staatl. Hochschule für Musik, 30175 Hannover, Germany.

THIEME, Ulrich; Professor of Recorder and Musicologist; b. 5 Aug. 1950, Hamm, Germany. *Education:* State Diploma, Music Teaching, 1973; Concert Diploma, Recorder, 1974; PhD, Musicology. *Career:* Television appearances with broadcasts for several German stations, 1969–; Recorder Teacher at Academy of Music in Cologne, 1973–78 and Academy of Music at Hannover, 1978–; Concert tours throughout Europe, Eastern Asia and South America and 50 concerts with recorder and lute-guitar duo in Germany; mem, Vice-President, ERTA, European Recorder Teachers Association, German Section. *Recordings:* Jürg Baur's Tre Studi per Quattro; Bach's Brandenburg Concertos; Baroque Recorder Music by various composers including Delalande, Bonocini and Mancini. *Publications:* Studien zum Jugendwerk A Schoenbergs, 1979; Affektenlehre im Barocken Musikdenken, 1984. *Contributions:* Editor of Baroque Recorder Music (Castello, Monteclair); TIBIA. *Honours:* 1st Prize, German Young Musicians Competition, 1967. *Address:* c/o Staatliche Hochschule für Musik, D-3 Hannover, Germany.

THIOLLIER, François-Joël; concert pianist; b. 12 Nov. 1943, Paris, France; m. Beatrice Fitch 1978; one s. *Education:* studied in Paris with Robert Casadesus, Juilliard Preparatory College. *Career:* many concerts in over 30 countries including appearances with the Orchestre de Paris, Nouvel Orchestre Philharmonique, Moscow and Leningrad Philharmonic Orchestras, the Hague Residentie Orkest, Tokyo and Berlin Philharmonics and RAI in Italy; Concert halls include Amsterdam Concertgebouw, Théâtre des Champs Elysées, Teatro Real of Madrid, Accademia di Santa Cecilia, Rome, and Victoria Hall Geneva; Played the Busoni Concerto in Berlin. *Recordings:* Complete works of Rachmaninov and Gershwin; Beethoven Sonatas Op 27 No. 2, Op 13 and Op 57; Liszt Sonata and Complete Songs for Tenor and Piano; Brahms Sonata Op 5; Paganini Variations; Mozart Sonata K330 and Quintet K452. *Honours:* Prizewinner at International Piano Competitions: Viotti, Casella, Busoni, Pozzoli, Montreal, Tchaikovsky Moscow, Marguérite Long, Paris, Queen Elisabeth, Brussels. *Current Management:* Patricia Garrasi, Via Manzoni, 20121 Milan, Italy.

THOMAS, Augusta (Read); Composer; b. 24 April 1964, Glen Cove, New York, USA. *Education:* Studied at Northwestern University (1983–87) and with Jacob Druckman at Yale University (MM 1988); Postgraduate studies at the Royal Academy of Music, London 1988–89. *Career:* Freelance composer; Faculty member, Eastman School of Music, Rochester, New York, 1993–2001; Prof. of Music, Northwestern University, Chicago, IL; Mead Composer-in-Residence, Chicago Symphony Orchestra, 1997–(2006); mem., Bd of Dirs, American Music Center, 2000–. *Compositions include:* Vigil for cello and chamber orchestra, 1992; Ligeia, chamber opera, 1994 (Int. Orpheus Prize); Words of the Sea, for orchestra, 1996; Orbital Beacons, for orchestra, 1997; Ritual Incantations, cello concerto, 1999; Ceremonial, for orchestra, 1999; Daylight Divine, 2001; Prayer Bells, for orchestra, 2001; In My Sky at Twilight, 2002; Silver Chants the Litanies, homage to Luciano Berio, for solo horn and ensemble; Tangle, for orchestra; Galaxy Dances, ballet for orchestra; Gathering Paradise, for solo soprano and orchestra; Grace Notes, for orchestra. *Honours:* International Orpheus Prize for Opera, Spoleto Italy, 1994; Charles Ives Fellowship, 1994; Rockefeller Foundation Grant, 1997; New York State Artist Fellowship, 1998; Koussevitzky Award, 1999; Siemens Award, 2000; American Academy Award, 2001. *Address:* c/o PO Box 769, Lee, MA 01238, USA. *Website:* www.augustareadthomas.com.

THOMAS, Caryl; Harpist; b. 23 Oct. 1958, Aberystwyth, Dyfed, Wales; m. Huw Williams, 22 Oct 1985. *Education:* Welsh College of Music and Drama; MA, New York University, USA; Associate, Royal College of Music. *Career:* Debut: Carnegie Hall, NY, 1981; Freelance Harpist, concentrating on solo and concert work with great emphasis on BBC

Radio 3 and Channel 4 television broadcasting; Appearances include London debut at Wigmore Hall, concerto soloist with BBC National Orchestra of Wales in 1982, and Mozarteum Orchestra at Salzburg, Austria in 1984. *Recordings:* Mozart Concerto for Flute and Harp with London Philharmonic Orchestra, flautist Jonathan Snowden and conducted by Andrew Litton, 1987; French Impressions with Prometheus Ensemble. *Address:* Hendre'r Wenallt, St Athan Road, Cowbridge, South Glamorgan CF71 7LT, Wales.

THOMAS, David; British singer; b. 26 Feb. 1943, Orpington; m. Veronica Joan Dean 1982; three d. *Education:* St Paul's Cathedral Choir School, London, King's School, Canterbury, King's Coll., Cambridge. *Career:* has performed all over the world in most of the maj. concert halls with leading conductors, particularly works of the Baroque and Classical period; Chair. Artistic Advisory Cttee; mem. Bd Blackheath Concert Halls. *Works include:* more than 100 records, including Handel's Messiah, Athalia, La Resurrectione, Suzanna, Orlando, Bach's B Minor Mass, Cantata 'Ich habe genug', St John Passion, St Matthew Passion, Haydn's Creation, Mozart's Requiem; solo record Aria for Montagnana. *Current Management:* Allied Artists, 42 Montpelier Square, London, SE10 8HP; 74 Hyde Vale, Greenwich, London, SE10 8HP, England.

THOMAS, Gwion; Singer (Baritone); b. 1954, Wales. *Education:* Studied at the Royal Northern College of Music. *Career:* Appearances with Welsh National Opera, Royal Opera Garden Venture, Kent Opera and the Aldeburgh Festival (in the title role in the premiere of Lefanu's Wildman, 1995); Other roles include Orestes, Mozart's Don Giovanni, Count and Papageno, and Britten's Tarquinius, Billy Budd and Ned Keene; Television appearances in Weir's Night at the Chinese Opera and Scipio's Dream; Concerts with the BBC Symphony Orchestra, London Philharmonic Orchestra.

THOMAS, Matthew (Elton); Singer (Baritone); b. 1963, Canada. *Career:* Performances as Kuligin in Katya Kabanova for the Canadian Opera Company, and Marcello in La Bohème at Vancouver; Mozart's Count, Guglielmo and Don Giovanni at the Banff Centre of the Performing Arts; Ourrais in Gounod's Mireille and Le Conte in Massenet's Grisélidis for Opera in Concert, Toronto; British performances include Rigoletto for Clonter Opera Farm and English Touring Opera (1996); Rossini's Figaro for ETO, Belcore (L'Elisir d'amore) for Mid Wales Opera and Valentin in Faust for Dublin Grand Opera Society; Further appearances as Hercules/The Herald in Gluck's Alceste for Scottish Opera and Don Giovanni for Opera on a Shoestring, Glasgow; Concert repertoire includes Carmina Burana, Messiah, Elijah, and the Requiems of Brahms, Fauré and Duruflé. *Address:* c/o English Touring Opera, 250a Kennington Lane, London, SE11 5RD, England.

THOMAS, Michael Tilson; Conductor, Pianist and Composer; b. 21 Dec. 1944, Los Angeles, California, USA. *Education:* Studied at University of Southern California with Ingolf Dahl, John Crown and Alice Ehlers. *Career:* Conducted the Young Musicians Foundation Orchestra; Pianist and Conductor at Monday Evening Concerts, assisting the composers with premieres of works by Copland, Stockhausen, Kraft, Stravinsky and Boulez and with Boston Symphony Chamber Players; Conducted Boston Symphony Orchestra from 1969, being Principal Guest Conductor, 1972–74; Music Director of Buffalo Philharmonic 1971–79; Directed the Young People's Concerts of the New York Philharmonic, 1971–77; Principal Guest Conductor of Los Angeles Philharmonic, 1981–85; US premiere of Berg's Lulu (3 act version) at Santa Fe, 1979; Regular Conductor of Chicago, Pittsburgh and Philadelphia Orchestras; Directed a new production of Der fliegende Holländer in France, Janáček's The Cunning Little Vixen, New York, 1980, Fidelio at Houston and Tosca at Chicgao Lyric Opera; US premiere of Steve Reich's Desert Music, 1984; Engagements with various international orchestras; Principal Conductor of London Symphony Orchestra, 1988–95; BBC television productions of 'Discovery' concerts, Channel 4 BMG series of Concerto!; Founder and Music Director of New World Symphony, 1988, a national fellowship orchestra for young professionals; Music Director of San Francisco Symphony, 1995–; Conducted the London Symphony Orchestra in Last Works concert series, London Barbican, 1997; Tours with San Francisco Symphony Orchestra include USA, 1996, 2003, Europe, 1996, 1999, 2002, 2003 Japan, Hong Kong, 1997; Carnegie Hall Perspectives Series, 2003–04. *Recordings include:* Mahler Symphonies 1, 3 and 6 with San Francisco Symphony Orchestra; Four-hand version of Stravinsky's Rite of Spring with Ralph Grierson; Charles Ives's 2nd Symphony with Concertgebouw Orchestra; Complete Works of Carl Ruggles with Buffalo Philharmonic; Various musicals by Weill and Gershwin. *Honours:* Koussevitzky Conducting Prize at Berkshire Music Center, 1968; Many Grammy nominations and international awards for his recordings. *Address:* c/o Van Walsum Management Ltd 4 AddisonBridge Place, London W14 8XP England.

THOMAS, Nova; Singer (Soprano); b. 1960, North Carolina, USA. *Education:* Studied at the University of Bloomington with Eileen Farrell. *Career:* Debut: Mimi in La Bohème at North Carolina;

Appearances at opera houses in Cologne, Hamburg, Belfast (Opera Northern Ireland), St Louis, Seattle, San Diego, Detroit and New York City Opera; Season 1991–92 in Cologne and Paris as Giulia in La Scala di Seta; Roles have included Violetta, the Four Heroines in Les Contes d'Hoffmann, the Trovatore Leonora and Anna Bolena; Further engagements as Mozart's Constanze for Cologne Opera, Norma with Seattle Opera and Hoffmann under Richard Bonynge; Sang Adalgisa in Norma at Philadelphia, 1998. *Recordings include:* Title role in The Bohemian Girl, under Bonynge. *Honours:* Winner, Metropolitan Opera National Council Auditions, 1984. *Address:* c/o Opera Co of Philadelphia, 510 Walnut Street, Suite 1600, Philadelphia, PA 19106, USA.

THOMAS, Peter; Violinist; b. 1944, South Wales. *Education:* Studied in England, winning the Menuhin Prize at Bath Festival, 1958. *Career:* Second Violinist of the Allegri Quartet, 1963–68; Co-Founder of Orion Piano Trio, becoming resident ensemble at Southampton University; Leader of BBC National Orchestra of Wales, 1972, then Philharmonia; Leader of City of Birmingham Symphony Orchestra and Artistic Director of Birmingham Ensemble; String Adviser to Gustav Mahler Youth Orchestra, Vienna; Purcell Room, London, recital 1993, with works by Schubert, Berio (Sequenza VIII), Schoenberg and Busoni (2nd Sonata). *Honours:* With Orion Piano Trio: BBC Prize for British and Commonwealth Ensembles. *Address:* Camerata Artists, 4 Margaret Road, Birmingham B17 0 EU, England.

THOMAS, Steven Murray, BA, DipMus; Canadian stage producer and television producer; b. 26 June 1946, Peterborough, ON; m. Irene Wronski 1985. *Education:* University of Western Ontario, Royal Conservatory of Toronto. *Career:* debut with New Jersey State Opera in 1976; Producer, Artistic Director, Actor, Dramatic Theatre, 1964–72; Producer and Stage Director for Opera (freelance), 1972–78; Production Manager, Opera Festival at National Arts Centre, Ottawa, 1978–79; Artistic Director for Opera Hamilton, 1979–86; Producer, television opera, CHCH-TV, Hamilton, 1979–86; Operas produced for television include La Bohème, La Traviata, Madama Butterfly, The Barber of Seville, Rigoletto, Aida, Manon Lescaut, The Marriage of Figaro, Hansel and Gretel and Carmen. *Honours:* CANPRO Awards for Excellence in the Performing Arts, Canadian Television National Competition, for La Bohème, 1980, La Traviata, 1981, The Barber of Seville, 1983, and Aida, 1985; Canadian Music Council Award for television, La Traviata, 1983. *Address:* 226 Westmount Avenue, Toronto, ON M6E 3M8, Canada.

THOMASCHKE, Thomas Michael; German concert and opera singer (bass); b. 2 Aug. 1943, Pirna; m. 1964; one s. one d. *Education:* Dresden Hochschule für Musik. *Career:* debut in Freiberg, Germany, in Tosca, 1963; Sang in Leipzig, Dresden, and at the Komische Oper Berlin in the 1960s; La Scala, Bavarian State Opera, Glyndebourne, Covent Garden, Paris, Lisbon, Buenos Aires, Vienna, Edinburgh, Cape Town, Rome, Florence and Amsterdam; Has sung Figaro, Don Giovanni, Rocco (Fidelio), Sarastro (Magic Flute), Gurnemanz (Parsifal); Sang Ramphis in Aida at Cape Town, 2000; Artistic Director of Festival Mitte Europa. *Recordings include:* Bach and Handel, conducted by Nikolaus Harnoncourt; Weber, Freischütz, Philips, Colin Davis; Beethoven 9th Symphony, Yehudi Menuhin. *Publications:* contrib. to Opernwelt. *Honours:* Schumanpreis, 1966; Tschaikowskypreis, 1970; 1st Prize, Preis Hertogenbosch, 1971. *Address:* Fliederweg 108, 50859 Cologne, Germany.

THOME, Diane; Composer, Pianist, University Professor and Lecturer; b. 25 Jan. 1942, Pearl River, New York, USA. *Education:* Studied piano with Dorothy Taubman, New York, composition with Robert Strassburg, Darius Milhaud at Aspen, Colorado, Roy Harris at Inter-American University, PR; PhD in Music, Princeton University, 1973; Alexander Boscovich (Israel); Milton Babbitt, Princeton. *Career:* Taught music at Princeton University, New Jersey, 1973–74; Taught theory and 20th century music at SUNY, Binghampton, 1974–77; Professor of Theory and Composition at University of Washington School of Music, Seattle; mem, SCI Inc; BMI; CMS. *Compositions include:* Chamber: 3 Pieces, 1958, 3 Movements, 1958, Sonatine, 1960, Suite, 1961, Quartet, 1961, Constellations, 1966; Electronic music: Le Berceau De Miel, 1968, Spectrophonie, 1969, Polyvalence, 1972, January Variations, 1973, Los Nombres, 1974, Alexander Boscovich Remembered, 1975, Anais, 1976, Sunflower Space, 1978, Winter Infinities, 1980, To Search The Spacious World, 1986, The Ruins Of The Heart for Soprano, Orchestra and Tape, 1991, Angels for Virtual Reality Artwork, 1992, The Palaces Of Memory for Large Chamber Ensemble or Chamber Orchestra and Tape, 1993; Masks of Eternity, 1994; Unseen Buds, for chorus and tape, 1995; Unfold, Entwine, 1998; Like a Seated Swan, for viola and tape, 2000; Multimedia works: In My Garden, 1956, Caprice, 1957, Night Passage, 1973; Anais; Bright Air/Brilliant Fire; Levadi (Alone); Unfold Entwine; Unseen Buds; Orchestral: 3 Movements, 1962, S'Embarquement, 1971, The Golden Messengers, 1984, Lucent Flowers, 1988; Piano works: Sonatine, 1959, Pianismus; Sacred works: Three Psalms, 1979; Vocal: Ash On An Old Man's Sleeve, 1962, Spring And Fall: To A Young Child, 1962, Cantata, 1964, Songs On Chinese Verses, 1964, The Yew Tree, 1979, 3 Sonnets By Sri Aurobindo: Settings for Soprano and Orchestra,

1984; Lucent Flowers; Celestial Canopy, 1999. *Recordings include:* Palaces of Memory, electro-acoustic music; The Ruins of the Heart; Three Psalms; Pianismus; The Yew Tree; The Palaces of Memory, 1995; Bright Air/Brilliant Fire, 2000. *Address:* University of Washington School of Music, Box 353450, Seattle, WA 98195, USA.

THOMPSON, Adrian; Singer (tenor); b. 1954, London, England. *Education:* Guildhall School of Music and Drama, London. *Career:* opera engagements with the Glyndebourne Festival, Scottish Opera, Handel Opera Society and at the Buxton, Aldeburgh, Wexford, Lausanne and Göttingen Festivals; roles include Ariodante, Snout and Flute in A Midsummer Night's Dream, Albert Herring, Podesta, Pedrillo in Die Entführung, Le nozze di Figaro, Così fan tutte, Bardolph in Falstaff, Conti's Don Quixote in Sierra Morena, the Simpleton in Boris Godunov and Nurse in L'Incoronazione di Poppea; sang Alfred in Die Fledermaus at Belfast, 1990, the title role in Haydn's Orlando Paladino at Garsington Manor, Oxford, and Britten's Flute at Sadler's Wells, 1990 (Snout at Glyndebourne, 1989); concert performances throughout Europe and the UK in works by Purcell, Bach, Handel, Berlioz, Schoenberg and Tippett; Britten repertoire includes Les Illuminations, The Serenade, Nocturne, Canticles and Song Cycles; appearances with leading British orchestras, the Netherlands Chamber Orchestra, Nash Ensemble and Stockholm Bach Choir; frequent Promenade Concerts and recitals at the Aldeburgh, Bath, Lichfield and Buxton festivals; has sung Schubert's Die schöne Müllerin at the Wigmore Hall and songs by Schubert and Schoenberg at South Bank; recitals in Israel, Canada, Germany, France and Switzerland; recitals in USA, Salome in Netherlands, Handel's Tamerlano at Karlsruhe and Irus in Monteverdi's Ulisse at the Coliseum, London, 1992–93; sang Grimoaldo in Rodelinda with Broomhill Opera, 1996; Schoolmaster in Janáček's Vixen at Spoleto, 1998; Albert Gregor in The Makropulos Case at Cologne, 2000. *Recordings include:* Gurney's Ludlow and Teme; Beggar's Opera. *Current Management:* Caroline Phillips Management, The Old Brushworks, Pickwick Road, Corsham, Wiltshire, SN13 9BX, England. *Telephone:* (1249) 716716. *Fax:* (1249) 716717. *E-mail:* cphillips@caroline-phillips.co.uk. *Website:* www.caroline-phillips.co.uk/thompson.

THOMPSON, Arthur; Singer (Baritone); b. 27 Dec. 1942, New York City, USA. *Education:* Studied at the Manhattan School of Music, Hartt College and the Juilliard School. *Career:* Debut: Chautauqua as Papageno in 1964; Performances with Metropolitan Opera Studio, 1966–71; Over 50 comprimario roles with the Metropolitan Opera, New York, from 1970 including Mandarin in Turandot in 1970; Many performances of Porgy and Bess in America and abroad; Sang at Covent Garden in 1987 as Mel in The Knot Garden. *Recordings include:* Four Saints in Three Acts by Virgil Thomson; Jake in Porgy and Bess conducted by Lorin Maazel; Sang Britten's Tarquin at Rio de Janeiro, 1998. *Address:* Metropolitan Opera House, Lincoln Center, NY 10023, New York.

THOMPSON, Donald (Prosser); University Professor, Conductor and Writer; b. 28 Feb. 1928, Columbus, Ohio, USA; m. Ana Christina Figueroa Laugier, 23 Jan 1972, 2 s., 1 d. *Education:* AB, University of Missouri, 1952; MA, University of Missouri, 1954; Akademie für Musik, Vienna, Austria; Eastman School of Music; PhD, University of Iowa, 1970. *Career:* Retired as Professor and Chair, Department of Music, University of Puerto Rico, 1956–85; Conductor, opera, music theatre, television, San Juan, Puerto Rico, 1956–; Music Critic San Juan Star, 1957–60, 1975–94; Consultant in Arts Management, 1985–. *Contributions:* Manual para monografias musicales, 1980; The New Grove Dictionary of Music, 1980; The New Grove Dictionary of American Music, 1986; Music Research in Puerto Rico, 1982; The Puerto Rico Symphony Orchestra, 1985; The New Grove Dictionary of Opera, 1992; El joven Tavarez; nuevos documentos y nuevas perspectivas, 1993; Diccionario de musica espanola e hispanoamericana, 1994. *Contributions:* Revista musical chilena, 1984; African Music, 1975–76; Inter American Music review, 1989; Revista musical de Venezuela, 1989; Bibliografia musicologica latinoamericana, 1992, 1993; Latin American Music Review, 1983, 1985, 1990, 1993. *Address:* Calle Acadia N-64, Rio Piedras, Puerto Rico.

THOMPSON, (Robert) Ian, MA, ARCM, ARCO; singer (tenor), harpsichordist, conductor and artistic director; b. 5 April 1943, Bradford, England; m. Judith Welch 1970. *Education:* Queens' College, Cambridge, Royal College of Music, London; singing with Campogalliani, Italy. *Career:* BBC Chorus, 1966–67; Vicar Choral, St Paul's Cathedral, London, 1967–77; Opera and Concert Singer: Kent Opera; Opera North; Debut, Royal Opera House, Covent Garden, 1993; Since debut at the Rossini Festival, Pesaro, 1991, has appeared regularly at leading European theatres including, La Scala (Milan), San Carlo (Naples), Regio (Turin), Bastille and Châtelet (Paris), Strasbourg, Bordeaux and Lyon; Broadcasts in most European countries; Visiting Lecturer, RSAMD, Glasgow, 1996–; Artistic Director, Lonsdale Music; 60e Parallèle with Philippe Mancury; Ariadne auf Naxos, with Giuseppe Sinopoli; mem, Incorporated Society of Musicians; Royal College of Organists; The Alpine Club;

Amaryllis Consort. *Recordings:* With Pro Cantione Antiqua, Early Music Consort, Società Cameristica di Lugano and Capella Clementina; Dr Wittkop in 60 Paranèle; Scaramuccio in Ariadne auf Naxos. *Current Management:* Athole Still International Management, Forresters Hall, 25–27 Westow Street, London, SE19 3RY, England. *Telephone:* (20) 8771-5271. *Fax:* (20) 8768-6600. *Website:* www.atholestill.com. *Address:* Hill Top, Tearnside, Kirkby Lonsdale, Cumbria LA6 2PU, England.

THOMPSON, Lesleigh (Karen); Composer and Pianist; b. 8 Nov. 1966, Bulawayo, Rhodesia (now Zimbabwe), Australian resident since 1977. *Education:* BMus 1991, MMus 1994, The University of Melbourne. *Career:* Lecturer in Music Techniques at the University of Melbourne, 1993–96; Studied with Brenton Broadstock, 1989–93; Stephen Ingham, 1994–97; Examiner, Australian Music Examinations Board, 1997–. *Compositions include:* Toccata for piano, 1989; Captive, for ensemble, 1991; Enost, for string quartet, 1992; Sonata for Piano: Mad Men, Mad Times, 1992; Sphygmus for piano, 1992; Exuviae for piano, 1993; Facade for guitar, 1994; Clandestine, for orchestra, 1994; Sweet Talk, for guitar and cello, 1995; Roulette, for piano, 1996. *Honours:* New Audience Award for Composition, 1990; Albert H Maggs Award, 1993. *Address:* c/o APRA, 1A Eden Street, Crows Nest, NSW 2065, Australia.

THOMPSON, Margaret; Singer (Mezzo-soprano); b. 26 Aug. 1962, Glenlovee, New York. *Education:* New England Conservatory, Boston and University of Delaware; Salzburg Mozarteum with Grace Bumbry. *Career:* Sang Carmen, and Orlofsky in Die Fledermaus, in USA; Koblenz and Pforzheim opera houses, from 1991, and Bielefeld Opera from 1995; Roles have included Rosina, Cherubino, Strauss's Composer, Eboli, Charlotte in Werther, Queen of the Spirits in Marschner's Hans Heiling, Britten's Oberon, Suzuki, and Margaretha in Schumann's Genoveva (Bielefeld 1995); Mahler's Rückert Lieder at Salzburg, 1996; Other concert repertory in works by Bach, Handel, Haydn, Mozart and Penderecki; Sang in German, premiere of Blond Eckbert, by Judith Weir, at Bielefeld. *Honours:* Winner Sylvia Geszty Competition; Luxembourg, 1995. *Address:* c/o Bühnen der Stadt Bielefeld, Brunhenstrasse 3–9, Pf. 220, 4800 Bielefeld, Germany.

THOMPSON, Martin; Singer (Tenor); b. 1956, USA. *Career:* Many appearances at leading European and American opera houses; Roles have included Werther, Hoffmann, Gounod's Roméo, Edgardo, Pinkerton, Peter Grimes, Don José, Lensky, Rodolfo, and Orombello in Bellini's Beatrice di Tenda; Concerts include Beethoven's Ninth Symphony at San Francisco, Cherubini's Mass in D Minor (Stuttgart) and Britten's War Requiem; Season 1997–98 with Covent Garden and Metropolitan Opera debuts (as the Duke of Mantua, and Pinkerton), Hoffmann in Philadelphia and Pinkerton at Santa Fe; Other repertory includes Tom Rakewell (Philadelphia, 1997), the title role in Mozart's Mitridate (Wexford Festival, 1988), Nadir in Les pêcheurs de Perles and the title role in Argento's Voyage of Edgar Allan Poe (Dallas Opera); Santa Fé Opera 1999–2000, as Don José, Pinkerton and the Duke of Mantua; Puccini's Des Grieux for ENO 2000, Foresto in Attila at Chicago and Rodolfo in Luisa Miller for the Deutsche Oper Berlin. *Address:* c/o Metropolitan Opera, Lincoln Center, New York, NY 10023, USA.

THOMPSON, Michael; Horn Player; b. 7 Jan. 1954, London. *Education:* Studied at the RAM, London, with Ifor James. *Career:* Principal of the BBC Scottish Symphony Orchestra, 1972–75; Philharmonia Orchestra, London, 1975–85; Professor at the Royal Academy, 1984–; Concert repertory includes concertos of Haydn and Mozart, Sea Eagle by Maxwell Davies, and Des Canyons aux Etoiles, by Messiaen; Premieres of works by Benedict Mason, Simon Bainbridge and Anthony Powers. *Recordings include:* Standard Concertos, and the Quintets of Franz Danzi and Antoine Reicha. *Address:* c/o Royal Academy of Music, Marylebone Road, London W1, England.

THOMPSON, Terence; Composer, Teacher, Clarinettist and Saxophonist; b. 19 Jan. 1928, Staffordshire, England. *Education:* ABSM, performer and teacher; ABSM, (T T D), Birmingham School of Music. *Career:* Music master, West Bromwich Technical High School, 1950–59; Clarinet tutor, Birmingham School of Music, 1954–55; Head of Music, March End School; mem, Performing Right Society; British Academy of Composers and Songwriters; Musicians' Union; Central Composers' Alliance; Birmingham Conservatoire Asscn (Alumnus). *Compositions:* Boogie and Blues; Suite Chalumeau Swing; Suite City Scenes; Back to Bach; Two syncopated dances. *Recordings:* London Saxophone Quartet in digital; Two Light Pieces, 1999; A Cumbrian Voluntary, 2000. *Publications:* Romance in Sepia, 1985; Something Blue, 1983; Song and Dance, 1994. *Address:* 58 Willenhall Road, Bilston, West Midlands WV 14 6NW, England.

THOMSON, Brian Edward; Australian film, theatre and opera designer; b. 5 Jan. 1946, Sydney; s. of Austin Thomas Thomson and Adoree Gertrude Thomson. *Education:* Applecross Sr High School, Perth Tech. Coll., Univ. of New South Wales. *Career:* Supervising Designer, closing ceremony of Olympic Games, Sydney 2000; Production Designer, Centennial of Fed. Ceremony 2001. *Musicals:* Hair, Jesus

Christ Superstar (London and Australia), The Rocky Horror Show (original London production and worldwide), Chicago, The Stripper, Company, Chess, The King and I (Broadway production 1996, London Palladium), How to Succeed in Business Without Really Trying, South Pacific, Hello, Dolly!, Merrily We Roll Along, Grease, Happy Days. *Theatre:* Housewife Superstar!!! (London and New York); The Threepenny Opera (opening season, Drama Theatre, Sydney Opera House); Big Toys (the Old Tote); A Cheery Soul, Chinchilla, Macbeth, The Doll Trilogy, The Ham Funeral, A Midsummer Night's Dream, The Crucible, The Homecoming, Uncle Vanya, Death and the Maiden, Coriolanus, Falsettos, King Lear, Arcadia, Medea, Mongrels, Third World Blues, After the Ball, White Devil (also at Brooklyn Acad. of Music), Up for Grabs (all for Sydney Theatre Co.); Arturo Ui, Rock-Ola (Nimrod); Lulu, Shepherd on the Rocks Crow (State Theatre Co. of S Australia); Ghosts, The Tempest, The Master Builder, Buzz, Frogs, Aftershocks, Radiance, Up the Road, Burnt Piano, The Laramie Project (Company B Belvoir); Angels in America (Melbourne Theatre Co.); Soulmates, One Day of the Year (Sydney Theatre Co.), My Zinc Bed, Buried Child (Company B Belvoir). *Film and television:* Barlow and Chambers, Shadow of the Cobra (both mini-series); Shirly Thompson vs. the Aliens, The Rocky Horror Picture Show, Starstruck, Rebel, Night of Shadows (also dir), Ground Zero, Turtle Beach, Frauds. *Dance:* Synergy, Fornicon (Sydney Dance Co.), Tivol (Sydney Dance Co. and Australian Ballet). *Opera:* Death in Venice, The Makropulos Affair (Adelaide Festival); Turandot, Aida, Summer of the Seventeenth Doll (Vic. State Opera); Voss, Death in Venice, Tristan und Isolde, Katya Kabanova, The Eighth Wonder (The Australian Opera); Billy Budd (Welsh Nat. Opera, Opera Australia, Canadian Nat. Opera), Sweeney Todd (Lyric Opera of Chicago). *Honours:* Australian Film Inst. Award for production design, Rebel 1985, Ground Zero 1987, Sydney Theatre Critics' Award for Best Designer 1989, 1992, 1993, 1994, Mo Award 1994, 1995, Tony Award for The King and I 1996. *Address:* 5 Little Dowling Street, Paddington, NSW 2021, Australia. *Telephone:* (2) 9331-1584. *Fax:* (2) 9360-4314. *E-mail:* bt@brianthomson.biz (office). *Website:* www.brianthomson.biz (office).

THOMSON, Heather; Opera Singer (Soprano); b. 7 Dec. 1940, Vancouver, Canada; m. Perry Price. *Education:* Studied at the Toronto Conservatory with Herman Geiger-Torel and Irene Jessner. *Career:* Debut: Toronto in 1962 in Hansel and Gretel; Debut with Sadler's Wells as Micaela followed by Mimi, Marguerite in Faust and Anne Trulove in The Rake's Progress; Canadian Opera Company roles include Manon, Rosalinda in Die Fledermaus, Donna Anna and Donna Elvira in Don Giovanni, Ellen in Peter Grimes, Marguerite in Faust, Mother in Hansel and Gretel, Mimi in La Bohème, Tatyana in Eugene Onegin, Lady Billows in Albert Hessing, and world premieres of Heloise and Abelard by Wilson, and Mario and The Magician by Sommers and the title role in Beatrice Cenci, by Goldschmidt in Magdeburg, Germany; Has sung with Welsh National Opera as well as throughout the British Islies, Holland, Czech Republic, Germany, Chile, Monterideo, Poland, Norway, China, the Phillipines and in USA; Roles with New York City Opera include Violetta, Nedda, Donna Anna and Donna Elvira, Marguerite, Rosalinda, and Agathe in Der Freischütz; 1993–94 season as Lady Macbeth in Chemnitz in Germany, Violetta in La Traviata in Toledo, Ohio, Hanna in The Merry Widow at Victoria BC and concerts in Germany and Canada; Sang Rosalinda in Die Fledermaus in Regina, Sash in 2002; Teacher at the School of Music, University of British Columbia in Vancouver and at the New England Vocal Studios, which she established with her husband Perry Price in 1997 in Danbury, CT, USA. *Recordings:* Sang Manon for CBC television; Lady Billows in Albert Herring for CBC and BBC radio; Mother in Hansel and Gretel for CBC-Radio. *Address:* c/o Canadian Opera Company, 227 Front Street East, Toronto, M5A 1E8, Canada.

THOMSON, Neil; Conductor; b. 1966, London, England. *Education:* Studied at the Royal Academy of Music with George Hurst and at the Royal College with Norman del Mar and Christopher Adey. *Career:* Director, Manson Ensemble at RAM giving many performances during the Messiaen Festival in 1987 and the Henze Festival in 1988; Conducted major orchestral and instrumental works of Paul Patterson at venues around the United Kingdom; Founded the contemporary music group, Terre Nova in 1986, with its debut at St John's Smith Square; Concerts at the Purcell Room, South Bank and the Huddersfield Contemporary Music Festival; Worked with such soloists as Christopher Bunting in Dvořák's Cello Concerto and the Brahms Double Concerto with Emanuel Hurwitz; And Suddenly It's Evening by Elisabeth Lutyens with Philip Langridge, and Philip Gammon with Saint-Saëns's 2nd Concerto; Concerts with the Royal Tunbridge Wells Symphony Orchestra; Music Director, Sadler's Wells Youth Ballet Workshop; Concerts with the Bombay Chamber Orchestra in India. *Honours:* Bursary for Conductors, National Association of Youth Orchestras.

THORBURN, Melissa Rachel, BMus, MMus; American opera and concert singer (mezzo-soprano); b. 9 July 1956, Monmouth, IL; m. Timothy Richard Sobolewski 1985; one s. *Education:* Louisiana State University, New England Conservatory, studied with Yvonne Lefèbure in Paris. *Career:* Handel's Messiah with Philadelphia Orchestra, 1987–91, annually; Sang in Berlioz's L'Enfance du Christ with Seattle Symphony, WA, in 1987, Gounod's Faust as Siebel with Deutsche Oper Berlin in 1988, Pergolesi's Stabat Mater with the Puerto Rico Symphony in 1988, Mozart's Le nozze di Figaro as Cherubino with Sarasota Opera, FL, in 1988; Mozart's Requiem with Los Angeles Philharmonic in 1991, and Handel's Messiah with National Symphony in 1992; Mozart's Requiem and Schubert's Mass in E flat with Indianapolis Symphony conducted by Richard Hickox, 1994; Bach's Mass in B Minor with Winter Park Bach Festival, Florida, 1994; Bach's Christmas Oratorio and Cantata No.78 with Baldwin-Wallace Bach Festival, Ohio, 1995; Mendelssohn's Lobgesang with Vancouver Symphony and recitals at the Bermuda Festival, 1996; Mendelssohn's A Midsummer Night's Dream with Philadelphia Orchestra conducted by Charles Dutoit, 1997, and with St Louis Symphony, 1998. *Recordings:* Vaughan Williams's Serenade to Music with the New York Virtuosi Chamber Symphony; Sousa's Désirée. *Current Management:* Thea Dispeker Inc. Artists Representative, 59 E 54th Street, New York, NY 10022, USA. *Address:* c/o Music Department, SUNY, 222 Baird Hall, Buffalo, NY 14260, USA.

THORN, Benjamin; Composer, Editor and Recorder Player; b. 31 Jan. 1961, Canberra, Australia. *Education:* BA (Hons), University of Sydney, 1983, PhD, 1989; Studied with Larry Sitsky and Donald Hollier, 1977–78. *Career:* University of Sydney, 1986; National Printing Industry Training Council, 1991; Performances as recorder player with the Renaissance Players, and other groups. *Compositions include:* Visioni di Cavoli for ensemble, 1985; Pipistrelli Gialli for bass recorder and live electronics, 1985; Chasing for 3 recorders, 1985; Croutons II for clarinet, 1985; Magnificat for chorus, 1985; The Voice of the Crocodile for bass clarinet, 1988; The Pobble for chorus, 1988; Chick Peas for two mandolins, 1990; Two Diagonals and a Squiggle for recorder and percussion, 1991; Missa Sine Verbum, 1991; Croutons III for baroque flute, 1992; Croutons IV for harpsichord, 1992; Songs for my father's wedding, bass recorder, 1995. *Publications:* Editor, two vols of recorder music, Recorders at Large, Works of Sitsky, Strozzi and Castello. *Honours:* Co-winner, Fellowship of Australian Composers' Competition, 1991. *Address:* c/o APRA, 1A Eden Street, Crows Nest, NSW 2065, Australia.

THORN, Penelope; Singer (soprano); b. 19 Sept. 1957, Kent, England. *Education:* Guildhall School of Music and studied with Tito Gobbi in Italy. *Career:* Sang with Karlsruhe Opera from 1980 as Adriana Lecouvreur, Alice Ford, Amelia in Ballo in Maschera, Princess in Rusalka, Giorgetta in Il Tabarro, Freia, Giulietta and Armida in Handel's Rinaldo, also at Barcelona; Sang at Düsseldorf and Mannheim, then appeared at Hannover from 1985 as Tosca, Abigaille and Jenůfa; Freia and Gutrune in Der Ring des Nibelungen for Deutsche Oper am Rhein; Guest appearances at Giessen in Menotti's Mara Golovin, 1986 and at Bielefeld as the Forza Leonora and Asteria in Boito's Nerone; Zürich as Freia and Gutrune and at Nice as Minnie in La Fanciulla del West; Has sung Senta at Freiburg, Lyon and Mannheim, Strauss's Empress at Karlsruhe and Bremen and Third Norn in Götterdämmerung at Munich Staatsoper and in Berlin, under Christian Thielemann; Appearances at Saarbrücken as Aida, Salome, Leonore, Butterfly and Elsa; Sang Third Norn in Götterdämmerung at the Deutsche Oper Berlin, 2000. *Honours:* Winner Voci Verdiane at Bussetto, 1985; Engaged as Salome at Stuttgart, 1996. *Current Management:* Athole Still International Management, Forresters Hall, 25–27 Westow Street, London, SE19 3RY, England. *Telephone:* (20) 8771-5271. *Fax:* (20) 8768-6600. *Website:* www.atholestill.com.

THORNER-MENGEDOTH, Jane; Singer (Soprano); b. 1955, Seattle, USA. *Education:* Studied at Seattle, Munich, Milan, and Geneva. *Career:* Sang in concert at Vienna, with Schreker's Das Spielwerk und die Prinzessin and Pfitzner's Von deutscher Seele; Geneva Opera, 1984, as Alceste; Season 1985 as Salome at Seattle, Leonore at Lucerne, Tippett's Andromache at Nancy and Schreker's Princess at Wuppertal; Sang Abigaille in Nabucco at the Bregenz Festival, 1993–94; Other roles include Cherubini's Medea, and Wagner's Senta, Sieglinde and Gutrune; Festival engagements at Lucerne, Basle and Lausanne; Concerts with the Berlin Philharmonic Orchestra, Metropolitan Orchestra Tokyo and Orchestra of the Santa Cecilia, Rome. *Address:* c/o Bregenz Festival Theatre, Postfach 311, 6901 Bregenz, Austria.

THORNTON-HOLMES, Christopher; Singer (baritone); b. 1959, England. *Education:* Royal Northern College of Music. *Career:* Glyndebourne Tour and Festival from 1985, as Morales in Carmen, Jankel in Arabella, Paolo in Simon Boccanegra, Narumov in The Queen of Spades and Zaretsky in Eugene Onegin (1994); Engagements with Scottish Opera Go Round as Puccini's Sharpless, and Don Giovanni, Amonasro for New Sussex Opera and Verdi's Renato and Rigoletto, Mozart's Count

and Eugene Onegin; Further engagements at the Royal Opera, Covent Garden, and La Scala Milan. *Recordings:* Emilia di Liverpool by Donizetti (Opera Rava).

THORPE, Marion; Pianist and Writer and Musical Administrator and Teacher; b. (Marion Stein), 1926, Vienna, Austria; m. 1st The Earl of Harewood; 2nd Rt Hon. Jeremy Thorpe, three s., one step-s. *Education:* Private study with Franz Osborn. *Career:* Lectures, talks and interviews; Programme notes; mem., Aldeburgh Productions; Co-Founder, Leeds International Pianoforte Competition; Trustee, Britten-Pears Foundation; Friends of Covent Garden. *Publications:* Editor: Form and Performance by Erwin Stein, 1962; Classical Songs for Children, 1964; Series of 19 vols of Piano Lessons and Pieces, The Waterman/Harewood Series, 1967–. *Address:* 2 Orme Square, London W2 4RS, England.

THORSEN, Marianne; Concert Violinist; b. 1972, Trondheim, Norway. *Education:* Studied in Norway, at the Suzuki Institute, London, the Purcell School, and the Royal Academy in London with György Pauk. *Career:* Solo performances in Berlin, with the Slovak Chamber Orchestra, Philharmonia, BBC Symphony Orchestra and orchestras throughout Norway; Recitals at the Bergen International Festival; Member of the Leopold String Trio. *Recordings:* Svendsen's Romance with the Stavanger Symphony Orchestra; Albums with the Trondheim Soloists. *Address:* c/o BLH Artists Management, Strindvegen 38, N–7502 Trondheim, Norway. *E-mail:* blh@c2i.net.

THURLOW, Sarah; Clarinettist; b. 29 May 1974, Bromley, Kent, England. *Education:* BMus, MMus, PGDipRCM, DipRCM, ARCM, with Robert Hill, Stephen Trier and Michael Harris, Royal College of Music; Study with Hans Deinzer, Scuola Internazionale di Perfezionamento Musicale, Bobbio, Italy; Private study with Andrew Marriner and Nicholas Bucknall. *Career:* Debut: St John's Smith Square, 1996; Philharmonia/David Parry Recital Debut, accompanied by Nigel Clayton, Purcell Room, 1999; Solo recitals: Kirckman concerts, Park Lane Group broadcast; Fresh Young Musicians, Purcell Room; Numerous appearances for music clubs and societies; Concertos: including touring with European Union Chamber Orchestra; Orchestral: Freelance with London Symphony Orchestra, Academy of St Martin in the Fields, Sinfonia 21, London Chamber Orchestra, Age of Enlightenment, BBC Philharmonic, Manchester Camerata, Viva; Chamber: Founded Contemporary Consort in 1998; Performances at Cheltenham, Brighton, Kings Lynn and York Late Music Festivals. *Address:* 64A South Eden Park Road, Beckenham, BR3 3BG, England.

THURMER, Harvey; Violinist; b. 1950, Vienna, Austria. *Education:* Vienna Acad. of Music. *Career:* mem. of the Franz Schubert Quartet, 1983–90; many concert engagements in Europe, USA, and Australia including showings in the Amsterdam Concertgebouw, the Vienna Musikverein and Konzerthaus, the Salle Gaveau Paris and the Sydney Opera House; visits to Zürich, Geneva, Basle, Berlin, Hamburg, Rome, Rotterdam, Madrid and Copenhagen; festival engagements include Salzburg, Wiener Festwochen, Prague Spring Schubertiade at Hohenems, the Schubert Festival at Washington DC and Belfast and Istanbul Festivals; tours of Russia, Australasia and USA, and frequent concert tours of the UK; featured in the Quartet Concerto by Spohr with the Liverpool Philharmonic at the Liverpool Festival Hall; Wigmore Hall series includes Master Concerts, Russian Series, Summer Nights, and Coffee Concerts; performance of Alun Hoddinott's Quartet at the 1989 Cheltenham Festival featured on BBC Welsh television; teacher at the Vienna Conservatory and Graz Musikhochschule; masterclasses at the Royal Northern Coll. of Music and at the Lake District Summer Music. *Recordings include:* Schubert's Quartet in G, D877; Complete Quartets of Dittersdorf.

THWAITES, Penelope (Mary); Pianist and Composer; b. 18 April 1944, Chester, England; m. Edward Jackson, 5 Dec 1981, one s., one d. *Education:* BMus, 1st class Hons, Melbourne University, Australia, 1965; Postgraduate study: Piano with Albert Ferber, Composition with William Reed. *Career:* Debut: Wigmore Hall, London, 1974; Regular concerts and broadcasts in London; Tours on 5 continents; Concertos with leading orchestras, Australia, the United Kingdom, America; Lectures, lecture recitals, radio, television and video appearances; Artistic Director, First London International Grainger weekend, 1998; Founder and Chairman, Performing Australian Music Competition, London, 2001. *Compositions include:* Ride! Ride!, 1976; Dancing Pieces, 1989; A Lambeth Garland, 1990; Instrumental and organ works. *Recordings:* Australian Piano Music, 1981; Percy Grainger: complete original music for 4 hands, with John Lavender, Vol. 1, 1989, Vol. II, 1991, Vol. III, 1993; Percy Grainger: Chosen Gems for Piano, solo, 1992; Her own songs recorded, 1985, 1991; Ten recordings in Chandos Grainger Edition; Musical, Ride, Ride, 1999. *Contributions:* The Singer, 1996; BBC Music Magazine, 1997. *Honours:* Order of Australia (AM) 2001; International Grainger Society Medallion 1991. *Current Management:* Siva Oke Music Management. *Address:* 23 Lyndale Avenue, Child's Hill, London NW2 2QB, England.

THYM, Jürgen; Musicologist; b. 2 July 1943, Bremervörde, Germany; m. Peggy Dettwiler, 6 June 1992. *Education:* Diploma in School Music, Hochschule für Musik, Berlin, 1967; PhD, Musicology, Case Western Reserve University, 1974; Studies in theory and composition with Reinhard Schwarz Schilling, counterpoint with Ernst Pepping, 12-tone technique with Josef Rufer and musicology with Reinhold Brinkmann, Rudolph Stephen and Jon G Suess. *Career:* Visiting Instructor at Oberlin College, USA, 1973; Instructor, Assistant Professor, Associate Professor, Professor, 1973–, Chair of Musicology, 1982–, Eastman School of Music, Rochester, NY. *Publications:* The Solo Song Settings of Eichendorff's Poems by Schumann and Wolf, 1974; Translations of Kirnberger's The Art of Strict Musical Composition, 1982, and Schenker's Counterpoint, 1987; 100 Years of Eichendorff Songs, 1983; Schoenberg Collected Works Edition, vol. XIV, 1988, vol. XIII, 1993. *Contributions:* Articles in Journal of Music Theory, Notes, American Choral Review, Comparative Literature, Journal of Musicological Research, Fontes Artis Musicae, Musica Realtà and Aurora, Eichendorff year book, among others; Essays on Mendelssohn and Schumann.

TIBBELS, Nicole; Singer (Soprano); b. 1960, England. *Education:* Sheffield University and the Guildhall School, London. *Career:* Sang with the Swingle Singers and has made many concert appearances in music by Berio; Other repertory includes Dies by Wolfgang Rihm, Mason's Concerto for Viola Section, Nenia by Birtwistle, and songs by Stravinsky; Opera engagements as the Queen of Night with Richard Hickox, and the European Chamber Opera, Alice Ford and Rossini's Clorinda for Pimlico Opera, Serpina in La Serva Padrona for Broomhill Opera and Mozart's Constanze for Perth Festival Opera; Royal Opera Covent Garden debut 1997, as La Comtesse in Massenet's Chérubin; 1997–98 appearances as La Folie in Platée by Rameau and Fido in Paul Bunyan; Premieres of works by Maxwell Davies, Bainbridge, Berio, Michael Finnissy, Jonathan Lloyd and Nigel Osborne. *Recordings include:* Berio's Sinfonia, and works by Bryars, Smalley, Cage and Stockhausen. *Address:* c/o Allied Artists, 42 Montpelier Square, London, SW7 1JZ, England.

TICHY, Georg; Singer (Baritone); b. 9 June 1944, Vienna, Austria. *Education:* Studied with Hilde Zadek in Vienna. *Career:* Debut: Vienna Staatsoper in 1973 in Tristan und Isolde; Sang in Vienna in operas by Verdi, Rossini, Mozart, Puccini, Britten and Wagner; Sang at Maggio Musicale Florence in 1984 as Rigoletto and at Bregenz Festival in 1986 as Papageno; Sang in Schubert's Fierrabras and Wagner's Lohengrin at Vienna in 1990; Sang Ned Keene in the house premiere of Peter Grimes, Vienna Staatsoper, 1996; Season 2000–01 at Covent Garden as Faninal in Der Rosenkavalier, Don Carlo in Ernani and Verdi's Renato for the Vienna Staatsoper; Frequent concert appearances. *Recordings:* Ariadne auf Naxos; Parsifal; Alfonso und Estrella by Schubert. *Address:* c/o Vienna Staatsoper, Opernring 1, Vienna, Austria.

TIEBOUT, Torsten; Violist; b. 21 Sept. 1963, Kassel, Germany. *Education:* Music studies in Hamburg, Hannover, Trossingnen and Helsinki with Prof Stanley Weiner, Hatto Beyerle, Emile Cantor, Hermann Voss and Teemu Kupiainen; Masterclasses with Csaba Erdlyi, Kim Kashkashian, Bruno Giuranna, Tabea Zimmermann, Rainer Moog and Wolfram Christ. *Career:* Debut: As Soloist, with Helsinki University Orchestra in first performance in Finland of revised version of Bart ók's Viola Concerto, conductor John Storgårds, 13 April 1996; Member of Finnish Radio Symphony Orchestra, 1991–95; Principal of Tampere Philharmonic Orchestra, 1995–96; Principal Violist of Helsinki Philharmonic Orchestra, 1996–. *Recordings:* Numerous radio recordings as chamber musician with Cable Quartet, especially contemporary music. *Address:* Paciuksenkatu 4 A 24, 00290 Helsinki, Finland.

TIEPPO, Giorgio; Singer (Tenor); b. 1953, Varese, Italy. *Education:* Studied at the Giuseppe Verdi Conservatory, Milan, and with Pier Miranda Ferraro. *Career:* Sang in concert from 1977 and made opera debut at Pavia 1983, as Don Ruiz in Donizetti's Maria Padilla; Appeared as Don Ruiz in Parma and Ravenna and sang further in La Bohème and Lucia di Lammermoor at Bergamo; Pinkerton in Butterfly at Genoa, Bologna, Turin and New Orleans; Vienna, Mannheim and Dublin debuts as Cavaradossi; Verona Arena in Nabucco, Il Trovatore, Un Ballo in Maschera, Norma and Aida; Appearances at the Zürich Opera as Rodolfo (season 1996–97), Cavaradossi, and Luigi in Il Tabarro; Further engagements in New York, Dallas, Berlin, Rome and Helsinki. *Honours:* Winner, Voci Nuove Verdiane Competition, Bergamo; Voci Verdiane in Busseto. *Address:* c/o Opernhaus Zürich, Falkenstrasse 1, 8008 Zürich, Switzerland.

TIERNEY, Vivian; Singer (soprano); b. 26 Nov. 1957, London, England. *Career:* Sang as Principal Soprano with D'Oyly Carte Opera Company; Freelance, 1982–, at first with Sadler's Wells Opera Company in Kalman's The Gypsy Princess and Lehar's The Count of Luxembourg; Edwige in Offenbach's Robinson Crusoe for Kent Opera; Hanna Glawari in Die Lustige Witwe for Opera North; English National Opera from 1987 as Frasquita, Euridice in Orpheus in the Underworld and Regan in the British premiere of Reimann's Lear, 1989; Sang title role in world premiere of Robin Holloway's Clarissa, 1990; Has sung with Freiburg Opera as Lady Macbeth of Mtsensk, Ellen Orford and Giulietta (Les Contes d'Hoffmann); Has appeared in Handel's Alceste at Versailles; Mimi in La Bohème at Montpellier Festival; Euridice in Milhaud's Les Malheurs d'Orphée at Frankfurt; Donna Anna for Flanders Opera; Sang in Sullivan's cantata The Golden Legend for Colorado Springs Orchestra; Appearance with Opera 80 as Donna Anna; Marie in Wozzeck (Almeida Festival, 1988); Other roles include the Marschallin in Der Rosenkavalier, Jenny (in Mahagonny), Rosalinde in Die Fledermaus, and Malinka in The Excursions of Mr Brouček; Mimi in La Bohème for English National Opera, 1992; Gypsy Princess (Los Angeles); Sang Ellen Orford in a new production of Peter Grimes at Glyndebourne, 1992; Renata in The Fiery Angel in Freiburg, 1993; Berg's Marie for Opera North, 1993; Sang Gutrune in Götterdämmerung at Covent Garden, 1996; Season 1998 with Jitka in Smetana's Dalibor for Scottish Opera; Season 2000 as Korngold's Marietta at Cologne, Ellen Orford at Glyndebourne and Mrs Foran in the premiere of The Silver Tassie, by Turnage, for ENO. *Current Management:* Athole Still International Management, Forresters Hall, 25–27 Westow Street, London, SE19 3RY, England. *Telephone:* (20) 8771-5271. *Fax:* (20) 8768-6600. *Website:* www.atholestill.com.

TIKKA, Kari (Juhani); Conductor and Composer; b. 13 April 1946, Siilinjärvi, Finland; m. Eeva Relander, 18 May 1979, 3 s., 1 d. *Education:* Oboe Diploma, Conducting Diploma, Sibelius Academy, Helsinki; Private study with Arvid Jansons and Luigi Ricci. *Career:* Debut: Helsinki, 1968; Conductor: Tampere Theatre, 1969–70; Finnish National Opera, Helsinki, 1970–72, 1979–; Finnish Radio Symphony Orchestra, 1972–76; Royal Swedish Opera, Stockholm, 1975–77; Symphony Orchestra Vivo, Helsinki, 1986–97; Guest Conductor, Scandinavia, Western and Eastern Europe, Israel and USA. *Compositions:* Frieda, opera; Luther, opera; Two Aphorisms; Due Pezzi; Many songs; Cantatas; The Prodigal Son, oratorio; Concerto for Cello; Music for choir; Chamber music. *Recordings:* Vivo-Tikka; Triplet; Jumala on rakkaus; Armolaulu: Armolaulu, VIVO Finlandia. *Address:* Mannerheimintie 38 A 4, 00100 Helsinki, Finland. *E-mail:* kari.tikka@kolumbus.fi.

TILLEY, David; Singer (Baritone); b. 1960, England. *Education:* Studied with Mark Wildman and David Mason. *Career:* Appearances in Das Liebesverbot by Wagner at Wexford and Howard Goodall's Silas Marner for CBTO; Lesbo in Handel's Agrippina at Cambridge, Frost King in Purcell's King Arthur at Croydon and Adonis in Blow's Venus and Adonis; Other roles include Leporello and parts in Purcell's Fairy Queen (English Bach Festival, 2001) and Jonathan Dove's Tobias and the Angel for the Almeida Festival; Further roles in Rigoletto and Die Zauberflöte. *Address:* c/o English Bach Festival, 15 South Eaton Place, London, SW1W 9ER, England.

TILLI, Johann; Singer (Bass); b. 11 Nov. 1967, Kerimäki, Finland. *Education:* Studied at the Sibelius Academy, Helsinki. *Career:* Appearances at the Savonlinna Festival, Finland, as Sarastro, the King in Aida, Banquo and Landgraf and other roles; National Opera, Helsinki, as Lodovico and High Priest Baal (Nabucco); Commendatore and Rossini's Basilio at Oslo, with further engagements at Amsterdam, Brussels, Tel-Aviv and Hannover; Member of the Hamburg Opera from 1990; First Bass with Düsseldorf Oper, 1996–97; Has worked with many conductors including Abbado, Cillario, de Burgos, Fricke, Harnoncourt, Steinberg, Sawallisch and Wallberg; Three Bass Concert with Matti Salminen, Jaakko Ryhänen and conductor Leif Segerstam in Helsinki, 1995; Wotan in Die Walküre at Helsinki, 1998; Season 2000–01 as Fasolt at Bayreuth, Gremin for Cologne Opera and Colonna in Wagner's Rienzi at Dresden (concert). *Recordings include:* Gazzaniga's Don Giovanni (Sony Classics); Mahler's 8th Symphony; Schumann Genoveva; Dessau: Haggaddah; Highlights from Savonlinna; Lady Macbeth of the Mtsensk District (DGG). *Address:* c/o Hamburg Staatsoper, Grosse Theaterstrasse 34, Pf 302448, 20354 Hamburg, Germany.

TILLIKAINEN, Sauli; Singer (Baritone); b. 7 Dec. 1952, Finland. *Education:* Studied at the Sibelius Academy Helsinki and in Vienna with Anton Dermota and Hans Hotter. *Career:* Debut: Sang in concert from 1981; Sang with the Finnish National Opera from 1984 and as guest at the Moscow Bolshoi, Stockholm, Dresden and Copenhagen; Roles have included Guglielmo, Don Giovanni, Escamillo, Mozart's Count, Germont, Eugene Onegin, Ruprecht in The Fiery Angel and the title roles in Lionardo by Werle and Thomas by Rautavaara; Kennedy Center, Washington, in Ein Deutsches Requiem and the Kullervo Symphony by Sibelius; Sang Valmonte in Sallinen's The Palace, Savonlinna Festival, 1996; Season 2000–01 as Helsinki as Edgar in the premiere of Sallinen's Lear, and Germont in Traviata; Lieder recitals in music by Schubert and Schumann. *Address:* Finnish National Opera, Bulevardi 23–27, 00180 Helsinki 18, Finland.

TILLING, Camilla; Singer (soprano); b. 1972, Sweden. *Education:* Gothenburg University; Royal College of Music, with Margaret Kingsley. *Career:* Debut: Camiletta and Mergelina, in intermezzi by Jommelli, Vadstena Summer Opera; Appearances in Gothenburg as Offenbach's Olympia, Sophie in Der Rosenkavalier, and Rossini's Rosina (2000–01); Mozart's Blonde and Susanna in London and Aix; Corinna in Il Viaggio a Reims for New York City Opera, Purcell's Belinda in Geneva and Nannetta in Falstaff at the New York Met (2001); Concerts include Handel's Saul in Brussels, and engagements with the London Mozart Players, King's Consort and Corydon Singers; Glyndebourne Festival debut 2000, as First Niece in Peter Grimes.

TILNEY, Colin; Harpsichordist; b. 31 Oct. 1933, London, England. *Education:* Studied harpsichord with Mary Potts at Cambridge and with Gustav Leonhardt in Amsterdam. *Career:* Soloist and ensemble player in the United Kingdom and Europe from the early 1960s; US debut in 1971; Repertoire has included music by Renaissance and Baroque composers; Has performed on various clavichords, harpsichords, virginals and early pianos, employing both historical instruments and modern copies. *Recordings include:* Parthenia, a collection of pieces by Byrd, Bull and Gibbons published in 1611; Complete Keyboard Works of Matthew Locke and the Suites of Purcell and Handel; CD of Bach's Toccatas, 1990. *Publications include:* Edition of the harpsichord music of Antoine Forqueray. *Address:* c/o Conifer Records, Horton Road, West Drayton, Middlesex UB7 8JL, England.

TIMARU, Valentin; Composer; b. 16 Oct. 1940, Sibiu, Romania; m. Maria Chisbora, 20 May 1976, 1 s., 1 d. *Education:* Licence in Musical Pedagogy, 1964, Licence in Musical Composition, 1972, George Dima Conservatory, Cluj; Doctor of Musicology, 1982. *Career:* Debut: As Author of Musical Portrait, 30 Jan 1970; Music Teacher, Buftea, Bucharest, 1964–68; Music Inspector for Cultural Department of Cluj District, 1968–70; University Assistant in Musical Theory, 1970; University Lecturer in Musical Forms, 1977; University Professor of Musical Forms, 1990. *Compositions:* 2 String Quartets, 1968, 1992; 4 Cantatas for Choir and Orchestra, 1971, 1976, 1980, 1992; Symphony No. 1, 1972, No. 2, 1988, No. 3, 1988, No. 4, 1990, No. 5, 1999; Violin Concerto, 1976; Double Concerto for Double Bass and Percussion, 1980; 3 Oratorios, 1981, 1984, 1999; Lorelei, opera, 1989; Liturgy for Mixed Choir (Liturgy of Ioan Chrysostomos), 1994; The Ciuleandra Ballet (after the novel of Liviu Rebreanu), 1998; Lieder, works for choirs, miscellaneous chamber music. *Publications:* Musical Form Theory, vol. I, 1990, vol. II, 1994, vol. III, 1998; Enescian Symphonism (Analysis of Enescu's Symphonies), 1992; The Art of Musical Ensemble (Orchestral and Vocal), 1998; Our Holy Music, 2001; Dictionary of Notions and Terminology, 2003; Musical Analysis between Genre Conscience and Form Conscience, 2003. *Honours:* Romanian Composers' Union Prize, 1986, 1992, 1995, 2003; Romanian Acad. Prize, 1995. *Address:* Gheorghe Dima Music Academy, 25 I.C. Bratianu Street, PO Box 195, 400750 Cluj-Napoca, Romania. *E-mail:* v_timaru@yahoo.com.

TINNEY, Hugh; pianist; b. 28 Nov. 1958, Dublin, Ireland. *Education:* Trinity College, Dublin, 1976–79; Private piano studies with Mabel Swainson, Louis Kentner, Bryce Morrison and Maria Curcio; LRSM Diploma, 1974. *Career:* debut, Purcell Room, London in 1983; Performed concertos and recitals in 30 countries in 4 continents; Radio broadcasts in 12 countries and 2 recitals for Irish television, RTE; Concerto appearances on Irish, Italian and Spanish television; Recitals at Queen Elizabeth Hall in London, Musikverein, Vienna, Kennedy Center, Washington; Appearances at festivals include Newport, Rhode Island, Granada, and Prague Spring Festival; Performances with Gulbenkian, Lisbon, Spanish National, Spanish Radio, and Brazil Symphony Orchestras; Proms debut in 1989 with BBC National Orchestra of Wales; Other performances with British orchestras such as London Philharmonic, Philharmonia, Royal Philharmonic, Royal Liverpool Philharmonic, City of Birmingham and Royal Scottish Orchestras. *Recordings:* Liszt Recital–Dante Sonata, Benediction de Dieu dans La Solitude; Harmonies Poétiques et Réligieuses, Liszt, 1993. *Current Management:* Tennant Artists, Unit 2, 39 Tadema Road, London, SW10 0PZ, England. *Telephone:* (20) 7376-3758. *Fax:* (20) 7351-0679. *E-mail:* info@tennantartists.demon.co.uk. *Address:* 258b Camden Road, London NW1 9AB, England.

TINSLEY, Pauline; Singer (Soprano); b. 27 March 1928, Wigan, England. *Education:* Northern School of Music, Manchester, LRAM 1949; Opera School, London; Further study with Eva Turner and Eduardo Asquez. *Career:* Professional engagements in the United Kingdom from 1961 include London debut as Desdemona, Rossini's Otello; leading roles in Verdi's I Masnadieri, Ernani, Il Corsaro and Bellini's Il Pirata; Welsh National Opera from 1962 as Susanna, Elsa, Lady Macbeth, Sinaide (Rossini's Moses), Abigaille, Aida, Tosca, Turandot, Kostelnicka (Jenůfa), Elektra and Dyer's Wife (Frau Ohne Schatten) 1981; Sadler's Wells/English National Opera from 1963 as Gilda, Elvira (Ernani), Fiordiligi, Queen of Night, Countess, Donna Elvira, Beethoven's Leonore and Fidelio, Leonora (Force of Destiny),

Elizabeth (Mary Stuart), 1973, Mother/Witch (Hansel and Gretel), 1987, Kabanicha (Katya Kabanova), 1989; Covent Garden from 1965 as Overseer (Elektra), Amelia (Ballo in Maschera), 1971, Helmwige and 3rd Norn (The Ring), Santuzza, 1976, Mère Marie (Carmélites), 1983, Lady Billows (Albert Herring), 1989; Various roles with Scottish Opera including Kostelnicka and Opera North (Fata Morgana in Love for 3 Oranges) and with Handel Opera Society; From 1966, performed abroad in Germany, Netherlands, Italy, USA, Canada, Switzerland, Czechoslovakia, Spain and Belgium; Concerts, recitals, broadcasts and television operas; Wexford Festival as Lady Jowler in The Rising of the Moon, 1990; Sang Lady Billows at Garsington, 1996; Sang Grandmother Burya in Jenůfa, for Opera North, 1995 and 2002, and for Netherlands Opera 1997 and 2001. *Recordings include:* Electra in Idomeneo (Philips). *Address:* c/o Music International, 13 Ardilaun road, Highbury, London N5 2QR, England.

TIPO, Maria; Pianist; b. 23 Dec. 1931, Naples, Italy. *Education:* Studied with her mother, Ersilla Cavallo. *Career:* Debut: Public piano performance aged four; Many solo engagements from 1949 throughout Europe, USA, Central and South America, Africa, Russia, Japan and the Middle East, including many performances in the USA after discovery by Arthur Rubinstein in 1952; Teacher at the Bolzano, Florence and Geneva Conservatories; Performances of works by Clementi, Scarlatti and other Italian composers, Beethoven, Mozart, Schumann, Ravel, Debussy, Chopin, Brahms; Has performed with the Berlin Philharmonic, Vienna Philharmonic, Boston Symphony, London Philharmonic, Concertgebouw Orchestra in Amsterdam, Czech Philharmonic, Orchestre de Paris, Salzburg Mozarteum, La Scala in Milan, S Cecilia in Rome and many others; Chamber music performances with the Amadeus Quartet, Salvatore Accardo and Uto Ughi; Judge at many international competitions; President, Centro Studi Musicali F Busoni. *Recordings include:* Piano Sonatas by Clementi; Bach's Goldberg Variations; Eighteen Scarlatti Sonatas. *Honours:* Many awards include: Prizewinner at the 1949 Geneva and 1952 Queen Elisabeth of the Belgians Competitions; First Music Critics Prize, 1985; Gargano Award; Ernest Hemingway Award; Personality of the Year Award. *Address:* c/o Accademia Santa Cecilia, Via Vittoria 6, 00187 Rome, Italy.

TIPTON, Thomas; Singer (Baritone); b. 18 Nov. 1926, Wyandotte, Michigan, USA. *Education:* Studied at Michigan State College with Herbert Swanson and at Ann Arbor with Chase Baromeo. *Career:* Debut: New York City Opera in 1954 as Bob in The Old Maid and The Thief by Menotti; Sang two seasons in New York, then visited Europe; Sang at Mannheim Opera, 1960–63, Stuttgart, 1964–66, and Bayerische Staatsoper Munich from 1966; Guest appearances in Vienna, Berlin and Hamburg; Sang at Salzburg Festival, 1964–65, Bayreuth Festival in 1967 as Wotan and the Herald in Lohengrin, and at Covent Garden, 1972–74 as Rigoletto; Other roles included Nabucco and Macbeth; Concert appearances in North and South America. *Publications:* Thomas Tipton ein Leben in Bildern, Munich, 1987. *Address:* c/o Bayerische Staatsoper, Postfach 745, 8000 Munich 1, Germany.

TIRIMO, Martino; Concert Pianist and Conductor; b. 19 Dec. 1942, Larnaca, Cyprus; m. Mione J Teakle, 1973, 1 s., 1 d. *Education:* Royal Academy of Music, London; Vienna State Academy. *Career:* Debut: Recital, Cyprus, 1949; Conducted La Traviata 7 times at Italian Opera Festival, Cyprus, 1955; London debut, 1965; Concerto performances with most major orchestras, and recitals, television and radio appearances in the United Kingdom, Europe, USA, Canada, South Africa and the Far East from 1965; Gave public première of complete Schubert Sonatas, London, 1975, 1985; Public première of Beethoven concertos directing from the keyboard, Dresden and London, 1985, 1986; Gave several premières of Tippett Piano concerto from 1986; Four Series of Beethoven's 32 sonatas, 2000; Two Series dedicated to major piano works of Robert and Clara Schumann, 2001. *Compositions include:* film score for the Odyssey in 8 episodes for Channel 4 television, 1998. *Recordings:* Brahms Piano Concertos; Chopin Concertos; Tippett Piano Concerto (with composer conducting); Rachmaninov Concertos; Complete Debussy piano works; Complete Schubert Piano Sonatas; Various other solo recordings with mixed repertoire. *Publications:* Schubert: The Complete Piano Sonatas, 3 vols, edited for Wiener Unitext Edition (with own completions to the unfinished movements), 1997–99. *Honours:* Gold Medal, Associated Board of the Royal Schools of Music; Liszt Scholarship, Royal Academy of Music; 11 other Prizes at Royal Academy of Music including Macfarren Medal; Boise Foundation Scholarship, 1965; Gulbenkian Foundation Scholarship, 1967–69; Joint Winner, Munich International Competition, 1971; Winner, Geneva International Competition, 1972; ARAM, 1968; FRAM, 1979; Silver Disc, 1988; Gold Disc, 1994. *Current Management:* Music Partnership Ltd. *Address:* 1 Romeyn Road, London SW16 2NU, England.

TISCHENKO, Leonid; Singer (Bass); b. 1969, Kiev, Ukraine, Russia. *Education:* Studied at the Moscow and Kiev Conservatories. *Career:* Has sung with the National Opera of the Ukraine at Kiev as Pimen

(Boris Godunov), Verdi's King Phillip and Gremin in Eugene Onegin; Concerts at Strasbourg 1999, in the Mozart Requiem, and at the Concertgebouw Amsterdam in Rossini's Stabat Mater; further engagements with the Verdi Requiem and other works in Germany, Italy, the USA, Austria, France and Hungary; has also conducted the Ukraine State Symphony Orchestra. *Address:* National Opera of the Ukraine, Kiev, Ukraine.

TISHCHENKO, Boris; Composer; b. 23 March 1939, Leningrad, USSR; m. Irene Donskaya 1977, thee s. *Education:* Leningrad with Ustvolskaya, Salmanov, Voloshinov and Evlachov; with Logovinsky as a pianist; Later study with Shostakovich. *Career:* Freelance composer; Pianist; Teacher at Leningrad (later St Petersburg) Conservatory 1965, Assistant Professor 1980, Full Professor at Leningrad Conservatory, 1986; mem, Union of Composers of Russian Federation. *Compositions:* Stage: The Twelve, ballet 1963; Fly-bee, ballet 1968; The Stolen Sun, opera 1968; A Cockroach, musical comedy 1968; The Eclipse (Yaroslavna), ballet 1974; Beatriche Ballet, 2004; Orchestral: 7 Symphonies, 2nd Marina with mixed chorus to verses by Tsvetayeva, 1961–1994; 1st Violin Concerto 1958; Piano Concerto 1962; 1st Cello Concerto 1963; Pushkin's Symphony, 1967, rev. 1998; Sinfonia Robusta 1970; Concerto for flute, piano and strings 1972; Harp Concerto 1977; 2nd Cello Concerto, 1969; 2nd Violin Concerto 1981; Concerto allamarcia for 16 soloists, 1989; Symphony The Siege Chronicle 1984; Vocal: Lenin is Alive, cantata to verse by Mayakovsky, 1959; Requiem to text by Akhmatova 1966; To my Brother for soprano, flute and harp to verse by Lermontov 'The Will', 1986; The Will for soprano, harp and organ to verse by Zabolocky, 1986; Garden of Music, cantata in 2 parts to verses by Kushner, 1987; Chamber music including 5 String Quartets 1957–84; Quintet for strings and piano 1985; 10 Piano sonatas, 1957–97; 2 sonatas for violin solo 1957, 1975; Rondo, Capriccio and Fantasy for Violin and Piano 1956, 1965, 1994; 3 sonatas for cello solo 1960, 1979; Dog Heart, novelettes for chamber ensemble, 1988; Incidental music for plays; Concerto for clarinet and piano trio, 1990; Vocal cycles, Music for films, Orchestral suites; Pieces for different instruments, songs, works for chorus a capella; Egosuite for piano, 1957; The Chelom Wise Men, a vocal instrumental quartet for violin, soprano, bass and piano, Words by O Driz, 1991; Twelve Inventions for organ, 1964; Twelve portraits for organ, 1992; The French Symphony, 1958–93; Eight Portraits for piano in 4 hands, 1996; The Whims, suite for piano, 1958–98; Sonata for family of flutes and organ, 1999; Orchestrations: Monteverdi, Coronation of Poppea, 1967; Shostakovich, Satires, words by Chorny, 1980; Four Poems by Captain Lebjadkin, words by Dostoevsky, 1986; Antiformalistic Little Paradise, 1989; Grieg: Four Romances, 1991; Mahler: 8 songs, 1993; Prokofiev: 3 choruses, 1972. *Honours:* 1st prize, on the International Contest of Young Composers in Prague, 1966; State Prize of Russian Federation named by Glinka, 1978; Prize of Mayor of St Petersburg, 1995; The title, People's Artist of Russia, 1987; The Gold Pushkin's Medal, 1999; The Order for merits for Homeland IVth Degree, 2002; The prize of the Union of Composers of RF named by Shostakovich, 2002; The Honour Prize of Russian Author's Society, 2003. *Address:* Rimsky-Korsakov Avenue, 79-10, St Petersburg 190121, Russia.

TISNE, Antoine; Composer; b. 29 Nov. 1932, Lourdes, France. *Education:* Studied at the Paris Conservatoire with Riviere and Darius Milhaud, among others. *Career:* Inspector of Music for the French Ministry of Culture, 1967–92; Inspector for the municipal conservatories of Paris, from 1992; Professor of compositions and orchestration at the Paris Conservatoire. *Compositions include:* 4 piano concertos, 1959, 1961, 1962, 1992; 4 string quartets, 1956, 1979, 1979, 1989; Cantique de Printemps, 1960; Wind Quintet, 1961; Violin Sonata, 1963; Cosmogonies for 3 orchestras, 1967; Violin Concerto, 1969; Ondes Flamboyantes, for strings, 1973; Impacts for ondes martenots and 2 string orchestras, 1973; Isle de Temps for ondes martenot sextet, 1980; La Ramasseuse de sarments, music theatre, 1982; Instant, ballet, 1985; L'Heure des Hommes, oratorio, 1985; Reliefs irradiants de New York, for orchestra, 1979; Le Chant des Yeux, oratorio, 1986; Les Voiles de la nuit, 1991; De la Nuit et L'Aurore, for oboe and strings, 1991; La Voix de l'Ombre, for flute and string trio, 1991; Dans la lumière d'Orcival, for chorus, 1992; Invocation, for baritone and orchestra, 1993; Pour l'amour d'Alban, opera. *Honours:* Grand Prix Musical of the City of Paris, 1979. *Address:* c/o SACEM, 225 Avenue Charles de Gaulle, 92521 Neuilly sur Seine Cédex, France.

TITOV, Alexander; Conductor; b. 1950, St Petersburg, Russia. *Education:* Graduated St Petersburg Conservatoire, 1981. *Career:* Assistant conductor to Gennadi Rozhdestvensky and Mstislav Rostropovich; Conductor at the Kirov Opera and Ballet, St Petersburg from 1991; Repertoire has included La Traviata, Prokofiev's The Gambler and Love for Three Oranges, Stravinsky's Rossignol, Katerina Izmailova and Ruslan and Lyudmila; Ballets include Chopiniana, The Sleeping Beauty, The Firebird and Schéhérazade; Conducted the Kirov Ballet in summer season at Covent Garden, 2000; Professor at the St

Petersburg Conservatoire. *Honours:* Winner, International Minon Competition, Tokyo, 1988. *Address:* c/o Kirov Opera, Mariinsky Theatre, St Petersburg, Russia.

TITTERINGTON, David Michael; Concert Organist; b. 10 Jan. 1958, Oldham, England. *Education:* BA, 1980, Organ Scholar, 1977–81, Pembroke Coll., Oxford; studied under Marie-Claire Alain, Conservatoire National de Rueil-Malmaison, Paris, 1982–85;. *Career:* debut, Royal Festival Hall, 1986; recitals in cathedrals and halls throughout the UK; concert tours of Germany, Scandinavia, France, USA, Far East, New Zealand and Australia; appearances at major international festivals at Hong Kong, Harrogate, Istanbul, Adelaide, Sydney and Brighton; concert hall appearances include Wigmore Hall, Royal Festival Hall, Munich, Acad. for Performing Arts, Hong Kong; television appearances on BBC 2 and Anglia television; Prof. of Organ, Royal Academy of Music, London, 1990–; Concertos with Berlin Symphony, BBC Symphony Orchestra, City of London Sinfonia and English Sinfonia; Recitals, Concertos and Masterclasses world-wide at major venues and festivals including BBC Proms, Hong Kong, Sydney, New Zealand, Tokyo; Head of Organ Studies, Royal Acad. of Music, 1996–. *Recordings:* Messiaen; La Nativité du Seigneur; Eben; Job; Eberlin; Toccatas; over 30 recordings for BBC and networks world-wide. *Publications:* edited works of Petr Eben; Organ Works (ed.). *Current Management:* Denny Lyster Artists' Management, PO Box 155, Stanmore, Middlesex HA7 3WF, England. *Telephone:* (20) 8954-5521. *Fax:* (20) 8954-9168. *E-mail:* artists@dennylyster.co.uk. *Website:* www.dennylyster.co.uk.

TITUS, Alan; Singer (baritone); b. 28 Oct. 1945, New York, NY, USA. *Education:* Studied with Askel Schiotz at the Colorado School of Music and with Hans Heinz at Juilliard. *Career:* Debut: Washington DC in 1969 in La Bohème; Sang the Celebrant in the premiere of Bernstein's Mass at Washington DC, 1971; Sang at New York City Opera in 1972 in Summer and Smoke; European debut at Amsterdam in 1973 in Debussy's Pelléas; Sang at Metropolitan Opera in 1976 as Harlekin in Ariadne auf Naxos, Glyndebourne in 1979 as Guglielmo, Deutsche Oper am Rhein Düsseldorf in 1984 as Don Giovanni, and Santa Fe in 1985 in Strauss's Intermezzo; Engagements at Aix-en-Provence, Hamburg and Frankfurt; Sang at Maggio Musicale Florence in 1987 as Olivier in Capriccio; Sang Dandini at San Francisco in 1987, at Munich as Valentin and sang in Mathis der Maler in 1989, Bologna 1990 as Storch in the Italian premiere of Intermezzo; Sang Kovalyov in The Nose by Shostakovich at Frankfurt in 1990; Season 1992–93 in Arabella at La Scala, the title role in Donizetti's Il Duca d'Alba at Spoleto, and Hans Sachs at Frankfurt; Sang the title role in Hindemith's Mathis der Maler at Covent Garden, 1995; Sang Pizarro in Fidelio at Rome, 1996; Altair in Strauss's Aegyptische Helena at the Festival Hall, 1998; Season 2000–01 as Kurwenal at Covent Garden and Strauss's Barak for the Dresden Staatsoper; Sang Wotan in The Ring at Bayreuth, 2001. *Recordings include:* Haydn's La Feldeltà Premiata; La Bohème; L'Elsir d'Amore; Don Giovanni; La Wally; Le nozze di Figaro; Falstaff; Paradies und die Peri; Genoveva; Carmen. *Current Management:* L. S. Artists, Lydia Störle, Orlando Strasse 8, 8000 Munich 2, Germany.

TITUS, Graham; Singer (Baritone); b. 15 Dec. 1949, Newark, Nottinghamshire, England. *Education:* MA, Clare College, Cambridge University (Organ Scholar); FRCO; Cologne Musikhochschule. *Career:* Debut: Purcell Room, London in 1974; Appearances with New Opera Company, Handel Opera and English National Opera; Radio recitals from 1974 and appearances on Dutch radio and television; Concert tour of South America; Recital and oratorio work throughout the United Kingdom including the Aldeburgh Festival in 1975 and the Glyndebourne Festival in 1979 as Guglielmo. *Honours:* Winner of Young Musicians Competition, 1974 and 's-Hertogenbosch Competition, 1977. *Address:* c/o English National Opera, St Martin's Lane, London WC2N 4ES, England.

TOCZYSKA, Stefania; Singer (Mezzo-Soprano); b. 19 Feb. 1943, Gdansk, Poland. *Education:* Gdansk Conservatory with Barbara Iglikovska. *Career:* Debut: Danzig in 1973 as Carmen; Sang in Poland as Azucena, Leonora in La Favorita and Dalila; Western debut in 1977 as Amneris at Basle Opera; Sang at Vienna Staatsoper in 1977 as Ulrica in Un Ballo in Maschera returning as Carmen and as Verdi's Azucena, Eboli and Preziosilla; Sang at Munich and Hamburg in 1979 as Eboli in Don Carlos, San Francisco Opera as Laura in La Gioconda, Amneris and in Roberto Devereux, Royal Opera Covent Garden, 1983–84 as Azucena and Amneris, Bregenz Festival and Chicago Lyric Opera in 1986 as Giovanna Seymour in Anna Bolena, Houston Opera in 1987 as Adalgisa and Amneris, and Barcelona in 1987 and Hamburg in 1990 as Venus in Tannhäuser; Sang Laura in La Gioconda at the Metropolitan Opera in 1989, at Washington and Houston in 1990 as Amneris and Dalila and appeared in Aida at the Caracalla Festival at Rome in 1990; Season 1992 as Azucena at Munich, Massenet's Dulcinée at Toulouse, Donizetti's Maria Stuarda at Barcelona and Carmen at the Munich Festival; Sang Amneris at the Met, 1997; Season 2000–01 as Amneris at Maastricht, and in Moniuszko's The Haunted Castle, at Warsaw. *Address:* c/o Metropolitan Opera, Lincoln Center, New York, NY 10023, USA.

TODD, Will, BA, MMus; British Composer; b. 14 Jan. 1970, Durham, England; s. of Derek and Iris Todd; m. Bethany Halliday, one s., one d. *Education:* MMus, Bristol Univ. with Raymond Warren and Adrian Beaumont, 1988–93. *Compositions:* opera, Isambard Kingdom Brunel, premiered at Colston Hall, Bristol, 1993; Midwinter, for chorus, 1994; oratorio, St Cuthbert, premiered at Durham Cathedral, 1996; The Burning Road commissioned for Crouch End Festival Chorus, 1996; musical, The Screams of Kitty, with librettist David Simpatico performed at Boston Conservatory 2001; opera, The Blackened Man, with librettist Ben Dunwell, Linbury Studio Theatre Covent Garden (prizewinner, International Giuseppe Verdi Competition), 2002. *Recordings:* The Burning Road (Silva Classics), Saint Cuthbert (Northumbrian Anthology). *Address:* 39 Grover House, Vauxhall Street, London, SE11 5LJ, England (office); 1 Blue Coat Court, Claypath, Durham, DH1 1TX, England (home). *Telephone:* (20) 7793-7013 (office); (191) 383-1101 (home). *E-mail:* will@willtodd.com (office). *Website:* tyalgumpress.com.

TODISCO, Nunzio; Singer (Tenor); b. 1942, Italy. *Career:* Has sung in Italy and at Orange, Lisbon, Rome and Zürich from 1970; US debut at San Francisco in 1978 as Pollione in Norma; Sang Loris in Fedora at the Metropolitan Opera and in Naples, 1989; Sang at Verona Arena in 1989 as Ismaele in Nabucco; Other roles include Verdi's Carlo in I Masnadieri, Foresto in Attila, Arrigo in La Battaglia di Legnano, Manrico, Ernani and Radames, Puccini's Dick Johnson, Luigi and Cavaradossi and Licinius in La Vestale by Spontini; Sang Ismaele at Verona in 1992. *Address:* c/o Arena di Verona, Piazza Brà 28, 37121 Verona, Italy.

TODOROV, Nedyalcho (Georgiev); Violinist and Professor; b. 27 Oct. 1940, Plovdiv, Bulgaria; m. Veneta Assenova Todorova, 26 Nov 1967, 1 s., 1 d. *Education:* MA, State Academy of Music, Sofia, 1964; Gnessini State Music Pedagogy Institute, Moscow, 1973–74. *Career:* Violin Teacher, Secondary School of Music, Plovdiv, 1964–67; Violin Professor, Deputy Rector, 1974–79, Rector, 1979–83, Academy of Music and Dance Art, Plovdiv; Director, 1970–72, Concertmaster, 1976–79, Plovdiv Philharmony; 1st Violinist, Plovdiv String Quartet, 1978–; Director, Educational Department, Ministry of Culture, Sofia, 1983–91; Recitals, soloist with orchestra, chamber music concerts; Repertoire includes concertos of Bach, Mozart, Beethoven, Mendelssohn, Bruch, Hindemith, Shostakovich, V Stoyanov, Ivan Spassov; sonatas, pieces, duos, trios, quartets. *Recordings:* Luigi Boccherini: String Quartet Op 33 No. 6, A major; Quintet for oboe, violins, viola and violoncello Op 45 No. 1, G major, Quintet Op 45 No. 2, F major, Quintet Op 45 No. 3, D major with Plovdiv String Quartet and Boryu Pamoukchiev, oboe, 1988; 4 concertos for violin, oboe and orchestra: Telemann, C minor, Fasch, D minor, Vivaldi, B flat major, Bach, D minor, soloists: self, violin, Pamoukchiev, oboe, with Jambol Chamber Orchestra, conductor N Sultanov, 1988. *Publications:* 1st performances, recordings, editions (pieces for violin and piano, duos for 2 violins and chamber ensembles by modern Bulgarian composers), 6 vols, 1977–88; Recordings, editions (collections of classical concertos for oboe and violin), 1990; Bulgarian Violin Literature (editor), catalogue, 1992; Avramov Catalogue, 1999. *Address:* Complex Hippodrome, Block 139, Entr A, Apt 33, 1612 Sofia, Bulgaria. *E-mail:* todorov@inet.bg.

TODOROVIC, Nicholas; Singer (Bass-Baritone); b. 1965, Christchurch, New Zealand. *Education:* University of Canterbury and Queen's Conservatorium of Music. *Career:* Appearances with Mercury Opera, Auckland, as Hermann in The Queen of Spades and Morales in Carmen; Don Giovanni with the Lyric Opera of Queensland and Papageno with Victoria State Opera; British debut as the villains in Les Contes d'Hoffmann, for Stowe Opera; Season 1996–97 as Masetto for Victoria State Opera and Johnny Dowd in the premiere of Summer of the Seventeenth Doll by Richard Mills, at the Melbourne International Arts Festival; Masetto in Don Giovanni for Auckland Opera (with Kiri Te Kanawa) and Schaunard in La Bohème at Melbourne; Resident in the United Kingdom. *Address:* c/o Victoria State Opera, 77 Southbank Blvd, Melbourne, VIC3205, Australia.

TODOROVICH, Zoran; Singer (Tenor); b. 1962, Bulgaria. *Education:* Belgrade Conservatoire and in Zagreb with Zinka Milanov. *Career:* National Theatre, Belgrade, from 1985 as Rossini's Almaviva, Shuisky in Boris Godunov and Donizetti's Tonio; State Opera Hanover 1994–99; Pinkerton at the Vienna and Berlin State Operas, 1997–98, Faust at the Deutsche Oper, Berlin; Season 1999–2000 as Leopold in La Juive (Vienna), US debut as Rodolfo at San Francisco, Lensky for Nice Opera and Alfredo in La Traviata at Zürich; Season 2000–01 as Lensky in Tokyo, Rodolfo at Hamburg and the Berlioz Faust in Zürich; Further engagements in Roberto Devereux by Donizetti in Munich, Edgardo and the Duke of Mantua for Hamburg Opera and Alfredo at Frankfurt; Concerts include the Verdi Requiem (Munich), Gounod's Mors et Vita and Rossini's Stabat Mater. Other opera roles include Mozart's Titus (at

Madrid). *Recordings include:* Mors et Vita. *Address:* c/o Theateragentur Dr G. Hilbert, Maximilianstrasse 22, 80539 Munich, Germany.

TOFFOLUTTI, Ezio; Stage Designer; b. 1941, Venice, Italy. *Education:* Studied set design and art at the Accademia delle Belle Arti, Venice. *Career:* Designer at the Volksbuhne, Berlin, 1971–79; Collaboration with such opera producers as Harry Kupfer, Johannes Schaaf and Jerome Savary (Rossini's Le Comte Ory at the 1997 Glyndebourne Festival, also televised); Engagements also include Rigoletto in Berlin, Die Meistersinger at La Scala, and Idomeneo at the Salzburg Festival; Grand Theatre, Geneva, with Così fan tutte and at the Palais Garnier, Paris; Season 1997–98 with Il Matrimonio Segreto in Vienna and Die Entführung aus dem Serail at Trieste. *Address:* c/o Grand Théâtre de Gènève, 11 Boulevard de Théâtre, 1211 Geneva 11, Switzerland.

TOIVANEN, Heikki; Singer (Bass); b. 1947, Mikkeli, Finland; m. Ingrid Haubold. *Education:* Studied at the Sibelius Academy, Helsinki, and in Germany. *Career:* Sang at the Finnish National Opera, 1973–74, Wuppertal, 1974–76, and Karlsruhe, 1977–84; Bayreuth Festival, 1977–78, as Fasolt and Titurel; Guest appearances throughout Europe and in South America; Many concert engagements. *Address:* Staatstheater Karlsruhe, Baumeisterstrasse 11, Pf 1449, W-7500 Karlsruhe, Germany.

TOKODY, Ilona; Singer (Soprano); b. 27 April 1953, Szeged, Hungary. *Career:* Has sung at the Hungarian National Opera from 1973; Engaged at Bratislava and the Vienna Staatsoper from 1978; Further appearances in Munich, Hamburg, Leningrad, Moscow, Prague, Naples, Barcelona and Cologne; Covent Garden debut in 1986 as Mimi; Sang at San Diego in 1986 as Desdemona and at Los Angeles in 1989, and Boston in 1989 as Mimi; Other roles include Violetta, Tosca, Asteria in Boito's Nerone, Rachel in La Juive, Suor Angelica, Giselda in I Lombardi, Leonora in Il Trovatore and La Forza del Destino and Puccini's Lauretta, Liu and Butterfly; Sang the Trovatore Leonora at Madrid in 1992; Liu in Turandot at Budapest, 1998 and Desdemona, 2000. *Recordings include:* Suor Angelica; Nerone; La Fedeltà Premiata by Haydn; Strauss's Guntram; Erkel's Hunyádi Lászlo; Respighi's La Fiamma; Mascagni's Iris. *Address:* c/o Allied Artists, 42 Montpelier Square, London SW7 1JZ, England.

TOLE, Vasil S.; Albanian composer and musicologist; b. 22 Nov. 1963, Përmet. *Education:* Tirana Conservatory, Folkwang Hochschule, Essen, Athens Univ. *Career:* Music Dir, Naïm Frashëri Palace of Culture 1988–91; Artistic Dir, Elrena Gjika Ensemble 1988–91; Lecturer, Tirana Conservatory 1991–; founder, New Albanian Music Asscn 1993; founder, Ton de Leeuw Int. Competition for New Music, Tirana 1997; Dir, Theatre of Opera and Ballet, Tirana 1997–99; Dir, State Ensemble of Folk Songs and Dances 1997–99. *Compositions include:* Suite 1986, Symphonic Poem 1987, Kontrast 1989, Concerto for Orchestra 1990, Epitaf dhe britmë 1992–93, Pheromones 1993, Genotype 1996, Trias 1996, RIP 1997, Dikotomi 2000, Eumenides (opera) 2004. *Recordings:* Trias 1997, Epitaf dhe britmë 1998. *Publications:* Music and Literature 1997, SAZET 1998, Albanian folk polyphony 1999, Etnostructure and Etnosemantic 2000, Encyclopedia of Albanian Folk Music 2001, The Albanian National Anthem 2003, The Albanian Intangible Heritage 2004, Cluster, Musicology and Composition 2004. *Honours:* Asscn of Albanian Composers Prix des Jeunesses Musicales 1990, Ministry of Culture MUZA Prize 2001. *Address:* Rr 'Sitki Çiço', Pallatet 9 kate, Shkalla 2, Ap. 4, Tirana, Albania. *Telephone:* 4 374127. *Fax:* 4 222857. *E-mail:* tole@vasiltole.com. *Website:* www.vasiltole.com.

TOLIVER, Edmund; Singer (Bass); b. 1947, Greenport, USA. *Education:* Michigan University (MM) and in Vienna. *Career:* Vienna Staatsoper as Pistol in Falstaff, Nightwatchman in Die Meistersinger and Hector in Les Troyens; Coburg Opera, 1985–87; Graz Opera, 1987–92, Dortmund from 1992; Sang Fasolt, Fafner, Hunding and Hagen in Ring cycles at Graz and Salzburg Landestheaters, 1988–89; Detroit, 1985, as the King in Aida, Linz, 1988, as Boito's Mefistofele; Paris Châtelet, 1994, as Hunding and Fafner, and 1996 in The Rake's Progress; Sang King Marke in Tristan at Enschede, 1999; Further appearances in Berlin, Munich, Zürich and New York; Frequent concert engagements. *Recordings include:* Bonze in Madama Butterfly. *Address:* c/o Châtelet Théâtre Musical, 2 Rue Edouard Colonne, 75001 Paris, France.

TOMASSON, Tomas; Singer (bass); b. 1968, Iceland. *Education:* Studied at the Reykjavík College of Music and the Royal College of Music Opera School, London. *Career:* Sang at first with Icelandic Opera, as Sparafucile (Rigoletto), Mozart's Sarastro and Lodovico in Otello; Further engagements as Arasse in Handel's Siroe at the RCM, the Commendatore at Valencia, Masetto at Covent Garden (1996) and in Copenhagen, Colline in La Bohème at the Royal Albert Hall (1997) and Pimen in Boris Godunov at Turin; Further Handel roles include Cadmus and Somnus in Semele at the Berlin Staatsoper, and Christian in Rinaldo at Geneva; Concerts include Haydn's Nelson Mass, Mozart's Coronation Mass and Requiem, Tippett's A Child of our Time with the Icelandic Symphony Orchestra, Bach's St Matthew Passion at the

United Kingdom Handel Festival and Verdi's Requiem at the Mayfield Festival. *Current Management:* Athole Still International Management, Forresters Hall, 25–27 Westow Street, London, SE19 3RY, England. *Telephone:* (20) 8771-5271. *Fax:* (20) 8768-6600. *Website:* www .atholestill.com.

TOMASZEWSKI, Rolf; Singer (Bass); b. 18 March 1940, Deutzen, Leipzig, Germany. *Education:* Studied in Dresden with Johannes Kemter. *Career:* Debut: Wittenberg in 1959 as Baculus in Lortzing's Der Wildschütz; Teacher until 1971 then sang in opera at Dresden-Radebeul, 1971–75; Performances at the Dresden Staatsoper and elsewhere in Germany from 1975 as Sarastro, Osmin, the Commendatore, Don Alfonso, Kaspar in Der Freischütz, the Landgrave in Tannhäuser, King Henry in Lohengrin and buffo roles; Many concert appearances. *Address:* c/o Semper-Oper, Dresden 01067, Germany.

TOMITA, Yo, BMus, MMus, PhD; University Lecturer; b. 17 Dec. 1961, Fukushima, Japan. *Education:* Musashino Academia Musical, Tokyo, Univ. of Leeds. *Career:* Postdoctoral Research Fellow, Queen's Univ., Belfast 1995–; Lecturer, Queen's Univ., Belfast 2000–; Reader, Queen's Univ., Belfast 2001; mem. Royal Musical Asscn, Neue Bach-Gesellschaft, American Bach Soc., Soc. for Musicology in Ireland, Japan Musicological Soc.. *Publications:* J. S. Bach's Das Wohltemperierte Clavier II, 1993, 1995; editions of Fugal Composition: A guide to the study of Bach's 48 by Joseph Groocock, Bach studies from Dublin with Anne Leahy; contrib. to Oxford Composer Companions: J. S. Bach 1999, many journals. *Honours:* Martha Goldsworthy Arnold Fellowship at the Riemenschneider Bach Institute, Berea, Ohio, USA 2002. *Address:* School of Music, Queen's University, Belfast, BT7 1NN, Northern Ireland (office). *Telephone:* (28) 90975206 (office). *Fax:* (28) 90975053 (office). *E-mail:* y.tomita@qub.ac.uk (office). *Website:* www.music.qub.ac .uk/tomita (office).

TOMLINSON, Ernest, FRCO; Composer; b. Sept. 1924, Rawtenstall, England; m.; four c. *Education:* composition, organ, piano and clarinet, Royal Manchester Coll. of Music, Manchester Univ., 1941; MusB, Composition; ARMCM, Organ, 1947. *Career:* mem., Rossendale Male Voice Choir; arranger, group of music publishers, 1947; Organist, Church in Mayfair; Dir, Church choir; Musical Dir, Chingford Amateur Dramatic and Operatic Society, 1951–53; broadcast with his own orchestras and singers, 1995–; conducted his own compositions, Royal Festival Hall, Royal Albert Hall, London, Tchaikovsky Hall, Moscow; founder, Northern Concert Orchestra; Rossendale Male Voice Choir, 1976–81; co-founder, Rossendale Festival Choir; founder, Ribble Vale Choir, Longridge, 1989; Conductor, Slovak Radio Symphony Orchestra, Bratislava; Conductor, RTE Concert Orchestra, Dublin; New Zealand Symphony Orchestra, Wellington; mem., Composers' Guild of Great Britain (exec. cttee, Chair., 1964), Performing Right Society (Composer-Dir, 1965–94), Light Music Society (Chair.). *Compositions:* Overtures; Suites; Rhapsodies; two symphonies for combined jazz and symphony orchestras; three concertos; one-act opera, Head of the Family; background music for use in films, television; brass band and wind band and organ music; Fantasia on Auld Lang Syne; Fantasia on North-Country Tunes, commissioned by the Hallé Orchestra, 1977. *Recordings:* conducted on five albums, British Light Music, 1991–. *Honours:* Ivor Novello Award, 1974; Special Composers' Guild Award. *Address:* Lancaster Farm, Chipping Lane, Longridge, Preston, Lancashire PR3 2NB, England.

TOMLINSON, John; Singer (Bass); b. 22 Sept. 1946, Oswaldtwistle, Lancashire, England; m. Moya Joel, 1969, 1 s., 2 d. *Education:* BSc, Civil Engineering, Manchester University, England; Royal Manchester College of Music. *Career:* Since beginning career with Glyndebourne in 1970 has sung over 150 operatic bass roles with English National Opera and Covent Garden and in Geneva, Lisbon, Milan, Paris, Stuttgart, San Diego, Vancouver (Hagen and Hunding), San Francisco, Bordeaux, Aix-en-Provence, Avignon and Copenhagen; English National Opera from 1975 as Masetto, Wagner's Pogner, Fasolt and Mark, Bart ók's Bluebeard, Rossini's Moses, Mephistopheles, Padre Guardiano and Baron Ochs; Bayreuth Festival in 1988 as Wotan in Das Rheingold and Die Walküre; Sang the Wanderer in Siegfried in 1989; Opera North in 1991 as Attila, Covent Garden in 1991 as Hagen and as the Green Knight in the premiere of Birtwistle's Gawain and sang in the Reginald Goodall Memorial Concert in London, 1991; Season 1992–93 as Boris Godunov for Opera North, Wotan and Wanderer at Bayreuth and Gurnemanz at the Berlin Staatsoper; Season 1993–94 as Hans Sachs at Covent Garden, Baron Ochs for ENO and Wotan in a new production of The Ring at Bayreuth; Videos of The Ring from Bayreuth; Returned to English National Opera for Ochs, 1997; Sang Wotan for the Royal Opera at the Albert Hall, 1998; Season 1999 as Golaud in Pelléas et Mélisande at Glyndebourne; Seasons 1999–2001 as Schoenberg's Moses, and Gurnemanz, at the Met, Gounod's Mephisto at Munich, Baron Ochs at Dresden and Pfitzner's Borremeo for the Royal Opera; Sang Hagen in Götterdämmerung, Bayreuth 2001; Gurnemanz at Covent Garden, 2002; Dvořák's Stabat mater and Handel's Samson at

the London Proms, 2002; Wotan and the Wanderer in new production of Die Walküre and Siegfried at Munich, 2002; Dutchman at Bayreuth, 2003. *Recordings:* Roles in Donizetti's Maria Stuarda, Handel's Hercules, Rameau's Nais, Thomas' Hamlet, Martinů's Greek Passion and Verdi's Macbeth. *Honours:* Manchester Evening News Opera Award, 1989; Singer of the Year, Royal Philharmonic Society, 1991, 1998; Grammy Award, Best Classical Album, 1993; Reginald Goodall Award, Wagner Society, 1996; Honorary Fellowship, Royal Northern College of Music, 1996; Honorary Doctorates, Universities of Sussex, 1997, Manchester, 1998; South Bank Show Award, 1998; Evening Standard Opera Award, 1998. *Address:* c/o Music International, 13 Ardilaun Road, Highbury, London N5 2QR, England.

TOMMASI, Carlo; Stage Designer; b. 1950, Italy. *Education:* Brera Academy. *Career:* Designs for Rigoletto at Munich, in production by Roman Polanski, Carmen in Tokyo, Otello at Bregenz and Tannhäuser in Frankfurt; Premiere production of Berio's La Vera Storia (La Scala, 1982), La Cenerentola in Brussels (1983) and L'Incoronazione di Poppea at Nancy; Further designs at La Monnaie for The Cunning Little Vixen, Der Rosenkavalier, Der fliegende Holländer and Der Freischütz; Collaborations with Nicholas Joël at Théâtre du Capitole, Toulouse, for Falstaff (1991) and Roméo et Juliette (1993 also at the Royal Opera, Covent Garden); Further work includes Leonore at Genoa and Les Contes d'Hoffmann at Toulouse. *Address:* c/o Théâtre du Capitole, Place du Capitole, 31000 Toulouse, France.

TOMOWA-SINTOW, Anna; Singer (Soprano); b. 22 Sept. 1943, Stara Zagora, Bulgaria. *Education:* Studied at the Sofia Conservatory with Zlatew Tscherkin. *Career:* Debut: Stara Zagora as Tatiana in Eugene Onegin; Sang at Leipzig in 1967 as Abigaille in Nabucco, Berlin in 1972 as Butterfly becoming member of the company, 1972–76; Discovered by Karajan and sang in the premiere of De Temporum Fine Comoedia by Orff at Salzburg in 1973; Appearances at Milan, Brussels, Munich, San Francisco and at Covent Garden London in her debut in 1975 as Fiordiligi; Sang at Salzburg Easter and Summer Festivals in 1976 as Elsa and Countess Almaviva, Vienna Staatsoper from 1977, Metropolitan Opera from 1978 as Donna Anna, Elsa and Aida, the Marschallin and Amelia Boccanegra, Salzburg in 1983 as the Marschallin, Paris Opéra in 1984 as Elisabeth in Tannhäuser, and Salzburg, 1987–89 as Donna Anna and Tosca; Sang in Der Rosenkavalier at Florence in 1989 and Chicago in 1990; Appeared as Yaroslavna in a new production of Prince Igor at Covent Garden in 1990; Season 1992–93 as Tosca at Helsinki and Strauss's Helen in Athens; Sang Ariadne at Lisbon, 1996; Salome in concert at Barcelona, 1998; Engaged as Tosca at the Berlin Staatsoper, 2000; Sang the Marschallin at Covent Garden and Strauss's Empress for the Deutsche Oper Berlin, 2000. *Recordings:* Beethoven's 9th Symphony and Missa Solemnis; Verdi's Requiem; Ein Deutsches Requiem; De Temporum Fine Comoedia; Don Giovanni; Der Rosenkavalier; Mozart's Requiem and Coronation Mass; Bruckner's Te Deum and Lohengrin; Le nozze di Figaro; Ariadne auf Naxos; Die Frau ohne Schatten from Covent Garden, 1992; Capriccio from Salzburg, Barcelona, Berlin and Vienna, 1985, 1986, 1990; Also recordings with H von Karajan, 4 Last Songs and Capriccio by Strauss; Korngold, Das Wunder der Heliane. *Honours:* Prizewinner, International Competition, Sofia, 1970; Winner, Rio de Janeiro Competition, 1971; Made Kammersängerin in Berlin. *Address:* Teatro Nacional de São Carlos, Rua Serpa Pinto 9, 1200 Lisbon, Portugal.

TOMTER, Lars Anders; Violist; b. 30 Nov. 1959; 1 d. *Education:* Piano, 5 years, Violin, 8 years, Violin and Viola, Conservatory, 13 years, Max Rostal Bern Conservatory, 3 years, Sándor Végh, Mozarteum, Salzburg, 2 years. *Career:* Solo Performances, USA, Germany, Vienna, Scandinavia, Madrid, Budapest, Frankfurt, Cologne, Paris, London; Soloist with such orchestras as Academy of St Martin-in-the-Fields, City of Birmingham and Frankfurt Radio Symphony Orchestra, Philharmonic Orchestra of Frankfurt, Hungarian National Philharmonic Orchestra, Los Angeles Chamber Orchestra, Oslo and Bergen Philharmonics, Danish Radio Symphony Orchestra, Stockholm New Chamber Orchestra, Gavleborg, Norwegian Radio, Trondheim and Stavanger Symphony Orchestras; Proms debut with RPO, 1998; Artistic Director, Risar Chamber Music Festival; Walton's concerto at the London Proms, 2002. *Recordings:* Walton Concertos; Franck and Vieuxtemps Sonatas; Mozart's Sinfonia Concertante with Norwegian Chamber Orchestra and Iona Brown; Schumann and Brahms Sonatas with Pianist Leif Ove Andsnes. *Honours:* Numerous awards and prizes. *Address:* c/o Martin Muller, Vintrup 4, 59320 Ennigerloh Ostenfelde, Germany.

TONE, Yasunao; American composer and multimedia artist; b. 31 March 1935, Tokyo, Japan. *Education:* Japanese National University, Chiba, Tokyo University of the Arts. *Career:* founded performance group Ongaku at Tokyo, 1960; Wrote tape pieces Geography, and Music performed by Merle Cunningham Dance Company; Settled in New York 1972, participating in avant garde and computer music festivals in North America and Europe, FLUXUS festivals 1979–87 and Venice Biennale (1990). *Compositions include:* Intermedia Art Festival, 1969;

Multi Performance, 1972; Voice and Phenomenon, 1976; The Wall and the Books, 1982; Word of Mouth, 1988. *Publications include:* Can Art be Thought, 1970. *Honours:* New York Foundation for the Arts Fellowship, 1987.

TOOLEY, Sir John, Kt; Theatre Administrator; b. 1 June 1924, Rochester, Kent, England; m. (1) Judith Craig Morris, 1951, dissolved, 1965, 3 d., (2) M. Patricia Janet Norah Bagshawe, 1968, 1 s. *Education:* Magdalene College, Cambridge. *Career:* Served in the Rifle Brigade, 1943–47; Secretary to the Guildhall School of Music, 1952–55; Assistant to General Administrator, 1955–60, Assistant General Administrator, 1960–70, General Administrator, 1970–80, General Director, 1980–87, Royal Opera House, Covent Garden, London; Governor, The Royal Ballet and The Royal Ballet School, also Repton School; Director, Royal Opera House Trust; mem, Garrick Club; Arts. *Publications:* In House, Covent Garden. *Honours:* Commendatore, Italian Republic, 1976; Honorary Fellow, Royal Academy of Music and Honorary Member, Guildhall School of Music and the Royal Northern College of Music. *Address:* c/o Royal Opera House, Covent Garden, London, WC2, England.

TOOVEY, Andrew; Composer; b. 21 Feb. 1962, London, England. *Education:* Studied at the Universities of Surrey and Sussex with Jonathan Harvey and at Dartington with Morton Feldman. *Career:* Music has been performed by Alan Hacker, Michael Finnissy, the Mistry Quartet and the Endimion Ensemble; Director of Ixion, founded in 1987, giving performances of works by Cage, Feldman, Ferneyhough, Finnissy, James Dillon and Xenakis; Composer in Residence at the Banff Centre, Canada, 1997. *Compositions:* Chamber and ensemble: Winter Solstice, 1984, String Quartet, 1985, Cantec for Viola and Piano, 1986, Ate, 1986, Shining for Violin and Cello, 1987, Shining Forth, 1987, Shimmer Bright for String Trio, 1988, White Fire, 1988, Snow Flowers, 1988, Black Light, 1989, An Die Musik, 1989, Adam, 1989; Solo instruments: Veiled Wave 1 and 2, for Flute and Clarinet, 1985, Artaud for Piano, 1986, Fragments After Artaud, 1988, Lament, Strathspey, reel for Violin, 1988, Out Jumps Jack Death and Down There By The Sea for Piano, 1989, UBU, opera in 2 acts (five scenes), 1990–92, The Juniper Tree, opera in one act (4 scenes), 1993; The Moon Falls through the Autumn, for piano, 1995; Out!, for two pianos and orchestra, 1995; Red Icon, for large symphony orchestra, 1996; Oboe Concerto, 1997; In the Shallow Grave, opera, 1999. *Recordings include:* Artaud; Out Jumps Jack Death; Red Icon and The Juniper Tree, 1998. *Honours:* Tippett Prize for Untitled String Quartet; Terra Nova Prize for Ate; Bernard Shore Composition Award for Cantec; Young Concert Artists Trust Associate Composer, 1993–. *Current Management:* Ycat. *Address:* 57B Station Road, Willesden, London NW10 4UX, England.

TÖPPER, Hertha; Singer (Mezzo-Soprano); b. 19 April 1924, Graz, Austria. *Education:* Studied at the Graz Conservatory. *Career:* Debut: Graz in 1945 as Ulrica in Un Ballo in Maschera; Sang in Graz, 1945–52, at Munich Staatsoper from 1952 notably in the 1957 premiere of Hindemith's Die Harmonie der Welt, at Bayreuth Festival from 1951 as Brangaene and Fricka, and visited Covent Garden with the Munich Company in 1953 as Clairon in Capriccio; Sang at San Francisco in 1960 and Metropolitan Opera in 1962 as Octavian in Der Rosenkavalier, and at Munich in 1972 in the premiere of Isang Yun's Sim Tjong; Other roles included Verdi's Eboli and Amneris, Mozart's Dorabella, Magdalena in Die Meistersinger and Nancy in Martha; Sang Branhaene with Bayreuth Company in Osaka; Retired from stage in 1981; Often heard in sacred music by Bach; Professor at the Munich Musikhochschule from 1971. *Recordings:* Die Meistersinger; Bluebeard's Castle; Oedipus Rex; Schoenberg's Gurrelieder; Bach's B minor Mass; Octavian in Der Rosenkavalier from London's Covent Garden. *Address:* Knöbelstrasse 2, 80538 München, Germany.

TORADZE, Alexander; Pianist; b. 1955, Tbilisi, Georgia. *Education:* Graduated the Tchaikovsky Conservatory Moscow 1978. *Career:* Resident in the USA from 1983, giving concerts in every major centre and appearing with such conductors as Ashkenazy, Dutoit, Eschenbach, Masur, Mehta, Ozawa and Rattle; European engagements with the Kirov Orchestra (under Valery Gergiev) Rotterdam Philharmonic Orchestra, London Symphony and Philharmonic, CBSO and Philharmonia Orchestra; Season 1997 with the Los Angeles Philharmonic Orchestra under Esa-Pekka Salonen, Toronto Symphony Orchestra under Jukka-Pekka Saraste, the Orchestra National de France and the Rotterdam Philharmonic Orchestra under Gergiev; Festival appearances at the London Proms, Hollywood Bowl, St Petersburg White Nights, Saratoga and Schleswig-Holstein; From 1991, Martin Endowed Professor in Piano at Indiana University South Bend; Prokofiev's concerto No. 3 in C major at the London Proms, 2002. *Recordings include:* Prokofiev's 7th Sonata, Ravel's Miroirs, Three Movements from Petrushka, Pictures at an Exhibition, Gaspard de la Nuit (EMI/Angel); Prokofiev Concertos, with the Kirov Orchestra and Gergiev (Philips Classics). *Current Management:* Askonas Holt Ltd, Lonsdale Chambers, 27 Chancery Lane, London, WC2A 1PF, England. *Telephone:* (20) 7400-

1700. *Fax:* (20) 7400-1799. *E-mail:* info@askonasholt.co.uk. *Website:* www.askonasholt.co.uk.

TORCHINSKY, Yuri; Violinist; b. 1949, Kharkiv, Ukraine (United Kingdom resident from 1991); 1 s. *Education:* Tchaikovsky Conservatory Moscow, 1975–80; Postgraduate Conservatory Assistant, 1980–83. *Career:* Debut: Brahms Violin Concerto with the Kharkov Philharmonic Orchestra conducted by Vakhtang Gordania; Leader of the Bolshoi Theatre in Moscow with numerous performances, concerts and tours, as soloist and orchestra leader, world-wide including the Metropolitan Opera in New York and at many opera theatres and concert halls in USA, Italy, Austria, France, Netherlands, Germany, Japan and elsewhere; Radio appearances with recitals in Moscow and on television in Yugoslavia; Several appearances at the Albert Hall in London, television and radio recordings of Promenade Concerts performance, at the Barbican Hall, Royal Festival Hall, New Symphony Hall and Town Hall in Birmingham; Many concerts and radio and CD recordings as guest leader of London Symphony Orchestra as well as tours to France, Switzerland, Austria, Portugal and Italy; Solo appearances at Royal Opera House, 1995; Guest Leader with such orchestras as BBC National Orchestra of Wales, Philharmonia, Royal Philharmonic, and BBC Manchester; Leader of the Royal Ballet Symphonia Orchestra of the Birmingham Royal Ballet. *Address:* 14 Ellery Road, Upper Norwood, London SE19 3QG, England.

TORKE, Michael; Composer and Pianist; b. 22 Sept. 1961, Milwaukee, Wisconsin, USA. *Education:* Graduated from Eastman School of Music, Rochester, 1984. *Career:* Commissions from New York City Ballet and The Huddersfield Festival; European performances with the Danish Radio Symphony Orchestra, the Ensemble Intercontemporain, London Sinfonietta and Lontano; As Pianist has recorded on several labels. *Compositions:* Laetus for Piano Solo, 1982; Ceremony of Innocence for Flute, Clarinet, Violin, Cello and Piano, 1983; Ecstatic Orange for Ensemble, 1984; Vanada for Keyboards, Brass and Percussion, 1984; The Yellow Pages, 1984; Bright Blue Music for Ensemble, 1985; Verdant Music for Ensemble, 1986; The Directions, one-act opera based on The Yellow Pages, 1986; Adjustable Wrench for Ensemble, 1987; Black And White for Wind Instruments, Percussion and Synthesizer, 1988; Copper for Brass Quintet and Orchestra, 1988; Ash for Orchestra or Chamber Orchestra, 1989; Slate, ballet for Concertante Group and Orchestra, 1989; Rust for Piano and Wind Instruments, 1989; Run for orchestra 1992; Four Proverbs for voice and ensemble 1993; Book of Proverbs for soprano, baritone, chorus and orchestra, 1996; Overnight Mail and Change of Address for ensemble, 1997; Brick Symphony, 1997; Pentecost for soprano, organ and strings, 1997; King of Hearts, 1994 and Strawberry Fields, 1999, chamber operas; Opera, The House of Mirth, for the New York City Opera, 2004. *Honours:* Prix de Rome; Koussevitsky Foundation Award. *Address:* c/o Boosey and Hawkes Ltd, 295 Regent Street, London W1R 8JH, England.

TÖRNQUIST, Pirkko; Singer (Soprano); b. 1955, Finland. *Education:* Helsinki Conservatory and Sibelius Academy; With Vera Rozsa in London, Nicolai Gedda in Stockholm and with Anitta Välkki. *Career:* Many appearances as opera and concert singer throughout Finland and Europe; Finnish National Opera at Helsinki from 1990, as Amelia in Ballo in Maschera, Tosca, Tatiana in Eugene Onegin, Mozart's Countess and Elsa in Lohengrin; Maija in Pohjan's Daughter, by Merikanto; Savonlinna Festival, 1990–91, as Aida; Sang Sieglinde in Die Walküre at Helsinki, 1998. *Honours:* Prize Winner, 1993 Competition, Vienna Belvedere. *Address:* c/o Finnish National Opera, PO Box 176, Helsinkikatu 58, 00251 Helsinki, Finland.

TORRES, Victor; Singer (Baritone); b. 1965, Buenos Aires, Argentina. *Education:* Studied in Buenos Aires and with Gerard Souzay. *Career:* Debut: Bilbao, 1991, as Germont; Sang in South Africa as Verdi's Posa and Luna; Teatro Col ón, Buenos Aires, from 1993, as Masetto in Don Giovanni and Paolo Orsini in Rienzi; Season 1993–94 at the Châtelet, Paris, and Lyon as Germont; Further appearances as Donizetti's Enrico at the Paris Opéra and as Purcell's Aeneas and Bart ók's Bluebeard at San Francisco; Season 1997–98 as Don Alfonso in Così fan tutte at the Berlin Staatsoper and Germont at Opéra de Nancy; Many concert engagements, notably in Bach's St John Passion, Messiah, Haydn's Creation and Schumann's Scenes from Faust; Sang Yeletzky in The Queen of Spades at Florence, 1999. *Recordings include:* Monteverdi Vespers.

TORRES-SANTOS, Raymond; Composer, Arranger, Keyboardist, Conductor and Music Educator and Music Critic; b. 19 June 1958, Puerto Rico. *Education:* BA, Puerto Rico University and Conservatory of Music, 1980; MA 1982, PhD 1986, University of California, Los Angeles; Ferienkurse für Neue Musik, 1982; CCRMA, Stanford University, 1985; Centro di Sonologia Computazionale, Padua University, Italy, 1988. *Career:* Arranger, Music Director, for best American singers and entertainers; Composer of film music, studio musician in Hollywood; Professor, California State University, San Bernardino, 1986–91;

Chairman of Music Department, University of Puerto Rico, 1991–93; Chancellor, Puerto Rico Conservatory of Music, 1994–98; Visiting Professor, CUNY, 2000–01. *Compositions include:* Sinfonietta Concertante for Orchestra, 1980; Summertime, Clarinet Consort, 1982; Exploraciones for String Orchestra, 1982; Areytos: a Symphonic Picture, 1985; Enchanted Island, Piano and Tape, 1986; Monchin del Alma: Ballet, 1988; El Pais de los Cuatro Pisos: A Symphonic Overture, 1988; Viaggio Senza Destinazione for Tape, 1988; Danza for Orchestra, 1991; La Cancion de las Antillas: A Symphonic Poem, 1992; Fantasia Caribena, for Orchestra, 1992; Salsa y tres Sones, for piano or harp solo; Requiem for Mezzo-Soprano, Baritone, Mixed Chorus, Children's Choir and Orchestra, 1995; Odalisque, ballet, 1997; Concertino for clarinet, French horn, piano, percussion and strings, 1998; Trio for clarinet, cello and piano, 1998; Overture for Orchestra, 1998; Conversation with Silence, for soprano and ensemble, 1999; Millennium Symphony for orchestra, 2000; Jersey Polyphony for chorus, 2000; Juris Oratorio, for chorus, 2000; Performed and/or commissioned by the Casals Festival, Vienna Philharmonic, New Jersey Chamber Music Society, Continuum, Bronx Arts Ensemble, Quintet of the Americas, Paquito de Rivera, Inter-American University, Youth Symphony of the Americas, San Juan Ballet and Pops Orchestra; American Composers Orchestra; Boston Pops; Symphony Orchestra from Puerto Rico, Queens, London, Virginia, Pacific, Northwestern University and University of California at Los Angeles. *Recordings:* 25 as Arranger and/or Conductor. *Address:* PO Box 361743, San Juan, Puerto Rico 00936-1743, USA.

TORTELIER, Yan Pascal; Conductor; b. 19 April 1947, Paris, France; m. Sylvie Burnet-Moret, 1970, 2 s. *Education:* Paris Conservatoire, general musical studies with Nadia Boulanger; Conducting studies with Franco Ferrara. *Career:* Has conducted all major British orchestras and toured extensively in the USA, Canada, Japan, Australia, Scandinavia, Eastern and Western Europe; Leader and Associate Conductor, Orchestre du Capitole in Toulouse, 1974–83; Opera debut, 1978; Principal Conductor and Artist Director, Ulster Orchestra, Northern Ireland, 1989–92; Principal Conductor, BBC Philharmonic, 1992–; Conducted Stravinsky-Lutoslawski concert at York University, 1997; London Proms, 1999 with Sibelius's Second (CBSO) and Elgar's Cello Concerto (BBC Philharmonic); Béatrice et Bénédict with European Union Opera, 1998; Conducted the BBC Philharmonic at the London Proms, 2002; Principal Guest Conductor of Pittsburgh Symphony Orchestra, 2005–. *Recordings:* Numerous including complete symphonic works of Debussy and Ravel with Ulster Orchestra and highly acclaimed series of Hindemith and Henri Dutilleux with BBC Philharmonic; Several labels. *Publications:* Premiere orchestration of Ravel's Piano Trio, 1992. *Honours:* Honorary Doctor of Letters, University of Ulster, 1992. *Current Management:* IMG Artists. *Address:* c/o IMG Artists, Lovell House, 616 Chiswick High Road, London W4 5RX, England.

TORZEWSKI, Marek; singer (tenor); b. 1960, Poland. *Education:* Poznan Academy of Music. *Career:* debut, Łódź Opera 1984 as Edgardo in Lucia di Lammermoor; Sang in Idomeneo at the Théâtre de la Monnaie Brussels, 1984; Appearances in La Finta Giardiniera at Vienna, Salzburg, Amsterdam, Berlin and New York, 1985; Further engagements at Brussels and in Hamburg, Montpellier, Philadelphia and Lausanne; Season 1989–90 in L'Incoronazione di Poppea in Paris, Rosenkavalier, Così fan tutte and Fierrabras by Schubert in Brussels, Don Ottavio at Toulouse and Glyndebourne Festival debut as Fenton in Falstaff; Season 1991–92 as Tamino at Lausanne, Alfredo for Scottish Opera and the Mozart Requiem under Muti at La Scala, Milan; Debut with the Berlin Philharmonic 1992, singing in Nono's Il Canto Sospeso, under Abbado; Opera National de Lisbon, Eugene Onegin–Lensky, Staatsoper Leipzig, Così fan tutte–Ferrando, 1993; Théâtre Municipal de Lausanne, Iphigénie en Tauride–Pylade, 1994. *Recordings include:* Il Canto Sospeso (Deutsche Grammophon). *Current Management:* Robert Gilder & Co., Enterprise House, 59–65 Upper Ground, London, SE1 9PQ, England. *Telephone:* (20) 7928-9008. *Fax:* (20) 7928-9755. *E-mail:* rgilder@robert-gilder.com.

TOTENBERG, Roman; Violinist and Conductor; b. 1 Jan. 1911, Łódź, Poland; m. 30 July 1941, 3 d. *Education:* Baccalaureate, Warsaw; Chopin School, Warsaw; Chopin School of Music Diploma, Warsaw, Gold Medal, 1929; Hochschule für Musik with Carl Flesch, Berlin, Mendelssohn Prize, 1932; Paris Institut Instrumentale with Georges Enesco, 1933. *Career:* Soloist with most major orchestras, Europe, USA, South America; Formerly Director Chamber Music radio station WQXR New York and Director of Longy School, Cambridge, Massachusetts; Professor of Music, Boston University, 1962–; Summers: Kneisel Hall Blue Hill, Maine, 1975–; Formerly Music Academy of the West, Salzburg Mozarteum, Berkshire Music Centre and Aspen Festival; Co-Chairman, String Department, Boston University. *Recordings:* Brahms and Lipinski Concertos, Titanic, 1990; Beethoven and Szymanowski Concertos, VGR, 1992; Bloch Concerto, Vanguard, 1992; All Bach Sonatas and Partitas, Schumann Sonatas, German Baroque

Concerti, Musical Heritage. *Publications:* Cadenzas to Mozart concerti, co-author, 1998. *Address:* 329 Waverley Avenue, Newton, MA 02458, USA.

TOVEY, Bramwell; Conductor and Composer; b. 1955, England. *Career:* Many concerts in a broad repertoire throughout Canada and Europe; Former Music Director of the Winnipeg Symphony Orchestra and Artistic Director of Winnipeg New Music Festival: premieres of more than 250 works in 10 years; Music Director of the Vancouver Symphony Orchestra, 2000–; Season 2000–01 engaged with the Toronto Symphony, New York Philharmonic, Royal Scottish National Orchestra and London Philharmonic. *Compositions include:* Cello Concerto, premiered at Winnipeg New Music Festival, 2001. *Address:* c/o IMG Artists, Lovell House, 616 Chiswick High Rd, London, W4 5RX, England.

TOWER, Joan (Peabody); Composer, Pianist and Teacher; b. 6 Sept. 1938, New Rochelle, New York, USA. *Education:* BA, Bennington College, 1961; MA, 1964, DMA, 1978, Columbia University. *Career:* Co-founder and Pianist of Da Capo Chamber Players, New York, 1969–84; Faculty, Bard College, Annandale on Hudson, 1972–; Composer-in-Residence, St Louis Symphony Orchestra, 1985–87. *Compositions include:* Orchestral: Sequoia, 1980; Island Rhythms, 1985, Concerto for Flute and Orchestra, 1989, Concerto for Orchestra, 1991, Violin Concerto, 1992, Stepping Stones, ballet, 1993, Duets for Chamber Orchestra, 1995; 2 piano concertos, 1985, 1996; Chamber: Percussion Quartet, 1963, revised 1969, Breakfast Rhythms l and ll, 1974–75, Petroushskates, 1980, String Quartet, Night Fields, 1994, Fifth Fanfare for The Uncommon Woman for 4 Trumpets, 1994; Solo Instruments: Wings for solo clarinet, Hexachords for Solo Flute, 1972, Fantasy... Harbour Lights, for clarinet and piano, 1983, Elegy for Trombone and String Quartet, 1994, Tres Lent for Cello and Piano, 1994; Turning Points, clarinet quintet, 1995; Valentine Trills, for flute, 1996. *Recordings include:* CDs: Platinum Spirals with violinist Joel Smirnoff, Cello Concerto, with Lynn Harrell on Cello, Clarinet Concerto with Robert Spring and Eckhart Selheim, and Chamber Works, 1995; Island Rhythms with Louisville Orchestra; Clocks with Sharon Isbin on guitar; Silver Ladders, Fanfare for The Uncommon Woman with St Louis Symphony. *Address:* c/o Music Department, Bard College, Annandale on Hudson, NY 12504, USA.

TOWSE, David; Violinist; b. 1956, Bridlington, England. *Education:* Studied piano and violin from 1961; Royal College of Music from 1974 with Leonard Hirsch, Peter Element and Herbert Howells. *Career:* Leader of the East Riding County Youth Orchestra and British Youth Symphony Orchestra, 1972; Leader of the London Youth String Ensemble while at the Royal College of Music; Freelance in and around London before joining the Royal Philharmonic Orchestra in 1978 and Associate Leader, 1982; Performances of Piano Quintets and Quartets with the Forellen Ensemble (members of the RPO) at music clubs and festivals throughout the United Kingdom; Left RPO, 1998; Freelance in and around London: Guest leading, directing and coaching ensembles, teaching and performing as a soloist, also chamber music both for concerts and private functions. *Address:* 47 Abbotswood Road, London SW16 1AJ, England.

TOZZI, Giorgio; singer (bass); b. 8 Jan. 1923, Chicago, Illinois, USA. *Education:* Studied with Rosa Raisa, Giacomo Rimini and John Daggert Howell. *Career:* Debut: Tarquinus in The Rape of Lucretia, on Broadway, 1948; Studied further in Italy and sang Rodolfo in La Sonnambula at the Teatro Nuovo Milan, 1950; La Scala 1953, in La Wally by Catalani; Metropolitan Opera from 1955, as Alvise (La Gioconda), Sparafucile, Pimen, Boris Godonov, Mozart's Figaro, Daland, Pogner, Sachs, Rocco and Philip II; Created the Doctor in Barber's Vanessa (1958); San Francisco from 1955, as Ramfis, Calkas in Troilus and Cressida and Archibaldo (L'Amore dei tre Re); Salzburg Festival 1958, 1961 in Vanessa and as Fiesco in Simon Boccanegra; Hollywood Bowl 1956, in the US premiere of David by Milhaud; La Scala 1962, in a revival of Les Huguenots; Appearances in Florence, Palermo, Hamburg, Frankfurt, Lisbon and Munich as Sarastro, Padre Guardiano, Don Giovanni, Gurnemanz, Arkel and Gremin; Boston Opera 1977, in the US premiere of Ruslan and Lyudmila by Glinka; Active in films, television and musical comedy. *Recordings:* Rigoletto, Guillaume Tell; Der fliegende Holländer; Vanessa; La Forza del Destino; Aida; La Bohème; Le nozze di Figaro; Luisa Miller; Il Trovatore, La Fanciulla del West, Rigoletto.

TRACEY, Edmund; Translator, Administrator and Librettist; b. 14 Nov. 1927, Preston, England. *Career:* Music Critic for The Observer 1958–65; Sadler's Wells (later English National Opera) Director from 1965, as dramaturg and repertory planner; Translated for ENO such texts as Les contes d'Hoffmann 1970, Aida, 1978 and Manon, 1979; La Finta Giardiniera by Mozart for English Music Theatre at Sadler's Wells, 1976; Librettist for Malcolm Williamson's Lucky-Peter's Journey (after Strindberg), Sadler's Wells 1969. *Address:* English National Opera, St Martin's Lane, London WC2N 4ES, England.

TRACK, Gerhard; Conductor and Composer; b. 17 Sept. 1934, Vienna, Austria; m. Micaela Maihart, 3 Aug 1958, 2 s. *Education:* Music Theory, Conducting and Piano, Academy of Music and Performing Arts, Vienna, Austria; Teacher Training College, Vienna, Austria, 1953; Member, Vienna Boys Choir, 1942–48. *Career:* Debut: Conductor, Vienna Boys Choir, 1953; Conductor, Vienna Boys Choir, 1953–58; Music Director, St John's Symphony Orchestra, Associate Professor, Music, St John's University, Men's Chorus, Minnesota, USA, 1958–69; Music Director, Metropolitan Youth Symphony Orchestra, Minneapolis, Minnesota, USA, 1965–69; Music Director, Pueblo Symphony Orchestra, Chorale and Youth Symphony; Founder, annual Mozart Festival, Pueblo, Colorado, USA; Thatcher Professor of Music, University of Southern Colorado, Pueblo, Colorado, 1969–86; Music Director and Conductor, Choral Society of Young Vienna (Jung-Wien), 1986–96; Orchester Pro Musica International and Vienna Serenade Orchestra, Vienna, 1986–; Teacher: Conservatory of the City Vienna and Hochschule (University) for Music and Performing Arts. Vienna, 1987–89; Director, Conservatory of the City of Vienna, 1989–99; President, Austrian Composers Society, 1988–92; Music Director, Vienna Male Choral Society, 1990–2003; International Guest Conductor, Europe, USA, Asia and Australia; President and Founder, PMI Music Publication, California. *Compositions:* Over 600 compositions, orchestral works, choral compositions and arrangements, 1 opera, chamber music, songs, 3 children's operas, 11 Masses, published in Europe and USA. *Recordings:* Many for major recording companies. *Contributions:* Sacred Music; Oesterreichische Musikzeitschrift. *Honours:* Golden Honorary Cross for Merits, Republic of Austria,Golden Honorary Cross of Vienna and Honarary Cross for Science and Art, 1st Class Austria. *Current Management:* PMI, 10730 Riverside Drive, North Hollywood, CA 91602, USA. *Address:* Praterstrasse 76/8, 1020 Vienna, Austria.

TRAMA, Ugo; Singer (bass); b. 4 Aug. 1932, Naples, Italy. *Education:* Studied with Emilia Gubitosi in Naples, at the Accademia Chigiana in Siena and at the Accademia di Santa Cecilia Rome. *Career:* Debut: Spoleto Festival 1951, as Banquo in Macbeth; Sang in Cairo and the Italian provinces; Holland Festival 1960, as Fiesco in Simon Bocanegra; Wexford festival 1961, as Silva in Ernani; Dallas Opera 1961; San Francisco Opera 1965; Appearances at the Maggio Musicale Florence, Teatro Liceo Barcelona and Strasbourg; Glyndebourne 1964–79, as Asdrubale in La Pietra del Paragone, Giove and Pane (Calisto), Atinoo and Tempo (Il Ritorno d'Ulisse), Bartolo (Le nozze di Figaro), Pistol (Falstaff) and Farfallo (Die schweigsame Frau). *Recordings include:* Ramphis in Aida; La Cenerentola (Deutsche Grammophon); Il Ritorno d'Ulisse (CBS).

TRAN, Quang Hai; Ethnomusicologist, Educator, Musician and Composer; b. 13 May 1944, Viet Nam; m. Bach-Yen Quach, 17 June 1978, one d. *Education:* National Conservatory of Music, Saigon, 1961; Sorbonne, Paris, 1963; Institut d'Ethnologie, 1964; Diploma, Centre d'Etudes de Musique Orientale, Institut de Musicologie, Paris, 1969; State Diploma, Professor of Traditional Music, 1989. *Career:* Ethnomusicologist, Musée National des Arts et Traditions Populaires, 1968–87, Musée de l'Homme, Paris, 1968–; Professor, Centre d' Etudes de Musique Orientale, 1970–75; Lecturer, Universities of Paris X and Nanterre, 1987; Over 2000 concerts in 45 countries, 1966–; Played at many international music festivals and in films including Le chant des Harmoniques (co-author, principal actor, composer), 1989. *Compositions include:* 300 pop songs; Ve Nguon, electro-acoustic, 1975; Shaman, 1982; Nui Ngu Sông Huong, monochord, 1983; Voyage chamanique, voice, 1986; Solo Thai, zither, 1989; Tambours 89, percussion, tape, 1989; Vinh Ha Long, 1993; Hôn Viêtnam, 1993; For Jew's harp: Nostalgie au Pays Mông, 1997; Vietnam Mon Pays, 1997; Tuva Tuva (with overtone singing), 1997; Ambiance des Hauts Plateaux du Vietnam, 1997. *Recordings:* Numerous records on Vietnamese music including: Landscape of the Highlands, 1997; Jew's Harps of the World, 1997; Vietnam Music of the Mountains, 1997; Over 150 television programmes throughout the world; Over 250 radio programmes, the latest with BBC Radio 3 on World Routes in December 2003 and January 2004. *Publications:* Am Nhac Viet Nam, 1989; Musique du Monde (with Michel Asselineau and Eugène Bérel), 1993, in English, 1994; Tuyen tap 50 cakhuc (Book of 50 Songs) with Vo My Ngoc, 1999. *Contributions:* Numerous to New Grove Dictionary of Music and Musicians, Encyclopedia Universalis, others. *Honours:* Grand Prix of the Academy of the Charles Cros, Paris, 1983; Gold Medal of the Academy of Asia, 1986; Grand Prize of the International Scientific Film, Parnu, Estonia, 1990; Prize of Best Ethnomusicological Film, Parnu, Estonia, 1990; Prize of Best Film on Scientific Research, International Film Festival, Palaiseau, France, 1990; Grand Prize of the 2nd International Scientific Film Festival, Montreal, Canada, 1991; Special Prize of Overtone Singing, Kyzyl, Tuva, 1995; Medal of Cristal, 1996; Grand Prize of the Academy Charles Cros, 1997; Medal of Honour of the City of Limeil Brevannes, France, 1998; Special Prize of Jew's Harp Performer, Je's Harp International Festival, Molln, Austria, 1998; Knight of the Legion of Honour, 2002. *Address:* 12 rue Gutenberg, 94450

Limeil Brevannes, France. *E-mail:* tranquanghai@hotmail.com. *Website:* www.tranquanghai.org; www.tranquanghai.net; www .ethnomus.org; tranquanghai.phapviet.com.

TRANTER, John; singer (bass); b. 1946, Chesterfield, Derbyshire, England. *Education:* London Opera Centre, singing with John Dethick in Sheffield. *Career:* debut, Hobson in Peter Grimes, Châtelet Opera in Paris; Opera for All; Kent Opera as the Commendatore in Don Giovanni and Seneca in L'Incoronazione di Poppea; ENO from 1976 as Sarastro, Colline, Monterone in Rigoletto, Verdi's Grand Inquisitor Opera North as Zaccaria in Nabucco, Rossini's Don Basilio, Daland in Der fliegende Holländer, Gremin in Eugene Onegin, Pogner in Die Meistersinger and Trulove in The Rake's Progress; WNO as Wagner's Fasolt and Hagen, and Grigoris in The Greek Passion; other engagements in Nancy, Nîmes, Wellington and Lausanne; other roles include Oroveso (Norma), Ramphis (Aida), Nourabad (Les pêcheurs de Perles), Henry VIII (Anna Bolena) and Tiresias (Oedipus Rex); Fafner at Covent Garden and Pope Leone in Attila at Covent Garden 1990; Banquo in Metz, France, and engagements in Marseille; debut in Pittsburgh as Varlaam (Boris) 1991; season 1992 as Melchtal in Guillaume Tell at Covent Garden and Monterone for Opera North; has sung in concert at the Royal Albert Hall, Royal Festival Hall, Canterbury Cathedral, York Minister and Leeds Town Hall; also sang with the Scottish Opera as Gremin, King in Aida and in Billy Budd, Pearl Fishers; sang Fafner in Siegfried and the King in Aida at Santiago 1996–98; Hobson in Peter Grimes at La Scala 2000. *Current Management:* Music International, 13 Ardilaun Road, Highbury, London, N5 2QR, England.

TRAUBOTH, Andrea; German singer (soprano); b. 2 April 1959, Seefeld, Munich, Germany. *Education:* studied in Munich. *Career:* sang with the Dortmund Opera 1983–86, Munich Staatsoper from 1986 and Cologne Opera from 1988; Dresden 1986–87, notably as Musetta and Donna Anna; sang Pamina at Essen 1990, and Elsa at Kiel 1992; further appearances at the Komische Oper, Berlin, La Scala, Milan and in Madrid, as Agathe, Senta, Rusalka and Micaela; concerts in Netherlands, Greece, France and England; season 1999–2000 at Cologne as Agathe and First Lady in Die Zauberflöte. *Address:* c/o Hochschule für Musik Köln, Theaterstraße 2–4, 52062 Aachen, Postfach 1265, 52013 Aachen, Germany.

TRAVIS, Roy (Elihu); Composer; b. 24 June 1922, New York, NY, USA; m. 3c. *Education:* Studied with Otto Luening at Columbia University; MA 1951; Schenkerian studies privately with Felix Salzer, 1947–50; Studied with Bernard Wagenaar at Juilliard; MS, 1950; and with Darius Milhaud, Conservatoire National, Paris, on a Fulbright grant, 1951–52. *Career:* Teacher at Columbia University, 1952–53, Mannes College of Music 1952–57 and the University of California at Los Angeles, 1957–91, Professor 1968–91. *Compositions include:* Symphonic Allegro 1951; First Piano Sonata, 1954; Songs from Shakespeare's Tempest, 1954; String Quartet 1958; African Sonata, 1966; Duo Concertante for violin and piano 1967; The Passion of Oedipus, opera, Los Angeles 1968; Collage for orchestra 1968; Piano Concerto 1969; Barma, Septet, 1968; Switched-On Ashanti for flute, piccolo and tape (including African instruments and synthesized sounds), 1973; Songs and Epilogues for bass and orchestra, 1975; The Black Bacchants, opera, 1982; Dover Beach for bass and piano, 1983; Concerto for violin, tabla and orchestra. 1988; Various piano pieces and songs. *Publications include:* Five Preludes for piano; Songs and Epilogues for bass and piano; African Sonata; Duo Concertante; Piano Concerto Collage; Toward a New Concept of Tonality, 1959; Tonal Coherence in the First Movement of Bartók's Fourth String Quartet, 1970; The Recurrent Figure in the Britten/Piper Opera Death in Venice, 1987; Traditional Ashanti Dances as a Compositional Resource: Tachema-chema and Sikyi, 1995. *Address:* 16680 Charmel Lane, Pacific Palisades, CA 90272, USA.

TREACHER, Graham; Conductor, Composer and Lecturer; b. 1932, England. *Career:* Conducted the London New Music Singers 1958–63, with the first performances of works by Davies and Bennett, British premieres of works by Penderecki and Schoenberg; Tours of Europe, Henry Wood Promenade Concerts; Conductor at Morley College, London, Holst Choir and Opera Group; Director of the Thaxted Festival, Essex until 1963; Assistant Chorus Master Royal Opera House, Covent Garden 1962–64 for the British premiere of Schoenberg's Moses und Aron; Associate conductor of the BBC Scottish Symphony Orchestra and Chorus, 1964–67; Director of the Purcell School, London, 1968–70; Director of Music at the University of Warwick, 1969–70; Lecturer in Style, Interpretation and Conducting, University of York, 1972–85; Founder of the Amati Ensemble, baroque quartet, playing harpsichord and chamber organ, 1978–85; Director and conductor, Northern Music Theatre 1980–84, with first performances of works by Vic Hoyland, Philip Grange and British premieres of Kagel and Henze; Artistic Director of the John Loosemore Early Music Centre, Devon, 1988–92. *Compositions include:* Music for children, vocal and instrumental music including music for Strings, Percussion and Celestine, for the 1990

Orkney Summer Festival; Choral music with settings of Chaucer and Christmas music. *Publications include:* Editions of Gesualdo (Cantiones Sacrae 1603) and Pallavicino's three act Carnival opera Messalina, for performance at the Vadstena International Opera Festival, Sweden; Dixit Dominus by Pallavicino. *Address:* Warren Cottages, Hippenscombe, Nr Marlborough, Wilts SNB 3NN, England.

TREE, Michael; Concert Violinist and Violist; b. 19 Feb. 1934, Newark, New Jersey, USA; m. Johanna Kreck, 1 s., 1 d. *Education:* Diploma, Curtis Institute of Music, 1955. *Career:* Debut: Carnegie Hall, 1954; Soloist with major American orchestras; Solo and chamber music appearances at major festivals, including Israel, Athens, Spoleto, Casals, Marlboro; Founding member, Guarneri String Quartet; Faculty member, Curtis Institute of Music University of Maryland, Rutgers University, Manhattan School of Music; Repeated appearances on the Today Show and first Telecast of Chamber Music Live from Lincoln Center; mem, President of the First American String Quartet Congress at University of Maryland and Smithsonian Institute, 1989. *Recordings:* Over 60 chamber music works on Columbia, Nonesuch, Philips and RCA labels; Complete Beethoven quartets, 10 works for piano and strings, with Artur Rubinstein; Collaborations with Emanuel Ax, Jaimie Laredo, Leonard Rose, Alexander Schneider, Rudolf Serkin and Pinchas Zuckerman. *Honours:* New York City Seal of Recognition, 1982; Honorary degress, Doctor of Fine Arts, University of South Florida, State University of New York at Binghampton. *Current Management:* Herbert Barrett Management.

TREFAS, György; Hungarian singer (bass); b. 6 Oct. 1931, Budapest; m. Szabó Katalin 1972. *Education:* studied with Werner Alajos, Makai Mihály, Lendvay Andor, Hetényi Kálmán. *Career:* debut in Csokonai Theatre, Debrecen, Hungary; bass characters of operas: Verdi's King Philip, Don Carlos, Attila and De Silva in Ernani; Rocco, Fidelio; Duke Bluebeard, Bartók: Duke Bluebeard's Castle – radio recording, Dresden, Antwerp, Zaccaria, Nabucco, Sofia; Magdeburg, Mephisto, Faust; Ibert; Angelica; King Nero television film; Sarastro, Zauberflöte; Osmin, Entführung; Family portrait film, Hungarian television. *Address:* Bethlen-U 42-44, 4026 Debrecen, Hungary.

TREKEL, Roman; Singer (Baritone); b. 1962, Pirna, Saxony, Germany. *Education:* Studied at the Berlin Musikhochschule 1980–86 and with Siegfried Lorenz and Hans Hotter. *Career:* Sang with the Berlin Staatsoper from 1986, notably in Erwin and Elmire by Reichardt 1987 and Ullmann's Emperor of Atlantis 1989; Many roles in operas by Mozart in Berlin and elsewhere; Season 1992 as Ulysses in Erendira by Violet Dinescu and as Tarquinius in The Rape of Lucretia with the Berlin Kammeroper; Concerts and Lieder recitals in Germany, Belgium, Austria, Czechoslovakia, Sweden and England; Berlin Staatsoper 1999–2001, as Leonhard in Die Brautwahl by Busoni, Ottokar in Der Freischütz and Don Alfonso. *Recordings include:* Title role in Telemann's Orpheus. *Honours:* Prizewinner, Dvořák Competition, 1985; Karlovy Vary, 1987; DDR Competition Germany; 1989 International Lieder Competition Walter Gruner in London. *Address:* Stuttgart Staatsoper, Oberer Schlossgarten 6, 7000 Stuttgart 1, Germany.

TREKEL-BURCKHARDT, Ute; Singer (Mezzo-soprano); b. 3 Nov. 1939, Pirna, Saxony, Germany. *Education:* Studied in Berlin with Rita Meinl-Weise. *Career:* Debut: Komische Oper Berlin 1963, as the Page in Salome; Sang at the Komische Oper until 1978, then joined the Staatsoper Berlin; Guest appearances in Vienna, Cologne, Brussels, Madrid and Dresden; Cologne 1984, as Renata in The Fiery Angel by Prokofiev; Nancy 1985, as The Woman in Schoenberg's Erwartung; Created Queen Marguerite in Sutermeister's Le roi Bérenger at Munich in 1985; Other roles include the Countess Geschwitz in Lulu, Mozart's Sextus and Cherubino, Verdi's Eboli, Amneris and Ulrica, Strauss's Nurse (Die Frau ohne Schatten), Composer and Octavian, and Wagner's Fricka, Kundry and Ortrud (Wiesbaden 1988); Sang Venus in Tannhäuser as guest with the Berlin Staatsoper at Las Palmas in 1986; Sang Clytemnestra in Elektra at the Komische Oper Berlin, 2000; Many concert appearances. *Address:* Deutsche Staatsoper, Unter den Linden 7, 1086 Berlin, Germany.

TRELEAVEN, John; Singer (tenor); b. 10 June 1950, Cornwall, England. *Education:* Studied in London and Naples. *Career:* With Welsh National Opera has sung Tamino, Alfredo (La Traviata), Pinkerton, Nadir (Les Pêcheurs de Perles) and Mark in The Midsummer Marriage); At English National Opera his roles have included Don José, Cavaradossi, Faust (Berlioz), Erik in Der fliegende Holländer, the Prince in Rusalka, Hoffmann, Don Carlos and Wozzeck in a new production of Berg's Opera (1990); Royal Opera, Covent Garden, debut as Tamino, followed by Froh in Das Rheingold and Peter Grimes, 1989; Appearances with Scottish Opera have included Florestan, Jenik (The Bartered Bride), Werther and Radames; Opera North as Dick Johnson (La Fanciulla del West), Cavaradossi, Radames and Peter Grimes; Further engagements in The Damnation of Faust at the Adelaide Festival, Pylades (Iphigénie en

Tauride) at the Paris Opéra, Verdi's Attila at the Concertgebouw, Amsterdam and Prince Golitisin (Khovanshchina) at the San Francisco Opera, 1990; Concert performances include a 1981 debut at the Festival Hall in Puccini's Messa di Gloria and Rossini's Stabat Mater; Verdi Requiem under Nello Santi at the 1984 Festival de la Mediterranée; Dream of Gerontius 1989, with the Scottish National Orchestra; Concert performance of Bernstein's Candide at the Barbican in London, 1989; Season 1992 as Erik at Buenos Aires, Essex in Gloriana at Mainz (Siegmund 1993) and Weill's Jimmy Mahoney in Karlsruhe; Debut as Walther in Die Meistersinger at Mainz, 1997; Title role in Siegfried at Kiel, 1998; Sang Lohengrin at Barcelona, 2000; Season 2000 at Karlsruhe, as Apollo in Daphne, Siegmund and Tristan; Siegfried at Mannheim and Chemnitz; Sang Weill's Jim Mahonney at Genoa and Tristan in Amsterdam, 2001; Tristan for the BBC SO at the Barbican, 2002–03. *Recordings include:* Solo parts: Le Prophète, Meyerbeer, conducted by Henry Lewis; L'Assedio di Calais, Donizetti; Il Trovatore, Colin Davis, with José Carreras; Il Tabarro, Maazel with Placido Domingo; Rachmaninov Vespers, Candide, Leonard Bernstein; Videos of Rusalka for English National Opera; Richard Dauntless in Ruddigore; Candide. *Current Management:* Athole Still International Management, Forresters Hall, 25–27 Westow Street, London, SE19 3RY, England. *Telephone:* (20) 8771-5271. *Fax:* (20) 8768-6600. *Website:* www .atholestill.com.

TRETYAKOV, Victor; Violinist; b. 1946, Siberia, Russia. *Education:* Studied at the Irkutsk Music School and the Moscow Conservatoire. *Career:* Many concert tours of Europe, the USA and Latin America; Leader of the State Chamber Orchestra of Moscow, from 1983; Carnegie Hall recital and appearances with the Pittsburgh, Detroit and Atlanta Symphony Orchestras; Soloist with the St Petersburg Philharmonic Orchestra on tour to US, 1990; Season 1995 included concerts in Harrogate and Wiesbaden with the Oslo Philharmonic; Lucerne and Locarno Festivals with the St Petersburg Philharmonic Orchestra; British tour with the Philharmonia under Mikhail Pletnev, 1996–97, and concerts with the London Philharmonic; Philharmonia and Ulster Orchestra concerts, 1997–98. *Recordings include:* Tchaikovsky Concerto; Brahms Concerto. *Honours:* People's Artist of the USSR. *Current Management:* Askonas Holt Ltd, Lonsdale Chambers, 27 Chancery Lane, London, WC2A 1PF, England. *Telephone:* (20) 7400-1700. *Fax:* (20) 7400-1799. *E-mail:* info@askonasholt.co.uk. *Website:* www .askonasholt.co.uk.

TREW, Graham Donald, MVO, FRSA; Singer (baritone), Teacher and Adjudicator; b. 18 July 1948, Epping, England. *Education:* Guildhall School of Music and Drama, AGSM with distinction; MMus, Univ. of London; Postgraduate Certificate in Adjudication, Bretton Hall. *Career:* performed, English Opera Group, Nottingham Music Theatre, Cockpit Opera Workshop (20 productions and title role in video of Marriage of Figaro); recitals, Wigmore Hall, Purcell Room, Queen Elizabeth Hall, Barbican, Royal National Theatre; oratorio and concerts throughout England, Europe, USA, Caribbean and South Africa; English song recitals for BBC Radio 3, Music Night Is Music Night, Songs from the Shows, Melodies for You, for BBC Radio 2; Gentleman of Her Majesty's Chapel Royal, St James's Palace, 1975–2002; teaches privately and at Tonbridge School; Assoc. Teacher, Trinity Coll. of Music; guest Lecturer, Royal Acad. of Music lieder class and Birmingham Conservatoire; adjudicates throughout England, including Adjudicator, British Federation of Music Festivals; mem., Equity, Royal Society of Musicians; mem. Royal Metropolitan Order. *Recordings:* English song recordings for Meridian and Hyperion with Roger Vignoles; recordings for Priory Records and the British Music Society with John Alley; Marcello-Cantatas; Rodolphe, Florence; The Holy Boy, with Simon Weale, James Bowman and Richard Lewis. *Honours:* Gold Medal, Guildhall School of Music, 1973; Vocal Record of the Year Award for A Shropshire Lad, Gramophone Magazine, 1980; Queen's Silver Jubilee Medal; Queen's Golden Jubilee Medal. *Address:* Melin-y-Grogue, Llanfair Waterdine, Knighton, Powys LD7 1TU, Wales.

TRIFONOVA, Olga; Singer (soprano); b. 1969, St Petersburg, Russia. *Education:* St Petersburg Conservatoire. *Career:* Appearances at the Mariinksy Theatre, St Petersburg, from 1994 as Mozart's Queen of Night and Barbarina, Rosina, Lucia di Lammermoor, Xenia in Boris Godunov, Frasquita in Carmen and Louisa in Prokofiev's Betrothal in a Monastery; Salzburg debut 1998, as Flowermaiden in Parsifal, New York Met 1999, in The Queen of Spades; Sang the title role in The Snow Maiden by Rimsky-Korsakov (Concert) with the Kirov Opera at Covent Garden, 2000; Other roles include Stravinsky's Nightingale, Amina in La Sonnambula, Gilda, Glinka's Lyudmila and Chloë/Prilepa in The Queen of Spades. *Recordings include:* Le Rossignol (London Philharmonic under Robert Craft). *Address:* c/o Kirov Opera, Mariinsky Theatre, 1 Theatre Square, St Petersburg, Russia.

TRIMARCHI, Domenico; Singer (Bass-Baritone); b. 21 Dec. 1940, Naples, Italy. *Education:* Studied at the Naples Conservatory and with Gino Campese. *Career:* Debut: Teatro La Fenice Venice 1964, as

Belcore in L'Elisir d'amore; Has sung widely in Italy (Verona Arena 1975–78), Edinburgh, London, Stuttgart, Frankfurt, Chicago and Dubrovnik; Teatro Regio Parma 1987, as Falstff in the operas by Salieri and Verdi; Repertoire also includes Leporello, Alfonso, Papageno, Arbace and Count Almaviva (Mozart); Varlaam (Mussorgsky); Germont, Paolo and Fra Melitone (Verdi); Dulcamara, Belcore, Don Pasquale, Malatesta, Enrico and Alfonso (Donizetti); Dallapiccola's Job; Marcello, Sharpless and Gianni Schicchi (Puccini); Sang Donizetti's Mamma Agata at Luga di Romagna, 1988; Marchese in Linda di Chamounix at Trieste, 1989, Leporello at Parma; Sang in Wolf-Ferrari's Quattro Rusteghi at Geneva, 1992. *Recordings:* Haydn's La Vera Costanza, L'Incontro Improvviso and Il Mondo della Luna, Il Barbiere di Siviglia, Vivaldi's Tito Manlio, Tosca (Philips); Elisa e Claudio by Mercadante; La Straniera by Bellini; La Cenerentola (CBS); Pimpinone by Albinoni. *Address:* Foresters Hall, 25–27 Westow Street, London SE19 3RY, England.

TRITT, William; Concert Pianist; b. 1950, Canada. *Education:* Studied at the Ecole Vincent d'Indy in Montreal with Lucille Brassard and Yvonne Hubert; Further study with Yvonne Lefèbure in Paris and György Sebok at Indiana University. *Career:* First solo appearance aged 15 with the Little Orchestra Society at Avery Fisher Hall, New York; Further engagements with the Montreal Symphony and the CBS Orchestra in Quebec; Boston Pops Orchestra and the Chicago Symphony at the Ravinia Festival; Cincinnati and Houston Symphony Orchestras; Nationwide appearances in Canada, including Toronto, Edmonton, Winnipeg and Halifax; London recital debut 1981, Wigmore Hall. *Recordings include:* Bach D minor Concerto; Beethoven C major Concerto and Schumann A minor; Liszt Totentanz. *Honours:* Winner of all major competitions in Canada, 1966–71.

TROITSKAYA, Natalia Leonidovna; Singer (Soprano); b. 18 May 1956, Moscow, Russia. *Education:* Studied in Moscow and Belgrade. *Career:* Debut: Sang Tosca at Barcelona, 1991, with Placido Domingo; Aida at Macerata and Liège, 1982; Vienna Staatsoper from 1984; Amelia in Ballo in Maschera at the Paris Opéra and Adriana Lecouvreur at Rome; Deutsche Oper Berlin, 1988–89, as Desdemona and Tosca; Covent Garden, 1986 as Tosca and US debut at Washington DC, 1989, as Lisa in The Queen of Spades; Other roles include Manon Lescaut, Leonora in Il Trovatore and Elisabeth de Valois (San Francisco, 1990). *Honours:* Winner of Competitions at Toulouse, Vercelli, and Barcelona. *Address:* c/o Deutsche Oper Berlin, Richard Wagner Str 10, 10585 Berlin, Germany.

TROJAHN, Manfred; Composer; b. 22 Oct. 1949, Cremlingen, Brunswick, Germany. *Education:* Studied at the Niedersächsische Musikschule, Brunswick, 1966–70; Composition at the Hamburg Hochschule, 1970–77. *Career:* Freelance composer including Residency at the Villa Massimo in Rome, 1979–80; Teacher of composition at the Robert Schumann Hochschule, Düsseldorf, 1991. *Compositions include:* Opera Enrico (1991); 4 symphonies, 1973, 1978, 1985, 1992; 3 string quartets, 1976, 1980, 1983; Fünfsee-Bilder für messosopran und orchester, 1979–83; Flute Concerto, 1983; Requiem, 1985;... une campagne noire de soleil, 7 ballet scenes for chamber ensemble, 1983–93; Sonatas for violin and cello, 1983; Variations for orchestra, 1987; Cinq Epigraphes for orchestra, 1987; Fragmente für Antigone, 6 pieces for string quartet, 1988; Transir for orchestra, 1988; Aubade for 2 sopranos, 1990; Ave Maria for chorus, 1991; Grodek for baritone and 8 instruments, 1991; Quattro Pezzi for orchestra, 1992; Divertissement for oboe and chamber orchestra, 1993; Cornisches Nachtlied for orchestra, 1994; Was ihr Wollt (As You Like It), opera, 1997–98. Liebeslieder, for soprano and orchestra, 1997; Palinsesto, for soprano and string quartet, 1997; Violin Concerto, 1999; La Clemenza di Tito by Mozart with newly composed recitatives by Trojahn, premièred Netherlands Opera, Amsterdam, 2002; Limonen aus Sizilien: Drei italienische Geschichten (opera), premièred Cologne City Theatre, 2003; Occhi mie for tenor, 2002; Three Songs by John Keats for Mezzo-soprano and six instruments, 2002; Rhapsodie for Clarinet and Orchestra, 2001/02. *Address:* 44 rue Dauphine, 75006 Paris, France.

TROPP, Vladimir; Pianist; b. 9 Nov. 1939, Moscow, Russia; m. Tatiana Zelikman 1961; one s. *Education:* Gnessin Children's Music School; Gnessin Specialized Music School; Gnessin Institute. *Career:* concert tours in Russia, Netherlands, USA, Italy, Japan, Finland, Germany, Ireland, Costa Rica, Republic of Korea, Czechoslovakia, Cuba; masterclasses and concerts in American univs, conservatories of Holland and Ireland, London Royal Acad. of Music, Italy, France, Japan; numerous chamber music festivals; performances on radio and television in Russia, Netherlands, Germany, USA, Finland, Costa Rica; performances with major orchestras; Prof. of Piano, Dept of Russian, Gnessin Acad. of Music, Chief of Piano Dept. *Recordings include:* works by Chopin, Brahms, Tchaikovsky, Rachmaninov, Scriabin, Medtner. *Contributions:* articles in magazines and newspapers in Russia. *Address:* Dmitry Ulianov Str 4, Block 2, Apt 251, Moscow 117333, Russia.

TROST, Rainer; Singer (Tenor); b. 1966, Stuttgart, Germany. *Education:* Munich Hochschule, with Adalbert Kraus. *Career:* Member of the Hanover Staatstheater, 1991–95; Sang Ferrando in Così fan tutte at the Hamburg Opera 1992 and toured in Mozart's opera with the Monteverdi Choir and Orchestra; Sang Ferrando at Munich 1993, Don Ottavio at Dresden and Vienna, Tamino in Geneva and Berlin (1994) and Eginhard in Schubert's Fierrabras at Florence (1995); Further engagements at the Cologne Opera, Opéra National de Paris, as Belmonte in Vienna and Hamburg and as Ferrando at Covent Garden, Glyndebourne, 1994 (debut role), returning 1997; Season 1998–99 sang Orsino in the premiere of Manfred Trojahn's Was ihr Wollt, Munich, Entführung, Don Giovanni and Zauberflöte in Vienna, Don Giovanni in Hamburg and concerts of Tristan und Isolde with the Berlin Philharmonic under Abbado; Season 1999–2000 included Zauberflöte and Fidelio in Munich, Così fan tutte at Salzburg Festival with Abbado, Katya Kabanova for Netherlands Opera and concerts for Gesellschaft der Musikfreunde in Vienna; Season 2001 as Fenton and Ferrando in Munich, Belmonte at Hannover and Des Grieux in Henze's Boulevard Solitude at Covent Garden; Further engagements include Don Giovanni, Zauberflöte, Così fan tutte, Fidelio and Falstaff in Munich, Zauberflöte at Vienna State Opera and Così fan tutte in Salzburg, with concert engagements of Fidelio in Munich and Katja Kabanowa in Brussels and Barcelona; Concerts include Mozart's Mass in C Minor, with the Monteverdi Choir and Orchestra; Die Schöpfung, with the Hamburg Philharmonic Orchestra and the Cologne Radio Symphony Orchestra, Bach's Christmas Oratorio (NDR SO) and the St Matthew Passion, with the Concertgebouw Orchestra. *Recordings include:* CD and video of Così fan tutte (DGG). *Address:* c/o Haydn Rawstron Ltd, 36 Station Road, London SE20 7BQ, England.

TROTTER, Thomas (Andrew); Concert Organist; b. 4 April 1957, Birkenhead, England. *Education:* ARCM, Royal College of Music, London, 1976; MA, Cambridge University, 1979; Conservatoire Rueil-Malmaison, France, 1979–81. *Career:* Debut: Royal Festival Hall, 1980; Regular broadcasts on Radio 2 and 3; Performances at festivals throughout Europe; Proms debut in 1986; Concert tours of USA, Australia and Japan; Organist for St Margaret's Church, Westminster, London, 1982–, City of Birmingham, 1983–; Messiaen recitals, Edinburgh Festival, 1994. *Recordings:* The Grand Organ of Birmingham Town Hall; Liszt Organ Works and Reubke Sonata; Jehan Alain Organ Works; Charles-Marie Widor Organ Works; Antonio Soler Concertos for 2 Organs; Olivier Messiaen Organ Works; The Ride of the Valkyries: Organ Transcriptions; Liszt Organ Works vol. 2; Mozart Organ Works. *Honours:* Scholar, RCM; Organ Scholar, St George's Chapel, Windsor and King's College, Cambridge (John Stewart of Rannock Scholarship in Sacred Music, 1979); Walford Davies Prize, RCM, 1976; 1st Prize and Bach Prize, St Alban's International Organ Competition, 1979; Prix de Virtuosite, 1981. *Current Management:* Karen McFarlane Artists Inc, 12429 Cedar Road, Cleveland Heights, OH 44106, USA. *Address:* c/o Town Hall, Birmingham, B3 3DQ, England.

TROUP, Malcolm; Concert Pianist, Professor Emeritus of Music, City University and Former Director of Music, Guildhall School of Music and Drama; b. 22 Feb. 1930, Toronto, Canada; m. (1) Carmen Lamarca Subercaseaux, 1 d., (2) Wendela Lumley. *Education:* DPhilMus. University of York; Associate, Royal Conservatory of Music (ARCT), Toronto; FGSM; LLD, Memorial University of Newfoundland; Hon D.Mus, City University. *Career:* Debut: With CBC Symphony Orchestra, Toronto, aged 17; Recitals and Concertos with leading orchestras in Europe, North and South America; Premieres, important modern works; Frequent broadcaster with the BBC; External Examiner, Universities of York, Keele, London; Member of International Juries: Chopin Competition of Australia, CBC National Talent Competition, Young Musician of the Year; 1st Dvořák International Piano Competition, 1997; Rome 1997 and 2002 International Piano Competition and 1st Claudio Arrau International Piano Competition, Chillan, Chile, 2003; Vice President, World Piano Competition, London; President of Jury, 1st EPTA International Piano Competition, Zagreb, 1999, Reykjavík, 2000; Founder and Vice-President Asociación Latinoamericana de Profesores de Piano (ALAPP/Chile); Director, London International String Quartet Competition; President, Oxford International Piano Festival, 1999–; Governor of Music Therapy Charity; Chairman of European Piano Teachers Association; Chairman of Beethoven Piano Society of Europe; Trustee of Jewish Music Trust; Freeman of the City of London, 1971; Liveryman of Worshipful Company of Musicians, 1973; Court Member, 1991, Master 1999. *Recordings:* Major record labels. *Publications:* Editor, The Piano Journal. *Contributions:* The Messiaen Companion, London: Faber and Faber, 1995; The Science and Psychology of Music Performance, New York: OUP, 2002. *Honours:* Medal Winner in the Harriet Cohen International Awards, 1965; Liszt Medal of the American Liszt Society, 1998. *Address:* 86 Lexham Gardens, London W8 5JB, England.

TROWELL, Brian (Lewis); Professor of Music; b. 21 Feb. 1931, Wokingham, Berkshire, England; m. Rhianon James, 1958, 2 d. *Education:* Christ's Hospital; MA 1959, PhD 1960, Gonville and Caius College, Cambridge. *Career:* Assistant Lecturer later Lecturer in Music, Birmingham University, 1957–62; Freelance Scholar, Conductor, Opera Producer, Lecturer and Editor, 1962–67; Head of BBC Radio Opera, 1967–70; Regents' Professor, University of California, Berkeley, USA, 1970; Reader in Music, 1970 then Professor of Music, 1973, KCL; Visiting Gresham Professor of Music, City University, 1971–74; King Edward Professor of Music, University of London, King's College, 1974–88; Chairman of Editorial Committee, Musica Britannica, 1983–93; President, Royal Musical Association; Chairman, Handel Institute Trust and Council, 1987–98; Heather Professor of Music, University of Oxford, 1988–96; Professor Emeritus, 1996–. *Publications:* The Early Renaissance, Pelican History of Music, vol. II, 1963; Four Motets by John Plummer, 1968; Joint Editor, John Dunstable: Complete Works, Editor, M F Bukofzer, 2nd revised edition, 1970; Editor, Invitation to Medieval Music, vol. 3, 1976, vol. 4, 1978; Opera translations. *Contributions:* Dictionaries of music and articles in books and learned journals including: Libretto II, The New Grove Dictionary of Opera, London, 1992, Acis, Galatea and Polyphemus: a serenata a tre voci?, Music and Theatre: Essays in Honour of Winton Dean, 1987, Elgar's Use of Literature in Edward Elgar Music and Literature, 1993. *Address:* Faculty of Music, Oxford University, St Aldate's, Oxford OX1 1 DB, England.

TRPČESKI, Simon; pianist; b. 1979, Skopje, Macedonia. *Education:* University of St Cyril and St Methodius, Skopje and with Boris Romanov. *Career:* concert appearances in Romania, Bulgaria, Italy, France, Portugal and Korea; played Prokofiev's Third Concerto at the World Piano Competition, London 2000; Piano aux Jacobins Festival, Toulouse 2000; further concerts in Russia, Yugoslavia, Czech Republic, Turkey, Canada, Switzerland, Norway, UK, Australia and USA; repertoire centres on Russian music, and Chopin; Season 2001–2002 with Wigmore Hall, London debut, Saint-Saëns Concerto no. 2 with the Bournemouth Symphony Orchestra and concerts in Australia and Malaysia; Royal Festival debut with the Philharmonia Orchestra; Recent engagements include collaborations with Sydney and Melbourne Symphony Orchestras, the Tonhalle Orchestra, the Bergen Philharmonic, Seattle Symphony, Royal Liverpool Philharmonic, Scottish Chamber Orchestra, Stockholm Philharmonic Orchestra and the Hallé Orchestra. *Honours:* Winner, Yamaha Music Foundation of Europe, Skopje, 1998; Second Prize, World Piano Competition, London, 2000; Young Artist Award by the Royal Philharmonic Society; Gramophone Award for his EMI debut CD. *Current Management:* IMG Artists, Lovell House, 616 Chiswick High Road, London, W4 5RX, England. *E-mail:* Cdyer@imgworld.com.

TRUAX, Barry; Composer; b. 10 May 1947, Chatham, Ontario, Canada. *Education:* Studied physics and mathematics at Queen's University Kingston, BS, 1969; MM, Electronic music at the University of British Columbia, 1971, and at the Institute of Sonology, University of Utrecht, 1971–73. *Career:* Collaboration with Murray Schafer at World Soundscape Project in Vancouver; Director of Sonic Research Studio, and Professor in Communication Department, Simon Fraser University, 1976–, and School for the Contemporary Arts. *Compositions include:* Four Sonic Landscapes, 1971–79; Gilgamesh, for voices, chorus, ensemble and tape, 1974; Nautilus for percussion and tape, 1976; East Wind for amplified recorder and tape, 1981; Nightwatch for marimba and tape, 1982; Etude for cello and tape, 1983; Divan, and Wings of Nike, for computer images and tape, 1985–87; Tongues of Angels for English horn and oboe d'amore, 1988; Dominion for chamber ensemble and tape, 1991; Song of Songs, for oboe d'amore, tape and computer images, 1993; Bamboo, Silk and Stone, for Asian instruments and tape, 1994; Inside, for bass oboe and tape, 1995; Wings of Fire, for cello and tape, 1996; Androgyne, Mon Amour, for double bass and tape, 1997; Powers of Two, for singers, dancers, video and tape, 1995–99; Twin Souls, Islands. *Recordings:* Digital Soundscapes, Pacific Rim, Song of Songs, Inside. *Publications include:* Handbook for Acoustic Ecology (1978) CD-ROM, 1999, and Acoustic Communication (1984), 2001. *Honours:* Magisterium, International Electro-acoustic Competition, Bourges, 1991. *Address:* c/o School of Communication, Simon Fraser University, Burnaby, BC V5A 1S6, Canada. *Website:* www.sfu .ca\~truax.

TRUBASHNIK, Simon; Oboist; b. 16 Sept. 1939, Odessa; Divorced, 1 d. *Education:* Central Music School for Gifted Children, Moscow Conservatoire; Diploma, 1953, Graduate Diploma, Moscow Conservatoire, 1958. *Career:* Debut: Solo, Youth Festival, Berlin, 1955; Principal Oboe, Moscow Philharmonic Orchestra, 1955–72; Principal Oboe, Moscow Chamber Orchestra, 1958–72; Associate Principal Oboe, Israel Philharmonic Orchestra, 1972–75; Principal Oboe, Belgium National Opera, 1976–85; Principal Oboe, Halifax Symphony, Canada, 1986–87; Professor, Royal Conservatory of Music, Toronto, 1987–; Solo with Moscow

Philharmonic and Moscow Chamber Orchestras (World Tours); Radio Luxembourg Orchestra of Belgium; Mozart Chamber Orchestra, Brussels; Opera Orchestra of Ghent; Toronto Chamber Players; Kingston Philharmonic; McGill Chamber Orchestra; mem, American Federation of Musicians. *Recordings:* Bach Concerto (with David Oistrakh) and Concertos by Mozart and Strauss with Moscow Philharmonic Orchestra; Italian Baroque Concerts with Luxembourg Radio Orchestra; 100 Orchestral Records with Moscow Philharmonic Orchestra. *Honours:* Gold Medal, Moscow Conservatoire, 1958. *Current Management:* Sol Hurock Management. *Address:* 100 Upper Madison #610, North York, Ontario M2N 6M4, Canada.

TRUEFITT, Alison; Singer (Soprano); b. 1958, England. *Education:* Studied at London University and the Royal Academy of Music. *Career:* Debut: Sang at the Purcell Room, London, 1979; Has appeared in recital with the Songmakers' Almanac and with the BBC in songs by Britten, Bart ók, Fauré, Holst, Milhaud, Poulenc, and Tippett; With orchestra or ensemble in works by Gerald Finzi, Stephen Dodgson and Frank Martin; Promenade Concerts debut in La Forza del Destino; Sang Gluck's Iphigenia with Opera Factory, 1985, and created Kathe in John Metcalf's The Crossing (tours of the USA, the United Kingdom and Canada); Sang in the British stage premiere of Schubert's Fierrabras, Oxford University 1986; English National Opera 1988, as Manassah in Salome; Sang Donizetti's Rita, Madame Herz in Mozart's Impresario and Musetta with London Chamber Opera 1988; Appearances with London Chamber Opera 1988; Appearances as the Queen of Night with Birmingham Touring Opera, 1988–89; Other repertory includes Leila in Les pêcheurs de Perles, the Governess in The Turn of the Screw, Britten's Phaedra and Major Stone in Weill's Happy End; Translated Orfeo for Opera North, 1990, and has provided several sets of surtitles for Covent Garden. *Address:* c/o Royal Opera House, Covent Garden, London WC2E 9 DD, England.

TRUSSEL, Jacques; Singer (Tenor); b. 7 April 1943, San Francisco, California, USA. *Education:* Studied at Ball State University, Muncie, Indiana and in New York. *Career:* Sang at first in concert then made opera debut at the Oberlin Festival 1970, as Pinkerton; Has appeared in Boston, Dallas, Houston, Santa Fe, New Orleans, Chicago (from 1976), Pittsburgh (1979), Washington (1981) and San Francisco (Loge in Das Rheingold 1990); Sang Don José at Cincinnati 1988 and has appeared as Rodolfo, Cavaradossi, Berg's Alwa, Araquil in La Navarraise by Massenet, Števa in Jenůfa, Max (Der Freischütz) and Nero in L'Incoronazione di Poppea (Geneva 1989); Sang at Houston in the title role of Hugh the Drover by Vaughan Williams (US premiere 1973) and in the 1974 word premiere of The Seagull by Pasatieri; European debut Spoleto Festival 1976, as Hermann in The Queen of Spades; Sang Alwa at Florence 1985 and at Chicago 1987; Covent Garden and Nancy 1989, as Peter Grimes and as Sergei in the French premiere of Lady Macbeth of Mtsensk by Shostakovich; Appeared with Greater Miami Opera 1990, as Pollione in Norma; London appearances 1991, as Don José; Season 1991/92 as Alexey in the US premiere of The Gambler, at Chicago; Sergei at the Opéra Bastille, Monteverdi's Nero in Florence, Don José in Birmingham and Roderick in The Fall of the House of Usher by Philip Glass at the Maggio Musicale; Sang Golitsin in Khovanschina at Brussels, 1996; Herod in Salome at Vancouver, 1998 and at Cincinnati, 2000. *Address:* c/o Vancouver Opera, Suite 500, 845 Cambie Street, Vancouver British Columbia V6B 4Z9, Canada.

TRYON, Valerie; Pianist and Associate Professor, McMaster University, Hamilton, Ontario; b. 1934, Portsmouth, England. *Education:* Studied at the Royal Academy of Music and with Jacques Fèvrier in Paris. *Career:* Debut: Wigmore Hall, 1954; Has appeared at the Cheltenham Festival and in all the major concert halls in the United Kingdom with leading conductors and orchestras; Recitals in Europe and Africa and in North America; Repertoire ranges from Bach to contemporary composers, with 50 concertos; Noted for playing of Chopin, Liszt and Rachmaninov; Frequent broadcasts for the BBC and other radio stations and regular chamber music concerts; Adjudicator and performer at many music festivals and competitions in Europe and North America; Fellow of the Royal Academy of Music; Associate Professor of Music at McMaster University, Hamilton, Ontario. *Recordings:* Albums for Pye (Virtuoso Series), BBC Enterprises, Omnibus, Argo, Lyrita, Educo and the CBC; Dorian Records: Tchaikovsky CDs; Brahms (The Rembrandt Trio); Dvořák, Trio; Bloemendaal, Tryon, Kantarjian; Naxos (Liszt), Appian (Scarlatti and Ravel). *Honours:* Harriet Cohen Award; Ferenc Liszt Medal of Honour; Juno Award, 1994. *Address:* Department of Music, McMaster University, 1280 Main Street West, Hamilton, Ontario, Canada.

TRYTHALL, (Harry) Gilbert, BA, MMus, DMA; composer and teacher; b. 28 Oct. 1930, Knoxville, TN, USA; m.; two d. *Education:* University of Tennessee, Northwestern University, Cornell University; studied with David Van Vactor, Wallingford Riegger, Robert Palmer and Donald Grout. *Career:* Assistant Professor of Music, Knox College, Galesburg, Illinois, 1960–64; Professor of Music Theory and Composition, 1964–75;

Chairman, School of Music, George Peabody College for Teachers, Nashville, Tennessee, 1973–75; Professor of Music, 1975–, Dean, Creative Arts Center, 1975–81, Virginia University, Morgantown, West Virginia; Guest Lecturer at various universities and colleges. *Compositions:* Operas: The Music Lesson, 1960; The Terminal Opera, 1982, revised 1987; The Pastimes of Lord Caitanya, chamber opera, 1992; Orchestral: A solemn Chant for strings, 1955; Symphony No. 1, 1958, revised 1963; Harp Concerto, 1963; Dionysia, 1964; Chroma I, 1970; Cindy the Synthe (Minnie the Moog) for synthesizer and strings, 1975; Chamber: Flute Sonata, 1964; A Vacuum Soprano for brass quintet and tape, 1966; Entropy for brass, harp, celesta, piano and tape, 1967; Echospace for brass and tape, 1973; Choral music; Piano pieces; Organ music; Electronic scores; Mixed media pieces; Film music. *Publications:* Principles and Practice of Electronic Music, 1974; Eighteenth Century Counterpoint, 1993; Sixteenth Century Counterpoint, 1994. *Address:* 41 W Main, Morgantown, WV 26505, USA.

TSCHAIKOV, Basil (Nichols); Clarinettist; b. 30 May 1925, London, England; m. (1) 2 d., (2) Dorothy Gallon, July 1966. *Education:* Royal College of Music. *Career:* London Philharmonic Orchestra, 1943–47; Royal Philharmonic Orchestra, 1947–55; Philharmonia Orchestra, 1958–79; Visiting Lecturer, Middlesex Polytechnic, England, 1959–79; Professor, Royal College of Music, 1964–84; Director, National Centre for Orchestral Studies, London University, Goldsmiths' College, 1979–89; Artistic and Executive Director, Orchestra for Europe, 1989–90; Chairman, Music Performance Research Centre, 1987–; Editor in Chief, Musical Performance, Harwood Academic Publishers, 1993–2001; mem. Musicians Union; Chair. Music Preserved (formerly Music Performance Research Centre) 1987–2003; President Emeritus, Music Preserved, 2003–. *Compositions:* First Tunes and Studies; Play the Clarinet. *Recordings:* Various chamber ensembles. *Publications:* Play the Clarinet Teachers Handbook; How to Be a Musician. *Honours:* Honorary RCM;Fellow, Royal Society of Arts. *Address:* Hillside Cottage, Hillbrow, Liss, Hampshire GU33 7PS, England. *E-mail:* bnt@dial.pipex.com (home).

TSCHAMMER, Hans; Singer (Bass); b. 1945, Schlesien, Germany. *Education:* Würzburg Musikhochschule and Salzburg Mozarteum. *Career:* Sang at the Deutsche Oper am Rhein from 1975, notably as Pogner, Hagen, Daland, the Landgrave in Tannhäuser and Gurnemanz; Guest appearances at Hamburg, Zürich and San Francisco (Hunding, 1983); Bayreuth Festival, 1985–86; Further appearances at the New York Metropolitan, 1983, Bregenz Festival as Daland, 1990, and Covent Garden as Rocco, 1991; Other roles include the Commendatore in Don Giovanni and Prince Gremin (Toulouse, 1990 and 1993); Season 1994–95 as Sarastro at Turin and Gurnemanz at Montpellier; Season 1998 as King Marke for Flanders Opera and at Monte Carlo; Sang Rocco in Fidelio at Rome, Daland in Dresden and Pogner for the Deutsche Oper Berlin, 2000; Concerts include Mozart's C minor Mass. *Address:* c/o Opéra et Concert, Rue Volney, 75002 Paris, France.

TSCHERGOV, Michail; Bulgarian singer (tenor, baritone); b. 1 Oct. 1928, Novo Selo. *Education:* studied in Sofia. *Career:* sang with the Vraza Opera, 1952–53 (debut as Nemorino), at Rostock, 1966–68, as Max, Alvaro and Dimitri; Sang widely in Eastern Europe as Otello, Canio, Des Grieux and Pedro in Tiefland; Other roles have included Calaf, Don José, Florestan, Tannhäuser, Siegmund and Rodolfo; Sang Otello at Frankfurt, 1988, and from 1990 such baritone roles as Verdi's Rigoletto and Renato. *Address:* c/o Bulgarian National Opera, Boul Dondoukov 58, 1000 Sofia, Bulgaria.

TSONEVA, Plamena, MA, MAS; Bulgarian musicologist and art manager; b. 19 Nov. 1954, Baltchik. *Education:* Dobris Hristov High School of Music, Varna, Pancho Vladigerov Music Acad., Sofia, Acad. for Music and Dance, Plovdiv, Int. Centre for Culture and Management, Salzburg and Linz Univ., Austria. *Career:* Dept of Culture, Dobrich Municipality 1978–85; Bulgarian Nat. Inst. of Culture, Branch Dobrich 1985–88; musicologist and Production Man., Varna Summer Int. Music Festival and Int. Summer Music Acad.; recent projects include Balkan Musicians in the Varna Summer Festival 2002, Varna Summer Int. Music Acad., with assistance from the British Council, Folkwang Hochschule, Essen, Germany 2002; meeting point of Young Talents supported by the EC Cultural 2000 Program; participation in, as representative of the Varna Festival, projects initiated by the European Festivals Asscn 1998–2003. *Publications:* catalogues and brochures for Varna Summer Int. Music Festival, texts and articles about the festival image, programmes and performers 1989–2000, Varna Summer Int. Festival and Creative Urban Policy summary, 'The Balkan City – Stage for the End of the XX Century' in conference book for Yugoslav Performing Arts Centre, Belgrade 2000, script for a documentary 'Choir Singing in Dobrich (Bulgarian Nat. TV/Branch Varna) 2002, contrib. to Das Musiktheater in Exil und Diktatur und seine Rezeption – Salzburg 2003 with paper, Bulgarian Opera during the period 1944–89, Journeys of Expression II, in cultural festivals/events and tourism Vienna 2003, Centre for Tourism and Cultural Change Sheffield Hallam Univ., in asscn with

IFEA Europe, The City and the Festival, 'A must or muse' Rotterdam 2001, Boekman Foundation, Topic Arts and Culture in Education – Policy and Practice in Europe, Analysis of the Situation in Bulgaria. *Address:* Varna Summer International Music Festival, Varna Municipality, 43 Osmi Primorski Polk Blvd., 9000 Varna, Bulgaria (office). *Telephone:* (359) 52222425 (office). *Fax:* (359) 52220101 (office). *E-mail:* plconeva@varna.bg (office). *Website:* www.varnasummerfest.org.

TSONTAKIS, George; Composer; b. 24 Oct. 1951, New York, USA. *Education:* Studied with Roger Sessions (1974–79), at the Juilliard School (1978–86) and with Karlheinz Stockhausen in Rome, 1981. *Career:* Freelance Composer; Assistant in Electronic Music at Juilliard (1978) and Assistant Professor at the Brooklyn College Conservatory, 1986–87. *Compositions include:* Scenes from the Apocalypse for soloists, chorus and orchestra, 1978; The Epistle of James, Chapter I for narrator, chorus and orchestra, 1980; Erotkritos, oratorio for chorus and orchestra, 1982; Five Signs and a Fantasy for orchestra, 1985; Fantasia Habanera for orchestra, 1986; 4 string quartets, 1980, 1984, 1986, 1989; Bird-wind Quintet, 1983; Brass Quintet, 1983; Brass Quintet, 1984; Saviours for soprano, chorus and orchestra, 1985; The Past, The Passion, for 15 players, 1987; Galway Kinnell Songs for mezzo, piano and string quartet; The Sowers of the Seed for orchestra, 1989; Heartsounds, quintet for piano and strings, 1990; Stabat Mater, for soprano, chorus and orchestra, 1990; 4 Symphonic Quartets, 1992–96; Gemini for horn, violin, cello and piano, 1996; Dust, for horn, violin and piano, 1998; Violin Concerto, 1998. *Honours:* Koussevitszky Foundation Commission, 1987. *Address:* c/o ASCAP, ASCAP Building, 1 Lincoln Plaza, New York, NY 10023, USA.

TSOUPAKI, Calliope; Composer and Pianist; b. 27 May 1963, Piraeus, Greece. *Education:* Studied at the Hellinicon Conservatory, Athens and at Nikos Skalkottas Conservatory (1985); With Louis Andriessen at the Hague Royal Conservatory; Summer courses at Darmstadt with Iannis Xenakis, Olivier Messiaen and Pierre Boulez (1985–88). *Career:* Freelance composer and pianist; Gaudeamus International Music Week at Amsterdam, 1991 and 1993; Composer in residence at the 1993 Budapest Young Artists Foundation; Featured composer at 1995 San Francisco Other Minds Festival. *Compositions include:* Eclipse for orchestra, 1986; Earinon for 8 horns and percussion, 1986; Revealing Moment for alto flute, 1987; Moments I and II for piano, 1988; For Always for female voice, tape and lights, 1989; Your Thouht for voice, tape and lighting, 1989; Silver Moments for 2 pianos and 2 percussion players, 1989; Mania for amplified violin, 1989; Visions of the Night, for amplified chamber ensemble, 1989; Sappho's Tears for violin, tenor recorder, and female voice, 1990; When I was 27, for amplified viola and double bass, 1990; Song for Four, for string quartet, 1991; Echoing Purple for violin and ensemble, 1992; Eros and Psyche, for wind octet and double bass, 1992; Orphic Fields for flute, 2 harps and 2 pianos, 1993; Phantom for tuba, 1994; Her Voice for harp, 1994; Ethra for flute, string trip and harp, 1995; Epigramma for chorus and orchestra, 1995; Lineos for chorus and ensemble, 1995; Hippolutos, music theatre after Euripides, 1996; Medea, stage, 1996; Interface, for ensemble, 1996; Siren, for narrator and chamber orchestra, 1997; No Name I, for oboe and violin, 1997; E guerre morte, after Tasso, for chorus and ensemble, 1997.

TSUTSUMI, Tsuyoshi; Concert Cellist and Professor of Music; b. 28 July 1942, Tokyo, Japan; m. Harue Saji, 14 May 1978, 1 s., 1 d. *Education:* Toho Gakuen High School of Music, Tokyo, 1961; Artist Diploma, Indiana University, USA, 1965. *Career:* Debut: Tokyo, Japan, 1955; Soloist (Iwaki), European Tour, NHK Symphony Orchestra of Tokyo, 1960; Soloist (Ozawa), Chicago Symphony, Ravinia Festival, Ravinia Park, Chicago, Illinois, USA, 1967; Soloist (Ozawa), American and European Tour, New Japan Philharmonic, 1974; Soloist (Akiyama), American Symphony, New York City, 1978; Soloist (Ceccato), Czech Philharmonic, Prague, Czechoslovakia, 1984; Professor of Music, School of Music, University of Illinois, Urbana, Illinois, USA; Professor of Music, School of Music, Indiana University, Bloomington, Indiana, USA; Pres. Toho Gakuen School of Music Tokyo 2004. *Recordings:* Bach, Unaccompanied Suites, complete; Beethoven, Sonatas and Variations (Turini, piano); Dvořák Concerto, Czech Philharmonic (Košler, conductor); Haydn, Concertos, English Chamber Orchestra; Yashiro Concerto, Tokyo Symphony Orchestra, conducted by Ohtomo. *Publications:* An Illinois Diary (The Cello and I), 1991, My Life with Celllo 2003. *Address:* 2715 Bluff Court, Bloomington, IN 47401, USA.

TSYDYPOVA, Valentina; Singer (soprano); b. 1955, Buritia, Russia. *Education:* Graduated the Novosibirsk Conservatory 1984. *Career:* Sang at the Ulan-Ude Opera Theatre 1984–89; Novosibirsk Opera Theatre 1989–92; Kirov Opera St Petersburg from 1992, notably on tour to Italy, Israel, Spain, the Met Opera in New York, France, Finland and Germany; Guest appearances as Butterfly at the Opéra Bastille, Paris (1993) and in Hamburg and Berlin, Tosca at the Savonlinna Festival and Gorislava in Ruslan and Lyudmila at San Francisco; Other roles include Tchaikovsky's Tatiana, Maria (Mazeppa) and Lisa, Elisabeth de

Valois, Desdemona, Aida, Santuzza and Yaroslavna; Concerts include Wigmore Hall recital (1995) and the Verdi Requiem at the Bastille Opéra. *Recordings include:* Rimsky's Sadko and Glinka's Ruslan and Lyudmila, with the Kirov Opera (Philips). *Honours:* People's Artist of the Buriatian Republic. *Current Management:* Askonas Holt Ltd, Lonsdale Chambers, 27 Chancery Lane, London, WC2A 1PF, England. *Telephone:* (20) 7400-1700. *Fax:* (20) 7400-1799. *E-mail:* info@askonasholt.co.uk. *Website:* www.askonasholt.co.uk.

TSYPIN, George; Set Designer; b. 1954, Russia. *Education:* Studied architecture in Moscow and set design in New York. *Career:* Collaborations with producer Peter Sellars include premiere of Osborne's The Electrification of the Soviet Union (1987) and Handel's Theodora (1996) at Glyndebourne; Premiere production of The Death of Klinghoffer by John Adams seen at Brussels, San Francisco, Lyon and New York, 1991; Messiaen's St Francois d'Assise (1992) and Le Grand Macabre by Ligeti (1997) at the Salzburg Festival; First staging by British company of Hindemith's Mathis der Maler, Covent Garden 1995; Further engagements with Salome and Katerina Izmailova at the Kirov, St Petersburg; The Gambler at La Scala, Die Zauberflöte in Florence and Orfeo and Euridice in Zürich; Oedipus Rex in Japan, Rigoletto for Canadian Opera with further work on Tannhäuser, Don Giovanni and Pelléas et Mélisande; Engaged for The Ring at Netherlands Opera (concluding with Götterdämmerung, 1999).

TUCAPSKY, Antonin; Composer, Conductor and Professor; b. 27 March 1928, Opatovice, Czechoslovakia; m. Beryl Musgrave, 13 Oct 1972, 1 s., 1 d. *Education:* PhDr, Teachers' training College, Masaryk University, Brno; Music Education, Conducting, choral singing, composition, Janáček Academy of Music, Brno. *Career:* Debut: Ostrava; Conductor of various choirs, 1954–65; Children's Radio Choir, Ostrava, 1960–62; Chief Conductor, Moravian Teachers Choir, 1964–73; Appearances on Czech Radio, Supraphon Records, BBC radio and television, Belgian radio; Professor of Composition at Trinity College, London. *Compositions:* In Honorem Vitae; Lauds; 5 Lenten Motets, choral cycles; The Time of Christmas; The Sacrifice, cantatas; Four Dialogues, clarinet and piano; Pocket Music, wind quintet; Adieu; Moravian Polka, orchestra; Missa Serena, oratorio; Stabat Mater, oratorio; The Undertaker, opera; Triptychon, symphony orchestra, 1991; Concertino, for piano and string orchestra, 1992; Concerto, for violin and orchestra, 1993; String Quartet No.2, 1993; Viola Concerto, 1996; Piano Trio No.2 'Eclogues' 1996; Oboe Quintet, 1997; Clarinet Concerto, 1999; Te Deum, 1999. *Recordings:* Choral Music; Comoedia, Cantata, Veni Sancte Spiritus, BBC Recordings; Viola Concerto. *Publications:* Sightreading and Sightsinging, 1969; Janáček's Male Choruses and Their Interpretation, 1971. *Address:* 50 Birchen Grove, Kingsbury, London NW9 8 SA, England.

TUCCI, Gabriella; Singer (Soprano); b. 4 Aug. 1929, Rome, Italy. *Education:* Studied at the Accademia di Santa Cecilia and with Leonardi Filoni. *Career:* Debut: Teatro Giglio Lucca 1951, as Violetta; Spoleto Festival 1952, as Leonora in La Forza del Destino; Florence 1953, as Cherubini's Médée; Tour of Australia 1955; La Scala Milan from 1959, as Mimi and in the Italian premiere of A Midsummer Night's Dream; Verona Arena 1959–69; US debut San Francisco 1959, as Madeleine in Andrea Chénier; Metropolitan Opera, 1960–73 as Butterfly, Aida, Euridice, Leonora in Trovatore and La Forza del Destino, Violetta and Marguerite; Covent Garden 1960, as Tosca; Appearances at Buenos Aires, Sydney, Oslo, Johannesburg, Dallas, New Orleans and Philadelphia; Other roles include Desdemona, Anaide in Mosé by Rossini, Luisa Miller, Micaela and Elvira in I Puritani; Teacher at Indiana University from 1983. *Recordings:* Pagliacci; Il Trovatore; Requiems by Bellini and Donizetti. *Address:* Music Faculty, Indiana University, Bloomington, IN 47405, USA.

TUCEK, Rene; Singer (baritone); b. 8 Jan. 1936, Plzeň, Czechoslovakia. *Education:* Studied in Plzeň with M. Gartnerova and in Vienna with F. Schuch-Tovini. *Career:* Debut: Brno 1960, as Count Luna in Il Trovatore; Sang first in Brno, Plzeň and Ceske Budejovice; Prague National Theatre from 1971, in the standard repertory and in operas Prokofiev, Martinů, Gershwin and Myslivicek; Guest appearances in Spain, Austria, Bulgaria, Luxembourg and Cuba; Has sung in concert and in song recitals; Teacher at the Prague Conservatory from 1973. *Recordings:* The Jacobin by Dvořák and operas by Smetana. *Address:* c/o National Theatre, PO Box 865, 112 30 Prague 1, Czech Republic.

TUCKER, Mark; Singer (tenor); b. 10 Aug. 1958, England. *Education:* Studied at Cambridge and the Guildhall School of Music and Drama. *Career:* Active as concert and opera singer throughout Europe under such conductors as Michel Corboz, John Eliot Gardiner, Ton Koopman, Roger Norrington and Sigiswald Kuijken; Appearances at the Salzburg Festival in Monteverdi's Vespers of 1610 under Harnoncourt and under John Eliot Gardiner at St Mark's in Venice; Other notable concert engagements have included a tour of China with the Academy of London singing Les Illuminations, 1994; Operatic engagements include notably the title role in Monteverdi's Orfeo at the Bruges Festival and at the

Arena di Verona, at the Liceu, Barcelona in 1993 and at the Palazzo Ducale, Mantua; Has also sung productions of Monteverdi's Il ritorno d'Ulisse in patria and L'incoronazione di Poppea in Amsterdam, New York, and on tour in Italy, 1993; In addition has sung numerous tenor roles, Tom Rakewell (The Rake's Progress), in a new production for Opera Factory, 1994 and Lysander (A Midsummer Night's Dream) in Turin, 1995; Royal Opera, Covent Garden debut in 1995 as The Novice (Billy Budd); Highlights in 1995 included Gomatz (Zaide) at La Monnaie, in Strasbourg and in Kolmar, a tour of the Netherlands with the Niuew Sinfonietta Amsterdam under Mark Wigglesworth singing Les Illuminations; 1996 included a return to Netherlands Opera (Il ritorno d'Ulisse in patria), Messiah in Marseille and a performance of Elijah at the Proms; Season 1997 with Judas Maccabaeus in Vienna and Ravel's L'Enfant with the London Symphony Orchestra; Sang Marzio in Mozart's Mitridate at the Paris Châtelet and Ecclitico in Haydn's Il mondo della luna, 2000. *Recordings include:* Fennimore and Gerda by Delius (1997). *Current Management:* Harrison/Parrott Ltd, 12 Penzance Place, London, W11 4PA, England. *Telephone:* (20) 7229 9166. *Fax:* (20) 7221 5042. *Website:* www.harrisonparrott.com.

TUCKWELL, Barry (Emmanuel); Horn player and Conductor; b. 5 March 1931, Melbourne, Australia. *Education:* Studied at the Sydney Conservatorium. *Career:* Principal horn of the London Symphony Orchestra 1955–68; formed Tuckwell Wind Quintet 1968 and played with London Sinfonietta in modern repertory: Thea Musgrave, Iain Hamilton and Don Banks have written works for him; premiered Oliver Knussen's Concerto at Tokyo, 1994; season 1994/5 included concerts with the London Symphony and Hallé Orchestras, Saint Louis Symphony and orchestras in Germany, France and Netherlands; Music Director of the Maryland Symphony and guest conductor of the Northern Sinfonia from 1992. *Recordings include:* Concerto by Robin Holloway; Mozart with the Philharmonia and Strauss with the Royal Philharmonic. *Honours:* Order of the British Empire, 1965. *Address:* Northern Sinfonia, Sinfonia Centre, 41 Jesmond Vale, Newcastle, NE1 1PG.

TULACEK, Thomas; Violinist; b. 26 April 1955, Prague. *Education:* Studied at the Prague Conservatory, the Prague Academy of Musical Arts and the Guildhall School of Music. *Career:* First Violin Section, BBC Scottish Symphony Orchestra, 1985–89; Leader, New Chamber Orchestra, Oxford, 1990–; Associate Professor, Trinity College of Music, London, 1991; Recital work has taken him to countries such as Italy, Switzerland, France, Israel and the Czech Republic and has recorded for Czech Radio and Radio Vatican; Since 1990 has been performing regularly with the English pianist Steven Wray and they have formed a piano trio with Jaroslav Ondracek; Concerto performances have included works by Prokofiev, Bruch, Haydn, Mozart and most recently Nielsen, with the Teplice Symphony Orchestra, in the Czech Republic. *Address:* 1 Brookes Court, Longley Road, London SW17 9LF, England.

TUMA, Jaroslav; Czech organist; b. 1956. *Education:* Prague Academy of Arts with Milan Sleehta and Zuzana Ruzicková, summer school at Haarlem, Netherlands with Hans Haselböck, studied improvisation and Bach interpretation with Piet Kee. *Career:* Laureate of organ competitions in Prague, Linz, Leipzig, Nuremberg and Haarlem; Festival appearances by Nuremberg, Linz, Prague and Mechelen; Engagements in Europe, Japan and the USA; Concerts with Czech Philharmonic Orchestra, Three years cycle of complete organ works by J. S. Bach in Prague; Repertoire includes works by Bach, Franck, Liszt, Reger, Hoffhaimer, Sweelinck, Isaac and Husa; Accompanies major soloists on the harpsichord. *Recordings:* L. and H. Hassler, Muffat; Handel; Series organs of Bohema I–IV, Czech compositions for harpsichord. *Current Management:* Bohemia-Concert, PO Box 5, 100 05 Prague, Czech Republic. *Address:* c/o Prague Academy of Arts, Dominumilc, Alsovo náb e i 12, 110100 Prague 1, Czech Republic.

TUMAGIAN, Eduard; Singer (Baritone); b. 1944, Bucharest, Romania. *Career:* Sang at Bucharest from 1968 as Papageno, Alfonso, Mozart's Count, and Wolfram in Tannhäuser; Opéra du Rhin Strasbourg from 1974, as Germont, Iago, Enrico in Lucia di Lammermoor, Scarpia, Marcello, Belcore, Escamillo and Eugene Onegin; Guest appearances at Lyon, Stuttgart, Karlsruhe and Orange; Sang Rigoletto at Basle 1981 and appeared further with Welsh and English National operas, Frankfurt (Renato 1983), Nice (I Puritani and Vespri Sicilaini (Montfort), I Due Foscari and Riccardo III by Flavio Testi; Paris Opéra 1985, as Germont; US debut 1986 at Pittsburgh as Don Carlo in La Forza del Destino; Carnegie Hall New York in concert performances of Béatrice et Bénédict and Nabucco; Recent appearances at the Deutsche Oper Berlin, Staatsoper Hamburg, Vienna Staatsoper (Scarpia in season 1988–89), Toulouse (La Franciulla del West) and Oviedo Festival (Simon Boccanegra and La Favorita); Season 1991 as Nabucco at Trieste and Buenos Aires, Rigoletto at Philadelphia; Sang Vaudémont in Iolanta and Verdi's Germont at Orange and Baltimore, 1999; Concert repertoire includes music by Bach, Handel, Beethoven, Mussorgsky, Britten and Shostakovich (14th Symphony at the 1984 Salzburg

Festival). *Recordings include:* Miller in video of Luisa Miller from Opéra de Lyon; Napoleon in War and Peace; Turandot.

TUMANYAN, Barseg; Singer (bass baritone); b. 1958, Jerevan, Armenia. *Education:* Studied at the Komitas Conservatoire and at La Scala, Milan; Further study with Evgeny Nesterenko at the Moscow Conservatoire, 1985. *Career:* Sang with the Spenderian Opera (Armenia) from 1980; Performances of Basilio at the Teatro San Carlo Naples 1988; Appeared in Gala Concert for Armenia at Covent Garden 1989, and invited back to sing in La Bohème, Les Contes d'Hoffmann and Carmen; US debut with Boston Opera as Ramfis in Aida, 1989; Appearances in USA, 1989 with the Armenian State Opera; Sang Colline in La Bohème at Covent Garden and Monte Carlo, 1990; King Philip in Don Carlos at Los Angeles; Wigmore Hall recital, June 1990; Sang Moser in I. Masnadieri with the Royal Opera, 1998; Sang Ramphis in Aida at Dublin, and Gounod's Mephisto at Lyon, 2000. *Honours:* Prizewinner, Bussetto Competition, 1983; 2nd Prize, Tchaikovsky Competition, Moscow 1986; Joint First Prize, Rio de Janeiro Competition, 1987. *Current Management:* Askonas Holt Ltd, Lonsdale Chambers, 27 Chancery Lane, London, WC2A 1PF, England. *Telephone:* (20) 7400-1700. *Fax:* (20) 7400-1799. *E-mail:* info@askonasholt.co.uk. *Website:* www.askonasholt.co.uk.

TUNLEY, David (Evatt); Emeritus Professor of Music; b. 3 May 1930, Sydney, New South Wales, Australia; m. Paula Patricia Laurantus, 26 May 1959, one s., two d. *Education:* Diploma, New South Wales State Conservatorium of Music, 1949–51; BMus, University of Durham, England, 1957; MMus, 1963, DLitt, 1970, University of Western Australia. *Career:* Music Master, Fort Street Boys High School, Sydney, 1952–57; University of Western Australia, 1958–; Emeritus Professor of Music. *Compositions:* Concerto for Clarinet and Strings, recorded. *Publications:* Monographs: The 18th Century French Cantata, 1974, 1997; Couperin, 1982; Harmony in Action, 1984; The French Cantata Facsimile, 17 vols, 1990–91; Romantic French Song 1830–1870, 6 vols, 1994–95; The Bel Canto Violin: The Life and Times of Alfredo Campoli 1906–1991, 1999; Salons, Singers and songs: A Background to Romantic French Song 1830–70, 2001; François Couperin and 'The Perfection of Music, 2004. *Contributions:* New Grove Dictionary; New Oxford History of Music, vols 6 and 9. *Honours:* Honorary D.Mus, University of Western Australia, 2001. *Address:* 100 Dalkeith Road, Nedlands, Western Australia 6009, Australia. *E-mail:* dtunley@eyllene.uwa.edu.au.

TUNNELL, Jonathon; Cellist; b. 1955, England. *Career:* Debut: Wigmore Hall, 1984, with Peter Pears; Member of the Tunnell Trio; Co-founded the Brindisi String Quartet at Aldeburgh 1984; Concerts in a wide repertory throughout the United Kingdom and in France, Germany, Spain, Italy and Switzerland; Festival engagements at Aldeburgh (residency 1990), Arundel, Bath, Brighton, Huddersfield, Norwich and Warwick; First London performance of Colin Matthews's 2nd Quartet, 1990, premiere of David Matthews's 6th Quartet 1991; Quartet by Mark Anthony Turnage 1992; Many BBC recitals and resident artist with the University of Ulster. *Recordings include:* Quartets by Britten, Bridge and Imogen Holst; Works by Pierné and Lekeu. *Honours:* Prizewinner, Third Banff International String Quartet Competition in Canada, 1989, with Brindisi Quartet. *Address:* c/o Owen-White Management, 14 Nightingale Lane, London N8 7QU, England.

TUOMELA, Tapio (Juhani); Composer and Conductor; b. 11 Oct. 1958, Kuusamo, Finland; m. Helena Tuovinen, 7 Sept 1985, 3 d. *Education:* Diplomas: Piano, 1982, Orchestra Conducting, 1987, Sibelius Academy, Helsinki; MMus in Composition, Eastman School of Music, Rochester, New York, USA, 1990. *Career:* Debut: Concert of own compositions, Helsinki Festival, 1991; Performances of own works: UNM Festivals (Young Scandinavian Composers), 1985–89; Scandinavian Music Days, 1990, 1994, 1996; Time of Music Festival, Viitasaari, 1993, 1997; Tampere Biennale, 1994, 1996; Performances in the USA, Germany, Russia, Hungary, Netherlands, all Scandinavian countries; Also active as a Conductor including numerous first performances in Scandinavia. *Compositions:* L'échelle de l'évasion for chamber orchestra, 1989; Symphony, 1991; The Ear's Tale, chamber opera (Finnish National Opera commission), 1993; Jokk for orchestra, 1995; Mirage for ensemble, 1997; Mothers and Daughters, Opera from the Kalevala, premiered 1999. *Recordings:* Symmetry, quintet; L'échelle de l'évasion; Conductor, world premiere recording of ballet music Maa, by K Saariaho and some late pieces for string orchestra by Sibelius, 1995. *Address:* Temppelikatu 14 A 12, 00100 Helsinki, Finland.

TURBAN, Ingolf; Violinist; b. 17 March 1964, Munich, Germany; m. Barbara Meier, 28 July 1994, 2 s. *Education:* Studied at the Munich Musikhochschule with Gerhart Hetzel and at Aspen, Colorado with Dorothy DeLay and Jens Ellerman. *Career:* Debut: Munich, 1986, with the Munich Philharmonic; National Symphony Orchestra, Washington DC, USA, 1991; Leader of the Munich Philharmonic, 1985–88; Solo career since 1988 in Europe, USA, Canada and Israel; Professor,

Stuttgart Musikhochschule, 1995–. *Compositions:* Cadenzas to numerous violin concertos; a Niccolò, for 5 violins, 1998. *Recordings:* Numerous including: World premieres, Paganini Caprices with piano accompaniment by Schumann; Hartmann Solo Sonatas and Suites; Ernst Pieces; Respighi with English Chamber Orchestra; Marek with the Philharmonia, London. *Current Management:* Art Productions, Marbachstrasse 19A 81369 Munich, Germany. *Address:* Nordstrasse 4, 82131 Stockdorf, Munich, Germany.

TURBET, Richard Beaumont, BA, MLitt; Librarian; b. 5 Feb. 1948, Ilford, England; m.; two s. *Education:* Bancroft's School, Woodford, Essex, Univ. Coll. London, Leeds Polytechnic, Aberdeen Univ. *Career:* trainee asst librarian, Dundee Univ. 1969–70; graduate teaching asst, Univ. of Calgary 1971–72; Asst Librarian, National Central Library 1972–74; Librarian, Prison Service Coll., Wakefield 1974–77; Asst Librarian, Aberdeen Univ. 1977–90, Sub-Librarian 1990–; Layclerk, Wakefield Cathedral 1976–77, Aberdeen Cathedral 1977–92; mem. Royal Musical Asscn, Int. Asscn of Music Libraries, British Music Soc., Viola da Gamba Soc., Friends of Cathedral Music. *Publications:* William Byrd: A guide to research 1987, Tudor Music: a research and information guide 1994, William Byrd: Lincoln's Greatest Composer 1993, 1999, Byrd Studies (ed with Alan Brown) 1992, Music Librarianship in the United Kingdom (ed) 2003; contrib. to sundry music books (Festschrift for O. W. Neighbour 1993), Aspects of British Song 1992, Branches of Literature and Music 2000, New Grove Dictionary of Music and Musicians (second edn), Oxford Dictionary of National Biography, over 100 articles in journals and British Catalogue of Music Periodicals. *Honours:* C. B. Oldman Prize 1994. *Address:* 140 Newburgh Road, Bridge of Don, Aberdeen, AB22 8QY, Scotland (home). *Telephone:* (1224) 704601 (home). *E-mail:* r.turbet@abdn.ac.uk (office).

TURCHI, Guido; Composer; b. 10 Nov. 1916, Rome, Italy. *Education:* Studied at the Rome Conservatory and with Pizzetti at the Accademia di Santa Cecilia. *Career:* Taught at the Rome Conservatory, Director, Parma and Florence Conservatories 1967–72; Artistic Director, Accademia Filarmonica Romana 1963–66, and Teatro Comunale Bologna, 1968–70; Artistic Director, Accademia di Santa Cecilia from 1972–75; Accademia Musicale Chigiana do Siena, 1978–88. *Compositions include:* Opera II buon soldato Svejk, La Scala Milan 1962; Trio for flute, clarinet and viola 1945; Invettiva for small chorus and 2 pianos 1946; Concerto for string orchestra 1948; Piccolo concerto notturno 1950; 3 Metamorfosi for orchestra 1970; Dedalo, ballet, Florence 1972; Dedica for flute 1972; Adagio for orchestra, 1983; Parabola for orchestra, 1993; Exil, for singers and chamber orchestra, 1996; Te Lucis Ante-Terminum, for chorus and string orchestra, 1988; 6 Bagatelles, for chamber orchestra, 1999; Fantasia, for string quintet, 1999; Choruses, songs and incidental music. *Recordings:* Exil, 1995; Fantasia, 1990; 6 Bagatelles, 1999. *Address:* Cannaregio 233, 30121 Venice, Italy.

TURCO, Enrico; Singer (Bass); b. 1962, Genoa, Italy. *Education:* Studied at the Accademia di Santa Cecilia, Rome. *Career:* Sang at first in concert and made stage debut in 1987, as King Philip in Don Carlos; Macerata Festival, 1991, as Leporello, and Frankfurt Alte Oper in a concert of Franchetti's Cristoforo Colombo; Guest appearances at La Scala, Turin, Parma and the Scottish Opera; Sang Capello in Bellini's Capuleti at Reggio Emilia, 1998. *Address:* c/o Teatro alla Scala, Via Filodrammatici 2, 20121 Milan, Italy.

TURETZKY, Bertram (Jay); Double Bass Player and Composer; b. 14 Feb. 1933, Norwich, Connecticut, USA. *Education:* Studied at the Hartt School of Music (graduated 1955), at New York University (musicology with Curt Sachs) and with David Walter; Further study at the University of Hartford, MM 1965. *Career:* Played double bass in various orchestras and ensembles; Solo debut at Judson Hall, New York, Oct 1064, with works by Donald Erb and Barney Childs; Novel performing techniques have been exploited by such composers as Donald Martino, Richard Felciano, Paul Chihara, Kenneth Gaburro, George Perle and Ben Johnston. *Compositions:* Collages I–IV 1976–81; Reflections on Ives and Whittier for double bass and tape 1979–81; In memoriam Charles Mingus 1979; Baku for tape 1980. *Publications include:* The Contemporary Contrabass 1974; Editions of double bass studies for the American String Teachers Association; Editor of series published by the University of California Press on contemporary performance techniques. *Address:* ASCAP, ASCAP Building, 1 Lincoln Plaza, New York, NY 10023, USA.

TURKOVIC, Milan; Austrian Bassoonist; b. 14 Sept. 1939, Zagreb, Yugoslavia. *Education:* Studied in Vienna. *Career:* Performed with the Philharmonia Hungarica, then soloist with the Bamber Symphony and member of the Bamberg Wind Quintet; Soloist with the Vienna Symphony from 1967, with freelance concert performances from 1984; Further concerts at the Salzburg Mozarteum and with Concentus Musicus at Vienna, under Harnoncourt; Created Helmut Eder's concerto in 1968 and with Helmut and Wolfgang Schulz formed the

Vienna Trio. *Address:* c/o Salzburg Mozarteum Orchestra, Erzbischof-Gebhardstrasse 10, 5020 Salzburg, Austria.

TURNAGE, Mark-Anthony; British composer; b. 10 June 1960, Corringham, Essex; s. of Roy Turnage and Patricia Knowles; m. 1st Susan Shaw 1989 (divorced 1990); m. 2nd Helen Reed 1992; two s. *Education:* Hassenbrook Comprehensive School, Palmers Sixth Form, Grays, Royal Coll. of Music with Oliver Knussen and John Lambert and Tanglewood, USA with Henze and Gunther Schuller. *Career:* studied composition at RCM with Oliver Knussen and John Lambert; Mendelssohn scholarship to study with Gunther Schuller and Hans Werner Henze in Tanglewood, USA 1983; first opera, Greek, premiered at first Munich Biennale 1988; Composer in Asscn with City of Birmingham Symphony Orchestra, composing three major works 1989–93; Composer in asscn with ENO 1995–99; Assoc. Composer in asscn with BBC Symphony Orchestra 2000–03; Momentum, BBC 3 composer weekend dedicated to his music, Barbican Hall, London 2003. *Compositions include:* Night Dances for orchestra 1980, Lament for a Hanging Man for soprano and ensemble 1983, Sarabande for soprano saxophone and piano 1985, On All Fours for chamber ensemble 1985, Release for eight players 1987, Greek opera in two acts 1987, Three Screaming Popes for orchestra 1988, Greek Suite for mezzo soprano, baritone and ensemble 1989, Kai for solo cello and ensemble 1989, Some Days 1989, Momentum for orchestra 1990, Killing Time television scena 1991, Drowned Out 1992, Your Rockaby saxophone concerto 1992, Blood on the Floor for large ensemble 1994, Dispelling the Fears 1994, Twice Through the Heart for mezzo and 16 players 1997, Country of the Blind 1997, Four-Horned Fandango 1997, The Silver Tassie opera in four acts 1997, Silent Cities for orchestra 1998, About Time for two orchestras 1999, Evening Songs for orchestra 2000, Another Set To for trombone and orchestra 2000, Fractured Lines for two percussionists and orchestra 2000, Scorched for jazz trio and orchestra (with John Scofield) 2000, On Opened Ground concerto for viola and orchestra 2000, Bass Inventions for double bass and ensemble 2001, The Torn Fields for orchestra 2001, Dark Crossing 2001, A Quick Blast 2001, The Game is Over for orchestra 2002. *Honours:* Guinness Prize for Composition 1982, Benjamin Britten Young Composers' Prize 1983, BMW Music Theatre Prize 1988, Laurence Olivier Award 2001. *Current Management:* Van Walsum Management Ltd, 4 Addison Bridge Place, London, W14 8XP, England. *Telephone:* (20) 7371-4343. *Fax:* (20) 7371-4344. *E-mail:* vwm@vanwalsum.co.uk (office). *Website:* www.vanwalsum.co.uk (office).

TURNER, Bruno; Choral Director; b. 7 Feb. 1931, London. *Education:* studied Gregorian chant and Renaissance choral music. *Career:* many performances of Medieval and Renaissance music, notably as Dir of Pro Cantione Antiqua; liturgical reconstruction of the Missa Tecum Principium by Robert Fayrfax, 1962; Iberian, English and Franco-Flemish choral music of the 15th and 16th centuries. *Recordings include:* albums of early choral music on various labels. *Publications include:* Mapa Mundi Editions. *Address:* Apdo 172, Garrucha 04630, Almeria, Spain. *E-mail:* bruno.t@freedom255.com.

TURNER, Charles (Lloyd); Musicologist, Bibliographer and Performer; b. 10 July 1948, Houston, Texas, USA. *Education:* BMus, 1970; MMus, 1976; MSLS, 1979, University of Texas; D.Mus, Indiana University, 1986. *Career:* Founding Director, La Primavera, Early Music Ensemble; Concert tours of Texas, California, Southwest USA; Tour of Mexico sponsored by US State Department; Musicologist, Director of Hartt Early Music Ensemble, Hartt School, University of Hartford. *Recordings:* Popular Elizabethan Music; The Greater Passion Play from Carmina Burana. *Publications:* Bibliographer, Medieval Music, 1986; The Isorhythmic Motet in Continental Europe, Proportion and Form, 1986; Articles in Journal of the Lute Society of America, Lute Society Quarterly, Journal of the American Musicological Society, Journal of the International Trumpet Guild, Early Music, Notes and Music Analysis; Reviews in Notes; Associate Editor,Notes 2001–03;. *Address:* Hartt School, University of Hartford, 200 Bloomfield Avenue, West Hartford, CT 06117, USA.

TURNER, Claramae; Singer (Contralto); b. 28 Oct. 1920, Dinuba, California, USA. *Education:* Studied with Nino Comel, Armando Angini and Giacomo Spadoni at San Francisco and with Dick Marzollo in New York. *Career:* Debut: San Francisco 1942, in Les Contes d'Hoffmann; Sang at the Metropolitan Opera 1946–50, notably as Amneris; Sang in the premieres of Menotti's The Medium (1946), The Tender Land by Copland (1954) and Bomarzo by Ginastera (1967); Teatro Liceo Barcelona 1957–58; Chicago Lyric Opera 1956, as Azucena; Sang Diego 1967, in the US premiere of Der junge Lord by Henze; Appearances in Buenos Aires, Mexico City, Venice, Monte Carlo, Boston, Dallas, Houston, Baltimore, Philadelphia and Pittsburgh. *Recordings:* Un Ballo in Maschera, conducted by Toscanini; Bomarzo.

TURNER, Jane; Singer (Mezzo Soprano); b. 1960, County Durham, England. *Education:* Guildhall School of Music; Opera Studio, London.

Career: West German debut as Wellgunde and Siegrune in The Ring at Bayreuth, 1984, as a Flower Maiden and Flosshilde; British Opera debut 1985 as Carmen with the Glyndebourne Tour; Flora in Peter Hall's production of Traviata at the Festival, 1987; Covent Garden debut 1987, as Ann Who Strips in the Hytner production of The King Goes Forth to France; returned as a Flower Maiden in Parsifal and as Flosshilde in Das Rheingold; English National Opera as Maddalena in Rigoletto and as Lola in Cavalleria Rusticana; Sang Siebel in Faust at Dublin, 1995. *Address:* c/o English National Opera, St Martin's Lane, London, WC2, England.

TURNER, Margarita; Singer (Soprano); b. 11 March 1943, Perth, Australia. *Education:* Studied in London and West Germany. *Career:* Debut: Krefeld 1969, as Micaela; Appearances in opera at Cologne, Saarbrucken, Wiesbaden and Wuppertal; 15 year career at the Essen Opera as Fiordiligi, Pamina, Marguerite, Martha, Marenka, Violetta, Marzelline (Fidelio), Mélisande, Eva, Concepcion and Nedda; Sophie in Der Rosenkavalier, Mimi, Liu, Rosalinde and Luise in Der Junge Lord by Henze; Frequent concert engagements; Teacher at the Essen Musikhochschule; Season 2000–01 at Essen, in Elektra, Faust and Jenůfa. *Address:* c/o Theater, Rolandstrasse 10, 4300 Essen, Germany.

TURNER, Paul; Composer; b. 16 April 1948, Morwell, Victoria, Australia. *Education:* BMus, 1977, Mus, 1980, University of Melbourne; Study with Barry Conyngham. *Career:* Composer-in-the-Community, Hamilton, Victoria, 1981; Faculty Member, University of Adelaide, 1987–92. *Compositions include:* Panels II for violin, clarinet and piano, 1974; Grand Pocket Sonata in B Minor for piano, 1986; Herbivores for piano, 1987; Sonata, for tape, 1994; A Spangled Pandemonium Escapes from the Zoo, for ensemble; Chronic Interludes I–III for saxophone and piano; Geraniums or Nasturtiums for saxophone and piano; Instrumental Rationality, for various combinations; Icarus Flying, for guitar or tape; Machines I–III for harp and tape; Phrygian Misery for saxophone and piano. *Address:* c/o APRA, 1A Eden Street, Crows Nest, NSW 2065, Australia.

TURNER, Robert; Composer; b. 6 June 1920, Montreal, Canada; m. 2 s., 1 d. *Education:* BMus, McGill University, 1943; D.Mus, 1953; Overseas scholar, Royal College, 1947–48; MMus, George Peabody College, 1950. *Career:* Music producer, Canadian Broadcasting Corp, Vancouver, 1952–68; Lecturer in Music, UBC, 1955–57; Assistant Professor, Music Acadia University, Wolfville, 1968–69; Professor, Composition, University of Manitoba, Winnipeg, 1969–1985; Professor Emeritus, Manitoba, 1985; Composer in residence, MacDowell Colony, Peterborough, NH, 1987; mem., Music Publishers of Canada; Canadian League of Composers; Canadian Music Centre. *Compositions:* 2 operas; 3 symphonies; 4 concertos; A Group of Seven for viola, reciter and orchestra; Johann's Gift to Christmas, for narrator and orchestra; The Third Day, Easter Cantata for soloists, chorus and orchestra; The River of Time for chorus and orchestra; Shades of Autumn, orchestra; Manitoba Memoir for strings, 1989; The Phoenix and the Turtle; Time for Three; and Four Last Songs; House of Shadows, 1994; Festival Dance, 1997; Diverti-memento, for chamber orchestra, 1997. *Recordings:* RCI Anthology of Canadian Music; Sonata for violin, piano; 5 Canadian Folksongs; Vestiges for piano. *Publications:* Opening Night, Theatre overture, 1960; String quartet no. 2, 1963; Eidolons, 1977; Chamber Concerto for bassoon and 17 instruments, 1977; Two Choral Pieces, 1990. *Honours:* Fellow, Canada Council, 1966–67; Mem. of the Order of Canada, 2003; Commemorative Medal for 125th Anniversary of Confed. of Canada, 1993; Queen's Golden Jubilee Award, 2003. *Address:* 1725 Beach Drive, Apt 465, Victoria, BC, V8R 6H9, Canada.

TURNOVSKY, Martin; Conductor; b. 29 Sept. 1928, Prague, Czechoslovakia. *Education:* Music Academy, Prague; Studied Conducting with Dedecek and Ančerl, Prague Academy of Music, 1948–52; Private studies in conducting with Szell, 1956. *Career:* Conductor, Czech Army Symphony Orchestra, 1955–60; State Philharmonic Orchestra, Brno, 1960–63; Music Director, Plzeň Radio Orchestra, 1963–66; Dresden State Opera and State Orchestra, 1966–68; Guest Conductor with numerous well-known orchestras including Radio Orchestra, Berlin; Cleveland Orchestra; New York Philharmonic Orchestra; Detroit Symphony Orchestra; Toronto Symphony; Stockholm Philharmonic Orchestra; BBC Northern Orchestra, Manchester 1968; Music Director, Norwegian Opera, Oslo 1975–80; Music Director, Bonn Opera, 1979–83; Opera engagements with the Deutsche Oper Berlin, Welsh National Opera, (British opera debut, Eugene Onegin, 1988); Staatsoper Stuttgart, Royal Opera Stockholm and the Savonlinna Festival, Finland; Season 1992/93 appointed as Music Director of the Prague Symphony Orchestra and conducted Otello and Un Ballo in Maschera at the Prague State Opera; American opera debut with Jenůfa at Cincinnati, 1998; Seattle Opera, Dvořák's Rusalka. *Recordings:* Has made many recordings for Supraphon including 4th Symphony of Bohuslav Martinů, Grand Prix du Disque 1968. *Honours:* Recipient, 1st Prize, International Competition for Conductors, Besancon, France 1958; Österreichisches Ehrenkreuz für Wissenschaft und Kuust 1.

Klasse. *Current Management:* G. Baron Management, Dornbacher Strasse 41/111/2, 1170 Vienna, Austria.

TUROK, Paul (Harris); Composer; b. 3 Dec. 1929, New York City, USA; m. Susan Kay Frucht, 24 Mar 1967. *Education:* BA, Queens College, 1950; MA, University of California, Berkeley, 1951; Special studies at Juilliard School of Music, 1951–53; MS, Baruch College, 1986. *Career:* Music Director, Experimental television, US Army, Augusta, GA, 1954; Music Director, KPFA, Berkeley, 1955–56; Lecturer, City College of New York, 1960–63; Visiting Professor, Williams College, 1964. *Compositions:* Operas: Richard III, A Secular Masque, Scene Domestic; Orchestral: American Variations, Chartres West, Ultima Thule, Great Scott!, Joplin Overture, Sousa Overture, Danza Viva, Concertos for Violin, English Horn, Trombone, Cello, Oboe, Symphony; Chamber Music: 4 String Quartets, English Horn Quintet, Sonatas for Flute, Bassoon, Horn, Trumpet, Viola, Cello, Harp, Harpsichord; Numerous other works; Organ: Toccata; Piano: Passacaglia, Transcendental Etudes; Brass: Elegy, Quintet; Vocal: Lanier Songs, Evocations, To Music, Three Popular Songs. *Address:* c/o G Schirmer Incorporated, 24 East 22nd Street, New York, NY 10010, USA.

TURPIN, Kathryn; Singer (Mezzo-soprano); b. 1968, England. *Education:* History of Art, New Hall, Cambridge; Opera School, Royal College of Music; Samling Foundation; Welsh Arts Council Scholar. *Career:* Lady de Hautdesert in Birtwistle's Gawain at the Royal Opera House; Margaretha in Schumann's Genoveva at Garsington; Bizet's Djamileh at Cap Ferrat; Lucretia in The Rape of Lucretia for Music Theatre Wales; Carmen at the Festival de la Vezère; Cherubino at Neuchâtel; Ulisse in Deidamia, London Handel Society; Madame Popova in The Bear at Cambridge; Conductors worked for include Simon Rattle, Neville Marriner, David Willcocks, Elgar Howarth, Matthew Best and Martyn Brabbins; Orchestras include CBSO, Orchestra of the Age of Enlightenment, London Sinfonietta, Bournemouth Sinfonietta, London Mozart Players, Hanover Band, Orchestre National de Lille, Orchestre de Besançon, National Youth Orchestra of Wales, Academy of St Martin in the Fields. *Recordings:* In The Beginning, Copland, with the Choir of St John's College, Cambridge; Duruflé Requiem; Broadcasts for BBC Radio 3 and Classic FM. *Address:* 109 Sugden Road, London SW11 5 ED, England.

TURSKA, Joanna (Lucja); Flautist; b. 16 Oct. 1958, Warsaw, Poland; m. Roman Siczek, 28 June 1986, 1 d. *Education:* MMus, Flute Performance, Warsaw Academy of Music; Postgraduate Studies; Royal Conservatory, The Hague, Netherlands; Conservatories in Creteil and Paris, France; Teachers include E Gajewska, F Vester, A Marion (flute), S T Preston, P Sechet (baroque flute). *Career:* Appearances at recitals, chamber music concerts and as soloist with orchestras in Europe and America including: Germany, France, Italy, Switzerland, Austria, Netherlands, Belgium, Luxembourg, Poland, Cuba, USA; Performances at such festivals as Paris, Youth Music Festival (Bayreuth, Germany), Warsaw Autumn, New Music Festival and Early Music Festival (Chicago, USA). *Recordings:* Solo, chamber music and orchestral performances recorded by Polish radio and television, Belgian radio, French radio, and US radio, television Classical and ethnic channels; Album for winners of Premio Ancona competitions. *Address:* 1426 Portsmouth, Westchester, IL 60153, USA.

TUSA, Andrew; singer (tenor); b. 1966, England. *Education:* New College, Oxford, Pears-Britten School. *Career:* sang in the Play of Daniel at the Queen Elizabeth Hall 1989, followed by Asterion in Rameau's Nais for the English Bach Festival; Concert engagements include Messiah with the Leicester Bach Choir, St John Passion in Krefeld, soloist with Gothic Voices in Milan and Second Shepherd in Monteverdi's Orfeo at the 1990 Salzburg Festival; Appearances with the Gabrieli and Taverner Consorts, Christmas Oratorio under Andrew Parrott in Oslo, Masses by Mozart in Barbican Hall, 1991, St Matthew Passion with Birmingham Bach Society and Messiah with the Stavanger Symphony in Norway. *Recordings include:* Mozart's Salzburg Masses with the Winchester College Choir and Monteverdi Madrigals with I Fagiolini. *Current Management:* Robert Gilder & Co., Enterprise House, 59–65 Upper Ground, London, SE1 9PQ, England. *Telephone:* (20) 7928-9008. *Fax:* (20) 7928-9755. *E-mail:* rgilder@robert-gilder.com.

TUTINO, Marco; Composer; b. 30 May 1954, Milan, Italy. *Education:* Studied at the Giuseppe Verdi Conservatory, Milan. *Career:* Works performed at the 1976 Gaudeamus Festival in Amsterdam; Operas produced in Genoa, Alessandria, Livorno and Modena. *Compositions:* A synthesis between 19th century procedures and more modern methods. *Compositions include:* Operas Pinnochio, Genoa 1985; Cirano, commedia lirica, Alessandria 1987; La lupa, Livorno 1990; Le vite immaginarie, chamber opera, Modena 1990. *Address:* c/o Sezione Musica, Viale della Letteratura n.30, 00144 Roma (EUR), Italy.

TUVÅS, Linda; Singer (Soprano); b. 1972, Stockholm, Sweden. *Education:* Studied at Stockholm University, the Birkagarden School of Music

and the Guildhall School, London. *Career:* Engagements as Mozart's Donna Anna and Fatima in Grétry's Zémire et Azor at Drottningholm and the Théâtre Champs-Elysées, Paris; Kate Pinkerton, Jano in Jenůfa and Micaela (Carmen) for Gothenburg Opera; Further roles as Musetta for Welsh National Opera, Tatiana for British Youth Opera and the title role in Il Segretto di Susanna for Newbury Opera; Also sings Massenet's Grisélidis, Arminda in La Finta Giardiniera by Mozart, and Offenbach's Giulietta; Sang Barbarina in Le nozze de Figaro at the 1997 Glyndebourne Festival; Season 1998 as Amor in Poppea for WNO, Varvara (Katya Kabanova) for the Glyndebourne Opera. *Address:* c/o Neil Dalrymple, Music International, 13 Ardilaun Road, London N5 2QR, England.

TWARDOWSKI, Romuald; Composer; b. 17 June 1930, Wilno, Poland; m. Alice Stradczuk, 16 June 1981, 1 s. *Education:* Diplomas, Composition and Piano, Wilno Conservatory, 1957; Diploma, Composition, Higher School of Music, Warsaw; Postgraduate studies, Nadia Boulanger, Paris, 1963. *Career:* Professor, Academy of Music, Warsaw. *Compositions:* Operas including: Cyrano de Bergerac, 1963; Tragedy, 1969; Lord Jim, 1976; Maria Stuart, 1979; Story of St Catherine, 1985; Also numerous works for orchestra, choirs, theatre, cinema, most recent include: Old Polish Concerto for strings; Little Concerto for vocal orchestra; Michelangelo Sonnets for baritone and piano; Lithuanian Variations for winds/quartet, all 1988; Niggunim, for violin and orchestra, 1991. *Recordings include:* Gershwin, Variations for symphony orchestra, Polish Radio, Kraków, 1980; Spanish Fantasy for cello and orchestra, Polish Radio, Warsaw; Alleluia for mixed choir, 1990; Espressioni for violin and piano, 1990; Niggunim, chassidim tunes for violin and piano or orchestra; Numerous recordings, own compositions. *Address:* ul Miaczynska 54 m 61, 02-637 Warsaw, Poland.

TYL, Noel; Singer (Baritone); b. 31 Dec. 1936, West Chester, Pennsylvania, USA. *Career:* Studied with Gibner King in New York. *Address:* New York City Opera, Lincoln Center, New York, NY 10023, USA.

TYLER, James; Lutenist and Viol Player; b. 3 Aug. 1940, Hartford, CT, USA. *Education:* Hartt College of Music. *Career:* Debut: New York Pro Musica, 1962; Appearances with early music ensembles in USA and Europe, including Studio der Frühen Musik, Munich; Early Music Consort, London, and Musica Reservata from 1969; Co-founded the Consort of Musicke and was co-director until 1972; Julian Bream Consort, 1974–; Founded London Early Music Group 1976, with performances of Renaissance Music, Director of Early Music Program at UCLA, from 1986. *Publications include:* The Early Guitar, 1980; A Brief Tutor for the Baroque Guitar, 1984; Edition, Gasparo Xanetti's II scolaro, 1984; Mixed ensembles, in A Performer's Guide to Renaissance Music, 1994. *Address:* c/o Early Music Program, University of California LA, 5151 State University Drive, Los Angeles, CA 90032, USA.

TYLER, Marilyn; Singer (soprano); b. 6 Dec. 1928, New York, NY, USA. *Education:* studied with Friedrich Schorr in New York and with Toti dal Monte in Venice. *Career:* sang first in operetta; Basle Opera 1948; Netherlands Opera 1955, as Violetta; sang title role in Die Entführung; Bayreuth; Bayreuth 1961, Brünnhilde in Die Walküre; appearances in Italy, Germany, North America and Israel. *Recordings include:* Die Zauberflote, Die Entführung, Serse by Handel, Stravinsky's Pulcinella.

TYNAN, Kathleen; Soprano; b. 1960, Ireland. *Education:* Royal Irish Academy of Music, Dublin; Guildhall School of Music and Drama, London. *Career:* Selected by RTE, representative Ireland, Cardiff Singer of the World Competition, 1987; Sang for Opera Theatre Company, Expo '98, Lisbon; Cork Opera House; Performed songs with pianist Dearbhla Collins and Irish Piano Trio in recitals, Theatre Royal, Wexford, Belfast Waterfront Hall, RHA Gallery, Dublin, Boyle Arts Festival, St James's, Picadilly; New work for voice and electronics by Fergus Johnston, 2000; Opera Ireland; Wexford Festival Opera; RTE television production Riders to the Sea; Opera South, Cork; Olympia Theatre, Dublin; Opera Theatre Company, Dublin; Queen Elizabeth Hall, London; Toured France; Bermuda Festival for MidSummer Opera; Sang Marzelline for new adaptation in English, Zulu and Afrikaans, Broomhill Opera/Opera Africa, with Northern Sinfonia; Toured the United Kingdom extensively; Extensive concert and song recital; London Festival orchestra; St John's Smith Square; Liverpool Cathedral Festival; National Symphony Orchestra, Ireland; Concerts with RTE Concert Orchestra; Presented recitals for music network, Ireland; Broadcasts for BBC Radio Ulster. *Recordings:* Debut CD, Romancing Rebellion. *Address:* 63 Dominic Street, Shandon, Ireland.

TYNES, Margaret; Singer (Soprano); b. 11 Sept. 1929, Saluda, Virginia, USA. *Education:* Studied with Emil Cooper in New York and with Tullio Serafin in Italy. *Career:* Debut: New York City Opera 1952, as Fata Morgana in The Love for Three Oranges; Montreal 1959, as Lady Macbeth; Has sung in Spoleto (as Salome), Vienna, Budapest, Toronto, Milan, Prague, Naples and Bologna; Metropolitan Opera debut 1973, as Jenůfa; Other roles have included Norma, Aida, Desdemona, Dido and Marie in Wozzeck; Many concert appearances.

TYREN, Arne; Singer (Bass-Baritone); b. 27 Feb. 1928, Stockholm, Sweden. *Education:* Studied with Ragnar Hulten at the Stockholm Opera School. *Career:* Debut: Royal Opera Stockholm 1955, as Bartolo in Le Nozze di Figaro; Has sung in Scandinavia as Leporello, Baron Ochs, the Grand Inquisitor, Sarastro and Wozzeck; Drottningholm Festival from 1955, as Bartolo in Paisiello's Il Barbiere di Siviglia, Don Alfonso, Il Maestro di Capella, Buonafede in Haydn's Il Mondo della luna and Seneca in L'Incoronazione di Poppea; Sang at Stockholm in the premieres of Blomdahl's Aniara (1959) and Herr von Hancken (1965) and Tintomara by Werle (1973); Edinburgh Festival 1959, Wozzeck; Further engagements in Hamburg, Cologne, Turin, Lisbon and Tel-Aviv; Director of the Stockholm Opera School from 1977. *Recordings include:* Aniara (Columbia). *Honours:* Swedish Court Singer 1978. *Address:* Opera School, Kungliga Teatern, PO Box 16094, 10322, Stockholm, Sweden.

TYRRELL, John; Musicologist; b. 17 Aug. 1942, Salisbury, Southern Rhodesia. *Education:* BMus, University of Cape Town, 1963; Oxford. *Career:* Former associate editor of the Musical Times; Editorial staff, New Grove Dictionary of Music until 1980; Lecturer, Nottingham University 1976, Reader in Opera Studies 1989; Executive Editor, The New Grove Dictionary of Music and Musicians, 2nd edition, 1996–2001; Professorial Research Fellow at Cardiff University in 2000; Professor, School of Music, Cardiff University, 2003. *Publications include:* Leoš Janáček: Kát'a Kabanová, 1982; Czech Opera, 1988, Czech edition, 1992; Janáček's Operas: A Documentary Account, 1992; Intimate Letters: Leoš Janáček to Kamila Stösslová (Ed and Translator), 1994; Leoš Janáček: Jenůfa (Brno Version 1908), (Co-ed.) 1996; Janáček's Works: A Catalogue of the Music and Writings of Leoš Janáček, (Co-author), 1997; My Life with Janáček: The Memoirs of Zdenka Janáčková (Ed and Translator), 1998. *Honours:* Hon. Doctorate, Masaryk Univ. of Brno, 2002. *Address:* School of Music, University of Cardiff, 31 Corbett Road, Cardiff CF1 3EB, England.

TYRRELL, Lisa (Jane); Soprano; b. 7 June 1967, Salford. *Education:* Chetham's School of Music, Manchester: Entered as a singer aged 11 years, 2nd study, piano; Drama, Guildhall School of Music, London; Banff Centre, School of Fine Arts, Canada. *Career:* Debut: Pamina in Die Zauberflöte, English Touring Opera, 1990; Zerlina in Don Giovanni with the English Touring Opera; Lace Seller in Death in Venice at Glyndebourne Festival Opera; Semire in Les Boreádes, Birmingham Touring Opera; Judith in European Story, Garden Venture (Covent Garden); Naiad in Ariadne auf Naxos, Garsington Opera; Euridice in Orfeo, Scottish Opera-go-Round; Debut at the Welsh National Opera in The Doctor of Myddfai; as the Child, a new opera written by Peter Maxwell Davies; Debut at the Royal Opera, Covent Garden as Barbarina in The Marriage of Figaro; Concerts include: St John Passion in Salzburg, Handel's Messiah in St John's Smith Square; Concerts with Fretwork at St John's; Monteverdi Vespers; Ariadne auf Naxos at Endellion Festival, with Richard Hickox; Vivaldi's Gloria at St Paul's Cathedral and Brazil; Brahms' Requiem; The Fairy Queen, ENO Bayliss Programme; New commission by Peter Maxwell Davies, with Scottish Chamber Orchestra, 1997; Janáček's Vixen with City of Birmingham Touring Opera, 1998. *Honours:* Associate (with distinction) of G S M D, 1989; Wyburd Trust Award (for advanced lieder study), 1990; Wingate Scholar, 1996; Channel 4 at G S M D; Also BBC Film with Peter Skellern, Where Do We Go From Here, following students of Chetham's. *Address:* c/o Music International, 13 Ardilaun Road, London, N5 2QR, England.

TZINCOCA, Remus; Conductor and Composer; b. 1920, Iassy, Romania; m. Anisia Campos. *Education:* Iassy Conservatory of Music, Conservatoire National Superieur de Musique de Paris; disciple and musical assistant of George Enescu. *Career:* debut, led Colonne Orchestra with George Enescu as soloist, Paris; Conducted major orchestras in Europe and North America including: London Philharmonic, Zürich Tonhalle, Lamoureux, Pasdeloup and Colonne in Paris, Radiotelevision Francaise, New York Philharmonic, Cleveland Orchestra, CBC Orchestra, Bucharest Philharmonic; Radio Television and Bucharest Opera; Founder, Musical Director, Newport Music Festival, Rhode Island, USA; Founder, Musical Director, New York Orchestra da Camera, with concerts at Metropolitan Museum, Carnegie Hall and Town Hall; Discovered with Anisia Campos, original version, in Romanian, of Bartók's Cantata Profana, in New York Bartók Archives and gave premiere in Bucharest with the Philharmonic Orchestra, 1984. *Compositions:* oratorios, symphonies, lieder and a Byzantine Mass. *Address:* 632 Avenue Herve-Beaudry, Laval, QC H7E 2X6, Canada.

U

UCHIDA, Mitsuko; Japanese pianist; *Artist-in-Residence, Cleveland Orchestra*; b. 20 Dec. 1948, Tokyo; d. of Fujio Uchida and Yasuko Uchida. *Education:* Vienna Acad. of Music with Prof. R. Hauser. *Career:* debut Vienna 1963; Co-Dir Marlboro Music Festival; Artist-in-Residence, Cleveland Orchestra 2002–. *Performances:* recitals and concerto performances with all maj. London orchestras, Chicago Symphony, Boston Symphony, Cleveland Orchestra, Berlin Philharmonic, Vienna Philharmonic, New York Philharmonic, LA Philharmonic and others; played and directed the cycle of 21 Mozart piano concertos with the English Chamber Orchestra in London 1985–86; gave US premiere of piano concerto Antiphonies by Harrison Birtwistle 1996; Perspectives recital series at Carnegie Hall 2003. *Recordings include:* Mozart Complete Piano Sonatas and 21 Piano Concertos (English Chamber Orchestra and Jeffrey Tate), Chopin Piano Sonatas, Debussy 12 Etudes, Schubert Piano Sonatas, Beethoven Piano Concertos, Schoenberg Piano Concerto. *Honours:* Hon. CBE 2001; First Prize Beethoven Competition Vienna 1969, Second Prize Chopin Competition Warsaw 1970, Second Prize Leeds Competition 1975, Gramophone Award (Mozart Piano Sonatas) 1989, Gramophone Award (Schoenberg Piano Concerto) 2001. *Current Management:* Van Walsum Management Ltd, 4 Addison Bridge Place, London, W14 8XP, England. *Telephone:* (20) 7371-4343 (office). *Fax:* (20) 7371-4344 (office). *E-mail:* chouse@vanwalsum.com (office).

UDAGAWA, Hideko; Violinist; b. 1960, Japan. *Education:* Tokyo University of Arts; Studied with Milstein, London and Juilliard School of Music, New York. *Career:* Debut: At age 15; Television appearances and radio broadcasts, Europe; Concerts in USA, many European countries; Recitals, Queen Elizabeth Hall; Lincoln Center; Concerto performances with London Symphony Orchestra, the Philharmonia, the Royal, London and Liverpool Philharmonics, the City of Birmingham Symphony, the English Chamber and the Polish Chamber Orchestras; Toured the United Kingdom and Ireland with Berlin Symphony and the Bucharest Philharmonic Orchestra. *Recordings:* Virtuoso violin pieces for EMI Japan; Heifetz Transcriptions for ASV; Brahms and Bruch Concertos with Charles Mackerras and London Symphony for Chandos.

UDALOVA, Irina; Singer (Soprano); b. 1957, Nikolaevsk na, Amur, Russia. *Education:* Studied at the Kishinev Conservatory. *Career:* Sang in opera at Aschchabad, Turkmenistan, notably as Tatiana, Iolanta, Amelia (Ballo in Maschera) and Nedda; Bolshoi Opera, Moscow, from 1985, as Militrissa in The Tale of Tsar Sultan, and Tchaikovsky's Lisa and Maid of Orleans; Guest with the Bolshoi at Glasgow 1990 and elsewhere as Voyslada in Rimsky's Mlada. *Recordings include:* Judith by Serov (Melodya). *Address:* c/o Bolshoi Theatre, 103009 Moscow, Russia.

UGORSKI, Anatol; Pianist; b. 28 Sept. 1942, Leningrad, Russia. *Education:* Studied at the Leningrad Conservatoire. *Career:* From 1962 has given many concerts and recitals, including works by Boulez, Messiaen, Berg and Schoenberg; Teacher at the Leningrad Conservatoire from 1982, Resident in Germany, 1990.

UHLIK, Tomislav; Composer and Conductor; b. 24 Oct. 1956, Zagreb, Croatia; m. Lidija; one s. one d. *Education:* Theory of Music, 1981, Conducting, 1989, Zagreb Music Acad. *Career:* Music Dir, Lado Folklore Ensemble, 1983–85; Conductor, Komedija Theatre, Zagreb, 1992–; regular guest conductor of the symphonic wind orchestra of the Croatian army; mem., Croatian Composers' Asscn. *Compositions:* Six Episodes for Wind Quintet, 1986; The Body of Our Lord (liturgical cantata for folk choir and tambouras), 1990; Divertimento for Strings, 1991; Melancholy Variations for Harp Solo, 1991; Don Quixote and Dulcinea, for cello and double bass; Concerto for Horn and Wind Orchestra, 1997. *Honours:* First Prize for the Nocturne, for mixed choir a cappella, Matetic Days Festival in Ronjgi, 1988; Croatian Ministry of Culture Award, for Hymne for Soprano and Orchestra. *Address:* 10010 Zagreb, Varicakova 4, Croatia.

UHRMACHER, Hildegard; singer (soprano); b. 15 Dec. 1939, Mönchen Gladbach, Germany. *Education:* Studied in Waldniel and Düsseldorf. *Career:* debut, Deutsche Oper am Rhein, 1964, as Vespina in Haydn's L'Infedeltà delusa; Sang at Kassel Opera, 1967–73, Hamburg from 1974, Munich, 1970–78; Further appearances at Vienna, Amsterdam, Florence and Cardiff; Staatsoper Stuttgart, 1981–89; Roles have included Salome, The Queen of Night, Constanze, Zerbinetta, Gilda, Traviata, Musetta and Flotow's Martha; Düsseldorf, 1995, as Hanna Glawari and Mannheim, 1996 in Amandas Traum by Harold Weiss; Modern repertoire also includes Zimmermann's Die Soldaten (Hanover, 1989) and works by Dessau and Britten.

ULBRICH, Andrea (Edina); Singer (Mezzo-soprano); b. 1964, Budapest, Hungary. *Education:* Studied at the Budapest Music Academy. *Career:* Has sung with the Hungarian National Opera at Budapest from 1988,

notably as Nicklausse in Les Contes d'Hoffmann, Sextus in Clemenza di Tito, Mercédès in Carmen and as Flotow's Nancy; Frankfurt, 1991, in a concert of Franchetti's Cristoforo Colombo; Guest at Ludwigshafen, 1992, as Cherubino; Dorabella (Così fan tutte), Olga (Onegin), Judith (Bluebeard's Castle), Octavian (Der Rosenkavalier), Rosina (Barber of Seville), Dryad (Ariadne auf Naxos), Priestess (Aida), Mirinda in Cavalli's Ormindo, Angelina (La Cenerentola), Lolette (La Rondine-Puccini) and others; Guest at Deutsche Oper Berlin, Oper Frankfurt, Brüssel, Klagenfurt, Wiener Konzerthaus, appearing as Amneris in Verdi's Aida, Eboli in Verdi's Don Carlos, Cuniza in Verdi's Oberto and Melibea in Rossini's Il Viaggio a Leims; Has sung with the Deutsche Operam Rhein from 1996. *Recordings include:* La Canterina, Haydn; Donizetti and Rossini songs and duets; Opera Gala, Berlin; Die Hochzeit des Camacho, Mendelssohn; Serenata, Scarlatti. *Honours:* Prizewinner at the Dvořák Competition, Prague and Paris competition; Belvedere Competition, Vienna; Mandi Prize Fondation from Hungarian State Opera, 1989; Grand Prix, Brussels Bel Canto competition, 1990; Béla Bartók-Pasztory Ditta Prix, 1992; Mihaly Szekely Prize, 1994. *Address:* c/o Hungarian National Opera, Népöztársaság utja 22, 1061 Budapest, Hungary.

ULEHLA, Ludmila; Composer and Pianist; b. 20 May 1923, Flushing, NY. *Education:* Manhattan School of Music, with Vittorio Giannini. *Career:* Professor of Manhattan School from 1947; Chairperson of Composition Department, 1970–89. *Compositions include:* Piano Concerto, 1947; Violin Concerto, 1948; Two Piano Sonatas, 1951, 1956; String Quartet, 1953; Music for Minstrels, 1969; Michelangelo: A Tone Portrait, 1970; Five Around for ensemble, 1972; In Memoriam, piano trio, 1972; Fountains, Castles and Gardens, for soprano, clarinet and keyboard, 1977; The Great God Pan for chorus and flute, 1979; Temple at Abydos for trombone, harp, woodwind and strings, 1981; Inspirations from Nature, for piano, 1985; Symphony in Search of Sources, 1990; Bassoon Sonata, 1992; Sybil of the Revolution, chamber opera, 1993; Mississippi for flute, trombone, guitar and percussion, 1995; Visions, for ensemble, 1997; Undersea Fantasy, for orchestra, 1997; Vivo, for orchestra, 1999. *Honours:* Awards and Grants from ASCAP. *Address:* c/o ASCAP, ASCAP Building, One Lincoln Plaza, New York, NY 10023, USA. *Telephone:* 001 212 621 6000. *Fax:* 001 212 724 9064.

ULFUNG, Ragnar; Singer (Tenor); b. 28 Feb. 1927, Oslo, Norway; Opera Producer. *Education:* Studied at the Oslo Conservatory and in Milan. *Career:* Debut: Sang in concert from 1949; first stage role in Menotti's The Consul, Oslo, 1952; Member of Royal Opera Stockholm from 1958; Sang Renato in Un Ballo in Maschera at Covent Garden 1960; Sang Don Carlos at Covent Garden for two seasons, 1963–64; Returned in the premiere of Maxwell Davies's Taverner, 1972 and as Mime in the Götz Friedrich production of the Ring, 1974–6; Metropolitan Opera debut 1972, as Mime; Later sang Strauss's Herod, Wagner's Loge, Berg's Captain and Weill's Fatty in New York; Other appearances include Strauss's Liebe der Danaë and Penderecki's Die schwarze Maske in Santa Fe, as Kent in Reimann's Lear in San Francisco and Tom Rakewell in The Rake's Progress; Concert performances of Messiaen's St Francois d'Assise in London and Lyon; Sang Herod in Salome at San Francisco 1986; Paris Opéra and Geneva 1988, as Shuisky (Boris Godunov) and in The Fiery Angel; Alfred in Die Fledermaus as Oslo, 1988; Festival Hall London 1989, Aegisthus in Elektra; Herod at Los Angeles; Valzacchi in Der Rosenkavalier at Santa Fe 1989; Sang Goro in Butterfly at Lyon, 1990; Season 1992 as the Witch in Hansel and Gretel at Los Angeles, Fatty in Mahagonny at Geneva and Valzacchi in Rosenkavalier at the Santa Fe Festival; Debut as stage director Santa Fe 1973, with La Bohème; Other stagings include Lulu for Santa Fe, Otello in Stockholm and Der Ring des Nibelungen in Seattle; Sang Hauk in The Makropulos Case, Chicago, 1995; Bill Poster in US premiere of A Dream Play by Lindberg, Santa Fe, 1998; Sang Aegisthus in Elektra at Santa Fe, 2000. *Recordings include:* Monostatos in Ingmar Bergman's version of Die Zauberflöte. *Address:* c/o Santa Fe Opera, PO Box 2408, Santa Fe, NM 87504, USA.

ULIVIERI, Nicola; Singer (Baritone); b. 1972, Italy. *Education:* Graduated Claudio Monteverdi Conservatory, 1992. *Career:* Debut: Wolf-Ferrari's I Quattro Rusteghi, 1993; Appearances from 1995 as Conte Robinson in Il matrimonio Segreto and Don Giovanni; Rotta's La notte di un nevrastenico at Cosenza and Spoleto; Guido in Mercadante's Elena da Feltre at the 1997 Wexford Festival; Season 1998 as Publio in La Clemenza di Tito at Ferrara and Don Giovanni at Cologne and on tour in Europe. *Recordings include:* Dottor Mangiacarta in Spontini's Li puntigli delle donne; Guido in Elena da Feltre. *Honours:* Winner, 1995 Belli Competition at Spoleto and Riccardo Zandonai Competition at Rovereto. *Address:* c/o AMP Productions, Conso di Porta Ticinese 89, 1–20123 Milan, Italy.

ULLMANN, Elisabeth; Organist; b. 20 April 1952, Zwettl, Austria; m. Professor Bigenzahn, 1981, 1 s. *Education:* Music studies in Vienna, London and Salzburg. *Career:* Debut: First Prize, Bach Competition, Leipzig, 1976; Has given numerous recitals and performed on radio and television; Artistic Dir, 20th Anniversary Int. Stift Zwettl Organ Festival, Austria. *Recordings:* Muffat, Apparatus Complete (Diapason Award); Hindemith Organ Sonatas; Mozart, Complete Church Sonatas; Haydn, Great Organ Mass; Wagenseil, Concerti per organo; Gottlieb Muffat, Selected keyboard music. *Contributions:* Fono Forum. *Honours:* First Prize, Bruckner Competition, 1978. *Address:* Bennoplace 8/28, 1080 Vienna, Austria. *E-mail:* elisabeth.bigenzahn-ullmann@moz.ac.at.

ULLMANN, Jakob; Composer and Organist; b. 12 July 1958, Freiberg, Germany. *Education:* Studied in Naumburg, 1975–78, and School of Sacred Music, Dresden, 1979–82; Influenced by Schoenberg and John Cage. *Compositions include:* Komposition for string quartet, 1985; Symmetries on Aleph Zero, 1–3, for ensemble, 1987; Ensemblekomposition, theatre music, 1986–; Alakata, for ensemble, 1989; Due Frammenti, for orchestra, 1990; Komposition I–III for orchestra, 1991, 1993, 1994; Meeting John Cage under the Tropic of the late Eighties, graphic score, 1990; Disappearing Musics, 1990; Pianissimo, for viola and electronics, 1990; Echoing A Distant Sound, for ensemble, 1991–93; A Catalogue of Sounds for 13 solo strings, 1996; Voice Books and Fire I–III, graphic score, 1990–. *Address:* c/o GEMA, Rosenheimstr. 11, 8166 Munich, Germany. *Telephone:* 0049 89 480 0300. *Fax:* 0049 89 480 03495.

ULLMANN, Marcus; Singer (Tenor); b. 1970, Olbernhau, Germany. *Education:* Dresden Kreuzchor and Musikhochschule; Lieder classes with Dietrich Fischer-Dieskau. *Career:* Concerts and opera with Helmuth Rilling (Bach B minor Mass), Sylvain Cambreling, Leopold Hager and Peter Schreier; Orchestras include Bamberg SO, Staatskapelle Berlin and Dresden, Gewandhaus Orchestra, Munich PO and Salzburg Mozarteum; Sang in Schoenberg's Moses and Aron, under Kent Nagano, at the Vienna Konzerthaus, 2001; Festival appearances at Milan, Savonlinna, Philadelphia, Madrid, Utrecht and Salzburg. *Address:* c/o Wiener Konzerthaus, A–1010 Vienna, Austria.

UNDERWOOD, John; Violist; b. 11 Oct. 1932, Luton, Bedfordshire, England. *Education:* Studied with Frederick Riddle at the Royal College of Music. *Career:* Co-principal viola of the RPO under Beecham, 1962–62; Co-founder of the Delmé Quartet 1962; Many performances in the United Kingdom and Europe in the classical and modern repertory; Concerts at the Salzburg Festival and the Brahms Saal of the Musikverein Vienna; Season 1990 included Haydn's Seven Last Words in Italy and elsewhere, three Brahms programmes at St John's Smith Square with Iain Burnside, piano; Concerts at St David's Hall Cardiff with quartets by Tchaikovsky and Robert Simpson (premiere of 13th quartet); Appearances in Bremen, Hamburg and Trieste, followed by festival engagements, 1991; Other repertory includes works by Paul Patterson, Daniel Jones, Wilfred Josephs, Iain Hamilton and Bernard Stevens. *Recordings include:* Haydn Seven Last Words; Vaughan Williams On Wenlock Edge and Gurney's Ludlow and Teme; Simpson quartets 1–9 and String Trio (Hyperion); Daniel Jones 3 quartets and Bridge No. 2 (Chandos); Bliss Nos 1 and 2; Josef Holbrooke Piano Quartet and Clarinet Quintet (Blenheim); Brahms Clarinet Quintet and Dvořák F major (Pickwick); Verdi Quartet and Strauss A major Op 2 (Hyperion). *Address:* c/o J Williams, 33 Whittingstall Road, Fulham, London SW6, England.

UNG, Chinary; American composer; b. 24 Nov. 1942, Prey Lovea, Cambodia. *Education:* studied clarinet at the Manhattan School of Music; studied composition with Chou Wen-Chung at Columbia Univ. DMA, 1974. *Career:* Regents Prof. at Arizona State Univ., Tempe, 1987–95; Prof. of Music at Univ. of California at San Diego, 1995–. *Compositions include:* Tall Wind for soprano and ensemble, after e. e. cummings, 1969; Anicca for chamber orchestra, 1970; Mohori for mezzo and ensemble, 1974; Khse Buon for cello, 1979; Child Song I–VII for various instrumental ensembles, 1979–89; Inner Voices for chamber orchestra (Grawemeyer Award 1989), 1986; Grand Spiral 'Desert Flowers Bloom' for orchestra, 1993; Water Rings for chamber orchestra, 1993; Antiphonal Spirals for orchestra, 1995; '…Still Life after Death' for high voice and ensemble, 1995. *Honours:* Kennedy Center Friedheim Award, 1991; Koussevitszky Foundation Commission, 1992. *Address:* c/o ASCAP, ASCAP Building, 1 Lincoln Plaza, New York, NY 10023, USA.

UNGER, Gerhard; Singer (Tenor); b. 26 Nov. 1916, Bad Salzungen, Thuringia, Germany. *Education:* Studied at Eisenach and the Berlin Musikhochschule. *Career:* Sang lyric roles at Weimar from 1947, Tamino, Pinkerton and Alfredo; Bayreuth Festival 1951–52 as David in Die Meistersinger; Guest appearances at the Dresden Opera as Tamino and Pinkerton; Engaged at the Berlin Staatsoper from 1952, Stuttgart from 1982; Member of the Hamburg Staatsoper 1962–73, appearing also in Vienna, Milan, Paris, Metropolitan New York and London (Alwa in Lulu at Sadler's Wells, 1966); Salzburg Festival 1961–64, as Pedrillo in Die Entführung and Brighella in Ariadne auf Naxos; Character roles later in career (Captain in Wozzeck, Mime and Shuratov in From the House of the Dead) in Europe and North and South America (Mime at Dallas 1984); Bregenz Festival 1980 as Pedrillo, Stuttgart 1987 as Mime (last major role). *Recordings include:* Der Waffenschmied, Steuermann in Fliegende Holländer, Die Meistersinger, Alwa in Lulu; Die Entführung, Die Meistersinger; Fidelio, Königskinder by Humperdinck, Die Zauberflöte, Carmina Burana, Elektra, Ariadne auf Naxos, Der Rosenkavalier, Tannhäuser (EMI); La Finta Giardiniera. *Address:* c/o Stuttgart Staatsoper, Oberer Schlossgarten 6, 7000 Stuttgart, Germany.

UNGVARY, Tamas; Composer, Conductor, Double Bass Player and Teacher; b. 12 Nov. 1936, Kalocsa, Hungary; 1 d. *Education:* Philosophy, Budapest; Conducting Diploma, Mozarteum in Salzburg; Double Bass at Béla Bartók Conservatory, Budapest. *Career:* Solo Double Bass, Camerata Academica, Salzburg, 1967–69; As Composer at 4 ISCM Festivals; All major European radios; Lecturer on Computer Music; Artistic Manager, EMS, Stockholm, Sweden and Director of Kineto-auditory Communication Research at Royal Institute of Technology, Stockholm. From 1992, Leader of EA-Music Courses at Vienna University of Music and Performing Art; *Compositions include:* Seul; Traum des Einsamen; Akonel No. 2 for Flute and Tape; Interaction No. 2 for Organ and Tape; Ite missa est; Dis-Tanz for Ensemble and Tape; Istenem Uram! for Tape; Sentograffito, live computer music, 1993; Grattis for Tape, 1994. *Address:* Hagalundsgatan 31, 16966 Solna, Sweden.

UNRUH, Stan; Singer (Tenor); b. 20 Nov. 1938, Beaver, Oklahoma, USA. *Education:* Studied at the Juilliard School, New York. *Career:* Debut: Geneva 1970, as Melot in Tristan; Appearances at Paris, Orange, Rouen, Bordeaux (Lohengrin 1979 and Aeneas 1980) and Toulouse; Member of the Krefeld Opera 1977–85, notably in Der Ring des Nibelungen; New York City Opera, 1976, as Erik in Der fliegende Holländer, Strasbourg 1977, as Parsifal; Further guest appearances at Barcelona, 1978, Brunswick and Innsbruck 1983, Buenos Aires, 1985 (Siegfried in Götterdämmerung) and Freiburg 1986, in the premiere of Hunger und Durst by Violeta Dinescu; Sang at the Staatstheater Kassel, 1989–90; Other roles include Wagner's Tristan, Siegmund, Loge and Walther von Stolzing, Florestan, Shuratov in From the House of the Dead, Max, Don José, Samson, Stravinsky's Oedipus and Bacchus. *Address:* Staatstheater, Friedrichplatz 15, 3500 Kassel, Germany.

UNWIN, Nicholas; Concert Pianist; b. 1962, Cambridge, England. *Education:* Studied at the Royal College of Music and with Philip Fowke. *Career:* Played Bartók, Lambert and McCabe at the Purcell Room, London, 1986; Bartók's 2nd Concerto at St John's Smith Square (also on Radio 3); Wigmore Hall recital, 1987; BBC recital, 1989, followed by Birmingham University and Leeds Town Hall; Artist-in-Residence at the King's Lynn Festival, 1989, with Nights in the Gardens of Spain and Ravel's G major Concerto; BBC documentary on Michael Tippett, 1990, playing the Second Sonata; Specialised in Spanish music, culminating in Images of Iberia at Blackheath Concert Halls; Performed Tippett in Madrid and Radio France, also at the Barbican's Tippett Festival, 1994; First work written for him by Luis De Pablo, 1997. *Recordings:* Tippett Sonata 4, with Robert Saxton and Colin Matthews, 1995; Tippett Sonatas 1–3, 1995; Joaquin Nin: Piano Works, 1998. *Honours:* Chappell Gold Medal and Cyril Smith Recital Prize, Royal College of Music; Winner, Lambeth Music Award, Hastings Concerto Festival, and the Brant Piano Competition; Schott Award, 1990. *Address:* Old Mill House, Langham, Colchester CO4 5NU, England.

UPPMAN, Theodor; Singer (Baritone); b. 12 Jan. 1920, San Jose, California, USA; m. Jean Seward, 31 Jan 1943, 1 s., 1 d. *Education:* Curtis Institute of Music, 1939–41; Stanford University, Opera Department, 1941–42; University of Southern California, 1949–50. *Career:* Debut: Pelléas with San Francisco Symphony, Monteux, 1947; Title role in Billy Budd premiere, Royal Opera House, Covent Garden, 1951 and in USA premiere, NBC television Opera, 1952; Leading Baritone at Metropolitan Opera, 1953–78 as Masetto, Papageno, Sharpless, Guglielmo, Pelléas, Paquillo in La Périchole, Taddeo, Harlekin in Ariadne auf Naxos, Kothner in Die Meistersinger, Eisenstein in Die Fledermaus; Recitals throughout USA and Canada; Sang in US premiere of Britten's Gloriana, Cincinnati May Festival, 1956 Sang in the premieres of Floyd's The Passion of Jonathan Wade at New York City Opera in 1962 and Yerma by Villa-Lobos in Santa Fe in 1971; Appearances with opera companies in USA and Europe including Traveller in Death in Venice, Geneva Opera in 1983, and soloist with most major USA orchestras; Appearances on radio and television; Faculty, Manhattan School of Music, Mannes College of Music and Britten-Pears School for Advanced Musical Studies; Sang in world premiere of Bernstein's A Quiet Place, at Houston, Texas, 1983, La Scala, 1984, and Vienna Staatsoper, 1986; mem, Professional Committee, Regional Auditions for Metropolitan Opera; National Association of

Teachers of Singing; Sullivan Foundation. *Recordings include:* Fauré Requiem, with Roger Wagner Chorale, 1952; Songs and Arias with orchestra, 1954–56; World premiere performance of Billy Budd, Covent Garden, 1951. *Honours:* Musical Prizes: Atwater Kent Auditions, Gainsborough Award; Honorary Director of Britten-Pears School for Advanced Musical Studies. *Address:* 201 West 86th Street, New York, NY 10024, USA.

UPSHAW, Dawn, MA; American singer (soprano); b. 17 July 1960, Nashville, TN; m. Michael Nott 1986; one d. *Education:* Illinois Wesleyan Univ. and Manhattan School of Music, Metropolitan Opera School. *Career:* sang in the US premiere of Hindemith's Sancta Susanna 1983; joined young artists devt program at the Metropolitan Opera, New York after winning int. auditions sponsored by Young Concert Artists 1984; sang at the Met, appearing as Countess Ceprano, Echo (Ariadne), Adina, Despina, Susanna, Sophie (Werther), the Woodbird and Zerlina 1985–; has performed with major orchestras, opera cos and chamber groups in the USA and Europe, including the Netherlands Opera Co., Vienna opera, Hamburg (Germany) opera, Berlin Philharmonic, Los Angeles Philharmonic, Rotterdam Philharmonic (Netherlands) and Chicago Symphony Orchestras; festival appearances include Salzburg Festival as Barbarina 1987, as L'Ange in St Francois at Salzburg 1992, 1998, Clemene in Saariaho's L'Amour de loin 2000, Aix-en-Provence as Despina and Pamina 1988–89, Anne Trulove 1992, sang Pamina at the London Proms 1990, Judith Weir's Natural History 1999, sang Theodora at Glyndebourne 1996; appearances include at the Barbican and at Covent Garden, London, at the Paris Châtelet; other roles include Marzelline (Fidelio), Constance in Les Dialogues des Carmélites, Mozart's Cherubino, Daisy in Harbison's The Great Gatsby, Janáček's Vixen. *Operas include:* Rigoletto, Simon Boccanegra, Khovanshchina, Carmen, La Clemenza di Tito, Dialogues of the Carmelites, The Magic Flute 1985, Death in the Family 1986, Alice in Wonderland, The Marriage of Figaro (also on TV), L'elisir d'amore 1988, Così fan Tutte 1988, Idomeneo 1988–89, Werther 1988–89, Don Giovanni 1989–90. *Recordings include:* Ariadne auf Naxos, songs by Rachmaninov, Hugo Wolf, Richard Strauss, Charles Ives and Kurt Weill, songs and pieces by Samuel Barber, John Harbison, Stravinsky and Gian-Carlo Menotti (Grammy Award for Best Classical Vocal Soloist 1990), Bach's Magnificat and Vivaldi's Gloria 1989, Lucio Silla, L'elisir d'amore. *Honours:* jt first prize Naumburg Competition 1985. *Current Management:* IMG Artists, Lovell House, 616 Chiswick High Road, London, W4 5RX, England.

URBAIN, Mady; Singer (Mezzo-soprano); b. 27 April 1946, Montegnée, Belgium. *Education:* Studied at the Liège Conservatoire and in Vienna and Salzburg. *Career:* Sang at the Liège Opera from 1967, and made many guest appearances elsewhere in Belgium and throughout France; Roles have included Amneris, Preziosilla, Mistress Quickly, Carmen, Marcellina, Charlotte, Puccini's Princess and Suzuki, Strauss's Adelaide and Mère Marie in The Carmélites; Concerts include Messiah, Bach's B Minor Mass, the Verdi Requiem and Beethoven's Ninth; Professor at the Grètry Academy, Liège, from 1970. *Address:* c/o Opéra de Wallonie, 1 Rue des Dominicains, 4000 Liège, Belgium.

URBANNER, Erich; Composer and Conductor; b. 26 March 1936, Innsbruck, Austria. *Education:* Vienna Music Academy, with Hans Swarowsky; Darmstadt courses, with Bruno Maderna and Karl-Heinz Stockhausen. *Career:* Professor at Vienna Music Academy, 1969–; Director of Institut für Electroakustik und Experimentelle Musik, 1986–89. *Compositions include:* String quartets nos 2 and 3, 1957, 1972; Piano Concerto, 1958; Flute Concertino, 1959; Der Gluckreich, comic opera, 1963; Oboe Concerto, 1966; Violin Concerto, 1971; Concerto "Wolfgang Amadeus," 1972; Sinfonietta 79, 1979; Cello Concerto, 1981; Requiem 1983; Ninive, oder Das Leben geht weiter, opera, 1987; Concerto for saxophone quartet and orchestra, 1989; Quasi una fantasia, for 15 instruments, 1993; Zyklus, for organ, 1993; Begegnung for 12 instruments, 1996; Formen in Wandel, piano, 1996. *Address:* c/o AKM, Baumannstr 10. 1031 Wien, Postfach 259, Austria. *Telephone:* 00431 717 140. *Fax:* 00431 717 14107/262/195.

URBANOVA, Eva; Singer (soprano); b. 1963, Slany, Prague, Czechoslovakia. *Career:* Plzeň Opera, 1987–89; National Theatre, Prague, from 1990, as Verdi's Leonoras, Donna Anna, Tosca, Norma, Suor Angelica and Santuzza; New York Metropolitan Opera, 1998–99, as Ortrud in Lohengrin; La Scala debut as Gioconda; Further engagements in Britten's War Requiem at the London Proms, Tosca at the Met, and Abigaille in Nabucco at Zürich; Season 1999 as Libuše by Smetana at Prague, Milada in Dalibor at Cagliari and the Trovatore Leonora in Canada; Season 2000–01 as Gioconda and the Forza Leonora at the Deutsche Oper Berlin; the Kostelnička in Jenůfa for Washington Opera; Concerts throughout Europe and the Americas. *Recordings include:* Libuše and Dalibor; Janáček's Glagolitic Mass and Dvořák's Rusalka. *Address:* c/o Music International, 13 Ardilaun Road, London N5 2QR, England.

URIA-MONZON, Beatrice; Singer (Mezzo-soprano); b. 28 Dec. 1963, Agen, France. *Education:* Studied in Marseille and the Opera School of the Paris Opéra. *Career:* Debut: Nancy, 1989, as Cherubino; Lyon and Aix, 1989, as Smeraldine in The Love for Three Oranges by Prokofiev; Sang Mignon at Avignon, 1990, Charlotte in Werther, 1991; Berlioz's Béatrice at Toulouse and Marguerite in La Damnation de Faust at Bregenz, 1992; Carmen at the Opéra Bastille, 1993, at Buenos Aires and Verona; New productions of Carmen at St Etienne, and Toulouse (1997); Season 2000–01 as Carmen at Houston and the Vienna Staatsoper, Offenbach's Giulietta for the Festival d'Orange and Massenet's Hérodiade at St Etienne. *Recordings include:* Beethoven's Ninth; The Love for Three Oranges; Carmen. *Address:* c/o Théâtre du Capitole, Place du Capitole, 31000 Toulouse, France.

URMANA, Violeta; Lithuanian singer (mezzo-soprano); b. 1959. *Education:* Vilnius and Munich High Schools for Music. *Career:* sang at the Munich Opera from 1992; State Opera of Stuttgart 1994; Lucerne Opera as Princess Eboli, and Bayreuth as Waltraute 1994; Opéra Bastille and Ravenna Festival 1995, as Fenena in Nabucco; Season 1996 at La Scala as Wagner's Fricka and La Haine in Gluck's Armide; Azucena at the Deutsche Oper Berlin; further roles include Santuzza, Preziosilla and Eboli in Don Carlos (Vienna Staatsoper); concerts include Das Lied von der Erde in Bologna and Bach's B minor Mass at Wuppertal 1996; Season 1998 as Kundry at the Deutsche Oper Berlin, Eboli with the Royal Opera at Edinburgh, Bartók's Judith at Aix; Act II of Parsifal with Placido Domingo at St Petersburg; Season 2000–01 as Azucena at La Scala, Adalgisa in Seville, Santuzza at Florence, Amneris in Geneva, Waltraute for the Bayreuth Festival and Kundry at the Met (debut role); sang Kundry at Covent Garden 2002. *Current Management:* Caecilia Lyric Department, Rennweg 15, 8001 Zürich, Switzerland. *Telephone:* (1) 221 33 88. *Fax:* (1) 211 71 82. *E-mail:* caecilia@caecilia-lyric.ch. *Website:* www.caecilia.ch.

URRILA, Irma; Singer (Soprano); b. 29 Jan. 1943, Helsinki, Finland. *Education:* Studied in Helsinki, Milan and Essen. *Career:* Debut: Helsinki 1964, as Mimi in La Bohème; Sang with the Finnish National Opera, notably as Pamina, and in the 1975 premiere of The Last Temptations by Jonas Kokkonen; Premiere of Antonio Bilbalo's Macbeth, Oslo, 1990; Sang throughout Scandinavia in concert and opera; Many broadcast appearances; Pamina in the film version of Die Zauberflöte, directed by Ingmar Bergman. *Recordings include:* Die Zauberflöte; The Last Temptations (DGG). *Honours:* Prize-winner in Competitions at Lonigo (1965) and Parma (1996). *Address:* c/o Finnish National Opera, PO Box 176, Helsingkatu 58, 002 51 Helsinki, Finland.

URROWS, David Francis; Composer and Music Historian; b. 25 Oct. 1957, Honolulu, Hawaii, USA. *Education:* AB, Brandeis University, 1978; MMus, University of Edinburgh, 1980; DMA, Boston University, 1987. *Career:* Compositions performed, commissioned and broadcast in USA, Asia and Europe; Lecturer at several American Universities. *Compositions:* String Quartet, 1978; Piano Sonata, 1979; Quintet for Winds, 1981; Three Vailima Episodes, Soprano and String Orchestra, 1984; A New England Almanack, Baritone and Piano, 1985; Sonata for Oboe and Harp, 1985; Partita: Nun Komm, der Heiden Heiland, Organ, 1985; Sonata, San Angelo, 2 Violas, 1986; Ricordanza dell Umbria, Piano, 1987; Winterreise, Soprano and Chamber Orchestra, 1988; Sonata for Violin and Piano, 1991; Opera: A Midsummer Night's Dream, 1980; Oratorio: Lycidas, 1987; Epiphany Cantata, 1993; Many songs and anthems. *Publications include:* Sea Ballads and Songs in Whalsay, Shetland, 1983; The Choral Music of Christopher le Fleming, 1986; Randall Thompson: A Bio-Bibliography, 1991. *Address:* Department of Music and Fine Arts, Hong Kong Baptist University, Kowloon Tong, Hong Kong.

URSULEASA, Mihaela; Concert Pianist; b. 1978, Brasov, Romania. *Education:* Brasov Music School from 1985, with Stela Dragulin; Vienna Musikhochschule, with Heinz Medjimorec. *Career:* Salzburg Festival debut with the Mozarteum Orchestra, 1998; Tour of Germany with the Academy of St Martin in the Fields under Sir Neville Mariner, 2000; London debut at South Bank Centre, Harrods International Piano Series, 2002; European tour with the Gothenburg Symphony Orchestra under Neeme Järvi, 2003; Debut with RAI Torino, Hallé Orchestra, Bournemouth Symphony Orchestra, 2003, Wigmore Hall debut, 2004. *Honours:* winner, Clara Haskil International Piano Competition, 1995. *Address:* c/o Schmid UK, 4 Addison Bridge Place, London W14 8XP, England.

URTEAGA, Irma; Composer and Pianist; b. 7 March 1929, San Nicolas, Argentina. *Education:* National Conservatory and Instituto del Teatro Colón, Buenos Aires. *Career:* Professor at National Conservatory and at Teatro Colón 1984–93, Coach at Teatro Colón, 1974–1978; Director of opera workshop at Teatro Colón, 1984; Professor at Teatro Colón Institute Summer Courses, 1985–1993. *Compositions:* Piano Sonata, 1969; String Quartet, 1969; Ambitos, for orchestra, 1970; Paolo e Francesca for soprano, tenor and chamber orchestra, 1971; L'Inferno, for chorus and orchestra, 1971; Expectacion for soprano and chorus, 1977; Suenos de Yerman, for mezzo and ensemble, 1986; La maldolida, chamber opera, 1987; El mundo del ser, for mezzo and orchestra, 1990; Escalénicas for piano, 1992; Cánticos para sõnar, 1993; Marimba Concerto, 1994; Tiempo de memorias for clarinet, violin and piano, 1996; Variaciones sobre un tema de Beatriz Sosnik, for piano, 1997. *Address:* Rio Bamba 944, 6–C, 1118 Buenos Aires Argentina. *Telephone:* 54 11 4813 0435.

USHAKOVA, Natalia; Singer (Soprano); b. 1969, Tashkent, Russia. *Education:* Graduated Munich Conservatoire, 1999. *Career:* Appearances with the Kirov Opera, St Petersburg, from 1998, as Maria in Mazeppa, Lyubka in Prokofiev's Semyon Kotko, Tatiana (Eugene Onegin) and Mozart's Countess and Donna Elvira; Sang with the Kirov Opera in Summer season at Covent Garden, 2000. *Honours:* Prizewinner, Wroclaw International (1993), 1st Pechkovsky, St Petersburg (1994) and Volkswagen (1997) Competitions. *Address:* c/o Kirov Opera, Mariinsky Theatre, 1 Theatre Square, St Petersburg, Russia.

USPENSKY, Vladislav Aleksandrovich; Russian composer and academic; *Professor of Composition, Leningrad State Conservatory*; b. 7 Sept. 1937, Omsk; s. of Alexander Grigoryevich Kolodkin and Vera Pavlovna Uspenskaya; m. Irina Yevgenyevna Taimanova 1963. *Education:* Leningrad State Conservatory. *Career:* postgrad. studies under Dmitri Shostakovich; teacher of music theory Leningrad State Conservatory 1965–67, Dean of Musicology 1967–72, Prof. of Composition 1982–; Guest Composer-in-Residence Seoul Univ., Korea 1995, Lima Univ., Peru 1997, Boston Univ. USA; Chair. Music Council of Cultural Cttee, St Petersburg Govt 1996–; Vice-Pres. Union of Composers of St Petersburg 1972–; Gen. Dir Int. Musical Children's Festival 1995–. *Compositions:* Phantasmagoria, Vepres, Requiem, Liturgie, Temperaments, Toccata, Sonata-Phantasia, States, Sonata for the Violin and Piano, Anna Karenina (musical), Trombone Concertino 1963, Double Piano Concerto 1965, Music for Strings and Percussion 1967, The War Against Salamanders (opera) 1967, To the Memory of a Hero (ballet) 1969, Intervention (opera) 1970, A Road to the Day (ballet) 1974, Symphonic Frescoes 1977, For You to the Sea (ballet) 1978, Nocturne for low voice and orchestra 1980, Expectation 1982, With You and Without You (oratorio) 1984, Cranes Flying (ballet) 1984, Towards the Light

(symphony) 1985, Dedication (symphony) 1988, The Mushroom's Alarm (ballet) 1990, All Night Vigil 1990, The Departure of the Soul (funeral service) 1992, A Dithyramb of Love for two pianos and orchestra 1995, Trombone Concerto 1995, Concerto for low voice and orchestra 1997, Casanova in Russia (musical) 1998, Temptation of Jeanna (musical) 1999; music for plays, including Revizor, over 100 songs, music for films, theatre and TV productions. *Publication:* D. Shostakovich in My Life. *Honours:* People's Artist of Russia, D. Shostakovich Prize 1997, Order of Merit of Homeland 1998, Order of Catherine the Great 2002; music festival in his honour, St Petersburg autumn 2002. *Address:* Composers' Union, B. Morskaia 45, St Petersburg (office); Admiralteysky canal 5 Apt. 26, St Petersburg, Russia (home). *Telephone:* (812) 117-35-48 (office); (812) 117-74-35 (home). *Fax:* (812) 117-35-48 (office).

USTVOLSKAYA, Galina; Composer; b. 17 June 1919, Petrograd, Russia; m. Bagrenin Konstantin, 23 Dec 1966. *Education:* Rimsky-Korsakov Conservatory until 1939–47; Postgraduate courses in composition, Leningrad Conservatory, 1947–50. *Career:* Tutor in Composition at Leningrad Conservatory College, 1948–77; Visited Amsterdam, 1995; mem, Russian Composers Union. *Compositions include:* Concerto for piano, string orchestra and timpani, 1946; Sonata for piano No. 1, 1947; Trio for clarinet, violin and piano, 1949; Sonata No. 2 for piano, 1949; Bylina 'Stepan Razin's Dream' for bass and orchestra, 1949; Octet for 2 oboes 4 violins, timpani, and piano, 1949–50; Sonata for piano No. 3, 1952; Sonata for violin and piano, 1952; 12 Preludes for piano, 1953; Symphony No. 1, in 3 movements, for 2 boy's voices and Orchestra, 1955; Suite for orchestra, 1955; Sonata for piano No. 4, 1957; Poem for orchestra No. 1, 1958; Symphonic Poem, No. 2, 1959; Duet for violin and piano, 1964; Dona Nobis Pacem for piccolo, tuba and piano, 1970–71; Dies Irae for 8 double basses, percussion and piano, 1972–73; Benedictus, Qui Venit for 4 flutes, 4 bassoons and piano, 1974–75; Symphony No.2 True and Eternal Bliss, 1979; Symphony No. 3 Jesus Messiah, Save Us!, 1983; Sonata No. 5 for piano, 1986; Symphony No. 4 Prayer, 1985–87; Sonata No. 6 for piano, 1988; Symphony No. 5 Amen, 1989–90. *Recordings include:* 3 Sonatas, 1947, 1952 and 1957; Grand Duet for violoncello and piano, 1959. *Honours:* Heidelberger Kunstlerinnenpreis, 1992. *Address:* Gagarina Avenue 27-72, St Petersburg 196135, Russia.

V

VACCHI, Fabio; Italian composer; b. 19 Feb. 1949, Bologna. *Education:* Bologna Conservatory, 1968–74; Accademia Musicale, Siena, with Franco Donatoni; Tanglewood, USA. *Career:* Active in Venice, 1975–92; Lecturer at Milan Conservatory, from 1992. *Compositions:* Les soupirs de Genève, for 11 strings, 1975; Sinfonia in Quattro Tempi, 1976; Il cerchio e gli inganni, for ensemble, 1981; Trois Visions de Genève, for low voice and 11 strings, 1981; Girotondo, opera, 1982; Piano Concerto, 1983; Quintet, 1987; Il Viaggio, opera, 1989; Quartetto a Bruno Maderna, 1989; Danae for orchestra, 1989; Otteto a Luigi Nono, 1991; Settimino, for ensemble, 1992; String Quartet, 1992; La station thermale, comic opera, 1993; Dai calanchi di Sabbiuno, for ensemble, 1995; In alba mia dir, for cello, 1995; Faust, choreographic poem, 1995; Sacer Sanctus, for chorus and ensemble, 1996; Wanderer-Ocktett, 1997; Dionisio germogliatore, ballet, 1996–98; Briefe Büchners for baritone and piano, 1996; Les Oiseaux de passage, opera 1998. *Honours:* Koussevitsky Prize for Composition, Tanglewood, 1974. *Address:* c/o SIAE (Sezione Musica), Viale delle Letteratura 30, 00144 Rome, Italy. *Telephone:* 00396 59901. *Fax:* 0039 659 6470552.

VACEK, Milos; Composer; b. 20 June 1928, Horni Roven, Pardubice, Czechoslovakia. *Education:* Studied at the Prague Conservatory, 1942–47; Academy of Musical Arts, 1947–51. *Career:* Freelance composer from 1954. *Compositions include:* Operas Jan Zelivsky, composed 1956–58, performed Olomouc 1984; Brother Zak, Ostrava, 1982; Romance of the Bugle, Ceske Budejovice 1987; Mikes the Tomcat, Brno 1986; Ballets: The Comedian's Fairytale, 1958, Wind in the Hair, 1961, The Mistress of the Seven Robbers 1966, Meteor, 1966; Lucky Sevens, 1966; Musicals: The Night is my Day (on Bessie Smith) 1962; The Emperor's New Clothes, 1962; Madame Sans Gene, 1968; Wind from Alabama, 1970; Orchestral: Sinfonietta, 1951; Spring Suite for wind instruments and strings, 1963; Serenade for Strings, 1965; May Symphony, 1974; Poem of Fallen Heroes for alto and orchestra, 1974; Olympic Flame, symphonic poem, 1975; A Solitary Seaman, symphonic picture, 1978; World's Conscience, in memory of Lidice, 1981; Trombone Concerto, 1986; Symphony No.2, 1986; Chamber and piano music. *Address:* Spojovaci 401, 252 45 Zvole u, Prague, Czech Republic.

VADUVA, Leontina; Singer (Soprano); b. 1 Dec. 1960, Rosiile, Romania. *Education:* Studied with mother and at Bucharest Conservatory. *Career:* Debut: Sang Manon at Toulouse 1987, conducted by Michel Plasson; Appeared as Ninetta in La Gazza Ladra at the Théâtre des Champs Elysées, Paris, July 1988, followed by Manon at Covent Garden; Returned to London in a production of Rigoletto by Nuria Espert, and sang Drusilla at Théâtre du Châtelet, Paris, and at the Grand Théatre, Geneva; Engagements for season 1990–91 included appearances in Les Pêcheurs de Perles and L'Elisir d'amore at Toulouse; Manon at Montpellier, Bordeaux, Avignon, Paris (Opéra Comique) and Vienna; Rigoletto at Bonn; Donizetti's Il Campanello di Notte at Monte Carlo; Les Contes d'Hoffmann in Paris (Théâtre du Châtelet) and London (Covent Garden); Ismene in Mitridate by Mozart at the Châtelet, conducted by Jeffrey Tate; Micaela in Carmen at Covent Garden (returned 1996, as Mimi); Season 1998 with Mimi for Opera Pacific and Adina at Barcelona; Sang Marguerite and Mimi at Los Angeles, Poulenc's Blanche at La Scala, Offenbach's Antonia for Festival d'Orange and Adina at Savonlinna, 2000; Season 2003–04 engaged as Euridice at Barcelona, as Marguérite in Turin, Alice Ford for Bordeaux Opera and Mimi on tour of Japan for Catania Opera. *Recordings include:* Mitridate; Le nozze di Figaro, conducted by John Eliot Gardiner (1993). *Honours:* Winner, Concours de Chant, Toulouse, 1986; Winner, 's-Hertogenbosch Competition, Netherlands, 1987; Laurence Olivier Prize, London 1989. *Address:* Stafford Law Associates, 6 Barham Close, Weybridge KT13 9 PR, England.

VAGGIONE, Horacio; Composer; b. 21 Jan. 1943, Cordoba, Argentina. *Education:* Composition, Arts School, National University of Cordoba. *Career:* Co-Founder, Experimental Music Centre, University of Cordoba, 1964–69; Alea Electronic Music Group, Madrid, Spain, 1969–74; Computer Music Project, University of Madrid, 1970–73; Guest Composer, IRCAM/Centre Georges Pompidou, 1981–85 Groupe de Musique Experimentale de Bourges, France, 1983; Technische Universität, West Berlin, 1987–88; Director, Electro-acoustic Music Studio, University of Paris VIII, 1985–. *Compositions:* 48 including symphonic, chamber and electronic music; Myr-S, for cello and electronics, 1996; Frauyage for violin, cello and tape, 1997; Nodal for tape; Performances of works at Festivals of Warsaw, Stockholm, Berlin, Kassel, Frankfurt, Amsterdam, Helsinki, Oslo, Paris, Venice, La Rochelle, Bourges, Geneva, Lausanne, Milan, Turin, Rome, Madrid, Athens and at UNESCO's Rostrum of Composers, World Music Days, Los Angeles Olympic Arts Festival, ICMC (Rochester, Illinois, The Hague, Venice, Paris, Cologne), British Arts of London, Berlin Kulturstadt Europas 88,

Darmstadt Ferienkurse für Neue Musik. *Recordings:* ADDA, Paris; Le Chant du Monde, Paris; WERGO, Germany. *Address:* Editions Salabert, 22 Rue Chauchat, 75009 Paris, France.

VAJDA, Janos; Composer; b. 8 Oct. 1949, Miskole, Hungary. *Education:* Franz Liszt Academy, Budapest, 1968–75; Amsterdam Conservatory. *Career:* Professor, Budapest Academy, from 1981. *Compositions:* De Angelis, wind quintet, 1978; Stabat Mater, 1978; Barabbas, opera, 1978; Farewell, for orchestra, 1980; Sinfonia Retrograde, 1980; Mario and the Magician, opera, 1980–85; The Moment of Truth, ballet, 1981; Don Juan, ballet, 1981; Via Crucis, for chorus, 1983; The Circus is Coming, ballet, 1984; Duo, for violin and cello, 1989–91; Double Concerto, violin and cello, 1993; Leonce and Lena, opera, 1990–95; Violin Concerto, 1995; Two String Quartets, 1995, 1997; Piano Sonata, 1996; O Magnum Mysterium, for chorus, 1999. *Honours:* Erkel Prize, 1981. *Address:* c/o ARTISJUS, Mészáros u. 15–17, H–1539 Budapest 114, POB 593, Hungary. *Telephone:* 0036 1212 1553. *Fax:* 0336 1212 1544.

VAJNAR, Frantisek; Conductor; b. 15 Sept. 1930, Strasice u Rokycan, Czechoslovakia. *Education:* Studied violin and conducting at the Prague Conservatoire. *Career:* Played in the orchestra of the Prague National Theatre; 1950–53, conducted the ensemble of Czech Army, 1953–55; Conducted at the State Theatre of Karlina 1955–60, Ostrava 1960–62; Director of the Nejedly Theatre Usti nad Labem 1962–73, with operas by Smetana (complete), Dvořák, Janáček, Wagner, Verdi, Puccini, Strauss, Prokofiev, Henze and Hartmann; Conductor at the National Theatre Prague 1973–79, Artistic Director from 1985; Chief Conductor of the Czech Radio Symphony Orchestra 1979–85, Guest Conductor of the Czech Philharmonic; Director of the Collegium Musicum Pragense and guest conductor in Australia, Brazil, Germany, France, Greece, Italy, Japan, Poland, Scandinavia, Russia and Switzerland; Festival appearances at Salzburg, Vienna, Prague; Conducted Prokofiev's Betrothal in a Monastery at the 1979 Wexford Festival; Teacher at Prague Academy of Arts. *Recordings include:* Smetana The Kiss; Shostakovich 10th and 15th Symphonies (Czech Philharmonic); Beethoven Overtures; Brixi Organ Concertos; Mozart arranged Wendt Le nozze di Figaro; Dvořák's The Cunning Peasant. *Address:* c/o National Theatre, PO Box 865, 11230 Prague 1, Czech Republic.

VAKARELIS, Janis; Concert Pianist; b. 1950, Greece. *Education:* Studied at the Vienna Music Academy with Nikita Magaloff and Bruno Leonardo Gelber. *Career:* Engagements from 1979 with the Gewandhaus Orchestra, Mozarteum Orchestra of Salzburg, Zürich Chamber, Monte Carlo Philharmonic, Berlin Symphony, Stuttgart Philharmonic, Staatskapelle Dresden and BBC Symphony; Conductors have included Rattle, Weller, Masur, Kurt Sanderling, Ashkenazy, Litton and Rowicki; Recitals at the Concertgebouw in Amsterdam and the Teatro Real Madrid; Festival appearances at Spoleto and Athens, BBC Prom Concerts 1986. *Recordings include:* Prokofiev's 3rd Concerto and works by Brahms and Liszt; Labels include RCA, ASV and RPO. *Honours:* Winner, 1979 Queen Sofia Competition, Madrid; Pan-Hellenic Piano Competition and the Prix d'Academie d'Athenes. *Address:* c/o Primusic, Herrengasse 6–8/2/22, A–1010 Vienna, Austria.

VALADE, Pierre-André; Conductor; b. 14 Oct. 1959, Brive, France; m. 5 May 1990. *Education:* As a flautist: Michel Debost's Private Class, Paris, 1979–81; Occasional lessons from Marcel Moyse, Maxence Larrieu and Alain Marion. *Career:* Flautist 1979–95; Numerous stage including ensemble, chamber music and soloist appearances in repertoire from Mozart 1982–95; Soloist: numerous world premieres including Eolia by Philippe Hurel, Paris, Radio-France, 1983; Jupiter by Philipe Manoury on Flute-4x, IRCAM, Paris, 1987; ...explosante-fixe... by Pierre Boulez, for Flute, Computer and Ensemble, Paris, 1991; Concerts with Ensembles: Ensemble Musique Oblique, 1983–93; Ensemble InterContemporain, 1985–90, including London Proms, 1985, US Tour with Pierre Boulez 1986; ...explosante-fixe... in New York, Carnegie Hall, with P. Boulez, 1993; Director, Collection Pierre-André Valade, Edition Henry Lemoine, Paris, 1985–95; Career as a Conductor: Co-Founder and Musical Director of Court-circuit Ensemble, Paris, 1991–; Guest Conductor: West Australian Symphony Orchestra, 1995, 1996,1998; Melbourne Symphony Orchestra, 1998; London Sinfonietta, 1999, 2000; Ensemble InterContemporain, 2000–(05); Ensemble Modern, 2001–04; Philharmonia Orchestra, 2003–04, BBC Symphony Orchestra, 2001–04; Tonhalle Orchester, Zürich, 2003–04; Orchestre Symphonique de Montréal, 2003; Major Festivals: Festival of Perth, Australia (1996, 1998); Ultima Festival, Oslo Norway, 1998–2004; Festival de Strasbourg, 1995–2003; Festival of Bath, UK, 1999; Aldeburgh, UK, 2002; Festival Présence de Radio-France, Paris, 1998, 1999; Festival Agora, Ircam, Paris, 1998–2002; London Proms, 2002; Llucerne Festival, 2002, 2004; Salzburg Easter Festival, 2002; mem, International Contemporary Music Society. *Recordings:* A

Schoenberg: Pierrot Lunaire, Harmonia Mundi, 1992; A Jolivet: The Complete Works for Flute, 1993. *Publications:* La Flute dans le Repertoire du XXe Siècle pour Ensemble Instrumental, 1987; Flute et Creations, 1991. *Honours:* Chevalier dans l'Ordre des Arts et des Lettres, 2001; Grand Prix de la Nouvelle Académie du Disque Francais. *Current Management:* Allied Artists, 42 Montpelier Square, London SW7 1JZ, England. *Telephone:* (20) 7589-6243. *E-mail:* andrew@alliedartists.co.uk.

VALCARCEL, Edgar; Pianist and Composer; b. 4 Dec. 1932, Puno, Peru; m. Carmen Pollard, 1 Jan 1958, 2 s., 2 d. *Education:* Catholic University, Lima, Peru; National Conservatory of Music, Lima; Instituto Torcuato de Tella, Buenos Aires, Argentina; Columbia Princeton University, New York, USA. *Career:* As Pianist: Soloist, National Symphony Orchestras of Lima, Rio de Janeiro and La Habana; As Composer: Commissions, V Inter-American Festival, Washington DC, 1971, Rochester Festival, 1972, Maracaibo Festival, Venezuela, 1977; Works premiered at Panamerican Union Peer International Corporation, 1968, Tonos, Darmstadt, 1977, Veracruz University, Mexico, 1983; Head of Music Department, Newton College, Lima. *Compositions:* Dichotomy III, for 12 instruments, 1968; Montaje 59, for chamber ensemble, 1977; Chegan IV, for choir, 1977; Karabotasat Cutintapata, for orchestra, 1977; 4 Children's Songs, 1983. *Recordings:* American Contemporary Music, EDS-030-Stereo; Edul, Organization of American States; Antologia Music Peruana Siglo XX, Vol. III, Edubanco. *Honours:* Professor honoris causa, Puno University, Peru; National Award for Composition Award, Caracas, Venezuela, 1981. *Address:* Avenida Angamos (Oeste) 862-C, Miraflores, Lima 18, Peru.

VALDES, Maximiano; Conductor; b. 17 June 1949, Santiago, Chile. *Education:* Studied in Santiago, at the Santa Cecilia Rome and with Franco Ferrara. *Career:* Assistant conductor at La Fenice, Venice, 1976–80; Principal guest with the Spanish National Orchestra from 1984 and music director of the Buffalo Philharmonic, USA, from 1989; Guest appearances in England, Scandinavia and France (Paris Opéra). *Honours:* Prizewinner at the 1978 Rupert Foundation Competition, London, and the 1980 Nikolai Malko Competition, Copenhagen. *Address:* c/o Cramer/Marder Artists, 3436 Springhill Road, Lafayette, CA 94549, USA.

VALEK, Vladimír; Conductor; b. 1935, Czechoslovakia. *Education:* Graduated, Prague Academy of Performing Arts, 1962. *Career:* Conductor, Czech Radio Studio Orchestra in Prague, 1965–75; Founder and Leader, Dvořák Chamber Orchestra; Conductor, Prague Symphony Orchestra, 1977–88; Chief Conductor, Prague Radio Symphony Orchestra, 1985–; Conductor, Czech Philharmonic Orchestra, 1996–; Guest performances with the Czech Philharmonic in USA, Russia, Japan, the United Kingdom, Germany, Austria, Netherlands, Switzerland, Korea and Taiwan; Festival engagements at Lucerne, Interlaken, Montreux, Berlin, Linz, Istanbul, Prague and Bratislava. *Recordings include:* Bartók's Concerto for Orchestra and Prokofiev's Romeo and Juliet Ballet Suites with the Czech Philharmonic; Dvořák's Symphonies Nos 8 and 9, and Slavonic Dances, Schubert's Mass in A flat, Sibelius's Symphony No. 2, Saint-Saëns's Symphony No. 3, Martinů's Symphony No. 6 with the Prague Radio Symphony Orchestra; Martinů's The Frescoes, Stravinsky's Petrushka and Rite of Spring, Dvořák's Symphonies Nos 5 and 7 and Suk's Symphony Asrael with the Prague Radio Symphony Orchestra. *Current Management:* Lubomir Herza, Struharov 667, 251 68 Czech Republic. *Address:* Na Vápenné m 6, 147 00 Prague 4, Czech Republic.

VALENTE, Benita; Singer (Lyric Soprano); b. 19 Oct. 1934, Delano, California, USA; m. Anthony Phillip Checchia, 21 Nov 1959, 1 s. *Education:* Graduated, Curtis Institute of Music, 1960; Studied with Chester Hayden, Martial Singher, Lotte Lehmann, Margaret Harshaw. *Career:* Debut: Freiburg Opera, 1962; Metropolitan Opera, 1973, as Pamina; Leading roles Orfeo, Rigoletto, Traviata, Idomeneo, Marriage of Figaro, Faust, La Bohème, Turandot, Magic Flute, Rinaldo, The Governess in The Turn Of the Screw, Anne Trulove in The Rake's Progress; Appeared throughout USA and Europe in operas and symphonies; has sung in New York as Countess, Susanna, Pamina, Ilia, Nannetta and Almirena in Rinaldo, 1985; Santa Fe, as Ginevra in Ariodante 1985; Sang in the premiere of Vanqui by L.S. Burrs for Columbus Opera, 1999. *Recordings:* Many recordings for international recording companies. *Honours:* Winner, Metropolitan Opera Council auditions, 1960; First singer to receive Richard D. Bogomolny National Service Award, Chamber Music America, 1999. *Address:* c/o Anthony P Checchia, 135 S 18th Street, Philadelphia, PA 19103, USA.

VALERA, Roberto; Composer; b. 21 Dec. 1938, Havana, Cuba. *Education:* Havana Conservatory; Warsaw School of Music, 1965–67. *Career:* Professor of Composition, Instituto Superior de Arte, Havana, 1975–. *Compositions include:* Toccata, for piano, 1965; Conjuro for soprano and orchestra, 1967; Devenir for orchestra, 1969; Iré a Santiago, for mixed chorus, 1969; Tres Impertinencias, for 12 instruments, 1971; Quisiera for mixed chorus, 1971; Es rojo, for baritone, flute and piano, 1979; Violin Concerto, 1982; Concierto por la paz, for saxophone and orchestra, 1985; Ajiaco, tape, 1989; Nadie oye, female chorus, 1990; Palmas tape, 1991; Tierra de sol, cielo y tierra, for ensemble, 1992; Periodo espacial, tape, 1993; Yugo y estrella, for soprano, baritone, chorus and orchestra, 1995; Hic et Nunc, tape, 1996; Concierto de Cojimer, for guitar and orchestra, 1998. *Address:* c/o ACDAM, Calle 6 no. 313 entre 13y15, Vedado La Habana CP–10400, Cuba.

VALJAKKA, Taru; Singer (soprano); b. 16 Sept. 1938, Helsinki, Finland. *Education:* Studied with Antti Koskinen in Helsinki, with Gerald Moore in Stockholm and London, Erik Werba in Vienna and Conchita Badia in Santiago. *Career:* debut, Helsinki, 1964, as Donna Anna in Don Giovanni; Linzer Theater, 1977; Sang in Helsinki at premiere of Sallinen's The Red Line, 1978; Budapest, Oslo, Prague and Berlin; Kiel Opera, 1980 in the German premiere of The Horseman by Sallinen; Bluthochzeit and Tannhauser at Linz, 1982; Metropolitan Opera, 1983, in The Horseman with the Helsinki Company; Savonlinna Festival Finland, 1983, as Senta in Der fliegende Holländer; Other roles include the Trovatore Leonora, Aida, Countess Almaviva, Fiordiligi, Desdemona, Pamina and Mélisande; Teatro Colón Buenos Aires, 1987, as Senta; Numerous recitals in the songs of Sibelius; Singing Professor, Tallinn Music Academy, 1995–; Sang Marthe in Faust at Savonlinna, 1999. *Recordings include:* Joonas Kokkonen, The Last Temptation; Lady Macbeth of Mtsensk; Juha by Merikanto; The Horseman. *Address:* Bulevardi 19A2, 00120 Helsinki, Finland.

VÄLKKI, Anita; Singer (Soprano); b. 25 Oct. 1926, Saakmaki, Finland. *Education:* Studied with Tynne Haase, Jorma Huttunen and Lea Piltti in Helsinki. *Career:* Performed first as an actress and sang in operettas at theatre in Kokkola; Sang at the Helsinki National Opera from 1955; Royal Opera Stockholm from 1960, as Aida, Santuzza and Brünnhilde; Covent Garden 1961–64, as Brünnhilde; Metropolitan Opera 1962–66, Senta, Turandot, Venus, Brünnhilde, Kundry; Bayreuth Festival 1963–64; Guest appearances in Mexico City, Palermo and Philadelphia; Savonlinna Festival Finland 1983, as Mary in Der fliegende Holländer; sang at Helsinki 1986, in Juha by Merikanto. *Recordings include:* Third Norn in Götterdämmerung, conducted by Solti (Decca); The Horseman by Sallinen. *Address:* c/o Finnish National Opera, Bulevardi 23–27, SF 00180 Helsinki 18, Finland.

VALLE, José (Nilo); Conductor, Composer and Teacher; b. 20 Feb. 1946, Santa Catarina State, Brazil. *Education:* Paraná Music College (Music License and Fine Arts Degrees); National School of Music, Federal University of Rio de Janeiro (Graduate degrees in Composition and Conducting; MMusic and DMA in Orchestral Conducting, University of Washington School of Music, USA. *Career:* Debut: Federal University of Rio de Janeiro Symphony Orchestra, 1983; Teacher, Music Theory, Parana Music College; Assistant Conductor, Federal University of Rio de Janeiro, 1981–83; Conductor of the Florianópolis Choral Association, 1985–86; Assistant Conductor at the University of Washington, 1989–91; Conductor and Founder, Proconart Ensemble for Contemporary Music, University of Washington, 1989–91; Conductor, Founder, Camerata Simfonica, Seattle, Washington, 1989–91; Founder, and since 1993 Music Director and Conductor, Santa Catarina Symphony Orchestra, Florianópolis, Santa Catarina State, Brazil; President Director of the Santa Catarina Cultural Association. *Address:* CP 1004, 88010-970 Florianopólis, Santa Catarina State, Brazil.

VALLER, Rachel; Pianist; b. 14 Sept. 1929, Sydney, Australia; m. Walter Travers, 28 Feb 1965. *Education:* BA, 1952; DipEd, 1960; LTCL, 1947; Conservatorium of Music, Sydney; University of Sydney; Pupil of Ignaz Friedman. *Career:* Debut: Sydney, 1940; Soloist, Associate Artist Chamber Ensembles, ABC radio and television; Appearances with Sydney, Melbourne and Queensland Symphony Orchestras; Toured with cellist André Navarra, with Violinists Wanda Wilkomirska, Stoika Milanova, Zvi Zeitlin, Erick Friedman, Erich Gruenberg, Thomas Zehetmair and bassoonist George Zukerman. *Recordings:* Lesser known piano works of Beethoven issued to mark Beethoven bicentenary, 1970; Schubert's Sonatinas with violinist Susanne Lautenbacher to commemorate 150th anniversary of his death, Germany, 1978. *Honours:* Harriet Cohen Commonwealth Medal, 1956; O A M Medal of the Order of Australia, 1995. *Address:* 22 Allen's Parade, Bondi Junction, New South Wales 2022, Australia. *E-mail:* waltrav@bigpond.com.

VAN ALLAN, Richard; Opera Singer (bass baritone); b. 28 May 1935, Clipstone, Nottinghamshire, England; (divorced); 2 s., 1 d. *Education:* Dip Ed Science, Worcester College of Education; Birmingham School of Music. *Career:* Debut: Glyndebourne Festival Opera, 1964; sang in 1970 premiere of Maw's The Rising of the Moon: other appearances as Osmano in L'Ormindo, Leporello, Osmin, Trulove, the Speaker in Die Zauberflöte and Melibeo in La Fedeltà Premiata; Welsh National Opera; English National Opera; Royal Opera House, Covent Garden, London; Scottish Opera; Paris Opéra, France; Boston, San Diego, and Miami Operas, USA; Metropolitan Opera, New York; Brussels Opera, Belgium;

Buenos Aires Opera, Argentina; Director, National Opera Studio, 1986–; Sang Don Alfonso at the Metropolitan 1990, Pooh-Bah in The Mikado for ENO; Glyndebourne Festival 1990, as Budd in Albert Herring and Pistol in Falstaff; Season 1992 as Tiresias in the premiere of Buller's Bacchae at ENO and in Osborne's Terrible Mouth; Sang the Grand Inquisitor in Don Carlos for Opera North, 1993, Don Jerome in the world stage premiere of Gerhard's The Duenna (Madrid 1992); Appeared in title role of Don Quichotte by Massenet at Victoria State Opera, Melbourne, Australia, 1995, and for English National Opera, 1996; Season 1998 as Morenigo in Caterina Cornaro at the Queen Elizabeth Hall and in Dove's Flight at Glyndebourne; mem, Elected to Board of Directors, English National Opera Company, 1995. *Recordings include:* Brander, La Damnation de Faust, conductor, Colin Davis; Don Alfonso, Così fan tutte, Colin Davis; Leporello, Don Giovanni, conductor, Bernard Haitink. *Honours:* Grand Prix du Disque, La Damnation de Faust; Grammy Award, Così fan tutte; Grammy Nomination, Don Giovanni; Gloriana conducted by Charles Mackerras Decca, 1992; C.B.E., 2002. *Current Management:* Askonas Holt Ltd, Lonsdale Chambers, 27 Chancery Lane, London, WC2A 1PF, England. *Telephone:* (20) 7400-1700. *Fax:* (20) 7400-1799. *E-mail:* info@askonasholt.co .uk. *Website:* www.askonasholt.co.uk.

VAN APPLEDORN, Mary Jeanne, BM, MM, PhD; American composer and academic; *Paul Whitfield Horn Professor of Music Theory and Composition, Texas Technical University;* b. 2 Oct. 1927, Holland, MI; d. of John and Elizabeth Rinck. *Education:* Eastman School of Music, University of Rochester, New York. *Career:* solo piano debut, Weill Recital Hall, New York City, 1956; solo performer, Concerto Brevis for piano, American University, Washington DC, 1960; piano accompaniment, Concerto for trumpet and piano, with Robert Birch, trumpet for International Trumpet Guild, Albuquerque, New Mexico, 1985; Paul Whitfield Horn Professor of Music Theory and Composition, School of Music, Texas Tech University, Lubbock 1950–; ASCAP, Standard Panel Awards, 1980–2004. *Compositions:* Rhapsody, for violin and orchestra, 1996; Incantations for Oboe and Piano, 1998; Galilean Galaxies for flute, bassoon and piano, 1998; Five Psalms for tenor, trumpet and piano, 1998; Gestures for clarinet quartet, 1999; Meliora for symphony orchestra, 1999 and Meliora for symphonic band 2002; Commission from San Francisco Women's Symphony for Year 2000 Millennium performances; Symphony for Percussion Orchestra, 2000; Fanfare for trumpets, drums and cymbals, 2001; A Symphony of Celebration for Youth Orchestra 2002; Passages III for Clarinet, Cello and Piano 2003; Sonata for Guitar 2003. *Publications:* Cycles of Moons and Tides 1995; Trio Italiano, 1996. *Address:* 1629 16th Street, Apt 216, Lubbock, TX 79401, USA (home).

VAN ASPEREN, Bob; Harpsichordist; b. 8 Oct. 1947, Amsterdam, Netherlands. *Education:* Studied at the Amsterdam Conservatoire, with Gustav Leonhardt. *Career:* From 1971 many concerts as soloist and in concert; Appearances with La Petite Bande and Quadro Hotteterre; Founded the ensemble Melante 81, for the tercentenary of Telemann; Teacher at the Hague Conservatoire, 1973–88, Professor at the Hague Conservatoire from 1987. *Address:* Berlin Hochschule für Musik, Ernst Reuter Platz 10, 1000 Berlin 10, Germany.

van BARTHOLD, Kenneth; pianist and teacher; b. 10 Dec. 1927, Surabaya, Java, Indonesia; m. 1st Prudence; m. 2nd Sarianne; m. 3rd Gillian; two s. two d. *Education:* Bryanston School, Paris National Conservatoire of Music with Yves Nat. *Career:* debut, Bournemouth Municipal Orchestra 1944; Wigmore Hall 1956; frequent recitals in London Piano Series, Queen Elizabeth Hall and throughout the UK; concerts in Canada, France, Israel and Ireland, including broadcasts; concert appearances with many orchestras, including London Symphony Orchestra, English Chamber Orchestra, London Classical Players and Polyphonia under the conductors Sir Adrian Boult, Raymond Leppard, Sir Roger Norrington and Bryan Fairfax; Director of Studies, Victoria Coll. of Music 1953–1959; Prof. of Piano, Trinity Coll. of Music 1959–65; Head of Music, City Literary Inst. 1960–1983; Univ. of Edinburgh annual masterclasses during Int. Festival 1968–; Sr Piano Tutor, ILEA 1983–90; Lecturer on 19th- and 20th-Century Opera, Wimbledon Coll. of Art 1983–94; masterclasses in Israel, Canada and throughout the UK; int. juror in France and Canada; has written and presented 21 hour-long documentaries on TV, including first ever full-length studio documentary (BBC) 1964; further frequent appearances interviewing, linking, profiling and performing on both BBC and ITV. *Recordings:* Mozart Recital, Sonatas K284 and K332, Chopin Recital–Ballade No. 4, Mazurkas, Etudes etc, Schumann Recital, Couronne Competition, Liszt Sonata, Hommage à Pierre Max Dubois. *Publications:* The Story of the Piano (co-author) 1976; reviewer for BBC Music Magazine, various articles. *Honours:* Critics Award (television) 1972. *Address:* Arvensis, Stour Lane, Stour Row, Shaftesbury, Dorset SP7 0QJ, England. *E-mail:* kvanbarthold@aol.com.

VAN BLERK, Gerardus J. M.; Concert Pianist; b. 14 May 1924, Tilburg, Netherlands; m. A. Van den Brekel. *Education:* Studied Piano with Professor W. Andriessen, Amsterdam Conservatory; Piano-Soloist (Prix d'excellence); Studied with Yves Nat, Paris, France 1950–52. *Career:* Solo concerts with Concertgebouw Orchestra, Residentie Orchestra, The Hague, Rotterdam Philharmonic Orchestra with Haitink, Jochum, Fournet; Recitals, Chamber Music, Accompaniments (instrumental and singers); Professor of Piano, Royal Conservatory, The Hague. *Recordings:* Hindemith, Kammermusik Number 2, Klavierkonzert, op 36 Number 1; Chopin, Grand duo Concertant, Polonaise brillante op 3, Sonata in G minor op 65 with Anner Bylsma (violoncellist); Max Reger; Sonata for Cello and Piano, Caprice and Romance with Anner Bylsma; Brahms Lieder with Jard Van Nes (Alto); French violin sonatas; works of M Ravel. *Address:* Prinsengracht 1095, 1017 Amsterdam, Netherlands.

VAN BOER, Bertil Herman, Jr; Musicologist and Conductor; b. 2 Oct. 1952, Florida, USA; m. Margaret Fast 1977. *Education:* PhD, Uppsala University, Sweden, 1983. *Career:* Musical Director, Opera Kansas, 1989–; Assistant/Associate/Full Professor, Wichita State University, 1987–; Assistant Professor of Music, Brigham Young University, UT, 1983–87; Instructor, Shasta College, 1981–83. *Publications:* Dramatic Cohesion in the Works of Joseph Martin Kraus, 1989; Joseph Martin Kraus: Systemtisch-thematiches Werkverzeichnis, 1988; Joseph Martin Kraus Der Tod Jesu, 1987; The Symphony: Richter, Sweden I and II, 1983–86; Gustav III and the Swedish Stage, 1993. *Contributions:* Articles in Fontes, Svensk tidskrift for Musikforskning, Journal of Musicology, Journal of Musicological Research. *Address:* 316 S Belmont, Wichita, KS 67218, USA.

VAN BUREN, John (Hidden); Composer; b. 21 Sept. 1952, Portland, Oregon, USA; m. Margret Ulrike Schaal, 9 June 1988. *Education:* Reed College, Portland, 1970–72; Oregon State University, 1972–74; Composition with Milko Kelemen, Piano with Edgar Trauer, Electronic Music with Erhard Karkoschka, 1973–79, Diploma, Composition, 1979, Staatliche Hochschule für Musik, Stuttgart, Germany. *Career:* His works broadcast on various German radio stations, 1974–; Other performances of his works include ZDF national television, 1979. St ädtisch Bühne Mainz Ballet, 1981, American Composers' Orchestra, in Carnegie Hall, 1987, Deutsche Sinfonie Orchester, Berlin, 1994; Organiser, new music concerts, Stuttgart, notably as Artistic Director and Manager, Musica Nova Society; Has taught music at Ludwigsburg University, John-Cranko Ballet School of Stuttgart State Opera, City School of Music, Stuttgart; Dozent, Hochschule für Music Nürnberg-Augsburg, Augsburg; Taught International Masterclass in Verulà, Spain. *Compositions include:* Streichquartett, 1981; Fünf Gesänge nach Catull, 1984–85; Les Nuages de Magritte for violin, cello, piano, 1989 Mementos, Symphony No. 1, 1989–90; Aufbruch for orchestra, 1992. *Recordings:* Mementos, 1994; String Quartet Nr 2, 1996; Night Scenes for orchestra, 1996; Flute Concerto, 1998; Luxe, Calme et Volupté for violoncello and Piano, 1998; All major works recorded by Süddeutscher, Westdeutscher, Hessischer Südwest and Sender Freies Berlin radio stations. *Address:* Daimlerstrasse 29, 70372 Stuttgart, Germany.

VAN DAM, José; Singer (Bass); b. 25 Aug. 1940, Brussels, Belgium. *Education:* Brussels Conservatory with Frederic Anspach. *Career:* Debut: Liège 1960, as Basilio; Paris Opéra 1961–65, debut in Les Troyens; Geneva Opera 1965–67, taking part in the premiere of Milhaud's La m ère coupable, 1966; Deutsche Oper Berlin from 1967, as Verdi's Attila, Mozart's Leporello and Don Alfonso and Paolo in Simon Boccanegra; Sang Escamillo at his US debut (Santa Fe 1967) and at Covent Garden in 1973; Salzburg from 1968, in La Rappresentazione di Anima e di Corpo by Cavalieri, as Jochanaan in Salome, the villains in Les Contes d'Hoffmann, Mozart's Figaro and Amfortas in Parsifal; Vienna Staatsoper debut 1970, as Leporello; Metropolitan Opera debut 1975, as Escamillo; returned to New York as Golaud in Pelléas and Mélisande; Berg's Wozzeck and Jochanaan; Other appearances in Venice, Stockholm, Lisbon and Munich; Salzburg Easter Festival 1982, as the Flying Dutchman; Paris Opéra 1983 as St Francis of Assisi, in the premiere of Messiaen's opera; Sang Hans Sachs in Paris, 1990, Jochanaan in Salome at Lyons; Simon Boccanegra at Brussels; Sang as Falstaff at the Salzburg Festival, 1993; Season 1992/93 as Figaro (Mozart) in Brussels, Dapertutto at the Opéra Bastille, Don Quichotte at Toulouse and Saint Francois at Salzburg; Philip II in Don Carlos, London and Paris, 1996; Wagner's Dutchman at Rome, 1997; Debut as Boris Godunov at Toulouse, 1998; Season 2000–01 as Claudius in Hamlet at the Châtelet, Paris, Hans Sachs in Brussels, and as King Philip at Naples; Concert appearances in Chicago, Boston, Tokyo, Los Angeles and London. *Recordings:* Roles in: Carmen, Fidelio, Salome, Pelléas et Mélisande, Così fan tutte, Simon Boccanegra, Louise, Mireille and La jolie fille de Perth (HMV); Un Ballo in Maschera, La Damnation de Faust, Le nozze di Figaro (Decca); Parsifal, Die Zauberflöte (Deutsche Grammophon); Don Giovanni (CBS); Pénélope, Dardanus (Erato); Also heard in the Requiems of Brahms and Verdi and Bach's B Minor Mass. *Address:* c/o Théâtre Royal de la Monnaie, 4 Léopoldstrasse, 1000 Brussels, Belgium.

VAN DE VATE, Nancy (Hayes); Composer and Record Producer; b. 30 Dec. 1930, Plainfield, New Jersey, USA; m. (1) Dwight Van de Vate Jr, 9 June 1952, 1 s., 2 d., (2) Clyde Arnold Smith, 23 June 1979 (died 1999). *Education:* Eastman School of Music, University of Rochester, 1948–49; AB, Wellesley College, 1952; MM, University of Mississippi, 1958; D.Mus, Florida State University, 1968; Postdoctoral study, Electronic Music, Dartmouth and University of New Hampshire, 1972. *Career:* Opera premieres: In the Shadow of the Glen, Cambridge, Mass, USA, 1999; All Quiet on the Western Front (Acts II & III), NY City Opera, 2003; Im Westen nichts Neues, Osnabrück, Germany, 2003; Orchestral premieres: Distant Worlds, Concerto for Percussion and Orchestra, Concertpiece for Cello and Small Orchestra all premiered by Polish Radio Symphony Orchestra of Kraków, Szymon Kawalla conductor, 1987–89; Premieres, Musica Viva Festival, Munich, Aspekte, Salzburg, Poznan Spring Festival, Poland; Chernobyl, for orchestra, Vienna 1994; Dark Nebulae, Vienna Musikverein, 2000; Vice-President and Artistic Director of Vienna Modern Masters. *Compositions:* Cocaine Lil, 5 singers, percussion; Teufelstanz, percussion ensemble; A Night in the Royal Ontario Museum, soprano, tape; Pura Besakih for large orchestra; Nine Preludes for Piano; Twelve Pieces for Piano; Trio for Violin, Violoncello and Piano; Many choral, vocal, brass and solo string works; Viola Concerto; Four Sombre Songs, for mezzo and orchestra; Premieres: Katyn, 1989, Polish Radio Symphony Orchestra and Chorus, S Kawalla, Conductor; Concerto for Violin and Orchestra, 1992, Vienna Konzerthaus, Vienna Musiksommer; Operas: Nemo: Jenseits von Vulkania; In the Shadow of the Glen; All Quiet on the Western Front; Where the Cross is Made. *Recordings:* Operas Nemo: Jenseits von Vulkania, All Quiet on the Western Front, and In the Shadow of the Glen. Orchestral works, Polish Radio Symphony Orchestra of Kraków; Many solo and chamber works also commercially recorded; Violin Concerto No. 2, 1996; Suite from Nemo for Orchestra, 1996. *Address:* Margaretenstrasse 125/15, 1050 Vienna, Austria.

VAN DEN HOEK, Martijn; Concert Pianist; b. 1955, Rotterdam, Netherlands. *Education:* Studied at the Rotterdam Conservatory, in Moscow with Valeri Kastelskii, in Budapest with Pal Kadosa and in Weimar with Ludwig Hofmann; New York with Joseff Raieff and Eugene Liszt; Further study in Vienna with Paul Angerer. *Career:* Has performed as soloist with the Amsterdam Concertgebouw Orchestra, the Wiener String Quartet and the National Hungarian Post Orchestra; Performances in Belgium, France, Germany, Austria, Portugal, USA, Japan and Hong Kong; Recital with the BBC, London; Repertoire includes concertos by Bach, Bart ók, Beethoven, Chopin, Haydn, Hummel, Mozart and Schumann; Sonatas by Beethoven, Berg, Brahms, Chopin, Haydn, Mozart, Scarlatti, Schubert, Impromptus and Moments Musicaux, Schoenberg's Op 23; Schumann's Kreisleriana and Faschingsschwank aus Wien; Liszt Consolations, Sonata, Spanish Rhapsody, Valses oubliées and Opera transcriptions. *Honours:* Prix d'Excellence and Goethe Prize, 1978; Public Prize of the City of Amsterdam, 1981; First Prize, International Liszt Competition in Utrecht, 1986.

VAN DER LINDE, Clint; Singer (Countertenor); b. 1976, South Africa. *Education:* Boy soprano in Drakenberg Boys' Choir School, S. Africa, 1988; University of Pretoria, 1996; Eton College; Choral College of Music, with Ashley Stafford; Bach studies with Peter Schreier. *Career:* Appearances with the Orchestra of the Age of Enlightenment in Bach's B minor Mass; Title roles in Lotario, Ottone and Flavio for the London Handel Festival (1999, 2000, 2001); St Matthew Passion at St George's Hanover Square, 2001. *Honours:* Queen Elizabeth, the Queen Mother Scholarship, RCM; Kathleen Ferrier Bursary for Young Singers. *Address:* c/o Royal College of Music, Prince Consort Road, London, SW7, England.

VAN DER MEER, Ruud; Singer; b. 23 June 1936, The Hague, Netherlands; m. Annetje Schonk, 12 May 1979, 1 s., 2 d. *Education:* Royal Conservatory, The Hague; Mozarteum, Salzburg; With Pierre Bernac, Paris. *Career:* Debut: Concertgebouw, Amsterdam, 1967; Concerts, recitals and oratorio, USA, Western and Eastern Europe; Regular BBC radio recitals, Dutch and German radio stations; Now retired; Since 1991 Director of the Princess Christina Concours in the Netherlands. *Recordings include:* Bach Cantatas with Harnoncourt, Vienna; Bach St Matthew Passion with Royal Concertgebouw Orchestra; Duparc, Schumann and Brahms Lieder. *Honours:* Knight, Order of Orange Nassau; Order of the Dutch Lion, 2001. *Address:* L V Leeuwesteyn 71, 2271 HJ Voorburg, Netherlands.

VAN DER ROOST, Jan (Frans Joseph); Composer; b. 1 March 1956, Duffel, Belgium; m. Bernadette Johnson, 16 May 1980, 2 s., 2 d. *Education:* Lemmens Institute, Leuven; Royal Academy of Music, Antwerp and Ghent; Graduated in Music Theory, Harmony, Counterpoint, Fugue, Musical History, Trombone, Choral Conducting and Composition; Professor at the Lemmensinstituut in Leuven; Guest Professor, Shobi Institute of Education, Tokyo; Nagoya Univ. of Arts. *Compositions:* Divertimento, for piano, 1982; Canzona Gothica, for trombone and piano, 1982; Melopee e Danza, for 2 guitars, 1982; Per Archi, for string orchestra, 1983; 3 Bagatels, for flute and piano, 1984; Rikudim, for band, orchestra or string orchestra, 1985; Van Maan en Aarde (Of the Moon and the Earth), for mixed choir, 1985; Mozaieken (Mosaics), for orchestra, 1986; Concerto Grosso, for cornet, trombone and brass band, 1986; Jaargang (Turning of the Year), for choir and piano, 1986–87; Puszta, for band, 1987; Excalibur, for brass band, 1987; Elckerlyc (Everyman), Oratorio for soloists, choir and orchestra, 1987; Obsessions, for brass instrument and piano, 1987–88; Arghulesques, for clarinet quartet, 1988; Spartacus, for band, 1988; Symphony, for orchestra, 1988–89; Chemical Suite, for trombone quartet, 1990; Amazonia, for band, 1990; Met Annie in Toverland, for children's choir and ensemble, 1990; Olympica for band, 1992; Stonehenge for brass band, 1992; A Year has Four Lives, for female choir and guitar, 1993; Exodus, Oratorio, for soloists, choir, organ and brass band, 1994; Concierto de Homenaje for guitar and orchestra, 1995; Rhapsody for horn, winds and percussion, 1995; Poème Montagnard for band, 1996; canTUBAllada for solo tuba, 1997; Contrasto Grosso for recorder quartet and string quartet, 1997; Et in Terra Pax for band, 1998; Credentium for band, 1998; Canti d'Amore for baritone and chamber orchestra, 1999; Concerto Doppio for 2 clarinets and string orchestra, 1999; Sinfonia Hungarica for band, 2000; Albion for brass band, 2001; Concerto per Tromba for trumpet, cembalo and string orchestra, 2001; I Continenti for recorder quartet, 2002; Partita for guitar quartet, 2002; Sirius for orchestra, 2002; Sinfonietta for band, 2003; Contemplations for choir and organ, 2003. *Recordings include:* Per Archi, Canti D'Amore, Contrasto Grosso and Concerto Doppio (EMI Classics). *Address:* Albrecht Rodenbachlaan 13, 2550 Kontich, Belgium.

VAN GOETHEM, Patrick; Singer (Counter-tenor); b. 1968, Belgium. *Education:* Private studies. *Career:* Flemish Schola Cantorum Cantate Domingo; Member of various ensembles; Appearances with Laudantes Consort; Permanent soloists' ensemble; Performed with Ricercar Consort, Les Rumeurs Souterraines and Akademia; Appearances at festivals all over Europe; Passau Mozart Festival; Festival van Vlaanderen, Bruges; Ensemble Vocal Regional de Champagne-Ardenne; Dresden State Theatre; Bach weekends of the European Music Festival; Musica Antiqua Köln; Concentus Musicus Wien; Freiburger Barokorchestra and Hasse; Dresden Chamber Choir; Baroque Orchestra; Sang alto solos in Rotterdam; Sang with Orquesta Ciudad de Malaga; Netherlands Bach Society; Netherlands Handel Society; Concerto Köln; Baroque cantatas; Bach cantatas in Leipzig, as part of the Bach 250 celebrations. *Recordings:* 3 Bach cantatas; Monteverdi 1610 Vespers; Zelenka Te Deum; Heinichen Mass Opus 9; Scheidt Magnificat. *Address:* Kloosterstraat 114, 9420 Erpe-Mere, Belgium.

VAN HOVE, Luc; Composer; b. 3 Feb. 1957, Wilrijk, Belgium. *Education:* Antwerp Conservatory, with Wiilem Kersters. *Career:* Lecturer at Antwerp Conservatory and Lemmens Institute, Leuven, from, 1984. *Compositions:* Wood-Wind Quintet, 1982; Trois poèmes (Verlaine) for soprano, chorus and chamber orchestra, 1984; Two symphonies, 1989, 1997; Septet, 1989; Cello Sonata, 1991; Aria, for cello, 1992; Triptych, oboe concerto, 1993; String Quartet, 1994; Piano Concerto, 1995; Nonet, 1995; Strings, 1997. *Address:* c/o SABAM, Rue d'Arlon 75–77, B–1040 Brussels, Belgium. *Telephone:* (2) 2868211. *Fax:* (2) 2311800.

VAN IMMERSEEL, Jos; Harpsichordist and Conductor; b. 2 April 1928, Monaco. *Education:* Studied at the Antwerp Conservatoire, notably with Flor Peeters and Kenneth Gilbert. *Career:* Professor at the Anvers Conservatoire from 1972 and Artistic Director at the Sweelinck Conservatoire Amsterdam, 1981–85; Founded the Baroque Orchestra Anima Eterna, 1985 and Professor of Piano at the Paris Conservatoire from 1992; Many recitals and concerts throughout France; Conductor of the ensemble Anime Eterna and let it in Handel's Serse for Flanders Opera, 1996. *Address:* Conservatoire National, 14 Rue de Madrid, 75008 Paris, France.

VAN KEULEN, Isabelle; violinist and violist; b. 16 Dec. 1966, Mijdrecht, Netherlands. *Education:* Sweelinck Conservatoire, Amsterdam, Salzburg Mozarteum with Sándor Végh, masterclasses with Max Rostal and Vladimir Spivakov. *Career:* debut as violist 1992; has appeared from 1983 with Berlin Philharmonic, Vienna, Detroit, Minnesota and BBC National Orchestra of Wales, NHK of Tokyo and the Concertgebouw; Conductors have included Baumgartner, Chailly, Colin Davis, Dutoit, Ehrling, Leitner, Leppard, Marriner, Neumann, de Waart and Zinman; Appearances at the Salzburg Festival and tours with the Bamberg Symphony and Gidon Kremer's Lockenhaus Soloists; BBC Proms debut 1990, in Mozart with the Rotterdam Philharmonic; Strauss's Concerto with the BBC Philharmonic and the Dutilleux Concerto with the Concertgebouw; Other repertoire includes concertos by Bach, Haydn, Henkemans, Schnittke, Spohr and Stravinsky, in addition to the standard items; Messiaen's Quartet for the End of Time at the 1999 London Prom concerts; as violist has collaborated with the Hagen, Orlando and Borodin Quartets. *Recordings include:* Saint-Saëns and Vieuxtemps Concertos, London Symphony; Schubert's Octet; Shostakovich Sonatas for Violin and Viola (Fidelio). *Honours:* Silver Medal, International Yehudi Menuhin Violin Competition, 1983; Winner, Eurovision Young Musician of the Year Competition, 1984. *Current Management:* Georgina Ivor Associates, 66 Alderbrook Road, London SW12 8AB, England.

VANAUD, Marcel; Singer (Baritone); b. 1952, Brussels, Belgium. *Education:* Studied at the Brussels Conservatoire and at Liège. *Career:* Sang at the Liège Opera 1975–83, notably as Papageno, Escamillo, Alfonso in La Favorita, Renato and Ourrais in Mireille; Guest appearances at Pittsburgh and New Orleans 1984; New York City Opera 1985 as Zurga in Les Pêcheurs de Perles; Théâtre de la Monnaie Brussels as Raimund in Comte Ory and Mozart's Figaro; Season 1987–88 as Lescaut at Montreal, Posa in Don Carlos at Tulsa, Figaro at Santa Fe and Raimbaud at Toulouse; La Scala Milan 1989 in the premiere of Doktor Faustus by Manzoni; Returned to Liège 1992 as Mephistopheles in La Damnation de Faust and sang Germont at Los Angeles; Festival de Radio France at Montpellier 1992, as Sacchini's Oedipus and in Chateau des Carpathes by Philippe Hersant; Season 2000–01 as Count Luna at Montpellier, Amonasro in Geneva, and the Dutchman at Liège. *Recordings include:* Les contes d'Hoffmann and Franck's Les Béatitudes; Karnac in Le Roi d'Ys.

VANDERSTEENE, Zeger; Singer (Tenor); b. 5 June 1940, Ghent, Belgium. *Career:* Sang at first in concert and appeared in opera from 1980; Théâtre de la Monnaie at Brussels, 1981–84, as Evandre in Alceste and Steuermann in Fliegende Holländer; Théâtre du Châtelet, Paris, 1983, in Rameau's Les Indes Galantes; Bologna, 1987, in Gluck's La Danza; Sang Aegisthus in Elektra at Antwerp, 1990; Song recitals in works by Schubert, Schumann and Fauré. *Recordings include:* Castor et Pollux by Rameau (Telefunken); Armide by Lully (Erato). *Address:* Antwerp Opera, Ommeganchshtrasse 59, 2018 Antwerp, Belgium.

VANDERVELDE, Janika; Composer; b. 26 May 1955, Ripon, WI, USA. *Education:* University of Wisconsin; University of Minnesota, with Dominick Argento (PhD 1983). *Career:* Commissions from Minnesota Orchestra, St Paul CO and Dale Warland Singers; Faculty, Minnesota Center for Arts Education, 1990–; Composer-in-residence, Minnesota Chorale, 1999–2002. *Compositions:* Genesis I, for oboe and piano (1983), II, piano and trio (1983), III, flute, viola and harp (1984), IV, for violin, clarinet and piano (1987), V, four guitars (1987), VI, string trio (1988), VII, for saxophone, piano and percussion (1989); Clockwork Concerto, for viola and orchestra, 1987; Hildegard, video opera, 1989; O viridissima virga, for chorus and percussion, 1992; Polyhymnia for chorus and orchestra, 1992; Seven Sevens, opera, 1993; Echoes across the Stara Planina, for female chorus and orchestra, 1995; The Dreamweaver, for speaker and orchestra, 1996; Cafés of Melbourne, for accordion and orchestra, 1997; Beijing Cai Hong, for chorus and pipa, 1997; Wataridori, for chorus and oboe, 1997; Pacific Transit for pipa and orchestra, 1998; Cosmos for speaker and orchestra, 1999; Tutti for Earth and Heaven for chorus and organ, 1999; Cançao de Embalar for chorus, 2000; Dance Ablaze! for chorus and percussion, 2001; Adventures of the Black Dot for speaker, 4 instruments and chorus, 2001; O factura dei for chorus, percussion and electric bass, 2002; Birds of Oz for chorus, 2003. *Address:* c/o Hothouse Press, 1631 Highland Parkway, Saint Paul, MN 55116, USA. *Telephone:* (651) 690-3000. *Fax:* (651) 690-4559. *E-mail:* janikav@visi.com. *Website:* www.janikavandervelde.com.

VANDOR, Ivan; Composer; b. 13 Oct. 1932, Pecs, Hungary. *Education:* Diploma in Composition, S Cecilia; MA Ethnomusicology, UCLA, 1970. *Career:* Member, Musica Elettronica Viva, 1966–68; Member, Nuova Consonanza Improvis Group, 1967–68; Research in Tibetan Buddhist Music, 1970–71; Director, International Institute for comparative Music Studies, Berlin, 1977–83; Founder, Director, Scuola Interculturale di Musica, 1979–; Professor, Composition, Conservatory of Music, Bologna, 1979–; Professor of Music, Conservatory of Music S Cecilia. *Compositions:* Quartetto Per Archi, 1962; Moti, 1963; Serenata, 1964; Dance Music, 1969; Esercizi, 1966; Winds, 1970; Cronache, 1981; Cronache II, 1989; Concerto for Violoncello and orchestra, 1991; Fantasie for piano and orchestra, 1992; Offrande II, 1993; some short pieces for Harpsichord. *Publications:* La Musique du Bouddhisme Tibetain, 1976; Die Musik des Tibetischen Buddhismus, 1978; Editor, The World of Music, 1975–85. *Address:* Viale Parioli 73, 00197 Rome, Italy.

VANEEV, Vladimir; Singer (Bass); b. 1961, Russial. *Education:* Graduated Gorky Conservatoire, 1986. *Career:* Sang with the Mussorgsky Opera, St Petersburg, 1986–97; Kirov Opera from 1997, as Verdi's Philip II and Grand Inquisitor Boris and Pimen in Boris Godunov and Prince Gremin in Eugene Onegin; Further appearances as Dosifei in Khovanshchina, Ruslan, Wagner's Wotan and Dutchman and Boris in Katerina Izmailova; Sang Ivan Khovansky in Khovanshchina with the Kirov at Covent Garden, 2000; Other roles include Prince Galitsky and Khan Konchak in Prince Igor, Monterone (Rigoletto), Remeniuk in Prokofiev's Semyon Kotko and Kochubei in Mazeppa; Sang

Klingsor in Parsifal, with the Kirov at the Royal Albert Hall, 1999. *Honours:* Honoured Artist of Russia; Prize Winner Voce Verdiani, All-Russian Chaliapin and Russian State Competitions. *Address:* c/o Kirov Opera, Mariinksy Theatre, 1 Theatre Square, St Petersburg, Russia.

VANELLI, Adriana; Singer (Soprano); b. 1957, Detroit, USA. *Education:* Cleveland Institute of Music. *Career:* Sang at New York Grand Opera as Butterfly, Mimi and Aida, Liu in Turandot and Nedda in Pagliacci for Stamford State Opera, Mozart's Countess in Nevada and Tosca for New Jersey Opera; Violetta for Connecticut Grand Opera 1985 and Desdemona at Providence, 1986; European debut as Liu, at Hamburg; Tatiana in Eugene Onegin for Netherlands Opera, Manon Lescaut at Wiesbaden (1985) and Tosca at Nice (1986); Deutsche Oper Berlin 1986-89; Sang Annina in Menotti's The Saint of Bleecker Street, 1989; Concert engagements in Europe and North America. *Address:* c/o Deutsche Oper, Richard Wagner Strasse 10, D-10585 Berlin, Germany.

VANESS, Carol; Singer (Soprano); b. 27 July 1952, San Diego, California, USA. *Education:* Studied in California with David Scott and in 1976 won the San Francisco Opera Auditions. *Career:* San Francisco 1977, as Vitellia in La Clemenza di Tito; New York City Opera from 1979, as Alcina, Antonia in Les Contes d'Hoffmann, Vitellia, Flotow's Frau Fluth, Mimi, and Leila in Les pêcheurs de Perles, Rigoleto (Gilda), Traviata (Violetta); Donna Anna; Glyndebourne Opera from 1982, as Donna Anna, Electra in Idomeneo, Fiordiligi and Amelia Boccanegra (1986); Covent Garden debut 1982, as Mimi: returned for Vitellia and Dalila in Handel's Samson; Countess Almaviva, 1989; Rosalinda in Der Fledermaus; Metropolitan Opera from 1984, as Armida in Rinaldo, Fiordiligi, Electra and the Countess in Figaro, Manon; Australian Opera 1985, Amelia in Un Ballo in Maschera; Seattle Opera 1986, as Massenet's Manon; Desdemona, 1986; Violetta, 1988; Leonora in Trovatore, 1989; Concert appearances in the Choral Symphony in Paris, the Verdi Requiem in Philadelphia and at the Lincoln Center New York with Pavarotti; Sang in Beethoven Missa solemnis at the Barbican Hall, London, 1989; Royal Opera, Vitellia in La Clemenza di Tito 1989; Trovatore 1990 at the Metropolitan Opera and Faust (Marguerite); Don Giovanni (Anna) at Covent Garden, 1992; Season 1992/93 as Iphigénie en Tauride at La Scala, Mathilde in Guillaume Tell at San Francisco and Olympia at the Met; Sang Desdemona at the Metropolitan, 1994; Norma at Seattle, 1994, (Amelia, Ballo in Maschera, 1995); Fiordiligi at the Met, 1997; Elisabeth de Valois at the Opéra Bastille, 1998; Season 2000–01 as Donna Elvira for San Francisco Opera, the Trovatore Leonora in Washington and Mathilde in Guillaume Tell for the Vienna Staatsoper; Sang Tosca at Covent Garden, 2002. *Recordings include:* Donna Anna in the Glyndebourne production of Don Giovanni conducted by Bernard Haitink; Masses by Haydn; Glyndebourne, Haitink, Così fan tutte; Beethoven's Ninth with Dohnányi and Cleveland Orchestra; Missa Solemnis with Tate and the ECO; Don Giovanni (Elvira), conducted by Muti, EMI; Tosca, Philips; Rossini, Stabat Mater, Philips (Bychkov). *Address:* c/o Herbert H Breslin, 119 West 57th Street, NY 10019, USA.

VÄNSKÄ, Osmo; Conductor; b. 28 Feb. 1953, Sääminki, Finland. *Education:* Sibelius Academy, Helsinki, with Jorma Panula, 1977–79. *Career:* Co-principal clarinet with Helsinki PO, 1977–82; Principal Guest Conductor, Lahti SO, 1985 (Music Director from 1988); Music Director Iceland SO 1993–96, Tapiola Sinfonietta 1990–92; Chief Conductor BBC Scottish SO until 2002; Music Director Minnesota Orchestra, 2003–; Guest conductor with Chicago SO, Cleveland Orchestra, Boston SO, San Francisco SO, Detroit, Houston and Saint Louis Symphonies; Munich PO, Leipzig Gewandhaus Orchestra, Oslo PO, Concertgebouw Orchestra, BBC SO, Czech PO, Orchestre National de France; Symphonic cycles of Beethoven, Sibelius and Nielsen with BBC Scottish SO: Tapiola by Sibelius and Nielsen's 4th at the 2002 London Proms. *Recordings include:* Sibelius Edition, with Lahti SO (BIS); Albums of Kalevi Aho; Sofia Gubaidulina, Kokkonen and Rautavaara; Nielsen Symphonies. *Honours:* Royal Philharmonic Society Award, 2002. *Current Management:* Harrison/Parrott Ltd, 12 Penzance Place, London, W11 4PA, England. *Telephone:* (20) 7229 9166. *Fax:* (20) 7221 5042. *Website:* www.harrisonparrott.com.

VARADY, Julia; Singer (soprano); b. 1 Sept. 1941, Oradea, Romania; m. Dietrich Fischer-Dieskau, 1977. *Education:* Studied in Cluj with Emilia Popp and in Bucharest with Arta Florescu. *Career:* Debut: Cluj 1962, as Fiordiligi; Guest appearances at the Budapest and Bucharest Operas; Moved to Frankfurt, 1972; Sang Violetta at Cologne, 1972; Munich from 1973, as Vitellia in La Clemenza di Tito, Lady Macbeth, Butterfly, Giorgetta (Il Tabarro), Elektra in Idomeneo, Santuzza, Liu, Leonora (La Forza del Destino), Elisabeth de Valois and Cordelia in the premiere of Lear by Reimann (1978); Scottish Opera 1974, as Gluck's Alceste; Metropolitan Opera 1978, Donna Elvira; Tours of Japan, Israel and the USA; Appearances at the Berlin, Edinburgh, Munich and Salzburg Festivals and at the Promenade Concerts London; La Scala Milan 1984, in Idomeneo; Other roles include Countess Almaviva, Judith (Bluebeard's Castle), Tatiana, Desdemona and Rosalinde; Sang Wagner's

Senta at Munich 1990, Covent Garden 1992; Vitellia in La Clemenza di Tito at the Queen Elizabeth Hall, 1990; Appeared as Abigaille in Nabucco at the 1990 Munich Festival; Season 1992/93 as the Trovatore Leonora at Munich, in concert performances with the Glyndebourne Company of Fidelio and Elisabeth de Valois at the Deutsche Oper Berlin; Returned to Berlin 1997, as Senta; Aida at the 1997 Munich Festival; Featured Artist (People No. 181), Opera Magazine, 1992; Concert repertoire includes arias by Mozart and Beethoven, Vier Letzte Lieder by Strauss, Britten's War Requiem, the Verdi Requiem, the Faust oratorios of Schumann and Berlioz; Requiem by Reimann (premiere 1982); Soloist in the Verdi Requiem at Berlin, 2000; Recital in Madrid, 2003. *Recordings include:* Lucio Silla by Mozart); Die Fledermaus; Il Matrimonio Segreto; Lear; Idomeneo; La Clemenza di Tito; Duke Bluebeard's Castle; Gli Amori di Teolinda by Meyerbeer; Cavalleria Rusticana; Les Contes d'Hoffmann, Arabella; Don Giovanni; Handel's Saul. *Current Management:* Askonas Holt Ltd, Lonsdale Chambers, 27 Chancery Lane, London, WC2A 1PF, England. *Telephone:* (20) 7400-1700. *Fax:* (20) 7400-1799. *E-mail:* info@askonasholt.co.uk. *Website:* www.askonasholt.co.uk.

VARCOE, Stephen; Singer (baritone); b. 19 May 1949, Lostwithiel, Cornwall, England; m. Melinda Davies 1972; three s. (one deceased) two d. *Education:* Cathedral Choir School and King's School, Canterbury; MA, King's College, Cambridge; Guildhall School of Music, London. *Career:* concerts in most major British and European festivals; specialist in Lieder, French Mélodies and English song; many appearances on British, French and German radio stations; sang Sarastro in Die Zauberflöte at the Mozart Experience, London, 1989; Haydn's L'Infedeltà Delusa at Antwerp in 1990; created Zossima in the premiere of Tavener's Mary of Egypt, Aldeburgh, 1992; Peri's Eurydice in Drottningholm, 1997; sang Bartley in Riders to the Sea, Vaughan Williams Festival, London, 1997. *Recordings:* over 130 albums including: Purcell's Indian Queen, Fairy Queen, King Arthur and The Tempest; Handel's Partenope, L'Allegro, Triumph of Time and Truth, Alessandro and Israel in Egypt; Bach's B Minor Mass, Masses, Cantatas and Matthew and John Passions; Fauré's Requiem; Finzi's Songs of Thomas Hardy; Rameau's Motets, French Mélodies; Britten's Cantata Misericordium and Tavener's Mary of Egypt; Schubert's Lieder. *Publication:* Sing English Song, 2000. *Contribution:* Cambridge Companion to Singing, 2000. *Honours:* Gulbenkian Foundation Fellowship, 1977. *Current Management:* Caroline Phillips Management, The Old Brushworks, Pickwick Road, Corsham, Wiltshire, SN13 9BX, England. *Telephone:* (1249) 716716. *Fax:* (1249) 716717. *E-mail:* cphillips@caroline-phillips.co.uk. *Website:* www.caroline-phillips.co.uk/varcoe.

VARGA, Balint (Andras); Music Publisher and Music Interviewer; b. 3 Nov. 1941, Budapest, Hungary; m. Katalin Zsoldos, 14 Jan 1977, 2 d. *Education:* Teacher's degree, English and Russian, University of Budapest, 1960–65; Hungarian Journalists' School, 1966–67; Studied piano privately for 13 years. *Career:* Regular radio programmes in Budapest, 1965–; Some foreign radio programmes; Occasional programmes on Hungarian Television; Head of Promotion, Editio Musica Budapest, 1971–; Deputy Director of the Hungarian Cultural Institute, Berlin, 1991–. *Publications:* Conversations with Lutoslawski, 1974; Conversations with Iannis Xenakis, 1980; Conversations with Luciano Berio, 1981; 4 other anthologies of musical interviews published in Hungarian 1972, 1974, 1979, 1986; Translated Aaron Copland's The New Music into Hungarian 1973, also two books published in English and one published in German. *Contributions:* Regular articles in Muzsika. *Address:* 1020 Berlin, Fischerinsel, 10301, Germany.

VARGA, Gilbert; Conductor; b. 17 Jan. 1952, London, England; m. 2 children. *Education:* Studied with Franco Ferrara, Sergiu Celibidache and Charles Bruck. *Career:* Principal Conductor, Hofer Symphoniker, 1980–85; Chief Conductor of the Philharmonia Hungarica, 1985–90; Principal Guest Conductor, Stuttgart Chamber Orchestra, 1992–1996; Principal Guest Conductor, Malmö Symfoniorkester, 1997–99; Music Director Orquestre Sinfonica de Euskadi, 1998–; Guest engagements include Orchestre de Paris, Rotterdam Philharmonic, Hallé Orchestra, City of Birmingham Symphony, BBC Philharmonic, Bavarian Radio, Gürzenich Orchestra Cologne, Toronto Symphony, Indianapolis Symphony, Sydney Symphony Orchestra; Yomiuri Nippon Symphony, Tokyo; Scottish Chamber ORchestra; Orchestre de la Suisse Romande; Göteborg Symphony Orchestra; Cologne Radio; Minnesota Orchestra; Santa Caecilia Roma; Saint Louis Symphony; RAI Torino. *Recordings include:* Symphony No. 6 of Anton Rubinstein and solo cello concertos with BBC Philharmonic and Rolland; Ravel recording with Orquestre Sinfonica de Euskadi and recordings with Munich Chamber Orchestra and Bamberg Symphony. *Address:* c/o Intermusica Artists Management Ltd, 16 Duncan Terrace, London N1 8BZ, England.

VARGAS, Milagro; Singer (Mezzo-soprano); b. 1958, USA. *Education:* Studied at Oberlin College and the Eastman School of Music with Jan DeGaetani. *Career:* Member of the Stuttgart Staatsoper 1983–88, notably in the premiere of Akhnaten by Philip Glass (1984) and as Cherubino, Nancy in Albert Herring, Orlofsky, and Lybia in Jommelli's Fetonte; Komische Opera Berlin as Cherubino, Heidelberg Festival as Ramiro in La Finta Giardiniera; Sang Charlotte in Zimmermann's Die Soldaten at Strasbourg and Stuttgart, 1988; Sang Ravel's Shéhérazade at the Cabrillo Festival 1986 and has appeared elsewhere in concert at the Aspen and Marlboro Festivals, with the Philadelphia Orchestra and the Rochester Philharmonic; Season 2000–01 as Nemorino at Houston, Lensky in Florence, Donizetti's Roberto Devereux for the Vienna Staatsoper and Don Carlos for Washington Opera; Duke of Mantua at Covent Garden, 2002. *Recordings include:* Akhnaten; Die Soldaten. *Address:* c/o Staatsoper Stuttgart, Oberer Schlossgarten 6, 7000 Stuttgart 1, Germany.

VARGAS, Ramon; Singer (Tenor); b. 1959, Mexico City, Mexico. *Career:* Has sung in opera a Mexico City as Fenton in Falstaff, Nemorino, Don Ottavio and Count Almaviva; Sang Gelsomino in Il Viaggio a Reims at the Vienna Staatsoper, 1987; Pesaro and Salzburg Festivals, 1987, Mexico City 1988 as Tamino: Further appearances at Lucerne 1989, Zürich 1990 as Lorenzo in Fra Diavalo and Enschede Holland, as Fenton; Season 1991–92 as Leicester in Rossini's Elisabetta at Naples, Almaviva at Rome, Rodrigo in a concert performance of La Donna del Lago at Amsterdam and Paolina in Il Matriomonio Segreto at Martina Franca; Sang Rossini's Almaviva at the Verona Arena, 1996; Alfredo Germont at the Opéra Bastille, 1998–99; Rodolfo in La Bohème at Covent Garden, 1999 and at the New York Met, 2002; London Proms, 2002. *Recordings include:* Rossini's Il Turco in Italia; Massenet's Werther. *Address:* c/o Opernhaus Zürich, Falkenstrasse 1, 8008 Zürich, Switzerland.

VARGYAS, Lajos (Karoly); Musical Folklorist and Ethnographer; b. 1 Feb. 1914, Budapest, Hungary; m. 17 Dec 1949. *Education:* Pupil of Kodály in Musical Folklore, Budapest University; Church Music at Budapest Music Academy, 1936–37; Doctor of Ethnography, Linguistics and Hungarian Literature, 1941; Academic D.Mus, 1963. *Career:* Assistant Professor at Budapest University, 1952–54; Director of Folk Music Research Group, Hungarian Academy, 1970–73; President, Committee for Scientific Classification in Musicology and Ethnography, Hungarian Academy; Music Committee, Hungarian Academy. *Recordings:* Mongolian Folk Music, UNESCO, 1971. *Publications include:* Aj falu zenei élete (The Musical Life of the Village Aj), 1941; Compiler, Kodály: A Magyar népzene; A peldatart szerkesztette Vargyas Lajos (The Hungarian Folk Music: Collection of Tune Examples by L Vargyas), 1952; A magyar vers ritmusa (The Rhythm of the Hungarian Verse), 1952; Author and Editor, Studia Memoriae Belae Bartók Sacra, 1956, 1957 and 1959; Aj falu zenei anyaga (The Tune Material of The Village Aj), 1960, 1961 and 1963; Magyar vers–Magyar Nyelv (Hungarian Verse–Hungarian Language), 1966; Researches into The Mediaeval History of Folk Ballad, 1967; Zoltan Kodály: Folk Music of Hungary, 2nd revised and enlarged edition, 1971; Balladaskonyv (Books of Ballads with their tunes), 1979; Hungarian Ballads and The European Ballad Tradition, in Hungarian, 1976, English 1983; A magyarság népzenéje (Folkmusic of the Hungarians), 1981, 1993; Keleti hagyomany–nyugati kultura, Tanulmanyok (Eastern Traditions–Western Culture, Essays), 1984; Magyar Néprajz V Népköltészet (Hungarian Ethnography Folkpoetry), 1988; Kodály hatrahagyott foljegyzesei l (Kodály's Records Left Behind), editor, 1989, 1993; Corpus Musicae Popularis Hungaricae VIII/A-B, editor, 1993; Kerítésen kivül (Emlékek életemböl) (Memoirs), 1993; Magyar népballadák (Hungarian Folkballads), 1994. *Honours:* Erkel Prize, 1980; Széchényi Prize, 1991. *Address:* 1022 Budapest, Szemlohegy Str 4/B, Hungary.

VARNAY, Astrid; Singer (soprano, mezzo-soprano); b. 25 April 1918, Stockholm, Sweden; m. Hermann Weigert, 19 May 1944. *Education:* Studied with Paul Althouse and Herman Weigert in New York. *Career:* Debut: Metropolitan Opera 1941, as Sieglinde; Sang at the Metropolitan until 1956, as Brünnhilde, Isolde, Senta, Elsa, Elisabeth, Kundry, Venus, Ortrud, the Marschallin, Amelia Boccanegra, Santuzza and Salome; Sang in the premiere of Menotti's The Island God, 1942; Chicago Opera debut 1944, Sieglinde; San Francisco Opera 1946–51, notably as Gioconda and Leonore; Mexico City 1948, as Aida and Santuzza; Covent Garden debut 1948, as Brünnhilde in Siegfried: returned to London 1951, 1958–59 and 1968 (Kostelnicka in Jenůfa); Bayreuth Festival 1951–67, as Brünnhilde, Isolde, Ortrud, Kundry and Senta; Paris Opéra and La Scala Milan as Isolde, 1956, 1957; Stuttgart 1959, as Jocasta in the premiere of Oedipus der Tyrann by Orff; Mezzo roles from 1962: Clytemnestra, Herodias and the title role in Einem's Der Besuch der Alten Dame; Salzburg Festival 1964–65, as Elektra; Professor at the Düsseldorf Musikhochschule from 1970; Returned to the Metropolitan 1974, as the Kostelnicka, then sang Herodias, Clytemnestra and Begbick in Mahagonny. *Recordings:* Der fliegende Holländer, Lohengrin (Decca); Oedipus der Tyrann (Deutsche Grammophon); Cavalleria Rusticana (HMV); Private recordings from Bayreuth and the Metropolitan; Der Ring des Nibelungen conducted by Clemens Krauss, Bayreuth 1953; Sang in recordings released 1984–85 by Decca:

Andrea Chénier and The Rake's Progress; Götterdämmerung, Bayreuth, 1951, released 1999; Salome, 1953, Orfeo; Schoenberg's 2nd Quartet, conducted by Dimitri Mitropoulos. *Publications include:* 55 Years in Five Acts (co-author), 2000. *Honours:* Maximilansorden, Bavaria, 1980; Wilhelm-Pitz Medal, Bayreuth, 1988. *Address:* c/o Bayerische Staatsoper, Max.Joseph-Platz 2, 80539 Munich, Germany.

VARONA, Luciano; Argentine stage designer and costume designer; b. 14 Aug. 1930, Mendoza. *Education:* Escuela Superior de Bellas Artes, Buenos Aires. *Career:* debut at Teatro Colón, Buenos Aires 1959, Prokofiev's The Love for Three Oranges; Collaborated with Tito Capobianco at the New York City 1966–73, with Giulio Cesare, The Golden Cockerel, Manon, Lucia di Lammermoor and Donzetti's Tudor trilogy; Handel's Ariodante for the opening of the Kennedy Center at Washington, DC, 1971; San Francisco and Vancouver Opera 1972–73, with Norma and Lucrezia Borgia; further association with Capobianco at the Deutsche Oper Berlin and the Netherlands Opera 1971–74, Attila, Aida, Rodelinda and La Traviata; Returned to the Teatro Colón 1981–88, with designs for Romeo et Juliette, Die Zauberflöte, Carmen and Die Entführung. *Address:* c/o Teatro Colón, Cerrito 618, 1010 Buenos Aires, Argentina.

VARPIO, Marja-Leena; Singer (Soprano); b. 1956, Helsinki, Finland. *Education:* Munich Musikhochschule and Salzburg Mozarteum. *Career:* Vienna Kammeroper 1985-87, as Paisiello's Rosina, Susanna, and Blondchen in Die Entführung; Vienna Volksoper 1987-90, as Mozart's Despina and Papagena; Festival appearances as Schwetzingen, Vienna and Savonlinna (Telemann's Pimpinone, 1990); Premiere of Adriana Hölszky's Bremer Freiheit, Munich 1998; Season 1993-94 as Axiniain in Katerina Izmailova at Stuttgart and Musetta for Finnish National Opera; Other roles include Mozart's Countess, and Lucia in Hindemith's The Long Christmas Dinner; Frequent engagements in operetta; Concerts include Mozart's Requiem, Beethoven's Ninth, Masses by Haydn, and Carmina Burana. *Address:* c/o Finnish National Opera, PO Box 176, Helsingkatu 58, 002 51 Helsinki, Finland.

VARVISO, Silvio; Conductor; b. 26 Feb. 1924, Zürich, Switzerland. *Education:* Studied at the Zürich Conservatory and in Vienna with Clemens Krauss. *Career:* Debut: St Gallen 1944, Die Zauberflöte; Assistant, then Principal Conductor of Basle Opera, 1950–62; Conducted opera in Berlin and Paris, 1958; San Francisco Opera from 1959 (US premiere of A Midsummer Night's Dream, 1961); Metropolitan Opera from 1961, Lucia di Lammermoor, Die Walküre, Die Fledermaus, Die Meistersinger, and Italian repertory; Glyndebourne and Covent Garden 1962, Le nozze di Figaro and Der Rosenkavalier; Principal Conductor of the Royal Opera, Stockholm 1965–71; Bayreuth Festival 1969–74; Die Meistersinger, Der fliegende Holländer and Lohengrin; Conducted new production of La Bohème at Covent Garden, 1974; Musical Director at Stuttgart 1972–80; has led performances of Rossini, Donizetti, Bellini, Strauss, Mozart and Wagner; Musical Director of the Paris Opéra 1980–85; Conducted Lohengrin at Stuttgart 1990, Manon Lescaut at Barcelona; Season 1992/93 with Tosca at Antwerp and Die Frau ohne Schatten in Florence; Conducted La Fanciulla del West at Ghent, 1996; Turandot at Antwerp, 1998. *Address:* c/o Staatstheater Stuttgart, Oberer Schlossgarten 6, 7000 Stuttgart 1, Germany.

VASARY, Támás; Pianist and Conductor; b. 11 Aug. 1933, Debrecen, Hungary; m. Ildiko Kovacs, 15 Mar 1967. *Education:* Franz Liszt Music Academy, Budapest, 1951. *Career:* Debut: First Concert, aged 8; Performed in major music centres, world-wide; Festivals include: Salzburg, Edinburgh, Berlin; Conducting Debut in 1970; conducted over 70 orchestras; Music Director, Northern Sinfonia, 1979–83; Principal Conductor, Music Director, Bournemouth Sinfonietta, 1989–97; Musical Director of Hungarian Radio Orchestra, 1993; Conducted Die Zauberflöte at the Thalia Theatre, Budapest, 1998. *Recordings:* Chopin; Liszt; Debussy; Brahms; Mozart; Rachmaninov. *Honours:* Paris, Marguérite Long, 1950; Queen Elisabeth of Belgium, 1956; Rio de Janeiro International Competition, 1956; Bach and Paderewski medals, 1960. *Address:* 9 Village Road, London N3 1TL, England.

VASILYEVA, Alla; Concert Cellist; b. 1933, Moscow, Russia. *Education:* Studied at the Central Music School and at the Moscow State Conservatoire, with Rostropovich. *Career:* Joined the Moscow Chamber Orchestra under Rudolf Barshai 1958 and remains as principal cellist; many tours with the Moscow Chamber Orchestra and as solo recitalist, notably in modern Russian works; Plays her own arrangements of works by Respighi and Vivaldi. *Recordings:* Works by Bach, Geminiani, Vivaldi, Moshei Wainberg, Boris Tchaikovsky, Khrennikov and Shostakovich. *Address:* c/o Sonata, 11 Northpark Street, Glasgow G20 7AA, Scotland.

VASKS, Peteris; Composer; b. 16 April 1946, Aizpute, Latvia. *Education:* Studied double bass at Lithuanian Conservatory, Vilnius, 1964–70; Composition at Latvian Conservatory, Riga, until 1978. *Career:* Double bassist in orchestras throughout Latvia and Lithuania, 1963–74;

Lecturer at Riga Music School, 1989–. *Compositions:* Music for Fleeting Birds, wind quintet, 1977; Three string quartets, 1997, 1984, 1995; In Memoriam for two pianos, 1997; Cantabile for strings, 1979; Book for Cello, 1979; In Memory of a Friend, wind quintet, 1982, Message for orchestra, 1982; Piano Trio, 1985; Double Bass Sonata, 1986; Latvija, chamber cantata, 1987; English Horn Concerto, 1989; Symphony, Voices, for strings, 1991; Litene, for 12 voices, 1992; Cello Concerto, 1994; Violin Concerto, 1997; Dona nobis pacem, for chorus and seven instruments, 1997; Symphony No. 2, 1998. *Address:* c/o AKKA/LAA, 12 Kr, Barona Str, Riga PDP, LV-1426, Latvia.

VASSAR, Frédéric; Singer (Baritone); b. 1948, France. *Education:* Studied at the Opera Studio of the Théâtre de la Monnaie, Brussels. *Career:* Sang first as bass in Opera at Brussels from 1973 (Alberich), then at Ghent (Wotan, Hoffmann, Boccanegra) and for French Radio; Sang Mephistopheles in Faust at Marseilles, 1977, followed by visits to Strasbourg, Avignon, Dublin and Orange; Engagements at Liège, 1985–86 as (Escamillo, Ourrais in Mireille), Angers, Metz (Golaud), Don Giovanni and the Villains in Hoffmann); Season 1989–90, as Mephistopheles at Avignon, Lescaut at Nantes, Telramund at Limoges and Scarpia for Opera Northern Ireland in Belfast. *Honours:* Winner, 1976 Voix d'or Enrico Caruso and Henri Duparc, France; Winner, Toti dal Monte.

VASSILEV, Vasko; violinist and concertmaster; b. 1965, Sofia, Bulgaria. *Education:* studied in Moscow. *Career:* after early competition success, joined Orchestra of Royal Opera House, 1991, as youngest ever leader and Concertmaster; solo career in Europe, North America and the Far East; European tour with the Royal Opera Orchestra 1998, with Mendelssohn and Tchaikovsky Concertos; Artistic Director of the Soloists of the Royal Opera House Orchestra 1998; Laureate of the String Ensemble. *Recordings include:* Solo and chamber music including Brahms Sonatas and Concerto by John Adams (Harmonia Mundi; Trittico Classics and Erato); Tartini Devil's Trill Sonata and The Original Four Seasons, with the Royal Opera String Ensemble and Vanessa Mae. *Honours:* prizewinner at Jacques Thibaud, Carl Flesch and Paganini Competitions. *Address:* c/o Royal Opera House (Contracts) Covent Garden, London WC2, England.

VASSILIEV, Alexandre; Singer (Bass); b. 20 March 1970, St Petersburg, Russia. *Education:* Tchaikovsky Conservatory, Moscow, 1989–93, with Evgeny Nesterenko; Masterclasses with Ernst Haefliger in Moscow, Hanna Ludwig at Salzburg and Astrid Varnay at Munich. *Career:* Appearances at the Bavarian State Opera, Munich, 1994–95, and the Freiburg Opera 1995–97; Role have included Bottom in Britten's Midsummer Night's Dream, Alidoro in Rossini's Cenerentola and Mozart's Figaro; Achillas in Handel's Giulio Cesare for Bavarian Radio; Concerts include Bach's B Minor Mass and Mozart's Requiem under Helmuth Rilling in Moscow; Beethoven's Missa Solemnis at Landshut, Oedipus Rex at Stuttgart and Suppé's Requiem in Freiburg; Season 1997–98 include appearances at Cologne Opera with Colline in La Bohème, Mesner in Tosca and Pistola in Falstaff; Performances of Sciarrino's Die tödliche Blume at the Schwetzingen and Vienna Festivals; Concerts and recitals in Freiburg, Stuttgart, Strasbourg and Cologne. *Address:* c/o Haydn Rawstron Ltd, 36 Station Road, London SE20 7BQ, England.

VASSILIEVA, Elena; Singer (Soprano); b. 1956, France. *Education:* Studied at the Paris Conservatoire. *Career:* Won various awards in the early 1980s and sang in Henze's Boulevard Solitude at Paris, 1984; Has sung in operas by Puccini, Massenet, Verdi, Strauss and Mozart and notably as Tatiana in Eugene Onegin; Saffi in Der Zigeunerbaron at Liège; Many concert appearances, including modern repertory and songs by Russian composers. *Address:* Opéra de Wallonie, 1 Rue des Dominicains, 4000 Liège, Belgium.

VATER, Wolfgang; Singer (Bass-baritone); b. 1949, Bremerhaven, Germany. *Education:* Hanover Musikhochschule, 1969–75. *Career:* Sang at Bielefeld from 1975, notably as Leporello; Bremen Opera from 1986; Gelsenkirchen, 1987, as Faber in Tippett's The Knot Garden; Season 1991 at Bielefeld in the premiere of Katharina Blum by Tilo Medek; Kothner in Die Meistersinger at Wiesbaden and Wiedehopf in Die Vögel by Braunfels; Other roles include Mephistopheles in Faust, Don Alfonso in Così fan tutte and Gessler in Guillaume Tell; Many concert and oratorio appearances. *Recordings include:* Werther; Strauss's Daphne. *Address:* c/o Buhnen der Stadt Bielefeld, Bruhnenstrasse 3–9, Pf 220, 4800 Bielefeld, Germany.

VAUGHAN, Denis (Edward); Orchestral Conductor and Organist; b. 6 June 1926, Melbourne, Australia. *Education:* BMus, University of Melbourne, 1947; Royal College of Music, London, England, 1947–50. *Career:* Debut: As Conductor, Royal Festival Hall, London, 1953; Annual harpsichord concerts, Royal Festival Hall, 1948–58; Concert to honour Toscanini, with Bernstein, Klemperer, Celibidache and Maazel, Parma, 1959; Adviser to UNESCO and Berne Union on musical aspects of copyright matters, 1962–67; Music Director, Australian Elizabethan

Theatre Trust, 1966; Orchestral concerts, operas in Europe, Australia, USA, Canada, 1970–2002; Munich State Opera House, 1972–80; Musical Director, State Opera of South Australia, 1981–84; Operas conducted include Così fan tutte, Faust, Fidelio, Falstaff, Boris Godunov, The Rake's Progress, Giulio Cesare; Concert in Vienna to celebrate the Austrian Millennium, 1996. *Recordings include:* 23 with Orchestra of Naples, including complete Schubert symphonies, 12 Haydn, 11 Mozart, Re Pastore etc, RCA Victor/BMG. *Publications:* Le Discrepanze Nei Manoscritti Verdiani, La Scala, 1959; Preface on organ articulation and phrasing, Stanley Voluntaries, 1959; Puccini's Orchestration, Royal Musical Association, 1961; The Evaluation of Errors and Omissions in Dvořák's Manuscripts, Prague, 1999. *Current Management:* Hazard Chase Ltd, Norman House, Cambridge Place, Cambridge, CB2 1NS, England. *Telephone:* (1223) 312400. *Fax:* (1223) 460827. *Website:* www.hazardchase.co.uk. *Address:* 41 Floral Street, London WC2E 9DG, England. *Telephone:* (20) 7836-7399. *Fax:* (20) 7836-2289. *E-mail:* denisvaughan2001@yahoo.co.uk.

VAUGHAN, Elizabeth; Singer (Soprano); b. 12 March 1937, Llanfyllin, Montgomeryshire, Wales. *Education:* Royal Academy of Music; FRAM. *Career:* Debut: Welsh National Opera, 1960, as Abigaille in Nabucco; Covent Garden from 1961, as Mimi, Liu (Turandot), Teresa (Benvenuto Cellini), Gayle (The Ice Break, world premiere), Andromache and Hecuba (King Priam), Mozart's Elvira and Electra, Madama Butterfly, and Verdi's Amelia (Boccanegra), Abigaille, Alice (Falstaff), Leonore (Trovatore), Gilda and Violetta; Opera North as Tosca, Lady Macbeth and Abigaille; Welsh National Opera as Tosca, Leonora (La Forza del Destino) and Maddalena in Andrea Chénier; English National Opera as Aida, Penelope Rich (Gloriana) and Beethoven's Leonore; Metropolitan Opera debut, 1972, as Donna Elvira; Guest engagements in Vienna, Berlin, Paris, Hamburg, Munich and Prague; Appearances in Australia, Canada, South America, Japan; Toured USA with English National Opera, 1984; Now Mezzo with major companies, roles of Herodias, Kabanicha (Katya Kabanova), and the Witch in Hansel and Gretel; Sang the Overseer in Elektra at Covent Garden, 1997; La Frugola in Il Tabarro for ENO, 1998; Season 1999 Princess in Suor Angelica and Old Prioress in Carmélites; Sang Herodias in Salome for Scottish Opera, 2000. *Honours:* Honorary D.Mus, University of Wales. *Current Management:* IMG Artists Europe, London, England. *Address:* c/o IMG Artists Europe, Lovell House, 616 Chiswick High Road, London W4 5RX, England.

VAUGHAN WILLIAMS, (Joan) Ursula Penton, FRCM; writer; b. 15 March 1911, Valletta, Malta; m. 1st Michael Forrester Wood 1933; m. 2nd Ralph Vaughan Williams 1953. *Career:* writer of songs, song cycles, libretti for cantatas and opera libretti; cttees: RVW Ltd., Ralph Vaughan Williams Trust. *Publications:* A biography of Ralph Vaughan Williams 1964, Paradise Remembered – An Autobiography 2002; seven vols of poems, three novels, two books of photographs of Ralph Vaughan Williams. *Honours:* Hon. FRAM, RNCM. *Address:* 66 Gloucester Crescent, London, NW1 7EG, England.

VAVILOV, Gennadi (Alekseevich); Composer and Professor; b. 7 May 1932, Russia; m. Natalia Romanenko, 17 Mar 1971, 1 s. *Education:* Musical High School, 1958; Theory on Music and Composing, Leningrad Conservatory, 1966; Moscow Conservatory, 1973–83; Petrozavodsk University, 1978. *Career:* Debut: Performing of Cantata for Choir and Symphony Orchestra, Moscow, 1959; Composer, 1958; Teacher of Theory of Music and Composition, 1958; Professor of Theory of Music, Instruments and Scores of Symphony Orchestra, 1989; Lecturer of Music, 1982; Music Accompaniment, 1982. *Compositions include:* Symphony No. 1, Voroneh, 1982; Philadelphia, USA, 1992; Symphony No. 4, Finland, 1990; Sochi, Russia, 1996; Symphony No. 3, Moscow, 1973; Sonata No. 2 for piano, Paris, France, 1996; Piano music: Allegro Barbaro, Dreams... Bushnell, USA, 1998; Original musical themes, traditions of Russian classical music, intonations characteristic for Karelian and Finnish Folk Tunes. *Recordings:* 3 records, Symphonietta for full symphony orchestra, Sonata for piano, Karellia tunes for symphony orchestra; Songs About Karelia, 1985; More than 13 works recorded to Gold Fund of Radio Russia. *Contributions:* Typical Features of Opera Orchestra by Mussorgsky, 1984; Some Problems in the Usage of Folk in Composing, 1985; Polifonia forms in the Symphony Music, 1985. *Honours:* 2nd place in the competitions of Young Composers, Moscow, 1958; Television Competition of the USSR, Moscow, 1959. *Address:* Lenin Street 13-3, 185000 Petrozavodsk, Russia.

VAVRINECZ, Béla; Composer, Conductor and Ethnomusicologue-historian; b. 18 Nov. 1925, Budapest, Hungary; m. Amalia Endrey, 1950, 1 s., 6 d. *Education:* Diploma in Composition, 1950, Diploma in Conducting, 1952, Budapest Academy of Music. *Career:* Debut: Budapest Academy of Music, 1949; First Conductor, Philharmonic Orchestra, Györ, 1957–58; Chief Conductor, Ministry of Home Affairs Symphony Orchestra, Budapest, 1961–73; Artistic Director, Dance Ensemble Budapest, 1974–83; Artistic Director, Ensemble Duna Budapest, 1983–85; Works frequently performed on radio and television. *Compositions:* 2 operas; 2

ballets; 112 musical pieces for dance theatre; 12 incidental works; 4 oratoria; Gisela, 1991; Chronicle of Somogy, 1999; 6 cantatas; 18 works for choir and orchestra; 20 works for symphony orchestra, including Symphonie, 1955; 6 works for chamber orchestra; 7 concerts; 45 chamber music works; Solo pieces; 33 choral works; 1 Mass; Songs; Arrangements; Music for wind bands. *Recordings:* Numerous. *Publications:* Kodály Memorial Book, 1953. *Address:* Cinkotai utca 39, 1141 Budapest, Hungary.

VEALE, John, MA; British composer; b. 15 June 1922, Shortlands, Kent, England; m. Diana Taylor 1944 (divorced 1971); one s. two d. (one deceased). *Education:* Repton School and Univ. of Oxford, studied with Thomas Armstrong, Egon Wellesz, Roger Sessions, Roy Harris. *Career:* Commonwealth Fellowship, USA 1949–51; Research Fellowship, Corpus Christi Coll., Oxford 1952–54; film correspondent, Oxford Mail 1964–80; copy ed., Oxford Univ. Press 1968–87; mem. Performing Right Soc. Ltd, British Acad. of Composers and Songwriters, Royal Philharmonic Soc.. *Compositions:* Symphonies 1, 2 and 3 1947, 1965, 1996, Clarinet Concerto, Violin Concerto, Panorama for orchestra, Metropolis concert overture for orchestra, Elegy for flute, harp and strings, String Quartet, Kubla Khan for baritone solo, mixed chorus and orchestra, Song of Radha for soprano and orchestra, Demos Variations for orchestra, Apocalypse for chorus and orchestra, Triune for oboe/cor anglais and orchestra, Encounter for two guitars, Three Sydney Streetscenes for chorus and instrumental ensemble 1994, Triptych for recorder and string quartet. *Recordings:* Clarinet Concerto, Three Sydney Streetscenes, Violin Concerto. *Publications:* contrib. articles and reviews to various publications. *Address:* 7 Nourse Close, Woodeaton, Oxford, OX3 9TJ, England. *Telephone:* (1865) 558156.

VEASEY, Josephine, CBE; British voice teacher and retd singer (mezzo-soprano); b. 10 July 1930, London, England; m. (divorced); one s. one d. *Career:* joined chorus of Royal Opera House, Covent Garden, 1949, a Principal there, 1955–82 (interval on tour in opera for Arts Council); Singer, Royal Opera House, Glyndebourne, Metropolitan (New York), La Scala and in France, Germany, Spain, Switzerland, South America; Operatic roles included: Octavian in Der Rosenkavalier; Cherubino in Figaro; Name role in Iphigénie en Tauride; Dorabella in Così fan tutte; Amneris in Aida; Fricka in Die Walküre; Fricka in Das Rheingold; Name role in Carmen; Dido and Cassandra in The Trojans; Marguerite in The Damnation of Faust; Charlotte in Werther; Eboli in Don Carlos; Name role in Gluck's Orfeo; Adalgisa in Norma; Rosina in The Barber of Seville; Kundry in Parsifal; Gertrude in Hamlet, 1980; Concerts, 1960–70; Aix Festival, 1967; Various works of Mahler; 2 tours of Israel with Solti; Sang in Los Angeles with Mehta; Handel's Messiah in England, Munich, Oporto and Lisbon; Berlioz Romeo and Juliette, London and Bergen Festival; Emperor in 1st performance of Henze's We Come to the River, Covent Garden, 1976; Final appearance at Covent Garden, 1982, as Herodias; Private Teacher, 1982–; Teacher of Voice Production and Interpretation, Royal Academy of Music, 1983–84; Voice Consultant to English National Opera, 1985–94. *Contributions:* Time Well Spent (profile), to Opera Magazine, July 1990. *Honours:* Hon. RAM 1972. *Address:* 2 Pound Cottage, St Mary Bourne, Andover, Hampshire, England.

VECCIA, Angelo; Singer (Baritone); b. 1963, Rome, Italy. *Education:* Studied at the Santa Cecilia Academy, Rome, and the Juilliard School, New York. *Career:* Debut: Sang Mozart's Figaro at Juilliard; Gave concerts at the Lincoln Center, New York, and elsewhere in America, and appeared in Tosca with Placido Domingo; Appearances throughout Italy as Rossini's Figaro, Belcore, Marcello (at Verona, Venice and Florence) and Silvio; Further roles in Gluck's Iphigénie en Tauride at La Scala, Rimsky's Golden Cockerel at Rome and Schoenberg's Moses und Aron in Florence; Zürich Opera as Sharpless (Madama Butterfly), Gianni Schicchi and Marcello; Season 1997 in Bohème and Turandot at Tel-Aviv, Il Barbiere di Siviglia at Zürich and Lucia di Lammermoor at La Scala; Sang as guest in Aida at Berlin and in the 1996 Christmas Concert under Riccardo Chailly at the Amsterdam Concertgebouw. *Address:* c/o Opernhaus Zürich, Falkenstrasse 1, 8008 Zürich, Switzerland.

VEDERNIKOV, Alexander; Conductor; b. 1964, Moscow, Russia. *Education:* Studied at Central Music School Moscow and at the Tchaikovsky Conservatoire with Mark Ermler. *Career:* Moscow Musical Theatre from 1989, conducting La Finta Glardiniera, Le nozze di Figaro, Cav and Pag, Il Barbiere di Siviglia, La Traviata, Eugene Onegin, The Queen of Spades, Boris Godunov and ballets by Tchaikovsky; Assistant Conductor at the Moscow Radio Symphony Orchestra 1990; Conductd the Junge Deutsche Philharmonie 1990, contract with the Rome Opera, 1991, debut with The Nutcracker; led the Moscow Radio Symphony at the Athens and Ankara Festivals 1992 and in Scotland, featuring music by Frank Martin, Glinka, Shostakovich and Vaughan Williams; Tours to the USA and Japan in season 1992–93; Guest engagements with orchestras in the United Kingdom. *Address:* c/o Sonata, 11 Northpark Street, Glasgow G20 7AA, Scotland.

VEDERNIKOV, Alexander (Filoppovich); Singer (Bass); b. 23 Dec. 1927, Mokino, nr Kirov, USSR. *Education:* Studied in Moscow with Alpert-Khasina. *Career:* Debut: Bolshoi Theatre Moscow 1957, as Ivan Susanin in Glinka's A Life for the Tsar; Appearances in Moscow, Leningrad, Tbilisi and Kiev as Boris and Varlaam in Boris Godunov, Dosifey (Khovanshchina) and Konchak in Prince Igor; Engagements with the company of the Bolshoi at Paris, New York and Milan as Philip II and the Grand Inquisitor in Don Carlos and Massimilione in Verdi's I Masnadieri; Toured West Germany with the Bolshoi 1987; Other roles include Daland in Der fliegende Holländer, Prince Gremin (Eugene Onegin), Kutuzov in War and Peace and Mephistopheles (Faust). *Recordings include:* The Stone Guest by Dargomyzhsky; Rimsky-Korsakov's The Snow Maiden, Pimen in a video of Boris Godunov from the Bolshoi (National Video Corporation). *Address:* c/o Bolshoi Theatre, Pr Marxa 8/2, 103009 Moscow, Russia.

VEERHOFF, Carlos; Composer; b. 3 June 1926, Buenos Aires, Argentina. (German national). *Education:* Berlin Hochschule für Musik with Hermann Grabner and Boris Blacher, in Cologne with Walter Braunfels, and in Switzerland with Hermann Scharchen. *Career:* Freelance composer in Munich (from 1952), Stuttgart, Argentina and Paris. *Compositions:* Pavane royal, ballet, 1950; Sinfonische Invention for Orchestra, 1951; Sinfonia panta-rhei, 1954; Sinfonischer Satz for Orchestra, 1954; Targusis, Opera 1955–57; Symphony, 1956, Symphonie Spirales 1958; El porquerizo del rey, ballet, 1958; Mirages for orchestra, 1961; Die goldene Maske, opera 1962–63, rev. 2002; Tanz des lebens, puppet opera, 1962; Five Bagatellen for Brass Orchestra, 1965; Akroasis for orchestra, 1965; Gesänge auf dem Wege for Baritone and Orchestra, 1966; Textur, for orchestra, 1970; Symphony no. 2, 1972; Es gibt doch Zebrastreifen, opera, 1972; Two Violin Concertos, 1976, 1992; Dualis, ballet 1975; Nonett, 1976; Gesänge aus Sanfsâra, 1976, rev. 1984; Piano Concerto no. 1, 1979; Dorefamie for Orchestra, 1980; Pater noster for chorus and orchestra, 1985; Concerto for cello, double bass and orchestra, 1988; Piano Concerto no. 2, 1989 rev. 1998; Concerto for percussion solo and orchestra, 1994; Desiderata, for chorus, solo voices and orchestra (Symphony No. 6), 1996; Burleske, for chorus, 1982, rev. 1998. *Address:* c/o GEMA, Rosenheimer Str. 11, 81667 Munich, Germany. *Telephone:* 0049 89480 0300. *Fax:* 0049 89480 03495.

VEIRA, Jonathan; Singer (Bass Baritone); b. 1960, England. *Education:* Studied at Trinity College of Music, London; The National Opera Studio. *Career:* Debut: Soloist, Wexford, 1986; At Glyndebourne appeared as Lemokh in the premiere of The Electrification of the Soviet Union; Die Entführung and Capriccio; Other engagements include a tour with Opera 80; Antonio, in Le nozze di Figaro at the Prom concerts and Tippett's New Year for the Glyndebourne Tour; Broadcasts of Mahagonny and Rossini's Tancredi for the BBC; Television appearances in La Traviata, The Electrification of the Soviet Union and Death in Venice; Engagements with Opera Factory, London; As a concert artist has performed at many major London venues; Has broadcast Leoncavallo's La Bohème and Königskinder for RTE Dublin; Television appearances include The Marriage of Figaro, La Traviata and Death in Venice; In 1993 he sang his first Papageno in a new production of The Magic Flute conducted by Jane Glover at the Covent Garden Festival; Sang Bartolo (Barber of Seville) for Opera Northern Ireland and at Garsington Festival in 1994; Other performances include a premiere of a new opera by Stuart Copeland in the Barbados Festival, Bottom (A Midsummer Night's Dream), for Covent Garden Festival and Scarpia in a concert performance of Tosca for the opening of the 1994 Bournemouth International Festival; In 1995 he sang Dulcamara (L'Elisir d'amore) for Opera Northern Ireland, Dr Bartolo (The Marriage of Figaro), Melitone (La Forza del Destino) and Calchas (La Belle Hélène) for Scottish Opera; Engagements in 1996 included Leporello (Don Giovanni) for Auckland Opera with Kiri Te Kanawa, Melitone with the Royal Danish Opera, Dr Bartolo for Opéra de Nice; Banker (Lulu) and roles for Glyndebourne Festival Opera; 1997 with Bartolo for Welsh National Opera; Sharpless (Madama Butterfly), Dr Bartolo (Le Nozze di Figaro) for Opera Ireland; Dr Kolonaty (The Makropulos Case) for Glyndebourne at the Proms, Royal Albert Hall; Engagements in 1998 included Baron Zeta, The Merry Widow, for Royal Opera; Dr Bartolo, The Marriage of Figaro, Zürich Opera; Vaarlam, Boris Gedonov, Welsh National Opera; Tonio, Pagliacci, Opera Ireland; Jake, Porgy and Bess, BBC Proms; Engagements in 1999–2000 included Talum Hadjo in Delius's Godunov, The Magic Fountain at Scottish Opera; Title role in Falstaff, Royal Danish Opera, Copenhagen, Mustafà, The Italian Girl in Algiers, Garsington Festival; Kecal, The Bartered Bride, Glyndebourne Festival and tour; Season 2000–01 as Leporello with GTO, Bunoafede in Haydn's Il mondo della luna at Garsington and Janáček's Kolenaty at the Academy of Music, New York. *Recordings:* Two solo albums; Featured soloist on recording of operatic excerpts for Opera Rara; Elgar's The Spanish Lady, CD. *Honours:* Winner, Peter Pears Singing Competition; Anna Instone Memorial Award. *Address:* 4 Lincoln Road, Guildford, Surrey GU2 6JT, England.

VEJZOVIC, Dunja; Singer (soprano); b. 20 Oct. 1943, Zagreb, Yugoslavia. *Education:* Studied in Zagreb, Stuttgart, Weimar and Salzburg. *Career:* Sang first at Zagreb, then in Frankfurt, Düsseldorf, Vienna, Hamburg and Stuttgart; Bayreuth Festival 1978–80, as Kundry in Parsifal: also sang the role at the Salzburg Easter Festival; Metropolitan Opera 1978–79, as Venus in Tannhäuser; Paris Opéra 1982, Ortrud; Teatro Liceo Barcelona 1983 in the title role of Hérodiade by Massenet; La Scala Milan 1984, as Venus; Théâtre de la Monnaie, Brussels 1984, Senta in Der fliegende Holländer; Also sings Chimène in Le Cid by Massenet; sang Ortrud at the Vienna Staatsoper, 1990; Season 1992 as Kundry in Robert Wilson's production of Parsifal at Houston. *Recordings:* Parsifal, conducted by Karajan (Deutsche Grammophon); Christus by Liszt; Lohengrin and Der fliegende Holländer (EMI). *Address:* c/o Allied Artists Agency, 42 Montpelier Square, London SW7 1JZ, England.

VELAZCO, Jorge; Conductor and Music Director; b. 12 Jan. 1942, Mexico City, Mexico. *Education:* General Law degree, National University of Mexico; Student of Conrado Tovar (Piano), Antonio Gomezanda (Piano, Music Theory), Rodolfo Halffter (Composition, Music Analysis), Lukas Foss, Franco Ferrara at Accademia Musicale Chigiana, Siena, Herbert von Karajan (Conducting). *Career:* Assistant Chairman, Mexico Federal Government's Music Department, 1972–73; Professor, National Conservatory, Mexico City, 1973–84; Chairman, Music Department, 1973–74, Vice-President for Cultural Affairs, 1974–76, Researcher in Music, 1974–, National University of Mexico; Visiting Professor, Wyoming and Michigan State Universities, Phoenix College, University of Houston, University of Oviedo (Spain), 1975–94; Associate Conductor, 1977–81, Music Director, 1985–89, UNAM Philharmonic; Assistant to Herbert von Karajan at Salzburg Easter Festival, 1977; Founder, Music Director, Minería Symphony Orchestra, 1978–84; Principal Guest Conductor, Florence Chamber Orchestra, Italy, 1990–; Director, International Studies, Texas Music Festival, Houston, 1992–; Artistic Director and Conductor, Mineria Symphony Orchestra, 1995–; Guest Conductor, National Orchestra of Spain, Interamerican Music Festival Orchestra, several major US and European orchestras; mem, Sociedad Española de Musicología; Royal Musical Association, London; International Musicological Society. Cedros 18, San Miguel Ajusco, Tlalpan DF, Mexico 14700. *Recordings:* Several with Berlin Radio Symphony Orchestra, Florence Chamber Orchestra, Berlin Symphony and Sinfonietta RIAS. *Publications:* Edgard Varèse, Perfil de un Revolucionario, 1975; De Música y Músicos, 1981; Dos Músicos Eslavos, 1981; El Pianismo Mexicano del Siglo XIX, 1983–84; Federico II, El Rey Músico, 1986; La Versión Original de 'Janitzio' de Silvestre Revueltas, 1986; La Música por Dentro, 1988; Antonio Gomezanda y el Nacionalismo Romántico Mexicano, 1991. *Honours:* Guggenheim Fellow, 1987; Wortham Chair in Performing Arts, University of Houston, 1991, 1994.

VELIS, Andrea; Singer (Tenor); b. 7 June 1932, New Kensington, Pennsylvania, USA. *Education:* Studied with Louise Taylor in Pittsburgh, at the Royal College of Music, London, and at the Accademia di Santa Cecilia, Rome. *Career:* Debut: Pittsburgh 1954, as Goro in Madama Butterfly; Appearances in Chicago, Cincinnati, Philadelphia and San Francisco; Metropolitan Opera from 1961 in 1,600 performances of 50 operas, including La Fanciulla del West, Death in Venice, Hansel and Gretel, Eugene Onegin, The Ring (Mime), Les Contes d'Hoffmann, Otello, Der Rosenkavalier, Tosca and Boris Godunov; Sang Mardian in the premiere of Barber's Antony and Cleopatra, 1966. *Recordings include:* Tosca (HMV). *Address:* c/o Metropolitan Opera, Lincoln Center, New York, NY 10023, USA.

VELLA, Joseph; Composer and Conductor; b. 9 Jan. 1942, Gozo, Malta. *Education:* Accademia Musicale, Siena, with Franco Donatoni and Franco Ferrara; University of Durham, until 1970. *Career:* Guest appearances as conductor in Europe, USA, Asia; Musical Dir, Astra Opera House, Gozo, 1970–; Associate Professor, Univ. of Malta, 1994–. *Compositions:* Over 150 works including Trio for violin, horn and piano, 1968; Sinfonia De profundis, 1969; Clarinet Quintet, 1973; The Seasons, Madrigal cycle, 1980; String Quartet, 1981; Piano concerto 1984; Sinfonietta, for strings, 1984; A Canticle Cantata, 1985; Sinfonia No. 2, 1989; Blood on the Verna, oratorio, 1989; Brass Quintet, 1992; Love Textures, for baritone and orchestra, 1993; Violin Concerto, 1993; Cello Concerto, 1995; Flute Concerto, 1996; Concerto Barocco for bassoon and orchestra, 1998; Concerto for 2 pianos solo, 2000; Sinfonietta for 13 woodwind players, 2001; Symphony No. 3 (The Apocalypse Verses), 2003. *Address:* c/o Music Dept, University of Malta, Sliema, Malta. *E-mail:* joseph.vella@um.edu.mt.

VELLA, Richard; Composer and Professor of Music; b. 1 Dec. 1954, Melbourne, Victoria, Australia. *Education:* BA 1978, MA 1981, La Trobe University. *Career:* General Editor, Music Currency Press, 1989–; Professor, La Trobe University, 1996–97; Advisory Professor, 1998–99; Artistic Director, Calculated Risks Opera Productions, 1990–. *Compositions include:* Tales of Love, opera, 1990; A Piano Reminisces, 1991;

Remember, Unending Love, for chorus, 1992; The Last Supper, opera, 1993; Concerto for Trombone, 1995; Commissions from Astra Choir, One Extra Dance Company, The Elizabethan Theatre Trust, and others. *Publications:* Musical Environments, 2000. *Honours:* Commonwealth Postgraduate Research Award, 1979. *Address:* c/o Red House Editions, PO Box 2123, Footscray, Vic 3011, Australia.

VENGEROV, Maxim; Israeli violinist and violist; b. 20 Aug. 1974, Novosibirsk, Western Siberia, USSR; s. of Alexander Vengerov and Larissa Vengerov. *Career:* studied with Galina Tourchaninova and Zakhar Bron; first recital aged five; debut Moscow, playing Schubert's Rondo Brillant 1985; US debut with New York Philharmonic 1990; performs concerts and recitals with all maj. int. orchestras including Concertgebouw, Russian State Symphony, Berlin Philharmonic, London Philharmonic, St Petersburg Philharmonic, Chicago Symphony, Los Angeles Philharmonic, Mozarteum, Vienna Philharmonic, Hallé and English Chamber Orchestras; worked with Abbado, Mehta, Simonov, Barenboim, Menuhin; solo recital programme of Bach, Ysaÿe, Shchedrin and Paganini 2002–03; Prof. of Violin, Musikhochschule des Saarlandes; Prof. of Violin, Saarbrücken Univ.; apptd. UNICEF Envoy for Music 1997. *Recordings include:* Sonatas by Beethoven and Brahms and Paganini 1st Concerto 1992, Sonatas by Mozart, Beethoven and Mendelssohn 1992, Virtuoso Violin Pieces, Bruch and Mendelssohn Violin Concertos, Britten Violin Concerto and Walton Viola Concerto 2002 (Classical BRIT Critics' Award 2004). *Honours:* 1st Prize Jr Wieniawski Competition Poland 1984, Winner Carl Flesch Int. Violin Competition 1990, Gramophone Young Artist of the Year 1994, Ritmo Artist of the Year 1994, Gramophone Record of the Year 1996, Edison Award 1997, Gramophone Artist of the Year 2002. *Current Management:* Askonas Holt Ltd, Lonsdale Chambers, 27 Chancery Lane, London, WC2A 1PF, England. *Telephone:* (20) 7400-1780. *Fax:* (20) 7400-1799. *E-mail:* info@askonasholt.co.uk. *Website:* www.askonasholt .co.uk.

VENN, Edward John, BA, MA, PhD, LRSM; Lecturer; b. 31 Oct. 1974, Watford, England. *Education:* Univ. of Birmingham. *Career:* Lecturer, Dept of Music, Lancaster Univ. 2001–; cttee mem., Soc. for Music Analysis 2004–. *Publications:* 'Idealism and Ideology in Tippett's writings', in Michael Tippett: Music and Literature (ed. Suzanne Robinson), The Music of Hugh Wood. *Address:* Department of Music, Lancaster University, Lancaster, LA1 4YW, England (office). *Telephone:* (1524) 593105 (office). *E-mail:* e.venn@lancaster.ac.uk (office). *Website:* www.lanc.ac.uk/staff/venn (office).

VENTRE, Carlo; Singer (Tenor); b. 23 Feb. 1969, Montevideo, Uruguay. *Education:* Studied in Uruguay and in Italy (from 1991). *Career:* Appearances at La Scala Milan under Riccardo Muti as the Duke of Mantua, and Ismaele in Nabucco; Further engagements at Rome, Ravenna, Trieste, Athens, Tokyo and Cologne; Wexford Festival 1995, in Pacini's Saffo; Season 1996–97 included British debut, as Rodolfo with Welsh National Opera, and American debut as the Duke of Mantua for Opera Pacific; Engaged as the Duke by Michigan Opera, as Pinkerton in Trieste and Edoardo di Sanval in Un Giorno do Regno by Verdi at Parma. *Recordings include:* Pacini's Saffo. *Honours:* Gino Becchi Prize at the 1990 Francisco Vinas Competition; Winner, 1995 Luciano Pavarotti Competition, Philadelphia. *Address:* c/o IMG Artists, Lovell House, 616 Chiswick High Road, London W4 5RX, England.

VENTRIGLIA, Franco; Opera Singer (Bass); b. 20 Oct. 1927, Fairfield, Connecticut, USA; m. 1945. *Education:* American Theatre Wing, Toti Dal Monte International School of Bel Canto in Rome and Venice. *Career:* Debut: Teatro Massimo Palermo, Italy, Meistersinger, Tullio Serafin, Conductor; Appearances in various operas, Academia Di S Cecilia, Rome; La Scala, Vienna Staatsoper, Berlin Staatsoper; San Carlo; Regio di Parma; Regio di Torino; Comunale di Firenze; King's Theatre, Edinburgh; Chicago Lyric; Dallas Opera; Wexford Festival; La Fenice Venezia; Arena di Verona; Teatro de L'Opera Roma; Milwaukee; Concertgebouw, Amsterdam; Dutch Radio; Roles have included Rossini's Basilio, Raimondo, Elmiro (Otello by Rossini), Walter and Wurm in Luisa Miller, Loredano (I due Foscari), the Grand Inquistor, Alvise, Colline and Sparafucile (Rigoletto); mem, AGMA. *Recordings:* La Traviata, RCA; Manon Lescaut, EMI; Angelium, Vedette Records. *Contributions:* Opera News.

VENTRIS, Christopher; Singer (Tenor); b. 5 May 1960, London, England. *Education:* Studied at the Royal Academy of Music. *Career:* Joined Glyndebourne Festival Chorus, 1987; Touring opera debut, 1988 as Vanya in Katya Kabanova; Later appearances as Tom Rakewell with Glyndebourne Festival Opera and The Porter in Death in Venice, Jacquino in Fidelio, and Steva in Jenůfa with GTO; Opera work with Opera North, ENO and Royal Opera; Performed in: Magic Flute, 1993 in Geneva, King Priam and Eugene Onegin, 1994 at Antwerp and Flying Dutchman, 1992 and Salome, 1995 at Leipzig; Concert work throughout Europe includes: Beethoven 9th Symphony, Mendelssohn's Second Symphony, (Lobgesang) and Elijah, and Tippett's Child of Our Time;

Further engagements include: Steuermann at Amsterdam in 1995, Midsummer Marriage with Royal Opera, Title role in Parsifal at Antwerp; Debut at La Scala as Max in Der Freischütz, 1998; Engaged as Parsifal at San Francisco, 2000, and Siegmund in Die Walküre at Cologne, 2001. *Recordings:* Caritas, Saxton; Blonde Eckbert, Weir. *Honours:* Esso GTFO Singers Award, 1988–89; John Christie Award, Glyndebourne; Associate of Royal Academy of Music, 1993. *Address:* c/o IMG Artists Europe, Lovell House, 616 Chiswick High Road, London W4 5RX, England.

VENUTI, Maria; Singer (Soprano); b. 1953, New York, USA. *Education:* Eastman School, Rochester, and Detmold Musikhochschules with Helmut Kretzschmar and Gunter Weissenborn. *Career:* Sang at the Vienna Staatsoper from 1976, Lyric Opera Chicago from 1978; Appearances throughout Europe in operas by Mozart, Amor in Orfeo ed Euridice, Oscar (Un ballo in Maschera), Sophie in Der Rosenkavalier and Bizet's Micaela; Engagements at Augsburg, Kassel (Mozart's Ilia, 1984), Salzburg and Brussels; Concert repertoire has included Schubert's Lazarus, Utrecht Te Deum by Handel, and the Mozart Requiem. *Recordings include:* Inez, in Il Trovatore, under Karajan (EMI). *Address:* Augsburg Opera, Kasernstrasse 4-6, Of 111949, D-86044, Augsburg, Germany.

VENZAGO, Mario; Conductor; b. 1 July 1948, Zürich, Switzerland. *Education:* Studied at the University of Zürich and the Zürich and Vienna Conservatories, notably with Hans Swarowsky. *Career:* Conductor of the Collegium Musicum at Winterthur from 1977, general music director at Heidelberg from 1986, then principal conductor of the Graz Philharmonic; Further concerts with the Swiss Radio Lugano and Suisse Romande orchestras; Principal Conductor of the Gothenburg Symphony Orchestra, 2004–. *Recordings:* Works by Schumann, Janáček and others. *Address:* Bulmer and Dixon Ltd, Granitweg 2, 8002 Zürich, Switzerland.

VERA-RIVERA, Santiago Oscar; Professor and Composer; b. 2 Nov. 1950, Santiago, Chile; m. Maria Angelica Bustamante, 25 May 1974, 2 s., 1 d. *Education:* University of Chile; Doctorate in Musicology, University of Oviedo, Spain, 1991. *Career:* Professor, University of Chile, 1974–81, University of Tarapaca, 1984; Acad Pedag Santiago, 1981–85; University Metropolitana, 1986; Escuela Moderna de Musica, 1976–87; Intem/OAS, 1984. *Compositions:* Choral, piano, electronic, percussion, guitar and orchestral pieces include: Apocaliptika II, 1988; Silogistika I for flute and guitar, 1989; Silogistika II for voice, clarinet, violin, violoncello and piano, 1989; Silogistika III for voice and orchestra. *Recordings include:* Tres Temporarias, 1987; Cirrus, 1987; Tres acuareskas, 1989; Chiloé, Tierra de Agua, 1989; CD: Musica Para el Fin de Siglo. *Publications:* Harmony for two voices, 1990; Contributor to Dictionary of Music, Hispano Americano and Espanola, 1989–92; Informúsica, Spain, 1992; Voices for Hispano-Americano and Española, Dictionary of Music of Ten Chilean Composers; Complete Catalogue of Chilean and Latin American Classical Music. *Address:* San Juan 4967, Santiago, Chile.

VERBITSKY, Leonid; Composer, Conductor and Arranger; b. 9 Dec. 1930, Kharkov, USSR. *Education:* Musical Secondary School, Kiev, Russia, 1938–49; Conservatoire (Evening Department), Kiev, Russia, 1949–53. *Career:* Singing Teacher, Secondary School, Kiev, Russia, 1953–55; Member of Orchestra and Arranger, Republican State Variety Orchestra, 1955–66; Conductor, Kiev State Russian Dramatic Theatre, 1966–71; Conductor and Arranger, Ukrainian Masters of Arts Concert Team, Kiev State Opera and Ballet Theatre, 1971–74; Leader of the Orchestra, Music Ensembles Union, Kiev, 1974–79; Moved to USA and settled in New York City, 1979–; Numerous tours of Russia conducting variety orchestras; Many performances on television and radio. *Compositions:* Over 400 compositions include: Music for 9 cartoons; 3 theatrical plays; Several television and radio plays; More than 300 songs and romances including: The Girl is Going; Blue Roses; The Cranes; The Black Eyes' Charm; It is Good When It is Good. *Recordings:* 20 compositions recorded. *Publications:* More than 200 compositions published by different publishing houses. *Address:* 200 Corbin Place, #6F, Brooklyn, NY 11235, USA.

VERBITSKY, Vladimir, PhD; Russian conductor; b. 24 Oct. 1943, Leningrad; m. Ninel; one s. one d. *Education:* studied piano, choral, operatic and symphony conducting, Leningrad Conservatoire. *Career:* various orchestral appointments, including Chief Conductor and Music Dir, Voronezh Philharmonic, Voronezh 1972–; Guest Conductor, State Orchestra of the USSR, Moscow 1976–89; Chief Conductor, Slovak Philharmonic Orchestra, Bratislava, Czechoslovakia 1982–84; Music Dir, State Orchestra of Victoria, Melbourne, Australia 1987–88; Guest Conductor 1987–91, Principal Guest Conductor 1992–97, Conductor Laureate 1997–, West Australian Symphony Orchestra. *Honours:* Herbert von Karajan Int. Young Conductors' Competition diploma, Berlin 1973, Laureate Villa Lobos Int. Young Conductors' Competition, Rio de Janeiro 1975, Laureate Hungarian Radio and Television Int.

Conductors' Competition, Budapest 1976, People's Artist of the Russian Federation 1993; Order of Honour USSR Govt 1980. *Address:* West Australian Symphony Orchestra, PO Box Y3041, East St Georges Tce, Perth, WA 6832, Australia. *E-mail:* VNVerbitsky@aol.com.

VERBRUGGEN, Marion; Recorder Player and Teacher; b. 2 Aug. 1950, Amsterdam, Netherlands. *Education:* Study with Kees Otten, Amsterdam Conservatory, 1966; With Frans Brüggen, Muziek Lyceum, Amsterdam, and Royal Conservatory, The Hague, 1967; B Diploma, 1971; Solo degree cum laude, 1973. *Career:* Performances with various ensembles and solo concerts; Netherlands, USA, Canada, Japan, most European countries; Regular guest, Gustav Leonhardt, Amsterdam Baroque Orchestra, Musica Antiqua, Cologne, Tafelmusik Toronto, many others; Plays at Holland Festival of Early Music; Television appearances, Netherlands, Norway, Belgium, Italy, Federal Republic of Germany, USA; Teacher: Royal Conservatory, The Hague; Utrecht Conservatory; Guest Teacher, Malmö Conservatory, Sweden; Masterclasses and workshops, Stanford University, Toronto, Montreal, New York, Philadelphia, Malmö, Trondheim, Copenhagen, Jerusalem. *Recordings:* For EMI, Philips/Seon, Titanic, Hungaroton, ASV London, L'Oiseau Lyre, Monumenta Belgicae Musicae; Archiv, Harmonia Mundi. *Address:* Vondelstraat 99, 1054 GM Amsterdam, Netherlands.

VERBY, Theo; Composer; b. 5 July 1959, Delft, Netherlands. *Education:* Royal Conservatory, The Hague, 1978–85. *Career:* Lecturer in Composition; Amsterdam Sweelinck Conservatory, 1997–; Commissions from London Sinfonietta, Residentie-Orkest and Royal Concertgebouw Orchestra. *Compositions:* Caprice Symphonique, 1976; Triplum for wind instruments, 1982; Random Symphonies. electronic, 1985; Contrary motion, for orchestra, 1986; Inversie, for ensemble, 1987; Expulsie, for ensemble, 1990; De Peryton, for seven wind instruments, 1990; Triade for orchestra, 1991, rev. 1994; Whitman, for soprano and orchestra, 1992; Notturno, for oboe, two horns and strings, 1995; Conciso, for ensemble, 1996; Alliage for orchestra, 1996; Six Rilke Lieder for baritone and small orchestra, 1998. *Honours:* Amsterdam Art fund Award, 1987. *Address:* c/o BUMA, PO Box 725, 1180 AS Amstelveen, Netherlands. *Telephone:* 0031 20540 7911. *Fax:* 0031 20540 7496.

VERCO, Wendy; Singer (Mezzo-soprano); b. 1945, Melbourne, Australia. *Education:* Studied at Sydney Conservatory and in London at Opera Studio. *Career:* Debut: Opera 80, 1982, as Orlofsky in Die Fledermaus; Appearances with Opera 80 as Dorabella and with Welsh National Opera as Maddalena in Rigoletto and Meg Page in Falstaff; Glyndebourne Festival from 1981, in Poppea, Idomeneo and Arabella; Opera North, 1985, as Irene in Tamerlano, Covent Garden, 1986, as Rossweise in Die Walküre; Welsh National Opera on tour to Japan, 1990; Sang Clytemnestra in Gluck's Iphigénie operas at the Théâtre des Champs Elysées, Paris, 1991; Concerts with the City of Birmingham Symphony Orchestra and the London Mozart Players. *Recordings:* Videos of Poppea, Arabella and Idomeneo from Glyndebourne.

VERCOE, Elizabeth (Walton); Composer; b. 23 April 1941, Washington DC, USA; 1 s., 1 d. *Education:* BA in Music, Wellesley College, 1962; MMus in Composition, University of Michigan, 1963; Doctor of Musical Arts in Composition, Boston University, 1978. *Career:* Instructor of Musical Theory, Westminster Choir College, 1969–71; Assistant Professor of Music, Framlingham State College, Massachusetts, 1973–74; Composer, Cité Internationale des Arts, Paris, France, 1983–85 and Charles Ives Center for American Music, 1984, 1992; Co-Director of Women's Music Festival, Boston, 1985, MacDowell Colony, 1992, and St Petersburg, Russia, Spring Music Festival, 1993; Director, Society of Composers Festivals, 1995–96; Lecturer Regis College, Weston Massachusetts, 1997–; Residency, Civitella Ranieri Center, Italy, 1998; Acuff Chair of Excellence, Austin Peay State Univ., TN, 2003. *Compositions include:* Fantasy for piano; Duo for violin and cello; Sonario for cello; Three Studies for piano; Irreveries from Sappho for SSA and piano or soprano and piano; Herstory II for soprano, piano and percussion; Herstory III; Persona for piano; Rhapsody for violin and orchestra; Despite our Differences No. 1 for piano trio, No. 2 for piano and orchestra, 1988; Plucked String Editions: A la Fin tout seul for mandolin and optional piano; A Dangerous Man for baritone and piano, 1990; Changes for chamber orchestra, 1991; Four Humors for clarinet and piano, 1993; Herstory IV for soprano and mandolin or marimba, 1997; Umbrian Suite for piano 4-hands, 1999; Kleemation for flute and piano, 2003; To Music for solo flute, 2003. *Recordings:* Herstory III, on Owl; Herstory II; 13 Japanese Lyrics for soprano, piano and percussion; Fantasy for Piano; Irreveries from Sappho for voice and piano; Fantasia for flute and percussion. *Publications:* Various works published. *Contributions:* The Lady Vanishes?, in Perspectives of New Music, 1982; A Composer's View, in the Journal of Early Music America, 1990. *Address:* 74 Judy Farm Road, Carlisle, MA 01741, USA.

VERGARA, Victoria; Singer (Mezzo-soprano); b. 1948, Santiago, Chile. *Education:* Studied in Santiago and in New York with Nicola Moscona, and Anton Guadagno, and at the Juilliard School with Daniel Ferro and Rose Bampton. *Career:* Sang minor roles in the USA, before New York City Opera debut, 1977; Sang at Detroit from 1977, Santiago 1978; Houston Grand Opera from 1980; Has sung Carmen at San Francisco, Cincinnati, Zürich, Lisbon, Vancouver, Philadelphia, Seattle, New Orleans and Berlin; Chicago Lyric Opera 1982, Vienna Staatsoper 1984, as Amneris; Washington Opera 1987, as the Duchess of Alba in the premiere of Menotti's Goya, opposite Placido Domingo; Metropolitan Opera debut 1988, as Carmen; Teatro Liceo Barcelona 1989, in the premiere of Cristobal Colon by Leonardo Balada, with Caballé and Carreras; Season 1990 sang Herodias (Salome) at Santiago and at the Zarzuela Theatre Madrid in El viajero indiscreto, as Dona; Other roles include Donna Elvira, Cherubino, Federica in Luisa Miller, Maddalena, Rosina, Dalila, Nicklausse, Charlotte and Massenet's Dulcinée. *Recordings include:* Maddalena in Rigoletto. *Address:* c/o IM Röhrich 55, 6702 Bad Dürkheim 2, Germany.

VERMEERSCH, Jef; Singer (Baritone); b. 7 Feb. 1928, Bruges, Belgium. *Education:* Studied in Bruges, Ghent and Antwerp, 1960, as Wotan in Das Rheingold; Sang at Gelsenkirchen from 1966; Member, Deutsche Oper Berlin from 1973; Guest appearances in Germany and Brussels, Amsterdam, Lyon, Venice, Lisbon, Prague, Geneva, San Francisco, Barcelona and Stockholm; Salzburg Easter Festival 1973, as Kurwenal in Tristan and Isolde, conducted by Karajan; Bayreuth Festival 1981–83, Kothner in Die Meistersinger; Other roles included Hans Sachs, Amfortas, the Dutchman, Boris Godunov, Golaud, Pizarro, Kaspar, the title role in Giulio Cesare by Handel, Leporello, Jochanaan, Kepler in Hindemith's Die Harmonie der Welt, Falstaff, Amonasro and St Just in Von Einem's Dantons Tod; Sang Kothner at Bayreuth 1988; Kurwenal at Wuppertal 1989;*Address:* Wuppertal Bühnen, Spinnstrasse 4, 5600 Wuppertal.

VERMILLION, Iris; Soprano; b. 1960, Bielefeld, Germany. *Education:* Studied flute at first then voice with Mechthild Bohme and Judith Beckmann. *Career:* Debut: Brunswick in 1986 as Zulma in L'Italiana in Algeri and as Barbara in Eine Nacht in Venedig; Sang Dorabella and Octavian in Brunswick; Deutsche Oper Berlin from 1988 as a Rhinemaiden, Hansel and Cherubino; Darmstadt in 1988 as Judith in Duke Bluebeard's Castle; Sang Dorabella with Netherlands Opera in Amsterdam in 1990; Salzburg Festival in 1990 as Clairon in Capriccio; Other roles include Werther, Charlotte and Mozart's Sextus; Also sings in the St Matthew Passion and Mozart's Davidde Penitente; Sang Bianca in Zemlinsky's Florentinische Tragödie at Florence, 1995; Season 2000 as Strauss's Composer at La Scala, Waltraute for the Vienna Staatsoper, premiere of Rihm's St Luke Passion at Stuttgart and Adriano in Wagner's Rienzi at Dresden (concert). *Recordings include:* Second Lady in Die Zauberflöte under Neville Marriner. *Honours:* Prize Winner at Cardiff Singer of World Competition. *Address:* c/o Deutsche Oper Berlin, Richard Wagnerstrasse 10, 1000 Berlin, Germany.

VERNEROVA-NOVAKOVA, Ludmila; Singer (Soprano); b. 6 Dec. 1962, Prague, Czechoslovakia; m. Pravomil Novák, 1 d. *Education:* Academy of Musical Arts, Prague. *Career:* Debut: National Theatre, Prague, 1987; Bach Academy at Stuttgart, Germany, three times: Handel, Messiah; Bach Mass in B Minor; Mozart Festival at Citta del Castello, Italy, 1991; Mozart's Missa C Major; Sommerfestspiele at Stuttgart, 1993; Festival at Marbella, Spain, 1994: Beethoven's Missa Solemnis; Festival Prague Spring, 1995: Mozart's Concert Arias; Festival in Ludwigsburg, Germany, 1995: Mozart's Requiem; Music Festival Bratislava, Slovakia, 1997: Mozart's Missa C Minor; Festival Prague Autumn, 1997; Other repertory includes: Myslivecek's Isaac; Purcell's Dido and Aeneas (Dido, Belinda); Britten's Beggar's Opera; Mozart's Nozze di Figaro (Countess), Don Giovanni (Donna Anna); Bizet's Carmen (Micaela); Sang under conductors V Neumann, H Rilling, G Delogu, W Gönnenwein, F Bernius, G Albrecht, Ch Dohnányi and others in most European countries; Her repertoire also includes Handel's Samson, Judas Maccabaeus, Rodelinda, Alcina, Jephtha, several cantatas; Beethoven's 9th Symphony and Songs; Bach's St John Passion, St Mark Passion, Mass in B minor, Magnificat, numerous cantatas; Haydn's Die Schöpfung, Stabat Mater, Vier Jahreszeiten and Masses; Schubert's Stabat Mater, Masses, Salve Regina, Erstes Offertorium (Op 45); Brahms' Ein Deutsches Requiem, Songs; Dvořák's Stabat Mater, Mass in D, Songs; also music by Mendelssohn, Schumann, Rameau, Pergolesi, Carissimi, Vivaldi, Zelenka, Buxtehude and others. *Recordings:* 42 CDs include: Dvořák's Stabat Mater; Haydn's Nelson Mass, Stabat Mater; Schubert's Mass No. 3 BFlat; Pergolesi's Stabat Mater; J. S. Bach's St John Passion; Mozart's Coronation Mass, Vesperae Solemnes. *Address:* Kafkova 8, Prague 6-Dejvice, CZ 160 00.

VERNET, Isabelle; Singer (Soprano); b. 1966, Paris, France. *Education:* Studied with Regine Crespin in Paris. *Career:* Sang in Der Rosenkavalier at Paris, 1989; Season 1991 as Fauré's Pénélope at Nancy and in La Vie Parisienne at Geneva; Opéra de Lyon, 1993–95, as Offenbach's Giulietta and Donna Elvira; Frankfurt, 1994, as Gluck's Iphigénie en Tauride; Season 1996 as Alceste at Scottish Opera and Nice, Phèdre in Hippolyte et Aricie at the Palais Garnier, Paris; Season 1998 as Vitellia in La Clemenza di Tito for Welsh National Opera; Engaged as Iphigénie at Bordeaux, 2000; Sang the Trovatore Leonora at Montpellier and Mozart's Elettra in Toronto, 2000. *Recordings include:* Oedipe by Enescu; Le Domino Noir by Auber. *Address:* c/o OIA, 16 ave Franklin Roosevelt, 75008 Paris, France.

VERNHES, Alain; Singer (Baritone); b. 1944, France. *Career:* Sang at the Opéra de Lyon, 1969–72, and made many appearances throughout France; Opéra d'Avignon, 1982–85, with such singers as Caballé, Aragall and Bruson; Orange Festival, 1987, as Vitellius in Massenet's Herodiade, and Opéra du Rhin, Strasbourg, as Zuniga in Carmen; Avignon, 1992, as Ourrais in Gounod's Mireille; Has also sung Puccini's Marcello and Scarpia in concert performances; Sang Melitone in La Forza del Destino at Orange, 1996; Marquis in The Carmélites at Amsterdam, 1998; Season 2000–01 as Massenet's Des Grieux at Monte Carlo, in Chausson's Le Roi Arthus at Edinburgh and Ramon in Gounod's Mireille for Opéra de Nice; Massenet's Sancho Panza for Washington Opera and Lothario in Mignon at Toulouse. *Address:* Opéra d'Avignon, Rue Racine, 84000 Avignon, France.

VERNON, Richard; Singer (Bass); b. 1950, Memphis, Tennessee, USA. *Education:* Studied at Memphis State University. *Career:* Debut: Memphis 1972, as Pimen in Boris Godunov; Has sung with Houston Opera Studio from 1977, in operas by Verdi; Appearances with Washington Opera and Pittsburgh Opera; Metropolitan Opera from 1981, in L'Enfant et les Sortilèges, and as Titurel (Parsifal) and the Commendatore (Don Giovanni); Sang Foltz in a new production of Die Meistersinger at the Metropolitan, 1993. *Address:* c/o Metropolitan Opera, Lincoln Center, New York, NY 10023, USA.

VERONELLI, Ernesto; Singer (Tenor); b. 1948, Milan, Italy. *Education:* Studied at the Giuseppe Verdi Conservatory, Milan. *Career:* Has sung in operas by Verdi, Puccini, Massenet and Giordano at Paris, Zürich, Berlin, Barcelona, Vienna and Verona; Debut with the Royal Opera Covent Garden as Cavaradossi, 1983, later singing Chevalier Roland in Esclarmonde, opposite Joan Sutherland; Season 1985–86 sang Canio at the Metropolitan, Cavaradossi in Pretoria and Pinkerton at the Cologne Opera; Calaf in Detroit and Radames at Toronto; Other roles have been Verdi's Macduff, Carlo (Giovanna d'Arco), Don Carlos and Manrico.

VERRETT, Shirley; Singer (Soprano and Mezzo Soprano); b. 31 May 1931, New Orleans, USA. *Education:* Studied in Los Angeles with Anna Fitziu and Hall Johnson and at the Juilliard School with Madame Szekely-Freschl. *Career:* Debut: Yellow Springs Ohio, 1957 as Britten's Lucretia; New York City Opera, 1958 as Irina in Lost in the Stars by Weill; European debut 1959 in Rasputins Tod by Nabokov; First major success as Carmen at Spoleto in 1962, New York City Opera in 1964 and La Scala in 1966; Covent Garden from 1966 as Ulrica, Azucena, Amneris, Eboli, Carmen, Orpheus and Selika in L'Africaine; Metropolitan Opera from 1968 as Carmen, Eboli, Cassandra and Dido in Les Troyens, Judith in Bluebeard's Castle, Adalgisa, Norma, Neocle in L'Assedio di Corinto and Leonore in La Favorita; Sang at Florence in 1969 as Elisabetta in Maria Stuarda, Paris Opéra in 1983 in Moïse by Rossini, and Verona Arena in 1984 as Carmen; Appearances at Salzburg, Dallas Opera, Moscow, Kiev and San Francisco; Other roles include Lady Macbeth, Tosca, Dalila and Fréderica in Luisa Miller; Sang Dido in the opening production of the Bastille Opéra, Paris in 1990; Season 1991–92 as Azucena at Genoa and Leonora in La Favorita at Madrid; Recital repertoire includes songs by Mahler, Brahms, Schubert and Milhaud. *Recordings:* Orpheus; Un Ballo in Maschera; La Forza del Destino; Luisa Miller; Lucrezia Borgia; Don Carlos; L'Africaine; Macbeth; Video of L'Africaine at San Francisco.

VERROT, Pascal; Conductor; b. 9 Jan. 1959, Lyon, France. *Education:* Studied at the Sorbonne and Conservatoire, Paris. *Career:* Assistant to Seiji Ozawa at the Boston Symphony, from 1985, giving concerts at Symphony Hall Boston and Tanglewood; Further concerts with the Boston Chamber Players; Guest engagements in Japan, throughout North America and France; Music director of the Quebec Symphony Orchestra from 1991. *Honours:* Prizewinner at the 1985 Tokyo International Competition. *Address:* Quebec Symphony Orchestra, 130 West Grand-Allée, Québec, Province Québec G1R, Canada.

VERROUST, Denis; Flautist and Musicologist; b. 21 Feb. 1958, Vincennes, France; m. Marguerite Sopinski, 27 Dec 1986. *Education:* Baccalaureate A, 1975; DEUG, Economics, 1979; Graduate, Saint-Maur CNR; DE, flute teacher, 1988. *Career:* Appearances, St Malo Festival, Brittany, 1980–; Several tours in France, Germany, Netherlands with Cologne Chamber Orchestra, as soloist; Radio programme for Radio-France, 1982; Invited Lecturer in several American Universities. *Publications:* 5 titles proposed and edited for the Billaudot Edition, Paris, 1980 and 1982; J. S. Bach: Sinfonia from Cantata BWV 209; 4 characteristic XIXth Century pieces by W Popp, F Doppler and A Fürstenberg; Principal editor and director of collections for the Stravaganza Edition, Paris; Mozart, Haydn, Rossini (Opera overtures

for 2 flutes); A Hugot (Trios for 2 flutes and bass); Jean-Pierre Rampal, over 40 years of recordings 1946–1989; The Flute in France from Devienne to Faffanel (150 years 1770–1920) in progress; Complete Catalogue of XIXth Century Flute Literature, in progress; The Romantic Flute, in progress; Exhaustive Researchers and Leading Authority on the Late Classical and Romantic Flute Repertoire. *Contributions:* Numerous articles to professional journals. *Address:* 16 Avenue Aubert, 94300 Vincennes, France.

VERSCHRAEGEN, Herman (Elie Bertha); Organist, Director of Music and Organ Master; b. 4 April 1936, Ghent, Belgium; m. Genevieve Van Hove, 2 July 1963, 1 s., 1 d. *Education:* Several First Prizes and Higher Diploma in Organ, Royal Conservatory of Music, Ghent, 1960; Virtuosity Prize, Organ, 1965. *Career:* Debut: Ghent, 1957; Organist, St Josef Church, Antwerp, 1962; Master of Music Theory and History, Music Academy of Wilrijk, 1963–73; Organ Master, Music Academy of Aalst, 1965–73 and Music Academy of Geel, 1966–73; Director, Music Academy of Wilrijk-Antwerp, 1974–; Organ Master, Royal Conservatory of Music, Brussels, 1976–; Over 700 organ concerts and recitals in Austria, Belgium, Czechoslovakia, Denmark, Germany, France, Netherlands, Israel, Italy, Japan, Poland, South Africa, Sweden, Switzerland, England, USA, Philippines; Several seminars about C Franck and the Flemish Organ School and also masterclass in Japan; Member of Jury of International Organ Contests, Nuremberg 1970, Lokeren 1972; Recitals for International Broadcasting Corporations Belgium, Denmarks Radio, Suddeutscher Rundfunk, Hessischer Rundfunk, Bayerischer Rundfunk, Sender Freies Berlin, Sudwestfunk, NDR, Czechoslovakia, Sweden, Radio Geneva, Bern, Zürich, Suisse Romande, USA, South Africa. *Compositions:* Fantasy for Organ. *Recordings:* Handel, Bach, Couperin, Van den Gheyn (Polydor). *Address:* 5 Schansweg, 2610 Wilrijk-Antwerpen, Belgium.

VEZNIK, Vaclav; Stage Director; b. 1 Aug. 1930, Brno, Moravia, Czechoslovakia; m. Helena Rozsypalova, 28 Sept 1957, 1 s., 1 d. *Education:* The Masaryk State University (Philosophy), 1949–50; The Janáček Academy of Music, 1950–54; Operatic Production, Stage Director; Private study of violin and singing. *Career:* Debut: Donizetti's Don Pasquale, State Theater Brno, 1955; Stage Director, State Theater, Brno, 1954; Guest Directors at all theatres in Czech Republic and Slovakia, 1955–97; Guest directions in Norway, Germany, Switzerland, Italy, Spain, Belgium, Austria, Yugoslavia, 1968–95: 173 operatic productions include: Janáček's Fate (world premiere), 1958; Martinů's The Marriage (Czech premiere), 1960; Fischer's Rome, Julia and the Darkness (world premiere), 1962; Martinů's The Voice of the Forest (World Stage Production), 1964; Martinů's Alexander bis (Czech premiere), 1964; Von Einem's Dantons Tod (Czech premiere), 1966; Gershwin's Porgy and Bess (Czech premiere), 1968; Szokolay's The Blood Wedding (Czech premiere), 1971; Television productions: Prokofiev's Duenna, Prague, 1972; Janáček's Jenůfa, Brno, 1972; Rimsky-Korsakov's The Golden Cockerel, Prague, 1973; Janáček's The Excursions of Mr Brouček, Brno, 1978; Janáček's The Cunning Little Vixen, Brno, 1979; Verdi's Simon Boccanegra, Brno, 1984; Verdi's Nabucco, Brno, 1989; Professor at The Janáček Musik Academy, Brno, 1990–. *Contributions:* Many articles about opera productions in Program (journal of the Janáček Opera, Brno). *Honours:* Bedrich Smetana Medal, 1974, Leoš Janáček Medal, 1978–79, Czech Ministry of Culture. *Address:* Brenkova 3, Brno 613 00, Czech Republic.

VIALA, Jean-Luc; Singer (Tenor); b. 5 Sept. 1957, Paris, France. *Education:* Studied in Paris with Michel Sénèchal. *Career:* Debut: Paris Opéra-Comique 1983 in Pomme d'Apis by Offenbach; Sang at the Opéra-Comique in César Franck's Stradella and has made many appearances at provincial French opera houses; Glydebourne Festival 1986, as the Italian Singer in Capriccio, Dublin 1987, Aix-en-Provence Festival 1989, as the Prince in the Love of Three Oranges; Recent engagements at the Opéra de Lyon including Rodolfo 1990; Sang in Sacchini's Oedipe à Colone for the Festival de Radio France at Montpellier, 1992; Other roles include Paolino in Il Matrimonio Segreto, Giannetto (La Gazza Ladra), Fenton, George Brown in La Dame Blanche and Iopas in Les Troyens; Sang Belfiore in Il Viaggio a Reims at Liège, 2000. *Recordings include:* Guercoeur by Magnard and Les Brigands by Offenbach; Narraboth in the French version of Salome, Osmin in Gluck's La Rencontre Imprévue and Bénédict in Béatrice et Bénédict, all with the Lyon Opéra; The Love for Three Oranges; Engaged as George Brown in La Dame Blanche at St Etienne, 1996–97; Rossini's Otello at the Theater an der Wien, Vienna, 1998. *Address:* c/o Opéra de Lyon, 9 Quai Jean Moulin, 69001 Lyon, France.

VICAR, Jan; Musicologist and Composer; b. 5 May 1949, Olomouc, Czechoslovakia; m. 1st Anna Betkova, 11 August 1979, 2 s; m. 2nd Eva Slavickova, 17 November, 2001, 1 d. *Education:* Accordion, Conservatory in Ostrava, 1972; Music, Palacky University, Olomouc, 1972; Composition, Academy of Music and Performing Arts, Prague, 1981. *Career:* Lecturer, Department of Music, Palacky University, 1973–85; Editor-in-Chief, Hudebni Rozhledy, 1986–89; Senior Lecturer, Academy of Music and Performing Arts, Prague, 1985–; Professor, Head, Department of Musicology, Palacky University, 1990–98; Professor of Theory and History of Music at the Academy of Music in Prague, 1998–; Fulbright Scholar-in-Residence, 1998–99; mem, Czechoslovak Society of Arts and Sciences. *Compositions:* String Quartet, 1978; Music For Strings and Timpani, 1980; The Cry, 1981; Japanese Year, 1979; Night Prayer, 1996; Instructions of Surruppak, 1996; Choruses and Songs For Children, 1997; Three Marches for Dr Kabyl for brass band, 1999; Vivat universitas!, 2000; Preludes/ Phantasms, 2000. *Publications:* Akordeon a Jeho Hudebni Uplatneni, 1981; Vaclav Trojan, 1989; Hudebni Kritika A Popularizace Hudby, 1997; Music Aesthetics with Roman Dykast, 1998. *Honours:* Prizes, Japanese year, 1980. *Address:* Malostranske Nam 1, 118 00 Prague 1, Mala Strana, Czech Republic.

VICK, Graham; Opera Producer; b. 30 Dec. 1953, Liverpool, England. *Career:* Productions for the ENO include Ariadne auf Naxos, the Rape of Lucretia, Madama Butterfly, Eugene Onegin, Timon of Athens by Stephen Oliver, (world premiere 1991), and the Marriage of Figaro; For Opera North, Così fan tutte, Die Zauberflöte and Katya Kabanova; For Glyndebourne Festival, Queen of Spades, Lulu, Eugene Onegin and Manon Lescaut; Artistic Director, City of Birmingham Touring Opera; European engagements in Brussels, Bonn, Venice, Netherlands, Berlin, Paris, Italy and St Petersburg; Covent Garden debut in 1989 with the British premiere of Un Re in Ascolto by Berio, returning for Mozart's Mitridate, 1991 and Die Meistersinger, 1993, The Midsummer Marriage at Royal Opera House, 1996; Parsifal for the Opéra Bastille, Paris, 1997; Season 1998–99 with Don Carlos at the Opéra Bastille, Così fan tutte at Glyndebourne, Ernani in Vienna and Moses and Aron at the Met in New York; Il Trovatore at the Met, 2001; Television works include Il Segreto di Susanna for Scottish television, The Rape of Lucretia for Channel Four, a live BBC television Broadcast of War and Peace from St Petersburg, and Queen of Spades from Glyndebourne;. *Honours:* Premi Abbiati Award as Best Director for Mahagonny at the Teatro Communale in Florence and a SWET Olivier Award for Mitridate at the Royal Opera, Covent Garden; Chevalier of the Ordre des Arts et Lettres, France; Honorary Professor of Music, Birmingham University. *Current Management:* Ingpen & Williams Ltd, 7 St George's Court, 131 Putney Bridge Road, London, SW15 2PA, England.

VICKERS, Jon; Singer (Tenor); b. 29 Oct. 1926, Prince Albert, Saskatchewan, Canada; m. Henrietta Outerbridge, 1953, 3 s., 2 d. *Career:* Concert and Opera Singer, Canada; Joined Royal Opera House, Covent Garden, London 1957–84 as Riccardo, Don Carlos, Radames, Florestan, Giasone (Médée), Samson (Handel and Saint-Saëns), Aeneas, Siegmund and Tristan; Sang at Bayreuth Festival, Vienna State Opera, San Francisco, Chicago Lyric Opera, Metropolitan Opera, La Scala, Milan, Paris Opéra, Boston, Buenos Aires, Athens, Ottawa, Houston, Dallas, Hamburg, Berlin, Munich, Athens Festival, Salzburg Festival, Festival of Orange, Tanglewood Festival, Rio de Janeiro; Biography, Jon Vickers: a Hero's Life, published, 2000; mem, Royal Academy of Music, London. *Recordings:* Messiah; Otello; Aida; Die Walküre, Samson and Delilah; Fidelio; Italian Arias; Verdi's Requiem; Peter Grimes; Das Lied von der Erde; Les Troyens; Tristan und Isolde; Films include, Carmen; Pagliacci; Norma; Otello; Peter Grimes. *Honours:* Honorary LLD, Saskatchewan; Honorary CLD, Bishop's University; Mus D, Brandon University, University of Western Ontario; LLD, University of Guelph; Civ LD, University of Laval; D.Mus, University of Illinois; Critics Award, London, 1978; Grammy Award, 1979. *Address:* c/o Metropolitan Opera, Lincoln Center, New York, NY 10029, USA.

VIDAL, Elizabeth; Singer (Soprano); b. 1961, Nice, France. *Education:* Studied in Paris with Elisabeth Grümmer and Eric Tappy. *Career:* Sang at Opéra de Lyon from 1985, as Nannetta, Mozart's Blondchen, Charpentier's Glauce (Médée) and Paisiello's Rosina; Aix-en-Provence, 1987, in Lully's Psyché, Spoleto, 1989, as Offenbach's Olympia; Season 1991 as Auber's Manon Lescaut at the Paris Opéra Comique and Strauss's Sophie at Montpellier; Queen of Night at Avignon and Olympia at Covent Garden; Sang Oscar in Un Ballo in Maschera at Santiago, 1996; Sophie in Massenet's Werther at Venice, 1998; Concerts include Mozart's Requiem and Haydn's Creation. *Recordings include:* Scylla et Glaucus by Leclair.

VIDOVSZKY, Lászlá; Composer; b. 25 Feb, 1944, Békéscsaba, Hungary. *Education:* Franz Liszt Academy, Budapest, 1962–67; Further study with Messiaen in Paris, 1970–71. *Career:* Co-founded Budapest New Music Studio, 1970; Lecturer at Pécs University, 1984–93; Professor at Pécs University, 1993–; Professor at Franz Lisxt Academy, Budapest, 1999–. *Compositions:* Music for Györ, for orchestra, 1971; Double for two prepared pianos, 1968–72; Autokoncert, 1972; Circus, electronic, 1975; Schroeder's Death for Piano, 1975; Encounter, Melodrama, 1980; Narcissus and Echo, opera, 1981; Motetta, for chorus and horn, 1981; Une Semaine de beauté, synthesizer, 1983–89; Romantic Readings for Ensemble or Orchestra, 1985; Twelve Duos for Violin and Viola, 1989; Danses Allemandes for String Quartet, 1989;; Etudes for MIDI-piano, 1989–93; Lear, ballet, 1988; German Dances, for orchestra, 1990; Soft

Errors, for ensemble 1990; Black Quartet, percussion, 1993–97, Cinema, for ensemble and tape, 1993; Nine Little Greeting Chorales to Kurtág, for piano, 1996; Ady: the Black Piano, for orchestra, 1997; Flute Sonata, 1997; Silly Old Muzak, Electronic, 1997; Zwölf Streichquartette, for String Quartet, 2000; Sonata for Violin and Radio, 2001;. *Address:* c/o ARTISJUS, Mészáros u. 15–17, H–1539 Budapest 114, POB 593, Hungary. *Telephone:* 00361 212 1553. *Fax:* 00361 212 1544. *E-mail:* vid@art.pte.hu.

VIER, Michael; Singer (Bass-baritone); b. 27 Aug. 1963, Hamburg, Germany. *Education:* Studied in Hamburg and Paris. *Career:* Sang Mozart's Count at Pforzheim, then at Bielefeld from 1986, as Nelusko in L'Africaine, as Spohr's Faust and in Gerhard's Duenna; Bernstein's Songfest, with the composer, in London and Moscow; Season 1993–94 as the Herald in Lohengrin at Kiel and Papageno at Zürich; Cologne Opera from 1995, as Papageno, Sharpless and Elviro in Handel's Xerxes; Melot in Tristan und Isolde, 1998; Season 1999–2000 at Cologne in Der König Kandaules by Zemlinsky, Die Vogel by Braunfels, and as Guglielmo and Marcello. *Recordings include:* Spohr's Faust and Lortzing's Ali Pascha von Janina. *Address:* Oper der Stadt Köln, Offenbachplatz Pf 180241, 50505 Cologne, Germany.

VIGAY, Denis; Cellist; b. 14 May 1926, Brixton, London, England; m. Greta Vigay, 24 July 1952, 1 s., 2 d. *Education:* Royal Academy of Music, London. *Career:* Debut: BBC, 1941; Principal Cello, Royal Liverpool Philharmonic Orchestra; BBC Symphony Orchestra; Soloist, Promenade Concerts, Royal Albert Hall; Soloist, Principal Cello, Academy of St Martin-in-the-Fields. *Recordings:* Complete Chamber Works of Handel; Schubert Octet; Beethoven Septet; Mendelssohn Octet; Complete Boccherini Guitar Quintets; Mozart Clarinet Quintet; Mozart Oboe Quartet; Mozart Horn Quintet; Fantasia on a Theme of Corelli, Michael Tippett. *Honours:* FRAM, 1972. *Address:* 12 Chesterfield Road, Finchley, London N3 1 PR, England.

VIGNOLES, Roger (Hutton); Pianoforte Accompanist and Conductor; b. 12 July 1945, England; m. (1) Teresa Ann Elizabeth Henderson 1972, diss 1982, (2) Jessica Virginia Ford, 1982. *Education:* Canterbury Cathedral Choir School; Sedbergh School; BA, BMus, Magdalene College, Cambridge; Royal College of Music, London (ARCM). *Career:* Accompanist of national and international reputation, regularly appearing with the most distinguished international singers and instrumentalists, in London and provinces and at major music festivals including Aldeburgh, Cheltenham, Edinburgh, Brighton, Bath, Salzburg, Prague, etc; Broadcasting for BBC Radio 3 and television; International tours include USA, Canada, Australia, New Zealand, Hong Kong, Scandinavia; Recitals at Opera Houses of Cologne, 1982; Brussels, 1983; Frankfurt, 1984; Lincoln Center, New York, 1985; San Francisco, 1986; Tokyo, 1985 and 1987; Repetiteur, Royal Opera House, Covent Garden, 1969–71; English Opera Group, 1968–74; Australian Opera Company, 1976; Professor of Accompaniment, Royal College of Music, 1974–81; Conducted Handel's Agrippina at the 1992 Buxton Festival; Accompanist to Inger Dam-Jensen in Strauss, Poulenc and Nielsen at the V & A, London, 1999; London Proms Chamber Music, 2002. *Recordings include:* English song, various, with Graham Trew, Baritone; Lieder by Schumann and Brahms/Dvořák; Cabaret Songs by Britten, Gershwin and Dankworth with Sarah Walker, Mezzo; Premiere recording of The Voice of Love (Nicholas Maw); Franck and Grieg cello sonatas with Robert Cohen, Cello; The Sea, songs and duets with Sarah Walker and Thomas Allen, Baritone; Parry Violin Sonatas with Erich Gruenberg, Violin. *Honours:* Honorary RAM, 1984. *Address:* 1 Ascham Street, Kentish Town, London NW5 2PB, England.

VIGNON, Lucille; Singer (Mezzo-soprano); b. 1963, Paris, France. *Education:* Studied in Paris and Venice and with Isabel Garcisanz. *Career:* Debut: Treviso, 1988, as Tisbe in Cenerentola; Appearances throughout France and Italy as Cenerentola, Rosina, and Pippo in La Gazza Ladra; Sara in Donizetti's Roberto Devereux at Montpellier and Bologna; Season 1991 as Fenena at Caracalla and Anne Boleyn in Henry VIII by Saint-Saëns at Compiègne; Other roles include Maddalena in Rigoletto, Nicklausse in Les Contes d'Hoffmann and Léonor in La Favorite, at Nantes; Oreste in La Belle Hélène at Montpellier and at Zürich, 1994–95; Concerts include works by Berio, and the Verdi Requiem. *Address:* c/o Opernhaus Zürich, Falkenstrasse 1, 8008 Zürich, Switzerland.

VIHAVAINEN, Ilkka; Singer (Bass-baritone); b. 18 Oct. 1960, Finland. *Education:* Studied at the Sibelius Academy, Helsinki, 1984–87, and in Berlin and Zürich. *Career:* Sang with the Zürich Opera as Lord Walton in I Puritani, Belcore, Garibaldo in Rodelinda and Nick Shadow in The Rake's Progress; Royal Opera Stockholm, 1988, as the Commendatore in Don Giovanni, and the Savonlinna Festival in Sallinen's The King goes forth to France; Concert appearances in Bach, Mozart's Requiem and Haydn's Creation. *Address:* Finnish National Opera, Bulevardi 23–27, 00180 Helsinki 18, Finland.

VIHAVAINEN, Satu; Singer (Soprano); b. 1958, Finland. *Education:* Graduated Sibelius Academy, Helsinki, 1982. *Career:* Sang in concert from 1981, Finnish National Opera from 1982; Roles have included Micaela, Nedda, Donna Elvira, Susanna, Mimi and Marguerite; Savonlinna Festival from 1981, as First Lady and Pamina in Zauberflöte, Priestess in Aida and Marzelline in Fidelio; Guested at Los Angeles, 1992, in premiere of Sallinen's Kullervo; Sang Freia in Das Rheingold at Helsinki, 1996; Sang Wagner's Gutrune at Helsinki, 1999; Many concert engagements. *Address:* Finnish National Opera, Bulevardi 23–27, 00180 Helsinki 18, Finland.

VILÉGIER, Jean Marie; Stage Director; b. 1940, France. *Education:* Ecole Normale Supérieure Paris. *Career:* Lecturer at the Theatre Studies department, University of Nancy; Director of Théâtre National de Strasbourg, 1990–93; Founder and Director of L'Illustré Théâtre; Opera productions have included La Cenerentola (1983), Lully's Atys (1986), La fée Urgèle by Duni and Favart (1991), Charpentier's Médée (1993) and Rameau's Hippolyte et Aricie, 1996; Tours of Atys, Médée and Hippolyte to the Brooklyn Academy, New York; Further collaborations, with William Christie include Handel's Rodelinda at Glyndebourne, 1998. *Recordings include:* Rodelinda (video).

VILJAKAINEN, Raili; Singer (Soprano); b. 1954, Helsinki, Finland. *Education:* Studied at the Sibelius Academy, 1973–78; Further study with Luigi Ricci in Rome. *Career:* Has sung in Stuttgart from 1978 as Aennchen in Der Freischütz, Sophie, Pamina, Ilia, Micaela, Mimi, Liu, Eva, Freia in Das Rheingold and Countess in Figaro; Guest appearances at the Savonlinna Festival, Salzburg and the Saratoga Springs Festival; Concert appearances in works by Bach, Mozart, Beethoven, Handel and Mahler; Has sung at Carnegie Hall, New York and in Finland, throughout Germany, Austria, USA, Australia, France and Spain; Sang Pamina at the Savonlinna Festival, 1981–90, Tatiana in Eugene Onegin and Desdemona in Otello at Helsinki; Contemporary music in Paris, Biennale Helsinki, Opera in Bonn, and in Sciarrino's Lohengrin; Sang Ellen Orford in Helsinki and Berlin, 1999. *Recordings:* Aennchen in Der Freischütz. *Honours:* 1st Prize, Timo Callio Competition at Savonlinna Festival, 1976; 1st Prize, 's-Hertogenbosch Competition, Netherlands, 1977. *Address:* c/o Finnish National Opera, Helsinginkatu 58, 00260 Helsinki, Finland.

VILLA, Edoardo; Singer (Tenor); b. 19 Oct. 1953, Los Angeles, USA. *Education:* Studied at the University of Southern California and with Martial Singher, Horst Gunter and Margaret Harshaw. *Career:* Many appearances in opera throughout the USA and abroad; Paris Opéra 1986, as Don Carlos, Houston 1988, as Don José; Sang at the Munich Staatsoper, 1989, and has appeared widely in Canada; Sang Jacopo Foscari in I Due Foscari with the Opera Orchestra of New York, 1992; Other roles include Corrado in Il Corsaro, Ruggero in La Rondine, Hoffmann, the Italian Singer in Rosenkavalier and Albert Herring; Season 1999–2000 as Enzo in La Gioconda for Miami Opera and Radames at Heidenheim. *Recordings include:* Le Roi d'Ys by Lalo.

VILLAROEL, Veronica; Singer (Soprano); b. 1962, Chile. *Education:* Studied in Chile and the USA. *Career:* Debut: Santiago, 1988, as Marguerite in Faust; Sang Antonia at the 1989 Spoleto Festival, Fiordiligi at Barcelona, 1990 (returned for Violetta 1992); Season 1991 as Nedda at Miami, Traviata at Milwaukee and Mimi at Opéra de Lyon; Los Angeles and Théâtre du Châtelet, Paris, as Violetta; Sang Nedda in Paggliacci at Los Angeles; Season 2000 as Desdemona for Washington Opera, Nedda and Boito's Margherita at the Met, Hélène in Verdi's Jérusalem at Genoa and the Trovatore Leonora for the Teatro Col ón, Buenos Aires; London Proms, 2002; Many concert engagements. *Address:* 256 West 85th Street #2C, New York, NY 10024, USA.

VILLARS, John; Singer (Tenor); b. 1965, Panama City, Florida, USA. *Education:* Juilliard Opera School, New York. *Career:* Sang Midir in Boughton's The Immortal Hour at Juilliard, 1994; Season 1997-98 as the Drum Major in Wozzeck at Salzburg and Bacchus in Ariadne auf Naxos at Florence; Season 1998-99 as Calaf for Canadian Opera, Apollo in Strauss's Daphne at the Deutsche Oper Berlin and the Drum Major in Gurlitt's Wozzeck, Enée in Les Troyens at Salzburg, 2000; Other roles include Strauss's Emperor, Werther, Stravinsky's Oedipus Rex, Cavaradossi and Don José; Concerts include Mahler's 8th Symphony, at the London Proms, 2002. *Recordings include:* Video of Ariadne auf Naxos, Dresden 1999. *Honours:* Winner, National Competition for Young Opera Singers, New York, 1994. *Address:* c/o Staatsoper Dresden, Theaterplatz 2, D-01067 Dresden, Germany.

VILMA, Michele; Singer (Mezzo-soprano); b. 23 Feb. 1932, Rouen, France. *Education:* Studied at the Rouen Conservatoire. *Career:* Debut: Sang Léonor in La Favorite at Verviers; Appearances at the Rouen Opera, notably as Dalila, and elsewhere in France as Charlotte, Carmen, Herodiade, Azucena and Dulcinée in Don Quichotte by Massenet; Paris Opéra from 1970 as Eboli, Fricka and the Kostelnicka in Jenůfa; Marseille Opéra as Laura in La Gioconda, Fricka at Bayreuth and Brangaene at the Metropolitan; Sang Clytemnestra in Elektra at

the Opéra de Toulouse. *Address:* c/o Opéra de Paris, Théâtre National, 8 Rue Scribe, 75009 Paris, France.

VINCO, Ivo; Singer (Bass); b. 8 Nov. 1927, Verona, Italy; m. Fiorenza Cossotto. *Education:* Studied at the Liceo Musicale Verona and at La Scala Opera School with Ettore Campogalliani. *Career:* Debut: Verona 1954, as Ramfis in Aida; Appearances at La Scala and in Rome, Naples, Bologna, Venice, Turin and Florence; Sang at the Verona Arena almost every year from 1954; Further appearances in Vienna, Hamburg, Berlin, Buenos Aires, Paris, Lisbon, Barcelona, Monte Carlo, Moscow, Chicago, Miami and Seattle; Metropolitan Opera debut 1969; Roles include Raimondo (Lucia di Lammermoor), Alvise (La Gioconda), the Grand Inquisitor, Oroveso (Norma), Sparafucile (Rigoletto), Ferrando (Il Trovatore) and Bartolo (Le nozze di Figaro); Sang Alvise in La Gioconda at Barcelona, 1988; Ramphis at Palma, 1992. *Recordings include:* Lucia di Lammermoor, Il Trovatore, Rigoletto, Don Carlos; La Gioconda, Le nozze di Figaro; Iris by Massenet; Norma. *Address:* c/o Arena di Verona, Piazza Bra 28, 37121 Verona, Italy.

VINE, Carl; Composer, Pianist and Conductor; b. 8 Oct. 1954, Perth, Australia. *Education:* studied with Stephen Dornan and John Exton at the Univ. of Western Australia. *Career:* co-founder of contemporary music ensemble Flederman, 1979; appearances as conductor and pianist in the UK, Europe and the USA; resident composer with the Sydney Dance Co, 1979, London Contemporary Dance Theatre, 1979, Australian Chamber Orchestra, 1987 and Univ. of Western Australia, 1989; Lecturer in Electronic Music at the Queensland Conservatorium, 1980–82; Artistic Dir of Musica Viva Australia since 2001. *Compositions include:* Cafe Concertino, 1984; Canzona, 1985; Love Song for trombone and tape, 1986; Six Symphonies (no. 6 Choral Symphony), 1986–96; Defying Gravity for 4 percussion, 1987; Percussion Concerto, 1987; Piano Sonata, 1990; The Tempest, ballet, 1991; String Quartet No. 3, 1993; Esperance for chamber orchestra, 1994; Five Bagatelles for piano, 1994; Inner World for cello and tape, 1994; Gaijin for koto, strings and electronics, 1994; Oboe Concerto, 1996; Flag Handover Music (for Atlanta Olympic Games), 1996; Metropolis, for Melbourne Symphony Orchestra, 1997; Piano Concerto, for Sydney Symphony Orchestra, 1997; Piano Sonata No. 2, 1998; Pipe Dreams (flute concerto), 2002; V (an orchestral fanfare), 2002. *Honours:* John Bishop Memorial, 1990. *Address:* c/o Faber Music Ltd, 3 Queen Square, London, WC1N 3AU, England. *E-mail:* info@carlvine.au.nu. *Website:* www.carlvine.au.nu.

VINE, David; Conductor and Harpsichordist; b. 1943, London, England. *Education:* Royal College of Music, London, 1961–65; Studied piano with Cornelius Fischer, Bernard Roberts, Eric Harrison, piano accompaniment with Joan Trimble, harpsichord with Millicent Silver, baroque ensemble playing with Hubert Dawkes, conducting with Adrian Boult; ARCM; BMus 1st Class Honours, Harpsichord Performance, Canterbury University. *Career:* Tutored in Baroque Music, Guildhall School of Music and City Literary Institute; Founder of London Telemann Ensemble; Settled in New Zealand in 1974; Conductor of New Zealand National Youth Orchestra, Wellington Polytechnic Orchestra, Dunedin Sinfonia and Schola Cantorum, Amici Chamber Orchestra, Christchurch Symphony Orchestra, Orpheus Choir, and Cantoris; Musical Director of Gisborne Choral Society, Christchurch Operatic Society, Jubilate Singers, Perkel Opera, Academy Chamber Orchestra and Ensemble Divertimento; Orchestral keyboard: New Zealand Symphony Orchestra; Recitalist, presenter and announcer with Radio NZ 's Concert FM; Musical Director, Phoenix Choir and Academy Opera, conducting 7 New Zealand premieres of Handel, Mozart and Puccini operas; Has lectured at universities of Canterbury, Auckland, Waikato, and is at Massey University of Wellington. *Recordings:* Serenata. *Publications:* Handel: Suite in C minor, reconstruction for 2 keyboards, 1992; A Caldara, 16 Sonatas for cello and continuo, Doblinger, Vienna, 1996–. *Honours:* 1st Prize, 3 times, Northampton Eisteddfod Piano Section; Acknowledged one of New Zealand's finest harpsichordists, piano accompanists and conductors. *Address:* Academy Trust, PO Box 12675,Thorndon, Wellington, New Zealand. *E-mail:* david.vine@paradise.net.nz.

VINIKOUR, Jory; Harpsichordist; b. 12 May 1963, Chicago, Illinois, USA. *Education:* Peabody Conservatory, 1981–83; BA, 1986, MA, 1988, Mannes College of Music, 1986; Doctoral studies, Rutgers University, 1988–90; Artist Diploma, Conservatoire Nationale Supérieure de Musique de Paris, 1990–93; Medaille d'Or, Prix d'Excellence, 1991; Prix de Virtuosité, 1992, Conservatoire Nationale de Musique de Rueil-Malmaison. *Career:* Recitals at festivals in Deauville, Paris, Monaco, Prague, London, USA; Soloist with Rotterdam Philharmonic, Flanders Opera Orchestra, Orchestre de Chambre de Grenoble, Moscow Chamber Orchestra; Important contemporary music concerts in France, Germany and Netherlands; Major performances of contemporary works including Amsterdam Festival of Contemporary Harpsichord Music; Featured soloist, Festival Presence, Radio France; French and Belgian premieres of Michael Nyman's harpsichord concerto. *Recordings:* Soloist–Chaconne; Toccatas of Bach; Soundtrack, Jefferson in Paris; Continuist, Les

Arts Florissants, Les Musiciens du Louvre, L'Ensemble Orchestral de Paris, Mahler Chamber Orchestra. *Honours:* Fulbright Award, 1990; Nadia et Lily Boulanger Foundation, 1994; First prize, International Harpsichord Competition of Warsaw, 1993; First prize, International Harpsichord Competition of Prague, 1994. *Address:* 39 Rue Manin, 75019 Paris, France.

VINK, Elena; Singer (Soprano); b. 1962, Netherlands. *Education:* Studied at the Hague Conservatory. *Career:* Broadcast performances with conductors Jean Fournet, Kenneth Montgomery and Hans Vonk; Netherlands Opera as Lucia di Lammermoor, Constanze, Gilda, Poppea and Oscar; Mozart's Queen of Night at Lausanne, Brussels, the Berlin Staatsoper and the Opéra Bastille, Paris (1994); Sang in Mozart's Sogno di Scipione at Aix, 1991; Bath Festival, 1992, as Musetta; Amsterdam from 1994, as Aminta in Il Re Pastore, in The Nose by Shostakovich and as the Dove in Heppener's A Soul of Wood, 1998. *Recordings include:* Donna Anna in Don Giovanni.

VINTON, John; Writer on Music; b. 24 Jan. 1937, Cleveland, Ohio, USA. *Education:* Ohio State University, 1954–58; New York University, 1958–63; University of Southern California, 1965–66. *Career:* Editorial and Research Assistant, Bela Bart ók Archives, New York, 1962–65; General Manager, Dance Theatre Workshop, New York, 1971–73; Assistant Music Critic, Washington Star-News, 1966–67; Left music field and specialized in story telling in literature of Adirondack mountains. *Publications:* Dictionary of Contemporary Music, 1974; Published in England as Dictionary of 20th Century Music; Essays after a Dictionary, 1977; A Treasury of Great Adirondack Stories, 1991. *Contributions:* Music Quarterly; Music Review; Music and Letters; Journal of the American Musicological Society; Arte Musical; Studia Musicologica; Sohlmans Musiklexikon; Notes. *Honours:* Research on Béla Bart ók won bronze medal from Hungarian Academy of Sciences, 1981. *Address:* 167 Hicks Street, Brooklyn, NY 11201, USA.

VINZING, Ute; Singer (Soprano); b. 9 Sept. 1936, Wuppertal, Germany. *Education:* Studied with Martha Mödl. *Career:* Sang at Lubeck 1967–70, notably as Marenka in The Bartered Bride and Senta in Der fliegende Holländer; Wuppertal Opera 1971–76, sang Brünnhilde in Der Ring des Nibelungen; Has sung in Hamburg, Munich, Vienna, Buenos Aires, Geneva, and Seattle (as Brünnhilde); Paris Opéra 1977, 1985, as Brünnhilde and Isolde; Teatro Liceo 1983; Metropolitan Opera from 1984, debut as Elektra; Other roles include Ortrud, Kundry, Leonore and the Dyer's Wife in Die Frau ohne Schatten; Teatro Col ón, Buenos Aires 1987, as Elektra; Sang Isolde at Florence 1988; Elektra at Marseilles 1989; Sang Ortrud at Buenos Aires 1991. *Recordings include:* Elektra; Die Frau ohne Schatten, conducted by Sawallisch.

VIOTTI, Marcello; conductor; *Music Director, La Fenice, Venice;* b. 29 June 1954, Vallorbe (Vaud), Switzerland. *Education:* Lausanne Conservatory, Geneva. *Career:* Kapellmeister for three years, Opera Regio, Turin; appointed Artistic Dir, Lucerne Opera at age 32; Gen. Music Dir, City of Bremen Opera 1990–93; Chief Conductor, Symphony Orchestra of the Saarländische Rundfunk for five years; Principal Conductor, MDR Symphony Orchestra, Leipzig 1996–99; Chief Conductor, Bayer-ische Rundfunk Orchestra 1998–2000; orchestras conducted include Berlin Philharmonic, Vienna Symphony Orchestra, Tonhalle Orchestra Zürich, Oslo Philharmonic, Munich Philharmonic, Japan Philharmonic, Bamberger Symphoniker, English Chamber Orchestra and all the German Radio Symphony Orchestras; directed first concert with the Vienna Philharmonic during the Mozart Week in Salzburg 1997; opera engagements include all major int. opera houses, including Vienna Staatsoper, Deutsche Oper Berlin and the operas of Munich, Hamburg and Zürich; Dir of numerous new productions at La Scala, Milan, Monnaie, Brussels, Paris Opéra, Vienna Staatsoper, Deutsche Oper Berlin, Zürich Opera and Metropolitan Opera, New York; Music Dir, Gran Teatro La Fenice, Venice 2002–. *Honours:* first prize Gino Marinuzzi Conductors' Competition, San Remo, Italy 1982, Ehrenkrauz der Republik Oesterreich 2004. *Address:* c/o Teatro La Fenice di Venezia, Campo S. Fantin 2519, 30100 Venice, Italy. *E-mail:* info@teatrolafenice.org. *Website:* www.teatrolafenice.it; www.marcello-viotti .com.

VIR, Param; Composer; b. 6 Feb, 1952, Delhi, India. (British national). *Education:* Delhi University; Dartington Summer School, 1983–84, with Peter Maxwell Davies; Guildhall School, London, with Oliver Knussen. *Career:* Composition Fellow at Tanglewood, 1986; Broken Strings and Snatched by the Gods commissioned by Hans Werner Henze for the Munich Biennale, 1992; Ion premiered at Aldeburgh, 2000. *Compositions:* The Demons of Bara Tooti, music theatre, 1980; Besura Desh, theatre, 1982; Fall Out, musical, 1984; Contra-pulse, for ensemble, 1985; Pragati, concertante, 1986; Antiphons and Elegies, for chamber orchestra, 1986; Before Krishna, for strings, 1987; Krishna, children's opera, 1988; Brahma, Vishnu Sita, for six solo voices, 1988; Snatched by the Gods, chamber opera, 1900; Broken Strings chamber opera, 1992; Horse Tooth White Rock, for orchestra, 1994; The Comfort

of Angels, for two pianos, 1995; Tender Light for viola da gamba, 1996; Ultimate Words: Infinite Song, for baritone, six percussion and piano, 1997; Ion, opera after Euripides, 2000. *Honours:* Tippett Composition Award, Britten Prize, 1987. *Address:* c/o PRS Ltd, 29–33 Berners St, London, W1T 3 AB, England. *Telephone:* (20) 7580-5544. *Fax:* (20) 7306-4455.

VIRAGH, Endre; Professor of Organ and Orchestra Conductor; b. 23 March 1928, Vasvár, Hungary; m. Margit Piláth, 21 Sept 1958. *Education:* Graduated in Organ playing, Liszt Ferenc Academy of Music, Budapest, 1955; Studied with J Reinberger, Prague, 1958–59, with M Dupré, Paris, 1960, and with Germani, Rome and Siena, 1965, 1967, 1968. *Career:* Debut: Bart ók Conservatoire, Miskolc, 1955; Principal Parish Church, Budapest, 1961; Regularly appears as soloist at concert on Hungarian radio and television; Organ recitals in Brune and Siena; Permanent interpreter at prestigious organ concerts; Extensive repertoire includes all organ works of J. S. Bach, Liszt, and César Franck, sonatas of Mendelssohn and Hindemith, organ works by modern composers such as Dupré, Messiaen, Janáček and Kodály, and organ concertos including Vivaldi's 2nd; mem, Saint Cecilia OMCE; Ferenc Liszt Society; Zoltán Kodály Society; Lajos Bardos Society. *Recordings:* Video: Assisi, Italy, 1982; Castelgandolfo, Italy, 1991; Professor of Organ at Miskolc from 1955, and at Belá Bartók Conservatoire, Budapest, from 1969. *Honours:* Diploma of Honour, Siena, 1967; Pro-Arte Prize, 1980; Eminent Pedagogue of Organ, 1991; Rectorate Honourable Mention, 1992. *Address:* Róbert-Károly krt 12 a, 1138 Budapest, Hungary.

VIRKHAUS, Taavo; Symphony Orchestra Conductor; b. 29 June 1934, Tartu, Estonia; m. Nancy Ellen Herman 1969. *Education:* BM, University of Miami, Florida, 1951–55; MM 1957, DMA 1967, Eastman School of Music, Rochester, New York; Pierre Monteux Masterclass 1960 and 1961; Fulbright Grant to Cologne, Germany, 1963–64. *Career:* Debut: Conducting the Miami Ballet Guild Orchestra, 1956; Director of Music, University of Rochester, 1966–77; Music Director and Con-ductor, Duluth-Superior Symphony Orchestra, Duluth, Minnesota, 1977–94; Huntsville AL Symphony Orchestra, 1990–2003, Conductor Emeritus, 2003–; Guest Conductor with Rochester Philharmonic; Baltimore Symphony; Estonian SSR State Symphony; Minnesota Orchestra; Music Director and Conductor of Huntsville, Alabama, Symphony Orchestra, 1990–. *Compositions:* 5 Symphonies, 2 Violin Concerti. *Honours:* Howard Hanson Prize, 1966. *Current Management:* Joanne Rile Artists Management, Philadelphia, Pennsylvania, USA. *Address:* 111 Lake Shore Drive, Madison, AL 35758, USA.

VIRSALADZE, Eliso; Concert Pianist; b. 14 Sept. 1942, Russia. *Education:* Studied with Anastasia Virsaladze, then at Tblisi Con-servatory. *Career:* Since winning prizes at competitions in Moscow and Leipzig (1962, 1966) she has played all over the world, including Japan, Germany, Italy, Austria, Poland and Bulgaria; Tours of America and Europe with the Leningrad Philharmonic; British recital debut at the Queen Elizabeth Hall 1981, followed by concerto debut with the Royal Philharmonic and Yuri Temirkanov; Season 1983–84 toured England with USSR Symphony Orchestra; Returned 1987–88 with the Bourne-mouth Symphony, the Royal Philharmonic under Dorati, the Royal Liverpool Philharmonic, BBC Philharmonic, City of Birmingham Symphony and the Philharmonia under Kurt Sanderling; Season 2002–03: appearances at the Wigmore Hall, London, in Paris, Barcelona, Munich, Moscow, St Petersburg and throughout Italy. Toured Japan with St Petersburg Philharmonic and Yuri Temirkanov. *Honours:* Winner, Soviet Competition of Performing Musicians, 1961; Bronze Medal, Tchaikovsky Competition Moscow, 1962; Prize Winner at 1966 Schumann Competition Leipzig. *Address:* Edward Schwich Str. 30 8 54 München, Germany.

VISCONTI, Piero; Singer (Tenor); b. 1947, Valenze, Piedmont, Italy. *Education:* Studied in Rome. *Career:* Debut: Naples, 1975, as Rodolfo in La Bohème; Sang at Miami, 1979, Rome Opera from 1978 (debut as Ernani); Vienna Staatsoper 1980, as Edgardo, the Duke of Mantua at the 1981 Verona Arena, Barcelona and Mannheim from 1982; US appearances at Houston and Philadelphia, Verdi Requiem in London, 1985, and Sydney Opera, 1986; Other roles include Almaviva, Arturo in La Straniera, Pollione in Norma, Nemorino, Foresto, Gabriele Adorno, Pinkerton, Calaf, Enzo and Andrea Chénier. *Address:* Opéra de Montpellier, 11 Boulevard Victor Hugo, 3400 Montpellier, France.

VISHNEVSKAYA, Galina; Singer (Soprano); b. 25 Oct. 1926, Leningrad, Russia; m. Mstislav Rostropovich, 1955, 2 d. *Education:* Studied with Vera Garina. *Career:* Toured with Leningrad Light Opera Company, 1944–48, with Leningrad Philharmonic Society, 1948–52; Joined Bolshoi Theatre 1952; Concert appearances in Europe and USA, 1950–; Has often sung in the 14th Symphony of Shostakovich, including first performance, 1969; First appeared at Metropolitan Opera, New York, USA, 1961; Roles included Leonore in Fidelio; Tatiana in Eugene Onegin, Iolanta; Aida; Sang in England at Festival Hall, Aldeburgh

Festival, Edinburgh Festival, Covent Garden, Rostropovich Festival, Snape; Made concert tours with husband; Member of Jury, Cardiff Singer of the World, 1991; Opera on her life, Galina, by Marcel Landowski, premiered at Lyon 1996. *Recordings:* Numerous recordings. *Publications:* Galina (autobiography). *Current Management:* Victor Hochhauser, 4 Holland Park Avenue, London W11 3QU, England.

VISSE, Dominique; Singer (Counter-Tenor); b. 30 Aug. 1955, Lisieux, France; m. Agnès Mellon. *Education:* Chorister at Notre Dame in Paris; Organ and Flute Studies at the Versailles Conservatory; Further study with Alfred Deller, René Jacobs and Nigel Rogers, 1976–78. *Career:* Debut: Opera debut at Tourcoing 1982, in Monteverdi's Poppea; Sang Flora in the first modern performances of Vivaldi's L'Incoronazione di Dario at Grasse, 1984; Charpentier's Actéon at Edinburgh 1985, Nirenus in Nicholas Hytner's production of Giulio Cesare at the Paris Opéra 1987 and Delfa in Cavilli's Giasone at the 1988 Innsbruck Early Music Festival; Created Geronimo in the premiere of Le Rouge et Noir by Claude Prey, Aix 1989; Sang Annio in Gluck's La Clemenza di Tito at Lausanne, 1991; Sang the Nurse in Monteverdi's Poppea at Buenos Aires, 1996; Season 1998–99 with La Calisto at the Berlin Staatsoper, the Salzburg Festival, the Barcelona Opera and the New York Lincoln Center; At La Scala Milan in Luciano Berio's latest opera, Outis; Instrumentalist in medieval and Renaissance music; Founded the Ensemble Clement Janequin and sang with Les Arts Florissants under William Christie; Sang Narciso in Handel's Agrippina at Brussels (2000) and Nirenus at the Paris Palais Garnier, 2002. *Recordings include:* L'Incoronazione di Dario by Vivaldi; Charpentier's Acteon, Les Arts Florissants and David et Jonathan; Cavalli's Xerxes and Giasone; Octavia's Nurse in L'Incoronazione di Poppea; Rameau's Anacréon and Hasse's Cleofide. *Current Management:* Satirino. *Address:* c/o Ian Malkin, Satirino, 59 rue Orfila, 75020 Paris, France. *E-mail:* info@satirino.fr.

VISSER, Lieuwe; Singer (Bass); b. 23 Aug. 1940, Diemen, Netherlands. *Education:* Studied with Jo van de Meent in Amsterdam and at the Accademia di Santa Cecilia, Rome with Giorgio Favaretto. *Career:* Debut: Netherlands Opera Amsterdam, as Don Basilio in Il Barbiere di Siviglia; Has sung with Netherlands Opera in the 1974 premiere of The Picture of Dorian Gray by Kox and as Masetto, 1984; Glyndebourne Festival 1981, in A Midsummer Night's Dream; Centre France Lyrique Paris 1983, in the stage premiere of Frankenstein by Gruber. *Recordings include:* Lucrezia Borgia by Donizetti.

VITALI, Marisa; Singer (Soprano); b. 1964, South Africa. *Education:* Studied in Cape Town and New York. *Career:* Sang at Bonn Opera from 1989, as Rosina, Strauss's Composer, Wellgunde and Donna Elvira; Guest appearances elsewhere in Germany as Traviata, Liu in Turandot, Suor Angelica, Micaela, Mélisande and Offenbach's Antonia; Fiora in Montemezzi's L'Amore dei tre Ré at Hanover, 1993, and Despina at Catania; Season 1995–96 as Nedda in Pagliacci at Verona, Maria in Guglielmo Ratcliff by Mascagni at Livorno, and Donna Elvira at the Deutsche Oper Berlin. *Honours:* Winner, Francisco Viñas Competition, Barcelona, 1989. *Address:* c/o Deutsche Oper Berlin, Richard Wagner Str 10, 10585 Berlin, Germany.

VITMAN, Yelena; Singer (Mezzo-Soprano); b. 1969, Russia. *Education:* St Petersburg Conservatoire. *Career:* Appearances at the Mariinsky Theatre, Kirov Opera, from 1996; Roles have included Lyubava in Sadko and Lyubasha in The Tsar's Bride, both by Rimsky-Korsakov; Olga in Eugene Onegin, Puccini's Suzuki, Konchakovna in Prince Igor and Siebel in Faust; Sang with the Kirov Opera in summer season at Covent Garden, 2000; Other roles include Clarice in The Love for Three Oranges, and Maria Bolkonskaya in War and Peace. *Honours:* Prizewinner at Wroclaw (1992) and St Petersburg (1994) Vocal Competitions. *Address:* c/o Kirov Opera, Mariinsky Theatre, 1 Theatre Square, St Petersburg, Russia.

VLAD, Marina (Marta); Composer; b. 8 March 1949, Bucharest, Romania; m. Ulpiu Vlad, 15 Sept 1973, 1 s. *Education:* Music High School, Bucharest, 1960–65; High School, T L Caragiale, 1965–67; Graduate in Composition, The C Porumbescu Academy of Music, 1973. *Career:* University Assistant at the C Porumbescu Academy of Music, 1973–91; Professor at The University of Music, Bucharest, 1991; mem, Union of Composers of Romania. *Compositions:* Recorded at the Romanian Radio: Sonata for Violin and Piano, 1978; Rondo for Piano, 1978; Symphony Movement, 1979; Images for String Orchestra, 1980; Sonata for Piano, 1981; String Quartet No. 1, 1981; String Quartet No. 2, 1982; Legend and In Search of The Game for Piano, 1983; String Trio No. 1, Inscriptions for Peace, 1984; String Trio No. 2, 1985; String Trio No. 3, 1986; This Country's Land, cantata for Solo Voice, Choir and Orchestra, a verse by Jon Brad, 1987; Light Rays, trio for Flute, Oboe and Clarinet, 1988; Thoughts for the Future, quartet for Flute, Violin, Viola and Cello, 1989; In Search of The Game No. 2 for Piano, 1994; Still Life I for oboe solo, 1996; Still Life II for clarinet solo, 1997; Still Life III for piano solo, 1997; Still Life IV for violin solo, 1998;

Still Life V for Viola solo, 1999; Still Life Vi (cello, 2000), and VII (flute, 2000). *Recordings:* String Quartet No. 2 and Sonata for Piano, 1984. *Publications:* Sonata for Violin and Piano, 1982; Rondo for Piano, 1983; String Trio No. 1, Inscriptions for Peace, 1986; Dream of Peace, String Trio No. 2, 1988; Light Rays, trio for Flute Oboe and Clarinet, 1989. *Honours:* Prize granted by the Conservatory of Music, C Porumbescu for The Cantata Resonance, 1972. *Address:* Str Andrei Popovici 18, Bl 8A, Sc c et IV, Apt 39, 71254 Bucharest, Romania.

VLAD, Roman; composer and writer on music; b. 29 Dec. 1919, Cernauti (now Uczaina), Romania. *Education:* Cernauti Conservatory and in Rome with Casella. *Career:* active as a pianist and lecturer from 1939; Artistic Director of the Accademia Filarmonica in Rome, 1955–58 and 1966–69; President, Accademia Filarmonica, Rome; Artistic Director of the Maggio Musicale Fiorentino, 1964 and of the Teatro Comunale, Florence, 1968–72; Taught at Dartington Summer School, 1954–55; Co-Editor of the Enciclopedia dello Spettacolo, 1958–62 and the Nuova Rivista Musicale Italiana, 1967–; President of the Italian section of the ISCM, 1960–83; Professor of Composition at the Perugia Conservatory, 1968; Supervisor of the Turin Radio Symphony Orchestra, 1973–80; Artistic Adviser of the Turin Settembre Musica Festival from 1985; President of Society of Italian Authors and Publishers (SIAE) from 1987, Governmental Commissioner 1992–94; President of CISAC, 1982–84, 1992–96; Artistic Director, Teatro alla Scala, Milan, 1994–96. *Compositions:* Ballets: La Strada sul caffé, 1943; La Dama delle Camelie, 1945; Fantasia, 1948; Masques Ostendias, 1959; Die Wiederkehr, 1962; Il Gabbiano, 1968; Il Sogno, 1973; Operas: Storia di una Mamma, 1951; Il Dottore di Vetro, 1960; La Fantarca, 1967; Orchestral: Sinfonietta, 1941; Suite, 1941; Sinfonia all'antica, 1948; Variazioni Concerti su una Serie di 12 Note dal Don Giovanni di Mozart for Piano and Orchestra, 1955; Musica per Archi, 1957; Musica Concertata for Harp and Orchestra, 1958; Ode Super Chrysae Phorminx for Guitar and Orchestra 1964; Divertimento Sinfonico, 1967; Vocal: 3 Cantatas, 1940–53; Lettura di Michelangelo for Chorus, 1964; Immer Wieder for Soprano and 8 Instruments, 1965; Piccolo Divertimento Corale, 1968; Lettura di Lorenzo Magnifico for Chorus, 1974; La Vespa di Toti for Boys' Voices and Instruments, 1976; Chamber: Divertimento for 11 Instruments, 1948; String Quartet, 1957, Serenata for 12 Instruments, 1959; Il Magico Flauto di Severino for Flute and Piano, 1971; Cinque elegie su testi biblici, 1990; Melodia variata, 1990; Stagioni giaponesi, 24 Haiku, 1993–94; Piano Music; Music for more than 100 films. *Publications include:* Collected Essays, 1955; Luigi Dallapiccola, 1957; Storia della Dodecafonia, 1958; Stravinsky, 1958, revised 1973 and 1979; Essays on Busoni, Schoenberg and Stravinsky; Introduzione alle cultura musicale, 1988; Capire la musica 1989. *Address:* Via XXIV Haggio N 51, 00187 Rome, Italy.

VLAD, Ulpiu; Composer; b. 27 Jan. 1945, Zarnesti, Romania; m. Marina Marta Vlad, 15 Sept 1973, 1 s. *Education:* Music High School, Bucharest, 1958–64; Academy of Music C Porumbescu, Bucharest, 1964–71; Seminar in Composition, Conservatory of Music, Santa Cecilia, Rome. *Career:* Debut: Septet for Winds and Piano, 1970, Conservatory of Music C Porumbescu; Researcher in Romanian Folk Music, Academy of Music, Bucharest, 1972–77; Researcher in Romanian Folk Music, Institut de Cercetari Etnologice si Dailectologice, Bucharest, 1977–80; Editor, 1980–84, Manager, 1984–92, Romanian Musical Publishing Company; Music Department Director, Romanian Ministry of Culture, 1992–93; Professor at The Academy of Music, Bucharest, 1990–; Romanian television and radio appearances; mem., Union of Composers and Musicologists, 1973. *Compositions include:* Sonata for oboe and piano (harpsichord), 1969; This is Earth, cantata foro mixed choir and orchestra, verse by Eugen Frunz, 1970; As Hardly from Depths, symphonie concertante for violoncello, pianoforte and orchestra, 1971, revised 1981; First Symphony Roads in The Light, 1979; Lights in The Sunset, symphonic work, 1991; The Secret of Dreams, quintet for Winds No. 2, 1992; The Time of Mirrors, for chamber orchestra, 1974; Mosaic, chamber-vocal-symphonic cycle, with unlimited possibilities of combinations between the different instruments of the orchestra and a vocal quartet, 1974–78; Flowers for peace, string quartet, 1982; Voices of peace, quintet for winds and tape, 1986; String trio, 1987; Sun-lit Landscape, string trio no. 2, 1987; On this Sunny Land, string trio no. 3, 1988; String Trio, 1990; The Joy of the Passage, string trio no. 4, 1991; The Joy of Dreams I, quintet for flute, violin, viola, cello and percussion, 1990; From the Joy of Dreams, Concerto for string orchestra, 1991; The Game of Dreams I, Concerto for chamber orchestra, 1992; The Time of Dreams, quartet for flute, clarinet, piano and percussion, 1993; Suddenly Dreams, concerto for Chamber Orchestra, 1994; The Legend of Dreams, septet for flute, oboe, clarinet, piano, bassoon, percussion, violin and cello, 1994; The Light of Dreams, symphonic work, 1995; Beyond Dreams, music for wind, string and keyboard, 1996; The Secret of Dreams III, septet for flute, oboe, clarinet, bassoon, horn, percussion and piano, 1996; Resonances in the future, solo pieces for flute, oboe, clarinet, bassoon, horn, percussion, violin, viola, cello, piano, harp, 1997–2001; Interlocking Dreams, for 3 flutes, oboe, clarinet, bassoon, horn, violin, viola and accordion, 1997; Interlocking Dreams II, 3 pieces for wind quintet, string quartet, trumpet, percussion, piano and harp, 1998; Resonances on White Background, quartet for saxophones, trombone, percussion and piano, 1998; Interlocking Dreams III, 3 pieces for wind quintet, string trio, saxophone, trumpet, percussion, piano, soprano and improvising ensemble, 1999; Mauve, 2000, Light Blue, 2000, Green, 2001; Resonances on Pale Background – Concerto for harp and string orchestra, 2002; The Poetry of Dreams, 3 pieces for chamber ensemble and tape (dedicated to victims of the Holocaust), 2003. *Recordings:* Mosaic, 2 versions, 1980; Dreams 1; The Joy of Achievement – Wedding Songs; Beyond Dreams III, 1998; Suddenly Dreams, 2000. *Publications include:* Mosaic, 1982; 1st Symphony, Roads in The Light, 1985; 2nd Symphony, From our Hearts, 1988; Inscriptions in Hearts, 1989; Dreams ll, 1992; The Spring, String Trio No. 1, 1994. *Honours:* Oboe Prize, Festival of Young Performers of Romania, 1964; Special Prize of Univ. of Music, Bucharest, 1971; Medal for Distinction in Culture (2nd Class), 1983; George Enescu Prize of the Acad. of Romania, 1985; First Prize, Union of Composers and Musicologists, Nat. Festival of Song, Romania, 1987; Prize, Union of Romanian Composers and Musicologists, 1991, 1995, 2000. *Address:* Str. Andrei Popovici 18, Bl 8A, Sc c et IV Apt 39, 71254 Bucharest, Romania. *Telephone:* (21) 2306712. *E-mail:* romanvlad@dnt.ro. *Website:* composers21.com/compdocs/vladu.htm.

VLATKOVIC, Radovan; Horn Player; b. 1962, Zagreb, Croatia. *Education:* Zagreb Academy of Music and the Northwest German Music Academy at Detmold. *Career:* Principal of the Berlin Radio Symphony Orchestra, 1982–90; Solo engagements from 1979, notably at Salzburg 1984, the Vienna Konzerthaus, the Barbican, the Théâtre de la Ville in Paris, Pushkin Museum Moscow, Metropolitan Museum New York, Orchestra Hall Chicago and Suntory Hall, Tokyo; Soloist with leading orchestras and chamber music performer with Gidon Kremer, Heinz Holliger, András Schiff and Aurèle Nicolet; Professor of Horn, Stuttgart Hochschule für Musik, 1992–. *Recordings include:* Mozart's Four Concertos and R Strauss Concertos with the English Chamber Orchestra conducted by Jeffrey Tate. *Honours:* Prizes at the Wind Instruments Competition in Ancona, 1979; Horn Competition in Liège, 1981; 1st Prize, International ARD Competition in Munich, 1983; German Music Critics' Prize three times for recordings of solo (Mozart) and chamber music (Gubaidulina, Hindemith) Repertoire. *Current Management:* Ingpen & Williams Ltd, 7 St George's Court, 131 Putney Bridge Road, London, SW15 2PA, England.

VLIJMEN, Jan van; Composer and Administrator; b. 11 Oct. 1935, Rotterdam, Netherlands. *Education:* Studied composition with Kees van Baaren. *Career:* Director of the Amersfoort Music School, 1961–65; Lecturer in Theory at Utrecht Conservatory, 1965–67; Deputy Director of the Royal Conservatory, The Hague, 1967, Director, 1971; General Manager of Netherlands Opera, 1985–88; Director of the Holland Festival, 1991–97. *Compositions include:* Strijkkwartet No. 1, 1956 and No. 2, 1958 both for String Quartet; Gruppi for Orchestra, 1962, revised 1980; Sonata for Piano and Large Ensemble, 1966; Quintetto a fiati No. 2 for Wind Quintet, 1972; Axel, opera with Reinbert de Leeuw, 1977; Faithful for Viola, 1984; Nonet for Ensemble, 1985; Solo II for Clarinet, 1986; R Escher–Summer Rites at Noon for 2 Orchestras, 1987; Such a Day of Sweetness for Soprano and Orchestra, 1988; Un Malheureux Vêtu de Noir, opera, 1990; Concerto for Piano and Orchestra, 1991; Tombeau (Solo III), for Violoncello, 1991; Inferno (Dante), cantate for Choir and Large Ensemble, 1993; A Schoenberg–6 Kleine Klavierstücke, Op 19 arrangement for Orchestra (published), 1993; After Schoenberg Op 19: Solo IV, against that time, for flute and contralto, 1994–95; Quintetto for strings, 1995–96; Monumentum for large orchestra and mezzo-soprano, 1998; Sei pezzi for violin and piano, 1998; Choeurs for chamber choir and several instruments, 1999; Gestures I and II for violin and piano, 1999; Arrangements of Schoenberg and Zemlinsky. *Recordings:* Un malheureux de Noir; Sonata, Omaggio a Gesualdo and Inferno; Concerto. *Honours:* Officier des Arts et des Lettres, France; Officier in de orde van de Nederlandse Leeuw, Netherlands; State Prizes; Prizes from the City of Amsterdam. *Address:* Eerste Breeuwerstraat 24, 1013 MK Amsterdam, Netherlands.

VODICKA, Leo (Marian); Singer (Tenor); b. 1950, Brno, Czechoslovakia. *Education:* Studied at the Janáček Academy of Arts with Josef Valek. *Career:* Has sung in most Czech opera houses, notably the Janáček Opera Brno and the Prague National Theatre; Guest engagements in Bologna, Rome, Milan, Geneva, Zürich, Berne, Graz, Salzburg, Cologne, Paris, Nice, Tokyo, Osaka and in Bulgaria, Hungary, the former Soviet Union and East Germany; Major roles have included Verdi's Rigoletto, Don Carlos, Manrico and Otello; Puccini's Cavaradossi, Des Grieux, Pinkerton and Rodolfo; Janáček's Laca and Boris, the Prince in Rusalka and Smetana's Jenik and Dalibor; Don José and Stravinsky's Oedipus; Concert repertoire includes Verdi Requiem; Dvořák Stabat Mater and Requiem; Janáček Amarus, Glagolitic Mass, Diary of One Who Disappeared and Everlasting Gospel; Martinů's Field Mass and Bart

ók's Cantata Profana; Staatsoper Vienna for role of Prince in Rusalka by Dvořák, 1990; Vienna, L Janáček-Glagolitic Mass and Osud (Fate), 1990; Solo tour in Japan/Tokyo, Koriyama, Kumamoto, Matsuyama with airs from Carmen, Andrea Chénier, La Forza del Destino, Otello, Tosca, Traviata, conducted by Shigeo Genda, 1992; Season 2000 as Don José, Max in Der Freischütz and Cavaradossi, at the Prague State Opera. *Recordings:* Smetana The Kiss, The Secret and Libuše; Dvořák The Cunning Peasant; Foerster Eva; Janáček Amarus conducted by Charles Mackerras (Supraphon); Antonin Dvořák–Dimitrij, title role, conducted by Gerd Albrecht, Supraphon, 1989; London BBC, Diary of One Who Disappeared, with Radoslav Kvapil-piano, 1993. *Current Management:* Pragokoncert, Maltézské nam 1, Prague 1, Czech Republic. *Address:* Zlichovska 6, Prague, Czech Republic.

VOGEL, Siegfried; Singer (Bass); b. 6 March 1937, Chemnitz, Germany. *Education:* Studied in Dresden with H Winkler and J Kemter. *Career:* Debut: Dresden Staatsoper 1959, as Zizell in Si j'etais roi by Adam; Sang Mozart roles in Dresden; Sarastro, Osmin and the Commendatore; Berlin Staatsoper from 1965 as Leporello, Alfonso, Hunding, Basilio, Count Almaviva, Escamillo, Kecal and Ochs; Guest appearances in Moscow, Paris, Lausanne (Hans Sachs and Baron Ochs 1983), Brussels and Vienna; Further engagements at La Scala and in Venice, Stockholm, Helsinki, Amsterdam and Cairo; Bayreuth Festival 1985–86, as Biterolf in Tannhäuser; Sang Kaspar, Rocco and the King Henry in Lohengrin, 1986 at the Berlin Staatsoper; Metropolitan debut 1986, as Hunding, sang Morosus in Die schweigsame Frau at Palermo, 1988; Bayreuth 1989, as Fasolt, Biterolf and Titurel; Toronto Opera 1990, as the Doctor in Wozzeck; Sang the Athlete in Lulu at the Semper Oper Dresden, 1992; Concert repertoire includes sacred music by Bach and Handel; Sang Rocco in Fidelio at the 1996 Edinburgh Festival; Sang Saul in the premiere of Weill's The Eternal Road, Chemnitz 1999; Fafner in The Ring at the Berlin Staatsoper, 2001. *Recordings:* Der Freischütz; Ariadne auf Naxos, Die Meistersinger, Zar und Zimmermann, Genoveva, Rienzi; St Matthew Passion; Karl V by Krenek. *Address:* c/o Berlin Staatsoper, Unter den Linden 7, 1086 Berlin, Germany.

VOGEL, Volker; Singer (Tenor); b. 13 Oct. 1950, Karlsruhe, Germany. *Education:* Studied at the Hanover Musikhochschule. *Career:* Sang at the Dortmund Opera, then at Freiburg, 1984–85, and the Vienna Volksoper, 1984–90; Zürich Opera from 1991; Guest appearances in Barcelona, Berlin, Bregenz and Verona; Vienna, 1990, in the premiere of Einem's Tuliphant; Salzburg and London, 1992, in Weill's Sieben Todsünden; Other roles include Mozart's Pedrillo and Beethoven's Jacquino; Season 1999–2000 as Herod in Salome and Shuisky in Boris Godunov, at Dublin; Wagner's Melot and Mime for Zürich Opera. *Recordings include:* Zemlinsky's Kleider machen Leute; Monostatos in Die Zauberflöte. *Address:* Opernhaus Zürich, Falkenerstrasse 1, 8008 Zürich, Switzerland.

VOGLER, Jan; Cellist; b. 18 Feb. 1964, Berlin, Germany. *Education:* Hanns Eisler Hochschule für Musik, Berlin; Basle Music Academy, Switzerland, Teachers Josef Schwab, Heinrich Schiff. *Career:* Concert Master, cello, Staatskapelle Dresden, 1985–; Concerts as soloist, orchestras including Berlin Radio Orchestra 1986, 1987, 1989, Staatskapelle Dresden, Berlin Chamber Orchestra, Dresden Chamber Orchestra, Virtuosi Saxoniae; US debut, Chicago 1987; Marlboro Festival, USA 1988, 1989; Numerous radio broadcasts, live recordings; Recitals, many countries. *Current Management:* Kunstleragentur, Krausenstrasse 9/10, 1080 Berlin. *Address:* Bahnhofstrasse 47, 1123 Berlin, Germany.

VOGT, Lars; concert pianist; b. 8 Sept. 1970, Düren, Germany; m. Tatiana Komarova. *Education:* Hanover Conservatoire with Prof. Kämmerling. *Career:* numerous concerto and recital performances throughout Europe, Asia and North America; London debut, Royal Albert Hall 1990; work with numerous British orchestras, including Philharmonia, London Symphony, Royal Scottish Nat. and all BBC Orchestras; Berlin concerto debut with Deutsches Symphonie-Orchester under Leonard Slatkin; performed with LA Philharmonic, including Hollywood Bowl under Simon Rattle; played 16-concert tour of Australia 1997; Far East tour, including performances with NHK Symphony, Tokyo 1998; season 1998–99 included engagements with Salzburg Mozarteum Orchestra, Leipzig Gewandhaus, City of Birmingham Symphony; played Mostly Mozart Festival, New York; debut with Atlanta and Montreal Symphony Orchestras; recitals in London, Salzburg, Berlin, Rome, Amsterdam and Bilbao; played Brahms with Skampa Quartet, Wigmore Hall, London; Beethoven concerto cycle with Gurzenich Orchestra under James Conlon; founder, chamber music festival in Heimbach, Germany 1998; season 1999–2000 included engagements with the Komische Oper Berlin, Dresden Philharmonic, BBC Nat. Orchestra of Wales; Lutoslawski's Piano Concerto in Zürich, Dresden, Stuttgart, Bremen and Vienna; recitals in London, Los Angeles and Montreaux and chamber concerts in London, Vienna, Salzburg, Lucerne and Frankfurt; premiere of a new concerto by

Tatiana Komarova 2001; Schumann's concerto in A minor at the London Proms 2002. *Recordings:* Schumann Concerto, Grieg Concerto with City of Birmingham Symphony and Simon Rattle, first two Beethoven concertos with Simon Rattle, 19th and 20th century Russian works, Haydn sonatas and Schumann's Kreisleriana and Bunte Blätter, Beethoven Sonatas op 10 No. 1 and Op 111, Prokofiev and Shostakovich cello sonatas with Truls Mork, Hindemith piano concerto No. 1 with Berlin Philharmonic and Claudio Abbado. *Honours:* Diapason d'Or for Prokofiev and Shostakovich cello sonatas. *Current Management:* Askonas Holt Ltd, Lonsdale Chambers, 27 Chancery Lane, London, WC2A 1PF, England. *Telephone:* (20) 7400-1700. *Fax:* (20) 7400-1799. *E-mail:* info@askonasholt.co.uk. *Website:* www.askonasholt.co.uk.

VOICULESCU, Dan; Composer, Musicologist and Professor of Counterpoint and Composition; b. 20 July 1940, Saschiz-Sighisoara, Romania. *Education:* diplomas in composition and piano, Acad. of Music Gh. Dima, Cluj, 1958–64; classes with V. Mortari, Venice, Italy, 1968, K. Stockhausen, Cologne, Germany, 1971–72; DMus, 1983. *Career:* Prof. of Counterpoint and Composition, Acad. of Music, Cluj, 1963–2000, National Univ. of Music, Bucharest, 2000–; Ed., Lucrari de Muzicologie (Musicological Works), Cluj, 1979–91; mem., Union of Romanian Composers. *Compositions:* Sinfonia Ostinato, 1963; Visions Cosmiques, 1968; Music for strings, 1971; Pieces for orchestra, 1973; Suite from Codex Caioni for strings, 1996; Inflorescences, for strings, 2001; Fables, Dialogues, Sonata, Croquis, Sonantes, Spirals, 3 Toccatas for piano solo, 6 Sonatas for flute solo, Sonata for clarinet solo; Sketches and Sonata for oboe solo; Fiorituri for violin and piano; Dilemmas, for seven; Concertant Diptych, for Baroque ensemble; Cantata for baritone, choir and orchestra, 1977; Homage to Blaga for mixed choir; Mass for children's choir; Four vols choral music for children; Book Without End, 3 vols of piano pieces for children; 50 Lieder for voice and piano; The Bald Chanteuse, chamber comic opera, 1993. *Publications:* Polyphony of Baroque in the Works of J. S. Bach, 1975; Polyphony of the 20th Century, 1983; Bachian Fugue, 1986. *Honours:* Union of Romanian Composers Prizes, 1972–1978, 1995; G. Enescu Prize from the Romanian Acad., 1984. *Address:* Str. Carol Davila 67, 050452 Bucharest, Romania.

VOIGT, Deborah; Singer (soprano); b. 4 Aug. 1960, Chicago, USA. *Education:* San Francisco Opera's Merola Program. *Career:* debut, Shostakovich's 14th Symphony, San Francisco Chamber Symphony; European engagements include Schubert's Fierrabras at Brussels, Electra in Idomeneo for Finnish National Opera, 1991, and Elvira in Ernani for Chelsea Opera Group, 1990; Other opera performances in concert include Das Rheingold with the Minnesota Orchestra, Weber's Agathe in New York, Die Walküre, La Wally and Il Piccolo Marat for Dutch Radio; Season 1990–91, with Amelia, Ballo in Maschera, at San Francisco and Strauss's Ariadne with the Boston Lyric Opera; Metropolitan Opera debut 1991, as Amelia; Season 1992–93 included Leonora in Il Trovatore with the Metropolitan Opera and as Amelia in Un ballo in maschera with the Lyric Opera of Chicago; Highlights of the 1993–94 season included her debut with the Berlin Philharmonic in Zemlinsky's Lyrische Symphonie, performances of the Verdi Requiem and her debut with the Philadelphia Orchestra in a series of highly acclaimed Wagner concerts in Philadelphia and Carnegie Hall; Made her first concert appearance with Luciano Pavarotti in Lincoln Center's Pavarotti Plus! gala, 1994; European engagements in 1995–96 included Senta in Wagner's Der fliegende Holländer with the Vienna Staatsoper and a gala concert in Tel-Aviv under Daniel Oren, and as Amelia, Covent Garden (debut), 1995; Amelia at the Metropolitan, 1997; Season 1998 with Sieglinde on Act I of Die Walküre at St Petersburg and Strauss's Aegyptische Helena for the Royal Opera, London, in concert; season 2002 as Danae in Die Liebe der Danae at the Salzburg Festival, Ariadne in Ariadne auf Naxos at San Francisco Opera, in Elektra at the New York Met, and in Tosca at Vienna State Opera. *Recordings include:* Strauss's Ariadne auf Naxos; La Forza del Destino; Strauss's Die Frau ohne Schatten. *Honours:* Prizewinner, Metropolitan Opera Auditions and the Pavarotti International Competition at Philadelphia; Winner, 1989 Bussetto Verdi Competition and 1990 Tchaikovsky International at Moscow; Opera Debut of the Year, New York Times, 1991; Title role in Strauss's Die Liebe der Danaë, Salzburg Festival 2002. *Current Management:* Prima International Artists Management, Piazza de' Calderini 2/2, 40124 Bologna, Italy. *Telephone:* (051) 264056. *Fax:* (051) 230766. *E-mail:* prima@primartists.com. *Website:* www.primartists .com. *Address:* IMG Artists, Lovell House, 616 Chiswick High Road, London, W4 5RX, England. *Telephone:* (20) 8233-5800. *Fax:* (20) 8233-5801. *E-mail:* artistseurope@imgworld.com. *Website:* www.imgartists .com; www.deborahvoigt.com.

VOKETAITIS, Arnold; Singer (Bass); b. 11 May 1931, New Haven, Connecticut, USA. *Education:* Studied in New York. *Career:* Debut: New York City Opera 1958, as Vanuzzi in Die schweigsame Frau; Sang in New York as Britten's Theseus, Creon in Oedipus Rex and the Father in the local premiere of Douglas Moore's Carrie Nation, 1968; Guest

engagements at Houston, Miami, Pittsburgh, Mexico City, San Antonio, Montreal and Vancouver; Chicago 1968–73 in Le Rossignol, Madama Butterfly, Carmen, I Due Foscari, Werther and Billy Budd; Other roles have included Don Magnifico (Metropolitan Opera National Touring Company), Don Pasquale, Dulcamara, Basilio and John Hale in The Crucible by Robert Ward, Milwaukee 1976. *Recordings:* Le Cid by Massenet.

VOLANS, Kevin; Irish composer; b. 26 July 1949, Pietermaritzburg, South Africa. *Education:* Universities of Witwatersrand and Aberdeen; Hochschüle für musik, Cologne, 1975–79, with Karl-Heinz Stockhausen, Mauricio Kagel and Alois Kontarsky. *Career:* Lecturer in Composition at University of Natal, 1981–85; Composer-in-Residence at Queen's University, Belfast, 1986–89; Princeton University, 1992; many commissions. *Compositions include:* White Man Sleeps, for two harpsichords, bass viol and percussion, 1982 (arranged as String Quartet no. 1, 1986); Walking Song, for ensemble, 1984; She Who Sleeps with a Small Blanket, for percussion, 1985; Kneeling Dance, for two pianos, 1985 (version, for six pianos, 1992); Into the Darkness, for ensemble, 1987; Hunting, Gathering, string quartet no. 2, 1987; The Songlines, string quartet no. 3, 1988, rev, 1993; Chevron, dance, 1990; The Ramanujan Notebooks, string quartet no. 4, 1990; The Man with Footsoles of Wind, chamber opera, 1993; Plane-song, film music, 1993; Concerto, for piano and wind, 1995; Blue, Yellow, dance, 1995; Dancers on a Plane, string quartet, 1995; Slow, for piano and wind, 1996; Asanga, for percussion, 1997; Violin Concerto, 1997; Double Violin Concerto, 1999; Piano Trio, 2001; Concerto for Double Orchestra, 2002; Strip Weave for orchestra, 2002; Trumpet and String Quartet 1 & 2, 2002; String Quartet No. 7 (Similarity 1), 2002; Confessions of Zeno, 2002. *Current Management:* c/o Van Walsum Management, 4 Addison Bridge Place, London W14 8DS, England. *Telephone:* (20) 7371-4343. *Fax:* (20) 7371-4344.

VOLKERT, Gudrun; Singer (Soprano); b. 1942, Brno, Czeckoslovakia. *Education:* Studied at the Linz Conservatory. *Career:* Sang dramatic roles at Klagenfurt 1966–67, Kiel 1967–74, Bielefield 1974–83; Guest appearances at Brunswick 1983–88, Kassel from 1984, Hamburg 1986 and Turin 1987; Performances as Brünnhilde in Der Ring des Nibelungen at Rotterdam, 1988, Warsaw 1988–89, and Seattle 1991; Sang Cherubini's Médée at Wuppertal 1988, followed by Isolde 1989; Metropolitan Opera 1990, as Brünnhilde; Scottish Opera 1991, as Leonore in a new production of Fidelio; Other roles include Senta, Ortrud, Salome, the Marschallin, Gioconda, Tosca, Turandot and the Countess in Die Soldaten. *Address:* c/o Seattle Opera Association, PO Box 9248, WA 98109, USA.

VOLKONSKY, Andrey Mikhaylovich; Composer and Harpsichordist; b. 14 Feb. 1933, Geneva, Switzerland. *Education:* Studied with Nadia Boulanger and Dinu Lipatti in Paris; Moscow Conservatory, 1950–53. *Career:* Associated with Rudolf Barschai and Chamber Orchestra of Moscow; Performances of his music by Pierre Boulez in London and Berlin (1967) after ban by Soviet authorities; Emigrated to France 1973 and worked for Belaieff Foundation, in aid of needy musicians. *Compositions:* String trio, 1951; Concerto for Orchestra, 1953; Piano Quintet, 1955; Two string quartets, 1955, 1958; Serenade for an Insect, for chamber orchestra, 1958; Les plaintes de Shchaza for soprano and ensemble, 1961; Itinerant Concerto, for low voice and ensemble, 1963–67; Les mailles du temps for three instrumental groups, 1969; Immobile, for piano and orchestra, 1978; Was noch lebt, for mezzo and string trio, 1985; Psalm 148, 1989; Crossroads for synthesizer and ensemble, 1992. *Publications include:* The Foundation of Temperament, Moscow, 1998. *Address:* c/o SACEM, 225 avenue Charles de Gaulle, 92521 Neuilly Sur Seine Cédex, France.

VOLKOV, Solomon; American musicologist; b. 17 April 1944, Ura-Tyube, Tajikistan. *Education:* Leningrad Conservatory. *Career:* Artistic Dir, Leningrad Experimental Studio of Chamber Opera 1965–70; staging of Fleischmann's Rothschild's Violin, completed by Shostakovich; research at Russian Inst., Columbia Univ. 1976. *Publications:* Young Composers of Leningrad 1971, Remembrance of the 'Leningrad Spring' 1974, Testimony: The Memoirs of Dmitri Shostakovich (ed.) 1979, Scissors and Music: Music Censorship in the Soviet Union 1983, Balanchine's Tchaikovsky 1985, Yevgeny Mravinsky, Leningrad's Master Builder 1988, From Russia to the West: the Musical Memoirs of Nathan Milstein (with N. Milstein) 1990, St Petersburg: A Cultural History 1995, Conversations with Joseph Brodsky 1998, Shostakovich and Stalin 2004; contrib. articles in journals and newspapers 1959–. *Address:* c/o Alfred A. Knopf, 1745 Broadway, New York, NY 10019, USA.

VOLKOVA, Svetlana; Singer (Soprano); b. 1950, Russia. *Career:* Many appearances throughout Russia in concerts and opera; Kirov Opera, St Petersburg, from 1990, as Pauline in The Gambler by Prokofiev, Sonya in War and Peace, the Hostess in The Fiery Angel and Fata Morgana in The Love for Three Oranges; Sang with the Kirov Opera in summer season at Covent Garden, 2000; Other roles include Tisbe in Cenerentola, Susanna (Khovanshchina), Herodias in Salome, Mozart's Marcellina, Fricka in Das Rheingold, Larina (Eugene Onegin) and Skomoroshina in Sadko by Rimsky-Korsakov. *Address:* c/o Kirov Opera, Mariinksy Theatre, 1 Theatre Square, St Petersburg, Russia.

VOLLE, Michael; Singer (Baritone); b. 1959, Germany. *Education:* Studied in Stuttgart and Trossingen with Joseph Metternich and Rudolf Piernay. *Career:* Sang first at Mannheim, then three seasons at Bonn as Mozart's Guglielmo, Count, Don Giovanni and Papageno, Marcello in La Bohème and Rossini's Figaro; Further engagements at Hanover, Wiesbaden, Dresden, Düsseldorf, Leipzig and Paris; Season 1997–98 with Covent Garden and La Scala debuts, as the Herald in Lohengrin and the Speaker in Die Zauberflöte; Other roles include Silvio, Don Fernando (Fidelio) and Ottokar in Der Freischütz; Don Giovanni at the 1998 Schwetzingen Festival; Season 2000–01 as Billy Budd, Eugene Onegin and Mozart's Count at Cologne, Don Giovanni at the Berlin Staatsoper and Ford in Falstaff at Brussels; Bach's St Mathew Passion at the London Proms, 2002; Many concert appearances. *Recordings include:* Britten's War Requiem; Schubert's Mass in A-flat and Bach's Christmas Oratorio. *Honours:* Winner of numerous competitions. *Address:* c/o Oper der Stadt Bonn, Am Boeselagerhof 1 Pf 2440, 5300 Bonn, Germany.

VOLODOS, Arcadi; concert pianist; b. 24 Sept. 1972, St Petersburg, Russia. *Education:* St Petersburg and Moscow Conservatories, Paris Conservatoire with Jacques Rouvier, Madrid Conservatory with Dmitri Bashkirov. *Career:* frequent recital and concerto engagements in Russia and Europe; Carnegie Hall, New York debut 1998; Salzburg Festival debut 2002; repertoire includes Bach, Mozart, Schumann and Russian Masters. *Recordings include:* Mozart's Rondo alla Turca, transcriptions of songs by Rachmaninov, Scriabin Sonata No. 10 and Schumann Bunte Blätter, Schubert Sonatas D157 and D894. *Current Management:* Columbia Artists Management International, Albrechtstrasse 18, Berlin 10117, Germany. *Telephone:* (30) 20 64 8078. *Fax:* (30) 20 45 3480.

VOLZ, Manfred; Singer (Bass-baritone); b. 1949, Darmstadt, Germany. *Career:* Sang in concert from 1972; Stage debut as Mozart's Figaro at Trier, 1980; Further appearances as Melitone in La Forza del Destino and Papageno; Engaged at Aachen 1981–83, Kassel from 1985, as Alberich, Ford, Amonasro, Mozart's Count, and Faninal; Bad Gandersheim 1986, as the King in Der Kluge by Orff; Sang Alberich in Ring cycles at Rotterdam 1988 and Dortmund 1991; Season 2000–01 at Kassel as Banquo, Faninal in Der Rosenkavalier, Berg's Dr Schön and Rangoni in Boris Godunov; Concert repertoire includes Verdi's Requiem. *Address:* c/o Opernhaus, Kuhstrasse 12, 4600 Dortmund, Germany.

VON DER WETH, Alexandra; Singer (Soprano); b. 1972, Coburg, Germany. *Education:* Studied in Munich. *Career:* Debut: Leipzig 1993, in Grétry's Zémire et Azor; Appearances with the Deutsche Oper am Rhein, Düsseldorf, from 1996 as Mozart's Pamina and Sandrina, Manon, Lucia di Lammermoor and Alcina; Season 1999–2000 as Micaela at Cologne, Fiordiligi at the Glyndebourne Festival and Musetta for the Vienna Staatsoper; Lulu and Violetta at Düsseldorf; Season 2000–01 with Lucia at Santa Fe, Musetta at the New York Met and Violetta in Chicago; Covent Garden debut 2001, as Manon Lescaut in Henze's Boulevard Solitude; Engaged as Strauss's Daphne at Covent Garden (Concert), 2002. *Recordings include:* Concert arias by Mozart and Beethoven; Lieder by Clara Schumann. *Address:* c/o Deutsche Oper am Rhein, Heinrich Heine Allee 16a, 40213 Düsseldorf, Germany.

VON DOHNÁNYI, Christoph; German conductor; *Principal Conductor, Philharmonia Orchestra;* b. 8 Sept. 1929, Berlin; s. of Hans von Dohnányi and Christine (née Bonhoeffer) von Dohnányi; brother of Klaus von Dohnányi; m. 1st Renate Zillessen; one s. one d.; m. 2nd Anja Silja 1979; one s. two d. *Education:* Munich Musikhochschule. *Career:* abandoned legal training to study music 1948; studied in USA under grandfather, Ernst von Dohnányi 1951; répétiteur and conductor under Georg Solti, Frankfurt Oper 1952–56; Gen. Music Dir Lübeck 1957–63, Kassel 1963–66; London debut with London Philharmonic Orchestra 1965; Chief Conductor of Cologne Radio Symphony Orchestra 1964–69; Gen. Music Dir and Opera Dir, Frankfurt 1968–77; Chief Conductor and Intendant, Hamburg State Opera 1977–84; Music Dir (desig.) Cleveland Orchestra 1982–84, Music Dir 1984–; Prin. Guest Conductor Philharmonia Orchestra 1994, Prin. Conductor 1997–; numerous guest appearances; numerous recordings of symphonies with Cleveland Orchestra and opera recordings. *Honours:* Dr hc (Kent State Univ., Case Western Univ., Oberlin Coll., Eastman School of Music, Cleveland Inst. of Music); Commdr, Ordre des Arts et des Lettres; Commdr's Cross, Order of Merit (Germany); Commdr's Cross (Austria); recipient Richard Strauss Prize, Bartok Prize, Goethe Medal, Frankfurt, Arts and Science Prize, City of Hamburg, Abraham Lincoln Award. *Current Management:* Harrison/Parrott Ltd, 12 Penzance Place, London, W11 4PA,

England. *Telephone:* (20) 7229-9166. *Fax:* (20) 7221-5042. *Website:* www .harrisonparrott.com.

VON MAGNUS, Elisabeth; Singer (Mezzo-soprano); b. Vienna, Austria. *Education:* Drama School, Salzburg; Vocal studies with Hertha Töpper, Munich, and S Schouten, Netherlands. *Career:* Own programme on Austrian Radio; Soloist in nearly all European countries, Japan and the USA; Venues include the Alte Oper, Frankfurt, the Barbican Centre, London, the Vienna Musikverein, the Concertgebouw, Amsterdam, the Berlin Philharmonic and the Cologne Philharmonic; Has sung with conductors such as Abbado, Harnoncourt, Weill, Hans Vouk; N. Marnines; Adam Fischer, Herreweghe, and Ton Koopman; US debut in 1991 with St Matthew Passion with the Los Angeles Philharmonic under Peter Schreier; Salzburg Festival debut in Mozart's C Minor Mass, Monteverdi's L'Incoronazione di Poppea and Vespers of 1610, 1993; Has appeared in many and varied roles at several leading opera houses and music festivals with recitals of songs ranging from Haydn to Berg and Weill; Has featured on numerous radio and television broadcasts including Mozart's Le nozze di Figaro from Zürich Opera House; Sang Piramus in Hasse's Piramo e Tisbe, Wiener Schauspielhaus, 2001. *Recordings include:* Zigeunerbaron; Stabat mater; Bach's Christmas Oratorio and Magnificat; Shostakovich, Sieben Romanzen with Stononi Trio; Arianna and Canzonettes by Haydn (Challenge Records). *Address:* Künstleragentur Dr Raab and Dr Böhm, Plankeng 7, 1010 Vienna, Austria.

VON OTTER, Anne-Sofie; Swedish singer (mezzo-soprano); b. 9 May 1955, Stockholm. *Education:* Conservatorium, Stockholm, studied interpretation with Erik Werba (Vienna) and Geoffrey Parsons (London), vocal studies with Vera Rozsa. *Career:* mem. Basel Opera, Switzerland 1982–85; début France at Opéra de Marseille (Nozze di Figaro—Cherubino) and Aix-en-Provence Festival (La Finta Giardiniera) 1984, Rome, Accad. di Santa Cecilia 1984, Geneva (Così fan tutte—Dorabella) 1985, Berlin (Così fan tutte) 1985, USA in Chicago (Mozart's C minor Mass) and Philadelphia (Bach's B minor Mass) 1985, London at Royal Opera, Covent Garden (Le Nozze di Figaro) 1985, Lyon (La Finta Giardiniera) 1986, La Scala, Milan (Alceste) 1987, Munich (Le Nozze di Figaro) 1987, Stockholm (Der Rosenkavalier) 1988, The Metropolitan Opera, New York (Le Nozze di Figaro) 1988, The Royal Albert Hall, London (Faust) 1989, Handel's Ariodante 1997; Glyndebourne (Carmen) 2002, Théâtre des Champs Elysées (Handel's Serse) 2003; repertoire extends from baroque music, German lieder through opera to 20th century music; recorded For the Stars with Elvis Costello 2001; has given recitals in New York, Paris, Brussels, Geneva, Stockholm, Vienna and London. *Honours:* Hon. DSc (Bath) 1992. *Current Management:* IMG Artists, Lovell House, 616 Chiswick High Road, London, W4 5RX, England. *Telephone:* (20) 8233-5800. *Fax:* (20) 8233-5801. *E-mail:* info@imgartists.com. *Website:* www.imgartists.com.

VON STADE, Frederica; Singer (mezzo-soprano); b. 1 June 1945, Somerville, New Jersey, USA; m. Peter Elkus 1973 (divorced), 2 d; m. 2nd Michael Gorman, 1990. *Education:* Noroton Academy; Studied with Sebastian Engelberg, Paul Berl and Otto Guth, Mannes College of Music. *Career:* Apprenticeship, Long Wharf Theater, New Haven, Connecticut; Metropolitan Opera debut, New York, 3rd Boy, Die Zauberflöte, 1970; Cherubino, Opera House, Versailles Palace, 1973; Covent Garden debut, London, England as Rosina, 1975; Appearances with many of the world's major opera companies; Various festival engagements; Soloist with orchestras, recitalist; Member, Chamber Music Society of Lincoln Center, New York; Operatic roles include Mozart's Idamante and Dorabella; Bellini's Adalgisa; Massenet's Charlotte; Debussy's Mélisande; Strauss's Octavian; Created roles in several operas including Nina in Pasatieri's The Seagull, 1974; Tina in Argento's The Aspern Papers, 1988; Sang Massenet's Charlotte at Milan (La Scala) and the Vienna Staatsoper, 1988; Cherubino at Los Angeles, 1990, Rosina at Chicago 1989 and at the Metropolitan, 1992; Season 1992–93 as Rosina at the Met and San Francisco, Cherubino at the Met and Mélisande at Covent Garden; Sang Offenbach's Périchole at the 1996 Metropolitan Opera gala; Countess Geschwitz in Lulu at San Francisco, 1998; Mélisande at Buenos Aires, 1999; Season 2000 as Hanna Glawari at the Met and Joe's Mother in the premiere of Dead Man Walking, by Jake Heggie, at San Francisco; Appearances in many operatic films; Crossover artist, Broadway musical recordings. *Honours:* Honorary DMus, Yale University 1985. *Current Management:* IMG Artists, 825 Seventh Avenue, New York, NY 10019, USA. *Telephone:* (212) 489-8300. *Website:* www.fredericavonstade.com.

VONDRÁCEK, Lukás; Concert Pianist; b. 1986, Ostrava, Czech Republic. *Education:* Academy of Music, Latowice; Vienna Musikhochschule and Ostrava University. *Career:* Debut: First public recital aged four; British appearances at Ribble Valley Piano Week, Warwick, Leamington, Buxton and Ryedale Festivals; Season 2001–02 with the Czech PO and Ashkenazy in Prague and Italy and with St Petersburg PO; Season 2002–03 with recitals at Gilmore and Ravinia Festivals and New York International Series; Debuts in London at the Queen Elizabeth Hall and

Carnegie Hall, NY, with the Czech PO; Tour with the NHK SO in Japan; Further appearances in Chicago, Washington, Paris and Brussels; Repertory includes Prokofiev's First Concerto, Liszt's Hungarian Rhapsody no. 12 and Variations Serieuses by Mendelssohn. *Address:* c/o Harrisson Parrot Ltd, 12 Penzance Place, London, W11 4 PA, England. *Telephone:* (20) 7229 9166. *Fax:* (20) 7221 5042.

VOSCHEZANG, Hans; Singer (baritone); b. 1970, Netherlands. *Education:* Utrecht School of Arts; Guildhall School, London. *Career:* Appearances in Netherlands and London as Masetto in Don Giovanni, Purcell's Aeneas, Nick Shadow, Silvio (Pagliacci), Argante in Rinaldo, Ctésippe in Faure's Pénélope, Gianni Schicchi, and Esteban Montejo in Henze's El Cimarrón; Concerts in Wuppertal, with the Brabants Orchestra, the Orchestre Symphonique de la Monnaie under Marc Soustrot and the Academy of Ancient Music with Paul Goodwin. *Honours:* Prizewinner, Hertogenbosch International Singing Competition, Netherlands, 2000. *Current Management:* Askonas Holt Ltd, Lonsdale Chambers, 27 Chancery Lane, London, WC2A 1PF, England. *Telephone:* (20) 7400-1700. *Fax:* (20) 7400-1799. *E-mail:* info@askonasholt.co.uk. *Website:* www.askonasholt.co.uk.

VOSS, Ealynn (Elverta Lynn); Opera Singer (Soprano); b. 10 March 1949, Pittsburgh, Pennsylvania, USA. *Education:* BS, Vocal Performance major, Oberlin Conservatory of Music, 1971. *Career:* Operatic appearances at various US venues, and in Canada, Australia, Spain, Japan, Netherlands and Denmark; Frequent appearances in Turandot title role include Arizona Opera (1988), Opera Carolina, 1990, Miami Opera, 1990, the Australian Opera (1991, 1994) New York City Opera (1991, 1992), Arena di Verona in Japan (1991) Baltimore Opera, 1992, San Francisco, 1993, Michigan Opera, 1994, Houston Grand Opera, 1994 and Copenhagen Opera, Denmark (1996); Sang the Foreign Princess in Rusalka at the Spoleto Festival, USA, 1988, and again at Seattle Opera, 1990; Ariadne (Ariadne auf Naxos) at Victoria State Opera, Australia, 1988, and Los Angeles Music Center Opera, 1992, where she also sang Chrysothemis in Elektra, 1991, 1994, Amelia (Un Ballo in Maschera), 1991, 1994, and Senta (Der fliegende Holländer), 1995; Manitoba Opera, Canada, 1989, as Lady Macbeth, returning as Amelia (1992); Other appearances include Elvira (Ernani) at the Oviedo Festival, Spain, 1991, Tove in Gurre-Lieder at the Concertgebouw Amsterdam, 1995, and Brünnhilde in Götterdämmerung at the Aspen Festival; Concerts include Beethoven's 9th with Santa Barbara Symphony and Verdi's Requiem with Pasadena Symphony; Debut with the Rome Opera singing Turandot in 1996. *Recordings:* Video, Turandot with Australian Opera, 1991. *Current Management:* Columbia Artists Management Inc. *Address:* 508 South First Avenue, Elizabeth, PA 15037-1320, USA.

VOSS, Friedrich; Composer; b. 12 Dec. 1930, Halberstadt, Germany; m. Erna Lewann, 10 Dec 1965, 1 s. *Education:* Abitur, Gymnasium Halberstadt, 1949; Studied composition and piano, Hochschule für Musik, West Berlin, 1949–54. *Career:* Performances with: Berlin Philharmonic Orchestra, under Karajan; Radio Symphony Orchestra, Berlin, under Maazel; Japan Philharmonic Orchestra, under James Loughran; in Germany, Western Europe, USA, Australia, Asia, South Africa, Latin America; Television performances in Madrid, Johannesburg, Adelaide (Australia). *Compositions include:* Over 75 works: 5 symphonies; 2 violin concertos; 1 cello concerto; 1 cello concertino; 5 string quartets; 1 saxophone quartet; concertino for organ, strings and timpani; 2 works for choir; Hamlet overture; Dithyrambus for Orchestra; Metamorphosis for Orchestra; ballet, Die Nachtigall und die Rose; opera, Leonce und Lena; Cantata of Psalms for soloists, choir and orchestra; Missa MM (Versöhnungsmesse) for soloists, chorus and orchestra (Composers' Prize, Catholic and evangelical churches in Baden-Württemberg, 2001. *Recordings:* About 100 broadcasting recordings in Germany and Western Europe; CD: CTH 2069, THOROFON (4 works). *Honours:* 1st place, Composers' Competition, Munich Chamber Orchestra, 1955; Stuttgart Music Prize, 1960; Berlin Art Prize (Young Generation), 1961; Düsseldorf Robert Schumann Prize, 1962; Villa Massimo Award, 1964, 1977; Johann Wenzel Stamitz Prize, Mannheim, 1985. *Address:* Hoppenstedts Weg 5, 29308 Winsen/Aller, Germany.

VOSS, Hermann; Violist; b. 9 July 1934, Brunen, Germany. *Education:* Studied in Düsseldorf with Maier and in Freiburg with Végh. *Career:* Former Member of Karl Munchinger's Stuttgart Chamber Orchestra in Heibronn; Co-Founded the Melos Quartet of Stuttgart, 1965; First concert tours sponsored by the Deutsches Musikleben Foundation and represented West Germany at the Jeunesse Musicales in Paris, 1966; International concert tours from 1967; Bicentenary concerts in the Beethoven House at Bonn, 1970, and soon toured the USSR, Eastern Europe, Africa, North and South America, the Far East and Australia; British concerts and festival appearances from 1974; Cycle of Beethoven quartets at Edinburgh Festival, 1987; Wigmore Hall, St John's Smith Square and Bath Festival, 1990; Associations with Rostropovich in the Schubert Quintet and the Cleveland Quartet in works by Spohr and

Mendelssohn; Teacher at the Stuttgart Musikhochschule. *Recordings:* Complete quartets of Beethoven, Schubert, Mozart and Brahms; Quintets by Boccherini with Narcisco Ypes and by Mozart with Franz Beyer. *Honours:* (with members of the Melos Quartet) Grand Prix de Disque and Prix Caecilia from the Academie du Disque in Brussels.

VOSTRIAKOV, Alexander; Singer (Tenor); b. 1948, Kurgan Region, Russia. *Education:* Studied in Kursk and at the Kharkov Institute of the Arts. *Career:* Member of the Kharkov Opera from 1973, then Dnepropetrovsk Opera Theatre until 1983; Principal of the Kiev National Opera from 1983, notably as Lohengrin and Ismaele in Nabucco; Tour of the United Kingdom in 1996 with the Perm State Opera as Lensky in Eugene Onegin. *Address:* c/o Sonata Ltd, 11 North Park Street, Glasgow G20 7AA, Scotland.

VOYTIK, Viktor Antonovich; Composer; b. 3 Oct. 1947, Grodno, Belarus. *Education:* Conservatories of Belarus and Moscow. *Career:* Lecturer at Conservatory of Belarus from 1980. *Compositions:* Two Symphonies. 1972, 1974; How the Gnat went Wooing, Cantata, 1972; Remembering Khatin, oratorio, 1973; Suite in the Olden Style for orchestra, 1973; Cossack songs, cantata, 1974; Paraphrases, Suite for orchestra, 1975; Day of the Homeland, oratorio, 1977; Sonata for two cimbaloms, 1979; String Quartet, 1979; Clarinet Concerto, 1984; Cimbalom Concerto, 1988; Suite, for male voices, 1990; Patriotic Chant for chorus and orchestra, 1991; The Last Autumn of the Poet for soprano, baritone and ensemble, 1992; Spring Song, opera, 1995; Journey to the Alphabet Castle, 1996. *Address:* c/o RAO, 6a B. Bronnya, Moscow 103670, Russia. *Telephone:* 007095 203 3777/200. *Fax:* 00 7095 200 1263.

VRIEND, Jan; Composer, Conductor and Pianist; b. 10 Nov. 1938, Benningbroek, Netherlands. *Education:* Conservatory of Amsterdam, 1960–67; Paris, GRM/ORTF and Schola Cantorum, 1967–68; Institute of Sonology, Utrecht, 1965–66; Self taught in mathematics. *Career:* Founder and first conductor of ASKO-Amsterdam, 1964; Conductor of choirs orchestras and ensembles, 1961–70; Conductor of Stroud Symphony Orchestra, 1989–94; Lectured on many topics concerning composition, the use of mathematics in composition and philosophy of music. *Compositions include:* Paroesie for 10 Instruments, 1963–67; Huantan for organ and 4 groups of wind instruments, 1968; Ensembles for mixed choir, 1971; Elements of Logic for wind orchestra, 1972; Heterostase for piano, flute and bass clarinet, 1980; Gravity's Dance for piano, 1983; Jets d'Orgue, I, II and III, 1984–90; Hallelujah I for large orchestra, 1986–97; Hallelujah II for 26 instruments, 1987; 3 Songs for Soprano and Orchestra, 1991; Symbiosis for 9 instruments, 1992; Khepera for altoflute and altoclarinet, 1997; Du-Dich-Dir for mixed choir, 1998; Piano Quintet, 1999; Choirbook part 1 for male choir, 1999; In Paradisum for large ensemble, 2000; Grosse Fuge for 6 percussion and organ, 2001. *Publications:* Essays on the music of Xenakis and Varèse and on musical life in Netherlands, published in Netherlands and France. *Honours:* Schnittger Organ Prize for Herfst, 1966; Prize for Composition, Amsterdam Conservatory, 1967; International Gaudeamus Prize, 1970. *Address:* 22 Pooles Lane, Selsley, Stroud GL5 5JT, England.

VRIES, Hans de; Oboist; b. 31 Aug. 1941. *Education:* Studied in Amsterdam. *Career:* Soloist with the Concertgebouw Orchestra, and Netherlands Chamber Orchestra; Founder member, Netherlands Wind Ensemble, 1960; Danzi Wind Quintet from 1973; Concerto soloist and chamber music collaborations throughout Europe, America and the Far East; Premiered Bruno Maderna's Third Concerto, and works by Morton Feldman and Louis Andriessen; Lecturer at Amsterdam Conservatory, from 1964. *Recordings include:* Albums of music by Bach, Mozart and Telemann. *Address:* c/o Sweelinck Conservatorium, Van Baerlesstraat 27, 1071 AN Amsterdam, Netherlands. *Telephone:* 0031 20540 7911. *Fax:* 0031 20540 7496.

VRIES, Klass de; Composer; b. 15 July 1944, Terneuzen, Netherlands. *Education:* Rotterdam Conservatory, with Otto Ketting; Stuttgart Hochschule für Musik. *Career:* Lecturer at Rotterdam Conservatory, 1979–; Guest Composer at Tanglewood, 1995. *Compositions:* Refrains, for two pianos and orchestra, 1970; Difficulties, for ensemble, 1977; Movements, for 15 instruments, 1979; Areas, for mixed chorus, wind ensemble and orchestra, 1980; Discantus, for orchestra, 1982; Eréndira, opera, 1984; Phrases, for soprano, mixed chorus, wind ensemble and orchestra, 1986; Piano sonata, 1987; Diafonia, la creación for two female voices and ensemble, 1988; Songs and Dances I–IV, for violin and piano, 1989; Eclipse, for ensemble, 1991; De Profundis, for wind orchestra, 1991; String Quartet, 1994; A King, Riding, Scenic oratorio after The Waves by Virginia Woolf, 1996. *Honours:* Mathijs Vermeulen Prize, 1983. *Address:* c/o BUMA, PO Box 725, AS Amstelveen, Netherlands. *Telephone:* 0031 20540 7911. *Fax:* 0031 20540 7496.

VRONSKY, Petr; Conductor; b. 4 March 1946, Prague, Czechoslovakia; 1 d. *Education:* Violin, Conservatoire Plzeň, 1967; Conducting, Academy of Music Arts, Prague, 1972. *Career:* debut, Prague, 1971; Opera, Plzeň,

1971; Opera, Usti Nad Labem, Aussig, 1974; State Philharmonic Orchestra, Brno, 1979–91; Senior Lecturer, Prague, 1990; Kammeroper Wien, 1991; Dance Theatre, Haag, 1995; Guest Conductor, Czech Philharmonic Orchestra, Prague, Symphony Orchestra, Prague, National Theatre, Prague, State Opera, Prague, Metropolitan Orchestra, Tokyo, Radio Symphony Orchestra, Munchen, Philharmonic Orchestra, Dortmund; mem, Association of Music Scientists and Musicians, Prague. *Honours:* Conducting Competition Prizes, Olomouc, 1970, Besancon, 1971, Berlin, 1973. *Address:* Majerskeho 2049, PO Box 124, 14900 Prague 4, Czech Republic.

VROOMAN, Richard van; Singer (Tenor); b. 29 July 1936, Kansas City, Missouri, USA. *Education:* Studied at the Kansas City Conservatorium and with Max Lorenz at the Salzburg Mozarteum. *Career:* Debut: Bregenz Festival 1962, as Lorenzo in Fra Diavalo; Many appearances in West Germany, Austria and Switzerland, notably at the Zürich Opera 1964–78; Guest engagements at Salzburg 1964–65, Aix-en-Provence, with the Deutsche Oper am Rhein and the Paris Opéra and in Lisbon, Geneva, Frankfurt, Hamburg, Rome, Bordeaux and Marseille; Glyndebourne Festival 1968, as Belmonte in Die Entführung; Best known in operas by Mozart, Rossini and Donizetti and in the Baroque repertoire; Many concert appearances. *Recordings:* Wozzeck (CBS); Mozart Davidde Penitente and Handel Acis and Galatea (Schwann); Doktor und Apotheker by Dittersdorf; Cimarosa Requiem (Philips); Haydn Salve Regina (EMI). *Address:* c/o Opernhaus Zürich, Falkenstrasse 1, 8008 Zürich, Switzerland.

VUORI, Harri; Composer; b. 10 Jan. 1957, Lahti, Finland. *Education:* Sibelius Academy, 1978–89, with Eino Rautavaara. *Career:* Department of Musicology, Helsinki University, 1993–; Composer-in-residence, Hyvinkää Orchestra, 1997. *Compositions:* Piano Sonata, 1976; In Natural State, for ensemble, 1978; String Quartet, 1979; The Seasons, in Natura Naturally, for four female voices and ensemble, 1982; Like a Bird's footprints in the Sky, chamber opera, 1983; Mystical metamorphoses nocturnae, for two sopranos and ensemble, 1985; Kri, for orchestra, 1988; Songs of Dreaming and Death, for soprano and cello, 1990; Interrupted Movements, for chamber orchestra, 1991; Above and Below, for wind and percussion, 1995; Violin Sonata, 1996; The Mandelbrot Echoes, for orchestra, 1996; Sky Line, electro-acoustic, 1997; Invitation to a Nocturnal Dance, for two viols and harpsichord, 1997; Awakenings, for chorus, 1997. *Address:* c/o TEOSTO, Lauttasaarentie 1, SF–00200 Helsinki, Finland. *Telephone:* 00358 0681 011. *Fax:* 00358 9677 134.

W

WAAGE, Lars; Danish singer (bass-baritone); b. 1948, Århus. *Education:* Århus Conservatory. *Career:* sang with the Lubeck Opera, 1975–80, as King Henry in Lohengrin and Wagner's Gurnemanz; Jyske Opera at Århus from 1980, notably as Wotan and Gunther in The Ring; guest appearances as Sharpless, Iago, Pizarro, Mephistopheles and Kurwenal; Concert singer in France, Germany and Italy. *Address:* Århus Opera, Thomas Jensens Allee, 8000 Århus, Denmark.

WÄCHTER, Erich; Conductor; b. 3 July 1945, Bielefeld, Germany. *Education:* Hochschule für Musik, Berlin. *Career:* Repetiteur at Kaiserslautern, 1969–71, Kapellmeister der Opera, 1971–74; Kapellmeister at the Saarbrucken State Opera, 1974–77; Musical Director of the Saarbrucken City Choir; Musical Assistant, Bayreuth, 1975 (and conducted Der fliegende Holländer and Die Zauberflöte at Tbilisi); Conductor at the Baden State Opera in Karlsruhe, 1977–85; Guest Conductor, Wiesbaden (with Der Rosenkavalier, Carmen and La Forza del Destino); Lecturer in Music at State Music Academy, Karlsruhe, 1980; Kapellmeister at Darmstadt, 1985–87 and National Theatre at Mannheim, 1987–90; General Music Director, Lübeck Opera, 1987–; Also engaged by the Stuttgart Opera, Vienna Volksoper, Oslo, Munich State Opera, Hamburg, Leipzig, Dresden, Stockholm and Antwerp, and Zürich Opera; Leiter des Hochschulorchesters und Leiter der Dirigierabteilung Musikhochschule Lübeck, 1993.

WADDINGTON, Henry; Singer (Bass); b. 1968, Kent, England. *Education:* Royal Northern College of Music, with Barbara Robotham. *Career:* Debut: As Bottom in A Midsummer Night's Dream, at the RNCM; Glyndebourne Touring Opera from 1992, in The Rake's Progress, and in the premiere of Birtwistle's The Second Mrs Kong (1994); Appearances in Le Comte Ory and Tchaikovsky's The Enchantress for New Sussex Opera, as Colline for GTO, Farlaf in Ruslan and Lyudmila for Dorset Opera, as Falstaff for Opera North and Fiorello in Il Barbiere di Siviglia for Royal Opera House; Count Lamoral in Arabella and Mozart's Antonio at the Glyndebourne Festival, 1996–97; Season 1998 with Major Domo in Capriccio at Glyndebourne, Verdi's Ribbing for WNO, Don Magnifico in Cenerentola for English Touring Opera, Count Horn in Ballo in Maschera for WNO and Oroe in Semiramide for Chelsea Opera Group; 1999, Banquo in Macbeth for ETO; Concerts include: Mozart's Requiem with the English CO at the Barbican Hall, Sir John in Love for British Youth Opera, the Verdi Requiem, and The Rake's Progress with the BBC Symphony Orchestra at the Festival Hall (1997). *Current Management:* Ingpen & Williams Ltd, 7 St George's Court, 131 Putney Bridge Road, London, SW15 2PA, England.

WADE, Simon; Composer; b. 28 Aug. 1958, Devonport, Tasmania, Australia. *Education:* BA (Mus), Tasmanian Conservatory, 1979; Master of Creative Arts, Film and Communications Diplomas, 1995. *Career:* Tasmanian Conservatory, 1980; University of Sydney, 1988; Rare Birds Productions Co, 1993; Commissions from Tasmanian Opera Co, New England String Quartet, and others. *Compositions include:* Saxophone Quartet, 1984; Extracts for saxophone and piano, 1984; Songs from Shakespeare, for chorus and orchestra, 1984; Introduction to the String Quartet, 1985; The Other Meaning, song cycle for tenor and piano, 1985; Sequences for clarinet and piano, 1985; The Watching Clock, chamber opera, 1992; The Herald Angel, for alto trombone and piano, 1993; Computer-generated music for film and theatre, 1993–. *Address:* c/o APRA, 1A Eden Street, Crows Nest, NSW 2065, Australia.

WADSWORTH, Matthew; British lutenist. *Education:* Chetham School of Music, RAM, Royal Conservatory, The Hague. *Career:* founder mem., Ricordo Ensemble 1997–; Wigmore Hall solo debut 2003; US concert tour 2005; continuo player and chamber musician with leading early music ensembles; lute song recitals with Faye Newton; workshops with Live Music Now! for visually impaired children; guest tutor, Royal Northern Coll. of Music. *Recordings:* Away Delights (lute solos and songs from Shakespeare's England), 14 Silver Strings (music by Kapsberger and Piccinini). *Honours:* London Student of the Year Award for development of Braille lute tablature 1997. *Current Management:* Chameleon Arts Management, 32 St Michael's Road, Sandhurst, GU47 8HE, England. *Telephone:* (20) 8521-4959. *E-mail:* concerts@matthewwadsworth.com. *Website:* www.matthewwadsworth.com.

WADSWORTH, Stephen; Stage Director, Translator and Librettist; b. 3 April 1953, Mount Kisco, New York, USA. *Career:* Artistic Director and Stage Director of the Skylight Opera in Milwaukee; Productions of Monteverdi's three principal operas, from 1982; Wrote libretto for Bernstein's A Quiet Place 1983 and has directed productions of it at La Scala, Milan and in Vienna; For Seattle Opera has directed Jenůfa, Fliegende Holländer, and Gluck's Orphée; Handel's Xerxes at Milwaukee 1985 and Partenope at Omaha, 1988; Fidelio and La Clemenza di Tito for Scottish Opera, 1991, Die Entführung at San Francisco 1990,

other productions include Le nozze di Figaro and Alcina (St Louis) and Simon Boccanegra (Netherlands Opera); Head of the Opera Program at the Manhattan School of Music, 1991; Translations of Monteverdi's Orfeo and Handel's Xerxes, Alcina and Partenope; Covent Garden debut 1992, Handel's Alcina; Staging of Xerxes seen at Santa Fe, Los Angeles and Boston (1996). *Honours:* Chevalier, Ordre des Arts et des Lettres. *Address:* c/o Boston Lyric Opera, 114 State Street, Boston, MA 02109, USA.

WAGEMANS, Peter-Jan; Composer; b. 7 Sept. 1952, The Hague, Netherlands. *Education:* Studied at the Hague Conservatory, and with Klaus Huber in Freiburg. *Career:* Lecturer at Hague Conservatory, 1978–84; Rotterdam Conservatory, 1982–; Promoter of modern music concerts at Rotterdam, from 1990. *Compositions include:* Symphony, 1972; Wind Quintet, 1973; Musiek, I–IV, 1974, 1977, 1985, 1988; Cantata, 1979; Octet, 1980; Trio, for clarinet, violin and piano, 1985; Klang, for orchestra 1986; Wie, for alto, two clarinets and two horns, 1987; Walk on Water, for trumpet and ensemble, 1988; Rosebud, for orchestra and female chorus, 1988; Requiem for strings and percussion, 1992; Panthalassa, for wind, 1994; Wind Quintet no. 2, 1994; Concerto for two pianos, 1994, rev, 1997; Nachtvlucht for soprano and orchestra, 1997; String Quartet, 1998. *Honours:* Matthijs Vermeulen Prize, 1990. *Address:* c/o BUMA, PO Box 725, 1180 AS Amstelveen, Netherlands. *Telephone:* 0031 20540 7911. *Fax:* 0031 20540 7496.

WAGENAAR, Diderik; Composer; b. 10 May 1946, Utrecht, Netherlands. *Education:* Royal Conservatory, The Hague. *Career:* Lecturer at Royal Conservatory. 1969–. *Compositions include:* Canzonas, for 15 brass instruments, double bass and two pianos, 1976, Tam Tam, for ensemble 1978; Canapé, for clarinet, violin, cello and piano 1980, Metrum, for four saxophones and orchestra, 1984; Limiet, for string quartet, 1985; Triforium, for wind ensemble and percussion, 1988; Tessituur, for orchestra, 1990; Solenne, for six percussion, 1992; Cat Music, for two violins, 1994; Trios Poèmes en prose, for soprano and orchestra, 1995; Rookery Hill, for ensemble, 1998; Galilei, for chamber orchestra, 1999; Arrangement of Berg's Altenberglieder for medium voice and ensemble, 1985. *Honours:* Matthijs Vermeulen Prize, 1996. *Address:* c/o BUMA, PO Box 725, 1180 As Amstelvven, Netherlands.

WAGENFUHRER, Roland; Singer (Tenor); b. 1964, Hof/Saale, Germany. *Education:* Studied at the Nuremberg Conservatory, from 1982. *Career:* Member of the Bavarian State Opera Studio 1987–89, as Ferrando and as Chlestakov in Der Revisor; Landestheater Coburg 1989–95, as Jenik in The Bartered Bride, Lensky, Don José and Wagner's Erik; Dresden Semper Oper from 1995, as Max, Laca (Jenůfa), Desportes in Zimmermann's Soldaten and Dionysos in The Bassarids by Henze; Guest appearances as Florestan at the Bregenz Festival (1995–96), Tamino in Cologne, Walther von Stolzing in Lubeck and Erik at the Vienna Staatsoper; Season 1997–98 as Florestan at the Komische Oper Berlin and Hoffmann at Cologne; Engagements for 1998 in The Bartered Bride in Munich, Fliegender Holländer at the Bayreuth Festival and New York Met, and Freischütz/Max in Vienna; Lohengrin at Bayreuth, 1999; Further engagements include Elijah in Zürich, Beethoven's 9th in Brussels and Duisburg, Bruch's Moses-Oratorium in Berlin and Munich, and Berlioz's Faust Studies in Paris; Season 2000–01 as Florestan at Munich and Dresden, Lohengrin for the Bayreuth Festival and Wagner's Erik at the Met. *Address:* c/o Theateragentur Dr G. Hilbert, Maximillianstr 22, D–80539 Munich, Germany.

WAGNER, James; Singer (Tenor); b. 1949, New Orleans, Louisiana, USA. *Education:* Studied at Rochester University and in Vienna. *Career:* Sang at the Frankfurt Opera, 1975–76, Kassel, 1976–80, New York City Opera, 1981–82, Vienna Volksoper, 1983–84; Theater am Gärtnerplatz, Munich, 1985–88, and elsewhere, as Almaviva, Xerxes, Belmonte, Giasone in Cherubini's Médée, Florestan, Edgardo, and Dionysos in Henze's Bassarids; Guest appearances in Berne, Bologne (1987), Venice (1990) and Greece; Season 2000–01 in the Verdi Requiem in Vienna and as Rossini's Otello (concert) at Halle. *Recordings include:* Amadis de Gaule by J C Bach (Hanssler). *Address:* Theater am Gärtnerplatz, Gärtnerplatz 3, W-8000 Munich 5, Germany.

WAGNER, Wolfgang; Opera Director; b. 30 Aug. 1919, Bayreuth, Germany; (1) Ellen Drexel, 11 April 1943, 1 s., 1 d., (2) Gudrun Armann, 1 d. *Career:* Stage Manager, Bayreuth Festival, 1940; Assistant, Preussische Staatsoper, Berlin, 1940–44; Director, annual Wagner operatic festival, 1951–; Numerous guest appearances and international tours; Productions include, Andreasnacht, Berlin, 1944; Das Rheingold, Naples, 1952; Die Walküre, Naples, 1952 and 1953, Barcelona 1955, Venice 1957, Palermo 1962, Osaka 1967; Lohengrin, Bayreuth, 1953 and 1967, Taormina, 1991, Tokyo, 1997; Siegfried,

Naples 1953, Brussels 1954, Venice 1957, Bologna 1957; Der fliegende Holländer, Bayreuth, 1955, Dresden 1988; Tristan und Isolde, Barcelona 1955, Bayreuth 1957, Venice 1958, Palermo 1960, Osaka 1967, Milan 1978; Parsifal, Barcelona 1955, Bayreuth 1975, 1989; Don Giovanni, Brunswick, 1955; Die Meistersinger von Nurnberg, Rome 1956, Bayreuth 1968, 1981, 1996 and Dresden 1985, Der Ring des Nibelungen, Venice 1957, Bayreuth 1960 and 1970; Götterdämmerung, Venice, 1957; Tannhäuser, Bayreuth, 1985. *Address:* PO Box 100262 Bayreuther Festspiele, 95402 Bayreuth, Germany.

WAHLGREN, Per-Arne; Singer (Baritone); b. 1953, Sweden. *Education:* Studied at the opera school of the Royal Opera Stockholm. *Career:* Debut: Norrland Opera 1978, as Don Giovanni; Sang at the Stora Teater Gothenburg from 1979 as Germont and Belcore; Guest appearances at the Theater an der Wien, Vienna 1980, in the premiere of Jesu Hochzeit by Gottfried von Einem; Royal Opera Stockholm from 1981, as Mozart's Count and Guglielmo, Marcello, Sharpless and Wolfram; Humbert Humbert in the premiere of Rodion Shchedrin's Lolita under the direction of M Rostropovich, 1994; Further engagements at Nice in Tannhäuser and The Queen of Spades, and in Madrid in Mendelssohn's Elijah; Stockholm 1986 in the premiere of Christina by Hans Gefors; Drottningholm Court Theatre 1991, as Orestes in a revival of Electra by J C F Haeffner; Sang Frank in Korngold's Die tote Stadt, Stockholm, 1995. Concert repertory includes Bach's Passions, Christmas Oratorio and Cantatas, the Brahms Requiem, Messiah, Utrecht Te Deum by Handel, the Fauré Requiem, Lieder eines fahrenden Gesellen and Carmina Burana. *Recordings include:* Dido and Aeneas. *Address:* Kungliga Teatern PO Box 16094, 10322 Stockholm, Sweden.

WAHLUND, Sten; Singer (Bass); b. 1943, Stockholm, Sweden. *Education:* Stockholm Music High School, 1964–70, with Erik Saéden. *Career:* Debut: Royal Opera Stockholm, 1969, as Sarastro; Appearances in Stockholm and at the Drottningholm Baroque Theatre, as the Commendatore, Rossini's Basilio, the Grand Inquisitor in Don Carlos, and Don Pasquale; Premieres of Christina by Hans Gefors, 1986, and Doktor Glas by Arne Mellnäs, 1994; Season 1995–96 at Stockholm as Gurnemanz in Parsifal and Pimen in Boris Godunov; Other roles include Mephistopheles in Faust, Fafner, and King Henry in Lohengrin; Sang King Marke in Tristan at Karlstad, 2000; Frequent concert engagements in Scandinavia and elsewhere. *Address:* Royal Opera, Stockholm, PO Box 16094, 10322 Stockholm, Sweden.

WAKASUGI, Hiroshi; Conductor; b. 31 May 1935, Tokyo, Japan. *Education:* Studied conducting with Hideo Sati and Nobori Kaneko. *Career:* Conducted the Kyoto Symphony Orchestra from 1975; Regular concerts with the Berlin Philharmonic, Vienna Symphony, Munich Philharmonic, Toronto Symphony, Montreal Symphony, Pittsburgh Symphony, NHK Symphony, Bavarian Radio Symphony and the Frankfurt Museum Society; Chief Conductor of the Cologne Radio Symphony 1977–83; US debut 1981, with the Boston Symphony Orchestra; Music Director of the Deutsche Oper am Rhein Düsseldorf, 1981–86; Principal Guest Conductor of the Dresden State Opera and the Dresden Staatskapelle, 1982–1991; Chief Conductor, Tokyo Metropolitan Orchestra; Chief Conductor and Artistic Director of the Tonhalle Orchestra Zürich, from 1987, 1987–91; 1986–1995 Music Director and 1987–1995 Principal Conductor of Tokyo Metropolitan Symphony Orchestra; From spring 1995 Permanent Conductor of NHK Symphony Orchestra; Music Director, 1988–95 and Principal Conductor, 1987–95, of the Tokyo Metropolitan Symphony Orchestra; Has conducted first Japanese performances of Schoenberg's Gurrelieder and Pelléas und Mélisande, Wagner's Parsifal, Der fliegende Holländer, Rheingold and Siegfried, Strauss's Capriccio and Ariadne auf Naxos, and many contemporary works; Lohengrin at Tokyo, 1998. *Honours:* Suntory Prize, 1987. *Address:* c/o Astrid Schoerke, Kunstler Sekretariat, Mönchebergallee 41, 3000 Hannover, Germany.

WAKEFIELD, John; Professor of Singing and Singer (Tenor); b. 21 June 1936, Yorkshire, England; m. Rilla Welborn, 2 s., 1 d. *Education:* Royal Academy of Music, FRAM; Honorary FTCL. *Career:* Debut: Welsh National Opera, 1960; Macduff, Glyndebourne, 1964; Rinuccio at Royal Opera House, 1965; Other roles included: Fenton, Tamino, Paris, Don Ottavio, Ferrando, Belmonte, Idamante, Rodolfo, Orfeo, Cavalli's Ormindo, Essex in Britten's Gloriana and Saul; mem, Equity; NATFHE. *Recordings:* La Traviata, Ormindo; The Mikado; Messiah. *Honours:* Kathleen Ferrier Scholarship, 1958; Tenor Prize, 's-hertogenbosch, 1959. *Address:* 12 Avenue Gardens, Teddington, Middlesex TW11 0BH, England.

WALACINSKI, Adam; Composer; b. 18 Sept. 1928, Kraków, Poland. *Education:* Studied at the Kraków Conservatory, 1947–52; Private studies in composition with Stefan Kisielewski. *Career:* Violinist in the Kraków Radio Orchestra, 1948–56; Teacher at the Kraków Conservatory, 1972–92, Professor, 1993–96, Prorector; Music Critic, Dziennik Polski, 1962–; Collaborates with PWM Music Cyclopedia as Area Editor

of 20th Century composers; Member of the Grupa Krakowska, for promotion of the New Music; Chairman, Kraków section, Polish Composers Union, 1971–87. *Compositions include:* Alfa for orchestra, 1958; String Quartet, 1959; Intrada for 7 players, 1962; Canto Tricolore for flute, violin and vibraphone, 1962; Horizons for chamber orchestra, 1962; A Lyric Before Falling Asleep for soprano, flute and 2 pianos, 1963; Concerto de Camera for violin and strings, 1964; Fogli volanti for string trio, 1985; Canzona for cello, piano and tape, 1966; Epigrams for chamber ensemble, 1967; Refrains and Reflections for orchestra, 1969; Notturno 70 for 24 strings, 3 flutes and percussion; Torso for orchestra, 1971; Divertimento interrotto for 13 players, 1974; Mirophonies for soprano and ensemble, 1974; Ballada for flute and piano, 1986; Little Autumn Music for flute and string trio, 1986; Drama e Burla for orchestra, 1988; Pastorale, for flute, oboe, violin, 1992; La vida es sueno, reminiscences from Calderon, for flute, guitar and viola, 1998; Aria for orchestra, 1998; Spirale of Time for 15 players, 2000; Music for theatre, cinema and television. *Honours:* State Award, 1966; Prize of the City of Kraków, 1976. *Address:* ul Arciszewskiego 4, 30-138 Kraków, Poland.

WALDHANS, Jiri; Conductor; b. 17 April 1923, Brno, Czechoslovakia. *Education:* Studied at the Brno Conservatory until 1948 and with Igor Markevitch in Salzburg. *Career:* Repetiteur and Chorus Master at the Ostrava Opera, 1949–51; Conducted the Brno State Philharmonic, 1951–54, Ostrava Symphony Orchestra 1955–62; Returned to the Brno State 1962–80; Janáček Academy at Brno from 1980; Guest Conductor in Czechoslovakia and elsewhere in Europe. *Recordings include:* Dvořák Cello Concerto with the Czech Philharmonic (Supraphon); 15 Pages after Dürer's Apocalypse by Luboš Fišer; Janáček's Lachian Dances, Jealousy (Jenůfa) Overture, The Fiddler's Child and The Ballad of Blanik Hill; Suites from Martinů's Ballets Istar and Spalicek; Cello Concertos by Milhaud, Beethoven's Piano Arrangement of his Violin Concerto and early Concerto in E flat 1784, with Felicia Blumenthal. *Address:* Slezske divadlo, Marketing Manager, Ales Waldhans, Horni Namesti 13, 749 69 Opava, Czech Republic.

WALENDOWSKI, Dario; Singer (Tenor); b. 1 Aug. 1955, Łódź, Poland. *Career:* Debut: Łódź, 1980, as Alfredo in La Traviata; National Opera Warsaw from 1982, as Donizetti's Edgardo, Nadir in Les Pêcheurs de Perles, Tamino, Captain, Tebaldo (Capuleti ed i Montecchi) and Shuisky in Boris Godunov; Engagements in Austria from 1985 and Germany, 1989; Oberhausen and Giessen Operas as Count Almaviva, the Duke of Mantua, Rodolfo, Jontek (Halka), Edgardo, Des Grieux, Macduff, Romeo, Jenik (Bartered Bride), Don José, Hoffmann and Pinkerton; Staatstheater Schwerin from 1993, as Cavaradossi, Pedro (Tiefland), Sly, Radames, Faust, Nemorino, and Manrico; Guest appearances at the Bolshoi (Moscow), Mannheim, Berlin, Madrid, Hamburg, Barcelona and Paris; Form 1996 guest appearances at Lübeck and Rostock as Alva (Lulu), Don Alvaro (La Forza del Destino); Modern repertory includes Jedidia in Penderecki's The Black Mask; Der schöne Herr Herrmann (Hindemith's Neues vom Tage), Sandy (The Lighthouse), Pierrot/Soldât. *Address:* c/o Mecklenburgisches Staatstheater, Alte Garten, 2751 Schwerin, Germany.

WALKER, David; Stage Designer; b. 18 July 1934, Calcutta, India. *Education:* Studied at the Central School of Arts and Crafts, London, 1952–56. *Career:* Designs for Joan Littlewood's Theatre from 1955; Opera designs for Werther and La Bohème at Glyndebourne, 1966–67; Royal Opera House designs (some in collaboration with producer John Copley), 1965–82, Suor Angelica, Così fan tutte, Don Giovanni and Semele; Costumes for Carmen at the Metropolitan, 1972; Manon Lescaut at Palermo and Lucia di Lammermoor at La Fenice, Venice; Production designs for La Traviata and Der Rosenkavalier at English National Opera, 1973, 1975; Sets and costumes for Donizetti's Roberto Devereux at the Teatro dell'Opera Rome, 1988 and at Naples, 1998; Collaborated with John Conkin on designs for Der Rosenkavalier at Santa Fe, 1989; ENO designs for La Traviata seen at Philadelphia, 1992. *Address:* c/o English National Opera, St Martin's Lane, London WC2N 4ES, England.

WALKER, Diana; Singer (Soprano); b. 1958, Salt Lake City, Utah, USA. *Career:* Has sung at the New York City Opera, 1983–, as Leila (Les Pêcheurs de Perles), Gilda, Adele, Micaela, Barbara (Argento's Casanova) and Ninetta (The Love of Three Oranges); Seattle Opera in the title roles of The Ballad of Baby Doe and Lucia di Lammermoor; Utah Opera as the Queen of Night; European debut as Blondchen in Die Entführung with Nice Opera; Modern repertory includes Laetitia in The Old Maid and the Thief with St Louis Opera, Abigail in The Crucible by Robert Ward and Ariel in Lee Hoiby's The Tempest (Kansas City); Performances of the ballet Alice, after Del Tredici's In Memory of a Summer Day, in Toronto, Chicago, Washington DC, Florida, California, New York (Metropolitan Opera) and London; Sang Lakmé for Chicago Opera Theatre, 1990; Premieres of Victoria Bond's Travels in Virginia, 1995; Concert repertory includes, Messiah, Handel's Joshua and Rinaldo (at Kennedy Center) and Mahler's 4th Symphony; Further roles include Donizetti's Norina, Adina and Marie; Gluck's Iphigénie;

Mozart's Mme Silberklang, Blondchen and Susanna; Strauss's Sophie and Zerbinetta; Verdi's Nannetta and Ophelia in Hamlet by Thomas; Guest artist with Miami Chamber Symphony, Brooklyn Symphony, New York, Utah Symphony, Kansas City Philharmonic, Roanoke, Virginia Symphony, Aspen Symphony. *Current Management:* c/o Anthony George Management, 250 W 77th Street, No. 304, New York City, NY 10024, USA.

WALKER, George Theophilus, Jr, BMus, DMA; American composer, pianist and educator; *Professor Emeritus of Music, Rutgers University*; b. 27 June 1922, Washington, DC; two s. *Education:* Oberlin Coll., Curtis Inst. of Music, Univ. of Rochester. *Career:* first professional concert, Shiloh Baptist Church, Washington, DC 1939; organist Oberlin Theological Seminary 1939–41; debut as pianist at Town Hall, New York 1945; numerous recitals world-wide; teacher, Dillard Univ., New Orleans 1953–54, Dalcroze School of Music, New York 1960–61, New School for Social Research, New York 1960–61, Smith Coll., Northampton, MA 1961–68, Peabody Inst. Conservatory at Johns Hopkins Univ., Baltimore 1975–78; Visiting Prof. of piano and piano literature, Univ. of Colorado at Boulder 1968–69; Distinguished Prof. of Music, Univ. of Delaware, Newark 1975–76; teacher of piano, theory, music history and composition, Rutgers Univ., Newark, NJ 1969–92, Chair of Music Dept 1975–77, Prof. Emeritus 1992–; John Hay Whitney Fellowship 1958; Bok Foundation grant for European concerts 1963; Bennington Composers Conference Fellowships 1967, 1968; Guggenheim Fellowships 1969, 1988; MacDowell Colony Fellowships 1966–69; Yaddo Fellowship 1969; Rutgers Univ. Research Council grant 1969; Rockefeller Fellowships 1971, 1974; NEA grants 1971, 1975, 1978, 1984. *Compositions include:* Lyric for Strings 1947, 18 songs for voice and piano 1941–94, arrangements of spirituals for voice and piano 1947–62, five piano sonatas, two string quartets, two sonatas for violin and piano, concertos for cello, trombone, violin and piano, Concerto for piano and orchestra, Concerto for trombone and orchestra, Cantata for soprano, tenor boys' choir and chamber orchestra, Mass for chorus and orchestra, Address for orchestra, three Sinfonias for orchestra, Serenata for chamber orchestra, Sonata for cello and piano, Music for Brass, Poem for soprano and chamber ensemble, Variations for orchestra, Antifonys for chamber orchestra, Orpheus for chamber orchestra 1994, Lilacs for soprano or tenor and orchestra (Pulitzer Prize 1996) 1995, Pageant and Proclamation for orchestra 1997, Tangents for chamber orchestra 1999, Wind Set for woodwind quintet 1999, Modus for two guitars, winds and strings 1999. *Recordings include:* George Walker in Recital 1994, George Walker A Portrait 1994, George Walker (Chamber Works) 1995, George Walker plays Bach, Schumann, Chopin and Poulenc 1997, The Music of George Walker 1997, George Walker: Works for Chamber Orchestra. *Publications:* Make Room for Black Classical Music, New York Times, 1992; The Lot of the Black Composer, 1992; Recordings of Solo Piano Works: George Walker in Recital, George Walker Plays Bach, Schumann, Chopin and Poulenc, George Walker In Concert. *Honours:* Univ. of Rochester Distinguished Scholar medal 1996, Dr hc (Lafayette Coll., Easton) 1982, (Oberlin Coll.) 1983, (Curtis Inst.) 1997, (Montclair State Univ.) 1997, (Bloomfield Coll.) 1997; Religious Arts Festival Award 1961, Carnegie Mellon Inst. Harvey Gaul Prize 1963, Koussevitzky Award 1988. *Address:* 323 Grove Street, Montclair, NJ 07042, USA.

WALKER, Helen; Singer (Soprano); b. 1952, Tunbridge Wells, England. *Education:* Guildhall School, London, with Noelle Barker. *Career:* Sang Verdi's Giovanna d'Arco, 1977; Glyndebourne Festival as Fiordiligi, Monteverdi's Poppea 1984, and Helena in A Midsummer Night's Dream; Glyndebourne Touring Opera as Pamina, Ann Trulove in The Rake's Progress, and Ninetta in The Love of Three Oranges; Opera North as Pamina, and Fenena in Nabucco; Helena at Aldeburgh and Covent Garden; Handel roles include Polissena in Radamisto (Handel Opera Society) and Teseo, for the English Bach Festival at Sadler's Wells Theatre; Foreign engagements in Hong Kong and Nancy (with Glyndebourne Touring Opera), Montpellier and La Fenice, Venice (as Anne Trulove); Sang a Maid in Elektra at Covent Garden, 1990; Freia, Sieglinde and Gutrune in the City of Birmingham Touring Opera version of the Ring; Premiered Leaving by Turnage, Symphony Hall and Radio 3, 1992. *Recordings:* Dido and Aeneas (1st Witch), Philips. *Honours:* Winner, Susan Longfield Competition, 1977; Ricordi Prize for Opera; Mozart Memorial Prize, 1978; South East Arts Young Musicians Platform; Glyndebourne Touring Award; Christie Award, Glyndebourne.

WALKER, John (Edward); Singer (Tenor); b. 19 Aug. 1933, Bushnell, Indiana. *Education:* Studied at the Universities of Denver, Urbana and Bloomington. *Career:* Debut: Berne 1963, as Tamino; Appearances in Europe at Zürich, Cologne, Frankfurt, Stuttgart and Brussels; US engagements at San Francisco, Dallas, Santa Fe, Chicago, Seattle, San Diego, Omaha and Portland; Other roles have included Mozart's Belmonte, Don Ottavio and Ferrando, Nadir, Almaviva, Alfredo, Fenton, Ernesto, Nemorino, Werther, Lensky and Britten's Lysander;

Has also sung Jenik in The Bartered Bride, Nureddin in the Barber of Baghdad, Albert Herring, and David in Die Meistersinger; Many concert and oratorio engagements. *Address:* c/o Staatsoper Stuttgart, Oberer Schlossgarten 6, 7000 Stuttgart 1, Germany.

WALKER, Malcolm; Singer (Baritone); b. 1958, USA. *Career:* Sang Pelléas at the Opéra du Rhin, Strasbourg, and Monteverdi's Orfeo at Milan; Glyndebourne, 1985, as Morales in Carmen and 1987–88 in L'Enfant et les Sortilèges; Don Giovanni on tour to Hong Kong; Lille Opéra in The Rake's progress and Geneva Opera in Manon; Pelléas at the Vienna Staatsoper, La Scala, Florence, Seattle (1993) and Venice (1995); Other roles include Varbel in Cherubini's Lodoiska, at Montpellier, Fürst in Guillaume Tell at Théâtre des Champs Elysées, and Massenet's Lescaut at Opéra-Comique (1999). *Recordings include:* Gluck's Les Pèlerins de la Mecque; Chabrier's Le Roi malgré Lui. *Address:* c/o Seattle Opera Association, PO Box 9248, Seattle, WA 98109, USA.

WALKER, Nina; Pianist, Opera Coach and Chorus Master; b. 30 May 1926, Hyde, Cheshire, England; m. Francis Barnes, 2 s., 1 d. *Education:* Pianoforte, Composition, Royal Manchester College of Music, 1945–50; Studied with Alfred Cortot 1953, Lausanne, Bridget Wild, 1965. *Career:* Accompanist and Solo Pianist, Arts Council Recitals, Germany, Italy, Sweden, Greece; Solo Pianist, Marquis de Cuevas Ballet, Paris, 1957; Accompanist, Caballé, La Scala, Milan, Spain, Japan, Germany, Royal Opera House, 1975–90; Masterclasses, Pavarotti, etc.; Chorus Master, Royal Choral Society 1970–75, Huddersfield Choral Society 1980–83; Music Staff, Royal Opera House, 1974–83; Chorus Master 1981–83; Founder, Director, Nimbus Records, 1973. *Recordings:* Nimbus Records, Schubert Song Cycles, Shura Gehrman; Argentinian Songs, Raul Gimenez; Rossini, Soirées Musicales, June Anderson; Complete Schubert Piano Duets, Adrian Farmer; Fauré and Duparc Songs, Shura Gehrman; Mussorgsky (Songs and Dances of Death) Songs I Love, Jenny Drivala, Soprano (Somm Records). *Honours:* Open Scholarship, RMCM, 1946; LRAM, 1948; ARMCM, 1948; Hilary Haworth Memorial Prize, 1949; Edward Hecht Prize, 1949; FRMCM, 1970. *Address:* 12 Ainsdale Road, Ealing, London W5 1JX, England.

WALKER, Penelope; singer (mezzo-soprano); b. 12 Oct. 1956, Manchester, England; m. Phillip Joll, two c. *Education:* GSMD, 1974–78 (AGSM and advanced studies); National Opera Studio, 1979–80. *Career:* debut, Royal Albert Hall, 1976; Prom Debut, Grimgerde in Die Walküre with Gwyneth Jones and the National Youth Orchestra, 1989; Canada with Regina Symphony Orchestra, 1993, singing Wesendonck Lieder, and Chausson's Poème de l'amour et de la mer; Royal Opera House, Covent Garden, Die Walküre, 1994; BBC television and radio, including Elgar documentary with Simon Rattle and CBSO, Operatic debut in Paris, 1982 with Opéra-Comique; London debut at Camden Festival, Maria Tudor (Pacini) Opera Rara; ENO, Siegrune (Die Walküre), Kate Pinkerton (Madama Butterfly) and Madame Sosostris (Midsummer Marriage); Opera North, Madame Sosostris; Welsh National Opera, Fricka (Das Rheingold and Die Walküre), Anna in The Trojans, Madame Larina in Eugene Onegin, Tornrak-Main Protagonist in Metcalf Opera; Geneviève, Pelléas; Zürich Opera, 1991, 3rd Lady; Hedwig (William Tell); Mozart Requiem; Grimgerde (Die Walküre), Chatelêt Ring, 1994; Debut at La Scala, 1994; Rossweisse, Covent Garden, 1994; Sang Handel's Riccardo Primo at the 1996 Göttingen Festival. *Recordings:* London Opera, Hippolyta (Midsummer Night's Dream), Virgin, Hickox; Schwertleite (Die Walküre) C. Dohnányi, Cleveland Symphony, Decca; Flosshilde and Fricka, Das Rheingold, Operavox Animated Opera, television; Geneviève, (Pelléas et Mélisande) WNO Video, Peter Stein production, Pierre Boulez; New Israeli Opera, Mamma Lucia (Cavalleria Rusticana). *Current Management:* Robert Gilder & Co., Enterprise House, 59–65 Upper Ground, London, SE1 9PQ, England. *Telephone:* (20) 7928-9008. *Fax:* (20) 7928-9755. *E-mail:* rgilder@robert-gilder.com.

WALKER, Robert (Ernest); Composer; b. 18 March 1946, Northampton, England. *Education:* Chorister at St Matthew's Church, Northampton; Choral Scholar, Organ Scholar, at Jesus College, Cambridge. *Career:* Organist and Schoolmaster in Lincolnshire; Freelance Composer from 1975; Featured Composer at 1982 Greenwich Festival; Living composer, Eastern Orchestral Board 1990–91; Works performed by Royal Philharmonic Orchestra at Chichester and Exeter Festivals; Regular broadcasts on BBC Radio 3. *Compositions:* Orchestral, Pavan for violin and strings 1975, At Bignor Hill 1979, Chamber Symphony No. 1 1981, Variations on a Theme of Elgar 1982, Charms and Exultations of Trumpets 1985, Symphony No. 1 1987; Vocal, The Sun on the Celandines 1973, Psalm 150 1974, Requiem 1976, The Norwich Service 1977, Canticle of the Rose 1980, The Sun Used to Shine for tenor, harp and strings 1983, Magnificat and Nunc Dimittis in D 1985, Missa Brevis 1985, Singer by the Yellow River for soprano, flute and harp 1985, Five Summer Madrigals 1985, Jubilate 1987, English Parody Mass for choir and organ 1988; Instrumental, String Quartet No. 1 1982, Five Capriccios 1 and 2 1982–85, Piano Quintet 1984, Passacaglia for 2 pianos, Serenade for flute, harp, violin and cello, Journey into Light, A Choral Symphony 1992 and Music for BBC1, BBC2 and Channel 4; Melelivida, after Catullus, for chorus, percussion, piano and strings, 1997. *Address:* c/o PO Box 46, UBVD 80571, Bali, Indonesia.

WALKER, Sandra; Singer (Mezzo-soprano); b. 1 Oct. 1948, Richmond, Virginia, USA. *Education:* Studied at the University of North Carolina and the Manhattan School of Music, New York. *Career:* Debut: San Francisco 1972, as Flosshilde in Das Rheingold; Sang in opera at Philadelphia, Chicago and the New York City Opera; European engagements at Gelsenkirchen, 1985 and Wiesbaden, 1987; Sang the Nurse in Ariane et Barbe-bleue at Amsterdam, 1989; San Francisco Opera 1989 and 1992, as Bradamante in Vivaldi's Orlando Furioso and Hedwige in Guillaume Tell; Lyric Opera Chicago 1990–91, as Olga in Eugene Onegin and Marta in Mefistofele; Other roles include Carmen, Suzuki, Lola, the Marquise in La Fille du Régiment and Frugola in Il Tabarro; Hostess in Boris Godunov at the New York Met, 1998. *Address:* c/o San Francisco Opera, War Memorial Opera House, San Francisco, CA 94102, USA.

WALKER, Sarah; Singer (Mezzo Soprano); b. 11 March 1943, Cheltenham, England; m. Graham Allum. *Education:* Royal College of Music; Hon LRAM. *Career:* Debut: Diana/Giove, Cavalli's La Calisto, Glyndebourne Festival Opera, 1971; Glyndebourne, Scottish, Royal Opera House, Covent Garden, Chicago, San Francisco, Geneva, Brussels, Vienna Staatsoper; Metropolitan Opera, New York; Kent and English National Operas; Roles include: Didon, Les Troyens; Marguerite, La Damnation de Faust; Ottavia, Poppea and Penelope; Monteverdi; Maria Stuarda; Dorabella; Fricka; Herodias; Charlotte; Baba the Turk; Dejanira, Hercules; Mistress Quickly, Queen Elizabeth I, Gloriana; Frequent recitals and performances of contemporary music in the United Kingdom, Australia, New Zealand, USA and Europe; Concerts include appearances with Ozawa, Colin Davis, Mackerras, Bernstein, Rozdestvensky, Solti and Boulez with the Orchestre de Paris, London Symphony Orchestra, Royal Philharmonic Society; Sang Astron in The Ice Break at the 1990 Promenade concerts; Mrs Sedley in Peter Grimes at Geneva, 1991; Katisha in The Mikado for ENO, 1990; Cornelia in Giulio Cesare at the Metropolitan, 1988; Sang Stravinsky's Faun and Shepherdess and Britten's Phaedra at the Festival Hall, London, 1997; Sang Mrs Sedley at La Scala, 2000; mem, Incorporated Society of Musicians. *Recordings include:* Voices (Henze) and Baba the Turk with the London Sinfonietta; Dejanira in Hercules, with the Monteverdi Choir and Orchestra; Numerous recitals with Roger Vignoles and Graham Johnson including first recording of Britten's Cabaret Songs and complete Fauré songs with Malcolm Martineau; Video recordings include Gloriana, Julius Caesar and King Priam. *Honours:* Recipient of various awards and honours including: FRCM, 1988; Hon GSM, 1989; C.B.E., 1991; President of Cheltenham Bach Choir.

WALKER, Thomas; Music Historian; b. 5 Nov. 1936, Malden, Massachusetts, USA; m. Barbara Bland, 30 Jan 1965, 1 d. *Education:* AB, Harvard University, 1961; Fulbright Scholarship, Copenhagen, 1961–62; Graduate Study, University of California, Berkeley. *Career:* Assistant Professor, State University of New York, Buffalo, 1968–73; Lecturer, University of London King's College, 1973–80; Professor Ordinario di Storia della Musica, Universita della Calabria, 1980–81; Universita di Ferrara, 1981–; mem, Consiglio Direttivo, Societa Italiana di Musicologia; Responsible for Rivista Italiana di Musicologia. *Publications:* Edited to date (with Giovanni Morelli and Reinhard Strohm), 8 vols of Drammaturgia Musicale Veneta, Milan, Ricordi, 1983–. *Contributions:* Musica Disciplina, Journal of the A.M.S Musica/Realta, Rivista Italiana di Musicologia; Concert Criticism for The Times and other London newspapers, 1973–77.

WALKER, Timothy Alexander, AM, BA, DipEd, MusA, DipFinMgt; Arts Administrator; b. 23 Nov. 1954, Hobart, Australia. *Education:* Univ. of Tasmania, Univ. of New England. *Career:* Concert Man., Canberra School of Music 1981–87; Marketing and Development Man., Australian Chamber Orchestra 1987–89; Gen. Man., Australian Chamber Orchestra 1989–99; Chief Exec., World Orchestra 1999–2003; Chief Exec. and Artistic Dir, London Philharmonic Orchestra 2003–; mem. Int. Soc. for Performing Arts, Royal Philharmonic Soc.. *Honours:* Sidney Myer Performing Arts Awards 1999, Nugget Award, Australian Institue of Arts Management 2000. *Address:* London Phiharmonic Orchestra, Level 4, 89 Albert Embankment, London, SE1 7TP, England (office). *Telephone:* (20) 7840-4218 (office). *Fax:* (20) 7840-4201 (office). *E-mail:* timothy.walker@lpo.org.uk (office). *Website:* www.lpo.org.uk (office).

WALKER, William; Singer (Baritone); b. 29 Oct. 1931, Waco, Texas, USA. *Education:* Studied at the Texas Christian University in San Antonio. *Career:* Debut: Fort Worth Opera 1955, as Schaunard in La Bohème; Appearances at Opera Houses in New Orleans, Santa Fe, Milwaukee, San Antonio, Vancouver, Washington and Fort Worth; Metropolitan Opera New York from 1962, as Mozart's Guglielmo and Papageno, Malatesta, Verdi's Germont, Ford, Amonasro and Rigoletto,

Valentin, Rossini's Figaro, Marcello, Alfio, Tonio, Escamillo. Noted Concert Artist. *Address:* c/o Metropolitan Opera, Lincoln Center, New York, NY 10023, USA.

WALLACE, Ian Bryce, OBE, MA; British singer, actor and broadcaster; b. 10 July 1919, London; s. of the late Sir John Wallace and Mary Temple; m. Patricia Gordon Black 1948; one s. one d. *Education:* Charterhouse and Trinity Hall, Cambridge. *Career:* debut, Schaunard in Puccini's La Bohème, London 1946; appeared at Glyndebourne 1948–61 with roles, including Masetto in Don Giovanni, Bartolo in Le nozze di Figaro and Il Barbiere di Siviglia, Don Magnifico in La Cenerentola and Matteo in Arlecchino; continued to appear in opera in Britain and briefly in Italy until 1970s, appearances including Berlin Festwoche 1954, Teatro Reale, Rome 1955, Scottish Opera 1966–75; later appeared on concert platforms and also in plays, reviews, musicals and pantomimes, as well as in many television and radio shows, notably My Music (BBC) 1966–93; Pres. Inc. Soc. of Musicians 1979–80, Council for Music in Hospitals 1987–99. *Film appearances include* Plenty, Tom Thumb. *Radio:* panellist, 'My Music' (BBC). *Television appearances include:* The Mikado, Singing for Your Supper (opera series, Scottish TV), Porterhouse Blue. *Recordings:* Ian Wallace—My Music, Mikado, Iolanthe, Your Hundred Favourite Hymns, Glyndebourne recordings of Le nozze di Figaro, La Cenerentola, Il Barbiere di Siviglia, Le Comte Ory. *Publications:* I Promise Me You'll Sing Mud (autobiog., vol. I) 1975, Nothing Quite Like It (autobiog., vol. II) 1982, Reflections on Scotland 1988. *Honours:* Hon. MusD (St Andrews Univ.) 1991; Hon. mem. RAM, Royal Coll. of Music. *Current Management:* PFD, Drury House, 34–43 Russell Street, London, WC2B 5HA, England. *Telephone:* (20) 7344-1000. *Fax:* (20) 7836-9539. *E-mail:* postmaster@pfd.co.uk. *Website:* www.pfd.co.uk.

WALLACE, Stephen; Singer (counter-tenor); b. 1970, England. *Education:* Royal Northern College of Music. *Career:* Appearances as Athamas in Handel's Semele for English National Opera and the Staatsoper Berlin; Gluck's Orpheus for English Touring Opera, Orlofsky in Die Fledermaus for Dublin Lyric Opera and Anfinomus in Monteverdi's Ulysses for Opera North; Athamas, and Hasse's Solimano at the Innsbruck Early Music Festival; Madam Bubble in The Pilgrim's Progress by Vaughan Williams at Manchester and Bach's Magnificat for Israel Camerata; Season 2001 with James the Less in Birtwistle's The Last Supper, at Glyndebourne, Monteverdi's Orfeo in Brussels, Gassmann's L'Opera Seria in Paris and Death in Venice for Opera Zuid; Concerts with Les Arts Florissants and Akadamie für Alte Musik Berlin. *Recordings:* Dido and Aeneas (Harmonia Mundi).

WALLACE, William; Composer and Educator; b. 25 Nov. 1933, Salt Lake City, Utah, USA; m. Harriette Kippley, 7 June 1957, 2 s. *Education:* BMus, 1957, PhD, 1962, University of Utah; University of Oxford, 1958–59. *Career:* Educator, Rutgers and McMaster Universities; mem, Canadian League of Composers; Canadian Music Centre. *Compositions:* Concerto Variations for orchestra; Concertos for Piano and Orchestra, Clarinet, Violin and Orchestra, Clarinet, Violin, Piano and Orchestra; Several chamber works. *Recordings:* Dances and Variations, with London Symphony; Luminations, Epilogue, with Warsaw Chamber Orchestra; Concerto for Clarinet, Violin, Piano and Orchestra, with Janáček Symphony Orchestra; Concerto for Clarinet, Violin and Orchestra, with Martinu Symphony Orchestra. *Publications:* Concerto Variations, 1990; Symphonic Variations, 1990; Dance Suites: Introduction and Passacaglia, 1990. *Honours:* Phi Beta Kappa, 1957; Commissioned concerti, 1995, 1996, 1998, 1999. *Address:* Box 203, Wilson, WY 83014-0203, USA. *E-mail:* wwallcomp@aol.com.

WALLAT, Hans; Conductor; b. 18 Oct. 1929, Berlin, Germany. *Education:* Studies at the Conservatory of Scherwin. *Career:* Debut: Metropolitan Opera, 1971; Conductor at Stendal 1950–51; Meiningen 1951–52; Schwerin Opera, 1953–56; Conductor at Leipzig Opera, 1958–61; Stuttgart, 1961–64; Deutsche Oper Berlin, 1964–65; Music Director at Bremen, 1965–70; Mannheim, 1970–80; Regular appearances at the Vienna Staatsoper from 1968; Bayreuth from 1970; Music Director at Dortmund, 1979–85; Deutsche Oper am Rhein, Düsseldorf, from 1986; Conducted new production of Macbeth, 1988; Led the Company in Schreker's Die Gezeichneten at the 1989 Vienna Festival: Many engagements at the Hamburg Staatsoper. *Address:* c/o Deutsche Oper am Rhein, Heinrich-Heine Allee 16, 4000 Düsseldorf, Germany.

WALLÉN, Martti; Opera Singer (Bass); b. 20 Nov. 1948, Helsinki, Finland. *Education:* Sibelius Academy, Helsinki. *Career:* Debut: Helsinki; Finnish National Opera, 1973–75; Principal Bass, Royal Opera, Stockholm, 1975–; Roles include Colline (Bohème), Ferrando, Philip II (Don Carlos), Sparafucile (Rigoletto), Spirit Messenger (Die Frau ohne Schatten), Dikoy (Katya Kabanova), Baron Ochs, Marke, Landgraf, Daland, Orestes, Pimen, Falstaff; Roles in Finnish modern operas such as The Last Temptations (Paavo), The Horseman (Judge); Sang Fasolt in Das Rheingold at Helsinki, 1996. *Address:* c/o Finnish National Opera, Bulevardi 23–27, 00180 Helsinki 18, Finland.

WALLER, Adalbert; Singer (baritone); b. 1932, Danzig, Germany. *Education:* Studied in Frankfurt. *Career:* Opera appearances at Bielefeld, 1958–59; Passau, 1962–65; Aachen, 1968–74, as Rigoletto, Scarpia, Alfio; Sang Telramund in Lohengrin, 1976–77; Sang Wozzeck in the Brazilian premiere of Berg's opera, São Paulo, Cologne, 1981, as the Dutchman; Member of Frankfurt Opera Company, from 1981; Brunswick, 1985 as Reimann's Lear and Antwerp 1982, as Dr Schön in Lulu; Further engagements as Alberich in Der Ring des Nibelungen at Buenos Aires, 1982; Kurwenal at Bologna, 1984; Season 2000–01 in Reimann's Gespenstersonate, at Berlin, and Schigolch in Lulu at the Vienna Staatsoper; Other centres as Hans Sachs, Wotan, Falstaff, Count Luna.

WALLEZ, Jean-Pierre; French violinist and conductor; b. 18 March 1939, Conservatoire de Lille, Conservatoire Nat. Supérieure de Musique, Paris, France. *Education:* Lille and Paris Conservatories. *Career:* Founder and leader of the Ensemble Instrumental de France, 1968–83; Leader of the Orchestre de Paris, 1975–77; Founder and Dir, Ensemble Orchestral de Paris, 1978–87; First guest conductor, Sonderjyllands Symfoniorkester, Denmark; Musical Dir, Orchestre Royal de Chambre de Wallonie, Örebro Orchestra, Sweden; Principal Guest Conductor, Orchestra Ensemble Kanazawa, Japan, 1994–2000; Orchestre Pasdeloup, Paris, France, 1996–2002; Artistic Dir, Albi Music Festival, 1974–91; Premiered works by Landowski, Bondon, Martinů, Jolivet, Florentz, Finzi, Sciortino, Loussier, Hersant, Capdenat, Bon; Prof. of Violin, Geneva Conservatory, 1987–. *Honours:* Commandeur dans l'Ordre Nat. du Mérite, Chevalier de la Légion d'Honneur, Officier des Arts et des Lettres. *Current Management:* Agence Artistique Monique Cazeneuve, 5–7 avenue Mac-Mahon, 75017 Paris, France. *Telephone:* 1-43-80-15-86. *Fax:* 1-46-22-58-76. *E-mail:* cazeneuve@noos.fr. *Website:* www.monique-cazeneuve.com.

WALLFISCH, Elizabeth; violinist; b. 28 Jan. 1952, Melbourne, Australia. *Career:* began performing on 'modern' violin; Early professional engagements included concerto performances with orchestras in Australia and the United Kingdom, including the London Mozart Players and the Royal Liverpool Philharmonic Orchestra; Concerts, recordings and broadcasts, both as concerto soloist (often directing from the violin), and as a recitalist with the Locatelli Trio which she founded in 1989 with Paul Nicholson and Richard Tunnicliffe; Regularly leads the Orchestra of the Age of Enlightenment and the Raglan Baroque Players, director Nicholas Kraemer and, occasionally, the London Classical Players under Roger Norrington; Has performed works from the later periods include Spohr's Concerto No. 8 for the BBC with the Ulster Orchestra under Roy Goodman; The Brahms Double Concerto with her husband Raphael Wallfisch; The Viotti Concerto No. 22 with the Hanover Band and the Brahms Violin Concerto with the Orchestra of the Age of Enlightenment under Charles Mackerras; Regular visits to her native Australia where, in 1992, she was welcomed as Artist-in-Residence at Melbourne University, returned in September 1993 with the Locatelli Trio for four week tour and in 1995 toured as soloist; Featured soloist and leader of orchestra at the annual Carmel and Boulder Bach Festivals in the USA; The Locatelli Trio made USA debut at the Frick Collection in January 1994; Visited Utrecht, Irsee and Amsterdam Locatelli Festivals, 1995; Has directed the Britten-Pears Orchestra, Hanover Band, Les Musiciens du Louvre, Nordwestdeutsche Philharmonie, Camerata of Athens, Israel Chamber Orchestra, American Bach Soloists, Brandywine Baroque, Australian Chamber Orchestra, Queensland Philharmonic, Melbourne Chamber Orchestra, the Acad. of Melbourne, Brandenburg Orchestra of Australia; Recent enagements include debut with MDR Orchestra Leipzig performing Myslivecek Concerto and directing from the violin; Handel Concertos with the Orchestra of the Age of Enlightenment; Vivaldi's L'Estro Armonico with Les Musiciens du Louvre; Concertos with Netherlands Bach Soc., Staatstheater Wiesbaden and Tafelmusik, Toronto. *Recordings:* Complete Violin Concerti by Bach (including those reconstructed from Bach's Harpsichord Concertos in D minor and G minor); Haydn, including the Sinfonia Concertante; Recently recorded a series of early Italian Violin Sonatas with the Locatelli Trio; Current releases include, Locatelli, Tartini (2 CDs) and Corelli (Double CD Set), with Albinoni and Veracini; Trio have also recorded Handel Sonatas Op 1; Locatelli Violin Concertos Op 3, 'L'Arte del Violino' performed by Elizabeth Wallfisch with Raglan Baroque Players under Nicholas Kraemer; Locatelli Concerti Grossi, also with Raglan Baroque Players, and Locatelli Opus 8 Sonatas with The Locatelli Trio; Solo recording of Bach Solo Sonatas and Partitas. *Current Management:* Early Music Agency, 22 Michael Road, London, E11 3DY, England.

WALLFISCH, Lory; Pianist, Harpsichordist and Professor of Music; b. 21 April 1922, Ploesti, Romania; m. Ernst Wallfisch, 12 Nov 1944, deceased 1979, 1 s. *Education:* Royal Academy of Music, Bucharest; Studied with Florica Muzicescu and M Jora. *Career:* Debut: Duo with Ernst Wallfisch, Bucharest, 1943; Taught: Bucharest; Switzerland; Cleveland, USA; Detroit; Smith College, Northampton, Massachusetts, 1964–, Professor

of Music; Visiting Professor, International Menuhin Music Academy, Switzerland; Masterclasses and lectures, USA and abroad; Lecture-performances on Enescu, Lipatti, other Romanian composers; Formerly Pianist-Harpsichordist, Wallfisch Duo with violist husband; Concerts, television appearances, radio recordings, USA, Canada, Europe, North Africa, Israel; Occasional appearances as soloist and in chamber music; Participated in music festivals, Western Europe and the United Kingdom; In recent years has played in premieres of Lipatti's works in Switzerland, Italy, Germany and Moscow; Member of Jury, International Piano Festival and Competition, University of Maryland, 1986. *Recordings:* For various labels; Several CDs as pianist of the Wallfisch-Duo (with late husband) reissued; All-ENESCU: solo, piano sonata and cello sonata with cellist Julius Berger. *Address:* 7 Jay Court, Avon CT 06001, USA.

WALLFISCH, Raphael; Concert Cellist; b. 15 June 1953, London, England. *Education:* Studies with Amarylis Fleming; Amadeo Baldavino, in Rome; Derek Simpson at the Royal Academy; Gregory Piatigorsky, in California. *Career:* Since winning the 1977 Gaspar Cassado International Cello Competition in Florence, appeared widely in Europe; Australia; USA, Indianapolis Symphony Orchestra, 1988; Chamber music formerly with Heifetz in California; With Amadeus Quartet: Recitals with his father, Peter Wallfisch; Solti on television; Piano Trio concerts with Ronald Thomas and Anthony Goldstone; Performances with most major British orchestras, including Prokofiev's Sinfonia Concertante at the Festival Hall; Promenade Concerts, London, August 1989; James Macmillan's Concerto at the 1999 Proms. *Recordings:* Tchaikovsky's Rococo Variations, Strauss's Don Quixote and Romanze, Britten's Cello Symphony, Prokofiev's Sinfonia Concertante, Concertos by Shostakovich, Barber, Kabalevsky, Khachaturian, Finzi, Bax, Moeran, Bliss, Dvořák and Brahms on Chandos; Delius Violin and cello concerto, with Tasmin Little and Cello concerto, EMI. *Address:* Clarion-Seven Muses, 64 Whitehall Park, London N19 3 TN, England.

WALLIS, Delia; singer (mezzo-soprano); b. 1944, Chelmsford, Essex, England. *Education:* Guildhall School of Music, London. *Career:* debut at Wexford Festival, 1968, as Annius in La Clemenza di Tito; Welsh National Opera from 1968, as Hansel and Cherubino, Covent Garden, from 1970; Glyndebourne, 1971–72, 1976, as Cathleen in Maw's The Rising of the Moon; Composer in Ariadne auf Naxos and Cherubino; Has sung at the Hamburg Staatsoper, from 1973. *Recordings:* Manon Lescaut, EMI.

WALLSTRÖM, Tord; Singer (Baritone); b. 1952, Sweden. *Education:* Stockholm Music Academy. *Career:* Engagements at the Royal Opera, Stockholm, the Drottningholm Theatre, and at Gothenburg; Appearances in Soliman II by J M Kraus and as Masetto in Don Giovanni; Essen Opera and Stockholm from 1985, as Telramund in Lohengrin, Don Giovanni, Cecil in Roberto Devereux, Tonio in Pagliacci and Klingsor in Parsifal (1995); Guest appearances in Scandinavia and Germany as Handel's Giulio Cesare and Arsamenes (Xerxes), Mandryka in Arabella and Fra Melitone in La Forza del Destino; Frequent concert engagements. *Recordings include:* Soliman II by Kraus, and Don Giovanni.

WALMSLEY-CLARK, Penelope; Singer (Soprano); b. 19 Feb. 1949, London, England. *Career:* Sang the Queen of Night in Die Zauberflöte at Covent Garden; Returned for British premiere of Berio's Un Re in Ascolto, 1989; Glyndebourne Festival in The Electrification of the Soviet Union by Nigel Osborne; Has sung the Queen of Night for Geneva Opera, and English National Opera, 1989; Ligeti's Le Grand Macabre in Vienna; Concert engagements include the Brahms Requiem at the City of London Festival; Carmina Burana with the London Symphony Orchestra; Elijah in Liverpool with Marek Janowski; Shostakovich Symphony No. 14, with City of London Sinfonia; Title roles in Maria Stuarda and Norma, Leonora in La Forza del Destino and Il Trovatore, all with Scottish Opera; Concert performances of the operas Moses und Aron at the Festival Hall and Elegy for Young Lovers at La Fenice, Venice; Further appearances in Vienna, Berlin, Salzburg, Frankfurt, Czechoslovakia and Russia; Conductors include Birtwistle, Boulez, Colin Davis, Charles Groves, Haitink, Norrington and Leppard; Sang as Guinevere in the world premiere of Birtwistle's Gawain at Covent Garden, 1991; Donna Anna for English National Opera, 1995; Hecuba in King Priam for Flanders Opera, 1996. *Recordings:* A Mind of Winter by George Benjamin with London Sinfonietta; Song Offerings by Jonathan Harvey, with London Sinfonietta; Gawain, complete opera, under Elgar Howarth; Le Grand Macabre, by Ligeti. *Address:* c/o Allied Artists, 42 Montpelier Square, London SW7 1JZ, England.

WALSH, Louise; Singer (Soprano); b. 16 March 1966, Dublin, Ireland. *Education:* Trinity College, and College of Music, Dublin; Royal Northern College of Music, and National Opera Studio, London. *Career:* Opera engagements as Susanna, and La Fée in Cendrillon, for RNCM; Britten's Tytania for the Broomhill Trust, Janáček's Vixen for Opera

Northern Ireland and in Handel's Tamerlano for the Covent Garden Festival; Stuttgart Opera (contract 1995–97) in Hansel and Gretel, as Serpina in La Serva Padrona, Servilia in La Clemenza di Tito, Pauline in La Vie Parisienne for Stuttgart Opera, Xenia in Boris Godunov and Musetta in La Bohème, 1997; Adele in Die Fledermaus, for Opera Ireland, 1998, and Carl Rosa opera company, 1999; Rosina in Sarlatan by P. Hass, for Wexford Festival Opera, 1998; Anne Trulove in The Rake's Progress for Opera Theatre, 1999; Concerts include Bach's St John Passion and Mass in B Minor, Elijah, Carmina Burana, Messiah and Mozart's Mass in C Minor; Engaged as a Flowermaiden at Brussels, 1998 (production of Parsifal). *Honours:* Prizewinner, 1994 Vienna Belvedere International Singing Competition; Elizabeth Harwood Memorial Scholarship, Curtis Gold Medal for Singing and Ricordi Prize for Opera, at the RNCM. *Current Management:* Neil Dalrymple at Music International. *Address:* 89 Ridgemount Gardens, London WC1E 7AY, England.

WALT, Deon van der; Singer, (Tenor); b. 28 July 1958, Cape Town, South Africa. *Education:* Studied at the University of Stellenbosch. *Career:* Debut: Sang Jacquino in Fidelio at the Nico Malan Opera House, Cape Town, 1981; From 1982, has sung at Stuttgart, Munich, Gelsenkirchen and Hanover. Covent Garden from 1985, as Almaviva in Il Barbiere di Siviglia; Hermes in King Priam; Belmonte in Die Entführung aus dem Serail; Sang in concert at Salzburg, 1985, returning 1989, as Tamino and Tonio in La fille du regiment; Metropolitan opera debut, 1995, as Tamino; Sang Idomeneo at Florence, 1996; Piquillo in La Perichole at Zürich, 1998; Season 2000 as Gluck's Orpheus for Zürich Opera, Tamino at Barcelona and Mozart's Tito in Santiago. *Recordings:* Ferrando in Così fan tutte, from Ludwigsburg Festival, Harmonia Mundi; Massimila Doni by Schoeck, Schwann.

WALTER, Bertrand; Violinist; b. 17 March 1962, Metz, France. *Education:* Studied at the Metz and Paris Conservatories. *Career:* After study with Franco Gulli at the University of Indiana (1985–86) became co-leader of the Orchestre Philharmonique de France; With violist Laurent Verney and cellist Dominique de Williencourt founded the string trio BWV and has given many recital concerts throughout France. *Honours:* Prizes at the Paris Conservatoire and the 1980 Paganini International Competition. *Address:* Orchestre Philharmonique de France, 116 Avenue de Pres Kennedy, 75786 Paris, Cédex 16, France.

WALTER, Horst; Musicologist; b. 5 March 1931, Hannover, Germany; m. Liesel Roth, 1959, 2 s. *Education:* Musicology, German Philology, Philosophy, University of Cologne; DPh. *Career:* Scientific Co-operator, Joseph Haydn Institute, Cologne, 1962–92; Director of the Institute, 1992–96. *Publications include:* Music History of Lüneburg, from end 16th Century to Early 18th Century, Tutzing, 1967; Editor, Complete Haydn Edition Symphonies i/4, i/17. 1964, 1966; Baryton trios xiv/5, 1968; La Vera Costanza xxv/8, 1976; Keyboard Concertos xv/2, 1983; Accompanied Keyboard Divertimenti and Concertini xvi, 1987; Wind-band Divertimenti and Scherzandi viii/2, 1991; String Quartets op.76, op.77 and op.103, xii/6, 2003; G van Swieten's Manuscript Notebooks of The Creation and The Seasons; Haydn Studies i/4, 1967; Haydn's Pianos, Haydn Studies, ii/4, 1970; The Biographical Relationship Between Haydn and Beethoven, Report of Bonn Conference, 1970, 1973; An Unknown Schütz Autograph in Wolfenbüttel, Festschrift K G Fellerer, 1973; The Posthorn Signal in the Works of Haydn and Other 18th Century Composers, Haydn Studies iv/1, 1976; Haydn's Pupils at the Esterhazy Court, Festschrift H Hüschen, 1980; Haydn Bibliography, 1973–83, Haydn Studies v/4, 1985; Haydn Bibliography 1984–90, Haydn Studies vi/3, 1992; Hanky-panky Around Haydn, Haydn Studies, vi/4, 1994; String Quartets Dedicated to Haydn, Tradition and Reception, Report of the Gesellschaft für Musikforschung Köln 1982, 1985; On Haydn's "Characteristic" Symphonies, Internationales Musik-wissen- schaftliches Symposium Eisenstadt 1995, Eisenstadt 2000. *Contributions:* Music Past and Present, MGG; New Grove Dictionary; Proceedings International Haydn Conference, Washington DC, USA 1975, 1981; International Haydn Congress, Vienna 1982, 1986. *Address:* Herkenfelder Weg 146, 51467 Bergisch Gladbach, Germany.

WALTER, Rudolf, DPhil; professor of musicology; b. 24 Jan. 1918, Gross Wierau, Silesia; m. Marianne Marx 1946; one s. three d. *Education:* Universities of Breslau, Strasbourg and Mainz, College of Stuttgart, University of Mainz. *Career:* founder and conductor of Kissinger Kantorei and Cappella Palatina Heidelberg; radio broadcasts in Germany, Austria, Switzerland, Czechoslovakia and France; Professor of Musicology at University of Mainz. *Recordings:* 12 Organ records; 1 Choral record of Monteverdi's Mass for 4 Voices. *Publications include:* Books: M Brosig, Dülmen, 1988, J C F Fischer, Frankfurt, 1990; Musikgeschichte der Zisterzienserabtei Grüssau von 1700 bis zur Aufhebung 1810 mit Musikinventar, 1996; Book articles on Southern German Organ Music; Austrian Musicology; Organs of J A Silbermann; Organs of J Ph Seuffert; The Organ of O Messiaen; Max Reger's Sacred Music; Silesian Musicology; Editor of Sueddeutsche Orgelmeister des Barock, 21 vols; Orgelwerke von Schlick, Tunder, Sweelinck, Reichardt,

Merulo, Fasolo, Trabaci, Gottlieb Muffat; Organum in missa cantata, 3 vols; Sacred vocal works of German, English, French, Spanish and Italian Masters; J. C. F. Fischer, Psalmi vespertini, J. C. Fischer, Litaniae Lauretanae, and T. Fritsch, Novum et insigne opus musicum, 120 motets in 2 vols, all in Erbe Deutscher Musik; F X A Murschhauser, Vespertinus... cultus in Denkmäler der Tonkunst in Bayern; J J Fux, 8 Offertoria and 10 Offertoria in 2 vols in Gesamtausgabe der Werke; Musikinventare der Breslauer Kathedrale von 1761 u. 1825, 1988; Musikinventare der Kreuzheren in Neisse von 1825, 1997; Musikin-ventare der Jesuiten u. Pfarrkirche Glatz, 1997; Musik zur Verehrung der hl Hedwig aus Schlesien, Oldenburg, 1995; Die Rezeption der Kirchenmusik Carl Ditters von Dittersdorfs in Schlesien, 1997; Das Reimoffizium der hl Hedwig, Würzburg, 1997; (Studie in Festschrift J J Menzel, 1998): Joseph Ignaz Schnabels Figuralmusik zur Vesper (30 Druckseiten mit Noteninzipits), 1998; Ein schlesisches Reise-Diarium zum Zisterzienser-Generalkapitel 1771, 1999; New Grove, London, 2001; Zur Kirchenmusikpflege an Hl. Geist, Heidelberg, 17–20 Jh, in Jahrbuch zur Geschichte von Heidelberg, Band 8–10, 2003. *Address:* Lessing Strasse 3, 69214 HD-Eppelheim, Germany.

WALTHER, Ute; Singer (Mezzo-soprano); b. 23 June 1945, Jena, Germany. *Education:* Musikhochschule, Berlin. *Career:* Debut: Schwerin, 1968, as Octavian in Der Rosenkavalier; Sang at Rostock, 1974–80, Dresden Staatsoper from 1980 and Deutsche Oper Berlin, 1986; Tours of Japan with the Vienna Staatsoper and Deutsche Oper companies, as Fricka and Waltraute in The Ring; Guest appearances at Warsaw, Cologne (Brangaene in Tristan, 1990), the Moscow Bolshoi, Edinburgh Festival and Madrid; Season 1995–96 at Berlin as Brangaene, Dorabella, Cherubino, Carmen, Eboli in Don Carlos, Amneris, and the Hostess in Boris Godunov; Sang the Witch in Hansel and Gretel, season 1997–98; Season 2000 at the Deutsche Oper as Brangaene, Wagner's Mary, Nicolai's Frau Fluth and Meg Page in Falstaff; Many concert appearances, notably in music by Bach. *Address:* c/o Deutsche Oper Berlin, Richard Wagner Str 10, 10585 Berlin, Germany.

WALZ, Melanie; Singer (Soprano); b. 1965, Stuttgart, Germany. *Career:* Many appearances in concert and opera throughout Europe, notably in contemporary music; Sang in Einstein on the Beach and The Fall of the House of Usher by Philip Glass, at Stuttgart; Hamburg, Staatsoper 1997, in the premiere of Helmut Lachenmann's Mädchen mit den Schwefelhölzern; Engagements at the Vienna Konzerthaus in Luigi Nono's La fabbrica illuminata and Intolleranza, Noti by Heinz Holliger, and Schoenberg's Moses und Aron (2001); Basle Theatre from 1998, as Mozart's Blondchen and Sophie in Der Rosenkavalier. *Address:* Hamburgische Staatsoper, Grosse Theatestrasse 34, D-20354 Hamburg, Germany.

WANAMI, Takoyoshi; Concert Violinist; b. 1945, Tokyo, Japan; m. Mineko Tsuchiya. *Education:* Studied with Kichinouska Tsuji, Saburo Sumi and Toshiya Eto. *Career:* Debut: Played the Glazunov Concerto with the Japan Philharmonic, 1963; Performed with orchestras including the Leipzig Gewandhaus, City of Birmingham Symphony, Bournemouth Symphony, BBC Philharmonic, BBC National Orchestra of Wales, London Mozart Players, Zürich Chamber, Festival Strings Lucerne, Vienna Chamber, Slovak Chamber and Boston Pops; Conductors include R Barshai, G Bertini, R Fruhbeck de Burgos, K Masur, T Otaka and S Ozawa; Collaborated with pianists including S Lorenzi, B Canino, E Lush, G Pratley and H Barth; Duo partnership with the pianist Mineko Tsuchiya since 1980; Festivals: Lucerne International Music Festival 1980 and 1988; Festival Estivalde in Paris, 1981; Schaffhausen Bach Festival, 1982; Seon Bach Festival, 1984; Japan Week in Cairo, 1986; Meiningen Summer Festival, 1991; Tours: USA, 1973, 1981, 1989; Soviet Union, 1983, 1989, 1991; Egypt and Morocco, 1986; Gave numerous recitals at Queen Elizabeth Hall, Purcell Room and Wigmore Hall in London including a Solo Recital of 20th Century Violin Music in 1987; In Tokyo, directing Izumigoh Festival Orchestra, 1991; Annual recital entitled, Christmas Bach Series, 1991–; Two performances with Academy of St Martin in the Fields under Neville Marriner in Japan, 1994; Performed Brahms' Concerto in Budapest, 1994; Recital with Mineko Tsuchiya at St John's Smith Square in London, 1995; Fiftieth Birthday Concert in Tokyo in April 1995; Recital at St Johns, London, 1997. *Recordings include:* Tchaikovsky, Bruch and Mendelssohn Concertos with the Philharmonia; Bach Concertos with the London Mozart Players; Brahms and Schumann Concertos with London Philharmonic; Bach Solo Sonatas and Partitas (Complete) Ysaÿe Six Solo Sonatas; Brahms Violin Sonatas with Mineko Tsuchiya. *Publications:* Autobiography, The Gift of Music, 1994. *Honours:* Suntory Music Award, 1995; Prize Winner at the 1965 Long-Thibaud Competition and the Carl Flesch International, London 1970; Ysaÿe Medal, 1970; Mobil Music Award, 1993. *Address:* 61 Woodhill Crescent, Kenton, Harrow HA3 0LU, England.

WANG, Jian; Cellist; b. 1969, Shanghai, China. *Education:* Shanghai Conservatoire Yale School of Music. *Career:* Debut: Saint-Saëns

Concerto with Shanghai SO, 1980; Solo appearances in USA from 1982; Concerts with Central PO of China on tour to North America, 1987; Season 2000–2001 with Stockholm PO, and Scottish Chamber Orchestra; Brahms Double Concerto with Chicago Symphony and Cleveland Orchestras; Further engagements with Concertgebouw Orchestra, and playing the Shostakovich First Concerto in Rome; Dvořák Concerto with Minnesota Orchestra, and in Wales with Richard Hickox; Recitals in Paris, Vancouver, Hong Kong and Tokyo; Chamber music with Isaac Stern at the Mostly Mozart Festival, New York and Shanghai Quartet at Carnegie Hall, Trio partnership with Augustin Dumay and Maria João Pires. *Recordings include:* Haydn Concertos with Gulbenkian Orchestra, Messiaen Quartet for the End of Time with Myung Whun Chung, Gil Shaham and Paul Meyer; Brahms, Mozart and Schumann Trios (DGG). *Current Management:* Askonas Holt Ltd, Lonsdale Chambers, 27 Chancery Lane, London, WC2A 1PF, England. *Telephone:* (20) 7400-1700. *Fax:* (20) 7400-1799. *E-mail:* info@askonasholt.co.uk. *Website:* www.askonasholt.co.uk.

WANGEMANN, Hendrikje; Singer (Soprano); b. 1961, Kropstädt, Germany. *Education:* Leipzig Musikhochschule. *Career:* Debut: Armida in Handel's Rinaldo at Halle; Sang at Halle, 1987–91, as Asteria in Handel's Tamerlano, Gilda, Susanna, Marzelline in Fidelio, Nannetta in Falstaff and Micaela in Carmen; Leipzig Opera from 1991, as Musetta, Zerlina (1994) and Amanda in Ligeti's Le Grand Macabre; Guest appearances in Austria, Switzerland, Hungary and Germany; Other roles include Mozart's Pamina and Servilia, Baroness in Lortzing's Der Wildschütz and Jenny in Weill's Mahagonny; Season 1996 in Greek by Marc Anthony Turnage, at Leipzig. *Recordings include:* Deutsche Sinfonia by Hanns Eisler.

WANGENHEIM, Volker; Conductor, Composer and Professor; b. 1 July 1928, Berlin, Germany; m. Brigitte Antweiler; one d. *Education:* Musikhochschule, Berlin. *Career:* Founder, Principal Dir, Berlin Mozart Orchestra 1950–59; Conductor, Dir of Studies, Mecklenburg State Opera, Schwerin 1951–52; Conductor, Orchestra Berlin Musikfreunde 1952–55, Berlin Academic Orchestra 1954–57; first concert with Berlin Philharmonic Orchestra 1954; guest conductor, Germany and worldwide 1953–; Music Dir, City of Bonn; Principal Conductor, Orchestra of Beethovenhalle and Philharmonic Choir, Bonn; Artistic Dir, Bonn Beethoven Festivals 1957; Gen. Music Dir, Bonn 1963–78; Prof., Musikhochschule, Cologne 1972–99; international conducting class; Dean, Artistic Dept I 1991–93; mem. of the Bd, German Music Council 1980–88; jury mem., international music competitions, Besançon 1991, Copenhagen 1995, Geneva 1996; co-founder, Principal Conductor, Artistic Dir, German National Youth Orchestra 1969–84; co-founder, German National Student Orchestra. *Recordings:* classical, Baroque, chamber orchestra, symphonic and choral. *Compositions:* Sonatina for orchestra, Sinfonietta Concertante, Concerto for strings, Sinfonia Notturna, Sinfonie 1966, Klangspiel I and II, Hymnus Choralis for String Quintet, Choral works a cappella, Mass: Stabat Mater, Pater Noster, Nicodemus Iesum nocte visitat, Cantus de cognitione, Canticum sponsae, Hymnus Matriae, Parvulus natus est nobis, Domine, probasti me, Non moriar, sed vivam, Quid est homo, Deus caritas est, Dei iudiciorum altitudo, Antiphonae Marianae, Cantus de luce, Cantica de pace, Altenkirchener Hymnar, Te Deum, Pange Lingua, Veni Creator, Veni Sancte Spiritus, O Lux beata Trinitas, Lucis Creator optime, Nolite thesaurizare, Lucerna corporis tui, Lex charitatis, Emitte Lucem tuam, Pacem relinquo vobis, Psalms 1, 23, 62, 67, 70, 90, 93, 103, 121, 123, 130, 131, German and European folk songs. *Address:* Gerhart-Hauptmann-Strasse 12, 57610 Altenkirchen, Germany.

WARD, David W. B.; Musician, Pianist, Conductor, Teacher and Lecturer; b. 28 Dec. 1942, Sheffield, Yorkshire, England; m. Elizabeth Gladstone 1963, 1 s., 1 d. *Education:* Music Scholar at Bryanston School, Dorset, 1956–61; Music Exhibitioner, Caius College, Cambridge, 1962–63; Royal College of Music, London, 1963–67; Studied with Nadia Boulanger, Paris, 1968–69. *Career:* Debut: Purcell Room, London, 1972; Many concerts as soloist in the United Kingdom, Netherlands, France, Germany, America and Australia; Conductor of La Spiritata Chamber Orchestra and others; Professor at Royal College of Music, 1969–; Well-known for interpretation of Mozart; Now playing harpsichord and more especially the fortepiano; Teacher of fortepiano, Birmingham Conservatoire; Examiner, Associated Board of Royal Schools of Music; Much recital work in the United Kingdom and Netherlands. *Recordings:* Mozart Piano Music, 3 records; Tapes of Duets with Susan Rennie and Solo Works; Aslo radio recordings with BBC, RTE and ORTF; Mozart piano and violin sonatas with Yossi Zivoni; Haydn Trios and Piano Solos with Badinage, on fortepiano and original instruments; Duets and solos by J. C. and C. P. E. Bach, Haydn and first recording of a new piece by David Stoll for two fortepianos with Marejka Smit-Sibinga, Amsterdam; Mozart Keyboard Music on fortepiano; David Stoll Chamber Music, including a Piano Sonata and a Two Piano Sonata with Noel Skinner. *Address:* 4 Patten Road, London SW18 3RH, England.

WARD, Joseph; Singer (Tenor) and Vocal Consultant; b. 22 May 1942, Preston, Lancashire, England. *Education:* Studied at the Royal Manchester College of Music; FRMCM; FRNCM. *Career:* Debut: Royal Opera House, Covent Garden, 1962; Many appearances in opera in the USA, London, Germany, Portugal, France and Austria; Formerly Head of vocal studies at the Royal Northern College of Music; Formerly Principal Tenor, Royal Opera House, Covent Garden; Consultant in Opera and Vocal Studies at the Hong Kong Academy for performing arts; Director of Opera, Freelance; Course Director, European Opera Centre, Manchester from 1998 (Tosca and Mozart's Lucio Silla); Many BBC broadcasts. *Recordings:* Norma, Beatrice di Tenda, Montezuma, Wuthering Heights, Pilgrim's Progress and Albert Herring; Numerous others for major labels. *Honours:* O.B.E., 1991. *Address:* c/o Royal Northern College of Music, 124 Oxford Road, Manchester, M13 9RD, England.

WARD, Nicholas; Violinist; b. 1954, England. *Education:* Royal Northern Coll. of Music and in Brussels. *Career:* joined the Royal Philharmonic in 1977 and is co-leader of the City of London Sinfonia and Dir of the Northern Chamber Orchestra, Manchester; mem. of the Instrumental Quintet of London, with repertoire including works by Jongen, Mozart, Debussy and Villa-Lobos; mem. of the Melos and Radcliffe Ensembles. *Current Management:* Upbeat Classical Management, PO Box 479, Uxbridge, UB8 2ZH, England. *Telephone:* (1895) 259441. *Fax:* (1895) 259341. *E-mail:* info@upbeatclassical.co.uk. *Website:* www.upbeatclassical.co.uk.

WARD JONES, Peter Arthur, MA, FRCO; Music Librarian, Musicologist, Organist and Harpsichordist; b. 30 March 1944, Chester, England; m. Shirley Bailey 1978 (died 2001); one s. one d. *Education:* Balliol Coll., Oxford. *Career:* part-time Prof., Royal Coll. of Music 1967–69; music librarian, Bodlian Library, Oxford 1969–; harpsichordist, City of Oxford Orchestra 1968–99; conductor, Oxford Harmonic Soc. 1971–2000; mem. of editorial bd, Leipzig Mendelssohn edition 1993; mem. Royal Coll. of Organists, Royal Musical Asscn, Mendelssohn-Gesellschaft. *Publications:* Catalogue of the Mendelssohn Papers in the Bodlian Library Oxford Vol. 3 1989, Revision of P. Radcliffe's Mendelssohn 1990, The Mendelssohns on Honeymoon 1997, Mendelssohn: an Exhibition 1997; contrib. to Music and Letters, Brio, Mendelssohn-Studien, RMA Research Chronicle, New Grove Dictionary of Music and Musicians 1980, 2000, Die Musik in Geschichte und Gegenwart (second edn), Festschrift Rudolf Elvers, The Encyclopaedia of Oxford. *Honours:* F. J. Read prize (FRCO) 1962. *Address:* 25 Harbord Road, Oxford, OX2 8LH, England.

WARD-STEINMAN, David; Composer; b. 6 Nov. 1936, Alexandria, Louisiana, USA; m. 1st Susan Diana Lucas, 28 Dec 1956, 1 (divorced) s., 1 d m. 2nd Patrice Dawn Madura, 28 May 2001. *Education:* BMus, cum laude, Florida State University, 1957; MM, University of Illinois, 1958; DMA, University of Illinois, 1961; Postdoctoral Visiting Fellow, Princeton University, 1970; National Music Camp, Interlochen, summers, 1952–53; Aspen Music School, summer, 1956; Berkshire Music Center, Tanglewood, 1957; Paris, 1958–59; Fulbright Senior Scholar in Music to Australia, 1989–90. *Career:* Professor of Music, San Diego State University, 1961–; Composer-in-Residence, Brevard Music Centre, North Carolina; University Research Lecturer, San Diego State University, 1986–87; Faculty, California State Summer School for the Arts, Loyola Marymount University, Los Angeles, 1988; Numerous commissions; Major orchestral performances of his work include those by Chicago Symphony; Japan Philharmonic; New Orleans Philharmonic; San Diego Symphony; Orchestra USA; Belgrade Radio Orchestra, Yugoslavia and the Seattle Symphony; Joffrey Ballet, San Diego Ballet Company, California Ballet Co. *Compositions:* Major works for orchestra; ballet; band; chamber groups; Vocal ensembles, over 50 works published. *Recordings:* Concerto No. 2 for chamber orchestra; Fragments from Sappho; Duo for cello and piano; Brancusi's Brass Beds; Child's Play; 3 Songs for Clarinet and Piano; Sonata for Piano; The Tracker; Scorpio; Western Orpheus Concert Suite; Sonata for Piano Fortified, Moiré; Cello Concerto; Chroma Concerto; Cinnabar Concerto; Prisms and Reflections; Borobudur; Night Winds; Sonata for Piano Fortified. *Address:* 9403 Broadmoor Place, La Mesa, CA 91942, USA.

WARFIELD, Sandra; Singer (Mezzo-Soprano); b. 6 Aug. 1929, Kansas City, Missouri, USA; m. James McCracken, died 1988. *Education:* Studied at the Kansas City Conservatory with Harold von Duze; Further study with Irran Petina, Elsa Seyfart and Joyce McClean. *Career:* Debut: Metropolitan Opera, 1953, in Le nozze di Figaro; Sang in New York until 1957, as Marcellina, Madelon in Andrea Chénier, La Cieca and Ulrica, then moved to Europe; Sang at the Zürich Opera from 1959, notably in the premiere of The Greek Passion by Martinů and as Fides, Azucena, Dalila, Amneris and Léonor in La Favorita; San Francisco Opera, 1963, Dalila; Appearances in Berlin, Vienna, Perugia and elsewhere in Europe as Carmen and Fricka; Metropolitan Opera, 1972; Samson et Dalila, with James McCracken. *Recordings:* Les Contes d'Hoffmann; Le nozze di Figaro.

WARING, Kate; Composer; b. 22 April 1953, Alexandria, Louisiana, USA; m. 22 May 1981, 1 s., 1 d. *Education:* BMus, Flute Performance, 1975, MMus, Composition, 1977, Louisiana State University; Doctorate Science Humaine, Sorbonne, Paris, France, 1984. *Career:* Solo Flute Recitals in Italy, France, Germany, USA; Original Compositions performed in USA, Italy, France, Switzerland and Germany; Radio Performances of Compositions on Swiss, German and USA Radio; Founder of annual American Music Week in Germany concert series; Appearances on American PBS and Worldnet Television. *Compositions:* Over 60 Works; Variations, Flute and Harpsichord, 1984; Assemblages, Soprano, Flute, Trombone, Percussion and Piano, 1977; 3 Act Ballet, Acteon, for large Orchestra, 1983; Chamber Opera, Rapunzel, 1988; Remember the Earth Whose Skin You Are, an Oratorio, 1994. *Address:* Zum Kleinen Oelberg 41, 53639 Königswinter, Germany.

WARNER, Deborah; British theatre and opera director; b. 12 May 1959, Oxford; d. of Ruth Warner and Roger Warner. *Education:* Sidcot School, Avon, St Clare's, Oxford, Cen. School of Speech and Drama, London. *Career:* Artistic Dir Kick Theatre Co 1980–86; Resident Dir RSC 1987–89; Assoc. Dir Royal Nat. Theatre 1989–98; Assoc. Dir Abbey Theatre, Dublin 2000; has also staged productions at ENO (Bach's St John Passion and Janacek's Diary of One Who Disappeared), Glyndebourne Festival Opera (Don Giovanni 1994, Fidelio 2001), Royal Opera at the Barbican (Britten's Turn of the Screw), Opera North (Wozzeck), London Proms (concert of Honegger's Jeanne d'Arc au Bûcher), and has staged productions for Fitzroy Productions, Odeon Theatre, Chaillot and Bobigny Theatre, Paris, Salzburg Festival (Coriolan), LIFT and Perth Int. Arts Festival, Lincoln Center Festival, New York; engaged for The Rape of Lucretia at Munich 2004; Dir Fitzroy Productions. *Productions include:* Titus Andronicus (RSC), King John (RSC), Electra (RSC), Hedda Gabler (Abbey Theatre, Dublin/West End), The Good Person of Simvan (Royal Nat. Theatre), King Lear (Royal Nat. Theatre), Richard II (Royal Nat. Theatre), The Powerbook (Royal Nat. Theatre), The Waste Land (Fitzroy Productions), Medea (Abbey Theatre/West End/Broadway). *Films:* The Waste Land 1996, The Last September 1999. *Television includes:* Richard II (BBC), Hedda Gabler (BBC), Don Giovanni (Channel 4). *Honours:* Officier, Ordre des Arts et Lettres 2000; Evening Standard Award 1988, 1998, 2002, Laurence Olivier Award 1989, 1992, New York Drama Desk Award 1997, South Bank Arts Award 1998, OBIE Award 2003. *Address:* c/o Conway van Gelder Ltd, 18–21 Jermyn Street, London, SW1Y 6HP; c/o Askonas Holt, Lonsdale Chambers, 27 Chancery Lane, London, WC2A 1PF, England. *Telephone:* (20) 7287-0077 (Conway van Gelder Ltd); (20) 7400-1700 (Askonas Holt). *Fax:* (20) 7287-1940 (Conway van GelderLtd).

WARNER, Keith; Stage Director; b. 6 Dec. 1956, England. *Education:* Studied in London, at Bristol University and at Bayreuth. *Career:* Early work in fringe theatre; Staff Producer at English National Opera from 1981; Associate Director, 1984–89, staging Rossini's Moïse, Dargomizhsky's Stone Guest, Pacific Overtures and Werther; With David Pountney co-produced A Midsummer Marriage, The Flying Dutchman and The Queen of Spades; Associate Director of Scottish Opera, with Carmen, Tosca, Werther, Die Zauberflöte and Iolanthe; Handel's Flavio at Florence and Batignano; Further productions of Trovatore at Dortmund, Norma in Bielefeld and Un Ballo in Maschera with the Canadian Opera Company; Madama Butterfly and Casken's Golem at Omaha, The Queen of Spades in Madrid and Carmen for the Brighton Festival, My Fair Lady for Houston: Production of Janáček's The Makropulos Case in Oslo, 1992; Director, Designer, Der fliegende Holländer in Minneapolis, transferring to Omaha and Portland; Weill's Lost in the Stars for the Brighton Festival; Head of Productions for Omaha Fall Opera and the Omaha festival from 1992 (Eugene Onegin and Weisgall's Gardens of Adonis, 1992); Directed Tosca for English National Opera 1994; Pagliacci and Cavalleria Rusticana at the Berlin Staatsoper, From the House of the Dead for Opéra du Rhin and Carmen at Turin, 1996; Carmen for Minnesota Opera and La Finta Giardinera for Opera Zuid, 1997; The Turn of the Screw at La Monnaie, Brussels, 1998; Der fliegende Holländer for Opera Pacific, Il Trittico for Spoleto Festival, USA and Lohengrin for Bayreuth Festival, 1999; Season 2000 with Der fliegende Holländer for de Vlaamse Opera; The Cunning Little Vixen for Portland Opera; Manon Lescaut for English National Opera; Lohengrin for Bayreuth Festival and God's Liar for La Monnaie, Brussels (for which he also wrote the Libretto); Engaged for Wagner's Ring at Covent Garden, from 2005. *Current Management:* Athole Still International Management, Forresters Hall, 25–27 Westow Street, London, SE19 3RY, England. *Telephone:* (20) 8771-5271. *Fax:* (20) 8768-6600. *Website:* www.atholestill.com.

WARRACK, John; Musicologist; b. 9 Feb. 1928, London; m. Lucy Beckett, 1970, 4 s. *Education:* Winchester College 1941–46; Royal College of Music, 1949–52. *Career:* Freelance oboist, 1951–54; Assistant Music Critic, Daily Telegraph, 1954–61; Chief Music Critic, Sunday Telegraph, 1961–72; Director, Leeds Musical Festival, 1977–83; University Lecturer in Music and Fellow, St Hugh's College, Oxford, 1984–93;

Editorial Board, Cambridge Opera Journal, New Berlioz Edition, Neue Weber Gesamtausgabe; mem, Royal Musical Association. *Publications:* Concise Oxford Dictionary of Opera 1964, Carl Maria von Weber 1968, Tchaikovsky Symphonies and Concertos 1969, Tchaikovsky 1973, Tchaikovsky Ballet Music 1979, Carl Maria von Weber: Writings on Music (ed.) 1981, Oxford Dictionary of Opera (ed.) 1992, concise version 1996, Richard Wagner: Die Meistersinger von Nürnberg 1994, German Opera 2001. *Contributions:* Musical Times; Music and Letters; Opera; Gramophone; International Record Review; Opera translations; Articles in the New Grove Dictionary of Music and Musicians, 1980. *Honours:* Colles Prize, Royal College of Music, 1951; ARCM, 1952; MA, Oxon, 1984; D.Litt, Oxon, 1989. *Address:* Beck House, Rievaulx, Helmsley, York YO62 5LB, England. *E-mail:* warrack@aelred.demon.co.uk.

WARREN, Raymond (Henry Charles); Composer and University Professor of Music; b. 7 Nov. 1928, Weston-super-Mare, England; m. Roberta Smith, 9 April 1953, three s., one d. *Education:* Studied at Corpus Christi College, Cambridge with Robin Orr, 1949–52, then with Michael Tippett and Lennox Berkeley. *Career:* Teacher, Queen's University of Belfast from 1955, Professor of Composition, 1966; Professor of Music, Bristol University, 1972–94; mem, ISM; BACS. *Compositions:* Incidental music for 11 plays by W B Yeats: The Lady of Ephesus, chamber opera, Belfast, 1959; Finn and the Black Hag, children's opera, Belfast, 1959; Graduation Ode, opera in 3 acts, Belfast, 1963; Church operas, Let my People Go, Liverpool, 1972, St Patrick, Liverpool, 1979, and In the Beginning, Bristol, 1982. *Compositions include:* Oratorio, The Passion, 1962, Violin Concerto, 1966, Three Symphonies, 1965, 1969, 1996, Three String Quartets, 1965, 1975 and 1977, Oratorio Continuing Cities, 1989, Violin Sonata, 1993; Song cycles: The Pity of Love (Yeats) 1965; Songs of Old Age (Yeats) 1968; In My Childhood (MacNeice) 1998; Two Wind Quintets 2003; Ballet shoes, ballet, 2001. *Publications:* Book: Opera Workshop, 1995. *Address:* 4 Contemporis Court, Merchants Road, Bristol, BS 8 4HB, England.

WARREN-GREEN, Christopher; Violinist and Educator; b. 30 July 1955, Cheltenham, England. *Education:* Royal Academy of Music. *Career:* Debut: Solo, Berlin; London, 1984; Leader, BBC National Orchestra of Wales, 1977; Philharmonia Orchestra, 1980; Academy of St Martin-in-the-Fields, 1985; Music Director, London Chamber Orchestra, 1987; Tours a soloist, 1983–; Television Presenter, BBC Music and Arts; Professor, Royal Academy of Music, 1985–. *Recordings:* Mozart Violin concerti; Vivaldi Four Seasons; 4 records Haydn Concerti, Philharmonia; Mendelssohn Concerto; Tchaikovsky; Exclusive to Virgin Classics, 1987–; Berlin Chamber Akademie. *Honours:* Honorary ARAM, 1983.

WASCHINSKI, Jörg; Singer (Countertenor); b. 1966, Berlin, Germany. *Education:* Trained in Church Music, then at the Berlin Music College, Masterclasses with Barbara Schlick and Peter Schreier. *Career:* Many appearances in Germany and elsewhere in Europe in the Baroque music repertory; Operas by Jommelli at Stuttgart. *Recordings include:* Title role in Jommelli's Il Vologeso. *Honours:* Second Prize, International J H Schmetzer Competition for Baroque Music, Melk, 1996; Prize of the German State Association at the State Singing Competition, Berlin. *Address:* c/o Orfeo International Music GmbH, 8000 Munich, Germany.

WASSERTHAL, Elfriede; Singer, (Soprano); b. 12 March 1911, Lubeck, Germany. *Career:* Debut: Stettin 1935, as Marzelline in Fidelio; Sang in Essen and Düsseldorf, then at the Deutsche Oper Berlin, Charlottenburg, debut as Fiordiligi; Sang at Düsseldorf, 1941, in the premiere of Die Hexe von Passau by Gerster; Hamburg Staatsoper 1947–64, notably as Tosca, Desdemona, Jenůfa and Magda Sorel in The Consul; Visited Edinburgh Festival with the Hamburg Company 1952, for the British stage premiere of Mathis der Maler by Hindemith; Staatsoper Berlin 1951, as Selika in L'Africaine; Sang at Covent Garden as Eva, Sieglinde, Donna Elvira, Elsa and Marie in Wozzeck; Copenhagen, 1960; Frequent concert appearances.

WASSILJEV, Nikolai; Singer (Tenor); b. 1957, Leningrad, Russia. *Education:* Studied in Leningrad. *Career:* Has sung with the Bolshoi Opera from 1982, with guest appearances at La Scala Milan and the Metropolitan Opera, New York; Roles have included Alfredo, Cavaradossi, Turiddu, Lensky, Prince Gvidon in Rimsky's Tale of Tsar Saltan, Vladimir in Prince Igor and Dimitri in Boris Godunov; Sang in Mlada at New York, 1991. *Honours:* Prizewinner at the 1984 Glinka Competition and the 1986 Voci Verdiane at Busseto. *Address:* c/o Bolshoi Opera, 103009 Moscow, Russia.

WASSON, Jeffrey; Musicologist; b. 24 Aug. 1948, Illinois, USA. *Education:* BMus, 1970, MMus, 1973, PhD, Music History and Literature, 1987, Northwestern University; Boston College, 1989; Brandeis University, 1995; Boston University, 2000. *Career:* Instructor, 1980–85, Visiting Associate, 1990, 1993, Northwestern University; Professor of Music, Director of Music, Barat College, Lake Forest, Illinois, 1985–2001; Barat College of De Paul University, 2001–; Director of Music, St Mary of the Angels Church, Chicago, 1992–97;

Lecturer at Universities of Yale, Michigan, Minnesota, Brandeis, Boston, De Paul, Michigan State, Loyola of Chicago and Nebraska. *Recordings:* Jacket Annotations. *Publications include:* Editor, A Compendium of American Musicology: Essays in Honour of John F Ohl; Self Study Modules of History of Music in the Middle Ages and Renaissance; First Mode Gradual Salvum fac Servum: Modal Practice Reflected in a Chant that Begins on B-Flat. *Contributions:* The Hymnal, 1982; Companion and Reader's Guide to Music History and Theory; Encyclopaedia of the Romantic Era. *Address:* 1500 Oak Avenue, Evanston, IL 60201, USA.

WATERHOUSE, William; Bassoonist and Author; b. 18 Feb. 1931, London, England. *Education:* Studied at the Royal College of Music with Archie Camden, Gordon Jacob. *Career:* Played first with the Philharmonia Orchestra, 1951–53; Royal Opera House Orchestra, 1953–55; First bassoon, Italian-Swiss Radio Orchestra in Lugano, 1955–58; First bassoon, London Symphony Orchestra, 1958–64; BBC Symphony, 1964–82; Member of the Melos Ensemble from 1959, including tours of Europe and USA; Many solo appearances; Tutor in Bassoon, 1966–96, Fellow, 1991–, Royal Northern College of Music; Curator, RNCM Collection of Historic Musical Intruments, 1996–; Honorary Archivist of the Galpin Society, 1983; Visiting Faculty at Indiana University, 1972, Melbourne, 1983, Sarasota, 1985, Haus Marteau, Lichtenberg, 1986–98; Banff 1987, Victoria, 1988; Tanglewood, 1999; Competition Juror at Munich, 1965, 1975, 1984, 1990, Prague, 1986, Eindhoven, 1988, Markneukirchen, 1990, Victoria, British Columbia, 1993, Potsdam, 1996 and 1998; Member of Arts Council of Great Britain Music Advisory Panel, 1983–85; Joint President of the British Double Reed Society, 2002; Honorary member of the International Double Reed Society, 2003; Honorary member of the I D R S , Deutschland, 2001; Dedicatee of works by Gordon Jacob, Jean Françaix, Elliott Schwartz and other composers. *Recordings:* Numerous with Melos Ensemble and various orchestras; First recording of Anton Liste Sonata, 1999. *Publications:* Numerous editions of wind music; Translations; Articles for New Grove Dictionary; Bibliography of Bassoon Music, 1962; Joint Editor of Universal Bassoon Edition; The New Langwill Index: a Dictionary of Musical Wind-Instrument Makers and Inventors, 1993; Yehudi Menuhin Music Guides: The Bassoon, 2003. *Address:* 86 Cromwell Avenue, London N6 5 HQ, England.

WATERMAN, David Allen Woodrow; Cellist; b. 24 March 1950, Leeds, England. *Education:* MA, PhD in Philosophy, Trinity Coll., Cambridge; musical studies with Martin Lovett, William Pleeth, Jane Cowan and Sándor Végh, International Musicians Seminar; research scholar, Trinity Coll., Cambridge. *Career:* cellist, Endellion Quartet (founded 1979); appearances at Kennedy Center, Washington DC, Ambassadors Auditorium, Los Angeles, many times at London, Bath Festival, Concertgebouw, Amsterdam, Lucerne and Gstaad Festivals, Switzerland, Spoleto and Fiesole Festivals, South Bank Festival, City of London Festival, Aldeburgh Festival; tours of USA, Australia, New Zealand and most major European centres and radio stations; award-winning recordings of Quartetto Intimo, John Foulds; tours of South Africa, South America and Western Europe, with Endellion Quartet. *Recordings:* complete Britten Chamber Music; Haydn, Mozart, Dvořák, Smetana, Bartók, Martinů, Walton and Frank Bridge; Thomas Ades, Arcadia. *Contributions:* European String Teachers' Association Magazine; chapter in Cambridge Companion to the String Quartet. *Current Management:* Hazard Chase Ltd, Norman House, Cambridge Place, Cambridge, CB2 1NS, England. *Telephone:* (1223) 312400. *Fax:* (1223) 460827. *Website:* www.hazardchase.co.uk. *Address:* 27 Lancaster Grove, London NW3 4EX, England.

WATERMAN, Dame Fanny, DBE, FRCM; British pianist and piano teacher; *Chairwoman, Leeds International Pianoforte Competition;* b. 22 March 1920, Leeds, England; d. of Myer and Mary (née Behrmann) Waterman; m. Geoffrey de Keyser 1944; two s. *Education:* Allerton High School (Leeds) and Royal Coll. of Music (London) with Tobias Matthay and Cyril Smith. *Career:* co-founder (with Marion Harewood) Leeds Int. Pianoforte Competition 1961, Chair. 1963–, Chair. of Jury 1981–; Vice-Pres. European Piano Teachers Asscn 1975–; Trustee Edward Boyle Memorial Trust 1981–; Gov Harrogate Festival 1983; mem. Int. Juries, Vienna 1977, 1993, Terni (Italy) 1978, Munich 1979, 1986 and Leipzig (Germany) 1980, 1984, Calgary (Canada) 1982, Salt Lake City (USA) 1982, 1984, Viña del Mar (Chile) 1982, 1987, 1992, Maryland (USA) 1983, Cologne (Germany) 1983, 1986, Pretoria (S Africa) 1984, 1992, Santander (Spain) 1984, Rubinstein 1986, 1989, Moscow 1986, Vladigerov (Bulgaria) 1986, Lisbon 1987, 1991, CBC Toronto (Canada) 1989. *Television:* Piano Progress (series on ITV, Channel 4). *Publications:* Piano Tutors (series, with Marion Harewood) 1967–, Fanny Waterman on Piano Playing and Performing 1983, Young Violinists Repertoire (series, with Paul de Keyser) 1984, Music Lovers' Diary 1984–86, Merry Christmas Carols 1986, Christmas Carol Time 1986, Nursery Rhyme Time 1987, Piano for Pleasure (books 1–2) 1988, Me and My Piano: Repertoire and Duets (books 1–2) 1988, Animal Magic 1989, Piano

Competition: the story of Leeds (jtly) 1990. *Honours:* Hon. MA (Leeds) 1966, Hon. MusDoc (Leeds) 1992, Hon. DUniv (York) 1995. *Address:* Woodgarth, Oakwood Grove, Leeds, LS8 2PA, England. *Telephone:* (113) 265-5771.

WATERMAN, Ruth (Anna); Violinist; b. 14 Feb. 1947, Harrogate, Yorkshire, England. *Education:* Juilliard School, New York; Royal Manchester College of Music,. *Career:* Recitals and concerts throughout Europe and USA, radio and television, lecture-recitals, lecturing, coaching; Concerts include Bath Festival with Yehudi Menuhin as Conductor, 1966; Televised Prom, 1966; New York recital debut, International Artists series, Carnegie Hall Corporation, 1974; Concertos with London Symphony, BBC Symphony, BBC Scottish, English Chamber, Orpheus Chamber Orchestra and others; Festivals include Aldeburgh, Montreux; BBC Radio 3, complete Bach Sonatas, 1992; Lecture-recitals at Wigmore Hall, South Bank, Great Performers at Lincoln Center, New York, 2000, Avery Fisher Hall, New York, 1997; Recital at Hermitage Museum, St Petersburg, 2001; Radio interviews and talks for BBC, WNYC New York, Bayerischer Rundfunk, 1996; Professor, Queens College, City University of New York, 1975–92; Faculty Member, New York University, Royal Academy of Music; Masterclasses and lectures: Oxford University, 1994, Juilliard School, 2000, Royal Northern College of Music, New England Conservatory, Menuhin School; St Petersburg Conservatoire; mem. ISM; Fellow, George Bell Institute. *Recordings:* Bach Brandenburg Concertos, 1985; Bach Sonatas with Keyboard, 1997. *Publications:* Articles on interpretation and reviews for The Strad, BBC Music Magazine. *Honours:* Critic's Choice, Gramophone, 1997. *E-mail:* j.craxton@ruthwaterman .com.

WATERS, Rosalind; Singer (Soprano); b. 1965, Somerset. *Education:* Welsh College of Music and Drama, Cardiff and Royal College of Music. *Career:* Appearances with Musicians of the Globe, under Philip Pickett, the Gabrieli Consort, Corydon Singers and the Monteverdi Choir (tours of Europe); Handel's Saul in France, Mozart's Requiem in Madrid and Gubaidulina's The Canticle of the Sun in London, with Mstislav Rostropovich; Further engagements at the Purcell Room and Elizabeth Hall, London, and at the Strasbourg Festival; Elizabethan Lute Songs in Tel-Aviv; Tour of Spain, France and Turkey with Florilegium. *Recordings:* Albums with the New London Consort and the Philharmonia Orchestra (Suor Angelica). *Address:* c/o New London Consort, 8/9 Rust Square, London SE5 7 LG, England.

WATERS, Susannah; Singer (Soprano); b. 1965, England. *Education:* Studied at Guildhall School of Music and Drama, graduated 1989. *Career:* Debut: Sang Belinda, in Dido and Aeneas at Symphony Place, NY, 1986; The Princess in L'Enfant et les Sortilèges at 1989 Aldeburgh Festival and Louise in German production of Henze's The English Cat; Season 1990–91: Nannetta in Falstaff, Scottish Opera, Papagena at Glyndebourne, Philine in Thomas' Mignon at the Vienna Volksoper and Cherubino for Opera Factory, London, Many recital and oratorio appearances; Season 1991–92: Despina in Così fan tutte, Zerlina in Don Giovanni for Opera Factory, London; Martha, Sarasota Opera, USA; 1st Niece, in Peter Grimes for Glyndebourne Festival Opera; Dorlinda, in Orlando for Musica nel Chiostro, Italy; Season 1992–93: Gilda in Rigoletto for Opera Northern Ireland, Pamina in The Magic Flute, Scottish Opera, Susanna, in The Marriage of Figaro for Opera Factory, Cunegonde in Candide at Musica nel Chiostro; Season 1993–94: Fairy Godmother, in Cendrillon and Dalinda, in Ariodante, Welsh National Opera, Blonde, in Abduction from the Seraglio, for Sante Fe Opera; Season 1994–95: Atlanta, in Xerxes, LA Music Center Opera, Cupidon and Nereid, in King Arthur at Théâtre du Châtelet, Paris and Covent Garden; Despina, Welsh National Opera; Belinda for Royal Opera of Stockholm at Drottningholm; Elizabeth, in Elegy for Young Lovers at Lausanne and on South Bank, London, 1997; Sang Salome in Stradella's San Giovanni Battista, Batignano, 1996; New York City Opera and Los Angeles 1997, as Atlanta in Serse and Countess in Fedora. *Recordings:* As Evato in King Arthur, with William Christie and Les Arts Florissants. *Current Management:* IMG Artists Europe, Tom Graham. *Address:* c/o 4 Tremadoc Road, London SW4 7NE, England.

WATERS, Willie Anthony; Conductor; b. 1952, Miami, Florida, USA. *Education:* Studied at the University of Miami. *Career:* Assistant Conductor of the Memphis Opera, 1973–75; Music Assistant to Kurt Herbert Adler at San Francisco Opera, 1975–79; Music Director of the San Antonio Festival, 1983–84; Artistic Director of the Greater Miami Opera for whom he has conducted La Gioconda, L'Italiana in Algeri, Madama Butterfly, Ernani, 1984–85, Of Mice and Men by Floyd, Rigoletto, Cav and Pag, 1985–86, Salome, La Traviata, Hamlet, Aida, 1986–87, Bellini's Bianca e Falliero, Tosca, Otello, 1987–88, Le nozze di Figaro, Die Walküre, La Forza del Destino, 1988–89, I Vespri Siciliani, Idomeneo, Elektra, 1989–90, Così fan tutte and Falstaff, 1990–91; Has also worked with the Detroit Symphony Orchestra, Fort Worth Opera, Miami City Ballet, Florida Symphony Orchestra, Cincinnati, Chautaqua and Connecticut Opera Companies, Australian Opera Sydney, Cologne Opera, Sudwestfunk Orchestra and Essen Philharmonic, debuts 1990–91; Season 1991–93 conducting Aida with Connecticut Opera, Greater Miami Opera, SWF Sinfonieorchester, Baden-Baden, Florida Philharmonic Orchestra, and Macbeth with Charlotte Opera; Led an all-black Bohème at Cape Town, 1997–98.

WATKIN, David Evan; British cellist; b. 8 May 1965, Crowthorne. *Education:* studied with Sharon McKinley, Wells Cathedral School with Margaret Moncrieff and Amaryllis Fleming, St Catherine's Coll., Cambridge with William Pleeth. *Career:* St John's Smith Square debut recital 1989; Lincoln Centre, New York debut 1999; principal cello, Orchestre Révolutionaire et Romantique, English Baroque Soloists, Orchestra of the Age of the Enlightenment, Acad. of Ancient Music, Philharmonia Orchestra 2002–; revived the realization of figured bass on the cello; mem., Eroica Quartet 1999–. *Recordings include:* Corelli Op. 5 Violin Sonatas (realized figured bass, with Trio Veracini), Farewell to Hirta (music by Francis Pott), Vivaldi Cello Sonatas, Beethoven Cello Sonatas. *Publications:* article on the Beethoven Cello Sonatas, in Performing Beethoven. *Current Management:* c/o Eroica Quartet, Early Music Agency, 22 Michael Road, London, E11 3DY, England. *E-mail:* louise@earlymusicagency.com (office).

WATKINS, Glenn; Musicologist; b. 30 May 1927, McPherson, Kansas, USA. *Education:* BA 1948, MMus 1949, University of Michigan; PhD, University of Rochester, 1953; Diploma, American Conservatory, Fontainebleau, 1956. *Publications:* Gesualdo, Complete Works, co-editor, 1959–66; Gesualdo: The Man and His Music, 1973, 2nd edition, 1991; S D'India, Complete Works, co-editor, 1980–; Soundings Music in 20th Century, 1988; Pyramids at the Louvre, 1994; Proof Through the Night: Music and the Great War, 2003. *Honours:* Fulbright, England, 1953–54; National Book Award Nominee, 1974; Senior Fellow, National Endowment for the Humanities, 1976–77. *Address:* 1336 Glendaloch Circle, Ann Arbor, MI 48104, USA.

WATKINS, Michael Blake; Composer; b. 4 May 1948, Ilford, Essex, England; m. Tessa Marion Fryer 1975; two d. *Education:* studied guitar and lute with Michael Jessett, 1964–67, composition with Elisabeth Lutyens, 1966–70 and Richard Rodney Bennett, 1970–75. *Career:* appointed Fellow in Television Composition with London Weekend Television, 1981–83. *Compositions:* orchestral Works: Clouds and Eclipses for Guitar and Strings, 1973, Aubade for Brass Band, 1973, Horn Concerto, 1974, Violin Concerto, 1977, Etalage for Symphony Orchestra, 1979, Trumpet Concerto, 1988, Cello Concerto, 1992, Viola Concerto, 1998; chamber works: Somnial for Guitar Solo, 1968, Solus for Guitar Solo, 1975, The Wings of Night for Solo Violin, 1975, All That We Read in Their Smiles for Tenor, Horn and Piano, 1977, The Spirit of The Universe for Soprano and Ensemble, 1978, The Spirit of The Earth for Guitar Solo, 1978, String Quartet, 1979, The Magic Shadow Show for Cello and Ensemble, 1980, Sinfonietta for 12 Instruments, 1982, Clarinet Quintet, 1984, La mort de l'aigle for Solo Trumpet, 1993; Piano quintet, 1995; The River of Time for guitar trio, 1996; Viola Concerto, 1998. *Recordings:* Trumpet Concerto with Håkan Hardenberger and the BBC Philharmonic Orchestra conducted by Elgar Howarth; La mort de l'aigle with trumpet played by Håkan Hardenberger; The River of Time, Zagreb Guitar Trio. *Honours:* Menuhin Prize, 1975; Carl Flesch Composition Prize, 1976; Guinness Prize, 1978. *Current Management:* Novello Publishing Limited, 8–9 Frith Street, London, W1D 3JB, England. *Telephone:* (20) 7434-0066. *Fax:* (20) 7287-6329. *Website:* www.chesternovello.com. *Address:* Acacia House, Uxbridge Road, Hillingdon, Middlesex UB10 0LF, England. *E-mail:* michael@blakewatkins.freeserve.co.uk.

WATKINS, Sara (Van Horn); Oboist and Conductor; b. 12 Oct. 1945, Chicago, Illinois, USA; m. John Shirley Quirk, 29 Dec 1981, 1 s., 2 d. *Education:* BMus, Oberlin Conservatory of Music, 1967; Studied with Ray Still, Marc Lifschey, Marcel Moyse; Fellowship student at Tanglewood Music Festival, 1967. *Career:* Principal Oboist, American National Opera Company, 1967; Honolulu Symphony Orchestra, 1969–73; National Symphony Orchestra, 1973–81; Professor of Oboe, University of Hawaii, 1969–73; Catholic University, 1973–81; Oberlin Conservatory, 1984; In residence, Scottish Academy of Music, 1985; Oboe Soloist, Conductor, 1981–; Oboe Soloist at Aldeburgh, Sofia, Spoleto Festivals, Vienna, The Hague, Moscow, Leningrad, London, São Paulo, New York and other major US cities; Recent conducting appearances in Glasgow, Cambridge, London Queen Elizabeth Hall, Britten-Pears School, Snape Maltings, Paris, New York Glimmerglass Opera; mem, Musicians' Union of Chicago and London; Conductors' Guild, USA. *Recordings:* CDs: Britten Chamber Music with John Shirley-Quirk, Osian Ellis, Philip Ledger; Handel Cantatas, Arias and Sonatas with Yvonne Kenny, John Shirley-Quirk, Martin Isepp. *Current Management:* Columbia Artists Management. *Address:* 51 Wellesley Road, Twickenham, Middlesex TW2 5RX, England.

WATKINSON, Andrew; Musician; b. 1955, England. *Career:* founder member and leader of the Endellion String Quartet from 1979; many concerts in Amsterdam, Frankfurt, Paris, Munich, Rome and Salzburg; appeared at South Bank Haydn Festival in 1990, the Wigmore Hall Beethoven Series and the Quartet Plus Series in 1994; Quartet-in-Residence at the Univ. of Cambridge from 1992 and Residency at MIT, USA 1995. *Recordings include:* works by Haydn, Bartók, Barber, Dvořák, Smetana and Walton. *Current Management:* Hazard Chase, Norman House, Cambridge Place, Cambridge CB2 1NS, England. *Telephone:* (1223) 312400. *Fax:* (1223) 460827. *Website:* www.hazardchase.co.uk.

WATKINSON, Carolyn; Singer (Mezzo-soprano); b. 19 March 1949, Preston, Lancashire, England. *Education:* Royal Manchester College of Music; Muzieklyceum, The Hague, Netherlands. *Career:* Early specialisation in Baroque music, and sang with Syntagama Musicum, Grande Ecurie de la Chambre du Roi, with Jean-Claude Malgoire and Gächinger Kantorei, under Helmuth Rilling; Sang Phèdre in Hippolyte et Aricie at Covent Garden and Versailles, 1978, English Bach Festival; Nero in L'Incoronazione di Poppea with Netherlands Opera, 1979; Guest in Stuttgart as Rossini's Rosina and at Ludwigsburg as Mozart's Cherubino, 1980; 1981 as Handel's Ariodante at La Scala, Milan; 1982 Edinburgh Festival, Ariodante; Glyndebourne Festival debut, 1984, as Cherubino, returned as Cenerentola; Aix-en-Provence debut, 1985, as the Messenger in Monteverdi's Orfeo; Concerts include Mahler's 3rd and 8th Symphonies, conducted by Haitink, Das Lied von der Erde, and appearances with the Royal Liverpool Philharmonic, BBC Symphony, Scottish Chamber and National Orchestras and the Philharmonia; Sang with Boston Symphony at Tanglewood, 1985; Engagements in Paris, Vienna, San Francisco, Washington DC, Madrid, Barcelona; Toured Australia, 1987, and appeared at Sydney Opera; Sang in Gloucester Cathedral performance of St John Passion, shown by BBC television on Good Friday, 1989; Sang Nero in L'Incoronazione di Poppea at Montpellier, 1989; Purcell's Dido conducted by John Eliot Gardiner at Salerno Cathedral, 1990; Nero at the 1990 Innsbruck Festival. *Recordings:* Handel Messiah (Hogwood), Rinaldo and Xerxes; Solomon (Gardiner); Mozart Requiem; Bach B Minor Mass (Schreier) and St Matthew Passion; Solo album recorded live at her debut, Wigmore Hall recital, London. *Address:* c/o Opéra et Concert, 1 Rue Volney, F–75002 Paris, France.

WATSON, Janice; Singer (Soprano); b. 1964, England. *Education:* Studied at the Guildhall School, further study with Johanna Peters. *Career:* Concert repertory has included the Four Last Songs of Strauss, Stravinsky's Pulcinella, Les Nuits d'Eté by Berlioz, Mahler's 4th Symphony and Berio's Sinfonia (Barbican Hall, London); Has sung the Brahms Requiem with Dulwich Choral Society, Haydn's Nelson Mass and Seasons at the Usher Hall, Edinburgh; Bach's Magnificat, Christmas Oratorio and St Mark Passion on South Bank, Britten's Les Illuminations at Salisbury Cathedral; Elgar's The Spirit of England with the Hallé Orchestra; Messiah in St Alban's Cathedral and Beethoven's Missa Solemnis with the Chichester Singers; Hummel's E flat Mass and Schubert's Stabat Mater at the Queen Elizabeth Hall; Mendelssohn's Elijah with the Bristol Bach Choir; Further repertory includes Handel's Saul, Mendelssohn's Hymn of Praise (2nd Symphony), Vaughan Williams's Pastoral Symphony and Beethoven's Mass in C (Barcelona Palace of Music); Recitals with the Songmakers' Almanac and in the crush bar at Covent Garden; Opera engagements at Glyndebourne, in Monteverdi's L'Incoronazione di Poppea at the City of London Festival and Musetta in La Bohème at Covent Garden (1990); With Welsh National Opera has sung Musetta, Fiordiligi, Micaela, Adèle in Le Comte Ory, Pamina and Rosalinde (Die Fledermaus); US and Canadian debuts in Messiah, conducted by Trevor Pinnock, 1990; Eugene Onegin for Welsh National Opera and recently Lucia di Lammermoor, Daphne for San Francisco Opera and at Santa Fe (1996), Les Illuminations by Benjamin Britten at the Proms, Messiah at the Barbican with Richard Hickox; Engaged as Pamina at the Berlin Staatsoper and Arabella at San Francisco, 1998; Beethoven's Choral Symphony with the London Symphony Orchestra at the 1999 London Proms; Season 1999–2000 as Mozart's Elettra at Santa Fe, Micaela for Chicago Lyric Opera, Governess in The Turn of the Screw for ENO and Ellen Orford at Amsterdam; Mendelssohn's Elijah at the London Proms, 2002. *Address:* Elm Cottage, Portsmouth Road, Milford, Godalming, Surrey, GU8 5DU.

WATSON, Lillian; Singer (Soprano); b. 4 Dec. 1947, London, England. *Education:* Studied at the Guildhall School of Music and the London Opera Centre. *Career:* Sang first at the Wexford Festival, then with the Welsh National Opera; Glyndebourne from 1976, as Susanna, Despina, Sophie, Tytania in A Midsummer Night's Dream and Blondchen (1988); Covent Garden debut, 1971, as Barbarina in Le nozze di Figaro; Appearances in die Entführung, Der Rosenkavalier and Arabella; Guest engagements with English National Opera and Scottish Opera and in Munich, Paris, Rouen, Marseilles and Bordeaux; Salzburg Festival,

1982, as Marzelline in Fidelio; Vienna Staatsoper in Le nozze di Figaro; Sang Strauss's Sophie at the Théâtre des Champs-Elysées, 1989; Norina in Don Pasquale at Amsterdam; Title role in The Cunning Little Vixen at Covent Garden, 1990; Sadler's Wells Theatre, 1990, as Britten's Tytania; Television engagements in Don Pasquale and Orpheus in the Underworld. Sang Fairy Godmother in Massenet's Cendrillon for Welsh National Opera, 1993 and at Ghent, 1998; Bella in The Midsummer Marriage at Covent Garden, 1996; Despina, 1997; Sang Britten's Tytania at Rome 1999 and Naples 2001. *Recordings:* Carmen; Le nozze di Figaro; Monteverdi Madrigals and Handel's Israel in Egypt; Die Entführung aus dem Serail; The Cunning Little Vixen; Così fan tutte; Britten's A Midsummer Night's Dream. *Address:* c/o IMG Artists, Lovell House, 616 Chiswick High Road, London W4 5RX, England.

WATSON, Linda; Singer (Soprano and Mezzo-soprano); b. 1959, San Francisco, USA. *Education:* New England Conservatory, Boston; Vienna, with Erik Werba and Waldemar Kmentt; Berlin, with Hannelore Kuhse. *Career:* Sang in Vienna from 1986; Aachen Opera 1992-1995, as Jezibaba in Rusalka, Santuzza, and Offenbach's, Giulietta; Essen and Leipzig 1995-97, as Wagner's Venus and Brangaene, Azucena Marina in Boris Godunov and Sieglinde in Die Walküre; Guest appearances in Prague (the Marschallin, 1996), Vienna Staatsoper (Venus, 1997) and Hamburg; Deutsche Oper am Rhein as Sieglinde, Kundry and Isolde, from 1997; Bayreuth Festival 1998, as Kundry in Parsifal; Further engagements in London, Moscow, Tokyo, Boston and Amsterdam (Venus 1998); Season 1998-99 as Leonore in Fidelio at Dusseldorf, Brünnhilde in Siegfried at Bonn and Isolde for the Maggio Musicale, Florence Elisabeth in Tannhäuser at Toulouse; Complete Ring cycles, as Brünnhilde, at Barcelona, Vienna and Amsterdam, from 2003. *Address:* c/o IMG Artists, Lovell House, 616 Chiswick High Road, London, W4 5RX, England.

WATT, Alan; Singer (Baritone); b. 1947, Aberdeen, Scotland. *Education:* Scottish Academy of Music, Glasgow. *Career:* Debut: Scottish Opera, Glasgow, 1970; Sang as Háry János by Kodály at the 1971 Buxton Festival; Glyndebourne Festival and Touring Opera from 1973, as Marcello, Guglielmo and Figaro; Appearances in The Cunning Little Vixen, Strauss's Intermezzo and The Visit of the Old Lady by Einem; Covent Garden, 1976, in the premiere of Henze's We Come to the River; Wexford Festival, 1978, as Ernesto in Haydn's Il mondo della luna; Sang Guglielmo at Venice, 1983, and Strasbourg, 1989, Figaro at Vienna, 1986, and for Welsh National Opera, 1987; Papageno at Tel-Aviv, 1991; Festival Hall, London, 1998, as Pish-Tush in The Mikado; Many concert and oratorio engagements. *Address:* c/o D'Oyly Carte Opera Co, Valley Park, Cromer Gardens, Wolverhampton WV 6 0UA, England.

WATTS, André; Pianist; b. 20 June 1946, Nuremberg, Germany. *Education:* Studied with Genia Robiner, Doris Bawden and Clement Petrillo, Philadelphia Musical Academy; Artist's Diploma, Peabody Conservatory of Music, Baltimore, 1972, and with Leon Fleisher. *Career:* Debut: Soloist, Haydn's Concerto in D Major, Philadelphia Orchestra Children's Concert, 1955; Soloist, Franck's Symphonic Variations, Philadelphia Orchestra, 1960; Soloist, Liszt's Concerto No. 1, with Bernstein and New York Philharmonic Orchestra, 1963; European debut, London Symphony Orchestra, 1966; New York recital debut, 1966; World tour, 1967; First pianist to play a recital on live network television in USA, New York, 1976; Celebrated 25th anniversary of debut as soloist with New York Philharmonic Orchestra, Liszt Concerto No. 1, the Beethoven Concerto No. 2 and Rachmaninov Concerto No. 2, telecast nationwide, 1988; Rachmaninov's concerto No. 2 in C minor at the London Proms, 2002. *Recordings:* Various. *Honours:* Honorary Doctorates from Yale University, 1973, Albright College, 1975; Film documentary of his career; Avery Fisher Prize, 1988. *Address:* c/o Columbia Artists' Management Inc., 165 West 57th Street, New York, NY 10019, USA.

WATTS, Andrew; Singer (Countertenor); b. 1967, Middlesex, England. *Education:* Royal Academy of Music. *Career:* Appearances at the Almeida and Montepulciano Festivals in works by Smirnov, McQueen and Henze; Opera roles include Tolomeo in Giulio Cesare, Lidio in Cavalli's L'Egisto, Handel's Sosarme, Scarlatti's Tigrane and Britten's Oberon, Arsamenes in Xerxes, and Monteverdi's Orfeo (1999–2000) for English National Opera; Double bill of Dido and Aeneas and Venus and Adonis for De Vlaamse Opera; Season 1998–99 as Gluck's Orpheus at Sydney and for ENO, and in Cesti's Il Pomo d'Oro at Batignano; Season 2000 in Birtwistle's Gawain at Covent Garden and premiere of Guarnieri's Passione Secondo Matteo at La Scala; Concerts include Bach's Passions and Magnificat, Chapentier's Te Deum (at Lourdes), Purcell's Indian Queen in France, Messiah at Oxford, Handel's Jephtha on tour to Italy and Judas Maccabaeus in France. *Address:* Music International, 13 Ardilaun Road, London N5 2QR, England.

WATTS, Helen; Singer (contralto); b. 9 Dec. 1927, Milford Haven, Wales. *Education:* Royal Academy of Music with Caroline Hatchard and Frederick Jackson. *Career:* Sang in the BBC Chorus; Solo engagements

from 1953, including Gluck's Orpheus; Promenade Concerts, 1955, singing Bach Arias with Malcolm Sargent; Sang with Handel Opera Society from 1958, as Didymus in Theodora, Ino and Juno in Semele and Rinaldo; Toured with the English Opera Group to Russia, 1964, performing Britten's Lucretia under the composer; Covent Garden, 1965–71, as First Norn in Götterdämmerung, Erda and Sosostris in The Midsummer Marriage; Welsh National Opera, 1969, as Mistress Quickly; US debut, New York Philharmonic Hall, 1966, in A Mass of Life, by Delius; Carnegie Hall, 1970, in Kindertotenlieder by Mahler with the Chicago Symphony under Solti; Repertoire included music by Strauss, Schoenberg, Stravinsky, Mendelssohn, Elgar and Berlioz. *Recordings:* Handel's Sosarme and Semele; Bach B Minor Mass; First Norn in Götterdämmerung; A Midsummer Night's Dream; Béatrice et Bénédict; Messiah; St Matthew Passion; The Apostles by Elgar; Handel's Samson. *Honours:* C.B.E., 1976. *Current Management:* Askonas Holt Ltd, Lonsdale Chambers, 27 Chancery Lane, London, WC2A 1PF, England.

WAYENBERG, Daniel (Ernest Joseph Carel); Pianist and Composer; b. 11 Oct. 1929, Paris, France. *Education:* Studied with his mother and with Marguérite Long. *Career:* Played in private houses, 1939–46; Public debut, Paris, 1949; Opening recital of the Chopin Centenary Festival, Florence, 1949; Besançon Festival, 1951; US debut, Carnegie Hall, 1953, conducted by Mitropoulos; Numerous concerto appearances throughout the world (tours of USA and Indonesia, 1955); Repertoire centres on 19th century classics but also plays Haydn and Stockhausen; Teacher at Conservatory of Rotterdam. *Compositions:* Ballet Solstice, 1955; Sonata for violin and piano; Concerto for 5 wind instruments and orchestra; Capella, symphony; Concerto for 3 pianos and orchestra, 1975. *Recordings:* Numerous concertos including Brahms, Tchaikovsky, Beethoven, Gershwin and Rachmaninov. *Current Management:* Concert Director, Samama 8C, Netherlands. *Address:* 17 rue Thibault, 94520 Mandres-Les Roses, France.

WEAVER, James (Merle); Harpsichordist, Pianist and Fortepianist; b. 25 Sept. 1937, Champaign, Illinois, USA. *Education:* BA, 1961, MM, 1963, University of Illinois, Urbana-Champaign; Studied with Gustav Leonhardt, Sweelinck Conservatory, Amsterdam, 1957–59. *Career:* Many appearances as keyboard artist; Curator of historic instruments at the Smithsonian Institution, Washington DC, USA, 1967; Co-founder of Smithsonian Chamber Players, 1976; Teacher, Cornell University and American University; Various masterclasses in 18th century performance practice. *Recordings include:* Smithsonian Collection. *Address:* c/o Smithsonian Chamber Players, Smithsonian Institution, Washington DC 20560, USA.

WEAVING, John (Weymouth); Singer (Tenor); b. 23 Feb. 1936, Melbourne, Australia. *Education:* Studied with Browning Mummery in Melbourne, Audrey Langford in London and Ken Neate in Munich. *Career:* Debut: Sadler's Wells in 1960 as Eisenstein in Die Fledermaus; Has sung in operas by Wagner with the English National Opera; Engagements at opera houses in Kiel, Essen, Hanover, Lyon, Wiesbaden and Munich; Other roles included Florestan, Huon in Oberon, Alvaro in La Forza del Destino, Otello, Don José, Bacchus, Herman in The Queen of Spades, and Sali in A Village Romeo and Juliet; Many concert appearances. *Address:* c/o English National Opera, St Martin's Lane, London WC2N 4ES, England.

WEBB, Jonathan; Conductor; b. 1963, England. *Education:* University of Manchester. *Career:* Appearances with New Israel Opera with Jenůfa, Così fan tutte, Midsummer Night's Dream, Faust, Carmen, Don Pasquale, Butterfly, Der Freischütz, Hoffmann, Samson et Dalila, Cavalleria Rusticana, Pagliacci, Traviata, L'Elisir d'amore, Cenerentola and Lucia di Lammermoor; Head of Music, Opera Ireland; Resident Conductor New Israeli Opera; Festival appearances in Turin and Rome; Don Pasquale, Der Zigeunerbaron and Die Zauberflöte at the Vienna Volksoper; Peter Grimes in Genoa and Balfe's The Rose of Castile at Wexford; Figaro, The Rape of Lucretia, Falstaff and L'Histoire du Soldât in Ireland; Co-production between Kirov Opera and New Israel Opera of Lady Macbeth of Mtsensk; Season 1999–2000 with L'Italiana in Algeri, Tosca, La Juive, Macbeth and Eugene Onegin in Tel-Aviv; Mahagonny for the Deutsche Oper Berlin, La Traviata in Cologne and Turandot for the Caesarea Festival; Season 2000–01 with Tancredi in Venice and Carmen at the Deutsche Oper, Berlin. *Address:* Music International, 13 Ardilaun Road, London N5 2QR, England.

WEBB, Peter; Composer and Conductor; b. 29 Feb. 1948, Melbourne, Victoria, Australia. *Education:* BA, University of Melbourne, and Teaching Certificate, 1970. *Career:* Oboe and Cor Anglais in the Adelaide Symphony Orchestra, 1975–95; Conductor and Teacher; Commissions from ABC, Adelaide Harmony Choir, Unley Chamber Orchestra, and others. *Compositions include:* Songs of the Wind, song cycle for soprano and orchestra, 1978; Quintet for Brass, 1980; Sonata for Clarinet and Piano, 1981; Songs of the Shadows, song cycle for mezzo soprano and orchestra, 1985; The Christmas Kangaroo for narrator and orchestra, 1986; Sextet for pairs of horns, clarinets and bassoons, 1987; Sonata for bassoon and piano, 1987; Five Blake Songs for chorus and orchestra, 1988; Trio for clarinet, bassoon and piano, 1989; Sinfonietta for orchestra, 1990; Trio for 2 oboes and piano, 1992; Trio for flute, oboe and piano, 1992; Sonata for Cor Anglais and piano, 1995; Sonata for cello and piano, 1998; Retrospection for 8 cellos, 1999; Sonata for flute and piano, 2001. *Address:* c/o APRA, 1A Eden Street, Crows Nest, NSW 2065, Australia. *E-mail:* pjwebb@senet.com.au.

WEBBER, Oliver; Violinist; b. 1969, Essex, England. *Education:* Wells Cathedral; Cambridge; The Hague, Netherlands. *Career:* Appearances from 1995 with the Charivari Agréable Sinfonie, Gabrieli Consort and Florilegium; Violin and Viola with the Revolutionary String Quartet, Red Priest and the Consort of Musicke; Soloist with Florilegium, the Avison Baroque Ensemble, La Serenissima and London Musical Arts; Exponent of early and Baroque music performance practice, including ornamentation and the use of gut strings; European tour with the London Handel Festival, 2001. *Address:* c/o Florilegium, 21 Village Road, Finchley, London N3 1TL, England.

WEBER, Margit; Pianist; b. 24 Feb. 1924, Ebnat-Kappel, St Gallen, Switzerland. *Education:* Studied organ with Heinrich Funk in Zürich and piano with Max Egger and Walter Lang at the Zürich Conservatory. *Career:* Frequent concert tours of the USA and Europe; Festival appearances at Lucerne, Munich, Venice, Berlin and Vienna; Has given the premieres of Martinů's Fantasia Concertant, 1958, Stravinsky's Movements in 1960, and Tcherepnin's Bagatelles and 5th Piano Concerto; Has performed Moeschinger's Piano Concerto in 1962, Schibler's Ballade for Piano and Strings in 1963, Fortner's Epigrams for Piano in 1964, Vogel's Horformen for Piano and Strings in 1972; Concert classes at the Zürich Musikhochschule from 1971. *Recordings include:* Mozart Concerto K414 under Baumgartner; Nights in the Gardens of Spain; Franck Symphonic Variations; Weber's Konzertstück; Stravinsky's Movements with the Berlin Radio Symphony Orchestra under Fricsay. *Honours:* Hans Georg Nägeli Medal of Zürich, 1971.

WEBER, Peter; Singer (Baritone); b. 1955, Vienna, Austria. *Education:* Diploma, Hochschule für Musik, Vienna. *Career:* Engaged by the Studio of the Vienna Staatsoper, 1976; Member of ensemble of the Vienna Staatsoper, 1978; Engaged at the Nuremberg Opera in 1980 and Hanover Staatsoper in 1982; Regular appearances at the Salzburg Festival and the Vienna Festwochen from 1977; Appeared at Glyndebourne Festival 1985–89 as Mandryka in Arabella and Olivier in Capriccio; Debut at the Teatro Col ón in Buenos Aires in 1986 as Mozart's Count; Debuts at the Teatro Liceo Barcelona and the Teatro dell'Opera Rome in 1988; Guest engagements in Hamburg, Düsseldorf, Geneva, Paris and Milan; Sang Mandryka at Covent Garden in 1990; USA debut as Amonasro at Dallas Opera in 1991; Contracted to Vienna State Opera in 1992; Other roles include Silvio, Sharpless, Malatesta, Falke and the Secretary in Der Junge Lord by Henze, Don Giovanni, Don Alfonso, Telramund, Pizarro, Amfortas, Eisenstein, Onegin; Debuts as Wagner's Gunther and Strauss's Barak at Hanover in 1993; Concerts and recitals in Europe and the USA; Radio and television appearances; Engaged as the Count in Capriccio, Vienna 1996–97; Season 2000–01 as Wozzeck at La Scala, the Speaker in Die Zauberflöte, Kurwenal and the Chosen One in Schoenberg's Die Jakobsleiter, at the Vienna Staatsoper; Hindemith's Mathis at Hannover. *Recordings:* Ariadne auf Naxos; Un Ballo in Maschera; Die Frau ohne Schatten; Die Zauberflöte; Schoeck Penthesilea; Schubert Alfonso und Estrella; Haydn's Die Feuerbrunst. *Honours:* Prizewinner, Hugo Wolf Competition in Salzburg in 1976; Interpretation Prize from the Mozartgemeinde Vienna in 1976; International Schubert-Wolf Competition, Vienna in 1978. *Address:* c/o Vienna State Opera, Ringstrasse, Vienna, Austria.

WEBSTER, Beveridge; Pianist; b. 30 May 1908, Pittsburgh, USA. *Education:* Studied at the Pittsburgh Conservatory and with Isidor Philipp at the Paris Conservatoire; Graduated in 1926; Further study with Artur Schnabel. *Career:* Many solo, orchestral and recital engagements in USA and abroad; Associated with Ravel and performed Tzigane in 1924; US debut in 1934 in MacDowell's 2nd Concerto with New York Philharmonic; Many appearances with Curtis, Juilliard, Kolisch, Fine Arts and Pro Arte String Quartets; Often heard in modern American music and works by Debussy and Ravel; Jury member for numerous important competitions and awards; Gives lecture-concerts and masterclasses at leading colleges and universities throughout USA; Teacher at New England Conservatory, 1940–46; Professor of Piano at the Juilliard School from 1946; Music Editor for International Music Co; Gave recital at Juilliard in 1978 to celebrate 70th birthday; mem, National Society of Literature and Arts, 1975–. *Recordings:* For various labels. *Honours:* 1st Prize in Piano at the Paris Conservatoire; NAAAC Award for Outstanding Services to American Music; Honorary D.Mus, University of New Hampshire in 1962. *Address:* Juilliard School of Music, Piano Faculty, Lincoln Center Plaza, New York, NY 10023, USA.

WEBSTER, Gillian; Singer (soprano); b. 2 May 1964, Scotland; m. Brian Kay. *Education:* Studied at the Royal Northern College of Music, graduate, 1987; National Opera Studio. *Career:* Appearances with the English Bach festival, Scottish Opera, Glyndebourne Festival and English National Opera; Roles include Micaela, Pamina, Agilea (Handel's Teseo) and Ilia in Idomeneo; Sang Klim (debut) in The Making of the Representative from Planet 8 by Philip Glass for ENO; Covent Garden from 1988 as Servilia in La Clemenza di Tito and in Rigoletto, Peter Grimes, Médée, Elektra and Prince Igor; Other Royal Opera roles include Micaela and Euridice; Sang Micaela with Welsh National Opera, 1990; Television appearances include Gluck's Euridice at Covent Garden; Sang Mozart's Countess with the Royal Opera at the Shaftesbury Theatre, 1998. *Honours:* John Noble Award from Scottish Opera, 1986. *Current Management:* Athole Still International Management, Forresters Hall, 25–27 Westow Street, London, SE19 3RY, England. *Telephone:* (20) 8771-5271. *Fax:* (20) 8768-6600. *Website:* www.atholestill.com.

WEDD, Peter; Singer (Tenor); b. 1970, England. *Education:* Graduated Guildhall School, 1996, and National Opera Studio, 1998. *Career:* Season 1998–99 in Die Lustige Witwe and Paul Bunyan for the Royal Opera, Pavel Haas's Sarlatan and Zandonai's I Cavalieri di Ekebù at Wexford; Don José for Welsh National Opera, Britten's Lysander at Singapore, Tamino for European Chamber Opera and Federico in L'Arlesiana for Opera Holland Park; Covent Garden season 1999–2000 in Gawain, Der Rosenkavalier, The Greek Passion, Die Meistersinger and La Battaglia di Legnano; Concerts include Mozart's Requiem, Haydn's Mass in Time of War, Messiah, the Glagolitic Mass, St John Passion and The Dream of Gerontius; Britten's Serenade at Neuchâtel. *Address:* Music International, 13 Ardilaun Road, London N5 2QR, England.

WEGMAN, Rob Cornelis, MPhil, PhD; Dutch musicologist; b. 26 Jan. 1961, Emmen; m. Helene van Rossum; one s. one d. *Education:* Univ. of Amsterdam. *Career:* Asst Lecturer, Univ. of Amsterdam 1983–85; Researcher, Univ. of Amsterdam 1987–91; Weston Jr Research Fellow, Univ. of Oxford 1991–93, British Acad. Post-Doctoral Research Fellow 1993–95, concentrating on 15th-century polyphony; Asst Prof., Princeton Univ. 1995–2000, Assoc. Prof. 2000–. *Publications include:* edn of Choirbook of the Burgundian Court Chapel 1989, Born for the Muses: The Life and Masses of Jacob Obrecht 1994, 'Who was Josquin?' (chapter in The Josquin Companion) 2001, 'Historical Musicology: Is it Still Possible?' (chapter in A Critical Introduction to the Cultural Study of Music), The Crisis of Music in Early Modern Europe 1470–1530. *Honours:* Westrup Prize 1990, Music and Letters Award 1992, American Musicological Soc. Alfred Einstein Award 1996, Royal Musical Asscn Edward J. Dent Medal 1998. *Address:* Department of Music, Woolworth Center of Musical Studies, Princeton University, Princeton, NJ 08544, USA (office). *Telephone:* (609) 258-4248 (office). *Fax:* (609) 258-6793 (office). *E-mail:* rwegman@phoenix.princeton.edu (office). *Website:* www.princeton.edu (office).

WEGNER, John; Singer (Bass-baritone); b. 1950, Germany. *Education:* Victorian College of the Arts, Australia. *Career:* Australian Opera, 1981–92, as Britten's Theseus, Collatinus and Swallow, Mozart's Commendatore and Leporello, Escamillo, Baron Ochs, Banquo and Boris Godunov; Falstaff for Queensland Opera; 1992–95 with Karlsruhe Opera as Orestes, Wotan, Cardillac (Hindemith), Prince Igor and Iago; Wagner's Dutchman at Berne and Leipzig, Scarpia at Sydney and Copenhagen; Wotan and the Wanderer in The Ring, at Adelaide, 1999; Bayreuth debut, 1997, as Donner in Das Rheingold; Season 1999–2000 as Escamillo and Scarpia for Opera Australia, Wotan at Toulouse and Alberich in Götterdämmerung at Stuttgart; Season 2000–01 as the Dutchman, Boris and Wotan at Düsseldorf, Scarpia in Brussels, Kurwenal for Opera North in Leeds and on tour to Germany; Jochanaan in Salome at the Berlin Staatsoper and Telramund at Sydney. *Recordings:* Wotan/Wanderer in The Ring, from Stuttgart (Bella Music). *Honours:* Mo Award as Operatic Performer of the Year 1998–89 from the Australian Entertainment Industry. *Address:* Music International, 13 Ardilaun Road, London N5 2QR, England.

WEHOFSCHITZ, Kurt; Singer (Tenor); b. 3 May 1923, Vienna, Austria. *Education:* Studied at the Vienna Music Academy. *Career:* Debut: Linz in 1948 as Wilhelm Meister; Sang at Kiel, 1953–54, Munich, 1956–59 notably as Ulrich Greiner-Mars in the premiere of Hindemith's Harmonie der Welt in 1957; Sang at Düsseldorf, 1959–64, Frankfurt, 1964–66 notably in The Photo of the Colonel by Humphrey Searle, Düsseldorf in 1960 as Creon in the German premiere of Oedipe Re by Enescu; Guest appearances at Zürich, Lisbon, Rio de Janeiro and the Vienna Staatsoper; Sang at the Vienna Volksoper until 1980; Other roles have included Mozart's Belmont and Basilio, Leandro in Haydn's Mondo della Luna, Strauss's Leukippos and Flamand, Alfredo, Germont, Don Carlos, Riccardo and Tom Rakewell. *Recordings include:* Carmen.

WEIDENAAR, Reynold (Henry); Composer and Video Artist; b. 25 Sept. 1945, East Grand Rapids, Michigan, USA. *Education:* BMus, Composition, Cleveland Institute of Music, 1973; MA, 1980, PhD, 1989, Composition, New York University; Studied composition with Donald Erb and Brian Fennelly. *Compositions include:* Between The Motion And The Act Falls The Shadow, 1981; Love Of Line, Of Light And Shadow: The Brooklyn Bridge, 1982; Night Flame Ritual, 1983; The Stillness, 1985; The Thundering Scream Of The Seraphim's Delight, 1987; Long River, 1993; Long into the Night, Heavenly Music Flowed Out Of the Street, 1995; Swing Bridge, 1997. *Recordings:* The Tinsel Chicken Coop, 1978, 1982; Twilight Flight, 1986; Harmony, 1986; Imprint: Footfalls To Return, 1986; Night Flame Ritual, 1986. Bass Bars, videotape, 1988; Long River, for piano and tape, 1993; Magic Music from the Telharmonium, 1997; Swing Bridge, clarinet and tape, 1997. *Publications:* Magic Music From The Telharmonium, 1995. *Contributions:* New Music America: A Moveable Fest, in The Independent, 1984; Down Memory Lane: Forerunners of Music and The Moving Image and So You Want to Compose for The Moving Image, in Ear Magazine, 1985; Live Music and Moving Images: Composing and Producing The Concert Video, in Perspectives of New Music, 1986; The Alternators of the Telharmonium, 1986, in Proceedings of the International Computer Music Conference, 1991. *Address:* William Paterson University, Department of Communication, Wayne, NJ 07470, USA.

WEIDINGER, Christine; Opera Singer (Dramatic Coloratura); b. 31 March 1946, Springville, New York, USA; m. Kenneth Smith, 7 July 1976. *Education:* BA, Music, Grand Canyon College, Phoenix; Studied singing with Marlene Delavan, Phoenix, 1967–70, Adrian de Peyer, Wuppertal, and Dean Verhines in Los Angeles. *Career:* Debut: Musetta in La Bohème at the Metropolitan in 1972; Sang at Metropolitan Opera, 1972–76, Stuttgart and Bielefeld Operas, Germany, 1981–; Guest Artist at La Scala, State Opera, Vienna, Barcelona, Venice, Bologna, West Berlin and others; Regular Guest in Marseille; Specialist for bel-canto roles of Bellini and Donizetti; Interpreter of Constanze in Abduction from the Seraglio; Repertoire includes: Norma, Donna Anna, Electra in Idomeneo, Queen Elizabeth in Roberto Devereux, Gilda, Leonora in Trovatore, Mimi, Liu; Sang Constanze at Monte Carlo in 1988, Adèle in Le Comte Ory at Montreal in 1989, and Vitellia in La Clemenza di Tito at La Scala in 1990; Appeared at Cincinnati Opera in 1990 as Lucia di Lammermoor; Sang Violetta for San Diego Opera in 1991. *Recordings:* Handel's Rinaldo with Marilyn Horne; L'Africaine with Caballé and Domingo; Die Freunde von Salamanka by Schubert; Médée with Caballé and Lima; Mitridate by Mozart. *Honours:* National 1st Prize, Metropolitan Opera Auditions, 1972. *Current Management:* Robert Lombardo Associates. *Address:* c/o Robert Lombardo, 1 Harkness Plaza, 61 West 62nd Street, Suite 6F, New York 10023, USA.

WEIGLE, Jorg-Peter; Conductor; b. 1953, Greifswald, Germany. *Education:* Studied at the Thomasschule, Leipzig, 1963–71; Hochschule für Musik, East Berlin from 1973. *Career:* First kapellmeister at the State Symphony Orchestra of Neubrandenburg, 1978–80; Conductor of the Leipzig Radio Chorus, 1980; Chief Conductor of the Dresden Philharmonic Orchestra; Repertoire has included Bach's Christmas Oratorio, St John Passion and B Minor Mass, symphonies by Beethoven, Haydn, Mozart, Shostakovich and Schubert, and Janáček's Sinfonietta; Visited Wales and the West Country with the Dresden Philharmonic in 1989, with works by Beethoven, Brahms, Weber and Tchaikovsky, Hamburg and Spain in 1989 and Czechoslovakia in 1990; Season 1990–91 included Mahler's Das klagende Lied, Haydn's Symphony No. 92, Mozart's Requiem and Concertante K364, Sibelius's Symphonies 2, 3 and 7, Brahms' 2nd Symphony and D Minor Concerto, Berg's Violin Concerto; Concert performance of Meyerbeer's Il Crociato in Egitto, to celebrate the bicentenary of the composer's birth. *Recordings:* Albeniz' Iberia Suite; Falla's Three Cornered Hat; Mozart's Horn Concertos, Arias and Duets; Ravel's Rhapsodie Espagnole; Reger's Böcklin Tone Pictures and Mozart Variations. *Address:* Dresden Philharmonic Orchestra, Kulturpalast am Altmarkt, 8012 Dresden, Germany.

WEIKERT, Ralf; Conductor; b. 10 Nov. 1940, St Florian, Linz, Austria. *Education:* Studied at the Bruckner Conservatory Linz, the State Academy Vienna with Hans Swarowsky. *Career:* Coach, Conductor at the Landestheater Salzburg 1963; Concerts in Austria, Scandinavia from 1965; Conductor at the Bonn Opera 1966, Music Director 1968; Salzburg Festival (concert) 1971; Guest Conductor, Royal Opera Copenhagen, 1972; with works by Mozart, Verdi, Stravinsky; Hamburg Staatsoper from 1975, with Don Quichotte, works by Mozart, Puccini and Donizetti; Vienna Staatsoper debut 1974, Il Trovatore; Zürich Opera 1976–80, with Le nozze di Figaro, Arabella, Fidelio, La Cenerentola and Il Barbiere di Siviglia; Deutsche Oper Berlin 1978–80, Figaro and Don Pasquale; US debut 1980, with the City Opera's Giulio Cesare in New York and Los Angeles; Teatro La Fenice Venice 1981, Tancredi by Rossini; Further engagements in Barcelona, Munich, Vienna, 1968–88, Rosenkavalier, Carmen, Die Entführung and L'Elisir d'amore; Metropolitan Opera 1987–90, Elisir, Barbiere and Bohème; Finnish National Opera 2001–2004: La Fanciulla del West, Die Entführung aus dem Serail; Arabella; Der Ring des Nibelungen; Arena di Verona 1987, La Traviatza; Concert engagements with leading orchestras in Berlin, Vienna, Scandinavia, Paris, Hungary, West Germany, the United Kingdom (English Chamber Orchestra, Welsh National Orchestra, Academy of St. Martin in the Fields); Festival appearances at Salzburg (Mozart Matinées, Serenades and Cenerentola), Aix-en-Provence, Orange, Bregenz and Lucerne; Conducted Offenbach's Barbe Bleue at Stuttgart, 1996 and Fidelio at Catania, 1998. *Recordings:* Rossini Tancredi, Schoeck Lebendig Begraben; James Morris Recital; Love Duets Araiza-Lind; Barbiere di Siviglia, Metropolitan Opera; Alexander von Zemlinsky: kleider machen Leute, opera; Eugen d'Albut: Die totum Angem, Opera. *Address:* Neubruchstrasse 5, 8127 Zürich, Switzerland. *E-mail:* ralf.wekert@bluewin.ch.

WEIKL, Bernd; Singer (Baritone); b. 29 July 1942, Vienna, Austria. *Education:* Hannover Musikhochschule. *Career:* Sang Ottokar in Der Freischütz, Hannover, 1968; Appeared at Deutsche Oper am Rhein, Düsseldorf, 1970–73, Bayreuth Festival from 1972, as Wolfram, Amfortas and Hans Sachs, more than 160 performances in all; Member of Deutsche Oper Berlin from 1974, debut as Eugene Onegin; Covent Garden debut in 1975 as Rossini's Figaro; Later sang Giordano's Gerard and Strauss's Mandryka in London; Sang at Vienna Staatsoper in 1976 at premiere of Von Einem's Kabale und Liebe; Metropolitan Opera debut in 1977 as Wolfram with later New York appearances as Mandryka, Jokanaan in Salome and Beethoven's Don Fernando; Guest engagements at La Scala Milan, Bavarian State Opera, Hamburg State Opera and Salzburg Festival; Further appearances as Hans Sachs under Sawallisch at La Scala and under Dohnányi at Covent Garden in 1990; Sang Iago at Stuttgart in 1990, Boccanegra at Hamburg in 1991 and Dutchman at Bayreuth in 1990; Sang Sachs in a new production of Die Meistersinger at the Metropolitan in 1993; Jochanaan at San Francisco, 1997; Kurwenal in Tristan and Isolde at Munich, 1998; Season 2000–01 as the Dutchman at Covent Garden, Kurwenal in Hamburg, Hans Sachs at the Deutsche Oper Berlin and Falstaff in Munich; Also sings lieder and oratorio; Television appearances include Mendelssohn's Elijah, from Israel, 1983. *Recordings:* Opera sets include L'Elisir d'amore, Tristan und Isolde, Palestrina, Der Freischütz, Don Giovanni, Alceste, and Lohengrin; Solo in Ein Deutsches Requiem by Brahms. *Address:* c/o Theateragentur Dr G. Hilbert, Maximillianstrasse 22, D–80539 München, Germany.

WEIL, Bruno; Conductor; b. 24 Nov. 1949, Hahnstatten, Germany. *Education:* Studied with Franco Ferrara in Italy and with Hans Swarowsky in Vienna. *Career:* Conducted at the opera houses of Wiesbaden and Brunswick; Debut with the Berlin Radio Symphony Orchestra in 1977; Concerts with the Berlin Philharmonic from 1979; Music Director of Augsburg Opera, 1979–89; Debut at the Deutsche Oper Berlin in 1980 with Weill's Die Sieben Todsünden; Salzburg Festival from 1982 including Don Giovanni at the 1988 Festival; Conducted Fidelio for Radio France in Paris, 1984, and led the Yomiuri Nippon Symphony Orchestra in Japan; In 1985 conducted Aida at the Vienna Staatsoper and Ariadne auf Naxos at Bordeaux, and in 1986 Le nozze di Figaro at Trieste; Initiated series of Mozart operas in joint production with the Vienna Volksoper and Austrian television, 1987; Conducted Die Entführung aus dem Serail in Bonn and Die Zauberflöte in Karlsruhe, 1987; US debut in 1988 in a Schubertiade in New York; Concerts in Netherlands with the Residentie Orchestra and Rotterdam Philharmonic; Concerts with the Los Angeles Philharmonic and the BBC Scottish Symphony from season 1988–90; Tour of Germany with the English Chamber Orchestra; Season 1990–91 with the Orchestre National de France and the Montreal Symphony; Conducted Brahms with the Orchestra of the Age of Enlightenment, London, 1997. *Recordings:* Various albums with the Deutsche Philharmonie. *Honours:* Second Prize, Herbert von Karajan Conductors' Competition in 1979. *Current Management:* Ingpen & Williams Ltd, 7 St George's Court, 131 Putney Bridge Road, London, SW15 2PA, England.

WEIL, Tibor V.; Singer (baritone), Pianist, Cellist, Impresario and Economist; b. 16 May 1942, Hungary. *Education:* Economist, Mackenzie University, São Paulo, Brazil; MA, New York University, USA; Pianist and cellist, Budapest Music High School, Salvador Music High School, Pro Arte Music High School. *Career:* Debut: Piano and Cello in 1960; Concerts, television appearances in São Paulo, Rio de Janeiro, and Salvador, 1958–; Regular chamber music performances; Frequent concerts as lieder and light opera singer, sacred music and requiems, 1989–; mem, Pro Arte, São Paulo; Managing Adviser, Centro de Musica Brasiliera. *Honours:* Viscua Konservatoire Scholarship, 1956; Pro Arte Scholarship, 1959. *Address:* TAW Promotions SP, Rua Angatuba 80, Bairro, Pacaembu, CEP 01247 São Paulo SP, Brazil.

WEILERSTEIN, Donald; Violinist; b. 14 March 1940, Washington DC, USA. *Education:* BS; MS, Juilliard School of Music, 1966. *Career:* Debut: New York, 1963; Founding First Violinist, Cleveland Quartet, 1969–89; Professor of Violin and Chamber Music; Cleveland Institute of

Music, 1967–71, 1989–, SUNY at Buffalo, 1971–76, Eastman School of Music, NY, 1976–89; mem, American String Teachers' Association. *Recordings:* Complete Brahms Quartets; Complete Beethoven Quartets; Schubert 2 cello Quintet; Schubert Trout Quintet; Mendelssohn and Schubert Octets; Complete Violin and Piano and Solo Violin Works of Ernest Bloch; Sonatas of Dohnányi and Janáček; The Complete Sonatas of Robert Schumann with pianist Ulvian Hornik Weilerstein, 1995; The Complete Sonatas and Partitas of J. S. Bach, 2000. *Publications:* Chapter on Violin Technique in Medical Problems of Instrumental Musicians, 2000. *Honours:* NEA Grant; Grammy nominations for recorded works; Prizewinner, Munich Competition for violin and piano duo. *Current Management:* Jane Deckoff. *Address:* 2645 Fairmount Blvd, Cleveland Heights, OH 44106, USA.

WEIN, Erika; Singer (Mezzo-Soprano); b. 2 Sept. 1928, Vienna, Austria. *Education:* Studied at the Vienna Music Academy with Erik Werba. *Career:* Sang at the Vienna Volksoper, 1952–53, Bremen, 1953–59, and Düsseldorf, 1959–64; Engagements at the Zürich Opera, 1964–80, notably in the premieres of Sutermeister's Madame Bovary in 1967, and Kelterborn's Ein Engel Kommt nach Babylon, 1977; Guest appearances in Berlin, the State Operas of Munich, Hamburg, Stuttgart, Frankfurt and Cologne, at the Holland Festival, Florence, Lyon, Buenos Aires, Paris, San Francisco and Turin; Roles included: Carmen, Azucena, Amneris, Eboli, Ulrica, Ortud, Fricka, Brangane, Venus, Orpheus, Marina in Boris Godunov, Clytemnestra and Berg's Marie; Concert showings in works by Bach, Beethoven and Brahms; Lieder recitals and concerts in Germany, Switzerland, Spain and Austria. *Recordings include:* Highlights from Rigoletto and Nabucco. *Address:* c/o Opernhaus Zürich, Falkenstrasse 1, 8008 Zürich, Switzerland.

WEINGARTNER, Elisabeth; Singer (Mezzo-Soprano); b. 23 Jan. 1938, Sissach, Switzerland. *Education:* Studied in Basle and with Res Fischer in Stuttgart. *Career:* Sang at the Basle Opera, 1973–81 and made guest appearances at Nantes, Paris, Trier and Cannes; Roles have included Dorabella in Così fan tutte by Mozart, Carmen by Bizet, Isabella in L'Italiana in Algeri, Idamantes in Idomeneo, Geneviève in Pelléas, Annina, and the Hostess in Boris Godunov; Sang at Strasbourg in 1984 in the premiere of H H Ulysse by Prodromidès; Concert and lieder engagements in France and Switzerland and at Liège, Stuttgart and Vienna; Sang in Verdi's Requiem in Paris with Orchestra Lamoureux and Dvořák's Requiem at San Sebastian in Spain. *Recordings include:* H H Ulysse. *Address:* Opéra du Rhin, 19 Place Brogile, 67008 Strasbourg Cédex, France.

WEINSCHENK, Hans-Jorg; Singer (Tenor); b. 14 Nov. 1955, Stuttgart, Germany. *Career:* Sang in Opera at Heidelberg, 1974–76, and Wuppertal, 1976–80; Member of the Zürich Opera, 1981–85, and Theater am Gärtnerplatz Munich from 1984; Guest appearances at Lausanne in 1985, and the Grand Opera Paris in 1986; Sang in the premiere of Der Meister und Margarita by Kunad, Karlsruhe, 1986; Roles have included such buffo and character repertory as Pedrillo, the Witch in Hansel and Gretel, Monostatos, David in Die Meistersinger and the Steuermann in Fliegende Holländer; Frequent concert engagements; Sang in The Cunning Little Vixen at Karlsruhe, 1996 and in Hindemith/Milhaud/Weill/Toch programme, 1998; Season 2000–01 as Flaminio in A. Scarlatti's Il trionfo dell'onore, at Halle, Victorin in Die tote Stadt, Mozart's Basilio and Finn in Ruslan and Lyudmila, at Karlsruhe. *Address:* c/o Badische Staatstheater Karlsruhe, Baumersterstrasse, 11, Pf 1449, W-7500 Karlsruhe, Germany.

WEIR, Dame Gillian Constance; Concert Organist; b. 17 Jan. 1941, New Zealand; m. Lawrence I. Phelps 4 Aug. 1972. *Education:* Royal College of Music, London; further studies with Nadia Boulanger, Marie-Claire Alain and Anton Heiller. *Career:* debut, Poulenc Concerto at First Night of the London Proms, and solo recital, Royal Festival Hall, 1965; concerto appearances with leading British and foreign orchestras; regular appearances at international festivals in Edinburgh, Aldeburgh, Proms, and Europalia, performing at the Royal Festival and Albert Halls, Lincoln and Kennedy Centers, Palais des Beaux Arts and Sydney Opera House; frequent radio and television appearances worldwide, including the BBC series The King of Instruments, as presenter and performer, 1989; adjudicator at international competitions; Artist-in-Residence at several univs, giving lectures and masterclasses internationally; Poulenc's Concerto at the Last Night of the 1999 London Proms. *Recordings include:* Poulenc Concerto, 1990–96; Complete Organ Works of Olivier Messiaen, 1994 (re-issued 2003), Cesar Franck, 1997; The Art of Gillian Weir (5 CDs), 1999; Organ Masters (3 CDs), 2001; Poulence/Barber/Petit Concertos, 2002. *Publications:* chapter on organ works of Messiaen in The Messiaen Companion, 1996; professional journals. *Honours:* CBE, 1989; DBE, 1996; Hon. DMus, Univ. of Victoria, NZ, 1983, Univ. of Hull, 1999, Univ. of Exeter, 2001; Hon. DLitt, Univ. of Huddersfield, 1997; Hon. DUniv, Univ. of Central England, 2001; Hon. mem., RAM, 1989; Hon. Fellowship, Royal College of Music, 2000; Hon. DMus (Leicester), 2003; Evening Standard Award, 1998–99; Silver Medal of the Albert

Schweitzer Asscn, Sweden, 1998. *Current Management:* Denny Lyster Artists' Management, PO Box 155, Stanmore, Middlesex HA7 3WF, England; Karen McFarlane Artists Inc., 2385 Fenwood Road, Cleveland, OH 44118-3803, USA. *Website:* gillianweir.com.

WEIR, Judith; Composer; b. 11 May 1954, Cambridge, England. *Education:* Studied composition with John Tavener; King's College, Cambridge, 1973–76 with Robin Holloway; Tanglewood, 1975 with Gunther Schuller. *Career:* Southern Arts Association's Composer-in-Residence, 1976–79; Music Department, Glasgow University, 1979–82; Creative Arts Fellowship at Trinity College, Cambridge, 1983–85; Composer-in-Residence, Royal Scottish Academy of Music and Drama, 1988–91; Fairbairn Composer in Association with The City of Birmingham Symphony Orchestra, 1995–97. *Compositions:* Stage: The Black Spider, opera in 3 acts, 1984, The Consolations of Scholarship, musical drama, 1985, A Night at The Chinese Opera, opera in 3 acts, 1986, The Vanishing Bridegroom, opera, 1990, Blond Eckbert, opera, 1993; Orchestral: Music Untangled, 1991–92, Heroic Strokes of The Bow, 1992, Moon and Star, 1995; Forest, 1995; Piano Concerto, 1997; Certum ex incertis, 1998; Natural History, 1998; We Are Shadows, chorus and orchestra, 1999; Vocal: King Harald's Saga, 1979, Missa del Cid, 1988, Heaven Ablaze in His Breast, for Voices, 2 Pianos and 8 Dancers, 1989; Scipio's Dream, 1991; Combattimento II, 1993; Our Revels now are Ended for female voices and ensemble, 1995; All the Ends of the Earth, for chorus and percussion, 1999; All the Ends of the Earth, 1999; woman.life.song, for soprano and orchestra, 2000; The welcome arrival of rain, for orchestra, 2001. *Recordings:* A Night at the Chinese Opera. *Honours:* Critics' Circle Award for the Most Outstanding Contribution to British Musical Life, 1994. *Address:* c/o Chester Music, 8–9 Frith Street, London W1D 3JB, England.

WEIR, Scot; Singer (Tenor); b. 1954, New Mexico, USA. *Education:* Studied at Colorado University and in Graz. *Career:* Sang at the Gelsenkirchen Opera, 1981–85, notably as Don Ottavio, Lenski and Xerxes; Wiesbaden Opera, 1985–89, as Almaviva, Medoro in Haydn's Orlando Paladino, Belfiore in La finta giardiniera, and Veit in Lortzing's Undine; Sang Hylas in Les Troyens at Brussels (1992) and has appeared as guest in Canada, Israel, Japan and the USA; Sang Monteverdi's Ulisse at Vienna, 1998. *Recordings include:* Franck's Les Béatitudes; Mozart C minor Mass. *Address:* Théâtre Royale de la Monnaie, 4 Leopoldstrasse, 1000 Brussels, Belgium.

WEISBERG, Arthur; Bassoonist, Conductor and Teacher; b. 4 April 1931, New York City, USA. *Education:* Studied bassoon with Simon Kovar, conducting with Jean Morel, Juilliard School of Music, New York. *Career:* Bassoonist with Houston Symphony Orchestra, Baltimore Symphony Orchestra, and Cleveland Orchestra; Member of New York Woodwind Quintet, 1956–70; Founder-Director of Contemporary Chamber Ensemble, NY, 1969–; Chief Conductor, Iceland Symphony Orchestra, Reykjavík, 1987–88; Guest Conductor with various orchestras including New York Philharmonic, 1983, 1984; Teacher, Juilliard School of Music, 1960–68, State University of New York, Stony Brook, 1971–89, Yale University, 1975–89. *Publications:* The Art of Wind Playing, 1973. *Address:* 12008 South 35th Ct, Phoenix, AZ 85044, USA.

WEISBROD, Annette; Pianist; b. 9 Dec. 1937, Blackburn, Lancashire, England; m. Charles Kirmess, 21 Jan 1967. *Education:* Teaching Diploma, Chamber Music Diploma, Zürich Conservatory; Soloist and Concert Diploma, Basle Conservatoire. *Career:* Debut: Wigmore Hall in London, 1960; Concert appearances world-wide; Radio and television appearances in Switzerland, Germany, England, France, the former Yugoslavia and China; Professor at Berne Conservatoire; mem, Swiss Tonkünstler Verein; Swiss Musikpädagogischer Verein; International Piano Teachers Association; Soroptimist International, Zürich; Business and Professional Women, Zürich. *Recordings:* Over 50 albums including: Haydn Trios with the Swiss Festival Trio; Complete Works for Piano and Cello by Beethoven; Several piano concertos and many piano works. *Address:* Heuelstr 33, 8032 Zürich, Switzerland.

WEISE, Klaus; Conductor; b. 30 Jan. 1936, Kolpin, Poland. *Education:* Studied at Berlin, Dresden and Leipzig. *Career:* Conducted first at Wuppertal, then principal conductor of the Essen Opera; Musical director at Fribourg Opera, 1978–81, Kiel, 1981–85, and Dortmund, 1985–90; Director of the Nice Opera and Philharmonic Orchestra, from 1990. *Address:* Théâtre de l'Opéra de Nice, 4 and 6 Rue St François de Paule, 06300 Nice, France.

WEISEL-CAPSOUTO, Robin; Singer (Soprano); b. 1952, USA. *Education:* Studied at Oberlin College, University of Illinois, with Jennie Tourel in Jerusalem and with Heather Harper in London. *Career:* Debut: Sang Vivaldi's Gloria with the Jerusalem Symphony Orchestra in 1974; Sang in Mahler's 4th with Israel Philharmonic, 1976; Opera engagements in USA and Israel as Gluck's Amor, Lucy in The Beggar's Opera, and in La Voix Humaine, Le Roi David, Bacchus and Ariadne by Thomas Arne and Rameau's Les Fêtes d'Hébé; Sang Zerlina with New England Opera Company in 1984, and The Governess in The Turn of

The Screw for New Israeli Opera in 1992; Concert repertoire includes Bach's B minor Mass, Carissimi's Jephté, Solomon and other oratorios by Handel.

WEISS, Ferdinand; Composer and Educator; b. 6 June 1933, Vienna, Austria; m. Ingeborg Scheibenreiter, 16 Sept 1967, 2 s. *Education:* Diplomas: Music, 1958, Composition (prize) 1960, Conducting (prize) 1961, Flute, Viennese Academy of Music. *Career:* Debut: As Composer, Eisenstadt, 1957; Freelance composer, private teacher of music theory, conductor and orchestra musician, 1960–; Music Master, Vienna Conservatory and Baden Pedagogische Academie; Manager, Concert Chamber Ensemble, Lower Austria Composer's Society; President of Inoek. *Compositions:* About 245 works including: 3 Symphonies, Concertos for Flute, Oboe, Clarinet, Trumpet and Trombone, Chamber music, Lieder; About 1000 performances, concerts and radio in Austria, USA, Italy, Argentina, Germany, France, Netherlands, Hungary, Sweden, Azerbaijan, Peru, Syria, Bulgaria, Turkey, Belgium, Portugal, Spain, Norway, Poland, England, Switzerland, Finland, Australia and Japan; Quattrofonia for Saxophone Quartet at Carnegie Hall; 5 Scènes pour Quatuor De Guitares in Paris; a sa fin for orchestra, 1994; Avec un Souffle du Tristesse, for flute and string orchestra, 1997; Quartetto Egiziano, Première at Opera House, Cairo, 2002. *Address:* Christalnigg-Gasse 11, 2500 Baden, Austria.

WEISS, Howard A., BM, MM; American violinist, conductor, concert-master and educator; b. 1935, Chicago, IL. *Education:* Chicago Musical College, Roosevelt University. *Career:* founder, Music Director, Conductor, Rochester Philharmonic Youth Orchestra, 1970–89, with 12 tours including England, Scotland, 1984, Germany, Austria, Switzerland, 1986, Dominican Republic, 1987, Alaska, 1988; Jamaica, 1989, also on Voice of America; Advisory Board, Young Audiences of Rochester, 1975–; Rochester Chamber Orchestra, 1981–; Professor, Violin: Eastman School of Music, Rochester, 1981–, Nazareth College, Rochester, 1983–85; Concertmaster: Chicago Chamber Orchestra, 1962–70, San Francisco Ballet Orchestra, 1962, Virginia Symphony, 1964, Rochester Philharmonic, 1967–87 (Concertmaster Emeritus, 1987–), Eastern Music Festival, Greensboro, North Carolina, 1976–80, Grand Teton Music Festival Seminar, Jackson Hole, Wyoming, 1983–86, Rochester Oratorio Society, 1987–, Bear Lake Music Festival, Utah, 1992–93; Music Director, Conductor String Orchestra, Siena Festival, Italy, 1998–; 1st Violinist, Cleveland Orchestra, 1965–67; Violin Soloist, over 45 concerti with Cleveland Orchestra, Rochester and New Orleans Philharmonics, Chicago Grant Park Symphony, Cincinnati, Chicago and Rochester Chamber Orchestras, Siena Festival, Italy; Violin soloist with conductors James Levine, David Zinman, Alexander Schneider, Walter Hendl and Gerard Schwarz; Soloist in the US premiere of the Carl Nielsen Violin Concerto, 1967; Soloist in the Rochester, New York premieres of the violin concertos of Berg, Nielsen and Vaughan Williams; Soloist, complete concerti for violin and orchestra of J. S. Bach (5), Rochester Bach Festival, of Haydn (3), Rochester Chamber Orchestra; Violinist of Brockport Piano Trio, 1971–74; Leader, Hartwell String Quartet, 1975–78; Participant, Casals Festival, Puerto Rico, 1975–80; Chamber music with Misha Dichter, Leonard Rose, Lynn Harrell, Yo-Yo Ma; Elly Ameling, Jaime Laredo, Walter Trampler, Lillian Fuchs, James Buswell, Gary Karr, Alan Civil, Lukas Foss. *Recordings:* Amram Elegy for Violin and Orchestra, David Zinman, Rochester Philharmonic; Music Director, Conductor, Rochester Philharmonic Youth Orchestra. *Honours:* Outstanding Graduate of 1966, Roosevelt University, 1973; Monroe County (New York) Medallion, 1986. *Address:* 228 Castlebar Road, Rochester, NY 14610, USA.

WEISSENBERG, Alexis; Pianist; b. 26 July 1929, Sofia, Bulgaria. *Education:* Piano and composition studies with Pancho Viadiguerov at age 3, Olga Samarov, Juilliard School of Music, New York, USA, 1946. *Career:* Debut: Concert with New York Philharmonic under George Szell at Carnegie Hall, New York; 1st orchestral concert in Israel in 1944; Concert tour to South Africa in 1944; USA coast to coast tour and concerts in Paris, Vienna, Madrid, Milan, with Philadelphia Orchestra under Eugene Ormandy in 1951; Soloist playing Tchaikovsky's 1st Piano Concerto with Berlin Philharmonic Orchestra under Herbert von Karajan in 1966; Invited performer for many leading conductors and orchestras world-wide including Abbado, Bernstein, Karajan and Ormandy, 1967–; Played at Royal Festival Hall in London in 1974; Various world tours with New Philharmonic Orchestra under Maazel. *Recordings include:* Music by Beethoven, Chopin, Tchaikovsky, Rachmaninov, Bach and Schumann. *Address:* c/o Michal Schmidt, Thea Dispeker Inc, 59 East 54th Street, New York, NY 10022, USA.

WEITHAAS, Antje; Concert Violinist; b. 1966, Germany. *Education:* Hanns Eisler Hochschule, Berlin. *Career:* frequent concerts with the Deutsches Symphony Orchestra and Vladimir Ashkenazy, Leipzig Gewandhaus Orchestra, Suisse Romande and Acad. of St Martin in the Fields; Los Angeles Philharmonic Orchestra, Boston Symphony Orchestra and Minneapolis Orchestra; Philharmonia, BBC Symphony Orchestra, Dresdner Staatskapelle and Scottish Chamber Orchestra; Season 1995–96 with recitals at the Bath Festival and Wigmore Hall, London, San Francisco Symphony Orchestra Debut Series and in Toronto; Season 1996–97 with the Orchestre de Paris, Zürich Tonhalle, Gothenburg Symphony Orchestra, BBC Symphony Orchestra, and tour of Germany with the Bournemouth Symphony Orchestra; Season 1998–99 with Scottish Chamber Orchestra, English Northern Philharmonic and BBC Symphony Orchestra; other engagements with the Royal Liverpool Philharmonic Orchestra and the Hallé Orchestra; with the Trio Ex Aequo, resident at the Vancouver Festival; Season 1999–2000 with the Royal Liverpool Philharmonic, Brabant and Residentie Orchestras, Orchestra de Palermo and the Malaysian Philharmonic; Season 2001–02 with the Tokyo Metropolitan, Copenhagen Philharmonic, Ulster, Capetown Philharmonic and Swedish Chamber Orchestras; Season 2002–03 with the Gothenburg Symphony, BBC Philharmonic, Scottish Chamber and Lisbon Gulbenkian Orchestras; regularly performs chamber music with the Ex Aequo Trio, Vancouver Festival resident 1998–99; festivals include Kuhmo, Bath, Vancouver, Heimbach, Mondsee, Risör and Delft; plays Peter Greiner violin, 2001. *Honours:* winner of Wieniawski, Kreisler and Joseph Joachim Competitions. *Current Management:* CLB Management, 28 Earlsmead Road, London, NW10 5QB, England. *Telephone:* (20) 8964-4513. *Fax:* (20) 8964-4514. *Website:* www.clbmanagement.co.uk.

WELBORN, Tracey; Singer (Tenor); b. 1967, Stoneville, North Carolina, USA. *Education:* Curtis Institute of Music, Philadelphia. *Career:* School teacher until 1989; Opera engagements with Lausanne Opera, Boston Lyric Opera, Spoleto USA, Opera Co of Philadelphia and Portland Opera; Season 1993–94 with Rossini's Lindoro for Utah Opera, Ernesto and Tamino for Canadian Opera and Gluck's Pylade at Strasbourg; Season 1994–95 with Paris in La Belle Hélène for Scottish Opera, Ferrando at Pittsburgh and Jupiter in Semele at Spoleto, Italy; Concerts include Candide with the San Francisco Symphony Orchestra, Messiah with the Baltimore Symphony Orchestra, Honegger's King David, and Mozart's Requiem; Phoenix Symphony Orchestra in Bach's St Matthew Passion; Season 1997 with Mozart's Belmonte at Edmonton, Don Ottavio at Costa Mesa and in Prokoviev's The Duenna at Geneva; title role in Rossini's Le Comte Ory, at Glyndebourne; Season 1998 with Bernstein's Candide at Turin and in Prokofiev's Duenna at Geneva. *Recordings include:* Paolo in Il Matrimonio Segreto. *Honours:* Winner, Washington International Competition and Mario Lanza Competition. *Address:* c/o Allied Artists, 42 Montpelier Square, London SW7 1JZ, England.

WELCHER, Dan; Composer and Conductor; b. 2 March 1948, Rochester, New York, USA. *Education:* BMus, 1969, Eastman School at Rochester (composition with Samuel Adler); MM, 1972, Manhattan School of Music and postgraduate studies in electronic music at the Aspen Music School, 1972. *Career:* Bassoonist with the Rochester Philharmonic Orchestra, 1968–69, and US Military Band at West Point, 1969–72; Louisville Orchestra, 1972–78; Assistant Conductor with the Austin, Texas Symphony Orchestra (1980–90); Faculty of University of Texas 1978, Full Professor from 1989; Faculty of Aspen Music Festival, 1976–93. *Compositions include:* Flute Concerto, 1974; 2 Wind Quintets, 1972, 1977; Concerto da Camera for bassoon and chamber orchestra, 1975; Trio for violin, cello and piano, 1976; The Visions of Merlin for orchestra, 1980; Partita for horn, violin and piano, 1980; Vox Femina for soprano and ensemble, 1984; Quintet for clarinet and strings, 1984; Prairie Light for orchestra, 1985; Arches: An Impression for concert band, 1985; Evening Scenes: Three Poems of James Agee, 1985; Della's Gift, opera, 1986; The Yellowstone Fires for wind ensemble, 1988; Clarinet Concerto, 1989; Bridges, 5 pieces for strings, 1989; 2 string quartets, 1987, 1992; 2 symphonies, 1992, 1994; Violin Concerto, 1993; Piano Concerto, Shiva's Drum, 1994; Zion for wind ensemble, 1994; Bright Wings, for orchestra, 1996; Brass Quintet, 1983; Oratorio, JFK: The Voice of Peace, 1999; Oboe Concerto Venti di Mare, 1999; Orchestral works: Beyond Sight, 1999; Zion, 2000; Wind Ensemble Works: Symphony #3 (Shaker Life), 1998; Perpetual Song, 2000; Songs without Words, 2001; Minstrels of the Kells, 2002; Glacier, 2003. *Honours:* Residencies, MacDowell Colony, 1989, and Bellagio, 1997; Composer-in-Residence with the Honolulu Symphony Orchestra, 1990–93; Guggenheim Fellowship, 1997; 3 National Endowment for the Arts awards;Artistic Advisory Board, Lotte Lehmann Foundation, 01–. *Address:* c/o ASCAP, ASCAP Building, One Lincoln Plaza, New York, NY 10023, USA.

WELKER, Hartmut; Opera Singer (Bass-Baritone); b. 27 Oct. 1941, Velbert, Rhineland, Germany; m. Edeltraut, 2 July 1982, 1 s., 1 d. *Education:* Studied for technical career, took up singing, 1972. *Career:* Debut: Opera, Aachen, 1974; British debut, Edinburgh Festival with London Symphony Orchestra/Abbado, 1983; Aachen Opera, 1974–80; Since then has had 3-year contract with Karlsruhe Opera; Sang at La Scala (Lohengrin with Abbado), Geneva, Paris (Khovanshchina); Sang Don Pizarro (Fidelio), Madrid and at Maggio Musicale, Florence, Italy and for Scottish Opera, 1984; Appeared in Hamburg, Munich and Stuttgart; Boris Godunov in North America with Chicago Symphony Orchestra/Abbado; Vienna State Opera, Berlin and Hamburg in productions of Fidelio, Flying Dutchman, Salome, Lohengrin; Covent Garden debut in Fidelio, 1986; Sang also with Philharmonia Orchestra/ Muti, also at Turin, Vienna, Madrid, Bologna, Naples, Tokyo, Chicago; Season 1988 included appearances in San Francisco, Berlin, Geneva, with further visits to La Scala, Covent Garden and Salzburg; Sang in London, 1986–89, as Pizarro and Kaspar; Theater an der Wien and Turin, 1989 in Schubert's Fierrabras and as Wozzeck; Telramund in Lohengrin at the Vienna Staatsoper and the Deutsche Oper Berlin, 1990; Other roles include Kurwenal, Klingsor, Macbeth, Carlos in La Forza del Destino; Amonasro, Barnaba and Scarpia; Sang Pizarro in Fidelio at the Metropolitan, 1991; Sang Wozzeck at Catania, 1996; Pizarro in Beethoven's Leonore at the Théâtre de Champs Elysées, Paris, 1998; Season 2000 as Alberich at Cologne and Scarpia at Essen; Kurwenal, Amonasro and Wotan for Karlsruhe Opera. *Recordings include:* Zemlinksy's Der Traumgörge as Kaspar/Hans; Notre Dame by F. Schmidt as Archidiakonus; Fierrabras, Brutamonte, 1992, Fidelio (Pizarro), Lohengrin (Telramund); Das Wunder der Heliane, Korngold, 1992; Season 1997–98, Semperoper, Dresden as Kurwenal, Holländer, Pizarro; Further roles as Amfortas in Parsifal, and Wotan and Alberich in Wagner's Ring, Bayreuth, 2000. *Recordings:* Arcesius in Die toten Augen, d'Albert, 1997. *Address:* Frühlingstrasse 10, 76327 Pfintzal/ Wöschbach, Germany.

WELLEJUS, Henning; Composer; b. 23 Aug. 1919, Roskilde, Denmark; m. Inge Osterby, 2 c. *Education:* Studied with composer Svend Erik Tarp and conductor Giovanni Di Bella; University of Copenhagen. *Career:* Debut: Copenhagen; mem, Danish Composers Society. *Compositions include:* 3 Symphonies; 4 Concerts for violin and orchestra, oboe and orchestra, cello and orchestra, and piano and orchestra; Symphonic Fantasies: The History of the Year, Nina; Our Childhood's Friends and from Hans Christian Anderson's picturebook, 2 suites from ballet, The Swan; Wind Quintet; Flute Serenade Just for Fun, for flute, violin, viola and cello; 2 String Quartets; Several Songs; Trio for clarinet, viola and piano; The Dream, ballet; Passacaglia for orchestra; A Freedom Overture; Copenhagen Rhapsody; A Danish Summer Pastorale; Grates Nune Omnes Reddamus Domini, for soprano, chorus and orchestra; A Danish Requiem for soprano, baritone and orchestra; A Trio for Piano, Violin and Oboe; 3 Symphonic Fantasies, Dionysia, A Summer Morning in Hornboek and the Distant Morningsong of the Stars; a Trio for Violin, Viola and Cello; Operas; The Changed Bridegroom and Barbara; Several songs and numerous other works. *Recordings:* CD of music of his concert for violin and orchestra; CD of orchestra music; CD of Wind Quintet. *Honours:* Lange-Müller Stipendich, 1956; Aksel Agerbys Mindelegat, 1957; Det Anckerske Legat, 1958; Aügüst and Theodore Kassels Familie-og, Künstnerlegat, 1987; Cross, Order of Knighthood, Denmark. *Address:* Godthaabsvej 99, 2000 Frederiksberg, Denmark.

WELLER, Dieter; Singer (Bass Baritone); b. 25 May 1937, Essen, Germany; m. Dorte Fischer. *Education:* Studied with Erwin Rottgen in Essen; Further study in Cologne. *Career:* Debut at Bremerhaven, 1963–66 as Padre Guardiano in La Forza del Destino; Member of the Frankfurt Opera from 1966; Appeared in San Francisco in 1974 as Wurm in Luisa Miller; Further appearances in Berlin, Düsseldorf, Hamburg, Brussels and Edinburgh; Sang at Teatro Regio Turin in 1983 in Berg's Lulu, at Metropolitan Opera in 1985 as the Music Master in Ariadne auf Naxos; Season 2000 as Joe in Mahagonny at Hamburg and Reimann's Lear for the Dresden Staatsoper; Many appearances in operas by Rossini, Lortzing, Weber, Smetana, Wagner and Wolf-Ferrari; Frequent concert engagements. *Recordings:* Der Freischütz and Martha; Der Zwerg by Zemlinsky.

WELLER, Walter; Conductor and Violinist; b. 30 Nov. 1939, Vienna, Austria; m. Elisabeth Samohyl, 1966, 1 s. *Education:* Studied violin at High School for Music and Dramatic Art, Vienna. *Career:* Member, 1946–, Soloist, 1951–, Violinist, Concertmaster, 1956–69, Vienna Philharmonic Orchestra; Founder and Director of Weller Quartet touring Europe, Asia and North America; Conductor, Vienna State Opera, 1969–, touring USA, Scandinavia, Israel, Italy, Netherlands, Spain, Switzerland, Belgium and France; Principal Conductor, Artistic Adviser, Royal Liverpool Philharmonic Orchestra, 1977–80; Principal Conductor, Royal Philharmonic Orchestra, London, 1980–85; President of the Rodewald Concert Society in England, 1984–, touring Japan, Germany, Scotland, Hong Kong, and Russia; Chief Guest Conductor of Royal Philharmonic Orchestra, London, 1985–; Conductor, Royal Scottish National Orchestra 1991–96; Chief Guest Conductor, National Orchestra of Spain, 1987–; Conducted Prince Igor at the Deutsche Staatsoper, Berlin, 1989; Principal Guest Conductor of the Royal Flanders Philharmonic Orchestra in Belgium, 1990; Music Director and Chief Conductor of the Basle Theatre and Symphony Orchestra from 1994; Has conducted Fidelio and Der Rosenkavalier for Scottish Opera, Der fliegende Holländer and Ariadne auf Naxos for English

National Opera; Der Freischütz at Bologna and Holländer at La Scala, Milan; Die Zauberflöte at Basle, 1996. *Honours:* Grand Prix du Disque Charles Cros; Beethoven Gold Medal; Mozart Interpretation Prize; Medal of Arts and Science, Austria, 1968; Great Silver Cross of Honour, for Services to the Republic of Austria, 1998. *Current Management:* Harrison/Parrott Ltd, 12 Penzance Place, London, W11 4PA, England. *Telephone:* (20) 7229 9166. *Fax:* (20) 7221 5042. *Website:* www .harrisonparrott.com.

WELLINGTON, Christopher Ramsay, MA, ARCM; British violist and viola d'amore player; b. 5 Feb. 1930, London, England; m. 1st Joanna Donat 1954; one s. one d.; m. 2nd Eileen Darlow 1988. *Education:* Univ. of Oxford, Royal College of Music. *Career:* Sadler's Wells Opera Orchestra, 1954–58; Philharmonia Orchestra, 1958–65; Principal Viola, London Bach Orchestra, Philomusica of London, Tilford Bach Orchestra; Principal Viola of Southern Pro Musica; Viola player of Zorian String Quartet, Amici String Quartet, Nemet Piano Quartet, Music Group of London, Rasumovsky String Quartet; Frequent soloist at Queen Elizabeth Hall; Professor of Viola, University College, Chichester; Warden, Solo Performers Section, 1986–87 Incorporated Society of Musicians. *Recordings:* Elegiac Meditation by Robin Milford; Works of Haydn, Rubbra, Charles Ives, Shostakovich with Amici Quartet; Works by Elgar, Vaughan Williams, Frank Bridge, Schubert with Music Group of London. *Publications:* Editor of Concerto for Viola and Orchestra by William Walton, Vol. 12, 2002. *Address:* 7 Fraser Gardens, Emsworth, Hants PO10 8PY, England. *Telephone:* (1243) 378300. *Fax:* (1243) 378300.

WELLS, Jeffrey; Singer (Bass-baritone); b. 1957, USA. *Career:* Sang Donizetti's Raimondo at New Orleans in 1985; Season 1986–87 as Assur in Semiramide and Ferrando in Il Trovatore at Washington; Sang Stravinsky's Nick Shadow at Glyndebourne, 1989, and Rossini's Basilio at Toronto; Metropolitan Opera from 1990, in Semiramide, Billy Budd, Carmen (as Zuniga), and A Midsummer Night's Dream, 1996; Guest appearances at Washington as Enrico in Anna Bolena, 1993, at Bonn as Escamillo, 1994, Detroit as Don Giovanni, 1995, and San Francisco, 1996–98, as Glinka's Ruslan, and Escamillo; Sang the Rheingold Wotan at San Francisco, 1999; Britten's Claggart in Seattle and Toronto, 2001. *Recordings include:* Il Trovatore. *Address:* San Francisco Opera, War Memorial House, Van Ness Avenue, San Francisco, CA 94102, USA.

WELSBY, Norman; Singer (Baritone); b. 7 Feb. 1939, Warrington, Cheshire, England. *Education:* Studied at the Royal College of Music in Manchester and with Gwilym Jones and Otakar Kraus in London. *Career:* Debut: Sadler's Wells Opera, London in 1968 as Masetto; Many appearances at Covent Garden and with English National Opera in the standard repertoire and in modern works; Sang Gunther in The Ring, under Reginald Goodall, 1973–74; Sang in the premiere (concert) of The Magic Fountain by Delius, BBC, 1977; Sang Pentheus in the British premiere of The Bassarids for ENO in 1974 and The General in the premiere of We Come to The River, at Covent Garden in 1976; Many concert appearances. *Recordings include:* The Ring of the Nibelung conducted by Reginald Goodall; The Magic Fountain. *Address:* c/o English National Opera, London Coliseum, St Martin's Lane, London WC2N 4ES, England.

WELSER-MÖST, Franz; Conductor; b. 16 Aug. 1960, Linz, Austria. *Education:* Completed music studies with Professor Balduin Sulzer. *Career:* Principal Conductor of the Austrian Youth Orchestra until 1985; Mahler's 1st Symphony and Bruckner's 5th Symphony in the Musikverein, live recording with the London Philharmonic Orchestra; Salzburg Festival debut, 1985; British debut, 1986 with the London Philharmonic; European tour with the orchestra to Vienna, Berlin and Amsterdam; Guest engagements with the Zürich Tonhalle, Vienna Symphony, New York Philharmonic, Boston Symphony, Philadelphia Orchestra, Chicago Symphony, Cleveland, St Louis and Los Angeles Philharmonic, Bayerischer Rundfunk, Berlin Philharmonic; 2 tours to South Africa with the London Philharmonic Orchestra, 1983, 1994; Opera debut in October 1987 with a new production of L'Italiana in Algeri at the Vienna State Opera; Così fan tutte at the Deutsche Oper, Berlin; Formerly Chief Conductor in Norrkoeping and Winterthur; London Philharmonic Orchestra, 1990; Season 1991–92 with La Clemenza di Tito at the Deutsche Oper Berlin and Rosenkavalier at Zürich; Season 1993–94 with Tristan und Isolde at the Festival Hall, London, and Peter Grimes at Glyndebourne; Music Director, Zürich Opera, September 1995–; Music Director, London Philharmonic Orchestra, 1990–96; Elektra at Linz; Die Lustige Witwe, Glyndebourne Company at the Festival Hall; Die Fledermaus, Un Ballo in Maschera and Dvořák's Rusalka at Zürich; Glyndebourne Festival 1996, Così fan tutte; Appointed Director of the Cleveland Orchestra, 1999; Led Jenůfa at Zürich, 1998; Conducted new production of Schubert's Fierrabras at Zürich, 2002. *Recordings include:* Lehar's Die Lustige Witwe, 1994; Bruckner's Symphony No. 5; Beethoven's Symphony No. 5; Mozart's C Minor Mass. *Current Management:* IMG Artists Europe. *Address:* c/o

Cleveland Orchestra, Severance Hall, 1101 Euclid Ave, Cleveland, OH 44106, USA.

WELSH, Moray Meston, BA, LRAM, ARCM, GradDip; British cellist; *Principal Cellist, London Symphony Orchestra*; b. 1 March 1947, Haddington, Scotland; s. of D. A. Welsh and C. Welsh (née Meston); pnr, Jonathan Papp. *Education:* York Univ. and Moscow Conservatoire. *Career:* debut, Wigmore Hall 1972; cello solo appearances in UK, USA, USSR, Europe and Scandinavia; appeared with major UK orchestras, including London Symphony Orchestra, Royal Philharmonic Orchestra, BBC Symphony; festivals at Bath, Edinburgh, Aldeburgh, Bergen and Helsinki; appeared as soloist internationally under Colin Davis, Previn, De Burgos, Haitink; chamber music performances with Previn, Bashmet, Midori, Galway and Chung; Prin. Cellist, London Symphony Orchestra (LSO) 1992–. *Recordings include:* concertos by Boccherini, Vivaldi, Alexander Goehr, Hoddinott, Hugh Wood (Sunday Times record of the year); recorded with James Galway, Kyung-Wha Chung, Allegri Quartet, Alberni Quartet; cello and orchestra music by Herbert Howells with LSO; Rachmaninov Complete Works for Cello and Piano. *Radio:* frequent broadcasts on BBC Radio 3. *Honours:* British Council Scholarship 1969, Gulbenkian Fellowship 1970. *Address:* 32 Dartmouth Road, London, NW2 4EX, England. *Telephone:* (20) 8933-3032. *Fax:* (20) 8933-3032. .

WEN, De-Qing; Composer; b. 10 July 1958, Jian Yang, Fujian, China. *Education:* Art Department, Fujian Normal University, 1978–82; China Conservatory of Music, Beijing, 1988–90; Conservatoire de Musique de Genève, Switzerland, 1992–96; Conservatoire National Supérieur de Musique de Lyon, France, 1993–94. *Career:* debut as composer, Ningxia Ensemble, China, 1984; Concert Portrait performed by Ningxia Ensemble, Xining, 1986; Music for Fan Jun's film My Childhood in Ruijing, 1990; Concert Portrait performed by Ensemble Contrechamps and Ensemble CIP, Geneva, 1995; Concert Portrait performed by Quatuor du Temps, La Chaux-de-Fonds, 1998; Concert Portrait tour in China, 1999. *Compositions:* Ji I and Ji II for piano, 1992–93; Complainte for 1 speaker of Beijing Opera and 3 percussionists, 1994; Le souffle for 6 instruments, 1994; String Quartet No. 1, 1995; Spring, River, Flowers, Moon, Night for 12 women's voices, 1995; Traces II for 9 instruments, 1996; Divination for 6 instrumentalists, 1997; Petit Chou variation for erhu and string quartet, 1997; String Quartet No. 2, 1997; Ballade, for pipa and string quartet, 1998; Kung-fu, for percussion solo, 1998; Quatre Poésies for chamber orchestra, 1999. *Recordings:* De-qing Wen, Ensemble Contrechamps and CIP, Quatuor du Temps, recorded for Radio Suisse Romande, Espace 2, 1996. *Publications:* Musical Works, China, 1997, Switzerland, 1998. *Address:* 36 Avenue de la Roseraie, 1205 Geneva, Switzerland.

WENKEL, Ortrun; German singer (mezzo-soprano, alto); b. 25 Oct. 1942, Buttstadt, Thuringia; m. Peter Rothe 1966. *Education:* Franz Liszt Hochschule Weimar, Hochschule für Musik, Frankfurt, Lohmann masterclass and operatic studies with Cavelti. *Career:* debut concert, as student, in London, 1964; Opera in Heidelberg, 1971; Performed at opera houses throughout Europe including Milan Scala, Covent Garden, Bayerische Staatsoper, Hamburg, with appearances at the Salzburg Festival, Munich Opera Festival and festivals of Schwetzingen, Edinburgh, Berlin and Vienna, notably as Penelope in the Zürich production of the Monteverdi Cycle; Has given numerous lieder recitals and made guest appearances with symphony orchestras in New York, London, Berlin, Vienna, Paris, Bayreuth, Amsterdam, Buenos Aires and Rio de Janeiro among others; Alto part of Erda in Wagner's Rheingold and Siegfried; Debuts in new mezzo soprano roles as Adriano in Wagner's Rienzi, Staatsoper Prague, Fricka in Wagner's Rheingold and Walküre, Herodias in Salome and Klytämnestra in Elektra by Richard Strauss, Spring Festival, Budapest, 1999; Magda Schneider in Kühr/Turrini's Tod und Teufel, world premiere, Graz, Steirischer Herbst, 1999; Beroe in Henze's The Bassarids at New York and Moscow; Bernarda in Reimann's Bernarda Albas Haus, Swiss premiere, Bern, 2002; Numerous concert engagements. *Recordings include:* Boulez Bayreuth Centenary Ring, The Ring with Dresdner Staatskapelle; Mahler's 3rd Symphony and 8th Symphony; Mozart's Requiem; The Magic Flute; Schoenberg's Jacob's Ladder; Dvořák's Stabat Mater; Handel's Xerxes; Solo recitals of Italian Baroque music; St Matthew Passion by Bach and several of his cantatas; Zemlinsky Lieder, Schreker and Shostakovich Lieder; Henze's The Bassarids; Wagner's Ring with Badische Staatskapelle, 1995. *Honours:* Grammy Award for Wagner's Ring des Nibelungen, principal soloist, 1982; Deutscher Schallplattenpreis for Mozart's Requiem, 1983. *Address:* Eichendorffstrasse 25, 69493 Hirschberg-Leutershausen, Germany.

WENKOFF, Spas; Singer (Tenor); b. 23 Sept. 1928, Tirnovo, Bulgaria. *Education:* Studied with J Jossifov in Sofia, Madame Saffiriva in Russe and Johannes Kemter in Dresden. *Career:* Debut: Tirnovo 1954, in Keto and Kote by Dolidse; Sang in Russe, Bulgaria, 1962–65; East Germany from 1965, Dobben, Madgeburg, Halle and the Staatsoper Berlin; Sang Tristan at Dresden Staatsoper in 1975, and Tristan and Tannhäuser at

Bayreuth Festival, 1976–83; Has sung roles in operas by Verdi and Puccini as well as leading parts in operas by Wagner; Sang Tannhäuser at Vienna Staatsoper in 1982; Further appearances at the Deutsche Oper Berlin in 1984, Munich and Cologne; Sang Tannhäuser at Berne in 1987.

WENNBERG, Siv (Anna Margareta); Dramatic Soprano; b. 18 Sept. 1944, Timrå, Sweden. *Education:* Ingesunds Musikskola, Sweden; Musikaliska Akademien Stockholm; Qualified Pianist, Organist and Music Director. *Career:* Debut: Royal Opera House, Stockholm in 1972; Opera performances from 1972 throughout Europe; Extensive concert appearances with roles including Brünnhilde in Siegfried and Die Walküre, Empress in Die Frau ohne Schatten (television), Amelia in Ballo in Maschera (television), Alice in Falstaff, Puccini's Tosca, Leonora in Fidelio, Mozart's Donna Elvira, Daisy Doody in Aniara, Euridice in Orpheus in the Underworld and Beatrice in von Suppé's Boccaccio; Television and radio appearances in Sweden, throughout Europe and the USA; Permanent member of the Royal Opera Stockholm; Sang Verdi title role, Aida and Lady Macbeth; Wagner: Senta, Elisabeth, Elsa and Sieglinde; Strauss: Elektra, Salome, Ariadne. *Recordings:* Scandinavian Songs with Geoffrey Parsons; Wagner's Rienzi, Irene, with Dresden Staatskapelle; Royal Opera Stockholm Gala excerpt from Aida, 1995; Schubert and Strauss songs with Jan Eyron, 1997. *Honours:* First prizes at Jussi Björling Competition and Scandinavian Singing Contest, 1971; Swedish Opera Prize for Wagner's Isolde, 1988; Appointed Court Singer by King Carl Gustaf XVI of Sweden, 1994. *Current Management:* Svenska Konsertbryån, Jungfrugatan 45, 11444, Stockholm, Sweden. *Address:* Odengatan 32, 11351 Stockholm, Sweden.

WENZINGER, August; Cellist, Conductor and Educator; b. 14 Nov. 1905, Basle, Switzerland; m. Ilse Hartmann. *Education:* Studied cello at the Basle Conservatory, 1915–27; Studied in Cologne with Jarnach and Grummer, 1927–29. *Career:* First Cellist of the Bremen Orchestra, 1929–34, Basle Allgemeine Musikgesellschaft, 1936–70; Cellist in the Basle String Quartet, 1933–47; Co-founded the Schola Cantorum Basiliensis in 1933, teaching viola da gamba, ensemble and ornamentation there; Co-leader, Kammermusikkreis Scheck-Wenzinger, 1936–43; Lectured at Harvard University on performance practice and viola da gamba playing, 1953; Directed the Capella Coloniensis for West German Radio in Cologne, 1954–58; Directed performances of baroque operas at Herrenhausen, 1958–66; Founded the viola da gamba trio of the Schola Cantorum Basiliensis, 1968; Musical Director of Baroque concerts at Oberlin, OH; Guest Professor for Viola Da Gamba at the Hochschule für Musik, Vienna, 1976–; Concert tours of Europe, Asia and the USA; Gave the premieres of Martin's Ballade for Cello and Schoeck's Cello Concerto. *Publications include:* Bach Solo Suites for Cello; JCF Bach Sonata in A; Monteverdi's Orfeo, 1955. *Honours:* Honorary D.Mus. University of Basle, 1960; Fellow, Royal Swedish Academy of Music, 1965; Honorary D.Mus, Berlin College, 1981. *Address:* 3 Zehntenfreistrasse, 4103 Bottmingen, Switzerland.

WERDER, Felix; Australian composer; b. 24 Feb. 1922, Berlin, Germany. *Career:* settled in Australia, 1941; Adult Education Class Music Lecturer, 1956–; music critic, The Age, Melbourne, 1960–77; Founder and Dir, Australia Felix Ensemble, presenting new Australian works by young composers. *Compositions include:* Kisses for a Quid, opera, 1960; En Passant, ballet, 1964; The General, opera, 1966; Agamemnon, opera, 1967; The Affair, opera, 1969; The Vicious Square, opera, 1971; The Conversation, opera, 1973; Banker, music theatre, 1973; La Belle Dame sans Merci, ballet, 1973; Quantum, ballet, 1973; Cranach's Hunt, horn concerto, 1974; Six Symphonies, 1948–79; Sans souci, flute concerto, 1974; Synorgy for synthesizer, winds and organ, 1974; The Tempest, electronic music for V100, 1974; Index for chamber ensemble, 1976; Bellyful, music theatre, 1976; The Director, music theatre, 1980; Board Music, for piano, 1983; The Medea, opera, 1985; Opening for contrabass and flute, 1987; Concerto for Orchestra, 1987; Concert Music for bass clarinet and orchestra, 1987; Renunciation for viola and orchestra, 1987; Business Day, music theatre, 1988; Two Fantasias for string trio, 1988; Saxophone Quintet, 1988; Belzaser, choral cantata, 1988; Off Beat for cello and piano, 1990; Four Violin Sonatas, 1958–88; Los Dramas, for soprano and chamber ensemble, 1990; The Wenzel Connection, clarinet concerto, 1990; Music for a While, for chamber orchestra, 1991; Taffelmusik, for clarinet, cello and piano, 1991; Piano Quartet, 1991; Symphony No. 7 (Pique Dame), 1992; Sisiphus, for solo cello and string orchestra, 1993; Hawthorn Konzert, for solo violin, percussion and string orchestra, 1994; Gryphiusad, for voice and orchestra, 1995; Catullus and John Donne, Songs, 1996; San Souci, sinfonia concertante, 1997; Uber die Maniere for full orchestra, 1998; Klav**4, for 4-handed piano. *Recordings:* No. 3, Laocoon; Tower Concerto; Concerto for Violin; String Quartets 4, 6, 9; Requiem, for soprano and ensemble; Aspect, collection of works. *Publications:* More than Music, 1991; Music and More, 1994. *Address:* c/o Locked Bag 3665, St Leonards, NSW 2065, Australia.

WERRES, Elisabeth; Singer (soprano); b. 1954, Bonn, Germany; m. Anthony Bramall (conductor). *Education:* Cologne Conservatory under D. Jacob. *Career:* Debut age 22, Cologne Opera in small roles for one season; Resident soprano, Staatstheater Karlsruhe, 1978–80: roles included Rosina, Marguerite in Gounod's Faust, Adele, Eurydice, Frau Fluth; Resident soprano, Dortmund Opera, 1980–82: roles included Nedda, Susanna, Musetta, Gilda, Aminta, Adina; Resident soprano, Staatsoper Hannover, 1989–1997: roles included Tatjana, Rosalinde, Musetta, Freia, Merry Widow, Marschallin, Mazenka, Helmwige; Guest engagements in over 30 theatres in Europe including Staatsoper Hamburg, Staatsoper Munich, Deutsche Oper Berlin, Cologne Opera, Komische Oper Berlin, Essen, Leipzig, Zürich, Mannheim, Strasbourg, Wiesbaden, Weimar, Dortmund, Karlsruhe, Amsterdam, Vienna Volksoper: roles included Rosalinde, Marie in Wozzeck, Turandot by Busoni, The Merry Widow, Milada in Dalibor, Chrysothemis in Elektra, Arabella, Countess in Figaro, Elena in I Vespri Siciliani and especially Feldmarschallin in Der Rosenkavalier; Concerts in Barcelona, Chicago, Tokyo, Hamburg, Essen, Stuttgart, Karlsruhe, Strasbourg, Luxembourg, Vienna, Munich, Cologne, Zürich, Luzern, Berlin: Beethoven's 9th, Strauss' 4 Last Songs, Weill's Seven Deadly Sins, Wozzeck Fragments, opera and operetta galas; Prof. of voice, Univ. of the Arts, Berlin, 2003–. *Recordings:* Laura in Hindemith's opera Neues Vom Tage, conductor Jan Latham-Koenig; Offenbachiade: Gala for opening of Cologne Philharmonic, conductor Pinchas Steinberg. *Honours:* Special Award, Mozart Competition Würzburg, 1977. *Address:* Wehrastr. 11, 76199 Karlsruhe, Germany.

WERTHEN, Rudolf; Violinist and Conductor; b. 16 July 1946, Malines, Belgium. *Education:* Studied at the Ghent and Brussels Conservatories, with André Gertler. *Career:* Soloist with the NDR Symphony Orchestra at Hamburg and professor at the Robert Schumann Institute, Detmold; Flanders Chamber Orchestra from 1977 and musical director of Flanders Opera at Antwerp, from 1992; Has rediscovered and premiered the 7th Concerto of Vieuxtemps and the Russian Concerto of Lalo. *Honours:* Prizewinner of competitions at Vienna, Amsterdam and Brussels. *Address:* Robert Schumann Institute and Hochschule für Musik, Allee 22, 4930 Detmold, Germany.

WEST, Ewan Donald, BA, MA, MBA, DPhil; writer on music; b. 9 Aug. 1960, Cheltenham, Gloucestershire, England. *Education:* Exeter College, Oxford, Cranfield School of Management. *Career:* Lecturer, History of Music, Worcester College, Oxford, 1986–94; Junior Research Fellow, Mansfield College, Oxford, 1988–92; Director of Studies in Music, Somerville College, Oxford, 1989–94; mem, American Musicological Society; Royal Musical Association. *Publications:* The Hamlyn Dictionary of Music, 1982; The Oxford Dictionary of Opera, with John Warrack, 1992; The Concise Oxford Dictionary of Opera, 3rd edition, with John Warrack, 1996; contrib. to Music and Letters; Austrian Studies. *Honours:* James Ingham Halstead Scholar, University of Oxford, 1985–87. *Address:* 14 Moorhouse Road, London W2 5DJ, England.

WEST, John; American singer (bass); b. 25 Oct. 1938, Cleveland, OH. *Education:* Curtis Institute with Martial Singher, in New York with Beverley Johnson. *Career:* debut in San Francisco in 1963 as Sarastro; Many appearances at US opera centres including Houston, Philadelphia, Seattle, Santa Fe, Portland, San Francisco, Washington and Fort Worth; Guest engagements at Vancouver, Mexico City, Hanover and Spoleto; Other roles have included Don Alfonso, Oroveso in Norma, Basilio, Mephistopheles of Gounod and Berlioz, Boris Godunov, Ramphis, Arkel, Ochs, La Roche in Capriccio, Hunding and Tiresias; Frequent concert engagements. *Address:* c/o San Francisco Opera, War Memorial Opera House, San Francisco, CA 94102, USA.

WEST, John Frederic; singer (tenor); b. 4 March 1952, Dayton, OH, USA. *Education:* Manhattan School of Music and American Opera Center at Juilliard, New York. *Career:* sang Tamino and Stravinsky's Tom Rakewell at Glens Falls, 1975; Scottish Opera, 1980, as Gabriele Adorno; Season 1982–83 as Manrico at Frankfurt and Calaf at the New York City Opera; Waldemar in Schoenberg's Gurrelieder at the Edinburgh Festival; Toronto, 1986, as Apollo in Strauss's Daphne, Bacchus in Ariadne auf Naxos at Washington and the Metropolitan Opera, 1993; Wagner's Tristan at the reopening of the Prinzregententheater, Munich, 1996; Season 1997–98 as Tannhäuser at the Metropolitan and Tristan at the Nationaltheater, Munich; Tristan at Covent Garden, 2001; Engaged as Siegfried in The Ring at the Deutsche Oper, Berlin, 2003. *Recordings include:* DVD of Tristan, from Munich. *Current Management:* Robert Gilder & Co., Enterprise House, 59–65 Upper Ground, London, SE1 9PQ, England. *Telephone:* (20) 7928-9008. *Fax:* (20) 7928-9755. *E-mail:* rgilder@robert-gilder.com.

WEST, Kevin; Singer (Tenor); b. 1960, England. *Education:* Studied at the Guildhall School with Walter Gruner. *Career:* Sang first with the D'Oyly Carte Opera Company; Appearances with Opera 80 as Sellem in The Rake's Progress and Don Ottavio, and Britten's Peter Quint for Music Theatre Wales; Engagements with Opera Restor'd in English Baroque Music and throughout the United Kingdom; Sang Monteverdi's Orfeo at the Prom Concerts in London; English National Opera debut, 1989 as David in The Mastersingers; Has also sung with English National Contemporary Opera Studio, Opera Factory as Trimalchio in Maderna's Satyricon in 1990 and the Montepulciano Festival in Henze's The English Cat in 1990; Appeared with Opera Northern Ireland in 1991 as Mozart's Don Basilio (repeated for Opera North, 1996); Sang in Bernstein's Candide at Turin, 1997; Concert repertoire includes Bach's St John Passion and Easter Oratorio, works by Handel, Mozart and Schubert and Tippett's A Child Of Our Time at South Bank in London.

WEST, Stephen; Singer (bass-baritone); b. 1950, New York, USA. *Education:* Curtis Inst., Philadelphia, and with Jerome Hines in New Jersey. *Career:* debut, Bonze in Butterfly at Philadelphia 1973; sang with the Metropolitan Opera, Chicago, Washington, Seattle and many others; New York City Opera from 1995, as Boito's Mefistofele and Verdi's Attila; Deutsche Staatsoper, Berlin as Weber's Kaspar and Paris Bastille as Berg's Dr Schön; concert appearances with the Philadelphia Orchestra at Carnegie Hall, and with the Denver and Montreal Symphony Orchestras; season 1997–98 as Adams in the premiere of Amistad by Anthony Davis at Chicago, and Kolenaty in The Makropulos Case by Janáček at the New York Metropolitan; further engagements as King Henry in Lohengrin at Bayreuth, Dr Schön at the Met, Gounod's Mephistopheles at Baltimore and Massenet's Comte des Grieux for Dallas Opera; season 2000–01 as Mars in Henze's Venus and Adonis, at Santa Fe and Acrobat in Lulu at the Met. *Honours:* prizewinner at Met Audition and Tchaikovsky Competition. *Current Management:* Herbert Barrett Management, 266 W 37th Street, 20th Floor, New York, NY 10018, USA. *Telephone:* (212) 245-3530. *Fax:* (212) 397-5860. *Website:* www.herbertbarrett.com.

WESTERGAARD, Peter; Composer and Professor of Music; b. 28 May 1931, Champaign, Illinois, USA. *Education:* AB, Magna cum Laude, Harvard College, 1953; MFA, Princeton University, 1956; Studied Composition with Walter Piston, Darius Milhaud, Roger Sessions, and Wolfgang Fortner. *Career:* Assistant Professor 1963–66, Columbia College; Visiting Lecturer with rank of Associate Professor, Princeton University, 1966–67; Associate Professor, Amherst College, 1967–68; Princeton University, 1968–71; Professor, Princeton University, 1971–; Chairman, Department of Music, Princeton University, 1974–78, 1983–86; Director, Princeton University Orchestra, 1968–73; Board of Directors: American Music Centre, 1969–72; International Society for Contemporary Music, 1970–74; Director, Princeton University Opera Theatre, 1970–; Visiting Professor, University of British Columbia, 1987; Lecturer, International Music Seminar, University of Bahia, Brazil, 1992; Interdepartmental Committee for the Program in Musical Performance, Princeton University, 1992–93; William Shubael Conant Professor of Music, Princeton University, 1995–, Acting Chair, Department of Music, 1995. *Compositions include:* 5 Movements for Small Orchestra, 1959; Cantata II, 1959, III, 1966; Quartet for Violin, Vibraphone, Clarinet and Violoncello, 1961; Variations for 6 Players, 1967; Mr and Mrs Discobbolos, 1967; Divertimento on Discobbolic Fragments, 1967; Noises, Sounds and Sweet Airs, 1968; Tuckets and Sennets, 1969; Cantata I, 1956; Two Rhymes, for soprano and violin, 1979, 1997; Ariel Music, 1987; Ode, 1989; The Tempest, Opera in Three Acts after William Shakespeare, 1990; Ringing Changes, 1996; All 4s, 1996; anyone lived in a pretty how town, 1996; Byzantium for baritone and percussion quartet on poems by Yeats, 1997; Chicken Little, an opera for children, 1997; Cantata VI, To The Dark Lady, 1998; Chaconne, 1999; Epithalamium, 2000; Singing Translations of The Magic Flute, Don Giovanni, Der Freischütz, Fidelio (original version of 1805), Così fan tutte, The Marriage of Figaro, Cinderella and The Coronation of Poppea. *Address:* 40 Pine Street, Princeton, NJ 08542, USA.

WESTERN, Hilary; Singer (Soprano); b. 1948, Cardiff, Wales. *Education:* Studied at the Royal Academy of Music and the London Opera Centre. *Career:* Sang at the Wexford and Glyndebourne Festivals and in Angers as Mimi and Toulouse as Frasquita; Appearances as Fiordiligi in Grenoble, Anchorage and Britain; Sang Mimi, Papagena and Diana for Opera North; Ariadne, Louise, Micaela, Christine in Blake's Toussaint, Musetta and Diana; Sang at Almeida Festival in 1990 in the world premiere of Europeras III and IV by John Cage; Performances of Birtwistle's Punch and Judy, The Beggar's Opera and Orfeo with Opera Factory; Schoenberg's Pierrot Lunaire for Ballet Rambert; Has sung in the musicals, chess and A Little Night Music, in the West End and at the Chichester Festival in Born Again. *Honours:* Arts Council Award, to study with Martin Isepp in New York.

WESTLAKE, Nigel; Composer and Clarinettist; b. 6 Sept. 1958, Perth, Western Australia. *Education:* Clarinet with Don Westlake, 1970–78; Bass Clarinet with Harry Sparnay, 1983; Composition self taught. *Career:* Freelance clarinettist from 1975; Principal of Australia Ensemble, 1987–92, with tours throughout Australia and abroad;

Tour of Australia and England 1992, with John Williams' group, Attaca; Film and television music. *Compositions include:* Onomatopoeia for bass clarinet and digital delay, 1984; Omphalo Centric Lecture, for 4 percussion, 1984; Entomology, for chamber ensemble and tape, 1988; Refractions at Summercloud Bay, for bass clarinet, flute and string trio, 1989; Malachite Glass, for bass clarinet and percussion quartet, 1990; Antarctica Suite, for guitar and orchestra (from the film score), 1992; Tall Tales But True, for 2 guitars and ensemble, 1992; Songs from the Forest, for guitar duo, 1994; High Tension Wires, for string quartet, 1994; Invocations, concerto for bass clarinet and orchestra, 1995; Babe: orchestral excerpts from the film, 1996; Piano Sonata, 1997. *Honours:* Gold Medal, New York radio festival, 1987; APRA Award, Babe, Best Film Score, 1996. *Address:* c/o APRA, PO Box 576, Crows Nest, NSW 2065, Australia.

WETHERELL, Eric (David); Composer and Conductor; b. 30 Dec. 1925, Tynemouth, Northumberland, England; m. (1) Jean Bettany, 4 July 1949, 1 s., 1 d., (2) Elizabeth Major, 16 Jan 1976, 2 d. *Education:* BA, BMus, The Queen's College, Oxford, 1945–47; Royal College of Music, 1948–49. *Career:* Horn Player, 1949–59; Repetiteur, Royal Opera House, Covent Garden, 1960–63; Assistant Music Director, Welsh National Opera, 1963–69; Music Director, HTV, 1969–76; Chief Conductor, BBC Northern Ireland Orchestra, 1976–81; Senior Music Producer, BBC Bristol, 1981–85. *Compositions:* Choral, Solo Songs, Orchestral including Airs and Graces and Welsh Dresser for Orchestra, Bristol Quay for String Orchestra, Your Gift to Man for Chorus; Music for television plays and films. *Publications:* Life of Gordon Jacob, 1995; Arnold Cooke, 1996; Patrick Hadley, 1997; Albert Sammons, 1998. *Address:* c/o British Music Information Centre, 11 Stratford Place, London, W1, England.

WETHERILL, Linda; Flautist; b. 1950, USA. *Career:* Recital and concerto Soloist in major cities of Europe, Canada, USA; Principal Flautist with the orchestras of Hessischer Rundfunk Frankfurt and of Pierre Boulez's IRCAM at Pompidou Centre, Paris, France; Repertoire includes Baroque, Classic, Romantic and Impressionist works; Performed and premiered the flute music of Luciano Berio, Pierre Boulez, Elliott Carter, Olivier Messiaen, Goffredo Petrassi and Karl-Heinz Stockhausen; Taught master classes in English, French, German, Spanish and American Conservatories. *Recordings:* Numerous for DTR and Deutsche Grammophon. *Honours:* Won New York Young Artists debut, 1979; First American and first flautist to be featured artist, 35 year running World Peace Festival, Llangollen, Wales, 1982; Selected by West German Broadcasting Association for a 10 country European Concerto debut, 1975.

WEWEL, Gunter; Singer (Bass); b. 29 Nov. 1934, Arnsberg, Sauerland, Germany. *Education:* Studied with Johannes Kobeck in Vienna, Rudolf Watzke in Dortmund, Emmi Muller in Krefeld. *Career:* Member of the Dortmund Opera from 1963; Guest appearances in Düsseldorf, Cologne, Karlsruhe, Hanover, Budapest, Paris, Zürich, Salzburg, Munich; Radio and Television engagements in Germany, France; Roles include Wagner's Daland, Titurel, Fafner, King Mark, Landgrave and King Heinrich; Philip II in Don Carlos, Gremin in Eugene Onegin and Beethoven's Rocco; Mozart's Sarastro, Osmin and Commendatore; Nicolai's Falstaff and Rossini's Bartolo. *Recordings include:* Die Zauberflöte conducted by Sawallisch; Schumann's Paradies und die Peri under Henryk Czyz; Suppé's Boccaccio with Willi Boskovsky; Die Königskinder, Mendelssohn's Die Beiden Pädagogen, Les Contes d'Hoffmann and Millöcker's Gasparone, conducted by Heinz Wallberg; La Vie Parisienne, with Willy Mattes.

WHEATLEY, Patrick; Singer (Baritone); b. 1950, Hinckley, Leicestershire, England. *Education:* Studied at London Opera Centre, 1973. *Career:* Appeared with English National Opera, 1974–80, as Germont, Amonasro, Marcello, Sharpless, Donner, Gunther, De Bretigny (Manon), Albert (Werther), Schelkalov (Boris Godunov) and the King in Dalibor; Guest appearances as Escamillo, Kothner, Hans Sachs and Talbot and Cecil in Maria Stuarda; Other roles include Renato (Northern Ireland Opera Trust); Ezio in Attila (University College Opera); Falstaff and Papageno (City of Birmingham Touring Opera); Zurga in Les Pêcheurs de Perles (Scottish Opera); Jochanaan, and Yeletsky in The Queen of Spades (Chelsea Opera Group); Nabucco (Opera West); Mercutio in Roméo et Juliette (Las Palmas); Don Pasquale (Neath Opera); Rigoletto (Welsh National Opera); Sang Wotan and the Wanderer in a version of Wagner's Ring for the City of Birmingham Touring Opera, 1990–91; Concert engagements in Italy, Belgium and Spain and at the Promenade Concerts, London. *Address:* Music International, 13 Ardilaun Road, London N5 2QR, England.

WHEELER, Antony, BMus, MPhil; composer, clarinettist and saxophonist; b. 9 Aug. 1958, Dunedin, New Zealand. *Education:* Queensland Conservatory, Shanghai Conservatory, Hong Kong University, studied with Ann Boyd. *Career:* clarinettist with Queensland Symphony Orchestra and Philharmonic Orchestra 1980–82, ABC Sinfonia

1983–85, Sydney Symphony Orchestra 1983–85; Freelance Teacher and Performer, 1987–95; Lane Cove Public School, 1992–99; Trinity Grammar School, 1996–99; Australian Institute of Music, 1992–99; Active in wide range of performance styles, including traditional Chinese music, contemporary, improvisation, using clarinet, saxophone, qin, ruan; mem. APRA; Musicians' Union of Australia; Australian Music Centre. *Compositions include:* many for Chinese instruments; Piano Variations, 1982; Incidental Music for Ubu the King, for ensemble, 1983; Sarabande and Fugue, brass quintet, 1984; Winter, 1986; Bodhisattva of the Silk Road, 1986; Cold Moon Shines South of the River, 1987; Approach to Peace, for Chinese orchestra, 1988; Snake, 1988; Wind Quintet in Five Movements, 1988; Love Songs of the Grasslands for chorus and string orchestra, 1989; Rising, for Chinese orchestra, 1990; Hearing Thunder on the Fishing Boat, for Chinese percussion ensemble, 1990; Back to the Bush for clarinet, saxophone and piano, 1990; Birthday Variations, wind quintet, 1991; Now Close the Windows, for tenor and piano, 1991; Jin Beng Bong, for Chinese ensemble, 1998. *Address:* c/o APRA, 6–12 Atchison Street, St Leonards, NSW 2065, Australia.

WHELAN, Paul; Singer (Baritone); b. 29 Sept. 1966, Christchurch, New Zealand. *Education:* Studied at the Wellington Conservatoire and the Royal Northern College of Music. *Career:* Concerts and Recitals in New Zealand, the USA and Europe; Nielsen's 3rd Symphony under Simon Rattle, Messiah in Russia with Yehudi Menuhin and in London with the London Mozart Players; Vaughan Williams's Five Mystical Songs and Sea Symphony, Messiah at the Albert Hall under Charles Farncombe; Opera engagements include roles in Death in Venice for Glyndebourne Opera, Schaunard in La Bohème at Stuttgart, Masetto in Bordeaux, 1993, Britten's Demetrius for Australian Opera and on tour in France and Guglielmo for Dublin Grand Opera; Welsh National and Scottish Opera debuts 1994, as Timur in Turandot and Mozart's Figaro; Messiah with Hallé Orchestra, conductor Roger Vignoles; Verdi, Requiem, Budapest Symphony Orchestra, conductor Paolo Olmi; Recitals at Blackheath and Wigmore Halls, London; Sang Demetrius at the Edinburgh Festival, 1994 and Schaunard for Netherlands Opera; Covent Garden debut 1996, as Schaunard; Don Giovanni for Opera Australia, 1997; Season 1998–99 included Guglielmo and the baritone roles in Death in Venice; Marcello at the Bastille; Apollo in Gluck's Alceste at Netherlands Opera; Gil in Il Segreto di Susanna; Tarquinius in The Rape of Lucretia; The Count in Figaro with Scottish Opera; Escamillo in Carmen with Welsh National Opera; Season 2000–01 as Christus in Bach's St John Passion for ENO, Mephisto in The Damnation of Faust, with the BBC Philharmonic, and the Villains in Hoffmann, in New Zealand; Concert engagements with RIAS Berlin Chamber Choir for Messiah. *Honours:* Brigitte Fassbaender Award for Lieder. *Address:* c/o IMG Artists, Lovell House, 616 Chiswick High Road, London W4 5RX, England.

WHETTAM, Graham (Dudley); Composer; b. 7 Sept. 1927, Swindon, Wiltshire, England; m. (1) Rosemary B. Atkinson, 20 Nov 1948, (2) Janet Rosemary Lawrence, 31 Mar 1959, 4 s., 1 d. *Education:* Self-taught Composer. *Career:* Debut: Concert: C.B.S.O., Birmingham, 1950; Radio: BBC 3rd Programme, 1951; Works in concert and broadcast in the United Kingdom and abroad; Has withdrawn recognition of works written mostly prior to 1959. *Compositions include:* Orchestra: Clarinet Concertos No. 1, 1959, No. 2, 1982; Introduction and Scherzo Impetuoso, 1960; Sinfonia Contra Timore, 1962; Cello Concerto, 1962; Sinfonia Intrepida, 1976; Sinfonia Drammatica, 1978; Hymnos for Strings, 1978; Symphonic Prelude, 1985; Ballade for Violin and Orchestra, 1988; Choral: The Wounded Surgeon Plies the Steel, 1960; Magnificat and Nunc Dimmitis, 1962; Do Not Go Gentle Into That Good Night, 1965; Consecration, 1982; A Mass for Canterbury, 1986; Chamber Music: 3 String Quartets, 1967, 1978, 1980; Sextet for Wind and Piano, 1970; Quintetto Concertato, Wind Quintet, 1979; Percussion Partita for Six Players, 1985; Quartet for Four Horns, 1986; Piano, Prelude, Scherzo and Elegy, 1964, revised 1986; Prelude and Scherzo Impetuoso, 1967; Night Music, 1969; Solo Violin Sonatas No. 1, 1957, revised 1987, No. 2, 1972; Solo Violin Sonata No. 3, 1989; Suite for Timpani, 1982; Solo Cello Sonata, 1990; Andromeda for Percussion Quartet, 1990; Concerto Ardente for Horn and Strings, 1992; Les Roseaux au Vent for Two Oboes, Cor Anglais and Strings, 1993; Romanza for Solo Violin (also arr. for Solo Viola and Solo Cello), 1993; Les Roseaux au Vent, for 2 oboes, bassoon and strings, 1993; Concert for Brass Quintet, 1993; Three Shakespearian Elegies, 1994; Evocations, for orchestra, 1995; Concerto drammatico for cello and orchestra, 1998; Promethean Symphony, 1999. *Recordings:* Quartet for Four Horns, 1989. *Contributions:* Listener; Times Educational Supplement; Guardian. *Address:* Meriden Music, The Studio Barn, Silverwood House, Woolaston, Nr Lydney, Gloucestershire GL15 6PJ, England.

WHITE, (Edwin) Chappell, BA, BMus, MFA, PhD; educator and musicologist; b. 16 Sept. 1920, Georgia, USA; m. Barbara Tyler 1959; one s. two d. *Education:* Emory University, Westminster Choir College, Princeton

University. *Career:* Instructor, Agnes Scott College, 1950–52; Instructor and Associate Professor, Emory University, 1952–74; Professor, Kansas State University, 1974–91 now retired; Violist with Atlanta Symphony, 1950–57; Music Critic, Atlanta Journal, 1959–72; Visiting Professor, University of Georgia, 1970–71, Indiana University, 1972–73; Brown Foundation Fellow, University of the South, 1993; mem, College Music Society, President, 1979–80; American Musicological Society; Visiting Professor, University of the South , 1993–2002. *Publications:* G B Viotti: A Thematic Catalogue of His Works, 1985; Intro to Life and Works of R Wagner, 1969; Editor, 4 Concertos by G B Viotti, 1976, and 3 Concertos by J Myslivecek, 1994; From Vivaldi to Viotti: A History of The Classical Violin Concerto, 1992. *Contributions:* 15 articles in New Grove Dictionary, 1980; Journal of American Musicological Society; Fontes Artis Musiche; Musical Quarterly. *Honours:* Research Grant, NEH, 1982–83. *Address:* 150 Bobtown Circle, Sewanee, TN 37375, USA.

WHITE, Frances, BMus, MA; composer; b. 30 Aug. 1960, Philadelphia, USA. *Education:* University of Maryland, Princeton University. *Career:* technical asst to John Cage 1985–87, collaborating on works for computer-generated tape; freelance composer. *Compositions include:* Ogni pensiero vola, for tape, 1985; Chiaroscura, for percussion and tape, 1986; Design for an Invisible City for tape, 1987; Valdrada, 1988; Still Life with Piano, for piano and tape, 1989; Resonant Landscape, interactive computer-music, 1990; Trees for 2 violins, viola and tape, 1992; Nocturne, 1992; Walks Through Resonant Landscapes 1–5 for tape, 1992; Winter Aconites (commission from ASCAP in memory of John Cage) for clarinet and ensemble, 1993. *Honours:* First Prize, programme music category, 18th Bourges International Electro-Acoustic Music Competition, 1990; ASCAP Awards, 1990, 1993, 1994.

WHITE, Harry; University Professor of Music; b. 4 July 1958, Dublin, Republic of Ireland; m. Eithne Graham 1980; two s. *Education:* Univ. Coll. Dublin; Univ. of Toronto; Trinity Coll., Dublin. *Career:* part-time Lecturer, St Patrick's Coll., Maynooth, 1984–85; Asst Lecturer in Music, 1985–88, Coll. Lecturer, 1988–93, Prof. of Music, 1993–, Univ. Coll. Dublin; Visiting Prof. of Music, Univ. of Western Ontario, 1996; Visiting Prof. of Musicology, Ludwig-Maximilians-Universität, Munich, 1999; General Ed., Irish Musical Studies (Dublin), 1990–; Foreign Corresponding Ed., Current Musicology (New York), 1996–; mem., Irish RILM Cttee (Chair. 1992–), Editorial Board of the International Review of the Aesthetics and Sociology of Music (Zagreb, 2001–), Society for Musicology in Ireland (founding mem., 2003–). *Publications:* Johann Joseph Fux, Il Trionfo della Fede (ed.), 1988; Musicology in Ireland (co-ed.), 1990; Johann Joseph Fux and the Music of the Austro-Italian Baroque (ed.), 1992; Music and the Church (co-ed.), 1993; Music and Irish Cultural History (co-ed.), 1995; The Maynooth International Musicological Conference: Selected Proceedings (co-ed.), 1996; The Keeper's Recital: Music and Cultural History in Ireland 1770–1970, 1998; Musical Constructions of Nationalism (co-ed.), 2001. *Contributions:* Acta Musicologica, Bach, Fontes Artis Musicae, International Review of the Aesthetics and Sociology of Music, Irish University Review, Eighteenth Century Ireland, Irish Review, Journal of American Studies, Kirchenmusikalisches Jahrbuch, Canadian Journal of Irish Studies, Modern Drama, Journal of Musicology, Studies in Music from the University of Western Ontario, College Music Symposium, Atti del Antiquae Musicae Italicae Studiosi, Music and Letters, The New Grove Dictionary of Music and Musicians (revised edn, 2001). *Address:* Department of Music, University College Dublin, Belfield, Dublin 4, Ireland.

WHITE, Ian David; Violist; b. 16 Sept. 1941, London; m. Annelise White, 16 Feb 1987, 4 c. *Education:* Royal College of Music, 1956–60; Viola making with Dr Arthur Councell, 1957–62; Decoration in Baroque music with Dr Carl Dolmetsch, 1967–72. *Career:* Debut: With Royal Philharmonic Orchestra, 1960; First appearance in Wigmore Hall, 1966, Purcell Room, 1967, Smith Square, 1969; Music for A Man for All Seasons; Chamber music on BBC television; Performances with English Chamber Orchestra, with Benjamin Britten; Hold the Front Page; Lectures at Royal College of Music and Guildford University; mem, Viola d'Amore Society of Great Britain; American Viola d'Amore Society; Principal Viola, BBC London Studio Strings, March 1970– March 1987; Principal Viola L'estro Armonico, 64 Haydn Symphonies CBS Masterworks 1976–90; Leader of the Misbourne Orchestra 1982–94. *Compositions:* Arrangements of Trio in E flat for Viola, Cello and Bass, by Michael Haydn, Concertos for Viola d'Amore by Vivaldi, Böhm, Carl Stamitz and W F Rust, Pfeiffer Trio, Quantz Trios. *Recordings:* Brandenberg Concertos with English Chamber Orchestra and Benjamin Britten; Nisi Dominus by A Vivaldi; Christmas Story, Heinrich Schütz; St John Passion, J. S. Bach, at King's College, Cambridge– Instruments with Sympathetic Strings. *Publications:* Arrangements: Lute and Viola d'Amore Concerto, Vivaldi, 1978; Divertimento for Viola d'Amore, by Karl Stamitz; La Chasse by Hraczek; Trios by Pfeiffer and Graupner. *Contributions:* Profile in the Strad, 1968; Articles in Bucks Examiner. *Honours:* Alfred Gibson Viola Prize and Percy Carter Buck

Prize, Royal College of Music, 1958–60. *Current Management:* Viola d'Amore Society. *Address:* 4 Constable Road, Felixstowe, Suffolk IP11 7 HH, England.

WHITE, Jeremy; Singer (bass-baritone); b. 1953, Liverpool, England. *Education:* Studied at Queen's College and Christ Church, Oxford; Singing Studies with David Johnston, Elisabeth Fleming. *Career:* Many performances with early music ensembles in the United Kingdom and Europe; Acis and Galatea for Swiss Television, debut at the Amsterdam Concertgebouw in Bach cantatas under Ton Koopman; Performances in Vienna, Budapest and Turku (Finland); Bach's St John Passion in England and Spain with The Sixteen; CPE Bach's Oratorio Auferstehung und Himmelfahrt Jesu, in Munich; Bach's Magnificat and Christmas Oratorio in Oxford and London with King's College Choir and English Chamber Orchestra; Handel/Mozart Messiah in Paris and Lucerne; Bach's Passions in English Cathedrals; Modern concert repertoire includes Abraham and Isaac by Stravinsky, and music by Berio and Taverner; Has sung in The Lighthouse by Maxwell Davies, Walton's The Bear (title role), Pfitzner's Palestrina (Cardinal Morone), Les Troyens and Der Rosenkavalier (the Notary, Aix-en-Provence Festival); Roles in operas by Mozart and Rossini; Recent engagements 1993: Tour of Verdi's Requiem, including Paris and the Flanders Festival; Series of performances of Arvo Pärt's Passio in Jerusalem, Seville and throughout Poland and Finland, Berio in Helsinki conducted by the composer and Beethoven's Ninth Symphony for Swiss Radio; Sang Don Prudenzio in Rossini's Il Viaggio a Reims, Covent Garden, 1992; Sang Webern's Second Cantata with Pierre Boulez in a broadcast from Birmingham Symphony Hall; Season 1993–94: Contemporary Music Network tour as Peter in Jonathan Harvey's Passion and Resurrection, followed by a return to the Royal Opera to sing Benoit in La Bohème; Visit to Brazil with the Scottish Chamber Orchestra; Return to Swiss Radio in Lugano; Concert appearances with The Sixteen and The Taverner Players in Beethoven and Schütz in Germany, Norway and Switzerland, and Handel's La Resurrezione in Paris and Bourges; Concerts in London and the provinces; Sang in Pfitzner's Palestrina at Covent Garden, 1997; Season 1998 with Talbot in Verdi's Giovanna d'Arco in London and Leeds; Sang Colonna in Wagner's Rienzi for Chelsea Opera Group, 1999; Season 2000–01 as Rossini's Selim for ENO and Mesner in Tosca at Covent Garden. *Recordings include:* John Tavener's Great Canon of St Andrews; Monteverdi's Vespers, with The Sixteen; Handel Israel in Egypt conducted by Andrew Parrott. *Current Management:* Musicmakers International Artists Representation, Tailor House, 63–65 High Street, Whitwell, Hertfordshire SG4 8AH, England. *Telephone:* (1438) 871708. *Fax:* (1438) 871777. *E-mail:* musicmakers@compuserve.com. *Website:* www.operauk.com. *Address:* c/o Royal Opera, Contracts, Covent Garden, London WC2, England.

WHITE, John; Musician and Professor of Viola; b. 28 May 1938, Leeds, Yorkshire, England; m. Carol Susan Shaw, 29 August 1964, 1 s., 1 d. *Education:* Charles Oldham Scholar, 1959–63, Royal Academy of Music; Huddersfield Technical College, Music Department, 1953–57. *Career:* Member, Alberni String Quartet, 1960–67, Stadler Trio 1967–76; Professor of Viola, Junior Department, Royal Academy of Music, 1967–76; Senior Lecturer, Hockerill College of Education, 1970–78; Tutor, RNCM, 1974; Professor of Viola RAM 1975–2002; Head of Instrumental Studies RAM 1984–1991; President of RAM Club 2001–02; Viola Tutor European Union Youth Orchestra 1984–1992; gave masterclasses at Beijing Conservatory, China, 1997 and also in Greece, Holland, Sweden and Ireland; Jury Member, International William Primrose Viola Competition, 1999; mem, Royal Society of Musicians; British Federation of Music Festivals; Special Services Award from International Viola Congress, Sweden, 2000. *Recordings:* Haydn String Quartets; Rawsthorne String Quartets. *Publications include:* Editor: Sonatina for Viola and Piano by Alan Bush, Three Miniature String Quartets by Richard Stoker, Ballade for Viola and Piano, Minna Keal, Scales and Arpeggios for viola players, Watson Forbes, Sonata Impromtu Violin and Viola by William Alwyn, Pastoral Fantasia Viola and Strings (piano) William Alwyn; Nocturne Viola and Cello, Gordon Jacob, Sussex Lullaby, Autumn Sketches, Intrada, Rhapsody by Alan Richardson; A Book of Daily Exercises by Watson Forbes; Introduction and Andante Op 5, for six violas, Phantasy for viola and piano, Rhapsody, for viola and piano, Viola Concerto by York Bowen; English Dance by Dale/Bowen for Viola and Piano; Slavonic Dance by Dvořák/Harding for Viola and Piano op. 46 no. 4; Trio Sonata for Bass Clarinet, Viola and Piano and Three Pieces for Oboe, Viola and Piano by Alan Richardson; Handel (Dennison) The Arrival of the Queen of Sheba for six-part Viola Ensemble; Gordon Jacob concert Piece for Viola and Orchestra and Viola and Piano; Author: An Anthology of British Viola Players, 1997; A Biography of Lionel Tertis, forthcoming. *Honours:* FRAM; ARAM; ARCM, Assoc. of the Inst. of Education, London. *Address:* 36 Seeleys, Harlow, Essex CM 17 0AD, England.

WHITE, John; Composer; b. 5 April 1936, Berlin, Germany. *Education:* Studied with Elisabeth Lutyens at the Royal College of Music, 1954–57. *Career:* Music Director of the Western Theatre Ballet, 1959–60; Teacher of Composition at the Royal College of Music, 1961–66; Tuba Player with the London Gabrieli Brass Ensemble, 1971–72. *Compositions include:* 136 Piano Sonatas, 1957–96; 26 Symphonies 1965–90; 35 Ballets 1957–93; Music for Films and Television; Operas Stanley and the Monkey King, London 1975, and the Trial; Orpheus: Eurydice, London 1976; Music Theatre Man-Machine Interface. *Address:* c/o PRS Ltd, Member Registration, 29–33 Berners Street, London W1P 4AA, England.

WHITE, John David; Composer and Cellist; b. 28 Nov. 1931, Rochester, Minnesota, USA; m. Marjorie Manuel 1952, 2 s., 1 d. *Education:* BA, University of Minnesota 1953; MA 1954; PhD 1960; Eastman School of Music, University of Rochester, 1960. *Career:* University of Wisconsin, Kent State University, Music Department, Chair, Whitman College, 1978–80; Dean, School of Music, Ithaca College 1973–75; Professor and Head of Composition and Theory, University of Florida 1980–; Active Cellist in recital and chamber music; Soloist with Atlanta, Rochester, Madison and Akron Orchestras; Composer of 50 works, performances by Cleveland, Atlanta, Rochester, Madison and Akron Orchestras; Music published by G. Schirmer, Galaxy, Carl Fischer, Lawson-Gould; Author of Five Books; Taught at University of Michigan. *Compositions:* Symphony No. 2, 1960; Symphony No. 3; Legend of Sleepy Hollow, 1962; 3 Choruses from Goethe's Faust; 3 Madrigals for Chorus and Orchestra; Numerous choral works, 1960–87; Variations for Clarinet and Piano; Zodiac, Chorus and Piano; Music for Oriana, 1979 (for Violin, Cello and Piano); Pied Beauty, Chorus and Piano; Eiseleic Madrigals; Sonata for Cello and Piano, 1982; Music for Violin and Piano, 1983; Concerto for Flute and Wind Ensemble, 1984; Symphony for Wind Band, 1985; Dialogues for Trombone and Piano, 1984; Symphony for A Saint, 1987; Songs of the Shulamite, 1988; Mirrors for Piano and Orchestra, 1990. *Recordings:* Variations for Clarinet and Piano, Advent 5005. *Publications:* Understanding and Enjoying Music, 1968; Music in Western Culture, 1972; Guidelines for College Teaching of Music Theory, 1981; The Analysis of Music, 2nd Edition, 1984. *Contributions:* Journal of Music Theory; Journal for Musicological Research; Music and Man. *Address:* 5715 NW 62nd Court, Gainesville, FL 32606, USA.

WHITE, Wendy; Singer (Mezzo-soprano); b. 1959, USA. *Career:* Sang Valencienne in The Merry Widow at Washington, 1984, Carmen at Cincinnati, 1985; New York City Opera, 1986, as Charlotte in Werther (also at Nice, 1990); Chicago Lyric Opera from 1987, as Siebel in Faust, Charmian in Barber's Antony and Cleopatra, and Suzuki in Butterfly (1998); Metropolitan Opera from 1990, in La Traviata, Rusalka, Les Troyens (as Anna), Otello and Andrea Chénier (1996); Magdalena in Die Meistersinger, 1998; Sang Cherubino in Corigliano's The Ghosts of Versailles, Metropolitan and Chicago, 1995; Sang Mascagni's Lola, Annina in Der Rosenkavalier and Fenena (Nabucco) at the Met, 1999–2001. *Recordings include:* Parsifal, and Bernstein's A Quiet Place. *Address:* c/o Metropolitan Opera, Lincoln Center, New York, NY 10025, USA.

WHITE, Sir Willard Wentworth, Kt, CBE, BA; Jamaican/British opera singer (bass); b. 10 Oct. 1946, Ewarton, St Catherine, Jamaica; s. of Egbert White and Gertrude White; m. Gillian Jackson 1972; three s. one d. *Education:* Excelsior School, Kingston and Juilliard School of Music, NY. *Career:* debut with New York City Opera as Colline in La Bohème 1974–75; European debut as Osmin with Welsh Nat. Opera 1976; has performed in most int. opera houses, including Royal Opera House, Covent Garden, England, La Scala, Italy, Glyndebourne, England, Scotland; roles include: Porgy, Orestes, Banquo, King Henry (Lohengrin), Pizarro, Wotan, Mephistopheles, Boris Godunov, Golau, Leporello, Prince Kovansky, Napoleon; extensive concert appearances; appeared as Othello, RSC, Stratford-upon-Avon; Falstaff at Aix Festival 2001, Klingsor in Parsifal, Covent Garden 2001, Bartok's Bluebeard 2002, Messiaen's St Francis, San Francisco 2002, Wotan in the Ring, Aix and Salzburg 2005. *Recordings include:* Porgy and Bess, Mozart Requiem, Orfeo, Die Aegyptische Helena, Acis and Galatea. *Honours:* Prime Minister of Jamaica's Medal of Appreciation 1987. *Current Management:* IMG Artists Europe, 616 Chiswick High Road, London, W4 5RX, England.

WHITEHEAD, Gillian; Composer; b. 23 April 1941, Whangarei, New Zealand. *Education:* University of Auckland; BMus, University of Wellington; MMus, University of Sydney, New South Wales; Studied with Peter Maxwell Davies in Adelaide, then in the United Kingdom. *Career:* Lived in the United Kingdom and Europe, 1967–81; Appointed 1st Composer-in-Residence, Northern Arts, Newcastle upon Tyne, England, 1978; Lecturer in Composition, Sydney Conservatorium of Music, New South Wales, Australia, 1981; Various commissions funded by Music Board of Australia Council, Arts Council of Great Britain, New Zealand Arts Council. *Compositions:* Published and/or Recorded: Missa Brevis, 1963; Qui Natus Est, Carol, 1966; Fantasia on Three Notes,

Piano Solo, 1966; Whakatau-Ki, Chamber Music with Voice, 1970; La Cadenza Sia Corta, Piano Solo, 1974; Tristan and Iseult, for 4 Singers, Mimes and Puppets, Instrumental Ensemble, 1975; Voices of Tane, Piano Solo, 1976; At Night the Garden Was Full of Flowers, for 4 Recorders, 1977; The Tinker's Curse, Children's Opera, 1979; Requiem, for Male Soprano and Organ (Dance Score), 1981; The King of the Other Cowboy, chamber opera, 1984; The Pirate Moon, chamber opera, 1986; Resurgences, for orchestra, 1989; Angels Born at the Speed of Light, 1990, for string quartet; Moments, for chorus, 1993; The Art of Pizza, chamber opera, 1995. *Honours:* Recipient of numerous grants including New Zealand Queen Elizabeth II Arts Council and Vaughan Williams Trust. *Current Management:* Helen Lewis. *Address:* c/o Helen Lewis, 10 John Street, Woollahra, New South Wales 2025, Australia.

WHITEHOUSE, Frank, Jr; Emeritus Professor; b. 20 Nov. 1924, Ann Arbor, Michigan, USA; m. Helen Alice Schimkat, 1 s., 3 d. *Education:* AB, University of Michigan, College of Literature, Science and the Arts, 1953; MD, University of Michigan Medical School, 1953. *Career:* Active duty, World War II, 1942–46, Pilot B-29; Internship, Blodgett Memorial Hospital, Michigan, 1953–54; Faculty Member, University of Michigan Dept of Microbiology and Immunology, 1954–95; Visiting Scientist, Queen Victoria Hospital, East Grinstead, England, 1971; Senior Fulbright Lecturer, Bahrain University, 1979; Retired, 1995; Composer of religious and secular music; mem, ASM. *Compositions:* Religious music: Hymn for the Human Family; Memorial Day Anthem; Scottish Advent Carol; Meditation for Mary; Master Builder; Easter Anthem; All Children at Play; The Gift of the Church is Love; Introit; Amen; The Genius of Jesus; Secular music: The Lioness March; Big Time Flo' from Kokomo; Here's To You Maize and Blue; Dr Chase Patent Medicine Show. *Recordings:* Here's To You Maize and Blue on the University of Michigan Marching Band CD, The Spirit of Michigan. *Publications:* Numerous publications, subjects include microbiology and immunology; Civil War Surgeon's Diary, in progress. *Honours:* Hopwood Literary Award, University of Michigan, 1947; Departmental and Medical School Award for distinguished contributions to medical and undergraduate education, 1995; Air Medal USAAF, 1995. *Address:* 3411 Woodland Road, Ann Arbor, MI 48104-4257, USA.

WHITFIELD, John (Peter); Conductor, Musical Director and Bassoonist; b. 21 March 1957, Darlington, County Durham, England. *Education:* Chetham's School of Music, 1973–75; Keble College, Oxford, 1975–78; National Youth Orchestra, 1973–77; European Community Youth Orchestra, 1978; International Youth Orchestra; Bassoon Studies with Charles Cracknell, Martin Gatt and Mordechai Rechtmann, Tel-Aviv. *Career:* Debut: South Bank Conducting Debut, 27 March 1983; Israel Chamber Orchestra; City of London Sinfonia; English Baroque Orchestra; London Sinfonietta; London Symphony Orchestra, also tours; London Symphony Orchestra Israel Chamber Orchestra; Founder and Musical Director of Endymion Ensemble; Many concerts in London and the United Kingdom festivals as bassoonist, conductor, with soloists; commissioned and conducted premieres of works by David Bedford, Dominic Muldowney, Nigel Osborne, Michael Nyman, Giles Swayne, Anthony Payne; Assistant Conductor for Spitalfields Festival Production and EMI recording of Armide (Gluck) with Felicity Palmer in title role; Assistant to Richard Hickox; Stage Debut as Conductor of Birtwistle's Down by the Greenwood Side at the Bath Festival, also broadcast by Radio 3. *Recordings:* Stravinsky record including Symphonies of Wind and Dumbarton Oaks and Britten Record with Gomez and Palmer on EMI. *Current Management:* Music & Musicians Artists Management, London. *Address:* 45 Chalcot Road, London NW1 8lS, England.

WHITICKER, Michael; Composer; b. 1954, Gundagai, New South Wales, Australia. *Education:* Degree, Composition, New South Wales Conservatorium of Music, 1982; Studied with Richard Troop; Postgraduate Composition Studies, West Germany with Isang Yun and Witold Szalonek. *Compositions:* Orchestral Works: Ad Marginem, 1986; Tartengk, 1985; Tya, 1984; Works for the Stage: The Bamboo Flute, 1982; Gesualdo, 1987; Ensemble Works: Hunufcu, 1979; Korokon, 1983; Quidong, 1983; Kwa, 1986; Winamin, 1986; Orpheus and Persephone, 1987; Plangge, 1987; Venus Asleep, 1987; Min-amé, 1988; Ad Parnassum, 1989; Redror, 1989; Solo Instrumental Works: Vibitqi, 1980; Tulku, 1982; If Buifs, 1981; Kiah, 1986; The Hands, The Dream, 1987; In Prison Air, 1988; On Slanting Ground, 1988; Vocal Works: A Voice Alone, 1982; Night Swimming, 1984; Sheaf Tosser, 1984; As Water Bears Salt, 1989; Works for Students: Boinko the Billio, 1979; Homage to Alban Berg, 1980; Liexliu, 1980; Introduction for Concert Band, 1985; Karobaan, 1985; Taldree, 1985; The Bankstown Pageant, 1985; The Hollow Crown, 1985; The Serpent Beguiles, 12985; Three Episodes, 1985; Works for Tape Alone: Cement Mounted Inlays, 1981; Model Sequence II, 1981; Slid PC, 1982; Ballets: Factor X, 1980; Passion, 1989; Film Scores: Atlantis, 1981; Conferenceville, 1982; The Bus Trip, 1982; Man, The Skin Cancer of the Earth, 1991 for Three Voices, Sax, Percussion and Tape; Jellingroo, 1990 for Didjeridoo, Flute and Cello;

Encircled by Lillies, 1991, for Soprano, Tenor and Piano. *Address:* c/o Australian Music Centre, PO Box 49, Broadway 2007, Australia.

WHITTALL, Arnold; Musicologist; b. 11 Nov. 1935, Shrewsbury, England. *Education:* Emmanuel College, Cambridge (BA 1959, doctorate 1963). *Career:* Senior Lecturer at University College, Cardiff, 1971–75; Reader at King's College, London, 1976–81; Professor of Musical Theory and Analysis, King's College, 1981–96; Visiting Professor at Yale University, 1985. *Publications include:* Post-Twelve Note Analysis, 1968; Stravinsky and Music Drama, 1969; Schoenberg Chamber Music, 1972; Music Since the First World War, 1977; The Music of Britten and Tippett, 1982, 1990; Romantic Music, 1987; Wagner's Later Stage Works, 1990, The Emancipation of Dissonance: Schoenberg and Stravinsky, 1993; Musical Composition in the Twentieth Century, 1999; Exploring Twentieth Century Music, 2003. *Address:* Professor Arnold Whittall, 10 Woodway Crescent, Harrow HA1 2NG, England.

WHITTLESEY, Christine; Singer (soprano); b. 12 Jan. 1950, New York City, USA. *Education:* Studied in Boston. *Career:* Sang with opera companies in Boston, Washington and Santa Fe; Concerts with the New York Pro Musica Antique and other Chamber Ensembles; Resident in Europe from 1981: Concert engagements with the Sudwestfunk and Austrian Radio, conducted by Boulez and Michael Gielen; Tours of Russia and South America with Ensemble Modern; Ensemble Intercontemporain in Paris and Ensemble Kontrapunkte in Vienna; Debut with the BBC Symphony 1988, in Pli selon Pli under Boulez; Sang in Dallapiccola's Ulisse with the BBC Symphony Orchestra under Andrew Davis and appeared at the Henze Festival at the Barbican Centre, London, 1991, with the BBC Philharmonic and the Scottish Chamber Orchestra; Further concerts in Berlin, Salzburg, Strasbourg and Warsaw; Season 1992–93 with Debussy's Damoiselle Elue in the Netherlands and Russian songs in Paris; Performs at all major music festivals. *Recordings include:* Homage to T. S. Eliot by Gubaidulina; Schoenberg: String Quartet No. 2; Harrison Birtwistle: Three Celan Settings; Benedict Mason: Self-Referential Songs and Realistic Virelais; Mahler Symphony No. 4; Dieter Schnebel: Dahlemer Messe. *Current Management:* Ingpen & Williams Ltd, 7 St George's Court, 131 Putney Bridge Road, London, SW15 2PA, England.

WHITWORTH-JONES, Anthony; Administrator; b. 1945, England. *Education:* Wellington College; Edinburgh University; Qualified as Chartered Accountant. *Career:* Administrative Director of London Sinfonietta, 1972–80, including Schoenberg/Gerhard series, Webern and Stravinsky festivals and tours of Europe, Australasia and North America; Opera Manager of Glyndebourne Festival and Administrator of Glyndebourne Touring Opera, 1981–88; From 1983 responsible for new opera policy, commissioning such works as Knussen/Sendak double bill: Where the Wild Things Are and Higglety Pigglety Pop! (1985), Osborne's Electrification of the Soviet Union (1987), Tippett's New Year (British premiere, 1990), Birtwistle's The Second Mrs Kong (1994), Jonathan Dove's Flight (1998) and Birtwistle's The Last Supper (2000); Presided over rebuilding of Festival Theatre, 1993–94; General Director, Glyndebourne Festival Opera, 1989–98; General Director, The Dallas Opera, 2000–2002; Chairman, Michael Tippett Musical Foundation, 1998–; Trustee, Spitalfields Festival, 2003; Artistic Director of the Casa da Música in Oporto, 2004–. *Address:* 81 St Augustine's Road, London NW1 9RR, England.

WIBAUT, Frank; Concert Pianist; b. 10 Nov. 1945, London, England; m. Kay Alexander. *Education:* Studied at the Royal College of Music; ARCM. *Career:* Debut: Wigmore Hall, London, 1969; Concert performances in Netherlands, Belgium, Denmark, Germany, Ireland, Spain and Malta; Frequent broadcaster on radio and television; Member, The Camirilla Ensemble; mem, Musicians Union; Incorporated Society of Musicians. *Recordings:* The Romantic Chopin; Favourite Piano Classics; Elgar's From the Bavarian Highlands (in original form); Piano Quintets by Elgar, Suk and others. *Honours:* Senior Foundation Scholarship, Leverhulme Scholarship and Countess of Munster Award, Royal College of Music; 1st Prize, Chopin Competition, London; Chappell Gold Medal; BBC Piano Competition, 1968. *Address:* Highfield Lodge, 68 Harborne Road, Edgbaston, Birmingham B15 3 HE, England.

WICH, Gunther; Conductor; b. 23 May 1928, Bamberg, Germany. *Education:* Studied in Freiburg, 1948–52. *Career:* Conducted at the Freiburg Town Theatre, 1952–59; Opera Director at Graz, 1959–61; General Music Director at Hanover, 1961–65; Conducted the first production of Schoenberg's three one-act operas as a triple bill, 1963; General Music Director, Deutsche Oper am Rhein, Düsseldorf/Duisburg, 1965–87; Took the Company to Edinburgh, 1972, for the British premiere of Zimmermann's Die Soldaten; Covent Garden debut 1968, Die Zauberflöte; Professor of Conducting, Musikhochschule, Würzburg, 1982–94; Guest Conductor with major orchestras in Europe, Japan and the USA; Has led the Capella Colonsiensis on tours to North and South America. *Recordings include:* Handel's Concerti Grossi Op 3 and

Alexander's Feast; Haydn's Symphonies Nos 82 and 85; Serenades by Dvořák, Mozart and Tchaikovsky; Early Mozart Piano Concertos with Martin Galling; Pfitzner's Violin Concerto with Susanne Lautenbacher, 21. *Address:* c/o Spitalrain 10, 97234 Reichenberg, Germany.

WICKS, Camilla; Concert Violinist and Professor of Violin; b. 1925, USA; m. 5 c. *Education:* Fellowship to Juilliard School aged 10. *Career:* Debut: New York Town Hall aged 13; Solo appearances with the Hollywood Bowl Orchestra, the Los Angeles and New York Philharmonic Orchestras and the Chicago Symphony; Many concerts with European Orchestras from age 18; Played the Sibelius Concerto before the composer in Helsinki and has also featured the Bloch Concerto in addition to the standard repertory; Frequent engagements in Norway and elsewhere in Scandinavia; Teaching appointments 1960s–; notably faculties of North Texas State University, California State College at Fullerton, San Francisco Conservatory of Music, Banff Centre for the Performing Arts, University of Washington and University of Southern California; Professor and Head of the String Department, Royal Academy of Music, Oslo; Professor of Violin, University of Michigan School of Music, 1984; Shepherd School of Music at Rice University, Houston, Texas, 1988–; Continuing performances in recital and as orchestral soloist and in Chamber Music Concerts. *Recordings:* Several albums, including the Sibelius Concerto. *Address:* Shepherd School of Music, Rice University, Houston, Texas, USA.

WIDDICOMBE, Gillian; Music Critic and Journalist; b. 11 June 1943, Aldham, Suffolk, England; m. Sir Jeremy Isaacs, 1988. *Education:* Studied at the Royal Academy of Music and Gloucester Cathedral. *Career:* Music Division, BBC, 1966; Glyndebourne Festival Opera, 1969; Critic and Journalist, various publications including Financial Times, 1970–76; The Observer, 1977–93; Sub-titles for television opera productions; Opera Consultant, Channel Four television, 1983–88; Arts Editor, The Observer, 1988–93; Feature Writer, The Independent, 1993–95; Director, Jeremy Isaacs Productions, 1995–; Production Executive, Cold War, 1998; Associate Producer, Millennium, 1999; From 2000 Producer of Artsworld TV Programmes including Star Recitals with Paco Peña, Amanda Roocroft and Simon Preston; Poulenc, A Human Voice, for BBC 2. *Honours:* ARAM; Prix Italia 1982; BP Award for Arts Journalism, 1986. *Address:* 80 New Concordia Wharf, Mill Street, Bermondsey, London SE1 2BB, England.

WIDMANN, Jörg; Composer and Clarinettist; b. 19 June 1973, Munich, Germany. *Education:* Studied clarinet with Professor Gerd Starke at the Hochschule für Musik and with Charles Neidich at the Juilliard School, New York; Studied composition with Hans Werner Henze, Wilfried Hiller and Wolfgang Rihm. *Career:* Debut: As soloist in Mozart's Clarinet Concerto with members of Munich Philharmonic on a tour of Japan (aged 12); Soloist with orchestras including: Münchener Rundfunkorchester, Sinfonia Varsovia, Capella Istropolitana. *Compositions include:* Absences, 1990; La Verrière Lilas, 1991; Jardin du Luxembourg, 1992; Carillon, 1992–93; Kreisleriana, 1993; 180 Beats per minute, 1993; Tränen der Musen, 1993; Stimmbruch, 1994; Nickel List, 1994; Badinerie, 1994; Wunder Verwirklichen, 1995; Knastgesänge, 1995; Trauergesang und Frühlingsmusik, 1995–96; Three Rilke Fragments, 1996; Beitrage, Lea and Rachel, Lilith, 1996; Fleurs du Mal, 1996–97; Fünf Bruchstücke, 1997; Mullewapp, 1997; Sieben Abesänge Auf Eine Tote Linde, 1997; Insel der Sirenen, premiere, with Isabelle Faust on violin in Warsaw, Autumn 1997; Kleine Morgenstern-Szene for Soprano, Cymbalon and Schlagzeug, 1997; Werk für Klarinette, Streichquartett und Klavier, 1997; Sieben Miniaturen; Pas de deux, Ritual, für zwei Flöten und Orchester, 1997. *Recordings:* As composer and clarinettist, Honours: Kulturfördpreis of city of Munich, 1996; 1st Prize, Wettwerb deutscher Musikhochschulen, Berlin, 1996; 1st Prize, Carl Maria Von Weber Competition, Munich, 1996; Bavarian State Prize for Young Artists, 1997. *Address:* Barerst 3, 80333 München, Germany.

WIDMER, Oliver; Singer (Baritone); b. 1965, Zürich, Switzerland. *Education:* Studied at the Basle Music Academy with Kurt Widmer; Masterclasses with Fischer-Dieskau in Berlin, 1986 and 1989. *Career:* Concert appearances at the Salzburg Festival, Festival de Musique de Strasbourg, the Vienna Musikverein, the San Francisco Symphony Hall and the Leipzig Gewandhaus; Recitals at the Schubertiade in Hohenems, the Wigmore Hall, London, the Residenz in Munich, Alte Oper Frankfurt, Fêtes Musicales de Touraine, Louvre de Paris, the Vienna Konzerthaus and the 1992 Aldeburgh Festival; Zürich Opera from 1991 as Mozart's Papageno and Guglielmo, Olivier in Capriccio and Harlequin in Ariadne auf Naxos; Salzburg Festival 1993, conducted by Harnoncourt; Season 2000–01 as Guglielmo for Zürich Opera, Rocco in Pa ër's Leonora at Wintherthur and Christus in the St Matthew Passion at La Scala. *Recordings:* Die Zauberflöte and Schreker's Die Gezeichneten. *Honours:* Prizewinner at ARD Competition Munich, Hugo Wolf International Competitions Stuttgart and the Othmar Schoeck Competition in Lucerne. *Address:* c/o R & B Kunstleragentur, Plankengasse 7, A–1010 Vienna, Austria.

WIEDSTRUCK, Yvonne; Singer (soprano); b. 1960, Potsdam, Germany. *Education:* Studied in Germany. *Career:* Sang first at Altenburg, in Rusalka, Hänsel und Gretel, La Bohème and Faust; Komische Oper Berlin as Despina, Zerlina, Euridice, Susanna, Micaela, the Daughter in Hindemith's Cardillac and Stella in Goldschmidt's Der Gewaltige Hahnrei; Schwetzingen Festival, 1992, in the premiere of Desdemona und ihre Schwestern, by Siegfried Matthus; Appearances as Octavian in Der Rosenkavalier at the Deutsche Oper Berlin and Covent Garden (1995); La Scala debut 1996, in Das Rheingold under Riccardo Muti, and debut as Beethoven's Leonore at Essen Opera, 1997; Engaged as the Composer in Ariadne auf Naxos, Bayerische Staatsoper Munich, 1998; Resident artist at the Deutsche Oper Berlin from 1996; Concert repertory includes Bach's St Matthew Passion (under Kurt Masur), Schubert's E-flat Mass, Pergolesi's Stabat Mater and Les Illuminations by Britten; Pfitzner's choral fanatasia Das Dunkle Reich under Rolf Reuter; Season 2000–01 at the Deutsche Oper as Rossini's Zulma, Octavian and Gertrude in Hans Heiling; Waltraute at Bayreuth (2002) and Brangaene at Glyndebourne, 2003. *Recordings include:* Songs by Shostakovich.

WIEGOLD, Peter (John); Composer, Conductor and Teacher; b. 29 Aug. 1949, Ilford, Essex, England. *Education:* BMus, MMus, University College of Wales, Aberystwyth; PhD, University of Durham. *Career:* Director of Gemini, regular tours of the United Kingdom including many broadcasts; Many residencies involving local participation in shared concerts; Artistic Director, Performance and Communication Skills Project, Guildhall School of Music; Has directed many workshops in music and music theatre including those with London Sinfonietta, Royal Opera House, English National Opera, Scottish Chamber Orchestra and City of London Sinfonia; Junge Deutsche Philharmonie in Greece, Canada, Spain and Sweden; London Symphony Orchestra; mem, Past Member, Council and Executive Committee of SPNM. *Compositions include:* Gemini; Sing Lullaby; The Flowers Appear on the Earth; Preludes I–V; The Dancing Day; Songs from Grimm; Half-hour opera commissioned by the Royal Opera House, performed 1989; the Seventh Wave for cello and tape, 1997; Earth Receive/an Honoured Guest, for cor anglais and string trio, 1998; Kalachakrá, for 18 players, 2000; Farewells Take Place in Silence, Octet, 2001. *Honours:* Several Arts Council awards. *Address:* 82 Lordship Park, London N16 5UA, England.

WIENER, Otto; Singer (Baritone); b. 13 Feb. 1913, Vienna, Austria. *Education:* Studied in Vienna with Kuper and Hans Duhan. *Career:* Sang in Concert from 1939; Stage debut Graz 1953, as Simon Boccanegra; Sang at the Salzburg Festival from 1952; in Pfitzner's Palestrina 1955 and in the stage premiere of La Mystère de la Nativité by Martin, 1960; Deutsche Oper am Rhein Düsseldorf, 1956–59; Bayreuth Festival from 1957, as Hans Sachs, Gunther and the Dutchman; Member of the Vienna Staatsoper from 1957, Munich Staatsoper, 1960–70; Guest appearances in Paris, London, Rome and Brussels, often in operas by Wagner; Glyndebourne Festival 1964, as La Roche in Capriccio; Retired from stage 1976 and led an Opera School at the Vienna Staatsoper. *Recordings include:* Missa Solemnis, conducted by Klemperer; Faninal in Der Rosenkavalier; Lohengrin; St Matthew Passion. *Address:* c/o Staatsoper, Opernring 2, 1010 Vienna, Austria.

WIENS, Edith; Singer (soprano); b. 1950, Canada. *Career:* concert engagements with orchestras in Berlin, London, Israel, Munich, New York (Philharmonic), and with Cleveland, Philadelphia, San Francisco, Montréal and London Symphony Orchestras; broadcasts on Bavarian Radio, Dresden Staatskapelle, Leipzig Gewandhaus Orchestra; conductors include Barenboim, Georg Solti, Colin Davis, Haitink, Kurt Masur, Marriner, Sawallisch and Tennstedt; Salzburg debut 1984, with the Boston Symphony under Ozawa, with whom she has also sung Mozart's Ilia in Japan; other operatic roles include Donna Anna (at Glyndebourne under Haitink, in Paris and at Amsterdam under Harnoncourt) and Mozart's Countess (Buenos Aires); St Matthew Passion in Paris and Salzburg under Masur, with whom she also appeared in Mendelssohn's Elijah in New York; L'Enfant et les Sortilèges at Carnegie Hall; Mahler's 4th Symphony in Munich; recitals in Paris, Vienna, Florence, Buenos Aires, New York and Montréal; Concertgebouw, Amsterdam, and the Pushkin Museum, Moscow; Jury Member of International Competitions; Rotarian, 2001; Prof. of Voice at the Hochschule für Musik, Augsburg, and at the Hochschule für Musik und Theater München, 2000. *Recordings include:* Schubert, Schumann, Strauss and Zemlinsky Lieder, the title role in Schumann's Das Paradies und die Peri, which won a Grammy in 1990 and the Maurice Fleuret (Paris) Prize in 1991; Flowermaiden in Parsifal, conducted by Barenboim; Mahler's 8th Symphony, conducted by Tennstedt; Haydn's Creation conducted by Neville Marriner; Brahms Lieder, Zemlinsky's Lyrical Symphony with the Swiss Romande Orchestra. *Honours:* DMus, hc, Oberlin Coll., USA 1997; Officer of the Order of Canada, 2000. *Address:* Georg-Schuster-Str. 10, 82152 Krailling, Germany.

WIESE, Henrik; Flautist; b. 22 July 1971, Vienna, Austria. *Education:* Studied with Ingrid Koch, Roswitha Staege and Paul Meisen at Musikhochschule Hamburg and Musikhochschule Munich. *Career:* Engaged as 1st Principal Flautist, Bavarian State Opera, Munich, 1995–; Solo concerts with various orchestras including Berlin Radio Symphony Orchestra, Orchestra of the Beethovenhalle in Bonn, Polish Chamber Philharmonic, others; Solo concerts with Berlin Radio Symphony Orchestra, Hanover Radio-Philharmonie of NDR, Lower Saxonian State Orchestra. *Recordings:* Chamber music works including Mozart, Flute Quartets and Overtures arranged for flute and string quartet, with Artemis; Bach Flute Sonatas with Anikó Soltész. *Publications:* Several editions at Henle Edition. Contributions to Mozart-Jahrbuch, 1997. *Honours:* Prizewinner at national compositions, such as German Music Competition, 1995; , Elise Meyer Competition, 1996; Prizewinner at international competitions such as Kobe International Flute Competition 1997, Markneukirchen and Munich International Music Competition 2000. *Address:* Franziskaner-strasse 2, 81669 Munich, Germany. *Website:* www.henrikwiese.de.

WIGGLESWORTH, Mark; Music Director and Conductor; b. 19 July 1964, Ardingly, Sussex, England. *Career:* Associate Conductor, BBC Symphony Orchestra, 1991–93; Music Director, Opera Factory, 1991–94; Music Director, Premiere Ensemble, 1989–; Music Director, BBC National Orchestra of Wales, 1996–2000; Principal Guest Conductor, Swedish Radio Orchestra, 1988–2001; Worked in the United Kingdom with BBC Symphony, BBC Scottish Symphony, London Philharmonic, London Symphony, Bournemouth Symphony, English and Scottish Chamber Orchestras, Royal Scottish National Orchestra, European Community Youth Orchestra; Conducted Premiere Ensemble and BBC National Orchestra of Wales in Centenary Season of BBC Proms; Guest Conductor in Europe including Berlin Philharmonie and Deutsches-Symphonie Orchester Berlin; Conductor, BBC National Orchestra of Wales; Mahler Festival at the Concertgebouw, Amsterdam, 1995 with the 10th Symphony, Completed by Deryck Cooke; Royal Concertgebouw Orchestra; Rotterdam Philharmonic, Residentie Orchester, Radio Philharmonie and Netherlands Wind Ensemble, Netherlands; Welsh National Opera; English National Opera; Santa Cecilia of Rome; Israel Philharmonic; European engagements include: Oslo Philharmonic; Swedish Radio Orchestra; Tour with Deutsche Kammerphilharmonie; Mozarteum Orchestra at Salzburg Festival; Chicago, Cleveland, Philadelphia, Minnesota and Los Angeles Philharmonic Orchestras; St Louis, Toronto and San Francisco Symphony Orchestras and at Hollywood Bowl; Engaged for debut with Sydney Symphony Orchestra, New York Philharmonic and at Glyndebourne with Peter Grimes, 2000; Covent Garden debut 2002, Die Meistersinger. *Honours:* 1st Prize, International Kondrashin Competition, Netherlands, 1989. *Current Management:* Askonas Holt Ltd, Lonsdale Chambers, 27 Chancery Lane, London, WC2A 1PF, England. *Telephone:* (20) 7400-1700. *Fax:* (20) 7400-1799. *E-mail:* info@askonasholt.co.uk. *Website:* www.askonasholt.co.uk.

WILBRAHAM, John; Trumpet Player; b. 15 April 1944, Bournemouth, England; m. Susan Drake. *Education:* Royal Academy of Music, London; LRAM; ARCM. *Career:* New Philharmonia Orchestra, 1966–68; Royal Philharmonic Orchestra, 1968–72; BBC Symphony Orchestra from 1972; Many appearances as soloist in the trumpet concerto repertory; mem, Savage Club; ISM. *Recordings include:* Concertos by Haydn, Hummel, Mozart, Telemann and Torelli. *Honours:* Silver Medal, Worshipful Company of Musicians, 1965. *Address:* 14b Elizabeth Mews, London NW3, England.

WILBY, Philip; Composer; b. 18 July 1949, Pontefract. *Education:* Leeds Grammar School, with Herbert Howells and at Keble College, Oxford. *Career:* Violinist with the Covent Garden Orchestra and City of Birmingham Symphony Orchestra; Senior Lecturer at Leeds University from 1972. *Compositions:* Orchestral Sunstudy; The Wings of Morning, 1988; Vocal: Et Surrexit Christus for 3 Sopranos and Ensemble, 1979; Ten Songs of Paul Verlaine for Baritone and Piano, 1983; The Temptations of Christ for Soprano and Ensemble, 1983; Winter Portrait in Grey and Gold for Voice and Ensemble, 1977–85; Cantiones Sacrae: In Darkness Shine, 1987; Magnificat and Nunc Dimittis, 1988; Easter Wings for Soprano and Ensemble, 1989; A Passion of our Times, 1997; Chamber: Little Symphony for Brass, 1985; The Night and All The Stars, Horn Quintet, 1985; Sonata Sacra: In Darkness Shine for Clarinet, Viola and Piano, 1986; And I Move Around The Cross for Double Wind Quintet, 1985; Two Concert Studies for Violin and Piano, 1986; Capricorn Suite for 4 Trombones, 1987; Parables for Cello and Piano, 1988; Classic Images, Partita for Brass Quintet, 1988; Concert music for Winds, 1988; Green Man Dancing, Wind Quintet, 1988; Breakdance for Recorder and Tape, 1988; Wind Band: Firestar, 1983; Symphonia Sacra: In Darkness Shine, 1986; Catcher of Shadows, 1988; Laudibus in sanctis, 1994; Keyboard: Roses for the Queen of Heaven, 1982; Two Preludes on English Tunes, 1987; Lifescape-Mountains, 1987;... Aunque es de Noche, 1989; Mozart Reconstructions include

Concerto for Violin and Piano K315f and Concerto for Violin, Viola, Cello and Orchestra K320e, for the Philips Mozart Edition; Commissions include Symphony for the BBC Philharmonic. *Address:* c/o Chester Music, 8/9 Frith Street, London W1V 5TZ, England.

WILD, Earl; Pianist, Composer and Teacher; b. 26 Nov. 1915, Pittsburgh, Pennsylvania, USA. *Education:* Carnegie Technical College, 1930–34; Studied Piano with Egon Petri, Selmar Jansen, Paul Doguereau. *Career:* Debut: New York City, 1934; Pianist, KOKA Radio, Pittsburgh, 1930–35; Pianist, NBC Symphony Orchestra, under Toscanini, 1937–44; Soloist with Toscanini and NBC Symphony, 1942; Staff Pianist, Composer, Conductor, ABC TV, New York City, 1945–68; Teacher, Juilliard School of Music, 1977–; Teacher, Manhattan School of Music, 1981–83. *Compositions:* 14 Rachmaninov song transcriptions; 7 Gershwin song transcriptions, Porgy and Bess Fantasy; Dance of the Four Swans, Tchaikovsky's Swan Lake. *Recordings:* Liszt the Virtuoso, Transcriber and Poet; Beethoven Sonatas Op 22, Op 31 No. 3; Rachmaninov Concertos; Fauré Cello Sonatas Nos 1 and 2; Chopin Record. *Publications:* 2 vols of Liszt Piano Music, 1986. *Honours:* Performed for US Presidents Hoover, Roosevelt, Truman, Eisenhower and Kennedy; Performed for Kennedy at his inauguration, 1961. *Current Management:* Judd Concert Bureau, New York City, USA.

WILDE, David (Clark); Pianist, Composer, Conductor and Professor of Piano; b. 25 Feb. 1935, Manchester, England; m. (1) Jeanne Lukey, 23 May 1956, 1 s., 1 d., (2) Jane Heller, 14 June 1984. *Education:* Privately, Solomon/Reizenstein, 1945–47; Royal Manchester College of Music, Piano (Elinson), Composing (Hall), Conducting (Cohen), 1948–53; Nadia Boulanger, privately and American Conservatoire, Fontainebleau; Caird Foundation Scholar, 1963–64. *Career:* Concerts, USA, Canada, Australia, New Zealand, India, Brazil, France, Belgium, Netherlands, Spain, Germany, Hungary, Russia; International recording and concert artist for BBC, 1961–; Henry Wood Proms from 1961; Soloist, Royal concert in HM the Queen's presence, Royal Festival Hall, and at BBC television inaugural concert, Manchester (Hallé Orchestra, Barbirolli), 1962; Edinburgh, Cheltenham, Three Choirs, Perth (Australia) festivals; Tours, all leading British orchestras; Conductor, Worthing Symphony, season 1967–68; Writer, narrator, pianist, BBC television Liszt and Bartók documentary programmes, 1972–73; Guest Conductor, Royal Philharmonic, 1975; Liszt in Weimar, film, Granada television, 1986; Soloist, Tippett's Concerto, BBC Philharmonic, conducted Tippett (Manchester), Edward Downes (London Proms), 1988. *Compositions:* Love, song for baritone and cello, 1981; Jens, Heidi und die Schneekönigin, 1984; Vocalise, mezzo soprano, guitar; Die Jahreszeiten, song cycle, 1986; Mandala, solo viola, 1986; Piano trio, 1987–88; String quartet, 1991; The Cellist of Sarajevo, solo cello, 1992; Suite, Cry Bosnia-Herzogovina, violin, piano, 1993. *Recordings include:* Schumann Fantasie; Liszt Sonata; Complete Beethoven Sonatas with Gruenberg, violin. *Publications:* Transcriptions for piano, chapter in Franz Liszt, The Man and His Music, 1970; Liszt's Consolations, complete (editor), 1978. *Address:* c/o J Audrey Ellison International Artists' Management, 135 Stevenage Road, Fulham, London SW6 6PB, England.

WILDE, Mark; Singer (tenor); b. 1960, Dundee, Scotland. *Education:* Read Music, University of East Anglia; Choral Scholar, Norwich Cathedral Choir; Foundation Scholar, Royal College of Music; Thomas Allen Scholar, RCM. *Career:* Lay Clerk, Queen's Free Chapel of St George, Windsor Castle; Performs regularly throughout the United Kingdom and abroad in oratorio and recital; Bach's St Matthew Passion, Helsinki; Britten's War Requiem, Westminster Cathedral, Norwich Cathedral; Berlioz Te Deum, Orleans Cathedral; Mozart's Requiem, Israel; Monteverdi Vespers, Norway; Handel's Arminio, RCM; Maxwell Davies' The Lighthouse and Vivaldi's Ottone in Villa and Giustino for BBC Radio 3; Ferrando, Royal Academy of Music and Pimlico Opera Tour; Many recitals and oratorio appearances, including appearances with Osmo Vanska, Liège Philharmonic Orchestra, Southend Festival Choir, The Aldeburgh Music Club, Birmingham Festival Choral Society; Solo recitals in London and Aberdeen; Title role in Albert Herring, Perth Festival, 1998; Buxton Festival and appearances in recital and oratorio, 1999. *Recordings:* Requiem with the National Youth Choir of Great Britain and music by Wren Baroque Ensemble. *Current Management:* Hazard Chase, Norman House, Cambridge Place, Cambridge CB2 1NS, England. *Telephone:* (1223) 312400. *Fax:* (1223) 460827. *Website:* www .hazardchase.co.uk. *Address:* St Michael's Cottage, Church Lane, Bray SL6 2AF, England.

WILDING, Simon, BMus; British singer (bass); b. b. 10 May 1970, Leigh, Lancashire, England. *Education:* Royal Northern College of Music with Robert Alderson, and with Patrick Mcguigan. *Career:* at Royal Northern College of Music, sang Quince and Snug in separate productions of Britten's Midsummer Night's Dream; Geronimo in Il Matrimonio Segreto; and Walter Raleigh in Donizetti's Roberto Devereux; Luka in Walton's The Bear at Manchester and the UK/LA Festival at Los Angeles; Sang Count Ceprano in Rigoletto for English National Opera;

and Foltz in Die Meistersinger (ROH debut), ein Brabantische Edle in Lohengrin, and the Cappadocian in Salome at Covent Garden; Also covered and performed roles including Theseus in A Midsummer Night's Dream; The Drunken Poet in The Fairy Queen; The Speaker in The Magic Flute; Kotwitz in The Prince of Homburg; General in Die Soldaten; 5th Jew in Salome; Angelotti in Tosca; Other roles include Jove in La Calisto and roles in Il Pomo d'Oro for the Batignano Festival; Sang Fasolt in Das Rheingold and Hagen in Götterdämmerung for the Mastersingers and Wagner Soc.. *Recordings include:* Cappadocian in Salome (ROH); Lt Ratcliffe in Billy Budd (Hallé); Dick Deadeye in HMS Pinafore (D'Oyle Carte). *Honours:* Wagner Bursary Award for most promising singer of Wagner, 1991. *Current Management:* Robert Gilder & Co., Enterprise House, 59–65 Upper Ground, London, SE1 9PQ, England. *Telephone:* (20) 7928-9008. *Fax:* (20) 7928-9755. *E-mail:* rgilder@robert-gilder.com. *E-mail:* simon@wilding608.freeserve.co.uk.

WILDING-WHITE, Raymond, MM, DMA; composer and teacher; b. 9 Oct. 1922, Caterham, Surrey, England. *Education:* Juilliard School, New England Conservatory, Tanglewood with Copland and Dallapiccola, Boston University with Gardner Read. *Career:* teacher at Case Institute of Technology, Cleveland, 1961–67 and De Paul University, Chicago (1967–88); Founder and Director of the Loop ensemble, 1969–89, for the performance of contemporary music; Many music education broadcasts on WFMT-FM, Chicago, including series Our American Music, 1976, and a memorial tribute to John Cage 1992. *Compositions include:* Piano Concerto, 1949; The Tub, chamber opera, 1952; The Selfish Giant, television fable, 1952; Even Now for baritone and orchestra, 1954; Paraphernalia for chorus and five instruments, 1959; The Lonesome Valley, ballet, 1960; Yerma, opera, 1962; Concertante for viola, violin, horns and strings, 1963; Bandmusic, 1966; Encounters, ballet, 1967; 6 string quartets, 1948–88; Violin Concerto, 1978; Beth, musical, 1989 (renamed Trio 1994); Gifts, liturgical drama, 1993; Symphony of Symphonies, 1995.

WILKE, Elisabeth; Singer (Mezzo-Soprano); b. 19 May 1952, Dresden, Germany. *Education:* Studied at the Musikhochschule Dresden. *Career:* Debut: Dresden 1974, as Hansel; Appearances with the Dresden Staatsoper-Semper Oper in Germany and on tour as Dorabella, Amastris in Handel's Serse, Olga (Eugene Onegin) and Tisbe in Cenerentola, 1992; Sang Veronika in the premiere of Der Goldene Topf by E Mayer, 1989; Zulma in L'Italiana in Algeri at Dresden, 1997; Soloist in the St Matthew Passion at Magdeburg, 2000. *Recordings include:* Symphoniae Sacrae by Schütz (Capriccio); Saint-Saëns Christmas Oratorio; Missa Brevis by C P E Bach; J. S. Bach's St Matthew Passion. *Address:* c/o Semper Oper, 8012 Dresden, Germany.

WILKENS, Anne; Singer (Mezzo-Soprano); b. 1 July 1947, Romford, England. *Education:* Guildhall School of Music; London Opera Centre; Further Study with Eva Turner. *Career:* Sang in Verdi's Ernani at the Festival Hall, 1972; The Nose by Shostakovich for the New Opera Company, 1973; Sang with English Opera Group in operas by Britten, in Aldeburgh, Venice and Brussels; Sang in world premieres of Death in Venice, 1973, and Musgrave's The Voice of Ariadne, 1974; Member of the Royal Opera Company, Covent Garden, 1974–78, as Olga in Eugene Onegin, Maddalena in Rigoletto, and in the world premiere of Henze's We Come to the River, 1976; Appearances with Handel Opera Society: Handel roles include Julius Caesar, Dejanaira (Hercules) and Ezio; Welsh National Opera 1979, as Brangaene in Tristan und Isolde; Guest appearances in Frankfurt (Azucena), Marseille and Stuttgart (Brangaene); Bayreuth 1983, in the Solti/Hall production of The Ring; Karlsruhe from 1983, as Eboli in Don Carlos and as Wagner's Venus, Fricka, Ortrud and Waltraute; Sang in the premiere of Der Meister und Margarita by Kunaud, Karlsruhe, 1986; Sang Neris in Cherubini's Médée for Opera North, 1996; Mme Larina in Eugene Onegin for ENO, 1997; Season 2000–01 as Wagner's Mary at Covent Garden and in Dublin; Concert engagements with the London Symphony Orchestra, Hallé Orchestra, Bournemouth Symphony and in Netherlands, Spain, Brussels and Stockholm. *Recordings include:* Tristan und Isolde, conducted by Reginald Goodall. *Address:* c/o English National Opera, St Martin's Lane, London, EC 2, England.

WILKINS, Caroline; Composer; b. 31 July 1953, Somerset, England. *Education:* BMus, Royal College of Music, London, 1975; Cologne Music Academy, with Mauricio Kagel, 1987–88. *Career:* Composer and performer with new music projects in Australia, 1984–86; Freelance composer in Germany, 1989–; Commissions from Ensemble Köln (1991), the Hilliard Ensemble (1994) and others; Festival Participation at Darmstadt, Rheinland, Zürich and Witten, 1990–94. *Compositions include:* Piece for Accordion and Phonograph, 1988; Piece for Accordion with Screens, 1988; Arias for Phonograph and Singers, 1988; Piece for 17 Tones, for 2 pianos, 1990; Piece for Player Piano and Piano, 1990; Loquela, for 1 to 8 female voices, 1991; Automatophone, for ensemble, 1991; The Bird Organ is Made of Wood for Percussion, 1991; Camera Aeolia for organ, 1992; Auroram Lucifer for chorus, 1993; For These My Friends and Yours for 4 male voices, 1994; With Circle and Axis, for string quartet, 1998. *Honours:* First Prize, Frauenmusik-Forum, Berne, 1992. *Address:* c/o Ms F. Zimmermann, Edition Modern, Tre Media Musikverlage, Karlsruhe, Germany. *Website:* www .tremediamusicedition.de.

WILKINS, Margaret (Lucy); Composer and Music Educator; b. 13 Nov. 1939, Kingston upon Thames, England; m. Nigel E Wilkins, 11 Aug 1962 (divorced 1977), 2 d. *Education:* Trinity College of Music, London, 1952–57; BMus, University of Nottingham, 1957–60, 1987–90; LRAM, 1960; A.Mus.D, University of Nottingham, 1995. *Career:* Debut: BBC; Works performed world-wide, South Bank, and Wigmore Hall, London, England, Scotland, Canada, Germany, Italy, Switzerland, Bulgaria, Austria, Netherlands, America, Spain, Romania and Poland; Commissions: BBC SSO, University of St Andrews, New Music Group of Scotland, William Byrd Singers, John Turner, Julie Wilson, Goldberg Ensemble, Kirklees Cultural Services; Philip Mead; Festivals: Durham, Edinburgh, Huddersfield, Nottingham, Donne in Musica, Llangollen Eistedfodd, ISCM, World Music Days, Poland, Middelburg, Netherlands; New Music, Bucharest; Music Teacher, Mansfield Grammar School, Nottingham, UK, 1961–62; Private teacher of piano and theory, St. Andrews, Scotland, 1964–1976; Founder-Member and Performer of Scottish Early Music Consort, 1970–76; Principal Lecturer, Music, University of Huddersfield, 1999–2003; Senior Lecturer, Huddersfield Polytechnic/ University of Huddersfield, 1976–1999; Subject Leader in Composition, University of Huddersfield, UK, 1984–92; Artistic Director, Polyphonia, 1989–95; Maude Clarke Visiting Professor at Queen's University, Belfast, 1995; External Assessor for BA Performing Arts, Anglia Polytechnic University, UK, 1997–2001; Module Area Leader in Composition, University of Nottingham, UK, 1997–2003; MA in Music Composition Course Leader, University of Huddersfield, UK, 1990–2003; CALMA Fellowship, University of Huddersfield, UK, 2000; External Examiner for PhD, Edinburgh University, Scotland, 2000; Doctoral Commission, University of Music, Bucharest, Romania, 2001; External Examiner for PhD, Leeds University, 2002. *Compositions include:* Struwwelpeter, 1973; Hymn to Creation, 1973; Etude, 1974; Circus, 1975; Ave Maria, 1975; Music of the Spheres, 1975; Gitanjali, 1981; Aspects of Night, 1981; Epistola da San Marco, 1987; Réve, Réveil, Révélations, Réverbérations, 1988; Revelations of the Seven Angels, 1988; Symphony, 1989; Kanal, 1990; Musica Angelorum, 1991; Stringsing, 1992; L'Attente, 1994; Study in Black and White No. 3, 1996; Folk Works, 1996; Fearful Apathy, 1997; Ring Out, Wild Bells, 1998; Rituelle, 1999; Trompettes de Mort, 2003. *Recordings:* Study in Black and White Nos 1 and 2, Ananda Sukarlan, solo piano; The Pentatonic Connection, 1994. *Honours:* Scottish Arts Council Bursary for Composers, 1970; Winner of The New Cantata Orchestra of London's Competition for Young British Composers (Concerto Grosso), 1970; Winner of the Cappiani Prize for Women Composers (The Silver Casket), 1971; First Prize in the Halifax (Canada) International Competition for Teaching Music (Instrumental Interludes), 1973; Hinrichsen Foundation Award for Composers, UK, 1979; Arts Council of Great Britain, Bursary for Composers, 1981–82; First Prize, Miriam Gideon International Prize for Composers (Struwwelpeter), 2000; LTSN Palatine Development Award, UK, 2002. *Address:* 4 Church Street, Golcar, Huddersfield HD7 4AH, West Yorkshire, England. *E-mail:* margaretlucywilkins@btinternet.com. *Website:* composers21.com/ compdocs/wilkinsm.htm.

WILKINSON, Katie; Violist; b. 1960, England. *Career:* Debut: Wigmore Hall 1984, with Peter Pears; Co-Founded the Brindisi String Quartet at Aldeburgh, 1984; Concerts in a wide repertory throughout the United Kingdom and in France, Germany, Spain, Italy and Switzerland; Festival engagements at Aldeburgh (residency 1990), Arundel, Bath, Brighton, Huddersfield, Norwich and Warwick; First London Performance of Colin Matthews's 2nd Quartet 1990, premiere of David Matthews's 6th Quartet, 1991; Quartet by Mark Anthony Turnage, 1992; Many BBC recitals and Resident Artist with the University of Ulster. *Recordings include:* Quartets by Britten, Bridge and Imogen Holst; Works by Pierné and Lekeu. *Honours:* (with Brindisi Quartet) Prizewinner at the Third Banff International String Quartet Competition in Canada, 1989. *Address:* c/o Owen-White Management, 14 Nightingale Lane, London N8 7QU, England.

WILKOMIRSKA, Wanda; Violinist; b. 11 Jan. 1929, Warsaw, Poland; m. 2 s. *Education:* Studied with Irena Dubiska, Łódź Conservatory; Studied with Ede Zathureczky, Budapest, Hungary; Studied with Henryk Szeryng, Paris, France. *Career:* Debut: Age 7; With orchestra, Kraków, Poland, age 15; Appears frequently with most major orchestras throughout the world; Defected whilst on tour of Federal Republic of Germany, 1982. *Recordings:* Numerous. *Honours:* Polish State Prize, 1952 and 1964; Several Foreign prizes including Bach Competition Award; Officer's Cross of Polonia Restituta, 1958; Order of Banner of Labour 2nd Class 1959, 1st Class 1964; Minister of Culture and Arts Prize, Polish Musicians' Association, 1979.

WILKOMIRSKI, Jozef, MA; Conductor, Composer, Broadcaster, Lecturer and Journalist; b. 15 May 1926, Kalisz, Poland; m. Margaret Zasinska 1980, 1 d. *Education:* State High School of Music, Warsaw, Warsaw Univ. *Career:* debut, Warsaw Philharmonic 1950; Asst Conductor, Kraków Philharmonic 1950–51; Conductor, Poznan Philharmonic 1954–57; Dir and Chief Conductor of State Philharmonic M. Karlowicz in Szczecin 1957–71; founder, Chief Man. and Artistic Dir of Sudettic Philharmonic in Walbrzych 1978–, later renamed the Sudettic Philharmonia; guest conductor in numerous countries in Europe, Asia and America; composer from 1968; numerous radio and television programme appearances. *Compositions:* 2 Sinfoniettas; Symphonic Poems; Symphonic Suite, Royal Castle in Warsaw; Sonatas for Violin, Cello, and Double Bass; Harp Concerto; Concerto for Violin and Cello; Trio; Songs. *Publications:* over 400 articles and pieces of journalism. *Honours:* Gold Medal of Pomeranian Gryphon 1960, Musical Prize of the City Szczecin 1961, Medal for Merit in Culture 1967, Prize for Public Cultivation of Music 1970, Prize of the City Walbrzych 1979, Prize of Low Silesia Press 1982, Prize of the Province Walbrzych 1983, Medal of National Education 1984, Cultural Award of the City Walbrzych 1999; Cross of Warsaw Insurrection 1985, Order of the Banner of Labour (First Class) 1986, Cross of the Home Army 1995, Medal of the Veteran of the War for Independence 1995, Commander's Cross with the Star of the Order Polonia Restituta 1998. *Address:* Sudettic Philharmonia, ul Slowackiego 4, 58-300 Walbrzych, Poland. *Telephone:* 74 842-28-73. *Fax:* 74 842-28-73. *E-mail:* filharmonia@pako.pl. *Website:* www .filharmonia.pako.pl.

WILL, Jacob; Singer (Bass); b. 8 June 1957, Hartsville, South Carolina, USA. *Education:* Studied at the Cincinnati Conservatory and at San Francisco Opera Studio. *Career:* Sang Masetto at San Francisco, followed by appearances with Long Beach and Anchorage Operas, as Basilio in Il Barbiere di Siviglia; Carmel Beach Festival as Mozart's Figaro; Appearances throughout the USA as Don Giovanni, Frank in Die Fledermaus, and Dulcamara; Sang in Europe from 1986, Zürich Opera from 1988 as Basilio and Melcthal in Guillaume Tell; St Gallen as Sparafucile and Raimondo in Lucia di Lammermoor, Barnaba in Andrea Chénier, 1989; Vancouver 1990, as Oroveso, Bregenz Festival 1992, as Zuniga in Carmen; Concert engagements include Rossini's Petite Messe Solennelle, Lincoln Center, 1989; Sang the Speaker in Die Zauberflöte at Zürich and Giachino in Pa ër's Leonora at Winterthur, 2000. *Recordings include:* Zemlinsky's Kleider Machen Leute. *Address:* c/o Opernhaus Zürich, Falkenstrasse 1, 8008 Zürich, Switzerland.

WILLCOCK, Christopher John; Composer; b. 8 Feb. 1947, Sydney, New South Wales, Australia. *Education:* BMus (Hons), University of Sydney, 1974; Theological Doctorates at Paris, 1987. *Career:* Trinity Mass for Cantor, chorus, congregation and organ, 1977; Psalms for Feasts and Seasons, 1977; Convict and the Lady, for chorus and chamber ensemble, 1978; Lines from Little Gidding for chorus and organ, 1978; Friday 3.30 for chorus and string orchestra, 1986; Easter Moon for chorus and brass instruments, 1988; Two Pastorals for voice and harpsichord, 1990; Duo for Oboe and Harpsichord, 1992; Plaint Over Dili for oboe and harpsichord, 1992; The Frilled Lizard for viola and harp, 1993; Here be Dragons, for harpsichord, 1994. *Honours:* Dr Percy Jones Award for Outstanding Services to Liturgical Music, 1993. *Address:* c/o APRA, 1A East Street, Crows Nest, NSW 2065, Australia.

WILLCOCKS, Sir David (Valentine), Kt; Conductor; b. 30 Dec. 1919, Newquay, Cornwall, England; m. Rachel Blyth, 8 Nov 1947, two s., 1 deceased, two d. *Education:* Chorister at Westminster Abbey; King's Coll., Cambridge; Royal Coll. of Music. *Career:* Organist, Salisbury Cathedral, 1947–50; Organist, Worcester Cathedral, 1950–57; Conductor, City of Birmingham Choir, 1950–57; Fellow and Organist, King's Coll. Cambridge, 1957–73; Univ. Lecturer, 1957–74, Univ. Organist, 1958–74, Cambridge; Conductor, Cambridge Univ. Musical Society, 1958–73; Musical Dir, The Bach Choir, 1960–98; Dir, The Royal Coll. of Music, 1974–84. *Compositions:* Many choral and orchestral works. *Recordings:* Many with The Bach Choir, Royal Coll. of Music Chamber Choir, Choir of King's College, Cambridge and the principal London orchestras. *Honours:* MC 1944, FRCM 1965, Hon. RAM 1965, FRCCO 1967, CBE 1971, Hon. MA 1973, Hon. FTCL 1976, FRSCM 1977, Hon. Fellow King's Coll. Cambridge 1979, Hon. GSM 1980, Freeman of the City of London 1981, FRSAMD 1982, Hon. DLitt 1982 & 2003, Hon. DSL 1985, Hon. Dr of Fine Arts 1998, Hon. LLD 2001 Hon. DMus from 7 institutions 1976–1999. *Address:* 13 Grange Road, Cambridge CB3 9AS, England. *E-mail:* david_willcocks@dvvcambs.freeserve.co.uk.

WILLEN, Niklas Olov; Conductor; b. 30 March 1961, Stockholm, Sweden; m. Anna Schulze, 26 July 1997, 3 s., 1 d. *Education:* Royal College of Music, Stockholm. *Career:* Debut: Gavleborg Symphony Orchestra, Sweden, 1988; Royal Opera, Stockholm; Gothenburg Opera; Principal Conductor, The Sundsvall Chamber Orchestra, Sweden, 1993–97; Principal Guest Conductor, Royal Stockholm Philharmonic Orchestra, 1993–96; Guest Appearances in Norway, Finland, Denmark, Germany, England, Scotland, Ireland, USA; mem, Swedish Society of

Musical Artists. *Compositions:* Lux Aeterna for Choir, 1983; Bassoon Concerto, 1988; Wind Quintet, 1993. *Recordings:* Symphonies by Hugo Alfrein with Royal Scottish National Orchestra on Naxos; Several other recordings for major labels. *Honours:* 2nd Prize, Nordic Competition, 1990. *Current Management:* Patrick Garvey Management. *Address:* Top Floor, 59 Lansdowne Place, Hove, East Sussex BN3 1 FL, England.

WILLI, Herbert; Composer; b. 7 Jan. 1956. *Education:* Abitur; MPhil, University of Innsbruck; Diploma in Composition and MA, Mozarteum, Salzburg; Studies with Helmut Eder and Boguslav Schaeffer. *Compositions:* Opera Schlafes Bruder (libretto by Robert Schneider); Orchestral works: Der Froschmäusekrieg–for sprechgesang, 3 orchestral groups and tape, 1989; Räume für Orchester, 1991; Konzert für Orchester, 1991–92; Flötenkonzert, 1993; Chamber music: Stück für Flöte solo, 1985, 1986; Streichquartett, 1986; Trio für Violine, Horn und Klavier, 1992; Concerto for Orchestra, 1992; Flute Concerto, 1993; Begegnung, for orchestra, 1999; *Performances of his works:* New York (Carnegie Hall), London (Royal Albert Hall), Vienna (Konzerthaus/Musikverein), Salzburg Festival (Grosses Festspielhaus), Berlin Philharmonic Hall, performed by international orchestras Vienna Philharmonic, Berlin Philharmonic, Cleveland Orchestra, conducted by Claudio Abbado and Christoph von Dohnányi. *Honours:* Prize of the Republic of Austria, 1986; Rome Prize, 1987, 1988; Rolf Liebermann Scholarship, 1990; Ernst-von-Siemens Prize, 1991; Composer in Residence, Salzburg Festival, 1992. *Current Management:* Schott Musik International.

WILLIAM, Louis Hagen; Singer (Bass-Baritone); b. 1950, New Orleans, USA. *Education:* Studied at University of Los Angeles Opera Workshop and at Paris Conservatoire. *Career:* With Lyon Opéra sang Sarastro, Daland and the Landgrave in Tannhäuser, Paris Opéra Company in Turandot and L'Heure Espagnole; Other roles include Mephistopheles, Nilakanta in Lakmé, Rossini's Bartolo and the villians in Les Contes d'Hoffmann; Has sung in various versions of Porgy and Bess with the Royal Liverpool Philharmonic, the Scottish Chamber Orchestra under Carl Davis, the Ulster Orchestra under Yan Pascal Tortelier, and the Hallé and Royal Philharmonic Orchestras; Has also sung in Handel's Judas Maccabaeus and on French Radio and Television. *Recordings include:* Negro Spitituals (Quantum) and Mozart Concert Arias. *Honours:* First Prizes for Opera and Concert Singing at the Paris Conservatoire.

WILLIAMS, Adrian; Composer and Pianist; b. 30 April 1956, Watford, Hertfordshire, England. *Education:* Royal College of Music, London. *Career:* Composer-in-Residence, Charterhouse, 1980–82; Founder Director, Presteigne International Festival, 1983–92. *Compositions:* Sonata for Solo Cello, 1977; String Quartet No. 2, 1981; Tess, Orchestral Poem, 1982; Cantata: September Sky, 1985; Mass, 1986; Chaconne for Guitar, 1986; Images of a Mind, Cello and Piano, 1986; Cantata: Not Yet Born, 1986; Leaves from the Lost Book, 1987; Dies Irae, 1988; Music for the Film Gernika, 1987; Cantata: The Ways of Going, 1990; String Quartet No. 3, 1991; The King of Britain's Daughter, 1993. *Honours:* Menuhin Prize, 1978; Guinness Prize, 1986. *Address:* c/o BMI, 79 Harley House, Marylebone Road, London, NW1, England.

WILLIAMS, Bradley; Singer (tenor); b. 1965, Texas, USA. *Education:* University of Texas and Cincinnati Conservatory of Music. *Career:* Debut: As Ernesto in Don Pasquale with the Metropolitan Opera Guild, 1991; Performances include Korngold's Die Tote Stadt with New York City Opera and Zimmermann's Die Soldaten; Opera Orchestra of New York as Georges in Boieldieu's La Dame Blanche; Don Ramiro in La Cenerentola and Giannetto in La Gazza Ladra at Gran Teatro del Liceu in Barcelona; 1992 included Italian debut as Salvini in world premiere of Bellini's Adelson e Salvini at Teatro Massimo Bellini; Beppe in Pagliacci for New York City Opera; Canadian debut as Ernesto in Don Pasquale in Edmonton; Arturo in I Puritani in Malaga; Carmina Burana at Teatro Regio Torino under Hubert Soudant; Alphonse in Hérold's Zampa at the Wexford Festival; 1995, created role of Scott for Houston Grand Opera's world premiere of Wallace and Korie's Harvey Milk; Count Almaviva in Il Barbiere di Siviglia; Performances of Handel's Judas Maccabaeus and Messiah with Collegiate Chorale for Carnegie Hall debut; Australian debut as Tonio in Fille du Régiment with Opera Australia, 1997; Connecticut Opera debut as Ernesto; Ernesto for Opéra de Québec and Ferrando in Così fan tutte for Dayton Opera; Lindoro in l'Italiana in Algeri for Garsington Opera Festival, Oxford; Season 1998–99 included Duke in Rigoletto in Anchorage, Alaska, debut at Strasbourg's Opéra du Rhin as Tonio in Fille du Régiment and Edgardo in Lucia di Lammermoor in Anchorage. *Recordings:* Salvini in Adelson e Salvi; Harvey Milk with San Francisco Opera. *Current Management:* Athole Still International Management, Forresters Hall, 25–27 Westow Street, London, SE19 3RY, England. *Telephone:* (20) 8771-5271. *Fax:* (20) 8768-6600. *Website:* www .atholestill.com.

WILLIAMS, Camilla; American singer; *Professor of Voice, Indiana University*; b. 8 Oct. 1922, Danville, VA; m. Charles T. Beavers 1950.

Education: Virginia State Coll., studied with Marion Szekely-Freschl. *Career:* sang role of Madama Butterfly as first black singer, New York City Centre 1946; sang Aida, New York City Centre 1948; New York performance of Mozart's Idomeneo, Little Orchestra Soc. 1950; tour of Alaska 1950; European tour (London) 1954; performance of Menotti's Saint of Bleecker Street 1955; American Festival, Belgium 1955; African tour for US State Dept (14 countries) 1958–59; tour of Israel 1959; guest of Pres. Eisenhower, Concert for Crown Prince of Japan 1960; tour of Formosa, Australia, New Zealand, Korea, Japan, Philippines, Laos, South Viet Nam 1962; New York performance of Handel's Orlando 1971; tour of Poland 1974; appearances with orchestras, including the Royal Philharmonic, Vienna Symphony, Zürich, Tonhalle, Berlin Philharmonic, New York Philharmonic, Chicago Symphony, Philadelphia Orchestra, BBC Orchestras, Stuttgart Orchestra, Geneva, Belgium; Prof. of Voice, Brooklyn Coll. 1970–73, Bronx Coll. 1970–, Queens Coll. 1974–, Indiana Univ., Bloomington 1977–. *Address:* School of Music-Studio MU104B, Indiana University, Bloomington, IN 47405, USA.

WILLIAMS, Daniel Lewis; Singer (bass); b. 1960, USA. *Education:* University of Utah, Salt Lake City; Musikhochschule, Munich and with Kurt Böhme and Kurt Moll. *Career:* Many appearances at opera houses throughout Germany and Italy, with roles including Ramphis in Aida, Gremin, Sarastro, Hunding, Rocco and Daland; Baron Ochs in Der Rosenkavalier at Frankfurt, Palermo, Munich and Genoa; Season 2000–2001 as King Marke at Genoa, Fafner and Hagen in The Ring at Marseille, Claggart in Billy Budd at Venice, Sarastro in Weimar and Daland for Opera di Trieste; Concerts include the Verdi Requiem in Nuremberg, Schoenberg's Gurrelieder, Shostakovich Symphony no. 14, Stravinsky's Threni and Beethoven's Mass in C (both in Venice). *Current Management:* Athole Still International Management, Forresters Hall, 25–27 Westow Street, London, SE19 3RY, England. *Telephone:* (20) 8771-5271. *Fax:* (20) 8768-6600. *Website:* www .atholestill.com.

WILLIAMS, Edgar Warren; Professor, Composer and Conductor; b. 12 June 1949, Orlando, Florida, USA; m. Christine Anderson, 19 June 1971, 1 s., 1 d. *Education:* BA, Duke University, 1971; MA, Columbia University, 1973; MFA 1977; PhD 1982, Princeton University. *Career:* Teaching Assistant, Columbia University, 1972–73; Assistant in Instruction, Princeton University, 1977–78; Visiting Lecturer in Music, University of California, Davis, 1978–79; Assistant Professor, The College of William and Mary, Williamsburg, Virginia, 1979–82; Associate Professor, 1982; Guest Conductor with orchestras including Bennington Composers Conference Ensemble, 1969–70 and Columbia Composers Ensemble, 1973; Conductor, William and Mary Orchestra, 1979–82. *Compositions:* Numerous published including: Three Songs, 1977; Across a Bridge of Dreams, 1979–80; Amoretti, 1980; Some Music for Merry Wives, 1982; Landscapes With Figure, 1983; Now Showing, for wind and percussion, 1993; Pentimenti, for chamber orchestra, 1993; String Quartet II, 1996; String Quartet III, 1997; Nosferata: A Symphony of Horror, for large orchestra, 1998; Lone, for solo saxophone, 1998. *Publications:* Harmony and Voice Leading, with Taylor and Miller, 1993; Introduction to Music, 1993. *Contributions:* In Theory Only; 19th Century Music. *Address:* Department of Music, College of William and Mary, Williamsburg, VA 23185, USA.

WILLIAMS, Harriet; Singer (Mezzo-soprano); b. 1969, London; m., 1 c. *Education:* Guildhall School with Johanna Peters; Studied with Hazel Wood. *Career:* Welsh National Opera from 1993 in operas by Mozart, Strauss, Berlioz, Verdi and Janáček; Purcell's Dido at Bath, Suzuki in Butterfly at the Mananan Festival and Cenerentola for Clonter Opera; Other roles include Mozart's Cherubino and Dorabella; Concerts include the Mozart and Verdi Requiems, St Matthew Passion, Haydn's Nelson and St Theresa Masses and Mahler's Rückert Lieder; Season 1998–99 with Poppea for Welsh National Opera and The Dream of Gerontius with the Liverpool Philharmonic; Season 2003 Carmen for English Pocket Opera; Storge in Handel's Jephtha with Konzertcher Darmstadt with performances in Baberihausen, Frankfurt, Amorbach and Darmstadt. *Address:* 18 Clarence Road, London, E12 5BB, England. *E-mail:* harriet.williams@btopenworld.com.

WILLIAMS, Helen; Singer (Soprano); b. 1959, Merseyside. *Education:* Royal Northern College of Music. *Career:* Appearances with Glyndebourne Festival and Tour in 1980s, including Sashka in Osborne's The Electrification of the Soviet Union, and Emme in Albert Herring on tour to Italy; Engagements from 1994 include Handel's Rodelinda in Dublin and in Jephtha with The Sixteen in Rome and London; Dalinda in Ariodante and Amor in Gluck's Orfeo, for English National Opera; Britten's Helena for Opera North and Flaminia in Hayden's Mondo della luna for Netherlands Opera; Sang Naiad in Ariadne auf Naxos and Mozart's First Lady for Scottish Opera; Concerts include The Poisoned Kiss by Vaughan Williams (London and Birmingham), Messiah at the Albert Hall and Handel's Israel in Egypt at St John's Smith Square (2000); Season 2000–2001 with Polinesso in Handel's Radamisto for Opera North and Rodelinda at Aldeburgh and New York. *Recordings* *include:* Gianetta in L'Elisir d'amore and Frasquita in Carmen (Chandos). *Address:* c/o Opera North, 26 New Briggate, Leeds, Yorkshire, LS1 6NU, England.

WILLIAMS, Howard; Conductor; b. 25 April 1947, Hemel Hempstead, Hertfordshire, England; m. Juliet Solomon 1977, 1 s, 1 d. *Education:* King's School, Canterbury; BA, New College, Oxford; BMus, Liverpool University; Advanced conducting course, Guildhall School of Music and Drama. *Career:* Conducted over 40 opera productions with English National Opera and elsewhere, including Punch and Judy and The Knot Garden for Channel 4 television; Other modern repertory includes the premieres of Holloway's Liederkreis and Concertino No. 1, Hamilton's Anna Karenina, and Cowie's Choral Symphony and Concerto for Orchestra; Many productions with Royal Ballet at Covent Garden and abroad; Regular Guest Conductor with BBC Symphony Orchestra, BBC National Orchestra of Wales; Regular appearances with Royal Philharmonic, Scottish National, Bournemouth Symphony, Northern Sinfonia, English Chamber, London Sinfonietta and Royal Liverpool Philharmonic; Regular visitor overseas to orchestras in France, Belgium, Netherlands, Sweden and Hungary; Principal Conductor, Pècs Symphony Orchestra, Hungary, 1989–, being first British conductor to hold appointment in Hungary; Led Chelsea Opera group in Massenet's Esclarmonde, 1998; Season 2000–01 as Chief Conductor of Oxford Orchestra da Camera, concerts with Prague and Portuguese Symphony Orchestras and Bavarian Radio Symphony Orchestra. *Compositions:* Shadowdance, 1991. *Recordings include:* three vols of music by Frank Bridge, including his opera The Christmas Rose; Bizet's Ivan The Terrible. *Current Management:* Connaught Artists Management Ltd, 2 Molasses Row, Plantation Wharf, London, SW11 3UX, England. *Telephone:* (20) 7738 0017. *Fax:* (20) 7738 0909. *E-mail:* classicalmusic@connaughtartists.com. *Website:* www.connaughtartists .com.

WILLIAMS, Huw; Organist; b. 2 June 1971, Swansea, Wales. *Education:* Organ Scholar, Christ's College, Cambridge; 2 years Postgraduate at RAM; Organ Scholar, St Paul's Cathedral, London; Organ lessons, Netherlands. *Career:* Assistant Organist, Hereford Cathedral; Three Choirs Festival; Sub-Organist, St Paul's Cathedral; BBC broadcasts with both Cathedral Choirs; mem, ISM. *Recordings:* 10 recordings with Cathedral Choirs, Hereford and St Paul's. *Honours:* Fellow of Royal College of Organists; Limpus Prize, 1991; Music degree, Cambridge, 1992; Countess of Munster Music Scholar, 1993–95; Ian Fleming Musical Trust Scholar, 1994–95; Associate of the Royal Academy of Music, 2001. *Address:* 4A Amen Court, London EC 4M 7BU, England.

WILLIAMS, Janet; Singer (Soprano); b. 1965, Detroit, USA. *Career:* Debut: San Francisco Opera, 1989, as Despina in Così fan tutte; Roles at San Francisco have included Adele in Die Fledermaus, Nannetta, Musetta, and Elvira in L'Italiana in Algeri; Guest at Los Angeles as Mozart's Blondchen and at Wexford as Rezia in Gluck's La Rencontre imprévue, 1991; Season 1992–93, as Zerlina in Lyon and Rosina at Washington; Berlin Staatsoper from 1992, as Pamina, Graun's Cleopatra, and Oresia in Telemann's Orfeo; Deutsche Oper Berlin, 1996, as Handel's Semele; Verdi's Oscar at the Paris Opéra Bastille and Elisa in Mozart's Il Re Pastore at Nice, 1994; Adele in Die Fledermaus at the New York Met, 1996; Season 1997–98 in Opera Gala at San Francisco, and as Manon in Henze's Boulevard Solitude at Frankfurt; Sang Poppea in Handel's Agrippina at Graz, 2000; Concerts include Tippett's A Child of our Time at Berlin and Mozart's Requiem at New York. *Recordings include:* Messiah and Graun's Cesare e Cleopatra. *Address:* c/o San Francisco Opera, War Memorial House, Van Ness Avenue, San Francisco, CA 94102, USA.

WILLIAMS, Jeremy Huw; Singer (Baritone); b. 1965, England. *Education:* St John's College, Cambridge; National Opera Studio, and with April Cantelo. *Career:* Debut: Guglielmo in Così fan tutte, with Welsh National Opera; Appearances with L'Opéra de Nantes as Papageno, Olivier in Capriccio and title role in Karetnikov's Till Eulenspiegel; Escamillo, Germont, and Marcello in La Bohème for WNO; Further engagements for Music Theatre Wales, Opera Ireland and the City of Birmingham SO; Buxton Festival, Holland Park Opera and Ulm, Germany; Sang M. Gaye in the Lully/Molière Bourgeois Gentilhomme, for the English Bach Festival at the Linbury Theatre, Covent Garden, 2001. *Address:* c/o English Bach Festival, 15 South Eaton Place, London, SW1W 9ER, England.

WILLIAMS, John, AO, OBE; guitarist; b. 24 April 1941, Melbourne, Australia; s. of Len Williams and Melaan Ket; m. 1st Linda Susan Kendall 1964 (divorced); one d.; m. 2nd Sue Cook 1981 (divorced); one s.; m. 3rd Kathleen Panama 2000. *Education:* Friern Barnet Grammar School and Royal Coll. of Music, London. *Career:* studied guitar with father, Segovia and at Accad. Chigiana, Siena; has toured widely and appears frequently on TV and radio; numerous transcriptions and gramophone recordings as solo guitarist and with leading orchestras; f. The Height Below (ensemble) with Brian Gascoigne 1974, John

Williams and Friends (ensemble) and Founder-mem. groups Sky 1979–84 and John Williams' Attacca 1991–; Artistic Dir South Bank Summer Music Festival 1984–85, Melbourne Arts Festival 1987. *Films:* composed and played music for film Emma's War. *Honours:* Hon. FRCM, FRAM, FRNCM; Dr hc (Melbourne). *Current Management:* Askonas Holt Ltd, 27 Chancery Lane, London, WC2A 1PF, England. *Telephone:* (20) 7400-1700. *Fax:* (20) 7400-1799.

WILLIAMS, John Towner; American composer; b. 8 Feb. 1932, Flushing, NY. *Education:* Juilliard School, UCLA. *Career:* pianist Columbia Pictures; jazz pianist working with Henry Mancini on television scores; conductor Boston Pops Orchestra 1980–98. *Film scores:* The Secret Ways 1961, Diamond Head 1962, None But the Brave 1965, How to Steal a Million 1966, Valley of the Dolls 1967, The Cowboys 1972, The Poseidon Adventure 1972, Tom Sawyer 1973, Earthquake 1974, The Towering Inferno 1974, Jaws (Acad. Award) 1975, The Eiger Sanction 1975, Family Plot 1976, Midway 1976, The Missouri Breaks 1976, Raggedy Ann and Andy 1977, Black Sunday 1977, Star Wars (Acad. Award) 1977, Close Encounters of the Third Kind 1977, The Fury 1978, Jaws II 1976, Superman 1978, Dracula 1979, The Empire Strikes Back 1980, Raiders of the Lost Ark 1981, E.T.: The Extra Terrestrial (Acad. Award) 1982, Return of the Jedi 1983, Indiana Jones and the Temple of Doom 1984, The River 1985, Space Camp 1986, The Witches of Eastwick 1987, Empire of the Sun (BAFTA Award for Best Score) 1988, 1941 1989, Always 1989, Born on the Fourth of July 1989, Indiana Jones and the Last Crusade 1989, Stanley and Iris 1990, Presumed Innocent 1990, Home Alone 1990, Hook 1991, JFK 1993, Far and Away 1993, Home Alone 2: Lost in New York 1993, Jurassic Park 1993, Schindler's List (Acad. Award) 1993, Sabrina 1995, The Reivers 1995, Nixon 1995, Sleepers 1996, Rosewood 1996, Land of the Giants 1997, Seven Years in Tibet 1997, The Lost World: Jurassic Park 1997, Amistad 1997, Lost in Space 1997, Time Tunnel 1997, Saving Private Ryan 1998, The Phantom Menace 1999, Angela's Ashes 1999, Harry Potter and the Sorcerer's Stone 2001, Attack of the Clones 2001, Minority Report 2002, Harry Potter and the Chamber of Secrets 2002, Catch Me if You Can 2002, Harry Potter and the Prisoner of Azkaban 2004, The Terminal 2004. *Recordings:* John Williams Plays The Movies 1996, Music From The Star Wars Saga 1999, Jane Eyre 1999, Themes From Academy Award Winners, Over The Rainbow: Songs From The Movies 1992, John Williams Conducting The Boston Pops 1996, The Hollywood Sound 1997, From Sousa To Spielberg, Best Of John Williams 1998, Treesong 2001, Call Of The Champions (official theme of 2002 Winter Olympics, Salt Lake City) 2001, John Williams Trumpet Concerto 2002, American Journey 2002; recordings of film scores. *Honours:* numerous hon. degrees; two Emmy Awards, three Golden Globes, 16 Grammy Awards, recipient of Kennedy Center Honors 2004. *Current Management:* Michael Gorfaine, Gorfaine & Schwartz, 13245 Riverside Drive, Suite 450, Sherman Oaks, CA 91423, USA. *Website:* www.johnwilliams.org.

WILLIAMS, Julius (Penson); Composer and Conductor; b. 22 June 1954, Bronx, New York, USA; m. Lenora B Williams, 7 Aug 1977, 1 s., 1 d. *Education:* Music major, Andrew Jackson High School, 1972; BS, Herbert H Lehman College, City University of New York, 1977; MM, Hartt School of Music, 1980; Aspen Music School, 1984; Professional Fellow, Aspen, 1985. *Career:* Debut: Premiere of A Norman Overture, New York Philharmonic and Zubin Mehta, 1985; Music Director, CPTV, 1984–85; Arts Award Guest Conductor, Connecticut Opera, 1983, Dallas Symphony, 1986, Savannah Symphony, 1987; Assistant Conductor, Aspen Music Festival, 1985; Conductor, Composer-in-Residence, Nutmeg Ballet, Connecticut, 1986–88; Guest Conductor, New Haven Symphony, May 1987; Guest Conductor, Amor Artist Chamber Orchestra, 1987; Artistic Director, New York State Summer School of the Arts (Choral Studies), 1988–; Principal Guest, School of Orchestral Studies; Associate Professor, University of Vermont; Artist-in-Residence, Saratoga Arts Festival, Aug 1988; National television, CBS Sunday Morning with Charles Kuralf, 11 Sept 1988. *Compositions:* A Norman Overture; Toccatina for Strings; Incommendation of Music; The Spring; Rise Up Shepherd and Follow; Vermont's Escape; Alison's Dream; The Fall, Summers Good Ecelin. *Contributions:* American Choral Directors' Journal Choral Review, 1982. *Current Management:* Euphonia Artist Management, PO Box 809, Cambridge, MA 02238, USA. *Address:* Henderson, 7th Ave, Apt 4K, New York, NY 10026-2231, USA.

WILLIAMS, Laverne; Singer (Tenor); b. 1935, San Francisco, California, USA. *Education:* Master's Degree, University of California; Alfred Hertz Memorial Scholarship and Rockefeller Foundation Scholarship for studies in Europe. *Career:* Concerts and Opera appearances ranging from Baroque to Contemporary; L'Incoronazione di Poppea, Salome, Idomeneo and Porgy and Bess, Switzerland; Appeared with Jessye Norman in Great Day in the Morning, Paris; Porgy and Bess, Glagolitic Mass and Jenůfa under Simon Rattle, United Kingdom; Appearances with most major orchestras in London and the United Kingdom including London Symphony, Royal Philharmonic and the Royal Liverpool Philharmonic Orchestra; Directed and sung in an experimental evening of spirituals, Almeida Theatre; Performed Virgil Thomson's Four Saints in Three Acts, Almeida Theatre; European Opera appearances include Zürich, Lyon and Brussels operas; Television and Radio appearances include: Gershwin's Blue Monday in Switzerland; Hermann Prey Show for German television; Here Comes the Classics and excerpts from Carmen Jones, BBC television; Club Mix, Channel 4; Leading role, European premiere of Carmen Jones; Weber's Oberon, Edinburgh Festival, Tanglewood and Frankfurt, 1986. *Recordings:* Great Day in the Morning, with Jessye Norman. *Honours:* Competition successes in 'S-Hertogenbosch, Rio de Janeiro and Barcelona.

WILLIAMS, Louise; Violist; b. 23 Sept. 1955, England. *Education:* Royal Academy of Music; Juilliard School of Music, New York. *Career:* Co-founder and second violinist Endellion Quartet, 1979–83; Violist Chilingirian Quartet, 1987–92; Member, Raphael Ensemble, 1996–2003; Quintet partner, Lindsay Quartet, 1995–; Founder-member, Merel Quartet, 2002–; Freelance chamber musician and soloist. *Recordings:* Complete Quartets of Bartók and Dvořák; Bartók Piano Quintet; Dvorak Quintets; Mozart Flute Quartets; Beethoven Serenade; Haydn Quartets; Prokofiev Quartets; Mendelssohn Viola Quintets; Bridge Sextet, Quintet and Viola Duo; Bridge Music for Viola and Piano. *Address:* 10a Paultons Street, London SW3 5DP, England. *E-mail:* louisevla@ukonline.co.uk.

WILLIAMS, Peter Fredric, BA, MusB, MA, PhD, LittD; musicologist, academic, writer, organist and harpsichordist; b. 14 May 1937, Wolverhampton, Staffordshire, England; m. Rosemary Seymour 1982; three s. one d. *Education:* Birmingham Inst., St John's Coll., Cambridge. *Career:* Lecturer 1962–72, Reader 1972–82, Prof. 1982–85, Dean 1984, Univ. of Edinburgh; Dir, Russell Coll. of Harpsichords, Edinburgh 1969; Founder-Ed., The Organ Yearbook 1969–; Arts and Sciences Distinguished Prof. 1985–95, Dir, Graduate Center for Performance Practice Studies 1990–96, Duke Univ., Durham, NC, USA; John Bird Prof., Univ. of Wales, Cardiff 1996–2002; mem. British Inst. of Organ Studies (chair.). *Publications:* The European Organ 1450–1850 1966, Figured Bass Accompaniment (two vols) 1970, Venta/Peeters the Organ of the Netherlands (trans.) 1971, Bach Organ Music 1972, A New History of the Organ From the Greeks to the Present Day 1980, The Organ Music of J. S. Bach (three vols) 1980–84, Bach, Handel and Scarlatti: Tercentenary Essays (ed.) 1985, Playing the Works of Bach 1986, The Organ 1988, Playing the Organ Music of Bach 1988, Mozart: Perspectives in Performance (ed. with L. Todd) 1991, The Organ in Western Culture 750–1250 1992, The King of Instruments: How Do Churches Come to Have Organs? 1993, The Chromatic Fourth During Four Centuries of Music 1995, Cambridge Studies in Performance Practice (series ed., four vols) –1995, Music to Hear, or Fears for Higher Music Study 2001, Bach: The Goldberg Variations 2001; several vols of keyboard music by Bach and Handel; contrib. to scholarly books and journals. *Honours:* Hon. Fellow, Royal Scottish Acad. of Art, Research Fellow, Cornell Univ., New York, Curt Sachs Award, American Musical Instrument Soc. 1996. *Address:* c/o Department of Music, Corbett Road, University of Wales, Cardiff, Cardiff, CF10 3EB, Wales.

WILLIAMS, Sioned; Harpist; b. 1 July 1953, Mancot, Clwyd, North Wales; m. Kim A L Sargeant, 6 August 1977. *Education:* Welsh College of Music and Drama, 1971–74; Recital Diploma, Royal Academy of Music. *Career:* Debut: Purcell Room, Park Lane Group Young Artists/20th Century Music, 1977; Carnegie Hall, New York, USA (Concert Artists Guild Award), 1980; Appearances world-wide with London Symphony Orchestra, Philharmonia, London Philharmonic Orchestra, RPO, BBC Symphony Orchestra, BBC Philharmonic, CBSO, Royal Ballet, London Sinfonietta, Royal Opera House, ENO, WNO, SNO; Solo and Concerto performances, premiering over 80 works; Chamber Music with Uroboros, Gemini, Spectrum, Endymion, Divertimenti, Koenig, Grosvenor, Circle; Theatre, radio, television and festival appearances; Professor of Harp, Royal College of Music Junior Department, 1976–85; Royal Academy of Music, 1983–84; London College of Music, 1985–86; Trinity College of Music, 1986–; Adjudicator at major Welsh Eisteddfods, 1981–. *Compositions:* Cyfres i'r Delyn, 1973 (special prize, 17th International Harp Week); Serenata e Danza, 1983. *Recordings:* Harp Music, John Thomas; Harp Music, John Parry; Spun Gold for Flute and Harp; Ceremony of Carols, Britten; Nielsen with James Galway. *Publications:* Editor, John Parry: Four Sonatas, 1982; Four Sonatas, 1982; J. S. Bach: Suite BMV1006a, 1986. *Honours:* Numerous Prizes, Awards and Scholarships including Bursary, Arts Council Advanced Training Scheme, 1982. *Address:* 181 Gloucester Road, Cheltenham, Gloucester GL51 8NQ, England.

WILLIAMS, Wayne; Singer (Tenor); b. 1960, Cleveland, Ohio, USA. *Education:* Studied at the Cleveland Music Settlement and with Gerard Souzay in Geneva. *Career:* Concert appearances with the Suisse Romande, Chamber Orchestra of Lausanne, Berne Symphony, Tonhalle

Zürich, YMSO (London), Orchestra Haydn (Italy) and the Shanghai Symphony (China); Conductors have included Armin Jordan, Peter Maag, Horst Stein, Lopez-Cobos, James Blair, Paul Angerer and Herbert Handt; Recitals throughout the USA and Europe with Dalton Baldwin; Appearances in Paris in Dvořák's Requiem and Stabat Mater, Switzerland in The Creation and St Matthew Passion; Opera repertoire includes Schubert's Fierrabras, L'Elisir d'amore, La Traviata and A Midsummer Night's Dream. *Recordings include:* Poulenc Gloria; Great Day in the Morning, with Jessye Norman; Dvořák Stabat Mater.

WILLIAMS-KING, Anne; Singer (Soprano); b. 1960, Wrexham, Wales. *Education:* Studied at the Royal Northern College of Music and the National Opera Studio in London. *Career:* Sang with the Welsh National Opera as Lenio in The Greek Passion by Martinů, Mimi, Gilda, Fiordiligi, Marzelline in Fidelio and Micaela; Covent Garden debut in 1988 as Freia in Das Rheingold; Appearances with Opera North as Mimi and in Rebecca by Josephs and A Village Romeo and Juliet by Delius; Scottish Opera as Freia and Violetta, invited to return as Jenůfa, Madama Butterfly and Mimi; Foreign engagements include Anne Trulove in The Rake's Progress at Berne; Frequent concert appearances with leading British orchestras and on television; Sang Butterfly with Scottish Opera at Edinburgh, 1990; Suor Angelica for ENO, 1998; Season 1999–2000 as Lisa in The Queen of Spades, at Antwerp, and Janáček's Emilia Marty at Osnabrück. *Address:* c/o Stafford Law Associates, 6 Barham Close, Weybridge, Surrey, England.

WILLIS, Helen; Singer (Mezzo-Soprano); b. 25 July 1959, Newport, Gwent, Wales; m. Robert Venn, 17 Dec 1983. *Education:* Diploma, Royal Academy of Music, 1977–83. *Career:* Debut: Wigmore Hall, London, 1983; Member of Glyndebourne Festival Chorus, 1983–85; Solo Operatic debut with Welsh National Opera as Siegrune in Die Walküre in 1984; Concerts and recitals throughout the United Kingdom and abroad; Broadcasts include Sea Pictures and Wesendonck Lieder with BBC National Orchestra of Wales. *Honours:* Triennial Young Welsh Singer of the Year, 1982.

WILLIS, Nuala; Singer (mezzo-soprano); b. 1950, England. *Career:* Worked as Designer and Costumier and as Actress in England in North America; Sang with Opera Studio in Brussels and small roles with the Glyndebourne Tour; Aldeburgh Festival in Eugene Onegin and A Midsummer Night's Dream; Guest appearances at Nancy, Metz, Marseilles (Herodias in Salome), Geneva (Larina in Eugene Onegin), Marseilles (Jezibab in Rusalka) and Zürich (The Hostess in Boris Godunov); At Covent Garden appeared in A Midsummer Night's Dream, Eugene Onegin and Faust as Martha; In Ireland has sung Widow Bebick (Mahagonny) at Wexford and Clytemnestra in Elektra conducted by Janos Fürst, in Dublin; Season 1989–90 included Herodias in the Swedish Folkopera's Salome at the Edinburgh Festival; Ulrica in Un Ballo in Maschera for Canadian Opera in Toronto; Royal National Theatre in Sondheim's Sunday in the Park with George; Engagements with the D'Oyly Carte Opera; Sang the Elephant in Paran Vir's Broken Strings at the Almeida Theatre, 1996; Older Woman in the premiere of Dove's Flight, Glyndebourne, 1998; Season 1999–2000 as Stravinsky's Mother Goose at Lausanne and Glyndebourne and premiere of Ion by Param Vir, at Aldeburgh. *Current Management:* Athole Still International Management, Forresters Hall, 25–27 Westow Street, London, SE19 3RY, England. *Telephone:* (20) 8771-5271. *Fax:* (20) 8768-6600. *Website:* www.atholestill.com.

WILLS, Arthur; Composer and Cathedral Organist; b. 19 Sept. 1926, Coventry, England; m. Mary Elizabeth Titterton, 14 Nov 1953, 1 s., 1 d. *Education:* St John's School, Coventry; St Nicholas College, Canterbury; FRCO, 1948; ADCM, 1951; BMus, 1952; D.Mus, 1958; Hon RAM, 1974; FRSCM, 1977. *Career:* Organist, Ely Cathedral, 1958–90; Professor, Royal Academy of Music, 1964–92; Organ Recitals in Europe, USA, Australia and New Zealand; mem, Royal Academy of Music. *Compositions:* Organ Concerto, 1970; An English Requiem, 1971; Guitar Sonata, 1974; Three Poems of E. E. Cummings for Tenor, Oboe and Piano, 1974; Love's Torment (Four Elizabethan Love Songs) for Alto and Piano, 1975; The Fenlands (Symphonic Suite for Brass Band and Organ), 1981; Overture: A Muse of Fire for Brass Band, 1983; Concerto Lirico for Guitar Quartet, 1987; When the Spirit Comes (Four Poems of Emily Brontë for Mezzo Soprano and Piano), 1985; Piano Sonata '1984'; The Dark Lady (Eight Sonnets of Shakespeare for Baritone and Piano), 1986; Sacrae Symphonia: Veni Creator Spiritus, 1987; Choral Concerto: The Gods of Music, 1992; Eternity's Sunrise, Three Poems by William Blake, 1992; A Toccata of Galuppi's, Scena for Countertenor and String Quartet, 1993. *Recordings:* Arthur Wills CDs available 2004: Missa Sancti Stephani; Missa Incarnationis; Music for Organ and Brass, Hyperion; The Praises of the Trinity, Herald; Full Stops, Meridian; Music of Six Centuries, Meridian; Wondrous Machine!–Organ Music of Arthur Wills, Guild. *Publications:* Organ, Menuhin Music Guide Series, 1984 and 1993. *Contributions:* Musical Times. *Honours:* O.B.E., 1990. *Address:* Paradise House, 26 New Barns Road, Ely, Cambridgeshire CB 7 4PN, England.

WILSON, Catherine; Singer (soprano); b. 1936, Glasgow, Scotland. *Education:* Royal Manchester Coll. of Music with Elsie Thurston; further study with Ruth Packer in London and Maria Carpi in Geneva. *Career:* debut, Sadler's Wells, London in 1960 as Angelina in La Cenerentola; Glyndebourne in 1960 in Die Zauberflöte; Sadler's Wells in 1965 in the premiere of Bennett's The Mines of Sulphur; Scottish Opera in the 1977 Edinburgh Festival, title role in Thea Musgrave's Mary Queen of Scots; Scottish Opera in 1974 in the premiere of Hamilton's The Catiline Conspiracy; guest appearances in Aldeburgh, Cologne, Geneva, Boston, Houston, Louisville and ENO in London, and Santa Fe; often heard in operas by Mozart, Rossini, Puccini, Strauss and Britten and as a concert singer; teacher at Royal Northern Coll. of Music, 1980–91; performance coach, William Walton Trust, 1990–95. *Recordings include:* Albert Herring by Britten, The Merry Widow, Dido and Aeneas. *Honours:* Fellow, Royal Manchester Coll. of Music. *Address:* 18 St Mary's Grove, London, N1, England.

WILSON, Charles; Composer; b. 8 May 1931, Toronto, Canada. *Education:* Studied with Godfrey Ridout at the Toronto Conservatory; D.Mus, Toronto University in 1956; Further study with Lukas Foss and Carlos Chavez at the Berkshire Music Center. *Career:* Head of the Music Department at Guelph Collegiate Institute, 1962–70; Composer-in-Residence at Canadian Opera Company from 1972, and at the University of Guelph in Ontario; Chorusmaster, Canadian Opera Company; mem, Associate Composer, Canadian Music Centre; Canadian League of Composers. *Compositions include:* 4 String Quartets, 1950, 1968, 1975, 1983; The Strolling Clerk From Paradise, chamber opera, 1952; Symphony in A, 1954; Sonata de Chiesa for Oboe and Strings, 1960; String Trio, 1963; The Angels Of The Earth, oratorio, 1966; En Guise for Baritone and Strings, 1968; Concert 5x4x3 for String Quintet, Woodwind Quartet and Brass Trio, 1970; Johnny Fibber, operetta, 1970; Phrases From Orpheus, multi media opera, 1971; The Summoning Of Everyman, church opera, 1973; Heloise and Abelard, opera in 3 acts, 1973; The Selfish Giant, children's opera, 1973; Sinfonia for Double Orchestra, 1973; Image Out Of Season for Chorus and Brass Quintet, 1973; Christo Paremus Canticum for Chorus and Orchestra, 1973; Symphonic Perspectives: Kingsmere for Orchestra, 1974; Missa Brevis for Chorus and Organ, 1975; Psycho Red, opera in 2 acts, 1980; Kamouraska, opera in 3 acts, 1979; Revelations to John: A Festival Cantata for 3 choirs and organ; Symphony No. 1, 1998; Seasons of Life–song cycle for contralto and piano, 1998; Cantata for Palm Sunday for choir, soli and piano, 1998; Images for contralto and flute, 1999; Cantata for Tenebrae, 1999; Song cycle for Contralto and piano, The Cave, 2000. *Publications:* Dona Nobis Pacem, for choir and brass sextet, 1972. *Address:* 610 Wildwood Crescent, Gabriola , BC V0R 1X4, Canada.

WILSON, Christopher; lutenist and vihuela player; b. 1951, England. *Education:* Royal College of Music with Diana Poulton. *Career:* specialised in the performance of Renaissance music throughout the United Kingdom; concert tours of Europe, Scandinavia, USA, the Baltic States, Russia and the Far East; as well as working with his own group Kithara, interest in the lute song repertoire has led him to work with such song recitalists as countertenor Michael Chance and the tenor Rufus Müller; performs with Fretwork, Gothic Voices, the Consort of Musicke and the English Baroque Soloists; Concerts 1993–94 included tours to Sweden, Hong Kong and Japan, Poland and Taiwan. *Recordings:* appeared on over 50 recordings and on solo recordings.

WILSON, Christopher R., BA, MA, DPhil; University Lecturer; b. 1 Oct. 1952, Hull, England; m. Christine; three c. *Education:* Univ. of Oxford. *Career:* Temporary Lecturer, Univ. of St Andrews 1978; Lecturer, Univ. of Reading 1979; Senior Lecturer, Univ. of Reading 2001; mem. Royal Musical Asscn (council 1989–92, 2001–03), Finzi Trust Friends. *Publications:* Campion, A Critical Study 1989, Campion and Coprario Treatises 2003; contrib. to A Shakespeare Music Catalogue 1991, Grove Opera 1992, New Oxford Companion to Music 2002, Music and Letters 1979–, Early Music 1981–. *Honours:* Louise Dyer Award 1978, Research project grant, Leverhulme Trust 2001–04. *Address:* The University of Reading Department of Music, 35 Upper Redlands Road, Reading, RG1 5JE, England (office). *Telephone:* (118) 3788415 (office). *Fax:* (118) 3788412 (office). *E-mail:* c.r.wilson@rdg.ac.uk (office). *Website:* www.rdg.ac.uk/music (office).

WILSON, Elisa, AMusA; Australian singer (soprano); b. 22 Oct. 1965, Perth, Western Australia; d. of Cyril William Wilson and Gloria Elwyn Stitfold; m., three s. *Education:* WA Conservatorium, Perth; Univ. of Western Australia. *Career:* debut: Despina in Cosí fan Tutte, WA Opera, and Adele in Die Fledermaus; Other engagements throughout Australia for Western Australia Opera Company include Nanetta in Falstaff, the Sandman and Dew Fairy in Hansel & Gretel, Micaela in Carmen, Pamina in The Magic Flute, Gilda in Rigoletto, Susanna in The Marriage of Figaro, Norina in Don Pasquale, Adina in The Elixir of Love, Musetta in La Bohème, Leila in The Pearl Fishers, Alice Ford in Falstaff and world premieres, Nanette in The Eureka Stockade and Heloise in HEloise and Abelard. Also performed Greta in Brian Howard's Metamorphosis and Mrs Green in Harrison Birtwistle's Down by the Greenwood Side for other companies in WA; Donna Elvira in Don Giovanni and The Girl in The Emperor of Atlantis for Victoria State Opera; Echo in Ariadne auf Naxos, Spoleto Festival, Melbourne; debut with Opera Australia as Helena in A Midsummer Night's Dream at Edinburgh Festival, 1994 and in Sydney; Handel's Alcina in Sydney and Melbourne; Rosalilnda in Die Fledermaus and Musetta in La Bohème at Sydney Opera House; Concert appearances as soloist with Australian Symphony Orchestra and other Australian orchestras, with Vienna Male Voice Choir and Opera Australia; live broadcasts of operas Rita and Susanna's Secret for ABC. *Recording:* Bruckner's Mass in D Minor (soprano soloist). *Leisure interests:* martial arts, genealogy. *Honours:* Creative Development Fellowship ArtsWA, 1994; Armstrong-Martin Opera Award, 1992; Dame Mabel Brookes Award, 1992; ABC Prize, 1992. *Current Management:* Patrick Togher Artists Management, Suite 25, 450 Elizabeth Street, Surry Hills, NSW 2010, Australia. *Telephone:* (2) 9319-6255 (office). *Fax:* (2) 9319-7611 (office). *E-mail:* pjtogher@ozemail.com.au (office). *Website:* www.patricktogher.com.

WILSON, Fredric (Woodbridge); Musicologist; b. 8 Sept. 1947, Point Pleasant, New Jersey, USA. *Education:* BA, Music, Lehigh University, Bethlehem, Pennsylvania, 1969; MA, Musicology, New York University, 1977. *Career:* Director, The Wall Choirs, New Jersey, 1969–81; Editor, Allaire Music Publications, 1980–; Curator, The Pierpont Morgan Library, New York City, 1981; Professor of Museum Studies, Graduate School of Arts and Science, New York University, 1994–; Musical and Textual Consultant to opera companies. *Compositions:* More than 50 musical editions published, including motets by Gallus, Charpentier, mass by Lotti. *Publications:* Introduction to the Gilbert and Sullivan Operas, 1989; Index to the Opus Musicum of Jacob Handl, 1992; General Editor, The W S Gilbert Edition, 1986–; Complete Savoy Opera Libretti, Folio Society, 1994. *Contributions:* New Grove Dictionary of Opera; Many papers and articles to various publications; Organised conferences in English Opera, New York, 1985, Gilbert and Sullivan, New York, 1989, Purchase College, 1994; Organised exhibitions at Pierpont Morgan Library, 1985, 1989, Kentucky Center for the Arts, 1987, 1988, Purchase College, 1994. *Address:* Pierpoint Morgan Library, 29E 36th Street, New York, NY 10016, USA.

WILSON, Gordon; Singer (Tenor); b. 1968, Scotland. *Education:* Studied at the Royal Scottish Academy. *Career:* Appearances at Covent Garden, Glyndebourne, Scottish Opera, Opera North and the Buxton Festival; Sang Philidor's Tom Jones at Drottningholm and in Massenet's Chérubin at Covent Garden; Roles have included Nathaniel in Hoffmann, Alfredo, the Duke of Mantua, Riccardo in Oberto, Jenik in The Bartered Bride and Walton's Troilus; Concerts with the Ulster Orchestra, Northern Sinfonia and Manchester Camerata.

WILSON, Ian, BMus, DPhil; Northern Irish composer; b. 26 Dec. 1964, Belfast. *Education:* Univ. of Ulster. *Career:* AHRB Research Fellow in Creative and Performing Arts, Univ. of Ulster 2000–03; featured composer at Presteigne Festival 2005. *Compositions include:* Prime 1987, Running, Thinking, Finding 1989, BIG 1991, Drive 1992, Winter's Edge (String Quartet No. 1) 1992, Rise 1993, The Capsizing Man and other stories 1994, Rich Harbour 1994–95, I Sleep at Waking 1995, The Seven Last Words (Piano Trio No. 2) 1995, Six Days at Jericho 1995, For Eileen, after rain 1995, Catalan Tales (Piano Trio No. 3) 1996, Towards the Far Country 1996, From the Book of Longing 1996, A Haunted Heart 1996, Lim 1998, Spilliaert's Beach 1999, In Blue Sea or Sky 2000, Verschwindend 2001, Winter Finding 2005. *Recordings:* Winter's Edge, Spilliaert's Beach, In Blue Sea or Sky, The Seven Last Words, Catalan Tales and Six Days at Jericho, Winter's Edge, The Capsizing Man and other stories and Towards the Far Country, String Quartets 1–3, From the Book of Longing, Drive, Spilliaert's Beach, BIG, For Eileen, after rain, Verschwindend, Lim and A Haunted Heart. *Honours:* Ultima Festival, Oslo composition prize 1991, Macaulay Fellowship 1992, elected to Aosdána 1998. *E-mail:* mail@ianwilson.org.uk. *Website:* www.ianwilson.org.uk.

WILSON, James; Composer; b. 27 Sept. 1922, London, England. *Education:* Studied at Trinity College of Music, London. *Career:* Resident in Ireland from 1948; Freelance Composer of music for stage and other works. *Compositions:* Three symphonies; The Hunting of the Snark, children's opera, 1965; Twelfth Night, opera in 3 acts, 1969; Letters to Theo, opera in one act, 1984; Grinning at the Devil, opera in 2 acts, 1989; The King of the Golden River, 1990; A Passionate Man, Opera in 2 acts, 1995; Virata, opera in 4 scenes; Numerous concerti including those for viola, violin, wind quintet, clarinet, harpsichord; Chamber music; Choral works; Numerous song cycles. *Address:* 10a Wyvern, Killiney Hill, Co Dublin, Ireland.

WILSON, Paul; Singer (tenor, baritone); b. 1952, Gloucester, England. *Education:* Studied at Jesus College Oxford and at the Royal College of Music. *Career:* British appearances with English National, Welsh National and Scottish Opera companies, Kent Opera, Glyndebourne

Festival, Chelsea Opera and Opera North; Foreign engagements with the Opera Factory Zürich, Pocket Opera Nürnberg and Nairobi Opera; Roles include Tom Rakewell, Andrea Chénier, Bacchus, Mark in The Wreckers, and Don José; Royal Opera Covent Garden in Handel's Samson, Ariadne auf Naxos, King Priam and Der Rosenkavalier; Welsh National Opera debut in 1987 as Florestan, and English National Opera debut in 1988 as Monostatos; Sang in the world premieres of Golem by John Casken and Cage's Europeras III and IV (Almeida Festival, 1989–90) and Oliver's Timon of Athens (ENO, 1991); Opera North from 1990 in Gianni Schicchi and L'Heure Espagnole; Sang Siegmund and Siegfried in Birmingham Touring Opera's truncated Ring performances in the United Kingdom, 1990–91; Concert repertory includes The Dream of Gerontius, the Glagolitic Mass, Verdi's Requiem and Beethoven's 9th Symphony, conducted by Roger Norrington; Performance of Stravinsky's Les Noces with the National Youth Orchestra of Spain; Aldeburgh Festival in 1990 in Goehr's Triptych; Garsington Manor Opera in Ariadne auf Naxos in 1993; Kong in Harrison Birtwistle's The Second Mrs Kong, Glyndebourne, 1995; Now sings as a baritone; Retired from full-time performing, 1996; Director of Drama, Whitgift School, Croydon, England. *Recordings:* Golem, John Gasken, 1991; Caritas, Robert Saxton, 1992; Four Seafarers' Songs, Alan Bush, 1999. *Honours:* First Wagner Society Bayreuth Bursary, 1983; Arts Council Bursary. *Address:* 76 Avondale Road, S Croydon CR2 6JA, England.

WILSON, Richard E.; Composer, Pianist and Professor of Music; b. 15 May 1941, Cleveland, Ohio, USA; m. Adene Stevenson Green 1971, 1 s., 1 d. *Education:* AB, Harvard University, 1963; MA, Rutgers University, 1966; Cello studies with Ernst Silberstein, piano with Leonard Shure, composition with Robert Moevs. *Career:* Works performed in New York, London, Tokyo, San Francisco, Los Angeles, Bogota, Stockholm, The Hague, Vienna, Aspen, Boston, Chicago; Assistant Professor, 1966, Associate Professor, 1970, Professor, 1976–, Mellon Chair in Music, 1988–, Vassar College, Poughkeepsie, New York; Composer in Residence, American Symphony, 1992–; Commissions from The Library of Congress; Naumburg, Koussevitzky and Fromm Foundations; Chamber Music America; The Chicago Chamber Musicians. *Compositions include:* String Quartets 1–4; Symphonies 1–2; Opera: Aethelred the Unready; Concertos for violin, bassoon, piano and Triple Concerto for horn, bass clarinet and marimba; Eclogue, Fixations, Intercalations for solo piano; The Ballad of Longwood Glen for tenor and harp. *Recordings include:* Bassoon Concerto; Piano Concerto; Symphony No. 1; Aethelred the Unready; complete choral works; String Quartets 3 & 4; Affirmations for chamber ensemble; Transfigured Goat for 2 singers and instruments. *Publications include:* entire catalogue. *Honours:* Stoeger Prize for Chamber Music Composition, 1994. *Address:* 27 Vassar Lake Drive, Poughkeepsie, NY 12603, USA. *E-mail:* riwilson@vassar.edu.

WILSON, Robert; Playwright, Stage Director and Designer; b. 4 Oct. 1941, Waco, Texas, USA. *Education:* University of Texas, 1959–65; BFA, Architecture, Pratt Institute, NY. *Career:* Produced plays from 1969, firstly in New York then in Europe including the 12 hour play, The Life and Times of Joseph Stalin at Copenhagen in 1973; Collaboration with Philip Glass in Einstein On The Beach, premiered at Avignon in 1976 and repeated at the Metropolitan Opera; Further music theatre work with Glass and Gavin Bryars on Civil Wars in 1984; Directed Charpentier's Médée and Medea by Bryars, at Lyon in 1984; Designed the opening concert of the Opéra de Bastille in Paris, 1989; Premiere of Louis Andriessen's Die Materie at Amsterdam, 1989; Produced and designed Gluck's Alceste, for Chicago Lyric Opera in 1990 with Jessye Norman, Lohengrin for Zürich Opera in 1991; Palace of Arabian Nights with music by Philip Glass, produced at Lisbon and the Seville World Fair in 1992, and Parsifal at Houston in 1992; Directed Nono's Prometeo at Brussels, 1997; Season 1998 with Lohengrin at the Met and collaboration with Philip Glass on Monsters of Grace, Los Angeles and London. *Address:* c/o Lyric Opera of Chicago, 20 North Wacker Drive, Chicago, IL 60606, USA.

WILSON, Timothy; singer (countertenor); b. 18 July 1961, England. *Education:* Royal Academy of Music. *Career:* operatic engagements include Handel's Orlando and Britten's Death in Venice for Scottish Opera, Dido and Aeneas in Frankfurt, Gluck's Orfeo in Kassel, L'Incoronazione di Poppea in Gelsenkirchen, The Fairy Queen in Florence, A Midsummer Night's Dream in Kentucky, the modern premiere of Cesti's Il Pomo d'Oro in Vienna, and the world premieres of Maxwell Davies's Resurrection in Darmstadt, and Luis de Pablo's El Viajero Indiscreto in Madrid; Season 1990–91 with Vivaldi in Prague, Messiah in Valencia, Bach in the Philippines and the title role in Handel's Xerxes at Innsbruck; Covent Garden debut in 1992 as Oberon in A Midsummer Night's Dream; Sang in Agrippina at Buxton Festival, Alcina at the Halle Festival and Giulio Cesare at Ludwigshafen, 1992–93; Further concert appearances with Mackerras, Hickox, Pinnock, Herreweghe, Leonhardt, Norrington and Parrott; Venues include Netherlands, France, Germany, Austria, Spain, Italy and the

United Kingdom including the Promenade Concerts. *Recordings include:* Alcina, Purcell's Come Ye Sons of Art Away and Handel's Israel in Egypt.

WILSON-JOHNSON, David; Singer (baritone); b. 16 Nov. 1950, Northampton, England. *Education:* St Catharine's College, Cambridge; Royal Academy of Music, London. *Career:* Royal Opera House, Covent Garden, from 1976 in Le Rossignol, L'Enfant et les Sortilèges, Boris Godunov, Die Zauberflöte, Werther, Turandot, Roméo et Juliette; Appearances with Welsh National Opera and Opera North, in operas by Delius, Rossini and Mozart; Concerts under Boulez, Giulini, Harnoncourt, Masur and Mehta; Sang title part in the first British performance of Messiaen's St François d'Assise, Royal Festival Hall, 1988; King Fisher in a televised production of Tippett's A Midsummer Marriage, 1989; Tours with David Owen Norris in Schubert's Winterreise; Lev in The Ice Break at the 1990 Promenade Concerts; Sang Choregos in Birtwistle's Punch and Judy for Netherlands Opera, 1993; Billy Budd, Arianna at Royal Opera House; Albert Herring, Billy Budd and Peter Grimes with Geneva Opera; Die Glückliche Hand and Von Heute auf Morgen by Schoenberg with the Netherlands Opera, 1995; Sang in Pfitzner's Palestrina at Covent Garden, 1997; Borée in Les Boréades by Rameau at the 1999 London Proms; Swallow in Peter Grimes, at Amsterdam, 2000; Oliver Knussen's Where the Wild Things Are and Higglety, Pigglety, Pop! at the London Proms, 2002. *Recordings include:* Mozart Masses; Winterreise; Tippett's King Priam; Birtwistle's Punch and Judy; Walton's Belshazzar's Feast; B Minor Mass; Von Heute auf Morgen. *Current Management:* Askonas Holt Ltd, Lonsdale Chambers, 27 Chancery Lane, London, WC2A 1PF, England. *Telephone:* (20) 7400-1700. *Fax:* (20) 7400-1799. *E-mail:* info@askonasholt.co.uk. *Website:* www.askonasholt.co.uk.

WIMBERGER, Peter; Singer (Bass-Baritone); b. 14 May 1940, Vienna, Austria. *Education:* Studied at the Vienna Music Academy with Paul Schöffler and Adolf Vogel. *Career:* Debut: Dortmund 1963, as Pietro in Simon Boccanegra; Appearances in the opera houses of Frankfurt, Karlsruhe, Kassel, Düsseldorf, Munich, Warsaw and Copenhagen; Barcelona 1985, as the Wanderer in Siegfried; Festivals of Bregenz and Florence; Repertoire includes principal roles in operas by Mussorgsky, Mozart, Wagner, Rossini, Verdi and Strauss; Sang at Palermo and Naples, 1988, as Amfortas; Rangoni at the Vienna Staatsoper, 1988; Kuno in Der Freischütz, 1996; mem, Vienna Staatsoper from 1968. *Recordings:* Haydn's Harmoniemesse; Spirit Messenger in Die Frau ohne Schatten by Strauss. *Address:* c/o Landestheater, Promenade 39, A 4010 Linz, Austria.

WINBECK, Heinz; Composer and Teacher; b. 11 Feb. 1946, Piflas, Landshut, Germany. *Education:* Studied piano and conducting at the Munich Richard Strauss Conservatory, 1964–67; Composition with Harald Genzmer and Gunter Bialas at the Munich Hochschule, 1963–73. *Career:* Conductor and Composer at Ingolstadt and Wunsiedel, 1974–78; Teacher at the Munich Hochschule 1980–88, Professor of Composition at the Würzburg Hochschule, from 1988; Composer in Residence at the Cabrillo, California, Music Festival, 1985. *Compositions include:* In Memorian Paul Celan, for soprano, flute, piano and percussion, 1970; Sie Tanzt for baritone and ensemble, 1971; Sonosillent, for cello and strings, 1971; Musik for wind quintet, 1971; Espaces, for 4 percussionists, piano and flute, 1972; Nocturne I for chamber ensemble, 1972; Lenau-Fantasien for cello and chamber orchestra, 1979; 3 String Quartets, 1979, 1980, 1984; Chansons a Temps, for women's voices and 13 instruments, 1979; 4 Symphonies, 1983, 1987, 1988, 1993; Blick in den Strom, for String Quintet, 1993. *Honours:* Music Prize of the Akademie der Schonen Kunste, Berlin, 1985. *Address:* c/o GEMA, Rosenheimer Str 11, 81667 Munchen, Germany.

WINDMULLER, Yaron; Singer (Baritone); b. 1956, Israel. *Education:* Studied in Tel-Aviv, Munich with Ernst Haefliger and in Vicenza with Malcolm King; Further study at the Opera Studio of the Bayerische Staatsoper. *Career:* Debut: City of London Festival in 1982, in Gluck's Armide; Sang as soloist with the Israel Philharmonic, and as member of Theater am Gärtnerplatz, Munich, from 1986, as Purcell's Aeneas, Mozart's Count, Guglielmo, Don Giovanni and Papageno, Wolfram, Marcello, Hans Jürgen von Bose's Werther and Kaspar in Der Zaubergeige by Werner Egk; Sang Trinity Moses in Weill's Mahagonny at Frankfurt in 1990; Sang Paolo in Simon Boccanegra at Wellington, 2000; Many concert appearances and Lieder recitals. *Address:* c/o Staatstheater am Gärtnerplatz, Gartnerplatz 3, 8000 Munich 1, Germany.

WINKLER, Hermann; Singer (Tenor); b. 3 March 1924, Duisburg, Germany. *Education:* Studied at the Hanover Conservatory. *Career:* Sang at the Bayreuth Festival from 1957, notably as the Steersman in Der fliegende Holländer in 1965 and Parsifal, 1976–77; Member of the Zürich Opera from 1970; Frankfurt Opera, 1970 as Lohengrin and Florestan; Munich in 1972 as Mozart's Don Ottavio and Idomeneo; Salzburg Festival and Deutsche Oper Berlin, 1976, 1981 in Idomeneo;

USA debut in 1980 as Don Ottavio; Sang Florestan in USA and Japan in 1981; Covent Garden debut in 1984 as the Captain in Wozzeck; Zürich Opera in 1985 as the Emperor in Die Frau ohne Schatten; Guest appearances in Vienna and Hamburg; Sang Herod in Salome at La Scala, 1987, and Loge at Bologna; Season 1987–88 at the Teatro Real Madrid in Wozzeck and Lulu; Marseilles and Barcelona in 1989 as Aegisthus in Elektra; Sang in Peter Grimes at Zürich in 1989; Many appearances in the concert hall, often in Das Lied von der Erde by Mahler. *Recordings:* Arabella; Mahler's 8th Symphony; Idomeneo; Drum Major in Wozzeck.

WINKLER, Peter; Composer and Editor; b. 26 Jan. 1943, Los Angeles, USA. *Education:* BA 1960, University of California at Berkeley (study with Andrew Imbrie and Lalo Schifrin); MFA 1967, Princeton University (study with Milton Abbitt and Earl Kim). *Career:* Teacher at State University of New York, Stony Brook, from 1971; Editor of Journal of Popular Music Studies, 1992–. *Compositions include:* String Quartet, 1967; Praise of Silence for soprano, chorus, Renaissance ensemble and tape, 1969; Symphony, 1971–78; Clarinet Bouquet; Four Concert Rags, 1976–80; No Condition is Permanent, for flute and piano, 1990; Waterborne, for violin and tape, 1991; Sing Out the Old Sing in The New for men's chorus, tuba and violin, 1992; Saboreando el Gusto Cubano, for violin, piano and percussion, 1994; One Light, for men's chorus, piano and percussion, 1994; Tingle-Tangle: A Wedekind Cabaret, collaboration with William Bolcom and A Black, 1994. *Honours:* MacDowell Colony Fellowship, 1971. *Address:* c/o ASCAP, ASCAP Building, 1 Lincoln Plaza, New York, NY 10023, USA.

WINKLER, Wolfgang; Musicologist; b. 12 June 1945, Graz, Austria; m. Elisabeth; one d. *Education:* Universität Graz. *Career:* Brucknerkonservatorium Linz, Bibliothek und musikwissenschaftliches Referat 1978; Referent für U. Musik im ORF Landesstudio 1979; Head of Music, ORF 1985; Artistic Dir and CEO, LIVA 1998. *Publications:* contrib. to Musik in Österreich (Gottfried Kraus Verlag), Musicolociga austriaca 11, Umkunst (Publikation der Hochschule für künstlerisches und industrielle Gestaltung, Linz), 20 Jahre Bruckenhaus, Gedanken zu Balduin Sulzer (Musikarchiv der Österreichisch Nationalbibliothek), Musikgeschichte Österreichs, Neue Musik und Medien, echt falsch Will die Welt betrogen werden? (Kremayr und Scheriau). *Address:* Untere Donaulände 7, Linz, 4020, Austria (office). *Telephone:* (732) 7612 2025 (office). *Fax:* (732) 7612 2030 (office). *E-mail:* w.winkler@liva.co.at (office). *Website:* www.wolfgang-winkler.at (office).

WINSCHERMANN, Helmut; Oboist and Conductor; b. 22 March 1920, Munich, Germany. *Education:* Studied in Essen and Paris. *Career:* Principal with the Frankfurt Radio Symphony Orchestra, 1945–51; Co-founded Collegium Instrumental Detmold, 1954, and became professor at the Detmold Academy, 1956; Appearances with the Capella Coloniensis and Stuttgart Chamber Orchestra; Founded the Deutsche Bachsolisten, giving many performances throughout Europe and elsewhere; Premiered La tomba di Igor Stravinsky by Giselher Klebe, 1979. *Address:* Detmold Hochschule für Musik, Allee 22, 4930 Detmold, Germany.

WINSLADE, Glenn; Singer (Tenor); b. 1958, Australia. *Education:* Studied at the New South Wales Conservatorium and at Vienna Conservatory. *Career:* Has sung with English National Opera as Ferrando, Victoria State Opera as Belmonte, Walter von der Vogelweide and Don Ottavio, Scottish Opera as Mozart's Titus and Australian Opera as Oronte in Alcina; Covent Garden debut in 1990 as Vogelgesang in Die Meistersinger; Further appearances with Glyndebourne Festival and Touring Opera, New Sadler's Wells Opera in Merry Widow, Freiburg Opera, Semper Oper Dresden as Belmonte, Stuttgart Opera and the Netherlands Opera in Idomeneo; Other roles include Tamino, The Prince in The Love of Three Oranges, Stroh (Intermezzo), Elemer in Arabella, Amenophis in Mosè, Ernesto and Nemorino, Fracasso in La Finta Semplice, Lindoro and Alfredo, Jacquino in Fidelio, Steuermann in Der fliegende Holländer and Jason in Cherubini's Médée; Mozart's Titus for Welsh National Opera; Engaged as Wagner's Rienzi at the Vienna Staatsoper, 1998; Strauss's Emperor at Covent Garden, 2001; Sang in Mahler's 8th at Vienna, 2002; Concert engagements with the Musica Antiqua Vienna, Duke University, NC, RAI Milan and The BBC. *Recordings include:* Messiah with the Scottish Chamber Orchestra; Merry Widow. *Honours:* Winner, Australian Opera Auditions, Esso/Glyndebourne Touring and John Christie Glyndebourne Awards. *Address:* c/o Musiespana, c/José Marañon, 10-40 Izqda, E–28010 Madrid, Spain.

WINSTIN, Robert; Composer, Conductor and Pianist; b. 6 June 1959, Chicago, Illinois. *Education:* Advanced Studies, Chicago Musical College; Roosevelt University; University of Colorado. *Career:* Debut: Pianist, Carnegie Hall, 1986; First American composer to have work ad perform in mainland China, 1995; Shanghai and Beijing, piano concerto No. 2; Music Director and Principal Conductor, Metropolis Youth Symphony; Music Director and Principal Conductor, Derriere Guard

Festival Orchestra; Musical Director and Principal Conductor, Millennium Symphony; Executive Director, Foundation for Music; mem, ASCAP; NARAS; Derriere Guard Society. *Compositions:* Dedo, opera; Scherto Burlesque; Symphony No. 2; Symphony No. 5; Piano concerto No. 2; Cello Concerto, Millennium Symphony. *Recordings:* Piano Art; Simple Songs; Piano concerto No. 2; Favourites; Dedo. *Publications:* Scherzo Burlesque, 1988; Symphony No. 2, 1989; Piano Art, 1995; Symphony No. 5, 1996; Etudes, 1993; Cello Concerto, 1997; Piano concerto, 1994. *Contributions:* Music editor, Nit and Wit magazine, 1985–88; Radio producer and writer, Nuovo Voce, 1990–. *Honours:* Joseph Jefferson Citations Wing Recommendation for Oedipus Requiem, 1989; Concours Caveat Prim Palm D'Or, 1992; Barrettson Prize in American Music, Piano concerto No. 1, 1998. *Current Management:* ERM. *Address:* c/o ERM 3712 N Broadway #264, Chicago, IL 60613, USA.

WINTER, Louise; Singer (mezzo-soprano); b. 29 Nov. 1959, Preston, Lancashire, England; m. Gerald Finley. *Education:* Studied at Chetham's School of Music and at the Royal Northern College of Music with Frederick Cox. *Career:* With Glyndebourne Touring Opera (from 1982) has sung Tisbe in La Cenerentola, Dorabella in Così fan tutte and Mercédès in Carmen; Sang Zerlina on Glyndebourne's tour to Hong Kong, Nancy in Albert Herring at the 1986 summer festival and in the Ravel double bill in 1987–88; Covent Garden debut in 1988 as a Flowermaiden in Parsifal; Has sung Janáček's Varvara and Ravel's Concepcion for Opera North; Netherlands Opera as Rosina in Il Barbiere di Siviglia and Second Lady in Die Zauberflöte; Glyndebourne Festival, 1988–90, in Katya Kabanova, Il Barbiere di Siviglia and the Ravel double bill; Appearances with the Canadian Opera Company in Eugene Onegin and as Dorabella in Così fan tutte in 1991; Concert engagements with the König Ensemble and in the Choral Symphony conducted by Simon Rattle; Season 1997 with Carmen and the Berlioz Marguerite for English National Opera and Jocasta in Oedipus Rex at the Festival Hall; Season 1998 with Eduige in Rodelinda at Gyndebourne and Marina in Boris Gounov for New Sussex Opera, Berlioz's Damnation of Faust in Sydney and Mahler's Des Knaben Wunderhorn in Kuala Lumpur with Malaysian Philharmonic Orchestra; Britten's Phaedre at the 1999 London Proms; Sang Carmen for ENO, 2001; London Proms, 2002. *Recordings:* Songs of Frank Bridge, 1997; Lucia di Lammermoor with Hanover Band, conducted by Charles Mackerras. *Current Management:* Askonas Holt Ltd, Lonsdale Chambers, 27 Chancery Lane, London, WC2A 1PF, England. *Telephone:* (20) 7400-1700. *Fax:* (20) 7400-1799. *E-mail:* info@askonasholt.co.uk. *Website:* www.askonasholt.co.uk.

WINTER, Nils Tomas; Composer; b. 1 March 1954, Arboga, Sweden. *Education:* University studies in archaeology, law, Spanish and Portuguese; Studied composition with Werner Wolf Glaser, 1980–94, Daniel Börtz, 1981, and Miklós Maros, 1995. *Career:* Debut: Swedish National Radio programme, Monologue No. 10 for Bassoon and Monologue No. 2 for Guitar, 1982; FST, 1998–; Society of Swedish Composers. *Compositions:* Sargasso for saxophone quartet, 1995–96; Istros for string quartet, 1996–97; Symphony No. 1 1998–99; Piano trio, 2000. *Honours:* Three scholarships, 1997–2001. *Address:* Tunadalsgatan 34 D, 731 40 Köping, Sweden.

WINTER, Quade; Composer and Singer (Tenor); b. 1950, Oregon, USA. *Career:* Debut: Sang Max in Der Freischütz at San Francisco; Has sung the Duke of Mantua for Eugene Opera, Canio at Anchorage, Don Ottavio at the Carmel Bach Festival and Ishmael in Nabucco for San Francisco Opera; Appeared in US premiere of The Excursions of Mr Brouček, with the Berkeley Symphony; Concerts have included Beethoven's Ninth with the Stockton Symphony and the Verdi Requiem at the San Francisco Festival of Masses, conducted by Robert Shaw; European debut as Hermann in The Queen of Spades with Graz Opera in 1982; La Scala Milan in 1982 as Cherubini's Anacréon; Roles with the Stadtheater Würzburg have included Don Carlos, Lensky, Herod, Rodolfo and Canio; Has sung Parsifal at Graz and Herod in Heidelberg and Seattle; Scottish Opera debut as Mark in The Midsummer Marriage, in 1989; Music for Gilbert and Sullivan's Thespis performed by Ohio Light Opera, 1996. *Address:* Music International, 13 Ardilaun Road, London N5 2QR, England.

WINTER, Sidonie; Singer (Soprano); b. 1965, England. *Education:* University of East Anglia, Royal Academy of Music and National Opera Studio. *Career:* Frequent concerts throughout the United Kingdom, including Wigmore Hall, St John's Smith Square and South Bank; Proms debut as Lady Angela in Patience; Other concerts include Messiah and Handel's Dixit Dominus, the Mass in D Minor by Haydn, Beethoven's Mass in C and Elgar's Apostles; Opera debut as Leila in Iolanthe for D'Oyly Carte Opera; Other roles include Siebel in Faust, Elena (Aroldo), Sofia (Lombardi) and Priestess (Aida, Covent Garden, 1996); Fiordiligi at Ischia for the Walton Trust, Geisha in Mascagni's Iris for Chelsea Opera Group, Mozart's Countess and Donna Elvira at

Aldeburgh; Lady Billows in Rheinsberg Sieglinde for Wagner Society. *Address:* 12 Pond Road, Stratford, London E15 3 BE, England.

WIRKKALA, Merja; Singer (Soprano); b. 7 Oct. 1954, Kaustinen, Finland. *Education:* Studied at the Sibelius Academy, Helsinki. *Career:* Sang with the Helsinki Opera from 1976, notably as Nannetta, Zerlina, Despina, Susanna, Kaisa in Merikanto's Juha, and Siebel; Sang Marzelline in Fidelio at the Vienna Staatsoper (1980), Zerlina at Covent Garden, 1981, and the title role in the premiere of Elina by Liukolas at Helsinki, 1992; Guest in Juha at the Edinburgh Festival, 1987. *Address:* Finnish National Opera, Bulevardi 23–27, 00180 Helsinki 18, Finland.

WIRTZ, Dorothea; Singer (Soprano); b. 13 March 1953, Tuttlingen, Germany. *Education:* Studied in Berlin with Hugo Diez and in Munich with Hanno Blaschke. *Career:* Sang at the Munich Staatsoper, 1979–80, Kassel, 1980–84; Member of the Zürich Opera from 1984; Guest appearances in Düsseldorf, Venice, Naples, Lisbon, Bologna, Berlin, Cologne, Wiesbaden, Florence and Strasbourg; Roles include Olympia in Les Contes d'Hoffmann, Blondchen, the Queen of Night, Zerlina, Despina, Ilia in Idomeneo, Rosina, Sophie in Der Rosenkavalier, Zerbinetta, Norina, Adina, Marzelline and the Woodbird in Siegfried; Sang Blondchen at Buenos Aires in 1987; Professor at the Freiburg Musikhochschule, from 2000; Concert Repertoire includes works by Handel, Mozart, Bach and Schumann including Paradies und die Peri. *Recordings include:* Strauss's Daphne. *Address:* c/o Operhaus Zürich, Falkerstrasse 1, 8008 Zürich, Switzerland.

WISE, Patricia; Singer (Soprano); b. 31 July 1944, Wichita, Kansas, USA. *Education:* Studied at Kansas University, Santa Fe, and in New York with Margaret Harshaw. *Career:* Debut: Susanna in The Marriage of Figaro, Kansas City in 1966; Appearances at the Houston Opera, New York City Opera, New Orleans, Philadelphia, Chicago, San Francisco, Washington, Miami, Baltimore, San Antonio and Pittsburgh; Carnegie Hall, New York in 1971 in Handel's Ariodante, Covent Garden, London in 1971 as Rosina in Rossini's Barber of Seville with New York City Opera; Glyndebourne in 1972 as Zerbinetta in Ariadne auf Naxos; Vienna Staatsoper in 1983 as Pamina, Nannetta and Sophie; Sang at the 1984 Salzburg Festival in the premiere of Un Re in Ascolto by Berio; 1st appearance in Geneva in 1985 as Lulu; Repertoire includes roles in operas by Donizetti, Gounod, Gluck, and Verdi's Gilda; Sang with the Vienna Staatsoper, 1976–91, in 300 performances, many of which were Strauss or Mozart operas; Since 1985 has appeared in five other productions of Berg's 3 act Lulu, from Berlin to Paris; Sang Lulu at Madrid in 1987, Sophie in Der Rosenkavalier at Budapest, 1989, Gilda in Rigoletto at Madrid, 1989, Fiordiligi in Mozart's Così fan tutte, and Violetta in Verdi's Traviata, 1990; Guest appearances in European opera houses including La Scala, Munich, Berlin, Hamburg, Barcelona, Geneva, Glyndebourne and at Salzburg Festival. *Honours:* Kammersängerin, Vienna Staatsoper, 1996. *Address:* c/o Vienna Staatsoper (Artist Contracts), Opernring 2, 1010 Vienna, Austria.

WISEMAN, Debra (Debbie), MBE, GGSM; British composer and conductor; b. 10 May 1963, London; d. of Paul and Barbara Wiseman; m. Tony Wharmby 1987. *Education:* Trinity Coll. of Music, Kingsway Princeton/Morley Coll., Guildhall School of Music and Drama, London. *Career:* composer and conductor of music for film and TV productions 1989–; Visiting Prof. of Film Composition, Royal Coll. of Music 1995–; mem. Performing Right Soc., BAFTA, Musicians' Union, British Acad. of Composers and Songwriters. *Compositions include:* Inside Looking Out 1989, Squares and Roundabouts 1989, Echoes of Istria 1989, The Guilty, Lighthouse, Female Perversions, The Dying of the Light, Shrinks (Silents to Satellite Award for Best Original TV Theme Music 1991), The Good Guys (Television and Radio Industries Club Award for TV Theme Music of the Year 1993), Tom and Viv 1994, The Project, Judge John Deed, P.O.W., Wilde Stories, The Upper Hand, The Churchills, Serious and Organised, The Second Russian Revolution, Little Napoleons, Children's Hospital, Death of Yugoslavia, Haunted 1995, Wilde 1997, The Fairy Tale of the Nightingale and the Rose 1999, The Fairy Tale of the Selfish Giant 1999, It Might be You, A Week in Politics, People's Century, What Did You Do In The War, Auntie?, The Cuban Missile Crisis, Vet's School, The Missing Postman, Tom's Midnight Garden, Absolute Truth, My Uncle Silas 2001, Othello 2001, Warriors (Royal TV Soc. Award) 2000, Oscar Wilde Fairy Stories 2002, Freeze Frame 2004, He Knew He Was Right 2004, The Truth About Love 2004, Arsène Lupin 2004. *Current Management:* c/o Roz Colls, Music Matters International, Crest House, 102–104 Church Road, Teddington, Middx TW11 8PY, England. *Telephone:* (20) 8979-4580. *Fax:* (20) 8979-4590. *E-mail:* dwiseman10@aol.com. *Website:* www .debbiewiseman.co.uk.

WISHART, Trevor; Composer; b. 11 Oct. 1946, Leeds, England; m. Jacqueline Joan Everett, 2 d. *Education:* BA Music, Oxford University; MA, Analysis of Contemporary Music, Nottingham University; DPhil, Composition, York University. *Career:* Foreign tours: Scandinavia, Australia, Japan, USA, Netherlands, Spain, Germany, IRCAM commis-

sion, Vox-5, 1986; Vox cycle performed at London Proms, 1988; Sound Designer, Jorvik Viking Centre Museum, York; Special Professor of Music, University of Nottingham, 1990–92; Visiting Fellow, Bretton Hall College of the University of Leeds, 1994; Research Fellow, University of Birmingham; Chair, Sonic Arts Network, 1990–92; Founder, Composers Desktop Project. *Compositions:* Red Bird; Anticredos; The Vox Cycle; Pastorale–Walden 2; Beach Singularity; Tongues of Fire, 1994; Fabulous Paris, 1997. Two Women, for DAAD, Berlin, 1998: American Triptych, for French Ministry of Culture, 1999. *Recordings:* Vox; Vox 5; Red Bird; Anticredos; October Music; Audible Design, 1994. *Publications:* Sounds Fun, educational music games, 1974 also in Japanese; On Sonic Art, 1985; Audible Design, 1994; Sun, Creativity and Environment; Sun-2, A Creative Philosophy; Whose Music, A Sociology of Musical Language. *Contributions:* Contact; Musics; Ear Magazine, New York; Interface, Utrecht; Computer Music Journal, USA; Musica Realta, Milan. *Honours:* Prizewinner: Bourges International Electro-Accoustic Music Festival, 1978, Gaudeamus International Festival, Netherlands, 1979, Linz Ars Electronica, 1985, 1995.

WISLOCKI, Leszek; Composer and Pianist; b. 15 Dec. 1931, Chorzow, Poland; m. Renata Krumpholz, 9 July 1968, 2 s. *Education:* Piano, 1955, Composition, 1957, Conducting, 1962, Academy of Music, Wroclaw. *Career:* Concerts as Pianist and Composer, Polish Radio and Television. *Compositions:* Andante and Presto for xylophone and piano; Two Miniatures for violin and cello; Sonata for oboe and cello; Ostinato and Toccatina for piano solo; Polonaise for piano solo; Suita Lubuska for wind orchestra; Songs for choir a cappella (male and female); 4 symphonies; Rhapsody for the great symphonic orchestra, 1996; 3 concerts for instruments (piano, oboe, bassoon) and orchestra; 2 compositions for 46th International Eucharistic Congress, Wroclaw: Diledissimo Papae Iohanni Paulo Secundo ad honorem maximum, for 10 brass instruments and 4 kettle drums, Cantata, The Shepherd Goes, for choir and symphonic orchestra, 1997; VIth Piano Trio, 1997; XIth String Quartet, 2002; Two sonnets for Baritone and Piano, 2002 (text: John Gracen-Brown). *Recordings:* Many tapes, Radio-Wrocław; Andante and Presto for xylophone and piano. *Address:* ul Komandorska 48-8, 53-343 Wrocław, Poland.

WISPELWEY, Pieter; Concert Cellist; b. 1965, Netherlands. *Career:* Appearances with the Rotterdam Philharmonic, under Kent Nagano, L'Orchestre des Champs Elysées (Philippe Herreweghe), BBC SO, Netherlands Radio SO (Frans Brüggen), and the Camerata Academica Salzburg (Roger Norrington); Further engagements in Argentina, Japan, South Africa and Australia; Bach-Marathon concerts with the six solo suites throughout Europe, 2000, including the Wigmore Hall; Tours with National Orchestra of Lille and Baseler Kammerorchester, 2001; With piano partner Dejan Lazic performed complete Beethoven cello sonatas, Edinburgh Festival 2001; Repertoire also includes works by Kagel, Carter and Schnittke. *Recordings include:* Suites by Bach, Britten and Reger; Sonatas by Schubert, Brahms and Beethoven; Concertos by Haydn, Vivaldi, Elgar, Dvořák and Schumann (Channel Classics). *Honours:* Netherlands Music Prize; Diapason d'Or. *Address:* c/o Ariën Arts, de Boeystraat 6, B–2018 Antwerp, Belgium.

WIT, Antoni; Conductor; b. 7 Feb. 1944, Kraków, Poland; m. Zofia Cwikilewicz, 12 Oct 1977. *Education:* Law, Jagiellonian University, Kraków, 1969; Conducting, Kraków Academy of Music, 1967. *Career:* Debut: Concert with Kraków Philharmonic Orchestra, 1964; Assistant Conductor, National Philharmonic, Warsaw, 1967–70; Engagements at the Grand Theatre, Warsaw, 1970–80; Conductor, Poznan Philharmonic, 1970–72; Artistic Director, Principal Conductor, Pomeranien Philharmonic in Bydgoszcz, 1974–77; Artistic Director, Principal Conductor, Kraków Radio Symphony and Choir, 1977–83; Artistic Director, Principal Conductor, National Polish Radio Symphony Orchestra, Katowice, 1983–2000; Artistic Director, later Principal Guest Conductor, Philharmonic Orchestra, Gran Canaria, 1987–91; Professor of Conducting, Academy of Music, Warsaw, 1997–. *Recordings:* Over 100 CDs. *Honours:* 2nd Prize, Herbert von Karajan Competition, Berlin, 1971; Diapason d'or and the Grand Prix du Disque 92 for Piano Concertos Nos 1–5 by Prokofiev recorded for Naxos, 1993. *Current Management:* Konzertdirektion Hans Adler, Berlin; Musicaglotz, Paris; World-wide Artists, London. *Address:* ul. Emilii Plater 22, 05-500 Piaseczno, Poland.

WITT, Kerstin; Singer (Mezzo-soprano); b. 1960, Altentreptow, Brandenburg, Germany. *Education:* Hanns Eisler Conservatory, Berlin, 1977–85. *Career:* Appearances at the Dresden Staatsoper from 1988, as Donna Elvira, Strauss's Clairon (Capriccio), Octavian and Composer (Ariadne), Medea in Handel's Teseo, Leonore in Fidelio and Offenbach's Nicklauss; Modern repertory includes the Mother in Janáček's Osud, Countess Geschwitz in Lulu and Bart ók's Judith; Guest appearances at Montpellier, Venice and elsewhere; Wagner roles include Brangaene in Tristan, and Magdalena in Die Meistersinger; Concerts include the Wesendoncklieder and Kindertotenlieder and Dvořák's Gypsy Songs;

Sang Brangaene at Enschede (1999) and Herodias in Salome for the Dresden Staatsoper, 2001. *Recordings include:* Herodias in Salome.

WITZENMANN, Wolfgang; Composer; b. 26 Nov. 1937, Munich, Germany; m. Renata Di Salvo 1977; one s. one d. *Education:* Privatmusiklehrer Diplom, Musikhochschule Stuttgart 1960; DPhil History of Music, Universitaet Tübingen 1965. *Career:* as composer: Gaudeamus-Festival, Netherlands 1967, 1968, 1970, 1971, Internationale Ferienkurse für Neue Musik, Darmstadt, Germany 1969, Autunno Musicale, Como, Italy 1975, Festival Internazionale Nuova Consonanza, Rome 1985, Festival Internazionale Terenzio Gargiulo, Naples 1986; founded Wolfgang Witzenmann Musikverlag 2003. *Compositions:* Choirs, Oden I–V for voice and piano, 6 cycles of Lieder, Operas Nivasio, Mary and Sappho, Oratorio Christus and Gilgamesh, Eigenklänge Natur Deutschland-Lieder for orchestra, Sinfonia 1 and 2 for orchestra, Violin Concerto, Antiphonales Konzert for trumpet and orchestra, piano and organ music, chamber music, and music for early instruments; arrangements from original works by Macque, Gesualdo, Bellini. *Recordings:* Monographic 1989. *Publications:* Domenico Mazzocchi (1592–1665), Dokumente und Interpretationen 1970. *Contributions:* Analecta Musicologica, Acta Musicologica, Die Musikforschung, Recercare, Rivista Italiana di Musicologica, Studi Musicali. *Address:* Via Mario Fascetti 67, 00136 Rome, Italy. *E-mail:* wo_witzenmann@msn.com.

WIXELL, Ingvar; Baritone; b. 7 May 1931, Lulea, Sweden. *Education:* Studied in Stockholm with Dagmar Gustavson. *Career:* Debut: Sang at Gavle in 1952; Stockholm in 1955 as Papageno; Member of the Royal Opera Stockholm from 1956; Appeared with the company in Alcina at Covent Garden in 1960; Glyndebourne Festival in 1962 as Guglielmo in Così fan tutte; US debut at Chicago Lyric Opera in 1967 as Belcore in L'Elisir d'amore; Salzburg Festival 1966–69, as Count Almaviva and Pizarro; Hamburg Staatsoper in 1970 as Rigoletto and Scarpia; Covent Garden, 1972–77 as Simon Boccanegra, Scarpia, Belcore and Mandryka in Arabella; Metropolitan Opera from 1973 as Rigoletto, Germont, Amonasro, Marcello and Renato in Un Ballo in Maschera; Other roles include Don Carlo in La Forza del Destino, Count Luna, Posa and Pentheus in The Bassarids by Henze; Sang Amonasro at Houston in 1987; Covent Garden, 1987–90 as Rigoletto and Belcore; Stuttgart Staatsoper, 1990 as Scarpia; Sang in Tosca at Earl's Court in London, 1991; Sang Falstaff at Copenhagen, 1997; Scarpia at Malmö, 2000. *Recordings:* Le nozze di Figaro, Don Giovanni, Zaide, La Bohème, Un Ballo in Maschera, Tosca, Un Giorno di Regno, Il Trovatore, L'Elisir d'amore; Video of Tosca. *Address:* c/o Opéra et Concert, 1 Rue Volney, F–75002 Paris, France.

WLASCHIHA, Ekkerhard; Singer (Baritone); b. 28 May 1938, Pirna, Germany. *Education:* Studied at the Franz Liszt Musikhochschule in Leipzig and with Helene Jung. *Career:* Debut: Gera in 1961 as Don Fernando in Fidelio; Sang in Dresden and Weimar, 1964–70; Leipzig Opera from 1970 as Scarpia, Pizarro, Alfio, Tonio, Dr Coppelius, and Jochanaan in Salome; Sang in the premieres of Greek Wedding by Hannell in 1969 and The Shadow by Fritz Geissler in 1975; Lausanne Opera and Staatsoper Berlin in 1983 as Kurwenal and Telramund; Sang Kaspar in Der Freischütz at the reopening of the Semper Opera House in Dresden, 1985; Bayreuth Festival in 1986 as Kurwenal; Appeared on Russian television in Fidelio by Beethoven; Sang Telramund at the Berlin Staatsoper in 1990, and Alberich in a new production of Siegfried at Covent Garden in 1990; Returned to London 1997, as Bishop Ercole in Pfitzner's Palestrina and 1998 as Alberich at the Albert Hall; Season 2000–01 as Alberich and Klingsor at the Met, Pizarro in Dresden and Biterolf in Tannhäuser for the Munich Staatsoper. *Address:* c/o Allied Artists Agency, 42 Montpelier Square, London SW7 1JZ, England.

WOHLER, Rudiger; Singer (Tenor); b. 4 May 1943, Hamburg, Germany. *Education:* Studied at the Hamburg Musikhochschule. *Career:* Sang at Darmstadt, 1968–71; Sang at Zürich 1971–74 as Mozart's Belmonte, Ferrando, Tamino and Don Ottavio; Sang at Stuttgart from 1974 and has made guest appearances in Hamburg, Munich, Vienna and Frankfurt; Schwetzingen Festival in 1975 as Belmonte; Deutsche Oper Berlin from 1977; Sang Tamino at the 1981 Salzburg Festival; La Scala Milan in 1983 as Ferrando in Così fan tutte; Sang in Cavalli's L'Ormindo at the Hamburg Staatsoper 1984 and toured with the company to Japan; Stuttgart in 1984 as Don Ottavio in the newly restored opera house; Other roles include Fenton in Die Lustigen Weiber von Windsor, Lionel in Martha, Nemorino, Lensky and Almaviva in Il Barbiere di Siviglia; Many concert engagements and lieder recitals; Sang Idomeneo with the English Bach Festival at Covent Garden in 1990. *Recordings:* Jacquino in Fidelio; Cantatas by Bach, Fux and Scarlatti; Die Schöpfung by Haydn. *Address:* c/o Hamburgische Staatsoper, Grosse Theaterstrasse 34, 2000 Hamburg 36, Germany.

WOHLHAUSER, René Claude; Composer; b. 24 March 1954, Zürich, Switzerland; 2 s., 2 d. *Education:* Diploma as Teacher of Music Theory, Basel Conservatory, 1975–79; Composition courses with Kazimierz

Serocki, Mauricio Kagel, Herbert Brün and Heinz Holliger; Study with Klaus Huber, Staatliche Musikhochschule, Freiburg, 1980–81; Composition with Brian Ferneyhough, 1982–87. *Career:* Works played by Arditti String Quartet, Basel, Biel and Luzern Symphony Orchestras, also at Schweizer Tonkünstlerfeste and International Darmstädter Ferienkurse für Neue Musik, Notre Dame de Paris, Toronto, Newcastle, Baku, Klangforum Wien and Schauspielhaus Berlin; Portraits and works on radio programmes; Lectures on musical and philosophical aspects of his works at Darmstadt, Winterthur and Basel; Founder, Komponistenforum Basel and Co-founder of Adesso, contemporary music of independently published composers. *Compositions include:* Duometrie, for flute and bass clarinet, 1985–86; Adagio assai for String Quartet, 1982–88; In statu mutandi, for orchestra, 1991–93; Vocis Imago for Flute, Clarinet, Percussion, Piano, Violin and Cello, 1993–95. *Recordings:* Wer den Gesang nicht kennt; Drei Stücke für Klavier; Portrait. *Address:* Schillerstrasse 5, 4053 Basel, Switzerland.

WOLF, Gerd; Singer (Bass); b. 18 April 1940, Floha, Saxony, Germany. *Education:* Studied at the Berlin Musikhochschule. *Career:* Debut: Dresden Radesbeul in 1970 as the Hermit in Der Freischütz; Sang at Dresden and elsewhere in East Germany until 1982, Berlin Staatsoper from then as Mozart's Osmin, Leporello and Bartolo, Nicolai's Falstaff, Bett in Zar und Zimmerman, Geronimo in Il Matrimonio Segreto and the Doctor in Wozzeck; Guest appearances in Leipzig, Karlsruhe and with the Berlin Staatsoper company at Naples, Messina, Prague, Bratislava, Japan and Netherlands; Season 2000–01 in Berlin as Mozart's Bartolo and Kuno in Der Freischütz. *Recordings include:* Pfitzner's Palestrina; Graf Mirabeau by Siegfried Matthus; Ariadne auf Naxos. *Address:* Deutsche Staatsoper Berlin, Unter den Linden 7, 1086 Berlin, Germany.

WOLF, Markus; Violinist and Violist; b. 28 May 1962, Vienna, Austria; 2 s. *Education:* Violin studies at Wiener Musikhochschule with Edith Bertschinger and Guenter Pichler, 1968–83; Diploma with Honours, 1983; Further studies with Max Rostal, Klagenfurt and Bern; Masterclasses with Nathan Milstein and Oscar Shumsky. *Career:* Debut: Wiener Musikverein, 1976, Wigmore Hall, London, 1987, Suntory Hall, Tokyo, 1990, Carnegie Hall (Weill Hall), New York, 1996; Violist, String trio with brothers Reinhold and Peter Wolf, 1973–; Appearances with the Alban Berg Quartet, 1986; Violinist, Assistant of Guenter Pichler, Wiener Musikhochschule, 1983–89; Principal Concertmaster, Wiener Symphoniker, 1987–88; Principal Concertmaster, Bavarian State Opera in Munich, 1989–; Guest Leader, London Symphony Orchestra, 1997–; Founder of Beethoven Trio Wien in 1981; Member and Teacher of Junge Muenchner Philharmonie, 1999–2002; Teacher at Richard Strauss Conservatory, Munich, 2000–. *Recordings:* Mozart with Alban Berg Quartet; Tchaikovsky, Beethoven, Mendelssohn, Mozart, Schubert, Dvořák, Smetana, Suk, Mahler, Schoenberg and Korngold with Beethoven Trio; Webern with Jérôme Granjon; Wagner with Wolfgang Sawallisch; Schoenberg with Zubin Mehta; Mendelssohn with Munich Youth Orchestra. *Address:* Bayerisches Staatsorchester München, Max Joseph Platz 2, 80539 Munich, Germany.

WOLF, R. Peter; Musicologist and Harpsichordist; b. 5 Dec. 1942, Washington DC, USA. *Education:* AB, Harvard University, 1965; MPhil, 1969; PhD, 1977, Yale University; Studied harpsichord with Gustav Leonhardt at Amsterdam Conservatorium, 1965–66 and with Ralph Kirkpatrick at Yale School of Music, 1966–70. *Career:* Debut: Carnegie Recital Hall, NY, 1975; Numerous concerts as harpsichord soloist and continuo player; Musician-in-Residence, NC State University, Raleigh; 2 television shows, NC Educational Network, 1972; Instructor in Music, SUNY, Stony Brook, 1972–78; Assistant Professor of Music, University of Utah, 1978–80, and at Rutgers University, 1980–85; Editor, Brouda Brothers Ltd, 1985–89; Director of Development, Hoboken Chamber Orchestra, 1989–; Member of Bowers-Wolf Duo, Salt Lake Chamber Ensemble, Apollo's Banquet, and New York Baroque. *Recordings:* Telemann's Instrumental Chamber Music with Concertmasters Ensemble; Private recording of works by Rameau, J. S. Bach, C. P. E. Bach; Violin Sonatas by Biber, 1681, with Sonya Monosoff and Judith Davidoff. *Publications include:* Joint Editor, ms Bauyn, New York; Editor, Rameau, Les Paladins, New York and Paris; Editor, facsimile edition of Rameau, Les Paladins, 1986. *Contributions:* The Scriblerian; Actes; Colloque International Rameau, Dijon, 1983; The Musical Quarterly; Journal of The American Musical Instrument Society; Recherches; Early Music; Journal of The American Musicological Society. *Address:* 37A Phelps Avenue, New Brunswick, NJ 08901, USA.

WOLF, Reinhold (Michael); Violinist; b. 23 May 1956, Vienna, Austria. *Education:* Piano lessons at age 6; 1st Violin instruction at Wiener Musikakademie at age 8, later chamber music lessons with Alban Berg Quartet; Kuenstlerische Diplompruefung mit Auszeichnung, 1976; Violin studies with G Poulet in Paris and Max Rostal in Cologne; Chamber music with Amadeus Quartet; Konzert-Examen mit Auszeichnung Cologne, 1981. *Career:* Established the Wolf Trio with brothers Markus on Viola and Peter on Violoncello; Concertmaster, World Youth Orchestra with L Bernstein at Tanglewood, USA at age 18; Concertmaster, Orchestra of the Deutsche Oper Berlin, 1982–; Soloist with various European orchestras; Appeared as Double Concerto partner of H Szeryng with Vienna Symphony Orchestra; Established ensemble, Contraste in Berlin, 1989. *Honours:* Special Prize, Jeunesse Musicales Austria for the Wolf Trio, 1973; 1st Prize as Soloist, Jugend Musiziert Competition, Austria, 1975. *Address:* c/o Deutsche Oper Berlin, Orchesterdirektion, Richard Wagnerstrasse 10, 10585 Berlin, Germany.

WOLF, Sally; Singer (Soprano); b. 1957, USA. *Career:* Santa Fe Opera from 1982, as the Queen of Night, in the premiere of Eaton's The Tempest (1985) and in Sallinen's The King goes forth to France; Has sung the Queen of Night throughout North America, at Covent Garden (1986) and with Opera North at Leeds (1987); Seattle Opera, 1992, as Lucia di Lammermoor, Netherlands Opera, 1990, as Constanze, and San Francisco, 1991, as Giunia in Mozart's Lucio Silla; Other roles include Eternita in La Calisto (at Santa Fe), Gilda, Violetta and Oscar; Sang Donna Anna at the 1996 Munich Festival and Mozart's Queen of Night at Los Angeles, 1998; Season 1999–2000 as Donna Elvira in Los Angeles, Amalia in Verdi's Masnadieri at Carnegie Hall and Mme Cortese in Il Viaggio a Reims at the New York City Opera. *Address:* Santa Fe Opera, PO Box 2408, Santa Fe, NM 87504, USA.

WOLFF, Beverly; Singer (Mezzo-Soprano); b. 6 Nov. 1928, Atlanta, Georgia, USA. *Education:* Studied with Sidney Dietch and Vera McIntyre at The Academy of Vocal Arts in Philadelphia. *Career:* Debut: Sang Dinah in a television production of Bernstein's Trouble In Tahiti, 1952; Has sung with the New York City Opera from 1958, with debut as Dinah; Appeared on NBC television in the premiere of Menotti's Labyrinth, 1963; Stage engagements in Mexico City, Cincinnati, Boston, Houston, Washington and San Francisco as Carmen, Adalgisa, Cherubino, Kabanicha in Katya Kabanova, Radamisto, Dalila and Sesto in Handel's Giulio Cesare; Concert appearances as Dalila and Sesto; Sang in the Premieres of Douglas Moore's Carrie Nation in 1966 and Menotti's The Most Important Man in 1971; Concert appearances with leading American orchestras. *Recordings:* Roberto Devereux by Donizetti; Rossini's La Pietra del Paragone; Giulio Cesare. *Honours:* Winner, Youth Auditions, Philadelphia, 1952.

WOLFF, Christian; Composer; b. 8 March 1934, Nice, France. *Education:* Influenced by John Cage, Morton Feldman and Earle Brown after moving to the USA; Studied classics at Harvard, PhD in 1963. *Career:* Taught at Harvard University, 1962–76; Teacher of Classics and Music at Dartmouth College from 1976; Strauss Professor of Music, Professor of Classics, Dartmouth College, New Hampshire, USA. *Compositions include:* Nine for Ensemble, 1951; Suite for Prepared Piano, 1954; Duo for Pianists l and ll, 1957–58; Music For Merce Cunningham, 1959; Duo for Violin and Piano, 1961; Summer for String Quartet, 1961; In Between Pieces for 3 players, 1963; Septet, 1964; Quartet for 4 Horns, 1966; Elec Spring I–III, 1966–67; Toss for 8 or more players, 1968; Snowdrop for Harpsichord, 1970; Burdocks for 1 or more Orchestras or 5 or more Players, 1971; Accompaniments, 1972; Lines for String Quartet, 1972; Changing The System, 1973; Exercises 1–24, 1973–84; Wobbly Music for Mixed Chorus and Instruments, 1976; Bread And Roses for Piano and for Violin, 1976; Dark As A Dungeon for Clarinet, 1977, for Trombone and Double Bass, 1977; The Death Of Mother Jones for Violin, 1977; Stardust Pieces for Cello and Piano, 1979; Isn't This A Time for Saxophone, 1981; Eisler Ensemble Pieces, 1983; Piano Song–I Am A Dangerous Woman, 1983; Peace March 1–3, 1983–84; I Like To Think Of Harriet Tubman for Female Voice, Treble and Alto, 1984; Piano Trio, 1985; Bowery Preludes, 1986; Long Peace March, for chamber ensemble, 1987; From Leaning Forward, songs, 1988; Rosas, for piano and percussion, 1990; Ruth, for piano and trombone, 1991; Merce, for percussion ensemble, 1993; Two Pianists, 1994; Memory, octet, 1994; Percussionist Songs, 1995; Percussionist Dances, 1997; John, David, for orchestra, 1998; Pebbles for violin and piano, 1999; Cello Suite Variation, 2000. *Recordings:* For Ruth Crawford; Stones; Bread and Roses; I Like to Think of Harriet Tubman. *Publications:* Cues: Writing and Conversations, book, 1998. *Honours:* John Cage Award for Music, 1996; Fromm Foundation Commissioning Grant, 1998. *Address:* 104 South Main Street, Hanover, NH 03755, USA.

WOLFF, Hugh (MacPherson); Conductor; b. 21 Oct. 1953, Paris, France; M. Judith Kogan, 3 c. *Education:* Piano lessons from Fleisher and Shure; Studied composition with Crumb and Kirchner; BA, Harvard University, 1975; Studied composition with Messiaen; Piano with Sancan; Conducting with Bruck; MM, Piano, 1977, MM, Conducting, 1978, Peabody Institute. *Career:* Exxon/Arts Endowment Conductor, 1979–82, Associate Conductor, 1982–85, National Symphony Orchestra, Washington DC; Music Director, Northeastern Pennsylvania Philharmonic Orchestra, 1981–86; European debut with London Philharmonic Orchestra in 1982; Music Director, New Jersey Symph-

ony Orchestra, Newark, 1985–; Principal Conductor, St Paul Chamber Orchestra, Minn, 1988–; Chief conductor of the Frankfurt Radio Symphony Orchestra, 1997; Guest Conductor with various North American and European orchestras. *Honours:* Frank Huntington Beebe Fellow, 1975–76; Annette Kade Fellow, 1978; Co-Recipient, Affiliate Artist's Seaver Conducting Award, 1985; Cannes Classical Award, 2001. *Address:* c/o ICM Artists Ltd, 40 West 57th Street, New York, NY 10019, USA.

WOLFF, Jean-Claude; Composer; b. Oct. 1946, Paris, France. *Education:* Studied Composition, Analysis, History of Music, at L'Ecole Normale de Musique de Paris, then at Conservatoire National Supérieur de Musique de Paris with Henri Dutilleux, Jean-Pierre Guezec, Michel Philippot, Ivo Malec; Electro-acoustic classes with Jean-Etienne Marie, Centre International de Recherches Musicales; Spent 3 summers following Composition courses with Franco Donatoni, Accademia Chigiana, Siena, Italy; Laureate, Académie de France, Rome (Villa Medici), 1978–80. *Compositions include:* About 40 works performed at various festivals and concerts of contemporary music in France (Radio-France, International Musical Weeks in Orleans, Angers Music Festival, Contemporary Music Meetings at Metz) and abroad in Italy, Switzerland, Denmark, Spain, Netherlands; For several years has concentrated mainly on chamber music; Working on four pieces for piano solo or with violin or violoncello; Symphony for voices and large orchestra. *Honours:* 1st Prize, Vienna Modern Masters, 1991. *Address:* 39 rue Bouret, 75019 Paris, France. *E-mail:* jeanclaude.wolff@free.fr.

WOLFF, Marguerite; Concert Pianist; b. 1930, London, England; m. Derrick Moss, deceased, 2 d. *Education:* FTCL, Royal Academy of Music, with Thomas Khatt; Trinity College of Music, with Gertrude Agulkyi, and with pianist Louis Kentner. *Career:* Soloist, London Symphony Orchestra, Royal Philharmonic Orchestra, Philharmonia, Bournemouth and Birmingham Orchestras; Radio and television broadcasts with major orchestras; Toured USA, Europe and Far East; 9 tours of Far East (Nepal, Delhi, Bombay, Calcutta, Malaysia, Indonesia, Singapore, Hong Kong), East Africa, Mexico, Peru and North America; 10 tours of South America. *Recordings:* Bliss Piano Sonata; Liszt Society Recording, Liszt recording, Wright Society. *Honours:* HONFTCL, UK and O.B.E. *Address:* Flat T, 82 Portland Place, London W1B 1 NS, England.

WOLLENBERG, Susan L. F.; BA, MA, DPhil; University Teacher; b. 28 April 1949, Lancashire, England; m. L. Wollenberg; one s. one d. *Education:* Withington Girls' School, Manchester, Royal Northern Coll. of Music, Lady Margaret Hall, Oxford. *Career:* Clara Sophie Deneke Music Scholar, Lady Margaret Hall 1966–69; Halstead Postgraduate Scholar, Faculty of Music, Oxford 1969–72; Univ. Lecturer in Music, Faculty of Music, Oxford 1972–2002; Reader in Music, Faculty of Music, Oxford 2002–; Fellow and Tutor in Music, Lady Margaret Hall 1972–; Lecturer in Music, Brasenose Coll., Oxford 1987–; mem. Royal Musical Asscn, Oxford Architectural and Historical Soc.. *Compositions include:* The Survivor (song cycle). *Publications:* Music at Oxford in the 18th and 19th Centuries, Concert Life in 18th Century Britain (ed. with S. McVeigh); contrib. to New Grove Dictionary of Music and Musicians, Oxford Dictionary of National Biography, various musical journals. *Address:* 131 Eynsham Road, Botley, Oxford, OX2 9BY, England (home). *Telephone:* (1865) 276125 (office). *Fax:* (1865) 276128 (office). *E-mail:* office@music.ox.ac.uk (office).

WOLOVSKY, Leonardo; Singer (Bass-Baritone); b. 1922, York, Pennsylvania, USA. *Education:* Studied at Oberlin College, Ohio. *Career:* Sang at first in concert then appeared with Maria Callas in Norma at Catania, 1952; Engaged at Wiesbaden Opera, 1953–57, Nuremberg, 1957–73; Guest appearances at Frankfurt, 1959–73, Bayerische Staatsoper Munich, 1961–69, Hanover, 1961–73, Hamburg, 1956–60; Sang also at Graz, Essen, Amsterdam, Zürich, Paris, Barcelona and Athens; Bielefeld 1988, as Simon Mago in Nerone by Boito; Other roles have included Enrico (Lucia di Lammermoor); Oroveso, King Philip, Nabucco, the Dutchman, Hans Sachs, the Wanderer in Siegfried and Boris Godunov; Concert repertoire included Beethoven's Ninth, the Verdi Requiem and Bach's Christmas Oratorio. *Address:* St ädtische Buhnen, Brunnenstrasse 3, 48000 Berlin 1, Germany.

WOLPE, Michael, MA; Israeli composer; b. 4 March 1960, Tel-Aviv. *Education:* Rubin Acad., Jerusalem, Univ. of Cambridge. *Career:* founder regional music school, Sdeh Boker kibbutz; teacher, High School of Sciences and the Arts 1991–, Rumin Acad., Jerusalem 1996–; Head of Music Dept, Israeli Arts and Sciences Acad. 1999–; founder and Artistic Dir, Sounds in the Desert festival. *Compositions include:* Capella Kolot 1988, Stabat Mater 1994, Concerto for flutes and orchestra 1995, Trio 1996, Songs of Memory 1998, Hatarat Nedarim 2002, Songs of the Land (cycle of symphonic poems), Kaprisma Nos 1–9 for the Jerusalem Ensemble Kaprisma. *Recordings:* Kaprisma No. 8. *Address:* c/o Israeli Arts and Sciences Academy, Massuah Road, Jerusalem 96408, Israel (office).

WOLVERTON, Joseph; Singer (tenor); b. 1970, Chicago, USA. *Education:* Juilliard School, New York; American Conservatory of Music, Chicago. *Career:* Appearances with Minnesota Opera as Alfredo, Leicester in Maria Stuarda and Mozart's Ferrando for Chautauqua Opera, and Bellini's Pollione with Toledo Opera; Faust and Hoffmann for Michigan Opera, Edgardo and Riccardo (Ballo in Maschera) at Knoxville, the Duke of Mantua at Seattle, and Pinkerton for New York City Opera; European engagements as Nemorino at Hamburg, Werther in Malaga and Pinkerton for Dublin Opera; Concerts include Beethoven's Ninth and Missa Solemnis, Berlioz Requiem, Mahler's Eighth and the Verdi Requiem; Season 2001–2002 as Cavaradossi at Brussels, Nemorino at Montreal and the Duke for Tulsa Opera; Other roles include Macduff, Rinuccio in Gianni Schicchi, Turiddu, and Mascagni's Silvano. *Current Management:* Athole Still International Management, Foresters Hall, 25–27 Westow Street, London, SE19 3RY, England. *Telephone:* (20) 8771-5271. *Fax:* (20) 8768-6600. *Website:* www.atholestill.com.

WONG, Randall (Kevin); Singer (Male soprano and Countertenor); b. 10 April 1955, Oakland, California. *Education:* Doctor of Musical Arts, Stanford University, California; Master of Arts in Music; Bachelor of Music; Magna cum laude, San Francisco State University, California. *Career:* Debut: Opera debut, Bernabei's Ascanio, Teatro Olimpico, Vicenza, Italy; San Francisco Opera; NY City Opera; Houston Grand Opera in Harvey Milk; Houston Grand Opera in Monk's Atlas; JC Bach's Endimione at the Carmel Bach Festival and Jommelli's Demofoonte at the Schwetzingen Festival; mem, AGMA; NARAS. *Recordings:* Hasse's Cleofide; Meredith Monk's Atlas; Wallace and Korie's Harvey Milk; Wallace and Korie's Kabbalah; Solo soprano cantatas of Vivaldi; Classical music composed by computer. *Publications:* Barbara Strozzi entry in Women Composers: Music Through The Ages vol. 2, GK Hall & Co, 1996. *Honours:* NY Dance and Performance Award, 1997; Recipient of the California Arts Council Touring Grant, 1986–. *Current Management:* California Artists Management. *Address:* 140 Beulah St, San Francisco, CA 94117, USA.

WOOD, Hugh; Composer; b. 27 June 1932, Parbold, Lancashire, England. *Education:* Studied at Oxford University and in London with W S Lloyd Webber; Further study with Anthony Milner, Iain Hamilton and Matyas Seiber. *Career:* Professor of Harmony at the Royal Academy of Music, 1962–65; Teacher at Morley College, 1958–67; Research Fellow in Composition, Glasgow University, 1966–70; Lecturer in Music, Liverpool University, 1971–73 and at Cambridge University from 1976; Talks on BBC Radio 3; Piano Concerto premiered at the 1991 Promenade Concerts. *Compositions:* Songs For Springtime for Chorus and Piano, 1954; Suite for Piano, 1956; String Quartet, 1957; Variations for Viola and Piano, 1958; Laurie Lee Songs, 1959; Songs To Poems By Christopher Logue, 1961; Trio for Flute, Viola and Piano, 1961; String Quartet No. 1, 1962; Scenes From Comus for Soprano, Tenor and Chorus, 1965; 3 Choruses, 1966; Songs To Poems By D H Lawrence, 1966; Capriccio for Organ, 1967; Quintet for Clarinet, Horn and Piano Trio, 1967; The Horses, song cycle, 1967; The Rider Victory, song cycle, 1968; Cello Concerto, 1969; String Quartet No. 2, 1970; Chamber Concerto, 1971; Violin Concerto, 1972; 2 Choruses, 1973; Songs To Poems By Robert Graves, 1973; Songs To Poems By Pablo Neruda for High Voice and Chamber Orchestra, 1973; String Quartet No. 4, 1978; Symphony, 1979–82; Piano Trio, 1984; Comus Quadrilles, 1988; Horn Trio, 1987–89; Cantata for Chorus and Orchestra, 1989; Marina for High Voice and Ensemble, 1989; Piano Concerto, 1990; Funeral Music (brass quintet), 1992; String Quartet No. 3, 1993; Poem, for violin and piano, 1993; The Kingdom of God, anthem, 1994; Variations for orchestra, 1997; Clarinet Trio, 1997; Greek Songs, 1998; Serenade and Elegy for string quartet and orchestra, 1999; String Quartet No. 5, 2001. *Address:* c/o Churchill College, Cambridge CB 3 ODS, England.

WOOD, James (Peter); Composer, Conductor and Percussionist; b. 27 May 1953, Barton-on-Sea, Hampshire, England; m. Penny Irish, 25 June 1977, 1 s., 1 d. *Education:* Radley College, 1966–71; ARCO, 1969; FRCO, 1971; Sidney Sussex College, Cambridge, 1972–75; BA, Music, 1975; Studied with Nadia Boulanger in Paris, 1971–72; RAM, 1975–76. *Career:* Conductor, Schola Cantorum of Oxford, 1977–81; Founder and Conductor of New London Chamber Choir, 1981; Professor of Percussion, Internationale Ferienkurse, Darmstadt, 1982–; Regular radio and television appearances; Artistic Adviser to Percussion Foundation and Percussion 88 and 90 Festivals; Founder and Director, Centre for Microtonal Music, 1990–; Director of Barbican's Annual Weekend of Microtonal Music. *Compositions include:* Phaedrus; Oreion, BBC Symphony Orchestra commission, premiered at 1989 Promenade Concerts; Stoicheia, Darmstadt commission; Ho Shang Yao; T'ien Chung Yao; Choroi Kaithaliai; Spirit Festival With Lamentations; Village Burial With Fire; Incantamenta; The Parliament of Angels, for 18 instruments, 1995; Children at a Funeral, for prepared piano, 1996; The Parliament of Angels, 1996; Séance, 1996; Mountain Language, 1998; Jodo, 1999; Journey of the Magic, 2000. *Recordings include:*

Stoicheia; Music for Percussion and Voices; Stravinsky's Les Noces and other choral works; Bergman's Choral Works; 15th Century Flemish Choral Works, 2 records. *Contributions:* A New System for Quarter-Tone Percussion, in Musical Times and Percussive Notes. *Honours:* Lili Boulanger Prize, 1975; Lili Boulanger Memorial Award, 1980; Holst Foundation Award, 1995. *Current Management:* Colin Boyle. *Address:* Bancroft, Rectory Lane, Fringford, Bicester, Oxfordshire OX6 9DX, England.

WOOD, Jeffrey (Neal); Composer and University Professor; b. 3 Oct. 1954, Allentown, Pennsylvania, USA; 1 s. *Education:* BMus, Oberlin College Conservatory of Music, 1976; MMus, 1978, MA, 1980, PhD, 1982, State University of New York, Stony Brook. *Career:* Visiting Lecturer, University of New Mexico, Albuquerque, New Mexico Institute of Mining and Technology, 1983–84, Austin Peay State University, Clarksville, TN, 1984–. *Compositions:* Duo for Cello and Piano, 1982 (recorded); In Memoriam Magistri for Brass Quintet, 1982; Sonata for Cello and Piano, 1984; String Quartet No. 2, 1985; MCMXIV for Tenor and Piano, 1985; Now The Most High Is Born, 1985; Trio-Sonata for Cello, Piano and Percussion, 1986; The Dream Of The Rood for Tenor Solo, Chorus and Organ, 1986; Swifts for Violin and Cello, 1986; First Essay for Orchestra, 1986; Music for Concert Band, 1987; Comedies for Woodwind Quintet, 1988; Quartet for Flute, Violin, Cello and Piano, 1988; Lay Your Sleeping Head My Love for Soprano, Tenor and Piano, 1987; Kreigeslieder for Mezzo-Soprano and Piano, 1988; Time Let Me Hail And Climb for Chorus, Brass Quintet and Piano, 1990; The Killing for Tenor and Piano, 1989; Four Deadly Serious Songs for Baritone and Piano, 1990; Ballads For The Goodly Fere for Voice and Piano, 1991; Dances for 2 Pianos, 1992; Preludes for Piano Solo, 1992; Ghosts for Clarinet, Viola and Piano, 1993. *Recordings:* Comedies, by Quintet of the Americas, 1991. *Contributions:* In Theory Only, vol. 7, 1983. *Current Management:* Broadcast Music Inc. *Address:* Department of Music, Austin Peay State University, Clarksville, TN 37044, USA.

WOODLAND, Rae, FRSA; British singer (soprano) and teacher of singing; b. 1930, Nottingham, England; m. Denis Stanley. *Education:* Opera School, London and private studies with Roy Henderson, Joan Cross and Vittorio Gui. *Career:* debut, Sadler's Wells Theatre, as Queen of the Night in Mozart's Magic Flute; notable appearances include Covent Garden debut in Sonnambula 1965, sang Diana in the Olympians at the Royal Festival Hall, soloist in the first performance of Angels of the Mind at Lancaster Univ., sang Handel's Messiah at Church of the Nativity, Bethlehem, sang in the productions of The Unknown Island for the Royal Festival Ballet and La Fête Étrange for the Royal Ballet, sang in Der Rosenkavalier at Glyndebourne before announcing her retirement from public performances; numerous broadcasts with the BBC; roles include Venus in Tannhäser, Naiade in Ariadne auf Naxos, Fiordiligi in Così fan Tutte, Odabella in Atilla, Electra in Idomeneo, Giselda in I Lombardi, Mimi in La Bohàme, Donna Anna and Donna Elvira in Don Giovanni, Constanze in Entführung, Luisa in Luisa Miller, Marguerite in Mefistofele, Mistress Ford in Falstaff, Helmwige in Walküre, Flower Maiden in Parsifal, Female Chorus in Rape of Lucretia, Lady Billows in Albert Herring, Miss Jessel in Turn of the Screw, Eugenie in Nicholas Maw's Rising of the Moon, Frau I I I in Von Einem's Visit of the Old Lady, Guinone in The Return of Ulysses, Dama in Macbeth; performances with opera companies including Scottish Opera, WNO, ENO, Glyndebourne Festival Opera, Sadler's Wells, Royal Opera Covent Garden, and several companies world-wide; numerous appearances at festivals, including Glyndebourne, Aix-en-Provence, Amsterdam, Edinburgh, Aldeburgh, Rome, Wiesbaden, Antwerp, Geneva, Lyon, Bergen, Brussels, Three Choirs Festival; Prof. of Singing, Royal Acad. of Music, London; vocal consultant, Britten Pears School, Snape; guest lecturer in Edinburgh, the Univs of Aberdeen, East Anglia and Nottingham; international adjudicator and examiner, Royal Acad. of Music, Guildhall School of Music, Royal Northern Coll. of Music, Royal Welsh School of Music, Trinity Coll. and the Royal Scottish Acad. of Music; adviser to Arts Council of Great Britain, Eastern Arts; Patron of Erin Arts; mem. Music Panel of the English Speaking Union, Aldeburgh Music Club (Pres.), Royal Acad. of Music Guild, Asscn of Teachers of Singing, Incorporated Soc. of Musicians, Equity. *Recordings include:* Messiah, John Tobin-Handel Society; Arthur Bliss's Birthday; Midsummer Night's Dream, Haitink; Montezuma, by Gunn, Bonynge; Idomeneo, Davis; Mahler No. 2, Stokowski; Glyndebourne, Macbeth and Ritorno d'Ulisse; the Queen of Night, BBC Proms, Glyndebourne. *Honours:* Hon. RAM. *Address:* Brackendale, Priory Lane, Snape, Saxmundham, Suffolk IP17 1SD, England (home). *E-mail:* raewoodlandsnape@aol.com. *Website:* www.impulse-music.co.uk/woodland.htm.

WOODROW, Alan; Singer (tenor); b. 1952, Toronto, Canada. *Education:* Studied at the Royal Conservatory in Toronto and at the London Opera Centre. *Career:* From 1976 sang with English National Opera as Pedrillo, Don Ottavio, Froh (Das Rheingold), Lindoro, Vasek, Monostatos, Canio, Hermann, Don José, Edmund in Reimann's Lear and

Walther von Stolzing; Recent London appearances as the Prince in The Love of Three Oranges, the Captain in Wozzeck, Herod in Salome and Siegmund in Die Walküre, season 1992–93; Has also sung Sergei in Lady Macbeth of Mtsensk at La Scala and the Bastille, Paris; Season 1998 as Tannhäuser at Naples and Huon in Oberon at the Barbican Hall, London; Concert engagements in Canada with the Mozart and Verdi Requiems; The Choral Symphony and Mahler's Eighth; A Mass of Life by Delius; Kodály's Psalmus Hungaricus; Season 1999–2000 as Don José for ENO, Siegfried in The Ring at the Tyrol Festival, and Strauss's Emperor for the Munich Staatsoper; Bacchus in Naples, Peter Grimes at Aldeburgh and in Henze's Venus and Adonis, at Toronto. *Recordings include:* Siegfried and Götterdämmerung, from the Tyrol Festival. *Current Management:* Athole Still International Management, Forresters Hall, 25–27 Westow Street, London, SE19 3RY, England. *Telephone:* (20) 8771-5271. *Fax:* (20) 8768-6600. *Website:* www .atholestill.com.

WOODS, Elaine; Singer (Soprano); b. 1958, Lancashire, England. *Education:* Studied at Oxford University and at the Royal Manchester College of Music with Elsie Thurston; Further study with Marjorie Thomas. *Career:* Debut: With Kent Opera as Violetta in 1979 at the Edinburgh Festival; Sang in Handel's Tolomeo at the Batigniano Festival in Italy, 1980; German debut in 1981 as Mimi in Mannheim; Bremen Opera from 1982 as Fiordigili, Tatiana, Eva, Liu and the Countess in Capriccio; In 1983 sang in JC Bach's Lucio Silla in Frankfurt and Acis and Galatea at Karlsruhe; Appeared as Pamina at the 1986 Bregenz Festival and sang Belinda in a new production of Dido and Aeneas at Frankfurt; With Welsh National Opera has sung Donna Elvira, Fiordigili and Mozart's Countess; Concert repertoire includes the Verdi and Mozart Requiems, Haydn's Creation and Seasons, Messiah and Beethoven's Missa Solemnis and Ninth Symphony. *Honours:* Prizewinner at the 1978 's-Hertogenbosch Competition. *Current Management:* Ingpen & Williams Ltd, 7 St George's Court, 131 Putney Bridge Road, London, SW15 2PA, England.

WOODS, Thomas; Australian conductor; b. 1959, Tanzania. *Education:* Western Australian Conservatorium, Perth and with Vladimir Ponkin at the Gnessin Institute, Moscow. *Career:* Asst Conductor with West Australian Opera Company for productions of Don Pasquale and Madama Butterfly, 1982–93; Asst Chorus Master and Conductor at the Australian Opera, 1994–, leading Il Barbiere di Siviglia, A Midsummer Night's Dream, La Traviata and The Gondoliers; with La Fille du Régiment in Sydney, Il Barbiere in Sydney and La Traviata in Perth, 1997. *Honours:* Cultural Exchange Scholarship, 1989.

WOODWARD, Donna; Opera Singer and Voice Teacher; b. 2 June 1946, Baltimore, Maryland, USA; m. Juergen Stadtmueller, 28 Dec 1983. *Education:* AA degree, Virginia Intermont College; BMus, College Conservatory of Music, University of Cincinnati; Postgraduate work in Cincinnati and at University of Hamburg, Germany. *Career:* Coloratura and Lyric Soubrette at Stadtheater Darmstadt, 1971–73; Stadttheater, Heidelberg, 1973–75; Nationaltheater, Mannheim, 1975–86 Frequently guesting in (Nationaltheater) Munich, Cologne, Karlsruhe and Stuttgart; Freelance since 1986; Apearances in Germany, Switzerland, France and Belgium; Teacher of Voice since 1991; Voice Department, University of Mainz, 1991–2001; Hochschule für Musik, Heidelberg/Mannheim, 1992–97; Private studio in Frankfurt, Germany, 1999–; mem, Delta Omicron; NATS. *Recordings:* Rosalia in Karl von Dittersdorf's Doktor und Apotheker. *Honours:* Giorno Memorial Prize, 1969; Stipend from Corbett Foundation for study in Europe, 1969. *Address:* Auf der Weide 4A, 65550 Limburg, Germany; 1694 Wayah Drive, Charleston, SC, USA. *E-mail:* woodstadt@aol.com.

WOODWARD, Roger Robert, OBE; Australian conductor, composer and pianist; b. 20 Dec. 1942, Sydney; one s. one d. *Education:* DSCM, Sydney Conservatory of Music; Warsaw Academy, Poland. *Career:* Debut: Royal Festival Hall in London, 1970; His career has been closely associated with leading composers including Xenakis, Boulez, Stockhausen, Takemitsu, Bussotti, Berio, Feldman, Dillon, Meale, Boyd, Sitsky, Conyngham and Cage with works specially written for him; Has worked with many leading conductors including Boulez, Leinsdorf, Masur and Mehta; Has performed throughout Europe, USA and Australia and has appeared at international festivals and with major orchestras worldwide; Founder Member of contemporary music series in London in 1972 and in Australia in 1975; Performed historic series of 16 concerts presenting the complete works of Chopin in 1985; World premiere of Xenakis' Keqrops, conceived for him with New York Philharmonic under Mehta, 1986; Music Director, Xenakis' ballet, Kraanerg, by Sydney Dance Company, 1988; Founded Alpha Centuri Ensemble, 1989; Founder and Director of Sydney Spring (1989), Kotschach-Mauthner Musiktage (1990) and Joie et Lumière (Burgundy, 1997) Festivals; Chair of Music, University of New England, Australia. *Recordings include:* Rachmaninov Preludes; Australian Contemporary Music; Barraqué Sonata and music by Bussotti; Werder 3rd Sonata, 1969; 2

Beethoven Sonatas; Shostakovich's 24 Preludes and Fugues, double album; Liszt's transcription of Beethoven's Eroica; Brahms' 1st Piano Concerto under Masur. *Honours:* Fellow, Chopin Institute, Warsaw, 1976; KT (Breffni), 1985. *Current Management:* Patrick Togher Artists. *E-mail:* pjtogher@ozemail.com.au; woodward@metz.une.edu.au.

WOOF, Barbara; Composer; b. 2 Sept. 1958, Sydney, New South Wales, Australia. *Education:* BMus (Hons), University of Sydney, 1981; Royal Conservatory, The Hague; Study with Peter Sculthorpe and Jan van Vlijman. *Career:* Faculty Member, Utrecht School of Arts, the Netherlands, 1988–; Resident Composer with the Sydney Symphony Orchestra, 1992. *Compositions include:* Maldoror, for violin, 1983; Caoine, for alto saxophone, 1985; Hymns and Melodies, for saxophone quartet, 1989; Soundings, for gamelan, 1990; Banshee's Dance, for orchestra, 1992; Night Crossing, for orchestra, 1993; Táragató-Ray, for chamber ensemble, 1998; Alchimien du verbe, for voice and chamber orchestra, 1999; Naxos revisited, for soprano and 4 channel tape, 2003; Traumland, for sporano and chamber orchestra, 2003. *Recordings:* Soundings, for Gamelan. *Honours:* Winner, Martin Codex Composition Competition, Spain, 1985. *Address:* c/o DONEMUS, Paulus Potterstraat 16, 1016-CZ Amsterdam, Netherlands.

WOOLFENDEN, Guy (Anthony); Composer and Conductor; b. 12 July 1937, Ipswich, England; m. Jane Aldrick, 29 Sept 1962, 3 s. *Education:* Westminster Abbey Choir School; Whitgift School; Christ's College, Cambridge; MA (Cantab); LGSM; FBSM; Honorary LCM. *Career:* Head of Music, Royal Shakespeare Company, Stratford-upon-Avon and London, composed more than 150 scores for this company, 1963–98; Also composed scores for Burgtheater, Vienna; Comédie Française, Paris; Teatro di Stabile, Genoa and National Theatre, Norway; Also for films, radio, television; Conducted concerts with most British Symphony Orchestras; Conducted concerts and ballet in Canada, Germany, Japan, USA, Hong Kong, and France; Conducted opera for BBC radio, television and 3 productions with Scottish Opera; Conductor of Birmingham Conservatoire Wind Orchestra; Arranged and composed music for four full-length ballets by choreographer André Prokovsky: Anna Karenina, The Three Musketeers, La Traviata and The Queen of Spades, all now in the repertory of the world's major companies; Conducted Russian premiere of Anna Karenina with Kirov Ballet in St Petersburg, 1993; Artistic Director, Cambridge Festival, 1986–91. *Compositions:* composed 3 musicals; Comedy of Errors for RSC; A Children's Opera, The Last Wild Wood Sector 88 with Adrian Mitchell; Works for the Concert Hall include: Concertos, Chamber Music and Several works for Symphonic Band; Bassoon Concerto, 1999. *Recordings:* Music for Royal Shakespeare Company; Music for The Winter's Tale; Songs of Ariel; Gallimaufry featuring the wind music of Guy Woolfenden; Sweet Swan of Avon; Video: The Comedy of Errors, Antony and Cleopatra, Macbeth. *Address:* Malvern House, Sibford Ferris, Banbury, Oxon OX15 5RG, England.

WOOLLAM, Kenneth Geoffrey; Opera Singer (tenor); b. 16 Jan. 1937, Chester, England; m. Phoebe Elizabeth Scrivenor; four d. *Education:* Chester Cathedral Choir School; Royal Coll. of Music. *Career:* debut, Sadler's Wells, London, 1972; appearances with Royal Opera Copenhagen, Saul and David, David; Florestan in Frankfurt; ENO roles include Rienzi, Radames, Aida; sang with Scottish Opera, Royal Opera, Ghent, Opera du Nord, Warsaw Philharmonic Orchestra in various roles including Walther in Die Meistersinger, Siegfried in The Ring, Laca in Jenůfa; sang Husband in world premiere of John Tavener's Gentle Spirit at Bath; three film appearances as Canio, Alfredo and Hoffmann; concerts and oratorios with leading societies; sang in the premieres of Hamilton's Royal Hunt of The Sun and Blake's Toussaint L'Ouverture, 1977; Covent Garden debut 1988, as Aegisthus; Prof. of Singing at Royal Coll. of Music; vocal consultant to David Puttnam's film, Meeting Venus, 1990; appointed vocal consultant to DeVlaamse Opera in Antwerp and Ghent, Belgium, 1995; Pierre (War and Peace, Prokofiev); Tristan; mem., Incorporated Society of Musicians, Savage Club, Glass Circle; hon. mem., Royal Coll. of Music, 1992. *Recordings:* Delius's Margot-La-Rouge; Berlioz's La Mort d'Orphée, conductor Jean Fournet, 1987; television, Songfest by Bernstein; BBC television, Elgar's Gerontius, conducted by Vernon Handley, 1987; Gurre-Lieder, Bergen International Festival, televised; Herod in Salome at Edinburgh Festival, 1989. *Address:* 33 Marlborough Crescent, Bedford Park, Chiswick, London W4 1HE, England.

WOOLLETT, Elizabeth; Singer (soprano); b. 13 March 1959, Hillingdon, Middlesex, England. *Education:* Studied at Royal Academy of Music from 1977. *Career:* Sang Magda in La Rondine and Irene in Donizetti's Belisario at the RAM; Opera North from 1984, as the Owl in The Cunning Little Vixen, Papagena, Kate Pinkerton, Mermaid in Oberon at Le Fenice, Venice, Anna in Intermezzo and Second Maid in the British premiere of Strauss's Daphne; Scottish Opera debut 1989, as Mozart's Susanna; Buxton festival, 1990, as Amenaide in Tancredi; Debut, Royal Opera House, Covent Garden, 1991, as Clorinda in La Cenerentola; Other roles include Adina (L'Elisir d'amore), Cherubino,

Micaela, Bella (The Midsummer Marriage) and Despina; Isabella in L'Assedio di Calais by Donizetti for the Wexford Festival, 1991; Sang Weber's Agathe for Chelsea Opera Group, South Bank, 1997; Season 1998 as Musetta for ENO and Violetta for Castleward Opera; Has also sung for the BBC Radio 3 and has recorded works by Gilbert and Sullivan for TER records. *Honours:* Alec Redshaw Memorial Award. Grimsby, 1986. *Current Management:* Musicmakers International Artists Representation, Tailor House, 63–65 High Street, Whitwell, Hertfordshire SG4 8AH, England. *Telephone:* (1438) 871708. *Fax:* (1438) 871777. *E-mail:* musicmakers@compuserve.com. *Website:* www .operauk.com.

WOOLLEY, Robert; Harpsichordist and Organist; b. 8 Jan. 1954, London, England. *Education:* Royal College of Music 1970–75 with Ruth Dyson. *Career:* Harpsichordist, Organist, Member of the Purcell Quartet, debut concert at St John's Smith Square, London in 1984; Professor, The Royal College of Music; Extensive tours and broadcasts in France, Belgium, Netherlands, Germany, Austria, Switzerland, Italy and Spain; British appearances include four Purcell concerts at the Wigmore Hall, 1987, later broadcast on Radio 3; Tours of USA and Japan, 1991–92; Repertoire includes music on the La Folia theme by Vivaldi, Corelli, CPE Bach, Marais, Scarlatti, Vitali and Geminiani, instrumental songs by Purcell, music by Matthew Locke, John Blow and fantasias and airs by William Lawes, 17th century virtuoso Italian music by Marini, Buonamente, Gabrieli, Fontana, Stradella and Lonati, J. S. Bach and his forerunners Biber, Scheidt, Schenk, Reinken and Buxtehude; Many Concerts with other ensembles and as soloist. *Recordings include:* Complete Keyboard works of Henry Purcell; Solo recordings of Bach, Scarlatti, Frescobaldi, Couperin and Gibbons. *Address:* 11 Sterry Drive, Thames Ditton, Surrey KT 7 0YN, England.

WOOLRICH, John; Composer; b. 3 Jan. 1954, Cirencester, England. *Education:* English at Manchester University; Composition with Edward Cowie at Lancaster University. *Career:* Northern Arts Fellow in Composition at Durham University, 1982–85; Composer-in-Residence, National Centre for Orchestral Studies, 1985–86; Animateur of various educational and music-theatre projects; Visiting Lecturer and Composer-in-Residence, Goldsmiths College, London, 1987–88; Artistic Director, Composers Ensemble, 1989–; Tutor at Guildhall School of Music, 1990–91; Composition Teacher, Dartington Summer School, 1991–93; Professor, Stage Internacional de Musica de Cambra, 1992; Visiting Lecturer, Reading University, 1993; Lecturer, Royal Holloway University of London, 1994–98; Visiting Fellow, Clare Hall, Cambridge, 1999–2001. *Compositions include:* Four Songs After Hoffmann for Soprano and Clarinet, 1981; Spalanzani's Daughter for Instrumental Ensemble, 1983; Black Riddle for Soprano and Chamber Orchestra, 1984; The Barber's Timepiece for Orchestra, 1986; Dartington Doubles for Chamber Ensemble, 1988; Night Machines for Instrumental Ensemble, 1988; The Turkish Mouse for Soprano and Ensemble, 1988; Barcarolle for 6 Players, 1989; Lending Wings, 1989; The Ghost In The Machine, 1990; Berceuse, 1990; Quicksteps, 1990; The Death Of King Renaud, 1991; The Theatre Represents A Garden: Night, 1991; It Is Midnight, Dr Schweitzer, 1992; A Farewell, 1992; String Quartet, 1995; In the House of Crossed Desires, opera, 1996; Oboe concerto, 1996; String Trio, 1996; Cello Concerto, 1998; Little Walserings, for chorus, 1999; Accord, for mixed orchestra, 1999; Wind Sextet, 1999; A Shadowed Lesson, for piano and strings, 1999; Bitter Fruit for 16 players, 2000; Fanfarronda, for chamber orchestra, 2002; Watermark, for violin and bass clarinet, 2002; Good Morning-Midnight, five songs, for soprano and piano, 2002; Arcangelo Homage to Corelli, 2003. *Recordings:* Lending Wings; Ulysses Awakes; The Ghost In The Machine. *Honours:* Honorary Fellow, Trinity College, London, 1996. *Address:* c/o Faber Music Ltd, 3 Queen Square, London WC1N 3AU, England.

WORDSWORTH, Barry; Conductor; b. 20 Feb. 1948, Surrey, England. *Education:* Studied at the Royal College of Music, London; Conducting with Adrian Boult in London and harpsichord with Gustav Leonhardt in Amsterdam. *Career:* Debut: Soloist in Frank Martin's Harpsichord Concerto at the Royal Opera House, for Kenneth Macmillan's ballet, Las Hermanas; Freelance conductor with the Royal Ballet, the Australian Ballet and the National Ballet of Canada (including performances at the Metropolitan, New York); Music Director of the BBC Concert Orchestra and the Brighton Philharmonic in 1989; Music Director of the Royal Ballet and the Birmingham Royal Ballet in 1991; Debut with the Royal Opera at Covent Garden with Carmen in 1991; Conducted the BBC Concert Orchestra at the 1991 Promenade Concerts; Piano Concerto by Bliss, Malcolm Arnold's Guitar Concerto, Vaughan Williams's 8th Symphony, and Act 3 of Sleeping Beauty; Conducted Last Night of The Proms, with the BBC Symphony Orchestra in 1993; Conducted New Queen's Hall Orchestra at the 1995 Proms; Raymond Gubay's Carmen at the Albert Hall, 1997; Poulenc's Les Biches and Roussel's 3rd Symphony at the 1999 London Proms; Conducted the BBC Concert Orchestra at the London Proms, 2002. *Recordings include:* Series of

British music with the BBC Concert Orchestra, 1990–91. *Address:* ICM Artists, Oxford House, 76 Oxford Street, London W1R 1RB, England.

WORKMAN, Charles; Singer (Tenor); b. 1965, Arkansas, USA; m. Alexandra Harwood. *Education:* Studied at the Juilliard School, New York. *Career:* Appearances in operas by Mozart and Rossini at the New York Met, English National Opera, Geneva, Nice, Amsterdam and the Spoleto Festival; Further roles as Henn Smith in Bizet's Jolie Fille de Perth, Jupiter in Semele and Fenton in Falstaff; Season 1998 in Semele for Flanders Opera, as Giocondo in La Pietra del paragone at Garsington and Iago in Rossini's Otello at Pesaro; Season 1999–2000 as Alamar in Donizetti's Alahor in Granata, Ferrando at Ferrara and Monteverdi's Orfeo for the Munich Staatsoper; Don Ottavio at Salzburg, Cherubini's Anacréon in Venice and Belfiore in Il Viaggio a Reims, at La Coruña. *Recordings include:* Renaud in Gluck's Armide. *Address:* c/o Music International, 13 Ardilaun Road, London N5 2QR, England.

WORTON-STEWARD, Andrew; Composer, Organist and Lecturer; b. 20 Feb. 1948, Kent, England. *Education:* BA, DMus, Cincinnati Conservatory, USA, 1976; Diploma of Education; LLCM. *Career:* performances of own music world-wide including New York, Long Island, Milan, London, Manchester, Sydney, Australia; Music Adviser for Somerset Univ., England; recital tour on organ, Texas Gulf, USA, 1985, New York, 1986; concert of choral works, New York, 1986; BBC radio broadcast, 1987; concerts, Paris, 1987, Purcell Room, 1987; Organist at Holy Trinity, New York, 1987–88; commissions for Chichester Cathedral, 1987, Hove Festival, 1987, Hanover, 1988; Choral masterclass, Tallahassee, FL, USA, 1988; Organ recitals, St Thomas, and St James, New York, 1988; TVS documentary, Requiem, in the series Music Makers, 1989; course tutor and Lecturer, Open Univ.; ARCO. *Compositions (recorded):* Chamber Music, 1978; Soli 3, 1980; Via Crucis, 1983; My Eyes For Beauty Pine; Oecumuse. *Publications:* piano music published. *Address:* c/o White Lodge, 105 Pembroke Crescent, Hove, Sussex, England.

WOSNITZA, Cornelia; Singer (Soprano); b. 28 Nov. 1960, Dresden, Germany. *Education:* Studied at the Dresden Musikhochschule. *Career:* Sang Yniold in Pelléas and the Shepherd Boy in Tannhäuser at Dresden, 1979; Has appeared throughout Germany and in Russia, Amsterdam and elsewhere as Aennchen, Gretel, Blondchen, Norina, Susanna, Zerlina, Papagena and Musetta; Concert appearances in works by Bach, Handel, Mozart, Schumann, Strauss and Orff (Carmina Burana). *Honours:* Prizewinner at the 1981 Robert Schumann Competition at Zwickau and the 1985 Mozart Competition at Salzburg. *Address:* Dresden Staatsoper, Theaterplatz 2, 8010 Dresden, Germany.

WOTTRICH, Endrik; Singer (Tenor); b. 1964, Celle, Germany. *Education:* Studied both violin and voice in Würzburg with Ingeborg Hallstein, and in New York at the Juilliard School. *Career:* Debut: Wiesbaden, 1992, as Cassio in Otello; Berlin Staatsoper from 1993, as Tamino in Die Zauberflöte, Alfredo in La Traviata, Sänger in Rosenkavalier and Capriccio and Gernando in Haydn's L'isola disabitatà; Vienna Staatsoper, 1994, as Wagner's Steuermann and Théâtre du Châtelet, Paris, as Andres (Wozzeck) and in Fidelio, 1995–97; Bayreuth since 1996, as David in Die Meistersinger; Concerts include Verdi Requiem with Zubin Metha in Berlin; Das Lied von der Erde by Mahler, Matthäus Passion by Bach, Faustszenen by Schumann with Abbado and Harnoncourt; Season 1999–2000 as David at Bayreuth, Jacquino in Fidelio at La Scala and Don Carlos for Bonn Opera; Steuermann in Der fliegende Holländer at Chicago and Konrad in Hans Heiling for the Deutsche Oper, Berlin, 2001. *Recordings:* Many recordings including Braunfels's Die Vögel, Der Freischütz with Berlin Philharmonic (both Grammy nominated), Korngold, Ring des Polykrates, Kalman's Herzogin von Chicago as well as Beethoven's 9th Symphony. *Address:* Berlin Staatsoper, Unter den Linden 7, 1060 Berlin, Germany.

WOYKE, Andreas; Pianist; b. 28 April 1966, Siegen, Germany; m. Beate, 1 s., 1 d. *Education:* Jugendmusikschule Siegen, with Pál Molnar, Aldo Antognazzi, Julio Largacha, Siegfried Fiedler; Musikhochschule Cologne with Pavel Gililov; Musikhochschule Vienna, with Rudolf Kehrer. *Career:* Concerts in Germany at Philharmonie Cologne, Gasteig Munich, Tonhalle Düsseldorf; Concerts in Austria at Konzerthaus Vienna, Musikverein Vienna, Schloá Eggenberg Graz; Concerts throughout Europe and in USA, Canada, South Africa, Russia and Chile; Radio appearances in Germany, Austria, USA, Canada, South Africa; Television appearances in Germany, Switzerland and South Africa; mem, Studienstiftung des Deutschen Volkes, 1988–92. *Recordings:* Bach Concertos for 2, 3 and 4 pianos; Bremen Competition: Ginastera, Danzas Argentinas. *Honours:* First Prize, Bremen Piano Competition, 1987; First Prize, International Brahms Competition, Hamburg, Germany, 1992; Second Prize, UNISA-Transnet International Piano Competition, Pretoria, South Africa, 1996; First Prize, Knezkova-Hussey International Piano Competition, Bathurst, Canada, 1996. *Address:* Farmi 85, 8511 Greisdorf, Austria.

WRAY, Steven (Donald); Pianist; b. 10 June 1959, Bolton, Lancashire, England. *Education:* BA, Honours, Queen's College, Oxford, 1976–79; Private studies with Dorothea Law and Ruth Nye; International Summer Musical Academy at Salzburg, masterclasses with Hans Graf and Carmen Graf-Adnet, 1985–86; Further studies at Hochschule für Musik und Darstellende Kunst, Vienna. *Career:* Live Music Now! solo artist, 1985; Solo recital, Park Lane Group, Young Artists and Twentieth Century Music series, Purcell Room in London, 1988; Formation of duo with Czech violinist Tomas Tulacek in 1990; Concert and festival appearances, solo and duo recitals, and ensemble and concerto engagements in Austria, Czechoslovakia, Slovenia, the United Kingdom, Israel and Portugal. *Current Management:* Chameleon Arts Management. *Address:* 1 Brookes Court, Longley Road, London SW17 9LF, England.

WRIGHT, Brian (James); Conductor; b. 4 Aug. 1946, Tonbridge, Kent, England. *Education:* Gulbenkian Scholar, Guildhall School of Music; Guildhall School of Music; Studied with George Hurst and Jascha Horenstein; Munich Music Academy, Germany. *Career:* Debut: Royal Festival Hall, London, 1972 (Messiah); Professional singer (Tenor) with English Opera Group; Recitals Wigmore Hall 1971, Purcell Room 1972; Associate Conductor Goldsmith's Choral Union 1972; Musical Director 1973; Conductor Highgate Choral Society 1972; Assistant Conductor London Symphony Orchestra 1974–75; Conductor BBC Symphony Orchestra Chorus 1976–84; Berlioz Requiem 1982; Liszt's Christus, 1985–; guest Conductor with British orchestras: London Symphony (Mendelssohn 3, Sibelius 2); Philharmonia (Beethoven 6); Hallé (Brahms 2); Bournemouth Symphony (A Child of our Time, Verdi Requiem); Scottish National (Dvořák Requiem); Royal Liverpool Philharmonic (Hugh Wood Symphony); World and British premieres of works by Robert Simpson, Wilfred Josephs, Penderecki and Lutoslawski; First complete performance of Furtwängler's 3rd Symphony; Season 1988–89 conducted Tippett's Mask of Time on South Bank and Stravinsky's Pulcinella for BBC television; Season 1990 with the Bach B Minor Mass at the Barbican, the Verdi Requiem at the Festival Hall, and concerts with the RPO, BBC Symphony Orchestra and BBC National Orchestra of Wales; mem, ISM. *Honours:* Silver Medal, Cantelli Competition, Milan 1975. *Current Management:* Worldwide Artists. *Address:* c/o World-wide Artists, 6 Petersfield Crescent, Coulsdon, Surrey CR5 2JQ, England.

WRIGHT, Peter Anthony, BA, BMus, MA, PhD; Musicologist; b. 14 April 1953, Vienna, Austria; m. Joanne Frew; two d. *Education:* Pembroke Coll., Oxford, Nottingham Univ. *Career:* freelance teacher and writer 1975–77, 1981–85; Lecturer, Exeter Univ. 1987–88; Lecturer, Nottingham Univ. 1988, Reader in Music 2000–; specialist in 15th-century music, especially source study; mem. Royal Musical Asscn (council 2001–04, cttee for Early English Church Music 2002–), American Musicological Soc., Plainsong and Mediaeval Music Soc., Royal Musical Asscn. *Publications:* The Related Parts of Trent, Museo Provinciale d'Arte, MSS 87 (1374) and 92 (1379) 1989, I codici musicali trentini 2 (ed.) 1996; contrib. to Early Music (ed.), Early Music History, Leading Notes, Music and Letters, Music and Musicians, Plainsong and Medieval Music, Revised New Grove Dictionary of Music and Musicians, Die Musik in Geschichte und Gegenwart. *Honours:* The Westrup Prize 1995. *Address:* Department of Music, University of Nottingham, University Park, Nottingham, NG7 2RD, England (office). *Telephone:* (115) 9514760 (office). *Fax:* (115) 9514756 (office). *E-mail:* p.a.wright@nottingham.ac.uk (office).

WRIGHT, Rosemarie; Concert Pianist; b. 12 Dec. 1931, Chorley, Lancashire, England; m. Michel Brandt, 28 Oct 1961, 2 s. *Education:* Royal Academy of Music, London; Staatsakademie, Vienna; Masterclasses with Edwin Fischer, Pablo Casals and Wilhelm Kempff. *Career:* Debut: Grosser Musikvereinssaal, Vienna, 1960; Concerts throughout Europe, USA, Far East, Australasia; Broadcasts world-wide; Concertos with London Philharmonic, English Chamber Orchestra, London Mozart Players, BBC Orchestras, Vienna Symphony Orchestra, and Danish and French Radio; Professor of Piano: Royal Northern College of Music, Manchester, 1973–78, Royal Academy of Music, London, 1978–97; Pianist-in-Residence, Southampton University 1972–80; mem, British Federation of Festivals for Music, Dance and Speech, Adjudicator. *Recordings:* Piano Music by Edward Macdowell; Vols 1, 2 and 3, and Double CD of Haydn Sonatas on 1799 Broadwood Fortepiano. *Honours:* Chappell Silver Medal, 1953; Tobias Matthay Fellowship, 1954; Haydn Prize, Vienna, 1959; Bösendorfer Prize, 1960. *Address:* 84 Filsham Road, Hastings, East Sussex TN 38 0PG, England.

WRIGHT, William George; pianist; b. 14 Dec. 1936, Airdrie, Scotland; m. Janette Montgomery Rose 1961; two s. one d. *Education:* Royal Scottish Academy of Music and Drama. *Career:* Liszt scholar; gives lectures and recitals in Belgium, Canada, Hungary, and the USA; numerous radio and television appearances; mem, Liszt Society, London; American Liszt Society. *Recordings:* BBC Scotland world premiere recording of Liszt's Piano Piece in A flat S189, 1987; First

modern performance (BBC recording) of Liszt/de Swert Consolations I and IV and 'Enchaînement' de F. Liszt D11 for Cello and Piano, with Mark Bailey, 1991; First modern performance (BBC recording) of Liszt's Die Vätergruft, 1886 version, for Baritone and Piano, with Christopher Underwood, 1998. *Publications:* More Light on Young Liszt: Liszt 2000, 2000; Liszt's Chamber Compositions and Transcriptions: The Liszt Companion, 2002; contrib. New Letters of Liszt, Journal of the American Liszt Society, vols 31 and 33; Letters from the Royal Library, Copenhagen: Liszt Saeculum Nr. 54, 1995; New List Letters, The Hungarian Quarterly, vol 44, no 170, Summer 2003. *Address:* 24 Ayr Road, Giffnock, Glasgow G46 6RY, Scotland. *E-mail:* wright24@bigfoot.com.

WROBLEWSKI, Patryk; Singer (Baritone); b. 4 Dec. 1956, Mishawaka, Indiana, USA. *Career:* Debut: Sang Malatesta at the 1980 Blossom Festival; Recent appearances as Fernando in La Gazza Ladra at Philadelphia, Silvio, Valentin and Monteverdi's Orfeo at Dallas; Lyric Opera of Chicago as Germont and Marcello and in Satyagraha by Glass; Opera Grand Rapids as Don Giovanni; Season 1991–92 with debut at New York City Opera as Zurga in Les pêcheurs de perles and as Silvio; Puccini's Lescaut with Greater Miami Opera and Silvio at the Munich Staatsoper (European stage debut); Season 1992–93 as Zurga in Holland, Taddeo in L'Italiana in Algeri at Dublin, and Marcello and Rossini's Figaro for the New Israel Opera; Concert appearances with the Chicago Symphony under Leppard and the Grant Park Concerts under Leonard Slatkin; Santa Fe Opera in Henze's Young Lord; Weill, The Protagonist; Dublin Grand Opera, Marcello in La Bohème; Manitoba Opera, Zurga, Carmen. *Honours:* Grand Prize, 1984 Rosa Ponselle International Competition; Winner, Luciano Pavarotti Competition, 1985. *Address:* c/o Opera Ireland, John Player House, 276–288 South Circular Road, Dublin 8, Ireland.

WU, Mary Mei-Loc; Pianist; b. 22 Dec. 1964, Hong Kong; m. James Wong, 4 July 1992. *Education:* Yehudi Menuhin School, 1976–83; Performer's Diploma of Royal College of Music, London, 1983–87; Banff Center of Fine Arts, Winter School Diploma, Canada, 1987–88; Master of Music, 1988–89, Doctorate of Musical Arts, 1989–92, State University of New York at Stony Brook, USA. *Career:* Debut: Queen Elizabeth Hall, London, 1979; Beethoven Sonata with Yehudi Menuhin in Germany, 1985; Bach Double Concerto with Vlado Perlemuter, London South Bank, 1986; Solo Recital, Wigmore Hall, London, 1994; Artist-in-Residence, Chinese University, Hong Kong, 1997. *Recordings:* Fantasias; Chinese Contemporary Piano Music; Piano Classico. *Address:* 135 Stevenage Road, Fulham, London SW6 6PB, England.

WU, Zuqiang; Professor; b. 24 July 1927, Peking, China; m. Zheng Liqin 1953, 1 s., 1 d. *Education:* Graduate in Composition, China's Central Conservatory of Music, 1952; Graduate, Tchaikovsky Music Conservatory, Moscow, 1958. *Career:* Teacher, 1952, Senior Lecturer, 1962, Associate Professor, 1978, Deputy President, 1978–81, President, 1982–88, Professor, 1983–, Supervisor of Doctoral Work, 1986–, Central Conservatory of Music; Head of Composition Section, China's Central Philharmonic Orchestra, 1972–75; Vice-Executive Chairman, China Federation of Literary and Art Circles, 1988–; Board of Directors, China's Copyright Agency Corporation, 1988–; Adviser, Chinese Music Copyright Association, 1993–; Adjudicator of many Chinese and foreign music competitions; mem, Vice-President, Chinese Musicians Association, 1985–; Executive Vice-Chairman, China Symphony Development Foundation, 1994–. *Compositions:* String Quartet, 1957; The Mermaid, dance drama, 1958; Red Woman's Detachment, ballet, 1964; Moon Reflected in the Erquan Pool for String Orchestra, 1976; Young Sisters of the Grassland, pipa concerto, 1973–76. *Publications:* Analysis of Music Form and Composition, textbook. *Honours:* Excellent Textbook Prize, National Universities and Colleges, 1987. *Address:* Central Conservatory of Music, 43 Baojia Street, Beijing 100031, People's Republic of China.

WULKOPF, Cornelia; Singer (Contralto); b. 1952, Braunschweig, Germany. *Education:* Detmold Music Academy, with Gunther Weissenborn,. *Career:* Debut: Sang Sieglinde and Flosshilde at the 1977 Bayreuth Festival, in The Ring conducted by Pierre Boulez; Sang at the Bavarian State Opera from 1977, notably as Erda and Waltraute in The Ring, 1978; Lieder and Oratorio concerts from 1981, at Munich and elsewhere; Schmidt's Das Buch mit Sieben Siegeln, Salzburg, 1981; Cornelia in Giulio Cesare at the 1993 Schwetzingen Festival; Brangaene in Tristan at Hamburg, 1996; Sang Erda in Das Rheingold for Cologne Opera, and Amelfa in The Golden Cockerel at Bregenz, 2000; Wagner's Mary at Trieste 2001; Further concerts include Schubert's Lazarus, Vier Ernste Gesänge by Brahms and the Verdi Requiem. *Recordings include:* Mozart's Apollo et Hyacinthus. *Address:* c/o Hamburg Staatsoper, Grosse Theaterstrasse 34, 20354 Hamburg, Germany.

WULSTAN, David; Professor of Music; b. 18 Jan. 1937, Birmingham, England; m. Susan Nelson Graham, 9 Oct 1967, 1 s. *Education:* BSc,

College of Technology, Birmingham; BA, 1st Class, Music, 1963, Fellow, 1964, MA, 1966, Magdalen College, Oxford. *Career:* Founder and Director, The Clerkes of Oxenford, 1961–; Numerous appearances on BBC television and Radio 3, Thames television, NWDR, BRT, Cheltenham, York, Bologna, Holland and Flanders Festivals, Proms and various films; Visiting Professor, University of California, Berkeley, 1977; Professor of Music, University College, Cork, 1980; Professor of Music, University College, Aberystwyth, Wales, 1983–90; Research Professor, 1991–; Consulting Ed., Spanish Academic Press; Council, Plainsong and Mediaeval Music Society; Fellow, Royal Soc. of Musicians. *Compositions:* Various Christmas carols, hymns, chant and film music. *Recordings:* Tallis; Sheppard; Gibbons: Church Music; Play of Daniel; Robert White. *Publications include:* Early English Church Music, vol. 3, 1964, vol. 27, 1979; Anthology of Carols, 1968; Anthology of English Church Music, 1971; Play of Daniel, 1976; Coverdale Chant Book, 1978; Sheppard: Complete Works, 1979–; Tudor Music, 1984; The Emperor's Old Clothes, 2001; The Poetic and Musical Legacy of Heloise and Abelard, 2003; Music from the Paraclete, 2004; Play of Daniel (3rd edn), 2004. *Contributions:* Journal of Theological Studies; Journal of the American Oriental Society; Music and Letters; Galpin Society Journal; Musical Times, Iraq; English Historical Review; Plainsong and Medieval Music; Cantigueiros; Al-Masāq. *Address:* Ty Isaf, Llanilar, Aberystwyth SY23 4NP, Wales.

WUORINEN, Charles; Composer; b. 9 June 1938, New York City, USA. *Education:* Attended Columbia University, BA 1961, MA 1963. *Career:* Founded the Group for Contemporary Music 1962; Teacher at Columbia University 1964–71; Professor of Music, Rutgers University, 1984–; Visiting Professor, New York University, 1990; Visiting Professor, State University of New York at Buffalo, 1989–94; San Francisco Symphony (and New Music Adviser to Music Director Herbert Blomstedt), 1985–89; American Academy in Rome, 1990. *Compositions include:* Stage: The Politics of Harmony 1968 and The W of Babylon; Opera: Haroun and the Sea of Stories, 2001; Orchestral: Music for orchestra 1956; Orchestral and Electronic Exchanges 1965; 3 Piano Concertos 1966, 1975, 1984; Contrafactum 1969; Grand Bamboula 1971; Concerto for amplified violin and orchestra 1972; A Reliquary for Igor Stravinsky, 1975; Tashi, 4 soloists and orchestra, 1976; Two-Part Symphony, 1978; The Magic Art: An Instrumental Masque, after Purcell, 1978; Short Suite, 1981; Crossfire, 1984; Bamboula Squared, 1984; Movers and Shakers, 1984; Rhapsody for violin and orchestra, 1984; The Golden Dance, 1986; Five, concerto for amplified cello and orchestra, 1987 Microsymphony, 1991–92; The Mission of Virgil, 1993; Concerto for Saxophone Quartet and Orchestra, 1993; The River of Light, 1995–96; The Great Procession, 1995; Symphony Seven, 1997; Chamber Music includes 3 String Quartets, 1971, 1979, 1987; String Trio, 1968; On Alligators, for 8 players, 1972; Speculum Speculi, 1972; Hyperion, 1975; Fortune, 1975; Fast Fantasy for cello and piano, 1977; Archaeopteryx, 1978; New York Notes, 1981; Sonata for violin and piano, 1988; String Sextet, 1989; Piano Quartet, 1994; Sonata for guitar and piano 1995; Horn Trio, 1981 and 1985; (Wuorinen) Cello variations III, 1997; Brass Quintet, 1999; An Orbicle of Jasp for cello and piano, 1999; String Quartet No. 4, 2000; Cyclops for chamber orchestra; Vocal Music includes: Genesis for chorus and orchestra, The Celestial Sphere, oratorio, 1980; Mass for soprano, chorus, violin 3 trombones and organ; Piano and Organ music; Many keyboard works including 3 Sonatas; A Winter's Tale (2 versions), soprano and chamber and w/piano, 1991, 1992; Fenton songs, for soprano and piano trio, 1997; Electronic: Time's Encomium, 1970. *Publications:* Charles Wuorinen, a Bio-Bibliography by Richard Burbank. *Honours:* Joseph Bearns Prize 1958, and Letters Award 1967; Guggenheim Fellowship, 1968–72; Pulitzer Prize for Time's Encomium, 1970; Rockefeller Foundation Fellowship, 1979, 1981, 1982; American Academy of Arts and Letters, 1985; MacArthur Foundation Fellowship, 1986–91. *Current Management:* c/o Howard Stokar Management. *Address:* c/o Howard Stokar Management, 870 West End Avenue, New York, NY 10025, USA.

WÜTHRICH, Hans; Composer; b. 3 Aug. 1937, Aeschi, Switzerland; m. Beatrice Mathez, 6 May 1977, 1 d. *Education:* Piano and Violin studies at Conservatory of Music, Berne, 1957–62; Studies of composition with Klaus Huber, Academy of Music, 1968–74; Doctor's Degree, University of Zürich, 1973. *Career:* Lecturer of Linguistics, Zürich University, 1971–85, and Teacher, Winterhur Conservatory, 1985–; Performances of compositions in Donaueschingen, 1978, 1985, at ISCM World Music Festival, Bonn in 1977 and at Athens in 1979. *Compositions:* Kommunikationsspiele, 1973; Das Glashaus, 1974–75; Netz-Werke I, II, 1983–85; Annaeherungen an Gegenwart, 1986–87; Procuste Deux Etoiles, 1980–81; Supplement: Netz-Werk III, 1987–89; Chopin Im TGV Basel-Paris, 1989; Wörter Bilder Dinge, 1990–91; Leve, 1992; Ah! Vous voila!, 1994; Happy Hour, 1995–97. *Recordings:* Procuste Deux Etoiles, 1980–81; Annäherungen an Gegenwart, 1986–87; Chopin im TGV Basel-Paris, 1989; Wörter Bilder Dinge, 1990–91. *Address:* Kirchgasse 4, 4144 Arlesheim, Switzerland.

WYN-DAVIES, Catrin; British singer (soprano); b. 1969, England. *Education:* Guildhall School of Music. *Career:* roles with Welsh National Opera (1994–96) have included Mozart's Ilia, Zerlina and Susanna, and Anne Trulove in The Rake's Progress; Season 1996–97 with Gilda for WNO, First Flower Maiden in Parsifal at the Paris Châtelet and Handel's Acis and Galatea with the English Concert; Concerts have included Soprano Solo in Schoenberg's Moses und Aron with the Philharmonia (1996), Handel's Orlando, Elijah with David Willcocks and Bach's Christmas Oratorio with René Jacobs on tour to Europe; Wigmore Hall debut recital 1994; Further opera roles included Kristine in The Makropulos Case and Monteverdi's Poppea (for WNO), 1998; Leader of the Flower Maidens in Parsifal at the Festival Hall, 1998; Engaged for the Beggar's Opera at Strasbourg; Sang Ginevra in Ariodante for ENO, London, 2002; Engaged as Jenůfa for WNO, 2003. *Recordings include:* Sacred music by Vivaldi with the King's Consort; Weill's Der Silbersee under Marcus Stenz; Beethoven Folk Songs, with Malcolm Martineau. *Honours:* Kathleen Ferrier Decca Award 1994. *Current Management:* IMG Artists, Lovell House, 616 Chiswick High Road, London, W4 5RX, England. *Telephone:* (20) 8233-5800. *Fax:* (20) 8233-5801. *E-mail:* info@imgartists.com. *Website:* www.imgartists.com.

WYN-ROGERS, Catherine; Singer (contralto); b. 1958, England. *Education:* Studied at the Royal College of Music with Meriel St Clair and later with Ellis Keeler and Diane Forlano. *Career:* Regular concerts with the Bach Choir under David Willcocks in London and abroad; Frequent appearances with the United Kingdom's major orchestras; Tours with English Concert and Trevor Pinnock including Messiah in Germany and Vivaldi's Gloria in Rome for TV/Deutsche Grammophon recording; Appearances at the Proms with the Sixteen, the National Youth Orchestra and the English Concert Opera including Il Ritorno d'Ulisse for English National Opera and Stuttgart, Maddalena in Rigoletto in Nantes, La Gioconda for Opera North, Die Zauberflöte for the ROH and Salzburg Festival; Sang First Norn in Götterdämmerung at Covent Garden, 1995; Sang in Palestrina and Pfitzner recital at Covent Garden, 1997; Mary Magdalene in The Kingdom by Elgar at the 1999 London Prom Concerts; Bach's Magnificat with the Sixteen, 2000; Season 2000–01 in the St John Passion and as La Cieca in La Gioconda for ENO, Adelaide in Arabella at Munich and Hero in Béatrice et Bénédict for WNO; Dvorák's Stabat mater at the London Proms, 2002. *Recordings:* Vaughan Williams's Serenade To Music and Magnificat with Matthew Best; Teixera Te Deum and Bach's Christmas Oratorio with the Sixteen; Elgar's Dream of Gerontius with Vernon Handley and the Royal Liverpool Philharmonic. *Honours:* College Song Recital Prize; Dame Clara Butt Award; Grantee, Countess of Munster Trust, RCM. *Current Management:* Askonas Holt Ltd, Lonsdale Chambers, 27 Chancery Lane, London, WC2A 1PF, England. *Telephone:* (20) 7400-1700. *Fax:* (20) 7400-1799. *E-mail:* info@askonasholt.co.uk. *Website:* www.askonasholt.co.uk. *Address:* 67 Whiteley Road, Upper Norwood, London, SE19 1JU, England.

WYNER, Susan (Davenny); Singer (Soprano); b. 17 Oct. 1945, New Haven, Connecticut, USA. *Education:* Graduated from Cornell University, 1965; Vocal studies with Herta Glaz, 1969–75. *Career:* Debut: Carnegie Hall recital in 1972; Alice Tully Hall recital in 1973; Orchestral debut with the Boston Symphony in 1974; Engagements with all leading orchestras in USA and Canada and with Israel Philharmonic and London Symphony; Repertoire includes Baroque and contemporary works; Operatic debut as Monteverdi's Poppea, New York City Opera, 1977; Metropolitan Opera in 1982 as Woglinde in Das Rheingold; Has sung in the premieres of Del Tredici's Adventures Underground in 1975 and Carter's A Mirror On Which To Dwell in 1965, and in the premieres of Memorial Music and Fragments from Antiquity by Yehudi Wyner; Also sings works by Rochberg (Quartet No. 2) and Reimann (Inane).

WYNER, Yehudi; Composer, Pianist and Conductor; b. 1 June 1929, Calgary, Alberta, Canada; m. Susan Davenny Wyner. *Education:* Studied at the Juilliard School then at Yale University with Paul Hindemith gaining BMus in 1951 and MMus in 1953; Further study with Walter Piston at Harvard University gaining MA in 1952. *Career:* American Academy in Rome, 1953–56; Performed and recorded contemporary music in New York; Directed the Turnau Opera; Teacher at Yale School of Music from 1963, Chairman of Composition, 1969–73; Music Director of the New Haven Opera Society and keyboard player with the Bach Aria Group; Berkshire Music Center, 1975; Professor of Music at State University of New York, Purchase, 1978, Dean of Music, 1978–82. *Compositions include:* Piano Sonata, 1954; 3 Informal Pieces for Violin and Piano, 1961; Torah Service, 1966; Cadenza for Clarinet and Harpsichord, 1969; Canto Cantabile for Soprano and Band, 1972; Memorial Music for Soprano and 3 Flutes, 1971–73; Intermedio for Soprano and Strings, 1974; Fragments From Antiquity for Soprano and Orchestra, 1978–81; Romances for Piano Quartet, 1980; On This Most Voluptuous Night for Soprano and 7 Instruments, 1982; Wind Quintet, 1984; String Quartet, 1985; Toward The Center for Piano, 1988; Il Cane

Minore for 2 Clarinets and Bassoon, 1992; Concerto for Cello and Orchestra, 1994; Lyric Harmony, for orchestra, 1995; A Mad Tea Party, for soprano, 2 baritones and ensemble 1996; Horn Trio, 1997; The Second Madrigal for soprano, string quartet, wind quintet and percussion, 1999. *Honours:* Guggenheim Fellowship, 1958–59, 1977–78; NEA Grant, 1976; Commissions from the Ford Foundation, Delos String Quartet and the Aeolian Chamber Players; American Academy of Arts and Letters, 1999. *Address:* c/o ASCAP, ASCAP Building, 1 Lincoln Plaza, New York, NY 10023, USA.

WYSOCKI, Zdzislaw; Composer; b. 18 July 1944, Poznań, Poland; m.; one s. one d. *Education:* Piano studies at the Music School, Poznan, 1951–58; Music High School in Poznan, final examinations in music theory and piano, 1958–63; Composition at the University of Music in Poznan, 1963–68; Scholarship from the Austrian Ministry of Education at University of Music in Vienna, 1969–70. *Career:* Debut: Poznan, 1963; Performances in Austria, Poland, Germany, France, the United Kingdom, Italy, Denmark, Portugal, Hungary, Ukraine, Slovakia, former Yugoslavia, Soviet Union, USA, Canada, Brazil, Japan; Festivals in Germany, Brazil, Slovakia, Austria, Hungary, Italy, Portugal, Poland; World premieres: Double Concerto, Berkeley Symphony Orchestra under Kent Nagano, 2002; Concerto Doppio, Ensemble Wiener Collage/René Staar, Salzburg Festival, 2003; Radio transmissions recordings in Poland, Austria, Germany, Japan, USA, France, Denmark; Television, Poland. *Compositions:* Missa in honorem Ioannis Pauli secundi op 30; orchestra and chamber works, Quasi concerto grosso op 36; Quartetto op 46; Quasi Divertimento op 49; Trio op 51; De finibus temporum op 52, 1994; Etudes, chamber ensemble op 54, 56, 60, 1996–2001; Fantasia op 33; Gespräch mit einem guten Menschen, opera, 1992; Musica de la passione, for strings, 1999. *Recordings:* Austrian contemporary music, works of Z Wysocki op 46, 49, 51, 52, Ensemble Wiener Collage; Klang debuts Ensemble Graz, St Petersburg; Etudes op 54/7,9; Guitar recital performed by Leo Witoszynskyj, Due Caratteri op 29; Violoncellomusik des 20 Jahrhunderts performances by Adalbert Skocic, Walter Delahunt, Fantasia op 33. *Publications:* Quartetto, 1990; Quasi Divertimento op 49, 1993; Etudes op 54/4-10, 1995; Movimento Saxophonquartet op 47, 1991; Double Concerto, op.63, 2002; In Memoriam, op. 66, 2002; Concerto Doppio, op. 67, 2003. *Address:* Pfarrgasse 34-44/16/7, 1232 Vienna, Austria.

WYZNER, Franz; Singer (Bass); b. 1932, Vienna, Austria. *Education:* Studied in Vienna. *Career:* Sang at the Landestheater in Salzburg, 1958–59, Gelsenkirchen, 1959–64, Wuppertal, 1964–85, notably in the German premiere of Crime and Punishment by Petrovic, 1971, and the first performance of The Gamblers by Shostakovich in the arrangement by K Meyer, 1986; Guest appearances at the Schwetzingen Festival, 1970, Vienna Volksoper in the Austrian premiere of The Burning Fiery Furnace by Britten in 1977, Salzburg Festival in Dantons Tod, 1983, Buenos Aires as Alberich in 1983, and Cologne in 1985; Other roles have included Mozart's Leporello, Figaro, Papageno and Alfonso, Kaspar in Der Freischütz, Don Magnifico, Mephistopheles, the Doctor in Wozzeck, and Kecal in The Bartered Bride. *Recordings include:* Dantons Tod, Orfeo. *Address:* Theater am Gärtnerplatz, Gärtnerplatz 3, 8000 Munich 1, Germany.

X

XIA, Liping; Composer and Music Educator; b. Feb. 1935, China; m. 1963, 3 s. *Education:* Music Institute of China, graduated 1958. *Career:* Music Editor, radio station of Hainan, China; Leader, music group at radio station, Guangdong, China for 21 years; Music Professor, Hainan Normal Institute and Guangdong University of Foreign Studies for 20 years. *Compositions:* Song of Spring Ploughing, 1965; Song of Rubber Forest, 1981; Joy Over a Bumper Harvest, 1989; Having Classes, 1993; Dance Music in Praise of Youth, 1993. *Recordings:* The Pass to South Guangdong, 3rd part of the music programme series Along Today's Long March, 1986. *Publications:* Appreciation of Chinese Classical Music, 1993; Appreciation and Analysis of Ancient Chinese Melodies, 1993; A Music Course for College Students, 1999. *Contributions:* Chief Editor, University Music Education, Guangdong. *Address:* 388-5 Dong-Hua Doag Road Rm# 703, Guangzhou, People's Republic of China.

XIONG, Jihua; Chinese professor of conducting and composition; b. 24 Feb. 1932, Beijing; m. Cai Rengi 1953; two d. *Education:* Chengdu Arts School, studied conducting with Russian and German teachers. *Career:* debut conducting Shanghai Symphony Orchestra, 1958; debuted several new works including Recollection of the past on the Grassland (Gao Weijie, Tang Qingshi) and Symphonic Suite (Zou Lu) and Symphonic Poem, Chant of the River (Li Zhongyong); Conducted various master works including Bruch, Violin Concerto No. 1 in G minor; Chopin, Piano Concerto No. 1 in E Minor; Rachmaninov, Piano Concerto No. 2 in C minor, Beethoven, Symphony No. 3 (Eroica) and Symphony No. 5 (Fate); Dvořák, Symphony No. 9 New World; Tchaikovsky Symphony Pathétique; Rimsky-Korsakoff, Symphony Suite Scheherezade; Conducted orchestras for numerous films and plays; Conducted 200 dance theatres; Conducted several broadcast symphony concerts; Invited participant, 20th Century Classical Music Works Chinese Composers; Conducted all the major Chinese orchestras. *Compositions:* Wan Xi Sha, symphony, 1962; Die Lian Hua, orchestra piece, 1964; A Stormy October, film music, 1979; Mystic Giant Buddha, film music, 1981; The Soul of Hua Xia, television series of plays, 1984; Welcoming the New Year, solo works for pipa; Morning Song, solo for violin; Pour Out One's Heart, piano solo. *Recordings:* Recollections of the Past on Grassland. *Publications:* Article, How to Read the Orchestra Score. *Address:* c/o Sichuan Conservatory of Music, 6 Xinsheng Road, Chengdu, Sichuan 610021, China.

Y

YAHR, Carol; singer (mezzo-soprano); b. 1959, USA. *Career:* Sang at the Cologne Opera, 1987, as Venus in Tannhäuser, Théâtre des Champs-Elysées, 1988, as Fricka in The Ring; Nice Opéra, 1988–89, as Geneviéve in Pelléas and Dido in Les Troyens; Seattle, 1989, as Wagner's Eva, Leonore at Innsbruck, 1990, and with Glyndebourne Tour; Scottish Opera and Innsbruck, 1991, as Sieglinde and Elisabeth; Sang the Walküre Brünnhilde at Wiesbaden, 1993; Sang Brünnhilde in The Ring for Norwegian Opera, 1996; Sang Isolde for Hawaiian Opera, 2000. *Address:* c/o Der Norske Opera, PO Box 8800, Youngstorget, 0028 Oslo, Norway.

YAKAR, Rachel; Singer (Soprano); b. 3 March 1938, Lyon, France. *Education:* Studied at the Paris Conservatoire and with Germaine Lubin. *Career:* Sang with Deutsche Oper am Rhein, Düsseldorf from 1964 in roles including Antonia in Les Contes d'Hoffmann; Sang at Aix-en-Provence in 1966 in Ariadne auf Naxos, Strasbourg Opera in 1967 in a new production of Der Junge Lord by Henze, Amsterdam, 1968–69 as Cleopatra in Giulio Cesare and as Marguerite, at Düsseldorf in 1969, and Paris Opéra in 1970 as Gilda and Micaela; Baroque repertoire from 1971 includes Deidamia by Handel; Munich Festival in 1974 as Donna Elvira, Bayreuth Festival in 1976 as Freia and Gerhilde in Patrice Chéreau's centenary production of Der Ring des Nibelungen, Glyndebourne Festival, 1977, 1980 as Donna Elvira and the Marschallin, Strasbourg and Düsseldorf in 1978 as Mélisande; Sang Cycle of operas by Monteverdi at Zürich in 1978; Geneva Opera in 1981 as Janácek's Jenúfa; Guest appearances in San Francisco, East Berlin, Edinburgh, Lausanne, Monte Carlo and Santiago; Other roles include Mozart's Ilia and Fiordigili; Sang Madame Lidoine in Dialogues des Carmélites at Lyon, 1990; Climène in Lully's Phaëton at Lyon, 1993. *Recordings include:* Rameau's Les Indes Galantes, and Pygmalion; Idomeneo; Monteverdi's Orfeo; Dido and Aeneas; Bach B minor Mass; Lully's Armide; Schütz's Christmas Story and Magnificat; Fux's and Scarlatti's Baroque Cantatas; Die Zauberflöte, from the Salzburg Festival conducted by James Levine.

YAMASHITA, Kazuhito; Japanese guitarist; b. 25 March 1961, Nagasaki; s. of Toru Yamashita. *Education:* Nagasaki Guitar Acad., studied with Kojiro Kobune, J. Thomas, Narciso Yepes, Andres Segovia, Toru Takemitsu. *Career:* debut recitals in Tokyo 1978, Paris 1979; concert at the Toronto Guitar Festival with his guitar transcription of Mussorgsky's Pictures at an Exhibition 1984; transcribed and performed Stravinsky's Firebird Suite, Dvořák's 'New World' Symphony for solo guitar, and Beethoven's Violin Concerto for guitar and orchestra; duo tour of USA with James Galway 1987; mem., Nagasaki Guitar Ensemble; 'The World of Kazuhito Yamashita' recital series, Casals Theatre, Tokyo 1989, 1994, 1999. *Compositions include:* Imaginary Forest for solo guitar 1982. *Recordings:* transcriptions of Mussorgsky's Pictures at an Exhibition, Stravinsky's Firebird Suite, Dvořák's 'New World' Symphony, J. S. Bach's Sonatas, Partitas and Suites for unaccompanied flute, violin, cello and lute, the complete works of Fernando Sor, Giuliani and Ponce. *Honours:* winner All-Japan Guitar Competition 1976, Ramirez competition, Spain 1977, Alessandria competition, Italy 1977, Concours International de Guitare, Paris 1977. *Address:* c/o Allegro Music Tokyo Inc, Meisen Bldg 502, 7-17-20 Roppongi, Minato-ku, Tokyo 106-0032, Japan (office).

YANAGIDA, Takayoshi; Composer; b. 27 March 1948, Sapporo, Hokkaido, Japan; m. Keiko Tsuhako 1973; one s. one d. *Education:* Musashino Music Coll., and Graduate School; Musik Hochshule, München. *Career:* debut, Iino Hall, Tokyo, 1969; Prof. of Music, Bunkyo Univ.; Composer for the Music of NHK Educational Program; mem., ISME, JSCM, JFC. *Compositions:* Mixed Chorus Suite, Kitano-kawa, MCS Pony of Stars; Seen in the Twilight, for flute, violin and piano; Beside a Stream, for piano. *Recordings:* Concert Tableau for wind orchestra; Johi-haku-un. *Publications:* Orchestra Project '93; Libretto on a Dreamy Vision for flute and orchestra (recorded and sent on the air by NHK), 1993; Selections from a Literary Calendar for clarinet and orchestra, 1998. *Honours:* First Prize in the 38th Japan Music Competition, Composition Division, 1969. *Address:* 7-23-13, Higashi-urawa, Midori-ku, Saitama-shi 336-0926, Japan.

YANAGITA, Masako; Violinist; b. 30 March 1944, Tokyo, Japan; m. Abba Bogin. *Education:* Artist Diploma, Mannes College of Music, New York City, USA; Studied with Eijin Tanaka, Louis Graeler, William Kroll. *Career:* Debut: Tokyo, 1966; Concert appearances throughout USA, Europe, Near and Far East; Soloist, orchestras in Japan, the United Kingdom, Germany, Philippines, USA; 1st Violinist, toured with Vieuxtemps String Quartet; Faculty Member, Mannes College of Music. *Recordings include:* Complete Schubert violin and piano repertoire (with Abba Bogin, pianist). *Honours:* Silverstein Prize, Berkshire Music Center, Massachusetts, 1966; Carl Flesch Competition, London,

England, 1968; Paganini Competition, Genoa, Italy, 1968; Munich International Competition, 1969. *Current Management:* Raymond Weiss Artists Management, New York City, USA. *Address:* 838 West End Avenue, New York, NY 10025, USA.

YANG, Guang; Singer (mezzo-soprano); b. 1970, Peking, China. *Education:* Central Conservatory, Peking. *Career:* Concerts at Carnegie Hall, New York, Bournemouth, London, Newcastle and Stockholm; Verdi Requiem at the Wales National Eisteddfod; Philharmonic Orchestra at Symphony Hall, Birmingham, 1999; Opera roles include Rossini's Rosina (Welsh National Opera, 1999) and Mozart's Dorabella; Celebrity recital at the 1999 International Eisteddfod. *Honours:* Winner, 1997 Cardiff Singer of the World Competition. *Current Management:* Harlequin Agency Ltd, 203 Fidlas Road, Cardiff CF4 5NA, Wales.

YANG, Liqing; Composer; b. 30 April 1942, Sichuan, China; Divorced; one d. *Education:* BA, Shenyang Conservatory, 1970; MA in Composition, Shanghai Conservatory, 1980; Diplomas of composition and piano, Musikhochschule, Hannover, Germany, 1983. *Career:* Debut: Violin concerto, White Hair Girls, Shenyang Conservatory of Music, 1970; 24th Tage der Neuen Musik Hannover, poems from Tang Dynasty, Germany, 1982; Musique en Scene, France, 1997; Glocke Musikhall, Bremen, Germany, 1998; 17th Asian Art Festival, Hong Kong, 1997. *Compositions:* Grievances at Wujiang, 1986; Festive Overture, 1987; Prelude, Interlude and Postlude, 1991; Elegy, 1991, 1998. *Recordings:* Grievances at Wujiang, 1986; Taiwan, Linfair, 1995; Yang Liqing's Orchestral Works; Elegy. *Publications:* The Composition Techniques of Olivier Messiaen, 1989; Style Evolution in Orchestration, 1986–87; On Postmodernism in Contemporary Western Music, 1994; Contemporary Instrumentation Techniques, 2001. *Contributions:* Interview with Composer Yang Liqing, Chinese Music Yearbook, 1993. *Address:* 1855 Tianshan Road, Apt. 1710#, Shanghai 200051, Shanghai, People's Republic of China.

YANG, Simon; Singer (Bass); b. 1960, Seoul, South Korea. *Education:* Cologne Musikhochschule, with Kurt Moll. *Career:* Debut: Düsseldorf, 1992, as Giorgio in I Puritani; Sang at Karlsruhe Opera, 1993–95, then with the Hamburg Staatsoper; Roles have included Mozart's Sarastro and Commendatore, King Philip in Don Carlos and Padre Guardiano in La Forza del Destino; Fasolt and Fafner in The Ring at Karlsruhe; Concerts include Beethoven's Ninth, the Verdi Requiem and Schumann's Paradies und der Peri; Sang Osmin in Die Entführung at Vienna Schönbrunn, 1998; Season 2000–01 at Hamburg as Mozart's Bartolo, Varlaam in Boris Godunov and in Donizetti's Roberto Devereux (concert). *Recordings include:* Wagner's Ring. *Honours:* Winner, Vienna Belvedere Competition. *Address:* c/o Hamburg Staatsoper, Grosse Theaterstrasse 34, 20354 Hamburg, Germany.

YANG, Sungsic; Concert Violinist; b. 1966, Korea. *Education:* Studied at the Paris Conservatoire and with Yfrah Neaman at the Guildhall School of Music, 1987. *Career:* Debut: Recital in Seoul in 1977; Solo appearances throughout Europe including tour with the Seoul Philharmonic; Tchaikovsky and Mendelssohn Concertos with the Moscow Philharmonic at Seoul for the Olympic Festival in 1988; Paris concerto debut with Orchestre National de France, conducted by Lorin Maazel, 1988; BBC radio recording, 1988; Appearances with National Symphony Orchestra, RTE, Dublin, and Gävleborgs Symfoniorkester, Sweden, 1991; Plays a Joseph Guarneri del Gesu of 1720; Repertoire also includes concertos by Bach, Brahms, Bruch, Beethoven, Mozart, Prokofiev, Saint-Saëns, Sibelius and Wieniawski; Solo works by Bach, sonatas by Brahms, Beethoven, Debussy, Fauré, Franck, Tartini and Ysaÿe, and Stravinsky's Suite Italienne. *Honours:* Prizewinner in Paganini Competition, Genoa, Long-Thibaud Paris, and Indianapolis, USA; 1st Prize, Carl Flesch Competition, London, 1988.

YANG, Tianjie; Composer; b. 5 Sept. 1952, Changsha City, Hunan Province, China; m. Shuyun He, 9 June 1979, 1 d. *Education:* Graduate, Composing Department, Shanghai Conservatory of Music; Studies at Beijing Broadcast College. *Career:* debut, The Legend of Mountains, orchestral music played at Beijing Music Hall, 1979; Started professional composing, 1972; Created more than 1,000 pieces of music, many of which have been performed in the USA, Russia, Austria, Poland, Hong Kong and elsewhere; mem, Chinese Musicians' Institute, 1990–; Manager of China International Famous Association, 1999. *Compositions:* Orchestral Music: The Carnival of the Miaos; Spring of the Yao Shan; Symphony: Linhai Cuts Firewood; Erhu Concerto: Yearning; Dance Drama: Border Town; Opera: The Remote Days. *Recordings:* Music for the television serial, Nuo Yao. *Recordings:* Border Town, 1990; The Carnival of the Miaos, 1993; Spring of Yao Shan, 1994; Children Sing Ancient Poetries, 1994. *Publications:* On Opera Music's Reforming, 1991; Chinese Theatre: A Talk on the Music Creation of Dance Drama,

Border Town, 1996. *Honours:* Title of National First Degree Composer; Wenhua Award (the most prestigious art award in China), 1996; World Cultural Celebrities' Achievement Award, 1998. *Address:* The Song and Dance Theatre of Hunan, 9 Ren Min Road, Changsha City, Hunan Province 410011, People's Republic of China.

YANG, Youqing; Conductor and Pianist; b. 10 Dec. 1952, Shanghai, China. *Education:* BA in Conducting, Shanghai Conservatory of Music, 1984; MA, 1997, DMA in Orchestral Conducting, 2000, School of Music, Michigan State University, USA; Studied with Distinguished Professor Leon Gregorian. *Career:* Debut: Brahms Symphony No. 4, Mozart Piano Concerto No. 20 and Berlioz Overture to Benvenuto Cellini, with Guangzhou Symphony Orchestra, 1984; Conductor, Symphony Orchestra of China National Opera Theatre, 1984–, appearances including World Premiere of opera Savage Land at 1st China Arts Festival in Beijing, 1987; Has appeared since 1986 as Guest Conductor for Shanghai Philharmonic Orchestra, Shangdong Symphony Orchestra, Central Philharmonic Orchestra of China, China Broadcasting Symphony Orchestra, China Film Philharmonic Orchestra and at Zhou Xiaoyan Opera Centre, Shanghai; In 1995, Music Director of Chinese Musicians' Delegation Concert Tour in Europe, and Guest Conductor of Das Saarlandisches Staatsorchester Saarbrucken, with concerts at Kunst und Ausstellungshalle der Bundesrepublik Deutschland and Saarlandisches Staatstheater, Germany, at the Classic Open-Air in Solothurn, Switzerland, and the Municipal Theatre, Luxembourg; mem, Chinese Musicians' Association. *Contributions:* Looking for Perfect Combination of Mind and Music, interview in Contemporary China magazine, 1991. *Honours:* Merit Fellowship and Scholarship, Shanghai Conservatory of Music, 1982, 1983, 1984. *Address:* c/o Shanghai Symphony Orchestra, 105 Hunan Lu, Shanghai 200031, People's Republic of China.

YANNAY, Yehuda; Composer; b. 26 May 1937, Timisoara, Romania. *Education:* Graduated Rubin Academy of Music, Tel-Aviv, 1964; MFA, Brandeis University, USA, 1966 (study with Berger, Shapero and Krenek); DMA University of Illinois at Urbana, 1974. *Career:* Resident in Israel from 1951; Teacher of theory and composition at University of Wisconsin, Milwaukee, 1970–; Music from Almost Yesterday concert series, 1971–. *Compositions include:* Spheres for soprano and 10 instruments, 1963; Two Fragments for violin and piano, 1966; Wraphap, theatre music, 1969; Coloring Book from the Harpist, 1969; Concert for Audience and orchestra, 1971; The Hidden Melody for cello and horn, 1977; Concertino for violin and chamber orchestra, 1980; Celan Ensembles: Augentanz and Galgenlied for tenor and instruments, 1986–; In Madness There is Order for voice, projections and synthesizers, 1988–92; The Oranur Experiment, music video, Part 1, Journey to Orgonon for actor, projections and synthesizer, 1991; Five Pieces for Three Players for soprano saxophone, clarinet and marimba, 1994; Exit Music at Century's End, for orchestra, 1995; Geometry of Aloneness, for low voice, glass harmonica and slide projections, 1996; Marrakesh Bop, for flute and guitar, 1999. *Address:* c/o ASCAP, 1 Lincoln Plaza, New York, NY 10023, USA.

YANOV-YANOVSKY, Dmitri Feliksovich; Uzbekistan composer; b. 24 April 1963, Tashkent. *Education:* Tashkent State Conservatory. *Career:* founder and Artistic Dir, Int. Festival of Contemporary Music ILKHOM-XX, Tashkent. *Compositions include:* Bagatelles 1982, Piano Concerto 1983, Anno Domini 1985, Chang-Music I–V 1990–94, Lacrymosa 1991, Awakening 1993, Ritual 1994, Conjunctions 1995, Takyr 1995, Come and Go (for theatre) 1995, Hommage à Gustav Mahler 1996, The Little Match-Girl (ballet) 1996–97, Lux aeterna 1997, Music of Dreams 1999, Eh Joe (chamber opera) 2001, Twilight Music 2002, scores for over 40 films. *Recordings:* Chang-Music V (with Kronos Quartet), Lacrymosa, Dawn upshaw (with Kronos Quartet), Music of Dreams (with Elisabeth Chojnacka), Opus 111. *Honours:* second prize Int. Competition de Musique Sacrée, Fribourg 1991, ALEA III Int. Prize, Boston 1992, Cannes Int. Film Festival Special Award of Nantes 1992. *Address:* C-1 47-ap. 42, 700000 Tashkent, Uzbekistan. *Telephone:* 711 361382. *Fax:* 712 560296. *E-mail:* yanovsky@mail.tps.uz.

YARBOROUGH, William; Symphony Conductor; b. 3 Jan. 1926, Wilmington, North Carolina, USA; m. Ruth M Feldt, 29 Jan 1955. *Education:* BM, Chicago Musical College and University of Chicago; MM, Indiana University; Studied with Nadia Boulanger, Vittorio Rieti and Serge Koussevitsky; Studied at Peabody Conservatory and Berkshire Music Center. *Career:* Debut: As Conductor, aged 19, American Symphony in Paris; As Concert Violinist, aged 8; Music Director and Conductor, American Symphony Orchestra, Paris, France; Richmond Philharmonic Orchestra, Richmond, Virginia; CBS Radio broadcasts; Music Director, Conductor, Michigan Bach-Mozart Festival; Performances with Touring American Opera Company and American Chamber Orchestra at present; Music Director, Conductor, American Chamber Orchestra, Washington DC since 1980; Director, Wolf Trap American University Program for the Performing Arts, Washington, DC; Guest Conductor of many of the major symphonies in Europe and

USA including Royal Philharmonic, Vienna Symphony, St Cecilia Orchestra in Rome, Boston Symphony and Philadelphia Orchestra; Numerous radio and television appearances; Speaker, Chicago Adult Education Council; Music Adviser, Old Dominion Symphony Council. *Contributions:* Journal of the American Musicological Society. *Address:* American Chamber Orchestra Society, 4201 Cathedral Avenue NW, Suite 706-E, Washington, DC 20016, USA.

YARON, Gilah; Singer (Soprano); b. 1941, Tel-Aviv, Israel. *Education:* Studied in Tel-Aviv with Tuerk Bernstein and with Gunter Reich, George London and Elisabeth Schwarzkopf. *Career:* Sang with the Israel Philharmonic and other orchestras from 1970; Israel Festival in 1972 in Bach's Magnificat; Sang in Switzerland and other European centres from 1975 including concert at Berlin Festival with works by Hindemith and Webern; Guest appearances in Austria, Belgium, Netherlands, Italy, Denmark and England; Sang Psaumes Hebraiques by Markevitch and Poèmes pour Mi by Messiaen; Other repertoire includes Penderecki's St Luke Passion, Mahler's 2nd Symphony and Mendelssohn's music for A Midsummer Night's Dream; Singing Teacher at The Rubin Academy of Music and Dance, Jerusalem, 1982–. *Address:* c/o PO Box 2179, Bat Yam 59121, Israel.

YASSA, Ramzi; Pianist; b. 15 March 1948, Cairo, Egypt; m. Brigitte Chevrot, 7 June 1978, 1 s., 1 d. *Education:* Lycee of Heliopolis; Diploma, Cairo Conservatory, 1968; Tchaikovsky Conservatory, Moscow, 1969–74; FTCL, 1972; Licence de Concert, Ecole Normale, Paris, 1977. *Career:* Appearances at The Barbican in London with Royal Philharmonic Orchestra, conductor Charles Groves, Kennedy Center, Mann Auditorium with IPO, conductor Zubin Mehta, Musikverein, Palau, Barcelona, Théâtre des Champs Elysées and South Bank, London; Television Mondovision with Zubin Mehta in 1987; Inaugural concert, Cairo Opera House, 1988; BBC recordings and live broadcasts; Adjudicator for international piano competitions; Appearances with Yehudi Menuhin as conductor; Director of the Cairo Opera House, 1998–; Special Adviser for Music to the Egyptian Minister of Culture, 1999–. *Recordings:* Tchaikovsky's The Seasons, Ades, France; Prokofiev's Cinderella, 2nd Sonata, Belgium; Chopin's Ballades and Opus 22, Belgium; Beethoven Appassionata/Waldstein/Lieder von Goethe; Beethoven 5 Piano Concertos and Choral Fantasy Op 80. *Address:* 14 Rue Sainte Cecile, 75009 Paris, France.

YASUNAGA, Toru; Violinist; b. 14 Nov. 1951, Fukuoka, Japan. *Education:* Studied at the Toho Music Academy, Tokyo, and with Michael Schwalbe in Berlin. *Career:* Many appearances in Europe and the Far East as recitalist and in concert; Joined Berlin Philharmonic Orchestra, 1977, and became leader. *Honours:* Winner, Leu Cadia prize at the All Japan Music Competition, 1971. *Address:* c/o Berlin Philharmonic Orchestra, Philharmonie, Matthaikirchestrasse 1, W-10785 Berlin, Germany.

YAUGER, Margaret; Singer (Mezzo-Soprano); b. 1947, Birmingham, Alabama, USA; m. Malcolm Smith, 4 Oct 1975. *Education:* BM, Converse College; MM, New England Conservatory of Music; Special studies at American Opera Centre, Juilliard School of Music, New York City, and Goldovsky Opera Studio. *Career:* Debut: American National Opera Company, Sarah Caldwell, Conductor; Performances with New York City Opera, 1973–75, Lake George Opera Festival, 1972–74, Central City Opera Festival, 1973–76, Boris Goldovsky Opera Tour, 1973–74, Mexico City Opera, Teatro Regio Turin, Italy; Sang at Knoxville with Tennessee Opera, Birmingham Alabama Civic Opera, Fort Worth, Texas Opera; Deutsche Oper am Rhein, Düsseldorf, Germany, 1977–86; Sang at Krefeld, Hanover, Karlsruhe, Freiburg, Wiesbaden and Gelsenkirchen Opera Houses and with Solingen, Duisburg, Münchengladbach-Krefeld, and Trier Symphonies; Appearances on East Berlin Radio and with Dresden Philharmonic; Sang Fricka in Das Rheingold, Washington National Symphony, Margret in Wozzeck, with Boston Symphony Orchestra, 3rd Magd, Elektra with London Symphony Orchestra; Heidelberg Schloss, Festspiele, 1992; Sang in Verdi Requiem, Delaware Symphony Orchestra, 1993; Mahler Symphony No. 2, Roanoke Symphony, 1994; Choral Arts Society of Washington tour of France, 1996; Youngstown Symphony, 1996; Cincinnati Opera, 1996; Portland Maine Symphony, Cesky Krumlov Summer Festival, Czech Republic; Voice Teacher, University of Southern Maine, 1999–; mem, AGMA. *Recordings:* Beethoven Symphony No. 9, alto part, with Mexico City Symphony; Live recording of Rigoletto, New York City Opera. *Honours:* Miss Alabama Competition Scholarship; 3 Scholarships, William Mathis Sullivan Foundation. *Current Management:* Thea Dispecker, Artists' Representative, 59 East 54th Street, New York, NY 10022, USA. *Address:* 12 Locksley Road, Cape Elizabeth, ME 04107, USA.

YEEND, Frances; Singer (Soprano); b. 28 Jan. 1918, Vancouver, Washington, USA. *Education:* Studied at Washington State University. *Career:* From 1943 sang in musicals and on the radio; Concert tour of USA in 1944; Sang Ellen Orford in the US premiere of Peter Grimes, at

Tanglewood in 1946; World tour in 1947 with Mario Lanza and George London, as Bel Canto Trio; New York City Opera, 1948–65, as Violetta, Eva in Die Meistersinger, Micaela, Mozart's Countess and Marguerite; Metropolitan Opera, 1961–64, as Chrysothemis in Elektra and Gutrune in Götterdämmerung; European engagements in Barcelona, Edinburgh in 1951, London in Mimi in 1953, Munich, Verona in Turandot in 1958, and Vienna. *Recordings include:* Micaela in Carmen; Ein Deutsches Requiem by Brahms.

YEN, Wen-hsiung, BA, MA; American musician (piano, erhu), composer and conductor; *Music Director, Chinese Music Orchestra of Southern California;* b. 26 June 1934, Tainan, Taiwan; m. Yuan Yuan 1961; three s. *Education:* Nat. Taiwan Normal Univ., Chinese Culture Univ., Univ. of California at Los Angeles, World Univ., studied piano with Qing-Yan Zhou, Fu-Mei Lee, composition with Paul Chihara Hsu, Chang-Houei and Mike Mitacek. *Career:* instructor, Taiwan Provincial Taichung Teacher Coll. 1961–62; Prof., Chinese Culture Univ. 1964–69; founder and Music Dir, Chinese Music Orchestra of Southern California 1974–; founder, Chinese Culture School, Los Angeles 1976–; Lecturer, West Los Angeles Coll. 1978–82; Faculty, Dept of Music, Univ. of Maryland 1982–83; instructor, Los Angeles City Coll., California State Univ., Los Angeles 1984–, California State Univ., Northridge and Santa Monica City Coll. 1986–; founder and Pres., Chinese Musicians' Asscn of Southern California 1990–; conducted the orchestra for the Dragon Boat Festival at the Chinese Cultural Center in Los Angeles' Chinatown 1993 and for the opening ceremony of the annual Chinese Writers' Asscn of Southern California Conference 1993; mem. Soc. for Ethnomusicology, Int. Council for Traditional Music, Soc. for Asian Music. *Compositions:* Drinking Alone in the Moonlight (words L. Bai), Song of 911, Pure Even Tune (words L. Bai), Roc Flies Ten Thousand Miles, Mother Earth – Four Seasons, The Phoenix Hair Pin (words Lu You). *Publications:* Taiwan Folk Songs Vol. I 1967, Vol. II 1969, A Dictionary of Chinese Music (co-author) 1967, A Collection of Wen-hsiung Yen's Songs Vol. I 1968, Vol. II 1987, Vol. III 2002, Chinese Musical Culture and Folk Songs 1989, A Study of Si Xiang Qi (article) 1989, Silk and Bamboo Expresses Emotion of Meaning 2000. *Honours:* Confucius Commemorative Day Ceremony Outstanding Teacher Award, Los Angeles 1984. *Address:* c/o Chinese Cultural School of Los Angeles, 615 Las Tunas Drive, Suite B, Arcadia, CA 91007, USA.

YERNA, Alexise; Singer (Mezzo-soprano); b. 1959, Belgium. *Education:* Studied at the Brussels Conservatoire with Jules Bastin. *Career:* Sang in operas by Handel, Chabrier and Puccini at the Brussels opera studio; Opéra Wallonie at Liège from 1982, as Orlofsky and in operettas by Offenbach; Has appeared throughout Belgium and France at Lola, Pepa in Goyescas, Fenena (Nabucco) and the Priestess in Aida; Many concert engagements. *Address:* c/o Opéra de Wallonie, 1 Rue des Dominicains, 4000 Liège, Belgium.

YEROFEEVA, Yelena; Cellist; b. 1960, Moscow, Russia. *Education:* Studied at the Moscow Conservatoire with Alexei Shislov. *Career:* Co-founded the Glazunov Quartet 1985; Many concerts in the former Soviet Union and recent appearances in Greece, Poland, Belgium, Germany and Italy; Works by Beethoven and Schumann at the Beethoven Haus in Bonn; Further engagements in Canada and Netherlands; Teacher at the Moscow State Conservatoire and Resident at the Tchaikovsky Conservatoire; Repertoire includes works by Borodin, Shostakovich and Tchaikovsky, in addition to the standard works. *Recordings include:* The six quartets of Glazunov. *Honours:* (with the Glazunov Quartet) Prizewinner of the Borodin Quartet and Shostakovich Chamber Music Competitions. *Address:* c/o Sonata (Glazunov Quartet), 11 Northpark Street, Glasgow G20 7AA, Scotland.

YIM, Jay Alan, BA, MMus; Composer; b. 24 April 1958, St Louis, MO, USA. *Education:* University of California, Royal College of Music, London, England; studied at Dartington, England and Tanglewood. *Career:* Lecturer, Director of Electronic Music Studio, University of California, Santa Barbara, 1978–80; Composer-in-Residence, Cummington School of the Arts, 1984; Major festival performances at Huddersfield, 1982, International Computer Music Conference, 1985, Tanglewood in 1986 and 1987, and Gaudeamus in 1987. *Compositions:* Orchestral: Askesis, 1980–81, Eastern Windows, 1981, Karénas, 1986; Chamber: Palimpsest, 1979, Piak, 1981, Autumn Rhythm, 1984–85, Moments Of Rising Mist, 1986, Mille Graces, 1986, Geometry And Delirium, 1987; Solo instrument: Timescreen for Pianoforte No. 1, 1984, No. 2, 1983, Furiosamente for Piccolo, 1985, Más Furiosamente for Flute, 1985; Electronic: Kinkakuji, 1984, Shiosai, 1984. *Address:* c/o ASCAP, ASCAP Building, 1 Lincoln Plaza, New York, NY 10023, USA.

YING, Shi Zhen; Piano Professor; b. 29 Nov. 1937, China; m. Pan Yi Ming 1960, 2 s. *Education:* Bachelor Degree, 1960, Masters Degree, 1962, Central Conservatory of Music, Beijing. *Career:* Debut: Seven years of age; Piano teacher, Department of Central Conservatory of Music, Beijing, 1962–91; Performed numerous piano recitals and concerts in China and around the world; Recitals, The Tchaikovsky Conservatory of

Moscow and other cities in Russia; Lecturer, many Chinese Conservatories including Hong Kong University, 1984; Music Adviser, Singapore Yamaha Music Academy, Singapore, 1991–; Examiner, Guildhall School of Music and Drama, England. *Compositions:* Many piano examination pieces. *Publications:* The Methods of Piano Teaching and Performance, 1990; Over 10 articles in magazines in China; Text books. *Honours:* 1st prize, Conservatory Piano Competition, 1961. *Address:* Blk 38, 14-2406 Upper Boon, Kent Road, 5380038, Singapore.

YOES, Janice; Singer (Soprano); b. 1947, USA. *Career:* Debut: New York City Opera in 1973 as Santuzza; Sang at the Augsburg Opera, 1975–77, Saarbrucken, 1976–77, and Karlsruhe, 1977–78; Engaged at Nuremberg, 1978–84, with guest appearances at Graz, 1980–83; Sang Strauss's Elektra at the Vienna Staatsoper, Marseilles, Madrid, the Deutsche Oper Berlin, Seattle and Santiago in 1984; Bregenz Festival in 1977 as Reiza in Oberon; Appearances as Brünnhilde in Der Ring de Nibelungen at Naples, Lisbon and Seattle, 1982–86; Further engagements at Basle, Trieste, Brunswick and Pretoria, 1987–88; Other roles have included Isolde, Salome and Lady Macbeth. *Address:* Opera of the Performing Arts Council, Transvaal PO Box 566, Pretoria 0001 Transvaal, South Africa.

YORDANOV, Luben; Violinist; b. 6 Dec. 1926, Sofia, Bulgaria. *Education:* Studied at the Paris Conservatoire, with Pierre Pasquier. *Career:* Has performed throughout Europe as concert soloist from 1951; Leader of the orchestra of the Monte Carlo Opera, 1958–67; Orchestre de Paris, 1967–91; Premiered the Concerto by André Jolivet, 1973, and became professor of chamber music at the Paris Conservatoire, 1987. *Address:* Conservatoire National Superieur de Musique et de Danse de Paris, 209 Avenue Jean-Jaures, Paris 75019, France.

YORK, Deborah; Singer (soprano); b. 9 Nov. 1964, Sheffield, Yorkshire, England. *Education:* Manchester University and the Guildhall School of Music, with Laura Sarti; Further study with Janice Chapman. *Career:* Opera engagements with Glyndebourne Touring Opera as Servilia in La Clemenza di Tito, Mirror in Birtwistle's The Second Mrs Kong; Emilia in Handel's Flavio for Dublin Touring Opera; Mozart's Barbarina at Covent Garden and Fortuna in Monteverdi's Poppea for Netherlands Opera (1995–96); Concerts include Pergolesi's Stabat Mater under Marc Minkowski, Purcell's Tempest with Ivor Bolton, Handel's Israel in Egypt with the Brandenburg Consort and Dixit Dominus with the Hallé Orchestra; Purcell's King Arthur with the King's Singers in Italy and with the English Concert at the 1995 London Proms; Further concerts with the Collegium Vocale, Ghent, under Phillipe Herreweghe; Other broadcasts include music by Purcell with the King's Consort for the BBC, and with the Gabrieli Players in France; Music for the Mona Lisa on Radio 3; Season 1997–98 with Gianetta in L'Elisir d'amore at Covent Garden, Semele at Berlin, Anne Trulove in concert with the London Symphony Orchestra and Handel's Jephtha at the 1997 London Proms; Acis and Galatea in Spain and the St John Passion at Montpellier; Sang Alceste in Handel's Admeto at Beaune, 1998; Season 2000–01 with Almirena in Handel's Rinaldo at Munich and Anne Trulove at Teatro Colón, Buenos Aires. *Current Management:* IMG Artists, Lovell House, 616 Chiswick High Road, London, W4 5RX, England. *Telephone:* (20) 8233-5800. *Fax:* (20) 8233-5801. *E-mail:* artistseurope@imgworld.com. *Website:* www.imgartists.com.

YORK, John; Pianist; b. 20 March 1949, Eastbourne, England; m. Fiona Osborne, 5 Sept 1981, 1 s., 1 d. *Education:* AGSM Diploma, Guildhall School of Music and Drama, London, 1971; Studied in Paris with Jacques Février, 1971–72; Vienna Hochschule with Dieter Weber, 1972–74. *Career:* Debut: Wigmore Hall, 1974; Recitals and concerts in the United Kingdom, Ireland, France, throughout Europe, USA, Canada, Brazil, Bermuda, Singapore, Malaysia; Australia; Partner to Raphael Wallfisch, cello; Member of York 2 Piano Duo; Classic FM, BBC radio, and CBC television and radio. *Recordings:* Many albums on several labels including: 3 albums of York Trio; Eminence and Black Box with Raphael Wallfisch. *Publications:* Selector and assistant in new issue of Mikrokosmos (Bartók); Fingers and Thumbs, 1993; 20th Century Collections, 1998. *Contributions:* Reviewer for Piano Magazine, The Strad. *Honours:* Debussy Prize, Paris, 1973. *Current Management:* Clarion/Seven Muses, London, England. *Address:* 38 Caterham Road, Lewisham, London SE13 5 AR, England. *Telephone:* (20) 8318-1824. *E-mail:* john@yorkpiano.freeserve.co.uk.

YORK, Richard, BEd; British musician and music historian; b. 15 May 1953, Northampton, England; m. Elizabeth York; two d. *Education:* Culham Coll., Abingdon and Northampton Coll. *Career:* freelance education workshop leader in schools and museums; music historian and interpreter at museums and heritage sites, including Victoria & Albert museum, London, Greenwich Foundation, English Heritage and Nat. Trust properties, and Elgar's birthplace museum; plays a large collection of instruments from medieval clarsach to Victorian concertina and hammer dulcimer; mem. Incorporated Soc. of Musicians, Int. Museum Theatre Alliance Europe, Assn for Historical Interpretation.

Address: 1 Exmoor Close, Northampton, NN3 3AU, England (home). *Telephone:* (1604) 639581 (home). *E-mail:* richard@richard-york.co.uk (office). *Website:* www.richard-york.co.uk (office).

YOSHINO, Naoko; Harpist; b. 1967, London, England. *Education:* Studied with Susan McDonald of Indiana University from 1974. *Career:* Soloist with leading orchestras from 1977, notably the Israel Philharmonic under Mehta in 1985, the Philadelphia Orchestra under Frühbeck de Burgos in 1987, and in Japan with Seiji Ozawa and Wolfgang Sawallisch; New York recital debut at Merkin Hall in 1987 and chamber concert with members of the Berlin Philharmonic; Soloist with the Berlin Philharmonic under Ozawa in 1988; Classic Aid concerts with Lorin Maazel in Paris, 1988, and Yehudi Menuhin at Gstaad Festival in 1988; London debut with James Galway in Mozart's Concerto K299 in 1990; London recital debuts in 1990; English Chamber Orchestra at the Barbican under Menuhin in 1990; Played at the World Harp Festival at Cardiff in 1991. *Recordings:* Album with the English Chamber Orchestra under Menuhin; 5 Other albums recorded: 3 as solo artist, 1 with flute and 1 concerto album. *Honours:* Second Prize, First International Harp Contest, Santa Cecilia Academy in Rome, 1981; 1st Prize, 9th International Harp Contest in Israel, 1985. *Current Management:* Kajimoto Concert Management Ltd. *Address:* Kajimoto Concert Management Ltd, Kahoku Building 8-6-25 Ginza, Chuo-Ku, Tokyo, Japan.

YOST, Ricardo; Singer (Bass-baritone); b. 1943, Chile. *Education:* Studied in Santiago. *Career:* Sang at the Teatro Colón Buenos Aires from 1973, notably as Guglielmo, Rigoletto, Amonasro, Iago, Renato, Malatesta, Escamillo and Napoleon in Prokofiev's War and Peace; Has appeared throughout South America and in bass roles such as Mephistopheles and Rossini's Basilio; Sang Amonasro at Buenos Aires, 1996; Sang in Francesca da Rimini at Buenos Aires, 2000. *Address:* Teatro Colón, Cerrito 618, 1010 Buenos Aires, Argentina.

YOUN, Kwangchul; Singer (Bass); b. 1970, Korea. *Education:* Chong-Ju University; Sofia Music School and Berlin Hochschule der Künste, with Herbert Brauer. *Career:* Sang in concert at Seoul from 1998; South Korean State Opera 1988-90; Engaged at the Deutsche Oper Berlin from 1993; Bayreuth Festival debut 1996, in Die Meistersinger; Sang the Priest in Schoenberg's Moses und Aron, Vienna Konzerthaus 2001; Season 2001–02 with concerts in Berlin and Lyon, Mozart's Bartolo at Barcelona and High Priest in Idomeneo at the Salzburg Festival. *Address:* c/o Deutche Oper Berlin, Richard Wagnerstrasse 10, D-10568 Berlin, Germany.

YOUNG, Douglas; Composer, Pianist, Conductor, Writer and Broadcaster; b. 18 June 1947, London, England; m. Susan Anne Devlin, 22 Nov 1980, 1 d. *Education:* Trinity College of Music, Junior Exhibitioner, 1957–66; ATCL, Piano Performance, 1963; BMus, London Royal College of Music, 1969. *Career:* Debut: As Pianist, Royal Festival Hall, London, 1970; Works with Ronald Hynd, choreographer for Royal Ballet and München Staatsoper Ballet, 1970–; Fellow, Commoner in The Creative Arts, Trinity College, Cambridge, 1973–75; Composer-in-Residence, Leicester Education Authority, 1975–77; Founded internationally renowned ensemble, Dreamtiger, 1975; Trustee, LAMA; SPNM; BMIC. *Compositions include:* Works in all genres including several inspired by Apollinaire, Lewis Carroll, Joyce, Virginia Woolf and Borges; Series of Concerti, Night Journeys Under The Sea; Ludwig–Fragments Eines Rätsels, ballet in 2 acts, 1986; Mr. Klee Visits the Botanical Gardens, for string quartet, 1993; Herr Schoenberg Plays Ping-Pong, for piano, 1992–99; The Excursions of M. Jannequin, for piano, 1997–; The Eternal Waterfall, for cello and piano, 1998; The Lost Puzzle of Gondwana, stage, 1999. *Recordings include:* Virages–Region One for Cello and Large Orchestra; Trajet, Inter Lignes, 1980; The Hunting Of The Snark, 1982; Third Night Journey Under The Sea, 1980–82; Rain, Steam And Speed, 1982; Dreamlandscapes, Portrait Of Apollinaire, 1983; Dreamlandscapes Book ll, 1986. *Contributions:* Tempo; Music Teacher; Composer. *Honours:* Cobbett Prize for Chamber Music, 1968; Karl Rankl Prize for Orchestral Composition, Musica Nova, 1970–71. *Address:* c/o BMI, 79 Harley House, Marylebone Road, London, NW1, England.

YOUNG, Josephine; Cellist; b. 1960, Auckland, New Zealand. *Education:* Studied at the New England Conservatory, and in London with Christopher Bunting. *Career:* Debut: Concert in Wellington, 1988; Chamber musician and soloist in New Zealand; Co-founder of the New Zealand String Quartet in 1987 under the auspices of the Music Federation of New Zealand; Concerts at the Tanglewood School in USA, the Banff International Competition in Canada and performances with the Lindsay Quartet at the 1990 International Festival of the Arts, Wellington; Soloist with the New Zealand Symphony Orchestra and artist-in-residence at Victoria University, Wellington; Tour to Australia in 1990 for Musica Viva Australia; Tours of New Zealand in 1992 and concerts in New York, 1993. *Recordings:* Various albums.

YOUNG, Julianne; Singer (Mezzo-soprano); b. 1973, Cape Town, South Africa. *Education:* Royal College of Music, with Lillian Watson. *Career:* Concert engagements include Mozart's Requiem at King's College Chapel, Bach's Passions at St John's Smith Square (St John Passion with Peter Schreier, 2000) and Rossini's Petite Messe in Glasgow; Opera roles include Adalberto in Ottone and Vitige in Flavio, for the London Handel Festival, 2000–2001; Baba the Turk in The Rake's Progress; Further concerts include Linbury Theatre, Covent Garden, recital (2000), master class with Barbara Bonney, concert tour of Japan with the BBC Concert Orchestra and engagement with the Cape Town Symphony Orchestra, 2000. *Honours:* Winner, Lady Maud Warrender and Cuthbert Smith Prizes, RCM; John McCormack Golden Voice Competition, Ireland. *Address:* Royal College of Music, Prince Consort Road, London SW7, England.

YOUNG, La Monte Thornton; Composer and Performer; b. 14 Oct. 1935, Bern, Idaho, USA; m. Marian Zazeela, 1963. *Education:* Studied at Los Angeles City College, 1953–56, Los Angeles State College, 1956–57 and UCLA with Robert Stevenson; Further study with Andrew Imbrie at the Stockhausen masterclasses at Darmstadt and electronic music at the New School for Social Research, NY. *Career:* Performed and taught Kirana style of North Indian classical vocal music, with Pran Nath; Collaborations with Marian Zazeela; Associations with the Fluxus and Minimalist movements of artistic endeavour; Returned to California in 1959 and became Music Director of the Ann Halprin Dance Company, 1959–60; With Marian Zazeela made tours of USA and Europe with the Theatre of Eternal Music, 1969–75; Director of the Kirana Center for Indian Classical Music, 1971; Dream House maintained by the Dia Art Foundation's programme at Harrison Street, NY, 1979–85. *Compositions include:* Various pieces for electronic and mixed-media forces, 1959–67; Trio for Strings, 1958; Studies I–III, 1959; Arabic Numeral, 1960; Death Chant for Male Voices and Carillon, 1961; The Well-Tuned Piano, ongoing series of pieces for Prepared Piano; Orchestral Dreams, 1985; The Subsequent Dreams of China, 1993; The Empty Base, Sound environments, 1991–. *Publications include:* An Anthology, 1963, revised, 1970; Selected Writings, 1969. *Honours:* Woodrow Wilson Fellowship, 1959; Guggenheim Fellowship, 1966; Creative Arts Public Service Grants; Commission from the Dia Art Foundation, 1975–85. *Address:* c/o ASCAP, ASCAP Building, 1 Lincoln Plaza, New York, NY 10023, USA.

YOUNG, Richard; Violist; b. 1945, USA. *Education:* Studied at Indiana University and Catholic University; Teachers included Josef Gingold, Aaron Rosand and William Primrose. *Career:* Performed at Queen Elisabeth of Belgium Competition aged 13; Member of Faculty at Oberlin Conservatory of Music, 1972–84; Performances with the Rogeri Trio and the Hungarian Quartet in the USA, Europe, South America, Africa and Australia; Member of the Vermeer Quartet from 1985; Performances at all major US centres and in Europe, Israel and Australia; Festival engagements at Tanglewood, Aspen, Spoleto, Edinburgh, Mostly Mozart in New York, Aldeburgh, South Bank, Santa Fe, Chamber Music West and the Casals Festival; Resident quartet for Chamber Music Chicago; Annual masterclasses at the Royal Northern College of Music, Manchester; Member of the Resident Artists Faculty of Northern Illinois University; Producer of the Vermeer Quartet's Grammy-nominated CD of Haydn's the Seven Last words of Christ; Mozart K421 and Beethoven op 95 with the Vermeer Quartet at the 2001 Bath Festival. *Recordings include:* Quartets by Beethoven, Dvořák, Verdi and Schubert; Brahms Clarinet Quintet with Karl Leister. *Address:* Allied Artists, 42 Montpelier Square, London SW7 1JZ, England.

YOUNG, Simone; Conductor; b. 21 March 1961, Sydney, New South Wales. *Career:* Appearance with Australian Opera before European debut with Cologne Opera, 1987; Komische Oper, Berlin, 1992; First woman conductor at Vienna State Opera and Paris Opéra; Vienna Staatsoper debut, La Bohème, 1993; Covent Garden debut 1994, Rigoletto; Season 1997–98 with Macbeth at Houston, Hoffmann at the Met and Traviata at Covent Garden; Falstaff for Opera Australia, 1999; Ring Cycle at Vienna, 1997; Season 2000–01 at Covent Garden, with Der fliegende Holländer and Katya Kabanova; also worked with Bayerische Staatsoper, Munich; Metropolitan Opera, New York; Opéra de la Bastille, Paris; Staatsoper Hamburg; LA Opera; Houston Grand Opera; Concerts include Munich and New York Philharmonic Orchestras; Maggio Musicale, Florence; ORF Radio Orchestra, Vienna; NDR Hannover; NHK Symphony Orchestra, Japan; Hamburg and Stuttgart Philharmonic Orchestras; Nat. Orchestre de Lyon Staatskapelle Dresden; Chief Conductor, Bergen Philharmonic Orchestra, 1999–2002; Music Director, Opera Australia, 2001–03; Gen. Manager and Music Dir, Hamburg State Opera; Music Dir, Philharmonic State Orchestra Hamburg, (2005–). *Honours:* Chevalier des Arts et des Lettres; Hon. doctorates (Monash University, 1998; Univ. of NSW, 2001); Australian Mo Award for Classical Performer of the Year, 2002.

Address: c/o Arts Management Pty Ltd, 420 Elizabeth Street, Surry Hills, NSW 2010, Australia.

YOUNG, Thomas; Singer (Tenor); b. 1962, USA. *Career:* Debut: Sang the Inspector in the premiere of Under the Double Moon, by Anthony Davis, St Louis, 1989; New York City Opera from 1990, as Schoenberg's Aron, Molqi in The Death of Klinghoffer by John Adams (also in Brussels and San Francisco) and in Zimmermann's Die Soldaten; Season 1992 as Frère Elie in Messiaen's St François d'Assise, at Salzburg, and in Birtwistle's Punch and Judy at Amsterdam; Florence Maggio Musicale 1994, as Aron; Chicago Lyric Opera, 1997, as the Trickster God in the premiere of Amistad, by Anthony Davis; Concerts include Mendelssohn's Elijah, and modern repertory. *Recordings include:* The Death of Klinghoffer. *Address:* c/o Chicago Lyric Opera, 20 North Wacker Drive, Chicago, IL 60606, USA.

YTTREHUS, Rolv; Composer; b. 12 March 1926, Duluth, USA. *Education:* BS in music at University of Minnesota, 1950; MM with Ross Lee Finney, at University of Michigan, 1955; Further study with Brustad in Oslo, Boulanger in Paris, Sessions at Princeton (1957–60) and Petrassi in Rome, 1960–61. *Career:* Teacher at the University of Wisconsin, Oshkosh, 1969–77; State University of New Jersey, Rutgers, from 1977. *Compositions include:* Six Haiku for flute, cello and harp, 1959; Music for Winds, Percussion and Viola, 1961; Expression for orchestra, 1962; Sextet for 6 instruments, 1969; Music for winds, percussion, cello and voices, 1969; Angstwagen for soprano and percussion, 1971; Quintet, for flute, violin, clarinet, cello and piano, 1973; Gradus ad Parnassum, for soprano and chamber orchestra, after Nietzsche and Fux, 1979; Explorations for piano, 1985; Cello Sonata, 1988; Raritan Variation for piano, 1989; Symphony, 1995. *Address:* c/o ASCAP, 1 Lincoln Plaza, New York, NY 10023, USA.

YU, Chun Yee; Pianist; b. 12 July 1936, Shanghai, China; m. (1) Isabella Miao, Dec 1963, 2 s., (2) Jung Chang, June 1982. *Education:* Royal College of Music, England under Kendall Taylor; Agostic, Italy; Tagliaferro, France. *Career:* Examiner to the Associated Board of Royal School of Music; Professor of Piano, Royal College of Music; Represented Singapore at the First Asian Music Festival in Hong Kong; First appeared at the Royal Festival Hall in 1963 as soloist with London Philharmonic Orchestra; Has played extensively in the Far East and throughout the United Kingdom; Recently toured Taiwan and China. *Honours:* Recordi Prize for Conducting; Prizewinner, International Piano Competition; Scholarship to study in Siena under Agosti. *Address:* c/o Royal College of Music, London, SW7, England.

YU, Julian Jing-Jun; Composer; b. 2 Sept. 1957, Beijing, China; m. Marion Hazel Gray, 9 Nov 1984. *Education:* Diploma of Music, Central Conservatory of Music, Beijing, 1977; Postgraduate Diploma in Composition, Tokyo College of Music, 1982; Graduate Diploma in Music, Queensland Conservatorium of Music, 1987; MA, Music (Composition), La Trobe University, Melbourne, 1994. *Career:* Emigrated to Australia in 1985; Tanglewood Fellow, 1988; Victorian Ministry for The Arts Music Advisory Panel, 1991–93 and 1995–96; Work commissioned by Australian Broadcasting Corporation, Australia Ensemble, Intercontemporain, Chamber Made Opera, Australia Ensemble, Synergy Percussion; The City of Munich and the BBC Proms; Jury Member for BMW Music Theatre Prize at 3rd Munich Biennale, 1992; Works performed at Huddersfield Contemporary Music Festival, 1990; ISCM World Music Days in Zürich, 1991 and New Mexico in 1993. *Compositions:* Impromptu; Wu-Yu for Orchestra, 1987; Scintillation I, II and III, 1987; Great Ornamented Fuga Canonica, 1988; Medium Ornamented Fuga Canonica; Reclaimed Prefu I and II, 1989; The White Snake, 1989; First Australian Suite, 1990; In the Sunshine of Bach, 1990; Hsiang-Wen (Filigree Clouds), for orchestra, 1991; Philopentatonia for chamber orchestra, 1994; Three Symphonic Poems, 1994; Sinfonia Passacaglissima, 1995; Marimba Concerto, 1996; Lyrical Concerto for flute and orchestra, 1996; Fresh Ghosts, opera, 1997; Concerto for zheng and orchestra, 1999; Nor a Stream but and Ocean for orchestra, 1999. *Recordings:* Vienna Modern Masters; Scintillation II; Wu-Yu; Jangled Bells; Scintillation III; Impromptu (Tall Poppies); Trio for violin, cello and piano; Classical Allusion: Selected Works by Julian Yu (Move); Dovetailing (ABC Classics); Tea Chinese Folk and Art Songs (ABC). *Address:* Australian Music Centre, PO Box N690, Grosvenor Place, NSW 1220, Australia.

YU, Long; Conductor; b. 1965, China. *Career:* Many appearances with leading orchestras in Europe and the Far East; Artistic Director of the Peking International Festival, 1998–; Founder of the China Philhar-

monic Orchestra, 2000; Engagements with soloists including Frank-Peter Zimmermann (violin), Tiziana Fabbricini (soprano) and Nelson Freire (piano) in Australia, France, Germany and Hungary; Further concerts in Hong Kong, Poland, Singapore, Slovakia, Switzerland and China. *Recordings include:* Albums with the China Philharmonic (Deutsche Grammophon). *Current Management:* IMG Artists, Lovell House, 616 Chiswick High Road, London W4 5RX, England.

YUASA, Takuo, BMus; Japanese conductor; b. Osaka. *Education:* Univ. of Cincinnati, USA, in France with Igor Markevich, Hochschule, Vienna with Hans Swarowsky, in Siena with Franco Ferrara. *Career:* fmr Asst to Lovro von Matacic in Monte Carlo, Milan and Vienna; fmrly Principal Conductor Gumma Symphony Orchestra, Japan, Principal Guest Conductor BBC Scottish Symphony Orchestra; currently Principal Guest Conductor Ulster Orchestra, Northern Ireland –(2005); regularly performs throughout Europe and the Far East; has played with orchestras, including the Adelaide Symphony, BBC Scottish Symphony Orchestra, Berliner Symphoniker, Bournemouth Symphony Orchestra, Brabants Orkest, Gelders Orkest, Hallé Orchestra, Hong Kong Philharmonic, London Philharmonic, Luxembourg Philharmonic, Nat. Symphony Orchestra of Ireland, New Zealand Symphony Orchestra, North Netherlands Orchestra, Norwegian Radio Orchestra, Oslo Philharmonic, Polish Radio Nat. Symphony Orchestra, Queensland Orchestra, Royal Liverpool Philharmonic Orchestra, Royal Scottish Nat. Orchestra, Sonderjyllands Symphony Orchestra, Sydney Symphony Orchestra, Trondheim Symphony, Ulster Orchestra, Warsaw Nat. Philharmonic. *Honours:* Fitelberg Int. Conducting Competition special award, Katowice, Poland. *Current Management:* Patrick Garvey Management, Cedar House, 10 Rutland Street, Filey, North Yorkshire YO14 9JB, England. *Telephone:* (1723) 516613. *Fax:* (1723) 514678. *E-mail:* patrick@patrickgarvey.com. *Website:* www.patrickgarvey.com.

YUEN, Nancy; Singer (Soprano); b. 1965, Hong Kong. *Education:* Royal Academy of Music, London; Scholarship to study Lieder, Germany. *Career:* Extensive concert repertoire; 11 operatic roles; Worked with: Welsh National Opera; English National Opera; Mid-Wales Opera; Los Angeles Music Centre Opera; West Australian Opera; New Zealand International Festival of the Arts; Singapore Lyric Opera; Barbados Festival, 1995; Further engagements with ENO, Hong Kong Arts Festival, Singapore Lyric Opera and Kentish Opera; Extensive tour of Middle East and Far East; Regularly performs at Royal Festival Hall, Queen Elizabeth Hall and the Purcell Room; Recent engagements with: Opera Northern Ireland; Concerts in France and around the United Kingdom; Touring production in the Middle East and Far East; Festival of the Asian Performing Arts, Singapore; Singapore Lyric Theatre; Royal Albert Hall; Performances in Manchester and Sheffield; Lyric Opera productions, National concert Hall, Dublin; Toured France with London City Opera; Sang for Opera Queensland; Royal Albert Hall; Lyric Opera, NCH. *Recordings:* Recorded for BBC radio, Television Hong Kong, Radio FM, New Zealand. *Address:* 16 Maygrove Road, London NW6 2EB, England.

YURISICH, Gregory; Singer (Baritone); b. 13 Oct. 1951, Mount Lawley, Western Australia, Australia. *Education:* Studied in Perth. *Career:* Debut: Paolo in Simon Boccanegra for Australian Opera at Sydney, 1978; Roles in Australia have included Mozart's Masetto and Don Alfonso, Verdi's Germont and Melitone, Alberich in The Ring, Varlaam in Boris Godunov, Beethoven's Pizarro and Wagner's Dutchman; European debut, Frankfurt, 1989, as Bottom in A Midsummer Night's Dream; Covent Garden debut, 1990, as William Tell, returning as Dr Bartolo, the villains in Les Contes d'Hoffmann, Don Profondo in a new production of Il Viaggio a Reims, 1992; Pizarro in Fidelio and Scarpia in Tosca; For English National Opera has sung in two world premieres: Alcibiades in Timon of Athens by Stephen Oliver, 1991, and Cadmus in Bakxai by John Buller, 1992; Sang Stankar in a new production of Verdi's Stiffelio at Covent Garden, 1993; Other roles include Escamillo, Leporello (Glyndebourne 1991), King Henry in Anna Bolena, and Verdi's Iago, Simon Boccanegra, Rigoletto and Nabucco; Further engagements include: San Francisco and Geneva (Germont Père in La Traviata); Covent Garden (title role in Nabucco); Australia (title role in Falstaff); Vienna (Balstrode in Peter Grimes and title role in Rigoletto); Munich (title role in Nabucco); Sang in opening gala concert of Belfast Concert Hall, 1997; Tonio in Pagliacci at Washington; Sang the High Priest in Samson et Dalila at Los Angeles, 1999. *Recordings:* Leporello with Roger Norrington. *Address:* c/o English National Opera, St Martin's Lane, London, WC2, England.

ZABARA, Maksim; Bassoonist; b. 12 April 1957, Minsk, Belarus. *Education:* Belorus Lyceum of Music, 1982–91; Kiev Special Music School Lisenko, 1991–94; National Academy of Music, Ukraine, 1994–97. *Career:* Many recital and concert appearances in Belarus, Ukraine, Germany, Netherlands and Canada. Repertory includes CP Bach Sonatas, Concertos by Devienne, Françaix, Hummel, Mozart, Vivaldi and Weber; Sonatas by Glinka, Saint-Saëns and Schubert (arrangement of Arpeggione Sonata); Beethoven's Trio op 11 (arranged), Kreutzer's Trio op 43 and the Trio Pathétique by Glinka. *Honours:* Second Prize, Belarus Youth Woodwind Competition, 1991; Diploma of the International Woodwind Competition, Minsk, 1994. *Address:* c/o NWB Apollon & Hermes, PR-Arts-Media Services Production, Im Flögerhof 12, 53819 Neunkirchen-Cologne, Germany.

ZABILIASTA, Lydia; Singer (Soprano); b. 1959, Oleno-Koshorivka, Kirovohrad, Ukraine. *Education:* Studied in Kirovgrad and at the Kiev State Conservatoire; Further study with Giulietta Simionato at La Scala. *Career:* Principal at the National Opera in Kiev from 1982, with such roles as Elsa, Tatiana, Nedda, Xenia in Boris Godunov and Mimi; Tours to North and South America, Japan, Australia and the United Kingdom (with Perm Opera, 1996), adding roles of Abigaille in Nabucco and Madama Butterfly. *Honours:* Gold Medal, Tchaikovsky Singing Competition, Moscow, 1982. *Address:* c/o Sonata Ltd, 11 North Park Street, Glasgow G20 7AA, Scotland.

ZABLOCKI, Jerzy; Conductor; b. 25 July 1928, Lublin, Poland; m. 4 Jan 1968, 1 s. *Education:* Studied Musicology at University of Wroclaw, conducting at Faculty of Composition, Theory and Conducting, Academy of Music, Wroclaw, 1955. *Career:* Teacher in schools, college and at Academy of Music since 1948; Conductor, Polish Radio Orchestra; Over 400 pieces performed and recorded including 120 own compositions and arrangements for orchestra and choir with orchestra, 1953–58; Operetta Theatre, Wroclaw, 1959–62; Conductor, Wroclaw State Opera, 1970–77, Bydgoszcz State Opera, 1981–82 and Warsaw Operetta, 1982–84; Recently Professor in Warsaw Academy of Music and Bydgoszcz Academy of Music, Director of postgraduate study for choir conductors; Other positions have included chairman, music critic and journalist. *Compositions:* 120 recorded works including 20 folk songs of Lower Silesia and 50 Polish folk songs and dances. *Recordings:* 400 Pieces, Polish radio and television. *Address:* Marszalkowska 68-70 m 6, Warsaw, Poland.

ZACCARIA, Nicola; Singer (Bass); b. 9 March 1923, Athens, Greece. *Education:* Studied at the Royal Conservatory, Athens. *Career:* Debut: Athens in 1949 as Raimondo in Lucia di Lammermoor; Has sung at many Italian centres; La Scala debut in 1953 as Sparafucile in Rigoletto; Sang in Milan in the standard bass repertory until1974, and created the Third Knight in the premiere of Pizzetti's Assassino nella Cattedrale, 1958; Vienna Staatsoper from 1956; Salzburg Festival from 1957 as the Minister in Fidelio, the Monk in Don Carlos, the Commendatore in Don Giovanni and Ferrando in Il Trovatore; Covent Garden in 1957 and 1959, as Oroveso in Norma, and Creon in Médée, both with Maria Callas; Further appearances in Brussels, Cologne, Geneva, Moscow, Rio di Janeiro, Mexico City, Berlin, Monte Carlo, Edinburgh, Aix and Orange; Dallas in 1976 as King Marke in Tristan and Isolde; Sang Colline in La Bohème at Macerata in 1982; Other roles included Verdi's Zaccaria in Nabucco and Silva in Ernani, Rodolfo in La Sonnambula and Sarastro in Die Zauberflöte. *Recordings include:* Norma; Aida; Un Ballo in Maschera; Il Trovatore; La Sonnambula; Rigoletto; Turandot; Barbiere di Siviglia; La Bohème; Falstaff; L'Italiana in Algeri; La Navarraise; Orlando Furioso; Mignon by Thomas; Beethoven's Missa Solemnis.

ZACHARIAS, Christian; pianist; b. 27 April 1950, Tamshedpur, India. *Education:* studied with Irene Slavin in Karlsruhe, Germany, with Vlado Perlemuter in Paris, France. *Career:* US debut with the Boston Symphony; appeared in the USA with the Boston Symphony, Cleveland Orchestra and New York Philharmonic, in Canada with the Montreal Symphony; regular appearances in the UK, including the Edinburgh Festival 1985 with the Polish Chamber Orchestra and Jerzy Maksymiuk; engagements at major European festivals include Salzburg and the piano festival at La Roque d'Antheron; chamber concerts with the violinist Ulf Hoelscher, the cellist Heinrich Schiff and the Alban Berg Quartet; British concerts include appearances with the London Symphony Orchestra, BBC Nat. Orchestra of Wales and Royal Liverpool Philharmonic. *Recordings:* Schubert, Scarlatti and Mozart Sonatas, Concertos by Beethoven with the Dresden Staatskapelle. *Honours:* won prizes in Geneva and in the Van Cliburn Competition 1969, won the European Broadcasting Union Ravel Prize 1975. *Current Management:* Kunstlersek A. Schoerke, Grazer Strasse 30, 30519 Hannover, Germany.

ZACHARIASSEN, Mathias; Singer (Tenor); b. 1968, Stockholm, Sweden. *Education:* Stockholm College of Opera, with Nicolai Gedda. *Career:* Debut: Eurimedes in Telemann's Orfeo, at the Staatsoper Berlin and Innsbruck Festival of Early Music, 1994; Opera engagements as the Singer in Der Rosenkavalier at Stockholm and Oslo, Mozart's Ferrando and Idamante at Brussels, Lenski and Elemer in Arabella at the 1996 Glyndebourne Festival; Season 1996–97 with Ferrando and Tamino at Graz, Don Ottavio in Oslo; Season 1998 with Jacquino in Leonore and Fidelio, Théâtre des Champs Elysées, Paris; Concerts have included Mozart's C Minor Mass in Oslo and Gothenburg, the Requiem with the Danish Radio Symphony Orchestra and Schubert's A-flat Mass; Verdi Requiem at Norrkoping; Further concerts in Helsinki, Trondheim, Bad Kissingen and Amsterdam. *Address:* c/o Svenska Konsertbyran AB, Jungfrugatan 45, S–114 44 Stockholm, Sweden.

ZACHER, Gerd; Concert Organist; b. 6 July 1929, Meppen, Germany. *Education:* Studied at Detmold with Gunter Bialas and in Hamburg. *Career:* Worked at the German Church, Santiago, before position as organist at the Lutheran Church, Hamburg Wellingsbutel, 1957–70; Director of the Church Music Institute at the Essen Hochschule and interpreter of many modern works; Has premiered music by John Cage (Variations, 1963), Mauricio Kagel (Phantasie, 1967), Ligeti (Two Studies, 1967) and Isang Yun (Fragment, 1975); Also a noted performer of works by Bach, Frescobaldi, Liszt and Cabezon.

ZAGORZANKA, Barbara; Singer (Soprano); b. 31 July 1938, Kazimierzow, Poland. *Career:* Sang at the Bydgoszcz Opera, 1960–67 as Butterfly, Gilda, Tosca and Tatiana, Poznan from 1967 as Halka, Micaela, Elisabeth de Valois, Marguerite, Odabella in Attila, Mozart's Countess and Fiordiligi, and Lucia, and Warsaw Opera from 1967 as Aida, Liu, Leonore, Norma, Abigaille, Sieglinde and Roxana in Szymanowski's King Roger; Has sung Halka on tour to the USA and Roxana in Vienna in 1989; Concert of Penderecki's Utrenja at Frankfurt in 1992; Further guest appearances in Paris including Lisa in The Queen of Spades, and Wiesbaden. *Address:* Polish National Opera, Grand Theatre, Plac Teatrainy 1, 00-950 Warsaw, Poland.

ZAGROSEK, Lothar; Conductor and Composer; b. 13 Nov. 1942, Waging, Germany. *Education:* Studied in Vienna with Hans Swarowsky and with Karajan and Bruno Maderna. *Career:* Appointments at opera houses in Salzburg, Kiel and Darmstadt, 1967–73; Frequent appearances with the London Sinfonietta from 1978, conducting music by Weill, Ligeti, Messiaen and Stravinsky; Engagements in USA, notably San Diego and Seattle, from 1984; Guest Conductor for BBC Symphony Orchestra; Musical Director, Paris Opéra, 1986–88; Glyndebourne debut in 1987 with Così fan tutte; Conducted the premiere of Krenek's oratorio, Symeon Stylites, at the 1988 Salzburg Festival; Conducted the Paris Opéra Orchestra in York Höller's Der Meister und Margarita in 1989, the last new production at the Paris Opéra, Palais Garnier, before the opening of the Opéra de la Bastille; Conducted the BBC Symphony Orchestra at the 1989 Promenade Concerts in music by Markevitch, Mozart, Mendelssohn, Kodály and Brahms' Ein Deutsches Requiem; Conducted Peter Sellars production of Die Zauberflöte at Glyndebourne in 1990; Promenade Concerts in 1991; Season 1997–98 with King Roger, Die Entführung and Tosca at Stuttgart; Double bill of Bluebeard's Castle and Erwartung at Covent Garden, 2002. *Recordings include:* Jonny spielt auf (Krenek), Goldschmidt's Der gewaltige Hahnrei and Die Vögel by Braunfels, Gruber's Cello Concerto, Schnittke's Piano Concerto, Haydn's 47th Symphony, Brahms No. 1 and Mendelssohn's Violin Concerto; Appointed Music Director at the Stuttgart State Opera, 1996; Chief Conductor of the Städtische Theater, Leipzig; Led the premiere of Das Mädchen by Lachenmann, Hamburg, 1997. *Address:* Staatsoper Stuttgart, Oberer Schossgarten 6, Stuttgart, Germany.

ZAHORTSEV, Volodymr Mykolayovych; Composer; b. 27 Oct. 1944, Kiev, Ukraine. *Education:* Tchaikovsky Conservatory, Kiev. *Career:* Joined avant-garde group of post-Stalinist composers in Kiev; mem, The Composers Union of the Ukraine. *Compositions include:* Priskaski, song cycle, 1963; Violin Sonata, 1964; String Quartet, 1964; Sizes for 5 Instruments, 1965; Graduations for Chamber Group, 1966; Games for Chamber Orchestra, 1968; Symphony No. 1, 1968; Music for 4 Strings, 1968; Sonata for Strings, Piano and Percussion, 1969; Rhythms for Piano, 1970; Symphony No. 2 for Soprano, Tenor and Orchestra, 1978; Oboe Sonata, 1978; Music for 4 Strings, No. 2, 1978; A Day In Pereyaslavl for Soloists, Chorus and Orchestra, 1979; In The Children's Room, cantata, 1979; Chamber Concertos 1–4, 1981; Maty (Mother), Lvov, opera, 1985; Chamber Concerto No. 5, 1997; Epitaph No. 1, No. 2, No. 3, 1998; Sonata for piano No. 3, 1999. *Honours:* Zyatoshinsky Prize, 1997. *Address:* c/o Music Information of the Composers Union of the Ukraine, Ul Sofiuska 16/16, 252001 Kiev 1, Ukraine.

ZAIDEL, Nahum; Musician and Conductor; b. 20 Sept. 1933, Russia; m. 30 Aug 1976. *Education:* Graduated as Orchestra Soloist, Chamber Music Performer, and Teacher, P I Tchaikovsky State Conservatoire, Moscow, 1957; Studied conducting with Igor Markevitch and Genady Rozhdestvensky, 1963–66. *Career:* Solo Flautist, Moscow Chamber Orchestra under Rudolf Barschai, 1957–58, Moscow Radio Symphony Orchestra under Rozhdestvensky, 1959–72, and Jerusalem Symphony Orchestra, Israel, 1972–; Professor, Rubin Music Academy, Jerusalem, 1972–; Masterclasses for flute and appearances as guest conductor. *Recordings:* Works by Handel, Bach, Beethoven, Gluck, Hindemith, Prokofiev, Doppler, Vivaldi, Stamitz, Cimarosa, Salieri, Chaminade, Bloch, Dvořák, Stravinsky and Kurt Weill, for record and radio. *Honours:* 1st Prize for Flute, International Competition in Moscow, 1957. *Address:* Haviv Avshalom 4-7, Jerusalem 93802, Israel.

ZAJICK, Dolora; Singer (Mezzo-Soprano); b. 24 March 1952, Salem, Oregon, USA. *Education:* Studied at the University of Nevada with Ted Puffer and at the Manhattan School of Music with Helen Vanni and Lou Galtiero; Further study with Donald Hall. *Career:* Debut: San Francisco Opera in 1986 as Azucena; Metropolitan Opera debut in 1988 as Azucena; Season 1988–89 with further debuts at Lyric Opera of Chicago, Vienna Staatsoper, Rome's Caracalla Festival and the Verona Arena; Sang Rossini's Stabat Mater at the Cincinnati May Festival and Mahler's 8th Symphony at Washington DC under Rostropovich, Verdi's Requiem at Carnegie Hall and in Paris and London, Mahler's 2nd Symphony in Paris under Lorin Maazel; Season 1989–90 as Amneris and Azucena at the Metropolitan, Tchaikovsky's Maid of Orleans at Carnegie Hall, Il Trovatore in Toulouse and Florence, Aida in Reno, the Verona Arena and at the Caracalla Festival, as Marfa in Khovanshchina at San Francisco Opera, 1990, Eboli in Don Carlo at the Metropolitan, La Scala and in Reno, 1990; Sang Principessa in Adriana Lecouvreur at San Carlo, Naples, 1992, and Jezibaba in Rusalka at the Metropolitan in 1993; Other opera houses include Barcelona, Houston, Florence, Orange Festival, and Covent Garden with debut in 1994; Sang Amneris at the Verona Arena, 1996; Sang in Cav and Pag double bill, Met 1997; Paris Opéra Bastille debut 1998 as Eboli; Season 2000–01 as Azucena at the Met; Etoli at the Munich and Vienna State Opera and Verdi Requiem in Munich. *Recordings include:* La Forza del Destino and Verdi Requiem under Muti; Aida; Il Trovatore, 1991; Don Carlo, under Levine; Alexander Nevsky, under Rostropovich. *Honours:* Bronze Medal, Tchaikovsky International Competition, Moscow, 1982. *Address:* Edgar Vincent-Patrick Farrell Associates, 157 West 57th Street, Suite 502, New York, NY 10019, USA.

ZAK, Jerzy, MA, ARCM; Polish musician, musicologist and specialist in historical plucked instruments, lute and guitar; b. 31 March 1954, Łódź. *Education:* Higher School of Music, Łódź, Conservatorio Superior de Musica, Alicante, Early Music Centre, London. *Career:* chamber musician and basso continuo player on lute, theorbo and guitar; chamber concerts, recitals and participation or directing opera performances in Poland, several European countries and in Canada; Several broadcasts on Polish radio, and television appearances, 1980–; Assistant, Academy of Music, Łódź, 1983–; Lecturer, Academy of Music, Kraków, 1993–, taught at international summer courses in Wilanów, Poland (Early Music), 1993–94, and in Szczawno Zdrój, Poland (guitar), 1992–99; Artistic Director, Days of Guitar Music, International Festival, Łódź, 1984, 1986; Consultant, Akademie Weiss-Institute for Lute Studies, Parc de Schoppenwihr, France, 1992–; founder and Director of the Kleine Kammer-Musik ensemble, 1993–; researcher, chamber music with plucked instruments. *Recordings include:* A. Scarlatti, San Casimiro, Re di Polonia, oratorio (Direction); A. Cesti, Chamber Sonatas (Continuo and direction); Jacob Polak, Complete Works (Lute solo). *Address:* Pustola 32A m 6, 01-107 Warsaw, Poland.

ZAKAI, Mira; Singer (Contralto); b. 1942, Jerusalem. *Education:* Studied in Tel-Aviv with Jennie Tourel. *Career:* Debut: Vienna in 1976 with Mahler's Rückert Lieder; Further concerts with the Philharmonia Orchestra, Berlin Philharmonic (Mahler No. 2 under Abbado), in New York (Bach B minor Mass), and throughout Germany (Das Lied von der Erde and Mahler No. 3, 1987); Sang with Israel National Opera from 1990 in The Medium and Hansel and Gretel; Sang at Bonn in 1992 in Beethoven's Ninth; Opera includes Gluck's Orpheus with Scottish Opera, and Anne in Les Troyens with Opéra de Lyon; Has also sing with the following conductors: Guillini, Leinsdorf, Kubelik, Mehta, the premiere of Berio's orchestrations for Mhler Songs under Berio, Andrew Davis, Bertini, Menuhin in a concert for Pope John Paul in Castel Gandolfo, Rome, Zedda, Rizzi, Groves etc.; Collaborations with pianists including: Mikael Eliasen, Graham Johnson, Cristian Ivaldi, Andras Schiff and others; Professor at the Tel Aviv Rubin Academy of Music, part of the Tel Aviv University, teaching voice and heading the Lied and Oratorio Department. *Recordings include:* Mahler 2nd Symphony with the Chicago Symphony Orchestra and George Solti. *Honours:* Grammy Award for recording of Mahler's 2nd Symphony with the Chicago Symphony Orchestra and Sir George Solti; Special Prize for contribu-

tion to Israeli Music given by the ministry of education; BA Hebrew Literature and Theatre Arts from Tel Aviv University; BMus and MMus in singing from Tel Aviv University. *Address:* 6 Patai St. Givatayim 53203 Israel. *E-mail:* mzakai@post.tau.ac.il.

ZALEWSKI, Wlodzimerz; Singer (Bass-Baritone); b. 1949, Poland. *Career:* Sang at the Łódź Opera, 1975–82 and Gelsenkirchen from 1982; Bregenz Festival in 1978 as the Dutchman, and Philadelphia in 1988 as Don Alfonso in Così fan tutte; Professor at the Łódź Music Academy from 1981; Sang in the 1989 premiere of Michael Kohlhaas by Karl Kogler at the Landestheater, Linz; Appearances at Łódź and elsewhere as Boris Godunov; Other roles have included Hindemith's Cardillac, Kaspar in Der Freischütz, Basilio, Mustafà, Wotan and Scarpia; Frequent concert appearances.

ZAMBELLI, Marco; Conductor; b. 1965, Genoa, Italy. *Education:* organ and composition, Geneva Conservatoire. *Career:* Chorus Master at the Grasse Boys Choir, 1988–89, Opéra de Lyon 1989–92 (including the premiere of Debussy's Rodrigue et Chimène); other repertory includes all major operas of Mozart, L'Elisir d'amore, La Bohème, Butterfly, Poppea, Orfeo and Il Trovatore; asst with such conductors as John Eliot Gardiner (Manon Lescaut at Glyndebourne and other repertory with Monteverdi/EBS), Luciano Berio and Woldemar Nelsson; Season 1996–97 with Pergolesi/Cimarosa double bill at Messina, La Cenerentola at Ascoli and Don Giovanni for Opera Zuid; Haydn's Creation in Cogliou, 1996; Madama Butterfly, 1996, and Don Pasquale and Rigoletto, 1997, at the Tenerife Opera Festival; Luisa Miller and Madama Butterfly for Opera North and Manon Lescaut at the 1997 Glyndebourne Festival; Così fan tutte.

ZAMBELLO, Francesca, BA; American opera producer and musical director; b. 24 Aug. 1956, New York. *Education:* American School of Paris, Colgate Univ. *Career:* Asst Dir Lyric Opera of Chicago 1981–82, San Francisco Opera 1983–84; Artistic Dir Skylight Music Theatre 1984–; guest producer San Francisco Opera, Teatro La Fenice, Savonlinna Festival, Houston Grand Opera, Nat. Opera of Iceland, Seattle Opera, San Diego Opera, Opera Theatre of St Louis, Rome Opera, Théâtre Municipal de Lausanne, Teatro Regio, Greater Miami Opera, Pesaro Festival, Parma and Wexford Festival. *Works directed include:* La Traviata (San Francisco Opera) 1983, La Voix Humaine (San Francisco Opera) 1986, Faust (San Francisco Opera) 1986, La Bohème (San Francisco Opera) 1988, Lucia di Lammermoor (New York Metropolitan Opera) 1992, Arianna (Royal Opera House, Covent Garden) 1994–95, Billy Budd (Royal Opera House, Covent Garden, Opéra Bastille) 1995–96, Khovanshchina (ENO) 1995–96, Tannhäuser (Copenhagen) 1995–96, Modern Painters (Santa Fe Opera) 1995–96, Prince Igor (San Francisco Opera) 1996, Lady in the Dark (Nat. Theatre, London) 1997, Iphigènie en Tauride (Glimmerglass Festival) 1997, Salammbô (Opéra Bastille) 1998, Tristan (Seattle) 1998, Napoleon (Shaftesbury Theatre, London) 2000, The Bartered Bride (Royal Opera House, Covent Garden) 2001, Don Giovanni (Royal Opera House, Covent Garden) 2002, Guillaume Tell (Opéra Bastille) 2003. *Honours:* several Olivier Awards, Nat. Opera Inst. grant. *Current Management:* Columbia Artists, 165 W 57th Street, New York, NY 10019, USA.

ZAMBORSKY, Stanislav; Pianist; b. 12 April 1946, Kosice; m. Zlata Olachova, 8 July 1972, 2 d. *Education:* Konservatorium Kosice; Academy of Music and Dramatic Arts, Bratislava; Franz Liszt Academy, Budapest; Doctor Degree, Academy of Arts, Bratislava. *Career:* Debut: Bratislava Music Festival; Many Concerts with Orchestra and Recitals in Netherlands, France, Bulgaria, Poland, Soviet Union, Germany, Italy, Sweden, Spain, Belgium, Kuwait, Cuba, Korea, Jerusalem. *Recordings:* Mozart, Haydn Concertos; Schumann, Sonata G minor; Liszt, Liebersträume, Au bord d'une source, Death of Isolde; Hummel Works for 4 hands piano; Sixta Piano Sonata; Bokes Piano concerto; Parik Dropping Foliage Songs, Hrusovsky Sonata No. 2; Mozart Piano Sonatas; Grieg Piano Concerto. *Honours:* 2nd Prize, Prague, 1968; 4th Prize, Utrecht, 1969; Frico Kafenda Prize, Excellent Interpretation, Slovak Music, Bratislava, 1995; Complete Musical Critic Prix, Bratislava, 1996. *Address:* Bieloruska 52, 821 06 Bratislava, Slovakia.

ZAMIR; singer (high tenor); b. 1953, USA. *Education:* Univ. of Massachusetts at Amherst, Univ. of Maine at Portland-Gorham, Chicago and San Francisco Conservatories of Music. *Career:* has appeared since 1985 in major cities of Israel, USA, Iceland, Germany, England and Cyprus in wide range of concert and operatic music; Conductors include Marc Minkowski, Christopher Hogwood, Nicholas McGegan, and Richard Westenberg; Has performed as Male Soprano, Countertenor and Baritone as well as Tenor, specializing as high tenor, Tenore di Grazia; Has sung in Die Fledermaus in 1977, Cendrillon in 1986, A Midsummer Night's Dream in 1987, La Bohème in 1988, Lucia di Lammermoor, Mefistofele, Attila, Platée and Cavalleria Rusticana in 1988, La Clemenza di Tito and Alcina in 1990, and Riccardo Primo with the English Bach Festival at Covent Garden in 1991.

ZAMPARINO, Cesare; Singer (Tenor); b. 1969, Italy. *Career:* Sang Alfredo in Traviata at Rieti (1992) followed by the Duke of Mantua at Buenos Aires; Teatro San Carlo Naples from 1993, as Alfredo and as Alfred in Fledermaus; other repertory includes Rodolfo, Nemorino, Elvino (La Sonnambula), Edgardo, Ernesto and Cavaradossi. *Address:* c/o Atholl Still Ltd, Foresters Hall, 25–27 Westow Street, London SE19 3RY, England.

ZAMPIERI, Maria; Singer (Soprano); b. 24 May 1941, Padua, Italy. *Education:* Studied at the Padua Conservatory. *Career:* Debut: Pavia in 1972; La Scala Milan from 1977 as Amalia in I Masnadieri, Leonora in Il Trovatore and Elisabeth de Valois; Trieste as Elvira in Ernani; Lisbon as Amelia Boccanegra; Vienna Staatsoper from 1979 in Il Giuramento, Attila and Macbeth; Deutsche Oper Berlin and Verona Arena as Aida; Covent Garden debut in 1984 as Tosca; Other engagements in Munich, Buenos Aires, San Francisco, Bregenz, Bonn and Frankfurt; Sang Francesca da Rimini at Karlsruhe in 1986; Season 1987–88 as Norma at Nîmes and Lady Macbeth at Spoleto; Stuttgart Staatsoper in 1990 as Tosca, Bregenz Festival in 1990 in the title role of La Wally; Debut as Salome at Vienna, 1991; Sang Suor Angelica at Zürich, 1996; Verdi's Elena and Lady Macbeth at the Vienna Staatsoper, 1999. *Recordings include:* Il Giuramento; Attila; Belisario by Donizetti; Macbeth. *Address:* Allied Artists, 42 Montpelier Square, London SW7 1JZ, England.

ZAMUSZKO, Slawomir; Composer, Viola Player and Teacher of Music Theory; b. 30 Dec. 1973, Łódź, Poland. *Education:* H. Wieniawski State Music Lyceum, Łódź, Poland, 1986–92; Graduated in Viola and in Composition with Distinction, The Academy of Music, Lódz, 1992–99; Postgraduate Composition studies with Professor Marian Borkowski, F. Chopin Academy of Music, Warsaw, Poland, 2000–. *Career:* Debut: As composer, Stage Music for David Mercer's Flint, with flute, horn, trombone, strings and synthesizer, 'Stake' Theatre Studio, Lódz, 1993; Viola player with Strings of Lódz Chamber Orchestra, 1990–93; Polish Camerata Orchestra, 1993–94; 1st and Solo Violist, Young Austrian Philharmony, 1996–99; Contribution to Justus Frantz's Philharmony of Nations, 1998; mem, Candidate member, Polish Composers' Society. *Compositions include:* Instrumental and vocal instrumental: Suite for viola solo, 1995; Sonatina for percussion quartet, 1995; Controversies, an instrumental theatre for 2 flutes, 1996; 46–Tema con Variazioni for flute, oboe, clarinet and bassoon, 1996; 4 a.m., for trumpet solo, 1996; Portal 1 for horn and piano, 1996; Kaja Got Wet, for voice or 1-voiced children's choir and piano (text by Joanna Kulmowa), 1998; Concerto for clarinet and string orchestra, 1998; An die unsterbliche Geliebte, cantata (after Beethoven) for baritone and orchestra, 1998; Portal 2 for viola, cello and orchestra, 1999; Preludes for piano, 2000; Requiem (text by Anna Akhmatova) for alto and string quartet, 2000; Allegro con brio for string quartet, 2000; Re-percussions, for 2 trumpets and 2 percussion groups, 2001; Permeatings, for string orchestra, 2001; Vocal: A Head Grows Up, song for 4-voiced male choir a capella (text by Jan Kochanski), 1999; Lingvariations on theme of John Cage, for speaking voice, 2001; Electronic: Babel FM for tape, 1997; Play-tin for tape, 1997; Controversies 2 for flute and tape, 1999; Other: Music for the spectacles of 'Stake' Theatre Studio in Lódz and pictures realised by students of Film/Television Directing and Cinematography Departments of Leon Schiller Polish National Film, Television and Theatre School in Lódz. *Recordings:* Portal 1 for horn and piano, 2000. *Contributions:* Muzyka 21, 2000–, Koneser, 2001–. *Honours:* Scholarship, Ministry of Culture and Arts, 1997–98; 1st Prize International Composers' Competition, Cottbus, Germany, 2000. *Address:* Piotrkowska 204/210 m 106, 90-369 Łódź, Poland. *E-mail:* zamek@mnc.pl. *Website:* www.mnc.pl/~zamek/zamek.htm#utwory.

ZANABONI, Giuseppe, DipMus; Italian organist, conductor and composer; b. 25 Nov. 1926, Pontelagoscuro; m. Clelia Losi 1951; one s. one d. (deceased). *Career:* debut 1945; major solo organ concerts world-wide; masterclasses in Europe and America; chamber and symphonic orchestra conductor, Italy; Dir of State Music Conservatorium, Piacenza 1968–93; Artistic Dir, V. L. Ciampi instrumental group for diffusion of ancient music; founder and Dir, Group V. Legrenzio Ciampi chamber music ensemble, Piacenza. *Compositions include:* Lyric Opera: Alcesti, 1949; Myrica, 1949; La Regina delle Nevi, 1953; Casello 83, 1956; De Placentiae Synodo, 1995–96; Cantatas: Apoteosi di S Giovanni B de la Salle, 1950; Cantata a Roma; I Bambini di Terezin, 1991; Chamber Music: Quartetto in Do for strings, 1949; Improvviso Drammatico, 1953; Meditazione for strings and organ, 1968; Luna Park, 1968; Quatuor for strings, 1988; Con Pincchio nel Regno della Fantasia, 1990; Menhir studio, 1992; Immagini e Suoni, 1993; Fantasia in Epidiapente, 1993; Tiphyscolon, impressioni sinfoniche su Cristoro Colombo, 1992; Choral Music: Missa Laudate Pueri Dominum, 1941; Requiem Aeternam, 1943; Missa Domine Non Sum Dignus, 1944; Esaltazione del Volto di S Corrado, 1994; La Fravezzosa, carme madricalis, 1984; For Organ: Toccata, 1966; Profilo di un Organo, 2nd suite, 1988; Musiche Nuove per un Organo Antico, 1985. *Recordings:* 10 albums of organ music in series,

Antichi Organi Italiani, and instrumental music. *Publications:* Ciampi, 30 anni di musica a Piacenza, 1987. *Address:* Via Giulio Alberoni 33, 29100 Piacenza, Italy.

ZANASI, Mario; Singer (Baritone); b. 8 Jan. 1927, Bologna, Italy. *Education:* Studied at the Conservatorio Martini, Bologna; La Scala Opera School. *Career:* Debut: Cesena in 1954 in Lohengrin; Sang widely in Italy and at opera houses in Portugal, France, Belgium and Germany; Metropolitan Opera from 1958 as Sharpless in Butterfly, Escamillo, Marcello in La Bohème, Amonasro and Enrico in Lucia di Lammermoor; Sang at Covent Garden in 1958 and Verona Arena, 1957–72; Further appearances in Paris, Vienna, Chicago, Dallas, Miami, San Francisco and Munich. *Recordings:* Giulietta e Romeo by Zandonai; Madame Sans-Gêne by Giordano; Madama Butterfly; Maria di Rohan by Donizetti.

ZANAZZO, Alfredo; Singer (Bass); b. 14 Oct. 1946, Imperia, Italy. *Education:* Studied with Tancredi Pasero. *Career:* Debut: Verona Arena in 1981 as the King in Aida; Verona Arena, 1982–89, as Ramphis and Timur; Sang Wagner's Dutchman at Treviso in 1981, La Scala Milan in 1982 as Narbal in Les Troyens, and the King of Scotland in Ariodante; Season 1986–87 as Colline in La Bohème at the Paris Opéra, Padre Guardiano at Rome, Zaccaria and Masetto at Turin and Ramphis at the Metropolitan; Appearances at Luxor and the Vienna Staatsoper as Ramphis, Macerata Festival as Raimondo in Lucia di Lammermoor; Zürich Opera in 1988 as Banquo and Walter Furst in Guillaume Tell; Further engagements at the Geneva Opera as Pluto in Monteverdi's Orfeo, at Frankfurt as Raimondo, in Toronto as Procida in Les Vêpres Siciliennes and at Las Palmas as Alvise in La Gioconda; Teatro Margherita Genoa in 1991 as Roucher in La Gioconda; Sang Pagano in I Lombardi at Piacenza, 1995. *Address:* c/o Opernhaus Zürich, Falkenstrasse 1, 8008 Zürich, Switzerland.

ZANCANARO, Giorgio; Singer (Baritone); b. 9 May 1939, Verona, Italy. *Career:* Debut: Teatro Nuovo Milan in I Puritani; Sang widely in Italy from 1971; International career from 1977, notably in London, Frankfurt, Rome, Hamburg, Paris and Zürich; Milan La Scala debut in 1981 as Ford in Falstaff; Metropolitan Opera debut in 1982 as Renato in Un Ballo in Maschera; Macerata Festival in 1983 as Posa in Don Carlos; Florence, 1984–85 as Germont and Posa; Covent Garden in 1985 as Gerard in Andrea Chénier; Other roles include Verdi's Rigoletto, Luna and Ezio in Attila, Escamillo, Tonio in Pagliacci and Albert in Werther; Hamburg and La Scala in 1988 as Count Luna and Guillaume Tell; Sang Ezio in Attila at Covent Garden in 1990, and in Donizetti's Parisina d'Este in Florence in 1990; Sang Michele in Il Tabarro at Zürich, 1996 and Nabucco there in 1998; Season 1999–2000 as Verdi's Renato in Venice and the High Priest in Samson et Dalila for Zürich Opera. *Recordings include:* Il Trovatore, conducted by Giulini; Andrea Chenier (G. Patane); La Traviata (Kleiber); La Forza del Destino, Rigoletto, Guillaume Tell, Attila, I Vespri Siciliani and Tosca all with Muti. *Address:* c/o Theateragentur Luisa Petrov Glauburgstr. 95. D–60318 Frankfurt am Main, Germany.

ZANDER, Benjamin; Conductor; b. 1943, England. *Education:* studied with Benjamin Britten and Imogen Holst at Aldeburgh, at Florence with cellist Gaspar Cassado, at the Academica Chigiana in Siena, the State Conservatory Cologne and London Univ.; graduate work at Harvard and in New York. *Career:* faculty mem., New England Conservatory 1968–85, conducting the Youth Philharmonic Orchestra and the Conservatory's Symphony Orchestra; ten international tours with the Youth Philharmonic Orchestra, including South America, 1995; Artistic Dir, New England Conservatory at Walnut Hill School, 1986–; guest conductor with American orchestras and in the Far East, Russia, Italy, Germany and Israel; founding Dir of the Boston Philharmonic, leading it in many concerts; debut with the London Philharmonic Orchestra, 1995, with Mahler's Sixth, returning for the Ninth Symphony. *Recordings include:* Mahler's Sixth Symphony, Beethoven's Ninth and The Rite of Spring, with the Boston Philharmonic Orchestra. *Address:* c/o Boston Philharmonic Orchestra, 295 Huntingdon Avenue, Suite 210, Boston, MA 02115–4433, USA.

ZANETTOVICH, Renato; Violinist; b. 28 July 1921, Trieste, Italy; m. Bianca Negri, 28 June 1947, 3 s. *Education:* Violin Diploma. *Career:* Debut: With the Trio Di Trieste in 1933; Concerts and records with Trio Di Trieste world-wide; Violin Teacher at Conservatories of Bolzano, 1950–55, Trieste, 1955–70 and Venice, 1970–86; mem, Rotary Club, Trieste. *Recordings:* Numerous recordings for major record companies. *Publications:* Revision of Etudes by Kayser Op 20, Mazas Op 36, Dont Op 37, Sitt Op 32; Scale and Arpeggio Exercises, 5 books. *Honours:* Accademico di S Cecilia; Grande Ufficiale dell'Ordine Al Merito della Repubblica Italiana; He is now teaching at Accademía Musicale Chigiana in Siena and at Scuola Superiore Internazinale di Musica da Camera del Trio di Trieste in Duino. *Address:* Via Catraro 9, Trieste, Italy.

ZANNINI, Laura; Singer (Mezzo-Soprano); b. 4 April 1937, Trieste, Italy. *Education:* Studied at the Conservatorio Benedetto Marcello in Venice, with Gilda dalla Rizza, and with Bruno Maderna. *Career:* Debut: Spoleto in 1955 as Isabella in L'Italiana in Algeri; Sang leading roles at La Scala Milan, Genoa, Palermo, Naples, Parma, Venice, Turin and Trieste; Sang at Verona Arena in 1957, 1967, 1979–80, 1986, and Piccola Scala in 1966 in the premiere of Flavio Testi's Albergi dei Poveri; Further appearances at the Maggio Musicale Fiorentino, the State Operas of Vienna and Munich, the Paris Opéra, Brussels, Bordeaux, Wiesbaden, Copenhagen, London, Edinburgh, Moscow and Budapest; Sang Alisa in Lucia di Lammermoor at Bari and Tisbe in La Cenerentola at Glyndebourne, 1983; Also sang in operas by Henze, Britten, Menotti, Poulenc, Stravinsky, Schoenberg and Zandonai; Sang Caterina in L'Amico Fritz at Livorno, 1996. *Recordings:* Tisbe in La Cenerentola; Flora in La Traviata with Callas; Mascagni's Isabeau.

ZANOLLI, Silvana; Singer (Soprano); b. 14 Oct. 1928, Fiume, Italy; m. Otello Borgonova. *Education:* Studied at the Milan Opera School and with Luciano Tomerilli and Tomaso Japelli. *Career:* Debut: La Scala Milan in 1951 in La Buona Figliuola, by Piccinni; Appearances in leading roles at Rome, Palermo, Bologna, Parma, Turin, Trieste, Naples and Venice; Festival engagements at Florence and Rome with guest showings at Buenos Aires, the State Operas of Vienna, Stuttgart and Munich, at Brussels, Cologne, Rio de Janeiro, Geneva, Barcelona, Lisbon and London Covent Garden; Verona Arena, 1957–58 and Glyndebourne, 1959–60 as Clorinda in La Cenerentola; Also sang in Mexico City, Monte Carlo and New York at Metropolitan Opera. *Recordings:* Amelia al Ballo by Menotti; Cimarosa's Il Matrimonio Segreto; Il Campiello by Wolf-Ferrari.

ZANOTELLI, Hans; Conductor; b. 1927, Wuppertal, Germany; m. Ingeborg Schlosser. *Education:* Student in Cologne. *Career:* Choirmaster, Solingen, 1945; Conductor, Wuppertal in 1950, Düsseldorf, 1951–54, Bonn, 1954–55, Hamburg State Opera, 1955–57; General Music Director, Darmstadt, 1957–63, Augsburg, 1963–72; Chief Conductor, Stuttgart Philharmonic Orchestra, 1971–; Guest Conductor, Dresden Staatskapelle, 1964–67, Bavarian State Opera, 1968–71; Wurttemberg State Opera; Tours of many European countries; Conducted Der Rosenkavalier at Dresden for 300th anniversary and Verdi's Requiem at Dresden for anniversary of destruction of city in World War II. *Recordings:* Many. *Address:* Stuttgarter Philharmoniker, Leonhardplatz 28, 7000 Stuttgart, Germany.

ZAROU, Jeannette; Singer (Soprano); b. 1942, Ramallah, Palestine. *Education:* Studied at The Royal Conservatory of Music in Toronto with Irene Jessner, Halina Wyszkowski and Herman Geiger-Torel. *Career:* Debut: Priestess in Aida with Canadian Opera at Toronto, 1964; Sang Liu in Turandot for Canadian Opera in 1965; Member of the Deutsche Oper am Rhein, Düsseldorf, from 1967; Guest appearances in Toronto, Deutsche Oper Berlin, Hamburg and Munich State Opera, Cologne, Frankfurt, Karlsruhe, Nuremberg, Bordeaux and Rouen; Other roles have included Mimi, Marguerite, Ilia in Idomeneo, Pamina, and Sophie in Rosenkavalier; Modern repertoire has included Miss Wordsworth in Albert Herring and Blanche in Dialogues des Carmélites; Many concert appearances. *Recordings include:* Requiem by Draeske.

ZARTNER, Rose Marie; Pianist; b. 14 Sept. 1939, Nuremberg, Germany; m. Wolfgang Schwabe, 1 s., 1 d. *Education:* Studied in Nuremberg with Ernst Gröschel, Frankfurt am Main with Brauka Musulin; Concert Examen, Cologne, with Bruno Seidlhofer. *Career:* Many solo concert engagements and tours, in Germany and abroad; Numerous appearances as lieder accompanist in chamber engagements; Performed at recitals at Beethoven and Reger festivals, Bonn, Palais Schaumburg, German Federal Chancellery, Minsk and Bucharest; Concerts with Berlin Philharmonie, in Vienna, Salzburg, Nuremberg, Mannheim; Schwetzingen Musik Festival and Haydn Festival in Burgenland; Concerts with numerous orchestras including Bamberg and Nuremberg Symphonies, Symphony Orchestra of Romania, Orchester of Beethovenhalle and Classical Philharmonie, Bonn; Extensive classic repertory including works of Haydn and Mozart, also modern and unknown works; Numerous radio performances at home and in Europe; Many works dedicated to her; As member of Bonn Ensemble, appearances at International Music Days in Bonn and at Royal Danish Opera, Copenhagen, and in Seoul; Docent, Music School, Bonn and private tuition. *Recordings:* Works of Schumann, Haydn, Schubert, Dittersdorf, Reger. *Honours:* Cultural Prize, Sudetendeutsche Landsmannschaft, 1975; Grand Cultural Prize, 1997. *Address:* Im Ringelsacker 49, 53123 Bonn, Germany.

ZARZO, Jose; French Horn Player; b. 6 Aug. 1966, Mexico City; m. Mari Carmen Lobeira, 23 Aug 1992, 1 s., 1 d. *Education:* Started music lessons at 7, Solfège, with father, Vicente; At 10 horn lessons with Vicente; Studied at Royal Conservatory of the Hague, Netherlands with Professor Vicente Zarzo; Attended Masterclasses with Professor Radovan Vlatkovic and Professor Dale Clevenger. *Career:* Debut:

Orlando Festival, with Orlando String Quartet, Heinz Holliger, 1983; Appeared on Dutch Television with Punto's Horn Concerto No. 5; Has performed with almost all Dutch symphony orchestras, 1989–; Principal Horn, Gran Canaria Philharmonic Orchestra, performing solo and recording major symphony repertoire; Tours of major cities in Austria, Switzerland, Germany; Founding Member of Chamber Music Group, Ensemble Isola, with principals from Gran Canaria Philharmonic Orchestra and pianist Juan Francisco Parra; mem, International Horn Society. *Recordings:* Virtuoso Bläsermusik; Gustav Mahler's Symphony No. 5; Gustav Mahler's Symphony No. 4 with Gran Canaria Philharmonic Orchestra, Adrian Leaper, Conductor. Choros of Villa Lobos. *Address:* Montana de Humiaga 30, 35411 Arucas, Spain.

ZAWADZKA, Barbara; Composer; b. 21 Sept. 1951, Warsaw, Poland. *Education:* MA, Academy of Music in Kraków; Studied composition with Krzysztof Penderecki; French Government Scholarship to CNSM to study composition, theory and analysis with Guy Riebel, 1983–85; Studied composition and electro-acoustic and computer music at IRCAM, Paris, 1989. *Career:* Debut: Sixth International Wettgewerb–GEDOK, Mannheim, Germany, 1976; Lecturer at Kraków Music Academy since 1980; Has participated at the major music festivals in Poland, France, Germany, Norway, Switzerland and Hong Kong, 1988–; ISCM World Music Days. *Compositions:* Greya for tape; Monodrama for violin; Esperanza for tape; '4+1' quintet for oboe, cor anglais, clarinet, bass clarinet and piano; Sources for tape, 80 projectors and percussion; Games for clarinet, saxophone, cello, percussion and tape; Stabat Mater for choir; Locus Solus for piano; Motif of Space for strings. *Recordings include:* cassette, 1990; CD, 2000. *Publications:* Ruch Muzyczny, 1988; Ars Electronica, 1988; Boswil, 1988. *Address:* Academy of Music, Tomasza 43, 31-027 Kraków, Poland. *E-mail:* zbzawadz@cyf-kr.edu.pl.

ZAWADZKA-GOLOSZ, Anna; Composer; b. 1 Dec. 1955, Kraków, Poland; m. Jerry Golosz, 6 July 1986. *Education:* Diploma in Theory of Music, Academy of Music, Kraków, 1981; Studies in composition at the Academy of Music, Kraków under Krystyna Moszumanska-Nazar; Diploma, Academy of Music, Kraków and at the Hochschule für Musik, Theater und Tanz in Essen under Wolfgang Hufschmidt. *Career:* Teacher of Theory of Music, 1981–; Assistant at Academy of Music in Kraków; Performances in Poland and abroad including Warsaw Autumn–International Festival of Contemporary Music, 1986; mem, Polish Section of ISCM. *Compositions:* A Duo for Double Bass and Tape, 1980; Esoterikos for Soprano and Oboe Quartet, 1984; Senza for Double Bass, 1984; Girare for Percussion and Tape, 1986; Obraz w Pieciu Ujeciach (The Picture In Five Aspects), 1987; Vitrail ll for Clarinet, Cello, Accordion and Vibraphone, 1988. *Address:* ul Basztowa 5-28, 31-134 Kraków, Poland.

ZAZOFSKY, Peter; Concert Violinist; b. 1955, Boston, USA. *Education:* Studied with Joseph Silverstein, Dorothy DeLay and Ivan Galamian and at the Curtis Institute of Music. *Career:* Frequent appearances from 1977 with such orchestras as the Berlin and Rotterdam Philharmonics, the Vienna Symphony and the Amsterdam Concertgebouw Orchestra; North American engagements at Atlanta, Baltimore, Boston, Minnesota, Montreal, Philadelphia, San Francisco, Toronto and Vancouver; Tour of the USA with the Danish Radio Orchestra and recitals at the Kennedy Center and New York's Carnegie Hall; Further concerts in Israel and throughout Europe with such conductors as Dutoit, Zinman, Ormandy, Tennstedt and Ozawa; 1978 recital tour of South America; Season 1995–96 with concertos by Bart ók and Mendelssohn in Germany and Belgium; Also plays Nielsen and Bernstein (Serenade). *Honours:* Prizewinner at the 1977 Wieniawski Competition, 1978 Montreal International and 1980 Queen Elisabeth of the Belgians Competition, Brussels; Avery Fisher Career Grant, 1985. *Address:* c/o Künstler Sekretariat am Gasteig, Rosenheimerstr 52, 81669 Munich, Germany.

ZAZZO, Lawrence; Singer (Counter-tenor); b. 1970, Philadelphia, USA. *Education:* King's College, Cambridge, and Royal College of Music, with David Lowe. *Career:* Concerts include Bach Cantatas at the 1997 Lufthansa Festival, London, Vivaldi Nisi Dominus and Handel's Messiah with the Israel Camerata, Season 1996–97; Opera debut as Oberon in A Midsummer Night's Dream at the RAM, London, 1996; Title role in Handel's Arminio and Alessandro Severo for the London Handel Festival, Bacco in Goehr's Arianna at Cambridge, 1996; Athamas in Semele at Santa Fe Opera; 1998 season included Unulfo in Rodelinda at the Karlsruhe Handel Festival and with the Glyndebourne Touring Opera, title role in Cavalli's Giasone at the Spoleto Festival in Charleston, South Carolina. *Recordings include:* Purcell's Jubilate, Britten's Rejoice in the Lamb, Bernstein's Chichester Psalms and Pergolesi's Stabat Mater. *Address:* c/o Portland Wallis, 50 Great Portland Street, London W1N 5AH, England.

ZEANI, Virginia; Singer (Soprano); b. 21 Oct. 1925, Solovastru, Romania; m. Nicola Rossi-Lemeni, 1957 (deceased 1991). *Education:* Studied in Bucharest with Lucia Angel and Lydia Lipkovska, and with

Aureliano Pertile in Milan. *Career:* Debut: Bologna, 1948, as Violetta; London debut, Stoll Theatre, 1953, as Violetta; La Scala, 1956, as Cleopatra in Giulio Cesare; Sang Blanche in premiere of Dialogues des Carmélites, 1957; Vienna and Paris debuts, 1957; Verona Arena, 1956–63; Took part in revivals of Donizetti's Maria di Rohan (Naples 1965), Rossini's Otello (Rome 1968), Verdi's Alzira (Rome 1970); Further appearances at Covent Garden, 1959, Metropolitan, 1966, and Budapest, Bucharest, Mexico City, Rio de Janeiro, Zürich, Amsterdam, Belgrade, Moscow, Madrid; Other roles included Aida, Desdemona, Tosca, Manon and Manon Lescaut, Lucia di Lammermoor, Elvira (I Puritani), Magda Sorel in The Consul (Menotti); Further engagements, Barcelona, Lisbon, Leningrad, Houston, Philadelphia, Berlin and New Orleans, 1966; Sang at Barcelona, 1977–78, as Giordano's Fedora; Sang 67 roles, 648 times Traviata around the world; Professor of Voice, 1980–, Distinguished Professor, 1994–, Emeritus Professor, 1995–, Indiana University School of Music, USA; mem, Accademia Tiberina-Roma; Commendatore of Italian Republic; Soroptimist Club of Rome. *Recordings:* La Traviata; Rossini's Otello; Elisa e Claudio by Mercadante; Rossini's Zelmira; Alzira; La Serva Padrona. *Honours:* 34 awards including: Gold Medal, Egypt, 1951; Gold Medal, Barcelona, 1963; Maschera d'Argento, 1965–70; Arena d'Oro, 1966; Diapason d'Oro, 1968; Viotti D'Oro, 1999; Una Vita per la Lirica, San Remo, 1999. *Address:* 2701 Robins Bow, Bloomington, IN 47401, USA.

ZEAVIN, Carol; Violinist; b. 2 May 1948, San Bernardino, California, USA. *Education:* Studied in New York. *Career:* Co-Founder of Columbia String Quartet, 1977, initially called Schoenberg String Quartet; Many performances in the standard and modern repertory, including the premieres of Wuorinen's Archangel and Second Quartet, 1978, 1980, Roussaki's Ephemeris, 1979, and quartets by Morton Feldman, 1980, Wayne Peterson, 1984, and Larry Bell, 1985; In 1979 at Abraham Goodman House, New York, played in the premiere of Berg's Lyric Suite with recently discovered vocal finale. *Recordings include:* String Quartet No. 3 by Lukas Foss and Ned Rorem's Mourning Song.

ZEBINGER, Franz; Composer, Harpsichordist and Organist; b. 29 April 1946, Styria; m. 2 s., 1 d. *Education:* Musikhochschule Graz, Organ, Harpsichord; University of Graz, Archaeology; Linguistics. *Career:* Harpsichord and organist with Gamerith Consort; Ljubljana Barocni Trio; Ramovs Consort; Concilium Musicum; Many recordings for the radio, television; Concerts as a soloist, organ and forte piano; mem, Steirischer Tonkünstlerbund; President, Komponisten und Interpreten Burgenlands, 2000–. *Compositions:* Carmen Miserabile, 1988; Drachenkampf, 1995; Markuspassion, 1996; Heller als die Sonn, 1998; Dies Illa, 1999; Bruder Sonne, Schwester Hond, 2002. *Recordings:* Gamerith Consort, 1989; Dedications for Sax, 1993; Stay a Weill, 1994; Haydn Keyboard Trios, 1994; Spectaculars, 1997; Barré en Bloc, 1999; Haydn music for Forte Piano on original instruments, 2002; Franz Zebinger compositions, 2000. *Publications:* Ikonographie zum Musikleben der Etrusker, Dissertation, Graz, 1982. *Address:* 7423 Kroisegg Nr 25, Austria. *Telephone:* 0664 505 4805. *E-mail:* franz_zebinger@web.de. *Website:* www.kibu.at.

ZECCHILLO, Giuseppe; Singer (Baritone); b. 18 Dec. 1929, São Paulo, Brazil. *Education:* Studied at the Conservatorio Giuseppe Verdi at Milan and with Aureloano Pertile and Carlo Tagliabue. *Career:* Debut: Teatro Nuovo Milan in 1953 as Germont in La Traviata; Leading roles at La Scala, Rome, Bologna, Naples, Palermo, Parma, Turin, Trieste and Venice; Festival engagements at Caracalla, Verona, 1972–85, as Sharpless in Butterfly in 1983 and Florence, Maggio Musicale; Further appearances at the New York City Opera and in San Francisco and Monte Carlo; Distinguished in contemporary as well as standard repertory. *Recordings include:* Nina by Paisiello.

ZECHBERGER, Gunther; Composer and Conductor; b. 24 April 1951, Zams, Tyrol, Austria. *Education:* Studied at the Innsbruck Conservatory, 1968–74 and at University of Innsbruck with Witold Rowicki and Boguslaw Schaeffer. *Career:* Founder and Conductor of the Tyroler Ensemble für Neue Musik, 1984. *Compositions include:* Trio for Clarinet, Horn and Bassoon, 1973; Trio for Violins, 1975; Das Neue Preislied for Women's Chorus and Speaker, 1975; Schlus Stuck for Mixed Chorus and Orchestra, 1979; Mass for Mixed Chorus and Orchestra, 1979; Trombone Quartet, 1980; Stabat Mater for Mixed Chorus, 1981; Im Nebel for Mezzo and Orchestra, 1982; Study for 12 Strings, 1983; Hendekegon for 26 Instruments, 1984; Tieferschuttert for Mezzo, Trombone and Guitar, 1984; String Quartet, 1985; Chorus for 5 Musicians, 1985; Stabat Mater ll for Mezzo and Ensemble, 1985–88; Kammermusik for Conductor and 5 Musicians, 1986; Dear Mr J, 1987; Interview for Tape, 1987; Guitar Concerto, 1988; Duet for Guitars, 1988. *Address:* c/o AKM, III Baumanstrasse 8-10, Postfach 334-338, 1031 Vienna, Austria.

ZECHLIN, Ruth; Composer, Harpsichordist and Organist; b. 22 June 1926, Grosshartmannsdorf, Germany. *Education:* Studied composition with Johann Nepomuk David, organ with Karl Straube and Gunther

Ramin, 1943–49. *Career:* Lecturer in Music from 1950 and Professor of Composition from 1969 at the Berlin Musikhochschule; Member of the Akademie der Künste Berlin in 1970; mem, Akademie der Künste Berlin; Freie Akademi der Künste Mannheim. *Compositions include:* Reineke Fuchs, opera for actors, 1967; Ballet, La Vita, 1983; Opera Die Salamandrin und Die Bildsäule, 1989; Opera Die Reise, 1991; Orchestral: 2 Violin Concertos, 1963, 1990, 3 Symphonies, 1965, 1966, 1971, 19 Great Mixed Chamber Music, 1966–93, 2 Chamber Symphonies, 1967, 1973, Piano Concerto, 1974; 4 Organ Concertos, 1974, 1975, 1980, 1984; 2 Harpsichord Concertos, 1975, 1986, Briefe, 1978, Situationen, 1980, Musik für Orchester, 1980, Metamorphosen, 1982, Musik Zu Bach, 1983, Kristallisation, 1987, Stufen, 1993; Varianten zu Goethes Märchen for chamber orchestra, 1998; Triptychon 2000 for orchestra, 1999; Triptychon zu Angelus Suesius for soprano, flute, strings, 1999; Chamber: 7 String Quartets, 1959–95, Reflexionen for 14 Strings, 1979, Konstellationen for 10 Winds, 1985, Akzente Und Flächen for 5 Percussions, 1993, Circulations for 8 Percussions, 1994; 5 Studien and 1 collage for chamber ensemble, 1996; Musikalische Antworten auf J. S. Bach for flute and organ, 1999; Vocal: Lidice Kantante, 1958, Canzoni alla Notte for Baritone and Orchestra, 1974, Der Sieg Von Guernica for 4 Voices, 1975, Das Hohelied for Tenor and Orchestra, 1979, Das A Und Das O for Mezzo Solo, 1990; Geistliche Kreise for 24 voice choir, 1995; Sonnengesang des Franz von Assisi for 8 voice choir, 1996; Stabat Mater for tenor and organ, 1999; Dies Irae for alto and organ, 1999; Scheyerer Messe for 4 voice choir, 1999; Piano, harpsichord and organ music. *Honours:* Gothepreis Berlin, 1962; Kunstpreis, 1965; Hanns-Eisler-Preis, 1968; Nationalpreis der DDR, 1975, 1982; Heidelberger Künstlerinnenpreis, 1996; Verdienstkreuz 1st class; BRD. *Address:* Adolf-Rebl-Str 1, 85276 Pfaffenhofen a. d. J1M, Germany.

ZEDNIK, Heinz; Tenor; b. 21 Feb. 1940, Vienna, Austria. *Education:* Studied with Marga Wissmann and at the Vienna Conservatory. *Career:* Debut: Graz in 1964 in La Forza del Destino; Vienna Staatsoper from 1964, notably in the 1976 premiere of Von Einem's Kabale und Liebe; Guest appearances in Nice, Moscow, Montreal and Baden; Bayreuth Festival from 1970 as David, the Steersman, Mime and Loge; Salzburg Festival in 1984 in the premiere of Berio's Un Re in Ascolto; Other roles include Mozart's Pedrillo and Monostatos, Beethoven's Jacquino and Peter the Great in Zar und Zimmermann; Salzburg Festival in 1986 in the premiere of Penderecki's Die schwarze Maske; Pedrillo, 1987–89; Mime at New York Metropolitan, 1989–90, also televised; Sang Baron Laur in Weill's Silbersee at the 1996 London Proms; Season 2000 at the Vienna Staatsoper as Bob Boles in Peter Grimes, the Villians in Les Contes d' Hoffmann, the Captain in Wozzeck, and Monk in Schoenberg's Die Jakobsleiter. *Recordings:* Parsifal; Lustige Weiber Von Windsor; Le nozze di Figaro; Wozzeck; Salome; Wiener Blut; Die Zauberflöte; Das Rheingold and Siegfried from Bayreuth. *Address:* c/o Allied Artists, 42 Montpelier Square, London, SW7 1JZ, England.

ZEFFIRELLI, G. Franco Corsi; Italian theatrical, opera and film producer and designer; b. 12 Feb. 1923, Florence. *Education:* Liceo Artistico, Florence and School of Architecture, Florence. *Career:* designer Univ. Productions, Florence; actor Morelli Stoppa Co.; collaborated with Salvador Dali on sets for As You Like It 1948; designed sets for A Streetcar Named Desire, Troilus and Cressida, Three Sisters; producer and designer of numerous operas at La Scala, Milan 1952– and worldwide; Senator Forza Italia 1994–2002, cultural collaborator, Italian Ministry of Culture and Arts. *Exhibition:* Zeffirelli - The Art of Spectacle (Tokyo, Athens, Florence, Milan). *Operas include:* Lucia di Lammermoor, Cavalleria Rusticana, Pagliacci (Covent Garden) 1959, 1973, Falstaff (Covent Garden) 1961, L'elisir d'amore (Glyndebourne) 1961, Don Giovanni, Alcina (Covent Garden) 1962, Tosca, Rigoletto (Covent Garden) 1964, 1966, 1973, (Metropolitan, New York) 1985, Don Giovanni (Staatsoper-Wien) 1972, (Metropolitan, New York) 1990, Otello (Metropolitan, New York) 1972, Antony and Cleopatra (Metropolitan, New York) 1973, Otello (La Scala) 1976, La Bohème (Metropolitan, New York) 1981, Turandot (La Scala) 1983, 1985, (Metropolitan, New York) 1987, Don Carlos 1992, Carmen 1996, Aida (New Theatre, Tokyo) 1997, (Busseto) 2000, La Traviata (Metropolitan, New York) 1998, Tosca (Rome) 2000, Il Trovatore (arena di Verona) 2001, Aida (arena di Verona) 2002, La Bohème (La Scala) 2003, Carmen (arena di Verona) 2003. *Theatre:* Romeo and Juliet (Old Vic, London) 1960, Othello (Stratford) 1961, Amleto (Nat. Theatre, London) 1964, After the Fall (Rome) 1964, Who's Afraid of Virginia Woolf (Paris) 1964, (Milan) 1965, La Lupa (Rome) 1965, Much Ado About Nothing (Nat. Theatre, London) 1966, Black Comedy (Rome) 1967, A Delicate Balance (Rome) 1967, Saturday, Sunday, Monday (Nat. Theatre, London) 1973, Filumena (Lyric, London) 1977, Six Characters in Search of an Author (London) 1992, Absolutely Perhaps! (London) 2003. *Films:* The Taming of the Shrew 1966, Florence, Days of Destruction 1966, Romeo and Juliet 1967, Brother Sun and Sister Moon 1973, Jesus of Nazareth 1977, The Champ 1979, Endless Love 1981, La Traviata 1983, Cavalleria Rusticana 1983, Otello 1986, The Young Toscanini 1987, Hamlet 1990,

Sparrow 1994, Jane Eyre 1995, Tea with Mussolini 1998, Callas Forever 2002. *Ballet:* Swan Lake 1985; produced Beethoven's Missa Solemnis, San Pietro, Rome 1971. *Publication:* Zeffirelli by Zeffirelli (autobiog.) 1986. *Honours:* Hon. KBE; Prix des Nations 1976 and numerous others. *Address:* Via Lucio Volumnio 45, 00178 Rome, Italy. *Fax:* (06) 7184213.

ZEHETMAIR, Thomas; Concert Violinist; b. 23 Nov. 1961, Salzburg, Austria. *Education:* Studied at the Salzburg Mozarteum; Masterclasses with Max Rostal and Nathan Milstein. *Career:* Concert appearances with the Boston, Chicago, Cleveland, Minnesota and San Francisco Orchestras, Philharmonia, English and Scottish Chamber, BBC Symphony, City of Birmingham, Rotterdam Philharmonic and Concertgebouw, Stockholm Philharmonic and Leipzig Gewandhaus; Conductors have included Blomstedt, Eschenbach, Harnoncourt, Horst Stein, Sawallisch, Leppard, Dohnányi, Marriner, Rattle and Norrington; Guest engagements at international music festivals; Chamber music with Gidon Kremer at Lockenhaus; London recital debut at Wigmore Hall in 1993; Concerto engagements with the BBC Philharmonic, Bournemouth Symphony, Northern Sinfonia and Scottish Chamber Orchestra, 1993; Edinburgh Festival, 1995 with Bach's works for solo violin; Berlioz Harold in Italy, London Proms, 1997; Repertoire includes concertos by Szymanowski, Bach, Bart ók, Henze, Berg and Prokofiev, in addition to the standard works; Founder of the Zehetmair Quartet. *Recordings:* Beethoven's Kreutzer and Spring Sonatas, Concertos by Brahms, Joseph and Michael Haydn, Mendelssohn, Mozart, Schumann and Sibelius; Berg's Chamber Concerto and Schoenberg's Violin Concerto under Heinz Hoffiger; Szymanowski, Concertos no 1 and 2 with Simon Rattle; Bartók Concertos no 1 and 2 with Ivan Fischer. *Address:* c/o Sue Lubbock Concert Management, 25 Courthope Road, London NW3 2LE, England.

ZEHNDER, Kaspar; Flautist and Conductor; b. 27 Aug. 1970, Bern, Switzerland. *Education:* Flute, with Heidi Indermühler, 1978–, Piano, with Agathe Rytz-Jaggi, 1981–, Theory and Conducting with Arthur Furer and Dr Ewald Körner, 1985, Berne Conservatory; Bachelor Type A, Ancient Languages, High College, Bern, Switzerland; Studies at Berne Music Academy, 1986–; Swiss School for Orchestra and Opera Conductors, 1991; Masterclasses with Ralf Weikert and Horst Stein, 1991–93; Private lessons and masterclasses, with Aurèle Nicolet, Basel and Siena, 1993–; Studies in Paris, free assistance with Charles Dutoit, Orchestre National de France, 1994; Member European Mozart Academy, 1995. *Career:* Soloist with Bern Symphony, 1988; Conductor, Basel Symphony, 1993; Conducting, Tchaikovsky Symphony Orchestra, Moscow, 1999–; Artistic Director Murten Classics Festival, 1999; Artistic director Swiss Chamber Opera, 2001–; Concerts throughout Europe with orchestras including: Capella Istropolitana, Bratislava, 2000; Prague Philharmonia, 2001; Bucharest Symphony Orchestra, 2001; Appeared at festivals including: Mecklenberg-Vorpommern, Germany and Le stelle del futuro, Venice, 1996; President, Swiss Brahms Society, 2000–; Swiss Musicians Society. *Recordings:* French Music for flute and piano; Sonatas for flute and piano by Franck, Martinů, Prokofiev. *Honours:* Swiss Youth Competition, 1984, 1986; Migros Foundation Scholarship, 1994; Honour Diploma, Accademia Chigiana, Siena, 1994, 1998. *Address:* Junkerngasse 13, 3011 Bern, Switzerland. *E-mail:* kaspar.zehnder@datecomm.ch.

ZEITLIN, Zvi; Concert Violinist and Professor of Violin; b. 21 Feb. 1923, Dubrovno, USSR; m. Marianne Langner, 1 s., 1 d. *Education:* Juilliard School of Music; Hebrew University, Jerusalem. *Career:* Debut: New York, 1951; Professor, Eastman School of Music, University of Rochester, New York; Head of Violin Department, Music Academy of the West, Santa Barbara, California; Concert tours world-wide; Appearances with leading world symphony orchestras; Broadcasts on radio and television; Editor, newly discovered Nardini Concerto, 1958; Working on six other Nardini concertos; mem, The Bohemians, New York; University of Rochester Faculty Club; New York State Teachers' Association; American Federation of Musicians. *Recordings:* Schoenberg Violin Concerto; Rochberg Variations; Schumann Sonatas; Schubert, Glinka and Tchaikovsky Trios with Eastman Trio, 1976–82. *Honours:* American Israel Society Award for furthering cultural relations between USA and Israel, 1957; Commissions of violin concertos by Gunther Schuller, Carlos Surinach and Paul Ben Haim; American Israel Cultural Foundation; 1st Kilbourn Professor, Eastman School of Music. *Current Management:* Thea Dispeker, New York City, USA. *Address:* 204 Warren Avenue, Rochester, NY 14618, USA.

ZELJENKA, Ilja; Composer; b. 21 Dec. 1932, Bratislava, Czechoslovakia; m. Maria Kimlickova, 13 April 1957, 1 d. *Education:* Gymnasium 1943–51; Compositions studies at Academy of Music and Drama, Bratislava, 1951–56. *Career:* Debut: 1956; Dramaturgist of the Slovak Philharmony, 1957–61; With Slovak Radio, 1961–68; Freelance Composer, 1968–90; Chairman of the Slovak Music Union, 1990–91; President of the International Festival of Contemporary Music, Melos-Ethos, 1991. *Compositions:* 5 Symphonies, 6 string quartets, 4 piano sonatas, 2 piano concertos, clarinet concerto, violin concerto, Dualogues

for Violoncello and Chamber String Orchestra, Oswienczym Cantata, 2 piano quartets, Polymetric Music for 4 String Quintets, music for clarinet, piano and percussion, Metamorphoses XV for Chamber Ensemble and Reciter, Galgenlieder for Soprano, String Quartet, Clarinet, Flute and Piano, Mutations for Soprano, Bass, Wind Quintet and Percussion, Astecian Songs for Soprano, Piano and Percussion, and Plays for 13 Singers and Percussion. *Address:* 11A Zeljenka, Slavicie udolie 14, 81102 Bratislava, Slovakia.

ZELTSER, Mark; Concert Pianist; b. 3 April 1947, Kischiniev, Russia. *Education:* Graduated Moscow Conservatory, 1971. *Career:* Resident in USA from 1976; Played at the 1977 Salzburg Festival under Karajan and performed in Berlin with the Philharmonic in 1979; Debut with the New York Philharmonic, 1980; Further appearances with leading orchestras in Europe and America. *Address:* c/o Berlin Philharmonic Orchestra, Philharmonie, Matthaikirchstrasse 1, W-1000 Berlin, Germany.

ZELTZER, Sandra; Singer (Soprano); b. 1972, Paris, France. *Education:* Paris Conservatoire with Christiane Eda-Pierre, Guildhall School, London. *Career:* Covent Garden recital 1995, with appearances in Così fan tutte and Elektra 1997; Further engagements at Tatiana at the Paris Conservatoire, Linda di Chamounix at the Guildhall, Micaela for Mid Wales Opera and Bizet's Leila for English Touring Opera; Arminda, La Finta Giardiniera for Opera Zuid in the Netherlands; Sang Melia in Mozart's Apollo et Hyacinthus, Britten Theatre, London, 1998; Micaela (Carmen) and Donna Elvira (Don Giovanni) with Opéra Comique in Paris; Spoleto Festival, 1999, Lauretta (Gianni Schicchi); Versailles, 1999, Il Viaggio a Reims (Rossini); Carmen (Micaela) Opéra de Nancy, 1999–2000; Engaged as Donna Elvira at Glyndebourne Festival, 2000. Concerts include Gounod's Requiem in France and recitals in Oxford and at the Wigmore Hall, London; Recital at the Opéra-Comique, 1999; Sang Natasha in new production of War and Peace for ENO, 2001; Anacreón by Cherubini. *Recordings:* Recital recording of songs, 2001. *Honours:* 1994 James Gulliver Prize; Bourse Lavoisier Scholarship; Prize Winner at the 1995 Maggie Teyte Competition. *Current Management:* Ingpen & Williams Ltd, 7 St George's Court, 131 Putney Bridge Road, London, SW15 2PA, England.

ZEMTSOVSKY, Izaly (Iosifovich); Ethnomusicologist; b. 22 Feb. 1936, St Petersburg, Russia; m. Alma Kunanbay, 29 Jan 1982. *Education:* MA, Philology, University of Leningrad, 1958; Diploma, Russian Folklore, Musicology and Composition, Leningrad Conservatoire, 1955–60, 1961; MA, PhD. *Career:* Debut: 1958; Senior Research Fellow, Head of Folklore Department, Leningrad State Institute of Theatre, Music and Cinema (now Russian Institute of History of the Arts, 1990–), 1960–95; Head, Department of Traditional Culture, Russian Pedagogic University, 1989–93; Vice-President, Jewish Musical Society of St Petersburg, 1992–96; Vice President, International Delphic Council, 1994–96; President, Delphic Movement in Russia, 1995–97; Fellow, Institute for Research in the Humanities, University of Wisconsin-Madison, 1995–; Visiting Professor in Slavic and E Bloch Professor in Music, University of California, Berkeley, 1997–99. *Publications include:* Russian Folk Song, 1964; The Russian Drawn-Out Song, 1967; Songs of Toropets: Songs of The Homeland of Moussorgsky, 1967; Song Hunters, 1967; The Poetry of Peasant Holidays, 1970; The Melodics of Calendar Songs, 1975; Folklore and The Composer, 1978; Tracing the Melody Vesnianka from P Tchaikovsky's Piano Concerto: The Historical Morphology of the Folk Songs, 1987; Russian Folk Music, in Grove's Dictionary of Music and Musicians, 1980; Boris Asaf'yev on Folk Music, 1987; Jewish Folk Songs: An Anthology, 1994; An Attempt at a Synthetic Paradigm, 1997. *Address:* 2550 Dana Street Apt 9B, Berkeley, CA 94704, USA.

ZENATY, Ivan; Concert Violinist; b. 1960, Czechoslovakia. *Education:* Studied at the Prague Conservatoire and the Academy of Arts, Weimar with André Gertler, Zürich with Nathan Milstein. *Career:* Solo appearances with all leading Czech orchestras in Austria, Bulgaria, England, Finland, Netherlands, Italy, Poland, Spain, Russia, Switzerland and Yugoslavia; Festival engagements in Prague, Dubrovnik, Moscow, Sofia, Berlin and Havana; Repertoire includes concertos by Bach, Haydn, Mozart, Vivaldi, Myslivicek, Sibelius, Dvořák, Vieuxtemps and Kalabis, Bach solo sonatas and Telemann solo fantasies, sonatas by Mozart, Beethoven, Vanhal, Schubert, Schumann, Brahms, Prokofiev, Dvořák, Janáček and Martinů. *Recordings:* Various albums. *Honours:* First Prize, Prague Spring Festival Competition, 1987. *Address:* c/o Prague Conservatory, na Rejdi ti 1, 110 00 Prague, Czech Republic.

ZENDER, Johannes Wolfgang Hans; composer and conductor; b. 22 Nov. 1936, Wiesbaden, Germany; m. Gertrud Achenbach. *Education:* diplomas in conducting, piano and composition, Academy of Music, Freiburg. *Career:* Conductor, Freiburg, 1959; Principal Conductor, Bonn, 1964; General Music Director, City of Kiel, 1969; Principal Conductor, Saar Broadcasting, 1971–83; Chief Conductor, Hamburg

State Opera House, 1984–87; Guest Conductor for Berlin Philharmonic, London Symphony Orchestra, BBC, Residentie-Orkest, ORF Vienna, Tonhalle Zürich, Opera Houses of Munich, and Bayreuth (Parsifal); Chief Guest Conductor of the National Opera Orchestra, Brussels with Fidelio, 1989; Professor of Composition, Musikhochschule, Frankfurt, 1988; Guest Conductor, SWF Symphony Orchestra, until 1999. *Compositions include:* Vexilla Regis; Quartel: for Flute, Cello, Piano and Percussion; Trifolium for Flute, Cello and Piano; Les Sirènes Chantent for Soprano and Instruments; Muji No Kyo for Trio and Instruments; Bremen Wodu, electronic; Schachspiel for Orchestra; Zeitstrome for Orchestra; Cantos I–V for Voices and Instruments; Hölderlin Lesen for String Quartet and Voice; Modelle I–XII for Orchestral Groups; Loshu I–VII for Flute and Instruments; Dialog Mit Haydn; Stephen Climax, 1979–84; Hölderlin II, for viola and electronics; Hölderlin Lesen Ill for string quartet and gramophone; Jours de Silence for baritone and orchestra; Furin No Kyo, for soprano and ensemble; Animula for female choir, instruments and electronics; Schumann-Fantasiecs for large orchestra; Römer VIII for Soprano, alto and organ; Joh Ill for a capella choir. *Recordings include:* Elemente; Litanei; Mondschrift; Cantos 1, 11, V, VI, VIII; Dialogue with Haydn; Furin No Kyo; Zeitsröme; Stephen Climax; Schubert's Winterreise; Hölderlin Lesen 1-111. *Current Management:* Astrid Schoerke, Moernckebergallee 41, 30453 Hannover, Germany.

ZENTAI, Csilea; Singer (Soprano); b. Hungary. *Education:* Studied at Budapest, and in Stuttgart. *Career:* Debut: Stuttgart Opera School, 1969, in Ibert's Angelique; Sang at Ulm Opera, 1969–1972, Bremen, 1973–79, Deutsche Oper am Rhein from 1979; Guest appearances at the State Operas of Stuttgart, Hamburg and Munich, Vienna Staatsoper as Mozart's Countess and Fiordigili, Luise (Junge Lord); Zürich as the Marschallin, Deutsche Oper Berlin as Elvira and Blumenmädchen 1, and Cologne Opera as Fiordigili, Agathe, Butterfly, Rosalinde, Countess and Marenka; Further engagements at Bordeaux, Brussels, Salzburg as Donna Anna in concert performance of Don Giovanni, and Moscow; Other roles have included Violetta, Composer, Jenůfa, Pamina, Rosalinde, Marguerite and Amaranta in La Fedeltà Premiata by Haydn, Konstanze, Susanna, Jlica, Donna, Elviva, Marzelline; Leonore (Fidelio and Troubadour), Tosca, Traviata, Lucia, Mimi, Nedde, Euydice, Antonia, Martha, Michaela; Concert appearances in Germany, Netherlands, Belgium, Italy, Spain, Mexico and Hungary; Title of Kammersängerin of the Deutsche Oper am Rhein, 1990–; Professor, Folkwang Musikhochschule, 1991–. *Honours:* First Prize in s'Hertogeubosch (1968); Internqtional Vocal Competition; Silvermedallion in Toulouse (1968); First Prize in the "Francisco Viñas" Vocal Competition in Barcelona (1969). *Address:* c/o Deutsche Oper am Rhein, Heinrich Heine Allee 16, 40667 Dusseldorf, Germany.

ZENZIPER, Arkadi; Pianist; b. 10 April 1958, Leningrad, Russia; m. Tatjana Zenzipér, 10 Aug 1990, 3 s., 2 d. *Education:* Specialised Music School at Leningrad Conservatory, with T. Orlovsky; Final Examination with distinction, Leningrad Conservatory, 1981, after studying with N. Perlmann and G. Sokolov; Master's degree, 1984. *Career:* Debut: Television piano recital in Vilnius, Lithuania, 1982; Major concerts with orchestras: Berlin Symphonic Orchestra, 1990, Munich Klaviersommer, 1994, Ljubljana Festival, 1994; Stuttgart Chamber Orchestra, 2002; Krakauer Philharmonic Orchestra, 2001, 2002, 2004; Major chamber music concerts: Schleswig-Holstein Music Festival, 1989, 1990, Lucerne Festival, 1989, Concertgebouw, Amsterdam, 1990, 1991, Berlin Philharmonic Hall, 1992, and frequently at Berlin Konzerthaus; Radio performance of Prokofiev 4th and 5th Piano Concertos with Berlin Radio Orchestra, 1992; Television portrait and recording of Rachmaninov with Staatskapelle Dresden; La Chaise Dieu Music Festival with Orchestre Nat. de Lyon, 1998, 1999, 2000; Chamber music: Rheingau Festival, 1996; Dresdner Musikfestspiele, 1996; Tibor Varga Festival Sion, 1997; Beethovenhaus Bonn, 1997; Hitzacker-Festival, 1997; Prague Spring Festival, 2003; Rostica Music Festival London, 2003; Concerts with soloists of the Israeli Philharmonic Orchestra, 2003; Art Dir, Dreiklang Music Festival, 2001–; Regular Professor, Dresden Musikhochschule, 1993–. *Recordings:* Radio recordings of chamber music with RIAS-Berlin, Hessischer Rundfunk, South German Radio, Deutschland Radio; 9 CDs. *Current Management:* Pressando Musikagentur, Feuerbachstrasse 1, 04105 Leipzig, Germany. *Telephone:* (341) 4623088. *Fax:* (341) 4623089. *E-mail:* patrizia.meyn@t-online.de.

ZERBINI, Antonio; Singer (Bass); b. 1928, Italy. *Career:* Debut: Sang in La Forza del Destino at Spoleto in 1952; Sang at the Verona Arena, 1958–71 with debut as Ramphis in Aida; Further appearances at La Scala Milan, Moscow, Buenos Aires and the Paris Opéra; Théâtre de la Monnaie Brussels, 1960, 1962, 1969, and 1979 as the King in Aida, Mozart's Commendatore, Angelotti in Tosca, Timur in Turandot and Padre Guardiano in La Forza del Destino; Also sang in Nice and Monte Carlo in 1979; Verona Arena in 1981 as Sparafucile in Rigoletto; Sang Hieros in a revival of L'Assedio di Corinto by Rossini at Florence in 1982. *Recordings:* Tosca; Aida; Don Giovanni; L'Arlesiana; Donizetti's Maria

Stuarda; I Lombardi; La Forza del Destino; Manon; Lucia di Lammermoor.

ZETTERSTROM, Rune; Singer (Bass); b. 1936, Vasteras, Sweden. *Education:* Studied at the opera school of the Stora Teatern, Gothenburg, 1963–66. *Career:* Debut: Gothenburg 1966, as Mozart's Bartolo; Guest engagements: Oslo, 1970, Bergen, 1972, 1975, Copenhagen, 1976, London, 1977; Major roles have been: Seneca, in L'Incoronazione di Poppea, Rossini's Basilio, Verdi's Renato, bass in Tintomara by Werle, Timur in Turandot, Puccini's Colline; Sang the Lion in Werle's Animalen with the Stora Teatern at the Wiesbaden Festival, 1981; Further roles include: Mozart's Figaro, Sarastro, Leporello, Osmin, Philip, in Don Carlos; Guest engagements, in Semperoper in Dresden, 1988 with Osmin; Sang Leporello at Stockholm, 1996; Louis in the premiere production of Marie Antoinette by D Börtz, Stockholm and Brighton, 1998. *Recordings include:* Tintomara. *Address:* c/o Kungliga Teatern, PO Box 16094, S–10322, Stockholm, Sweden.

ZHADKO, Victoria; Conductor; b. 1967, Kiev, Ukraine. *Education:* Studied at the Kiev Conservatoire. *Career:* Deputy Conductor of the Kiev Radio Symphony Orchestra in 1993; Performances of Ukrainian music with the St Petersburg Philharmonic and guest engagements with the Rotterdam Philharmonic, Netherlands Radio, Helsinki, Wroclaw and Poznan Philharmonics; Repertoire includes the Viennese classics, Strauss, Tchaikovsky, Brahms, Liszt and Ravel; Teacher at the Kiev School of Arts and Odessa Conservatoire. *Address:* c/o Sonata Ltd, 11 North Park Street, Glasgow G20 7AA, Scotland.

ZHANG, Jianyi; Singer (tenor); b. 3 Aug. 1959, Shanghai, China. *Education:* Shanghai Conservatory of Music, 1981–86; The Juilliard School, 1986–89. *Career:* Debut: As the Lover in Amelia al Ballo, 1987; Appeared as the Duke of Mantua in Rigoletto at Teatro Comunale di Firenze, 1989; As Rodolfo in La Bohème at New York City Opera and Werther at Opera de Nice, 1990–91; Performed Nadir in the Pearl Fishers at Washington Opera and Opera Pacific, 1991–92; Roldolfo at Opéra de Lyon and Opera Nice and Des Grieux in Manon at Opéra Comique Paris, 1992–93; Season 1993–94 as Don José in Carmen at the National Opéra de Paris Bastille; Faust in Paris, Washington, Michigan Opera Theatre and Miami Grand Opera, 1994–95; As Alfredo in La Traviata at Staatsoper Hamburg and Rodolfo at Stattsoper Stuttgart, 1995–96; Season 1996–97 as Faust at the Metropolitan Opera and The Duke of Mantua in Rigoletto at the Montreal Opera and as Nemorino in L'Elisir D'Amore at the New Israeli Opera; Sang Rodolfo and Alfredo at New York City Opera and as Des Grieux at the Metropolitan Opera, 1997–98; Appearances as Rodolfo at Dallas Opera and Alfredo at Vancouver Opera and Tamino in The Magic Flute at Florentine Opera, Faust at Savonlinna Opera Festival at the Seattle Opera, 1998–99; From 1999 sang Meyerbeer's Robert for Deutsche Staatsoper, Berlin, Gerald in Lakmé at Montreal, Massenet's Des Grieux in Madrid and Cavaradossi at Hong Kong. *Honours:* The First Prizewinner in the Belvedere International Opera Singer Competition in Vienna, 1984; The Grand Winner in the Luciano Pavarotti International Voice Competition in Philadelphia, 1988. *Address:* c/o 62-54 97th Place Apt PH-1, Rego Park, NY 11374, USA.

ZHAO, Pingguo; Professor of Piano and Pianist; b. 1934, China; m. Ling Yuan 1956, 1 s., 1 d. *Education:* Graduated, Piano, Central Conservatory of Music, 1951; Studied at Central Conservatory of St Petersburg with Aram Taturan and Tachiana Kravchenko. *Career:* Joined Piano Faculty, Central Conservatory of Music, 1951; Took part in International Tchaikovsky Piano Competition, 1962; Professor of Piano; Performance tour of Japan with promising pupil, 1996; Numerous piano concert performances; Repertoire includes Beethoven Sonatas; Chopin pieces; Mozart Concertos; Tchaikovsky Concertos; Numerous lectures in cities world-wide including Russia, Ukraine, Los Angeles, Japan; Judge, several piano competitions; Grader, National Examinational Piano Playing. *Address:* Central Conservatory of Music, 43 Bao Jia Street, Beijing, People's Republic of China.

ZHAO, Xiaosheng; Composer, Pianist, Musicologist and Music Professor; b. 27 July 1945, Shanghai, China. *Education:* BA, Piano, 1967, MA, Composition, 1981, Shanghai Conservatory of Music. *Career:* Visiting Scholar, Visiting Professor, UMC, USA, 1981–84; Over 100 piano recitals in 20 main cities of China, in USA and Hong Kong; Created Taiji Composition, 1987, Tone-sets Motion Theory, 1991; Guest Host, Radio Shanghai, Oriental Radio Shanghai, STV and OTV, Shanghai; Editor-in-Chief, Shanghai Piano Guild, 1994, 1995; Vice Editor-in-Chief, Piano Artistry magazine. *Compositions include:* Six Concert Etudes for piano, 1976; 2 String Quartets, 1980, 1981; The Goddess of Hope, Piano Concerto, 1985; Four Movements of Jian, 1986; Taiji, piano solo, 1987; Three Movements of Yin-Yang for 16 players, 1987; Bi Xiao Pai Yun for flute, 1988; Double Concerto for Gaohu and Erhu and Chinese Orchestra, 1988; LuYao, pipa solo, 1989; Ting Qin for Erhu and Piano, 1989; Huan Feng, sheng solo, 1989; Hui Liu, quartet, 1989; Three Symphonic Suites, 1990; The Song of Earth, Sound of Man, Sacrifice to

Heaven, ballet, 1990; Liao Yin, piano concerto, 1991; The Sun of Wilderness, ballet, 1991; Shi Lou for Chinese Chamber Orchestra, 1994; Pieces for piano solo: Stephen Hawking's View of Cosmos; Filter; Eight Scenes of West Lake; Qin Yun; Xiao Xue; A-Bing Sui Xiang (Capriccio from Blind Abing); Blake and White; Drum and Bell; 62343314; Echoes from Empty Valley; Ancient Sound of Mt Yu, 1999; More than 30 improvisations. *Recordings:* Music from His Heart–Zhao Plays His 14 Own Piano Pieces, 2CD album, 1999; How to Play The 'Music Note Book for Anna Magdalena Bach', 2VCD album, 1999. *Address:* Composition Department, Shanghai Conservatory of Music, 20 Fenyang Lu, Shanghai 200031, People's Republic of China.

ZHIDKOVA, Elena; Singer (Mezzo-soprano); b. 1972, Russia. *Education:* St Petersburg Conservatory and Opera Studio of Hamburg State Opera. *Career:* Mascagni's Lola and Maddalena in Rigoletto at Hamburg; Deutsche Oper Berlin as Olga in Eugene Onegin, Hansel, and Siebel in Faust; Guest appearances in Japan, at Théâtre du Châtelet, Paris, New York Lincoln Center and Barbican Hall, London; Season 2000–01 as Fides in Le Prophète at Kiel, Schwertleite in Die Walküre at Bayreuth and in The Ring at the Deutsche Oper; Concerts include Mahler's 8th Symphony in Rome, under Myung-Whun Chung. *Honours:* Prize Winner, Dvořák Competition, Prague. *Address:* c/o Theateragentur Dr G. Hilbert, Maximilianstrasse 22, 80539 Munich, Germany.

ZHIKALOV, Yuri; Singer (Tenor); b. 1948, Russia. *Education:* Graduated St Petersburg Conservatoire, 1972. *Career:* Many engagements in concerts and opera throughout Russia; Kirov Opera, St Petersburg, from 1977 as Lensky in Eugene Onegin, Mozart's Monostatos, Andrei in Mazeppa and Khovanshchina, and Finn in Ruslan and Lyudmila; Sang with the Kirov in summer season at Covent Garden, 2000; Other roles include Prince Guidon in The Tale of Tsar Saltan by Rimsky-Korsakov, Norman in Lucia di Lammermoor, Mikhail and Nikita in Rimsky's The Maid of Pskov and Platon in War and Peace. *Address:* c/o Kirov Opera, Mariinsky Theatre, 1 Theatre Square, St Petersburg, Russia.

ZHISLIN, Grigory; Violinist and Violist; b. 7 May 1945, St Petersburg, Russia. *Education:* Studied at the Central Music School and the State Conservatoire in Moscow. *Career:* Many appearances with such leading ensembles as the Leipzig Gewandhaus, Dresden Staatskapelle, Vienna Symphony, Warsaw National Philharmonic, Berlin Philharmonic and all the major Russian orchestras: Conductors have included Moshe Atzmon, Neeme Järvi, Herbert Blomstedt, Mariss Jansons, Leif Segerstram, Kurt Sanderling, Kyrill Kondrashin and Yuri Temirkanov; Concerts at such festival at the Warsaw Autumn, Prague Spring, Maggio Musicale, Istanbul, Bergen and Kuhmo; Performances of such contemporary composers as Schnittke, Gubaidulina, Denisov and Penderecki (tours with the Kraków Philharmonic to the United Kingdom and Europe 1990, playing the Penderecki Violin and Viola concertos which were written for him); Assistant Professor at the Moscow Conservatoire 1969–71; Teacher at the Gnessin Institute, Moscow, and masterclasses in Kraków, Oslo, Montreal and Genoa (students have included Dimitri Sitkovetsky); Professor of Violin and Viola at the Royal Academy of Music, London from 1991. *Honours:* Gold Medal of the International Paganini Competition at Genoa, 1967; Silver Medal at the Queen Elisabeth Competition in Brussels, 1968. *Address:* c/o Sonata, 11 Northgate Street, Glasgow G20 7AA, Scotland.

ZHIVOPISTEV, Vladimir; Singer (Baritone); b. 1960, Dobrush, Byelorussia. *Education:* Odessa State Conservatoire. *Career:* Appearances at the Maly Opera Theatre, St Petersburg; Kirov Opera, Mariinsky Theatre, from 1996; Roles have included Giorgio Germont, Yeletsky in The Queen of Spades, Eugene Onegin, Rossini's Figaro and Goro in Madama Butterfly; Sang in War and Peace, Khovanshchina and Semyon Kotko (British premiere) with the Kirov at Covent Garden, 2000; Other roles include Robert in Tchaikovsky's Iolanta, the Indian Guest in Rimsky's Sadko, Spoletta in Tosca and Bayan in Ruslan and Lyudmila. *Honours:* Prize Winner, Lysenko International Vocal Competition. *Address:* c/o Kirov Opera, Mariinksy Theatre, 1 Theatre Square, St Petersburg, Russia.

ZHU, Ai-La; Singer (soprano); b. 1957, Nanking, China. *Education:* studied in Peking and Berlin and at the Hartt School of Music. *Career:* sang first with the Peking Central Opera notably as Butterfly, Violetta and Mimi; sang Micaela with Texas Opera, Mimi and Marguerite with Virginia Opera and Xola in the premiere of Under The Double Moon by A. Davis, with the St Louis Opera; appeared at Pepsicosummerfare as Zerlina in the Peter Sellars production of Don Giovanni; season 1990–92 as Violetta at Boston, Gilda at Philadelphia and Leila with Minnesota Opera; sang at Glyndebourne Festival 1990–91 as Pamina; also features in Lieder recitals.

ZHU, Jian-Er; Composer and Professor of Composition; b. 18 Oct. 1922, Tianjin, China; m. Qun Shu 1949, 2 s., 1 d. *Education:* Graduated, Moscow State Conservatory, 1960; Studied with Professor Sergey Balasanian. *Career:* Composer, Art Troupe, New 4th Army, 1945–49; Conductor, Brass Band, 1946–49; Composer, Shanghai and Peking Film Studios, 1949–63; Shanghai Opera House, 1963–75; Shanghai Symphony Orchestra, 1975–; Professor of Composition, Shanghai Conservatory of Music. *Compositions:* Main Works: Orchestral: Festival Overture, 1958; In Memorian, for Strings, 1978; Symphonic Fantasia, 1980; Sketches in Mountains of Guizhou, 1982; The Butterfly Fountain for Er-hu and Orchestra, 1983; A Wonder of Naxi, 1984; Symphonies No. 1, 1986; No. 2, 1987; No. 3 Tibet, 1988; No. 4, 1990; No. 5, 1991; No. 6, 1994; No. 7, 1994; No. 8, 1994; No. 9, 1999; No. 10, 1998; Sinfonietta, 1994; Concerto for Sona and Orchestra, 1989; Hundred Year Vicissitudes, 1996; Choral: Salute 1946, 1945; Gada-meilin, 1958; Symphony-Cantata Heroic Poems, 1960; A Cappella Cycle The Green, Green Water Village, 1981; Piano: Preludes, 1955; Theme and Var, 1956; Ballade, 1958; Five Yunnan Folk Songs, 1962; Quintet, 1992; Folk Instrumental Ensemble Day of Liberation, 1953; Song of the Spring, for Oboe and Piano, 1956; Numerous Songs. *Address:* 105 Hu Nan Road, Shanghai Symphony Orchestra, Shanghai 200031, People's Republic of China.

ZHU, Kunqiang; Musician (French horn); b. 10 April 1963, Bengbu, Anhui Province, People's Republic of Chinab. *Education:* Music Department, Army Art Academy of China. *Career:* Principal French Horn, Symphony Orchestra of the Chinese Army, 1983; Toured Russia, Hungary, Poland, Romania and Germany, 1988; Performed at the Hong Kong Arts Festival with the China Youth Symphony Orchestra, 1991; Macao Music Festival with the China Chamber Music Orchestra, 1995; Principal French Horn with the China National Symphony Orchestra, 1996–; Has toured China, and abroad, including Hong Kong Arts Festival, 1997, 1998 and 2000, Germany, the United Kingdom and Austria, 1998, Japan and the Osaka International Music Festival, 1999, Mexico, 2000, and Hong Kong and Macao, 2001; Co-founded and performs with the Wuxing Brass Quintet; mem, International Horn Society; Chinese Musician's Association. *Recordings include:* numerous works for television and film with the China Radio Symphony Orchestra and the China Film Orchestra; Chinese Folk Song Collection with the Wuxing Brass Quintet; Many Chinese and Western symphonic works with the China National Symphony Orchestra. *Honours:* First Prize at the Second Chinese Horn Competition, 1991. *Address:* c/o The China National Symphony Orchestra, 11-1 Hepingjie, Chaoyang District, Beijing 100013, People's Republic of China.

ZHU XIAO MEI; French (b. Chinese) concert pianist; *Professor of Piano, Conservatoire National Supérieur de Paris*; b. b. Shanghai. *Education:* Nat. Music School for Gifted Children. *Career:* made first radio and TV appearances in Peking at age of six; sent to labour camp in Inner Mongolia at age of ten following Cultural Revolution 1970–76; continued playing piano in secret; left China for USA following visit of Isaac Stern in 1979; won several prizes in USA and began concert career; moved to Paris 1985, French citizenship 2000; Prof. of Piano, Conservatoire Nat. Supérieur de Paris; divides her time between teaching and worldwide concert schedule; regular guest performer at Théâtre de la Ville, Paris 1994–. *Recordings include:* major piano works of Bach, Scarlatti, Mozart, Schubert and Schumann. *Address:* 4 rue de Nevers, 75006 Paris, France. *Telephone:* 1-46-33-61-31. *Fax:* 1-46-33-61-31.

ZHUKOV, Sergei; Composer; b. 30 Aug. 1951, Zhytomyr, Ukraine; m. Natalia Zhukova, 4 Mar 1982, 2 d. *Education:* Musical College, Zhitomir, 1973–; Graduated, Department of Composition, 1978, Post-graduate Course, 1980, Moscow State Conservatory. *Career:* Debut: Chamber Music Concert, Maliy Hall, Moscow Conservatory, 1973; Participated, All-Union and International Concerts, Festivals, Symposia, including: Moscow Autumn Musical Festival, 1981, 1982, 1983, 1984; Warsaw Autumn, 1988; International Musical Festival, Leningrad, 1989; Charles Ives Festival, USA, 1990; Week Van de Hedendaagse Musiek, Belgium, 1991; Works performed on ITV, Radio: Symphony, All-Union Radio, 1987; Moments, running in succession, oratorio, All-Union Television, 1987; Partita for violin solo, Donderdag, Dutch Radio, 1990; Landscape for Clarinet Solo, BRT-3, Belgium Radio; Solaris, fantasic ballet, Ukrainian television recording, 1991; Teaching, Department of Theory and Composition, Moscow State Conservatory, 1991; mem, Union of Composers of Russia, 1980. *Compositions:* Spivanochki, Chamber Cantata to Traditional Words, 1975, published 1983; Partita for Violin Solo, 1983, published 1986; Refracted Sounds, Wind Quintet, 1984; Symphony, 1985; Sonata-Bussanda for Piano, 1988; Concerto for Orchestra and Solo Percussions, 1990; Image and Transfiguration, for Organ, 1991; Concerto-Partes for String Orchestra, 1992; Lot of Nemisida, Choreographic Composition for Clarinetist, Dancer, Magnetic Tape, 1993; Concerto-Mystery for Piano, Violin, Violoncello and Orchestra, 1994; Insomnia, ballet after Pushkin, 1999. *Contributions:* Some aspects of Creation of Musical Compositions, article, 1980; Series of Articles for The Musical Encyclopedia, 1991. *Address:* Studencheskaja Str 44-28, Apt 128, 121165 Moscow, Russia.

ZIEGLER, Delores; Singer (Mezzo-Soprano); b. 4 Sept. 1951, Atlanta, Georgia, USA. *Education:* Studied at the University of Tennessee. *Career:* Sang at first in concert then made stage debut as Flora in

Traviata at Knoxville, Tennessee, 1978; Sang Maddalena in Rigoletto at St Louis in 1979; Bonn Opera from 1981 as Emilia in Otello, Dorabella and Octavian; Member of the Cologne Opera from 1982, notably as Cherubino, Orlofsky and Octavian; La Scala Milan, 1984–87 in Bellini's Romeo; Guest engagements in Munich, Oslo, San Diego, Toronto, Hamburg and at the Glyndebourne Fesival as Dorabella in 1984; Maggio Musicale Florence in 1989 as Idamantes; Salzburg Festival in 1988 as Mozart's Sextus; Metropolitan Opera, 1989–91 as Siebel and Octavian; Sang in Der Rosenkavalier with the Canadian Opera Company at Toronto, 1990; Sang Dorabella at Washington DC, 1996; Sang Mozart's Marcellina at the Met (1999) and in Rameau's Hippolyte et Aricie at Saint Louis, 2001; Many concert engagements. *Recordings include:* Bach's B minor Mass; Così fan tutte; Mozart's Mass in C; Second Lady in Die Zauberflöte; Le Roi d'Ys by Lalo. *Address:* c/o Cote Artists Management, 150 West 57th Street, Suite 803, New York, NY 10019, USA.

ZIELINSKA, Lidia; Composer; b. 30 Oct. 1953, Poznań, Poland; m. Zygmunt Zielinski, 3 Aug 1974, 1 d. *Education:* MA, State Higher School of Music, Poznan; Studied composition with Andrzej Koszewski. *Career:* Collaborated in Electronics Music Studio in Kraków, 1978–; Composers Workshops in Poland, Netherlands, France and Switzerland, 1979–87; Polish Radio Experimental Studio, 1980–81, 1986–, and Studio IPEM, Ghent, 1985; Polish Center of Art for Children and Youth, Artistic Group, Artificial Cult; Co-organised Multimedia Art Meetings, Obecnosc, Poznan; Festivals, Young Polish Music, Szczecin; Concerts and performances in Europe, Asia and USA; Assistant Professor, Academy of Music, Poznan, 1983–. *Compositions include:* Violin Concerto, 1979; Farewell Mr Toorop for Orchestra, 1981; Lullaby Gagaku for Double Bass, 1984; Sonnet On The Tatras for 4 Musicians, 1985; Music For Stanislaw Wyspianski for Tape, 1985; Glossa for Viola or Violin, 1986; Polish Dances for Tape after Father Baka, 1986; Pleonasmus for Oboe, Violin and String Orchestra, 1986; Kaleidoscope, Passacaglia for Percussion, Slides and Clapping Hands, for children, 1987; Concrete Music for Choir and Orchestra, 1987; The Same, 1988; Little Atrophic Symphony, 1988; Musica Humana or How Symphonies Are Born, radio piece, 1989; Jacquard Loom for 15 Musicians, 1991; Fago for Bassoon, Double Bass and Accordion or Electronic Keyboard, 1992; Venture Unknown, ballet, 1995; The Plot Theory of Sound, installation, 1996; Expandata, for percussion and tape, 1997. *Recordings:* Numerous. *Address:* ul Poplinskich 7-9, 61-573 Poznań, Poland.

ZIESAK, Ruth; Singer (Soprano); b. 9 Feb. 1963, Hofheim, Taunus, Germany. *Education:* Studied with Christoph Pregardien, at the Frankfurt Musikhochschule with Elsa Cavelti, and at the Frankfurt Opera School. *Career:* Debut: Heidelberg in 1988 as Valencienne in Die Lustige Witwe; Sang at Heidelberg as Pamina, Gilda, Sesto in Giulio Cesare and Despina; Deutsche Oper am Rhein in 1989 as Marzelline; Tour of Tokyo, Osaka and Kyoto with the Ludwigsburg Festival Ensemble, singing in Messiah and Mozart's Requiem, 1989; Sang Susanna at the Opéra Bastille, Paris, and Pamina, 1991, and at the Salzburg Festival, 1993; Season 1993–94 as Sophie in Rosenkavalier at the Deutsche Oper Berlin, 1993; Sang Ighino in Pfitzner's Palestrina at Covent Garden, 1997; Aennchen in Der Freischütz at La Scala, 1998; Season 2000–01 as Marzelline in Fidelio at Munich, and Aennchen in Der Freischütz; Mozart's Countess at Glyndebourne, 2003. *Recordings include:* Servilia in La Clemenza di Tito, under Harnoncourt. *Address:* c/o IMG Artists, Lovell House, 616 Chiswick High Road, London W4 5RX, England.

ZIESE, Christa-Maria; Singer (Soprano); b. 13 July 1924, Aschersleben, Germany; m. Rainer Ludeke. *Education:* Studied with Gottlieb Zeithammer and Josef-Maria Hausschild in Leipzig. *Career:* Debut: Leipzig in 1947 as Gretel; Sang at the Leipzig St ädtische Theater, 1951–77 notably as Fidelio, Santuzza, Tosca, Salome, Aida, Carmen, Turandot, Senta, Isolde and Venus; Guest appearances in Weimar, 1951–54, Dresden, Komische Oper Berlin, Moscow Bolshoi, Düsseldorf, Hamburg, Nice, Zürich and Brno; Many concert appearances. *Recordings:* Many. *Honours:* Bach Competition Dresden and International Competition in Prague, 1949.

ZIKMUNDOVÁ, Eva; Opera Singer (Soprano); b. 4 May 1932, Kromeriz, Czechoslovakia; Divorced, 1 s. *Education:* State Conservatory, Brno; Music Academy, Prague. *Career:* Debut: Opera House, Ostrava; Member of Opera Company of National Theatre, Prague, 1958–92; Assistant Producer, State Opera, Prague, 1992–95; Guest appearances at State Opera, Berlin, Hannover, Mannheim, Germany, Venice, Genoa, Naples, Italy, Lausanne, Switzerland, Vienna, Austria, Edinburgh, Scotland, Amsterdam, Netherlands, Warsaw, Poland, Budapest, Hungary, Sofia, Bulgaria, and Brussels, Belgium; Recitals for Czech Radio and Television; Professor of Singing at State Conservatory, Teplice. *Recordings:* Dvořák's St Ludmila and Moravian duets; Janáček's The Cunning Little Vixen; Numerous recordings of arias and duets. *Publications:* Translations into Czech of: Martienssen-Lohmann, Der wissende Sänger and Das bewusste Singen, 1994; Rodolfo Celletti:

Storia del belcanto, 1998. *Honours:* Supraphon Annual Award for Cunning Little Vixen, 1974; Merited Member of The National Theatre, Ministry of Culture. *Current Management:* Pragokoncert, Prague 1, Czech Republic. *Address:* Mánesova 23, Prague 2, Czech Republic.

ZILBERSTEIN, Lilya; Concert Pianist; b. 19 April 1965, Moscow, Russia; m. Alexander Gerzenberg, 27 Aug 1988, 2 s. *Education:* Moscow Gnessin Special Music School with Ada Traub, 1972–83; Gnessin Music Pedagogical Institute, with Alexander Satz, 1983–90. *Career:* St Louis Symphony, Chicago Symphony, Berlin Philharmonic, London Symphony, Royal Philharmonic, Dresden Staatskapelle, Moscow Philharmonic, Finnish Radio; Montreal Symphony Orchestra; Teatro La Scala, 1999. *Recordings:* 8 CD's, 6 Recitals include: Concertos Nos 2, 3 by Rachmaninov with the Berlin Philharmonic and Claudio Abbado; Concerto by Grieg with Gothenburg Symphony and Neeme Järvi. *Honours:* 1st Prize, Busoni International Piano Competition, 1987; International Prize of Academia Musicals Chigiana in Siena, Italy. *Current Management:* Konzertdirektion Dr Goette, Hamburg. *Address:* c/o Konzertdirektion Dr Goette, Brahmsallee 6, 20144 Hamburg, Germany.

ZILIO, Elena; Singer (Soprano); b. 1941, Bolzano, Italy; m. Stillo Burchiellaro. *Education:* Studied at the Conservatorio Monteverdi in Bolzano, at the Accademia Chigiana in Siena and the Accademia di Santa Cecilia, Rome. *Career:* Debut: At Spoleto in 1963 as Sofia in Rossini's Il Signor Bruschino. Career. Has sung at La Scala Milan, Rome, Genoa, Palermo, Naples, Turin, Trieste, Venice and Verona Arena in 1970, 1973, 1978; Festivals at Caracalla and Florence; Sang Lisa in La Sonnambula at Geneva in 1982; Chicago Opera in 1983 as Suzuki in Madama Butterfly; Milan at La Scala and Piccola Scala in 1983 as Amore in Cherubini's Anacréon and Dardane in La Rencontre Imprévue by Gluck; Sang Smeaton in Anna Bolena at Bergamo in 1983, returning in 1988 as the Page in Donizetti's Gianni di Parigi; With the company of the San Carlo Naples sang Giustinio in Pergolesi's Flaminio at Versailles and Spoleto, USA, 1983 and Wiesbaden in 1985; Cologne Opera in 1984 as Pippo in La Gazza Ladra: Returned to La Scala in 1985 in a revival of Rossi's Orfeo; Further appearances in Brussels, at Paris Opéra, in Boston, San Antonio, Montreal, Bregenz and Dubrovnik; Sang Elena in La Gazza Ladra at Palermo, 1996; Marquise in La Fille du Régiment at Rome, 1998; Sang Mistress Quickly in Falstaff at Lyon and Frankfurt, 1999–2000. *Recordings:* La Buona Figliola by Piccinni; La Straniera by Bellini; Un Giorno di Regno by Verdi. *Address:* c/o Teatro alla Scala, Via Filodrammatici, 1-20121 Milan, Italy.

ZIMANSKY, Robert; Violinist; b. 20 April 1948, Iowa City, USA; m. Lucia Borsatti, 9 April 1979. *Education:* University of Iowa, 1960–66; Juilliard School of Music, 1966–71; Masterclasses with various teachers, 1970–74. *Career:* Debut: Orchestra Hall, Chicago with Civic Symphony Orchestra; Resident Europe, 1972–; Leader of Symphonie-Orchester Graunke, 1972–73, Suddeutsche Rundfunk, 1974, and Orchestre de la Suisse Romande, 1975–99; Professor of Advanced Classes, Geneva Conservatory, 1980–; Soloist with Wolfgang Sawallisch, Horst Stein, Charles Dutoit, Leif Segerstam, David Zinman, George Cleve and Herbert Blomstedt; mem, Board of Directors, Association des Musiciens Suisses. *Recordings:* X and P Scharwenka Violin Sonatas; Bach 5th Brandenberg; Albéric Magnard Sonata; Schumann 3 Sonatas (award); Reger, Sonatas op 72 and 84; Schubert, Octet and Janáček complete violin works. *Honours:* Grand Prix du Disque, Academie Charles Cros, 1986. *Current Management:* Wismer-Casetti, 30, CH Du Vieux-Vesenaz, 1222 Vesenaz. *Address:* 6 Tour de Champel, 1206 Geneva, Switzerland.

ZIMERMAN, Krystian; Concert Pianist; b. 5 Dec. 1956, Zabrze, Poland; m., 1 s., 1 d. *Education:* Studied at the Music Academy in Katowice. *Career:* Concerts in Vienna and all world's music centres; Concerts and recordings with such conductors as Bernstein, Giulini and Karajan, and more recently Witold Lutoslawski dedicated his Piano Concerto to Zimerman who gave its premiere in 1989; Repertoire extends through solo piano music, concertos and chamber music. *Recordings include:* Beethoven Nos 1–5, Piano Concertos; Brahms Piano Concertos No. 1 and 2; Liszt B minor Sonata. *Honours:* Youngest ever winner of the Chopin Piano Competition, Warsaw, 1975; Grammy Award; Gramophone Award. *Address:* Kernmattstr 8B, 4102 Binningen, Switzerland.

ZIMMERMAN, Christopher; Conductor; b. 1957, England. *Education:* Studied at Yale and the University of Michigan; Further study with Nadia Boulanger and at the Pierre Monteux School of Conducting, Maine. *Career:* Music Director of the Yale Bach Society, 1980; Conducted the Michigan University Symphony Orchestra in the USA and Europe; Worked with the Toronto Symphony, the Czech Philharmonic, 1983–85; London 1985, leading concerts with the Royal Philharmonic and the London Symphony Orchestras; Appearances with the Royal Liverpool Philharmonic and at the Concertgebouw in Amsterdam; Prague 1987, with the Prague Symphony Orchestra; Conducted the Seoul Philharmonic in Korea, 1989; Guest Music

Director at Mexico City Opera; Music Director, City of London Chamber Orchestra, 1988–93; Most recent Guest Engagements: Edmonton Symphony Orchestra, 1993, Waterbury Symphony Orchestra, 1994; Further engagements in Finland and Venezuela; Music Director, Bangor Symphony Orchestra, Bangor Maine, and Music Director, Concert Orchestra, Cincinnati College Conservatory of Music, Cincinnati, Ohio, USA; mem, A S O L. *Current Management:* Kenneth Wentworth, Jonathan Wentworth & Associates Ltd. *Address:* Artist Management, Suite 503, 100 Stevens Avenue, Mount Vernon, New York 10550, USA.

ZIMMERMAN, Franklin B., BLitt, PhD; Musician, Conductor and Musicologist; b. 20 June 1923, Wanneta, Kansas, USA; m. 1988, 1 s., 5 d. *Education:* University of Southern California, Oxford University; studied French Horn with Aubrey Brain, conducting with Ernest Read, orchestration with Leon Kirchner and Ingolf Dahl. *Career:* Created Music SoundScapes, a 3–dimensional, animated and colo-coded new graphic musical notation; Debut: London in 1957; Founder and Director, Pennsylvania Pro Musica playing over 520 concerts; mem, AMS; IMS. *Recordings:* Handel L'Allegro ed Il Penseroso, 1981. *Publications:* Henry Purcell: Analytical Catalog, 1963; Henry Purcell: Life and Times, 1967, 1983; Henry Purcell: Thematic Index, 1973; Words to Music, 1965; Facsimile Editions: An Introduction to the Skill of Musick by John Playford, 12th edition corrected and amended by Henry Purcell, with index, introduction and glossary, 1972; The Gostling Manuscript, compiled by John Gostling, Foreword by Franklin B Zimmerman, 1977; Henry Purcell: a Guide to Research, 1989; Henry Purcell (1659–1695): Analytical Essays on his Music, 2001; Visible Music Sound-Scapes: A New Approach to Musical Notation and Understanding; Purcellian Melodies Indexed: A Thematic Index to the Complete Work of Henry Purcell. *Contributions:* numerous articles and monographs. *Honours:* Arnold Bax Medal for Musicology, 1958. *Address:* Visible Music SoundScapes, Inc.Suite 1A, 225 South 42nd Street, Philadelphia, PA 19104, USA. *E-mail:* musica@dca.net. *Website:* visiblemusics.com/new.

ZIMMERMAN, Willi; Violinist; b. 1955, Switzerland. *Education:* Studied with the Alban Berg Quartet in Vienna. *Career:* Leader, Amati String Quartet, 1981–; Further study with members of the Amadeus and Bartók Quartets, and with Walter Levin; Many performances in Switzerland, USA and elsewhere in the classical repertoire, and in works by Szymanowski, Tailleferre, Cui, Steuermann, Vladimir Vogel, Kelterborn and Robert Suter; Recitals at Basle in 1986 and tours of the United Kingdom, 1990–91; Menuhin Festival at Gstaad in 1991; Recitals with Bruno Canino, Malcolm Frager, Bruno Giuranna, Karl Leister among others. *Honours:* With Amati Quartet: Grand Prix, Concours International at Evian, 1982, Art Prize of the Lions Club in 1985, and 1st Prize, Karl Klinger Competition in Munich, 1986. *Address:* c/o Dönch Amati Quartet, Eckenheimer Landstrasse 483, D–60435 Frankfurt, Germany.

ZIMMERMANN, Frank Peter; Concert Violinist; b. 27 Feb. 1965, Duisburg, Germany. *Education:* Studied with Valery Gradov at Folkwang Musikhochschule Essen, Staatliche Hochschule Berlin with Saschko Gawrilloff and from 1980 with Hermann Krebbers in Amsterdam. *Career:* Debut: Duisburg in 1975 playing Mozart's Concerto K216; engagements in all major venues and festivals in Europe, USA, Japan, South America and Australia; Appearances with many international orchestras including Vienna Philharmonic, London Symphony Orchestra, English Chamber Orchestra, Boston Symphony, under such conductors as Maazel, Barenboim, Haitink, Sanderling, Sawallisch, and Ozawa; Festival engagements include Lucerne, 1979, and Salzburg, from 1983; USA debut in 1984 with the Pittsburgh Symphony; Tour of USA with Chamber Orchestra of Europe under Lorin Maazel, 1986; Performed at the Mostly Mozart in New York, Tanglewood and Ravinia Festivals in 1987; Season 1988–89 playing at Germany, London, Boston, Munich, Milan and Oslo; Sibelius Concerto at the Helsinki Festival and the Beethoven Concerto with the Berlin Philharmonic; Highlights during 1993–94 included extensive tours in Japan and Australia; Concerts with Munich Philharmonic and Christoph von Dohnányi; Engagements with the Vienna Philharmonic Orchestra and Lorin Maazel, the Gustav Mahler Jugend Orchester and Bernard Haitink, the Tonhalle Orchestra Zürich and Claus Peter Flor and the Rotterdam Philharmonic Orchestra; Philadelphia Orchestra and Wolfgang Sawallisch; The English Chamber Orchestra, on tour in Japan; The Orchestre de Paris and David Zinman and the orchestra of the Bayerische Rundfunk and Lorin Maazel; Boston Symphony Orchestra and Bernard Haitink; Season 2001–02 with the Pittsburgh Orchestra, Los Angeles Philharmonic Orchestra and Berlin Philharmonic Orchestra; Premiere of Ligeti Concerto, 2001 and Matthias Pintscher's Concerto, 2003; engagements include Los Angeles Philharmonic Orchestra and Antonio Pappano; Chicago Symphony Orchestra and Manfred Honeck; Nat. Symphony Orchestra of Washington and Leonard Slatkin; Berlin Philharmonic Orchestra and Bernard Haitink; Philharmonia Orchestra and Wolfgang Sawallisch; Symphony Orchestra of Bavarian Radio and

Mariss Jansons. *Recordings include:* Concertos of Berg, Beethoven, Brahms, Dvořák, Glazunov, Mendenssohn, Mozart, Prokofiev, Ravel (Tzigane), Sain-Saëns No. 3, Sibelius, Stravinsky, Tschaikovsky and Weill; all Mozart and Prokofiev sonatas, with pianist Alexander Lonquich; works by Ravel, Debussy and Janáček; 6 solo sonatas of Eugène Ysaÿe; Ligeti's violin concerto. *Honours:* Premio del Accademia Musicale Chigiana, Siena, 1990; Rheinischer Kulturpreis, 1994. *Address:* c/o Riaskoff Concert Management, 34 avenue du Beau Séjour, 1180 Brussels, Belgium.

ZIMMERMANN, Margarita; Singer (Mezzo-Soprano); b. Aug. 1942, Buenos Aires, Argentina. *Education:* Studied in Buenos Aires. *Career:* Debut: Teatro Colón Buenos Aires, as Orpheus in the opera by Gluck, 1977; European debut at the Landestheater in Salzburg, as Carmen and Ulrica in Un Ballo in Maschera; Covent Garden debut in 1980 as Cherubino; US appearances at Miami as Dalila in 1979 and San Francisco as Rosina in 1982; Further engagements at Naples, Bologna, Venice, Rome, Lyon, Geneva and Paris; Further roles include Mozart's Sextus, Idamante and Zerlina, Handel's Giulio Cesare and Agrippina, Juno in Cavalli's Ercole Amante and Wagner's Fricka; In 1988 sang at Piacenza and Madrid as Massenet's Charlotte and as Andromache in Rossini's Ermione; Appeared as Thérèse in the opera by Massenet at Opéra de Monte Carlo, 1989. *Recordings include:* The Singer in Manon Lescaut.

ZIMMERMANN, Margrit; Composer; b. 7 Aug. 1927, Bern, Switzerland. *Education:* Studied piano and theory with Jeanne Bovet and Walter Furrer in Bern, with Denise Bidal in Lausanne, and masterclasses with Alfred Cortot; Diploma in Pianoforte; Composition studies under Arthur Honegger, Ecole Normale de Musique de Paris; Study as conductor with Ewald Korner, Municipal Theatre of Bern; International masterclasses with Igor Markevitch, Monte Carlo, and Hans Swarowsky, Ossiach; Diploma in Composition, Giuseppe Verdi Conservatorium, Milan. *Career:* Music teacher, Bern; Composer. *Compositions:* Numerous including symphonic and scenic works, chamber music for a wide range of instruments, vocal and solo works for piano, strings, wind, percussion and guitar; Works include Panta Rhei, Op 39, 1987, Cloccachorda, Op 40, 1987, Die Gestundete Zeit, Op 52, 1987; Piano Time, Op 46, 1987; Quadriga, Op 51, 1987; Murooji, Op 57, for Guitar Solo; Trptychon, Op 58; Pianorama, Op 59; In Urbis Honorem, symphony for Orchestra and Choir; Jubilation, concert for Orchestra. *Recordings:* Cloccachordia; Piano Time; Quadriga; Pensieri; Orphische Taenze; Quartetto d'Archi. *Address:* Ostermundigenstrasse 22, 3006 Bern, Switzerland.

ZIMMERMANN, Tabea; Concert Violist; b. 8 Oct. 1968, Lahr, Germany. *Education:* Studied with Ulrich Koch and Sándor Végh. *Career:* Professor at the Conservatoire in Frankfurt, 1994–; Frequent concerts with such soloists as Gidon Kremer, Heinz Holliger, Thomas Zehetmair, Steven Isserlis and Heinrich Schiff; Appearances at Prades, Schleswig-Holstein, Lockenhaus, Marlboro and other chamber music festivals; Regular recitals with pianist Hartmut Holl; Concert engagements include Mozart's Sinfonia Concertante in Amsterdam, and at the Salzburg Festival; Has also performed with the Bamberg Symphony under Christoph Eschenbach, at Frankfurt with Gary Bertini, Penderecki's Concerto with the composer conducting the Munich Philharmonic and concerts in Hamburg, Tokyo, Rome, Copenhagen, Helsinki and Israel; Gave the world premieres of concertos by Mark Koptyman and Volker David Kirchner in 1992; Premiere of Ligeti's Viola Sonata at Cologne in 1993; Alexander Goehr's Schlussgesang at the 1997 Aldeburgh Festival and Berio's Concerto for Clarinet and Viola (1996) with Paul Meyer; Recent engagements include the Mahler Chamber Orchestra; Recitals in Italy, France and Belgium; Scottish Chamber Orchestra, Royal Concertgebouw, CBSO, Orchestre National de Lyon; Season 2002 with premieres of Recicanto by Heinz Holliger and Concerto by Sally Beamish. *Recordings:* Mozart's Concertante K364; Bach Trio Sonatas; Gubaidulina Hommage; Chamber works by Bruch, Mozart and Schumann; The Concerto in Europe; Double Concertos and works by Penderecki. *Honours:* First Prize at competitions in Geneva, Budapest and awarded the Vatelot Viola at Paris; Frankfurter Musikpreis, 1995; Accademia Musicale Chigiana, Sienna, 1997. *Current Management:* Harrison/Parrott Ltd, 12 Penzance Place, London, W11 4PA, England. *Telephone:* (20) 7229 9166. *Fax:* (20) 7221 5042. *Website:* www.harrisonparrott.com.

ZIMMERMANN, Udo; Composer and Conductor; b. 6 Oct. 1943, Dresden, Germany. *Education:* Studied composition with J. P. Thilman at the Dresden Musikhochschule, 1962–68; Masterclasses at the Akademie der Kunste East Berlin, 1968–70. *Career:* Composer and Producer at the Dresden State Opera, 1970; Founded the Studio for New Music in Dresden 1974; Professor of Composition at the Dresden Hochshule für Musik 1978; Professor of Experimental Music Theatre at Dresden, 1982; Conducted the Bavarian Radio Symphony Orchestra in the premiere of Hartmann's Sinfonia Tragica, Munich 1989; Premiere of Bernhard Jesl's Opera Der König Stirbt at Bonn in 1990; Intendant of the Leipzig State Opera from 1990, Deutsche Oper –2002. *Compositions include:*

Operas: Die Weisse Rose, 1967, Levins Muhle, 1973, Die Wundersame Schusterfrau, 1982; 5 songs for Baritone and Orchestra, 1964; Musik für Streicher, 1967; String Quartet, 1967; Sieh, Meine Augen for Chamber Orchestra, 1970; Mutazioni for Orchestra, 1972; Choreographien Nach Edgar Degas for 21 Instruments, 1974; Hymnus An Die Sonne, after Kleist, for Soprano, Flute and Harpsichord, 1976; Pax Questuosa for 5 Soloists, 3 Choirs and Orchestra, 1980. *Current Management:* AWA, Storkower Strasse 134, 1055 Berlin, Germany.

ZIMMERMANN, Walter; Composer; b. 15 April 1949, Schwabach, Germany. *Education:* Studied piano, violin and oboe; Composition with Werner Heider and Otto Laske at Utrecht; Ethnological Centre Jaap Kunst in Amsterdam, 1970–73; Computer music in the USA, 1974. *Career:* Pianist in the Ars-Nova Ensemble of Nuremberg, 1968–70; Founded Beginner Studio at Cologne, 1977; Lecturer at Darmstadt, 1982, and Liège Conservatory from 1982; Professor of Composition, HDK Berlin. *Compositions include:* Lokale Musik, 15 works for various forces, 1977–81; Uber Die Dörfer, dramatic song for Soprano, Chorus and Orchestra, 1986; Fragmente der Liebe for Saxophone and String Quartet, 1987; Beginners Mind for piano, 1975; Wüstenwanderung for 1986; Festina lente for string quartet; Diastasis/Diastema for 2 orchestras without conductor, 1992; Distentio for string trio, 1990; Affeklenlehre for ensemble, 1995–. *Address:* c/o GEMA, Postfach 80 07 67, 81607 Munich, Germany.

ZIMMERMANN, Wolfram; Singer (Bass-Baritone); b. 17 April 1920, Stuttgart, Germany. *Education:* Studied with his father, at the Stuttgart and Vienna Academies and with Anna Bahr-Mildenburg. *Career:* Debut: Stuttgart in 1947 as Rossini's Basilio; Radio broadcasts in Germany and Austria; Sang Beckmesser in Die Meistersinger, under Furtwängler, at La Scala, 1952; Created title role in Titus Feuerfuchs by Heinrich Sutermeister for television in Austria, 1959; Vienna Staatsoper 1958–63, notably as Leporello, Mozart's Papageno and the Doctor in Wozzeck by Berg; Rome Opera in 1956, Graz in 1958, Barcelona, 1958–63, and Mexico City in 1966 as Beckmesser; Other roles include the title roles in Mozart's Figaro, Gounod's Mephistopheles and Donizetti's Don Pasquale; mem, Honorary Cavalier, Deutschcherrn-Ritterbund Norimberga. *Recordings:* Zar und Zimmermann by Lortzing; Tannhäuser by Wagner. *Honours:* Diploma, International Song, Geneva, 1949; Bach Prize, Leipzig, 1950; Gold Medal, Accademia Italia, 1980. *Address:* Erbisleiten 6, 91227 Weissenbrunn, Gemeinde Leinburg, Germany.

ZINKLER, Christiane; Singer (Mezzo-Soprano); b. 23 Nov. 1947, Coburg, Germany. *Education:* Studied with Willi Domgraf-Fassbaender in Nuremberg and with Clemens Kaiser-Breme in Essen. *Career:* Debut: Deutsche Oper am Rhein, Düsseldorf, in 1968 as Messenger in Dallapiccola's Job; Member of the Dortmund Opera notably as Gluck's Orpheus, Erda and Fricka in Der Ring des Nibelungen, Ulrica, Hansel, Monteverdi's Poppea, Anina in Der Rosenkavalier, Cherubino and Dorabella; Guest appearances in Hamburg, Essen, Copenhagen, Wiesbaden and Florence; Many concert appearances. *Address:* c/o Opernhaus, Kuhstrasse 12, 4600 Dortmund, Germany.

ZINMAN, David Joel; Conductor; b. 9 July 1936, New York City, USA; m. Mary Ingham. *Education:* Violin at Oberlin Conservatory, 1954–58; MA, Composition, University of Minnesota; Pierre Monteux's assistant at his summer school in Maine, 1961–63. *Career:* Debut: Holland Festival in 1963; Philadelphia Orchestra, 1967; Music Director, Netherlands Chamber Orchestra, 1964–77, Rotterdam Philharmonic Orchestra, 1979–82, Rochester Philharmonic Orchestra, 1974–85, Baltimore Symphony Orchestra, 1985–99 (Music Director Emeritus 1999–2001), Tonhalle Orchestra, Zürich, 1995–; Music Director of the Aspen Music Festival and School, 1998–. *Recordings:* More than 80 records including Janáček's Sinfonietta, Chopin's Les Sylphides, Tchaikovsky's Serenade for Strings, Grieg's Holberg Suite, C. P. E. Bach's Complete Flute Concerti, J. C. Bach's Symphonies, Chopin's Concerto No. 2 in F minor for Piano and Orchestra, Mozart's Piano Concerto No. 12 in A, K414, Dvořák's Legends, Op 59, Berlioz's Overture to Benvenuto Cellini, Love Scene from Roméo et Juliette, Three Excerpts from La Damnation de Faust, Minuet of the Will-o-the-Wisps, Dance of the Sylphs, Rákóczy March, Le Corsaire Overture, Trojan March, Royal Hunt and Storm from Les Troyens, La Marseillaise; Masterworks–Britten's Symphony for Cello and Orchestra, Op 68; Barber's Concerto for Cello and Orchestra, Op 22; Roussel's Symphony No. 1; Mozart's Piano Concerto No. 22, K482, and No. 23, K488. *Honours:* Named by Time Magazine as One of the Five For the Future, 1982; 2 Grand Prix du Disque Awards; 2 Edison Prizes; 5 Grammy Awards; Deutsche Schallplattenpreis; Gramophone Award; Ditson Award from Columbia University, 1997; City of Zurich Art Prize, 2002; Title of Chevalier de l'Ordre des Arts et des Lettres. *Current Management:* ICM Artists Ltd, 40 West 57th Street, New York, NY 10019, USA. *Address:* Harrison/Parrott Ltd, 12 Penzance Place, London, W11 4PA, England. *Telephone:* (20) 7229 9166. *Fax:* (20) 7221 5042. . *Website:* www.harrisonparrott.com.

ZINOVENKO, Yuri; Singer (Bass); b. 1955, Simferopol, Ukraine. *Education:* Studied in Tashkent. *Career:* Sang first at the Kirov Opera, St Petersburg; Croatian National Opera, Zagreb, 1981–87; Further engagements at the Frankfurt Opera and the Staatstheater, Darmstadt; Guest appearances in Italy, Israel, Austria, Russia and the USA; Roles have included the Hermit in Der Freischütz, Water Sprite in Rusalka, Prince Gremin (Eugene Onegin), and Kochubey in Tchaikovsky's Mazeppa; Verdi roles include Zaccaria and Lodovico; Sang The Prophet in the first production this century of Zemlinsky's first opera, Sarema (Trier Opera, 1996); Concerts include Mozart's Requiem and Shostakovich's 13th Symphony, Babi-Yar. *Recordings include:* Sarema (Koch International). *Address:* c/o Theater der Stadt Trier, Am Augustinerhof, 5500 Trier, Germany.

ZINSSTAG, Gérard; composer; b. 9 May 1941, Geneva, Switzerland; m. 1984; one s. one d. *Education:* CNSM, Paris, Chigiana Acad., Siena, Musikhochschule, Zürich, studied with H. U. Lehmann, Helmut Lachenmann. *Career:* composer-in-residence, Berlin 1981 (DAAD); orchestral musician touring Europe, 1964–67; solo flute, Orchestra of Zürich, Tonhalle, 1967–75; participation in summer course, Darmstadt, 1976–78; seminar at University of California, Berkeley, 1979 and several in New York; founder of Festival of Zürich, Tage für neue Musik Zürich, 1986–; tour of Russia, Moscow and Baku, 1990; several conferences and lectures in Moscow, Taipeh, Paris (Sorbonne and IRCAM), Salzburg, Geneva, Zürich, Bamberg etc.; mem. Suisa, Composers' Forum, New York, ISCM. *Compositions:* Déliements; Wenn Zum Biespiel; Tatastenfelder; Suono Reale; Innanzi; Foris; Perforation; Altération; Trauma; Edition Modern Munich; Cut Sounds; Incalzando, 1981; Artifices, 1982–83; Sept Fragments, 1982–83; Stimuli, 1984; Tempi Inquieti, 1984–86; Eden Jeden, 1987; Artifices ll, 1988; Tempor, 1992; String Quartet no. 2, 1995; Tahir, 1995; Ergo, 1996; Hommage à Charles Racine, for mezzo and ensemble, 1997; Ubu Cocu, opéra bouffe, 2000; Passage, for orchestra, 2002; String Quartet no. 3. *Recordings:* Foris, Innanzi, etc; Tempor; Diffractions. *Publications:* Pro Musica, 1988; Revue Musicale Suisse, 1979–80. *Address:* Seefeldstr. 191, 8008 Zürich, Switzerland; 4 place Victor Basch, 30400 Ville-lés-Avignon, France.

ZITEK, Vaclav; Singer (Baritone); b. 24 March 1932, Tisa, Czechoslovakia. *Education:* Studied in Prague with Adrian Levicky. *Career:* Debut: Prague Opera Studio in 1957 as Germont in La Traviata; Member of the National Theatre, Prague, in operas by Mozart, Verdi, Tchaikovsky, Smetana, Dvořák, Martinů, Puccini, Strauss and Prokofiev; Guest appearances at the Bolshoi Theatre Moscow, the Staatsoper and Komische Oper Berlin, National Opera in Bucharest and the Bordeaux Opera; Sang at Prague National Theatre in 1983 as Premysl in Smetana's Libuše; Frequent concert and oratorio engagements. *Recordings:* Operas by Smetana, Dvořák's Jacobin and Šarka by Fibich; Šiškov in From the House of the Dead, and Jenůfa with the Vienna Philharmonic conducted by Charles Mackerras; Don Giovanni, Don Carlos, Trovatore, Pelléas et Mélisande, Faust, Macbeth, The Queen of Spades, Pagliacci; Smetana/Dalibor, Libuše, The Kiss, The Secret, The Devil's Wall; The Makropulos Case; From the House of the Dead; Jenůfa; The Cunning Little Vixen; Don Giovanni; Luisa Miller. *Honours:* Laureate of the State Prize, 1981; National Artist of Czechoslovakia, 1985; Prize of the National Academy of Recording and Science, Šiškov, in Janáček's From the House of the Dead, with the Vienna Philharmonic conducted by Charles Mackerras, 1981. *Address:* Ke skalkam 2450, 106 00 Prague 10, Czech Republic.

ZIVA, Vladimir P.; Russian conductor; b. 7 March 1957, Arkhangelsk; m. Ziva Anna; two s. *Education:* Leningrad State Conservatory, Moscow State Conservatory. *Career:* asst to principal conductor Symphony Orchestra of Moscow Philharmonics 1984–87; teacher Moscow State conservatory 1988–89; Artistic Dir and chief conductor Nizhne-Novgorod Philharmonic Orchestra 1988–2000; principal conductor St Petersburg Mussorgsky Theatre of Opera and Ballet 1990–92; Artistic Dir and principal conductor Moscow Symphony orchestra 2000–; co-founder Krasnodar Opera Co. 2003–; repertoire comprises classical and modern music; opera stage productions, in collaboration with B. Pokrovsky, include The Turn of the Screw, Albert Herring by B. Britten, Snow Maiden by P. Tchaikovsky. *Honours:* Hon. Artist of Russia, Conductor of the Year 1996, 1997; State Prize of Russian Federation 1995. *Address:* Kazanskaya str. 8/10 apt. 42, St Petersburg 191186, Russia (home). *Telephone:* 812-117 2337 (home).

ZIVONI, Yossi; Violinist; b. 2 Dec. 1939, Tel-Aviv, Israel; m. Jeanne 1962; one d. *Education:* Israel Acad. of Music, Tel-Aviv, Conservatoire Royal de Musique de Bruxelles, Belgium. *Career:* debut, Amsterdam, Netherlands 1964; concert tours in Europe, Israel, Australia, Canada, Far East and South America; Principal Tutor, Royal Northern Coll. of Music, Manchester; Prof. of Violin, Royal Coll. of Music, London; Leader of the Gabrieli String Quartet, 1995–2000; mem. Royal Society of Musicians of Great Britain. *Recordings:* Mozart Sonatas, Bach Sonatas and Partitas, Mendelssohn Sonatas, Bartók Sonata for solo violin and violin duos.

Honours: Paganini International Competition 1960, Bavarian Radio International Competition, Munich 1961, Queen Elisabeth International Competition, Brussels, Belgium 1963, Fellow, Royal Northern Coll. of Music. *Current Management:* Anglo-Swiss Management Ltd, Suite 6, 72 Fairhazel Gardens, London, NW6 3SR, England. *Address:* 18 Midholm, London, NW11 6LN, England.

ZLATKOVA, Sonia; Singer (Soprano); b. 1963, Tolbuchin, Bulgaria. *Education:* Studied in Varna and Sofia. *Career:* Sang in concert in France in 1988 and made her stage debut at Ruse in 1989 as Despina; Sang at Bulgarian National Opera at Sofia from 1989 as Gilda, Lucia, the Queen of Night and Rosina; Guest appearances at Bregenz in 1991 as Frasquita, at St Gallen as Oscar and at Kaiserslautern as the Queen of Night; Sang Pamina at Schönbrunn, Vienna, 1996; Sang Zerlina and Nannetta for Graz Opera, 1999–2001. *Address:* Bulgarian National Opera, Boulevard Dondoukov 58, 1000 Sofia, Bulgaria.

ZNAIDER, Nikolaj; Violinist; b. 1975, Denmark. *Education:* Royal Danish Academy; Juilliard School of Music; Vienna Conservatory with Boris Kuschnir. *Career:* Appearances with the Cleveland, Leipzig Gewandhaus and St Petersburg Philharmonic Orchestras; Engaged season 1999–2000 with the Berlin Philharmonic Orchestra under Daniel Barenboim, London Symphony under Rostropovich at the Barbican and on tour to Japan and London Philharmonic with Kurt Masur at the Royal Festival Hall; Los Angeles Philharmonic, Czech, Oslo and Munich Philharmonics, BBC Symphony and Budapest Festival Orchestra; Yehudi Menuhin Memorial Concert at the Albert Hall; Engaged for tour of Australia, 2000; Nielsen's concerto at the London Proms, 2002; Recitals in New York, Paris, Amsterdam and Lucerne; Frequent guest with the ChicagoSymphony Orchestra, Cleveland Orchestra, Detroit Symphony, National Symphony, New York Philharmonic Orchestra and the Philadelphia Orchestra; He has collaborated with Daniel Barenboim, Herbert Blomstedt, Myung Whun Chung, Sir Colin Davis, Charles Dutiut, Valery Gergiev, Mariss Jansons, Neeme Jarvi, Lorin Maazel, Kurt Masur, Zubin Mehta, Mstislav Rostropovich, Leonard Slatkin and Yuri Temirkanov. *Recordings:* Bruch No. 1 and Nielsen Concertos with the London Philharmonic and Lawrence Foster. *Honours:* Winner, Queen Elisabeth Violin Competition, Brussels, 1997; First Prize at the 1992 Carl Nielson International Violin Competition. *Address:* c/o IMG Artists, Lovell House, 616 Chiswick High Road, London W4 5RX, England. *E-mail:* tcarrig@imgworld.com.

ZOBEL, Ingeborg; Singer (Soprano); b. 31 July 1928, Gorlitz, Schlesien, Germany. *Education:* Studied at the Dresden State Music Academy with Eduard Plate. *Career:* Debut: As Amelia in Un Ballo in Maschera, Cottbus, 1952; Sang in Schwerin, 1955–57, Rostock, 1957–66, and Weimar, 1966–72; Dresden Staatsoper from 1972, notably as Wagner's Brünnhilde, Isolde and Ortrud, the Marschallin, Tosca, Santuzza, Lady Macbeth and Leonore in Fidelio; Guest appearances in Leningrad, Barcelona, Budapest, Wiesbaden, Prague, Belgrade and Sofia; Teacher at the Franz Liszt Musikhochschule in Weimar. *Recordings:* Various albums. *Address:* c/o Dresden Staatsoper, 8012 Dresden, Germany.

ZOGHBY, Linda; Singer (Soprano); b. 17 Aug. 1949, Mobile, Alabama, USA. *Education:* Studied at Florida State University and with Elena Nikolaii. *Career:* Sang at first in concert; Stage debut at Houston in 1974 as Donna Elvira in Don Giovanni; Dallas Opera in 1976 as Giulietta in I Capuleti e i Montecchi; Glyndebourne Festival from 1978 as Mimi and in Haydn's La Fedeltà Premiata; Metropolitan Opera in 1982 and 1986 as Mimi and as Ilia in Idomeneo; Other roles include Mozart's Fiordigili and Pamina. *Recordings:* Haydn's L'Isola Disabitata and L'Incontro Improvviso.

ZOLLER, Karlheinz; Flautist; b. 24 Aug. 1928, Hohr-Grenzhausen, Germany. *Education:* Studied at the Detmold and Frankfurt Musikhochschule. *Career:* Many performances as concert soloist and chamber musician from 1950; Soloist with the Berlin Philharmonic, 1960–69, and teacher at the Berlin Musikhochschule; Professor at Hamburg before returning to Berlin; Has premiered the Double Concerto by Ligeti (1972) and the flute concerto by Isang Yun (1977). *Address:* Berlin Philharmonic Orchestra, Philharmonie, Matthaikirchstrasse, W-1000 Berlin, Germany.

ZOLLMAN, Ronald; Conductor; b. 8 April 1950, Antwerp, Belgium; m. Dominique G. Mols. *Education:* Diploma in Conducting, Brussels Conservatoire; Diploma, Academy Chigiana. *Career:* Has conducted throughout Europe, North and South America, and in Australia; Head of Conducting Faculty at the Royal Brussels Conservatory of Music; Musical Director of the Philharmonic Orchestra of UNAM, Mexico. *Recordings:* Belgian Music for Ministry of Culture, Brussels; various recordings with the National Orchestra of Belgium, the World Orchestra, the London Sinfonietta, Basle Symphony Orchestra, Northern Sinfonia, Barcelona Orchestra and Northern Sinfonia. *Honours:* Premio Firenze for Conductors, 1972. *Current Management:* Konsert-

bolaget, Kungsgatan 32, 11132, Stockholm, Sweden. *Address:* Rue Général de Gaulle 36, 1310 La Hulpe, Belgium.

ZOUHAR, Vit; Composer and Musicologist; b. 13 March 1966, Brno, Czechoslovakia; m. Karla Zemanová, 28 June 1997. *Education:* Master, 1989, Postgraduate degree, 1993, Composition, Janáček University of Music and Dramatic Arts, Brno; Composition, University of Music and Dramatic Arts, Graz, Accademia Chigiana, Siena; Master, Musicology, Masaryk University, Brno, 1996; Doctorate 2001, Janáček University of Music and Dramatic Arts, Brno. *Career:* Teacher, Musical Theory, State Conservatory, Brno, 1989; Assistant, Palacky University, Olomouc, 1992–; Teacher, 1992–, Guest Composer, 1993, Institute of Electronic Music, Graz, Austria; Guest Composer, Werkstadt Graz, 1994; Co-Founder, Teacher, Computer Music Study Room, Ostrava University, 1996; Works performed by State Philharmonic Orchestra Brno, Moravian Symphony Orchestra, DAMA DAMA percussion ensemble, Sonata a Tre, also many concerts, festivals, radio, television, including: Hörgänge Wien; Experimental Music Festival, Prague; IST alles, ballet, Czech television, 1992; The Garden, Forfest Music Festival, 1995; Like Water Is, ballet, Janáček Theatre, Brno, National Theatre, Prague, 1996; Wide Crossing, ballet, Graz Opernhaus, 1997; Prague Spring; Europalia Brussel; EXPO; Vice-Dean of the Pedagogical Faculty Palacký University Olomuc, 2003. *Compositions include:* Le Vedute di Bruna for string quartet, 1985; Agastia for large orchestra, 1988; The Sun Gate for 4 percussionists and large orchestra, 1989; Es scheint mir aber immer for violin, clarinet and piano, 1992; Ist alles for 2 guitarists, 1992; Close Encounters of Those Wild at Heart for stereo-orchestra, 1993; Like Water Is for clarinet, bassoon and piano, 1994; Wide Crossing, 1994; Il Pendolo for chamber ensemble, 1998; Coronide, chamber opera, 2000; Petite sirène, for four percussionists 2001; Rings of Levels, for a recorder quartet, 2003; Torso, chamber opera together with Tomáš Hanzlík, 2003. *Address:* CZ-67907 Kotvrdovice 175, Czech Republic.

ZOUHAR, Zdenek; Composer and Musicologist; b. 8 Feb. 1927, Kotvrdovice, Czechoslovakia. *Education:* PhD, Brno University, 1967; Studied composition at Brno Janáček Academy, 1967. *Career:* Head of Music Section at Brno University Library, 1953–61; Editor for Czech Radio, 1961–70; Professor at Brno Janáček Academy, 1962–. *Compositions include:* Sonatina for piano, 1948; Spring Suite for 3 violins, 1949; Partita for organ, 1956; Midnight Mass, 1957; '151' Music for wind quintet I, 1958; Trio for flute, contralto and bass clarinet, 1961; Divertimento I for 4 winds and percussion, 1965; Music for strings, 1966; 2 String Quartets, 1966, 1983; Symphonic Triptych, 1967; Music for wind quintet II, 1982; Triple Concerto for clarinet, trumpet, trombone and orchestra, 1970; Chamber radio opera, Metamorphosis, 1971; Variations On A Theme By B Martinů for symphonic orchestra, 1979; Musica Giocosa Per Archi, 1981; Brass Quintet, 1985; Comic opera, A Great Love, 1986; Oratorio, The Flames Of Constance, 1988; Divertimento III for Brno Brass Band, 1993; Pavel Haas Symphony (1941) completed by Šdenek Zouhar, 1994. *Address:* Halasovo ná m 4, CZ 638 00 Brno-Lesná, Czech Republic.

ZSCHAU, Marilyn; Singer (Soprano); b. 9 Feb. 1944, Chicago, Ilinois, USA. *Education:* Juilliard School of Music, 1961–65; Further study with John Lester in Montana. *Career:* Toured with Metropolitan National Company, 1965–66; Debut at Vienna Volksoper as Marietta in Die Tote Stadt, 1967; Vienna Staatsoper in 1971 as the Composer in Ariadne auf Naxos; New York City Opera from 1978, as Puccini's Minnie and Butterfly, Odabella in Attila, and Maddalena in Andrea Chénier; Metropolitan Opera debut in 1985 as Musetta in La Bohème; La Scala debut in 1986 as the Dyer's Wife in Die Frau ohne Schatten; Appearances world-wide in operatic roles including Aida, Leonora, Desdemona, Butterfly, Brünnhilde in Die Walküre and Götterdämmerung, Salome, Elektra, Prokofiev's Renata in The Fiery Angel, Shostakovich's Katerina in Lady Macbeth of Mtsensk, Santuzza and Manon Lescaut; Sang Puccini's Minnie at Reggio Emilia and Chicago in 1990, and The Fiery Angel at the 1990 Holland Festival; Other roles include: Janáček's Vixen and Kostelnicka in Jenůfa, the Marschallin and Octavian in Der Rosenkavalier, Mozart's Fiordigili, Countess and Pamina, Lucille in Dantons Tod, and Tatiana in Eugene Onegin; Sang Elektra at Buenos Aires, 1996; Season 1998 as Kostelnicka in Jenůfa at Santiago; Sang Elektra with New Israeli Opera at Savonlinna, 2000. *Recordings include:* Video of Covent Garden performance of La Bohème. *Honours:* Martha Baird Rockefeller Foundation Scholarships, 1962, 1963. *Address:* c/o Janine Meyer and Associates, Suite 1C, 201 West 54th Street, New York, NY 10019, USA.

ZSIGMONDY, Denes; Violinist; b. 9 April 1922, Budapest, Hungary; m. Anneliese Nissen, pianist, Aug 1947, 2 d. *Education:* Baccalaureate, University of Budapest; Franz Liszt Academy, Budapest; Studied with Geza de Kresz, Leo Weiner, Imre Waldbauer and others. *Career:* Soloist with Vienna and Berlin Symphonies, Tokyo, Budapest and Munich Philharmonies, Radio Orchestras ABC Sydney, Melbourne and Munich, Stuttgart Chamber Orchestra, and Salzburg Camerata; Performed with

BBC Radio London, NHK Tokyo, Radio Paris and others; World premieres of works by Bialas, Eder, Genzmer, Rozsa and others; Professor, University of Washington, Seattle, USA, 1971–; Occasional masterclasses including New England Conservatory; Established annual Holzenhausen Festival in Ammerland, Bavaria with concerts and violin courses, 1978–; Visiting Professor, Boston University, 1981–82; Courses at the Summer Academy, Salzburg-Mozarteum, Austria and in Germany, Italy, Hungary, Poland and others, 1986–. *Recordings include:* The Virtuoso Violin; The Romantic Violin; Zsigmondy Plays Bartók, vols 1 and 2; Sonatas by Beethoven, Brahms, Grieg, Franck, Debussy and all Mozart and Schubert violin-piano music. *Address:* Bonselweg 10, 8193 Ambach, Bavaria, Germany.

ZUKERMAN, Eugenia; Flautist; b. 25 Sept. 1944, Cambridge, MA, USA; m. (1) Pinchas Zukerman, divorced, (2) David Seltzer, 1988. *Education:* Juilliard School, New York with Julius Baker. *Career:* Debut: New York Town Hall in 1971; Has played with most major orchestras in the USA and Canada; Tour of US with English Chamber Orchestra; European performances with the Royal Philharmonic, Israel Chamber Orchestra and the Hamburg Bach Solisten; Participation in Festival of Two Worlds at Spoleto, London's South Bank Festival and the Edinburgh Festival; Collaborations with Jean-Pierre Rampal at Carnegie Hall in 1976, and James Galway; Music Commentator on CBS News's Sunday Morning. *Address:* c/o 10 Barley Mow Passage, London, W4 4PH, England.

ZUKERMAN, Pinchas; Conductor, Violist, Violinist and Teacher; b. 16 July 1948, Tel-Aviv, Israel; m. (1) Eugenia Zukerman, divorced, (2) Tuesday Weld, divorced, 2 d. *Education:* Israel Conservatory and Academy of Music, 1956; Juilliard School, New York, 1961 with Ivan Galamian. *Career:* Won 1967 Leventritt Competition and soon appeared with most of the world's leading orchestras in the standard repertoire; 1969 with New York Philharmonic and at Brighton Festival; Debut as conductor in London, 1970; Guest appearances include English Chamber Orchestra, Philadelphia Orchestra, Boston Symphony and Israel Philharmonic; Artistic Director, South Bank Summer Music, London, 1978–80; Music Director of St Paul Chamber Orchestra, 1980–86; Principal Guest Conductor of Dallas International Music Festival, 1990–94; Music Director, Baltimore Symphony Orchestra Summer MusicFest, 1997–99; Music Director, National Arts Centre Orchestra, Canada, 1999–; Noted in chamber music repertory in which he also plays viola; Concerts with Daniel Barenboim, Jacqueline du Pré, Isaac Stern, Yo-Yo Ma, Itzhak Perlman and Jean-Pierre Rampal; Participant in many television specials including Alexander's Bachtime Band, with Stern and Alexander Schneider; Premieres of Boulez, Kraft, Lutoslawski, Neikrug, Takemitsu and Picker. *Recordings include:* Over 90 recordings including, Bach with English Chamber Orchestra as director and soloist, Beethoven and Mozart Sonatas with Marc Neikrug, Mozart Quintets with Tokyo String Quartet. *Honours:* Numerous including, Doctorate of Brown University, Achievement Award from International Centre, NY, and Medal of Arts Award presented by President Reagan, 1983; Isaac Stern Award for Artistic Excellence from National Arts Awards, 2002. *Address:* c/o Kirshbaum Demler Associates Inc, 711 West End Avenue #5KN, New York, NY 10025, USA.

ZUKOFSKY, Paul; Violinist and Conductor; b. 22 Oct. 1943, Brooklyn, New York, USA. *Education:* BM, 1964, MS, 1964, Juilliard School of Music. *Career:* Creative Associate, SUNY, Buffalo, 1964–65; Various positions as violinist, and violin teacher, 1965–75; President, Musical Observations Inc, 1975–; Principal Investigator, Project Director, Limits, 1976–82; Conductor with various orchestras, 1977–79; Programme Co-ordinator, American Portraits, concert series at John F Kennedy Center, 1980–; Conductor, Contemporary Chamber Ensemble at Juilliard School of Music, 1984–; Founder, Principal Conductor, Sinfoniuhljomsveit Aeskunnar, 1985–; Director of Chamber Music Activities, The Juilliard School, 1987–89; Artistic Director, Summer Garden Concert Series, Museum of Modern Art, NYC, 1987–. *Recordings include:* As conductor: Various Icelandic Orchestral Works, 1987, Sixteen Dances by Cage, 1984; As violinist: Penderecki's Capriccio for Violin and Orchestra, 1968, Babbitt and Milton Sextets, 1972, Glass's Strung Out, 1977, Cage's Cheap Imitation, 1981, Sonata for Solo Violin, 1983, For John Cage, Feldman, Morton, 1984. *Contributions:* Articles in professional journals including The Psychology of Music, with Sternberg and Knoll. *Honours:* Nominee for Grammy Awards, 1972; Pick of the Pack, Time Magazine, 1975; ASCAP Community Orchestra Award, 1979; ASCAP Citation, 1979; Guggenheim Fellowship, 1983–84; National Endowment for The Arts Fellowship, 1983; Knight's Cross, Icelandic Order of the Falcon. *Address:* c/o The Juilliard School of Music (Violin Faculty), Lincoln Plaza, New York, NY 10023, USA.

ZUPKO, Ramon; Composer; b. 14 Nov. 1932, Pittsburgh, Pennsylvania, USA. *Education:* Studied with Vincent Persichetti at Juilliard (BS 1956, MS 1957) and with Schiske at the Vienna Academy of Music, 1958–59; Electronic music at Columbia University, and with Koenig at the University of Utrecht. *Career:* Teacher of Theory and Director of Electronic Music at the Chicago Musical College of Roosevelt Uni-

versity, 1967–71; Professor of Composition and Director of Electronic Music at Western Michigan University, Kalamazoo, 1971–97; Gilmore Foundation Commission, 1990. *Compositions include:* Variations for orchestra, 1961; Violin Concerto, 1962; Translucents, for strings, 1967; Tangents, for 18 bass instruments, 1967; Radiants, for orchestra, 1971; Proud Music of the Storm, multimedia theatre, 1976; Wind Song, piano concerto, 1979; Life Dances, for orchestra, 1981; Where the Mountain Crosses, song cycle for mezzo and piano, 1982; Canti Terrae, for orchestra, 1982; 2 Symphonies, 1984, 1986; Series of twelve Chamber Pieces, Fluxus, for various instrumental combinations (1977–94); Vox Naturae, Concerto for Brass Quintet and Orchestra, 1992; Chaconne for piano, 1995; The Nightingale, Opera, 1998. *Honours:* NEA Grants, Koussevitzky Foundation Award and Guggenheim Fellowship (1981–82). *Address:* 1540 North 2nd Street, Kalamazoo, MI 49009, USA.

ZUR, Menachem, DipEd, BMus, MFA, DMusA; Israeli composer and teacher of theory and composition; b. 6 March 1942, Tel-Aviv. *Education:* College for Teachers of Music, Jerusalem, Rubin Academy of Music, Mannes College of Music, NY, USA, Sarah Lawrence College, Columbia University. *Career:* Musical Adviser to the Israel Museum, Jerusalem; Chairman of the Music Education Department of the Rubin Academy of Music, 1991; Chairperson, Israeli Composers' League, 1992–94, 2000–; Chair, Israeli Composers' League, 2000–. *Compositions include:* Fantasy for Piano; Sonata for Cello and Piano; Several works for Tape; Prisma for two pianos; Double Concerto for Bassoon, French Horn and Chamber Orchestra; Clarinet Quintet; Piano Concerto; Tuba Concerto; Violin Concerto, Concerto Grosso; Centres, string quartet; Pygmalion, chamber opera; Sonata for Violin and Piano; 3 Symphonies; Prelude for Band; The Golem for 11 Instruments and Baritone Solo; Horn Trio; 2 Sonatas for Cello and Piano; Fantasy for Brass Quintet; Circles of Time for Piano Solo; Pieces for Choir: Hallelujah, Kedushah, Shiluvium, A Tale of Two Sandals; concerto for piano 4 hands and orchestra, 1997; String Sextet, 1998; Prisma for piano duet, 1999. *Recordings include:* Chants and Horizons for Magnetic Tape; Sonata No. 1 for Cello and Piano; Clarinet Quintet, electro-acoustic music. *Publications:* Keyboard Harmony (co-author) 1980; contrib. to Musical Quarterly. *Honours:* Acum Prize for Life Achievements, 2001; Prime Minister Prize for Composition, 2001. *Address:* Rubin Academy of Music, Givat-Ram, Jerusalem, Israel.

ZVETANOV, Boiko; Singer (Tenor); b. 14 June 1955, Sofia, Bulgaria. *Education:* Studied at the Sofia Conservatory. *Career:* Sang with the Bulgarian National Opera from 1982 as the Duke of Mantua, Foresto in Attila, Fernando in La Favorita, Pollione and Radames; Concerts in Russia, Czechoslovakia and France (Verdi's Requiem at Paris), and the Italian Singer in Der Rosenkavalier at the Vienna Staatsoper; Sang at St Gallen in 1991 as Riccardo in Un Ballo in Maschera, Opernhaus Zürich as Lensky, Alvaro in Forza del Destino, Arnold in Guillaume Tell and Rodolfo; 1992 included Capriccio, Wiener Staatsoper, La Forza del Destino in Zürich, Guillaume Tell, La Bohème and Il Pirata in Zürich; 1993 included Hérodiade in Zürich, Cavalleria rusticana in Wiesbaden and Capriccio in Dresden; La Forza del Destino in Karlsruhe in 1993–94; Season 1994–95 included Rosenkavalier and Ballo in Maschera with Deutsche Oper Berlin; Lucia di Lammermoor at Teatro Principal in Valencia with L Alberti, 1995; Rosenkavalier, Oper der Stadt Bonn, director Spiros Argiris, 1995; Season 1999–2000 as Arvino in I Lombardi for Zürich Opera and Manrico at the Prague State Opera; Don Carlos in Mainz, 2002. *Recordings:* CDs of arias and duets from Verdi's operas. *Address:* Opernhaus Zürich, Falkenstrasse 1, 8008 Zürich, Switzerland.

ZWEDEN, Jaap; Violinist and Conductor; b. 1960, Amsterdam, Netherlands. *Education:* Amsterdam Conservatory and with Dorothy DeLay at Juilliard, New York. *Career:* Leader of the Royal Concertgebouw Orchestra from 1979; Solo performances under conductors Haitink, Giulini, Solti and Bernstein; Conductor from 1995 including tours with the Berlin Symphony Orchestra, the Salzburg Mozarteum, the Israel CO and the Japanese CO; Music Director of the Netherlands Symphony Orchestra from 1997; Buenos Aires Philharmonic Orchestra in Argentina and on tour to Europe; US debut with the St Louis Symphony Orchestra, 1997; Principal guest conductor of the Brabant Orchestra, 1997; Season 1999–2000 with Netherlands Symphony Orchestra on tour to USA and debut with the London Philharmonic; Principal Conductor of the Residentie Orchestra, The Hague, from 2000. *Honours:* First prize, 1977 Dutch National Violin Competition. *Address:* c/o IMG Artists, Lovell House, 616 Chiswick High Road, London W4 5RX, England.

ZWIAUER, Florian; Violinist; b. 1954, Vienna, Austria. *Education:* Studied at the Vienna Academy of Music. *Career:* Co-founded the Franz Schubert Quartet, 1974; Won the European Broadcasting Union's International String Quartet Competition in Stockholm, 1974; Appearances at Amsterdam Concertgebouw, Vienna Musikverein and Konzerthaus, the Salle Gaveau, Paris, and Sydney Opera House; Visits to Zürich, Geneva, Basle, Berlin, Hamburg, Rome, Rotterdam, Madrid,

Copenhagen, Stockholm, Dublin, Manchester, Munich, Lisbon and many more; Festival engagements include Salzburg, Wiener Festwochen, Prague Spring, Bregenz Festival, Schubertiade at Hohenems, the Schubert Festival at Washington DC and the Belfast and Istanbul Festivals; Tours of Australasia, USSR and USA; British debut at the Queen Elizabeth Hall, 1979; Frequent appearances at Wigmore Hall and Cheltenham Festival; 1st Leader of Vienna Symphony Orchestra, 1989–; Teacher at the Vienna Conservatory and Graz Musikhochschule; Masterclasses at the Royal Northern College of Music and at the Lake District Summer Music. *Recordings include:* Schubert's Quartet in G, D887; Complete quartets of Dittersdorf; Haydn's 3 Last String Quartets; The 10 late Mozart String Quartets; Complete Tchaikovsky string chamber music; Complete string quartets of Franz Schmidt, Erich Wolfgang Korngold; Complete string quartets of Hans Pfitzner. *Honours:* As Soloist won 2nd Prize at the W A Mozart International Violin Competition in Salzburg, 1978. *Current Management:* Künstleragentur Dr Raab and Dr Böhm, Plankengasse 7, 1010 Vienna, Austria. *Address:* Alszeile 15/14, 1170 Vienna, Austria.

ZWILICH, Ellen Taaffe; Composer; b. 30 April 1939, Miami, Florida, USA; m. Joseph Zwilich, 22 June 1969, deceased 1979. *Education:* BMus, 1960, MMus, 1962, Florida State University; DMA, Juilliard School of Music, 1975; Other study with various teachers. *Career:* Violinist with American Symphony, NY, 1965–73; Freelance Composer, 1973–, works performed include: Premier Symposium for Orchestra, Pierre Boulez, NYC, 1975, Chamber Symphony and Passages, Boston Musica Viva, 1979, 1982, Symphony No. 1, Gunther Schuller, American Composers Orchestra, 1982; mem, Honorary Life Member, American Federation of Musicians; Past Board, Past Vice President, American Music Centre; International League of Women Composers. *Compositions include:* Orchestral and Chamber Music includes: Sonata In 3 Movements, 1973–74, String Quartet No. 1, 1974; Chamber Symphony, 1979, String Trio, 1982, Cello Symphony, 1985, Concerto Grosso, 1985, Images for 2 Pianos and Orchestra, 1987, Piano Trio, 1987, Symbolon for Orchestra, 1987, Trombone Concerto, 1988, Flute Concerto, 1990, Oboe Concerto, 1990; Concerto for violin, cello and orchestra, 1991; Bassoon Concerto, 1992; 3rd Symphony, 1992; Concerto for horn and strings, 1993; American Concerto for trumpet and orchestra, 1994; A Simple Magnificat, 1995; Triple Concerto, 1996; Piano Concerto, 1997; Violin Concerto, 1997; String Quartet No.2, 1998; Symphony No.4, for choruses and orchestra, 1999. *Honours:* Numerous honours and awards including: Elizabeth S Coolidge Chamber Music Prize, 1974, Viotti Gold Medal, Italy, 1975, Pulitzer Prize, 1983, Award, National Institute of Arts and Letters, 1984, Arturo Toscanini Music Critics Award, 1987, Honorary D.Mus, Oberlin College, 1987. *Current Management:* Music Associates of America, 224 King Street, Englewood, NJ 07631, USA. *Address:* Hainburger Strasse 47, 1030 Vienna, Austria.

ZYKAN, Otto M.; Composer and Pianist; b. 29 April 1935, Vienna, Austria. *Education:* Vienna Academy of Music. *Career:* many concert appearances, performing contemporary works. *Compositions:* Opera, Auszahireim, 1986; Sonata for cello and piano, 1958; String Quartet, 1958; Piano Concerto, 1958; Kyryptomnemie for winds, percussion,

piano, 1963; Schon der Reihe ballet, 1966; Kurze Anweisung for orchestra, 1969; Miles Smiles, chamber music theatre, 1974; Symphonie der heilen welt, scenic concerto, 1977; Trio for violin, 1977; Ausgesucht Freundliches, concerto for 2 soloists, chorus, orchestra, 1979; Kunst Kommt von Gonnon, opera, 1980; Cello concerto, 1982; 3 String Quartets, with speaker, 1984; Krüppelsprache, for 5 voices, 1984; Engels Engel, scenic concerto, 1988; Wahr ist, dass der Tigerfrisst, choral opera, 1994; Piano Trio, 1997; Wanderers Nachtlied, for chorus, string quartet and tape, 1997; String Quartet, 2002; Messe! fur 12 Selipten, Chor und Orchester, 2003; Cello Koncert, 2004; Violin Koncert, 2004. *Honours:* Winner, Darmstadt Competition for pianist, 1958. *Address:* c/o AKM, III Baumanstrasse 8–10, Postfach 334-338, 1031 Vienna, Austria.

ZYLIS-GARA, Teresa; Singer (Soprano); b. 23 Jan. 1935, Landvarov, Vilna, Poland. *Education:* Studied at the Łódź Academy with Olga Ogina. *Career:* Debut: Kraków, 1957, as Halka in Moniusko's opera; Sang in Oberhausen, Dortmund, Düsseldorf, 1960–70. Glyndebourne Festival, 1965, 1967 as Octavian and Donna Elvira; Covent Garden, from 1968 (debut as Violetta); Salzburg Festival, 1968; Metropolitan Opera, from 1968, as Mozart's Elvira and Fiordiligi, Verdi's Desdemona, Wagner's Elisabeth and Elsa, Strauss's Marschallin, Puccini's Suor Angelica and Manon Lescaut and Tatiana in Eugene Onegin; Vienna Staatsoper, from 1972; Barcelona, 1973–74; Orange Festival, 1979, as Liu in Turandot; Guest engagements in Hamburg, Paris, Berlin and Warsaw; Concert appearances in Bach, Chopin, Handel, Mozart and Brahms; Sang at the Hamburg Staatsoper, 1988, as Desdemona. *Recordings:* Mosè in Egitto by Rossini; Songs by Chopin; Il Giuramento by Mercadante; Bach's Easter and Christmas Oratorios, St Matthew Passion, Cavalieri's Rappresentazione di Anima e di Corpo, Mozart's Requiem; Ariadne auf Naxos, Electrola. *Honours:* Winner, International Singing Competition, Munich, 1960; Mozart Gold Medal, Mexico City; Polish National Award, great distinction of artistic achievement. *Address:* Hamburg State Opera, Grosse Theaterstrasse 34, 2000 Hamburg 36, Germany.

ZYSSET, Martin; Singer (Tenor); b. 1965, Solothurn, Switzerland. *Education:* Studied at the Berne Conservatory and with Ernst Haefliger, Edith Mathis and Roland Hermann. *Career:* Debut: Selzach Summer Festival, 1992, as Pedrillo in Die Entführung; Appearances at the Zürich Opera, 1992–, as Scaramuccio in Ariadne auf Naxos, Monostatos in Die Zauberflöte, Count Hohenzollern (Henze's Der Prinz von Homburg), Cassio, Jacquino and Tamino; Vienna Festival, 1994, in the premiere of Ein Narrenparadies by Ofer Ben-Amots; Further engagements with the Radio della Svizzera Italiana, in Antwerp and in Luxembourg (concert performance of Fidelio, under Leopold Hager); Other roles include Don Ottavio, Goro in Butterfly and Spoletta in Tosca; Season 2000–01 at Zürich as Johann Strauss's Simplicius Simplicissimus (also televised) and in Tosca, The Queen of Spades, Lulu and Carmen. *Honours:* Prizewinner at the 1990 Pro Arte Lyrica Competition, Lausanne. *Address:* c/o Opernhaus Zürich, Falkenstrasse 1, 8008 Zürich, Switzerland.

Directory

Directory

APPENDIX A: ORCHESTRAS

Argentina

Orquesta Filarmónica de Buenos Aires: Cerrito 618, 0101 Buenos Aires; tel. 54 1 383 5199; fax 54 1 383 6167.

Orquesta Sinfónica Nacional: Córdoba 1155, 1055 Buenos Aires; tel. 54 1 45 4252.

Armenia

Armenian Philharmonic Orchestra: Aram Khachaturian Concert Hall, Mashtotz 46, 375002 Yerevan; tel. 3741 560645; fax 3741 564965; e-mail apo@arminco.com; website www.apo.am; Gen. Man. Nika Babayan.

Armenian State Symphony Orchestra: Mashtotz 46, 375019 Yerevan; tel. 37 885 256 4965; fax 37 885 258 1142; Music Dir Loris Tjeknavorian; Man. George Avedissian.

Australia

Adelaide Symphony Orchestra: PO Box 2131, Adelaide, SA 5081; tel. 61 8 8343 4834; fax 61 8 8343 4808; e-mail aso@aso.com.au; website www.aso.com.au; Gen. Man. Robert Clarke.

Australian Brandenburg Orchestra: 159A New South Head Road, Edgecliff, NSW 2027; tel. 61 2 9363 2899; fax 61 2 9327 2593; e-mail mail@brandenburgorchestra.org.au; Music Dir Bruce Applebaum.

Australian Opera and Ballet Orchestra: PO Box 291, Strawberry Hills, NSW 2021; tel. 61 2 9699 3184; Music Dir Simone Young.

Canberra Symphony Orchestra: PO Box 1919, Second Floor, Hobart Place, Canberra, ACT 2601; tel. 61 6 247 9191; fax 61 6 247 9026; e-mail info@cso.org.au; website www.cso.org.au; CEO Ian McLean.

Melbourne Symphony Orchestra: PO Box 9994, Melbourne, Vic. 3001; tel. 61 3 9626 1111; fax 61 3 9626 1101; e-mail mso@mso.com.au; website www.mso.com.au; Conductor Laureate: Hiroyuki Iwaki; Chief Conductor Marcus Stenz; Gen. Man. Steven Porter.

Queensland Orchestra: GPO Box 9994, Brisbane, Qld 4001; tel. (7) 3377-5000; fax (7) 3377-5001; e-mail info@thequeenslandorchestra.com.au; website www.thequeenslandorchestra.com.au.

State Orchestra of Victoria (Orchestra Victoria): PO Box 836, S Melbourne, Vic. 3205; tel. 61 3 9694 3600; fax 61 3 9694 3611; e-mail dana.moran@orchestravictoria.com.au; website www.stateorchestra.com.au; Man. Dir Peter Garnick; Admin. Officer Dana Moran.

Sydney Symphony: GPO Box 4338, Sydney, NSW 2001; tel. 61 2 9334 4644; fax 61 2 9334 4646; e-mail info@sydneysymphony.com; website www.sydneysymphony.com; Chief Conductor and Artistic Dir Gianluigi Gelmetti; Man. Dir Libby Christie.

Tasmanian Symphony Orchestra: Australian Broadcasting Corporation, PO Box 9994, Hobart, TAS 7001; tel. 61 03 6235 3646; fax 61 03 6235 3651; e-mail tso@tso.com.au; website www.tso.com.au; Chief Conductor David Porcelijn; Gen. Man. Julie Warn.

Victorian Concert Orchestra: 1 Treasury Place, Third Floor, Melbourne, Vic. 3002; Music Dir Martin Rutherford.

West Australian Symphony Orchestra: PO Box 9994, 191 Adelaide Terrace, Perth, WA 6000; tel. 61 8 9326 0011; fax 61 8 9220 0099; website www.waso.com.au; Music Dir Vernon Handley; Gen. Man. Henk Smit.

Austria

Austro-Hungarian Haydn Orchestra: Favoritenstrasse 139/20, 1100 Vienna; tel. and fax 43 69 9 1032 4797; website www.haydnphil.com; Dir Adam Fischer.

Bruckner-Orchester: Promenade 39, 4020 Linz; tel. 43 70 761 1194; fax 43 70 761 1315; e-mail office@bruckner-orchester.at; website www.bruckner-orchester.at; Chief Conductor Martin Sieghart; Man. C.-F. Steiner.

Grazer Philharmonisches Orchester: Kaiser-Josef-Platz 10, 8010 Graz; Man. Dr Gerhard Brunner.

The Haydn Academy: Wiener Str 14, 2100 Linz; tel. 43 2 2627 2662; e-mail anton.gabmayer@gmx.net; Music Dir Anton Gabmayer.

Haydn Sinfonietta Wien: 1130 Vienna, Bossi Gasse 76; tel. 43 1 877 5208; fax 43 1 877 5208-17; e-mail haydn.sinfonietta@utanet.at; Music Dir Manfred Huss.

Mozarteum Orchester: Erzbischof-Gebhyardstrasse 10, 5020 Salzburg; tel. 43 66 284 3571; fax 43 66 284 357123; e-mail info@mozarteum.orchester.at; website www.mozarteum.orchester.at; Music Dir Hubert Soudant; Exec. Dir Dr Peter Ramsauer.

Niederösterreichisches Tonkünstler-Orchester: Elisabethstrasse 22/9, 1010 Vienna; Chief Conductor Fabio Luisi; Gen. Man. Peter Roczek.

Orchester Pro Musica International: Praterstrasse 76/8, 1020 Vienna; tel. 43 1 216 7333; fax 43 1 216 7333; Music Dir Gerhard Track; Man. Joanna Lewis.

Österreichisches Rundfunk Symphonie Orchester: Argentinierstrasse 30, 1040 Vienna; tel. 01 50101/18241; fax 01 50101/18358; e-mail rso-wien@orf.at; website www.rso-wien.orf.at; Chief Conductor Pinchas Steinberg; Gen. Man. Dr Andrea Seebohm.

Wiener Kammerorchester (Vienna Chamber Orchestra): Schachnerstrasse 27, 1220 Vienna; tel. 43 1 203 6357; fax 43 1 204 3750; e-mail wiener@kammerorchester.com; website www.kammerorchester.com; Chief Conductor Philippe Entremont; Gen. Man. Christian Buchmann.

Wiener Musica Antiqua Ensemble: Minoritenplatz 2, Arkadentrakt, 1010 Vienna; Music Dir Bernhard Kiebel.

Wiener Philharmoniker: Bösendorferstrasse 12, 1010 Vienna; tel. 43 1 505 6525; e-mail philoffice@wienerphilharmoniker.at; www.wienerphilharmoniker.at; Man. Peter Pecha.

Wiener Symphoniker: Lehargasse II, 1060 Vienna; tel. 43 1 591 8916; e-mail office@wiener-symphoniker.at; website www.wiener-symphoniker.at; Chief Conductor Vladimir Fedoseyev; Man. Rainer Bischof.

Azerbaijan

Azerbaijan Symphony Orchestra: Baku.

Belarus

State Academic Symphony Orchestra of Byelorussia: Pr Skoriny 50, 220005 Minsk, Belarus; tel. 17 2 315547; fax 17 2 319050; e-mail presto@belarustoday.com; Orchestra Dir Iosif Turko.

Belgium

Belgian Chamber Orchestra: Buizenbergstrasse 1, 9830, St-Martens-Latem; Conductor Rudolf Werthen; Man. Dries Sel.

Collegium Instrumentale Brugense: Vijversdreef 9b, 8310 Bruges; tel. 32 50 353717; fax 32 50 362717; Music Dir Patrick Peire; Admin. Dir Lieve Geerolf.

Collegium Vocale Gent: Drongenhof 42, 9000 Gent, Belgium; tel. 32 9 265 90 50; fax 32 9 265 90 51; e-mail org@collegiumvocale.com; website www.collegiumvocale.com; Man. Stephane Leys.

Ensemble Musique Nouvelle: Place de Vingt Août 16, 4000 Liège; Music Dir Patrick Davin; Man. Michel Schoonbrood.

Filharmonisch Orkest van der BRT: Magdalenazaal Duquesnoystr. 14, 1000 Brussels; Music Dir Frank Shipway; Man. André Laporte.

Grand Orchestre d'Harmonie de la Ville de Charleroi: rue Biavent A, 6208 Charleroi; tel. 00 32 71 36 38 73; fax 00 32 31 39 38 73; Dir Christian Delcoux.

Het Nieuw Belgisch Kamerorkest: Bondgenteniaan 114, 3000 Leuven; Music Dir Jan Caeyers; Man. Jan Roekens.

Koninklijk Filharmonisch Orkest van Vlaanderen: Britselei 80, 2000 Antwerp; tel. 32 3 231 3737; fax 32 2 231 9126; website www.kfovv.be; Music Dir Walter Van Den Eeckhout.

La Petite Bande: Vital Decosterstraat 72, 3000 Leuven; tel. 32 1 623 0830; fax 32 1 622 7610; e-mail info@lapetitebande.be; website www.lapetitebande.be; Music Dir Sigiswald Kuijken.

Orchestre National de Belgique: Galerie Ravenstein, 28 Boite 6, 1000 Brussels; tel. 32 2 552 0460; fax 32 2 552 0465; e-mail info@nob-onb.be; website www.onb.be; Music Dir Mikko Franck.

Orchestre Philharmonique de Liège et de la Communauté Française: Salle Philharmonique, Blvd Piercot 25, 4000 Liège; tel. 31 4 220 0000; fax 31 4 220 0001; website www.opl.be; Music Dir Pierre Bartholomée; Man. Paul-Emile Mottard.

Orchestre Royal de Chambre de Wallonie et de la Communauté Française: rue de Nimy 106, 7000 Mons; tel. 65 584 7044; fax 6 532 1158; Music Dir Georges Octors; Man. Robert Leleu.

Orchestre Symphonique de la RTBF: Place Eugène Flagey 18, 1050 Brussels.

Orchestre Symphonique du Théâtre Royal de la Monnaie: 4 rue Léopold, 1000 Brussels; tel. 32 2 229 1227; fax 32 2 229 1386; Man. Bernt Sandstad.

Philharmonische Vereniging van Antwerpen: De Boeystraat 6, 2018 Antwerp; tel. 3 218 6975; fax 3 230 3523; Man. Albrecht Klora.

Bosnia and Herzegovina

Sarajevo Philharmonic Orchestra: Obala Kulina Bana 9, 71000 Sarajevo; tel. 666-519; fax 666-521; e-mail sarphore@bsh.net.ba.

Sarajevo Radio and Television Symphony Orchestra: Sarajevo Radio and Television, 71000 Sarajevo.

Brazil

Orquestra Filarmônica do Rio de Janeiro: Rua das Marrecas 25, Sala 901, Centro, 20013-120 Rio de Janeiro; tel. 55 21 240 7354; fax 55 21 262 4269; e-mail orquestra@filarmonica-rio.com.br; website www .filarmonica-rio.com.br; Music Dir Florentino Dias; Man. Regina Helena Macedo.

Orquestra Sinfônica Brasileira: Avenida Rio Branco 135, Room 918, 20040 Rio de Janeiro; tel. 55 21 225 2 6330; fax 55 21 250 8 9592; website.www.osb.com.br; Music Dir Isaac Karabtchevsky.

Orquestra Sinfônica do Teatro Nacional de Brasilia: Avenida N2, Anexo do Teatro Nacional de Brasilia, 70000 Brasilia; Conductor Silvio Barbato.

Bulgaria

Bulgarian Radio and Television Symphony Orchestra: 4 Dragan Tsankov Blvd, Sofia; tel. and fax 359 2 661812; Music Dir Milen Natcher.

Sofia Philharmonic Orchestra: Benkovski str 1, 1000 Sofia; tel. 359 2 883197; fax 359 2 874072; website www.sofiaphilharmonie.bg; Music Dir Emil Tabakov; Admin. Vassil Kostov.

Vidin Philharmonic Orchestra: 4 Gradinska Street, 3700 Vidin; tel. 359 94 24675; e-mail sinfonia@vidin.net; Music Dir Nayden Todorov; Man. Miroslav Krastev.

Vratza State Philharmonic Orchestra: 1 Bolev Square, 3000 Vratza; tel. 359 922 3434/3261; fax 359 926 0053; e-mail vratzaphil@mbox.digsys .bg; Principal Conductor Valeri Vatchev; Man. Dir Dimitar Panov.

Canada

Calgary Philharmonic Orchestra: 205 Eighth Avenue, Calgary, AB T2G 0K9; tel. 1 403 571 0270; fax 1 403 294 7424; e-mail info@cpo-live.com; website www.cpo-live.com; Music Dir Hans Graf.

Edmonton Symphony Orchestra: Winspear Centre, Winston Churchill Square NW, Edmonton, AB T5J 4X8; tel. 1 403 428 1108; fax 1 403 425 1067; website www.edmontonsymphony.com; Music Dir Gregorz Nowak; Man. Dir Robert McPhee.

Hamilton Philharmonic Orchestra: Effort Trust Building, 105 Main Street E, Suite 1515, Hamilton, ON L8N 1G6; tel. 1 905 526 1677; fax 1 905 526 0616; e-mail office@hamiltonphilharmonic.org; website www .hamiltonphilharmonic.org; Artistic Dir Michael Reason; Gen. Man. Jack Nelson.

Kingston Symphony: PO Box 1616, Kingston, ON K7L 5C8; tel. 1 613 546 9729; fax 1 613 546 8580; e-mil info@kingstonsymphony.on.ca; Music Dir Glen Fast; Gen. Man. Andrea Haughton.

Kitchener-Waterloo Symphony Orchestra: 101 Queens Street N, Kitchener, ON N2H 6P7; tel. 1 519 745 4711; fax 1 519 745 4474; e-mail mail@kwsymphony.on.ca; website www.kwsymphony.on.ca; Music Dir Chosei Komatsu; Man. Dir Mark Jarnison.

National Arts Centre Orchestra: PO Box 1534, Station B, Ottawa, ON K1P 5W1; tel. (613) 947-7000; fax (613) 943-1400; website www.nac-cna .ca; Man. Dir Christopher Deacon.

Orchestra London Canada: 520 Wellington Street, London, ON N6A 3R1; tel. 1 519 679 8558; fax 1 519 679 8914; e-mail olc.info@orchestra .london.on.ca; website www.orchestralondon.ca; Music Dir Timothy Vernon; Exec. Dir Robert Gloor.

Orchestre Symphonique de Montréal: 260 de Maisonneuve Blvd W, Second Floor, Montréal, QC H2X 1Y9; tel. 1 514 842 9951; fax 1 514 842 0728; website www.osm.ca; Music Dir Charles Dutoit; Man. Dir Robert Spickler.

Orchestre Symphonique de Québec: 130 Grande Alleé W, Québec, QC G1R 2G7; tel. 1 418 643 5598; fax 1 418 646 9665; e-mail info@osq.org; website www.osq.org; Artistic Dir Yoav Talmi; Man. Louis Laplante.

Regina Symphony Orchestra: 200 Lakeshire Drive, Regina, SK S4P 3V7; tel. 1 306 586 9555; fax 1 306 586 2133; e-mail rso2@sk.sympatico.ca; website www.reginasymphonyorchestra.sk.ca; Music Dir Vladimir Conta; Exec. Dir Pat Middleton.

Saskatoon Symphony Orchestra: Suite 703, Delta Bessborough Hotel, 601 Spadina Crescent E, Saskatoon, SK S7K 3G8; tel. 306 665-6414; fax 306 652- 3364; e-mail saskatoonsymphony@sasktel.net; website www .saskatoonsymphony.org; Artistic Dir Douglas Sanford; Gen. Man. Karen Conway.

Thunder Bay Symphony Orchestra: PO Box 2004, Thunder Bay, ON P7B 5E7; e-mail info@tbso.ca; website www.tbso.ca; Music Dir Geoffrey Moull; Gen. Man. Erik Perth.

Toronto Symphony: Suite 550, 212 King Street W, Toronto, ON M5H 1K5; tel. 1 416 593 7769; fax 1 416 977 2912; website www.tso.on.ca; Music Dir Designate Peter Oundjian; Man. Dir Max Tapper.

Vancouver Symphony Orchestra: 601 Smithe Street, Vancouver, BC V6B 5G1; tel. 1 604 684 9100; fax 1 604 684 9264; e-mail reachus@ vancouversymphony.ca; website www.vancouversymphony.ca; Music Dir Bramwell Tovey.

Victoria Symphony Orchestra: 846 Broughton Street, Victoria, BC V8W 1E4; tel. 1 250 385 9771; fax 1 250 385 7767; e-mail administration@ victoriasymphony.bc.ca; website www.victoriasymphony.bc.ca; Music Dir Tania Miller; Gen. Man. Michael Aze.

Winnipeg Symphony Orchestra: Centennial Concert Hall, 555 Main Street, Room 101, Winnipeg, MB R3B 1C3; tel. 1 204 949 3950; fax 1 204 956 4271; website www.wso.mb.ca; Musical Dir Andrey Boreyko; Exec. Dir Howard Jang.

Chile

Orquesta Filarmónica de Santiago: San Antonio 149, PO Box 18, Santiago; tel. 56 2 639 9735/9736; fax 56 2 633 7214; e-mail andrespinto@ municipal.cl; Man. Andrés Pinto.

People's Republic of China

Central Philharmonic Orchestra: Beijing.

Shanghai Symphony Orchestra: 105 Hunan Lu, Shanghai 200031; tel. and fax 86 21 6433 3752; Conductor Chen Xie-Yang; Gen. Man. Cao Yiji.

Colombia

Orquesta Filarmónica de Bogotá (Bogota Philharmonic Orchestra): Calle 39A, No. 14-57, PO Box 16034, Bogotá; tel. 57 1 340 6643; fax 57 1 288 3162; e-mail info@filarmonicabogota.org.co; website www .filarmonicabogota.gov.co; Music Dir Francisco Rettig; Exec. Dir Maria Cristina Sánchez.

Orquesta Sinfónica de Colombia: Teatro Colón, Calle 10, No. 5-32, Bogotá; tel. 57 243 5316; fax 57 820 854; Music Dir Federico Garcia Vigil; Man. Blanca Cecilia Carreno.

Costa Rica

Orquesta Sinfónica Nacional: PO Box 1035, San José 1000; Music Dir Irwin Hoffman; Gen. Man. Gloria Waissbluth.

Croatia

Croatian Radio and Television Symphony Orchestra: Dezmanova 10, 41000 Zagreb.

Zagreb Philharmonic Orchestra: Trg Stjepana Radica 4 pp909, Zagreb; tel. 385 1 606 0103; fax 385 1 611 1577; e-mail zqfilhar@zqf.hr; website www.zqf.hr; Dir Berislav Sipus.

Czech Republic

Brno State Philharmonic Orchestra: Komenského nám 8, 602 00 Brno; tel. and fax 420 5 4221 2300; e-mail info@sfb.cz; website www.sfb.cz; Conductor Aldo Ceccato.

Hradec Králové State Symphony Orchestra: Náb e í Elí ino 777, 500 03 Hradec Králové tel. 495 211375; fax 495 211952; e-mail fhk@fhk.cz; website www.fhk.cz; Chief Conductor Frantisek Vajnar; Man. Radomir Malý.

Janácek Philharmonic Orchestra: 28 rijna 124, 702 00 Ostrava 1; tel. 420 69 661 9914; fax 420 69 661 9997; e-mail office@jfo.cz; website www.jfo .cz; Chief Conductor Christian Arming; Man. Miroslav Snyrich.

Karlovy Vary Symphony Orchestra: Náb e í CSP 1, 360 01 Karlovy Vary; website www.kso.cz; Music Dir Douglas Bostock; Man. Peter Kuli.

Kosice State Philharmonic Orchestra: Dom Umenia, Moyesova 66, 041 23, Kosice; tel. 421 95 622 4514.

Moravian Philharmonic Orchestra: Horni nám sti 23, 772 00 Olomouc; tel. 420 585 206 520; fax 420 585 220 124; website www.mfo.cz; Dir Vladislav Kvapil.

National Theatre of Moravia and Silesia in Ostrava: Csl., Legil, 701 04, Ostrava; tel. 420 69 6125144; fax 420 69 6112881; Dir Ludek Golat; Man. Dr G. Coates-Gibson.

Plzeňská filharmonie (Radio Symphony Orchestra Pilsen): náměstí Míru 10, 301 00 Plzeň; tel. and fax 420 377423336; e-mail plzenska .filharmonie@softech.cz; Chief Conductor: Hynek Farkač; Dir: Jan Motlík.

Prague Radio Symphony Orchestra: Vinohradská 12, 12099 Prague 2; tel. 420 2 2155 1412; fax 420 2 2155 1413; e-mail socr@cro.cz; Chief Conductor Vladimir Válek; Man. Lubomir Herza.

Prague Symphony Orchestra (FOK): Obecni dum, nám Republiky 5, 110 21 Prague 1; tel. 420 2 2231 5981/200 2425; fax 420 2 2231 0784; e-mail pso@fok.cz; website www.fok.cz; Principal Guest Conductor Libor Pesek; Man. Dir Petr Polivka.

South Bohemian State Orchestra: Ceská ul 1, 370 21 Ceske Budejovice; Chief Conductor Ondrej Kukal; Dir Milan Kraus.

West Bohemian Symphony Orchestra: Tída Odborá u 51, 353 21 Mariánské Lazn; tel. 420 165 2141; fax 420 68 5228 511; Music Dir Radomil Elika; Man. Nadjda Domanjová.

Denmark

Ålborg Symfoniorkester: Kjellerupsgade 14, 9000 Ålborg; tel. 45 98 131955; fax 45 98 130378; e-mail info@aalborgsymfoniorkester.dk; website www.aalborgsymfoniorkester.dk; Gen. Man.: Palle Kjeldgaard; Principal Chief Conductors: Lan Shui, Ari Rasilainen.

Århus Symfoniorkester: Musikhuset Århus, Thomas Jensens Allé, 8000 Århus; tel. 45 89 404040; fax 45 89 409091; e-mail symf@aarhus.dk; website www.aarhussymfoni.dk; Chief Conductor Giancarlo Andretta.

Danish National Symphony Orchestra: Rosenørns Allé 22, 1999 Copenhagen; tel. 45 3520 3040; fax 45 3520 6121; website www.dr.dk/rso; Chief Conductor: Thomas Dausgaard; Man.: Per Erik Veng; Principal Guest Conductor: Yuri Temirkanov.

Odense Symphony Orchestra: Claus Bergs Gade 9, 5000 Odense C; tel. 45 66 12 00 57; fax 45 65 91 00 47; e-mail orchestra@odensesymfoni.dk; website www.odensesymfoni.dk; Gen. Man. Per Holst.

Royal Danish Orchestra: PO Box 2185, 1017 Copenhagen; tel. 45 33 096701; fax 45 33 696767; e-mail admin@kgl-teater.dk; Principal Conductor Paavo Berglund.

Sjaellands Symphony Orchestra: Bernstorffsgade 9, 1577 Copenhagen V; Man. Maria Sørensen.

Søndersyllands Symfoniorkester (Danish Philharmonic Orchestra, South Jutland): Skovvej 16, 6400, Sønderborg; tel. 45 74 426161; fax 45 74 426106; e-mail info@sdisymfoni.dk; website www.sonderjyllands -symfoniorkester.dk; Gen. Man. Henrik Wenzel Andreasen.

Tivoli Symphony Orchestra: Tivoli, Vesterbrogade 3, 1620 Copenhagen V.

West Jutland Symphony Orchestra: Islandsgade 50, 6700 Esbjerg; tel. 45 75 139339; fax 45 75 133242; Admin. Dir Leif Pedersen.

Dominican Republic

Orquesta Sinfónica Nacional: Palacio de Bellas Artes, Santo Domingo; Music Dir Carlos Piantini; Man. Sofia de Sturla.

Ecuador

Orquesta Sinfónica Nacional: Casilla 2844, Calle Venezuela 666, Quito; Music Dir Alvaro Manzano; Man. G. Sáenz.

Egypt

Cairo Symphony Orchestra: Egyptian Opera House, Geziro, Cairo 11211; tel. 202 342 0601; fax 202 342 0599; e-mail csorchestra@yahoo.com; website www.cairo-symphony.com.eg; Music Dir Ahmed Elsaedi.

Estonia

Eesti Riikliku Sümfooniaorkestri—ERSO (Estonian National Symphony Orchestra): Estonia PO Box 4, 10143 Tallinn; tel. 372 6147787; fax 372 6313133; e-mail erso@erso.ee; website www.erso.ee; Dir Andres Sitan.

Finland

Finnish Radio Symphony Orchestra: PO Box 14, 00 024 Yleisradio, Helsinki; tel. 358 9 1480 4366; fax 358 9 1480 3551; e-mail tuula.sarotie@ yle.fi; website www.yle.fi/rso; Conductor of Honour Jukka-Pekka Saraste; Chief Conductor Sikari Oramo; Gen. Man. Tuula Sarotie.

Helsinki Philharmonic Orchestra: Finlandia Hall, Karamzininkatu 4, 00100 Helsinki; tel. 358 9 4024 265; fax 358 9 406484; website www.hel.fi/ filharmonia; Chief Conductor Leif Segerstam; Man. Helena Ahonen.

Tampere Philharmonic Orchestra: PL 16, 31 101 Tampere; tel. 358 3 243 4111; fax 358 3 243 4400; e-mail orchestra@tampere.fi; website www .tampere.fi; Artistic Dir Eri Klas; Gen. Man. Maritta Hirvonen.

Turku Philharmonic Orchestra: Sibeliuksenkatu 2 A, 20 110 Turku; tel. 358 21 2314 577; fax 358 21 250 0480; e-mail orchestra@turku.fi; website www3.turku.fi/orkesteri; Man. Kalevi Kuosa.

France

Association des Concerts Colonne: 2 rue Edouard Colonne, 75001 Paris; Music Dir Antonello Allemandi; Gen. Man. Guy Arnaud.

Association des Concerts Lamoureux: 252 rue de Faubourg St-Honoré, 75008 Paris; tel. 33 1 45 63 44 34; fax 33 1 45 62 05 41; Man. Annie Foultier.

Association des Concerts Pasdeloup: 18 rue de Berne, 75008 Paris; Man. Roger Landy.

Ensemble Ars Nova: 16 rue des Fossés St Jacques, 75005 Paris; tel. 33 1 43 26 74 84; fax 33 1 46 3334 59; Music Dir Marius Constant.

Ensemble Instrumental de Grenoble: 1 rue du Vieux Temple, 38000 Grenoble; Dir Marc Tardue; Man. Jean-Peter Roeber.

Ensemble Intercontemporain: 223 avenue Jean Jaurès, 75019 Paris; tel. 33 1 44 84 44 50; fax 33 1 44 84 44 61; website www.ensembleinter.com; Music Dir David Robertson; Man. Claude Le Cleach.

Ensemble Orchestral de Haute-Normandie: 50 ave de la Porte des Champs, 76000 Rouen; Music Dir Jean-Pierre Berlingen; Admin. Jean-Michel Bernard.

Ensemble Orchestral de Paris: 37 rue Anatole-France, 92309 Levallois-Perret Cedex, 75008 Paris; e-mail contact@eop.com.fr; website www .ensemble-orchestral-paris.com; Conductor John Nelson; Man. Alain Guillon.

Ensemble Orchestral Harmonia Nova: 74 rue de Faubourg St Denis, 75010 Paris; Music Dir Didier Bouture; Man. Daniel Gutenberg.

La Chapelle Royale/Orchestre des Champs Elysees: 10 rue Coquilliere, 75001 Paris; tel. 33 1 40 26 58 00; fax 33 1 40 26 38 37; website www .lachapelleroyale.com; Music Dir Philippe Herreweghe.

La Grande Ecurie et la Chambre du Roy: 19 rue de Biercy Vanry, 77640 Jouarre; tel. 33 1 60 22 98 45; fax 33 1 60 22 03 13; Music Dir Jean-Claude Malgoire.

Les Arts Florissants: 2 rue de Saint-Petersburg, 75008 Paris; tel. 33 1 43 87 98 88; fax 33 1 43 87 37 31; e-mail contact@arts-florissants.com; website www.arts-florissants.com; Music Dir William Christie; Gen. Admin. Luc Bouniol Laffont.

Musique en Sorbonne: 2 rue Francis de Croisset, 75018 Paris; tel. 33 1 42 62 71 71; fax 33 1 42 51 69 11; website www.musique-en-sorbonne.org; Gen. Man. Jim Houdayer.

Nouvel Orchestre Philharmonique: Radio France, 116 avenue du Président Kennedy, 75786 Paris Cédex 16; tel. 33 1 42 30 36 30; fax 33 1 42 30 47 48; Music Dir Marek Janowski; Artistic Dir Yvon Kapp.

Opera de Rouen: 7 rue du Docteur Rambert, 76 000, Rouen; tel. 33 2 35 98 50 98; fax 33 2 35 15 33 49; website www.operaderouen.com; Musical Dir Oswald Sallaberger; Dir Laurent Langlois.

Orchestra Symphonique de Tours: Grand Théâtre, 34 rue de la Scellerie, 37000 Tours; tel. 33 247 60 20 00; fax 33 247 60 20 40; e-mail theatre@ville-tours.fr; Dir: Jean-Yves Ossonce; Admin.: Luc Cavalier.

Orchestre d'Auvergne: 2 rue Urbain II, 63000 Clermont-Ferrand; tel. 04 73 14 47 47; fax 04 73 14 47 46; e-mail orchestre.d.auvergne@wanadoo.fr; Admin. Alain Riviere.

Orchestre de Bretagne: 42A rue St-Melaine, BP 30823 Rennes, Céedex 3; tel. 33 2 99 275 285; fax 33 2 99 275 276; e-mail administration@ orchestre-de-bretagne.com; website www.orchestre-de-bretagne.com; Dir Jean-Marc Bador; Man. Jean-François Jeandet.

Orchestre de Caen: 1 rue du Carel, 14050 Caen Cédex 4; tel. 33 2 31 30 46 88; fax 33 2 31 30 46 87; website www.caen.fr/OrchestredeCaen; Music

Dir Jean-Marc Laureau; Man. Delphine Chevallier; Artistic Dir Stephane Bechy.

Orchestre de Chambre de Versailles: 3 rue Descartes, 92310 Sèvres; Music Dir M. B. Wahl.

Orchestre de Chambre Jean-François Paillard: 50 rue Laborde, 75008 Paris; Music Dir Jean-François Paillard; Admin. Richard Siegel.

Orchestre de Chambre Jean-Louis Petit: 34 rue Corot, 92410 Ville d'Avray; tel. 33 1 47 09 22 82; fax 33 1 47 50 53 90; Music Dir Jean-Louis Petit.

Orchestre de Chambre National de Toulouse: 4 rue Clémence Isaure, 31000 Toulouse; tel. 33 5 62 30 34 40; fax 33 5 62 30 34 41; e-mail ocnt .ocnt@wanadoo.fr; website www.espritsnomades.com/onct.html; Dir Alain Moglia; Man. Jean-Pierre Paragon.

Orchestre de Chambre Paul Kuentz: 144 rue du Faubourg St Antoine, 75012 Paris; Music Dir Paul Kuentz.

Orchestre de Paris: 25 rue de Mogador, 75009 Paris; tel. 33 1 56 35 12 00; fax 33 1 42 89 24 49; website www.orchestredeparis.com; Music Dir Christoph Eschenbach; Gen. Dir Georges-François Hirsch.

Orchestre des Concerts Lamoureux: 53 rue des Orteaux, 75020 Paris; tel. 33 1 58 39 30 30; fax 33 1 58 39 30 31; e-mail orchestrelamoureux@ wanadoo.fr; website www.orchestrelamoureux.com; Chief Principal Yutaka Sado; Pres. Lionel Evans.

Orchestre des Pays de Savoie: 6 rue Metropole, 73000 Chambéry; tel. 33 4 79 33 42 71; fax 33 4 79 33 43 00; e-mail orchestrepayssavoie@ wanadoo.fr; website www.savoie-culture.com; Music Dir Graziella Contra-tto; Pres. Andre Fumex; Admin. Dir Odile Ollagnon.

Orchestre Français des Jeunes: Maison de Radio France, 116 avenue du Président Kennedy, 75220 Paris Cédex 16; tel. 33 1 56 40 49 45; fax 33 1 56 40 49 90; e-mail ofjeunes@aol.com; website www.ofj.asso.fr; Music Dir Emmanuel Krivine; Admin. Dir Pierre Barrois; Man. Aude le Cleh.

Orchestre Jean-François Gonzales: 32 rue du Maréchal Joffre, Residence 7, 78000 Versailles; tel. 33 01 39 51 66 05; Music Dir J.-F. Gonzales-Hamilton.

Orchestre Lyrique de Région Avignon Provence: 258 chemin des Rémouleurs, Zl de Courtine, PO Box 967, 84093 Avignon Cédex 9; website www.ars-dom.com/olrap; Music Dir François Bilger.

Orchestre National Bordeaux-Aquitaine: PO Box 95, 33025 Bor-deaux; tel. 33 5 56 00 85 20; fax 33 5 56 81 93 66; e-mail courrier@opera -bordeaux.com; website www.opera-bordeaux.com/artistes/onba.htm; Admin. Daniel Dourneau-Gabory; Music Dir Hans Graf.

Orchestre National d'Ile de France: 19 rue des Ecoles, 94140 Alfortville; tel. 33 1 41 79 03 40; fax 33 1 41 79 03 50; e-mail courrier@ orchestre-ile.com; website www.orchestre-ile.com; Music Dir Jacques Mercier; Gen. Dir Marc-Olivier Dupin.

Orchestre National de France: Radio France, 116 avenue du Président Kennedy, 75786 Paris Cédex 16; tel. 33 1 42 30 26 03; fax 33 1 42 30 43 33; Music Dir Charles Dutoit; Gen. Man. Patrice d'Ollone.

Orchestre National de Lille: 30 place Mendès-France, PO Box 119, 59027 Lille Cédex; tel. 33 03 20 128240; fax 33 03 20 782910; e-mail jbrochen@orlille.com; website www.orlille.com; Man. Jacqueline Brochen.

Orchestre National de Lyon: 82 rue de Bonnel, 69431 Lyon Cédex 3; tel. 33 4 78 95 95 00; fax 33 4 78 60 13 08; website www.orchestrelyon.com; Music Dir David Robertson; Dir-Gen. Anne Poursin.

Orchestre National de Montpellier: Le Corum, PO Box 9056 34041, Montpellier Cédex 1; tel. 33 4 67 61 67 21; fax 33 4 67 61 67 20; website www.orchestre-montpellier.com; Musical Dir Friedemann Layer; Admin. Sophie Cuvillier.

Orchestre National du Capitole de Toulouse: Halle aux Grains, place Dupuy, 31000 Toulouse; tel. 33 5 61 63 13 13; fax 33 5 62 27 49 49; website www.onct.mairie-toulouse.fr; Music Dir Michel Plasson; Man. George Schneider.

Orchestre Philharmonique de Lorraine: 25 avenue Robert Schuman, 57008 Metz; tel. 33 3 87 55 12 02; fax 33 3 87 65 69 36; website www .orchestrenatinoal-lorraine.fr; Artistic Dir Jacques Mercier; Gen. Admin. Pascal Schwan.

Orchestre Philharmonique de Montpellier: Le Corum, PO Box 9056, 34041 Montpellier Cédex 01; tel. 33 04 67 61 67 21; fax 33 04 67 61 66 82; Music Dir Friedemann Layer; Dir Gen. René Koering; Admin. Jany Macaby.

Orchestre Philharmonique de Nice: 4 rue St François de Paule, 06300 Nice; tel. 33 4 92 17 4 0 00; fax 33 4 93 80 34 83; Music Dir Marcello Parni; Man. Pierre Medecin.

Orchestre Philharmonique de Radio France: 116 avenue du Président Kennedy, 75220, Paris Cédex 16; tel. 1 42 30 36 30; fax 1 42 30 47 48; e-mail philhar@radiofrance.com; Musical Dir Myung-Whun Chung; Admin. Jean-François Jeandet; Artistic Delegate Eric Montal-betts.

Orchestre Philharmonique de Strasbourg: Palais de la Musique et des Congrès, avenue Schutzenberger, 67000 Strasbourg Cédex; tel. 33 03 88 15 09 00; fax 33 03 88 15 09 01; e-mail opstrasbourg@aol.com; website www.philharmonique-strasbourg.com; Music Dir Ian Latham Koenig; Dir-Gen. Patrick Minard.

Orchestre Philharmonique des Pays de la Loire: 26 avenue Montaigne, PO Box 15246, 49052 Angers Cédex 2; tel. 33 41 24 11 20; fax 33 41 87 80 52; website www.onpl.fr; Music Dir Hubert Soudent; Gen. Admin. Maryvonne Lavigne.

Orchestre Régional de Cannes-Provence Alpes Côte d'Azur: 104 avenue Francis Tonner, PO Box 46, 06150 Cannes La Bocca Cédex; tel. 33 4 93 48 61 10; fax 33 4 93 90 27 79; Dir Philippe Bender; Man. Catherine Morschel.

Orchestre Régional Poitou-Charentes: 3 place Prosper Mérimée, PO Box 422, 86000 Poitiers Cédex; tel. 33 5 49 55 91 10; fax 33 5 49 60 12 21; Dir Charles Frey.

Orchestre Symphonique de la Garde Républicaine: 12 blvd Henri IV, 75004 Paris; Music Dir Roger Boutry.

Orchestre Symphonique de Rhin-Mulhouse: 38 Passage du Théâtre, 68100 Mulhouse; Music Dir Luca Pfaff; Man. Jean-Luc Fischer.

Orchestre Symphonique et Lyrique de Nancy et de Lorraine: 1 rue Sainte Catherine, 54000 Nancy; tel. 33 83 85 33 20; fax 33 83 85 30 66; Music Dir Sebastian Lang-Lessing; Man. Astrid Chepfer.

Société des Concerts du Conservatoire: 1 rue de la Bibliothèque, 13000 Marseille.

Germany

Akademie Hamburger Solisten: Seilerstrasse 41, 20355 Hamburg; Music Dir Joachim Kerwin.

Bach Collegium München e V: Elisabethstrasse 9, 8000 Munich; Music Dir Florian Sonnleitner.

Badische Staatskapelle Karlsruhe: Baumeisterstrasse 11, 7500 Karlsruhe; Gen. Music Dir Anthony Brawall.

Bamberger Symphoniker: Mussstrasse 1, 96047 Bamberg; tel. 49 951 964 7100; fax 49 951 964 7123; e-mail intendanz@bamberger-symphoniker .de; website www.bamberger-symphoniker.de; Chief Conductor Jonathon Nott; Principal Guest Conductor Ingo Metzmacher.

Bayerisches Staatsorchester: Max-Joseph-Platz 2, 80539 Munich; tel. 49 89 218501; fax 49 89 2185 1003; website www.staatsorchester.de; Musical Dir Zubin Mehta; Gen. Dir Peter Jonas.

Berliner Barock-Orchester: Arnold-Knoblauch-Ring, 64, Pf 173, 1000 Berlin; Music Dir Konrad Latte.

Berliner Philharmonisches Orchester: Philharmonie, Matthäikirch-strasse 1, 14057 Berlin; tel. 49 30 254 880; fax 49 30 261 4887; website www.berliner-philharmoniker.de; Man. Elmar Weingarten; Music Dir Sir Simon Rattle.

Berliner Sinfonie-Orchester: Gendarmenmarkt, 1086 Berlin; Music Dir Michael Schønwandt; Man. Frank Schneider.

Berliner Symphoniker: Christstrasse 30, 14059 Berlin; tel. 49 30 321 1017; fax 49 30 325 5326; e-mail kontakt@berlin-symphoniker.de; website www.berliner-symphoniker.de; Music Dir Alun Francis; Chief Conductor Lior Shambadal; Man. Jochen Thärichen.

Bochumer Symphoniker: Prinz-Regent-Strasse 50-60, 44795 Bochum; tel. 49 02 34 910 8622; fax 49 02 34 910 8616; website www.bochum.de/ symphonie; Gen. Music Dir Steven Sloane.

Brandenburger Symphoniker: Brandenburger Theater, Graben-strasse 14, 14776 Brandenburg/Havel; tel. 3381 511 131; fax 3381 511 160; e-mail info@brandenburgertheater.de; website www .brandenburgertheater.de; Music Dir Michael Helmrath.

Brandenburgische Philharmonie: Zimmerstrasse 10, 1570 Potsdam; Music Dir Stefan Sanderling.

Brandenburgisches Kammerorchester e V, A Thiemig: Schopen-hauerstrasse 9, 7513 Cottbus; e-mail bko@bko-berlin.de; website www.bko -berlin.de; Music Dir Rainer Johannes Kimstedt.

Bremen Filharmoniker: Wüstestätte 11, 28195 Bremen; tel. (421) 361 41 78; fax (421) 361-41-94; e-mail info@bremerphilharmoniker.de; website www.bremerphilharmoniker.de; Gen. Music Dir Lawrence Renes.

Collegium Aureum: Nordstrasse 2, 7800 Freiburg; Music Dir Franzjosef Maier.

Concerto Grosso Frankfurt e V: Ludwigstrasse 66, 6050 Offenbach; Music Dir Irina Edelstein.

Detmolder Kammerorchester e V: Bruchstrasse 25, Pf 1404, 32756 Detmold; tel. 05231 31603; fax 05231 31606; e-mail info@detmolder -kammerorchester.de; website www.detmolder-kammerorchester.de; Music Dir Christoph Poppen.

Deutsche Bachsolisten: Goddardstrasse 28, 5300 Bonn; Music Dir Helmut Winschermann.

Deutsche Kammerakademie: Oberstrasse 17, Pf 101452, 41460 Neuss 1; tel. 02131 904116; fax 02131 904127; Music Dir Johannes Goritzki.

Deutsche Kammerphilharmonie: Schwedlerstrasse 2–4, 60320 Frankfurt am Main 1.

Deutsches Kammerorchester Frankfurt am Main: Hans-Bredow-Strasse 42B, 6200 Wiesbaden; tel. 0611 464 619; fax 0611 464 755; e-mail concmanag@aol.com; website www.deutscheskammerorchester-frankfurt .com; Conductor Rista Savic.

Deutsches Kammerorchester: Lietzenburger Strasse 51, 1000 Berlin; e-mail info@dko-berlin.de; website www.dko-berlin.de; Music Dir Fritz Weisse.

Deutsches Symphonie Orchester Berlin: Charlottenstrasse 56, 10117 Berlin; tel. 49 30 2029 8711; fax 49 30 2029 8729; website www.dso-berlin .de; Chief Conductor Kent Nagano; Orchestral Dir Dr Thomas Schmidt.

Dresdner Kammerorchester: c/o Sächsische Staatskapelle Dresden, Theaterplatz 2, 8010 Dresden.

Dresdner Philharmonie: Kulturpalast am Altmarkt, Pf 120424, 01005 Dresden; tel. 49 351 486 6202/6287; fax 49 351 486 6306/6286; website www.dresdnerphilharmonie.com; Gen. Music Dir Rafael Frühbeck de Burgos; Artist Man. Dr Olivier von Winterstein.

Duisburger Sinfoniker: Beckarstrasse 1, 4100 Duisburg 1; Gen. Music Dir Bruno Weil.

Düsseldorfer Symphoniker: Ehrenhof 1, 40479 Düsseldorf; tel. 49 211 899 3606; fax 49 211 892 9143; Music Dir John Fiore; Man. Thomas Stuhrk.

Folkwang Kammerorchester Essen e V: Hollestrasse 1g, 45127 Essen; tel. 49 201 230034; fax 49 201 200696; e-mail fko.essen@web.de; website www.folkwang-kammerorchester.de; Man. Dir Ralph Sistermanns; Music Dir Stefan Fraas.

Freies Kammerorchester Berlin e V: Antonstrasse 25, 1000 Berlin; Music Dir Christoph Hagel.

Gewandhausorchester zu Leipzig: Augustusplatz 8, 04109 Leipzig; tel. 49 341 1270; fax 49 341 12 70200; website www.gewandhaus.de; Principal Conductor Herbert Blomstedt.

Göttinger Symphonie-Orchester: Godehardstrasse 19–21, 3400 Göttingen; Music Dir Christian Simonis.

Gürzenich-Orchester: Bischofsgartenstrasse 1, 50667 Cologne 1; tel. 0221 22122437; fax 0221 22123800; Gen. Music Dir James Conlon.

Hamburger Mozart-Orchester: Helgolandstrasse 12, 2000 Wedel; Music Dir Robert Stehli.

Hamburger Symphoniker: Dammtorwall 46, 20355 Hamburg; tel. 49 40 344851; fax 49 40 353788; website www.hamburger-symphoniker.de; Music Dir Miguel Gómez Martínez.

Händelfestspielorchester: Universitätsring 24, 06108 Halle an der Saale; tel. 49 345 511 10300; fax 49 345 511 0303; Music Dir Roger Epple; Orchestral Man. Bruno Scharnberg.

Hofer Symphoniker: Klosterstrasse 9–11, 95028 Hof; tel. 0049 9281 7200; fax 0049 9281 7272; e-mail info@hofer-symphoniker.de; website www.hofer-symphoniker.de; Man. Wilfried Anton.

Hohner-Akkordeonorchester 1927 Trossingen e V: Neuenstrasse 29, 78647 Trossingen-Schura; tel. 490 7425 20212; fax 490 7425 20462; e-mail mkeller@hohner.de; Pres. Matthias Keller.

Jenaer Philharmonie: Volkshaus Carl-Zeiss-Platz 15, 07743 Jena; tel. 0049 3641 590010; fax 0049 3641 590026; e-mail philharmonie@jena.de; website www.jenaer-philharmonie.de; Man. Bruno Scharnberg.

Kammerorchester Merck: Stefan Reinhardt, Pf 4119, 6100 Darmstadt.

Kammerorchester Musica Juventa Halle: Hegelstrasse 9, 06109 Halle an der Saale; Music Dir Roger Epple.

Kammerorchester Schloss Werneck e V: Balthasar-Neumann-Platz 8, Pf 65, 97440 Werneck; tel. 490 9722 91610; fax 490 9722 91611; e-mail

info@tammerorchester.de; website www.kammerorchester.de; Music Dir Ulf Klausenitzer.

Klassische Philharmonie Telekom Bonn: Theaterstrasse 10, 5300 Bonn 1; Music Dir Heribert Beissel.

Kölner Kammerorchester e V: Schlosstrasse 2, 5040 Bruhl; Music Dir Helmut Müller-Bruhl.

Kölner Rundfunk-Sinfonie-Orchester: Appellhofplatz 1, 50600; Principal Conductor Semyon Bychkov; Dir of Music Programming: Hermann Lang.

Kürpfalzisches Kammerorchester: D 6, 2, 6800 Mannheim 1; Music Dir Jiri Malát.

Landessinfonieorchester Thüringen-Gotha: Reinhardsbrunner Strasse 23, 5800 Gotha; Music Dir Hermann Breuer.

Landestheaterorchester Coburg: Coburger Landestheater, Schlossplatz 6, 96450 Coburg; tel. (49) 9561 898900; website www.landestheater .coburg.de; Gen. Music Dir: Alois Seidlmeier.

Magdeburgische Philharmonie: Theater der Landeshauptstadt Magdeburg, Pf 1240, 39002 Magdeburg; tel. 03 91 540 6500; Gen. Music Dir Mathias Husmann.

Mainzer Kammerorchester e V: Friedrich Naumann Str 9, 55131 Mainz; tel. 06131 839 198; fax 06131 834 128; e-mail info@mainzer -kammerorchester.de; website www.mainzer-kammerorchester.de.

MDR Sinfonieorchester: Augustusplatz 9a, 04105 Leipzig; tel. 49 341 300 8705; fax 49 300 8701; e-mail mdr-lkangkoerper@mdr.de; website www.mdr.de/konzerte; Gen. Man. Mario Plath; Chief Conductor Fabio Luisi.

Mecklenburgische Staatskapelle: Alter Garten, 2750 Schwerin; e-mail info@mecklenburgische-staatskapelle.de; website www .mecklenburghische-staatskapelle.de; Musical Dir Matthias Foremny.

Münchener Kammerorchester e V: Wittelsbacherplatz 2, 80333 Munich; tel. 089-636-35972; fax 089-280-171; e-mail hans-joachim -litzkow@muenchener.de; website www.muenchener-kammerorchester .de; Music Dir Christoph Poppen.

Münchener Philharmonie: Gasteig Kulturzentrum, Kellerstrasse 4/III, 81667 Munich; tel. 49 89 4809 8509; fax 49 89 4809 8513; e-mail philharmoniker@ muenchen.de; website www.muencher-philharmoniker .de; Gen. Music Dir James Levine; Man. Bernd Gellermann.

Münchener Symphoniker e V: Drachslstrasse 14, 81541 Munich; tel. 08944 11960; fax 08944 119615; e-mail info@muenchner-symphoniker.de; website www.muenchner-symphoniker.de; Music Dir Christoph Stepp.

Musica Antiqua Köln: Brüsseler Str. 94, 50672 Köln; tel. 221 9232030; fax 221 9232031.

Nationaltheater-Orchester Mannheim: Mozartstrasse 11, 68161 Mannheim; tel. 49 0621 26044; fax 49 0621 23182; Musical Dir Adam Fischer.

NDR-Sinfonieorchester: Norddeutscher Rundfunk Hamburg, Rothenbaumchaussee 132, 20149 Hamburg; tel. 49 40 4156 2401/3545; fax 49 40 4156 3758/7569; e-mail sinfonie@ndr.de; website www.ndr.de/sinfonie; Chief Conductor Herbert Blomstedt; Dir of Music Programming Bernhard Hansen.

Neubrandenburger Philharmonie: Pfaffenstrasse 22, 17033 Neubrandenburg; tel. 49 39 5569 9811; fax 49 39 5582 6179; e-mail philharmonie .NB@t-online.de; website www.philharmonie-online.de; Chief Conductor Stefan Malzew; Man. Horst Beitz.

Niederrheinische Sinfoniker: Theater Mönchengladbach, Odenkirchener Strasse 78, 41236 Mönchengladbach; tel. 2166-6151-128; fax 2166-6151-134; e-mail gmd@theater-kr-mg.de; website www.theater-krefeld -moenchengladbach.de; Gen. Music Dir Graham Jackson.

Niedersächsisches Staatsorchester: Opernplatz 1, 3000 Hannover 1; Gen. Music Dir Christof Prick.

Norddeutsche Philharmonie Rostock: Patriotischer Weg 33, 18057 Rostock; tel. 49 38 1381 4650; fax 49 38 1381 4659; Gen. Music Dir Wolf-Dieter Hauschild.

Nordwestdeutsche Philharmonie: Stiftbergstrasse 2, 32049 Herford; tel. 39 52 198380; fax 5221 983821; e-mail info@nwd-philharmonie.de; website www.nwd-philharmonie.de; Music Dir Michail Jurowski.

Nürnberger Symphoniker: Bayernstrasse 100, 90471 Nürnberg; tel. 39 91 1474 0140; fax 39 91 1474 0150; e-mail info@nuernbergersymphoniker .de; website www.nuernbergersymphoniker.de; Man. Lucius A. Hemmer.

Oldenburgisches Staatsorchester: Theaterwall 28, 26122 Oldenburg; tel. 0441/2225-111; fax 0441/2225-221; website www.oldenburg .staatstheater.de; Gen. Music Dir Alexander Rumpf.

Opernhaus-und Museumsorchester Frankfurt am Main: Untermainanlage 11, 60320 Frankfurt am Main; Gen. Music Dir Sylvain Cambreling.

Orchester der Beethovenhall Bonn: Verwaltung, Wachsbleiche 2, 53111 Bonn 1; tel. 0228 630031; fax 0228 630376; e-mail info@beethoven -orchester.de; website www.beethoven-orchester.de; Gen. Music Dir Roman Kofman.

Orchester der Deutschen Oper Berlin: Richard-Wagner-Strasse 10, 10585 Berlin; tel. 49 30 34381; fax 49 30 348 8232; e-mail info@ deutscheoperberlin.de; website www.deutscheoperberlin.de/orchester; Gen. Music Dir Christian Thielemann.

Orchester der Elbe-Saale Bühnen: Thomas-Müntzer-Strasse 14/15, 4600 Wittenberg; Music Dir Klaus Hofmann.

Orchester der Hansestadt Lübeck (Philharmonisches Orchester der Hansestadt Lübeck): Beckergrube 16, 23552 Lübeck; tel. 0451 70880; website www.theater.luebeck.de; Gen. Music Dir Roman Brogli-Sacher.

Orchester der Komischen Oper Berlin: Behrenstrasse 55–57, 10117 Berlin; tel. 49 30 202600; fax 49 30 2026 0405; e-mail info@komische-oper -berlin.de; website www.komische-oper-berlin.de; Gen. Music Dir Kirill Petrenko.

Orchester der Landesbühnen Sachsen: Meissner Strasse 152, 8122 Radebeul; Music Dir Joachim Widlak; Man. Christian Schmidt.

Orchester der Musikalischen Komödie Leipzig: Dreilindenstrasse 30, 7033 Leipzig; Music Dir Roland Seiffarth.

Orchester der Staatsoperette: Pirnaer Landstrasse 131, 01257 Dresden; tel. 0351 207990; e-mail info@staatsoperette-dresden.de; website www.staatsoperette-dresden.de; Music Dir Volker Munch.

Orchester der Stadt Ulm: Ulmer Theater, Herbert-von-Karajan-Platz 1, 89073 Ulm; tel. 0049/0731/161-4500; fax 0049/0731/161-1619; e-mail PhilharmonieUlm@aol.com; website www.theater.ulm.de; Gen. Music Dir Alicja Mounk; Public Relations Karin Mayer.

Orchester des Friedrichstadtpalastes Berlin: Friedrichstrasse 107, 10117 Berlin; tel. 49 30 2326 2264/2265; fax 49 30 282 4578; website www .friedrichstadtpalastes.de; Music Dir Detlef Klemm; Man. Julian Herrey.

Orchester des Hessischen Staatstheater Wiesbaden: Christian-Zais-Strasse, 65022 Wiesbaden; tel. 61 113 2255; fax 61 113 2236; Gen. Music Dir Oleg Caetani.

Orchester des Landestheaters Dessau: Fritz-Hesse-Platz 1, 4500 Dessau; Gen. Music Dir Daniel Lipton.

Orchester des Landestheaters Detmold: Landestheater Detmold, Theaterplatz, 37256 Detmold; tel. 5231 97460; fax 5231 974701; e-mail info@landestheater-detmold.de; website www.landestheater-detmold.de.

Orchester des Landestheaters Mecklenburg: Friedrich-Ludwig-Jahn-Strasse, 2080 Neustrelitz; Music Dir Golo Berg.

Orchester des Meininger Theaters: Bernhardstrasse 5, 98617 Meiningen; tel. 03693 451222; fax 03693 451301; e-mail kasse@das-meininger -theater.de; website www.das-meininger-theater.de; Music Dir Wolfgang Hocke.

Orchester des Pfalztheaters Kaiserslautern: Fruchthallstrasse, 6750 Kaiserslautern; Gen. Music Dir Lior Shambadal.

Orchester des Staatstheaters am Gärtnerplatz: 80469 Munich; tel. 089 20241 1; fax 089 20241-237; website www.staatstheater-am -gaertmerplatz.de; Music Dir: David Stahl; Man.: Prof. Klaus Schultz.

Orchester des Staatstheaters Darmstadt: Auf dem Marienplatz, 6100 Darmstadt.

Orchester des Staatstheaters Kassel: Staatstheater Kassel, Friedrichsplatz 15, 3500 Kassel; Gen. Music Dir Georg Schmöhe.

Orchester des Theaters der Altmark-Landestheater Sachsen-Anhalt Nord: Karlstrasse 4–6, 3500 Stendal; Music Dir Frank Jaremko.

Orchester des Theaters des Westens: Kantstrasse 12, 1000 Berlin 12; Music Dir Peter Keuschnig.

Orchester des Theaters Nordhausen: Kathe-Kollwitz-Strasse 15, 5500 Nordhausen; Music Dir Kurt Schafer.

Orchester des Theaters Zwickau: Gewandhausstrasse 7, Pf 308, 9541 Zwickau; Music Dir Welisar Gentscheff.

Orchester des Vogtland-Theaters Plauen: Theaterplatz 1–3, 9900 Plauen; Music Dir Paul Theissen.

Osnabrücker Symphonieorchester: Städtische Bühnen Osnabrück, Domhof 10/11, 49086 Osnabrück; tel. 0049 541 3233355; fax 0049 541 3233751; e-mail musikbuero.theateros@t-online.de; Music Dir Lothar Koenigs.

Philharmonia Hungarica: Lord Menuhin-Haus, Hochstrasse 34, 45768 Marl; tel. 02365 13031; fax 02365 15877; e-mail philharmonia-hungarica@ t-online.de; website www.philharmonia-hungarica.com; Gen. Music Dir Jun Märkl.

Philharmonic Essen: Aatlo Musiktheater, Opernplatz 10, 45128 Essen; website www.theater-essen.asp.de; Gen. Music Dir Stefan Soltesz.

Philharmonisches Kammerorchester Hamburg e V: Musikhalle, Karl-Muck-Platz, 20355 Hamburg; Music Dir Wilfried Laatz.

Philharmonisches Kammerorchester München e V: Connolly-Strasse 15, 8000 Munich; Music Dir Michael Helmrath.

Philharmonisches Kammerorchester Wernigerode GmbH: Bahnhofstrasse 16, 38855 Wernigerode; tel. (3943) 94-95-14; fax (3943) 94-95-29; website www.kammerorchester-wr.de; Music Dir Christian Fitzner.

Philharmonisches Orchester Augsburg: Kasernstrasse 4–6, 86152 Augsburg; tel. 49 821 324 4935; fax 49 821 324 4935; Gen. Music Dir Rudolf Piehlmayer; Man. Matthias Gress.

Philharmonisches Orchester der Landeshauptstadt Kiel: Rathausplatz 4, 24103 Kiel; tel. 49 431 901 2856; fax 49 431 901 6288; website www .theater-kiel.de; Gen. Music Dir Georg Fritzsch.

Philharmonisches Orchester der Staatstheaters Cottbus: Lausitzer-Strasse 33, 03046; website www.staatstheater-cottbus.de; Gen. Music Dir Reinard Petersen.

Philharmonisches Orchester der Stadt Bielefeld: Brunnenstrasse 3, 4800 Bielefeld 1; website www.bielefelder-philharmoniker.de; Gen. Music Dir Peter Kuhn.

Philharmonisches Orchester der Stadt Dortmund: Kuhstrasse 12, 4600 Dortmund 1; Gen. Music Dir Moshe Atzmon.

Philharmonisches Orchester der Stadt Gelsenkirchen: Musiktheater im Revier, 4650 Gelsenkirchen; Gen. Music Dir Neil Varon.

Philharmonisches Orchester der Stadt Nürnberg: Städtische Bühnen Nürnberg, Musiktheater, Richard-Wagner-Platz 2–10, Nürnberg; Gen. Music Dir Eberhard Kloke.

Philharmonisches Orchester des Staatstheaters Mainz GmbH: Gutenbergplatz 7, 6500 Mainz 1; Gen. Music Dir Peter Erckens.

Philharmonisches Orchester Erfurt: Placidus-Muth-Strasse 1, 99084 Erfurt; tel. 0361 22330; website www.theater-erfurt.de; Gen. Music Dir Walter E. Gugerbauer.

Philharmonisches Orchester Frankfurt an der Oder: Collegienstrasse 7, 1200 Frankfurt an der an Oder; Gen. Music Dir Nikos Athinäos.

Philharmonisches Orchester Freiburg: Bertoldstrasse 46, 79098 Freiburg; tel. 49 761 2012807; website www.theater.freiburg.de; Music Dir Kwamé Ryan.

Philharmonisches Orchester Gera: Bühnen der Stadt Gera, Küchengartenalle 2, 07548 Gera; tel. 365 82790; fax 365 827 9135; Music Dir Wolfgang Wappler.

Philharmonisches Orchester Hagen: Elberfelder Strasse 65, 58095 Hagen 1; website www.theater.hagen.de; Gen. Music Dir Gerhard Markson.

Philharmonisches Orchester Heidelberg: Friedrichstrasse 5, 69117 Heidelberg; e-mail info@heidelberger-philharmoniker.de; website www .heidelberger-philharmoniker.de; Gen. Music Dir Thomas Kalb.

Philharmonisches Orchester Regensburg: Bismarckplatz 7, 08468 Regensburg; Gen. Music Dir Hilary Griffiths.

Philharmonisches Staatsorchester Halle: Kleine Brauhausstrasse 26, 06108 Halle an der Saale; tel. 49 345 221 3001; fax 49 345 221 3010; e-mail philharmonie@halle.de; website www.staatsorchester-halle.de; Gen. Music Dir Hendrik Vestmann.

Philharmonisches Staatsorchester Hamburg: Grosse Theaterstrasse 34, 20354 Hamburg; e-mail info@philharmonisches-staatsorchester -hamburg.de; website www.philharmnisches-staatsorchester-hamburg .de; Gen. Music Dir Ingo Metzmacher; Man. Peter Ruzicka.

Pro Arte Ensemble Mainz e V: Werderstrasse 8, 6200 Wiesbaden; Music Dir Juan Levy.

Radiokammerorchester Hamburg: Zum Forellenbach 11, 22113 Oststeinbek; tel. 040 712 3701; fax 040 713 8525; Music Dir Karl Henke.

Radio-Sinfonie-Orchester Frankfurt: Bertramstrasse 8, 60320 Frankfurt; tel. 069 155 2071; fax 069 155 2720; e-mail rso-frankfurt@hr-online .de; website www.rso-frankfurt.de; Orchestra Man. Medi Gasteiner-Girth.

Radio-Sinfonieorchester Stuttgart des SWR: 70150 Stuttgart; tel. 49 711 929-2590; fax 49 711 929-4053; Chief Conductor Roger Norrington; Orchestra Man. Felix Fischer.

Remscheider Symphoniker: Stadt Remscheid, Kulturverwaltungsamt, Konrad-Adenauer-Strasse 31/33, 5630 Remscheid; Gen. Music Dir Reinhard Seifried.

Reussisches Kammerorchester: Bühnen der Stadt Gera, Küchengartenalle 2, 6500 Gera; Music Dir Herbert Voigt.

Rheinisches Kammerorchester Köln: Steinfelder Gasse 11, 5000 Cologne 1; Music Dir Jan Corazolla.

Robert Schumann Philharmonie: Pf 756, 09007 Chemnitz.

Robert-Schumann-Philharmonie: Chemnitz, Käthe-Kollwitz-Strasse 7, 09111 Chemnitz; website www.theater-chemnitz.de; Gen. Music Dir Niksa Bareza.

Rundfunkorchester des Hessischen Rundfunks: Bertramstrasse 8, 60320 Frankfurt am Main 1; Music Dir Peter Falk; Dir of Music Programming Leo Karl Gerhartz.

Rundfunkorchester des Südwestfunks: Fliegerstrasse 36, 6750 Kaiserslautern; Music Dir Klaus Arp; Dir of Music Programming Dr Reimund Hess.

Rundfunkorchester Hannover: Rudolf-von-Benningsen-Ufer 22, 3000 Hannover; Chief Conductor Bernhard Klee.

Rundfunk-Sinfonieorchester Berlin: Haus des Rundfunks, Masurenallee 8–14, 14057 Berlin; website www.rso-berlin.com; Chief Conductor Marek Janowski.

Rundfunk-Sinforneorchester Saarbrücken: Funkhaus Halberg, Pf 1050, 6600 Saarbrücken; Chief Conductor: Günther Henbig; Dir of Music Programming: Dr Sobine Tomek.

Saarländisches Staatsorchester Saarbrücken: Schillerplatz, 6600 Saarbrücken; Gen. Music Dir Jun Märkl.

Sächsische Staatskapelle Dresden: Theaterplatz 2, 8010 Dresden.

Schleswig-Holsteinisches Sinfonieorchester: Rathausstrasse 22, 24937 Flensburg; tel. 0461 141000; website www.sh-landestheater.de; Gen. Music Dir Gerard Oskamp.

Sinfonieorchester des Theaters der Hansestadt Stralsund: Olaf-Palme-Platz, 2300 Stralsund; Music Dir Daniel Kleiner.

Sinfonieorchester Wuppertal: Spinnstrasse 4, 5600 Wuppertal; e-mail info@sinfonieorchester-wuppertal.de; website www.sinfonieorchester -wuppertal.de; Gen. Music Dir George Hanson.

Sinfonietta Köln: Auf der Kuhle 11, 5250 Engelskirchen; Music Dir Cornelius Frowein.

Städtisches Orchester Aachen: Stadttheater, 5100 Aachen.

Städtisches Orchester Bremerhaven: Theodor-Heuss-Platz, Pf 12051, 2850 Bremerhaven; Gen. Music Dir Leo Plettner.

Städtisches Orchester Trier: Am Augustinerhof, 5500 Trier; Gen. Music Dir Reinhard Petersen.

Städtisches Philharmonisches Orchester Würzburg: Theaterstrasse 21, 8700 Würzburg; Gen. Music Dir Jonathan Seers.

Staatliches Orchester Sächsen: Chemnitzer Strasse 46, 9125 Grüna.

Staatskapelle Berlin: Unter den Linden 7, 10117, Berlin; tel. 49 30 2035 4555; fax 49 30 2035 4480; website www.staatsoper-berlin.de; Gen. Music Dir Daniel Barenboim.

Staatskapelle Weimar: Theaterplatz 2, 99423 Weimar; website www .nationaltheater-weimar.de; Gen. Music Dir Julia Miehe.

Staatsorchester Braunschweig: Orchestervarstand Am Theater, 38100 Braunschweig; website www.staatsorchesterbraunschweig.de; Gen. Music Dir Jonas Alber.

Staatsorchester Rheinische Philharmonie: Eltzerhostrasse 6a, 56068 Koblenz; tel. 0261 30 12272; fax 0261 3012 277; e-mail info@rheinische -philharmonie.de; website www.rheinische-philharmonie.de; Gen. Music Dir Shao-Chia Lü Man. Hans Richard Stracke.

Staatsorchester Stuttgart: Oberer Schlossgarten 6, 70173 Stuttgart; website www.staatstheater-stuttgart.de; Gen. Music Dir Gabriele Ferro.

Staatsphilharmonie Rheinland-Pfalz: Heinigstrasse 40, 67059 Ludwigshafen; tel. 621 5990999; fax 621 5990950; website www .staatsphilharmonie.de; Music Dir Ari Rasilainen; Man. Raimund Gress.

Stuttgarter Kammerorchester e V (Stuttgart Chamber Orchestra): Johann-Sebastian-Bach-Platz, 70178 Stuttgart; tel. 49 711 6192121; fax 49 711 6192122; e-mail info@stuttgarter-kammerorchester.de; website www .stuttgarter-kammerorchester.de; Music Dir: Dennis Russell Davies; Man. Dir: Timan Kuttenkeuler.

Stuttgarter Philharmoniker: Leonhardblatz 28, 70182 Stuttgart; tel. 0711 216 7843; e-mail philharmoniker@stuttgart.de; website www .stuttgart.de/philharmoniker; Gen. Music Dir Jörg-Peter Weigle.

Südwestdeutsche Philharmonie Konstanz: Spanierstrasse 3, 7750 Konstanz; Gen. Music Dir Petr Altrichter.

Südwestdeutsches Kammerorchester Pforzheim (South-West German Chamber Orchestra, Pforzheim): Westliche Karl-Friedrich-Strasse 257a, 75172 Pforzheim; tel. 49 7231 464644; fax 49 7231 464643; e-mail swdko-pforzheim@t-online.de; website www.swdko.de; Music Dir: Sebastian Tewinkel; Man.: Andreas Herrmann.

Südwestfälische Philharmonie: Im Langen Feld 2, Pf 1320, 5912 Hilchenbach; Music Dir Hiroshi Kodama; Man. Volker Mattern.

SWF-Sinfonieorchester Baden-Baden: Hans-Bredow-Strasse, 7570 Baden-Baden; Chief Conductor Michael Gielen; Man. Mathias Weigmann.

Symphonieorchester der Stadt Münster: Neubrückenstrasse 63, 4400 Münster; Gen. Music Dir Will Humburg.

Symphonieorchester der Stadt Solingen: Konrad-Adenauer-Strasse 71, 5650 Solingen; Gen. Music Dir Christian Süss.

Symphonieorchester des Bayerischen Rundfunks: Rundfunkplatz 1, 8000 Munich; Chief Conductor Zubin Mehta.

Telemann-Kammerorchester Sachsen-Anhalt: Institut für Auffuhrungspraxis Michaelstein, Pf 24, 3720 Blankenburg; Music Dir Eitelfriedrich Thom.

Theaterorchester Senftenberg: Rathenaustrasse 6/8, 7840 Senftenberg; Music Dir Michael Keschke.

Thüringen Philharmonie Suhl: Bahnhofstrasse 8–10, Pf 306, 6000 Suhl; Gen. Music Dir Olaf Koch.

Thüringer Symphoniker Saalfeld/Rudolstadt: Thüringer Landestheater Rudolstadt, Anger 1, 6820 Rudolstadt; Music Dir Oliver Weder.

Thüringisches Kammerorchester Weimar: Theaterplatz 2, 5300 Weimar; Conductors Max Pommer, Claus Gebauer.

Virtuosi Saxoniae: Welterstrasse 16, 8029 Dresden; Music Dir Ludwig Güttler.

Vogtlandphilharmonie: Weinholdstrasse 7, 9800 Reichenbach; Music Dir Stefan Fraas.

Waiblinger Kammerorchester e V: Friedemann Enssle, Lindauer Strasse 40, 7150 Backnang; Music Dir Gerd Budday.

Westdeutsche Sinfonia: Am Kreispark 32, Pf 310154, 5090 Leverkusen; Music Dir Dirk Joeres.

Württembergische Philharmonie Reutlingen: Wilhelmstrasse 69, 7410 Reutlingen; Gen. Music Dir Roberto Paternostro.

Württembergisches Kammerorchester Heilbronn: Pf 3830, 7100 Heilbronn; Music Dir Jörg Faerber.

Greece

Athens Radio Symphony Orchestra: 432 Messioghion Street, 15310 Athens; tel. 30 1 639 2721; fax 30 1 639 6012; Chair. Mikis Theodorakis.

Athens State Orchestra: 17-19 Vas. Georgious B'Str, 10675 Athens; tel. 30 2 1072576013; fax 30 2 10 72 57 600; Artistic Dir Aris Garoufalis.

Orchestra of Colours: 18 Alexandrou Soutsou, 10671 Athens; tel. 30 1 362 8074; fax 30 1 362 1477; Artistic Dir George Kouroupos.

Thessaloniki State Symphony Orchestra: 21 Ippodromiou Street, 54630 Thessaloniki; tel. 30 31 589156; fax 30 31 604854; e-mail koth@ otenet.gr; Dir Mikis Michaelides; Pres. Konstantinos A. Yakoumis.

Tsakalof Symphony Orchestra and Opera: Platia G. Stavrou 5, 45444 Ioannina; tel. 30 651 33300; fax 30 651 70714; Principal Conductor George Chlitsios; Gen. Dir Aspasia Zerva.

Guatemala

Orquesta Sinfónica Nacional: 3a Avenida 4-61, Zona 1, Guatemala City.

Honduras

Orquesta Sinfónica Nacional: PO Box 4087, Tegucigalpa; tel. 504 220 7206; website www.osnh.hn; Music Dir Ramiro Soriano-Arce; Exec. Dir Jim Andonie.

Hong Kong

Hong Kong Philharmonic Orchestra: Level 8, Administration Building, Hong Kong Cultural Centre, 10 Salisbury Road, Kowloon; tel. 852 2721-2030; fax 852 2311-6229; website www.hkpo.com; Chief Conductor and Artistic Dir: Edo de Waart; CEO: Paul S. W. Leung.

Hungary

Budapest Chamber Orchestra Franz Liszt: Kiskorona utca 7, 1036 Budapest; tel. 1 250 4938; fax 1 270 0846; Dir János Rolla.

Budapest Concert Orchestra MAV: Muzeum utca 11, 1088 Budapest; tel. 36 1 338 2664; fax 36 1 338 4085; e-mail bcorch.mav@matavnet.hu; website www.bmc.hu/mav; Music Dir Tamás Gál; Man. Dir Géza Kovécs.

Budapest Festival Orchestra: Vörösmarty tér 1, 1369 Budapest; Music Dirs Ivan Fischer, Zoltán Kocsis; Man. Ildikó Gedényi.

Budapest Philharmonic Orchestra: Hajos utca 8–10, 1061 Budapest; tel. 36 1 3319 478; fax 36 1 138 8910; website www.bpo.hu; Music Dir Rico Saccani.

Budapest Symphony Orchestra of the Hungarian Radio: Brody Sandor utca 5–7, 1800, Budapest; tel. 36 1 328 8326; fax 36 1 328 8910; e-mail kelenta@iroda.radio.hu; Chief Musical Dir Tamas Vasary; Man. Dir Apor Héthy.

Debrecen Philharmonic Orchestra: Simonffy utca 1/c, 4025 Debrecen; tel. and fax 36 52 412 395; Artistic Dir Imre Kollar.

Hungarian National Philharmonic Orchestra: Vörösmarty tér 1, 1364 Budapest; tel. 36 1 411 6600; fax 36 1 422 6699; website www .hunphilharmonic.org.hu; Music Dir Gilbert Varga.

Hungarian Symphony Orchestra: 10–12 Pava utca, 1094, Budapest; tel. 36 1 215 5770; fax 36 1 215 5462; e-mail btg@tza.hu; website www .orchestra.matav.hu; Music Dir Tamás Vásáry.

Nord Hungarian Symphony Orchestra Miskolc: Fábián utca 6a, 3525 Miskolc; tel. 36 46 323488; fax 36 46 351497; Music Dir László Kovács; Man. László Sir.

Pécs Symphony Orchestra: Kossuth Lajos utca 19, 7621 Pécs; Music Dir Nicolas Pasquet; Admin. Péter Szkladányi.

Savaria Symphony Orchestra: Thököly utca 14, 9700 Szombathely; tel. 36 94 314 472; fax 36 94 316 808; website www.savaria-symphony.hu; Music Dir Robert Houlihan; Man. Tibor Menyhárt.

Szeged Symphony Orchestra: Festö utca 6, 6721 Szeged; tel. 36 62 420 256; fax 36 62 426 102; e-mail orch@symph-szeged.hu; website www .symph-szeged.hu; Dir and Principal Conductor: Sandor Gyüdi.

Iceland

Iceland Symphony Orchestra: Háskólabió v/Hagatorg, PO Box 7052, 127 Reykjavík; tel. 354 545 2500; fax 354 562 4475; e-mail sinfonia@ sinfonia.is; website www.sinfonia.is; Music Dir Rico Saccani; Man. Runólfur Birgir Leifsson.

Reykjavík Chamber Orchestra: Hauhlid 14, 105 Reykjavík; Man. Rut Ingolfsdottir.

India

Kolkata Symphony Orchestra: 6B Sunny Park, Kolkata 700019.

Delhi Symphony Orchestra: 2 Humayun Road, New Delhi 110003; tel. 4623431; fax 24361918.

Ireland

Irish Chamber Orchestra: Foundation Building, University of Limerick, Castletroy, Limerick; tel. 353 61 202620; fax 353 61 202617; e-mail ico@ul.ie; website www.icorch.com; Chief Exec. John Kelly; Artistic Dir Nicholas McGegan.

Radio Telefis Éireann (RTÉ) Concert Orchestra: Radio Telefis Éireann, Donnybrook, Dublin 4; tel. 353 1 208 2779; fax 353 1 208 2511; e-mail Anthony.Long@rte.ie; website www.rte.ie/music; Gen. Man.: Anthony Long; Principal Conductor: Laurent Wagner.

Radio Telefis Éireann (RTÉ) National Symphony Orchestra: National Concert Hall, Earlsfort Terrace, Dublin 2; tel. 353 1 208 2530; fax 353 1 208 2160; e-mail westerm@rte.ie; Exec. Dir Martyn Westermann.

Israel

Israel Chamber Orchestra: Amot Mishpat House, 8 Shaul Ha'melech Blvd, 64733 Tel-Aviv; tel. 972 3 696 1167; fax 972 3 691 0104; e-mail ico2000@netvision.net.iz; Music Dir: Noam Sheriff; Gen. Dir: Arie Bar-Droma; Chair.: Avigdor Levin.

Israel Kibbutz Orchestra: 60990 Shefayim; tel. 972 9 9503715; fax 972 9 9523643; Music Dir Noam Yeny; Man. Aharon Kidron; formerly Kibbutz Chamber Orchestra.

Israel Northern Symphony Haifa: PO Box 6746, 1a Keller Street, 34483 Haifa; tel. 972 4 836 3131; fax 972 4 837 6355; Music Dir Ronald Zollman.

Israel Philharmonic Orchestra: PO Box 23500, 1 Huberman Street, 61231 Tel-Aviv; tel. 972 3 629 3345; fax 972 3 629 0097; Music Dir Zubin Mehta; Gen. Sec. Avi Shoshani.

Israel Pro-Musica Orchestra: PO Box 7191, 31071 Haifa; Music Dir Dalia Atlas.

Israel Sinfonietta: Derech Hameshachrerim 12, 84299 Beer Sheva; tel. 7 623 1616; fax 7 623 5412;Artistic Dir Uri Mayer; Man. Misha Grass.

Jerusalem Symphony Orchestra: PO Box 4640, 91040 Jerusalem; tel. 972 2 5660211; fax 972 2 5669117; Music Dir David Shallon; Man. Dir Zusia Rodan; Artistic Dir Gideon Paz.

Netanya Orchestra: PO Box 464, 42103 Netanya; Music Dir Samuel Lewis; Gen. Man. Yafe Duek.

Ramat Gan Chamber Orchestra: PO Box 138, 13 Hertzel Street, Ramat Gan; Music Dir Zeev Steinberg; Man. Sarah Lash-Yolowitz.

Rishon Le-Zion Symphony Orchestra: 5 Habanim Street, 75254 Rishon Le-Zion; tel. 972 3 948 4842; fax 972 3 948 4843; Music Dir Asher Fisch; Gen. Dir Menachem Shai; Asst Conductor Ilan Schul.

Technion Symphony Orchestra: Churchill Auditorium, 32000 Haifa; Music Dir Dalia Atlas.

Young Israel Philharmonic: PO Box 11292, 1 Huberman Street, 61112 Tel-Aviv; Music Dir Ze-ev Dorman; Admin. Dir Yaffa Sharett.

Italy

I Solisti Veneti: Piazzale Pontecorvo 4A, 35121 Padua; tel. 49 666 128; fax 49 875 2598; Conductor Claudio Scimone; Man. Mirella Gualandi.

Orchestra Alessandro Scarlatti di Napoli della Radiotelevisione Italiana: Via Marconi 5, 80125 Naples; Artistic Dir Massimo Fargnoli.

Orchestra da Camera di Padova e del Veneto: Via Marsilio da Padova 19, 35139 Padua; website www.pvorchestra.org; Artistic Sec. Cecilia Montovani.

Orchestra della Toscana: Via Verdi 20, 50122 Florence; tel. 39 55 234 0710; fax 39 55 200 8035; e-mail info@orchestradellatoscana.it; website www.orchestradellatoscana.it;

Artistic Dir Sergio Sablich; Principal Conductor Lu Jia.

Orchestra Filarmonica Marchigiana: Vicolo Aranci 2, 60121 Ancona; tel. 39 071 206168; fax 39 071 206730; e-mail filarmonica.marche@libero.it; Artistic Dir Gustav Kuhn.

Orchestra Sinfonica dell'Accademia Nazionale de Santa Cecilia: Via Vittoria 6, 00187 Rome; Music Dir Daniele Gatti.

Orchestra Sinfonica di Milano della Radiotelevisione Italiana: Via Conservatorio 12, 21011 Milan; Artistic Dir Mario Messinis.

Orchestra Sinfonica di San Remo: Corso Cavallotti 51, 18038 San Remo; Artistic Dir Giovanni Guglielmo.

Orchestra Sinfonica di Torino della Radiotelevisione Italiana (RAI): Piazza Fratelli Rossaro 15, 10124 Turin; tel. 39 11 812 3424; fax 39 11 817 7410; Artistic Dir Daniele Spini; Orchestral Man. Maria Sciavolino; Principal Conductor Eliahu Inbal.

Orchestra Sinfonica Haydn di Bolzano e Trento: Via Gilm 1A, 39100 Bolzano; tel. 0471 975 031; fax 0471 327868; e-mail haydn@dnet.it; website www.haydn-orchestra.com; Artistic Dir Hubert Stuppner.

Orchestra Sinfonica Nazionale della RAI: Piazza Rossaro, 10124 Torino; tel. 39 011 4961; fax 39 011 817 7410; Artistic Dir Daniele Spini.

Orchestra Sinfonica Siciliana: Via G. La Farina 29, 90141 Palermo; tel. 39 91 300609; fax 39 91 300155; Artistic Dir Giuseppe Catalso; Conductor Gabriele Ferro.

Orchestra Sinfonico dell'Emilia Romagna Arturo Toscanini: Via G. Tartini 13, 43100 Parma; tel. 39 521 274417; fax 39 251 272134.

Japan

Hiroshima Symphony Orchestra: 15-10 Hatchobori, Naka-ku, Hiroshima 730; tel. 81 82 222 8448; fax 818 2222 8447; Music Dir Kazuyoshi Akiyaima.

Japan Philharmonic Orchestra: 1-6-1 Umezato, Suginami-ku, Tokyo 166; tel. 81 3 5378 6311; fax 81 3 5378 6161; e-mail office@japanphil.or.jp; website www.jphil.or.jp; Music Dir Kenichiro Kobayashi; Man. Dir Shuhei Deguchi.

Kanagawa Philharmonic Orchestra: Hanami-dai 4-2, Hodogaya-ku, Yokohama 240; tel. 81 45 331 4001; fax 81 45 331 4022; website www.kanaphil.com; Music Dir Yuzo Toyama; Exec. Dir Yutaka Ueno.

Kansai Philharmonic Orchestra: 7F Harp Oak 26h, 1-2-4 Benten, Minato-ku, Osaka-shi, Osaka; tel. 06 557 1381; fax 06 557 1383; Conductor Uri Mayer.

Kobe Philharmonic Orchestra: 1-9-1 San-no-miya-cho, Chuo-ku, Kobe-shi 650; Conductor Chitaru Asahina.

Kunaicho Gakuba (Imperial Court Orchestra): Imperial Palace, Tokyo 100.

Kyoto Symphony Orchestra: 103 Izumoji Tatemoto-cho, Kita-ku, Kyoto 603-8134; tel. 81 75 222 0331; fax 81 75 222 0332; website www.city.kyoto.jp/bunshi/symphony; Chief Conductor: Naoto Otomo; Chief Guest Conductor: Hiroyuki Iwaki; Artistic Man. Mitsuru Yoshida; f. 1956; performs some 90 concerts each year, including 15 subscription concerts with world-famous conductors and soloists, and a series of concerts for children.

Kyushu Symphony Orchestra: 1-11-50 NoNaKuma, Jonan-ku, Fukuoka-shi 814-01; tel. 092 822 8855; fax 092 822 8833; Music Dir Ishimaru Hiroshi; Chair. Kenzou Tanaka.

Nagoya Philharmonic Orchestra: Nagoya City Music Plaza 4f 1-4-10, Kanayama Naka-ku Nagoya 460-0022; tel. 81 52 322 2774; fax 81 52 322 3066; e-mail eigyou@nagoya-hil.or.jp; Conductor Iimori Tajjiro; Man. Susumu Nonoyama.

New Japan Philharmonic Orchestra: Sumia Triphony Hall, 1-2-3 Kinshi, Sumida-ku, Tokyo 130-0013; tel. 813 5610 3820; fax 813 3822 0729; Hon. Artistic Dir Seiji Ozawa; Man. Chiyoshige Matsubara.

NHK (Japan Broadcasting Corporation) Symphony Orchestra: 2-16-49 Takanawa, Minato-ku, Tokyo 108; tel. 81 3 5793 8111; fax 81 3 3443 0278; Music Dir Charles Dutoit; Exec. Dir Takeshi Hara.

Orchestra Ensemble Kanazawa: Hirosaka 1-7-1, Kanazawa 920; tel. 076 232 0171; fax 076 232 0172; e-mail office@oek.jp; website www.oek.jp; Music Dir Hiroyuki Iwaki; Man. Dir Masayuki Yamada.

Osaka Philharmonic Orchestra: 1-1-44 Kishinosato, Nishinari-ku, Osaka 557-0041; tel. 81 6 6656 7711; fax 81 6 6656 7714; Music Dir Takashi Asahina; Sec.-Gen. Shoji Onodera.

Osaka Symphony Orchestra: 4-3-9 203 Tezukayama naka, Sumiyoshi-ku, Osaka 558; Music Dir Thomas Sanderling; Gen. Man. Tetsuo Shikishima.

Sapporo Symphony Orchestra: c/o Kyoiku Bunka Kaikan, Nishi 13-chome, Kita 1-jo, Chuo-ku, Sapporo 060; tel. 011 251 4774; fax 011 251 4776; Conductor Kazuyoshi Akiyama; Pres. Hideji Kitagawa.

Shinsei Nihon Symphony Orchestra: Maruishi Building, 3-16-4 Nishi Ikebukuro, Toshima-ku, Tokyo 171; Music Dir Ryusuke Numjiri; Exec. Dir Saburo Kurematsu.

Tokyo City Philharmonic Orchestra: 1-19-1-2-3 Sumiyoshi Koutu-ku, Tokyo, 135-0002; tel. 813 5624 4001; fax 813 5624 4114; e-mail mail@cityphil.gr.jp; website www.cityphil.jp; Music Dir Naohiro Totsuka; Exec. Dir Tatatsugu Kuwahata.

Tokyo Metropolitan Symphony Orchestra: c/o Tokyo Bunkakaikan, 5-45 Ueno Park, Taito-ku, Tokyo 110-0007; tel. 81 3 3822 0727; fax 81 3 3822 0729; Chief Conductor Koizumi Kauhiro; Exec. Dir Hiroshi Kainuma.

Tokyo Philharmonic Symphony Orchestra: Eiritsu Building, 3-3 Kanda Kajicho, Chiyoda-ku, Tokyo 10; tel. 81 3 3256 9696; fax 81 3 3256 9698; Conductor Kazushi Ohno; Dir Shogo Matsuki.

Tokyo Symphony Orchestra: 2-23-5 Hyakunin-cho, Shinjuku-ku, Tokyo 169-0073; tel. 03 3369 1661; fax 03 3360 8249; e-mail tokyosymphony@musicinfo.com; website www.tokyosymphony.com; Music Dir Kazuyoshi Akiyama; Gen. Man. Shigteto Kanayama.

Yomiuri Nippon Symphony Orchestra: 7F Daiichi Nurihiko Bldg, 2-9-2 Kyobashi Chuo-ku, Tokyo 104-0031; tel. 81 3 3562-1540; fax 81 3 3562-1544; e-mail yomikyo@k3.dion.ne.jp; website yomikyo.yomiuri.co.jp; Principal Conductor: Gerd Albrecht; Dir Gen.: Takao Ohuchi.

Republic of Korea

Busan Philharmonic Orchestra: 848-4 Daeyon 4 Dong, Nam-gu, Pusan; tel. 82 51 625 8130; fax 82 51 625 8138; e-mail 61pwc@hanmail.net; Music Dir Sung Kwak; Gen. Man. Won-Chul Park.

Korean Broadcasting System (KBS) Symphony Orchestra: 18 Yoido-dong, Youngdungpo-gu, Seoul 150-790; website www.kbsso.kbs.co.kr; Chief Conductor Othmar Maga.

Seoul Philharmonic Orchestra: 81-3 Sejong-Ro, Chong Ro-Gu, Seoul 110-050; tel. 82 2 736 2721; fax 82 2 738 0948; website www.seoulphilharmonic.org; Music Dir Kyung-Soo Won.

Latvia

Latvian National Symphony Orchestra: 6 Amatu St, 1664 Riga; tel. 371 722 9357; fax 371 722 4850; e-mail secretary@lnso.lv; website www.lmuza.lv; Music Dir Olan Eits; Gen. Man. Ilona Brege.

Latvian Philharmonic Chamber Orchestra: Iagrera Str, Riga, 1050; tel. 371 9223201; fax 371 2451038; Man. Dir Linda Liepzig.

Latvian Radio and Television Symphony Orchestra: c/o Latvian Radio and Television, Riga.

Riga Chamber Orchestra: Kalku St 11a, 226350 Riga.

Liepaja Symphony Orchestra: Graudu 50, 3401, Liepaja; tel. 371 342 5538; fax 371 348 1478; e-mail lsovija@mail.anet.lv; Artistic Dir Imants Resnis.

Lithuania

Lithuanian National Symphony Orchestra: Ausroz Vartu 5, 2001 Vilnius; tel. 370 2 627 047; fax 370 2 622 859; e-mail info@filharmonija.lt; Artistic Dir and Chief Conductor Juozas Domarkas.

Lithuanian State Symphony Orchestra: Zygimantu 6, 2600 Vilnius; tel. 370 2 628127; fax 370 2 220966; e-mail lvso@lvso.lt; website www.lvso.lt/en; Music Dir Gintaras Rinkevicius; Gen. Dir Gintautas Kevisas.

Luxembourg

Orchestre Philharmonique du Luxembourg: BP 2243, 1022 Luxembourg; tel. 352 22 99 01205; fax 352 22 99 98; e-mail info@opl.lu; website www.opl.lu; Chief Conductor: Bramwell Tovey; Man. Benedikt Fohr.

Malaysia

Malaysian Philharmonic Orchestra: Level 2, Tower 2, Petronas Twin Towers, Kuala Lumpur; tel. 603 581 3208; fax 603 581 3216; Musical Dir Kees Bakels.

Mexico

National Symphony Orchestra of Mexico: Regina 52, Centro, 06080 Mexico City, DF; tel. 52 5 709 8118; fax 52 5 709 3533; Musical Dir Enrique Arturo Diemecke; Gen. Man. Aleiandro Toledano.

Orquesta de Cámera de Bellas Artes: Extemplo de Santa Teresa La Antigua, Lic Verdad 8 y Moneda, Centro, 06060 Mexico City, DF; Music Dir Ildefonso Cedillo; Man. Maricarmen Guerrero Meneses.

Orquesta Filarmónica de Jalisco: Teatro Degollado, 44100 Guadalajara, Jalisco; tel. 33 3658 3812; fax 52 614 9366; website www.ofj.com.mx; Music Dir José Guadalupe Flores; Man. Silvia Susana Hernández Huerta.

Orquesta Filarmónica de la Ciudad de México: Periférico Sur 5141, Sala Ollin Yoliztli, 14030 Mexico City, DF; tel. 52 905 606 8933; fax 52 905 606 8401; Principal Conductor Luis Herrera de la Fuente.

Orquesta Filarmónica de la Universidad Autónoma de México: Avda Insurgentes Sur 3000, Sala Nezahualcóyotl, 04510 Mexico City, DF, Coyoacán; Music Dir Ronald Zollman; Gen. Man. Maricarmen Costero.

Orquesta Sinfónica del Estado de México: Plaza Fray Andrés de Castro, Edificio C, 1°, Toluca, Mex C.P. 5000; tel. 52 72 44 5219; fax 52 72 45 6216; Music Dir Enrique Bátiz; Gen. Man. Maria Dolores Castillo.

State of Mexico Symphony Orchestra: Avenida José Vicente Villada No. 406 1er Piso, Col. Centro, 50000 Toluca; tel. 52 7 214 5219; fax 52 7 215 6216; Musical Dir Enrique Batiz; Admin. Dir Alfredo Higuera Hernandez.

Moldova

Symphony Orchestra of the National Philharmonic of Moldova: 78 Mitropolitul, Varlaam Str., 2012 Chisinau; tel. 373 244 5879; fax 373 223 3509; e-mail somnph@ch.moldpac.md; Chief Conductor Valentin Doni.

Monaco

Orchestre Philharmonique de Monte Carlo: BP 139, Place du Casino, 98007 Monte Carlo; tel. 00 377 92 16 23 17; fax 00 377 92 15 08 71; e-mail info@opmc.mc; website www.opmc.mc; Music Dir Marek Janowski; Dir René Croesi; Artistic Dir Chandler Cudlipp.

Netherlands

Amsterdam Baroque Orchestra: Meerwag 23, 1405 BC Bussum; website www.tonkoopman.nl; Music Dir Ton Koopman; Gen. Man. Hans Meijer.

Arnhem Philharmonic Orchestra: Velperbuitensingel 12, PO Box 1180, 6801 BD Arnhem; tel. 31 26 442 2632; fax 31 26 443 9966; e-mail info@hetgeldersorkest.nl; Principal Conductor Lawrence Renes.

Brabants Philharmonisch Orkest: J. Van Lieshoutstraat 5, 5611 EE Eindhoven; tel. 31 40 265 5699; fax 31 40 246 3459; e-mail info@brabantsorkest.nl; Man. Dir Stan Paardehooper; Chief Conductor Marc Soustrot.

Forum Filharmonisch: PO Box 1321, 7500 BH Enschede; Gen. Man. J. M. Bal.

Het Gelders Orkest: Velperbuitensingel 12, 6828 CV Arnhem; tel. 31 26 442 2632; fax 31 26 443 9966; website www.hetgeldersorkest.nl; Principal Conductor Martin Sieghart; Gen. Admin. H. Hierck.

Koninklijk Concertgebouworkest: Jacob Obrechstraat 51, 1071 KJ Amsterdam; tel. 31 20 20 679 2211; fax 31 20 676 3331; e-mail info@concertgebouworkest.nl; website www.concertgebouworkest.nl; Chief Conductor Riccardo Chailly.

Limburgs Symphonie Orkest: Statenstraat 5, 6211 TB Maastricht; tel. 043 350 7000; fax 043 350 7025; e-mail info@lso.nl; website www.lso.nl; Chief Conductor Ed Spanjaard.

Metropole Orkest: PO Box 125, 1200 AC Hilversum; tel. 31 0 35 67 14 160; fax 31 0 35 67 14 171; website www.metropoleorchestra.com; Music Dir Dick Bakker; Man. Fred Dekker.

Nederlands Philharmonisch Orkest: Beurs van Berlage, Damrak 213, 1012 ZH Amsterdam; tel. 31 020 521 75 00; fax 31 20 622 9939; website www.orkest.nl; Music Dir Hartmut Haenchen; Man. Dr J. W. Loot.

Noordhollands Philharmonisch Orkest: Klokhuisplein 2A, 2011 HK Haarlem; tel. 31 235 319248; fax 31 235 32 8533; Music Dir Lucas Vis; Man. Casper Vogel.

Noord-Nederlands Orkest: Emmaplein 2, PO Box 818, 9700 AV Groningen; tel. 31 35 6714 140; fax 31 35 6714 171; website www.noordnederlandsorkest.nl; Man. A. L. E. Verberne.

Radio Filharmonisch Orkest Holland: Heuvellaan 33, PO Box 125, 1200 AC Hilversum; tel. 31 35 6714 130; fax 31 35 6714 171; e-mail rfo@mco.nl; website www.rfo.nl; Chief Conductor Edo de Waart; Man. Stefan Rosu.

Radio Kamerorkest: PO Box 125, 1200 JB Hilversum; tel. 31 35 6714150; fax 31 35 6714171; Conductor Frans Bruggen; Man. Ferdinand L. J. Vrijma.

Radio Symphonie Orkest: Heuvellaan 33, PO Box 125, 1200 AC Hilversum; tel. 31 0 35 671 41 40; fax 31 0 35 671 41 71; e-mail rso@mco.nl; website www.nl-rso.org; Chief Conductor Eri Klas; Gen. Man. Henk Smit.

Residentie Orkest: PO Box 11543, 2502 AM The Hague; tel. 31 070 88 00 200; fax 31 070 36 519 07; e-mail info@residentieorkest.nl; website www.residentieorkest.nl; Chief Conductor Jaap van Zweden; Man. H. Van den Akker.

Rotterdams Philharmonisch Orkest: PO Box 962, 3000 AZ Rotterdam; tel. 31 10 217 1760; fax 31 10 411 6215; e-mail art.dir@rpho.nl; Chief Conductor Valery Gergiev; Man. Paul Zeegers.

New Zealand

Auckland Philharmonia: PO Box 56024, Dominion Road, Auckland, New Zealand; tel. 649 639 7073; fax 649 630 9687; e-mail ap@akl-phil.co.nz; website www.akl-phil.co.nz; Music Dir Miguel Harth Bedoya.

Auckland Philharmonic Orchestra: PO Box 56-024, Mount Eden, Auckland; tel. 9 638 7073; fax 9 630 9687; Gen. Man. Lloyd Williams.

Christchurch Symphony Orchestra: St Elmos Court, 47 Hereford Street, Christchurch; tel. 64 3 379 3886; fax 64 3 379 3861; e-mail office@chsymph.co.nz; website www.csymph.co.nz; Music Dir: Marc Taddei.

New Zealand Symphony Orchestra: PO Box 6640, Wellington 6001; tel. 64 4 801 3890; fax 64 4 801 3891; e-mail info@nzso.co.nz; website www.nzso.co.nz; Musical Dir James Judd; Chief Exec. Mark Keyworth.

Southern Sinfonia: PO Box 5571, Dunedin; tel. 03 477 5623; fax 03 477 5628; e-mail sinfonia@earthlight.co.nz; Gen. Man. Philippa Harris.

Wellington Sinfonia: Level 2, Municipal Office Bldg, 101 Wakefield Street, Wellington; tel. 64 4 801 3882; fax 64 4 801 3888; website www.wellingtonsinfonia.co.nz; Gen. Man. Christine Pearce.

Norway

Bergen Filharmoniske Orkester: Grieghallen, Lars Hilles Gate 3a, 5015 Bergen; tel. 47 5521 6228; fax 47 5531 8534; website www.harmonien.no; Principal Conductor: Andrew Litton; Gen. Man.: Lorentz Reitan; f. 1765, one of Norway's two national orchestras; puts on some 70–90 concerts each year, international and national tours.

Norsk Kammerorkester (Norwegian Chamber Orchestra): Pilestredet 7, 0180 Oslo; tel. 47 2242 0770; fax 47 38 022991; e-mail post@kso.no; Artistic Dir Iona Brown.

Oslo Filharmoniske Orkester: PO Box 1607 Vika, 0119 Oslo; tel. 47 2201 4900; fax 47 2201 4901; website www.oslophil.com; Chief Conductor Mariss Jansons; Man. Trond Okkelmo.

Stavanger Symfoniorkester: Sandvigå 27, Bjergsted, 4007 Stavanger; tel. 47 51508830; fax 47 51508839; e-mail post@sso.no; website www.sso.no; Admin. Dir Thorstein Granly; Man. Dir Erik Landmark.

Trondheim Symfoniorkester: PO Box 774, 7001 Trondheim; tel. 47 7353 9800; fax 47 7353 9801; e-mail post@tso.no; website www.tso.no; Artistic Dir Roar Leinan; Chief Conductor Daniel Harding.

Panama

Orquesta Sinfónica Nacional: Apto 9190, Panama City 6; Conductor Eduardo Charpentier de Castro.

Paraguay

Orquesta Sinfónica de la Ciudad de Asunción: México 145, Asunción; tel. 595 21 492416; e-mail sfa@pol.com.py; website www.sfa.org.py; Music Dir Luis Szarán.

Philomúsica de Asunción: Guillermo Arias 884 y Dr Paiva, Asunción; tel. and fax 595 21 424005; e-mail szaran@pol.com.py; website www.szaran.org.py; Contact Glenda Campos.

Peru

Orquesta Sinfónica Nacional: Avda Javier Prado Este 2465, Lima 41; tel. and fax 225-8882; e-mail osnperu@telefonica.net.pe; Artistic Dir and Conductor: Armando Sánchez Málaga.

Philippines

Manila Symphony Orchestra: Manila Metropolitan Theater, Liwasang Bonifacio, PO Box 664, Manila; Music Dir Alfredo Buenaventura.

National Philharmonic Orchestra: PO Box 2650, Makati, Metro, Manila; tel. 63 817 2601; fax 63 815 3483; Music Dir Redentor Romero.

Philippine Philharmonic Orchestra: Cultural Center of the Philippines, Roxas Blvd, Manila; tel. 63 2 832 1125; fax 63 2 832 3683; Music Dir Oscar Yatco; Exec. Dir Amelita Guevara.

Poland

Baltic State Philharmonic Orchestra: Aleja Zwyci stwa 15, 80-219 Gdańsk.

Białystok State Philharmonic Orchestra: Podlesna 2, 15-227 Białystok; Music Dir Miroslaw Blaszczyk.

Chopin Chamber Orchestra: 25/54 ul Gabrieli Zapolskiej, 30-126 Kraków; tel. 12 637 0684; Music Dir and Man. Boguslaw Dawidów.

Czestochowa Philharmonic Orchestra: Wilsona 16, 42-202 Czestochowa; tel. 48 034 3244230; fax 48 034 34 37; e-mail filharmonia@filharmonia.com.pl; website www.filharmonia.com.pl; Man. Dir: Leszek F. Hadrian; Music Dir: Jerzy Swoboda.

Filharmonia Poznańska im. Tadeusza Szeligosdkiego (Tadeusz Szeligowski Poznań Philharmonic Orchestra): ul. Św. Marcin 81, 61-808 Poznań; tel. 61 852 47 08; fax 61 852 34 51; e-mail filharmonia@filharmonia.poznan.pl; website www.filharmonia.poznan.pl; Gen. and Artistic Dir: José Maria Florêncio.

Jelenia Gora State Philharmonic Orchestra: ul 22-go Lipca 60, 58-500 Jelenia Gora; Music Dir Tadeusz Wicherek; Dir Zuzanna Dziedzic.

Kraków Philharmonic Orchestra Karol Szymanowski: Zwierzyniecka 1, 31-103 Kraków; tel. and fax 48 12 422 4312; e-mail fk@filharmonia.krakow.pl; website www.filharmonia.krakow.pl; Music Dir and Chief Conductor: Tomasz Bugay; Man.: Anna Oberc.

National Polish Radio Symphony Orchestra: Plac Sejmu Slaskiego 2, 40-032 Katowice; tel. 48 32 2518903; fax 48 32 2571384; e-mail nospr@nospr.org.pl; website www.nospr.org.pl; Gen. and Programme Dir: Joanna Wnuk-Nazarowa.

New Polish Radio Orchestra: J. P. Woronicza 17, 00-950 Warsaw; Artistic Dir and Principal Conductor Tadeusz Strugala.

Polish Chamber Orchestra: Centrum Sztuki Studio, Palac Kultury i Nauki, 00901 Warsaw; tel. 48 22620 0138; e-mail imp@sinfoniavarsovia.com; Music Dir Franciszek Wybranczyk.

Polska Filharmonic Baltycka: ul Olowianka 1, 80-751 Gdańsk; tel. 48 58 30 52 040; fax 48 58 30 52 040.

Pomeranian State Philharmonic Orchestra Ignacy Paderewski: Libelta 16, 85-080 Bydgoszcz; tel. 52 21 09 20; fax 52 21 07 52.

Rzeszów State Philharmonic Orchestra Artur Malawski: Chopina 30, 35-055 Rzeszów; Music Dir Adam Natanek.

Silesian State Philharmonic Orchestra: Sokolska 2, 40-084 Katowice; tel. 48 32 597571; fax 48 32 589885; Music Dir Jerzy Swoboda.

Sinfonia Varsovia: Centrum Sztuki Studio, Palac Kultury i Nauki, 00901 Warsaw; e-mail imp@sinfoniavarsovia.com; Artistic Dir Krysztof Penderecki; Music Dir and Man. Franciszek Wybranczyk.

Sudettic Philharmonic Orchestra: Slowackiego 4, 58-3000 Walbrzych; tel. 842 41 80; fax 842 28 93; Artistic Dir and Chief Man. Jozef Wilkomirski.

Szczecin State Philharmonic Orchestra Mieczyslaw Karlowicz: Dzierzy skiego 1, 70-455 Szczecin; Music Dir Stefan Marczyk; Man. Jadwiga Igiel.

Warsaw Chamber Orchestra: ul Freta 28/8, 00-227 Warsaw; tel. 22 31 63 63; fax 22 48 76 66; Artistic Dir Marek Sewen.

Warsaw Philharmonic Orchestra: ul. Jasna 5, 00 950 Warsaw; tel. 48 22 5517101; fax 48 22 5517200; e-mail filharmonia@filharmonia.pl; website www.filharmonia.pl; Artistic and Gen. Dir: Antoni Wit; national orchestra of Poland.

W. Lutoslawski Philharmonic in Wrocław: ul. Pilsudskiego 19, 50-044 Wrocław; tel. 4871 342 20 01; fax 4871 342 89 80; e-mail biuro@filharmonia.wroclaw.pl; website www.filharmonia.wroclaw.pl; Gen. Dir: Lidia Geringer d'Oedenberg; Artistic Dir: Mariusz Smolij.

Zielona Góra State Philharmonic Orchestra: Plac Powsta ców Wielkopolskich 10, 65-075 Zielona Góra; Music Dir Czeslaw Grabowski.

Portugal

Orquestra Gulbenkian: Fundação Calouste Gulbenkian, Serviço de Música, Avda de Berna 45a, 1067-001 Lisbon; tel. 351 21 782 3000; fax 351 21 782 3041; e-mail musica@gulbenkian.pt; Principal Conductor and Artistic Dir: Lawrence Foster.

Orquestra Sinfónica do Porto: Radiodifusao Portuguesa, Rua Candido Reis 74/10, 4000 Porto; Music Dir Gunther Arglebe.

Orquestra Sinfónica Portuguesa: Rua Serpa Pinto 9, 1200 Lisbon; tel. 351 1 343 1734; fax 351 1 343 1735; Chief Conductor and Artistic Dir Alvaro Cassuto.

Romania

Bucharest Chamber Orchestra: Allée Ioanid 4, Bucharest 70259; Music Dir Ion Voicu; Man. Madeleine Cretu.

Bucharest State Philharmonic Orchestra George Enescu: Ateneul Roman, Franklin Str 1, Bucharest.

Iasi Philharmonic: Str Cuza Voda 29, 6600 Iasi; tel. 240 32 114601; fax 240 32 214160; e-mail filarmonicais@mail.dntis.ro; Artistic Dir Bujor Prelipcean.

Rumanian Radio and Television Symphony Orchestra: Str Nuferilor 62-64, 79756 Bucharest.

Russia

Bolshoi Symphony Orchestra: Bolshoi Theater, Petrovka St 1, Moscow; tel. 7 095 292 6570; fax 7 095 292 9032; Music Dir and Conductor Mark Ermler.

Ensemble XXI Moscow (Moscow International Chamber Orchestra): Voznesensky Per 8/5, Moscow 103009; tel. and fax 7095 299 1221; e-mail info@ensemblexxi.org; website www.ensemblexxi.org; Artistic Dir and Conductor Lygia O'Riordan.

Moscow Chamber Orchestra: Ul Gorkogo 37, Moscow; tel. 7095 956 7677; e-mail info@moscowchamberorchestra.com; website www.moscowchamberorchestra.com; Musical Dir Constantine Orbelian.

Moscow Philharmonic Orchestra: Ul Gorkogo 37, Moscow; Chief Conductor Vassily Sinaisky.

Russian National Symphony Orchestra: Studio Moscow, Alexeya Tolstovo St 26-33, 103001 Moscow; tel. 7 095 290 6262; fax 7 095 292 6511; Conductor Mikhail Pletnev.

Russian State Philharmonic Orchestra: 18 Murmansky Proezd, App 77, 129075, Moscow; tel. 7095 233 8996; Chief Conductor Valery Poljansky.

St Petersburg Chamber Orchestra: ul Brodskogo 2, St Petersburg.

St Petersburg Philharmonic Orchestra: Mikhailovskaya St 2, 219011 St Petersburg; tel. 7 812 311 7331; fax 7 812 311 2126; Chief Conductor Yuri Temirkanov.

State Radio and Television Symphony Orchestra: 24 Malaya Nikitskaya, 12812 Moscow; tel. 095 290 05 01; fax 095 573 61 75; e-mail letter@rtvsymphony.ru; Chief Dir Anatoly Nemudrov.

State Symphony Orchestra of Russia: Arbat 35, 121835 Moscow; Chief Conductor Evgeny Svetlanov.

Serbia and Montenegro

Belgrade Philharmonic Orchestra: Studentski Trg 11, 11000 Belgrade; tel. 38111187533; fax 38111187533; Gen. Man. Branka Cvejic-Mezei.

Belgrade Radio and Television Symphony Orchestra: Hilendarska 2, 11000 Belgrade.

Singapore

Singapore Symphony Orchestra Ltd: 11 Empress Place, Second Floor, Victoria Memorial Hall, 179558 Singapore; tel. 65 6336 4417; fax 65 6336 6382; e-mail ssonet@singnet.com.sg; website www.sso.org.sg; Music Dir Lan Shui.

Slovakia

Capella Istropolitna: Schillerove 23, 811 04 Bratislava; Music Dir Ewald Daniel; Man. Karol Kopernický.

Musica Aeterna: 816 01 Bratislava; Chief Conductor Peter Zajicek.

Slovak Chamber Orchestra: 816 01 Bratislava; Chief Conductor Bohdan Warchal.

Slovak Philharmonic Orchestra: 816 01 Bratislava; tel. 00 421 25443 3351; website www.filharm.sk; Chief Conductor Ondrej Lenárd; Man. Tatiana Schoeferová.

Slovak State Philharmonic, Kosice: Dom Umenia, Moyzesova 66, 04123 Kosice; tel. 421 55 622 7216; e-mail sfk@sfk.sk; Chief Conductor Tomás Koutnik; Exec. Dir Julius Klein.

Symphony Orchestra of the Slovak Radio: Mýtna 1, 812 90 Bratislava; tel. 421 7/57273475; fax 421 7/57273386; Chief Conductor Robert Stankovsky; Man. Dir Milos Jurkovic.

Slovenia

Slovenian Philharmonic Orchestra: Kongresni trg 10, 61000 Ljubljana; tel. 386 01 24 10 800; fax 386 01 24 10 900; e-mail slo-filharmonija@filharmonija.si; website www.filharmonija.si; Artistic Dir Marko Letonja.

Slovenian Radio and Television Symphony Orchestra: Tavcarjeva 17, 61000 Ljubljana.

South Africa

Cape Town Philharmonic Orchestra: PO Box 4040, Cape Town 8000; tel. 27 21 418 9809; fax 27 21 425 1009; e-mail capephil@artscape.co.za; Principal Conductor Bernhard Ejueller.

Cape Town Symphony Orchestra: City Hall, Darling Street, Cape Town 8001.

Kwa Zulu-Natal Philharmonic Orchestra: PO Box 5353, Durban 4000; tel. 27 31 369 9438; fax 27 31 369 9559; e-mail kznpomar@iafrica.com; website www.kznpo.co.za; Artistic Dir Bongani Tembe.

The National Orchestra: PO Box 566, Pretoria 0001; Principal Conductor Carlo Franci; Gen. Man. Stephen Wikner.

New Arts Philharmonic Orchestra (NAPOP): PO Box 566, Pretoria 0001; tel. 27 12 322 1665; fax 27 12 322 3913; Principal Conductor Gerard Korsten.

Spain

Joven Orquesta Nacional de España: Príncipe de Vergara, 28002 Madrid; Principal Conductor Edmon Colomer; Man. Juan Wesolowski y Fernández-Heredia.

Orquesta Ciudad de Barcelona: Via Laietan a 41, pral, 08003 Barcelona; Music Dir Garcia Navarro; Man. Jaume Masferrer.

Orquesta del Principado de Asturias: Corrado del Obispo s/n, Edificio del Conservatorio de Música Eduardo Martínez Torner, 33003 Oviedo; Music Dir Maximiano Valdes.

Orquesta Nacional de España: Príncipe de Vergara 146, 28002 Madrid; Principal Conductor Aldo Ceccato; Man. Dir Tomas Marco.

Orquesta Pablo Sarasate: 6° Izquierda, 31002 Pamplona; tel. 34 948 229217; fax 34 948 211948; e-mail pablosarasate@retemail.es; website www.pablosarasate.com/orquesta.htm; Artistic Dir Jacques Bodmer; Man. José Maria Montes Navio; Admin. Ricardo Salcedo.

Orquesta Sinfónica de Baleares: Calle Vicente Juan Rossello 22-B, 07013 Palma; tel. 34 971 287 565; fax 34 971 287 758; e-mail informacio@simfonica-de-balears.com; Music Dir Luis Remartínez Gómez; Man. Carlos Rubic.

Orquesta Sinfónica de Barcelona i Nacional de Catalunya (OBC): Via Laietana 41, 08003 Barcelona; tel. 34 3 317 1096; fax 34 3 317 5439; website www.obc.es; Artistic Dir Lawrence Foster.

Orquesta Sinfónica de Euskadi (Basque National Symphony Orchestra): Paseo Miramon 214, 20 140 San Sebastian, Basque Country; tel. 34 943 01 32 32; fax 34 943 30 83 24; e-mail medios@orquestadeeuskadi.es; website www.orquestadeeuskadi.es; Gen. Dir: Germán Ormazábal Artolazábal; Music Dirs: Gilbert Varga, Cristian Mandeal.

Orquesta Sinfónica de Málaga: Calle Ramos Marin s/n, 29012 Málaga; Music Dir Octav Calleya.

Orquesta Sinfónica de Radiotelevisión Española: Sor Angela de la Cruz 2, 7°, 28020 Madrid; Chief Conductor Sergiu Comissiona.

Orquesta Sinfónica de Sevilla: Cerrajeri 10, 2° izquierda, 41004 Seville; Music Dir Vjekoslav Sutej; Gen. Man. Francisco José Senra Lazo.

Orquesta Sinfónica de Tenerife: Pim. Cabildo de Tenerife, Plaza de España 1, 38001 Santa Cruz de Tenerife; tel. 34 922 23 9801; fax 34 922 23 9617; e-mail info@sinfonicadetenerife.com; website www.sinfonicadetenerife.com; Music Dir Victor Pablo Pérez; Gen. Man. Enrique Rojas.

Orquestra de Valencia: Palau de la Música, Paseo de la Alameda 30, 46023; tel. 34 96 337 5020; fax 34 96 337 0988; Conductor Miguel Angel Gohez Martínez.

Sri Lanka

Tamil Service Orchestra: c/o Sri Lanka Broadcasting Corporation, Torrington Square, Colombo 7; tel. 1 697 491 10; fax 1 695 488.

Sweden

Gävle Symfoniorkester: PO Box 1071, Kungsbacksvagen 22, 80134, Gävle; tel. 46 26 1729 30; fax 46 26 17 2935; e-mail gavle.symfoniorkester@gavle.se; website www.gavle.se/symfoniorkester; Music Dir Hannu Koivula; Gen. Man. Haukur F. Hannesson.

Göteborgs Symfoniker (Gothenburg Symphony Orchestra): Götaplatsen, 412 56 Göteborg; tel. 46 31 726 5300; fax 46 31 726 5370; e-mail info@gso.se; website www.gso.se; Principal Conductor: Neeme Järvi; the national orchestra of Sweden.

Helsingborgs Symfoniorkester: Konserthuset, 25221 Helsingborg; tel. 46 10 42 70; fax 42 12 31 97; e-mail konserthuset@helsingborg.se; website www.hso.nu; Music Dir Hannu Lintu.

Malmö Symfoniorkester: 205 80 Malmö tel. 46 40 34 35 10; fax 46 40 611 7505; e-mail office@mso.se; website www.mso.se; Music Dir: Christoph König; Gen. Man.: Lennart Stenkvist.

Norrköpings Symfoniorkester: PO Box 2144, 600 02 Norrköping; tel. 46 11 1551 50; fax 46 11 1551 55; website www.symfoniorkester.nu; Music Dir: Lü Jia; Man. Dir: Hans Barksjö.

Norrlands Symphony Orchestra: PO Box 360, 90108, Umea; tel. 46 0 90154300; fax 46 0 90125845; Marketing Asst Felicia Wipp.

Orebro Symphony Orchestra and Swedish Chamber Orchestra: Konserthuset, Farriksgatan 2, 702 10 Orebro; Music Dir Goran Nilson; Man. Karl Friman.

Royal Baltic Symphony Orchestra: Kungliga Slottet, 111 30 Stockholm; tel. 46 8 102247; fax 46 8 215911; Music Dir Mats Liljefors; Programme Man. Mathias Walin.

Stockholms Filharmoniska Orkester: PO Box 7083, 103 87 Stockholm; tel. 46 8 7860200; fax 46 8 50667720; website www.konserthuset.se; Chief Conductor: Alan Gilbert; Exec. and Artistic Dir: Stefan Forsberg.

Sveriges Radios Symfoniorkester: Berwaldhallen, Strandvägen 69, 105 10 Stockholm; tel. 46 8 784 1801; fax 46 8 784 5150; e-mail orkestern@bwh.sr.se; Gen. Man. Michael Tyden; Principal Conductor Manfred Honeck.

Uppsala Kammarorkester: PO Box 1510, 751 45 Uppsala; Music Dir Kjell Söderqvist; Man. Nils-Olof Sondell.

Västeras Musiksällskap: Sangargatan 3, 722 20 Västeras; Man. Ulf Stenberg.

Switzerland

Basler Kammerorchester: PO Box 4001, 4051 Basel.

Berner Symphonieorchester: Münzgraben 2, 3000 Bern 7; tel. 41 31 328 2424; fax 41 31 328 2425; e-mail info@bernorchester.ch; website www.bernorchester.ch/ index3.htm; Chief Conductor Dmitri Kitaenko; Man. Margrit Lenz.

Camerata Bern: Mayweg 4, 3007 Bern; tel. 031 371 86 88; fax 031 371 38 35; Conductor Thomas Füri; Gen. Sec. Rose Brügger.

Camerata Zürich: Bergstrasse 50-G, 8712 Stáfa; Conductor Räto Tschupp; Sec. Rosemarie Kleinert.

Collegium Academicum de Genève: PO Box 539, 1211 Geneva 4; Music Dir Thierry Fischer; Man. Janine Mariz.

Collegium Musicum Zürich: Konzertgesellschaft, Steinwiesstrasse 2, 8032 Zürich; Man. Barbara Oehninger.

Festival Strings Lucerne: Dreilindenstrasse 93, 6006 Lucerne; tel. 41 420 62 63; fax 41 420 62 73; e-mail info@festivalstringslucerne.org; website www.festivalstringslucerne.org; Artistic Dir: Achim Fiedler; Man. Dir: Samuel Steinemann; concerts and tours throughout the world.

Orchester Musikkollegium Winterthur: Rychenbergstrasse 94, 8400 Winterthur; tel. 41 52 268 1560; fax 41 52 268 1570; Music Dir Jac van Steen; Dir Karl Bossert.

Orchestra della Radiotelevisione della Svizzera Italiana: 6903 Lugano.

Orchestre de Chambre de Lausanne: Chemin du Devin 72, 1010 Lausanne; Music Dir Jesús López-Cobos; Chair. Jean-Jacques Rapin.

Orchestre de la Suisse Romande: Promenade du Pin 3, 1211 Geneva; tel. 41 22 807 0017; fax 41 22 807 0018; e-mail music@osr.ch; website www.osr.ch; Chief Conductor Armin Jordan; Artistic Dir Fabio Luisi; Gen. Man. Jean Cordey.

Radio-Sinfonie-Orchester: Münsterplatz 18, 4051 Basel; Chief Conductor Nello Santi.

Sinfonieorchester Basel: Barfüsserplatz 8, Stadtcasino Basel, 4051 Basel; tel. 41 61 205 0095; fax 41 61 205 0099; e-mail info@sinfonieorchesterbasel.ch; website www.sinfonieorchesterbasel.ch; Dir: Franziskus Theurillat.

Sinfonieorchester der Allgemeinen Musikgesellschaft Luzern: Moosstrasse 15, 6003 Lucerne; Music Dir Olaf Henzold; Man. Peter Keller.

Sinfonieorchester St Gallen: Museumstrasse 1, 9004 St Gallen; tel. 41 071 242 05 05; website www.sinfonieorchestersg.ch; Music Dir: Jin Kout; Man.: Florian Scheiber.

Sinfonietta Wetzikon: Lindenhofstr 12a, 8624 Grüt; tel. 41 1 972 1898; fax 41 1 972 1897; Artistic Dirs Werner Bärtsch, Matthias Ziegler; Sec. Pauline d'Hooghe.

Symphonisches Orchester Zürich: PO Box 1923, 8021 Zürich; Music Dir Daniel Schweizer; Man. Paul Trachsel.

The Masterplayers: Via Losanna 12, 6900 Lugano; Conductor Richard Schumacher; Man. Dr D. V. Zschinsky.

Tonhalle Orchester Zürich: Gotthardstrasse 5, 8002 Zürich; tel. 41 1 206 34 44; fax 41 1 206 34 73; e-mail pr-marketing@tonhalle.ch; Exec. Dir: Trygve Nordwall; Artistic Dir: David Zinman; Dir of Admin.: Jürg Keller; Artistic Admin.: Etienne Reymond.

Züricher Kammerorchester: Muhlebachstrasse 86, PO Box 1011, 8032 Zürich; tel. 41 1 388 3600; fax 41 1 388 3610; Music Dir Howard Griffiths; Gen. Man. Thomas Pfiffner.

Taiwan

Taipei City Symphony Orchestra: 25 Pa Teh Road, Sec 3, Taipei 10560; tel. 886 2 752 3731; fax 886 2 751 8244; Music Dir Chen Chiu-sen.

Taiwan Symphony Orchestra: 292 Ming-Sheng Road, Wu Feng, T'aichung; Conductor Tze-shiou Liu; Man. Po-chou Chang.

Thailand

Bangkok Symphony Orchestra: Tejapaibil Building, Fifth Floor, 16 Plubplachai Road, Bangkok 10100; tel. 662 22308715; fax 662 6215751; e-mail bso_bangkok@hotmail.com; Music Dir John Georgiadis; Gen. Man. Witaya Tumornsoontorn.

Turkey

Istanbul State Symphony Orchestra: Atatürk Kültür Merkezi-80090 Taksim, Istanbul; tel. 90 212 243 1068; fax 90 212 251 0507; e-mail istsymph@hotmail.com; Conductor Erol Erdinc; Man. Ozer Sezgin; Dir Turkmen Goner; Programme Controller Orhan Topguoglu.

Izmir State Symphony Orchestra: Büro SSK Ishani C Blok 4, Kat Konak, 352260 Izmir; tel. 90 232 484 8343; fax 90 232 484 5172; Music Dir Iosif Conta; Dir Numan Pekdemir.

Presidential Symphony Orchestra: Talatpasa Bulvari 38A, 06330 Ankara; tel. 90 312 309 1343; fax 90 312 311 7548; Music Dir Gürer Aykol.

Ukraine

Crimea State Symphony Orchestra: PO Box 53, 98600 Yalta; tel. 380 654 32 5070; Chief Conductor Aleksey Goulianitsky.

Crimean State Philharmonic: 13 Litkens Street, 334200 Yalta.

Karhkiv Philharmonic Orchestra: Rymarskaya Street 21, 61057 Kharkiv; tel. 380 572 470527; fax 380 572 631212; e-mail itl360@online.kharkov.ua; Music Dir Yuriy Yanko; Exec. Dir Nicolai A. Saltovsky.

Kiev Chamber Orchestra: Volodymyrskiy Uzviz 2, 252001 Kiev.

National Symphony Orchestra of Ukraine: Volodymyrskiy Uzviz 2, 252001 Kiev; tel. and fax 380 44 229 6842; Artistic Dir and Conductor Theodore Kuchar.

Odesa Chamber Orchestra: 15 R. Vul. I. Bunina, 65026 Odesa.

Odesa Philharmonic Orchestra: 15 R. Vul. I. Bunina, 65026 Odesa; tel. and fax 7 048 222 6349.

Ukrainian State Symphony Orchestra: Khrestchatyk 26, 01001 Kiev; tel. 380 44 235 5272; fax 380 44 229 3322; e-mail radio_na@c-mail.ru; Chief Conductor V. Blinov.

United Kingdom

Academy of Ancient Music: 10 Brookside, Cambridge CB2 1JE; tel. 1223 301509; fax 1223 327377; e-mail aam@aam.co.uk; website www.aam.co.uk; Dir Christopher Hogwood; Assoc. Conductor Paul Goodwin; Gen. Man. Christopher Lawrence.

Academy of London: Studio 26, Building 56, Magnet Road, GEC East Lane Estate, Wembley, Middlesex HA9 7RG; tel. 20 8908 4348; fax 20 8908 4713; Conductor Richard Stamp; Gen. Man. Elaine Baines.

Academy of St Martin-in-the-Fields: Raine House, Raine Street, Wapping, London E1W 3RJ; tel. 20 7702 1377; fax 20 7481 0228; e-mail info@asmf.org; website www.academysmif.co.uk; Life Pres. Neville Marriner; Man. Gillian Brierley; Artistic Dir Kenneth Sillito.

All Souls Orchestra: All Souls Music Office, St Paul's Church, Robert Adam Street, London W1M 5AH; tel. 20 7487 3508; fax 20 7224 6087; Principal Conductor Noël Tredinnick.

Ambache Chamber Orchestra: 9 Beversbrook Road, London N19 4QG; tel. (20) 7263-4027; e-mail polmear.ambache@telinco.co.uk; website www.ambache.co.uk; Music Dir Diana Ambache; Gen. Man. Sue Sharpe; specialists in the music of Mozart and female composers of the last 250 years, performing collaboratively without a conductor.

Amici Chamber Orchestra: 55 Rosedale, Welwyn Garden City, Hertfordshire AL7 1DP; tel. and fax 1438 715740; Conductor Nigel Springthorpe.

Barbican Chamber Orchestra: 10 Acacia Road, London E17 8BW; Principal Conductor Gregory Rose; Man. Paul Thomas.

Basildon Symphony Orchestra: 101 Queens Park Avenue, Bournemouth BH8 9LJ; Conductor and Artistic Dir Richard Studt.

BBC Concert Orchestra: BBC Hippodrome, North End Road, London NW11 7RP; tel. 20 7765 4010; fax 20 7765 4929; e-mail concert.orch@bbc.co.uk; website www.bbc.co.uk/orchestras; Principal Conductor Barry Wordsworth; Gen. Man. Ian Maclay.

BBC National Orchestra of Wales: Broadcasting House, Llandaff, Cardiff CF5 2YQ, Wales; tel. 02920 322442; fax 02920 322575; e-mail now@bbc.co.uk; website www.bbc.co.uk/wales/now/index.htm; Principal Conductor Richard Hickox; Orchestra Man. Byron Jenkins.

BBC Philharmonic Orchestra: New Broadcasting House, Oxford Road, Manchester M60 1SJ; tel. 161 244 4001; fax 161 244 4211; e-mail philharmonic@bbc.co.uk; website www.bbc.co.uk/orchestras/philharmonic; Principal Conductor Gianandrea Noseda; Conductor Laureate:Yan Pascal Tortelier; Man. Peter Marchbank.

BBC Scottish Symphony Orchestra: Broadcasting House, Queen Margaret Drive, Glasgow G12 8DG; tel. (141) 338 2606; fax (141) 307 4312; e-mail bbcsso@bbc.co.uk; website www.bbc.co.uk/bbcsso; Chief Conductor: Ilan Volkov; Dir: Hugh Macdonald; Man.: Alan Davis; f. 1935; plays world-wide.

BBC Symphony Orchestra: Maida Vale Studios, Delaware Road, London W9 2LG; tel. 20 7765 2956; fax 20 7286 3251; e-mail bbcso@bbc.co.uk; website www.bbc.co.uk/orchestras/so/; Chief Conductor Leonard Slatkin; Gen. Man. Paul Hughes.

Ben Uri Chamber Orchestra: 5 Bradby House, Carlton Hill, London NW8 9XE; tel. 20 7624 1756; Conductor Sydney Fixman.

Birmingham Contemporary Music Group: CBSO Centre, Berkley Street, Birmingham, B1 2LF; tel. 121 616 2616; fax 121 616 2622; e-mail info@bcmg.org.uk; website www.bcmg.org.uk; Artistic Dir Stephen Newbould.

Birmingham Sinfonietta: 41 St Agnes Road, Birmingham B13 9PJ; tel. 121 449 0225; Music Dir Jeremy Ballard; Man. Susan Savage.

Blackheath Haus: 23 Lee Road, London, SE3 9RQ; tel. 20 8318 9758; fax 20 8852 5154; Artistic Dir Peter Conway.

Bournemouth Sinfonietta: 2 Seldown Lane, Poole, Dorset BH15 1UF; tel. 1202 670611; fax 1202 687235; Principal Conductor Alexander Polianichko.

Bournemouth Symphony Orchestra: 2 Seldown Lane, Poole, Dorset BH15 1UF; tel. 1202 670611; fax 1202 687235; e-mail contact@bsolive.com; website www.bsolive.com; Principal Conductor Marin Alsop; Conductor Laureate Andrew Litton; Man. Dir Michael Henson.

Brandenburg Consort: Crooked Cottage, Dunkerton, Bath, Avon BA2 8BG; tel. 1761 431535; fax 1761 431538; Musical Dir Roy Goodman; Man. Charlotte de Grey.

Brighton Philharmonic Orchestra: 50 Grand Parade, Brighton, East Sussex BN2 2QA; tel. 1273 622900; fax 1273 697887; website www.brightonphil.co.uk; Principal Conductor Barry Wordsworth; Gen. Man. Ivan Rockey.

Bristol Philharmonic Orchestra: 11 Windsor Court, Victoria Terrace, Bristol BS8 4LJ; tel. 117 929 7597; fax 117 925 1301; website www.3sixty.co.uk/bristolphil/; Artistic Dir Derek Bourgeois; Gen. Man. Kenneth H. Gibbs.

Britten Sinfonia: 13 Sturton Street, Cambridge CB1 2SN; tel. 1223 300795; fax 1223 302092; e-mail info@brittensinfonia.co.uk; website www.brittensinfonia.co.uk; Concerts Dir Nikola White; Chief Exec. David Butcher.

BT Scottish Ensemble: Centre for Contemporary Arts, 350 Sauchiehall Street, Glasgow, G2 3JD; tel. 141 332 4747; fax 141 332 3555; website www.scottishensemble.co.uk; Artistic Dir Clio Gould; Gen. Man. Heather Duncan.

Cantelli Chamber Orchestra: 13 Cotswold Mews, 12–16 Battersea High Street, London SW11 3JB; Conductor Philip Ellis; Man. Alexander Waugh.

Chamber Orchestra of Europe: 8 Southampton Place, London WC1A 2EA; tel. 20 7831 2326; fax 20 7831 8248; e-mail redbird@coeurope.org; Artistic Adviser Claudio Abbado; Gen. Man. June Megennis.

Cheltenham Chamber Orchestra: 5 Deans Quarry, Burleigh, Stroud, GL5 2PQ; tel. (1453) 882268; fax (1453) 887262; e-mail piccpeter@aol.com; Orchestral Man. Peter Tomlinson.

City of Birmingham Symphony Orchestra: CSBO Centre, Berkley Street, Birmingham B1 2LF; tel. 121 616 6500; fax 121 616 6518; e-mail information@cbso.co.uk; website www.cbso.co.uk; Principal Conductor Sakari Oramo; Chief Exec. Stephen Maddock; Gen. Man. Mike Buckley.

City of London Sinfonia: 11 Drum Street, London E1 1LH; tel. 20 7480 7743; fax 20 7488 2700; e-mail info@cls.co.uk; website www.cityoflondonsinfonia.co.uk; Music Dir Richard Hickox; Gen. Man. Stephen Carpenter.

City of Oxford Orchestra: Midsummer Cottage, Boars Hill, Oxford OX1 5DG; tel. and fax 1865 744457; e-mail info@cityofoxfordorchestra.co.uk; website www.cityofoxfordorchestra.co.uk; Artistic Dir Roger Payne; Man. Dir John King.

Collegium Musicum 90 Ltd: 71 Priory Road, Kew, Surrey TW9 3DH; tel. 20 8940 7086; fax 20 8332 0879; Man. Francesca McManus.

East of England Orchestra: Derby College at Wilmorton, Pentagon Centre, Beaufort Street, Derby, DE21 6AX; tel. 1332 207570; fax 1332 207569; Principal Conductor Nicholas Kok.

English Bach Festival Orchestra and English Bach Festival Baroque Orchestra: 15 South Eaton Place, London SW1W 9ER; tel. 20 7730 5925; fax 20 7730 1456; Dir Lina Lalandi.

English Baroque Orchestra: 57 Kingswood Road, London SW19 3ND; tel. 20 8542 1661; fax 20 8540 1103; Music Dir Leon Lovett; Man. Robert Porter.

English Baroque Soloists: 61 Wandsworth High Street, SW18 2PT; tel. 20 8871 4750; fax 20 8871 4751; Music Dir John Eliot Gardiner; Gen. Man. Michael B. MacLeod.

English Camerata: 14 Dunstarn Drive, Leeds, LS16 8EH; tel. and fax 113 267 5821; Musical Dir Elizabeth Altman; Admin. John Harris.

English Chamber Orchestra: 2 Coningsby Road, London W5 4HR; tel. 20 8840 6565; fax 20 8567 7198; e-mail mail@englishchamberorchestra.co .uk; website www.englishchamberorchestra.co.uk; Principal Conductor Ralf Gothóni; Dir Pauline Gilbertson.

English Classical Players: 25B Epsom Lane South, Tadworth, Surrey KT20 5TA; tel. 1737 813273; fax 1737 215676; e-mail ecp@classicconcerts .co.uk; Artistic Dir Jonathan Brett; Exec. Dir Lyn Mumford.

The English Concert: 8 St George's Terrace, London NW1 8XJ; tel. 20 7911 0905; fax 20 7911 0904; e-mail ec@englishconcert.co.uk; website www .englishconcert.co.uk; Artistic Dir Andrew Manze; Man. Felix Warnock.

English Festival Orchestra: 151 Mount View Road, London N4 4JT; tel. 20 8341 6408; fax 20 8802 0595; e-mail tford@aol.com; Gen. Man. Trevor Ford.

English National Opera Orchestra: London Coliseum, St Martin's Lane, London WC2N 4ES; tel. 20 7836 0111; fax 20 7845 9277; website www.eno.org; Orchestra Man. Richard Smith; Music Dir Paul Daniel.

English Northern Philharmonia: Opera North, Grand Theatre, Leeds LS1 6NU; tel. (113) 243-9999; fax (113) 244-0418; e-mail info@operanorth .co.uk; website www.operanorth.co.uk; Principal Conductor Steven Sloane; Gen. Dir Richard Mantle.

English Sinfonia: 1 Wedgwood Court, Stevenage, Hertfordshire SG1 4QR; tel. 1438 350990; fax 1438 350930; e-mail info@englishsinfonia.org .uk; website www.englishsinfonia.org.uk; Chief Exec. Lucy Potter; Principal Conductor Nicolae Moldoveanu.

English Sinfonietta: The Barn, Layston Park, Royston, Hertfordshire SG8 9DS; tel. 1763 2424847; fax 1763 248048; Principal Conductor Steuart Bedford; Gen. Man. Graham Pfaff.

English String Orchestra: Rockliffe House, Church Street, Malvern, Worcestershire WR14 2AZ; tel. (1684) 560696; fax (1684) 560656; e-mail info@eso.co.uk; website www.eso.co.uk; Artistic/Music Dir: William Boughton; Admin.: Kate Hodson.

English Symphony Orchestra: Rockliffe House, Church Street, Malvern, Worcestershire WR14 2AZ; tel. (1684) 560696; fax (1684) 560656; e-mail info@eso.co.uk; website www.eso.co.uk; Artistic/Music Dir: William Boughton; Admin.: Kate Hodson.

Esterhazy Orchestra: 278 Kew Road, Richmond, Surrey TW9 3EE; tel. 20 8948 6140.

European Union Chamber Orchestra: Hollick, Yarnscombe, Devon EX31 3LQ; tel. 1271 858249; fax 1271 858375; e-mail eucorch1@aol.com; website www.etd.gb.com; Dir Gen. Ambrose Miller.

European Union Youth Orchestra: 65 Sloane Street, London SW1X 9SH; tel. 20 7235 7671; fax 20 7235 7370; e-mail info@euyo.org.uk; website www.euyo.org.uk; Music Dir Vladimir Ashkenazy; Gen. Man. Huw Humphreys.

Gabrieli Consort and Players: 372 Old Street, London EC1V 9LT; tel. 20 7613 4404; fax 20 7613 4414; e-mail info@gabrieli.com; Gen. Man. Ole Backhoej.

Guildford Philharmonic Orchestra: Millmead House, Millmead, Guildford, Surrey GU2 5BB; tel. 1483 444666; fax 1483 444732; e-mail guildfordphil@guildford.gov.uk; website www.guildfordphilharmonic.co .uk; Principal Conductor En Shao.

Guildhall String Ensemble: 41 Belmont Lane, Stanmore, Middlesex, HA7 2PU; tel. 20 8954 1380; fax 20 8954 9212; Dir Robert Salter.

Hallé Orchestra: The Bridgewater Hall, Manchester M1 5HA; tel. 161 237 7000; fax 161 237 7029; e-mail info@halle.co.uk; website www.halle.co .uk; Music Dir Mark Elder; Chief Exec. David Richardson.

Hanover Band: The Old Market, Upper Market Street, Hove, East Sussex BN3 1AS; tel. 1273 206978; fax 1273 329636; website www .hanoverband.com; Artistic Dir Caroline Brown.

Henry Wood Chamber Orchestra: 64 Ashley Gardens, Ambrosden Avenue, London, SW1P 1QG; Music Dir John Landor; Admin. William Corke.

The King's Consort: 34 St Mary's Grove, London W4 3LN; tel. 20 8995 9994; fax 20 8995 2115; e-mail info@tkcworld.com; website www.tkcworld .com; Artistic Dir Robert King.

Kreisler String Orchestra: 57 Sunnyside Road, Chesham, Buckingham-shire HP5 2AR; tel. and fax 1494 792572; Man. Robert Woollard.

Langham Chamber Orchestra: 9 Weylea Avenue, Burpham, Guildford, Surrey GU4 7YN; tel. 1483 573705; Orchestra Man. Peter Holt.

Little Symphony of London: 14 Beaumont Road, Purley, Surrey CR8 2EG; tel. and fax 20 8668 5883; Artistic Dir Darrell Davison.

Liverpool Sinfonietta: 40 Caulfield Drive, Greasby, Wirral, Merseyside L49 1SW; Music Dir Anthony Ridley.

London Bach Orchestra: c/o Goldberg Ensemble, 1 Rowsley Avenue, West Didsbury, Manchester M20 2XD; tel. and fax 161 446 2170; Artistic Dir Nicholas Kraemer.

London Camerata: 21 Halstead Road, Mountsorrel, Leicestershire LE12 7HD; tel. 116 230 3674; Conductor Paul Hilliam.

London Chamber Orchestra: c/o The London Chamber Society Ltd, 6 Hambalt Road, London SW4 9EB; tel. 20 8772 9741; fax 20 8772 9742; e-mail info@lco.co.uk; website www.lco.co.uk; Music Dir Christopher Warren-Green; Gen. Man. Step Parikian.

London Chamber Players: PO Box 84, London NW11 8AL; tel. 20 8455 9200; fax 20 8455 6799; e-mail london-players@excite.com; Conductor Adrian Sunshine; Admin. Sheila Genden.

London Chamber Symphony: Toynbee Studios, 28 Commercial Street, London E1 6LS; tel. 20 7247 2950; fax 20 7247 2956; Conductor Odalaine de la Martinez; Co-Dir Sophie Langdon.

London Chanticleer Orchestra: Tickerage Castle, Pound Lane, Fram-field, Uckfield, East Sussex TN22 5RT; tel. 1825 890348; Sec. H. J. Graty.

London City Chamber Orchestra: 3/5 Bridge Street, Hadleigh, Ipswich, Suffolk IP7 6BY; tel. 1473 822596; fax 1473 824175; e-mail thomas.mcintosh@minstrelmusic.demon. co.uk; Conductor Thomas McIn-tosh; Gen. Man. Miranda Reckitt.

London Concert Orchestra: 29–31 East Barnet Road, New Barnet, Hertfordshire EN4 8RN; tel. 20 8216 3000; fax 20 8216 3001; Admin. Raymond Gubbay.

London Festival Orchestra: 13 Theed Street, London SE1 8ST; tel. 20 7928 9250; fax 20 7928 9252; e-mail orchestra@lfo.co.uk; website www.lfo .co.uk; Music and Artistic Dir Ross Pople; Man. Anne Storrs.

London Handel Orchestra: 32 Wolverton Gardens, London W6 7DX; tel. 20 8563 0618; fax 20 8741 5233; Musical Dir Denys Darlow; Admin. Joya Logan.

London Jupiter Orchestra: 57 White Horse Road, London E1 0ND; tel. 20 7790 5883; fax 20 7265 9170; Conductor Gregory Rose.

London Mozart Players: Suite 306, Park House, Park Street, Croydon CR0 1YE; tel. (20) 8686-1996; fax (20) 8686-2187; e-mail info@lmp.co.uk; website www.lmp.co.uk; Man. Dir: Antony Lewis-Crosby; Music Dir: Andrew Parrott.

London Philharmonic Orchestra: 89 Albert Embankment, London, SE1 7TP; tel. 20 7840 4200; fax 20 7840 4201; e-mail admin@lpo.org.uk; website www.lpo.co.uk; Artistic Dir Serge Dorny; Principal Conductor Kurt Masur.

London Pro Arte Baroque: 17b St Augustine's Avenue, South Croydon, Surrey CR2 6JN; tel. (20) 8688-2901; fax (20) 8654-9137; e-mail office@ londonproarte.co.uk; website www.londonproarte.co.uk; Artistic Dir Mur-ray Stewart; Orchestra Man. Richard Thomas.

London Pro Arte Orchestra: 17b St Augustine's Avenue, South Croydon, Surrey CR2 6JN; tel. (20) 8688-2901; fax (20) 8654-9137; e-mail office@londonproarte.co.uk; website www.londonproarte.co.uk; Artistic Dir Murray Stewart; Orchestra Man. John Cobb.

London Repertoire Orchestra and Chamber Orchestra: 56 Alexan-dra Road, Croydon, Surrey CR0 6EU; Conductor Francis Griffin.

London Sinfonietta: Dominion House, 101 Southwark Street, London SE1 OJF; tel. (20) 7928-0828; fax (20) 7928-8557; e-mail info@ londonsinfonietta.org.uk; website www.londonsinfonietta.org.uk; Conductor Laureate: Oliver Knussen; Artistic Dir: Gillian Moore; Man. Dir: Cathy Graham.

London Soloists' Chamber Orchestra: PO Box 100, East Horsley KT24 6WN; tel. 1483 282666; fax 1483 284777; e-mail info@londonsoloists.com; website www.londonsoloists.com; Conductor David Josefowitz; Man. Nick Bomford.

London String Orchestra: 37 St Davids Road, Clifton Campville, nr Tamworth, Staffordshire B79 0BA; tel. 1827 373586; Conductor James Maddocks.

London Symphony Orchestra: Barbican Centre, Silk Street, London EC2Y 8DS; tel. 20 7588 1116; fax 20 7374 0127; e-mail admin@lso.co.uk; website www.lso.co.uk; Principal Conductor Colin Davis; Man. Dir Clive Gillinson.

Manchester Camerata: Zion Arts Centre, Stretford Road, Manchester M15 5ZA; tel. 161 226 8696; fax 161 226 8600; Principal Conductor and Artistic Dir: Douglas Boyd; Principal Guest Conductor: Nicholas Kraemer.

Manchester Mozart Orchestra: 30 Derby Road, Fallowfield, Manchester M24 6UW; Man. John Whibley.

Melos Ensemble: 35 Doughty Street, London WC1N 2AA.

Monteverdi Choir and Orchestra: Fourth Floor, 11 Westferry Circus, Canary Wharf, London E14 4HE; tel. (20) 7537-4004; fax (20) 7517-9874; Gen. Man.: Per Hedberg.

Musiciens du Roi: 6 Aldersmead Road, Beckenham, Kent BR3 1NA; Dir Lionel Sawkins.

National Chamber Orchestra: Fir Tree Lodge, Jumps Road, Churt, nr Farnham, Surrey GU10 2JY; tel. 1252 792315; fax 1252 795120.

National Philharmonic Orchestra: 7 Lowlands, 218 Eton Avenue, Hampstead, London NW3 3EJ; tel. 20 7722 1078; fax 1689 852311; Dir Sidney Sax.

National Symphony Orchestra: Fir Tree Lodge, Jumps Road, Churt, nr Farnham, Surrey GU10 2JY; tel. 1252 792315; fax 1252 795120.

National Symphony Orchestra of London: 177 John Ruskin Street, London SE5 0PQ; tel. 20 7703 3148; fax 20 7701 9479; e-mail enquiries@nso.co.uk; website www.nso.co.uk; Principal Conductor Martin Yates; Man. Dir/Joint Artistic Dir Anne Collis.

New English Concert Orchestra: 23 Hitchin Street, Biggleswade, Bedfordshire SG18 8AX; tel. 1767 316521; fax 1767 317221; e-mail neco@lindsaymusic.co.uk; Music Dir Douglas Coombes; Admin. Rose Miles.

New English Orchestra: 4 Link Road, Edgbaston, Birmingham B16 0EP; website www.newenglishorchestra.org; Principal Conductor: Nigel Swinford; Company Sec.: Julie Fry.

New London Orchestra: 4 Lower Belgrave Street, London SW1W 0LJ; tel. 20 7823 5523; fax 20 7823 6373; e-mail admin@nlo.co.uk; website www.nlo.co.uk; Artistic Dir Ronald Corp; Gen. Man. Julian Knight.

New Queen's Hall Orchestra: Trees, Ockham Road, South East Horsley, Surrey KT24 6QE; tel. 1483 281300; fax 1483 281811; e-mail info@nqho.com; website www.nqho.com; Artistic Dir John Boyden; Gen. Admin. James Thomson.

Northern Ballet Theatre Orchestra: West Park Centre, Spen Lane, Leeds LS16 5BE; tel. 113 274 5355; fax 113 274 5381; website www.nbt.co.uk; Music Dir John Pryce-Jones.

Northern Chamber Orchestra: 799 Wilmslow Road, Didsbury, Manchester M20 2RR; tel. 161 247 2220; fax 161 247 6899; e-mail info@norch.co.uk; website www.ncorch.co.uk; Music Dir Nicholas Ward; Gen. Man. Jonathan Thackeray; presents concerts in north-west England, associated education programmes.

Northern Sinfonia of England: The Sinfonia Centre, 41 Jesmond Vale, Newcastle upon Tyne NE1 1PG; tel. 191 240 1812; fax 191 240 2668; e-mail nsinfonia@ndirect.co.uk; website www.nsinfonia.ision.co.uk; Music Dir Thomas Zehetmair; Chief Exec. John Summers.

Orchestra da Camera: 41 Mill End, Kenilworth, Warwickshire CV8 2HP; tel. (1926) 858187; e-mail enquiries@orchestradacamera.com; website www.orchestradacamera.com; Artistic Dir: Rosalind Page.

Orchestra of Sadler's Wells Royal Ballet: Sadler's Wells Theatre, Rosebery Avenue, London EC1R 4TN; Man. Wendy Hacker.

Orchestra of St John's, Smith Square: The White House, Eltham College, Grove Park Road, London SE9 4QF; tel. 20 8857 8579; fax 20 8857 9340; e-mail info@osj.org.uk; Principal Conductor John Lubbock; Chief Exec. Nicky Goulder.

Orchestra of the Age of Enlightenment: Third Floor, 33 Henrietta Street, Covent Garden, London WC2E 8NA; tel. 20 7836 6690; fax 20 7836 6692; e-mail info@oae.co.uk; website www.oae.co.uk; Chief Exec.: Marshall Marcus; Dir of Planning: Charlotte Wadham; Dir of Development and Marketing: Katy Shaw; Chair.: Greg Malgaard.

Orchestra of the Royal Opera House: Covent Garden, London WC2E 9DD; tel. 20 7304 4000; fax 20 7212 9460; e-mail webmaster@roh.org.uk; website www.royalopera.org; Music Dir Antonio Pappano.

Orchestra of Welsh National Opera: c/o Welsh National Opera Ltd, Wales Millennium Centre, Bay Chambers, West Bute Street, Cardiff, CF10 5GG; tel. (29) 2040 2000; fax (29) 2040 2001; e-mail info@wmc.org.uk; website www.wno.org.uk, www.wmc.org.uk; Orchestra Dir Peter Harrap.

Orchestre Revolutionnaire et Romantique: 61 Wandsworth High Street, Tower Place, London SW18 2PT; tel. 20 8871 4750; fax 20 8871 4751; e-mail info@monteverdi.org.uk; Music Dir Sir John Eliot Gardiner; Gen. Man. Michael MacLeod.

Per Musica Chamber Orchestra: 50 Cranfield Court, Homer Street, London W1; Music Dir Julian Reynolds; Admin. Joan Cruickshank.

Philharmonia Orchestra: First Floor, 125 High Holborn, London WC1V 6QA; tel. 20 7242 5001; fax 20 7242 4840; e-mail info@philharmonia.co.uk; website www.philharmonia.co.uk; Principal Conductor Christoph von Dohnányi; Man. Dir David Whelton.

Purcell Orchestra: 86 Park Hill, Carshalton Beeches, Surrey SM5 3RZ; tel. and fax 20 8669 4358; Artistic Dir Robin Page.

Raglan Baroque Players: 140 Muswell Hill Road, London N10 3JD; tel. 20 8444 2507; fax 20 8444 1795; e-mail raglanadmin@compuserve.com; Music Dir Nicholas Kraemer.

Regent Sinfonia of London: 17 Parliament Hill, London NW3 2TA; tel. 20 7435 5965; fax 20 7435 9166; Artistic Dir George Vass.

Rossini Chamber Orchestra: 10A Radipole Road, Fulham, London SW6 5DL; tel. 20 7736 3821; fax 20 8449 1664; Music Dir and Conductor Alexander Bryett.

Royal Liverpool Philharmonic Orchestra: Philharmonic Hall, Hope Street, Liverpool L1 9BP; tel. 151 210 2895; fax 151 210 2902; e-mail info@liverpoolphil.com; website www.liverpoolphil.com; Music Dir Gerard Schwarz.

Royal Philharmonic Orchestra: 16 Clerkenwell Green, London EC1R 0QT; tel. 20 7608 8800; fax 20 7608 8801; e-mail info@rpo.co.uk; website www.rpo.co.uk; Music Dir Daniele Gatti; Man. Dir John Manger.

Royal Scottish National Orchestra: 73 Claremont Street, Glasgow G3 8EP; tel. 141 225 3500; fax 141 225 3505; e-mail admin@rsno.org.uk; website www.rsno.org.uk; Principal Conductor Alexander Lazarev; Chief Exec. Paul Hughes; Marketing Man. Fiona Brownlee.

Scottish Chamber Orchestra: 4 Royal Terrace, Edinburgh EH7 5AB; tel. 131 557 6800; fax 131 557 6933; e-mail info@sco.org.uk; website www.sco.org.uk; Principal Conductor Joseph Swensen; Man. Dir Roy McEwan.

Sinfonia 21: 14 Prince's Gardens, London, SW7 1NA; tel. 20 7584 2759; fax 20 7581 0970; e-mail info@sinfonia21.co.uk; Chief Exec. Oliver Rivers; Gen. Man. Claire Wright.

Sinfonia of London: 27 Grove Road, Beaconsfield, Buckinghamshire HP9 1UR; tel. (1494) 677934; fax (1494) 670433; e-mail info@sinfonia-of-london.com; website www.sinfonia-of-london.com; Exec. Dir: Peter Willison.

South Yorkshire Symphony Orchestra: Springfield Close, Eckington, Sheffield S21 4GS; tel. 1246 431562; website www.syso.co.uk/orchestra.htm; Music Dir Paul Scott.

St James's Baroque: 120 Chewton Road, London E17 7DN; tel. (20) 8223-0772; fax (20) 8926-2979; e-mail petermccarthy@waitrose.com; Dir: Ivor Bolton; Man.: Peter McCarthy.

Taverner Players: Ibex House, 42–46 Minories, London EC3N 1DY; tel. 44 1717 481 2103; fax 44 1717 481 2865; Conductor Andrew Parrott; Admin. Victoria Newbert.

Ulster Orchestra: Elmwood Hall at Queens, 89 University Road, Belfast BT7 1NF; tel. 44 028 9066 4535; fax 44 028 9066 2761; website www.ulster-orchestra.org.uk; Gen. Man. Roger Lloyd; Principal Conductor and Artistic Dir Thierry Fischer; Chief Exec. David Byers.

Vivaldi Concertante: 35 Laurel Avenue, Potters Bar, Hertfordshire EN6 2AB; tel. and fax 1707 643366; Conductor Joseph Pilbery.

Welsh Chamber Orchestra: 100 Ystrad Fawr, Bridgend, Mid-Glamorgan CF31 4HW; tel. and fax 1656 658891.

Worthing Symphony Orchestra: Connaught Theatre, Union Place, Worthing, Sussex, BN11 ILG; tel. 1903 231799; fax 1903 215337; Chief Conductor John Gibbons.

Yorkshire Philharmonic Orchestras: Torridon House, 104 Bradford Road, Wrenthorpe, Wakefield, West Yorkshire WF1 2AH; tel. 1924 371496; Gen. Man. Brian Greensmith.

United States of America

Albany Symphony Orchestra: 19 Clinton Avenue, Albany, NY 12207; tel. (518) 465-4755; fax (518) 465-3711; e-mail info@albanysymphony.com; website www.albanysymphony.com; Music Dir David Alan Miller.

American Composers Orchestra: 37 W 65th Street, Sixth Floor, New York, NY 10023; Music Dir Dennis Russell Davies; Exec. Dir Jesse Rosen.

American Symphony Orchestra: 850 Seventh Avenue, Suite 1106, New York, NY 10019; Music Dir Leon Botstein; Exec. Dir Eugene Carr.

Anchorage Symphony Orchestra: 400 D Street, Suite 230, Anchorage, AK 99501; tel. 274 8668; fax 272 7916; e-mail aso@corecom.net; website www.anchoragesymphony.org; Music Dir Randall Craig Fleischer; Exec. Dir Sherri Reddick.

Ann Arbor Symphony Orchestra: 527 E Liberty Suite 208B, Ann Arbor, MI 48104; tel. 1 734 994 4801; fax 1 734 994 3949; website www .a2so.com/main.html; Music Dir Samuel Wong; Exec. Dir Mary Blaske.

Arkansas Symphony Orchestra: PO Box 7328, 2417 N Tyler, Little Rock, AR 72217; tel. 1 501 666 1761; fax 1 501 666 3193; Music Dir David Itkin; Exec. Dir JoAnn Greene.

Aspen Festival Orchestra and Chamber Symphony: PO Box AA, Aspen, CO 81612; Gen. Man. Thomas Eirman.

Atlanta Symphony Orchestra: 1293 Peachtree Street NE, Suite 300, Atlanta, GA 30309; tel. 1 404 733 4900; fax 1 404 733 4901; e-mail aso -info@woodruffcenter.org; website www.atlantasymphony.org; Music Dir Robert Spano; Pres. Allison Vulgamore.

Austin Symphony Orchestra: Symphony Square, 1101 Red River, Austin, TX 78701; tel. 1 512 476 6064; fax 1 512 476 6242; e-mail contact@ austinsymphony.org; website www.austinsymphony.org; Music Dir Peter Bay; Exec. Dir Kenneth K. Caswell.

Baltimore Symphony Orchestra: Joseph Meyerhoff Symphony Hall, 1212 Cathedral Street, Baltimore, MD 21201; tel. 1 410 783 8000; fax 1 410 783 8077; e-mail webmaster@baltimoresymphony.org; website www .baltimoresymphony.org; Music Dir Yuri Temirkanov; Exec. Dir John Gidwitz.

Berkeley Symphony Orchestra: 1942 University Avenue, Suite 207, Berkeley, CA 94704-1073; tel. 1 510 841 2800; fax 1 510 841 5422; e-mail mail@berkeleysymphony.org; website www.berkeleysymphony.org/index .htm; Music Dir Kent Nagano; Exec. Dir Kelly Johnson.

Boise Philharmonic: 516 S Ninth Street, Boise, ID 83702; tel. 1 208 344 7849; fax 1 888 300 7849; e-mail info@boisephilharmonic.org; website www .boisephilharmonic.org; Music Dir James Ogle; Gen. Man. Margie Stoy.

Boston Symphony Orchestra: Symphony Hall, 301 Massachusetts Avenue, Boston, MA 02115; tel. (617) 266-1492; fax (617) 638-9367; website www.bso.org; Music Dir: James Levine; Man. Dir: Mark Volpe.

Brooklyn Philharmonic Symphony Orchestra: 30 Lafayette Avenue, Brooklyn, NY 11217; Music Dir Robert Spano; Exec. Dir Joseph Horowitz.

Buffalo Philharmonic Orchestra: 71 Symphony Circle, Buffalo, NY 14201; tel. 1 716 885 0331; fax 1 716 885 9372; e-mail amanton@bpo.org; website www.bpo.org; Music Dir Joann Falletta; Exec. Dir John Bauser.

Cedar Rapids Symphony Orchestra: 205 Second Avenue SE, Cedar Rapids, IA 52401; e-mail webmaster@crsymphony.org; website www .crsymphony.org; Music Dir Christian Tiemeyer; Exec. Dir Kathy Hall.

Charleston Symphony Orchestra: 160 E Bay Street, Charleston, SC 29401; tel. (843) 723-7528; fax (843) 722-3463; e-mail info@ charlestonsymphony.com; website www.charlestonsymphony.com; Music Dir David Stahl; Exec. Dir Sandra Ferencz.

Chautauqua Symphony Orchestra: Chautauqua, NY 14722; tel. 1 716 357 6200; fax 1 716 357 9014; e-mail cso@ciweb.org; website symphony .ciweb.org; Music Dir Uriel Segal; Gen. Man. Marty W. Merkley.

Chicago Chamber Orchestra: 332 S Michigan Avenue, Suite 1143, Chicago, IL 60604; tel. 1 312 922 5570; fax 1 312 922 9290; Music Dir Dieter Kober; Gen. Man. Magdalene Lornez.

Chicago Symphony Orchestra: Symphony Center, 220 S Michigan Avenue, Chicago, IL 60604; tel. 1 312 294 3000; fax 1 312 294 3329; website www.chicagosymphony.org; Music Dir Daniel Barenboim; Exec. Dir Henry Fogel.

Cincinnati Symphony Orchestra: 1241 Elm Street, Cincinnati, OH 45202-7531; tel. (513) 621-1919; fax (513) 744-3535; website www .cincinnatisymphony.org; Music Dir: Paavo Jarvi; Pres.: Steven I. Monder.

Cleveland Orchestra: Severance Hall, 11001 Euclid Avenue, Cleveland, OH 44106; tel. 1 216 231 7300; fax 1 216 231 0202; e-mail info@ clevelandorchestra.com; website www.clevelandorch.com; Music Dir Franz Welser-Möst; Exec. Dir Thomas W. Morris.

Colorado Springs Symphony Orchestra: PO Box 1692, Colorado Springs, CO 80901; Music Dir Christopher Wilkins.

Columbus Symphony Orchestra: 55 E State Street, Columbus, OH 43215; tel. 1 614 228 9600; fax 1 614 224 7273; website www.csobravo.com; Music Dir Alessandro Siciliani; Music Dir Designate Franz Welser-Most; Exec. Dir Susan Franano.

Colorado Symphony Orchestra: Denver Place, North Tower, 999 18th Street, Suite 2055, Denver, CO 80202; tel. 1 303 292 5566; fax 1 303 293 2649; e-mail administration@coloradosymphony.org; website www .coloradosymphony.org; Music Dir Laureate Marin Alsop.

Dallas Symphony Orchestra: 2301 Flora Street, Suite 300, Dallas, TX 75201; tel. 1 214 692 0203; website www.dallassymphony.com; Music Dir Andrew Litton; Exec. Dir Eugene Bonelli.

Dayton Philharmonic Orchestra: 125 E First Street, Dayton, OH 45422; website www.daytonphilharmonic.com; Music Dir Isaiah Jackson; Exec. Dir Curtis Long.

Delaware Symphony Orchestra: PO Box 1870, Wilmington, DE 19899; e-mail info@desymphony.org; website www.desymphony.org; Music Dir Stephen Gunzenhauser; Exec. Dir Curtis Long.

Detroit Symphony Orchestra: 3633 Woodward Avenue, Detroit, MI 48201; tel. 1 313 576 5700; fax 1 313 576 5101; website www .detroitsymphony.com; Music Dir Neeme Järvi; Exec. Dir Mark Volpe.

Eastern Philharmonic Orchestra: PO Box 22026, Greensboro, NC 27420; Music Dir Sheldon Morgenstern.

Eugene Symphony Orchestra: 45 W Broadway, Suite 201, Eugene, OR 97401; tel. 1 541 687 9487; website www.eugenesymphony.org/directory .htm; Music Dir and Conductor Miguel Harth-Bedoya; Exec. Dir Stuart Weiser.

Fairbanks Symphony Orchestra: PO Box 82104, Fairbanks, AK 99708; tel. 1 907 474 5733; e-mail symphony@fairbankssymphony.org; website www.fairbankssymphony.org; Musical Dir Eduard Ziberkant; Exec. Dir Jane Aspnes.

Florida Orchestra: 101 S Hoover Blvd, Suite 100, Tampa, FL 33609; tel. 1 813 286 1170; fax 1 813 286 2316; e-mail admin@floridaorchestra.org; website www.floridaorchestra.org; Music Dir Stefan Sanderling; Exec. Dir Kathryn Holm.

Florida Philharmonic Orchestra: 3401 NW Ninth Avenue, Fort Lauderdale, FL 33309; tel. 1 954 938 6700; Music Dir James Judd; Exec. Dir John Graham.

Florida Symphonic Pops: 120 NE First Avenue, Boca Raton, FL 33432; Artistic Dir Derek Stannard; Exec. Vice-Pres. Carol Simmons.

Florida West Coast Symphony Orchestra: 709 N Tamiami Trail, Sarasota, FL 34236; tel. 1 941 953 4252; fax 1 941 953 3059; e-mail marketing@fwcs.com; website www.fwcs.org; Music Dir Leif Bjalanf; Exec. Dir Gretchen Serrie.

Fort Worth Symphony Orchestra: 330 E Fourth Street, Suite 200, Fort Worth, TX 76102; tel. 1 817 665 6500; fax 1 817 665 6600; e-mail admin@ fwsymphony.org; Music Dir John Giordano; Exec. Dir Ann Koonsman.

Fresno Philharmonic Orchestra: 2610 W Shaw Avenue, Suite 103, Fresno, CA 93711; tel. (559) 261-0600; fax (559) 261-0700; e-mail info@ fresnophil.org; website www.fresnophil.org; Exec. Dir David H. Gaylin; Music Dir Theodore Kuchar.

Glendale Symphony Orchestra: PO Box 4626, Glendale, CA 91203; tel. 1 818 500 8720; e-mail info@glendalesymphony.org; website www .glendalesymphony.org; Music Dir Norman Henry Mamey.

Grand Rapids Symphony Orchestra: 169 Louis Campari Promenade, Suite 1, Grand Rapids, MI 49503; tel. 1 616 454 9451; fax 1 616 454 7477; website www.grsymphony.org; Music Dir David Lockington; Exec. Dir Peter W. Smith.

Grant Park Symphony Orchestra: 425 E McFetridge Drive, Chicago, IL 60605; Principal Conductor Hugh Wolff.

Greater Bridgeport Symphony Orchestra: 446 University Avenue, Bridgeport, CT 06604; tel. 1 203 576 0263; fax 1 203 367 0064; website www.bridgeportsymphony.org; Music Dir Gustav Meier; Gen. Man. Jena Maric.

Greater Trenton Symphony Orchestra: 28 W State Street, Suite 201, Trenton, NJ 08608; tel. 1 609 394 1338; fax 1 609 394 1394; website www

.trentonsymphony.org; Exec. Dir and Principal Conductor John Peter Holly.

Handel and Haydn Society: Horticultural Hall, 300 Massachusetts Avenue, Boston, MA 02115; tel. 1 617 262 1815; fax 1 617 266 4217; e-mail info@handelandhaydn.org; website www.handelandhaydn.org; Music Dir Grant Llewellyn; Conductor Laureate Christopher Hogwood; Exec. Dir Mary A. Deissler.

Hartford Symphony Orchestra: 228 Farmington Avenue, Hartford, CT 06105; tel. 1 860 246 8742; fax 1 860 249 5430; e-mail website www.hartfordsymphony.org; Music Dir Edward Cumming; Exec. Dir Charles H. Owens.

Honolulu Symphony Orchestra: 650 Iwilei Road, Suite 202, Honolulu, HI 96817; tel. 1 808 524 0815; fax 1 808 524 1507; website www.honolulusymphony.com; Music Dir Samuel Wong.

Houston Symphony Orchestra: 615 Louisiana Street, Houston, TX 77002; tel. 1 713 224 4240; fax 1 713 222 7024; website www.houstonsymphony.org; Music Dir Hans Graf; Exec. Dir David M. Wax.

Hudson Valley Philharmonic Orchestra: 35 Market Street, Poughkeepsie, NY 12601; tel. website www.bardavon.org/hvp.htm; Music Dir Randall Fleischer; Man. Dir Karen Deschere.

Huntsville Symphony Orchestra: PO Box 2400, Huntsville, AL 35804; website www.hso.org; Music Dir Carlos Prieto; Exec. Dir Samuel Woodward.

Indianapolis Chamber Orchestra: 4603 Clarendon Road, Suite 36, Indianapolis, IN 46208; Music Dir Kirk Trevor; Exec. Dir Chad Miller.

Indianapolis Symphony Orchestra: 32 E Washington Street, Suite 600, Indianapolis, IN 46204-2919; tel. (317) 262-1100; fax (317) 262-1159; website www.indianapolissymphony.org; Music Dir: Mario Venzago; Pres. and CEO: Richard R. Hoffert.

Jacksonville Symphony Orchestra: 300 Westwater Street, Suite 200, Jacksonville, FL 32202; tel. 1 904 354 5547; fax 1 904 354 9238; website www.jaxsymphony.org; Music Dir Fabio Mechetti; Conductor Laureate Roger Nierenberg; Exec. Dir David Pierson.

Kalamazoo Symphony Orchestra: 359 South Kalamazoo Mall, Suite 100, Kalamazoo, MI 49007; tel. 1 269 349 7759; fax 1 269 349 9229; website www.kalamazoosymphony.com; Music Dir Raymond Harvey; Exec. Dir Stacy Ridenour.

Kansas City Symphony Orchestra: 1020 Central, Suite 300, Kansas City, MO 64105; tel. 1 816 471 1100; fax 1 816 471 0976; website www.kcsymphony.org; Conductor Timothy Hankewich; Gen. Man. Susan Franano.

Knoxville Symphony Orchestra: 406 Union Avenue, Suite 100, Knoxville, TN 37902; tel. 1 865 523 1178; fax 1 865 546 3766; website www.knoxvillesymphony.org; Music Dir Lucas Richman; Exec. Dir Constance Harrison.

Long Beach Symphony Orchestra: 110 W Ocean Blvd, Suite 22, Long Beach, CA 90802; website www.lbso.org; Music Dir: Enrique Arturo Diemecke; Exec. Dir: Jack A. Fishman.

Long Island Philharmonic Orchestra: 1 Hungtington Quadrangle, Suite LL 09, Melville, NY 11747; Music Dir Enrique Arturo Diemecke; Exec. Dir Jack Fishman.

Los Angeles Chamber Orchestra: 707 Wiltshire Blvd, Suite 1850, Los Angeles, CA 90017; tel. 1 213 622 7001; fax 1 213 955 2071; e-mail laco@laco.org; website www.laco.org; Artistic Adviser Jeffrey Kahane; Exec. Dir Ruth L. Eliel.

Los Angeles Philharmonic Orchestra: 151 S Grand Avenue, Los Angeles, CA 90012; tel. 1 213 972 7300; fax 1 213 617 3065; website www.laphil.org; Music Dir Esa-Pekka Salonen.

Louisiana Philharmonic Orchestra: 305 Baronne Street, Suite 600, New Orleans, LA 70112; tel. (504) 523-6530; fax (504) 595-8468; website www.lpomusic.com; Music Dir Klauspeter Seilbel; Exec. Dir Sharon Litwin.

Louisville Orchestra: 300 W Main Street, Suite 100, Louisville, KY 40202; tel. 1 502 587 8681; fax 1 502 589 7870; e-mail info@louisvilleorchestra.org; website www.louisvilleorchestra.org; Music Dir Uriel Segal; Exec. Dir Wayne S. Brown.

Maryland Symphony Orchestra: 13 S Potomac Street, Hagerstown, MD 21740; tel. 1 301 797 4000; fax 1 301 797 2314; website www.marylandsymphony.org; Music Dir Elizabeth Schulze; Man. Dir Cassandra H. Wantz.

Memphis Symphony Orchestra: 3100 Walnut Grove, Suite 501, Memphis, TN 38111; tel. 1 901 324 3627; fax 1 901 324 3698; website www.memphissymphony.org; Music Dir David Loebel; Exec. Dir Martha Maxwell.

Michigan Chamber Orchestra: 60 Farnsworth, Detroit, MI 48202; Principal Conductor Andrew Massey; Gen. Man. Virginia Catanese.

Milwaukee Symphony Orchestra: 330 E Kilbourn Avenue, Suite 900, Milwaukee, WI 53202; tel. 1 414 291 6010; fax 1 414 291 7610; website www.milwaukeesymphony.org; Music Dir Andreas Delfs; Exec. Dir Joan Squire.

Minnesota Orchestra: 1111 Nicollet Mall, Minneapolis, MN 55403; tel. 612 371 5600; fax 1 612 371 0838; e-mail info@mnorch.org; website www.minnesotaorchestra.org; Music Dir Osmo Vänskä; Pres. David J. Hyslop.

Mississippi Symphony Orchestra: 201 E Pascagoula Street, Jackson, MS 39201; tel. 1 601 960 1565; website www.msorchestra.com; Music Dir Crafton Beck; Exec. Dir Philip K. Messner.

Music Academy of the West Summer Festival Orchestra: 1070 Fairway Road, Santa Barbara, CA 93108; tel. (805) 969-4726; fax (805) 969-0686; website www.musicacademy.org; Pres. David L.Kuehn; Vice-Pres. and Dean W. Harold Laster.

Music of the Baroque Orchestra: 343 S Dearborn, Suite 1716, Chicago, IL 60604; Music Dir Thomas Wikman.

Naples Philharmonic: 5833 Pelican Bay Blvd, Naples, FL 33963; e-mail info@thephil.org; website www.thephil.org; Music Dir Christopher Seaman; Pres. and CEO Myra Janco Daniels.

Nashville Symphony Orchestra: 2000 Glen Echo Road, Suite 204, Nashville, TN 37215; tel. 1 615 783 1200; fax 1 615 255 5656; website www.nashvillesymphony.org; Music Dir Kenneth Schemerhorn; Exec. Dir Stephen R. Vann.

National Gallery Orchestra: Sixth Street and Constitution Avenue NW, Washington, DC 20565; Music Dir George Manos.

National Repertory Orchestra: PO Box 38, Keystone, CO 80435; e-mail nro@NROMusic.com; website www.nromusic.com; Conductor Carl Topilow.

National Symphony Orchestra: John F. Kennedy Center for the Performing Arts, 2700 F Street NW, Washington, DC 20566; tel. 1 202 416 8000; fax 1 202 416 8105; website www.kennedy-center.org/nso; Music Dir Leonard Slatkin; Gen. Man. Richard Hancock.

New Hampshire Symphony Orchestra: 1087 Elm Street, Manchester, NH 03101; tel. (603) 669-3559; fax (603) 623-1195; e-mail info@nhso.org; website www.nhso.org; Exec. Dir: Douglas A. Barry; Music Dir: Kenneth Kiesler; f. 1974; .

New Haven Symphony Orchestra: 70 Audubon Street, New Haven, CT 06510; tel. (203) 865-0831; fax (203) 789-8907; website www.newhavensymphony.org; Music Dir: Jung-Ho Pak; Exec. Dir: Michael MacLeod.

New Jersey Symphony Orchestra: 2 Central Avenue, Newark, NJ 07102; tel. 1 201 624 3713; fax 1 201 624 2115; e-mail information@njsymphony.org; website www.njsymphony.org; Music Dir Zdenek Macal; Exec. Dir Lawrence Tamburri.

New Mexico Symphony Orchestra: 4407 Menaul Blvd NE, Albuquerque, NM 87190; tel. 1 505 881 9590; website www.nmso.org; Music Dir Guillermo Figueroa; Exec. Dir Kevin Hagen.

New World Symphony: 541 Lincoln Road, Third Floor, Miami Beach, FL 33139; tel. 1 305 673 3330; fax 1 305 673 6749; e-mail email@nws.org; website www.nws.org; Artistic Dir Michael Tilson Thomas; Artistic Admin. John Duffy.

New York Chamber Symphony: 92nd Street Y, 1395 Lexington Avenue, New York, NY 10128; Music Dir Gerard Schwarz; Man. Tom Gaitens.

New York Philharmonic Orchestra: Avery Fisher Hall, 10 Lincoln Center Plaza, Lincoln Center for the Performing Arts, Broadway at 65th St, New York, NY 10023; tel. 1 212 875 5900; fax 1 212 875 5717; website www.newyorkphilharmonic.org; Music Dir Lorin Maazel; Man. Dir Deborah Borda.

New York Virtuosi Chamber Symphony: C. W. Post College, Greenvale, NY 11548; website www.newyorkvirtuosi.org; Music Dir Kenneth Klein; Exec. Dir Yolanda Padula.

North Carolina Symphony Orchestra: 2 E South Street, Raleigh, NC 27601; tel. 1 919 733 2750; fax 1 919 733 9920; website www.ncsymphony.org; Music Dir Gerhardt Zimmerman; Exec. Dir Banks C. Talley Jnr.

Oakland East Bay Symphony Orchestra: 1999 Harrison Street, Suite 2030, Oakland, CA 94612; Music Dir Michael Morgan.

Oklahoma City Philharmonic Orchestra: 428 W California, Suite 210, Oklahoma City, OK 73102; website www.okcphilharmonic.org; Music Dir Joel Levine; Gen. Man. Alan D. Valentine.

Omaha Symphony Orchestra: 1605 Howard Street, Suite 310, Omaha, NE 68102; tel. 1 402 342 3836; fax 1 402 342 3819; website www.omahasymphony.org; Music Dir Bruce Hangen; Exec. Dir Roland Valliere.

Oregon Symphony Orchestra: 711 SW Alder, Suite 200, Portland, OR 97205; tel. 1 503 228 4294; fax 1 503 228 4150; website www.orsymphony.org; Music Dir Carlos Kalmar; Pres. Don Roth.

Orpheus Chamber Orchestra: 490 Riverside Drive, New York, NY 10027; tel. (212) 896-1700; fax (212) 896-1717; e-mail orpheusnyc@orpheusnyc.org; website www.orpheusnyc.org; Man. Dir: Ronnie Bauch.

Pacific Symphony Orchestra: 3631 S Harbor Blvd, Suite 100, Santa Ana, CA 92704; tel. 1 714 755 5788; fax 1 714 755 5789; e-mail pso@pso.org; website www.pacificsymphony.org; Music Dir Carl St Clair; Exec. Dir John E. Forsyte.

Pasadena Symphony Orchestra: 2500 E Colorado Blvd, Suite 260, Pasadena, CA 91107; tel. 1 626 793 7172; fax 1 626 793 7180; website www.pasadenasymphony.org; Music Dir Jorge Mester; Exec. Dir Wayne Shilkret.

Philadelphia Orchestra: Academy of Music, 260 S Broad Street, Suite 1600, Philadelphia, PA 19102; tel. 1 215 893 1900; fax 1 215 893 7649; e-mail philadelphia_orchestra@philadelphiaorchestra.org; website www.philorch.org; Music Dir Christoph Eschenbach; Pres. and COO Joseph H. Kluger.

Philharmonia Baroque Orchestra: 180 Redwood Street, Suite 200, San Francisco, CA 94102; tel. 1 415 252 1288; fax 1 415 252 1488; e-mail info@philharmonia.org; website www.philharmonia.org; Music Dir Nicholas McGegan; Exec. Dir George Gelles.

Philharmonia Virtuosi: PO Box 645, North Salem, NY 10560-0645; e-mail bkapp@pvmusic.org; website pvmusic.org; Exec. Dir Barbara Kapp.

Phoenix Symphony Orchestra: 455 N Third Street, Suite 390, Phoenix, AZ 85004; tel. 1 602 495 1117; fax 1 602 253 1772; e-mail info@phoenixsymphony.org; website www.phoenixsymphony.org; Principal Guest Conductor Hermann Michael; Pres. and CEO Conrad Kloh; Music Dir James Sedares.

Pittsburgh Symphony Orchestra: Heinz Hall, 600 Penn Avenue, Pittsburgh, PA 15222-3259; tel. (412) 392-4900; fax (412) 392-4909; e-mail ldonnermeyer@pittsburghsymphony.org; website www.pittsburghsymphony.org; Music Dir: Mariss Jansons; Pres. and CEO: Lawrence Tamburri.

Portland Symphony Orchestra: 477 Congress Street, Mezzanine, Portland, ME 04104; tel. 1 207 773 6128; fax 1 207 773 6089; e-mail psobox@portlandsymphony.com; website www.portlandsymphony.com; Music Dir Toshiyuki Shimada; Exec. Dir Jane E. Hunter.

Puerto Rico Symphony Orchestra: PO Box 41227, San Juan, PR 00940; tel. 787 721 7727; fax 787 726 4009; website www.sinfonicapr.gobierno.pr; Music Dir Eugene Kohn; Gen. Dir Félix Rosas Crespo.

Rhode Island Philharmonic Orchestra: 222 Richmond Street, Providence, RI 02903; tel. 1 401 831 3123; fax 1 401 831 4577; e-mail information@ri-philharmonic.org; website www.ri-philharmonic.org; Music Dir Larry Rachleff; Exec. Dir David M. Wax.

Richmond Symphony Orchestra: The Berkshire, 300 W Franklin Street, Richmond, VA 23220; tel. 1 804 788 4717; fax 1 804 788 1541; website www.richmondsymphony.com; Music Dir Mark Russell Smith; Exec. Dir David Fisk.

Rochester Philharmonic Orchestra: 108 East Avenue, Rochester, NY 14604; tel. (585) 454-7311; fax (585) 423-2256; e-mail rpo@rpo.org; website www.rpo.org; Music Dir: Christopher Seaman; Pres. and CEO: Richard Nowlin.

Sacramento Symphony Orchestra: 77 Cadillac Drive, Suite 101, Sacramento, CA 95825; Music Dir Geoffrey Simon.

San Antonio Symphony Orchestra: 222 E Houston Street, Suite 200, San Antonio, TX 78205; tel. 1 210 554 1000; fax 1 210 554 1008; website www.sasymphony.org; Music Dir Larry Rachleff; Exec. Dir David Schillhammer.

San Francisco Symphony: Louise M. Davies Symphony Hall, 201 Van Ness Avenue, San Francisco, CA 94102; tel. 1 415 552 8000; fax 1 415 431 6857; website www.sfsymphony.org; Music Dir Michael Tilson Thomas; Exec. Dir Peter Pastreich.

San Jose Symphony Orchestra: 99 Almaden Blvd, Suite 400, San Jose, CA 95113; tel. 1 408 287 7383; fax 1 408 286 6391; Music Dir Leonid Grin.

Santa Barbara Symphony Orchestra: 1900 State Street, Suite G, Santa Barbara, CA 93101; tel. 1 805 898 9626; fax 1 805 898 9326; e-mail info@thesymphony.org; website www.thesymphony.org; Music Dir Gisèle Ben-Dor; Gen. Man. James L. Wright.

Savannah Symphony Orchestra: PO Box 9505, Savannah, GA 31412; website www.savannahsymphony.org; Music Dir Philip Greenberg; Gen. Man. Gregg W. Gustafson.

Seattle Symphony Orchestra: 200 University Street, Seattle, WA 98111; tel. 1 206 215 4700; fax 1 206 215 4701; e-mail info@seattlesymphony.org; website www.seattlesymphony.org; Music Dir Gerard Schwarz; Exec. Dir Deborah Card.

South Dakota Symphony Orchestra: 300 N Dakota Avenue, Suite 116, Sioux Falls, SD 57104; tel. 1 605 335 7933; fax 1 605 335 1958; e-mail sdsymphony@sdsymphony.org; website www.sdsymphony.org; Music Dir Henry Charles Smith; Exec. Dir Tom Bennett.

Spokane Symphony Orchestra: 818 W Riverside, Suite 100, Spokane, WA 99201; tel. 1 509 624 1200; website www.spokanesymphony.org; Music Dir Fabio Mechetti; Exec. Dir Richard Early.

St Louis Symphony Orchestra: Powell Symphony Hall, 718 N Grand Blvd, St Louis, MO 63103; tel. 1 314 533 2500; fax 1 314 286 4142; website www.slso.org; Music Dir David Robertson; Exec. Dir Bruce Coppock.

The Saint Paul Chamber Orchestra: 408 Saint Peter Street, Third Floor, Saint Paul, MN 55102-1497; tel. (651) 292-3248; fax (651) 292-3281; e-mail info@spcomail.org; website www.thespco.org; Pres. and Man. Dir Bruce Coppock.

Stockton Symphony Orchestra: 46 W Fremont Street, Stockton, CA 95202; tel. 1 209 951 0196; fax 1 209 951 1050; e-mail admin@stocktonsymphony.org; website www.stocktonsymphony.org; Music Dir Peter Jaffe; Exec. Dir George A. Sinclair.

Syracuse Symphony Orchestra: 411 Montgomery Street, Suite 40, Syracuse, NY 13202; tel. 1 315 424 8222; fax 1 315 424 1131; website www.syracusesymphony.org; Music Dir Daniel Hege; Exec. Dir Jeffry Comanici.

Theater Chamber Players of Kennedy Center: John F. Kennedy Center for the Performing Arts, Washington, DC 20566; Dirs Leon Fleisher, Dina Koston.

Toledo Symphony Orchestra: 1838 Parkwood Avenue, Suite 310, Toledo, OH 43624; tel. 1 419 246 8000; fax 1 419 321 0890; website www.toledosymphony.com; Principal Conductor Stefan Sanderling; Man. Dir Robert Bell.

Tucson Symphony Orchestra: Tucson Symphony Center, 2175 N Sixth Avenue, Tucson, AZ 85705; tel. 1 520 792 9155; website www.tucsonsymphony.org; Music Dir George Hanson; Exec. Dir Susan Franano.

Utah Symphony Orchestra: 123 W South Temple, Salt Lake City, UT 84101; tel. 1 801 533 5626; fax 1 801 521 6634; Music Dir Keith Lockhart; Artistic Admin. Cecil Cole.

Virginia Symphony Orchestra: 861 Glenrock Road, Suite 200, Norfolk, VA 23502; tel. 1 757 466 3060; fax 1 757 466 3046; website www.virginiasymphony.org; Music Dir JoAnn Falletta; Exec. Dir John Morison.

West Virginia Symphony Orchestra: PO Box 2292, Charleston, WV 24328; e-mail info@wvsymphony.org; website www.wvsymphony.org; Music Dir Thomas Conlin; Exec. Dir Paul A. Helfrich.

Wichita Symphony Orchestra: 225 W Douglas, Suite 207, Wichita, KS 67202; tel. 1 316 267 5259; fax 1 316 267 1937; e-mail symphony@wso.org; website www.wso.org; Music Dir Andrew Sewell; Gen. Man. Mitchell A. Berman.

The Women's Philharmonic: 44 Page Street, Suite 604D, San Francisco, CA 94102; tel. 1 415 437 0123; fax 1 415 437 0121; e-mail info@womensphil.org; website www.womensphil.org; Exec. Dir Shira Cion.

Uruguay

Orquesta Sinfónia del SODRE: Calle Sarandi 450, Montevideo 1100; Music Dir Roberto Montenegro; Pres. Escribano Ramiro Llana.

Venezuela

Orquesta Sinfónica Municipal de Caracas: PO Box 17390, Parque Central, Caracas 1015-A; Dir Carlos Riazuelo.

Simón Bolívar Symphony Orchestra of Venezuela: Torre Oeste, 1°, Parque Central, Caracas; Music Dir José Antonio Abreu.

APPENDIX B: OPERA COMPANIES

Argentina

Teatro Colón: Cerrito 618, 1010 Buenos Aires; tel. 54 1 382 8924; fax 54 1 111232; website www.teatrocolon.org.ar; Gen. and Artistic Dir Gabriel Senanes.

Australia

Opera Australia: PO Box 291, Strawberry Hills, NSW 2012; tel. 61 2 9699 1099; fax 61 2 9699 3184; e-mail online@opera-australia.org.au; website www.opera-australia.org.au; Gen. Man. Donald McDonald; Artistic Dir Moffat Oxenbould.

Opera Australia: PO Box 389, South Melbourne, Vic. 3205; tel. 61 3 9685 3777; fax 61 3 9686 1441; e-mail online@opera-australia.org.au; website www.opera-australia.org.au; Public Affairs Man. Sonja Chambers.

Opera Queensland: Queensland Conservatorium, 16 Russell Street, South Bank, Qld 4101; tel. 61 7 3875 3030; fax 61 7 3844 5352; e-mail info@operaqueensland.com.au; website www.operaqueensland.org.au; Gen. Dir: Chris J. Mangin; Gen. Man. Suzannah Conway.

State Opera of South Australia: 216 Marion Road, Netley, SA 5037; tel. 61 8 226 4790; fax 61 8 226 4791; e-mail info@saopera.sa.gov.au; website www.saopera.sa.gov.au; Artistic Dir Bill Gillespie; Gen. Dir Stephen Phillips.

Victoria State Opera: 77 Southbank Blvd, Melbourne, Vic. 3205; Gen. Man. Ken Mackenzie-Forbes; Artistic Admin. Kate Stevenson.

West Australian Opera: His Majesty's Theatre, 825 Hay Street, Perth, WA 6850; tel. 08 9321 5869; fax 08 9324 1134; website www.waopera.asn .au; Gen. Man. Carolyn Chard; Artistic Dir Richard Mills; Head of Music Marilyn Phillips.

Austria

Landestheater: Promenade 39, 4010 Linz; tel. 43 732 761 1100; fax 43 732 761 1105; Dir Roman Zeilinger.

Landestheater: Schwarstrasse 22, 5020 Salzburg; tel. 43 662 871512; fax 43 662 87151213; Dir Lutz Hochstraate.

Raimund Theater: Wallgasse 18–20, 1060 Vienna.

Sommertheater: Wiesingerstrasse 7, 4820 Bad Ischl; Music Dir Eduard Macku; Man. Silvia Müller.

Stadttheater: Rathausplatz 11, 3100 St Pölten; Dir Perter Wolsdorff.

Stadttheater: Theaterplatz 4, 9020 Klagenfurt; Dir Dietmar Pflegerl.

Stadttheater: Theaterplatz 7, 2500 Baden bei Wien; Dir Helmuth Brandstätter.

Tiroler Landestheater: Rennweg 2, 6020 Innsbruck; tel. 43 512 520744; fax 43 512 52074333; Dir Dominique Mentha.

Vereinigte Bühnen Wien GmbH: Linke Wienzeile 6, 1060 Vienna; tel. 43 1 588 30 200; fax 43 1 588 30 33; e-mail info@vbw.at; website www .musicalvienna.at; CEO: Franz Häussler; consists of three theatres: Theater an der Wien, Raimund Theater and Etablissement Ronacher.

Vereinigte Bühnen: Kaiser Josef Platz 10, 8010 Graz; tel. 43 316 8000; fax 43 316 8565; website www.theater-graz.com; Dir Gerhard Brunner.

Volksoper: Währingerstrasse 78, 1090 Vienna; tel. 43 1 514 443318; website www.volksoper.at; Dir Ioan Holender.

Wiener Kammeroper: Fleischmarkt 24, 1010 Vienna; tel. 43 1 512 0100; fax 43 1 512 010010; e-mail information@wienerkammeroper.at; website www.wienerkammeroper.at; Music Dir Daniel Hoyem-Cavazza; Gen. Mans Isabella Gabor, Holger Bleck.

Wiener Staatsoper: Opernring 2, 1010 Vienna; tel. and fax 43 1 51444; e-mail information@wiener-staatsoper.at; website www.wiener -staatsoper.at; Dir Ioan Holender.

Belgium

Opéra Royal de Wallonie: 1 rue des Dominicains, 4000 Liège; tel. 32 4 221 4720; fax 32 4 221 0201.

Opera voor Vlaanderen: Schouwburgstraat 3, 9000 Ghent; tel. 32 9 225 2425; Music Dir Marc Minkowski; Gen. Man. Marc Clémeur.

Théâtre Royal de la Monnaie: 4 rue Léopold, 1000 Brussels; tel. 32 2 229 1200; fax 32 2 229 1330; website www.demunt.be; Dir Bernard Foccroulle.

Vlaamse Opera: Van Ertbornstraat 8, 2018 Antwerp; tel. 32 3 202 1011; fax 32 3 232 2661; website www.vlaamseopera.be.

Bosnia and Herzegovina

National Theater Opera: Obala 9, 71000 Sarajevo.

Bulgaria

Bourgas State Opera: K1, Ohridski St 2, 8000 Bourgas.

Plovdiv State Opera: 4000 Plovdiv.

Sofia National Opera: 30 Dondoukov Blvd, 1000 Sofia; tel. 359 2 988 5869; fax 3592 987 7998; Chief Conductor Gueorgui Notev; Gen. Man. Plamen Kartaloff.

Stara Zagora State Opera: 6000 Stara Zagora.

Stefan Makedonski Musical Theater: 3P Volov Street, 1500 Sofia.

Varna State Opera: 1 Nezavisimost Square, 9000 Varna; tel. 35952 602086; fax 35952 602088; e-mail opera.varna@mbox.actbg.bg; Gen. Dir Hristo Ignatov.

Canada

Calgary Opera: 601 237-8 Avenue SE, Calgary, AB T2G 5C3; tel. 1 403 262 7286; fax 1 403 263 5428; website www.calgaryopera.com; Gen. Dir/ CEO W. R. McPhee.

Canadian Opera Company: 227 Front Street E, Toronto, ON M5A 1E8; tel. 1 416 363 6671; fax 1 416 363 5584; e-mail info@coc.ca; website www .coc.ca; Gen. Dir Richard Bradshaw.

Edmonton Opera: Winspear Centre, 9720 102nd Avenue NW, Edmonton, AB T5J 4B2; tel. 1 780 424 4040; fax 1 780 429 0600; e-mail edmopera@ edmontonopera.com; website www.edmontonopera.com.

Edmonton Opera Association: 320-10232 112th Street, Edmonton, AB T5K 1M4; tel. 1 403 423 424 4040/1000; fax 1 403 423 429 0600; Gen. Dir Richard Mantle.

Manitoba Opera: 380 Graham Avenue, Winnipeg, MB RC3 4K2; tel. 1 204 942 7479; fax 1 204 949 0377; e-mail mbopera@manitobaopera.mb.ca; website www.manitobaopera.mb.ca; Dir Larry Desrochers.

Opéra de Montréal: 260 Blvd de Maisonneuve W, Montréal, QC H2X 1V9; tel. 1 514 985 2222; fax 1 514 985 2219; e-mail info@operademontreal .com; website www.operademontreal.com; Artistic and Gen. Dir David Moss.

Opéra de Québec: 1220 Avenue Taché, Québec, QC G1R 3B4; tel. 1 418 529 4142; fax 1 418 529 3735; e-mail operaqc@mediom.qc.ca; website www .operadequebec.qc.ca; Gen. and Artistic Dir Grégoire Legendre.

Opera Mississauga: Living Arts Centre, 4141 Living Arts Drive, Mississauga, ON L5B 4B8; tel. 1 905 306 0060; fax 1 905 306 9976; e-mail info@royaloperacanada.com; website www.royaloperacanada.com; Gen. and Artistic Dir Dwight Bennett.

Opera Ontario: 110 King Street W, Second Floor, Hamilton, ON L8P 4S6; Artistic Dir Daniel Lipton.

Pacific Opera Victoria: 1316b Government Street, Victoria, BC V8W 1Y8; tel. 1 250 382 1641; fax 1 250 382 4944; website www.pov.bc.ca; Artistic Dir Timothy Vernon; Gen. Man. David Devan.

Royal Opera Canada: Toronto Centre for the Arts, 5040 Yonge Street, Toronto, ON M2N 6R8; tel. 1 416 322 0456; fax 1 416 482 7044; e-mail info@royaloperacanada.com; website www.royaloperacanada.com; Gen. and Artistic Dir Dwight Bennett.

Vancouver Opera: 835 Cambie Street, Vancouver, BC V6B 2P4; tel. 1 604 682 2871; fax 1 604 682 3981; website www.vanopera.bc.ca; Music/ Artistic Admin. Jonathan Darlington; Gen. Dir James W. Wright.

Chile

Opera del Teatro Municipal: San Antonio 149, Santiago Centro; tel. 56 2 4631002; fax 56 2 6337214; e-mail giesen@ctcreuna.cl; website www .municipal.cl; Gen. Dir Cristobal Giesen.

People's Republic of China

Central Opera Theater: Dongzhimenwai, Zuojiazhuang, Beijing 100028; tel. 86 465 2317; Dir Wang Shi-guang.

China Peking Opera Theater: Beijing; Pres. Zhang Dong-Chuan.

Shanghai Opera House: Lane 100, Changshu Road, Shanghai 200040; tel. 86 216 248 5359; fax 86 216 249 8127.

Colombia

Compañia Nacional de Opera: Teatro Colón, Calle 10, No. 5-32, Bogotá.

Costa Rica

Compañía Lirica Nacional: PO Box 1035, San José 1000; Dir Gloria Waissbluth.

Czech Republic

Moravian State Theatre: Tr Svobdy 33, 771 07 Olomouc; tel. 420 68 522 5727; fax 420 68 522 5781.

National Theatre: Dvo ákova 11, 657 70 Brno; tel. 420 5 4232 1285; fax 420 5 4221 3746.

National Theatre: PO Box 865, 112 30 Prague 1; tel. 420 2 24 910312/901227; fax 420 2 24 911524.

Ostrava State Theatre: Pabla Nerudy 14, 701 04 Ostrava.

Silesian Theatre: Horní nám sti 13, 74669 Opava.

State Opera: Legerova 75, CRIII 21 Prague; tel. 420 22 4 227 6396; fax 420 22 423 0410/29437.

Stavovske Divadlo (Theatre of the Estates): Ostrovni, PO Box 865, 11230 Prague 1; tel. 44 2 24 215001/26 7797/901520; fax 44 2 24 91 1530.

J. K. Tyl Theatre: Prokopova 14, 304 11 Pize.

Z nejedlý State Theatre: Kralova Vý ina 10, 400 00 Ustí nad Labem.

Denmark

Den Jyske Opera (Danish National Opera): Musikhuset Århus, Thomas Jensens Alle, 8000 Århus; tel. 45 89 409110; fax 45 86 133710; e-mail post@jyske-opera.dk; website www.jyske-opera.dk; Gen. Dir Troels Kold; Admin. Tony Borup Mortenson.

Det Kongelige Teater (Royal Danish Opera): PO Box 2185, 1017 Copenhagen K; tel. 45 33 696933; fax 45 33 696767; website www.kgl-teater.dk; Artistic Dir Kasper Bech Holten; Man. Michael Christiansen.

Musikdramatisk Teater: Ernst Meyersgade 8, 1772 Copenhagen V.

Estonia

Estonian National Opera: Estonia Blvd 4, 10148 Tallinn; tel. 372 6831 201; fax 372 6313 080; e-mail info@opera.ee; website www.ooper.ee; Artistic Dir: Arvo Volmer.

Finland

Finnish National Opera: PO Box 176, Helsingkatu 58, 00251 Helsinki; tel. 358 9 403021; fax 358 9 40302305; website www.operafin.fi; Gen. Dir Erkki Korhonen.

France

Atelier du Rhin: 6 Route d'Ingersheim, PO Box 593, 68008 Colmar; tel. 33 3 89 41 71 92; fax 33 3 89 41 33 26; e-mail info@atelierdurhin.com; website www.atelierdurhin.com; Dir Matthew Jocelyn.

Atelier Lyrique de Tourcoing: 82 Blvd Gambetta, 59200 Tourcoing; tel. 33 3 20 26 66 03; fax 33 3 20 27 91 19; e-mail atelierlyriquedetourcoing@nordnet.fr; Gen. Dir Jean-Claude Malgoire; Gen. Admin. Catherine Noel.

Châtelet Théâtre Musical: 2 rue Edouard Colonne, 75001 Paris; tel. 33 1 40 28 28 28; fax 33 1 42 36 89 75; website www.chatelet-theatre.com; Gen. Dir Jean-Pierre Brossmann.

Chorégies d'Orange: PO Box 205, 84107 Orange Cedex; tel. 33 90 51 83 83; fax 33 90 34 87 67; e-mail info@choregies.asso.fr; website www.choregies.asso.fr.

Ecole Art Lyrique de l'Opéra: 5 rue Favart, 75009 Paris; Dir Michel Sénéchal; Admin. Francis Meunier.

Grand Théâtre de Reims: 13 rue Chanzy, 51100 Reims; tel. 33 3 26 50 31 00; fax 33 3 26 84 90 02.

L'Opéra Comique: 5 rue Favart, 75002 Paris; tel. 33 1 42 44 45 40/5; fax 33 1 49 26 05 93; website www.opera-comique.com; Dir Jérôme Savary.

L'Opéra de Dijon: Service Location, 2 rue Longpierre, 21000 Dijon; tel. 33 80 67 23 23; Dir Pierre Filippi.

Opéra d'Avignon: Regie Municipale, PO Box 111, 84007 Avignon; tel. 33 90 82 42 42; fax 33 90 85 04 23.

Opéra de La Bastille: 120 rue de Lyon, 75012 Paris; tel. 33 1 40 01 17 89; fax 33 1 44 73 13 00; website www.opera-de-paris.fr; Conductor James Conlon; Gen. Admin. Hugues Gall.

Opéra de Lille: Théâtre de l'Opéra, 2 rue des Bons Enfants, 59800 Lille; tel. 33 3 20 14 99 20; fax 33 3 20 14 99 27; website www.opera-lille.fr; Artistic Dir Ricardo Szwarcer; Admin. Michel Default.

Opéra de Lyon: 1 Place de la Comedie, 69001 Lyon; tel. 334 72 00 45 00; fax 334 72 00 45 01; website www.opera-lyon.com; Gen. Dir Serge Dorny; Deputy Dir Patrice Armengau.

Opéra de Marseille: 2 rue Molière, 1321 Marseille Cédex 01; tel. 33 4 91 55 21 12.

Opéra de Nancy et de Lorraine: 1 rue Ste Catherine, 54000 Nancy; tel. 33 83 85 33 20; fax 33 83 85 30 66; Dir Antoine Bourseiller; Admin. Christophe Bezzone.

Opéra de Nantes: 1 rue Molière, 44000 Nantes; tel. 33 40 41 90 60; fax 33 40 41 90 77; Dir Philippe Goderfroid; Admin. Serge Cochelin.

Opéra de Tours: Grand Théâtre, 34 rue de la Scellerie, 37000 Tours; tel. 33 247 60 20 00; fax 33 247 60 20 40; e-mail theatre@ville-tours.fr; Dir: Jean-Yves Ossonce; Admin.: Luc Cavalier.

Opéra du Rhin: 19 Place Broglie, 67008 Strasbourg Cédex; tel. 33 3 88 75 48 23; fax 33 3 88 24 09 34; website www.opera-national-du-rhin.com; Gen. Dir Laurent Spielmann; Admin. Lucien Colinet.

Opéra National de Bordeaux: Grand Théâtre, place de la Comédie, BP 95, 33025 Bordeaux Cédex; tel. 33(0)5 56 00 85 20; fax 33(0)5 56 81 93 66; website www.opera-bordeaux.com; Dir Thierry Fouquet.

Opéra National de Montpellier: 11 Blvd Victor Hugo, 34967 Montpellier, Cédex 2; tel. 04 67 60 19 80; fax 04 67 60 19 90; website www.opera-montpellier.com; Gen. Dir Henri Maier; Admin. Renée Panabière.

Opéra Théâtre de Metz: 4–5 Place de la Comédie, 57000 Metz; tel. 03 87 55 51 71; fax 03 87 31 32 37; e-mail smtp.theatre@maine-metz.fr; Admin. Daniel Lucas.

Opera de Rouen: 7 rue du Docteur Rambert, 76000 Rouen; tel. 33 2 35 98 50 98; fax 33 2 35 15 33 49; website www.operaderouen.com; Dir Laurent Langlois; Musical Dir Oswald Sallaberger.

Théâtre de Caen/Atelier Lyrique de Caen: PO Box 217, 14007 Caen Cédex; Dir Jean Malraye.

Théâtre de l'Opéra de Nice: 4/6 rue St François de Paule, 06300 Nice; tel. 33 492 17 40 62; fax 33 492 17 40 65; e-mail olivier-cautres@ville-nice.fr; Music Dir: Marco Guidarini; Man. Paul-Emile Fourny.

Théâtre des Arts: 76177 Rouen Cédex; Dir Marc Adam.

Théâtre des Champs-Elysées: 15 Avenue Montaigne, 75008 Paris; tel. 33 1 49 52 50 00; fax 33 1 49 52 07 41; website www.theatrechampselysses.fr; Gen. Dir Alain Durel; Admin. Francis Lepigeon.

Théâtre du Capitole: Place du Capitole, 31000 Toulouse; tel. 33 61 23 21 35; website www.theatre-du-capitole.org; Artistic Dir Nicolas Joel; Admin. Robert Gouaze.

Théâtre Musical d'Angers: 7 rue Duboys, 49100 Angers.

Théâtre National de l'Opéra de Paris: 8 rue Scribe, 75009 Paris.

Germany

Bühnen der Hansestadt Lübeck: Fischergrube 5-21, 2400 Lübeck; Gen. Music Dir Erich Wächter; Gen. Man. Dietrich von Oertsen.

Bühnen der Stadt Bielefeld: Brunhenstrasse 3–9, Pf 220, 4800 Bielefeld; tel. 49 521512502; fax 49 521 513430; Gen. Music Dir Rainer Koch; Man. Heiner Bruns.

Bühnen der Stadt Gera: Küchengartenalle 2, 6500 Gera; Music Dir Wolfgang Wappler; Man. Eberhard Kneipel.

Badisches Staatstheater Karlsruhe: Baumeisterstrasse 11, Pf 1449, 7500 Karlsruhe; Gen. Music Dir Günter Neuhold; Gen. Man. Günter Könemann.

Bayerische Kammeroper: Rathaus, Gemeinde Veitshöchheim, 8707 Veitshöchheim; Music Dir Siegfried Köhler; Man. Blagoy Apostolov.

Bayerische Staatsoper-Nationaltheater: Max-Joseph-Platz, 80539 Munich; tel. 49 89 2185 1000; fax 49 89 2185 1003; website www.staatstheater.bayern.de; Gen. and Artistic Dir: Sir Peter Jonas; Man. Dir: Dr Roland Felber.

Berliner Kammeroper eV: Kottbusser Damm 79, 10967 Berlin; tel. 49 30 693 1054; fax 49 30 692 5201; Music Dir Brynmor Llewelyn Jones; Artistic Dir Henry Akina.

Big Bang Theater München: Dachauer Strasse 192, 8000 Munich 50; Music Dir Walter Waidosch.

Brandenburg Theater: Grabenstrasse 14, 1800 Brandenburg; Music Dir Heiko Mathias Förster; Man. Ekkehard Phophet.

Bremen Theater: Pf 101046, 2800 Bremen.

Comédia Opera Instabile: Holzstrasse 11, 8000 Munich 5.

Das Meininger Theater: Bernhardstrasse 5, 6100 Meiningen; Music Dir Wolfgang Hocke; Man. Ulrich Burkhard.

Deutsche Oper am Rhein: Theatergemeinschaft Düsseldorf-Duisburg, Opernhaus; website www.deutsche-oper-am-rhein.de.

Deutsche Oper Berlin: Richard Wagner Str 10, 10585 Berlin; tel. 49 30 343 8401; fax 49 30 343 84232; website www.deutscheoperberlin.de; Gen. Music Dir Christian Thielemann.

Deutsche Staatsoper Berlin: Unter den Linden 7, 1060 Berlin; tel. 49 30 20 354555; fax 49 30 20 354481; Gen. Music Dir Daniel Barenboim; Man. Georg Quander.

Deutsch-Sorbisches Volkstheater Bautzen: Seminarstrasse 12, 8600 Bautzen; Music Dir Dieter Kempe; Man. Michael Grosse.

Düsseldorf Heinrich-Heine-Alle 16a, 40213 Düsseldorf; tel. 49 211 89080; fax 49 211 890 8389 Gen. Music Dir Zoltan Pesko; Gen. Man. Kurt Horres.

Eduard-von-Winterstein-Theater: Buchholzer Strasse 67, 9300 Anna-berg-Buchholz; Music Dir Ulrich Sprenger; Man. Hans-Hermann Krug.

Elbe-Saale-Bühnen Wittenberg-Bernburg: Thomas-Müntzer-Strasse 14–15, 4600 Wittenberg; Music Dir Klaus Hofmann; Man. Helmut Blass.

Hamburgische Staatsoper: Grosse Theaterstrasse 34, 20354 Hamberg, Germany; tel. tel. 040 3568-0; website www.hamburgische-staatsoper.de.

Hans Otto Theater Potsdam: Berliner Strasse 27a (Schiffbauergasse), 14467 Potsdam; tel. 49 331 9811 0; fax 49 331 9811 280; e-mail hansottotheater@t-online.de; website www.hot.potsdam.de; Man. Dir Volkmar Raback; Art Dir Ralf-Günter Krolkiewicz.

Hessisches Staatstheater: Christian-Zais-Strasse 3–5, Pf 3247, 6200 Wiesbaden; Gen. Music Dir Oleg Caetani; Man. Claus Leininger.

Kammeroper Frankfurt: Nordenstrasse 60, 6000 Frankfurt am Main; tel. and fax 49 69 55 6189; Music Dir Martin Krähe; Artistic Dir Rainer Pudenz.

Kammeroper-Niedersachsen: Eibenstrasse 5c, 3012 Langenhagen; Music Dir Wolfgang M. Sieben; Man. Helmut M. Erlwein.

Kleist-Theater: Gerhart-Hauptmann-Strasse, 1200 Frankfurt an der Oder; Gen. Music Dir Nikos Athinäos; Maria-Luise Preuss.

Komische Oper Berlin: Behrenstrasse 55–57, 10117 Berlin; tel. 49 30 20 2600; fax 49 30 20 260405; Gen. Music Dir: Kirill Petrenko; Man.: Andreas Homoki.

Landesbühne Sachsen-Anhalt Lutherstadt Eisleben: An der Land-wehr 5, 4250 Eisleben; Music Dir Paul Sergiou; Man. Frank Hofmann.

Landesbühnen Sachsen: Meissner Strasse 152, 01445 Dresden; tel. 49 351 704; fax 49 351 704201; Music Dir Joachim Widlak; Man. Christian Schmidt.

Landestheater Altenburg: Theaterplatz 19, 7400 Altenburg; Man. Georg Mittendrein.

Landestheater Coburg: Schlossplatz 6, 8630 Coburg; Gen. Music Dir Christian Fröhlich; Man. Ernö Weil.

Landestheater Dessau: Fritz-Hesse-Platz 1, 4500 Dessau; Man. Johannes Felsenstein.

Landestheater Detmold: Theaterplatz 1, 4930 Detmold; Man. Ulf Reiher.

Landestheater Mecklenburg: Friedrich-Ludwig-Jahn-Strasse, 2080 Neustrelitz; Music Dir Golo Berg; Man. Manfred Straube.

Landestheater und Landeskapelle Eisenach: Theaterplatz 4–7, 5900 Eisenach; Gen. Music Dir Harke de Roos; Man. Jürgen Fabritius.

Münchner Opernbühne (Deutsches-Tourneetheater): Dambor-strasse 11, 8900 Augsburg; Conductors Paul Popescu, Tams Sulyok; Man. Kurt Rösler.

Mecklenburgisches Staatstheater Schwerin: Alter Garten, 2751 Schwerin.

Minipolitan-Eschweges Kleine Schaubühne e V: Niederhoner Strasse 2, 3440 Eschwege; Conductors Andreas Paetzold, Andreas Worm.

Musiktheater im Revier: Kennedyplatz, Pf 101854, 4650 Gelsen-kirchen; tel. 49 209 4097-138; fax 49 209 4097-262; website www .musiktheater-im-revier.de; Gen. Music Dir Neil Varon; Gen. Man. Ludwig Baum.

Musiktheater Oberlausitz/Niederschlesien GmbH: Demianiplatz 2, 02826 Görlitz; tel. 49 3581-47 47 21; e-mail info@theater-goerlitz.de; website www.theater-goerlitz.de; Music Dir Eckehard Stier; Man. Dr Michael Wieler.

Nationaltheater Mannheim: Mozartstrasse 9, 68161 Mannheim; tel. 49 621 16800; fax 49 621 21540; Chief Conductor Jun Märkl; Man. Klaus Schultz.

Neuburger Kammeroper: Willstätter Strasse 18, 8070 Ingolstadt.

Neue Flora: Stresemannstrasse 159a, 2000 Hamburg 50; Music Dir David Caddick.

Niedersächsische Staatstheater Hannover: Opernhaus, Opernplatz 1, 30159 Hannover; tel. 49 511168 6161; fax 49 511 368 1768/363; Gen. Music Dir Christof Prick; Man. Hans-Peter Lehmann.

Offenbach-Theater Köln: Vietorstrasse 70, 5000 Cologne 91; Dir Karl-Wolfgang Saalmann.

Oldenburgisches Staatstheater: Theaterwall 18, 2900 Oldenburg; Gen. Music Dir Knut Mahike; Gen. Man.; Hans Häckermann.

Oper der Stadt Bonn: Am Boeselagerhof 1, Pf 2440, 53111 Bonn; tel. 49 228 7281; fax 49 228 728371; Man. Gian-Carlo del Monaco.

Oper der Stadt Köln: Offenbachplatz, Pf 180241, 50505 Cologne; tel. 49 221 221 8282/8400; Gen. Music Dir James Conlon; Man. Michael Hampe.

Oper Frankfurt: Untermainanlage 11, 6000 Frankfurt; tel. 49 69 37 333; fax 49 69 237 330; website www.oper-frankfurt.de; Gen. Music Dir Sylvain Cambreling; Press and Information Brigitta Mazamec.

Oper Leipzig-Musikalische Komödie: Dreilindenstrasse 30, 04109 Leipzig; tel. 49 341 12610; fax 49 341 12 61387; Music Dir Roland Seiffarth; Man. Udo Zimmermann.

Oper Leipzig-Opernhaus: Augustusplatz 12, 7010 Leipzig; website www.oper-leipzig.de; Man. Udo Zimmermann.

Operettenhaus Hamburg: Spielbudenplatz 1, 2000 Hamburg 36; Music Dir Koen Schoots.

Opernhaus Halle: Universitätsring 24, 4020 Halle an der Saale; Music Dir Wolfgang Balzer; Man. Klaus Froboese.

Pfalztheater Kaiserslautern: Willy Brandt-Platz 4–5, 67657 Kaiser-slautern; tel. 631-36750; e-mail info@pfalztheater.bv-pfalz.de; website www.pfalztheater.de; Gen. Music Dir Francesco Corti; Man. Johannes Reitmeier; opera, operetta, musical, ballet.

Pocket Opera Company Nürnberg: Gertrudstrasse 21, 90429 Nürn-berg; tel. 49 911 329047; fax 49 911 314606; e-mail info@pocket-opera.com; website www.pocket-opera.com; Artistic Dir Peter B. Wyrsch.

Sächsische Staatsoper Dresden (Semperoper): Theaterplatz 2, 01067 Dresden; tel. 49 351 49110; fax 49 351 491 1691; Music Dir Giuseppe Sinopoli; Man. Christoph Albrecht.

Süddeutsche Kammeroper: Am Eselsberg 10–12, 7900 Ulm.

Südostbayerisches Städtetheater (Fürstbischöfliches Oper-nhaus): Gottfried-Schäffer-Strasse 2, 8390 Passau; Music Dir Jeanpierre Faber; Man. Klaus Schlette.

Saarländisches Staatstheater: Schillerplatz, 66111 Saarbrücken; tel. 49 681 30920; fax 49 681 309 2325.

Schleswig-Holsteinisches Landestheater und Sinfonieorchester: Rathausstrasse 22, 2390 Flensburg; Gen. Music Dir Gerhard Schneider; Gen. Man. Dr Horst Mesalla.

Sorbisches National-Ensemble Bautzen: Aussere Lauenstrasse 2, 8600 Bautzen; Music Dir Jan Bulank; Man. Detlef Kobjela.

Städtebundtheater: Schützenstrasse 8, 8670 Hof an der Saale; Music Dir Klaus Straube; Man. Reinhold Röttger.

Städtische Bühnen Dortmund: Kuhstrasse 12, 4600 Dortmund; tel. 00 49 231 5027222; Gen. Music Dir Moshe Atzmon; Gen. Man. Horst Fechner; Artistic Dir John Dew.

Städtische Bühnen Freiburg: Bertoldstrasse 46, 79098 Freiburg im Breisgau; tel. 49 761 2012807; Music Dir Kwamé Ryan.

Städtische Bühnen Münster: Neubrückenstrasse 63, 4400 Münster; Gen. Music Dir Will Humburg; Gen. Man. Achim Thorwald.

Städtische Bühnen Nürnberg: Richard-Wagner-Platz 2–10, 90443 Nürnberg; tel. 49 911 231 3500; fax 49 911 231 3571; Gen. Man. Lew Bogdan.

Städtische Bühnen Osnabrück GmbH: Domhof 110-1, 4500 Osnabrück; Gen. Music Dir Jean-François Monnard; Man. Norbert Kleine-Borgmann.

Städtische Bühnen Regensburg: Bismarckplatz 7, 93047 Regensburg; tel. 49 941 507 1422; fax 49 941 507 4429; Gen. Music Dir Hilary Griffiths; Man. Marietheres List.

Städtische Theater Chemnitz: Theaterplatz 2, 9001 Chemnitz; Gen. Music Dir Dieter-Gerhardt Worm; Gen. Man. Jörg Liljeberg.

Städttheater Würzburg: Theaterstrasse 21, 8700 Würzburg; Gen. Music Dir Jonathan Seers; Man. Dr Tebbe Harms Kleen.

Staatsoperette Dresden: Pirnaer Landstrasse 131, 8045 Dresden; Music Dir Volker Münch; Man. Elke Schneider.

Staatstheater am Gärtnerplatz 3: 80469 Munich; tel. 089 20241 1; fax 089 20241-237; website www.staatstheater-am-gaertnerplatz.de; Music Dir: David Stahl; Man.: Prof. Klaus Schultz.

Staatstheater Braunschweig: PO Box 4539, 38100 Braunschweig; tel. 49 531 484 2700; fax 49 531 484 2727; Gen. Music Dir Jonas Alber; Gen. Man. Jürgen Flügge.

Staatstheater Cottbus: Karl-Liebknecht-Strasse 136, 7500 Cottbus; Gen. Music Dir Frank Morgenstern; Man. Johannes Steurich.

Staatstheater Darmstadt: PO Box 111432, 64229 Darmstadt; tel. 49 6151 28111; fax 49 6151 281 1226; Man. Peter Girth.

Staatstheater Mainz: Gutenbergplatz 7, 55116 Mainz; Gen. Music Dir Catherine Rückhardt; Man. Georges Delnon.

Staatstheater Stuttgart: Oberer Schlossgarten 6, 70173 Stuttgart; tel. 49 711 203 2520; fax 49 711 203 2514; website www.staatstheater .stuttgart.de; Music Dir Lothar Zagrosek; Gen. Dir Klaus Zehlein.

Stadttheater Aachen: Theaterplatz, 5100 Aachen; Music Dir Marcus R. Bosch; Gen. Man. Dr Paul Esterhazy.

Stadttheater Bremerhaven: Theodor-Heuss-Platz, Pf 120541, 27519 Bremerhaven; tel. 49 471 482 0645; fax 49 471 482 0682; Gen. Music Dir Leo Plettner; Man. Dirk Böttger.

Stadttheater Döbein: Theaterstrasse, 7300 Döbein; Music Dir Harald Weigel; Man. Wolfram Jacobi.

Stadttheater Freiberg: Borngasse 1, 9200 Freiberg; Music Dir Jany Renz; Man. Rüdiger Bloch.

Stadttheater Giessen GmbH: Berliner Platz, 65390 Giessen; tel. 0641 79 57 12; fax 0641 79 57 26; e-mail stadttheater-giessen.intendanz@t -online.de; website www.stadttheatergiessen.de; Gen. Music Dir Carlos Spierer; Man. Cathérine Miville.

Stadttheater Hildesheim GmbH: Theaterstrasse 6, 3200 Hildesheim; Music Dir Werner Seitzer; Man. Klaus Engeroff.

Stadttheater Lüneburg: An den Reeperbahnen 3, 2120 Lüneburg; Music Dir Michael Dixon; Man. Jan Aust.

Stadttheater Pforzheim: Am Waisenhausplatz 5, 75217 Pforzheim; tel. 7231 391488; fax 7231 391485; e-mail theater@stadt-pforzheim.de; website www.theater-pforzheim.de; Gen. Music Dir and Artistic Dir: Jari Hämäläinen.

Starlighttheater Bochum: Stadionring 24, 4630 Bochum; Music Dir Phil Edwards.

Thüringer Landestheater: Anger 1, 6820 Rudolstadt; Music Dir Konrad Bach; Man. Peter P. Pachl.

Theater an der Rott: Pfarrkirchener Strasse 70, 8330 Eggenfelden; Music Dir Lutz Teschendorf; Man. Adi Fischer.

Theater Augsburg: Kasernstrasse 4–6, 86152 Augsburg; tel. 49 821 32449; fax 49 821 3244544; e-mail theater@augsburg.de; website www .theater.augsburg.de; Gen. Music Dir: Rudolf Piehlmayer; Man.: Dr Ulrich Peters.

Theater der Hansestadt Stralsund: Olof-Palmer-Platz, 2300 Stralsund; Music Dir Daniel Kleiner; Man. Thomas Bayer.

Theater der Landeshauptstadt Magdeburg: Pf 1240, 39002 Magdeburg; tel. 49 391 540 6500; fax 49 391 540 6599; Gen. Music Dir Mathias Husmann; Gen. Man. Max K. Hoffmann.

Theater der Stadt Gummersbach: Reininghause Strasse, 5270 Gummersbach; Music Dir and Man. Gus Anton.

Theater der Stadt Heidelberg: Friedrichstrasse 5, 69117 Heidelberg; tel. 49 6221 583502; fax 49 6221 583599; Gen. Music Dir: Thomas Kalb; Man.: Günther Beelitz.

Theater der Stadt Koblenz: Clemensstrasse 1, 5400 Koblenz 1; Gen. Music Dir Christian Klutting; Man. Hannes Houska.

Theater der Stadt Trier: Am Augustinerhof, 5500 Trier; Gen. Music Dir Reinhard Petersen.

Theater des Westens Berlin: Kantstrasse 12, 1000 Berlin; Music Dir Peter Keuschnig; Man. Helmut Baumann.

Theater Greifswald: Anklamer Strasse 106, 2200 Greifswald; Chief Conductor Ekkehard Klemm; Man. Dieter Wagner.

Theater Hagen: Elberfelder Strasse 65, 58095 Hagen; Artistic Dir: Rainer Friedemann; Music Dir: Antony Hermus.

Theater Halberstadt: Spiegelstrasse 20a, 3600 Halberstadt; Music Dir Christian Hammer; Man. Gero Hammer.

Theater-Hof: Kulmbacherstrasse 5, 95030 Hof; e-mail info@theater-hof .com; website www.theater-hof.com.

Theater Kiel: Rathausplatz 4, 24103 Kiel; tel. 49 431 901 2880; fax 49 431 901 2838; e-mail info@theater-kiel.de; website www.kiel.de/buehnen; Artistic Dir (Opera): Anette Berg; Gen. Music Dir: Georg Fritesch.

Theater Nordhausen: Käthe-Kollwitz-Strasse 15, Pf 109, 5500 Nordhausen; Man. Hubert Kross.

Theater und Philharmonie Essen: Rolandstrasse 10, 4300 Essen 1; Gen. Music Dir Wolf-Dieter Hauschild.

Theater Zeitz: August-Bebel-Strasse 2, 4900 Zeitz; Music Dir Hans-Frieder Liebmann; Man. Wolfgang Eysold.

Theater Zwickau: Gewandhausstrasse 7, Pf 308, 9541 Zwickau; Music Dir Albrecht Hofmann; Man. Horst-Dieter Brand.

Ulmer Theater: Olgastrasse 73, 7900 Ulm; Gen. Music Dir Alicja Mounk; Man. Dr Bernd Wilms.

Vereinigte Städtische Bühnen Krefeld und Mönchengladbach: Theater Mönchengladbach, Odenkirchener Strasse 78, 41236 Mönchengladbach; tel. 2166-6151; fax 2166-420110; website www.theater-krefeld -moenchengladbach.de; Gen. Dir Jens Pesel.

Vogtland-Theater Plauen: Theaterstrasse 1–3, 9900 Plauen; Music Dir Paul Theissen; Man. Dieter Roth.

Volkstheater Rostock: Patriotischer Weg 33, 2500 Rostock; Gen. Music Dir Michael Zilm; Gen. Man. Berndt Renne.

Wuppertaler Bühnen: Bundesallee 260, 42103 Wuppertal; tel. 49 202 563 4261; fax 49 202 563 8078; Gen. Music Dir George Hanson; Gen. Man. Gerd Leo Kuck.

Greece

Greek National Opera: 18-A Harilaou Trikoupi St, 106 79 Athens; tel. 30 1 363 3105; fax 30 1 360 0224; e-mail info@nationalopera.gr; website www .nationalopera.gr; Chief Conductor L. Karytinos.

Hungary

Csokonai Szinház (Csokonai Theatre): PO Box 79, 4001 Debrecen.

Magyar Állami Operaház (Hungarian State Opera House): Andrássy út 22, 1061 Budapest; tel. (1) 312-4642; fax (1) 332-7331; e-mail opera@opera.hu; website www.opera.hu; Gen. Dir Miklós Szinetár; Music Dir Emil Petrovics.

Pécsi Nemzeti Szinhás (Pécs National Theatre): PO Box 126, 7601 Pécs.

Szegedi Nemzeti Szinház (Szeged National Theatre): PO Box 69, 6701 Szeged.

Iceland

The Icelandic Opera: Ingolfsstraeti, PO Box 1416, 121 Reykjavík; tel. 354 511 6400; fax 354 552 7384; e-mail opera@opera.is; website www.opera .is; Gen. Dir: Bjarni Danielsson; Music Dir: Kurt Kopecky.

Ireland

Opera Ireland: The Schoolhouse, 1 Grantham Street, Dublin 8; tel. 353 1 478 6041; fax 353 1 478 6046; e-mail info@opera-ireland.ie; website www .operaireland.com; Exec. Dir David Collopy; Artistic Dir Dieter Kaegi.

Opera Theatre Company: Temple Bar Music Centre, Curve Street, Dublin 2; tel. 353 1 679 4962; fax 353 1 679 4963; e-mail info@opera.ie; website www.opera.ie; Dir James Conway.

Israel

New Israeli Opera: 28 Leonardo da Vinci St, PO Box 33321, Tel-Aviv 61332; tel. 972 3 6927803; fax 972 3 6954886; e-mail opera@mail.israel-opera.co.il; website www.israel-opera.co.il; Music Dir Asher Fisch.

Italy

Arena di Verona: Piazza Bra 28, 37121 Verona; tel. 390 45 590109; fax 390 45 590201/8011566; website www.arena.it.

Teatro Alighieri: Piazza Garibaldi 5, 48100 Ravenna; website www.teatroalighieri.org.

Teatro alla Scala di Milano: Via Filodrammatici 2, 20121 Milan; tel. 39 2 88 791; fax 39 2 887 9331; website www.lascala.milano.it; Artistic Dir Roman Vlad; Musical Dir Riccardo Muti.

Teatro Arena Sferisterio: Piazza Mazzini 10, 62100 Macerata; tel. 39 733 26 1335; fax 39 733 26 1449.

Teatro Coccia: Via Fratelli Resselli 4, 28100 Novara; website www.teatrococcia.it; Artistic Dir Carlo Pesta.

Teatro Comunale del Giglio: Piazza del Giglio, 55100 Lucca; tel. 39 583 44 2101.

Teatro Comunale dell'Opera de Genoa: Passo al Teatro 4, 16121 Genoa; tel. 39 10 53811.

Teatro Comunale di Bologna: Largo Respighi 1, 40126 Bologna; tel. 390 51 52 9901; fax 390 51 52 9934/9905; website www.bolognacomunale.it; Chief Conductor Danielle Gatti.

Teatro Comunale di Firenze: Via Solferino 15, 50123 Florence; tel. 390 55 27791; fax 390 55 239 6954; Principal Conductor Zubin Mehta.

Teatro Comunale G. B. Pergolesi: Piazza della Repubblica, 60035 Jesi; tel. 39 731 59788; website www.teatropergolesi.org.

Teatro Comunale G. Verdi: Via Palestro 40, 56200 Pisa; website www.teatrodipisa.pi.it.

Teatro Comunale: TEATRI spa, Piazza San Leonardo 1, 31100 Treviso; tel. 0422 513 300; fax 0422 513 306; e-mail teatrispa@fondazionecassamarca.it; website www.teatrispa.it.

Teatro Comunale: Corso Vittorio Emanuele 52, 26100 Cremona; tel. 39 372 407273.

Teatro Comunale: G. Verdi di Trieste, Riva Novembre 1, 34121 Trieste; tel. 39 40 6722111; fax 39 40 6722 249.

Teatro Comunale: Corso Giovecca 12, 44100 Ferrara; website www.teatrocomunaleferrara.it.

Teatro Comunale: Via del Teatro 8, 41100 Modena; tel. 39 059 225 443; website www.teatrocomunalemodena.it.

Teatro dell'Opera di Roma: Piazza B. Gigli 8, 00184 Rome; tel. 39 648 81601; fax 39 6 488 1253.

Teatro Donizetti: Piazza Cavour 14, 24100 Bergamo.

Teatro Grande: Via Paganora 19, 25121 Brescia; tel. 39 030 29 79 311.

Teatro La Fenice di Venezia: Campo S. Fantin 2519, 30100 Venice; website www.teatrolafenice.it.

Teatro Lirico G. Pierluigi da Palestrina di Cagliari: Viale Regina Margherita 6, 09100 Cagliari.

Teatro Massimo Bellini: Via Perrotta 12, 95131 Catania; website www.teatromassimobellini.it.

Teatro Massimo di Palermo: Via R. Wagner 2, 90139 Palermo; tel. 39 91 605 3111; fax 39 91 605 3324/5.

Teatro Municipale Romolo Valli: Piazza Martiri 7 Luglio, 42100 Reggio Emilia; tel. 39 052 245 8811; fax 39 052 245 8922.

Teatro Municipale: Via Verdi 41, 29100 Piacenza; tel. 39 523 49 2254.

Teatro Petruzzelli: Via Cognetti 26, 70100 Bari.

Teatro Politearna Greco: Via XXV Luglio 30, 73100 Lecce.

Teatro Regio di Torino: Piazza Castello 215, 10124 Turin; tel. 39 011 88151; fax 39 011 881 5214.

Teatro Regio: Via Garibaldi 16, 43100 Parma; tel. 39 521 218912; fax 39 521 206156.

Teatro San Carlo di Napoli: Via San Carlo, 80132 Naples; tel. 39 81 797 2111; fax 39 81 797 2309; Artistic Dir Carlos Mayer.

Teatro Sociale: Piazza Cavollotti, 46100 Mantua; tel. 39 037 632 3860; fax 39 037 636 2739.

Teatro Sociale: Piazza Garibaldi 14, 45100 Rovigo.

Teatro Sociale: Via Bellini 3, 22100 Como; website www.teatrosocialecomo.it.

Japan

Kansai Nikkai Opera Company: 3-3-9 Bingo-cho, Chyno-ku, Osaka; Dir Makoto Kikawada.

Kansai Opera Group: 3-57 Kyobashi, Higashi-ku, Osaka; Dir Takashi Asahina.

Nihon Opera Shinkokai (Japanese Opera Foundation): Nishiazabu 28, Mori Building, 4-16-13 Nishiazabu, Minato-ku, Tokyo 106; tel. 81 3 5466 3181; fax 813 5466 3186; Chair. Seiya Matsumoto.

Republic of Korea

National Opera Group: c/o The National Theatre, Jangchoong-dong, Choong-ku, Seoul.

Latvia

Latvian National Opera: Aspazijas Blvd 3, 1050 Riga; tel. 371 707 3715; fax 371 722 8930; e-mail info@opera.lv; website www.opera.lv; Gen. Dir: Andrejs Zagars; Principal Conductor: Andris Nelsons.

Lithuania

Lithuanian State Opera and Ballet Theatre: Vienuolio 1, 232600 Vilnius; tel. 370 2 620093; fax 370 2 623503; Chief Conductor Rimas Geniuas; Admin. Zigmas Pieaitis.

Luxembourg

Théâtre Municipal: 2525 Luxembourg; Dir Jeannot Comes.

Mexico

Compañía Nacional de Opera Palacio de Bellas Artes: Avda Hidalgo 1, 3°, Centro, Mexico City, DF 06050; tel. 525 521 3668; fax 525 521 6776; Gen. Dir Gerardo Kleinburg.

Monaco

Opera de Monte Carlo: Place du Casino, 98000 Monte Carlo; tel. 377 92 162318; fax 377 92 16 37 77; website www.opera.mc; Dir John Mordler.

Netherlands

De Nederlandse Opera: Waterlooplein 22, 1011 PG, Amsterdam; tel. 31 20 551 8922; fax 3120 551 8311; e-mail info@nederlandse-opera.nl; website www.dno.nl; Artistic Dir Pierre Audi; Man. Dir Truze Lodder.

Nationale Reisopera: PO Box 1321, 7500 GH, Enschede; tel. 3153 4878500; fax 31 53 4321882; website www.reisopera.nl.

New Zealand

Auckland Opera Company: PO Box 77066, Mount Albert, Auckland 1; tel. 64 9 846 7433; fax 64 9846 7141; Gen. Man. Stephen Morrison.

Canterbury Regional Opera Trust: PO Box 176, Christchurch 1; Chair. Lewis Brown.

Dunedin Opera Company: PO Box 533, Dunedin; Chair. Ian Page.

National Opera: State Opera House, PO Box 6588, Te Aro, Wellington; tel. 64 4 384 4434; fax 64 4 384 3333; Man. Patricia Hurley.

NBR New Zealand Opera: PO Box 6478, Wellesley Street, Auckland; tel. 64 9 379 4068; fax 64 9 3794066; website www.nzopera.com; Gen. Dir Alex Reedijk.

Norway

Den Norske Opera: PO Box 8800 Youngstorget, 0028 Oslo; tel. 47 22 42 9475; fax 47 22 33 4027; website www.operaen.no; Artistic Dir Sven Olaf Eliasson.

Opera Bergen: Komediebakken 9, 5010 Bergen; tel. 47 55 32 3856; fax 47 55 32 24 35; e-mail vno@cdi.net; Artistic Dir Anne Randine Øverby.

Operaen i Kristiansund: PO Box 401, 6501 Kristiansund N; tel. 47 71 677733; fax 47 71 676657.

Trondheim Opera: Kongsgårdsgt 2, 7013 Trondheim; tel. 47 73 52 56 65.

Poland

Baltic Opera: Al Zwyciêstwa 15, 80-219 Gdańsk; tel. 48 58 763 4912; fax 48 58 763 4914; website www.operabaltycka.pl.

Kraków Music Theatre: Senacka 6, 31-002 Kraków.

Łódz Grand Theatre: Plac Dâbrowskiego, 90-249 Łódz.

Opera Nova: 20 Gdanska St, 85-006 Bydgoszcz; tel. 0048 52 322 4985; fax 0048 52 3225950; e-mail promacja@opera.bydgoszcz.pl; website www .opera.bydgoszcz.pl; Artistic and Gen. Dir Maciej Figas.

Poznán Grand Theatre: Fredry 9, 60-967 Poznán.

Silesian Opera: Moniuszki 21, 41-902 Bytom; tel. 48 32 281 3431; fax 48 32 281 4335.

The National Opera: Grand Theatre, Plac Teatrainy 1, 00-950 Warsaw; tel. 48 22 826 3289; fax 48 22 826 0423.

Warsaw Chamber Opera: Nowogrodzka 49, 00-695 Warsaw; tel. 48 22 628-30-96; fax 48 22 629-32-33; e-mail artmgmt@wok.pol.pl; website www .wok.pol.pl; Man. and Artistic Dir Stefan Sutkowski; Deputy Man. and Artistic Dir Edward Pallasz; repertoire spans wide range of musical styles and genres; also holds annual festivals and numerous concerts.

Wroclaw State Opera: Swidnicka 35, 50-066 Wroclaw.

Portugal

Companhia de Opera do Teatro Nacional Sao Carlos: Rua Serpa Pinto 9, 1200 Lisbon; tel. 35 1 346 8408.

Teatro Nacional de Sao Carlos: Rua Serpa Panto noG, 1200 442 Lisbon; tel. 3 51 21 34 68 408; fax 3 51 21 34 71 738; website www2.saocarlos.pt.

Romania

Bucharest State Operetta: Str Operetei 4, Bucharest.

Cluj-Napoca Hungarian Opera: Str 1 Mai 26-28, Cluj-Napoca.

Cluj-Napoca Romanian Opera: Piata Stefan cel Mare 24, 3400 Cluj-Napoca.

Iasi Musical Theatre: Str 9 Mai nr 18, 6600 Iasi.

Romanian State Opera: Blvd Mihail Kogainiceanu 70–72, 70609 Bucharest.

Timisoara State Opera: Str M r sesti 2, Timisoara.

Russia

Bolshoi Theatre: 1 Teatralnaya Square, Moscow; tel. 7 095 292 9986; website www.bolshoi.ru; Music Dir Mark Ermler.

Kirov Opera: 1 Theatre Square, St Petersburg; tel. 7 812 314 9083; Chief Conductor Valery Gergiev.

Maly Opera: St Petersburg; Artistic Dir N. Boyarchicov.

Serbia and Montenegro

Narodno Pozoriste (National Theatre Opera Company): Francuska 3, 11000 Belgrade; tel. 381 11 624565; fax 381 11 622560; e-mail npozor@ eunet.yu; Gen. Man. and Principal Conductor Dejan Saviá.

Slovakia

Bratislava Chamber Opera: Fuikova 3, 816 01 Bratislava; Musical Dir Marián Vach.

Kosice State Theatre Opera: robárova 14, PO Box E-47, 042 77 Kosice; Musical Dir Igor Dohovic.

Slovak National Theatre Opera: Gorkého 4, 815 06 Bratislava; tel. 00421 7 544 35085; fax 00421 7 544 35072; Artistic Dir Ondrej Lenard; Dir of the Opera Juraj Hrubant.

Slovenia

Slovenian National Theatre Opera: Zupanciceva 1, 61000 Ljubljana; website www.sngdrama-lj.si.

South Africa

Johannesburg Operatic and Dramatic Society: PO Box 7010, Johannesburg 2000.

Opera of the Cape Performing Arts Board: PO Box 4107, Cape Town 8000; tel. 27 21 215470; fax 27 21 215 448.

Opera of the Natal Performing Arts Council: PO Box 5353, Durban 4000, Natal.

Opera of the Orange Free State Performing Arts Council: PO Box 1292, Bloemfontein 9300; Gen. Dir Fred Sharp.

Opera of the Performing Arts Council, Transvaal: PO Box 566, Pretoria 0001; tel. 2712 322 1665; fax 2712 322 3913; Gen. Man. Johan Maré.

Spain

Gran Teatre del Liceu: La Rambla 51–59, 08002 Barcelona; tel. 34 93 4859900; fax 34 93 4859918; website www.liceubarcelona.com; Artistic Dir Joan Matabosch; Music Dir Bertrand de Billy.

Madrid Opera: Teatro Real, Plaza de Oriente s/n, 28013 Madrid; tel. 34 91 5160600; fax 34 91 5160651; e-mail info@teatro-real.com; website www .teatro-real.com; Gen. Dir Inés Argüelles; Artistic Dir Emilio Sag.

Teatro de la Zarzuela: Jovellanos, 28014, Madrid; tel. 34 1 429 8225; fax 34 1 429 7157; website www.teatrodelazarzuela.mcu.es.

Sweden

Drottningholms Slottsteater: PO Box 15417, 10465 Stockholm; tel. 46 8 556 931 00; fax 46 8 556 931 01; website www.drottningholmsslottsteater .dtm.se; Artistic Dir Per Erik Ohrn.

Folkoperan: Hornsgatan 72, 118 21 Stockholm; tel. 46 8 616 0750/0700; fax 46 8 44146; website www.folkoperan.se; Music Dir Kerstin Nerbe.

Göteborgs Operan: Christina Nilssons Gatan, 411 04 Göteborg; tel. 46 31 1080; fax 46 31 1080 30; Man. Dir Dag Hallberg.

Kungliga Operan AB (Royal Swedish Opera): PO Box 16094, 103 22 Stockholm; tel. 46 8 791 4300; fax 46 8 791 4444; website www.operan.se; Gen. Man. Bengt Hall.

Malmö Stadsteater: PO Box 17520, 200 10 Malmö; Dir Lars Rudolfsson.

Norriandsoperan: PO Box 360, 901 08 Umea; tel. 46 0 90154300; fax 46 0 90126845; Artistic Dir Jonas Forsell.

Switzerland

Grand Théâtre de Genève: 11 Blvd du Théâtre, 1211 Geneva 11; tel. 41 22 418 3000; fax 41 22 418 3001; website www.geneveopera.ch; Gen. Dir Renée Auphan.

Opéra de Lausanne: PO Box 3972, 1002 Lausanne; tel. 41 21 310 1616; fax 41 21 310 1690; e-mail opera@lausanne.ch; website www.opera -lausanne.ch.

Opernhaus Zürich: Falkenstrasse 1, 8008 Zürich; tel. 41 1 268 6400/ 6666; fax 41 1 268 6401/6555; website www.opernhaus.ch; Chief Conductor Franz Welser-Möst.

Stadttheater Bern: Nägeligasse 1, 3011 Bern; tel. 41 31 329 5111; fax 41 31 329 5100; website www.staadtheaterbern.ch; Admin. Ernst Gosteli.

Stadttheater Biel: Burggasse 19, 2502 Biel; tel. 41 32 328 8970; fax 41 32 328 8967; website www.ensemble-theater.ch; Admin. Mario Bettoli.

Stadttheater Lucerne: Theaterstrasse 2, 6002 Lucerne; tel. 4141 210 6618/9; fax 4141 210 3367; Music Dir Jonathan Nott.

Stadttheater St Gallen: Museumstrasse 24, 9000 St Gallen; tel. 41 71 242 0505; fax 41 71 242 0506; website www.theatersg.ch; Dir Werner Signer.

Theater Basel: Elisabethenstrasse 16, 4010 Basel; tel. 41 61 295 1460; fax 41 61 295 1590; website www.theater-basel.ch; Chief Conductor Julia Jones.

Turkey

Istanbul State Opera and Ballet: Atatürk Merkezi, Taksim, 80090 Istanbul; tel. 90 212 245 16 36.

Izmir State Opera and Ballet: Izmir; website www.izdob.gov.tr.

Turkish State Opera and Ballet: Opera Binasi, Ankara.

Ukraine

Lviv S. Krushelnytskyi State Academic Opera: 79000 Lviv, pr. Svobody; tel. (322) 72-85-62; internet www.lvivopera.org; f. 1900; Dir Tadei O. Eder; Artistic Dir Myron Yusypovych.

Odesa State Academic Opera: 65026 Odesa, prov. Chaikovskoho 1; e-mail opera-ballet@tm.odessa.ua; website www.opera-ballet.tm.odessa .ua.

Ukrainian National Opera: 01034 Kiev, vul. Volodymrska 50.

United Kingdom

Abbey Opera: 68 Queens Gardens, London W2 3AH; tel. 020 7262 9023; Conductor Antony Shelley; Artistic Dir Mary Hill.

Birmingham Opera Company: 205 The Argent Centre, 60 Frederick Street, Birmingham B1 3HS; tel. (121) 2466644; fax (121) 2466633; Gen. Man.: Jean Nicholson; Artistic Dir: Graham Vick.

Buxton Festival Opera: 5 The Square, Buxton, Derbyshire SK17 6AZ; tel. 01298 70395; e-mail info@buxtonfestival.co.uk; website www.buxtonfestival.co.uk; Gen. Man. Glyn Foley.

Dorset Opera: 26 Central Acre, Yeovil, Somerset BA20 1NU; tel. 01935 479297; fax 01935 412210; e-mail info@dorsetopera.com; website www.dorsetopera.com; Music Dir Patrick Shelley; Admin. Joy Liddiard.

D'Oyly Carte Opera Company: The Power House, 6 Sancroft Street, London SE11 5UD; tel. 020 7793 7100; fax 020 7793 7300; website www.doylycarte.org.uk.

Early Opera Project: 112b High Street, Hungerford, Berkshire RG17 0NB; Musical Dirs Roger Norrington, Kay Lawrence.

English National Opera—ENO: London Coliseum, St Martin's Lane, London WC2N 4ES; tel. 020 7836 0111; fax 020 7845 9277; website www.eno.org; Music Dir Paul Daniel.

Glyndebourne Festival Opera: Glyndebourne, PO Box 2624, Lewes, East Sussex BN8 5UW; tel. (1273) 813813; fax (1273) 814686; website www.glyndebourne.com; Chair.: Gus Christie; Gen. Dir: David Pickard; Music Dir: Vladimir Jurowski.

Glyndebourne on Tour: Glyndebourne, Lewes, East Sussex BN8 5UU; tel. 01273 812321; fax 01273 812783; website www.glyndebourne.com; Music Dir: Edward Gardner; Admin.: Helen McCarthy.

London Chamber Opera: 82 Redcliffe Gardens, London SW10 9HE; tel. 020 7373 8535; Music Dir David Wordsworth.

Midsummer Opera: 90 Grange Road, London W5 3PJ; tel. 020 8579 7477/8840 9560; Music Dir David Roblou; Producer Alan Privett; Chair. David Skewes.

Music Theatre Wales: 5 Llandaff Road, Cardiff CF11 9NF; tel. 029 2023 0833; fax 029 2034 2046; e-mail enquiries@musictheatrewales.org.uk; website www.musictheatrewales.org.uk; Music Dir Abigail Pogson.

Musica nel Chiostro: 377 Liverpool Road, London N1; Dir Adam Pollock.

New Sadler's Wells Opera: Sadler's Wells Theatre, Roseberry Avenue, London EC1R 4TN; Dir Joseph Karaviotis.

New Sussex Opera: 22 Bradford Road, Lewes, East Sussex BN7 1RB; tel. and fax 01273 471851; e-mail mail@newsussexopera.com; website www.jjj.eurobell.co.uk; Gen. Dir David James.

Nexus Opera: 16 Kennington Park Road, London SE11 4AS; tel. 020 7582 0980; fax 020 7582 1444; website www.nexusopera.com; Artistic Dir Delia Lindon.

Opera Anglia: 3–5 Bridge Street, Hadleigh, Suffolk, IP7 6BY; tel. 01473 822596; fax 01473 824175; e-mail thomas.mcintosh@minstrelmusic.demon.co.uk; Artistic Dir Thomas McIntosh.

Opera Brava Ltd: Morley House, 67 Franklynn Road, Haywards Heath, West Sussex, RH16 4DT; tel. 01444 443060; fax 01444 443060; e-mail admin@operabrava.co.uk; website www.operabrava.co.uk; Artistic Dir Bronek Pomorski.

Opera Italiana: 10a Radipole Road, Fulham, London SW6 5DL; tel. 020 7736 3821; fax 020 8447 1664; Artistic Dir Alexander Bryett.

Opera North: Grand Theatre, 46 New Briggate, Leeds, Yorkshire LS1 6NU; tel. (113) 243-9999; fax (113) 244-0418; e-mail info@operanorth.co.uk; website www.operanorth.co.uk; Gen. Dir Richard Mantle; Chair. Michael Beverly; Music Dir Richard Farnes.

Opera Northern Ireland: 35 Talbot Street, Belfast, Northern Ireland BT1 2LD; tel. 01232 322538; fax 01232 32291; Artistic Dir Stephen Barlow; Gen. Man. Tim Kerr.

Opera on the Move: 47 Queen's Drive, London N4 2SZ; Dirs Odaline de la Martinez, Linda Hirst.

Opera Rara Ltd: 134–146 Curtain Road, London EC2A 3AR; tel. 020 7613 2858; fax 020 7613 2261; website www.opera-rara.com; Artistic Dir Patric Schmid.

Opera Restor'd: 54 Astonville Street, London SW18 5AJ; tel. (20) 8870-7649; fax (20) 8516-6313; e-mail info@operarestord.co.uk; website www.operarestord.co.uk; Man.: Caroline Anderson; Music Dir: Peter Holman; Stage Dir: Jack Edwards.

Pavilion Opera Company: Thorpe Tilney Hall, Thorpe Tilney, nr Lincoln LN4 3SL; tel. 01526 378231; fax 01526 378315; Music Dir Peter Bailey; Gen. Man. Freddie Stockdale.

Pisa Opera Group: Flat 2, 79 Linden Gardens, London W2 4EU; tel. 020 7229 7060; Dir Stella J. Wright.

Scottish Opera: 39 Elmbank Crescent, Glasgow G2 4PT; tel. 0141 248 4567; fax 0141 221 8812; e-mail info@scottishopera.org.uk; website www.scottishopera.org.uk; Chief Exec. Chris Barron.

Telemann Opera: 1a Warwick Chambers, Pater Street, London W8 6EN; Artistic Dir Jill Watt.

Thameside Opera: 11 Arden Mhor, Pinner, Middlesex HA5 2HR; tel. 020 8866 3272; fax 020 8429 1179; e-mail thameside.opera@virgin.net; Gen. Man. Maurice F. Maggs; Musical Dir George Badacsonyi.

The Royal Opera: Royal Opera House, Covent Garden, London WC2E 9DD; tel. 020 7212 9502; fax 020 7212 9502; website www.royalopera.org; Music Dir Antonio Pappano; Chair. Colin Southgate; Exec. Chief Tony Hall; Opera Dir Elaine Padmore.

Travelling Opera: 114 St Mary's Road, Market Harborough, Leicestershire LE16 7DT; tel. 01858 434677; fax 01858 463617.

Welsh National Opera: Wales Millennium Centre, Bay Chambers, West Bute Street, Cardiff, CF10 5GG; tel. (29) 2040 2000; fax (29) 2040 2001; e-mail info@wmc.org.uk; website www.wno.org.uk, www.wmc.org.uk; Music Dir Carlo Rizzi; Gen. Dir Anthony Freud.

Wessex Opera: 11 Luccombe Hill, Redland, Bristol BS6 6SN; Music Dir Paul Webster; Gen. Man. Richard Evans.

United States of America

Abilene Opera Association: PO Box 6611, Abilene, TX 79608; tel. 1 915 676 7372; fax 1 915 690 6660.

Albuquerque Civic Light Opera Association: 4201 Ellison NE, Albuquerque, NM 87109; Exec. Dir Linda E. McVey.

American Chamber Opera: PO Box 909, New York, NY 10023; Exec. Dir Doug Anderson.

Anchorage Opera Company Inc: 1507 Spar Avenue, Anchorage, AK 99501; tel. 1 907 279 2557; fax 1 907 279 7798; website www.anchorageopera.org; Dir Peter H. Brown.

Arizona Opera Company: 3501 N Mountain Avenue, Tucson, AZ 85719; tel. 1 520 293 4336; fax 1 520 293 5097; website www.azopera.com; Gen. Dir Clynn Ross; Artistic Dir Joel Revzen.

Ash Lawn-Highland Opera Company: Route 6, PO Box 37, Charlottesville, VA 22901; Gen. Man. Judith H. Walker.

Aspen Music Festival: PO Box AA, Aspen, CO 81612; tel. 1 970 925 3254; fax 1 970 925 3802; Music Dir Lawrence Foster; Pres. and CEO Robert Harth.

Atlanta Opera: 728 Peachtree Street NW, Atlanta, GA 30308; tel. 1 404 881 8801; fax 1 404 881 1711; website www.atlantaopera.org; Artistic Dir William Fred Scott; Gen. Man. Alfred D. Kennedy.

Augusta Opera Company: PO Box 3865, Hill Station, Augusta, GA 30904; Gen. Dir Edward Bradberry.

Austin Lyric Opera: PO Box 984, Austin, TX 78767; tel. 1 512 472 5927; fax 1 512 472 4143; website www.austinlyricopera.org; Artistic Dir Richard Buckley; Man. Dir Tamara Hale.

Baltimore Opera Company Inc: 110 W Mt Royal Avenue, Suite 306, Baltimore, MD 21201; tel. 1 410 625 1600; fax 1 410 625 6474; website www.baltimoreopera.com; Gen. Dir Michael Harrison; Music Dir William Yannuzzi.

Baton Rouge Opera Inc: PO Box 2269, Baton Rouge, LA 70821; Artistic Dir Marioara Trifan.

Beaumont Civic Opera: 1030 Harriot Street, Beaumont, TX 77705; Conductor L. Randolph Babin; Business Man. Delores Black.

Berkeley Opera: 715 Arlington, Berkeley, CA 94707; website www.berkeleyopera.org; Artistic Dir Jonathan Khuner.

Berkshire Opera Company: PO Box 598, 17 Main St, Lee, MA 01238; Artistic Dir Joel Revzen.

Boise Opera Inc: 516 S Ninth Street, Suite B, Boise, ID 83702.

Boston Lyric Opera Company: 45 Franklin Street, Fourth Floor, Boston, MA 02110; tel. 1 617 542 4912; fax 1 617 542 4913; website www.blo.org; Gen. Dir Janice DelSesto; Artistic Dir Leon Major; Music Dir Stephen Lord.

Bronx Opera Company: 5 Minerva Place, Bronx, NY 10468; website www.bronxopera.org; Artistic Dir Michael Spierman.

Casa Italiana Opera Company: 5959 Franklin Avenue, Suite 212, Hollywood, CA 90028; website www.casaitaliana.org; Gen. Dir Mario E. Leonetti.

CCM Opera/Musical Theater: University of Cincinnati College, Conservatory of Music, Cincinnati, OH 45221; Artistic Dir Malcolm Fraser.

Central City Opera: 400 S Colorado Blvd, Suite 530, Denver, CO 80246; tel. (303) 292-6500; fax (303) 292-4958; e-mail admin@centralcityopera.org; website www.centralcityopera.org.

Chattanooga Opera: 630 Chestnut Street, Chattanooga, TN 37402; tel. 1 423 267 8583; fax 1 423 265 6520; website www.chattanoogasymphony.org; Artistic Dir Robert Bernhardt; Man. Dir Donal L. Andrews.

Chautauqua Opera: Chautauqua Institution, Chautauqua, NY 14722; tel. 1 716 357 6200; fax 1 716 357 9014; website opera.ciweb.org; Artistic and Gen. Dir Jay Lesenger.

Chicago Opera Theater: 70 E Lake Street, Suite 540, Chicago, IL 60601; tel. 1 312 704 8420; fax 1 312 704 8421; website www.chicagooperatheater.org; Gen. Dir Brian Dickie.

Cincinnati Opera Association: Music Hall, 1241 Elm Street, Cincinnati, OH 45210; tel. 1 513 621 1919/241 2742; fax 1 513 621 4310; Artistic Dir James de Blasis.

Cleveland Opera: 1422 Euclid Avenue, Suite 1052, Cleveland, OH 44115; tel. (216) 575-0903; fax (216) 575-1918; e-mail mail@clevelandopera.org; website www.clevelandopera.org; Gen. Dir Robert Chumbley.

Connecticut Grand Opera: 61 Atlantic Street, Stamford, CT 06901; Artistic Dir Laurence Gilgore.

Connecticut Opera Association: 226 Farmington Avenue, Hartford, CT 06105; tel. 1 860 527 0713; fax 1 860 293 1715; website www.connecticutopera.org; Gen. and Artistic Dir Willie Anthony Waters.

Dallas Opera: The Centrum, 3102 Oak Lawn Avenue, Suite 450, LB-130, Dallas, TX 75219; website www.dallasopera.org; Music Dir Graeme Jenkins; Gen. Dir Plato Karayanis.

Dayton Opera Association: 138 N Main Street, Dayton, OH 45402; tel. 1 937 228 7591; fax 1 937 449 5068; e-mail info@daytonopera.org; website www.daytonopera.org; Artistic Dir Thomas Bankston; Gen. Dir Jane Nelson.

Des Moines Metro Opera Inc: 106 W Boston Avenue, Indianola, IA 50125; tel. 1 515 961 6221; fax 1 515 961 8175; e-mail dmmo@dmmo.org; website www.dmmo.org; Artistic Dir Robert L. Larsen.

Eugene Opera: PO Box 11200, Eugene, OR 97440; tel. 1 541 485 3895; fax 1 541 683 3783; website www.eugeneopera.com; Artistic Dir Robert Ashens.

Fargo-Moorhead Civic Opera Company: 1104 Second Avenue S, Fargo, ND 58103; tel. 1 701 239 4558; Artistic Dir David F. Martin.

Florentine Opera Company: 700 N Water Street, Suite 950, Milwaukee, WI 53202; tel. 1 414 291 5700; fax 1 414 291 5706; website www.florentineopera.org; Gen. Dir Dennis Hanthorn.

Florida Grand Opera: 1200 Coral Way, Miami, FL 33145; tel. 1 305 854 1643; fax 1 305 856 1042; website www.fgo.org; Music Dir Stewart Robertson; Gen. Man. Robert M. Heuer.

Florida Lyric Opera Association/Lyric Opera Theater: 1183 85 Terrace N, Suite D, St Petersburg, FL 33702-3333; tel. 1 727 578 1657; Gen. Man. Rosalia Maresca.

Fort Worth Opera: 3505 W Lancaster, Fort Worth, TX 76107; website www.fwopera.org; Gen. Dir William Walker.

Fullerton Civic Light Opera: 218 W Commonwealth, Fullerton, CA 92632; website www.fclo.com; Gen. Man. Griff Duncan.

Glimmerglass Opera: PO Box 191, Cooperstown, NY 13326; tel. (607) 547-5704; fax (607) 547-6030; e-mail info@glimmerglass.org; website www.glimmerglass.org; Dir of Artistic Operations: Nicholas G. Russell.

Greensboro Opera Company: PO Box 29031, Greensboro, NC 27429; website www.greensboroopera.org; Conductor Norman Johnson.

Gulf Coast Opera Theatre Inc: PO Box 118, Biloxi, MS 39552; tel. 1 228 436 6514; Pres. Dr Laurence M. Oden.

Hawaii Opera Theater: 987 Waimanu Street, Honolulu, HI 96814; tel. 1 808 596 7372; fax 1 808 596 0379; website www.hawaiiopera.org; Gen. Dir J. Mario Ramos.

Houston Grand Opera Association: 510 Preston Avenue, Houston, TX 77002; Gen. Dir R. David Gockley.

Indiana Opera Theater: 7515 E 30th Street, Indianapolis, IN 46219; Exec./Artistic Dir Elaine Morgan Bookwalter.

Indiana University Opera Theater: School of Music, Indiana University, Bloomington, IN 47405.

Indianapolis Opera: 250 E 38th Street, Indianapolis, IN 46205; tel. 1 317 283 3531; fax 1 317 923 5611; e-mail info@indyopera.org; website www.indyopera.org; Artistic Dir James Caraher.

Ithaca Opera: 116 N Cayuga Street, Ithaca, NY 14850; tel. 1 607 272 0168.

Juilliard Opera Center: The Juilliard School, Lincoln Center for the Performing Arts, New York, NY 10023; Artistic Dir Frank Corsaro.

Kentucky Opera: 101 S Eighth Street, Louisville, KY 40202; tel. 1 502 584 4500; fax 1 502 584 7484; e-mail info@kyopera.org; website www.kyopera.org; Gen. Dir Deborah Sandler; Music Dir Robin Stamper.

Knoxville Opera Company: PO Box 16, Knoxville, TN 37901; tel. 1 865 524 0795; fax 1 865 524 7384; website www.knoxvilleopera.com; Gen. Dir Francis Graffeo.

Lake George Opera Festival: PO Box 2172, Glens Falls, NY 12801; website www.lakegeorgeopera.org; Artistic Dir Joseph Illick.

Lancaster Opera Company: PO Box 8382, Lancaster, PA 17604; tel. 1 717 392 0885; website www.lancasteropera.com; Artistic Dir Dorothy Rose Smith.

Light Opera Works: 927 Noyes Street, Evanston, IL 60201; tel. 1 847 869 6300; fax 1 847 869 6388; website www.light-opera-works.org; Artistic Dir Philip A. Kraus.

Lincoln Opera: 2456 N Surrey Court, Chicago, IL 60614; Artistic Dir Norma M. Williams.

Long Beach Civic Light Opera: PO Box 20280, Long Beach, CA 90801; Exec. Dir J. Phillip Keene III.

Long Beach Opera: PO Box 14895, Long Beach, CA 90853; tel. 1 562 439 2580; fax 1 562 439 2109; website www.longbeachopera.org; Gen. Dir Andreas Mitisek.

Los Angeles Concert Opera: 2250 Gloaming Way, Beverly Hills, CA 90210; Gen. Dir Loren L. Zachary.

Los Angeles Music Center Opera: 135 N Grand Avenue, Los Angeles, CA 90012; tel. 1 213 972 7219; fax 1 213 687 3490; website www.losangelesopera.com; Artistic Dir Placido Domingo.

Lyric Opera Cleveland: PO Box 93046, Cleveland, OH 44101; tel. 1 216 685 5976; website www.lyricoperacleveland.org; Exec. Dir Michael McConnell.

Lyric Opera of Chicago: 20 N Wacker Drive, Chicago, IL 60606; tel. 1 312 332 2244; fax 1 312 419 8345; website www.lyricopera.org/inc; Gen. Dir William Mason; Artistic Dir Matthew Epstein; Music Dir Andrew Davis.

Lyric Opera of Dallas: 8111 Preston Blvd, No. 818, Dallas, TX 75225; Gen. Dir Charles Kuba.

Lyric Opera of Kansas City: 1029 Central, Kansas City, MO 64105; tel. 1 816 471 7344; fax 1 816 471 0602; website kc-opera.org; Gen. Artistic Dir Russell Patterson.

Lyric Theater of Oklahoma: 1727 NW 16th Street, Oklahoma City, OK 73106; tel. 1 405 524 9310; fax 1 405 524 9316; website www.lyrictheatreokc.com; Artistic Dir Nick Dermos.

Madison Opera: 333 Glenway Street, Madison, WI 53705; tel. 1 608 238 8085; fax 1 608 233 3431; e-mail info@madisonopera.org; website www.madisonopera.org; Music Dir Roland Johnson; Man. Ann Stanke.

Manhattan Opera Association: PO Box 475, Planetarium Station, New York, NY 10024; Artistic Dir and Pres. Barbara Norcia.

Metro Lyric Opera: 40 Ocean Avenue, Allenhurst, NJ 07711; tel. 1 732 531 2378; website www.metrolyricopera.org; Gen. and Artistic Dir Erq M. Tognoli.

Metropolitan Opera: Lincoln Center for the Performing Arts, New York, NY 10023; tel. 1 212 799 3100/362 6000; fax 1 212 874 2569; website www.metopera.org; Artistic Dir James Levine; Gen. Dir Joseph Volpe.

Michigan Opera Theater: Detroit Opera House, 1526 Broadway, Detroit, MI 48226; tel. 1 313 961 3500; fax 1 313 237 3412; website www.metopera.org; Gen. Dir David DiChiera.

Milwaukee Opera Company: 820 E Knapp Street, Milwaukee, WI 53202; Exec. Dir Josephine Busalacchi.

Minnesota Opera: 620 N First Street, Minneapolis, MN 55401; tel. (612) 333-2700; fax (612) 333-0869; e-mail staff@mnopera.org; website www.mnopera.org; Pres. and CEO Kevin Smith.

Mississippi Opera: PO Box 1551, Jackson, MS 39215; tel. 1 601 960 2300; fax 1 601 960 1526; website www.msopera.org; Artistic Dir Carroll Freeman.

Mobile Opera Inc: 257 Dauphin Street, Mobile, AL 36602; tel. 1 251 432 6772; e-mail info@mobileopera.org; website www.mobileopera.org; Artistic Dir Jerome Shannon; Gen. Man. Pelham G. Pearce Jr.

National Lyric Opera Company: 5332 Sherrier Place NW, Washington, DC 20016; Gen. Man. Nikita Wells.

National Opera Company: PO Box 12800, Raleigh, NC 27605; Artistic Dir Don Wilder.

Nevada Opera Association: PO Box 3256, Reno, NV 89505; tel. 1 702 786 4046; fax 1 702 786 4063; Artistic Dir Ted Puffer.

New England Lyric Operetta Inc: PO Box 1007, Darien, CT 06820; tel. 203 655 0566; fax 203 655 8066; Pres. William H. Edgerton.

New Jersey State Opera: 50 Park Place, 10th Floor, Newark, NJ 07102; tel. 1 973 539 8970; Gen. Dir Alfredo Silipigni.

New Orleans Opera Association: 305 Baronne Street, Suite 500, New Orleans, LA 70112; tel. 1 504 529 2278; fax 1 504 529 7668; website www .neworleansopera.org; Gen. Dir Robert Tannebaum.

New York City Opera: New York State Theater, Lincoln Center for the Performing Arts, New York, NY 10023; tel. 1 212 870 5633/5600; website www.nycopera.com; Music Dir George Manahan.

New York Gilbert and Sullivan Players Inc: 251 W 91st Street, No. 4c, New York, NY 10024; website www.nygasp.org; Artistic Dir Albert Bergeret.

New York Grand Opera: 154 W 57th Street, Suite 125, New York, NY 10019; website www.newyorkgrandopera.org; Artistic Dir Vincent LaSelva.

North Miami Beach Opera: 5225 La Gorce Drive, Miami Beach, FL 33140; Music Dir Laurence Siegal.

North Star Opera: 75 W Fifth Street, Suite 414, St Paul, MN 55102; website www.northstaropera.org; Artistic Dir Steve Stucki; Admin. Dir Irma Wachtler.

Oakland Lyric Opera: PO Box 20709, Oakland, CA 94620; website www .oaklandlyricopera.org; Gen. Dir Marilyn Kosinski.

Opera Carolina: 345 N College Street, Suite 409, Charlotte, NC 28202; tel. 1 704 332 7177/372 1000; fax 1 704 332 6448/1154; website www .operacarolina.org; Gen. Dir and Principal Conductor James Meena.

Opera Colorado: 695 S Colorado Blvd, Suite 20, Denver, CO 80222; tel. 1 303 778 1500; fax 1 303 778 6533; website www.operacolorado.org; Gen. Dir Peter Russell.

Opera Columbus: 177 E Naghten Street, Columbus, OH 43215; tel. 1 614 461 8101; website www.operacols.org; Artistic Dir William Boggs; Gen. Dir Philip M. Dobard.

Opera Company of Boston Inc: PO Box 50, Boston, MA 02112; Artistic Dir Sarah Caldwell.

Opera Company of Mid-Michigan: 215 Washington Square, Suite 135, Lansing, MI 48933; Exec. Dir Theresa Weller.

Opera Company of Philadelphia: 1420 Locust Street, Suite 210, Philadelphia, PA 19102; tel. 1 215 893 3600; fax 1 215 893 7801; website www.operaphilly.com; Gen. Dir Robert Driver.

Opera Delaware Inc: 4 S Poplar Street, Wilmington, DE 19801; tel. 1 302 658 8063; fax 1 302 658 4991; website www.operade.org; Gen. Dir Leland Kimball, III.

Opera Grand Rapids: 161 Ottawa NW, Suite 205-B, Grand Rapids, MI 49503; tel. 1 616 451 2741; website www.operagr.org; Gen. Dir Robert Lyall.

Opera Memphis: 6745 Wolf River Parkway, Memphis, TN 38120; website www.operamemphis.org; Artistic Dir Michael Ching.

Opera Northeast: 530 E 89th Street, New York, NY 10128; Artistic Dir Donald Westwood.

Opera Orchestra of New York: 239 W 72nd Street, No. 2r, New York, NY 10023; tel. 1 212 799 1982; fax 1 212 721 9170; website www.oony.org; Music Dir Eve Queler; Man. Alix Barthelmes.

Opera Pacific: 9 Executive Circle, Suite 190, Irvine, CA 92714; website www.operapacific.org; Gen. Dir David DiChiera.

Opera Roanoke: 541 Luck Avenue, Suite 209, Roanoke, VA 24016; tel. 1 540 982 2742; fax 1 540 982 3601; website www.operaroanoke.org; Exec. Dir Judith Clark.

Opera San Jose: 12 S First Street, Suite 207, San Jose, CA 95113; website www.operasj.org; Gen. Dir Irene Dalis.

Opera Southwest: 515 15th Street NW, Albuquerque, NM 87104; tel. 1 505 243 0591; Artistic and Music Dir Richard Boldrey.

Opera Theater of Connecticut: PO Box 733, Clinton, CT 06413; website www.operatheater-ct.org; Admin. Dir Kate A. Ford.

Opera Theater of Pittsburgh: PO Box 110108, Pittsburgh, PA 15232; tel. 1 412 624 3500; fax 1 412 624 3525; website www .operatheaterpittsburgh.org; Artistic Dir Gary Race.

Opera Theater of Saint Louis: PO Box 191910, 539 Garden Avenue, St Louis, MO 63119; tel. 314 961 0171; fax 314 961 7463; e-mail info@opera .stl.org; website www.opera-stl.org; Gen. Dir Charles MacKay.

Opera Theatre at Wildwood: PO Box 25202, Little Rock, AR 72221; Artistic Dir Ann Chotard.

Opera Theatre of Northern Virginia: 2700 S Lang Street, Arlington, VA 22206; Artistic Dir John Edward Niles.

Opera/Omaha Inc: 1613 Farnam, Suite 200, Omaha, NE 68101; tel. 1 402 346 4398/0357; fax 1 402 346 7323; website www.operaomaha.org; Gen. Dir Mary Robert.

Operaworks Ltd: 170 W 73rd Street, New York, NY 10023; Dir Joel P. Casey.

Orlando Opera Company Inc: c/o Dr Phillips Center for Performing Arts, 1111 N Orange Avenue, Orlando, FL 32804; Gen. Dir Robert Swedberg.

Palm Beach Opera Inc: 415 S Olive Avenue, West Palm Beach, FL 33401; tel. 1 407 833 7888; fax 1 561 833 8294; website www.pbopera.org; Artistic Dir Anton Guadagno; Gen. Dir Herbert P. Benn.

Pamiro Opera Company: 115 S Jefferson Street, No. 301-A, Green Bay, WI 54301; website www.pamiro.org; Artistic and Music Dir Miroslav Pansky.

Pittsburgh Opera Inc: 711 Penn Avenue, Eighth Floor, Pittsburgh, PA 15222; website www.pbhopera.org; Gen. Dir Tito Capobianco.

Portland Opera Association: 1515 SW Morrison Street, Portland, OR 97205; tel. 503 241 1407; fax 503 241 4212; e-mail aom@portlandopera.org; Gen. Dir Robert Bailey.

Potomac Valley Opera Company: 2218 N Kensington Street, Arlington, VA 22205; Dir Richard Wilmer.

Rimrock Opera Company: PO Box 11, Billings, MT 59103; website www .rimrockopera.org; Artistic Dir Douglas Nagel; Exec. Dir John Baber.

Sacramento Opera Company: PO Box 161027, Sacramento, CA 95816; tel. (916) 264-5181; fax (916) 737-1032; e-mail info@sacopera.org; website www.sacopera.org; Exec. Dir: Rod Gideons.

Salt Lake Opera Theatre: 44 W 3000 South American Towers, No. 8075, Salt Lake City, UT 84101; Gen. Dir Robert Zabriskie.

San Barnardino Civic Light Opera Association: PO Box 606, San Bernardino, CA 92402; Gen. Man. Keith Stava.

San Diego Civic Light Opera Association: Starlight, PO Box 3519, San Diego, CA 92103; Exec. Dir Leon Drew.

San Diego Comic Opera Company: 545 Market Street, PO Box 1726, San Diego, CA 92101; Man. Dir Kathleen Switzer.

San Diego Opera: 18th Floor, Civic Center Plaza, 1200 Third Avenue, San Diego, CA 92101-4112; tel. 619 232 7636; fax 619 231 6915; e-mail sdostaff@sdopera.com; website www.sdopera.net; Gen. Dir Ian D. Campbell.

San Francisco Opera: War Memorial Opera House, San Francisco, CA 94102; tel. 1 415 565 6431/864 3300; fax 1 415 621 7508; website www .sfopera.com; Music Dir Donald Runnicles.

San Jose Civic Light Opera: 4 N Second, No. 100, San Jose, CA 95113; Artistic Dir Dianna Shuster.

Santa Fe Opera: PO Box 2408, Santa Fe, NM 87504; tel. 1 505 986 5955; fax 1 505 986 5999; Gen. Dir John Crosby.

Sarasota Opera Association: 61 N Pineapple Drive, Sarasota, FL 34236; tel. 1 941 366 8450; fax 1 941 955 5571; Artistic Dir Victor De Renzi; Exec. Dir Deane C. Allyn.

Seattle Opera Association: PO Box 9248, Seattle, WA 98109; tel. 1 206 389 7600; fax 1 206 389 7651; website www.seattleopera.org; Gen. Dir Speight Jenkins.

Shreveport Opera: 212 Texas Street, Suite 101, Shreveport, LA 71101; tel. 1 318 227 9503; fax 1 318 227 9518; Gen. Dir Gayle Norton; Artistic Dir Joseph Illick.

Skylight Opera Theatre: 158 N Broadway, Milwaukee, WI 53202; tel. 1 414 291 7811; website www.skylightopera.com.

Sorg Opera Company: 65 South Main Street, Middletown, OH 45044; tel. (513) 425-0180; fax (513) 425-0181; e-mail sorgopera@core.com; website www.sorgopera.org; Gen. Dir Curtis Tucker; professional opera productions.

Spanish Lyric Theatre: 1032 Coral Street, Tampa, FL 33602; Artistic Dir Rene Gonzalez.

Springfield Regional Opera: 109 Park Central Square, Springfield, MO 65806; Man. Artistic Dir James Billings.

Stockton Opera: PO Box 7883, Stockton, CA 95267; Artistic Dir George Buckbee.

Summer Opera Theatre Company: c/o Benjamin T. Rome School of Music, 620 Michigan; Gen. Man. Elaine R. Walter.

Syracuse Opera Company: PO Box 1223, Syracuse, NY 13202; tel. 1 315 475 5915; fax 1 315 475 6319; Artistic Dir Richard McKee.

Tacoma Opera: PO Box 7468, Tacoma, WA 98406; tel. 1 253 627 7789; fax 1 253 627 1620; website www.tacomaopera.com; Exec. Dir Kathryn Smith.

Tampa Bay Opera: 2035 Arbor Drive, Clearwater, FL 34620; Artistic Dir Mario Laurenti; Gen. Man. Cynthia Youkon.

Teatro de la Opera Inc: PO Box 40734, Minillas Station, Santurce, PR 09940; Artistic Dir Alberto Esteves.

Tennessee Opera Theatre: 5924 Sedberry Road, Nashville, TN 37205; Artistic Dir Daniel Killman.

Toledo Opera Association: 425 Jefferson Avenue, Suite 415, Toledo, OH 43604; tel. 1 419 255 7464; website www.toledo-opera.com; Principal Conductor and Gen. Dir James Meena.

Triangle Opera Theater Association: 120 Morris Street, Durham, NC 27701; Gen. Man. Rebecca Siegel.

Tri Cities Opera Co Inc: 315 Clinton Street, Binghamton, NY 13905; tel. (607) 729-3444; fax (607) 797-6344; e-mail info@tricitiesopera.com; website www.tricitiesopera.com; Artistic Dir Duane Skrabalak; Exec. Dir Reed W. Smith.

Tulsa Opera: 1610 S Boulder Avenue, Tulsa, OH 74119; Exec. Dir Gayle Pearson.

Utah Symphony & Opera: Abravanel Hall, 123 West South Temple, Salt Lake City, UT 84101; tel. (801) 533-5626; fax (801) 521-6634; website www.utahopera.org; Gen. Dir Anne Ewers.

Virginia Opera: PO Box 2580, Norfolk, VA 23501; Gen. Dir Peter Mark.

Washington Concert Opera: 1690 36th Street NW, Suite 411, Washington, DC 20007; Gen. Man. Stephen Crout.

Washington Opera: John F. Kennedy Center for the Performing Arts, Washington, DC 20566; tel. 1 202 416 7890; fax 1 202 298 6008; Artistic Dir Placido Domingo; Gen. Dir Martin Feinstein; Music Dir Heinz Fricke.

West Bay Opera: PO Box 1714, Palo Alto, CA 94302; Gen. Dir Maria Holt.

West Coast Opera Theatre: PO Box 166, Palm Desert, CA 92661; Gen. Dir Josephine Lombardo.

Western Opera Theater: War Memorial Opera House, San Francisco, CA 94102; Dir Christopher Hahn.

Wolf Trap Opera Company: 1624 Trap Road, Vienna, VA 22182; tel. 1 703 255 1935; fax 1 703 255 1924; Admin. Dir Peter Russell.

Venezuela

Opera de Caracas: Museo del Teclado, Parque Central, Edif. Tacaqua, Mezzanina, Caracas 1010; Dir José Ignacio Cabrujas.

APPENDIX C: FESTIVALS

Argentina

Festival Internacional de Música de San Juan: 25 de Mayo y Urquiza, 5400 San Juan.

Australia

Adelaide Festival of Arts: PO Box 8116, Station Arcade, Adelaide, SA 5000; tel. 61 8 8216 4444; fax 61 8 8216 4455; e-mail afa@adelaidefestival .net.au; website www.adelaidefestival.com.au; Artistic Dir Stephen Page; biennial festival held in Feb.–March.

Australian Festival of Chamber Music: PO Box 5871, Townsville, Qld 4810; tel. 61 7 4771 4144; fax 61 7 4771 4122; e-mail afcm@afcm.com.au; website www.afcm.com.au; July.

Brisbane Warana Festival: PO Box 3611, South Brisbane, Qld 4101; tel. 61 7 3852 2323; Sept.–Oct.

Melbourne International Festival of Organ and Harpsichord: PO Box 92, Parkville, Vic. 3052; tel. 61 3 9347 0447; Easter Week.

Melbourne International Festival of the Arts: 35 City Road, Melbourne, Vic. 3205; tel. 61 3 9662 4242; Oct.

Musica Nova: PO Box 9994, Brisbane, Qld 4001; Aug.

Sydney Festival: Level 2, 18 Hickson Road, The Rocks, Sydney, NSW 2000; tel. 61 2 8248 6500; fax 61 2 8248 6599; e-mail mail@sydneyfestival .org.au; website www.sydneyfestival.org.au; Jan.

UWA Perth International Arts Festival: UWA Festival Centre, 3 Crawley Avenue, Crawley, WA 6009; tel. 61 8 9380 2000; fax 61 8 9380 8555; e-mail festival@perthfestival.com.au; website www.perthfestival .com.au; Feb.–March.

Austria

Ars Electonica: Museumsgesellschaft mbH, Haupstrasse 2, 4040 Linz; tel. 43 732 7272 75; fax 43 732 7272 77; e-mail festival@aec.at; website www.aec.at; Festival Prod. Katrin Emler; June.

Aspekte Salzburg: Lasserstrasse 6, 5020 Salzburg; tel. 43 662 881547; fax 43 662 882143; e-mail office@aspekte-salzburg.at; website www .aspekte-salzburg.at; contemporary music festival held in Feb.–March; also monthly concerts.

Bregenz Festival: Platz der Wiener Symphoniker 1, 6900 Bregenz; tel. 43 5574 407224; fax 43 5574 407223; e-mail info@bregenzerfestspiele.com; website www.bregenzerfestspiele.com; July–Aug.

Carinthian Summer: Stift Ossiach, 9570 Ossiach; tel. 43 4243 2510; fax 43 4243 2353; website www.carinthischersommer.at; June–Aug.

Chamber Music Festival Austria: Germergasse 16, 2500 Baden; Aug.–Sept.

Easter Festival Salzburg: Herbert von Karajan Platz 9, 5020 Salzburg; tel. 43 662 8045-361; fax 43 662 8045-790; website www.osterfestspiele -salzburg.at.

Festival Wien Modern: PO Box 140, Lothringerstrasse 20, 1037 Vienna; tel. 43 1 242 00; e-mail office@wienmodern.at; website www.wienmodern .at; Oct.–Nov.

Festival Wiener Klassik: Preindlgasse 1, 1130 Vienna; April, July and Dec.

Haydnfestival: Schloss Esterhazy, 7000 Eisenstadt; tel. 43 2682 61 866; fax 43 2682 61 805; e-mail office@haydnfestival.at; website www .haydnfestival.at; Sept.

Innsbruck Festival of Early Music: Haspingerstrasse 1, 6020 Innsbruck; June–Sept.

International Competition of Choral Singing: Burgplatz 1, 9800 Spittal an der Drau; July.

International Cultural Days and Symposium: PO Box 18, 8692 Neuberg an der Mürz; July–Aug.

International Youth and Music Festival: Kongresszentrum, 1014 Vienna; July.

Internationale Brucknerfest Linz: Untere Donaulände 7, 4010 Linz; Sept.–Oct.

Internationale Musikwochen Millstatt: PO Box 27, 9872 Millstatt/ See; May–Oct.

Kitzbüheler Sommerkonzerte: Stadtgemeinde, 6730 Kitzbühel; July–Aug.

Mozart Festival Week: Getreidegasse 14/2, 5020 Salzburg; Jan.

Operetta Weeks: Wiesingerstrasse 7, 4820 Bad Ischl; July–Aug.

Salzburg Palace Concerts: Makartplatz 9, 5020 Salzburg; Jan.–Dec.

Salzburger Kulturtage: PO Box 42, Waagplatz 1a, 5010 Salzburg; tel. 43 662 845346; fax 43 662 842665; e-mail kulturvereinigung@salzburg.com; held in Oct.

Salzburger Operetten Konzerte: Lerchenstrasse 33, 5023 Salzburg; May–Oct.

Schubertiade Feldkirch: Schubertplatz 1, PO Box 625, 6803 Feldkirch; June–July.

Seefestspiele Mörbisch: Schloss Esterhazy, 7000 Eisenstadt; June–Aug.

Steirische Kulturveranstaltungen: Palais Attems, Sackstrasse 17, 8010 Graz; tel. 43 316 812941; fax 43 316 82500015; e-mail info@styriarte .com; website www.styriarte.com; held in June–July.

Styrian Autumn: Sackstrasse 17/1, 8010 Graz; Oct.

Szene: International Theatre and Dance Festival: Anton Neumayr-Platz 2, 5020 Salzburg.

Vienna Festival: Lehargasse 11, 1060 Vienna; website www.festwochen .at; May–June.

Vienna Music Summer: Laudongasse 29, 1080 Vienna; June–Sept.

Belgium

Ars Musica: The Spring of Contemporary Music: 18 Pl Eugène Flageyplein 18, Rm 245, 1050 Brussels; website www.arsmusica.be; March–April.

Europalia: 10 rue Royale, 1000 Brussels; website www.europalia.be; Sept.–Dec. of odd-numbered years.

Festival de Wallonie: 29 rue du Jardin Botanique, 4000 Liège; website www.festivaledewallonie.be; June–Nov.

Festival Van Vlaanderen, Antwerpen: Kortrijksesteenweg 90 h, 9830 Sint-Martens-Latem; Stadhuis, website www.festivale-van-vlaanderen .be; Aug.–Sept.

Festival Van Vlaanderen, Brugge: Collaert Mansionstraat 30, 8000 Bruges; tel. 050 33 22 83; fax 050 34 52 04; e-mail musica-antiqua@unicall .be; website www.musica-antiqua.com; held in July–Aug; includes annual competition.

Week of Contemporary Music: Muzikon vzw, Hoogpoort 64, 9000 Ghent; tel. 32 9 225 15 15; Feb.

Bermuda

Bermuda Festival: PO Box HM 297, Hamilton, HM AX; tel. 441 295 1291; e-mail bdafest@ibl.bm; website www.bermudafestival.com; Jan.–Feb.

Brazil

Bienal de Música Contemporânes Brasileira: Sala Cecilia Meireles, Largo da Lapa 47, Lapa, 20021 Rio de Janeiro; Nov.

Festival Música Nova de Santos: Sociedade Ars Viva, Rua Barâo de Paranapiacaba 31, 11050 Santos.

Festival Villa-Lobos: Rua Sorocaba 200, 22271 Rio de Janeiro; Nov.

Petrópolis Summer Festival: Rua Franio Peixoto 134, Bingen, 25600; Jan.–Feb.

Petrópolis Winter Festival: Petrópolis; June–Aug.

Bulgaria

Apollonia: 54/B Korab Planina St, 1125 Sofia; April, Sept. and Oct.

Chamber Music Festival: PO Box 387, 1090 Sofia; June.

March Music Days, Sofia Music Weeks: PO Box 387, 1090 Sofia; May–June.

Varna Summer: Municipal Council BG, 9000 Varna; website www.varna .bg/kult/v_summer/lmf.htm; June–July.

Canada

Banff Festival of the Arts: Box 1020, Station 28, Banff, Alta, T0L 0C0; June–Aug.

Charlottetown Festival: PO Box 848, Charlottetown, PE C1A 7L9; June–Oct.

Festival International de Lanaudière: 1500 Base-de-Roc Blvd, Joliette, QC J6E 3Z1; June–Aug.

Festival International de Musique Baroque: PO Box 644, Lameque, NB E0B 1V0; July.

Festival of the Sound: PO Box 750, Parry Sound, ON P2A 2Z1; July–Aug.

Guelph Spring Festival: PO Box 1718, Guelph, ON N1H 6Z9; May.

Scotia Festival of Music: 1541 Barrington St, Suite 317, Halifax, NS B3J 1Z5; May–June.

Shaw Festival: PO Box 774, Niagara-on-the-Lake, ON L0S 1J0; April–Nov.

Vancouver Early Music Summer Festival: 1254 W Seventh Avenue, Vancouver, BC V6H 1B6; July–Aug.

Croatia

Zagreb Musical Biennale Festival of Contemporary Music: HD Skladatelja, Berislaviceva, 1000 Zagreb.

Czech Republic

Brno International Music Festival: Uvoz 39, 602 00 Brno; tel. 420 543 233 116; fax 420 543 233 358; e-mail mhfb@arskoncert.cz; website www.mhfb.cz; Sept.–Oct.

Prague Autumn Festival: Sekaninova 26, 120 00 Prague 2.

Prague Cultural Summer: nam Republiky 5, 110 00 Prague 1; June–Sept.

Prague Easter Festival: Sonus Pod Smuký kou 1049, 150 00 Prague 5.

Prague Festival: Sonus Pod Smuký kou 1049, 150 00 Prague 5; Sept.–Oct.

Prague Spring International Music Festival: Hellichova 18, 118 00 Prague 1; tel. 420 257 320 468; fax 420 257 313 725; e-mail info@festival.cz; website www.festival.cz; Dir: Roman Belor; Marketing and PR: Alena Svobodova; held in May–June.

Denmark

Århus Festival: Vester Allé 3, 8000 Århus; website www.aarhusfestuge.dk; Aug.–Sept.

Fanø Music Festival: Toftestein 21, Sønderho, 6720 Fanø; June, July and Aug.

Lerchenborg Music Days: Tuborgvej 99, 2900 Hellerup; July–Aug.

Royal Danish Ballet and Opera Festival: PO Box 2185, 1017 Copenhagen.

Estonia

Tallinn International Organ Festival: Niguliste Str, 13, 0001 Tallinn; tel. 372 614 7737; fax 372 614 7709; July–Aug.; Artistic Dir Andres Uibo.

Finland

Finland Festivals: PO Box 56, 00101 Helsinki; website www.festivals.fi; year-round.

Helsinki Festival: Lasipalatsi, Mannerheimintie 22–24, 00100 Helsinki; tel. 358 9 6126 5100; fax 358 9 6126 5161; e-mail info@helsinkifestival.fi; website www.helsinkifestival.fi; Aug.–Sept.; Dir Risto Nieminen.

Joensuu Song Festival: Koskikatu 1, 80100 Joensuu; June.

Jyväskylä Arts Festival: Asemakatu 6, 40100 Jyväskylä; website www.jyvaskyla.fi/kesa/info; July; Festival Man. Tanja Rasi.

Kangasniemi Music Festival: Kulttuuritoimisto, 51200 Kangasniemi; June–July.

Karjaa Music Festival: Rantatie 1, 10300 Karjaa; June–July.

Korsholm Music Festival: Festival Office, 65610 Korsholm; tel. 358 6 322 2390; fax 358 6 322 2393; e-mail music.festival@korsholm.fi; website www.korsholm.fi/music; June–July.

Kuhmo Chamber Music Festival: Torikatu 39, 88900 Kuhmo; tel. 358 8 652 0936; fax 358 8 652 1961; e-mail kuhmo.festival@kuhmofestival.fi; website www.kuhmofestival.fi; July–Aug.

Lahti Organ Festival: Kirkkokatu 5, 15110 Lahti; tel. 358 3 782 3184; fax 358 3 783 2190; e-mail lof@pp.phnet.fi; website www.lahtiorgan.net; held in Aug.

Oulu Music Festival: Lintulammentie 1 K, 90140 Oulu; Jan.–May.

Naantali Music Festival: PO Box 46, 21101 Naantali; tel. 358 2 4345363; fax 358 2 4345425; e-mail tiina.tunturi@naantali.fi; website www.naantalimusic.com; Artistic Dir Arto Noras; Exec. Dir Tiina Tunturi; held in June.

Savonlinna Opera Festival: Olavinkatu 27, 57130 Savonlinna; tel. 358 15 476750; fax 358 15 4767540; e-mail info@operafestival.fi; website www.operafestival.fi; Gen. Man.: Jan Hultin; held in June–July.

Suvisoitto-Porvoo Summer Sounds: Erottajankatu 19 D 21, 00130 Helsinki; June–July.

Tampere Biennale: Tullikamarinaukio 2, 33100 Tampere; tel. 358 3 3146 6136; fax 358 3 223 0121; e-mail music@tampere.fi; website www.tampere.fi/biennale; Exec. Dir: Jouni Auramo; held in 31 March–4 April 2004, 5–9 April 2006.

Time of Music: Kunnantalo, 44500 Vitasaari; July.

Turku Music Festival: Uudenmaankatu 1 A 20500 Turku; tel. 358 2 251 1162; fax 358 2 231 3316; e-mail info@turkumusicfestival.fi; website www.turkumusicfestival.fi; Aug.

France

Academie Internationale d'Art Musicale, Tours: 17 rue des Ursulines, 37000 Tours; July.

Avignon Festival: 8 bis rue de Mons, 84000 Avignon; website www.festival-avignon.com; July–Aug.

Biennale de la Musique Française: Maison de Lyon, Place Bellecour, 69002 Lyon; Sept. of odd-numbered years.

Chorégies d'Orange: 18 Place Silvain, PO Box 205, 84107 Orange Cédex; July–Aug.

Festival d'Aix: Palais de l'Ancien Archevêché, 13100 Aix-en-Provence; tel. 33 442 17 34 00; fax 33 442 96 12 61; website www.festival-aix.com; June–July.

Festival d'Art Sacré de la Ville de Paris: 17 rue de l'Arbe Sec, 75001 Paris.

Festival d'Automné à Paris: 156 rue de Rivoli, 75001 Paris; website www.festival-automne.com; Sept.–Dec.

Festival de Chartres/Grandes Orgues de Chartres: 75 rue de Grenelle, 75007 Paris; July and Sept.

Festival de Colmar: 4 rue des Unterlinden, 68000 Colmar; tel. 33 389 20 68 97; fax 33 389 413 413; e-mail infofestival@ot-colmar.fr; website www.colmar-festival.com; July.

Festival de la Rochelle: 26 rue Washington, 75008 Paris; June–July.

Festival de L'Ile de France: 26 rue de Gramont, 75002 Paris; Sept.–Oct.

Festival de Paris: 2 rue Edouard Colonne, 75001 Paris; May–June.

Festival de Prades: rue Victor Hugo, 66500 Prades; July–Aug.

Festival de Versailles: Maire de Versailles, RP 144, 78011 Versailles; May–June.

Festival de Ville d'Avray: 10 rue de Marnes, 92410 Ville d'Avray; May–June.

Festival des Instruments Anciens: 58 rue Viollet-la-Duc, 94210 St Maur La Varenne; March–April.

Festival des Nations Europeennes: PO Box 60, 68140 Munster; July.

Festival du Comminges: Academie Internationale, 31260 Mazeres-sur-Salat; website www.festival-du-comminges.com; July–Aug.; Artistic Dir Jean-Patrice Brosse.

Festival Estival de Paris: 20 rue Geoffroy l'Asnier, 75004 Paris; July–Sept.

Festival International Atlantique: 7 quai de Versailles, 44000 Nantes Cédex; June–Aug.

Festival International d'Art Lyrique et de Musique: Palais de l'Ancien Archevêché, 13100 Aix-en-Provence; July–Aug.

Festival International d'Eté de Nantes: Porte St Pierre, rue de l'Evêché, 44000 Nantes; July.

Festival International de Besançon et Franche-Comte: 2d rue Isenbart, 25000 Besançon; Aug.–Sept.

Festival International de Carpentras: La Charité, rue Cottier, PO Box 113, 84204 Carpentras Cédex; July–Aug.

Festival International de Chant Choral de Nancy: PO Box 3335, 54000 Nancy; tel. 33 383 27 56 56; fax 33 383 27 55 66; website www.fest .chantchoral.free.fr; May.

Festival International de Musique Sacrée de Lourdes: Place du Champ Commun, 65100 Lourdes; Easter.

Festival International de Musique de Toulon: Palais de la Bourse, Avenue Jean-Moulin, 83000 Toulon; tel. 33 494 93 52 84; June–July.

Festival International des Musiques d'Aujourd'hui: 9 rue de Général Frère, 67000 Strasbourg; Sept.–Oct.

Festival J. S. Bach: Palais Delphinal, 26260 Saint-Donat-sur-Berbasse; July–Aug.

Festival Mediterranéen: PO Box 4, 13129 Salin de Giraud; June–Aug.

Festival Musique en Sorbonne: 2 rue Francis de Croisset, 75018 Paris; June–July.

Festival Radio France Montpellier: Le Corum 9214, 34043 Montpellier Cédex 01.

Festival 'Synthèse', International Festival of Electronic Music and Creations, Bourges: place André Malraux, PO Box 39, 18000 Bourges; tel. 33(0)2 20 41 87; fax 33(0)2 48 20 45 51; e-mail administration@ime -bourges.org; website www.imeb.net. Festival programme of 30 concerts, presenting music from 24 countries, masterclasses, demonstrations of electronic art.

Fêtes Musicales en Touraine: Hôtel de Ville, 37032 Tours Cédex; June.

Lille Festival: 64 Avenue President J. F. Kennedy, 59800 Lille; Oct.–Dec.

Nuits de la Fondation Maeght: Fondation Maeght, 06570 St Paul-de-Vence; July.

Recontres d'Eté de la Chartruese: La Chartreuse, PO Box 30, 30400 Villeneuve-les-Avignon; July.

Recontres internationales de la Guitare: Hôtel de Ville, PO Box 114, 65013 Tarbes Cédex; July.

Rencontres Musicales d'Evian: Château de Blonay, 74500 Evain les Bains; May.

Strasbourg International Festival: Wolf Musique, 24 rue de la Mésange, 67000 Strasbourg; June–July.

Germany

Augsburger Mozart-Sommer: Kulturamt, Maximilianstrasse 36, 8900 Augsburg; tel. 49 821 324 2727; Aug.–Sept.

Bach Festival Berlin: Rathaus, 2120 Lüneburg; June.

Bachwoche Ansbach: PO Box 1741, 8800 Ansbach; website www .bachwocheansbach.de; July–Aug. of odd-numbered years.

Bad Hersfeld Festival Concerts and Opera: Nachtigallenstrasse 9, 6430 Bad Hersfeld; tel. 49 6621 2109; June–Aug.

Bayreuth Festival: PO Box 100262, 95402 Bayreuth; tel. 49 9217 8780; website www.bayreuther-festspiele.de; July–Aug.

Berliner Festwochen/Berliner Festspiele GmbH: PO Box 301648, 10748 Berlin; tel. 49 30 254 890; fax 49 30 254 89111; e-mail info@ berlinerfestspiele.de; website www.festwochen.de; Sept.–Nov.

Bodensee Festival: Olgastrasse 21, 88045 Friedrichshafen; tel. 49 75 4120 33300; fax 49 75 4120 33310; website www.bodfest.de; April–May.

Bonner Herbst: Wachsbleiche 21, 5300 Bonn 1; tel. 49 228 77 45 33; Oct.–Nov.

Brühler Schlosskonzerte eV: Schlosstrasse 2, 5040 Brühl; May–Sept.

Cloister Concerts: Kurverwaltung Alpirsbach, 7297 Alpirsbach; June–Aug.

Collegium Musicum Schloss Pommersfelden: Austrasse 10, 90559 Burgthann; tel. 49 9183 8245; fax 49 9183 7814; July–Aug.

Corveyer Musikwochen: Stadtverwaltung/Stadthaus am Petritor, 3470 Höxter 1; May–June.

Dollart Festival: PO Box 1580, 26585 Aurich; tel. 49 41 179 967; fax 49 41 179 975; website www.dollart-festival.de.

Donaueschingen Festival of Contemporary Music: Südwestfunk Baden-Baden, PO Box 820, 7570 Baden-Baden; Oct.

Dresdner Musikfestspiele: PO Box 202723, 01193 Dresden; tel. 49 351 478560; fax 49 351 website www.musikfestspiele.de; May–June.

Dresdner Tage der Zeitgenössischen Musik: Schevenstrasse 17/150-05, 8054 Dresden; Oct.

Ettingen Schloss-Festspiele: PO Box 0762, 7505 Ettingen; June–Aug.

European Festival: Dr Hans Kaptingerstrasse 22, 94032 Passau; June–July.

Festliche Sommer in der Wies: Bahnhofstrasse 44, 8920 Schongau; June–Aug.

Festspiele am Roten Tor: Kasernstrasse 4-6, 8900 Augsburg; July.

Feuchtwangen Kreuzgangspiele: Marktplatz, 91555 Feuchtwangen; tel. 9852 904 44; fax 9852 904 260; e-mail kulturamt@feuchtwangen.de; held in May–Aug.

Gandersheimer Donfestspiele: Barfüsserkloster 15, 3353 Bad Gandersheim; June–Aug.

Gewandhaus-Festtage Leipzig: Aug.usplatz 8, 7010 Leipzig; tel. 49 341 12700; June.

Göttingen Handel Festival: Hainholzweg 3–5, 3400 Göttingen; May–June.

Händelfestspiele in Halle: Gorsse Nikolaistrasse 5, 06108 Halle; tel. 49 345 5009 0222; June.

Heidelberg Castle Festival: Friedrichstrasse 5, 6900 Heidelberg; tel. 49 6221 583 521; July–Aug.

Herbstliche Musiktage Bad Urach: PO Box 1240, 7432 Bad Urach; tel. 49 7125 15 61 51; Sept.–Oct.

Hitzacker Summer Music Festival: Barkhausenweg 12, 2000 Hamburg; July–Aug.

International Castle Concerts: Schloss, 8851 Leitheim bei Donauwörth; April–Oct.

Internationale Fasch-Festtage Zerbst: Wikhaus Breiteskin, PO Box 1113, 39251, Zerbst.

International May Festival: PO Box 3247, 6200 Wiesbaden; tel. 49 611 1321; May.

International Organ Festival: Jacobikirchof 3, 3400 Göttingen; Oct. of odd-numbered years.

Internationale Bachakademie Stuttgart: Johann-Sebastian-Bach-Platz, 70178 Stuttgart; tel. 0711 6192132; fax 0711 6192130; e-mail office@bachakademie.de; website www.bachakademie.de; organizes the annual Stuttgarter Bachwoche festival in Feb.–March.

Internationale Festspiele Baden-Württemberg: Marstallstrasse 5, 71634 Ludwigsburg; tel. 49 7141 9396-0; fax 49 7141 9396-77; e-mail info@ schlossfestspiele.de; website www.schlossfestspiele.de; held in June–Sept.; Man. Dir Prof. Hans-Peter Schmitt.

Internationale Orgelwoche Nürnberg-Music Sacra: Bismarckstrasse 46, 8500 Nürnberg; tel. 49 911 231 3528; June–July.

Internationales Beethovenfest Bonn: Wachsbleiche 21, 5300 Bonn; triennial.

Kissinger Summer Music Festival: PO Box 2260, 8730 Bad Kissingen; June–July.

Leitheim Schloss Concerts: Schloss Leitheim, 8851 Kaisheim; May–Oct.

Limburger Organ Vespers: Städtisches Verkehrsamt, 6250 Limburg an der Lahn; April–Aug.

Ludwigsburger Schlossfestspiele: Marstallstrasse 5, 71634 Ludwigsburg; tel. 49 7141 9396-0; fax 49 7141 9396-77; e-mail info@ schlossfestspiele.de; website www.schlossfestspiele.de; held in June–Sept.; Man. Dir Prof. Hans-Peter Schmitt.

Münchener Biennale: Rindermarkt 3–4, 8000 Munich 2; tel. 49 89 290 41 83; April.

Munich Opera Festival: Bayerische Staatsoper, Max Jospeh Platz 2, 80539 Munich; July–Aug.

Music in the 20th Century: PO Box 1050, 6600 Saarbrücken; tel. 49 681 602 2210; May.

Musica Bayreuth: Ludwigstrasse 26, 8580 Bayreuth; tel. and fax 49 921 67367; website www.musica-bayreuth.de; held in May.

Musikfest Hamburg: Grosse Theaterstrasse 34, 2000 Hamburg 36; Sept.

Musiksommer Obermain: Bambergerstrasse 25, 8623 Staffelstein; May–Dec.

Neue Bachgesellschaft e V: Postfach 10 07 27, 04007 Leipzig; tel. 0341 9601463; fax 0341 2248182; e-mail info@neue-bachgesellschaft.de; website www.neue-bachgesellschaft.de; holds the annual Bach festival in June–July.

Opera Festival Eutiner Sommerspiele GmbH: PO Box 112, 2420 Eutin/Holstein; tel. 49 4521 2161; July–Aug.

Palace Courtyard Serenade Concerts: Friedrichstrasse 5, 6900 Heidelberg; June–July.

Pro Musica Nova: Heinrich-Hertzstrasse 13, 2800 Bremen; May.

Ruhrfestival-Europäisches Festival: Otto Burrmeister Alle 1, 4350 Recklinghausen; tel. 49 2361 9180; May–June.

Schleswig-Holstein Music Festival: PO Box 2655, 23514 Lubeck; June–Aug.

Schloss Elmau: Schloss Elmau, 8101 Klais/Oberbayern.

Schwetzingen Festival: SWR Funkhaus Baden-Baden, Hans-Bredow-Strasse, 76530 Baden-Baden; held in April–June.

Tage Alter Musik: PO Box 100903, 93009 Regensburg; tel. 49 941 507 4410/11/12; fax 49 941 507 4419; website www.tage-alter-musik.allmusic.de; June.

Tage für Neue Musik: Kornbergstrasse 32, 7000 Stuttgart 1; Oct.–Nov.

Tage Neuer Kammermusik Braunschweig: Steintorwall 3, 3300 Braunschweig; Nov.–Dec.

Telemann-Festtage: Liebigstrasse 10, 3010 Magdeburg; website www.musikfeste.de; March.

Witten Festival of Contemporary Chamber Music: Bergerstrasse 25, 5810 Witten; tel. 49 2302 581 2424; April.

Würzburg Bach Festival: Hofstallstrasse 5, 8700 Würzburg; Nov.

Würzburg Mozart Festival: Haus zum Falken, 8700 Würzburg; June.

Greece

Athens Festival: 23 Hadjichristou and Makriyianni, 11742 Athens; tel. 30 1 92 82 900; fax 30 1 92 82 941; website www.hellenicfestival.gr; June–Sept.

Iraklion Summer Festival: 71202 Iraklion, Crete; tel. 30 81 282 221.

Patras International Festival: PO Box 1184, 26110 Patras; tel. 30 61 278 730; June–Aug.

Hong Kong

Hong Kong Arts Festival: 12/F Hong Kong Arts Centre, 2 Harbour Road, Wanchai, Hong Kong; tel. 852 2824 3555; fax 852 2824 3798/3722; website www.hk.artsfestival.org; Jan.–Feb.

Hungary

Beethoven Concerts: Vörösmarty tér 1, 1364 Budapest; tel. 36 1 176 222; June–Aug.

Budapest Autumn Festival: PO Box 95, Rákóczi u. 65, VI 66, 1081 Budapest; tel. 36 1 210 2795; Oct.–Nov.

Esztergom International Guitar Festival: PO Box 38, 2501 Esztergom; tel. 36 33 313 808; July–Aug.

Open Air Theatre-Summer Festival: PO Box 95, 1525 Budapest; tel. 36 1175 5922; June–Aug.

Sopron Early Music Days: PO Box 80, 1366 Budapest; tel. 36 1 117 9838; June–July.

Iceland

Dark Music Days: Laufásvegur 40, 101 Reykjavík; Jan.–Feb.

Reykjavík Arts Festival: PO Box 88, 121 Reykjavík; website www.artsfest.is; June.

Ireland

Adare Festival: Adare Manor, Adare, County Limerick; July.

Cork International Choral Festival: PO Box 68, Cork; tel. 353 21 484 7277; fax 353 21 484 7278; e-mail chorfest@iol.ie; website www.corkchoral.ie; April–May.

Dublin International Organ and Choral Festival: 18 Eustace Street, Dublin 2; tel. 353 1 633 7392; e-mail organs@diocf.iol.ie; website www.dublinorganfestival.com; Sept.

Galway Arts Festival: Black Box Theatre, Dyke Road, Galway; tel. 353 91 509 700; fax 353 91 562 655; e-mail info@galwayartsfestival.ie; website www.galwayartsfestival.ie; July.

Kilkenny Arts Week: 92 High Street, Kilkenny; tel. 353 56 776 3663; fax 353 56 775 1704; e-mail info@kilkennyarts.ie; website www.kilkennyarts.ie; Aug.

Waterford International Festival of Light Opera: George's Street, Waterford; tel. 353 51 872639; fax 353 51 876002; website www.waterfordfestival.com; Sept.–Oct.

Wexford Festival Opera: Theatre Royal, High Street, Wexford; tel. 353 53 22400; fax 353 53 24289; e-mail info@wexfordopera.com; website www.wexfordopera.com; Oct.

Israel

Ein Gev Music Festival: Ein Gev, 14940 Kibbutz Ein Gev; Passover.

Israel Festival: Jerusalem Theatre, PO Box 4409, 91040 Jerusalem; tel. 972 2 561 1438; May–June.

Kol-Israel, Upper Galilee Chamber Music Days: Hakirya, 61070 Tel-Aviv; July–Aug.

Vocalisa 90: PO Box 515, 20101 Carmiel; April.

Italy

Antidogma Musica Festival: Via Alberto Nota 3, 10122 Turin; Sept.–Oct.

Aterforum: Piazzetta Santa Anna 3, Int 8, 44100 Ferrara; June–July.

Autunno Musicale a Como: Via Cantoni 1, 22100 Como; Sept.–Oct.

Batignano Musica nel Chiostro: Santa Croce, Comune di Grosseto, 58041 Batignano; tel. 39 564 33 80 96; fax 39 564 33 80 85; July–Aug.

Biennale di Venezia, Festival Internazionale di Musica Contemporanea: Ca'Giustinian, S Marco, 30100 Venice; website www.labiennale.com; Sept.–Oct.

Canto delle Pietro-Musiche Sacre e Spiritual: Via Cantoni 1, 22100 Como; April–June.

Ente Autonomo Spettacoli Lirici Arena di Verona: Piazza Bra 28, 37121 Verona; tel. 39 045 805 18 11; July–Aug.

Estate Maceratese: Arena Sferisterio, 62100 Macerata; July.

Festa Musica Pro Mundo Uno: Via di Villa Maggiorani 20, 00168 Rome; July–Aug.

Festival Barocco: Corso Massimo d'Azeglio, 10126 Turin; May and Sept.

Festival dell'Opera Siciliana e Taormina: Via Cavour 117, 90133 Palermo; Oct.

Festival di Musica Antica: Via Zeffirino Re 2, 47023 Cesena; July.

Festival di Musica Sacra: Villa Igea, 90142 Palermo.

Festival de Opera Barga: Via della Fornacetta 11, 55051 Barga Lucca; July–Aug.

Festival Internazionale di Musica Antica: Via Confalonieri 5, 00195 Rome; July.

Festival Internazionale di Musica Classica e Contemporanea: PO Box N95, 16038 Santa Margherita Ligure; June–July.

Festival Mozart in Lombardia: Via Cantoni 1, 22100 Como; Sept.–Nov.

Festival of Contemporary Music Nuovi Spazi Musicali: Via Divisione Torino 139, 00143 Rome; tel. and fax 39 6 5021208; e-mail ada.gentile@tin.it; Art Dir: Ada Gentile; Gen. Man.: Franco Mastroviti; held annually in the autumn, with five or six concerts dedicated to performers and composers from all over the world.

Festival of Two Worlds: Via Cesare Beccaria 18, 00196 Rome; June–July.

Festival Pontino: Viale le Corbusier 379, 04100 Latina; tel. 0773 605551; fax 0773 628498; e-mail campus.musica@panservice.it; website www.campusmusica.it; held in June–July.

Festival Romaeuropa: Via Sistina 48, 00187 Rome; May–July.

Festival Spaziomusica: Via Liguria 60, 09127 Cagliari; tel. 39 070 400844; fax 39 070 485439; e-mail info@festivalspaziomusica.it; website www.festivalspaziomusica.it; held in Oct.–Nov.

Gli Incontri Musicale Romani: Largo Nazzareno 8, 00187 Rome.

Gubbio Festival: Corso Garibaldi 88, 06024 Gubbio; Sept.

Incontri con La Nuova Musica: PO Box 196, 25100 Brescia; Nov.–Dec.

International Chamber Music Festival of Asolo: Via Browning 141, 31011 Asolo; Aug.–Sept.

Lucca in Villa Festival: Via Turati 31, 55049 Viareggio, Lucca; Aug.

Maggio Musicale Fiorentino: Via Solferino 15, 50123 Florence; tel. 39 055 27791; fax 39 055 2396954; e-mail protocollo@maggiofiorentino.com; website www.maggiofiorentino.com; Gen. Man.: Giorgio van Straten; Artistic Dir: Gianni Tangucci; held in April–July.

Musica 2000 Festival: 8 Via Alpi, 60131 Ancona; April.

Musica Verticale Festival: Via Lamarmora 18, 00185 Rome; Oct.–Nov.

Puccini Festival: Piazza Belvedere Puccini 4, 55048 Lucca; tel. 39 584 350567; fax 39 584 341657; e-mail fpuccini@nodalisfree.it; website www.puccinifestival.it; July–Aug.

Rassegna di Nuova Musica: Arena Sferisterio, CP 92, 62100 Macerata; May–June.

Ravenna Festival: Via Dante Alighieri 1, 48100 Ravenna; tel. 39 544 249211; fax 39 544 36303; website www.ravennafestival.org; June–July.

Rome Festival: Via Francesco Duodo 49, 00136 Rome; tel. 39 328 411 7977; May–Aug. and Oct.–Nov.

Rossini Opera Festival: Via Rossini 37, 61100 Pesaro; tel. 39 721 380 0291; fax 39 721 380 0220; website www.rossinioperafestival.it; Aug.

Sagra Musicale al Tempio Maiatestiano: 47037 Rimini; Sept.

Sagra Musicale Umbra: PO Box 341, 06100 Perugia; website www.sagramusicaleumbra.com; Sept.

Settembre Musica: Piazza S Carlo 161, 10123 Turin; Aug.–Sept.

Settimane Musicali di Stresa: Via Carducci 38, 28838 Stresa; tel. 39 0323 31095; fax 39 0323 33006; e-mail info@settimanemusicali.net; website www.settimanemusicali.net; held in Aug.–Sept.

Settimane Musicali Senese: Via di Città 89, 53100 Siena; July.

I Suoni del Tempo: Via Zeffirino Re 2, 47023 Cesena; July.

Taormina Arte: Via Pirandello 31, 98039 Taormina; July–Sept.

Triest Prima, Incontri internazionale: Via Settefontane 30, 34141 Trieste; Sept.

Veneto Festival: Piazzale Pontecorvo 4a, 35100 Padua; May–July.

Verdi Festival: Via Farini 34, 43100 Parma; Sept.

Verona Festival: Piazza Brà 28, 37121 Verona; July–Sept.

Japan

Kusatsu International Summer Music Academy and Festival: Wako Bldg 2f, 14-3 Motoyoyogi-cho, Shibuya-ku, Tokyo 151-0062; tel. 81 3 5790-5561; fax 81 3 5790-5562; e-mail info@kusa2.jp; website www.kusa2.jp; Music Dir: Kazuyuki Toyama; Sec.-Gen.: Hiroshi Isaka; held annually in the last two weeks of Aug.

Min-On Contemporary Music Festival: 1-32-13 Kita-Shinjuku, Shinjuku-ku, Tokyo 169; website www.min-on.org; June.

National Arts Festival: Ministry of Education, Tokyo 100; Oct.–Nov.

Osaka International Festival Society: New Asahi Building, Nakanoshima 2-3-18, Kita-ku, Osaka 530; April.

Pacific Music Festival: c/o Sapporo Concert Hall, 1-15 Nakajima-Koen, Chuo-ku, Sapporo 064; July–Aug.

Tokyo City Arts Festival: 3–5 Marunouchi, Chiyoda-ku, Tokyo; Jan.–March.

Tokyo International Chamber Music Festival: 32-11-411 Kamikitazawa 4-chome, Setagaya-ku, Tokyo; April–May.

Tokyo Summer Festival: Copacabana Building, 5F, 3-6-4 Akasaka, Minato-ku, Tokyo 107; July.

Republic of Korea

Autumn Music Festival in Seoul: Dong-Hwa Building, Suite 210, 43-1, Pil-Dong 1-Ga, Choong-gu, Seoul 100-271; Oct.–Nov.

Seoul International Music Festival: Korean Broadcasting System, 18 Yoido-dong, Youngdungpo-gu, Seoul 150-790; Oct.–Nov.

Lithuania

Baltic Music Festival: Mickevi iaus 29, 2600 Vilnius; tel. 370 2 220939; Oct.

Luxembourg

Festival Européen de Wiltz-Luxembourg: Château de Wiltz, 9516 Wiltz; July.

Festival International Echternach, Luxembourg: Parvis de la Basilique 9, 6486 Echternach; May–June.

Macao

International Music Festival of Macao: Avda Aviso Goncalves Zarco, s/n, First Floor, Macao; Oct.

Mexico

Festival de Música de Cámara de San Miguel de Allende: Calle Hernández Macias 75, San Miguel de Allende; July–Aug.

Festival de San Miguel de Allende: Hospicio 48, San Miguel de Allende; tel. 52 415 2 5911; Dec.

Festival Internacional Cervantino: Alvaro Obregón 273, 06700 Mexico, DF; Oct.

Gran Festival Ciudad de México: Alvaro Obregón 73, 06700 Mexico, DF; July.

Monaco

Printemps des Arts de Monte Carlo: rue Louis Notari, MC 98000 Monaco; April–May.

Netherlands

Festival Amsterdam Chamber Music Society: Ceintuurbaan 376, 1073 EM Amsterdam; tel. 31 20 626 9069; March and Nov.

Festival Nieuwe Muziek: PO Box 15, 4330 AA Middleburg; tel. 31 118 623650; fax 31 118 624754; June–July.

Haarlem Organ Festival: PO Box 3333, 2011 Haarlem; July.

Holland Festival: Kleine-Gartmanplantsoen 21, 1071 RP Amsterdam; website www.hollandfestival.nl; June.

Holland Festival Early Music Utrecht: PO Box 734, 3500 AS Utrecht; tel. 31 (0)30 2303838; fax 31 (0)30 2303839; e-mail info@oudemuziek.nl; website www.oudemuziek; Artistic Dir Jan van den Bossche; held in Aug.–Sept.

International Choir Festival: Plompetorengracht 3, 3512 CA Utrecht; tel. 31 30 233 56 00; fax 31 30 233 56 80; e-mail unisono@amateurmuziek.nl; website www.amateurmuziek.nl; Man. Dir: Jeroen Schrijner; held in June.

International Gaudeamus Music Week: Swammerdamstr 38, 1090 RV Amsterdam; Sept.

New Music Festival Maastricht: St Maartenspoort 23, 6221 BA Maastricht; tel. 31 43 25 0511; Sept.

New Zealand

New Zealand International Arts Festival: PO Box 10113, Wellington 6036; tel. 64 4 473 0149; fax 64 4 471 1164; e-mail nzfestival@festival.co.nz; website www.nzfestival.telecom.co.nz; Feb.–March.

Norway

Bergen International Festival: Strandgt 18, PO Box 183, 5001 Bergen; website www.fib.no; May.

Elverum Festival: PO Box 313, 2401 Elverum; Aug.

Northern Norway Festival: PO Box 901, 9401 Harstad; June.

Oslo Sommeropera: Grev Wedels Plass 2, 0151 Oslo; June.

St Olav Festival: PO Box 2045, 7410 Trondheim; tel. 47 73 84 14 50; fax 47 73 84 14 51; e-mail per.uddu@olavsfestdagene.no; Festival Dir: Per Kvistad Uddu; held in July–Aug.

Stord International Choir Festival: PO Box 433, 5401 Stord; June.

Philippines

Philippine Music Festival: NAMCYA-FAT, CCP Complex, Roxas Blvd, Manila; Oct.–Nov.

Poland

Festival of Early Music of Central and Eastern Europe: Libelta 16, 85-080 Bydgoszcz; Sept.

Henryk Wieniawski Days: Tadeusza Ko ciuszki nr 19, 58-310 Szczawno-Zdrój; June.

International Music and Arts Festival: Rynek-Ratusz 24, 50-1010 Wroclaw; Sept.

Music in Old Kraków: ul. Zwierzyniecka 1, 31-103 Kraków; tel. 48 12 4214566; fax 48 12 4294328; e-mail amadeusz@capellacracoviensis.art.pl; website www.capellacracoviensis.art.pl; held in Aug.

Polish and International Music Festival: Chopina 30, 35-055 Rzeszów; May.

Warsaw Autumn International Festival of Contemporary Music: Rynek Starego Miasta 27, 00-272 Warsaw; tel. 48 22 8311634; fax 48 22 6359138; e-mail festival@warsaw-autumn.art.pl; website www.warsaw-autumn.art.pl; Dir: Tadeusz Wielecki; held in Sept.

Romania

Cluj-Napoca Musical Autumn: Str E de Martonne 1, 3400 Cluj-Napoca; Oct.

George Enescu International Festival: Artexim, Calea Victoriei 155, Bl D1, Sc 8 et 2, 71012 Bucharest; website www.festivalenescu.ro; Sept.

Tirgu Mures Musical Days: 2 Enescu Str, 4300 Tirgu Mures; May.

Russia

December Nights: Volkhona 12, 121019 Moscow; Dec.

Festival Moscow: Ul Kalantchovskaya 15, Moscow; July–Aug.

International Music Festival St Petersburg Spring: Herzena 45, 190000 St Petersburg; April.

Moscow International Music Festival: RosInterFest, 12 Sadovaya Triumfalnaya Str, 103006 Moscow; May.

St Petersburg Palaces International Chamber Music Festival: c/o M & N Artists Ltd, 400 W 43rd Street 19A, New York, NY 10036, USA; June.

White Nights: Fontanki 41, St Petersburg; June.

Serbia and Montenegro

Belgrade Music Festival: Terazije 41, 11000 Belgrade; Oct.

Singapore

Singapore Festival of Arts: PSA Building, 35th Storey, 460 Alexandria Road, Singapore 0511; June of even-numbered years.

Slovakia

Bratislava Cultural Summer: Suché Mýto 17, 812 93 Bratislava; July–Aug.

Evenings of New Music: Fucikova 29, 811 02 Bratislava; June.

Slovenia

Ljubljana Festival: Trg Francoske Revolucije 1–2, 1000 Ljubljana; tel. 386 1 241 60 00; fax 386 1 241 60 37; e-mail info@festival-lj.si; website www.festival-lj.si; held in July–Aug.

Spain

Curso de Música Barroca y Rococo: Acuerdo 17-1 A, 28015 Madrid; Aug.

Festival de Música de Canarias: Leon y Castillo 427-3, 35007 Las Palmas de Gran Canaria; tel. 34 928 24 74 42; fax 34 928 27 60 42; website socaem.com; Jan.–Feb.

Festival Internacional de Guitarra Andres Segovia: Ramon Llull 2, 07001 Palma de Mallorca; Nov.

Festival Internacional de Música y Danza de Granada: PO Box 64, 18080 Granada; June–July.

Festival Internacional de Música Castell de Peralada: Pere de Moncada 1, 08034 Barcelona; tel. 34 935 03 86 46; website www.festivalperalada.com; July–Aug.

Festival Internacional de Música Contemporánea de Alicante: Santa Isabel 52, 28012 Madrid; Sept.

Festival Internacional de Música de Barcelona: Via Laietana, 41 pral, 08003 Barcelona.

Festival Internacional de Organo: Calle La Paloma 7, 24003 Leon; tel. 34 87 25 78 37; Sept.–Oct.

Festival Internacional de Santander: Avda Calvo Sotelo 15, 5°, 39004 Santander; website www.festival-int-santander.org; July–Sept.

Semana de Música de Cámara Festival internacional de Segovia: San Facundo 5, Segovia; July.

Serenatas Musicales de Valencia: Avellanas 603a, 46003 Valencia; tel. 34 6 391 90 48; July.

Sweden

Drottningholm Court Theatre Festival: Drottningholms Slottsteater, Box 15417, 104 65 Stockholm; held in May–Sept.

Electro-Acoustic Music Festival: PO Box 101, 739 22 Skinnskatteberg; June.

Helsingborg Summerfestival: Konserthuset, 252 21 Helsingborg; Aug.

Royal Palace Music Festival: Royal Palace, 111 30 Stockholm; July–Aug.

Stockholm New Music: PO Box 1225, 111 82 Stockholm; March.

Umeå International Festival of Chamber Music: 901 78 Umeå; June.

Visby Festival: Tranhusgatan 47, 621 55 Visby; July–Aug.

Switzerland

Estate Musicale internazionale de Lugano: Via Losanna, 6900 Lugano; Aug.

European International Festival: 10 rue des Eaux-Vives, 1207 Geneva; May–July.

Festival de Musique Sacrée de Fribourg: PO Box 292, 1701 Fribourg; July.

Festival d'Eté, A Swiss Summer: PO Box 10, 1211 Geneva; July–Aug.

Festival de Sion Tibor Varga: PO Box 1429, 1951 Sion; tel. 0041 27 323 4317; fax 0041 27 323 4662; July–Sept.; Sec.-Gen. Fabienne Gapany.

Interlakner Festwochen: PO Box, 3800 Interlaken; Aug.

International Bach Festival: Stadthaus, 8201 Schaffhausen; tel. 41 52 632 52 11; May.

International Festival of Music, Lucerne: Hirschmattstrasse 13, PO Box, 6002 Lucerne; Aug.–Sept.

International Festival of Organ Music: Ente Turistico del Gambarogno, 6574 Vira; tel. 41 91 795 12 14; June–July.

Montreux Choral Festival: CP 1526, 1820 Montreux; tel. 41 21 966 55 50; fax 41 21 966 55 69; e-mail montreuxchoralfestival@bluewin.ch; website www.choralfestival.ch; Pres.: Daniel Schmutz; held in April; choirs from around the world sing classical, popular and folk repertoires.

Montreux-Vevey Music Festival: rue du Théâtre 5, PO Box 162, 1820 Montreux; Aug.–Oct.

Settimane Musicale d'Ascona: Via Lido 24, 6612 Ascona; tel. 41 91 791 00 90; Aug.–Oct.

Tage für Neue Musik Zürich: Hegibachstrasse 38, 8032 Zürich; Nov.

Taiwan

Taipei Music Festival: 25 Pa Teh Road, Sec 3, 10560 Taipei; Sept.–Oct.

Turkey

Ankara International Festival: Tunali Hilmi Cad 114/43, 06700 Kavaklidere/Ankara; April.

Istanbul International Festival: Istiklal Caddesi 146, Luvr Apt, Beyoglu, 80070 Istanbul; website www.istfest.org; June–July.

Izmire International Festival: 1442 Sok No. 4/6, 35220 Alsancak, Izmir; June–July.

United Kingdom

Aberdeen International Youth Festival: Linksfield Community Centre, 520 King Street, Aberdeen, Scotland AB24 5SS; tel. 01224 494400; fax 01224 494114; e-mail admin@aiyf.org; website www.aiyf.org; Chief Exec. Stephen Stenning; Aug.

Aldeburgh/Almeida Opera: 3 Dean Trench Street, London SW1P 3HB; tel. (20) 7340-0662; fax (20) 7222-0082; website www.almeida.co.uk; Prod.: Patrick Dickie; Gen. Admin.: Régis Cochefert.

Aldeburgh Britten Festival: Aldeburgh Productions, Snape Maltings Concert Hall, Snape, Suffolk IP17 1SP; tel. 01728 687100; fax 01728 687120; e-mail enquiries@aldeburgh.co.uk; website www.aldeburgh.co.uk; Oct.

Aldeburgh Easter Festival: Aldeburgh Productions, Snape Maltings Concert Hall, Snape, Suffolk IP17 1SP; tel. 01728 687100; fax 01728 687120; e-mail enquiries@aldeburgh.co.uk; website www.aldeburgh.co.uk; Easter Week.

Aldeburgh Festival of Music and the Arts: Aldeburgh Productions, Snape Maltings Concert Hall, Snape, Saxmundham, Suffolk IP17 1SP; tel. (1728) 687100; fax (1728) 687120; e-mail enquiries@aldeburgh.co.uk; website www.aldeburgh.co.uk; June.

Arundel Festival: 3 Castle Mews, Arundel, Sussex, BN19 9DG; website www.arundelfestival.co.uk; Aug.

Bath International Festival of Music and the Arts: Bath Festivals Trust, 2 Church Street, Abbey Green, Bath, Avon BA1 1NL; tel. 01225 463362; website www.bathmusicfest.org.uk; May--June.

Bath Mozartfest: 110 Gloucester Avenue, London NW1 8JA; Nov.

BBC Henry Wood Promenade Concerts: 16 Langham Street, Room 425, London W1A 1AA; website www.bbc.co.uk/proms; July--Sept.

Belfast Festival at Queen's: 25 College Gardens, Belfast, Northern Ireland BT9 6BS; tel. 028 9027 2600; website www.belfastfestival.com; Nov.

Birmingham Early Music Festival: 42 Beech Avenue, Worcester WR3 8PY; July.

Bournemouth Live! Music Festival: Visitor Information Bureau, Westover Road, Bournemouth BH1 2BU; tel. (1202) 451700; website www.bournemouth.co.uk; held in June--July.

Bournemouth Musicmakers Festival: Westover Road, Bournemouth BH1 2BU; held in June--July.

Brighton Festival: 54 Old Steine, Brighton, Sussex BN1 1EQ; website www.brighton-festival.org.uk; May.

Bromsgrove Festival: Festival Office, Bromsgrove Museum and Tourist Information Centre, 26 Birmingham Road, Bromsgrove B61 8AB; tel. 01527 876504; fax 01527 575366; April–May.

Buxton Festival: 5 The Square, Buxton, Derbyshire SK17 6AZ; tel. 01298 70395; e-mail info@buxtonfestival.co.uk; website www.buxtonfestival.co.uk; July--Aug.

Cambridge Summer Music Festival: Cambridge Arts Theatre, 6 St Edward's Passage, Cambridge CB2 3PJ; tel. 01223 503333; website www.cambridgesummermusic.com; Dir Juliet Abrahamson; July--Aug.

Canterbury Festival: Festival Office, Christ Church Gate, The Precincts, Canterbury, Kent CT1 2EE; tel. 01227 452853; e-mail info@canterburyfestival.co.uk; website www.canterburyfestival.co.uk; Oct.

Cardiff Festival of Music: St David's Hall, The Hayes, Cardiff, Wales CF1 2SH; Sept.–Oct.

Cheltenham International Festival of Music: Town Hall, Imperial Square, Cheltenham, Gloucestershire GL50 1QA; website www.cheltenhamfestivals.co.uk; Artistic Dir Michael Berkeley; July.

Chester Summer Music Festival: 8 Abbey Square, Chester CH1 2HU; July.

Chichester Festivities: Canon Gate House, South Street, Chichester, Sussex PO19 1PU; e-mail info@chifest.org.uk; website www.chifest.org.uk; July.

City of Leeds College of Music Festival: Cookridge Street, Leeds, Yorkshire LS2 8B; Feb.–March.

City of London Festival: Bishopsgate Hall, 230 Bishopsgate, London EC2M 4QH; tel. 020 7377 0540; fax 020 7377 1972; e-mail admin@colf.org; website www.colf.org; Dir Kathryn McDowall; June--July.

Dartington International Summer School: The Barn, Dartington Hall, Totnes, Devon TQ9 6DE; tel. (1803) 847080; fax (1803) 847087; e-mail info@dartingtonsummerschool.org.uk; website www.dartingtonsummerschool.org.uk; Admin.: Sophie Bradford; offers some 50 courses spanning western musical repertoire and music of other cultures; masterclasses, workshops, exhibitions and concerts; next held 24 July–28 Aug. 2004

East Anglia Summer Music Festival: The Old School, Bridge Street, Hadleigh, Suffolk IP7 6BY; July–Aug.

Edinburgh International Festival: The Hub, Castlehill, Edinburgh, Scotland EH1 2NE; tel. 0131 473 2001; website www.eif.co.uk; Aug.

Evening Standard Holland Park Theatre Festival: Central Library, Phillimore Walk, Kensington, London, W8 7RX.

Exeter Festival: Exeter City Council, Civic Centre, Paris Street, Exeter EX1 1JN; tel. 01392 265205; fax 01392 265366; e-mail festival@exeter.gov.uk; website www.exeter.gov.uk/festival; July.

Fishguard International Music Festival: Festival Office, Fishguard, Pembrokeshire, Wales SA65 9BJ; tel. and fax 01348 873612; e-mail fishguard-imf@cwcom.net; July.

Garsington Opera Festival: Garsington Opera, Garsington, Oxfordshire, OX44 9DH; June–July.

Glyndebourne Festival Opera: Glyndebourne, PO Box 2624, Lewes, East Sussex BN8 5UW; tel. (1273) 813813; fax (1273) 814686; website www.glyndebourne.com; Chair.: Gus Christie; Gen. Dir: David Pickard; Music Dir: Vladimir Jurowski.

Harrogate International Festival: 1 Victoria Avenue, Harrogate, Yorkshire HG1 1EQ; tel. 01423 562303; fax 01423 521264; e-mail info@harrogate-festival.org.uk; website www.harrogate-festival.org.uk; July--Aug.

Haslemere Festival: Jesses, Grayswood Road, Haslemere, Surrey GU27 2BS; July.

Henley Festival of Music and the Arts: 14 Friday Street, Henley-on-Thames RG9 1AH; tel. 01491 843400; fax 01491 410482; e-mail info@henley-festival.co.uk; website www.henley-festival.co.uk; July.

Huddersfield Contemporary Music Festival: University of Huddersfield, Queensgate, Huddersfield HD1 3DH; tel. 01484 425082; fax 01484 472957; e-mail info@hcmf.co.uk; website www.hcmf.co.uk; Artistic Dir Susanna Eastburn; Nov.

International East Anglian Summer Music Festival: 3–5 Bridge Street, Hadleigh, Suffolk, IB7 6BY; tel. 01473 822596; fax 01473 824175.

International Organ Festival: PO Box 80, St Albans AL3 4HR; July.

King's Lynn Festival: 29 King Street, King's Lynn, Norfolk PE30 1HA; July.

Lake District Summer Music: 92 Stricklandgate, Kendal, Cumbria LA9 4PU; tel. 01539 724441; fax 01539 741882; e-mail info@ldsm.org.uk; website www.ldsm.org.uk; July--Aug.

Leamington Festival: Pageant House, 2 Jury Street, Warwick CV34 4EW; tel. (1926) 410747; fax (1926) 409050; e-mail admin@warwickarts.org.uk; website www.warwickarts.org.uk; Festival Dir Richard Phillips; held in May; includes chamber music concerts, Leamington Jazz Weekend, New Music Day, world music, puppets and literary events.

Lichfield Festival: 7 The Close, Lichfield, Staffordshire WS13 7LD; tel. 01543 306270; e-mail lichfield.fest@lichfield-arts.org.uk; website www.lichfieldfestival.org; July.

Llandaff Summer Festival: 1 St Mary's, Cardiff, Wales CF5 2EB; May–July.

Llangollen International Musical Eisteddfod: Royal International Pavilion, Abbey Road, Llangollen, LL20 8SW; tel. 01978 862000; fax 01978 862002; e-mail info@ international-eisteddfod.co.uk; website www.international-eisteddfod.co.uk; July.

London New Wind Festival: 119 Woolstone Road, Forest Hill, London SE23 2TQ; tel. 20 8699 1101; fax 20 8699 2219; Music Dir Catherine Pluygers; Man. Jonathan Lindridge.

Lufthansa Festival of Baroque Music: 71 Priory Road, Kew Gardens, Surrey TW9 3DH; website www.lufthansa-festival.org.uk; June.

Malvern Festival: Rockliffe House, 40 Church Street, Malvern, Worcestershire WR14 2AZ; May–June.

Manchester-Hallé Proms Festival: Hallé Concerts Society, Heron House, Albert Square, Manchester M2 5HD; June–July.

Mayfest: 18 Albion Street, Glasgow, Scotland G1 1LH; April–May.

Musicfest Aberystwyth: Aberystwyth Arts Centre, Penglais Campus, Aberystwyth, Ceredigion SY23 3DE; website www.musicfest-aberystwyth.org; Artistic Dir David Campbell; July--Aug.

Newbury Spring Festival: 1 Bridge Street, Newbury, Berkshire RG14 5BE; tel. 01635 32421; fax 01635 528690; website www.newburyspringfestival.org.uk; Festival Dir Mark Eynon; May.

Norfolk and Norwich Festival: 42-58 St George's Street, Norwich NR3 1AB; tel. 01603 614921; fax 01603 632303; e-mail info@n-joy.org.uk; website www.nnfest.demon.co.uk; Artistic Dir Peter Bolton; Oct.

North Wales Music Festival: High Street, St Asaph, Clwyd, North Wales LL17 0RD; Sept.

Perkshore Festival: Manor House Barn, Fladbury, Perkshore, Worcestershire WR10 2QN; June–July.

Perth Festival of the Arts: 2 High Street, Perth, Scotland; May.

Peterborough Cathedral Festival: The Cathedral Shop, 24 Minster Precincts, Peterborough PE1 1XZ; July.

Presteigne Festival of Music and the Arts: 17 Parliament Hill, London, NW3 2TA.

Royal National Eisteddfod of Wales: 40 Parc Ty Glas, Llansihen, Cardiff, Wales CF4 5WU; Aug.

St Albans International Organ Festival: PO Box 80, St. Albans, Hertfordshire, AL3 AHR; July (odd numbered years).

St Endellion Easter and Summer Festivals of Music: Churchtown Farmhouse, Michaelstow, Bodmin, Cornwall PL30 3PD; April and Aug.

Salisbury Festival: 75 New Street, Salisbury SP1 2PH; tel. 01722 332977; fax 01722 410552; website www.salisburyfestival.co.uk; May–June.

Sheffield Chamber Music Festival: 65 Rawcliffe Lane, Clifton, York YO3 6SJ; May.

Spitalfields Festival: 75 Brushfield Street, London E1 6AA; tel. 020 7377-0287; fax 020 7247-0494; e-mail info@spitalfieldsfestival.org.uk; website www.spitalfieldsfestival.org.uk; Artistic Dir Jonathan Dove; Exec. Dir Judith Serota; held in June.

Stratford-upon-Avon Music Festival: Pageant House, 2 Jury Street, Warwick CV34 4EW; tel. (1926) 410747; fax (1926) 409050; e-mail admin@warwickarts.org.uk; website www.warwickarts.org.uk; Festival Dir Richard Phillips; held in Oct.; includes chamber music concerts, early music, and other types of music.

Swansea Festival of Music and the Arts: The Guildhall, Swansea SA1 4PE; Sept.–Nov.

Three Choirs Festival: Comunity House, College Green, Gloucester GL1 2LZ; Aug.

Tilford Bach Festival: Fairlawne, Kiln Way, Grayshott GU26 6JF; tel. (1428) 713338; e-mail sa.greaves@tiscali.co.uk; website www.tilford-bach.org.uk; held in May–June.

Vale of Glamorgan Festival: St Donat's Castle, Llantwit Major, Wales CF6 9WF; Aug.

Walsingham Variations: The Grove, 61 Bracondale, Norwich, Norfolk NR1 2AT; Aug.

Warwick Festival: Pageant House, 2 Jury Street, Warwick CV34 4EW; tel. (1926) 410747; fax (1926) 409050; e-mail admin@warwickarts.org.uk; website www.warwickarts.org.uk; Festival Dir Richard Phillips; held in June–July; includes orchestral, choral and chamber music concerts.

Windsor Festival: Dial House, Englefield Green, Egham, Surrey TW20 0DU; Sept.–Oct.

York Early Music Festival: National Centre For Early Music, St Margaret's Church, Walmgate, York YO1 9TL; tel. 01904 632220; fax 01904 612631; e-mail info@ncem.co.uk; website www.ncem.co.uk; July.

United States of America

American Music Festival: National Gallery of Art, Sixth Street and Constitution Avenue NW, Washington, DC 20565; April–May.

Ames Festival: PO Box 1243, Ames, IA 50010.

An Appalachian Summer: ASU Office of Cultural Affairs, PO Box 32045, Boone, NC 28608; tel. 1 828 262 4046; fax 1 828 262 2848; website www.appsummer.com; July.

Ann Arbor May Festival: Burton Memorial Tower, Suite 100, Ann Arbor, MI 48109; May.

Artpark: 450 S Fourth Street, Lewiston, NY 14092; tel. 1 716 754 9000; fax 1 716 754 2741; website www.artpark.net; May–Sept.

Arts Festival of Atlanta: 999 Peachtree Street, Suite 140, Atlanta, GA 30309; Sept.

Art Song Festival: Cleveland Institute of Music, 11021 East Blvd, Cleveland, OH 44106; tel. 1 216 791 5000; fax 1 216 791 3063; website www.cim.edu; May.

Aspen Music Festival: 2 Music School Road, Aspen, CO 81611; tel. 1 970 925 3254; fax 1 970 920 1643; e-mail festival@aspenmusic.org; website www.aspenmusicfestival.com; June–Aug.

Aston Magna Festival: PO Box 28, Great Barrington, MA 01230; tel. (413) 528-3595; e-mail info@astonmagna.org; website www.astonmagna.org; held in July–Aug.

Atlanta Symphony Orchestra: Summer Concerts: 1293 Peachtree Street, NE, Suite 300, Atlanta, GA 30309; June–Aug.

Bay Chamber Concerts: PO Box 228, Rockport, ME 04856-0228; tel. (207) 236-2823; website www.baychamberconcerts.org; summer festival held in July–Aug.; performing arts series held in Oct.–June.

Baltimore Symphony Orchestra Summerfest and Oregon Ridge Concert Series: 1212 Cathedral Street, Baltimore, MD 21201; June–Aug.

Bard Music Festival: PO Box 5000, Bard College, Annandale-on-Hudson, NY 12504; tel. 1 845 758 7410; e-mail bm@bard.edu; Aug.

Berkeley Festival and Exhibition: 101 Zellerbach Hall, University of California at Berkeley, Berkeley, CA 94720; website www.bfx.berkeley.edu/bfx; June.

Berkshire Choral Festival: 245 N Undermountain Road, Sheffield, MA 01257; tel. (413) 229-8526; fax (413) 229-0109; e-mail bcf@choralfest.org; website www.chorusfest.org; Exec. Dir: Trudy Weaver Miller; held in July–Aug.

Bethlehem Musikfest Association: 22 Bethlehem Plaza, Bethlehem, PA 18018; website www.musikfest.org; Aug.

Big Sky Arts Festival: PO Box 160308, Big Sky, MT 59716; July.

Binghamton Summer Music Festival: PO Box 112, Binghamton, NY 13903; tel. 1 607 777 4777; fax 1 607 777 6780; e-mail bsmf1@yahoo.com; website summermusic.binghamton.edu; July–Aug.

Boston Early Music Festival and Exhibition: PO Box 1286, Cambridge, MA 02238; tel. 1 617 424 7232; fax 1 617 267 6539; e-mail bemf@bemf.org; website www.bemf.org; Artistic Dir Paul O'Dette; June.

Boston Pops: Symphony Hall, 301 Massachusetts Avenue, Boston, MA 02115; website www.bso.org; May–June.

Boston Symphony Orchestra Tanglewood Festival: Symphony Hall, 301 Massachusetts Avenue, Boston, MA 02115; tel. (617) 266-1492; fax (617) 638-9367; website www.bso.org; Music Dir: James Levine; Man. Dir: Mark Volpe; held in June–Aug.

Bravo! Colorado Music Festival at Vail, Beaver Creek: 953 South Frontage Road, Suite 104, Vail, CO 81657; tel. 1 970 949 1999; July–Aug.

Brevard Music Festival: PO Box 312, 10000 Probart Street, Brevard, NC 28712; tel. 1 828 862 2100; fax 1 828 884 2036; e-mail bmc@brevardmusic.org; website www.brevardmusic.org; June–Aug.

Britt Festivals, Music and Performing Arts Festivals: PO Box 1124, Medford, OR 97501; tel. 1 541 779 0847; fax 1 541 776 3712; website www.brittfest.org; June–Sept.

Cabrillo Music Festival: 104 Walnut Lane, Suite 206, Santa Cruz, CA 95060; tel. 1 831 426 6966; e-mail info@cabrillomusic.org; website www.cabrillomusic.org; Aug.

Cape May Music Festival: PO Box 340, Cape May, NJ 08204; May–June.

Caramoor International Music Festival: PO Box R, Katonah, NY 10536; June–Aug.

Carmel Bach Festival: PO Box 575, Carmel-by-the-Sea, CA 93921; tel. (831) 625-1521; fax (831) 624-2788; e-mail info@bachfestival.org; website www.bachfestival.org; Music Dir: Bruno Weil; Man. Dir: Willem Wijnbergon; 23 days of concerts and recitals in July–Aug.; Baroque and Classical repertoire.

Castle Hill Festival: PO Box 563, Ipswich, MA 01938; July–Sept.

Chamber Music Northwest: 522 SW Fifth Avenue, Suite 725, Portland, OR 97204; tel. 1 503 223 3202; fax 1 503 294 1690; e-mail info@cmnw.org; website www.cmnw.org; June–July.

Chautauqua Institution: PO Box 28, Chautauqua, NY 14722; tel. 1 716 357 6200; fax 1 716 357 9014; website www.ciweb.org; June–Aug.; Dir of Programming Marty W. Merkley.

Cincinnati May Festival: Music Hall, 1241 Elm Street, Cincinnati, OH 45202; tel. 1 513 621 1919; fax 1 513 744 3535; website www.mayfestival.com; May–June.

Cincinnati Opera Association Summer Festival: 1241 Elm Street, Cincinnati, OH 45202; tel. 1 513 241 2742; fax 1 513 744 3530; website www.cincinnatiopera.org; June–July.

Cincinnati Symphony and Pops Orchestras at Riverbend: 1241 Elm Street, Cincinnati, OH 45202; website www.cincinnatisymphony.org; June–Aug.

Cleveland Orchestra at the Blossom Music Center: PO Box 1000, Cuyahoga Falls, OH 44223; May–Sept.

Colorado Music Festival: 1035 Pearl Street, Suite 303, Boulder, CO 80302; website www.coloradomusicfest.com; June–Aug.

Columbia Festival of the Arts: 5575 Sterrett Place, Suite 280, Columbia, MD 21044; tel. 1 410 715 3044; fax 1 410 715 3056; e-mail info@columbiafestival.com; website www.columbiafestival.com; June.

Connecticut Early Music Festival: PO Box 329, New London, CT 06320; tel. 1 860 444 2419; website www.ctearlymusic.org; June; Artistic Dir John Metz.

Dallas Symphony Orchestra EDS International Summer Music Festival: 2301 Flora Street, Dallas, TX 75201; tel. 1 214 692 0203; website www.dallassymphony.com; June–July.

Des Moines Metropolitan Opera: 106 W Boston Avenue, Indianola, IA 50125; tel. 1 515 961 6221; fax 1 515 961 8175; website www.dmmo.org; June–July.

Eastern Music Festival: PO Box 22026, Greensboro, NC 27420; tel. 1 336 333 7450 ext. 21; fax 1 336 333 7454 ext. 21; e-mail emfinfo@bellsouth.net; website www.easternmusicfestival.com; June–July.

Fanfare: Southeastern Louisiana University, PO Box 797, Hammond, LA 70402; Oct.

Festival at Sandpoint: PO Box 695, Sandpoint, Idaho 83864; website www.festivalatsandpoint.com; July–Aug.

Festival Casals: PO Box 41227, Minillas Station, Santurce, Puerto Rico 09940; tel. 1 787 721 7727; fax 1 787 723 5843; website www.festcasalspr.gobierno.pr; June.

Festival Miami: University of Miami School of Music, PO Box 248165, Coral Gables, FL 33124; tel. 1 305 284 4940; website www.music.miami.edu/festivalmiami; Sept.–Oct.

Festival Music Society of Indiana: 6471 Central Avenue, Indianapolis, IN 46220; tel. 1 317 251 5190; e-mail merfms@msn.com; website www.emindy.org; June–July.

Festival of Young Orchestras of the Americas: PO Box 41227, Minillas Station, Santurce, Puerto Rico 00940; June.

Firefly Festival for the Performing Arts: 202 S Michigan Street, Suite 845, South Bend, IN 46601; website www.fireflyfestival.com; June–Aug.

Flagstaff Festival of the Arts: PO Box 1607, Flagstaff, AZ 86002; July–Aug.

Flathead Music Festival: PO Box 1780, Whitefish, MT 59937; tel. 1 406 257 0787; July.

Florida International Festival: PO Box 1310, Daytona Beach, FL 32115-1310; tel. 1 386 681 2410; fax 1 386 238 1663; website www.fif.lso.org; Aug. (odd-numbered years).

Garden State Arts Center: PO Box 116, Holmdel, NJ 0733; June–Sept.

Gina Bachauer International Piano Festival: 138 W Broadway, Suite 220, Salt Lake City, UT 84101; tel. (801) 297-4250; fax (801) 521-9202; e-mail gina@bachauer.com; website www.bachauer.com; Artistic Dir: Paul Pollei; Man.: Tracey Harty; held in June, rotating annually between four age groups (11–13, 14–18, 19–32 and 33–100).

Glimmerglass Opera: PO Box 191, Cooperstown, NY 13326; tel. 1 607 547 5704; website www.glimmerglass.org; July–Aug.; Gen. Dir Joanne Cossa; Artistic Dir Paul Kellogg.

Grand Canyon Chamber Music Festival: PO Box 1332, Grand Canyon, AZ 86023; tel. 1 928 638 9215; e-mail gcmf@infomagic.net; website grandcanyonmusicfest.org; Sept.

Grand Teton Music Festival: 4015 W Lake Creek Drive, Suite 1, Wilson, WY 83014; tel. (307) 733-3050; fax (307) 739-9043; e-mail gtmf@gtmf.org; website www.gtmf.org; Exec. Dir: Donald Reinhold; held in June–Aug.

Grant Park Music Festival: Chicago Park District Administration Bldg, 425 E McFetridge Drive, Chicago, IL 60605; June–Aug.

Hartwood Music and Dance Festival: 1520 Pennsylvania Avenue, Pittsburgh, PA 15222; May–Sept.

Hollywood Bowl Summer Festival: PO Box 1951, 2301 N Highlands Avenue, Hollywood, CA 90078; tel. 1 323 850 2000; July–Sept.

Houston International Festival: 7413-B Westview Drive, Houston, TX 77055; tel. 1 713 654 8808; fax 1 713 654 1719; e-mail contactus@iFest.org; website www.iFest.org; April.

Huntington Summer Arts Festival: 213 Main Street, Huntington, NY 11743; tel. 1 516 271 8442; June–Aug.

Indiana University School of Music Summer Festival: Indiana University School of Music, Bloomington, IN 47405; tel. 1 812 855 1583; website www.music.indiana.edu; June–Aug.

Indianapolis Symphony Orchestra, Marsh Symphony on the Prairie: 32 E Washington Street, Suite 600, Indianapolis, IN 46204; tel. 1 317 236 2040; fax 1 317 236 2038; website www.indianapolissymphony.org; June–Aug.

Inter-American Festival of the Arts: PO Box 41227, Minillas Station, Santurce, Puerto Rico 00940; Sept.–Oct.

Interlochen Arts Festival: PO Box 199, Interlochen, MI 49643; tel. 1 231 276 7200; fax 1 231 276 6321; website www.michiweb.com/interlochen; June–Aug.

Irving S. Gilmore International Keyboard Festival: The Epic Center, 359 S Kalamazoo Mall, Suite 101, Kalamazoo, MI 49007; website www.gilmore.org; April–May (even-numbered years).

Kent/Blossom Music: Kent State University, E101 M&S, PO Box 5190, Kent, OH 44242; tel. (330) 672-2613; fax (330) 672-7837; e-mail jlacorte@kent.edu; website dept.kent.edu/blossom; Dir: Jerome LaCorte; f. 1968; professional training ground for young musicians embarking on professional careers; emphasis on chamber music and orchestral audition preparation; held in June–Aug.

La Jolla Chamber Music Society: 7946 Ivanhoe Avenue, Suite 309, La Jolla, CA 92037; tel. 1 858 459 3724; fax 1 858 459 3727; website www.ljcms.org; Aug.

Lake George Opera Festival: 480 Broadway, Suite 336, Saratoga Springs, NY 12866; tel. 1 518 584 6018; fax 1 518 584 6775; e-mail lgopera@aol.com; website www.lakegeorgeopera.org; July–Aug.; Gen. Dir William Florescu.

Lakeside Summer Festival: 236 Walnut Avenue, Lakeside, OH 43440; tel. 1 419 798 4461; website www.lakesideohio.com; June–Sept.

Lancaster Festival: PO Box 1452, Lancaster, OH 43130; tel. (740) 687-4808; fax (740) 687-1980; e-mail lanfest@lanfest.org; website www.lanfest.org; Dir: Lou Ross; held in July.

Library of Congress Summer Chamber Festival: Library of Congress, Washington, DC 20540; June.

Lincoln Center Out-of-Doors: 70 Lincoln Center Plaza, Ninth Floor, New York, NY 10023; website www.lincolncenter.org; Aug.

Los Angeles Festival: PO Box 5210, Los Angeles, CA 90055; Sept.

Manchester Music Festival: PO Box 33, Manchester, VT 05254; tel. 1 802 362 1956; e-mail info@mmfvt.org; website www.mmfvt.org; July–Aug.

Mann Music Center: 1617 J. F. Kennedy Blvd, Philadelphia, PA 19103; website www.manncenter.org; June–Sept.

Marlboro Music Festival: Box K, Marlboro, VT 05344; tel. 1 802 254 2394; fax 1 802 254 4307; e-mail info@marlboromusic.org; website www.marlboromusic.org; July–Aug.

Mendocino Music Festival: PO Box 1808, Mendocino, CA 95460; tel. (707) 937-2044; fax (707) 937-1045; e-mail music@mendocinomusic.com; website www.mendocinomusic.com; held in July.

Michigan Bach Festival: 400 Town Center Drive, Suite 300, Dearbon, MI 48126; March–April.

Midsummer Mozart Festival: 3661 Buchanan Street, Suite 200, San Francisco, CA 94123; tel. 1 415 292 9620; fax 1 415 292 9622; e-mail amadeus@midsummermozart.org; website www.midsummermozart.org; July–Aug.

Minnesota Orchestra Viennese Sommerfest: 1111 Nicollet Mall, Minneapolis, MN 55403; tel. 1 612 371 5656; July–Aug.

Missouri River Festival of the Arts: PO Box 1776, Boonville, MO 65233; Aug.

Monadnock Music: PO Box 255, Peterborough, NH 03458; tel. 1 603 924 7610; fax 1 603 924 9403; e-mail mm@monadnockmusic.org; website www.monadnockmusic.org; July–Aug.; Dir James Bolle.

Mostly Mozart Festival: 70 Lincoln Center Plaza, Ninth Floor, New York, NY 10023; July–Aug.

Music Academy of the West Summer Concert Season: 1070 Fairway Road, Santa Barbara, CA 93108; tel. (805) 969-4726; fax (805) 969-0686; website www.musicacademy.org; Pres. David L.Kuehn; Vice-Pres. and Dean W. Harold Laster; held in June–Aug.

Music Festival of Arkansas: PO Box 1243, Fayetteville, AR 72702; June.

Music From Angel Fire: PO Box 502, Angel Fire, NM 87710; website www.musicfromangelfire.org; Aug.–Sept.; Artistic Dir Ida Kavafian.

Music in the Mountains: 530 Searls Avenue, Nevada City, CA 95959; tel. 1 530 265 6173; fax 1 530 265 6810; e-mail mim@musicinthemountains .org; website www.musicinthemountains.org; June–July.

National Symphony Orchestra: Concerts at the Capitol: John F. Kennedy Center for the Performing Arts, Washington, DC 20566; Memorial Day and Labor Day weekends, and Fourth of July.

New England Bach Festival: 38 Walnut Street, Brattleboro, VT 05301; tel. 1 802 257 website www.bmcvt.org/nebf; Sept.–Oct.

New Hampshire Music Festival: Festival House, 52 Symphony Lane, Center Harbour, NH 03226; tel. 1 603 279 3300; e-mail info@nhmf.org; website www.nhmf.org.

New Jersey Festival of American Music Theatre: 1650 Broadway, New York, NY 10019; June–Aug.

Newport Music Festival: PO Box 3300, Newport, RI 02840; tel. (401) 846-1133; fax (401) 849-1857; e-mail staff@newportmusic.org; website www.newportmusic.org; Gen. Dir: Dr Mark P. Malkovich III; 17 days with 64 concerts, festival of little-known chamber music, debuts of works by international artists.

New York Festival of American Music Theatre: 1650 Broadway, New York, NY 10019; July–Aug.

Norfolk Chamber Music Festival: 165 Elm Street, Suite 101, PO Box 208246, New Haven, CT 06520; tel. 1 203 432 1966; fax 1 203 432 2136; e-mail norfolk@yale.edu; website www.yale.edu/norfolk; June–Aug.

North County Chamber Players Summer Festival: PO Box 904, Littleton, NH 03561; tel. 603 444-0309; e-mail nccp@ncia.net; July–Aug.; Exec. Dir Linn Downs.

Ohio Light Opera: College of Wooster, Wooster, OH 44691; tel. 1 330 263 2336; fax 1 330 263 2272; e-mail OH_LT_OPERA@wooster.edu; website www.wooster.edu/ohiolightopera; June–Aug.

Ojai Festival: PO Box 185, Ojai, CA 93024; tel. 1 805 646 2094; website www.ojaifestival.com; June; Artistic Dir Thomas W. Morris; Music Dir Kent Nagano.

Oklahoma Mozart International Festival: PO Box 2344, Bartlesville, OK 74005; June.

Opera Festival of New Jersey: 55 Princeton-Highstown Road, Princeton Junction, NJ 08550; June–July.

Opera Theatre of St Louis: PO Box 191910, St Louis, MO 63119; website www.opera-stl.org; May–June.

Oregon Bach Festival: University of Oregon School of Music, Eugene, OR 97403; tel. 1 800 457 1486; fax 1 541 346 5669; e-mail bachfest@ darkwing.uoregon.edu; website bachfest.uoregon.edu; June–July.

Ravinia Festival: 1575 Oakwood Avenue, Highland Park, IL 60035; website www.ravinia.org; June–Sept.

Redlands Bowl Summer Music Festival: PO Box 466, Redlands, CA 92373; June–Aug.

Rio Grande Valley International Music Festival: PO Box 2315, McAllen, TX 78502; Feb.

Riverbend Festival: PO Box 886, Chattanooga, TN 37401; website www .riverbendfestival.com; June.

Rockport Chamber Music Festival: PO Box 312, Rockport, MA 01966; tel. (978) 546-7391; fax (978) 546-7391; e-mail rcmf.info@verizon.net; website www.rcmf.org; Artistic Dir: David Deveau; held in June.

Round Top Festival: PO Box 89, Round Top, TX 78954-0089; tel. 1 979 249 3129; fax 1 979 2495078; e-mail info@festivalhill.org; June–July; Founder James Dick; Programme Dir Alain Declert.

Rutgers SummerFest: Rutgers Arts Center, New Brunswick, NJ 08903; June–July.

Saint Louis Symphony Orchestra Queeny Pops: 718 N Grand Blvd, St Louis, MO 63103; July–Aug.

St Petersburg Palaces International Chamber Music Festival: c/o M & N Artists Ltd, 400 W 43rd Street 19A, New York, NY 10036; June.

San Luis Obispo Mozart Festival: PO Box 311, San Luis Obispo, CA 93406; tel. 1 805 781 3008; fax 1 805 781 3011; website www.mozartfestival .com; Aug.; Exec. Dir Curtis Pendleton.

Santa Fe Chamber Music Festival: PO Box 2227, Santa Fe, NM 87504-2227; tel. (505) 983-2075; fax (505) 986-0251; e-mail info@sfcmf.org; website www.sfcmf.org; held over six weeks in July–Aug.

Santa Fe Opera Festival: PO Box 2227, Santa Fe, NM 87504-2408; website www.santafeopera.org; July–Aug.

Sarasota Music Festival: 709 N Tamiami Trail, Sarasota, FL 34236; tel. (941) 952-9634; website www.fwcs.org/sarasota; May–June; Artistic Dir Paul Wolfe.

Saratoga Performing Arts Center: 108 Avenue of the Pines, Saratoga Springs, NY 12866; tel. (518) 584-9330; fax (518) 584-0809; e-mail elinehan@spac.org; website www.spac.org; f. 1966; numerous festivals and events held throughout the year.

Seattle Chamber Music Festival: 10 Harrison Street, Suite 306, Seattle, WA 98109; tel. 1 206 283 8710; fax 1 206 283 8826; e-mail info@ seattlechambermusic.org; website www.scmf.org; June–July; Artistic Dir Toby Saks.

Seattle Opera Summer Festival: PO Box 9248, Seattle, WA 98109; July–Aug.

SMU Conservatory Summer Music Festival: Southern Methodist University, Dallas, TX 75275; June.

Southeastern Music Center: PO Box 8348, Columbus, GA 31908; tel. and fax 1 706 568 2465; July.

Spoleto Festival USA: PO Box 157, Charleston, SC 29402; website www .spoletousa.com; May–June.

Stern Grove Midsummer Music Festival: 44 Page Street, Suite 604-D, San Francisco, CA 94102; June–Aug.

Summer Music at Harkness Park: 300 State Street, Suite 400, New London, CT 06320; tel. 1 860 442 9199; fax 1 860 442 9290; e-mail info@ summer-music.org; website www.summer-music.org; July–Aug.

Sun Valley Music Festival: PO Box 656, Sun Valley, ID 83353; July–Aug.

Texas Music Festival: University of Houston School of Music, Houston, TX 77204; website www.texasmusicfestival.org; June–July.

Three Rivers Arts Festival: 707 Penn Avenue, Pittsburgh, PA 15222; tel. 1 412 281 8723; fax 1 412 281 8722; website www.artsfestival.net; June.

Tweeter Center for the Performing Arts: PO Box 810, Mansfield, MA 02048; tel. 1 508 339 2331; website www.tweetercenter.com; June–Sept.

Vermont Music Festival: PO Box 512, Burlington, VT 05402; July–Aug.

Waterloo Festival: Village of Waterloo, Stanhope, NJ 07874; July–Aug.

Winter Park Bach Festival: Rollins College, PO Box 2763, Winter Park, FL 32789; tel. 1 407 646 2182; website www.bachfestivalflorida.org; Feb.–March.

Wolf Trap Foundation: 1645 Trap Road, Vienna, VA 22182; website www.wolf-trap.org; May–Sept.

Woodstock Mozart Festival: PO Box 734, Woodstock, IL 60098; e-mail contactus@mozartfest.org; website www.mozartfest.org; July–Aug.; Gen. Dir Anita Whalen; Artistic Dir Mark Peskanov.

Worcester Music Festival: Memorial Auditorium, Worcester, MA 01608.

APPENDIX D: MUSIC ORGANIZATIONS

Albania

Albanian National Music Committee: Lidya e Shrkrimtare de Artistere, R. Kavojes Nr4, Tirana; tel. and fax 355 42 27471; Contact Dr Vasil S. Tob.

Argentina

Asociación Argentina de Interpretes (SADEM): Avda Belgrano 3655, 1210 Buenos Aires; tel. 54 11 4957 4062/4932 5769.

Consejo Argentino de la Música: PO Box 5532, Correo Central, 1000 Buenos Aires.

Fundación Encuentros Internacionales de Música Contemporánea: PO Box 1008, Correo Central, 100 Buenos Aires; tel. 54 11 4822 1383.

Sociedad Argentina de Autores y Compositores de Música (SADAIC): Lavalle 1547, 1048 Buenos Aires; tel. 54 11 4379 8600; fax 54 11 4379 8633; website www.sadaic.org.ar.

Australia

Australasian Mechanical Copyright Owners Society Ltd (AMCOS): Locked Bag 3665, St Leonards, NSW 2065; tel. 61 2 9935 7900; fax 61 2 9935 7999; website www.amcos.com.au.

Australasian Performing Right Association (APRA): Locked Bag 3665, St Leonards, NSW 2065; tel. 61 2 9935 7900; fax 61 2 9935 7999; website www.apra.com.au.

Australia Council for the Arts: 372 Elizabeth Street, Surry Hills, NSW 2010; tel. 61 2 9215 9302; e-mail mail@ozco.gov.au; website www.ozco.gov .au.

Australian Copyright Council (ACC): 245 Chalmers Street, Redfern, NSW 2016; tel. 61 2 9318 1788; fax 61 2 9698 3247; e-mail info@copyright .com.au ; website www.copyright.com.au.

Australian Music Centre Ltd: Level 4, The Arts Exchange, 18 Hickson Road, The Rocks, Sydney, NSW 2000; tel. 61 2 9247 4677; fax 61 2 9241 2873; e-mail info@amcoz.com.au; website www.amcoz.com.au.

Australian Music Publishers Association Ltd (AMPAL): Locked Bag 3665, St Leonards, NSW 2065; tel. 61 2 9935 7900; fax 61 2 9935 7999; website www.apra.com.au.

Australian Record Industry Association Ltd—ARIA: PO Box Q20, QVB Post Office, Sydney, NSW 1230; tel. 61 2 9267 7996; fax 61 2 9264 5589; e-mail aria@aria.com.au; website www.aria.com.au.

Australian Society for Keyboard Music: 42/35 Orchard Street, Chatswood, NSW 2067; tel. 61 2 9406 5131.

Confederation of Australasian Performing Arts Presenters: PO Box 4274, Sydney, NSW 2001.

International Society for Contemporary Music (Australian Section)—ISCM: c/o University of Sydney Music Department, Sydney, NSW 2006.

Musica Viva Australia: PO Box 1687, Strawberry Hills, NSW 2012; tel. 61 2 8394 6666; fax 61 2 9698 3878; e-mail musicaviva@mva.org.au; website www.mva.org.au.

Phonographic Performance Company of Australia Ltd—PPCA: PO Box Q20, QVB Post Office, Sydney, NSW 1320; tel. 61 2 8569 1100; fax 61 2 8569 1183; e-mail ppca@ppca.com.au; website www.ppca.com.au.

Youth Music Australia: PO Box Q186, QVB Postshop, NSW 1230; tel. 61 2 9283 7216; fax 61 2 9283 7217; e-mail youthmusic@yma.com.au.

Austria

Arnold Schöenberg Center Privatstiftung: Schwarzenbergplatz 6, 1030 Vienna; tel. 431 712 18 88; fax 431 712 18 88-88; e-mail direktion@ schoenberg.at; website www.schoenberg.at; Dir: Dr Christian Meyer; houses the legacy of Arnold Schönberg, including archive and library; organizes concerts, symposia and exhibitions.

Gesellschaft der Musikfreunde in Wien: Bösendorferstrasse 12, 101 Vienna; tel. 43 1 505 8190; website www.musikverein.at; Sec.-Gen.: Dr Thomas Angyan; promotes classical concerts.

Gesellschaft für Forschungen zur Aufführungspraxis: Zuckerkanlg 14 A, 1190 Vienna.

Gewerkschaft Kunst: Medien, Freie Berufe, Sektion Musiker, Maria Theresienstrasse 11, 1090 Vienna; website www.kmsfb.at.

Herbert von Karajan Stiftung: Prof. Peter Csobádi, Seestrasse 13, 5322 Hof bei Salzburg.

IFDI Landesgruppe Österreich: Habsburgergasse 6–8/18, 1010 Vienna.

International Music Centre Vienna (IMZ): Filmstadt Wien, Speisinger Strasse 121-127, 1230 Vienna; tel. 43 1 889 03 15; fax 43 1 889 03 15 77; e-mail office@imz.at; website www.imz.at.

Internationale Bruckner Gesellschaft: Rathausplatz 3, 1010 Vienna.

Internationale Gesellschaft für Neue Musik: Ungargasse 9/3, 1030 Vienna.

Internationale Gustav Mahler Gesellschaft: Wiedner Guertel 6, 1040 Vienna; tel. and fax 43 1 505 7330; website www.gustav-mahler.org.

Internationale Hugo Wolf Gesellschaft: Latschkagasse 4, 1090 Vienna.

Internationale Schönberg Gesellschaft: Bernhardgasse 6, 2340 Mödling.

Literar-Mechana (Wahrnemungsgesellschaft für Urheberrechte): Linke Wienzelle 18, 1060 Vienna; tel. 43 1 587 21 61; fax 43 1 587 21 619; website www.literar.at.

Musikalische Jugend Österreichs—Jeunesse: Administration Office, Lothringerstrasse 20, 1030 Vienna; tel. 7103616; fax 7103617; e-mail mail@jeunesse.at; website www.jeunesse.at; Sec.-Gen. Angelika Möser; f. 1949, mem. of Jeunesse Musicale International; organizes about 700 concerts a year for young people, contemporary music, world music, classical chamber music, orchestral concerts and jazz; organizes music camps and a Jeunesse Festival.

Musikverleger Union Österreich: Baumannstrasse 10, 1030 Vienna.

Österreichischer Komponistenbund (OKB): Ungargasse 9/3, 1030 Vienna.

Staatlich Gesellschaft der Autoren Komponisten und Musikverleger: Baumannstrasse 8-10, 1030 Vienna.

Belgium

Association des Arts et de la Culture: rue royale 10, 1000 Brussels; website www.adac.be.

Association des Artistes Professionnels de Belgique: rue Paul Lauters 1, 1050 Brussels.

Association Internationale du Théâtre Lyrique: rue des Dominicains 1, 4000 Liège.

Association pour la Diffusion de la musique Belge: rue d'Arlon 75–77, 1040 Brussels.

Atelier Créatif de Musique Électroacoustique—ACME: PO Box 19, 1170 Brussels; website www.cahiersacme.org.

Centre Belge de Documentation Musicale: rue d'Arlon 75–77, 1040 Brussels; tel. 02 230 9430; fax 02 230 9437; e-mail info@cebedem.be; website www.cebedem.be; Dir Alain Van Kerikhoven.

Centre International d'Echanges Musicaux: rue des Patriotes 60, 1040 Brussels.

Chambre Syndicale des Agents Artistiques et Impresario de Belgique: rue Rogier 3, 6040 Charleroi.

Confédération musicale de Belgique: rue du Loncin 22, 4430 Alleur; Pres. S. Coucke.

Conseil de la Musique de la Communauté française de Belgique: Blvd Reyers 52, 1044 Brussels; Pres. Dr Robert Wangermée.

Fondation pour la Promotion des Arts: rue aux Choux 47, 1000 Brussels.

Jeunesses musicales de la Communaute française de Belgique: rue Royale 10, 1000 Brussels.

Royale Union Artistique et Littéraire: rue du Tombeux 52A, 1801 Stembert.

Société Belge de Musicologie: rue de la Régence 30, 1000 Brussels; Contact Dr Robert Wangermée.

Société Belge des Auteurs, Compositeurs et Editeurs—SABAM: rue d'Arlon 75–77, 1040 Brussels; website www.sabam.be.

Société Cesar Franck de Belgique: rue des Foulons 11, 400 Liège.

Sociéte Culturel des Arts Dramatiques et Musicaux: rue F. Ferrer 37, 1360 Tubize.

Société des Auteurs et Compositeurs Dramatiques: Avenue Jeanne 29, 1050 Brussels.

Société Liégoise de Musicologie: Les Enclos 13, 4080 Werbomont.

Union de la Presse Musicale Belge: Avenue C. Woeste 140, 1090 Brussels.

Union des Artistes: rue du Marché aux Herbes 105, 1000 Brussels.

Union des Compositeurs Belges—UCB: rue d'Arlon 75–77, 1040 Brussels; tel. and fax 00322 2868381; Pres. Jacques Leduc.

Union Royale Belge des Éditeurs de Musique: rue F. Neuray 8, 1060 Brussels.

Union Wallonne des Organistes: rue Romainville 25a, 5228 Bas-Oha/Wanze.

Bolivia

Sociedad Boliviana de Autores and Compositores de Música: Figueroa 788, Departamento 1, 2nd Floor, La Paz.

Brazil

Associacao Brasileira dos Produtores de Discos—ABPD: Rua Marques de Sao Vicente 99-1, Gavea, 22451 Rio de Janeiro, RJ; tel. 55 21 2512 9908; fax 55 21 2259 4145; e-mail abpd@abpd.org.br; website www.abpd.org.br.

Associacao de Canto Coral: Rua das Marrecas 40, 9th Floor, 20080-010 Rio de Janeiro, RJ.

Fundaçao de Educaçao Artistica: Rua Gonçalves Dias 320, 30000 Belo Horizonte, MG.

Instituto Brasileiro de Arte e Cultura: Rua de Imprensa 16, 20030 Rio de Janeiro, RJ.

Juventude Musical do Brasil: PO Box 62626, 22257 Rio de Janeiro, RJ.

Sindicato dos Músicos Profissionals do Estado de Sao Paulo: Largo Paissandu, Sao Paulo.

Sindicato dos Músicos Profissionals do Estado de Rio de Janeiro: Rua Alvaro Alvim 24, Grupo 401, 20031 Rio de Janeiro, RJ.

Sociedada Brasileira de Autores Teatrais: Avda Almirante Barroso 97, 3rd Floor, PO Box 1503, 20031-002 Rio de Janeiro, RJ.

Sociedada Brasileira de Música Contemporânea: SQS 105, Bloco B, PO Box 506, 70344-020 Brasilia, DF.

Sociedada Brasileira de Realizçoes Artistico-Culturais: Avda Franklin Roosevelt 23, Room 310, 20021 Rio de Janeiro, RJ.

Sociedad de Cultura Artistica: Rua Nestor Pestana 196, CEP 01303 Sao Paulo.

Sociedada Independente de Compositores and Autores Musicals: Largo Paissandú 51, 10th, 11th, 16th Floors, 01034 Sao Paulo.

Uniao Brasileira de Compositores: Rua Visconde de Inhaúma-Centro, 20091-000 Rio de Janeiro; Chief Exec. Dr Vanisa Santiago.

Uniao dos Músicos do Brasil: Avda Rio Branco 185, Rio de Janeiro, RJ.

Bulgaria

Bulgarian Association of Music Producers—BAMP: 7 Reznyovete Str, bl 128, entr B, app 27, Sofia Lozenets 1421; tel. 359 2 866 8120/0104; fax 359 2 963 2757; e-mail office@bamp-bg.org

Union of Bulgarian Composers: 2 Ivan Vazoz Str, 1000 Sofia.

Canada

Alliance for Canadian New Music Projects—ACNMP: 20 St Joseph Street, Toronto, ON M4Y 1J9; tel. 1 416 963 5937; fax 1 416 961 7198; website www.acnmp.ca; Pres. Janet Fothergill.

American Federation of Musicians of the United States and Canada: 75 The Donway W, Suite 1010, Don Mills, ON M3C 2E9; Vice-Pres. (Canada) Ray Petch.

Association of Canadian Women Composers—ACWC: 20 St Joseph Street, Toronto, ON M4Y 1J9; tel. 1 416 239 5195; Chair. Lorraine Johnson.

Association of Cultural Executives: 720 Bathurst Street, Suite 503, Toronto, ON M5S 2R4.

Canadian Amateur Musicians/Musiciens Amateurs du Canada—CAMMAC: 85 Cammac Road, Harrington, QC J8G 2T2; tel. 1 819 687 3938; website www.cammac.ca; Dir-Gen. Barry Crago.

Canada Council/Conseil des Arts du Canada: PO Box 1047, 350 Albert Street, Ottawa, ON K1P 5V8; tel. 1 613 566 4414; fax 1 613 566 4390; website www.canadacouncil.ca; Dir Roch Carrier.

Canadian Association of Artists Managers: 117 Ava Road, Toronto, ON M6C 1W2.

Canadian Association of Arts Administration Educators: Simon Fraser University, 515 W Hastings Street, Vancouver, BC V6B 5K3; Pres. Letia Richardson.

Canadian Bureau for the Advancement of Music: Exhibition Place, Toronto, ON M6K 3C3.

Canadian League of Composers: Chalmers House, 20 St Joseph Street, Toronto, ON, M4Y 1J9; Pres. Patrick Cardy.

Canadian Music Centre/Centre de Musique Canadienne: 20 St Joseph Street, Toronto, ON M4Y 1J9; tel. 1 416 961 6601; fax 1 416 961 7198; e-mail info@musiccentre.ca; website www.musiccentre.ca; Exec. Dir Simone Auger.

Canadian Music Educators' Association/L'Association canadienne des éducateurs de musique—CMEA: 1207 Staffordshire Road, London, ON N6H 5R1; tel. (519) 474-6877; website www.musiceducationonline.org/cmea.index.html; Pres.: Gregg Bereznick; membership enquiries to: Betty Hanley, Faculty of Education, Box 3010, University of Victoria, Victoria, BC V8W 3N4.

Canadian Music Publishers Association—CMPA: 56 Wellesley Street W, Suite 320, Toronto, ON M5S 2S3; tel. 1 416 926 1966; fax 1 416 926 7521; e-mail dbaskin@cmpa.ca; website www.cmmra.ca; Pres. Mark Altman.

Canadian Musical Reproduction Rights Agency Ltd—CMRRA: 56 Wellesley Street W, Suite 320, Toronto, ON M5S 2S3; tel. 1 416 926 1966; fax 1 416 926 7521; website www.cmmra.ca; Gen. Man. David A. Basskin.

Canadian Recording Industry Association—CRIA: 890 Yonge Street, Suite 1200, Toronto, ON M4W 3P4; tel. 1 416 967 7272; fax 1 416 967 9415; e-mail info@cria.ca; website www.cria.ca; Pres. Brian Robertson.

Canadian Resource Centre for Career Performing Artists: PO Box 188, Station A, Toronto, ON M5W 1B2; Pres. Ann Summers.

Canadian University Music Society—CUMS: PO Box 507, Station Q, Toronto, ON M4T 2M5; tel. 1 416 483 7282; fax 1 416 489 1713; website www.cums/smuc.ca; Pres. Dr Eugene Cramer.

Jeunesses Musicales du Canada: 305 Avenue Mont-Royal E, Montréal, H2T 1P8; tel. 1 514 845 4108; fax 1 514 845 8241; website www.jeunessesmusicales.com; Gen. Dir Nicolas Desjardins; Artistic Dir Jacques Marquis.

Ontario Choral Federation: 20 St Joseph Street, Toronto, ON M4Y 1J9; Exec. Dir Bev Jahnke.

Orchestras Canada: 56 The Esplanade, Suite 203, Toronto, ON M5E 1A7; tel. (416) 366-8834; fax (416) 366-1780; e-mail info@oc.ca; website www.oc.ca; Exec. Dir Daniel Donaldson.

Organization of Canadian Symphony Musicians—OCSM: 455 Gérard Morisset, No. 6, Québec, QC G1S 4V5; Chair. Evelyne Robitaille.

Saskatoon Symphony Society: 703-601, Spading Crescent E, Saskatoon, SK S7K 3G8; tel. 306 6656414; fax 306 6523364; Gen. Man. Catherine McKeenan.

Society of Composers, Authors and Music Publishers of Canada—SOCAN: 41 Valleybrook Drive, Don Mills, Toronto, ON M3B 2S6; tel. 1 416 445 8700; fax 1 416 445 7108; website www.socan.ca; Gen. Man. Michael Rock.

Chile

Asociación Nacional de Compositores—ANC: Almirante Moritt 453, Santiago; website www.anc.scd.cl.

Instituto de Música: Universidad Católica de Chile, Jaime Guzman E 3 300, Santiago.

Juventudes Musicales: Universidad de Chile, Facultad de Artes, Compañía 1264, 4°, Santiago.

Sociedad Chilena del Derecho de Autor—SCD: Condell 346, Providencia, Santiago; website www.musica.cl.

Sociedad de Autores Teatrales de Chile: San Diego 246, Santiago.

People's Republic of China

Association of Chinese Musicians: Nong zhanguan Nan Li, No 10, Beijing 100026; tel. 86 10 65389265; fax 86 10 65004524.

Colombia

Asociación Colombiana de Músicos Profesionales: Calle 17, No. 10–16, Oficina 607, Bogotá, DE.

Asociación Colombiana de Productores de Fonogramas: Avenida 15 No. 123–29, Torre C, Jorge Baron Oficina 208, AA 101540, Santa Fe de Bogota, DC; tel. 57 1 612 0350/0390; fax 57 1 612 0310.

Asociación de Artistas de Colombia: Calle 13, No. 9-63, Interior 104, PO Box 24627, Bogotá, DE.

Centro de Documentación Musical, Instituto Colombiano de Cultura: Calle 11, No. 5-51, 2°, Bogotá, DE.

Instituto Colombiano de Cultura-Colcultura: Calle 11, No. 5-51, 2°, Santafé de Bogotá, DC.

Juventudes Musicales de Colombia: PO Box 089436, Carrera 16A No. 202, Bogotá 8.

Sociedad de Autores y Compositores de Colombia: Carrera 19, No. 40-72, PO Box 6482, Santafé de Bogotá, DC ZP1.

Costa Rica

Juventudes Musicales de Costa Rica: PO Box 1035, San José 1000.

Croatia

Croatian Composers' Society—HDS: Berislaviceva 9, 41000 Zagreb, Croatia; tel. 385 1 423 463; fax 385 1 422 850.

Cuba

Centro de Información y Promoción de la Música Cubana Odilio Urfé: Calle 17 esq. E, Vedado, Havana.

Centro de Investigación y Desarrollo de la Música Cubana: Calle G, No. 505 esq. 21 y 23, Vedado, Havana.

Centro Nacional de Derecho de Autor—CENDA: Calle Línea No. 365 (altos), esq. G, Vedado, Havana; website www.cenda.cu.

Centro Nacional de Música de Concierto: Calle Línea No. 365, esq. G, Vedado, Havana.

Centro Nacional de Música Popular: Avda 1a, esq. 10 y 12, Playa, Havana.

Editora Musical de Cuba: San Rafael No. 104, esq. Consulado, Centro Habana, Havana.

Empresa de Grabaciones y Ediciones Musicales—EGREM: Calle 3ra 1008 e, 10 y 12, Miramar, Havana; tel. 1 537 209 0687; fax 1 537 209 0688; website www.egrem.com.cu.

Instituto Cubano de la Música: Calle 15 No. 452, esq. F, Vedado, Havana.

Unión de Escritores y Artistas de Cuba (Music Section)—UNEAC: Calle 17 No. 351, esq. H, Vedado, Havana; website www.uneac.com.

Czech Republic

Authors' Association of Protection for Rights on Musical Works: Armády 20, 160 56 Prague 6.

Confederation of Arts and Culture: Senovážné nám. 23, 110 00 Prague 1; tel. 420 224 142 555; fax 420 224 142 512; e-mail odborykuk@volny.cz; Pres.: Adriena Jirková.

Czech Music Fund: Besední 3, 118 00 Prague 1; tel. 420 2 57320008; fax 420 2 57312834; e-mail nchf@gts.cz; website www.nchf.cz; Dir Miroslav Drozd.

Czech Music Information Centre: Besední 3, 118 00 Prague 1; tel. 420 2-5731 2422; fax 420 2-5731 7424; e-mail his@vol.cz; website www.musica .cz; Dir: Miroslav Pudlak; documentation and information centre for Czech contemporary composers and events; funded principally by the Czech Music Fund; publications include Czech Music, Musical Events, HIS VOICE.

Czech Music Society: Radlická 99, 150 00 Prague 5; tel. 420 2 51552382; 420 2 51552453; e-mail czechmusiksoc@hotmail.com; Pres. Míla Smetáck-ová.

Czech Society for Chamber Music: Korunní 98, 101 00 Prague 10.

International Federation of Phonogram and Videogram Producers: Gorkého nam. 23, 112 82 Prague 1.

International Music Council (National Committee): Valdstejnske nám. 1, Prague 1.

Denmark

Choir Conductors' Society: Astrugårdsvej 12, 2650 Hvidovre.

Danish Choral Association: Slagelsegade 9, 2100 Copenhagen O.

Danish Composers' Society: Gråbrødretorv 16, 1154 Copenhagen K; tel. 45 33 13 54 05; fax 45 33 14 32 19; website www.komponistforeningen .dk.

Danish Cultural Institute: Kultorvet 2, 1175 Copenhagen K; tel. 45 33 13 54 48; fax 45 33 15 10 91; e-mail dankultur@dankultur.dk; website www .dankultur.dk.

Danish Jazz Center: Boripvej 66, 4683 Rønnede.

Danish Music Information Centre: 48 Vimmelskaftet, 1161 Copenhagen K; website www.mic.dk.

Danish Musicians' Union: Vendersgade 25, 1363 Copenhagen K.

Danish Musicological Society: Department of Musicology, University of Copenhagen, Klerkegade 2, 1308 Copenhagen K; Chair: Best Morten Michelsen.

Danish Organists' and Precentors' Society: Flegmade 14, 7100 Vejle.

Danish Society of Composers, Authors and Editors: Maltegårdsvej 24, 2820 Gentofte.

Danish Society of Jazz, Rock, and Folk Composers: Klerkegade 19, 1308 Copenhagen K.

Danish Soloists' Association: Sundholmsvej 49, 2300 Copenhagen S.

Dansk Arbeider Sanger-og Musikforbund: Skovgade 6, 5500 Mid-delfart.

Dansk kapelmesterforening: Rosenvangsvej 47, 2670 Greve Strand.

Det dansk orgelselskab (Danish Organ Society): Willemoesgade 85, 1.th., 2100 Copenhagen; website www.detdanskeorgelselskab.dk.

International Society for Contemporary Music (Danish Section): Valkendorfsgade 3, 1151 Copenhagen K.

Samrået for Musikundervisning: Vallerod-skolen, Stadion Allé, 2960 Rungsted Kyst.

Society of Danish Church Singing: Hoyrups Allé 7, 2900 Hellerup.

State Music Council: Vesterbrodgade 24, 1620 Copenhagen V.

Union of Danish Singers: Norre Sovej 26 A, 8800 Viborg.

Ecuador

Juventudes Musicales: Casilla Correo, 8162, Sucursal 8, Quito.

El Salvador

Centro Nacional de Artes: 2a Avda Norte Pje. Contreras, No. 145, San Salvador.

Estonia

Jeunesses Musicales Eestis: Estonia pst 4 tuba 410, 200105 Tallinn.

Finland

Association of Finnish Conservatories: Fredrikinkati 34 B, 00100 Helsinki.

Association of Finnish Music Schools—SML: Fredrikinkatu 25 B 26, 00120 Helsinki; tel. 358 9 646 122/646 116; fax 358 9 6843 8910; e-mail smlfmf@smlfmf.fi; website www.kolumbus.fi/smlfmf.

Association of Finnish Operas: Iso-Roobertinkatu 20-22 A 76, 00120 Helsinki.

Association of Finnish Soloists: Museokatu 3 B 12, 00100 Helsinki.

Association of Finnish Symphony Orchestras: Aninkaistenkatu 3 B, 20110 Turku.

Association of Military Conductors: Helsingin varuskuntasoitto-kunta, PL 13, 00251 Helsinki.

Association of Music Libraries in Finland: PO Box 148, 01301 Vantaa.

Association of Swedish Speaking Church Musicians: 10210 Ingå.

Concert Centre: Urho Kekkosen katu 8 C 30, 00100 Helsinki.

Federation for Church Music in Finland: Tollinpolku 1 C, 00410 Helsinki.

Federation for Finnish Traditional Music: Raumantie 1, 00350 Helsinki.

Federation of Music Teachers in Finland: Asemamiehenkatu 4, 00520 Helsinki.

Finland Festivals: PO Box 56, 00100 Helsinki.

Finlands svenska sång-och musikförbund r.f.: Handelsespladen 23 B, 65100 Vasa.

Finnish Composers' Copyright Society—TEOSTO: Lauttasaarentie 1, 00200 Helsinki; tel. 358 9 681011; fax 358 9 677134; e-mail teosto@teosto .fi: website www.teosto.fi; Man. Kalle Jamsen.

Finnish Jazz Federation: Arabiankatu 2, 00560 Helsinki; tel. 358 9 757 2077; fax 358 9 757 2067; Exec. Man. Timo Vahasilta.

Finnish Music Information Centre: Runeberginkatu 15 A, 00100 Helsinki.

Finnish Music Publishers' Association: Runeberginkatu 15 A 12, 00100 Helsinki; website www.musiikkikustantajat.fi.

Finnish Musicians' Union: Pieni Roobertinkatu 16, 00120 Helsinki.

Finnish Performing Music Promotion Centre: Pieni Roobertinkatu 16, 00100 Helsinki; tel. 358 9 6803 4040; fax 358 9 6803 4033; e-mail esek@ gramex.fi.

Finnish Society for Ethnomusicology: Mannerheimintie 40 C 69, 00100 Helsinki.

Folk Music Institute: 69600 Kaustinen.

Foundation for the Promotion of Finnish Music: Runeberginkatu 15 A 6, 00100 Helsinki.

Guild of Light Music Composers and Authors in Finland: Runeberginkatu 15 A 11, 00100 Helsinki.

Head Organization of Finnish Traditional Music: 39170 Jumesniemi.

IFPI (Finnish National Group): Yrjonkatu 3, 00120 Helsinki.

International Music Council (Finnish Section): Ukonkivenpolku 4 D 28, 01610 Vantaa.

Institute of Accordion Music in Finland: Kvrösselänkatu 3, 39599 Ikaalinen.

Korvat Aukiry (Society for Young Contemporary Composers): Kurkisuontie 12 D 35, 00940 Helsinki.

Music Artists Organization: Kuususaarenkuia 9, 00340 Helsinki.

Musicological Society of Finland: Töölönkatu 28, 00260 Helsinki.

Sibelius Museum: Biskopsgatan 17, 20500 Åbo; tel. 358 2 2154494; fax 358 2 2518528; e-mail jbrusila@abo.fi; Curator Johannes Brusila.

Society of Finnish Composers: Runeberginkatu 15 A 11, 00100 Helsinki; tel. 358 9 445589; fax 358 9 440181; e-mail saveltajat@compose .pp.fi; Exec. Dir Annu Mikkonen.

SULASOL (Federation of Amateur Musicians in Finland): Fredrikinkatu 51–53B, 00100 Helsinki; tel. 358 9 41361100; fax 358 9 41361122; e-mail info@sulasol.fi; website www.sulasol.fi.

Workers' Institute of Music: Mannerheimintie 40 C 74, 00100 Helsinki.

Workers' Musical Organization in Finland: Hämeenpuisto 33 B 25, 33200 Tampere.

France

Académie du Disque Français et du Film musical: 68 Blvd de Courcelles, 75017 Paris.

American Center: 51 rue de Bercy, 75592 Paris Cédex 12; tel. 33 1 44 73 77 77; fax 33 1 44 73 77 55.

Association des Festivals Internationaux de France: 16 Place du Havre, 75009 Paris.

Association Nationale de Diffusion Culturelle: 5 rue Bellart, 75015 Paris.

Association pour le Developpement des Echanges Artistique et Culturels—ADEAC: 101 Blvd Raspail, 75006 Paris.

Bibliothèque Bozidar Kantuser, Centre International d'Information de Musique Contemporaine: Conservatoire Supérieur de Paris—, 14 rue de Madrid, 75008 Paris; tel. 33 1 44 70 64 21; Pres.: Didier Duclos; fmrly the Bibliothèque Internationale de Musique Contemporaine.

Bibliothèque-Musée de l'Opera de Paris: 8 rue Scribe, 75009 Paris; tel. 33 1 47 42 07 02; fax 33 1 42 65 10 16.

Bureau International d'Enregistrement et de Reproduction Méchanique–BIEM: 14 rue Lincoln, 75008 Paris; tel. 33 1 53 93 67 00; fax 33 1 45 63 06 11; e-mail info@biem.org.

Centre de Documentation de la Musique Contemporaine—CDMC: 225 Avenue Charles de Gaulle, 92521 Neuilly-sur-Seine Cédeamerican center parisx; website www.cdmc.asso.fr; Dir Marianne Lyon.

Centre de Documentation de Musique Internationale: 116 Avenue du Président Kennedy, 75016 Paris.

Chambre Syndicale de l'Edition Musicale—CSDEM: 62 rue Blanche, 75009 Paris; Pres. Jean Devoust.

Chambre Syndicale de la Facture Instrumentale: 62 rue Blanche, 75009 Paris; Pres. Bernard Maillot.

Chambre Syndicale des Editeurs de Musique: Editions Choudens, 38 rue Jean Mermoz, 75008 Paris.

Comite National de la Musique—CNM: 252 rue de Faubourg St Honoré, Salle Pleyel, 75008 Paris; Gen. Man. Jacques Masson-Forestier.

Commission d'Attribution de la Carte de Critique: 6 bis rue Gabriel Laumain, 75010 Paris.

Confédération Internationale des Sociétés d'Auteurs et Compositeurs—CISAC: 11 rue Keppler, 75116 Paris.

Fédération Nationale de la Musique: 62 rue Blanche, 75009 Paris; Pres. Pierre Henry.

Groupe de l'Edition Audiovisuelle et Electronique—HAVE: 35 rue Gregoire de Tours, 75006 Paris.

Groupment des Industries Electroniques—GIEL: 11 rue Hamelin, 75783 Paris Cédex 16.

Institut de Recherche et Coordination Acoustique/Musique: 31 rue Saint-Merri, 75004 Paris; Dir Laurent Bayle; Hon. Dir Pierre Boulez.

International Music Council (UNESCO): 1 rue Miollis, 75732 Paris Cédex 15; tel. 33 1 45 68 25 50; fax 33 1 43 06 87 98; Sec.-Gen. Guy Huot.

International Music Critics Association: 11 Avenue de Lena, 75016 Paris.

Jeunesses Musicales de France: 20 rue Geoffroy l'Asnier, 75004 Paris; website www.lesjmf.org; Dir Robert Berthier.

Médiathèque Musicale Gustav Mahler: 11 bis rue de Vézelay, 75008 Paris; tel. 1 53 89 09 10; fax 1 43 59 70 22; website www .mediathequemahler.org.

Musicora: Salon de la Musique, 62 rue de Miromesnil, 75008 Paris.

Société Alkan: 9bis Avenue Médicis, 94100 St Maur de Fosses; e-mail alkan.association@voila.fr; Chief Officer Laurent Martin; Sec. François Luguenot.

Société des Auteurs et Compositeurs Dramatiques—SACD: 11 bis rue Ballu, 75009 Paris; tel. 33 1 40 23 44 44; fax 33 1 45 26 74 28; website www.sacd.fr; Chief Officer Jean-Jacques Plantin.

Société des Auteurs, Compositeurs et Editeurs—SACE: 62 rue Blanche, 75009 Paris; Pres. Wladimir Walberg.

Société des Auteurs, Compositeurs et Editeurs de Musqiue— SACEM: 225 Avenue Charles de Gaulle, 92521 Neuilly-sur-Seine Cédex; tel. 33 1 47 15 47 15; fax 33 1 47 45 12 94; Dir-Gen. Jean-Loup Tournier.

Société pour l'Administration de Droit de Reproduction Méchanique des Auteurs, Compositeurs et Editeurs—SDRM: 225 Avenue de Charles de Gaulle, 92521 Neuilly-sur-Seine Cédex.

Syndicat des Artistes de Variétés-Syndicat des Artistes Lyriques: 29 rue Jean Jacques Rousseau, 75001 Paris.

Syndicat des Artistes Musiciens Professionnels de Paris—SAMUP: 14–16 rue des Lilas, 75019 Paris; Sec.-Gen. François Nowak.

Syndicat des Industries de Materiels Audiovisuels Electroniques—SIMAVELEC: 11 rue Hamelin, 75783 Paris Cédex 16.

Syndicat Francais des Artistes Interprétes—SFA: 21 bis rue Victor Massé, 75009 Paris.

Syndicat National des Artistes Musiciens de France—SNAM: 14–16 rue des Lilas, 75019 Paris; Sec.-Gen. François Nowak.

Syndicat National des Auteurs et des Compositeurs de Musique: 80 rue Taitbout, 75442 Paris Cédex 09.

Syndicat National des Chefs d'Orchestre: 3 rue Chateau d'Eau, 75010 Paris.

Union des Artistes: 21 bis rue Victor Massé, 75009 Paris.

Germany

AG Song-Arbeitsgemeinschaft Der Liedermacher: Mailaender Strasse 14/92, 60598, Frankfurt Am Main; tel. 069 686269.

Akademie der Künste Berlin: Hanseatenweg 10, 1000 Berlin 21; website www.adk.de; Pres. Prof. Dr Walter Jens.

Allgemeiner Cäcilien-Verband für Deutschland (ACV Deutschland): Andreasstrasse 9, 93059 Regensburg; tel. and fax 49 941 84339; Pres. Dr Wolfgang Bretschneider.

Arbeitsgemeinschaft der Leiter Musikpädagogischer Studiengänge: Hochschule der Künste Berlin, Fachbereich 8/KWE 2, Fasanenstrasse 1, 10623 Berlin; tel. 49 303 185 2399; Speaker Prof. Dr Ulrich Mahlert.

Arbeitsgemeinschaft der Musikakademien, Konservatorien und Hochschulinstitute: Ludwigshöhstrasse 120, 64285 Darmstadt; tel. 49 6151 96640; fax 49 6151 966413; Chair. Hartmut Gerhold.

Arbeitsgemeinschaft Deutsche Saxophonisten e V (ARDESA): Rötenäcktstrasse 2, 8500 Nürnberg 90; Chair. Günter Priesner.

Arbeitsgemeinschaft Deutscher Chorverbände (ADC): Adersheimer Strasse 60, 38304 Wolfenbüttel; tel. 49 5331 46018; fax 49 5331 43723; Chair. Lore Auerbach; Man. Rolf Pasdzierny.

Arbeitsgemeinschaft Deutscher Musikakademien und Konservatorien: Richard-Strauss-Konservatorium, Kellerstrasse 6, 81667 Munich; tel. 89 48098415; fax 89 48098417; e-mail sekretariat@rsk.musin.de; Pres. Martin Maria Krüger.

Arbeitsgemeinschaft Deutscher Studentenorchester: Wilhelmstrasse 30, 7400 Tübingen; Chair. Helmut Calgéer.

Arbeitsgemeinschaft Deutscher Zupfinstrumenten-Verbände (AZV): Rissweg 22, 7507 Pfinztal 2; Chair. Adolf Mössner.

Arbeitsgemeinschaft Freikirchlicher Chorwerke in Europa (AFC): Westfalenweg 207, 5600 Wuppertal 1; Chair. Pastoe Frieder Ringeis.

Arbeitsgemeinschaft für Mittelrheinische Musikgeschichte e V: Musikwissenschaftliches Institut der Universität Mainz, Arbeitsstelle für landeskundliche Musikforschung, Welderweg 18, PO Box 3980, 6500 Mainz; Chair. Prof. Dr Christoph-Hellmut Mahling.

Arbeitsgemeinschaft für rheinische Musikgeschichte e V: Musikwissenschaftliches Institut der Universität Köln, Albertus-Magnus-Platz, 5000 Cologne; Chair. Prof. Dr Siegfried Kross.

Arbeitsgemeinschaft Musik in der Evangelischen Jugend e V (AG Musik): Dorfstrasse 4, 24250 Löptin; tel. 49 4302 96780; fax 49 4302 967820; Chair. Carl-Walter Petersen.

Arbeitsgemeinschaft Schulmusik an den Hochschulen für Musik: Musikhochschule Lübeck, Grosse Peters-grube 17-29, 2400 Lübeck; Chair. Prof. Dr Wilfried Ribke.

Arbeitskreis der Musikbildungsstatten in der Bundesrepublik Deutschland: Landesakademie für die musikierende Jugend in Baden-Württemberg, Dr Hans-Bruno Ernst, Schlossbezirk 6, PO Box 1180, 7955, Ochsenhausen.

Arbeitskreis der Orgelsachverständigen: Hohenstrasse 19, 7541 Straubenhardt 6 (Langenalb); Chair. Heinrich R. Trötschel.

Arbeitskreis für Schulmusik und allgemeine Musikpädagogik e V (AFS): Gründgensstrasse 16, 2000 Hamburg 60; Chair. Prof. Dr Volker Schütz.

Arbeitskreis Musik in der Jugend e V (AMJ): Adersheimer Strasse 60, 38304 Wolfenbüttel; tel. 5331-46016; fax 5331-43723; e-mail amjmuiskinderjugend@t-online.de; website www.amj-musik.de; Chair. Helmut Steger; Gen. Sec. Martin Koch.

Arbeitskreis Musikpädagogische Forschung e V (AMPF): Nycolaystrasse, 4790 Paderborn-Dahl; Chair. Dr Georg Maas.

Bayerische Akademie der Schönen Künste: Max-Joseph-Platz, 8000 Munich 22; Pres. Heinz Friedrich.

Bayerischer Landesverein für Heimatpflege e V: Beratungsstelle für Volksmusik, Ludwigstrasse 23, Rgb., 8000 Munich 22; Chair. Max Streibl.

Bayerischer Musiklehrer-Verband e V: Willibaldstrasse 49, 8000 Munich 21; Chair. Roland Sieber.

Berufsverband der Musiktherapeuten Deutschlands e V (BMD): Waldhüterofad 38, 1999 Berlin 37; Chair. Herbert Lunkenheimer.

Berusfverband für Kunst-, Musik-und Tanztherapie: Grüner Hang 16, 4400 Münster; Chair. Prof. Dr Georg Hörmann.

Berufsverband Klinischer Musiktherapeuten in der Bundesrepublik Deutschland e V: Stader Weg 31, 2800 Bremen; Chair. Ilse Wolfram.

Bildungswerk Rhythmik eV (BWR): Kalscheurer Weg S Nr. 12, 5000 Cologne 1; Chair. Christine Humpert.

Bogenforschungsgesellscaft: Ankerstrasse 34, 5205 Sankt Augustin; Chair. Rudolf Gahler.

Brahmsgesellschaft Baden-Baden e V: PO Box 1609, 7560 Gaggenau; Chair. Dr Werner Hoppe.

Brandenburgisches Colloquiem für Neue Musik e V: Clara-Zetkin-Strasse 1, 1276 Buckow.

Bruder-Busch-Gesellschaft e V: Untere Wiesenstrasse 33, 5912 Hilchenbach; Business Man. Wolfgang Burbcah.

Bund der Theatergemeinden e V: Bonner Talweg 10, 5300 Bonn 1; Pres. Friedrich von Kekulé.

Bund Deutscher Blasmusikverbände e V (BDB): Am Märzengraben 6, 7800 Freiburg im Breisgau; Pres. Dr Norbert Nothhelfer.

Bund Deutscher Liebhaberorchester e V (BDLO): Schlegelstrasse 14, 8500 Nürnberg; Chair. Dr Joachim Conradi.

Bund Deutscher Orgelbaumeister e V (BDO): Frankfurter Ring 243, 8000 Munich 40; Chair. Hans-Gerd Klais.

Bund Deutscher Zupfmusiker e V (BDZ): Huulkamp 26, 22397 Hamburg; tel. 49 40 6088 9013; fax 49 40 6088 9014; Chair. Rüdiger Grambow.

Bundes-Eltern-Vertretung e V der Musikschulen des VdM: Ossietzkyring 55, 3000 Hanover 91; Chair. Dieter Fröhling.

Bundesinnungverband für das Musikinstrumenten-Handwerk (BIV): Kreishandwerkerschaft Köln, Frankenwerft 35, Cologne; Chair. Johann Scholtz.

Bundesverband der Deutschen Musikinstrumenten-Hersteller e V (BdMH): Tennelbachstrasse 25, 65193 Wiesbaden; tel. 49 611 954 5885; fax 49 611 954 5886; Man. Dir Winfried Baumbach.

Bundesverband der deutschen Volksbühnen-Vereine e V: Am Handelshof 9, 4300 Essen 1; Chair. Axel Wolters.

Bundesverband der Phonographischen Wirtschaft e V (Bundesverband Phono): Oranienburger Strasse 67–68, 10117 Berlin; tel. 030 590038; fax 030 590038; Chair. Gerd Gebhardt; Gen. Man. Peter Zombik.

Bundesverband Deutscher Gesangspädagogen e V (BDG): Waldeck 7, 4930 Detmold; Pres. Prof. Helmut Kretschmar.

Bundesverband für Tanztherapie Deutschland e V: Hostrasse 16, Marienburg, 4019 Monheim; Chair. Wally Kaechele.

Bundesverband Rhythmische Erziehung e V (BRE): Akademie Remscheid, Küppelstein 34, 5630 Remscheid 1; Chair. Prof. Brigitte Steinmann.

Bundesverband Studentische Kulturarbeit e V (BSK): Kaiserstrasse 32, 5300 Bonn 1.

Bundesvereinigung der Musikveranstalter e V: Kronprinzenstrasse 46, 5300 Bonn 2; Pres. Leo Imhoff.

Bundesvereinigung Deutscher Blas-und Volksmusikverbände e V (BDBV): König-Karl-Strasse 13, 70372 Stuttgart; tel. 49 711 568397; fax 49 711 552523; Pres. Minister Gerhard Weiser.

Bundesvereinigung Deutscher Orchesterverbände eV (BDO): Rudolf-Maschke-Platz 6, 78647 Trossingen; tel. 49 7425 8312; fax 49 7425 21519; Pres. Ernst Burgbacher MdB; Dir Erik Hörenberg.

Bundesvereinigung Kulturelle Jugendbildung e V (BKJ): Küppelstein 34, 5630 Remscheid; Chair. Prof. Bruno Tetzner.

Carl-Orff-Stiftung: Königinstrasse 25, 8000 Munich 22; Chair. Liselotte Orff.

Chopin-Gesellschaft in der Bundesrepublik Deutschland e V: Kasinostrasse 3 (J. F. Kenedy-Haus), 6100 Darmstadt 11; Pres. Maciej Lukasz.

Christlicher Sängerbund e V (CS): Westfalenweg 207, 5600 Wuppertal 1.

Club Deutscher Drehorgelfreunde e V: Wilfried Hömmerich, Brusseler Strasse 20, PO Box 170103, 5300 Bonn 1; Chair. Wilfried Hömmerich.

Deutsche Angestellten-Gewerkschaft (DAG): Karl-Marx-Platz 1, PO Box 301230, Hamburg.

Deutsche Arbeitsgemeinschaft für Akustik (DAGA): Hauptstrasse 5, 5340 Bad Honnef 1; Chair. Prof. Dr H. Kuttruff.

Deutsche Disc-Jockey-Organization (DDO): Kaiser-Friedrich-Alle 1–3, 5100 Aachen; Contact Klaus Quirini.

Deutsche Forschungsgemeinschaft e V (DFG): Kennedyalle 40 PO Box 205004, 5300 Bonn 2; Pres. Prof. Dr Wolfgang Fruhwald.

Deutsche Frank-Martin-Gesellschaft e V: Hochschule für Musik Köln, Dagobertstrasse 38, 5000 Cologne 1; Pres. Dirk Schortemeier.

Deutsche Gesellschaft für Flote e V: Eschenheimer Anlage 30, 6000 Frankfurt am Main 1; Pres. András Adorján.

Deutsche Gesellschaft für Musik bei Behinderten e V (DGMB): Frangenheimstrasse 4, 5000 Cologne 41; Chair. Prof. Dr Helmut Moog.

Deutsche Gesellschaft für Musikpsychologie e V (DGfM): Meisenweg 7, 3008 Garbsen 1; Chair. Prof. Dr Klaus-Ernst Behne.

Deutsche Gesellschaft für Musiktherapie e V (DGMT): Libauerstrasse 17, 10245 Berlin; e-mail info@musiktherapie.de; website www .musiktherapie.de; Chair. Franz Mecklenbeck.

Deutsche Gesellschaft für Volkstanz e V (DGV): Anni Herrmann, Paul-Lincke-Ufer 25, 1000 Berlin 36; Chair. Gerhard Palmer.

Deutsche Glockenspiel-Vereinigung e V: Pfortenstr. 30, 07318 Saalfeld; Chair. Knut Schieferdecker.

Deutsche Johann-Strauss-Gesellschaft e V: Untere Anlage 2, 8630 Coburg; Chair. Arthur Kulling.

Deutsche Mozart-Gesellschaft e V (DMG): Karlstrasse 6, 8900 Augsburg.

Deutsche Musikinstrumentenstiftung: Emil-Nolde-Weg 29, 37085 Göttingen; tel. 0049 551 72198; Chair. Prof. Dr Jürgen Costede.

Deutsche Orchestervereinigung e V in der DAG (DOV): Heimhuder Strasse 5, 2000 Hamburg 13; Chair. Dr Rolf Dünnwald.

Deutsche Phono-Akademie e V (DPhA): Grelckstrasse 36, 22529 Hamburg; tel. 49 40 581935; fax 49 40 580533; Chair. Gerd Gebhardt.

Deutsche Richard-Wagner-Gesellschaft e V: Schlosstrasse 9a, 1000 Berlin 28; Chair. Prof. Uwe Faerber.

Deutsche Rossini-Gesellschaft e V: Hohenheimerstrasse 84, 7000 Stuttgart 1; Chair. Gustav Kuhn.

Deutsche Sängerschaft (Weimarer CC): Cranachweg 9, 7320 Göppingen; Chair. Franz Jedlitschka.

Deutsche Schubert-Gesellschaft e V (DSG): Handelstrasse 6, 4100 Duisburg 14 (Rheinhausen); Chair. Günter Berns.

Deutsche Sektion der Gesellschaft für Elektroakustische Musik: Treuchtlinger Strasse 8, Berlin; Chair. Folkmar Hein.

Deutsche Stiftung Musikleben (DSM): Herrengraben 3, 2000 Hamburg 11; Pres. Erhard Bouillons.

Deutsche Suzuki Gesellschaft e V: Ankerstrasse 34, 5205 Sankt Augustin 1; Chair. Rudolf Gahler.

Deutscher Akkordeonlehrer-Verband e V (DALV): PO Box 11 35, 78635 Trossingen; tel. 49 7425 20249; fax 49 7425 20448; Chair. Wolfgang Eschenbacher; Man. Matthias Keller.

Deutscher Allgemeiner Sängerbund e V (DAS): Barbarastrasse 7, 44357 Dortmund; tel. 49 231 336558; fax 49 231 333352; Pres. Fritz Neuhaus.

Deutscher Berufsverband für Tanzpadagogik e V: Hollestrasse 1g, 4300 Essen 1; Chair. Ulrich Roehm.

Deutscher Bühnenverein-Bundesverband deutscher Theater e V (DBV): Quatermarkt 5, 5000 Cologne 1; Contact Rolf Golwin.

Deutscher Bundesverband Tanz e V (DBT): Küppelstein 34, 5630 Remscheid; Chair. Annmargret Pretz.

Deutscher Chorverband Pueri Cantores: Zwölfling 12, 4300 Essen 1; Pres. Georg Sump.

Deutscher Feuerwehrverband e V: Fachgebiet Musik, Koblenzer Strasse 133, 5300 Bonn 2; Pres. Heinrich Struve.

Deutscher Harmonika-Verband e V (DHV): Rudolf-Maschke-Platz 6, PO Box 1150, 7218 Trossingen 1; Pres. Ernst Pfister.

Deutscher Hotel-und Gaststättenverband (DEHOGA): Fachabteilung musikveranstaltende Betriebe, Kronprinzenstr. 46, Bonn; Chair. Otto Manfred Lamm.

Deutscher Komponisten-Verband e V (DKV): Kadettenweg 80b, 12205 Berlin; tel. 49 30 8431 0580; fax 49 30 8431 0582; Pres. Karl Heinz Wahren.

Deutscher Kulturrat: Adenaueralle 7, 5300 Bonn 1.

Deutscher Musikrat e V (DMR): Nationalkomitee der Bundesrepublik Deutschland im Internationalen Musikrat, Am Michaelshof 4a, 5300 Bonn 2; Pres. Prof. Dr Franz Müller-Heuser.

Deutscher Musikverleger-Verband e V (DMV): Friedrich-Wilhelm-Strasse 31, 53113 Bonn; Gen. Man. Dr H. H. Wittgen.

Deutscher Rockmusiker-Verband e V: Kolbergerstrasse 30, 2120 Lüneburg; Chair. Ole Seelenmeyer.

Deutscher Sängerbund e V (DSB): Bernhardstrasse 166, 50968 Koln; Pres. Dr Heinz Eyrich.

Deutscher Schützenbund e V: Fachgruppe Musik, Niedersächsischer Sportschützenverband, Wunstorfer Landstrasse 57, 3000 Hannover 91.

Deutscher Tanzrat/Deutscher ballettrat e V: Bonner Künstlerhaus, Graurheindorfer Strasse 23, 5300 Bonn 1; Chair. Iskra Zankova.

Deutscher Textdichter-Verband e V: Dohlenweg 5, 5020 Frechen; Pres. Heinz Korn.

Deutscher Zithermusik-bund e V (DZB): Ulrich Oesterle, Steigäcker 4, 7140 Ludwigsburg.

Deutsches High-Fidelity Institut e V (DHFI): Karlstrasse 19–21, 6000 Frankfurt am Main 1; Chair. Karl Breh.

Deutsches Tubaforum e V: Saarbrückener Stasse 26, 3000 Hannover 71; Chair. Prof. Klemens Propper.

Die Kunstlergilde e V: Hafenmarkt 2, 73725 Esslingen; tel. 49 711 3969 0123; fax 49 711 3969 010; Chair. Albrecht Baehr.

Dr Hanns-Simon-Stiftung: Bedaplatz, 5520 Bitburg.

Dramatiker-Union e V (DU): Bismarckstrasse 107, 1000 Berlin 12; Pres. Prof. Giselher Klebe.

Dramaturgische Gesellschaft e V: Tempelhofer Ufer 22, 1000 Berlin 61; Chair. Dr Klaus Pierwoss.

Dresdner Zentrum für zeitgenössischen Musik: Schevenstrasse 17/ 150-05, 8054 Dresden; Dir Prof. Udo Zimmermann.

Emil-Berliner-Stiftung in der Deutschen Phono-Akademie e V: Grelckstrasse 36, 2000 Hamburg 54; Chair. Richard Busch.

EPTA-Gesellschaft der Padagogik für Tasteninstrumente e V: Bult 6, 4590 Cloppenburg; Chair. Prof. Edith Picht-Axenfeld.

Ernst-Pepping-Gesellschaft e V: Jebensstrasse 3, 1000 Berlin 12; Chair. Prof. Dr Heinrich Poos.

Ernst-von-Siemens-Stiftung: Zug (Schweiz), Wittelsbacherplatz 2, 8000 Munich 2.

Eugen-Jochum-Gesellschaft e V: Marktplatz 14, Kulturamt, 8942 Ottobeuren; Pres. Dr Georg Simnacher.

Europa Cantat-Europäische Föderation Junger Chöre e V (EC-EFJC): Grosser Hillen 38, 3000 Hannover 71; Sec.-Gen. Hans Dieter Reinecke.

Europäische Arbeitsgemeinschaft Schulmusik—EAS (European Association for Music in Schools): c/o Prof. Dr Franz Niermann, University of Music and Performing Arts Vienna, Institute for Music Education, Metternichgasse 8, 1030 Vienna; tel. (1) 71155-3700; fax (1) 71155-3799; e-mail niermann@mdw.ac.at; website www.musiceducation .at.

Europäische Union der Musikwettbewerbe für die Jugend: Herzog-Johann-Strasse 10, 8000 Munich 60; Contact Dr Eckart Rohlfs.

European Guitar Teachers Association (EGTA): Marblicksweg 55, 59555 Lippstadt; tel. 49 2941 60445; fax 49 2941 658029; Chair. Reinhard Froese, Michael Koch.

European String Teachers Association (ESTA): Dagmar klevenhusen, Friedenweg 6, 2807 Achim.

Evangelischer Sängerbund e V (ESB): Bremer Strasse 2, 5600 Wuppertal 1; Chair. Rudolf Steege.

Fachverband Deutsche Klavierindustrie e V (FDK): Friedrich-Wilhelm-Strasse 31, 53113 Bonn; tel. 49 228 539700; fax 49 228 539 7070; Gen. Man. Dr Hans-Henning Wittgen.

Fachverbad Deutscher Berufscholeiter e V (FDB): Unkenweg 19, 4330 Müllheim/Ruhr.

Fachverband Historische Tasteninstrumente e V (FHT): Untermarkt 40, 8190 Wolfratshausen; Chair. Reinhard Hoppe.

Ferenc-Fricsay Gesellschaft e V (FFG): Heerstrasse 70, 1000 Berlin 19; Chair. Prof. Dr Wolfgang Geisler.

Förderkreis Hugo Herrmann e V: Ringinger Tal 26, 7453 Burladingen; Chair. Werner Zintgraf.

Förderkreis Instrumentales Musizieren e V: Friedrich-Wilhelm-Strasse 31, 5300 Bonn 1; Chair. Alfred Döll.

Förderkreis Unterhaltungsmusik e V (FKU): Ringstrasse 4, 46562 Voerde; tel. 49 2855 2112; fax 49 2855 4514; Chair. Kurt Althans.

Förderverein der Klassischen Gesangskunst in Deutschland e V: PO Box 101516, 7000 Stuttgart 10; Chair. Prof. Sylvia Geszty.

Fonds Darstellende Künste e V: Am Handelshof 9, 4300 Essen 1; Chair. Prof. Dr Jürgen-Dieter Waidelich.

Fonds Soziokultur e V: Stirnband 10, 5800 Hagen 1; Chair. Dr Olaf Schwencke.

Franz-Grothe-Stiftung: Rosenheimer Strasse 11, 8000 Munich 80; Chair. Hans Schröpf.

Franz-Liszt-Gesellschaft e V Weimar: Platz der Demokratie 2–3, 5300 Weimar; Pres. Prof. Dr Detlef Altenburg.

Frau und Musik-Internationaler Arbeitskreis e V Geschäftsstelle: Adelheid Klammt, Vogesort 8 F, 3000 Hannover 91; Chair. Prof. Siegrid Ernst.

Freie Akademie der Künste Hamburg: Ferdinandstor la, 2000 Hamburg; Pres. Prof. Armin Sandig.

Freunde der Querflöte: Körnerstrasse 51, 5820 Gevelsberg; Chair. Elli Edler-Busch.

Freunde der Tonkunst und Musikerziehung e V: Landsberger Strasse 425, 8000 Munich 60; Chair. Dr Rüdiger von Canal.

Friedrich-Kiel-Gesellschaft e V: Ithstrasse 20, 31863 Coppenbrügge; tel. 49 5156 1637; fax 49 5156 1637; Chair. Dr Hartmut Wecker.

Fritz-Büchtger-Kuratorium: Musica Sacra Viva, PO Box 750202, 8000 Munich 75; Chair. Andreas Weymann.

GEMA-Stifung: Rosenheimer Strasse 11, 8000 Munich 80; Chair. Prof. Dr Reinhold Kreile.

Genossenschaft Deutscher Bühnenangehöriger (GDBA) in der DAG: Feldbrunnenstrasse 74, 20148 Hamburg; tel. 49 40 443870; fax 49 40 459352; Pres. Hans Herdlein.

Georg Hesse Stiftung: Am Brühl 13, 7825 Lenzkirch 3 (Kappel); Chair. Hannelore Hesse-Mange.

Georg-Friedrich-Händel-Gesellschaft-Internationale Vereinigung e V: Grosse Nikolaistrasse 5, 06108 Halle an der Saale; Pres. Prof. Dr Wolfgang Ruf.

Gesamtverband Deutscher Musikfachgeschäfte e V (GDM): Friedrich-Wilhelm-Strasse 31, 53113 Bonn; tel. 49 228 539700; fax 49 228 539 7070; Gen. Man. Dr H. H. Wittgen.

Gesellschaft der Orgelfreunde e V (GdO): Josestrasse 6, 6642 Mettlach 1; Chair. Prof. Alfred Reichling.

Gesellschaft für Alte Musik e V (GAM): Birkenstrasse 18, 7218 Trossingen; Chair. Prof. Dr Ludger Lohmann.

Gesellschaft für Bayerische Musikgeschichte e V: PO Box 100611, 8000 Munich 1; Chair. Prof. Dr Theodor Göllner.

Gesellschaft für Musikforschung (GfM): Heinrich-Schütz-Allee 35, 34131 Kassel; tel. 49 561 310 5240; fax 49 561 31050; Pres. Prof. Dr Klaus W. Niemöller.

Gesellschaft für Musikpädagogik e V (GMP): Von-der-Tann-Strasse 38, 8400 Regensburg; Chair. Prof. Dr Reinhard Schneider.

Gesellschaft für Neue Musik e V: (GNM)-Sektion Bundesrepublik Deutschland der Internationalen Gesellschaft für Neue Musik (IGNM), Schwedlerstrasse 2–4, 6000 Frankfurt am Main 1; Pres. Friedrich Goldmann.

Gesellschaft für Selbstspielende Musikinstrumente e V: Heiligenstock 46, 5060 Bergisch Gladbach 2; Chair. Dr Jürgen Hocker.

Gesellschaft für Theatergeschichte e V: Mecklenburgische Strasse 56, 1000 Berlin 33; Chair. Prof. Dr Peter Spengel.

Gesellschaft zur Förderung der Berufsbildung junger Künstler e V (GFBK): Eichkatzweg 25, 3107 Hambuhren.

Gesellschaft zur Förderung der Westfalischen Kulturarbeit e V: Landschaftverband Westfalen-Lippe, Warendorfer Str 14, Münster; Chair. Reinhold Brauner.

Gotthard-Schierse-Stiftung: Bundesallee 1-12, 1000 Berlin 15; Chair. Horst Göbel.

Günter Henle Stiftung München: G Henle Verlag, Forstenrieder Allee 122, PO Box 710466, 8000 Munich 71; Chair. Anne Liese Henle.

Hamburger, Internationaler Verein für die Musik der Bach-Sohne (HBG): Durchschnitt 25, Hamburg; Chair. Prof. Edith Picht-Axenfeld.

Hamburger Telemann-Gesellschaft e V: Haus der Patriotischen Gesellschaft, Trostbrücke 4, 2000 Hamburg 11; Chair. Eckart Klessmann.

Hamburgische Kulturstiftung: Chilehaus C, 20095 Hamburg; tel. 49 040 33 90 99; fax 49 040 32 69 58.

Hans-Breuer-Stiftung zur Pflege und Förderung des deutschen Liedgutes e V: Hochschule für Musik and Theater, Harvestehuder Weg 10–12, 2000 Hamburg 13; Chair. Prof. Dr Hermann Rauhe.

Hans-Pfitzner-Gesellschaft e V: Mauerkircher Strasse 8, 8000 Munich 80; Chair. Gen. Music Dir Prof. Rolf Reuter.

Heinrich-Heine-Gesellschaft e V (HHG): Bolkerstrasse 53, PO Box 1120, 4000 Düsseldorf 1; Chair. Gerd Högener.

Heinrich-Kaminski-Gesellschaft e V: Storchen-Apotheke, Hauptstrasse 20, 7890 Waldshut-Tiengen 2; Chair. Jürgen Klein.

Industriegewerkschaft Medien-Druck und Papier, Publizistik und Kunst (IG Medien): Friedrichstrasse 15, 70174 Stuttgart; Man. Heinrich Bletcher.

Institut für Bildung und Kultur e V (IBK): Küppelstein 34, 5630 Remscheid; Chair. Prof. Bruno Tetzner.

Institut fur Musiktherapie: Waldhuterpfad 38, 14169 Berlin; tel. 030 8135080; fax 030 8135080.

Institut für Neue Musik und Musikerziehung e V: Grafenstrasse 35, 6100 Darmstadt; Chair. Dr Susanne Liegler.

Institut für Studien der Musikkultur des Portugiesischen Sprachraumes: An Der Münze 1, 50668 Cologne; Contact Dr Harald Hülskath.

Interessenverband Deutscher Komponisten e V (IDK): Willinghusener Landstrasse 70, 2000 Barsbüttel; Chair. Gustav Kneip.

Interessenverband Deutscher Konzertveranstalter und Künstlervermittler e V (IDKV): Lenhartstrasse 15, 20249 Hamburg; tel. 49 40 460 5028; fax 49 40 484443; website www.idkv.com; Pres. Jens Michow.

International Association of the Wagner Societies: Sonnhalde 123, 79104 Frieburg; tel. 49 761 53756; fax 49 761 53756; Pres. Josef Lienhart.

International Association of Music and Education: Heinrich-Schutz Allee 33, 34131, Kassel; tel. 49 561 93 51 70; fax 49 561 313772.

International Federation of the Phonographic Industry (IFPI)-Deutsche Landesgruppe: Grelckstrasse 36, 2000 Hamburg 54; Chair. Helmut Fest.

Internationale Andreas-Werckmeister-Gesellschaft e V: Kulturamt der Stadt Halberstadt, Dominikanerstrasse 16, Halberstad; Pres. Dr Rüdiger Pfeiffer.

Internationale Arbeitsgemeinschaft der Theaterbesucher organisationen (IATO): Am Handelshof 9, Essen; Pres. Prof. Dr Jurgen-Dieter Waidelich.

International Carl-Maria-von-Weber-Gesellschaft e V: Staatsbibliothek zu Berlin (Preussischer Kulturbesitz), Musikabteilung, Unter den Linden 8, PO Box 1312, 1086 Berlin; Chair. Dr Ute Schwab.

Internationale Discotheken Organisationen: Deutsche Diskotheken-Unternehmer, Kaiser-Friedrich-Allee 1–3, 5100 Aachen; Contact Halga Quirini.

Internationale Draeseke-Gesellschaft e V: Matthias-Grünewald-Strasse 5, 6720 Speyer; Chair. Dr Helmut Loos.

Internationale Fasch-Gesellschaft e V: Wiekhaus Breitestein, PO Box 1113, 39251 Zerbst; Pres. Dr Konstanze Musketa.

Internationale Föderation für Chormusik-International Federation for Choral Music (IFCM): Burgstrasse 33, Bonn; Pres. Dr H. Royce Saltzmann.

Internationale Gesellschaft für Musik in der Medizin e V (ISFMIM): Paulmannshöher Strasse 17, 5880 Ludenscheid; Chair. Dr Roland Droh.

Internationale Gesellschaft für Musikerziehung (ISME): Deutsche Sektion, Deutscher Musikrat/AGMM, Am Michaelsahof 4 a, 5300 Bonn 2.

Internationale Gesellschaft für musikpädagogische Fortbildung e V (IGMF): Johannes-Hummel-Weg 1, 57392 Schmallenberg; tel. 49 2974 9110; fax 49 2974 911100; Chair. Prof. Dr Hans-Walter Berg.

Internationale Gesellschaft für Urheberrecht e V (INTERGU): Rosenheimer Strasse 11, 8000 Munich 80.

Internationale Gitarristische Vereinigung Freiburg e V (IGVF): Lessingstrasse 4, 7800 Freiburg im Breisgau; Chair. Jörg Sommermeyer.

Internationale Heinrich-Schütz-Gesellschaft e V (ISG): Heinrich-Schütz-Allee 35, 5300 Kassel; Chair. Prof. Dr Arno Forchert.

Internationale Hugo-Wolf-Akademie für Gesang-Dichtung-Liedkunst e V: Neckarstrasse 86, 7000 Stuttgart 1; Chair. Dr Rainer Wilhelm.

Internationale Johann-Nepomuk-David-Gesellschaft E V (IDG): Fichenstrasse 19, 7336 Uhingen; Chair. Wolfgang Dallmann.

Internationale Joseph Martin Kraus-Gesellschaft e V: PO Box 1422, 74713 Buchen (Odenwald); tel. 49 6281 8898; fax 49 6281 556898; e-mail info@kraus-gesellschaft.de; website www.kraus-gesellschaft.de; Chair.: Prof. Dr Reinhard Wiesend.

Internationale Louis Spohr Gesellschaft e V: Schöne Aussicht 2, 3500 Kassel; Pres. Wolfgang Windführ.

Internationale Meyerbeer-Gesellschaft e V: Tristanstrasse 10, 8034 Germering; Chair. Karl Zelenka.

Internationale Posaunenvereinigung (IPV)-Sektion Deutschland: Launhardt, Hahnenstrasse 18, 5024 Pulheim; Pres. Prof. Johannes Doms.

Internationale vereinigung der Musikbibliotheken und: Dr Bettina Seyfried, Gärtnerstrasse 25-32, PO Box 450229, 12207 Berlin; Pres. Dr Joachim Jaenecke.

Internationale Viola-Gesellschaft: c/o Dr Ronald Schmidt, Gechtemer Weg 52, 53332 Bornheim; fax 221 400 75283.

Internationaler Arbeitskreis für Musik e V (IAM): Am Kloster 1a, 49565 Bramsche-Halgarten; tel. 49(0) 5461 9963-0; Exec. Dir Peter Koch.

Internationaler Verein Freund behinderter Tonkünstler e V: Melchiorstrasse 74, 8000 Munich 71; Chair. Elisabeth Stöcklein-Weiss.

Internationales Forum Junge Chormusik Rotenburg (Wümme) e V: Rathaus, Grosse Strasse 1, Rotenburg/Wümme; Pres. Prof. Dr Guy Maneveau.

Jacques-Offenbach-Gesellschaft e V Bad Ems (JOG): Waldstrasse 3, 5427 Bad Ems; Contact Dr Günther Obst.

Jean Sibelius Gesellschaft Deutschland e V: Trivstrasse 19, 8000 Munich 19; Pres. Prof. August Everding.

Jeunesses Musicales Deutschland: Marktplatz 12, 97990 Weikersheim; tel. 49 7934 280; fax 49 7934 8526; website www .JeunessesMusicales.de; Gen. Sec. Thomas Rietschel.

Johann Adolph Hasse-Gesellschaft München e V: Ursula Biehl, Landsberger Strasse 55, 8080 Fürstenfeldbruck; Chair. Ursula Biehl.

Johannes-Brahms-Gesellschaft Internationale e V: Trostbrücke 4, 2000 Hamburg 11; Pres. Detlef Kraus.

Jospeh-Haas-Gesellschaft e V (JHG): Veroneserstrasse 4, 8000 Munich 90; Pres. Prof. Dr Siegfried Gmeinwieser.

Jospeh-Suder-Gesellschaft e V: Grünwalderstrasse 250, 8000 Munich 90; Chair. Reinhold Pfandzelter.

Jürgen Ponto-Stiftung zur Förderung junger Künstler: Jürgen-Ponto-Platz 1, 60301 Frankfurt am Main; tel. 49 69 263 52 396; fax 49 69 263 54 732; e-mail ponto-stiftung@dresdner-bank.com; website juergen -ponto-stiftung.de; Principal Man. Karin Heyl.

Karg-Elert-Gesellschaft e V (KEG): Lortzingstrasse 11, 7980 Ravensburg; Chair. Prof. Dr Wolfgang Stockmeier, Johannes Michel.

Karl-Klingler-Stiftung e V: Siemens AG, Dr Rüdiger v Canal, Wittelsbacherplatz 2, 8000 Munich 2.

Kodály-Gesellschaft e V: Conrad W. Mayer, Grabenstrasse 22, 7812 Bad Krozingen.

Körber-Stiftung: Kampchaussee 10, PO Box 800660, 2050 Hamburg 80; Chair. Ulrich Voswinckel.

Kulturinstitut Komponistinnen gestern-heute e V: Theaterstrasse 11, 69117 Heidelberg; tel. 49 6221 166861; fax 49 6221 182072; Chair. Roswitha Sperber. .

Kulturkreis im Bundesverband der Deutschen Industrie e V: Gustav-Heinemann-Ufer 84–88, 5000 Cologne 51; Chair. Dr Arend Oetker.

Kulturpolitische Gesellschaft e V: Stirnband 8–10, 5800 Hagen 1; Pres. Dr Olaf Schwencke.

Kulturstiftung des Landes Schleswig-Holstein: Ministerium für Bildung, Wissenschaft, Jugend und Kultur, Gartenstrasse 6, 2300 Kiel 1; Chair. Dr Peter Joachim Kreyenberg.

Kunststiftung Baden-Württemberg GmbH: Gerokstrasse 37, 7000 Stuttgart 1; Chair. Dr Christof Müller-Wirth.

Kurt-Weill-Vereinigung Dessau: Stadtverwaltung Dessau, Dezernat IV, Kulturamt, Zerbster Strasse 1, 4500 Dessau; Chair. Dr Jürgen Schebera.

Landgraf-Moritz-Stiftung (LMST): Heinrich-Schütz-Allee 35, PO Box 100329, 3500 Kassel; Chair. Walter Olbrich.

Lohmann-Stiftung Wiesbaden e V: Prinz-Nikolas-Strasse 26, 6200 Wiesbaden; Chair. Prof. Hildegund Lohmann-Becker.

Medizinische Gesellschaft für Kunstschaffende-Musikkorthopädie und Kunstmedizine V: Universität Ulm, Am Hochstrasse 8, PO Box 4066, Ulm. Dr A. Lahme.

Mendelssohn-Gesellschaft e V: Zerbster Strasse 59, 1000 Berlin 45; Chair. Ernst Thamm.

Musica Reanimata: Förderverein zur Wiederentdeckung NS-verfolgter Komponisten, Heidi Tamar Hoffmann, Johannisberger Strasse 12A, 1000 Berlin 33; Chair. Dr Albrecht Dümling.

Musik + Tanz + Erziehung: Orff-Schulwerk-Gesellschaft Deutschland e V, Hermann-Hummel-Strasse 25, 82166 Lochham; tel. 49 89 854 2953; fax 49 89 854 2851; Chair. Gerhard Kuhn.

Musikalische Jugend Deutschlands e V (MJD): Marktplatz 12, 6992 Weikersheim; Chair. Dr Michael Jenne.

Musikfonds für Musikurheber e V: Adenauerallee 134, 5300 Bonn 1; Chair. Prof. Dr Peter Ruzicka.

Musiktherapie e V: Von-Esmarch Strasse 111, 4400 Münster; Chair. Prof. Dr Karl Hörmann.

Neue Bachgesellschaft e V (NBG): Internationale Vereinigung, Thomaskirchhof 16, PO Box 727, Leipzig; Chair. Prof. Dr H. C. Helmuth Rilling.

Neue Deutsche Händel-Gesellschaft e V: Im Brögen 4 b, 5204 Lohmar 21; Pres. Prof. Dr Albert Scheibler.

Neue Zentralstelle der Bühnenautoren und Bühnenverleger GmbH: Bismarckstrasse 107, 1000 Berlin 12; Chair. Dr Maria Müller-Sommer.

NRW Zentrum für Popularmusik und Kommunikationstechnologie: Rottscheidter Strasse 6, PO Box 201414, 5600 Wupppertal 11; Contact Dieter Gorny.

ORPLID internationale Gesellschaft für Musiktheater und Architektur e V: Hohenheimer Strasse 84, 7000 Stuttgart; Chair. Wilhelm Keitel.

Oscar-und-Vera-Ritter-Stiftung: Bundesstrasse 4, 2000 Hamburg 13; Chair. Jürgen Wittekind.

PE-Förderkreis für Studierende der Musik e V: Dr Ralph Landsittel, Otto-Back-Strasse 46, 6800 Mannheim 1; Chair. Angelika Milos-Engelhorn.

Percussion Creativ e V: Hastverstr. 31, 90408 Nurnberg; tel. and fax 49 911 365 9768; Chair. Prof. Werner Thärichen.

Posaunenwerk in der Evangelischen Kirche in Deutschland e V: Hinter der Grambker Kirche 5, 2820 Bremen 77; Chair. Günther Schulz.

Pro Musica Viva-Maria Strecker-Daelen-Stiftung (PMV): PO Box 3146, 55021 Mainz; fax 06131-366432; e-mail Pro.MusicaViva@t-online .de.

ProFolk, Dachverband für Folkmusik e V: Brigitte Kempe, Oberachernerstrasse 93, 7590 Achern 2; Chair. Jens Peter Müller.

Rachmaninoff-Gesellschaft e V Wiesbaden: PO Box 4853, 6200 Wiesbaden; Pres. Richard Henger.

Ralph-Vaughan-Williams-Gesellschaft e V: Jugendmusik-u Kunstschule, Elberfelder Strasse 20, 5630 Remscheid; Chair. Dr Lutz-Werner Hesse.

Rektorenkonferenz der Musikhochschulen in der BRD: Hochschule für Musik Köln, Dagobertstr 38, 50668 Cologne; fax 49 221 131204; Contact Isabel Pfeiffer-Poensgen.

Richard-Strauss-Gesellschaft München e V: Viktualienmarkt 3, 8000 Munich 2; Chair. Prof. Wolfgang Sawallisch.

Richard-Wagner-Verband International e V—RWVI (International Association of Wagner Societies): Sonnhalde 123, 79098 Freiburg im Breisgau; Chair. Josef Lienhart; 136 societies, with some 37,000 members.

Robert-Schumann-Gesellschaft e V: Bilker Strasse 4–6, 4000 Düsseldorf 1; Chair. Dr Herbert Zapp.

Robert-Schumann-Gesellschaft Zwickau e V: Robert-Schumann-Haus, Hauptmarkt 5, 8540 Zwickau; Chair. Dr Martin Schoppe.

Robert-Stolz-Stiftung e V: Steinhauser-Strasse 3, 8000 Munich 80; Chair. Thomas M. Stein.

Rudolf-Eberle-Stiftung: c/o Akademie Schloss Solitude, Solitude 3, 70197 Stuttgart; tel. 711 99 6 19 471; Chair. Michael Russ.

Sängerbund der Deutschen Polizei e V (SbdDP): Rosenfelder Strasse 20, 2300 Kiel 14; Chair. Werner Busche.

Schostakowitsch-Gesellschaft e V: Klaustalerstrasse 2, 1100 Berlin; Chair. Hilmar Schmalenberg.

Schütz-Akademie e V: Heinrich-Schütz-Strasse 1, PO Box 22, 07586 Bad Kostritz; tel. 036605 36198; fax 036605 36199; e-mail heinrich-schutz -haus@t-online.de; Dir Friederike Böcher.

Sinfonima-Stiftung: Mannheimer Versicherung AG, Augstaanlage 66, PO Box 102161, 6800 Mannheim 1.

Sonderhauser Verband akademisch-musikalischer Verbindungen (SV): Hilger Schallen, Bahnweg 85, 6500 Mainz 42; Chair. Gerhard Seher.

Spitzenverband Deutsche Musik e V (SPIDEM): Adenauerallee 134, 5300 Bonn 1; Pres. Prof. Dr H. C. Erich Schulze.

Stiftung Bayerischer Musikfonds: Salvatorstrasse 2, 8000 Munich 2.

Stiftung 100 Jahre Yamaha e V—Verein zur Popularisierung der Musik: Siemensstrasse 22–34, 25462 Rellingen; Chair. Masahito Kato.

Stiftung fur Kutturell Weiterbildung und Kulturberatung: Jägerstrasse 51m, 1080 Berlin; Chair. Prof. Dr Hermann Glaser.

Stiftung Kulturfonds: Molkenmarkt 1–3, PO Box 240, 1020 Berlin.

Stiftung Kunst und Kultur des landes Nordrhein-Westfalen: Haus der Stiftungen in NRW, Rosstrasse 133, 4000 Düsseldorf 30; Chair. Johannes Rau.

Stiftung Ostdeutscher Kulturrat (OKR): Kaiserstrasse 113, 5300 Bonn 1; Pres. Dr Herbert Hupka.

Stiftung Preussischer Kulturbesitz: Von-der-Heydt-Strasse 16–18, 10785 Berlin; tel. 49 (0)30 25463-0; fax 49 (0)30 25463-268; e-mail info@hv .spk-berlin.de; website www.preussischer-kulturbesitz.de; Pres. Prof. Dr hc Klaus-Dieter Lehmann; cultural organization with museums, the State Library, State Archive, research institutes, and various collections; administers various annual awards.

Stiftung Rheinland-Pfalz für Kultur: Ministerium für Wissenschaft, Weiterbildung, Forschung und Kulter, Mittlere Bleiche, 55116 Mainz; Chair. Minister Pres. Kurt Beck.

Stiftung Volkslied (STV): Heinrich-Shütz-Allee 33, 3500 Kassel; Chair. Alfred Peters.

Sudetendeutscher Sängerbund e V (SDS): Hans-Schitzer-Weg 19, 8960 Kempten; Chair. Gunther Wohlrab.

Telemann-Gesellschaft e V Internationale Vereinigung: Liebigstrasse 10, 3010 Magdeburg; Pres. Prof. Dr Martin Ruhnke.

Union Deutscher Jazz-Musiker e V (UDJ): Am Michaelshof 4a, 5300 Bonn 2; Chair. Prof. Joe Viera.

Verband der Deutschen Konzertdirektionen e V: Liebigstrasse 39, 8000 Munich 22; Pres. Michael Russ.

Verband der deutschen Kritiker e V: Andreas Richter, Prinz-Fr-Leopold Strasse 34a, 1000 Berlin 38; Chair. Hartmut Krug.

Verband der Musikpädagogen e V (VMP): Von-der-Tann-Strasse 38, 8400 Regensburg; Chair. Dr Lothar Schubert.

Verband der Vertriebe von Musikinstrumenten und Musikelektronik: Heinstrasse 169, Stuttgart; Chair. Werner Sonderwald.

Verband Deutscher Bühnenverleger e V: Bismarckstrasse 107, 1000 Berlin 12; Chair. Stefani Cremer-Hunzinger.

Verband Deutscher Geigenbauer e V (VDG): Oho-Devrient-Str 14, 07743 Jena; tel. 0049 3641 447804; fax 0049 3641 824884; Chair. Hieronymus Köstler.

Verband Deutscher Komponisten: An der Kolonnade 15, 1080 Berlin; Chair. Hans J. Wenzel.

Verband Deutscher KonzertChöre e V (VDKC): Kempener Strasse 5, 41749 Viersen; tel. 49 2162 67058; Pres. Hans-Heinrich Grosse-Brockhoff.

Verband Deutscher Musikschaffender (VDM): Kaiser-Friedrich-Allee 1–3, 5100 Aachen; Pres. Klaus Quirini.

Verband Deutscher Musikschulen e V (VDM): Plitterdorfer Strasse 93, 53173 Bonn; tel. 49 228 957060; website www.musikschulen.de; Chair. Reinhart von Gutzeit.

Verband Deutscher Schulmusiker (VDS): Weihergarten 5, PO Box 3640, 55116 Mainz; tel. 49 6131 234049; fax 49 6131 246823; website www .vds-musik.de; Chair. Prof. Dr Dieter Zimmerzchied.

Verband Deutscher Tonmeister e V (VDT): Masurenallee 8–14, 1000 Berlin 19; website www.tonmeister.de; Pres. Günter Griewisch.

Verband evangelischer Kirchenchöre Deutschlands e V (VEK): Hasenburger Weg 67, 2120 Lüneburg; Pres. Dr Hans-Christian Drömann.

Verband evangelischer Kirchenmusiker Deutschlands (VeM): Domplatz 5, 6720 Speyer; Pres. KMD Prof. Hermann Rau.

Verein zur Förderung der Nordoff/Robbins Musiktherapie e V: Dorfstrasse 22, 58099 Hagen; tel. 2304 642104; e-mail nordoff.robbins .verein@freenet.de.

Verein zur Förderung Historischer Harfen e V: Rainer m Thurau, Helenenstrasse 10, 6200 Wiesbaden; Chair. Elena Polonska.

Vereinigung deutscher Harfenisten e V: Vera Munkel-Remann, Goldammerweg 183, 5000 Cologne 30; Chair. Therese Reichling.

Vereinigung Deutscher Musik-Bearbeiter e V: Kiesstrasse 44a, 12209 Berlin; tel. and fax 030 772 6241.

Vereinigung Deutscher Opernchöre und Buhnentanzer: Bismarckstrasse 14–16, 5000 Cologne 1; Chair. Heinz Mersch.

Villa Musica: Stiftung zur Förderung der Musik, Auf der Bastei, 6500 Mainz; Chair. Mindirig Ernst Maurer.

Walcker-Stiftung für orgelwissenschaftliche Forschung: PO Box 1128, 6601 Kleinblittersdorf 2; Chair. Klaus Walcker.

Walter Kaminsky-Stiftung: Kösener Strasse 4, 1000 Berlin 33.

Walther-Hensel-Gesellschaft e V: Ob dem Staeffele 2, 71364 Winnenden; tel. 7195 2631; fax 7195 1397300; e-mail post@walther-hensel -gesellschaft.de; website www.walther-hensel-gesellschaft.de; Chair. Herbert Preisenhammer.

Werkgemeinschaft Musik e V: Carl-Mosterts-Platz 1, 40477 Düsseldorf; tel. 49 211 4693 191; fax 49 211 4693 159; website www .werkgemeinschaft-musik.de; Chair. Prof. Karl Berg.

Wilhelm-Furtwängler-Gesellschaft e V: Schwelmer Strasse 4, 1000 Berlin 45; Chair. Dr Friedhelm Schöning.

Wilhelm-Petersen-Gesellschaft e V: Brahmsweg 4, 6100 Darmstadt.

Wissenschaftliche Sozietät Musikpädagogik e V (WSMP): Fachbereich Erziehungswissenschaft, Insitut für Musikpadagogik, Von-Melle-Park 8, 2000 Hamburg 13; Chair. Prof. Dr Hermann J. Kaiser.

Xaver and Philipp Scharwenka-Gesellschaft e V: Prassekstrasse 5, 23566 Lübeck; tel. 49 (0)451 6 4264; fax 49 (0)451 6 5098; e-mail ETrenkner@aol.com; website www.scharwenka.de; Chair. Prof. Evelinde Trenkner.

Zentralverband Katholischer Kirchenangestellter Deutschlands e V (ZKD): Am Kielshof 2, PO Box 990125, 5000 Cologne 91; Chair. Franz Kopecky.

Zentrum Bundesrepublik Deutschland des Internationalen Theaterinstituts: Bismarckstrasse 107, 100 Berlin 12; Pres. Prof. August Everding.

Zentrum für Kunst und Medientechnologie Karlsruhe (ZKM): Institut für Musik und Akustik, Ritterstrasse 42, Karlsruhe; Dir Prof. Dr Heinrich Klotz.

Greece

International Music Council (Greek Section): 38 Mitropleos St, 105 63 Athens; Gen. Sec. Apostolos Kositios.

Jeunesses Musicales de Grece/Musique Pour l'Enfant: Stratigou Kallari 52, Psychico, 154 52 Athens; Pres. Domini Sarris.

Société Hellenique pour la Protection de la Proprieté intellectuelle: 14 Delighianni Street, 106 83 Athens; Man. Dir George Galanakis.

Tsakalof Cultural Centre: Platia G, Stavrou 5, 45444 Ioannina; Pres. Aspasia Zerva.

Guatemala

Asociación Guatemalteca de Autores y Compositores (AGAYC): 14 Calle 11-42, Zona 1, 01001 Guatemala City.

Juventudes Musicales de Guatemala: Diagonal 6, Calle Real de la Villa 13-46, Zona 10, Guatemala City; Pres. Francisco Saravia.

Hong Kong

Hong Kong Arts Administrators Association Ltd: c/o ARIC, Room 301, 3/F Hong Kong Arts Centre, 2 Harbour Road, Wanchai.

Hong Kong Government Music Office: 25/F Wanchai Tower One, 12 Harbour Road, Wanchai; website www.usd.gov.hk/musicoffice.

Hungary

Artisjus Hungarian Bureau for the Protection of Authors' Rights: PO Box 593, 1539 Budapest; tel. 36 1 212 1543; website www.artisjus.com; Pres. János Bródy; Gen. Dir Dr Péter Gyertyánfy.

F. Liszt Society: Vörösmarty u. 35, 1064 Budapest; tel. 36 1 342 15 73; Pres.: Prof. Istvan Lantos; Sec.-Gen.: Klara Hamburger.

Hungarian Arts Foundation, Music Department: Báthori-utca 10, 1054 Budapest; Dir of the Music Dept Kálmán Strém.

Hungarian Composers Union: 1051 Budapest, Vorosmarty Ter 1; tel. 36 1 338 4139; fax 36 1 338 4139; Pres. Maie Hoilos.

International Kodály Society: PO Box 8, 1502 Budapest.

Jeunesses Musicales of Hungary: PO Box 80, 1366 Budapest, Vörösmarty tér 1, 1051 Budapest; Sec.-Gen. Beáta Schanda.

Magyar Tudományos Akadémia Zenetudományi Intézet (Institute for Musicology of the Hungarian Academy of Sciences): PO Box 28, 1250 Budapest; Táncsics Mihály u. 7., 1014 Budapest; tel. 361 214 6770; fax 361 375 9282; e-mail info@zti.hu; website www.zti.hu; Dir Dr Tibor Tallián; research in music history, folk music and dance; holds the Bartók archives, Dohnányi archives, and publishes the Studia Musicologica, Musicalia Danubiana, CAO-ECE and Cantus Planus.

Magyar Zenei Tanacs (Hungarian Music Council): PO Box 47, 1364, Budapest; tel. 36 1 318 4243; fax 36 1 317 8267; e-mail hmc@holdon.hu; Pres.: Adrienne Csengery; Exec. Sec. Agnes Paldy.

Music Information Centre of Hungary: Lónyay u. 54, fsz.3., 1097 Budapest.

National Centre of International Music Competitions and Festivals: PO Box 80, 1366 Budapest, Vörösmarty tér 1, 1051 Budapest; Dir Tamás Klenjánszky.

Trade Union of Hungarian Musicians: Gorkij Fasor 38, 1068 Budapest.

Iceland

Association of Icelandic Composers: Laufásvegi 40, Reykjavík.

Association of Light Composers and Songwriters: Háteigsvegur 28, 105 Reykjavík.

Association of Music School Directors: Kennarasamband Islands, Grettisgata 89, 105 Reykjavík.

Association of Music School Teachers: Kennarasamband Islands, Grettisgata 89, 105 Reykjavík.

Iceland Music Information Centre: Sidumuli 34, 108 Reykjavík; Dir Bergljót Jónsdóttir.

Icelandic Musicians' Union: Raudagerdi 27, 108 Reykjavík.

International Society for Contemporary Music, Icelandic Section: Tonskaldafelag Islands, Laufásvegur 40, Reykjavík.

Reykjavík Music Society: Garoastraeti 17, 101 Reykjavík.

Society of Icelandic Musicians: Laufásvegur 40, 101 Reykjavík.

Union of Authors and Copyright Owners: Laufásvegur 40, 101 Reykjavík.

India

Delhi Symphony Society: 2 Humanyum Road, New Delhi 110003; tel. 11 6512091; fax 11 24361918.

Inter-National Cultural Centre: 205 Tansen Marg, New Delhi 1.

National Centre for the Performing Arts: Nariman Point, Mumbai 400021; tel. 11 22 285 4309; fax 11 22 283 3737.

Ireland

Arts Council (An Chomhairle Ealaion): 70 Merrion Square, Dublin 2; tel. 353 1 618 0200; fax 353 1 676 1302/661 0349; website www.artscouncil .ie.

Contemporary Music Centre: 19 Fishamble Street, Temple Bar, Dublin 8; tel. 353 1 6731922; fax 353 1 6489100; e-mail info@cmc.ie; website www .cmc.ie; Promotion Man. Karen Hennessy.

International Songwriters Association Ltd: Raheen, Limerick City.

Irish Composers Centre: Liberty Hall, Room 804, Dublin 1.

Irish Federation of Musicians and Associated Professions: 63 Lower Gardiner Street, Dublin 1; tel. and fax 353 1 874 4645.

Irish Music Rights Organization (IMRO): Copyright House, Pembroke Row, Lower Baggot Street, Dublin 2; tel. 353 1 661 4844; fax 353 1 676 3125; website www.imro.ie.

Mechanical Copyright Society Ltd (MCPS): Copyright House, Pembroke Row, Lower Baggot Street, Dublin 2; tel. 353 1 676 6940; fax 353 1 661 1316.

Israel

Independent Musicians Union: 6 Rabin Square, 64591 Tel-Aviv; Chair. Dany Gottfried.

International Music Council (Israeli Section): Ministry of Education and Culture, Devora Hanaviah Street 2, 91911 Jerusalem; Chief Officer Raaya Zimran.

International Society for Contemporary Music (Israeli Section): c/o Israel Composers' League, PO Box 45068, 61450 Tel-Aviv.

Israel Composers' League: PO Box 45068, 61450 Tel-Aviv; Chair. Manachem Zur.

Israel Music Institute (IMI): 144 Hayarkon Street, 63451 Tel-Aviv; tel. 972 3 527 0219; fax 972 3 524 5276; Dir Paul Landau.

Israeli Musicians' Union: 6 Rabin Square, Tel-Aviv 64951; tel. 972 3 695 9355; fax 972 3 696 3528; Pres.: Dan Gottfried.

Jerusalem Music Centre: PO Box 4568 Mishkanot Sha'ananim, Jerusalem 91045; Dir Benny Gal-Ed; Chair. Issac Stern.

Jeunesses Musicales d'Israel: 8 Sderot Chen, 64071 Tel-Aviv.

Music Information Centre of Israel: 144 Hayarkon Street, PO Box 3004, 63451 Tel-Aviv; tel. 972 3 524 6475; fax 972 3 524 5276; Dir Paul Landau.

National Council for Culture and Arts: 16 Hanatziv Street, 67018 Tel-Aviv; Chief Officer David Sinai.

Society of Authors, Composers, and Music Publishers in Israel—ACUM: 9 Tyval Street, Ramat-Gan 52117; Chair. Hana Goldberg.

Italy

Accademia Luigi Boccherini: Piazza Insurrezione 10, 35129 Padua.

Accademia Tartiniana: Piazzale Pontecorvo 4/A, 35121 Padua.

Associazione Antiquae Musicae Italicae Studiosi: Via Remorsella 5/A, 40125 Bologna.

Associazione Centro Studi Carusiani: Via Omboni 1, 20129 Milan.

Associazione dei Fonografici Italiani (AFI): Via Vittor Pisani 10, 20124 Milan.

Associazione dei Rappresentanti Italiani di Artisti di Concerti e Spettacoli: Via Cappuccio 11, 20123 Milan.

Associazione di Informatica Musicale Italiana (AIMI): c/o La Biennale di Venezia, Settore Musica, San Marco, Ca Giustinian, 30124 Venice; website aimi.dist.unige.it.

Associazione Festival Teatrali: Musicali e Cinematografici (Federfestival), c/o AGIS, via di Villa Patrizi 10, 00161 Rome.

Associazione Generale Italiana dello Spettacolo (AGIS): Via di Villa Patrizi 10, 00161 Rome.

Associazione Internazionale Biblioteche Musicali (AIBM): Italian Section, c/o Conservatorio Giuseppe Verdi, via Conservatorio 12, 20111 Milan.

Associazione Internazionale Studi di Canto Gregoriano: Via Battaglione 58, 26100 Cremona.

Associazione Italiana Archivi Sonori e Audiovisivi: c/o Istituto di Ricerca per il Teatro Musicale, via Francesco Tamagno 65, 00168 Rome; tel. 39 066147277; fax 39 066144371; e-mail irtem@mclink.it; website www .irtem.it.

Associazione Italiana Biblioteche (AIB): c/o Biblioteca Nazionale, via le Castro Pretorio 105, 00186 Rome.

Associazione Italiana Degli Editori di Musica (AIDEM): Via Enrico Tito 4, 20123 Milan.

Associazione Italiana delle Scuole di Musica: Villa La Torraccia, via delle Fontanelle 24, 50016 San Domenico di Fiesole (FI).

Associazione Italiana di Acustica (AIA): Via Cassia 1216, 00189 Rome.

Associazione Italiana Operatori Musicali (ASSIOM): c/o Centro di Ricerca e Sperimentazione per la Didattica Musicale, Villa La Torraccia, via delle Fontanelle 24, 50016 San Domenico di Fiesolo (FI).

Associazione Italiana per la Musica Sacra S. Cecilia (AISC): Piazza S. Apollinare 49, 00186 Rome.

Associazione Italiana Studi di Musicoterapia (AISMt): Via Brignole De Ferrari 6, 16122 Genoa.

Associazione Liutariana Italiana (ALI): Piazza Cavour 5, 26100 Cremona.

Associazione Nazionale Agenti Teatrali (ANAT): Via Assietta, 00141 Rome.

Associazione Nazionale Artisti Lirici Primarii Italiani (ANALPI): Corso Venezia 61, 20121 Milan.

Associazione Nazionale Bande Italiane Musicali (AMBIMA): Via Marianna Dionigi 43, 00193 Rome.

Associazione Nazionale Critici Musicali: Via Cardinale Mimmi 32, 70124 Bari.

Associazione Nazionale delle Cooperative Culturali: Via dei Alpi 32, 00198 Rome.

Associazione Nazionale Insegnanti di Danza (ANID): Via A. Gramsci 36, 00197 Rome.

Associazione Nazionale Liuteria Artistica Italiana (ANLAI): Piazza Venezia 11, 00187 Rome.

Associazione Nazionale Musicisti di Jazz (AMJ): Via Vallerozzi 77, 53100 Siena.

Associazione Pro Musica Studium: Via Ferdinando Martini 23/8, 00137 Rome.

Centre International de Recherche sur la Presse Musicale (CIRPEM): Via del Conservatorio 31/B, 43100 Parma.

Centro di Sonologia Computazionale: c/o Università di Padova, via San Francesco 11, 35121 Padua.

Centro di Studi Donizettiani: c/o Ateneo di Scienze, Lettre ed Arti, via Torquato Tasso 4, 24121 Bergamo.

Centro di Studi Musicali Ferruccio Busoni: Piazza della Vittoria 16, 50053 Empoli (F1).

Centro Internazionale per la Divulgazione della Musica Italiana: Via Sistina 48, 00187 Rome.

Centro Internazionale per la Ricerca Strumentale: Cannaregio 3099, 30121 Venice.

Centro Studi Giovanni Paisiello: Via Euclide 15, 74100 Taranto.

Centro Studi Rinascimento Musicale: Villa Medicea La Ferdinanda, 50040 Artimino (F1).

Centro di Studi Spontiniani: c/o Comune, via Spontini, 60030 Maiolati Spontini (AN).

CIDIM-National Music Committee of Italy (IMC-UNESCO): Via Vittoria Colonna 18, 00193 Rome.

Civico Instituto di Studi Paganiani: c/o Comune di Genova, Settore Promozione della Città, Via Sottoripa 5, 16124 Genoa; tel. 39 0105574349; fax 39 0105574326; e-mail violinopaganini@comune.genova.it; website www.comune.genova.it.

Editori Muscali Associati (EMA): Piazza Liberty 2, 20121 Milan.

Ente Nazionale Previdenza e Assistenza per i Lavoratori dello Spettacolo: Viale Regina Margherita 206, 00198 Rome.

Federazione Industria Musicale Italiana (FIMI): Via Vittor Pisani 10, 20124 Milan.

Federazione Informazione Spettacolo (FIS)CISL): Via Boncompagni 19, 00187 Rome.

Federazione Italiana dei Compositori de Musica Contemporanea: Via Cavalieri di Vittorio Veneto 34, 56121 Cascina (PI).

Federazione Italiana della Musica (FEDERMUSICA): Via Vittor Piasni 10, 20124 Milan.

Federazione Italiana Lavoratori informazione e Spettacolo (FILISCGIL): Piazza Sallustio 24, 00187 Rome.

Federazione Italiana Lavoratori Stampa: Spettacolo, Informazione e Cultura (FILSIC-UIL), via Belisario 7, 00187 Rome.

Federazione Italiana Tradizioni Popolari (FITP): Via E. Gattamelata 25, 00176 Rome.

Federazione Nazionale delle Cooperative Culturali: Piazza della Libertà, 00192 Rome.

Federazione Nazionale Italiana delle Associazioni Regionali Corali: Via Castellana 44, 30174 Venezia Mestre.

Federazione Nazionale Lavoratori Spettacolo (CISNAL): Via Principe Amedeo 42, 00185 Rome.

Fondazione Claudio Monteverdi: Via Pallavicino 7, 26100 Cremona.

Fondazione Giacomo Puccini: c/o Teatro del Giglio, corte San Lorenzo 9, 55100 Lucca.

Fondazione Giorgio Cini: Instituti per la Musica, Isola di San Giorgio Maggiore, 30124 Venice.

Fondazione Giovanni Pierluigi da Palestrina: Vicolo Pierluigi 3, 0036 Palestrina, Rome.

Fondazione Rossini: Piazza Olivieri 5, 61100 Pesaro.

Fondazione Ugo e Olga Levi: Centro di Cultura Musicale Superiore, Palazzo Giustinian-Lolin, San Marco 2893, 30124 Venice.

Fondazione Vincenzo Bellini: c/o Università degli Studi di Catania, via Biblioteca 13, 95124 Catania.

Fondo Ottorino Respighi: c/o Fondazione Giorgio Cini, Isola San Giorgio Maggiore, 30124 Venice.

International Center of New Musical Sources: Via Alberto Nota 3, 10122 Turin.

International Dance Organization (IDO): Via Bronzino 117, 50142 Florence.

Istituto di Bibliografia Musicale: c/o Biblioteca Nazionale, viale Casteo Pretoria 105, 00185 Rome.

Istituto di Paleografia Musicale: circonvallazione Casilini 122, 00176 Rome.

Istituto di Ricerca per il Teatro Musicale: Via Francesco Tamagno 65, 00168 Rome; tel. 39 066147277; fax 39 066144371; e-mail irtem@mclink.it; website www.irtem.it; Pres.: Carlo Marinelli; f. 1984; non-profit, publicly-financed institute sponsoring research into the fields of musical theatre, 20th century music, ethnomusicology and music-media relations; organizes annual international conference, and adminsters archives.

Istituto di Studi Organologici: Via monte Zebio 33, 00195 Rome.

Istituto di Studi Rinascimentali: Palazzo Paradiso, via delle Scienze 17, 44100 Ferrrara.

Istituto Internazionale Luigi Cherubini: Via Giovanni Secchi 3, 00136 Rome.

Istituto Italiano Antonio Vivaldi: c/o Fondazione Giorgio Cini, Isola di San Giorgio Maggiore, 30124 Venice; tel. 041 2710220; fax 041 5238540; e-mail vivaldi@cini.it; Dir Dr Francesco Fanna.

Istituto Italiano per la Storia della Musica: Via Vittoria 6, 00187 Rome.

Istituto Mutualistico tra Artisti Interpreti Esecutori (IMAIE): Via Piave 66, 00187 Rome.

Istituto Nazionale di Studi Verdiani: Strada della Repubblica 56, 43100 Parma.

Istituto di Studi Pucciniani: Piazza Buonarroti 29, 20149 Milan.

Pontificio Instituto Ambrosiano di Musica Sacra: Viala Gorizia 5, 20144 Milan.

Pontificio Instituto di Musica Sacra: Via di Torre Rossa 21, 001165 Rome.

Sindacato Musicisti Italiani (SMI): Via Goito 39, 00185 Rome.

Sindacato Nazionale Instruzione Artistica: Via Antonio Pio 40, 00145 Rome.

Sindacato Nazionale Musicisti (SNM): Via Pinelli 100, 10144 Turin.

Società Italiana degli Autori ed Editori (SIAE): Via le della Letteratura 30, 00144 Rome; website www.siae.it.

Società Italiana della Viola da Gamba: Via dei Servi 51, 50122 Florence.

Società Italiana di Etnomusicologia (SIE): c/o Centro Flog Tradizioni Popolari, via Maestri del Lavoro 1, 50134 Florence.

Società Italiana di Musicologia (SldM): Via Galliera 3, 40125 Bologna.

Società Italiana Musica Contemporanea (SIMC): Via F. Juvara 11, 21029 Milan.

Società Italiana per l'Educazione Musicale (SIEM): Via Guerrazzi 20, 40125 Bologna.

UNION-Operatori Indipendenti: c/o I Soluzionisti, via Trionfale 85, 00136 Rome.

Unione Folclorica Italiana (UFI): Via Mazzini 22, 33081 Aviano (PN).

Unione Nazionale Arte Musica Spettacolo (UNAMS): Viale delle Provincie 18, 00162 Rome.

Unione Nazionale Editori di Musica Italiani (UNEMI): Via Teulada 52, 00195 Rome.

Japan

Concert Managers Association of Japan: Mitoko Building, 6-2-4 Akasaka, Minato-ku, Tokyo 107; Chair. Naoyasu Kajimoto.

Electronic Industries Association of Japan: Tokyo Shoko Kaigisho Building, 3-2-2 Marunouchi, Chiyoda-ku, Tokyo 100; Chair. Dr Tadahiro Sekimoto.

Japan Audio Society: Mori Building, 1-14-34 Jingumae, Tokyo 150; Sec.-Gen. Sho Nagasawa.

Japan Conductors Association: 4-18-20 Ogikubo Suginami-ku, Tokyo 167; Pres. Takashi Asahina.

Japan International League of Artists: 2-3-16-607 Shinjuku, Shinjuku-ku, Tokyo 160; Chief Officer Kazuhiko Hattori.

Japanese Composers Society: Ogawa Building, 3-7-15 Akasaka, Minatoku, Tokyo 107.

Japanese Society for Rights of Authors, Composers and Publishers: 1-7-13 Nishishimbashi, Minato-ku, Tokyo 105.

Music for Youth Inc: Kowa Building, No. 24, 3-1-1 Roppongi, Minato-ku, Tokyo 106; Pres. Eloise Cunningham.

Recording Industry Association of Japan: 2-8-9 Tsukiji, Chuo-ku, Tokyo 104.

Republic of Korea

Asian Composers League (Korean Committee): PO Box 874, Seoul 110-062; Dir Sung-Jae Lee.

Federation of Artistic and Cultural Organizations of Korea: 1-117 Dongsoong-dong, Chongro-ku, Seoul.

Jeunesses Musicales of Korea: PO Box 10980, Seoul.

Korean Cultural Foundation Inc: 25 Neung-Dong, Sung-ku, Seoul 133-180; Dir No Hi Pak.

Music Association of Korea: 1-117 Dongsoong-dong, Chongro-ku, Seoul; Pres. Sang-Hyun Cho.

Luxembourg

Luxemburger Gesellschaft für Neue Musik: PO Box 828, 2018 Luxembourg; Pres. Marcel Wengler.

Union Grand-Duc Adolphe: 2 rue Sosthène Weis, 2722 Luxembourg.

Macao

Instituto Cultural de Macao: Rua Pedro Coutinho 27, Third Floor, Macao.

Mexico

Asociación Mexicana de Productores de Fonogramas y Videogramas AC: Francisco Petrarca 223-503, Chapultepec Morales, 11560 México.

Juventudes Musicales de México: Santisimo 25, San Angel, 01000 México 20, DF.

Sociedad de Autores y Compositores de Música SA (SACM): San Felipe 143, Col. General Anaya, 03330 México, DF.

Netherlands

BUMA (Composers Rights Society): Prof. E. M. Meijerslaan 3, 1183 AV Amsterdam; website www.bumastemra.nl; Chief Officer: G. P. Willemsen.

CNM (Center for Netherlands Music): PO Box 1634, 1200 PB Hilversum; Chief Officer: J W ten Broeke.

Foundation Gaudeamus (Center of Contemporary Music): Swammerdamstraast 38, 1091 RV Amsterdam; Dir Henk Heuvelmans.

Gentootschap van Nederlandse (Society of Netherlands Composers): Prof. E. M. Meijerslaan 3, 1183 AV Amsterdam; Pres. Gilius van Bergejik.

International Society for Contemporary Music (Netherlands Section): Swammerdamstraat 38, 1091 RV Amsterdam; Pres. H. Reiziger.

Jeugd en Musiek Nederland: Roemer Visscherstraat 42, 1054 EZ Amsterdam; Pres. Jur Naessens.

Katholieke Dirigenten en Organisten Vereniging—KDOV: Donkere Begijnhof 5, 2011 HG Haarlem; e-mail gemcoe@cs.com; Sec.: Gemma Coebergh.

Koninklijke Nederlandse Toonkunstenaars Vereniging: Keizersgracht 480, 1017 EG Amsterdam; Chief Officer H. Luif.

KNTV: Keizersgracht 480, 1017 EG Amsterdam; tel. 31 020 5221020; fax 31 20 6200229.

Muziek Groep Nederland: Paulus Potterstraat 14, 1071 CZ Amsterdam; tel. 31 20 3058900; fax 31 20 6733588; e-mail info@muziekgroep.nl; website www.muziekgroep.nl.

NTB (Nederlandse Toonkunstenaars Bond): Herengracht 272, 1016 BW Amsterdam.

Nederlandse Vereniging van Grammofoondetallhandelaren: Die Noord 3, 1452 PS Ilpendam; Chair. J. F. T. Hotzenbosch.

Netherlands Committee of the International Music Council: Rubenslaan 200, 3582 JJ Utrecht.

Netherlands Theater Institute: PO Box 19304, 1000 GH Amsterdam; Chief Officer Ton Offerman.

STEMRA (Mechanical Rights Society): Prof. E. M. Meijerslaan 3, 1183 AV Amsterdam; website www.bumastemra.nl; Chief Officer: G. P. Willemsem.

Stichting Contactorgaan Electronische Muziek: Swammerdamstraat 38, 1091 RV Amsterdam; Chief Officer Henk Heuvelmans.

Stichting voor Kamermuziek: Sijzenlaan 6, 2566 WG The Hague.

Vereniging voor Nederlandse Muziekgeschiedenis: PO Box 1514, 3500 BM Utrecht.

New Zealand

Australasian Performing Right Association Ltd (APRA): PO Box 6315, 92 Parnell Road, Auckland 1; website www.apra.co.nz; Gen. Man. Bernie Darby.

Composers Association of New Zealand: PO Box 4065, Wellington; Pres. Denise Hulford.

Music for Youth: 26 Patanga Crescent, Wellington 6001; Chair. Beverley Wakem.

Music Trades Association (NZ) Inc: PO Box 386, Auckland; Exec. Officer Dean Reynolds.

New Zealand Composers Foundation: PO Box 633, Wellington; Chair. Ashley Heenan.

New Zealand Music Centre Ltd: SOUNZ New Zealand, PO Box 102, The Terrace, Wellington; Exec. Dir Nicholas McBryde.

New Zealand Musicians Union: 35–39 George Street, Kingsland, Auckland; tel. 09 375 2680; fax 09 375 2681; Sec. Peter Shannon.

Phonographic Performances (New Zealand) Ltd: PO Box 9241, Wellington; Gen. Man. Tony Chance.

Queen Elizabeth II Arts Council of New Zealand: PO Box 3806, Wellington; Dir Peter Quin.

Recording Industry Association of New Zealand Inc: 11 York Street, PO Box 37442 Parnell, Auckland; tel. 64 9 3080510; fax 64 9 3064977; website www.rianz.org.nz; Chief Exec. Terence O'Neill.

Service Workers Union: Musicians Division, Private Bag 68-914, Newton, Auckland; Sec. Peter Shannon.

Norway

International Music Council (National Committee): c/o Statens Musikkrad, Toftesgate 69, 0552 Oslo.

International Society for Contemporary Music (Norwegian Section): c/o Ny Musikk, Toftesgate 69, 0552 Oslo.

Jeunesses Musicales (Norwegian Section): c/o Landslaget Musikk i Skolen, Toftesgate 69, 0552 Oslo.

Landslaget Musikk i Skolen (Youth and Music): Toftesgate 69, 0552 Oslo.

New Music (Ny Musikk): Toftesgate 69, 0552 Oslo.

NASOL (Norwegian Association of Symphony Orchestras): Toftesgate 69, 0552 Oslo.

Norsk Tonekunstnersamfund (Norwegian Association of Musical Artists): Bogstadvn 66, 0366 Oslo.

Norwegian Archives for Folk and Popular Songs: Toftesgate 69, 0552 Oslo.

Norwegian Cultural Council: Militaerhospitalet, PO Box 101, Sentrum, 0102 Oslo.

Norwegian Music Information Centre: Toftesgate 69, 0552 Oslo; Man. Jostein Simble.

Norwegian Musicians' Union: Youngsgate 11, 0181 Oslo; Pres. Tore Nordvik.

Norwegian Society of Composers: PO Box 9171, Grønland, 0134 Oslo; tel. 47 22 05 72 00; fax 47 22 05 72 50; e-mail tono@tono.no; website www.tono.no.

Norwegian Song and Music Council: Toftesgate 69, 0552 Oslo.

Rikskonsertene (Norwegian State Travelling Concerts Organization): PO Box 7613, Skillebekk, 0205, Oslo.

Paraguay

Juventudes Musicales: c/o Saul Gaona, RI 3 Corrales 516, Asunción.

Sociedad Filarmónica de Asunción: Mexico 145 (Estación del Ferrocarril), Asunción; Chair. Luis Szaran.

Peru

Asociación Peruana de Autores y Compositores (APDAYC): Avda Petit Thouars No. 5038, Miraflores, Lima 18; website www.apdayc.pe; Chair. Armando Masse.

Juventudes Musicales: Garcilaso de la Vega 1746, Lima 14; Pres. Oscar Zamora.

Philippines

Andres Bobifacio Music Foundation: Union Village, Tandang Sora, Quezon City.

Choral Conductors Association of the Philippines: c/o University of the Philippines, College of Music, Quezon City.

Eliseo Pajaro Foundation Inc: c/o Cultural Center of the Philippines, Roxas Blvd, Manila.

Filipino Society of Composers, Authors and Publishers (FILS-CAP): 308 RCBC Building, Buendia Extension, Makati, Metro Manila.

Kodály Society of the Philippines: c/o St Paul's College, Herran Street, Manila.

League of Filipino Composers: c/o Cultural Center of the Philippines, Roxas Blvd, Manila.

Music Theater Foundation: c/o University of the Philippines, College of Music, Diliman, Quezon City.

Musika: 9-A Manga Road, New Manila, Quezon City.

National Music Council of the Philippines: c/o University of the Philippines, College of Music, Diliman, Quezon City.

Organisasyon ng Pilipinong Mang-aawit (OPM): Zeta Building, Suite 65, 191 Salcedo Street, Legaspi Village, Makati, Metro Manila.

Piano Teachers' Guild of the Philippines: c/o St Scholasticas's College, Leon Guinto, Malate, Manila.

Philippine Musicians Guild: 409 Unlad Condominium, Taft Avenue and General Malvar Street, Malate, Manila.

Philippine Society for Music Education: c/o Philippine Normal College, Music and Arts Department, Taft Avenue, Manila.

Samahan ng mga Manunuri at Manunulat ng Musika sa Pilipinas (SAMMPI): Aurora Pijuan Street, Blvd 5, Lot 1, BF Resort Village, Pamplona, Las Pinas, Metro Manila.

University of the Philippines Musical Arts and Research Management Inc: University of the Philippines, College of Music, Abelardo Hall, Diliman, Quezon City.

Poland

Association of Polish Violin Makers: Krakowskie Przedmie cie 16/18, 00-325 Warsaw.

Chopin Society of Music: Okólnik 1, 00-368 Warsaw.

Jeunesses Musicales de Pologne: ul. Hoza 50–51, 00-682 Warsaw; tel. 48 22 6254984; fax 48 22 6255810.

Karol Szymanowski Music Association: 34-500 Zakopane, Willa Atma, ul. Kasprusie 1; tel. and fax 48 18 2014554.

Polish Composers' Union: Rynek Starego Miasta 27, 00-272 Warsaw; tel. and fax 48 22 8311741; e-mail zkp@zkp.org.pl; website www.zkp.org.pl; Pres.: Jerzy Kornowicz.

Polish Composers' Union, Musicological Section: Rynek Starego Miasta 27, 00-272 Warsaw; tel. and fax 48 22 8311741; e-mail zkp@zkp.org.pl; website www.zkp.org.pl; Pres.: Katarzyna Dadak-Kozicka.

Polish Music Information Centre: Rynek Starego Miasta 27, 00-272 Warsaw; tel. 48 22 8311634; fax 48 22 8310607; e-mail polmic@polmic.pl; website www.polmic.pl; Dir: Mieczyslaw Kominek.

Polish Union of Artist Violin Makers: ul. Krakowskie Przedm. 16–18, 00-325 Warsaw; tel. and fax 48 22 826 71 52; Dir Anna Kucharska.

Society of Authors ZAIKS: Hipoteczna 2, 00-092 Warsaw; Gen. Man. Witold Kolodziejski.

Society of Music Education: Koszykowa 24/7a, 00-553 Warsaw; Pres. Adrianna Poniecka-Piekutowska.

Society of Polish Librarians: Music Libraries Section, c/o Warszawskie Towarzystwo Muzyczne, Bibliotéka Zakroczymska 2, 00-225 Warsaw.

Society of Polish Musicians: Krucza 24–26, 00-526 Warsaw.

Szymanowski Society of Music: Kasprusie 19, willa Atma, 34-500 Zakopane.

Union of Polish Lyric Writers and Composers of Light Music ZAKR: Hipoteczna 2, 00-092 Warsaw.

Warsaw Music Society: Morskie Oko 2, 02-511 Warsaw.

Wieniawski Society of Music: Sweitos awska 7, 61-840 Poznań.

Portugal

Fundaçâo Calouste Gulbenkian: Serviço de Música, Avda de Berna 45a, 1067-001 Lisbon; tel. 351 21 782 3000; fax 351 21 782 3041; e-mail musica@gulbenkian.pt; Dir of Music Dept: Luis Pereira Leal.

Juventude Musical Portuguesa: Rua Rosa Araujo 6, Third Floor, 1200 Lisbon; Pres. Miguel Henriques.

Sindicato dos Músicos: Avda D. Carlos I 72, Second Floor, 1200 Lisbon.

Sociedade Portuguesa de Autores (SPA): Avda Dugue de Louié 31, 1098 Lisbon Codex; Pres. Luis Francisco Rebelo.

Romania

Jeunesses Musicales: Str Lipscani 53, Bucharest.

Union of Romanian Composers and Musicologists: Calea Victoriei 141, Sector 1, 70149 Bucharest; tel. 40 21 2127966; fax 40 21 2107211; e-mail ucmr@itcnet.ro; Pres.: Prof. Dr Adrian Iorgucescu.

Russia

Intercultcentre (International Center for Festivals and Competitions): Arbat Str 35, 121835 Moscow; Dir Gen. Suren Shaumian.

International Union of Musicians: ul Gertsena 14/2, 103009 Moscow; Pres. Irina Arkhipova.

State Academic Mariinsky Theatre: Teatralnaya Square 1, 190000, St Petersburg; tel. 812 1143039; fax 812 2141744; Artistic and Gen. Dir Katia Sirakanian.

Union of Composers of Russia: Brusov Pereulok 8–10, 103009 Moscow; Chair. V Kazenin.

VAAP (Russian Copyright Agency): ul Bolshaia Bronnaia 6A, GSP K 104, 103670 Moscow.

Serbia and Montenegro

International Society for Contemporary Music (Yugoslav section): PO Box 213, 11000 Belgrade.

Union of Yugoslav Composers: Misarska 12–14, 11000 Belgrade.

Yugoslav Music Information Center of Sokoj: Misarska 12–14, 11 000 Belgrade; tel. and fax 381 11 3245 192; Dir Ana Koievska.

Singapore

Musicians and Singers Association: Block 3, 03-628, Rochor Centre, Rochor Road, Singapore 0718; Chief Officer Stephen Gomez.

National Arts Council: PSA Building, 35th Storey, 460 Alexandria Road, Singapore 0511.

Slovakia

Music Centre Slovakia: Michalská 10, 815 36 Bratislava 1; tel. (2) 5920-4811; fax (2) 5443-0379; e-mail hc@hc.sk; website www.hc.sk; Dir Olga Smetanová.

Slovak Music Association: Afárikova nám 4, 811 02 Bratislava.

Slovak Music Fund: Fucikova 29, 811 02 Bratislava.

Slovak Music Union: Michalská 10, 815 36 Bratislava.

Slovkoncert (Slovak Artistic and Publicity Agency): Michalská 10, 815 36 Bratislava.

South Africa

Association of the South African Music Industry: 150 Hendrils Verwoerb Drive, Frn Republic Road, Johannesburg; Chief Exec. Des Dubery; Gen. Man. Nhlamhla Sibisi.

Dramatic, Artistic, and Literary Rights Organization Ltd (DALRO): PO Box 9292, Johannesburg; Man. Dir Gideon Ross.

Foundation for the Creative Arts: PO Box 91122, Auckland Park 2006; Exec. Man. Herman Van Niekerk.

Recording Industry of South Africa: PO Box 367, Randburg 2194; tel. 27 11 886 1342; fax 27 11 886 4169; website www.risa.org.za

South African Music Rights Organization Ltd (SAMRO): 73 Juta Street, Braamfontein, Johannesburg 2001; tel. 011 489 5000; fax 011 403 1934; Man. Dir Gideon Ross; CEO Rob Hooijer.

South African Recording Rights Association Ltd (SARRAL): PO Box 4378, Johannesburg 2000; Chief Officer George Hardie.

South African Society of Music Teachers: PO Box 5318, Walmer 6065.

Spain

Asociación Cultural Laboratorio de Interpretación Musical (LIM): Seco 12, 28007 Madrid; Pres. Jesús Villa Rojo.

Asociación de Música en Compostela: Pablo Aranda 6, 28006 Madrid; Pres. Margarita Pastor Zacharias.

Centro Para la Difusión de la Música Contemporánea: Santa Isabel 52, 28012 Madrid; Dir Tomas Marco.

Direccion General de Música y Teatro: Ministerio de Cultura, Paso del Rey 1, 28071 Madrid.

International Society for Contemporary Music (Spanish Section): Avda de America 58-5, 28028 Madrid; Sec.-Gen. José Maria Franco Gil.

Instituto de Bibliografica Musical: penulas 12, 12p 28071 Madrid; Pres. Jacinto Torres Mulas.

Joventuts Musical de Barcelona: Pau Claris 139, Fourth Floor, 1a, 08009 Barcelona.

Juventudes Musicales: Girona 10, 3, Barcelona.

Sociedad de Conciertos: Altamira 3, 03002 Alicante; Dir Margarita Berenger.

Sociedad Española de Musicologia (SEM): Canos del Peral 7, 28013 Madrid; Pres. Ismael Fernández de la Cuesta.

Sociedad General de Autores de España (SGAE): Fernando VI 4, 28004 Madrid; tel. 34 913 499 550; fax 34 913 499 500; website www.sgae.es; Pres. Manuel Gutierrez Aragón

Sweden

International Society for Contemporary Music (Swedish Section): c/o FST, PO Box 27327, 102 54 Stockholm.

Society of Music Teachers in Sweden: c/o Nordstedt, Otroftagatan 37, 216 20 Malmö.

Society of Swedish Church Musicians: c/o S. Henriksson, Storgatan 36, 520 40 Floby.

Society of Swedish Composers: PO Box 27327, 102 54 Stockholm; Chair. Sten Melin.

Sveriges Orkesterförbund (Association of Swedish Orchestras): Stockholm; website www.orkester.nu; f. 1999; represents some 327 orchestras; Gen. Man.: Magnus Eriksson

Swedish Artists and Musicians Interest Organization: Mosebacke Torg 16, 116 20 Stockholm.

Swedish Choral Association: PO Box 38014, 100 64 Stockholm.

Swedish Music Information Center: PO Box 27327, 102 54 Stockholm; Dir Roland Sandberg.

Swedish Musicians' Union: PO Box 49144, 100 29 Stockholm; Chair. Roland Almlén.

Swedish Performing Rights Society: PO Box 27327, 102 54 Stockholm; tel. 46 8 783 88 00; fax 46 8 662 62 75; website www.stim.se; Dir Gunnar Petri.

Swedish Piano Teachers Association: Solbacken 9, 131 42 Nacka.

Swedish Society for Musicology: c/o Statens Musiksamlingar, PO Box 16326, 103 26 Stockholm.

Swedish Society of Light Music Composers: PO Box 27327, 102 54 Stockholm.

Swedish Union of Professional Musicians: Drottninggatan 55, 111 21 Stockholm.

Switzerland

Association of Concert Giving Societies of Switzerland: Münsterplatz 18, 4051 Basel.

Association of Swiss Musicians: Avenue du Grammont 11 bis, PO Box 177, 1000 Lausanne 13; Gen. Sec. Hélène Petitpierre.

European Association of Amateur Orchestras: Heimstrasse 24, 3018 Berne; tel. and fax 0041 319912270; Vice-Pres.: Kathi Engel Pignolo.

European Association of Music Festivals: 120B, rue de Lausanne, 1202 Geneva; Sec. Dr Henry Siegwart.

Federation of International Music Competitions: 104 rue de Carouge, 1205 Geneva.

Gesellschaft der Freunde alter Musikinstrumente: Mühlebachstrasse 174, 8008 Zürich.

Goethe Foundation of Arts and Sciences: Münstergasse 9, 8001 Zürich.

International Federation of Musicians: Hofackerstrasse 7, 8032 Zürich.

International Music Council (National Committee): Bahnhofstrasse 78, 5000 Aarau.

International Musicological Society: PO Box 1561, 4001 Basel.

International Society for Contemporary Music: Association of Swiss Musicians, Avenue du Grammont 11 bis, PO Box 177, 1000 Lausanne 13.

Jeunesses Musicales de Suisse: rue Merle d'Aubigné 25, 1207 Geneva.

National Association of Orchestras: Wattenwylweg 30, 3006 Bern.

National Association of Singers: Burgstrasse 1, 4143 Dornach.

National Music Association: 3946 Turtmann.

Performing Right Society of Switzerland (SUISA): Bellariastrasse 82, 8038 Zürich.

Romand Centre of Sacred Music: PO Box 204, Champel, 1211 Geneva.

Schweiz Chorvereinigung: Scheuchzerstrasse 14, 8006 Zürich.

SUISA Music Foundation (Music Information Centre): Passage Maxmililien-de-Meuron 4, PO Box 409, 2001 Neuchâtel; website www .suisa.se; Man. Dir P. Liechti.

SUISA Swiss Society for Rights of Authors of Musical Works: Bellariastrasse 82, PO Box 782, 8038, Zurich; tel. 41 1 4856666; fax 41 1 4824333; website www.suisa.se.

Swiss Association for Concert Managers: 7 rue de la Fontaine, 1204 Geneva; Sec. and Pres. Jack Yfar.

Swiss Association for Church Singing: Hirschengraben 50, PO Box, 8025 Zürich.

Swiss Association of Mixed Choirs: Rainallee 68, 4125 Riehen.

Swiss Association of Professional Conductors: Stutzstrasse 9, 8834 Schindellegi.

Swiss Association of Professional Musicians: Elisabethenstrasse 2, 4051 Basel.

Swiss Music Council: Haus der Musik, Gönhardweg 32, 5000 A A RAU; tel. 41 62 822 9423; fax 41 62 822 9407.

Swiss Music Education Association: Forchstrasse 376, 8008 Zürich.

Swiss Music Interpreters Society: Mittelstrasse 49, 8008 Zürich.

Swiss Music Teachers Association: Forchstrasse 376, 8008 Zürich.

Swiss Society of Music Teachers: Alpstrasse 34, 6020 Emmenbrücke.

Swiss Society for Musical Research: PO Box 231, 4020 Basel.

Swiss Society for Popular Music: c/o SUISA, Bellariastrasse 82, 8038 Zürich.

Swiss Workers' Music Association: PO Box 29, 3000 Bern 9.

World Federation of International Music Competitions: rue de Carouge 104, 1205 Geneva; tel. 41 22 321 36 20; fax 41 22 781 14 18.

United Kingdom

Alkan Society: 21 Heronswood, Salisbury, Wiltshire SP2 8DH; website www.alkansociety.org; Hon. Sec. Peter Grove.

Amateur Music Association: Medlock School, Wadeson Road, Manchester M13 9UR; Gen. Sec. Ian Clarke.

Arts Council of Great Britain: 2 Pear Tree Court, London EC1R 0DS; tel. 020 7608 6100; fax 020 7608 4100; e-mail enquiries@artscouncil.co.uk; website www.artscouncil.org.uk; Sec.-Gen. Anthony Everitt.

Association for the Advancement of Teacher Education in Music: 16 Ullswater Ave, Cardiff CF2 5PT; Chair. Dr William Salaman.

Association of British Choral Directors: 15 Granville Way, Sherborne, Dorset DT9 4AS; tel. 01935 389482; fax 0870 128 4085; website www.abcd.org.uk; Gen. Sec. Rachel Greaves.

Association for British Music: 2 Union Place, Boston, Lincolnshire PE21 6PS; Hon. Sec. Estelle Stiles.

Association of British Orchestras: 8 Gerrard Street, London W1D 5PJ; tel. 020 7287 0333; fax 020 7287 0444; e-mail info@abo.org.uk; website www.abo.org.uk; Dir Russell Jones.

Association for Business Support of the Arts: 2 Chester Street, London SW1X 7BB; Dir Colin Tweedy.

Association of Entertainment and Arts Management: 3a–5a Stanley Street, Southport, Merseyside PR9 0BY; Gen. Sec. J. B. A. Sharples.

Association of Teachers of Singing: Weir House, 108 Newton Road, Burton-on-Trent, Staffs DE15 0TT; tel. and fax 01283 542198; website www.aotos.co.uk; Membership Sec. Coral Gould.

Association of Woodwind Teachers: Hilltop, Gravel Hill, Chartham Hatch, Canterbury, Kent CT4 7NH; tel. 01227 730923; website www.awt .org.uk; Sec. Sheila Wyver.

Audio Engineering Society Ltd (British Section): PO Box 645, Slough SL1 8BJ; tel. (1628) 663725; fax (1628) 667002; website www.aes .org.

Bantock Society: 48 Ravenswood Road, Redland, Bristol BS6 6BT; tel. 0117 924 0506; website www.musicweb.uk.net/bantock; Chair. Ron Bleach.

Barbirolli Society: 2 Cedar Close, Uttoxeter, Staffs ST14 7NP; Chair. Pauline Pickering.

Benslow Instrument Loan Scheme: Little Benslow Hills, Benslow Lane, Hitchin, Hertfordshire SG4 9RB; tel. (1462) 420748; fax (1462) 440171; e-mail loanscheme@benslow.org; website www.benslow.org; Man. Liz Clark; Development Co-ordinator Clare Talbot; high quality string/ woodwind instruments loaned to talented young players and students who cannot afford the calibre of instrument needed for further development.

Benslow Music Trust: Little Benslow Hills, Benslow Lane, Hitchin, Hertfordshire SG4 9RB; tel. (1462) 459446; fax (1462) 440171; e-mail info@ benslow.org; website www.benslow.org; Chief Exec. Lisa J. Railton; Dir of Music David Matthews; year-round residential and day music courses for adult amateur musicians of all ages and standards; also puts on concerts and has facilities for hire.

Boughton Trust: 14–15 Craven Street, London WC2N 5AD; tel. 020 7925 0303.

Bowen Society: Cairnbield, Gordon, Berwickshire; Chair. John Lindsay.

Brighton and Hove Philharmonic Society: 50 Grand Parade, Brighton, BN2 2QA; tel. 01273 622900; fax 01273 697887; website www .brightonphil.org.uk.

British-American Arts Association: Third Floor, 116–118 Commercial Street, London E1 6NF; tel. 020 7247 5385; Dir Jennifer Williams.

British Arts Festivals Association: Third Floor, Whitechapel Library, 77 Whitechapel High Street, London E1 7QX; Co-ordinator Gwyn Rhydderch.

British Association of Symphonic Bands and Wind Ensembles (BASBWE): 12 Wilshaw House, Creekside, Deptford, London SE8 4SF; website www.basbwe.org; Sec. Samuel Becker.

British Broadcasting Corporation (BBC): Broadcasting House, London W1A 1AA; website www.bbc.co.uk.

British Copyright Council: 29–33 Berners Street, London W1T 3AB; website www.britishcopyright.org.uk; Sec. Geoffrey Adams.

British Council: Arts Group, 10 Spring Gardens, London SW1A 2BN; tel. 020 7389 3194; fax 020 7389 3199; e-mail artweb@britishcouncil.org; website www2.britishcouncil.org; Dept of Music Dir John Acton.

British Federation of Audio (BFA) Ltd: PO Box 365, Farnham, Surrey GU10 2BD; tel. 01428 714616; fax 01428 717599.

British Federation of Brass Bands (BFBB): Unit 12, Maple Estate, Stocks Lane, Barnsley S75 2BL; tel. 01226 771015; website www.bfbb.co .uk; Registry and Office Man. Colin Johnson.

British Federation of Music Festivals: Festivals House, 198 Park Lane, Macclesfield, Cheshire SK11 6UD; tel. 01625 428297; fax 01625 503229; Sec. Eileen Craine.

British Flute Society: 41 Devon Avenue, Twickenham, Middlesex TW2 6PN; tel. 020 8241 7572; e-mail secretary@bfs.org.uk; website www.bfs.org .uk; Contact Julie Wright.

British Horn Society: c/o Paxman Ltd, 116 Long Acre, London WC2E 9PA; website www.british-horn.org; Contact Mike Fage.

British Institute of Organ Studies: 39 Church Street, Haslingfield, Cambridge, CB3 7JE; tel. 01223 872190; website www.bios.org.uk; Sec. Jose Hopkins.

British Kodály Society: 31 Woodlands Road, London SW13 0JZ.

British Music Information Centre (BMIC): 10 Stratford Place, London W1C 1BA; tel. 020 7499 8567; fax 020 7499 4795; e-mail info@bmic.co.uk; website www.bmic.co.uk; Man. Elizabeth Yeoman.

British Music Society: 8b Melton Drive, Hunstanton, PE36 5DD; tel. (1485) 534282; e-mail david.burnett@btinternet.com; Hon. Sec.: David Burnett.

British Phonographic Industry (BPI) Ltd: Riverside Building, County Hall, Westminster Bridge Road, London SE1 7JA; tel. 020 7803 1300; fax 020 7803 1310; e-mail general@bpi.co.uk; website www.bpi.co.uk; Dir-Gen. John Deacon.

British Society for Electronic Music: 277 Putney Bridge Road, London SW15 2PT; Sec. Dr Peter Zinovieff.

British Suzuki Institute: 39 High Street, Wheathampstead, St Albans, Herts AL4 8BB; tel. (1582) 832424; fax (1582) 834488; e-mail bsi@ suzukimusic.force9.co.uk; website www.britishsuzuki.com; CEO: Landa Melrose.

Cathedral Organists' Association: Cleveland Lodge, Westhumble, Dorking, Surrey, RH5 6BW; tel. 01306 872800; fax 01306 887260; e-mail coa@rscm.com; Hon. Sec. Prof. John Harper.

Celfyddydau Cymru (Arts Council of Wales): 9 Museum Place, Cardiff CF10 3NX; tel. 02920 376500; fax 02920 221447; website www .artswales.org; Senior Arts Development Officer, Music Simon Lovell-Jones.

Choir Schools' Association: Westminster Cathedral Choir School, Ambrosden Avenue, London SW1P 1QH; website www.choirschools.org.uk; Hon. Sec. P. Hannigan.

City of London Society of Organists: Hill House, 17 Hans Place, London SW1X 0EP; Chair. and Sec. Richard Townend.

Clarinet and Saxophone Society of Great Britain: 15 Springwell, Ingleton, Co Durham, DL2 3JJ; Membership Sec. Susan Moss.

Concert Artistes' Association: 20 Bedford Street, London WC2E 9HP; tel. 020 7836 3172; Sec. Jo Palmer.

Critics' Circle: 51 Vartry Road, London N15 6PS; e-mail info@criticscircle.org.uk; website www.criticscircle.org.uk; Sec. Peter Hepple.

Crotch Society: 74 Pembroke Road, London W8 6NX; Sec. Jonathan Rennert.

Dalcroze Society (UK) Inc: 100 Elborough Street, London SW18 5DL; tel. 020 8870 1986; e-mail admin@dalcroze.org.uk; Chair. Ruth Stewart.

Delius Society: 21 Woodlands Drive, Brooklands, Sale, Cheshire M33 3PQ; tel. (161) 2823654; website www.delius.org.uk; Sec.: Ann Dixon.

Delius Trust: 16 Ogle Street, London W1W 6JA; tel. (20) 7436-4816; fax (20) 7637-4307; website www.delius.org.uk; Chair. David Lloyd-Jones; Sec. Marjorie Dickinson.

Dolmetsch Concertante: Lower Flat, 6 Junction Place, Haslemere, Surrey GU27 1LE; Sec. Pat Dutton.

Donizetti Society: 56 Harbut Road, London SW11 2RB; website www.donizettisociety.com; Hon. Sec. J. R. Carter.

Dvořák Society: 32 Glebe Way, Burnham-on-Crouch, Essex CM0 8QJ; Sec. Shawn Pullman.

Early Music Centre Ltd: Charles Clore House, 17 Russell Square, London WC1B 5DR; Admin. Frederik Martin.

Electro-Acoustic Music Association of Great Britain: 10 Stratford Place, London W1N 9AE; Admin. Charol Butler.

Elgar Society: 20 Geraldine Road, Malvern, Worcs WR14 3PA; website www.elgar.org.

English Folk Dance and Song Society (EFDSS): 2 Regents Park Road, London NW1 7AY; tel. 020 7485 2206; website www.efdss.org; Man. Dir Brenda Godrich.

European Piano Teachers' Association (UK) Ltd: Archpool House, High Street, Handcross, Haywards Heath, W Sussex, RH17 6BJ; tel. 01444 400852; fax 01444 401443; Chair. Frank Martin.

European String Teachers' Association (ESTA): 10 Swanns Meadow, Bookham, Leatherhead, Surrey KT23 4JX; website www.estaweb.org.uk; Sec. Leonie Anderson.

Federation of Master Organ Builders: Petersfield GU32 3AT; Sec. D. M. van Heck.

Federation of Recorded Music Societies Ltd: c/o The Secretary, 67 Galleys Bank, Whitehill, Kidsgrove, Staffs ST7 4DE; Sec. M. Williamson.

Fellowship of Makers and Researchers of Historical Instruments: London Guildhall University, 41–71 Commercial Road, London E1 1LA; tel. 020 7320 1841; fax 020 7320 1830; e-mail ljones@lgu.ac.uk; Hon. Sec. Lewis Jones.

Galpin Society: 37 Townsend Drive, St Albans, Herts AL3 5RF; Admin. Maggie Kilbey.

Gilbert and Sullivan Society: 273 Northfield Avenue, London W5 4UA.

Percy Grainger Society: 6 Fairfax Crescent, Aylesbury, Bucks HP20 2ES; tel. and fax 01296 428609/581185; website www.percygrainger.org.uk; Sec. Barry P. Ould.

Guild of Professional Musicians: 48 Chalcot Road, London NW1 8LS; Admin. Ian Bonner.

Haydn Society of Great Britain: c/o University of Lancaster, Department of Music, Lancaster LA1 4YW; e-mail d.mccaldin@lancaster.ac.uk; website www.haydnsocietyofgb.netfirms.com; Dir Denis McCaldin.

Hazard Chase Ltd: Norman House, Cambridge Place, Cambridge CB2 1NS; tel. 01223 312400; fax 01223 460827; website www.hazardchase.co.uk.

Hymn Society of Great Britain and Ireland: The Vicarage, 7 Paganel Road, Minehead, Somerset, TA24 5ET; website www.dsg.freeispshares.co.uk/Hsoc; Sec. Rev. Geoffrey Wrayford.

Incorporated Association of Organists: 17 Woodland Road, Northfield, Birmingham B31 2HU; tel. and fax (121) 475-4408; e-mail w.j.stormont@btinternet.com; website www.iao.org.uk; Gen. Sec.: John Stormont.

Incorporated Society of Musicians: 10 Stratford Place, London W1C 1AA; tel. (20) 7629-4413; fax (20) 7408-1538; e-mail membership@ism.org; website www.ism.org; CEO Neil Hoyle; professional body for all musicians: performers, composers, teachers, conductors, organists, etc.; represents musicians' interests, raise professional standards, and provide services (insurance, legal advice, etc.) to members.

Incorporated Society of Organ Builders (ISOB): Smithy Steads, Cragg Vale, Hebden Bridge, W Yorkshire, HX7 5SQ; tel. and fax 0870 139 3645; website www.isob.co.uk.

Institute of Musical Instrument Technology (IMIT): Northfield House, 11 Kendal Avenue South, Sanderstead, Croydon, Surrey CR2 0QR; website www.imit.org.uk; Hon. Sec. Malcolm Dalton.

International Artist Managers' Assen—IAMA: 23 Garrick Street, Covent Garden, London WC2E 9BN; tel. (20) 7379-7336; fax (20) 7379-7338; e-mail info@iamaworld.com; websites www.iamaworld.com, www.classicalmusicartists.com.

International Association of Music Libraries, Archives and Documentation Centres (United Kingdom and Ireland Branch): c/o Music Library, Edinburgh City Libraries, 9 George IV Bridge, Edinburgh EH1 1EG; website www.iaml.info; Gen. Sec. Peter Baxter.

International Council for Traditional Music: Flat 1, 30 Holland Park, London W11 3TA; Sec. Philippa Heale.

International Federation of Musicians: 29 Catherine Place, Buckingham Gate, London SW1E 6EH.

International Federation of Phonogram and Videogram Producers: 54 Regent Street, London W1R 5PJ.

International Society for Contemporary Music: British Section, c/o West Heath Studios 174 Mill Lane, London NW6 1TB; Admin. Richard Steele.

Ireland Trust: 35 St Mary's Mansions, St Mary's Terrace, London W2 1SQ; tel. 20 7723-6376; fax 20 7724-8362; website www.musicweb.uk.net/ireland/trust.htm; Hon. Sec.: M. Taylor.

Kempe Society: 135 Stevenage Road, London SW6 6PB; Treasurer-Sec. J. Audrey Ellison.

Korngold Society: 12 Townhead Terrace, Paisley, Renfrewshire PA1 2AX; Sec. Konrad Hopkins.

Liszt Society Ltd: 135 Stevenage Road, London SW6 6PB; Sec. Audrey Ellison.

London Artfest: PO Box 34904, London SW6 6GX; tel. and fax 020 7736 4717; Artistic Dir Lana Bezanov.

Lute Society: Southside Cottage, Brook Hill, Albury, Guildford GU5 9DJ; tel. 01483 202159; fax 01483 203088; e-mail lutesoc@aol.com; website www.lutesoc.co.uk; Sec. Christopher Goodwin.

Making Music (The National Federation of Music Societies): 7–15 Rosebery Avenue, London EC1R 4SP; tel. 0870 903 3780; fax 0870 903 3785; e-mail info@makingmusic.org.uk; website www.makingmusic.org.uk; Chief Exec. Robin Osterley.

Massenet Society: Flat 2, 79 Linden Gardens, London W2 4EU; tel. 020 7229 7060; Dir Stella J. Wright.

Mechanical Copyright Protection Society/Performing Rights Society (MCPS/PRS) Alliance: 29–33 Berners Street, London W1T 3AB; tel. 020 7306 4777; fax 020 7631 8957; website www.mcps-prs-alliance.co.uk; Chief Exec. John Hutchinson.

Music Advisers' National Association: Education Department, Avon House North, St James Barton, Bristol BS99 7EB; Sec. Carl Sidgreaves.

Music Industries Association (MIA): Ivy Cottage Offices, Finch's Yard, Eastwick Road, Great Bookham, Surrey KT23 4BA; tel. 01372 750600; fax 01372 750515; e-mail office@mia.org.uk; website www.mia.org.uk.

Music Masters' and Mistresses' Association (MMA): Steepcot, Bedales School, Petersfield, Hants GU32 2DG; website www.mma-online.org.uk; Hon. Sec. Jonathan Willcocks.

Music Publishers Assen—MPA: Third Floor, Strandgate, 20 York Bldgs, London WC2 6JU; tel. (20) 7839-7779; fax (20) 7839-7776; e-mail info@mpaonline.org.uk; website www.mpaonline.org.uk; CEO Sarah Faulder; Asst Chief Exec. Jenny Goodwin; trade organization representing music publishers in the UK, advising or assisting members in the promotion and protection of music copyright.

Music Retailers Association: PO Box 249, London W4 5EX; Sec. Arthur Spencer-Bolland.

Music for Youth: 102 Point Pleasant, London SW18 1PP; tel. 020 8870 9624; fax 020 8870 9935; e-mail mfy@mfy.org.uk; website www.mfy.org.uk; Exec. Dir Larry Westland.

Musicians' Union: 60–62 Clapham Road, London SW9 0JJ; tel. 020 7582 5566; fax 020 7582 9805; website www.musiciansunion.org.uk; Gen. Sec. John Smith.

National Association of Art Centres: The Arts Centre, Room 110, Vane Terrace, Darlington DL3 7AX.

National Association for Education in the Arts: c/o University of Exeter, School of Education, St Luke's, Exeter EX1 2LU; Sec. Beryl Phillips.

National Association of Teachers in Further and Higher Education: 27 Britannia Street, London WC1X 9JP; tel. 020 7837 3636; fax 020 7837 4403; website www.natfhe.org.uk; Gen. Sec. Paul Mackney.

National Association of Youth Orchestras: Central Hall, West Tollcross, Edinburgh EH3 9BP; tel. 0131 221 1927; fax 0131 229 2921; website www.nayo.org.uk; Hon. Sec. John Clarkson.

National Campaign for the Arts: Pegasus House, 37–43 Sackville Street, London W1S 3EH; tel. 020 7333 0375; fax 020 7333 0660; e-mail nca@artscampaign.org.uk; website www.artscampaign.org.uk; Dir Victoria Todd.

National Early Music Association (NEMA): 137 Preston Road, Wembley, Middx HA9 8NW; website www.nema-uk.org; Sec. Jane Beeson.

National Federation of Gramophone Societies: Withyfeld, 192c Woodrow Forest, Melksham, Wilts SN12 7RF; Chair. J. R. Shaw.

National Operatic and Dramatic Association (NODA): 58–60 Lincoln Road, Peterborough PE1 2RZ; tel. 0870 770 2480; fax 0870 770 2490; website www.noda.org.uk; Chief Exec. Mark Pemberton.

National School Band Association (NSBA): 52 Hall Orchard Lane, Frisby on the Wreake, Melton Mowbray, Leicestershire, LE14 2NH; Chair. Alan Winwood.

Northern Sinfonia Concert Ltd: The Sinfonia Centre, 41 Jejmundvale, Newcastle Upon Tyne, NE2 1PG; tel. 0191 240 1812; fax 0191 240 2668.

Open University Arts Faculty: Walton Hall, Milton Keynes MK7 6AA; tel. 01908 653280; website www.open.ac.uk; Contacts: Prof. D. Burrows, Prof. T. Herbert.

Orff Society: 7 Rothesay Avenue, Richmond, Surrey TW10 5EB; website www.orff.co.uk; Sec. Margaret Murray.

Organ Club: 10 Roxburgh Court, 69 Melrose Road, London SW18 1PG; Gen. Sec. Adrian Mumford.

Personal Managers' Association: c/o Rooke Holt and Co, 83 Elbury Street, London SW1; Chair. Peter Dunlop.

Plainsong and Mediaeval Music Society: c/o RSCM, Cleveland Lodge, Westhumble, Dorking, Surrey RH5 6BW; tel. 01306 872800; fax 01306 887260; e-mail pmms@rscm.com.

Pro Corda: Leiston Abbey House, Leiston, Suffolk IP16 4TB; tel. 01728 831354; fax 01728 832500; website www.procorda.com; Music Dir: Dr Ioan Davies; Admin. Mererid Crump.

The Rawsthorne Trust: The Alpines, Main Street, Hemingbrough, Selby YO8 6QF; tel. and fax (1757) 630256; website www.musicweb.uk.net/rawsth/index.htm; Chair.: John M. Belcher.

Robert Farnon Society: Stone Gables, Upton Lane, Seavington St Michael, Ilminster, Somerset TA19 0PZ; website www.rfsoc.org.uk; Sec.: David Ades.

Royal College of Organists: Kensington Gore, London SW7 2QS; website www.rco.org.uk; Hon. Sec. Stephen Cleobury.

Royal Musical Association: St Aldates, Faculty of Music, Oxford OX1 1DB; website www.rma.ac.uk; Sec. Dr Ewan West.

Royal Philharmonic Society: 10 Stratford Place, London W1C 1BA; tel. (20) 7491 8110; fax (20) 7493 7463; e-mail admin@royalphilharmonicsociety.org.uk; website www.royalphilharmonicsociety.org.uk; Chair.: Tony Fell; Admin.: Rosemary Johnson.

Royal School of Church Music (RSCM): Cleveland Lodge, Westhumble, Dorking, Surrey RH5 6BW; tel. 01306 872800; fax 01306 887260; website www.rscm.com; Dir Dr Lionel Dakers.

The Royal Society of Musicians of Great Britain: 10 Stratford Place, London, W1C 1BA; tel. and fax 020 7629 6137; Sec. Maggie Gibb.

Schools Music Association: 71 Margaret Road, New Barnet, Herts EN4 9NT; tel. and fax 020 8440 6919; website www.schoolsmusic.org.uk; Hon. Sec. Maxwell Pryce.

Schubert Society of Great Britain: Garden Flat, 125 Grosvenor Avenue, London N5 2NL; Sec. Alan Tabelin.

Scottish Arts Council: 12 Manor Place, Edinburgh EH3 7DD; tel. (131) 226-6051; fax (131) 225-9833; website www.sac.org.uk; Head of Music: Nod Knowles.

Scottish Music Information Centre: 1 Bowmont Gardens, Glasgow G12 9LR; tel. (141) 334-6393; fax (141) 337-1161; e-mail info@scottishmusiccentre.com; website www.scottishmusiccentre.com.

Simpson Society: 3 Engle Park, London NW7 2HE; Secs John Brooks, Sylvia Brooks.

Society for the Promotion of New Music (SPNM): Fourth Floor, 18–20 Southwark Street, London SE1 1TJ; tel. 020 7407 1640; website www.spnm.org.uk; Admin. Richard Steele.

Society for the Research in the Psychology of Music: Westminster College, N Hinksey, Oxford OX2 9AT; Sec. Dr Janet Mills.

Spohr Society of Great Britain: 123 Mount View Road, Sheffield S8 8PJ; Sec. Chris Tutt.

Stokowski Society: 7 Priestfields, Rochester, Kent ME1 3AG; Sec. Andrew Barker.

United Kingdom Harpists Association: 4 Fairlawn Park, Sydenham, London SE26 5RU; tel. 39 Villiers Close, Surbiton, Surrey KT5 8DN; website www.ukha.org.

Viola da Gamba Society: 93A Sutton Road, London N10 1HH; website www.vdgs.demon.co.uk; Admin. Caroline Wood.

Wagner Society: 15 David Avenue, Wickford, Essex SS11 7BG; website www.wagnersociety.org; Sec. Jeremy D. Rowe.

Peter Warlock Society: 32a Chipperfield House, Cale Street, London SW3 3SA; tel. 020 7589 9595; website www.peterwarlock.org; Sec. Malcolm Rudland.

Welsh Amateur Music Federation: Ty Cerdd, 15 Mount Stuart Square, Docks, Cardiff, CF10 5DP; tel. 029 2046 5700; fax 029 2046 2733; Dir Keith Griffin.

Welsh Music Guild: Bronyfelin, 17 Penyrheol Drive, Heol Felinfoel, Llanelli, Carmarthenshire, SA15 3NX; website www.welshmusic.org.uk.

Welsh Music Information Centre: Ty Cerdd, 15 Mount Stuart Square, Cardiff, CF10 5DP; tel. 02920 465700/462855; fax 02920 462733; Dir A. J. Howard Rees.

Workers' Music Association: 17 Prideaux House, Prideaux Place, London WC1; Sec. Anne Gilman.

Worshipful Company of Musicians: Sixth Floor, 2 London Wall Buildings, London Wall, London EC2M 5PP; tel. 020 7496 8990; fax 020 7588 3633; website www.wcom.org.uk; Clerk W. R. I. Crewdson.

United States of America

Amateur Chamber Music Players Inc: 1123 Broadway, Room 304, New York, NY 10010-2007; tel. 1 212 645 7424; fax 1 212 741 2678; website www.amcp.net; Chair. Susan M. Lloyd.

American Academy and Institute of Arts and Letters: 633 W 155th Street, New York, NY 10032; Exec. Dir Virginia Dajani.

American Academy of Teachers of Singing: Hotel Ansonia, Studio No. 5-517, 2109 Broadway, New York, NY 10023; website www.voiceteachersacademy.org; Chair. Donald Read.

American Accordionists' Association Inc: 580 Kearny Avenue, Kearny, NJ 07032; tel. 1 201 991 2233; fax 1 201 991 1944; website www.ameraccord.com; Pres. Dr. Carmelo Pino.

American Arts Alliance: 1156 15th Street NW, Suite 820, Washington, DC 20005-1726; tel. 1 202 387 8300; fax 1 202 833 2686; website www.americanartsalliance.org.

American Music Therapy Association Inc. (AMTA): 8455 Colesville Road, Suite 1000, Silver Spring, MD 20910; tel. 1 301 589 3300; fax 1 301 589 5175; e-mail info@musictherapy.org; website www.musictherapy.org.

American Beethoven Society: San Jose State University, 1 Washington Square, Ira F. Brilliant Center for Beethoven Studies, San Jose, CA 95192; Contact William Meredith.

American Berlin Opera Foundation Inc: 6 87th Street, New York, NY 10128; tel. and fax 1 212 534 5383; e-mail gala@operafoundation.org; website www.operafoundation.org; Chief Officer Christa Drechsler.

American Brahms Society: University of Washington, School of Music, PO Box 353450, Seattle, WA 98195-3450; tel. 1 206 543 0400; fax 1 206 284

0111; e-mail brahms@u.washington.edu; website brahms.unh.edu; Exec. Dir George S. Bozarth.

American Cello Council Inc: 340 W 55th Street, New York, NY 10019; tel. 1 212 586 7137; Admin. and Treasurer Esther Prince.

American Choral Directors' Association (ACDA): 502 SW 38th Street, Lawton, OK 73505; tel. 1 580 355 8161; fax 1 580 248 1465; website www.acdaonline.org; Exec. Dir Gene Brooks.

American College of Musicians: PO Box 1807, 808 Rio Grande Street, Austin, TX 78701; tel. 1 512 478 5775; Pres. Richard Allison.

American Composes Alliance and Edition: 170 W 74th Street, New York, NY 10023; Pres. Richard Brooks.

American Federation of Musicians: 1501 Broadway, Suite 600, New York, NY 10036; tel. 1 212 869 1330; fax 1 212 764 6134; website www.afm .org; Pres. Mark Tully Massagli.

American Federation of Television and Radio Artists (AFTRA): 260 Madison Avenue, New York, NY 10016; tel. 1 212 532 0800; website www .aftra.org; National Exec. Dir Gregory Hessinger.

American Federation of Violin and Bow Makers Inc (AFVBM): 33 North B Street, No. 8, San Mateo, CA 94401; website www.afvbm.com; Sec. John Montgomery.

American Guild of Music: PO Box 599, Warren, MI 48090; tel. 1 248 336 9388; e-mail agm@americanguild.org; website www.americanguild.org; Registered Agent E. D. Herrick.

American Guild of Musical Artists (AGMA): 1430 Broadway, 14th Floor, New York, NY 10018; tel. 1 212 265 3687; fax 1 212 262 9088; e-mail AGMA@MusicalArtists.org; website www.musicalartists.org; National Exec. Dir Alan S. Gordon.

American Guild of Organists: 475 Riverside Drive, Suite 1260, New York, NY 10115; tel. 1 212 870 2310; fax 1 212 870 2163; e-mail info@agohq .org; website www.agohq.org; Exec. Dir Daniel N. Colburn.

American Harp Society Inc: 6331 Quebec Drive, Los Angeles, CA 90068; website www.harpsociety.org; Pres. Molly Hahn.

American Liszt Society Inc: 210 Devonshire Drive, Rochester, NY 14625; website www.americanlisztsociety.org; Pres. Fernando Laires.

American Matthay Association: 46 Popular Street, Pittsburgh, PA 15205; website www.matthay.org; Pres. Thomas C. Davis.

American Mechanical Rights Agency Inc (AMRA): 150 S Barrington Avenue, Suite 1, Los Angeles, CA 90049; tel. 1 310 440 8778; fax 1 310 440 0059; website www.amermecrights.com; Chief Officer Patricia Bente.

American Music Center Inc: 30 W 26th Street, Suite 1001, New York, NY 10010; tel. 1 212 366 5260; fax 1 212 366 5265; website www.amc.net; Exec. Dir Nancy C. Clarke.

American Music Conference: 5790 Armada Drive, Carlsbad, CA 92008; tel. 1 760 431 9124; fax 1 760 438 7327; website www.amc-music.com; Exec. Dir Robert Morrison; Contact Sharon McLaughlin.

American Musical Instrument Society: c/o Shrine to Music Museum, 414 E Clark Street, Vermilliom, SD 57069; website www.amis.org.

American Musicians Union: 8 Tobin Court, Dumont, NJ 07628; tel. 1 201 384 5378; Pres. Ben Intorre.

American Musicological Society: 201 S 34th Street, Philadelphia, PA 19104; tel. 1 215 898 8698; fax 1 215 573 3673; website www.ams-net.org; Exec. Dir Ruth Steiner.

American New Music Consortium: 87-27 Santiago Street, Holliswood, NY 11423; Exec. Dir Dinu Ghezzo.

American Orff-Schulwerk Association: PO Box 391089, Cleveland, OH 44139; tel. 1 440 543 5366; website www.aosa.org.

American Society of Composers, Authors and Publishers (ASCAP): 1 Lincoln Plaza, New York, NY 10023; tel. 1 212 621 6000; fax 1 212 724 9064; website www.ascap.com; Pres. Marilyn Bergman.

American String Teachers Association Inc: 4153 Chain Bridge Road, Fairfax, VA 22030; tel. 1 703 279 2113; fax 1 703 279 2114; website www .astaweb.com; Exec. Admin. Galen Wixson.

American Symphony Orchestra League: 910 17th Street NW, Washington, DC 20006; tel. 1 202 776 0215; fax 1 202 776 0224; website www.symphony.org; CEO Catherine French.

American Viola Society: 13140 Coit Road, Suite 320, LB 120, Dallas, TX 75240-5737; tel. 1 972 233 9107 ext 204; website www .americanviolasociety.org; Pres. Alan de Veritch.

American Women Composers Inc: George Washington University, Washington, DC 20052; Pres. Stephania de Kenessey.

Americans for the Arts: 1000 Vermont Avenue NW, Sixth Floor, Washington DC 20005; tel. 1 202 371 2830; fax 1 202 371 0424.

Arts International Program: Institute of International Education, 809 UN Plaza, New York, NY 10017; Dir Jane M. Gullong.

The Asia Society: 725 Park Avenue, New York, NY 10021; tel. 1 212 288 6400; fax 1 212 517 8315; e-mail info@asiasoc.org; website www .asiasociety.org; Dir Rhoda Grauer.

Associated Male Choruses of America Inc: PO Pox 771, Brainerd, MN 56401; website www.amcachorus.org; Exec. Sec. John Fleming.

Association for Recorded Sound Collections Inc: PO Box 543, Annapolis, MD 21404; website www.asrc-audio.org; Exec. Dir Peter Shambarger.

Association of Arts Administration Educators (AAAE) Inc: c/o American Council for the Arts, 1 E 53rd Street, New York, NY 10022; Pres. J. Dennis Rich.

Association of Performing Arts Presenters: 1112 16th Street NW, Suite 400, Washington, DC 20036; Exec. Dir Susan Farr.

Audio Engineering Society Inc: 60 E 42nd Street, Lincoln Building, Room 2520, New York, NY 10165; Exec. Dir Donald J. Plunkett.

Broadcast Music Inc: 320 W 57th Street, New York, NY 10019; tel. 1 212 586 2000; website www.bmi.com; Pres. and CEO Frances W. Preston.

Bruckner Society of America Inc: 2150 Dubuque Road, Iowa City, IA 52240; Pres. Charles L. Eble.

Business Committee for the Arts Inc: 29-27 Queens Plaza N, Fourth Floor, Long Island City, New York, NY 10001; tel. 1 718 482 9900; fax 1 718 482 9911; e-mail info@bcainc.org; website www.bcainc.org; Pres. Judith A. Jedlicka.

Chamber Music America: 305 Seventh Avenue, Fifth Floor, New York, NY 10001; tel. 1 212 242 2022; fax 1 212 242 7955; website www.chamber -music.org; Pres. Bonnie Hampton.

Chopin Foundation of the United States: 1440 79th Street Causeway, Suite 117, Miami, FL 33141; tel. 1 305 868 0624; fax 1 305 868 5150; e-mail info@chopin.org; website www.chopin.org.

Choristers' Guild: 2834 W Kingsley Road, Garland, TX 75041; tel. 1 972 271 1521; fax 1 972 840 3113; website www.choristersguild.org; Exec. Dir Jim Rindelaub.

Chorus America: Association of Professional Vocal Ensembles, 1156 15th Street NW, Suite 310, Washington, DC 20005; tel. 1 202 331 7577; website chorus.america.org; Exec. Dir Kenneth Garner.

College Band Directors National Association: University of Texas, PO Box 8028, Austin, TX 78713; website www.cbdna.org; Sec.-Treasurer Richard L. Floyd.

The College Music Society Inc: 312 E Pine Street, Missoula, MT 59802; tel. 1 406 721 9616; fax 1 406 721 9419; e-mail cms@music.org; website www.music.org; Exec. Dir Robby D. Gunstream.

Composers' Forum Inc: 73 Spring Street, Suite 506, New York, NY 10012.

Composers Guild: PO Box 586, Farmington, UT 84025; Pres. Ruth Gatrell.

Composers' Resources Inc: PO Box 19935, Atlanta, GA 30325; Pres. Howard Weshil.

Concert Music Broadcasters Association: Hotel St Francis, 335 Powell Street, San Francisco, CA 94102.

Conductors' Guild Inc: 5300 Glenside Drive, Suite 2207, Richmond, VA 23228; tel. 1 804 553 1378; fax 1 804 553 1876; website www .conductorsguild.org; Exec. Sec. Judy Ann Voois.

Creative Audio and Music Electronics Organization: 7753 State Blvd Ext, Meridan, MS 39305; Pres. Larry Blakely.

Delta Omicron (International Music Fraternity): 841 W Cherokee Drive, Jefferson City, TN 37760; website www.delta-omicron.org.

Early Music America (EMA): 2366 Eastlake Avenue E, Suite 429, Seattle, WA 98102; tel. 1 206 720 6270; website www.earlymusic.org.

George Enescu Society of the United States Inc: 4 Barrett Place, Northampton, MA 01060.

Guitar Foundation of America: PO Box 1240, Claremont, CA 91711; website www.guitarfoundation.org; Gen. Man. Gunnar Eisel.

Gustav Mahler Society USA: 1616 N Sierra Bonita Avenue, Los Angeles, CA 90046.

The Hymn Society in the United States and Canada: 745 Common-wealth Avenue, Boston, MA 02215; fax 1 617 353 7322; website www.hymnsociety.org; Exec. Dir W. Thomas Smith.

Independent Composers Association: PO Box 45134, Los Angeles, CA 90045; Pres. Burt Goldstein.

Institute for Music, Health and Education: PO Box 4179, Boulder, CO 80306; Dir Don G. Campbell.

Institute of Audio Research: School of Audio and Video Technology, 64 University Place, Greenwich Village, New York, NY 10003; tel. 1 212 777 8550; fax 1 212 677 6549; e-mail contact@audioschool.com; website www.audioschool.com; Dir Miriam Friedman.

International Association of Auditorium Managers: 4425 West Airport Freeway, Suite 590, Irving, TX 75062; Exec. Dir John S. Swinburn.

International Computer Music Association: 2040 Polk Street, Suite 330, San Francisco, CA 94109; website www.computermusic.org; Pres. Allen Strang.

International Double Reed Society: University of North Texas, School of Music, Denton, TX 76203; website www.idrs.org; Pres. Charles Veazey.

International Federation of Festival Organizations: 4230 Stansbury Avenue, No. 105 Sherman Oaks, CA 91423; Sec.-Gen. Armando Moreno.

International Horn Society: 2220 N 1400 E, Provo, UT 84604; website www.hornsociety.org; Exec. Sec. Ellen Powley.

International Society of Bassists: 4020 McEwen, Suite 105, Dallas, TX 75244; tel. 1 972 233 9107; website www.isbworldoffice.com; Gen. Man. Madeleine Crouch.

International Society of Performing Arts Administrators: 2920 Fuller Avenue, NE, Suite 205, Grand Rapids, MI 49505; Exec. Dir Michael C. Hardy.

International Teleproduction Society Inc: 350 Fifth Avenue, Suite 2400, New York, NY 10118; Exec. Dir Janet Luhrs.

International Ticketing Association (INTIX): 330 W 38th Street, Suite 605, New York, NY 10018; tel. 1 212 629 4036; fax 1 212 629 8532; e-mail info@intix.org; website www.intix.org.

Jeunesses Musicales of the USA: c/o Trinity University, 715 Stadium Drive, San Antonio, TX 78284; Dir Gerald Benjamin.

Keyboard Teachers Association International Inc: 361 Pin Oak Lane, Westbury, NY 11590; Pres. Albert DeVito.

League of Composers: International Society of Contemporary Music, PO Box 1205, New York, NY 10276; tel. 1 718 442 5225; e-mail league-iscm@league-iscm.org; website www.league-iscm.org; Exec. Dir Geoffrey Kidde.

Leschetizky Association: 105 W 72nd Street, New York, NY 10023; website www.leschetizky.org; Pres. Genia Robinor.

Lincoln Center for the Performing Arts: 70 Lincoln Center Plaza, New York, NY 10023; tel. 212 875 5000; fax 212 875 5745; website www.lincolncenter.org.

Lute Society of America: PO Box 1328, Lexington, VA 24450.

The Masterwork Music and Art Foundation Inc: Morristown, NJ 07962; tel. 1 909 781 5669; Exec. Dir Shirley S. May.

Moravian Music Foundation Inc: 457 S Church Street, Box L, Winston-Salem, NC 27108; tel. 1 336 725 0651; fax 1 336 725 4514; website www.moravianmusic.org; Pres. M. Keith Kapp.

Mu Phi Epsilon: 2212 Mary Hills Drive, Minneapolis, MN 55422; website home.muphiepsilon.org; Pres. Katherine Doepke.

Music Association of America: 224 King Street, Englewood, NJ 07631; Exec. Dir George Sturm.

Music Critics Association Inc: 7 Pine Court, Westfield, NJ 07090; website www.mcana.org; Man. Albert H. Cohen.

Music Educators National Conference: 1806 Robert Fulton Drive, Reston, VA 22091.

Music Library Association Inc: 8551 Research Way, Suite 180, Middleton, WI 53562; tel. 1 608 836 5825; fax 1 608 831 8200; website www.musiclibraryassoc.org.

Music Publishers' Association of the United States: 711 Third Avenue, New York, NY 10017; website www.mpa.org.

Music Teachers National Association Inc: 441 Vine Street, Suite 505, Cincinnati, OH 45202; tel. (513) 421-1420; fax (513) 421-2503; e-mail mtnanet@mtna.org; website www.mtna.org; Exec. Dir Gary L. Ingle.

National Academy of Recording Arts and Sciences Inc: 3402 Pico Blvd, Santa Monica, CA 90405; Pres. Michael Greene.

National Assembly of State Arts Agencies: 1010 Vermont Avenue NW, Suite 920, Washington, DC 20005; Exec. Dir Jonathan Katz.

National Association for Music Therapy Inc: 8455 Colesville Road, Suite 930, Silver Spring, MD 20910; tel. 1 301 589 3300; website www.musictherapy.org.

National Association of Broadcasters: 1771 N Street NW, Washington, DC 20036; tel. 1 202 429 5300; fax 1 202 429 4199; website www.nab.org; Pres. and CEO Edward Fritts.

National Association of Negro Musicians: 11551 S Laflin Street, Chicago, IL 60643; Exec. Sec. Ona Campbell.

National Association of Pastoral Musicians: 962 Wayne Avenue, Suite 210, Silver Spring, MD 20910; tel. 1 240 247 3000; fax 1 240 247 3001; website www.npm.org; Pres. Virgil C. Funk.

National Association of Performing Arts Managers and Agents (NAPAMA) Inc: 459 Columbus Avenue, Suite 133, New York, NY 10024; e-mail info@napama.org; website www.napama.org.

National Association of Recording Merchandisers Inc: 9 Eves Drive, Suite 120, Marlton, NJ 08053; tel. 1 856 596 2221; fax 1 856 596 3268; website www.narm.org; Exec. Vice-Pres. Pam Horovitz.

National Association of Schools of Music: 11250 Roger Bacon Drive, Suite 21, Reston, VA 22090; Exec. Dir Samuel Hope.

National Association of Teachers of Singing Inc: 2800 University Blvd N, Jacksonville, FL 32211; website www.nats.org.

National Choral Council: 1650 Broadway, New York, NY 10019; tel. 1 212 333 5333; fax 1 212 315 2420; website www.nationalchorale.org; Exec. Dir Martin Josman.

National Council of Acoustical Consultants: 66 Morris Avenue, Suite 1a, Springfield, NJ 07081; tel. 1 973 564 5859; fax 1 973 564 7480; e-mail info@ncac.com; website www.ncac.com; Exec. Sec. Virginia Marguire.

National Federation of Music Clubs: 1336 N Delaware Street, Indianapolis, IN 46202; website www.nfmc-music.org; Chief Officer D. Clifford Allison.

National Foundation for Advancement in the Arts: 800 Brickell Avenue, Suite 500, Miami, FL 33131; website www.nfaa.org; Pres. William H. Banchs.

National Guild of Community Schools of the Arts Inc: PO Box 8018, Englewood, NJ 07631; website www.nationalguild.com; Exec. Dir Lolita Mayadas.

National Music Council: 711 Third Avenue, Eighth Floor, New York, NY 10017; website www.musiccouncil.org.

National Music Publishers' Association (NMPA) Inc: 475 Park Avenue S, 29th Floor, New York, NY 10016; tel. 1 646 742 1651; fax 1 646 742 1779; e-mail pr@nmpa.org; website www.nmpa.org; Pres. Edward P. Murphy.

National Opera Association: Northwestern University, School of Music, 711 Elgin Road, Evanston, IL 60208; website www.noa.org.

National Orchestral Association: 245 Park Avenue, 15th Floor, New York, NY 10167.

National School Orchestra Association: PO Box 1087, Mill Valley, CA 94942.

National Women Composers Resource Center: 330 Townsend Street, Suite 218, San Francisco, CA 94107.

Network for New Music: PO Box 27556, Philadelphia, PA 19118; tel. 1 215 848 7647; e-mail info@networkfornewmusic.org; website www.networkfornewmusic.org; Artistic Dir Linda Reichert.

New Music Alliance: 508 Woodland Terrace, Philadelphia, PA 19104; Pres. Tina Davidson.

New York Consortium for New Music: 215 W 90th Street, New York, NY 10024; Pres. Patricia Spencer.

OPERA America Inc: 1156 15th Street NW, Suite 810, Washington DC 20005; tel. 1 202 293 4466; fax 1 202 393 0735; website www.operaam.org; Exec. Vice-Pres. and CEO Marc A. Scorca.

Percussive Arts Society: 701 NW Ferris Avenue, Lawton, OK 73507; tel. 1 580 353 1455; fax 1 580 353 1456; e-mail percarts@pas.org; website www.pas.org; Admin. Man. Steve Beck.

Piano Manufacturers Association International: National Piano Foundation, 4020 McEwen, Suite 105, Dallas, TX 75244; tel. 1 214 233 9107; fax 1 214 240 4219; Exec. Dir Donald W. Dillon.

Piano Technicians Guild Inc: 3930 Washington, Kansas City, MO 64111; Exec. Dir Larry Goldsmith.

Recording Industry Association of America (RIAA): 1330 Connecticut Avenue NW, Suite 300, Washington, DC 20036; tel. 1 202 775 0101; fax 1 202 775 7253; website www.riaa.com; Pres. Jason S. Berman.

SESAC Inc: 55 Music Square E, Nashville, TN 37203; tel. 1 615 320 0055; fax 1 615 329 9627; website www.sesac.com.

Society for Ethnomusicology Inc: Indiana University, Morrison Hall 005, Bloomington, IN 47405.

Society of Composers Inc: PO Box 450, Old Chelsea Station, New York, NY 10113; website www.societyofcomposers.org.

Songwriters Guild of America: 1500 Harbor Blvd, Weehawken, NJ 07087; website www.songwriters.org; Pres. George David Weiss.

Sonneck Society for American Music: PO Box 476, Canton, MA 02021.

Suzuki Association of the Americas Inc: PO Box 17310, Boulder, CO 80308; tel. 1 303 444 0948; e-mail info@suzukiassociation.org; website www.suzukiassociation.org; Pres. Jeffrey Cox.

Theatre Communications Group Inc: 355 Lexington Avenue, New York, NY 10017; tel. 1 212 697 5230; website www.tcg.org; Dir Peter Zeisler.

Tubists Universal Brotherhood Association: University of Texas at Austin, Austin, TX 78712.

United States Information Agency, Arts America Program: 301 Fourth Street SW, Washington, DC 20547.

Viola da Gamba Society of America: University of Colorado, Dept of Music, Boulder, CO 80302; website vdgsa.org; Pres. Gordon Sandford.

Violin Society of America: 48 Academy Street, Poughkeepsie, NY 12601; tel. 1 845 452 7557; website www.vsa.to; Pres. Hans E. Tausig.

Violoncello Society Inc: 127 W 72nd Street, No. 2R, New York, NY 10023; Exec. Admin. Esther Prince.

Kurt Weill Foundation for Music Inc: 7 E 20th Street, Third Floor, New York, NY 10003; website www.kwf.org; Pres. Kim H. Kowalke.

Young Audiences Inc: 115 E 92nd Street, New York, NY 10128; tel. 1 212 831 8110; fax 1 212 289 1202; website www.youngaudiences.org; Exec. Dir Richard Bell.

Uruguay

Asociación General de Autores del Uruguay: Canelones 1122, PZ 11100 Montevideo; Pres. Antonio Italiano.

Asociación, Uruguay de Musicos: Calle Maldonado 983, PO Box 11100 Montevideo; Pres. Alfonson Coronel.

Centro Cultural de la Música: PO Box 5, Avda 18 de Julio 1006, 6°, Montevideo; Dir Jorge Calvetti.

Juventudes Musicales del Uruguay: Sarandi 444, 1°, Edificio SODRE, Montevideo; Pres. Maria Tania Siver.

Sociedad Uruguay de Interpretes: Canelones 1090, Montevideo; Pres. José Maria Lorenzo.

Sociedad Uruguay de Música Contemporánea: Casilla de Correo 1328, 11000 Montevideo; Pres. Diego Legrand.

Venezuela

Sociedad de Autores y Compositores de Venezuela: Avda Andres Bello, Ede, Vam Torre Oeste, 10°, Caracas; Pres. Guillermo Carrasco.

APPENDIX E: MAJOR COMPETITIONS AND AWARDS

Value of awards, restrictions on entrants, dates, etc. may vary from year to year and interested readers are advised to contact the sponsoring organizations directly for complete information. It should also be noted that many institutions listed in Appendix F also maintain competitions, awards and scholarship programmes.

Australia

Australian Broadcasting Corporation Young Performers' Awards: PO Box 9994, Sydney, NSW 2001. Annual awards for singers and instrumentalists to the age of 30 who have been in continuous residence in Australia for one year. Must compete in state of residence. Award of $A 19,500 plus concert engagements.

Australian Singing Competition: PO Box A2325, Sydney South, NSW 1235; tel. 61 2 9231 4293; fax 61 2 9221 8201; e-mail asc@aussing.com.au; website www.aussing.com.au; Annual awards for operatic and classical singers. Must be an Australian or New Zealand citizen under the age of 26 for classical singers and under the age of 35 for operatic singers. Mathy and opera awards totalling $A 100,000.

Sydney International Piano Competition of Australia: PO Box 420, Double Bay, Sydney, NSW 1360; tel. 61 2 9326 2405; fax 61 2 9326 2604; e-mail info@sipca.com.au; website www.sipca.com.au. Quadrennial competition open to pianists of all nationalities between the ages of 17 and 30. Prizes include 1st prize of $A 25,000 and various other prizes totalling $120,000; next competition in 2004.

Austria

Ludwig van Beethoven International Piano Competition: Anton-von-Webern-Platz 1, 1030 Vienna; tel. 43 1 71155 6050; fax 43 1 71155 6059; e-mail info@beethoven-comp.at; website www.beethoven-comp.at. Quadrennial competition open to pianists of all nationalities between the ages of 17 and 32. Prizes include: 1st prize of 80,000 Schillings, a Bösendorfer piano, and concert engagements; 2nd prize of 60,000 Schillings; 3rd prize of 50,000 Schillings; and three further prizes of 20,000 Schillings.

International Anton Bruckner Organ Competition: Untere Donaulande 7, 4010 Linz. Quadrennial competition open to organists of all nationalities to the age of 35. Prizes include 1st prize of 50,000 Schillings, 2nd prize of 40,000 Schillings and 3rd prize of 30,000 Schillings.

International Belvedere Competition for Opera Singers: Fleischmarkt 24, 1010 Vienna. Annual competition for singers to the age of 35. Prizes totalling 50,000 Schillings.

International Fritz Kreisler Competition: PO Box 76, 1030 Vienna; tel. 43 1 711 55 6021; fax 43 1 711 55 6029; e-mail office@fritz-kreisler .music.at; website www.fritz-kreisler.music.at. Quadrennial competition for violin and viola. Prizes include 1st prize of 150,000 Schillings, 2nd prize of 125,000 Schillings and 3rd prize of 100,000 Schillings.

International Mozart Competition of the Universität Mozarteum: Universität Mozarteum Salzburg, Alpenstrasse 48, 5020 Salzburg; tel. 43 662 6198; fax 43 662 6198-3033; website www.moz.ac.at. Quadrennial competition open to musicians of all nationalities. Prizes include the Mozart Prize from the Austrian Ministry of Science and Research, as well as other prizes and concert engagements. Next competition (for voice) in 2006.

Internationaler Chorwettbewerb: Kulturreferat der Stadtgemeinde, 9800 Spittal. Annual competition for Choirs. Prizes include money and documents.

Prix Ars Electronica: Museumsgesellschaft mbH, Hauptstrasse 2, 4040 Linz; tel. 43 732 72720; fax 43 732 72722; e-mail info@aec.at; website www .aec.at. Annual competition for the computer arts open to individuals, groups, and organizations. Prizes include money and awards.

Nancy Van de Vate International Composition Prize for Opera: Margaretenstrasse 125/15, 1050 Vienna. Annual competition open to all female composers of opera and music theatre.

Vienna International Competition for Composers: Casinos Austria, Dr Karl-Lueger Ring 14, 1015 Vienna. Annual competition open to composers to the age of 40, who submit a composition not previously accepted for performance, or performed in public, or awarded a prize in another competition.

Belgium

Concours International de Chant de Verviers: Rue des Dominicains 1, 4000 Liège. Biennial competition open to singers of all nationalities.

Concours International de Guitare: c/o Le Printemps de la Guitare asbl, Place du Chef Lieu 9, 6040 Charleroi; tel. and fax 32-71 35 5320; e-mail info@printemps-guitare.be; website www.printemps-guitare.be. Biennial competition open to solo classical guitarists of all nationalities to the age of 32. Prizes include 1st prize of 5,000 euros, 2nd prize of 3,700 euros, 3rd prize of 2,500 euros, 4th prize of 1,500 euros, 5th prize of 800 euros, and 6th prize of 500 euros.

Festival Van Vlaanderen, Brugge: Collaert Mansionstraat 30, 8000 Bruges; tel. 050 33 22 83; fax 050 34 52 04; e-mail musica-antiqua@unicall .be; website www.musica-antiqua.com; Annual competition open to harpsichord and fortepiano players (2004), solo singers and solo instrumentalists (2005), organ players and ensembles (2006), categories rotating annually on a triennial schedule. Prizes total 30,000 euros.

Queen Elizabeth International Music Competition of Belgium: 20 rue Aux Laines, 1000 Brussels. Competition for, Compostition and Piano in 2002, Singing in 2003 and Violin in 2004. 1st prize of 500,000 Belgian francs.

Bulgaria

Boris Christoff International Competition for Young Opera Singers: 56 rue Alabin, 1000 Sofia. Quadrennial competition open to men up to the age of 35 and to women up to the age of 33. Prizes include a Grand Prize, 1st prize, 2nd prize, 3rd prize, medals and diplomas.

Canada

Banff International String Quartet Competition: c/o Banff Centre School of Fine Arts, PO Box 1020, Banff, AB T1L 1H5; tel. 1 403 762 6180; e-mail bisqc@banffcentre.ca; website www.banffcentre.ca/bisqc. Triennial competition open to quartets whose members are under 35 years of age at the time of the competition. Prizes include C $20,000, $12,000, $8,000, $5,000, $500, set of bows, Canadian tour, and Banff Centre residency.

Canada Council/Conseil des Arts du Canada Grants and Awards: PO Box 1047, 350 Albert Street, Ottawa, ON K1P 5V8; tel. 1 613 566 4414; fax 1 613 566 4390; website www.canadacouncil.ca; Grants and awards to artists of Canadian citizenship and to non-profit arts organizations.

Canadian Music Competition: 1450 City Councillors Street, Suite 220, Montréal, QC H3A 2E6; tel. 1 514 284 5398; fax 1 514 284 6828; e-mail mus@cmcnational.com; website www.cmcnational.com. Annual competition for pianists, string players, wind players and singers. Open to Canadian citizens or those holding a Landed Immigrant Certificate or those studying with a Canadian teacher for the last three years, between the age of seven and 31.

Concours Orchestre Symphonique de Montréal: 85 St Catherine West, Montréal, QC H2X 3P4. Annual competition open to Canadian citizens or those holding a Landed Immigrant Certificate featuring piano and voice one year and strings and wind the following year; piano: category A for between the ages of 18 and 25 and category B for those under 18; voice: for those between the ages of 18 and 30; strings: category A for those between the ages of 18 and 25 and category B for those under 18; wind: for those between the ages of 16 and 25. Prizes totalling C $15,500 and an appearance on the regular subscriptions series of the Orchestre Symphonique de Montréal.

Eckhardt-Gramatté National Music Competition: Queen Elizabeth II Music Building, Brandon University, 270 18th Street, Brandon, MB R7A 6A9; tel. (204) 728-8212; fax (204) 729-9085; e-mail eckhardt@ brandonu.ca; website www.brandonu.ca/egre; Admin. Officer: Nancy Nehring. Annual competition open to Canadian citizens or Canadian residents, alternating annually between voice, strings and piano. Prizes include 1st prize of C $5,000 and a concert tour, 2nd prize of $3,000 and 3rd prize of $2,000.

Glenn Gould Prize: The Glenn Gould Foundation, PO Box 190, 260 Adelaide Street E, Toronto, ON M5A 1N1. Triennial honour to individuals of all nationalities who have made an exceptional contribution to music and its communication through the use of any communication technology. Previous laureates include R. Murray Schafer, Lord Menuhin, Toru Takemitsu, Yo-Yo Ma and Pierre Boulez. Any person may nominate a potential laureate by sending a complete rationale, in writing, to the

Foundation office. Next laureate named in 2005, nominations accepted between April and Oct. 2004.

Kamloops Symphony Orchestra New Celebrity Competition: PO Box 57, Kamloops, BC V2C 5K3; tel. 1 250 372 5000; fax 1 250 372 5089; e-mail info@kamloopssymphony.com; website www.kamloopssymphony .com. Annual competition open to Canadian citizens or those holding a Landed Immigrant Certificate. Prizes include 1st prize of C $1,000 and 2nd prize of $500, with the two finalists appearing in concert with the Kamloops Symphony Orchestra.

Montréal International Music Competition: Place des Arts, 1501 Jeanne-Mance Street, Montréal QC H2X 1Z9. Competition for violin (2002), piano (2003), and voice (2004); violin and piano for those between the ages of 16 and 30, and voice for those between the ages of 20 and 35. Prizes totalling C $40,500.

Czech Republic

Prague Spring International Music Competition: Hellichova 18, 118 00 Prague 1; tel. 42 2 533474; fax 42 2 536040. Annual competition open to performers of all nationalities with categories changing annually in five-year cycles. Prizes include money and an appearance at the Prague Spring International Music Festival.

Denmark

Carl Nielsen International Music Competitions: Claus Bergs Gade 9, 5000 Odense C; tel. 45 66 12 00 57; fax 45 65 91 00 47; e-mail carlnielsencompetition@odensesymfoni.dk; website www.odensesymfoni .dk/cncomp. Quadrennial competitions open to violinists (2004), clarinet-tists (2005) and flautists (2006) of all nationalities to the age of 30. Prizes include a minimum of 340,000 kroner.

International Organ Competition, Odense: Kultursekretariatet, Vindegade 18, 5000 Odense C; tel. and fax 45 65914318; e-mail kultur .ksf@odense.dk; website home13.inet.tele.dk/organcmp. Biennial competi-tion open to organists of all nationalities to the age of 34. Prizes include 1st prize of 40,000 kroner, 2nd prize of 15,000 kroner, 3rd prize of 10,000 kroner, 4th prize of 5,000 kroner, and a special prize of 5,000 kroner.

Nicolai Malko International Competition for Young Conductors: c/o Danmarks Radio, Rosenoerns Alle 22, 1999 Frederiksberg C. Triennial competition open to conductors between the ages of 20 and 31. Prizes include money.

Finland

Jean Sibelius International Violin Competition: PO Box 31, 00101 Helsinki; tel. 358 9 4114-3443; fax 358 10 850-4760; e-mail violin .competition@kolumbus.fi. Quinquennial competition for violinists born in or after 1975. Next competition in 2005. Prizes totalling about 48,000 euros.

Mirjam Helin International Singing Competition: c/o Finnish Cultural Foundation, PO Box 203, Bulevardi 5 A, 00121 Helsinki; tel. 358 9 6128 1248; fax 358 9 640 474; e-mail mh@skr.fi; website www.skr.fi. Quinquennial competition open to singers of all nationalities, women born in or after 1973 and men born in or after 1971. Prizes separate for men and women, including four prizes totalling 100,000 euros. Next competition in July–Aug. 2004.

Paulo Cello Competition: PO Box 1105, 00101 Helsinki; tel. 358 40 528 4876; fax 358 9 2243 2879; e-mail cello@paulo.fi; website www .cellocompetitionpaulo.org; Quinquennial competition for young cellists of all nationalities. Prizes include money.

France

Concours International d'Ensembles de Musique de Chambre de Colmar: c/o Service des Activités Culturelles, Hôtel de Ville, 68000 Colmar. Triennial competition for chamber music ensembles for perfor-mers to the age of 35. Prizes include 30,000 French francs, 15,000 francs and 10,000 francs.

Concours International d'Orgue Grand Prix de Chartres: 75 rue de Grenelle, 75007 Paris; tel. 33 145 48 31 74; fax 33 145 46 14 34; e-mail orgues.chartres@free.fr; website orgues.chartres.free.fr. Biennial compe-tition open to all organists born after 1 Jan 1961. Prizes include two grand prizes of 20,000 French francs each, one for interpretation and one for improvisation, and two 2nd prizes of 5,000 francs each, one for interpretation and one for improvisation.

Concours International de Chant de La Ville de Toulouse: c/o Théâtre du Capitole, 31000 Toulouse; tel. 33 61 23 21 35; fax 33 61 22 24 34. Annual competition open to singers between the ages of 18 and 33. Prizes totalling 135,000 French francs.

Concours International de Chant de Paris: 8 rue du Dôme, 75116; tel. 33 147 04 76 38; fax 33 147 27 35 03. Biennial competition open to singers, women to the age of 32 and men to the age of 34. Prizes include 120,000 French francs and concert engagements.

Concours International de Chant Offenbach: 79 rue Jouffroy, 75017 Paris. Biennial competition open to singers of all nationalities and all ages. Prizes include appearances in European theatres and festivals.

Concours International de Clavecin: c/o Festival Estival de Paris, 20 rue Geoffroy l'Asnier, 75004 Paris. Biennial competition open to harpsichordists to the age of 32. Prizes include money.

Concours International de Flute Jean-Pierre Rampal: 5 rue Bellart, 75015; Open to flautists up to the age of 30.

Concours International de Guitare: c/o Radio France, 116 Ave du President Kennedy, 75786 Paris Cédex 16. Annual competition open to classical guitarists of all nationalities to the ages of 30 and biennial competition open to composers of all nationalities. Prizes include money, concerts and recitals.

Concours International de Jeunes Chefs d'Orchestre: Square Saint Amour 3 bis, rue Léonel de Moustier, 25000 Besançon; tel. 33 381 25 05 85; fax 33 381 81 52 15. Annual competition open to conductors under the age of 35. Prizes include Emile Vuillermoz Prize.

Concours International de Musique de Chambre: Rue de Dôme 10, 75116 Paris. Biennial competition open to instrumentalists and singers to the age of 35. Prizes include 62,500 French francs.

Concours International de Trompette Maurice André: 5 rue Bellart, 75015 Paris. Competition for young trumpeters. Prizes include four grand prizes.

Concours International de Violon Yehudi Menuhin: 5 rue Bellart, 75015 Paris; tel. 33 1 47 83 33 58; fax 33 143 06 68 79. Competition for young violinists. Prizes include a grand prize and three other prizes.

Concours International de Violoncelle Rostropovich: 146 rue de Rennes, 75006 Paris. Competition for cellists of all nationalities to the age of 33. Prizes include money and public performances.

Concours International du Festival de Musique de Toulon: 117 avenue Lazare Carnot, 83000 Toulon. Annual competition open to instrumentalists between the ages of 18 and 30 with categories rotating annually. Prizes include 1st prize of 20,000 French francs, 2nd prize of 12,000 francs and 3rd prize of 8,000 francs.

Concours International Marguerite Long-Jacques Thibaud: 32 Ave Matignon, 75008 Paris; tel. 33 1 42 66 66 80; fax 33 1 42 66 06 43; website www.concours-long-thibaud.org. Triennial competition open to pianists and violinists between the ages of 16 and 30. Prizes include 250,000 French francs for winners in each category.

Florilège Vocal de Tours: PO Box 1452, 37014 Tours Cédex; tel. 33 2 47 21 65 26. Annual competition open to choral and vocal performers and composers. Prizes include 18 prizes totalling 100,000 French francs.

Fondation des Etats-Unis Harriet Hale Woolley Scholarships: 15 Blvd Jourdan, 75690 Paris Cédex 14. Annual scholarships open to single American instrumentalists or artists between the ages of 21 and 30 for study in Paris. Scholarships include from four to five US $8,500 awards.

International Rostropovich Cello Competition: c/o Association pour la Création et la Diffusion Artistique, 3 rue des Couronnes, 75020 Paris; tel. 1 40 33 45 35; fax 1 40 33 45 38; e-mail rostro@civp.com; website www .civp.com. Next competition in Nov. 2005.

Yvonne Lefébure International Piano Competition: 131–135 boule-vard Carnot, BP 23, 78110 Le Vesinet; tel. 33 1 39 76 76 44; fax 33 1 39 76 27 31. Biennial competition open to pianists of all nationalities to the age of 35. Prizes include money and public performances.

Prix Musical International Arthur Honegger: c/o Fondation de France, 40 Avenue Hoche, 75008 Paris; tel. 33 1 44 21 31 00; fax 33 1 44 21 31 01. Biennial competition open to all composers. Prizes include 50,000 French francs.

Rencontres Musicales d'Evian International String Quartet Com-petition: 6 rue Téhéran, 75008 Paris or Château de Blonay, 74500 Evian les Bains. Biennial competition open to string quartets of all nationalities whose average age does not exceed 33 years of age. Prizes total over 500,000 French francs.

World Music Masters International Piano Competition: Salle Gaveau, 45 rue La Boétie, 75008 Paris. Annual competition open only to pianists who have been finalists in other international competitions. Prizes include US $30,000 and concert engagements.

Germany

Hannover International Violin Competition: Stiftung Niedersachsen, Ferdinandstrasse 4, 30175 Hannover. Triennial competition to violinists of all nationalities between the ages of 16 and 30. Next competition in 2006. Prizes include money, a recording, and concert engagements.

International Johann Sebastian Bach Competition: Thomaskirchhof 16, 04109 Leipzig. Quadrennial competition open to pianists, organists, violinists, harpsichordists and singers of all nationalities. Age limitations: 16–34. Prizes include money.

International Kuhlau Wettbewerb für Flotisten: Herzogenplatz 5, PO Box 2061, 29525 Uelzen; tel. 49 581 800 227; fax 49 581 800 108. Triennial competition for solo flute and flute with piano, two flutes or two flutes with piano, or three or four flutes. Age limit: up to 32.

International Music Competition of the Broadcasting Corporations of Germany: c/o Bayerischer Rundfunk, Rundfunkplatz 1, 80300 Munich. Annual competition open to solo instrumentalists, string quartets, and singers with categories changing annually.

International Piano Competition of Cologne: c/o Foundation Tomassoni, Dagobertstrasse 38, 50668 Cologne. Triennial competition open to pianists of all nationalities between the ages of 18 and 29. Prizes include 1st prize of 15,000 Deutsche Marks, 2nd prize of 10,000 DM and 3rd prize of 5,000 DM.

International Robert Schumann Contest: Muenzstrasse 12, 08056 Zwickau; tel. 49 375 21 26 36; fax 49 375 83 41 30. Quadrennial competition open to pianists to the age of 25 and to singers to the age of 32. Prizes include money.

International Violin Competition Louis Spohr: Burgunderstrasse 4, 79104 Freiburg. Triennial competition open to violinists of all nationalities to the age of 32. Prizes include 1st prize of 12,000 Deutsche Marks, 2nd prize of 8,000 DM and 3rd prize of 5,000 DM.

Internationaler Wettbewerb für Junge Pianisten Ettlingen: Pforzheimerstrasse 25a, 76275 Ettlingen; tel. 7243 101-311; fax 7243 101-436; e-mail info@pianocompetition.org; website www.pianocompetition.org; Dir Frank Reich. Biennial competition open to pianists of all nationalities; category A for those born on or after 7 August 1988, or category B for those born on or after 7 August 1983; next competition in Aug. 2004.

Internationaler Wettbewerb für Komponistinnen: Elisabethstrasse 5, Mannheim. Quadrennial competition open to female composers of all nationalities. Prizes include money.

Karl Klingler Wettbewerb: c/o Internationaler Musikwettbewerb, z.Hd. Frau Ingeborg Krause, Bayerischer Rundfunk, 80300 München. Triennial competition open to string quartets whose total age is at least 128 years with no members over the age of 37. Prizes include money.

Greece

Dmitris Mitropoulos International Competition: 18 Alex Soutaou, 10671 Athens; tel. 30 210 36 27 412; fax 30 210 36 21 477; website www.mitropouloscompetition.gr. Annual competition.

International Maria Callas Music Competition: Amerikis Street 8, 10671 Athens. Biennial competition open to singers (opera, oratorio, lieder) and pianists with the categories alternating annually. Prizes include money.

Hungary

Budapest International Music Competition: c/o InterArt Festivalcenter, Vorosmarty ter 1, 1051 Budapest; tel. 36 1 117 9838; fax 36 1 317 9910. Annual competition with categories changing annually.

International Conductors' Competition of Hungarian Television: Vorasmarty tér 1, 1051 Budapest. Triennial competition open to conductors of all nationalities under the age of 35.

Ireland

AXA Dublin International Piano Competition Ltd: AXA Insurance, Dublin Road, Bray, Co. Wicklow; tel. 353 1 272 1523; fax 353 1 252 1508; website www.axadipc.ie. Triennial competition open to pianists between the ages of 17 and 30. Prizes include 1st prize of 12,000 euros, debut recitals in London, Vienna, Paris and New York, and concert engagements with major international orchestras, 2nd prize of 9,000 euros, 3rd prize of 6,000 euros, and other prizes; next competition in 2006.

Israel

International Harp Contest in Israel: 4 Aharonowitz Street, 63566 Tel-Aviv; tel. 972 3 528 0233; fax 972 3 629 9524; website www.harpa.com/israel-harp-contest.htm. Triennial competition open to harpists of all nationalities. Prizes include 1st prize of a Lyon & Healy concert harp, 2nd prize of US $6,000, 3rd prize of $4,000; next contest in 2006.

Arthur Rubinstein International Piano Master Competition: PO Box 6018, 61060 Tel-Aviv; tel. 972 3 685 6684; fax 972 3 685 4924; website www.arims.org.il. Triennial competition open to pianists of all nationalities between the ages of 18 and 32. Prizes include 1st prize of the Arthur Rubinstein Award Gold Medal and US $10,000, 2nd prize of the Silver Medal and $5,000, 3rd prize of the Bronze Medal and $3,000, and 4th, 5th, and 6th prizes of $1,000 each.

Italy

Associazione Concorisi & Rassegno Musicali (ACERM): Borgo Albizi, 50122 Florence; tel. and fax 39 55 240672. Annual competition open to chamber music instrumentalists to the age of 32. Prizes totalling some 30,000,000 Italian lire.

Valentino Bucchi Competition: Via Ubaldino Peruzzi 20, 00139 Rome. Annual competition open to performers and composers. Prizes totalling some 100,000,000 Italian lire.

Enrico Caruso International Competition for Young Tenors: c/o Associazione Enrico Caruso, Via Degli Omenoni 2, 20121 Milan. Biennial competition open to tenors between the ages of 18 and 28.

Alessandro Casagrande Concorso Pianistico Internazionale: Comune de Terni, Vico S. Lorenzo 1, 05100 Terni. Biennial competition open to pianists born after 1 January 1970. Prizes include 1st prize of 12,000,000 Italian lire, 2nd prize of 8,000,000 lire and 3rd prize of 5,000,000 lire.

Gaspar Cassadó International Cello Competition: Via Solferino 15, 50123 Florence. Biennial competition open to cellists.

Concorso Internazionale di Chitarra Classica Città di Alessandria: Piazza Garibaldi 16, 15100 Alessandria. Annual competition open to solo classical guitarists of all nationalities. Prizes include money.

Concorso Internazionale di Composizione 2 Agosto: c/o Studio Colliva e Nannucci, Via Savioli 24, 40137 Bologna.

Concorso Internazionale di Composizione Camilo Togni: c/o Associazione Nuovi Spazi Sonori, PO Box 196, 25100 Brescia. Biennial competition open to composers of all nationalities born after 31 December 1960. Prizes include 1st prize of 10,000,000 Italian lire, plus publication and performance of winning composition.

Concorso Internazionale di Composizione Goffredo Petrassi: Fondazione Arturo Toscanini, Palazzo Marchi, Strada della Repubblica 57, 43100 Parma; tel. 39 521 391322; fax 1 39 521 391321; website www.fondazione-toscanini.org. Biennial competition open to composers of all nationalities born after 6 Nov. 1964 for an unpublished symphonic composition not exceeding 30 minutes in length. Prizes include 1st prize of 15,000,000 Italian lire.

Concorso Internazionale di Composizione Guido d'Arezzo Fondazione: Corso Italia 102, 52100 Arezzo. Annual competition for polyvocal composition not previously published or performed, of at least five minutes' duration.

Concorso Internazionale di Direzione d'Orchestra Arturo Toscanini: Fondazione Arturo Toscanini, Palazzo Marchi, Strada della Repubblica 57, 43100 Parma; tel. 39 521 391322; fax 1 39 521 391321; website www.fondazione-toscanini.org. Triennial competition open to conductors of all nationalities to the age of 32. Prizes include 1st prize of 15,000,000 Italian lire, 2nd prize of 10,000,000 lire and 3rd prize of 6,000,000 lire.

Concorso Internazionale di Violino Alberto Curci: Fondazione Alberto Curci, Via Santa Brigida 68, 80132 Naples; tel. 39 81 5513030/7649370; fax 39 81 7649370; e-mail curcicompetition@libero.it. Competition open to violinists to the age of 32.

Concorso Internazionale di Violino Premino N. Paganini: Via Sottoripa 5, 16124 Genoa; tel. 39 10 5574215.

Concorso Internazionale Luigi Russolo per Giovani Compositori: c/o Fondazione Russolo-Pratella, Via G Bagaini 6, 21100 Varese. Annual competition open to composers of all nationalities to the age of 35, for electroacoustic, analogue and digital music compositions.

Concorso Internazionale per Contrabasso Giovanni Bottesini: c/o Conservatorio di Musica Arrigo Boito, Via del Conservatorio 27, 43100 Parma. Triennial competition open to double bass players of all nationalities between the ages of 16 and 32. Prizes include 1st prize of 10,000,000 Italian lire, 2nd prize of 6,000,000 lire and 3rd prize of 4,000,000 lire.

Concorso Internazionale per La Conquista Della Chitarra Classica: CP 10673, 20125 Milan. Annual competition open to classical guitarists of all ages. Prizes include money, gold medals and guitars.

Concorso Internazionale per Quartetto d'Archi Premio Paolo Borciani: c/o Teatro Municipale Valli, Piazza Martiri del 7 luglio, 42100 Reggio Emilia; tel. (39) 0522 458811; fax (39) 0522 458822; e-mail premioborciani@iteatri.re.it; website www.premioborciani.iteatri.re.it. Triennial competition open to string quartets of all nations whose members' total age does not exceed 128 years on 12 June 2005. Prizes include 1st prize of 19,000 euros, 2nd prize of 13,800 euros, 3rd prize of 6,600 euros, and a special prize for the best performance of a new quartet, awarded by Sir Peter Maxwell Davies, of 2,500 euros.

Concorso Internazionale per Voci Verdiane: Fondazione Arturo Toscanini, Palazzo Marchi, Strada della Repubblica 57, 43100 Parma; tel. 39 521 391322; fax 1 39 521 391321; website www.fondazione-toscanini .org.

Concorso Internazionale Pianistico Liszt Premio Mario Zanfi: c/o Conservatorio di Musica Arrigo Boito, Via del Conservatorio 27, 43100 Parma. Triennial competition open to pianists of all nationalities between the ages of 16 and 32. Prizes include 1st prize of 10,000,000 Italian lire, 2nd prize of 6,000,000 lire and 3rd prize of 4,000,000 lire.

Concorso Pianistico Internazionale Alfredo Casella: Via del Parco Margherita 49, pal 5, 80121 Naples. Biennial competition open to pianists of all nationalities.

Concorso Pianistico Internazionale Ettore Pozzoli: Segreteria, Via Paradiso 6, 20038 Seregno; tel. and fax 39 0362 222 914; e-mail info@ concorsopozzoli.it; website www.concorsopozzoli.it. Biennial competition open to pianists of all nationalities born on or after 1 Jan. 1973. Prizes include 1st prize of 10,000 euros and recording and release of a CD, 2nd prize of 5,000 euros, 3rd prize of 2,500 euros, two special prizes of 1,000 euros and two special prizes of 500 euros; next competition in 2005.

Fondazione Concorso Pianistico Internazionale Ferruccio Busoni: Piazza Domenicani 25, 39100 Bolzano. Biennial competition open to pianists of all nationalities between the ages of 15 and 28. Prizes include 1st prize of 22,000 euros and concert engagements, 2nd prize of 10,000 euros, 3rd prize of 5,000 euros, 4th prize of 4,000 euros, 5th prize of 3,000 euros, and 6th prize of 2,500 euros.

International Competition of the Teatro Alla Scala: Dino Ciani Prize: c/o Teatro alla Scala, Fondazione di Diritto Privato, Ufficio Assunzioni, PO Box 1611, 20101 Milan. Triennial competition open to pianists of all nationalities born after 31 December 1975. Prizes include 1st prize of 20,000,000 Italian lire, 2nd prize of 8,000,000 lire and 3rd prize of 3,000,000 lire, with medals and performances for each.

Rodolfo Lipizer International Violin Contest: Via Don Giovanni Bosco 91, 34170 Gorizia; tel. 39 481 34775/532551/533264; fax 39 481 536710; e-mail lipizer@lipizer.it; website www.lipizer.it. Annual competition open to violinists of all nationalities born after 17 Sept. 1966. Prizes include money and concert appearances.

Niccolò Paganini Premio Internazionale di Violino: Palazzo Doria, Via Garibaldi 9, 16124 Genoa. Annual competition open to violinists of all nationalities under the age of 35. Prizes include 1st prize of 20,000,000 Italian lire, 2nd prize of 10,000,000 lire, 3rd prize of 6,000,000 lire, 4th prize of 4,000,000 lire, 5th prize of 3,000,000 lire, and 6th prize of 2,000,000 lire.

Antonio Pedrotti International Competition for Orchestra Conductors: Via San Croce 67, 38100 Trento; tel. 39 461 231223; fax 39 461 232592. Biennial competition open to conductors between the ages of 18 and 33. Prizes include 1st prize of 10,000,000 Italian lire and engagements with Italian Orchestras, 2nd prize of 7,000,000 lire and 3rd prize of 5,000,000 lire.

Premio Musicale Città di Trieste: Concorso Internazionale di Composizione Sinfonica: Palazzo Municipale, Piazza dell'Italia 4, 34121 Trieste. Biennial competition open to composers of all nationalities. Prizes include 1st prize of 5,000,000 Italian lire and performance of composition, 2nd prize of 2,500,000 lire and 3rd prize of 1,500,000 lire.

Rassegna della Canzone d'Autore-Premio Tenco: Via Meridiana 7, 18038 San Remo. Annual competition open to singers who are lyricists and composers, by invitation only.

Toti dal Monte International Singing Competition: Ente Teatro Comunale, Corso del Popolo 31, Via Diaz 7, 31100 Treviso.

G. B. Viotti Concorso Internazionale di Musicale: PO Box 127, 13100 Vercelli; tel. 39 0161 252667; fax 39 0161 255575; e-mail info@ concorsoviotti.it; website www.concorsoviotti.it. Annual competition for singers and pianists.

Vittorio Gui International Chamber Music Competition: ACRM, Borgo degli Albizi 15, 50122 Florence; tel. and fax 39 55 240672; e-mail acrm@frenze.net.

Japan

International Music Competition of Japan: West Park Building 4F, 1-10-16, Ebisunhishi, Sibuya-ku, Tokyo 150. Triennial competition open to instrumentalists of all nationalities between the ages of 17 and 32. Prizes include money, medals, and concert appearances.

Reiko Takahashi IRINO (Irino Prize Foundation): c/o JML Seminar Yoshiro Irino Institute of Music, 5-22-2 Matsubara, Setagaya-ku, Tokyo 156-0043; tel. 3 3323-0646; fax 3 3325-5468; e-mail jml-irinopz@nyc.odn.ne .jp; website www.jml-irino.jp/IrinoPrize/index.html. Annual prize open to composers of all nationalities under the age of 40, rotating annually between an orchestral and a chamber music composition. Prizes include 650,00 yen for an orchestral composition and 200,000 yen for a chamber music composition.

Tokyo International Competition for Chamber Music Composition: c/o Japan International Artists, 2-3-16-607 Shinjuku, Shinjuku, Tokyo. Competition open to composers of chamber music of all ages and nationalities. Prizes include 1st prize of 300,000 yen, 2nd prize of 150,000 yen and 3rd prize of 100,000 yen.

Tokyo International Music Competition: 1-32-13 Kita-Shinjuku, Shinjuku-ku, Tokyo 169; website www.min-on.or.jp. Annual competition open to performers of all nationalities with categories changing annually. Prizes include 1st prize of 1,000,000 yen and a medal, 2nd prize of 700,000 yen and a medal, 3rd prize of 500,000 yen, a medal and a certificate of honourable mention, and 4th prize of 200,000 yen and a medal.

Monaco

Prix de Composition Musicale Prince Pierre de Monaco: Centre Administratif, rue Louis Notari, 098000 Monaco. Annual prize awarded to the best musical composition of the year prize of 50,000 French francs.

Netherlands

BG S-Hertogenbosch International Singing Competition: PO Box 1225, 5200 BG's-Hertogenbosch; tel. 31 736 900999. Annual competition open to singers. Prizes include money.

César Franck Organ Competition: Leeghwaterstraat 14, 2012 GD Haarlem; tel. 31 235 327070.

Delft Chamber Music Festival: 0.2. Voorburgwal 72, 1012 GE Amsterdam; tel. 31 20 643 2043; fax 31 20 640 3961; e-mail mbrinks@ xs4all.nl; website www.delftmusicfestival.nl.

I K F International Choir Festival: Plompetorengracht 3, 3512 CA Utrecht; tel. 31 302 313174; fax 31 302 318137. Quadrennial prizes awarded to choirs.

International Competition for Early Music Ensembles: Singel 308-sous, 1016 AE Amsterdam; tel. 31 206 391390; fax 31 206 227118. Annual competition open to young professional early music ensembles consisting of two to eight performers.

International Competition for Organ Improvisation: PO Box 3333, 2001 DH Haarlem; tel. 31 231 60574; fax 31 231 60576. Annual competition open to concert organists experienced in improvisation. Prizes include money.

International Franz Liszt Piano Competition: Muziekcentrum Vredenburg, PO Box 550, 3500 AN Utrecht; tel. 31 302 330233; fax 31 302 316522. Triennial competition open to pianists of all nationalities between the ages of 16 and 30. Prizes include money and engagements for the 1st prize winner.

International Gaudeamus Composers' Competition: Gaudeamus Foundation, Swammerdamstraat 38, 1091 RV Amsterdam; tel. 31 206 947349; fax 31 206 947258. Annual competition open to composers to the age of 30. Prizes include money.

International Gaudeamus Interpreters' Competition: Gaudeamus Foundation, Swammerdamstraat 38, 1091 RV Amsterdam; tel. 31 206 947349; fax 31 206 947258. Annual competition open to instrumentalists and singers of contemporary music. Prizes include money, with a 1st prize of 10,000 florins.

International Kirill Kondrashin Competition for Young Conductors: c/o NOS, PO Box 26444, 1202 JJ Hilversum; tel. 31 357 75453; fax 31 357 74311. Quinquennial competition open to conductors to the age of 36. Prizes include guest conducting engagements with major orchestras.

Scheveningen International Music Competition: Gevers Deynootweg 970 Z, 2586 BW Scheveningen; tel. 31 20 6947349; fax 31 20 6947258. Annual competition open to instrumentalists to the age of 30. Prizes include money.

New Zealand

Lexus New Zealand International Violin Competition: PO Box 10-113, Wellington. Quadrennial competition open to violinists of all nationalities between the ages of 18 and 28. Prizes include money.

Norway

Queen Sonja International Music Competition: PO Box 5190, Majorstua, 0302 Oslo 1; tel. 47 22 464055; fax 47 22 463630. Triennial competition open to instrumentalists or singers. Prizes include money and concert engagements.

Poland

Fryderyk Chopin International Piano Competition: ul Okólnik 1, 00-368 Warsaw. Quinquennial competition open to pianists of all nationalities born between 1977 and 1988. Prizes include 1st prize of US $25,000 and a gold medal, 2nd prize of $20,000 and a silver medal, 3rd prize of $15,000 and a bronze medal, and three other money prizes; next competition in 2005.

Grzegorz Fitelberg International Competition for Conductors: Sokolska 2, 40-084 Katowice; tel. and fax 48 32 596074. Quadrenial competition open to conductors to the age of 35. Prizes include money and medals.

International Composers' Competition Kasimierz Serocki: ul Mazowiecka 11, 00-052 Warsaw. Triennial competition open to composers of all nationalities. Prizes include money.

International Henryk Wieniawski Competition for Violinists, Composers, and Violin Makers: Swietoslawska St 7, 61-840 Poznan; tel. 48 61 522642; fax 48 61 528991. Quinquennial competition open to violinists of all nationalities to the age of 30. Prizes include money.

International Stanislaw Moniuszko Competition for Young Vocalists: c/o Warsaw Philharmonic Orchestra, ul. Jasna 5, 00 950 Warsaw; tel. 48 22 5517101; fax 48 22 5517200; e-mail filharmonia@filharmonia.pl; website www.filharmonia.pl. Triennial competition open to young vocalists. Prizes include money.

International Witold Lutoslawski Composers' Competition: c/o Warsaw Philharmonic Orchestra, ul. Jasna 5, 00 950 Warsaw; tel. 48 22 5517101; fax 48 22 5517200; e-mail filharmonia@filharmonia.pl; website www.filharmonia.pl. Biennial competition open to composers of all nationalities and all ages. Prizes include money and performances by the Warsaw Philharmonic.

Portugal

Porto International Music Competition: Rua Azevedo Coutinho 195, 4100 Porto; tel. 35 126 095099; fax 35 126 004307. Annual competition.

Romania

George Enescu International Piano, Violin and Singing Competition: Calea Victoriei 155, Blvd D1, sc.8, et.2, 71012 Bucharest.

Russia

International Tchaikovsky Competition: 15 Neglinnaya St, Moscow. Quadrennial competition open to pianists, violinists, cellists and singers of all nationalities. Prizes include money and medals.

Singapore

Rolex Music Performance Awards: The Rolex Centre, 302 Orchard Road, 01-01 Tong Building, Singapore 0923. Biennial competition open to pianists and violinists who are citizens or permanent residents of Singapore, Malaysia, Brunei, Indonesia, Thailand, the Philippines or Hong Kong. Prizes include money.

Spain

Concurso Internacional de Canto Julián Gayarre: Calle Santo Domingo 6, 31001 Pamplona; tel. 34 48 106072; fax 34 48 223906. Biennial competition open to singers of all nationalities, women between the ages of 18 and 32, and men between the ages of 20 and 35. Prizes include money.

Concurso Internacional de Ejecución Musical Maria Canals de Barcelona: Gran Via de les Corts Catalanes 654, 08010 Barcelona; tel. and fax 34 33 187731. Annual competition open to instrumentalists between the ages of 18 and 32. Prizes include money.

Concurso Internacional de Piano Frederic Chopin: Conservatorio Professional de Música de Baleares, Calle Hospital 4, 07012 Palma de Mallorca; tel. 34 71 711157. Biennial competition open to pianists of all nationalities to the age of 35. Prizes include 1st prize of 1,000,000 pesetas and recitals, 2nd prize of 500,000 pesetas, and 3rd prize of 250,000 pesetas.

Concurso Internacional de Piano José Iturbi: Plaza de Manises 4, 46003 Valencia; tel. 34 63 882500; fax 34 63 882775. Biennial competition open to pianists of all nationalities under the age of 31 on the date of the competition. Prizes include 1st prize of 18,100 euros, 2nd prize of 12,100 euros, 3rd prize of 6,100 euros, with recitals for each category.

Concurso Internacional de Piano Premio Jaén: c/o Instituto de Estudios Giennenses, 23002 Jaén. Annual competition open to pianists of all nationalities, except winners of the Jaén Prize. Prizes include 1st prize of 2,000,000 pesetas, a gold medal and concert engagements, 2nd prize of 1,000,000 pesetas, 3rd prize of 400,000 pesetas, and the Rose Sabater Prize of 500,000 pesetas for the best interpreter of Spanish music.

Palpma O'Shea Santander International Piano Competition: Calle Hernán Cortés 3, 39003 Santander; fax 34 42 314816. Triennial competition open to pianists of all nationalities between the ages of 17 and 30. Prizes include money totalling 15,000,000 pesetas, recordings, concerts and travel grants.

Premio Internacional de Canto Fundación Guerrero: Gran Via 78, 28013 Madrid. Biennial competition open to singers of all nationalities and ages. Prizes include 1st prize of 2,500,000 pesetas and a prize of 600,000 pesetas for the best interpreter of the music of Jacinto e Inocencio Guerrero.

Premio Internacional de Piano Fundación Guerrero: Gran Via 78, 28013 Madrid. Biennial competition open to pianists of all nationalities and ages. Prizes include 1st prize of 2,500,000 pesetas.

Pablo Sarasata International Violin Competition: Calle Santo Domingo 6, 31001 Pamplona; tel. 34 48 106072/106500; fax 34 48 223906. Biennial competition open to violinists.

Francisco Viñas International Singing Contest: Bruc 125, 08037 Barcelona. Annual competition open to singers, women between the ages of 18 and 32 and men between the ages of 20 and 35. Prizes for both include 1st prize of 8,000 euros, 2nd prize of 5,000 euros, 3rd prize of 4,000 euros, and medals and special prizes.

Sweden

Jussi Björling Tenor Competition: Borlänge Kommun 781, 81 Borlänge, Höbergstatan 76B, 11856 Stockholm; tel. 46 8 243 7400; fax 46 8 243 66208.

Switzerland

Concours Géza Anda: Bleicherweg 18, 8002 Zürich; tel. 0041 1 205 14 23; fax 0041 1 205 14 29; e-mail info@gezaanda.ch; website www.gezaanda.ch. Triennial competition open to pianists to the age of 32. Prizes include money and major concert engagements. Next competition in June 2006.

Concours International d'Execution Musicale: 104 rue de Carouge, 1205 Geneva. Annual competition open to performers of all nationalities with categories changing annually. Prizes totalling 130,000 Swiss francs.

Concours Suisse de l'Orgue: Place du Prieur, 1323 Romainmôtier. Annual competition open to organists of all nationalities and ages.

Clara Haskil Piano Competition: 40 rue du Simplon, PO Box 234, 1800 Vevey; tel. 41 21 922 6704; fax 41 21 922 6734. Biennial competition open to pianists to the age of 30. Prizes include 20,000 Swiss francs and concert engagements.

International Competition in Composition of Sacred Music: PO Box 292, 1701 Fribourg. Biennial competition open to composers of all nationalities and ages. Prizes include 10,000 Swiss francs and the premiere of the winning work at the Fribourg Festival of Sacred Music.

International Violin Competition Sion-Valais: PO Box 1429, 1951 Sion; tel. 41 27 323 43 61; fax 41 27 323 46 62; e-mail info@sion.festival.ch; website www.sion.festival.ch. Annual competition open to violinists between the ages of 15 and 32. Prizes totalling 30,000 Swiss francs.

Musical Prize Contest Queen Marie-José: PO Box 19, 1252 Meinier, Geneva. Biennial competition open to composers of all nationalities and ages who submit an unpublished composition. Prizes include 10,000 Swiss francs.

Swiss Organ Competition: Place du Prieur, 1323 Romainmôtier; tel. 41 24 531718; fax 41 24 531150.

United Kingdom

BBC Television Young Musician of the Year Competition: c/o BBC TV, Kensington House, Richmond Way, London W14 0AX; website www.bbc.co.uk. Biennial televised competition open to British resident performers to age 18 and composers to age 21. Prizes totalling £32,000.

Cardiff Singer of the World Competition: c/o BBC Wales, Music Department, Broadcasting House, Llandaff, Cardiff, Wales CF5 2YQ;

website www.bbc.co.uk. Biennial competition open to singers 18 years of age or older. Prizes include £5,000 and concert engagements.

City of London Carl Flesch International Violin Competition: c/o City Arts Trust, Bishopsgate Hall, 230 Bishopsgate, London EC2M 4QH. Biennial competition open to violinists of all nationalities under the age of 28. Prizes include 1st prize of £6,000, 2nd prize of £4,000, 3rd prize of £3,000, 4th prize of £1,750, 5th prize of £1,250, and 6th prize of £750, with five additional prizes of £500 each.

City of London Walter Gruner International Lieder Competition: c/o City Arts Trust, Bishopsgate Hall, 230 Bishopsgate, London EC2M 4QH. Biennial competition open to singers to the age of 28. Prizes include 1st prize of £3,500 and a debut recital in London, 2nd prize of £2,250, 3rd prize of £1,250, and 4th prize of £750, with an accompanists' prize of £1,250.

Donatella Flick Conducting Competition: PO Box 34227, London NW5 1XP; fax 020 7482 1353; website www.conducting.org. Biennial competition open to European Community nationals under 35.

Folkestone Menuhin International Violin Competition: 72 Leopold Road, London SW19 7JQ. Biennial competition open to violinists. Prizes totalling £15,700.

Great Grimsby International Competition for Singers: 23 Enfield Ave, New Waltham, Great Grimsby, South Humberside DN36 5RD. Triennial competition open to singers between the ages of 20 and 30 with accompanists to age 26. Prizes include 1st prize of £2,000, 2nd prize of £1,000 and 3rd prize of £500, with an accompanists' prize of £500.

Kathleen Ferrier Awards: Kathleen Ferrier Memorial Scholarship Fund, Courtyard House, Neopardy, Crediton, Devon EX17 5EP; tel. 01363 777844; fax 01363 777845; e-mail info@ferrierawards.org.uk; website www.ferrierawards.org.uk. Annual competition open to British and Commonwealth singers aged 21-28. 1st prize £10,000 and Wigmore Hall recital.

Leeds Conductors' Competition: Music Department, Leeds Leisure Service, Town Hall, The Headrow, Leeds, LS1 3AD; tel. 0113 247 8336; website www.leedsconductors.com.

Leeds International Pianoforte Competition: Piano Competition Office, University of Leeds, Leeds LS2 9JT; tel. 0113 244 6586; website www.leedspiano.com. Triennial competition open to professional pianists under the age of 30. Prizes include money totalling £60,000 and concert engagements worldwide; next competition in Sept. 2006.

London International Piano Competition: 28 Wallace Road, London N1 2PG; tel. (20) 7354-1087; fax (20) 7704-1053; e-mail ldn-ipc@dircon.co.uk; website www.ldn-ipc.dircon.co.uk. Triennial competition open to pianists of all nationalities to the age of 29. Prizes include money totalling £30,000, concert engagements and scholarships; next competition in 2005.

London International String Quartet Competition: 62 High St, Fareham, Hampshire PO16 7BG. Triennial competition open to string quartets whose aggregate ages do not exceed 120 years. Prizes include 1st prize of £8,000 and the Amadeus Trophy, 2nd prize of £4,800, 3rd prize of £3,200, 4th prize of £2,400, and 5th prize of £1,600, with the Menuhin Prize of £750 and the Audience Prize of £500.

Newport International Competition for Young Pianists: Civic Centre, Newport, Gwent NP20 4UR; tel. 01633 662666; website www.newport.gov.uk/piano. Triennial competition open to pianists to the age of 25. Prizes include money and concerts; next competition in 2006.

Performing Right Society Electroacoustic Composition Prize: c/o Electroacoustic Music Association of Great Britain, 10 Stratford Place, London W1N 9AE. Biennial competition open to composers.

Royal Over-Seas League of Music Competition: Over-Seas House, Park Place, St James's St, London SW1A 1LR. Annual competition open to Commonwealth and former Commonwealth citizens, for instrumentalists to the age of 28 and for singers to the age of 30. Various prizes.

Scottish International Piano Competition: c/o SIPC Office, The Mitchell Library, 201 North Street, Glasgow G3 7DN; tel. 0141 287 2857; fax 0141 287 2858; website www.sipc2004.org. Triennial competition open to pianists of all nationalities to the age of 32. Prizes include £8,000.

Tunbridge Wells International Young Concert Artists (TWIYCA) Competition: Paddock Wood, Kent TN12 6PA. Biennial competition open to performers to the age of 25. Prizes totalling £9,000.

Wigmore Hall International Song Competition: Room 616a, Langham House, 308 Regent Street, London W1B 3AT; e-mail whisc@wigmore-hall.org.uk; website www.wigmore-hall.org.uk

Yehudi Menuhin International Competition for Young Violinists: c/o Royal Academy of Music, Marylebone Road, London, NW1 5HT; website www.geniusoftheviolin.org. Biennial competition open to violi-

nists of any nationality under the age of 22. Prizes totalling £20,000. The competition forms part of the Genius of the Violin Festival.

United States of America

ALEA III International Composition Prize: c/o Boston University School of Music, 855 Commonwealth Ave, Boston, MA 02215; tel. 1 617 353 3340; website www.aleaiii.com. Annual competition open to composers of all nationalities under the age of 40. Submitted composition must not have been published, publicly performed, or awarded any prize.

ASCAP Foundation Grants to Young Composers: 1 Lincoln Plaza, New York, NY 10023; tel. 1 212 621 6219; website www.ascap.com. Annual grants to composers who are citizens or permanent residents of the USA and have not reached their 30th birthday by 15 March.

American Academy and Institute of Arts and Letters: 633 W 155th St, New York, NY 10032. Various awards are given in the field of music.

American Academy in Rome: 7 E 60th Street, New York, NY 10022; tel. 1 212 751 7200; fax 1 212 751 7220; e-mail info@aarome.org; website www.aarome.org. Annual residents' programme to support distinguished artists and scholars as residents at the academy for a year and annual Rome Prize Fellowships for American composers to study at the academy.

American Berlin Opera Foundation Inc: 6 E 87th Street, New York, NY 10128; tel. 1 212 534 5383; e-mail ABOF@operafoundation.org; website www.operafoundation.org. Annual scholarships for American singers who are citizens or permanent residents between the ages of 18 and 32, to study at the Deutsche Oper Berlin. Prizes include a scholarship of US $15,000 and a round trip flight.

American Guild of Organists (AGO)/National Young Artists Competition in Organ Performance: 475 Riverside Drive, Suite 1260, New York, NY 10115; tel. 1 212 870 2310; fax 1 212 870 2163; e-mail info@agohq.org; website www.agohq.org. Biennial competition open to organists between the ages of 22 and 32.

American Musicological Society Inc: 201 South 34th St, Philadelphia, PA 19104. Noah Greenberg Award of up to US $2,000 for a distinguished contribution to the study and/or performance of music prior to 1700. Otto Kinkeldey Award of $400 and a scroll to a US or Canadian writer of the most notable full-length study in musicology. Alfred Einstein Award of $400 to a young scholar who has published an article on a musicological subject in the preceding year.

American Pianists' Association National Fellowship Piano Auditions: Clowes Memorial Hall, Butler University, 4600 Sunset Ave, Indianapolis, IN 46208; e-mail apainfo@americanpianists.org; website www.americanpianists.org. Biennial fellowships open to American classical pianists between the ages of 18 and 30. Prizes include three-year fellowship, US $10,000, sponsorship at an international competition, and US concert engagements.

Artists International's Annual New York Debut Award Auditions: 521 Fifth Ave, Suite 1700, New York, NY 10017; tel. 1 212 292 4257. Annual auditions open to performers of all nationalities who have not given a New York recital debut or who have not received a New York review for a solo recital. Prizes include New York recital debut at Carnegie Recital Hall, Merkin Concert Hall or Alice Tully Hall at the Lincoln Center.

Artists International's Distinguished Artists Award Auditions: 521 Fifth Ave, Suite 1700, New York, NY 10017; tel. 1 212 292 4257. Annual auditions open to soloists or chamber groups who have received at least one review from a major New York publication and have no management. Prizes include recital engagement in New York.

Broadcast Music Inc (BMI) Student Composers Awards: 320 W 57th St, New York, NY 10019; website www.bmi.com. Annual awards open to student composers who are citizens or permanent residents of a country in the western hemisphere, to the age of 25. Prizes totalling US $16,000.

Johann Sebastian Bach International Competition: 1211 Potomac St NW, Washington, DC 20007. Competition open to performers of the works of J S Bach between the ages of 20 and 40. Prizes include money and concert engagements.

Gina Bachauer International Piano Competition: 138 W Broadway, Suite 220, Salt Lake City, UT 84101; website www.bachauer.com. Triennial competition open to pianists between the ages of 19 and 32. Prizes include 1st prize of a grand piano and New York and Los Angeles debut concerts; other prizes include Gold, Silver, and Bronze medals, money prizes, concerts and recitals, with finalists appearing with the Utah Symphony Orchestra. Also a junior section for pianists between the ages of 8 and 18.

Baltimore Opera Vocal Competition for American Operatic Artists: 101 W Read St, Suite 605, Baltimore, MD 21201. Annual competition open to operatic singers between the ages of 20 and 35. Prizes include 1st prize of US $10,000, 2nd prize of $8,000, 3rd prize of $4,500, 4th prize of $2,500, 5th prize of $2,000, 6th prize of $1,200, and 7th prize of $1,000, with an additional prize of $1,000 awarded by the audience.

Barlow International Competition: c/o Brigham Young University, Harris Fine Arts Center, Provo, UT 84602. Annual competition open to composers of all nationalities; composition must not have won any other competition. Prizes totalling US $10,000.

Joseph H Bearns Prize in Music: c/o Columbia University, Department of Music, 703 Dodge Hall, New York, NY 10027; tel. 1 212 854 3825. Annual competition open to American composers between the ages of 18 and 25. Prizes include money.

Frank Huntington Beebe Fund for Musicians: 290 Huntington Ave, Boston, MA 02115; tel. 1 617 262 1120. Annual scholarships open to American post-graduate music students for study abroad.

Simone Belsky Music Award Competition: 153 North St, PO Box 1112, Litchfield, CT 06759; tel. 1 860 567 4162; fax 1 860 567 3592. Biennial competition open to pianists over 30 years old. Prizes include 1st prize of US $1,500 and concert engagements.

Boston Classical Orchestra Youth Competition: 551 Tremont St, Boston, MA 02116; tel. 1 617 423 3883. Annual competition open to high school seniors in New England and New York who wish to pursue a career as an instrumentalist. Prizes include a four-year merit scholarship to the Boston University School of Music and an appearance as soloist with the Boston Classical Orchestra at a youth concert.

Brandeis University Creative Arts Awards: Brandeis University, PO Box 549110, Waltham, MA 02254; tel. 1 781 736 2027; fax 1 781 736 3457; e-mail arts50@brandeis.edu. Annual prizes open to established artists in various fields, including music. Prizes include a medal and an honorarium.

Benjamin Britten Memorial Fund: 135 E 83rd St, Suite 4/5-C, New York, NY 10028. Annual scholarships open to American students for study at the Britten-Pears School for Advanced Musical Studies in Aldeburgh, Suffolk, England.

Bryan International String Competition: North Carolina Symphony Orchestra, PO Box 28026, Raleigh, NC 27611. Quadrennial competition open to violinists, violists, and cellists between the ages of 18 and 30. Prizes include 1st prize of US $12,000, 2nd prize of $6,000 and 3rd prize of $3,000.

Grace Bumbry Student Assistance Award: c/o AGMA Relief Fund, 1727 Broadway, New York, NY 10019. Study grant for American classical singers between the ages of 18 and 25. Prizes include 1st prize of US $2,000.

William C Byrd Young Artist Competition: c/o Flint Institute of Music, 1025 E Kearsley St, Flint, MI 48503; website www.byrdartists.com. Annual competition open to performers with categories changing annually. Prizes include 1st prize of US $2,500 and an appearance with the Flint Symphony Orchestra.

CRS National Festival for the Performing Arts: 724 Winchester Road, Broomall, PA 19008. Annual competition with prizes including fellowships, recording contracts, national appearances and artist representation.

Carmel Chamber Music Competition: PO Box 221458, Carmel, CA 93922; tel. 1 831 625 2212. Annual competition open to non-professional chamber groups of three to six players averaging under the age of 26. Prizes include money.

Carmel Music Society Competition: PO Box 1144, Carmel, CA 93921; tel. 1 831 625 9938; fax 1 831 625 6823; e-mail carmelmusic@sbcglobal.net; website www.carmelmusic.org. Annual competition open to musicians who are residents or full-time students in California. Prizes include money and an appearance at a Carmel Chamber Music concert.

Center for Contemporary Opera International Opera Singers Competition: PO Box 1350, Gracie Station, New York, NY 10028; tel. 1 212 308 6728; fax 1 212 308 6744. Annual competition open to singers who have not attained a major operatic career. Prizes include money.

Chamber Music America: Commissioning Program, 305 Seventh Ave, 5th Floor, New York, NY 10001-6008; tel. 1 212 242 2022; fax 1 212 242 7955. Annual ASCAP Awards for various activities devoted to the performance and promotion of chamber music.

Chopin Foundation of the National Chopin Piano Competition of the United States: 1440 79th St Causeway, Suite 117, Miami, FL 33141; tel. 1 305 868 0624; fax 1 305 868 5150; e-mail info@chopin.org; website www.chopin.org. Quinquennial competition open to American pianists between the ages of 16 and 18, to enable them to participate in the International Chopin Piano Competition in Warsaw. Prizes include 1st

prize of US $15,000, 2nd prize of $9,000, 3rd prize of $6,000, 4th prize of $3,500, 5th prize of $2,500, and 6th prize of $2,000.

Civic Orchestra of Chicago Soloist Competition: 220 S Michigan Ave, Chicago, IL 60604. Annual competition open to soloists between the ages of 19 and 30. Prizes include US $1,000 and concert engagements.

Cleveland International Piano Competition: 1988 Ford Drive, Cleveland, OH 44106; tel. 1 216 707 5397; fax 1 216 707 0224; e-mail ClevePiano@aol.com; website piano.wclv.com. Biennial competition open to pianists between the ages of 17 and 32. Prizes include money and concert engagements.

Van Cliburn International Piano Competition: 2525 Ridgmar Blvd, Suite 307, Fort Worth, TX 76116; tel. 1 817 738 6536; fax 1 817 738 6534; website www.cliburn.org. Quadrennial piano competition open to pianists between the ages 18 and 30. Prizes include 1st prize of US $15,000, Carnegie Hall recital and orchestral debuts, US recital and orchestral tour, and European recital and orchestral tour, 2nd prize of $10,000, New York debut, and US tour, 3rd prize of $7,500 and US tour, 4th prize of $5,000, 5th prize of $3,500, and 6th prize of $2,000.

Coleman Chamber Ensemble Competition: Coleman Chamber Music Association, 202 S Lake Avenue, Suite 201, Pasadena, CA 91101; tel. (626) 793-4191; fax (818) 787-1294; e-mail krfccma@aol.com; website coleman .caltech.edu/2004comp.pdf. Annual competition open to non-professional chamber ensembles whose members' average age is under 26, and prepared by a coach. Prizes include US $6,000 (2004 only), $4,000, $4,000, $3,000 and $2,000.

Composers Guild Annual Competition Contest: 40 North 100 West, PO Box 586, Farmington, UT 84025; tel. 1 801 451 2275. Annual competition open to composers. Prizes include money.

Concert Artists Guild International New York Competition: 850 Seventh Ave, Suite 1205, New York, NY 10019. Annual competition open to instrumentalists, chamber ensembles and singers. Prizes include money, concert engagements, recordings and free management services.

Concerto Competition of the Rome Festival Orchestra: Empire State Building, Suite 3304, New York, NY 10118; tel. 1 212 971 9702. Annual competition open to North American performers of violin, viola, cello, double bass, oboe and horn. Prizes include five tuition fellowships and solo appearance in Rome.

Corporation of Yaddo: PO Box 395, Union Ave, Saratoga Springs, NY 12866; tel. 1 518 584 0746; fax 1 518 584 1312; website www.yaddo.org. Room, board and studio for professional composers of all nationalities. Residency up to two months.

Council for International Exchange for Scholars-Fulbright Scholar Program: 3007 Tilden St NW, Suite 5M, Washington, DC 20008; tel. 1 202 686 4000; fax 1 202 362 3442; website www.cies.org. Annual grants for university lecturing and/or advanced research abroad by Americans, including several in the field of music.

D'Angelo Young Artist Competition: c/o Mercyhurst College, 501 E 38th St, Erie, PA 16546; tel. 1 814 824 2394. Annual competition open to performers under the age of 35 with categories rotating annually. Prizes include 1st prize of US $10,000 and concert engagements, 2nd prize of $5,000 and 3rd prize of $3,000, with $1,000 to all finalists.

Kenneth Davenport National Competition for Orchestral Works: c/o State University of New York, College of New Paltz, New Paltz, NY 12561; tel. 1 814 257 3860; fax 1 814 257 3859. Annual competition open to composers who are American citizens or permanent residents. Prizes include US $1,500 and performance of composition.

Delius Composition Contest: c/o Jacksonville University, College of Fine Arts, Jacksonville, FL 32211; tel. 1 904 745 7370; fax 1 904 745 7375. Annual competition open to composers. Prizes include 1st prize of US $500, $100 for the best vocal, keyboard, and instrumental composition, and high school composition category of 1st prize of $200 and 2nd prize of $100.

Delta Omicron International Music Fraternity Triennial Composition Competition: 8009 Volk Dr., Dayton, OH 45415; website www .delta-omicron.org. Triennial competition open to American composers of college age or older. Prizes include US $500 and premiere of composition.

Detroit Symphony Orchestra Fellowship Program: 400 Buhl Building, 535 Griswold St, Detroit, MI 48226; website www .detroitsymphony.com. One-year residency for African-American orchestral players with the Detroit Symphony Orchestra.

Murray Dranoff International Two Piano Competition: 180 NE 39th Street, Suite 207, Miami, FL 33137; tel. 1 305 572 9900; fax 1 305 572 9922; e-mail mail@dranoff2piano.org; website www.dranoff2piano.org. Biennial competition open to duo pianists between the ages of 18 and 35. Prizes include 1st prize of US $10,000, 2nd prize of $5,000 and 3rd prize of $2,000, plus concert engagements.

East and West Artists International Auditions for New York Debut: 310 Riverside Dr., Suite 313, New York, NY 10025; tel. 1 212 222 2433. Annual competition open to performers who have not given a New York debut recital. Prizes include debut at Weill Recital Hall at Carnegie Hall, money, radio and concert engagements.

Fischoff National Chamber Music Competition: 303 Brownson Hall, University of Notre Dame, Notre Dame, IN 46556; fax 1 574 631 2903; e-mail info@fischoff.org; website www.fischoff.org. Annual competition open to instrumental ensembles of three to five members to the age of 18. Prizes include money.

Avery Fisher Artist Program: Lincoln Center, 140 W 65th St, New York, NY 10023; tel. 1 212 875 5540; fax 1 212 875 5539. Career grants open to American instrumental soloists by a recommendation board and chosen by the executive committee. No applications accepted. Prizes include Avery Fisher Career Grant of US $10,000 and Avery Fisher Prize of $25,000.

Fort Collins Symphony Association Young Artists Competition: PO Box 1963, Fort Collins, CO 80522; tel. 1 970 482 4823; fax 1 970 482 4858; website www.fcsymphony.org. Annual competition open to instrumentalists. Prizes include US $2,000 Adeline Rosenberg Memorial Prize.

Fort Smith Symphony Association Young Artist Competition: PO Box 3151, Fort Smith, AR 72913; tel. 1 479 452 7575; website www .fortsmithsymphony.org. Annual competition open to string, brass and woodwind players to the age of 18. Prizes include 1st prize of US $1,000 and an apppearance with the Fort Smith Symphony Orchestra.

Fromm Music Foundation: Harvard University, Department of Music, Cambridge, MA 02138; tel. 1 617 495 2791; fax 1 617 496 8081. Sponsorship of composers, performers and concerts of contemporary music.

Harvey Gaul Composition Contest: c/o Duquesne University, School of Music, Pittsburgh, PA 15282. Biennial competition open to American composers of unpublished and unperformed compositions. Prizes include US $3,000 and performance of composition.

Florida Grand Opera Young Artist/Technical/Apprentice Programs: 1200 Coral Way, Miami, FL 33145; tel. 1 305 854 1643; fax 1 305 856 1042; website www.fgo.org. Annual seven-month programme (October-April) open to singers to work with the Greater Miami Opera.

Charles Tomlinson Griffes American Music Composers Competition: 5 Joseph Wallace Dr., Croton-on-Hudson, NY 10521. Annual competition open to American or permanent resident composers between the ages of 12 and 18 whose submitted composition has not won any other competition. Prizes include money and performance of composition.

John Simon Guggenheim Memorial Foundation: 90 Park Ave, New York, NY 10016; tel. 1 212 687 4470; fax 1 212 697 3248; e-mail fellowships@gf.org; website www.gf.org. Annual fellowships in music open to composers and scholars who have demonstrated previous outstanding ability. Fellowships in two categories: For citizens or permanent residents of the USA and Canada, and for citizens or permanent residents of Latin America and the Caribbean.

Haddonfield Symphony Young Instrumentalists Solo Competition: PO Box 212, Haddonfield, NJ 08033; tel. 1 856 429 1880; fax 1 856 428 5634; e-mail symphony@haddonfield-symphony.org; website www .haddonfield-symphony.org. Annual competition open to solo instrumentalists resident in one of the 11 northeastern states or the District of Columbia between the ages of 16 and 25. Prizes include 1st prize of US $2,500 and an appearance with the Haddonfield Symphony, and 2nd prize of $750.

Hobin Harp Competition: c/o Greater Trenton Symphony Orchestra Foundation, 28 W State St, Suite 201, Trenton, NJ 08608. Annual competition open to American harpists who are college students. Prizes include 1st prize of US $1,600.

Joanna Hodges International Piano Competition: see Virginia Waring International Piano Competition.

Ima Hogg National Young Artist Audition: c/o Houston Symphony Orchestra, 615 Louisiana St, Houston, TX 77002. Annual competition open to instrumentalists between the ages of 19 and 27. Prizes include 1st prize of US $5,000 and an appearance with the Houston Symphony, 2nd prize of $2,500 and an appearance with the Houston Symphony, and 3rd prize of $1,000.

Henry Holt Memorial Scholarship: PO Box 1714, Palo Alto, CA 94302. Annual scholarship open to singers between the ages of 18 and 26. Prizes include 1st prize of US $1,000 and 2nd prize of $500.

Holtkamp/American Guild of Organists Award in Organ Composition: 475 Riverside Dr., Suite 1260, New York, NY 10115. Biennial competition open to composers of organ compositions. Prizes include US $2,000 and publication and performance of composition.

Houston Opera Studio Auditions: c/o Houston Grand Opera, 510 Preston, Houston, TX 77002; website www.houstongrandopera.org. Annual auditions to work with the Houston Opera Studio.

Indiana State University Contemporary Music Festival Competition: c/o Louisville Orchestra, 609 W Main St, Louisville, KY 40202. Annual competition open to composers who have not won the competition within the previous five years.

Institute of International Education/Fulbright and Other Graduate Study Scholarships: 809 United Nations Plaza, New York, NY 10017; website www.iie.org. Annual scholarships open to Americans with a BA or equivalent, for graduate study abroad.

International Horn Society Composition Contest: c/o University of Missouri at Kansas City, Conservatory of Music, 4949 Cherry, Kansas City, MO 64110. Annual competition open to composers. Prizes include money.

International Trombone Association Ensemble Composition Contest: c/o University of North Texas, School of Music, Denton, TX 76203. Biennial competition open to composers. Prizes include US $1,000.

International Violin Competition of Indianapolis: 32 E Washington Street, Suite 1320, Indianapolis, IN 46204; tel. 1 317 637 4574; fax 1 317 637 1302; e-mail ivci@violin.org; website www.violin.org. Quadrennial competition open to violinists of all nationalities between the ages of 18 and 30. Prizes include money totalling more than US $200,000, medals, concert engagements in North America and Europe, and recordings.

Ivo Pogorelich International Solo Piano Competition (USA): c/o Kantor Concert Management, 67 Teignmouth Road, London NW2 4EA, England. Open to prizewinners and finalists in any previous international competition. 1st prize US $100,000.

Kennedy Center Friedheim Awards: John F Kennedy Center for the Performing Arts, Washington, DC 20577. Annual award to a living American composer of orchestral or chamber music. Prizes include 1st prize of US $5,000, 2nd prize of $2,500, 3rd prize of $1,000 and 4th prize of $500.

Kingsville International Young Performers' Competition: PO Box 2873, Kingsville, TX 78363; tel. 1 361 592 2374; website www .kingsvillemusic.com. Annual competition open to pianists and orchestral instrumentalists to the age of 26. Prizes totalling more than US $20,000, with highest ranking winner receiving a minimum of $5,000 and an appearance with the Corpus Christi Symphony.

Kate Neal Kinley Memorial Fellowship: c/o University of Illinois, 110 Architecture Building, 608 E Lorado Taft Dr., Champaign, IL 61820; tel. 1 217 333 1661; website www.faa.uiuc.edu. Annual fellowship open to graduates under the age of 25 for advanced study in the USA or abroad. Fellowship of US $7,000.

Irving M. Klein International String Competition: California Music Center, 3260 Harrison Street, San Francisco, CA 94110; tel. 1 415 282 7160; e-mail info@kleincompetition.org; website www.kleincompetition .org. Annual competition open to string players between the ages of 15 and 23. Prizes include 1st prize of US $10,000 and appearances with the Peninsula and Santa Cruz Symphony Orchestras.

Kosciuszko Foundation Chopin Piano Competition: 15 E 65th St, New York, NY 10021; tel. 1 212 734 2130; fax 1 212 628 4552; e-mail info@ thekf.org; website www.kosciuszkofoundation.org. Annual competition open to pianists who are American citizens or permanent residents of the USA or full-time foreign students with valid visa, between the ages of 17 and 23. Prizes include US $2,500, $1,500 and $1,000.

Olga Koussevitsky Young Artist Awards Competition: 165 W 66th St, New York, NY 10023. Annual competition open to performers between the ages of 16 and 26 with categories rotating annually. Prizes totalling US $3,500, concert engagements and auditions.

Eleanor Lieber Awards for Young Singers: 1516 SW Alder, Portland, OR 97205. Biennial awards open to singers who are residents of Oregon, Washington, Idaho, Montana or Alaska, between the ages of 20 and 31. Prizes include money.

Liederkranz Foundation Scholarship Awards: 6 E 87th St, New York, NY 10128. Annual awards open to singers and pianists. Prizes totalling some US $35,000.

Luciano Pavarotti International Voice Competition: 1616 Walnut St, Suite 2115, Philadelphia, PA 19103. Triennial competition.

Macallister Award for Opera Singers: c/o Indiana Opera Theatre, 7515 E 30th St, Indianapolis, IN 46206. Annual audition open to opera singers. Prizes include 1st prize of US $10,000, 2nd prize of $5,000, 3rd prize of $3,000, 4th prize of $1,500, and 5th prize of $1,000.

MacDowell Colony Inc: 100 High St, Peterborough, NH 03458; tel. 1 603 924 3886; fax 1 603 924 9142; e-mail info@macdowellcolony.org; website www.macdowellcolony.org. Awards residency fellowships for composers and other creative artists.

Quinto Maganini Award in Composition: 37 Valley View Road, Norwalk, CT 06851. Biennial competition open to American composers of orchestral music not publicly performed. Prizes include US $2,500 and premiere by the Norwalk Symphony Orchestra.

Marguerite McCammon Voice Competition: 422 Coombs Creek Dr., Dallas, TX 75211. Biennial competition open to singers between the ages of 21 and 32. Prizes include 1st prize of US $3,000 and operatic engagements.

Louise D McMahon International Music Competition: c/o School of Fine Arts, Cameron University, 2800 W Gore Blvd, Lawton, OK 73505. Competition open to instrumentalists and singers over 25 years old. Prizes include money and solo performance with orchestra.

Marian Anderson Award: The Ives Center, PO Box 2957, Danbury, CT; e-mail info@marianandersonaward.org; website www.marianandersonaward.org. A significant financial award to an American singer of concert and opera, by recommendation.

Meadows Foundation Young Artists Auditions Competition: 8 Drake Road, Somerset, NJ 08873; website www.mfi.org. Annual competition open to performers in three divisions: Junior Division (Junior High School), High School Division and Senior Division (to the age of 35). Prizes include money, recitals, concert and chamber music engagements.

Metropolitan Opera National Council Auditions: Lincoln Center, New York, NY 10023; tel. 1 212 870 4515; fax 1 212 870 7606; e-mail ncouncil@mail.metopera.org; website www.metopera.org. Annual competitive auditions open to singers between 20 and 30 years of age. Prizes include money and study grants.

Midland-Odessa Symphony and Chorale Inc, National Young Artist Competition: PO Box 60658, Midland, TX 79711; tel. 1 432 563 0921; e-mail symphony@mosc.org; website www.mosc.org. Biennial competition open to performers. Prizes include money and appearances with the Midland-Odessa Symphony and Chorale.

Missouri Southern International Piano Competition: Missouri Southern State University, 3950 E Newman Road, Joplin, MO 64801; tel. (417) 625-9755; fax (417) 625-9798; e-mail msipc@mssu.edu; website www.mssc.edu/msipc. Biennial competition open to pianists of all nationalities to the age of 30. Prizes include 1st prize of US $10,000 and appearance at Carnegie Recital Hall.

Mu Phi Epsilon International Competition: 4858 Stallcup Dr., Mesquite, TX 75150; website home.muphiepsilon.org. Triennial competition open to members of Mu Phi Epsilon who have appeared in recital and/or as soloist with orchestra, but are not under contract to professional management. Prizes include two-year concert engagements.

Museum in the Community Composer's Award: PO Box 251, Scott Depot, WV 25560. Biennial competition open to American composers of a composition for string quartet not previously performed in public. Prizes include US $5,000 and performance of composition.

Music Teachers National Association-CCP/ Belwin Student Composition Competition: c/o Eastman School of Music, 26 Gibbs St, Rochester, NY 14604; website www.mtna.org. Annual competition open to American composers who are in college, high school, junior high school or elementary school, who are studying with an active member of the Music Teachers National Association. Prizes include money.

Naftzger Young Artists Auditions and Music Awards: c/o Wichita Symphony Society, 225 W Douglas, Suite 207, Wichita, KS 67202; tel. (316) 267-5259; fax (316) 267-1937. Annual competition open to instrumentalists between the ages of 18 and 26 and to singers between the ages of 20 and 28. Entrants must be residents of/attend a university or college in Missouri, Oklahoma or Kansas. Prizes include US $5,000 Naftzger Young Artist Award and $2,000 in each of various categories.

National Association of Teachers of Singing Artist Award Competition: 4745 Sutton Park Court, Suite 201, Jacksonville, FL 32224; tel. 1 904 992 9101; fax 1 904 992 9326; e-mail info@nats.org; website www.nats.org. Competition held every 18 months. Open to singers between the ages of 21 and 35 whose most recent teacher has been a member of the National Association of Teachers of Singing. Prizes include 1st prize of US $10,000, Carnegie Hall concert and AIMS scholarship, and 2nd prize of $2,500.

National Competition for Performing Artists: c/o Contemporary Recording Society, 724 Winchester Road, Broomall, PA 19008. Annual competition open to performers. Prizes include recording.

National Endowment for the Arts, Music Program Office: 1100 Pennsylvania Ave NW, Washington, DC 20506; tel. 1 202 682 5400; website www.nea.gov. Lends organizational assistance to professional music organizations and gives fellowships to composers and performers.

National Endowment for the Humanities: 1100 Pennsylvania Ave NW, Washington, DC 20506; website www.neh.fed.us. Awards fellowships and grants for various projects in the field of music.

National Federation of Music Clubs: 1336 N Delaware St, Indianapolis, IN 46202; tel. 1 317 638 4003; fax 1 317 638 0503; e-mail info@nfmc-music.org; website www.nfmc-music.org. Provides various annual awards and fellowships.

National Symphony Orchestra Young Soloists' Competition, College Division: 5931 Oakdale Road, McLean, VA 22101. Annual competition open to high school graduates studying music in the Washington metropolitan area or Washington residents studying elsewhere. Prizes include money and appearances with the National Symphony Orchestra.

Walter W Naumburg Foundation International Competition: 60 Lincoln Center Plaza, New York, NY 10023. Annual competition open to performers of all nationalities with categories rotating annually. Prizes include 1st prize of US $5,000, concert engagements and a recording, 2nd prize of $2,500, and 3rd prize of $1,000.

New Jersey Symphony Orchestra Young Artists Auditions: Robert Treat Center, 2 Central Ave, Newark, NJ 07102. Annual competition open to instrumentalists under the age of 20, resident in New Jersey. Prizes include 1st prize of an appearance with the New Jersey Symphony Orchestra; prizes range from US $3,000 to $500.

New York Foundation for the Arts Artists' Fellowship Program: 155 Ave of the Americas, New York, NY 10013. Biennial fellowships for non-students of two or more years' residency in New York State. Prizes include grants.

Omaha Symphony Guild New Music Competition: 8723 N 57th St, Omaha, NE 68152; website www.omahasymphony.org. Annual competition open to composers of chamber orchestra compositions. Prizes include US $2,000.

Opera at Florham Guild Vocal Competition: PO Box 343, Convent Station, NJ 07961. Competition open to all singers between the ages of 18 and 35. Prizes include 1st prize of US $3,000 and a recital.

Opera/Columbus Vocal Competition: 177 E Naghten Street, Columbus, OH 43215; tel. 1 614 469 0939; e-mail info@operacolumbus.org; website www.operacols.org. Competition open to singers who are residents of Ohio. Prizes for senior level (ages 24 to 35) include 1st prize of US $2,000 and a scholarship to the American Institute of Musical Studies in Graz, Austria.

Oratorio Society of New York Solo Competition: Carnegie Hall, Suite 504, 881 Seventh Ave, New York, NY 10019; website www.oratoriosocietyofny.org. Annual competition open to solo oratorio singers under the age of 40. Prizes include US $10,000.

Palm Beach Invitational International Piano Competition: PO Box 3094, Palm Beach, FL 33480; tel. 1 561 833 8817; fax 1 561 833 6735. Annual competition open to 25 young pianists, each from a different nation and each the winner of an international competition. Prizes totalling US $50,000, including 1st prize of $15,000 and a concert at Alice Tully Hall in New York.

Palm Beach Opera Vocal Competition: 415 S Olive Ave, West Palm Beach, FL 33401; tel. 1 561 833 8924; fax 1 561 833 8294. Annual competition open to singers with Junior Division between the ages of 18 and 23 and Senior Division between the ages of 24 and 30. Prizes include money totalling US $43,000 and performances.

Performing Arts Assistance Corporation: PO Box 1296, Ansonia Station, New York, NY 10023. Gives seminars for performers.

Gregor Piatigorsky Seminar for Cello: c/o University of Southern California School of Music, Los Angeles, CA 90089. Seminar open to cellists.

Rosa Ponselle International Vocal Competition for the Vocal Arts: Windsor, Stevenson, MD 21153. Biennial competition open to singers to the age of 25. Prizes include study grants between US $20,000 and $25,000, medallions and training in Italy and France.

Pro Musicis International Award: 140 W 79th St, No 9F, New York, NY 10024. Annual career development award. Prizes include major recitals in New York, Los Angeles, Washington, DC, Boston, Paris and Rome.

Pulitzer Prize in Music: c/o Columbia University, 702 Journalism Building, New York, NY 10027. Annual prize of US $3,000 to an American composer for a major composition premiered in the USA during the year.

Queens Opera Vocal Competition: 313 Bay 14 St, Brooklyn, NY 11214. Annual competition open to singers who have appeared in one opera performance. Prizes include 1st prize of money and an appearance in a full opera performance.

Rome Prize Fellowships of the American Academy in Rome: 41 E 65th St, New York, NY 10021; website www.aarome.org/prize.htm. Annual fellowships for American composers with a BA or equivalent degree. Fellowships include one year residency at the American Academy in Rome, stipend, and travel allowance.

San Antonio International Keyboard Competition: PO Box 39636, San Antonio, TX 78218; tel. 1 210 655 0766; fax 1 210 822 6056. Triennial competition open to pianists between the ages of 20 and 32. Prizes include 1st prize of US $5,000 and gold medal, 2nd prize of $2,500 and silver medal, 3rd prize of $1,000 and bronze medal, and 4th prize of $500.

San Francisco Opera Center National Auditions: c/o War Memorial Opera House, San Francisco, CA 94102. Annual competitive auditions for singers, sopranos between the ages of 20 and 30 and all other singers between 20 and 34. Prizes include awards given in the Merola Opera Program totalling US $28,000. Participants may also apply for the Adler Fellowship Program.

San Jose Symphony Young Pianist Concerto Competition: 99 Almaden Blvd, Suite 400, San Jose, CA 95113. Annual competition open to pianists to the age of 30. Prizes include grand prize of US $5,000 and an appearance with the San Jose Symphony.

Santa Barbara Symphony and the Esperia Foundation Young Artists' Competition: 214 E Victoria St, Santa Barbara, CA 93101. Competition open to string players and pianist alternating between instruments annually. Prizes include money and an appearance with the Santa Barbara Symphony.

Friedrich Schorr Memorial Performance Prize in Voice: 110 S Madison St, Adrian, MI 49221. Annual competition open to all professional singers. Prizes include $10,000 in performance awards/stipends.

Sewanee Music Festival International Scholarships: 735 University Ave, Sewanee, TN 37375. Annual scholarships for musicians of all nationalities between the ages of 16 and 25.

Shreveport Symphony/Nena Plant Wideman Annual Piano Competition: PO Box 205, Shreveport, LA 71162. Annual competition open to pianists between the ages of 18 and 28. Prizes include 1st prize of US $2,500, 2nd prize of $1,000 and 3rd prize of $500.

Sinfonia Foundation: c/o Phi Mus Alpha Sinfonia Fraternity, 10600 Old State Road, Evansville, IN 47711. Commissions to composers and annual research grants for scholarly research on music in America or American music.

Sorantin Young Artists Award: PO Box 5922, San Angelo, TX 76902.

Sound Research Residencies: c/o Yellow Springs Institute for Contemporary Studies and the Arts, 1645 Art School Road, Chester Springs, PA 19425. Annual 10-day residency for composers with at least three years of professional experience.

Southwestern Youth Music Festival Competition: PO Box 41104, Los Angeles, CA 90041; website www.symf.org. Annual competition open to pianists to the age of 18, whose teacher must become a member of the festival. Prizes include US $10,000 and orchestral appearances.

James Spencer Memorial Performance Prize in Composition: 110 S Madison St, Adrian, MI 49221. Open to American composers. Prizes include travel and housing allowance, lecture stipend, and performance and recording by the Adrian Symphony Orchestra.

Spivey International Performance Competition: Clayton State College, Morrow, GA 30260. Annual competition for performers. Prizes include 1st prize of US $5,000.

Stewart Awards National Operatic Voice Competition: PO Box 18321, Oklahoma City, OK 73154. Biennial competition open to American singers between the ages of 20 and 32. Prizes include money totalling US $14,000.

Stravinsky Awards International Piano Competition for Children Aged 18 and Under: 1003 W Church Street, Champaign, IL 61821; tel. (217) 352-0688; fax (217) 352-8707; Exec. Dir: Roger Shields. Biennial competition open to pianists of all nationalities in age divisions ranging from small children to 22.

Julius Stulberg International String Competition: PO Box 107, Kalamazoo, MI 49005; tel. 1 616 372 6237; fax 1 616 372 7513. Annual

competition open to string players to the age of 19. Prizes include money and performances.

Louis and Virginia Sudler International Wind Band Composition Contest: c/o US Marine Bane, Eighth and First Sts SE, Washington, DC 20390. Biennial competition open to composers of wind music. Prizes include 1st prize of US $12,000.

William Matheus Sullivan Musical Foundation Inc: PO Box 189, Kent, CT 06757; tel. 1 860 927 3572; fax 1 860 927 1680; e-mail info@sullivanfoundation.org; website www.sullivanfoundation.org. Annual assistance programme for professional young singers.

Trebas Institute Scholarships: 6464 Sunset Blvd, No. 1180, Hollywood, CA 90028. Annual scholarships for educational opportunities in the music business, and the recording arts and sciences.

Richard Tucker Music Foundation: 1790 Broadway, Suite 715, New York, NY 10019; tel. 1 212 757 2218; fax 1 212 757 2347; website www .richardtucker.org. Annual awards to American singers by recommendation. Prizes include the Richard Tucker Award of US $30,000, four career grants of $6,500, and other grants.

USA International Harp Competition: PO Box 5157, Bloomington, IN 47407. Triennial competition open to harpists of all nationalities, born between 1969 and 1985. Prizes include eight awards.

Unisys African-American Composers Forum and Symposium: DSOH Education Department, 400 Buhl Building, 535 Griswold St, Detroit, MI 48226. Encourages performances of orchestral compositions by African-American composers by major professional symphony orchestras.

United States Information Agency Artistic Ambassador Program: 301 Fourth St SW, Room 216, Washington, DC 20547. Annual programme for American musicians at least 21 years old, to serve as artistic ambassadors abroad at government expense, for four to six weeks.

University of Louisville Grawemeyer Award for Music Composition: c/o University of Louisville, School of Music, Grawemeyer Music Award Committee, Louisville, KY 40292. Annual award for outstanding achievement by a composer. Compositions may not be submitted by the composer but must be sponsored by a professional music organization or individual. Award totalling US $150,000, paid in five annual instalments of $30,000.

University of Maryland International Competitions: c/o University of Maryland, College Park, MD 20742. Annual competition open to pianists, cellists and singers of all nationalities. Prizes include 1st prize of US $20,000 and concert engagements, 2nd prize of $10,000 and 3rd prize of $5,000.

Elizabeth Harper Vaughan Concerto Competition: 1200 E Center St, Kingsport, TN 37660; tel. 1 423 392 8423; fax 1 423 392 8428. Annual competition open to performers of classical music to the age of 26. Prizes include US $1,000 and an appearance with the Kingsport Symphony Orchestra.

Women's Association of the Minnesota Orchestra (WAMSO) Young Artist Competition: c/o Minnesota Orchestra, 1111 Nicollet Mall, Minneapolis, MN 55403; tel. 1 612 371 5654; fax 1 612 371 7176; website www.wamso.org. Annual competition open to instrumentalists to the age of 25. Various prizes.

Virginia Waring International Piano Competition: College of the Desert, 43500 Monterey Avenue, Palm Desert, CA 92260; tel. (760) 773-2575; fax (760) 776-0168; website www.vwipc.org; Admin. Dir: Terri Fleck. Fmrly the Joanna Hodges International Piano Competition. Quadrennial competition. Next competition 10 Jan.–5 Feb. 2005. No minimum age, maximum age 35. Performance prizes include solo and orchestral performances, including Carnegie Hall, Rome and Vienna.

Washington International Competition: 4530 Connecticut Ave, PO Box 704, Washington, DC 20008. Annual competition open to performers between the ages of 18 and 32 with categories rotating annually. Prizes include money.

Abby Whiteside Foundation Inc: 8 E 83rd Street, New York, NY 10028; website www.abbywhiteside.org; purpose to make the teaching principles of piano teacher Abby Whiteside better known; sponsors a series of piano recitals at Weill Hall, Carnegie Hall; Pres. Sophia Rosoff.

Andrew Wolf Chamber Music Award: PO Box 191, Camden, ME 04843; Newton Music School, 321 Chestnut St, West Newton, MA 02165. Biennial award given to an American chamber music pianist under the age of 40. Award includes US $10,000 and concert appearances.

Young Concert Artists Inc: 250 W 57th Street, Suite 1222, New York, NY 10107; tel. (212) 307-6655; e-mail yca@yca.org; website www.yca.org;

Dir Susan Wadsworth. Annual auditions for solo performers and string quartets.

Loren L Zachary Society Opera Awards National Vocal Competition: 2250 Gloaming Way, Beverly Hills, CA 90210; tel. 1 310 276 2731; fax 1 310 275 8245; Pres. and Dir Nedra Zachary. Annual competition open to professional opera singers seeking contracts for leading roles in European opera houses; for women between the ages of 21 and 33 and for men between the ages of 21 and 35. Prizes totalling about US $25,000 and a round trip flight to Europe for auditioning purposes.

Uruguay

Concurso Internacional de Piano Ciudad de Montevideo: Santiago Vásquez, Montevideo. Triennial competition open to pianists to the age of 32.

APPENDIX F: MUSIC LIBRARIES

Afghanistan
Kabul Public Library: Kabul.

Albania
Biblioteka Kombetare (National Library): Tirana.

Algeria
Bibliothèque Nationale: Avenue Frantz Fanon, Algiers.

Bibliothèque Universitaire: Rue Didouche Mourad, Algiers.

Argentina
Academia Nacional de Bellas Artes: Biblioteca, Sanchez de Bustamante 2663, 1425 Buenos Aires.

Biblioteca Nacional: México 564, 1097 Buenos Aires.

Fondo Nacional de las Artes: Biblioteca, Alsina 673, 1087 Buenos Aires.

Australia
Australia Music Centre Ltd Library: First Floor, Argyle Centre, 18 Argyle Street, The Rocks, NSW 2000.

City of Sydney Public Library: Town Hall House, Level 3, 456 Kent Street, Sydney, NSW 2000; tel. 61 2 9265 9470; fax 61 2 9265 9157; e-mail library@cityofsydney.nsw.gov.au.

National Library of Australia: Music and Dance Division, Parkes Place, Canberra, ACT 2600; tel. (2) 6262-1111; fax (2) 6273-5081; e-mail infoserv@nla.gov.au; website www.nla.gov.au.

National Music Library: Australian Broadcasting Corporation, PO Box 9994, Sydney, NSW 2001; tel. 61 2 8333 1627; fax 61 2 8333 1684.

State Library of New South Wales: Music Division, Macquarie Street, Sydney, NSW 2000; tel. 61 2 9273 1414; website www.sl.nsw.gov.au; Music Archivist: Meredith Lawn.

State Library of Queensland: Music Division, PO Box 3488, South Brisbane, Qld 4000; tel. 61 7 3840 7666; fax 61 7 3846 2421; website www.slq.qld.gov.au.

State Library of South Australia: Music Division, North Terrace, PO Box 419, Adelaide, SA 5001; tel. 61 8 8207 7200; fax 61 8 8207 7247; website www.slsa.sa.gov.au.

State Library of Tasmania: Music Division, 91 Murray Street, Hobart, TAS 7000; tel. 61 3 6233 7511; fax 61 3 6231 0927; website www.statelibrary.tas.gov.au.

State Library of Victoria: Music Division, 328 Swanston Street, Melbourne, Vic. 3000; tel. 61 3 8864 7000; website www.state.library.vic.gov.au.

State Library of Western Australia: Music Division, Alexander Library Building, Perth Cultural Centre, Perth, WA 6000; tel. 61 8 9427 3111; website www.liswa.wa.gov.au.

Austria
Büchereien der Stadt Linz: Zentrale und Hauptbücherei, Museumstrasse 15, 4020 Linz.

Burgenländische Landesbibliothek: Landhaus Freiheitsplatz 1, 7001 Eisenstadt.

Gesellschaft der Musikfreunde in Wien: Archiv und Bibliothek, Bösendorferstrasse 12, 1010 Vienna; tel. 43 1 505 81 90; fax 43 1 505 81 90 94; website www.musikverein.at.

Haus des Buches: Hauptbücherei, Skodagasse 20, 1080 Vienna; tel. 43 1 400 08 45 00.

Kammer für Arbeiter und Angestel.lte: Volksbüchereien, Bahnhofplatz 3, 9021 Klagenfurt.

Musik Informations Zentrum Österreich: Stiftgasse 29, 1070 Vienna.

Österreichische Akademie der Wissenschaften: Bibliothek, Dr Ignaz Seipelplatz 2, 1010 Vienna 1.

Österreichische Gesellschaft für Musik: Bibliothek, Hanuschgasse 3, 1010 Vienna.

Österreichische Nationalbibliothek: Josefplatz 1, PO Box 308, 1015 Vienna; e-mail onb@onb.ac.at; website www.onb.ac.at.

Österreichische Gewerkschaftsbund: Bibliothek, Grillparzerstrasse 14, 1010 Vienna.

Stadtbücherei: Schloss Mirabell, 5020 Salzburg.

Stadtbücherei: Herzog Leopoldstrasse 21, 2700 Wiener Neustadt.

Stadtbücherein: Landhausgasse 2, 8010 Graz.

Universitätsbibliothek der Universität für Musik und darstellende Kunst Wien: Lothringerstrasse 18, 1030 Vienna; tel. (1) 71155-8101; website www.mdw.ac.at; Dir: Dr Susanne Eschwé.

Wiener Stadt-und Landesbibliothek: Rathaus, 1082 Vienna; tel. 43 1 400 08 49 20; website www.stadtbibliothek.wien.at.

Belgium
Academie royale des sciences, des lettres et des beaux arts de Belgique, Bibliothèque: Palais des Académies, 1 rue Ducale, 1000 Brussels; tel. 32 2 550 22 55; fax 32 2 550 22 65; website www.armb.be.

Bibliothèque Centrale: En Hors Chateau 31, 4000 Liège.

Bibliothèque Provinciale du Degré Moyen: rue des Croisiers 15, 4000 Liège.

Bibliothèque Royale Albert ler: Blvd de l'Empereur 4, 1000 Brussels.

Centre Belge de Documentation Musicale ASBL: rue d'Arlon 75–77, 1040 Brussels.

Koninklijke Academie voor Wetenschappen: Defacqzstraat 1 bus 3, 1000 Brussels; tel. 32 2 538 02 11; fax 32 2 539 23 53.

Stadsbibliotheek: Hendrik Conscienceplein 4, 2000 Antwerp; website www.stadsbibliotheek.antwerpen.be.

Bolivia
Biblioteca y Archivo Nacional de Bolivia: Calle España 25, PO Box 338, Sucre; tel. 591 64 1481.

Brazil
Biblioteca Nacional: Fundaçao Nacional Pro-Memoria, Avda Rio Branco 219–239, 20040 Rio de Janeiro; tel. 21 2220 9367; fax 21 2220 4173; website www.bn.br.

Bulgaria
Nacionalna Biblioteka: Kiril i Metodij, F. Tolbuhin 11, 1504 Sofia.

Union of Bulgarian Composers: lv Vazov 2, 1000 Sofia; website www.ubc-bg.com.

Cambodia
Bibliothèque Nationale: 4, Phnom Penh.

Canada
Bibliothèque Municipale de Montréal: 1210 Sheerbrooke Street East, Montréal, QC H2L 1L9.

Bibliothèque Municipale de Québec: 37 rue Sainte-Angéle, Québec, QC G1R 4G5.

Bibliothèque Nationale du Québec (BNQ): 2275 Holt, Montréal, QC H2G 3H1; tel. 1 514 873 1100; fax 1 514 873 7510; website www.bnquebec.ca.

Calgary Public Library, Music Division: 616 Macleod Trail SE, Calgary, AB T2G 2M2; website www.calgarypubliclibrary.com.

Canadian Music Centre: 20 St Joseph Street, Toronto, ON M4Y 1J9; tel. 1 416 961 6601; website www.musiccentre.ca.

Edmonton Public Library, Music Division: 7 Sir Winston Churchill Square, Edmonton, AB T5J 2V4; tel. 1 780 496 7000; website www.epl.ca.

Greater Victoria Public Library, Music Division: 735 Broughton Street, Victoria, BC V8W 3H2; tel. 1 250 382 7241; fax 1 250 382 7125; website www.gvpl.ca.

Guelph Public Library, Music Division: 100 Norfolk Street, Guelph, ON N1H 4J6; tel. 1 519 824 6220; website www.library.guelph.on.ca.

Halifax City Regional Library, Music Division: 5381 Spring Garden Road, Halifax, NS B3J 1E9; tel. 1 902 421 6980.

Hamilton Public Library, Music Division: 55 York Blvd, Hamilton, ON L8R 3K1; tel. 1 905 546 3200; website www.hpl.hamilton.on.ca.

Kingston Frontenac Public Library, Music Division: 130 Johnson Street E, Kingston, ON K7L 1X8; website www.kfpl.ca.

Kitchener Public Library, Music Division: 85 Queen Street N, Kitchener, ON N2H 2H1; tel. 1 519 743 0271; website www.kpl.org.

National Library of Canada, Music Division: 395 Wellington Street, Ottawa, ON K1A 0N4; tel. 1 613 995 9481; website www.nlc-bnc.ca.

Ottawa Public Library: 120 Metcalfe Street, Ottawa, ON K1P 5M2; website www.opl.ottawa.on.ca.

Regina Public Library, Music Division: 2311 12th Avenue, PO Box 2311, Regina, SK S4P 3Z5; website www.reginalibrary.ca.

Saskatoon Public Library, Music Division: 311 23rd Street E, Saskatoon, SK S7K 0J6; website www.publib.saskatoon.sk.ca.

Toronto Public Library, Music Division: 789 Yonge Street, Toronto, ON M4W 2G8; tel. 1 416 393 7131; website www.tpl.toronto.on.ca.

Vancouver Public Library, Music Division: 350 W Georgia Street, Vancouver, BC V6B 6B1; tel. 1 604 331 3603; website www.vpl.vancouver.bc.ca.

Windsor Public Library, Music Division: 850 Ouellette Avenue, Windsor, ON N9A 4M9; tel. 1 519 255 6770; website www.windsorpubliclibrary.com.

Winnipeg Public Library, Music Division: 251 Donald Street, Winnipeg, MB R3C 3P5; website www.wpl.winnipeg.ca.

Chile

Biblioteca Nacional: Avda Bernardo O'Higgins 651, Santiago.

People's Republic of China

National Library of China: 39 Baishiqiao Road, Haidian District, Beijing 100 081.

Colombia

Biblioteca Nacional de Colombia: C24, 5-60, PO Box 27600, Bogotá.

Costa Rica

Biblioteca Nacional: C 15-17, Avda 3Y 3b, PO Box 10008, San José.

Cuba

Biblioteca Nacional José Marti: PO Box 3, Avda de Independencia 3, 20 de Mayo y Arangusen, Plaza de la Revolución José Marti, Havana.

Czech Republic

Mstská knihovna v Praze (City Library of Prague): Knihovna Bedricha Smetany, Dr V. Vacka 1, 115 72 Prague.

Music Information Centre: Besední 3, 118 00 Prague 1.

Státni knihovna (State Library): Klementinum 190, 110 01 Prague 1.

Denmark

Danish Music Information Centre: 48 Vimmelskaftet, 1161 Copenhagen K.

Det Kongelige Bibliotek (Royal Library): Christians Brygge 8, PO Box 2149, 1219 Copenhagen K; tel. 1 33 93 01 11.

Musikhistorisk Museum and Carl Claudius' Samling: Åbenrå 30, 1124 Copenhagen K; tel. 45 33 11 27 26; fax 45 33 11 60 44; e-mail info@musikhistoriskmuseum.dk; website www.musikhistoriskmuseum.dk.

Dominican Republic

Biblioteca Nacional: César Nicolás Penson 91, Plaza de la Cultura, Santo Domingo.

Ecuador

Biblioteca Nacional de Ecuador: 12 de Octubre 555, PO Box 67, Quito.

Egypt

Egyptian National Library: Sharia Corniche El-Nil, Bulaq, Cairo.

El Salvador

Biblioteca Nacional: 8A Avda Norte y Calle Delgado, San Salvador.

Ethiopia

National Library and Archives of Ethiopia: PO Box 1907, Addis Ababa.

Finland

Finnish Music Information Centre: Lauttasaarenti 1, 00120 Helsinki; tel. 358 9 6810 1313; website www.fimic.fi.

France

Bibliothèque centrale de prêt du Doubs et du Territoire de Belfort: 24 Avenue de l'Observatoire, 25000 Besançon.

Bibliothèque centrale de prêt du Pas-de-Calais: 13 Place Guy Mollet, 62000 Arras.

Bibliothèque de la ville de Caen: Place Guillouard, 14027 Caen Cédex.

Bibliothèque de la ville et du musée Fabre: 37 Blvd Bonnes-Nouvelles, 34000 Montpellier.

Bibliothèque municipale: 32–34 rue Edouard-Delesalle, 59043 Lille Cédex; tel. 03 20 15 97 25; fax 03 20 63 94 59; e-mail dqueneutte@mairie-lille.fr.

Bibliothèque municipale: 30 Blvd Vivier-Merle, 69431 Lyon Cédex 03; website www.bm-lyon.fr.

Bibliothèque municipale: 38 rue du 141 Ria, 13001 Marseille Cédex 3.

Bibliothèque municipale: 1 Cour Elie Fleur, 57000 Metz; tel. 03 87 55 53 33.

Bibliothèque municipale: 19 Grand rue, 68090 Mulhouse Cédex.

Bibliothèque municipale: 43 rue Stanislas, 54000 Nancy; tel. 03 83 37 38 83.

Bibliothèque municipale: 37 rue Gambetta, 44041 Nantes Cédex.

Bibliothèque municipale: 1 rue Dupanloup, 45043 Orléans Cédex.

Bibliothèque municipale: 1 rue de La Borderie, 35042 Rennes Cédex; tel. 02 99 87 98 88.

Bibliothèque municipale: rue Jacques Villon, 76043 Rouen Cédex.

Bibliothèque municipale: 3 rue Kuhn, 67000 Strasbourg Cédex.

Bibliothèque municipale: 1 rue de Périgord, 31070 Toulouse; tel. 05 61 22 21 78.

Bibliothèque municipale: 2 bis Quai d'Orléans, 37042 Tours Cédex; tel. 02 47 05 47 33.

Bibliothèque municipale: 5 rue de l'Indépendence Américaine, 78000 Versailles.

Bibliothèque municipale classée: 3 rue Mably, 33075 Bordeaux, Cédex.

Bibliothèque municipale classée: 43 Place Charles-de-Gaulle, 86000 Poitiers.

Bibliothèque municipale classée: 2 Place Carnegie, 51100 Reims Cédex; website www.bm-reins.fr.

Bibliothèque municipale d'étude et d'information: Blvd Maréchal-Lyautey, PO Box 1095 RP, 38021 Grenoble Cédex.

Bibliothèque municipale d'études: 21 bis Blvd Dubouchage, 06047 Nice Cédex.

Bibliothèque-Musée de l'Opéra: rue Scribe, 75009 Paris; tel. 1 40 01 23 39; fax 1 42 65 10 16; e-mail pierre.vidal@bnf.fr; Dir Pierre Vidal; library located in Place de l'Opéra, Paris.

Bibliothèque Musicale Gustav Mahler: 11 bis rue Vézelay, 75008 Paris.

Bibliothèque Nationale: Department de la Musique, 2 rue Louvois, 75084 Paris.

Institut de France, Acádemie des Beaux-Arts: 23 Quai de Conti, 75006 Paris.

Germany

Akademie der Künste: Robert-Koch-Platz 7, Berlin; website www.adk.de.

Bayerische Staatsbibliothek: Ludwigstrasse 16, 80539 Munich; tel. 49 89 286 38 23 22; website www.bsb-muenchen.de.

Bibliothek der Hansestadt Lübeck: Hundestrasse 5-17, Lübeck.

Bibliothek des Handel-Houses Halle: Grosse Nikolaiste 5, 06108, Halle.

Bischöfliche Zentralbibliothek: Proskesche Musikabteilung, Dr Raymond Dittrich, St Petersweg 11–13, 93047 Regensburg; tel. 0941 59532-2510; fax 0941 59532-2521; e-mail rdittrich.biblio@bistum-regensburg.de; website www.bistum-regensburg.de/bibliothek.

Deutsche Bibliothek: Frankfurt am Main, Adickesallee 1, 60322 Frankfurt am Main; website www.ddb.de.

Deutsche Bücherei: Deutscher Platz, Leipzig.

Hamburger Öffentliche Bücherhallen: Grosse Bleichen 23–27, 20354 Hamburg; tel. 040 35 60 61 23.

Hessische Landes-und Hochschulbibliothek: Schloss 6, 64283 Darmstadt; tel. 06151 16 58 50.

Hochschule fur Musik 'Franz Liszt' Hochschulbibliothek: Platz der Demokratie 2–3, 99423 Weimar.

Kreisbibliothek: Leipzig-Land, Karl-Rothe-Strasse 13, Leipzig.

Kreisbibliothek Schwerin-Land: Wismarsche Strasse 144, Schwerin.

Landesbibliothek: Schlossplatz 1, Schloss Ehrenburg, Coburg; tel. 09561 76757/8; fax 09561 99622; website www.bib-bvb.de/Landesbibliothek/home.htm.

Lippische Landesbibliothek: Hornschestrasse 41, 32756; Detmold; tel. 49 5231 92 6600; website www.lib-detmold.de.

Münchner Städtische Bibliotheken: Rosenheimerstrasse 5, Munich.

Musikbibliothek de Stadt Leipzig: Ferdinand-Lassale-Strasse 21, Leipzig.

Öffentliche Bibliothek der Stadt Aachen: Couvenstrasse 15, Pf 1210, Aachen.

Offentliche Bücherei: Hintern Brudern 23, Braunschweig.

Ratsbücherei: Am Marienplatz 3, PO Box 2540, Lüneburg.

Sächsische Landesbibliothek: Marienalle 12, Dresden.

Staatsbibliothek: Neue Residenz, Domplatz 8, 96049 Bamberg; tel. 49 951 955 030; website www.staatsbibliothek-bamberg.de.

Staatsbibliothek: Luitpoldplatz 7, PO Box 2840, Bayreuth.

Staatsbibliothek zu Berlin Preussischer Kulturbesitz (Berlin State Library): Haus Unter den Linden 8, 10117 Berlin; tel. 49 (0)30 266 1700; fax 49 (0)30 266 1751; e-mail generaldir@sbb.spk-berlin.de; website www.staatsbibliothek-berlin.de; Head: Barbara Schneider-Kempf; Head of Music Dept: Dr Helmut Hell.

Staatsbibliothek: 24 Berlin-Preussischen Kulturbesitz, Musikabteilung, Pf 1312 Berlin.

Staats-und Stadtbibliothek: Schaezlerstrasse 25, PO Box 111909, Augusburg.

Staats-und Universitätsbibliothek: Bibliothekstrasse, PO Box 330160, Bremen.

Stadtarchiv und Stadtbibliothek: Am Steine 7, Hildesheim.

Stadtarchiv und Wissenschaftliche Stadtbibliothek: Berliner Platz 2, Bonn.

Stadtbibliothek: Langestrasse 43, 76530 Baden-Baden; website www.baden-baden.de.

Stadtbibliothek: Wilhelmstrasse 3, PO Box 181, Bielefeld; website www.stadtbibliothek-bielfeld.de.

Stadtbibliothek: Schusterstrasse 7, Brandenburg.

Stadtbibliothek: Steintorwall 15, PO Box 3309, Braunschweig.

Stadtbibliothek: Schwachhauser Heerstrasse 30, Bremen; website www.stadtbibliothek-bremen.de.

Stadtbibliothek: Zerbsterstrasse 10, 06844 Dessau; tel. 0340 213264.

Stadtbibliothek: Düsseldorfer Strasse 5–7, 47049 Duisburg; website www.stadtbibliothek.duisburg.de.

Stadtbibliothek: Hollestrasse 3, 45127 Essen; tel. 0201 88 42001; website www.stadtbibliothek.essen.de.

Stadtbibliothek: Münsterplatz 17, 79098 Freiburg; tel. 0761 201 2207; fax 0761 201 2299; website www.stadtbibliothek.freiburg.de.

Stadtbibliothek: Jochmannstrasse 2–3, Görlitz.

Stadtbibliothek: Gotmarstrasse 8, PO Box 3842, Göttingen.

Stadtbibliothek: Hildesheimer Strasse 12, PO Box 125, 30169 Hannover; tel. 0511 168 42169; website www.stadtbibliothek.hannover.de.

Stadtbibliothek: Im Weiterbuldungszentrum, Klosterstrasse 8, 67655 Kaiserslautern; tel. 0631 365 1421; fax 0631 365 1429.

Stadtbibliothek: Ständehausstrasse 2, 76133 Karlsruhe; website www.karlsruhe.de/Bildung/Bib.

Stadtbibliothek: Rathaus, 34117 Kassel; tel. 49 561 787 4013.

Stadtbibliothek: Kornpforstrasse 15, PO Box 2064, Koblenz.

Stadtbibliothek: Bismarckstrasse 44–48, PO Box 212125, Ludwigshafen; tel. 0621 504 2601.

Stadtbibliothek: Rheinalle 3b, 55116 Mainz; tel. 06131 122649; fax 06131 04187 648.

Stadtbibliothek: Blücherstrasse 6, PO Box 85, Mönchengladbach.

Stadtbibliothek: Zentralbibliothek, Egidienplatz 23, 90403 Nuremberg; tel. 49 911 231 2790; fax 49 911 231 5476; website www.stadtbibliothek.nuernberg.de.

Stadtbibliothek: Nauwieser Strasse 5, Saarbrücken.

Stadtbibliothek: Weinhof 12, 89073 Ulm; tel. 49 731 161 4100; fax 49 731 161 1633; website www.stadtbibliothek.ulm.de.

Stadtbibliothek: Steubenstrasse 1, Weimer.

Stadtbibliothek: Rathauspassage, Wiesbaden.

Stadtbibliothek: Kolpingstrasse 8, 42103 Wuppertal; tel. 49 202 563 2162; fax 49 202 306 594; website www.wuppertal.de/stadtbib/welcome.htm.

Stadtbibliothek: Dr Friedrichs-Ring 19, 08056 Zwickau; tel. and fax 49 375 241 651.

Stadtbücherei: Gutenbergstrasse 2, 86150 Augsburg; tel. 49 821 324 2754; fax 49 821 324 2707.

Stadtbücherei: Friedrichstrasse 2, Bamberg.

Stadtbücherei: Rathausplatz 2–6, PO Box 102269-2270, Bochum.

Stadtbücherei Bonn: Bottlerplatz 1, Bonn.

Stadtbücherei Köln: Zentralbibliothek, Josef-Haubrich-Hof 1, Pf 108020, 50676 Cologne; tel. 49 221 221 3894; fax 49 221 221 3933; website www.stbib-koeln.de.

Stadtbücherei: Markt 12, PO Box 907, Dortmund.

Stadtbücherei: Marktplatz 1, PO Box 3160, Erlangen.

Stadtbücherei: Zentralbibliothek, Zeil 17–19, PO Box 102113, 60313 Frankfurt am Main; tel. 49 692 123 4482; fax 49 692 123 7949.

Stadtbücherei: Ebertstrasse 19, Gelsenkirchen.

Stadtbücherei: Deutschordenshof, Kirchbrunnenstrasse 12, 74072 Heilbronn; tel. 49 713 156 2663; fax 49 713 196 2931; website www.stadtbuecherei.stadt-heilbronn.de.

Stadtbucherei: Hallstrasse 2–4, 85049 Ingolstadt; tel. 49 841 305 1830; fax 49 841 305 1849.

Stadtbücherei: Holstenbrücke 1, PO Box 4140, 24103 Kiel; tel. 49 431 901 3434; fax 49 431 901 3450; website www.kiel.de/stadtbuecherei.

Stadtbücherei: N 3, 4 (Dalberghaus), PO Box 5868, 68161 Mannheim; tel. 49 621 293 8930; fax 49 621 239 8908; website www.stadtbuecherei.mannheim.de.

Stadtbücherei: Friedrich-Ebert-Strasse 47, PO Box 011620, 45468 Mülheim; tel. 49 208 455 4189; fax 49 208 455 4125.

Stadtbücherei: Alter Steinweg 7, PO Box 5909, Münster.

Stadtbücherei: Langemarkstrasse 19–21, Oberhausen.

Stadtbücherei: Haidplatz 8, 93047 Regensburg; tel. 49 941 507 2473; fax 49 941 507 4479.

Stadtbücherei: Konrad-Adenauer-Strasse 2, Stuttgart.

Stadtbücherei: Brunnenstrasse 3, Tübingen.

Städtbucherei: Max-Heim-Bücherei, Marktplatz 9, Haus zum Falken, 97070 Würzburg; tel. 49 931 372 444; fax 49 931 373 638.

Stadtbüchereien: Berliner Alle 59, PO Box 1120, Düsseldorf.

Stadt-und Bezirksbibliothek: Haus am Schillerplatz, Chemnitz.

Stadt-und Bezirksbibliothek: Salzgrafenstrasse 2, Halle.

Stadt-und Bezirksbibliothek: Mozartstrasse 1, Leipzig.

Stadt-und Bezirksbibliothek: Weitlingstrasse 1a, Magdeburg.

Stadt-und Berzirksbibliothek: Kröpeliner Strasse 82, Rostock.

Stadt-und Kreisbibliothek Heinrich Heine: Orangerie, Gotha.

Stadt-und Kreisbibliothek: Strasse d DSF 8, Ludwigslust.

Stadt-und Kreisbibliothek: Strasse des Friedens 54, Oranienburg.

Stadt-und Kreisbibliothek: August-Wolf-Strasse 10, Quedlinburg.

Stadt-und Kreisbibliothek: Ernestiner Strasse 38, Meiningen.

Stadt-und Kreisbibliothek: Mühlhausen.

Stadt-und Kreisbibliothek: Schulplatz 13, Rudolstadt.

Stadt-und Kreisbibliothek: Schloss Sondershausen.

Stadt-und Landesbibliothek: Königswall 18, 44137 Dortmund; tel. 49 231 502 3225; fax 49 231 502 3199; website www.dortmund.de/ bibliotheken.

Stadt-und Universitätsbibliothek: Bockenheimer Landstrasse 134–138, 60325 Frankfurt; tel. 49 692 123 9244; fax 49 692 123 7398; website www.stub.uni-frankfurt.de/musik.htm.

Ghana

Central Reference and Research Library: PO Box 1633, Accra; tel. 233 21 21 162.

Greece

Ethnike Bibliotheke tes Hellados: Odos Venizelou 32, 10679 Athens; tel. 30 1 361 4413.

Guatemala

Biblioteca Nacional de Guatemala: 5a Avda 7-26, Guatemala City; tel. 502 2 539 071; fax 502 2 322 443.

Haiti

Bibliothèque Nationale d'Haiti: 193 rue du Centre, Port-au-Prince; tel. 509 223 2148; fax 509 223 2029.

Honduras

Biblioteca Nacional de Honduras: 6a Avda Salvador Mendieta, Tegucigalpa; tel. 504 228 577.

Hungary

Állami Gorkij Könyvtar (Gorky State Library): Molnár u 11, 1056 Budapest.

Institute for Musicology of Hungarian Academy of Sciences: PO Box 28, 1250, Budapest.

Magyar Tudományos Akadémia Zenetudományi Intézete: Táncsis M u 7, 1014 Budapest.

Music Information Centre of the Hungarian Council: POB 47, 1367 Budapest.

Országos Széchémyi Könyvtar (National Széchémyi Library): 1 Budavári Palota Fépület, 1827 Budapest; tel. 36 1 375 7533; fax 36 1 375 6167; website www.ozhk.hu.

Iceland

Landsbokasafn Islands (National Library of Iceland): Arngrimsgötu 3, IS-107 Reykjavik; tel. 354 1 563 5600; fax 354 1 563 5615; website saga .bok.hi.is.

India

National Library: Belvedere, Kolkata, West Bengal 700027; tel. 91 33 455 381.

Indonesia

Perpustakaan Nasional (National Library of Indonesia): J1 Salemba Raya 28, PO Box 3624, Jakarta 10002; tel. 62 21 310 1411.

Iran

National Library of Iran: Niavaran Street, Tehran; tel. 98 21 228 0937.

Iraq

National Library: Bab-el-Muaddum, Baghdad.

Ireland

National Library of Ireland: Kildare Street, Dublin 2; tel. 353 1 603 0200; fax 353 1 661 2523; website www.nli.ie.

Royal Irish Academy of Music: 36–38 Westland Row, Dublin 2.

Israel

AMLI Library of Music: 23 Arlosoroff Street, Haifa.

The Felicja Blumental Music Center & Library: PO Box 4882, 26 Bialik Street, 61048 Tel-Aviv; tel. 972 3 5250499; fax 972 3 5281032; e-mail ryna_k@tzion.tel-aviv.gov.il; Dir: Irit Schoenhorn.

Jewish National and University Library: PO Box 503, 91004 Jerusalem.

Italy

Archivio di Stato di Ancona: Via Maggini 80, 60127 Ancona.

Archivio di Stato de Bari: Via Pasubio 137, 70124 Bari.

Archivio di Stato di Bologna: Piazza dei Celestini 4, 40123 Bologna.

Archivio di Stato di Cagliari: Via Gallura 2, 09125 Cagliari.

Archivio di Stato di Catania: Via Vittorio Emanuele 156, 95131 Catania.

Archivio di Stato di Firenze: Loggiato degli Riffizi, 50100 Florence.

Archivio di Stato di Genova: Via Tommaso Reggio 14, 16123 Genoa; tel. 39 010 246 8373; fax 39 010 246 8992; website archivi.beniculturali.it/ ASGE.

Archivio de Stato di Milano: Via Senato 10, 20121 Milan; tel. 39 02 774 2161; fax 39 02 7742 16230.

Archivio di Stato di Napoli: Via Grande Archivio 5, 80138 Naples; tel. 39 081 563 8111; fax 39 081 563 8300; website archivi.beniculturali.it/ ASNA/index.htm.

Archivio di Stato di Palermo: Corso Vittorio Emanuele 31, 90133 Palermo.

Archivio Centrale dello Stato: Piazzale degli Archivi, 00144 Rome.

Archivio di Stato di Trieste: Via Lamarmora 17, 34139 Trieste; tel. 39 040 390 020; fax 39 040 394 461.

Archivio de Stato di Torino: Sezioni Riunite, Via Piave 21, 10122 Turin; tel. 39 011 540 382 / 460 4111; fax 39 011 546 176 / 436 4795; website www .multix.it/asto.

Associazione Culturale Archivi del Sud: Via Giovanni Spano 5, 07041 Alghero.

Biblioteca Augusta del Domune di Perugia: Palazzo Conestabile della Staffa, Via delle Prome 15, 06100 Perugia.

Biblioteca Centrale della Regione Siciliana: Corso Vittorio Emanuele 431, 90134 Palermo; tel. 39 091 581 602; fax 39 091 696 7644.

Biblioteca Civica: Via Tripoli 16, 15100 Alessandria.

Biblioteca Civica: Via Arte Botanico 5, 35123 Padua.

Biblioteca Civica: Piazza, Petrarca 2, 27100 Pavia.

Biblioteca Civica: Via Cappello 43, 37121 Verona; tel. 39 045 807 9710; fax 39 045 800 5701; website www.comune.verona.it/internet/ Bibliotecaciv.

Biblioteca Civica Angelo Mai: Piazza Vecchia 15, 24100 Bergamo; tel. 39 035 399 111; fax 39 035 240 555; website www.bibliotecamai.org.

Biblioteca Civica Bertoliana: Via Riale 5–13, 36100 Vicenza.

Biblioteca Civica Gambalunga: Via Gambalunga 27, 47037 Rimini; tel. 39 0541 704 311.

Biblioteca Civiche e Raccolte Storiche: Via Cittadella 5, 10122 Turin; tel. 39 011 57 651; fax 39 011 442 9830.

Biblioteca Comunale: Via Independenza 87, 22100 Como.

Biblioteca Comunale: Via Roberto Ardigò 13, 46100 Mantua.

Biblioteca Comunale Sormani: Palazzo Sormani, Corso di Porta Vittoria 6, 20133 Milan; tel. 39 02 8846 3350; fax 39 02 8846 3353; website www.comune.milano.it/biblioteche/sub_sorman.

Biblioteca Comunale: Piazza Brunaccini, 90134 Palermo; tel. 39 091 331 274.

Biblioteca Comunale: Via Madruzzo 26, 38100 Trento; tel. 39 0461 2321 7123; fax 39 0461 985 166.

Biblioteca Comunale: Borgo Cavour 18, 31100 Treviso.

Biblioteca Comunale A Saffi: Corso della Repubblica 72, 47100 Forli.

Biblioteca Comunale Arisotea: Via delle Scienze 17, 44100 Ferrara; tel. 39 0532 418 200; fax 39 0532 204 296; website www.comune.fe.it/biblio.

Biblioteca Comunale Classense: Via Baccarini 3, 48100 Ravenna.

Biblioteca Comunale degli Intronati: Via della Sapienza 5, 53100 Sienna; tel. 39 0577 280 704.

Biblioteca Comunale Forteguerriana: Piazza della Sapienza 1, PO Box 177, Pistoia.

Biblioteca Comunale Joppi: Piazza Marconi 8, 33100 Udine.

Biblioteca Comunale Labronica F. D. Guerrazzi: Viale del Forte San Pietro 15, 57100 Livorno; tel. 39 0586 219 265; fax 39 0586 219 151; website www.comune.livorno.it/txt/labronica.html.

Biblioteca Comunale Luciano Benincasa: Via Bernabei 32, 60121 Ancona; tel. 39 071 222 5020-2; fax 39 071 222 2109.

Biblioteca Comunale Passerini Landi: Via Neve 3, 29100 Piacenza.

Biblioteca del Civico Museo Correr: Piazza San Marco 52, Procuratie Nuove, 30100 Venice.

Biblioteca dell'Archivio di Stato di Trento: Via Rome 51, Trento.

Biblioteca della Città di Arezzo: Via dei Pileati-Palazzo Pretorio, 52100 Arezzo.

Biblioteca Durazzo Giustiniani: Via Balbi 1, 16126 Genoa.

Biblioteca Estense: Palazzo dei Musei, Piazzo San Agostino 309, 41100 Modena.

Biblioteca Medicea-Laurenziana: Piazza San Lorenzo 9, 50123 Florence; tel. 39 055 210 760; fax 39 055 230 2992.

Biblioteca Municipale A. Panizzi: Via Farini 3, 42100 Reggio Emilia; tel. 39 0522 456 078; fax 39 0522 456 081.

Biblioteca Nazionale Centrale: Piazza Cavalleggeri 1B, 50122 Florence; tel. 39 055 249 191; fax 39 055 234 2482; website www.bncf.firenze.sbn.it.

Biblioteca Nazionale Marciana: Palazzi della libreria Vecchia e della Zecca, San Marco 7, 30124 Venice; tel. 39 041 520 8788.

Biblioteca Nazionale Sagarriga-Visconti-Volpi: Palazzo Ateneo, Piazza Umberto, 70122 Bari; tel. 39 080 521 1298; fax 39 080 521 1298.

Biblioteca Nazionale Vittorio Emanuele III: Palazzo Reale, 80132 Naples; tel. 39 081 407 921; fax 39 081 403 820.

Biblioteca Palatina: Via del Conservatorio 27, 43100 Parma; tel. 39 0521 289 429; fax 39 0521 235 662.

Biblioteca Reale: Piazzo Castel.lo 191, 10100 Turin; tel. 39 011 545 305; fax 39 011 543 855.

Biblioteca Regionale Universitaria: Via dei Verdi 73, 98100 Messina; tel. 39 090 771 908.

Biblioteca Regionale Universitaria: Piazza Università 2, 95124 Catania; tel. 39 095 321 725; fax 39 095 326 862.

Biblioteca Riunita Civica e A Ursino Recupero: Via Biblioteca 13, 95124 Catania.

Biblioteca Statale e Libreria Civica: Via Ugolani Dati 4, 26100 Cremona; tel. 39 0732 413 543; fax 39 0732 413 544.

Biblioteca Statale di Lucca: Via San Maria Corteorlandini 12, 55100 Lucca; tel. 39 0583 491 271; fax 39 0583 46 770; website www.bslu.librari.beniculturali.it.

Biblioteca Universitaria: Via Università 32A, 09100 Cagliari.

Biblioteca Universitaria: Palazzo dell'Università, 27100 Pavia.

Biblioteca Universitaria: Via Curtatone e Montanara 15, 56100 Pisa; tel. 39 050 24 506.

Biblioteca Universitaria: Via Aurelio Saffi 2, 61029 Urbino.

Civica Biblioteca Queriniana: Via Mazzini 1, 25100 Brescia.

Istituto di Ricerca per il Teatro Musicale: Via Francesco Tamagno 65, 00168 Rome; tel. 39 066147277; fax 39 066144371; e-mail irtem@mclink.it; website www.irtem.it; Pres.: Carlo Marinelli; f. 1984; non-profit, publicly-financed institute sponsoring research into the fields of musical theatre, 20th century music, ethnomusicology and music-media relations; organizes annual international conference, and adminsters archives.

Istituto Nazionale di Studi Verdiani: Strada della Repubblica 56, 43100 Parma.

Istituto Storia Musica: Via Vittoria 6, 00187 Roma.

Raccolte storiche del Comune di Milano: Biblioteca e Archivio, Palazzo De Marchi, Via Borgonuovo 23, 20121 Milan.

Universitaria di Bologna Biblioteca: Via Zamboni 35, 40126 Bologna; tel. 39 051 243 420; fax 39 051 252 110; website www.bub.unibo.it.

Jamaica

Institute of Jamaica Library: 12–16 East Street, Kingston; tel. 1 876 9220 6207; fax 1 876 922 1147.

Japan

Documentation Centre of Modern Japanese Music: 4-19-6 Nishi Azabu; Minato-ku, Tokyo 106; tel. 81 3 400 0079.

Hiroshima Prefectural: 2020 Kami-Nobori-machi, Hiroshima.

Kyoto Prefectural Library: Okazaki Park, Kyoto Shi, Kyoto.

National Diet (Parliament) Library: 10-1 Nagatacho 1-chome, Chiyoda-ku, Tokyo 100.

Osaka Prefectural Nakanoshima Library: 1-2-10 Nakanoshima, Kita-ku, Osaka 530; tel. 81 6 203 0474.

Tokyo Metropolitan Central Library: 5-7-13 Minami-Azabu, Monato-ku, Tokyo 106; tel. 81 3 3442 8451; fax 81 3 3447 8924.

Jordan

Greater Amman Public Library: PO Box 182181, Amman; tel. 962 6 637 111.

Kenya

Central Government Archives: PO Box 30050, Nairobi.

Kenya National Archives: PO Box 49210, Moi Ave, Nairobi.

Democratic Republic of Korea

Grand People's Study House (National Library): PO Box 200, Pyongyang.

Republic of Korea

National Central Library: 60-1, Panpo-Dong, Seocho-Gu, Seoul; tel. 82 2 535 4142; fax 82 2 599 6942.

Laos

Bibliothèque Nationale: PO Box 122, Vientiane; tel. 856 21 212 452; fax 856 21 213 029.

Lebanon

Bibliothèque Nationale du Liban: Place de l'Etoile, Beirut; tel. 961 1 486 374; fax 961 1 374 079.

Libya

National Library of Libya: PO Box 9127, Benghazi.

Luxembourg

Bibliothèque Nationale: 37 Blvd F. D. Roosevelt, 2450 Luxembourg; tel. 352 229 755; fax 352 475 672; website www.etat.lu/BNL.

Malaysia

Perpustakaan Negara Malaysia (National Library of Malaysia): Lot G1 8 G2, Block A, Exchange Square, 50572 Kuala Lumpur; tel. 60 3 255 3144; fax 60 3 291 7436.

Mexico

Asociación Musical Manuel M. Ponce: AC, Bucareli No. 12, Desp 411, Mexico City.

Biblioteca Nacional de México: Insurgentes Sur s/n, Centro Cultural, Ciudad Universitaria, Coyoacán, 04510.

Monaco

Bibliothèque Louis Notari: 8 rue Louis Notari, 98000 Monte Carlo; tel. 377 9315 2940; fax 377 9315 2941.

Morocco

Bibliothèque Générale et Archives: PO Box 1003, Avenue ibn Battouta, Rabat; tel. 212 7 771 890; fax 212 7 776 062.

Myanmar

National Library: Six Storeyed Building, Strand Road, Yangon; tel. 95 1 72 058.

Netherlands

Gemeenschappelijke Openbare Bibliotheek: Piazza 201, 5611 AG Eindhoven.

Gemeenschappelijke Openbare Bibliotheek: Ridderstraat 29, 6511 TM Nijmegen.

Gemeentebibliothek: Hoogstraat 110, 3011 PV Rotterdam.

Gemeentel.ijke Utrechtse Openbare Bibliotheek: Oude Gracht 167, 3511 AL Utrecht.

Koninklijke Bibliotheek (Royal Library): PO Box 90407, Prins Willem-Alexanderhof 5, 2509 LK, The Hague; tel. 31 70 314 0911; fax 31 70 314 0450; website www.kb.nl.

Maatschappij tot Bevordering der Toonkunst: le jac Van Campenstraat 59, 1072 BD Amsterdam.

Openbare Bibliotheek: Brink 70, 7411 BW Deventer.

Openbare Bibliotheek: H. B. Blijdensteinstichting, Pijpennstraat 15, 7511 GM Enschede.

Openbare Bibliotheek: Doelenplein 1, 2011 XR Haarlem; tel. 31 23 157 600; fax 31 23 157 669.

Openbare Bibliotheek: Bilderdijkstraat 103, 2513 CM The Hague.

Openbare Bibliotheek: Koningsplein 1, 5038 WG Tilburg.

Openbare Bibliotheken (Public Library): Centraale Bibliotheek, Prinsengracht 587, 1016 HT Amsterdam.

Rotterdamsch Leeskabinet, Bibliotheek: Burg Oudlaan 50 (16), PO Box 1738, 3000 DR Rotterdam.

Stadsbibliotheek: Nieuwenhofstraat 1, 6211 KG Maastricht; tel. 31 43 329 3259; fax 31 43 329 2795.

Stichting Arnhemse Openbare en Gelderse Wetenschappelijke Bibliotheek: Koningstaat 26, 6801 DG Arnhem.

Stichting Centrale Bibliotheekdienst voor Friesland: Zuiderkruisweg 2, PO Box 530, 8901 BH Leeuwarden.

Stichting Openbare Bibliotheek: PO Box 30004, 9700 RE Groningen.

Stichting Openbare Bibliotheek: Hinthamerstraat 72, 5211 MR Hertogenbosch.

Stichting Openbare Bibliotheken: Gravelandseweg 55, 1217 EH Hilversum.

Stichting Samenwerkende Openbare Bibliotheken: Kruissstraat 71, 2611 ML Delft.

New Zealand

Auckland City Libraries: Lorne Street, PO Box 4138, Auckland 1; tel. 64 9 377 0209; fax 64 9 307 7741.

Canterbury Public Library: Orford Terrace and Gloucester Street, PO Box 1466, Christchurch 1.

Centre for New Zealand Music Ltd (SOUNZ New Zealand): PO Box 10 042, Level 3, 15 Brandon Street, Wellington.

Dunedin Public Library: 230 Moray Place, PO Box 5542, Dunedin; tel. 64 3 474 3690; fax 64 3 474 3660.

National Library of New Zealand, Music Room: PO Box 1467, Wellington; tel. 4 474 3000; fax 4 474 3035; website www.natlib.govt.nz; located at 70 Molesworth Street, Wellington.

Wellington Public Library: 65 Victoria Street, PO Box 1992, Wellington 1; tel. 64 4 801 4040; fax 64 4 801 4047.

Nicaragua

Biblioteca Nacional: Calle del Triunfo 302, PO Box 101, Managua.

Nigeria

National Library of Nigeria: 4 Wesley Street, Private Mail Bag 12626, Lagos; tel. 234 1 656 590.

Norway

Bergen offentlige bibliotek: Hordaland fylkesbibliotek, Strømgaten 6, 5015 Bergen; tel. 47 5556 8560.

Deichmanske Bibliotek: Henrik Ibsensgate 1, 0179 Oslo; tel. 47 2220 4335; fax 47 2211 3389.

Drammen folkebibliotek: Gamle Kirke Plass 7, PO Box 1136, 3001 Drammen.

Kristiansands folkebibliotek: Radhusgate 11, PO Box 476, 4601 Kristiansand.

Norsk Musikksamling (National Music Collection), Nasjonalbiblioteket (National Library of Norway): PO Box 2674 Solli, 0203 Oslo; tel. 47 23 27 60 43; fax 47 23 27 60 49; e-mail musikk-nbo@nb.no; website www.nb.no; collection of Norwegian printed music, manuscript music, sound recordings, books and papers; library located at Observatoriegt 2, Oslo.

Norsk Visearkiv (Norwegian Folk and Popular Song Archives): Tollbugt 28, 0157 Oslo.

Norwegian Music Information Centre: 28 Tollbugate, 10157 Oslo; tel. 47 2242 9090; fax 47 2242 9095; website www.notam.uio.no/nmi.

Rogaland folkebibliotek: Haakon VII's gate 11, PO Box 310/320, 4001 Stavanger.

Sør-Trøndelag folkebibliotek: Søndregate 5 og Kongensgate 2, PO Box 926, 7001 Trondheim.

Pakistan

National Library of Pakistan: H 558, Street 83, Sector G-6/4, Islamabad; tel. 92 51 822 449.

Punjab Public Library: Library Road, Lahore 1884.

Panama

Biblioteca Nacional: PO Box 2444, Panama City 1892; website www.binal.ac.pa.

Paraguay

Biblioteca y Archivo Nacionales: Mariscal Estigarriba 95, Asunción.

Peru

Biblioteca Nacional del Perú: Avda Abancay s/n, PO Box 2335, Lima; tel. 51 1 428 7690; fax 51 1 427 7331.

Philippines

National Library: Ermita, T. M. Kalaw Street, Ermita, Manila 1000; tel. 63 2 582 511.

Poland

Biblioteka Narodowa: ul Niepodległości 213, PO Box 36, 00973 Warsaw; tel. 48 22 259 271; fax 48 22 255 251.

Biblioteka Publiczna m st Warszawy: ul Koszykowa 26, 00950 Warsaw; tel. 48 22 628 2001; fax 48 22 621 1968.

Biblioteka Slaska (Silesian Library): ul Francuska 12, 529, 40956 Katowice; tel. 48 3 155 4305; fax 48 3 156 4953.

Biblioteka Uniwersytecka w Warszawie, Gabinet Zbiorów Muzycznych: ul Dobra 56–66, 00312 Warsaw.

Biblioteka w Krakowie PAN (Library of the Polish Academy of Sciences): ul Slawkowska 17, 31016 Kraków.

Library of the Polish Composers' Union: Rynek Starego Miasta 27, 00-272 Warsaw; tel. 48 22 8311634; fax 48 22 8310607; e-mail polmic@polmic.pl; website www.polmic.pl.

Miejska Biblioteka Publiczna (City Library): ul Franciskanska 1, 31004 Kraków.

Miejska Biblioteka Publiczna im Edwards Rqaczynskiego: Pl Wolnosci 19, 60967 Poznań.

Miejska Biblioteka Publiczna im L. Warynskiego: 90508 ód, Gdańsk 102.

Towarzystwo im Fryderyka Chopina (Frederic Chopin Society): Ostrogski Castle, 1 Okolnik Street, 00-368 Warsaw; tel. (48 22) 826-59-35; fax (48 22) 827-95-99; e-mail info@chopin.pl; website www.chopin.pl; Chair.: Kazimierz Gierzod; houses the Chopin Museum, Library, and archive of historical data and recordings.

Wojewódzka Biblioteca Publiczna i Ksiaeznica miejska: ul J Slowackiego 8, 87100 Torun.

Wojewódzka i Miejska Biblioteka Publiczna: ul Warszawska 45, 40010 Katowice.

Wojewódzka i Miejska Biblioteka Publiczna im H. Lopacinskiego: ul Narutowicza 4, 20950 Lublin.

Wojewódzka i Miejska Biblioteka Publiczna im St Staszica: ul Podgórna 15, 70952 Szczecin.

Wojewódzka i Miejska Biblioteka Publiczna im T. Mikulskiego: Rynek 58, 50116 Wrocław.

Portugal

Biblioteca Municipal Central: Largo do Campo Pequeno, Palácio Galveias, 1000 Lisbon.

Biblioteca Nacional: Rua Ocidental do Campo Grande 83, 1751 Lisbon; tel. 351 21 798 2000; fax 351 21 798 2140; website www.ibl.pt.

Romania

Academia Românía Library: Calea Victoriei 196, 71104 Bucharest; tel. 40 21 650 5680.

Biblioteca central de stat: Str Ion Ghica 4, Bucharest.

Russia

Moscow State Library: Vozdvizhenka 3, 101000 Moscow.

St Petersburg State Library: St Petersburg.

Singapore

National Library: c/o National Library Board, 1 Temasek Avenue, Suite 06-00 Millenia Tower, Singapore 039192; tel. (65) 6332 3133; fax (65) 6332 3611; website www.nlb.gov.sg.

Slovakia

Matica slovenska Kni ica (Slovak National Library): ulice Ladislava Novomeského 32, 03652 Martin; tel. 421 43 31 371.

South Africa

Cape Town City Libraries: Mayor's Garden, Longmarket Street, PO Box 4728, Cape Town 8000.

Durban Municipal Library: Smith Street, City Hall, PO Box 917, Durban 4000; tel. 27 31 309 4405; fax 27 31 309 6033.

Performing Arts Library: Central Johannesburg Library, Private Bag X 93, Marshalltown, Johannesburg 2107; tel. 27 011 870 1247; fax 27 11 870 1252; e-mail kalieB@joburg.org.za; Performing Arts Librarian: P. J. Burger.

Pretoria Public Library: 159 Andries Street, Pretoria 0002.

South African Library: Queen Victoria Street, PO Box 496, Cape Town 8001; tel. 27 21 246 320; fax 27 21 244 848.

State Library: 239 Vermeulen Street, PO Box 397, Pretoria 0001; tel. 27 12 218 931; fax 27 12 325 5984.

Spain

Biblioteca de Menéndez Pelayo: Rubio 6, Santander.

Biblioteca del Ministerio de Cultura: Calle San Marcos 40, 5A, 28004 Madrid; tel. 34 9142 924 44; website www.mec.es/mec/publicaciones/p_public.html.

Biblioteca Municipal del Ayuntamiento: Fuencarral 78, Madrid 4.

Biblioteca Nacional: Avda Calvo Sotelo, 28022 Madrid; website www.bne.es.

Biblioteca Provincial: Paseo del Misadero, Toledo.

Biblioteca Pública: F. Bonnemaison de Verdaguer i Callis, Baja de San Pedro 7, Barcelona.

Biblioteca Pública: Ramón Llull 3, Palma de Mallorca.

Biblioteca Pública de la Ciudad: Plaza de los Sitios 5, Zaragoza.

Biblioteca Pública del Estado: Jardines del Salón, s/n, Apdo Oficial, Granada.

Biblioteca Pública del Estado: Santa Nonia 5, Casa de Cultura, León.

Biblioteca Pública del Estado: Alfonso XII 19, 41001 Seville.

Biblioteca Pública e Archivo Distrital de Ponta Delgada: Rua Ernest do Canto, Ponta Delgada, San Miguel.

Biblioteca Pública Provincial: Plaza de San Juan, Burgos.

Biblioteca Pública Provincial: Avda Ramón Carranza 16, Cádiz.

Biblioteca Pública Provincial: Paseo de la Florida 9, Victoria.

Centro de Documentación Música y de la Danza: Torregalindo 10, 28016 Madrid; tel. 34 91 353 14 80; fax 34 91 353 13 73; e-mail cdmyd@inaem.mcu.es; website cdmyd.mcu.es.

Real Academia de Bellas Artes de San Fernando: Biblioteca, Alcala 13, 28014 Madrid; tel. 34 9153 190 53; website rabasf.onsde.es.

Sri Lanka

National Museum Library: Sr Marcus Fernando Mawatha, PO Box 854, Colombo 7.

Sweden

Gävle stadsbibliotek: Södra Strandgatan 6, Box 801, 80130 Gävle.

Göteborgs stadsbibliotek: Box 5404, 40229 Göteborg.

Helsingborgs stadsbibliotek: Bolbrogatan, 25225 Helsingborg.

Kungliga Biblioteket (Royal Library): Humlegården, PO Box 5039, 10241 Stockholm; tel. 46 8 679 5040; fax 46 8 611 6956; website www.kb.se.

Malmö stadsbibliotek: Regementsgatan 3, 21142 Malmö.

Norrköpings stadsbibliotek: Södra Promenaden 105, 60181 Norrköping.

Örebros stadsbibliotek: Nabbtorgsgatan 12, 70114 Örebro.

Swedish Music Information Centre: PO Box 27327, 79 Sandhamnsgatan, 10254 Stockholm; tel. 46 8 783 8800; fax 46 8 783 9510; website www.mic.stim.se.

Uppsala stadsbibliotek: Östra Ågatan 19, PO Box 643, 75127 Uppsala.

Västerås stadsbibliotek: Biskopsgatan 2, PO Box 717, 72187 Västerås; tel. 46 21 390000; fax 46 21 394680; e-mail musikinfo@vasteras.se; website www.bibliotek.vasteras.se; extensive media collection.

Switzerland

Allgemeine Bibliotheken der GGG: Gerbergasse 24, 4001 Basel; tel. 41 61 264 1111; fax 41 61 264 1190.

Berner Volksbücherie: Monbijoustrasse 45a, PO Box 2267, 3001 Bern.

Bibliothèque municipale: 11 Place Chauderon, 1003 Lausanne.

Bibliothèque publique et universitarie: 3 Place Numa-Droz, 2000 Neuchâtel.; tel. 41 38 207 300; fax 41 38 207 309.

Bibliothèques municipales: 16 Place de la Madeleine, 1204 Geneva.

Pestalozzi-Bibliothek: Zahingerstrasse 17, 8001 Zürich.

Stadtbibliothek: Dufourstrasse 26, 2502 Biel.

Stadtbibliothek: Hauptgasse 12, 4600 Olten.

Stadtbibliothek: Kauffmannweg 4, 6003 Lucerne.

Stadtbibliothek: Goldsteinstrasse 15, PO Box 91, 82025 Schaffhausen.

Stadtbibliothek: Museumstrasse 52, 8401 Winterthur; tel. 41 52 267 5145; fax 41 52 267 5140.

Syria

Al Maktabah Al Wataniah (National Library): Bab El-Faradj, Aleppo.

Al Zahiriah National Library: Bab el Barid, Damascus.

Thailand

Ho Samut Haeng Chat (National Library of Thailand): Samsen Road, Bangkok 10300; tel. 66 2 281 5212; fax 66 2 281 0263; website www.natlib.moe.go.th.

Tunisia

Dar al-Katub Al-Watanlyya/Bibliothèque Nationale: Ministere des Affaires Culturelles, 20 souk El Attarine, 1008 Tunis.

Turkey

Beyazit Deviet Kütüyshanesi (Beyazit State Library): Imaret Sok 18, Istanbul; tel. 90 212 522 2488; fax 90 212 526 1133.

Milli Kütüphane (National Library): Bahçelievier, 06490 Ankara; tel. 90 312 222 3812; fax 90 312 223 0451; website www.mkutup.gov.tr.

United Kingdom

Aberdeen Central Library: Rosemount Viaduct, Aberdeen, AB25 1GW, Scotland; tel. 01224 652511.

Belfast Public Library: Royal Ave, Belfast, BT1 1EK, Northern Ireland; tel. 028 9024 323.

Birmingham Central Library: Chamberlain Square, Birmingham B3 3HQ; tel. 0121 303 4511; fax 0121 233 4458.

Bristol Central Library: College Green, Bristol BS1 5TL; tel. 0117 903 7202.

British Library Music Collections: 96 Euston Road, London NW1 2DB; tel. (20) 7412-7772; e-mail music-collections@bl.uk; website www.bl.uk; Head of Music Collections: Chris Banks.

British Library Sound Archive: 96 Euston Road, London NW1 2DB; tel. 020 7412 7676; fax 020 7412 7441; website www.bl.uk.

British Music Information Centre: 10 Stratford Place, London W1C 1BA; tel. 020 7499 8567; fax 020 7499 4795; website www.bmic.co.uk.

Cardiff Central Library: Frederick Street, Cardiff, CF10 2DU, Wales; tel. (29) 2038-2116; Music Librarian: Sheila Basford.

Carmarthen Public Library: St Peter's Street, Carmarthen, SA31 1LN, Wales; tel. 01267 224830.

Dundee Central Library: The Wellgate, Dundee, DD1 1DB, Scotland; tel. 01382 431500; fax 01382 431558.

Edinburgh Central Library: George IV Bridge, Edinburgh, EG1 1EG, Scotland; tel. 0131 242 8000.

English Folk Dance and Song Society: Cecil Sharp House, Library, 2 Regent's Park Road, London NW1 7AY; tel. 020 7485 2206; website www .efdss.org.

Leeds Central Library: Calverley Street, Municipal Building, Leeds LS1 3AB; tel. 0113 247 8911.

Liverpool Central Library: William Brown Street, Liverpool L3 8EW; tel. 0151 225 5463; fax 0151 207 1342.

Llyfrgell Genedlaethol Cymru (National Library of Wales): Aberystwyth, Ceredigion, SY23 3BU, Wales; tel. (1970) 632800; fax (1970) 615709; e-mail holi@llgc.org.uk; website www.llgc.org.uk.

Manchester Central Library: St Peter's Square, Manchester M2 5PD; tel. (161) 2341976; fax (161) 2341961; e-mail music@libraries.manchester .gov.uk.

Mitchell Library: North Street, Glasgow, G3 7DN, Scotland; tel. 0141 248 7030; fax 0141 305 2815; website www.mitchelllibrary.org.

National Library of Scotland: George IV Bridge, Edinburgh, EH1 1EW, Scotland; tel. (131) 226-4531; fax (131) 622-4803; e-mail music@nls.uk; website www.nls.uk/collections/music/index.html; Head of Music: Almut Boehme.

Newcastle upon Tyne City Library: Princess Square, Newcastle upon Tyne NE99 1DX; tel. 0191 261 0691.

University of Birmingham: Department of Music, Barber Institute, Edgbaston, Birmingham B15 2TT; website www.bham.ac.uk.

United States of America

American Music Center: 30 W 26th Street, Suite 1001, New York, NY 10010-2011; tel. 1 212 366 5260; fax 1 212 366 5265; website www.amc.net.

Atlanta-Fulton Public Library: 1 Margaret Mitchell Square NW, Atlanta, GA 30303; website www.af.public.lib.ga.us.

Austin Public Library: 800 Guadalupe Street, PO Box 2287, Austin, TX 78768; website www.cityofaustin.org/library.

Birmingham Public Library: 2100 Park Place, Birmingham, AL 35203; tel. 1 205 226 3610; website www.bplonline.org.

Boston Public Library: 700 Boylston Street, Boston, MA 02116; tel. 1 617 536 5400; website www.bpl.org.

Buffalo and Erie County Public Library: 1 Lafayette Square, Buffalo, NY 14203; tel. 1 716 858 8900; fax 1 716 858 6211; website www.buffalolib .org.

California State Library: PO Box 942837, Sacramento, CA 94237; website www.library.ca.gov.

Carnegie Library of Pittsburgh: 4400 Forbes Avenue, Pittsburgh, PA 15213; tel. 1 412 622 3114; website www.clpgh.org.

Chicago Public Library: 400 S State Street, Chicago, IL 60605; tel. 1 312 747 4882; fax 1 312 747 4887; website www.chipublib.org.

City of Phoenix Public Library: 1221 N Central Avenue, Phoenix, AZ 85004; tel. 1 602 261 8836; website www.ci.phoenix.az.us.

Cleveland Public Library: 325 Superior Avenue, Cleveland, OH 44114-1271; tel. 1 216 623 2881; fax 1 216 623 2935; website www.cpl.org.

Columbus Metropolitan Library: 28 S Hamilton Road, Columbus, OH 43213.

Connecticut State Library: 231 Capitol Avenue, Hartford, CT 06106.

Dallas Public Library: 1515 Young Street, Dallas, TX 75201.

Denver Public Library: 1357 Broadway, Denver, CO 80203; tel. 1 303 640 8880; fax 1 303 595 3034; website www.denver.lib.co.us.

Detroit Public Library: 5201 Woodward Avenue, Detroit, MI 48202; tel. 1 313 833 1460; fax 1 313 833 5039; website www.detroit.lib.mi.us.

Enoch Pratt Free Library: 400 Cathedral Street, Baltimore, MD 21201.

Free Library of Philadelphia: Logan Square, Philadelphia, PA 19103; tel. 1 215 686 5322; fax 1 215 563 3628; website www.library.phila.gov.

Houston Public Library: 500 McKinney Avenue, Houston, TX 77002.

Illinois State Library: Springfield, IL 62756.

Indiana State Library: 140 N Senate Avenue, Indianapolis, IN 46204.

Indianapolis-Marion County Public Library: 40 E St Clair Street, PO Box 211, Indianapolis, IN 46406.

Kansas City Public Library: 311 E 12th Street, Kansas City, MO 64106.

Library of Congress, Music Division: James Madison Building, LM 113, Washington, DC 20540; tel. 1 202 287 5507; website www.loc.gov.

Library of Michigan: 702 W Kalamazoo Street, PO Box 30740, Lansing, MI 48909; tel. 1 517 373 1300.

Library of Virginia: 800 E Broad Street, Richmond, VA 23219.

Los Angeles Public Library: 630 W Fifth Street, Los Angeles, CA 90071; tel. 1 213 612 3263; fax 1 213 612 0536.

Louisville Free Public Library: 301 York Street, Louisville, KY 40203.

Memphis and Shelby County Public Library: 1850 Peabody Avenue, Memphis, TN 38104.

Miami-Dade Public Library: 101 W Flagler Street, Miami, FL 33130; tel. 1 305 375 1505; fax 1 305 375 4436.

Milwaukee Public Library: 814 W Wisconsin Avenue, Milwaukee, WI 53233; tel. 1 414 286 3000; fax 1 414 286 2794; website www.mpl.org.

Minneapolis Public Library: 300 Nicollet Mall, Minneapolis, MN 55401; tel. 1 612 630 6000; fax 1 612 630 6210; website mpls.lib.mn.us.

Missouri State Library: 2002 Missouri Blvd, Jefferson City, MI 65102.

New Hampshire State Library: 20 Park Street, Concord, NH 03301.

New Jersey State Library: 185 W State Street, Trenton, NJ 08625.

New Mexico State Library: 325 Don Gaspar, Santa Fe, NM 87503.

New Orleans Public Library: 219 Loyola Avenue, New Orleans, LA 70140; tel. 1 504 596 2500.

New York Public Library: 40 Lincoln Center Plaza, New York, NY 10023-7498; tel. 1 212 870 1639; fax 1 212 787 3852; website www.nypl.org.

New York State Library: Cultural Education Center, Empire State Plaza, Albany, NY 12230; tel. 1 518 474 5930; fax 1 518 474 5786; website www.nysl.nysed.gov.

Newark Public Library: 5 Washington Street, PO Box 630, Newark, NJ 07101; tel. 1 973 733 7840; fax 1 973 733 5648; website www.npl.org.

Oregon State Library: State Library Building, Salem, OR 97310.

Providence Public Library: 225 Washington Street, Providence, RI 02903; tel. 1 401 455 8000; fax 1 401 455 8080; website www.provlib.org.

Public Library of Cincinnati and Hamilton County: 800 Vine Street, Library Square, Cincinnati, OH 45202; tel. 1 513 369 6955; fax 1 513 369 6067.

Richmond Public Library: 101 E Franklin Street, Richmond, VA 23219.

Rochester Public Library: 115 South Avenue, Rochester, NY 14604.

Sacramento Public Library: 1010 Eighth Street, Sacramento, CA 95814.

St Louis Public Library: 1301 Olive Street, St Louis, MI 63103; tel. 1 314 241 2288; fax 1 314 241 3840.

St Paul Public Library: 90 W Fourth Street, St Paul, MN 55102.

San Diego Public Library: 820 East Street, San Diego, CA 92101.

San Francisco Public Library, Art and Music Center: Civic Center, San Francisco, CA 94102; tel. 1 415 557 4400; fax 1 415 557 4524.

Seattle Public Library: 1000 Fourth Avenue, Seattle, WA 98104.

State Library of Massachusetts: 341 State House, Boston, MA 02133.

State Library of Ohio: 65 S Front Street, Columbus, OH 43215.

State Library of Pennsylvania: 333 Market Street, Harrisburg, PA 17105-1745.

United States Information Agency: Arts America Program, 301 Fourth Street, Room 568, Washington, DC 20547.

Washington State Library: Olympia, WA 98504.

Uruguay

Biblioteca Nacional del Uruguay: 18 de Julio 1790, Casilla 452, Montevideo; tel. 598 2 496 011.

Venezuela

Biblioteca Nacional: Bolsa a San Francisco, PO Box 68350, Caracas 106.

Viet Nam

National Library of Viet Nam: 31 Trang-Thi, 10000 Hanoi.

National Library II: 69 Gia-Long St, Ho Chi Minh City 1976.

APPENDIX G: MUSIC CONSERVATOIRES

Argentina

Conservatorio Provincial de Música de Bahia Blanca: Belgrano 446, 800 Bahia Blanca, Provincia de Buenos Aires.

Conservatorio de Música Julián Aguirre: Gral Rodríguez 7672, Banfield, Provincia de Buenos Aires.

Conservatorio Municipal de Música Manuel de Falla: Sarmiento 1551, 1042 Buenos Aires.

Conservatorio Nacional de Música: Carlos López Buchardo, Calle 1521, 1024 Buenos Aires.

Pontificia Universidad Católica Argentin Santa Maria de los Buenos Aires: Faculty of Arts and Music, Juncal 1912, Buenos Aires 1116.

Australia

Canberra School of Music: National Institute of the Arts, Australian National University, Building 105B, Canberra, ACT 0200; tel. 61 2 6125 5700; fax 61 2 6248 0997; website www.anu.edu.au/ITA/music.

New South Wales State Conservatorium of Music: Macquarie St, Sydney, NSW 2000.

Newcastle Conservatorium of Music: Auckland Street, Newcastle, NSW 2300; tel. 61 2 4921 8900; fax 61 2 4921 8958; e-mail conservatorium@newcastle.edu.au; website www.newcastle.edu.au.

Queensland Conservatorium of Music: Griffith University, PO Box 3428, South Brisbane, Qld 4101; website www.gu.edu.au.

Tasmanian Conservatorium of Music: University of Tasmania, PO Box 63, Hobart, TAS 7001; tel. 61 3 6226 7314; fax 61 3 6266 7333; website www.utas.edu.au/music.

University of Adelaide: Elder Conservatorium of Music, PO Box 498, Adelaide, SA 5001; website www.adelaide.edu.au.

University of Melbourne: Faculty of Music, Parkville, Vic. 3010; tel. 61 3 8344 5256; fax 61 3 8344 5346; e-mail enquiries@music.unimelb.edu.au; website www.music.unimelb.edu.au.

University of Queensland: Faculty of Music, Qld 4072; website www.uq.edu.au.

University of Sydney, Department of Music: Sydney, NSW 2006; tel. 61 2 9351 2222; website www.usyd.edu.au.

University of Western Australia: School of Music, 35 Stirling Highway, Crawley, WA 6009; website www.uwa.edu.au.

Victorian College of the Arts: 234 St Kilda Road, Southbank, Melbourne, Vic. 3006; tel. 61 3 9685 9300; fax 61 3 9682 1841; website www.vca.unimelb.edu.au.

Wollongong Conservatorium: Gleniffer Brae: Murphys Avenue, PO Box 62, Keiraville, NSW 2500; tel. 61 2 4228 1122; fax 61 2 4226 6942; website www.wollconmusic.nsw.edu.au.

Austria

Bruckner-Konservatorium des Landes Oberösterreich: Wildbergstrasse 18, 4040 Linz; tel. 43 70 70 10000; fax 43 70 70 1000 30; website www.bk-linz.at.

Hochschule für Musik und Darstellande Kunst: Leonhardstrasse 15, 8010 Graz; tel. 43 316 389.

Hochschule für Musik und Darstellende Kunst: Universität für Musik und darstellende Kunst Wien, Anton-von-Webern-Platz 1, 1030 Vienna; tel. (1) 71155; website www.mdw.ac.at.

Horak-Konservatorium für Musik und Darstellende Kunst: Hegelgasse 3, 1010 Vienna.

Kärntner Landeskonservatorium: Miesstalerstrasse 8, 9021 Klagenfurt.

Konservatorium der Stadt Innsbruck: Museumstrasse 17a, 6020 Innsbruck.

Konservatorium der Stadt Wien: Johannesgasse 4a, 1010 Vienna 1.

Konservatorium für Musik und Dramatische Kunst: Mühlgasse 28–30, 1040 Vienna.

Universitat Mozarteum Salzburg: Alpenstrasse 48, 5020 Salzburg; tel. 43 662 6198; fax 43 662 6198-3033; website www.moz.ac.at.

Belgium

Chapelle Musicale Reine Elisabeth: Chaussée de Tervuren 445, 1410 Argenteuil-Waterloo; tel. 32 2 352 0110; fax 32 2 351 1024; e-mail info@cmre.be; website www.cmre.be.

Conservatoire de Musique de Charleroi: 1 rue Adolphe Biarrent, 6000 Charleroi.

Conservatoire de Musique de Grand: 54 rue de la Hoogpoort, 9000 Ghent.

Conservatoire de Musique de Huy: 11-13 rue du Palais de Justice, 5200 Huy.

Conservatoire de Musique de Ostende: 36 rue de Rome, 8400 Ostend.

Conservatoire de Musique de Tournai: 2 Place Reine Astrid, 7500 Tournai.

Conservatoire de Musique de Verviers: 6 rue Chapuis, 4800 Verviers; website users.skynet.be/conservatoire/.

Conservatoire de Musique: Chaussée de Louvain 121, 5000 Namur.

Conservatoire Royal de Musique de Bruxelles: 30 rue de la Régence, 1000 Brussels; tel. 32 2 511 0427; website www.conservatoire.be.

Conservatoire Royal de Musique de Liège: 14 rue Forgeur, 4000 Liège; tel. 32 4 222 0306.

Conservatoire Royal de Musique de Mons: 7 rue de Nimy, 7000 Mons.

Institut de Musique Sacrée: 28 rue Juppin, 5000 Namur.

Koninklijke Beiaardschool Jef Denyn: Fredrik de Mersdestraat 63, 2800 Mechelen; tel. 32 15 20 47 92; fax 32 15 203176; e-mail beiaardschool@yucom.be; website www.beiaardschool.be.

Koninklijk Musiekconservatorium van Gent: Hoogpoort 64, 9000 Ghent.

Koninklijk Muziekconservatorium van Brussel: Regentschapstraat 30, 1000 Brussels.

Koninklijk Vlaams Conservatorium van Antwerpen: Desguinler 25, 2018 Antwerp.

Stedelijk Conservatorium: Dirk Boutslaan 60–62, 3000 Leuven; tel. 016 22 21 21; fax 016 31 08 28; e-mail conservatorium@leuven.be; website www.leuven.be; Contact: Cathérine Legaey.

Stedelijk Muziekconservatorium: Melaan 3–5, 2800 Mechelen; tel. 015 28-29-80; fax 015 28-29-89; e-mail conservatorium.mechelen@skynet.be; Dir Jan de Maeyer.

Stedelijk Muziekconservatorium: Sint-Jacobsstratt 23, 8000 Bruges.

Bolivia

Academia de Música Hohner: Calle Goitia 162, La Paz.

Conservatorio Nacional de Música: Avda 6 de Agosto, No. 2092, La Paz.

Escuela Superior de Bellas Artes: Calle Rosendo Gutiérrez 323, La Paz.

Brazil

Conservatorio Brasileiro de Música: Avda Graça Aranha 57, No. 12, 20030 Rio de Janeiro; website www.cbm-musica.org.br.

Conservatorio Dramático e Musical de Sao Paulo: Avda Sao Joao 269, São Paulo.

Escola de Música e Belas Artes do Paraná: rue Emilian Perneta 179, 80000 Curitiba, Paraná.

Escola de Música-Minas Gerais: rue Santa Catarina 466, 30000 Belo Horizonte, Mina Gerais.

Faculdade de Música Mae de Deus: Avda Sao Paulo 651, CP106, 86100 Londrina, Paraná.

Faculdade de Música Sagrado Coracao de Jesus: Rua Caraibas 882, CP 8383, Villa Pompéia, São Paulo.

Faculdade Santa Marcelina: Rua Dr Emilio Ribas 89, 05006 São Paulo; tel. 11 3824 5800; e-mail fasm@fasm.edu.br; website www.fasm.com.br.

Fundaçao Universidade de Brasília: Institute of Arts and Communication, Campus Universitário, Asa Norte, 70910 Brasilia, DF.

Instituto de Letras a Artes: Rua Marechal Floriano 179, 96100 Pelotas, RS.

Instituto de Música de Bahia: Universidade Catolica de Salvador, Rua Carlos Gomes 400, Centro, 4000 Salvador, Bahia.

UNESP-Universidade Estadual Júlio de Mesquita Filho: Instituto do Artes do Planalto, Dept of Music, Rua Dom Luis Lasagna 400, São Paulo.

Universidade de Sao Paulo (USP): Department of Music, Cidade Universitaria, Butanta, 05508 São Paulo; website www.usp.br.

Universidade do Rio de Janeiro: Letters and Arts Center, Avda Pasteur 296, 22290 Rio de Janeiro; website www.uerj.br.

Universidade Federal de Bahia: Escola de Música, Parque Universitario Edgard Santos, Canela, 40140, Salvador, Bahia; website www.ufba.br.

Universidade Federal de Minas Gerais: Escola de Música, Avda Antônio Carlos 6627, Pampulha, 3000 Belo Horizonte, Minas Gerais; website www.ufmg.br.

Universidade Federal de Paraiba: Department of Music, Cidade Universitária, 5800 Joao Pessôa, Paraiba; website www.ufpb.br.

Universidade Federal do Rio de Janeiro: Escola de Música, Rua do Passeio 98, Rio de Janeiro; website www.ufrj.br.

Bulgaria

Academy of Music and Dance: Ul. Todor Samodumov 2, PO Box 117, 4025 Plovidiv; tel. (32) 601-441; fax (32) 631-668; e-mail amti_sekretar@evrocom.net; Rector Prof. Anastas Slavchev; faculties of Music Pedagogy, Music Folklore and Choreography, and Language and Special Training.

Conservatoire Bulgare d'Etat: Sofia 1505.

Canada

Acadia University, School of Music: Wolfville, NS B0P 2R6; tel. 1 902 585 2001; website www.acadiau.ca.

Banff Centre, School of Fine Arts: PO Box 1020, Banff, AB T1L 1H5; tel. 1 403 762 6100; website www.banffcentre.ca.

Brandon University, School of Music: 270-18 Street, Brandon, MB R7A 6A9; website www.brandonu.ca.

Carleton University, School for Studies in Art and Culture, Music Programme: 1125 Colonel By Drive, Ottawa, ON K1S 5B6; tel. (613) 520-5770; fax (613) 520-3905; website www.carleton.ca.

Concordia University, Department of Music: 1455 de Maisonneuve Blvd W, Montréal, QC H3G 1M8; tel. 1 514 848 2424; website www.concordia.ca.

Conservatoire de Musique de Québec: 270 St Amable, QC G1R 5G1.

Dalhousie University, Department of Music: Arts Centre, Room 514, Halifax, NS B3H 4R2; tel. 1 902 494 2211; website www.dal.ca.

Maritime Conservatory of Music: 6199 Chebucto Road, Halifax, NS B3H 1X8; tel. 1 902 423 6995.

McGill University, Faculty of Music: 555 Sherbrooke Street W, Montréal, QC H3A 1E3; tel. 1 514 398 4455; website www.mcgill.ca.

McMaster University, Department of Music: 1280 Main Street W, Hamilton, ON L8S 4M2; website www.mcmaster.ca.

Mount Allison University, Department of Music: Sackville, NB E4L 1A6; website www.mta.ca.

Queen's University, School of Music: Kingston, ON K7L 3N6; website www.queensu.ca.

Royal Conservatory of Music: 273 Bloor Street W, Toronto, ON M5S 1W2; tel. (416) 408-2824; fax (416) 408-3096; website www.rcmusic.ca; Pres.: Dr Peter Simon. f. 1886. Largest and oldest independent arts educator in Canada, serving more than 500,000 active participants each year. Offers opportunities for learning and development through music and the arts, in all Canadian provinces and in a number of international locations.

Simon Fraser University, School for the Contemporary Arts: 8888 University Drive, Burnaby, BC V5A 1S6; tel. (604) 291-3363; fax (604) 291-5907; e-mail ca@sfu.ca; website www.sfu.ca/sca.

St Francis Xavier University, Department of Music: PO Box 108, Antigonish, NS B2G 1C0; website www.stfx.ca.

Université de Moncton, Department of Music: Moncton, NB E1A 3E9; website www.umoncton.ca.

Université de Montréal, Faculty of Music: 2900 Blvd Edouard-Montpetit, Montréal, QC H3C 3J7; website www.umontreal.ca.

Université Laval, Faculté de musique: Pavillon Louis-Jacques-Casault, Cité Universitaire, Québec, QC G1K 7P4; tel. 1 418 656 2131; fax 1 418 656 2809; website www.ulaval.ca.

University of Alberta, Department of Music: Edmonton, AB T6G 2C9; website www.ualberta.ca.

University of British Columbia (UBC), School of Music: 6361 Memorial Road, Vancouver, BC V6T 1W5; website www.ubc.ca.

University of Calgary, Department of Music: 2500 University Dr., NW Calgary, AB T2N 1N4; tel. 1 403 220 5110; website www.ucalgary.ca.

University of Guelph College of Arts, Department of Music: Room 207, Guelph, ON N1G 2W1; website www.uogelph.ca.

University of Lethbridge, Department of Music: 4401 University Dr., Lethbridge, AB T1K 3M4; website www.uleth.ca.

University of Manitoba, School of Music: 65 Dafoe Road, Winnipeg, MB R3T 2N2; tel. 1 204 474 8880; website www.umanitoba.ca.

University of Ottawa, Department of Music: 550 Cumberland, Ottawa, ON K1N 6N5; tel. 1 613 562 5700; website www.music.uottawa.ca.

University of Regina, Department of Music: 3737 Wascana Pkwy, Regina, SK S4S 0A2; website www.uregina.ca.

University of Saskatchewan, Department of Music: Saskatoon, SK S7N 0W0; tel. 1 306 966 4343; website www.usask.ca.

University of Toronto, Faculty of Music: Edward Johnson Building, Room 238, 80 Queen's Park Circle, Toronto, ON M5S 1A1; tel. 1 416 978 2011; website www.utoronto.ca.

University of Victoria, School of Music: PO Box 1700, Victoria, BC V8W 2Y2; website www.uvic.ca.

University of Western Ontario, Don Wright Faculty of Music: London, ON N6A 3K7; tel. (519) 661-2043; fax (519) 661-3531; e-mail music@uwo.ca; website www.uwo.ca; Dean: Dr Robert Wood.

University of Windsor, School of Music: 401 Sunset Ave, Windsor, ON N9B 3P4; tel. 1 519 253 4232.

Vancouver Academy of Music: Music Centre, Vanier Park, 1270 Chestnut Street, Vancouver, BC V6J 4R9; tel. 1 604 734 2301; fax 1 604 731 1920; website www.vam.bc.ca.

Victoria Conservatory of Music: 901 Pandora Ave, Victoria, BC V8V 3P4; tel. 1 250 386 5311; fax 1 250 386 6602; website www.vcm.bc.ca.

Wilfrid Laurier University, Faculty of Music: 75 University Ave W, Waterloo, ON N2L 3C5; tel. 1 519 884 1970; fax 1 519 886 9351; website www.wlu.ca.

York University, Department of Music: 4700 Keele Street, North York, ON M3J 1P3; tel. 1 416 736 2100; website www.yorku.ca.

Chile

Conservatorio Nacional de Música: Compañia, 1264, Santiago.

Pontificia Universidad Católica de Chile: Faculty of Architecture and Fine Arts, Avda Alameda 340, PO Box 114-D, Santiago; website www.puc.cl.

Universidad Católica de Valparaiso, Conservatorio de Música: Avda Brasil 2950, Valparaiso; website www.ucv.cl.

Universidad de Chile, Faculty of Fine Arts: Avda Bernardo O'Higgins 1058, Casilla 10-D, Santiago; website www.uchile.cl.

People's Republic of China

Central Conservatory of Music: 43 Baojiajie, Beijing; website www.ccom.edu.cn.

Conservatory of Chinese Music: 17 Qianhaixijie, Beijing.

Guangzhou Xinghai Conservatory of Music: 48 Xianliedonghenglu, Guangzhou.

Harbin Normal University, Department of Music: Harbin.

Nanjing Arts College: 15 Hujubeilu, Nanjing.

Northwest Teacher's College, Department of Music: Lanzhou.

Shandong Academy of Arts, Music Division: Shandong.

Shanghai Conservatory of Music: 20 Fen Yang Road, Shanghai 200031.

Shengyang Conservatory of Music: No. 1, Section 2, San Hao Street, Peace District, Shengyang.

Sichuan Conservatory of Music: Xinnanmenwai, Chengdu.

Tianjin Conservatory of Music: 5, 11th Meridian Road, Tianjin.

Wuhan Conservatory of Music: 255 Jiefanglu, Wuchang District, Wuhan.

Xian Conservatory of Music: 118 Changanzhonglu, Xian 710061.

Colombia

Conservatorio Nacional de Música: Departmento de Música, Facultad de Artes, Universidad Nacional, Bogotá.

Universidad del Atlántico, Conservatorio de Música: Carrera 43, Nos 50–53, Apdo Nacional 148, Aéreo 1890, Barranquilla.

Costa Rica

Universidad de Costa Rica (UCR), School of Fine Arts: San José website www.ucr.ac.cr.

Cuba

Instituto Superior de Arte, Facultad de Música: Calle 120, No. 1110, Havana.

Czech Republic

Janá kova Akademie Mûzick ch Umeni (Janá ek Academy of Music and Dramatic Arts): Komenskeho nam 6, 662 15 Brno.

Konservato v Brne (Brno Conservatory): Trida Kpt Jarose 43–45, Brno.

Konservato v Otrave (Ostrava Conservatory): Hrabakova 1, Ostrava.

Prazska Konservator (Prague Conservatoire): Na Rejdisti 1, 110 00 Prague 1; tel. 420 222 319 102; fax 420 222 326 406; e-mail conserv@prgcons.cz; website www.prgcons.cz; Dir: Veroslav Neumann.

Vysoká Skola Mûzick ch Umeni v Praha (Academy of Music and Dramatic Arts Prague): D m um lc, Alsovo náb e í 12, 1101 00 Prague 1.

Denmark

Carl Nielsen Academy of Music Odense: Islandsgade 2, 5000 Odense C; tel. 45 66 11 06 63; fax 45 66 17 77 63; e-mail dfm@adm.dfm.dk; website www.dfm.dk.

Det Fynske Musikkonservatorium (The Funen Conservatory of Music): Islandsgade 2, 5000 Odense C; tel. 45 66 11 06 63; fax 45 66 17 77 63; e-mail dfm@adm.dfm.dk; website www.dfm.dk.

Det Jyske Musikkonservatorium (Royal Academy of Music, Århus): Fuglesangs Allé 26, PO Box 1300, 8210 Århus V; tel. 45 8948 3388; fax 45 8948 3322; website www.musik-kons.dk.

Det Kongelige Danske Musikkonservatorium (The Royal Danish Conservatory of Music): Niels Brocksgade 7, 1574 Copenhagen V; tel. 45 33 69 22 69; fax 45 33 69 22 79; e-mail dkdm@dkdm.dk; website www.dkdm.dk.

Nordjysk Musikkonservatorium (North Jutland Conservatory of Music): Ryesgade 52, 9000 Ålborg; tel. 45 98 12 77 44; fax 45 98 11 37 63; website www.nordkons.dk.

University of Copenhagen, Department of Music: Frue Plads, 1168 Copenhagen K; website www.ku.dk.

Vestjysk Musikkonservatorium (West Jutland Conservatory of Music): Islandsgade 50, 6700 Esbjerg; website www.vmk.dk.

Dominican Republic

Conservatorio Nacional de Música: Cesar Nicolas Penson, Santo Domingo.

Ecuador

Conservatorio Nacional de Música, Quito: Madrid 11-59, Quito.

Egypt

Cairo Conservatoire of Music: Academy of Arts, Japan Street, Al Giza, Cairo; tel. 202 5613451; fax 202 561-1034; e-mail caiconserv@idsc.net.eg; Dean: Dr Rageh Daoud; part of the Academy of Arts; studies at all levels.

El Salvador

Centro Nacional de Artes CENAR, Department of Music: 6A Avda Norte 319, San Salvador.

Estonia

Tallinn State Conservatory: Vabaduse Pst 130, 200015 Tallinn.

Finland

Helsinki Conservatory of Music: Ruoholahdentori 6, 00180 Helsinki; tel. 358 5860580; fax 358 58605868; e-mail rea.warme@stadia.fi; Rector: Rea Warme.

Jyväskylä Polytechnic, School of Music: Pitkäkatu 18–22, 40700 Jyväskylä; tel. 358 14 444 7371; fax 358 14 444 7399; e-mail music@jypoly.fi; website www.jypoly.fi.

Kuopion Konservatorio: Kuopionlahdenkatu 23 C, 70200 Kuopio; tel. 358 17 262 3617; website www.kuopionkonservatorio.net.

Oulun Kaupungin Konservatorio: Lintulammentie 1 K, 90140 Oulu; tel. 358 8 314 1951.

Paijat-Hameen Konservatorio: Sibeliuksenkatu 8, 15110 Lahti; tel. 358 3 752 0161.

Sibelius Academy of Music: Töölönkatu 28, 00260 Helsinki; website www.siba.fi.

Sibeliusmuseum Misikvetenskapliga Institutionen vid Åbo Akademi (Sibelius Museum, Musicological Institution at Åbo Academy): Biskopsgatan 17 20500, Åbo 50.

Tampereen Konservatorio: F. E. Sillanpään Katu 9, 33230 Tampere; tel. 358 3 245 2500; fax 358 3 245 2501; website www.tampereenkonservatorio.net.

France

Conservatoire de Caen: 1 rue du Carel, 14027 Caen Cédex.

Conservatoire National de Région: Bordeaux, 22 Quai Saint Croix, 33800 Bordeaux; tel. 33 5 56 92 96 96; fax 33 5 56 92 22 30.

Conservatoire National de Région, Dijon: 24 Blvd Clemenceau, 21000 Dijon; tel. 33 3 80 73 22 43.

Conservatoire National de Région, Grenoble: 6 Chemin de Gordes, 38100 Grenoble; tel. 33 4 76 46 48 44.

Conservatoire National de Région, Lille: 48 Place du Concert, 59800 Lille; tel. 33 3 20 74 57 50.

Conservatoire National de Région, Limoges: 9 rue Fritz-James, 87000 Limoges; tel. 33 5 55 79 71 81.

Conservatoire National de Région, Marseille: 2 Place Carli, 13001 Marseille; tel. 33 4 91 55 35 72.

Conservatoire National de Région, Metz: 2 rue Paradis, 57036 Metz; tel. 33 3 87 55 54 56; fax 33 3 87 61 51 08.

Conservatoire National de Région, Montpellier: 14 rue Eugene Lisbonne, 34000 Montpellier; tel. 33 4 67 60 79 33.

Conservatoire National de Région, Nancy: 3 rue Michel Ney, 54000 Nancy; tel. 33 3 83 25 27 95; fax 33 3 83 36 47 85.

Conservatoire National de Région, Nantes: rue Gaëtan Rondeau Ile Beaulieu, 44200 Nantes; tel. 33 2 51 25 00 02.

Conservatoire National de Région, Nice: 24 Blvd de Cimiez, 06000 Nice; tel. 33 4 93 53 01 17.

Conservatoire National de Région, Poitiers: 5 rue Franklin, 86000 Poitiers; tel. 33 5 49 01 83 67; fax 33 5 49 01 19 94.

Conservatoire National de Région, Reims: 14 rue Carnot, 51100 Reims; tel. 33 3 26 86 77 00.

Conservatoire National de Région, Rennes: 26 rue Hoche, 35000 Rennes; tel. 33 2 99 28 55 72.

Conservatoire National de Région, Rouen: 50 Ave de la Porte des Champs, 76000 Rouen; tel. 33 2 32 08 13 50; fax 33 2 32 08 13 59.

Conservatoire National de Région, Rueil-Malmaison: 182 Ave Paul Doumer, 92500 Rueil-Malmaison; tel. 33 1 47 49 74 45.

Conservatoire National de Région, Strasbourg: 10 rue du Hohwald, 67000 Strasbourg; tel. 33 3 88 15 08 88.

Conservatoire National de Région, Toulouse: 3 rue Labéda, 31000 Toulouse; tel. 33 5 61 22 28 62.

Conservatoire National de Région, Tours: 17 rue des Ursulines, 37000 Tours; tel. 33 2 47 05 57 64.

Conservatoire National de Région, Versailles: 24 rue de la Chancellerie, 78000 Versailles; tel. 33 1 39 50 24 53.

Conservatoire National Supérieur de Musique de Lyon: 3 rue de l'Angile, 69005 Lyon.

Conservatoire National Supérieur de Musique: 209 avenue Jean Jaurès, 75019 Paris; tel. 33 1 40 40 46 46/47; fax 33 1 40 40 47 27; website www.cnsmdp.fr.

École Normale de Musique: 114 bis Blvd Malesherbes, 75017 Paris.

Institut International de Musique Electroacoustique de Bourges—IMEB: place André Malraux, PO Box 39, 18000 Bourges; tel. 33(0)2 20 41 87; fax 33(0)2 48 20 45 51; e-mail administration@ime-bourges .org; website www.imeb.net. f. 1970 (as GMEB until 1994); composition, research, diffusion, training, bibliographic and phonographic editions, archives, studies of electroacoustic music.

Schola Cantorum, École Supérieure de Musique de Danse et d'Art Dramatique: 269 rue St Jacques, Paris.

Georgia

Tbilisi State Conservatoire: Tbilisi; e-mail tbil_conservatory@hotmail .com; Rector: Prof. Manana Doijashvili.

Germany

Bayerisches Staatskonservatorium für Musik: Mergentheimer-strasse 76, Würzburg.

Hochschule der Künste, Berlin: Ernst-Feuter-Platz 10, 10587 Berlin; website www.hdk-berlin.de.

Hochschule für Musik Carl Maria von Weber: Wettiner Platz 13, 01067 Dresden; tel. 49 351 492 3600; website www.hfmdd.de.

Hochschule für Musik Detmold: Willi-Hofmann-Strasse 5, 32756 Detmold; tel. 5231 9755; fax 5231 975972; e-mail info@hfm-detmold.de; website www.hfm-detmold.de.

Hochschule für Musik Felix Mendelssohn-Bartholdy: Grassistrasse 8, 04107 Leipzig; tel. 49 341 214 455; fax 49 341 21 44 503; website www .hmt-leipzig.de.

Hochschule für Musik Franz Liszt: Platz der Demokratie 2–3, 99423 Weimar; tel. 49 3643 5550; fax 49 3643 555 117; website www.hfm-weimar .de.

Hochschule für Musik Hanns Eisler: Charlottenstrasse 55, 10117 Berlin; tel. 49 30 90269700; fax 49 30 90269701; e-mail rektorat.hfm@ berlin.de; website www.hfm-berlin.de; Dir Prof. Christhard Gössling; Vice-Dir Prof. Michael Vogler.

Hochschule für Musik und Darstellende Kunst, Frankfurt am Main: Eschersheimer Landstrasse 29–39, 60322 Frankfurt am Main; tel. 49 69 154 007-0; fax 49 69 154 007-108; website www.jfmdk-frankfurt.de.

Hochschule für Musik und Darstellende Kunst, Hamburg: Harvest-ehuder Weg 12, 20148 Hamburg.

Hochschule für Musik und Theater, Hannover: Emmichplatz 1, 30175 Hannover; website www.hmt-hannover.de.

Hochschule für Musik und Theater, München: Arcisstrasse 12, 80333 Munich; tel. 49 89 28903; fax 49 89 28927419; e-mail verwaltung@ musikhochschule-muenchen.de; website www.musikhochschule -muenchen.de; Rector: Prof. Dr Siegfried Mauser.

Konservatorium der Stadt Nürnberg, Fachakademie für Musik: Am Katharinenkloster 6, 90403 Nürnberg.

Leopold-Mozart-Konservatorium, Augsburg: Maximilianstrasse 59, 86150 Augsburg.

Musikhochschule des Saarlandes: Bismarckstrasse 1, 66111 Saar-brücken; tel. 49 681 967 310; fax 49 681 967 3130; website www.hmt .saarland.de.

Musikhochschule, Lübeck: Grosse Petersgrube 17–29, 23552 Lübeck.

Richard-Strauss-Konservatorium: Ismaningerstrasse 29, 81667 Munich.

Staatliche Hochschule Düsseldorf: Robert-Schumann-Institut, Fischerstrasse 110, 40416 Düsseldorf; tel. 49 211 49 180; fax 49 211 49 11 618; e-mail rsh@rsh-duesseldorf.de; website www.rsh-duesseldorf.de.

Staatliche Hochschule für Musik Köln, Aachen: Grenzland-Institut, Aachen, Theaterstrasse 2–4, 52062, Aachen; tel. 49 241 455 03; fax 49 241 455 499; website www.mhs-aachen.de.

Staatliche Hochschule für Musik Köln: Abteilung Wuppertal: Institut Wuppertal, Friedrich-Ebert-Strasse 141, 42117 Wuppertal; tel. 49 202 371 500; fax 49 202 371 5040; website www.mhs-wuppertal.de.

Staatliche Hochschule für Musik Köln: Dagobertstrasse 38, 50668 Cologne; website www.mhs-koeln.de.

Staatliche Hochschule für Musik und Darstellende Kunst: Urban-strasse 25, 70182 Stuttgart; tel. 49 711 212 4620; website www.mh -stuttgart.de.

Staatliche Hochschule für Musik, Freiburg im Breisgau: Schwarz-waldstrasse 141, 79102 Freiburg im Breisgau.

Staatliche Hochschule für Musik, Heidelberg-Mannheim: Frie-drich-Ebert-Anlage 62, Heidelberg.

Staatliche Hochschule für Musik, Trossingen: Schultheiss-Koch-Platz 3, 78647 Trossingen.

Staatliche Hochschule für Musik: PO Box 6040, 76040 Karlsruhe.

Staatliches Institut für Musikforschung Preussischer Kulturbe-sitz (State Institute for Music Research): Tiergartenstrasse 1, 10785 Berlin; tel. 49 (0)30 25481-0; fax 49 (0)30 25481-172; e-mail sim@sim.spk -berlin.de; website www.sim.spk-berlin.de; Head: Dr Thomas Ertelt; Head of Museum of Musical Instruments: Prof. Dr Conny Restle.

Theater Erfurt: Generalintendant, Dietrich Taube, PSF 244, 99005 Erfurt.

Wiesbadener Musikakademie: Bodenstedtstrasse 2, 65189 Wiesbaden.

Greece

Epirotic Conservatory Tsakalof: Platia G, Stavrou 5, 45444 Ioannina.

Kratikon Odeion Thessaloniki: Leondos Sofou 16, 54625 Thessaloniki.

Odeion Athenon: Odos Rigillis and Vassileos Georgiou 17–19, Athens.

Odeion Ethnikon: Odos Maizonos 8, 108 Athens.

Odeion Hellenikon: Odos Phidiou 3, Athens.

Skalkotas Conservatory: Agias Lavras 78, Ano Patisia, 11141 Athens.

Guatemala

Conservatorio Nacional de Música: 3a Avda 4-61, Zona 1, Guatemala City.

Honduras

Escuela Nacional de Música: 2a Avda, 307, Tegucigalpa.

Hong Kong

Hong Kong Academy for Performing Arts, School of Music: 1 Gloucester Road, Wanchai, Hong Kong; website www.hkapa.edu.

University of Hong Kong, Faculty of Music: Pokfulam Road, Hong Kong; tel. 852 2859 2111; fax 852 2858 2549; website www.hku.hk.

Hungary

Liszt Ferenc Zenemüves-zeti Föiskola (Franz Liszt Academy of Music): PO Box 206, Liszt Ferenc tér 8, 1391 Budapest VI; website www .liszt.hu.

Iceland

Tónlistarskólinn i Rekyavík (Reykjavík College of Music): Skipholt 33, 105 Reykjavík.

India

Bhavan's Bharatiya Sangeet and Nartan Skikshapeeth (Academy of Music and Drama): Cahupatty Road, Mumbai 4000007.

Delhi School of Music: 8 Nyaya Marg, New Delhi 110021.

Indira Kala Sangit Vishwavidyalaya (University of Music and Fine Arts): Khairagarth, Madhya Pradesh 491881.

Kalakshetra: Tiruvanmiyur, Chennai 600041.

Music Academy: Teachers' College of Music, 306 TTK Road, Chennai 600041.

Rabindra Bharati University, Department of Music: 6–4 Dwaraka-nath Tagore Lane, Kolkata 700007; website www .rabindrabharatiuniversity.net.

Sangeet Natak Akademi (National Academy of Music, Dance and Drama): Rabindra Bhavan, Feroze Shah Road, New Delhi 11001.

University of Madras, Department of Indian Music: University Centenary Building, Chepauk, Triplicane, Tamil Nadu, Chennai 600005; website www.unom.ac.in.

Indonesia

Academi Seni Tari Indonesia: Jl Buahbatu 212, Bandung.

Institute Kesenian Jakarta: Taman Ismial Marzuki, Jalan Cikini, Jakarta.

Ireland

Conservatory of Music and Drama: Dublin Institute of Technology, Rathmines Road, Dublin 2; e-mail conservatory@dit.ie.

Royal Irish Academy of Music: 36–38 Westland Row, Dublin 2; tel. 353 1 676 4412/3; fax 353 1 662 2798; website www.riam.ie.

Israel

Israel Conservatory of Music: 19 Shtriker St, Tel-Aviv.

Jerusalem Academy of Music and Dance: Givat-Ram Campus, 91904 Jerusalem; tel. 972 2 675 9911; fax 972 2 652 7713; website www.jmd.ac.il.

Levinsky Teachers College, Music Teachers Seminary: 15 Shoshana Persitz St N, PO Box 48130, Tel-Aviv.

Rubin Academy of Music: University of Tel-Aviv, Faculty of Fine Arts, PO Box 39040, Ramat Aviv, Tel-Aviv.

Samuel Rubin Conservatory of Music: 9 Haparsim St, Haifa; tel. 972 4 8521530; fax 972 4 8514405; e-mail ns_sigiw@bezegint.net; Contact: Stella Wenkert.

Italy

Accademia Musicale Chigiana: Via di Città 89, 53100 Siena; tel. 0577 22091; fax 0577 288124; e-mail accademia.chigiana@chigiana.it.

Accademia Musicale di Milano: Viale dei Mille 17, Milan.

Accademia Musicale Napoletana: Via del Parco Margherita 49, pal 5, 80121 Naples.

Accademia Nazionale di Santa Cecilia: Via Vittoria 6, 00187 Rome.

Conservatorio Statale di Musica Antonio Vivaldi: Via Parma 1, Alessandria; website www.conservatoriovivaldi.it.

Conservatorio Statale di Musica Arcangelo Corelli: Via Bonino 1, 98100 Messina.

Conservatorio Statale di Musica Arrigo Boito: Via del Conservatorio 27, 43100 Parma; website www.conservatorio.pr.it.

Conservatorio Statale di Musica Benedetto Marcello: Palazzo Pisani, San Marco 2809, 30124 Venice.

Conservatorio Statale di Musica Cesare Pollini: Via Eremitani 6, 35121 Padua.

Conservatorio Statale di Musica Claudio Monteverdi: Piazza Domenicani 19, 39100 Bolzano.

Conservatorio Statale di Musica Francesco Morlacchi: Piazza Mariotti 2, 06100 Perugia; website www.conservatorio.pg.it.

Conservatorio Statale di Musica Gioachino Rossini: Piazza Olivieri 5, 61100 Pesaro.

Conservatorio Statale di Musica Giovanni Battista Martini: Piazza Rossini 2, 40126 Bologna.

Conservatorio Statale di Musica Giovanni Pierluigi da Palestrina: Via Bacaredda, 09100 Cagliari; website www.conservatorioca.it.

Conservatorio Statale di Musica Girolamo Frescobaldi: Via Previati 22, 44100; website www.commune.ferrara.it/conservatorio

Conservatorio Statale di Musica Giuseppe Tartini: Via Carlo Ghega 12, 34132 Trieste; website www.conservatorio.trieste.it.

Conservatorio Statale di Musica Giuseppe Verdi: Via del Conservatorio 12, 20122 Milan.

Conservatorio Statale di Musica Giuseppe Verdi: Via Mazzini 11, Piazza Bodoni, 10123 Turin; website www.arpnet.it/conservatorio.

Conservatorio Statale di Musica Luigi Cherubini: Piazza delle Belle Arti 2, 50122 Florence; tel. 39 055 292-180; fax 39 055 239-6785; e-mail direttore@conservatorio.firenze.it; website www.conservatorio.firenze.it; Dir: Mario Pazzaglia.

Conservatorio Statale di Musica Niccòlo Paganini: Via Albaro 38, 16145 Genoa.

Conservatorio Statale di Musica Niccolo Piccinni: Via Brigata Bari 26, 70124 Bari; website www.conservatoriopiccinni.it.

Conservatorio Statale di Musica San Pietro a Majella: Via San Pietro a Majella 35, 80138 Naples.

Conservatorio Statale di Musica Santa Cecilia: Via del Greci 18, 00187 Rome.

Conservatorio Statale di Musica Vincenzo Bellini: Via Squarcialupo 45, 90133 Palermo.

Istituto Musicale Pareggiato Luigi Boccherini: Piazza S. Ponziano, 55100 Lucca.

Liceo Musicale Giovanni Battista Viotti: Casella Postale 127, 13100 Vercelli.

Pontificïo Istituto di Musica Sacra: Via di Torre Rossa 21, 00165 Rome.

Japan

Elizabeth University of Music: 4-15 Nobori-cho, Naka-ku, Hiroshima 730.

Kunitachi College of Music: 5-5-1 Kashiwa-cho, Tachikawa-shi, Tokyo 190; website www.kunitachi.ac.jp.

Kyoto City University of Fine Arts and Music: 13-6 Ohe Kutsukake-cho, Nishikyo-ku, Kyoto 610-11; website www.kcua.ac.jp.

Musashino Ongaku Daigaku (Musashino College of Music): 1-13-1 Hazawa, Nerima-ku, Tokyo 176.

Osaka College of Arts: 469 Higashiyama, Kanan-cho, Minamilawachi-gun, Osaka 561.

Osaka Ongaku Daigaku (Osaka College of Music): 1-1-8 Saiwaima-chi, Shonai, Toyonaka, Osaka 561.

Toho Gakuen School of Music: 1-41-1 Wakaba-cho, Chofu-shi, Tokyo 182-8510.

Tokyo College of Music: 3-4-5 Minami-Ikebukuro, Toshima-ku, Tokyo 171.

Tokyo Daigaku (University of Tokyo) Faculty of Musicology: 7-3-1 Hongo, Bungyo-ku, Tokyo 113; website www.u-tokyo.ac.jp.

Tokyo Geijutsu Daigaku (Tokyo National University of Fine Arts and Music): 12-8 Ueno-koen, Taito-ku, Tokyo 110-8714.

Ueno Gakuen College, Department of Music: 4-24-12 Higashiueno, Taito-ku, Tokyo 110.

Republic of Korea

Korean Union College, Department of Music: Cheongryang, PO Box 18, Seoul.

Korea University: 1 5-KA, Anamdong, Sungbukku, Seoul 136-701; website www.korea.ac.kr.

Kyung Hee University, College of Music: 1 Hoegi-dong, Tongadae-mun-gu Seoul 131; website www.kyunghee.ac.kr.

National Academy of Arts, Department of Music: 1 Sejongno, Chongno-gu, Seoul.

Seoul National University, College of Music: San 56-1, Shinrim-dong, Kwanak-gu, Seoul 151; website www.snu.ac.kr.

Yonsei University, College of Music: 134 Shinchon-dong, Sodaemun-gu, Seoul 120; website www.yonsei.ac.kr.

Latvia

Latvian Y Vitol State Conservatory: Ul Krisyana Barona 1, 226050 Riga.

Lithuania

Lithuanian State Conservatory: 232001 Vilnius.

Luxembourg

Conservatoire de Musique d'Esch-sur-Alzette: 10 rue de l'Eglise, PO Box 145, 4002 Esch-sur-Alzette.

Conservatoire de Musique de la Ville de Luxembourg: 33 rue Charles Martel, 2134 Luxembourg.

Mexico

Conservatorio Nacional de Música de México: Avda Presidente Masaryk 582, Mexico City 5, DF.

Facultad de Música: Universidad Veracruzana, Barragán No. 32, Xalapa Veracruz CP 91000.

Universidad Nacional Autónoma de México: Escuela Nacional de Música, Xicotencat 126, Coyoacán, Mexico City 04100, DF.

Monaco

Académie de Musique Prince Rainier III de Monaco: 1 Blvd Albert, 98000 Monte Carlo.

Morocco

Conservatoire de Tangier: Tangier.

Conservatoire National de Musique: de Danse, et d'Art Dramatique, Rabat.

Conservatorie de Musique: Marrakesh.

Ecole Nationale de Musique: 133 Ave Ziraoui, Casablanca.

Ecole Nationale de Musique: 22 rue Marrakchia, Kaa Ouarda, Meknes.

Netherlands

Akademie voor Muziek: Koninginneweg 25, 1217 KR Hilversum.

Amsterdamse Hogeschool voor de Kunsten: Afdeling Conservatorium van Amsterdam, PO Box 78022, 1070 LP Amsterdam; tel. 020-5277550; fax 020-6761505; e-mail info@cva.ahk.nl; website www.cva.ahk.nl; Dir: Lucas Vis.

Brabants Conservatorium voor Muziek en Dans: Kempenbaan 27, 5022 KC Tilburg; website www.fontys.nl/bc.

Christelijke Hogeschool voor de Kunsten Constantijn Huygens: Aan de Stadsmuur 88, 8011 VD Zwolle.

Hilversums Conservatorium: Snelliuslaan 10, 1222 TE Hilversum.

Hogeschool Enschede sector Conservatorium: Van Essengaarde 10, 7511 PN Enschede.

Hogeschool voor de Kunsten Arnhem: Fakulteit Muziek, Weverstraat 40, 6811 EM Arnhem.

Hogeschool voor Muziek en Dans Rotterdam: Kruisplein 26, 3012 CC Rotterdam; tel. 10-217 11 00; fax 10-217 11 01; e-mail hmd@hmd.nl; website www.hmd.nl.

Koninklijk Conservatorium voor Muziek en Dans: Juliana van Stolberglaan 1, 2595 CA The Hague.

Rijkshgeschool Maastricht: Subfaculteit Conservatorium, Bonnefanten 15, 6211 KL Maastricht.

Rijkshogeschool Groningen sector Kunstvakopleidingen afdeling Conservatorium: Veemarkstraat 76, 9724 GA Groningen.

Stedelijke Muziekpedagogische Akademie: Eewal 56–58, Leeuwarden.

Toonkunst Conservatorium: Mathenesserlaan 219, Rotterdam.

Utrechts Conservatorium: Mariaplaats 28, 3511 LL Utrecht.

New Zealand

University of Auckland, Faculty of Music: Private Bag 92019, Auckland 1020; tel. 64 9 373 7999; website www.auckland.ac.nz.

University of Canterbury, Faculty of Music: Private Bag 4800, Christchurch 8020; tel. 64 3 366 7001; fax 64 3 264 2999; website www.canterbury.ac.nz.

University of Otago, School of Language, Literature and Performing Arts, Division of Humanities: PO Box 56, Dunedin; website www.otago.ac.nz.

Victoria University of Wellington, Faculty of Music: PO Box 600 Wellington; website www.vuw.ac.nz.

Nicaragua

Escuela Nacional de Musica: Antigua Hacienda el Retiro, Managua.

Norway

Bergen Musikkonservatorium: Lars Hilles Gate 3, 5015 Bergen; tel. 47 5532 4950; fax 47 5532 3033.

Kunsthøgakolen i Oslo (Oslo National College of the Arts): Department of Operatic Art, PO Box 6853, St Olavs plass, 0130 Oslo; tel. 47 2299 55 00; fax 47 2299 55 02; e-mail khio@khio.no.

Østlandets Musikkonservatorium: Vetlandsveien 45, 0685 Oslo 6.

Rogaland Musikkonservatorium: Bjergsted, 4007 Stavanger.

Trondelag Musikkonservatorium: Homebergvn 1, 7038 Trondheim.

Panama

Escuela Nacional de Música: PO Box 1414, Panama City.

Paraguay

Conservatorio Municipal de Música: Mcal Estigarribia, E-Pai Perez y Curupayty, Asunción.

Escuela Municipal de Canto: Dr Eduardo Victor Haedo 682, Asunción.

Peru

Conservatorio Nacional de Música: Emancipación 180, Lima 1.

Philippines

St Paul College, College of Music: 680 Pedro Gil Street, Malate, Manila; website www.spcm.edu.ph.

St Scholastica's College, School of Music: 2560 Leon Guinto Sr Street, Malate, Manila.

University of San Augustin: Conservatory of Music, General Luna Street, Iloilo City 5901; website www.usa.edu.ph.

University of Santo Tomas, Conservatory of Music: Espana, Manila; website www.ust.edu.ph.

Poland

Akademia Muzyczna im Feliksa Nowowiejskiego w Bydgoszczy: Ul J Slowackiego 7, 85-008 Bydgoszcz; website www.amuz.bydgoszczy.pl.

Akademia Muzyczna im Fryderyka Chopina w Warzawie: Ul Okólnik 2, 00-368 Warsaw.

Akademia Muzyczna im Karola Szymanowskiego w Katowice: UL Zacisze 3, Katowice; website www.am.katowice.pl.

Akademia Muzyczna im Stanislaw Moniuszko w Gdansku: Lagiewniki 3, 80-847 Gdańsk; website www.amuz.gda.pl.

Akademia Muzyczna Poznań iu: Ul Czerwonej Armii 87, 61-808 Poznań.website www.amuz.poznan.pl

Akademia Muzyczna w Krakówie: Ul Bohaterów Stalingradu 3, 31-038 Kraków; website www.amuz.krakow.pl.

Akademia Muzyczna w Łódz: Ul Gdanska 32, 90-716 Łódz.

Akademia Muzyczna Wroclawiu: Ul Powstancow Laskich 204, 53-140 Wroclaw.

Portugal

Academia de Amadores de Musica: R. Nova da Trindade 18, 2°, E, 1200 Lisbon.

Conservatório de Musica: Rua de Maternidade 13, 4000 Oporto.

Conservatório Regional de Coimbra: Rua do Brasil, 3000 Coimbra.

Escola Superior de Musica: Conservatório Nacional, Rua dos Caetanos 29, 1200 Lisbon.

Romania

Conservatorul de Muzic Ciprian Porumbescu: Str Stirbei Voda 33, 70732 Bucharest.

Conservatorul de Muzic Georges Enescu: Str Closca 9, 6600 Iasi.

Conservatorul de Muzic Gheorghe Dima: Str 23 August 25, 3400 Cluj-Napoca.

Russia

Moscow Conservatory: Ul. B. Nikitinskaya 13, 103009 Moscow; website www.mosconsv.ru.

St Petersburg Conservatory: Teatralnaya Pl 3, 192041 St Petersburg.

Singapore

School of Arts and Language: 469 Bukit Gimah Road, Singapore 1025.

Slovakia

Bratislava Konzervatorium: Tolstého 11, 811 06 Bratislava.

Vysoká Skola Mûzick ch Umeni v Bratisaave (Academy of Music and Dramatic Arts Bratislava): Jiráskova 3, 81301 Bratislava.

South Africa

University of Cape Town, College of Music: Private bag, Rondebosch 7700, Cape Town; website www.uct.ac.za.

University of KwaZulu-Natal, School of Music: Durban 4041; tel. 27 31 2603351; fax 27 31 2601048; e-mail hodges@nu.ac.za; website www.nu.ac.za/und/music.

University of Pretoria, Department of Music: Pretoria 0002; website www.up.ac.za.

University of South Africa, Department of Music: PO Box 392, Pretoria 0001; website www.unisa.ac.za.

University of Stellenbosch, Department of Music: Stellenbosch 7600; website www.sun.ac.za.

University of the South Africa Free State, Department of Music: PO Box 339, Bloemfontein 9300; tel. 51 401 28 10; fax 51 448 44 02; e-mail lampregp.hum@mail.uovs.ac.za; website www.uovs.ac.za; Head of Dept: Prof. Deon Lamprecht.

University of the Witwatersrand, Wits School of Music: Jan Smuts Ave, Johannesburg 2001; website www.wits.ac.za.

Spain

Conservatorio de Música Manuel de Falla: Calle del Tinte 1, Cadiz.

Conservatorio Superior de Música de Barcelona: Calle Bruche 112, Barcelona 9.

Conservatorio Superior de Música y Escuela de Arte Dramatico y Danza: Calle Angel de Saavedra 1, 14003 Cordoba.

Conservatorio Superior de Música y Escuela de Arte Dramatico: Calle Jesús del Gran Poder 49, Seville 41002.

Conservatorio Superior de Música y Escuela de Arte Dramatico y Danza: Plaza San Esteban 3, Valencia.

Conservatorio Superior de Música: Easo 39, San Sebastian 20006.

Escuela Superior de Música Sagrada y de Pedagogia Musical Escolar: Victor Pradera 65 bis, Madrid 8.

Real Conservatorio Nacional de Música y Declamacion: San Bernardo 44, Madrid.

Real Conservatorio Superior de Música: Plaza de Isabell II s/n, Madrid 28013.

Sri Lanka

Institute of Aesthetic Studies: 21 Albert Crescent, Colombo 7.

Sweden

Göteborgs Universitet, Musikhögskolan: PO Box 3174, 400 10 Göteborg; website www.gu.se.

Kungliga Musikaliska Academien (Royal Swedish Academy of Music): Blasieholmstorg 8, 11148 Stockholm; tel. 46 8 407 1800; fax 46 8 611 8718; e-mail adm@musakad.se; website www.musakad.se.

Musikhögskolan och teaterhögskolan: PO Box 135 15, Ystadvägen 25, S-200 44 Malmö.

Musikhögskolan: Valhallavägen 103-109, 115 31 Stockholm.

Switzerland

Conservatoire de Musique de Genève: Place Neuve, 1204 Geneva.

Conservatoire de Musique de La Chaux-de-Fonds-Le Locie: Ave Léopold-Robert 34, 2300 La Chaux-de-Fonds.

Conservatoire de Musique de Lausanne: rue de la Grotte 2, PO Box 2427, 1002 Lausanne; tel. 41 21 321 3535; fax 41 21 321 3536; website www.regart.ch/cml

Conservatoire de Musique de Neuchâtel: 106 Faubourg de l'Hopital, 2000 Neuchâtel.

Conservatoire de Musique de Vevey: 4 rue des Communaux, 1800 Vevey.

Conservatoire et Académie de Musique: 228-A rue Pierre Aeby, 1700 Fribourg.

Institute Jaques-Dalcroze: 11 rue Sillem, 1207 Geneva; website www.dalcroze.ch.

Konservatorium für Musik und Theater: Kramgasse 36, 3011 Bern.

Konservatorium Luzern: Dreilindenstrasse 93, 6006 Lucern.

Konservatorium und Musikhochschule Zürich: Birchstrasse 95, 8050 Zürich.

Musik-Akademie der Stadt Basel: Leonhardsstrasse 6, 4501 Basel.

Musikakademie Zürich: Florastrasse 52, 8008 Zürich.

Musikschule und Konservatorium Schaffhausen: Rosengasse 16, 8200 Schaffhausen.

Musikschule und Konservatorium Winterthur: Tössertobelstrasse 1, 8400 Winterthur.

Stadtische Musikschule und Konservatorium: Ring 12, 2500 Biel.

Stadtische Musikschule: 4600 Olten.

Taiwan

National Institute of the Arts, Music Department: 172 Chung Cheng Road, Ru Chow, Taipei.

National Taiwan Academy of Arts: 59, Section 1, Ta Kuan Road, Pan-Chiao Park, Taipei.

Tunisia

Institut Superieure de Musique: 20 Ave de Paris, Tunis.

Turkey

Ankara State Conservatory: Hacettepe Üniversitesi, Hacetlepe Parki, Ankara.

Istanbul State Conservatory of Music: Mimar Sinan Üniversitesi, Findikli, Istanbul.

Turkish Conservatory of Music: Istanbul Teknik Üniversitesi, Aya-zaga, Istanbul.

United Kingdom

Birmingham Conservatoire: UCE Birmingham, Paradise Place, Birmingham B3 3HG; tel. (121) 331-5901; fax (121) 331-5906; e-mail conservatoire@uce.ac.uk; website www.conversatoire.uce.ac.uk; Principal: Prof. George Caird; f. over 100 years ago, national college of music performance and composition.

Chetham's School of Music: Long Millgate, Manchester M3 1SB; tel. 0161 834 9644; fax 0161 839 3609; e-mail chets@chethams.com; website www.chethams.com.

City of Belfast School of Music—CBSM: 99 Donegal Pass, Belfast, Northern Ireland BT7 1DR; tel. (28) 9032-2435; fax (28) 9032-9201; e-mail music.belb@btinternet.com; website www.cbsm.org.uk; Principal: Dr Joe McKee.

Dartington College of Arts, Department of Music: Totnes, Devon TQ9 6EJ; tel. (1803) 862224; fax (1803) 863569; e-mail registry@dartington.ac.uk; website www.dartington.ac.uk; Dir of Music: Dr Trevor Wiggins; specialises in contemporary music and arts.

Department of Music, King's College London: Strand, London WC2R 2LS; tel. 020 7836 5454; website www.kcl.ac.uk.

Guildhall School of Music and Drama: Silk Street, Barbican, London EC2Y 8DT; tel. 020 7628 2571; fax 020 7256 9438; website www.gsmd.ac.uk.

Leeds College of Music: 3 Quarry Hill, Leeds LS2 7PD; tel. (113) 222-3416; e-mail enquiries@lcm.ac.uk; website www.lcm.ac.uk. The UK's largest music college. Courses range from post-16 education to undergraduate and postgraduate degrees.

London College of Music and Media: St Mary's Road, London W5 5RF; tel. 020 8231 2304; fax 020 8231 2546; website www.tvu.ac.uk.

London-City University, Department of Music: Northampton Square, London EC1V 0HB; tel. (20) 7040-8284; fax (20) 7040-8576; e-mail music@city.ac.uk; website www.city.ac.uk/music.

Middlesex University School of Arts 'Music': Trent Park Campus, Bramley Road, London N14 4YZ; tel. (20) 8411-5684; fax (20) 8411-5684; website www.mdx.ac.uk.

Purcell School: Aldenham Road, Bushey, Herts, WD23 2TS; tel. 01923 331100; fax 01923 331166; website www.purcell-school.org.

Queen's University of Belfast, School of Music: University Road, Belfast, Northern Ireland BT7 1NN; website www.qub.ac.uk.

Royal Academy of Music: Marylebone Road, London NW1 5HT; tel. (20) 7873-7373; fax (20) 7873-7374; e-mail go@ram.ac.uk; website www.ram.ac.uk; Principal: Prof. Curtis Price; Vice-Principal and Dir of Studies: Prof.

Jonathan Freeman-Attwood; Britain's foremost conservatoire, a college of the University of London.

Royal College of Music: Prince Consort Road, London SW7 2BS; tel. 020 7589 3643; fax 020 7589 7740; e-mail info@rcm.ac.uk; website www.rcm.ac.uk.

Royal Holloway and Bedford College, Department of Music: University of London, Egham, Surrey TW20 0EX; tel. 01784 443532; fax 01784 439441; e-mail music@rhul.ac.uk; website www.rhul.ac.uk/music.

Royal Military School of Music: Kneller Hall, Twickenham, Middlesex TW2 7DU; tel. 020 8744 8628.

Royal Northern College of Music: 124 Oxford Road, Manchester M13 9RD; tel. 0161 907 5200; website www.mcm.ac.uk.

Royal School of Church Music: Cleveland Lodge, Westhumble, Dorking, Surrey RH5 6BW; tel. 01306 872800; fax 01306 887260; e-mail enquiries@rscm.com; website www.rscm.com.

Royal Scottish Academy of Music and Drama—RSAMD: 100 Renfrew Street, Glasgow G2 3DB; tel. 0141 332 4101; fax 0141 332 8901; website www.rsamd.ac.uk.

Royal Welsh College of Music and Drama: Castle Grounds, Cathays Park, Cardiff, Wales CF10 3ER; tel. 029 2034 2854; fax 029 2039 1304; website www.rwcmd.ac.uk.

Salford College of Technology: Adelphi, Peru Street, Salford, Manchester M3 6EQ.

St Mary's Music School: Coates Hall, 25 Grosvenor Crescent, Edinburgh, EH12 5EL, Scotland; tel. (131) 538-7766; fax (131) 467-7289; e-mail info@st-marys-music-school.co.uk; website www.st-marys-music-school.co.uk; Headteacher: Jennifer Rimer; Dir of Music: John Grundy.

Trinity College of Music: King Charles Court, Old Royal Naval College, Greenwich, London SE10 9JF; tel. 020 8305 4444; fax 020 8305 9444; e-mail info@tcm.ac.uk; website www.tcm.ac.uk.

University of Birmingham, Department of Music: Barber Institute, Edgbaston, Birmingham B15 2TT; tel. 0121 414 3344; fax 0121 414 3971; website www.bham.ac.uk.

University of Cambridge, School of Music: 11 West Road, Cambridge CB3 9DP; website www.mus.cam.ac.uk.

University of Edinburgh, Faculty of Music: Old College, South Bridge, Edinburgh, Scotland EH8 9YL; tel. 0131 650 1000; fax 0131 650 2147; website www.ed.ac.uk.

University of Exeter, Department of Music: Northcote House, The Queen's Drive, Exeter EX4 4QJ; website www.ex.ac.uk.

University of Glasgow, Department of Music: Glasgow, Scotland G12 8QQ; tel. 0141 330 2000; website www.gla.ac.uk.

University of Hull, Department of Drama and Music: Cottingham Road, Hull HU6 7RX; tel. (1482) 346311; fax (1482) 465998; e-mail p.a.muse@hull.ac.uk; website www.hull.ac.uk/music; Dir of Studies: Dr Alastair Borthwick.

University of Lancaster, Department of Music: Bailrigg, Lancaster LA1 4YW; tel. 01524 65201; website www.lancs.ac.uk.

University of Leeds, Department of Music: Leeds LS2 9JT; tel. 0113 243 1751; fax 0113 244 3923; website www.leeds.ac.uk.

University of Leicester, Department of Music: University Road, Leicester LE1 7RH; tel. 0116 252 2522; fax 0116 252 2200; website www.le.ac.uk.

University of Liverpool, School of Music: 80 Bedford Street S, Liverpool L69 7WW; tel. 0151 794 2000; website www.liv.ac.uk; Head of School: Prof. J. G. Williamson.

University of London, Department of Music: Senate House, London WC1E 7AU.

University of Manchester, School of Music and Drama: Department of Music, Coupland Street, Manchester M13 9PL; tel. (161) 275-4982; fax (161) 275-4994; website www.art.man.ac.uk/music.

University of Oxford, Faculty of Music: St Aldate's, Oxford OX1 1DB; tel. 01865 276125; website www.music.ox.ac.uk.

University of Reading, Department of Music: 35 Upper Redlands Road, Reading RG1 5JE; website www.rdg.ac.uk.

University of Southampton, School for Humanities, Music: Highfield, Southampton SO17 1BJ; tel. 023 8059 5000; fax 023 8059 3939; website www.soton.ac.uk.

University of Sussex, Department of Music: Arts Building, Falmer, Brighton, East Sussex BN1 9QN; tel. 01273 606755; fax 01273 678335; website www.susx.ac.uk.

University of Wales, Bangor, School of Music: College Road, Bangor, Gwynedd LL57 2DG, Wales; tel. (1248) 382181; fax (1248) 370297; e-mail r.ley@bangor.ac.uk; website www.bangor.ac.uk/music.

University of Wales, Cardiff, School of Music: 31 Corbett Road, Cardiff, CF10 3EB, Wales; tel. 029 2087 4816; fax 029 2087 4379; e-mail music@cardiff.ac.uk; website www.cf.ac.uk/music; Head of School: Prof. Robin Stowell.

University of York, Department of Music: Heslington, York YO10 5DD; website www.music.york.ac.uk.

Yehudi Menuhin School: Stoke D'Abernon, Cobham, Surrey KT11 3QQ; fax 01932 864633; website www.yehudimenuhinschool.co.uk.

United States of America

92nd St Y School of Music: 1395 Lexington Ave, New York, NY 10128; tel. 1 212 415 5500; website www.92ndsty.org.

Aaron Copland School of Music: Queens College, City University of New York, 65-30 Kissena Blvd, Flushing, NY 11367; tel. 1 718 997 3800; fax 1 718 997 3849; website qcpages.qc.edu/music.

Abilene Christian University, Department of Music: PO Box 8274, Abilene, TX 79699; website www.acu.edu.

Academy of Vocal Arts: 1920 Spruce Street, Philadelphia, PA 19103; tel. (215) 735-1685; fax (215) 732-2189; website www.avaopera.org.

Adelphi University, Department of Music: Post Hall, Garden City, NY 11530; website www.adelphi.edu.

Alabama State University, School of Music: 915 S Jackson Street, Montgomery, AL 36101; website www.alasu.edu.

Albion College, Department of Music: Albion, MI 49224; website www.albion.edu.

Alcorn State University, Fine Arts Department: PO Box 29, Lorman, MS 39096; tel. 1 601 877 6100; website www.alcorn.edu.

Alderson-Broaddus College: Department of Music, PO Box 2126, Philippi, WV 26416; tel. (304) 457-1700; fax (304) 457-6239; website www.ab.edu.

Allegheny College, Department of Music: 520 N Main Street, Meadville, PA 16335; tel. 1 814 332 3100; website www.allegheny.edu.

Alverno College, Department of Music: 3400 S 43rd Street, Milwaukee, WI 53234; tel. 1 414 382 6000; website www.alverno.edu.

Amarillo College, Department of Music: PO Box 447, Amarillo, TX 79178; tel. 1 806 371 5000; website www.actx.edu.

American Conservatory of Music: 252 Wildwood Road, Hammond, IN 46324; tel. 1 219 931 6000; website www.americanconservatory.edu.

American University, Department of Performing Arts: Kreeger Building, 4400 Massachusetts Ave NW, Washington, DC 20016; tel. 1 202 885 3420; fax 1 202 885 1092; website www.american.edu.

Amherst College, Department of Music: Amherst, MA 01002; tel. 1 413 542 2000; website www.amherst.edu.

Anderson College, Department of Music: 316 Blvd, Anderson, SC 29621; tel. 1 864 231 2000; website www.anderson-college.edu.

Anderson University, Department of Music: 1100 E Fifth Street, Anderson, IN 46012; website www.anderson.edu.

Andrews University, Department of Music: Berrien Springs, MI 49104; tel. 1 269 471 7771; fax 1 269 471 6900; website www.andrews.edu.

Angelo State University, Department of Music: 2601 W Ave N, San Angelo, TX 76909; website www.angelo.edu.

Appalachian State University, Hayes School of Music: Broyhill Music Center, Boone, NC 28608; tel. (828) 262-3020; fax (828) 262-6446; website www.music.appstate.edu; Dean: Dr William G. Harbinson.

Arizona State University, Interdisciplinary Fine Arts Department: 4701 W Thunderbird Road, Phoenix, AZ 85069.

Arizona State University, School of Music: Tempe, AZ 85287; tel. 1 480 965 9011; website www.asu.edu.

Arkansas State University, Department of Music: PO Box 779, State University, AR 72467; website www.astate.edu.

Arkansas Tech University, Department of Music: 1509 N Boulder Ave, Russellville, AR 72801; tel. 1 479 968 0389; website www.atu.edu.

Ashland University, Department of Music: 401 College Ave, Ashland, OH 44805; website www.ashland.edu.

Aspen Music School: PO Box AA, Aspen, CO 81612.

Aston Magna Performance Practice Institute: PO Box 28, Great Barrington, MA 01230.

Atlantic Christian College, Fine Arts Department: Wilson, NC 27893.

Auburn University, Department of Music: Auburn, AL 36849; tel. 1 334 844 4000; website www.auburn.edu.

Augsburg College, Department of Music: 2211 Riverside Ave S, Minneapolis, MN 55454; tel. 1 612 330 1000; website www.augsburg.edu.

Augustana College, Department of Music: 639 38th Street, Rock Island, IL 61201; tel. 1 309 794 7000; website www.augustana.edu.

Austin College, Department of Music: 900 N Grand Ave, PO Box 1177, Sherman, TX 75090; website www.austincollege.edu.

Austin Peay State University, Department of Music: PO Box 4625, Clarksville, TN 37044; tel. 1 931 221 7011; website www.absu.edu.

Azusa Pacific University, School of Music: PO Box 7000, Azusa, CA 91702; website www.apu.edu.

Baldwin-Wallace College, Conservatory of Music: 275 Eastland Road, Berea, OH 44017; tel. (440) 826-2362; fax (440) 826-3239; e-mail thecon@bw.edu; website www.bw.edu/academics/conservatory.

Ball State University, School of Music: 2000 University Avenue, Muncie, IN 47306-0410; tel. (765) 285-5400; fax (765) 285-5401; website www.bsu.edu/music; Dir: Dr Peter A. McAllister.

Baptist College at Charleston, Department of Music: PO Box 10087, Charleston, SC 29411.

Baruch College, City University of New York, Department of Music: 1 Bernard Baruch Way, New York, NY 10010; tel. 1 646 312 1000; website www.baruch.cuny.edu.

Bates College, Department of Music: Lewiston, ME 04240; tel. 1 207 786 6255; website www.bates.edu.

Baylor University, School of Music: PO Box 7408, Waco, TX 76798; website www.baylor.edu.

Belmont College, School of Music: 1900 Belmont Blvd, Nashville, TN 37212; tel. 1 615 460 6785; website www.belmont.edu.

Beloit College, Department of Music: 700 College Street, Beloit, WI 53511; tel. 1 608 363 2000; website www.beloit.edu.

Bemidji State University, Department of Music: PO Box 53, 1500 Birchmont Dr. NE, No 53, Bemidji, MN 56601; tel. 1 218 755 2000; fax 1 218 755 4048; website www.bemidjistate.edu.

Benjamin T. Rome School of Music: The Catholic University of America, 620 Michigan Ave NE, Washington, DC 20064; tel. (202) 319-5414; fax (202) 319-6280; website music.cua.edu.

Bennington College, Department of Music: Jennings Hall, Bennington, VT 05201; website www.bennington.edu.

Berea College, Department of Music: CPO 1127, Berea, KY 40404; website www.berea.edu.

Berklee College of Music: 1140 Boylston St, Boston, MA 02215; website www.berklee.edu.

Bethany College, Department of Music: 421 N First St, Lindsborg, KS 67456.

Bethel College, Department of Music: 3900 Bethel Dr., St Paul, MN 55112; tel. 1 651 638 6400; website www.bethel.edu.

Bethel College, Department of Music: Drawer A, North Newton, KS 67117; website www.bethelks.edu.

Biola University, Department of Music: 13800 Biola Ave, La Mirada, CA 90639; tel. 1 562 903 6000; website www.biola.edu.

Black Hills State University, School of Arts and Humanities: PO Box 9003, Spearfish, SD 57783; website www.bhsu.edu.

Bluffton College, Department of Music: 280 W College Ave, Suite 1, Bluffton, OH 45817; tel. 1 419 358 3000; website www.bluffton.edu.

Bob Jones University, Music Division: PO Box 34533, Greenville, SC 29614; website www.bju.edu.

Boise State University, Department of Music: 1910 University Dr., Boise, ID 83725; tel. 1 208 426 1000; website www.boisestate.edu.

Boston Conservatory: Music Division, 8 The Fenway, Boston, MA 02215; tel. 1 617 536 6340; fax 1 617 536 3176; website www.bostonconservatory.edu.

Boston University, School of Music: 855 Commonwealth Ave, Boston, MA 02215; tel. 1 617 353 3350; website www.bu.edu/cfa/music.

Bowdoin College, Department of Music: Gibson Hall, Brunswick, ME 04011; website www.bowdoin.edu.

Bowling Green State University, College of Musical Arts: Bowling Green, OH 43403; tel. 1 419 372 2531; website www.bgsu.edu.

Bradley University, Department of Music and Theatre Arts: 1501 W Bradley Ave, Peoria, IL 61625; tel. (309) 677-2660; fax (309) 677-3505; website www.bradley.edu/theatre.

Brandeis University, Department of Music: South St, Waltham, MA 02254; website www.brandeis.edu.

Brevard College, Fine Arts Division: N Broad St, Brevard, NC 28712; website www.brevard.edu.

Brigham Young University, Department of Music: C-550 Harris Fine Arts Center, Provo, UT 84602; website www.byu.edu.

Brooklyn College, Conservatory of Music: Bedford Ave and Ave H, Brooklyn, NY 11210; tel. 1 718 951 5000; website www.brooklyn.cuny.edu.

Brooklyn Conservatory of Music: 58 Seventh Ave, Brooklyn, NY 11217; tel. 1 718 622 3300; website www.brooklynconservatory.com.

Brown University, Department of Music: PO Box 1924, 1 Young Orchard Ave, Providence, RI 02912; tel. 1 401 863 1000; website www.brown.edu.

Bucknell University, Department of Music: Moore Ave, Lewisburg, PA 17837; tel. 1 570 577 2000; website www.bucknell.edu.

Butler University, Jordan College of Fine Arts: 4600 Sunset Ave, Indianapolis, IN 46208; tel. 1 800 368 6852; fax 1 317 940 9930; e-mail info@butler.edu; website www.butler.edu.

California Institute of the Arts, School of Music: 24700 McBean Parkway, Valencia, CA 91355; tel. 1 661 255 1050; website www.calarts.edu.

California State Polytechnic University, Department of Music: 3801 W Temple Ave, Pomona, CA 91768; tel. 1 909 869 7659; website www.csupomona.edu.

California State University, Bakersfield, Fine Arts Department: 9001 Stockdale Highway, Bakersfield, CA 93311; tel. 1 661 664 2011; website www.csubak.edu.

California State University, Chico, Department of Music: 400 W 1st St, Chico, CA 95929; website www.csuchico.edu.

California State University, Dominguez Hills, Department of Music: 1000 E Victoria, Carson, CA 90747; tel. 1 310 243 3696; website www.csudh.edu.

California State University, Fresno, Department of Music: 5241 N Maple Ave, Fresno, CA 93740; tel. 1 559 278 4240; website www.csufresno.edu.

California State University, Fullerton, Department of Music: 800 N State College Blvd, Fullerton, CA 92834-6850; tel. (714) 278-2011; website www.fullerton.edu/arts/music.

California State University, Hayward, Department of Music: Hayward, CA 94542; tel. 1 510 885 3000; website www.csuhayward.edu.

California State University, Long Beach, Department of Music: 1250 Bellflower Blvd, Long Beach, CA 90840; tel. 1 562 985 4111; website www.csulb.edu.

California State University, Los Angeles, Department of Music: 5151 State University Dr., Los Angeles, CA 90032; tel. 1 323 343 3000; website www.calstatela.edu.

California State University, Northridge, Department of Music: 18111 Nordhoff St, Northridge, CA 91330; tel. 1 818 677 1200; website www.csun.edu.

California State University, Stanislaus, Department of Music: 801 Monte Vista Ave, Turlock, CA 95382; website www.csustan.edu.

Calvin College, Department of Music: Fine Arts Center, 1795 Knollcrest Circle SE, Grand Rapids, MI 49546-4404; tel. 1 616 526 6000; website www.calvin.edu.

Cameron University, Department of Music: Lawton, OK 73505; tel. 1 580 581 2200; website www.cameron.edu.

Campbell University, Fine Arts Division: PO Box 488, Buies Creek, NC 27506; tel. 1 800 334 4111; website www.campbell.edu.

Cantors Institute-Seminary College of Jewish Music of the Jewish Theological Seminary of America: 3080 Broadway, New York, NY 10027; tel. 1 212 678 8037.

Capital University, Conservatory of Music: 2199 E Main St, Columbus, OH 43209; tel. 1 614 236 6011; website www.capital.edu.

Carleton College, Department of Music: 1 N College St, Northfield, MN 55057; tel. 1 507 646 4000; website www.carleton.edu.

Carnegie Mellon University, School of Music: 5000 Forbes Avenue, Pittsburgh, PA 15213; tel. (412) 268-2372; website www.cmu.edu/cfa/music.

Carroll College, Department of Music: 100 NE Ave, Waukesha, WI 53186; website www.cc.edu.

Carson-Newman College, Music Division: PO Box 1839, Jefferson City, TN 37760; tel. 1 865 471 2000; website www.cn.edu.

Carthage College, Department of Music: 2001 Alford Park Drive, Kenosha, WI 53140; tel. 1 262 551 8500; website www.carthage.edu.

Case Western Reserve University, Department of Music: Haydn Hall, Cleveland, OH 44106; tel. 1 216 368 2000; website www.cwru.edu.

Catawba College, Department of Music: 2300 W Innes St, Salisbury, NC 28144; website www.catawba.edu.

Centenary College of Louisiana, Hurley School of Music: Shreveport, LA 71134; tel. 1 800 234 4448; website www.centenary.edu.

Center for Creative Studies: 200 E Kirby, Detroit, MI 48202; tel. 1 313 664 7400; fax 1 313 872 2739; website www.ccscad.edu.

Central Methodist College, Swinney Conservatory of Music: 411 CMC Sq., Fayette, MO 65248; website www.cmc.edu.

Central Michigan University, Department of Music: Powers Music Building, No 102, Mount Pleasant, MI 48859; tel. 1 989 774 4000; website www.cmich.edu.

Central Missouri State University, Department of Music: PO Box 800, Warrensburg, MO 64093; website www.cmsu.edu.

Central State University, Department of Music: 100 N University Dr., Edmond, OK 73034.

Central State University, Department of Music: Paul Robeson Cultural and Performing Arts Center, Room 218, Wilberforce, OH 45384; tel. 1 937 376 6011; website www.centralstate.edu.

Central Washington University, Department of Music: 400 E University Way, Ellensburg, WA 98926; website www.cwu.edu.

Chautauqua Institution Summer School of Music: PO Box 28, Chautauqua, NY 14722; website www.chautauqua-inst.org.

Chicago Musical College of Roosevelt University: 430 S Michigan Ave, Chicago, IL 60605; website www.roosevelt.edu.

Chicago State University: 95 State and King Dr., Chicago, IL 60628; website www.csu.edu.

Christopher Newport University, Department of Music: 1 University Place, Newport News, VA 23606; tel. 1 757 594 7000; website www.cnu.edu.

City College of New York, Department of Music: W 138th St and Convent Ave, New York, NY 10031; tel. 1 212 650 7000; website www.ccny.cuny.edu.

Claremont Graduate University, Department of Music: 150 E 20th St, Claremont, CA 91711; website www.cgu.edu.

Clemson University, Performing Arts Department: Clemson, SC 29634; tel. 1 864 656 3311; website www.clemson.edu.

Cleveland Institute of Music: 11021 East Blvd, Cleveland, OH 44106; tel. 1 216 791 5000; fax 1 216 791 3063; website www.cim.edu.

Cleveland Music School Settlement: 11125 Magnolia Dr., Cleveland, OH 44106; website www.thecmss.org.

Cleveland State University, Department of Music: 2121 Euclid Ave, Cleveland, OH 44115; tel. 1 216 687 2000; website www.csuohio.edu.

Coe College, Department of Music: 1220 First Ave NE, Cedar Rapids, IA 52402; tel. 1 319 399 8500; website www.coe.edu.

Coker College, Department of Music: 300 E College Ave, Hartsville, SC 29550; tel. 1 843 383 8000; website www.coker.edu.

Colgate University, Department of Music: Dana Arts Center, Hamilton, NY 13346; website www.colgate.edu.

College of Mount St Joseph, Department of Music: Delhi and Neeb Rds, Mount St Joseph, Cincinnati OH 45051; tel. 1 800 654 9314; website www.msj.edu.

College of St Benedict, Department of Music: 37 S College Ave, St Joseph, MN 56374; tel. 1 320 363 5011; website www.csbsju.edu.

College of St Catherine, Department of Music: 2004 Randolph Ave, St Paul, MN 55105; tel. 1 651 690 6000; website www.stkate.edu.

College of Staten Island, City University of New York, Department of Music: 130 Stuyvesant Place, Staten Island, NY 10301; tel. 1 718 982 2000; website www.csi.cuny.edu.

College of William and Mary, Department of Music: Williamsburg, VA 23185; website www.wm.edu.

College of Wooster, Department of Music: 1189 Beall Ave, Wooster, OH 44691; tel. 1 330 263 2000; website www.wooster.edu.

Colorado College, Department of Music: Packard Hall, Colorado Springs, CO 80903; tel. 1 719 389 6000; website www.coloradocollege.edu.

Colorado State University, Pueblo, Department of Music: 2200 Bonforte Blvd, Pueblo, CO 81001; tel. (719) 549-2552; fax (719) 549-2969.

Colorado State University, Department of Music: Fort Collins, CO 80523; website welcome.colostate.edu.

Columbia College, Department of Music: 1301 Columbia College Drive, Columbia, SC 29203; tel. 1 803 786 3871; website www.columbiacollegesc.edu.

Columbia University, Department of Music: 703 Dodge, New York, NY 10027; website www.columbia.edu.

Columbus College, Schwob Music Department: Columbus, GA 31993.

Community School of the Arts: 345 N College St, Suite 413, Charlotte, NC 28202; tel. 1 704 377 4187; website www.csarts.org.

Concordia College, Department of Music: Moorhead, MN 56560; website www.cord.edu.

Concordia University, Nebraska, Department of Music: 800 N Columbia Avenue, Seward, NE 68434; tel. (402) 643-7282; fax (402) 643-4073; e-mail music@cune.edu; website www.cune.edu; Chair, Dept of Music: Dr William Kuhn; institutional mem. of National Asscn of Schools of Music.

Conservatory of Central Illinois: 312 West Green, Urbana, IL 61801.

Conservatory of Music of Puerto Rico: PO Box 41227, Minillas Station, Santurce, PR 00940; tel. 1 787 751 0160.

Converse College, Petrie School of Music: 580 E Main Street, Spartanburg, SC 29301; website www.converse.edu.

Cornell College, Department of Music: Mount Vernon, IA 52314; website www.cornellcollege.edu.

Cornell University, Department of Music: Lincoln Hall, Ithaca, NY 14853; website www.cornell.edu.

Cornish College of Arts, Department of Music: 1000 Lenora St, Seattle, WA 98121; website www.cornish.edu.

Corpus Christi State University, Visual and Performing Arts Department: 6300 Ocean Dr., Corpus Christi, TX 78412.

Cumberland College, Department of Music: PO Box 7525, Williamsburg, KY 40769; tel. (606) 539-4332; e-mail jsmoak@cumberlandcollege.edu; website www.cumber.edu; Chair, Music Dept: Dr Jeff Smoak.

Curtis Institute of Music: 1726 Locust St, Philadelphia, PA 19103; tel. 1 215 893 5252; fax 1 215 893 9065; website www.curtis.edu.

Dalcroze School of Music: 161 E 73rd St, New York, NY 10021; website www.dalcroze.com.

Darlington School of Music, Arts, Dance & Drama: 977 Shavertown Road, Boothwyn, PA 19061; tel. 1 610 358 3632; website www.darlingtonarts.org.

Dartmouth College, Department of Music: Hopkins Center, Hanover, NH 03755; website www.dartmouth.edu.

Davidson College, Department of Music: PO Box 358, Davidson, NC 28036; website www.davidson.edu.

De Paul University, School of Music: 804 West Belden, Chicago, IL 60614; website www.depaul.edu.

Delaware Music School: PO Box 422, Milford, DE 19963; tel. 1 302 422 2043; website www.lewestoday.com/dms.

Delta State University, Department of Music: PO Box 3256, Cleveland, MS 38733; website www.deltastate.edu.

Denison University, Department of Music: Granville, OH 43023; website www.denison.edu.

DePauw University, School of Music: Performing Arts Center, Greencastle, IN 46135; tel. 1 765 658 4800; website www.depauw.edu.

Diller-Quaile School of Music Inc: 24 E 95th St, New York, NY 10128; tel. 1 212 369 1484; website www.diller-quaile.org.

Drake University, School of Fine Arts: Des Moines, IA 50311; tel. 1 515 271 2011; website www.drake.edu.

Drexel University, Performing Arts Department: 32 and Chestnut Sts, Philadelphia, PA 19104; website www.drexel.edu.

Duke University, Department of Music: Box 90665, Durham, NC 27708-0665; tel. (919) 660-3300; fax (919) 660-3301; e-mail duke-music@duke.edu; website www.duke.edu/music; Chair.: Scott Lindroth.

Duquesne University, School of Music: 600 Forbes Ave, Pittsburgh, PA 15282; tel. 1 412 396 6000; website www.duq.edu.

East Tennessee State University, Department of Music: PO Box 70267, Johnson City, TN 37614; tel. 1 423 439 1000; website www.etsu.edu.

East Texas Baptist University, Department of Music: 1209 North Grove, Marshall, TX 75670; tel. 1 903 935 7963; website www.etbu.edu.

Eastern Illinois University, Department of Music: Charleston, IL 61920; website www.eiu.edu.

Eastern Kentucky University, Department of Music: Richmond, NY 40475; website www.eku.edu.

Eastern Michigan University, Department of Music: N101 Alexander Music Building, Ypsilanti, MI 48197; website www.emich.edu.

Eastern Montana College, Department of Music: 1500 N 30th, Billings, MT 59101.

Eastern New Mexico University, School of Music: Station 16, Portales, NM 88130; tel. 1 505 562 1011; website www.enmu.edu.

Eastern Washington University, Department of Music: Cheney, WA 99004; website www.ewu.edu.

Eastman School of Music: University of Rochester, 26 Gibbs St, Rochester, NY 14604; website www.rochester.edu/ureastman.html.

Edinboro University of Pennsylvania, Department of Music: Heather Hall Music Building, Edinboro, PA 16444; tel. 1 814 732 2000; website www.edinboro.edu.

Elizabeth City State University, Department of Music: PO Box 820, Elizabeth City, NC 27909; website www.ecsu.edu.

Elizabethtown College, Fine and Performing Arts Department: Rider Hall, 1 Alpha Dr., Elizabethtown, PA 17022; website www.etown.edu.

Emory University, Department of Music: Humanities Building, Room 101, Atlanta, GA 30322; website www.emory.edu.

Emporia State University, Division of Music: 1200 Commercial St, Emporia, KS 66801; website www.emporia.edu.

Esther Boyer College of Music: Temple University, 13th and Norris Sts, Philadelphia, PA 19122; website www.temple.edu/boyer.

Evangel College, Department of Music: 1111 N Glenstone, Springfield, MO 65802; website www.evangel.edu.

Fairleigh Dickinson University, Fine Arts Department: 223 Montross Ave, Rutherford, NJ 07070; website www.fdu.edu.

Fairmont State College, Fine Arts Division: Fairmont, WV 26554; website www.fscwv.edu.

Fisk University, Music Department: 1000 17th Ave N, Nashville, TN 37208; tel. (615) 329-8702; fax (615) 329-8850; e-mail pautry@fisk.edu; website www.fisk.edu; Chair, Music Dept: Dr Philip E. Autry.

Flint School of Performing Arts, Dort Music Center: 1025 E Kearsley, Flint, MI 48503; website www.thefim.com/fspa.

Florida Agricultural and Mechanical University, Department of Music: Tallahassee, FL 32307; website www.famu.edu.

Florida Atlantic University, Conservatory of Music: College of Liberal Arts, 2912 College Ave, Boca Raton, FL 33314; website www.fau.edu.

Florida International University, Department of Music: University Park Campus, Miami, FL 33199; website www.fiu.edu.

Florida State University, School of Music: Tallahassee, FL 32306; website www.fsu.edu.

Fort Hays State University, Department of Music: 600 Park St, Hays, KS 67601; tel. 1 785 628 4000; website www.fhsu.edu.

Friends University, Fine Arts Division: 2100 University, Wichita, KS 67213; website www.friends.edu.

Furman University, Department of Music: Greenville, SC 29613; website www.furman.edu.

Garden State Academy of Music: 120 Jackson Ave, Rutherford, NJ 07070; tel. 1 201 933 5454; website www.gsamusic.org.

Gardner-Webb College, Fine Arts Department: Boiling Springs, NC 28017; website www.gardner-webb.edu.

George Mason University, Department of Music: 4400 University Dr., Fairfax, VA 22030; website www.gmu.edu.

George Washington University, Department of Music: B-144 Academic Center, Washington, DC 20052; website www.gwu.edu.

Georgia Southern University, Department of Music: PO Box 8052, Statesboro, GA 30460-8052; tel. (912) 681-5396; fax (912) 871-1295; e-mail music@georgiasouthern.edu; website www.gasou.edu.

Georgia State University, School of Music: University Plaza, Atlanta, GA 30303; website www.gsu.edu.

Gettysburg College, Department of Music: Gettysburg, PA 17325; website www.gettysburg.edu.

Goucher College, Department of Music: 1021 Dulaney Valley Road, Towson, MD 21204; website www.goucher.edu.

Grambling State University, Department of Music: Grambling, LA 71245; website www.gram.edu.

Grand Valley State University, Department of Music: Allendale, MI 49401; website www.gvsu.edu.

Gustavus Adolphus College, Department of Music: St Peter, MN 56082; website www.gac.edu.

Guy Fraser Harrison Academy for the Performing Arts: PO Box 60408, Oklahoma City, OK 73146; website www.harrisonacademy.org.

Haddonfield School of Creative and Performing Arts: PO Box 383, Haddonfield, NJ 08033; website www.haddonarts.org.

Hamline University, Department of Music: Hewitt Ave at Snelling, St Paul, MN 55104; website www.hamline.edu.

Hampton University, Department of Music: Hampton, VA 23668; website www.hamptonu.edu.

Hanover College, Department of Music: Hanover, IN 47243; website www.hanover.edu.

Hardin-Simmons University, School of Music: Drawer J Abilene, TX 79698; website www.hsutx.edu.

Harlem School of the Arts Inc: 645 St Nicholas Ave, New York, NY 10030; tel. 1 212 926 4100; website www.harlemschoolofthearts.org.

Harvard University, Department of Music: Music Building, Cambridge, MA 02138; website www.harvard.edu.

Hastings College, Department of Music: Seventh and Turner, Hastings, NE 68901; website www.hastings.edu.

Hebrew Union College, Jewish Institute of Religion, School of Sacred Music: 1 W Fourth St, New York, NY 10012; website www.huc.edu.

Henderson State University, Department of Music: 1100 Henderson St, Arkadelphia, AR 71923; website www.hsu.edu.

Herbert H Lehman College, City University of New York, Department of Music: Bedford Park Blvd W, Bronx, NY 10468; website www.lehman.cuny.edu.

Hiram College, Department of Music: Hiram, OH 44234; website www.hiram.edu.

Hochstein Memorial Music School: 50 N Plymouth Avenue, Rochester, NY 14614; tel. (585) 454-4596; fax (585) 454-4393; e-mail music@hochstein.org; website www.hochstein.org; Pres.: Margaret Quackenbush.

Hoff-Barthelson Music School: 25 School Lane, Scarsdale, NY 10583; tel. (914) 723-1169; fax (914) 723-0036; website www.hbms.org; Exec. Dir: Joan Behrens Bergman.

Hofstra University, Department of Music: 1000 Fulton Ave, Hempstead, NY 11550; website www.hofstra.edu.

Hollins College, Department of Music: PO Box 9642, Roanoke, VA 24020; website www.hollins.edu.

Hope College, Department of Music: Holland, MI 49423; website www.hope.edu.

Houghton College, School of Music: Houghton, NY 14744; website www.houghton.edu.

Houston Baptist University, College of Fine Arts: 7502 Fondren Road, Houston, TX 77074; website www.hbu.edu.

Howard Payne University, School of Music: 1000 Fisk St, Brownwood, TX 76801; tel. 1 325 649 8020; website www.hputx.edu.

Howard University, College of Fine Arts: Sixth and Fairmont Sts NW, Washington, DC 20059; website www.howard.edu.

Hunter College, City University of New York, Department of Music: 695 Park Ave, New York, NY 10021; tel. 1 212 772 4000; website www.hunter.cuny.edu.

Idaho State University, Department of Music: PO Box 8099, Pocatello, ID 83209; website www.isu.edu.

Illinois State University, Department of Music: Normal, IL 61761; website www.ilstu.edu.

Illinois Wesleyan University, School of Music: Presser Hall, Bloomington, IL 61702; website www.iwu.edu.

Immaculate College, Department of Music: Immaculate, PA 19345.

Incarnate Word College, Department of Music: 4301 Broadway, San Antonio, TX 78209; website www.uiw.edu.

Indiana State University, Department of Music: 217 N Sixth St, Terre Haute, IN 47809; website www.indstate.edu.

Indiana University of Pennsylvania, Department of Music: 101 Cogswell Hall, Indiana, PA 15705; website www.iup.edu.

Indiana University, School of Music: Music Building, Bloomington, IN 47405-2200; tel. 812 855 1583; website www.music.indiana.edu.

Indiana University-Purdue University at Indianapolis, Department of Music: 525 N Blackford St, Room 010, Indianapolis, IN 46202.

Interamerican University of Puerto Rico, Department of Music: Goodyear, PO Box 5100, San Germán, PR 00735.

Interlochen Center for the Arts, Department of Music: PO Box 199, Interlochen, MI 49643-0199; tel. 231 276 7200; fax 231 276 6321; e-mail ica@interlochen.k12.mi.us; website www.interlochen.org.

Iowa State University, Department of Music: 149 Music Hall, Ames, IA 50011; website www.iastate.edu.

Ithaca College, School of Music: Ithaca, NY 14850; website www.ithaca.edu.

Jackson State University, Department of Music: PO Box 17055, Jackson, MS 39217; website www.jsums.edu.

Jacksonville State University, Department of Music: Mason Hall, Jacksonville, AL 36265; website www.jsu.edu.

Jacksonville University, College of Fine Arts, Division of Music: Jacksonville, FL 32211; tel. 1 904 256 8000; website www.ju.edu.

James Madison University, School of Music: MSC 7301, Harrisonburg, VA 22807; tel. (540) 568-6714; website www.jmu.edu/music.

Jersey City State College, Music, Dance and Theatre Department: 2039 Kennedy Blvd, Jersey City, NJ 07305.

Juilliard School: 60 Lincoln Center Plaza, New York, NY 10023; tel. 1 212 799 5000; website www.juilliard.edu.

Kalamazoo College, Department of Music: 1200 Academy St, Kalamazoo, MI 49007; website www.kzoo.edu.

Kansas State University, Department of Music: McCain Auditorium, Room 109, Manhattan, KS 66506; tel. 1 785 532 6011; website www.ksu.edu.

Kearney State College, Department of Music: Kearney, NE 68847.

Kent State University, School of Music: Kent, OH 44242; website www.kent.edu.

Kentucky State University, Fine Arts Division: Frankfort, KY 40601; tel. 1 502 597 6000; website www.kysu.edu.

La Salle University, Fine Arts Department: Philadelphia, PA 19141; website www.lasalle.edu.

Lamar University, Department of Music: PO Box 10044, Beaumont, TX 77710; website www.lamar.edu.

Lawrence University, Conservatory of Music: PO Box 599, Appleton WI 54912; tel. 1 920 832 7000; website www.lawrence.edu.

Lebanon Valley College, Department of Music: Blair Music Center, Annville, PA 17003; website www.lvc.edu.

Lenoir-Rhyne College, Department of Music: PO Box 7355, Hickory, NC 28603; tel. 1 828 328 1741; website www.lrc.edu.

Levine School of Music: 1690 36th St NW, Washington, DC 20007; website www.levineschool.org.

Lewis and Clark College, Department of Music: 0615 SW Palatine Hill Road, Portland, OR 97219; website www.lclark.edu.

Liberty University, Department of Music: PO Box 20000, Lynchburg, VA 24506; website www.liberty.edu.

Limestone College, Fine Arts Division: 115 College Dr., Gaffney, SC 29340; website www.limestone.edu.

Lionel Hampton School of Music: University of Idaho, Moscow, ID 83843; website www.uidaho.edu/LS/Music.

Longwood University, Department of Music: 201 High St, Farmville, VA 23909; tel. 1 434 395 2000; website www.longwood.edu.

Longy School of Music Inc: 1 Follen St, Cambridge, MA 02138; website www.longy.edu.

Los Angeles City College, Department of Music: 855 N Vermont Ave, Los Angeles, CA 90029; tel. (323) 953-4000; fax (323) 953-4013; website www.lacitycollege.edu.

Louisiana College, Department of Music: 1140 College Drive, College Station, Pineville, LA 71360; tel. 1 318 487 7011; website www.lacollege.edu.

Louisiana State University, School of Music: Baton Rouge, LA 70803; website www.lsu.edu.

Louisiana Tech University, School of Performing Arts: PO Box 8608, Ruston, LA 71272; website www.latech.edu.

Loyola University, College of Music: 6363 St Charles Ave, New Orleans, LA 70118; website www.luc.edu.

Luther College, Department of Music: Decorah, IA 52101; website www.luther.edu.

Macalester College, Department of Music: 1600 Grand Ave, St Paul, MN 55105; website www.macalester.edu.

Malone College, Fine Arts Department: 515 25th St NW, Canton, OH 44709; website www.malone.edu.

Manchester College, Department of Music: College Ave, North Manchester, IN 46962; website www.manchester.edu.

Manhattan School of Music: 120 Claremont Ave, New York, NY 10027; tel. 1 212 749 2802; website www.mcmnyc.edu.

Manhattanville College, Department of Music: Purchase, NY 10577; website www.mville.edu.

Mannes College of Music: 150 W 85th St, New York, NY 10024; website www.mannes.edu.

Mansfield University, Department of Music: Butler Music Center, Mansfield, PA 16933; website www.mnsfld.edu.

Marietta College, Edward E MacTaggart Department of Music: Marietta, OH 45750; website www.marietta.edu.

Mars Hill College, Fine Arts Division: PO Box 530, Mars Hill, NC 28754; website www.mhc.edu.

Marshall University, Department of Music: Huntington, WV 25701; website www.marshall.edu.

Mary Washington College, Department of Music: Fredericksburg, VA 22401; website www.mwc.edu.

Marylhurst University, Music Department: PO Box 261, Marylhurst, OR 97036-0261; tel. (503) 699-6263; e-mail music@marylhurst.edu; website www.marylhurst.edu; Music Dept Chair: John Paul.

Maryville College, Fine Arts Department: PO Box 2805, Maryville, TN 37801; website www.maryvillecollege.edu.

Marywood College, Department of Music: 2300 Adams Ave, Scranton, PA 18509; website www.marywood.edu.

Mason Gross School of the Arts of Rutgers University: Marryott Music Building, Douglass Campus, 81 George Street, New Brunswick, NJ 08901; website www.masongross.rutgers.edu.

Mayville State University, Humanities and Social Science Division: Mayville, ND 58257; website www.masu.nodak.edu.

Memphis State University, Department of Music: Memphis, TN 38152.

Mercyhurst College, D'Angelo School of Music: Glenwood Hills, Erie, PA 16546; website www.mercyhurst.edu.

Meredith College: 3800 Hillsborough St, Raleigh, NC 27607; tel. 1 919 760 8600; website www.meredith.edu.

Messiah College, Department of Music: Grantham, PA 17027; website www.messiah.edu.

Metropolitan State College, Department of Music: 1006 11th St, PO Box 58, Denver, CO 80204; website www.mscd.edu.

Miami University, Department of Music: 121 Center for Performing Arts, Oxford, OH 45056; website www.muohio.edu.

Michigan State University, School of Music: Music Building, East Lansing, MI 48824; tel. 1 517 355 2308; fax 1 517 355 6473; website www.msu.edu.

Middle Tennessee State University, Department of Music: PO Box 47, Murfreesboro, TN 37132; website www.mtsu.edu.

Middlebury College, Department of Music: 326 Johnson Building, Middlebury, VT 05753; website www.middlebury.edu.

Midwestern State University, Department of Music: 3400 Taft, Wichita Falls, TX 76308; website www.mwsu.edu.

Millersville University of Pennsylvania, Department of Music: Northumberland House, Millersville, PA 17551.

Millikin University, School of Music: 1184 W Main St, Decatur, IL 62522; website www.millikin.edu.

Mills College, Music Department: 5000 MacArthur Blvd, Oakland, CA 94613; website www.mills.edu.

Minnesota State University Mankato, Department of Music: 202 Performing Arts Center, Mankato, MN 56001; tel. (507) 389-2118; fax (507) 389-2992; e-mail music@mnsu.edu; website www.mnsu.edu.

Minnesota State University Moorhead, Department of Music: 1104 Seventh Ave S, Moorhead, MN 56563; tel. (218) 477-2101; fax (218) 477-4097; e-mail music@mnstate.edu; website www.mnstate.edu/music.

Minot State University, Music Division: 500 Ninth Ave NW, Minot, ND 58701.

Mississippi College, Department of Music: PO Box 4206, Clinton, MS 39058; tel. 1 601 925 3000; website www.mc.edu.

Mississippi State University, Department of Music Education: Drawer F, Mississippi State, MS 39762; website www.msstate.edu.

Missouri Southern State University, Department of Music: 3950 E Newman Road, Joplin, MO 64801; tel. (417) 625-9755; fax (417) 625-9798; website www.mssc.edu.

Missouri Western State College, Department of Music: 4525 Downs Dr., St Joseph, MO 64507; website www.mwsc.edu.

Montana State University, Department of Music: Bozeman, MT 59717; website www.montana.edu.

Montclair State University, School of Fine and Performing Arts: Valley Road, Upper Montclair, NJ 07043; website www.montclair.edu.

Montgomery College, Department of Music: 51 Mannakee St, Rockville, MD 20850; website www.montgomerycollege.edu.

Moody Bible Institute, Sacred Music Department: 820 N LaSalle Drive, Chicago, IL 60610; tel. (312) 329-4082; fax (312) 329-4098; e-mail smdinfo@moody.edu; website www.moody.edu.

Morehead State University, Department of Music: Baird Music Hall, Room 106, Morehead, KY 40351; website www.morehead-st.edu.

Morgan State University, Department of Music: 1700 E Cold Spring Lane, Baltimore, MD 21251; tel. 1 443 885 3333; website www.morgan.edu.

Morningside College: 1501 Morningside Ave, Sioux City, IA 51106; website www.morningside.edu.

Mount Union College, Department of Music: 1972 Clark Ave, Alliance, OH 44601; website www.muc.edu.

Murray State University, Department of Music: University Station, Murray, KY 42071; website www.murraystate.edu.

Music Academy of the West: 1070 Fairway Road, Santa Barbara, CA 93108; tel. (805) 969-4726; fax (805) 969-0686; website www.musicacademy.org; Pres. David L.Kuehn; Vice-Pres. and Dean W. Harold Laster; organizes a summer school and festival.

Music and Arts Institute of San Francisco: 2622 Jackson St, San Francisco, CA 94115.

Music School of Brattleboro Music Center: 15 Walnut St, Brattleboro, VT 05301; tel. 1 802 257 4523.

Music/Arts Institute: 1010 South Pearl, PO Box 1141, Independence, MO 64051.

Musicians Institute: 1655 McCadden Place, Hollywood, CA 90028; website www.mi.edu.

Music School: 75 John St, Providence, RI 02906.

Muskingum College, Department of Music: New Concord, OH 43762; website www.muskingum.edu.

NcNeese State University, College of Liberal Arts, Department of Music: Ryan St, Lake Charles, LA 70609.

Nebraska Wesleyan University, Department of Music: 50 and St Paul St, Lincoln, NE 68504; website www.nebrweslyan.edu.

New England Conservatory of Music: 290 Huntington Ave, Boston, MA 02115; tel. 1 617 585 1100; website www.newenglandconservatory.edu.

New Mexico Highlands University, Creative and Performing Arts Department: Las Vegas, NM 87701; website www.nmhu.edu.

New Mexico State University, Department of Music: PO Box 30001, Las Cruces, NM 88003; website www.nmsu.edu.

New Orleans Baptist Theological Seminary, Church Music Ministries Division: 3939 Gentilly Blvd, New Orleans, LA 70126; website www.nobts.edu.

New School for Social Research, Department of Music: 66 W 12th St, New York, NY 10011.

New School of Music: 25 Lowell St, Cambridge, MA 02138; tel. 1 617 492 8105; fax 1 617 864 7318; website www.cambridgemusic.org.

New York University, Tisch School of the Arts: 721 Broadway, 4th Floor, New York, NY 10003; website www.nyu.edu.

Newberry College, Department of Music: 2100 College Street, Newberry, SC 29108; tel. (803) 321-5174; fax (803) 321-5175; e-mail scherrington@newberry.edu; website www.newberry.edu; Dept Chair: Dr Sally Cherrington.

Norfolk State University, Department of Music: 2401 Corprew Ave, Norfolk, VA 23504; website www.nsu.edu.

North Carolina Agricultural and Technological State University, Department of Music: 1601 E Market St, Greensboro, NC 27411; website www.ncat.edu.

North Carolina Central University, Department of Music: PO Box 19405, Durham, NC 27707; website www.nccu.edu.

North Carolina School of the Arts, School of Music: 200 Waughtown St, Winston-Salem, NC 27117; website www.ncarts.edu.

North Dakota State University, Music and Visual Arts Department: PO Box 5691, Fargo, ND 58105; website www.ndsu.nodak.edu.

North Park College, Department of Music: 3225 West Foster, Chicago, IL 60625; website www.northpark.edu.

Northeast Louisiana University, School of Music: 700 University, Monroe, LA 71209.

Northeastern State University, College of Arts and Letters: Tahlequah, OK 74464; tel. 1 918 456 5511; website www.nsuok.edu.

Northeastern University, Department of Music: 360 Huntington Ave, Boston, MA 02115; website www.northeastern.edu.

Northern Arizona University, Music Department: PO Box 6040, Flagstaff, AZ 86011; website www.nau.edu.

Northern Illinois University, School of Music: Music Building 140, DeKalb, IL 60115; website www.niu.edu.

Northern Michigan University, Department of Music: Fine Arts Building, C-130, Marquette, MI 49855; website www.nmu.edu.

Northern State University, School of Fine Arts: Aberdeen, SD 57401; website www.northern.edu.

Northwest Missouri State University, Department of Music: DeLuce Fine Arts Building, Maryville, MO 64468; tel. 1 800 633 1175; website www.nwmissouri.edu.

Northwestern State University of Louisiana, Department of Music: College Ave, Natchitoches, LA 71497; website www.nsula.edu.

Northwestern University, School of Music: 711 Elgin Road, Evanston, IL 60208; website www.northwestern.edu.

Nyack College, Music and Fine Arts Department: Nyack, NY 10960; website www.nyackcollege.edu.

Oakland University, Music, Theatre and Dance Department: Rochester, MI 48309; website www.oakland.edu.

Oberlin College Conservatory of Music: Oberlin, OH 44074; website www.oberlin.edu.

Odessa College, Department of Music: 201 W University Blvd, Odesa, TX 79764; website www.odessa.edu.

Ohio Northern University, Department of Music: 525 S Main Street, Ada, OH 45810; e-mail e-williams@onu.edu; website www.onu.edu; Chair, Dept of Music: Dr Edwin Williams.

Ohio State University, School of Music: 1866 College Road, Columbus, OH 43210; website www.osu.edu.

Ohio University, School of Music: Athens, OH 45701; website www.ohiou.edu.

Ohio Wesleyan University, Department of Music: Delaware, OH 43015; website www.owu.edu.

Oklahoma City University, School of Music and Performing Arts: 2501 North Blackwelder, Oklahoma City, OK 73106; tel. 1 405 521 5000; website www.okcu.edu.

Oklahoma State University, Department of Music: 132 Seretean Center, Stillwater, OK 74078; tel. 1 405 744 5000; website www.okstate.edu.

Old Dominion University, Department of Music: Norfolk, VA 23508; tel. 1 787 683 4154; website www.odu.edu.

Oral Roberts University, Fine Arts Department: Tulsa, OK 74171; website www.oru.edu.

Oregon State University, Department of Music: Benton 101, Corvallis, OR 97331; website www.oregonstate.edu.

Otterbein College, Department of Music: Battelle Fine Arts Center, Westerville, OH 43081; website www.otterbein.edu.

Pacific Lutheran University, Department of Music: Tacoma, WA 98447; website www.plu.edu.

Pacific University, Department of Music: Forest Grove, OR 97116; website www.pacificu.edu.

Pan American University, Department of Music: Edinburg, TX 78539; website www.panam.edu.

Park College, Department of Music: Parkville, Kansas City, MO 64152.

Pasadena Conservatory of Music: PO Box 91533, 1815 Queensberry Road, Pasadena, CA 91109; tel. 1 626 683 3355; website www.pasadenaconservatory.org.

Peabody Institute of the Johns Hopkins University: 1 E Mount Vernon Place, Baltimore, MD 21202; website www.peabody.jhu.edu.

Pembroke State University, Department of Music: Pembroke, NC 28372,

Pennsylvania State University, School of Music: 232 Music Building, University Park, PA 16802; website www.psu.edu.

People's Music School: 4750 N Sheridan, Suite 340, Chicago, IL 60640.

Pfeiffer University, Fine Arts Department: Misenheimer, NC 28109; website www.pfeiffer.edu.

Philadelphia College of Performing Arts: The University of the Arts, The School of Music, 250 S Broad St, Philadelphia, PA 19102.

Philips University, Department of Music: Division of Fine Arts, PO Box 2000, University Station, Enid, OK 73702.

Pittsburg State University, Department of Music: 1701 South Broadway, Pittsburg, KS 66762; tel. 1 620 231 7000; website www.pittstate.edu.

Plymouth State University, Department of Music: Plymouth, NH 03264; website www.plymouth.edu.

Pomona College, Department of Music: Thatcher Music Building, Claremont, CA 91711; website www.pomona.edu.

Portland State University, Department of Music: PO Box 751, Portland, OR 97207; website www.psx.edu.

Preucil School of Music: 524 N Johnson, Iowa City, IA 52245; website www.preucil.org.

Princeton University, Department of Music: Woolworth Center, Princeton, NJ 08544; website www.princeton.edu.

Providence College, Department of Music: River Ave and Easton St, Providence, RI 02918; website www.providence.edu.

Purdue University, Department of Music: 135 Hall of Music, W Lafayette, IN 47907; website www.purdue.edu.

Quachita Baptist University, School of Music: PO Box 37771, Arkadelphia, AR 71923; website www.obu.edu.

Queens College, Fine Arts Division and Music Department: 1900 Selwyn Ave, Charlotte, NC 28274; website www.queens.edu.

Radford University, Department of Music: E Norwood St, Radford, VA 24142; website www.radford.edu.

Rhode Island College, Department of Music: 600 Mount Pleasant Ave, Providence, RI 02908; website www.ric.edu.

Rhodes College, Department of Music: 2000 N Parkway, Memphis, TN 38112; tel. 1 901 843 3000; website www.rhodes.edu.

Rice University, Shepherd School of Music: PO Box 1892, Houston, TX 77251; tel. 1 713 348 0000; website www.rice.edu.

Richland College, Humanities Division: 12800 Abrams Road, Dallas, TX 75243; website www.rlc.dcccd.edu.

Ricks College, Department of Music: Rexburg, ID 83440.

Ripon College, Department of Music: 300 Seward St, PO Box 248, Ripon, WI 54971; website www.ripon.edu.

Roanoke College, Fine Arts Department: Olin Hall Center for Arts and Humanities, Salem, VA 24153; website www.roanoke.edu.

Roberts Wesleyan College, Fine Arts Division: 2301 Westside Dr., Rochester, NY 14624; website www.roberts.edu.

Rowan University, Department of Music: 201 Mullica Hill Road, Glassboro, NJ 08028; tel. 1 856 256 4000; website www.rowan.edu.

Rutgers University, Faculty of Arts and Sciences, Department of Music: Newark, NJ 07102; website www.rutgers.edu.

SacraCalifornia State University, Sacramento, Department of Music: 6000 Jay Ave, Sacramento, CA 95819.

Saint Louis Conservatory and Schools for the Arts: 560 Trinity at Delmar, St Louis, MO 63130.

Saint Louis University, Department of Music: 221 N Grand Blvd, St Louis, MO 63103; website www.slu.edu.

Saint Mary-of-the-Woods College, Department of Music: Saint Mary-of-the-Woods, IN 47876.

Saint Mary's College of Maryland, Arts and Letters Division: Saint Mary's City, MD 20686.

Saint Mary's College, Department of Music: Notre Dame, IN 46556.

Salem College, School of Music: Winston-Salem, NC 27108; website www.salem.edu.

Sam Houston State University, Department of Music: Huntsville, TX 77341; website www.shsu.edu.

Samford University, School of Music: 800 S Lakeshore Dr., Birmingham, AL 35229; tel. (205) 726-2778; fax (205) 726-2165; website www.samford.edu/schools/performingarts.

San Diego State University, Department of Music: 5300 Campanile Dr., San Diego, CA 92182; website www.sdsu.edu.

San Francisco Conservatory of Music: 1201 Ortega St, San Francisco, CA 94122; website www.sfcm.edu.

San Francisco State University, Department of Music: 1600 Holloway Ave, San Francisco, CA 94132; website www.sfsu.edu.

San Jacinto College North, Fine Arts Division: 5800 Uvalde Road, Houston, TX 77049.

San Jose State University, Department of Music: 1 Washington Sq., San Jose, CA 95192; website www.sjsu.edu.

Sarah Lawrence College, Department of Music: 1 Meadway, Bronxville, NY 10708; website www.slc.edu.

Seattle Pacific University, School of Fine and Performing Arts: 3307 Third Ave W, Seattle, WA 98119; website www.spu.edu.

Seton Hill College, Department of Music: Greensburg, PA 15601; website www.setonhill.edu.

Settlement Music School: 416 Queen St, Philadelphia, PA 19147; website www.smsmusic.org.

Shenandoah College and Conservatory: Winchester, VA 22601.

Sherwood Conservatory of Music: 1312 S Michigan Ave, Chicago, IL 60605; tel. 1 312 427 6267; website www.sherwoodmusic.org.

Shorter College, Fine Arts Division: PO Box 8, Rome, GA 30161; website www.shorter.edu.

Silver Lake College, Department of Music: 2406 S Alverno Road, Manitowoc, WI 54220; tel. (920) 686-6183; fax (920) 684-7082; e-mail mwagner@silver.sl.edu; website www.sl.edu/music; Chair: S. Marella Wagner.

Simpson College, Amy Robertson Music Centre: 701 North C Street, Indianola, IA 50125; tel. (515) 961-1637; e-mail dipalma@storm.simpson .edu; website www.simpson.edu; Chair, Dept of Music: Dr Maria DiPalma.

Sioux Falls College, Fine Arts Division: 1501 S Prairie Ave, Sioux Falls, SD 57105.

Skidmore College, Department of Music: Saratoga Springs, NY 12866; website www.skidmore.edu.

Slippery Rock University, Department of Music: Slippery Rock, PA 16057; website www.sru.edu.

Smith College, Department of Music: Northampton, MA 01063; website www.smith.edu.

South Carolina State College, Department of Music: PO Box 1917, Orangeburg, SC 29117; website www.scsu.edu.

South Dakota State University, Department of Music: Brookings, SD 57007.

Southeast Missouri State University, Department of Music: Brandt Music Hall, Cape Girardeau, MO 63701; website www.semo.edu.

Southeastern Louisiana University, Department of Music: PO Box 815, University Station, Hammond, LA 70402; website www.selu.edu.

Southeastern Oklahoma State University, Department of Music: PO Box 4173, Station A, Durant, OK 74701; website www.sosu.edu.

Southern Baptist Theological Seminary, School of Church Music: 2825 Lexington Road, Louisville, KY 40280.

Southern Illinois University at Carbondale, School of Music: Carbondale, IL 62901.

Southern Illinois University at Edwardsville, Department of Music: PO Box 1771, Edwardsville, IL 62026.

Southern Methodist University, Meadows School of the Arts: Owen Arts Center, Dallas, TX 75275; website www.smu.edu.

Southern Nazarene University, School of Music: 6729 NW 39 Expressway, Bethany, OK 73008; website www.snu.edu.

Southern Oregon State College, Department of Music: 1250 Siskiyou Blvd, Ashland, OR 97520; website www.sou.edu.

Southern University, Department of Music: PO Box 10215, Baton Rouge, LA 70813.

Southwest Baptist University, School of Fine Arts: 1601 S Spring-field St, Bolivar, MO 65613.

Southwest Missouri State University, Department of Music: 901 South National, Springfield, MO 65804.

Southwestern Baptist Theological Seminary, School of Church Music: PO Box 22000, Fort Worth, TX 76122.

Southwestern University, School of Fine Arts: Georgetown, TX 78626.

Spelman College, Department of Music: 350 Spelman Lane SW, Atlanta, GA 30314; website www.spelman.edu.

St Cloud State University, Department of Music: Performing Arts Center, Room 240, St Cloud, MN 56301.

St John's University, Department of Music: Collegeville, MN 56321.

St Mary's University of San Antonio, Department of Music: 1 Camino Santa Maria, San Antonio, TX 78284; website www.stmarytx.edu.

St Michael's College, Fine Arts Department: 56 College Farkway, Winooski, VT 05404.

St Norbert College, Department of Music: De Pere, WI 54115.

St Olaf College, Department of Music: Northfield, MN 55057.

Stanford University, Department of Music: Stanford, CA 94305; website www.stanford.edu.

State University of New York at Albany, Department of Music: 1400 Washington Ave, Albany, NY 12222; website www.albany.edu.

State University of New York at Binghamton, Department of Music: Vestal Parkway, Binghamton, NY 13901; website www .binghamton.edu.

State University of New York at Buffalo, Department of Music: Baird Hall, Room 226, Amherst Campus, Buffalo, NY 14260; website www .buffalo.edu.

State University of New York at Stony Brook, Department of Music: Stony Brook, L I, NY 11794; website www.sunysb.edu.

State University of New York, College at Brockport, Music and Theatre Department: Tower Fine Arts Center, Holley St, Brockport, NY 14420; website www.brockport.edu.

State University of New York, College at Buffalo, Performing Arts Department: 1300 Elmwood Ave, Buffalo, NY 14222.

State University of New York, College at Cortland, Department of Music: PO Box 2000, Cortland, NY 13045; website www.cortland.edu.

State University of New York, College at Fredonia, School of Music: Mason Hall, Fredonia, NY 14063; website www.fredonia.edu.

State University of New York, College at Geneseo, Department of Music: Geneseo, NY 14454; website www.geneseo.edu.

State University of New York, College at New Paltz, Department of Music: New Paltz, NY 12561; website www.newpaltz.edu.

State University of New York, College at Oneonta, Fine Arts Center: Oneonta, NY 13820; website www.oneonta.edu.

State University of New York, College at Oswego, Department of Music: Tyler Hall, Oswego, NY 13126; website www.oswego.edu.

State University of New York, College at Potsdam, Crane School of Music: Pierrepont Ave, Potsdam, NY 13676; website www.potsdam.edu.

State University of New York, College at Purchase, Music Division: Purchase, NY 10577; website www.purchase.edu.

Stephen F. Austin State University, Department of Music: PO Box 13043, Nacogdoches, TX 75962; tel. (936) 468-4602; fax (936) 468-5810; e-mail randerson@sfasu.edu; website www.music.sfasu.edu; Chair, Dept of Music: Ronald E. Anderson.

Stetson University, School of Music: De Land, FL 32720; website www .stetson.edu.

Sul Ross State University, Department of Music: Alpine, TX 79832; website www.sulross.edu.

Susquehanna University, Department of Music: Selinsgrove, PA 17870; website www.susqu.edu.

Sweet Briar College, Department of Music: Sweet Briar, VA 24595; website www.sbc.edu.

Syracuse University, School of Music: 215 Crouse College, Syracuse, NY 13244; website www.syr.edu.

Tanglewood Music Center: c/o Boston Symphony Orchestra, 301 Massachusetts Avenue, Boston, MA 02115; tel. (617) 638-9230; fax (617) 638-9342; e-mail tmc@bso.org; website www.bso.org.

Taylor University, Department of Music: Upland, IN 46989.

Tennessee State University, Department of Music: 3500 John A Merritt Blvd, Nashville, TN 37203; website www.tnstate.edu.

Tennessee Technological University, Department of Music: PO Box 5045, Cookeville, TN 38505; website www.tntech.edu.

Tennessee Temple University, Department of Music: 1815 Union Ave, Chattanooga, TN 37404; website www.tntemple.edu.

Tennessee Wesleyan College, Department of Music: PO Box 40, Athens, TN 37303; website www.tnwcnet.edu.

Texarkana College, Department of Music: Texarkana, TX 75501.

Texas A & I University, Department of Music: PO Box 174, Kingsville, TX 78363.

Texas A & M University, Department of Music: Commerce, TX 75428; website www.tamu-commerce.edu.

Texas Christian University, School of Music: PO Box 297500, Fort Worth, TX 76129.

Texas State University at San Marcos, School of Music: San Marcos, TX 78666; website www.swt.edu.

Texas Technical University, School of Music: PO Box 4239, Lubbock, TX 79409; website www.ttu.edu.

Texas Wesleyan University, School of Fine Arts: Fort Worth, TX 76105.

Texas Woman's University, Performing Arts Department: PO Box 23865, Denton, TX 76204; website www.twu.edu.

Towson State University, Department of Music: Baltimore, MD 21204.

Trenton State College, Department of Music: Hillwood Lakes, CN4700, Trenton, NJ 08650.

Trinity University, Department of Music: 715 Stadium Dr., San Antonio, TX 78284.

Troy State University, School of Fine Arts: Music Department, Long Hall, Troy, AL 36082.

Truman State University, Fine Arts Division: Kirksville, MO 63501; tel. 1 660 785 4000; website www.truman.edu.

Tufts University, Department of Music: 20 Professors Row, Medford, MA 02155.

Tulane University-Newcomb College, Department of Music: Dixon Hall, New Orleans, LA 70118; website www.tulane.edu.

Union University, Department of Music: 2447 Highway 45 Bypass, Jackson, TN 38305.

University of Akron, School of Music: 302 E Buchtel, Akron, OH 44325; website www.uakron.edu.

University of Alabama at Birmingham, Department of Music: 401 Humanities Building, Birmingham, AL 35294; website www.uab.edu.

University of Alabama, School of Music: PO Box 2876, Tuscaloosa, AL 35487; tel. 1 205 348 6010; website www.ua.edu.

University of Alaska, Anchorage, Music Department: 3211 Providence Dr., Anchorage, AK 99508; tel. 1 907 786 1800; website www.uaa.alaska.edu.

University of Alaska, Fairbanks, Music Department: 301 Fine Arts Complex, Fairbanks, AK 99775; website www.alaska.edu.

University of Arizona, School of Music: Tucson, AZ 85721; tel. 1 520 621 2211; website www.arizona.edu.

University of Arkansas at Little Rock, Department of Music: 2801 South University, Little Rock, AR 72204; website www.ualr.edu.

University of Arkansas, Department of Music: 201A Music Building, Fayetteville, AR 72701; website www.uark.edu.

University of Bridgeport, Department of Music: Arnold Bernhard Arts-Humanities Center, Bridgeport, CT 06602; tel. 1 203 576 4000; website www.bridgeport.edu.

University of California, Berkeley, Department of Music: Morrison Hall, Berkeley, CA 94720; website www.berkeley.edu.

University of California, Davis, Department of Music: 112 Music Building, Davis, CA 95616; website www.ucdavis.edu.

University of California, Irvine, School of Fine Arts, Department of Music: Irvine, CA 92717; website www.uci.edu.

University of California, Los Angeles (UCLA), Department of Music: 405 Hilgard Ave, Los Angeles, CA 90024; website www.ucla.edu.

University of California, Riverside, Department of Music: 900 University Ave, Riverside, CA 92521; website www.ucr.edu.

University of California, San Diego (UCSD), Department of Music: B-026, La Jolla, CA 92093; website www.ucsd.edu.

University of California, Santa Barbara, Department of Music: Santa Barbara, CA 93106; website www.ucsb.edu.

University of California, Santa Cruz, Department of Music: Porter College, Santa Cruz, CA 95064; website www.ucsc.edu.

University of Central Arkansas, Department of Music: PO Box 1726, Conway, AR 72032; tel. (501) 450-3163; fax (501) 450-5773; e-mail jshowell@uca.edu; website www.uca.edu/cfac/music.

University of Central Florida, Department of Music: Orlando, FL 32816; website www.ucf.edu.

University of Chicago, Department of Music: 5845 S Ellis Ave, Chicago, IL 60637; website www.uchicago.edu.

University of Cincinnati, College-Conservatory of Music: Cincinnati, OH 45221; website www.uc.edu.

University of Colorado, College of Music: PO Box 301, Boulder, CO 80309; website www.colorado.edu.

University of Connecticut, Department of Music: PO Box U-12, Room 228, 876 Coventry Road, Storrs, CT 06269; website www.uconn.edu.

University of Dayton, Music Division: 300 College Park Dr., Dayton, OH 45469; website www.udayton.edu.

University of Delaware, Department of Music: Newark, DE 19716; website www.udel.edu.

University of Denver, Lamont School of Music: 7111 Mountview, Denver, CO 80220; website www.du.edu.

University of Evansville, Department of Music: 1800 Lincoln Ave, Evansville, IN 47722; website www.evansville.edu.

University of Florida, Department of Music: 130 MUB, Gainesville, FL 32611; website www.ufl.edu.

University of Georgia, School of Music: 203 Fine Arts Building, Athens, GA 30602; website www.uga.edu.

University of The Hartt School: University of Hartford, 200 Bloomfield Avenue, West Hartford, CT 06117; tel. (860) 768-4454; fax (860) 768-4441; e-mail Harttadm@hartford.edu; website www.hartford.edu/hartt; f. 1920 as Julius Hartt, Moshe Paranov and Associated Teachers; one of three founding institutions of the University of Hartford in 1957; performing arts conservatory with degree programmes in music, dance and theatre; also a community arts school.

University of Hawaii, Department of Music: 2411 Dole St, Honolulu, HI 96822; website www.hawaii.edu.

University of Houston, School of Music: 4800 Calhoun, Houston, TX 77204; website www.uh.edu.

University of Illinois at Chicago, Department of Music: PO Box 4348, Chicago, IL 60680; website www.uic.edu.

University of Illinois, School of Music: 1114 W Nevada Street, Urbana, IL 60801; website www.music.uiuc.edu.

University of Indianapolis: 1400 E Hanna, Indianapolis, IN 46227; website www.uindy.edu.

University of Iowa, School of Music: Iowa City, IA 52242; website www.uiowa.edu.

University of Kansas, School of Fine Arts: 452 Murphy St, Lawrence, KS 66045; website www.ku.edu.

University of Kentucky, School of Music: 105 Fine Arts Building, Lexington, KY 40506; website www.uky.edu.

University of Louisville, School of Music: Louisville, KY 40292; website www.louisville.edu.

University of Lowell, College of Music: 1 University Ave, Lowell, MA 01854; website www.uml.edu.

University of Maine, Department of Music: 123 Lord Hall, Orono, ME 04469; website www.umaine.edu.

University of Maryland Eastern Shore, Fine Arts Department, Music Division: Princess Anne, MD 21853.

University of Maryland, Department of Music: Tawes Fine Arts Building, College Park, MD 20742; website www.umd.edu.

University of Massachusetts at Boston, Department of Music: Harbor Campus, Boston, MA 02125; website www.umb.edu.

University of Massachusetts, Music and Dance Department: Fine Arts Center, Amherst, MA 01003; website www.umass.edu.

University of Miami, School of Music: PO Box 248165, Coral Gables, FL 33124; website www.miami.edu.

University of Michigan, School of Music: Ann Arbor, MI 48109; website www.umich.edu.

University of Minnesota, Duluth, Department of Music: 10 University Dr., Duluth, MN 55812; website www.d.umn.edu.

University of Minnesota, Minneapolis, School of Music: 2106 Fourth St S, Minneapolis, MN 55455; website www.umn.edu.

University of Mississippi, Department of Music: 132 Meek Hall, University, MS 38677; website www.olemiss.edu.

University of Missouri at Columbia, Department of Music: 140 Fine Arts Center, Columbia, MO 65211; website www.missouri.edu.

University of Missouri at Kansas City (UMKC), Conservatory of Music: 4949 Cherry, Kansas City, MO 64110; website www.umkc.edu.

University of Missouri at St Louis, Department of Music: 8001 Natural Bridge, St Louis, MO 63121; tel. 1 314 516 5000; website www .umsl.edu.

University of Montana, Department of Music: Missoula, MT 59812; website www.umt.edu.

University of Montevallo, College of Fine Arts: Station 6670, Montevallo, AL 35115; website www.montevallo.edu.

University of Nebraska at Lincoln, School of Music: Westbrook Music Building 120, Lincoln, NE 68588; website www.unl.edu.

University of Nebraska at Omaha, Department of Music: College of Fine Arts, 60 and Dodge St, Omaha, NE 68182; website www.unomaha .edu.

University of Nevada, Las Vegas, Department of Music: 4505 S Maryland Parkway, Las Vegas, NV 89154; website www.unlv.edu.

University of Nevada, Reno, Department of Music: Reno, NV 89557; website www.unr.edu.

University of New Hampshire, Department of Music: Paul Creative Arts Center, 30 College Road, Durham, NH 03824; tel. (603) 862-2404; fax (603) 862-3155; e-mail music.info@unh.edu; website www.unh.edu/music; Dept Chair: Mark DeTurk.

University of New Mexico, Department of Music: College of Fine Arts, Albuquerque, NM 87131; website www.unm.edu.

University of New Orleans, Department of Music: Lakefront, New Orleans, LA 70148; website www.uno.edu.

University of North Carolina at Chapel Hill, Department of Music: Hill Hall CB3320, Chapel Hill, NC 27599; tel. 1 919 962 2211; website www .unc.edu.

University of North Carolina at Charlotte, Performing Arts Department: Charlotte, NC 28223; website www.uncc.edu.

University of North Carolina at Greensboro, School of Music: Greensboro, NC 27412; website www.uncg.edu.

University of North Carolina at Wilmington, Creative Arts Department: 601 S College Road, Wilmington, NC 28403; website www .uncwil.edu.

University of North Dakota, Department of Music: PO Box 8124, Grand Forks, ND 58202; website www.und.edu.

University of North Texas, School of Music: PO Box 13887, Denton, TX 76203; website www.unt.edu.

University of Northern Colorado, School of Music: Greeley, CO 80639; website www.unco.edu.

University of Northern Iowa, School of Music: Cedar Falls, IA 50614; website www.uni.edu.

University of Notre Dame, Department of Music: Crowley Hall of Music, Notre Dame, IN 46556; website www.nd.edu.

University of Oklahoma, School of Music: 560 Parrington Oval, No 109A, Norman, OK 73019; website www.ou.edu.

University of Oregon, School of Music: Eugene, OR 97403-1225; tel. (541) 346-3761; fax (541) 376-0723; e-mail mushelp@oregon.uoregon.edu; website www.uoregon.edu.

University of Pennsylvania, Department of Music: 201 S 34th St, Philadelphia, PA 19104; website www.upenn.edu.

University of Pittsburgh, Department of Music: 110 Music Building, Pittsburgh, PA 15260; website www.pitt.edu.

University of Portland, Performing and Fine Arts Department: 5000 N Williamette Blvd, Portland, OR 97203; website www.up.edu.

University of Puerto Rico, Department of Music: PO Box 23335, Rio Piedras, PR 00931; website www.upr.clu.edu.

University of Puget Sound, School of Music: 1500 North Warner, Tacoma, WA 98416; website www.ups.edu.

University of Redlands, School of Music: PO Box 3080, Redlands, CA 92373; website www.redlands.edu.

University of Rhode Island, Department of Music: Fine Arts Center, Kingston, RI 02881; website www.uri.edu.

University of Richmond, Department of Music: Richmond, VA 23173; website www.urich.edu.

University of St Thomas, Department of Music: 2115 Summit Ave, St Paul, NB 55105; tel. 1 651 962 5000; website www.stthomas.edu.

University of Sciences and Arts of Oklahoma: PO Box 3388, Chickasha, OK 73018.

University of South Alabama, Department of Music: 9 Faculty Court E, Mobile, AL 36688; website www.southalabama.edu.

University of South Carolina, School of Music: Columbia, SC 29208; website www.sc.edu.

University of South Dakota, Department of Music: Vermillion, SD 57069; tel. (605) 677-5274; fax (605) 677-5988; e-mail lschon@usd.edu; website www.usd.edu/cfa/music; Chair: Dr Larry B. Schon.

University of South Florida, Department of Music: Tampa, FL 33620; website www.usf.edu.

University of Southern California (USC), School of Music: University Park, Los Angeles, CA 90089; website www.usc.edu.

University of Southern Maine, Department of Music: College Ave, 102A Corthell Hall, Gorham, ME 04038; website www.usm.maine.edu.

University of Southern Mississippi, School of Music: PO Box 5081, Southern Station, Hattiesburg, MS 39406; website www.usm.edu.

University of Southwestern Louisiana, School of Music: PO Box 41207, Lafayette, LA 70505.

University of Tampa, Music Division: 401 W J F Kennedy Blvd, Tampa, FL 33606; website www.utampa.edu.

University of Tennessee at Chattanooga, Cadek Department of Music-1451: 308 Fine Arts Center, 615 McCallie Avenue, Chattanooga, TN 37403-2598; tel. (423) 425-4601; fax (423) 425-4603; website www.utc .edu/music.

University of Tennessee at Knoxville, Department of Music: 1741 Volunteer Blvd, Knoxville, TN 37996; website www.utk.edu.

University of Tennessee at Martin, Department of Music: 232 Fine Arts Building, Martin, TN 38238; website www.utm.edu.

University of Texas at Arlington, Department of Music: PO Box 19105, Arlington, TX 76019; website www.uta.edu.

University of Texas at Austin, Department of Music: Austin, TX 78712; website www.utexas.edu.

University of Texas at El Paso, Department of Music: University Ave at Hawthorne, El Paso, TX 79968; website www.utep.edu.

University of Texas at San Antonio, Music Division: San Antonio, TX 78285; website www.utsa.edu.

University of the Pacific, Conservatory of Music: 3601 Pacific Ave, Stockton, CA 95211; website www.uop.edu.

University of Toledo, Department of Music: 2801 W Bancroft St, Toledo, OH 43606; website www.utoledo.edu.

University of Tulsa, Department of Music: 600 South College, Tulsa, OK 74104; website www.utulsa.edu.

University of Utah, Department of Music: 204 Gardner Hall, Salt Lake City, UT 84112; website www.utah.edu.

University of Vermont, Department of Music: Music Building, Redstone Campus, Bulington, VT 05405; website www.uvm.edu.

University of Virginia, Department of Music: 112 Old Cabell Hall, Charlottesville, VA 22903; website www.virginia.edu.

University of Washington, School of Music: DN-10, Seattle, WA 98195; website www.washington.edu.

University of West Florida, Department of Music: Pensacola, FL 32514; website www.uwf.edu.

University of Wisconsin, Eau Claire, Department of Music: Fine Arts Center, Eau Claire, WI 54701; website www.uwec.edu.

University of Wisconsin, Green Bay, Department of Music: Green Bay, WI 54301; website www.uwgb.edu.

University of Wisconsin, La Crosse, Department of Music: 234 Fine Arts Building, La Crosse, WI 54601; website www.uwlax.edu.

University of Wisconsin, Madison, School of Music: 455 Park St, Madison, WI 53706; website www.wisc.edu.

University of Wisconsin, Milwaukee, Department of Music: PO Box 413, Milwaukee, WI 53201; website www.uwm.edu.

University of Wisconsin, Oshkosh, Department of Music: Arts and Communication Center, 800 Algoma Blvd, Oshkosh, WI 54901; website www.uwosh.edu.

University of Wisconsin, Parkside, Department of Music: 285 Communication Arts Building, Kenosha, WI 53141; website www.uwp.edu.

University of Wisconsin, Platteville, Department of Music: 1 University Plaza, Platteville, WI 53818; website www.uwplatt.edu.

University of Wisconsin, River Falls, Department of Music: River Falls, WI 54022; website www.uwrf.edu.

University of Wisconsin, Stevens Point, Department of Music: Stevens Point, WI 54481; website www.uwsp.edu.

University of Wisconsin, Superior, Department of Music: Superior, WI 54880; website www.uwsuper.edu.

University of Wisconsin, Whitewater, Department of Music: 800 W Main St, Whitewater, WI 53190; website www.uww.edu.

University of Wyoming, Department of Music: PO Box 3037, University Station, Laramie, WY 82071; tel. 307 766 1121; website www.uwyo.edu.

Utah State University, Department of Music: Logan, UT 84322; website www.usu.edu.

Valdosta State University, Department of Music: N Patterson St, Valdosta, GA 31698; website www.valdosta.edu.

Valley City State University, Department of Music: Valley City, ND 58072; website www.vcsu.edu.

Valparaiso University, Department of Music: Valparaiso, IN 46383; website www.valpo.edu.

Vanderbilt University, Blair School of Music: 2400 Blakemore Ave, Nashville, TN 37212; website www.vanderbilt.edu.

VanderCook College of Music: 3209 S Michigan Ave, Chicago, IL 60616; website www.vandercook.edu.

Vassar College, Department of Music: Raymond Ave, Poughkeepsie, NY 12601; website www.vassar.edu.

Virginia Commonwealth University, Department of Music: 922 Park Ave, Richmond, VA 23284; website www.vcu.edu.

Virginia Polytechnic Institute and State University, Department of Music: 256 Lane, Blacksburg, VA 24061; website www.vt.edu.

Virginia School of the Arts, Department of Music: 2240 Rivermont Ave, Lynchburg, VA 24503.

Virginia State University, Department of Music: PO Box 7, Petersburg, VA 23803.

Viterbo University, Department of Music: 815 S Ninth St, La Crosse, WI 54601; website www.viterbo.edu.

Wagner College, Department of Music: 631 Howard Ave, Staten Island, NY 10301; website www.wagner.edu.

Wake Forest University, Department of Music: 7345 Reynolds Station, Winston-Salem, NC 27109; website www.wfu.edu.

Walla Walla College, Department of Music: College Place, WA 99324; website www.wwc.edu.

Warren M Angell College of Fine Arts: Oklahoma Baptist University, 500 West University, Shawnee, OK 74801.

Wartburg College, Department of Music: PO Box 1003, 222 Ninth St NW, Waverly, IA 50677; tel. 1 800 772 2085; website www.wartburg.edu.

Washburn University, Department of Music: 17 and College, Topeka, KS 66621; website www.washburn.edu.

Washington State University, School of Music: Kimbrough Music Building, Pullman, WA 99164; website www.wsu.edu.

Washington University, Department of Music: Campus Box 1032, 1 Brookings Dr., St Louis, MO 63130; website www.wustl.edu.

Wausau Conservatory of Music: 404 Seymour St, PO Box 606, Wausau, WI 54402; tel. 1 715 845 6279; fax 1 715 842 3527; website www.wausauconservatory.org.

Wayne State University, Department of Music: 5451 Cass Ave, Room 105 Music, Detroit, MI 48202; website www.wayne.edu.

Weber State University, Performing Arts Department: 1905 University Circle, Ogden, UT 84408-1905; tel. (801) 626-6991; fax (801) 626-6811; e-mail mpalumbo@weber.edu; website www.weber.edu; Chair, Dept for Performing Arts: Michael A. Palumbo.

Webster University, Department of Music: 470 E Lockwoof, St Louis, MO 63119; website www.webster.edu.

Wesleyan University, Department of Music: Middletown, CT 06457; website www.wesleyan.edu.

West Georgia College, Department of Music: Carrolton, GA 30118.

West Liberty State College, Department of Music: Hall of Fine Arts, West Liberty, WV 26074; website www.wlsc.edu.

West Texas A & M University, Music and Dance Department: PO Box 870, Canyon, TX 79016; website www.wtamu.edu.

West Virginia State College, Department of Music: PO Box 4, Institute, WV 25112; website www.wvsc.edu.

West Virginia University, Department of Music: Creative Arts Center, Morgantown, WV 26506; website www.wvu.edu.

West Virginia Wesleyan College, Department of Music: PO Box 40, Buckhannon, WV 26201; website www.wvwc.edu.

Westchester Conservatory of Music: 20 Soundview Ave, White Plains, NY 10606; website www.musicconservatory.org.

Western Carolina University, Department of Music: Cullowhee, NC 28723; website www.wcu.edu.

Western Connecticut State University, Department of Music: 181 White St, Danbury, CT 06810; website www.wcsu.edu.

Western Illinois University, Department of Music: 122 Browne Hall, Macomb, IL 61455; website www.wiu.edu.

Western Kentucky University, Department of Music: 351 Fine Arts Center, Bowling Green, KY 42101; website www.wku.edu.

Western Michigan University, School of Music: Kalamazoo, MI 49008; website www.wmich.edu.

Western Oregon University, Creative Arts Division: Monmouth, OR 97361; website www.wou.edu.

Western Washington University, Department of Music: PA 273, Bellingham, WA 98225; website www.wwu.edu.

Westminster Choir College: Rider University, 101 Walnut Lane, Princeton, NJ 08540; website www.rider.edu/westminster.

Westminster College, Department of Music: New Wilmington, PA 16172; website www.westminster.edu.

Wheaton College, Conservatory of Music: 501 College Avenue, Wheaton, IL 60187; tel. (630) 752-5099; fax (630) 752-5341; e-mail music@wheaton.edu; website www.wheaton.edu/conservatory.

Whitman College, School of Music: 345 Boyer Ave, Walla Walla, WA 99362; website www.whitman.edu.

Whitworth College, Department of Music: Spokane, WA 99251; website www.whitworth.edu.

Wichita State University, School of Music: 1845 Fairmont, Wichita, KS 67260-0053; tel. (316) 978-3500; fax (316) 978-3625; website www.wichita.edu/music/index.asp.

Willamette University, Department of Music: 900 State St, Salem, OR 97301; website www.williamette.edu.

William Carey College, Winters School of Music: Tuscan Ave, Hattiesburg, MS 39401; website www.wmcarey.edu.

William Jewell College, Department of Music: Liberty, MO 64068; website www.jewell.edu.

William Paterson College of New Jersey, Department of Music: 300 Pompton Road, Wayne, NJ 07470.

Williams College, Department of Music: Bernhard Music Center, Williamstown, MA 01267.

Wilmington Music School: 4101 Washington St, Wilmington, DE 19802; website www.wilmingtonmusic.org.

Wingate University, Fine Arts Department: Wingate, NC 28174; website www.wingate.edu.

Winona State University, Department of Music: 145 Performing Arts Center, Winona, MN 55987; website www.winona.msus.edu.

Winston-Salem State University, Department of Music: PO Box 13176, Winston-Salem, NC 27101; website www.wssu.edu.

Winthrop University, Department of Music: 112 Conservatory of Music, Rock Hill, SC 29733.

Wisconsin Conservatory of Music: 1584 N Prospect Ave, Milwaukee, WI 53202; tel. 1 414 276 5760; fax 1 414 276 6076; website www.wcmusic .org.

Wittenberg University, Department of Music: Springfield, OH 45501; website www.wittenberg.edu.

Wright State University, Department of Music: Dayton, OH 45435; website www.wright.edu.

Xavier University of Louisiana, Department of Music: 7352 Palmetto St, New Orleans, LA 70125; website www.xula.edu.

Xavier University, Department of Music: 3800 Victory Parkway, Cincinnati, OH 45207; website www.xu.edu.

Yale University, School of Music: PO Box 2104A, Yale Station, New Haven, CT 06520; website www.yale.edu.

Youngstown State University, Dana School of Music: 1 University Plaza, Youngstown, OH 44555-3636; tel. (330) 941-3636; website www.ysu .edu; Dir: Dr Michael R. Crist.

Uruguay

Conservatorio Falleri-Balzo: Avda Uruguay 994, Montevideo.

Conservatorio Nacional de Música: 25 De Mayo 692, Montevideo.

Escuela Universitaria de Música: Paysandu 843, Montevideo.

Venezuela

Academia de Música Fischer: Edificio Léon de San Marco, Avda Ciencias y Calle Risques, Los Chaguaramos, Caracas.

Academia de Música Padre Sojo: 4A Avda Trans, 8AY9A, PO Box 60479 Este, Caracas.

Conservatorio Nacional de Música: Juan José Landeata, Urbanización Campo Alegre, 4A Avda, Caracas.

Conservatorio Italiano de Música: Calle Montesacro, Colinas de Bello Monte, Caracas.

Escuela de Música Lino Gallardo: Avda Principal de la Castellana, Entre 21 y 3a Transversales, Quinta Yudith, Caracas.

Escuela Nacional de Música Jose Angel Lamas: Veroes a Santa Capilla, Avda Urdaneta, Caracas.

Escuela Nacional de Opera: Este 2 con Sur 25, El Conde, Los Caobos, Caracas.